S0-BOJ-948

Greenland
(DENMARK)

Alaska
(U.S.A.)

REYKJAVÍK
ICELAND

C A N A D A

OTTAWA

UNITED STATES
OF AMERICA

Chicago

New York

WASHINGTON

*St Pierre &
Miquelon*
(FRANCE)

A t l a n t i c

Los Angeles

Bermuda
(U.K.)

O c e a n

MEXICO

Hawaii
(U.S.A.)

BAHAMAS

*Turks &
Caicos Is*
(U.K.)

*Puerto
Rico*
(U.S.A.)

British Virgin Is (U.K.)
U.S. Virgin Is (U.S.A.)
Anguilla (U.K.)
ST KITTS & NEVIS
ANTIGUA & BARBUDA
Montserrat (U.K.)
Guadeloupe (FRANCE)
DOMINICA
Martinique (FRANCE)
ST LUCIA
BARBADOS
ST VINCENT & THE GRENADINES
GRENADA

CAPE
VERDE

P a c i f i c

MEXICO
CITY

BELIZE

Cayman Is.
(U.K.)

CUBA

JAMAICA

HAITI

DOM.
REP.

Aruba
(NETH.)

*Neth.
Ant.*
(NETH.)

MARSHALL
IS

O c e a n

GUATEMALA
EL SALVADOR
NICARAGUA

HONDURAS

COSTA RICA

PANAMA

CARACAS

VENEZUELA

TRINIDAD
& TOBAGO

GUYANA
SURINAME

BOGOTÁ

COLOMBIA

French Guiana
(FRANCE)

NAURU

KIRIBATI

QUITO
ECUADOR

LOMON
LANDS

TUVALU

Tokelau
(N.Z.)

LIMA

PERU

B R A Z I L

VANUATU

*Wallis &
Futuna Is*
(FRANCE)

SÁMOA

*American
Samoa*
(U.S.A.)

Cook Is
(N.Z.)

LA PAZ

BRASÍLIA

FIJI

TONGA

Niue
(N.Z.)

French Polynesia
(FRANCE)

BOLIVIA

PARAGUAY

Pitcairn Is
(U.K.)

ASUNCIÓN

Rio de Janeiro

São Paulo

CHILE

Norfolk Is.
(AUSTRALIA)

A
R
G
E
N
T
I
N
A

URUGUAY

NEW ZEALAND

SANTIAGO

WELLINGTON

BUENOS
AIRES

MONTEVIDEO

*Falkland
Islands*
(U.K.)

*South Georgia & the
South Sandwich Islands*
(U.K.)

*Digital Cartography by: Map Creation Ltd
Woodlands Park Avenue,
Maidenhead, Berks, SL6 3LT*

DATE DUE

THE EUROPA
WORLD
YEAR BOOK
2003

THE EUROPA WORLD YEAR BOOK 2003

VOLUME II

KAZAKHSTAN–ZIMBABWE

Europa Publications
Taylor & Francis Group

LONDON AND NEW YORK

First published 1926

© Europa Publications 2003
11 New Fetter Lane, London, EC4P 4EE, England
(A member of the Taylor & Francis Group)

ISBN 1-85743-227-4 (The Set)
1-85743-197-9 (Vol. II)
ISSN 0071-2302
Library of Congress Catalog Card Number 59-2942

Typeset by Ignition UK and printed by Unwin Brothers Limited
The Gresham Press
Old Woking, Surrey

FOREWORD

THE EUROPA WORLD YEAR BOOK (formerly THE EUROPA YEAR BOOK: A WORLD SURVEY) was first published in 1926. Since 1960 it has appeared in annual two-volume editions, and has become established as an authoritative reference work, providing a wealth of detailed information on the political, economic and commercial institutions of the world.

Volume I contains a comprehensive listing of more than 1,650 international organizations and the first part of the alphabetical survey of countries of the world, from Afghanistan to Jordan. Volume II contains countries from Kazakhstan to Zimbabwe. An Index of Territories covered in both volumes can be found at the end of Volume II.

Each country is covered by an individual chapter, containing: an introductory survey including recent history, economic affairs, government, defence, education, and public holidays; an economic and demographic survey using the latest available statistics on area and population, health and welfare, agriculture, forestry, fishing, industry, finance, trade, transport, tourism, the media, and education; and a directory section containing names, addresses and other useful facts about government, political parties, diplomatic representation, judiciary, religious groups, the media, telecommunications, banks, insurance, trade and industry, development organizations, chambers of commerce, industrial and trade associations, utilities, trade unions, transport and tourism.

Launched simultaneously with publication of the 2003 edition of THE EUROPA WORLD YEAR BOOK is EUROPA WORLD ONLINE, incorporating sophisticated search and browse functions that allow access to the entire content of the print edition, as well as specially commissioned visual and statistical content. An ongoing programme of updates of key areas of information will ensure the currency of content, and will enhance the richness of the information for which THE EUROPA WORLD YEAR BOOK is renowned. Details of this prestigious new resource are available at www.europaworldonline.com.

Readers are referred to our annual regional surveys, AFRICA SOUTH OF THE SAHARA, CENTRAL AND SOUTH-EASTERN EUROPE, EASTERN EUROPE, RUSSIA AND CENTRAL ASIA, THE FAR EAST AND AUSTRALASIA, THE MIDDLE EAST AND NORTH AFRICA, SOUTH AMERICA, CENTRAL AMERICA AND THE CARIBBEAN, THE USA AND CANADA and WESTERN EUROPE, for additional information on the geography, history and economy of these areas. More detailed coverage of international organizations may be found in THE EUROPA DIRECTORY OF INTERNATIONAL ORGANIZATIONS.

The information is extensively revised and updated annually by a variety of methods, including direct mailing to all the institutions listed. Many other sources are used, such as national statistical offices, government departments and diplomatic missions. The editors thank the innumerable individuals and organizations throughout the world whose generous co-operation in providing current information for this edition is invaluable in presenting the most accurate and up-to-date material available.

May 2003.

ACKNOWLEDGEMENTS

The editors gratefully acknowledge particular indebtedness for permission to reproduce material from the following publications: the United Nations' *Demographic Yearbook, Statistical Yearbook, Monthly Bulletin of Statistics, Industrial Commodity Statistics Yearbook* and *International Trade Statistics Yearbook*; the United Nations Educational, Scientific and Cultural Organization's *Statistical Yearbook*; the Food and Agriculture Organization of the United Nations' Statistical Database and *Yearbook of Fishery Statistics*; the International Labour Office's Statistical Database and *Yearbook of Labour Statistics*; the World Bank's *World Bank Atlas, Global Development Finance, World Development Report* and *World Development Indicators*; the International Monetary Fund's Statistical Database and *International Financial Statistics* and *Government Finance Statistics Yearbook*; the World Tourism Organization's *Yearbook of Tourism Statistics*; and *The Military Balance 2002–2003*, a publication of the International Institute for Strategic Studies, Arundel House, 13–15 Arundel Street, London WC2R 3DX.

HEALTH AND WELFARE STATISTICS: SOURCES AND DEFINITIONS

Total fertility rate Source: WHO, *The World Health Report* (2002). The number of children that would be born per woman, assuming no female mortality at child-bearing ages and the age-specific fertility rates of a specified country and reference period.

Under-5 mortality rate Source: UNICEF, *The State of the World's Children* (2003). The ratio of registered deaths of children under 5 years to the total number of registered live births over the same period.

HIV/AIDS Source: UNAIDS. Estimated percentage of adults aged 15 to 49 years living with HIV/AIDS. < indicates 'fewer than'.

Health expenditure Source: WHO, *The World Health Report* (2002).
US $ per head (PPP)
International dollar estimates, derived by dividing local currency units by an estimate of their purchasing-power parity (PPP) compared with the US dollar. PPPs are the rates of currency conversion that equalize the purchasing power of different currencies by eliminating the differences in price levels between countries.
% of GDP
GDP levels for OECD countries follow the most recent UN System of National Accounts. For non-OECD countries a value was estimated by utilizing existing UN, IMF and World Bank data.
Public expenditure
Government health-related outlays plus expenditure by social schemes compulsorily affiliated with a sizeable share of the population, and extrabudgetary funds allocated to health services. Figures include grants or loans provided by international agencies, other national authorities, and sometimes commercial banks.

Access to water and sanitation Source: WHO, *Global Water Supply and Sanitation Assessment* (2000 Report). Defined in terms of the type of technology and levels of service afforded. For water, this includes house connections, public standpipes, boreholes with handpumps, protected dug wells, protected spring and rainwater collection; allowance is also made for other locally defined technologies. 'Access' is broadly defined as the availability of at least 20 litres per person per day from a source within 1 km of the user's dwelling. Sanitation is defined to include connection to a sewer or septic tank system, pour-flush latrine, simple pit or ventilated improved pit latrine, again with allowance for acceptable local technologies. Access to water and sanitation does not imply that the level of service or quality of water is 'adequate' or 'safe'.

Human Development Index (HDI) Source: UNDP, *Human Development Report* (2002). A summary of human development measured by three basic dimensions: prospects for a long and healthy life, measured by life expectancy at birth; knowledge, measured by adult literacy rate (two-thirds' weight) and the combined gross enrolment ratio in primary, secondary and tertiary education (one-third weight); and standard of living, measured by GDP per head (PPP US $). The index value obtained lies between zero and one. A value above 0.8 indicates high human development, between 0.5 and 0.8 medium human development, and below 0.5 low human development. A centralized data source for all three dimensions was not available for all countries. In some such cases other data sources were used to calculate a substitute value; however, this was excluded from the ranking. Other countries, including non-UNDP members, were excluded from the HDI altogether. In total, 173 countries were ranked for 2000.

CONTENTS

CONTENTS

ABBREVIATIONS

AB	Aktiebolag (Joint-Stock Company); Alberta	C	Centigrade	DE	Departamento Estatal; Delaware
Abog.	Abogado (Lawyer)	c.	circa; cuadra(s) (block(s))	Dec.	December
Acad.	Academician; Academy	CA	California	Del.	Delegación
ACP	African, Caribbean and Pacific (countries)	CACM	Central American Common Market	Dem.	Democratic; Democrat
ACT	Australian Capital Territory	Cad.	Caddesi (Street)	Dep.	Deputy
AD	anno Domini	CAP	Common Agricultural Policy	dep.	deposits
ADB	African Development Bank; Asian Development Bank	cap.	capital	Dept	Department
		Capt.	Captain	devt	development
ADC	aide-de-camp	CARICOM	Caribbean Community and Common Market	DF	Distrito Federal
Adm.	Admiral			Dgo	Durango
admin.	administration	CBSS	Council of Baltic Sea States	Diag.	Diagonal
AfDB	African Development Bank	CCL	Caribbean Congress of Labour	Dir	Director
AG	Aktiengesellschaft (Joint-Stock Company)	Cdre	Commodore	Div.	Division(al)
		CEMAC	Communauté économique et monétaire de l'Afrique centrale	DM	Deutsche Mark
AH	anno Hegirae			DMZ	demilitarized zone
a.i.	ad interim	Cen.	Central	DN	Distrito Nacional
AID	(US) Agency for International Development	CEO	Chief Executive Officer	Doc.	Docent
		CFA	Communauté Financière Africaine; Coopération Financière en Afrique centrale	Dott.	Dottore/essa
AIDS	acquired immunodeficiency syndrome			Dr	Doctor
				Dr.	Drive
AK	Alaska	CFP	Common Fisheries Policy; Communauté française du Pacifique; Comptoirs français du Pacifique	Dra	Doctora
Al.	Aleja (Alley, Avenue)			Dr Hab.	Doktor Habilitowany (Assistant Professor)
AL	Alabama				
ALADI	Asociación Latinoamericana de Integración			dr.(e)	drachma(e)
		Chair.	Chairman/person/woman	Drs	Doctorandus
Alt.	Alternate	Chih.	Chihuahua	DU	depleted uranium
AM	Amplitude Modulation	CI	Channel Islands	dwt	dead weight tons
a.m.	ante meridiem (before noon)	Cia	Companhia		
amalg.	amalgamated	Cía	Compañía	E	East; Eastern
Apdo	Apartado (Post Box)	CICP	Centre for International Crime Prevention	EBRD	European Bank for Reconstruction and Development
APEC	Asia-Pacific Economic Co-operation				
		Cie	Compagnie		
approx.	approximately	c.i.f.	cost, insurance and freight	EC	European Community
Apt	Apartment	C-in-C	Commander-in-Chief	ECA	(United Nations) Economic Commission for Africa
AR	Arkansas	circ.	circulation		
AŞ	Anonim Şrketi (Joint-Stock Company)	CIS	Commonwealth of Independent States	ECE	(United Nations) Economic Commission for Europe
A/S	Aktieselskab (Joint-Stock Company)	CJD	Creutzfeldt-Jakob disease	ECLAC	(United Nations) Economic Commission for Latin America and the Caribbean
		cm	centimetre(s)		
		cnr	corner		
ASEAN	Association of South East Asian Nations	CO	Colorado	ECO	Economic Co-operation Organization
		Co	Company; County		
asscn	association	c/o	care of	Econ.	Economist; Economics
assoc.	associate	Coah.	Coahuila	ECOSOC	(United Nations) Economic and Social Council
ASSR	Autonomous Soviet Socialist Republic	Col	Colonel		
		Col.	Colima; Colonia	ECOWAS	Economic Community of West African States
asst	assistant	COMESA	Common Market for Eastern and Southern Africa		
AU	African Union			ECU	European Currency Unit
Aug.	August	Comm.	Commission; Commendatore	Edif.	Edificio (Building)
auth.	authorized	Commdr	Commander	edn	edition
Ave	Avenue	Commdt	Commandant	EEA	European Economic Area
Avda	Avenida (Avenue)	Commr	Commissioner	EFTA	European Free Trade Association
Avv.	Avvocato (Lawyer)	Cond.	Condiminio		
AZ	Arizona	Confed.	Confederation	e.g.	exempli gratia (for example)
		Cont.	Contador (Accountant)	EIB	European Investment Bank
BC	British Columbia	Corp.	Corporate	eKv	electron kilovolt
BC	before Christ	Corpn	Corporation	EMS	European Monetary System
Bd	Board	CP	Case Postale, Caixa Postal, Casella Postale (Post Box); Communist Party	EMU	economic and monetary union
Bd, Bld, Blv., Blvd	Boulevard			eMv	electron megavolt
				Eng.	Engineer; Engineering
b/d	barrels per day	CPSU	Communist Party of the Soviet Union	EP	Empresa Pública
BFPO	British Forces' Post Office			ERM	exchange rate mechanism
Bhd	Berhad (Public Limited Company)	Cres.	Crescent	ESACA	Emisora de Capital Abierto Sociedad Anónima
Bldg	Building	CSCE	Conference on Security and Co-operation in Europe		
blk	block			Esc.	Escuela; Escudos; Escritorio
Blvr	Bulevar	CSTAL	Confederación Sindical de los Trabajadores de América Latina	ESCAP	(United Nations) Economic and Social Commission for Asia and the Pacific
BP	Boîte postale (Post Box)				
br.(s)	branch(es)				
Brig.	Brigadier	CT	Connecticut		
BSE	Bovine spongiform encephalopathy	CTCA	Confederación de Trabajadores Centro-americanos	ESCWA	(United Nations) Economic and Social Commission for Western Asia
BSEC	(Organization of) Black Sea Economic Co-operation	Cttee	Committee	esq.	esquina (corner)
		cu	cubic	est.	established; estimate; estimated
bte	boîte (box)	cwt	hundredweight		
BTN	Brussels Tariff Nomenclature			etc.	et cetera
bul.	bulvar (boulevard)	DC	District of Columbia; Distrito Capital; Distrito Central	EU	European Union
bulv.	bulvarīs (boulevard)			eV	eingetragener Verein

ABBREVIATIONS

excl. excluding
exec. executive
Ext. Extension

F Fahrenheit
f. founded
FAO Food and Agriculture Organization
f.a.s. free alongside ship
Feb. February
Fed. Federation; Federal
FL Florida
FM frequency modulation
fmr(ly) former(ly)
f.o.b. free on board
Fr Father
Fr. Franc
Fri. Friday
FRY Federal Republic of Yugoslavia
ft foot (feet)
FYRM former Yugoslav republic of Macedonia

g gram(s)
GA Georgia
GATT General Agreement on Tariffs and Trade
GCC Gulf Co-operation Council
Gdns Gardens
GDP gross domestic product
Gen. General
GeV giga electron volts
GM genetically modified
GmbH Gesellschaft mit beschränkter Haftung (Limited Liability Company)
GMT Greenwich Mean Time
GNI gross national income
GNP gross national product
Gov. Governor
Govt Government
Gro Guerrero
grt gross registered tons
Gto Guanajuato
GWh gigawatt hours

ha hectares
HE His/Her Eminence; His/Her Excellency
hf hlutafelag (Limited Company)
HI Hawaii
HIPC heavily indebted poor country
HIV human immunodeficiency virus
hl hectolitre(s)
HM His/Her Majesty
Hon. Honorary, Honourable
hp horsepower
HQ Headquarters
HRH His/Her Royal Highness
HSH His/Her Serene Highness

IA Iowa
IBRD International Bank for Reconstruction and Development (World Bank)
ICC International Chamber of Commerce; International Criminal Court
ICFTU International Confederation of Free Trade Unions
ICRC International Committee of the Red Cross
ICTR International Criminal Tribunal for Rwanda
ICTY International Criminal Tribunal for the former Yugoslavia
ID Idaho
IDA International Development Association
IDB Inter-American Development Bank
i.e. id est (that is to say)

IFC International Finance Corporation
IGAD Intergovernmental Authority on Development
IL Illinois
ILO International Labour Organization/Office
IMF International Monetary Fund
in (ins) inch (inches)
IN Indiana
Inc, Incorp.
 Incd Incorporated
incl. including
Ind. Independent
INF Intermediate-Range Nuclear Forces
Ing. Engineer
Insp. Inspector
Int. International
Inzå. Engineer
IPU Inter-Parliamentary Union
Ir Engineer
IRF International Road Federation
irreg. irregular
Is Islands
ISIC International Standard Industrial Classification
IT information technology
ITU International Telecommunication Union
Iur. Lawyer

Jal. Jalisco
Jan. January
Jnr Junior
Jr Jonkheer (Esquire); Junior
Jt Joint

kg kilogram(s)
KG Kommandit Gesellschaft (Limited Partnership)
kHz kilohertz
KK Kaien Kaisha (Limited Company)
km kilometre(s)
Kom. Komnata (Room)
kor. korpus (block)
KS Kansas
kv. kvartal (apartment block); kvartira (apartment)
kW kilowatt(s)
kWh kilowatt hours
KY Kentucky

LA Louisiana
lauk laukums (square)
lb pound(s)
Lic. Licenciado
Licda Licenciada
LNG liquefied natural gas
LPG liquefied petroleum gas
Lt, Lieut Lieutenant
Ltd Limited

m metre(s)
m. million
MA Massachusetts
Maj. Major
Man. Manager; managing
MB Manitoba
mbH mit beschränkter Haftung (with limited liability)
Mc/s megacycles per second
MD Maryland
ME Maine
Me Maître
mem.(s) member(s)
MEP Member of the European Parliament
Mercosul Mercado Comum do Sul (Southern Common Market)
Mercosur Mercado Común del Sur (Southern Common Market)

MEV, MeV mega electron volts
Méx. México
MFN most favoured nation
mfrs manufacturers
Mgr Monseigneur; Monsignor
MHz megahertz
MI Michigan
MIA missing in action
Mich. Michoacán
MIGA Multilateral Investment Guarantee Agency
Mil. Military
Mlle Mademoiselle
mm millimetre(s)
Mme Madame
MN Minnesota
MO Missouri
Mon. Monday
Mor. Morelos
MOU memorandum of understanding
MP Member of Parliament
MS Mississippi
MSS Manuscripts
MT Montana
MW megawatt(s); medium wave
MWh megawatt hour(s)

N North; Northern
n.a. not available
nab. naberezhnaya (embankment, quai)
NAFTA North American Free Trade Agreement
nám. náměstí (square)
Nat. National
NATO North Atlantic Treaty Organization
Nay. Nayarit
NB New Brunswick
NC North Carolina
NCO non-commissioned officer
ND North Dakota
NE Nebraska; North-East
NEPAD New Partnership for Africa's Development
NF Newfoundland
NGO non-governmental organization
NH New Hampshire
NJ New Jersey
NL Nuevo León
NM New Mexico
NMP net material product
no numéro, número (number)
no. number
Nov. November
nr near
nrt net registered tons
NS Nova Scotia
NSW New South Wales
NV Naamloze Vennootschap (Limited Company); Nevada
NW North-West
NY New York
NZ New Zealand

OAPEC Organization of Arab Petroleum Exporting Countries
OAS Organization of American States
OAU Organization of African Unity
Oax. Oaxaca
Oct. October
OECD Organisation for Economic Co-operation and Development
OECS Organisation of Eastern Caribbean States
Of. Oficina (Office)
OH Ohio
OIC Organization of the Islamic Conference
OK Oklahoma
ON Ontario
OPEC Organization of the Petroleum Exporting Countries

ABBREVIATIONS

opp. opposite
OR Oregon
Org. Organization
ORIT Organización Regional Interamericana de Trabajadores
OSCE Organization for Security and Co-operation in Europe

p. page
p.a. per annum
PA Palestinian Authority; Pennsylvania
Parl. Parliament(ary)
pas. passazh (passage)
per. pereulok (lane, alley)
PE Prince Edward Island
Perm. Rep. Permanent Representative
PF Postfach (Post Box)
PK Post Box (Turkish)
Pl. Plac, Plads (square)
pl. platz; place; ploshchad (square)
PLC Public Limited Company
PLO Palestine Liberation Organization
p.m. post meridiem (after noon)
PMB Private Mail Bag
PNA Palestinian National Authority
POB Post Office Box
pp. pages
PPP purchasing-power parity
PQ Québec
PR Puerto Rico
pr. prospekt (avenue)
Pres. President
PRGF Poverty Reduction and Growth Facility
Prin. Principal
Prof. Professor
Propr Proprietor
Prov. Province; Provincial; Provinciale (Dutch)
prov. provulok (lane)
PT Perseroan Terbatas (Limited Company)
Pte Private; Puente (Bridge)
Pty Proprietary
p.u. paid up
publ. publication; published
Publr Publisher
Pue. Puebla
Pvt. Private

QC Québec
Qld Queensland
Qro Querétaro
Q. Roo Quintana Roo
q.v. quod vide (to which refer)

Rag. Ragioniere (Accountant)
Rd Road
R(s) rand; rupee(s)
reg., regd register; registered
reorg. reorganized
Rep. Republic; Republican; Representative
Repub. Republic
res reserve(s)
retd retired
Rev. Reverend
RI Rhode Island
RJ Rio de Janeiro
Rm Room
RN Royal Navy
ro-ro roll-on roll-off
RP Recette principale
Rp.(s) rupiah(s)
RSFSR Russian Soviet Federative Socialist Republic
Rt Right

S South; Southern; San
SA Société Anonyme, Sociedad Anónima (Limited Company); South Australia
SAARC South Asian Association for Regional Co-operation
SAECA Sociedad Anónima Emisora de Capital Abierto
SADC Southern African Development Community
SAR Special Administrative Region
SARL Sociedade Anônima de Responsabilidade Limitada (Joint-Stock Company of Limited Liability)
SARS Severe Acute Respiratory Syndrome
Sat. Saturday
SC South Carolina
SD South Dakota
Sdn Bhd Sendirian Berhad (Private Limited Company)
SDR(s) Special Drawing Right(s)
SE South-East
Sec. Secretary
Secr. Secretariat
Sen. Senior; Senator
Sept. September
SER Sua Eccellenza Reverendissima (His Eminence)
SFRY Socialist Federal Republic of Yugoslavia
Sin. Sinaloa
SITC Standard International Trade Classification
SJ Society of Jesus
SK Saskatchewan
SLP San Luis Potosí
SMEs small and medium-sized enterprises
s/n sin número (without number)
Soc. Society
Sok. Sokak (Street)
Son. Sonora
Şos. Şosea (Road)
SP São Paulo
SpA Società per Azioni (Joint-Stock Company)
Sq. Square
sq square (in measurements)
Sr Senior; Señor
Sra Señora
Srl Società a Responsabilità Limitata (Limited Company)
SSR Soviet Socialist Republic
St Saint, Sint; Street
Sta Santa
Ste Sainte
str. strada, stradă (street)
str-la stradelă (street)
subs. subscriptions; subscribed
Sun. Sunday
Supt Superintendent
sv. Saint
SW South-West

Tab. Tabasco
Tamps Tamaulipas
TAŞ Turkiye Anonim Şirketi (Turkish Joint-Stock Company)
Tas Tasmania
TD Teachta Dàla (Member of Parliament)
tech., techn. technical
tel. telephone
TEU 20-ft equivalent unit
Thur. Thursday
TN Tennessee
Treas. Treasurer
Tue. Tuesday

TV television
TX Texas

u. utca (street)
u/a unit of account
UAE United Arab Emirates
UEE Unidade Económica Estatal
UEMOA Union économique et monetaire ouest-africaine
UK United Kingdom
ul. ulica, ulitsa (street)
UM ouguiya
UN United Nations
UNAIDS United Nations Joint Programme on HIV/AIDS
UNCTAD United Nations Conference on Trade and Development
UNDCP United Nations International Drug Control Programme
UNDP United Nations Development Programme
UNEP United Nations Environment Programme
UNESCO United Nations Educational, Scientific and Cultural Organization
UNHCHR UN High Commissioner for Human Rights
UNHCR United Nations High Commissioner for Refugees
UNICEF United Nations Children's Fund
Univ. University
UNRWA United Nations Relief and Works Agency for Palestine Refugees in the Near East
USA United States of America
USAID United States Agency for International Development
USSR Union of Soviet Socialist Republics
UT Utah

VA Virginia
VAT Value-added Tax
VEB Volkseigener Betrieb (Public Company)
v-CJD variant Creutzfeldt-Jakob disease
Ven. Venerable
Ver. Veracruz
VHF Very High Frequency
VI (US) Virgin Islands
Vic Victoria
Vn Veien (Street)
vol.(s) volume(s)
VT Vermont
vul. vulitsa (street)

W West; Western
WA Western Australia; Washington (State)
WCL World Confederation of Labour
Wed. Wednesday
WEU Western European Union
WFP World Food Programme
WFTU World Federation of Trade Unions
WHO World Health Organization
WI Wisconsin
WSSD World Summit on Sustainable Development
WTO World Trade Organization
WV West Virginia
WY Wyoming

yr year
YT Yukon Territory
Yuc. Yucatán

INTERNATIONAL TELEPHONE CODES

To make international calls to telephone and fax numbers listed in *The Europa World Year Book*, dial the international code of the country from which you are calling, followed by the appropriate country code for the organization you wish to call (listed below), followed by the area code (if applicable) and telephone or fax number listed in the entry.

	Country code	+ or − GMT*		Country code	+ or − GMT*
Afghanistan	93	+4½	Dominica	1 767	−4
Albania	355	+1	Dominican Republic	1 809	−4
Algeria	213	+1	Ecuador	593	−5
Andorra	376	+1	Egypt	20	+2
Angola	244	+1	El Salvador	503	−6
Antigua and Barbuda	1 268	−4	Equatorial Guinea	240	+1
Argentina	54	−3	Eritrea	291	+3
Armenia	374	+4	Estonia	372	+2
Australia	61	+8 to +10	Ethiopia	251	+3
Australian External Territories:			Fiji	679	+12
Australian Antarctic Territory	672	+3 to +10	Finland	358	+2
Christmas Island	61	+7	Finnish External Territory:		
Cocos (Keeling) Islands	61	+6½	Åland Islands	358	+2
Norfolk Island	672	+11½	France	33	+1
Austria	43	+1	French Overseas Departments:		
Azerbaijan	994	+5	French Guiana	594	−3
The Bahamas	1 242	−5	Guadeloupe	590	−4
Bahrain	973	+3	Martinique	596	−4
Bangladesh	880	+6	Réunion	262	+4
Barbados	1 246	−4	French Overseas Collectivité Départementale:		
Belarus	375	+2	Mayotte	269	+3
Belgium	32	+1	French Overseas Collectivité Territoriale:		
Belize	501	−6	Saint Pierre and Miquelon	508	−3
Benin	229	+1	French Overseas Territories:		
Bhutan	975	+6	French Polynesia	689	−9 to −10
Bolivia	591	−4	Wallis and Futuna Islands	681	+12
Bosnia and Herzegovina	387	+1	French Overseas Country:		
Botswana	267	+2	New Caledonia	687	+11
Brazil	55	−3 to −4	Gabon	241	+1
Brunei	673	+8	Gambia	220	0
Bulgaria	359	+2	Georgia	995	+4
Burkina Faso	226	0	Germany	49	+1
Burundi	257	+2	Ghana	233	0
Cambodia	855	+7	Greece	30	+2
Cameroon	237	+1	Grenada	1 473	−4
Canada	1	−3 to −8	Guatemala	502	−6
Cape Verde	238	−1	Guinea	224	0
The Central African Republic	236	+1	Guinea-Bissau	245	0
Chad	235	+1	Guyana	592	−4
Chile	56	−4	Haiti	509	−5
China, People's Republic	86	+8	Honduras	504	−6
Special Administrative Regions:			Hungary	36	+1
Hong Kong	852	+8	Iceland	354	0
Macao	853	+8	India	91	+5½
China (Taiwan)	886	+8	Indonesia	62	+7 to +9
Colombia	57	−5	Iran	98	+3½
The Comoros	269	+3	Iraq	964	+3
Congo, Democratic Republic	243	+1	Ireland	353	0
Congo, Republic	242	+1	Israel	972	+2
Costa Rica	506	−6	Italy	39	+1
Côte d'Ivoire	225	0	Jamaica	1 876	−5
Croatia	385	+1	Japan	81	+9
Cuba	53	−5	Jordan	962	+2
Cyprus	357	+2	Kazakhstan	7	+6
'Turkish Republic of Northern			Kenya	254	+3
Cyprus'	90 392	+2	Kiribati	686	+12 to +13
Czech Republic	420	+1	Korea, Democratic People's		
Denmark	45	+1	Republic (North Korea)	850	+9
Danish External Territories:			Korea, Republic (South Korea)	82	+9
Faroe Islands	298	0	Kuwait	965	+3
Greenland	299	−1 to −4	Kyrgyzstan	996	+5
Djibouti	253	+3			

	Country code	+ or − GMT*		Country code	+ or − GMT*
Laos	856	+7	Singapore	65	+8
Latvia	371	+2	Slovakia	421	+1
Lebanon	961	+2	Slovenia	386	+1
Lesotho	266	+2	Solomon Islands	677	+11
Liberia	231	0	Somalia	252	+3
Libya	218	+1	South Africa	27	+2
Liechtenstein	423	+1	Spain	34	+1
Lithuania	370	+2	Sri Lanka	94	+6
Luxembourg	352	+1	Sudan	249	+2
Macedonia, former Yugoslav republic	389	+1	Suriname	597	−3
Madagascar	261	+3	Swaziland	268	+2
Malawi	265	+2	Sweden	46	+1
Malaysia	60	+8	Switzerland	41	+1
Maldives	960	+5	Syria	963	+2
Mali	223	0	Tajikistan	992	+5
Malta	356	+1	Tanzania	255	+3
Marshall Islands	692	+12	Thailand	66	+7
Mauritania	222	0	Timor-Leste	670	+9
Mauritius	230	+4	Togo	228	0
Mexico	52	−6 to −7	Tonga	676	+13
Micronesia, Federated States	691	+10 to +11	Trinidad and Tobago	1 868	−4
Moldova	373	+2	Tunisia	216	+1
Monaco	377	+1	Turkey	90	+2
Mongolia	976	+7 to +9	Turkmenistan	993	+5
Morocco	212	0	Tuvalu	688	+12
Mozambique	258	+2	Uganda	256	+3
Myanmar	95	+6½	Ukraine	380	+2
Namibia	264	+2	United Arab Emirates	971	+4
Nauru	674	+12	United Kingdom	44	0
Nepal	977	+5¾	United Kingdom Crown		
Netherlands	31	+1	Dependencies	44	0
Netherlands Dependencies:			United Kingdom Overseas		
Aruba	297	−4	Territories:		
Netherlands Antilles	599	−4	Anguilla	1 264	−4
New Zealand	64	+12	Ascension Island	247	0
New Zealand's Dependent and Associated			Bermuda	1 441	−4
Territories:			British Virgin Islands	1 284	−4
Tokelau	690	−10	Cayman Islands	1 345	−5
Cook Islands	682	−10	Diego Garcia (British Indian		
Niue	683	−11	Ocean Territory)	246	+5
Nicaragua	505	−6	Falkland Islands	500	−4
Niger	227	+1	Gibraltar	350	+1
Nigeria	234	+1	Montserrat	1 664	−4
Norway	47	+1	Pitcairn Islands	872	−8
Norwegian External Territory:			Saint Helena	290	0
Svalbard	47	+1	Tristan da Cunha	2 897	0
Oman	968	+4	Turks and Caicos Islands	1 649	−5
Pakistan	92	+5	United States of America	1	−5 to −10
Palau	680	+9	United States Commonwealth		
Palestinian Autonomous Areas	970	+2	Territories:		
Panama	507	−5	Northern Mariana Islands	1 670	+10
Papua New Guinea	675	+10	Puerto Rico	1 787	−4
Paraguay	595	−4	United States External Territories:		
Peru	51	−5	American Samoa	1 684	−11
The Philippines	63	+8	Guam	1 671	+10
Poland	48	+1	United States Virgin Islands	1 340	−4
Portugal	351	0	Uruguay	598	−3
Qatar	974	+3	Uzbekistan	998	+5
Romania	40	+2	Vanuatu	678	+11
Russian Federation	7	+2 to +12	Vatican City	39	+1
Rwanda	250	+2	Venezuela	58	−4
Saint Christopher and Nevis	1 869	−4	Viet Nam	84	+7
Saint Lucia	1 758	−4	Yemen	967	+3
Saint Vincent and the Grenadines	1 784	−4	Zambia	260	+2
Samoa	685	−11	Zimbabwe	263	+2
San Marino	378	+1			
São Tomé and Príncipe	239	0			
Saudi Arabia	966	+3			
Senegal	221	0			
Serbia and Montenegro	381	+1			
Seychelles	248	+4			
Sierra Leone	232	0			

* Time difference in hours + or − Greenwich Mean Time (GMT). The times listed compare the standard (winter) times. Some countries adopt Summer (Daylight Saving) Time — i.e. + 1 hour — for part of the year.

KAZAKHSTAN

Introductory Survey

Location, Climate, Language, Religion, Flag, Capital

The Republic of Kazakhstan (until December 1991 the Kazakh Soviet Socialist Republic) is the second largest of the former Soviet republics, extending some 1,900 km (1,200 miles) from the Volga river in the west to the Altai mountains in the east, and about 1,300 km (800 miles) from the Siberian plain in the north to the Central Asian deserts in the south. To the south it borders Turkmenistan, Uzbekistan and Kyrgyzstan. To the east the border is with the People's Republic of China. There is a long border in the north with Russia and a coastline of 2,320 km (1,440 miles) on the Caspian Sea in the south-west. The climate is of a strongly continental type, but there are wide variations throughout the territory. Average temperatures in January range from –18°C (0°F) in the north to –3°C (27°F) in the south. In July average temperatures are 19°C (66°F) in the north and 28°C–30°C (82°F–86°F) in the south. Similarly, average annual rainfall in mountainous regions reaches 1,600 mm (63 ins), whereas in the central desert areas it is less than 100 mm (4 ins). The official language is Kazakh. The predominant religion is Islam, most ethnic Kazakhs being Sunni Muslims of the Hanafi school. Other ethnic groups have their own religious communities, notably the (Christian) Eastern Orthodox Church, which is attended mainly by Slavs. The national flag (proportions 1 by 2) consists of a light blue field, at the centre of which is a yellow sun (a disc surrounded by 32 rays), framed by the wings of a flying eagle, also in yellow, with a vertical stripe of national ornamentation in yellow near the hoist. In November 1997 the capital was moved from Almaty to Akmola (formerly Tselinograd), now known as Astana.

Recent History

After the February Revolution and the Bolshevik *coup d'état* in Russia in 1917, there was civil war throughout Kazakhstan, which had come under Russian control in the first half of the 18th century. Bolshevik forces finally overcame those of the anti-Bolshevik White Army, foreign interventionists and local nationalists. In 1920 the Kyrgyz Autonomous Soviet Socialist Republic (ASSR) was created within the Russian Soviet Federative Socialist Republic (the Russian Federation): the Kazakhs were known to the Russians as Kyrgyz, to distinguish them from the unrelated Cossacks. In 1925 the Kyrgyz ASSR was renamed the Kazakh ASSR; the Karakalpak region (now in Uzbekistan) was detached in 1930, and became an autonomous republic within the Uzbek Soviet Socialist Republic (SSR) in 1936. In December 1936 the Kazakh ASSR became a full Union Republic of the USSR, the Kazakh SSR.

Under Soviet rule parts of Kazakhstan were heavily industrialized. However, Kazakhstan was one of the worst-affected regions during the campaign in the early 1930s to collectivize agriculture and settle nomadic peoples, and more than 1m. people were estimated to have died as a result of starvation. There was severe repression from the 1930s, and Russian immigration was greatly increased. Many of those deported from parts of the USSR during the Second World War (including Germans, Crimean Tatars and Caucasian peoples) were sent to Kazakhstan, causing considerable local resentment. During Nikita Khrushchev's period in office as Soviet leader (1953–64) large areas of previously uncultivated land in Kazakhstan were transformed into arable land under the 'Virgin Lands' programme. This and other schemes, including nuclear-testing sites in eastern Kazakhstan, the Baikonur space centre at Leninsk (now Turatam) and the huge industrial complexes in the north and east, brought large numbers of ethnic Russians to Kazakhstan; the proportion of Russians increased from 19.7% of the population in 1926 to 42.7% in 1959.

Mikhail Gorbachev's accession to power in 1985 and his subsequent anti-corruption campaign, as well as the new policy of *glasnost* (openness), had important consequences in Kazakhstan. In December 1986 some 3,000 people took part in protests in the then capital, Almaty (Alma-Ata), after Gennadii Kolbin, an ethnic Russian, was appointed First Secretary of the Communist Party of Kazakhstan (CPK), in place of the populist, but corrupt, Dinmukhamed Kunayev, an ethnic Kazakh. Four people died when the protesters were dispersed by police. Kolbin subsequently dismissed many of Kunayev's former associates.

In September 1989 the Kazakh Supreme Soviet (parliament) adopted legislation establishing Kazakh as the official language of the republic, while Russian remained a language of inter-ethnic communication. However, the new law was opposed by many non-Kazakh residents. A local branch of the Russian nationalist organization, Yedinstvo (Unity), was established, and some members campaigned for annexation of Kazakhstan's northern regions by Russia.

Many of the unofficial, quasi-political groups established in Kazakhstan in the late 1980s were concerned with environmental issues, such as the harmful effects of nuclear testing near Semipalatinsk. A vigorous campaign to end nuclear testing was led by one of the largest such groups, Nevada-Semipalatinsk. In September 1990 an explosion in a factory producing nuclear fuel at Ulba, in eastern Kazakhstan, led to the contamination by toxic gases of a large area, including the nearby city of Ust-Kamenogorsk.

In June 1989 Kolbin was transferred to the Soviet and Russian capital, Moscow, and Nursultan Nazarbayev, a prominent ethnic Kazakh, who had been Chairman of the republic's Council of Ministers since March 1984, was appointed First Secretary of the CPK. Nazarbayev advocated economic reform, while emphasizing the need for political stability. Political and administrative changes were instituted in September 1989: a permanent Supreme Soviet was to be established, and elections were to be conducted on a multi-candidate basis. In addition, the state duties that had hitherto been the responsibility of the First Secretary of the CPK were transferred to the office of the Chairman of the Kazakh Supreme Soviet, to which post Nazarbayev was elected in February 1990. Many candidates stood unopposed at elections to the Supreme Soviet in March, and the system of reserved seats for CPK-affiliated organizations was retained, resulting in a substantial communist majority. In April the new body elected Nazarbayev to the newly established post of President of Kazakhstan.

On 25 October 1990 the Kazakh Supreme Soviet declared its sovereignty, asserting republican control over natural resources and the economy. Although the declaration emphasized ethnic equality, there were protests in the predominantly Slav-populated city of Ust-Kamenogorsk; Kazakh nationalist groups, meanwhile, judged the declaration too weak. Nazarbayev strongly supported a redefinition of the respective all-Union (Soviet) and republican powers, and the Kazakh Government participated in discussions on the new Union Treaty in early 1991. However, Nazarbayev also sought economic sovereignty for Kazakhstan, where some 90% of enterprises were under all-Union control.

In the referendum on the future of the USSR conducted in nine Soviet republics in March 1991, almost 90% of the electorate voted in Kazakhstan, of whom 94% endorsed the proposal to preserve the USSR as a 'union of sovereign states with equal rights'. In June the Kazakh Supreme Soviet voted, in principle, to adopt a draft Union Treaty, although Nazarbayev expressed reservations about certain aspects of the proposed federation. Kazakhstan was to sign the treaty in August, but the event was forestalled by the attempted *coup d'état* in Moscow. Nazarbayev did not initially condemn the coup, but subsequently denounced the group leading the *putsch* as illegal and harmful to economic and political progress. As the coup attempt collapsed, Nazarbayev resigned from the Politburo and Central Committee of the Communist Party of the Soviet Union (CPSU), in protest at the open support granted to the putschists by the CPSU leadership. The CPK was ordered to cease activities in state and government organs, and in September the party withdrew from the CPSU; it was re-formed as the independent Socialist Party of Kazakhstan (SPK).

In October 1991 Kazakhstan signed, with seven other republics, a treaty to establish an economic community, and in November agreed to the draft treaty of the new Union of Sovereign States. These accords were largely nullified by the Commonwealth of Independent States (CIS, see p. 172), agreed by the leaders of the three Slavic republics (Russia, Ukraine and Belarus) in December. Kazakhstan (despite initial reluctance) and the other Central Asian republics agreed to join the new Commonwealth. On 16 December 1991 Kazakhstan became the last of the republics to declare independence from the USSR, and was redesignated the Republic of Kazakhstan. The country was formally recognized as a co-founder of the CIS at the Almaty meeting on 21 December.

Kazakhstan's late declaration of independence was attributed to Nazarbayev's concern to preserve the delicate inter-ethnic balance between Russians and Kazakhs in the republic and also to prevent further discussion of the cession of Kazakhstan's northern territories to Russia. Furthermore, it was seen as evidence, together with his determination to retain many of the structures and personnel of the CPK (although re-formed as the SPK), of his view that economic reform should take precedence over political change. Nazarbayev was re-elected, with 98.8% of the votes cast, as President of Kazakhstan, on 1 December 1991.

Although Kazakhstan did not experience the inter-ethnic violence that affected several other former Soviet republics, some racial unrest was reported during 1992, particularly among Kazakhstan's ethnic Russian community (which constituted an estimated 38% of the total population, while ethnic Kazakhs comprised 40%). Russian interests demanded that the Russian language be guaranteed equal status with Kazakh in a new constitution, the content of which was widely debated. The Constitution, adopted in January 1993, invoked the law of 1989 (denoting Kazakh as the state language, with Russian as a language of inter-ethnic communication). The document also required that the President of the Republic be a fluent speaker of Kazakh. Meanwhile, increased emigration from the country, particularly by ethnic Germans (more than 300,000 of whom left Kazakhstan in the early 1990s) and Russians, was accompanied by the return of ethnic Kazakhs from, most notably, Kyrgyzstan, Mongolia, Tajikistan and Turkmenistan. According to official figures released by the Kazakh authorities in early 1998, a total of 1,652,700 emigrants left Kazakhstan in 1992–97; in May 1998 the number of ethnic Kazakhs who had returned in 1991–97 was officially said to exceed 100,000.

Opposition to Nazarbayev's administration became more pronounced during 1992. In June some 5,000 people demonstrated in Almaty against continued communist predominance in the Government and Supreme Kenges (as the legislature was now styled), demanding the formation of a new, coalition administration. In October the three most prominent nationalist opposition parties (the Azat movement, the Republican Party and the Dzheltoqsan National Democratic Party) united to form the Republican Party—Azat (RP—A). The Union of National Unity of Kazakhstan was established in February 1993, with a declared aim of promoting social harmony and countering radical nationalism. Nazarbayev (who had held no party affiliation since August 1991) became Chairman of the Union, which was reorganized as a political party, the People's Unity Party (PUP), later in 1993.

In December 1993 the Supreme Kenges voted to dissolve itself and to grant Nazarbayev the power to rule by decree pending elections to a new standing legislature, which was to be reduced in size from 360 to 177 seats. Kazakhstan's first multi-party elections were duly held on 7 March 1994, with the participation of 74% of the electorate. A number of irregularities were reported by international observers, with many prospective candidates allegedly being prevented from registering. Of the 754 candidates who successfully registered, the overwhelming majority (75%) were ethnic Kazakhs, prompting complaints of discrimination against the Russian community. The final composition of the new Kenges was 59% Kazakh and 28% Russian. The PUP obtained 33 seats, which, when combined with the 42 seats won by candidates from the so-called 'President's List' (candidates nominated by Nazarbayev) and those of pro-Nazarbayev independents, ensured that Nazarbayev's supporters emerged as the strongest force in the assembly. Other parties and groups achieved a significantly lower representation: the Confederation of Kazakh Trade Unions (CKTU) won 11 seats, the People's Congress Party of Kazakhstan (PCPK) nine and the SPK eight. After several unsuccessful attempts at re-establishment, the CPK was granted legal status in March. In May the CPK (claiming a membership of some 50,000) and other opposition parties, including the SPK, the PCPK and the RP—A, together with the CKTU, formed an opposition bloc in the Supreme Kenges, with the stated aim of acting as a guarantor against 'dictatorship by executive bodies'.

Divisions swiftly emerged between the Government and the Supreme Kenges: in May 1994 96 members of the Kenges endorsed a motion expressing 'no confidence' in the Government's economic, social and legal policies. In June Nazarbayev announced a major government reorganization, in an attempt to stimulate economic reform. The Government of Sergei Tereshchenko (the Prime Minister since 1991) resigned in October 1994, admitting its failure to reform the economy. Akezhan Kazhegeldin, an economist and First Deputy Prime Minister in the outgoing Council of Ministers, was appointed premier.

Meanwhile, in July 1994 the Supreme Kenges approved a proposal by Nazarbayev to transfer the capital to the northern city of Akmola (formerly Tselinograd) by 2000. Akmola's geographical advantages were emphasized, in contrast to Almaty's overcrowded conditions and its situation in an area vulnerable to earthquakes; however, there was widespread speculation that the move was designed to strengthen the Government's control over the largely Russian-populated northern regions.

A crisis arose in February 1995, when the Constitutional Court declared the result of the 1994 general election to be null and void, owing to 'procedural infringements'. Following an unsuccessful attempt by the Supreme Kenges to amend the Constitution in order to overrule the Court's decision, in March 1995 the legislature was forced to tender its resignation. (The Government was also obliged to resign, on the grounds that it had been approved by an unconstitutional parliament, but it was subsequently reinstated virtually unchanged.) Nazarbayev was thus effectively empowered to rule by decree pending a further legislative election, prompting opposition parties to allege that the situation had been orchestrated by him in order to remove an obstructionist parliament. At a national referendum on 29 April more than 95% of voters endorsed the extension of Nazarbayev's five-year mandate until 1 December 2000: the President had asserted that the measure was necessary to ensure political stability.

In May 1995 Nazarbayev ordered the establishment of a special council to prepare (under his guidance) a new constitution. Opposition activists denounced provisions whereby, they considered, the President would be guaranteed 'unchecked rule'. A final draft was approved by 89.1% of the electorate in a referendum on 30 August. The new Constitution preserved the extensive executive powers of the President, and abolished the post of Vice-President. The Supreme Kenges was replaced by a bicameral Parliament, comprising a 47-member Senate (the upper chamber—with 40 members elected by Kazakhstan's regional administrative bodies and seven appointed by the President) and a directly elected, 67-member Majlis (Assembly). The Constitutional Court was replaced by a Constitutional Council, the rulings of which would be subject to a presidential right of veto.

At elections to the Senate held on 5 December 1995, 38 of the 40 regionally elected seats were filled; Nazarbayev duly appointed seven senators. Direct elections were held to the Majlis on 9 December, with the participation of 80.7% of the electorate. However, the necessary two-thirds' quorum was not attained, as candidates succeeded in obtaining the requisite 50% of the votes in only 41 of the 67 constituencies. Further rounds of voting (contested by the two leading candidates from the first round) were held in the remaining 26 constituencies on 23 December and 4 February 1996, with 13 seats being filled at each round. A number of procedural violations in the elections to the Majlis were reported by foreign observers.

Popular dissatisfaction with the Government's economic and social policies became more pronounced in 1996. In April a new opposition movement, Azamat (Citizen), was established by a group of scientists, writers and public figures. (It was finally registered as a political party, the Azamat Democratic Party of Kazakhstan, in 1999.) Social tensions were exacerbated in late 1996 by widespread energy shortages. In October the leaders of Kazakhstan's two main trade-union federations organized rallies to protest at declining standards of living. Negotiations between political groups and parliamentary deputies followed, but requests for permission to organize a further rally in Almaty in November were refused by the city authorities. A silent demonstration proceeded, none the less, following which the organizers, including Petr Svoik (one of Azamat's leaders) and the Chairman of the Confederation of Free Trade Unions, Leonid Solomin, were briefly arrested. Prolonged delays in payments of wages, owing to the insolvency of numerous state-owned enterprises, were a principal cause of strikes and unauthorized demonstrations throughout 1997 and early 1998.

The ongoing reform of pensions' legislation also continued to provoke protests. Draft legislation regulating the pensions' system was approved by the Majlis in May 1997 and by Nazarbayev in June. Opponents of the new legislation (effective from January 1998) claimed that it would lead to the curtailment of many social guarantees. Meanwhile, demonstrations were held, in protest at the level of non-payment of pensions (amounting to some to US $500m. in May 1997). Payment of pensions' arrears commenced in August, apparently funded by revenue from the privatization of two Kazakh petroleum companies; in February 1998 it was announced that all such arrears had been cleared.

Meanwhile, from late 1996 employees from several ministries were relocated from Almaty to Akmola, marking the beginning of the transfer of the capital city. In November 1997 the new capital was officially inaugurated by Nazarbayev, and a joint session of both chambers of Parliament was held for the first time in Akmola in the following month. However, the costly transfer attracted widespread criticism, and it was reported that the initial stages had been poorly managed: in particular, an acute housing shortage in Akmola had not been adequately addressed. None the less, a ceremony was held in early June 1998 to mark the official opening of the capital under the new name of Astana (a presidential decree changing the name of the capital had been issued in May).

Nazarbayev undertook several far-reaching measures to restructure and rationalize the state administration in March 1997. The 48 ministries and other government agencies were reduced in number to 25. The Ministry of Petroleum and Natural Gas, headed by Nurlan Balgymbayev, was abolished and replaced by a new state company, KazakhOil, which was also led by Balgymbayev. In conjunction with the adoption of more liberal legislation on foreign investment, the State Committee for Investment became the sole body governing this area of the economy. The State Property Committee, which had been responsible for the management of all (and the divestment of most) state-owned enterprises, was dissolved. Seven government institutions—including the Ministries of Defence and of Internal Affairs and the newly established Agency for Control of Strategic Resources—became directly subordinate to the President. Nazarbayev continued the reform process by reducing the number of administrative regions from 19 to 14.

That Nazarbayev's governmental restructuring had been effected while Kazhegeldin was out of the country led to speculation that the President's confidence in the Prime Minister had begun to decline. Kazhegeldin's position appeared more precarious in August 1997, owing to an investigation by the National Security Committee (KNB) into alleged financial malpractice (although he was exonerated him of corruption charges). The Prime Minister's position was further undermined when, in the following month, a Russian newspaper published an admission by Kazhegeldin of his involvement, in the late 1980s, with the former Soviet state security service (KGB). In September 1997 it was announced that Kazhegeldin had resigned as Prime Minister, ostensibly for health reasons. He was replaced for a short interim period by Akhmetzan Yesimov, and in October Balgymbayev was named Prime Minister.

In January 1998, in an apparent attempt to counter increasingly vocal opposition to Nazarbayev, 17 political parties and movements signed a 'memorandum on mutual understanding and co-operation', pledging their support for the President's policies and reforms. However, political tensions were revived in April, when one of the leaders of the Workers' Movement of Kazakhstan, Madel Ismailov, was sentenced to one year's imprisonment, having been convicted of insulting the President during an unauthorized rally in November 1997. Meanwhile, in February 1998 Nazarbayev ordered a reshuffle of senior economic and financial posts. A further reorganization at the end of April included the appointment of a new President of KazakhOil.

In September 1998, in his annual address to Parliament, Nazarbayev outlined proposals for political reforms, including amendments to electoral procedures and enhanced legislative powers. In October, however, a joint session of Parliament rejected Nazarbayev's proposed constitutional reforms. The Head of State's expressed concern to transfer some presidential powers to the legislature was apparently interpreted by Parliament as an attempt by the President to mitigate his personal responsibility in the event of any future economic or political crisis. Moreover, the session subsequently voted in favour of a parliamentary amendment whereby the presidential election would take place before the expiry of Nazarbayev's extended mandate in 2000. Other amendments included an increase in the minimum age for presidential candidates from 35 to 40 years and the abolition of the upper age limit (of 65 years); parties were, henceforth, required to win at least 7% of the votes cast in a general election, in order to secure representation (previously, the minimum requirement was 10%). Although it was reported that Nazarbayev had agreed to an early presidential election only under threat of impeachment, there was considerable speculation that the dispute between the executive and legislature had been orchestrated by the President's supporters in order to facilitate Nazarbayev's re-election with an extended mandate.

During November 1998 several opposition figures were deemed ineligible to contest the presidency by the Central Electoral Commission, in accordance with a presidential decree, enacted in May, which prevented those convicted of an administrative offence in the 12 months prior to an election from registering as a candidate. The most prominent disqualification was that of former Prime Minister Kazhegeldin, on the grounds of attending a meeting of an unauthorized political organization, the Movement for Honest Elections; he had been widely considered to be Nazarbayev's principal rival. Kazhegeldin subsequently established a new political party, the Republican People's Party of Kazakhstan (RPPK), which was inaugurated in mid-December. A number of other opposition parties were formed in late 1998 and early 1999, although applications for registration by many of these were rejected by the Ministry of Justice. Among those to be accorded official status was a new pro-presidential party, Otan (Fatherland).

The Organization for Security and Co-operation in Europe (OSCE, see p. 283) was among international bodies to express serious concern at the conduct of the election campaign, in particular the exclusion of opposition candidates. Despite appeals for a postponement, voting proceeded on 10 January 1999, and resulted in a victory for the incumbent, with 81.0% of the votes cast. The rate of participation was 88.3% of the registered electorate. The OSCE immediately denounced the result, and other international monitors also criticized the poll. Nazarbayev was sworn in on 20 January, and a new Government, under Balgymbayev, was appointed two days later. In late May nine opposition parties and social movements signed a memorandum urging the establishment of a 'single bloc of democratic forces against authoritarianism and dictatorship in Kazakhstan', denouncing the recent presidential election, and criticizing measures adopted by Nazarbayev in recent years to extend his presidential powers.

In August 1999 the President of KazakhOil, Nurlan Kaparov, was dismissed, accused by Nazarbayev of having exceeded his powers. Earlier that month both the Minister of Defence, Gen. Mukhtar Altynbayev, and the Chairman of the KNB, Nurtay Abikayev, had been dismissed, after admitting responsibility for the attempted illegal sale of MiG-21 fighter aircraft to the Democratic People's Republic of Korea. Although Bakhytzhan Yertayev was subsequently appointed acting Minister of Defence he, too, was accused of involvement in the scandal; despite his acquittal in early February 2000, he was dismissed from his position as Chief of the General Staff in May.

In early September 1999 Kazhegeldin, who had been charged with tax evasion in April, was arrested at Moscow airport, but released following criticism of his detention by the OSCE. None the less, owing to the outstanding charges against him, Kazhegeldin—together with two other leading members of the RPPK—was barred from registering as a candidate for the parliamentary election in October. Further charges were brought against him in late February 2000.

At a partial election to the Senate, held on 17 September 1999, 29 candidates contested 16 seats, representing 14 oblasts and the cities of Astana and Almaty; the OSCE criticized the conduct of the election. In late September the RPPK announced that it would boycott the election to the Majlis, in protest at the severe restrictions imposed on opposition parties by the President, although some of the party's members would stand as independents. Elections to the Majlis (as well as to municipal and local councils) were held on 10 October. According to official reports, 65 candidates from nine political parties contested 10 seats allocated, for the first time, according to a party list system, and almost 500 candidates competed for the remaining 67 seats in single-mandate constituencies. Although all of the 10 party list seats were filled at the first round (with the pro-presidential Otan winning four seats and the CPK, the Agrarian Party of Kazakhstan and the Civic Party of Kazakhstan each taking two), only 20 of the 67 directly elected seats were filled, and a second round of voting was held on 24 October. (In three of the 47 'run-off' elections, voting was declared invalid and was repeated on 26 December.) Final results indicated that Otan was to be the largest political grouping in the new Majlis, with a total of 23 seats, with the Civic Party holding 13. Three other parties achieved representation, and 34 seats were taken by independent candidates. The rate of participation by voters was reported to be 62.6%. Observers from the OSCE cited numerous breaches of electoral law and claimed that its officials had been denied access to several key locations during the vote-counting.

In early October 1999, prior to the parliamentary election, Balgymbayev resigned the premiership and returned to his former position as President of KazakhOil. He was replaced as Prime Minister by Kasymzhomart Tokayev, a former Minister of Foreign Affairs. A government reorganization followed.

In May 2000 a new opposition party, the Party of Patriots of Kazakhstan (PPK), was formed by Gani Kasymov, a presidential candidate in January 1999. In late June 2000 a law was passed awarding President Nazarbayev certain guarantees and rights, as the first President of Kazakhstan, which were to remain in place even after the expiry of his term of office. Despite opposition protests, the Constitutional Court upheld the legislation in the following month. In September the President signed a decree, which authorized greater independence for the judiciary. In December President Nazarbayev carried out a government reorganization, including the abolition of a number of ministries and state agencies. A further, minor government reorganization was carried out in May 2001.

In mid-June 2001 a month-long amnesty was declared, to allow the return of capital that had been transferred abroad in violation of tax laws and other financial legislation; the Chairman of the National Bank consequently announced that US $480m. had been returned to domestic banks. However, the amnesty attracted criticism from exiled former Prime Minister Kazhegeldin, who claimed that the sale of petroleum alone had accounted for some $2,000m. in illegal transfers to Caribbean banks in 2000. In September 2001 Kazhegeldin, who had been tried *in absentia* on charges of abuse of power, tax evasion and the illegal possession of weapons, was sentenced to 10 years' imprisonment, amid allegations that his trial had been politically motivated.

In mid-September 2001, following the large-scale attacks on the USA, attributed to the al-Qa'ida (Base) organization of the Saudi-born militant Islamist, Osama bin Laden, President Nazarbayev expressed his support for US-led retaliatory attacks against al-Qa'ida militants and the regime of their hosts, the Taliban, in Afghanistan; Kazakhstan also offered the USA the use of airports, airspace and military bases. In response to subsequent increased discontent on the Afghan–Tajik border, the Majlis approved legislative amendments to facilitate the greater mobility of internal troops.

In mid-November 2001 Nazarbayev approved the resignation of Rakhat Aliyev as Deputy Chairman of the National Security Committee, amid accusations of abuse of power. Persistent reports that Aliyev, the husband of Nazarbayev's daughter, Dariga, controlled the majority of Kazakhstan's media outlets, and influenced their output, prompted the Akim (Governor) of Pavlodar Oblast, Galymzhan Zhakiyanov, and a number of other prominent political and business figures, including the Deputy Prime Minister, Uraz Dzhandosov, to announce the formation of a new political movement, the Democratic Choice of Kazakhstan (DCK), in late November. The DCK, which aimed to revive democratic reform, decentralize political power and ensure the freedom of the mass media, criticized the concentration of power among members of Nazarbayev's family and a small group of leading entrepreneurs. Prime Minister Tokayev subsequently announced that two attempts to assassinate the President had recently been averted, and threatened to tender his resignation unless the President dismissed Zhakiyanov, Dzhandosov, the Minister of Labour and Social Security, Alikhan Baymenov, and the Deputy Minister of Defence, whom he denounced as disloyal and accused of destabilizing the domestic situation, owing to their involvement in the formation of the DCK. Dzhandosov, Baymenov and two deputy ministers resigned shortly afterwards, announcing that they were unable to work with the Prime Minister; Nazarbayev dismissed Zhakiyanov on the same day. Meanwhile, at the end of November 16 opposition parties and groups, aligned in the Forum of Democratic Forces, met to demand publicly Nazarbayev's resignation. In the following month the Azamat Democratic Party, the PCPK and Akezhan Kazhegeldin's RPPK announced their intention to merge to form the United Democratic Party (UDP). The UDP, which was established in early 2002, declared its main aim to be the creation of a parliamentary republic, with a unicameral legislature and a new constitution, to be adopted by means of a referendum.

Meanwhile, in early December 2001 Gen. Mukhtar Altynbayev, who had been dismissed as Minister of Defence following a scandal in 1999 (see above), was reappointed to the post, replacing Lt-Gen. Sat Tokpakbayev. In January 2002 amendments to media legislation came into effect, which required 50% of all radio and television programmes to be broadcast in Kazakh, restricted the rebroadcast of foreign (mainly Russian) television programmes, and subjected internet sites to the same controls as print media. In mid-January a further assassination attempt against the President, attributed to international terrorist organizations, was reported to have been thwarted by the security services. In late January Prime Minister Tokayev announced his resignation; the entire Government duly resigned, in accordance with the Constitution. Some observers believed Tokayev's resignation to have been prompted by divisions within the political élite, and others agreed that the high-profile ministerial resignations of November 2001 had discredited the Prime Minister. Divisions also emerged within the DCK in late January 2002, when a number of its founding members, including Dzhandosov and Zhakiyanov, announced their intention to found a new opposition party, Ak Zhol (Light Road), which held its founding congress in mid-March. On 31 January a new Government was sworn in, led by a former Deputy Prime Minister, Imangali Tasmagambetov; Tokayev was appointed State Secretary and Minister of Foreign Affairs. At the same time the legislature approved amendments to the laws on terrorism and religion, imposing more severe sentences for attacks against state officials and restricting the operation of unregistered religious organizations.

In March 2002 a warrant was issued for the arrest of Zhakiyanov, on charges of abuse of power during his tenure as Governor of Pavlodar oblast. He subsequently sought refuge in the French embassy until early April, when an agreement was reached between the Government and the ambassadors of France, Germany, the United Kingdom and the USA that Zhakiyanov would be permitted to go free until an investigation into the allegations had been carried out. However, less than one week later he was arrested and flown from Almaty to Pavlodar, in contravention of the agreement, to assist the police there with their enquiries. In mid-May it was reported that Zhakiyanov had been admitted to hospital following interrogation by security officials.

Meanwhile, in early April 2002 Tasmagambetov admitted that a clandestine foreign bank account, funded by the sale of a 20% stake in the large Tengiz oilfield, had been established in 1996, in an attempt to avoid sudden large increases in consumer-price inflation. The Prime Minister stated that the account's foundation had been authorized by Kazhegeldin, and that money from the account had been used to settle pensions' arrears in 1997–98. The remaining funds had subsequently been transferred to the National Fund, which was officially established in 2001. In response to the revelations, opposition leaders from the oil-producing regions of western Kazakhstan announced their intention to establish a People's Oil Fund, to monitor the Government's economic activities and to promote transparency in its financial affairs.

At the end of April 2002 a new National Council was established by presidential decree, to function as an advisory and consultative body. In late May the Minister of Agriculture, Akhmetzhan Yesimov, was appointed to the additional position of Deputy Prime Minister. In the following month the former Minister of Transport and Communications, Abylai Myrzakhmetov, was arrested; he had been dismissed in April, owing to allegations of embezzlement during his previous role as General Director of Kazakhstan Railways, and replaced by Kazhmurat Nagmanov. In mid-July Nazarbayev signed into law controversial new legislation on political parties, which required a party to demonstrate that it had at least 50,000 members (rather than the previous 3,000), representing every region of the country, in order to qualify for registration. All parties were required to re-register. In the same month a former Minister of Energy, Industry and Trade and founding member of the DCK, Mukhtar Ablyazov, was sentenced to six years' imprisonment, having been found guilty of abuse of office. Zhakiyanov's trial commenced in July, and he was sentenced to a seven-year term in early August. Human rights organizations expressed alarm at the severity of the sentence, and there were claims that the charges against him had been politically motivated.

In late August 2002 Nazarbayev carried out a major reorganization of the Government, abolishing the Ministry of State Revenues, and establishing a new Ministry of Industry and Trade. Aleksandr Pavlov was appointed First Deputy Prime Minister. On 8 October partial elections to fill 16 seats in the Senate took place. Otan retained the largest representation in the Senate of any party, accounting for 18 of the upper chamber's 47 members. By-elections took place in late December, to fill three empty seats in the Majlis.

In early January 2003 it was reported that the leader of the moderate opposition party Ak Zhol, Uraz Dzhandosov, had been appointed as an aide to President Nazarbayev, suggesting to many observers, therefore, that the party was supportive of the incumbent leadership. In the same month the DCK's party registration was annulled by the Ministry of Justice, and in mid-January the establishment of a new opposition bloc, Democracy-Elections-Kazakhstan, was announced, with the aim of uniting those parties prevented from re-registering by the new legislation on political parties. In late January Sergei Duvanov, an independent journalist, was convicted of rape and sentenced to over three years' imprisonment. He had been arrested in October 2002, shortly before he was due to travel to the USA to speak about press freedoms and human rights issues. Duvanov's conviction prompted the US embassy to express concern about judicial procedure during his trial, and in mid-February 2003 the European Parliament adopted a resolution condemning the sentences awarded to Duvanov and the opposition politicians Ablyazov and Zhakiyanov, and demanding that an independent investigation into their trials be carried out. Ablyasov was pardoned in May, and subsequently announced his withdrawal from politics.

Relations between Kazakhstan and neighbouring Russia, the most influential CIS member, have periodically been strained by the issue of Kazakhstan's large Russian minority (comprising some 35.8% of the total population at the beginning of 1994). In early 1997 draft legislation to enhance the status of the Kazakh language attracted criticism from ethnic Russians resident in Kazakhstan. In July Parliament reconfirmed Kazakh as the state language, although Russian was to retain its parity with Kazakh in state organizations and as a language of inter-ethnic communication. According to official statistics, 72.4% of emigrants from Kazakhstan in 1997 departed for Russia.

The issue of the legal status of the Caspian Sea—and the division of the substantial mineral resources believed to be located in the seabed—was a further source of tension between Kazakhstan and Russia, as well as the other littoral states (Azerbaijan, Turkmenistan and Iran). Nevertheless, in July 1998 Nazarbayev and the Russian President, Boris Yeltsin, signed a bilateral agreement on the delineation of their respective boundaries of the Caspian seabed, by which Russia for the first time formally recognized Kazakhstan's claim to, and right to exploit, its offshore petroleum resources. The arrangement attracted particular criticism from Iran, which continued to assert that partitioning of the seabed required the consensus of all five littoral states. In October 2000 the Presidents of Kazakhstan and Russia signed an additional agreement, on the definition of the legal status of the Caspian Sea, and the 1998 agreement was further augmented in May 2002, when an accord was signed on the equal division of three oilfields in the northern Caspian, prompting condemnation by Iran. The accord was ratified by Nazarbayev in November. Russia and Kazakhstan have also signed a Treaty of Eternal Friendship and Co-operation, which provides for mutual military assistance in the event of aggression by a third party. In November 2001 Kazakhstan concluded a bilateral agreement with Azerbaijan on the two countries' respective mineral rights in the Caspian Sea, prompting further protests from Iran.

As the largest and most influential of the five Central Asian republics of the former USSR, Kazakhstan has been regarded as a potential guarantor of peace in the region. However, the issue of the formerly Soviet, subsequently Russian-controlled, nuclear warheads deployed in Kazakhstan (effectively making the country the fourth largest nuclear power in the world) was the focus of international concern. Following the dissolution of the USSR, Kazakhstan asserted its commitment to rid itself of its nuclear weapons, either by their destruction or transfer to Russia. In September 1992 the Kazakh legislature ratified the first Strategic Arms Reduction Treaty, signed by the USA and the USSR in July 1991, the provisions of which affected Kazakh-

stan as a (nuclear) successor state to the USSR. In December 1993 the Kazakh legislature ratified the Treaty on the Non-Proliferation of Nuclear Weapons (International Atomic Energy Agency, see p. 82). The USA provided Kazakhstan with substantial technical and financial aid for the dismantling of its nuclear arsenal. By April 1995 all nuclear warheads had been transferred to Russia, and in September 1996 Russia and Kazakhstan signed a final protocol governing the withdrawal of military units linked to the Russian nuclear weapons facilities in Kazakhstan. In November 2001 the Kazakh legislature ratified the Comprehensive Nuclear Test Ban Treaty. In late 2000, as a result of escalating conflict in Kyrgyzstan and Uzbekistan, Kazakhstan assumed a peace-making role, offering to provide military assistance to the two countries.

In April 2001, at a meeting of leaders of the Turkic-speaking countries, the Presidents of Azerbaijan, Kazakhstan, Kyrgyzstan, Turkey and Turkmenistan, and the Chairman of the Uzbek legislature signed an agreement on regional co-operation to combat terrorism and drugs-trafficking, to revive the old 'Silk Road' trade route between the People's Republic of China and Europe, and to ensure further protection of the environment. One month later the signatories of the CIS Collective Security Treaty—Armenia, Belarus, Kazakhstan, Kyrgyzstan, Russia and Tajikistan—agreed to form a Collective Rapid Reaction Force in Bishkek, Kyrgyzstan, to combat Islamist militancy in Central Asia; in January 2002 it was announced that the force was ready to undertake combat missions. An anti-terrorism centre became operational in Bishkek in August 2001. The US-led attacks against the al-Qa'ida organization and the Taliban regime in Afghanistan in late 2001 drew international attention to Central Asia, and the USA, in particular, acknowledged Kazakhstan's strategic importance. It was hoped that foreign interest in the region would lead to greater investment.

In July and October 1999 Russian craft exploded following their launch from the Baikonur space centre at Turatam, causing considerable damage to the surrounding area. The accidents provoked anger among local residents, environmentalists and the Kazakh Government, which responded by suspending launches of Russian-made rockets from Baikonur. In November Russia agreed to pay outstanding rental fees of US \$115m. and an undisclosed sum in compensation for the damage incurred and to improve facilities at Baikonur. The restriction on Russian launches was lifted in February 2000, and in June Kazakhstan and Russia reached agreement on the terms for Russia's continued use of the Baikonur space centre.

In 1992 Kazakhstan, together with other Central Asian states, joined the Economic Co-operation Organization (ECO, see p. 192), founded originally by Iran, Pakistan and Turkey). The Government, eager to establish good relations with the international community, explained that its intention was to facilitate economic activity, rather than to create an Islamist bloc. In early 1994 Kazakhstan and the neighbouring CIS states of Kyrgyzstan and Uzbekistan formed a trilateral economic area, and in February 1995 an Interstate Council was established to supervise its implementation. Several agreements to expand economic co-operation were signed by the three countries in 1996, and in December 1997 the Council met in Akmola (now Astana) to discuss the possibility of full economic integration. In March 1998 Tajikistan joined the alliance, which was renamed the Central Asian Co-operation Organization in March 2002. Meanwhile, in January 1995 Kazakhstan established a customs union with Russia and Belarus, and in March 1996 the three members of the customs union were joined by Kyrgyzstan in signing a treaty aimed at creating a 'community of integrated states'. The treaty provided for the closer integration of the signatories' economies, as well as of their cultural and social affairs; Tajikistan joined the union in April 1998. Kazakhstan, with other CIS countries, contributed troops to the peace-keeping force in Tajikistan. In October 2000 a new economic body, the Eurasian Economic Community (EAEC), was established to supersede the customs union. The EAEC was to have its own institutions, staff and budget, and had as its objective the creation of common policies on currencies, customs tariffs, employment and tax. In September 2002 President Nazarbayev and the President of Uzbekistan, Islam Karimov, signed a bilateral agreement on the delimitation of remaining sectors of their common border (another border agreement had been signed in the previous year).

Kazakhstan expressed concern at the underground nuclear tests carried out in the early 1990s by the People's Republic of China at Lop Nor in the Xinjiang Uygur Autonomous Region, which borders eastern Kazakhstan. In 1995 Nazarbayev made an official visit to China, where an agreement was signed to improve long-term stability between the two countries. Bilateral relations were further strengthened by two accords concluded in 1997, whereby China was granted permission to exploit two of the largest oilfields in Kazakhstan. The agreements, worth an estimated US $9,500m., provided, *inter alia*, for the construction of a petroleum pipeline connecting the two countries, although work on the project had not commenced by 2003. In July 1998 Nazarbayev and President Jiang Zemin of China signed an agreement concerning disputed areas of their joint border, and agreed to a 15-year programme of bilateral economic co-operation. The agreement was ratified by the Kazakh legislature in February 1999. In late November Nazarbayev made another state visit to China, which resulted in the signing of a communiqué on the full settlement of outstanding border issues, and of an agreement outlining future bilateral relations. In addition, China and Kazakhstan attended annual summit meetings of the heads of state of the so-called Shanghai Five (also comprising Kyrgyzstan, the Russian Federation and Tajikistan), which promotes economic co-operation and regional co-ordination on border and security issues. Members of the alliance, later known as the Shanghai Forum, and renamed the Shanghai Co-operation Organization, (see p. 351) upon the accession of Uzbekistan in mid-2001, signed the Shanghai Convention on Combating Terrorism, Separatism and Extremism in mid-June 2001.

Government

Under the terms of the 1995 Constitution (to which a number of amendments were made in October 1998), the President of the Republic is Head of State and commander-in-chief of the armed forces, and holds broad executive powers. The President is directly elected by universal adult suffrage for a seven-year term (and may serve a maximum of two consecutive terms). The Government, headed by the Prime Minister, is responsible to the President. The supreme legislative organ is the bicameral Parliament, comprising the 47-member Senate (upper chamber) and the 67-member Majlis (Assembly, lower chamber). Seven Senators are appointed by the President of the Republic, while the remaining 40 are elected for six years by regional assemblies. The deputies of the Majlis are directly elected every six years. The seven-member Constitutional Council is empowered to ensure the correct implementation of the Constitution; its rulings are subject to a presidential right of veto.

For administrative purposes, Kazakhstan is divided into 16 local governments (14 regions and the cities of Almaty and Astana). (The city of Leninsk—now Turatam—serving the Baikonur space centre, and formerly one of Kazakhstan's administrative units, was transferred to Russian jurisdiction in August 1995, for a period of 20 years.)

Defence

In May 1992 President Nazarbayev issued a decree on the establishment of Kazakhstan's armed forces (until independence, Kazakhstan had no armed forces separate from those of the USSR). By August 2002 the estimated strength of the national armed forces was 60,000 (army 41,000 and air force 19,000). In addition, there were 34,500 paramilitary troops (including an estimated 20,000 troops attached to the Ministry of Internal Affairs, and an estimated 12,000 border guards). In March 1998 the Kazakh Ministry of Defence reportedly announced that the strength of the armed forces was to be halved by reducing the period of military service for junior ranks from two years to one. Kazakhstan participates, with Russia, Azerbaijan and Turkmenistan, in the operation of the Caspian Sea Flotilla, a former Soviet force based, under Russian command, at Astrakhan (Russia). In mid-1992 Kazakhstan signed a Collective Security Treaty with five other members of the Commonwealth of Independent States; in May 2001 it was announced that the signatory countries were to form a Collective Rapid Reaction Force to combat Islamist militancy in Central Asia. A nuclear successor state to the USSR, Kazakhstan undertook to dismantle its nuclear capabilities, ratifying the first Strategic Arms Reduction Treaty in 1992 and the Treaty on the Non-Proliferation of Nuclear Weapons in 1993 (in the mean time, Kazakhstan's nuclear arsenal remained under Russian control). All nuclear warheads had been transferred to Russia by mid-1995, and a final protocol for the withdrawal of the Russian strategic-missile troops was signed in September 1996. In July 2000 the Semipalatinsk nuclear facility, once the world's largest nuclear-testing ground, was finally closed. In late 2001 Kazakhstan ratified the Comprehensive Nuclear Test Ban Treaty. In

May 1994 Kazakhstan joined NATO's 'Partnership for Peace' programme (see p. 273) of military co-operation. Kazakhstan also became a full member of the UN Conference on Disarmament in August 1999. The defence budget for 2001 was an estimated 34,900m. tenge.

Economic Affairs

In 2001, according to estimates by the World Bank, Kazakhstan's gross national income (GNI), measured at average 1999–2001 prices, was US $20,146m., equivalent to $1,360 per head (or $6,370 per head on an international purchasing-power parity basis). During 1990–2001, it was estimated, the population decreased at an average annual rate of 0.8%, while gross domestic product (GDP) per head decreased, in real terms, by an average of 1.7% per year. Overall GDP declined, in real terms, at an average annual rate of 2.2% in 1990–2001. However, GDP increased by 13.2% in 2001 and by 9.5% in 2002.

Agriculture (including forestry and fishing) contributed an estimated 8.7% of GDP in 2001, and the sector provided 22.0% of total employment in 1999. There are large areas of land suitable for agriculture, and Kazakhstan is a major producer and exporter of agricultural products. The principal crops include fruit, sugar beet, vegetables, potatoes, cotton and, most importantly, cereals. Livestock-breeding is also important, and Kazakhstan is a significant producer of karakul and astrakhan wools. The GDP of the agricultural sector decreased, in real terms, by an average of 5.9% per year in 1990–2001. However, agricultural GDP increased by 2.1% in 2001, and there was growth of 2.7% in 2002.

Industry (including mining, manufacturing, construction, and power) contributed an estimated 37.5% of GDP in 2001. The sector provided 18.3% of total employment in 1999. Measured by the gross value of output, the principal branches of industry in 1997 were the fuel industry (accounting for 27.7% of the total), metal-processing (23.9%), food-processing (15.4%) and electrical power generation (14.1%). Industrial GDP declined, in real terms, at an average annual rate of 5.5% in 1990–2001. However, the GDP of the sector increased by 15.5% in 2001, and there was growth of 9.8% in 2002.

Mining and quarrying provided 2.0% of employment in 1998. Kazakhstan possesses immense mineral wealth, and large-scale mining and processing industries have been developed. There are major coalfields (in the Karaganda, Turgai, Ekibastuz and Maikuben basins), as well as substantial deposits of iron ore, lead, zinc ore, titanium, magnesium, chromium, tungsten, molybdenum, gold, silver, copper and manganese. Petroleum is extracted, and Kazakhstan possesses what are believed to be among the world's largest unexploited oilfields (in the Caspian depression) and substantial reserves of natural gas. The discovery of major petroleum reserves at the offshore Kashagan oilfield was announced in mid-2000. At the end of 2001 Kazakhstan's proven total reserves (onshore and offshore) of petroleum and natural gas were estimated at 1,100m. metric tons and 1,840,000m. cu m, respectively.

Manufacturing provided 10.2% of employment in 1998, and an estimated 20.2% of GDP in 2001. The GDP of the manufacturing sector declined at an average annual rate of 23.2% in 1990–95.

In 1999 coal-fired thermal power stations provided about 72.0% of annual domestic electricity production, while hydro-electric power stations accounted for 12.9%. Kazakhstan was obliged to import some 6.6% of its annual fuel requirements in 2000.

The services sector contributed some 53.9% of GDP in 2001, and provided 59.8% of employment in 1999. During 1990–2001 the GDP of the services sector increased, in real terms, at an average annual rate of 2.3%. Services GDP increased by 7.4% in 2000 and by 5.8% in 2001.

In 2001 Kazakhstan recorded a visible trade surplus of US $1,175.0m., and there was a deficit of $1,240.3m. on the current account of the balance of payments. In 2001 the principal sources of imports were Russia (accounting for 45.0% of total imports), Germany and the People's Republic of China. The principal markets for exports in that year were Bermuda (16.1% of total exports), Russia, Germany, China, Switzerland and Italy. The main exports in 2000 were petroleum and gas condensate, metals (in particular rolled iron and steel and refined copper), and cereals. The principal imports in that year were machinery and electrical equipment, vehicles, non-food consumer goods and refined petroleum products.

In 2001 Kazakhstan recorded an overall budgetary deficit of 5,542m. tenge (equivalent to some 0.1% of GDP). Kazakhstan's total external debt was US $6,664m. at the end of 2000, of which

$3,602m. was long-term public debt. In that year the cost of debt-servicing was equivalent to 16.8% of the value of exports of goods and services. The annual rate of inflation averaged 112.8% during 1992–2001. However, the inflation rate slowed from the latter half of the 1990s; consumer prices increased by 8.4% in 2001 and by 6.6% in 2002. In 2001 10.4% of the labour force were unemployed.

In addition to its membership of the economic bodies of the CIS, Kazakhstan has joined the Asian Development Bank (ADB, see p. 143), is a 'Country of Operations' of the European Bank for Reconstruction and Development (EBRD, see p. 193), and is a member of the ECO.

Following independence in 1991, contraction in all sectors was recorded annually until 1995, when signs of an economic recovery emerged. Through a comprehensive programme of stabilization and reform (launched in 1993, with support from the international financial community), the Government succeeded in curbing a drastically high level of inflation (which had reached 1,877% in 1994), while rationalizing the banking and financial sectors. A large-scale programme of privatization was extended in 1996 to include the strategic hydrocarbons and metallurgical sectors, thereby raising the level of foreign direct investment (already the highest per head among the CIS countries). In 1998 the economy was severely affected by the economic crises in Russia and Asia, and the subsequent decline in world prices of Kazakhstan's principal exports. In April 1999, following a sharp decline in its value against the US dollar, the tenge was made freely convertible on foreignexchange markets. By mid-2000 Kazakhstan announced that it had been able to repay fully all outstanding debts owed to the IMF, seven years ahead of schedule, as the result of improved regional demand, increased world petroleum prices and prudent macroeconomic policies. Strong economic growth was recorded in 2001, despite that year's global economic downturn, and the high rate of growth continued in 2002. Kazakhstan's long-term economic prospects were considered to be highly favourable, owing to the country's immense, and largely unexploited, hydrocarbons and other mineral resources. Petroleum exports increased significantly, following the official opening, in November 2001, of a new, 1,500-km petroleum pipeline, connecting the onshore Tengiz field in western Kazakhstan with Novorossiisk, on the Russian Black Sea coast. Another development, which was expected to have great economic impact, was the discovery, announced in July 2000, of substantial petroleum deposits at the offshore Kashagan oilfield, thought to be the world's second largest. The extraction of petroleum and natural gas was expected to expand significantly as a result of bilateral agreements with Azerbaijan and Russia on the division of mineral resources in the Caspian seabed. The Government also hoped to implement a programme for the diversification of the economy, although growth in the non-petroleum sector remained highly dependent on the implementation of further structural reforms, the liberalization of trade and an improved business environment.

Education

General education (primary and secondary) is compulsory, and is fully funded by the state. Primary education begins at seven years of age and lasts for four years. Secondary education, beginning at 11 years of age, lasts for a further seven years, comprising a first cycle of five years and a second of two years. In 1996/97 total enrolment at primary schools was equivalent to 98% of the relevant age-group (males 97%; females 98%), and the comparable ratio for secondary enrolment was 87% (males 82%; females 91%). After completing general education, pupils may continue their studies at specialized secondary schools. In 2000/01 there was a total of 170 higher schools (including universities), with a total enrolment of 440,700 students. Ethnic Kazakhs form a greater proportion (64% in 1995/96) of students in higher education than in general education, since many ethnic Russians choose to study at universities outside Kazakhstan. None the less, the majority of higher education students (approximately 75% in 1997) are instructed in Russian. The number of private general schools in Kazakhstan increased from 18 in 1994/95 to 199 in 1999, as part of a government programme to encourage the private provision of education, although this figure had declined to 153 by 2000. In that year there were 117 private specialized secondary schools and 112 private higher schools (including universities). Government expenditure on education in 2001 was 105,024m. tenge (14.7% of total spending).

Public Holidays

2003: 1–2 January (New Year), 8 March (International Women's Day), 22 March (Nauryz Meyramy, Spring Holiday), 1 May (Day of Unity of Nationalities of Kazakhstan), 9 May (Victory Day, Day of Remembrance), 30 August (Constitution Day), 25 October (Republic Day), 16 December (Independence Day).

2004: 1–2 January (New Year), 8 March (International Women's Day), 22 March (Nauryz Meyramy, Spring Holiday), 1 May (Day of Unity of Nationalities of Kazakhstan), 9 May (Victory Day, Day of Remembrance), 30 August (Constitution Day), 25 October (Republic Day), 16 December (Independence Day).

Weights and Measures

The metric system is in force.

Statistical Survey

Source (unless otherwise stated): Agency on Statistics of the Republic of Kazakhstan, 480008 Almaty, pr. Abaya 125; tel. (3272) 62-66-45; fax (3272) 42-08-24; e-mail kazstat@mail.banknet.kz; internet www.stat.kz.

Area and Population

AREA, POPULATION AND DENSITY

Area (sq km)	2,717,300*
Population (census results)	
12 January 1989†	16,464,464
25 February–4 March 1999	
Males	7,201,785
Females	7,751,341
Total	14,953,126
Population (official estimates at 31 December)	
1999	14,896,100
2000	14,841,900
2001	14,820,900‡
Density (per sq km) at 31 December 2001	5.5

* 1,049,150 sq miles.

† Figure refers to the *de jure* population. The *de facto* total was 16,536,511.

‡ Provisional figure.

PRINCIPAL ETHNIC GROUPS

(permanent inhabitants, at 1999 census)

	Number*	%
Kazakh	7,985,000	53.4
Russian	4,479,600	30.0
Ukrainian	547,100	3.7
Uzbek	370,700	2.5
German	353,400	2.4
Tatar	249,000	1.7
Uigur	210,400	1.4
Belarusian	111,900	0.7
Korean	99,700	0.7
Azeri	78,300	0.5
Turkish	75,900	0.5
Others	392,100	2.6
Total	14,953,100	100.0

* Figures are rounded to the nearest 100 persons.

PRINCIPAL TOWNS
(population at 1999 census)

Astana* (capital)	313,000	Petropavlovsk	203,500
Almaty (Alma-Ata)	1,129,400	Uralsk	195,500
Karaganda	436,900	Temirtau	170,500
Chimkent	360,100	Kzyl-Orda	157,400
Taraz†	330,100	Aktau§	143,400
Ust-Kamenogorsk	311,000	Atyrau‖	142,500
Pavlodar	300,500	Ekibastuz	127,200
Semipalatinsk	269,600	Kokchetau	123,400
Aktobe‡	253,100	Rudniy	109,500
Kustanai	221,400		

* Formerly Akmola.
† Formerly Dzhambul.
‡ Formerly Aktyubinsk.
§ Formerly Shevchenko.
‖ Formerly Guriyev.

Mid-2000 (UN estimate, incl. suburbs): Almaty (Alma-Ata) 1,127,000 (Source: UN, *World Urbanization Prospects: The 2001 Revision*).

Mid-2001 (UN estimate, incl. suburbs): Astana 328,000 (Source: UN, *World Urbanization Prospects: The 2001 Revision*).

BIRTHS, MARRIAGES AND DEATHS

	Registered live births		Registered marriages		Registered deaths	
	Number	Rate (per 1,000)	Number	Rate (per 1,000)	Number	Rate (per 1,000)
1994	306,509	18.8	123,280	7.6	160,590	9.9
1995	277,006	17.2	116,380	7.2	168,885	10.5
1996	253,175	16.3	102,558	6.6	166,028	10.7
1997	232,356	15.2	101,874	6.6	160,138	10.4
1998	222,380	14.8	96,048	6.4	154,314	10.2
1999	209,039	14.0	85,872	5.8	144,450	9.7
2000	217,379	14.6	90,873	6.1	148,834	10.0
2001*	220,748	14.8	92,852	6.3	147,587	10.0

* Provisional figures.

Source: partly UN, *Demographic Yearbook* and *Population and Vital Statistics Report*.

Expectation of life (years at birth): 63.0 (males 58.8; females 67.2) in 2001 (Source: WHO, *World Health Report*).

ECONOMICALLY ACTIVE POPULATION
(annual averages, '000 persons)

	1997	1998	1999
Agriculture, forestry and fishing	1,542	1,360	1,342
Industry*	921	903	904
Construction	261	223	211
Trade, restaurants and hotels	1,382	1,405	1,398
Transport, storage and communications	646	560	576
Financing and insurance	37	38	36
Community, social and personal services	1,387	1,639	1,638
Activities not adequately defined	296	—	—
Total employed	6,472	6,128	6,105
Unemployed	968	925	950
Total labour force	7,440	7,053	7,055

* Including mining and quarrying, manufacturing, and electricity, gas and water.

Source: UN, *Statistical Yearbook for Asia and the Pacific*.

2000 (annual average, '000 persons): Total employed 6,201.0; Unemployed 906.4; Total labour force 7,107.4.

2001 (annual average, '000 persons): Total employed 6,698.8; Unemployed 780.3; Total labour force 7,479.1.

2002 (annual average, '000 persons): Unemployed 690.7.

Health and Welfare

KEY INDICATORS

Total fertility rate (children per woman, 2001)	2.0
Under-5 mortality rate (per 1,000 live births, 2001)	76
HIV/AIDS (% of persons aged 15–49, 2001)	0.07
Physicians (per 1,000 head, 2001)	3.46
Hospital beds (per 1,000 head, 2001)	7.44
Health expenditure (2000): US $ per head (PPP)	211
Health expenditure (2000): % of GDP	3.7
Health expenditure (2000): public (% of total)	73.2
Access to water (% of persons, 2000)	91
Access to sanitation (% of persons, 2000)	99
Human Development Index (2000): ranking	79
Human Development Index (2000): value	0.750

For sources and definitions, see explanatory note on p. vi.

Agriculture

PRINCIPAL CROPS
('000 metric tons)

	1999	2000	2001
Wheat	11,241.9	9,073.5	12,500.0*
Rice (paddy)	199.3	214.3	262.2*
Barley	2,264.9	1,663.6	2,287.0*
Maize	197.6	248.8	310.0*
Rye	16.6	48.3	66.4*
Oats	194.2	181.8	250.0*
Millet	43.8	62.3	85.6*
Buckwheat	16.1	28.7	40.0*
Other cereals	74.0	25.6	70.0*
Potatoes	1,694.7	1,692.6	2,192.0
Sugar beet	293.9	272.7	283.0
Dry beans*	9.0	7.4	9.2
Dry peas*	6.6	9.2	13.6
Sunflower seed	104.3	104.6	149
Safflower seed	34.0	25.4	25.0†
Cottonseed	249.4	287.1	420.0
Cabbages	215.4	262.7	303.5*
Tomatoes	300.6	387.0	447.2*
Cucumbers and gherkins*	162.0	190.6	220.2
Aubergines (Eggplants)*	18.0	21.5	24.8
Chillies and green peppers*	32	34.0	39.3
Dry onions*	280.0	302.0	348.9
Carrots	128.2	163.6	189.1*
Other vegetables*	285.4	316.0	214.1
Apples	64.0*	144.6	132.4*
Pears	7.5*	10.2	9.4*
Grapes	26.8	61.6	40.0†
Watermelons	369.6	421.6	450.0†
Tobacco (leaves)	8.0	16.2	19.0†
Cotton (lint)	66.7	83.0*	142.0*

* Unofficial figure(s).
† FAO estimate.

Source: FAO.

LIVESTOCK
('000 head, year ending September)

	1999	2000	2001
Horses	986	970	976
Asses*	29	30	30
Cattle	3,958	3,998	4,107
Buffaloes*	9	9	9
Camels	96	96	99†
Pigs	892	984	1,076
Sheep	8,691	8,725	8,939
Goats	835	931	1,042
Chickens	16,985	18,023	19,706
Rabbits*	58,000	60,000	61,500

* FAO estimates.
† Unofficial figure.

Source: FAO.

LIVESTOCK PRODUCTS
('000 metric tons)

	1999	2000	2001
Beef and veal	343.9	306.3	358.7*
Mutton and lamb*	94.7	87.2	117.5
Goat meat*	4.0	3.9	5.0
Horse meat	64.8	57.9	66.6*
Pig meat	97.7	133.4	81.2*
Poultry meat	29.3	33.3	24.7*
Rabbit meat*	0.4	0.4	0.5
Cows' milk	3,535.2	3,730.2	3,922.9
Sheeps' milk	31.6*	34.8*	35†
Goats' milk	9.9	9.7	10.5†
Cheese	6.3	6.8†	6.7†
Butter	3.2*	4.4	3.9
Hen eggs*	84.0	93.8	103.0
Wool: greasy	22.3	22.9	23.6
Wool: scoured	13.4	13.7	14.2
Cattle hides (fresh) . . .	37.8	34.8	39.9†
Sheepskins (fresh)	10.4	9.9	13.0†

* Unofficial figure(s).
† FAO estimate.

Source: FAO.

Forestry

ROUNDWOOD REMOVALS
('000 cubic metres, excl. bark)

	1995	1996	1997
Total (all fuel wood)	339	315	315

Source: FAO.

SAWNWOOD PRODUCTION
(unofficial figures, '000 cubic metres, incl. railway sleepers)

	1999	2000	2001
Coniferous (softwood)	191	261	261
Broadleaved (hardwood) . . .	146	199	199
Total	337	460	460

Source: FAO.

Fishing

('000 metric tons, live weight)

	1998	1999	2000
Capture	23.1	21.0	25.8
Freshwater bream*	9.8	8.9	10.9
Crucian carp*	2.1	1.9	2.3
Roaches*	1.3	1.2	1.4
Wels (Som) catfish* . . .	0.7	0.7	0.8
Pike-perch*	2.9	2.7	3.3
Azov sea sprat*	4.8	4.4	5.4
Aquaculture	1.1	1.2	1.2
Silver carp	1.0	1.1	1.1
Total catch	24.2	22.2	27.0

* FAO estimates.

Source: FAO, *Yearbook of Fishery Statistics*.

Mining
('000 metric tons, unless otherwise indicated)

	1998	1999	2000
Hard coal	68,058	58,378	74,872
Brown coal (incl. lignite) . . .	1,715		
Crude petroleum*	25,945	26,736	30,648
Natural gas (million cu m) . .	7,948	9,946	11,542
Iron ore (gross weight) . . .	8,693	9,617	13,829
Copper ore (metal content) . .	339	374	430
Nickel ore (metal content, metric tons)†	6,000	n.a.	3,000
Bauxite	3,437	3,607	3,730
Lead ore (metal content) . . .	30	34	39
Zinc ore (metal content) . . .	224	270	322
Manganese ore	399	563	720
Chromite	1,603	2,406	2,607
Titanium (metric tons) . . .	12,000	8,767	8,280
Vanadium (metal content, metric tons)†	1,000	1,000	1,000
Silver ore (metal content, metrictons)	726	905	927
Uranium (metal content, metric tons)	1,074	1,367	1,740
Gold (metal content, kg) . . .	18,100	20,236	28,171
Asbestos	155	139	233

* Including gas condensate.
† Estimates.

Source: mainly US Geological Survey.

Industry

SELECTED PRODUCTS
('000 metric tons, unless otherwise indicated)

	1998	1999	2000
Wheat flour	1,546	1,262	1,741
Raw sugar	230	228	280
Wine ('000 hectolitres) . . .	163	218	n.a.
Beer ('000 hectolitres) . . .	8,503	8,244	13,568
Mineral water ('000 hectolitres) .	475	549	n.a.
Cigarettes (million)	21,747	18,773	19,293
Cotton yarn	1.9	1.8	1.0
Woven cotton fabrics (million sq metres)	10	9	5
Sulphuric acid	605	685	635
Motor spirit (petrol)	1,732	1,298	1,255
Kerosene	229	71	63
Gas-diesel (distillate fuel) oils . .	2,495	1,830	1,954
Residual fuel oils	3,052	2,133	2,391
Cement	622	838	1,175
Pig-iron	2,594	3,438	4,010
Crude steel	3,116	4,105	4,799
Copper (unrefined)	335.0	384.2	n.a.
Electric energy (million kWh) . .	49,145	47,498	51,635

Sources: mainly UN, *Statistical Yearbook for Asia and the Pacific* and *Industrial Commodity Statistics Yearbook*.

Finance

CURRENCY AND EXCHANGE RATES

Monetary Units
100 tein = 1 tenge

Sterling, Dollar and Euro Equivalents (31 December 2002)
£1 sterling = 249.18 tenge
US $1 = 154.60 tenge
€1 = 162.13 tenge
1,000 tenge = £4.0.13 = $6.468 = €6.168

Average Exchange Rate (tenge per US $)
2000   142.13
2001   146.74
2002   153.28

Note: The tenge was introduced on 15 November 1993, replacing the old Russian (formerly Soviet) rouble at an exchange rate of 1 tenge = 500 roubles. On 18 November the rate was adjusted to 250 roubles per tenge. In April 1999 the tenge was allowed to 'float' on foreign exchange markets.

STATE BUDGET
(million tenge)

Revenue	1999	2000	2001*
Tax revenue	330,267	524,058	635,792
Other current revenue	26,896	38,602	70,539
Capital revenue	35,787	24,378	24,267
Official transfers	2,629	3,169	233
Repayment of debt principal	3,013	8,511	12,719
Total	398,592	598,746	743,550†

Expenditure‡	1999	2000	2001
General public services	28,856	35,114	47,771
Defence	17,198	20,379	32,347
Public order and security	32,507	47,738	63,681
Education	78,491	84,668	105,024
Health care	44,825	54,323	62,238
Social security and social assistance	159,064	171,065	186,641
Recreation and cultural activities	12,237	17,487	18,076
Housing and communal services	6,012	22,106	30,396
Economic affairs and services	48,794	87,761	132,188
Agriculture, forestry, water management, fishing and environmental protection	6,944	11,441	23,113
Mining and minerals (excl. fuel), manufacturing and construction	2,867	7,191	4,558
Transport and communications	12,865	37,804	41,651
Other purposes	19,442	35,541	37,764
Debt interest	19,442	35,541	37,764
Total	447,426	576,182	716,126

* Provisional figures.

† Including adjustment (28 million tenge).

‡ Excluding lending minus repayments (million tenge): 20,997 in 1999; 25,842 in 2000; 32,966 in 2001.

INTERNATIONAL RESERVES
(US $ million at 31 December)

	2000	2001	2002
Gold	501.5	510.7	585.6
IMF special drawing rights	—	—	1.0
Reserve position in IMF	0.01	0.01	0.1
Foreign exchange	1,594.1	1,997.2	2,549.7
Total	2,095.6	2,507.9	3,136.3

Source: IMF, *International Financial Statistics*.

MONEY SUPPLY
(million tenge at 31 December)

	2000	2001	2002
Currency outside banks	106,428	131,175	161,701
Demand deposits at commercial banks	126,124	137,014	219,423
Total money (incl. others)	236,163	270,009	381,935

Source: IMF, *International Financial Statistics*.

COST OF LIVING
(Consumer Price Index; base: 1992 = 100)

	1997	1998	1999
Food	50,946.3	53,208.3	57,161.7
Clothing	27,476.1	28,174.6	30,263.2
Rent	49,590.9	54,922.6	57,014.6
All items (incl. others)	62,775.9	67,245.5	72,833.6

2000: Food 66,302.0; All items 82,419.0.

Source: ILO.

2001: Food 73,894; All items 89,309 (Source: UN, *Monthly Bulletin of Statistics*).

NATIONAL ACCOUNTS
('000 million tenge at current prices)

Expenditure on the Gross Domestic Product

	1999	2000	2001*
Government final consumption expenditure	232.7	384.8	540.6
Private final consumption expenditure	1,460.1	1,620.2	1,926.1
Increase in stocks	32.2	21.3	102.4
Gross fixed capital formation	326.3	442.8	744.5
Total domestic expenditure	2,051.3	2,469.1	3,313.6
Exports of goods and services			
Less Imports of goods and services	47.3	246.4	−77.3
Sub-total	2,098.6	2,715.5	3,236.3
Statistical discrepancy†	−82.1	−115.6	49.1
GDP in purchasers' values	2,016.5	2,600.0	3,285.4
GDP at constant 1993 prices	24.4	26.7	30.2

* Provisional figures.

† Referring to the difference between the sum of the expenditure components and official estimates of GDP, compiled from the production approach.

Source: Asian Development Bank, *Key Indicators of Developing Asian and Pacific Countries*.

Gross Domestic Product by Economic Activity

	1999	2000	2001*
Agriculture, forestry and fishing	199.4	210.9	284.2
Industry†	569.1	864.7	1,051.9
Construction	95.7	134.6	178.6
Trade, restaurants and hotels	273.9	323.5	387.4
Transport, storage and communications	243.2	298.5	357.8
Other services			
Import duties			
Less Imputed bank service charges	635.2	767.8	1,025.5
GDP in purchasers' values	2,016.5	2,600.0	3,285.4

* Provisional figures.

† Including mining and quarrying, manufacturing, and electricity, gas and water.

Source: Asian Development Bank, *Key Indicators of Developing Asian and Pacific Countries*.

BALANCE OF PAYMENTS
(US $ million)

	1999	2000	2001
Exports of goods f.o.b.	5,988.7	9,288.1	9,024.8
Imports of goods f.o.b.	−5,645.0	−6,848.2	−7,849.8
Trade balance	343.7	2,439.9	1,175.0
Exports of services	932.5	1,132.8	1,279.6
Imports of services	−1,104.2	−2,156.6	−2,810.0
Balance on goods and services	172.0	1,416.1	−355.4
Other income received	108.6	138.8	233.8
Other income paid	−608.3	−1,333.0	−1,347.2
Balance on goods, services and income	−327.7	221.9	−1,470.0
Current transfers received	174.7	294.2	392.7
Current transfers paid	−18.0	−103.2	−163.0
Current balance	−171.0	412.9	−1,240.3
Capital account (net)	−234.0	−290.6	−197.3
Direct investment abroad	−3.6	−4.4	−15.5
Direct investment from abroad	1,587.0	1,282.5	2,763.0
Portfolio investment assets	−5.6	−85.5	−1,354.0
Portfolio investment liabilities	−39.9	30.7	31.7
Other investment assets	−778.4	43.6	514.5
Other investment liabilities	539.7	41.2	777.7
Net errors and omissions	−641.6	−1,122.7	−894.9
Overall balance	252.6	570.3	384.9

Source: IMF, *International Financial Statistics*.

External Trade

PRINCIPAL COMMODITIES
(US $ million)*

Imports c.i.f.	1998	1999	2000
Crude petroleum (incl. gas condensate)	146.9	21.3	79.9
Refined petroleum products . .	194.3	87.9	252.9
Electrical and non-electrical machinery	1,199.9	969.3	1,391.2
Foodstuffs	241.6	282.2	235.9
Non-food consumer goods . . .	356.0	410.8	427.6
Vehicles	434.0	629.9	564.8
Total (incl. others)	4,349.6	3,682.7	5,052.1

Exports f.o.b.	1998	1999	2000
Crude petroleum (incl. gas condensate)	1,650.5	2,040.2	4,502.4
Coal	323.2	152.0	168.5
Refined copper	507.9	525.6	669.1
Unrefined zinc	181.6	163.0	198.2
Iron ores and concentrates . . .	177.7	38.2	51.3
Ferro-alloys	224.0	212.9	293.4
Rolled iron and steel	515.7	599.9	764.1
Cereals	295.4	313.6	500.5
Total (incl. others)	5,435.8	5,592.2	9,139.5

* Figures refer to trade recorded by the customs authorities. After adjusting for operations excluded from customs statistics, shuttle transactions and, in the case of imports, other corrections (grants received, barter trade and a deduction for freight charges), the value of total trade (in US $ million), on an f.o.b. basis, was: Imports 6,726.1 in 1998, 5,645.0 in 1999, 6,849.8 in 2000; Exports 5,870.6 in 1998, 5,988.5 in 1999, 9,604.0 in 2000.

Source: IMF, *Republic of Kazakhstan: Selected Issues and Statistical Appendix* (March 2002).

2001 (US $ million): Total imports 5,787.4; Total exports 7,975.6.

PRINCIPAL TRADING PARTNERS
(US $ million)

Imports c.i.f.	1999	2000	2001
Belarus	39.0	39.9	46.1
China, People's Repub.	81.6	154.0	341.2
Finland	46.6	57.4	69.1
France	56.6	75.4	138.4
Germany	287.6	333.7	504.8
Italy	107.1	155.0	267.5
Japan	119.1	105.5	140.2
Korea, Repub.	48.8	82.5	118.8
Netherlands	101.2	64.7	126.0
Poland	63.2	58.8	59.3
Russia	1,350.6	2,459.8	2,798.6
Switzerland	42.8	54.3	65.8
Turkey	112.2	142.6	177.2
Ukraine	59.2	79.8	101.7
United Kingdom	232.9	219.4	140.2
USA	348.7	276.9	194.0
Uzbekistan	86.7	73.3	80.2
Total (incl. others) . . .	3,686.2	5,051.7	6,218.6

Source: mainly Asian Development Bank, *Key Indicators of Developing Asian and Pacific Countries.*

Exports f.o.b.	1999	2000	2001
Bermuda	780.0	1,358.1	1,936.2
British Virgin Islands . . .	376.9	n.a.	n.a.
China, People's Repub. . . .	473.1	670.3	910.6
Estonia	109.6	n.a.	n.a.
Germany	332.5	566.6	988.1
Iran	89.4	n.a.	n.a.
Italy	418.9	891.9	629.1
Kyrgyzstan	59.5	58.5	87.1
Lithuania	87.9	n.a.	n.a.
Netherlands	161.2	240.0	100.0
Poland	76.3	71.2	164.2
Russia	1,138.6	1,783.9	1,667.3
Switzerland	296.9	497.6	698.3
Ukraine	115.0	268.5	422.0
United Kingdom	189.1	231.0	116.6
USA	80.6	211.0	320.1
Uzbekistan	66.4	139.2	148.8
Total (incl. others) . . .	5,597.8	9,138.0	12,008.8

Source: mainly Asian Development Bank, *Key Indicators of Developing Asian and Pacific Countries.*

Transport

RAILWAYS
(estimated traffic)

	1999	2000	2001
Passenger-km (million) . . .	8,859	10,215	10,384
Freight net ton-km (million) . .	91,700	124,983	135,653

ROAD TRAFFIC
(motor vehicles in use at 31 December)

	1998	1999	2000
Passenger cars	971,170	987,724	1,000,298
Buses and coaches	44,295	43,421	45,666
Lorries and vans	270,198	247,693	233,045
Motorcycles and mopeds . .	200,637	155,850	112,742

Source: International Road Federation, *World Road Statistics.*

SHIPPING

Merchant Fleet
(registered at 31 December)

	1999	2000	2001
Number of vessels	18	20	21
Total displacement (grt) . . .	9,253	11,476	13,096

Source: Lloyd's Register-Fairplay, *World Fleet Statistics.*

CIVIL AVIATION
(traffic on scheduled services)

	1999	2000	2001
Passengers carried ('000) . .	800	800	900
Passenger-km (million) . . .	2,136	1,797	1,901
Total ton-km (million) . . .	64	118	44

Kilometres flown (million): 20 in 1996; 20 in 1997; 35 in 1998 (Source: UN, *Statistical Yearbook*).

Communications Media

	1998	1999	2000
Television receivers ('000 in use) .	3,890	3,900	3,910
Telephones ('000 main lines in use)	1,775.4	1,759.8	1,834.2
Facsimile machines (number in use)	1,636	2,045	n.a.
Mobile cellular telephones ('000 subscribers).	29.7	49.5	197.3
Internet users ('000)	20.0	70.0	100.0

Book production (incl. pamphlets, 1996): Titles 1,226; Copies 21,014,000.

Daily newspapers (1996): Titles 3; Average circulation 500,000.

Radio receivers ('000 in use, 1997): 6,470.

2001: Mobile cellular telephones ('000 subscribers) 582.0.

Sources: UNESCO, *Statistical Yearbook*; UN, *Statistical Yearbook*; International Telecommunication Union.

Education

(1999/2000, unless otherwise indicated)

	Institutions	Teachers	Students
Pre-primary	1,102	12,600	124,400
Primary	1,447	62,700	1,208,300
Secondary: general . .	8,309*	176,900	1,913,100
Secondary: vocational . . .	293*	n.a.	89,900
Higher: universities, etc. . .	170	27,189†	440,700
Higher: other		11,998‡	

* 2000/01.
† 1994/95.
‡ 1995/96.

Sources: partly Ministry of Education; UNESCO, *Statistical Yearbook*; UN, *Statistical Yearbook for Asia and the Pacific*.

Adult literacy rate (census results): 97.5% (males 99.1%; females 96.1%) in 1989 (Source: UNESCO, *Statistical Yearbook*).

Directory

The Constitution

The Constitution of the Republic of Kazakhstan was endorsed by 89% of the electorate voting in a national referendum on 30 August 1995, and was officially adopted on 6 September, replacing the Constitution of January 1993. A number of constitutional amendments were adopted on 8 October 1998. The following is a summary of the Constitution's main provisions:

GENERAL PROVISIONS

The Republic of Kazakhstan is a democratic, secular, law-based, unitary state with a presidential system of rule. The state ensures the integrity, inviolability and inalienability of its territory. State power belongs to the people, who exercise it directly through referendums and free elections, and also delegate the exercise of their power to state bodies. State power is separated into legislative, executive and judicial branches; these interact, with a system of checks and balances being applied.

Ideological and political diversity are recognized. State and private property are recognized and afforded equal protection. The state language is Kazakh. Russian is employed officially in state bodies and local government bodies on a par with Kazakh. The state creates the conditions necessary for the study and development of the languages of the peoples of Kazakhstan.

HUMAN AND CIVIL RIGHTS AND LIBERTIES

Citizenship of the Republic of Kazakhstan is acquired and terminated in accordance with the law. Citizenship of another state is not recognized for any citizen of Kazakhstan. The rights and liberties of the individual are recognized and guaranteed. No one may be subjected to discrimination on grounds of origin, sex, race, language, religious or other beliefs, or place of residence. No one may be subjected to torture, violence or other treatment or punishment that is cruel or degrading. All are entitled to use their native language and culture. Freedom of speech and creativity are guaranteed. Censorship is prohibited. Citizens are entitled to assemble and to hold meetings, rallies, demonstrations, marches and picket-lines peacefully and without weapons. Defence of the republic is the sacred duty and obligation of every citizen. Human and civil rights and liberties may be restricted only by law and only to the extent that is necessary to defend the constitutional system and to safeguard public order, and human rights and liberties. Any action capable of disrupting inter-ethnic accord is deemed unconstitutional. Restriction of civil rights and liberties on political grounds is not permitted in any form.

THE PRESIDENT OF THE REPUBLIC

The President of the Republic is the Head of State and highest official of Kazakhstan, who determines the main directions of the state's domestic and foreign policy and represents Kazakhstan within the country and in international relations. The President is symbol and guarantor of the unity of people and state power, the permanency of the Constitution and of human and civil rights and liberties. The President is elected for a seven-year term by secret ballot on the basis of general, equal and direct suffrage. No person may be elected to the office for more than two consecutive terms. A citizen of the republic by birth, who is at least 40 years of age, has a fluent command of the state language, and has lived in Kazakhstan for no less than 15 years, may be elected President.

The President addresses an annual message to the people; schedules regular and extraordinary elections to Parliament; signs and promulgates laws submitted by the Senate, or returns draft legislation for further discussion; with the consent of Parliament, appoints the Prime Minister and relieves him of office; on the recommendation of the Prime Minister, determines the structure of the Government, appoints its members to office and relieves them of office; presides at sessions of the Government on matters of particular importance; may cancel or suspend acts of the Government and of the akims (heads of regional administrative bodies); with the consent of Parliament, appoints to and relieves of office the Chairman of the National Bank; with the consent of the Senate, appoints to and relieves of office the Prosecutor-General and the Chairman of the National Security Committee; appoints and recalls the heads of diplomatic missions of the republic; decides on the holding of referendums; negotiates and signs international treaties; is supreme Commander-in-Chief of the armed forces; bestows state awards and confers honours; resolves matters of citizenship and of granting political asylum; in the event of aggression against the republic, imposes martial law or announces a partial or general mobilization; forms the Security Council, the Supreme Judicial Council and other consultative and advisory bodies.

The President may be relieved of office only in the event of his having committed an act of treason or if he exhibits a consistent incapacity to carry out his duties owing to illness. A decision on the President's early dismissal is adopted at a joint sitting of the chambers of Parliament by a majority of no less than three-quarters of the total number of deputies of each chamber. Dismissal of a treason indictment against the President at any stage shall result in the early termination of the powers of the Majlis members who initiated the consideration of the matter. The question of dismissal of the President may not be raised at the same time as he is considering early termination of the authority of Parliament.

PARLIAMENT

Parliament is the supreme representative body of the republic, exercising legislative functions. It consists of two chambers, the Senate (upper chamber) and the Majlis (assembly, lower chamber). The Senate comprises 47 members, of whom 40 are elected at joint sittings of the deputies of all representative bodies of the regions and the capital, while the remaining seven deputies are appointed by the President. The Majlis consists of 67 deputies elected from single-mandate constituencies by secret ballot on the basis of general, equal and direct suffrage and 10 elected by party lists. The Senate's term is six years, and that of the Majlis is five years. One-half of the elected deputies in the Senate are subject to election every three years.

THE GOVERNMENT

The Government exercises the executive power of the republic and is responsible to the President. The Government drafts the main areas of the state's socio-economic policy, defence capability, security and public order, and orders their implementation; presents to Parliament the republican budget and the report of its implementation, and ensures that the budget is implemented; submits draft legislation to the Majlis and provides for the implementation of laws; organizes the management of state property; formulates measures for the pursuit of Kazakhstan's foreign policy; directs the activity of Ministries, State Committees and other central and local executive bodies. The Prime Minister organizes and directs the activity of the Government and is personally responsible for its work.

THE CONSTITUTIONAL COUNCIL

The Constitutional Council consists of seven members whose term of office is six years. Former Presidents of the Republic are by right life members of the Constitutional Council. The Chairman and two members of the Council are appointed by the President of the Republic, two members are appointed by the Chairman of the Senate and two by the Chairman of the Majlis. One-half of the members of the Council are replaced every three years. The Council decides whether to hold a presidential or parliamentary election, or a republican referendum; prior to signature by the President, examines laws passed by Parliament for compliance with the Constitution; prior to ratification, examines international treaties.

LOCAL STATE ADMINISTRATION AND GOVERNMENT

Local state administration is exercised by local representative and executive bodies, which are responsible for the state of affairs on their own territory. The local representative bodies—the councils (maslikhat)—express the will of the population of the corresponding administrative-territorial units and, bearing in mind the overall state interest, define the measures necessary to realize this will and monitor the ways in which these are implemented. Councils are elected for a four-year term by a secret ballot of the public on the basis of general, equal and direct suffrage. The local executive bodies are part of the unified system of executive bodies of Kazakhstan, and ensure that the general state policy of the executive authority is implemented in co-ordination with the interests and development needs of the corresponding territory. Each local executive body is headed by the akim of the corresponding administrative-territorial unit, who is the representative of the President and the Government of the Republic.

The Government

HEAD OF STATE

President of the Republic of Kazakhstan: NURSULTAN A. NAZARBAYEV (elected 1 December 1991; re-elected 10 January 1999).

GOVERNMENT
(April 2003)

Prime Minister: IMANGALI TASMAGAMBETOV.

First Deputy Prime Minister: ALEKSANDR PAVLOV.

Deputy Prime Ministers: BAURZHAN MUKHAMEDZHANOV, KARIM MASIMOV.

Deputy Prime Minister and Minister of Agriculture: AKHMETZHAN YESIMOV.

Minister of Finance: ZEINULLA KAKIMZHANOV.

State Secretary and Minister of Foreign Affairs: KASYMZHOMART K. TOKAYEV.

Ministry of Economy and Budget Planning: KELIMBETOV KEYRAT NEMATOVICH.

Minister of Energy: VLADIMIR S. SHKOLNIK.

Minister of Defence: GEN. MUKHTAR ALTYNBAYEV.

Minister of Industry and Trade: MAZHIT YESENBAYEV.

Minister of Labour and Social Security: GULZHANA KARAGUSOVA.

Minister of Education and Science: SHAMSHA BERKIMBAYEVA.

Minister of Environmental Protection: AITKUL B. SAMAKOVA.

Minister of Internal Affairs: Col-Gen. KAIRBEK SULEIMENOV.

Minister of State Revenues: ZEINULLA K. KAKIMZHANOV.

Minister of Justice: GEORGI KIM.

Minister of Culture, Information and Social Accord: MUKHTAR A. KUL-MUKHAMMED.

Minister of Transport and Communications: KAZHMURAT NAGMANOV.

Minister of Public Health: ZHAKSYLYK DOSKALIYEV.

Head of Prime Minister's Office: ALTAI A. TLEUBERDIN.

HEADS OF GOVERNMENT BODIES

National Bank: GRIGORII MARCHENKO.

National Commission on Family and Women's Affairs: AITKUL B. SAMAKOVA.

National Security Committee: Col-Gen. NARTAI DUTBAYEV.

State Committee for Affairs of the Commonwealth of Independent States: ASAN KOZHAKOV.

State Committee for Aviation and Space: ALMAS KOSUNOV.

State Agency for Emergency Situations: ZAMANBEK NURKADILOV.

State Committee for Energy Supervision: MURAT RAMAZANOV.

State Agency for Financial Police: BOLATBEK BULGAKBAYEV.

State Agency for Management of Land Resources: BAKYT OSPANOV.

State Agency for Material Reserves: KABIDOLLA SAREKENOV.

State Agency for Migration and Demography: ALTYNSHASH DZHAGANOVA.

State Agency for the Protection of State Secrets: SERIK AKHMETOV.

State Agency on Regulation of Natural Monopolies, Protection of Competition and Support of Small Businesses: YERBOLAT DOSAYEV.

State Committee for State Property and Privatization: MAKSUTBEK RAKHANOV.

State Agency for Statistics: ALIKHAN SMAILOV.

State Agency for Tourism and Sports: DAULET TURLYKHANOV.

MINISTRIES

In 1998 ministries were relocated to Astana (formerly Akmola) from the old capital, Almaty.

Office of the President: 473000 Astana, Mira 11; tel. (3172) 32-13-99; fax (3172) 32-61-72; internet www.president.kz.

Office of the Prime Minister: 473000 Astana, Beibitshilik 11; tel. (3172) 32-31-04; fax (3172) 32-40-89.

Ministry of Agriculture: 473000 Astana, pr. Abaya 49; tel. (3172) 32-37-63; fax (3172) 32-62-99.

Ministry of Culture, Information and Social Accord: 437000 Astana, Beibitshilik 22; tel. (3172) 32-24-95; fax (3172) 32-32-91; e-mail newwave@mininfo.katelco.com.

Ministry of Defence: 473000 Astana, Beibitshilik 51A; tel. and fax (3172) 33-78-89.

Ministry of Economy and Budget Planning: 473000 Astana, Popeda 33; tel. (3172) 71-77-70; fax (3172) 71-77-12.

Ministry of Education and Science: 473000 Astana, Kenesary 83; tel. (3172) 32-25-40; fax (3172) 32-64-82.

Ministry of Energy: 473000 Astana, Beibitshilik 37; tel. (3172) 31-71-33; fax (3172) 31-71-64; e-mail ministr@minenergo.kegoc.kz; internet www.minenergo.kz.

Ministry of Finance: 473000 Astana, pl. Respubliki 60; tel. (3172) 28-00-65; fax (3172) 32-40-89; internet www.minfin.kz.

Ministry of Foreign Affairs: 473000 Astana; tel. (3172) 32-76-69; fax (3172) 32-76-67; internet www.mfa.kz.

Ministry of Industry and Trade: 473000 Astana.

Ministry of Internal Affairs: 473000 Astana, Manasa 4; tel. (3172) 34-36-01; fax (3172) 34-17-38.

Ministry of Justice: 473000 Astana, Pobeda 45; tel. (3172) 39-12-13; fax (3172) 32-15-54.

Ministry of Labour and Social Security: 473000 Astana, Manasa 2; tel. (3172) 15-36-02; internet www.enbek.banknet.kz.

Ministry of Environmental Protection: 475000 Kokchetau, Marks 81; tel. (31622) 54-265; fax (31622) 50-620.

Ministry of Public Health: Astana.

Ministry of Transport and Communications: 473000 Astana, pr. Abaya 49; tel. (3172) 32-62-77; fax (3172) 32-16-96.

President and Legislature

Presidential Election, 10 January 1999

Candidate	% of votes
Nursultan A. Nazarbayev	80.97
Serikbolsyn A. Abdildin	11.87
Gani Kasymov	4.68
Engels Gabbasov	0.77
Against all candidates	1.71
Total	**100.00**

PARLIAMENT

Parliament is a bicameral legislative body, comprising the Senate and the Majlis (Assembly). Elections to Parliament were held for the first time in December 1995.

Parliament: e-mail www@parlam.kz; internet www.parlam.kz.

Senate

Chairman: ORALBAI ABDYKARIMOV.

The Senate is the upper chamber of Parliament. It comprises 39 members: 32 elected by special electoral colleges (comprising members of local councils) in Kazakhstan's 14 regions and two cities, and seven appointed by the President of the Republic. At the first elections to the Senate, held on 5 December 1995, only 38 of the then 40 regionally elected seats were filled, necessitating further voting at a later date for the remaining two seats. The remaining seven Senators were appointed by President Nazarbayev. Elections are held every three years for one-half of the elected seats. Partial elections to the Senate were held on 17 September 1999 and 8 October 2002.

Majlis

Chairman: ZHARMAKHAN A. TUYAKBAYEV.

The Majlis is the 77-seat lower chamber of Parliament. The first direct elections to a 67-seat Majlis were held on 9 December 1995. Further direct elections to the Majlis were held on 10 October 1999, with the participation of 62.6% of the electorate. For the first time, an additional 10 seats were elected by party lists, bringing the total number of seats to 77. However, the required two-thirds' quorum was not achieved, as candidates succeeded in obtaining the requisite 50% of the votes in only 20 of the 67 single-mandate constituencies. A further round of voting took place in the remaining 47 constituencies on 24 October. Three of these results were subsequently declared to be invalid, thus necessitating a third round of voting in the three constituencies on 26 December.

General Election, 10 and 24 October and 26 December 1999

	Number of seats		
Party	Single-mandate constituencies	Party lists	Total
Independents and others	34	—	34
Otan	19	4	23
Civic Party of Kazakhstan	11	2	13
Communist Party of Kazakhstan	1	2	3
Agrarian Party of Kazakhstan	1	2	3
National Co-operative Party of Kazakhstan	1	—	1
Total	**67**	**10**	**77**

Political Organizations

A new law was introduced in July 2002, which required all parties to have a minimum of 50,000 members from among all the country's regions in order to qualify for official registration. The legislation was expected to cause considerable consolidation. By mid-April 2003 just seven parties were registered with the Ministry of Justice, compared with 19 in January.

Agrarian Party of Kazakhstan: Astana; e-mail agro@mail.kz; f. 1999 to support farmers and campaign for the introduction of private land ownership; centrist; re-registered in 2003; Leader ROMIN MADINOV; 45,000 mems.

Ak Zhol (Light Road) Party: Almaty; f. 2002 by former members of the Democratic Choice of Kazakhstan (q.v.); re-registered with the Ministry of Justice; Leader URAZ DZHANDOSOV; c. 65,000 mems.

Alash: Almaty; tel. (3272) 62-28-60; f. 1999, following split from Republican Party; radical nationalist Kazakh party; Leader SOVETKAZY AKATAYEV; 10,000 mems.

Aul (Village) Peasant and Social Democratic Party: Almaty; f. 2000; re-registered in 2003; Leader GANI KALIYEV.

Civic Party of Kazakhstan: Almaty; tel. (3272) 62-19-16; f. 1998; seeks strengthening of state system and improvements in the provision of social welfare; re-registered with the Ministry of Justice; Leaders AZAT PERUASHEV, DYUSEMBAY DUYSENOV; over 50,000 mems.

Communist Party of Kazakhstan (CPK): Almaty; tel. (3272) 65-13-09; suspended Aug. 1991, re-registered March 1994 and March 2003; Chair. SERIKBOLSYN A. ABDILDIN.

Democratic Choice of Kazakhstan (DCK): Almaty; f. 2001; advocates political liberalization, incl. the election of local government officials and members of the judiciary, and increased media freedom.

Justice Party of Kazakhstan: Astana; f. 1999; seeks to strengthen the state system with a socially-orientated market economy; Chair. TALGAT ZHANABAYEV.

National Co-operative Party: Almaty; tel. (3272) 62-34-94; f. 1994; promotes civil rights; Chair. UMIRZAK SARSENOV.

Otan (Fatherland): Almaty; tel. (3272) 62-24-83; e-mail party_otan@nursat.kz; internet www.otan.nursat.kz; f. 1999 by the People's Unity Party, the Kazakhstan–2030 Movement, the Liberal Movement of Kazakhstan and the Democratic Party of Kazakhstan; pro-presidential republican party; seeks to strengthen the state system and preserve political stability; mergers with the People's Co-operative Party of Kazakhstan and the Republican Labour Party reported in Sept. and Nov. 2002, respectively; re-registered with the Ministry of Justice; Chair. AMANGELDY ERMEGIYAYEV; Dep. Chair. KAZBEK KAZKENOV; 126,000 mems.

Party of Patriots of Kazakhstan (PPK): Almaty; f. 2000; re-registered with the Ministry of Justice; Leader GANI KASYMOV.

People's Front Movement: Almaty; f. 1998 by a leader of the Workers' Movement; Leader MADEL ISMAILOV.

People's Unity Party (PUP): 480013 Almaty, pl. Respubliki 13, Rm 501; tel. (3272) 63-77-89; f. 1993, originally as a socio-political movement, before becoming a political party; centrist; opposes radical nationalism, promotes social and ethnic harmony; Leader NURSULTAN A. NAZARBAYEV; Chair. of Political Bd SERIK ABDRAKHMANOV.

Renaissance Party of Kazakhstan (RNPK): Almaty; tel. (3272) 33-06-23; f. 1995; pro-presidential party, seeking moral and spiritual rebirth of Kazakhstan; Leader DZHAGANOVA ALTYNSHASH.

Republican Party—Azat (RP—A): Almaty; f. 1992 by merger of three nationalist opposition parties: the Azat (Freedom) movement, the Republican Party and the Dzheltoksan (December) National-Democratic Party; Chair. KAMAL ORMANTAYEV.

Slavic Movement—Lad (Concord): 480012 Almaty, Vinogradova 85, kv. 408; Astana; tel. (3272) 63-38-20; tel. (3172) 32-70-96; f. 1992; socio-cultural organization representing the rights of the Slavic communities; Chair. VIKTOR MIKHAILOV; 30,000 mems.

Socialist Party of Kazakhstan (SPK): Almaty; tel. (3272) 49-19-37; f. 1991 to replace Communist Party of Kazakhstan; Chair. ANATOLII ANTONOV; 50,000 mems.

United Democratic Party (UDP): Almaty; f. 2002 by the merger of the Azamat (Citizen) Democratic Party of Kazakhstan, the People's Congress Party of Kazakhstan and the Republican People's Party of Kazakhstan; advocates a parliamentary system of government with a unicameral legislature, the adoption of a new constitution by means of a referendum, the equitable distribution of mineral wealth, and the prevention of any member of the President's family from holding government office.

Smaller parties and organizations included the Justice Party, the Russian nationalist group, Yedinstvo (Unity), the anti-nuclear movement, Attan (Leader ASYLBEK AMANTAY), the Tabigat (Nature) party (Chair. MELS YELESIZOV), the Movement for Honest Elections, the Workers' Movement, the youth movement, For Kazakhstan's Future (f. 1998; Leader RAGANIN MEIRAM), the opposition Orleu (Progress) movement (Chair. SEYDAKHMET KUTTYKADAM), the pensioners' movement, Pokoleniye (Generation; Chair. IRINA SAVOSTINA), the Officers' Alliance, and Respublika-2000 (f. 1999).

Diplomatic Representation

EMBASSIES IN KAZAKHSTAN

Afghanistan: Almaty; tel. (3272) 28-68-71; Ambassador SAYD ZAHER SHAH AKHBARI.

Armenia: 480075 Almaty, Seifullina 579, 7th Floor; tel. and fax (3272) 69-29-08; e-mail akod100@hotmail.com; Ambassador Dr EDUARD SH. KHURSHUDIAN.

Australia: 480100 Almaty, Kazybek bi 20A; tel. (3272) 63-94-18; fax (3272) 581-16-01; Ambassador RUTH LAUREN PEARCE.

Bulgaria: 480002 Almaty, Makatayeva 13A; tel. (3272) 33-27-55; fax (3272) 30-27-55; Chargé d'affaires a.i. DIMITAR DEKOV.

Canada: 480100 Almaty, Karasai Batyr 34; tel. (3272) 50-11-51; fax (3272) 58-24-93; e-mail almat@dfait-maeci.gc.ca; Ambassador HECTOR COWAN.

China, People's Republic: Almaty, Furmanova 137; tel. (3272) 63-49-66; fax (3272) 63-82-09; Ambassador YAO PEISHENG.

Croatia: Almaty; tel. (3272) 62-57-03; fax (3272) 50-62-92; Chargé d'affaires a.i. KARINO HROMIN.

Cuba: 473005 Astana, Samal 10, kv. 1; tel. and fax (3172) 22-14-19; e-mail embacuba@cubakaz.com; internet www.cubakaz.com; Chargé d'affaires a.i. BLÁS NABEL PÉREZ CAMEJO.

Czech Republic: Almaty, Dostyk 212; tel. (3272) 64-16-06; fax (3272) 64-49-47; e-mail amaata@embassy.mzv.cz; Ambassador (vacant).

Denmark: Almaty; tel. (3272) 92-01-56; fax (3272) 92-19-97; e-mail rdecentrasia@umweb.dk; Ambassador B. DAN NIELSEN.

Egypt: 480100 Almaty, Zenkova 59; tel. (3272) 60-16-22; fax (3272) 61-10-22; Ambassador AYMAN HAMDI EL-KOUNI.

France: 480110 Almaty, Furmanova 173; tel. (3272) 50-62-36; fax (3272) 50-61-59; Ambassador GÉRARD PERROLET.

Georgia: Almaty, Gornaya 246; tel. (3272) 31-09-09; Ambassador TEMUR GOGOLADZE.

Germany: 480091 Almaty, Furmanova 173; tel. (3272) 50-61-55; fax (3272) 50-62-76; e-mail german_embassy_almaty@nursat.kz; internet www.deutschebotschaft-almaty.org; Ambassador ANDREAS R. KÖRTING.

Greece: 480051 Almaty, pr. Dostyka 216/1, Zavodskaya; tel. (3272) 50-39-61; fax (3272) 50-39-38; e-mail gr_embassy@kaznet.kz; Ambassador NIKOLAS HATOUPIS.

Holy See: 473000 Astana, Zelyonaya Alleya 20; tel. (3172) 24-16-03; fax (3172) 24-16-04; e-mail nuntius_kazakhstan@lycos.com; Apostolic Nuncio JÓZEF WESOŁOWSKI.

Hungary: Almaty, Tulebayeva 162, kv. 29; tel. (3272) 63-64-37; fax (3272) 50-70-99; Ambassador MIKLÓS JACZKOVITS.

India: 480091 Almaty, Maulenova 71; tel. (3272) 92-14-11; fax (3272) 92-67-67; e-mail ambind@netel.kz; Ambassador Dr V. S. VERMA.

Iran: Almaty, Kabanbai Batyr 119; tel. (3272) 67-78-46; fax (3272) 54-27-54; Ambassador MURTAZA SAFFARI.

Israel: Almaty, Zheltoksan 87; tel. (3272) 50-72-15; fax (3272) 50-62-83; e-mail emb_isr_almaty@kaznet.kz; Ambassador MOSHE KIMCHE.

Italy: 480100 Almaty, Kazybek bi 20A , 3rd Floor; tel. (3272) 91-00-07; fax (3272) 91-00-53; e-mail ambalma@nursat.kz; Ambassador DIEGO LONGO.

Japan: Almaty, Kazybek bi 41, 3rd Floor; tel. (3272) 60-86-00; fax (3272) 60-86-01; Ambassador TOSHIO TSUNOZAKI.

Korea, Democratic People's Republic: Almaty, Voronezhskaya 58; tel. (3272) 61-89-98; fax (3272) 25-27-66; Ambassador PAK UI CHUN.

Korea, Republic: Almaty, Jarkentskaya 2/77; tel. (3272) 53-26-60; fax (3272) 50-70-59; e-mail kzemb@hanmail.net; Ambassador TAE SUK-WON.

Kyrgyzstan: Almaty, Amangeldy 68A; tel. (3272) 63-33-09; fax (3272) 63-33-62; Ambassador AKBAR RYSKULOV.

Lebanon: Almaty, Sovkhoz 'Alatau', Naberezhnaya 20; tel. (3272) 48-71-51; Ambassador ASSIF NASSER.

Libya: Almaty, Satpaeva 10, kv. 2; tel. (3272) 62-67-17; fax (3272) 62-22-23; Chargé d'affaires a.i. OMAR ALI GEIT.

Lithuania: 480099 Almaty, Iskanderova 15; tel. (3272) 65-61-23; fax (3272) 65-14-60; e-mail lrambkaz@nursat.kz; Chargé d'Affaires a.i. JONAS VORONAVIČIUS.

Mongolia: Almaty, Kazybek bi 18; tel. (3272) 20-08-65; fax (3272) 60-17-23; Ambassador DANDIMZHAVYN DASHNYAM.

Netherlands: 480072 Almaty, Nauryzbai Batyr 103; tel. (3272) 50-37-73; fax (3272) 50-37-72; e-mail alm@minbuza.nl; internet www.nlembassy-almaty.org; Ambassador PETER VAN LEEUWEN.

Pakistan: 480004 Almaty, Tulebayeva 25; tel. (3272) 73-35-48; fax (3272) 73-13-00; e-mail parepalmaty@hotmail.com; Ambassador DURRAY SHAHWAR KURESHI.

Poland: 480099 Almaty, Dzharkentskaya 9–11, POB 228; tel. (3272) 58-15-51; fax (3272) 58-15-50; e-mail ambpol@mail.kz; Ambassador ZDZISŁAW NOWICKI.

Qatar: Almaty.

Romania: 480100 Almaty, Pushkina 97; tel. (3272) 63-57-72; fax (3272) 58-83-17; e-mail ambro@nursat.kz; Ambassador VASILE SOARE.

Russia: Almaty, Dzhandosova 4; tel. (3272) 44-64-91; fax (3272) 44-83-23; e-mail rfe@nursat.kz; Ambassador YURII MERZLYAKOV.

Saudi Arabia: Almaty, Gornaya 137; tel. (3272) 65-77-91; fax (3272) 50-28-11; Ambassador ALI AL-HAMDAN.

Spain: Almaty, Baitursinova 102; tel. (3272) 50-09-06; fax (3272) 50-35-30; e-mail embespkz@mail.mae.es; Ambassador FRANCISCO PASCUAL DE LA PARTE.

Tajikistan: Almaty, Jandosova 58; tel. and fax (3272) 44-20-89; Chargé d'affaires a.i. DAVLAT SIPINEROV.

Turkey: 480100 Almaty, Tole bi 29; tel. (3272) 61-81-53; fax (3272) 50-62-08; e-mail almatyturk@kaznet.kz; Ambassador KURTULUŞ TAŞKENT.

Turkmenistan: Astana, Emeleva 70; tel. and fax (3172) 61-17-60.

Ukraine: Astana, Aezova 57; tel. (3172) 32-60-42; e-mail embasy_ua@kepter.kz; Ambassador VASILIY G. TSUBENKO.

United Kingdom: 480110 Almaty, Furmanova 173; tel. (3272) 50-61-91; fax (3272) 50-62-60; e-mail british-embassy@nursat.kz; Ambassador JAMES LYALL SHARP.

USA: 480091 Almaty, Furmanova 97–99A; tel. (3272) 63-39-21; fax (3272) 63-38-83; e-mail usembassy-almaty@freenet.kz; internet www.usembassy-kazakhstan.freenet.kz; Ambassador JOHN HERBST.

Uzbekistan: 480100 Almaty, Baribayeva 36; tel. (3272) 61-02-35; fax (3272) 61-10-55; Ambassador TURDIKUL BUTAYAROV.

Judicial System

Chairman of the Constitutional Council: YURII KHITRIN.

Chairman of the Supreme Court: MAKSUT S. NARIKBAYEV.

Prosecutor-General: RASHID T. TUSUPBEKOV.

Religion

The major religion of the Kazakhs is Islam. They are almost exclusively Sunni Muslims of the Hanafi school. The Russian Orthodox Church is the dominant Christian denomination; it is attended mainly by Slavs. There are also Protestant Churches (mainly Baptists), as well as a Roman Catholic presence.

ISLAM

The Kazakhs were converted to Islam only in the early 19th century, and for many years elements of animist practices remained. Over the period 1985–90 the number of mosques in Kazakhstan increased from 25 to 60, 12 of which were newly built. By 1991 there were an estimated 230 Muslim religious communities functioning in Kazakhstan and an Islamic institute had been opened in Almaty. The Islamic revival intensified following Kazakhstan's independence from the USSR, and during 1991–94 some 4,000 mosques were reported to have been opened.

Mufti of Kazakhstan: ABSATTAR B. DERBISALIYEV, Almaty.

CHRISTIANITY

The Roman Catholic Church

Kazakhstan comprises the diocese of Karaganda and the three apostolic administrations of Almaty, Astana and Atyrau. Adherents to the Roman Catholic Church totalled an estimated 180,160 at 31 December 2000.

Bishop of Karaganda: Rt Rev. JAN PAWEŁ LENGA, 470077 Karaganda, Oktyabrskaya 25; tel. and fax (3212) 22-14-72; e-mail diocese-karaganda@city.krg.kz.

The Press

At July 2001 an estimated 950 newspaper and 342 periodical titles were published in Kazakhstan. In addition, 15 news agencies were operating in the country.

REGULATORY AUTHORITY

National Agency for the Press and Mass Information: 480013 Almaty, pl. Respubliki 13; tel. (3272) 63-93-97; fax (3272) 63-93-17; f. 1995; Dep. Chair. ALIBEK A. ASKAROV.

PRINCIPAL DAILY NEWSPAPERS

Almaty Asia Times: Almaty, Dzhandosova 60; tel. (3272) 44-74-50; fax (3272) 44-78-40.

Almaty Herald: Almaty, pr. Dostyk 85A; tel. and fax (3272) 63-36-55; internet www.herald.asdc.kz.

Ekspress–K: 480044 Almaty, Abdullinykh 6; tel. (3272) 59-60-00; fax (3272) 59-60-39; e-mail express-k@nursat.kz; internet www.ek.kz; f. 1922; 5 a week; in Russian; Editor-in-Chief IGOR SHAKHNOVICH; circ. 18,500.

Kazakhstanskaya Pravda (Truth of Kazakhstan): 480044 Almaty, Gogolya 39; Astana; tel. (3272) 63-65-65; fax (3272) 50-18-73; tel. (3172) 32-19-44; e-mail kpam@kaznet.kz; f. 1920; 5 a week; publ. by the Govt; in Russian; Editor-in-Chief V. MIKHAILOV; circ. 34,115.

Khalyk Kenesi (Councils of the People): Almaty; tel. (3272) 33-10-85; f. 1990; 5 a week; publ. by Parliament; in Kazakh; Editor-in-Chief ZH. KENZHALIN.

Vecherniy Almaty (Evening Almaty): Almaty, Ablai Khan 2; tel. (3272) 33-34-87; fax (3272) 39-64-24.

Yegemen Kazakhstan (Sovereign Kazakhstan): 480044 Almaty, Gogolya 39; Astana; tel. and fax (3272) 63-25-46; tel. (3172) 34-16-41; e-mail astegemen@nursat.kz; f. 1919; 6 a week; organ of the Govt; in Kazakh; Editor-in-Chief M. SERKHANOV; circ. 31,840.

OTHER PUBLICATIONS

Akikat (Justice): 480044 Almaty, Gogolya 39; tel. (3272) 63-94-33; fax (3272) 63-94-19; f. 1921; monthly; social and political; publ. by the Ministry of Culture, Information and Social Accord; circ. 1,484.

Aktsionerny (Stock Business Guide): 480004 Almaty, Chaikovskogo 11; tel. (3272) 32-96-09; fax (3272) 39-98-95; f. 1990; in Russian; twice a week; Editor-in-Chief VIKTOR SHATSKY.

Ana Tili (Native Language): 484044 Almaty, pr. Dostyk 7; tel. (3272) 33-22-21; fax (3272) 33-34-73; f. 1990; weekly; publ. by the Kazakh Tili society; in Kazakh; Editor-in-Chief ZH. BEISENBAY-ULY; circ. 11,073.

Ara-Shmel (Bumble-bee): 480044 Almaty, Gogolya 39; tel. (3272) 63-59-46; f. 1956; monthly; satirical; in Kazakh and Russian; Editor-in-Chief S. ZHUMABEKOV; circ. 53,799.

Arai (Dawn): Almaty, Furmanova 53; tel. (3272) 32-29-45; f. 1987; every two months; socio-political; Editor-in-Chief S. KUTTYKADAMOV; circ. 7,500.

Atameken (Fatherland): 484100 Almaty, pr. Dostyk 85; tel. (3272) 63-58-43; f. 1991; ecological; publ. by Ministry of Environmental Protection; circ. 25,063.

Aziya Kino (Asian Cinema): 480100 Almaty, Tole bi 23A; tel. (3272) 61-86-55; f. 1994; monthly; in Russian and Kazakh; Editor-in-Chief G. ABIKEYEVA.

Baldyrgan (Sprout): 480044 Almaty, pr. Zhibek zholy 50; tel. (3272) 33-16-73; f. 1958; monthly; illustrated; for pre-school and first grades of school; in Kazakh; Editor-in-Chief T. MOLDAGALIYEV; circ. 150,000.

Budem: 480004 Almaty, Chaikovskogo 11; tel. (3272) 39-97-04; f. 1997; monthly; in Russian; Editor-in-Chief R. GARIPOV.

Business World: Astana; tel. (3172) 75-17-51; e-mail areket-kz@hotmail.com; f. 1999; weekly; circ. 10,000.

Continent: Almaty; tel. (3272) 50-10-39; fax (3272) 50-10-41; e-mail continent@asdc.kz; f. 1999; policy and society journal; Editor-in-Chief ANDREI KUKUSHKIN; circ. 7,500.

Delovaya Nedelya (Business Week): 484044 Almaty, pr. Zhibek zholy 64; tel. (3272) 50-62-72; fax (3272) 33-91-48; e-mail rikki@kazmail.asdc.kz; f. 1992; weekly; in Russian; Editor-in-Chief O. CHERVINSKII; circ. 16,066.

Deutsche Allgemeine Zeitung: 480044 Almaty, pr. Zhibek zholy 50, Office 418; tel. (3272) 73-42-69; fax (3272) 73-92-91; e-mail daz@ok.kz; f. 1966; weekly; political, economic, cultural, social; in German; Editor-in-Chief IRINA ZIRENTSCHIKOWA; circ. 1,700.

Ekonomika i Zhizn (Economics and Life): Almaty; tel. (3272) 63-96-86; f. 1926; monthly; publ. by the Govt; in Russian; Editor-in-Chief MURAT T. SARSENOV; circ. 4,800.

Globe: 480009 Almaty, pr. Abaya 155, Rms 13/14; tel. (3272) 50-76-39; fax (3272) 50-63-62; e-mail ipa@mailonline.kz; internet www

.globe.kz; f. 1995; twice a week; in English and Russian; Editor-in-Chief NURLAN ABLYAZOV; circ. 5,550.

Golos Kazakha (Voice of Kazakhstan): Almaty, Zenkov 75; tel. (3272) 61-79-09; fax (3272) 61-94-47; f. 1989; weekly; organ of the Federation of Trade Unions of Kazakhstan; circ. 30,000.

Islam Nury (The Light of Islam): Semipalatinsk; f. 2000; every two weeks; Islamic.

Kakadu: 480004 Almaty, Chaikovskogo 11; tel. (3272) 39-97-04; f. 1995; monthly; in Russian; Editor-in-Chief L. GERTZY.

Karavan: 480004 Almaty, Chaikovskogo 11; tel. (3272) 32-08-39; fax (3272) 32-97-57; e-mail advertising@caravan.kz; internet www.caravan.kz; f. 1991; 20% of shares were reported to have been sold to a US investment co in 2001; weekly; in Russian; Editor-in-Chief ANDREI SHUKHOV; circ. 250,000.

Kazakh Adebiety (Kazakh Literature): 484091 Almaty, pr. Ablai-khana 105; tel. and fax (3272) 69-54-62; f. 1934; weekly; organ of the Union of Writers of Kazakhstan; in Kazakh; Editor-in-Chief A. ZHAKSYBAYEV; circ. 7,874.

Kazakhstan: 480044 Almaty, pr. Zhibek zholy 50; tel. (3272) 33-13-56; f. 1992; weekly; economic reform; in English; Editor-in-Chief N. ORAZBEKOV.

Kazakhstan Aielderi (Women of Kazakhstan): 480044 Almaty, pr. Zhibek zholy 50; tel. (3272) 33-06-23; fax (3272) 46-15-53; f. 1925; monthly; literary, artistic, social and political; in Kazakh; Editor-in-Chief ALTYNSHASH K. JAGANOVA; circ. 15,200.

Kazakhstan Business: 480044 Almaty, pr. Zhibek zholy 50; tel. (3272) 33-42-56; f. 1991; weekly; in Russian; Editor-in-Chief B. SUKHARBEKOV.

Kazakhstan Mektebi (Kazakh School): 480004 Almaty, pr. Ablai-khana 34; tel. (3272) 39-76-65; f. 1925; monthly; in Kazakh; Editor-in-Chief S. ABISHEVA; circ. 10,000.

Kazakhstan Mugalimi (Kazakh Teacher): 484100 Almaty, Dzhambula 25; tel. (3272) 61-60-58; f. 1935; weekly; in Kazakh; Editor-in-Chief ZH. TEMIRBEKOV; circ. 6,673.

Kazakhstan Zaman (Kazakh Time): 480002 Almaty, pr. Dostyk 106G; tel. (3272) 65-07-39; e-mail kazakistanzaman@mail.ru; f. 1992; in Kazakh and Turkish; weekly; publ. by the al-Farabi Foundation; circ. 15,000; Gen. Dir ERSIN DEMIRCI.

Khalyk Kongresi (People's Congress): Almaty; tel. (3272) 62-87-86; f. 1993; 3 a week; publ. by the People's Congress Party of Kazakhstan and the Nevada-Semipalatinsk anti-nuclear movement; in Kazakh (also appears in Russian, as *Narodnyi Kongress*); Editor-in-Chief SAYIN MURATBEKOV.

Korye Ilbo: 480044 Almaty, pr. Zhibek zholy 50; tel. (3272) 33-90-10; fax (3272) 63-25-46; f. 1923; weekly; in Korean and Russian; Editor-in-Chief YAN WON SIK.

Medicina (Medicine): Almaty, pr. Ablaikhana 63; tel. (3272) 33-48-01; fax (3272) 33-16-90; e-mail zdrav_kz@nursat.kz; f. 2000 (fmrly appeared as *Densaulik*); monthly; in Kazakh; Editor-in-Chief A. SH. SEYSENBAYEV.

Novoye Pokoleniye (New Generation): 480091 Almaty, Bogenbai Batyr 139; tel. (3272) 62-31-06; fax (3272) 63-96-45; e-mail np@asdc.kz; f. 1993; weekly; in Russian; Editor-in-Chief OLEG C. CHERVINSKY; circ. 50,000.

Panorama: 480013 Almaty, pl. Respubliki 15, Office 647; tel. (3272) 63-28-34; fax (3272) 63-66-16; e-mail panorama@kazmail.asdc.kz; internet www.panorama.kz; f. 1992; weekly; in Russian; Editor-in-Chief LERA TSOY; circ. 18,500.

Parasat (Intellect): 480044 Almaty, pr. Zhibek zholy 50; tel. (3272) 33-49-29; fax (3272) 33-64-58; f. 1958; socio-political, literary, illustrated; in Kazakh; Editor-in-Chief BAKKOZHA S. MUKAY; circ. 20,000.

Petroleum of Kazakhstan: 480091 Almaty, Bogenbai Batyr 139; tel. (3272) 62-31-06; fax (3272) 63-96-45; e-mail np@asdc.kz; every two months; in Russian and English; Editor-in-Chief OLEG C. CHERVINSKY; circ. 2,000.

Prostor (Expanse): 480091 Almaty, pr. Ablaikhana 105; tel. (3272) 69-61-87; e-mail info@prstr.samal.kz; internet prostor.samal.kz; f. 1933; monthly; literary and artistic; in Russian; Editor-in-Chief R. V. PETROV; circ. 1,800.

Russkii Yazyk i Literatura (Russian Language and Literature): 480091 Almaty, pr. Ablaikhana 34; tel. (3272) 39-76-68; f. 1962; monthly; in Russian; Editor-in-Chief B. S. MUKANOV; circ. 17,465.

Shalkar: 480044 Almaty, pr. Zhibek zholy 50; tel. (3272) 33-86-85; f. 1976; twice a month; in Kazakh (in the Arabic script); Editor-in-Chief A. KAIYRBEKOV; circ. 2,500.

Soldat: Almaty; f. 1999; weekly; indepedent, opposition publication; in Kazakh and Russian; Editor-in-Chief ERMURAT BAPI.

Soviety Kazakhstana (Councils of Kazakhstan): 480002 Almaty, pr. Zhibek zholy 15; tel. (3272) 34-92-19; f. 1990; weekly; publ. by Parliament; in Russian; Editor-in-Chief Yu. GURSKII; circ. 30,000.

Sport and ks: 480044 Almaty, pr. Zhibek zholy 50; tel. (3272) 33-92-90; f. 1959; weekly; in Kazakh and Russian; Editor-in-Chief NESIP ZHUNUSBAYEV; circ. 20,000.

Turkistan: 484012 Almaty, Bogenbai Batyr 150; tel. (3272) 69-61-54; fax (3272) 62-08-98; f. 1994; weekly; political; publ. by the Ministry of Culture, Information and Social Accord; in Kazakh; circ. 4,883.

Uigur Avazi (The Voice of Uigur): 480044 Almaty, pr. Zhibek zholy 50; tel. (3272) 33-84-59; f. 1957; 2 a week; publ. by the Govt; socio-political; in Uigur; Editor-in-Chief I. AZAMATOV; circ. 9,179.

Ukraine Novini (Ukraine News): 473000 Astana, pr. Respubliki 17; tel. (3172) 21-74-62; e-mail un_astana@mail.kz; internet ukrnovini.host.kz; f. 1994; weekly; in Ukrainian; CEO CHERNEGA TARAS; Editor-in-Chief A. GARKAVETS; circ. 1,200.

Ulan: 480044 Almaty, pr. Zhibek zholy 50; tel. (3272) 33-80-03; f. 1930; weekly; in Kazakh; Editor-in-Chief S. KALIYEV; circ. 183,014.

Vremya (Time): 480060 Almaty, Dzhandosova 60A; tel. (3272) 44-49-03; fax (3272) 45-51-44; internet www.time.kz; f. 1999; weekly; in Russian; Editor-in-Chief IGOR MELTSER; circ. 250,000.

Zerde (Intellect): 480044 Almaty, pr. Zhibek zholy 50; tel. (3272) 33-83-81; f. 1960; monthly; popular, scientific, technical; in Kazakh; Editor-in-Chief E. RAUSHAN-ULY; circ. 68,629.

Zhalyn (Flame): Almaty; tel. (3272) 33-22-21; f. 1969; monthly; literary, artistic, social and political; in Kazakh; Editor-in-Chief M. KULKENOV; circ. 2,196.

Zhas Alash (Young Generation): 480044 Almaty, Makatayeva 22; tel. (3272) 30-60-90; fax (3272) 30-24-69; internet www.zhasalash.kz; f. 1921; publ. by the Kazakhstan Youth Union; in Kazakh; Editor-in-Chief ZHUSIP NURTORE; circ. 133,000.

Zhuldyz (Star): 480091 Almaty, pr. Ablai-Khan 105; tel. (3272) 62-51-37; f. 1922; monthly; journal of the Union of Writers of Kazakhstan; literary, artistic, socio-political; in Kazakh; Editor-in-Chief MUKHTAR MAGAUIN; circ. 1,539.

NEWS AGENCY

Kazakh Information Agency (KazAAG): 480091 Almaty, pr. Ablaikhana 75; tel. (3272) 62-61-80; fax (3272) 69-58-39; e-mail arenov@nursat.kz; f. 1997; responsible to the Ministry of Culture, Information and Social Accord; provides information on government activities in Kazakhstan and abroad; Editor-in-Chief ARENOV M. MURAT.

Foreign Bureaux

Informatsionnoye Telegrafnoye Agentstvo Rossii—Telegrafnoye Agentstvo Suverennykh Stran (ITAR—TASS) (Russia): Almaty; Astana; tel. (3272) 33-96-81; tel. (3172) 32-42-02; Correspondent IGOR CHEREPANOV; Correspondent ORAL KAPISHEV.

Internews Network Agency (USA): Almaty; tel. (3272) 61-56-68.

Islamic Republic News Agency (IRNA) (Iran): Almaty; tel. (3272) 68-10-05; e-mail irna@irna.com; internet www.irna.com; Correspondent BAHARVAND ALI RAHMAD.

Reuters (United Kingdom): Astana; tel. (3172) 50-94-10.

Rossiiskoye Informatsionnoye Agentstvo—Novosti (RIA—Novosti) (Russia): Almaty; tel. (3272) 33-99-50; Correspondent REVMIRA VOSHENKO.

Xinhua (New China) News Agency (People's Republic of China): Almaty; tel. (3272) 24-68-68.

Publishers

Green Movement Centre (GMC): Taraz; tel. and fax (3262) 23-14-96; e-mail oasis97@kaznet.kz; f. 1988; education; environment; Chair. ALEX ZAGRIBELNY.

Gylym (Science): 480100 Almaty, Pushkina 111–113; tel. (3272) 91-18-77; fax (3272) 61-88-45; f. 1946; books on natural sciences, humanities and scientific research journals; Dir S. G. BAIMENOV.

Izdatelstvo Kazakhstan (Kazakhstan Publishing House): 480124 Almaty, pr. Abaya 143; tel. and fax (3272) 42-29-29; f. 1920; political science, economics, medicine, general and social sciences; Dir E. KH. SYZDYKOV; Editors-in-Chief M. D. SITKO, M. A. RASHEV.

Kainar (Spring): 480124 Almaty, pr. Abaya 143; tel. (3272) 42-27-96; f. 1962; agriculture, history, culture; Dir ORAZBEK S. SARSENBAYEV; Editor-in-Chief I. I. ISKUZHIN.

Kazakhskaya Entsiklopediya (Kazakh Encyclopaedia): Almaty; tel. (3272) 62-55-66; f. 1968; Editor-in-Chief R. N. NURGALIYEV.

Mektep: 480009 Almaty, pr. Abaya 143; tel. (3272) 42-26-24; fax (3272) 77-85-44; e-mail oao_mektep@nursat.kz; f. 1947; dictionaries, children's textbooks; fiction by young writers; Pres. E. SATYBALDIYEV; Editor-in-Chief SH. GUSAKOVA.

Oner (Art): 480124 Almaty, pr. Abaya 143; tel. (3272) 42-08-88; f. 1980; Dir S. S. ORAZALINOV; Editor-in-Chief A. A. ASKAROV.

Zhazushy (Writer): 480124 Almaty, pr. Abaya 143; tel. (3272) 42-28-49; f. 1934; literature, literary criticism, essays and poetry; Dir D. I. ISABEKOV; Editor-in-Chief A. T. SARAYEV.

Broadcasting and Communications

TELECOMMUNICATIONS

Beket: 480002 Almaty, Zhurgeneva 9; tel. (3272) 30-16-33; fax (3272) 30-01-43; mobile telecommunications services.

Kazakhtelekom: 480091 Almaty, pr. Abylai Khan 86; tel. (3272) 62-05-41; fax (3272) 63-93-95; internet www.itte.kz; f. 1994; national telecommunications corpn; 60% state-owned, 40% owned by Daewoo Corpn (Republic of Korea); Pres. SERIK BURKITBAYEV.

Satel: 480100 Almaty, Zenkov 22; tel. (3272) 63-64-32; fax (3272) 63-87-69; telecommunications services; joint venture between Telstra Corpn Ltd (Australia) and Kazakhtelecom; Man. Dir JERRY KOLETH.

BROADCASTING

In mid-2001 there were an estimated 124 television and radio stations.

Kazakh State Television and Radio Broadcasting Corporation: 480013 Almaty, Zheltoksan 175A; tel. (3272) 63-37-16; f. 1920; Pres. YERMEK TURSUNOV.

Radio

Kazakh Radio: 480013 Almaty, Zheltoksan 175A; tel. (3272) 63-19-68; fax (3272) 65-03-87; e-mail kazradio@astel.kz; internet www.kazradio.kz; f. 1921; broadcasts in Kazakh, Russian, Uigur, German and other minority languages; Gen. Dir TOREKHAN DANIYAR.

A number of private radio stations began operating in Kazakhstan in the 1990s.

Television

Khabar News Agency: 480013 Almaty, pl. Respubliki 13; tel. (3272) 63-83-69; fax (3272) 50-63-45; e-mail naz@khabar.almaty.kz; internet www.khabar.kz; f. 1959; international broadcasts in Kazakh, Uigur, Russian and German; two television channels; Dir DARIGA NAZARBAYEVA.

KTK (Kazakh Commercial Television): Almaty, pl. Respubliki 13; tel. (3272) 63-44-28; fax (3272) 50-66-25; e-mail ktkao@kzaira.com; f. 1990; independent; 20% of shares were reported to have been sold to a US investment co in 2001; Gen. Dir ANDREI SHUKHOV; Pres. SHOKAN LAUULIN.

NTK (Association of TV and Radio Broadcasters of Kazakhstan): 480013 Almaty, pl. Respubliki 13, 6th Floor; tel. (3272) 70-01-83; fax (3272) 70-01-85; e-mail kaztvradio@nursat.kz; f. 2000; privately owned; Pres. AIDAR ZHUMABAYEV.

There are several other private television companies operating in Kazakhstan.

Finance

(cap. = capital; res = reserves; dep. = deposits; m. = million; brs = branches; amounts in tenge, unless otherwise indicated)

BANKING

From 1994 the National Bank of Kazakhstan (NBK) effected a series of measures aimed at rationalizing the banking sector, in order to ensure a sound financial infrastructure. Numerous banks had their licences revoked: between 1995 and 1998 the number of commercial banks declined by almost one-half, and it continued to decline thereafter. In July 2001 the banking system comprised the NBK and 44 commercial banks. Of the commercial banks, only one was wholly state-owned, and 16 had some foreign participation. There were also 12 branches or representative offices of foreign banks. Some 42 banks were licensed to operate using the national currency, the tenge, as well as foreign currencies. The total registered capital of commercial banks in Kazakhstan at 1 July 2001 was 70,500m. tenge.

Central Bank

National Bank of Kazakhstan (NBK): 480090 Almaty, Koktem-3 21; tel. (3272) 50-46-25; fax (3272) 50-60-90; e-mail hq@ nationalbank.kz; internet www.nationalbank.kz; f. 1990; cap. 15,465.6m., res 113,099.2m., dep. 145,476.5m. (Dec. 2001); Chair. GRIGORII MARCHENKO; 19 brs.

Major Commercial Banks

Abidbank: 480100 Almaty, pr. Dostyka 85A; tel. (3272) 41-60-67; e-mail herald@mailbox.kz.

ABN AMRO Bank Kazakhstan CJSC: 480099 Almaty, Khadji Mukana 45; tel. (3272) 50-73-00; fax (3272) 50-72-98; e-mail abnamro@kaznet.kz; internet www.abnamro.com; f. 1994; 51%-owned by ABN AMRO Bank NV (the Netherlands); cap. 1,800.0m., res 58m., dep. 23,492m. (Dec. 2001); Chair. JAN WILLEM VAN DEN BOSCH; Gen. Man. OTBERT DE JONG; 1 br.

Alashbank: 480012 Almaty, Sharipova 84; tel. (3272) 92-60-08; e-mail alashbnk@online.ru; 1 br.

Alfa Bank Kazakhstan: 480012 Almaty, Masanchi 57A; tel. (3272) 92-00-12; fax (3272) 50-78-03; e-mail elerkh@alfabank.ru.

Almaty Commercial Bank: 480012 Almaty, Amangeldy 70; tel. (3272) 58-82-26; e-mail acb1@kaznet.kz.

Astana Bank: 487010 Turkestan, Aiteke bi 31; tel. (3252) 57-24-39; e-mail astanabnk@shym.kz.

ATF Bank: 480091 Almaty, Furmanova 100; tel. (3272) 50-30-40; fax (3272) 50-19-95; e-mail info@amb.kz; internet www.amb.kz; f. 1995 as Almaty Merchant Bank, name changed as above in June 2002; cap. 3,099.1m., res 1,151.8m., dep. 32,866.3m. (Dec. 2001); Chair. YERKEBLAN OKAYEV; 10 brs.

Bank Caspiyskiy OJSC: 480012 Almaty, Adi Sharipova 90; tel. (3272) 50-17-20; fax (3272) 50-95-96; e-mail office@bankcaspian.kz; internet www.bankcaspian.kz; f. 1997 by merger of Kazdorbank with Caspiyskiy; cap. 1,427.3m., res 281.4m., dep. 13,109.1m. (Dec. 2001); Chair. DENIS MILOVIDOV; 17 brs.

Bank Centercredit OJSC: 480072 Almaty, Shevchenko 100; tel. (3272) 58-41-58; fax (3272) 69-29-24; e-mail info@centercredit.kz; internet www.centercredit.kz; f. 1988 as Co-op Bank of the Almaty Union of Co-operatives; name changed to Centerbank 1991, to Centercredit 1996, to JS Centercredit 1998 (following merger with Zhilstroi Bank); cap. 2,588m., res 566m., dep. 21,373m. (Jan. 2002); Chair. of Council BAKHYTBEK R. BAYSEITOV; Chair. of Bd VLADISLAV S. LI; 19 brs.

Bank of Development of Kazakhstan: 473000 Astana, Samal 12; tel. (3172) 58-02-60; e-mail info@kdb.kz.

Bank Turan Alem: 480099 Almaty, Samal 2, Zholdasbekov 97; tel. (3272) 50-40-70; fax (3272) 50-02-24; e-mail post@bta.kz; internet www.bta.kz; f. 1997 by merger of Turanbank—Kazakh Corpn Bank and Alembank; privatized in 1998; cap. 16,091m., dep. 138,474m. (Dec. 2001); Chair. YERZHAN N. TATISHEV; 23 brs.

Central Asian Bank of Co-operation and Development: 480008 Almaty, pr. Abaya 115A; tel. (3272) 42-27-37; fax (3272) 42-27-37; e-mail cab@asdc.kz; f. 1994; Chair. GAMAL K. SOODANBEKOV; 1 br.

Citibank Kazakhstan: 480100 Almaty, Kazybek bi 41; tel. (3272) 60-84-00; fax (3272) 60-83-99; e-mail citibank.kazakhstan@citicorp .com; internet www.citibank.com/kazakhstan; f. 1998; cap. US $25m. (1998).

DanaBank: 637000 Pavlodar, Lenina 119; tel. (3182) 32-01-20; e-mail dana@dana1.kz.

Demir Kazakhstan Bank: 480091 Almaty, Kurmangazy 61A; tel. (3272) 50-85-50; fax (3272) 50-85-25; e-mail demirbank@demirbank .kz; internet www.demirbank.kz; f. 1997; cap. 1,000.0m., res 262.9m., dep. 697.4m. (Dec. 2001); Chair. IHSAN UGUR.

Eurasian Bank: 480002 Almaty, Kunayeva 56; tel. (3272) 50-86-07; fax (3272) 50-86-50; e-mail info@eurasian-bank.kz; internet www .eurasian-bank.kz; f. 1994; cap. 2,889.7m., res 1,377.1m., dep. 13,225.0m. (Dec. 2002); Chair. KIM INESSA; 3 brs.

Export–Import Bank of Kazakhstan (Eximbank): 480100 Almaty, Pushkina 118; tel. (3272) 63-43-00; fax (3272) 50-75-49; e-mail post_mail@eximbank.kz; f. 1994; cap. 6,091m. (March 2000); Chair. of Bd BEISENBAY IZTELEUOV.

Industrial Bank of Kazakhstan: 480020 Almaty, pr. Dostyka 264; tel. (3272) 93-51-99; fax (3272) 42-96-03; e-mail info@ibk.kz.

OJSC Kazakhstan International Bank: 480072 Almaty, Seifullina 597; tel. (3272) 92-99-62; fax (3272) 92-90-74; e-mail kib@kib .almaty.kz; f. 1993; cap. 887.8m., res 8.2m. Chair. ASKAR B. NASENOV.

Kazakhstan-Ziraat International Bank (KZI Bank): 480057 Almaty, Klochkova 132, POB 34; tel. (3272) 50-60-80; fax (3272) 50-60-82; e-mail kzibank@kzibank.com; f. 1993 as Kazkommerts Ziraat International Bank; name changed as above in 1999; cap. 1,058.3m., res 55.6m., dep. 957.6m. (Dec. 2001); Chair. SALIH CANGA; Gen. Man. HALIL TEKPINAR.

Kazkommertsbank: 480060 Almaty, Zh. Gagarina 135; tel. (3272) 58-52-81; fax (3272) 58-52-81; e-mail mailbox@kkb.kz; internet www .kkb.kz; f. 1991; assets US $1,293.9m., cap. $180.1m., dep. $735.6m. (June 2002); Chief Exec. NINA A. ZHUSSUPOVA; 23 brs.

Komirbank: 638710 Ekibastuz, Stroitelnaya 29; tel. (3183) 4-08-75; fax (3183) 4-03-41; e-mail komirbank@kaznet.kz; internet www .komirbank.kz; f. 1992 as JSC Ugolbank, name changed in 1996; merged with Latur Aliyans in 1999; cap. 1,500.0m., res 2.4m., dep. 2,186.2m. (Dec. 1999); Chair. of Bd SERIK SANSYZBAYEV.

Lariba-Bank: 480060 Almaty, Rozibakiyeva 181A; tel. (3272) 49-14-32; fax (3272) 49-64-21; e-mail lariba@kazmail.asdc.kz; 1 br.

Neftebank: 466200 Aktau, Microraion 9/23A; tel. (3292) 43-61-61; fax (3292) 43-61-45; e-mail nb@neftebank.kz; 5 brs.

OJSC Nurbank: 465050 Atyrau, Seifullina 5; tel. (3122) 25-41-75; fax (3122) 21-02-49; e-mail bank@nurbank.kz; internet www .nurbank.kz; f. 1992; cap. 2,700.0m., res 913.8m., dep. 19,829.6m. (Dec. 2001); Chair. of Bd ABILMAZHEN KUANYSHEVICH GILIMOV.

OJSC Temirbank: 480008 Almaty, pr. Abaya 68/74; tel. (3272) 58-78-88; fax (3272) 50-67-72; e-mail board@temirbank.kz; internet www.temirbank.kz; f. 1992; cap. 1,382.9m., res 251.1m., dep. 17,724.0m. (Dec. 2001); Chair. OLEG KONONENKO; 18 brs.

Tsesnabank: 473000 Astana, Beibitshilik 43; tel. (3172) 31-81-92; fax (3172) 31-82-58; e-mail tsesnabank_uavt@kepter.kz; internet www.tsesnabank.kz; f. 1992; cap. US $25,000.0, res $9,319.0m., dep. $198,263.6m. (Dec. 2001); Chair. of Bd VIKTOR FOGEL; 4 brs.

Savings Bank

Halyk (People's) Savings Bank of Kazakhstan: 480046 Almaty, Rozybakiyeva 97; tel. (3272) 59-00-00; fax (3272) 59-02-71; e-mail hsbk@halykbank.kz; internet www.halykbank.kz; f. 1936 as br. of Savings Bank of USSR, reorganized as joint-stock savings bank in 1994; fully privatized in Nov. 2001; cap. 7,222.6m., res 1,090.1m., dep. 113,246.9m. (July 2002); Chair. KAIRAT SATYLGANOV; Man. Dir KAIRAT RAKHMANOV; 611 brs.

Bankers' Organization

Commercial Banks' Association of Kazakhstan: Almaty; Pres. BAKHYTBEK BAISEITOV.

STOCK AND COMMODITY EXCHANGES

Kazakhstan Stock Exchange (KASE): 480091 Almaty, Aiteke bi 67; tel. (3272) 63-98-98; fax (3272) 63-89-80; e-mail info@kase.kz; internet www.kase.kz; f. 1993; Pres. and Chief Exec. AZAMAT M. DZHOLDASBEKOV.

Ken Dala Central Kazakhstan Commodity Exchange: 470074 Karaganda, pr. Stroitelei 28; tel. (3212) 74-27-80; fax (3212) 74-43-35; f. 1991; auth. cap. 6m. Pres. MADEGDA PAK.

Kazakhstan also has a Metal Exchange (f. 1992).

INSURANCE

At August 2000 there were 41 licensed insurance companies in Kazakhstan.

Almaty International Insurance Group: Almaty; tel. (3272) 50-12-31; e-mail aiig@world2.almaty.kz; internet www.aiig.escort.kz; Chair. SUREN AMBARTSUMIAN.

Dynasty Life Insurance Co: Almaty, Seifullina 410; tel. (3272) 50-73-95; e-mail dynasty@bta.nursat.kz; Chair. SERIK TEMIRGALEYEV.

Industrial Insurance Group (IIG): 480046 Almaty, Nauryzbai Batyr 65–69; tel. (3272) 50-96-95; fax (3272) 50-96-98; e-mail iig@ kaznet.kz; internet www.iig.kz; f. 1998; Pres. IVAN MIKHAILOV.

KazAgroPolicy: 480091 Almaty, Nauryzbai Batyr 49–61; tel. (3272) 32-13-24; fax (3272) 32-13-26; e-mail kazagropolise@mail .banknet.kz; Chair. YERMEK USPANOV.

Kazakhinstrakh: Almaty; tel. (3272) 33-73-49; fax (3272) 50-74-37; e-mail kiscentr@nursat.kz; Chair. NURLAN MOLDAKHMETOV.

Kazkommerts-Policy: 480013 Almaty, Satpayeva 24; tel. (3272) 58-48-08; fax (3272) 92-73-97; e-mail kkp@mail.kz; internet www .kkp.kz; Chair. SERGEI G. SUKHAREV; Dir TALGAT K. USSENOV.

MSCA Interteach: 480091 Almaty, Furmanova 111/48; tel. and fax (3272) 58-23-32; e-mail interteach@kaznet.kaz; internet www .interteachmsca.com; f. 1989; medical and travel insurance, health care, accident and employee liability insurance; 120 employees; 48 brs; Gen. Dir ERNST M. KURLEUTOV.

Interteach Assistance: 480091 Almaty, Kabanbai Batyra 122A; tel. and fax (3272) 69-58-31; e-mail interteach@kaznet.kz; internet www.interteachmsca.com; medical and travel insurance, health care; Gen. Dir ERNST M. KURLEUTOV.

West-Kazakhstan Insurance Firm: Uralsk, pr. Lenina 203; tel. (31122) 50-62-94; Chair. BOLAT DJUMAGALIYEV.

Trade and Industry

GOVERNMENT AGENCY

State Committee for Investment: Astana.

CHAMBERS OF COMMERCE

Union of Chambers of Commerce and Industry of Kazakhstan: 480091 Almaty, Masanchi 26; tel. (3272) 67-78-23; fax (3272) 50-70-29; e-mail tpprkaz@online.ru; internet www.ccikaz.kz; f. 1959; Chair. KHAMIT RAKISHEV.

Akmola Chamber of Commerce and Industry: 473000 Astana, Auezova 66, POB 1966; tel. (3172) 32-38-33; e-mail akmcci@dan.kz; Chair. TATYANA KONONOVA.

Aktobe Chamber of Commerce and Industry: 463000 Aktobe, Zhubanova 289/1; tel. (3132) 51-02-20; e-mail akbtpp@nursat.kz; Chair. ELENA RUDENKO.

Almaty Chamber of Commerce and Industry: 480091 Almaty, Tole bi 45; tel. (3272) 62-03-01; fax (3272) 62-14-04; e-mail alcci@nursat.kz; internet www.almatycci.kz; Chair. ZULFIYA AKHMETZHANOVA.

East Kazakhstan Chamber of Commerce and Industry: 492000 Ust-Kamenogorsk, Novatorova 3, POB 177; tel. (3232) 26-53-10; e-mail cci@ustk.kz; Chair. KAJRAT MUKEYEV.

Karaganda Chamber of Commerce and Industry: 470061 Karaganda, Mir Bulvar 31; tel. (3212) 56-32-32; e-mail ccikr@nursat.kz; f. 1994; Chair. NESIP SEITOVA.

Pavlodar Chamber of Commerce and Industry: 637002 Pavlodar, Toraigyrova 95/1; tel. (3182) 75-79-69; e-mail pav-cci@kaznet.kz; Chair. RAJHANGUL SATABAYEVA.

Semipalatinsk Chamber of Commerce and Industry: 490050 Semipalatinsk, Abaya 92/22; tel. (3222) 62-78-87; e-mail tpp@relcom.kz; Chair. TAMARA SOPOLEVA.

South Kazakhstan Chamber of Commerce and Industry: 486050 Chimkent, Tauke Khan 31; tel. (3252) 21-14-05; Chair. SYRLYBAJ ORDABEKOV.

Zhambyl Chamber of Commerce and Industry: 484039 Taraz, Karakhana 2; tel. (3262) 43-05-98; Chair. ADILKHAN ZHAPARBEKOV.

EMPLOYERS' ORGANIZATIONS

Kazakhstan Petroleum Association: 480100 Almaty, pr. Dostyk 38, Offices 516/7; tel. (3272) 50-18-16; fax (3272) 50-18-17; e-mail kpa@arna.kz; internet www.kpa.kz; f. 1998; Chair. Dr AHMED G. SALEH; 35 mem. cos.

Kazakhtrebsoyuz: Almaty, Komsomolskaya 57; tel. (3272) 62-34-94; union of co-operative entrepreneurs; Chair. UMIRZAK SARSENOV.

Union of Small Businesses: Almaty; f. 1991; Pres. CHINGIZ RYSEBEKOV.

UTILITIES

Electricity

Privatization of the electric power sector was undertaken from 1996. Many power-stations were withdrawn from the national electricity company and transformed into independent joint-stock companies; several power-supply network companies were established in the region. The state had completed the privatization of virtually all electricity producers and local distribution companies by the end of 2001.

State Committee for Energy Supervision: Chair. MURAT RAMAZANOV.

Kazakstanenergo (National Power System): 480008 Almaty, Shevchenko 162; tel. (3272) 62-62-00; fax (3272) 68-43-08; f. 1992; electricity co; Gen. Dir BERLIK ORAZBAYEV.

Kazakstan Electric Grid Operational Company (KEGOC): Almaty; f. 1997; technical electricity network operator; Pres. URAZ DZHANDOSOV.

Kazakhstan Energy and Power Market Operating Company (KEPMOC): Almaty; f. 2000 under a government resolution; electricity broker.

Water

Almaty Vodocanal: Almaty 480057, Jarokova 196; tel. (3272) 44-00-17; fax (3272) 44-84-02; f. 1937; state-owned co; responsible for water supply and sewerage in Almaty and surrounding villages; Gen. Dir SHARIPBEK SHARDARBEKOV.

STATE HYDROCARBONS COMPANIES

Aktobemunaigaz: Aktyubinsk; 25.1% state-owned; 60.3% owned by China National Petroleum Co (CNPC).

KazMunaiGaz National Co: Almaty; f. 2002 by merger of Kazakh-Oil and Transneftegas; Chair. UZAKBAI KARABALIN; Vice-Chair. TIMUR KULIBAYEV.

KazTransOil: transportation of petroleum; Dir-Gen. ASKAR SMANKULOV.

KazTransGas: transportation of natural gas; Dir-Gen. ABAY SADYKOV.

Munaigaz: Almaty; tel. (3272) 69-58-00; fax (3272) 69-52-72; f. 1991; petroleum and gas prospecting and producing; Pres. T. A. KHAZANOV.

Aktyubinskneft: 463022 Aktobe, Atynsarin 8; tel. (3132) 22-47-82; fax (3132) 22-93-21; f. 1993; produces petroleum and natural gas; Pres. S. P. ZIMIN; 10,500 employees.

JSC Mangistaumunaigaz: 466200 Mangistauskaya, Aktau, Mikrorayon 1; tel. (3292) 51-45-57; fax (3292) 43-39-19; 60% owned by Central Asian Petroleum (Indonesia), 10% owned by employees; production and transportation of petroleum and natural gas; Gen. Dir S. E. KRYMKULOV.

Pavlodar Petrochemical Joint Stock Co: 637043 Pavlodar, Khimkombinatovskaya 1; tel. (3182) 39-65-20; fax (3182) 39-60-98; e-mail bekturov@pnhz.kz; f. 1978; 51% owned by JSC Mangistaumunaigaz; processes petroleum from western Siberia (Russia); produces unleaded petroleum, diesel fuel, petroleum chemical gases, bitumen and petroleum coke; Exec. Dir RUSTEM BEKTUROV.

Tengizchevroil (TCO): 466440 Atyrau, Atyrau Airport, TCO Interim Office; tel. (312) 30-26-818; fax (312) 30-26-729; e-mail tiny@tengizchevroil.com; f. 1993; joint venture between the Govt (20%), Chevron Corpn (USA—with 50%), ExxonMobil (USA—25%) and LUKArco (a joint venture between LUKoil of the Russian Federation and Atlantic Richfield of the USA—5%); Gen. Dir KEN GODARD.

TRADE UNIONS

Confederation of Free Trade Unions of Coal and Mining Industries: Almaty; Chair. V. GAIPOV.

Federation of Trade Unions of Kazakhstan: 473000 Astana, pr. Abaya 94; tel. (3172) 216-68-14; fax (3172) 21-68-35; e-mail fprkastana@nursat.kz; internet www.trud.org/kazakhstan; 30 affiliated unions with 2,300,000 mems (2001); Chair. SIYAZBEK MUKASHEV.

Independent Trade Union Centre of Kazakhstan: f. 1991; 9 regional branches with 2,200 mems; Pres. LEONID SOLOMON.

National Trade Union of Journalists of Kazakhstan: Pres. MADRID RYSBEKOV.

Union of Manufacturers and Businessmen: Almaty; tel. (3272) 62-23-07; fax (3272) 66-54-90.

Transport

RAILWAYS

In 1996 the total length of rail track in use was 13,537 km (3,611 km of which were electrified). The rail network is most concentrated in the north of the country, where it joins the rail lines of the Russian Federation. From the former capital, Almaty, lines run north-eastward, to join the Trans-Siberian Railway, and west, to Chimkent, and then north-west along the Syr-Dar'ya river, to Orenburg in European Russia. From Chu lines run to central and northern regions of Kazakhstan, while a main line runs from Chimkent south to Uzbekistan. There is an international line between Druzhba, on the eastern border of Kazakhstan, and Alataw Shankou, in the People's Republic of China. Measures to restructure and privatize Kazakhstan's railways were announced in 1998, although it was stated that the main railway lines would remain under full state control.

In the late 1990s construction was under way of the first line of a new underground railway (metro) in Almaty. It was envisaged that the metro system, when completed, would comprise three lines (35.4 km in length).

Department of Railways (Ministry of Transport and Communications): 473000 Astana, pr. Abaya 49; tel. (3172) 32-62-77; fax (3172) 32-16-96; Dir I. P. SEGAL.

Kazakhstan Temir Zholy CJSC (Kazakhstan Railways): Astana, pr. Pobedy; tel. (3172) 14-44-00; fax (3172) 32-85-48; f. 1991 following break-up of former Soviet Railways (SZD); Gen. Dir YERLAN ATAMKULOV.

ROADS

In 2000 Kazakhstan's total road network was 81,331 km, including 22,063 km of main roads and 59,268 km of secondary roads. Some 94.7% of the network was hard-surfaced. In early 1999 the World Bank approved a US $100m. loan to enable Kazakhstan to repair important sections of its main roads, and to improve road maintenance systems. In early 2000 the Islamic Development Bank agreed to donate US $200m. towards the rehabilitation of the Karaganda–Astana road. Kazakhstan is linked by road with Russia (46 border crossings), Kyrgyzstan (seven), Uzbekistan (seven), and, via Uzbekistan and Turkmenistan, with Iran. There are six road connections with the People's Republic of China (including two international crossings, at Korgas and Bakhty). Government spending on the repair and construction of roads was to increase significantly, to some 42,000m. tenge, in 2002.

Department of Roads (Ministry of Transport and Communications): 473000 Astana, pr. Abaya 49; tel. (3172) 32-02-08; fax (3172) 32-16-96; Dir S. LARICHEV.

INLAND WATERWAYS

Kazakhstan has an inland waterway network extending over some 4,000 km. The main navigable river is the Irtysh, accounting for approximately 80% of cargo transported by river. The Kazakhstan River Fleet Industrial Association (Kazrechmorflot), comprising 11 water companies, administers river traffic.

Department of Water Transport (Ministry of Transport and Communications): 473000 Astana, pr. Abaya 49; tel. (3172) 32-03-58; fax (3172) 32-10-58; Dir JENYS M. KASYMBEK.

SHIPPING

Kazakhstan's ports of Atyrau and Aktau are situated on the eastern shores of the Caspian Sea. In 1997 a project was undertaken to upgrade the port of Aktau, at an estimated cost of US $74m. The first stage of the project was scheduled for completion in 1999, and it was forecast that by 2000 Aktau would handle more than 7.5m. metric tons of petroleum and up to 1m. tons of dry freight annually. In 1998 the port handled some 2m. tons of petroleum. A ferry port was inaugurated at Aktau in September 2001 as part of the Transport Corridor Europa—Caucasus—Asia (TRACECA) programme, with lines to Azerbaijan, Iran and Russia; the port was capable of processing some 10m. tons of petroleum and up to 30m. tons of dry goods per year. At 31 December 2001 Kazakhstan's merchant fleet comprised 21 vessels, with a combined total displacement of 13,096 grt.

Aktau Commercial Sea Port: Aktau, Umirzak; tel. (3292) 44-51-26; fax (3292) 44-51-01; e-mail seaport_akt@kaznet.kz; internet www.portaktau.kz; f. 1963; Dir TALGAT B. ABYLGAZIN; 407 employees.

Atyrauozenporty (Atyrau Port): tel. (3122) 25-45-63; fax (3122) 25-45-16; e-mail atr_info@asdc.kz.

CIVIL AVIATION

There are 18 domestic airports and three airports with international services (at Almaty, Aktau and Atyrau). In 1999 the airport at Astana was being upgraded, following that city's inauguration as the new capital in mid-1998. In 2002 plans were announced for the reconstruction of Atyrau airport, with the help of financial assistance from the European Bank for Reconstruction and Development. The national airline, Air Kazakhstan, was registered in January 1997, and replaced Kazakhstan Aue Zholy, which had been declared bankrupt in August 1996. There were over 50 airline companies registered in Kazakhstan in 2000, two-thirds of which were privately owned. In 2002 19 of the country's 56 air companies had their activities suspended and their licences revoked, in the interests of safety; it was envisaged that many of these companies would merge by the end of the year. Almaty airport has scheduled links with cities in Russia and other former Soviet republics, as well as with destinations in Europe, other parts of Asia and the Middle East.

Department of Aviation (Ministry of Transport and Communications): 473000 Astana, pr. Abaya 49; tel. (3172) 32-63-16; fax (3172) 32-16-96; Dir S. BURANBAYEV.

Aeroservice Kazakhstan Aviakompania: 480028 Almaty, Alga basskaya 2A; tel. (3272) 36-69-26; fax (3272) 52-93-45; f. 1991; provides charter services to Europe, the Middle East, Pakistan and the Republic of Korea.

Air Astana: Astana; f. 2001 jointly by the Government and BAE Systems (United Kingdom); domestic flights.

Air Kazakhstan CJSC (Kazakhstan Airlines): 480079 Almaty, Ogareva 14; tel. (3272) 57-29-82; fax (3272) 57-25-03; e-mail office@airkaz.com; internet www.airkaz.com; f. 1997, in succession to Kazakhstan Aue Zholy; state-owned; Pres. YERKIN KALIYEV.

Asiya Servis Aue Zholy (Asia Service Airlines): Almaty, Zheltoksan 59; tel. (3272) 33-63-49; operates services to Atyrau and Aktau.

Jana-Arka Air: 480012 Almaty, Ninogradova 85; tel. (3272) 63-28-74; fax (3272) 63-19-09; privately owned; provides both domestic and regional flights; Pres. YALKEN VALIN.

Sayakhat Air: 480091 Almaty, Bogenbai Batyr 124; tel. (3272) 62-26-28; fax (3272) 62-28-70; e-mail sayakhat@nursat.kz; internet www.sayakhat.com; f. 1989 as the country's first privately owned airline; commenced operations in 1991; passenger and cargo services to Africa, Asia and Europe; Pres. and Dir VLADIMIR KOUROPATENKO.

TOURISM

Tourism is not widely developed in Kazakhstan, owing to its Soviet legacy and infrastructural limitations. However, the country possesses mountain ranges, lakes and a number of historical sites, which the Government plans to promote.

State Agency for Tourism and Sport: 473000 Astana, Mukhtar Auezov 126; tel. (3172) 39-66-38; fax (3172) 39-64-68; e-mail turlykhanov@kazsport.kz; internet www.kazsport.kz; f. 2000; Chair. DAULET TURLYKHANOV.

KENYA

Introductory Survey

Location, Climate, Language, Religion, Flag, Capital

The Republic of Kenya lies astride the equator on the east coast of Africa, with Somalia to the north-east, Ethiopia and Sudan to the north, Uganda to the west and Tanzania to the south. The climate varies with altitude: the coastal region is hot and humid, with temperatures averaging between 20°C and 32°C (69°F–90°F), while inland, at more than 1,500 m (5,000 ft) above sea-level, temperatures average 7°C–27°C (45°F–80°F). The high-lands and western areas receive ample rainfall (an annual average of 1,000 mm–1,250 mm) but most of northern Kenya is very dry (about 250 mm). Kiswahili is the official language, while English is widely spoken and 22% and 13% of the population, respectively, speak Kikuyu and Luo as their mother tongue. Most of the country's inhabitants follow traditional beliefs. There is a sizeable Christian community, while Muslims form a smaller proportion of the population. The national flag (proportions 2 by 3) has three broad horizontal stripes, of black, red and green, separated by two narrow white stripes. Super-imposed in the centre is a red shield, with black and white markings, upon crossed white spears. The capital is Nairobi.

Recent History

Kenya was formerly a British colony (inland) and protectorate (along the coast). The first significant African nationalist organization was the Kenya African Union (KAU), founded in 1944, which was supported mainly by the Kikuyu, the largest ethnic group in Kenya. In 1947 Jomo Kenyatta, a Kikuyu, became President of the KAU. During 1952 a campaign of terrorism was launched by Mau Mau, a predominantly Kikuyu secret society that aimed to expel European (mainly British) settlers from Kenya. The British authorities declared a state of emergency in October 1952 and banned the KAU in 1953, when Kenyatta was imprisoned for alleged involvement with Mau Mau activities. The terrorist campaign ceased in 1956, and the state of emergency was revoked in January 1960.

Kenyatta was released from prison in 1961 and elected to the Legislative Council in 1962. Following general elections in May 1963, Kenya was granted internal self-government in June. The country became independent, within the Commonwealth, on 12 December 1963, and a republic exactly one year later. Kenyatta, then leader of the Kenya African National Union (KANU), was appointed Prime Minister in June 1963 and became the country's first President in December 1964. (He was subsequently re-elected to the presidency, unopposed, in 1969 and 1974.) In December 1966 Kenya's two parliamentary chambers, the Senate and the House of Representatives, were merged to form a unicameral National Assembly. The assassination in 1969 of Tom Mboya, a cabinet minister and the Secretary-General of KANU, led to civil unrest and the banning of the opposition Kenya People's Union. KANU was the only party to contest elections to the National Assembly in 1969 and 1974.

Kenyatta died in August 1978; the Vice-President, Daniel arap Moi, was proclaimed President in October, and was the sole candidate at a presidential election held (concurrently with a KANU-only general election) in November 1979. In June 1982 the National Assembly officially declared Kenya a one-party state. A series of political detentions and increasing press censorship were followed by an attempted coup in August, in which several hundred people were killed. Several cabinet ministers lost their seats at legislative elections in September 1983. Nevertheless, at a simultaneous presidential election Moi was returned unopposed for a second term. In August 1986 KANU approved an open 'queue-voting' system to replace the secret ballot in the preliminary stage of a general election. This new system was opposed by church leaders, on the grounds that it would discourage voting by those whose political impartiality was necessary for their work. In December the National Assembly adopted constitutional amendments that increased the power of the President by transferring control of the civil service to the President's office and by giving the Head of State the power to dismiss the Attorney-General and the Auditor-General without endorsement by a legal tribunal. In June 1987 it was announced that only members of the ruling party were to be entitled to vote during the preliminary stages of a general election.

In February 1988 Moi was nominated unopposed to serve a third term as President. In the same month preliminary elections under the 'queue-voting' system produced a KANU-approved list to contest 123 of the 188 elective seats in the National Assembly at a general election held in March (54 candidates received more than 70% of votes cast at the preliminary stage, and were thus deemed to have been elected, while 11 were elected unopposed). In an extensive cabinet reshuffle following the election, the Vice-President, Mwai Kibaki, was replaced by Josephat Karanja, hitherto an assistant government minister and a former High Commissioner to the United Kingdom. In July the National Assembly adopted constitutional amendments allowing the President to dismiss senior judges at will, and increasing from 24 hours to 14 days the legally permissible period of detention without trial for people suspected of capital offences. In December Kenneth Matiba, the Minister of Transport and Communications, resigned and was expelled from KANU, after criticizing the conduct of the party elections.

In April 1989 the National Assembly unanimously approved a motion of 'no confidence' in Karanja, following allegations that he had abused his position as Vice-President to further his own personal and tribal interests. Karanja, while denying the charges against him, resigned shortly afterwards, and was replaced by the Minister of Finance, Prof. George Saitoti. In June Moi released all political prisoners being held without trial, and offered an amnesty to exiled dissidents.

In February 1990 the Minister of Foreign Affairs and International Co-operation, Dr Robert Ouko, died in suspicious circumstances. Allegations that the Moi administration was implicated in his death led to anti-Government riots in Nairobi and the western town of Kisumu. In response, Moi banned all demonstrations and requested an investigation by British police into Ouko's death; the results of this were presented to the Kenyan authorities in September, and in October Moi ordered a judicial inquiry into the affair. In May a broad alliance of intellectuals, lawyers and clergy, under the leadership of Matiba, began to exert pressure on the Government to legalize political opposition to KANU. In July Moi ordered the arrests of Matiba and other prominent members of the alliance. Serious rioting ensued in Nairobi and its environs; more than 1,000 protesters were reportedly arrested. In August an Anglican bishop, who had publicly criticized the Government, died in a car crash, following threats to his life from cabinet members; the most senior of these, Peter Okondo, subsequently resigned as Minister of Labour. The Government ordered a public inquest into the bishop's death. In November the human rights organization Amnesty International reported that several hundred of those detained at the time of the July riots remained in custody and accused the Kenyan authorities of torturing some prisoners.

In December 1990 KANU abolished the system of 'queue-voting' and resolved to cease expelling party members, readmitting 31 expelled members in the following month. In June Matiba was released from prison, apparently on grounds of ill health. In the following month four of those who had been arrested during the July 1990 riots were found guilty of sedition and each sentenced to seven years' imprisonment. During July 1991 the human rights organization Africa Watch alleged that the Government was permitting the torture of detainees and exerting undue influence on the judiciary. In August six opposition leaders, including Oginga Odinga (Kenya's Vice-President in 1964–66), formed a new political movement, the Forum for the Restoration of Democracy (FORD); the Government outlawed the grouping, but it continued to operate.

In September 1991 the judicial inquiry into the death of Ouko was presented with evidence that he had been murdered; in November Moi dismissed the Minister of Industry, Nicholas Biwott, in response to widespread suspicion that the latter was implicated in the alleged assassination. Shortly afterwards Moi ordered the dissolution of the judicial inquiry. A suspect was eventually charged with the murder, but was acquitted in July 1994. (Biwott was reappointed to the Cabinet in 1997. In

December 2000 Biwott won a libel case against the British authors of a book that implicated him in the murder of Ouko.)

In November 1991 several members of FORD were arrested prior to a planned pro-democracy rally in Nairobi; protesters at the rally (which had been banned by the Government) were dispersed by the security forces. The Kenyan authorities were condemned internationally for suppressing the demonstration, and most of the opposition activists who had been detained were subsequently released. Bilateral and multilateral creditors suspended aid to Kenya indefinitely, pending the acceleration of both economic and political reforms. In December a special conference of KANU delegates, chaired by Moi, acceded to the domestic and international pressure for reform, resolving to permit the introduction of a multi-party political system. The National Assembly subsequently endorsed appropriate amendments to the Constitution.

Also in December 1991 Moi dismissed the Minister of Manpower Development and Employment, Peter Oloo Aringo, who had publicly criticized the Government; Aringo subsequently resigned as Chairman of KANU. Former Vice-President Mwai Kibaki resigned as Minister of Health later in the month, in protest against alleged electoral malpractice by KANU and against the unsatisfactory outcome of the judicial inquiry into the death of Ouko, and founded the Democratic Party (DP). Five other ministers and deputy ministers resigned their posts in subsequent weeks.

During the first half of 1992 some 2,000 people were reportedly killed in tribal clashes in western Kenya. In March the Government banned all political rallies, purportedly in order to suppress the unrest, and restrictions were placed on the activities of the press. Following a two-day general strike in April, organized by FORD, the Government ended the ban on political rallies. In August FORD split into two opposing factions, which were registered in October as separate political parties, FORD—Asili and FORD—Kenya, respectively led by Matiba and Odinga.

Multi-party presidential and legislative elections took place in December 1992. Prior to the elections opposition parties had protested that administrative and legal obstacles were effectively disenfranchising some sectors of the electorate. Moi was elected for a fourth term of office as President, winning 36.3% of the votes cast, ahead of Matiba (26.0%), Kibaki (19.5%) and Odinga (17.5%). Of the 188 elective seats in the National Assembly, KANU won 100 (including 16 uncontested); FORD—Asili and FORD—Kenya secured 31 seats each, and the DP took 23. Some 15 former cabinet ministers lost their seats. Votes were cast predominantly in accordance with ethnic affiliations, with the two largest tribes, the Kikuyu and Luo, overwhelmingly rejecting KANU. The leaders of FORD—Asili, FORD—Kenya and the DP initially campaigned to have the results declared invalid, alleging that there had been gross electoral irregularities. In January 1993, however, a Commonwealth monitoring group concluded that the outcome of the elections reflected 'the will of the people'. An extensive reshuffle of cabinet posts was effected.

Tribal clashes in western regions continued during 1993, escalating significantly in October. In November Africa Watch reiterated persistent accusations by the opposition that the Government was covertly inciting ethnic violence in order to discredit political pluralism in Kenya. During that month several people were arrested and charged with co-ordinating the unrest. Meanwhile, the international donor community agreed to resume the provision of aid to Kenya, in response to what it recognized as the Government's progress in implementing political and economic reforms.

In January 1994 Odinga died; he was succeeded as the Chairman of FORD—Kenya by Michael Wamalwa Kijana, hitherto the party's Vice-President. In June main opposition groups, excluding FORD—Asili, formed a loose coalition, the United National Democratic Alliance, which was, however, subsequently divided by disagreements. Disunity was also becoming apparent within individual opposition parties, with vying factions evident within both FORD—Kenya and FORD—Asili.

In May 1995 leading opposition activists formed a new political organization, Safina, under the chairmanship of Mutari Kigano, a lawyer specializing in human rights cases. Dr Richard Leakey, a prominent white Kenyan and former Director of the Kenya Wildlife Service (KWS), was appointed as Safina's Secretary-General. The party (which was refused registration) aimed to combat corruption and human rights abuses by the Kenyan authorities and to campaign for the introduction of an electoral

system of proportional representation. During August several Safina officials were attacked by members of KANU's youth wing. In October Koigi wa Wamwere, a founding member of Safina, was found guilty of attempted robbery and sentenced to four years' imprisonment. Opposition members of the National Assembly subsequently denounced the conduct of Wamwere's trial, claiming that the prosecution evidence had been fabricated. Wamwere's conviction was eventually overturned in November 1997.

During the mid-1990s Kenya's human rights record came under intense domestic and international scrutiny. In April 1995 the country's Roman Catholic bishops accused the Government of eroding judicial independence and of condoning police brutality and endemic corruption. In December Amnesty International alleged that the security forces were systematically torturing criminal suspects and opposition activists. In response to its critics (and apparently motivated by the need to ensure continuing inflows of foreign assistance), the Moi administration provisionally withdrew controversial draft legislation in January 1996 that would have severely restricted the freedom of the press and, in July, inaugurated a human rights committee to investigate alleged humanitarian abuses by the Kenyan authorities. During July and September, however, Moi announced that constitutional reforms would not be considered before the next elections, scheduled to take place in late 1997.

Divisions within opposition parties continued to undermine efforts to present a cohesive challenge to Moi and KANU prior to the 1997 elections. A renewed attempt to establish a coalition of opposition organizations, initiated in November 1995, was short-lived. Meanwhile, following an unsuccessful attempt to oust Wamalwa as Chairman of FORD—Kenya, Raila Odinga (the son of Oginga Odinga and a prominent opposition activist) left that party and subsequently became leader of the National Development Party (NDP). In October 1997 Matiba's faction of FORD—Asili registered as an independent party, the Forum for the Restoration of Democracy for the People (FORD—People); Matiba had resigned from the National Assembly in May, claiming that he no longer recognized the validity of the Moi administration. During the mid-1990s several opposition deputies, disaffected by these internal rivalries, defected to KANU. Within KANU itself rivalries began to emerge, not least because the Constitution permitted Moi to stand for only one further term as President.

In January 1997 Amnesty International accused the Moi administration of failing to halt the widespread torture of detainees. In the same month the reappointment to the Cabinet of Biwott (a principal suspect in the inquiry into the assassination of Robert Ouko in 1990) provoked considerable disquiet. In February 1997 Kenya became a signatory to the UN Convention Against Torture and Other Cruel, Inhuman and Degrading Treatment or Punishment.

During the first half of 1997 Moi repeatedly refused to accede to opposition demands for a review of the Constitution prior to the forthcoming elections. Opposition organizations protested that constitutional reforms and a reorganization of the supervisory Electoral Commission were essential in order to eliminate an in-built electoral advantage for the Moi administration. In April the National Convention Executive Council (NCEC) was established as a forum embracing representatives of non-governmental organizations, religious groups and opposition parties (excluding, however, supporters of Matiba and Odinga). Pressure for constitutional reform intensified in mid-June, when opposition parliamentarians disrupted the budget speech, in protest at the Moi administration's perceived intransigence, and anti-Government activists demonstrated in Nairobi. Illegal protest rallies in early July were brutally suppressed by the security forces, resulting in several fatalities and provoking strong condemnation from abroad. Eventually, in mid-July, Moi agreed to meet with opposition and religious leaders to discuss constitutional reform. It was subsequently announced that the opposition would henceforth be permitted to organize registered public meetings, and that a constitutional review commission would be established.

At the beginning of August 1997 the IMF suspended assistance to Kenya, pending the implementation of decisive action to eliminate official corruption and to improve the system of revenue collection; the Government consequently announced the inauguration of an anti-corruption body. The NCEC organized a one-day general strike in early August, in support of its demands for constitutional reform. In late August serious unrest erupted in and around Mombasa. While the Government blamed the NCEC for orchestrating the attacks, the NCEC alleged that the Government was inciting inter-ethnic conflict with the aim of depriving opposition supporters from the predominantly Luo region of the opportunity to vote in the forthcoming elections by forcing them to flee their homes. In the following month the National Assembly approved legislation that amended the Constitution with the stated aim of ensuring free and fair democratic elections. All political parties were granted equal access to the media, and detention without trial was prohibited. In addition, the new legislation enabled the opposition to participate in selecting the 12 nominated members of the National Assembly and 10 of the 12 members of the supervisory Electoral Commission.

The presidential and legislative elections, which took place concurrently on 29 December 1997, were undermined by allegations of widespread fraud and incompetence, as well as by logistical difficulties. Moi was re-elected President, winning 40.64% of the valid votes cast. Mwai Kibaki, the leader of the DP and former Vice-President, came second, with 31.49% of the votes cast. KANU secured 107 of the 210 elected seats in the enlarged National Assembly, while the remainder were divided between nine opposition parties, with the DP taking 39 seats, the NDP 21, FORD—Kenya 17 and the Social Democratic Party 15. Safina (which had finally been registered in November) won five seats. Moi was inaugurated for a fifth (and final) term as President in January 1998. Shortly afterwards Moi appointed a new Cabinet. However, he postponed the designation of a new Vice-President, evidently in order not to give an indication of his preferred successor to the presidency. No Kikuyu or Luo were appointed as ministers. The Cabinet was reorganized in February. Following the elections, Kibaki petitioned the High Court to declare Moi's re-election invalid. A group of independent Kenyan observers had, none the less, pronounced the electoral process 'satisfactory'.

In early 1998 inter-ethnic violence erupted once again in the volatile Rift Valley. The Moi administration blamed the conflict on bitterness in the Kikuyu and Luo communities at the outcome of the elections, while the latter alleged persecution both by the security forces and by smaller tribal groups that had voted predominantly for Moi and KANU. During January and February about 100 people were reported to have been killed in the unrest, while more than 300,000 were believed to have been displaced. Government troops reportedly embarked upon a programme of disarmament in the Rift Valley in May. In July the authorities organized a judicial inquiry into the causes of the ethnic disturbances of both 1992 and 1998. In August 2000 Fr John Kaiser, a US missionary known for his outspoken criticism of human rights abuses and government misconduct, was found shot dead. Amid fears that his killing had been politically motivated, agents from the US Federal Bureau of Investigation (FBI) travelled to Kenya to assist with the investigation into the death. It was reported that Fr Kaiser had documents linking two cabinet ministers to the ethnic disturbances of 1992 and 1998, which he had intended to present to a commission of inquiry into land issues established in November 1999. In April 2001, however, the FBI investigation concluded that Kaiser had committed suicide. This verdict was rejected by the Roman Catholic Church and Kenyan human rights groups, which subsequently demanded a public inquest into Kaiser's death. Tension between the Kikuyu and Kalenjin communities in the Rift valley remained, especially over disputed land vacated by the Kikuyu during the clashes.

During early 1998 an apparent *rapprochement* between Odinga and Moi caused considerable disquiet in both the NDP and KANU. A consultative forum on the constitutional review process was inaugurated in April, with the aim of organizing the long-anticipated constitutional review commission.

In early August 1998 a car-bomb exploded at the US Embassy in central Nairobi, concurrently with a similar attack on the US mission in Dar es Salaam, Tanzania. Some 254 people were killed in Nairobi, and more than 5,000 suffered injuries. The attacks were believed to have been co-ordinated by international Islamic fundamentalist terrorists and, in mid-August, the USA retaliated by launching air strikes against targets in Afghanistan and Sudan. In the aftermath of the bomb attacks, Kenyan investigators and US federal agents made extensive nation-wide inquiries, concentrating their search for the perpetrators particularly on the Muslim community in Mombasa and the surrounding coastal region. Evidence emerged during October that young Kenyan Muslims had been systematically recruited for military training by international Islamist guerrilla groups.

Meanwhile, the Government banned five local Islamic aid organizations, provoking strong resentment in the Muslim community. Four men were convicted of involvement in the bombings by a court in New York, USA, in May 2001 and were later sentenced to life imprisonment. A total of 22 people had been charged in connection with the bomb attacks; two were to be tried separately and three awaited extradition from the United Kingdom, while a further 13, including Osama bin Laden, the fugitive Saudi-born Islamist activist whom the US authorities held ultimately responsible for the bombings, were still at large.

In October 1998 Dr Leakey, evidently disappointed by the failure of the opposition to present a united and effective alternative to KANU, announced his intention to retire from politics; during the previous month he had been reappointed as Director of the KWS.

In mid-February 1999 Turkish agents in Nairobi captured Abdullah Öcalan, the leader of the Partiya Karkeren Kurdistan (Kurdistan Workers' Party), which was engaged in an armed struggle against the Turkish Government; Öcalan was returned to Turkey to face trial. He had reportedly entered Kenya clandestinely at the beginning of February, and had been sheltered at the Greek Embassy. The precise role of the Moi administration in Öcalan's arrest remained unclear. Subsequently several Kenyan diplomatic missions in Europe were occupied by Kurdish protesters. Shortly after the capture of Öcalan, Moi dismissed two leading members of the police force and a senior immigration official who had been implicated in the affair.

In February 1999 the Cabinet was reorganized. Most significantly the Minister of Finance, Simeon Nyachae, exchanged portfolios with the Minister of Industrial Development, Yekokanda Francis Masakhalia; this effectively represented a demotion for Nyachae, who had played a leading role in ongoing attempts to eliminate corruption and financial mismanagement from the public sector. Nyachae, claiming to have been victimized by senior government figures allegedly involved in corrupt activities, immediately resigned from his new post. In early April Saitoti was reappointed to the position of Vice-President (vacant since January 1998). Later in April 1999 a minor reshuffle of the Cabinet was effected. In July Moi appointed Dr Leakey as head of the civil service and Secretary to the Cabinet, with responsibility for combating corruption in the public services. In September Moi effected a major reorganization of the Cabinet, merging several ministries and reducing the number of government ministers from 27 to 15.

During early 2000 Moi appealed for international aid to combat a severe drought and resultant famine. Aid was pledged by various donors, including the World Bank and the IMF. However, in September the World Bank suspended its support for public-sector water projects, reportedly citing large-scale misappropriation of funds. The German Government pledged Ks. 150m. to assist famine victims, but insisted that it be channelled through international charitable organizations, stating that Germany would no longer support relief operations controlled by politicians.

In December 1999 the KANU-NDP majority in the National Assembly voted in favour of appointing a parliamentary select committee on constitutional review. However, a rival commission was established by an alliance of opposition and religious groups, known as Ufungamano, which intended to propose its own recommendations for constitutional change. Moi opposed the Ufungamano commission, although many Kenyans appeared to support it. In April 2000 the parliamentary committee, headed by Raila Odinga of the NDP, completed its review, proposing the establishment of a constitutional review commission, comprising 15 members, to be nominated by the National Assembly prior to their appointment by Moi. However, in November, following months of recriminations between the two rival commissions, Prof. Yash Pal Ghai, appointed by Moi to head the parliamentary commission, refused to be sworn into office. Ghai declared that he first wanted to negotiate with Ufungamano in an attempt to unite the two groups. Discussions between Ghai and Ufungamano followed, although the leaders of Ufungamano were divided over the issue. Nevertheless, the merger went ahead in May 2001; the new commission comprised 27 members, 12 of whom were drawn from Ufungamano. The commission was to complete its review of the Constitution in time for the 2002 elections, although there were fears that it might be delayed in its task by political infighting.

In July 2000 the civil service commenced the reduction of its work-force by some 25,000 in the first three-month phase of a programme of reforms to be effected over three years. Meanwhile, a parliamentary anti-graft committee was seeking the adoption by the National Assembly of a report in which the alleged perpetrators of corruption were named. (The Government later deleted the addendum containing the list of names, causing widespread outrage.) The committee also proposed legislation on economic crimes that would allow the anti-corruption authority (which had been established in 1997 at the insistence of the IMF) to prosecute alleged perpetrators of corruption without seeking permission from the Attorney-General. As a result of these measures, the IMF announced that it was to resume lending to Kenya. The Government agreed to a number of conditions, including the introduction of a law binding public officials to declare their wealth and liabilities and the enactment of the legislation on economic crimes. However, less than one month after the resumption of aid the High Court temporarily halted the retrenchment of civil servants, pending the final determination of a lawsuit on the issue, and ruled that all civil servants who had already been retrenched should be reinstated. (The court's ruling was later challenged by the Attorney-General.) The revelation in October that Leakey and his staff were earning approximately 50 times the basic civil-service wage, and that their salaries were being paid with loans from international donors, caused controversy. In January 2001 the IMF and the World Bank expressed concern over the setbacks in the reforms, particularly the failure to approve legislation on public-service ethics and economic crimes, and suspended aid to Kenya until the situation could be resolved. In August Kenyan deputies again refused to approve anti-corruption legislation, and the IMF suspended aid to Kenya indefinitely. Moi subsequently created a new police body to combat corruption. Meanwhile, in March Leakey resigned as head of the civil service and Secretary to the Cabinet (two months before the expiry of his contract) and was replaced by Dr Sally Kosgei, an ally of Moi. Leakey's departure, along with the dismissal of most of his colleagues, prompted a major reshuffle within the senior civil service. Many observers believed that Moi was now intent on gathering loyal followers around him in preparation for the 2002 elections.

In January 2001 Raila Odinga of the Luo-dominated NDP signed a memorandum of understanding with KANU, which allowed Moi to appoint ministers from the NDP. The agreement suggested that the two parties were intending to form an alliance to contest the 2002 elections. This prompted opposition parties to search for ways to counter such an alliance; members of smaller ethnic groups particularly feared losing representation. In June 2001 Moi reshuffled the Cabinet and appointed Odinga as Minister of Energy, thereby creating the first coalition Government in Kenya's history. Moi reshuffled the Cabinet again in November, introducing younger KANU ministers in an apparent attempt to provide suitable candidates for his succession; most notably Uhuru Kenyatta (son of the late President Jomo Kenyatta) and Cyrus Jirongo were appointed as Minister for Local Government and Minister for Rural Development, respectively. Saitoti remained Vice-President, while the Secretary-General of KANU, Joseph Kamotho, hitherto Minister of Local Government, was named Minister of the Environment. Furthermore, Moi appointed Chrisanthus Okemo, previously Minister of Finance, as co-Minister of Energy, which, effectively, amounted to a demotion for both Okemo and Odinga. In late November violent clashes erupted between the mainly Luo tenants of the Kibera slums in Nairobi and their predominantly Nubian landlords. The unrest was triggered by statements made by Moi and Odinga (a Luo) that rents in the area should be reduced; many observers suspected the violence was politically motivated, although there were conflicting views as to whether it was intended to strengthen or weaken Odinga's position.

The NDP was dissolved and absorbed into KANU in mid-March 2002, despite opposition from elements within both parties; Moi was elected as party Chairman, while Odinga was elected as Secretary-General, when the incumbent, Kamotho, withdrew from the contest. In June it emerged that the Government was considering using its parliamentary majority to extend the life of the National Assembly by one year, thereby delaying the elections. However, in response to fierce criticism, both domestic and international, Kanu abandoned the proposal in the following month. In July some 12 opposition parties, including the DP, FORD—Kenya and the National Party of Kenya, formed an electoral alliance, the National Alliance Party of Kenya (NAK).

In August 2002 Moi publicly announced that he favoured Uhuru Kenyatta as KANU's presidential candidate. However,

several senior KANU members, including Vice-President Saitoti and Odinga, subsequently announced their intention to seek the party's presidential nomination and formed the Rainbow Alliance to campaign within KANU for a democratic vote to select its candidate. Moi responded by dismissing the Vice-President. In mid-October, in protest at Moi's attempts to impose his preferred successor, members of the Rainbow Alliance resigned from their posts in the Government and from KANU, together with some 30 KANU deputies. The Rainbow Alliance subsequently boycotted the KANU conference, at which Kenyatta's presidential candidacy was endorsed. It was widely believed that Moi was hoping to extend his rule through Kenyatta, a close family friend of Moi, who was likely to protect Moi's wealth and shield him from prosecution. Later in October the Rainbow Alliance established a new party, the Liberal Democratic Party, and joined with the NAK to form the National Rainbow Coalition (NARC), with Mwai Kibaki as its presidential candidate. Shortly afterwards, and with nine more ex-KANU members in their ranks, the NARC proposed a vote of no confidence against Moi's Government, stating that the Government was illegally attempting to block the introduction of a new constitution, and citing Moi's failure to appoint a new Vice-President. However, Moi forestalled the tabling of the motion by dissolving the National Assembly on 25 October; thereby ensuring, moreover, that the elections would be held under the current Constitution.

At the presidential and legislative elections, held concurrently on 27 December 2002, the opposition secured an emphatic victory, with Mwai Kibaki winning 62.3% of the votes cast in the presidential election, and the NARC securing 125 of the 210 elected seats in the National Assembly, while Kenyatta received 31.2% of the votes cast for the presidency, and KANU won 64 seats in the legislature. The NARC were allocated a further seven appointed seats, increasing their representation to 132, and KANU a further four seats, bringing their total to 68. The electoral turn-out was 56.1%. Moi stepped down, as promised, and following his inauguration as President on 30 December, Kibaki promised reforms, including the adoption of a new constitution, under which certain powers would be transferred from the President to the legislature and the full independence of the judiciary guaranteed, the adoption of anti-corruption legislation, the privatization of state-owned companies and the dismissal of corrupt civil servants. In January 2003 Kibaki appointed a new Government, which abolished fees for primary education with immediate effect. However, the Government suffered a set-back in late January, when a charter aircraft near the Ugandan border crashed, killing Ahmed Mohamed Khalif, the new Minister of Labour and Human Resources Development, and injuring three other ministers who were also on board. Meanwhile, Kibaki himself was hospitalized to receive further treatment for injuries he sustained in a car crash during campaigning.

Meanwhile, on 28 November 2002 two simultaneous terrorist attacks were carried out in Kenya. In Mombasa, two surface-to-air missiles narrowly missed an Israeli charter aircraft as it took off from Mombasa airport, while in a nearby tourist resort suicide bombers attacked an Israeli-owned hotel, killing 18 people and injuring many more. The militant Islamist al-Qa'ida (Base) organization later claimed responsibility for the attacks. Agents from the US and Israeli intelligence services arrived in Kenya soon afterwards to assist the Kenyan authorities with their investigations, and by the end of the month 12 people had been arrested.

Kenya's relations with Tanzania were strained during the late 1970s. However, the Kenya–Tanzania border, which had been closed prior to the dissolution of the East African Community (EAC) in 1977, was reopened in November 1983, following an agreement on the distribution of EAC assets and liabilities between the three former members (Kenya, Tanzania and Uganda), and in December Kenya and Tanzania agreed to establish full diplomatic relations. Following the seizure of power by the National Resistance Army in Uganda in January 1986, Moi offered full co-operation to the new Ugandan President, Yoweri Museveni. After visits to Kenya by Museveni and President Ali Hassan Mwinyi of Tanzania in June, it was announced that joint commissions were to be formed to enhance co-operation between the three countries. In September, however, Ugandan authorities claimed that Kenya was harbouring anti-Museveni rebels, and stationed troops at the two countries' common border. These claims were denied, and in December, when Ugandan troops allegedly entered Kenya in pursuit of rebels, Ugandan and Kenyan armed forces exchanged fire across the border for several days; at least 15 people were reported to have been killed. Later in December Moi and Museveni agreed to withdraw troops from either side of the border. In July 1988 the Ugandan Government accused Kenya of complicity in smuggling weapons to rebels in Uganda. During 1988–89 the Kenyan authorities repeatedly accused the Ugandan armed forces of making incursions into Kenya. Moi visited Museveni in August 1990, indicating a renewed *détente* between Kenya and Uganda. In November 1994 Moi, Museveni and Mwinyi met in Arusha, Tanzania, and established a commission for co-operation; in March 1996 the Secretariat of the Permanent Tripartite Commission for East African Co-operation was formally inaugurated, with a view to reviving the EAC. A treaty for the re-establishment of the EAC, providing for the promotion of free trade between the member states, the development of the region's infrastructure and economy and the creation of a regional legislative assembly and court, was ratified by the Kenyan, Tanzanian and Ugandan Heads of State in November 1999. The new EAC (see p. 339) was officially inaugurated in Arusha in January 2001.

Relations between Kenya and Sudan deteriorated in mid-1988, as the two countries made mutual accusations of aiding rebel factions. In early 1989 Sudan renewed a long-standing dispute with Kenya over the sovereignty of territory on the Kenyan side of the two countries' common border, known as the 'Elemi triangle'. During the late 1990s Kenya hosted a series of peace talks between the Sudanese Government and opposition leaders, under the auspices of the Intergovernmental Authority on Development (see p. 242), in an attempt to resolve the conflict in southern Sudan. Further negotiations were held in Nairobi in September 2000 and June 2001, and in July 2002 the Sudanese Government and the opposition Sudan People's Liberation Army signed an accord in Machakos, Kenya, which provided for the holding of a referendum on self-determination for southern Sudan after a transitional period of six years.

Somalia has traditionally laid claim to part of north-eastern Kenya. During 1989 tension developed between the Kenyan authorities and ethnic Somalis from both sides of the Kenya–Somalia border, when Somalis were alleged to be largely responsible for wildlife-poaching and banditry in north-eastern Kenya. In September Moi protested strongly to the Somali Government, following an incursion into Kenya by Somali troops (reportedly pursuing Somali rebels), which resulted in the deaths of four Kenyans. The Kenyan Government closed the two countries' common border in mid-1999, in response to rising insecurity in the area. The border was reopened in April 2000. In September the Kenyan Minister of Foreign Affairs and International Co-operation, Dr Bonaya Godana, stated that, while the Government supported the peace process in Somalia, it had not, as had been reported, officially declared recognition of the interim Somali President, Abdulkasim Hasan, or his Government. Moi later agreed to mediate between the interim Government and opposing rebel factions in Somalia.

Relations between the Kenyan and Ethiopian Governments became strained in 1997, owing to an increased incidence of cross-border cattle-rustling, including an attack in March during which 16 members of the Kenyan security forces were killed. A number of communiqués were subsequently signed by representatives of the two countries, agreeing to reinforce border security, to take measures to prevent the smuggling of arms and drugs, and to enhance trade. In November 1998 some 189 people (mainly Somalis) were found to have been massacred in north-eastern Kenya; Ethiopian guerrillas were widely believed to be responsible. In January 1999 the Kenyan Government protested to the Ethiopian authorities, following an incursion into Kenya by Ethiopian security forces, who were alleged to be in pursuit of Ethiopian rebels. Kenya deployed additional troops at the two countries' common frontier in May, following a series of landmine explosions in the region, which had resulted in several fatalities. Ethiopian troops allegedly made a further infiltration into Kenyan territory in July. Bilateral relations deteriorated further during late 2000 after it was reported that some 50 Kenyans had been killed, allegedly by Ethiopian militia forces, in cross-border clashes. In January 2001 representatives from both countries met in Nairobi and agreed to initiate measures aimed at ending border disputes.

In October 1995, despite strong condemnation from foreign Governments, the Kenyan authorities refused to permit the international tribunal that was investigating war crimes committed in Rwanda during 1994 access to alleged Rwandan perpetrators of genocide who had fled to Kenya. In June 1996

the Moi Government closed the Rwandan embassy in Nairobi in protest at the Rwandan Government's refusal to waive diplomatic immunity for an embassy official who was suspected of plotting a murder in Kenya; the diplomat was deported. In September, however, the first arrest in Kenya was made of a Rwandan Hutu suspected of involvement in genocide. Kenya strongly denied accusations, in November, of supplying arms to Rwandan Hutu rebels operating from within Zaire (now the Democratic Republic of the Congo). Following the *coup d'état* in Burundi in July 1996, Kenya, along with other countries of the region, imposed full economic sanctions on the administration of Maj. Pierre Buyoya; these sanctions were subsequently relaxed, and eventually withdrawn in January 1999. In November and December 1996 regional summit meetings were held in Nairobi to discuss the crisis in the Great Lakes region. Relations between the Kenyan and Rwandan Governments improved during 1997, when further Rwandan Hutus were arrested by the Kenyan security forces to stand trial on charges of genocide at the UN tribunal in Arusha, Tanzania. During a visit by Moi to Rwanda in May 2000 the two countries agreed to reopen the Kenyan embassy in Kigali and to establish a joint commission for bilateral relations.

In early 1995 Kenya was reportedly sheltering about 200,000 refugees from the conflict in Somalia. The Moi Government, which claims that the refugees place an intolerable burden on the country's resources, has repeatedly requested the UN to repatriate the total refugee population. By mid-1998 an estimated 155,000 Somalis had been repatriated from Kenya, with assistance from the office of the UN High Commissioner for Refugees. However, continuing instability in Somalia resulted in further influxes of refugees to Kenya. Kenya's total refugee population stood at 239,221 at the end of 2001, including 144,349 from Somalia.

Government

Legislative power is vested in the unicameral National Assembly, with 224 members (210 elected by universal adult suffrage, the Attorney-General, the Speaker and 12 nominated members), who serve a term of five years, subject to dissolution. Executive power is held by the President, also directly elected for five years, who is assisted by an appointed Vice-President and Cabinet.

Defence

In August 2002 Kenya's active armed forces numbered 24,400, comprising an army of 20,000, an air force of 3,000 and a navy of 1,400, and the paramilitary Police General Service Unit had a membership of 5,000. Military service is voluntary. Defence was allocated Ks. 14,441m. in the budget for the financial year to 30 June 2002 (equivalent to 6.1% of total budgetary expenditure by the central Government). Military assistance is received from the United Kingdom and from the USA, whose Rapid Deployment Force uses port and onshore facilities in Kenya.

Economic Affairs

In 2001, according to estimates by the World Bank, Kenya's gross national income (GNI), measured at average 1999–2001 prices, was US $10,309m., equivalent to $340 per head (or $1,020 per head on an international purchasing-power parity basis). During 1990–2001, it was estimated, the population increased at an average annual rate of 2.5%, while gross domestic product (GDP) per head declined, in real terms, by an average of 0.9% per year. Overall GDP increased, in real terms, at an average annual rate of 1.6% in 1990–2001 Real GDP declined by 0.2% in 2000, but increased by 1.1% in 2001.

Agriculture (including forestry and fishing) contributed 20.8% of GDP and employed about 75.0% of the labour force in 2001. The principal cash crops are tea (which contributed 29.3% of total export earnings in 2000) and coffee (accounting for 9.8% of export earnings in 2000). Horticultural produce (Kenya is the world's fourth largest exporter of cut flowers), pyrethrum, sisal, sugar cane and cotton are also important. Maize is the principal subsistence crop. There is a significant dairy industry for domestic consumption and export. During 1990–2001, according to the World Bank, agricultural GDP increased at an average annual rate of 0.9%. Agricultural GDP declined by 2.3% in 2000, largely owing to severe drought, but increased by 3.0% in 2001.

Industry (including mining, manufacturing, construction and power) contributed 19.2% of GDP in 2001 and employed an estimated 19.8% of the total labour force in 1995. During 1990–2001, according to the World Bank, industrial GDP increased at an average annual rate of 1.4%. Industrial GDP declined by 1.3% in 2000, but increased by 1.4% in 2001.

Mining contributed 0.2% of GDP (at factor cost) in 2000. Soda ash is the principal mineral export. Fluorspar, iron ore, salt, limestone, gold, gemstones (including rubies and sapphires), vermiculite and lead are also mined. Kenya has substantial reserves of titanium.

Manufacturing contributed 13.4% of GDP in 2001. During 1990–2001, according to the World Bank, manufacturing GDP increased at an average annual rate of 1.9%. Manufacturing GDP declined by 1.5% in 2000, but increased by 1.4% in 2001.

Hydroelectric power accounted for 72.4% of total electricity generated in 1999, while a further 19.0% was derived from petroleum. Energy for domestic use is derived principally from fuel wood and charcoal. Prolonged drought led to severe power shortages in 2000. Some 347 KW of generating capacity was to be added to the national grid by 2003. In January 2001 it was announced that Kenya and Tanzania were to import electricity from Zambia under a cross-border energy project, which was expected to cost US \$153.5m. and to be completed by 2003. In 2000 imports of mineral fuels and lubricants (including crude petroleum intended for refining) comprised 26.2% of the value of total imports.

The services sector contributed 60.1% of GDP in 2001, and engaged 15.5% of the total labour force in 1991. Tourism makes an important contribution to Kenya's economy, and has been the country's principal source of foreign exchange since 1987. In 1998, however, a decline of 10.6% in tourist arrivals, to 894,300, was attributed partly to the effects of civil unrest in coastal areas during 1997. In 1999–2000 there was some recovery in tourism, with arrivals increasing to 1,036,628 in 2000. The GDP of the services sector increased at an average annual rate of 2.5% in 1990–2001, according to the World Bank. Services GDP increased by 1.0% in 2000, but decreased by 2.4% in 2001.

In 2001 Kenya recorded a visible trade deficit of US \$1,282.1m., and there was a deficit of \$317.8m. on the current account of the balance of payments. In 2000 the principal source of imports was the United Arab Emirates (which supplied 19.5% of total imports in that year); other major suppliers were the United Kingdom, South Africa, Saudi Arabia and Japan. Uganda was the principal market for Kenya's exports (purchasing 18.0%) in that year; other important purchasers were the United Kingdom, Tanzania, Pakistan and the Netherlands. The principal exports in 2000 were tea, vegetables and fruit, coffee and refined petroleum products. The principal imports in that year were petroleum and petroleum products, aircraft and parts, cereals and cereal preparations, and road vehicles and parts.

In the financial year ending 30 June 2001 there was a budgetary deficit of Ks. 14,705m., equivalent to 1.6% of GDP. In the financial year ending 30 June 2002 the deficit was Ks. 26,900m. The country's external debt was US \$6,295m. at the end of 2000, of which \$5,180m. was long-term public debt. In that year the cost of debt-servicing was equivalent to 17.3% of the value of exports of goods and services. The annual rate of inflation averaged 14.1% in 1990–2001; consumer prices increased by an average of 5.9% in 2000 and by 3.6% in 2001. Some 23% of the labour force were estimated to be unemployed in late 2000, and the rate of unemployment was reported to be approaching 30% by October 2001.

Kenya is a member of the Common Market for Eastern and Southern Africa (see p. 162) and, with Tanzania and Uganda, of the East African Community (see p. 339). The International Tea Promotion Association (see p. 337) is based in Kenya.

Kenya's economy is reasonably diversified, although most employment is dependent on agriculture. Agricultural development has been intermittently hindered by adverse weather conditions (generally low rainfall, although severe flooding occurred in 1997–98), resulting in sporadic food shortages, and also by rural ethnic unrest. Moreover, the country is highly vulnerable to fluctuations in international prices for its cash crops, most notably tea and coffee. A decline in economic growth in 2000 was attributed to the negative impact on production of prolonged drought; power rationing and increased energy costs; poor telecommunications and transport services; and inefficient institutions in the agricultural sector. Despite some rainfall in

late 2000, which led to a slight revival in the agricultural sector, the economy continued to perform poorly throughout the first half of 2001. However, by mid-2001 the Central Bank of Kenya was predicting a recovery later in the year, fuelled mainly by a resumption of regular and widespread rains and a consequent improvement in the availability of hydroelectric power. The ensuing growth in agriculture resulted in increased demand in the manufacturing sector and a reduction in the rate of inflation. Furthermore, improvements in Kenya's balance of payments led to an increase in the country's reserves of foreign exchange. However, unemployment continued to increase, and GDP growth in 2001, at 1.1%, was lower than initially forecast, owing, in part, to a decline in coffee production, low commodity prices and dwindling investor confidence. In July 1997 the IMF suspended assistance to Kenya, owing to concerns about corruption in the financial and public sectors and weak revenue collection. The IMF resumed aid to Kenya in July 2000, following promising signs of public-sector reform; however, funding was again withheld in January 2001, when the reform process suffered serious set-backs. Following the inauguration of the Kibaki administration, the IMF visited Nairobi in January 2003 for talks with the new Government; it was anticipated that discussions on a new IMF-supported programme for Kenya would commence by May. The new Government aimed to achieve annual GDP growth of 6%, to create 500,000 new jobs and to reduce the budget deficit within two years. The Government's stated priorities were to rebuild Kenya's infrastructure, improve the delivery of services, such as telecommunications and electricity, and to tackle the high levels of corruption. It was hoped that these measures would lead to the normalization of relations with donor countries and institutions, and consequently to a resumption of aid to Kenya, which was considered particularly important, as the new Government had inherited a deficit of US \$800m.—almost double the expected amount. The tourism industry, Kenya's largest source of foreign exchange, was expected to suffer as a result of the terrorist attacks in Mombasa in November 2002 (see Recent History), with some analysts predicting that it could take up to three years to recover.

Education

The Government provides, or assists in the provision of, schools. Primary education, which is compulsory, is provided free of charge. The education system involves eight years of primary education (beginning at six years of age), four years at secondary school and four years of university education. The total enrolment at primary schools increased from about 900,000 in 1963 to 5,544,998 in 1995. Primary enrolment in 1998/99 was equivalent to 90.7% of children in the relevant age-group (males 91.4%; females 90.0%). In the same year, however, secondary enrolment was equivalent to only 29.9% of the appropriate age-group (males 31.5%; females 28.2%), according to UNESCO estimates. There are five state universities and five chartered private universities. In 1998/99 there were 61,526 students enrolled at institutes of higher education. The education sector was allocated Ks. 52,277.4m. in the budget for 2001/02 (equivalent to 22.2% of total budgetary expenditure by the central Government).

Public Holidays

2003: 1 January (New Year's Day), 12 February* (Id al-Adha, Feast of the Sacrifice), 18–21 April (Easter), 1 May (Labour Day), 1 June (Madaraka Day, anniversary of self-government), 10 October (Moi Day), 20 October (Kenyatta Day), 26 November* (Id al-Fitr, end of Ramadan), 12 December (Independence Day), 25–26 December (Christmas).

2004: 1 January (New Year's Day), 2 February* (Id al Adha, Feast of the Sacrifice), 9–12 April (Easter), 1 May (Labour Day, anniversary of self-government), 1 June (Madaraka Day, anniversary of self-government), 10 October (Moi Day), 20 October (Kenyatta Day), 14 November* (Id al Fitr, end of Ramadan), 12 December (Independence Day), 25–26 December (Christmas).

*These holidays are determined by the Islamic lunar calendar and may vary by one or two days from the dates given.

Weights and Measures

The metric system is in use.

Statistical Survey

Source (unless otherwise stated): Central Bureau of Statistics, Ministry of Finance and Planning, POB 30266, Nairobi; tel. (20) 333971; fax (20) 333030.

Area and Population

AREA, POPULATION AND DENSITY

Area (sq km)	580,367*
Population (census results)†	
24 August 1989	21,443,636
24 August 1999	
Males	14,205,589
Females.	14,481,018
Total	28,686,607
Population (official estimates at mid-year)	
2000	29,573,434
2001	30,493,792
Density (per sq km) at mid-2001	52.5

* 224,081 sq miles. Total includes 11,230 sq km (4,336 sq miles) of inland water.
† Excluding adjustment for underenumeration.

PRINCIPAL ETHNIC GROUPS
(census of August 1989)

African	21,163,076	European		34,560
Arab	41,595	Other*		115,220
Asian	89,185	**Total**		21,443,636

* Includes persons who did not state 'tribe' or 'race'.

POPULATION BY PROVINCE
(census of August 1999)

Nairobi	2,143,254	Nyanza		4,392,196
Central	3,724,159	Rift Valley . . .		6,987,036
Coast	2,487,264	Western		3,358,776
Eastern	4,631,779	**Total**		28,686,607
North-Eastern . .	962,143			

PRINCIPAL TOWNS
(estimated population at census of August 1989)

Nairobi (capital) . .	1,346,000	Meru		78,100
Mombasa	465,000	Thika		57,100
Kisumu*	185,100	Kitale		53,000
Nakuru	162,800	Kisii		44,000
Eldoret*	104,900	Kericho		40,000
Nyeri*	88,600	Malindi*		35,200

* Boundaries extended between 1979 and 1989.

BIRTHS AND DEATHS
(UN estimates, annual averages)

	1985–90	1990–95	1995–2000
Birth rate (per 1,000)	46.2	38.1	35.4
Death rate (per 1,000)	11.1	10.5	12.1

Source: UN, *World Population Prospects: The 2000 Revision.*

Expectation of life (WHO estimates, years at birth): 48.9 (males 48.2; females 49.6) in 2001 (Source: WHO, *World Health Report*).

ECONOMICALLY ACTIVE POPULATION
(estimates, '000 persons, 1991)

	Males	Females	Total
Agriculture, etc.	4,587	3,270	7,857
Industry	657	159	816
Services	972	615	1,587
Total	6,216	4,044	10,260

Source: UN Economic Commission for Africa, *African Statistical Yearbook*.

Mid-2001 (estimates in '000): Agriculture, etc. 12,140; Total labour force 16,188 (Source: FAO).

Health and Welfare

KEY INDICATORS

Total fertility rate (children per woman, 2001).	4.3
Under-5 mortality rate (per 1,000 live births, 2001) . . .	122
HIV/AIDS (% of persons aged 15–49, 2001).	15.01
Physicians (per 1,000 head, 1995)	0.13
Hospital beds (per 1,000 head, 1990)	1.65
Health expenditure (2000): US $ per head (PPP)	115
Health expenditure (2000): % of GDP	8.3
Health expenditure (2000): public (% of total)	22.2
Access to water (% of persons, 2000).	49
Access to sanitation (% of persons, 2000)	86
Human Development Index (2000): ranking	134
Human Development Index (2000): value	0.513

For sources and definitions, see explanatory note on p. vi.

Agriculture

PRINCIPAL CROPS
('000 metric tons)

	1999	2000	2001
Wheat	190	181	180*
Rice (paddy)	65	55	55*
Barley*	50	45	45
Maize	2,300	2,200	2,700†
Millet	59	45	50*
Sorghum	110	133	133*
Potatoes*	470	500	500
Sweet potatoes	600	535	535*
Cassava (Manioc)*	930	950	950
Sugar cane*	5,200	4,750	5,150
Pulses*	240	230	230
Groundnuts (in shell)	31	30*	30*
Coconuts	64	63*	63*
Sesame seed*	11	10	10
Cottonseed*	15	13	13
Tomatoes*	31	30	30
Dry onions*	21	20	20
Green beans*	22	21	21
Other vegetables*	580	570	570
Bananas*	220	210	210
Plantains*	380	370	370
Oranges*	27	26	26
Grapefruits*	15	13	13
Mangoes*	24	22	22
Pineapples*	290	280	280
Other fruits (excl. melons)* . .	48	45	45
Coffee (green)	71	100	75†
Tea (made)	249	236	240†
Tobacco (leaves)	17	18	18*
Sisal	18	25*	25*

* FAO estimate(s).
† Unofficial figure.

Source: FAO.

LIVESTOCK
('000 head, year ending September)

	1999	2000	2001*
Cattle	13,392†	13,794†	12,500
Sheep*	7,500	7,000	6,500
Goats*	10,200	9,600	9,000
Pigs	301	315	315
Camels	811	825	830
Chickens	31	32	32

* FAO estimates.
† Unofficial figure.

Source: FAO.

LIVESTOCK PRODUCTS
('000 metric tons)

	1999	2000	2001*
Beef and veal	279	287	290
Mutton and lamb*	25	24	24
Goats' meat*	34	32	32
Pig meat*	10	12	12
Poultry meat	56*	54	54
Game meat*	13	14	14
Camel meat*	20	20	20
Cows' milk*	2,320	2,250	1,800
Sheeps' milk*	33	31	31
Goats' milk*	102	96	96
Hen eggs*	59	60	61
Honey	25*	25	25
Wool: greasy	2*	2	2
Cattle hides*	38	39	39
Goatskins*	11	10	10

* FAO estimate(s).

Source: FAO.

Forestry

ROUNDWOOD REMOVALS
(FAO estimates, '000 cubic metres, excluding bark)

	1999	2000	2001
Sawlogs, veneer logs and logs for sleepers*	460	460	460
Pulpwood*	357	357	357
Other industrial wood	1,160	1,160	1,160
Fuel wood	19,521	19,658	19,827
Total	21,498	21,635	21,804

* Annual output is assumed to be unchanged since 1989.

Source: FAO.

SAWNWOOD PRODUCTION
('000 cubic metres, including railway sleepers)

	1987	1988	1989
Total	195	188	185

1990–2001: Production as in 1989 (FAO estimates).

Source: FAO.

Fishing

('000 metric tons, live weight)

	1998	1999	2000
Capture	172.6	205.3	215.1
Silver cyprinid	42.3	48.8	49.6
Nile tilapia	14.7	17.5	19.3
Other tilapias	19.7	18.2	19.9
Nile perch	76.7	103.0	109.8
Aquaculture	0.2	0.3	0.5
Total catch	172.7	205.6	215.6

Note: Figures exclude crocodiles, recorded by number rather than by weight. The number of Nile crocodiles caught was: 714 in 1998; 3,350 in 1999; 2,460 in 2000.

Source: FAO, *Yearbook of Fishery Statistics*.

Mining

('000 metric tons)

	1998	1999	2000
Soda ash	242.9	245.7	238.2
Fluorspar	60.9	93.6	100.1
Salt	21.7	44.9	16.4
Limestone flux	32	32	32

Industry

SELECTED PRODUCTS
('000 metric tons, unless otherwise indicated)

	1998	1999	2000
Wheat flour	230	224	189
Raw sugar	449	470	402
Beer ('000 hectolitres)	2,630	1,884	2,029
Cigarettes (million)	7,599	7,231	6,009
Cement	1,453	1,421	1,146
Kerosene and jet fuels	355	337	400
Motor spirit (petrol)	296	285	335
Gas-diesel (distillate fuel) oils	429	431	511
Residual fuel oil	499	507	616
Electric energy (million kWh)	4,420	4,432	3,958

Finance

CURRENCY AND EXCHANGE RATES

Monetary Units
100 cents = 1 Kenya shilling (Ks.)
Ks. 20 = 1 Kenya pound (K£)

Sterling, Dollar and Euro Equivalents (31 December 2002)
£1 sterling = Ks. 124.22
US $1 = Ks. 77.07
€1 = Ks. 80.83
Ks. 1,000 = £8.0499 sterling = $12.975 = €12.372

Average Exchange Rate (Ks. per US $)
2000   76.176
2001   78.563
2002   78.749

Note: The foregoing information refers to the Central Bank's mid-point exchange rate. However, with the introduction of a foreign exchange bearer certificate (FEBC) scheme in October 1991, a dual exchange rate system is in effect. In May 1994 foreign exchange transactions were liberalized and the Kenya shilling became fully convertible against other currencies.

BUDGET
(Ks. million, year ending 30 June)

Revenue	1999/2000	2000/01	2001/02*
Tax revenue	151,359.5	169,759.2	179,008.0
Taxes on income and profits	53,317.0	54,796.1	59,952.0
Taxes on goods and services	69,437.3	81,165.4	87,407.0
Value-added tax	40,944.2	51,590.3	56,165.0
Excise duties	28,493.1	29,575.1	31,242.0
Taxes on international trade	28,605.2	33,797.7	31,649.0
Import duties	28,605.2	33,797.7	31,649.0
Non-tax revenue	26,061.3	26,759.5	25,171.5
Property income	5,988.4	6,452.8	5,701.0
Administrative fees and charges	20,072.9	20,306.7	19,470.5
Total	180,541.4	200,338.8	206,665.6

Expenditure	1999/2000	2000/01	2001/02*
General administration	41,426.6	81,611.6	69,926.4
Defence	10,427.2	14,266.1	14,441.0
Social services	60,286.0	67,054.6	70,387.0
Education	47,493.2	50,738.6	52,277.4
Health	10,054.2	13,500.9	14,066.9
Economic services	27,707.9	48,639.4	46,145.5
General administration	5,047.9	17,193.7	11,267.9
Agriculture, forestry and fishing	7,695.7	11,097.4	9,713.6
Roads	8,848.5	10,774.1	13,819.2
Interest on public debt	28,917.8	31,128.5	34,932.1
Total	168,765.5	242,700.2	235,832.0

* Forecasts.

INTERNATIONAL RESERVES
(US $ million at 31 December)

	2000	2001	2002
IMF special drawing rights . . .	0.3	1.0	0.8
Reserve position in IMF . .	16.2	15.8	17.1
Foreign exchange	881.2	1,048.1	1,050.0
Total	897.7	1,064.9	1,067.9

Source: IMF, *International Financial Statistics*.

MONEY SUPPLY
(Ks. million at 31 December)

	1999	2000	2001
Currency outside banks . . .	42,963	43,466	45,349
Demand deposits at commercial banks	56,849	65,206	76,220
Total money (incl. others) . . .	109,506	118,968	126,332

Source: IMF, *International Financial Statistics*.

COST OF LIVING
(Consumer Price Index for low-income group in Nairobi; annual averages; base: 1990 = 100)

	1999	2000	2001
Food, beverages and tobacco . .	408.5	421.8	431.9
All items (incl. others)	387.7	410.5	425.2

Source: ILO.

NATIONAL ACCOUNTS
(Ks. million at current prices)

Expenditure on the Gross Domestic Product

	1998	1999	2000
Government final consumption expenditure	113,568.4	125,943.0	142,133.6
Private final consumption expenditure	510,082.8	537,861.9	602,353.4
Increase in stocks	6,210.0	7,141.5	6,141.7
Gross fixed capital formation . .	113,858.0	112,923.1	116,555.2
Total domestic expenditure . .	743,719.2	783,869.5	867,183.9
Exports of goods and services . .	171,894.7	188,693.1	208,799.8
Less Imports of goods and services	224,771.9	232,232.6	287,066.7
GDP in purchasers' values* . .	690,842.0	740,330.0	788,917.0
GDP at constant 1982 prices .	116,444	n.a.	n.a.

Gross Domestic Product by Economic Activity
(at factor cost)

	1998	1999	2000
Agriculture, hunting, forestry and fishing	156,953	149,179	134,010
Mining and quarrying	823	994	1,143
Manufacturing	65,971	78,535	87,974
Electricity, gas and water . . .	6,962	7,368	7,624
Construction	23,933	27,070	29,134
Trade, restaurants and hotels . .	123,453	137,316	150,253
Transport, storage and communication	43,255	45,617	49,892
Finance, insurance, real estate and business services	105,623	109,469	106,798
Other services	66,380	81,815	105,393
Total*	593,353	637,362	672,219

* Based on unrounded data.

BALANCE OF PAYMENTS
(US $ million)

	1999	2000	2001
Exports of goods f.o.b.	1,756.7	1,782.2	1,894.0
Imports of goods f.o.b.	−2,731.8	−3,044.0	−3,176.1
Trade balance	−975.1	−1,261.7	−1,282.1
Exports of services	934.5	993.4	1,087.2
Imports of services	−570.4	−724.5	−825.5
Balance on goods and services	−611.0	−992.9	−1,020.4
Other income received	31.7	45.0	42.8
Other income paid	−190.9	−178.1	−190.3
Balance on goods, services and income	−770.2	−1,126.0	−1,167.8
Current transfers received . . .	685.3	926.6	850.0
Current transfers paid	−4.7	−4.2	—
Current balance	−89.6	−203.7	−317.8
Capital account	55.4	49.6	69.0
Direct investment from abroad . .	13.8	110.9	5.3
Portfolio investment assets . . .	—	−10.9	−7.3
Portfolio investment liabilities . .	−8.0	−6.0	2.4
Other investment assets . . .	−89.9	−55.7	−86.4
Other investment liabilities . .	249.7	116.5	167.2
Net errors and omissions . . .	−165.5	−10.0	117.0
Overall balance	−34.0	−6.8	−47.5

Source: IMF, *International Financial Statistics*.

External Trade

PRINCIPAL COMMODITIES
(distribution by SITC, Ks. million)

Imports c.i.f.	1998	1999	2000
Food and live animals . . .	18,905.4	13,093.0	21,332.6
Cereals and cereal preparations .	11,071.7	85,114.0	14,353.3
Crude materials (inedible) except fuels	6,299.3	5,788.4	6,364.0
Mineral fuels, lubricants, etc .	32,189.1	41,865.2	64,855.9
Petroleum, petroleum products, etc	31,628.5	41,332.5	64,358.0
Crude petroleum oils	15,036.6	22,355.3	41,907.2
Refined petroleum products . .	16,317.9	18,433.1	21,882.6
Animal and vegetable oils, fats and waxes	8,750.1	9,193.7	8,015.8
Chemicals and related products	30,018.1	31,987.3	32,796.7
Medicinal and pharmaceutical products	6,559.4	6,373.4	5,975.8
Artificial resins, plastic materials, etc	6,108.2	6,039.9	7,134.8
Basic manufactures	25,307.2	28,179.4	27,562.4
Iron and steel	7,899.7	9,102.6	8,603.8
Machinery and transport equipment	63,341.0	59,555.7	72,131.3
Power-generating machinery and equipment	5,760.0	6,045.0	12,142.8
Machinery specialized for particular industries	7,564.8	5,901.7	4,817.6
General industrial machinery, equipment and parts	8,735.8	8,524.0	8,831.9
Electrical machinery, apparatus, etc	6,310.7	6,410.1	6,685.3
Road vehicles and parts* . . .	17,737.0	15,004.5	12,546.1
Passenger motor cars (excl. buses)	6,458.8	5,289.2	4,764.9
Motor vehicles for goods transport and special purposes	6,062.5	4,798.5	2,798.1
Aircraft, associated equipment and parts*	8,545.7	8,838.5	14,972.7
Miscellaneous manufactured articles	12,002.4	15,290.0	13,353.8
Total (incl. others)	197,788.7	206,400.6	247,803.9

* Data on parts exclude tyres, engines and electrical parts.

Exports f.o.b.*	1998	1999	2000
Food and live animals . . .	63,285.0	63,471.2	66,953.7
Vegetables and fruit	9,384.0	11,147.8	13,420.8
Fresh or simply preseved			
vegetables	3,714.6	4,327.9	7,812.7
Coffee, tea, cocoa and spices . .	46,393.9	45,749.1	47,519.5
Coffee (green and roasted) . .	12,817.4	12,029.3	11,707.1
Tea	32,970.7	33,065.1	35,149.9
Crude materials (inedible)			
except fuels	10,196.7	11,578.9	13,575.9
Cut flowers and foliage	5,155.4	5,965.5	6,896.7
Mineral fuels, lubricants, etc. .	9,915.1	9,603.1	9,705.4
Petroleum, petroleum products,			
etc.	9,865.4	9,555.1	9,641.9
Refined petroleum products . .	9,671.5	9,392.4	9,441.3
Chemicals and related			
products	7,336.5	7,406.2	6,712.8
Basic manufactures	13,269.4	12,113.7	12,357.3
Iron and steel	3,823.7	2,257.5	2,605.1
Miscellaneous manufactured			
articles	4,868.4	5,637.6	5,736.1
Total (incl. others)	114,445.3	115,405.5	119,763.7

* Excluding re-exports.

PRINCIPAL TRADING PARTNERS
(Ks. million)

Imports c.i.f.	1998	1999	2000
Australia	1,724.7	2,692.3	2,611.4
Belgium-Luxembourg	3,277.4	3,152.8	n.a.
China	4,139.0	4,785.7	7,755.5
France	8,031.9	6,735.4	8,297.1
Germany	11,138.6	11,210.0	8,713.8
India	8,648.5	8,995.2	10,139.0
Indonesia	3,060.0	1,650.8	2,706.4
Italy	5,103.3	4,814.9	7,205.7
Japan	15,675.0	15,366.0	12,514.4
Netherlands	5,369.3	5,030.0	8,673.6
Saudi Arabia	12,384.4	10,872.7	15,004.5
Singapore	1,331.2	4,278.5	4,775.8
South Africa	14,197.6	17,134.1	16,585.6
Switzerland	2,386.5	2,945.9	2,671.0
United Arab Emirates	17,810.3	25,529.1	48,211.8
United Kingdom	24,354.5	23,122.8	25,135.8
USA	16,509.3	13,189.7	10,083.7
Total (incl. others)	197,788.7	206,400.6	247,803.9

Exports f.o.b.	1998	1999	2000
Belgium-Luxembourg . . .	1,717.3	1,590.4	1,911.5
Congo, Democratic Republic . .	2,014.8	2,031.0	3,042.5
Egypt	5,693.6	6,739.2	7,107.4
Ethiopia	1,535.0	1,412.4	2,056.9
France	1,889.9	2,290.1	2,143.4
Germany	5,550.2	5,773.0	5,577.4
Italy	1,747.6	1,650.3	1,518.7
Netherlands	5,284.4	6,152.0	7,292.6
Pakistan	8,276.0	9,019.9	9,986.2
Rwanda	3,037.2	3,110.3	3,504.1
Somalia	1,842.3	2,051.5	2,940.3
Sudan	2,989.5	2,705.4	2,191.4
Sweden	1,427.9	1,338.0	915.5
Tanzania	16,116.4	13,766.6	11,092.1
Uganda	19,466.3	21,189.1	24,186.1
United Kingdom	16,227.6	17,013.9	18,655.2
USA	3,053.4	2,761.2	2,803.8
Total (incl. others)	121,180.5	122,559.0	134,527.1

Transport

RAILWAYS
(traffic)

	1998	1999	2000*
Passenger-km (million)	432	306	302
Freight ton-km (million) . . .	1,111	1,492	1,557

* Provisional figures.

ROAD TRAFFIC
(estimates, motor vehicles in use)

	1998	1999	2000*
Motor cars	225,078	238,864	244,836
Light vans	148,832	155,465	159,450
Lorries, trucks and heavy vans .	54,172	56,335	57,796
Buses and mini-buses	36,367	37,961	38,930
Motorcycles and autocycles . . .	42,475	43,758	44,894
Other motor vehicles	29,842	31,029	31,820

* Provisional figures.

SHIPPING

Merchant Fleet
(registered at 31 December)

	1999	2000	2001
Number of vessels	38	38	36
Total displacement ('000 grt) . .	20.6	20.6	19.1

Source: Lloyd's Register-Fairplay, *World Fleet Statistics*.

International Sea-borne Freight Traffic
(estimates, '000 metric tons)

	1998	1999	2000*
Goods loaded	1,919	1,845	1,722
Goods unloaded	6,536	6,200	7,209

* Provisional figures.

CIVIL AVIATION
(traffic on scheduled services)

	1997	1998	1999
Kilometres flown (million) . . .	19	21	24
Passengers carried ('000) . . .	836	1,138	1,358
Passenger-km (million)	1,824	2,091	2,513
Total ton-km (million)	216	243	292

Source: UN, *Statistical Yearbook*.

Tourism

FOREIGN TOURIST ARRIVALS
(number of visitors by country of origin)

	1998	1999	2000
Austria	17,411	19,441	20,789
France	41,764	46,633	49,866
Germany	136,658	152,589	163,168
India	20,844	23,274	24,889
Italy	48,592	52,024	55,631
Sweden	32,034	33,535	35,860
Switzerland	34,145	38,126	40,769
Tanzania	108,310	109,016	116,574
Uganda	60,974	68,083	72,803
United Kingdom	132,811	148,293	158,574
USA	61,944	63,604	68,014
Total (incl. others)	894,300	969,419	1,036,628

Source: World Tourism Organization, *Yearbook of Tourism Statistics*.

Tourism receipts (Ks. million): 17,500 in 1998; 21,400 in 1999.

Communications Media

	1999	2000	2001
Television receivers ('000 in use) .	660	768	n.a.
Telephones ('000 main lines in use)	305	322	313
Mobile cellular telephones ('000 subscribers).	24	127	500
Personal computers ('000 in use) .	125	150	175
Internet users ('000)	35	200	500

Source: International Telecommunication Union.

Radio receivers ('000 in use, 1999): 6,383.

Facsimile machines (number in use, year ending 30 June 1995): 3,800.

Daily newspapers (1996): 4 titles (average circulation 263,000 copies).

Book production (titles, 1994): 300 first editions (excl. pamphlets).

Sources: UNESCO, *Statistical Yearbook*; UN, *Statistical Yearbook*.

Education

(1998/99, unless otherwise indicated)

	Institu-tions	Teachers	Pupils
Pre-primary	23,977	37,752	1,016,606
Primary	17,611	192,306	5,480,689
Secondary:			
general secondary	2,878*	43,694	1,139,569
technical†	36	1,147	11,700
teacher training	26*	808‡	18,992§
Higher	n.a.‖	n.a.‖	61,526

* 1995 figure.
† 1988 figures.
‡ 1985 figure.
§ 1992 figure.
‖ In 1990 there were four universities, with 4,392 teachers.

Sources: Ministry of Education, Nairobi; UNESCO Institute for Statistics.

Adult literacy rate (UNESCO estimates): 82.4% (males 88.9%; females 76.0%) in 2000 (Source: UN Development Programme, *Human Development Report*).

Directory

The Constitution

The Constitution was introduced at independence on 12 December 1963. Subsequent amendments, including the adoption of republican status on 12 December 1964, were consolidated in 1969. A further amendment in December 1991 permitted the establishment of a multi-party system. In September 1997 the National Assembly approved legislation which amended the Constitution with a view to ensuring free and fair democratic elections. All political parties were granted equal access to the media, and detention without trial was prohibited. In addition, the opposition was to participate in selecting the 12 nominated members of the National Assembly and 10 of the 12 members of the supervisory Electoral Commission. An amendment to the Constitution, approved by the National Assembly in November 1999, reduced the level of presidential control over the legislative process. The Constitution can be amended by the affirmative vote on Second and Third Reading of 65% of the membership of the National Assembly (excluding the Speaker and Attorney-General).

The central legislative authority is the unicameral National Assembly, in which there are 210 directly elected Representatives, 12 nominated members and two *ex-officio* members, the Attorney-General and the Speaker. The maximum term of the National Assembly is five years from its first meeting (except in wartime). It can be dissolved by the President at any time, and the National Assembly may force its own dissolution by a vote of 'no confidence', whereupon presidential and Assembly elections have to be held within 90 days.

Executive power is vested in the President, Vice-President and Cabinet. Both the Vice-President and the Cabinet are appointed by the President, who must be a member of the Assembly and at least 35 years of age. Election of the President, for a five-year term, is by direct popular vote; the winning candidate at a presidential election must receive no less than 25% of the votes in at least five of Kenya's eight provinces. If a President dies, or a vacancy otherwise occurs during a President's period of office, the Vice-President becomes interim President for up to 90 days while a successor is elected.

The Government

HEAD OF STATE

President: Mwai Kibaki (took office 30 December 2002).

CABINET
(April 2003)

Vice-President and Minister of National Reconstruction: Michael Kijana Wamalwa.

Minister of Finance: Daudi Mwiraria.

Minister of Foreign Affairs: Stephen Kalonzo Musyoka.

Minister of Roads, Public Works and Housing: Raila Amolo Odinga.

Minister of Education: Prof. George Saitoti.

Minister of Home Affairs: Moody Awory.

Minister of Planning and National Development: Prof. Peter Anyang' Nyongo.

Minister of Agriculture and Livestock: Kipruto Rono arap Kirwa.

Minister of Health: Charity Kaluki Ngilu.

Minister of Tourism: Raphael Tuju.

Minister of Transport and Communications: John Njoroge Michuki.

Minister of Local Government: Emmanuel Karisa Maitha.

Minister of Water Resources Management and Development: Martha Wangari Karua.

Minister of Energy: George Ochilo Mbogo Ayacko.

Minister of Trade and Industry: Dr Mukhisa Kituyi.

Minister of Lands and Settlement: Amos M. Kimunya.

Minister of the Environment, Natural Resources and Wildlife: Dr Newton W. Kulundu.

Minister of Labour and Human Resources Development: Najib M. Balala (acting).

Minister of Co-operative Development: Peter Njeru Ndwiga.

Minister of Gender, Sports, Culture and Social Services: Najib M. Balala.

Minister of Justice and Constitutional Affairs: Kiraitu Murungi.

Minister of State for Provincial Administration and National Security in the Office of the President: Christopher N. Murungaru.

Minister of State for Public Service in the Office of the President: Geoffrey Mepukori Parpai.

Minister of State in the Vice-President's Office: Lina Jebii Kilimo.

MINISTRIES

Office of the President: Harambee House, Harambee Ave, POB 30510, Nairobi; tel. (20) 227411; internet www.officeofthepresident.go.ke.

Office of the Vice-President and Ministry of National Reconstruction: Harambee Ave, POB 62345, Nairobi; tel. (20) 227411; internet www.vice-president.go.ke.

Ministry of Agriculture and Livestock: Kilimo House, Cathedral Rd, POB 30028, Nairobi; tel. (20) 718870; fax (20) 720586; internet www.agriculture.go.ke.

Ministry of Co-operative Development: Reinsurance Plaza, Taifa Rd, POB 30547, 00100 Nairobi; tel. (20) 339650; internet www .kenya.go.ke/cooperative.

Ministry of Education: Jogoo House 'B', Harambee Ave, POB 30040, Nairobi; tel. (20) 334411; e-mail elimul@africaonline.co.ke; internet www.education.go.ke.

Ministry of Energy: Nyayo House, Kenyatta Ave, POB 30582, Nairobi; tel. (20) 333551; internet www.energy.go.ke.

Ministry of the Environment, Natural Resources and Wildlife: Maji House, Ngong Rd, POB 49720, Nairobi; tel. (20) 716103; e-mail mec@nbnet.co.ke; internet www.environment.go.ke.

Ministry of Finance: Treasury Bldg, Harambee Ave, POB 30007, Nairobi; tel. (20) 338111; fax (20) 330426; e-mail info@treasury.go .ke; internet www.treasury.go.ke.

Ministry of Foreign Affairs: Treasury Bldg, Harambee Ave, POB 30551, Nairobi; tel. (20) 334433; e-mail mfapress@nbnet.co.ke; internet www.mfa.go.ke.

Ministry of Gender, Sports, Culture and Social Services: Jogoo House 'A', Taifa Rd, POB 30520, Nairobi; tel. (20) 228411; internet www.kenya.go.ke/gender.

Ministry of Health: Medical HQ, Afya House, Cathedral Rd, POB 30016, Nairobi; tel. (20) 717077; fax (20) 725902; internet www .health.go.ke.

Ministry of Home Affairs: Jogoo House 'A', Taifa Rd, POB 30520, Nairobi; tel. (20) 228411; internet www.homeaffairs.go.ke.

Ministry of Justice and Constitutional Affairs: State Law Office, Harambee Ave, POB 40112, Nairobi; tel. (20) 227461; internet www.kenya.go.ke/justice.

Ministry of Labour and Human Resources Development: Social Security House, Block 'C', Bishop Rd, POB 40326, Nairobi; tel. (20) 729800; fax (20) 726497; internet www.labour.go.ke.

Ministry of Lands and Settlement: Ardhi House, Ngong Rd, POB 30450, Nairobi; tel. (20) 718050; internet www.landsandsettlement .go.ke.

Ministry of Local Government: Jogoo House 'A', Taifa Rd, POB 30004, Nairobi; tel. (20) 217475; e-mail mlog@form-net.com; internet www.localgovernment.go.ke.

Ministry of Planning and National Development: Treasury Bldg, Harambee Ave, POB 30007, Nairobi; tel. (20) 338111; internet www.planning.go.ke.

Ministry of Roads, Public Works and Housing: Ministry of Works Bldg, Ngong Rd, POB 30260, Nairobi; tel. (20) 723101; fax (20) 720044; e-mail ps@roadsnet.go.ke; internet www.publicworks .go.ke.

Ministry of Tourism: Utalii House, 5th Floor, off Uhuru Highway, POB 30027, Nairobi; tel. (20) 333555; fax (20) 318045; internet www .tourism.go.ke.

Ministry of Trade and Industry: Teleposta Towers, Kenyatta Ave, POB 30430, Nairobi; tel. (20) 331030; internet www .tradeandindustry.go.ke.

Ministry of Transport and Communications: Transcom House, Ngong Rd, POB 52692, Nairobi; tel. (20) 729200; fax (20) 726362; internet www.transport.go.ke.

Ministry of Water Resources Management and Development: Maji House, Ngong Rd, POB 49720, Nairobi; tel. (20) 716103; internet www.kenya.go.ke/water.

President and Legislature

PRESIDENT

Election, 27 December 2002

Candidates	Votes	%
Mwai Kibaki (NARC)	3,646,409	62.3
Uhuru Kenyatta (KANU)	1,828,914	31.2
Simeon Nyachae (Ford—People)	345,378	5.9
James Orengo (SDP)	24,537	0.4
David Ng'ethe (CCU)	10,038	0.2
Total	**5,855,276**	**100.0**

NATIONAL ASSEMBLY

Speaker: Francis Xavier ole Kaparo.

General Election, 27 December 2002

Party	Seats
NARC	125
KANU	64
FORD—People	14
FORD—Asili	2
Safina	2
SKS	2
SPK	1
Total	**210***

*In addition to the 210 directly elected seats, 12 are held by nominees (NARC 7; KANU 4; FORD—People 1). The Attorney-General and the Speaker are, *ex officio*, members of the National Assembly.

Political Organizations

Chama Cha Uma (CCU): Nairobi; David Ng'ethe.

Democratic Party of Kenya (DP): Continental House, POB 56396, Nairobi; ; tel. (20) 340044; f. 1991; Chair. Mwai Kibaki; Sec. Joseph Munyao; rival faction led by Ngengi Muigai.

Forum for the Restoration of Democracy—Asili (FORD—Asili): Anyany Estate, POB 72595, Nairobi; f. 1992; Chair. George Nthenge; Sec. Martin J. Shikuku.

Forum for the Restoration of Democracy—Kenya (FORD—Kenya): Odinga House, POB 57449, Nairobi; tel. (20) 570361; f. 1992; predominantly Luo support; Chair. Michael Christopher Kijana Wamalwa; Sec. Gitobu Imanyara.

Forum for the Restoration of Democracy for the People (FORD—People): Nairobi; f. 1997 by fmr mems of FORD—Asili; Chair. Kimani wa Nyoike; Sec.-Gen. (vacant).

Kenya African National Union (KANU): KICC POB 72394, Nairobi; tel. (20) 332383; f. 1960; sole legal party 1982–91; absorbed the National Development Party (f. 1994) in 2002; Pres. and Chair. Daniel arap Moi; Sec.-Gen. Julius Sunkuli.

Kenya National Congress (KNC): POB 9474, Nairobi; f. 1992; Chair. Prof. Katana Mkangi; Sec.-Gen. Onesmus Musyoka Mbali.

Kenya National Democratic Alliance (KENDA): Wetithe House, Nkrumah St, POB 1851, Thika; tel. (151) 562304; f. 1991; Chair. Joram Gainye Kariuki; Sec. Patrick Ouma Kang'ethe.

Kenya Social Congress (KSC): POB 55318, Nairobi; f. 1992; Chair. George Moseti Anyona; Sec.-Gen. Kashini Maloba Fafna.

Labour Party Democracy: POB 7905, Nairobi; Chair. Geoffrey Mburu; Sec. David Mburi Ngachura.

Liberal Party: Chair. Wangari Maathai.

National Party of Kenya (NPK): f. 2001; Chair. Charity Kaluki Ngilu; Sec.-Gen. Fidelis Mweke.

National Rainbow Coalition (NARC): Mwenge House, Ole Odume Rd, off Gitanga Rd and near Methodist Guest House, Nairobi; tel. (20) 571506; internet www.narc-kenya.org; f. 2002; electoral alliance of the LDP and the NAK; Chair Titus Mbathi; Sec. Burudi Nabwera.

  Liberal Democratic Party (LDP): Nairobi; f. 2002 by fmr mems of KANU.

  National Alliance Party of Kenya (NAK): Nairobi; f. 2002; alliance of some 12 parties, including the DP, FORD—Kenya and the NPK.

Party of Independent Candidates of Kenya (PICK): Plot No 299/096 Kenyatta Ave, POB 21821, Nairobi; Chair. G. N. Musyimi; Sec. F. Ngugi.

Patriotic Pastoralist Alliance of Kenya: f. 1997; represents the interests of northern Kenyan pastoralist communities; Leaders Khalif Abdullahi, Ibrahim Woche, Jackson Laisagor.

People's Alliance for Change in Kenya (PACK): Nairobi; f. 1999; aims to unite diverse ethnic groups; Sec.-Gen. Olang Sana.

People's Union of Justice and New Order: Kisumu; Islamic support; Leader Wilson Owili.

Safina ('Noah's Ark'): POB 135, Nairobi; f. 1995; aims to combat corruption and human rights abuses and to introduce proportional representation; Chair. Clement Muturi Kigano; Sec.-Gen. Mwandawiro Mghanga.

Shirikisho Party of Kenya (SPK): POB 70421, Nairobi; Chair. Hamisi Saidi Jeffah; Sec. Omara Abae Kalasingha.

Sisi Kwa Sisi (SKS): Nairobi; f. 2001; Leader John Rukenya Kabugua.

Social Democratic Party of Kenya (SDP): POB 55845, Nairobi; tel. (20) 260309; f. 1992; Chair. JUSTUS NYAGAYA; Sec.-Gen. Dr APOLLO LUGANO NJONJO.

United Agri Party of Kenya: f. 2001; Chair. GEORGE KINYUA; Sec.-Gen. SIMON MITOBIO.

United Democratic Movement: Nairobi; Chair. FRED OKIKI AMAYO; Sec.-Gen. MAURICE KAMAU RUBIA.

United Patriotic Party of Kenya: POB 115, Athi River; Chair. JOSEPHAT GATHUA GATHIGA; Sec. MICHAEL NJUGUNA KIGANYA.

The following organizations are banned:

February Eighteen Resistance Army: believed to operate from Uganda; Leader Brig. JOHN ODONGO (also known as STEPHEN AMOKE).

Islamic Party of Kenya (IPK): Mombasa; f. 1992; Islamic fundamentalist; Chair. Sheikh KHALIFA MUHAMMAD (acting); Sec.-Gen. ABDULRAHMAN WANDATI.

Diplomatic Representation

EMBASSIES AND HIGH COMMISSIONS IN KENYA

Algeria: 37 Muthaiga Rd, POB 53902, Nairobi; tel. (20) 310430; fax (20) 310450; e-mail algerianembassy@mitsuminett.com.

Argentina: Posta Sacco, 6th Floor, University Way, POB 30283, Nairobi; tel. (20) 335242; fax (20) 217693; e-mail argentina@form-net.com; Ambassador JOSÉ MARÍA CANTILO.

Australia: ICIPE House, River Side Drive, off Chiromo Rd, POB 39341, Nairobi; tel. (20) 445034; fax (20) 444718; High Commissioner PAUL COMFORT.

Austria: City House, 2nd Floor, Wabera St, POB 30560, Nairobi; tel. and fax (20) 331792; e-mail austria@africaonline.co.ke; Ambassador FRANZ HÖRLBERGER.

Bangladesh: Lenana Rd, POB 41645, Nairobi; tel. (20) 583354; fax (20) 562817; High Commissioner Dr M. AFSARUL QADER.

Belgium: Muthaiga, Limuru Rd, POB 30461, Nairobi; tel. (20) 741564; fax (20) 442701; e-mail belgianembke@form-net.com; Ambassador LEO WILLEMS.

Brazil: Jeevan Bharati Bldg, 4th Floor, Harambee Ave, POB 30754, Nairobi; tel. (20) 332649; fax (20) 336245; Ambassador MÁRIO AGUSTO SANTOS.

Burundi: Development House, 14th Floor, Moi Ave, POB 44439, Nairobi; tel. (20) 575113; fax (20) 219005; Ambassador GERMAIN NKESHIMANA.

Canada: Comcraft House, 6th Floor, Haile Selassie Ave, POB 30481, Nairobi; tel. (20) 214804; fax (20) 226987; High Commissioner GERRY CAMPBELL.

Chile: International House, 5th Floor, Mama Ngina St, POB 45554, Nairobi; tel. (20) 331320; fax (20) 215648; e-mail echileke@form-net.com; Ambassador Dr VICENTE SÁNCHEZ.

China, People's Republic: Nairobi; tel. (20) 722559; fax (20) 746402; Ambassador AN YONGYU.

Colombia: International House, 8th Floor, POB 48494, Nairobi; tel. (20) 246770; fax (20) 246771; e-mail embcol@form-net.com; Ambassador Dr GERMÁN GARCÍA-DURÁN.

Congo, Democratic Republic: Electricity House, Harambee Ave, POB 48106, Nairobi; tel. (20) 229771; fax (20) 334539; Ambassador (vacant).

Cyprus: Eagle House, 5th Floor, Kimathi St, POB 30739, Nairobi; tel. (20) 220881; fax (20) 331232; High Commissioner PAVLOS HADJITOFIS.

Czech Republic: Embassy House, Harambee Ave, POB 48785, Nairobi; tel. (20) 210494; fax (20) 223447; e-mail zamini.cz@africaonline.co.ke; Ambassador VÁCLAV HUBINGER.

Denmark: HFCK Bldg, 11th Floor, Kenyatta Ave, POB 40412, Nairobi; tel. (20) 331088; fax (20) 331492; e-mail dkembnbo@africaonline.co.ke; Ambassador KLAUS DAHLGAARD.

Djibouti: Comcraft House, 2nd Floor, Haile Selassie Ave, POB 59528, Nairobi; tel. (20) 339640; Ambassador SALEH HAJI FARAH.

Egypt: Harambee Plaza, 7th Floor, Haile Selassie Ave, POB 30285, Nairobi; tel. (20) 570360; fax (20) 570383; Ambassador MOHAMMED ASIM IBRAHIM.

Eritrea: New Rehema House, 2nd Floor, Westlands, POB 38651, Nairobi; tel. (20) 443164; fax (20) 443165; e-mail eriembk@africaonline.co.ke; Ambassador MOHAMED ALI OMARO.

Ethiopia: State House Ave, POB 45198, Nairobi; tel. (20) 723027; fax (20) 723401; e-mail ethembnb@africaonline.co.ke; Ambassador TOSHOME TOGA.

Finland: International House, 2nd Floor, Mama Ngina St, POB 30379, Nairobi; tel. (20) 334777; fax (20) 335986; e-mail finland@form-net.com; Ambassador LAURI KANGAS.

France: Barclays Plaza, 9th Floor, Loita St, POB 41784, Nairobi; tel. (20) 339783; fax (20) 339421; e-mail ienkenya@form-net.com; Ambassador JACQUES DEPAIGNE.

Germany: Williamson House, 8th Floor, 4th Ngong Ave, POB 30180, Nairobi; tel. (20) 712527; fax (20) 714886; e-mail ger-emb@form-net.com; Ambassador JÜRGEN WEERTH.

Greece: Nation Centre, 13th Floor, Kimathi St, POB 30543, Nairobi; tel. (20) 228465; fax (20) 216044; Ambassador (vacant).

Holy See: Apostolic Nunciature, Manyani Rd West, Waiyaki Way, POB 14326, 00800 Nairobi; tel. (20) 4442975; fax (20) 4446789; e-mail nunciokenya@kenyaweb.com; Apostolic Nuncio Most Rev. GIOVANNI TONUCCI (Titular Archbishop of Torcello).

Hungary: Ole Odume Rd, POB 61146, Nairobi; tel. (20) 560060; fax (20) 560114; e-mail huembnai@africaonline.co.ke; Ambassador ANDRÁS TÓTH.

India: Jeevan Bharati Bldg, 2nd Floor, Harambee Ave, POB 30074, Nairobi; tel. (20) 225104; fax (20) 334167; e-mail hcindia@form-net.com; High Commissioner T. P. SREENIVASAN.

Indonesia: Menengai House, Upper Hill, POB 48868, Nairobi; tel. (20) 714196; fax (20) 713475; e-mail indonbi@arcc.or.ke; Ambassador TUPUCK SUTRISNO.

Iran: Dennis Pritt Rd, POB 49170, Nairobi; tel. (20) 720343; fax (20) 339936; Ambassador HAMID MOAYYER.

Iraq: Loresho Ridge, POB 49213, Nairobi; tel. (20) 580262; fax (20) 582880; Chargé d'affaires a.i. SABAH-TALAT KADRAT.

Israel: Bishop's Rd, POB 30354, Nairobi; tel. (20) 722182; fax (20) 715966; Ambassador MENASHE ZIPORI.

Italy: International House, 9th Floor, Mama Ngina St, POB 30107, Nairobi; tel. (20) 337356; fax (20) 337056; e-mail afra@form-net.com; Ambassador Dr ALBERTO BALBONI.

Japan: ICEA Bldg, 15th Floor, Kenyatta Ave, POB 60202, Nairobi; tel. and fax (20) 332955; Ambassador MORIHISA AOKI.

Korea, Republic: Anniversary Towers, 15th Floor, University Way, POB 30455, Nairobi; tel. (20) 333581; fax (20) 217772; e-mail emb-ke@mofat.go.kr; Ambassador KWON JONG RAK.

Kuwait: Muthaiga Rd, POB 42353, Nairobi; tel. (20) 761614; fax (20) 762837; e-mail kuwaitembassy@form-net.com; Chargé d'affaires a.i. JABER SALEM HUSSAIN EBRAHEEM.

Lesotho: Nairobi; tel. (20) 224876; fax (20) 337493; High Commissioner (vacant).

Malawi: Waiyaki Way (between Mvuli and Church Rds), POB 30453, Nairobi; tel. (20) 440569; fax 440568; High Commissioner J. P. A. NDISALE.

Mexico: Kibagare Way, off Loresho Ridge, POB 14145, Nairobi; tel. (20) 582850; fax (20) 581500; e-mail mexico@embamexken.co.ke; Ambassador LEANDRO ARELLANO.

Morocco: Diamond Trust House, 3rd Floor, Moi Ave, POB 61093, Nairobi; tel. (20) 222361; fax (20) 222364; e-mail embassymorocco@form-net.com; Chargé d'affaires a.i. DRISS KASSIMI.

Mozambique: Bruce House, 3rd Floor, Standard St, POB 66923, Nairobi; tel. (20) 221979; fax (20) 222446; High Commissioner PAULO ELIAS CIGARRO.

Netherlands: Uchumi House, 6th Floor, Nkrumah Ave, POB 41537, Nairobi; tel. (20) 227111; fax (20) 339155; e-mail holland@form-net.com; Ambassador RUUD J. TREFFERS.

Nigeria: Lenana Rd, Hurlingham, POB 30516, Nairobi; tel. (20) 564116; fax (20) 564117; High Commissioner CLARKSON N. UMELO.

Norway: International House, 1st Floor, Mama Ngina St, POB 46363, Nairobi; tel. (20) 341415; fax (20) 216009; e-mail emb.nairobi@mfa.no; Chargé d'affaires a.i. OVE DANBOLDT.

Pakistan: St Michel Rd, Westlands Ave, POB 30045, Nairobi; tel. (20) 443911; fax (20) 446507; High Commissioner (vacant).

Poland: Kabarnet Rd, off Ngong Rd, Woodley, POB 30086, 00100 Nairobi; tel. (20) 566288; fax (20) 727701; e-mail polambnairobi@form-net.com; Ambassador WOJCIECH JASINSKI.

Portugal: Reinsurance Plaza, 10th Floor, Aga Khan Walk, POB 34020, Nairobi; tel. (20) 338990; fax (20) 214711; Ambassador JOSÉ LAMEIRAS.

Romania: POB 63240, Nairobi; tel. (20) 743209; fax (20) 741696; e-mail roembken@wananchi.com; Chargé d'affaires a.i. PAUL FINANTU.

Russia: Lenana Rd, POB 30049, Nairobi; tel. (20) 728700; fax (20) 721888; e-mail russemb@swiftkenya.com; Ambassador BORIS SEPTOV.

Rwanda: International House, 12th Floor, Mama Ngina St, POB 48579, Nairobi; tel. (20) 560178; fax (20) 561932.

Saudi Arabia: Muthaiga Rd, POB 58297, Nairobi; tel. (20) 762781; fax (20) 760939; Chargé d'affaires IBRAHIM AMMAR.

Serbia and Montenegro: State House Ave, Nairobi; tel. (20) 720670.

Slovakia: Milimani Rd, POB 30204, Nairobi; tel. (20) 721896; fax (20) 721898.

Somalia: POB 30769, Nairobi; tel. (20) 580165; fax (20) 581683.

South Africa: Lonhro House, 14th Floor, Standard St, POB 42441, Nairobi; tel. (20) 32063100; fax (20) 32063236; e-mail sahc@africaonline.co.ke; High Commissioner L. M. MAKHUBELA.

Spain: Bruce House, 5th Floor, Standard St, POB 45503, Nairobi; tel. (20) 335711; fax (20) 332858; Ambassador FERMÍN PIETRO-CASTRO ROUMIER.

Sri Lanka: Rose Ave, off Lenana Rd, POB 48145, Nairobi; tel. (20) 227577; fax (20) 225391; e-mail slhckeny@user.africaonline.co.ke; internet www.lk/dipmissionf.html; High Commissioner J. D. A. WIJEWARDENA.

Sudan: Minet-ICDC Bldg, 7th Floor, Mamlaka Rd, POB 48784, Nairobi; tel. (20) 720853; fax (20) 721015; Ambassador OMER EL-SHEIKH.

Swaziland: Transnational Plaza, 3rd Floor, Mama Ngina St, POB 41887, Nairobi; tel. (20) 339231; fax (20) 330540; High Commissioner Prince MBILINI DLAMINI.

Sweden: International House, 10th Floor, Mama Ngina St, POB 30600, Nairobi; tel. (20) 229042; fax (20) 218908; e-mail ambassaden.nairobi@sida.se; Ambassador BO GÖRANSSON.

Switzerland: International House, 7th Floor, Mama Ngina St, POB 30752, Nairobi; tel. (20) 228735; fax (20) 217388; e-mail vertretung@nai.rep.admin.ch; Ambassador Dr ARMIN KAMER.

Tanzania: Continental House, Uhuru Highway, POB 47790, Nairobi; tel. (20) 721742; fax (20) 218269; High Commissioner MIRISHO SAM HAGGAI SARAKIKYA.

Thailand: Ambassador House, Rose Ave, POB 58349, Nairobi; tel. (20) 715800; fax (20) 715801; e-mail thainbi@form-net.com; Ambassador PONGSAK DISYATAT.

Turkey: Gigiri Rd, off Limuru Rd, POB 64748, Nairobi; tel. (20) 522562; fax (20) 522778; e-mail tcbenair@wananchi.com; Ambassador VAROL ÖZKOÇAK.

Uganda: Uganda House, 5th Floor, Kenyatta Ave, POB 60853, Nairobi; tel. (20) 330801; fax (20) 330970; High Commissioner J. TOMUSANGE.

United Kingdom: Upper Hill Rd, POB 30465, Nairobi; tel. (20) 714699; fax (20) 719486; e-mail bhcinfo@iconnect.co.ke; internet www.britain.or.ke; High Commissioner Sir JEFFREY JAMES.

USA: Mombasa Rd, POB 30137, Nairobi; tel. (20) 537800; fax (20) 537810; e-mail irc@pd.state.gov; internet us.state.gov/nairobi; Ambassador JOHNNIE CARSON.

Venezuela: Ngong/Kabarnet Rd, POB 34477, Nairobi; tel. (20) 574646; fax (20) 337487; e-mail embavene@africaonline.co.ke; Chargé d'affaires a.i. NOEL D. QUINTERO.

Yemen: cnr Ngong and Kabarnet Rds, POB 44642, Nairobi; tel. (20) 564379; fax (20) 564394; Ambassador AHMAD MAYSARI.

Zambia: Nyerere Rd, POB 48741, Nairobi; tel. (20) 724850; fax (20) 718494; High Commissioner ENESS CHISHALA CHIYENGE.

Zimbabwe: Minet-ICDC Bldg, 6th Floor, Mamlaka Rd, POB 30806, Nairobi; tel. (20) 721071; fax (20) 726503; High Commissioner LUCAS PANDE TAVAYA.

Judicial System

The Kenya Court of Appeal
POB 30187, Nairobi.

The final court of appeal for Kenya in civil and criminal process; sits at Nairobi, Mombasa, Kisumu, Nakuru and Nyeri.

Chief Justice: EVANS GICHERU.

Justices of Appeal: MATHEW MULI, J. M. GACHUHI, J. R. O. MASIME, SAMUEL BOSIRE, R. O. KWACH, EFFIE OWUOR.

The High Court of Kenya: Harambee Ave, POB 30041, Nairobi; tel. (20) 221221; e-mail hck-lib@nbnet.co.ke; has unlimited criminal and civil jurisdiction at first instance, and sits as a court of appeal

from subordinate courts in both criminal and civil cases. The High Court is also a court of admiralty. There are two resident puisne judges at Mombasa and at Nakuru, and one resident puisne judge at Eldoret, Kakamega, Kisumu, Nyeri, Kisii and Meru.

Resident Magistrates' Courts: have country-wide jurisdiction, with powers of punishment by imprisonment up to five years or by fine up to K£500. If presided over by a chief magistrate or senior resident magistrate the court is empowered to pass any sentence authorized by law. For certain offences, a resident magistrate may pass minimum sentences authorized by law.

District Magistrates' Courts: of first, second and third class; have jurisdiction within districts and powers of punishment by imprisonment for up to five years, or by fines of up to K£500.

Kadhi's Courts: have jurisdiction within districts, to determine questions of Islamic law.

Religion

Most of the population hold traditional African beliefs, although there are significant numbers of African Christians. The Arab inhabitants are Muslims, and the Indian population is partly Muslim and partly Hindu. The Europeans and Goans are predominantly Christian. Muslims are found mainly along the coastline; however, the Islamic faith has also established itself among Africans around Nairobi and among some ethnic groups in the northern districts. East Africa is also an important centre for the Bahá'í faith.

CHRISTIANITY

National Council of Churches of Kenya: Church House, Moi Ave, POB 45009, Nairobi; tel. (20) 242278; fax (20) 224463; f. 1943 as Christian Council of Kenya; 35 full mems and eight assoc. mems; Chair. Rev. JOSEPH WAITHONGA; Sec.-Gen. Rev. MUTAVA MUSYIMI.

The Anglican Communion
Anglicans are adherents of the Church of the Province of Kenya, which was established in 1970. It comprises 28 dioceses, and has about 2.5m. members.

Archbishop of Kenya and Bishop of Nairobi: Most Rev. Dr DAVID M. GITARI, POB 40502, Nairobi; tel. (20) 2714755; fax (20) 2718442; e-mail davidgitari@insightkenya.com.

Greek Orthodox Church
Archbishop of East Africa: NICADEMUS OF IRINOUPOULIS, Nairobi; jurisdiction covers Kenya, Tanzania and Uganda.

The Roman Catholic Church
Kenya comprises four archdioceses, 19 dioceses and one Apostolic Vicariate. At 31 December 2000 an estimated 24.9% of the total population were adherents of the Roman Catholic Church.

Kenya Episcopal Conference
Kenya Catholic Secretariat, POB 13475, Nairobi; tel. (20) 443133; fax (20) 442910; e-mail csk@users.africaonline.co.ke.

f. 1976; Pres. Rt Rev. JOHN NJUE (Bishop of Embu).

Archbishop of Kisumu: Most Rev. ZACCHAEUS OKOTH, POB 1728, Kisumu; tel. (35) 41765; fax (35) 62247; e-mail archdiocese-ksm@net2000ke.com.

Archbishop of Mombasa: Most Rev. JOHN NJENGA, Catholic Secretariat, Nyerere Ave, POB 83131, Mombasa; tel. (11) 471320; fax (11) 473166; e-mail msadio@africaonline.co.ke.

Archbishop of Nairobi: Most Rev. RAPHAEL NDINGI MWANA'A NZEKI, Archbishop's House, POB 14231, 00800 Nairobi; tel. (20) 4441919; fax 4447027; e-mail arch-nbo@wananchi.com.

Archbishop of Nyeri: Most Rev. NICODEMUS KIRIMA, POB 288, Nyeri; tel. (17) 30446; fax (17) 30435.

Other Christian Churches
Africa Inland Church in Kenya: Bishop Rev. Dr TITUS M. KIVUNZI.

African Christian Church and Schools: POB 1365, Thika; tel. (15) 47; f. 1948; Moderator Rt Rev. JOHN NJUNGUNA; Gen. Sec. Rev. SAMUEL MWANGI; 50,000 mems.

African Church of the Holy Spirit: POB 183, Kakamega; f. 1927; 20,000 mems.

African Israel Nineveh Church: Nineveh HQ, POB 701, Kisumu; f. 1942; High Priest Rt Rev. JOHN KIVULI, II; Gen. Sec. Rev. JOHN ARAP TONUI; 350,000 mems.

Baptist Convention of Kenya: POB 14907, Nairobi; Pres. Rev. ELIUD MUNGAI.

Church of God in East Africa: Pres. Rev. Dr BYRUM MAKOKHA.

Evangelical Fellowship of Kenya: Co-ordinator Rt Rev. ARTHUR GITONGA; Sec.-Gen. Dr WASHINGTON NG'ENG'I.

Evangelical Lutheran Church in Kenya: POB 874, Kisii; tel. (40) 31231; fax (40) 30475; e-mail elok@africaonline.co.ke; Bishop Rev. FRANCIS NYAMWARO ONDERI; 65,000 mems.

Methodist Church in Kenya: POB 47633, Nairobi; tel. (20) 724841; f. 1862; autonomous since 1967; Presiding Bishop Rev. Dr ZABLON NTHAMBURI; 854,000 mems (2000).

Presbyterian Church of East Africa: POB 48268, Nairobi; tel. (20) 504417; fax (20) 504442; e-mail pcea@africaonline.co.ke; Moderator Rt Rev. Dr JESSE KAMAU; Sec.-Gen. Rev. Dr PATRICK RUKENYA.

Other denominations active in Kenya include the Africa Gospel Church, the African Brotherhood Church, the African Independent Pentecostal Church, the African Interior Church, the Episcopal Church of Kenya, the Free Pentecostal Fellowship of Kenya, the Full Gospel Churches of Kenya, the Lutheran Church in Kenya, the National Independent Church of Africa, the Pentecostal Assemblies of God, the Pentecostal Evangelistic Fellowship of God and the Reformed Church of East Africa.

BAHÁ'Í FAITH

National Spiritual Assembly: POB 47562, Nairobi; tel. (20) 725447; mems resident in 9,654 localities.

ISLAM

Supreme Council of Kenyan Muslims (SUPKEM)
POB 45163, Nairobi; tel. and fax (20) 243109.

Nat. Chair. Prof. ABD AL-GHAFUR AL-BUSAIDY; Sec.-Gen. MOHAMMED KHALIF.

Chief Kadhi: NASSOR NAHDI.

The Press

PRINCIPAL DAILIES

Daily Nation: POB 49010, Nairobi; tel. and fax (20) 337710; e-mail nation@insightkenya.com; internet www.nationaudio.com; f. 1960; English; owned by Nation Media Group; Editor-in-Chief WANGETHI MWANGI; Man. Editor JOSEPH ODINDO; circ. 170,000.

East African Standard: POB 30080, Nairobi; tel. (20) 540280; fax (20) 553939; e-mail online@eastandard.net; internet www.eastandard.net; f. 1902; Group Man. Editor WARURU WACHIRO; circ. 60,000.

Kenya Leo: POB 30958, Nairobi; tel. (20) 332390; f. 1983; Kiswahili; KANU party newspaper; Group Editor-in-Chief AMBOKA ANDERE; circ. 6,000.

Kenya Times: POB 30958, Nairobi; tel. (20) 24251; f. 1983; English; KANU party newspaper; Group Editor-in-Chief AMBOKA ANDERE; circ. 10,000.

The People: POB 10296, 00100 Nairobi; tel. (20) 249686; fax (20) 253344; e-mail info@people.co.ke; f. 1993; Editor-in-Chief BEDAU MOUGUA; circ. 40,000.

Taifa Leo: POB 49010, Nairobi; tel. (20) 337691; Kiswahili; f. 1960; daily and weekly edns; owned by Nation Media Group; Editor ROBERT MWANGI; circ. 57,000.

Kenya has a thriving vernacular press, but titles are often short-lived. Newspapers in African languages include:

Kihooto (The Truth): Kikuyu; satirical.

Mwaria Ma (Honest Speaker): Nyeri; f. 1997; Publr Canon JAMLICK M. MIANO.

Mwihoko (Hope): POB 734, Muranga; f. 1997; Roman Catholic.

Nam Dar: Luo.

Otit Mach (Firefly): Luo.

SELECTED PERIODICALS

Weeklies and Fortnightlies

The Business Chronicle: POB 53328, Nairobi; tel. (20) 544283; fax (20) 532736; f. 1994; weekly; Man. Editor MUSYOKA KYENDO.

Coastweek: Oriental Bldg, 2nd Floor, Nkrumah Rd, POB 87270, Mombasa; tel. (11) 313767; fax (11) 225003; e-mail coastwk@africaonline.co.ke; internet www.coastweek.com; f. 1978; English; weekly; Editor ADRIAN GRIMWOOD; circ. 40,000.

The East African: POB 49010 Nairobi; tel. (20) 337710; fax (20) 213946; e-mail nation@insightkenya.com; internet www.nationaudio.com/news/eastafrican/current; f. 1994; weekly; English; owned by Nation Media Group; Editor-in-Chief WANGETHI MWANGI; Man. Editor MBATAU WA NGAI.

The Herald: POB 30958, Nairobi; tel. (20) 332390; English; sponsored by KANU; Editor JOB MUTUNGI; circ. 8,000.

Kenrail: POB 30121, Nairobi; tel. (20) 221211; fax (20) 340049; English and Kiswahili; publ. by Kenya Railways Corpn; Editor J. N. LUSENO; circ. 20,000.

Kenya Gazette: POB 30746, Nairobi; tel. (20) 334075; f. 1898; official notices; weekly; circ. 8,000.

Post on Sunday: Nairobi; weekly; independent; Editor-in-Chief TONY GACHOKA.

The Standard on Sunday: POB 30080, Nairobi; tel. (20) 540280; fax (20) 553939; English; Man. Editor FRED MUTISO; circ. 90,000.

Sunday Nation: POB 49010, Nairobi; f. 1960; English; owned by Nation Media Group; Man. Editor BERNARD NDERITU; circ. 170,000.

Sunday Times: POB 30958, Nairobi; tel. (20) 337798; Group Editor AMBOKA ANDERE.

Taifa Jumapili: POB 49010, Nairobi; f. 1987; Kiswahili; owned by Nation Media Group; Editor ROBERT K. MWANGI; circ. 56,000.

Taifa Weekly: POB 49010, Nairobi; tel. (20) 337691; f. 1960; Kiswahili; Editor ROBERT K. MWANGI; circ. 68,000.

Trans Nzoia Post: POB 34, Kitale; weekly.

The Weekly Review: POB 42271, Nairobi; tel. (20) 251473; fax (20) 222555; f. 1975; English; Man. Dir JAINDI KISERO; circ. 16,000.

What's On: Rehema House, Nairobi; tel. (20) 27651; Editor NANCY KAIRO; circ. 10,000.

Monthlies

Africa Law Review: Tumaini House, 4th Floor, Nkrumah Ave, POB 53234, Nairobi; tel. (20) 330480; fax (20) 230173; e-mail alr@africalaw.org; f. 1987; English; Editor-in-Chief GITOBU IMANYARA.

East African Medical Journal: POB 41632, 00100 Nairobi; tel. (20) 712010; fax (20) 724617; e-mail eamj@wanachi.com; English; f. 1923; Editor-in-Chief Prof. WILLIAM LORE; circ. 4,500.

East African Report on Trade and Industry: POB 30339, Nairobi; journal of Kenya Asscn of Mfrs; Editor GORDON BOY; circ. 3,000.

Executive: POB 47186, Nairobi; tel. (20) 530598; fax (20) 557815; e-mail spacesellers@wanachi.com; f. 1980; business; Publr SYLVIA KING; circ. 25,000.

Kenya Export News: POB 30339, Nairobi; tel. (20) 340010; fax (20) 218845; English; publ. for Kenya External Trade Authority, Ministry of Trade and Industry; Editor Prof. SAMUEL NJOROGE; circ. 5,000.

Kenya Farmer (Journal of the Agricultural Society of Kenya): c/o English Press, POB 30127, Nairobi; tel. (20) 20377; f. 1954; English and Kiswahili; Editor ROBERT IRUNGU; circ. 20,000.

Kenya Yetu: POB 8053, Nairobi; tel. (20) 250083; fax (20) 340659; f. 1965; Kiswahili; publ. by Ministry of Tourism; Editor M. NDAVI; circ. 10,000.

Nairobi Handbook: POB 30127, Accra Rd, Nairobi; Editor R. OUMA; circ. 20,000.

News from Kenya: POB 8053, Nairobi; tel. (20) 253083; fax (20) 340659; publ. by Ministry of Tourism.

PC World (East Africa): Gilgil House, Monrovia St, Nairobi; tel. (20) 246808; fax (20) 215643; f. 1996; Editor ANDREW KARANJA.

Presence: POB 10988, Nairobi; tel. (20) 568043; fax (20) 560420; e-mail emme-ken@africaonline.co.ke; f. 1984; economics, law, women's issues, fiction.

Sparkle: POB 47186, Nairobi; tel. (20) 530598; fax (20) 557815; e-mail spacesellers@wanachi.com; f. 1990; children's; Editor ANNA NDILA NDUTO.

Today in Africa: POB 60, Kijabe; tel. (25) 64210; English; Man. Editor MWAURA NJOROGE; circ. 13,000.

Other Periodicals

African Ecclesiastical Review: POB 4002, Eldoret; tel. (32) 61218; fax (32) 62570; e-mail gabapubs@net2000ke.com; f. 1969; scripture, religion and development; 6 a year; Editor AGATHA RADOLI; circ. 2,500.

Afya: POB 30125, Nairobi; tel. (20) 501301; fax (20) 506112; e-mail amrefkco@africaonline.co.ke; journal for medical and health workers; quarterly.

Busara: Nairobi; literary; 2 a year; Editor KIMANI GECAU; circ. 3,000.

East African Agricultural and Forestry Journal: POB 30148, Nairobi; f. 1935; English; quarterly; Editor J. O. MUGAH; circ. 1,000.

Eastern African Economic Review: POB 30022, Nairobi; f. 1954; 2 a year; Editor J. K. MAITHA.

Economic Review of Agriculture: POB 30028, Nairobi; tel. (20) 728370; f. 1968; publ. by Ministry of Agriculture and Livestock; quarterly; Editor OKIYA OKOITI.

Education in Eastern Africa: Nairobi; f. 1970; 2 a year; Editor JOHN C. B. BIGALA; circ. 2,000.

Finance: Nairobi; monthly; Editor-in-Chief NJEHU GATABAKI.

Inside Kenya Today: POB 8053, Nairobi; tel. (20) 340010; fax (20) 340659; English; publ. by Ministry of Tourism; quarterly; Editor M. NDAVI; circ. 10,000.

Kenya Education Journal: Nairobi; f. 1958; English; 3 a year; Editor W. G. BOWMAN; circ. 5,500.

Kenya Statistical Digest: POB 30007, Nairobi; tel. (20) 338111; fax (20) 330426; publ. by Ministry of Finance; quarterly.

Target: POB 72839, Nairobi; f. 1964; English; 6 a year; religious; Editor FRANCIS MWANIKI; circ. 17,000.

NEWS AGENCIES

Kenya News Agency (KNA): Information House, POB 8053, Nairobi; tel. (20) 223201; f. 1963; Dir S. MUSANDU.

Foreign Bureaux

Agence France-Presse (AFP): International Life House, Mama Ngina St, POB 30671, Nairobi; tel. (20) 230613; fax (20) 230649; e-mail afpkenya@net2000ke.com; Bureau Chief BERTRAND ROSENTHAL.

Agenzia Nazionale Stampa Associata (ANSA) (Italy): 12 Kyuna Rd, Spring Valley, Morningside, POB 20444, 00220 Nairobi; tel. (20) 583565; fax (20) 229383; e-mail ansake@africaonline.co.ke; Rep. Dr LUCIANO CAUSA.

Associated Press (AP) (USA): Chester House, Koinange St, POB 47590, Nairobi; tel. (20) 250168; fax (20) 221449; e-mail naiburo@ap.org; Bureau Chief SUSAN LINNÉE.

Deutsche Presse-Agentur (dpa) (Germany): Chester House, 1st Floor, Koinange St, POB 48546, Nairobi; tel. (20) 330274; fax (20) 221902; e-mail lapkya@form-net.com; Bureau Chief ANTJE PASSENHEIM.

Informatsionnoye Telegrafnoye Agentstvo Rossii– Telegrafnoye Agentstvo Suverennykh Stran (ITAR—TASS) (Russia): Likoni Lane, POB 49602, Nairobi; tel. and fax (20) 721978; e-mail itartass@swiftkenya.com; Correspondent ANDREI K. POLYAKOV.

Inter Press Service (IPS) (Italy): POB 54386, Nairobi; tel. (20) 335418; Correspondent HORACE AWORI.

Kyodo Tsushin (Japan): Koinange St, POB 58281, Nairobi; tel. (20) 243250; fax (20) 230448; e-mail kyodonew@africaonline.co.ke; Bureau Chief OHNO KEIICHIRO.

Newslink Africa (UK): POB 3325, Nairobi; tel. (20) 241339; Correspondent PAMPHIL KWEYUH.

Reuters (UK): Finance House, 12th Floor, Loita St, POB 34043, Nairobi; tel. (20) 330261; fax (20) 338860; e-mail nairobi.newsroom@reuters.com; Bureau Chief DAVID FOX.

United Press International (UPI) (USA): POB 76282, Nairobi; tel. (20) 337349; fax (20) 213625; Correspondent JOE KHAMISI.

Xinhua (New China) News Agency (People's Republic of China): Ngong Rd at Rose Ave, POB 30728, Nairobi; tel. and fax (20) 711685; Pres. and Editor-in-Chief Prof. FLAMINGO Q. M. CHEN.

Publishers

Academy Science Publishers: POB 24916, Nairobi; tel. (20) 884405; fax (20) 884406; e-mail asp@africaonline.co.ke; f. 1989; part of the African Academy of Sciences; Editor-in-Chief Prof. KETO E. MSHIGENI.

Amecea Gaba Publications: Amecea Pastoral Institute, POB 4002, Eldoret; tel. (32) 61218; fax (32) 62570; e-mail gabapubs@net2000ke.com; f. 1989; anthropology, religious; Dir Sister AGATHA RADOLI.

Camerapix Publishers International: POB 45048, Nairobi; tel. (20) 4448923; fax (20) 4448926; e-mail info@camerapix.com; internet www.camerapix.com; f. 1960; travel, topography, natural history; Man. Dir RUKHSANA HAQ.

East African Educational Publishers: cnr Mpaka Rd and Woodvale Grove, Westlands, POB 45314, Nairobi; tel. (20) 222057; fax (20) 448753; e-mail eaep@africaonline.co.ke; internet www.eastafricanpublishers.com; f. 1965 as Heinemann Kenya Ltd, present name adopted 1992; academic, educational, creative writing;

some books in Kenyan languages; Man. Dir and Chief Exec. HENRY CHAKAVA.

Evangel Publishing House: Lumumba Drive, Roysambu, POB 28963, Nairobi; tel. (20) 802033; fax (20) 860840; e-mail evanglit@maf.org; f. 1954; religious; Man. Dir D. TRASK.

Foundation Books: Nairobi; tel. (20) 765485; f. 1974; biography, poetry; Man. Dir F. O. OKWANYA.

Kenway Publications Ltd: POB 45314, Nairobi; tel. (20) 444700; fax (20) 448753; e-mail eaep@africaonline.co.ke; f. 1981; general, regional interests; Chair. HENRY CHAKAVA.

Kenya Literature Bureau: Bellevue Area, off Mombasa Rd, POB 30022, Nairobi; tel. (20) 506142; fax (20) 505903; f. 1977; parastatal body under Ministry of Education; literary, educational, cultural and scientific books and journals; Man. Dir S. C. LANG'AT.

Jomo Kenyatta Foundation: Industrial Area, Enterprise Rd, POB 30533, Nairobi; tel. (20) 557222; fax (20) 531966; e-mail publish@jomokenyattaf.com; f. 1966; primary, secondary, university textbooks; Man. Dir F. Z. K. MENJO.

Longman Kenya Ltd: Banda School, Magadi Rd, POB 24722, Nairobi; tel. (20) 891458; fax (20) 891307; f. 1966; textbooks and educational materials; Gen. Man. JANET NJOROGE.

Macmillan Kenya Publishers Ltd: Kijabe St, POB 30797, Nairobi; tel. (20) 220012; fax (20) 212179; e-mail dmuita@macken.co.ke; f. 1970; atlases, children's educational, guide books, literature; Man. Dir DAVID MUITA.

Newspread International: POB 46854, Nairobi; tel. (20) 331402; fax (20) 607252; f. 1971; reference, economic development; Exec. Editor KUL BHUSHAN.

Oxford University Press (Eastern Africa): Waiyaki Way, ABC Place, POB 72532, Nairobi; tel. (20) 440555; fax (20) 443972; f. 1954; children's, educational and general; Regional Man. ABDULLAH ISMAILY.

Paulines Publications-Africa: POB 49026, Nairobi; tel. (20) 447202; fax (20) 442097; e-mail paulines@iconnect.co.ke; f. 1985; children's, educational; religious; Pres. Sister MARIA PEZZINI; Dir Sister TERESA MARCAZZAN.

Transafrica Press: Kenwood House, Kimathi St, POB 48239, Nairobi; tel. (20) 331762; f. 1976; general, educational and children's; Man. Dir JOHN NOTTINGHAM.

Government Publishing House

Government Printing Press: POB 30128, Nairobi; tel. (20) 334075.

PUBLISHERS' ORGANIZATION

Kenya Publishers' Association: POB 42767, 00100 Nairobi; tel. (20) 3752344; fax (20) 339875; e-mail kenyapublishers@wananchi.com; f. 1971; Chair. JANET NJOROGE.

Broadcasting and Communications

TELECOMMUNICATIONS

KenCell Communications Ltd: Parkside Towers, City Sq., Mombasa Rd, POB 73146, 00200 Nairobi; e-mail info@kencell.co.ke; internet www.kencell.co.ke; f. 2000; operates a national mobile cellular telephone network; Man. Dir and CEO PHILLIPE VANDEBROUCK.

Telkom Kenya Ltd: Telposta Towers, Kenyatta Ave, POB 30301, Nairobi; tel. (20) 227401; fax (20) 251071; e-mail mdtelkom@kenyaeafix.net; f. 1999; operates a national fixed telephone network; privatization pending; Man. Dir AUGUSTINE CHESEREM.

Safaricom Ltd: Safaricom House, Waiyaki Way, Westlands, POB 46350, Nairobi; e-mail info@safaricom.co.ke; internet www.safaricom.co.ke; f. 1999; owned by Telkom Kenya Ltd and Vodafone Airtouch (UK); operates a national mobile telephone network; Gen. Man. and CEO MICHAEL JOSEPH.

Regulatory Authority

Communications Commission of Kenya (CCK): Kijabe St, Longonot Place, POB 14448, Nairobi; tel. (20) 240165; fax (20) 252547; e-mail info@cck.go.ke; internet www.cck.go.ke; f. 1999; Dir-Gen. and Chief Exec. SAMUEL K. CHEPKONG'A.

BROADCASTING

Radio

Kenya Broadcasting Corpn (KBC): Broadcasting House, Harry Thuku Rd, POB 30456, Nairobi; tel. (20) 334567; fax (20) 220675; e-mail kbc@swiftkenya.com; internet www.kbc.co.ke; f. 1989; state corpn responsible for radio and television services; Chair. Dr JULIUS KIANO; Man. Dir JOE M. KHAMISI.

Radio: National service (Kiswahili); General service (English); Vernacular services (Borana, Burji, Hindustani, Kalenjin, Kikamba, Kikuyu, Kimasai, Kimeru, Kisii, Kuria, Luo, Luhya, Rendile, Somali, Suba, Teso and Turkana).

Capital FM: Lonrho House, Standard St, POB 74933, Nairobi; tel. (20) 210020; fax (20) 332349; e-mail info@capitalfm.co.ke; internet www.capitalfm.co.ke; f. 1999; commercial station broadcasting to Nairobi and environs; Man. Dir LYNDA HOLT.

Citizen Radio: Ambank House, University Way, POB 45897, Nairobi; tel. (20) 249122; fax (20) 249126; commercial radio station broadcasting in Nairobi and its environs; Man. Dir S. K. MACHARIA.

IQRA Broadcasting Network: Islamia Bldg, Biashara St, POB 45163, Nairobi; tel. (20) 447624; fax (20) 243109; Islamic radio station broadcasting religious programmes in Nairobi; Man. Dir AHMED KHALIF MOHAMMED.

Kameme FM: Longonot Pl., Kijabe St, POB 49640, Nairobi; tel. (20) 217963; fax (20) 33129; e-mail rreach@form-net.com; commercial radio station broadcasting in Kikuyu in Nairobi and its environs; Man. Dir ROSE KIMOTHO.

Kitambo Communications Ltd: NSSF Bldg, POB 56155, Nairobi; tel. (20) 331770; fax (20) 212847; commercial radio and television station broadcasting Christian programmes in Mombasa and Nairobi; Man. Dir Dr R. AYAH.

Nation FM: Nation Centre, POB 49010, Nairobi; tel. (20) 337710; fax (20) 217112; internet www.nationalaudio.com; commercial radio station broadcasting in Nairobi and its environs; owned by Nation Media Group; Man. Dir CYRILLE NABUTOLA.

Radio Africa Ltd (KISS FM): Safina Towers, 16th Floor, University of Nairobi, POB 45897, Nairobi; tel. (20) 245368; fax (20) 245565; Man. Dir KIPRONO KITTONY.

Sauti ya Raheme RTV Network: Eldoret; POB 4139, Eldoret; Christian, broadcasts in Eldoret and its environs; Man. Dir Rev. ELI ROP.

Television

Kenya Broadcasting Corpn (KBC): see Radio.

Television: KBC–TV, financed by licence fees and commercial advertisements; services in Kiswahili and English; operates on five channels for c. 50 hours per week. KBC–II: private subscription service.

Citizen TV: POB 45897, Nairobi; tel. (20) 249122; fax (20) 249126; commercial station broadcasting in Nairobi and its environs.

Family TV: NSSF Bldg, POB 56155, Nairobi; tel. (20) 331770; fax (20) 212847.

Kenya Television Network (KTN–TV): Nyayo House, 22nd Floor, POB 56985, Nairobi; tel. (20) 227122; fax (20) 214467; e-mail ktn@form-net.com; f. 1990; commercial station operating in Nairobi and Mombasa; Man. Dir D. J. DAVIES.

Nation TV: POB 49010, Nairobi; e-mail nation@users.co.ke; f. 1999; commercial station; owned by Nation Media Group; Man. Dir CYRILLE NABUTOLA.

Stellagraphics TV (STV): NSSF Bldg, 22nd Floor, POB 42271, Nairobi; tel. (20) 218043; fax (20) 222555; f. 1998; commercial station broadcasting in Nairobi; Man. Dir HILLARY NGWENO.

Finance

(cap. = capital; res = reserves; dep. = deposits; m. = million;
brs = branches; amounts in Kenya shillings)

BANKING

Central Bank

Central Bank of Kenya (Banki Kuu Ya Kenya): Haile Selassie Ave, POB 60000, Nairobi; tel. (20) 226431; fax (20) 217940; e-mail info@centralbank.go.ke; internet www.centralbank.go.ke; f. 1966; bank of issue; cap. and res 6,861m., dep. 73,103m. (Dec. 2001); Gov. Dr ANDREW MULLEI.

Commercial Banks

African Banking Corpn Ltd: ABC-Bank House, Koinange St, POB 46452, Nairobi; tel. (20) 223922; fax (20) 222437; e-mail abc@form-net.com; f. 1995; cap. 300m., res 24m., dep. 2,488m. (Dec. 2000); Exec. Chair. ASHRAF SAVANI; Gen. Man. GHULAM HUSSAIN SHEIKH; 7 brs.

Akiba Bank Ltd: Fedha Towers, 2nd Floor, Muindi Mbingu St, POB 49584, Nairobi; tel. (20) 249633; fax (20) 225694; e-mail akiba.ho@akibabank.com; internet www.akibabank.com; cap. 500m., res 75m., dep. 1,800m. (Dec. 2000); Exec. Chair. L. J. PANDIT; Exec. Dir D. L. PANDIT; 3 brs.

Barclays Bank of Kenya Ltd: Barclays Plaza, Loita St, POB 30120, Nairobi; tel. (20) 332230; fax (20) 213915; e-mail bbk.fin@africaonline.co.ke; f. 1978; cap. 1,543m., res 7,195m., dep. 59,396m. (Dec. 1999); Chair. SAMUEL O. J. AMBUNDO; Man. Dir ISAAC TAKAWIRA; 87 brs.

Biashara Bank of Kenya Ltd: Jethalal Chambers, Biashara St, POB 30831, Nairobi; tel. (20) 221064; fax 221679; e-mail business@biasharabank.com; internet www.biasharabank.com; f. 1984; cap. 292m., res 100m., dep. 1,662m. (Dec. 2000); Chair. S. B. R. SHAH; CEO N. D. CHUDASAMA; 4 brs.

CFC Bank Ltd: CFC Centre, Chiromo Rd, POB 72833, Nairobi; tel. (20) 340091; fax (20) 223032; cap. 500m. (Dec. 1998); Chair. P. K. JANI; Man. Dir N. MAJMUDAR.

Chase Bank (Kenya) Ltd: Prudential Assurance Bldg, Wabera St, POB 28987, Nairobi; tel. (20) 244035; fax (20) 246334; e-mail chasebank@form-net.com; cap. 200m. (Dec. 1998); Chair. WILFRIED STROTHMANN; Man. Dir ZAFRULLAH KHAN.

Commercial Bank of Africa Ltd: Commercial Bank Bldg, cnr Wabera and Standard Sts, POB 30437, Nairobi; tel. (20) 228881; fax (20) 335827; e-mail cbacare@cba.co.ke; internet www.cba.co.ke; f. 1962; owned by Kenyan shareholders; cap. and res 1,489m., dep. 9,953m. (Dec. 1999); Chair. M. H. DA GAMA-ROSE; Man. Dir I. O. AWUONDO; 9 brs.

Consolidated Bank of Kenya Ltd: Consolidated Bank House, Koinange St, POB 51133, Nairobi; tel. (20) 340551; fax (20) 340213; e-mail consobank@iconnect.co.ke; f. 1989; state-owned; cap. 1,120m., res –271m., dep. 817m. (Dec. 1999); Chair. ANDREW N. LIGALE; Man. Dir E. K. MATHIU.

Delphis Bank Ltd: Finance House, Koinange St, POB 44080, Nairobi; tel. (20) 228461; fax (20) 219469; e-mail delphiskenya@iconnect.co.ke; internet www.delphisbank.com; f. 1991; cap. and res. 1,273m., dep. 1,227m. (Dec. 2002); Chair. G. V. SHAH; Man. Dir Y. M. SHUKLA.

Equatorial Commerce Bank Ltd: Sasini House, Loita St, POB 52467, Nairobi; tel. (20) 331122; fax (20) 331606; e-mail ecb@saamnet.com; internet www.sameer-group.com; cap. 306m. (Dec. 1999); Chair. S. M. C. THOMSON; Man. Dir T. N. KHWAJA.

Kenya Commercial Bank Ltd: Kencom House, Moi Ave, POB 48400, Nairobi; tel. (20) 223846; fax (20) 215565; e-mail kcbhq@kcb.co.ke; internet www.kcb.co.ke; f. 1970; 35% state-owned; cap. 1,496m., res 474m., dep. 52,077m. (Dec. 2001); CEO and Man. Dir GARETH A. GEORGE; 105 brs and sub-brs.

Middle East Bank Kenya Ltd: Mebank Tower, Milimani Rd, POB 47387, Nairobi; tel. (20) 723120; fax (20) 335168; e-mail mebkenya@nbnet.co.ke; f. 1981; 25% owned by Banque Belgolaise SA (Belgium), 75% owned by Kenyan shareholders; cap. and res 661m., dep. 3,038m. (Dec. 2000); Chair. A. A. K. ESMAIL; Man. Dir S. S. DINAMANI; 3 brs.

National Bank of Kenya Ltd (Banki ya Taifa La Kenya Ltd): National Bank Bldg, Harambee Ave, POB 72866, Nairobi; tel. (20) 339690; fax (20) 330784; e-mail nbkops@nbnet.co.ke; internet www.nationalbank.co.ke; f. 1968; 64.5% state-owned; cap. 1,000m., res 1,156m., dep. 19,588m. (Dec. 2000); Exec. Chair. JOHN P. N. SIMBA; Gen. Man. A. H. AHMED; 25 brs.

Stanbic Bank Kenya Ltd: Stanbic Bank Bldg, Kenyatta Ave, POB 30550, Nairobi; tel. (20) 335888; fax (20) 330227; e-mail stanbickenya@stanbic.com; internet www.stanbic.co.ke; f. 1992; 93% owned by Standard Bank Investment Corpn Ltd (Botswana), 7% state-owned; cap. 1,260m., res 128m., dep. 5,526m. (Dec. 2001); Chair. J. B. WANJUI; Man. Dir P. R. SOUTHEY; 3 brs.

Standard Chartered Bank Kenya Ltd: Stanbank House, Moi Ave, POB 30003, Nairobi; tel. (20) 330200; fax (20) 214086; e-mail nancy.oginde@ke.standardchartered.com; internet www.standardchartered.com/ke; f. 1987; owned by Standard Chartered Holdings (Africa) BV (Netherlands); cap. 824m., res 3,698m., dep. 34,939m. (Dec. 1999); Chair. HARRINGTON AWORI; CEO LES GIBSON; 43 brs.

Trans-National Bank Ltd: Transnational Plaza, 2nd Floor, Mama Ngina St, POB 34353, Nairobi; tel. (20) 224234; fax (20) 339227;

e-mail tnbl@form-net.com; f. 1985; cap. and res 711m., dep. 1,008m. (Dec. 1997); Chair. Mwakai Sio; Man. Dir Patrick Noble; 5 brs.

Trust Bank Ltd: Trustforte Bldg, Moi Ave, POB 46342, Nairobi; tel. (20) 226413; fax (20) 243538; e-mail gmupcountry@trustbnk.com; f. 1988; placed under statutory management Sept. 1998; cap. 10,821m. (Dec. 1999); Chair. Tarlok S. Nandhra; Man. Dir Bharat Jani; 21 brs.

Victoria Commercial Bank Ltd: Victor House, Kimathi St, POB 41114, Nairobi; tel. (20) 228732; fax (20) 220548; e-mail atul@vicbank.com; f. 1987 as Victoria Finance Co Ltd, name changed 1996; cap. 399m. (Dec. 1999), res 76m., dep. 3,097.8m. (Dec. 1998); Chair. Silvano Kola; Gen. Man. Yogesh Kanji Pattni.

Merchant Banks

Barclays Merchant Finance Ltd: Barclays Plaza, Loita St, POB 46661, Nairobi; tel. (20) 331324; fax (20) 331396; Man. Dir Gareth A. George.

Diamond Trust Bank of Kenya Ltd: Nation Centre, 8th Floor, Kimathi St, POB 61711, Nairobi; tel. (20) 210988; fax (20) 336836; f. 1945; cap. 318m. (Dec. 1999); Chair. James B. Galbraith; Man. Dir Alan P. Beauregard.

Kenya Commercial Finance Co Ltd: Kenyan House, 6th Floor, Moi Ave, POB 21984, Nairobi; tel. (20) 339074; fax (20) 215881; e-mail kcfc@kcb.co.ke; internet www.kcb.co.ke; f. 1971; cap. 300m. (Dec. 1999), dep. 4,042m. (1998); Chair. Peter C. J. O. Nyakiamo; Man. Dir James G. Chege.

Kenya National Capital Corpn Ltd: POB 73469, Nairobi; tel. (20) 336077; fax (20) 338217; f. 1977; 60% owned by National Bank of Kenya, 40% by Kenya National Assurance Co; cap. 80m., dep. 1,024m. (1996); Chair. R. Gitau; Gen. Man. C. M. Kibunja.

National Industrial Credit Bank Ltd (NIC): NIC House, Masaba Rd, POB 44599, Nairobi; tel. (20) 718200; fax (20) 718232; e-mail nic@iconnect.co.ke; cap. 412m. (Dec. 1999); Chair. N. Muriuki Mugwandia; Man. Dir M. N. Davidson.

Standard Chartered Financial Services Ltd: International House, 1st Floor, Mama Ngina St, POB 40310, Nairobi; tel. (20) 336333; fax (20) 334934; owned by Standard Chartered Bank Kenya; cap. and res 161.7m., dep. 1,700m. (Dec. 1992); Chair. A. Cleary; Man. Dir W. von Isenburg.

Foreign Banks

ABN AMRO Bank NV (Netherlands): Nyerere Rd, POB 30262, Nairobi; tel. (20) 710455; fax (20) 713391; e-mail info@abnamro.co.ke; internet www.abnamro.co.ke; Country Man. Adrian van der Pol; 2 brs.

Bank of Baroda (India): Bank of Baroda Bldg, cnr Mondlane St and Tom Mboya St, POB 30033, Nairobi; tel. (20) 228405; fax (20) 333089; e-mail barodabk_ho@form-net.com; Exec. Chair. C. K. Daiya; 6 brs.

Bank of India: Kenyatta Ave, POB 30246, Nairobi; tel. (20) 221414; fax (20) 229462; e-mail boilo@calva.com; CEO Pundarik Sanyal.

Citibank NA (USA): Citibank House, Upperhill Rd, POB 30711, 00100 Nairobi; tel. (20) 2711221; fax (20) 2714811; internet www.citibank.co.ke; f. 1974; Gen. Man. Sridhar Srinivasan.

Crédit Agricole Indosuez (France): Reinsurance Plaza, Taifa Rd, POB 69562, Nairobi; tel. (20) 211175; fax (20) 214166; Regional Man. Benoît Destoppelaire.

First American Bank of Kenya Ltd (USA): ICEA Bldg, 6th/7th Floors, Kenyatta Ave, POB 30691, Nairobi; tel. (20) 215936; fax (20) 333868; e-mail fabk@saamnet.com; f. 1987; cap. and res 950m., dep. 5,146m. (Dec. 2001); Chair. D. G. M. Hutchinson; Man. Dir Manlio Blasetti; 3 brs.

Habib Bank AG Zurich (Switzerland): National House, Koinange St, POB 30584, Nairobi; tel. (20) 334984; fax (20) 218699; e-mail habibbanks@form-net.com; Country Man. Iqbal Allawala.

MashreqBank PSC (UAE): ICEA Bldg, Kenyatta Ave, POB 11129, Nairobi; tel. (20) 330562; fax (20) 330792; e-mail m6cbd@gsm.net.com; Gen. Man. Syed Akhtar Iman.

Co-operative Bank

Co-operative Bank of Kenya Ltd: Co-operative Bank House, POB 48231, Nairobi; tel. (20) 32076000; fax (20) 249474; e-mail md@co-opbank.co.ke; internet www.co-opbank.co.ke; f. 1968; cap. 1,210m., res 403m., dep. 18,600m. (Dec. 2001); Chair. Hosea Kiplagat; Man. Dir Gideon Muriuki; 30 brs.

Development Banks

Development Bank of Kenya Ltd: Finance House, Loita St, POB 30483, Nairobi; tel. (20) 340401; fax (20) 338426; e-mail dbk@africaonline.co.ke; f. 1963 as Development Finance Co of Kenya,

current name adopted 1996; owned by Industrial and Commercial Devt Corpn (30.5%), govt agencies of Germany and the Netherlands (28.8% and 22.8% respectively), the Commonwealth Development Corpn (10.7%) and the International Finance Corpn, Washington (7.2%); cap. 348m., res 674m., dep. 895m. (Dec. 2001); Chair. Prof. Haroun Ngeny Kipkemboi Mengech; Gen. Man. John Vijedi Bosse.

East African Development Bank: Lonrho House, 12th Floor, Standard St, Nairobi; tel. (20) 340642; fax (20) 216651; Man. D. Horoho.

Industrial Development Bank Ltd (IDB): National Bank Bldg, 18th Floor, Harambee Ave, POB 44036, Nairobi; tel. (20) 337079; fax (20) 334594; e-mail idbkenya@swiftkenya.com; f. 1973; 49% state-owned; cap. 258m., res 489m., dep. 83m. (Dec. 2000); Chair. R. K. Cheshire; Man. Dir L. A. Masaviru.

STOCK EXCHANGE

Nairobi Stock Exchange (NSE): Nation Centre, 1st Floor, Kimathi St, POB 43633, Nairobi; tel. (20) 230692; fax (20) 224200; e-mail info@nse.co.ke; f. 1954; Chair. Bethuel Kiplagat; CEO Kibby Karrithi.

INSURANCE

American Life Insurance Co (Kenya) Ltd: POB 30364, 00100 Nairobi; tel. (20) 2711242; fax (20) 2711378; e-mail alicolife@alico-kenya.com; internet www.alico-kenya.com; f. 1964; life and general; Man. Dir Erwin Brewster.

Apollo Insurance Co Ltd: POB 30389, Nairobi; tel. (20) 223562; fax (20) 339260; e-mail insurance@apollo.co.ke; f. 1977; life and general; Chief Exec. Ashok K. M. Shah.

Blue Shield Insurance Co Ltd: POB 49610, Nairobi; tel. (20) 219592; fax (20) 337808; f. 1983; life and general.

Cannon Assurance (Kenya) Ltd: Haile Selassie Ave, POB 30216, Nairobi; tel. (20) 335478; fax (20) 331235; e-mail info@cannon.co.ke; internet www.cannon.co.ke; f. 1964; life and general; Man. Dir I. J. Talwar.

Fidelity Shield Insurance Ltd: POB 47435, Nairobi; tel. (20) 430635; fax (20) 445699.

Heritage AII Insurance Co Ltd: CFC Centre, Chiromo Rd, POB 30390, Nairobi; tel. (20) 749118; fax (20) 748910; e-mail info@heriaii.com; f. 1976; general; Man. Dir J. H. D. Milne.

Insurance Co of East Africa Ltd (ICEA): ICEA Bldg, Kenyatta Ave, POB 46143, Nairobi; tel. (20) 221652; fax (20) 338089; e-mail hof@icea.co.ke; internet www.icea.co.ke; life and general; Man. Dir J. K. Ndungu.

Jubilee Insurance Co Ltd: POB 30376, Nairobi; tel. (20) 340343; fax (20) 216882; f. 1937; life and general; Chair. Abdul Jaffer.

Kenindia Assurance Co Ltd: Kenindia House, Loita St, POB 44372, Nairobi; tel. (20) 333100; fax (20) 218380; e-mail kenindia@users.africaonline.co.ke; f. 1978; life and general; Exec. Dir R. S. Bedi.

Kenya Reinsurance Corpn Ltd (KenyaRe): Reinsurance Plaza, Taifa Rd, POB 30271, Nairobi; tel. (20) 240188; fax (20) 339161; e-mail kenyare@kenyare.co.ke; internet www.kenyare.co.ke; f. 1970; Man. Dir Johnson Githaka.

Lion of Kenya Insurance Co Ltd: POB 30190, Nairobi; tel. (20) 710400; fax (20) 711177; e-mail insurance@lionofkenya.com; f. 1978; general; CEO J. P. M. Ndegwa.

Mercantile Life and General Assurance Co Ltd: Nairobi; tel. (20) 218244; fax (20) 215528; e-mail mercantile@form-net.com; Gen. Man. Supriyo Sen.

Monarch Insurance Co Ltd: Chester House, 2nd Floor, Koinange St, POB 44003, Nairobi; tel. (20) 330042; fax (20) 340691; e-mail monarch@form-net.com; f. 1975; general; Exec. Dir R. A. Vadgama.

Pan Africa Insurance Co Ltd: POB 30065, Nairobi; tel. (20) 252168; fax (20) 217675; e-mail insure@pan-africa.com; f. 1946; life and general; Man. Dir William Olotch.

Phoenix of East Africa Assurance Co Ltd: Ambank House, University Way, POB 30129, Nairobi; tel. (20) 338784; fax (20) 211848; general; Man. Dir D. K. Sharma.

Prudential Assurance Co of Kenya Ltd: Yaya Centre, Argwings Kodhek Rd, POB 76190, Nairobi; tel. (20) 567374; fax (20) 567433; f. 1979; general; Man. Dir Joseph Murage.

PTA Reinsurance Co (ZEP-RE): Anniversary Towers, 13th Floor, University Way, POB 42769, Nairobi; tel. (20) 212792; fax (20) 224102; e-mail mail@zep-re.com; internet www.zep-re.com; f. 1992; Man. Dir S. M. Lubasi.

Royal Insurance Co of East Africa Ltd: Mama Ngina St, POB 40001, Nairobi; tel. (20) 717888; fax (20) 712620; f. 1979; general; CEO S. K. KAMAU.

Standard Assurance (Kenya) Ltd: POB 42996, Nairobi; tel. (20) 224721; fax (20) 224862; Man. Dir WILSON K. KAPKOTI.

UAP Provincial Insurance Co of East Africa Ltd: Old Mutual Bldg, Kimathi St, POB 43013, Nairobi; tel. (20) 330173; fax (20) 340483; f. 1980; general; CEO E. C. BATES.

United Insurance Co Ltd: POB 30961, Nairobi; tel. (20) 227345; fax (20) 215609; Man. Dir G. KARRUIKI.

Trade and Industry

GOVERNMENT AGENCIES

Export Processing Zones Authority: POB 50563, Nairobi; tel. (20) 712800; fax (20) 713704; e-mail epzahq@africaonline.co.ke; established by the Govt to promote investment in Export Processing Zones; CEO SILAS ITA.

Export Promotion Council: POB 40247, Nairobi; tel. (20) 228534; fax (20) 218013; f. 1992; promotes exports; CEO PETER MUTHOKA.

Investment Promotion Centre: National Bank Bldg, 8th Floor, Harambee Ave, POB 55704, Nairobi; tel. (20) 221401; fax (20) 336663; e-mail ipckenya@nbnet.co.ke; internet www.ipckenya.org; f. 1982; promotes and facilitates local and foreign investment; CEO LUKA E. OBBANDA.

Kenya National Trading Corpn Ltd: Yarrow Rd, off Nanyuki Rd, POB 30587, Nairobi; tel. (20) 543121; fax (20) 532800; f. 1965; promotes national control of trade in both locally produced and imported items; exports coffee and sugar; CEO S. W. O. OGESSA.

Settlement Fund Trustees: POB 30449, Nairobi; administers a land purchase programme involving over 1.2m. ha for resettlement of African farmers.

DEVELOPMENT ORGANIZATIONS

Agricultural Development Corpn: POB 47101, Nairobi; tel. (20) 338530; fax (20) 336524; f. 1965 to promote agricultural development and reconstruction; CEO Dr WALTER KILELE.

Agricultural Finance Corpn: POB 30367, Nairobi; tel. (20) 333733; a statutory organization providing agricultural loans; Gen. Man. G. K. TOROITICH.

Horticultural Crops Development Authority: POB 42601, Nairobi; tel. (20) 8272601; fax (20) 827264; f. 1968; invests in production, dehydration, processing and freezing of fruit and vegetables; exports of fresh fruit and vegetables; Chair. DOUDI TOYE; Man. Dir S. P. GACHANJA.

Housing Finance Co of Kenya Ltd: Rehani House, cnr Kenyatta Ave and Koinange St, POB 30088, 00100 Nairobi; tel. (20) 333910; fax (20) 334670; e-mail hfck@hfck.co.ke; internet www.hfck.co.ke; f. 1965; Chair. RICHARD KEMOLI; Man. Dir PETER LEWIS-JONES.

Industrial and Commercial Development Corpn: Uchumi House, Aga Khan Walk, POB 45519, Nairobi; tel. (20) 229213; fax (20) 333880; e-mail icdcexe@africaonline.co.ke; f. 1954; govt-financed; assists industrial and commercial development; Chair. JOHN NGUTHU MUTIO; Exec. Dir K. ETICH ARAP BETT.

Kenya Fishing Industries Ltd: Nairobi; Man. Dir ABDALLA MBWANA.

Kenya Industrial Estates Ltd: Nairobi Industrial Estate, Likoni Rd, POB 78029, Nairobi; tel. (20) 530551; fax (20) 534625; f. 1967 to finance and develop small-scale industries.

Kenya Industrial Research and Development Institute: POB 30650, Nairobi; tel. (20) 557762; f. 1942; reorg. 1979; restructured 1995; research and development in industrial and allied technologies including engineering, commodity technologies, mining and power resources; Dir Dr H. L. KAANE.

Kenya Tea Development Authority: POB 30213, Nairobi; tel. (20) 21441; f. 1964 to develop tea growing, manufacturing and marketing among African smallholders; in 1994/95 it supervised an area of 76,968 ha, cultivated by 289,270 registered growers; operates 45 factories; privatization pending; Chair. STEPHEN M. IMANYARA; Man. Dir EUSTACE G. KARANJA.

CHAMBER OF COMMERCE

Kenya National Chamber of Commerce and Industry: Ufanisi House, Haile Selassie Ave, POB 47024, Nairobi; tel. (20) 220867; fax (20) 334293; f. 1965; 69 brs; Nat. Chair. DAVID M. GITHERE; Chief Exec. TITUS G. RUHIU.

INDUSTRIAL AND TRADE ASSOCIATIONS

Central Province Marketing Board: POB 189, Nyeri.

Coffee Board of Kenya: POB 30566, Nairobi; tel. (20) 332896; fax (20) 330546; f. 1947; Chair. JOHN NGARI ZACHARIAH; Gen. Man. AGGREY MURUNGA.

East African Tea Trade Association: Tea Trade Centre, Nyerere Ave, POB 85174, Mombasa; tel. (11) 315687; fax (11) 225823; e-mail info@eatta.co.ke; internet www.eatta.co.ke; f. 1957; organizes Mombasa weekly tea auctions; Exec. Sec. LUCY MICHENI; 264 mems.

Fresh Produce Exporters' Association of Kenya: Nairobi; Chair. JAMES MATHENGE.

Kenya Association of Manufacturers: POB 30225, Nairobi; tel. (20) 746005; fax (20) 746028; e-mail kam@users.africaonline.co.ke; Chair. MANU CHANDARIA; Exec. Sec. LUCY MICHENI; 200 mems.

Kenya Dairy Board: POB 30406, Nairobi.

Kenya Flower Council: POB 24856, Nairobi; tel. and fax (20) 883041; e-mail kfc@africaonline.co.ke; internet www.kenyaflowers .co.ke; regulates production of cut flowers; Exec. Dir MICHAEL MORLAND.

Kenya Meat Corpn: POB 30414, Nairobi; tel. (20) 340750; f. 1953; purchasing, processing and marketing of beef livestock; Chair. H. P. BARCLAY.

Kenya Planters' Co-operative Union Ltd: Nairobi; e-mail gm@ kpcu.co.ke; coffee processing and marketing; Chair. J. M. MACHARIA; Gen. Man. RUTH MWANIKI.

Kenya Sisal Board: Mutual Bldg, Kimathi St, POB 41179, Nairobi; tel. (20) 223457; f. 1946; CEO J. H. WAIRAGU; Man. Dir KENNETH MUKUMA.

Kenya Sugar Authority: NSSF Complex, 9th Floor, Bishops Rd, POB 51500, Nairobi; tel. (20) 710600; fax (20) 723903; e-mail ksa@ users.africaonline.co.ke; Chair. LUKE R. OBOK; CEO F. M. CHAHONYO.

Mild Coffee Trade Association of Eastern Africa (MCTA): Nairobi; F. J. MWANGI.

National Cereals and Produce Board: POB 30586, Nairobi; tel. (20) 536028; fax (20) 542024; e-mail cereals@africaonline.co.ke; f. 1995; grain marketing and handling, provides drying, weighing, storage and fumigation services to farmers and traders, stores and manages strategic national food reserves, distributes famine relief; Chair. JAMES MUTUA; Man. Dir Maj. W. K. KOITABA.

Pyrethrum Board of Kenya: POB 420, Nakuru; tel. (37) 211567; fax (37) 45274; e-mail pbk@pyrethrum.co.ke; internet www .kenya-pyrethrum.com; f. 1935; 14 mems; Chair. J. O. MARIARIA; CEO J. C. KIPTOON.

Tea Board of Kenya: POB 20064, Nairobi; tel. (20) 572421; fax (20) 562120; internet www.teaboard.or.ke; f. 1950; regulates tea industry on all matters of policy, licenses tea planting and processing, combats pests and diseases, controls the export of tea, finances research on tea, promotes Kenyan tea internationally; 17 mems; Chair. JOHNSTONE O. MORONGE; CEO STEPHEN NKANATA.

EMPLOYERS' ORGANIZATIONS

Federation of Kenya Employers: Waajiri House, Argwings Kodhek Rd, POB 48311, Nairobi; tel. (20) 721929; fax (20) 721990; Chair. J. P. N. SIMBA; Exec. Dir TOM DIJU OWUOR.

Association of Local Government Employers: POB 52, Muranga; Chair. S. K. ITONGU.

Distributive and Allied Industries Employers' Association: POB 30587, Nairobi; Chair. P. J. MWAURA.

Engineering and Allied Industries Employers' Association: POB 48311, Nairobi; tel. (20) 721929; Chair. D. M. NJOROGE.

Kenya Association of Building and Civil Engineering Contractors: Nairobi; Chair. G. S. HIRANI.

Kenya Association of Hotelkeepers and Caterers: POB 46406, Nairobi; tel. (20) 726642; fax (20) 714401; f. 1944; Chair. P. MURIUKI.

Kenya Bankers' Association: POB 73100, Nairobi; tel. (20) 221792; e-mail kba@kenyaweb.com; Chair. (vacant).

Kenya Sugar Employers' Union: Kisumu; Chair. L. OKECH.

Kenya Tea Growers' Association: POB 320, Kericho; tel. (20) 21010; fax (20) 32172; Chair. M. K. A. SANG.

Kenya Vehicle Manufacturers' Association: POB 1436, Thika; Chair. C. PETERSON.

Motor Trade and Allied Industries Employers' Association: POB 48311, Nairobi; tel. (20) 721929; fax (20) 721990; Exec. Sec. G. N. KONDITI.

Sisal Growers' and Employers' Association: POB 47523, Nairobi; tel. (20) 720170; fax (20) 721990; Chair. A. G. COMBOS.

Timber Industries Employers' Association: POB 18070, Nairobi; Chair. H. S. BAMBRAH.

UTILITIES

Electricity

The Kenya Power and Lighting Co (KPLC): Stima Plaza, Kolobot Rd, POB 30099, Nairobi; tel. (20) 243366; fax (20) 337351; e-mail isd@form-net.com; state-owned; co-ordinates electricity transmission and distribution; Man. Dir SAMUEL GICHURU.

Kenya Electricity Generating Co Ltd (KenGen): Stima Plaza, Phase 3, Kolobot Rd, Parklands, POB 47936, Nairobi; tel. (20) 248833; fax (20) 248848; e-mail kengen@africaonline.co.ke; f. 1997 as Kenya Power Co, present name adopted 1998; generates 90% of Kenya's energy requirements; Man. Dir EDWIN WASUNNA.

TRADE UNIONS

Central Organization of Trade Unions (Kenya) (COTU): Solidarity Bldg, Digo Rd, POB 13000, Nairobi; tel. (20) 761375; fax (20) 762695; f. 1965 as the sole trade union fed. Chair. PETER G. MUTHEE; Sec.-Gen. JOSEPH J. MUGALLA.

Amalgamated Union of Kenya Metalworkers: POB 73651, Nairobi; tel. (20) 211060; Gen. Sec. F. E. OMIDO.

Bakers', Confectionary Manufacturing and Allied Workers' Union (Kenya): POB 57751, 00200 Nairobi; Lengo House, 3rd Floor, Room 20, Tom Mboya St, opposite Gill House, Nairobi; tel. (20) 330275; fax (20) 222735; e-mail bakers@form-net.com.

Communication Workers' Union of Kenya: POB 48155, Nairobi; tel. (20) 219345.

Dockworkers' Union: POB 98207, Mombasa; tel. (11) 491427; f. 1954; Gen. Sec. J. KHAMIS.

Kenya Airline Pilots' Association: POB 57505, Nairobi; tel. (20) 716986.

Kenya Building, Construction, Timber, Furniture and Allied Industries Employees' Union: POB 49628, Nairobi; tel. (20) 336414; Gen. Sec. FRANCIS KARIMI MURAGE.

Kenya Chemical and Allied Workers' Union: POB 73820, Nairobi; tel. (20) 338815; Gen. Sec. WERE DIBI OGUTO.

Kenya Electrical Trades Allied Workers' Union: POB 47060, Nairobi; tel. (20) 334655.

Kenya Engineering Workers' Union: POB 73987, Nairobi; tel. (20) 333745; Gen. Sec. JUSTUS MULEI.

Kenya Game Hunting and Safari Workers' Union: Nairobi; tel. (20) 25049; Gen. Sec. J. M. NDOLO.

Kenya Jockey and Betting Workers' Union: POB 55094, Nairobi; tel. (20) 332120.

Kenya Local Government Workers' Union: POB 55827, Nairobi; tel. (20) 217213; Gen. Sec. WASIKE NDOMBI.

Kenya National Union of Fishermen: POB 83322, Nairobi; tel. (20) 227899.

Kenya Petroleum Oil Workers' Union: POB 48125, Nairobi; tel. (20) 338756; Gen. Sec. JACOB OCHINO.

Kenya Plantation and Agricultural Workers' Union: POB 1161, Nakuru; tel. and fax (37) 212310; e-mail kpawu@africaonline.co.ke; Gen. Sec. FRANCIS ATWOLI.

Kenya Quarry and Mine Workers' Union: POB 332120, Nairobi; f. 1961; Gen. Sec. WAFULA WA MUSAMIA.

Kenya Railway Workers' Union: Rahu House, Mfangano St, POB 72029, Nairobi; tel. (20) 213091; f. 1952; Nat. Chair. FRANCIS O'LORE; Sec.-Gen. PETER GITONGA MUTHEE.

Kenya Scientific Research, International Technical and Allied Institutions Workers' Union: Ngumba House, Tom Mboya St, POB 55094, Nairobi; tel. (20) 215713; Sec.-Gen. FRANCIS D. KIRUBI.

Kenya Shipping, Clearing and Warehouse Workers' Union: POB 84067, Mombasa; tel. (11) 312000.

Kenya Shoe and Leather Workers' Union: POB 49629, Nairobi; tel. (20) 533827; Gen. Sec. JAMES AWICH.

Kenya Union of Commercial, Food and Allied Workers: POB 46818, Nairobi; tel. (20) 212545.

Kenya Union of Domestic, Hotel, Educational Institutions, Hospitals and Allied Workers: POB 41763, Nairobi; tel. (20) 336838.

Kenyan Union of Entertainment and Music Industry Employees: Nairobi; tel. (20) 333745.

Kenya Union of Journalists: POB 47035, 00100 Nairobi; tel. (20) 250888; fax (20) 250880; e-mail info@kujkenya.org; f. 1962; Gen. Sec. and CEO EZEKIEL MUTUA; Chair. TERVIL OKOKO.

Kenya Union of Printing, Publishing, Paper Manufacturers and Allied Workers: POB 72358, Nairobi; tel. (20) 331387; Gen. Sec. JOHN BOSCO.

Kenya Union of Sugar Plantation Workers: POB 36, Kisumu; tel. (35) 22221; Gen. Sec. ONYANGO MIDIKA.

National Seamen's Union of Kenya: Mombasa; tel. (11) 312106; Gen. Sec. I. S. ABDALLAH MWARUA.

Tailors' and Textile Workers' Union: POB 72076, Nairobi; tel. (20) 338836.

Transport and Allied Workers' Union: POB 45171, Nairobi; tel. (20) 545317; Gen. Sec. JULIAS MALII.

Independent Unions

Academic Staff Association: Nairobi; e-mail dorata@uonbi.ac.ke; Interim Chair. Dr KORWA ADAR.

Kenya Medical Practitioners' and Dentists' Union: not officially registered; Nat. Chair. GIBBON ATEKA.

Kenya National Union of Teachers: POB 30407, Nairobi; f. 1957; Sec.-Gen. AMBROSE ADEYA ADONGO.

Transport

RAILWAYS

In 1999 there were some 2,700 km of track open for traffic.

Kenya Railways Corpn: POB 30121, Nairobi; tel. (20) 221211; fax (20) 224156; f. 1977; privatization pending; Man. Dir A. HARIZ.

ROADS

At the end of 1996 there were an estimated 63,800 km of classified roads, of which 6,360 km were main roads and 19,600 km were secondary roads. Only an estimated 13.9% of road surfaces were paved. An all-weather road links Nairobi to Addis Ababa, in Ethiopia, and there is a 590-km road link between Kitale (Kenya) and Juba (Sudan). The rehabilitation of the important internal road link between Nairobi and Mombasa (funded by a US $165m. loan from the World Bank) was undertaken during the late 1990s.

Abamba Public Road Services: POB 40322, Nairobi; tel. (20) 556062; fax (20) 559884; operates bus services from Nairobi to all major towns in Kenya and to Kampala in Uganda.

East African Road Services Ltd: Nairobi; tel. (20) 764622; f. 1947; operates bus services from Nairobi to all major towns in Kenya; Chair. S. H. NATHOO.

Kenya Roads Board: Nairobi; tel. (20) 722865; f. 2000 to co-ordinate maintenance, rehabilitation and development of the road network; Chair. SHEM ODUOR NOAH.

Nyayo Bus Service Corpn: Nairobi; tel. (20) 803588; f. 1986; operates bus services within and between major towns in Kenya.

Speedways Trans-Africa Freighters: POB 75755, Nairobi; tel. (20) 544267; private road haulier; CEO HASSAN KANYARE.

SHIPPING

The major international seaport of Mombasa has 16 deep-water berths, with a total length of 3,044 m, and facilities for the off-loading of bulk carriers, tankers and container vessels. Mombasa port handled more than 8.5m. metric tons of cargo in 1998. In August 2000 it was announced that the container terminal at Mombasa port was to be privatized by 2003. An inland container depot with a potential full capacity of 120,000 20-ft (6-m) equivalent units was opened in Nairobi in 1984. Two further inland depots were scheduled to begin operating in the mid-1990s at Eldoret and Kisumu.

Kenya Ports Authority: POB 95009, Mombasa; tel. (11) 312211; fax (11) 311867; e-mail kpa_md@africaonline.co.ke; internet www.kenya.ports.com; f. 1978; sole operator of coastal port facilities, and operates two inland container depots; Chair. JONATHAN MTURI; Man. Dir BROWN M. M. ONDEGO.

Kenya Cargo Handling Services Ltd: POB 95187, Mombasa; tel. (11) 25955; division of Kenya Ports Authority; Man. Dir JOSHUA KEGODE.

Inchcape Shipping Services Kenya Ltd: POB 90194, Mombasa; tel. (11) 314245; fax (11) 314224; Man. Dir DAVID MACKAY.

Kenya Shipping Agency Ltd: POB 84831, Mombasa; tel. (11) 220501; fax (11) 314494; e-mail ksamba@africaonline.co.ke; f. 1967;

60% govt-owned, 40% owned by Southern Shield Group; dry cargo, container, bulk carrier and tanker agents; Chair. RAY KESTER; Man. Dir JONATHAN MTURI.

Mackenzie Maritime Ltd: Maritime Centre, Archbishop Makarios Close, POB 90120, Mombasa; tel. (11) 221273; fax (11) 316260; e-mail mml@africaonline.co.ke; shipping agents; Man. Dir M. M. BROWN.

Marship Ltd: Mombasa; tel. (11) 314705; fax (11) 316654; f. 1986; shipbrokers, ship management and chartering agents; Man. Dir MICHELE ESPOSITO.

Mitchell Cotts Kenya Ltd: Cotts House, Wabera St, POB 30182, Nairobi; tel. (20) 221273; fax (20) 214228.

Motaku Shipping Agencies Ltd: Motaku House, Tangana Rd, POB 80419, 80100 Mombasa; tel. (11) 312562; fax (11) 220777; e-mail motaku@africaonline.co.ke; f. 1977; ship managers and shipping agents; Man. Dir KARIM KUDRATI.

PIL (Kenya) Ltd: POB 43050, Mombasa; tel. (11) 225361; fax (11) 312296.

Shipmarc Ltd: POB 99553, Mombasa; tel. (11) 229241; fax (11) 315673; e-mail shipmarc@form-net.com.

Southern Line Ltd: POB 90102, Mombasa 80107; tel. (11) 229241; fax (11) 221390; e-mail shipmarc@africaonline.co.ke; operating dry cargo and tanker vessels between East African ports, Red Sea ports, the Persian (Arabian) Gulf and Indian Ocean islands.

Spanfreight Shipping Ltd: Cannon Towers, Moi Ave, POB 99760, Mombasa; tel. (11) 315623; fax (11) 312092; e-mail a23ke464@gncomtext.com; Exec. Dir DILIPKUMAR AMRITLAL SHAH.

Star East Africa Co: POB 86725, Mombasa; tel. (11) 314060; fax (11) 312818; shipping agents and brokers; Man. Dir YEUDA FISHER.

CIVIL AVIATION

Jomo Kenyatta International Airport (JKIA), in south-eastern Nairobi, Moi International Airport, at Mombasa, and Eldoret International Airport (which opened in 1997) all service international flights. Wilson Airport, in south-western Nairobi, and airports at Malindi and Kisumu handle internal flights. Kenya has about 150 smaller airfields. The rehabilitation and expansion of JKIA and Moi International Airport was undertaken during the late 1990s. A new cargo handling facility, The Nairobi Cargo Centre, opened at JKIA in June 1999, increasing the airport's capacity for storing horticultural exports.

Kenya Airports Authority: Jomo Kenyatta International Airport, POB 19001, Nairobi; tel. (20) 822950; fax (20) 822078; f. 1991; state-owned; responsible for the provision, management and operation of all airports and private airstrips; Man. Dir JANET WANGERA.

African Airlines International: POB 74772, Nairobi; tel. (20) 824333; fax (20) 823999; placed under receivership mid-1999; CEO Capt. MUSA BULHAN.

Airkenya Aviation: Wilson Airport, POB 30357, Nairobi; tel. (20) 605730; fax (20) 500845; e-mail info@airkenya.com; internet www.airkenya.com; f. 1985; operates internal scheduled and charter passenger services; Man. Dir JOHN BUCKLEY.

Blue Bird Aviation Ltd: Wilson Airport, Langata Rd, POB 52382, Nairobi; tel. (20) 506004; fax (20) 602337; e-mail bbal@form-net.com.

Eagle Aviation (African Eagle): POB 93926, Mombasa; tel. (11) 434502; fax (11) 434249; e-mail eaglemsa@africaonline.co.ke; f. 1986; scheduled regional and domestic passenger and cargo services; Chair. RAJA TANUJ; CEO Capt. KIRAN PATEL.

East African Safari Air: Mombasa; operates charter service.

Kenya Airways Ltd: Jomo Kenyatta International Airport, POB 19002, Nairobi; tel. (20) 823000; fax (20) 823757; e-mail gmurira@kenya-airways.com; internet www.kenyaairways.co.uk; f. 1977; in private-sector ownership since 1996; passenger services to Africa, Asia, Europe and Middle East; freight services to Europe; internal services from Nairobi to Kisumu, Mombasa and Malindi; also operates a freight subsidiary; Chair. ISAAC OMOLO OKERO; CEO RICHARD NYAGA.

CIVIL AVIATION AUTHORITY

Kenya Directorate of Civil Aviation: Jomo Kenyatta International Airport, POB 30163, Nairobi; tel. (20) 822950; f. 1948; under Kenya govt control since 1977; responsible for the conduct of civil aviation; advises the Govt on civil aviation policy; Dir J. P. AYUGA.

Kenya Civil Aviation Authority: POB 30163, 00100 Nairobi; tel. (20) 824557; fax (20) 824716; e-mail cav@insightkenya.com; f. 2002; regulatory and advisory services for air navigation; Dir Gen. C. A. KUTO.

Tourism

Kenya's main attractions for visitors are its wildlife, with 25 National Parks and 23 game reserves, the Indian Ocean coast and an equable year-round climate. A decline in the number of visitors in 1996–98 was attributed both to competition from other countries of the region, and to perceptions of high rates of crime and shortcomings in security within Kenya. There was a modest recovery in 1999–2000, with an estimated 1,036,628 foreign tourist arrivals recorded in 2000. Earnings from the sector totalled Ks. 21,400m. in 1999.

Kenya Tourism Board: Nairobi; internet www.kenyatourism.com; f. 1996; promotes Kenya as a tourist destination, monitors the standard of tourist facilities; Chair. UHURU KENYATTA.

Kenya Tourist Development Corpn: Utalii House, 11th Floor, Uhuru Highway, POB 42013, Nairobi; tel. (20) 330820; fax (20) 227815; e-mail info@ktdc.co.uk; internet www.ktdc.co.uk; f. 1965; Chair. PAUL KITOLOLO; Man. Dir JOHN A. M. MALITI.

KIRIBATI

Introductory Survey

Location, Climate, Language, Religion, Flag, Capital

The Republic of Kiribati (pronounced 'Kir-a-bas') comprises 33 atolls, in three principal groups, scattered within an area of about 5m. sq km (2m. sq miles) in the mid-Pacific Ocean. The country extends about 3,870 km (2,400 miles) from east to west and about 2,050 km (1,275 miles) from north to south. Its nearest neighbours are Nauru, to the west, and Tuvalu and Tokelau, to the south. The climate varies between maritime equatorial in the central islands and tropical in the north and south, with daytime temperatures varying between 26°C (79°F) and 32°C (90°F). There is a season of north-westerly trade winds from March to October and a season of rains and gales from October to March. Average annual rainfall, however, varies greatly, from 3,000 mm (118 ins) in the northern islands to 1,500 mm (59 ins) in Tarawa and 700 mm (28 ins) in the Line Islands. Droughts often occur in the central and southern islands. The principal languages are I-Kiribati (Gilbertese) and English, and the islands' inhabitants are mostly Christians. The national flag (proportions 1 by 2) depicts a golden frigate bird in flight, on a red background, above a rising sun and six alternating wavy horizontal lines of blue and white, representing the sea. The capital is the island of Bairiki, in Tarawa Atoll.

Recent History

In 1892 the United Kingdom established a protectorate over the 16 atolls of the Gilbert Islands and the nine Ellice Islands (now Tuvalu). The two groups were administered together by the Western Pacific High Commission (WPHC), which was based in Fiji until its removal to the British Solomon Islands (now Solomon Islands) in 1953. The phosphate-rich Ocean Island (now Banaba), west of the Gilberts, was annexed by the United Kingdom in 1900. The Gilbert and Ellice Islands were annexed in 1915, effective from January 1916, when the protectorate became a colony. The local representative of the WPHC was the Resident Commissioner, based on Tarawa Atoll in the Gilbert group. Later in 1916 the new Gilbert and Ellice Islands Colony (GEIC) was extended to include Ocean Island and two of the Line Islands, far to the east. Christmas Island (now Kiritimati), another of the Line Islands, was added in 1919, and the eight Phoenix Islands (then uninhabited) in 1937. The Line and Phoenix Islands, south of Hawaii, were also claimed by the USA. A joint British-US administration for two of the Phoenix group, Canton (now Kanton) and Enderbury, was agreed in April 1939. During the Second World War the GEIC was invaded by Japanese forces, who occupied the Gilbert Islands in 1942–43. Tarawa Atoll was the scene of some of the fiercest fighting in the Pacific between Japan and the USA.

As part of the British Government's programme to develop its own nuclear weapons, the first test of a British hydrogen bomb was conducted near Christmas Island in May 1957. Two further tests in the same vicinity followed later that year.

In 1963, to prepare the GEIC for self-government, the first of a series of legislative and executive bodies were established. In 1972 a Governor of the GEIC was appointed to assume almost all the functions previously exercised in the colony by the High Commissioner. The five uninhabited Central and Southern Line Islands, previously administered directly by the High Commissioner, became part of the GEIC at this time. In 1974 the Legislative Council was replaced by a House of Assembly, with 28 elected members and three official members. The House elected Naboua Ratieta as Chief Minister.

In October 1975 the Ellice Islands were allowed to secede from the GEIC to form a separate territory, Tuvalu (q.v.). The remainder of the GEIC was renamed the Gilbert Islands, and the House of Assembly's membership was reduced.

In 1975 the British Government refused to recognize as legitimate a demand for independence by the people of Ocean Island (Banaba), who had been in litigation with the British Government since 1971 over revenues derived from exports of phosphate. Open-cast mining had so adversely affected the island's environment that most Banabans had been resettled on Rabi Island, 2,600 km (1,600 miles) away in the Fiji group. The Banabans rejected the British Government's argument that phosphate revenues should be distributed over the whole territory of the Gilbert Islands. In 1976 the British High Court dismissed the Banabans' claim for unpaid royalties but upheld that for damages. An offer made by the British Government in 1977 of an *ex gratia* payment of $A10m., without admission of liability and on condition that no further judicial appeal would be made, was rejected.

The Gilbert Islands obtained internal self-government on 1 January 1977. Later in that year the number of elected members in the House of Assembly was increased to 36, and provision was subsequently made for a member appointed by the Rabi Council of Leaders. Following a general election in 1978, Ieremia Tabai, Leader of the Opposition in the previous House, was elected Chief Minister. On 12 July 1979 the Gilbert Islands became an independent republic within the Commonwealth, under the name of Kiribati. The House of Assembly was renamed the Maneaba ni Maungatabu, and Ieremia Tabai became the country's first President (Beretitenti). In September Kiribati signed a treaty of friendship with the USA, which relinquished its claim to the Line and Phoenix Islands, including Kanton and Enderbury. Kiribati did not become a member of the UN until September 1999, although it had previously joined some of the organization's agencies.

In 1981 the Banaban community on Rabi accepted the British Government's earlier *ex gratia* offer of compensation, but they continued to seek self-government. The 1979 Constitution provided for the establishment of an independent commission of inquiry to review the political status of the Banabans three years after Kiribati had achieved independence, but the inquiry was not commissioned until 1985.

The first general election since independence took place in March–April 1982. The members of the new Maneaba all sat as independents. In accordance with the 1979 Constitution, the legislature nominated from among its members candidates for the country's first presidential election, to be held on the basis of direct popular vote. President Tabai was confirmed in office at the election in May. The Government resigned in December, after the Maneaba had twice rejected proposals to increase salaries for civil servants. The legislature was dissolved, and a general election took place in January 1983. The formation of the new Maneaba necessitated a further presidential election in February, at which Tabai was re-elected for a third term of office. He was returned to office in May 1987 (following a general election in March). The May 1991 legislative election was followed by a presidential election in July, at which the former Vice-President, Teatao Teannaki, narrowly defeated Roniti Teiwaki to replace Tabai, who had served the maximum number of presidential terms permitted by the Constitution.

In 1992 the Maneaba approved an opposition motion urging the Government to seek compensation from Japan for damage caused during the Second World War. The intention to seek compensation was reiterated by President Teburoro Tito (see below) in late 1994.

In May 1994 the Government was defeated on a motion of confidence, following opposition allegations that government ministers had misused travel allowances. The Maneaba was dissolved, and at legislative elections in July five cabinet ministers lost their seats. Of the newly elected members, 13 were supporters of the Maneaban Te Mauri, while only eight were known to support the previously dominant National Progressive Party grouping. At the presidential election in September Teburoro Tito, of the Maneaban Te Mauri, was elected, receiving 51.1% of the total votes. The new President declared that reducing Kiribati's dependence on foreign aid would be a major objective for his Government. He also announced his intention to pursue civil and criminal action against members of the previous administration for alleged misuse of public funds while in office.

In 1995 a committee was created with the aim of assessing public opinion regarding possible amendments to the Constitution. In March 1998 more than 200 delegates attended a Constitutional Review Convention in Bairiki to consider the recommendations of a report presented to the Government in 1996, which included equalizing the status of men and women regarding the citizenship rights of foreigners marrying I-Kiribati and changes to the structure of the Council of State. Leaders of the Banaban community in Rabi, Fiji, were also consulted during 1998 as part of the review process.

A general election, held on 23 September 1998 and contested by a record 191 candidates, failed to produce a conclusive result, necessitating a second round of voting one week later, at which the Government and opposition each lost seven seats. The new Maneaba convened in October, when it selected three presidential candidates. At a presidential election on 27 November Tito was re-elected with 52.3% of total votes cast, defeating Dr Harry Tong, who obtained 45.8% of votes, and Ambreroti Nikora, with 1.8%.

In mid-1999 John Kum Kee, a member of the Maneaba, was sentenced to four years' imprisonment, having been convicted of bribing a customs official and evasion of customs duty. Controversy continued in 1999 regarding the renamed Millennium Island (previously Caroline Island). The island had been re-named in 1997 in an attempt to promote it as a tourist destination for the year 2000. In 1994 Kiribati had moved the international date-line to incorporate the Line and Phoenix Islands groups (including Millennium Island) in the same time zone as the Gilbert group, thus creating a large eastward anomaly in the date-line. Millennium Island's position as the first place to celebrate the New Year, however, was subsequently confirmed. In early 2000, however, opposition politicians severely criticized the Government for failing to attract the predicted numbers of tourists to the islands' millennium celebrations, despite expenditure of more than $A1m. Meanwhile, in April 1999 the Kiribati Government reiterated its desire to acquire Baker, Howland and Jarvis Islands (see US External Territories—Other Territories) from the USA, citing the potential economic value of their fishing resources.

In late 1999 concerns were expressed by a Pacific media organization after a New Zealand journalist working for Agence France-Presse was banned from entering Kiribati. The Kiribati Government claimed that a series of articles by the correspondent, unfavourable to Kiribati, which had been published in a regional magazine, were biased and sensationalist. In December former President Ieremia Tabai and a former member of the Maneaba, Atiera Tetoa, were fined, having been convicted of importing telecommunications equipment without a permit. They had launched Newair FM, an independent commercial radio station, 12 months previously; it had been immediately suspended and a criminal investigation was instigated by the police. Tabai subsequently established Kiribati's first private newspaper, the *Kiribati Newstar*, in an attempt to reduce the Government's control over the media in the islands. Its first published edition coincided with Media Freedom Week in May 2000.

In November 2000 the Vice-President and Minister for Home Affairs and Rural Development, Tewarika Tentoa, collapsed while addressing the Maneaba and died. The post of Vice-President was subsequently combined with the cabinet portfolio of finance and economic planning.

In mid-October 2002 Tito's administration suffered a rare defeat when a government bill aimed at amending the Constitution was rejected, after failing to gain the two-thirds support necessary. The proposed legislation, which received 20 parliamentary votes in favour and 13 against, included measures to replace the Chief Justice with the Attorney-General on the Council of State and amendments to the number of members of Parliament from each island. Opposition members criticized the proposals, which they claimed would favour the Government in the forthcoming general election.

Campaigning for the general election during November 2002 was characterized by numerous allegations of improper conduct. Observers noted that officials from the Chinese embassy in Tarawa, accompanied by government candidates, had been donating gifts to the local community in the weeks preceding the election. (The Government had recently amended the Elections Act to allow gifts to be distributed to the public by candidates during their electoral campaigns, a practice that had been banned hitherto.) The opposition, which had stated its intention to close the Chinese satellite-tracking station (based on South Tarawa—see below) if elected, claimed that this action constituted a clear attempt to influence voters. Moreover, under a newly amended Newspaper Registration Act, Tito ordered police to seize opposition election pamphlets in November. Further allegations that the Government was attempting to stifle

freedom of expression were made by former President Iremia Tabai, whoses private radio station was finally granted a licence to broadcast in December, following delays totalling almost four years in issuing the permit.

A total of 176 candidates contested the general election on 29 November 2002. The Government suffered significant losses with 14 of its members (including seven ministers) failing to retain their seats. The presidential election was postponed from its original date and finally took place on 25 February 2003. At the poll Tito received 14,160 votes, while the opposition candidate Taberannang Timeon secured 13,613. Tito was sworn in for his third term as President on 28 February and many of his former opponents in the legislature were expected to cross the floor to support him. However, in late March Tito was narrowly defeated on a motion of 'no confidence' and his Government was replaced by an interim administration, the Council of State (comprising the Speaker, the Chief Justice and the Public Service Commissioner). In accordance with the Constitution, another general election took place on 9 and 14 May, at which supporters of Tito secured a majority of seats. A presidential election was expected to take place in early June.

As a result of discussions held at the Pacific Islands Forum summit meeting in Kiribati in October 2000, Japan announced that it was willing to negotiate compensation claims with the islanders for damage caused during the Second World War. Furthermore, a six-day visit by President Tito to Japan in February 2001 resulted in a number of informal agreements aimed at enhancing relations between the two countries. These included a decision to try to resolve a dispute over tuna fishing, caused by Japan's refusal to sign a convention aimed at protecting tuna stocks in the central and western Pacific Ocean and agreements to address their differences over whaling and nuclear-fuel shipments. Tito also appeared to modify his position on nuclear energy following the visit to Japan, stating that emissions of harmful 'greenhouse gases' could be reduced by replacing fossil with nuclear fuel.

In September 1995 Kiribati severed relations with France, in protest at the French Government's decision to renew nuclear-weapons testing at Mururoa Atoll in French Polynesia.

In September 2001 Kiribati discussed with the Australian Government the possibility of establishing an offshore refugee-processing centre, in exchange for financial aid (see the chapter on Nauru. It was envisaged that Kanton Atoll might house up to 500 asylum seekers; however, negotiations collapsed in late November, reportedly owing to logistical reasons.

Reports that Palmyra Atoll (a privately owned uninhabited US territory some 200 km north of Kiribati's northern Line Islands) was to be sold and used by a US company for the storage of nuclear waste prompted a unanimous resolution of the Maneaba, in May 1996, urging the Government to convey to the US Government the islanders' concerns over the proposals. The islanders' anxieties centred largely on Palmyra's proximity to Kiribati, coupled with the belief that the atoll's fragility and porous structure make it an unstable environment for the storage of highly toxic materials. In November 2000, however, Palmyra was purchased by The Nature Conservancy, a conservation group that planned to preserve the natural state of the atoll.

Owing to the high rate of population growth within the territory (about 2% per year) and, in particular, the situation of over-population on South Tarawa and its associated social and economic problems, it was announced in 1988 that nearly 5,000 inhabitants were to be resettled on outlying atolls, mainly in the Line Islands. A further programme of resettlement from South Tarawa to five islands in the Phoenix group was initiated in 1995.

A Chinese satellite-tracking station was opened on South Tarawa in late 1997. Sea Launch, an international consortium led by the US Boeing Commercial Space Company, also announced plans to undertake a rocket-launching project from a converted oil-rig near the islands. A prototype satellite was launched in March 1999, and commercial operations began in late 1999. Kiribati, which, together with the South Pacific Regional Environmental Programme (SPREP), had expressed concerns regarding the potential negative environmental impact of the site, was not expected to benefit financially from the project, as the consortium had sought to carry out its activities in international waters near the outer limits of the islands' exclusive economic zone. The US authorities dismissed environmental concerns about the negative impact of the site (particularly the dumping of large quantities of waste fuel in the islands' waters), which were expressed by both the Government of Kiribati and SPREP in 1998. These fears were compounded in March 2000 after a rocket launched from the site crashed, and, furthermore, Sea Launch refused to disclose where it had landed. In November 1999 it was announced that the Government of Kiribati and the National Space Development Agency of Japan had reached agreement on the proposed establishment of a space-vehicle launching and landing facility on Kiritimati. In the following year the Japanese organization was also given permission by the Kiribati Government to use land and runway facilities on the island, free of charge, until 2020 and to construct a 100–150-room hotel.

In 1989 a UN report on the 'greenhouse effect' (the heating of the earth's atmosphere, and a resultant rise in sea-level as a result of pollution) listed Kiribati as one of the countries that would completely disappear beneath the sea in the 21st century, unless drastic action were taken. None of the land on the islands is more than two metres above sea-level, making the country extremely vulnerable to the effects of climate change. A rise in sea-level would not only cause flooding, but would also upset the balance between sea and fresh water (below the coral sands), rendering water supplies undrinkable. In late 1997 President Tito strongly criticized the Australian Government's refusal, at the Conference of the Parties to the Framework Convention on Climate Change (under the auspices of the UN Environment Programme, see p. 49) in Kyoto, Japan, to reduce its emission of gases known to contribute to the 'greenhouse effect'. In mid-1999 it was announced that two of Kiribati's uninhabited coral reefs had been submerged as a result of the 'greenhouse effect'. Meanwhile, a state of emergency was declared in early 1999, owing to one of the worst droughts ever recorded in the islands. Concern among the islanders intensified in early 2001 when many of the causeways linking villages on Tarawa atoll were flooded by high tides. A report released by the World Bank in 2000 listed the flooding and loss of low-lying areas, more intense cyclones and droughts, the failure of subsistence crops and coastal fisheries, the death of coral reefs and the spread of mosquito-borne diseases such as malaria and dengue fever as consequences of the 'greenhouse effect' on Pacific island nations. In April 2001 the USA's decision to reject the Kyoto Protocol to the UN's Framework Convention on Climate Change was widely criticized. In March 2002 Kiribati, Tuvalu and the Maldives announced their decision to take legal action against the USA for its refusal to sign the Kyoto Protocol.

Government

Legislative power is vested in the unicameral Maneaba ni Maungatabu. It has 39 members elected by universal adult suffrage for four years (subject to dissolution), one nominated representative of the Banaban community and, if he is not an elected member, the Attorney-General as an *ex-officio* member. The Head of State is the Beretitenti (President), who is also Head of Government. The President is elected by direct popular vote. The President governs with the assistance of the Vice-President and Cabinet, whom he appoints from among members of the Maneaba. Executive authority is vested in the Cabinet, which is responsible to the Maneaba.

Economic Affairs

In 2001, according to estimates by the World Bank, Kiribati's gross national income (GNI), measured at average 1999–2001 prices, was US $77m., equivalent to US $830 per head. During 1990–2001, it was estimated, the population increased by an average of 2.4% per year, while gross domestic product (GDP) per head increased, in real terms, by an estimated average of 0.2% per year. Overall GDP, according to revised estimates by the Asian Development Bank (ADB), expanded, in real terms, by 6.2% in 1999 but by only 0.2% in 2000.

According to official figures, agriculture (including fishing), which employs the majority of the working population, contributed an estimated 8.2% of monetary GDP in 2000. The principal cash crop is coconut, yielding copra—which accounted for an estimated 69.0% of domestic export earnings in 1999. Construction of a new copra mill, near Betio port, began in March 2002. The project, in partnership with Australian company Techso, was to extend copra production to the outer islands and produce oils and soaps for both local and international markets. Bananas, screw-pine (*Pandanus*), breadfruit and papaya are cultivated as food crops. The cultivation of seaweed began on Tabuaeran in the mid-1980s: seaweed provided an estimated 8.5% of domestic export earnings in 1999. Pigs and chickens are kept. The closure of the state fishing company was

announced in 1991, as a result of a dramatic decline in the fish catch: fish provided only 2.4% of export earnings in 1999 (compared with 46.2% in 1990); however, pet fish are a significant export commodity, contributing 13.6% of export earnings in 1999. The sale of fishing licences to foreign fleets (notably from South Korea, Japan, Taiwan and the USA) provides an important source of income: revenue from the sale of fishing licences reached a record US $22m. in 2001. An agreement was signed with the People's Republic of China in September 2001 licensing four vessels belonging to a Chinese company to fish in Kiribati waters. The GDP of the agriculture, fishing and seaweed sectors increased at an average annual rate of 0.8% in 1991–2000. According to the ADB, agricultural GDP rose by an estimated 8.8% in 1999 and by 7.9% in 2000.

Industry (including manufacturing, construction and power) contributed an estimated 6.0% of monetary GDP in 2000. Industrial GDP increased by an average of 0.5% per year in 1991–2000. Compared with the previous year, industrial GDP was estimated by the ADB to have expanded by 38.0% in 1999, but to have contracted by 32.4% in 2000.

Mining of phosphate rock on the island of Banaba, which ceased in 1979, formerly provided some 80% of export earnings. Interest from a phosphate reserve fund (the Revenue Equalization Reserve Fund—RERF), established in 1956, continues to be an important source of budgetary income, providing the Government with investment income equivalent to around 33% of GDP per year. In 2001 the ADB estimated that the value of the RERF was such that Kiribati had sufficient foreign reserves to cover the costs of 10 years of imports. By the end of 2001 the value of the fund was put at US $329m. The production of solar-evaporated salt for export to other islands of the Pacific (for use on fishing vessels with brine refrigeration systems) began on Kiritimati in 1985.

Manufacturing, which contributed an estimated 1.0% of monetary GDP in 2000, is confined to the small-scale production of coconut-based products, soap, foods, handicrafts, furniture, leather goods and garments. Manufacturing GDP increased by an annual average of 5.6% in 1991–2000. In 2000, compared with the previous year, the GDP of the manufacturing sector contracted by an estimated 42.1%, in contrast to the 51.2% increase recorded in 1999.

Production of electrical energy declined from 14.5m. kWh in 2000 to 12.6m. kWh in 2001. Mineral fuels accounted for an estimated 10.3% of total import costs in 1999. In August 2001 the European Union announced that it planned to fund the introduction of 1,500 new solar energy systems, valued at more than $A6m., to Kiribati.

Services provided 85.8% of monetary GDP in 2000. Tourism makes a significant contribution to the economy: the trade and hotels sector provided an estimated 16.6% of GDP in 2000. Tourist arrivals at Tarawa and Kiritimati rose from 3,112 in 1999 to 4,829 in 2000, in which year receipts from tourism reached $A2.2m. In December 2001 the Government announced its decision to lease a prop-jet which it intended to operate from Tarawa to the Marshall Islands, Tuvalu and Fiji. Air Nauru, meanwhile, provided Kiribati's only air links to Nauru and Fiji, but suspended its services in June, July and November 2001. The GDP of the services sector increased at an annual average rate of 5.1% in 1991–2000. According to revised estimates from the ADB, the services sector's GDP increased by 3.9% in 1999 and by 2.4% in 2000.

In 2000 Kiribati recorded a trade deficit of an estimated $A44.3m., and a surplus of $A29.5m. on the current account of the balance of payments. In 2000 Kiribati's trade deficit narrowed to 56.7% of GDP, as a decline in income from copra exports was more than offset by a fall in imports. In 2001 the principal sources of imports were Australia (25.1%), Poland (16.4%) and Fiji (15.5%). The principal recipients of exports in that year were Japan (44.4%) and Thailand (24.0%). The major imports in 1999 were food and live animals, machinery and transport equipment, manufactures, mineral fuels, beverages and tobacco, and chemicals. The major domestic exports were copra, pet fish and seaweed.

In 2001 the fiscal deficit increased sharply, to reach the equivalent of 37.5% of GDP. Budgetary expenditure for 2002, announced in December 2001, was projected at $A77.9m., 15% less than the revised estimates for 2001, and required a draw-down of $A16.7m. from the RERF. In April 2003 the interim administration enacted a budget providing for expenditure of $A32m. over the next five months. Kiribati's total external debt in 2001 was estimated by the ADB at US $8m., and the cost of debt-servicing was equivalent to 7.9% of revenue from exports of goods and services. The annual rate of inflation averaged 3.1% in 1990–2000. Consumer prices increased by an annual average of only 0.4% in 2000, but rose by 5.9% in 2001. About 2.8% of the labour force were unemployed in 1990. Only around 8,600 people, equivalent to less than 20% of the working-age population, were formally employed in 2001.

Kiribati is a member of the Pacific Community (see p. 304), the Pacific Islands Forum (see p. 306) and the Asian Development Bank (ADB, see p. 143); it is an associate member of the UN Economic and Social Commission for Asia and the Pacific (ESCAP, see p. 28), and is a signatory to the South Pacific Regional Trade and Economic Co-operation Agreement (SPAR-TECA, see p. 308) and to the Lomé Conventions and successor Cotonou Agreement (see p. 234) with the EU. The Council of Micronesian Government Executives, of which Kiribati was a founder member in 1996, aims to facilitate discussion of economic developments in the region and to examine possibilities for reducing the considerable cost of shipping essential goods between the islands.

According to UN criteria, Kiribati is one of the world's least-developed nations. The islands' vulnerability to adverse climatic conditions was illustrated in early 1999 when a state of national emergency was declared following a prolonged period of severe drought. Kiribati's extremely limited export base and dependence on imports of almost all essential commodities result in a permanent (and widening) trade deficit, which is in most years only partially offset by revenue from fishing licence fees, interest earned on the RERF and remittances from I-Kiribati working overseas. Although the value of the RERF had trebled within 10 years, the fund declined in value in 2001 as a result of the downturn in world stock markets (its assets being invested in offshore markets). The country is reliant on foreign assistance for its development budget. Official development assistance declined from a total of US $20.9m. in 1999 to US $17.9m. in 2000. In 2002/03 New Zealand provided $NZ3.0m. and Australia $A11.1m. in development assistance. In early 2003 Kiribati established a non-government body to secure US $840,000 in EU funding under the Cotonou Agreement, which would be spent on projects over the next five years. Dependence on external finance is widely regarded as having left Kiribati vulnerable to foreign exploitation. Moreover, concern has been expressed that, although foreign companies specializing in advanced technology (particularly telecommunications and satellite systems) are seeking to establish operations in the islands, Kiribati will not benefit significantly from the major investment involved in such projects. In 2000 the Government generated some US $400,000 of revenue through the sale of I-Kiribati

passports to investors in the islands. Further passport sales in 2001 were worth US $375,000 and, combined with sales of Kiribati Residential Permits, produced more than $A2.5m. in revenue. The Government's policy of subsidizing copra producers following a fall in world prices of the commodity, however, had a negative impact on the economy; in 2001 these subsidies totalled $A2m. The economy recovered somewhat in 2001, when the World Bank estimated that GDP had increased by 1.6%. This was largely as a result of a substantial increase in recurrent government expenditure, an improvement in copra production and the implementation of various development projects. The Government's National Development Strategy for 2000–03 sought to reform the public sector and promote private-sector development. Investors have in the past been deterred by the country's weak banking system and shortage of investment opportunities. It was estimated in 2001 that around 75% of capital belonging to Kiribati's companies and private citizens was invested abroad. The new proposals were intended to encourage greater investment in the country's private sector, which would allow the creation of jobs and the broadening of the islands' narrow base of exports.

Education

Education is compulsory for nine years between the ages of six and 15 years, comprising six years of primary school and three years of junior secondary school, an initiative introduced in 1998. Students may then continue at secondary school for a further three years. Every atoll is provided with at least one primary and junior secondary school. An estimated 92% of children aged six to 12 receive primary education. The Government administers a technical college and training colleges for teachers, nurses and seamen (the last, the Marine Training Centre, trains about 200 seamen each year for employment by overseas shipping companies). An extra-mural centre of the University of the South Pacific (based in Fiji) is located on South Tarawa. In 2000 the Government allocated $A12.8m. (equivalent to 19.9% of total budgetary expenditure) to expenditure.

Public Holidays

2003: 1 January (New Year), 18–21 April (Easter), 18 May (National Health Day), 11 July (National Church Day), 12–16 July (National Day Celebrations), 3 August (Youth Day), 10 December (Human Rights and Peace Day), 25–26 December (Christmas).

2004: 1 January (New Year), 9–12 April (Easter), 18 May (National Health Day), 11 July (National Church Day), 12–16 July (National Day Celebrations), 3 August (Youth Day), 10 December (Human Rights and Peace Day), 25–26 December (Christmas).

Statistical Survey

Source (unless otherwise stated): Statistics Office, Ministry of Finance and Economic Planning, POB 67, Bairiki, Tarawa; tel. 21082; fax 21307.

AREA AND POPULATION

Area: 810.5 sq km (312.9 sq miles). *Principal atolls* (sq km): Banaba (island) 6.29 Tarawa 31.02 (North 15.26, South 15.76); Abemama 27.37; Tabiteuea 37.63 (North 25.78, South 11.85); Total Gilbert group (incl. others) 285.52; Kanton (Phoenix Is) 9.15; Teraina (Fanning) 33.73; Kiritimati (Christmas—Line Is) 388.39.

Population: 77,658 at census of 7 November 1995; 84,494 (males 41,646, females 42,848) at census of 7 November 2000. *Principal atolls* (2000): Banaba (island) 276; Abaiang 5,794; Tarawa 41,194 (North 4,477, South—including Bairiki, the capital—36,717); Tabiteuea 4,582 (North 3,365, South 1,217); Total Gilbert group (incl. others) 78,158; Kanton (Phoenix Is) 61; Kiritimati 3,431; Total Line and Phoenix Is (incl. others) 6,336.

Density (November 2000): 104.2 per sq km.

Ethnic Groups (census of 2000): Micronesians 83,452; Polynesians 641; Europeans 154; Others 247; Total 84,494.

Principal Towns: (population in '000, 1990): Bairiki (capital) 18.1; Bikenibeu 5.1; Taburao 3.5; Butaritari 3.2. Source: Stefan Helders, *World Gazetteer* (internet www.world-gazetteer.com).

Births, Marriages and Deaths: Registered live births (1996) 2,299 (birth rate 29.5 per 1,000); Marriages (registrations, 1988) 352 (marriage rate 5.2 per 1,000); Death rate (estimate, 1995) 7 per 1,000.

Expectation of Life (WHO estimates, years at birth): 63.6 (males 61.7; females 65.8) in 2001. Source: WHO, *World Health Report*.

Employment (paid employees, 1995, provisional): Agriculture, hunting, forestry and fishing 487; Manufacturing 104; Electricity, gas and water 182; Construction 215; Trade, restaurants and hotels 1,026; Transport, storage and communications 710; Financing, insurance real estate and business services 349; Community, social and personal services 4,778; Total employed 7,848. Source: UN, *Statistical Yearbook for Asia and the Pacific*.

HEALTH AND WELFARE

Key Indicators

Total Fertility Rate (children per woman, 2001): 4.6.

Under-5 Mortality Rate (per 1,000 live births, 2001): 69.

Physicians (per 1,000 head, 1998): 0.30.

Hospital Beds (per 1,000 head, 1990): 4.27.

Health Expenditure (2000): US $ per head (PPP): 140.

Health Expenditure (2000): % of GDP: 8.1.

Health Expenditure (2000): public (% of total): 98.7.

Access to Water (% of persons, 2000): 47.

Access to Sanitation (% of persons, 2000): 48.
For sources and definitions, see explanatory note on p. vi.

AGRICULTURE, ETC.

Principal Crops (FAO estimates, '000 metric tons, 2001): Taro (Coco yam) 1.6; Other roots and tubers 7.0; Coconuts 96; Vegetables 5.5; Bananas 4.5; Other fruits 1.2.

Livestock (FAO estimates, '000 head, year ending September 2001): Pigs 11; Chickens 400. Source: FAO.

Livestock Products (FAO estimates, metric tons, 2001): Pig meat 820; Poultry meat 391; Hen eggs 210. Source: FAO.

Fishing ('000 metric tons, live weight, 1999): Capture 48.2 (Snappers 1.5; Percoids 24.6, Flyingfishes 2.5, Jacks and crevalles 1.9, Skipjack tuna 3.1, Sharks, rays, skates, etc. 3.0); Aquaculture 0.0; Total catch 48.2. Figures exclude aquatic plants ('000 metric tons): 9.4 (all aquaculture). Source: FAO, *Yearbook of Fishery Statistics*.

INDUSTRY

Copra Production (metric tons): 11,368 in 1998; 11,776 in 1999; 6,133 in 2000.

Electric Energy (million kWh): 12.9 in 1999; 14.5 in 2000; 12.6 in 2001.

FINANCE

Currency and Exchange Rates: Australian currency: 100 cents = 1 Australian dollar ($A). *Sterling, US Dollar and Euro Equivalents* (31 December 2002): £1 sterling = $A2.8467; US $1 = $A1.7662; €1 = $A1.8522; $A100 = £35.13 = US $56.62 = €53.99. *Average Exchange Rate* (US $ per Australian dollar): 0.4252 in 2000; 0.4063 in 2001; 0.4165 in 2002.

Budget ($A million, 2000): *Revenue*: Tax revenue 18.7 (Corporate tax 4.7, Import duties 13.9); Other current revenue 42.6 (Fishing licence fees 31.2, Fees and incidental sales 5.8); Capital revenue 0.0; Total 61.3. *Expenditure*: General public services 7.0; Public order and safety 4.7; Education 12.8; Health 8.8; Welfare and environment 1.1; Community amenities 1.5; Agriculture and fishing 2.3; Construction 1.9; Communication 1.7; Commerce 0.7; Labour affairs 1.7; Others 20.0; Total 64.3 (Current 53.9, Capital 10.4).

Cost of Living (Consumer Price Index for Tarawa; base: 1996 = 100): 107.5 in 1999; 107.9 in 2000; 114.3 in 2001.

Expenditure on the Gross Domestic Product ($A '000 at current prices, 1992): Government final consumption expenditure 25,039; Private final consumption expenditure 31,592; Increase in stocks 250; Gross fixed capital formation 25,750; *Total domestic expenditure* 82,631; Exports of goods and services 5,798; *Less* Imports of goods and services 52,625; Statistical discrepancy 10,456; GDP in purchasers' values 46,260. Source: UN, *Statistical Yearbook for Asia and the Pacific*.

Gross Domestic Product by Economic Activity ($A million at current prices, 2000): Agriculture 2.4; Fishing 2.6; Manufacturing 0.6; Electricity 0.9; Construction 2.2; Trade, hotels and bars 10.1; Transport and communications 8.5; Finance 3.5; Real estate 1.9; Government administration 25.6; Community and social services 2.6; *Sub-total* 60.8; Less Imputed bank service charge 3.1; *GDP at factor cost* 57.7; Indirect taxes less subsidies 14.0; *GDP in purchasers' values* 71.7. Figures exclude non-monetary GDP (6.4).

Balance of Payments (estimates, US $ million, 2001): *Trade balance* −27.6; Exports of services and income 39.3; Imports of services and income −21.5; *Balance on goods, services and income* −9.8; Current transfers received 13.0; Current transfers paid −1.4; *Current balance* 1.7; Capital account (net) 3.6; Direct investment (net) −0.5; Portfolio investment −5.7; *Overall balance* −0.9. Source: Asian Development Bank, *Key Indicators of Developing Asian and Pacific Countries*.

EXTERNAL TRADE

Principal Commodities (estimates, $A million, 1999): *Imports f.o.b.*: Food and live animals 18.0; Beverages and tobacco 4.9; Mineral fuels, lubricants, etc. 6.6; Chemicals 2.8; Basic manufactures 9.6; Machinery and transport equipment 14.4; Miscellaneous manufactured articles 4.6; Total (incl. others) 63.7. *Exports f.o.b.*: Copra 9.0; Seaweed 1.1; Pet fish 1.8; Total (incl. others) 13.0 (excl. re-exports 1.0).

Principal Trading Partners (US $ million, 2001): *Imports*: Australia 16.5; China, People's Republic 1.4; Cyprus 3.7; Fiji 10.2; Japan 5.5; New Zealand 1.4; Poland 10.8; USA 6.5; Total (incl. others) 65.7. *Exports* (incl. re-exports): Bangladesh 3.6; Brazil 1.2; Japan 17.6; Korea, Republic 4.1; Poland 0.8; Thailand 9.5; USA 1.1; Total (incl. others) 39.7. Source: Asian Development Bank, *Key Indicators of Developing Asian and Pacific Countries*.

TRANSPORT

Road Traffic (motor vehicles registered on South Tarawa, 2000): Motor cycles 702; Passenger cars 477; Buses 10; Trucks 267; Minibuses 392; Others 13; Total 1,861.

Shipping: *Merchant Fleet* (registered, at 31 December 2001): 8 vessels; total displacement 4,198 grt. (Source: Lloyd's Register-Fairplay, *World Fleet Statistics*). *International Sea-borne Freight Traffic*('000 metric tons, 1990): Goods loaded 15; Goods unloaded 26 (Source: UN, *Monthly Bulletin of Statistics*).

Civil Aviation (traffic on scheduled services, 1998): Passengers carried 28,000; Passenger-km 11 million. Source: UN, *Statistical Yearbook*.

TOURISM

Foreign Tourist Arrivals (at Tarawa and Kiritimati): 5,683 in 1998; 3,112 in 1999; 4,829 in 2000.

Tourism Receipts ($A million): 2.0 in 1998; 2.1 in 1999; 2.2 in 2000.

COMMUNICATIONS MEDIA

Radio Receivers (1997): 17,000 in use.

Television Receivers (1997): 1,000 in use.

Telephones (main lines in use, 2000): 3,353.

Facsimile Machines (1996): 200 in use.

Mobile Cellular Telephones (subscribers, 2000): 395.

Personal Computers ('000 in use, 2001): 2.

Internet Users ('000, 2001): 2.

Non-daily Newspapers (2002): 2; estimated circulation 3,600. Sources: UNESCO, *Statistical Yearbook*; UN, *Statistical Yearbook*; International Telecommunication Union; Australian Press Council.

EDUCATION

Primary (2001): 88 schools; 16,096 students; 627 teachers.

Junior Secondary (2001): 19 schools; 5,743 students; 324 teachers.

Secondary (2001): 14 schools; 5,743 students; 324 teachers.

Teacher-training (2001): 198 students; 22 teachers.

Vocational (2001): 1,303 students; 17 teachers.

Adult Literacy Rate (UNESCO estimates): 92.5% (males 93%; females 92%) in 2001. Source: UNESCO, *Assessment of Resources, Best Practices and Gaps in Gender, Science and Technology in Kiribati*.

Directory

The Constitution

A new Constitution was promulgated at independence on 12 July 1979. The main provisions are as follows:

The Constitution states that Kiribati is a sovereign democratic Republic and that the Constitution is the supreme law. It guaran-

tees protection of all fundamental rights and freedoms of the individual and provides for the determination of citizenship.

The President, known as the Beretitenti, is Head of State and Head of the Government and presides over the Cabinet which consists of the Beretitenti, the Kauoman-ni-Beretitenti (Vice-President), the Attorney-General and not more than eight other ministers appointed by the Beretitenti from an elected parliament known as the Maneaba ni Maungatabu. The Constitution provided that the pre-independence Chief Minister became the first Beretitenti, but that in future the Beretitenti would be elected. After each general election for the Maneaba, the chamber nominates, from among its members, three or four candidates from whom the Beretitenti is elected by universal adult suffrage. Executive authority is vested in the Cabinet, which is directly responsible to the Maneaba ni Maungatabu. The Constitution also provides for a Council of State consisting of the Chairman of the Public Services Commission, the Chief Justice and the Speaker of the Maneaba.

Legislative power resides with the single-chamber Maneaba ni Maungatabu, composed of 40 members elected by universal adult suffrage for four years (subject to dissolution), one nominated member (see below) and the Attorney-General as an *ex-officio* member if he is not elected. The Maneaba is presided over by the Speaker, who is elected by the Maneaba from among persons who are not members of the Maneaba.

One chapter makes special provision for Banaba and the Banabans, stating that one seat in the Maneaba is reserved for a nominated member of the Banaban community. The Banabans' inalienable right to enter and reside in Banaba is guaranteed and, where any right over or interest in land there has been acquired by the Republic of Kiribati or by the Crown before independence, the Republic is required to hand back the land on completion of phosphate extraction. A Banaba Island Council is provided for, as is an independent commission of inquiry to review the provisions relating to Banaba.

The Constitution also makes provision for finance, for a Public Service and for an independent judiciary (see Judicial System).

The Government

HEAD OF STATE

President (Beretitenti): TEBURORO TITO (elected 30 September 1994; re-elected 27 November 1998 and 25 February 2003).

Vice-President (Kauoman-ni-Beretitenti): BENIAMINA TIINGA.

COUNCIL OF STATE
(interim administration, appointed 2003)

Speaker: TAOMATI IUTA.

Chief Justice: ROBIN MILLHOUSE.

Public Service Commissioner: TION OTANG.

MINISTRIES

Office of the President (Beretitenti): POB 68, Bairiki, Tarawa; tel. 21183; fax 21145.

Ministry of Commerce, Industry and Tourism: POB 510, Betio, Tarawa; tel. 26158/26157; fax 26233; e-mail commerce@tskl.net.ki.

Ministry of Education, Training and Technology: POB 263, Bikenibeu, Tarawa; tel. 28091/28033; fax 28222.

Ministry of the Environment and Social Development: POB 234, Bikenibeu, Tarawa; tel. 28211/28071; fax 28334.

Ministry of Finance and Economic Planning: POB 67, Bairiki, Tarawa; tel. 21802/21805; fax 21307.

Ministry of Foreign Affairs: POB 68, Bairiki, Tarawa; tel. 21342; fax 21466; e-mail mfa@tskl.net.ki.

Ministry of Health and Family Planning: POB 268, Bikenibeu, Tarawa; tel. 28100; fax 28152.

Ministry of Home Affairs and Rural Development: POB 75, Bairiki, Tarawa; tel. 21092; fax 21133; e-mail homeaffairs@tskl.net .ki.

Ministry of Information, Communications and Transport: POB 487, Betio, Tarawa; tel. 26003/26435; fax 26193.

Ministry of Labour, Employment and Co-operatives: POB 69, Bairiki, Tarawa; tel. 21068/21071; fax 21452.

Ministry of Line and Phoenix Development: Kiritimati Island; tel. 21449/81213; fax 81278.

Ministry of Natural Resources Development: POB 64, Bairiki, Tarawa; tel. 21099; fax 21120.

Ministry of Works and Energy: POB 498, Betio, Tarawa; tel. 26192; fax 26172.

President and Legislature

PRESIDENT

Election, 25 February 2003

Candidate	Votes	%
Teburoro Tito	14,160	50.35
Taberannang Timeon	13,613	48.41
Bakeua Tekita	348	1.24
Total	28,121	100.00

A further presidential election was expected to take place in June 2003.

MANEABA NI MAUNGATABU
(House of Assembly)

This is a unicameral body comprising 40 elected members (most of whom formally present themselves for election as independent candidates), and one nominated representative of the Banaban community. A general election was held on 29 November 2002. However, in late March 2003, following its defeat on a motion of 'no confidence', the Government was replaced by an interim authority. A further general election was held on 9 and 14 May 2003, at which supporters of former President Teburoro Tito secured a majority of seats.

Speaker: TAOMATI IUTA.

Political Organizations

There are no organized political parties in Kiribati. However, loose groupings of individuals supporting similar policies do exist, the most prominent being the Maneaban Te Mauri (Protect the Maneaba), led by Teburoro Tito, the National Progressive Party, led by Teatao Teannaki, the Liberal Party, led by Tewareka Tentoa, and the Boutokan Te Koaua (Pillars of Truth), led by Dr Harry Tong.

Diplomatic Representation

EMBASSY AND HIGH COMMISSIONS IN KIRIBATI

Australia: POB 77, Bairiki, Tarawa; tel. 21184; fax 21440; e-mail AHC_Tarawa@dfat.gov.au; High Commissioner COLIN HILL.

China, People's Republic: POB 30, Bairiki, Tarawa; tel. 21486; fax 21110; e-mail prcembassy@tskl.net.ki; Ambassador YANG ZHIKUAN.

New Zealand: POB 53, Bairiki, Tarawa; tel. 21400; fax 21402; e-mail nzhc.tar@mfat.govt.nz; High Commissioner JOHN GOODMAN.

United Kingdom: POB 5, Bairiki, Tarawa; tel. 22501; fax 22505; e-mail ukrep@tskl.net.ki; internet www.ukinthepacific.bhc.org.fj; Dep. High Commissioner VERNON SCARBOROUGH.

Judicial System

There are 24 Magistrates' Courts (each consisting of one presiding magistrate and up to eight other magistrates) hearing civil, criminal and land cases. When hearing civil or criminal cases, the presiding magistrate sits with two other magistrates, and when hearing land cases with four other magistrates. A single magistrate has national jurisdiction in civil and criminal matters. Appeal from the Magistrates' Courts lies, in civil and criminal matters, to a single judge of the High Court, and, in matters concerning land, divorce and inheritance, to the High Court's Land Division, which consists of a judge and two Land Appeal Magistrates.

The High Court of Kiribati is a superior court of record and has unlimited jurisdiction. It consists of the Chief Justice and a Puisne Judge. Appeal from a single judge of the High Court, both as a Court of the First Instance and in its appellate capacity, lies to the Kiribati Court of Appeal, which is also a court of record and consists of a panel of three judges.

All judicial appointments are made by the Beretitenti (President).

High Court
POB 501, Betio, Tarawa; tel. 26007; fax 26149; e-mail highcourt@ tskl.net.ki.

Chief Justice: ROBIN MILLHOUSE.

Judges of the Kiribati Court of Appeal: RICHARD LUSSICK (President), Sir HARRY GIBBS (Vice-President), PETER DAVID CONNOLLY, KEVIN WILLIAM RYAN.

Religion

CHRISTIANITY

Most of the population are Christians: 53.4% Roman Catholic and 39.2% members of the Kiribati Protestant Church, according to the 1990 census.

The Roman Catholic Church

Kiribati forms part of the diocese of Tarawa and Nauru, suffragan to the archdiocese of Suva (Fiji). At 31 December 2000 the diocese contained an estimated 49,456 adherents. The Bishop participates in the Catholic Bishops' Conference of the Pacific, based in Suva (Fiji).

Bishop of Tarawa and Nauru: Most Rev. PAUL EUSEBIUS MEA KAIUEA, Bishop's House, POB 79, Bairiki, Tarawa; fax 21401; e-mail cathchurch@tskl.net.ki.

The Anglican Communion

Kiribati is within the diocese of Polynesia, part of the Anglican Church in Aotearoa, New Zealand and Polynesia. The Bishop in Polynesia is resident in Fiji.

Protestant Church

Kiribati Protestant Church: POB 80, Bairiki, Tarawa; tel. 21195; fax 21453; f. 1988; Moderator Rev. BAITEKE NABETARI; Gen. Sec. Rev. TIAONTIN ARUE; 29,432 mems in 1998.

Other Churches

Seventh-day Adventist, Church of God and Assembly of God communities are also represented, as is the Church of Jesus Christ of Latter-day Saints (Mormon).

BAHÁ'Í FAITH

National Spiritual Assembly: POB 269, Bikenibeu, Tarawa; tel. and fax 28074; e-mail emi@tskl.net.ki; 2,400 mems resident in 100 localities in 1995.

The Press

Butim'aea Manin te Euangkerio: POB 80, Bairiki, Tarawa; tel. 21195; e-mail kpc@tskl.net.ki; f. 1913; Protestant Church newspaper; weekly; a monthly publication Te Kaotan te Ota is also produced; Editor Rev. TOOM TOAKAI.

Kiribati Business Link: Bairiki, Tarawa; English.

Kiribati Newstar: POB 10, Bairiki, Tarawa; tel. 21652; fax 21671; e-mail newstar@tskl.net.ki; internet www.users.bigpond.com/kiribati_newstar; f. 2000; independent; weekly; English and I-Kiribati; Editor-in-Chief NGAUEA UATIOA.

Te Itoi ni Kiribati: POB 231, Bikenibeu, Tarawa; tel. 28138; fax 21341; f. 1914; Roman Catholic Church newsletter; monthly; circ. 2,300.

Te Uekera: Broadcasting and Publications Authority, POB 78, Bairiki, Tarawa; tel. 21162; fax 21096; f. 1945; weekly; English and I-Kiribati; Editor TIBWERE BOBO; circ. 5,000.

Broadcasting and Communications

TELECOMMUNICATIONS

Telecom Kiribati Ltd: Bairiki, Tarawa; Gen. Man. ENOTA INGINTAU.

Telecom Services Kiribati Ltd: POB 72, Bairiki, Tarawa; tel. 21446; fax 21424; e-mail ceo@tskl.net.ki; internet www.tski.net.ki; owned by Govt of Kiribati; Gen. Man. STUART EASTWARD; CEO CLIFF MACALPINE.

BROADCASTING

Regulatory Authority

Broadcasting and Publications Authority: POB 78, Bairiki, Tarawa; tel. 21187; fax 21096.

Radio

Radio Kiribati: Broadcasting and Publications Authority, POB 78, Bairiki, Tarawa; tel. 21187; fax 21096; f. 1954; statutory body; station Radio Kiribati broadcasting on SW and MW transmitters; programmes in I-Kiribati (90%) and English (10%); some advertising; Man. BILL REIHER.

Television

Television Kiribati: Broadcasting and Publications Authority, POB 78, Bairiki, Tarawa; tel. 21187; fax 21096; in process of establishing services.

Finance

(cap. = capital; dep. = deposits; res = reserves)

BANKING

The Bank of Kiribati Ltd: POB 66, Bairiki, Tarawa; tel. 21095; fax 21200; e-mail bankofkiribati@tskl.net.ki; f. 1984; 75% owned by ANZ Bank, 25% by Govt of Kiribati; dep. $A42.8m., res $A1.3m., total assets $A46.3m. (Sept. 1999); Chair. ALAN WALTER; Gen. Man. BOB COWLEY; 3 brs.

Development Bank of Kiribati: POB 33, Bairiki, Tarawa; tel. 21345; fax 21297; e-mail dbk@tskl.net.ki; f. 1986; took over the assets of the National Loans Board; identifies, promotes and finances small-scale projects; auth. cap. $A2m. Gen. Man. KIETAU TABWEBWEITI; 5 brs.

A network of lending entities known as 'village banks' operates throughout the islands, as do a number of credit unions under the management of the Credit Union League. In August 1995 there were 26 credit unions operating in Tarawa and seven in the outer islands with a total membership of 1,808 people.

INSURANCE

Kiribati Insurance Corpn: POB 38, Bairiki, Tarawa; tel. 21260; fax 21426; e-mail kirins@tskl.net.ki; f. 1981; govt-owned; only insurance co; reinsures overseas; Gen. Man. TEAIRO TOOMA.

Trade and Industry

GOVERNMENT AGENCIES

Kiribati Housing Corporation: Bairiki, Tarawa; tel. 21092; operates the Housing Loan and Advice Centre; Chair. TOKOREAUA KAIRORO.

Kiribati Provident Fund: POB 76, Bairiki, Tarawa; tel. 21300; fax 21186; f. 1977; total equity $A56.8m. (Dec. 1998); Gen. Man. TOKAATA NIATA.

CHAMBER OF COMMERCE

Kiribati Chamber of Commerce: POB 550, Betio, Tarawa; tel. 26351; fax 26351; Pres. WAYSANG KUM KEE; Sec.-Gen. TIARITE KWONG.

UTILITIES

Public Utilities Board: POB 443, Betio, Tarawa; tel. 26292; fax 26106; e-mail pub@tskl.net.ki; f. 1977; govt-owned; provides electricity, water and sewerage services in Tarawa; CEO TOKIA GREIG.

Solar Energy Company: Tarawa; e-mail sec@tskl.net.ki; a co-operative administering and implementing solar-generated electricity projects in North Tarawa and the outer islands.

CO-OPERATIVE SOCIETIES

Co-operative societies dominate trading in Tarawa and enjoy a virtual monopoly outside the capital, except for Banaba and Kiritimati.

The Kiribati Copra Co-operative Society Ltd: POB 489, Betio, Tarawa; tel. 26534; fax 26391; f. 1976; the sole exporter of copra; seven cttee mems; 29 mem. socs; Chair. RAIMON TAAKE; CEO RUTIANO BENETITO.

Bobotin Kiribati Ltd: POB 485, Betio, Tarawa; tel. 26092; fax 26224; replaced Kiribati Co-operative Wholesale Society; govt-owned; Gen. Man. AKAU TIARE.

TRADE UNIONS

Kiribati Trades Union Congress (KTUC): POB 502, Betio, Tarawa; tel. 26277; fax 26257; f. 1982; unions and asscns affiliated to the KTUC include the Fishermen's Union, the Co-operative Workers' Union, the Seamen's Union, the Teachers' Union, the Nurses' Asscn, the Public Employees' Asscn, the Bankers' Union, Butaritari Rural Workers' Union, Christmas Island Union of Federated Workers, the Pre-School Teachers' Asscn, Makim Island Rural Workers' Org., Nanolelei Retailers' Union, the Plantation

Workers' Union of Fanning Island and the Overseas Fishermen's Union (formed in 1998); 2,500 mems; Pres. Tatoa Kaiteie; Gen. Sec. Tamareti Taau.

Transport

ROADS

Wherever practicable, roads are built on all atolls, and connecting causeways between islets are also being built as funds and labour permit. A programme to construct causeways between North and South Tarawa was completed in the mid-1990s. Kiribati has about 670 km of roads that are suitable for motor vehicles; all-weather roads exist in Tarawa and Kiritimati. In 2000 there were about 1,468 motor vehicles registered in the islands, of which some 48% were motorcycles.

SHIPPING

A major project to rehabilitate the port terminal and facilities at Betio, with finance totalling some US $22m. from Japan, was completed in May 2000. There are other port facilities at Banaba, Kanton and English Harbour.

Kiribati Shipping Services Ltd: POB 495, Betio, Tarawa; tel. 26195; fax 26204; e-mail kssi@tskl.net.ki; operates five passenger/freight vessels on inter-island services; govt-owned; Man. Capt. Makeran Kwong.

MATS Shipping and Transport: POB 413, Betio, Tarawa; tel. 26355; operates a fortnightly passenger and cargo service to the outer islands and occasional longer journeys.

CIVIL AVIATION

There are five international airports (Bonriki on South Tarawa, Cassidy on Kiritimati, Antekana on Butaritari, as well as others on Kanton and Tabuaeran) and several other airfields in Kiribati. The airport at Bonriki was enlarged in the early 1990s, using a loan from the Bank of China. Air Nauru and Air Marshall Islands also operate international services to Tarawa, and Aloha Airlines operates a charter flight service between Kiritimati Island and Honolulu, Hawaii. In December 2001 the Government announced its decision to lease a prop-jet, which it intended to operate from Tarawa to the Marshall Islands, Tuvalu and Fiji.

Air Kiribati Ltd: POB 274, Bonriki, Tarawa; tel. 28088; fax 28216; e-mail airkiribati.admin@tsklnet.ki; f. 1977; fmrly Air Tungaru; national airline; operates scheduled services to 15 outer islands; Chair. Takei Taoaba; CEO Taniera Teibuako.

Tourism

Previous attempts to establish tourism have been largely unsuccessful, owing mainly to the remoteness of the islands. There were 14,211 visitor arrivals in 1998 (of whom fewer than 40% were tourists). Of total tourist arrivals in 1998, some 58.3% came from Asia and Oceania, and 26.9% came from the Americas. The number of tourist arrivals rose from 3,112 in 1999 to 4,829 in 2000. In 2000 the industry earned some $A2.2m. In 1996 there were 201 hotel rooms in the islands. In 1989 the Government adopted a plan to develop hotels in the Line Islands and to exploit sites of Second World War battles. A further Tourism Development Action Plan was introduced in 1997. Game-fishing and 'eco-tourism', particularly bird-watching, were promoted in the late 1990s in an attempt to increase tourist arrivals to Kiritimati. Kiribati also exploited the location of some of its islands in the Line and Phoenix group by marketing the area as a destination for tourists wishing to celebrate the year 2000. In 1997 Caroline Island, situated close to the recently realigned international date-line, was renamed Millennium Island in an attempt to maximize its potential for attracting visitors. In late 2000 an agreement was signed with the Norwegian Shipping Line company allowing large cruise ships to make weekly calls to the Line Islands from the end of 2001.

Kiribati Visitors Bureau: Ministry of Commerce, Industry and Tourism, POB 510, Betio, Tarawa; tel. 26157; fax 26233; e-mail commerce@tskl.net.ki; internet www.spto.com; Sec. Tinian Reiher; Senior Tourist Officer Tarataake Teannaki.

THE DEMOCRATIC PEOPLE'S REPUBLIC OF KOREA

Introductory Survey

Location, Climate, Language, Religion, Flag, Capital

The Democratic People's Republic of Korea (North Korea) occupies the northern part of the Korean peninsula, bordered to the north by the People's Republic of China and, for a very short section to the north-east, by the Russian Federation, and to the south by the Republic of Korea. The climate is continental, with cold, dry winters and hot, humid summers; temperatures range from –6°C to 25°C (21°F to 77°F). The language is Korean. Buddhism, Christianity and Chundo Kyo are officially cited as the principal religions. The national flag (proportions 33 by 65) is red, with blue stripes on the upper and lower edges, each separated from the red by a narrow white stripe. Left of centre is a white disc containing a five-pointed red star. The capital is Pyongyang.

Recent History

Korea was formerly an independent monarchy. It was occupied by Japanese forces in 1905 and annexed by Japan in 1910, when the Emperor was deposed. Following Japan's surrender in August 1945, ending the Second World War, Korea was divided at latitude 38°N into military occupation zones, with Soviet forces in the North and US forces in the South. A Provisional People's Committee, led by Kim Il Sung of the Korean Communist Party (KCP), was established in the North in February 1946 and accorded government status by the Soviet occupation forces. In July the KCP merged with another group to form the North Korean Workers' Party. In 1947 a legislative body, the Choe Ko In Min Hoe Ui (Supreme People's Assembly—SPA), was established, and Kim Il Sung became Premier. A new Assembly was elected in August 1948, and the Democratic People's Republic of Korea (DPRK) was proclaimed on 9 September. In the same year the Republic of Korea (q.v.) was proclaimed in the South. Initially, the DPRK was recognized only by the USSR and other communist countries. Soviet forces withdrew from North Korea in December 1948. In the following year, as a result of a merger between communists in the North and South, the Korean Workers' Party (KWP) was formed, under the leadership of Kim Il Sung; it has held power in North Korea ever since.

The two republics each claimed to have legitimate jurisdiction over the whole Korean peninsula. North Korean forces crossed the 38th parallel in June 1950, precipitating a three-year war between North and South. The UN mounted a collective defence action in support of South Korea, and the invasion was repelled. North Korean forces were supported by the People's Republic of China from October 1950. Peace talks began in July 1951 and an armistice agreement was concluded in July 1953. The cease-fire line, which approximately follows the 38th parallel, remains the frontier between North and South Korea. A demilitarized zone (DMZ), supervised by UN forces, separates the two countries.

Through the 'personality cult' of Kim Il Sung (the 'Great Leader') and of his son Kim Jong Il (the 'Dear Leader'), and a policy of strict surveillance of the entire population, overt opposition to the KWP has effectively been eliminated. The only organized opposition to the regime (albeit in exile) appears to be the Salvation Front for the Democratic Unification of Chosun, established by former military and other officials of the DPRK in the early 1990s, which has branches in Russia, Japan and the People's Republic of China. International human rights organizations have indicated that they believe there to be a number of concentration camps in North Korea, in which as many as 200,000 political prisoners may be held.

A new Constitution, adopted in December 1972, created the office of President, and Kim Il Sung was duly elected to the post. Kim Jong Il was appointed to several key positions within the KWP in 1980. In July 1984 Radio Pyongyang referred to Kim Jong Il, for the first time, as the 'sole successor' to his father, but there were reports of opposition to the President's heir, particularly among older members of the KWP.

Following elections to the eighth SPA, in November 1986 (when the 655 members were returned unopposed), Kim Il Sung was re-elected President, and a new Administration Council (cabinet) was formed. In March 1990 Kim Il Sung was returned to the post of President, and Kim Jong Il was appointed to his first state (as distinct from party) post, as First Vice-Chairman of the National Defence Commission. In February 1991 it was rumoured that there had been an unsuccessful military coup against Kim Jong Il. In December he was appointed Supreme Commander of the Korean People's Army (KPA), in place of his father, and in January 1992 he was reported to have been given control of foreign policy. In April Kim Jong Il was appointed to the rank of Marshal, while his father assumed the title of Grand Marshal.

In what was interpreted as a partial attempt to adapt to the change in international conditions following the collapse of communist regimes world-wide, the SPA (according to South Korean reports) made several amendments to the DPRK's Constitution in April 1992. Principal among these were the deletion of all references to Marxism-Leninism, and the promotion of 'economic openness' to allow limited foreign investment in North Korea (although the KWP's guiding principle of *Juche*, or self-reliance, was strongly emphasized). In September measures to address the deteriorating economic situation included a drastic devaluation of the national currency. In December changes were made to the hierarchy of the KWP, and a reshuffle of the Administration Council was effected. The extent of the DPRK's economic difficulties was indicated by the budget proposals for 1993, which envisaged substantial reductions in expenditure, and by persistent reports of food riots. In July Kim Il Sung's younger brother, Kim Yong Ju, unexpectedly returned to political life after a 17-year absence, and was subsequently elevated to the position of Vice-President and to membership of the Central Committee of the KWP's Politburo.

Kim Il Sung died of heart failure on 8 July 1994. One hundred days of national mourning were observed, but, contrary to expectations, Kim Jong Il was not appointed to the three leading posts of President of the DPRK, General Secretary of the KWP and Chairman of the KWP Central Military Commission. Although the official media now referred to Kim Jong Il as the 'Great Leader', he did not appear in public during this period, reviving earlier speculation that he was either in poor health or that a struggle for power was taking place. It was thought that Kim Il Sung's widow, Kim Song Ae, who was the stepmother of Kim Jong Il, favoured her eldest son Kim Pyong Il for the presidency. In February 1995 the Minister of the People's Armed Forces, Marshal O Jin U died; O had been a significant supporter within the military of Kim Jong Il's succession, and his death was seen as a potential set-back for Kim. Scheduled elections to the SPA did not take place in April 1995, and no session of the assembly was convened in 1996. Meanwhile, from the mid-1990s, the influence of the KPA expanded significantly, as Kim Jong Il increasingly relied upon the military to maintain his power. The 50th anniversary of the establishment of the KWP in October 1995 was dominated by the military rather than the party, and several generals were promoted. Kim Jong Il, however, failed to assume any new posts. In February 1996 Sung Hye Rim, a former wife of Kim Jong Il and mother of his eldest son, defected to a western European country. In February 1997 Premier Kang Song San, who had made no public appearance since early 1996, was dismissed, and replaced on an acting basis by Hong Song Nam. Deepening social unrest was indicated by an increase in the rate of defections. In February Hwang Jang Yop, a close adviser to Kim Jong Il, sought political asylum in the South Korean embassy in the People's Republic of China while returning from an official visit to Japan, and warned that the DPRK was preparing to launch a military assault on South Korea. Hwang's defection appeared to precipitate significant changes in the KWP and military high command, as did the deaths of the Minister of the People's Armed Forces, Marshal Choe Kwang, and also of his deputy, Kim Kwang Jin. Many senior figures in the formal hierarchy were replaced, and some 123 generals, including many allies of Kim Jong Il, were promoted in rank in April. In August two senior North Korean diplomats, including the ambassador to Egypt, defected to the USA. There were also rumours of unrest and coup attempts, and several senior figures disappeared from public view without explanation. The official mourning period for Kim Il Sung was formally declared to be at an end in July 1997, on the third anniversary of his death. It was announced that, henceforth, North Korea was to use the *Juche* calendar, with 1912, the year of Kim Il Sung's birth, designated the first year of the new calendar. On 8 October 1997, in accordance with the recommendations of recent municipal and provincial conferences of the KWP (including KPA delegates) Kim Jong Il was elected General Secretary of the KWP.

Elections to the SPA finally took place in July 1998, at which the single list of candidates received 100% of the votes cast. Some two-thirds of the 687 deputies were newcomers to the Assembly, while the military reportedly doubled its representation. The first session of the 10th SPA was convened in September, shortly before the 50th anniversary of the establishment of North Korea. However, the anticipated appointment of Kim Jong Il as President of the DPRK did not occur, as the post was effectively abolished under major amendments to the Constitution that extensively revised the structure of government. The deceased Kim Il Sung was designated 'Eternal President', thus remaining *de jure* Head of State, while Kim Jong Il, who had been re-elected to the Chairmanship of the National Defence Commission (now apparently the highest office in the state hierarchy), assumed the role of *de facto* Head of State. Vice-Marshal Jo Myong Rok, the Director of the General Political Bureau of the KPA, was appointed First Vice-Chairman of the Commission, becoming the *de facto* second-ranking official in the DPRK. The Cabinet, as the Administration Council was redesignated, assumed many of the functions of the Central People's Committee, which was abolished. A new Presidium of the SPA was established, the President of which was to represent the State in diplomatic affairs; Kim Yong Nam, hitherto Minister of Foreign Affairs, was appointed to this position. Hong Song Nam was formally appointed Premier of the new Cabinet. Two technocrats, Jo Chang Dok and Kwak Pom Gi, were appointed Vice-Premiers.

By late 1998 Kim Jong Il had come to rely on an informal group of senior military leaders, party technocrats, former classmates and members of his extended family (including his sister, Kim Kyong Hui, and her husband, Jang Song Taek) as his power base. His succession had been facilitated by the fact that many younger technocrats were themselves the sons and daughters of revolutionary leaders.

Elections to the Local People's Assemblies were held in March 1999; it was reported that all candidates were fully endorsed. In October 2000 the Minister of Finance, Rim Kyong Suk, and the President of the central bank, Jong Song Taek, were dismissed. They were replaced, respectively, by Mun Il Bong and Kim Wan Su. No reasons were given for their dismissal. The replacement of the Minister of Foreign Trade, Kang Chong Mo, in December, by Ri Kwang Gun, was also unexplained. The Minister of Agriculture was replaced in March 2001. Meanwhile, in October 2000 the 55th anniversary of the founding of the KWP was marked by a military parade, attended, *inter alia*, by an invited delegation from South Korea.

In January 2001 the Government urged a 'new way of thinking' to solve the country's economic and domestic problems and to complement the *Kangsong Taeguk* ('prosperous and powerful nation') philosophy adopted in the late 1990s. In April the fourth session of the 10th SPA was held, but lasted only a single day; the meeting approved the budget for the coming year. Meanwhile, the number of people defecting from the North to the South continued to increase, with nearly 650 such persons having settled in the latter since 1996.

During 2001 several senior officials died or were replaced. In February the Chairman of the General Association of Korean Residents in Japan (*Chongryon*), Han Dok Su, passed away, and was replaced by So Man Sul in May. Also in February, Pak Song Bong, a senior figure in the munitions industry, died. In May the Secretary-General of the Party Central Committee, Ri Song Bok, a senior aide to Kim Jong Il, died of cancer. In August Vice Marshal Jo Myong Rok, the First Vice-Chairman of the National Defence Commission, returned to Pyongyang after a kidney

transplant operation in Beijing. He subsequently received medical treatment in France in late September. At this time, South Korean intelligence reported a reshuffle in economy-related agencies in which younger technocrats assumed principal posts. In October Kim Gyong Ho replaced Ri Il Hwan as head of the Kim Il Sung Socialist Youth League.

In January 2002 official media urged that the *Kangsong Taeguk* principle be strengthened. In mid-February Kim Jong Il duly celebrated his 60th birthday, but the commemoration was less grandiose than expected, possibly so as not to overshadow the 90th anniversary of the birth of Kim Il Sung in mid-April. In late March the fifth session of the 10th SPA was held. In addition to announcing a new budget, the SPA also adopted a new land planning law, aimed at improving and intensifying land work. Prime Minister Hong Song Nam also urged improved trade and economic co-operation, including joint ventures with other countries and international organizations. In mid-April Kim Jong Il promoted some 55 military leaders, including Jang Song U, brother of Jang Song Taek. At the same time Shin Il Nam, hitherto a Vice-Minister of Public Security, was appointed Vice-Premier in charge of the Commission for Capital Construction.

At the end of April 2002 the authorities opened the long-awaited two-month *Arirang* festival held across the country, mainly to attract foreign visitors while South Korea co-hosted the 2002 football World Cup (see below).

The question of the succession of the next generation leadership became increasingly important during 2002–03, following Kim Jong Il's 60th birthday. Kim was initially believed to have been preparing his eldest son, Kim Jong Nam, eventually to succeed him. Kim Jong Nam had served in the Ministry of Public Security and as head of the country's information technology (IT) industry since the late 1990s; however, in May 2001 he was detained in Tokyo, Japan, on charges of entering the country with a false passport, and subsequently deported to China. The incident discredited Kim Jong Nam, and thenceforth it was reported that Kim Jong Il was preparing his youngest son, Kim Jong Chol, the son of his current wife, Ko Yong Hui. Kim Jong Nam spent much of 2002 in Russia, where his mother, Sung Hye Rim, died in July. Meanwhile, in August Japanese sources reported that Kim Jong Il's middle son, Kim Hyon (also known as Kim Hyon Nam) had been appointed head of the KWP's propaganda and agitation department, a post that Kim Jong Il himself had held in the 1960s when chosen as his father's successor.

In late September 2002 the Government designated the city of Sinuiju a 'Special Administrative Region' designed to attract foreign investment, and appointed Yang Bin, a Chinese-born Dutch citizen, as its first governor. However, within days of his appointment, Yang was arrested by the Chinese authorities on corruption charges, and he was unable to assume his post. None the less, the creation of the region was a significant development in the country's efforts to open up the economy. Under the 'Basic Law' establishing the region, Sinuiju would have its own government and legal system for a 50-year period, without interference from Pyongyang. In late 2002 the Government also established a special industrial zone in Kaesong, and a special tourist zone in the region of Mount Kumgang, although these did not have the same special status as Sinuiju. Despite these developments, a meeting of senior law enforcement officials was held in Pyongyang in early December during which Premier Hong urged the elimination of 'non-socialist elements'. In early 2003 it was reported that travel restrictions within the country had been reintroduced, in order to improve security.

The sixth session of the 10th SPA was held in late March 2003. Unlike previous sessions, Kim Jong Il did not attend the meeting, and South Korean observers noted that Kim had disappeared from public view for 50 days between February and early April. Furthermore, Vice-Marshal Jo Myong Rok received treatment for kidney disease in Beijing—although his visit was believed to be linked to discussions with China over the situation on the Korean Peninsula (see below). Several important events were scheduled to be held after mid-2003, namely the 50th anniversary of the end of the Korean War in late July, and elections to the SPA at the same time.

Meanwhile, North Korea's economic difficulties and widespread food shortages were exacerbated by unusually serious flooding in 1995 and 1996, forcing the DPRK to appeal to the UN and other international organizations for emergency food aid and flood relief. Assistance was provided by the USA, South Korea and Japan in 1995, but in early 1996 further shipments of cereals were halted, pending a positive response by North Korea to US proposals for peace negotiations (see below). Renewed appeals for emergency aid were issued by the UN in mid-1996, to which the USA, South Korea and Japan responded on humanitarian grounds. In January 1997 it was reported that the People's Republic of China had agreed to provide 500,000 metric tons of rice annually for five years. This was followed, in February, by an unprecedented admission from the DPRK that the country was experiencing 'temporary food problems' and that it had only one-half of the cereals necessary to feed its people.

In April and July 1997 the UN World Food Programme (WFP) issued two further appeals for food and medical supplies. UN representatives sent to North Korea to assess the extent of the crisis confirmed that chronic malnutrition was widespread, particularly among infants, and that the medical system was no longer able to provide even basic health care. The situation deteriorated in mid-1997, when severe drought devastated most of North Korea's maize crop; further damage was caused by a tidal wave on the western coast, which left many people homeless. In January 1998 WFP issued the largest appeal in the organization's history, requesting emergency aid valued at some US $380m. Agreement was reached with North Korea whereby additional UN staff were to be permitted to enter the country in order to monitor the distribution of aid, following allegations that supplies had been diverted to the army. Despite the provision of aid, severe food shortages persisted during 1998 and malnutrition was widespread among children. In December the UN issued an appeal for humanitarian aid. In January 1999 WFP announced that substantial food aid would be required for North Korea in that year. By mid-1999 WFP announced that increased aid had prevented starvation in North Korea for the time being, although poor infrastructure continued to hamper food distribution, and entry to 49 of the country's 211 counties was still forbidden. In August serious flooding destroyed large areas of farm land and caused severe damage to the communications network.

In late 1999 international attention was focused on the uncertain situation of the large number of North Koreans (estimated at some 30,000 by South Korean sources and at 200,000 by the voluntary organization Médecins Sans Frontières) who had crossed the border into the People's Republic of China in recent years. In early 2000 it was reported that China had returned some 10,000 escapees to North Korea during 1999. The number of migrants was thought to fluctuate, according to the season. During 2001 China took greater steps to reduce the number of North Korean refugees by forcibly sending back new arrivals, despite international protests. In 2002, however, an increasing number of North Korean asylum-seekers took refuge in foreign diplomatic missions in China. China allowed the group to travel to Seoul via the Philippines, despite an agreement with the DPRK that required such defectors to be repatriated. There were concerns that the incident would create a new precedent, and encourage China to take firm action against the thousands of North Korean escapees in the People's Republic (see below).

Severe weather conditions during 2000 exacerbated food shortages in North Korea, leaving it in increased need of international aid. In November 2000 the UN estimated North Korea's food shortage for 2001 at some 1.2m. metric tons. In December 2000 the organization appealed to the international community for aid worth some US $390m., including 810,000 tons of food. The total international assistance received by North Korea in 2000 was US $220.4m., of which South Korea provided 52%, including 500,000 tons of rice and corn, and 300,000 tons of fertilizer.

In February 2001 WFP agreed to provide 810,000 tons of food and US $93m. in aid. The UN subsequently urged members to provide $383m. in humanitarian aid in 2002. In April 2001 the head of WFP in North Korea stated that the most recent winter had been especially severe and could thus result in food shortages comparable to those of 1996–97. In May the South began deliveries of 200,000 tons of agricultural fertilizer, and in June WFP stated that the North had received 389,775 tons of food aid between January and May, but would require an additional 250,000 tons to prevent starvation later in the year. The official state media announced in June, meanwhile, that the country had experienced 100 days of continuous drought since March; WFP subsequently estimated that the 2001 grain harvest would fall to 2.57m. tons as a result, far less than the 4.8m. tons needed overall. The worst-affected drought areas were South Hwanghae, Kangwon, and South Pyongan Provinces. In October WFP delivered emergency food supplies to flood-stricken Kangwon

Province, and the Government began land rezoning programmes aimed at modernizing agricultural production in South Hwanghae Province. In November the head of the World Health Organization (WHO), Gro Harlem Brundtland, visited the DPRK and opened a permanent WHO office in Pyongyang. In December 2001 the Government launched an intensive campaign for potato and double-crop growing, in order to ease the famine.

In September–October 2002 FAO and WFP visited North Korea and released a special report on the food situation. According to the report, in 2002 the harvest was believed to have improved somewhat, with cereal production 4.9% higher than in the previous year. Overall food production was 49% higher than in 2001, but 6% below the levels of 1995/96. Total cereal production, including potato equivalents, for 2002/03 was expected to reach 3.8m. tons, whereas food requirements were forecast at 4.9m. tons, thus leaving a deficit of 1.1m. tons. Urban residents remained more vulnerable to food shortages than rural residents, and food consumption per caput per day was projected at 270g of cereal in cities, compared with 600g in rural areas. Thus, urban residents were forced to spend 75%–85% of income on food purchases. The introduction in July 2002 of a quasi-market pricing system caused a significant inflation of food prices, despite the concurrent increase in salaries. The FAO-WFP mission therefore recommended concentrating resources on assisting urban areas and vulnerable groups, such as children and pregnant women.

In 1971, meanwhile, talks took place for the first time between the Red Cross Societies of North and South Korea. Negotiations were, however, suspended in 1973, and hopes for better relations were undermined by a series of clashes between North and South Korean vessels in disputed waters during 1974. Propaganda campaigns, suspended by agreement in 1972, were resumed by both sides, and minor border incidents continued. In October 1978 the UN Command (UNC—under which troops are stationed in South Korea) accused North Korea of threatening the 1953 truce, after the discovery of an underground tunnel (the third since 1974) beneath the DMZ. During the 1980s the increasing prominence of Kim Jong Il, who advocated an uncompromising policy towards the South, appeared to aggravate the situation. In 1983 some 17 South Koreans, including four government ministers, were killed in a bomb explosion in Burma (now Myanmar), in what appeared to be an assassination attempt on the South Korean President, Chun Doo-Hwan. North Korea was held responsible for the attack, and Burma severed relations with Pyongyang. In January 1984, none the less, the DPRK suggested tripartite talks on reunification, involving North and South Korea and the USA; however the proposal was rejected by South Korea, which favoured bilateral talks. During 1984 the DPRK's propaganda campaign was moderated, and in September North Korea provided emergency relief to flood-stricken areas of the South. In November the first talks, on possible economic co-operation, were held, and negotiations continued in 1985. However, in February 1986, during the annual South Korean-US 'Team Spirit' military manoeuvres, North Korea suspended all negotiations with the South. North Korea denied accusations by the South of DPRK involvement in the explosion of a South Korean airliner over Burma in November 1987, despite the subsequent confession of an alleged North Korean agent. In his 1988 New Year message, none the less, Kim Il Sung reiterated proposals for the convening of a joint conference. In August three sessions of talks were held at the 'peace village' of Panmunjom (in the DMZ) between delegates of the legislatures of North and South Korea, although the discussions (the first formal contact between the two countries since 1986) produced no conclusive results. Further negotiations in 1989 were suspended by the DPRK.

Inter-Korean talks resumed in mid-1990, and in September the DPRK Premier visited the South Korean capital, Seoul, for discussions with his counterpart, the highest-level bilateral contact since the end of the Korean War. Subsequent discussions culminated in the signing of an 'Agreement on Reconciliation, Non-aggression and Exchanges and Co-operation between the South and the North', in Seoul in December 1991. Both states pledged, *inter alia*, to desist from mutual slander, vilification and sabotage, to promote economic and other co-operation and the reunion of families separated by the war, and to work towards a full peace treaty to replace the 1953 armistice agreement. In November 1992, however, the DPRK threatened a complete suspension of contacts with the South, in protest at the latter's decision to resume the 'Team Spirit' military exercises in March 1993. (The 1992 exercises had been cancelled, owing to the improvement in relations between the two states.) Relations had also been seriously impaired by the South's announcement, in October 1992, that an extensive North Korean espionage network had been discovered in South Korea, and by the North's repeated refusals to agree to simultaneous nuclear inspections in both countries (see below).

The controversy surrounding the DPRK's suspected nuclear programme prevented any improvement in inter-Korean relations during 1993 and the first half of 1994, and contacts were also strained by the DPRK's withdrawal, in May 1994, of its mission to the Military Armistice Commission (the Panmunjom-based body overseeing the maintenance of the 1953 truce). Following talks between Kim Il Sung and former US President Jimmy Carter, who visited the DPRK (on a private initiative) in June 1994, it was announced that the first summit meeting at presidential level between the two Korean states would be held in Pyongyang in July. However, the death of Kim Il Sung led to the indefinite postponement of the summit meeting. The DPRK was, furthermore, angered by South Korea's failure to express official condolences at Kim's demise. The signature of the US-DPRK nuclear accord in October (see below) caused South Korea to make renewed efforts to resume the inter-Korean negotiations, and in February 1995 the South announced the cancellation of the annual 'Team Spirit' manoeuvres (for the second consecutive year), as a gesture of goodwill.

Tension increased markedly in April 1996, when North Korea announced its decision to abandon the 1953 armistice. North Korean troops subsequently made a number of incursions into the DMZ, thereby violating the provisions of the agreement. Later in the month, in an attempt to revitalize the peace process and replace the armistice agreement with a formal peace treaty, President Bill Clinton of the USA and President Kim Young-Sam of South Korea proposed four-way talks, involving the two Koreas, the USA and the People's Republic of China. China responded positively, but the DPRK declared its willingness to hold discussions only with the USA. Following severe flooding in the DPRK in mid-1996, the USA, South Korea and Japan agreed to provide additional food aid to North Korea as an inducement to participate in the proposed quadripartite talks. North Korea, however, imposed conditions for its participation. Relations between the two Koreas deteriorated considerably in September, when a submarine from North Korea was discovered abandoned in South Korean waters. One of the two surviving crew members claimed that this was the fourth such mission undertaken by armed North Koreans. South Korea suspended all contact with the DPRK, including the provision of food aid, and the UN Security Council subsequently expressed 'serious concern' at the incident. Following protracted mediation by the USA, an unprecedented apology was broadcast in South Korea by the (North) Korean Central News Agency.

In March 1997 explanatory talks between delegates from the DPRK, South Korea and the USA were held in New York to discuss the proposed quadripartite negotiations. Following the talks, North Korea announced that its participation in full quadripartite negotiations was conditional upon the receipt of substantial food aid. In May representatives of the Red Cross organizations of North and South Korea (in the first such meeting for five years) reached agreement on the provision of grain to the DPRK, the distribution of which was to be monitored by South Korean Red Cross officials. Further supplies were pledged following meetings in July. Negotiations were concluded in October to allow foreign airlines, including those from South Korea, to use North Korean airspace. This was regarded as a significant breakthrough in bilateral relations.

Exploratory discussions on the proposed quadripartite negotiations were held at intervals throughout the first half of 1997. In July a military confrontation between North and South Korean troops in the DMZ jeopardized the progress of the discussions. Full quadripartite negotiations, aimed at concluding a peace treaty between North and South Korea, finally opened in Geneva, Switzerland, in December 1997. A second round of full discussions was held in March 1998, but proved unsuccessful, since North Korea continued to insist on the inclusion on the agenda of the withdrawal of US troops from the Korean peninsula. In December 1997, meanwhile, negotiations in Beijing between the South and North Korean Red Cross organizations foundered, owing to North Korea's reluctance to allow South Korean officials access to the DPRK to monitor the distribution of food aid. At a subsequent meeting, in March 1998, the provision of additional food aid was agreed.

Following the inauguration of the new South Korean President, Kim Dae-Jung, in February 1998, the DPRK urged 'dialogue and negotiation' with the South Korean administration. Nevertheless, a ministerial-level meeting held in Beijing, People's Republic of China, in April, to discuss the provision of fertilizer to North Korea (the first such direct contact for four years), broke down amid mutual accusations of inflexibility, when the South Koreans insisted that the DPRK enter into negotiations on the reunion of families. In that month, however, as part of Kim Dae-Jung's 'sunshine' policy of co-operation with the DPRK, the South Korean Government announced measures to encourage inter-Korean economic contacts, allowing the transfer of private funds to the North and relaxing legislation on investment. In June, in an historic development, Chung Ju-Yung, the founder of South Korea's Hyundai conglomerate, was permitted to cross the DMZ to deliver a gift of cattle to his home town; proposals for several other joint ventures were also discussed, including a plan to operate tour boats to Mount Kumgang, just north of the border. This improvement in relations seemed to be in jeopardy when, during the visit, a North Korean submarine was caught in the nets of a southern fishing boat; all nine crew members were found dead inside the vessel. The UNC condemned the incursion during a meeting with North Korean army officers in Panmunjom, the first such talks to be held in seven years. (North Korea had suspended direct contacts with UNC officers in 1991, in protest at the appointment of a South Korean general to command the force.) A further delivery of cattle was made by Chung Ju-Yung in October 1998, when he also met with Kim Jong Il, and in November some 800 tourists from South Korea participated in the first visit to Mount Kumgang. In December, during Chung's third visit to North Korea, a proposal for the construction of an industrial complex at Haeju was approved. Following further visits in early 1999, it was announced that these would continue on a monthly basis. Private and business-related inter-Korean contacts increased substantially during 1998. In December 1998 South Korean naval forces sank a suspected North Korean spy boat, after pursuing it into international waters.

Meanwhile, at a third session of quadripartite talks, held in Geneva in October 1998, agreement was reached on the creation of two sub-committees—one with a view to the establishment of a permanent peace mechanism for the Korean peninsula, and one to seek ways of easing tension. The sub-committees were formally inaugurated during the next round of negotiations in January 1999, although little substantive progress was reported. Proceedings were somewhat overshadowed by the reported defection of a North Korean diplomat in Germany, who was said to be seeking asylum in the USA, and by claims by the DPRK that the envoy had, in fact, been abducted by South Korean intelligence agents. In early February the North Korean authorities proposed senior-level political talks with South Korea, but attached a series of conditions that were unacceptable to the South, including the cessation of joint military exercises with foreign troops and the abrogation of South Korea's national security law. Later that month 17 North Korean political detainees, who had been imprisoned in South Korea for up to 41 years, were among more than 8,000 prisoners released in a special amnesty. In March South Korea announced that it would provide, via the Red Cross, humanitarian assistance in the form of fertilizers.

In June 1999 a week-long confrontation between North and South Korean naval forces in the Yellow Sea resulted in a brief gun battle, during which one North Korean torpedo boat was sunk and five other vessels were damaged. Two rounds of bilateral talks in Beijing in late June and early July ended in failure, after North Korean representatives demanded an apology for the sinking of the boat, and refused to discuss the issue of reunion of families until further fertilizer aid was delivered by the South. (South Korea had recently sent 100,000 metric tons of fertilizer, and had promised a second delivery if some agreement was reached at the talks.) Furthermore, Hyundai was forced to suspend tours to Mount Kumgang for more than a month, after a South Korean tourist was detained in late June for allegedly encouraging northern tour guides to defect. In September the DPRK declared invalid the Northern Limit Line (the maritime border that has separated the two Koreas since 1953), in protest at the UNC's refusal to renegotiate its demarcation. Meanwhile, no discernible progress had been achieved at sessions of the quadripartite talks held in April and August 1999. None the less, Hyundai proceeded with its plans for a number of projects in North Korea: in October the company concluded an agreement with the DPRK on the construction of the proposed industrial complex, which, it was envisaged, would comprise some 850 businesses, employing some 220,000 people, and would be capable of producing export goods worth an estimated US $3,000m. annually. In February 2000 foreign residents in South Korea were permitted to visit Mount Kumgang for the first time. In December 1999 another major South Korean company, Samsung Electronics, announced that it had signed a contract with the DPRK for the joint development of computer software and the manufacture of electronic products. In February 2000 the construction of a motor vehicle assembly plant, in a joint venture with the Pyonghwa Motor Company of South Korea, began in Nampo, south-west of Pyongyang. According to South Korean estimates, inter-Korean trade increased by 50.2% in 1999. A number of joint North-South cultural and sporting events took place in 1999. In March 2000 Kim Dae-Jung urged North Korea to develop economic contacts with the South at governmental level. In April, following a series of high-level bilateral contacts in Beijing, North and South Korea jointly announced that an historic summit meeting would take place between Kim Dae-Jung and Kim Jong Il in Pyongyang in June.

Following the presidential summit meeting on 13–15 June 2000, detailed agreements were signed pledging economic co-operation, the building of mutual trust and the resolution of reunification issues. In July ministerial-level delegations from both countries met in Seoul. This was the first visit to the South by North Korean officials since 1991. Although the two sides failed to reach an agreement on military matters, a joint communiqué was issued allowing for, *inter alia*, the reopening of liaison offices at Panmunjom which had been closed in 1996, and the reconnection of the inter-Korean Kyongui railway line. The construction of a highway to run alongside the railway from North to South was subsequently agreed. In September Kim Dae-Jung formally inaugurated the project to remove thousands of landmines (to be undertaken by soldiers from each side respectively) and rebuild the railway line and adjacent highway. Meanwhile, benefiting from the progress made at the summit meeting in June, in August 100 North Korean families travelled to Seoul and 100 South Korean families visited Pyongyang simultaneously to meet with relatives from whom they had been separated by the Korean War. The second ministerial meeting between the two sides was held in Pyongyang later that month. Negotiations were extended for one day because of an inability to agree on terms for beginning a dialogue between the two countries' military establishments. A compromise was reached after consultation with Kim Jong Il. It was agreed to hold two more cross-border family reunions by the end of 2000 and to commence talks on economic co-operation. In a symbolic display of unity, in September the two countries marched under the same flag in the opening ceremony of the Olympic Games in Sydney, Australia. In late September the DPRK's Minister of the People's Armed Forces, Vice-Marshal Kim Il Chol, visited the South and met his counterpart, Cho Seong-Tae, the first such ministerial meeting ever held. In October Kim Dae-Jung was awarded the Nobel Peace Prize in recognition of his reunification efforts. Further rounds of inter-ministerial, military and economic talks took place during 2000 and early 2001. In an indication of the improvement in relations, in December 2000 a meeting was also held between trade union representatives from the two countries.

Despite the increased level of dialogue and co-operation between the two countries, however, in December 2000 South Korea published its annual defence policy document, which described the North as its main enemy and alleged that it had expanded its military capacity along the DMZ. The DPRK was antagonized by its continued status as South Korea's most likely adversary. International analysts, however, felt that hostility was not imminent. North Korea was also angered in that month by the approval of a resolution by the South Korean legislature to demand the repatriation of prisoners of war who, it alleged, continued to be held by the North, despite the DPRK's denial of the existence of these prisoners.

In early 2001 the uncompromising attitude displayed by the new US administration towards North Korea threatened to undermine the reconciliation process. In March the DPRK unilaterally postponed scheduled cabinet-level talks following a visit to the USA by Kim Dae-Jung, raising speculation that Pyongyang wanted time to formulate a response to US criticism of its regime (see below), and in April North Korea denounced joint US-South Korean military exercises as a betrayal of the

goodwill surrounding the June 2000 summit meeting. Ministerial discussions resumed in Seoul in mid-September, the sixth round of which was concluded in mid-November (having been postponed from late October) without any agreement—the first unsuccessful such round since the presidential summit meeting. The North blamed the South, in particular the Minister of Unification, Hong Soon-Young, for the failure of the talks.

Meanwhile, during 2001 Kim Jong Il's long-awaited visit to Seoul for a second presidential summit meeting failed to materialize, and there was continued uncertainty as to when such a visit would take place. US President George W. Bush's reference in January 2002 to North Korea as part of an 'axis of evil' threatened to damage inter-Korean relations.

A stalemate in inter-Korean relations was broken in early April 2002, however, when the North received Kim Dae-Jung's special envoy, Lim Dong-Won. Following the visit, during which Lim met Kim Jong Il, the two sides agreed to further reunions for separated families (see below) and to continuing discussions on economic co-operation. North Korea also agreed to Lim's request that it renew dialogue with the USA and Japan. In mid-May Park Geun-Hye, a South Korean legislator and the daughter of former President Park Chung-Hee, visited the North and met Kim Jong Il. The visit was unusual because Northern agents had killed Park's mother in 1974 in a bid to assassinate her father. Despite the cordial visit, North Korea cancelled economic co-operation discussions with the South in May.

In May 2002 the increasing number of defectors from the North received international attention as several groups sought asylum at Canadian, Japanese and South Korean diplomatic buildings in China. They were eventually allowed to travel to the South, albeit via the Philippines. The South Korean Ministry of Unification reported in January 2003 that during 2002 some 1,141 North Koreans had defected to the South, compared with 583 in 2001.

At the end of June 2002 a gun battle between North and South Korean vessels in the Yellow Sea resulted in the sinking of a Southern patrol boat and the deaths of six crew members. South Korean military sources estimated that 30 Northern crewmen were also killed in the confrontation, which had started when two North Korean vessels accompanying a fishing boat reportedly crossed the Northern Limit Line. Following the incident, in July South Korea suspended rice shipments to the North and economic co-operation projects, reflecting widespread public anger there. None the less, Kim Dae-Jung maintained his 'sunshine' policy towards the North, and later expressed regret for the incident. Meanwhile, North Korean state television showed selected highlights of matches played by the South Korean football team in the 2002 football World Cup—although refrained from transmitting extensive coverage of the event, which was being co-hosted by Japan.

In mid-August 2002 North and South Korea held a seventh round of ministerial talks in Seoul, aimed at improving relations in the aftermath of the latest naval confrontation, and focusing on the issue of future family reunions, railway links (see below) and cultural exchanges. Regarding the latter, more than 300 North Korean athletes travelled to the South and participated in the Asian Games held in Busan during October. In late September the first inter-Korean military 'hotline' was inaugurated to allow for improved communications during sensitive occasions. Meanwhile, Pyongyang's revelation that it had abducted 12 Japanese citizens in the 1970s and 1980s (see below) highlighted the outstanding issue of several hundred missing South Korean citizens believed to have been abducted by the North.

The eighth round of ministerial talks was held in Pyongyang in late October 2002 and mainly focused on economic co-operation issues, despite the fact that the USA had earlier revealed the existence of a secret nuclear weapons programme in the North (see below). At the end of that month a North Korean economic delegation began a nine-day tour of the South, including several major industrial facilities in the itinerary. Noteworthy was the fact that the delegation included Jang Song Taek, Kim Jong Il's brother-in-law and one of his most trusted advisers, and also Kim Hi Taek, the first deputy head of the KWP's Central Committee. At the end of December 2002 South Korea's Ministry of National Defence published a 'white paper' which, for the first time, excluded any reference to the North as its main enemy.

By late 2002 some of the goodwill generated by the historic inter-Korean summit meeting in June 2000 had been undermined by the revelation that Kim Dae-Jung had arranged for the Korea Development Bank to give a Hyundai affiliate US $200m. to transfer to the North in order to arrange the summit. However, the election in December of Roh Moo-Hyun, the candidate of Kim's Millennium Democratic Party (MDP), as President of South Korea heralded a continuation of Kim's 'sunshine' policy. In early January 2003 representatives of Roh secretly met Northern officials in Beijing, and later in that month a ninth round of ministerial talks was held in Seoul. Kim also dispatched Lim Dong-Won to Pyongyang at the end of the month, but Lim failed to secure a meeting with Kim Jong Il, instead relaying a goodwill message through one of the latter's aides. Both North and South Korea were expected to continue efforts to improve relations with each other during 2003, despite a severe deterioration in relations between the North and the USA (see below). By March 2003 Roh was exploring a long-standing idea of developing gas pipelines between Sakhalin, Russia, and North Korea that would supply the latter with energy in return for an abandonment of its nuclear programme. North Korea hosted the 10th round of ministerial talks at the end of April. In mid-May, however, Pyongyang announced that it no longer recognized a joint declaration on the 'denuclear-ization' of the Korean peninsula, signed with the South in 1992 (see below).

The arrangements for further family reunions came under the auspices of the North and South Korean Red Cross organizations, which held several rounds of talks on the subject and co-ordinated the exchange of lists of potential candidates for reunion. In October 2000 South Korea accepted a DPRK proposal that the second exchange of family members should take place in late November–early December. Relations between the two sides subsequently deteriorated, casting doubt on the likelihood of the meetings taking place, when North Korea accused the head of the South Korean Red Cross of defaming the former's political system. The official was replaced in January 2001. The DPRK continued to dictate terms for reunions, asking South Korea to limit the amount of money and gifts transferred during the events, which took place in November–December 2000 and at the end of February 2001. It was subsequently reported that North Korean officials had confiscated money given to delegates for use as state funds. Meanwhile, in January 2001 an historic accord between the two sides allowed 300 separated families from the North and South each to exchange letters in mid-March. A fourth round of family reunions was initially scheduled for mid-October, but was cancelled owing to the heightened security situation following the terrorist attacks in the USA on 11 September. They were subsequently held at Mount Kumgang in late April 2002. A fifth round was held in mid-September 2002, again at Mount Kumgang, where officials from the two sides planned to build a centre for such meetings.

As the DPRK's financial situation worsened, economic issues played an important part in inter-Korean relations from 2000. There was speculation that Pyongyang's new openness was motivated by the necessity of securing increased assistance. In January 2001, however, a South Korean vessel carrying aid was refused permission to dock in the DPRK. Also in that month, it was reported that North Korea's energy shortages had reached crisis point, and that the country was desperately researching alternative power sources. A summit meeting took place between the two Koreas in February, at which the DPRK requested immediate and substantial electricity supplies to alleviate its pressing needs. Frustration resulted from South Korea's insistence on the necessity of on-site investigations prior to the commencement of deliveries. Meanwhile, in August 2000 Hyundai agreed to establish a technologically-advanced electronic industrial compound in Kaesong in the DPRK. Hyundai's financial problems, however, were likely to delay the implementation of the project. The company was also obliged to reduce its royalty payments to Pyongyang for the Mount Kumgang tourist initiative in 2000, owing to the attraction's failure to make a profit. In March 2001 the future of the initiative was jeopardized by its lack of profitability, and Hyundai appealed to the South Korean Government for assistance; the Government subsequently pledged 90,000m. won to maintain the tourist cruises. Hyundai founder Chung Ju-Yung died in late March, meanwhile, and his funeral was attended by a delegation sent by Kim Jong Il. On May Day workers from trade unions from the North and South attended a rally at Mount Kumgang. Bilateral talks held in October concerning the re-launch of the project and the opening of a connecting cross-border road, however, failed to make progress.

Negotiations to re-establish the inter-Korean rail link continued during 2001. It was hoped that such a link would create a new Eurasian transport corridor that would reduce the cost and time involved in the transit of goods from North-East Asia to European markets from 25 days to about 15 days, bringing economic benefits to all participants. In February 2001 a meeting was held at the DMZ to arrange regulations for troops and workers employed to rebuild the line, and a parallel highway. However, North Korea failed to attend a UN regional transport meeting held in Seoul in mid-November, following the failure of the sixth round of ministerial talks. A New Year's editorial in January 2002 described the upgrading of the railway as a priority during that year, and both Koreas agreed to accelerate the reconnection following bilateral talks in April 2002. Ground-breaking ceremonies for the reconnection of the railway and road links were held on both sides of the DMZ in late September 2002, and South Korea released a loan to the North to assist the funding of the work. In late 2002 South Korean officials attended the ground-breaking ceremony for the North's new industrial zone at Kaesong. In early February 2003 the first road reconnecting the North with the South was completed, on the eastern coast of the Korean peninsula.

In the early 1990s there was growing international concern that the DPRK had intensified its clandestine nuclear programme at Yongbyon, north of Pyongyang, and would soon be capable of manufacturing a nuclear weapon. During 1991 pressure was increasingly applied, by the USA and Japan in particular, for the DPRK to sign the Nuclear Safeguards Agreement (NSA) with the International Atomic Energy Agency (IAEA, see p. 80). This was required by the DPRK's signature, in 1985, of the Treaty on the Non-Proliferation of Nuclear Weapons (the Non-Proliferation Treaty—NPT), in order that IAEA representatives might be permitted to inspect the country's nuclear facilities. However, North Korea consistently refused to allow such inspections to take place unless there was to be a simultaneous inspection (or withdrawal) of US nuclear weapons sited in South Korea. Tension was eased considerably by the USA's decision, in October 1991, to remove all its tactical nuclear weapons from South Korea, and by South Korea's subsequent declaration that it would not manufacture, deploy or use nuclear, chemical or biological weapons. In December the South Korean Government stated that all US nuclear weapons had been withdrawn, and proposed that simultaneous inspections of military bases in the South and nuclear facilities in the North be conducted. Later in the month the two Korean states concluded an agreement 'to create a non-nuclear Korean peninsula', and in January 1992 the DPRK signed the NSA. In March delegates of North and South, meeting at Panmunjom, agreed to form a Joint Nuclear Control Commission (JNCC) to permit inter-Korean nuclear inspections to take place.

In May 1992 North Korea submitted to the IAEA an unexpectedly detailed report on its nuclear facilities, describing, *inter alia*, the Yongbyon installation as a research laboratory. In the same month IAEA inspectors were permitted to visit North Korean nuclear facilities (the first in a series of official visits during that year). Despite the findings of the inspectors (who concluded that the Yongbyon plant was 'primitive' and far from completion, although potentially capable of producing plutonium), suspicions persisted regarding the DPRK's nuclear ambitions. Moreover, North Korea repeatedly failed to agree to separate nuclear inspections by the JNCC, finally announcing in January 1993 its intention to boycott all future inter-Korean nuclear talks (in protest at the imminent resumption of the 'Team Spirit' manoeuvres). The situation became critical in February, when the DPRK refused to allow IAEA inspections of two 'undeclared' sites near Yongbyon, claiming that these were military installations unrelated to nuclear activities. In an unprecedented move, the DPRK announced in March that it was to withdraw from the NPT. In May the UN Security Council adopted a resolution urging the DPRK to reconsider its decision to withdraw from the NPT and calling on the country to allow an inspection by the IAEA of its nuclear facilities. Following negotiations with the USA in May and June, North Korea agreed to suspend its withdrawal from the NPT; in return, the USA agreed to assist the DPRK in the development of its non-military nuclear programme. International concern regarding the DPRK's arms programme was, meanwhile, heightened by the successful testing of a medium-range missile, the *Rodong-1*, in May. In response to US pressure, the DPRK subsequently agreed to further negotiations with the IAEA. Talks at the organization's headquarters in Vienna, Austria, in September

were, however, inconclusive, and further meetings were cancelled.

In February 1994, following further discussions between
North Korea and the USA, an agreement was reached whereby
the IAEA would be allowed to visit all the DPRK's declared
nuclear facilities. In March, however, the inspectors were
impeded in their efforts to remove samples from nuclear installations, and it was discovered that seals placed on nuclear
materials by IAEA representatives during previous visits had
been broken, leading the IAEA to conclude that North Korea
had, in all probability, produced more plutonium than had been
admitted. In June the DPRK again threatened to withdraw from
the NPT, and also to declare war against South Korea, if
economic sanctions were imposed by the UN. In August the USA
and North Korea reached an agreement on the replacement of
the DPRK's existing nuclear reactors by two light-water reactors, which were considered to be less easily adapted to the
production of nuclear weaponry. The agreement also recommended the establishment of a restricted form of diplomatic
representation between the two countries. However, the DPRK
discounted the possibility of an inspection by the IAEA of the
two contentious sites at Yongbyon. Further negotiations in
October led to the signing of an agreement whereby the USA
undertook to establish an international consortium to finance
and supply the light-water reactors, while North Korea agreed
to suspend operation of its existing reactors and halt construction at two further sites. To compensate for the DPRK's
consequent shortfall in energy production until the new reactors
were fully operational, the USA agreed to donate to North Korea
500,000 metric tons annually of heavy fuel oil. IAEA inspectors
subsequently travelled to Pyongyang to oversee the DPRK's
suspension of its nuclear programme.

In March 1995 several countries, led by the USA, South Korea
and Japan, created the Korean Peninsula Energy Development
Organization (KEDO), which insisted that the DPRK accept a
South Korean-designed reactor. This demand was opposed by
North Korea at renewed negotiations with the USA. However, in
August the North permitted a KEDO delegation (including
South Korean engineers) to visit Sinpo, on the east coast of the
DPRK, in order to assess its suitability as the site of the
proposed nuclear power station. Finally, in December North
Korea and KEDO reached agreement on the details of imple-
menting the October 1994 accord; this implied acceptance by the
DPRK of South Korean light-water reactors. In January 1996
the DPRK announced its willingness to permit routine inspections of its nuclear installations by the IAEA. In March the
Korea Electric Power Corporation (KEPCO), of South Korea,
was commissioned by KEDO as the principal contractor for the
construction of the light-water reactors. Discussions between
KEDO and the DPRK to negotiate the terms of repayment by
North Korea of the construction costs of the light-water reactors
were successfully concluded in April 1997, with North Korea
agreeing to reimburse KEDO over a 17-year period.

Meanwhile, US energy experts began the sealing of spent fuel
rods at the DPRK's nuclear facilities. However, North Korea's
continued refusal to grant IAEA inspectors access to several
contentious laboratories, despite meetings to negotiate the
implementation of the provisions of the NSA, again provoked
concern that the DPRK was developing its nuclear programme.
Preparation of the nuclear-reactor site at Sinpo formally began
in August 1997: the initial project involved the construction of
facilities to house the estimated 2,000 site employees. Negotiations held in early 1998 between the participants in KEDO
(which the European Union—EU—had joined in mid-1997) concerning the financing of the light-water reactors (estimated at
US $5,170m.) proved difficult, and were further complicated by
South Korea's financial problems, raising fears that progress on
the project would be hindered. In June 1998 the North Korean
Government admitted to having sold nuclear missiles abroad,
claiming that such exports were necessary, given ongoing US
economic sanctions against the DPRK, in order to earn foreign
currency. Some progress was made at talks between the USA
and the DPRK in New York, USA, in September, when North
Korea agreed to resume sealing of spent fuel rods (which had
been suspended earlier that year), while the USA promised to
deliver the delayed shipment of heavy fuel oil. The US Congress
was, however, increasingly reluctant to approve financing for
the purchase of fuel oil, obliging President Clinton personally to
authorize the disbursement of the necessary funds in October, in
order to safeguard the 1994 nuclear accord.

Concerns regarding a suspected nuclear-related underground
facility at Kumchang-ri, some 40 km north-west of Yongbyon,
dominated a series of senior-level talks between the USA and
the DPRK in late 1998 and early 1999. US attempts to gain
access to the site, which North Korea insisted was non-nuclear,
were unsuccessful, with the USA rejecting North Korean demands for compensation in return for an inspection of the site.
The North Korean authorities were angered by reports that
KEDO had decided, in January 1999, to delay commencing the
basic construction of the light-water reactors until mid-1999. In
March, following protracted negotiations in New York, agreement was finally reached permitting US access to the suspected
nuclear facility. The USA announced that it would donate
substantial food aid to the DPRK, in addition to agricultural
assistance, although it was emphasized that the aid was being
granted on purely humanitarian grounds and did not constitute
compensation. The US officials who inspected the Kumchang-ri
site in May found it to be incomplete and largely empty. (The
facility was reinspected in May 2000, and this finding was
confirmed.) At the same time the USA announced the provision
of an additional 400,000 metric tons of food aid for 1999.

In May 1999 William Perry, a former US Secretary of Defense
who had been appointed to review policy towards the DPRK,
visited Pyongyang, where he reportedly advised the North
Korean Government to abandon its nuclear ambitions in exchange for substantial economic and political benefits. Talks
held during mid-1999 between the USA and the DPRK to
discuss the latter's missile development programme culminated
in September in a decision by the USA to ease several long-
standing economic sanctions (principally on non-military trade,
travel and banking) against the DPRK. In return, North Korea
agreed to suspend missile test-firing for the duration of negotiations with the USA. Earlier in the month Perry had presented a
report recommending a comprehensive, long-term approach to
the establishment of normal relations with North Korea to the
US President and Congress. Discussions aimed at improving
US-North Korean relations were held in Beijing in November
1999 and January 2000. In March preparatory talks took place
in New York for a proposed higher-level meeting, scheduled to
be held in Washington, DC, in April. It was reported, however,
that disagreement had arisen over the DPRK's insistence on its
removal from the US list of countries supporting terrorism prior
to the Washington talks.

Meanwhile, in November 1999 it was reported that the IAEA
was supervising the final stage of the sealing of spent fuel rods
at Yongbyon. After several months of delays caused by disputes
over the division of the costs of the project, in December KEDO
and KEPCO finally signed the contract for the construction of
the two light-water reactors; in February 2000 it was reported
that construction of the reactors was unlikely to be completed
before 2007, some four years later than scheduled. In November
2000 North Korea, frustrated by the delay, threatened to restart
missile testing unless construction of the reactors was accelerated. The DPRK refuted the IAEA's claim that delays were
due to the former's refusal to allow nuclear inspections. Also in
that month, the EU agreed to provide US $130m. for the con-
struction of the reactors.

In June 2000 Pyongyang confirmed its moratorium on test
flights of ballistic missiles. Various rounds of discussion on the
missile issue took place throughout 2000, although no substantive progress had been achieved by the end of the year. In
July the USA rejected North Korea's demand for annual payments from the USA of US $1,000m. in return for the curtail-
ment of weapons exports. The fundamental issues of missile
development and export remained unresolved. A planned visit to
Pyongyang by the outgoing US President, Bill Clinton, was
cancelled in December when North Korea rejected a US proposal
that the two sides prepare a draft missile accord to form a basis
for talks. In early 2001 the new administration of George W.
Bush adopted a less conciliatory stance towards the DPRK,
officials reportedly referring to Kim Jong Il as a 'dictator', and
refusing to grant economic aid unless transparency in North
Korea's missile production and export was assured and verified.
Since the late 1990s elements in Bush's Republican Party had
been strongly arguing in favour of a planned 'national missile
defence' (NMD) system to protect the USA from attack, and had
frequently cited North Korea as a developer and exporter of such
missiles. US officials feared that the DPRK had developed an
intercontinental ballistic missile, the *Taepo Dong 2*, capable of
striking the west coast of the USA. Bush's commitment to
develop NMD was denounced by the DPRK, which responded by

threatening to abandon the 1994 framework, and to resume ballistic missile testing. In March the USA appointed Charles Kartman, a former special envoy to North Korea under the Clinton administration, as the new head of KEDO, and US Secretary of State Colin Powell suggested that revisions to the 1994 framework might be required. In May 2001 an EU delegation travelled to North Korea, in an effort to renew diplomatic initiatives aimed at advancing the process of détente. Discussions focused on North Korea's missile programme and on humanitarian issues. Kim Jong Il reportedly agreed to maintain the moratorium on the testing of missiles until at least 2003 and declared his willingness to attend another meeting with President Kim Dae-Jung. In June 2001 President Bush sought to broaden discussions with North Korea about its missile programme to include nuclear technology and a reduction of the country's conventional forces. The North responded that discussions on the latter would take place only following the withdrawal of the 37,000 US troops from the South, and that it was also seeking financial compensation for the delay in building KEDO's two light-water reactors, which were not expected to be completed until 2008 at the earliest. In October the North rejected suggestions by the head of the IAEA and later by US officials that inspections of its nuclear facilities were necessary; however, in December it agreed to limited international access to certain laboratories. Meanwhile, in November, a team of North Korean nuclear engineers visited power plants in the South, indicating their commitment to acquire southern-style reactors.

The DPRK's relations with Japan have long been dominated by continuing hostility towards the latter as a result of the atrocities committed in Korea during the Japanese occupation (1910–45). Pyongyang had demanded thousands of millions of dollars in compensation from Japan, before normal relations could be restored. In the 1980s, following the testimony of defectors, Japan began to suspect that North Korean agents had kidnapped a number of Japanese citizens during the late 1970s and early 1980s. Japan imposed sanctions on North Korea after its agents were accused of attempting to assassinate the South Korean President in Burma 1983. Following the destruction of a South Korean aircraft in 1987, allegedly by North Korean agents posing as Japanese citizens (see above) Japan reimposed sanctions during 1988; North Korea then severed diplomatic contacts with Japan, although mutual trade continued. From late 1990 there was a significant *rapprochement* between North Korea and Japan, and in January 1991 a Japanese government delegation visited Pyongyang for discussions concerning the possible normalization of diplomatic relations. The Japanese delegation offered apologies, on behalf of its Government, for Japanese colonial aggression on the Korean peninsula between 1910 and 1945. Moreover, the Japanese Government expressed its willingness to make reparations for Japanese abuses of human rights in Korea during this period. Subsequent negotiations in 1991 foundered, however, owing to the DPRK's demand for reparations for damage inflicted after 1945 (which the Japanese Government denied) and to Japan's insistence that North Korea's nuclear installations be opened to outside inspection; normalization talks collapsed in November 1992, as the North Korean delegation abandoned the proceedings. Relations with Japan were further strained after the DPRK's testing of the *Rodong-1* missile in the Sea of Japan in May 1993. The missile, according to US intelligence reports, would be capable of reaching most of Japan's major cities (and possibly of carrying either a conventional or a nuclear warhead). None the less, Japan, like South Korea, opposed the possible imposition of international economic sanctions on the DPRK, in response to North Korea's refusal to allow inspections of its nuclear facilities. Attempts failed to resume normalization talks in 1994, but in March 1995 a Japanese parliamentary group visited the DPRK and reached an agreement for the resumption of talks later that year. In May Japan agreed to North Korea's request for emergency rice aid, and later in the year Japan provided aid to help the DPRK overcome the effects of serious flooding (see above). In early 1996 Japan provided a shipment of fuel oil to alleviate the DPRK's energy shortfall.

Relations were complicated in 1997 by Japanese allegations that North Korea had abducted several Japanese citizens during the 1970s. However, in August 1997, for the first time since 1992, negotiations opened on the restoration of normal bilateral relations. The main focus of discussions was the issue of some 1,800 Japanese women married to North Koreans, who had never been permitted to leave the DPRK. An agreement was signed whereby the women were to be allowed to visit their relatives in Japan for short periods; the first such visits took place in November 1997 and January 1998. Moreover, in October 1997 the Japanese Government resumed the provision of aid to North Korea, suspended since mid-1996, donating food and medical supplies in response to the renewed appeals issued by the UN. Relations deteriorated in mid-1998, however, when the North Korean Government cancelled a third visit of the Japanese women to their homeland, following Japan's rejection of a North Korean investigation into the alleged abduction of Japanese nationals. The testing by the DPRK of a suspected *Taepo Dong-1* missile over Japanese territory, in August, further exacerbated tensions, prompting Japan to break off normalization talks, suspend food aid and postpone its contribution to the KEDO project. The DPRK subsequently claimed that the object launched was in fact a satellite. Tension between the two countries increased in March 1999, when Japanese naval forces pursued and opened fire on suspected North Korean spy ships that had infiltrated Japanese waters. Relations improved, however, following the DPRK's agreement with the USA, in September, to suspend its reported plans to test a new long-range missile. In October unofficial talks between North Korean and Japanese government officials were held in Singapore, and two weeks later Japan decided to allow the resumption of charter flights to the DPRK. In December, following a successful visit to the DPRK by a group of Japanese parliamentarians, Japan announced an end to its ban on food aid. Later in that month intergovernmental preparatory talks on re-establishing diplomatic relations were held in Beijing, and Japanese and North Korean Red Cross officials reached some agreement on humanitarian issues. Further progress was achieved by the two countries' Red Cross Societies at a meeting in March 2000. It was reported that North Korea had agreed to co-operate in a further investigation into the fate of some 10 missing Japanese nationals, while Japan had agreed to a search for Korean citizens who had disappeared prior to 1945. In addition, visits to their homeland by Japanese women married to North Koreans were to resume shortly, and Japan was to provide some 100,000 metric tons of rice to the DPRK through WFP. In late April Japanese charter flights to North Korea resumed. Meanwhile, following further informal contacts between the North Korean and Japanese Governments, full normalization talks commenced in April 2000; further rounds of discussions took place during the year, despite an announcement by Japan in September that relations between the two countries would not be normalized until the cases of Japanese citizens allegedly abducted by North Korean agents had been solved. In October, however, a further round of negotiations took place in Beijing, China. The two sides agreed to meet again, but no date was set. In November the DPRK rejected an offer by Japan to extend economic aid rather than grant wartime compensation. Meanwhile, in September the long-delayed third visits home by the Japanese wives of North Korean men took place. In October Japan decided, on humanitarian grounds, to provide 500,000 metric tons of rice to North Korea. Later that month meetings held with the USA and Japan focused on obtaining the extradition from the DPRK, in return for economic aid, of terrorist Japanese Red Army members, who had hijacked a Japanese aircraft and forced it to fly to Pyongyang in 1970 (later being granted political asylum in North Korea). No agreement was reached.

In December 2000 North Korea reiterated that normal relations with Japan could be restored only after the latter delivered an apology and compensation for its earlier colonial rule. However, at the same time former Japanese Prime Minister Tomiichi Murayama led a non-governmental delegation to Pyongyang, in an attempt to improve relations. In May 2001 Japan deported Kim Jong Nam, son of Kim Jong Il, for entering the country on a false passport (see above). In June North Korea condemned Japan's refusal to issue visas to North Koreans planning to attend a conference on Japanese compensation for Korea, held in Japan. In August North Korea demanded compensation for Korean victims of the atomic bombs dropped on Hiroshima and Nagasaki in 1945, and also for the collision of cargo ships from the two countries in July 2001.

North Korea was one of several Asian countries that strongly condemned Japanese Prime Minister Junichiro Koizumi's visit to the Yasukuni Shrine in August 2001. During late 2001 North Korea denounced Japan's military support for the USA's 'war on terrorism', stating that such support was aimed entirely at expanding Japan's military sphere of activities. In November

Japanese police arrested Kan Young Kwan, an executive of the Japan-based, pro-North Korean organization, *Chongryon*, on charges of diverting funds through the use of local credit unions. The incident highlighted the sometimes-illegal activities of the North Korean community in Japan.

In mid-December 2001 North Korea announced that it was abandoning efforts to locate missing Japanese nationals thought to have been abducted by North Korean agents. At the end of the month a suspected North Korean spy vessel was sunk by Japanese coastguard forces after it had been expelled from Japan's exclusive economic zone. North Korea condemned the incident, but denied any involvement, accusing Japan of seeking to mislead world opinion. Japanese coastguard forces searched the sunken vessel in May 2002, and raised it in September of that year. In February 2002 North Korea released a Japanese journalist who had been detained on spying charges since December 1999.

In an unexpected diplomatic move, Junichiro Koizumi visited Pyongyang in mid-September 2002, becoming the first incumbent Japanese Prime Minister to do so. His one-day visit, during which he held discussions with Kim Jong Il, was dominated by the latter's admission that North Korean agents had abducted 12 Japanese citizens in the 1970s and 1980s, of whom five were still alive. The remainder were said to have died of natural causes, although suspicions remained that they might have been executed, after Pyongyang failed to locate their graves. Kim apologized for the incidents, but attributed them to rogue elements within the security services. The admission led some sources to indicate that the total number of Japanese abductees might be as high as 100. The surviving captives were temporarily allowed to return to Japan in mid-October, although they had to leave behind any spouses or children. The Japanese authorities, however, refused to allow them to return to North Korea after the visit. Despite this, representatives from the two countries held the first round of resumed discussions on the restoration of normal diplomatic relations in Malaysia at the end of October, but failed to make any progress.

In October 2002 the alleged admission by North Korean officials to their visiting US counterparts that Pyongyang was pursuing a secret nuclear weapons programme alarmed Japan. Koizumi announced that Japan would halt further economic co-operation with North Korea until the issues of the abducted Japanese citizens and the nuclear programme were resolved. Pyongyang warned Japan that it would abandon its moratorium on missile testing if normalization talks failed to make any progress. In separate incidents in late February and early March 2003 North Korea test-launched two short-range ground-to-ship missiles in the Sea of Japan, and in early April tested a third missile in the Yellow Sea. However, it refrained from testing longer-range ballistic missiles, which Tokyo considered a threat to its security. The Director-General of Japan's Defence Agency warned North Korea that Japan could conduct a pre-emptive strike on North Korean missile facilities if necessary.

The DPRK has considered the USA to be its main enemy since the time of the Korean War and repeatedly accused South Korea of being a US 'puppet' state. Relations deteriorated after North Korea seized a US naval vessel, the *USS Pueblo*, in 1968 and detained its crew for several months. In 1969 the DPRK shot down a US reconnaissance aircraft which had apparently violated North Korean airspace, resulting in the deaths of 31 US servicemen. In 1987, in response to alleged North Korean involvement in the bombing of a South Korean airliner, the USA placed the DPRK on its list of countries supporting terrorism, and restricted contacts between US and North Korean diplomats. Relations with the USA in the 1990s were largely dominated by the DPRK's suspected nuclear ambitions (see above). In December 1994 it was announced that agreement had been reached to establish liaison offices in Washington, DC, and Pyongyang in 1995, in preparation for an eventual resumption of full diplomatic relations. The USA insisted, however, that normal relations would only be restored when North Korea ceased to export ballistic missiles and withdrew its troops from the border with South Korea; the DPRK, in turn, stated that liaison offices could only be opened when light-water nuclear reactors, in accordance with the October 1994 agreement between the DPRK and the USA, had been supplied. Relations faltered following the shooting-down of a US army helicopter which had apparently entered North Korean airspace; the DPRK initially refused to negotiate, but, after direct bilateral talks in December, the pilot was repatriated. In January 1995 the DPRK opened its ports to US commercial shipping and

removed restrictions on the import of goods from the USA. Following the severe flooding in North Korea in 1995 and 1996, the USA provided food aid and other flood relief.

The issue of four-way talks (see above) dominated relations between the USA and the DPRK in 1996, but parallel negotiations were conducted concerning the estimated 8,100 US soldiers who were listed as 'missing in action' following the Korean war. The USA agreed to provide funds to assist in locating the bodies, and it was reported that North Korea had requested additional food aid in return for its co-operation. In December, following the issuing of a (US-brokered) apology by North Korea for the submarine incursion in September, it was reported that the USA was prepared partially to revoke its economic sanctions against North Korea, and to allow the gradual expansion of bilateral trade. In early 1997 the USA responded to a renewed appeal issued by the UN for food aid and humanitarian assistance for North Korea, as a result of which the DPRK announced its intention to take part in exploratory discussions about the proposed quadripartite talks. Bilateral discussions with the USA during 1997 focused on the establishment of liaison offices, missile non-proliferation and procedures for the exhumation of the US servicemen listed as 'missing in action'. In August, however, the defection to the USA of two North Korean diplomats (the most senior officials yet to seek asylum in North America) resulted in the suspension of the third round of missile non-proliferation talks. North Korea was unsuccessful in attempting to make its participation in full quadripartite talks conditional upon the withdrawal of US forces from the Korean peninsula and upon the provision of food aid. None the less, the USA responded positively, on humanitarian grounds, to two further UN appeals for food aid during the year. Relations with the USA were dominated by nuclear issues and other concerns regarding the DPRK's missile development programme in 1998 and 1999 (see above). The exhumation of US soldiers listed as 'missing in action' proceeded, with 22 sets of remains returned to the USA in 1998. In October 1999 US officials visited Pyongyang to receive the remains of four soldiers, in the first such transfer to take place on North Korean territory without the involvement of the UNC. A further 15 sets of remains were returned in November 2000. Trade between the USA and the DPRK increased significantly following the partial revocation of economic sanctions against the latter in September 1999 (see above); US exports to North Korea increased massively in 1999. Meanwhile, the USA continued to provide emergency food aid to the DPRK.

Relations between North Korea and the USA were variable during 2000. In June the USA announced the partial easing of economic sanctions against North Korea. In August a round of talks with the USA in Washington on North Korea's removal from the list of terrorist sponsors ended without agreement, although the meeting was described as productive. In September, however, officials from North Korea declined to attend the UN Millennium summit meeting in New York, following a confrontation between the delegation and US security officials, who suspected the North Koreans of terrorism, at Frankfurt airport in Germany. The USA subsequently apologized, describing the incident as an 'innocent mistake' and refuting North Korea's claim of a 'brazen plot'. In October Kim Jong Il's special envoy, Vice-Marshal Jo Myong Rok, paid a state visit to the USA, the most senior North Korean official ever to do so. Later that month the US Secretary of State, Madeleine Albright, reciprocated the visit and in Pyongyang met Kim Jong Il, who agreed in principle to halt North Korea's long-range missile-testing programme. Talks were described as 'serious and constructive'. Shortly afterwards, however, tension arose when two US fighter aircraft participating in a US-South Korean joint manoeuvre briefly crossed the military demarcation line into North Korean airspace. The DPRK protested to the UN, demanding a formal apology and the implementation of measures to prevent a recurrence of the incident.

Relations between North Korea and the USA deteriorated during 2001 following the inauguration of George W. Bush as President of the latter. Bush adopted a tougher position towards the DPRK compared with his predecessor, and this also adversely affected inter-Korean relations (see above). The DPRK condemned the joint US-South Korean military exercises held in April. In May a non-governmental delegation from the USA visited North Korea to examine evidence of atrocities committed by US troops during the Korean War. In June Bush stated that he was willing to resume negotiations with the DPRK, albeit linking these to a reduction in North Korea's missile programme and military deployments—terms rejected by the North. In July the North Korean Minister of Foreign Affairs, Paek Nam Sun, failed to attend the Association of South East Asian Nations (ASEAN) forum in Viet Nam, also attended by the US Secretary of State. During his visit to Moscow in August, Kim Jong Il reiterated North Korea's long-standing demand for the withdrawal of US troops from the South.

Following the terrorist attacks on the USA in September 2001, the USA paid increasing attention to North Korea's biological, chemical and nuclear weapons programmes. Although North Korea had condemned those attacks, it subsequently opposed the US bombing of Afghanistan, and failed to provide any intelligence on terrorist networks to the USA. By late 2001 the DPRK was drawing increasing criticism from the USA, and in October the US State Department released its annual report on religious freedom, which included the DPRK on a list of countries suppressing such beliefs. In November Bush warned North Korea not to take advantage of the war in Afghanistan to increase tensions on the Korean peninsula. Despite signing two UN treaties against terrorism in November, the DPRK remained on the USA's list of states sponsoring terrorism.

In late January 2002 the DPRK's relations with the USA deteriorated further following President Bush's reference to North Korea as forming an 'axis of evil' with Iran and Iraq. Bush's comments were believed to reflect concern that the DPRK was exporting weapons technology to countries the USA considered to be 'rogue states'. (During the 1990s North Korea had exported missiles and related technology to countries such as Egypt, Iran, Libya, Pakistan and Syria, allegedly earning up to US $1,000m. a year.) However, when Bush visited the DMZ on a visit to the South, he urged the North to open up to the outside world. Although the USA ruled out any military action against North Korea, in March 2002 it was revealed that North Korea was one of seven nations considered a potential target for a US nuclear first strike, in the event of emergency circumstances. The DPRK responded by threatening to withdraw from existing agreements with the USA (see above). However, in April the North accepted a South Korean request to reopen dialogue with the USA, and invited a US envoy, Jack Pritchard, to discuss outstanding issues. At the same time the USA announced that it would release US $95m. to North Korea in order to accelerate the building of the replacement nuclear reactors—construction of which finally began in August 2002, with a view to completion in 2008. Pritchard himself attended the ground-breaking ceremony, but stated that the DPRK must accept international inspection of its nuclear facilities, a demand that Pyongyang stated was not mandatory until 2005.

Meanwhile, in July 2002 the Minister of Foreign Affairs, Paek Nam Sun, held an informal meeting with the US Secretary of State, Colin Powell, on the sidelines of the ASEAN Regional Forum (ARF) in Brunei—the highest-level contact between Pyongyang and the Bush Administration. In August North Korea rejected US demands for a significant reduction of its conventional military forces along its border with the South. The USA had long-feared that these could be used to attack the 15,000 US troops deployed between Seoul and the DMZ in the event of hostilities.

Relations between the DPRK and the USA deteriorated significantly from October 2002 after the USA announced that senior North Korean officials had admitted to the visiting US Assistant Secretary of State for East Asian and Pacific Affairs, James Kelly, that the DPRK was pursuing a secret nuclear weapons programme in violation of the 1994 agreement. The clandestine programme was allegedly based on uranium extraction, whereas the suspended programme had been based on plutonium extraction. The admission reportedly came after Kelly presented his Northern hosts with credible US intelligence reports about the programme, although Pyongyang later denied that it had made such an admission. Within days the USA declared the 1994 framework null and void and placed renewed pressure on the DPRK to halt its nuclear activities. The DPRK responded by stating that it would consider halting its nuclear programme if the USA would sign a non-aggression treaty guaranteeing the DPRK's sovereignty with Pyongyang—a demand rejected by the Washington. Pyongyang subsequently warned the USA of severe military measures if it continued to reject such a treaty. Meanwhile, Japan and South Korea in November agreed to maintain the KEDO project as the only viable mechanism for ending the new nuclear confrontation with Pyongyang. In the middle of that month, however, the USA finally halted petroleum shipments to North Korea, citing the latter's violation of the 1994 framework. Further confusion over Pyongyang's nuclear programme emerged on 17 November 2002 when North Korean radio reportedly admitted that the country already possessed nuclear weapons. However, the exact translation of the statement was in doubt, and most analysts concluded that the broadcast had stated that the DPRK was entitled to possess such weapons. At the same time it was widely reported that Pakistan had provided the technical expertise of North Korea's nuclear programme in exchange for ballistic missiles. Attention focused on the north-western city of Kusong, some 30 km north west of Yongbyon, as the centre of the secret programme.

The diplomatic crisis between the DPRK and the USA worsened in December 2002 when Pyongyang announced that it would restart its nuclear reactor at Yongbyon, and Washington accused North Korea of narcotics trafficking in order to raise money to support its ailing economy. Amid increasingly strong rhetoric from both sides, the former US President, Bill Clinton, revealed that he had come close to ordering airstrikes on the DPRK's nuclear facilities in 1994, and Spanish commandos, acting on intelligence supplied by the USA, seized a North Korean cargo vessel, the *So San*, carrying scud missiles to Yemen, in the Arabian Sea. However, the vessel was allowed to deliver its cargo after Yemen confirmed the legitimacy of the order. The incident was widely seen as a US warning to Pyongyang regarding its weapons proliferation. Later in that month the DPRK removed the IAEA's monitoring and surveillance equipment from the Yongbyon facility. The US Secretary of Defense, Donald Rumsfeld, warned Pyongyang not to take advantage of the USA's planned attack on Iraq (see the chapter on Iraq) to raise regional tensions, stating that the USA could fight against both countries simultaneously. Rumsfeld had earlier stated that the DPRK possessed nuclear weapons, and security analysts concluded that Pyongyang already possessed between two and five nuclear devices.

In late December 2002 the IAEA reported that North Korean technicians had transferred 1,000 fuel rods (out of 8,000 necessary to reactivate it) to the Yongbyon reactor, ostensibly for the production of electricity, but probably for the production of plutonium required to manufacture nuclear devices. The DPRK expelled the two remaining IAEA inspectors at the end of that year.

In early January 2003 the DPRK announced its withdrawal from the NPT, and the IAEA responded by adopting a resolution condemning Pyongyang's recent behaviour. However, President Bush indicated that the USA would resume food aid and petroleum deliveries if North Korea abandoned its nuclear weapons programme. He reiterated, however, that the 1994 framework was no longer valid and that a new arrangement would have to be reached. Pyongyang had earlier warned that any sanctions imposed on it would be tantamount to a declaration of war, but later in the month indicated that it would reverse its withdrawal from the NPT and readmit inspectors if the USA were to adopt a moderate attitude. Meanwhile, North Korean diplomats in January held unofficial discussions with the Governor of New Mexico, Bill Richardson, who had negotiated with Pyongyang in the past. In February Pyongyang stated that the Yongbyon reactor was operating normally, and that any US military build-up in the region could lead the North to launch a pre-emptive strike on US forces anywhere in the world. Pyongyang also threatened to withdraw from the 1953 armistice if the USA imposed a blockade on the DPRK. Despite these threats, the USA deployed long-range bombers to its bases on the Pacific island of Guam as a precautionary measure, and warned that although it favoured a peaceful resolution of the crisis, it had not ruled out any options—including military action.

In early March 2003 the USA and South Korea began their annual joint military exercises amid condemnation by the North, which announced at the end of the month that it was severing military contacts with the USA at the liaison office at the DMZ. Also in early March four North Korean fighter aircraft intercepted a US reconnaissance aircraft in international airspace and closely pursued its flight, the first such incident in 32 years. Between late February and the beginning of April 2003 North Korea also test-fired three short-range missiles, although refrained from testing its longer-range ballistic missiles. The commencement of the US-led war against Iraq in late March 2003 alarmed Pyongyang, which reportedly believed that the USA would target itself at some future date. By early April the USA had imposed new sanctions on the DPRK's Government and its Changgwang Sinyong Corporation, for exporting ballistic missiles to Pakistan. However, the sanctions were largely symbolic, since the USA had minimal economic links with the DPRK. Japanese sources reported that North Korean and US diplomats were quietly seeking a peaceful solution to the crisis.

Tensions between North Korea and the USA increased in late April 2003 after ambiguous statements by the North's official media in which it indicated it was preparing to reprocess, or was actually reprocessing, 8,000 spent fuel rods, a move that would enable it rapidly to produce nuclear weapons. Officials from North Korea, the USA and China held high-level discussions in Beijing during 23–24 April over Pyongyang's nuclear weapons programme. No agreements were reached, however, and US sources stated that the DPRK had, for the first time, admitted to possessing nuclear weapons and had threatened to carry out a nuclear test. In mid-May Pyongyang cited US behaviour against it as a reason for abandoning a 1992 commitment with the South on a nuclear-free peninsula.

During the years of the so-called Sino-Soviet dispute the DPRK fluctuated in its allegiance to each of its powerful northern neighbours, the People's Republic of China and the USSR. However, in the mid-1980s the DPRK placed increased emphasis on its relations with the USSR, culminating in a new arrangement for the supply of Soviet aircraft to North Korea, and an exchange visit by senior government officials. Kim Il Sung made several official visits to China in the late 1980s, which were interpreted by some Western observers as an attempt to establish closer relations in view of the erosion of communist power in many Eastern European countries. However, North Korea was aggrieved at China's establishment of full diplomatic relations with South Korea in August 1992. China appeared largely conciliatory with regard to North Korea's nuclear programme, and during 1993 and the first months of 1994 indicated that it would veto any attempt by the UN Security Council to impose economic sanctions on the DPRK. In 1997 China agreed to provide substantial food aid to North Korea to alleviate the effects of flooding. Later in that year China accepted US and South Korean proposals for quadripartite negotiations with North Korea to conclude a new peace agreement with the South, and between December 1997 and August 1999 it participated in all six rounds of these negotiations. Relations between North Korea and China remained close in 1998, with the latter donating grain, fertilizers and crude petroleum to Pyongyang over the course of the year. A high-level North Korean delegation visited China in June 1999. During the visit China announced that it would provide North Korea with 150,000 metric tons of food aid and 400,000 tons of coke over the following months. In October 1999 the Chinese Minister of Foreign Affairs, Tang Jiaxuan, participated in celebrations held in Pyongyang to commemorate the 50th anniversary of the establishment of diplomatic relations between the two countries. In February 2000 China permitted North Korea to open a consulate-general in Hong Kong. In the following month Kim Jong Il attended a function at the People's Republic of China's embassy in Pyongyang. This was his first visit to the mission for 15 years. In May Kim Jong Il visited China, his first official trip abroad for 17 years, in advance of the historic inter-Korean summit meeting. In late October Kim Jong Il met the visiting Chinese Minister of Defence, Chi Haotian. In mid-January 2001 the North Korean leader paid a second visit to the People's Republic. During this visit, Kim held extensive talks with Chinese leaders in Beijing, and also toured the new business zones of Shanghai and Shenzhen, where he observed joint-venture projects with foreign multinational corporations, telecommunications projects and the Shanghai Stock Exchange. It was widely believed that he was seeking inspiration for the revival of the DPRK's crisis-ridden economy and advice from Chinese leaders on developing Pyongyang's role within the international community.

In early September 2001 Chinese President Jiang Zemin paid an official visit to North Korea, his first such visit since 1990. Jiang promised an additional 200,000 tons of food aid and 30,000 tons of diesel oil as a gesture of goodwill to alleviate North Korea's economic crisis. Jiang also reportedly urged North Korea to resume discussions with the South. By early 2002 it was thought that North Korea was placing a renewed emphasis on relations with China in order to deflect criticism from the USA.

During 2002 the DPRK and China continued to seek the reconnection of the inter-Korean railway lines and their subsequent linking to China's own railway system. In May 2002, however, China's forcible removal of North Korean refugees

from South Korean embassies in the People's Republic brought the issue of the refugees to international attention. Several groups of North Korean refugees had, in 2002, fled to Western, Japanese and South Korean diplomatic offices in China, embarrassing the latter, since Beijing had signed a treaty with Pyongyang providing for the repatriation of refugees. In late June Beijing allowed 24 northern refugees who had been concealed in the embassy of South Korea to leave for that country. After that incident, Beijing began an operation against South Korean activists and missionaries who had been helping northerners to flee via China. It was estimated that as many as 300,000 North Korean refugees were already residing in China, with US sources stating that as many as 50,000 had fled to China in 2001 alone.

In October 2002 North Korea appointed a Chinese entrepreneur of Dutch citizenship, Yang Bin, as the new governor of its recently created Sinuiju Special Administrative Region; however, the Beijing authorities arrested him on charges of bribery and fraud (see above). By early 2003 China was becoming increasingly concerned about the growing diplomatic crisis between North Korea and the USA over the former's decision formally to restart its nuclear programme. In late February 2003 the President of the DPRK's SPA Presidium, Kim Yong Nam, visited Beijing and pledged to maintain strong bilateral relations. Beijing was expected to use its influence with Pyongyang to resolve the situation, albeit warning the UN Security Council not to involve itself in the matter.

In late April 2003 China hosted and participated in senior-level meetings between the DPRK and the USA over Pyongyang's nuclear weapons programme (see above). Immediately prior to the talks, Vice-Marshal Jo Myong Rok, Pyongyang's second-highest ranking official, led a military delegation to China, and held meetings with President Hu Jintao and senior military leaders.

The DPRK's diplomatic isolation became more pronounced in the early 1990s, as former communist bloc countries moved to foster relations with South Korea. Furthermore, the USSR announced that, from January 1991, its barter trading system with North Korea would be abolished in favour of trade in convertible currencies at world market prices. However, an agreement was reported to have been signed in May 1993 by the DPRK and the Russian Federation (which, following the dissolution of the USSR, had assumed responsibility for many of the USSR's international undertakings) on technological and scientific co-operation. Negotiations on the renewal of the 1961 bilateral treaty of friendship, co-operation and assistance, which expired in 1996 (but remained valid in the interim), opened in January 1997. Discussions on the rescheduling of the terms of repayment of North Korea's debt to Russia took place in October. In March 1999 a new bilateral treaty of friendship, good neighbourliness and co-operation was initialled in Pyongyang; a formal signing followed in February 2000, during a visit to Pyongyang by the Russian Minister of Foreign Affairs, Igor Ivanov. The treaty was ratified by North Korea in April. In July President Vladimir Putin became the first Russian (or Soviet leader) to visit North Korea. During the trip Kim Jong Il declared himself willing to halt missile development in exchange for access to space rocket technology funded by other countries, although he subsequently seemed to renege on this offer. Following Putin's visit, co-operation between Russia and the DPRK placed a strong emphasis on connecting the latter's rail system to the Trans-Siberian railway, with a view to creating a long-awaited Eurasian transport corridor, and in March 2001 the two countries signed a railway co-operation agreement.

In late April 2001 the DPRK's Minister of the People's Armed Forces, Vice-Marshal Kim Il Chol, visited Moscow and reportedly negotiated the acquisition of defensive weapons such as SU-27 aircraft, anti-aircraft systems and intelligence-gathering equipment, in addition to signing a military co-operation protocol.

In August 2001 Kim Jong Il paid a 24-day visit across Russia to Moscow, where he and President Putin signed a new declaration of co-operation in politics, the economy, military, science and technology, and culture. However, Russia also urged the DPRK to settle the latter's outstanding bilateral debt of as much as US $5,500m. North Korea had repaid some of this amount by sending hundreds of forced-labour woodcutters to work in Khabarovsk Krai (territory)—although such labour camps were reportedly closed down by late 2002. During his visit, Kim also toured industrial plants, including those manufacturing power equipment and tanks, a pig farm, beer brewery and the Krunichev Space Centre, outside Moscow. Kim reaffirmed the DPRK's moratorium on missile-testing until 2003, and urged the withdrawal of US troops from South Korea. Kim's visit suggested that North Korea was seeking closer relations with Russia, in addition to China, to strengthen its international standing. In late October 2001 the new Russian ambassador in Pyongyang, Andrei Karlov, held a banquet at which he spoke of strengthening bilateral ties. In December Kim had a meeting with Karlov.

The DPRK continued to maintain strong relations with Russia in 2002. In April two separate Russian delegations, one led by the Mayor of St Petersburg, Vladimir Yakovlev, the other by the Russian Presidential Representative in the Far Eastern Federal Okrug (district), Konstantin Pulikovskii, visited Pyongyang to discuss co-operation in all fields, particularly business. In May the Minister of Foreign Affairs, Paek Nam Sun, visited Moscow, in the first such visit in 15 years. In late July the Russian Minister of Foreign Affairs, Igor Ivanov, visited Pyongyang, and in late August Kim Jong Il visited the Russian city of Vladivostok, where he held discussions with Putin, mainly focusing on the reconnection of railway links across the Korean peninsula. At the same time North Korea and the Russian Oblast of Amur signed a co-operation agreement on agriculture and forestry. In October 2002 two North Korean military delegations visited Russia, and in December the Mayor of Moscow, Yurii Luzhkov, visited Pyongyang.

As the diplomatic crisis over the DPRK's nuclear weapons programme deteriorated in January 2003, Russia sought to defuse the situation by sending the Deputy Minister of Foreign Affairs, Aleksandr Losyukov, to Pyongyang, where he held discussions with Kim Jong Il. Losyukov, who had earlier visited China and subsequently the USA, urged a three-stage formula whereby the international community would accept a nuclear-free Korean peninsula, guarantees for the regime's security, and a resumption of humanitarian and economic aid. Pyongyang reiterated that the crisis could be resolved only through discussions with the USA. In February Kim Jong Il again visited the Russian embassy in Pyongyang, where a banquet was held on the occasion of his 61st birthday.

In late March 2003 a hitherto unrealized Russian proposal to supply North Korea with natural gas from the island of Sakhalin in return for Pyongyang's abandonment of its nuclear programme was raised by the South Korean Government.

The DPRK's unilateral application for UN membership, first announced in May 1991, represented a radical departure from its earlier insistence that the two Koreas should occupy a single UN seat. This development was welcomed by South Korea, and both countries were admitted separately to the UN in September of that year. In September 1999, for the first time in seven years, the North Korean Minister of Foreign Affairs attended and addressed the annual session of the UN General Assembly, in what was perceived as an attempt to end the DPRK's diplomatic isolation. Furthermore, in January 2000 Italy became the first of the G-7 group of Western industrialized nations (and the sixth member of the EU) to establish diplomatic relations with the DPRK, and in May Australia restored diplomatic ties with Pyongyang. Diplomatic relations were established with the Philippines in July and with the United Kingdom in December. During 2001 the DPRK further expanded its range of diplomatic partners, opening relations with the Netherlands, Belgium, Canada, Spain, Germany, Luxembourg, Greece, Brazil, New Zealand, Kuwait, the European Union, Bahrain, Turkey, and Liechtenstein. A number of these countries appointed chargés d'affaires to serve in Seoul prior to the foundation of embassies in Pyongyang. Relations with East Timor (now Timor-Leste) were establsihed in late 2002.

North Korea retained long-standing ties with many African countries, and had military advisers working in 12 of them. Pyongyang also maintained close links with a number of Arab and Middle Eastern countries, including Egypt, Libya, Syria and Iran, as well as Pakistan.

In April 2000 North Korea formally applied to join ASEAN (see p. 146). Following the DPRK's admittance to the ASEAN Regional Forum (ARF), a meeting in Thailand in July was attended for the first time by the North Korean Minister of Foreign Affairs, Paek Nam Sun, who held unprecedented meetings with his South Korean, Japanese and US counterparts. In November the Asia-Pacific Economic Co-operation (APEC, see p. 139) forum supported the DPRK's guest status of that organization. Full membership was expected to follow in 2007, upon the expiry of a 10-year moratorium on new members. In late July

2001 the President of the Presidium of the SPA, Kim Yong Nam, visited Viet Nam, Laos and Cambodia. In early March 2002 Kim visited Thailand and Malaysia, where he discussed mainly trade issues. Prime Minister Mahathir bin Mohamad of Malaysia accepted an invitation to visit the DPRK, and Indonesian President Megawati Sukarnoputri visited North Korea at the end of March 2002. Kim Yong Nam reciprocated Megawati's visit in July of that year, also visiting Libya and Syria. The President of Viet Nam, Tran Duc Luong, visited North Korea in May 2002 and signed several economic and legal co-operation agreements. In late 2002 the DPRK and Taiwan were exploring the possibility of establishing mutual liaison offices.

Government

The highest organ of state power is the unicameral Supreme People's Assembly (SPA), with 687 members, elected (unopposed) for five years by universal adult suffrage. The SPA elects, for its duration, the Chairman of the National Defence Commission, who, since the effective abolition of the presidency in September 1998, holds the most senior accessible office of state (although this is not formally stated in the Constitution). The SPA elects the Premier and, on the latter's recommendation, appoints other Ministers to form the Cabinet. The President of the SPA Presidium, whose members are elected by the SPA, represents the State in its relations with foreign countries.

Political power is held by the communist Korean Workers' Party (KWP), which is the most influential party in the Democratic Front for the Reunification of the Fatherland (comprising the KWP and two minor parties). The Front presents an approved list of candidates for elections to representative bodies. The KWP's highest authority is the Party Congress, which elects a Central Committee to supervise party work. The Committee elects a Political Bureau (Politburo) to direct policy. The Presidium of the Politburo is the KWP's most powerful policy-making body.

North Korea comprises nine provinces and two cities, each with an elected Local People's Assembly.

Defence

Military service is selective: army five to eight years, navy five to 10 years, and air force three to four years. The estimated total strength of the armed forces in August 2002 was 1,082,000: army 950,000, air force 86,000, and navy 46,000. Security and border troops numbered 189,000, and there was a workers' and peasants' militia ('Red Guards') numbering about 3.5m. In late 2002 it was reported that the DPRK was planning to make substantial reductions to its armed forces. The ratio of North Korea's armed forces to total population is believed to be the highest in the world. Defence expenditure for 2003 was budgeted at 15.4% of total spending, up from 14.9% (3,200m. won) in 2002. South Korean intelligence sources estimated the real level of defence spending at 43.5% of total spending in 2003.

Economic Affairs

In 2000, according to South Korean estimates, the DPRK's gross national income (GNI) was about US $16,800m., equivalent to some $757 per head. It was estimated that in 1998 the North Korean economy declined for a ninth successive year, contracting by 1.1%, in real terms. In 1999, however, it was estimated that the economy grew by 6.2%, and in 2000 by 1.3%. Growth was estimated at 3.7% in 2001 and anticipated at 0.3% in 2002. During 1990–2001, according to estimates by the World Bank, the population increased by an annual average of 1.0%.

Agriculture (including forestry and fishing) contributed an estimated 30.4% of gross domestic product (GDP) in 2000, according to South Korean sources. At mid-2000, according to FAO estimates, 30.1% of the labour force were employed in agriculture. The principal crops are rice, maize, potatoes, sweet potatoes and soybeans. The DPRK is not self-sufficient in food, and imports substantial amounts of wheat, rice and maize annually. Food shortages became a severe problem from the mid-1990s. By 1999 the food situation had improved to some extent, owing to fertilizer aid from international donors, agrarian reform and increased potato production, although shortages continued and were exacerbated by severe drought in 2000 and 2001, and subsequent typhoons and floods. It was estimated that North Korea's grain output declined by 15% to about 3.6m. metric tons in 2000, while potato production increased by some 25.8%. In December 2000 the Government launched an intensive campaign for potato growing and double-crop farming, and in November 2001 construction began on a 7,000-ha goat farm near Pyongyang. The raising of livestock (principally cattle and pigs), forestry and fishing are important. During 1985–90, according to the FAO, agricultural production increased by an annual average of 1.2%; during 1990–95, however, output declined by an average of 2.8% per year. In 2001, according to South Korean estimates, agricultural GDP increased by 6.8%, following a decline of 1.9% in 2000, and an increase of 9.2% in 1999.

In 2000, according to South Korean estimates, industry (including mining, manufacturing, construction and power) contributed 38.4% of GDP. At mid-1980 the industrial sector employed about 30% of the labour force. In 1995 the GDP of the mining and manufacturing sector declined by an estimated 4.6%, compared with 1994. According to North Korean reports, in the year to September 1999 industrial output increased by 20% (compared with the previous year).

Mining contributed 7.7% of GDP in 2000, according to South Korean estimates. The DPRK possesses considerable mineral wealth, with large deposits of coal, iron, lead, copper, zinc, tin, silver and gold. The country was formerly the second largest producer of magnesia products in the world, but output is believed to have declined significantly. According to official sources, there are unexploited offshore deposits of petroleum and natural gas. South Korean sources estimated that in 2001 output in the mining sector increased by 4.8%—although this was lower than growth rates of 14.1% in 1999 and 5.8% in 2000.

In 2000, according to South Korean estimates, the manufacturing sector contributed 17.7% of GDP (light industries 6.5% and heavy industries 11.2%). In the 1990s industrial development concentrated on heavy industry (metallurgy—notably steel production—machine-building, cement and chemicals). In the early 1980s the machine-building industry contributed about one-third of total industrial output. The textiles industry has provided significant exports. South Korean sources estimated that the GDP of the manufacturing sector increased by 3.5% in 2001, following an increase of 0.9% in 2000.

In 1998 it was estimated that nearly 84% of the DPRK's energy supply was derived from coal, followed in importance by hydroelectricity (12%) and petroleum (4%). A 30-MW nuclear reactor was believed to have been inaugurated in 1987. Light-water nuclear reactors were being constructed, for the purpose of electricity generation, in accordance with an agreement concluded with the USA in 1994 (see Recent History). Preparation of the site at Sinpo began in August 1997, although the construction of the reactors has been subsequently delayed. In 1998, according to South Korean sources, some 70% of the DPRK's electricity was generated by hydroelectric power stations, with most of the country's remaining requirements being provided by thermal power stations. During the 1990s the DPRK experienced increasing power shortages, as generation and transmission infrastructure deteriorated. Severe drought in the late 1990s and 2000 adversely affected the production of hydroelectric power. Petroleum is imported largely from the People's Republic of China, Russia and Iran: petroleum imports in 1993 totalled 2.3m. metric tons. Although South Korean sources estimated that electricity production increased by some 30% between 1986 and 1994, output is insufficient for the DPRK's needs, and there have been frequent reports of rationing in an effort to conserve fuel and energy. The DPRK's total electricity consumption in 1998 was only 61% of that in 1991. Shipments of fuel oil were provided by the USA, pending the construction of the light-water reactors, to meet part of North Korea's energy requirements. However, the USA suspended fuel oil shipments in late 2002, following Pyongyang's alleged admission that it was pursuing a secret nuclear programme. From the 1990s, and especially in early 2002, the DPRK sought greater foreign assistance in developing its offshore oilfields, located to the west in the Bohai Sea, and also in the north-east, near Chongjin city. A limited number of joint ventures were established with Asian oil companies.

South Korean sources estimated that in 2000 the DPRK's services sector accounted for 32.5% of GDP. In 2001 output in the sector was estimated to have declined by 0.3%, having increased by 1.2% in 2000, and decreased by 1.9% in 1999.

The trade deficit, including exchanges with South Korea, reached US $1,020.7m. in 2001. In 2001 total exports, excluding trade with South Korea, reached $650.2m. and imports totalled $1,620.3m., thus giving a trade deficit of $970.1m. (compared with a deficit of $840.7m. in the previous year). The DPRK's principal source of imports in 2001 was the People's Republic of China (accounting for 35.4% of total imports), followed by Japan (15.4%) and South Korea (14.0%). The principal market for

exports was Japan, which purchased 34.7% of total exports, followed by South Korea (27.0%). China was a source of crude petroleum, food and vehicles, while Japan was a destination for industrial and agricultural goods. Hong Kong had meanwhile become a centre for the re-export of North Korean goods, while Thailand emerged as a major trading partner in 2000. Inter-Korean trade increased by 28% in 2000, to reach US $425.1m. However, during the first nine months of 2001, this trade decreased by 11.8% compared with the corresponding period of the previous year, to $291.1m. During 2002, however, inter-Korean trade increased by 59.3% to $641.7m. Total trade (excluding exchanges with South Korea) increased by 33.1% to reach $1,970m. in 2000, and increased by 15.1% to reach $2,270m. in 2001. The principal exports in that year were live animals (24.4% of the value of total exports, excluding trade with South Korea), textiles (21.6%) and machinery and electrical equipment (15.0%). Other export commodities in the late 1990s included tobacco and silk. The principal imports in 2001 were machinery and electrical equipment (15.0% of the value of total imports, excluding trade with South Korea), mineral products (14.3%), vegetable products (13.6%), and textiles (12.6%). Other import items included road vehicles, chemicals and groceries. The 2002 budget envisaged revenue and expenditure balancing at 22,174m. won, compared with 21,571m. won in 2001. The state budgets for 1995–99 (inclusive) were not made public, a reflection of the extreme economic difficulties the country was experiencing, although a budgetary deficit of 38.7m. won was recorded in 2001. The DPRK's total external debt was estimated to be US $12,460m. in 2000. The average annual rate of inflation in 1993 was estimated to be 5%. However, following the introduction of market-orientated reforms in 2002, the inflation rate was said to have reached 4,000% in that year.

It is difficult to present an accurate economic profile of the DPRK, owing to the lack of reliable statistical data. North Korea's economic situation deteriorated sharply in the early 1990s, following the abandonment, in 1991 and 1992, respectively, of the barter trading system between the DPRK and the USSR (then its major trading partner) and China in favour of trade conducted exclusively in convertible currencies. The USSR also substantially reduced deliveries of crude petroleum and cereals, resulting in a severe decline in industrial production. The years 1994–97 were designated 'a period of adjustment in socialist economic construction', during which emphasis was to be transferred from traditional heavy industries to agriculture, light industry and trade. In 1996 it was believed that a measure of agricultural reform had been implemented, whereby farmers were permitted to sell a small proportion of their produce on the open market. Attempts to attract foreign capital into the Rajin-Sonbong Free Economic and Trade Zone, which was established in 1991 in the north-east of the country, have been largely unsuccessful. The severe food shortages in the mid-1990s prompted Pyongyang to appeal for international food aid and humanitarian assistance. The positive economic growth recorded in 1999 was mainly attributed to the effects of this aid and of foreign investment. Meanwhile, persistent reports suggested that many of North Korea's industries were operating well below capacity, although there had been an apparent improvement by early 2001. Defence industries retained their importance, with some Western estimates attributing 25% of GDP to the defence sector. The army was reported to be the DPRK's biggest foreign-exchange earner, with missile sales earning up to US $1,000m. each year, and servicemen engaged in numerous export-orientated projects, such as mining and herb collection. From the late 1990s North Korea slowly began to open up its economy to the outside world, developing trading relations with a number of European and Asian countries, and increasing the number of limited joint ventures with foreign firms. In October 2000 the DPRK reportedly established a research institute on capitalism, and it was believed that Kim Jong Il was seeking to introduce Chinese-style economic reforms following his visit to China in January 2001 (see above). North Korea also began developing its information technology (IT) industry, and by 2001 was operating six official websites. Joint IT ventures were established with institutes in the South, and in October the DPRK launched its first e-mail service provider. In May North Korea joined Intelsat (an international commercial satellite telecommunications organization), and in November the country agreed to adopt the global system for mobile communications (GSM) in the Rajin-Sonbong enterprise zone. At the 10th SPA in late March 2002, Prime Minister Hong Song Nam urged improved trade and economic co-operation, including joint ventures with other countries and international organizations. During the remainder of 2002, there were signs of a significant change in economic policy. In July the Government abandoned rationing, allowing farmers to sell produce at market prices, and wages were raised by a factor of 10–17, to take into account the concomitant price rises caused by the reforms. State assistance was reduced, and the value of the won decreased to as little as one-fiftieth of its previous value in relation to the US dollar. The other major reform of 2002 was the creation in September of a 'Special Administrative Region' in the city of Sinuiju (see Recent History), followed later in that year by a special industrial zone at Kaesong, and a new tourist zone at Mount Kumgang. All three were designed to attract new investment as part of the broader goal of opening up the economy. Meanwhile, a new 150-km waterway linking Pyongyang and Nampo was completed in October. From December 2002, in apparent displeasure with US policy towards the DPRK, the Government prohibited the use of the US dollar and adopted the euro as its official currency of foreign exchange. In March 2003 the Minister of Finance announced that the state budget's revenue would be 113.6% higher than in 2002, while expenditure would be 114.4% higher than in the previous year. The Government would also issue bonds for the first time in 50 years. However, analysts remained doubtful about Kim Jong Il's ability to restructure the economy without destabilizing the foundations of the ruling regime.

Education

Universal compulsory primary and secondary education were introduced in 1956 and 1958, respectively, and are provided at state expense. Free and compulsory 11-year education in state schools was introduced in 1975. Children enter kindergarten at five years of age, and people's school at the age of six. After four years, they advance to senior middle school for six years. In 1986 there were 519 university-level institutions and colleges; in the following year 325,000 students were enrolled in such institutions. In 1988 the Government announced the creation of new educational establishments, including one university, eight colleges, three factory colleges, two farmers' colleges and five special schools. English is compulsory as a second language at the age of 14. The adult literacy rate was estimated to be 99% in 1984.

Public Holidays

The *Juche* calendar was introduced in North Korea in 1997; 1912, the year of the late Kim Il Sung's birth, was designated the first year of the new calendar.

2003: 1 January (New Year), 16–17 February (Kim Jong Il's Birthday), 8 March (International Women's Day), 15 April (Day of the Sun, Kim Il Sung's birthday), 1 May (May Day), 15 August (Anniversary of Liberation), 9 September (Independence Day), 10 October (Anniversary of the foundation of the Korean Workers' Party), 27 December (Anniversary of the Constitution).

2004: 1 January (New Year), 16–17 February (Kim Jong Il's Birthday), 8 March (International Women's Day), 15 April (Day of the Sun, Kim Il Sung's birthday), 1 May (May Day), 15 August (Anniversary of Liberation), 9 September (Independence Day), 10 October (Anniversary of the foundation of the Korean Workers' Party), 27 December (Anniversary of the Constitution).

Weights and Measures

The metric system is in force.

Statistical Survey

Area and Population

AREA, POPULATION AND DENSITY*

Area (sq km)	122,762†
Population (census results)	
31 December 1993	
Males	10,329,699
Females.	10,883,679
Total	21,213,378
Population (UN estimates at mid-year)‡	
1999	22,110,000
2000	22,268,000
2001	22,428,000
Density (per sq km) at mid-2001.	182.7

* Excluding the demilitarized zone between North and South Korea, with an area of 1,262 sq km (487 sq miles).
† 47,399 sq miles.
‡ Source: UN, *World Population Prospects: The 2000 Revision.*

PRINCIPAL TOWNS
(population at 1993 census)

Pyongyang (capital) .	2,741,260	Wonsan	300,148
Nampo	731,448	Pyongsong . . .	272,934
Hamhung. . . .	709,730	Sariwon	254,146
Chongjin	582,480	Haeju	229,172
Kaesong	334,433	Kanggye	223,410
Sinuiju	326,011	Hyesan	178,020

Source: UN, *Demographic Yearbook.*

BIRTHS AND DEATHS
(UN estimates, annual averages)

	1985–90	1990–95	1995–2000
Birth rate (per 1,000)	20.6	20.8	18.6
Death rate (per 1,000)	5.8	7.0	10.4

Expectation of life (UN estimates, years at birth, 1995–2000): 63.1 (males 60.5; females 66.0).

Source: UN, *World Population Prospects: The 2000 Revision.*

ECONOMICALLY ACTIVE POPULATION
(ILO estimates, '000 persons at mid-1980)

	Males	Females	Total
Agriculture, etc.	1,484	1,870	3,355
Industry	1,654	719	2,373
Services	1,103	1,007	2,110
Total labour force	**4,241**	**3,597**	**7,838**

Source: ILO, *Economically Active Population Estimates and Projections, 1950–2025.*

Mid-2000 (estimates in '000): Agriculture, etc. 3,439; Total labour force 11,421 (Source: FAO).

Health and Welfare

KEY INDICATORS

Total fertility rate (children per woman, 2001).	2.1
Under-5 mortality rate (per 1,000 live births, 2001) . . .	55
HIV/AIDS (% of persons aged 15–49, 1994).	<0.01
Health expenditure (2000): US $ per head (PPP)	33
Health expenditure (2000): % of GDP	2.1
Health expenditure (2000): public (% of total)	77.3
Access to water (% of persons, 2000).	100
Access to sanitation (% of persons, 2000)	99

For sources and definitions, see explanatory note on p. vi.

Agriculture

PRINCIPAL CROPS
('000 metric tons)

	1999	2000	2001
Wheat	97*	50*	117
Rice (paddy)	2,343	1,690	2,060
Barley	55*	29*	61
Maize	1,235	1,041	1,482
Rye†	75	75	68
Oats†	10	11	11
Millet†	20	45	45
Sorghum†	10	10	10
Potatoes	1,473*	1,870	1,882
Sweet potatoes	490*	290*	350†
Pulses†	280	290	290
Soybeans (Soya beans)* . . .	340	350	350
Cottonseed†	34	35	35
Cabbages†	625	630	650
Tomatoes†	62	62	62
Pumpkins, squash and gourds† .	83	85	85
Cucumbers and gherkins† . .	64	64	64
Aubergines (Eggplants)† . .	42	43	43
Chillies and green peppers† .	55	55	55
Green onions and shallots† . .	90	90	90
Dry onions†	82	82	82
Garlic†	75	80	80
Other vegetables†	2,200	2,400	2,400
Apples†	650	650	650
Pears†	125	130	130
Peaches and nectarines† . .	110	110	110
Watermelons†	103	104	104
Cantaloupes and other melons† .	108	110	110
Other fruits and berries† . .	460	460	460
Tobacco (leaves)†	62	63	63
Hemp fibre†	12	13	13
Cotton (lint)†	12	12	12

* Unofficial figure(s).

† FAO estimate(s).

Source: FAO.

LIVESTOCK
('000 head, year ending September)

	1999	2000	2001
Horses*	45	46	46
Cattle	577	579	570
Pigs	2,970	3,120	3,137
Sheep	185	185	189
Goats	1,900	2,276	2,566
Chickens	11,200	15,733	16,894
Ducks	1,624	2,078	3,158
Rabbits	5,202	11,475	19,455

* FAO estimates.

Source: FAO.

LIVESTOCK PRODUCTS
(FAO estimates, '000 metric tons)

	1999	2000	2001
Beef and veal	20.0	20.0	21.5
Goat meat	9.0	10.2	10.5
Pig meat	133.8	140.0	145.0
Poultry meat	23.4	26.8	30.8
Cows' milk	86.0	90.0	90.0
Poultry eggs	95.0	110.0	120.0
Cattle hides (fresh)	2.8	2.8	3.0

Source: FAO.

Forestry

ROUNDWOOD REMOVALS
(FAO estimates, '000 cubic metres, excl. bark)

	1999	2000	2001
Sawlogs, veneer logs and logs for sleepers	1,000	1,000	1,000
Other industrial wood . . .	500	500	500
Fuel wood	5,429	5,503	5,561
Total	6,929	7,003	7,061

Sawnwood production ('000 cubic metres, incl. railway sleepers): 280 (coniferous 185, broadleaved 95) per year in 1970–2001 (FAO estimates).

Source: FAO.

Fishing

(FAO estimates, '000 metric tons, live weight)

	1998	1999	2000
Capture	220.0	210.0	200.9
Freshwater fishes	20.0	20.0	20.0
Alaska pollock	60.0	55.0	52.0
Other marine fishes . . .	114.9	109.9	104.3
Marine crustaceans . . .	15.0	15.0	14.3
Squids	10.0	10.0	9.5
Aquaculture	68.5	68.5	66.7
Molluscs	65.0	65.0	63.0
Total catch	288.5	278.5	267.6

Note: Figures exclude aquatic plants (FAO estimates, '000 metric tons, aquaculture only): 413.0 in 1998; 413.0 in 1999; 401.0 in 2000.

Source: FAO, *Yearbook of Fishery Statistics*.

Mining

(estimates, '000 metric tons, unless otherwise indicated)

	1999	2000	2001
Hard coal	30,000	27,000	24,000
Brown coal and lignite . . .	10,000	9,000	7,000
Iron ore: gross weight . . .	700	700	700
Iron ore: metal content . . .	300	300	300
Copper ore*	14	13	13
Lead ore*	60	60	60
Zinc ore*	100	100	100
Tungsten concentrates (metric tons)*	700	700	700
Silver (metric tons)*	40	40	40
Gold (kg)*	2,500	2,000	2,000
Magnesite (crude)	1,000	1,000	1,000
Phosphate rock†	350	350	350
Fluorspar‡	25	25	25
Barite (Barytes)	70	70	70
Salt (unrefined)	500	500	500
Graphite (natural)	33	30	25
Talc, soapstone and pyrophyllite	120	120	120

Note: No recent data are available for the production of molybdenum ore and asbestos.

* Figures refer to the metal content of ores and concentrates.

† Figures refer to gross weight. The phosphoric acid content (estimates, '000 metric tons) was: 105 in 1999; 105 in 2000; n.a. in 2001.

‡ Metallurgical grade.

Source: US Geological Survey.

Industry

SELECTED PRODUCTS
('000 metric tons, unless otherwise indicated)

	1995	1996	1997
Nitrogenous fertilizers * . . .	75	72	72
Motor spirit (petrol)† . . .	960	950	930
Kerosene†	205	200	190
Gas-diesel (Distillate fuel) oils† .	1,040	1,035	1,025
Residual fuel oils†	605	600	590
Coke-oven coke (excl. breeze)† .	3,500	3,450	3,400
Cement†‡	17,000	17,000	17,000
Pig-iron†‡	500	500	450
Crude steel†‡	1,500	1,000	1,000
Refined copper (unwrought)†‡ . .	27	28	28
Lead (primary metal)†‡ . . .	75	75	75
Zinc (primary metal)†‡ . . .	200	200	200
Electric energy (million kWh)† . .	36,000	35,000	33,990

* Output is measured in terms of nitrogen.
† Provisional or estimated figures.
‡ Data from the US Geological Survey.

Source: mainly UN, *Industrial Commodity Statistics Yearbook.*

1998 (estimates, '000 metric tons): Nitrogenous fertilizers 72; Cement 17,000; Pig-iron 250; Crude steel 1,000; Refined copper (unwrought) 28; Lead (primary metal) 75; Zinc (primary metal) 180 (Source: mainly US Geological Survey).

1999 (estimates, '000 metric tons): Cement 16,000; Pig-iron 250; Crude steel 1,000; Refined copper (unwrought) 25; Lead (primary metal) 70; Zinc (primary metal) 180 (Source: mainly US Geological Survey).

2000 (estimates, '000 metric tons): Cement 15,000; Pig-iron 250; Crude steel 1,000; Refined copper (unwrought) 25; Lead (primary metal) 70; Zinc (primary metal) 200 (Source: mainly US Geological Survey).

Finance

CURRENCY AND EXCHANGE RATES

Monetary Units
100 chon (jun) = 1 won

Sterling, Dollar and Euro Equivalents (31 December 2002)
£1 sterling = 245.880 won
US $1 = 152.550 won
€1 = 158.979 won
100 won = £0.41 = $0.66 = €0.63

Note: In August 2002 it was reported that a currency reform had been introduced, whereby the exchange rate was adjusted from US $1 = 2.15 won to $1 = 150 won: a devaluation of 98.6%.

BUDGET
(projected, million won)

	1992	1993	1994
Revenue	39,500.9	40,449.9	41,525.2
Expenditure	39,500.9	40,449.9	41,525.2
Economic development . .	26,675.1	27,423.8	28,164.0
Socio-cultural sector . . .	7,730.6	7,751.5	8,218.3
Defence	4,582.1	4,692.2	4,816.9
Administration and management	513.1	582.4	326.0

1998 (estimates, million won): Total revenue 19,790.8; Total expenditure 20,015.2.

1999 (estimates, million won): Total revenue 19,801.0; Total expenditure 20,018.2.

2000 (estimates, million won): Total revenue 20,955.0; Total expenditure 20,903.0.

2001 (projected, million won): Total revenue 21,571.0; Total expenditure 21,571.0.

2002 (projected, million won): Total revenue 22,174.0; Total expenditure 22,174.0.

NATIONAL ACCOUNTS

Gross Domestic Product by Economic Activity
(% of total)

	1997	1998	1999
Agriculture, forestry and fishing	28.9	29.6	31.4
Mining	6.7	6.6	7.3
Manufacturing	18.8	19.0	18.3
Electricity, gas and water . . .	4.3	4.2	4.5
Construction	6.3	5.1	6.1
Government services. . . .	25.1	25.3	22.8
Other services	9.9	10.2	9.6
Total	100.0	100.0	100.0

Source: Bank of Korea (Republic of Korea).

External Trade

PRINCIPAL COMMODITIES
(US $ million)*

Imports	1999	2000	2001
Live animals and animal products . . . . . . }	101.3 {	20.3	73.9
Vegetable products. . . . . }		159.0	221.0
Animal or vegetable fats and oils; prepared edible fats; animal or vegetable waxes . . . . . }			
	58.2	89.1	89.9
Prepared foodstuffs; beverages, spirits and vinegar; tobacco and manufactured substitutes . . }			
Mineral products	141.0	171.2	231.1
Products of chemical or allied industries.	96.4	108.4	123.4
Plastics, rubber and articles thereof	51.0	67.5	66.0
Textiles and textile articles . .	127.1	171.9	203.9
Base metals and articles thereof	59.0	85.2	100.4
Machinery and mechanical appliances; electrical equipment; sound and television apparatus . .	135.6	205.1	243.8
Vehicles, aircraft, vessels and associated transport equipment	102.2	146.2	88.4
Total (incl. others).	964.6	1,406.5	1,620.3

Exports	1999	2000	2001
Live animals and animal products	87.8	97.9	158.4
Vegetable products.	22.5	30.3	42.0
Mineral products	22.6	43.2	50.5
Products of chemical or allied industries. . . . . . }	39.9	44.9	44.6
Plastics, rubber and articles thereof . . . . . . }			
Wood, cork and articles thereof; wood charcoal; manufactures of straw, esparto, etc.	16.2	10.9	5.6
Textiles and textile articles . .	130.6	140.0	140.5
Natural or cultured pearls, precious or semi-precious stones, precious metals and articles thereof; imitation jewellery; coin	21.4	9.8	14.1
Base metals and articles thereof	46.5	43.9	60.2
Machinery and mechanical appliances; electrical equipment, sound and television apparatus . . .	81.3	105.2	97.9
Total (incl. others).	515.0	565.8	650.2

* Excluding trade with the Republic of Korea (US $ million): Imports 211.8 in 1999, 272.8 in 2000, 226.8 in 2001; Exports 121.6 in 1999, 152.4 in 2000, 176.2 in 2001.

Source: Korea Trade-Investment Promotion Agency (KOTRA), Republic of Korea.

PRINCIPAL TRADING PARTNERS
(US $ million)*

Imports	1999	2000	2001
China, People's Republic . . .	328.7	450.8	573.1
Germany	32.6	53.6	82.1
Hong Kong	60.5	68.5	42.6
India	98.0	142.9	154.8
Japan	147.8	206.8	249.1
Russia	48.5	42.9	63.8
Singapore	48.1	46.2	112.3
Spain	n.a.	15.3	31.6
Taiwan	11.7	n.a.	n.a.
Thailand	34.7	188.3	109.6
United Kingdom . . .	22.1	25.3	40.7
USA	11.3	n.a.	n.a.
Total (incl. others) . . .	964.6	1,406.5	1,620.3

Exports	1999	2000	2001
Bangladesh	24.2	n.a.	n.a.
China, People's Republic . .	41.7	37.2	166.7
Germany	23.7	25.6	22.8
Hong Kong	63.3	46.4	38.0
India	44.3	25.5	3.1
Japan	202.6	256.9	225.6
Spain	n.a.	12.7	12.6
Thailand	3.2	19.5	24.9
Total (incl. others) . . .	515.0	565.8	650.2

* Excluding trade with the Republic of Korea (US $ million): Imports 211.8 in 1999, 272.8 in 2000, 226.8 in 2001; Exports 121.6 in 1999, 152.4 in 2000, 176.2 in 2001.

Source: Korea Trade-Investment Promotion Agency (KOTRA), Republic of Korea.

Transport

SHIPPING

Merchant Fleet
(registered at 31 December)

	1999	2000	2001
Number of vessels	171	176	176
Total displacement ('000 grt) . .	657.8	652.6	697.8

Source: Lloyd's Register-Fairplay, *World Fleet Statistics*.

International Sea-borne Freight Traffic
(estimates, '000 metric tons)

	1988	1989	1990
Goods loaded	630	640	635
Goods unloaded	5,386	5,500	5,520

Source: UN, *Monthly Bulletin of Statistics*.

CIVIL AVIATION
(traffic on scheduled services)

	1995	1996	1997
Kilometres flown (million) . .	3	3	5
Passengers carried ('000) . .	254	254	280
Passenger-km (million) . . .	207	207	286
Total ton-km (million) . . .	22	22	30

Source: UN, *Statistical Yearbook*.

Tourism

	1996	1997	1998
Tourist arrivals ('000)	127	128	130

Source: World Tourism Organization, mainly *Yearbook of Tourism Statistics*.

Communications Media

	1994	1995	1996
Radio receivers ('000 in use) . .	2,950	3,000	3,300
Television receivers ('000 in use) .	1,000	1,050	1,090
Telephones ('000 main lines in use)*	1,100	1,100	1,100
Telefax stations (number in use) .	3,000*	n.a.	n.a.
Daily newspapers:			
number	11	11*	3
average circulation ('000 copies)*	5,000	5,000	4,500

* Estimate(s).

1997 ('000 in use): Radio receivers 3,360; Television receivers 1,200.

Sources: UNESCO, *Statistical Yearbook*; UN, *Statistical Yearbook*.

Education
(1987/88)

	Institutions	Teachers	Students
Pre-primary	16,964	35,000	728,000
Primary	4,810*	59,000	1,543,000
Secondary	4,840*	111,000	2,468,000
Universities and colleges . .	519†	23,000	325,000
Other tertiary	n.a.	4,000	65,000

* 1997 figure.
† Of which 46 were university-level institutions and 473 were colleges (1986).

Source: mainly UNESCO, *Statistical Yearbook*.

Directory

The Constitution

A new Constitution was adopted on 27 December 1972. According to South Korean sources, several amendments were made in April 1992, including the deletion of references to Marxism-Leninism, the extension of the term of the Supreme People's Assembly from four to five years, and the promotion of limited 'economic openness'. Extensive amendments to the Constitution were approved on 5 September 1998. The main provisions of the revised Constitution are summarized below:

The Democratic People's Republic of Korea is an independent socialist state; the revolutionary traditions of the State are stressed (its ideological basis being the *Juche* idea of the Korean Workers' Party), as is the desire to achieve national reunification by peaceful means on the basis of national independence. The Late President Kim Il Sung is the Eternal President of the Republic.

National sovereignty rests with the working people, who exercise power through the Supreme People's Assembly and Local People's Assemblies at lower levels, which are elected by universal, equal and direct suffrage by secret ballot.

The foundation of an independent national economy, based on socialist and *Juche* principles, is stressed. The means of production are owned solely by the State and socialist co-operative organizations.

Culture and education provide the working people with knowledge to advance a socialist way of life. Education is free, universal and compulsory for 11 years.

Defence is emphasized, as well as the rights of overseas nationals, the principles of friendly relations between nations based on equality, mutual respect and non-interference, proletarian internationalism, support for national liberation struggles and due observance of law.

The basic rights and duties of citizens are laid down and guaranteed. These include the right to vote and to be elected (for citizens who are more than 17 years of age), to work (the working day being eight hours), to free medical care and material assistance for the old, infirm or disabled, and to political asylum. National defence is the supreme duty of citizens.

THE STRUCTURE OF STATE

The Supreme People's Assembly

The Supreme People's Assembly is the highest organ of state power, exercises legislative power and is elected by direct, equal, universal and secret ballot for a term of five years. Its chief functions are: (i) to adopt, amend or supplement legal or constitutional enactments; (ii) to determine state policy; (iii) to elect the Chairman of the National Defence Commission; (iv) to elect the Vice-Chairmen and other members of the National Defence Commission (on the recommendation of the Chairman of the National Defence Commission); (v) to elect the President and other members of the Presidium of the Supreme People's Assembly, the Premier of the Cabinet, the President of the Central Court and other legal officials; (vi) to appoint the Vice-Premiers and other members of the Cabinet (on the recommendation of the Premier of the Cabinet); (vii) to approve the State Plan and Budget; (viii) to receive a report on the work of the Cabinet and adopt measures, if necessary; (ix) to decide on the ratification or abrogation of treaties. It holds regular and extraordinary sessions, the former being once or twice a year, the latter as necessary at the request of at least one-third of the deputies. Legislative enactments are adopted when approved by more than one-half of those deputies present. The Constitution is amended and supplemented when approved by more than two-thirds of the total number of deputies.

The National Defence Commission

The National Defence Commission, which consists of a Chairman, first Vice-Chairman, other Vice-Chairmen and members, is the highest military organ of state power, and is accountable to the Supreme People's Assembly. The National Defence Commission directs and commands the armed forces and guides defence affairs. The Chairman of the National Defence Commission serves a five-year term of office and has the most senior post in the state hierarchy.

The Presidium of the Supreme People's Assembly

The Presidium of the Supreme People's Assembly, which consists of a President, Vice-Presidents, secretaries and members, is the highest organ of power in the intervals between sessions of the Supreme People's Assembly, to which it is accountable. It exercises the following chief functions: (i) to convene sessions of the Supreme People's Assembly; (ii) to examine and approve new legislation, the State Plan and the State Budget, when the Supreme People's Assembly is in recess; (iii) to interpret the Constitution and legislative enactments; (iv) to supervise the observance of laws of State organs; (v) to organize elections to the Supreme People's Assembly and Local People's Assemblies; (vi) to form or abolish ministries or commissions of the Cabinet; (vii) to appoint or remove Vice-Premiers and other cabinet or ministry members, on the recommendation of the Premier, when the Supreme People's Assembly is not in session; (viii) to elect or transfer judges of the Central Court; (ix) to ratify or abrogate treaties concluded with other countries; (x) to appoint or recall diplomatic envoys; (xi) to confer decorations, medals, honorary titles and diplomatic ranks; (xii) to grant general amnesties or special pardon. The President of the Presidium represents the State and receives credentials and letters of recall of diplomatic representatives accredited by a foreign state.

The Cabinet

The Cabinet is the administrative and executive body of the Supreme People's Assembly and a general state management organ. It serves a five-year term and comprises the Premier, Vice-Premiers, Chairmen of Commissions and other necessary members. Its major functions are the following: (i) to adopt measures to execute state policy; (ii) to guide the work of ministries and other organs responsible to it; (iii) to establish and remove direct organs of the Cabinet and main administrative economic organizations; (iv) to draft the State Plan and adopt measures to make it effective; (v) to compile the State Budget and to implement its provisions; (vi) to organize and execute the work of all sectors of the economy, as well as education, science, culture, health and environmental protection; (vii) to adopt measures to strengthen the monetary and banking system; (viii) to adopt measures to maintain social order, protect State interests and guarantee citizens' rights; (ix) to conclude treaties; (x) to abolish decisions and directives of economic administrative organs which run counter to those of the Cabinet. The Cabinet is accountable to the Supreme People's Assembly.

Local People's Assemblies

The Local People's Assemblies and Committees of the province (or municipality directly under central authority), city (or district) and county are local organs of power. The Local People's Assemblies consist of deputies elected by direct, equal, universal and secret ballot. The Local People's Committees consist of a Chairman, Vice-Chairmen, secretaries and members. The Local People's Assemblies and Committees serve a four-year term and exercise local budgetary functions, elect local administrative and judicial personnel and carry out the decisions at local level of higher executive and administrative organs.

THE JUDICIARY

Justice is administered by the Central Court (the highest judicial organ of the State), local courts and the Special Court. Judges and other legal officials are elected by the Supreme People's Assembly. The Central Court protects state property, constitutional rights, guarantees that all state bodies and citizens observe state laws, and executes judgments. Justice is administered by the court comprising one judge and two people's assessors. The court is independent and judicially impartial. Judicial affairs are conducted by the Central Procurator's Office, which exposes and institutes criminal proceedings against accused persons. The Office of the Central Procurator is responsible to the Chairman of the National Defence Commission, the Supreme People's Assembly and the Central People's Committee.

The Government

HEAD OF STATE

President: (President KIM IL SUNG died on 8 July 1994 and was declared 'Eternal President' in September 1998).

Chairman of the National Defence Commission: Marshal KIM JONG IL.

First Vice-Chairman: Vice-Marshal JO MYONG ROK.

Vice-Chairmen: Vice-Marshal KIM IL CHOL, Vice-Marshal RI YONG MU.

Other members: Vice-Marshal KIM YONG CHUN, YON HYONG MUK, Marshal RI UL SOL, Vice-Marshal PAEK HAK RIM, JON BYONG HO, KIM CHOL MAN.

CABINET
(April 2003)

Premier: HONG SONG NAM.

Vice-Premiers: JO CHANG DOK, KWAK POM GI.

Vice-Premier and Chairman of the Commission for Capital Construction: Col-Gen. SHIN IL NAM.

Minister of Foreign Affairs: PAEK NAM SUN.

Minister of Public Security: Vice-Marshal PAEK HAK RIM.

Minister of the People's Armed Forces: Vice-Marshal KIM IL CHOL.

Chairman of the State Planning Commission: PAK NAM GI.

Minister of Power and Coal Industry: O GWANG HONG.

Minister of Extractive Industries: SON JONG HO.

Minister of Metal and Machine-Building Industries: JON SUNG HUN.

Minister of Construction and Building Materials Industries: JO YUN HUI.

Minister of the Electronics Industry: O SU YONG.

Minister of Railways: KIM YONG SAM.

Minister of Land and Marine Transport: KIM YONG IL.

Minister of Agriculture: KIM CHANG SHIK.

Minister of Chemical Industry: PAK PONG JU.

Minister of Light Industry: RI JU O.

Minister of Foreign Trade: RI KWANG GUN.

Minister of Forestry: RI SANG MU.

Minister of Fisheries: RI SONG UNG.

Minister of City Management: CHOE JONG GON.

Minister of Land and Environmental Protection: JANG IL SON.

Minister of State Construction Control: PAE TAL JUN.

Minister of Commerce: RI YONG SON.

Minister of Procurement and Food Administration: CHOE NAM GYUN.

Minister of Education: (vacant).

Minister of Post and Telecommunications: RI KUM BOM.

Minister of Culture: KANG NUNG SU.

Minister of Finance: MUN IL BONG.

Minister of Labour: RI WON IL.

Minister of Public Health: KIM SU HAK.

Minister of State Inspection: KIM UI SUN.

Chairman of the Physical Culture and Sports Guidance Committee: PAK MYONG CHOL.

President of the National Academy of Sciences: PYON YONG RIP.

President of the Central Bank: KIM WAN SU.

Director of the Central Statistics Bureau: KIM CHANG SU.

Chief Secretary of the Cabinet: JONG MUN SAN.

MINISTRIES

All Ministries and Commissions are in Pyongyang.

Legislature

CHOE KO IN MIN HOE UI
(Supreme People's Assembly)

The 687 members of the 10th Supreme People's Assembly (SPA) were elected unopposed for a five-year term on 26 July 1998. Its permanent body is the Presidium.

Chairman: CHOE TAE BOK.

Vice-Chairmen: CHANG CHOL, RYO WON GU.

President of the Presidium: KIM YONG NAM.

Vice-Presidents of the Presidium: YANG HYONG SOP, KIM YONG DAE.

Political Organizations

Democratic Front for the Reunification of the Fatherland: Pyongyang; f. 1946; a vanguard organization comprising political parties and mass working people's organizations seeking the unification of North and South Korea; Mems of Presidium PAK SONG CHOL, RYOM TAE JUN, YANG HYONG SOP, JONG TU HWAN, RI YONG SU, JONG SHIN HYOK, KIM PONG JU, PYON CHANG BOK, RYU MI YONG, RYO WON GU, KANG RYON HAK.

The component parties are:

Chondoist Chongu Party: Pyongyang; tel. (2) 334241; f. 1946; supports policies of Korean Workers' Party; follows the guiding principle of *Innaechon*(the realization of 'heaven on earth'); Chair. RYU MI YONG.

Korean Social Democratic Party (KSDP) (Joson Sahoeminju-dang): Pyongyang; tel. (2) 5211981; fax (2) 3814410; f. 1945; advocates national independence and a democratic socialist society; supports policies of Korean Workers' Party; Chair. KIM YONG DAE; First Vice-Chair. KANG PYONG HAK.

Korean Workers' Party (KWP): Pyongyang; f. 1945; merged with the South Korean Workers' Party in 1949; the guiding principle is the *Juche* idea, based on the concept that man is the master and arbiter of all things; 3m. mems; Gen. Sec. Marshal KIM JONG IL.

Sixth Central Committee

General Secretary: Marshal KIM JONG IL.

Politburo

Presidium: Marshal KIM JONG IL.

Full Members: KIM YONG NAM, PAK SONG CHOL, KIM YONG JU, KYE UNG TAE, JON BYONG HO, HAN SONG RYONG.

Alternate Members: HONG SONG NAM, YON HYONG MUK, YANG HYONG SOP, CHOE TAE BOK, KIM CHOL MAN, CHOE YONG RIM, RI SON SHIL.

Secretariat: Marshal KIM JONG IL, KYE UNG TAE, JON BYONG HO, HAN SONG RYONG, CHOE TAE BOK, KIM KI NAM, KIM KUK TAE, KIM JUNG RIN, KIM YONG SUN, JONG HA CHOL.

The component mass working people's organizations are:

General Federation of Trade Unions of Korea (GFTUK).

Kim Il Sung Socialist Youth League.

Korean Democratic Women's Union (KDWU).

Union of Agricultural Working People of Korea: See under Trade Unions.

There is one opposition organization in exile, with branches in Tokyo (Japan), Moscow (Russia) and Beijing (People's Republic of China):

Salvation Front for the Democratic Unification of Chosun: f. early 1990s; seeks the overthrow of the Kim dynasty, the establishment of democracy in the DPRK and Korean reunification; Chair. PAK KAP DONG.

Diplomatic Representation

EMBASSIES IN THE DEMOCRATIC PEOPLE'S REPUBLIC OF KOREA

Algeria: Munsudong, Taedongkang District, Pyongyang; tel. (2) 90372; Ambassador MOKHTAR REGUIEG.

Benin: Pyongyang; Ambassador A. OGIST.

Bulgaria: Munsudong, Taedongkang District, Pyongyang; tel. (2) 3827343; fax (2) 3817342; Ambassador YORDAN MUTAFCHIYEV.

Cambodia: Munsudong, Taedongkang District, Pyongyang; tel. (2) 3827459; fax (2) 3817625.

China, People's Republic: Kinmauldong, Moranbong District, Pyongyang; tel. (2) 3823316; fax (2) 3813425; Ambassador WU DONGHE.

Cuba: Munsudong, taedongkang District, Pyongyang; tel. (2) 3827380; fax (2) 3817703; Ambassador ESTEBAN LOBAINA ROMERO.

Czech Republic: Munsudong, Taedongkang District, Pyongyang.

Egypt: Pyongyang; tel. (2) 3817414; fax (2) 3817611; Ambassador AHMED RAMY AWAD ALHOSAINY.

Ethiopia: POB 55, Munsudong, Taedongkang District, Pyongyang; tel. (2) 3827554; fax (2) 3827550; Chargé d'affaires FEKADE S.G. MESKEL.

Finland: Munsudong, Taedongkang District, Pyongyang.

Germany: Munsudong, Taedongkang District, Pyongyang; tel. (2) 3827490; fax (2) 3817397.

India: Block 53, Munsudong, Taehak St, Taedongkang District, Pyongyang; tel. (2) 3817274; fax (2) 3817619; Ambassador R. P. SINGH.

Indonesia: 5 Foreigners' Bldg, Munsudong, Taedongkang District, Pyongyang; tel. (2) 3827439; fax (2) 3817620; e-mail kbripyg@public .east.cn.net; Ambassador BUCHARI EFFENDI.

Iran: Munhungdong, Monsu St, Taedongkang District, Pyongyang; tel. (2) 3817492; fax (2) 3817612; Ambassador MOHAMMAD GANJI-DOOST.

Laos: Munhungdong, Taedongkang District, Pyongyang; tel. (2) 3827363; fax (2) 3817722; Ambassador KHAMKENG SAYAKEO.

Libya: Munsudong, Taedongkang District, Pyongyang; tel. (2) 3827544; fax (2) 3817267; Secretary of People's Bureau AHMED AMER AL-MUAKKAF.

Mali: Pyongyang; Ambassador NAKOUNTE DIAKITÉ.

Mongolia: Munsudong, Taedongkang District, Pyongyang; tel. (2) 3827322; fax (2) 3817321; Ambassador J. LOMBO.

Nigeria: Munsudong, Taedongkang District, Pyongyang; tel. (2) 3827558; fax (2) 3817293; Ambassador ADOGA ONAH.

Pakistan: Munsudong, Taedongkang District, Pyongyang; tel. (2) 3827478; fax 3817622; Ambassador SULTAN HABIB.

Poland: Munsudong, Taedongkang District, Pyongyang; tel. (2) 3817327; fax (2) 3817634; Ambassador WOJCIECH KALUZA.

Romania: Munhungdong, Taedongkang District, Pyongyang; tel. (2) 3827336; fax (2) 3817336; Ambassador NICOLAE GIRBA.

Russia: Sinyangdong, Central District, Pyongyang; tel. (2) 3823102; fax (2) 3813427; Ambassador ANDREI KARLOV.

Syria: Munsudong, Taedongkang District, Pyongyang; tel. (2) 3827473; fax (2) 3817635; Ambassador YASSER AL-FARRA.

Thailand: Pyongyang; Ambassador NIKHOM TANTEMSAPYA.

United Kingdom: Munsudong, Taedongkang District, Pyongyang; tel. (2) 3817980; fax (2) 3817985; Ambassador DAVID SLINN.

Viet Nam: Munsudong, Taedongkang District, Pyongyang; tel. (2) 3817353; fax (2) 3817632; Ambassador LE XUAN VINH.

Judicial System

The judicial organs include the Central Court, the Court of the Province (or city under central authority) and the People's Court. Each court is composed of judges and people's assessors.

Procurators supervise the ordinances and regulations of all ministries and the decisions and directives of local organs of state power to ensure that they conform to the Constitution, laws and decrees, as well as to the decisions and other measures of the Cabinet. Procurators bring suits against criminals in the name of the State, and participate in civil cases to protect the interests of the State and citizens.

Central Court

Pyongyang.

the highest judicial organ; supervises the work of all courts.

President: KIM BYONG RYUL.

First Vice-President: YUN MYONG GUK.

Central Procurator's Office

supervises work of procurator's offices in provinces, cities and counties.

Procurator-General: CHOE YONG RIM.

Religion

The religions that are officially reported to be practised in the DPRK are Buddhism, Christianity and Chundo Kyo, a religion peculiar to Korea combining elements of Buddhism and Christianity. Religious co-ordinating bodies are believed to be under strict state control.

Korean Religious Believers Council: Pyongyang; f. 1989; brings together members of religious organizations in North Korea; Chair. JANG JAE ON.

BUDDHISM

In 1995, according to North Korean sources, there were some 60 Buddhist temples and an estimated 300 monks in the DPRK; the number of believers was about 10,000.

Korean Buddhists Federation: POB 77, Pyongyang; tel. (2) 43698; fax (2) 3812100; f. 1945; Chair. Cen. Cttee PAK TAE HWA; Sec. SHIM SANG RYON.

CHRISTIANITY

In 1995, according to North Korean sources, there were approximately 13,000 Christians (including 3,000 Roman Catholics) in the country, many of whom worshipped in house churches (of which there were about 500).

Korean Christians Federation: Pyongyang; f. 1946; Chair. Cen. Cttee KANG YONG SOP; Sec. O KYONG U.

The Roman Catholic Church

For ecclesiastical purposes, North and South Korea are nominally under a unified jurisdiction. North Korea contains two dioceses (Hamhung and Pyongyang), both suffragan to the archdiocese of Seoul (in South Korea), and the territorial abbacy of Tokwon (Tokugen), directly responsible to the Holy See.

Korean Roman Catholics Association: Changchung 1-dong, Songyo District, Pyongyang; tel. (2) 23492; f. 1988; Chair. Cen. Cttee JANG JAE ON; Vice-Chair. MUN CHANG HAK.

Diocese of Hamhung: Catholic Mission, Hamhung; 134-1 Waekwan-dong Kwan Eub, Chil kok kun, Gyeongbuk 718-800, Republic of Korea; tel. (545) 970-2000; Bishop (vacant); Apostolic Administrator of Hamhung and of the Abbacy of Tokwon Fr PLACIDUS DONG-HO RI.

Diocese of Pyongyang: Catholic Mission, Pyongyang; Bishop Rt Rev. FRANCIS HONG YONG HO (absent); Apostolic Administrator Most Rev. NICHOLAS CHEONG JIN-SUK (Archbishop of Seoul).

CHUNDO KYO

Korean Chundoists Association: Pyongyang; tel. (2) 334241; f. 1946; Chair. of Central Guidance Cttee RYU MI YONG.

The Press

PRINCIPAL NEWSPAPERS

Choldo Sinmun: Pyongyang; f. 1947; every two days.

Joson Inmingun (Korean People's Army Daily): Pyongyang; f. 1948; daily; Editor-in-Chief RI TAE BONG.

Kyowon Sinmun: Pyongyang; f. 1948; publ. by the Education Commission; weekly.

Minju Choson (Democratic Korea): Pyongyang; f. 1946; govt organ; 6 a week; Editor-in-Chief KIM JONG SUK; circ. 200,000.

Nongup Kunroja: Pyongyang; publ. of Cen. Cttee of the Union of Agricultural Working People of Korea.

Pyongyang Sinmun: Pyongyang; f. 1957; general news; 6 a week; Editor-in-Chief SONG RAK GYUN.

Rodong Chongnyon (Working Youth): Pyongyang; f. 1946; organ of the Cen. Cttee of the Kim Il Sung Socialist Youth League; 6 a week; Editor-in-Chief RI JONG GI.

Rodong Sinmun (Labour Daily): Pyongyang; f. 1946; organ of the Cen. Cttee of the Korean Workers' Party; daily; Editor-in-Chief CHOE CHIL NAM; circ. 1.5m.

Rodongja Sinmun (Workers' Newspaper): Pyongyang; f. 1945; organ of the Gen. Fed. of Trade Unions of Korea; Editor-in-Chief RI SONG JU.

Saenal (New Day): Pyongyang; f. 1971; publ. by the Kim Il Sung Socialist Youth League; 2 a week; Deputy Editor CHOE SANG IN.

Sonyon Sinmun: Pyongyang; f. 1946; publ. by the Kim Il Sung Socialist Youth League; 2 a week; circ. 120,000.

Tongil Sinbo: Kangan 1-dong, Youth Ave, Songyo District, Pyongyang; f. 1972; non-affiliated; weekly; Chief Editor JO HYON YONG; circ. 300,000.

PRINCIPAL PERIODICALS

Chollima: Pyongyang; popular magazine; monthly.

Choson (Korea): Pyongyang; social, economic, political and cultural; bi-monthly.

Choson Minju Juuiinmin Gonghwaguk Palmyonggongbo (Official Report of Inventions in the DPRK): Pyongyang; 6 a year.

Choson Munhak (Korean Literature): Pyongyang; organ of the Cen. Cttee of the Korean Writers' Union; monthly.

Choson Yesul (Korean Arts): Pyongyang; organ of the Cen. Cttee of the Gen. Fed. of Unions of Literature and Arts of Korea; monthly.

Economics: POB 73, Pyongyang; fax (2) 3814410; quarterly.

History: POB 73, Pyongyang; fax (2) 3814410; quarterly.

Hwahakgwa Hwahakgoneop: Pyongyang; organ of the Hamhung br. of the Korean Acad. of Sciences; chemistry and chemical engineering; 6 a year.

Jokook Tongil: Kangan 1-dong, Youth Ave, Songyo District, Pyongyang; organ of the Cttee for the Peaceful Unification of Korea; f. 1961; monthly; Chief Editor LI MYONG GYU; circ. 70,000.

Korean Medicine: POB 73, Pyongyang; fax (2) 3814410; quarterly.

Kunroja (Workers): 1 Munshindong, Tongdaewon, Pyongyang; f. 1946; organ of the Cen. Cttee of the Korean Workers' Party; monthly; Editor-in-Chief RYANG KYONG BOK; circ. 300,000.

Kwahakwon Tongbo (Bulletins of the Academy of Science): POB 73, Pyongyang; fax (2) 3814410; organ of the Standing Cttee of the Korean Acad. of Sciences; 6 a year.

Mulri (Physics): POB 73, Pyongyang; fax (2) 3814410; quarterly.

Munhwao Haksup (Study of Korean Language): POB 73, Pyongyang; fax (2) 3814410; publ. by the Publishing House of the Acad. of Social Sciences; quarterly.

Philosophy: PO Box 73, Pyongyang; fax (2) 3814410; quarterly.

Punsok Hwahak (Analysis): POB 73, Pyongyang; fax (2) 3814410; organ of the Cen. Analytical Inst. of the Korean Acad. of Sciences; quarterly.

Ryoksagwahak (Historical Science): Pyongyang; publ. by the Acad. of Social Sciences; quarterly.

Saengmulhak (Biology): POB, Pyongyang; fax (2) 3814410; publ. by the Korea Science and Encyclopedia Publishing House; quarterly.

Sahoekwahak (Social Science): Pyongyang; publ. by the Acad. of Social Sciences; 6 a year.

Suhakkwa Mulli: Pyongyang; organ of the Physics and Mathematics Cttee of the Korean Acad. of Sciences; quarterly.

FOREIGN LANGUAGE PUBLICATIONS

The Democratic People's Republic of Korea: Korea Pictorial, Pyongyang; f. 1956; illustrated news; Korean, Russian, Chinese, English, French, Arabic and Spanish edns; monthly; Editor-in-Chief HAN POM CHIK.

Foreign Trade of the DPRK: Foreign Trade Publishing House, Potonggang District, Pyongyang; economic developments and export promotion; English, French, Japanese, Russian and Spanish edns; monthly.

Korea: Pyongyang; f. 1956; illustrated; Korean, Arabic, Chinese, English, French, Spanish and Russian edns; monthly.

Korea Today: Foreign Languages Publishing House, Pyongyang; current affairs; Chinese, English, French, Russian and Spanish edns; monthly; Vice-Dir and Editor-in-Chief HAN PONG CHAN.

Korean Women: Pyongyang; English and French edns; quarterly.

Korean Youth and Students: Pyongyang; English and French edns; monthly.

The Pyongyang Times: Sochondong, Sosong District, Pyongyang; tel. (2) 51951; English, Spanish and French edns; weekly.

NEWS AGENCIES

Korean Central News Agency (KCNA): Potonggangdong 1, Potonggang District, Pyongyang; internet www.kcna.co.jp; f. 1946; sole distributing agency for news in the DPRK; publs daily bulletins in English, Russian, French and Spanish; Dir-Gen. KIM KI RYONG.

Foreign Bureaux

Informatsionnoye Telegrafnoye Agentstvo Rossii—Telegrafnoye Agentstvo Suverennykh Stran (ITAR—TASS) (Russia): Munsudong, Bldg 4, Flat 30, Taedongkang District, Pyongyang; tel. (2) 3817318; Correspondent ALEKSANDR VALIYEV.

The Xinhua (New China) News Agency (People's Republic of China) is also represented in the DPRK.

Press Association

Korean Journalists Union: Pyongyang; tel. (2) 36897; f. 1946; assists in the ideological work of the Korean Workers' Party; Chair. Cen. Cttee KIM SONG GUK.

Publishers

Academy of Sciences Publishing House: Nammundong, Central District, Pyongyang; tel. (2) 51956; f. 1953.

Academy of Social Sciences Publishing House: Pyongyang; Dir CHOE KWAN SHIK.

Agricultural Press: Pyongyang; labour, industrial relations; Pres. HO KYONG PIL.

Central Science and Technology Information Agency: Pyongyang; f. 1963; Dir RI JA BANG.

Education Publishing House: Pyongyang; f. 1945; Pres. KIM CHANG SON.

Foreign Language Press Group: Sochondong, Sosong District, Pyongyang; tel. (2) 841342; fax (2) 812100; f. 1949; Dir CHOE KYONG GUK.

Foreign Language Publishing House: Oesong District, Pyongyang; Dir SONG KI HYON.

Higher Educational Books Publishing House: Pyongyang; f. 1960; Pres. JU IL JUNG.

Industrial Publishing House: Pyongyang; f. 1948; technical and economic; Dir KIM TONG SU.

Kim Il Sung University Publishing House: Pyongyang; f. 1965.

Korea Science and Encyclopedia Publishing House: POB 73, Pyongyang; tel. (2) 18111; fax (2) 3814410; publishes numerous periodicals and monographs; f. 1952; Dir Gen. KIM YONG IL; Dir of International Co-operation JEAN BAHNG.

Korean People's Army Publishing House: Pyongyang; Pres. YUN MYONG DO.

Korean Social Democratic Party Publishing House: Pyongyang; tel. (2) 3818038; fax (2) 3814410; f. 1946; publishes quarterly journal *Joson Sahoemingjudang*(in Korean) and *KSDP Says*(in English); Dir CHOE WON JUN.

Korean Workers' Party Publishing House: Pyongyang; f. 1945; fiction, politics; Dir RYANG KYONG BOK.

Kumsong Youth Publishing House: Pyongyang; f. 1946; Dir HAN JONG SOP.

Literature and Art Publishing House: Pyongyang; f. by merger of Mass Culture Publishing House and Publishing House of the Gen. Fed. of Literary and Art Unions; Dir Gen. JO KYONG HWAN.

Transportation Publishing House: Namgyodong, Hyongjaesan District, Pyongyang; f. 1952; travel; Editor PAEK JONG HAN.

Working People's Organizations Publishing House: Pyongyang; f. 1946; fiction, government, political science; Dir PAK SE HYOK.

WRITERS' UNION

Korean Writers' Union: Pyongyang; Chair. Cen. Cttee KIM PYONG HUN.

Broadcasting and Communications

TELECOMMUNICATIONS

Korea Post and Telecommunications Co: Pyongyang; Dir KIM HYON JONG.

BROADCASTING

Regulatory Authorities

DPRK Radio and Television Broadcasting Committee: see Radio, below.

Pyongyang Municipal Broadcasting Committee: Pyongyang; Chair. KANG CHUN SHIK.

Radio

DPRK Radio and Television Broadcasting Committee: Jonsungdong, Moranbong District, Pyongyang; tel. (2) 3816035; fax (2) 3812100; programmes relayed nationally with local programmes supplied by local radio cttees; loudspeakers are installed in factories and in open spaces in all towns; home broadcasting 22 hours daily; foreign broadcasts in Russian, Chinese, English, French, German, Japanese, Spanish and Arabic; Chair. CHA SUNG SU.

Television

General Bureau of Television: Gen. Dir CHA SUNG SU.

DPRK Radio and Television Broadcasting Committee: see Radio.

Kaesong Television: Kaesong; broadcasts five hours on weekdays, 11 hours at weekends.

Korean Central Television Station: Ministry of Post and Telecommunications, Pyongyang; broadcasts five hours daily; satellite broadcasts commenced Oct. 1999.

Mansudae Television Station: Mansudae, Pyongyang; f. 1983; broadcasts nine hours of cultural programmes, music and dance, foreign films and news reports at weekends.

Finance

(cap. = capital; res = reserves; dep. = deposits; m. = million; brs = branches)

BANKING

During 1946–47 all banking institutions in North Korea, apart from the Central Bank and the Farmers Bank, were abolished. The Farmers Bank was merged with the Central Bank in 1959. The Foreign Trade Bank (f. 1959) conducts the international business of the Central Bank. Other banks, established in the late 1970s, are responsible for the foreign-exchange and external payment business of North Korean foreign trade enterprises.

The entry into force of the Joint-Venture Act in 1984 permitted the establishment of joint-venture banks, designed to attract investment into North Korea by Koreans resident overseas. The Foreign Investment Banking Act was approved in 1993.

Central Bank

Central Bank of the DPRK: Munsudong, Seungri St 58-1, Central District, Pyongyang; tel. (2) 3338196; fax (2) 3814624; f. 1946; bank of issue; supervisory and control bank; Pres. KIM WAN SU; 227 brs.

State Banks

Changgwang Credit Bank: Saemaeul 1-dong, Pyongchon District, Pyongyang; tel. (2) 18111; fax (2) 3814793; f. 1983; commercial, joint-stock and state bank; cap. 601.0m. won, res 1,194.2m. won, dep. 10,765.8m. won (Dec. 1997); Chair. KIM CHOL HWAN; Pres. KYE CHANG HO; 172 brs.

Credit Bank of Korea: Chongryu 1-dong, Munsu St, Otandong, Central District, Pyongyang; tel. (2) 3818285; fax (2) 3817806; f. 1986 as International Credit Bank, name changed 1989; Pres. LI SUN BOK; Vice-Pres. SON YONG SUN.

Foreign Trade Bank of the DPRK: FTB Bldg, Jungsongdong, Seungri St, Central District, Pyongyang; tel. (2) 3815270; fax (2) 3814467; f. 1959; deals in international settlements and all banking business; Pres. KIM JUN CHOL; 11 brs.

International Industrial Development Bank: Jongpyong-dong, Pyongchon District, Pyongyang; tel. (2) 3818610; fax (2) 3814427; f. 2001; Pres. SHIN DOK SONG.

Korea Daesong Bank: Segoridong, Gyongheung St, Potonggang District, Pyongyang; tel. (2) 3818221; fax (2) 3814576; f. 1978; Pres. RI HONG.

Koryo Bank: Ponghwadong, Potonggang District, Pyongyang; tel. (2) 3818168; fax (2) 3814033; f. 1989 as Koryo Finance Joint Venture Co, name changed 1994; co-operative, development, regional, savings and universal bank; Pres. RI CHANG HWAN; 10 brs.

Kumgang Bank: Jungsongdong, Central District, Pyongyang; tel. (2) 3818532; fax (2) 3814467; f. 1979; Chair. KIM JANG HO.

Joint-Venture Banks

Korea Commercial Bank: f. 1988; joint venture with Koreans resident in the USA.

Korea Joint Financial Co: f. 1988; joint venture with Koreans resident in the USA.

Korea Joint Bank: Ryugyongdong, Potonggang District, Pyongyang; tel. (2) 3818151; fax (2) 3814410; f. 1989; with co-operation of the Federation of Korean Traders and Industrialists in Japan; cap. US $1,932.5m. (1994); Chair PAK IL RAK; Vice-Pres. KIM SONG HWAN; 6 brs.

Korea Nagwon Joint Financial Co: f. 1987 by Nagwon Trade Co and a Japanese co.

Korea Rakwon Joint Banking Co: Pyongyang; Man. Dir HO POK DOK.

Korea United Development Bank: Central District, Pyongyang; tel. (2) 3814165; fax (2) 3814497; f. 1991; 51% owned by Zhongce Investment Corpn (Hong Kong), 49% owned by Osandok General Bureau; cap. US $60m. Pres. KIM SE HO.

Koryo Joint Finance Co: Pyongyang; Dir KIM YONG GU.

Foreign-Investment Banks

Golden Triangle Bank: Rajin-Sonbong Free Economic and Trade Zone; f. 1995.

Daesong Credit Development Bank: Potonggang Hotel, 301 Ansan-dong, Pyongchon District, Pyongyang; tel. (2) 3814866; fax (2) 3814723; f. 1996 as Peregrine-Daesong Development Bank; jt venture between Oriental Commercial Holdings Ltd (Hong Kong) and Korea Daesong Bank; Man. NIGEL COWIE.

INSURANCE

State Insurance Bureau: Central District, Pyongyang; tel. (2) 38196; handles all life, fire, accident, marine, hull insurance and reinsurance.

Korea Foreign Insurance Co (Chosunbohom): Central District, Pyongyang; tel. (2) 3818024; fax (2) 3814464; f. 1974; conducts marine, motor, aviation and fire insurance, reinsurance of all classes, and all foreign insurance; brs in Chongjin, Hungnam and Nampo, and agencies in foreign ports; overseas representative offices in Chile, France, Germany, Pakistan, Singapore; Pres. RI JANG SU.

Korea International Insurance Co: Pyongyang; Dir (vacant).

Korea Mannyon Insurance Co: Pyongyang; Pres. PAK IL HYONG.

Trade and Industry

GOVERNMENT AGENCIES

DPRK Committee for the Promotion of External Economic Co-operation: Jungsongdong, Central District, Pyongyang; tel. (2) 333974; fax (2) 3814498; Chair. KIM YONG SUL.

DPRK Committee for the Promotion of International Trade: Central District, Pyongyang; Pres. RI SONG ROK; Chair. KIM JONG GI.

Economic Co-operation Management Bureau: Ministry of Foreign Trade, Pyongyang; f. 1998; Dir KIM YONG SUL.

Korea International Joint Venture Promotion Committee: Pyongyang; Chair. RI KWANG GUN.

Korean Association for the Promotion of Asian Trade: Pyongyang; Pres. RI SONG ROK.

Korean International General Joint Venture Co: Pyongyang; f. 1986; promotes joint economic ventures with foreign countries; Man. Dir KANG JONG MO.

Korean General Merchandise Export and Import Corpn: Pyongyang.

INDUSTRIAL AND TRADE ASSOCIATIONS

Korea Building Materials Trading Co: Central District, Pyongyang; chemical building materials, woods, timbers, cement, sheet glass, etc; Dir SHIN TONG BOM.

Korea Cement Export Corpn: Central District, Pyongyang; f. 1982; cement and building materials.

Korea Cereals Export and Import Corpn: Central District, Pyongyang; high-quality vegetable starches, etc.

Korea Chemicals Export and Import Corpn: Central District, Pyongyang; petroleum and petroleum products, raw materials for the chemical industry, rubber and rubber products, fertilizers, etc.

Korea Daesong Jeil Trading Corpn: Potonggang District, Pyongyang; machinery and equipment, chemical products, textiles, agricultural products, etc.

Korea Daesong Jesam Trading Corpn: Potonggang District, Pyongyang; remedies for diabetes, tonics, etc.

Korea Ferrous Metals Export and Import Corpn: Potonggang District, Pyongyang; steel products.

Korea Film Export and Import Corpn: Daedongmundong, Central District, POB 113, Pyongyang; tel. (2) 180008034; fax (2) 3814410; f. 1956; feature films, cartoons, scientific and documentary films; Dir-Gen. CHOE HYOK U.

Korea First Equipment Export and Import Co: Central District, Pyongyang; tel. (2) 334825; f. 1960; export and import of ferrous and non-ferrous metallurgical plants, geological exploration and mining equipment, communication equipment, machine-building plant, etc. construction of public facilities such as airports, hotels, tourist facilities, etc. joint-venture business in similar projects; Pres. CHAE WON CHOL.

Korea Foodstuffs Export and Import Corpn: Tongdaewon District, Pyongyang; cereals, wines, meat, canned foods, fruits, cigarettes, etc.

Korea Fruit and Vegetables Export Corpn: Central District, Pyongyang; tel. (2) 35117; vegetables, fruit and their products.

Korea General Co for Economic Co-operation: Central District, Pyongyang; overseas construction, equipment for hydroelectric power plants, equipment for rice-cleaning mills.

Korea General Export and Import Corpn: Central District, Pyongyang; plate glass, tiles, granite, locks, medicinal herbs, foodstuffs and light industrial products.

Korea General Machine Co: Pyongyang; Dir RA IN GYUN.

Korea Hyopdong Trading Corpn: Central District, Pyongyang; fabrics, glass products, ceramics, chemical goods, building materials, foodstuffs, machinery, etc.

Korea Industrial Technology Co: Pyongyang; Pres. KWON YONG SON.

Korea International Chemical Joint Venture Co: Pyongyang; Chair. RYO SONG GUN.

Korea International Joint Venture Co: Pyongyang; Man. Dir HONG SONG NAM.

Korea Jangsu Trading Co: Potonggang District, Pyongyang; medicinal products and clinical equipment.

Korea Jeil Equipment Export and Import Corpn: Jungsongdong, Central District, Pyongyang; tel. (2) 334825; f. 1960; ferrous and non-ferrous metallurgical plant, geological exploration and mining equipment, power plant, communications and broadcasting equipment, machine-building equipment, railway equipment, construction of public facilities; Pres. CHO JANG DOK.

Korea Jesam Equipment Export and Import Corpn: Central District, Pyongyang; chemical, textile, pharmaceutical and light industry plant.

Korea Koryo Trading Corpn: Pyongyang; Dir KIM HUI DUK.

Korea Kwangmyong Trading Corpn: Central District, Pyongyang; dried herbs, dried and pickled vegetables; Dir CHOE JONG HUNG.

Korea Light Industry Import-Export Co: Juchetab St, Tongdaewon District, Pyongyang; tel. (2) 37661; exports silk, cigarettes, canned goods, drinking glasses, ceramics, handbags, pens, plastic flowers, musical instruments, etc. imports chemicals, dyestuffs, machinery, etc. Dir CHOE PYONG HYON.

Korea Machine Tool Trading Corpn: Pyongyang; Dir KIM KWANG RYOP.

Korea Machinery and Equipment Export and Import Corpn: Potonggang District, Pyongyang; tel. (2) 333449; f. 1948; metallurgical machinery and equipment, electric machines, building machinery, farm machinery, diesel engines, etc.

Korea Maibong Trading Corpn: Central District, Pyongyang; non-ferrous metal ingots and allied products, non-metallic minerals, agricultural and marine products.

Korea Manpung Trading Corpn: Central District, Pyongyang; chemical and agricultural products, machinery and equipment.

Korea Mansu Trading Corpn: Chollima St, Central District, POB 250, Pyongyang; tel. (2) 43075; fax (2) 812100; f. 1974; antibiotics, pharmaceuticals, vitamin compounds, drugs, medicinal herbs; Dir KIM JANG HUN.

Korea Marine Products Export and Import Corpn: Central District, Pyongyang; canned, frozen, dried, salted and smoked fish, fishing equipment and supplies.

Korea Minerals Export and Import Corpn: Central District, Pyongyang; minerals, solid fuel, graphite, precious stones, etc.

Korea Namheung Trading Co: Tongdaewon District, Pyongyang; high-purity reagents, synthetic resins, vinyl films, essential oils, menthol and peppermint oil.

Korea Non-ferrous Metals Export and Import Corpn: Potonggang District, Pyongyang.

Korea Okyru Trading Corpn: Central District, Pyongyang; agricultural and marine products, household goods, clothing, chemical and light industrial products.

Korea Ponghwa Contractual Joint Venture Co: Pyongyang; Dir RIM TONG CHON.

Korea Ponghwa General Trading Corpn: Central District, Pyongyang; machinery, metal products, minerals and chemicals.

Korea Publications Export and Import Corpn: Yokjondong, Yonggwang St, Central District, Pyongyang; tel. (2) 3818536; fax (2) 3814404; f. 1948; export of books, periodicals, postcards, paintings, cassettes, videos, CDs, CD-ROMs, postage stamps and records; import of books; Pres. RI YONG.

Korea Pyongchon Trading Co: Central District, Pyongyang; axles, springs, spikes, bolts and bicycles.

Korea Pyongyang Trading Co Ltd: Central District, POB 550, Pyongyang; pig iron, steel, magnesia clinker, textiles, etc.

Korea Rungra Co: Pyongyang; Dir CHOE HENG UNG.

Korea Rungrado Trading Corpn: Potonggang District, Pyongyang; food and animal products; Gen. Dir PAK KYU HONG.

Korea Ryongaksan General Trading Corpn: Pyongyang; Gen. Dir HAN YU RO.

Korea Samcholli General Corpn: Pyongyang; Dir JONG UN OP.

Korea Senbong Trading Corpn: Central District, Pyongyang; ferrous and non-ferrous metals, rolled steels, mineral ores, chemicals, etc.

Korea Somyu Hyopdong Trading Corpn: Oesong District, Pyongyang; clothing and textiles.

Korea Songhwa Trading Corpn: Oesong District, Pyongyang; ceramics, glass, hardware, leaf tobaccos, fruit and wines.

Korea Technology Corpn: Central District, Pyongyang; scientific and technical co-operation.

Korea Unha Trading Corpn: Tongdaewon District, Pyongyang; clothing and fibres.

Kwangmyong Trading Group of Korea: Pyongyang; Pres. CHOE JONG HUN.

TRADE UNIONS

General Federation of Trade Unions of Korea (GFTUK): POB 333, Pyongyang; fax (2) 3814427; f. 1945; 1.6m. mems (1986); six affiliated unions; Chair. RYOM SUN GIL.

  Metals, Engineering, Mining and Power Industries Workers' Union: Pyongyang; Chair. RI JU JIN.

  Light and Chemical Industries and Commerce Union: Pyongyang; Chair. MUN SOK NAM.

  Union of Public Employees: Pyongyang; Chair. PAK SEI HYOK.

  Union of Construction and Forestry Workers: Pyongyang; Chair. SON YONG JUN.

  Union of Educational and Cultural Workers: Pyongyang; Chair. PAK CHUN GEUN.

  Union of Transport Workers and Fishermen: Pyongyang; Chair. CHOE RYONG SU.

General Federation of Agricultural and Forestry Technique of Korea: Chung Kuyuck Nammundong, Pyongyang; f. 1946; 523,000 mems.

General Federation of Unions of Literature and Arts of Korea: Pyongyang; f. 1946; seven br. unions; Chair. Cen. Cttee CHANG CHOL.

Kim Il Sung Socialist Youth League: Pyongyang; fmrly League of Socialist Working Youth of Korea; First Sec. KIM GYONG HO.

Korean Architects' Union: Pyongyang; f. 1954; 500 mems; Chair. Cen. Cttee PAE TAL JUN.

Korean Democratic Lawyers' Association: Ryonhwa 1, Central District, Pyongyang; fax (2) 3814644; f. 1954; Chair. HAM HAK SONG.

Korean Democratic Scientists' Association: Pyongyang; f. 1956.

Korean Democratic Women's Union: Jungsongdong, Central District, Pyongyang; fax (2) 3814416; f. 1945; Chief Officer PAK SUN HUI.

Korean General Federation of Science and Technology: Jungsongdong, Seungri St, Central District, Pyongyang; tel. (2) 3224389; fax (2) 3814410; f. 1946; 550,000 mems; Chair. Cen. Cttee CHOE HUI JONG.

Korean Medical Association: Pyongyang; f. 1970; Chair. CHOE CHANG SHIK.

Union of Agricultural Working People of Korea: Pyongyang; f. 1965 to replace fmr Korean Peasants' Union; 2.4m. mems; Chair. Cen. Cttee SUNG SANG SOP.

Transport

RAILWAYS

Railways were responsible for some 62% of passenger journeys in 1991 and for some 74% of the volume of freight transported in 1997. At April 2000 the total length of track was 5,214 km, of which some 79% was electrified. There are international train services to Moscow (Russia) and Beijing (People's Republic of China). Construction work on the reconnection of the Kyongui (West coast, Sinuiju–Seoul) and East Coast Line (Wonsan–Seoul) began in September 2002; the former was expected to be completed by the end of that year, and the latter by September 2003. Reconnection work was subject to disruption by the changing political situation. Eventually the two would be linked to the Trans-China and Trans-Siberian railways respectively, greatly enhancing the region's transportation links.

There is an underground railway system in Pyongyang, comprising two lines with a combined length of 22 km. Unspecified plans to expand the system were announced in February 2002.

ROADS

In 2000, according to South Korean estimates, the road network totalled 23,407 km (of which only about 8% was paved), including 682 km of multi-lane highways.

INLAND WATERWAYS

The Yalu (Amnok-gang) and Taedong, Tumen and Ryesong are the most important commercial rivers. Regular passenger and freight services: Nampo–Chosan–Supung; Chungsu–Sinuiju–Dasado; Nampo–Jeudo; Pyongyang–Nampo.

SHIPPING

The principal ports are Nampo, Wonsan, Chongjin, Rajin, Hungnam, Songnim and Haeju. In 1997 North Korean ports had a combined capacity for handling 35m. tons of cargo. At 31 December 2001 North Korea's merchant fleet comprised 176 vessels, with a combined displacement of 697,804 grt.

Korea Chartering Corpn: Central District, Pyongyang; arranges cargo transportation and chartering.

Korea Daehung Shipping Co: Ansan 1–dong, Pyongchon District, Pyongyang; tel. (2) 18111 ext 8695; fax (2) 3814508; f. 1994; owns 6 reefers, 3 oil tankers, 1 cargo ship.

Korea East Sea Shipping Co: Pyongyang; Dir RI TUK HYON.

Korea Foreign Transportation Corpn: Central District, Pyongyang; arranges transportation of export and import cargoes (transit goods and charters).

Korean-Polish Shipping Co Ltd: Moranbong District, Pyongyang; tel. (2) 3814384; fax (2) 3814607; f. 1967; maritime trade mainly with Polish, Far East and DPRK ports.

Korea Tonghae Shipping Co: Changgwang St, Central District, POB 120, Pyongyang; tel. (2) 345805; fax (2) 3814583; arranges transportation by Korean vessels.

Ocean Maritime Management Co Ltd: Tonghungdong, Central District, Pyongyang.

Ocean Shipping Agency of the DPRK: Moranbong District, POB 21, Pyongyang; tel. (2) 3818100; fax (2) 3814531; Pres. O JONG HO.

CIVIL AVIATION

The international airport is at Sunan, 24 km from Pyongyang.

Chosonminhang/General Civil Aviation Bureau of the DPRK: Sunan Airport, Sunan District, Pyongyang; tel. (2) 37917; fax (2) 3814625; f. 1954; internal services and external flights by Air Koryo to Beijing and Shenyang (People's Republic of China), Bangkok (Thailand), Macao, Nagoya (Japan), Moscow, Khabarovsk and Vladivostok (Russia), Sofia (Bulgaria) and Berlin (Germany); charter services are operated to Asia, Africa and Europe; Pres. KIM YO UNG.

Tourism

The DPRK was formally admitted to the World Tourism Organization in 1987. Tourism is permitted only in officially accompanied parties. In 1999 there were more than 60 international hotels (including nine in Pyongyang) with 7,500 beds. Tourist arrivals totalled 128,000 in 1997. A feasibility study was undertaken in 1992 regarding the development of Mount Kumgang as a tourist attraction. The study proposed the construction of an international airport at Kumnan and of a number of hotels and leisure facilities in the Wonsan area. Local ports were also to be upgraded. It was hoped that the development, scheduled to cost some US $20,000m. and to be completed by 2004, would attract 3m. tourists to the area each year. In November 1998 some 800 South Korean tourists visited Mount Kumgang, as part of a joint venture mounted by the North Korean authorities and Hyundai, the South Korean conglomerate.

By November 2000 only 350,000 South Korean tourists had visited the attraction. In 1996 it was reported that proposals had been made to create a tourist resort in the Rajin-Sonbong Free Economic and Trade Zone, in the north-east of the country. It was announced that hotels to accommodate some 5,000 people were to be constructed, as well as an airport to service the area. There were reports in 1998 that a heliport had been opened in the Zone, and in 1999 the resort was completed. Mount Chilbo, Mount Kuwol, Mount Jongbang and the Ryongmum Cave were transformed into new tourist destinations in that year. In August 2000 plans were announced for the development, jointly with China, of the western part of Mount Paektu, Korea's highest mountain, as a tourist resort.

Korea International Tourist Bureau: Pyongyang; Pres. HAN PYONG UN.

Korean International Youth Tourist Co: Mankyongdae District, Pyongyang; tel. (2) 73406; f. 1985; Dir HWANG CHUN YONG.

Kumgangsan International Tourist Co: Central District, Pyongyang; tel. (2) 31562; fax (2) 3812100; f. 1988.

National Tourism Administration of the DPRK: Central District, Pyongyang; tel. (2) 3818901; fax (2) 3814547; e-mail nta@silibank.com; f. 1953; state-run tourism promotion organization; Dir RYO SUNG CHOL.

Ryohaengsa (Korea International Travel Company): Central District, Pyongyang; tel. (2) 3817201; fax (2) 3817607; f. 1953; has relations with more than 200 tourist companies throughout the world; Pres. CHO SONG HUN.

State General Bureau of Tourism: Pyongyang; Pres. RYO SUNG CHOL.

THE REPUBLIC OF KOREA

Introductory Survey

Location, Climate, Language, Religion, Flag, Capital

The Republic of Korea (South Korea) forms the southern part of the Korean peninsula, in eastern Asia. To the north, separated by a frontier which roughly follows the 38th parallel, is the country's only neighbour, the Democratic People's Republic of Korea (North Korea). To the west is the Yellow Sea, to the south is the East China Sea, and to the east is the Sea of Japan. The climate is marked by cold, dry winters, with an average temperature of –6°C (21°F), and hot, humid summers, with an average temperature of 25°C (77°F). The language is Korean. Confucianism, Mahayana Buddhism, and Chundo Kyo are the principal traditional religions. Chundo Kyo is peculiar to Korea, and combines elements of Shaman, Buddhist and Christian doctrines. There are some 17.5m. Christians, of whom about 83% are Protestants. The national flag (proportions 2 by 3) comprises, in the centre of a white field, a disc divided horizontally by an S-shaped line, red above and blue below, surrounded by four configurations of parallel, broken and unbroken black bars. The capital is Seoul.

Recent History

(For more details of the history of Korea up to 1953, including the Korean War, see the chapter on the Democratic People's Republic of Korea—DPRK.)

UN-supervised elections to a new legislature, the National Assembly (Kuk Hoe), took place in May 1948. The Assembly adopted a democratic Constitution, and South Korea became the independent Republic of Korea on 15 August 1948, with Dr Syngman Rhee, leader of the Liberal Party, as the country's first President. He remained in the post until his resignation in April 1960. Elections in July were won by the Democratic Party, led by Chang Myon, but his Government was deposed in May 1961 by a military coup, led by Gen. Park Chung-Hee. Power was assumed by the Supreme Council for National Reconstruction, which dissolved the National Assembly, suspended the Constitution and disbanded all existing political parties. In January 1963 the military leadership formed the Democratic Republican Party (DRP). Under a new Constitution, Gen. Park became President of the Third Republic in December.

Opposition to Park's regime led to the imposition of martial law in October 1972. A Constitution for the Fourth Republic, giving the President greatly increased powers, was approved by national referendum in November. A new body, the National Conference for Unification (NCU), was elected in December. The NCU re-elected President Park for a six-year term, and the DRP obtained a decisive majority in elections to the new National Assembly. In May 1975 opposition to the Government was effectively banned, and political trials followed. Elections to the NCU were held in May 1978, and the President was re-elected for a further six-year term in July. In October 1979 serious rioting erupted when Kim Young-Sam, the leader of the opposition New Democratic Party (NDP), was accused of subversive activities and expelled from the National Assembly. On 26 October Park was assassinated in an alleged coup attempt, led by the head of the Korean Central Intelligence Agency. Martial law was reintroduced (except on the island of Jeju), and in December the Prime Minister, Choi Kyu-Hah, was elected President by the NCU. Instability in the DRP and the army resulted in a military coup in December, led by the head of the Defence Security Command, Lt-Gen. Chun Doo-Hwan, who arrested the Army Chief of Staff and effectively took power. Nevertheless, President Choi was inaugurated on 21 December to complete his predecessor's term of office (to 1984).

Choi promised liberalizing reforms, but in May 1980 demonstrations by students and confrontation with the army led to the arrest of about 30 political leaders, including Kim Dae-Jung, former head of the NDP. Martial law was extended throughout the country, the National Assembly was suspended, and all political activity was banned. Almost 200 people were killed when troops stormed the southern city of Gwangju, which had been occupied by students and dissidents. In August Choi resigned, and Gen. Chun was elected President. Acting Prime Minister Nam Duck-Woo formed a new State Council (cabinet)

in September. In the same month the sentencing to death of Kim Dae-Jung for plotting rebellion was condemned internationally. (This sentence was subsequently suspended.) In October a new Constitution was overwhelmingly approved by referendum.

Martial law was ended in January 1981, and new political parties were formed. In the following month President Chun was re-elected: the start of his new term, in March, inaugurated the Fifth Republic. Chun's Democratic Justice Party (DJP) became the majority party in the new National Assembly, which was elected shortly afterwards. Amid opposition demands for liberalization, Chun pledged that he would retire at the end of his term in 1988, thus becoming the country's first Head of State to transfer power constitutionally.

During 1984, following an escalation of student unrest, the Government adopted a more flexible attitude towards dissidents. Several thousand prisoners were released, and the political 'blacklist' was finally abolished in March 1985. In January 1985 the New Korea Democratic Party (NKDP) was established by supporters of Kim Young-Sam and Kim Dae-Jung. At the general election to the National Assembly held in February, the DJP retained its majority, but the NKDP emerged as the major opposition force, boosted by the return from exile of Kim Dae-Jung. The new party secured 67 of the Assembly's 276 seats, while the DJP won 148 seats. Chun appointed a new State Council, with Lho Shin-Yong as Prime Minister. Before the opening session of the new National Assembly many deputies defected to the NKDP, increasing the party's strength to 102 seats.

In April 1987 internal divisions within the NKDP led to the formation of a new opposition party, the Reunification Democratic Party (RDP); Kim Young-Sam was elected to its presidency in May. In April Chun unexpectedly announced the suspension of the process of reform until after the Olympic Games (due to be held in Seoul in September 1988). While confirming that he would leave office in February 1988, Chun indicated that his successor would be elected by the existing electoral college system, precipitating violent clashes between anti-Government demonstrators and riot police.

In June 1987 Roh Tae-Woo was nominated as the DJP's presidential candidate. However, Roh subsequently informed Chun that he would relinquish both the DJP chairmanship and his presidential candidature if the principal demands of the opposition for constitutional and electoral reform were not satisfied. Under international pressure, Chun acceded, and negotiations on constitutional amendments were announced. In August the DJP and the RDP announced that a bipartisan committee had agreed a draft Constitution. Among its provisions were the reintroduction of direct presidential elections by universal suffrage, and the restriction of the presidential mandate to a single five-year term; the President's emergency powers were also to be reduced, and serving military officers were to be prohibited from taking government office. Having been approved by the National Assembly, the amendments were endorsed in a national referendum in October, and the amended Constitution was promulgated shortly thereafter.

Kim Dae-Jung joined the RDP in August 1987; in November, however, he became President of a new Peace and Democracy Party (PDP), and declared himself a rival presidential candidate. At the election, in December, Roh Tae-Woo won some 36% of the votes, while Kim Dae-Jung and Kim Young-Sam each achieved about 27%. Roh Tae-Woo was inaugurated as President on 25 February 1988, whereupon the Sixth Republic was established. At the general election to the National Assembly, in April, the DJP failed to achieve an overall majority, securing 125 of the 299 seats. The PDP achieved 70 seats, thus becoming the main opposition party; the remainder went to the RDP and the New Democratic Republican Party (NDRP—the revived and renamed DRP), led by Kim Jong-Pil.

During 1988 the Government granted greater autonomy to universities, permitted the formation of student associations, and eased restrictions on the press. The number of trade unions increased, and greater freedom to undertake foreign travel was granted to South Korean citizens.

In February 1990 the DJP merged with the RDP and the NDRP to form the Democratic Liberal Party (DLP). Roh was subsequently elected President of the DLP, while Kim Young-Sam and Kim Jong-Pil were elected as two of the party's three Chairmen. The DLP thus controlled more than two-thirds of the seats in the National Assembly. The PDP, effectively isolated as the sole opposition party, condemned the merger and demanded new elections. In March a new opposition group, the Democratic Party (DP), was formed, largely comprising members of the RDP who had opposed the merger.

In July 1990 a large rally was held in Seoul to denounce the adoption by the National Assembly of several items of controversial legislation, including proposals to restructure the military leadership and to reorganize the broadcasting media. Shortly afterwards all the opposition members of the National Assembly tendered their resignation, in protest at the legislation. Although the Assembly's Speaker refused to accept the resignations, the PDP deputies returned to the National Assembly only in November, following an agreement with the DLP that local council elections would take place in the first half of 1991, to be followed by gubernatorial and mayoral elections in 1992. The DLP also agreed to abandon plans for the transfer, by constitutional amendment, of executive powers to the State Council. The local elections (the first to be held in South Korea for 30 years) took place in March and June 1991, and resulted in a decisive victory for the DLP.

Meanwhile, in April 1991 the PDP merged with the smaller opposition Party for New Democratic Alliance to form the New Democratic Party (NDP). In September the NDP and the DP agreed to merge (under the latter's name) to form a stronger opposition front. A further opposition group, the Unification National Party (UNP), was established in January 1992 by Chung Ju-Yung, the founder and honorary chairman of the powerful Hyundai industrial conglomerate.

At elections to the National Assembly in March 1992 the DLP unexpectedly failed to secure an absolute majority, obtaining a total of 149 of the 299 seats. The remainder of the seats were won by the DP (97), the UNP (31) and independent candidates (21). In May Kim Young-Sam was chosen as the DLP's candidate for the presidential election, scheduled for December, and in August he replaced Roh as the party's President. Roh's decision to resign from the DLP altogether, in order to create a neutral government in anticipation of the election, was welcomed by opposition deputies. Serious divisions within the DLP led to defections from the party by opponents of Kim Young-Sam.

The presidential election, on 18 December 1992, was won by Kim Young-Sam, with some 42% of the votes cast. Kim (who was inaugurated on 25 February 1993) was the first South Korean President since 1960 without military connections. The defeated Kim Dae-Jung subsequently retired from political life. In February 1993 Chung Ju-Yung resigned as President of the United People's Party (UPP—as the UNP had been renamed), following allegations that he had embezzled Hyundai finances to fund his election campaign. Kim Young-Sam appointed Hwang In-Sung as Prime Minister, and a new State Council was formed.

Kim Young-Sam acted swiftly to honour his campaign pledge to eliminate corruption in business and political life; in all, during 1993, Kim's anti-corruption measures were reported to have resulted in the dismissal of, or disciplinary action against, some 3,000 business, government and military figures. One of Roh Tae Woo's former Ministers of National Defence, Lee Jong-Koo, was sentenced in November 1993 to three years' imprisonment, after having been convicted of accepting bribes from defence contractors. At the same time the announcement of measures to restrict the activities of the country's industrial conglomerates (*chaebol*) was accompanied by corruption proceedings against several prominent business executives. In November Chung Ju-Yung was sentenced to three years' imprisonment, although the sentence was suspended on account of his age (78) and past contribution to South Korea's economic development. Meanwhile, in August a presidential decree outlawed the opening of bank accounts under false names (a practice believed to have been used to conceal large-scale financial irregularities). In September the disclosure of the assets of some 1,500 public officials and the submission of these accounts for scrutiny by a government ethics committee prompted the resignation of several senior figures.

Hwang In-Sung resigned as Prime Minister in December 1993 and was succeeded by Lee Hoi-Chang, hitherto Chairman of the Board of Audit and Inspection (BAI). However, he resigned in

April 1994 and was replaced by Lee Yung-Duk, latterly the Deputy Prime Minister responsible for national unification.

In July 1994 the UPP and a smaller opposition party, the New Political Reform Party, merged to form the New People's Party (NPP). In October the Government announced that its inquiry into the role played by former Presidents Chun and Roh in the 1979 coup had found that both had participated in a 'premeditated military rebellion'. Prosecution proceedings were not initiated at this stage. In December 1994 Lee Hong-Koo (hitherto the Deputy Prime Minister responsible for national unification) was appointed Prime Minister, as part of a major restructuring of the State Council. Kim Deok, the new Deputy Prime Minister responsible for national unification, was obliged to resign in February 1995, following accusations that, in his former position as Director of the Agency for National Security Planning (South Korea's intelligence service), he had considered postponing the forthcoming local elections to allow for the revision of boundaries to the advantage of the DLP.

The DLP fared badly at elections for gubernatorial, mayoral and other municipal and provincial posts in May 1995 (the first full local elections to be held in South Korea for 34 years). A contributory factor to the DLP's poor performance was the success of a new party, the United Liberal Democrats (ULD), established in March by defectors from the DLP and led by Kim Jong-Pil (who had resigned as DLP Chairman earlier in the year). In September Kim Dae-Jung returned to political life, establishing his own party, the National Congress for New Politics (NCNP). The DP was severely undermined when many of its members left to join the NCNP.

A major scandal erupted in October 1995, when Roh Tae-Woo admitted in a televised address that he had amassed a large sum of money during his term of office. He was arrested in the following month; at his trial, which opened in December, Roh admitted to having received donations from South Korean businesses, but denied that these constituted bribes. Many senior political figures and business leaders were also detained and interrogated in connection with the affair. Kim Dae-Jung, meanwhile, unexpectedly admitted that his campaign for the 1992 presidential election had been supported by a donation of money from Roh's 'slush fund'. Kim Young-Sam denied opposition allegations that he too had benefited from a similar donation. In December 1995, in an effort to distance his party from the deepening scandal, Kim changed the DLP's name to the New Korea Party (NKP). A major reorganization of the State Council was effected, in which Lee Hong-Koo was replaced as Prime Minister by Lee Soo-Sung, the President of Seoul National University.

In late 1995 it was announced that Roh Tae-Woo and Chun Doo-Hwan were to be prosecuted for their involvement in the 1979 coup and 1980 Gwangju massacre. Chun was arrested in December 1995, and in the following month he was additionally accused of accumulating a huge political 'slush fund'. At the opening of his trial for corruption in February 1996 Chun denied charges that the fund had been amassed as a result of bribe-taking. Legal proceedings in connection with the events of 1979 and 1980 opened in March 1996: Chun was charged with mutiny for his organization of the 1979 coup, and with sedition in connection with the Gwangju massacre, while Roh was charged with aiding Chun. Meanwhile, also in March 1996, one of Kim Young-Sam's personal aides was arrested on bribery charges. Roh and Chun were convicted as charged in August. For their role in the *coup d'état* and Gwangju massacre, Chun was sentenced to death and Roh to 22½ years' imprisonment; each was heavily fined in the corruption cases. Several others were also convicted for their part in the events of 1979 and 1980. Following an appeal, in which their contribution to the country's impressive economic growth and to the establishment of democratic government were cited as mitigating factors, Chun's sentence was commuted to one of life imprisonment, while Roh's term of imprisonment was reduced to 17 years.

Elections to the National Assembly took place in April 1996. Contrary to widespread predictions, the NKP only narrowly failed to retain its parliamentary majority, winning a total of 139 of the 299 seats. One factor contributing to the NKP's success was believed to have been the recent incursions into the demilitarized zone (DMZ) by North Korean troops, which, although apparently intended to destabilize the electoral proceedings, in fact caused many voters to favour the ruling party out of concern for national security. The NCNP performed less well than had been expected, taking 79 seats; moreover, the party's leader, Kim Dae-Jung, failed to win a seat. The ULD obtained 50 seats and the DP only 15 (compared with 97 at the previous election); independent candidates won the remaining 16 seats. By the time the National Assembly convened in June, the NKP had secured a working majority with the support of several opposition and independent members. The opening of the Assembly was disrupted by opposition deputies, alleging electoral malpractice, but the boycott of the legislature was ended in July, following an agreement by the NKP to investigate the allegations.

The revision of South Korea's labour laws, with the aim of introducing greater flexibility into the labour market—a condition of the country's impending membership of the Organisation for Economic Co-operation and Development (OECD, see p. 277)—was initiated in May 1996. Disagreements over the extent of the labour reforms led to widespread strikes in the manufacturing industries in June. Reforms proposed by the Government in early December were severely criticized by trade unions and opposition parties. South Korea's principal workers' confederation, the Federation of Korean Trade Unions (FKTU), hitherto regarded as generally acquiescent to the Government, called a general strike in late December, after the Government convened a dawn session of the National Assembly, which approved the labour reform bill in the absence of opposition deputies. Controversial legislation was also passed to extend the powers of the Agency for National Security Planning. Many thousands of workers from key manufacturing industries, as well as public-sector employees, participated in the strike, which lasted for three weeks. Anti-Government demonstrators in Seoul and other major cities frequently clashed with riot police, and warrants were issued for the arrest of several leaders of the Korean Confederation of Trade Unions (KCTU), who were barricaded in the Roman Catholic Cathedral in Seoul. Concern was expressed that President Kim might be resorting to a more authoritarian style of leadership, particularly when it was alleged that North Korea was lending its support to the striking workers (a tactic used by the South Korean authorities in the past to justify the suppression of domestic dissent); furthermore, foreign labour officials, including a representative of OECD, were threatened with deportation for encouraging union action. By mid-January 1997 support for the strikes was abating; the KCTU proposed weekly one-day stoppages, in order to minimize financial losses, and suggested that it might accept a modification of the labour law, having previously insisted on its complete annulment. OECD issued a severe rebuke to the Government for failing to honour its pledges on the issue of labour reform, and, in a significant concession, Kim agreed to meet the leaders of the opposition parties to discuss amendments to the law; warrants for the arrest of union leaders were also suspended. In March the National Assembly approved a revised version of the legislation, whereby the implementation of certain proposals was delayed for two years, while the KCTU was granted immediate official recognition.

Meanwhile, political and economic scandals persisted throughout 1996, particularly concerning allegations of bribery, which resulted in several government resignations. The infiltration of a North Korean submarine into South Korean waters in September (see below) resulted in the dismissal of the Minister of Defence, Lee Yang-Ho. He was subsequently charged with divulging classified information and with receiving bribes in connection with the procurement of helicopters for the army, and in December was sentenced to four years' imprisonment. In January 1997 a further major scandal erupted when Hanbo, one of South Korea's largest steel and construction conglomerates, was declared bankrupt. Allegations were made that Hanbo had bribed the Government to exert pressure on banks to provide substantial loans to the conglomerate. The chief executives of several large Korean banks were arrested on charges of receiving bribes, and in February the Minister of Home Affairs, Kim Woo-Suk, resigned following allegations that he too had accepted payments from the company. President Kim issued an official apology for the loan scandal, and in March Lee Soo-Sung resigned as Prime Minister in a gesture of contrition. He was replaced by Goh Kun, hitherto President of Myongju University. In May the President's son, Kim Hyun-Chul, was arrested on charges of tax evasion and accepting bribes in return for influencing official appointments. The repercussions of the Hanbo affair widened further, implicating, among others, Kim Soo-Han, the Speaker of the National Assembly, and President Kim himself, whose 1992 election campaign was alleged to have been funded partially by the conglomerate. Kim Hyun-Chul was, however, formally cleared of any involvement. In June 1997 the former Chairman of Hanbo and several senior banking officials and politicians, including Kim Woo-Suk, were convicted on charges relating to the scandal.

In July 1997 Lee Hoi-Chang, former Prime Minister and Chairman of the NKP, was nominated as the ruling party's candidate for the presidential election, scheduled for December. Lee's candidacy was severely affected by various scandals surrounding the NKP and his family. Moreover, Rhee In-Je, the defeated challenger in the contest for the NKP nomination, decided to contest the presidency, subsequently forming his own political organization, the New Party by the People. In September Lee was elected President of the NKP, replacing Kim Young-Sam, who subsequently resigned from the party in order to ensure his neutrality in the forthcoming election. In October the NCNP and the ULD established an alliance, formulating a joint programme of proposed constitutional amendments and uniting behind the NCNP presidential nominee, Kim Dae-Jung, with the ULD to propose the Prime Minister in the event of victory. The conviction of Kim Hyun-Chul in October on charges of bribery and tax evasion was a further reverse for the NKP, which, in November, announced its merger with the DP, to form the Grand National Party (GNP).

Internal party politics were, however, overshadowed by the crisis experienced by the Korean economy in the latter half of 1997. Many of the conglomerates (*chaebol*) reported serious financial difficulties, having amassed huge debts which they were subsequently unable to service. Measures aimed at stabilizing the financial markets, announced in October, were unsuccessful. Moreover, in an unexpected reversal of its non-interventionist policy, the Government declared that part of the Kia Group, which was close to collapse, was to be nationalized, in an attempt to prevent further bankruptcies. Following the rejection by the legislature of the Government's financial liberalization measures, President Kim dismissed Kang Kyung-Shik, the Deputy Prime Minister and Minister of Finance and the Economy, in November, replacing him with Lim Chang-Yul, latterly Minister of Trade, Industry and Energy. An extensive economic stabilization programme, announced shortly afterwards, had little effect in curbing the depreciation of the national currency, the won, and the Government was forced to request the assistance of the IMF. This recourse to the IMF was condemned by opposition politicians and the media as a 'national shame'. The true extent of South Korea's economic crisis, described as the most serious in the country's history, became apparent upon the conclusion of negotiations with the IMF in early December 1997. In the IMF's largest ever rescue programme, worth US $57,000m., funds were to be allocated to prevent South Korea from defaulting on its repayments of external debt. Provision of the loans remained conditional upon the implementation of a programme of extensive financial and economic reforms.

The presidential election, held on 18 December 1997, was narrowly won by Kim Dae-Jung. Supporters of the ruling NKP were divided between Lee Hoi-Chang and Rhee In-Je, thus assuring victory for the NCNP-ULD alliance and the first peaceful transfer of power to an opposition politician in South Korea's history. Four other candidates contested the election. In a gesture to promote a sense of national unity, former Presidents Chun Doo-Hwan and Roh Tae-Woo were granted a presidential pardon and released from prison.

Legislation for financial reforms, to comply with the terms of the IMF agreement, was approved by the National Assembly in late December 1997. Discussions held throughout January 1998 with South Korea's overseas creditors to renegotiate the terms of the country's debt repayments were successfully concluded at the end of the month. An agreement was reached with labour leaders and business executives in early February to legalize redundancies (in return for which social welfare provisions would be improved); to permit unions to engage in political activities; and to allow state-employed teachers to form trade unions. Compulsory reform of the *chaebol*, which had been widely criticized for contributing to the debt-repayment crisis through their extensive borrowing, and legislation to allow foreign investors to acquire majority shareholdings in South Korean companies, were among reform measures promulgated in early 1998.

In addition to economic reform proposals, procedures to implement wide-ranging administrative reforms, including a reduction in government bureaucracy, were under discussion by the incoming leadership in early 1998. Constitutional amendments, including the replacement of the President by the Prime Minister as head of the Government, were also under consideration. Kim Dae-Jung was formally inaugurated as President in late February 1998. Despite resistance from the opposition, Kim Dae-Jung designated Kim Jong-Pil, the leader of the ULD, as acting Prime Minister, and a Cabinet was formed in early March, with the ministries divided equally between the NCNP and the ULD. Various administrative reforms were implemented, including the abolition of the two posts of Deputy Prime Minister, the merger of the Ministries for Home Affairs and Government Administration and a reduction in the powers of the Ministry of Finance and the Economy. The number of cabinet ministers was reduced to 17 (excluding the Prime Minister).

At the beginning of May 1998 a large rally organized by the KCTU in protest at job losses ended in violent clashes with riot police. Later that month a two-day strike was called to demand that the Government fully honour its pledge to improve unemployment benefits and to reform the *chaebol*; according to the KCTU, some 120,000 workers supported the first day of the strike. The NCNP and the ULD performed well in local elections in June, although the turn-out was low. As the economic recession deepened, with the unemployment rate rising above 7%, labour unrest increased. Tens of thousands participated in strikes in July to protest against unemployment, the Government's privatization proposals and plans from Hyundai Motor and Daewoo Motor for mass redundancies.

In August 1998 the National Assembly formally confirmed Kim Jong-Pil as Prime Minister, following months of legislative inactivity, during which the GNP had refused to support his nomination. The GNP, however, boycotted parliamentary sessions throughout September and into October, further delaying the consideration of urgent economic reforms, in protest at a government anti-corruption campaign, which it claimed was partisan and aimed at dividing the opposition. Several GNP members were placed under investigation on suspicion of illegally raising electoral campaign funds. In late October three former aides to Lee Hoi-Chang were charged in connection with an alleged attempt to bribe North Korean officials to organize a border incursion into the DMZ in December 1997, with the aim of aiding Lee's campaign for the presidency. The dispute escalated in December 1998, when a number of opposition deputies entered a room in the assembly buildings, which was being used by the intelligence agency, and removed confidential documents on 44 political figures. The GNP claimed that the agency had been carrying out surveillance of opposition deputies and subsequently boycotted legislative proceedings. In early January 1999, as the boycott continued, the ruling parties unilaterally passed 130 bills without debate, including legislation on banking reform and the endorsement of a controversial fishing agreement with Japan (see below). In mid-January, however, the ruling and opposition parties agreed that all issues relating to the affair be referred to the National Assembly's steering committee.

Tension arose within the ruling coalition in January 1999, when NCNP leaders proposed the postponement of plans for the introduction of a parliamentary, rather than presidential, system of government, with the Prime Minister assuming more power, as favoured by the ULD. Kim Young-Sam, who had refused to testify, was held responsible for the 1997 financial crisis in a report that was issued on the findings of parliamentary hearings held throughout February 1999. Meanwhile, the KCTU withdrew from a tripartite committee on management, labour and government (which had been established in early 1998), demanding an end to mass redundancies, a reduction in working hours and an improvement in the welfare system for the unemployed.

In late May 1999 a major reshuffle of the State Council was effected; an additional ministry was also created by the elevation to ministerial status of the Planning and Budget Commission. Kang Bong-Kyun, regarded as a strong advocate of reform, was appointed to the post of Minister of Finance and the Economy. In June, however, corruption scandals led to the replacement of two of the new ministers, and were believed to have contributed to the ruling coalition's failure to retain two parliamentary seats in by-elections held that month. Kim Tae-Joung, the Minister of Justice, was dismissed over allegations that, during his tenure as Prosecutor-General, a subordinate had encouraged a strike at a state-managed corporation. (An accusation that the minister's wife had accepted a gift from the wife of an insurance tycoon being investigated on allegations of fraud had also prompted demands for his dismissal.) Later that

month the new Minister of the Environment, Son Suk, an actress, resigned amid controversy over her acceptance of a gift of money during a recent theatre performance. In July Kim Dae-Jung and Kim Jong-Pil agreed not to seek a constitutional amendment on the adoption of a parliamentary system of government in 1999, despite protests from several senior ULD members.

Preparations for legislative elections (scheduled for April) dominated internal politics in early 2000. In January Kim Jong-Pil resigned as Prime Minister to chair the ULD, nominating Park Tae-Joon, the founder of Pohang Iron and Steel Company (the world's largest steel producer), as his successor. Kim Dae-Jung reshuffled the State Council, as a number of ministers resigned to concentrate on campaigning for parliamentary seats. Lee Hun-Jai, hitherto the Chairman of the Financial Supervisory Commission, was appointed as Minister of Finance and the Economy. There was speculation that by the appointments of Park and Lee, shortly before the elections, the ruling parties hoped to remind voters of the Government's relative success in overcoming the severe economic problems experienced by South Korea in 1997–98. Later in January 2000 Kim Dae-Jung established a new party, the Millennium Democratic Party (MDP), to succeed the ruling NCNP, having reportedly failed in attempts to effect a merger with the ULD. Meanwhile, civic groups exerting pressure on the main political parties to reform were receiving considerable popular support, in what was perceived as a reflection of increasing public discontent with South Korean party politics, following months of legislative inactivity. A grouping of some 470 civic organizations, styled the Citizens' Alliance for the 2000 General Elections, published a list of politicians whom it considered unfit to stand in the elections, largely on grounds of alleged corruption and incompetence. The ULD condemned the inclusion of Kim Jong-Pil on the list, accusing the MDP of involvement in its compilation. In February the National Assembly approved revisions to the election law, which reduced the number of legislative seats from 299 to 273 (227 directly elected and 46 allocated by proportional representation), and reversed a ban on campaigning by civic groups against candidates. A proposal by the MDP for the introduction of a two-ballot system was rejected by the National Assembly; the ULD was believed to have voted with the opposition GNP against its coalition partner. Lee Han-Dong, recently elected as President of the ULD, subsequently announced the party's withdrawal from the ruling coalition, claiming that the MDP had failed to fulfil its electoral pledges, although Prime Minister Park was to remain in the Government.

The elections to the National Assembly were held on 13 April 2000. The GNP, which won 133 of the 273 seats, retained its position as the largest party in the Assembly, but remained four seats short of a majority. The ruling MDP secured 115 seats, while the ULD suffered a serious reverse, taking only 17 seats (compared with 50 in the 1996 elections). Only two seats were won by the Democratic People's Party, which had been formed in February by defectors from the GNP who had failed to be nominated as parliamentary candidates by their former party. The New Korea Party of Hope won one seat, and independents five. In mid-May Park resigned as Prime Minister, amid increasing controversy over allegations of tax evasion. The designation of Lee Han-Dong as Park's successor indicated a restoration of MDP-ULD co-operation. Furthermore, the MDP's Lee Man-Sup was elected as Speaker of the National Assembly in early June, with the support of the ULD, the two smallest parliamentary parties and independents.

Amid criticism that reform of the *chaebol* was proceeding too slowly, Kim Dae-Jung effected a major government reorganization in August 2000, which primarily concerned the economic portfolios. Notably, Lee Hun-Jai was dismissed as Minister of Finance and was replaced by Jin Nyum, hitherto Minister of Planning and Budget. Later that month Song Ha resigned as Minister of Education following allegations of serious irregularities in his financial affairs.

While President Kim enjoyed increasing admiration and respect within the international community, in October 2000 being awarded the Nobel Peace Prize for his contribution to democracy and human rights (and particularly for his successful attempts at reconciliation with the Democratic People's Republic of Korea), his pursuit of reunification was criticized domestically by those who felt that South Korea, confronted by its own economic problems, could ill afford assistance to its northern neighbour, which was not perceived to be reciprocating in a magnanimous manner.

In November 2000 Kim Yong-Kap, a GNP member of the National Assembly, described the ruling MDP as a 'subsidiary of the North Korean KWP (Korean Workers' Party)'. The comments shocked and embarrassed both the MDP and the GNP, and the National Assembly was suspended. On the following day talks between the two parties were held, and it was agreed that the National Assembly would reconvene that evening, when the GNP would make a public apology for Kim's remarks and would strike them from the parliamentary record. Shortly after the legislature reconvened, however, the GNP walked out in protest at an MDP motion to dismiss Kim from his seat. A few days later there was renewed tension in the National Assembly as the GNP walked out again, this time prompted by the MDP's obstruction of a motion to impeach the Prosecutor-General, Park Soon-Yong, for alleged bias in the investigation of irregularities during the April elections. The GNP returned to the session one week later, citing the need for the Assembly to work to resolve the increasing economic difficulties and social instability. In December Kim Dae-Jung effected leadership changes in the MDP. Kim Joong-Kwon, Secretary to the President, was appointed Chairman in place of Suh Young-Hoon, who had resigned, and Park Sang-Kyu assumed the role of Secretary-General. Kim Dae-Jung rejected suggestions, both within and outside the party, that as Head of State he should relinquish the post of MDP President.

During 2000 and early 2001 dissatisfaction with the Government manifested itself on numerous occasions in the form of industrial and agricultural unrest. In late June 2000 doctors throughout South Korea participated in a strike to demonstrate their opposition to legislation depriving physicians of the right to prescribe drugs (which had been intended to restrict excessive prescription of medication and alleged profiteering by doctors). Several deaths were linked to the strike, which ended five days later following an offer by the Government to revise the legislation in July. Further action took place, however, in October, as a satisfactory compromise had not been reached. Mounting public anger obliged the abandonment of the renewed strike. In the following month farmers held a strike to demand that their debts be cancelled and that the Government intervene on their behalf at the World Trade Organization (WTO, see p. 323). Meanwhile, as the Daewoo Motor Company had been declared bankrupt, compounding anxieties for the future of other *chaebol*, some 15,000 workers protested in November 2000 in Seoul against government-led corporate restructuring which would result, it was feared, in large-scale retrenchment. Several more strikes in various sectors took place in late 2000, arising from fears of mass unemployment.

In January 2001 the State Council approved legislation providing for debt-relief loans to farmers and fishermen. At the end of that month a minor reorganization of the State Council was effected, when changes included Jin Nyum's elevation to the post of Deputy Prime Minister for Finance and the Economy. It was believed that the promotion would give Jin increased power to revitalize economic reform. Simultaneously, a government organization law came into effect that conferred the status of Deputy Prime Minister on the portfolios of Finance and Economy and of Education and Human Resources. Han Wang-Sang assumed the latter position. A Ministry of Gender Equality was also created, for which Han Myong-Sook was allocated responsibility. In late March there was a major reorganization of the State Council, following the resignation of the Minister of Foreign Affairs and Trade, Lee Joung-Binn, who had caused controversy by signing a joint statement with Russia criticizing the USA's planned 'national missile defence' (NMD) system. Han Seung-Soo, a member of the Democratic People's Party, replaced him. Lim Dong-Won, hitherto Chairman of the National Intelligence Service, was appointed Minister of Unification. He was widely recognized as having played a major role in Korean reunification efforts. Other changes included the replacement of the Ministers of National Defence and of Construction and Transportation. It was thought that the reshuffle was an attempt by President Kim to improve the public image of the Government, in the face of widespread dissatisfaction over its handling of economic and health reforms. The former Minister of Culture, Park Jie-Won, who had resigned in September 2000 following allegations of corruption, was appointed chief presidential policy adviser. Park had organized the historic inter-Korean summit in June 2000 (see below), and his appointment to this post reaffirmed Kim Dae-Jung's commitment to his 'sunshine' policy.

In early April 2001 the minor opposition Democratic People's Party joined the ruling MDP-led coalition, despite protests from within the MDP. Later that month the MDP suffered a defeat in local by-elections, and by May Kim Dae-Jung's popularity had fallen sharply, as voters grew disillusioned by his failure to implement political reforms. President Kim had also received criticism for his appointment of ministers and advisers from his home region of Jeolla, in the south-west, thereby antagonizing the south-eastern Gyeongsang region. In late May the newly appointed Minister of Justice, Ahn Dong-Soo, was forced to resign after having apparently pledged to support the MDP's forthcoming presidential election campaign. The pledge was embarrassing because it suggested that the leading investigative agencies were being manipulated against political opponents. Ahn was replaced by Choi Kyung-Won.

In June 2001 the KCTU organized a national strike involving 55,000 workers from 125 trade unions, who were protesting against decreasing wages and worsening working conditions. The strikes were joined by thousands of nurses and also airline pilots and ground staff, but denounced by President Kim as illegal. At the same time the country experienced its worst drought since 1904, adversely affecting agriculture and necessitating the mobilization of 130,000 troops to the most badly-stricken areas. The drought was followed by the worst floods in 37 years.

In July 2001 the Government's campaign against the alleged tax evasion and other financial dealings of the country's 23 news organizations (including major newspapers) led to accusations that President Kim was trying to stifle the media; one newspaper in particular, *Chosun Ilbo*, had been highly critical of Kim and his 'sunshine' policy. The National Tax Service had imposed fines totalling US $388m. in late June following a four-month investigation, which Kim defended as being part of ongoing anti-corruption campaigns but which opposition parties attributed to attempts by the MDP to boost its chances of winning the 2002 presidential election. Opinion polls showed the public to be generally supportive of the investigations and sceptical about the media, itself perceived as corrupt. In late August the owners of three newspapers, including *Chosun Ilbo*, were arrested for tax evasion.

Also in August 2001 the Minister of Construction and Transportation, Oh Jang-Seop, resigned after the US Federal Aviation Administration (FAA) downgraded the safety rating of South Korea's two main airlines and prevented them from flying to the USA. At the same time, Minister of Unification Lim Dong-Won came under heavy criticism from the opposition after delegates from several South Korean non-governmental organizations (NGOs) travelled to the North to mark the anniversary of Korean liberation from Japanese rule, on 15 August. In early September Lim was forced to resign after the National Assembly approved a motion of no-confidence in him, organized by the GNP and supported by the MDP's coalition partner, the ULD. The latter's actions effectively dissolved the ruling coalition, and President Kim appointed four new ministers: of Labour; Agriculture and Forestry; Construction and Transportation; and Maritime Affairs and Fisheries. In addition, Hong Soon-Young, hitherto ambassador to China, was appointed Minister of Unification. Lim was immediately appointed presidential adviser on reunification, national security and foreign affairs, reaffirming Kim's confidence in him. At the end of the month the new Minister of Construction and Transportation, Ahn Jung-Nam, resigned citing health reasons, and was replaced by Lim In-Taik. However, Ahn had been accused of corruption by the opposition.

In late October 2001 the GNP won three by-elections, increasing its seats in the National Assembly to 136—just one short of a majority. The opposition victory created new rifts within the ruling MDP between younger reformers and party veterans, and President Kim subsequently resigned from the party presidency in early November, ostensibly in order to administer state affairs without being involved in party disputes. He was succeeded, on an interim basis, by Han Kwang-Ok. Further infighting in the MDP ensued as senior party officials sought to strengthen their positions with a view to securing the party presidential nomination for the 2002 election. At the same time Park Jie-Won, the senior secretary for policy planning and a close aide of the president, also resigned. By early December some eight presidential candidates had emerged within the MDP and were forming political support networks.

In early January 2002 the MDP announced that it would hold a primary election in April to select its presidential candidate.

Also at this time, President Kim's reputation suffered a set-back when his nominee for the head of the newly created Presidential Commission for Anti-corruption, Kim Sung-Nam, was himself linked to a spy scandal in the 1980s.

In late January 2002 President Kim again reorganized the State Council , dismissing Minister of Unification Hong Soon-Young and reallocating seven other posts, as well as the positions of six of the eight senior presidential secretaries and his chief of staff. Hong was succeeded by Jeong Se-Hyun, hitherto a special assistant to the director of the National Intelligence Service (NIS), while Jeon Yun-Churl, hitherto Minister of Planning and Budget was appointed chief presidential secretary (chief of staff). Jeon was succeeded in his previous post by Chang Seung-Woo. Park Jie-Won returned as Kim's special aide for policy, emphasizing his close relationship with the President. The changes were intended to strengthen Kim's authority during his final year in office. Within days, the Minister of Foreign Affairs and Trade, Han Seung-Soo, was also dismissed, owing to Seoul's strained relations with the USA, and replaced by Choi Sung-Hong, hitherto Vice-Minister.

The contest for the MDP's presidential nomination intensified during February 2002 as putative reformist candidates sought to present a joint candidate, and opponents of the leading contender, Rhee In-Je, moved against him. The opposition GNP also experienced a power struggle, resulting in the party Vice-President, Park Geun-Hye (daughter of former military ruler Park Chung-Hee), leaving the party later in the month, initially with the intention of standing for the presidency as an independent candidate. Her decision undermined the chances of Lee Hoi-Chang, who had been leading in the opinion polls, and threatened to precipitate a political realignment. In May Park established a new party, the Korean Coalition for the Future (KCF), serving as its chairwoman.

Meanwhile, in late February 2002 the country suffered another general strike, by thousands of railway and energy workers, who were protesting against privatization plans and shortened working hours. In early April the KCTU cancelled a major strike after reaching a settlement with the Government. The KCTU leadership subsequently resigned *en masse*, following criticism that it had made too many concessions to the Government. However, limited strike action continued in May.

By late April 2002 Roh Moo-Hyun had secured the MDP presidential nomination, while the GNP remained mired in internal disputes; the party's eight vice-presidents all resigned on 24 March in order to 'renew the face of the party', and were succeeded by a collective leadership. Meanwhile, Lee Hoi-Chang had secured the GNP's nomination for the national presidency. Also in mid-April President Kim replaced the Deputy Prime Minister for Finance and the Economy, Jin Nyum, with Jeon Yun-Churl, hitherto the chief of staff to the President. Jeon was succeeded by Park Jie-Won.

In early May 2002 President Kim and six of his ministers resigned from the MDP in order to focus on state affairs during the final months of Kim's presidency. By that time, Kim had become increasingly embarrassed by the corruption scandals involving his second and third sons, Kim Hong-Up and Kim Hong-Gul respectively, and he publicly apologized for their behaviour. In early June Kim Hong-Gul was charged with bribery and tax evasion, and subsequently went on trial. Kim Hong-Up was arrested later that month, accused of receiving bribes from businessmen. A nephew of the President's wife, Lee Hyung-Taek, was also sentenced for receiving bribes. The scandals adversely affected the MDP's performance in local elections held in mid-June, in which the party secured only four posts (three of which were in Jeolla, its traditional support base), while the GNP won 11 posts and the ULD one post.

In early July 2002 President Kim reorganized the cabinet, appointing Chang Sang, hitherto President of Ewha Woman's University, as the country's first female Prime Minister. At the same time, six ministers were replaced. Notable new appointments were Lee Jun, a retired general, as Minister of National Defence, Kim Jung-Kil as Minister of Justice, and Kim Jin-Pyo as Minister of Government Policy Co-ordination. However, at the end of that month the National Assembly rejected Chang's appointment on the grounds of questionable property dealings and the fact that her son had adopted US citizenship. In her place, President Kim nominated Chang Dae-Whan, a former newspaper proprietor, but he too was rejected by the National Assembly in late August on the grounds of questionable financial practices. In September Kim nominated Kim Suk-Soo, a former Supreme Court judge and former Head of the National

Election Commission, as his candidate for the post of Prime Minister, and he was accepted by the National Assembly in early October, thus ending months of political paralysis.

Meanwhile, the popularity of Roh Moo-Hyun deteriorated so significantly after his nomination for the presidency that members of the MDP considered replacing him altogether. The MDP also suffered further set-backs in by-elections held in early August 2002 when the GNP won 11 out of 13 seats contested, giving it an overall majority in the National Assembly. In September Chung Mong-Joon, the sixth son of Hyundai founder Chung Ju-Yung, and who was also an independent legislator, President of the Korean Football Association and Vice-President of FIFA (the international football federation), announced that he was standing for the country's presidency. Chung's popularity had risen sharply following South Korea's successful co-hosting of the 2002 football World Cup and had surpassed that of Roh. In early November Chung formally launched his 'National Unity 21' party, receiving support from a broad political spectrum, including defectors from the MDP. However, later in that month Chung moved closer to Roh, and the two agreed to present a joint candidate for the presidency, namely Roh, in order to prevent Lee Hoi-Chang's election as President in December. Under the terms of the Roh-Chung partnership, there was to be a constitutional amendment whereby the powers of the presidency would be reduced in favour of those of the Prime Minister. A similar arrangement had been agreed between Kim Dae-Jung and Kim Jong-Pil in 1997 but never implemented.

The final months of 2002 witnessed the ruling MDP mired in further scandals. In October it emerged that President Kim and Chung Mong-Joon had arranged for a Hyundai subsidiary to transfer US \$200m. to North Korea via the (Southern) state-owned Korea Development Bank prior to the historic inter-Korean summit of June 2000 (see below), effectively 'buying' the meeting. Furthermore, Kim Hong-Up was sentenced to three-and-a-half years' imprisonment in early November for accepting bribes. Kim Hong-Gul was also sentenced, separately, to two years' imprisonment (with three years' suspension) for bribery and tax evasion. Both received heavy fines, and their convictions further undermined President Kim and the MDP.

None the less, the presidential election, held on 19 December 2002, was narrowly won by Roh Moo-Hyun, who received 48.9% of the votes cast, against Lee Hoi-Chang's 46.6%. Roh's victory came despite the last-minute withdrawal of Chung Mong-Joon's support, for which the latter subsequently apologized. It was generally acknowledged that Roh's victory was due to his uncompromising stance in favour of a foreign policy more independent from the USA, whereas Lee was widely seen as having very close relations with Washington, DC. The MDP in early December accused the USA of supporting Lee in the election, citing a meeting between him and the US ambassador. Relations with the USA (see below) had become a major election issue, as anti-American sentiment increased following several incidents involving US servicemen, and differences between the two countries emerged over how to resolve tensions with the North. As with past presidential elections, regionalism was manifested strongly in voting patterns, with some pro-Roh regions (Jeolla) voting 92% in his favour, while some pro-Lee regions (Gyeong-sang) voted 78% in his favour. Support for the two main candidates also indicated the emergence of a generational gap, with younger voters favouring Roh, while older voters supported Lee. Kwon Young-Gil of the Democratic Labour Party came a distant third, with 3.9% of the votes cast. The level of participation was estimated at 70.8%. Following his defeat, Lee Hoi-Chang retired from politics

In January 2003 President-elect Roh began making appointments to his new Government. Goh Kun, hitherto the president of Transparency International Korea, an anti-corruption agency, and himself a former Prime Minister, was reappointed to that post. Moon Hee-Sang, an MDP legislator, was appointed chief of staff, and concurrently Chairman of the Civil Service Commission, while Ryu In-Tae, a former legislator, was named presidential secretary for political affairs. Ra Jong-Yil, hitherto ambassador to the United Kingdom, was appointed national security adviser. President Kim meanwhile dissolved his *Donggyo-dong* faction of MDP loyalists in preparation for the transfer of power. Roh himself was inaugurated on 25 February 2003 and promptly appointed a new cabinet. Notable appointments included Kim Jin-Pyo as Deputy Prime Minister for Finance and Economy, Yoon Deok-Hong, hitherto President of Daegu University, as Deputy Prime Minister for Education and

Human Resources Development, and Kang Gum-Sil as Minister of Justice. Yoon Young-Kwan, hitherto professor of International Relations at Seoul National University, was appointed Minister of Foreign Affairs and Trade, while Gen. (retd) Cho Young-Kil became Minister of National Defence. Jeong Se-Hyun was retained as Minister of National Unification, indicating continuity of Kim Dae-Jung's 'sunshine' policy towards the North. The new cabinet contained four women, a record number thus far. President Roh also reorganized the military and intelligence services, appointing Gen. Kim Jong-Hwan as Chairman of the Joint Chiefs of Staff, and Ko Young-Koo, a human rights lawyer, as director of the National Intelligence Service (NIS). The latter appointment reflected Roh's determination to depoliticize the agency, which had been responsible for surveillance of political figures even after the transition to democracy.

Roh faced immediate challenges on assuming office, most notably the diplomatic crisis between North Korea and the USA, which had strained Seoul's relations with the latter. Other problems included the ongoing scandal surrounding Hyundai and the inter-Korean summit meeting of 2000, and a subway fire in Daegu in February 2003, which killed more than 200 people and highlighted the inadequacy of safety measures in public infrastructure. In the longer term Roh aimed to address regional imbalances and the disparity between rich and poor, to reduce corruption in business and the economy and to improve living standards and labour management.

In late April 2003 the GNP won two out of three seats in by-elections to the National Assembly, raising its total representation to 153. However, the victory of a reformist ally of the MDP, Rhyu Si-Min, was welcomed by the Government as an indication of support for the reform process.

The South Korean Constitution, meanwhile, stipulates that the Republic of Korea shall seek the peaceful unification of the Korean peninsula. During the 1980s relations with the DPRK were characterized by mutual suspicion, aggravated by various incidents—including the discovery of several pro-North Korean spy rings, and the death in October 1983 of four South Korean government ministers in a bomb explosion in Burma (now Myanmar), for which President Chun held the DPRK responsible. During 1985 representatives of the two states conferred on economic and humanitarian issues, but discussions were suspended in early 1986 when Kim Il Sung denounced the annual 'Team Spirit' military manoeuvres, held jointly with US troops in South Korea. Subsequent inter-Korean negotiations were likewise regularly suspended, owing to North Korean objections to the 'Team Spirit' exercises. In November 1987 the destruction of a South Korean airliner in flight over Burma, by a bomb that had allegedly been concealed aboard the aircraft by North Korean agents, caused a new outbreak of verbal hostility between the two countries.

However, with the appointment of Roh Tae-Woo as South Korean President in 1988, there appeared to be a greater willingness by the South to foster closer relations with the DPRK. Roh's announcement in early 1990 that the forthcoming 'Team Spirit' manoeuvres would be reduced in size and duration also contributed to an improvement in inter-Korean relations. In September of that year the North Korean Premier travelled to Seoul for discussions with his South Korean counterpart. The meeting represented the most senior-level contact between the two countries since the end of the Korean War in 1953. Further talks between the two premiers took place in late 1990. The DPRK's abandonment, announced in May 1991, of its long-standing position that the two Koreas should occupy a single seat at the UN was regarded as a significant concession. Accordingly, North and South Korea were admitted separately to the UN in September.

Prime-ministerial negotiations resumed in late 1991, and resulted in the signature of an 'Agreement on Reconciliation, Non-aggression and Exchanges and Co-operation between the South and the North'. At the end of December 1991 both states pledged to ban nuclear weapons from the Korean peninsula, and in early 1992 they agreed to form a joint commission to facilitate the simultaneous inspection of nuclear installations in the North and US military bases in the South. In recognition of the recent inter-Korean *rapprochement*, South Korea cancelled the 1992 'Team Spirit' exercises, and in the latter half of the year the DPRK permitted the inspection of its nuclear facilities by the International Atomic Energy Agency (IAEA, see p. 80). This apparent progress on military and nuclear issues was, however, reversed by the North's decision, in January 1993, to boycott all future inter-Korean nuclear talks, followed in March by its threatened withdrawal from the Treaty on the Non-Proliferation of Nuclear Weapons. Inter-Korean relations deteriorated further in early 1994, following the UN's announcement that it was considering the imposition of economic sanctions on North Korea: the DPRK, in turn, threatened to declare war on South Korea. The North Korean leadership was also incensed by South Korea's decision not to send a representative to the funeral, in July, of Kim Il Sung, and by its refusal to permit public mourning within South Korea. None the less, following the signing in October of the nuclear accord between the USA and the DPRK, the South Korean Government agreed to finance, in part, the construction and supply to the DPRK of light-water nuclear reactors, which are less easily adapted to the production of nuclear weapons (a key element of the accord), provided that reactors of a South Korean design were used.

The DPRK's announcement, in April 1996, that it was abandoning the 1953 armistice agreement was followed by a series of incursions by North Korean troops into the DMZ. The USA and South Korea proposed the holding of quadripartite negotiations with the People's Republic of China and North Korea; China subsequently agreed to the proposal, but the DPRK administration refused to commit itself to discussions. In September 1996 tension increased when a North Korean submarine was found abandoned near the South Korean coast; armed crew members in South Korean military uniforms were found dead near the submarine, others were killed by South Korean troops, and one was captured and interrogated. The South Korean Government denounced the incident and, demanding an apology, suspended all contacts with the North, including the provision of emergency food aid. In an unprecedented move, in December North Korea issued an apology for the incident and agreed to participate in preliminary talks about the proposed negotiations.

Exploratory discussions took place in New York, USA, in March 1997. Attempts by North Korea to link the progress of negotiations with the provision of food aid were unsuccessful. However, in May, in the first such meeting for five years, representatives of the Red Cross organizations of North and South Korea reached agreement on the provision of 50,000 metric tons of grain to the DPRK. In October negotiations to allow foreign airlines, including those from South Korea, to enter North Korean airspace reached a successful conclusion.

Despite a military confrontation between North and South Korean troops in the DMZ in July 1997 full quadripartite negotiations (with the USA and China), aimed at concluding a peace treaty between North and South Korea, opened in Geneva, Switzerland, in early December. Agreement was reached on procedural arrangements for future sessions, and a second round of full discussions was held in March 1998. A meeting held in Beijing, in April, between North and South Korean government ministers, the first such direct contact for four years, broke down following mutual accusations of inflexibility.

A further improvement in relations between North and South Korea followed Kim Dae-Jung's inauguration in February 1998. Private and business-related inter-Korean contacts increased substantially during 1998, following the South Korean Government's introduction, in April, of measures designed to facilitate such activity, as part of Kim's new 'sunshine' policy of engagement with the North. Chung Ju-Yung, the founder of the Hyundai Group, initiated a number of historic joint-ventures, including, in June and October, the delivery of cattle across the DMZ to his home town in North Korea and the organization, in November, of a visit of some 800 South Korean tourists to Mount Kumgang, just north of the border. Despite fears that this improvement in relations would be jeopardized by evidence of continued North Korean incursions, South Korea affirmed that it would continue to pursue a policy of conciliation.

At a third session of quadripartite talks, held in Geneva in late October 1998, agreement was reached on the creation of two sub-committees on the establishment of a permanent peace mechanism on the Korean peninsula and on ways of easing tension. The sub-committees were formally inaugurated during a further round of negotiations in January 1999. In February, as part of an amnesty, the South Korean Government released 17 North Korean long-term political detainees, who had refused to renounce their communist beliefs. In March the South Korean Government announced its provision of fertilizer to the DPRK, through the Red Cross. In June 1999 a brief gun battle took place between vessels from the two Koreas in the Yellow Sea following a week-long confrontation. Subsequent bilateral talks on family reunification issues made little progress in Beijing.

Meanwhile, no discernible progress was made at sessions of the quadripartite talks in April and August 1999.

None the less, private-level economic co-operation continued throughout 1999 and early 2000, and a number of joint cultural and sporting events also took place. In October 1999 Hyundai concluded an agreement with North Korea on the construction of an industrial complex, and in December Samsung Electronics announced it had signed a contract with the DPRK for the joint development of computer software and the manufacture of electronic products. Inter-Korean trade increased by some 50.2% in 1999. In March 2000, during a visit to Germany, Kim Dae-Jung urged North Korea to agree to government-level talks, and proposed the development of public-sector economic co-operation in areas such as agriculture, communications and the construction of infrastructure in the North. In April, following a series of high-level contacts in Beijing between officials of both countries, North and South Korea jointly announced that an historic summit meeting would take place between Kim Dae-Jung and Kim Jong Il in June 2000, during a three-day visit by the former to Pyongyang.

Following a delay of one day requested by North Korea for 'technical reasons' the presidential summit meeting took place on 13–15 June 2000. Detailed agreements were then signed pledging economic co-operation, the development of mutual trust and the resolution of reunification issues. In July ministerial-level delegations from both countries met in Seoul. This was the first visit to South Korea by Northern officials since 1991. Although the two sides failed to reach an agreement on military matters, a joint communiqué was issued allowing for, *inter alia*, the reopening of liaison offices at Panmunjom, which had been closed in 1996, and the reconnection of the inter-Korean Kyongui railway line. The construction of a highway to run alongside the railway from North to South was subsequently agreed. In September Kim Dae-Jung formally inaugurated the project to remove thousands of landmines (to be undertaken by soldiers from each side respectively) and rebuild the railway line and adjacent highway. (Final details for the restoration of the rail link were agreed in February 2001.) Meanwhile, benefiting from the progress made at the summit meeting in June, in August 100 South Korean families visited Pyongyang and 100 North Korean families travelled to Seoul simultaneously to meet with relatives from whom they had been separated by the Korean War. The second ministerial meeting between the two sides was held in Pyongyang later that month. Negotiations were extended for one day because of an inability to agree on terms for beginning a dialogue between the two countries' military establishments. A compromise was reached after consultation with Kim Jong Il. It was agreed to hold two more cross-border family reunions by the end of 2000 and to commence talks on economic co-operation. In a symbolic display of unity, in September the two countries marched under the same flag in the opening ceremony of the Olympic Games in Sydney, Australia. In late September the South Korean Minister of National Defence, Cho Seong-Tae, received his northern counterpart, Vice-Marshal Kim Il Chol, for discussions held on Jeju Island, the first such ministerial meeting ever conducted. Further rounds of inter-ministerial, military and economic talks took place during 2000 and early 2001. In an indication of the improvement in relations, in December 2000 a meeting was also held between trade union representatives from the two countries.

Despite this progress, in December 2000 South Korea published its annual defence policy document, which classified the DPRK as its main enemy, and alleged that it had expanded its military capacity along the DMZ, an accusation that angered the DPRK. International analysts, however, felt that hostility was not imminent. Also in that month a resolution was passed by the South Korean legislature to demand the repatriation of prisoners of war who it alleged continued to be held by the North, despite the DPRK's denial of the existence of these prisoners. The two incidents seemed to demonstrate the growing reluctance of many South Koreans to continue with the process of reunification as it stood, which they regarded as having become increasingly unbalanced to the detriment of the South.

In early 2001 the uncompromising attitude adopted by the new US Administration towards North Korea threatened to undermine severely the reconciliation process. In March the DPRK unilaterally postponed scheduled cabinet-level talks following Kim Dae-Jung's visit to the USA (see below), during which the latter had criticized Pyongyang's regime. Later that month, however, a member of the North Korean football team

was permitted to join a South Korean squad. In April the DPRK denounced joint US-South Korean military exercises as a betrayal of the goodwill surrounding the June 2000 summit meeting. Ministerial talks resumed in Seoul in mid-September, the sixth round of which was concluded in mid-November (having been postponed from late October) without any agreement—the first unsuccessful such round since the presidential summit meeting. North Korea blamed the South, particularly Unification Minister Hong Soon-Young, for the failure of the talks.

Meanwhile, Kim Jong Il's long-awaited visit to Seoul for a second presidential summit meeting failed to materialize during 2001, and there was continued uncertainty as to when such a visit would occur. US President George W. Bush's reference in January 2002 to North Korea as being part of an 'axis of evil' further jeopardized inter-Korean relations.

A stalemate in inter-Korean relations was broken in late March 2002, however, when the North agreed to receive Kim Dae-Jung's special envoy, Lim Dong-Won, in early April. Following the visit, during which Lim met Kim Jong Il, the two sides agreed to further reunions for separated families (see below), and to continuing talks on economic co-operation. North Korea also agreed to Lim's request that it renew dialogue with the USA and Japan. In mid-May Park Geun-Hye visited the North and met Kim Jong Il. The visit was unusual because Northern agents had killed Park's mother in 1974 in a failed bid to assassinate her father. Despite the cordial visit, North Korea cancelled economic co-operation discussions with the South in May.

In May 2002 the increasing number of defectors from the North to the South received international attention as several groups sought asylum at Canadian, Japanese and South Korean diplomatic buildings in China. They were eventually allowed to travel to the South, albeit via the Philippines. The South Korean Ministry of Unification reported in January 2003 that during 2002 some 1,141 North Koreans had defected to the South, compared with 583 in 2001.

At the end of June 2002 a gun battle between North and South Korean vessels in the Yellow Sea resulted in the sinking of a Southern patrol boat and the deaths of six crew members. South Korean military sources estimated that 30 Northern crewmen had also been killed in the confrontation, which had started when two North Korean vessels accompanying a fishing boat reportedly crossed the Northern Limit Line (the maritime border separating the two Koreas). Following the incident, in July South Korea suspended rice shipments to the North and economic co-operation projects, reflecting widespread public anger. None the less, Kim Dae-Jung maintained his 'sunshine' policy towards the North, which later expressed regret for the incident. Meanwhile, North Korean state television showed selected highlights of football matches played by the South Korean team in the 2002 World Cup, although it refrained from transmitting extensive coverage of the event, which was being co-hosted by Japan.

In mid-August 2002 North and South Korea held a seventh round of ministerial talks in Seoul, aimed at improving relations in the aftermath of the latest naval confrontation and focusing on the issue of future family reunions, railway links (see below) and cultural exchanges. Regarding the latter, more than 300 North Korean athletes travelled to the South and participated in the Asian Games held in Busan during October. In late September the first inter-Korean military 'hotline' was inaugurated to allow for improved communications during sensitive occasions. Meanwhile, Pyongyang's revelation that it had abducted 12 Japanese citizens in the 1970s and 1980s highlighted the outstanding issue of the whereabouts of several hundred missing South Korean citizens believed to have been abducted by the North.

The eighth round of ministerial talks was held in Pyongyang in late October 2002 and focused mainly on economic co-operation issues, despite the fact that the USA had earlier revealed the existence of a secret nuclear weapons programme in the North (see the chapter on the Democratic People's Republic of Korea). At the end of that month a North Korean economic delegation began a nine-day tour of the South, including several major industrial facilities. Noteworthy was the fact that the delegation included Jang Song Taek, Kim Jong Il's brother-in-law and one of his most trusted advisers, and also Kim Hi Taek, the first deputy head of the KWP's Central Committee. At the end of December 2002 South Korea's Ministry of National

Defence published a 'white paper' which, for the first time, excluded any reference to the North as its main enemy.

By late 2002 some of the goodwill generated by the historic inter-Korean summit meeting in June 2000 had been undermined by the revelation that Kim Dae-Jung had arranged for the Korea Development Bank to give a Hyundai affiliate US $200m. to transfer to the North in order to arrange the summit. However, the election in December of Roh Moo-Hyun as President of South Korea heralded a continuation of Kim's 'sunshine' policy. In early January 2003 representatives of Roh secretly met Northern officials in Beijing, and later in that month a ninth round of ministerial talks was held in Seoul. Kim also dispatched Lim Dong-Won to Pyongyang at the end of January, but Lim failed to secure a meeting with Kim Jong Il, instead relaying a goodwill message through one of the latter's aides. Both North and South Korea were expected to continue efforts to improve relations with each other during 2003, despite a severe deterioration in relations between the North and the USA. By March 2003 Roh was exploring a long-standing idea of developing gas pipelines from Sakhalin, Russia, to North Korea that would supply the latter with energy in return for an abandonment of its nuclear programme. North Korea hosted the 10th round of ministerial talks at the end of April. In mid-May, however, Pyongyang announced that it no longer recognized a joint declaration on the 'denuclearization' of the Korean peninsula, signed with the South in 1992.

The arrangements for further family reunions came under the auspices of the North and South Korean Red Cross organizations, which held several rounds of talks on the subject and co-ordinated the exchange of lists of potential candidates for reunion. In October 2000 South Korea accepted a DPRK proposal that the second exchange of family members should take place in late November–early December. Relations between the two sides subsequently deteriorated, when North Korea accused the head of the South Korean Red Cross of defaming the former's political system. The official was replaced in January 2001. The DPRK continued to dictate terms for reunions, asking South Korea to limit the amount of money and gifts transferred during the events, which took place in November–December 2000 and at the end of February 2001. It was subsequently reported that North Korean officials had confiscated money given to delegates for use as state funds. There was a notable decline in the level of enthusiasm for the reunions, which were proceeding slowly and on a small scale, among the South Korean populace (other than those who were directly involved). Meanwhile, in January 2001 an historic accord between the two sides allowed 300 separated families from the North and South each to exchange letters in mid-March. A fourth round of family reunions was initially scheduled for mid-October, but was cancelled owing to the heightened security situation following the terrorist attacks in the USA on 11 September. They were subsequently held at Mount Kumgang in late April 2002. A fifth round was held in mid-September 2002, again at Mount Kumgang, where officials from the two sides planned to build a centre for such meetings.

Of particular concern to those South Koreans who had begun to question the wisdom of extensive aid without firm preconditions was the fact that, as the DPRK's financial situation worsened, economic issues played an increasingly important part in inter-Korean relations during 2000 and 2001. There was speculation that Pyongyang's new openness was motivated by the necessity to secure greater assistance. South Korea provided 52% of the total international aid to North Korea in 2000. In January 2001, however, a South Korean vessel carrying aid was refused permission to dock in the DPRK. Also in that month, it was reported that North Korea's energy shortages had reached crisis point, and that it was desperately researching alternative power sources. A summit meeting took place between the two Koreas in February, at which the DPRK requested immediate and substantial electricity supplies to alleviate its pressing needs. South Korea, however, insisted that on-site investigations be conducted prior to the commencement of deliveries. Meanwhile, in August 2000 Hyundai agreed to establish a technologically-advanced electronic industrial compound in Kaesong in the DPRK. Hyundai's financial problems, however, were likely to delay the implementation of the project. The company was also obliged to reduce its royalty payments to Pyongyang for the Mount Kumgang tourist initiative in 2000, owing to the attraction's failure to make a profit. In March 2001 the future of the initiative was jeopardized by its lack of profitability, and Hyundai appealed to the South Korean Government for assistance; the Government subsequently pledged 90,000m.

won to maintain the tourist cruises. Hyundai founder Chung Ju-Yung died in late March 2001, meanwhile, and his funeral was attended by a delegation sent by Kim Jong Il. On May Day workers from trade unions from the North and South attended a rally at Mount Kumgang. Bilateral talks held in October concerning the re-launch of the project and the opening of a connecting cross-border road failed, however, to make progress.

Negotiations to reconnect the inter-Korean rail link continued during 2001. It was hoped that such a link would create a new Eurasian transport corridor that would reduce the cost and time of the transit of goods from North-East Asia to European markets from 25 days to about 15 days, bringing economic benefits to all participants. In February 2001 a meeting was held at the DMZ to arrange regulations for troops and workers employed to rebuild the line, and a parallel highway. However, North Korea failed to attend a UN Asian transport meeting held in Seoul in mid-November, following the breakdown of the sixth round of ministerial discussions. A New Year's editorial in the North in January 2002 described upgrading the railway as a priority during that year, and both Koreas agreed to accelerate the reconnection following bilateral talks in April 2002. Ground-breaking ceremonies for the reconnection of the railway and road links were held on both sides of the DMZ in late September 2002, and South Korea released a loan to the North to assist the funding of the work. In late 2002 South Korean officials attended the ground-breaking ceremony for the North's new industrial zone at Kaesong. In early February 2003 the first road reconnecting the North with the South was completed, on the eastern coast of the Korean peninsula.

Owing to its geographical position, Korea's foreign relations have long been dominated by its relations with the 'great powers' in the region—Russia, China, the USA and Japan. Following President Roh's inauguration in 1988, relations with the communist bloc showed signs of improvement. Trade with the USSR and the People's Republic of China expanded, and in 1990 full diplomatic relations were established with the USSR. These developments were denounced by the DPRK, its diplomatic isolation being compounded by South Korea's establishment of full diplomatic relations with the People's Republic of China (hitherto the North's principal ally) in August 1992. In August 1993 the Russian authorities published a new report into the shooting down, by Soviet forces, of a South Korean passenger aircraft in 1983, concluding that the airliner, which had been following an incorrect course, had been mistaken for a US aircraft engaged in espionage; previously, the Soviet authorities had maintained that the Korean aircraft was itself on a spying mission. In September 1993 it was announced that South Korea and Russia were to participate in joint naval exercises, and in 1994 it was reported that Russia was to supply South Korea with 'defensive missiles' in order to repay a part of its debt to South Korea. Further arrangements were made concerning the settlement of Russia's debt to South Korea, through the provision of commodities, in July 1997. There was speculation, however, that South Korea was no longer to receive the Russian defence systems, following pressure from the USA, hitherto South Korea's principal supplier of weaponry.

Relations were severely tested in mid-1998 by a diplomatic dispute, provoked by Russia's expulsion of a South Korean diplomat following allegations of espionage and bribery, which culminated in the resignation of the South Korean Minister of Foreign Affairs and Trade, Park Chung-Soo. During a state visit to Russia in May 1999, Kim Dae-Jung held a summit meeting with President Boris Yeltsin. Issues discussed included South Korea's engagement policy with North Korea, a proposed expansion of Moscow's role in regional affairs and bilateral economic co-operation. The Russian Minister of Defence visited Seoul in September 1999, and the two countries conducted their first joint naval exercises in April 2000. President Vladimir Putin of Russia paid a three-day state visit to South Korea in February 2001, during which the two nations confirmed their commitment to improving bilateral relations, and Putin agreed to proceed with a tripartite framework of co-operation between Russia and both Koreas. Arrangements were made for Russia to supply weapons to South Korea, which were to be partially paid for by the cancellation of some Soviet-era debt. South Korea and Russia also issued a joint statement supporting the 1972 Anti-Ballistic Missile (ABM) treaty; however, US displeasure with this led to the resignation of the Minister of Foreign Affairs and Trade, Lee Joung-Binn.

In mid-August 2001 a Russian diplomat, Valentin Moiseyev, was imprisoned for four-and-a-half years for passing secrets to

South Korea; however, the incident did not adversely affect bilateral relations.

A key area of co-operation between South Korea and Russia during 2001–02 remained the reconnection of the North–South Korea rail network, and its planned connection with the Trans-Siberian railway, thereby creating a Eurasian transport corridor. This would allow South Korea to become a major trading hub, linking Europe and Asia with the Americas. Meanwhile, in December 2002 South Korea agreed to receive US $534m. worth of military equipment from Russia as part of a 1995 agreement aimed at repaying Moscow's $2,000m. debt to South Korea. The transaction, the last of its kind, was to be completed by 2006.

In September 2002 in response to growing labour shortages in South Korea, the Government extended working visas for ethnic Korean residents of Russia and the former Soviet Union from three months to one year. It was expected that many of the estimated 40,000 ethnic Koreans in Sakhalin, Russia, would take advantage of the changes.

There were indications that Roh Moo-Hyun would seek to improve relations with Russia during his presidency, as part of a broader policy of reducing dependency on the USA. In March 2003 Roh revived the idea of building a 4,000-km pipeline that would provide North Korea with Russian natural gas from Sakhalin in exchange for the abandonment of its nuclear weapons programme.

Relations with China were strengthened in November 1998, when President Kim Dae-Jung paid an official visit to Beijing, meeting with Chinese President Jiang Zemin and Premier Zhu Rongji. Several accords were initialled during the visit. In August 1999 co-operative ties with China were further consolidated by the first visit of a South Korean defence minister to Beijing; a reciprocal visit to South Korea by the Chinese Minister of National Defence, Chi Haotian, took place in January 2000. The South Korean Government requested Chi's assistance in resolving the issue of seven North Korean defectors, who had recently been repatriated by China, despite South Korean protests. In October 2000 relations improved further when, during a visit to Seoul by Zhu Rongji, agreement was reached on the resumption of the quadripartite conference, incorporating the two Koreas, China and the USA, with the aim of establishing a peace mechanism for the Korean Peninsula. Later in the month, following strong opposition from Beijing, South Korea refused to grant a visa to the Dalai Lama, Tibet's spiritual leader, on the grounds that it would be 'inappropriate'.

During 2001 China continued to seek stability on the Korean peninsula. A diplomatic dispute arose between Seoul and Beijing in October, however, following the execution in China of a South Korean national and the alleged torture of another Korean prisoner, both convicted of drug-trafficking. In early November the ministers of economics, finance and foreign affairs from China, South Korea and Japan agreed to hold regular meetings to foster closer co-operation. In late 2001 there were concerns in South Korean business circles that China's admission to the WTO would divert investment and labour to the People's Republic and undercut the competitiveness of Korean goods. Nevertheless, the South Korean Minister of National Defence, Kim Dong-Shin, paid a week-long visit to China in December, where he sought closer military co-operation with his Chinese counterparts.

By 2002 economic and trade links were increasingly leading to closer relations between South Korea and China. During 2001 South Koreans invested more funding in China than in the USA, and in 2002 China displaced the USA as South Korea's largest trading partner (South Korea had already become China's third biggest trading partner). However, there was concern among domestic manufacturers that lower labour costs in China would undermine their competitiveness, and there were occasional trade disputes between the two countries.

In January 2002 China reacted with concern following the proposal to the South Korean National Assembly of legislation that would give special rights to ethnic Koreans living in China and elsewhere. In March the two countries announced the introduction of a new extradition pact, to take effect from April, and at the same time Wang Jiarui, the deputy head of the international liaison department of the Chinese Communist Party, visited Seoul.

Tensions between South Korea and China temporarily increased in mid-2002 when the Chinese authorities sought to prevent North Korean refugees from seeking asylum in various diplomatic buildings in China, including the South Korean embassy in Beijing, where a group of 23 had hidden. The members of the group, and others like them, were later permitted to travel to South Korea, but only via a third country—often the Philippines or Singapore. In response, the Chinese authorities increased efforts to combat South Korean NGOs and religious groups that were seeking to increase the number of North Korean refugees in China. In July and September Chinese military delegations visited Seoul to discuss bilateral military co-operation, and in August the Minister of Foreign Affairs and Trade received his Chinese counterpart in Seoul. In September Lee Hoi-Chang visited China and met President Jiang Zemin. In October the Minister of Finance proposed a three-way alliance comprising South Korea, China and Japan to manage the region's development. Also in that month the Government decided to extend working visas for ethnic Koreans in China to two years, with unlimited extensions. The move was designed to reduce the illegal trafficking of ethnic Koreans from China and its associated problems.

The growing diplomatic crisis over North Korea's nuclear programme in late 2002 and early 2003 led South Korea to seek China's assistance in persuading the North to work towards a peaceful solution. However, by April 2003 China had achieved only a minimal moderating influence over North Korea. Roh Moo-Hyun planned to visit China shortly afterwards.

Relations between South Korea and the USA were frequently strained in the late 1970s, in particular by the proposal to withdraw US ground troops from South Korea (which was abandoned in 1979) and by the trial of Kim Dae-Jung (see above). Disputes between South Korea and the USA in the late 1980s over trade issues had subsided by mid-1991. President George Bush of the USA visited South Korea in January 1992, and the two leaders agreed to cancel that year's 'Team Spirit' exercises. In December 1991 it had been announced that all US nuclear weapons had been withdrawn from South Korean territory. The 'Team Spirit' exercises were resumed in 1993. In July, during a visit to Seoul, President Clinton affirmed his country's continuing commitment to the defence of South Korea; he subsequently stated that an attack by the DPRK on South Korea would be tantamount to an act of aggression against the USA. In January 1994 it was announced that the USA was to deploy air-defence missiles on South Korean territory. In April 1996, during a visit to Seoul, Clinton issued a joint US-South Korean proposal for quadripartite negotiations with North Korea and the People's Republic of China (see above). In October 1997 the US Government asked the South Korean administration to reconsider its decision to order an air-defence missile system from France. South Korea, however, was seeking to reduce its dependence on the USA for military technology. Later in that year the USA pledged financial support for South Korea, following the conclusion of the agreement with the IMF.

President Kim Dae-Jung was warmly received on a state visit to the USA in June 1998, during which he outlined his 'sunshine' policy of engagement towards North Korea. A reciprocal visit was made by Clinton to Seoul in November. Meanwhile, occasional differences over trade issues persisted in 1998. In October agreement was reached on US access to the South Korean vehicle market, after a protracted dispute during which the USA had threatened to impose sanctions on imports from South Korea. In February 1999 the USA filed a complaint with the WTO over South Korea's refusal to allow foreign companies to tender for contracts for the construction of a new airport near Seoul. In March the South Korean Government welcomed a breakthrough in negotiations between North Korea and the USA on US access to a suspected nuclear site in North Korea (for further details, see the chapter on the DPRK). During a second visit by Kim Dae-Jung to the USA in July 1999, the US administration reaffirmed its support for the 'sunshine' policy. US-South Korean talks were held in late 1999 and early 2000 regarding South Korea's proposed extension of its missile range, from 180 km to 300 km for military purposes, and to 500 km for research and development. (In January 2001 a revised missile accord was signed between South Korea and the USA, permitting the former to develop missiles with greatly increased ranges and payloads.) In October 1999 the US and South Korean Governments began investigations into the alleged massacre of as many as 300 Korean refugees by US troops near Nogun-ri, in the South Korean province of North Chungcheong, shortly after the beginning of the Korean War. Revelations surrounding the use of defoliants in the DMZ in the late 1960s created further controversy in November 1999. The herbicides, which had apparently been provided by the USA but applied by South Korean troops, included Agent Orange, which had later been found to be highly toxic. The South Korean Government announced that it was prepared to compensate both soldiers and civilians adversely affected by the defoliants, but the USA reportedly refused to accept any liability. In December a lawsuit was filed against seven US chemical companies by a group of Koreans demanding compensation for damage they claimed to have suffered as a consequence of the herbicides.

In May 2000 there was further tension between the two countries when a US aircraft accidentally released several bombs close to a village south-west of Seoul, causing minor injuries and damage to property. Violent protests were held outside the US embassy in Seoul, and the USA subsequently agreed to cease using the Koon-ni range for such training missions. (Operations subsequently resumed, the USA citing a lack of suitable alternative facilities.) Following the incident, opposition politicians demanded a review of the Status of Forces Agreement (SOFA), which governed the 37,000 US troops stationed in South Korea. In August negotiations were held on the issue, and resulted in partial agreement. Further talks held in December successfully revised the agreement, which was signed in January 2001. South Korean civic groups, however, protested that the partnership between the two countries remained biased in favour of the USA. Also in December 2000, the WTO ruled that the USA had breached its rules in imposing 'anti-dumping' duties on South Korean exports of stainless steel, but did not recommend that the duties be revoked. In January 2001 outgoing US President Bill Clinton made an unprecedented statement of regret for the massacre near Nogun-ri. Many South Koreans, however, were angry that no apology was forthcoming. Later, in January 2002, a British Broadcasting Corporation (BBC) investigation revealed that US commanders had repeatedly ordered troops to fire on refugees at Nogun-ri and elsewhere during the opening months of the Korean War. Some South Korean historians were, in late 2001, also investigating the USA's possible role in the massacre by South Korean troops of 30,000 people on Jeju Island in a suppression of communist elements in late 1948 and early 1949. Meanwhile, the USA welcomed the improvement in inter-Korean relations during 2000. US Secretary of State Madeleine Albright visited Seoul in June and in October of that year to discuss developments. In March 2001 Kim Dae-Jung paid a visit to the new Bush administration in Washington, DC, hoping to secure support for his 'sunshine' policy. US President George W. Bush, however, took a firmer stance than his predecessor and declared that North Korea must prove its abandonment of its missile testing and development programme prior to any improvement in relations or release of aid.

In April 2001 a Seoul court ruled that the US air force's firing and bombing ranges near the village of Maehyang-ri caused damage and duress to inhabitants, and ordered the central Government to pay them compensation. In early May the US Deputy Secretary of State, Richard Armitage, visited South Korea, seeking Seoul's support for the USA's planned NMD system and urging the continuation of negotiations between North and South.

Disagreements between South Korea and the USA on how to deal with North Korea, however, continued to strain bilateral relations during 2001. In July Seoul refused to allow Hwang Jang Yop, the highest-ranking North Korean defector, to visit the USA and testify before Congress, fearing that such a move would exacerbate the already strained inter-Korean relations.

South Korea immediately pledged support to the USA following the terrorist attacks on the latter in September 2001, and in early December the National Assembly endorsed the deployment of non-combat troops to assist the US-led campaign in Afghanistan, mainly in a logistical capacity. Meanwhile, in November the USA and South Korea agreed to a major 'landswap' whereby existing US bases would relocate to other areas within the country, allowing a consolidation of bases and training facilities over the next 10 years.

In January 2002 South Korea reacted with concern to President Bush's reference to North Korea as being part of an 'axis of evil', a remark that further undermined Kim Dae-Jung's 'sunshine' policy. None the less the South Korean military planned to purchase US $800m. worth of surface-to-surface missiles capable of attacking most of North Korea, from US manufacturers. At the same time GNP leader Lee Hoi-Chang visited the USA and met senior US officials, his attitude to North Korea generally being closer to that of Bush than of Kim. Lee favoured a policy of 'strategic engagement' based on reciprocity and transparency. Bush himself visited South Korea in late Feb-

ruary and urged the North to change its ways, while ruling out any US invasion. South Korea feared that any US-induced stalemate might lead to a major crisis on the peninsula.

In March 2002 the USA announced plans to deploy a new mobile military force unit to South Korea by 2007. Some South Korean officials had previously indicated that US troops might remain in Korea even after any unification, possibly serving as peace-keepers in the North. Later in the month the USA agreed to sell a combat-radar system to South Korea, and the two countries held their biggest-ever joint military exercises, which antagonized the North. Also in that month South Korea reacted angrily to Bush's imposition of new tariffs on imported steel, since South Korea was a major steel exporter. At the end of the month the Ministry of National Defence announced that the Boeing Company of the USA had secured a US $4,500m. contract to supply South Korea with 40 F-15K fighter planes, having beaten rivals Dassault of France, the Eurofighter consortium and Sukhoi of Russia. Critics of the deal said that Daussault's *Rafale* aicraft offered greater technology transfer and value, as well as local manufacturing opportunities. South Korea hoped to develop an indigenous fighter aircraft by 2015.

Relations between South Korea and the USA deteriorated noticeably after an accident in June 2002 in which a US army vehicle killed two teenaged Korean girls. The US military charged two US soldiers with negligent homicide, and the South Korean authorities subsequently requested their submission for trial at a local court, but this was rejected by the US army. In November the two soldiers were acquitted by a US military court, leading to a significant increase in anti-US sentiment among the public. Although President Bush apologized for the incident, in mid-December hundreds of thousands of people attended anti-US rallies in Seoul and across the country, and there were several incidents of assaults on and hostility towards US troops and businesses. Although precipitated by the issue of the acquittals, the rallies became a forum of protest against the country's dependency on the USA and that country's policy towards North Korea. Meanwhile, in October a new joint base pact came into force whereby the US military would reduce the number of bases from 41 to 23 and return 50% of the land it used to South Korea. However, there had yet to be changes to the SOFA that governed the conduct of US troops in Korea— amendments to which had long been demanded by South Koreans. Public anger towards the USA was further raised by the crash of a U2 reconnaissance plane in January, causing destruction of property.

The election of Roh Moo-Hyun as President raised fears that South Korea's relations with the USA would be further undermined, since Roh had once called for the removal of US troops from South Korea (although he had subsequently rescinded such demands) and had campaigned for a foreign policy more independent from the USA. However, in January 2003 he indicated a more conciliatory stance, but nevertheless warned the USA against attacking North Korea, instead urging the USA to resume dialogue with Pyongyang. He also instructed the military to prepare contingency plans for the possible withdrawal of US troops, and the US Secretary of Defense, Donald Rumsfeld, in March stated that the troops could be reduced or withdrawn completely. The USA announced that it planned to remove its 15,000 troops stationed between Seoul and the DMZ and deploy them in the south of the country. Kim Dae-Jung had previously criticized the USA's policy of 'tailored containment' to isolate Pyongyang, warning that it would be ineffective.

In late February 2003 the commander of the United States Forces Korea, Gen. Leon LaPorte, stated that the USA and South Korea would review their 1953 Mutual Defense Treaty, with the possibility of ending provisions under the 'Combined Forces Command' for the transfer of control over South Korea's military to the USA in wartime. However, it was noted that South Korea's military still remained dependent on the USA for military intelligence. Despite disagreements, South Korea and the USA held their annual joint military exercises during March. In early April the US military announced that it would move its main base away from Seoul as part of a global redeployment of forces, and the two countries began major discussions on the long-term future of their alliance. The USA envisioned eventually consolidating its forces in two major hubs: the Osan-Pyeongtaek, and Daegu-Busan regions. Meanwhile, Roh arranged to send 700 non-combatant troops to Iraq in support of the USA, despite domestic protests. Roh visited President Bush in Washington, DC, in mid-May, and the two leaders agreed to work towards a peaceful solution to the crisis over North Korea's nuclear programme.

Relations between South Korea and Japan, which had long been strained, were eased by President Chun's official visit to Japan in September 1984 (the first such visit undertaken by a South Korean Head of State), during which Emperor Hirohito and Prime Minister Nakasone formally expressed their regret for Japanese aggression in Korea in the past. In May 1990, during President Roh's visit to Japan, Emperor Akihito offered official apologies for the cruelties of Japanese colonial rule in Korea. In January 1992 the Japanese Prime Minister, Kiichi Miyazawa, visited South Korea, where he publicly expressed regret at the enslavement during the Second World War of an estimated 100,000 Korean women, who were used by the Japanese military for sexual purposes ('comfort women'), but declined to state whether the Japanese Government would consider financial compensation. In late 1994 the Japanese Government announced that it would not make compensation payments directly to individuals, but would finance a programme to construct vocational training centres for the women concerned. In August 1995, on the 50th anniversary of the end of the Second World War, the Japanese Prime Minister, Tomiichi Murayama, issued a statement expressing 'deep reflection and sincere apologies' for Japanese colonial aggression. At the end of a summit meeting with President Kim in June 1996, the Japanese Prime Minister, Ryutaro Hashimoto, issued a public apology to the 'comfort women'. However, the South Korean Government regarded Japanese proposals to provide compensation through private sources of funding, rather than government money, as amounting to a denial of moral responsibility. The conclusion of new defence co-operation guide-lines between Japan and the USA in September 1997 was of concern for South Korea, which feared an expansion in Japanese military capability. Negotiations for a new fisheries agreement, under way since mid-1996, were unilaterally terminated by Japan in January 1998, following the continuing disagreement regarding sovereignty of a group of islets in the Sea of Japan, to which both countries laid claim. In April 1998 the South Korean Government announced its intention to make payments itself to surviving 'comfort women', apparently abandoning its attempts to gain compensation for the women from the Japanese Government. Later that month, however, a Japanese district court ordered the Government to pay compensation to three former 'comfort women' from the Republic of Korea. Another group of South Korean 'comfort women' was refused the right to recompense by the Japanese High Court in November 2000, and in March 2001 the 1998 compensation ruling was overturned by a regional High Court.

Relations with Japan improved considerably in October 1998, meanwhile, during a four-day state visit to Tokyo by President Kim Dae-Jung. A joint declaration was signed, in which Japan apologized for the suffering inflicted on the Korean people during Japanese colonial rule. In addition, South Korea agreed to revoke a ban on the import of various Japanese goods, while Japan promised financial aid to South Korea in support of its efforts to stimulate economic recovery. In November the two countries concluded negotiations on the renewal of their bilateral fisheries agreement, which came into effect in January 1999, despite the objections of the main South Korean opposition party, which protested that it failed positively to affirm South Korea's claim to sovereignty over the disputed islets. Differences over the accord and its implementation continued to create tension in early 1999, however, particularly in South Korea, where protests from fishermen, who were apparently suffering heavy losses because of the revised agreement, forced the resignation of the Minister for Maritime Affairs and Fisheries. In March increasing co-operation between the two countries was highlighted during a visit to South Korea by the Japanese Prime Minister, Keizo Obuchi, despite protests against Japan's military ties with the USA and failure fully to compensate the 'comfort women'. Both countries agreed to strengthen bilateral economic relations, and Japan pledged a further US $1,000m. in aid to South Korea. The Japanese Prime Minister, Yoshiro Mori, visited Seoul in May 2000 and met with Kim Dae-Jung. In November of that year the South Korean Minister of Foreign Affairs and Trade paid a visit to Tokyo to discuss ways of improving bilateral relations.

Relations with Japan deteriorated during 2001 following the publication in February of new Japanese history textbooks which sought to justify Japan's aggression towards its Asian neighbours during the Second World War, and neglected to mention the forced prostitution of Asian (mainly Korean) 'comfort women' by the Japanese army and the forcible transfer and use of Koreans as slave labour in Japan. Large-scale protests were held in Seoul, and the Japanese ambassador was summoned to the Ministry of Foreign Affairs and Trade. In April South Korea temporarily withdrew its ambassador from Japan. President Kim Dae-Jung urged Japan to adopt 'a correct understanding of history', and the South Korean National Assembly pressed the Government to reconsider any further opening of its markets to Japanese cultural products unless the books were abandoned. The South Korean Ministry of Foreign Affairs and Trade demanded 35 major revisions to the books, but in July Japan's Ministry of Education ruled out any further significant changes, prompting Kim Dae-Jung to refuse to receive a visiting Japanese delegation and the suspension of bilateral military co-operation. Protests also took place outside the Japanese embassy in Seoul. In mid-August South Korea was further outraged by the visit of the Japanese Prime Minister, Junichiro Koizumi, to the controversial Yasukuni Shrine in Tokyo honouring Japan's war dead. Koizumi's visit was seen as a sign of resurgent Japanese nationalism and was denounced by South Korea, as well as by Japan's other Asian neighbours. Koizumi visited Seoul in mid-October and delivered an apology for the suffering of Koreans under Japanese rule, but his visit was greeted by protests and he was forced to cancel a visit to the National Assembly owing to the hostile sentiment held by some legislators. However, both sides recognized the need to improve relations prior to co-hosting the football World Cup in 2002. In early January 2002, meanwhile, South Korea and Japan resolved a fishing dispute over access to waters claimed by Japan.

Along with China and North Korea, South Korea condemned Koizumi's visits to the Yasukuni Shrine in late April 2002 and mid-January 2003. However, Koizumi and Kim Dae-Jung in late March 2002 agreed to begin discussions on a possible bilateral free-trade agreement, and at the end of May Koizumi attended the opening ceremony of the 2002 football World Cup in Seoul. Also in attendance was Prince Takamado and his wife, who were making the first official visit to South Korea by a member of the Imperial family. The football tournament, a major source of prestige for both countries, passed off without incident. Any remaining mutual hostility between the two countries was overshadowed in 2002 by the need for co-operation in engaging with the North. In December 2002 Koizumi and South Korean President-elect Roh Moo-Hyun agreed to forge a united front when dealing with the North. Koizumi subsequently attended Roh's inauguration in late February 2003, and the two were expected to continue efforts towards reaching a free-trade agreement.

In November 2000, after eight years' suspension, the 25th Joint Conference of Korea-Taiwan Business Councils took place in Seoul. It was agreed that henceforth conferences would be held annually alternately in Seoul and Taipei. In the same month a Korean passenger aircraft flew from Seoul to Taipei for the first time since 1992, when diplomatic relations had been severed. South Korea also maintained close relations with South-East Asian countries, and Minister of Defence Kim Dong-Shin and Prime Minister Lee Han-Dong visited Viet Nam in December 2001 and April 2002 respectively. Security, economic and trade issues were the main topics of discussions. Viet Nam had already become the principal recipient of South Korean aid. In early 2003 a South Korean newspaper funded the opening of a peace park in southern Viet Nam, as a gesture of atonement for atrocities committed by South Korean soldiers, some 300,000 of whom had fought on behalf of South Viet Nam, during the Viet Nam war.

In February 2003 South Korea signed its first-ever free-trade agreement, with Chile, that would reduce tariffs on two-thirds of Korean goods. Seoul hoped to reach similar agreements with Mexico and Singapore.

Government

Under the Constitution of the Sixth Republic (adopted in October 1987), executive power is held by the President, who is directly elected for one term of five years by universal suffrage. The President appoints and governs with the assistance of the State Council (Cabinet), led by the Prime Minister. Legislative power is vested in the unicameral National Assembly (Kuk Hoe), popularly elected for a four-year term. The Assembly has 273 members.

Defence

Protection of the frontier separating North and South Korea is the responsibility of the UN. Military service lasts for 26 months in the army, and for 30 months in the navy and in the air force. In August 2002 the strength of the active armed forces was 686,000 (including an estimated 159,000 conscripts): army 560,000, navy 63,000, air force 63,000. Paramilitary forces included a 3.5m.-strong civilian defence corps. In August 2002 37,140 US troops were stationed in South Korea. Expenditure on defence was budgeted at 16,500,000m. won for 2002.

Economic Affairs

In 2001, according to estimates by the World Bank, South Korea's gross national income (GNI), measured at average 1999–2001 prices, was US $447,698m., equivalent to $9,400 per head (or $18,110 per head on an international purchasing-power parity basis). During 1990–2001, it was estimated, the population increased at an average annual rate of 1.0%, while gross domestic product (GDP) per head increased, in real terms, by an average of 4.9% per year. Overall GDP increased, in real terms, at an average annual rate of 5.9% in 1990–2001. GDP was estimated to have increased by 3.0% in 2001.

Agriculture (including forestry and fishing) contributed 4.4% of GDP in 2001, and engaged 10.3% of the employed labour force in that year. The principal crop is rice, but maize, barley, potatoes, sweet potatoes and fruit are also important, as is the raising of livestock (principally pigs and cattle). In 2000 the agricultural sector was adversely affected by an outbreak of foot-and-mouth disease. Fishing provides food for domestic consumption, as well as a surplus for export. In the late 1990s South Korea was one of the world's leading ocean-fishing nations. During 1990–2001, agricultural GDP increased by an average of 2.2% per year. Agricultural GDP increased by 2.0% in 2000. Growth was estimated at 1.4% in 2001.

Industry (including mining and quarrying, manufacturing, power and construction) contributed 41.4% of GDP in 2001, and engaged 28.1% of the employed labour force in 2000. Industry is dominated by large conglomerate companies (*chaebol*), with greatly diversified interests, especially in construction and manufacturing. During 1990–2001, industrial GDP increased at an average annual rate of 6.6%. Industrial GDP increased by 11.5% in 2000 and by 4.4% in 2001.

South Korea is not richly endowed with natural resources, and mining and quarrying contributed only 0.3% of GDP in 2001. In 2001 less than 0.1% of the employed labour force were engaged in the sector. There are deposits of coal (mainly anthracite); in 1998 coal-mining accounted for 19.2% of the total value of mining output, while the non-metallic mineral sector accounted for 61.4%. Other minerals include iron ore, lead, zinc, silver, gold and limestone, and sizeable offshore reserves of natural gas have been discovered. According to the ADB, mining GDP declined at an average annual rate of 1.4% in 1990–2000, decreasing by 23.9% in 1998 but increasing by 5.2% in 1999 and by 2.2% in 2000.

Manufacturing contributed 30.0% of GDP in 2001, and engaged 19.7% of the employed labour force in that year. The most important branches of manufacturing in include electrical machinery, transport equipment—mainly road motor vehicles and ship-building, non-electrical machinery, chemicals, food products, iron and steel, and textiles. During 1990–2001, manufacturing GDP increased by an average of 7.8% per year. The sector's GDP increased by 15.4% in 2000. Manufacturing GDP expanded by an estimated 4.0% in 2001.

Energy is derived principally from nuclear power, coal and petroleum. In 2001 27.0% of total electricity output was generated by nuclear power, while thermal and hydroelectric power provided 65.4% and 7.6%, respectively. A total of 14 nuclear power plants were to be constructed between 1993 and 2006. South Korea also produces liquefied natural gas for domestic and industrial consumption. Imports of petroleum and its products comprised an estimated 18.8% of the value of merchandise imports in 2001.

The services sector contributed 54.1% of GDP in 2001, and engaged 61.0% of the employed labour force in 2000. An important source of 'invisible' export earnings has been overseas construction work, mostly in the Middle East. Receipts from tourism are also significant (totalling $6,282.5m. in 2001). During 1990–2001, the GDP of the services sector increased at an average annual rate of 5.7%. The GDP of the sector increased by 8.3% in 2000. Growth was estimated at 2.1% in 2001.

In 2001 South Korea recorded a visible trade surplus of US $13,392m., and there was a surplus of $8,617m. on the current account of the balance of payments. Japan and the USA were the principal sources of imports in 2001 (accounting for, respectively, 18.9% and 15.9% of imports in that year); other important suppliers were the People's Republic of China and Saudi Arabia. Similarly, the USA (20.7%) and Japan (11.0%) were the principal markets for exports; other significant purchasers included the People's Republic of China and Hong Kong. The main exports in 2001 were electrical machinery, miscellaneous manufactured articles, road vehicles, textiles and chemical products. The principal imports in that year were machinery and transport equipment (especially electrical machinery), petroleum and petroleum products, basic manufactures and chemical products.

South Korea's budget surplus for 2003 was projected at the equivalent of 2.7% of GDP—the third consecutive year of surplus. The budget for 2003 envisaged expenditure of 111,500,000m. won. At the end of 2000 South Korea's total external debt was US $134,417m., of which $46,941m. was long-term public debt. In that year the cost of debt-servicing was equivalent to 10.9% of the value of exports of goods and services. The average annual rate of inflation was 5.1% in 1990–2000. Consumer prices increased by an average of 4.0% in 2001 and by 2.8% in 2002. The rate of unemployment declined from 3.8% of the labour force in 2001 to 3.1% in 2002.

South Korea is a member of the Asian Development Bank (ADB, see p. 143), Asia-Pacific Economic Co-operation (APEC, see p. 139), the Colombo Plan (see p. 339) and the Organisation for Economic Co-operation and Development (OECD, see p. 277).

In 1997 South Korea experienced its most serious economic crisis in 50 years. Several major *chaebol* collapsed, the won depreciated substantially against the US dollar and foreign-exchange reserves were almost depleted. The country was forced to seek extensive assistance from the IMF. President Kim Dae-Jung assumed office in February 1998, promising widespread economic reform, and accepted a three-year programme formulated by the IMF, which stipulated the implementation of stringent economic and financial liberalization measures. By the end of 1999 the economy appeared to have made a remarkable recovery, and in December 2000 the IMF ended its rescue programme, which it declared to have been a success. Economic difficulties however, mainly resulting from incomplete reform of the banking sector and *chaebol*, persisted. Official intervention was much in evidence in early 2001, reversing previous IMF-led policy, with many heavily-indebted companies receiving government aid. Vested interest groups with links to the *chaebol* continued to resist reform, and restructuring of the *chaebol* seemed to have stalled. Meanwhile, organized labour movements continued to arrange industrial action by workers fearing unemployment and seeking better working conditions, and strikes were held during 2001 and 2002. At the same time, declining job security led to reduced domestic consumption. Investor confidence remained low owing to a lack of clear evidence of reform, leading to fears that investment and jobs would be diverted to China and South-East Asia. Foreign direct investment declined by 27% to US $598m. in May 2001 from a year earlier, mainly owing to a reduction in spending by US and Japanese companies. Decreased demand from the USA, South Korea's principal export market, and the deceleration in the world economy substantially reduced South Korea's trade surplus and rate of growth in 2001. Sales of semiconductors, computers and other such goods were particularly badly affected, with exports decreasing by a record 19.4% in the year to August, although imports also declined, by 15.1%, over the same period. At only 3.0% in 2001, therefore, GDP growth failed to meet expectations and was substantially lower than in the previous year. However, GDP grew by a robust 6.3% in 2002, in part aided by a recovery in exports, with China emerging as the second most important destination. The corporate and financial sectors reported record profits in 2002, reflecting the success of reforms introduced during the preceding years. Although South Korea co-hosted the football World Cup with Japan in mid-2002, the overall economic benefits were limited, with much of the financing for infrastructure having been spent during the previous three years, and many businesses closing during major matches. Furthermore, far fewer foreign visitors attended the event than expected. In October the country experienced its worst typhoons in 40 years, resulting in nation-wide economic disruption and damage estimated at as much as US $1,000m. In particular, the damage to roads and railways disrupted the 'just-in-time' production lines of many industries, and was believed to have affected growth in the final quarter growth of 2002. Meanwhile, continued uncertainty over the North's nuclear programme was likely to reduce business confidence, especially among foreign investors. Domestic consumption decelerated in late 2002, further raising fears of a renewed slowdown. The rate of unemployment, however, continued to decline during 2002. President Roh was expected to continue reforms aimed at reducing the influence of the *chaebol*, and address the question of regional and social imbalances. Growth in 2003 was originally forecast at 5.1%. In April, however, the Bank of Korea revised downwards, to 4.1%, its forecast of the year's GDP growth.

Education

Education, available free of charge, is compulsory between the ages of six and 15. Primary education begins at six years of age and lasts for six years. In 1997 enrolment at primary schools included 93% of children in the appropriate age-group (males 92%; females 93%). Secondary education begins at 12 years of age and lasts for up to six years, comprising two cycles of three years each, the first of which is compulsory. Enrolment at secondary schools in 1996 included 97% of children in the appropriate age-group (males 97%; females 98%). In 2001 there

were 162 university-level institutions, with a student enrolment of 1,729,638. In that year there were 676 graduate schools, with a student enrolment of 243,270. Expenditure on education by the central Government totalled 17,779,200m. won in 1998 (representing 15.8% of total spending).

Public Holidays

2003: 1 January (New Year), 31 January–2 February (Lunar New Year), 1 March (Sam Il Jol, Independence Movement Day), 5 April (Arbor Day), 5 May (Children's Day), 8 May (Buddha's Birthday), 6 June (Memorial Day), 17 July (Constitution Day), 15 August (Liberation Day), 10–12 September (Juseok, Korean Thanksgiving Day), 3 October (National Foundation Day), 25 December (Christmas Day).

2004: 1 January (New Year), 21–23 January (Lunar New Year), 1 March (Sam Il Jol, Independence Movement Day), 5 April (Arbor Day), 5 May (Children's Day), 26 May (Buddha's Birthday), 6 June (Memorial Day), 17 July (Constitution Day), 15 August (Liberation Day), 27–29 September (Juseok, Korean Thanksgiving Day), 3 October (National Foundation Day), 25 December (Christmas Day).

Weights and Measures

The metric system is in force, although a number of traditional measures are also used.

Statistical Survey

Source (unless otherwise stated): National Statistical Office, Bldg III, Government Complex-Daejeon 920, Dunsan-dong, Seo-gu, Daejeon 302-701; tel. (42) 481-4114; fax (42) 481-2460; internet www.nso.go.kr.

Area and Population

AREA, POPULATION AND DENSITY*

Area (sq km)	99,313†
Population (census results)‡	
1 November 1995	44,608,726
1 November 2000	
Males	23,068,181
Females	22,917,108
Total	45,985,289
Population (official estimates at mid-year)	
2000	47,008,000
2001	47,343,000
2002	47,640,000
Density (per sq km) at mid-2002	479.7

* Excluding the demilitarized zone between North and South Korea, with an area of 1,262 sq km (487 sq miles).

† 38,345 sq miles. The figure indicates territory under the jurisdiction of the Republic of Korea, surveyed on the basis of land register.

‡ Excluding adjustment for underenumeration, estimated at 1.4% in 1995.

PRINCIPAL TOWNS
(population at 1995 census)

Seoul (capital)	10,231,217	Jeonju (Chonju)	563,153
Busan (Pusan)	3,814,325	Jeongju (Chongju)	531,376
Daegu (Taegu)	2,449,420	Masan	441,242
Incheon (Inchon)	2,308,188	Jinju (Chinju)	329,886
Daejeon (Taejon)	1,272,121	Kunsan	266,559
Gwangju (Kwangju)	1,257,636	Jeju (Cheju)	258,511
Ulsan	967,429	Mokpo	247,452
Seongnam		Chuncheon	
(Songnam)	869,094	(Chunchon)	234,528
Suwon	755,550		

2000 census: 9,853,972; Busan 3,655,437; Daegu 2,473,990; Incheon 2,466,338; Daejeon 1,365,961; Gwangju 1,350,948; Ulsan 1,012,110.

BIRTHS, MARRIAGES AND DEATHS*

	Registered live births		Registered marriages		Registered deaths	
	Number	Rate (per 1,000)	Number	Rate (per 1,000)	Number	Rate (per 1,000)
1993	723,924	16.4	402,593	9.0	240,468	5.4
1994	728,515	16.3	393,121	8.7	248,377	5.5
1995	721,074	16.0	398,484	8.7	248,089	5.4
1996	695,825	15.3	434,911	9.4	245,588	5.3
1997	678,402	14.8	388,591	8.4	247,938	5.3
1998	642,972	13.8	375,616	8.0	248,443	5.3
1999	616,322	13.2	362,673	7.7	246,539	5.2
2000	636,780	13.4	334,030	7.0	247,346	5.2

* Owing to late registration, figures are subject to continuous revision. The foregoing data refer to events registered by the end of 2000, tabulated by year of occurrence.

Expectation of life (WHO estimates, years at birth): 74.9 (males 71.2; females 78.7) in 2000 (Source: WHO, *World Health Report*).

ECONOMICALLY ACTIVE POPULATION*
(annual averages, '000 persons aged 15 years and over)

	1998	1999	2000
Agriculture, forestry and fishing .	2,480	2,349	2,288
Mining and quarrying	21	20	18
Manufacturing	3,898	4,006	4,244
Electricity, gas and water . . .	61	61	63
Construction	1,578	1,476	1,583
Trade, restaurants and hotels . .	5,571	5,724	5,943
Transport, storage and communications	1,169	1,202	1,260
Financing, insurance, real estate and business services	1,856	1,925	2,089
Community, social and personal services	3,339	3,499	3,551
Total employed (incl. others) . .	19,994	20,281	21,061
Unemployed	1,461	1,353	889
Total labour force	21,456	21,634	21,950
Males	12,893	12,889	12,950
Females	8,562	8,745	9,000

2001 ('000 persons aged 15 years and over): Agriculture, forestry and fishing 2,193; Manufacturing 4,199; Total employed 21,362; Unemployed 819; Total labour force 22,181 (Males 13,012; Females 9,169).

* Excluding armed forces.

Health and Welfare

KEY INDICATORS

Total fertility rate (children per woman, 2001)	1.5
Under-5 mortality rate (per 1,000 live births, 2001) . . .	5
HIV/AIDS (% of persons aged 15–49, 2001)	<0.10
Physicians (per 1,000 head, 1997)	1.36
Hospital beds (per 1,000 head, 1999)	5.5
Health expenditure (2000): US $ per head (PPP) . . .	909
Health expenditure (2000): % of GDP	6.0
Health expenditure (2000): public (% of total)	44.1
Access to water (% of persons, 2000)	92
Access to sanitation (% of persons, 2000)	63
Human Development Index (2000): ranking	27
Human Development Index (2000): value	0.882

For sources and definitions, see explanatory note on p. vi.

Agriculture

PRINCIPAL CROPS
('000 metric tons)

	1999	2000	2001
Rice (paddy)	7,032.8	7,124.8	7,453.0
Barley	330.6	226.6	382.8
Maize	79.3	64.2	57.0
Potatoes	678.3	704.6	730.0*
Sweet potatoes	428.1	344.9	273.1
Dry beans	22.8	21.0	20.0*
Chestnuts	95.8	92.8	90.0*
Soybeans (Soya beans) . . .	116.1	113.2	117.7
Sesame seed	24.1	31.7	31.0
Other oilseeds	37.3	34.7	n.a.
Cabbages	2,738.3	3,420.3	3,420.2
Lettuce	173.7	203.5	200.0*
Spinach	105.5	120.8	122.0*
Tomatoes	290.7	276.7	260.0*
Pumpkins, squash and gourds . .	217.0	240.5	240.5*
Cucumbers and gherkins . .	418.8	453.5	453.5*
Chillies and green peppers . .	436.6	391.3	380.0*
Green onions and shallots . .	606.6	657.9	657.9*
Dry onions	935.8	877.5	1,073.7
Garlic	483.8	474.4	406.4
Carrots	151.3	155.2	150.0*
Mushrooms	19.8	21.8	23.0*
Other vegetables	3,346.0	3,700.0	3,800.0*
Tangerines, mandarins, clementines and satsumas . .	624.2	563.5	640.0
Apples	490.5	489.0	403.6
Pears	259.1	324.2	417.2
Peaches and nectarines . . .	157.2	170.0	175.0*
Plums	43.7	51.7	55.0*
Strawberries	152.5	180.2	175.0*
Grapes	407.1	475.6	460.0*
Watermelons	936.7	922.7	900.0*
Cantaloupes and other melons . .	319.4	332.8	320.0*
Persimmons	273.8	287.8	290.0*
Other fruits	82.5	82.1	83.7*
Tobacco (leaves)	65.4	68.2	55.6

* FAO estimate.

Source: FAO.

LIVESTOCK
('000 head)

	1999	2000	2001
Cattle	2,486	2,134	1,954
Pigs	7,864	8,214	8,720
Goats	462	445	430*
Rabbits	462	436	600*
Chickens	94,587	102,547	102,393
Ducks	4,264	5,405	6,716

* FAO estimate.

Source: FAO.

LIVESTOCK PRODUCTS
('000 metric tons)

	1999	2000	2001
Beef and veal	342.4	305.0	226.0
Pig meat	996.3	915.9	927.7
Chicken meat	390.0*	373.6	377.1
Duck meat	39.3*	44.7*	48.0†
Other meat	9.1*	8.9*	10.1†
Cows' milk	2,243.9	2,252.8	2,338.9
Goats' milk†	3.5	4.6	4.4
Butter†	53.2	54.9	54.9
Hen eggs	461.9	478.8	460.0†
Other poultry eggs	20.2	21.3	22.5†
Honey	10.6	17.7	20.0†
Cattle hides (fresh)†	56.4	50.9	50.9

* Unofficial figure.
† FAO estimate(s).

Source: FAO.

Forestry

ROUNDWOOD REMOVALS
('000 cubic metres, excl. bark)

	1999	2000	2001
Sawlogs, veneer logs and logs for sleepers	621	420*	575*
Pulpwood .	410	552*	376*
Other industrial wood	663	620*	582*
Fuel wood	2,444	2,449*	2,454*
Total	4,138	4,041	3,987

* FAO estimate.

Source: FAO.

SAWNWOOD PRODUCTION
('000 cubic metres, incl. sleepers)

	1999	2000	2001
Coniferous (softwood)	3,648	4,044	4,330
Broadleaved (hardwood). . . .	652	500	90
Total	4,300	4,544	4,420

Source: FAO.

Fishing

('000 metric tons, live weight)

	1998	1999	2000
Capture	2,026.9	2,119.7	1,823.2
Alaska (walleye) pollock . . .	236.3	146.2	86.1
Croakers and drums . . .	89.0	114.2	67.6
Japanese anchovy	249.5	238.5	201.2
Skipjack tuna	143.4	109.8	137.0
Yellowfin tuna	73.4	43.3	49.5
Chub mackerel.	172.9	177.6	145.9
Largehead hairtail	74.9	64.4	81.1
Argentine shortfin squid . . .	92.4	271.7	150.1
Japanese flying squid	163.0	249.3	226.3
Aquaculture	327.5	303.1	323.2
Pacific cupped oyster	175.9	177.3	207.9
Other molluscs.	63.9	43.8	?
Total catch	2,354.4	2,422.8	2,146.4

Note: Figures exclude aquatic plants ('000 metric tons): 481.8 (capture 12.6, aquaculture 469.2) in 1998; 486.6 (capture 12.9, aquaculture 473.7) in 1999; 387.7 (capture 13.0, aquaculture 374.6) in 2000. Also excluded are aquatic mammals, recorded by number rather than by weight. The number of whales and dolphins caught was: 78 in 1998; 104 in 1999; 174 in 2000.

Source: FAO, *Yearbook of Fishery Statistics*.

Mining

('000 metric tons, unless otherwise indicated)

	1999	2000	2001
Hard coal (Anthracite) . . .	4,197	4,174	3,817
Iron ore: gross weight . . .	410	336	195
Iron ore: metal content . . .	230	188	109
Lead ore (metric tons)* . . .	1,822	2,724	988
Zinc ore (metric tons)* . . .	9,832	11,474	5,129
Kaolin	1,858.4	2,098.5	2,384.0
Feldspar	409.3	330.4	389.4
Salt (unrefined)†	750	800	800
Mica (metric tons)	24,733	65,249	109,339
Talc (metric tons)	15,313	11,344	47,712
Pyrophyllite	754.7	918.0	1,101.8

* Figures refer to the metal content of ores.

† Estimated production.

Source: US Geological Survey.

Industry

SELECTED PRODUCTS
('000 metric tons, unless otherwise indicated)

	1997	1998	1999
Wheat flour	1,750	1,722	1,834
Refined sugar.	1,691	1,132	1,182
Beer (million litres)	1,691	1,408	1,487
Cigarettes (million)	96,725	101,011	95,995
Cotton yarn—pure and mixed (metric tons)	276,411	n.a.	n.a.
Woven cotton fabrics—pure and mixed ('000 sq m)*	328,405	n.a.	n.a.
Plywood ('000 cu m)	995	587	664
Newsprint (metric tons). . .	1,583,303	1,699,164	1,737,753
Rubber tyres ('000)†	59,281	60,192	67,120
Caustic soda (metric tons) . .	959,217	1,069,308	1,163,413
Urea fertilizer (metric tons) . .	903,295	n.a.	n.a.
Liquefied petroleum gas (million litres)	3,897	4,238	4,893
Naphtha (million litres). . .	21,968	21,767	21,688
Kerosene (million litres). . .	11,308	9,809	15,071
Distillate fuel oil (million litres) .	41,694	37,622	35,157
Bunker C oil (million litres) . .	43,847	32,625	36,509
Residual fuel oil (million litres) .	1,079	710	812
Cement	60,317	46,791	48,579
Pig-iron	22,712	23,093	23,328
Crude steel	42,554	39,856	41,042
Television receivers ('000) . .	16,407	13,578	16,616
Passenger cars—assembled (number)	2,313,160	1,576,701	2,157,909
Lorries and trucks—assembled (number)	282,127	178,401	256,467
Electric energy (million kWh) . .	224,445	215,307	239,925

* After undergoing finishing processes.

† Tyres for passenger cars and commercial vehicles.

Shipbuilding (merchant ships launched, '000 grt): 7,156 in 1997; 6,974 in 1998; n.a. in 1999; 9,856 in 2000 (Source: UN, *Monthly Bulletin of Statistics*).

2000 ('000 metric ton): Cement 51,424; Pig-iron 24,938; Crude steel 43,107 (Source: US Geological Survey).

Finance

CURRENCY AND EXCHANGE RATES

Monetary Units
100 chun (jeon) = 10 hwan = 1 won

Sterling, Dollar and Euro Equivalents (31 December 2002)
£1 sterling = 1,911.9 won
US $1 = 1,186.2 won
€1 = 1,244.0 won
10,000 won = £5.230 = $8.430 = €8.039

Average Exchange Rate (won per US $)
2000   1,130.96
2001   1,290.99
2002   1,251.09

BUDGET
('000 million won)*

Revenue	1996	1997	1998
Taxation	72,385	78,434	78,310
Taxes on income, profits and			
capital gains	24,137	24,292	27,975
Income tax	14,767	14,868	17,194
Corporation tax	9,356	9,425	10,776
Social security contributions . .	7,425	8,506	10,512
Employees	2,804	3,433	n.a.
Employers	4,261	4,864	n.a.
Taxes on property	1,473	1,590	1,379
Domestic taxes on goods and			
services	27,478	30,650	27,159
Value-added tax	16,790	19,488	15,707
Excises	10,027	10,373	10,530
Import duties	5,309	5,798	3,836
Other current revenue . . .	11,791	13,639	17,480
Entrepreneurial and property			
income	4,600	5,634	9,854
Administrative fees and charges,			
non-industrial and incidental			
sales	1,518	1,394	1,530
Fines and forfeits	3,502	5,032	4,646
Capital revenue	1,352	1,295	883
Total	85,528	93,368	96,673

Expenditure	1996	1997	1998
General public services	7,847	9,039	10,841
Defence	12,553	13,159	13,621
Education	14,435	16,249	17,779
Health	682	777	957
Social security and welfare . . .	7,884	9,632	12,252
Housing and community amenities	7,077	6,677	7,336
Recreational, cultural and religious			
affairs and services . . .	534	679	788
Economic affairs and services . .	21,965	24,334	28,453
Interest expenditures . . .	2,241	2,258	3,399
Other	9,211	18,084	20,263
Total	84,429	100,888	115,689
Current	n.a.	62,812	70,631
Capital	n.a.	18,791	20,359
Net lending	n.a.	19,285	23,375
Other expenditures	n.a.	0	1,324

Source: IMF, *Republic of Korea: Statistical Appendix* (February 2000).

1999 ('000 million won)* Total revenue 107,923 (current 106,523; capital 1,386); Total expenditure (excl. net lending and other expenditures) 101,236 (current 76,798; capital 24,438) (Source: Bank of Korea, Ministry of Planning and Budget).

2000 ('000 million won)* Total revenue 133,584 (current 132,366; capital 1,218); Total expenditure (excl. net lending and other expenditures) 108,259 (current 82,667; capital 25,592) (Source: Bank of Korea, Ministry of Planning and Budget).

2001 ('000 million won)* Total revenue 139,890 (current 138,203; capital 1,697); Total expenditure (excl. net lending and other expenditures) 122,275 (current 99,755; capital 22,520) (Source: Bank of Korea, Ministry of Planning and Budget).

2002 ('000 million won)* Total revenue 151,873 (current 150,239; capital 1,633); Total expenditure (excl. net lending and other expenditures) 131,993 (current 109,123; capital 22,870) (Source: Bank of Korea, Ministry of Planning and Budget).

* Figures refer to the consolidated operations of the central Government, including extrabudgetary accounts, but excluding enterprise special accounts.

INTERNATIONAL RESERVES
(US $ million at 31 December)

	1999	2000	2001
Gold*	67.1	67.6	68.3
IMF special drawing rights . .	0.7	3.5	3.3
Reserve position in IMF . .	286.3	271.8	262.4
Foreign exchange	73,700.3	95,855.1	102,487.5
Total	74,054.4	96,198.1	102,821.6

* National valuation.

Source: IMF, *International Financial Statistics.*

MONEY SUPPLY
('000 million won at 31 December)

	1999	2000	2001
Currency outside banks	19,475	17,636	18,702
Demand deposits at deposit money			
banks	25,139	29,193	34,918

Source: IMF, *International Financial Statistics.*

COST OF LIVING
(Consumer Price Index; base: 2000 = 100)

	1998	1999	2001
Food	96.4	99.1	104.1
Housing	103.9	100.2	103.9
Fuel, light and water . . .	89.4	87.6	111.1
Furniture and utensils . . .	103.3	102.0	102.4
Clothing and footwear . . .	96.8	98.5	103.1
Medical treatment . . .	92.3	93.4	112.3
Education	93.5	95.3	104.4
Culture and Recreation . . .	101.1	100.1	99.7
Transport and communications .	95.7	97.2	102.0
All items (incl. others) . . .	97.0	97.8	104.1

NATIONAL ACCOUNTS
('000 million won at current prices)

National Income and Product

	1999	2000	2001*
Compensation of employees . .	210,411.5	229,605.2	244,898.2
Operating surplus . . .	149,183.2	160,338.7	157,458.2
Domestic factor incomes . .	359,594.7	389,943.9	402,356.4
Consumption of fixed capital .	60,904.2	61,655.9	63,184.5
Gross domestic product (GDP)			
at factor cost	420,498.9	451,599.8	465,540.9
Indirect taxes	63,552.8	71,811.8	80,938.7
Less Subsidies	1,307.5	1,452.4	1,466.3
GDP in purchasers' values .	482,744.2	521,959.2	545,013.3
Factor income from abroad . .	3,847.5	7,197.6	9,110.7
Less Factor income paid abroad	9,994.1	9,929.4	10,249.4
Gross national product . .	476,597.6	519,227.4	543,874.6
Less Consumption of fixed capital .	60,904.2	61,655.9	63,184.5
National income in market			
prices	415,693.4	457,571.5	480,690.0
Other current transfers from			
abroad (net)	2,223.9	644.3	-660.3
National disposable income .	417,917.3	458,215.8	480,029.7

* Provisional.

Expenditure on the Gross Domestic Product

	1999	2000	2001*
Government final consumption			
expenditure	50,089.4	52,479.7	56,785.2
Private final consumption			
expenditure	271,136.5	299,121.8	324,226.3
Increase in stocks . . .	-5,380.6	-1,033.7	-2,042.5
Gross fixed capital formation .	134,151.8	148,202.8	147,497.9
Statistical discrepancy . . .	-352.8	7,241.5	5,740.9
Total domestic expenditure .	449,644.3	506,012.1	532,207.8
Exports of goods and services .	204,377.6	233,791.7	233,857.1
Less Imports of goods and services	171,277.7	217,844.7	221,051.7
GDP in purchasers' values .	482,744.2	521,959.1	545,013.2
GDP at constant 1995 prices .	437,709.4	478,532.9	493,025.5

* Provisional.

Source: Bank of Korea.

Gross Domestic Product by Economic Activity

	1999	2000	2001*
Agriculture, forestry and fishing .	24,481.5	24,517.6	24,126.7
Mining and quarrying . . .	1,670.0	1,802.2	1,786.0
Manufacturing	148,402.9	163,283.2	163,334.9
Electricity, gas and water . .	13,014.0	14,374.4	15,845.8
Construction	42,149.3	41,788.0	44,879.3
Trade, restaurants and hotels . .	54,451.0	63,201.6	68,178.0
Transport, storage and communications . . .	32,976.3	34,901.1	35,039.8
Finance, insurance, real estate and business services	95,276.5	98,977.1	105,967.7
Government services. . . .	36,961.5	39,018.5	43,277.2
Other community, social and personal services . . .	24,806.0	27,484.8	32,410.9
Private non-profit services to households	11,470.6	12,320.7	13,514.3
Sub-total	485,659.6	521,669.2	548,360.6
Import duties	15,606.0	19,446.6	20,372.9
Less Imputed bank service charge	18,521.4	19,156.5	23,720.0
GDP in purchasers' values . .	482,744.2	521,959.2	545,013.3

* Figures are provisional.

BALANCE OF PAYMENTS
(US $ million)

	1999	2000	2001
Exports of goods f.o.b.	145,164	175,948	151,371
Imports of goods f.o.b.	−116,793	−159,076	−137,979
Trade balance	28,371	16,872	13,392
Exports of services	26,529	30,534	29,602
Imports of services	−27,180	−33,423	−33,129
Balance on goods and services	27,720	13,982	9,866
Other income received . . .	3,245	6,375	7,040
Other income paid	−8,404	−8,797	−7,926
Balance on goods, services and income	22,561	11,561	8,980
Current transfers received . . .	6,421	6,500	6,548
Current transfers paid . . .	−4,506	−5,820	−6,911
Current balance	24,477	12,241	8,617
Capital account (net) . . .	−389	−615	−443
Direct investment abroad . . .	−4,198	−4,999	−2,600
Direct investment from abroad. .	9,333	9,283	3,198
Portfolio investment assets . . .	1,282	−520	−5,499
Portfolio investment liabilities . .	7,908	12,697	11,856
Financial derivatives assets .	401	532	272
Financial derivatives liabilities	−915	−711	−378
Other investment assets . . .	−2,606	−2,289	7,458
Other investment liabilities . .	1,502	−1,268	−11,764
Net errors and omissions . . .	−3,536	−561	2,698
Overall balance	33,260	23,790	13,416

Source: IMF, *International Financial Statistics*.

External Trade

PRINCIPAL COMMODITIES
(distribution by SITC, US $ million)*

Imports c.i.f.	1999	2000	2001
Food and live animals . . .	5,551.3	6,496.7	6,789.3
Crude materials (inedible) except fuels	8,413.8	9,912.2	9,052.3
Mineral fuels, lubricants, etc. . .	22,874.9	38,076.6	34,069.3
Petroleum, petroleum products, etc.	17,906.0	30,535.4	26,485.6
Crude petroleum oils, etc. . .	14,782.7	25,215.6	21,367.8
Refined petroleum products . .	2,732.8	4,863.2	4,650.3
Gas (natural and manufactured)	3,003.2	5,355.2	5,236.6
Chemicals and related products	11,332.1	13,517.5	12,941.6
Organic chemicals	3,826.2	4,820.8	4,329.6
Basic manufactures . . .	15,080.0	18,290.9	16,683.8
Iron and steel.	4,003.2	5,315.7	4,420.0
Non-ferrous metals	3,770.1	4,449.8	3,894.9
Machinery and transport equipment.	43,608.9	59,078.9	47,911.0
Machinery specialized for particular industries . . .	3,370.9	5,510.0	3,713.1
General industrial machinery, equipment and parts . . .	4,000.7	4,942.4	4,594.2
Office machines and automatic data-processing machines .	4,330.5	7,711.0	5,640.8
Telecommunications and sound equipment	3,505.7	5,830.1	4,821.5
Other electrical machinery, apparatus, etc.	22,528.8	27,861.3	22,616.5
Thermionic valves and tubes, microprocessors, transistors, etc.	16,892.6	20,470.4	15,865.2
Electronic integrated circuits and microassemblies . . .	13,541.2	16,734.8	13,356.8
Miscellaneous manufactured articles	8,778.3	12,021.5	11,166.6
Total (incl. others)	119,752.3	160,481.0	141,097.8

Exports f.o.b.	1999	2000	2001
Mineral fuels, lubricants, etc.	5,810.9	9,375.5	8,009.1
Petroleum, petroleum products, etc.	5,569.9	9,172.8	7,892.7
Refined petroleum products	5,452.0	9,011.8	7,736.3
Chemicals and related products	10,756.7	13,783.7	12,523.8
Plastics in primary forms	4,173.5	5,147.8	4,633.2
Basic manufactures	27,915.8	30,380.1	26,789.5
Textile yarn, fabrics, etc.	11,617.8	12,710.4	10,940.8
Iron and steel	5,914.0	6,682.3	5,825.8
Machinery and transport equipment	77,953.8	100,275.2	86,694.8
Office machines and automatic data-processing machines	10,572.2	19,633.5	13,498.7
Automatic data-processing machines and units, etc.	7,156.7	9,290.5	7,484.9
Parts and accessories for automatic data-processing equipment	3,158.6	9,950.9	5,640.2
Telecommunications and sound equipment	10,502.8	14,363.9	15,943.6
Transmission apparatus for radio or television	3,756.7	5,672.7	7,483.6
Other electrical machinery, apparatus, etc.	27,678.0	31,836.0	21,694.0
Thermionic valves and tubes, microprocessors, transistors, etc.	21,843.4	24,688.1	14,741.9
Electronic integrated circuits and microassemblies	17,810.3	19,877.2	11,142.3
Road vehicles and parts†	13,424.8	15,436.1	15,363.1
Passenger motor cars (excl. buses)	9,969.0	11,896.0	12,029.4
Other transport equipment and parts†	7,949.6	8,946.1	10,229.9
Ships, boats and floating structures	7,490.3	8,229.4	9,699.2
Miscellaneous manufactured articles	13,918.9	12,432.5	11,247.0
Clothing and accessories (excl. footwear)	4,870.9	5,027.1	4,305.7
Total (incl. others)	143,685.5	172,267.5	150,439.1

* Figures exclude trade with the Democratic People's Republic of Korea (US $ million): Total imports 121.6 in 1999, 152.4 in 2000, 176.2 in 2001; Total exports 211.8 in 1999, 272.8 in 2000, 226.8 in 2001.

† Data on parts exclude tyres, engines and electrical parts.

Source: Korea Trade Information Services.

PRINCIPAL TRADING PARTNERS
(US $ '000)*

Imports c.i.f.	1999	2000	2001
Australia	4,672.4	5,958.7	5,534.1
Canada	1,792.9	2,107.8	1,821.3
China, People's Republic	8,886.7	12,798.9	13,302.7
France	1,823.1	2,243.8	2,092.3
Germany	3,826.0	4,624.7	4,473.4
Indonesia	3,986.9	5,286.9	4,473.5
Iran	1,505.8	2,392.8	2,099.3
Italy	1,269.0	1,637.8	1,787.5
Japan	24,142.0	31,827.9	26,633.4
Kuwait	1,416.4	2,716.0	2,250.7
Malaysia	3,155.3	4,878.0	4,125.0
Oman	944.4	1,744.7	2,310.9
Philippines	1,158.7	1,814.7	1,819.0
Qatar	868.4	2,292.1	2,572.1
Russia	1,590.5	2,058.3	1,929.5
Saudi Arabia	5,664.4	9,641.5	8,058.0
Singapore	2,311.7	3,722.9	3,011.5
South Africa	1,275.9	940.2	688.6
Taiwan	2,971.7	4,700.7	4,301.4
Thailand	1,067.8	1,630.9	1,589.2
United Arab Emirates	2,568.1	4,702.6	4,633.0
United Kingdom	2,098.2	2,575.7	2,353.5
USA	24,922.3	29,241.2	22,376.2
Total (incl. others)	119,752.3	160,481.0	141,097.8

Exports f.o.b.	1999	2000	2001
Australia	2,426.0	2,606.2	2,173.2
Brazil	1,209.3	1,724.1	1,611.2
Canada	1,638.5	2,426.7	2,035.7
China, People's Republic	13,684.6	18,454.5	18,190.2
France	1,654.1	1,713.3	1,541.2
Germany	4,184.9	5,153.8	4,321.8
Hong Kong	9,048.2	10,708.1	9,451.7
Indonesia	2,538.7	3,504.0	3,279.8
Italy	1,695.2	1,909.3	2,063.3
Japan	15,862.4	20,466.0	16,505.8
Malaysia	3,647.5	3,514.7	2,628.0
Mexico	2,016.9	2,391.4	2,148.9
Netherlands	2,143.6	2,657.9	2,532.1
Panama	1,812.8	1,247.0	1,719.0
Philippines	3,128.7	3,359.8	2,535.4
Singapore	4,921.8	5,648.2	4,079.6
Spain	1,490.5	1,533.1	1,518.2
Switzerland	1,840.7	515.8	431.9
Taiwan	6,345.5	8,026.6	5,835.3
Thailand	1,734.6	2,015.2	1,848.2
United Arab Emirates	1,550.6	1,991.5	2,169.1
United Kingdom	4,776.1	5,379.8	3,490.0
USA	29,474.7	37,610.6	31,210.8
Viet Nam	1,445.2	1,686.0	1,731.7
Total (incl. others)	143,685.5	172,267.5	150,439.1

* Excluding trade with the Democratic People's Republic of Korea.

Source: Korea Trade Information Services.

Transport

RAILWAYS
(traffic)

	1998	1999	2000
Passengers carried ('000)	829,050	823,563	814,472
Freight ('000 metric tons)	43,345	42,081	45,240

ROAD TRAFFIC
(motor vehicles in use at 31 December)

	1999	2000	2001*
Passenger cars	7,837,206	8,083,926	8,889,000
Goods vehicles	2,298,116	2,510,992	2,728,000
Buses and coaches	993,169	1,427,221	1,257,000
Motorcycles and mopeds	1,895,675	1,828,529	n.a.

* Figures are provisional.

SHIPPING

Merchant Fleet
(registered at 31 December)

	1999	2000	2001
Number of vessels	2,417	2,502	2,426
Total displacement ('000 grt)	5,734.8	6,199.8	6,395.0

Source: Lloyd's Register-Fairplay, *World Fleet Statistics.*

Sea-borne Freight Traffic
('000 metric tons)*

	1998	1999	2000
Goods loaded	254,449	268,728	282,768
Goods unloaded	446,561	506,302	550,811

* Including coastwise traffic loaded and unloaded.

CIVIL AVIATION

	1998	1999	2000
Domestic services:			
passengers ('000)	19,136	20,673	22,289
freight ('000 metric tons) . . .	356	381	428
International services:			
passengers ('000)	13,541	16,083	18,905
freight ('000 metric tons) . . .	1,359	1,604	1,865
mail ('000 metric tons) . . .	19	21	20

Tourism

FOREIGN VISITOR ARRIVALS*

Country of nationality	1999	2000	2001
China, People's Republic . . .	316,639	442,794	482,227
Hong Kong	234,087	200,874	204,959
Japan	2,184,121	2,472,054	2,377,321
Philippines	198,583	248,737	210,975
Russia	127,892	155,392	134,727
Taiwan.	110,563	127,120	129,410
USA	396,286	458,617	426,817
Total (incl. others)	4,659,785	5,321,792	5,147,204

* Including same-day visitors (excursionists) and crew members from ships.

† Including Korean nationals resident abroad: 301,027 in 1999; 277,523 in 2000; 286,585 in 2001.

Source: Korean National Tourism Organization.

Receipts from tourism (US $ million): 6,801.9 in 1999; 6,811.3 in 2000; 6,282.5 (estimate) in 2001 (Source: Bank of Korea).

Communications Media

	1999	2000	2001
Television receivers ('000 in use)	16,896	17,229	n.a.
Telephones ('000 main lines in use)	20,518.1	21,931.7	22,724.7
Mobile cellular telephones ('000			
subscribers).	23,442.7	26,816.4	29,045.6
Personal computers ('000 in use)	8,519	11,255	12,000
Internet users ('000).	10,860	19,040	24,380
Book production:			
titles.	25,910	25,632	25,146
copies ('000)	75,841	68,408	n.a.

1996: Facsimile machines (estimate, '000 in use): 400; Daily newspapers: Number 60, Circulation ('000 copies) 17,700 (estimate).

1997: Radio receivers ('000 in use) 47,500.

Sources: mainly UNESCO, *Statistical Yearbook*; UN, *Statistical Yearbook*; International Telecommunication Union.

Education

(2001)

	Institutions	Teachers	Pupils
Kindergarten	8,407	28,975	545,142
Primary schools	5,332	142,715	4,089,429
Middle schools	2,770	93,385	1,831,152
High schools	1,969	104,314	1,911,173
Junior vocational colleges. . .	158	11,897	952,649
Teachers' colleges	11	710	21,418
Universities and colleges . . .	162	43,309	1,729,638
Graduate schools	905	n.a.	243,270

Source: Ministry of Education, *Statistical Yearbook of Education*.

Adult literacy rate (UNESCO estimates): 97.8% (males 99.1%; females 96.4%) in 2000 (Source: UN Development Programme, *Human Development Report*).

Directory

The Constitution

The Constitution of the Sixth Republic (Ninth Amendment) was approved by national referendum on 29 October 1987. It came into effect on 25 February 1988. The main provisions are summarized below:

THE EXECUTIVE

The President

The President shall be elected by universal, equal, direct and secret ballot of the people for one term of five years. Re-election of the President is prohibited. In times of national emergency and under certain conditions the President may issue emergency orders and take emergency action with regard to budgetary and economic matters. The President shall notify the National Assembly of these measures and obtain its concurrence, or they shall lose effect. He may, in times of war, armed conflict or similar national emergency, declare martial law in accordance with the provisions of law. He shall lift the emergency measures and martial law when the National Assembly so requests with the concurrence of a majority of the members. The President may not dissolve the National Assembly. He is authorized to take directly to the people important issues through national referendums. The President shall appoint the Prime Minister (with the consent of the National Assembly) and other public officials.

The State Council

The State Council shall be composed of the President, the Prime Minister and no more than 30 and no fewer than 15 others appointed by the President (on the recommendation of the Prime Minister), and shall deliberate on policies that fall within the power of the executive. No member of the armed forces shall be a member of the Council, unless retired from active duty.

The Board of Audit and Inspection

The Board of Audit and Inspection shall be established under the President to inspect the closing of accounts of revenue and expenditures, the accounts of the State and other organizations as prescribed by law, and to inspect the administrative functions of the executive agencies and public officials. It shall be composed of no fewer than five and no more than 11 members, including the Chairman. The Chairman shall be appointed by the President with the consent of the National Assembly, and the members by the President on the recommendation of the Chairman. Appointments shall be for four years and members may be reappointed only once.

THE NATIONAL ASSEMBLY

Legislative power shall be vested in the National Assembly. The Assembly shall be composed of not fewer than 200 members, a number determined by law, elected for four years by universal, equal, direct and secret ballot. The constituencies of members of the Assembly, proportional representation and other matters pertaining to the Assembly elections shall be determined by law. A regular session shall be held once a year and extraordinary sessions shall be convened upon requests of the President or one-quarter of the Assembly's members. The period of regular sessions shall not exceed 100 days and of extraordinary sessions 30 days. The Assembly has the power to recommend to the President the removal of the Prime Minister or any other Minister. The Assembly shall have the authority to pass a motion for the impeachment of the President or any other public official, and may inspect or investigate state affairs, under procedures to be established by law.

THE CONSTITUTIONAL COURT

The Constitutional Court shall be composed of nine members appointed by the President, three of whom shall be appointed from persons selected by the National Assembly and three from persons nominated by the Chief Justice. The term of office shall be six years. It shall pass judgment upon the constitutionality of laws upon the request of the courts, matters of impeachment and the dissolution of political parties. In these judgments the concurrence of six members or more shall be required.

THE JUDICIARY

The courts shall be composed of the Supreme Court, which is the highest court of the State, and other courts at specified levels (for further details, see section on Judicial System). The Chief Justice and justices of the Supreme Court are appointed by the President, subject to the consent of the National Assembly. When the constitutionality of a law is a prerequisite to a trial, the Court shall request a decision of the Constitutional Court. The Supreme Court shall have the power to pass judgment upon the constitutionality or legality of administrative decrees, and shall have final appellate jurisdiction over military tribunals. No judge shall be removed from office except following impeachment or a sentence of imprisonment.

ELECTION MANAGEMENT

Election Commissions shall be established for the purpose of fair management of elections and national referendums. The National Election Commission shall be composed of three members appointed by the President, three appointed by the National Assembly and three appointed by the Chief Justice of the Supreme Court. Their term of office is six years, and they may not be expelled from office except following impeachment or a sentence of imprisonment.

POLITICAL PARTIES

The establishment of political parties shall be free and the plural party system guaranteed. However, a political party whose aims or activities are contrary to the basic democratic order may be dissolved by the Constitutional Court.

AMENDMENTS

A motion to amend the Constitution shall be proposed by the President or by a majority of the total number of members of the National Assembly. Amendments extending the President's term of office or permitting the re-election of the President shall not be effective for the President in office at the time of the proposal. Proposed amendments to the Constitution shall be put before the public by the President for 20 days or more. Within 60 days of the public announcement, the National Assembly shall decide upon the proposed amendments, which require a two-thirds majority of the National Assembly. They shall then be submitted to a national referendum not later than 30 days after passage by the National Assembly and shall be determined by more than one-half of votes cast by more than one-half of voters eligible to vote in elections for members of the National Assembly. If these conditions are fulfilled, the proposed amendments shall be finalized and the President shall promulgate them without delay.

FUNDAMENTAL RIGHTS

Under the Constitution all citizens are equal before the law. The right of habeas corpus is guaranteed. Freedom of speech, press, assembly and association are guaranteed, as are freedom of choice of residence and occupation. No state religion is to be recognized and freedom of conscience and religion is guaranteed. Citizens are protected against retrospective legislation, and may not be punished without due process of law.

Rights and freedoms may be restricted by law when this is deemed necessary for the maintenance of national security, order or public welfare. When such restrictions are imposed, no essential aspect of the right or freedom in question may be violated.

GENERAL PROVISIONS

Peaceful unification of the Korean peninsula, on the principles of liberal democracy, is the prime national aspiration. The Constitution mandates the State to establish and implement a policy of unification. The Constitution expressly stipulates that the armed forces must maintain political neutrality at all times.

The Government

HEAD OF STATE

President: ROH MOO-HYUN (took office 25 February 2003).

STATE COUNCIL
(April 2003)

Prime Minister: GOH KUN.

Deputy Prime Minister for Finance and the Economy: KIM JIN-PYO.

Deputy Prime Minister for Education and Human Resources Development: YOON DEOK-HONG.

Minister of Unification: JEONG SE-HYUN.

Minister of Foreign Affairs and Trade: YOON YOUNG-KWAN.

Minister of Justice: KANG GUM-SIL.

Minister of National Defence: Gen. (retd) CHO YOUNG-KIL.

Minister of Government Administration and Home Affairs: KIM DOO-KWAN.

Minister of Science and Technology: PARK HO-KOON.

Minister of Culture and Tourism: LEE CHANG-DONG.

Minister of Agriculture and Forestry: KIM YOUNG-JIN.

Minister of Commerce, Industry and Energy: YOON JIN-SHIK.

Minister of Information and Communication: CHIN DAE-JAE.

Minister of Health and Welfare: KIM HWA-JOONG.

Minister of the Environment: HAN MYUNG-SOOK.

Minister of Labour: KWON KI-HONG.

Minister of Gender Equality: JI EUN-HEE.

Minister of Construction and Transportation: CHOI JONG-CHAN.

Minister of Maritime Affairs and Fisheries: HUH SUNG-KWAN.

Minister of Planning and Budget: PARK BONG-HEUM.

Chairman of the Civil Service Commission: MOON HEE-SANG.

Chairman of the Financial Supervisory Commission: LEE JUNG-JAE.

Minister of Government Policy Co-ordination: LEE YOUNG-TAK.

Minister of the Government Information Agency: CHO YOUNG-DONG.

Chairman of the Korea Independent Commission Against Corruption: LEE EUN-YOUNG.

Note: From 2001 the romanization of place-names in South Korea was in the process of change, to be completed by 2005. Names of people and corporations were to remain unchanged for the time being.

MINISTRIES

Office of the President: Chong Wa Dae (The Blue House), 1, Sejong-no, Jongno-gu, Seoul; tel. (2) 770-0055; fax (2) 770-0344; e-mail president@cwd.go.kr; internet www.bluehouse.go.kr.

Office of the Prime Minister: 77, Sejong-no, Jongno-gu, Seoul; tel. (2) 737-0094; fax (2) 739-5830; internet www.opm.go.kr.

Ministry of Agriculture and Forestry: 1, Jungang-dong, Gwacheon City, Gyeonggi Prov. tel. (2) 503-7200; fax (2) 503-7238; internet www.maf.go.kr.

Ministry of Commerce, Industry and Energy: 1, Jungang-dong, Gwacheon City, Gyeonggi Prov. tel. (2) 503-7171; fax (2) 503-3142; internet www.mocie.go.kr.

Ministry of Construction and Transportation: 1, Jungang-dong, Gwacheon City, Gyeonggi Prov. tel. (2) 503-9405; fax (2) 503-9408; internet www.moct.go.kr.

Ministry of Culture and Tourism: 82-1, Sejong-no, Jongno-gu, Seoul 110-050; tel. (2) 7704-9114; fax (2) 3704-9119; internet www.mct.go.kr.

Ministry of Education and Human Resources Development: 77, 1-ga, Sejong-no, Jongno-gu, Seoul 110-760; tel. (2) 720-3404; fax (2) 720-1501; internet www.moe.go.kr.

Ministry of Environment: 1, Jungang-dong, Gwacheon City, Gyeonggi Prov. tel. (2) 2110-6576; fax (2) 504-9277; internet www.moenv.go.kr.

Ministry of Finance and the Economy: 1, Jungang-dong, Gwacheon City, Gyeonggi Prov. tel. (2) 503-9032; fax (2) 503-9033; internet www.mofe.go.kr.

Ministry of Foreign Affairs and Trade: 77, 1-ga, Sejong-no, Jongno-gu, Seoul; tel. (2) 3703-2555; fax (2) 720-2686; internet www.mofat.go.kr.

Ministry of Gender Equality: 520-3, Banpo-dong, Seocho-gu, Seoul 137-756; tel. (2) 2106-5000; fax (2) 2106-5145; internet www.moge.go.kr.

Ministry of Government Administration and Home Affairs: 77-6, Sejong-no, Jongno-gu, Seoul; tel. (2) 3703-4110; fax (2) 3703-5501; internet www.mogaha.go.kr.

Ministry of Health and Welfare: 1, Jungang-dong, Gwacheon City, Gyeonggi Prov. 427-760; tel. (2) 503-7505; fax (2) 503-7568; internet www.mohw.go.kr.

Ministry of Information and Communication: 100, Sejong-no, Jongno-gu, Seoul 110-777; tel. (2) 750-2000; fax (2) 750-2915; internet www.mic.go.kr.

Ministry of Justice: 1, Jungang-dong, Gwacheon City, Gyeonggi Prov. tel. (2) 503-7012; fax (2) 504-3337; internet www.moj.go.kr.

Ministry of Labour: 1, Jungang-dong, Gwacheon City, Gyeonggi Prov. tel. (2) 503-9713; fax (2) 503-8862; internet www.molab.go.kr.

Ministry of Maritime Affairs and Fisheries: 139 Chungjeong-no 3, Seodaemun-gu, Seoul 120-715; tel. (2) 3148-6040; fax (2) 3148-6044; internet www.momaf.go.kr.

Ministry of National Defence: 1, 3-ga, Yonsan-dong, Yeongsan-gu, Seoul; tel. (2) 795-0071; fax (2) 796-0369; internet www.mnd.go .kr.

Ministry of Planning and Budget: 520-3, Banpo-dong, Seocho-gu, Seoul 137-756; tel. (2) 3480-7716; fax (2) 3480-7600; internet www.mpb.go.kr.

Ministry of Science and Technology: 1, Jungang-dong, Gwacheon City, Gyeonggi Prov. tel. (2) 503-7619; fax (2) 503-7673; internet www.most.go.kr.

Ministry of Unification: 77-6, Sejong-no, Jongno-gu, Seoul 110-760; tel. (2) 720-2424; fax (2) 720-2149; internet www.unikorea.go .kr.

Civil Service Commission: Kolon Bldg, 35-34, Dongui-dong, Jongno-gu, Seoul 110-040; tel. (2) 3703-3633; fax (2) 3771-5027; internet www.csc.go.kr.

Financial Supervisory Commission: 27 Yeouido-dong, Yeong-deungpo-gu, Seoul; tel. (2) 3771-5000; fax (2) 785-3475; internet www.fsc.go.kr.

Korea Independent Commission Against Corruption: Seoul City Tower, 581, 5-ga, Namdaemun-no, Jung-gu, Seoul 100-095; tel. (2) 2126-0114; fax (2) 2126-0310; internet www.kicac.go.kr.

President and Legislature

PRESIDENT

Election, 19 December 2002

Candidate	Votes	% of total
Roh Moo-Hyun	12,014,277	48.9
Lee Hoi-Chang	11,443,297	46.6
Kwon Young-Gil	957,148	3.9
Lee Han-Dong	74,027	0.3
Kim Gil-Su	51,104	0.2
Kim Yeong-Kyu	22,063	0.1
Total	24,561,916	100.00

KUK HOE
(National Assembly)

1 Yeouido-dong, Yeongdeungpo-gu, Seoul; tel. (2) 788-2786; fax (2) 788-3375; internet www.assembly.go.kr.

Speaker: PARK KWAN-YONG.

General Election, 13 April 2000

Party	Elected representatives	Proportional representatives	Total seats
Grand National Party	112	21	133
Millennium Democratic Party	96	19	115
United Liberal Democrats	12	5	17
Democratic People's Party	1	1	2
New Korea Party of Hope	1	—	1
Independents	5	—	5
Total	227	46	273

Political Organizations

Democratic Labour Party (DLP): DooRay Bldg, 903, Yeouido-dong 24, Yeongdeungpo-gu, Seoul 151-010; tel. (2) 761-1333; fax (2) 761-4115; internet www.kdlp.org; f. 2000; Pres. KWON YOUNG-GIL.

Grand National Party (GNP) (Hannara Party): 17-7, Yeouido-dong, Yeongdeungpo-gu, Seoul 150-010; tel. (2) 3786-3373; fax (2) 3786-3610; internet www.hannara.or.kr; f. 1997 by merger of Democratic Party and New Korea Party; Pres. PARK HEE-TAE (acting); Exec. Chair. SUH CHANG-WON; Sec.-Gen. KIM YOUNG-IEL.

Korean Coalition for the Future: c/o National Assembly, Seoul; f. 2002 by defectors from the GNP; Chair. PARK GEUN-HYE.

Millennium Democratic Party (MDP): 15, Gisan Bldg, Yeong-deungpo-gu, Seoul; tel. (2) 784-7007; fax (2) 784-6070; internet www .minjoo.or.kr; f. 2000 following dissolution of National Congress for New Politics (f. 1995); Pres. CHYUNG DAI-CHUL; Chair. HAHN HWA-KAP; Sec.-Gen. LEE SANG-SOO.

United Liberal Democrats (ULD): Insan Bldg, 103-4, Shinsu-dong, Mapo-gu, Seoul 121-110; tel. (2) 701-3355; fax (2) 707-1637; internet www.jamin.or.kr; f. 1995 by fmr mems of the Democratic Liberal Party; Pres. KIM JONG-PIL.

Civic groups play an increasingly significant role in South Korean politics. These include: the People's Solidarity for Participatory Democracy (Dir Jang Hasung); the Citizens' Coalition for Economic Justice; and the Citizens' Alliance for Political Reform (Leader Kim Sok-Su).

Diplomatic Representation

EMBASSIES IN THE REPUBLIC OF KOREA

Algeria: 2-6, Itaewon 2-dong, Yeongsan-gu, Seoul 140-202; tel. (2) 794-5034; fax (2) 792-7845; e-mail sifdja01@kornet.net; internet www.algerianemb.or.kr; Ambassador AHMED BOUTACHE.

Argentina: Chun Woo Bldg, 5th Floor, 534 Itaewon-dong, Yeongsan-gu, Seoul 140-861; tel. (2) 793-4062; fax (2) 792-5820; Ambassador RODOLFO IGNACIO RODRÍGUEZ.

Australia: Kyobo Bldg, 11th Floor, 1, 1-ga, Jongno-gu, Seoul 110-714; tel. (2) 2003-0100; fax (2) 722-9264; internet www.australia.or .kr; Ambassador COLIN STUART HESELTINE.

Austria: Kyobo Bldg, Rm 1913, 1-1, 1-ga, Jongno, Jongno-gu, Seoul 110-714; tel. (2) 732-9071; fax (2) 732-9486; e-mail austroam@kornet .net; internet www.austria.or.kr; Ambassador Dr HELMUT BOECK.

Bangladesh: 7-18, Woo Sung Bldg, Dongbinggo-dong, Yeongsan-gu, Seoul; tel. (2) 796-4056; fax (2) 790-5313; e-mail dootrok@soback .kornet21.net; Ambassador HUMAYUN A. KAMAL.

Belarus: 432-1636 Sindang 2-dong, Jung-gu, Seoul; tel. (2) 2237-8171; fax (2) 2237-8174; e-mail consul_korea@belembassy.org; Ambassador ALYAKSANDR VIKTOROVICH SEMESHKO.

Belgium: 1-94, Dongbinggo-dong, Yeongsan-gu, Seoul 140-230; tel. (2) 749-0381; fax (2) 797-1688; e-mail seoul@diplobel.org; Ambassador KOENRAAD ROUVROY.

Brazil: Ihn Gallery Bldg, 4th and 5th Floors, 141 Palpan-dong, Jongno-gu, Seoul; tel. (2) 738-4970; fax (2) 738-4974; e-mail braseul@ soback.kornet21.net; Ambassador SÉRGIO B. SERRA.

Brunei: Gwanghwamun Bldg, 7th Floor, 211, Sejong-no, Jongnogu, Seoul 110-050; tel. (2) 399-3707; fax (2) 399-3709; e-mail kbnbd_seoul@yahoo.com; Ambassador Dato' ABD. RAHMAN HAMID.

Bulgaria: 723-42, Hannam 2-dong, Yeongsan-gu, Seoul 140-894; tel. (2) 794-8626; fax (2) 794-8627; e-mail ebdy1990@unitel.co.kr; Chargé d'affaires a.i. VALERY ARZHENTINSKI.

Cambodia: 657-162, Hannam-dong, Yeongsan-gu, Seoul 140–910; tel. (2) 3785-1041; fax (2) 3785-1040; e-mail camboemb@korea.com; Ambassador CHHEANG VUN.

Canada: Kolon Bldg, 10-11th Floors, 45, Mugyo-dong, Jung-gu, Seoul 100-662; tel. (2) 3455-6000; fax (2) 3455-6123; e-mail canada@ cec.or.kr; internet www.korea.gc.ca; Ambassador DENIS COMEAU.

Chile: Heungkuk Life Insurance Bldg, 14th Floor, 226 Sinmun-no 1-ga, Jongno-gu, Seoul; tel. (2) 2122-2600; fax (2) 2122-2601; e-mail echilekr@unitelkr; Ambassador FERNANDO SCHMIDT.

China, People's Republic: 54, Hyoja-dong, Jongno-gu, Seoul; tel. (2) 738-1038; fax (2) 738-1077; Ambassador LI BIN.

Colombia: Kyobo Bldg, 13th Floor, 1-ga, Jongno, Jongno-gu, Seoul; tel. (2) 720-1369; fax (2) 725-6959; Ambassador Dr MIGUEL DURÁN ORDÓÑEZ.

Congo, Democratic Republic: 702, Daewoo Complex Bldg, 167 Naesu-dong, Jongno-gu, Seoul; tel. and fax (2) 6272-7997; e-mail demcongoseoul@yahoo.fr; Chargé d'affaires N. CHRISTOPHE NGWEY.

Côte d'Ivoire: Chungam Bldg, 2nd Floor, 794-4, Hannam-dong, Yeongsan-gu, Seoul; tel. (2) 3785-0561; fax (2) 3785-0564; Ambassador HONORAT ABENI KOFFI.

Czech Republic: 1-121, 2-ga, Sinmun-no, Jongno-gu, Seoul 110-062; tel. (2) 725-6765; fax (2) 734-6452; e-mail seoul@embassy.mzv .cz; Ambassador IVAN HOTEK.

Denmark: Namsong Bldg, 5th Floor, 260-199, Itaewon-dong, Yeongsan-gu, Seoul 140-200; tel. (2) 795-4187; fax (2) 796-0986; e-mail selamb@um.dk; Ambassador LEIF DONDE.

Dominican Republic: Taepyeong-no Bldg, 19th Floor, 2-ga, 310 Taepyeong-no, Jung-gu, Seoul; tel. (2) 756-3513; fax (2) 756-3514; Ambassador JOSÉ M. NUNEZ.

Ecuador: Korea First Bldg, 19th Floor, 100 Gongpyeong-dong, Jongno-gu, Seoul; tel. (2) 739-2401; fax (2) 739-2355; e-mail mecuadorcor1@kornet.net; Ambassador FRANKLIN ESPINOSA.

Egypt: 46-1, Hannam-dong, Yeongsan-gu, Seoul; tel. (2) 749-0787; fax (2) 795-2588; internet www.mfg.gov.eg; Ambassador AMR HELMY.

El Salvador: Samsung Life Insurance Bldg, 20th Floor, Taepyeong-no 2-ga, Jung-gu, Seoul 100-716; tel. (2) 753-3432; fax (2) 753-3456; e-mail koembsal@hananet.net; Ambassador ALFREDO FRANCISCO UNGO.

Ethiopia: 657-26, Hannam-dong, Yeongsan-gu, Seoul; tel. (2) 790-8927; fax (2) 790-8929; Chargé d'affaires a.i. HAILE GEBRESELASSE.

Finland: Kyobo Bldg, Suite 1602, 1-1, 1-ga, Jongno, Jongno-gu, Seoul 110-714; tel. (2) 732-6737; fax (2) 723-4969; e-mail sanomat .seo@formin.fi; internet www.finlandembasy.or.kr; Ambassador LAURI KORPINEN.

France: 30, Hap-dong, Seodaemun-gu, Seoul 120-030; tel. (2) 3149–4300; fax (2) 3149–4328; e-mail ambfraco@elim.net; internet www .ambafrance-kr.org; Ambassador FRANÇOIS DESCOUEYTE.

Gabon: Yoosung Bldg, 4th Floor, 738-20, Hannam-dong, Yeongsan-gu, Seoul; tel. (2) 793-9575; fax (2) 793-9574; e-mail amgabsel@ unitel.co.kr; Ambassador EMMANUEL ISSOZE-NGONDET.

Germany: 308-5, Dongbinggo-dong, Yeongsan-gu, Seoul 140-230; tel. (2) 748-4114; fax (2) 748-4161; e-mail dboseoul@kornet.net; internet www.gembassy.or.kr; Ambassador HUBERTUS VON MORR.

Ghana: 5-4, Hannam-dong, Yeongsan-gu, Seoul (CPOB 3887); tel. (2) 3785-1427; fax (2) 3785-1428; e-mail ghana3@kornet.net; Ambassador EDWARD OBENG KUFUOR.

Greece: Hanwha Bldg, 27th Floor, 1, Janggyo-dong, Jung-gu, Seoul 100-797; tel. (2) 729-1401; fax (2) 729-1402; Ambassador GEORGE ASSIMACOPOULOS.

Guatemala: 3422, Lotte Hotel, 1, Sogong-dong, Jung-gu, Seoul; tel. (2) 771-7582; fax (2) 771-7584; Ambassador EMILIO R. MALDONADO.

Holy See: 2, Gungjeong-dong, Jongno-gu, Seoul (Apostolic Nunciature); tel. (2) 736-5725; fax (2) 739-2310; e-mail nunseoul@kornet .net; Apostolic Nuncio Most Rev. GIOVANNI BATTISTA MORANDINI (Titular Archbishop of Numida).

Honduras: Jongno Tower Bldg, 2nd Floor, 6, Jongno 2-ga, Jongno-gu, Seoul 110-160; tel. (2) 738-8402; fax (2) 738-8403; e-mail hondseul@kornet.net; Ambassador RENE FRANCISCO UMANA CHINCHILLA.

Hungary: 1-103, Dongbinggo-dong, Yeongsan-gu, Seoul 140-230; tel. (2) 792-2105; fax (2) 792-2109; e-mail huembsel@shinbiron.com; internet www.shinbiro.com/huembsel; Ambassador BÉLA LÁSZLÓ.

India: 37-3, Hannam-dong, Yeongsan-gu, CPOB 3466, Seoul 140-210; tel. (2) 798-4257; fax (2) 796-9534; e-mail eoiseoul@soback .kornet.nm.kr; Chargé d'affaires MOHINDER SINGH GROVER.

Indonesia: 55, Yeouido-dong, Yeongdeungpo-gu, Seoul 150-010; tel. (2) 783-5675; fax (2) 780-4280; e-mail bidpen@soback.kornet21.net; Ambassador ABDUL GHANI.

Iran: 726-126, Hannam-dong, Yeongsan-gu, Seoul; tel. (2) 793-7751; fax (2) 792-7052; e-mail iranssy@chollian.net; internet www.mfa.gov .ir; Ambassador MOHSEN TALAE'I.

Ireland: Daehan Fire and Marine Insurance Bldg, 15th Floor, 51-1, Namchang-dong, Jung-gu, Seoul; tel. (2) 774-6455; fax (2) 774-6458; e-mail hibernia@bora.dacom.co.kr; Ambassador PAUL MURRAY.

Israel: Dae-kong Bldg, 15th Floor, 823-21, Yeoksam-dong, Gangnam-gu, Seoul 135-080; tel. (2) 564-3448; fax (2) 564-3449; e-mail israeli@chollian.net; internet www.israelemb.or.kr; Ambassador UZI MANOR.

Italy: 1-398, Hannam-dong, Yeongsan-gu, Seoul 140-210; tel. (2) 796-0491; fax (2) 797-5560; e-mail ambseoul@italyemb.or.kr; Ambassador FRANCESCO RAUSI.

Japan: 18-11, Junghak-dong, Jongno-gu, Seoul; tel. (2) 2170-5200; fax (2) 734-4528; Ambassador TOSHIYUKI TAKANO.

Kazakhstan: 13-10, Seongbuk-dong, Seongbuk-gu, Seoul; tel. (2) 744-9714; fax (2) 744-9760; e-mail kazkor@chollian.net; Ambassador BORLAT K. NURGALIEV.

Kuwait: 309-15, Dongbinggo-dong, Yeongsan-gu, Seoul; tel. (2) 749-3688; fax (2) 749-3687; Ambassador FAWZI AL-JASEM.

Laos: 657-93, Hannam-dong, Yeongsan-gu, Seoul; tel. (2) 796-1713; fax (2) 796-1771; e-mail laoseoul@korea.com; Ambassador THONGSAVATH PRASEUTH.

Lebanon: 1-48, Dongbinggo-dong, Yeongsan-gu, Seoul 140-230; tel. (2) 794-6482; fax (2) 794-6485; e-mail emleb@nuri.net; Ambassador MOHAMAD NASRAT EL-ASSAAD.

Libya: 4-5, Hannam-dong, Yeongsan-gu, Seoul; tel. (2) 797-6001; fax (2) 797-6007; e-mail libyaemb@kornet.net; Ambassador AHMED MOHAMED TABULI.

Malaysia: 4-1, Hannam-dong, Yeongsan-gu, Seoul 140-210; tel. (2) 794-0349; fax (2) 794-5488; e-mail mwseoul@kornet.net; Ambassador Dato' VYRAMUTTU YOOGALINGAM.

Mexico: 33-6, Hannam 1-dong, Yeongsan-gu, Seoul 140-885; tel. (2) 798-1694; fax (2) 790-0939; Ambassador ROGELIO GRANGUILLHOME.

Mongolia: 33-5, Hannam-dong, Yeongsan-gu, Seoul; tel. (2) 794-1350; fax (2) 794-7605; e-mail monemb@uriel.net; internet www .mongoliaemb.or.kr; Ambassador URJINLHUNDEV PERENLEYN.

Morocco: S-15, UN Village, 270-3, Hannam-dong, Yeongsan-gu, Seoul; tel. (2) 793-6249; fax (2) 792-8178; e-mail sifamase@bora .dacom.co.kr; internet www.moroccoemb.or.kr; Ambassador JAAFAR ALJ HAKIM.

Myanmar: 724-1, Hannam-dong, Yeongsan-gu, Seoul 140-210; tel. (2) 792-3341; fax (2) 796-5570; e-mail myanmare@ppp.kornet.net; Ambassador U NYO WIN.

Netherlands: Kyobo Bldg, 14th Floor, 1-ga, Jongno, Jongno-gu, Seoul 110-714; tel. (2) 737-9514; fax (2) 735-1321; e-mail nlgovseo@ bora.dacom.co.kr; Ambassador HEIN J. DE VRIES.

New Zealand: Kyobo Bldg, 18th Floor, 1, 1-ga, Jongno, Jongno-gu, CPOB 1059, Seoul 100-610; tel. (2) 730-7794; fax (2) 737-4861; e-mail nzembsel@kornet.net; internet www.nzembassy.com/korea; Ambassador DAVID TAYLOR.

Nigeria: 310-19, Dongbinggo-dong, Yeongsan-gu, Seoul; tel. (2) 797-2370; fax (2) 796-1848; e-mail chancery@nigeriaembassy.or.kr; Ambassador AKPANG ADE OBI ODU.

Norway: 258-8, Itaewon-dong, Yeongsan-gu, CPOB 355, Seoul 100-603; tel. (2) 795-6850; fax (2) 798-6072; e-mail emb.seoul@mfa.no; internet www.norway.or.kr; Ambassador ARILD BRAASTAD.

Oman: 309-3, Dongbinggo-dong, Yeongsan-gu, Seoul; tel. (2) 790-2431; fax (2) 790-2430; e-mail omanembs@ppp.kornet.nm.kr; Ambassador MOOSA HAMDAN AL-TAEE.

Pakistan: 258-13, Itaewon 2-dong, Yeongsan-gu, Seoul 140-202; tel. (2) 796-8252; fax (2) 796-0313; e-mail heamb@pakistan-korea-trade .org; internet www.pakistan-korea-trade.org; Ambassador TARIQ OSMAN HYDER.

Panama: Hyundai Merchant Marine Bldg, 4th Floor, 66, Jeokseon-dong, Jongno-gu, Seoul; tel. (2) 734-8610; fax (2) 734-8613; e-mail panaemba@kornet.net; Ambassador FÉLIX PÉREZ ESPINOSA.

Papua New Guinea: 36-1, Hannam 1-dong, Yeongsan-gu, Seoul; tel. (2) 798-9854; fax (2) 798-9856; e-mail pngembsl@ppp.kornet.nm .kr; Ambassador DAVID ANGGO.

Paraguay: SK Bldg, 2nd Floor, 99 Seorin-dong, Jongno-gu, Seoul 110-728; tel. (2) 730-8335; fax (2) 730-8336; e-mail pyemc2@hananet .net; Ambassador LUIS FERNANDO AVALOS GIMÉNEZ.

Peru: Namhan Bldg, 6th Floor, 76-42, Hannam-dong, Yeongsan-gu, Seoul 140-210; tel. (2) 793-5810; fax (2) 793-3736; e-mail ipruseul@ uriel.net; Chargé d'affaires GUSTAVO LEMBCKE.

Philippines: Diplomatic Center, 9th Floor, 1376-1, Seocho 2-dong, Seocho-gu, Seoul; tel. (2) 577-6147; fax (2) 574-4286; e-mail phsk@ soback.kornet.net; Ambassador JUANITO P. JARASA.

Poland: 70 Sagan-dong, Jongno-gu, Seoul; tel. (2) 723-9681; fax (2) 723-9680; e-mail embassy@polandseoul.org; Ambassador TADEUSZ CHOMICKI.

Portugal: Wonseo Bldg, 2nd Floor, 171, Wonseo-dong, Jongno-gu, Seoul; tel. (2) 3675-2251; fax (2) 3675-2250; e-mail ambport@chollian .net; Ambassador FERNANDO MACHADO.

Qatar: 1-77, Dongbinggo-dong, Yeongsan-gu, Seoul; tel. (2) 790-1308; fax (2) 790-1027; Ambassador ABDUL RAZZAK AL-ABDULGHANI.

Romania: 1-42, UN Village, Hannam-dong, Yeongsan-gu, Seoul 140-210; tel. (2) 797-4924; fax (2) 794-3114; e-mail romemb@uriel .net; internet www.uriel.net/~romemb; Ambassador VIOREL ISTICIOAIA-BUDURA.

Russia: 34-16, Jeong-dong, Jung-gu, Seoul; tel. (2) 318-2116; fax (2) 754-0417; Ambassador TEYMURAZ. O. RAMISHVILI.

Saudi Arabia: 1-112, 2-ga, Sinmun-no, Jongno-gu, Seoul; tel. (2) 739-0631; fax (2) 732-3110; Ambassador SALEH BIN MANSOUR AL-RAJHY.

Singapore: Seoul Finance Bldg, 28th Floor, 84, 1-ga, Taepyeong-no, Jung-gu, Seoul 100-102; tel. (2) 774-2464; fax (2) 773-2465; e-mail singemb@unitel.co.kr; Ambassador CALVIN EU MUN HOO.

Slovakia: 389-1, Hannam-dong, Yeongsan-gu, Seoul 140-210; tel. (2) 794-3981; fax (2) 794-3982; e-mail slovakemb@yahoo.com; Chargé d'Affaires a.i. JÁN CHLÁDEK.

South Africa: 1-37, Hannam-dong, Yeongsan-gu, Seoul 140-210; tel. (2) 792-4855; fax (2) 792-4856; e-mail sae@saembasy.dacom.net; internet saembassy.dacom.net; Ambassador SYDNEY BAFANA KUB-HEKA.

Spain: 726-52 Hannam-dong, Yeongsan-gu, Seoul; tel. (2) 794-3581; fax (2) 796-8207; Ambassador ENRIQUE PANES CALPE.

Sri Lanka: Kyobo Bldg, Rm 2002, 1-1, 1-ga, Jongno, Jongno-gu, Seoul 110-714; tel. (2) 735-2966; fax (2) 737-9577; e-mail lankaemb@chollian.net; Ambassador K. C. LOGESWARAN.

Sudan: 653-24, Hannam-dong, Yeongsan-gu, Seoul; tel. (2) 793-8692; fax (2) 793-8693; Ambassador BABIKER A. KHALIFA.

Sweden: Seoul Central Bldg, 12th Floor, 136, Seorin-dong, Jongno-gu, KPO Box 1154, Seoul 110-110; tel. (2) 738-0846; fax (2) 733-1317; e-mail swedemb@swedemb.or.kr; internet www.swedemb.or.kr; Ambassador BO LUNDBERG.

Switzerland: 32-10, Songwol-dong, Jongno-gu, Seoul 110-101; tel. (2) 739-9511; fax (2) 737-9392; e-mail swissemb@elim.net; internet www.elim.net/~swissemb/; Ambassador CHRISTIAN MUEHLETHALER.

Thailand: 653-7, Hannam-dong, Yeongsan-gu, Seoul; tel. (2) 795-3098; fax (2) 798-3448; e-mail rteseoul@elim.net; Ambassador SOMBOON SANGIAMBUT.

Tunisia: 7-13, Dongbinggo-dong, Yeongsan-gu, Seoul 140-230; tel. (2) 790-4334; fax (2) 790-4333; e-mail tunseoul@att.co.kr; Ambassador MONDHER JEMAIL.

Turkey: Vivien Corpn Bldg, 4th Floor, 4-52, Seobinggo-dong, Yeongsan-gu, Seoul; tel. (2) 794-0255; fax (2) 797-8546; e-mail tcseulbe@kornet.net; Ambassador SELIM KUNERALP.

Ukraine: Diplomatic Center 905, 1376-1, Seocho 2-dong, Seocho-gu, Seoul; tel. (2) 578-6910; fax (2) 578-5514; e-mail ambassador@ukrembrk.com; Ambassador VOLODYMYR V. FURKALO.

United Arab Emirates: 5-5, Hannam-dong, Yeongsan-gu, Seoul; tel. (2) 790-3235; fax (2) 790-3238; Ambassador ABDULLA MOHAMED ALI AL-SHURAFA AL-HAMMADY.

United Kingdom: 4, Jeong-dong, Jung-gu, Seoul 100-120; tel. (2) 3210-5500; fax (2) 725-1738; e-mail bembassy@britain.or.kr; internet www.britain.or.kr; Ambassador CHARLES HUMFREY.

USA: 82, Sejong-no, Jongno-gu, Seoul; tel. (2) 397-4114; fax (2) 735-3903; internet usembassy.state.gov/seoul/wwwh418f.html; Ambassador THOMAS C. HUBBARD.

Uruguay: Daewoo Bldg, 1025, 541, 5-ga, Namdaemun, Jung-gu, Seoul; tel. (2) 753-7893; fax (2) 777-4129; e-mail uruseul@kornet.net; Ambassador JULIO GIAMBRUNO.

Uzbekistan: Diplomatic Center, Rm. 701, 1376-1, Seocho 2-dong, Seocho-gu, Seoul; tel. (2) 574-6554; fax (2) 578-0576; Ambassador VITALI V. FEN.

Venezuela: Garden Tower Bldg, 18th Floor, 98-78, Wooni-dong, Jongno-gu, Seoul; tel. (2) 741-0036; fax (2) 741-0046; e-mail emvesel@taeback.kornet.nm.kr; Chargé d'affaires KIDDER SALAZAR.

Viet Nam: 28-58, Samcheong-dong, Jongno-gu, Seoul 140-210; tel. (2) 738-2318; fax (2) 739-2064; e-mail vietnam@elim.net; Ambassador DUONG CHINH THUC.

Yemen: 11-444, Hannam-dong, Yeongsan-gu, Seoul 140-210; tel. (2) 792-9883; fax (2) 792-9885; e-mail yemensel@ppp.kornet21.net; internet www.gpc.org.ye; Chargé d'affaires YAHYA AHMED AL-WAZIR.

Judicial System

SUPREME COURT

The Supreme Court is the highest court, consisting of 14 Justices, including the Chief Justice. The Chief Justice is appointed by the President, with the consent of the National Assembly, for a term of six years. Other Justices of the Supreme Court are appointed for six years by the President on the recommendation of the Chief Justice. The appointment of the Justices of the Supreme Court, however, requires the consent of the National Assembly. The Chief Justice may not be reappointed. The court is empowered to receive and decide on appeals against decisions of the High Courts, the Patent Court, and the appellate panels of the District Courts or the Family Court in civil, criminal, administrative, patent and domestic relations cases. It is also authorized to act as the final tribunal to review

decisions of courts-martial and to consider cases arising from presidential and parliamentary elections.

Chief Justice: CHOI JONG-YOUNG, 967, Seocho-dong, Seocho-gu, Seoul; tel. (2) 3480-1002; fax (2) 533-1911; internet www.scourt.go.kr.

Justices: SONG JIN-HUN, SUH SUNG, CHO MOO-JEH, BYUN JAE-SEUNG, YOO JI-DAM, YOON JAE-SIK, LEE YONG-WOO, BAE KI-WON, KANG SHIN-WOOK, LEE KYU-HONG, LEE KANG-KOOK, SON JI-YOL, PARK JAE-YOON.

CONSTITUTIONAL COURT

The Constitutional Court is composed of nine adjudicators appointed by the President, of whom three are chosen from among persons selected by the National Assembly and three from persons nominated by the Chief Justice. The Court adjudicates the following matters: constitutionality of a law (when requested by the other courts); impeachment; dissolution of a political party; disputes between state agencies, or between state agencies and local governments; and petitions relating to the Constitution.

President: YUN YOUNG-CHUL, 83 Jae-dong, Jongno-gu, Seoul 110-250; tel. (2) 708-3456; fax (2) 708-3566; internet www.ccourt.go.kr.

HIGH COURTS

There are five courts, situated in Seoul, Daegu, Busan, Gwangju and Daejeon, with five chief, 78 presiding and 145 other judges. The courts have appellate jurisdiction in civil and criminal cases and can also pass judgment on administrative litigation against government decisions.

PATENT COURT

The Patent Court opened in Daejeon in March 1998, to deal with cases in which the decisions of the Intellectual Property Tribunal are challenged. The examination of the case is conducted by a judge, with the assistance of technical examiners.

DISTRICT COURTS

District Courts are established in 13 major cities; there are 13 chief, 241 presiding and 966 other judges. They exercise jurisdiction over all civil and criminal cases in the first instance.

MUNICIPAL COURTS

There are 103 Municipal Courts within the District Court system, dealing with small claims, minor criminal offences, and settlement cases.

FAMILY COURT

There is one Family Court, in Seoul, with a chief judge, four presiding judges and 16 other judges. The court has jurisdiction in domestic matters and juvenile delinquency.

ADMINISTRATIVE COURT

An Administrative Court opened in Seoul in March 1998, to deal with cases that are specified in the Administrative Litigation Act. The Court has jurisdiction over cities and counties adjacent to Seoul, and deals with administrative matters, including taxes, expropriations of land, labour and other general administrative matters. District Courts deal with administrative matters within their districts until the establishment of regional administrative courts is complete.

COURTS-MARTIAL

These exercise jurisdiction over all offences committed by armed forces personnel and civilian employees. They are also authorized to try civilians accused of military espionage or interference with the execution of military duties.

Religion

The traditional religions are Mahayana Buddhism, Confucianism and Chundo Kyo, a religion peculiar to Korea and combining elements of Shaman, Buddhist and Christian doctrines.

BUDDHISM

Korean Mahayana Buddhism has about 80 denominations. The Chogye-jong is the largest Buddhist order in Korea, having been introduced from China in ad 372. The Chogye Order accounts for almost two-thirds of all Korean Buddhists. In 1995 it had 2,426 out of 19,059 Buddhist temples and there were 12,470 monks.

Korean United Buddhist Association (KUBA): 46-19, Soosong-dong, Jongno-gu, Seoul 110-140; tel. (2) 732-4885; 28 mem. Buddhist orders; Pres. SONG WOL-JOO.

Won Buddhism

Won Buddhism combines elements of Buddhism and Confucianism. In 1995 there were 404 temples, 9,815 priests, and 86,823 believers.

CHRISTIANITY

National Council of Churches in Korea: Christian Bldg, Rm 706, 136-46, Yeonchi-dong, Jongno-gu, Seoul 110-736; tel. (2) 763-8427; fax (2) 744-6189; e-mail kncc@kncc.or.kr; internet www.kncc.or.kr; f. 1924 as National Christian Council; present name adopted 1946; eight mem. churches; Gen. Sec. Rev. PAIK DO-WOONG.

The Anglican Communion

South Korea has three Anglican dioceses, collectively forming the Anglican Church of Korea (founded as a separate province in April 1993), under its own Primate, the Most Rev. Matthew Chung Chul-Bum.

Bishop of Pusan (Busan): Rt Rev. JOSEPH DAE-YONG LEE, 455-2, Oncheon-1-dong, Dongnae-gu, Busan 607-061; tel. (51) 554-5742; fax (51) 553-9643; e-mail bpjoseph@hanmail.net.

Bishop of Seoul: Most Rev. MATTHEW CHUNG CHUL-BUM, 3, Jeong-dong, Jung-gu, Seoul 100-120; tel. (2) 738-6597; fax (2) 723-2640; e-mail bishop100@hosanna.net.

Bishop of Taejon (Daejeon): Rt Rev. PAUL YOON HWAN, 88-1, Sonhwa 2-dong, POB 22, Daejeon 300-600; tel. (42) 256-9987; fax (42) 255-8918.

The Roman Catholic Church

For ecclesiastical purposes, North and South Korea are nominally under a unified jurisdiction. South Korea comprises three arch-dioceses, 10 dioceses, and one military ordinate. At 31 December 2001 some 4,228,488 people (8.8% of the population) were adherents of the Roman Catholic Church.

Bishops' Conference

Catholic Bishops' Conference of Korea, 643-1, Junggok-dong, Gwangjin-gu, Seoul 143-912; tel. (2) 460-7500; fax (2) 460-7505; e-mail cbck@cbck.or.kr; internet www.cbck.or.kr.

f. 1857; Pres. Most Rev. ANDREAS CHOI CHANG-MOU (Archbishop of Gwangju).

Archbishop of Kwangju (Gwangju): Most Rev. ANDREAS CHOI CHANG-MOU, Archdiocese Office, 5-32, Im-dong, Buk-gu, Gwangju 500-868; tel. (62) 510-2838; fax (62) 525-6873; e-mail biseo@kjcatholic.or.kr.

Archbishop of Seoul: Most Rev. NICHOLAS CHEONG JIN-SUK, Archdiocesan Office, 1, 2-ga, Myeong-dong, Jung-gu, Seoul 100-022; tel. (2) 727-2114; fax (2) 773-1947; e-mail ao@seoul.catholic.or.kr.

Archbishop of Taegu (Daegu): Most Rev. PAUL RI MOON-HI, Archdiocesan Office, 225-1, Namsan 3-dong, Jung-gu, Daegu 700-804; tel. (53) 253-7011; fax (53) 253-9441; e-mail taegu@tgcatholic.or.kr.

Protestant Churches

Korean Methodist Church: 64-8, 1-ga, Taepyeong-no, Jung-gu, Seoul 100-101; KPO Box 285, Seoul 110-602; tel. (2) 399-4300; fax (2) 399-4307; e-mail bishop@kmcweb.or.kr; internet www.kmcweb.or.kr; f. 1885; 1,470,042 mems (2001); Bishop CHANG KWANG-YOUNG.

Presbyterian Church in the Republic of Korea (PROK): 1501, Ecumenical Bldg, 136-56, Yeonchi-dong, Jongno-gu, Seoul 110-470; tel. (2) 708-4021; fax (2) 708-4027; e-mail prok3000@chollian.net; internet www.prok.org; f. 1953; 332,915 mems (2001); Gen. Sec. Rev. Dr KIM JONG-MOO.

Presbyterian Church of Korea (PCK): Korean Church Centennial Memorial Bldg; 135, Yeochi-dong, Jongno-gu, Seoul 110-470; tel. (2) 741-4350; fax (2) 766-2427; e-mail thepck@pck.or.kr; internet www.pck.or.kr; 2,328,413 mems (2001); Moderator Rev. CHOI BYUNG-GON; Gen. Sec. Rev. Dr. KIM SANG-HAK.

There are some 160 other Protestant denominations in the country, including the Korea Baptist Convention and the Korea Evangelical Church.

CHUNDO KYO

A religion indigenous and unique to Korea, Chundo Kyo combines elements of Shaman, Buddhist, and Christian doctrines. In 1995 there were 274 temples, 5,597 priests, and 28,184 believers.

CONFUCIANISM

In 1995 there were 730 temples, 31,833 priests, and 210,927 believers.

TAEJONG GYO

Taejong Gyo is Korea's oldest religion, dating back 4,000 years, and comprising beliefs in the national foundation myth, and the triune god, Hanul. By the 15th century the religion had largely disappeared, but began a revival in the late 19th century. In 1995 there were 103 temples, 346 priests, and 7,603 believers.

The Press

NATIONAL DAILIES
(In Korean, unless otherwise indicated)

Chosun Ilbo: 61, 1-ga, Taepyeong-no, Jung-gu, Seoul 100-756; tel. (2) 724-5114; fax (2) 724-5059; internet www.chosun.com; f. 1920; morning, weekly and children's edns; independent; Pres. BANG SANG-HOON; Editor-in-Chief KIM DAE-JUNG; circ. 2,470,000.

Daily Sports Seoul: 25, 1-ga, Taepyeong-no, Jung-gu, Seoul; tel. (2) 721-5114; fax (2) 721-5396; internet www.seoul.co.kr; f. 1985; morning; sports and leisure; Pres. LEE HAN-SOO; Man. Editor SON CHU-WHAN.

Dong-A Ilbo: 139-1, 3-ga, Sejong-no, Jongno-gu, Seoul 100-715; tel. (2) 2020-0114; fax (2) 2020-1239; e-mail newsroom@donga.com; internet www.donga.com; f. 1920; morning; independent; Pres. KIM HAK-JOON; Editor-in-Chief LEE HYUN-NAK; circ. 2,150,000.

Han-Joong Daily News: 91-1, 2-ga, Myeong-dong, Jung-gu, Seoul; tel. (2) 776-2801; fax (2) 778-2803; Chinese.

Hankook Ilbo: 14, Junghak-dong, Jongno-gu, Seoul; tel. (2) 724-2114; fax (2) 724-2244; internet www.hankooki.com; f. 1954; morning; independent; Pres. CHANG CHAE-KEUN; Editor-in-Chief YOON KOOK-BYUNG; circ. 2,000,000.

Hankyoreh Shinmun (One Nation): 116-25, Gongdeok-dong, Mapo-gu, Seoul 121-020; tel. (2) 710-0114; fax (2) 710-0210; internet www.hani.co.kr; f. 1988; centre-left; Chair. KIM DOO-SHIK; Editor-in-Chief SUNG HAN-PYO; circ. 500,000.

Ilgan Sports (The Daily Sports): 14, Junghak-dong, Jongno-gu, Seoul 110-792; tel. (2) 724-2114; fax (2) 724-2299; internet www.dailysports.co.kr; morning; f. 1969; Pres. CHANG CHAE-KEUN; Editor KIM JIN-DONG; circ. 600,000.

Jeil Economic Daily: 24-5 Yeouido-dong, Yeongdeungpo-gu, Seoul; tel. (2) 792-1131; fax (2) 792-1130; f. 1988; morning; Pres. HWANG MYUNG-SOON; Editor LEE SOO-SAM.

JoongAng Ilbo (JoongAng Daily News): 7, Soonhwa-dong, Jung-gu, Seoul; tel. (2) 751-5114; fax (2) 751-9709; internet www.joins.com; f. 1965; morning; Pres. LEE JE-HOON; Man. Editor LEE CHANG-KYU; circ. 2,300,000.

Kookmin Ilbo: 12, Yeouido-dong, Yeongdeungpo-gu, Seoul; tel. (2) 781-9114; fax (2) 781-9781; internet www.kukminilbo.co.kr; Pres. CHA IL-SUK.

Korea Daily News: 25, 1-ga, Taepyeong-no, Jung-gu, Seoul; tel. (2) 2000-9000; fax (2) 2000-9659; internet www.kdaily.com; f. 1945; morning; independent; Publr and Pres. SON CHU-HWAN; Man. Editor LEE DONG-HWA; circ. 700,000.

Korea Economic Daily: 441, Junglim-dong, Jung-gu, Seoul 100-791; tel. (2) 360-4114; fax (2) 779-4447; internet www.ked.co.kr; f. 1964; morning; Pres. PARK YONG-JUNG; Man. Dir and Editor-in-Chief CHOI KYU-YOUNG.

The Korea Herald: 1-12, 3-ga, Hoehyeon-dong, Jung-gu, Seoul; tel. (2) 727-0114; fax (2) 727-0670; internet www.koreaherald.co.kr; f. 1953; morning; English; independent; Pres. KIM CHIN-OUK; Man. Editor MIN BYUNG-IL; circ. 150,000.

The Korea Times: 14, Junghak-dong, Jongno-gu, Seoul 110-792; tel. (2) 724-2114; fax (2) 732-4125; internet www.koreatimes.co.kr; f. 1950; morning; English; independent; Pres. CHO BYUNG-PIL; Man. Editor KIM MYONG-SIK; circ. 100,000.

Kyung-hyang Shinmun: 22, Jeong-dong, Jung-gu, Seoul; tel. (2) 3701-1114; fax (2) 737-6362; internet www.khan.co.kr; f. 1946; evening; independent; Pres. HONG SUNG-MAN; Editor KIM HI-JUNG; circ. 733,000.

Maeil Business Newspaper: 51-9, 1-ga, Bil-dong, Jung-gu, Seoul 100-728; tel. (2) 2000-2114; fax (2) 2269-6200; internet www.mk.co.kr; f. 1966; evening; economics and business; Pres. CHANG DAE-WHAN; Editor JANG BYUNG-CHANG; circ. 235,000.

Munhwa Ilbo: 68, 1-ga, Chungjeong-no, Jung-gu, Seoul 110-170; tel. (2) 3701-5114; fax (2) 722-8328; internet www.munhwa.co.kr; f. 1991; evening; Pres. NAM SI-UK; Editor-in-Chief KANG SIN-KU.

Naeway Economic Daily: 1-12, 3-ga, Hoehyon-dong, Jung-gu, Seoul 100; tel. (2) 727-0114; fax (2) 727-0661; internet www.naeway

.co.kr; f. 1973; morning; Pres. KIM CHIN-OUK; Man. Editor HAN DONG-HEE; circ. 300,000.

Segye Times: 63-1, 3-ga, Hangang-no, Yeongsan-gu, Seoul; tel. (2) 799-4114; fax (2) 799-4520; internet www.segyetimes.co.kr; f. 1989; morning; Pres. HWANG HWAN-CHAI; Editor MOK JUNG-GYUM.

Seoul Kyungje Shinmun: 19, Junghak-dong, Jongno-gu, Seoul 100; tel. (2) 724-2114; fax (2) 732-2140; internet www.sed.co.kr; f. 1960; morning; Pres. KIM YOUNG-LOUL; Man. Editor KIM SEO-WOONG; circ. 500,000.

Sports Chosun: 61, 1-ga, Taepyeong-no, Jung-gu, Seoul; tel. (2) 724-6114; fax (2) 724-6979; internet www.sportschosun.com; f. 1964; Publr BANG SANG-HOON; circ. 400,000.

LOCAL DAILIES

Cheju Daily News: 2324-6, Yeon-dong, Jeju; tel. (64) 740-6114; fax (64) 740-6500; internet www.chejunews.co.kr; f. 1945; evening; Pres. KIM DAE-SUNG; Man. Editor KANG BYUNG-HEE.

Chonbuk Domin Ilbo: 207-10, 2-ga, Deokjin-dong, Deokjin-gu, Jeonju, N Jeolla Prov. tel. (63) 251-7114; fax (63) 251-7127; internet www.domin.co.kr; f. 1988; morning; Pres. LIM BYOUNG-CHAN; Man. Editor YANG CHAE-SUK.

Chonju Ilbo: 568-132, Sonosong-dong, Deokjin-gu, Jeonju, N. Jeolla Prov. tel. (63) 285-0114; fax (63) 285-2060; f. 1991; morning; Chair. KANG DAE-SOON; Man. Editor SO CHAE-CHOL.

Chonnam Ilbo: 700-5, Jungheung-dong, Buk-gu, Gwangju, 500–758; tel. (62) 527-0015; fax (62) 510-0436; internet www.chonnamilbo.co.kr; f. 1989; morning; Pres. LIM WON-SIK; Editor-in-Chief KIM YONG-OK.

Chunbuk Ilbo: 710-5, Kumam-dong, Deokjin-gu, Jeonju, N. Jeolla Prov. tel. (63) 250-5500; fax (63) 250-5550; f. 1950; evening; Pres. SUH JUNG-SANG; Man. Editor LEE KON-WOONG.

Chungchong Daily News: 304, Sachang-dong, Hungduk-gu, Cheongju, N. Chungcheong Prov. tel. (43) 279-5114; fax (43) 262-2000; internet www.ccnews.co.kr; f. 1946; morning; Pres. SEO JEONG-OK; Editor IM BAIK-SOO.

Halla Ilbo: 568-1, Samdo 1-dong, Jeju; tel. (64) 750-2114; fax (64) 750-2520; internet www.hallailbo.com; f. 1989; evening; Chair. KANG YONG-SOK; Man. Editor HONG SONG-MOK.

Incheon Ilbo: 18-1, 4-ga, Hang-dong, Jung-gu, Incheon; tel. (32) 763-8811; fax (32) 763-7711; internet www.inchonnews.co.kr; f. 1988; evening; Chair. MUN PYONG-HA; Man. Editor LEE JAE-HO.

Jungdo Daily Newspaper: 274-7, Galma-dong, Seo-gu, Daejeon; tel. (42) 530-4114; fax (42) 535-5334; internet www.joongdo.com; f. 1951; morning; Chair. KI-CHANG; Man. Editor SONG HYOUNG-SOP.

Kangwon Ilbo: 53, 1-ga, Jungang-no, Chuncheon, Gangwon Prov. tel. (33) 252-7228; fax (33) 252-5884; internet www.kwnews.co.kr; f. 1945; evening; Pres. CHO NAM-JIN; Man. Editor KIM KEUN-TAE.

Kookje Daily News: 76-2, Goje-dong, Yeonje-gu, Busan 611-702; tel. (51) 500-5114; fax (51) 500-4274; e-mail jahwang@ms.kookje.co.kr; internet www.kookje.co.kr; f. 1947; morning; Pres. LEE JONG-DEOK; Editor-in-Chief JEONG WON-YOUNG.

Kwangju Ilbo: 1, 1-ga, Geumnam-no, Dong-gu, Gwangju; tel. (62) 222-8111; fax (62) 227-9500; internet www.kwangju.co.kr; f. 1952; evening; Chair. KIM CHONG-TAE; Man. Editor CHO DONG-SU.

Kyeonggi Ilbo: 452-1, Songjuk-dong, Changan-gu, Suwon, Gyeonggi Prov. tel. (31) 247-3333; fax (31) 247-3349; internet www.kgib.co.kr; f. 1988; evening; Chair. SHIN SON-CHOL; Man. Editor LEE CHIN-YONG.

Kyeongin Ilbo: 1121-11, Ingye-dong, Paldal-gu, Suwon, Gyeonggi Prov. tel. (31) 231-5114; fax (31) 232-1231; internet www.kyeongin.com; f. 1960; evening; Chair. SUNG BAEK-EUNG; Man. Editor KIM HWA-YANG.

Kyungnam Shinmun: 100-5, Sinwol-dong, Changwon, S. Gyeongsang Prov. tel. (55) 283-2211; fax (55) 283-2227; internet www.knnews.co.kr; f. 1946; evening; Pres. KIM DONG-KYU; Editor PARK SUNG-KWAN.

Maeil Shinmun: 71, 2-ga, Gyesan-dong, Jung-gu, Daegu; tel. (53) 255-5001; fax (53) 255-8902; internet www.m2000.co.kr; f. 1946; evening; Chair. KIM BOO-KI; Editor LEE YONG-KEUN; circ. 300,000.

Pusan Daily News: 1-10, Sujeong-dong, Dong-gu, Busan 601-738; tel. (51) 461-4114; fax (51) 463-8880; internet www.pusanilbo.co.kr; f. 1946; Pres. JEONG HAN-SANG; Man. Editor AHN KI-HO; circ. 427,000.

Taegu Ilbo: 81-2, Sincheon 3-dong, Dong-gu, Daegu; tel. (53) 757-4500; fax (53) 751-8086; internet www.tgnews.go.kr; f. 1953; morning; Pres. PARK GWON-HEUM; Editor KIM KYUNG-PAL.

Taejon Ilbo: 1-135, Munhwa 1-dong, Jung-gu, Daejeon; tel. (42) 251-3311; fax (42) 253-3320; internet www.taejontimes.co.kr; f. 1950; evening; Chair. SUH CHOON-WON; Editor KWAK DAE-YEON.

Yeongnam Ilbo: 111, Sincheon-dong, Dong-gu, Daegu; tel. (53) 757-5114; fax (53) 756-9009; internet www.yeongnam.co.kr; f. 1945; morning; Chair. PARK CHANG-HO; Man. Editor KIM SANG-TAE.

SELECTED PERIODICALS

Academy News: 50, Unjung-dong, Bundang-gu, Seongnam, Gyeonggi Prov. 463-791; tel. (31) 709-8111; fax (31) 709-9945; organ of the Acad. of Korean Studies; Pres. HAN SANG-JIN.

Business Korea: 26-3, Yeouido-dong, Yeongdeungpo-gu, Seoul 150-010; tel. (2) 784-4010; fax (2) 784-1915; f. 1983; monthly; Pres. KIM KYUNG-HAE; circ. 35,000.

Eumak Dong-A: 139, Sejong-no, Jongno-gu, Seoul 110-715; tel. (2) 781-0640; fax (2) 705-4547; f. 1984; monthly; music; Publr KIM BYUNG-KWAN; Editor KWON O-KIE; circ. 85,000.

Han Kuk No Chong (FKTU News): Federation of Korean Trade Unions, FKTU Bldg, 35, Yeouido-dong, Yeongdeungpo-gu, Seoul; tel. (2) 786-3970; fax (2) 786-2864; e-mail fktuintl@nownuri.net; internet www.fktu.or.kr; f. 1961; labour news; Publr LEE NAM-SOON; circ. 20,000.

Hyundae Munhak: Mokjung Bldg, 1st Floor, 1361-5, Seocho-dong, Seocho-gu, Seoul; tel. (2) 3472-8151; fax (2) 563-9319; f. 1955; literature; Publr KIM SUNG-SIK; circ. 200,000.

Korea Business World: Yeouido, POB 720, Seoul 150-607; tel. (2) 532-1364; fax (2) 594-7663; f. 1985; monthly; English; Publr and Pres. LEE KIE-HONG; circ. 40,200.

Korea Buyers Guide: Rm 2301, Korea World Trade Center, 159, Samseong-dong, Gangnam-gu, Seoul; tel. (2) 551-2376; fax (2) 551-2377; e-mail mkbg@buyersguide.co.kr; internet www.buykorea21.com; f. 1973; monthly; consumer goods; quarterly; hardware; Pres. YOU YOUNG-PYO; circ. 30,000.

Korea Journal: CPOB 54, Seoul 100-022; tel. (2) 776-2804; organ of the UNESCO Korean Commission; Gen. Dir CHUNG HEE-CHAE.

Korea Newsreview: 1-12, 3-ga, Hoehyeon-dong, Jung-gu, Seoul 100-771; tel. (2) 756-7711; weekly; English; Publr and Editor PARK CHUNG-WOONG.

Korean Business Review: FKI Bldg, 28-1, Yeouido-dong, Yeongdeungpo-gu, Seoul 150-756; tel. (2) 3771-0114; fax (2) 3771-0138; monthly; publ. by Fed. of Korean Industries; Publr KIM KAK-CHOONG; Editor SOHN BYUNG-DOO.

Korea and World Affairs: Rm 1723, Daewoo Center Bldg, 5-541, Namdaemun-no, Jung-gu, Seoul 100-714; tel. (2) 777-2628; fax (2) 319-9591; organ of the Research Center for Peace and Unification of Korea; Pres. CHANG DONG-HOON.

Literature and Thought: Seoul; tel. (2) 738-0542; fax (2) 738-2997; f. 1972; monthly; Pres. LIM HONG-BIN; circ. 10,000.

Monthly Travel: Cross Bldg, 2nd Floor, 46-6, 2-ga, Namsan-dong, Jung-gu, Seoul 100-042; tel. (2) 757-6161; fax (2) 757-6089; e-mail kotfa@unitel.co.kr; Pres. SHIN JOONG-MOK; circ. 50,000.

News Maker: 22, Jung-dong, Jung-gu, Seoul 110-702; tel. (2) 3701-1114; fax (2) 739-6190; e-mail hudy@kyunghyang.com; internet www.kyunghyang.com/newsmaker; f. 1992; Pres. JANG JUN-BONG; Editor PARK MYUNG-HUN.

Reader's Digest: 295-15, Deoksan 1-dong, Geumcheon-gu, Seoul 153-011; tel. (2) 866-8800; fax (2) 839-4545; f. 1978; monthly; general; Pres. YANG SUNG-MO; Editor PARK SOON-HWANG; circ. 115,000.

Shin Dong-A (New East Asia): 139, Chungjeong-no, Seodaemun-gu, Seoul 120–715; tel. (2) 361-0974; fax (2) 361-0988; f. 1931; monthly; general; Publr KIM HAK-JUN; Editor YOU YOUNG-EUL; circ. 170,000.

Taekwondo: Sinmun-no Bldg, 5th Floor, 238 Sinmun-no, 1-ga, Jongno-gu, Seoul 110-061; tel. (2) 566-2505; fax (2) 553-4728; e-mail wtf@unitel.co.kr; internet www.wtf.org; f. 1973; organ of the World Taekwondo Fed. Pres. Dr KIM UN-YONG.

Vantage Point: 85-1 Susong-dong, Jongno-gu, Seoul, 110-140; tel. (2) 398-3519; fax (2) 398-3539; e-mail kseungji@yna.co.kr; internet www.yna.co.kr; f. 1978; monthly; developments in North Korea; Editor KWAK SEUNG-JI.

Weekly Chosun: 61, Taepyeong-no 1, Jung-gu, Seoul; tel. (2) 724-5114; fax (2) 724-6199; weekly; Publr BANG SANG-HOON; Editor CHOI JOON-MYONG; circ. 350,000.

The Weekly Hankook: 14, Junghak-dong, Jongno-gu, Seoul; tel. (2) 732-4151; fax (2) 724-2444; f. 1964; Publr CHANG CHAE-KUK; circ. 400,000.

Wolgan Mot: 139, Sejong-no, Jongno-gu, Seoul 110; tel. (2) 733-5221; f. 1984; monthly; fashion; Publr KIM SEUNG-YUL; Editor KWON O-KIE; circ. 120,000.

Women's Weekly: 14, Junghak-dong, Jongno-gu, Seoul; tel. (2) 735-9216; fax (2) 732-4125.

Yosong Dong-A (Women's Far East): 139, Sejong-no, Jongno-gu, Seoul 110-715; tel. (2) 721-7621; fax (2) 721-7676; f. 1933; monthly; women's magazine; Publr KIM BYUNG-KWAN; Editor KWON O-KIE; circ. 237,000.

NEWS AGENCIES

Yonhap News Agency: 85-1, Susong-dong, Jongno-gu, Seoul; tel. (2) 398-3114; fax (2) 398-3257; internet www.yonhapnews.co.kr; f. 1980; Pres. KIM KUN.

Foreign Bureaux

Agence France-Presse (AFP): Yonhap News Agency Bldg, 3rd Floor, 85-1, Susong-dong, Jongno-gu, Seoul; tel. (2) 737-7353; fax (2) 737-6598; e-mail seoul@afp.com; Bureau Chief TIM WITCHER.

Associated Press (AP) (USA): Yonhap News Agency Bldg, 85-1, Susong-dong, Jongno-gu, Seoul; tel. (2) 739-0692; fax (2) 737-0650; Bureau Chief REID MILLER.

Central News Agency (Taiwan): 33-1, 2-ga, Myeong-dong, Jung-gu, Seoul; tel. (2) 753-0195; fax (2) 753-0197; Bureau Chief CHIANG YUAN-CHEN.

Deutsche Presse-Agentur (Germany): 148, Anguk-dong, Jongno-gu, Seoul; tel. (2) 738-3808; fax (2) 738-6040; Correspondent NIKOLAUS PREDE.

Informatsionnoye Telegrafnoye Agentstvo Rossii—Telegrafnoye Agentstvo Suverennykh Stran (ITAR—TASS) (Russia): 1-302, Chonghwa, 22-2, Itaewon-dong, Yeongsan-gu, Seoul; tel. (2) 796-9193; fax (2) 796-9194.

Jiji Tsushin (Jiji Press) (Japan): Joong-ang Ilbo Bldg, 7, Soonhwa-dong, Jung-gu, Seoul; tel. (2) 753-4525; fax (2) 753-8067; Chief Correspondent KENJIRO TSUJITA.

Kyodo News Service (Japan): Yonhap News Agency Bldg, 85-1, Susong-dong, Jongno-gu, Seoul; tel. (2) 739-2791; fax (2) 737-1776; Bureau Chief HISASHI HIRAI.

Reuters (UK): Byuck San Bldg, 7th Floor, 12-5, Dongja-dong, Yeongsan-gu, Seoul 140-170; tel. (2) 727-5151; fax (2) 727-5666; Bureau Chief ANDREW BROWNE.

Rossiiskoye Informatsionnoye Agentstvo—Novosti (RIA-Novosti) (Russia): 14, Junghak-dong, Jongno-gu, Seoul; tel. (2) 737-2829; fax (2) 798-0010; Correspondent SERGEI KUDASOV.

United Press International (UPI) (USA): Yonhap News Agency Bldg, Rm 603, 85-1, Susong-dong, Jongno-gu, Seoul; tel. (2) 737-9054; fax (2) 738-8206; Correspondent JASON NEELY.

Xinhua News Agency (People's Republic of China): B-1, Hillside Villa, 726-111, Hannam-dong, Yeongsan-gu, Seoul; tel. (2) 795-8258; fax (2) 796-7459.

PRESS ASSOCIATIONS

Korean Newspaper Editors' Association: Korea Press Center, 13th Floor, 25, 1-ga, Taepyeong-no, Jung-gu, Seoul; tel. (2) 732-1726; fax (2) 739-1985; f. 1957; 416 mems; Pres. SEONG BYONG-WUK.

Korean Newspapers Association: Korea Press Center, 13th Floor, 25, 1-ga, Taepyeong-no, Jung-gu, Seoul 100-745; tel. (2) 733-2251; fax (2) 720-3291; e-mail ccy73_2000@yahoo.co.kr; f. 1962; 49 mems; Pres. CHOE HAK-RAE.

Seoul Foreign Correspondents' Club: Korea Press Center, 18th Floor, 25, 1-ga, Taepyeong-no, Jung-gu, Seoul; tel. (2) 734-3272; fax (2) 734-7712; f. 1956; Pres. PARK HAN-CHUN.

Publishers

Ahn Graphics Ltd: 260-88, Seongbuk 2-dong, Seongbuk-gu, Seoul 136-012; tel. (2) 763-2320; fax (2) 743-3352; e-mail lbr@ag.co.kr; f. 1985; computer graphics; Pres. KIM OK-CHUL.

Bak-Young Publishing Co: 13-31, Pyeong-dong, Jongno-gu, Seoul; tel. (2) 733-6771; fax (2) 736-4818; f. 1952; sociology, philosophy, literature, linguistics, social science; Pres. AHN JONG-MAN.

BIR Publishing Co Ltd: 506, Sinsa-dong, Gangnam-gu, Seoul 135-120; tel. (2) 515-2000; fax (2) 514-3249.

Bobmun Sa Publishing Co: Hanchung Bldg, 4th Floor, 161-7, Yomni-dong, Mapo-gu, Seoul 121-090; tel. (2) 703-6541; fax (2) 703-6594; f. 1954; law, politics, philosophy, history; Pres. BAE HYO-SEON.

Bumwoo Publishing Co: 21-1, Kusu-dong, Mapo-gu, Seoul 121-130; tel. (2) 717-2121; fax (2) 717-0429; f. 1966; philosophy, religion, social science, technology, art, literature, history; Pres. YOON HYUNG-DOO.

Cheong Moon Gak Publishing Co Ltd: 486-9, Kirum 3-dong, Seongbuk-gu, Seoul 136-800; tel. (2) 985-1451; fax (2) 988-1456; e-mail cmgbook@cmgbook.co.kr; internet www.cmgbook.co.kr; f. 1974; science, technology, business; subsidiaries HanSeung Publishers, Lux Media; Pres. KIM HONG-SEOK; Man. Dir HANS KIM.

Design House Publishing Co: Paradise Bldg, 186-210, Jangchung-dong, 2-ga, Jung-gu, Seoul 100-392; tel. (2) 2275-6151; fax (2) 2275-7884; f. 1987; social science, art, literature, languages, children's periodicals; Pres. LEE YOUNG-HEE.

Dong-Hwa Publishing Co: 130-4, 1-ga, Wonhyoro, Yeongsan-gu, Seoul 140-111; tel. (2) 713-5411; fax (2) 701-7041; f. 1968; language, literature, fine arts, history, religion, philosophy; Pres. LIM IN-KYU.

Doosan Co-operation Publishing BG: 18-12, Ulchi-ro, 6-ga, Jeong-gu, Seoul 100-196; tel. (2) 3398-880; fax (2) 3398-2670; f. 1951; general works, school reference, social science, periodicals; Pres. CHOI TAE-KYUNG.

Eulyoo Publishing Co Ltd: 46-1, Susong-dong, Jongno-gu, Seoul 110-603; tel. (2) 733-8151; fax (2) 732-9154; e-mail eulyoo@chollian.net; internet www.eulyoo.co.kr; f. 1945; linguistics, literature, social science, history, philosophy; Pres. CHUNG CHIN-SOOK.

Hainaim Publishing Co Ltd: Minjin Bldg, 5th Floor, 464-41, Seokyo-dong, Mapo-gu, Seoul 121-210; tel. (2) 326-1600; fax (2) 333-7543; e-mail hainaim@chollian.net; f. 1983; philosophy, literature, children's; Pres. SONG YOUNG-SUK.

Hakwon Publishing Co Ltd: Seocho Plaza, 4th Floor, 1573-1, Seocho-dong, Seocho-gu, Seoul; tel. (2) 587-2396; fax (2) 584-9306; f. 1945; general, languages, literature, periodicals; Pres. KIM YOUNG-SU.

Hangil Publishing Co: 506, Sinsa-dong, Gangnam-gu, Seoul 135-120; tel. (2) 515-4811; fax (2) 515-4816; f. 1976; social science, history, literature; Pres. KIM EOUN-HO.

Hanul Publishing Company: 201, Hyuam Bldg, 503-24, Changcheon-dong, Seodaemun-gu, Seoul 120-180; tel. (2) 336-6183; fax (2) 333-7543; e-mail newhanul@nuri.net; f. 1980; general, philosophy, university books, periodicals; Pres. KIM CHONG-SU.

Hollym Corporation: 13-13, Gwancheol-dong, Jongno-gu, Seoul 110-111; tel. (2) 735-7554; fax (2) 735-7551; e-mail hollym@chollian.net; internet www.hollym.co.kr; f. 1963; academic and general books on Korea in English; Pres. HAM KI-MAN.

Hyang Mun Sa Publishing Co: 645-20, Yeoksam-dong, Gangnam-gu, Seoul 135-081; tel. (2) 538-5672; fax (2) 538-5673; f. 1950; science, agriculture, history, engineering, home economics; Pres. NAH JOONG-RYOL.

Hyonam Publishing Co Ltd: 627-5, Ahyun 3-dong, Mapo-gu, Seoul 121-013; tel. (2) 365-5056; fax (2) 365-5251; e-mail lawhyun@chollian.net; f. 1951; general, children's, literature, periodicals; Pres. CHO KEUN-TAE.

Il Ji Sa Publishing Co: 46-1, Junghak-dong, Jongno-gu, Seoul 110-150; tel. (2) 732-3980; fax (2) 722-2807; f. 1956; literature, social sciences, juvenile, fine arts, philosophy, linguistics, history; Pres. KIM SUNG-JAE.

Ilchokak Publishing Co Ltd: 9, Gongpyeong-dong, Jongno-gu, Seoul 110-160; tel. (2) 733-5430; fax (2) 738-5857; f. 1953; history, literature, sociology, linguistics, medicine, law, engineering; Pres. HAN MAN-NYUN.

Jigyungsa Publishers Ltd: 790-14, Yeoksam-dong, Gangnam-gu, Seoul 135-080; tel. (2) 557-6351; fax (2) 557-6352; e-mail jigyung@uriel.net; internet www.jigyung.co.kr; f. 1979; children's, periodicals; Pres. KIM BYUNG-JOON.

Jihak Publishing Co Ltd: 180-20, Dongkyo-dong, Mapo-gu, Seoul 121-200; tel. (2) 330-5220; fax (2) 325-5835; f. 1965; philosophy, language, literature; Pres. KWON BYONG-IL.

Jipmoondang: 95, Waryon-dong, Jongno-gu, Seoul 110-360; tel. (2) 743-3098; fax (2) 743-3192; philosophy, social science, Korean studies, history, Korean folklore; Pres. LIM KYOUNG-HWAN.

Jisik Sanup Publications Co Ltd: 35-18, Dongui-dong, Jongno-gu, Seoul 110-040; tel. (2) 738-1978; fax (2) 720-7900; f. 1969; religion, social science, art, literature, history, children's; Pres. KIM KYUNG-HEE.

Jung-Ang Publishing Co Ltd: 172-11, Yomni-dong, Mapo-gu, Seoul 121-090; tel. (2) 717-2111; fax (2) 716-1369; f. 1972; study books, children's; Pres. KIM DUCK-KI.

Kemongsa Publishing Co Ltd: 772, Yeoksam-dong, Gangnam-gu, Seoul 135-080; tel. (2) 531-5335; fax (2) 531-5520; f. 1946; picture books, juvenile, encyclopaedias, history, fiction; Pres. RHU SEUNG-HEE.

Ki Moon Dang: 286-20, Haengdang-dong, Seongdong-gu, Seoul 133-070; tel. (2) 2295-6171; fax (2) 2296-8188; f. 1976; engineering, fine arts, dictionaries; Pres. KANG HAE-JAK.

Korea Britannica Corpn: 117, 1-ga, Jungchung-dong, Seoul 100-391; tel. (2) 272-2151; fax (2) 278-9983; f. 1968; encyclopaedias, dictionaries; Pres. JANG HO-SANG, SUJAN ELEN TAPANI.

Korea University Press: 1-2, Anam-dong, 5-ga, Seongbuk-gu, Seoul 136-701; tel. (2) 3290-4231; fax (2) 923-6311; f. 1956; philosophy, history, language, literature, Korean studies, education, psychology, social science, natural science, engineering, agriculture, medicine; Pres. KIM JUNG-BAE.

Kum Sung Publishing Co: 242-63, Gongdeok-dong, Mapo-gu, Seoul 121-022; tel. (2) 713-9651; fax (2) 718-4362; f. 1965; literature, juvenile, social sciences, history, fine arts; Pres. KIM NAK-JOON.

Kyohak-sa Publishing Co Ltd: 105-67, Gongdeok-dong, Mapo-gu, Seoul 121-020; tel. (2) 717-4561; fax (2) 718-3976; f. 1952; dictionaries, educational, children's; Pres. YANG CHEOL-WOO.

Kyung Hee University Press: 1, Hoeki-dong, Dongdaemun-gu, Seoul 130-701; tel. (2) 961-0106; fax (2) 962-8840; f. 1960; general, social science, technology, language, literature; Pres. CHOE YOUNG-SEEK.

Kyungnam University Press: 28-42, Samchung-dong, Jongno-gu, Seoul 110-230; tel. (2) 370-0700; fax (2) 735-4359; Pres. PARK JAE-KYU.

Minumsa Publishing Co Ltd: 5/F Kangnam Publishing Culture Centre, 506, Sinsa-dong, Gangnam-gu, Seoul 135-120; tel. (2) 515-2000; fax (2) 515-2007; e-mail michell@bora.dacom.co.kr; f. 1966; literature, philosophy, linguistics, pure science; Pres. PARK MAENG-HO.

Munhakdongne Publishing Co Ltd: 6/F Dongsomun B/D 260, Dongsomundong 4-ga, Seongbuk-gu, Seoul 136-034; tel. (2) 927-6790; fax (2) 927-6793; e-mail etepluie@hotmail.com; internet www.munhak.com; f. 1993; art, literature, science, philosophy, non-fiction, children's, periodicals; Pres. KANG BYUNG-SUN.

Panmun Book Co Ltd: 923-11, Mok 1-dong, Yangcheon-gu, Seoul 158-051; tel. (2) 653-5131; fax (2) 653-2454; e-mail skliu@panmun.co.kr; internet www.medicalplus.co.kr; f. 1955; social science, pure science, technology, medicine, linguistics; Pres. LIU SUNG-KWON.

Sakyejul Publishing Ltd: 1-181, Sinmun-no-2-ga, Jongno-gu, Seoul 110-062; tel. (2) 736-9380; fax (2) 737-8595; e-mail sakyejul@soback.kornet.nm.kr; f. 1982; social sciences, art, literature, history, children's; Pres. KANG MAR-XILL.

Sam Joong Dang Publishing Co: 261-23, Soke-dong, Yeongsan-gu, Seoul 140-140; tel. (2) 704-6816; fax (2) 704-6819; f. 1931; literature, history, philosophy, social sciences, dictionaries; Pres. LEE MIN-CHUL.

Sam Seong Dang Publishing Co: 101-14, Non Hyun-dong, Gangnam-gu, Seoul 135-010; tel. (2) 3442-6767; fax (2) 3442-6768; e-mail kyk@ssdp.co.kr; f. 1968; literature, fine arts, history, philosophy; Pres. KANG MYUNG-CHAE.

Sam Seong Publishing Co Ltd: 1516-2, Seocho-dong, Seocho-gu, Seoul 137-070; tel. (2) 3470-6900; fax (2) 597-1507; internet www.howpc.com; f. 1951; literature, history, juvenile, philosophy, arts, religion, science, encyclopaedias; Pres. KIM JIN-YONG.

Segyesa Publishing Co Ltd: Dasan Bldg 102, 494-85, Yeongkandong, Mapo-gu, Seoul 121-070; tel. (2) 715-1542; fax (2) 715-1544; f. 1988; general, philosophy, literature, periodicals; Pres. CHOI SUN-HO.

Se-Kwang Music Publishing Co: 232-32, Seogye-dong, Yeongsan-gu, Seoul 140-140; tel. (2) 719-2652; fax (2) 719-2656; f. 1953; music, art; Pres. PARK SEI-WON; Chair. PARK SHIN-JOON.

Seong An Dang Publishing Co: 4579, Singil-6-dong, Yeong-deungpo-gu, Seoul 150-056; tel. (2) 3142-4151; fax (2) 323-5324; f. 1972; technology, text books, university books, periodicals; Pres. LEE JONG-CHOON.

Seoul National University Press: 56-1, Sinrim-dong, Gwanak-gu, Seoul 151-742; tel. (2) 889-0434; fax (2) 888-4148; e-mail snubook@chollian.net; f. 1961; philosophy, engineering, social science, art, literature; Pres. LEE KI-JUN.

Si-sa-young-o-sa, Inc: 55-1, 2-ga, Jongno, Jongno-gu, Seoul 110-122; tel. (2) 274-0509; fax (2) 271-3980; internet www.ybmsisa.co.kr; f. 1959; language, literature; Pres. CHUNG YOUNG-SAM.

Sogang University Press: 1, Sinsu-dong, Mapo-gu, Seoul 121-742; tel. (2) 705-8212; fax (2) 705-8612; f. 1978; philosophy, religion, science, art, history; Pres. LEE HAN-TAEK.

Sookmyung Women's University Press: 53-12, 2-ga, Jongpa-dong, Yeongsan-gu, Seoul 140-742; tel. (2) 710-9162; fax (2) 710-9090; f. 1968; general; Pres. LEE KYUNG-SOOK.

Tam Gu Dang Publishing Co: 158, 1-ga, Hanggangno, Yeongsan-gu, Seoul 140-011; tel. (2) 3785-2271; fax (2) 3785-2272; f. 1950; linguistics, literature, social sciences, history, fine arts; Pres. HONG SUK-WOO.

Tong Moon Gwan: 147, Gwanhoon-dong, Jongno-gu, Seoul 110-300; tel. (2) 732-4355; f. 1954; literature, art, philosophy, religion, history; Pres. LEE KYUM-NO.

Woongjin.com Co. Ltd: Woongjin Bldg, 112-2, Inui-dong, Jongno-gu, Seoul; tel. (2) 3670-1832; fax (2) 766-2722; e-mail lois.kim@email.woongjin.com; internet www.woongjin.com; children's; Pres. YOON SUCK-KEUM.

Yearimdang Publishing Co Ltd: Yearim Bldg, 153-3, Samseong-dong, Gangnam-gu, Seoul 135-090; tel. (2) 566-1004; fax (2) 567-9610; e-mail yearim@yearim.co.kr; internet www.yearim.co.kr; f. 1973; children's; Pres. NA CHOON-HO.

Yonsei University Press: 134, Sincheon-dong, Seodaemun-gu, Seoul 120-749; tel. (2) 361-3380; fax (2) 393-1421; e-mail ysup@yonsei.ac.kr; f. 1955; philosophy, religion, literature, history, art, social science, pure science; Pres. KIM BYUNG-SOO.

Youl Hwa Dang: 506, Sinsa-dong, Gangnam-gu, Seoul 135-120; tel. (2) 515-3141; fax (2) 515-3144; e-mail horang2@unitel.co.kr; f. 1971; art; Pres. YI KI-UNG.

PUBLISHERS' ASSOCIATION

Korean Publishers Association: 105-2, Sagan-dong, Jongno-gu, Seoul 110-190; tel. (2) 735-2702; fax (2) 738-5414; e-mail kpa@kpa21.or.kr; internet www.kpa21.or.kr; f. 1947; Pres. LEE JUNG-IL; Sec.-Gen. JUNG JONG-JIN.

Broadcasting and Communications

TELECOMMUNICATIONS

Dacom Corpn: Dacom Bldg, 706-1, Yeoksam-dong, Gangnam-gu, Seoul 135-610; tel. (2) 6220-0220; fax (2) 6220-0702; internet www.dacom.net; f. 1982; domestic and international long-distance telecommunications services and broadband internet services; CEO. PARK UN-SUH.

Daewoo Telecom Co Ltd: 14-34, Yeouido-dong, Yeongdeungpo-gu, Seoul; tel. (2) 3779-7114; fax (2) 3779-7500; internet www.dwt.co.kr; Pres. (vacant).

Hanaro Telecom: Kukje Electronics Center Bldg, 24th Floor, 1445-3, Seocho-dong, Seocho-gu, Seoul 137-728; tel. (2) 6266-4114; fax (2) 6266-4379; internet www.hanaro.com; local telecommunications and broadband internet services; CEO SHIN YUN-SIK.

Korea Mobile Telecommunications Corpn: 267, 5-ga, Namdae-mun-no, Jung-gu, Seoul; tel. (2) 3709-1114; fax (2) 3709-0499; f. 1984; Pres. SEO JUNG-UK.

Korea Telecom: 206 Jungja-dong, Bundang-gu, Seongnam-si, Gyeonggi Prov. 463-711; tel. (2) 727-0114; fax (2) 750-3994; internet www.kt.co.kr; domestic and international telecommunications services and broadband internet services; privatized in June 2002; Pres. LEE YONG-KYUNG.

Korea Telecom (KT) Freetel: Seoul; 33% owned by Korea Telecom; 3.17m. subscribers (1999); Pres. LEE SANG-CHUL.

KTF: KTF Tower, 890-20, Daechi-dong, Gangnam-gu, Seoul 135-280; tel. (2) 2016-1114; fax (2) 2016-0032; internet www.ktf.com; mobile telecommunications and wireless internet services; merged with KTm.com in May 2001; commenced (code division multiple access) commercial CDMA2000 1x services in May 2001, and (evolution data only) 1x EV-DO services in May 2002; 10m. subscribers (2002); CEO LEE KYUNG-JOON.

LG Telecom: LG Gangnam Tower, 19th Floor, 679 Yeoksam-dong, Gangnam-gu, Seoul 135-985; tel. (2) 2005-7114; fax (2) 2005-7505; internet www.lg019.co.kr; mobile telecommunications and wireless internet services; commenced commercial CDMA2000 1x service in May 2001; 4m. subscribers (2002); CEO NAM YONG.

Onse Telecom: 192-2, Gumi-dong, Bundang-gu, Seongnam-si, Gyeonggi Prov. 463-500; tel. and fax (31) 738-6000; internet www.onse.net; domestic and international telecommunications services; Pres. and CEO HWANG KEE-YEON.

SK Telecom Co Ltd: 99, Seorin-dong, Jongno-gu, Seoul 110-110; tel. (2) 2121-2114; fax (2) 2121-3999; internet www.sktelecom.com; cellular mobile telecommunications and wireless internet services; merged with Shinsegi Telecom in Jan. 2002; 16m. subscribers (2002); Chair. and CEO SON KIL-SEUNG.

BROADCASTING

Regulatory Authority

Korean Broadcasting Commission: KBS Bldg, 923-5, Mok-dong, Yangcheon-gu, Seoul 158-715; tel. (2) 3219-5117; fax (2) 3219-5371; Chair. KANG DAE-IN.

Radio

Korean Broadcasting System (KBS): 18, Yeouido-dong, Yeong-deungpo-gu, Seoul 150-010; tel. (2) 781-1000; fax (2) 781-4179; internet www.kbs.co.kr; f. 1926; publicly-owned corpn with 26 local broadcasting and 855 relay stations; overseas service in Korean, English, German, Indonesian, Chinese, Japanese, French, Spanish, Russian and Arabic; Pres. JUNG YUN-JOO.

Buddhist Broadcasting System (BBS): 140, Mapo-dong, Mapo-gu, Seoul 121-050; tel. (2) 705-5114; fax (2) 705-5229; internet www.bbsfm.ko.kr; f. 1990; Pres. CHO HAE-HYONG.

Christian Broadcasting System (CBS): 917-1, Mok-dong, Yang-cheon-gu, Seoul 158-701; tel. (2) 650-7000; fax (2) 654-2456; internet www.cbs.co.kr; f. 1954; independent religious network with seven network stations in Seoul, Daegu, Busan, Gwangju, Chonbuk, Jeonju and Chuncheon; programmes in Korean; Pres. Rev. KWON HO-KYUNG.

Educational Broadcasting System (EBS): 92-6, Umyeon-dong, Seocho-gu, Seoul 137-791; tel. (2) 526-2000; fax (2) 526-2179; internet www.ebs.co.kr; f. 1990; Pres. Dr PARK HEUNG-SOO.

Far East Broadcasting Co (FEBC): 89, Sangsu-dong, Mapo-gu, MPO Box 88, Seoul 121-707; tel. (2) 320-0114; fax (2) 320-0129; e-mail febcadm@febc.or.kr; internet www.febc.net; Dir Dr BILLY KIM.

> **Radio Station HLAZ:** MPO Box 88, Seoul 121-707; tel. and fax (2) 320-0109; e-mail febcadm@febc.or.kr; internet www.febc.net; f. 1973; religious, educational service operated by Far East Broadcasting Co; programmes in Korean, Chinese, Russian and Japanese; Dir Dr BILLY KIM.

> **Radio Station HLKX:** MPO Box 88, Seoul 121-707; tel. (2) 320-0114; fax (2) 320-0129; e-mail febcadm@febc.or.kr; internet www.febc.net; f. 1956; religious, educational service operated by Far East Broadcasting Co; programmes in Korean, Chinese and English; Dir Dr BILLY KIM.

Munhwa Broadcasting Corpn (MBC): 31, Yeouido-dong, Yeong-deungpo-gu, Seoul 150-728; tel. (2) 784-2000; fax (2) 784-0880; e-mail mbcir@imbc.com; internet www.imbc.com; f. 1961; public; Pres. KIM JOONG-BAE.

Pyong Hwa Broadcasting Corpn (PBC): 2-3, 1-ga, Jeo-dong, Jung-gu, Seoul 100-031; tel. (2) 270-2114; fax (2) 270-2210; internet www.pbc.co.kr; f. 1990; religious and educational programmes; Pres. Rev. PARK SHIN-EON.

Seoul Broadcasting System (SBS): 10-2, Yeouido-dong, Yeong-deungpo-gu, Seoul 150-010; tel. (2) 786-0792; fax (2) 780-2530; internet www.sbs.co.kr; f. 1991; Pres. SONG DO-KYUN.

US Forces Network Korea (AFN Korea): Seoul; tel. (2) 7914-6495; fax (2) 7914-5870; e-mail info@afnkorea.com; internet afnkorea.com; f. 1950; six originating stations and 19 relay stations; 24 hours a day.

Television

In late 1997 almost 40 domestic television channels were in operation.

Educational Broadcasting System (EBS): see Radio.

Inchon Television Ltd (ITV): 587-46, Hakik-dong, Nam-gu, Incheon; tel. (32) 830-1000; fax (32) 865-6300; internet www.itv.co.kr; f. 1997.

Jeonju Television Corpn (JTV): 656-3, Sonosong-dong, Deokjin-gu, Jeonju, N. Jeolla Prov. tel. (63) 250-5231; fax (63) 250-5249; e-mail jtv@jtv.co.kr; f. 1997.

Korean Broadcasting System (KBS): 18, Yeouido-dong, Yeong-deungpo-gu, Seoul 150-790; tel. (2) 781-1000; fax (2) 781-4179; f. 1961; publicly-owned corpn with 25 local broadcasting and 770 relay stations; Pres. JUNG YUN-JOO.

Munhwa Broadcasting Corpn (MBC-R/TV): 31, Yeouido-dong, Yeongdeungpo-gu, Seoul 150-728; tel. (2) 789-2851; fax (2) 782-3094; f. 1961; public; 19 TV networks; Pres. NOH SUNG-DAI.

Seoul Broadcasting System (SBS): see Radio.

US Forces Network Korea (AFN Korea): Seoul; tel. (2) 7914-2711; fax (2) 7914-5870; f. 1950; main transmitting station in Seoul; 19 rebroadcast transmitters and translators; 168 hours weekly.

Finance

(cap. = capital; res = reserves; dep. = deposits; m. = million; brs = branches; amounts in won, unless otherwise indicated)

BANKING

The modern financial system in South Korea was established in 1950 with the foundation of the central bank, the Bank of Korea.

Under financial liberalization legislation, adopted in the late 1980s, banks were accorded greater freedom to engage in securities or insurance operations. In March 1999 there were 87 commercial banks in South Korea, comprising 11 nation-wide banks, eight provincial banks and 68 branches of foreign banks. The Financial Supervisory Commission was formed in April 1998 to oversee and reorganize the operations of commercial banks and the financial services sector.

Specialized banks were created in the 1960s to provide funds for sectors of the economy not covered by commercial banks. There are also two development banks: the Korea Development Bank and the Export-Import Bank of Korea.

In late 1997 many merchant banks were forced to cease operations, after incurring heavy losses through corporate bankruptcies. In June 1998 five commercial banks were also required to cease operations.

Regulatory Authority

Financial Supervisory Commission: 27, Yeouido-dong, Yeong-deungpo-gu, Seoul; tel. (2) 3771-5234; fax (2) 3771-5190; internet www.fss.or.kr; Chair. LEE JUNG-JAE.

Central Bank

Bank of Korea: 110, 3-ga, Namdaemun-no, Jung-gu, Seoul 100-794; tel. (2) 759-4114; fax (2) 759-4139; e-mail bokdiri@bok.or.kr; internet www.bok.or.kr; f. 1950; bank of issue; res 4,613,900m., dep. 112,868,500m. (Dec. 2000); Gov. PARK SEUNG; Dep. Gov. LEE SEONG-TAE; 16 domestic brs, 7 overseas offices.

Commercial Banks

Chohung Bank: 14, 1-ga, Namdaemun-no, Jung-gu, Seoul 100-757; tel. (2) 733-2000; fax (2) 720-2882; internet www.chb.co.kr; f. 1897; merged with Chungbuk Bank in May 1999 and Kangwon Bank in Sept. 1999; cap. 3,395,400m., dep. 39,225,900m. (Dec. 2001); Pres. and CEO HONG SERCK-JOO; 446 domestic brs, 11 overseas brs.

Hana Bank: 101-1, 1-ga, Ulchi-no, Jung-gu, Seoul 100-191; tel. (2) 2002-1111; fax (2) 775-7472; e-mail webmaster@hanabank.com; internet www.hanabank.co.kr; f. 1991; merged with Boram Bank in Jan. 1999; cap. 853,549m., res 468,602m., dep. 39,139,314m. (Sep. 2002); Chair. and CEO KIM SEUNG-YU; 303 brs.

Kookmin Bank: 9-1, 2-ga, Namdaemun-no, Jung-gu, CPOB 815, Seoul 100-703; tel. (2) 317-2114; fax (2) 769-7229; e-mail kangseok@www.kookminbank.com; internet www.kookminbank.com; f. 1963 as Citizen's National Bank, renamed 1995; re-established Jan. 1999, following merger with Korea Long Term Credit Bank; merged with H&CB in November 2001; dep. 139,187.1m. (Jun. 2002); Chair. and Pres. KIM JUNG-TAE; 1,122 domestic brs, 6 overseas brs.

KorAm Bank: 39, Da-dong, Jung-gu, Seoul 100-180; tel. (2) 3455-2114; fax (2) 3455-2966; internet www.goodbank.com; f. 1983; jt venture with Bank of America; cap. 1,071,334m., res 170,871m., dep. 19,226,170m. (Dec. 2001); CEO and Chair. HA YUNG-KU; 222 domestic brs, 4 overseas brs.

Korea Exchange Bank: 181, 2-ga, Ulchi-no, Jung-gu, Seoul 100-793; tel. (2) 729-0114; fax (2) 729-9812; e-mail chan@koexbank.co.kr; internet www.keb.co.kr; f. 1967; merged with Korea International Merchant Bank in Jan. 1999; cap. 1,850,875m., res -168,034m., dep. 32,170,619m. (Dec. 2000); Pres. LEE KANG-WON; 261 domestic brs, 28 overseas brs.

Korea First Bank: 100, Gongpyeong-dong, Jongno-gu, Seoul 110-702; tel. (2) 3702-3114; fax (2) 3702-4901; e-mail master@kfb.co.kr; internet www.kfb.co.kr; f. 1929; 51% owned by Newbridge Capital Ltd (USA); cap. 980,584m., res 64,527m., dep. 17,388,790m. (Dec. 2000); Pres. and CEO ROBERT COHEN; 392 domestic brs, 4 overseas brs.

Seoulbank: 10-1, 2-ga, Namdaemun-no, Jung-gu, Seoul 100-746; tel. (2) 3709-5114; fax (2) 3709-6422; e-mail bos0216@chollian.net; internet www.seoulbank.co.kr; f. 1959; nationalized in Jan. 1998; cap. 554,900m., dep. 13,143,200m. (Dec. 2000); Pres. and CEO KANG CHUNG-WON; 291 domestic brs, 3 overseas brs.

Shinhan Bank: 120, 2-ga, Taepyeong-no, Jung-gu, Seoul 100-102; tel. (2) 756-0505; fax (2) 774-7013; internet www.shinhan.com; f. 1982; cap. 1,599,031m., res 660,995m., dep. 28,319,695m. (Dec. 2000); Pres. and CEO LEE IN-HO; 333 domestic brs, 8 overseas brs.

Woori Bank: 203, 1-ga, Hoehyeon-dong, Jung-gu, Seoul; tel. (2) 2002-3000; fax (2) 2002-5615; internet www.wooribank.com; f. 2002; following the merger of Hanvit Bank and Peace Bank of Korea; 100% owned by Government; cap. 2,764,400m., res 1,762,300m., dep. 51,806,200m. (Dec. 2001); Pres. LEE DUK-HOON; 688 domestic brs, 12 overseas brs.

Development Banks

Export-Import Bank of Korea: 16-1, Yeouido-dong, Yeongdeungpo-gu, Seoul 150-873; tel. (2) 3779-6114; fax (2) 3779-6732; e-mail kexim@koreaexim.go.kr; internet www.koreaexim.go.kr; f. 1976; cap. 2,675,755m., res 5,187m. (Dec. 2000); Chair. and Pres. LEE YOUNG-HOI; 8 brs.

Korea Development Bank: 16-3, Yeouido-dong, Yeongdeungpo-gu, Seoul 150-793; tel. (2) 787-4000; fax (2) 787-6191; internet www.kdb.co.kr; f. 1954; cap. 4,341m., res 66,059m., dep. 6,020m. (Dec. 1999); Gov. JUNG KEUN-YONG; 37 domestic brs, 9 overseas brs.

Specialized Banks

Asian Banking Corpn: Young Poong Bldg, 13th–14th Floors, 33, Seorin-dong, Jongno-gu, Seoul 110-752; tel. (2) 399-5500; fax (2) 399-5400; f. 1977; Pres. CHO KWAN-HAENG.

Industrial Bank of Korea: 50, 2-ga, Ulchi-no, Jung-gu, Seoul 100-758; tel. (2) 729-6114; fax (2) 729-6402; e-mail ifd@ibk.co.kr; internet www.ibk.co.kr; f. 1961 as the Small and Medium Industry Bank; cap. 2,291,385m., res 155,299m., dep. 33,233,163m. (Dec. 2000); Chair. and Pres. KIM JONG-CHANG; 387 domestic brs, 6 overseas brs.

Korea Merchant Banking Corpn: Daewoo Center Bldg, 2nd Floor, 541, 5-ga, Namdaemun-no, Jung-gu, Seoul 100-714; tel. (2) 3788-0114; fax (2) 753-9740; internet www.kmbc.co.kr; f. 1976; cap. 105,370m., dep. 1,904,762m. (March 1999); Pres. KIM IN-JU.

Korean-French Banking Corpn (SogeKo): Marine Center, 118, 2-ga, Namdaemun-no, Jung-gu, CPOB 8572, Seoul 100-092; tel. (2) 777-7711; fax (2) 777-7710; f. 1977; Pres. KIM DOO-BAE.

National Agricultural Co-operative Federation (NACF): 75, 1-ga, Chungjeong-no, Jung-gu, Seoul 100-707; tel. (2) 397-5114; fax (2) 397-5140; e-mail nacfico@nuri.net; internet www.nonghyup.com; f. 1961; cap. 2,564,400m., res 1,395,800m., dep. 64,063,500m. (2002); Chair. and Pres. HYUN EUI-SONG; 2,025 brs and member co-operatives.

National Federation of Fisheries Co-operatives: 11-6, Sincheon-dong, Songpa-gu, Seoul 138-730; tel. (2) 2240-2114; fax (2) 2240-3049; internet www.suhyup.co.kr; f. 1962; cap. 1,158,100m., res 301,900m., dep. 4,371,000m. (2002); Chair. and Pres. CHANG BYUNG-KOO; 120 brs.

National Livestock Co-operatives Federation: 451, Songnae-dong, Gangdong-gu, Seoul 134-763; tel. (2) 2224-8753; fax (2) 475-8253; internet www.nlcf.co.kr; f. 1981; cap. 96,718m., dep. 2,813,715m. (Dec. 1997); Chair. and Pres. PARK SOON-YONG; 35 brs.

Saehan Merchant Banking Corpn: Ankuk Insurance Bldg, 87, 1-ga, Ulchi-no, Jung-gu, CPOB 2723, Seoul 100-191; tel. (2) 754-1616; fax (2) 756-6093; internet www.smbc.co.kr; f. 1977; cap. 22,000m., res. 118,581m., dep. 112,894m. (March 1995); Pres. HUR MANN-GUI.

Provincial Banks

Cheju Bank: 1349, Ido-1-dong, Jeju 690-021, Jeju Prov. tel. (64) 734-1711; fax (64) 720-0183; f. 1969; cap. 55,500m., res. 30,700m., dep. 1,044,100m. (2002); merged with Central Banking Co in 2000; Chair. and Pres. KANG JOON-HONG; 29 brs.

Daegu Bank Ltd: 118, 2-ga, Susong-dong, Susong-gu, Daegu 706-712; tel. (53) 756-2001; fax (53) 740-6902; internet www.dgb.co.kr; f. 1967; cap. 602,100m., res 157,900m., dep. 10,551,500m. (2002); Chair. and Pres. KIM KUK-NYON; 183 brs.

Jeonbuk Bank Ltd: 669-2, Geumam-dong, Deokjin-gu, Jeonju 561-711, N Jeolla Prov. tel. (63) 250-7114; fax (63) 250-7078; internet www.jbbank.co.kr; f. 1969; cap. 165,300m., res 30,200m., dep. 2,784,100m. (2002); Chair. and Pres. HONG SUNG-JOO; 68 brs.

Kwangju Bank Ltd: 7-12, Daein-dong, Dong-gu, Gwangju 501-730; tel. (62) 239-5000; fax (62) 239-5199; e-mail kbjint1@nuri.net; internet www.kjbank.com; f. 1968; cap. 170,400m., res 72,600m., dep. 4,750,400m. (2002); Chair. and Pres. UM JONG-DAE; 119 brs.

Kyongnam Bank: 246-1, Sokjeon-dong, Hoewon-gu, Masan 630-010, Gyeongsang Prov. tel. (55) 290-8000; fax (55) 290-8199; internet www.knbank.co.kr; f. 1970 as Gyeongnam Bank Ltd, name changed 1987; cap. 259,000m., res 114,800m., dep. 5,643,700m. (2002); Chair. and Pres. KIM HYUNG-YUNG; 110 brs.

Pusan Bank: 830-38, Beomil 2-dong, Dong-gu, Busan 601-717; tel. (51) 640-4000; fax (51) 640-4099; e-mail psbkint@bora.dacom.co.kr; internet www.pusanbank.co.kr; f. 1967; cap. 475,226m., res – 68,601m., dep. 9,284,245m. (Dec. 2000); Pres. HOON SHIM; 143 brs.

Samyang Merchant Bank: 38-3, 3-ga, Gyongwon-dong, Wansan-gu, Jeonju 560-020; tel. (63) 83-7111; fax (63) 84-3056; f. 1979; cap. 30,254m., res 43,487m., dep. 400,426m. (March 1996); Pres. and CEO KIM PAIK-JOON.

Foreign Banks

ABN-AMRO Bank NV (Netherlands): Seoul City Tower Bldg, 11–12th Floors, 581, 5-ga, Namdaemun-no, Jung-gu, Seoul; tel. (2) 2131-6000; fax (2) 399-6554; f. 1979; Gen. Man. CHUNG DUCK-MO.

American Express Bank Ltd (USA): Gwanghwamun Bldg, 15th Floor, 64-8, 1-ga, Taepyeong-no, Jung-gu, CPOB 1390, Seoul 100-101; tel. (2) 399-2929; fax (2) 399-2966; f. 1977; Gen. Man. CHOE JAE-ICK.

Arab Bank PLC (Jordan): Daewoo Center Bldg, 22nd Floor, 541, 5-ga, Namdaemun-no, Jung-gu, CPOB 1331, Seoul 100-714; tel. (2) 317-9000; fax (2) 757-0124; Gen. Man. JO SEUNG-SHIK.

Australia and New Zealand Banking Group Ltd (Australia): Kyobo Bldg, 18th Floor, 1, 1-ga, Jongno, Jongno-gu, CPOB 1065, Seoul 110-714; tel. (2) 730-3151; fax (2) 737-6325; f. 1987; Gen. Man. PHIL MICHELL.

Bank Mellat (Iran): Bon Sol Bldg, 14th Floor, 144-27, Samseong-dong, Gangnam-gu, Seoul; tel. (2) 558-4448; fax (2) 557-4448; f. 2001; Gen. Man. ALI AFZALI.

Bank of America (USA): Hanwha Bldg, 9th Floor, 1, Janggyo-dong, Jung-gu, Seoul 100-797; tel. (2) 729-4500; fax (2) 729-4400; Gen. Man. BANG CHOON-HO.

Bank of Hawaii (USA): Daeyonkak Bldg, 14th Floor, 25-5, 1-ga, Jungmu-no, Jung-gu, Seoul 100-011; tel. (2) 757-0831; fax (2) 757-3516; Man. PARK YONG-SOO.

Bank of Nova Scotia (Canada): KCCI Bldg, 9th Floor, 45, 4-ga, Namdaemun-no, Jung-gu, Seoul 100-094; tel. (2) 757-7171; fax (2) 752-7189; e-mail bns.seoul@scotiabank.com; Gen. Man. HENRY YONG.

Bank of Tokyo-Mitsubishi Ltd (Japan): Young Poong Bldg, 4th Floor, 33, Seorin-dong, Jongno-gu, Seoul; tel. (2) 399-6474; fax (2) 735-4897; f. 1967; Gen. Man. KAZUMASA KOGA.

Bankers Trust Co (USA): Center Bldg, 10th Floor, 111-5, Sokong-dong, Jung-gu, Seoul; tel. (2) 3788-6000; fax (2) 756-2648; f. 1978; Man. Dir LEE KEUN-SAM.

BNP Paribas (France): Dong Yang Chemical Bldg, 8th Floor, 50, Sogong-dong, Jung-gu, Seoul 100-070; tel. (2) 317-1700; fax (2) 757-2530; e-mail bnppseoul@asia.bnparibas.com; f. 1976; Gen. Man. ALAIN PÉNICAUT.

Citibank NA (USA): Citicorp Center Bldg, 89-29, 2-ga, Sinmun-no, Jongno-gu, CPOB 749, Seoul 110-062; tel. (2) 2004-1114; fax (2) 722-3644; f. 1967; Gen. Man. SAJJAD RAZVI.

Crédit Agricole Indosuez (France): Kyobo Bldg, 19th Floor, 1, 1-ga, Jongno, Jongno-gu, CPOB 158, Seoul 110-714; tel. (2) 3700-9500; fax (2) 738-0325; f. 1974; Gen. Man. PATRICE COUVEGNES.

Crédit Lyonnais SA (France): You One Bldg, 8th–10th Floors, 75-95, Seosomun-dong, Jung-gu, Seoul 100-110; tel. (2) 772-8000; fax (2) 755-5379; f. 1978; Gen. Man. GEOFFROY DE LASSUS.

Deutsche Bank AG (Germany): Sei An Bldg, 20th–22nd Floors, 116, 1-ga, Sinmun-no, Jongno-gu, Seoul 110-700; tel. (2) 724-4500; fax (2) 724-4645; f. 1978; Gen. Man. KIM JIN-IL.

Development Bank of Singapore Ltd: Gwanghwamun Bldg, 20th Floor, 64-8, 1-ga, Taepyeong-no, Jung-gu, CPOB 9896, Seoul; tel. (2) 399-2660; fax (2) 732-7953; e-mail jeefun@dbs.com; f. 1981; Gen. Man. LOW JEE FUN.

First National Bank of Chicago (USA): Oriental Chemical Bldg, 15th Floor, 50, Sokong-dong, Jung-gu, Seoul 100-070; tel. (2) 316-9700; fax (2) 753-7917; f. 1976; Vice-Pres. and Gen. Man. MICHAEL S. BROWN.

Fuji Bank Ltd (Japan): Doosan Bldg, 15th Floor, 101-1, 1-ga, Ulchi-no, Jung-gu, Seoul 100-191; tel. (2) 311-2000; fax (2) 754-8177; f. 1972; Gen. Man. IKUO YAMAMOTO.

Hongkong and Shanghai Banking Corpn Ltd (Hong Kong): HSBC Bldg, 1-ga, Bongrae-dong, Jung-gu, CPOB 6910, Seoul 110-161; tel. (2) 2004-0000; fax (2) 381-9100; Gen. Man. G. P. S. CALVERT.

Indian Overseas Bank: Daeyungak Bldg, 3rd Floor, 25-5, 1-ga, Jungmu-no, Jung-gu, CPOB 3332, Seoul 100-011; tel. (2) 753-0741; fax (2) 756-0279; e-mail iobseoul@chollian.net; f. 1977; Gen. Man. K. P. MUNIRATHMAN.

Industrial and Commercial Bank of China (China): Taepyeong Bldg, 17th Floor, 310, 2-ga, Taepyeong-no, Seoul; tel. (2) 755-5688; fax (2) 779-2750; f. 1997; Gen. Man. ZHANG KEXIN.

ING Bank NV (Netherlands): Hungkuk Life Insurance Bldg, 15th Floor, 226, 1-ga, Sinmun-no, Jongno-gu, Seoul 110-061; tel. (2) 317-1800; fax (2) 317-1883; Man. YIM SANG-KYUN.

JP Morgan Chase Bank (USA): Chase Plaza, 34-35, Jeong-dong, Jung-gu, Seoul 100-120; tel. (2) 758-5114; fax (2) 758-5420; f. 1978; Gen. Man. KIM MYUNG-HAN.

Mizuho Bank Ltd (Japan): Nae Wei Bldg, 14th Floor, 6, 2-ga, Ulchi-no, Jung-gu, Seoul 100-192; tel. (2) 756-8181; fax (2) 754-6844; f. 1972; Gen. Man. TSUNEO KIKUCHI.

National Australia Bank Ltd: KDIC Bldg, 16th Floor, 33, Da-dong, Jung-gu, Seoul; tel. (2) 3705-4600; fax (2) 3705-4602; Gen. Man. MARK EDMONDS.

National Bank of Canada: Leema Bldg, 6th Floor, 146-1, Susong-dong, Jongno-gu, Seoul 110-140; tel. (2) 733-5012; fax (2) 736-1508; Vice-Pres. and Country Man. C. N. KIM.

National Bank of Pakistan: Kyobo Bldg, 12th Floor, 1, 1-ga, Jongno, Jongno-gu, CPOB 1633, Seoul 110-121; tel. (2) 732-0277; fax (2) 734-5817; f. 1987; Gen. Man. ABDUL GHAFOOR.

Overseas Union Bank Ltd (Singapore): Kyobo Bldg, 8th Floor, Suite 806, 1, 1-ga, Jongno, Jongno-gu, Seoul 110-714; tel. (2) 739-3441; fax (2) 732-9004; Vice-Pres. and Gen. Man. OOI KOOI KEAT.

Royal Bank of Canada: Kyobo Bldg, 22nd Floor, 1, 1-ga, Jongno, Jongno-gu, Seoul 110-714; tel. (2) 730-7791; fax (2) 736-2995; f. 1982; Gen. Man. THOMAS P. FEHLNER, Jr.

Société Générale (France): Sean Bldg, 10th Floor, 1-ga, Sinmun-no, Jongno-gu, Seoul 110-700; tel. (2) 2195-7777; fax (2) 2195-7700; f. 1984; CEO ÉRIC BERTHÉLEMY.

Standard Chartered Bank (UK): Seoul Finance Center, 22nd Floor, 84, 1-ga, Taepyeong-no, Jung-gu, Seoul; tel. (2) 750-6114; fax (2) 757-7444; Gen. Man. WILLIAM GEMMEL.

UBS AG (Switzerland): Young Poong Bldg, 10th Floor, 33, Seorin-dong, Jongno-gu, Seoul 110-752; tel. (2) 3702-8888; fax (2) 3708-8714; f. 1999; Gen. Man. LEE JAE-HONG.

UFJ Bank Ltd (Japan): Lotte Bldg, 22nd Floor, 1, 1-ga, Sogong-dong, Jung-gu, Seoul; tel. (2) 752-7321; fax (2) 754-3870; Gen. Man. HIDEKI YAMAUCHI.

Union Bank of California NA (USA): Kyobo Bldg, 12th Floor, 1, 1-ga, Jongno, Jongno-gu, CPOB 329, Seoul 110; tel. (2) 721-1700; fax (2) 732-9526; Gen. Man. KIM TAEK-JOONG.

Union de Banques Arabes et Françaises (France): ACE Tower, 3rd Floor, 1-170, Sunhwa-dong, Jung-gu, CPOB 1224, Seoul 100-742; tel. (2) 3455-5300; fax (2) 3455-5354; f. 1979; Gen. Man. PATRICK OBERREINER.

United Overseas Bank Ltd (Singapore): Kyobo Bldg, 20th Floor, 1, 1-ga, Jongno, Jongno-gu, Seoul 110-714; tel. (2) 739-3916; fax (2) 730-9570; Gen. Man. LIEW CHAN HARN.

Banking Association

Korea Federation of Banks: 4-1, 1-ga, Myeong-dong, Jung-gu, Seoul; tel. (2) 3705-5000; fax (2) 3705-5338; internet www.kfb.or.kr; f. 1928; Pres. CHONG CHUN-TAEK; Chair. LEE SANG-CHUL; Vice-Chair. LEE CHUNG-NYUNG.

STOCK EXCHANGE

Korea Stock Exchange: 33, Yeouido-dong, Yeongdeungpo-gu, Seoul 150-977; tel. (2) 3774-9000; fax (2) 786-0263; e-mail world@kse.or.kr; internet www.kse.or.kr; f. 1956; Chair. and CEO KANG YUNG-JOO.

Kosdaq Stock Market, Inc: 45-2, Yeouido-dong, Yeongdeungpo-gu, Seoul 150-974; tel. (2) 2001-5700; fax (2) 784-4505; e-mail webmaster@kosdaq.or.kr; internet www.kosdaq.or.kr; f. 1996; stock market for knowledge-based venture cos; 828 listed cos (Aug. 2002) with a market capitalization of US $39,945m. Pres. and CEO SHIN HO-JOO.

INSURANCE

In 2002 there were 22 life insurance companies and 13 non-life insurance companies.

Principal Life Companies

Allianz Jeil Life Insurance Co Ltd: 1303-35, Seocho 4-dong, Seocho-gu, Seoul 137-074; tel. (2) 3481-3111; fax (2) 3481-0960; f. 1954; Pres. LEE TAE-SIK.

Choson Life Insurance Co Ltd: 111, Sincheon-dong, Dong-gu, Daegu 701-620; tel. (53) 743-3600; fax (53) 742-9263; f. 1988; cap. 12,000m. Pres. LEE YOUNG-TAEK.

Daishin Life Insurance Co Ltd: 395-68, Sindaebang-dong, Dongjak-gu, Seoul 156-010; tel. (2) 3284-7000; fax (2) 3284-7451; internet www.dslife.co.kr; f. 1989; cap. 144,200m. (2002); Pres. PARK BYUNG-MYUNG.

Dong-Ah Life Insurance Co Ltd: Dong-Ah Life Insurance Bldg, 33, Da-dong, Jung-gu, Seoul; tel. (2) 317-5114; fax (2) 771-7561; f. 1973; cap. 10,000m. Pres. KIM CHANG-LAK; 900 brs.

Dongbu Life Insurance Co Ltd: Dongbu Bldg, 7th Floor, 891-10, Daechi-dong, Gangnam-gu, Seoul 135-820; tel. (2) 1588-3131; fax (2) 3011-4100; internet www.dongbulife.co.kr; f. 1989; cap. 85,200m. (2002); Pres. CHANG KI-JE.

Dongyang Life Insurance Co Ltd: 185, Ulchi-no 2-ga, Jung-gu, Seoul 100-192; tel. (2) 728-9114; fax (2) 771-1347; internet www.myangel.co.kr; f. 1989; cap. 340,325m. (2002); Pres. KU JA-HONG.

Doowon Life Insurance Co Ltd: 259-6, Sokjon-dong, Hoewon-gu, Masan 630-500; tel. (55) 52-3100; fax (55) 52-3119; f. 1990; cap. 10,000m. Pres. CHOI IN-YONG.

Han Deuk Life Insurance Co Ltd: 878-1, Bumchyun 1-dong, Busanjin-gu, Busan 641-021; tel. (51) 631-8700; fax (51) 631-8809; f. 1989; cap. 10,000m. Pres. SUH WOO-SHICK.

Hanil Life Insurance Co Ltd: 118, 2-ga, Namdaemun-no, Jung-gu, Seoul 100-770; tel. (2) 2126-7777; fax (2) 2126-7631; internet www.hanillife.co.kr; f. 1993; cap. 115,000m. (2002); Pres. LEE MYUNG-HYUN.

Hankuk Life Insurance Co Ltd: Daehan Fire Bldg, 51-1, Nam-chang-dong, Jung-gu, Seoul 100-060; tel. (2) 773-3355; fax (2) 773-1778; f. 1989; cap. 10,000m. Pres. PARK HYUN-KOOK.

Hansung Life Insurance Co Ltd: 3, Sujung-dong, Dong-gu, Busan 601-030; tel. (51) 461-7700; fax (51) 465-0581; f. 1988; Pres. CHO YONG-KEUN.

Hungkuk Life Insurance Co Ltd: 226, Sinmun-no 1-ga, Jongno-gu, Seoul 100-061; tel. (2) 2002-7000; fax (2) 2002-7804; internet www.hungkuk.co.kr; f. 1958; cap. 12,221m. (2002); Pres. RYU SEOK-KEE.

ING Life Insurance Co Korea Ltd: Sean Bldg, 116, Sinmun-no, Jongno-gu, Seoul 110-700; tel. (2) 3703-9500; fax (2) 734-3309; f. 1991; cap. 64,820m. (2002); Pres. JOOST KENEMANS.

Korea Life Insurance Co Ltd: 60, Yeouido-dong, Yeongdeungpo-gu, Seoul 150-603; tel. (2) 789-5114; fax (2) 789-8173; internet www.korealife.com; f. 1946; cap. 3,550,000m. (2002); Pres. LEE KANG-HWAN.

Korean Reinsurance Company: 80, Susong-dong, Jongno-gu, Seoul 110-733; tel. (2) 3702-6000; fax (2) 739-3754; internet www.koreanre.co.kr; f. 1963; Pres. PARK JONG-WON.

Kumho Life Insurance Co Ltd: 57, 1-ga, Sinmun-no, Jongno-gu, Seoul 110-061; tel. (2) 6303-5000; fax (2) 771-7561; internet www.kumholife.co.kr; f. 1988; cap. 211,249m. (2002); Pres. SONG KEY-HYUCK.

Kyobo Life Insurance Co Ltd: 1, 1-ga, Jongno, Jongno-gu, Seoul 110-714; tel. (2) 721-2121; fax (2) 737-9970; internet www.kyobo.co.kr; f. 1958; cap. 92,500m. Pres. and CEO CHANG HYUNG-DUK; 84 main brs.

Lucky Life Insurance Co Ltd: 3, Sujung-dong, Dong-gu, Busan 601-716; tel. (51) 461-7700; fax (51) 465-0581; internet www.luckylife.co.kr; f. 1988; cap. 139,054m. (2002); Pres. CHANG NAM-SIK.

MetLife Insurance Co of Korea Ltd: Sungwon Bldg, 8th Floor, 141, Samseong-dong, Gangnam-gu, Seoul 135-716; tel. (2) 3469-9600; fax (2) 3469-9700; internet www.metlifekorea.co.kr; f. 1989; cap. 97,700m. (2002); Pres. STUART B. SOLOMON.

Pacific Life Insurance Co Ltd: 705-9, Yeoksam-dong, Gangnam-gu, Seoul 135-080; tel. (2) 3458-0114; fax (2) 3458-0392; internet www.pli.co.kr; f. 1989; cap. 10,000m. Pres. KIM SUNG-MOO.

PCA Life Insurance Co Ltd: 142, Nonhyun-dong, Gangnam-gu, Seoul 135-749; tel. (2) 515-5300; fax (2) 514-3844; f. 1990; cap. 52,100m. (2002); Pres. MIKE BISHOP.

Prudential Life Insurance Co of Korea Ltd: Prudential Bldg, Yeoksam-dong, Gangnam-gu, Seoul; tel. (2) 2144-2000; fax (2) 2144-2100; internet www.prudential.or.kr; f. 1989; cap. 26,400m. Pres. JAMES C. SPACKMAN.

Samshin All State Life Insurance Co Ltd: Samwhan Bldg, 5th Floor, 98-5, Unni-dong, Jongno-gu, Seoul 110-742; tel. (2) 3670-5000; fax (2) 742-8197; Pres. KIM KYUNG-YOP.

Samsung Life Insurance Co Ltd: 150, 2-ga, Taepyeong-no, Jung-gu, Seoul 100-716; tel. (2) 751-8000; fax (2) 751-8100; internet www.samsunglife.com; f. 1957; cap. 100,000m. (2002); Pres. BAE JUNG-CHOONG; 1,300 brs.

Shinhan Life Insurance Co Ltd: 120, 2-ga, Taepyeong-no, Jung-gu, Seoul 100-102; tel. (2) 3455-4000; fax (2) 753-9351; internet www.shinhanlife.co.kr; f. 1990; Pres. HAN DONG-WOO.

SK Life Insurance Co Ltd: 168, Gongduk-dong, Mapo-gu, Seoul 121-705; tel. (2) 3271-4114; fax (2) 3271-4400; internet www.sklife.com; f. 1988; cap. 246,275m. (2002); Pres. KANG HONG-SIN.

Non-Life Companies

Daehan Fire and Marine Insurance Co Ltd: 51-1, Namchang-dong, Jung-gu, Seoul 100-778; tel. (2) 3455-3114; fax (2) 756-9194;

e-mail dhplane@daeins.co.kr; internet www.daeins.co.kr; f. 1946; cap. 19,500m. Pres. LEE YOUNG-DONG.

Dongbu Insurance Co Ltd: Dongbu Financial Center, 891-10, Daechi-dong, Gangnam-gu, Seoul 135-840; tel. (2) 2262-3450; fax (2) 2273-6785; e-mail dongbu@dongbuinsurance.co.kr; internet www.idongbu.com; f. 1962; cap. 30,000m. Pres. LEE SU-KWANG.

First Fire and Marine Insurance Co Ltd: 12-1, Seosomun-dong, Jung-gu, CPOB 530, Seoul 100-110; tel. (2) 316-8114; fax (2) 771-7319; internet www.insumall.co.kr; f. 1949; cap. 17,200m. Pres. KIM WOO-HOANG.

Green Fire and Marine Insurance Co Ltd: Seoul City Tower, 581, 5-ga, Namdaemun-no, Jung-gu, Seoul 100-803; tel. (2) 1588-5959; fax (2) 773-1214; internet www.greenfire.co.kr; KIM JONG-CHEN.

Haedong Insurance Co Ltd: 1424-2, Seocho-dong, Seocho-gu, Seoul; tel. (2) 520-2114; e-mail webmaster@haedong.co.kr; internet www.haedong.co.kr; f. 1953; cap. p.u. 12,000m. Chair. KIM DONG-MAN; CEO NAH BOO-WHAN.

Hankuk Fidelity and Surety Co Ltd: 51-1, Namchang-dong, Jung-gu, Seoul; tel. (2) 773-3355; fax (2) 773-1778; e-mail hfs025@unitel.co.kr; f. 1989; cap. 103,000m. Pres. CHO AM-DAE.

Hyundai Marine and Fire Insurance Co Ltd: 8th Floor, 140-2, Kye-dong, Jongno-gu, Seoul 110-793; tel. (2) 3701-8000; fax (2) 732-5687; e-mail webpd@hdinsurance.co.kr; internet www.hi.co.kr; f. 1955; cap. 30,000m. Pres. KIM HO-IL.

Korean Reinsurance Co: 80, Susong-dong, Jongno-gu, Seoul 100-733; tel. (2) 3702-6000; fax (2) 739-3754; e-mail service@koreanre.co.kr; internet www.koreanre.co.kr; f. 1963; cap. 34,030m. Pres. PARK JONG-WON.

Kukje Hwajae Insurance Co Ltd: 120, 5-ga, Namdaemun-no, Jung-gu, Seoul 100-704; tel. (2) 753-1101; fax (2) 773-1214; internet www.directins.co.kr; f. 1947; cap. 10,784m. Chair. LEE BONG-SUH.

Kyobo Auto Insurance Co Ltd: 76-4, Jamwon-dong, Seocho-gu, Seoul 137-909; tel. (2) 3479-4900; fax (2) 3479-4800; internet www.kyobodirect.com; Pres. SHIN YONG-KIL.

LG Insurance Co Ltd: LG Da-dong Bldg, 85, Da-dong, Jung-gu, Seoul 100-180; tel. (2) 310-2391; fax (2) 753-1002; e-mail webmaster@lginsure.com; internet www.lginsure.com; f. 1959; Pres. KOO CHA-HOON.

Oriental Fire and Marine Insurance Co Ltd: 25-1, Yeouido-dong, Yeongdeungpo-gu, Seoul 150-010; tel. (2) 3786-1910; fax (2) 3886-1940; e-mail webmaster@ofmi.co.kr; internet www.insuworld.co.kr; f. 1922; cap. 42,900m. Pres. CHUNG KUN-SUB.

Samsung Fire and Marine Insurance Co Ltd: Samsung Insurance Bldg, 87, 1-ga, Ulchi-no, Jung-gu, Seoul 100-191; tel. (2) 758-7948; fax (2) 758-7831; internet www.samsungfire.com; f. 1952; cap. 6,566m. Pres. LEE SOO-CHANG.

Seoul Guarantee Insurance Co: 136-74, Yeonchi-dong, Jongno-gu, Seoul 110-470; tel. (2) 3671-7459; fax (2) 3671-7480; internet www.sgic.co.kr; Pres. PARK HAE-CHOON.

Shindongah Fire and Marine Insurance Co Ltd: 43, 2-ga, Taepyeong-no, Jung-gu, Seoul; tel. (2) 6366-7000; fax (2) 755-8006; internet www.sdafire.com; f. 1946; cap. 60,220m. Pres. JEON HWA-SOO.

Ssangyong Fire and Marine Insurance Co Ltd: 60, Doryeom-dong, Jongno-gu, Seoul 110-716; tel. (2) 724-9000; fax (2) 730-1628; e-mail sfmi@ssy.insurance.co.kr; internet www.insurance.co.kr; f. 1948; cap. 27,400m. Pres. LEE JIN-MYUNG.

Insurance Associations

Korea Life Insurance Association: Kukdong Bldg, 16th Floor, 60-1, 3-ga, Jungmu-no, Jung-gu, Seoul 100-705; tel. (2) 2262-6600; fax (2) 2262-6580; internet www.klia.or.kr; f. 1950; Chair. BAE CHAN-BYUNG.

Korea Non-Life Insurance Association: KRIC Bldg, 6th Floor, 80, Susong-dong, Jongno-gu, Seoul; tel. (2) 3702-8539; fax (2) 3702-8549; internet www.knia.or.kr; f. 1946; 13 corporate mems; Chair. PARK JONG-IK.

Trade and Industry

GOVERNMENT AGENCIES

Fair Trade Commission: 1, Jungang-dong, Gwacheon-si, Gyeonggi Prov. 427-760; internet www.ftc.go.kr; Chair. LEE NAM-KEE.

Federation of Korean Industries: FKI Bldg, 2nd Floor, 28-1, Yeouido-dong, Yeongdeungpo-gu, Seoul 150-756; tel. (2) 3771-0114;

fax (2) 3771-0110; e-mail webmaster@fki.or.kr; internet www.fki.or.kr; f. 1961; conducts research and survey work on domestic and overseas economic conditions and trends; advises the Govt and other interested parties on economic matters; exchanges economic and trade missions with other countries; sponsors business conferences; 380 corporate mems and 65 business asscns; Chair. KIM KAK-CHOONG.

Korea Appraisal Board: 171-2, Samseong-dong, Gangnam-gu, Seoul; tel. (2) 555-1174; Chair. KANG KIL-BOO.

Korea Asset Management Corpn (KAMCO): 814, Yeoksam-dong, Gangnam-gu, Seoul; tel. (2) 3420-5049; fax (2) 3420-5100; internet www.kamco.co.kr; f. 1963; collection and foreclosure agency; appointed following Asian financial crisis as sole institution to manage and dispose of non-performing loans for financial institutions; Pres. CHUNG JAE-RYONG.

Korea Export Industrial Corpn: 33, Seorin-dong, Jongno-gu, Seoul; tel. (2) 853-5573; f. 1964; encourages industrial exports, provides assistance and operating capital, conducts market surveys; Pres. KIM KI-BAE.

Korea Export Insurance Corpn: 33, Seorin-dong, Jongno-gu, Seoul; tel. (2) 399-6800; fax (2) 399-6597; internet www.keic.or.kr; f. 1992; and official export credit agency of Korea; Pres. LIM TAE-JIN.

Korea Institute for Industrial Economics and Trade (KIET): 206-9, Cheongnyangni-dong, Dongdaemun-gu, Seoul; tel. (2) 3299-3114; fax (2) 963-8540; internet www.kiet.re.kr; f. 1976; economic and industrial research; Pres. PAI KWANG-SUN.

Korean Intellectual Property Office: Government Complex-Daejeon, Dunsan-dong, Seo-gu, Daejeon; tel. (42) 481-5027; fax (42) 481-3455; internet www.kipo.go.kr; Commissioner KIM GWANG-LIM.

Korea Industrial Research Institutes: FKI Bldg, 28-1, Yeouido-dong, Yeongdeungpo-gu, Seoul; tel. (2) 780-7601; fax (2) 785-5771; f. 1979; analyses industrial and technological information from abroad; Pres. KIM CHAE-KYUM.

Korea Trade-Investment Promotion Agency (KOTRA): 300-9, Yeomgok-dong, Seocho-gu, Seoul; tel. (2) 3460-7114; fax (2) 3460-7777; e-mail net-mgr@kotra.or.kr; internet www.kotra.or.kr; f. 1962; various trade promotion activities, market research, cross-border investment promotion, etc. 98 overseas brs; Pres. OH YOUNG-KYO.

CHAMBER OF COMMERCE

Korea Chamber of Commerce and Industry: 45, 4-ga, Namdaemun-no, Jung-gu, Seoul 100-743; tel. (2) 316-3114; fax (2) 757-9475; internet www.korcham.net; f. 1884; over 80,000m. mems; 63 local chambers; promotes development of the economy and of international economic co-operation; Pres. PARK YONG-SUNG.

INDUSTRIAL AND TRADE ASSOCIATIONS

Agricultural and Fishery Marketing Corpn: 191, 2-ga, Hangang-no, Yeongsan-gu, CPOB 3212, Seoul 140; tel. (2) 790-8010; fax (2) 798-7513; internet www.afmc.co.kr; f. 1967; integrated development for secondary processing and marketing distribution for agricultural products and fisheries products; Pres. AHN KYO-DUCK; Exec. Vice-Pres. KIM JIN-KYU.

Construction Association of Korea: Construction Bldg, 8th Floor, 71-2, Nonhyon-dong, Gangnam-gu, Seoul 135-701; tel. (2) 547-6101; fax (2) 542-6264; f. 1947; national licensed contractors' asscn; 2,700 mem. firms (1995); Pres. CHOI WON-SUK; Vice-Pres. PARK KU-YEOL.

Electronic Industries Association of Korea: 648, Yeoksam-dong, Gangnam-gu, CPOB 5650, Seoul 135-080; tel. (2) 553-0941; fax (2) 555-6195; e-mail eiak@soback.kornet.nm.kr; internet www.eiak.org; f. 1976; 328 mems; Chair. JOHN KOO.

Korea Automobile Manufacturers Association: 658-4. Deungchon-dong, Gangseo-gu, Seoul; tel. (2) 3660-1800; fax (2) 3660-1900; e-mail cwkim@kama.or.kr; internet www.kama.or.kr; f. 1988; Chair. KIM NOI-MYUNG.

Korea Coal Association: 80-6, Susong-dong, Jongno-gu, Seoul; tel. (2) 734-8891; fax (2) 734-7959; f. 1949; 49 corporate mems; Chair. JANG BYEONG-DUCK.

Korea Consumer Goods Exporters Association: KWTC Bldg, Rm 1802, 159, Samseong-dong, Gangnam-gu, Seoul; tel. (2) 551-1865; fax (2) 551-1870; f. 1986; 230 corporate mems; Pres. YONG WOONG-SHIN.

Korea Federation of Textile Industries: 944-31, Daechi-dong, Gangnam-gu, Seoul; tel. (2) 528-4001; fax (2) 528-4069; e-mail kofoti@kofoti.or.kr; internet www.kofoti.or.kr; f. 1980; 50 corporate mems; Pres. PARK SANG-CHUL.

Korea Foods Industry Association: 1002-6, Bangbae-dong, Seocho-gu, Seoul; tel. (2) 585-5052; fax (2) 586-4906; internet www.kfia.or.kr; f. 1969; 104 corporate mems; Pres. CHUN MYUNG-KE.

Korea Importers Association (KOIMA): 218, Hangang-no, 2-ga, Yeongsan-gu, Seoul 140-875; tel. (2) 792-1581; fax (2) 785-4373; e-mail info@aftak.com; internet www.aftak.or.kr; f. 1970; 11,903 mems; Chair. CHIN CHUL-PYUNG.

Korea International Trade Association: 159-1, Samseong-dong, Gangnam-gu, Seoul; tel. (2) 6000-5114; fax (2) 6000-5115; internet www.kita.org; f. 1946; private, non-profitmaking business org. representing all licensed traders in South Korea; provides foreign businessmen with information, contacts and advice; 80,000 corporate mems; Pres. KIM JAE-CHUL.

Korea Iron and Steel Association: 824, Yeoksam-dong, Gangnam-gu, Seoul; tel. (2) 559-3500; fax (2) 559-3508; internet www.kosa.or.kr; f. 1975; 39 corporate mems; Chair. YOO SANG-BOO.

Korea Oil Association: 28-1, Yeouido-dong, Yeongdeungpo-gu, Seoul; tel. (2) 3775-0520; fax (2) 761-9573; f. 1980; Pres. CHOI DOO-HWAN.

Korea Productivity Center: 122-1, Jeokseon-dong, Jongno-gu, Seoul 110-052; tel. (2) 724-1114; fax (2) 736-0322; internet www.kpc.or.kr; f. 1957; services to increase productivity of the industries, consulting services, education and training of specialized personnel; Chair. and CEO LEE HEE-BEOM.

Korea Sericultural Association: 17-9, Yeouido-dong, Yeongdeungpo-gu, Seoul; tel. (2) 783-6072; fax (2) 780-0706; f. 1946; improvement and promotion of silk production; 50,227 corporate mems; Pres. CHOI YON-HONG.

Korea Shipbuilders' Association: 65-1, Unni-dong, Jongno-gu, Seoul; tel. (2) 766-4631; fax (2) 766-4307; internet www.koshipa.or.kr; f. 1977; 9 mems; Chair. KIM HYUNG-BYUK.

Korea Textiles Trade Association: Textile Center, 16th Floor, 944-31, Daechi-dong, Gangnam-gu, Seoul; tel. (2) 528-5158; fax (2) 528-5188; f. 1981; 947 corporate mems; Pres. KANG TAE-SEUNG.

Korean Apparel Industry Association: KWTC Bldg, Rm 801, 159, Samseong-dong, Gangnam-gu, Seoul 135-729; tel. (2) 551-1454; fax (2) 551-1467; f. 1993; 741 corporate mems; Pres. PARK SEI-YOUNG.

Korean Development Associates: Seoul; tel. (2) 392-3854; fax (2) 312-3856; f. 1965; economic research; 25 corporate mems; Pres. KIM DONG-KYU.

Mining Association of Korea: 35-24, Dongui-dong, Jongno-gu, Seoul 110; tel. (2) 737-7748; fax (2) 720-5592; f. 1918; 128 corporate mems; Pres. KIM SANG-BONG.

Spinners and Weavers Association of Korea: 43-8, Gwancheol-dong, Jongno-gu, Seoul 110; tel. (2) 735-5741; fax (2) 735-5749; internet www.swak.org; f. 1947; 20 corporate mems; Pres. SUH MIN-SOK.

EMPLOYERS' ORGANIZATION

Korea Employers' Federation: KEF Bldg, 276-1 Daeheung-dong, Mapo-gu, Seoul 121-726; tel. (2) 3270-7336; fax (2) 701-2495; e-mail delee@kef.or.kr; internet www.kef.or.kr; f. 1970; advocates employers' interests with regard to labour and social affairs; 13 regional employers' asscns, 20 economic and trade asscns, and 4,000 major enterprises; Chair. KIM CHANG-SUNG.

UTILITIES

Electricity

Korea Electric Power Corpn (KEPCO): 167, Samseong-dong, Gangnam-gu, Seoul; tel. (2) 3456-3630; fax (2) 3456-3699; internet www.kepco.co.kr; f. 1961; transmission and distribution of electric power, and development of electric power sources; privatization pending; Pres. KANG DONG-SUK.

Gas

Korea Gas Corpn: 215, Jeongja-dong, Bundang-gu, Seongnam, Gyeonggi Prov. tel. (31) 710-0114; fax (31) 710-0117; internet www.kogas.or.kr; state-owned; proposed transfer to private-sector ownership announced in July 1998; Pres. KIM MYUNG-KYU.

Samchully Co Ltd: 35-6, Yeouido-dong, Yeongdeungpo-gu, Seoul; tel. (2) 368-3300; fax (2) 783-1206; internet www.samchully.co.kr; f. 1966; gas supply co for Seoul metropolitan area and Gyeonggi Prov. Chair. JIN JU-HWA.

Water

Korea Water Resources Corpn: 6-2, Yeonchuk-dong, Daedeok-gu, Daejeon; tel. (42) 629-3114; fax (42) 623-0963; internet www.kowaco.or.kr.

Office of Waterworks, Seoul Metropolitan Govt: 27-1 Hap-dong, Seodaemun-gu, Seoul; tel. (2) 390-7332; fax (2) 362-3653; f. 1908; responsible for water supply in Seoul; Head SON JANG-HO.

Ulsan City Water and Sewerage Board: 646-4, Sin-Jung 1-dong, Nam-gu, Ulsan; tel. (52) 743-020; fax (52) 746-928; f. 1979; responsible for water supply and sewerage in Ulsan; Dir HO KUN-SONG.

CO-OPERATIVES

Korea Computers Co-operative: Seoul; tel. (2) 780-0511; fax (2) 780-7509; f. 1981; Pres. MIN KYUNG-HYUN.

Korea Federation of Knitting Industry Co-operatives: 586-1, Sinsa-dong, Gangnam-gu, Seoul; tel. (2) 548-2131; fax (2) 3444-9929; internet www.knit.or.kr; f. 1962; Chair. JOUNG MAN-SUB.

Korea Federation of Non-ferrous Metal Industry Co-operatives: Backsang Bldg, Rm 715, 35-2, Yeouido-dong, Yeongdeungpo-gu, Seoul; tel. (2) 780-8551; fax (2) 784-9473; f. 1962; Chair. PARK WON-SIK.

Korea Federation of Small and Medium Business (KFSB): 16-2, Yeouido-dong, Yeongdeungpo-gu, Seoul 150-010; tel. (2) 2124-3114; fax (2) 782-0247; f. 1962; Chair. KIM YOUNG-SOO.

Korea Mining Industry Co-operative: 35-24, Dongui-dong, Jongno-gu, Seoul; tel. (2) 735-3490; fax (2) 735-4658; f. 1966; Chair. JEON HYANG-SIK.

Korea Steel Industry Co-operative: 915-14, Bangbae-dong, Seocho-gu, Seoul; tel. (2) 587-3121; fax (2) 588-3671; internet www.kosic.or.kr; f. 1962; Pres. KIM DUK-NAM.

Korea Woollen Spinners and Weavers Co-operatives: Rm 503, Seawha Bldg, 36, 6-ga, Jongno-gu, Seoul; tel. (2) 747-3871; fax (2) 747-3874; e-mail woollen@woolspd.or.kr; internet www.woolspd.or.kr; f. 1964; Pres. KIM YOUNG-SIK.

National Agricultural Co-operative Federation (NACF): 1, 1-ga, Chungjeong-no, Jung-gu, Seoul; tel. (2) 397-5114; fax (2) 397-5380; internet www.nacf.co.kr; f. 1961; international banking, marketing, co-operative trade, utilization and processing, supply, co-operative insurance, banking and credit services, education and research; Pres. WON CHUL-HEE.

National Federation of Fisheries Co-operatives: 11-6, Sin-cheon-dong, Songpa-gu, Seoul; tel. (2) 2240-3114; fax (2) 2240-3024; internet www.suhyup.co.kr; f. 1962; Pres. HONG JONG-MOON.

TRADE UNIONS

Federation of Korean Trade Unions (FKTU): FKTU Bldg, 35, Yeouido-dong, Yeongdeungpo-gu, Seoul; tel. (2) 782-3884; fax (2) 784-2864; e-mail fktuintl@nownuri.net; internet www.fktu.org; f. 1941; Pres. LEE NAM-SOON; affiliated to ICFTU; 29 union federations are affiliated with a membership of some 960,000.

Federation of Foreign Organization Employees' Unions: 5-1, 3-ga, Dangsan-dong, Yeongdeungpo-gu, Seoul; tel. (2) 2068-1645; fax (2) 2068-1644; f. 1961; Pres. KANG IN-SIK; 22,450 mems.

Federation of Korean Apartment Workers' Unions: 922-1, Bangbae-dong, Seocho-gu, Seoul; tel. (2) 522-6860; fax (2) 522-4624; f. 1997; Pres. LEE DAE-HYUNG; 3,670 mems.

Federation of Korean Chemical Workers' Unions: Sukchun Bldg, 2nd Floor, 32-100, 4-ga, Dangsan-dong, Yeongdeungpo-gu, Seoul; tel. (2) 761-8251; fax (2) 761-8255; e-mail fkcu@chollian.net; internet www.fkcu.or.kr; f. 1961; Pres. PARK HUN-SOO; 116,286 mems.

Federation of Korean Metalworkers' Unions: 1570-2, Sinrim-dong, Gwanak-gu, Seoul; tel. (2) 864-2901; fax (2) 864-0457; e-mail fkmtu@chollian.net; internet www.metall.or.kr; f. 1961; Pres. LEE BYUNG-KYUN; 130,000 mems.

Federation of Korean Mine Workers' Unions: Guangno Bldg, 2nd Floor, 10-4, Karak-dong, Songpa-gu, Seoul; tel. (2) 403-0973; fax (2) 400-1877; f. 1961; Pres. KIM DONG-CHUL; 6,930 mems.

Federation of Korean Printing Workers' Unions: 201, 792-155, 3-ga, Guro-dong, Guro-gu, Seoul; tel. (2) 780-7969; fax (2) 780-6097; f. 1961; Pres. LEE KWANG-JOO; 5,609 mems.

Federation of Korean Public Construction Unions: 293-1, Kumdo-dong, Sujong-gu, Seongnam-si, Gyeonggi-do; tel. (2) 2304-7016; fax (2) 230-4602; f. 1998; Pres. HONG SANG-KI (acting); 9,185 mems.

Federation of Korean Public Service Unions: Sukchun Bldg, 3rd Floor, 32-100, 4-ga, Dangsan-dong, Yeongdeungpo-gu, Seoul; tel. (2) 769-1330; fax (2) 769-1332; internet www.fkpu.or.kr; f. 1997; Pres. LEE KWAN-BOO; 15,641 mems.

Federation of Korean Rubber Workers' Unions: 830-240, 2-ga, Bumil-dong, Dong-gu, Busan; tel. (51) 637-2101; fax (51) 637-2103; f. 1988; Pres. CHO YUNG-SOO; 6,600 mems.

Federation of Korean Seafarers' Unions: 544, Donhwa-dong, Mapo-gu, Seoul; tel. (2) 716-2764; fax (2) 702-2271; e-mail fksu@chollian.net; internet www.fksu.or.kr; f. 1961; Pres. KIM PIL-JAE; 60,037 mems.

Federation of Korean State-invested Corporation Unions: Sunwoo Bldg, 501, 350-8, Yangjae-dong, Seocho-gu, Seoul; tel. (2) 529-2268; fax (2) 529-2270; internet www.publicunion.or.kr; f. 1998; Pres. JANG DAE-IK; 19,375 mems.

Federation of Korean Taxi & Transport Workers' Unions: 415-7, Janan 1-dong, Dongdaemun-gu, Seoul; tel. (2) 2210-8500; fax (2) 2247-7890; internet www.ktaxi.or.kr; f. 1988; Pres. KWAN OH-MAN; 105,118 mems.

Federation of Korean Textile Workers' Unions: 274-8, Yeom-chang-dong, Gangseo-gu, Seoul; tel. (2) 3665-3117; fax (2) 3662-4373; f. 1954; Pres. OH YOUNG-BONG; 6,930 mems.

Federation of Korean United Workers' Unions: Sukchun Bldg, 32-100, 4-ga, Dangsan-dong, Yeongdeungpo-gu, Seoul; internet www.fkuwu.or.kr; f. 1961; 51,802 mems.

Federation of Korean Urban Railway Unions: Urban Railway Station, 3-ga, Yeouido-dong, Yeongdeungpo-gu, Seoul; tel. (2) 786-5163; fax (2) 786-5165; f. 1996; Pres. HA WON-JOON; 9,628 mems.

Korea Automobile & Transport Workers' Federation: 678-27, Yeoksam-dong, Gangnam-gu, Seoul; tel. (2) 554-0890; fax (2) 554-1558; f. 1963; Pres. KANG SUNG-CHUN; 84,343 mems.

Korea Federation of Bank & Financial Workers' Unions: 88, Da-dong, Jung-gu, Seoul; tel. (2) 756-2389; fax (2) 754-4893; internet www.kfiu.org; f. 1961; Pres. LEE YUNG-DUK; 113,994 mems.

Korea Federation of Communication Trade Unions: 10th Floor, 106-6, Guro 5-dong, Guro-gu, Seoul; tel. (2) 864-0055; fax (2) 864-5519; internet www.ictu.co.kr; f. 1961; Pres. OH DONG-IN; 18,810 mems.

Korea Federation of Food Industry Workers' Unions: 106-2, 1-ga, Yanpyeong-dong, Yeongdeungpo-gu, Seoul; tel. (2) 679-6441; fax (2) 679-6444; f. 2000; Pres. BAEK YOUNG-GIL; 19,146 mems.

Korea Federation of Port & Transport Workers' Unions: Bauksan Bldg, 19th Floor, 12-5, Dongja-dong, Yeongsan-gu, Seoul; tel. (2) 727-4741; fax (2) 727-4749; f. 1980; Pres. CHOI BONG-HONG; 33,347 mems.

Korea National Electrical Workers' Union: 167, Samseong-dong, Gangnam-gu, Seoul; tel. (2) 3456-6017; fax (2) 3456-6004; internet www.knewu.or.kr; f. 1961; Pres. KIM JU-YOUNG; 16,741 mems.

Korea Professional Artist Federation: Hanil Bldg, 43-4, Donui-dong, Jongno-gu, Seoul; tel. (2) 764-5310; fax (2) 3675-5314; f. 1999; Pres. PARK IL-NAM; 2,395 mems.

Korea Tobacco & Ginseng Workers' Unions: 100, Pyeong-chon-dong, Daedeok-gu, Daejeon; tel. (42) 932-7118; fax (42) 931-1812; f. 1960; Pres. KANG TAE-HEUNG; 6,008 mems.

Korea Unions of Teaching and Educational Workers: Dongin Bldg, 7th Floor, 65-33, Singil 1-dong, Yeongdeungpo-gu, Seoul; tel. (2) 849-1281; fax (2) 835-0556; internet www.kute.or.kr; f. 1999; Pres. SON KYUNG-SOON; 18,337 mems.

Korean Communications Workers' Unions: 154-1, Seorin-dong, Jongno-gu, Seoul; tel. (2) 2195-1752; fax (2) 2195-1761; internet www.kpwu.or.kr; f. 1958; Pres. JEONG HYUN-YOUNG; 26,071 mems.

Korean Postal Workers' Union: 154-1, Seorin-dong, Jongno-gu, Seoul 110-110; tel. (2) 2195-1773; fax (2) 2195-1761; e-mail cheshin@chol.com; internet www.kpwu.or.kr; f. 1958; Pres. JUNG HYUN-YOUNG; 23,500 mems.

Korean Railway Workers' Union: 40, 3-ga, Hangang-no, Yeongsan-gu, Seoul; tel. (2) 795-6174; f. 1947; Pres. KIM JONG-WOOK; 31,041 mems.

Korean Tourist Industry Workers' Federation: 749, 5-ga, Namdaemun-no, Jung-gu, Seoul 100-095; tel. (2) 779-1297; fax (2) 779-1298; f. 1970; Pres. JEONG YOUNG-KI; 27,273 mems.

National Medical Industry Workers' Federation of Korea: 134, Sincheon-dong, Seodaemun-gu, Seoul; tel. (2) 313-3900; fax (2) 393-6877; f. 1999; Pres. LEE YONG-MOO; 5,610 mems.

Korean Confederation of Trade Unions: 139, 2-ga, Yeouido-dong, Yeongdeungpo-gu, Seoul; tel. (2) 635-1133; fax (2) 635-1134; internet www.kctu.or.kr; f. 1995; legalized 1999; Chair. DAN PYONG-HO; c. 600,000 mems.

Transport

RAILWAYS

At the end of 2001 there were 6,819 km (including freight routes) of railways in operation. Construction of a new high-speed rail system connecting Seoul to Busan (412 km) via Cheonan, Daejeon, Daegu, and Gyungju, was underway in 2001. The first phase, Seoul–Daejeon, was scheduled for completion in 2004. The second phase, Daejeon–Busan, was scheduled for completion in 2010. Construction work on the reconnection of the Kyongui (West coast, Sinuiju (North Korea)–Seoul) and East Coast Line (Wonsan (North Korea)–Seoul) began in September 2002; the former was expected to be completed by the end of that year, and the latter by September 2003. Reconnection work was subject to disruption by the changing political situation. Eventually the two would be linked to the Trans-China and Trans-Siberian railways respectively, greatly enhancing the region's transportation links.

Korean National Railroad: 920, Dunsan-dong, Seo-gu, Daejeon 302-701; tel. (42) 1544-7788; fax (42) 481-373; internet www.korail.go.kr; f. 1963; operates all railways under the supervision of the Ministry of Construction and Transportation; total track length of 6,819 km (2001); Admin. SON HAK-LAE.

City Underground Railways

Busan Subway: Busan Urban Transit Authority, 861-1, Bumchun-dong, Busan 614-021; tel. (51) 633-8783; e-mail ipsubway@buta.or.kr; internet subway.busan.kr; f. 1988; length of 71.6 km (2 lines, with a further 3rd line under construction); Pres. LEE HYANG-YEUL.

Daegu Metropolitan Subway Corpn: 1500 Sangin 1-dong, Dalseo-gu, Daegu; tel. (53) 640-2114; fax (53) 640-2229; e-mail webmaster@daegusubway.co.kr; internet www.daegusubway.co.kr; length of 28.3 km (1 line, with a further five routes totalling 125.4 km planned or under construction); Pres. YOON JIN-TAE.

Incheon Rapid Transit Corpn: 67-2, Gansok-dong, Namdong-gu, Incheon 405-233; tel. (32) 451-2114; fax (32) 451-2160; internet www.irtc.co.kr; length of 24.6 km (22 stations, 1 line), with two further lines planned; Pres. CHOUNG IN-SOUNG.

Seoul Metropolitan Rapid Transit Corporation: Seoul; internet www.smrt.co.kr; operates lines 5-8.

Seoul Metropolitan Subway Corpn: 447-7, Bangbae-dong, Seocho-gu, Seoul; tel. (2) 520-5020; fax (2) 520-5039; internet www.seoulsubway.co.kr; f. 1981; length of 134.9 km (115 stations, lines 1-4); Pres. KIM JUNG-GOOK.

Underground railways were also under construction in Daejeon and Gwangju.

ROADS

At the end of 2001 there were 91,396 km of roads, of which 76.7% were paved. A network of motorways (2,637 km) links all the principal towns, the most important being the 428-km Seoul–Busan motorway. Improvements in relations with North Korea resulted in the commencement of work on a four-lane highway to link Seoul and the North Korean capital, Pyongyang, in September 2000; construction of the road was scheduled for completion in 2003.

Korea Highway Corpn: 293-1, Kumto-dong, Sujong-gu, Seongnam, Gyeonggi Prov. tel. (822) 2230-4114; fax (822) 2230-4308; internet www.freeway.co.kr; f. 1969; responsible for construction, maintenance and management of toll roads; Pres. OH JUM-LOCK.

SHIPPING

In December 2001 South Korea's merchant fleet (2,426 vessels) had a total displacement of 6,394,994 grt. Major ports include Busan, Incheon, Donghae, Masan, Yeosu, Gunsan, Mokpo, Pohang, Ulsan, Jeju and Gwangyang.

Korea Maritime and Port Authority: 112-2, Inui-dong, Jongno-gu, Seoul 110; tel. (2) 3466-2214; f. 1976; operates under the Ministry of Maritime Affairs and Fisheries; supervises all aspects of shipping and port-related affairs; Admin. AHN KONG-HYUK.

Korea Shipowners' Association: Sejong Bldg, 10th Floor, 100, Dangju-dong, Jongno-gu, Seoul 110-071; tel. (2) 739-1551; fax (2) 739-1565; e-mail korea@shipowners.or.kr; internet www.shipowners.co.kr; f. 1960; 40 shipping co mems; Chair. HYUN YUNG-WON.

Korea Shipping Association: 66010, Dungchon 3-dong, Gangseo-gu, Seoul 157-033; tel. (2) 6096-2024; fax (2) 6096-2029; e-mail kimny@haewoon.co.kr; internet www.haewoon.co.kr; f. 1962; management consulting and investigation, mutual insurance; 1,189 mems; Chair. PARK HONG-JIN.

Principal Companies

Cho Yang Shipping Co Ltd: Chongam Bldg, 85-3, Seosomun-dong, Jung-gu, CPOB 1163, Seoul 100; tel. (2) 3708-6000; fax (2) 3708-6926; internet www.choyang.co.kr; f. 1961; Korea–Japan, Korea–China, Korea–Australia–Japan, Asia–Mediterranean–America liner services and world-wide tramping; Chair. N. K. PARK; Pres. J. W. PARK.

DooYang Line Co Ltd: 166-4, Samseong-dong, Gangnam-gu, Seoul 135-091; tel. (2) 550-1700; fax (2) 550-1777; internet www.dooyang .co.kr; f. 1984; world-wide tramping and conventional liner trade; Pres. CHO DONG-HYUN.

Hanjin Shipping Ltd: 25-11, Yeouido-dong, Yeongdeungpo-gu, Seoul; tel. (2) 3770-6114; fax (2) 3770-6740; internet www.hanjin .com; f. 1977; marine transportation, harbour service, warehousing, shipping and repair, vessel sales, harbour department and cargo service; Pres. CHOI WON-PYO.

Hyundai Merchant Marine Co Ltd: 66, Jeokseon-dong, Jongno-gu, Seoul 110-052; tel. (2) 3706-5114; fax (2) 723-2193; internet www .hmm.co.kr; f. 1976; Chair. HYUN YUNG-WON.

Korea Line Corpn: Dae Il Bldg, 43, Insa-dong, Jongno-gu, Seoul 110-290; tel. (2) 3701-0114; fax (2) 733-1610; f. 1968; world-wide transportation service and shipping agency service in Korea; Pres. JANG HAK-SE.

Pan Ocean Shipping Co Ltd: 51-1, Namchang-dong, Jung-gu, CPOB 3051, Seoul 100-060; tel. (2) 316-5114; fax (2) 316-5296; f. 1966; transportation of passenger cars and trucks, chemical and petroleum products, dry bulk cargo; Pres. CHIANG JIN-WON.

CIVIL AVIATION

There are seven international airports in Korea; at Incheon (Seoul), Gimpo (Seoul), Busan, Cheongju, Daegu, Gwangju, Jeju and Yangyang. The main gateway into Seoul is Incheon International Airport, which opened for service in March 2001. It is used by 30m. passengers annually, and has a capacity for 240,000 aircraft movements annually. The second phase began construction in 2002, with completion due by 2008. When complete, the airport will handle 44m. passengers and 4.5m. tons of cargo annually. The airport is located 52 km from Seoul. A new airport, Yangyang International Airport, opened in Gangwon province in April 2002.

Asiana Airlines Inc: 47, Osae-dong, Gangseo-gu, Seoul; tel. (2) 758-8114; fax (2) 758-8008; e-mail asianacr@asiana.co.kr; internet www.asiana.co.kr; f. 1988; serves 14 domestic cities and 36 destinations in 16 countries; CEO PARK SAM-KOO.

Korean Air: 1370, Gonghang-dong, Gangseo-gu, Seoul; tel. (2) 656-7092; fax (2) 656-7289; internet www.koreanair.com; f. 1962; by the Govt, privately owned since 1969; fmrly Korean Air Lines (KAL); operates domestic and regional services and routes to the Americas, Europe, the Far East and the Middle East, serving 73 cities in 26 countries; Pres. and CEO SHIM YI-TAEK.

Seoul Air International: CPOB 10352, Seoul 100-699; tel. (2) 699-0991; fax (2) 699-0954; operates domestic flights and routes throughout Asia.

Tourism

South Korea's mountain scenery and historic sites are the principal attractions for tourists. Jeju Island, located some 100 km off the southern coast, is a popular resort. In 2001 there were 5,147,204 visitors to South Korea, of whom about 46% came from Japan. Receipts from tourism in 2000 amounted to US $6,811m.

Korea National Tourism Organization: KNTO Bldg, 10, Da-dong, Jung-gu, CPOB 903, Seoul 100; tel. (2) 729-9600; fax (2) 757-5997; internet www.knto.or.kr; f. 1962 as Korea Tourist Service; Pres. LEE DEUK-RYUL.

Korea Tourism Association: Saman Bldg, 11th Floor, 945, Daechi-dong, Gangnam-gu, Seoul; tel. (2) 556-2356; fax (2) 556-3818; f. 1963; Pres. CHO HANG-KYU, KIM JAE-GI.

KUWAIT

Introductory Survey

Location, Climate, Language, Religion, Flag, Capital

The State of Kuwait lies at the north-west extreme of the Persian (Arabian) Gulf, bordered to the north-west by Iraq and to the south by Saudi Arabia. The State comprises a mainland region and nine small islands, of which the largest is Bubiyan and the most populous is Failaka. Immediately to the south of Kuwait, along the Gulf, lies a Neutral (Partitioned) Zone of 5,700 sq km, which is shared between Kuwait and Saudi Arabia. Much of Kuwait is arid desert, and the climate is generally hot and humid. Temperatures in July and August often exceed 45°C (113°F), and in the winter months are frequently above 20°C (68°F)—although there is often frost at night. Average annual rainfall is only 111 mm. The official language is Arabic, which is spoken by the majority of Kuwaiti nationals (estimated, by official definition, to have comprised 41.2% of Kuwait's population at mid-2000) and by many of the country's non-Kuwaiti residents. Apart from other Arabs, the non-Kuwaitis are mainly Iranians, Indians and Pakistanis. At the 1975 census 95.0% of the population were Muslims (of whom about 70% are now thought to belong to the Sunni sect), while 4.5% were Christians, Hindus or adherents of other faiths. The national flag (proportions 1 by 2) has three equal horizontal stripes, of green, white and red, with a superimposed black trapezoid at the hoist. The capital is Kuwait City.

Recent History

Kuwait became part of Turkey's Ottoman Empire in the 16th century. During the later years of Ottoman rule Kuwait became a semi-autonomous Arab monarchy, with local administration controlled by a Sheikh of the Sabah family, which is still the ruling dynasty. In 1899, fearing an extension of Turkish control, the ruler of Kuwait made a treaty with the United Kingdom, accepting British protection while surrendering control over external relations. Nominal Turkish suzerainty over Kuwait ended in 1918, with the dissolution of the Ottoman Empire.

Petroleum was first discovered in Kuwait in 1938, but exploration was interrupted by the Second World War. After 1945 drilling resumed on a large scale, and extensive deposits of petroleum were found. Sheikh Ahmad (ruler since 1921) was succeeded in 1950 by his cousin, Sheikh Abdullah as-Salim as-Sabah, who inaugurated a programme of public works and educational development, funded by petroleum revenues, which transformed Kuwait's infrastructure and introduced a comprehensive system of welfare services.

Kuwait became fully independent on 19 June 1961, when the United Kingdom and Kuwait agreed to terminate the 1899 treaty. The ruler took the title of Amir and assumed full executive power. Kuwait was admitted to the League of Arab States (the Arab League, see p. 260) despite opposition from Iraq, which claimed that Kuwait was historically part of Iraqi territory. Kuwait's first election took place in December 1961, when voters chose 20 members of a Constituent Assembly (the other members being cabinet ministers appointed by the Amir). The Assembly drafted a new Constitution, which was adopted in December 1962. A 50-member Majlis al-Umma (National Assembly) was elected, under a limited franchise (see Government, below), in January 1963. In the absence of formal political parties (which remain illegal), candidates contested the poll as independents, although some known opponents of the Government were elected. In the same month the Amir appointed his brother, Sheikh Sabah as-Salem as-Sabah (the heir apparent), to be Prime Minister. Iraq renounced its claim to Kuwait in October, and diplomatic relations were established.

In January 1965, following conflict between the paternalistic ruling family and the democratically-inclined Majlis, the powers of the Council of Ministers were strengthened. The Amir died in November 1965, and Sheikh Sabah succeeded to the throne. He was replaced as Prime Minister by his cousin, Sheikh Jaber al-Ahmad as-Sabah, who was named heir apparent in May 1966. The Neutral (Partitioned) Zone between Kuwait and Saudi Arabia was formally divided between the two countries in 1969: revenues from oil production in the area are shared equally.

As Kuwait's petroleum sector expanded during the 1960s, the country became increasingly wealthy. The Government effected an extensive redistribution of income, through public expenditure and a land compensation scheme, but there was some popular discontent concerning corruption and official manipulation of the media and the Majlis. A more representative legislature was elected in January 1971 (again under a limited franchise). A further general election took place in January 1975, but in August 1976 the Amir dissolved the Majlis, on the grounds that it was acting against the best interests of the State. Sheikh Sabah died on 31 December 1977 and was succeeded by Crown Prince Jaber. In January 1978 the new Amir appointed Sheikh Saad al-Abdullah as-Salim as-Sabah to be his heir apparent. The new Crown Prince, hitherto Minister of Defence and the Interior, became Prime Minister in the following month. In accordance with an Amiri decree of August 1980, a new Majlis was elected in February 1981, although only one-half of the eligible 6% of the population registered to vote.

The collapse of Kuwait's unofficial stock exchange, the Souk al-Manakh, in September 1982 caused a prolonged financial crisis, and eventually led to the resignations of the Ministers of Finance (in 1983) and of Justice (in 1985). The Majlis subsequently opposed several government measures, including proposed price increases for public services, educational reforms and legislation to restrict the press, and questioned the competence of certain ministers. In July 1986 the Council of Ministers submitted its resignation to the Amir, who then dissolved the Majlis and suspended some articles of the Constitution, declaring his intention to rule by decree. The Crown Prince was immediately reappointed Prime Minister. An Amiri decree accorded the Council of Ministers greater powers of censorship, including the right to suspend publication of newspapers for up to two years.

In late 1989 the Amir refused to accept a petition, signed by more than 20,000 Kuwaiti citizens, seeking the restoration of the Majlis. In January 1990 police dispersed two pro-democracy demonstrations, although later in the month the Government agreed to relax press censorship. In June 62% of eligible voters participated in a general election for 50 members of a 'provisional' National Council; a further 25 members were appointed by the Amir. The election was boycotted by pro-democracy activists, who continued to demand the full restoration of the Majlis.

Of all the Gulf states, Kuwait has been most vulnerable to regional disruption. Immediately after independence British troops (soon replaced by an Arab League force) were dispatched to support the country against the territorial claim by Iraq. The force remained until 1963, and relations between Kuwait and Iraq were stable until 1973, when Iraqi troops occupied a Kuwaiti outpost on their joint border. Kuwait none the less supplied aid to Iraq from the outbreak of the Iran–Iraq war in 1980. As a result, Kuwaiti petroleum installations and shipping in the Persian (Arabian) Gulf were targeted intermittently by Iranian forces, and by pro-Iranian groups within Kuwait, for much of the 1980s. A large number of Iranians were among 27,000 expatriates deported in 1985–86, and in 1987 the Government initiated a five-year plan to reduce the number of expatriates in the Kuwaiti work-force. Kuwait resumed diplomatic relations with Iran following the 1988 cease-fire between Iran and Iraq.

In July 1990 the Iraqi Government implicitly criticized Kuwait (among other states) for disregarding the petroleum production quotas stipulated by the Organization of the Petroleum Exporting Countries (OPEC, see p. 298). It also declared that Kuwait should cancel Iraq's war debt and compensate it for losses of revenue incurred during the war with Iran, and as a result of Kuwait's overproduction of petroleum—to which Iraq attributed a decline in international oil prices. In addition, Iraq alleged that Kuwait had established military posts and drilled oil wells on Iraqi territory. Despite regional mediation efforts, Iraq subsequently began to deploy armed forces on the Kuwait–Iraq border. Direct negotiations in Jeddah, Saudi Arabia, at the end of the month between Kuwaiti and Iraqi officials collapsed, and on 2 August some 100,000 Iraqi troops invaded Kuwait (whose total military strength was about 20,000): Iraq stated that it had entered at the invitation of insurgents who had overthrown the Kuwaiti Government. The Amir and other government members fled to Saudi Arabia, where they established a 'Government-in-exile', while Iraq declared that a provisional Government had been formed in Kuwait comprising Iraqi-sponsored Kuwaiti dissidents. The UN Security Council immediately adopted a series of resolutions, of which the first (Resolution 660) condemned the invasion, demanded the immediate and unconditional withdrawal of Iraqi forces from Kuwait, and appealed for a negotiated settlement of the conflict. A trade embargo was then imposed on Iraq and Kuwait. Meanwhile, the USA and member states of the European Community (now European Union—EU, see p. 199) froze all Kuwait's overseas assets to prevent their repatriation. Five days after the invasion US troops and aircraft were deployed in Saudi Arabia, with the stated aim of securing that country's borders with Kuwait in the event of further Iraqi territorial expansion. A number of European Governments, together with some Arab League states, agreed to provide military support for the US forces. The Iraqi Government subsequently announced the formal annexation of Kuwait, and ordered the closure of foreign diplomatic missions there. At the end of August most of Kuwait was officially declared to be the 19th Governorate of Iraq, while a northern strip was incorporated into the Basra Governorate.

In the months following the invasion apparent attempts at demographic manipulation—by settling Iraqis and Palestinians in Kuwait and by forcing Kuwaitis to assume Iraqi citizenship—were documented. The population was estimated to have decreased from approximately 2m. prior to the invasion to some 700,000, of whom Kuwaitis constituted about 300,000, Palestinians 200,000, and the remainder comprised other Arab and Asian expatriates. Many Kuwaitis, and Arab and Asian expatriates, had fled Iraq and Kuwait into Jordan, while most European and US expatriates were detained as hostages; by the end of 1990 it was claimed that all hostages had been released.

UN Security Council Resolution 678, adopted in November 1990, authorized the multinational force by now stationed in Saudi Arabia and the Gulf region to use 'all necessary means' to liberate Kuwait. It was implied that should Iraq not begin, by 15 January 1991, to implement the terms of 10 resolutions hitherto adopted regarding the invasion, military action would ensue. Renewed international diplomatic attempts failed to avert a military confrontation. On the night of 16–17 January the US-led multinational force launched an intensive aerial bombardment of Iraq. Ground forces entered Kuwait during the night of 23–24 February, encountering relatively little effective Iraqi opposition. Within three days the Iraqi Government had agreed to comply with the terms of all Security Council resolutions concerning Kuwait, and on 28 February the USA announced a suspension of military operations. Resolutions 686 and 687, adopted by the UN Security Council in March and April respectively, dictated the terms to Iraq for a permanent cease-fire: Iraq was required to release all allied prisoners of war and Kuwaitis detained as hostages, repeal all laws and decrees concerning the annexation of Kuwait, and recognize the inviolability of the Iraq–Kuwait border. Iraq promptly announced its compliance with both resolutions. Resolution 689, adopted in April, provided for the establishment of a demilitarized zone, to be supervised by a UN Iraq-Kuwait Observer Mission (UNIKOM, see p. 64).

Meanwhile, in October 1990, at a conference in Jeddah of some 1,000 prominent Kuwaitis, the exiled Crown Prince Saad agreed to establish government advisory committees on political, social and financial matters, and pledged to restore the country's Constitution and legislature and to organize free elections after Kuwait's eventual liberation. In February 1991, however, the Government-in-exile excluded the possibility of early elections, maintaining that the need to rebuild and repopulate the country took precedence over that for political reform. Immediately following liberation an Amiri decree imposed martial law in Kuwait, and in March the formation of a state security committee was announced: its objectives included the investigation of individuals suspected of collaboration with the Iraqi authorities in Kuwait, the prevention of unofficial acts of reprisal and the identification of those civilians relocated to Kuwait by Iraq. Palestinians in Kuwait were a particular target of reprisals, and it was alleged by several human rights organizations that they were subject to torture by Kuwaiti security forces. Kuwait's Palestinian population, which

had totalled around 400,000 prior to the Iraqi invasion, was estimated to have declined to less than 50,000 by early 1992.

The Amir, the Prime Minister and other members of the exiled regime returned to Kuwait in March 1991. The Council of Ministers resigned later that month, apparently in response to public discontent at the Government's failure to restore essential services. Although several specialists were appointed to strategic posts within the new Government named by Sheikh Saad in April (most notably to the finance, planning and oil portfolios), other important positions (including the foreign affairs, interior and defence ministries) were allocated to members of the as-Sabah family.

In May 1991 it was revealed that some 900 people were under investigation in Kuwait in connection with crimes committed during the Iraqi occupation; about 200 of these were accused of collaboration. The human rights organization Amnesty International expressed concern that trials were being conducted without the provision of adequate defence counsel, and alleged that torture had in some cases been used to extract confessions. The Government undertook to investigate such abuses. Martial law was ended in June, and 29 death sentences hitherto imposed on convicted collaborators were commuted to custodial terms. Outstanding trials relating to the occupation were to be referred to civilian courts, and in August a tribunal, said to guarantee defendants the right to greater legal protection as well as a right of appeal, was established to replace the martial law courts. Amid continuing international criticism of Kuwait's record on human rights, measures were subsequently taken to prevent clandestine deportations of alleged collaborators and to permit international supervision of the expulsion of foreign nationals. However, it was widely believed that Kuwait had been motivated to curb human rights abuses primarily in an attempt to procure international support for its efforts to secure the release of Kuwaiti nationals detained in Iraq.

It was announced in May 1991 that a US military presence would remain in Kuwait until September, by which time, it was envisaged, a regional defence force would be established. However, little progress was achieved in negotiations for such a force, and in August the USA announced that it would maintain 1,500 troops in Kuwait for several more months. In September the US and Kuwaiti Governments signed a 10-year military co-operation agreement, permitting the storage of US supplies and equipment in Kuwait, and providing for joint military training and exercises. (The agreement was renewed for a further 10 years in February 2001.) Defence accords were signed with both the United Kingdom and France in 1992.

In June 1993 the State Security Court was reported to have issued death sentences against 17 people who had been found guilty of collaborating with Iraq in 1990–91; Alaa Hussein Ali, the leader of the provisional Government installed by Iraq in August 1990, was convicted *in absentia*. In February 1994 Amnesty International again alleged serious violations of human rights in Kuwait, asserting that at least 120 alleged collaborators had been convicted by trials that failed to satisfy international minimum standards. Human rights organizations welcomed the endorsement by the Majlis, in August 1995, of government proposals to abolish the State Security Court. In January 1997 the Government announced the creation of a new human rights committee within the Ministry of the Interior.

Press censorship was partially relaxed in January 1992. Elections to the new Majlis, on 5 October, were contested by some 280 candidates, many of whom (although nominally independent) were affiliated to one of several quasi-political organizations. The franchise was again restricted, with only about 81,400 men eligible to vote. Anti-Government candidates, notably those representing Islamist groups, were unexpectedly successful, securing 31 of the Assembly's 50 seats. The Prime Minister subsequently formed a new Government, including six members of the Majlis, who were allocated, *inter alia*, the oil and justice portfolios; members of the ruling family retained control of foreign affairs, the interior and defence.

The Majlis voted in December 1992 to establish a commission of inquiry into the circumstances surrounding the 1990 invasion. The commission's report, published in May 1995, revealed profound negligence on the part of government and military officials, who had apparently ignored warnings of an imminent invasion. The report also claimed that the immediate flight of members of the royal family and the Council of Ministers had deprived the country of political leadership and military organization.

Meanwhile, in January 1993 legislation was enacted whereby the Majlis would have automatic access to the financial accounts of all state-owned companies and investment organizations, and stricter penalties would be imposed in cases of abuse of public funds. Demands for greater parliamentary scrutiny of the State's investments were largely prompted by revelations of the misappropriation of funds by the London-based Kuwait Investment Office (KIO), responsible for much of Kuwait's overseas investment portfolio (22 former KIO executives, including Sheikh Fahd Muhammad as-Sabah—its Chairman at the time of the Iraqi invasion—were reportedly implicated in the allegations), and also by emerging evidence of financial misconduct at the state-owned Kuwait Oil Tanker Co (KOTC). Sheikh Ali al-Khalifah as-Sabah, a former Minister of Finance and of Oil, and Abd al-Fatr al-Bader, a former Chairman of KOTC, were among five people brought to trial in connection with alleged embezzlement. In November 1995, however, a criminal court countermanded an earlier ruling by the Majlis that legal proceedings against government ministers need not be conducted in special courts. In July 1996 three former executives received prison sentences of between 15 and 40 years, having been convicted of corruption by the criminal court; they were ordered to repay embezzled funds, together with fines totalling more than US $100m. The fourth defendant was acquitted. In April 1997 the charges against the former minister were dismissed, on the grounds that the correct procedures had not been adhered to in referring his case for trial. However, following a ruling of the High Court in London, United Kingdom, in November 1998 that three former KOTC officials had defrauded the company of more than $130m., it was confirmed that the alleged role of Sheikh Ali al-Khalifa as-Sabah was to be investigated by the Kuwaiti authorities. In June 1999 the High Court in London ruled that Sheikh Fahd Muhammad as-Sabah and two other former KIO senior executives were guilty, *in absentia*, of conspiracy and fraud involving some $460m. against the KIO's Spanish subsidiary between 1988 and 1992.

The ruling family retained control of the foreign affairs, interior and defence portfolios following a reorganization of the Council of Ministers in April 1994. In June the Majlis approved legislation extending the franchise to sons of naturalized Kuwaitis. In July 1995 the Assembly approved a bill reducing from 30 years to 20 the minimum period after which naturalized Kuwaitis would become eligible to vote. In July 1996 the Ministry of the Interior announced that an electorate of just over 107,000 men was entitled to vote in the forthcoming elections to the Majlis, scheduled for 7 October. Pro-Government candidates were the most successful, securing the majority of the 50 seats. Sheikh Saad was reappointed Prime Minister; his new Council of Ministers included four newly elected deputies.

In March 1998 Sheikh Saad submitted his Government's resignation, after members of the Majlis proposed a motion of 'no confidence' in the Minister of Information, Sheikh Sa'ud Nasir as-Sa'ud as-Sabah, who had allowed what were deemed 'un-Islamic' publications to be exhibited at a book fair in Kuwait. The Amir immediately reappointed the Crown Prince as Prime Minister, and a new Government was named at the end of the month. The promotion of Sheikh Sa'ud Nasir as-Sa'ud as-Sabah to the post of Minister of Oil was controversial not only because of the recent action by the Majlis against him, but also because the oil portfolio was not customarily allocated to a member of the ruling family. An institutional crisis appeared imminent in June, when the Majlis sought to cross-examine the Minister of the Interior, Sheikh Muhammad Khalid al-Hamad as-Sabah, on issues including corruption, illicit drugs and human rights. However, the ministry in question was deemed by the Government to be 'sovereign' and therefore exempt from examination by the Majlis. Relations between the Government and the Majlis deteriorated further, necessitating intervention by the Amir to dispel rumours that the Assembly would be dissolved and a general election called. Tensions were swiftly revived in July, when the Government introduced amendments to legislation enacted in 1993 (and previously amended in 1995) regarding repayment of debts arising from the collapse of the Souk al-Manakh in 1982. Many deputies regarded new arrangements for the discharge of liabilities to be unduly favourable to debtors, many of whom were members of the ruling family, and boycotted an initial vote before reluctantly approving the amendments in August 1998. The Deputy Prime Minister and Minister of State for Cabinet Affairs, Nasir Abdullah ar-Rodhan, resigned in November. He was replaced in the following month by Abd al-Aziz ad-Dakhil, hitherto Minister of Commerce and Industry,

whose former post was allocated to Hisham al-Otaibi, President of the Kuwait Stock Exchange.

Confrontation persisted between the Government and the Majlis, which in February 1999 refused to refer to its finance committee government proposals for economic reform. In May the Amir dissolved the legislature and called fresh elections, after deputies had in the previous month questioned the Minister of Justice, Awqaf (Religious Endowments) and Islamic Affairs over errors that had appeared in copies of the Koran printed and distributed by his ministry. Some 80% of an eligible electorate of 113,000 Kuwaiti men voted in the election, which took place on 3 July. Pro-Government candidates recorded the greatest losses, taking only 12 seats; Islamist candidates won 20 seats, and liberals 14 seats, with the remaining four won by independents. Sheikh Saad was immediately reappointed Prime Minister, and a new Council of Ministers was inaugurated in mid-July. The ruling family retained control of the strategic foreign affairs, oil, interior and defence portfolios, although a number of liberal deputies joined the Government. Meanwhile, during the period between the dissolution of the Majlis and the election, the Government promulgated some 60 decrees (subject to legislative approval), most notably one proposing that women should be allowed to contest and to vote in elections from 2003. However, the law on female suffrage was defeated by a considerable majority when subjected to a vote in the new Majlis in November 1999, as liberal deputies, who supported women's enfranchisement, registered their protest at what they considered to be the unconstitutionality of legislation by decree by joining Islamist and conservative deputies in voting against the measure. Liberal deputies immediately submitted identical legislation regarding women's suffrage, but this was narrowly defeated in a vote at the end of the month.

In January 2000 Alaa Hussein Ali, leader of the provisional Government installed by Iraq in August 1990, who had been in self-imposed exile since Kuwait's liberation, returned to Kuwait in order to appeal against the death sentence pronounced in June 1993 (see above); the appeal hearing began at the Court of First Instance in February 2000. In May it was announced that Hussein had lost his appeal, and that he planned a further challenge to his sentence. The Court of Appeal upheld the previous ruling in July, but in March 2001 commuted Hussein's death sentence to one of life imprisonment.

In July 2000 unrest was reported in the Al-Jahra region, where a community of *bidoon* ('stateless' Arabs) form the majority of the population. (About 100,000 *bidoon* reside in Kuwait, but the authorities refuse to recognize their claims to Kuwaiti nationality.) The unrest followed the approval, in May, of a draft amendment to the Citizenship Law that would grant only a small number of *bidoon* the right to Kuwaiti citizenship. Some 1,000 *bidoon* obtained Kuwaiti citizenship in early 2001, leading to protests by those whose applications had been refused.

The issue of press freedom caused a renewed deterioration in relations between the Government and the Majlis in February 2000, when deputies criticized government efforts to suspend publication of two Kuwaiti newspapers, *Al-Watan* and *As-Seyassah*, for publishing reports of salary increases for the security forces. The Amir subsequently ordered that any planned action against the publications be abandoned. Later in the month a joint statement issued by several newspaper editors accused the Minister of Information of allowing actions that impeded press freedom. Amnesty International expressed concern in March that freedom of expression remained under threat in Kuwait, and urged the Government to end its practice of punishing journalists and authors for using what it deemed to be 'un-Islamic' language. In March 2001 the owner and editor-in-chief of the weekly *Al-Majaless*, Hedaya Sultan as-Salem, was killed by an unknown gunman in Kuwait City; as-Salem had been one of Kuwait's first female journalists and had played an influential role in the campaign for female suffrage. A police-officer was sentenced to death in February 2002, having been convicted of the murder.

In June 2000 Sheikh Sa'ud Nasir as-Sa'ud as-Sabah resigned as Minister of Oil, following two separate incidents at petroleum refineries (one of them Kuwait's largest refinery, at Mina al-Ahmadi) as a result of which eight people were killed and more than 50 injured; however, his resignation was rejected by the Majlis. In November the Amir accepted the resignation of the Minister of Information, Dr Saad Muhammad bin Teflah al-Ajmi. Sheikh Saad tendered his Government's resignation in January 2001. The Crown Prince denied that this constituted an attempt to prevent parliamentary scrutiny of the Minister of Justice and of Awqaf and Islamic Affairs, Saad Jasem Yousuf al-Hashil, relating to allegations of inefficiency and corruption in his ministry. The Amir immediately reappointed Sheikh Saad as Prime Minister, and a new 15-member Government was named in mid-February. The new administration included five younger members of the ruling family, as well as four members of the Majlis. The outgoing Deputy Prime Minister and Minister of Defence, Sheikh Salim Sabah as-Salim as-Sabah, left the Government, although the defence, foreign affairs and interior portfolios remained in the hands of the as-Sabah. A new minister, Ahmad Yaqub Bakir al-Abdullah, was named as Minister of Justice and of Awqaf and Islamic Affairs, while some controversy was caused by the allocation of the oil portfolio to Dr Adil Khalid as-Sabih, the minister previously responsible for the electricity, water and housing portfolios who had recently survived a parliamentary vote of 'no confidence' in respect of his business interests.

Kuwaiti women suffered a further reverse in their attempts to secure the right to contest and vote in elections in January 2001, when the Constitutional Court rejected a lawsuit brought by a male citizen against the State's election department for having failed to register the names of five women on electoral lists in his constituency. In March the Majlis rejected, on procedural grounds, draft legislation that would increase women's political rights.

During November 2000, as the crisis in Israeli–Palestinian relations deepened, 16 suspected Islamist militants (Kuwaitis and other Arab nationals) were arrested in Kuwait, accused of involvement in plotting bomb attacks on US military installations in the Gulf region in retaliation for perceived US support for Israel. The arrests of the alleged saboteurs followed reports that a Moroccan aide to the Saudi-born leader of the militant Islamist al-Qa'ida (Base) organization, Osama bin Laden, had entered Kuwait from Afghanistan; however, the aide subsequently fled to Iran. In June 2001 a senior Kuwaiti military official was convicted of concealing weapons to be used for terrorist purposes; he received a 10-year prison sentence, but in December this was reduced to seven years. (Eight of the suspected militants were given suspended sentences and ordered to pay fines; the remainder were acquitted.)

At the end of January 2002 four people died and about 19 were injured following a major explosion at Raudhatain, Kuwait's second largest oilfield, to the north of Kuwait City. Adil Khalid as-Sabih immediately submitted his resignation as Minister of Oil, stating that he accepted responsibility for the incident; he also ordered an investigation into the cause of the explosion. The minister's resignation was accepted a few days later and the Minister of Information, Sheikh Ahmad al-Fahd al-Ahmad as-Sabah, was named as acting Minister of Oil. However, a political crisis ensued after it proved impossible to find a permanent replacement for Dr as-Sabih, and Sheikh Ahmad was asked to remain in charge of the oil portfolio until the general election (scheduled for mid-2003). Meanwhile, several members of the Majlis demanded the resignation of the entire Government, alleging that the explosion at Raudhatain was the result of state corruption and mismanagement. In January 2003 the Amir accepted the resignation of the Minister of Finance, of Planning and Minister of State for Administrative Development, Dr Yousuf Hamad al-Ibrahim, who had been the object of severe parliamentary criticism. Dr al-Ibrahim, a leading reformist, had in July 2002 survived a vote of 'no confidence' instigated by Islamist Majlis deputies who accused him of poor management of the Government's fiscal affairs. The finance and planning portfolios were provisionally passed to the Minister of State for Foreign Affairs, Sheikh Muhammad Sabah as-Salim as-Sabah, and the Minister of Education and Higher Education, Dr Musaad Rashid al-Haroun, was given the position of Acting Minister of State for Administrative Development in addition to his existing responsibilities.

Friction between Kuwait and Iraq in the aftermath of the Gulf War was exacerbated by the issue of the demarcation of their joint border. The UN commission with responsibility for delineating the frontier formalized the land border as it had been defined by British administrators in 1932 (and officially agreed by Kuwait and Iraq in 1963). The boundary, the validity of which was now rejected by Iraq, was established some 570 m north of its pre-war position, dividing the Iraqi port of Umm Qasr, with the effect that Iraq retained the town and much of the harbour while Kuwait was awarded hinterland which included an abandoned Iraqi naval base; the border also situated several Iraqi oil

wells on Kuwaiti territory. In January 1993 the USA led air attacks on Iraq, and more than 1,000 US troops were dispatched to Kuwait, in response to a series of incursions by Iraqi forces into Kuwaiti territory in the days immediately preceding the designated entry into force of the new border; its formal delineation was completed in March, when the UN commission defined the maritime border along the median line of the Khawr Abd Allah waterway. Allegations made by Kuwait of Iraqi violations of the border, and of attempts to impede construction of a trench along the land border, intensified during the second half of 1993, and there were sporadic reports of exchanges of fire in the border region. In November a 775-strong armed UNIKOM reinforcement was deployed in northern Kuwait, with authorization (under specific circumstances) to use its weapons to assist the unarmed force already in the demilitarized zone.

In October 1994 Iraq deployed some 70,000 troops and 700 tanks near the border with Kuwait, in an apparent attempt to force an easing of UN economic sanctions. Kuwait immediately mobilized its army reserves, and dispatched some 20,000 troops to the border region. The USA committed almost 40,000 land, naval and air forces to the region; France and the United Kingdom deployed naval vessels, and the United Kingdom dispatched about 1,200 troops. Following Russian mediation, Iraq announced its willingness to recognize Kuwait's sovereignty and borders on condition that the UN ease sanctions against Iraq after six months. However, the UN Security Council adopted a resolution (No. 949) requiring Iraq's unconditional recognition of Kuwait's sovereignty and borders and restricting the movement of Iraqi troops in the border area. In November Iraq officially recognized Kuwait's sovereignty, territorial integrity and political independence, as well as its UN-defined borders. Most of the US and British reinforcements deployed in the region in October had been withdrawn by the end of the year. Kuwait's relations with Iraq deteriorated sharply in September 1996, after the Kuwaiti Government agreed to the deployment in Kuwait of US military aircraft and troops in support of a US operation to force the withdrawal of Iraqi armed forces from the Kurdish 'safe haven' in northern Iraq. In December the USA announced that some 4,200 US troops deployed in Kuwait during 1996 would be withdrawn by the end of the year, although the deployment of US F-117 *Stealth* fighter aircraft was to be extended.

Kuwait and Iraq made mutual accusations of territorial violations and attacks on shipping during 1997. Meanwhile, Kuwait continued to support the maintenance of international sanctions against Iraq, and to demand adherence by Iraq to all relevant UN resolutions adopted since the Gulf crisis. Furthermore, statements by the Iraqi Government that it was holding no Kuwaiti prisoners of war were refuted by Kuwait: the Kuwaiti authorities, asserting that some 600 Kuwaitis remained captive in Iraq, claimed in late 1997 to be in possession of documentation, passed by Iraq to the International Committee of the Red Cross (ICRC), relating to 126 Kuwaiti prisoners of war. As the crisis involving weapons inspections in Iraq by the UN Special Commission (see the Recent History of Iraq) deepened in February 1998, fears were expressed for Kuwait's security—in particular that an attack on Iraq might result in the use of chemical or other weapons of mass destruction against Kuwait. Although Kuwait was the only country in the region to announce its approval of the use of force against Iraq should diplomatic efforts fail, it emphasized that any military action would exacerbate hardship suffered by the Iraqi people and increase regional instability. The USA, supported by the United Kingdom, undertook a military deployment in the Gulf region at this time: by the end of the month, when the UN Secretary-General and the Iraqi Government reached a compromise agreement regarding weapons inspections, some 6,000 US ground troops had been dispatched to Kuwait. A series of air-strikes against targets in Iraq by US and British forces from December 1998 again increased tensions between Kuwait and Iraq. Iraq accused Kuwait of collaborating in the air attacks, and frequently reiterated claims to Kuwaiti territory. In response to perceived threats to its territorial integrity, in early 1999 Kuwait placed its armed forces on high alert, and the USA warned that any aggression against Kuwait would result in a renewed military offensive. In September Kuwait lodged an official protest over changes made to the final draft of an Arab League report to which, Kuwait asserted, references to the formation of a 'mechanism' to resolve the issue of Kuwaiti and other prisoners of war in Iraq had been added; Kuwait maintained that the ICRC was the only body empowered to deal with the issue. In November the Majlis established a committee to examine future relations with Iraq, and in December the Kuwaiti Government welcomed UN Security Council Resolution 1284 (establishing a new weapons inspectorate for Iraq, q.v.), which incorporated demands for the repatriation of Kuwaiti and other prisoners from Iraq, for Iraq's co-operation with the ICRC, and for the return of Kuwaiti property seized during the occupation.

In September 2000 ministers responsible for foreign affairs of the Co-operation Council for the Arab States of the Gulf (Gulf Co-operation Council—GCC, see p. 175) expressed concerns after the Iraqi leadership had repeatedly denounced both Kuwait and Saudi Arabia for allowing US and British military aircraft to use their airspace in order to conduct military attacks on Iraq, and had vowed to launch a new invasion of Kuwait. Iraq also renewed its long-standing accusation that Kuwait was drilling oil wells on Iraqi territory, and accused Kuwait and Saudi Arabia of inflicting, through the maintenance of UN sanctions, suffering on the Iraqi population. At the same time a number of small commercial vessels found to be entering or leaving Iraqi ports, allegedly in violation of the sanctions regime, were intercepted by Kuwaiti military units. In September and again in October Kuwait reinforced security along its border with Iraq, in the latter month to prevent a possible influx of *bidoon*, who had reportedly entered the demilitarized zone from Iraq and who were demanding the right of return to Kuwait (from where they had been excluded since the Gulf crisis).

In March 2001 a summit meeting of Arab League heads of state, held in Amman, Jordan, was considered as having made the most comprehensive effort hitherto in addressing divisions arising from the Gulf conflict. None the less, a draft resolution presented by the Iraqi delegation urging an end to UN sanctions and a resumption of civilian flights failed to secure adoption, owing to Iraq's unwillingness—on the grounds that it had already done sufficient to make clear its recognition of Kuwait's territorial integrity—to accede to a requirement of a specific guarantee that Iraq would not repeat the invasion of 1990. In November 2001 Kuwait issued a formal complaint to the UN following an alleged violation of its territory by Iraq. The incident occurred shortly after a senior Iraqi official had reiterated claims of sovereignty over Kuwait. In January 2002 the Kuwaiti leadership was reported to have rejected attempts by the Arab League to persuade it to accept Iraqi proposals apparently aimed at improving bilateral relations: as part of Iraq's diplomatic offensive to secure the support of the Arab world in view of the threat of US-led military action against Saddam Hussain's regime, the Iraqi leader had conveyed an appeal to Arab states to set aside their differences, referring specifically to the need to improve relations with Kuwait and Saudi Arabia; later in the month it was reported that Iraq had announced its preparedness to allow a delegation from Kuwait to visit Iraq to verify that no Kuwaiti prisoners of war were being held (Kuwait continued to assert that Iraq was detaining at least 90 Kuwaiti nationals). At the Arab League summit held in Beirut, Lebanon, in late March 2002, however, it was announced that Kuwait and Iraq had reached agreement on the resolution of outstanding differences. The summit's final communiqué welcomed Iraq's assurances that it would respect the 'independence, sovereignty and security' of Kuwait, and safeguard its 'territorial integrity'; Iraq was urged to co-operate in seeking a 'definitive solution' to issues of Kuwaiti prisoners and detainees, and of the return of property, while Kuwait was called upon to 'co-operate with what Iraq offers with respect to its nationals' reported as missing through the ICRC. Kuwait's First Deputy Prime Minister and Minister of Foreign Affairs was subsequently reported as having expressed his complete satisfaction with the agreement.

Relations with Iraq were profoundly affected by the political repercussions of the September 2001 suicide attacks against the mainland USA. Kuwait, which strongly condemned the attacks, subsequently assumed an important role in persuading other Gulf states to join the US-led 'coalition against terror'. US bases in Kuwait were subsequently used to provide logistical support to the US-led campaign against al-Qa'ida (held by the USA to be principally responsible for the attacks on New York and Washington, DC) and its Taliban hosts in Afghanistan during late 2001. Meanwhile, in October 2001 the Kuwaiti authorities revoked the citizenship of the official spokesman of al-Qa'ida, Sulayman Abu Ghaith, after remarks he had made via the Qatar-based *Al-Jazeera* television station. In late 2001 the Central Bank of Kuwait implemented measures designed to prevent Islamic charitable organizations from using Kuwait's financial institutions to channel funds to al-Qa'ida.

During the course of 2002 increased speculation that the US Administration of George W. Bush intended to extend the 'war against terror' to target the regime of Saddam Hussain in Iraq, exemplified not least by a series of visits to Kuwait by prominent US officials, threatened to fuel opposition to a continued US presence in the region and exacerbate an increasingly tense political situation in Kuwait. At the end of December some 12,000 US troops were stationed in Kuwait, and in early 2003 Kuwait's Ministry of Defence declared that the entire northern half of Kuwait would be designated a closed military zone from 15 February. Several US soldiers and civilians were killed in late 2002 and early 2003 in attacks by Kuwaitis, some of whom, it was alleged, had links to al-Qa'ida. In March an emergency meeting of the Arab League, hosted by Qatar, to discuss the deepening crisis descended into a bitter exchange of insults between, primarily, a senior Iraqi official and the Kuwaiti Minister of Information. Kuwait subsequently supported a proposal made by the President of the United Arab Emirates (UAE) for Saddam Hussain to go into exile in order to prevent a US-led war to remove his regime. At the outset of military action, which commenced on 20 March, US-led troops in Kuwait, the base for the main ground assault on Iraq, numbered some 140,000. Iraqi armed forces launched several missiles at Kuwaiti territory, although little damage was caused in the emirate during the course of the conflict. In April Kuwait announced that it had set up a reward fund of US $1m. for information to help uncover the fate of persons missing since the 1990–91 Gulf crisis, who were estimated to number more than 600.

Meanwhile, in May 1994 the governing body of the UN Compensation Commission (UNCC), responsible for considering claims for compensation arising from the Gulf crisis, approved the first disbursements (to 670 families or individuals in 16 countries), totalling US $2.7m. By late 1996 payments amounting to $3,000m. (to be partly financed by Iraqi oil revenues) had been endorsed by the UN, which had yet to consider claims for a further $190,000m. In December international arbitrators recommended that a payment of $610m. should be made to the Kuwait Oil Company (KOC), in compensation for the cost of extinguishing oil wells set alight by retreating Iraqi troops in early 1991. In March 1997 the Kuwaiti general committee responsible for evaluating war damages stated that it was to begin compensation payments, initially to some 4,500 citizens who had incurred losses valued at less than $100,000. The disbursement of a further $84m. to some 33,800 individuals was authorized by the UN in February 1999. In September 2000 the UN Security Council approved the payment to the Kuwait Petroleum Corporation (which controls the KOC) of $15,900m. in compensation for lost petroleum revenues arising from the Iraqi occupation; this was the largest claim to have been considered by the UNCC hitherto. However, the Security Council decided at the same time to reduce the share of Iraqi oil revenues to be paid into the compensation fund from 30% to 25%: France and Russia, which increasingly opposed the maintenance of sanctions against Iraq, had delayed a decision by the UNCC on the payment, and Russia had warned of its inclination to oppose Kuwaiti claims to reparations unless the levy on Iraqi oil revenues was reduced. By mid-2001 the majority of individual claimants (Kuwaitis and expatriates in Kuwait and Iraq during the Gulf war) had received compensation, with total disbursements being valued at some $12,000m. Meanwhile, the UNCC was considering a claim of $86,000m. by the Kuwait Investment Agency, principally in recompense for lost earnings during the conflict. In March 2002 the Commission approved further compensation payments totalling $1,500m. to Kuwaiti individuals, businesses and government ministries.

Relations with Jordan, which had deteriorated following that country's failure openly to denounce the Iraqi invasion, gradually eased in the mid-1990s. Flights between Kuwait and Jordan by both countries' national airlines, which had been suspended in 1990, resumed in July 1997, and the normalization of relations generally continued thereafter. Ministerial visits, which had not been undertaken since the Gulf crisis, were made by the Jordanian Minister of Planning and the Kuwaiti Deputy Prime Minister and Minister of State for Cabinet Affairs in June 1998 and January 1999, respectively, and in March 1999 the Jordanian embassy in Kuwait, which had been closed in 1990, was reopened. In September 1999 the new King Abdullah of Jordan made his first visit to Kuwait (his father, King Hussein, had not visited after 1990), where he held talks with the Amir. Jordan and Kuwait signed a bilateral free-trade agreement in December.

In July 2000 Kuwait and Saudi Arabia signed an agreement finalizing the delineation of their maritime borders. Kuwait subsequently commenced negotiations with Iran on the demarcation of respective rights to the continental shelf, following complaints by the Kuwaiti and Saudi authorities over Iran's decision to begin drilling for gas in a disputed offshore area. Iraq asserted that, as a concerned party, it should be included in the Kuwaiti-Iranian discussions. In December a defence agreement was signed by the six member states of the GCC.

Government

Under the 1962 Constitution, executive power is vested in the Amir, the Head of State (who is chosen by and from members of the ruling family), and is exercised through the Council of Ministers. The Amir appoints the Prime Minister and, on the latter's recommendation, other ministers. Legislative power is vested in the unicameral Majlis al-Umma (National Assembly), with 50 elected members who serve for four years (subject to dissolution). Only literate adult male Kuwaiti citizens, excluding members of the armed forces, may vote. The country is divided administratively into six governorates.

Defence

In August 2002 Kuwait's active armed forces numbered 15,500—a land army of 11,000 (including 1,600 foreign personnel), an air force of an estimated 2,500 and a navy of around 2,000—and there were reserve forces of 23,700. Paramilitary forces comprised a 6,600-strong national guard and a coastguard. There is a two-year period of compulsory military service (one year for university students). The defence budget for 2002 was estimated at KD 1,200m. Capital expenditure on defence procurement in 1992–2002 was to total some KD 3,500m.

A US force numbering 7,388 at August 2002 was stationed in Kuwait (5,000 army, 2,000 air force, 10 navy and 378 marines). The UN Iraq-Kuwait Observer Mission (UNIKOM, see p. 64) comprised 904 troops and 193 military observers at 1 August 2002.

Economic Affairs

In 2000, according to estimates by the World Bank, Kuwait's gross national income (GNI), measured at average 1998–2000 prices, was US $35,771m., equivalent to $18,030 per head (or $18,690 on an international purchasing-power parity basis). During 1990–2001, it was estimated, the population decreased at an average annual rate of 0.4%, while gross domestic product (GDP) per head increased, in real terms, by an average of 0.8% per year during 1992–2000. Overall GDP was estimated to have declined, in real terms, by some 10% annually in 1990–92. Following reconstruction, the gradual increase in oil production contributed to a renewed period of economic advance after 1992, with average annual GDP growth, in real terms, for the period 1992–2000 estimated at 5.1%. However, real GDP declined by 1.0% in 2001.

Agriculture (including hunting, forestry and fishing) contributed 0.4% of GDP in 2001. About 1.1% of the labour force were employed in the sector in mid-2001. The principal crops are potatoes, cucumbers, tomatoes, aubergines and dates. Owing to scarcity of water, little grain is produced, and the bulk of food requirements is imported. (Imports of food and live animals accounted for 14.9% of merchandise imports in 1999.) Livestock, poultry and fishing are also important. During 1993–97 agricultural GDP increased, in real terms, by an average of 21.3% per year. Agricultural production, which fell by some 84% in 1991, had recovered to pre-occupation levels by the mid-1990s; output increased at an average annual rate of 6.1% in 1995–2000.

Industry (including mining, manufacturing, construction and power) provided 51.5% of GDP in 2001, and employed 23.1% of the labour force in 1995. During 1993–97 industrial GDP increased, in real terms, at an average annual rate of 2.3%.

Mining and quarrying contributed 43.8% of GDP in 2001, although the sector engaged only 2.1% of the labour force in 1995. The production of petroleum and its derivatives is the most important industry in Kuwait, providing an estimated 91.3% of export revenue in 2002. At the end of 2001 the country's proven recoverable reserves of petroleum were 96,500m. barrels, representing about 9.2% of world reserves. According to oil industry figures, Kuwait's petroleum production averaged 2.14m. barrels per day (b/d) in 2001. With effect from 1 February 2003, Kuwait's production quota, as agreed by OPEC, was 1.97m. b/d. Kuwait aimed to increase its production capacity

from 2.5m. b/d in 2000 to 3.5m. b/d by 2005. There are significant reserves of natural gas (1,490,000m. cu m at the end of 2001) associated with the petroleum deposits. During 1993–97 the GDP of the mining sector increased, in real terms, at an average rate of 2.5% per year.

Manufacturing provided 6.4% of GDP in 2001, and employed 5.4% of the labour force in 1995. Petroleum refineries accounted for 75.9% of manufacturing activity, measured by gross value of output, in 1997. Of the other branches of manufacturing, the most important are the production of building materials (and related activities such as aluminium extrusion), fertilizer production, food processing and the extraction of salt and chlorine. During 1993–97 manufacturing GDP increased, in real terms, at an average annual rate of 5.3%.

Electrical energy is derived from Kuwait's own resources of petroleum (providing 77.3% of total electricity production in 1999) and both local and imported natural gas (22.7%). (The value of fuel imports in 2000 was equivalent to less than 1% of the value of total merchandise imports.) Total installed electricity-generating capacity increased from 6,898 MW in 1996 to 9,298 MW in 2000, following the completion of a 2,400-MW plant at Subiya; however, the proposed 2,500-MW az-Zour North plant was not scheduled for completion until 2006. Under the terms of an accord signed in early 2002, Qatar is to supply natural gas to the az-Zour plant from the end of 2005.

Services contributed 48.1% of GDP in 2001, and employed 74.8% of the labour force in 1995. Kuwait's second most important source of revenue is investment abroad (the total value of which was estimated to be in excess of US $45,000m. in the late 1990s), both in petroleum-related ventures and in other industries, chiefly in the USA, Western Europe and Japan; many such investments are held by the Reserve Fund for Future Generations (RFFG—to which 10% of petroleum revenues must by law be contributed each year, and which is intended to provide an income after hydrocarbon resources have been exhausted) and managed by the Kuwait Investment Authority. Prior to the Iraqi invasion the value of the RFFG was believed to have been some $100,000m. The combined GDP of the service sectors increased, in real terms, at an average rate of 0.5% per year during 1993–97.

In 2001 Kuwait recorded a visible trade surplus of US $9,241m., and there was a surplus of $8,566m. on the current account of the balance of payments. In 2000 the principal sources of imports were the USA and Japan, which provided, respectively, 10.9% and 9.8% of total imports; other important suppliers in that year were Germany, Saudi Arabia, the United Kingdom and Italy. The principal market for exports in 1987 was Japan (16.8%); other important purchasers in that year were Italy and the Netherlands. The major markets for non-petroleum exports in 2000 included Saudi Arabia (12.1%), Indonesia, the UAE and India. The principal exports are petroleum and petroleum products. The principal imports are machinery and transport equipment (particularly electrical machinery and road vehicles), which accounted for 39.7% of total imports in 1999, basic manufactures (especially iron and steel, and textiles) and other manufactured goods, food and live animals, and chemicals and related products.

A budget surplus of KD 6,43.5m. was recorded for the financial year ending 30 June 2001. Kuwait's total external debt in mid-1996 was estimated to be equivalent to 8.5% of GDP. The average annual rate of inflation in 1995–2002 was 1.2%; consumer prices increased by an annual average of 1.3% in 2002. National unemployment was estimated at only 1.4% in the mid-1990s and reported to be only 1% in 2001, the lowest rate in the region; however, underemployment was unofficially reported to be in excess of 50%.

Kuwait is a member of the GCC; the six GCC states established a unified regional customs tariff in January 2003, and it has been agreed to create a single market and currency no later than January 2010. Kuwait also belongs to the Organization of Arab Petroleum Exporting Countries (OAPEC, see p. 292) and to OPEC. Kuwait is a major aid donor, disbursing loans to developing countries through the Kuwait Fund for Arab Economic Development (KFAED) and the Arab Fund for Economic and Social Development (AFESD, see p. 136).

Despite its significant, oil-based wealth, Kuwait has a number of fundamental weaknesses in its economic structure: instability in its relations with Iraq have necessitated a high level of defence expenditure; reliance on oil revenues has impeded diversification into other industries; and its constitutional commitment to provide employment for all Kuwaitis has resulted in a heavy burden on government spending (an estimated 84% of the annual budget is allocated to salaries and subsidies). In 1999 the Government attempted to address this problem by proposing new taxes for companies and expatriate workers that would be used to create an employment fund to facilitate private-sector work for Kuwaitis. The value of shares quoted on the Kuwait Stock Exchange (KSE) declined during 1999–2001, apparently demonstrating a lack of investor confidence in the Government's economic reforms despite new legislation, enacted in May 2000, which allowed non-GCC investors to enter the market. However, by April 2003 the KSE share value was reported to be at its highest level ever recorded. During 2000–01 plans by the Kuwait Petroleum Corporation to allow foreign participation in a development project (known as 'Project Kuwait'), valued at US $7,000m., for the northern oilfields made slow progress; the project aimed to increase production from 400,000 b/d to 900,000 b/d by its completion date of 2005. Approval by the Majlis was also required, and, despite assurances that all reserves would remain Kuwaiti-owned, many Kuwaitis remained opposed to any foreign involvement in the petroleum sector. Nevertheless, in 2001 the Kuwaiti Government pursued legislation that would increase foreign investment in the economy, including the limited participation of international oil companies in the petroleum sector and measures that would permit foreign banks to operate in Kuwait. The recovery in world petroleum prices from late 1999 was the principal factor contributing to a budget surplus for 1999/2000 and 2000/01; although a deficit was predicted for 2001/02, a further surplus was forecast for 2002/03. Petroleum prices remained high until the latter part of 2001, when international markets were severely affected by the suicide attacks in the USA. A subsequent strengthening in prices (which reached very high levels in early 2003) most notably reflected uncertainty regarding oil supplies in the event of a US-led military campaign against the Iraqi regime of Saddam Hussain. Kuwait's heavy reliance on the volatile petroleum market was reflected in the economic downturn in 2001, and again led analysts to emphasize the need for structural reform in Kuwait, especially further privatization in order to increase state revenues. It was hoped that an increase in government expenditure in the 2003/04 budget would stim-ulate growth in the non-petroleum sector. In early 2002 a new Secretariat-General of Economic Reforms was being formed. In February the Majlis approved legislation imposing strict penalties for those convicted of money-laundering activities. On 1 January 2003 Kuwait pegged the dinar to the US dollar, as part of the GCC plan to create a single currency by 2010.

Education

Education is compulsory for eight years between the ages of six and 14. Although private schools exist, state education is free, and is graded into pre-primary (for children between four and six years of age), primary (for children aged six to 10), intermediate (10 to 14) and secondary (14 to 18). In 1996 enrolment at primary schools included 62% of children in the relevant age-group (males 62%; females 61%), while secondary enrolment included 61% of children in the relevant age-group (males 62%; females 61%). There is a teacher-training college, a technical college, and a university (where some 18,000 students were enrolled in 1998/99). In addition, more than 4,500 Kuwaiti students receive education abroad. Expenditure on education by the central Government in 2000/01 was budgeted at KD 331.5m. (10.4% of total expenditure).

Public Holidays

2003: 1 January (New Year's Day), 11 February* (Mount Arafat Day), 12 February* (Id al-Adha, Feast of the Sacrifice), 25 February (Kuwaiti National Day), 26 February (Liberation Day), 5 March* (Islamic New Year), 14 May* (Birth of the Prophet), 24 September* (Leilat al-Meiraj, Ascension of the Prophet), 26 November* (Id al-Fitr, end of Ramadan).

2004: 1 January (New Year's Day), 2 February* (Id al-Adha, Feast of the Sacrifice), 10 February* (Mount Arafat Day), 22 February* (Islamic New Year), 25 February (Kuwaiti National Day), 26 February (Liberation Day), 2 May* (Birth of the Prophet), 12 September* (Leilat al-Meiraj, Ascension of the Prophet), 14 November* (Id al-Fitr, end of Ramadan).

*These holidays are dependent on the Islamic lunar calendar and may vary by one or two days from the dates given.

Weights and Measures

The metric system is in force.

Statistical Survey

Sources (unless otherwise stated): Economic Research Department, Central Bank of Kuwait, POB 526, 13006 Safat, Kuwait City; tel. 2403257; fax 2440887; e-mail cbk@cbk.gov.kw; internet www.cbk.gov.kw; Central Statistical Office, Ministry of Planning, POB 26188, 13122 Safat, Kuwait City; tel. 2454968; fax 2430464; e-mail salah@mop.gov.kw; internet www.mop.gov.kw.
Note: Unless otherwise indicated, data refer to the State of Kuwait as constituted at 1 August 1990, prior to the Iraqi invasion and annexation of the territory and its subsequent liberation. Furthermore, no account has been taken of the increase in the area of Kuwait as a result of the adjustment to the border with Iraq that came into force on 15 January 1993.

Area and Population

AREA, POPULATION AND DENSITY

Area (sq km)	17,818*
Population (census results)†‡	
21 April 1985.	1,697,301
20 April 1995	
Males	913,402
Females.	662,168
Total	1,575,570
Population (official estimates at mid-year)†	
1999	2,107,195
2000	2,189,668
2001	2,274,980
Density (per sq km) at mid-2001	127.7

* 6,880 sq miles.

† Figures include Kuwait nationals abroad. The total population at the 1995 census comprised 653,616 Kuwaiti nationals (326,301 males; 327,315 females) and 921,954 non-Kuwaitis (587,101 males; 334,853 females).

‡ Excluding adjustment for underenumeration.

GOVERNORATES
(estimated population at mid-1998)

Governorate	Area (sq km)*	Population	Density (per sq km)	Capital
Capital . . .	199.8	305,694	1,530.0	Kuwait City
Hawalli . . }	368.4 {	496,245 }	2,700.4	{ Hawalli
Farwaniya . . }		498,584 }		{ Farwaniya
Al-Jahra . .	11,230.2	252,157	22.5	Jahra
Al-Ahmadi . .	5,119.6	313,424	61.2	Ahmadi City
Total. . .	16,918.0	1,866,104	110.3	

* Excluding the islands of Bubiyan and Warba (combined area 900 sq km).
Note: In November 1999 a sixth governorate, Great Mubarak, was created by dividing Hawalli.

PRINCIPAL TOWNS
(population at 1995 census)

Kuwait City (capital)	28,747	Subbah as-Salem .	54,608
Salmiya	129,775	Sulaibiah . . .	53,639
Jaleeb ash-Shuyukh .	102,169	Farwaniya . . .	52,928
Hawalli	82,154	Al-Kreen . . .	50,689
South Kheetan . .	62,241	Subahiya . . .	50,644

BIRTHS, MARRIAGES AND DEATHS

	Registered live births		Registered marriages		Registered deaths	
	Number	Rate (per 1,000)	Number	Rate (per 1,000)	Number	Rate (per 1,000)
1993	37,379	25.6	10,077	6.9	3,441	2.4
1994	38,868	24.0	9,550	5.9	3,464	2.1
1995	41,169	22.8	9,515	5.3	3,781	2.1
1996	44,620	23.6	9,022	4.8	3,812	2.0
1997	42,817	21.6	9,610	4.9	4,017	2.0
1998	41,424	20.4	10,335	5.1	4,216	2.1
1999	41,135	19.5	10,847	5.1	4,187	2.0
2000	41,843	19.1	10,785	4.9	4,227	1.9

Expectation of life (WHO estimates, years at birth): 75.3 (males 74.9; females 75.9) in 2001 (Source: WHO, *World Health Report*).

ECONOMICALLY ACTIVE POPULATION

(persons aged 15 years and over, census of April 1995)*

	Kuwaitis	Non-Kuwaitis	Total
Agriculture, hunting and fishing	216	15,140	15,356
Mining and quarrying	7,168	8,306	15,474
Manufacturing	997	39,107	40,104
Electricity, gas and water	32	137	169
Construction	1,415	113,804	115,219
Trade, restaurants and hotels	3,852	115,493	119,345
Transport, storage and communications	4,865	20,637	25,502
Finance, insurance, real estate and business services	4,139	53,077	57,216
Community, social and personal services	117,093	234,236	351,329
Activities not adequately defined	2,982	4,838	7,820
Total	142,759	604,775	747,534

* Figures exclude persons seeking work for the first time, totalling 14,086 (5,009 Kuwaitis; 9,077 non-Kuwaitis), but include other unemployed persons, totalling 15,919 (5,564 Kuwaitis; 10,355 non-Kuwaitis).

Mid-2000 (official estimates, persons aged 15 years and over): Total employed 1,197,887 (Kuwaitis 225,179; non-Kuwaitis 972,708); Unemployed 9,305 (Kuwaitis 2,351; non-Kuwaitis 6,954); *Total labour force* 1,207,192 (Kuwaitis 227,530; non-Kuwaitis 979,662).

Health and Welfare

KEY INDICATORS

Total fertility rate (children per woman, 2001)	2.7
Under-5 mortality rate (per 1,000 live births, 2001)	10
HIV/AIDS (% of persons aged 15–49, 1994)	0.12
Physicians (per 1,000 head, 1997)	1.9
Hospital beds (per 1,000 head, 1997)	2.76
Health expenditure (2000): US $ per head (PPP)	586
Health expenditure (2000): % of GDP	3.0
Health expenditure (2000): public (% of total)	87.2
Human Development Index (2000): ranking	45
Human Development Index (2000): value	0.813

For sources and definitions, see explanatory note on p. vi.

Agriculture

PRINCIPAL CROPS

('000 metric tons)

	1999	2000	2001
Potatoes	24.4	18.0	31.9
Cabbages	5.3	5.3	6.5
Lettuce	4.7	7.9	6.6
Tomatoes	32.1	36.7	41.1
Cauliflower	5.4	6.6	7.7
Pumpkins, squash and gourds	3.5	4.9	4.9*
Cucumber and gherkins	28.6	33.0	33.0*
Aubergines (Eggplants)	11.5	12.0	12.0*
Chillies and green peppers	5.1	5.5	6.8
Dry onions	3.7	6.6	4.9
Other vegetables*	23.5	25.0	25.3
Dates	7.9	10.2	10.4

* FAO estimate(s).

Source: FAO.

LIVESTOCK

('000 head, year ending September)

	1999	2000	2001
Cattle	20	21	15†
Camels*	9	9	9
Sheep	475	524	630
Goats	159	130	130
Poultry	29,204	33,000	32,463

* FAO estimates.
† Unofficial figure.

Source: FAO.

LIVESTOCK PRODUCTS

('000 metric tons)

	1999	2000	2001
Beef and veal	1.6*	1.7*	1.2†
Mutton and lamb*	38.0	35.7	35.7
Poultry meat	39.0	42.7	42.2
Cows' milk	33.7	30.1	39.6
Goats' milk	4.1	4.5	4.8
Hen eggs	18.2	20.1	22.5*
Sheepskins (fresh)*	13.4	12.6	13.5

* FAO estimate(s).
† Unofficial estimate.

Source: FAO.

Fishing

(metric tons, live weight)

	1998	1999	2000
Capture	7,799	6,271	6,300*
Hilsha shad	919	970	970*
Groupers	264	237	237*
Grunts and sweetlips	174	245	245*
Croakers and drums	1,211	1,385	1,385*
Yellowfin seabream	280	464	464*
Mullets	1,137	1,054	965*
Silver pomfret	501	259	259*
Indo-Pacific king mackerel	166	211	211*
Natantian decapods	1,598	720	720*
Aquaculture	250*	264	376
Total catch	8,049	6,535	6,676*

* FAO estimate.

Source: FAO, *Yearbook of Fishery Statistics*.

Mining*

	1999	2000	2001
Crude petroleum (million barrels) .	708	766	755
Natural gas (million cu metres)† .	8,688	9,600	9,500

* Estimates, including an equal share of production with Saudi Arabia from the Neutral/Partitioned Zone.
† On a dry basis.

Source: US Geological Survey.

Industry

SELECTED PRODUCTS
('000 metric tons, unless otherwise stated)

	1998	1999	2000
Wheat flour	155	159	162
Sulphur (by-product)*†	650	639	512
Chlorine	19	18	15
Caustic soda (Sodium hydroxide) .	22	21	19
Nitrogenous fertilizers‡	361	331	288
Motor spirit (petrol) ('000 barrels)*†§	17,520	17,000	10,000
Kerosene and jet fuels ('000 barrels)§	51,571	57,012	45,049
Gas-diesel (Distillate fuel) oils ('000 barrels)§	91,830	97,142	83,981
Residual fuel oils ('000 barrels)§	71,591	73,598	57,116
Petroleum bitumen (asphalt)*§	252	297	331
Liquefied petroleum gas§ . . .	3,124	3,228	2,997
Quicklime*†	40	40	40
Cement	2,310	947	n.a.
Electric energy (million kWh)§ .	29,988	31,576	32,323

2001†: Sulphur (by-product) 524; Motor spirit (petrol) ('000 barrels) 10,000§; Quicklime 40*.

* Provisional or estimated figure(s).
† Source: US Geological Survey.
‡ Production in terms of nitrogen.
§ Including an equal share of production with Saudi Arabia from the Neutral/Partitioned Zone.

Finance

CURRENCY AND EXCHANGE RATES

Monetary Units
    1,000 fils = 10 dirhams = 1 Kuwaiti dinar (KD)

Sterling, Dollar and Euro Equivalents (31 December 2002)
    £1 sterling = 482.84 fils
    US $1 = 299.56 fils
    €1 = 314.15 fils
    100 Kuwaiti dinars = £207.11 = $333.82 = €318.32

Average Exchange Rate (US $ per KD)
    2000   3.2600
    2001   3.2607
    2002   3.2906

GENERAL BUDGET
(KD million, year ending 30 June)

Revenue	1999/2000*	2000/01*†	2001/02*‡
Tax revenue	98.8	72.9	110.4
International trade and transactions . . .	75.9	58.6	81.4
Non-tax revenue	5,142.3	4,892.5	3,721.1
Oil revenue	4,794.4	4,528.0	3,236.3
Total operating revenue of government enterprises . .	270.3	222.1	337.0
Total	5,241.1	4,965.4	3,831.5

Expenditure	1998/99	1999/2000*	2000/01*†
Current expenditure	2,692.8	2,773.2	2,248.8
Defence, security and justice . .	887.9	921.2	733.7
Education	381.4	408.5	331.5
Health	265.7	257.2	203.0
Social and labour affairs . .	103.5	106.1	84.0
Electricity and water . . .	169.8	202.6	251.0
Communications	74.5	65.0	52.5
Capital expenditure	28.6	24.7	23.9
Development expenditure . .	376.6	313.6	214.4
Public works	73.2	76.0	66.9
Electricity and water . . .	238.7	187.5	103.3
Transfers to attached and public institutions	942.2	898.5	701.8
Total	4,040.2	4,010.0	3,188.1

* Approved budget figures.
† From 2001 the fiscal year was to end on 31 March, instead of 30 June. Consequently the budget for 2000/01 was for a nine-month period, from 1 July 2000 to 31 March 2001.
‡ Projections.

2001/02 (projection, KD million, year ending 31 March): Total expenditure 5,274.0.

2002/03 (projections, KD million, year ending 31 March): Total revenue 3,536 (oil revenue 2,984); Total expenditure 5,430.

INTERNATIONAL RESERVES
(US $ million at 31 December)

	2000	2001	2002
Gold*	103.9	103.1	106.0
IMF special drawing rights . .	90.9	108.0	132.9
Reserve position in IMF . . .	487.0	598.3	718.2
Foreign exchange	6,504.4	9,191.1	8,357.0
Total	7,186.3	10,000.5	9,314.1

* National valuation of gold reserves (2,539,000 troy ounces in each year).

Source: IMF, *International Financial Statistics*.

MONEY SUPPLY
(KD million at 31 December)

	2000	2001	2002
Currency outside banks . . .	416.6	401.2	442.2
Demand deposits at deposit money banks	1,051.1	1,240.2	1,624.6
Total money	1,467.7	1,641.4	2,066.8

Source: IMF, *International Financial Statistics*.

COST OF LIVING
(Consumer Price Index; base: 1980 = 100)

	1999	2000	2001
Food	171.6	172.9	171.9
Beverages and tobacco . . .	299.9	305.8	311.8
Clothing and footwear . . .	263.7	259.4	268.7
Housing services	200.4	204.3	206.6
All items (incl. others) . . .	205.5	209.2	211.7

NATIONAL ACCOUNTS
(KD million at current prices)

Expenditure on the Gross Domestic Product

	1999	2000	2001
Government final consumption expenditure	2,463	2,485	2,646
Private final consumption expenditure	4,490	4,633	4,801
Increase in stocks	1,335	827	866
Gross fixed capital formation . .			
Total domestic expenditure .	8,288	7,945	8,313
Exports of goods and services .	4,212	6,534	5,506
Less Imports of goods and services	3,616	3,488	3,762
GDP in purchasers' values .	8,884	10,991	10,057

Source: IMF, *International Financial Statistics*.

Gross Domestic Product by Economic Activity

	1999*	2000†	2001†
Agriculture, hunting, forestry and fishing	39.2	41.1	38.9
Mining and quarrying	3,328.6	5,543.1	4,587.2
Manufacturing	1,015.6	801.3	666.7
Electricity, gas and water . . .	−47.2	−101.9	−106.2
Construction	239.6	242.5	245.3
Trade, restaurants and hotels . .	692.5	676.7	695.6
Transport, storage and communications	451.3	506.4	507.7
Finance, insurance, real estate and business services	1,247.8	1,326.8	1,364.3
Community, social and personal services	2,278.3	2,363.4	2,467.9
Sub-total	9,245.7	11,399.4	10,467.4
Import duties . . . . . . ⎫	−361.7	−408.4	−410.4
Less Imputed bank service charges ⎭			
GDP in purchasers' values . .	8,884.0	10,991.0	10,057.0

* Revised figures.

† Provisional figures.

BALANCE OF PAYMENTS

(US $ million)

	1999	2000	2001
Exports of goods f.o.b.	12,276	19,478	16,173
Imports of goods f.o.b.	−6,708	−6,451	−6,932
Trade balance	5,568	13,027	9,241
Exports of services	1,560	1,822	1,788
Imports of services	−5,171	−4,923	−5,340
Balance on goods and services.	1,958	9,926	5,689
Other income received . . .	6,094	7,315	5,483
Other income paid	−985	−616	−525
Balance on goods, services and income.	7,066	16,626	10,647
Current transfers received . . .	99	85	52
Current transfers paid . . .	−2,102	−2,041	−2,133
Current balance	5,062	14,670	8,566
Capital account (net) . . .	703	2,217	2,933
Direct investment abroad . . .	−23	303	−323
Direct investment from abroad. .	72	16	−39
Portfolio investment assets. . .	−2,638	−12,923	−7,375
Portfolio investment liabilities. .	79	254	−78
Other investment assets . . .	−3,512	−1,108	431
Other investment liabilities . .	315	150	1,347
Net errors and omissions . . .	859	−1,311	−2,554
Overall balance	918	2,268	2,906

Source: IMF, *International Financial Statistics*.

External Trade

PRINCIPAL COMMODITIES

(distribution by SITC, KD million)

Imports c.i.f.	1997	1998	1999
Food and live animals . . .	342.4	356.3	345.6
Vegetables and fruit	78.1	88.9	83.8
Chemicals and related products	209.2	203.5	201.0
Basic manufactures	503.0	480.6	378.2
Textile yarn, fabrics, etc. . . .	80.0	75.0	63.2
Non-metallic mineral manufactures	93.5	92.8	80.2
Iron and steel.	128.5	133.2	77.4
Machinery and transport equipment.	964.7	1,081.9	920.4
Power-generating machinery and equipment	124.0	114.8	78.3
Machinery specialized for particular industries	109.0	104.1	107.6
General industrial machinery, equipment and parts	103.0	100.6	97.3
Telecommunications and sound equipment	69.4	78.8	85.5
Other electrical machinery, apparatus, etc.	107.7	96.2	91.0
Road vehicles and parts. . . .	384.7	421.0	372.6
Passenger motor cars (excl. buses).	244.4	254.8	223.6
Other transport equipment and parts.	17.4	115.1	38.4
Miscellaneous manufactured articles	352.9	359.6	325.0
Clothing and accessories (excl. footwear)	106.0	113.4	100.3
Total (incl. others)	2,501.6	2,626.2	2,318.3

2000 (KD million): Food and live animals 349.0; Chemicals and related products 207.9; Basic manufactures 395.2; Machinery and transport equipment 820.1; Miscellaneous manufactured articles 304.3; Total (incl. others) 2,195.4.

Exports f.o.b.	1998	1999	2000
Mineral fuels, lubricants, etc. .	2,598.0	3,356.8	5,581.3
Petroleum, petroleum products, etc.*	2,581.8	3,356.4	5,578.3
Chemicals and related products	180.2	213.7	255.0
Total (incl. others)*	2,911.6	3,702.8	5,962.7

2001 (KD million): Total imports c.i.f. 2,370.9; Total exports f.o.b. 4,948.4* (Petroleum, petroleum products, etc. 4,590.8*).

* Estimate(s) by the Central Bank of Kuwait.

2002 (KD million): Total imports c.i.f. 2,720.0; Total exports f.o.b. 4,683.2 (Petroleum, petroleum products, etc. 4,276.7) (Source: IMF, *International Financial Statistics*).

PRINCIPAL TRADING PARTNERS
(KD million)*

Imports c.i.f.	1998	1999	2000
Australia	58.4	74.6	64.9
Canada	42.4	47.6	52.6
China, People's Repub. . . .	72.1	75.3	85.8
France (incl. Monaco) . . .	97.4	86.1	70.8
Germany	183.1	178.3	178.4
India	91.8	86.8	82.8
Iran	22.1	31.5	35.3
Italy	151.9	135.2	117.1
Japan	356.8	296.7	214.1
Korea, Repub.	71.8	55.3	87.4
Malaysia	31.3	31.3	32.6
Netherlands	50.5	44.4	39.9
Saudi Arabia	163.2	143.6	154.4
South Africa	26.7	16.0	8.6
Spain	36.0	35.7	36.6
Switzerland-Liechtenstein . . .	53.1	43.3	37.0
Taiwan.	34.6	29.4	26.7
Thailand	29.2	29.9	27.4
Turkey.	38.4	36.6	35.5
United Arab Emirates . . .	56.5	73.2	79.5
United Kingdom	153.2	132.5	123.3
USA	404.9	284.8	239.3
Total (incl. others)	2,626.2	2,318.3	2,195.4

Exports f.o.b.†	1998	1999	2000
Bahrain	5.1	6.2	6.8
Belgium-Luxembourg	15.7	15.9	9.9
Canada	3.5	0.4	0.2
China, People's Repub. . . .	15.9	15.8	23.3
Egypt	17.0	8.5	11.8
India	23.5	31.2	26.8
Indonesia	2.1	13.5	30.9
Iran	2.7	3.3	4.5
Italy	1.0	4.1	3.3
Japan	4.5	4.0	5.7
Jordan	6.4	7.6	7.7
Lebanon	3.6	4.5	5.1
Malaysia	4.1	3.1	2.9
Oman	4.3	6.1	5.4
Pakistan	13.6	14.7	18.4
Philippines	7.4	7.9	7.0
Qatar	5.4	5.2	7.5
Saudi Arabia	38.7	41.6	46.7
Singapore	39.4	26.3	8.0
Switzerland	2.3	4.6	0.1
Syria	6.3	6.0	8.0
Taiwan.	5.8	4.2	4.3
Turkey.	5.6	3.5	4.9
United Arab Emirates . . .	30.6	33.9	27.7
USA	7.1	16.6	14.3
Total (incl. others)	329.8	362.7	386.6

* Imports by country of production; exports by country of last consignment.
† Excluding petroleum exports.

Transport

ROAD TRAFFIC
(motor vehicles in use at 31 December)

	1995	1996	1997
Passenger cars	662,946	701,172	747,042
Buses and coaches	11,937	12,322	13,094
Goods vehicles	116,813	121,753	127,386

1999: Buses and coaches 12,775; Goods vehicles 97,706.

2000: Buses and coaches 10,974; Goods vehicles 80,378.

SHIPPING

Merchant Fleet
(registered at 31 December)

	1999	2000	2001
Number of vessels	202	205	200
Displacement ('000 grt)	2,456.5	2,415.3	2,291.7

Source: Lloyd's Register-Fairplay, *World Fleet Statistics*.

International Sea-borne Freight Traffic
('000 metric tons)*

	1988	1989	1990
Goods loaded	61,778	69,097	51,400
Goods unloaded	7,123	7,015	4,522

* Including Kuwait's share of traffic in the Neutral/Partitioned Zone.

Source: UN, *Monthly Bulletin of Statistics*.

Goods loaded ('000 metric tons): 89,945 in 1997.

Goods unloaded ('000 metric tons): 746 in 1991 (July–December only); 2,537 in 1992; 4,228 in 1993; 5,120 in 1994; 5,854 in 1995; 6,497 in 1996; 6,049 in 1997.

CIVIL AVIATION
(traffic on scheduled services)

	1997	1998	1999
Kilometres flown (million) . . .	43	45	36
Passengers carried ('000) . . .	2,114	2,190	2,130
Passenger-km (million)	5,997	6,207	6,158
Total ton-km (million)	912	932	829

Source: UN, *Statistical Yearbook*.

Tourism

VISITOR ARRIVALS BY COUNTRY OF ORIGIN
(incl. excursionists)

	1998	1999	2000
Bahrain	43,692	49,658	50,024
Bangladesh	76,934	79,731	54,466
Egypt	227,127	226,262	219,553
India	215,087	226,629	225,642
Iran	80,716	93,801	100,328
Lebanon	45,817	48,001	48,642
Pakistan	74,601	78,206	74,429
Philippines	38,696	37,357	43,310
Saudi Arabia	524,873	574,924	641,691
Sri Lanka	60,506	54,816	54,804
Syria	142,850	146,084	143,020
Total (incl. others) . . .	1,762,641	1,883,633	1,944,233

Tourism receipts (US $ million): 207 in 1998; 243 in 1999.

Source: World Tourism Organization, *Yearbook of Tourism Statistics*.

Communications Media

	1999	2000	2001
Radio receivers ('000 in use) . .	1,200	n.a.	n.a.
Television receivers ('000 in use) .	910	930	n.a.
Telephones ('000 main lines in use)	455.6	467.1	472.4
Facsimile machines ('000 in use)	60	n.a.	n.a.
Mobile cellular telephones ('000 subscribers).	300.0	476.0	489.2
Personal computers ('000 in use)	230	250	260
Internet users ('000)	100	150	200
Book titles published	219	n.a.	n.a.

1996: Daily newspapers 8 (average circulation 635,000 copies); Non-daily newspapers 78.

Sources: UNESCO, *Statistical Yearbook*; UN, *Statistical Yearbook*; International Telecommunication Union.

Education

(state-controlled schools, 2000/01)

	Schools	Teachers	Students		
			Males	Females	Total
Kindergarten . .	153	3,379	22,142	22,128	44,270
Primary . . .	184	8,151	48,796	49,322	98,118
Intermediate . .	165	9,073	47,955	47,509	95,464
Secondary . . .	117	9,234	34,868	41,353	76,221
Religious institutes	7	351	n.a.	n.a.	2,454
Special training institutes . . .	33	756	n.a.	n.a.	543

Private education (1996/97): 63 kindergarten schools (598 teachers, 12,172 students); 80 primary schools (2,341 teachers, 47,111 students); 82 intermediate schools (1,860 teachers, 36,254 students); 66 secondary schools (1,576 teachers, 20,932 students).

2000/01 (private education): 112 schools; 7,324 teachers; 128,204 students.

Adult literacy rate (UNESCO estimates): 82.0% (males 84.0%; females 79.7%) in 2000 (Source: UNDP, *Human Development Report*).

Directory

The Constitution

The principal provisions of the Constitution, promulgated on 16 November 1962, are set out below. On 29 August 1976 the Amir suspended four articles of the Constitution dealing with the National Assembly, the Majlis al-Umma. On 24 August 1980 the Amir issued a decree ordering the establishment of an elected legislature before the end of February 1981. The new Majlis was elected on 23 February 1981, and fresh legislative elections followed on 20 February 1985. The Majlis was dissolved by Amiri decree in July 1986, and some sections of the Constitution, including the stipulation that new elections should be held within two months of dissolving the legislature (see below), were suspended. A new Majlis was elected on 5 October 1992 and convened on 20 October.

SOVEREIGNTY

Kuwait is an independent sovereign Arab State; its sovereignty may not be surrendered, and no part of its territory may be relinquished. Offensive war is prohibited by the Constitution.

Succession as Amir is restricted to heirs of the late Mubarak as-Sabah, and an Heir Apparent must be appointed within one year of the accession of a new Amir.

EXECUTIVE AUTHORITY

Executive power is vested in the Amir, who exercises it through the Council of Ministers. The Amir will appoint the Prime Minister 'after the traditional consultations', and will appoint and dismiss ministers on the recommendation of the Prime Minister. Ministers need not be members of the Majlis al-Umma, although all ministers who are not members of parliament assume membership *ex officio* in the legislature for the duration of office. The Amir also formulates laws, which shall not be effective unless published in the *Official Gazette*. The Amir establishes public institutions. All decrees issued in these respects shall be conveyed to the Majlis. No law is issued unless it is approved by the Majlis.

LEGISLATURE

A National Assembly, the Majlis al-Umma, of 50 members will be elected for a four-year term by all natural-born Kuwaiti males over the age of 21 years, except servicemen and police, who may not vote. Candidates for election must possess the franchise, be over 30 years of age and literate. The Majlis will convene for at least eight months in any year, and new elections shall be held within two months of the last dissolution of the outgoing legislature.

Restrictions on the commercial activities of ministers include an injunction forbidding them to sell property to the Government.

The Amir may ask for reconsideration of a bill that has been approved by the Majlis and sent to him for ratification, but the bill would automatically become law if it were subsequently adopted by a two-thirds' majority at the next sitting, or by a simple majority at a subsequent sitting. The Amir may declare martial law, but only with the approval of the legislature.

The Majlis may adopt a vote of 'no confidence' in a minister, in which case the minister must resign. Such a vote is not permissible in the case of the Prime Minister, but the legislature may approach the Amir on the matter, and the Amir shall then either dismiss the Prime Minister or dissolve the Majlis.

CIVIL SERVICE

Entry to the civil service is confined to Kuwaiti citizens.

PUBLIC LIBERTIES

Kuwaitis are equal before the law in prestige, rights and duties. Individual freedom is guaranteed. No one shall be seized, arrested or exiled except within the rules of law.

No punishment shall be administered except for an act or abstaining from an act considered a crime in accordance with a law applicable at the time of committing it, and no penalty shall be imposed more severe than that which could have been imposed at the time of committing the crime.

Freedom of opinion is guaranteed to everyone, and each has the right to express himself through speech, writing or other means within the limits of the law.

The press is free within the limits of the law, and it should not be suppressed except in accordance with the dictates of law.

Freedom of performing religious rites is protected by the State according to prevailing customs, provided it does not violate the public order and morality.

Trade unions will be permitted and property must be respected. An owner is not banned from managing his property except within the boundaries of law. No property should be taken from anyone, except within the prerogatives of law, unless a just compensation be given.

Houses may not be entered, except in cases provided by law. Every Kuwaiti has freedom of movement and choice of place of residence within the State. This right shall not be controlled except in cases stipulated by law.

Every person has the right to education and freedom to choose his type of work. Freedom to form peaceful societies is guaranteed within the limits of law.

The Government

HEAD OF STATE

Amir of Kuwait: His Highness Sheikh JABER AL-AHMAD AS-SABAH (acceded 31 December 1977).

COUNCIL OF MINISTERS
(April 2003)

Crown Prince and Prime Minister: Sheikh SAAD AL-ABDULLAH AS-SALIM AS-SABAH.

First Deputy Prime Minister and Minister of Foreign Affairs: Sheikh SABAH AL-AHMAD AL-JABER AS-SABAH.

Deputy Prime Minister and Minister of Defence: Sheikh JABER MUBARAK AL-HAMAD AS-SABAH.

Deputy Prime Minister and Minister of the Interior: Sheikh MUHAMMAD KHALID AL-HAMAD AS-SABAH.

Deputy Prime Minister, Minister of State for Cabinet Affairs and for National Assembly Affairs: MUHAMMAD DHAIFALLAH SHARAR.

Minister of Communications: Sheikh AHMAD ABDULLAH AL-AHMAD AS-SABAH.

Minister of Justice and of Awqaf (Religious Endowments) and Islamic Affairs: AHMAD YA'QUB BAQIR AL-ABDULLAH.

Minister of Information and Acting Minister of Oil: Sheikh AHMAD AL-FAHD AL-AHMAD AS-SABAH.

Minister of State for Foreign Affairs and Acting Minister of Finance and Planning: Sheikh MUHAMMAD SABAH AS-SALIM AS-SABAH.

Minister of Electricity and Water and Minister of Labour and Social Affairs: TALAL MUBARAK AL-AYYAR.

Minister of Commerce and Industry: SALEH ABD AR-REDA KHORSHED.

Minister of Public Works and Minister of State for Housing Affairs: FAHD DUWAYSAN AL-MAI'A.

Minister of Health: MUHAMMAD AHMAD AL-JARALLAH.

Minister of Education and Higher Education and Acting Minister of State for Administrative Development: Dr MUSAAD RASHID AL-HAROUN.

PROVINCIAL GOVERNORS

Al-Ahmadi: Sheikh ALI ABDULLAH AS-SALIM AS-SABAH.

Farwaniya: Dr IBRAHIM DUALJ AL-IBRAHIM AS-SABAH.

Great Mubarak: MUBARAK HUMUD AL-JABER AS-SABAH.

Hawalli: IBRAHIM JASEM AL-MUDHAF.

Al-Jahra: ALI JABER AL-AHMAD AS-SABAH.

Kuwait (Capital): Dr DAUD MUSAED AS-SALIH.

MINISTRIES

Ministry of Awqaf (Religious Endowments) and Islamic Affairs: POB 13, 13001 Safat, Kuwait City; tel. 2466300; fax 2449943; internet www.awkaf.net.

Ministry of Commerce and Industry: POB 2944, 13030 Safat, Kuwait City; tel. 2463600; fax 2424411.

Ministry of Communications: POB 318, 13004 Safat, Kuwait City; tel. 4819033; fax 4847058; e-mail webmaster@moc.gulfsat.com; internet www.moc.gulfsat.com.

Ministry of Defence: POB 1170, 13012 Safat, Kuwait City; tel. 4819277; fax 4846059.

Ministry of Education: POB 7, 13001 Safat, Hilali St, Kuwait City; tel. 4836800; fax 2423676; e-mail webmaster@moe.edu.kw; internet www.moe.edu.kw.

Ministry of Electricity and Water: POB 12, 13001 Safat, Kuwait City; tel. 4896000; fax 4897484.

Ministry of Finance: POB 9, 13001 Safat, al-Morkab St, Ministries Complex, Kuwait City; tel. 2468200; fax 2404025; e-mail webmaster@mof.gov.kw; internet www.mof.gov.kw.

Ministry of Foreign Affairs: POB 3, 13001 Safat, Gulf St, Kuwait City; tel. 2425141; fax 2430559; e-mail info@mofa.org; internet www.mofa.gov.kw.

Ministry of Health: POB 5, 13001 Safat, Arabian Gulf St, Kuwait City; tel. 4877422; fax 4865414.

Ministry of Higher Education: POB 27130, 13132 Safat, Kuwait City; tel. 2401300; fax 2456319.

Ministry of Information: POB 193, 13002 Safat, as-Sour St, Kuwait City; tel. 2415300; fax 2419642; e-mail info@moinfo.gov.kw; internet www.moinfo.gov.kw.

Ministry of the Interior: POB 11, 13001 Safat, Kuwait City; tel. 2524199; fax 2561268.

Ministry of Justice: POB 6, 13001 Safat, al-Morkab St, Ministries Complex, Kuwait City; tel. 2467300; fax 2466957; e-mail qht@moj .gov.kw; internet www.moj.gov.kw.

Ministry of Labour and Social Affairs: POB 563, 13006 Safat, Kuwait City; tel. 2464500; fax 2419877.

Ministry of Oil: POB 5077, 13051 Safat, Fahd as-Salem St, Kuwait City; tel. 2415201; fax 2417088.

Ministry of Planning: POB 15, 13001 Safat, Kuwait City; tel. 2428100; fax 2414734; e-mail info@mop.gov.kw; internet www.mop .gov.kw.

Ministry of Public Works: POB 8, 13001 Safat, Kuwait City; tel. 5385520; fax 5380829.

Legislature

MAJLIS AL-UMMA
(National Assembly)

Speaker: JASEM AL-KHARAFI.

Elections to the 50-seat Majlis took place on 3 July 1999: 20 seats were secured by Islamist candidates, 14 were won by liberals, 12 by pro-Government candidates and four by independents.

Political Organizations

Political parties are not permitted in Kuwait. However, several quasi-political organizations are in existence. Among those that have been represented in the Majlis since 1992 are:

Constitutional Group: supported by merchants.

Islamic Constitutional Movement: Sunni Muslim. moderate.

Kuwait Democratic Forum: internet www.kuwaitdf.org/df; f. 1991; secular; liberal.

National Democratic Rally (NDR): f. 1997; secular; liberal; Sec.-Gen. Dr AHMAD BISHARA.

National Islamic Coalition: Shi'a Muslim.

Salafeen (Islamic Popular Movement): Sunni Muslim.

Diplomatic Representation

EMBASSIES IN KUWAIT

Afghanistan: POB 33186, Rawdah, Surra, Block 6, Surra St, House 16, Kuwait City; tel. 5329461; fax 5326274; e-mail afg_emb_kuw@ hotmail.com; Chargé d'affaires Dr NASSER AHMAD NOOR.

Algeria: POB 578, 13006 Safat, Istiqlal St, Kuwait City; tel. 2519987; fax 2563052; Ambassador MUHAMMAD BURUBA.

Argentina: POB 1125, 45712 Surra, Kuwait City; tel. 5323014; fax 5323053; e-mail embargkuwait@hotmail.com; Chargé d'affaires a.i. ARMANDO MAURICIO BECHER.

Austria: POB 15013, Daiya, 35451 Kuwait City; tel. 2552532; fax 2563052; e-mail austremb@mail.qualitynet.net; Ambassador ROLAND HAUSER.

Bahrain: POB 196, 13002 Safat, Area 6, Surra Rd, Villa 35, Kuwait City; tel. 5318530; fax 5330882; e-mail 61116@kems.net; Ambassador ABD AR-RAHMAN M. AL-FADHEL.

Bangladesh: POB 22344, 13084 Safat, Khaldya, Block 6, Ali bin Abi Taleb St, House 361, Kuwait City; tel. 5316042; fax 5316041; e-mail bdoot@ncc.moc.kw; internet www.bdsociety.com/embassy; Ambassador AMINUL HOSSAIN SARKER.

Belgium: POB 3280, 13033 Safat, Salmiya, Baghdad St, House 15, Kuwait City; tel. 5722014; fax 5748389; Ambassador PHILIPPE-HENRI ARCQ.

Bhutan: POB 1510, 13016 Safat, Jabriya, Block 9, St 20, Villa 7, Kuwait City; tel. 5331506; fax 5338959; e-mail bhutankuwait@ hotmail.com; Ambassador TSHERING WANGDI.

Bosnia and Herzegovina: POB 6131, 32036 Hawalli, Kuwait City; tel. 5392637; fax 5392106; Ambassador EDHEM PASIĆ.

Brazil: POB 39761, 73058 Nuzha, Block 2, St 1, Jadah 1, Villa 8, Kuwait City; tel. 5328610; fax 5328613; e-mail brasemb@ncc.moc .kw; Ambassador (vacant).

Bulgaria: POB 12090, 71651 Shamiya, Jabriya, Block 11, St 107, Kuwait City; tel. 5314459; fax 5321453; e-mail bgembkw@qualitynet .net; Ambassador ANGEL N. MANTCHEV.

Canada: POB 25281, 13113 Safat, Diiya, Block 4, 24 al-Motawakell St, Villa 24, Kuwait City; tel. 2563025; fax 2563023; e-mail kwait@ dfait-maeci.gc.ca; Ambassador RICHARD MANN.

China, People's Republic: POB 2346, 13024 Safat, Dasmah, Sheikh Ahmad al-Jaber Bldgs 4 & 5, Kuwait City; tel. 5333340; fax 5333341; Ambassador ZENG XUYONG.

Czech Republic: POB 1151, 13012 Safat, Kuwait City; tel. 2529018; fax 2529021; e-mail kuwait@embassy.mzv; internet www .mzv.cz/kuwait; Chargé d'affaires a.i. Dr PETR KORBEL.

Egypt: POB 11252, 35153 Dasmah, Istiqlal St, Kuwait City; tel. 2519955; fax 2553877; Ambassador MAHMOUD WAJDI ABU ZEID.

Eritrea: POB 53016, 73015 Nuzha, Jabriya, Block 9, St 21, House 9, Kuwait City; tel. 5317426; fax 5317429; Ambassador MOUSA YASSIEN SHEIKH AD-DIN.

Ethiopia: POB 939, Surra, 45710 Safat, Kuwait City; tel. 5334276; fax 5331179; Ambassador RAZENE ARAYA.

Finland: POB 26699, 13127 Safat, Surra, Block 4, St 1, Villa 8, Kuwait City; tel. 5312890; fax 5324198; Ambassador MARKKU NII-NIOJA.

France: POB 1037, 13011 Safat, Mansouriah, Block 1, St 13, No. 24, Kuwait City; tel. 2571061; fax 2571058; Ambassador PATRICE PAOLI.

Germany: POB 805, 13009 Safat, Dahiya Abdullah as-Salem, Plot 1, St 14, Villa 13, Kuwait City; tel. 2520857; fax 2520763; e-mail 113061.3166@compuserve.com; Ambassador WERNER KREBS.

Greece: POB 23812, 13099 Safat, Khaldiya, Block 4, St 44, House 4, Kuwait City; tel. 4817101; fax 4817103; Ambassador ROCANAS CHAR-ALAMBOS.

Hungary: POB 23955, 13100 Safat, Qortuba, Area 2, Al-Baha'a bin Zuheir St 776, Kuwait City; tel. 5323901; fax 5323904; e-mail huembkwi@quality.net; Ambassador JENŐ FÖLDESI.

India: POB 1450, 13015 Safat, 34 Istiqlal St, Kuwait City; tel. 2530600; fax 2525811; e-mail indemb@ncc.moc.kw; Ambassador B. M. C. MYER.

Indonesia: POB 21560, 13076 Safat, Keifan, Block 5, As-Sebhani St, House 21, Kuwait City; tel. 4839927; fax 4819250; e-mail batik@ncc.moc.kw; Ambassador D. SOESJONO.

Iran: POB 4686, 13047 Safat, Daiyah, Embassies Area, Block B, Kuwait City; tel. 2560694; fax 2529868; Ambassador ALI JANNATI.

Italy: POB 4453, 13045 Safat, Shuwaikh 'B', Block 5, Villa 1, Kuwait City; tel. 4817400; fax 4817244; e-mail ambkuwa@ncc.moc.kw; Ambassador FRANCESCO CAPECE GALEOTA.

Japan: POB 2304, 13024 Safat, Jabriya, Area 9, Plot 496, Kuwait City; tel. 5312870; fax 5326168; Ambassador SHIGERU TSUMORI.

Jordan: POB 15314, 35305 Diiyah, Istiqlal St, Embassies Area, Kuwait City; tel. 2533500; Ambassador MUHAMMAD AL-QURAAN.

Korea, Republic: POB 20771, 13068 Safat, Rawda, Block 1, St 10, House 17, Kuwait City; tel. 2554206; fax 2526874; Ambassador CHOI JO-YOUNG.

Lebanon: POB 253, 13003 Safat, 31 Istiqlal St, Kuwait City; tel. 2562103; fax 2571682; Ambassador KHALED AL-KILANI.

Libya: POB 21460, 13075 Safat, 27 Istiqlal St, Kuwait City; tel. 2562103; fax 2571682; Chargé d'affaires IDRIS DAHMANI BU DIB.

Malaysia: POB 4105, 13042 Safat, Daiya, Diplomatic Enclave, Area 5, Istiqlal St, Plot 5, Kuwait City; tel. 2550394; fax 2550384; e-mail mwkuwait@qualitynet.net; Ambassador HUSNI ZAI BIN YAACOL.

Morocco: POB 784, 13008 Safat, Jabriya, Block 12, Villa 24, St 101, Kuwait City; tel. 4813912; fax 4814156; Ambassador DRISS KETTANI.

Netherlands: POB 21822, 13079 Safat, Jabriya, Area 9, St 1, Plot 40A, Kuwait City; tel. 5312650; fax 5326334; e-mail kwe@minbuza .nl; Ambassador HENK REVIS.

Niger: POB 44451, 32059 Hawalli, Salwa, Block 12, St 6, Villa 183, Kuwait City; tel. 5652943; fax 5640478; Ambassador AMADOU SEYNI.

Nigeria: POB 6432, 32039 Hawalli, Surra, Area 1, St 14, House 25, Kuwait City; tel. 5320794; fax 5320834; Ambassador MUHAMMAD ADAMU JUMBA.

Oman: POB 21975, 13080 Safat, Istiqlal St, Villa 3, Kuwait City; tel. 2561962; fax 2561963; Ambassador NASSER BIN KHALSAN AL-KHAROSSI.

Pakistan: POB 988, 13010 Safat, Jabriya, Plot 5, Block 11, Villa 7, Kuwait City; tel. 5327649; fax 5327648; Ambassador MUSHTAQ MEHR.

Philippines: POB 26288, 13123 Safat, Jabriya, Police Station St, Area 10, House 363, Kuwait City; tel. 5329316; fax 5329319; e-mail phembkt@ncc.moc.kw; Ambassador SUKARNO D. TANGGOL.

Poland: POB 5066, 13051 Safat, Jabriya, Plot 8, St 20, House 377, Kuwait City; tel. 5311571; fax 5311576; e-mail polamba@qualitynet .net; Ambassador WOJCIECH BOŻEK.

Qatar: POB 1825, 13019 Safat, Diiyah, Istiqlal St, Kuwait City; tel. 2513606; fax 2513604; Ambassador MUHAMMAD ALI AL-ANSARI.

Romania: 13574 Khaitan, Kuwait City; tel. 4843419; fax 4848929; e-mail ambsaat@ncc.moc.kw; Ambassador PATRA POPESCU.

Russia: POB 1765, 13018 Safat, Rawdah, Kuwait City; tel. 2560427; fax 2524969; Ambassador AZAMAT KULMUKHAMETOV.

Saudi Arabia: POB 20498, 13065 Safat, Istiqlal St, Kuwait City; tel. 2400250; fax 2426541; Ambassador AHMAD AL-HAMAD AL-YAHYA.

Senegal: POB 23892, 13099 Safat, Rawdah, Parcel 3, St 35, House 9, Kuwait City; tel. 2510823; fax 2542044; e-mail senegal_embassy@yahoo.com; Ambassador ABDOU LAHAD MBACKE.

Serbia and Montenegro: POB 20511, 13066 Safat, Jabriya, Block 7, St 12, Plot 382, Kuwait City; tel. 5327548; fax 5327568; e-mail yuembkuw@qualitynet.net; Ambassador ZORAN VEJNOVIĆ.

Somalia: POB 22766, 13088 Safat, Bayan, St 4, Block 4, Villa 4, Kuwait City; tel. 5394795; fax 5394829; e-mail som.emb@usa.net; Ambassador ABDUL KHADIR AMIN ABUBAKER.

South Africa: POB 2262, 40173 Mishref, Kuwait City; tel. 5617988; fax 5617917; e-mail saemb@southafrica.com; internet www .southafricaq8.com; Chargé d'affaires M. N. SLABBER.

Spain: POB 22207, 13083 Safat, Surra, Block 3, St 14, Villa 19, Kuwait City; tel. 5325827; fax 5325826; Ambassador JOSÉ LUIS ROSELLÓ.

Sri Lanka: POB 13212, 71952 Keifan, House 381, St 9, Block 5, Salwa; tel. 5612261; fax 5612264; e-mail lankemb@kuwait.net; Ambassador DARSIN SERASINGHE.

Sweden: POB 21448, 13075 Safat, Faiha, Area 7, ash-Shahba St, Kuwait City; tel. 2523588; fax 2572157; Ambassador THOMAS GANS-LANDT.

Switzerland: POB 23954, 13100 Safat, Qortuba, Block 2, St 1, Villa 122, Kuwait City; tel. 5340175; fax 5340176; e-mail vertretung@kow .rep.admin.ch; Ambassador JEAN-PHILIPPE TISSIÈRES.

Syria: POB 25600, 13116 Safat, Kuwait City; tel. 5396560; fax 5396509; Ambassador MUSTAFA HAJ ALI.

Thailand: POB 66647, 43757 Bayan, Surra, Area 3, Block 49, Ali bin Abi-Taleb St, Bldg No. 28, Kuwait City; tel. 5317531; fax 5317532; e-mail thaiemkw@ncc.moc.kw; Ambassador (vacant).

Tunisia: POB 5976, 13060 Safat, Nuzha, Plot 2, Nuzha St, Villa 45, Kuwait City; tel. 2542144; fax 2528995; e-mail tunemrku@ncc.moc .kw; Ambassador MUHAMMAD SAAD.

Turkey: POB 20627, 13067 Safat, Block 16, Plot 10, Istiqlal St, Kuwait City; tel. 2531785; fax 2560653; e-mail trkemb@ncc.moc.kw; internet www.turkish-embassy.org.kw; Ambassador AHMET ERTAY.

United Arab Emirates: POB 1828, 13019 Safat, Plot 70, Istiqlal St, Kuwait City; tel. 2528544; fax 2526382; Ambassador YOUSUF A. AL-ANSARI.

United Kingdom: POB 2, 13001 Safat, Arabian Gulf St, Kuwait City; tel. 2403336; fax 2426799; e-mail general@britishembassy-kuwait.org; internet www.britishembassy-kuwait .org; Ambassador RICHARD MUIR.

USA: POB 77, 13001 Safat, Bayan, Al-Masjeed Al-Aqsa St, Block 6, Plot 14, Kuwait City; tel. 5395307; fax 5380282; e-mail uskuwait@qualitynet.net; internet www.usembassy.gov.kw; Ambassador RICHARD H. JONES.

Venezuela: POB 24440, 13105 Safat, Block 5, St 7, Area 356, Surra, Kuwait City; tel. 5324367; fax 5324368; Chargé d'affaires ALBERTO ARMAS.

Zimbabwe: POB 36484, 24755 Salmiya, Kuwait City; tel. 5621517; fax 5621491; e-mail ZimKuwait@hotmail.com; Ambassador S. C. CHIKETA.

Judicial System

SPECIAL JUDICIARY

Constitutional Court: Comprises five judges. Interprets the provisions of the Constitution; considers disputes regarding the constitutionality of legislation, decrees and rules; has jurisdiction in challenges relating to the election of members, or eligibility for election, to the Majlis al-Umma.

ORDINARY JUDICIARY

Court of Cassation: Comprises five judges. Is competent to consider the legality of verdicts of the Court of Appeal and State Security Court; Chief Justice MUHAMMAD YOUSUF AR-RIFA'I.

Court of Appeal: Comprises three judges. Considers verdicts of the Court of First Instance; Chief Justice RASHED AL-HAMMAD.

Court of First Instance: Comprises the following divisions: Civil and Commercial (one judge), Personal Status Affairs (one judge), Lease (three judges), Labour (one judge), Crime (three judges), Administrative Disputes (three judges), Appeal (three judges), Challenged Misdemeanours (three judges); Chief Justice MUHAMMAD AS-SAKHOBY.

Summary Courts: Each governorate has a Summary Court, comprising one or more divisions. The courts have jurisdiction in the following areas: Civil and Commercial, Urgent Cases, Lease, Misdemeanours. The verdict in each case is delivered by one judge.

There is also a **Traffic Court,** with one presiding judge.

Attorney-General: MUHAMMAD ABD AL-HAIH AL-BANNAIY.

Advocate-General: HAMED AL-UTHMAN.

Religion

ISLAM
The majority of Kuwaitis are Muslims of the Sunni or Shi'a sects. The Shi'ite community comprises about 30% of the total.

CHRISTIANITY

The Roman Catholic Church

Latin Rite

For ecclesiastical purposes, Kuwait forms an Apostolic Vicariate. At 31 December 2001 there were an estimated 154,000 adherents in the country.

Vicar Apostolic: Mgr FRANCIS ADEODATUS MICALLEF (Titular Bishop of Tinisa in Proconsulari), Bishop's House, POB 266, 13003 Safat, Kuwait City; tel. 2431561; fax 2409981.

Melkite Rite

The Greek-Melkite Patriarch of Antioch is resident in Damascus, Syria. The Patriarchal Exarchate of Kuwait had an estimated 700 adherents at 31 December 1999.

Exarch Patriarchal: Archimandrite BASILIOS KANAKRY, Vicariat Patriarcal Greek-Melkite, POB 1205, Salwa Block 12, St No. 6, House 58, 22013 Salmiya, Kuwait City; tel. 5652802.

Syrian Rite

The Syrian Catholic Patriarch of Antioch is resident in Beirut, Lebanon. The Patriarchal Exarchate of Basra and Kuwait, with an estimated 1,200 adherents at 31 December 2000, is based in Basra, Iraq.

The Anglican Communion
Within the Episcopal Church in Jerusalem and the Middle East, Kuwait forms part of the diocese of Cyprus and the Gulf. The Anglican congregation in Kuwait is entirely expatriate. The Bishop in Cyprus and the Gulf is resident in Cyprus, while the Archdeacon in the Gulf is resident in Qatar.

Other Christian Churches

National Evangelical Church in Kuwait: POB 80, 13001 Safat, Kuwait City; tel. 2407195; fax 2431087; e-mail elc@ncc.moc.kw; Rev. NABIL ATTALLAH (pastor of the Arabic-language congregation), Rev. JERRY A. ZANDSTRA (senior pastor of the English-speaking congregation); an independent Protestant Church founded by the Reformed Church in America; services in Arabic, English, Korean, Malayalam and other Indian languages; combined weekly congregation of some 20,000.

The Armenian, Greek, Coptic and Syrian Orthodox Churches are also represented in Kuwait.

The Press

Freedom of the press and publishing is guaranteed in the Constitution, although press censorship was in force between mid-1986 and early 1992 (when journalists adopted a voluntary code of practice); in February 1995 a ruling by the Constitutional Court effectively endorsed the Government's right to suspend publication of newspapers (see History). The Government provides financial support to newspapers and magazines. In 1999 there were eight daily and 20 weekly newspapers, and 196 periodicals.

DAILIES

Al-Anbaa (The News): POB 23915, 13100 Safat, Kuwait City; tel. 4831168; fax 4837914; f. 1976; Arabic; general; Editor-in-Chief BIBI KHALID AL-MARZOOQ; circ. 85,000.

Arab Times: POB 2270, 13023 Safat, Kuwait City; tel. 4813566; fax 4833628; f. 1977; English; political and financial; no Friday edition; Editor-in-Chief AHMAD ABD AL-AZIZ AL-JARALLAH; Man. Editor MISHAL AL-JARALLAH; circ. 41,922.

Kuwait Times: POB 1301, 13014 Safat, Kuwait City; tel. 4833199; fax 4835621; e-mail info@kuwaittimes.net; internet www.kuwaittimes.net; f. 1961; weekend edition also published; English, Malayalam and Urdu; political; Owner and Editor-in-Chief YOUSUF ALYYAN; Gen. Man. BADRYA DARWISH; circ. 32,000.

Al-Qabas (Firebrand): POB 21800, 13078 Safat, Kuwait City; tel. 4812822; fax 4834355; e-mail alqabas@ncc.moc.kw; internet www.moc.kw/alqabas; f. 1972; Arabic; independent; Gen. Man. FOUZAN AL-FARES; Editor-in-Chief WALEED ABD AL-LATIF AN-NISF; circ. 60,000.

Ar-Ra'i al-'Aam (Public Opinion): POB 761, 13008 Safat, Kuwait City; tel. 4817777; fax 4838352; f. 1961; Arabic; political, social and cultural; Editor-in-Chief YOUSUF AL-JALAHMA; circ. 101,500.

As-Seyassah (Policy): POB 2270, Shuwaikh, Kuwait City; tel. 4816326; fax 4833628; e-mail alsyasah@qualitynet.net; f. 1965; Arabic; political and financial; Editor-in-Chief AHMAD ABD AL-AZIZ AL-JARALLAH; circ. 70,000.

Al-Watan (The Homeland): POB 1142, 13012 Safat, Kuwait City; tel. 4840950; fax 4818481; e-mail webmaster@alwatan.com.kw; internet www.alwatan.com.kw; f. 1962; Arabic; political; Editor-in-Chief MUHAMMAD ABD AL-QADER AL-JASEM; Gen. Man. YOUSUF BIN JASEM; circ. 91,726.

WEEKLIES AND PERIODICALS

Al-Balagh (Communiqué): POB 4558, 13046 Safat, Kuwait City; tel. 4818606; fax 4819008; f. 1969; weekly; Arabic; general, political and Islamic; Editor-in-Chief ABD AR-RAHMAN RASHID AL-WALAYATI; circ. 29,000.

Ad-Dakhiliya (The Interior): POB 71655, 12500 Shamiah, Kuwait City; tel. 2410091; fax 2410609; e-mail moipr@qualitynet.net; monthly; Arabic; official reports, transactions and proceedings; publ. by Public Relations Dept, Ministry of the Interior; Editor-in-Chief Lt-Col AHMED A. ASH-SHARQAWI.

Al-Hadaf (The Objective): POB 2270, 13023 Safat, Kuwait City; tel. 4813566; fax 4833628; f. 1964; weekly; Arabic; social and cultural; Editor-in-Chief AHMAD ABD AL-AZIZ AL-JARALLAH; circ. 268,904.

Hayatuna (Our Life): POB 26733, 13128 Safat, Kuwait City; tel. 2530120; fax 2530736; f. 1968; fortnightly; Arabic; medicine and hygiene; publ. by Al-Awadi Press Corpn; Editor-in-Chief ABD AR-RAHMAN AL-AWADI; circ. 6,000.

Al-Iqtisadi al-Kuwaiti (Kuwaiti Economist): POB 775, 13008 Safat, Kuwait City; tel. 805580; fax 2412927; e-mail kcci@kcci.org.kw; internet www.kcci.org.kw; f. 1960; monthly; Arabic; commerce, trade and economics; publ. by Kuwait Chamber of Commerce and Industry; Editor MAJED JAMAL AD-DIN; circ. 6,000.

Journal of the Gulf and Arabian Peninsula Studies: POB 17073, 72451 Khaldiya, Kuwait University, Kuwait City; tel. 4833215; fax 4833705; e-mail jotgaaps@kuc01.kuniv.edu.kw; f. 1974; quarterly; Arabic; English; Editor-in-Chief Prof. AMAL YOUSUF AL-ADBAI AS-SABAH.

Al-Khaleej Business Magazine: POB 25725, 13118 Safat, Kuwait City; tel. 2433765; e-mail aljabriya@gulfweb.com; Editor-in-Chief AHMAD ISMAIL BEHBEHANI.

Kuwait al-Youm (Kuwait Today): POB 193, 13002 Safat, Kuwait City; tel. 4842167; fax 4831044; f. 1954; weekly; Arabic; statistics, Amiri decrees, laws, govt announcements, decisions, invitations for tenders, etc. publ. by the Ministry of Information; circ. 5,000.

Al-Kuwaiti (The Kuwaiti): Information Dept, POB 9758, 61008 Ahmadi, Kuwait City; tel. 3989111; fax 3983661; e-mail kocinfo@kockw.com; f. 1961; monthly journal of the Kuwait Oil Co; Arabic; Editor-in-Chief ALI H. MURAD; circ. 6,500.

The Kuwaiti Digest: Information Dept, POB 9758, 61008 Ahmadi, Kuwait City; tel. 3980651; fax 3983661; e-mail kocinfo@kockw.com; f. 1972; quarterly journal of Kuwait Oil Co; English; Editor-in-Chief RA'AD SALEM AL-JANDAL; circ. 7,000.

Kuwait Medical Journal (KMJ): POB 1202, 13013 Safat, Kuwait City; tel. 5317972; fax 5312630; e-mail kmj@kma.org.kw; internet www.kma.org.kw/kmj; f. 1967; quarterly; English; case reports, articles, reviews; Editor-in-Chief Dr NAEL AN-NAQEEB; circ. 10,000.

Al-Majaless (Meetings): POB 5605, 13057 Safat, Kuwait City; tel. 4841178; fax 4847126; weekly; Arabic; current affairs; Editor-in-Chief (vacant); circ. 60,206.

Mejallat al-Kuwait (Kuwait Magazine): POB 193, 13002 Safat, Kuwait City; tel. 2415300; fax 2419642; f. 1961; monthly; Arabic; illustrated magazine; science, arts and literature; publ. by Ministry of Information.

Mirat al-Umma (Mirror of the Nation): POB 1142, 13012 Safat, Kuwait City; tel. 4837212; fax 4838671; weekly; Arabic; Editor-in-Chief MUHAMMAD AL-JASSEM; circ. 79,500.

An-Nahdha (The Renaissance): POB 695, 13007 Safat, Kuwait City; tel. 4813133; fax 4849298; f. 1967; weekly; Arabic; social and political; Editor-in-Chief THAMER AS-SALAH; circ. 170,000.

Osrati (My Family): POB 2995, 13030 Safat, Kuwait City; tel. 4813233; fax 4838933; f. 1978; weekly; Arabic; women's magazine; publ. by Fahad al-Marzouk Establishment; Editor GHANIMA F. AL-MARZOUK; circ. 10,500.

Sawt al-Khaleej (Voice of the Gulf): POB 659, Safat, Kuwait City; tel. 4815590; fax 4839261; f. 1962; politics and literature; Arabic; Editor-in-Chief CHRISTINE KHRAIBET; Owner BAKER ALI KHRAIBET; circ. 20,000.

At-Talia (The Ascendant): POB 1082, 13011 Safat, Kuwait City; tel. 4831200; fax 4840471; f. 1962; weekly; Arabic; politics and literature; Editor AHMAD YOUSUF AN-NAFISI; circ. 10,000.

Al-Yaqza (The Awakening): POB 6000, 13060 Safat, Kuwait City; tel. 4831318; fax 4840630; f. 1966; weekly; Arabic; political, economic, social and general; Editor-in-Chief AHMAD YOUSUF BEHBEHANI; circ. 91,340.

Az-Zamed: POB 42181, 13150 Safat, Kuwait City; tel. 4848279; fax 4819985; f. 1961; weekly; Arabic; political, social and cultural; Editor SHAWQI RAFA'E.

NEWS AGENCIES

Kuwait News Agency (KUNA): POB 24063, 13101 Safat, Kuwait City; tel. 4834546; fax 4813424; e-mail kuna@kuna.net.kw; internet www.kuna.net.kw; f. 1976; public corporate body; independent; also publishes research digests on topics of common and special interest; Chair. and Dir-Gen. MUHAMMAD AL-AJEERI.

Foreign Bureaux

Informatsionnoye Telegrafnoye Agentstvo Rossii—Telegrafnoye Agentstvo Suverennykh Stran (ITAR—TASS) (Russia): POB 1765, 13018 Safat, Kuwait City; tel. and fax 5639260; Correspondent CONSTANTINE MATHULSKI.

Middle East News Agency (MENA) (Egypt): POB 1927, Safat, Fahd as-Salem St, Kuwait City; Dir REDA SOLIMAN.

Reuters Middle East Ltd (UK): POB 5616, 13057 Safat, Mubarak al-Kabir St, Kuwait Stock Exchange Bldg, 4th Floor, Kuwait City; tel. 2431920; fax 2460340; internet www.reuters.com/gulf; Country Man. ISSAM MAKKI.

Xinhua (New China) News Agency (People's Republic of China): POB 22168, Safat, Sheikh Ahmad al-Jaber Bldg, 10 Dasman St, Kuwait City; tel. 4809423; fax 4809396; Correspondent HUANG JIANMING.

AFP (France), **Agence Arabe Syrienne d'Information**, **Anatolian News Agency** (Turkey), **AP** (USA), **dpa** (Germany), **JANA** (Libya), **QNA** (Qatar) and **RIA—Novosti** (Russia) are also represented.

PRESS ASSOCIATION

Kuwait Journalist Association: POB 5454, Safat, Kuwait City; tel. 4843351; fax 4842874; Chair. YOUSUF ALYYAN.

Publishers

Al-Abraj Translation and Publishing Co WLL: POB 26177, 13122 Safat, Kuwait City; tel. 2444665; fax 2436889; Man. Dir Dr TARIQ ABDULLAH.

Dar as-Seyassah Publishing, Printing and Distribution Co: POB 2270, 13023 Safat, Kuwait City; tel. 4813566; fax 4833628; internet www.contactkuwait.com/dar-alseyasa; publ. *Arab Times*, *As-Seyassah* and *Al-Hadaf*.

Gulf Centre Publishing and Publicity: POB 2722, 13028 Safat, Kuwait City; tel. 2402760; fax 2458833; Propr HAMZA ISMAIL ESSLAH.

Kuwait Publishing House: POB 29126, 13150 Safat, Kuwait City; tel. 2417810; Dir ESAM AS'AD ABU AL-FARAJ.

Kuwait United Advertising, Publishing and Distribution Co WLL: POB 29359, 13153 Safat, Kuwait City; tel. 4817111; fax 4817797.

At-Talia Printing and Publishing Co: POB 1082, Airport Rd, Shuwaikh, 13011 Safat, Kuwait City; tel. 4840470; fax 4815611; Man. AHMAD YOUSUF AN-NAFISI.

Government Publishing House

Ministry of Information: POB 193, 13002 Safat, as-Sour St, Kuwait City; tel. 2433038; fax 2434715; e-mail info@moinfo.gov.kw; internet www.moinfo.gov.kw.

Broadcasting and Communications

TELECOMMUNICATIONS

Plans to privatize the state telecommunications sector, and to reorganize the Ministry of Communications as a company, designated the Kuwaiti Communications Corporation, initiated in 1998, were completed by 2000, although their implementation was subject to political approval.

Mobile Telecommunications Co (MTC): POB 22244, 1308 Safat, Kuwait City; tel. 4842000; fax 4837755; e-mail mtcweb@mtc.com.kw; internet www.mtc.com.kw; f. 1983; Chair. and Man. Dir SALMAN YOUSUF AR-ROUMI.

National Mobile Telecommunications Co KSC (Wataniya Telecom): POB 613, 13007 Safat, Kuwait City; tel. 2435500; fax 2436600; internet www.wataniya.com; f. 1998; Chair. and Man. Dir FAISAL HAMAD AL-AYYAR; CEO and Gen. Man. DAVID MURRAY.

BROADCASTING

Radio

Radio of the State of Kuwait: POB 397, 13004 Safat, Kuwait City; tel. 2423774; fax 2456660; e-mail radiokuwait@radiokuwait.org; internet www.radiokuwait.org; f. 1951; broadcasts for 70 hours daily in Arabic, Farsi, English and Urdu, some in stereo; Dir of Radio Dr ABD AL-AZIZ ALI MANSOUR; Dir of Radio Programmes ABD AR-RAHMAN HADI.

Television

Kuwait Television: POB 193, 13002 Safat, Kuwait City; tel. 2413501; fax 2438403; internet www.moinfo.gov.kw/KTV/index.html; f. 1961; transmission began privately in Kuwait in 1957; transmits in Arabic; colour television service began in 1973; has a total of five channels; Head of News Broadcasting MUHAMMAD AL-KAHTANI.

Plans were announced in early 1998 for the establishment of a private satellite broadcasting television channel, with administrative offices in Kuwait and transmission facilities in Dubai, United Arab Emirates.

Finance

(cap. = capital; res = reserves; dep. = deposits; m. = million; brs = branches; amounts in Kuwaiti dinars unless otherwise stated)

BANKING

Central Bank

Central Bank of Kuwait: POB 526, 13006 Safat, Abdullah as-Salem St, Kuwait City; tel. 2449200; fax 2464887; e-mail cbk@cbk.gov.kw; internet www.cbk.gov.kw; f. 1969; cap. 5m., res 230.2m., dep. 1,643.1m. (March 2001); Governor Sheikh SALEM ABD AL-AZIZ SA'UD AS-SABAH.

National Banks

Al-Ahli Bank of Kuwait KSC: POB 1387, 13014 Safat, Ahmad al-Jaber St, Safat Sq., Kuwait City; tel. 2400900; fax 2424557; e-mail headoffice@abkuwait.com; f. 1967; wholly owned by private Kuwaiti interests; cap. 87.9m., res 71.3m., dep. 999.7m. (Dec. 2001); Chair. MORAD YOUSUF BEHBEHANI; Gen. Man. and CEO ERVIN B. KNOX; 13 brs.

Bank of Bahrain and Kuwait: POB 24396, 13104 Safat, Ahmad al-Jaber St, Kuwait City; tel. 2417140; fax 2440937; e-mail bbk@batelco.com.bh; internet www.bbkonline.com; f. 1977; owned equally by the Govts of Bahrain and Kuwait; cap. BD56.9m., res BD34.2m., dep. BD896.3m. (Dec. 1999); Chair. HASSAN KHALIFA AL-JALAHMA; Gen. Man. and CEO MURAD ALI MURAD.

Bank of Kuwait and the Middle East KSC: POB 71, 13001 Safat, Joint Banking Centre, East Tower, Darwazat Abd ar-Razzak, Kuwait City; tel. 2459771; fax 2461430; e-mail bkmekw@qualitynet.net; internet www.bkme.com; f. 1971; 49% state-owned; cap. 70.4m., res 56.6m., dep. 903.6m. (Dec. 2001); Chair. MUSTAFA JASIM ASH-SHEMALI; Gen. Man. PHILIP ANTHONY HALPIN; 16 brs.

Burgan Bank SAK: POB 5389, 12170 Safat, Ahmad al-Jaber St, Kuwait City; tel. 2439000; fax 2461148; e-mail mainbr@burgan.com.kw; internet www.burgan.com; f. 1975; cap. 78.1m., res 100.6m., dep. 1,226.8m. (Dec. 2001); Chair. and Man. Dir ABD AL-AZIZ IBRAHIM AN-NABHAN; Chief Gen. Man. ROD GOOM; 16 brs.

Commercial Bank of Kuwait SAK: POB 2861, 13029 Safat, Mubarak al-Kabir St, Kuwait City; tel. 2411001; fax 245010; e-mail cbkinq@banktijari.com; internet www.cbk.com; f. 1960 by Amiri decree; cap. 106.4m., res 120.9m., dep. 1,314.2m. (Dec. 2001); Chair. and Man. Dir Sheikh MUHAMMAD JARRAH AS-SABAH; Gen. Man. (acting) and CEO JAMAL AL-MUTAWA; 28 brs.

Gulf Bank KSC: POB 3200, 13032 Safat, Mubarak al-Kabir St, Kuwait City; tel. 2449501; fax 2445212; e-mail customerservice@ gulfbank.com.kw; internet www.gulfbank.com.kw; f. 1960; cap. 82.1m., res 122.0m., dep. 1,611.5m. (Dec. 2001); Chair. and Man. Dir BASSAM Y. ALGHANIM; 26 brs.

Industrial Bank of Kuwait KSC: POB 3146, 13032 Safat, Joint Banking Centre, Commercial Area 9, Kuwait City; tel. 2457661; fax 2462057; e-mail em.ibk@ncc.moc.kw; internet www.ibkuwt.com; 31.4% state-owned; f. 1973; cap. 20.0m., res 115.9m., dep. 49.4m. (Dec. 2001); Chair. and Man. Dir SALEH MUHAMMAD AL-YOUSUF; Gen. Man. ALI ABD AN-NABI KHAJAH.

Kuwait Finance House KSC (KFH): POB 24989, 13110 Safat, Abdullah al-Mubarak St, Kuwait City; tel. 2445050; fax 2455135; e-mail kfh@kfh.com.kw; internet www.kfh.com; f. 1977; Islamic banking and investment company; 45% state-owned; cap. 65.0m., res 174.8m., dep. 1,857.1m. (Dec. 2001); Chair. and Man. Dir BADER ABD AL-MOHSEN AL-MUKHAISEEM; Gen. Man. JASSAR D. AL-JASSAR; 27 brs.

Kuwait Real Estate Bank KSC: POB 22822, 13089 Safat, West Tower—Joint Banking Centre, Darwazat Abd ar-Razzak, Kuwait City; tel. 2458177; fax 2462516; e-mail kreb@yahoo.com; internet www.akaribank.com; f. 1973; wholly owned by private Kuwaiti interests; cap. 43.5m., res 57.2m., dep. 471.1m. (Dec. 2001); Chair. ESSA MUHAMMAD AL-MAZIDI; Man. Dir WALID SALEH AL-QATTAN; 2 brs.

National Bank of Kuwait SAK (NBK): POB 95, 13001 Safat, Abdullah al-Ahmad St, Kuwait City; tel. 2422011; fax 2431888; e-mail webmaster@nbk.com; internet www.nbk.com; f. 1952; cap. 147.4m., res 231.4m., dep. 3,834.9m. (Dec. 2001); Chair. MUHAMMAD ABD AR-RAHMAN AL-BAHAR; CEO IBRAHIM S. DABDOUB; 41 brs in Kuwait, 14 abroad.

Savings and Credit Bank: POB 1454, 13015 Safat, ash-Shuhada St, Kuwait City; tel. 2411301; f. 1965; auth. cap. 2,500m. Chair. and Gen. Man. Dr JASEM M. AD-DABBOUS.

INSURANCE

Al-Ahleia Insurance Co SAK: POB 1602, Ahmad al-Jaber St, 13017 Safat, Kuwait City; tel. 2448870; fax 2430308; f. 1962; all forms of insurance; cap. 11.7m. Chair. and Man. Dir SULAYMAN HAMAD AD-DALALI; Gen. Man. TALAL SAKIR AL-QATAMI.

Al-Ittihad al-Watani Insurance Co for the Near East SAL: POB 781, 13008 Safat, Kuwait City; tel. 4843988; fax 4847244; Man. JOSEPH ZACCOUR.

Arab Commercial Enterprises WLL (Kuwait): POB 2474, 13025 Safat, Kuwait City; tel. 2425995; fax 2409450; e-mail acekwt@ ace-ins.com; f. 1952.

Gulf Insurance Co KSC: POB 1040, 13011 Safat, Kuwait City; tel. 2423384; fax 2422320; f. 1962; cap. 11.3m. all forms of insurance; Chair. FAISAL HAMAD AL-AYYAR.

Kuwait Insurance Co SAK (KIC): POB 769, 13008 Safat, Abdullah as-Salem St, Kuwait City; tel. 2420135; fax 2428530; e-mail info@kic-kw.com; internet www.kic-kw.com; f. 1960; cap. US $64.6m. all life and non-life insurance; Chair. MUHAMMAD SALEH BEHBEHANI; Gen. Man. ALI HAMAD AL-BAHAR.

Kuwait Reinsurance Company: POB 21929, Munther Tower, Salhiya, 13080 Safat, Kuwait City; tel. 2432011; fax 2427823; e-mail kuwaitre@qualitynet.net; f. 1972; cap. 10.0m. (March 2003); Gen. Man. AMIR AL-MUHANNA.

Kuwait Technical Insurance Office: POB 25349, 13114 Safat, Kuwait City; tel. 2413986; fax 2413986.

Mohd Saleh Behbehani & Co: POB 370, 13004 Safat, Kuwait City; tel. 2412085; fax 2412089.

New India Assurance Co: POB 370, 13004 Safat, Kuwait City; tel. 2412085; fax 2412089.

The Northern Insurance Co Ltd: POB 579, 13006 Safat, Kuwait City; tel. 2427930; fax 2462739.

The Oriental Insurance Co Ltd: POB 22431, 13085 Safat, Kuwait City; tel. 2424016; fax 2424017; Man. JUGAL KISHORE MADAAN.

Sumitomo Marine & Fire Insurance Co (Kuwait Agency): POB 3458, 13055 Safat, Kuwait City; tel. 2433087; fax 2430853.

Warba Insurance Co SAK: POB 24282, 13103 Safat, Kuwait City; tel. 2445140; fax 2466131; internet www.kuwait.net/~warba; f. 1976; Chair. ABDULLAH HASSAN JARALLAH; 1 br.

Some 20 Arab and other foreign insurance companies are active in Kuwait.

STOCK EXCHANGE

Kuwait Stock Exchange: POB 22235, 13083 Safat, Mubarak al-Kabir St, Kuwait City; tel. 2423130; fax 2429771; e-mail borse@ qualitynet.net; internet www.kuwaitse.com; f. 1983; 96 companies and five mutual funds listed in March 2003; Dir-Gen. SAFAQ ABDULLAH AR-RUKAIBI.

Markets Association

Kuwait Financial Markets Association (KFMA): POB 25228, 13113 Safat, Kuwait City; internet www.kfma.org.kw; f. 1977; represents treasury, financial and capital markets and their members; Pres. THUNAYAN AL-GHANIM; Sec.-Gen. ZUHAIR AL-JUMA.

Trade and Industry

GOVERNMENT AGENCY

Kuwait Investment Authority (KIA): POB 64, 13001 Safat, Kuwait City; tel. 2439595; fax 2454059; e-mail webmaster@kia.gov .kw; internet www.kia.gov.kw; oversees the Kuwait Investment Office (London); responsible for the Kuwaiti General Reservecntry.sh kw 2469, Chair. Minister of Finance; Man. Dir SALEH MUBARAK AL-FALAH.

DEVELOPMENT ORGANIZATIONS

Arab Planning Institute (API): POB 5834, 13059 Safat, Kuwait City; tel. 4843130; fax 4842935; e-mail api@api.org.kw; f. 1966; 50 mems; publishes annual directory, *Journal of Development and Economic Policies* and proceedings of seminars and discussion group meetings, offers research, training programmes and advisory services; Dir ESSA ALGHAZALI.

Industrial Investments Company (IIC): POB 26019, 13121 Safat, Kuwait City; tel. 2429073; fax 2448850; f. 1983; invests directly in industry; partly owned by the Kuwait Investment Authority; privatization initiated in April 1996; Man. Dir TALEB A. ALI.

Kuwait Fund for Arab Economic Development (KFAED): POB 2921, 13030 Safat, cnr Mubarak al-Kabir St and al-Hilali St, Kuwait City; tel. 2468800; fax 2436289; e-mail info@kuwait-fund.org; internet www.kuwait-fund.org; f. 1961; cap. KD 2,000m. state-owned; provides and administers financial and technical assistance to the countries of the developing world, Chair. Minister of Finance; Dir-Gen. BADER M. AL-HUMAIDHI.

Kuwait International Investment Co SAK (KIIC): POB 22792, 13088 Safat, as-Salhiya Commercial Complex, Kuwait City; tel. 2438273; fax 2454931; 30% state-owned; cap. p.u. 31.9m., total assets KD 146.9m. (1988); domestic real estate and share markets; Chair. and Man. Dir JASEM MUHAMMAD AL-BAHAR.

Kuwait Investment Co SAK (KIC): POB 1005, 13011 Safat, 5th Floor, al-Manakh Bldg, Mubarak al-Kabir St, Kuwait City; tel. 2438111; fax 2444896; e-mail info@kic.com.kw; f. 1981; 88% state-owned, 12% owned by private Kuwaiti interests; total resources KD 50.1m. (1996); international banking and investment; Chair. and Man. Dir BADER A. AR-RUSHAID AL-BADER.

Kuwait Planning Board: c/o Ministry of Planning, POB 21688, 13122 Safat, Kuwait City; tel. 2428200; fax 2414734; f. 1962; supervises long-term development plans; through its Central Statistical Office publishes information on Kuwait's economic activity; Dir-Gen. AHMAD ALI AD-DUALJ.

National Industries Co SAK (NIC): POB 417, 13005 Safat, Kuwait City; tel. 4815466; fax 4839582; f. 1960; 22.7% owned by KIA; cap. p.u. KD 34.9m. has controlling interest in various construction enterprises; privatization initiated in March 1995; Chair. and Man. Dir SAUD M. AL-OSMANI.

Shuaiba Area Authority SAA: POB 4690, 13047 Safat, Kuwait City; POB 10033, Shuaiba; tel. 3260903; f. 1964; an independent governmental authority to supervise and run the industrial area and Port of Shuaiba; has powers and duties to develop the area and its industries which include an oil refinery, cement factory, fishing plant, power stations and distillation plants, chemical fertilizer and petrochemical industries, sanitary ware factory, asbestos plant and sand lime bricks plant; Dir-Gen. SULAYMAN K. AL-HAMAD.

CHAMBER OF COMMERCE

Kuwait Chamber of Commerce and Industry: POB 775, 13008 Safat, Chamber's Bldg, ash-Shuhada St, Kuwait City; tel. 805580; fax 2404110; e-mail kcci@kcci.org.kw; internet www.kcci.org.kw; f. 1959; 50,000 mems; Chair. ABD AR-RAZZAK KHALID ZAID AL-KHALID; Dir-Gen. AHMAD RASHED AL-HAROUN.

STATE HYDROCARBONS COMPANIES

Kuwait Petroleum Corpn (KPC): POB 26565, 13126 Safat, as-Salhiya Commercial Complex, Fahed as-Salem St, Kuwait City; tel. 2455455; fax 2467159; e-mail webmaster@kpc.com.kw; internet www.kpc.com.kw; f. 1980; co-ordinating organization to manage the petroleum industry; controls Kuwait Aviation Fuelling Co (KAFCO), Kuwait Foreign Petroleum Exploration Co (KUFPEC), Kuwait National Petroleum Co (KNPC), Kuwait Oil Co (KOC), Kuwait Oil Tanker Co (KOTC), Kuwait Petroleum International Ltd (KPI), Petrochemical Industries Co (PIC), Santa Fe International Corpn (SFIC); Chair. Minister of Oil; Deputy Chair. and CEO NADER HAMAD SULTAN.

Kuwait Aviation Fuelling Co KSC: POB 1654, 13017 Safat, Kuwait City; tel. 4330482; fax 4330475; Gen. Man. ABD AL-AZIZ AS-SERRI.

Kuwait Foreign Petroleum Exploration Co KSC (KUFPEC): POB 5291, 13053 Safat, Kuwait City; tel. 2421677; fax 2420405; f. 1981; state-owned; overseas oil and gas exploration and development; Chair. and Man. Dir BADER AL-KHASHTI.

Kuwait National Petroleum Co KSC (KNPC): POB 70, 13001 Safat, Ali as-Salem St, Kuwait City; tel. 2420121; fax 2433839; f. 1960; oil refining, production of liquefied petroleum gas, and domestic marketing and distribution of petroleum by-products; output of 855,000 b/d of refined petroleum in 1996/97; Chair. and Man. Dir HANI ABD AL-AZIZ HUSSEIN.

Kuwait Oil Co KSC (KOC): POB 9758, 61008 Ahmadi; tel. 3989111; fax 3983661; e-mail kocinfo@kockw.com; internet www.kockw.com; f. 1934; state-owned; Chair. and Man. Dir AHMAD AL-ARBEED.

Kuwait Petroleum International Ltd (Q8) (KPI): POB 1819, 13019 Safat, Chamber of Commerce and Industry Bldg, Al-Murgab, Mubarak al-Kabir St, Kuwait City; tel. 2404087; fax 2407523; internet www.q8.com; marketing division of KPC; controls 6,500 petrol retail stations in Europe, and European refineries with capacity of 235,000 b/d; Pres. KAMEL HARAMI.

UTILITIES

In 1998 there were plans to create regulatory bodies for each of Kuwait's utilities, with a view to facilitating their privatization.

Ministry of Electricity and Water: see Ministries (above); provides subsidized services throughout Kuwait.

TRADE UNIONS

Kuwait Trade Union Federation (KTUF): POB 5185, 13052 Safat, Kuwait City; tel. 5616053; fax 5627159; e-mail ktuf@hotmail.com.com; f. 1968; central authority to which all trade unions are affiliated.

KOC Workers Union: Kuwait City; f. 1964; Chair. HAMAD SAWYAN.

Federation of Petroleum and Petrochemical Workers: Kuwait City; f. 1965; Chair. JASEM ABD AL-WAHAB AT-TOURA.

Transport

RAILWAYS

There are no railways in Kuwait.

ROADS

Roads in the towns are metalled, and the most important are motorways or dual carriageways. There are metalled roads linking Kuwait City to Ahmadi, Mina al-Ahmadi and other centres of population in Kuwait, and to the Iraqi and Saudi Arabian borders, amounting to a total road network of 4,273 km in 1989 (280 km of motorways, 1,232 km of other major roads and 2,761 km of secondary roads). The total road network was estimated at 4,450 km in 1999.

Kuwait Public Transport Co SAK (KPTC): POB 375, 13004 Safat, Murghab, Safat Sq., Kuwait City; tel. 2469420; fax 2401265; e-mail info@kptc.com.kw; f. 1962; state-owned; provides internal bus service; regular service to Mecca, Saudi Arabia; Chair. and Man. Dir MAHMOUD A. AN-NOURI.

SHIPPING

Kuwait has three commercial seaports. The largest, Shuwaikh, situated about 3 km from Kuwait City, was built in 1960. By 1987 it comprised 21 deep-water berths, with a total length of 4 km, three shallow-water berths and three basins for small craft, each with a depth of 3.35 m. In 1988 3.6m. metric tons of cargo were imported and 133,185 tons were exported through the port. A total of 1,189 vessels passed through Shuwaikh in 1988.

Shuaiba Commercial Port, 56 km south of Kuwait City, was built in 1967 to facilitate the import of primary materials and heavy equipment, necessary for the construction of the Shuaiba Industrial Area. By 1987 the port comprised a total of 20 berths, plus two docks for small wooden boats. Four of the berths constitute a station for unloading containers. Shuaiba handled a total of 3,457,871 metric tons of dry cargo, barge cargo and containers in 1988.

Doha, the smallest port, was equipped in 1981 to receive small coastal ships carrying light goods between the Gulf states. It has 20 small berths, each 100 m long. Doha handled a total of 20,283 metric tons of dry cargo, barge cargo and containers in 1988.

The oil port at Mina al-Ahmadi, 40 km south of Kuwait City, is capable of handling the largest oil tankers afloat, and the loading of over 2m. barrels of oil per day. By 1987 the port comprised 12 tanker berths, one bitumen-carrier berth, two LPG export berths and bunkering facilities.

At 31 December 2001 Kuwait's merchant fleet numbered 200 vessels, with a total displacement of 2,291,672 grt.

Kuwait Ports Authority: POB 3874, 13039 Safat, Kuwait City; tel. 4812774; fax 4819714; f. 1977; Dir-Gen. ABD AR-RAHMAN AN-NAIBARI.

Principal Shipping Companies

Arab Maritime Petroleum Transport Co (AMPTC): POB 22525, 13086 Safat, OAPEC Bldg, Shuwaikh, Airport St, Kuwait City; tel. 4844500; fax 4842996; e-mail amptc@ncc.moc.kw; f. 1973; 7 tankers and 4 LPG carriers; sponsored by OAPEC and financed by Algeria, Bahrain, Egypt, Iraq, Kuwait, Libya, Qatar, Saudi Arabia and the UAE; Chair. Dr RAMADAN AS-SANUSSI BELHAG (Libya); Gen. Man. SULAYMAN I. AL-BASSAM.

Kuwait Maritime Transport Co KSC (KMTC): POB 25344, 13086 Safat, Nafisi and Khatrash Bldg, Jaber al-Mubarak St, Kuwait City; tel. 2449974; fax 2420513; f. 1981; Chair. FOUAD M. T. AL-GHANIM.

Kuwait Oil Tanker Co SAK (KOTC): POB 810, 13009 Safat, as-Salhiya Commercial Complex, Blocks 3, 5, 7 and 9, Kuwait City; tel. 2455455; fax 2445907; e-mail ysm@kotc.com.kw; internet www.kotc.com.kw; f. 1957; state-owned; operates six crude oil tankers, 16 product tankers and six LPG vessels; sole tanker agents for Mina al-Ahmadi, Shuaiba and Mina Abdullah and agents for other ports; LPG filling and distribution; Chair. and Man. Dir ABDULLAH HAMAD AR-ROUMI.

Kuwait Shipbuilding and Repairyard Co SAK (KSRC): POB 21998, 13080 Safat, Kuwait City; tel. 4830308; fax 4815947; e-mail mahmoud@ksrc.com.kw; internet www.ksrc.com.kw; ship repairs and engineering services, underwater services, maintenance of refineries, power stations and storage tanks; maintains floating dock for vessels up to 35,000 dwt; synchrolift for vessels up to 5,000 dwt with transfer yard; seven repair jetties up to 550 m in length and floating workshop for vessels lying at anchor; Chair. and Man. Dir MOUSA J. MARAFI; Commercial Man. MAHMOUD ASAD.

United Arab Shipping Co SAG (UASC): POB 3636, 13037 Safat, Shuwaikh, Airport Rd, Kuwait City; tel. 4843150; fax 4845388; e-mail gencom@uasc.com.kw; internet www.uasc.com.kw; f. 1976; national shipping company of six Arabian Gulf countries; services between Europe, Far East, Mediterranean ports, Japan and east coast of USA and South America, and ports of participant states on Persian (Arabian) Gulf and Red Sea; operates 24 container carriers and 27 general cargo vessels; subsidiary cos: Kuwait Shipping Agencies, Arab Transport Co (Aratrans), United Arab Chartering Ltd (United Kingdom), Middle East Container Repair Co (Dubai), Arabian Chemicals Carriers (Saudi Arabia), United Arab Agencies Inc. (USA) and United Arab Shipping Agencies Co (Saudi Arabia); Pres. and CEO ABDULLAH MAHDI AL-MAHDI.

CIVIL AVIATION

Kuwait International Airport opened in 1980, and is designed to receive up to 5.0m. passengers per year; in 2001 3.82m. arrivals and departures were recorded. The airport is undergoing a major programme of expansion, at a cost of some US $300m.

Directorate-General of Civil Aviation (DGCA): POB 17, 13001 Safat, Kuwait City; tel. 4335599; fax 4713504; e-mail isc@kuwait-airport.com.kw; internet www.kuwait-airport.com.kw; Pres. Sheikh JABER AL-MUBARAK AS-SABAH; Dir-Gen. YACOUB Y. AS-SAQER.

Kuwait Airways Corpn (KAC): POB 394, Kuwait International Airport, 13004 Safat, Kuwait City; tel. 4345555; fax 4314118; e-mail info@kuwait-airways.com; internet www.kuwait-airways.com; f. 1954; scheduled and charter passenger and cargo services to the Arabian peninsula, Asia, Africa, the USA and Europe; scheduled for privatization; Chair. and Man. Dir AHMAD FAISAL AZ-ZABIN.

Tourism

Attractions for visitors include the Kuwait Towers leisure and reservoir complex, the Entertainment City theme park, the Kuwait Zoological Garden in Omariya and the Khiran Resort tourist village near the border with Saudi Arabia, as well as extensive facilities for sailing and other water sports. In 2000 there were 20 hotels with a total of 2,857 beds for visitors.

Department of Tourism: Ministry of Information, POB 193, 13002 Safat, as-Sour St, Kuwait City; tel. 2463400; fax 2464460.

Touristic Enterprises Co (TEC): POB 23310, 13094 Safat, Kuwait City; tel. 5652775; fax 5657594; f. 1976; 92% state-owned; manages 23 tourist facilities; Chair. BADER AL-BAHAR; Vice-Chair. SHAKER AL-OTHMAN.

KYRGYZSTAN

Introductory Survey

Location, Climate, Language, Religion, Flag, Capital

The Kyrgyz Republic (formerly the Kyrgyz Soviet Socialist Republic and, between December 1990 and May 1993, the Republic of Kyrgyzstan) is a small, land-locked state situated in eastern Central Asia. The country has also been known as Kyrgyzia (or Kirghizia). It borders Kazakhstan to the north, Uzbekistan to the west, Tajikistan to the south and west, and the People's Republic of China to the east. There are distinct variations in climate between low-lying and high-altitude areas. In the valleys the mean July temperature is 28°C (82°F), whereas in January it falls to an average of −18°C (−0.5°F). Annual rainfall ranges from 180 mm (7 ins) in the eastern Tien Shan mountains to 750 mm–1,000 mm (30 ins–39 ins) in the Fergana mountain range. In the settled valleys the annual average varies between 100 mm and 500 mm (4 ins–20 ins). The state language is Kyrgyz; Russian additionally has the status of an official language. The major religion is Islam, with the majority of ethnic Kyrgyz being Sunni Muslims of the Hanafi school. The national flag (proportions 3 by 5) consists of a red field, at the centre of which is a yellow sun, with 40 counter-clockwise rays surrounding a red-bordered yellow disc, on which are superimposed two intersecting sets of three red, curved, narrow bands. The capital is Bishkek (called Frunze between 1926 and 1991).

Recent History

Following the October Revolution of 1917 in Russia, Kyrgyzia (which had been formally incorporated into the Russian Empire in 1876) experienced a period of civil war, with anti-Bolshevik forces, including the Russian 'White' Army and local armed groups (*basmachi*), fighting against the Bolshevik Red Army. Soviet power was established in the region by 1919. In 1918 the Turkestan Autonomous Soviet Socialist Republic (ASSR) was established within the Russian Soviet Federative Socialist Republic (the Russian Federation) and included Kyrgyzia until 1924, when the Kara-Kyrgyz Autonomous Oblast (Region) was created. (At this time the Russians used the term Kara-Kyrgyz to distinguish the Kyrgyz from the Kazakhs, then also known as Kyrgyz by the Russians.) In 1925 the region was renamed the Kyrgyz Autonomous Oblast, and it became the Kyrgyz ASSR in February 1926. On 5 December 1936 the Kyrgyz Soviet Socialist Republic (SSR) was established as a full union republic of the USSR.

During the 1920s considerable economic and social developments were made in Kyrgyzia, when land reforms resulted in the settlement of many of the nomadic Kyrgyz. The agricultural collectivization programme of the early 1930s was strongly opposed in the republic and prompted a partial revival of the *basmachi* movement.

Despite the suppression of nationalism under Stalin (Iosif V. Dzhugashvili—Soviet leader in 1924–53), many aspects of Kyrgyz national culture were retained. Leading members of the Kyrgyz Communist Party (KCP) attempted to increase the role of ethnic Kyrgyz in the government of the republic, but these so-called 'national communists' were expelled from the KCP and often imprisoned or exiled, particularly during the late 1930s. Tensions with the all-Union (Soviet) authorities continued following the death of Stalin in 1953. There were, notably, allegations that the murder in December 1980 of Sultan Ibraimov, the Chairman of the Kyrgyz Council of Ministers, was a result of his support for greater republican autonomy.

The election of Mikhail Gorbachev as Soviet leader in 1985, and his introduction of the policies of *perestroika* (restructuring) and *glasnost* (openness), led to the resignation of Turdakan Usubaliyev as First Secretary of the KCP. His successor, Absamat Masaliyev, accused Usubaliyev of corruption and nepotism, and dismissed many of his closest allies from office. However, Masaliyev's commitment to Gorbachev's reforms did not extend much beyond correcting the excesses of his predecessor. None the less, the republic's Supreme Soviet adopted Kyrgyz as the official language, and Russian was retained as a language of inter-ethnic communication. The conservative Kyrgyz leadership opposed the development of unofficial quasi-political groups, several of which were established with the aim of alleviating the republic's acute housing shortage by seizing vacant land. One such group, Ashar, was partially tolerated by the authorities and soon developed a wider political role.

Osh Aymaghi, a similar organization to Ashar, based in Osh Oblast, attempted to obtain land and housing provision for ethnic Kyrgyz in the region. (Osh had been incorporated into Kyrgyzia in 1924, although Uzbeks formed the majority of the population, and these had recently begun to demand the establishment of an Uzbek autonomous region there.) Disputes over land and homes in the crowded Fergana valley region of Osh precipitated violent confrontation between Kyrgyz and Uzbeks in 1990, in which, according to official reports, more than 300 people died (although other sources cited as many as 1,000 deaths). A state of emergency (which remained in force until 1995) and a curfew were introduced in the region, and the Uzbek–Kyrgyz border was closed.

Despite the growing influence of the nascent democratic movement, elections to the 350-member Kyrgyz Supreme Soviet (legislature) in February 1990 were conducted along Soviet lines, with KCP candidates winning most seats unopposed. In April Masaliyev was elected to the new office of Chairman of the Supreme Soviet. He favoured the introduction of an executive presidency, election to which was to be by the Supreme Soviet. The strong KCP majority in the legislature appeared to guarantee Masaliyev's election. However, by October, when an extraordinary session of the Supreme Soviet was convened to elect the President, Masaliyev had been seriously discredited by the conflict in Osh; moreover, the opposition, which had united as the Democratic Movement of Kyrgyzstan (DMK), had become a significant political force. In the first round of voting Masaliyev failed to achieve the requisite proportion of votes to be elected and he was refused permission to be renominated. In a further round Askar Akayev, the President of the Kyrgyz Academy of Sciences, was elected to the executive presidency. Akayev quickly allied himself with reformist politicians and economists, including leaders of the DMK. A State Committee for Economic Reform was appointed and plans were announced for an extensive programme of privatization. In December Masaliyev resigned as Chairman of the Supreme Soviet, and was replaced by Medetkan Sherimkulov. In that month, despite opposition from the KCP (and Masaliyev in particular), the Kyrgyz Supreme Soviet voted to change the name of the republic from the Kyrgyz SSR to the Republic of Kyrgyzstan. In February 1991, moreover, the capital, Frunze (named after the Red Army commander who had conquered much of Central Asia in the Civil War), reverted to its pre-1926 name of Bishkek. However, economic realities appeared to prevail against secession. In the referendum on the preservation of the USSR, held in nine republics in March, an overwhelming majority (87.7%) of eligible voters in Kyrgyzstan approved the proposal to retain the USSR as a 'renewed federation'.

In January 1991 Akayev replaced the unwieldy Council of Ministers with a smaller Cabinet, comprising mainly reformist politicians. However, his programme of political and economic reform had many opponents within the KCP and the security forces. In April, apparently owing to differences with Akayev, Masaliyev resigned as First Secretary of the KCP; he was replaced by Jumgalbek Amanbayev. Although Amanbayev appeared more sympathetic to Akayev's reform programme, there was much opposition within the KCP leadership to controversial plans for the 'departyization' (removal of KCP cells from workplaces) of government and the security forces.

In August 1991, when the State Committee for the State of Emergency (SCSE) announced that it had assumed power in the Russian and Soviet capital, Moscow, there was an attempt to depose Akayev in Kyrgyzstan. The KCP declared its support for the coup leaders, and the commander of the Turkestan Military District (which comprised the five Central Asian republics) threatened to dispatch troops and tanks to the republic. To pre-empt military action against him, Akayev dismissed the Chairman of the republican KGB (state security service), and ordered troops of the Ministry of Internal Affairs to guard strategic buildings in Bishkek. Akayev publicly denounced the coup and issued a decree prohibiting activity by any political party in government or state bodies. After the coup had collapsed in Moscow, Akayev and Vice-President German Kuznetsov renounced their membership of the Communist Party of the Soviet Union (CPSU), and the entire politburo and secretariat of the KCP resigned. On 31 August the Kyrgyz Supreme Soviet voted to declare independence from the USSR. Akayev (the sole candidate) was re-elected President of Kyrgyzstan by direct popular vote on 12 October, receiving 95% of the votes cast.

In October 1991 Akayev signed, with representatives of seven other republics, a treaty to establish a new economic community, and when Russia, Belarus and Ukraine proposed the creation of the Commonwealth of Independent States (CIS, see p. 172), Akayev was quick to announce his approval. On 21 December Kyrgyzstan was among the 11 signatories to the Almaty (Alma-Ata) Declaration, which formally established the CIS.

As in other former Soviet republics, a serious issue confronting Kyrgyzstan's Government following independence was the rapid increase in criminal activity—in particular the cultivation of, and trade in, illicit drugs. Akayev emphasized his commitment to combating both organized crime and official corruption, which he denounced as impediments to the reform process. Despite the deteriorating economic situation, Akayev's economic and political reforms (considered to be the most radical of those taking place in the Central Asian republics) appeared to enjoy continued popular support. However, his policies were increasingly opposed in the legislature, notably by nationalist and former communist elements. In mid-1992 the KCP was revived, with Amanbayev as its Chairman.

Discussions were held throughout 1992 to draft a new constitution, during which opposition forces demanded the restriction of the President's powers and a stronger role for the legislature. The Constitution, which was finally promulgated on 5 May 1993, provided for a parliamentary system of government, with the Prime Minister as head of the executive (the Government had hitherto been subordinate to the President). Legislative power was to be vested in a smaller (105-member) Zhogorku Kenesh, following a general election that was due to be held by 1995; in the mean time, the existing assembly would continue to act as the republic's parliament.

The new Constitution partly mitigated the growing concern among Kyrgyzstan's large Slav community and other ethnic groups that their civil rights were insufficiently protected. (In mid-1993 it was estimated that some 145,000 Russians had left the republic since 1989.) Despite attempts by nationalist deputies to retain Kyrgyz as the sole state language (there was no reference to Russian in the draft Constitution adopted in December 1992), in May 1993 the legislature voted to accord Russian the constitutional status of a language of inter-ethnic communication. However, the country's official name was changed from the Republic of Kyrgyzstan to the less ethnically neutral Kyrgyz Republic. Akayev's attempts to encourage non-Kyrgyz to remain in the republic suffered a serious reverse in July, when Kuznetsov (now the First Deputy Prime Minister), the most prominent Slav in government, announced his decision to return to Russia, claiming 'isolation' within the Kyrgyz administration.

Akayev's presidency was further destabilized during 1993 by a series of corruption scandals, which his supporters claimed were orchestrated by communist and nationalist forces, in an attempt to discredit the reformists. In March a commission of inquiry was appointed to investigate the business dealings of the Vice-President, Feliks Kulov. A second commission was established by the legislature later in the year to examine allegations that senior politicians—including the Prime Minister (since February 1992), Tursunbek Chyngyshev—had been involved in unauthorized gold exports. In December 1993 Kulov resigned as Vice-President 'for ethical reasons', urging the Government to do likewise. The legislature subsequently held a vote of confidence in Chyngyshev and his Government: the motion failed to achieve the required two-thirds' majority and Akayev dismissed the entire Cabinet. Later in the month the legislature approved a new Government, headed by Apas Jumagulov (Chairman of the Council of Ministers in 1986–91). The Government's composition was largely ethnic Kyrgyz, although it included one representative each of the Russian, German, Uzbek and Jewish communities. Amanbayev was appointed one of the six Deputy Prime Ministers and, following a parliamentary decree that

government ministers could not remain members of the legislature, he resigned his seat in the Kenesh, and also the leadership of the KCP. A referendum of confidence in the presidency was held (on Akayev's initiative) in January 1994, at which 96.2% of voters endorsed Akayev's leadership.

In June 1994, in an attempt to curb the rate of emigration from Kyrgyzstan (more than 100,000 people—mainly Russians —were reported to have left the country in that year), Akayev announced that Russian was henceforth to have the status of official language in regions predominantly populated by Russian-speakers, as well as in areas of economic importance. The procedure of application for dual citizenship was to be simplified and the equitable representation of ethnic Russians in the state administration was to be guaranteed. Akayev also requested that the Government delay the final date for the full establishment of Kyrgyz as the official state language from 1995 to 2000 (subsequently extended until 2005). A resolution based on Akayev's decree was adopted by the Zhogorku Kenesh in March 1996. This measure, together with the opening of a Slavonic university in Bishkek in 1993, probably contributed to the decline in the number of Russians emigrating from the republic, estimated at 20,000 in 1996.

Divisions within the legislature evolved into a parliamentary crisis in September 1994, when more than 180 pro-reform deputies announced their intention to boycott the next session of the Zhogorku Kenesh, in protest at the continuing obstruction by former communists of the economic reform process; they also demanded the dissolution of the Kenesh and the holding of fresh elections. The entire Government tendered its resignation, and Akayev announced that parliamentary elections would be held forthwith; opponents of the President suggested that the Government's resignation had been orchestrated in order to precipitate the removal of an obstructionist legislature. The Government was promptly reinstated by Akayev, who announced the holding of a referendum in October on constitutional amendments. Of the 87% of the electorate who participated, more than 70% endorsed proposals for a restructured Zhogorku Kenesh comprising a 70-member People's Assembly (upper chamber) to represent regional interests at twice-yearly sessions and a permanent 35-member Legislative Assembly (lower chamber) representing the population as a whole. The existing legislature was thus automatically dissolved.

More than 1,000 candidates, representing 15 ethnic groups, contested the elections to the two chambers of the new Zhogorku Kenesh, held on 5 February 1995, with the participation of some 62% of the electorate. However, only 16 seats were filled (since in many constituencies the large number of candidates prevented any individual from receiving the requisite minimum proportion of the votes cast). A second round was held on 19 February (again with a participation rate of 62%); however, voting did not take place in some constituencies, thus only 73 of the remaining 89 seats were filled. The Zhogorku Kenesh was, none the less, quorate, and its two chambers held their inaugural sessions on 28 March; Mukar Cholponbayev, a former Minister of Justice, was elected Speaker of the Legislative Assembly, while Almambet Matubraimov, a former First Deputy Prime Minister, was elected Speaker of the People's Assembly. The vacant seats in the lower chamber were subsequently filled. In April Jumagulov was reappointed Prime Minister and the remaining members of the Government (mostly ethnic Kyrgyz) were named later in the month.

An estimated 1.2m. signatures were collected by supporters of Akayev in August 1995, in favour of a proposal to hold a referendum on extending the President's term of office until 2001. The campaign appeared to have been inspired by similar votes held in 1994 and 1995 in the neighbouring Central Asian republics of Kazakhstan, Turkmenistan and Uzbekistan, as a result of which the respective Presidents had had their mandates extended without seeking re-election. In Kyrgyzstan, however, the referendum proposal was vetoed by the Legislative Assembly and a direct presidential election was scheduled for 24 December. Akayev emerged as the victor, receiving a reported 71.6% of the votes cast; Masaliyev (who had recently been reinstated as the leader of the KCP) won 24.4% of the votes. Some 82% of the registered electorate were reported to have voted.

Akayev was inaugurated on 30 December 1995. One of his first acts was to decree that a referendum be held on increasing the powers of the President's office, while limiting those of the legislature. A reported 96.6% of the electorate participated in the referendum, on 10 February 1996, of whom 94.3% endorsed the proposed amendments to the Constitution. The Government resigned later that month; Jumagulov was reinstated as Prime Minister in March and a new Government was appointed by Akayev shortly afterwards.

In September 1996, following an investigation into claims of government corruption, several leading officials were dismissed for serious financial impropriety, and senior members of the Government were severely reprimanded. The First Deputy Prime Minister was relieved of his duties in a government reorganization effected in December, amid speculation that he had been implicated in the scandal. Meanwhile, in November Cholponbayev was replaced as Speaker of the Legislative Assembly by Usup Mukambayev, after the Constitutional Court declared his election to have been invalid, since he had failed to obtain an overall majority vote.

Protests held in Bishkek in June 1997, against the imprisonment of two journalists of an independent opposition newspaper, who had been found guilty of libel against the Director of the state gold concern, Kyrgyzaltyn, resulted in clashes with security forces; the journalists' sentences were subsequently reduced. Legislation imposing reporting restrictions on the media, approved by the Zhogorku Kenesh in November, was criticized by the Kyrgyz Committee for Human Rights as a violation of press freedom. In January 1998 the promulgation of a new criminal code that included the abolition of the death penalty (with a moratorium on its implementation) was described by the Government as a measure to comply with international legal standards. However, the adoption by the Zhogorku Kenesh, in February, of draft legislation concerning the organization of public gatherings, whereby permission to hold a rally was to be sought from the local authorities at least 20 days prior to the planned event, appeared to be a further restriction of civil rights.

In March 1998 Jumagulov announced his retirement. The Zhogorku Kenesh endorsed the appointment of Kuvachbek Jumaliyev as the new Prime Minister, and a cabinet reorganization was effected. An extensive cabinet reshuffle undertaken in early April to accelerate economic and political reform included a reduction in the number of ministries and the abolition of two of the three posts of Deputy Prime Minister.

In July 1998 the Constitutional Court ruled in favour of allowing Akayev to seek a third term in the presidential election due to be held in 2000, following an appeal by a group of Zhogorku Kenesh deputies who claimed that, although the 1993 Constitution allowed a President to serve a maximum of two terms, Akayev's election in 1991 had taken place under the previous Soviet Constitution. In early September Akayev announced that a referendum would be held on proposed amendments to the system of parliamentary elections, prompting strong criticism from members of the Zhogorku Kenesh, which had not been advised of the planned changes. Early the following month the Ministry of Justice banned the Kyrgyz Committee for Human Rights, citing irregularities in the adoption of its 1996 charter. However, the Chairman of the organization, Ramazan Dyryldayev, alleged that the ban had been imposed as a result of the group's anti-Government stance, and to prevent it from acting as an observer at the referendum. The referendum took place on 17 October 1998, with the participation of about 96% of the electorate, and some 90% of voters approved the following constitutional amendments proposed by Akayev: the number of deputies in the Legislative Assembly was to increase to 60, and representation in the People's Assembly was to be reduced to 45; the electoral system was to be reformed; restrictions on parliamentary immunity were to be introduced; private land ownership was to be legalized; 'budgetary populism' (the presentation of unbalanced or unattainable budgets) was to be banned; and the adoption of any legislation restricting freedom of speech or of the press was to be prohibited. The Zhogorku Kenesh and the majority of political parties declared their opposition to the changes and, in particular, to the introduction of private land ownership, which they feared would result in the transfer of land to foreign owners. In August 1999 the Kyrgyz Committee for Human Rights was re-registered, following pressure from the international community. Facing arrest in July 2000, however, Dyryldayev fled to Vienna, Austria, from where he continued to oversee the work of the Committee.

It was announced in mid-December 1998 that a number of senior government officials, including three deputy ministers, had been arrested on charges of corruption and abuse of office. This action constituted an intensification of Akayev's campaign against financial crime and corruption, as a result of which 383

government officials had been dismissed since 1993. In late December 1998 the President dissolved the Government, on the grounds that it had failed to address the country's economic problems. Jumabek Ibraimov, hitherto the Chairman of the State Property Committee, was appointed to the office of Prime Minister and a new Cabinet was announced, although 10 ministers retained their portfolios. Akayev also issued a decree that extended the Prime Minister's powers, including the right to appoint and dismiss ministers and heads of departments (which had previously been the exclusive right of the President). In early April 1999, however, Ibraimov died; the nomination of Amangeldy Muraliyev, a former regional governor, as Prime Minister was approved by the Zhogorku Kenesh in late April.

At the end of May 1999 a new electoral law was introduced, whereby, henceforth, 15 of the seats in the Legislative Assembly were to be allocated on a proportional basis for those parties that secured a minimum of 5% of the votes; the legislation also banned the use of foreign and private funds in electoral campaigns. Meanwhile, new legislation on political parties came into effect in mid-June, banning political organizations considered to threaten Kyrgyzstan's stability and ethnic harmony. In July two new opposition parties were established: the Ar-Namys (Dignity) Party, which was to be led by the former Vice-President and Mayor of Bishkek, Feliks Kulov, and the Adilettuuluk (Justice) Party. In mid-August a group of communists, under the leadership of Klara Ajibekova, broke away from the KCP to form a rival organization, the Communist Party of Kyrgyzstan (CPK). Ajibekova stated that the KCP leader, Absamat Masaliyev, had betrayed the ideology of the party by defending several deputies who had been found guilty of corruption. Later in the month the Minister of Defence, Maj.-Gen. Murzakan Subanov, was removed from his post and replaced by the Chairman of the National Security Council, Maj.-Gen. Esen Topoyev; Subanov's dismissal followed claims that he had failed to ease a hostage crisis in the Osh region in August (see below). In mid-October another opposition party, the Republican Party of Kyrgyzstan (RPK), was established and officially registered with the Ministry of Justice. In the following month Akayev announced that a parliamentary election was to be held on 20 February 2000.

Several electoral alliances were forged prior to the legislative election. At the end of December 1999 three pro-presidential parties, the Social Democratic Party, the Birimdik Party and the Economic Revival Party, announced the establishment of a joint party list. A coalition of opposition parties and movements was formed in January 2000, which included the Ar-Namys Party, the Democratic Movement of Kyrgyzstan and the Republican Party of Kyrgyzstan (although the Democratic Movement subsequently withdrew from the ballot). As the election approached there were numerous accusations by opposition parties that the Government was impeding their campaigns. The head of one such party, El (Beibecharalai) Partiyasy, was arrested, although the authorities denied that the detention had a political motive. The Ar-Namys Party was prevented from contesting the election (since it had been in existence for only six months, rather than the required 12); however, Kulov was permitted to stand as an independent candidate.

At the election to both chambers of the restructured Zhogorku Kenesh, held on 20 February 2000, a total of six parties passed the 5% threshold required to secure party-list seats in the Legislative Assembly. The election was the first to take place since constitutional amendments had been approved by the referendum of October 1998 (see above). Although the Central Election Commission declared the election to have been 'free and fair', a number of electoral violations were reported by the Organization for Security and Co-operation in Europe (OSCE, see p. 283), which expressed particular concern regarding infringements to the freedom of the media and the election administration, as well as the alleged intimidation of opposition leaders. As a result of a second round of voting on 12 March, the KCP secured 27.7% of the votes cast, the Union of Democratic Forces 18.6%, the Democratic Women's Party of Kyrgyzstan 12.7%, the Party of Veterans of the War in Afghanistan and of Participation in other Local Conflicts 8.0%, the Ata-Meken (Fatherland) Socialist Party 6.5% and the My Country Party of Action 5.0%. In terms of seats, the Union of Democratic Forces achieved the greatest representation of any party or bloc in the combined Zhogorku Kenesh, once single-mandate constituency seats had been included, securing 12 seats, compared with the KCP's six. Independent candidates took 73 of the total 105 seats in the two chambers. Kulov, however, failed to win a seat, prompting opposition protests and allegations of official corruption. Later in March Kulov was arrested on charges of abuse of office while serving as Minister of National Security in 1997–98. Following his acquittal in August, Kulov intended to stand as a candidate in the presidential election scheduled for October. However, in September the Bishkek military court annulled its decision, and ordered a retrial. Moreover, Kulov refused to take the mandatory Kyrgyz language test for prospective presidential candidates (which the Constitutional Court had recently ruled to be legal), on the grounds that its introduction had been politically motivated. He was, therefore, effectively barred from participating in the election.

At the presidential election, held on 29 October 2000, the incumbent President defeated his opponents, securing 74.5% of the votes cast. Tekebayev won 13.9% of the votes and Almazbek Atambayev 6.0%. According to the Central Election Commission, an estimated 74% of the electorate participated. However, both before and during the election there were numerous reports of misconduct and the intimidation of presidential candidates. On the day of the election a criminal case opened in Bishkek following the discovery, by international observers, of several hundred ballot papers, marked in favour of Akayev, before polling had officially begun. In addition, opposition parties claimed that they had been prevented from taking part in media broadcasts during their election campaigns. Following severe criticism by the OSCE, the Chairman of the Central Election Commission was forced to concede that electoral violations had, indeed, taken place, leading to international condemnation. Mass protests took place, and demands were made for the election to be repeated. None the less, on 10 November the Constitutional Court formally endorsed the results of the election.

President Akayev was inaugurated for a third term on 9 December 2000. In accordance with the Constitution, the Government resigned shortly afterwards. On 21 December Kurmanbek Bakiyev, hitherto the Governor of Chui Oblast, was appointed the new Prime Minister. At the end of the month, under the guidance of the President, Bakiyev submitted to the Legislative Assembly a proposal for a revised structure of government, with a reduction in the number of ministries and state institutions, in an attempt to limit both bureaucracy and expenditure. A new Government was announced at the beginning of January 2001. Later in the same month Feliks Kulov was sentenced to seven years' imprisonment by the Bishkek military court. An appeal against his conviction was rejected in March, prompting Kulov's Ar-Namys Party to denounce his sentence as politically motivated. The Supreme Court upheld Kulov's sentence in July (although one charge of abuse of office was dismissed). In May 2002 Kulov was found guilty of further charges, of embezzlement.

In April 2001, in an attempt to combat Islamist extremism, the Government banned religious education in state schools and decreed that specialist religious schools would, henceforth, require a licence. In the same month the leaders of nine opposition parties formally announced the establishment of an alliance known as the People's Patriotic Movement, which stated its objectives to be the safeguarding of democracy and of human and constitutional rights. The movement organized demonstrations in the same month against the erosion of the independent media, and against the imprisonment of Feliks Kulov and another opposition leader, the Chairman of the Erkindik (Liberty) Party, Topchubek Turgunaliyev, who had been convicted in September 2000 of conspiring to assassinate the President in April 1999. (Turgunaliyev was pardoned by the President in August 2001.) In mid-October the President passed electoral amendments, which banned parties that had been registered for fewer than six months from participating in legislative elections and regulated the funding of election monitors. In early November opposition parties including the Ar-Namys Party, the Ata-Meken Socialist Party and Erkindik announced the formation of a new People's Congress, and elected Kulov as Chairman of the alliance. In the following month the President signed into law a constitutional amendment, granting Russian the status of official language, in what was considered an attempt to halt the emigration of ethnic Russians from Kyrgyzstan. (An amendment according the Russian language the status of second official language had been passed in May 2000, but had not been incorporated into the Constitution.)

In January 2002 the arrest of an opposition deputy and a former Chairman of the parliamentary committee on court reforms and legality, Azimbek Beknazarov, on charges of abuse

of power, prompted protesters to demand his release and to denounce his detention as politically motivated (Beknazarov had publicly criticized President Akayev's signature of the 1999 Sino-Kyrgyz border treaty—see below). International human rights organizations also expressed concern at what was perceived as the suppression of political dissent, and members of the People's Congress initiated a hunger strike in protest at the detention of both Kulov and Beknazarov (as a result of which one prominent human rights activist died). Nevertheless, Beknazarov's trial commenced in February (although it was adjourned until the following month). On 17–18 March large-scale protests took place in Jalal-Abad against the ongoing trial; six people were reported to have died, following clashes with security forces. Although the trial was subsequently suspended and Beknazarov was temporarily released, the Government accused the opposition of instigating the riots in an attempt to stage a *coup d'état* and maintained that the security forces had acted in self-defence. On his release, Beknazarov announced that he held the authorities responsible for the violence; witnesses supported his claims, alleging that security officials had shot at unarmed demonstrators without provocation or warning. The People's Congress demanded the resignations of both the President and the Government.

On 10 May 2002 the Legislative Assembly ratified the controversial Sino-Kyrgyz treaty, prompting two weeks of anti-Government demonstrations, hunger strikes and acts of civil disobedience. Protesters demanded that the Government accept responsibility for the violence of mid-March; rescind the ratification of the border treaty (which they claimed was signed illegally by President Akayev, since he had agreed to cede land to the People's Republic of China without the consent of the legislature); and close the criminal case against Beknazarov. Nevertheless, the treaty was ratified by the People's Assembly in mid-May, and subsequently signed into law by the President. Meanwhile, also in mid-May a state commission established to investigate the protests in Jalal-Abad issued its report to the President, in which it criticized all levels of government and the law-enforcement bodies for not having recognized the instability of the political situation and the rising levels of popular discontent in the region during Beknazarov's trial. The commission also stated the security forces' use of weapons to control the demonstrators to have been illegal. On 22 May Prime Minister Bakiyev tendered his resignation, and the entire Government duly resigned, in accordance with the Constitution. The Chief of the Presidential Administration also resigned, together with a senior prosecutor, and several senior police-officers were dismissed. The First Deputy Prime Minister, Nikolai Tanayev, was appointed Prime Minister (initially on an acting basis) and a new government was announced on 19 June. Meanwhile, in late May Beknazarov received a one-year, suspended prison sentence. An appeal against the sentence, heard in late June, was preceded by further large-scale demonstrations in Jalal-Abad, Kerben and Osh. Although the initial guilty verdict was upheld by the court of appeal, Beknazarov's sentence was annulled, enabling him to retain his parliamentary seat. In the same month Tanayev proposed an amnesty for those involved in the disturbances of mid-March. The amnesty, which was passed by the Legislative Assembly on 28 June, applied to opposition representatives and dozens of civilians arrested during the protests, as well as law-enforcement officials. Tanayev stated that he would release the remaining detainees provided that the organizers of the rallies agreed to a number of conditions, including the cessation of protests against the Sino-Kyrgyz treaty. None the less, in August the Prosecutor-General's Office announced that charges were to be filed against officials accused of mishandling the March protests, and in late December four former officials, including both the Prosecutor and the Police Chief of Jalal-Abad, were convicted of abuse of power and sentenced to terms of imprisonment.

In mid-January 2003 President Akayev announced that a referendum on several proposed constitutional amendments was to be held on 2 February. Despite opposition demands for the referendum's postponement, the amendments, providing *inter alia* for the introduction of a unicameral legislature from 2005, were duly approved by 76.6% of the electorate, and 78.7% of voters supported Akayev's remaining in office until 2005; the reported rate of participation was 86.7%. The hasty scheduling of the referendum attracted criticism from international human rights organizations, and there were also allegations of procedural violations. Nevertheless, the constitutional amendments were endorsed by the President, who insisted that the amendments would serve to reinforce democracy in the country, on 18 February.

Kyrgyzstan has sought to establish close relations with Arab and other Muslim states, in particular Turkey, with which it shares ethnic, cultural and linguistic ties. President Akayev has also stressed that, despite Islam being the dominant religion, Kyrgyzstan will remain a secular state, opposed to Islamist extremism. In 1992 the Kyrgyz Government participated in negotiations aimed at ending the civil conflict in neighbouring Tajikistan between forces of the Tajik Government and rebel Islamist groups. In January 1993, however, it was reported that groups of armed Tajiks had crossed into Kyrgyzstan, seeking to incite an Islamist insurrection among the local population. The Kyrgyz Government subsequently intensified controls along the border with Tajikistan and contributed troops to a CIS peace-keeping mission on the Tajik–Afghan border. Border tensions increased in mid-1996, and requests were made by the Kyrgyz Government for assistance from Tajikistan in the rehabilitation of an estimated 15,000 Tajik refugees who had fled to Kyrgyzstan. The peace agreement concluded in Tajikistan in June 1997 was welcomed by the Kyrgyz authorities, and in late 1999 Kyrgyzstan began to withdraw its peace-keeping troops from the Tajik–Afghan border. The Kyrgyz leadership remained concerned at the increase in drugs-trafficking across the Tajik–Kyrgyz border, and a customs accord was signed by Kyrgyzstan and Tajikistan in September 1998, with the aim of combating arms- and drugs-trafficking. (However, in March 2003 it was reported that drugs-trafficking from Afghanistan was increasing.) Border negotiations with Tajikistan, which had commenced in 1997, before being suspended, owing to the unstable political situation in that country, recommenced in December 2002.

Relations with Kyrgyzstan's other neighbouring Central Asian republics, Uzbekistan and Kazakhstan, deteriorated sharply in May 1993, following Kyrgyzstan's sudden introduction of its own currency, the som. The Uzbek Government, fearing a massive influx of roubles into Uzbekistan, closed its border with Kyrgyzstan, suspending trade and telecommunications links for several days. However, relations between the two states improved following talks in June. In January 1994 Kyrgyzstan joined the economic zone newly established by Kazakhstan and Uzbekistan, and in February 1995 an Interstate Council was formed to co-ordinate economic activity in the zone. Following the admission of Tajikistan in March 1998, in May the four countries were formally constituted as the Central Asian Economic Union (known as the Central Asian Co-operation Organization from March 2002).

Kyrgyzstan's campaign against Islamist extremism intensified in mid-1999 when Islamist groups believed to be based in Uzbekistan and Tajikistan held a number of people hostage in two separate events in the southern region of Osh. In early August four Kyrgyz officials were taken hostage by a group of armed fighters (presumed to be ethnic Uzbeks and Arabs belonging to an Islamist fundamentalist organization) who had entered the country from neighbouring Tajikistan. The hostages were released one week later, after the Kyrgyz authorities agreed to pay a ransom and to allow the fighters to pass into Uzbek territory. In mid-August Kyrgyz and Uzbek forces launched air-strikes against Tajik militants in the Osh region, in an attempt to prevent further acts of insurgency. However, later that month a senior Kyrgyz military commander was among more than 25 people kidnapped by a group of rebels, which captured three villages near the Tajik border. The rebels appeared to be members of the Islamist Movement of Uzbekistan (IMU), which demanded the release of Islamists imprisoned in that country. The hostage crisis intensified, with Kyrgyz government troops engaging in a large-scale military operation in order to defeat the rebels and free the hostages; fighting continued throughout September. It was announced in late October that all of the hostages had been released, following negotiations between Kyrgyz officials and members of the Islamist organization. (However, it was reported in mid-November that the body of a police-officer, taken hostage in late August, had been discovered.) From mid-August Islamist militants made a further series of incursions into Kyrgyzstan from Tajikistan, leading to armed conflict with government forces. The number of insurgents amassing on the Kyrgyz–Tajik border increased, despite intensive shelling and aerial bombardment by Kyrgyz troops. By the end of October, however, the Government claimed that all the rebels had left Kyrgyzstan and that it had regained full control of the regions bordering Tajikistan.

In April 2001 a local government official accused the Uzbek authorities of laying landmines along the Kyrgyz border, and demanded the removal of Uzbek troops, deployed in an effort to combat the incursions of Islamist militants and drugs-traffickers, from Kyrgyz border territories. Although it was announced in June that the mines were to be removed, there were claims in September that the laying of mines was continuing. As a result, the Kyrgyz Legislative Assembly refused to ratify an agreement with Uzbekistan on arms' supplies. Meanwhile, reports in May indicated that Islamist rebels were increasingly recruiting from southern Kyrgyzstan. One month later two members of the IMU, arrested during fighting in the Kyrgyz border territories in mid-2000, on charges that included murder and terrorism, were sentenced to death. The severity of the sentences was expected to act as a warning to other militants.

In April 2001, at a meeting of leaders of the Turkic-speaking countries, the Presidents of Azerbaijan, Kazakhstan, Kyrgyzstan, Turkey and Turkmenistan, and the Chairman of the Uzbek legislature signed an agreement on regional co-operation to combat terrorism and drugs-trafficking, to revive the old 'Silk Road' trade route between the People's Republic of China and Europe, and to ensure further protection of the environment. One month later the signatories of the CIS Collective Security Treaty—Armenia, Belarus, Kazakhstan, Kyrgyzstan, Russia and Tajikistan—agreed to form a Collective Rapid Reaction Force in Bishkek to combat Islamist militancy in Central Asia; in January 2002 it was announced that the force was ready to undertake combat missions. At 2003 the IMU and the Uzbek fundamentalist Hizb-ut-Tahrir al-Islami (Party of Islamic Liberation) continued to be regarded as threats to stability in Kyrgyzstan. The latter, which aimed to unite Muslim countries and establish Islamic law through peaceful means, had become the most widespread illegal movement in Kyrgyzstan, despite government attempts to suppress it.

Kyrgyzstan has strongly defended the preservation of the CIS, recognizing its dependence on the Commonwealth for economic viability. Among other agreements, Kyrgyzstan signed (in mid-1992) the Collective Security Treaty with five CIS members, and in early 1993 a charter on closer co-operation in all spheres was signed by six member states, including Kyrgyzstan. In March 1996 Kyrgyzstan signed a treaty with Russia, Belarus and Kazakhstan to create a 'community of integrated states', in an attempt not to restore in part the USSR, but rather to achieve closer economic, cultural and social integration. Kyrgyzstan also joined the customs union already established by the three other countries. Tajikistan joined the union in April 1998 and in October 2000 a new economic body, the Eurasian Economic Community (EAEC), was established to supersede the customs union.

Akayev has endeavoured to maintain good relations with the largest and most influential CIS member, Russia, and the issue of ethnic Russians in Kyrgyzstan (numbering some 603,000 in 1999) has been at the centre of discussions between the two countries. In June 1992 Akayev and the Russian President, Boris Yeltsin, signed a treaty of friendship, co-operation and mutual assistance, and the two countries signed a further declaration on friendship, alliance and partnership in July 2000. Military agreements, including a treaty of non-aggression, have also been concluded. An agreement concerning the expansion of Russian-Kyrgyz military co-operation was concluded in October 1997, whereby Russia was to lease four military installations in Kyrgyzstan in return for training Kyrgyz army recruits.

Kyrgyzstan reached a series of bilateral co-operation agreements with the People's Republic of China during 1996, the terms of which provided for the partial demarcation of their shared border, which was undertaken from mid-2001. Another border treaty was signed in August 1999, which ceded almost 95,000 ha of disputed territory to China. Akayev signed the agreement without the consent of the legislature, causing widespread protests upon its ratification in 2002 (see above). Meanwhile, an agreement signed in April 1997 with China, Russia, Kazakhstan and Tajikistan (which, together with Kyrgyzstan, constituted the so-called Shanghai Five, later known as the Shanghai Forum) aimed to improve joint border security. The alliance, renamed the Shanghai Co-operation Organization upon the accession of Uzbekistan, signed the Shanghai Convention on Combating Terrorism, Separatism and Extremism in mid-2001. In August an associated anti-terrorism centre became operational in Bishkek. The Presidents of Kazakhstan and Kyrgyzstan signed a border agreement in December. In March

2002 China agreed to provide Kyrgyzstan with military assistance worth some US $1.2m.

From early 1997 Kyrgyzstan was concerned by unrest on the country's border with the People's Republic of China, caused by members of an organization called For a Free Eastern Turkestan, which was seeking to create an Islamic state on the territory of China's Xinjiang Uygur (Uigur) Autonomous Region. Akayev assumed personal control of policies to prevent the proliferation of Islamist extremism and particularly Wahhabism, a conservative group within Sunni Islam. In May a group of Uigur separatists were arrested in Kyrgyzstan on charges including terrorism and the dissemination of Wahhabi propaganda; two of the activists were sentenced to terms of imprisonment in December. A draft law on religious freedom was adopted in March 1999, purportedly to prevent abuses by religious organizations attempting to 'destabilize' society under the original legislation, which had been in force since October 1991.

Following the large-scale suicide attacks on the US cities of New York and Washington, DC, on 11 September 2001, President Akayev announced that he was prepared to allow US military aircraft to have access to Kyrgyz airspace for the aerial bombardment of militants of the al-Qa'ida (Base) organization (held principally responsible by the USA for having co-ordinated the attacks), and its Taliban hosts in Afghanistan. In late November the Government agreed to give the US-led anti-terrorism coalition access to its military bases and, later, its main airport. Kyrgyzstan undertook joint exercises with US troops in February 2002, which aimed to facilitate attempts to counter insurgency in the country's mountainous regions (see below). In September Akayev met the US President, George W. Bush, and the US Secretary of State, Colin Powell, in Washington, where they discussed Kyrgyzstan's human rights record, the USA's declared 'war against terrorism', and economic issues.

Government

According to constitutional amendments approved at a referendum on 17 October 1998, supreme legislative power in the Kyrgyz Republic is vested in the bicameral 105-member Zhogorku Kenesh (Supreme Council), comprising a permanent 45-member Legislative Assembly (lower chamber) and a 60-member People's Assembly (upper chamber); the latter meets twice yearly to debate regional issues. The Zhogorku Kenesh is elected by universal suffrage for a term of five years. The President of the Republic, who is directly elected for a five-year term, is Head of State and Commander-in-Chief of the Armed Forces, and also holds extensive executive powers. The Prime Minister is appointed by the President, subject to the approval of the Zhogorku Kenesh; the remaining members of the Government are appointed by the President. The Prime Minister was also empowered to appoint and dismiss ministers and heads of departments. For administrative purposes, Kyrgyzstan is divided into seven regions (oblasts or dubans) and the municipality of Bishkek (the capital).

Defence

Kyrgyzstan began to raise a national army in 1992. In August 2002 Kyrgyzstan's total armed forces numbered 10,900 (army 8,500, air force 2,400). There are also an estimated 5,000 personnel in paramilitary forces. Military service is compulsory and lasts for 18 months. Kyrgyzstan joined the defence structures of the Commonwealth of Independent States (CIS) by signing, with five other member states, a collective security agreement in May 1992; in May 2001 it was announced that the signatory countries were to form a Collective Rapid Reaction Force to combat Islamist militancy in Central Asia. In June 1994 Kyrgyzstan joined NATO's 'Partnership for Peace' (see p. 273) programme of military co-operation. The country's defence budget for 2002 was some 1,100m. soms (US $23.5m.).

Economic Affairs

In 2001, according to estimates by the World Bank, Kyrgyzstan's gross national product (GNI), measured at average 1999–2001 prices, was US $1,386m., equivalent to $280 per head (or $2,710 per head on an international purchasing-power parity basis). During 1990–2001, it was estimated, the population increased by an annual average of 1.1%, while gross domestic product (GDP) per head declined, in real terms, at an average annual rate of 4.2%. Overall GDP declined, in real terms, at an estimated average annual rate of 3.2% in 1990–2001. Real GDP increased by 5.4% in 2000 and by 5.3% in 2001.

Agriculture contributed an estimated 35.6% of GDP in 2002, according to official figures. In 1999 52.4% of the labour force were employed in the sector. By tradition, the Kyrgyz are a pastoral nomadic people, and the majority of the population (some 65.2% in 1999) reside in rural areas. Livestock-rearing, once the mainstay of agricultural activity, is declining in importance. Only about 7% of the country's land area is arable; of this, some 70% depends on irrigation. The principal crops are grain, potatoes, vegetables and sugar beet. By 2002, according to government figures, collective farms accounted for only around 6% of agricultural production, while state farms accounted for just under 2%. The GDP of the agricultural sector increased, in real terms, by an average of 1.4% per year in 1990–2001; agricultural GDP increased by 6.8% in 2001, and output increased by 3.3% in 2002.

Industry contributed an estimated 31.7% of GDP in 2002. The industrial sector provided 11.6% of employment in 1999. Real industrial GDP declined at an average annual rate of 6.5% in 1990–2001; the GDP of the sector increased by 7.1% in 2001, but industrial GDP contracted by 13.1% in 2002, according to government figures.

In 1999 the mining and quarrying sector employed 4.7% of the industrial work-force. Kyrgyzstan has considerable mineral deposits, including coal, gold, tin, mercury, antimony, zinc, tungsten and uranium. In May 2001 the Government announced the discovery of new deposits of petroleum, estimated to total 70m. barrels, in an oilfield in the west. Production of gold from the Kumtor mine, which is believed to contain the eighth largest deposit of gold in the world, began in January 1997. As a result, Kyrgyzstan had become the 10th largest extractor and seller of gold in the world by 2001.

Manufacturing contributed an estimated 21.5% of GDP in 2000. In 2002 the principal branches of manufacturing, measured by gross value of output, were food products, beverages and tobacco (accounting for 34.0% of the total) and metallurgy (29.9%). According to World Bank estimates, real manufacturing GDP declined by an average of 13.4% per year in 1990–2001. However, manufacturing output revived from 1996, and output increased by 39.7% in 1997 and by 5.3% in 1998; the IMF estimated that the GDP of the manufacturing sector declined by 4.3% in 1999, before increasing by 6.0% in 2000.

Kyrgyzstan's principal source of domestic energy production (and also a major export) is hydroelectricity (generated by the country's mountain rivers). Hydroelectricity provided 92.3% of Kyrgyzstan's total energy requirements in 1999. Kyrgyzstan has insufficient petroleum and natural gas to meet its needs, and substantial imports of hydrocarbons are thus required; Kyrgyzstan exports electricity to Kazakhstan and Uzbekistan in return for coal and natural gas, respectively. Imports of mineral fuels comprised an estimated 21.8% of the value of total recorded imports in 2000. Exports of electricity contributed some 15.8% of the value of total exports in that year.

In 2002, according to official figures, the services sector contributed an estimated 32.7% of GDP. Services provided 36.1% of employment in 1999. In 1990–2001 the GDP of the sector declined, in real terms, by an average of 8.2% per year; however, services GDP increased by 13.0% in 2000 and by 0.8% in 2001.

In 2001 Kyrgyzstan recorded a visible trade surplus of US $39.1m., while there was a deficit of $52.6m. on the current account of the balance of payments. In 2001 the principal source of recorded imports (18.2%) was Russia; other major suppliers were Kazakhstan, Uzbekistan, the People's Republic of China, the USA and Germany. The main market for exports in that year was Switzerland (26.1%). Other principal markets were Germany, Russia, Uzbekistan and Kazakhstan. The main exports in 2000 were non-ferrous metallurgical products, electricity, machinery and metal-working products, unprocessed agricultural products and light industrial products. The principal recorded imports in that year were machinery and metal-working products, petroleum and natural gas, food and beverages, unprocessed agricultural products, light industrial products, chemicals, and medical products.

In 2002 Kyrgyzstan recorded an overall budgetary deficit of 798.1m. soms (equivalent to 1.1% of GDP). Kyrgyzstan's total external debt was US $1,829.1m. at the end of 2000, of which $1,223.6m. was long-term public debt. In that year the cost of debt-servicing was equivalent to 29.3% of the value of exports of goods and services. Annual inflation averaged 74.3% in 1992–2001. Consumer prices increased by 18.7% in 2000, by 6.9% in 2001, and, according to government figures, by 2.3% in 2002. At June 2002 3.1% of the population were officially registered as unemployed. However, the actual number of unemployed was estimated to be significantly higher, at around 8%, according to International Labour Organization methodology.

Kyrgyzstan participates in the economic bodies of the Commonwealth of Independent States (CIS, see p. 172), and has also joined the European Bank for Reconstruction and Development (EBRD, see p. 193), as a 'Country of Operations', and the Economic Co-operation Organization (ECO, see p. 192). In addition, Kyrgyzstan is a member of the Asian Development Bank (ADB, see p. 143). In 1994 Kyrgyzstan joined Kazakhstan and Uzbekistan in a trilateral economic area. In May 1998, following the admission of Tajikistan in March, the organization was constituted as the Central Asian Economic Union, which had been renamed the Central Asian Co-operation Organization by March 2002. In February 1995 Kyrgyzstan signed a 10-year 'partnership and co-operation' agreement with the European Union. In October 1998 Kyrgyzstan became the first CIS country to join the World Trade Organization (WTO, see p. 323). In October 2000 a new economic body, the Eurasian Economic Community (EAEC), was established to supersede a customs union established in the 1990s between Kyrgyzstan and Belarus, Kazakhstan, Russia and Tajikistan. The EAEC aimed to develop common policies on currencies, customs tariffs, employment and taxation.

Following independence in 1991, the Kyrgyz Government embarked on an ambitious programme of economic reforms to establish a market-based economy and achieve macroeconomic stabilization. Significant growth was registered in 1996–97, but the economy slowed considerably from mid-1998, owing to reduced growth in gold and agricultural production and the financial crisis in Russia. The crisis precipitated a 35% depreciation of the national currency, the som (introduced in 1993), which led to the rapid depletion of foreign reserves through large-scale intervention in the foreign exchange market. The privatization programme was relaunched in 1998, after its suspension in mid-1997, and in 2000 the Government approved a further two-year privatization programme to facilitate the sale of strategic enterprises. There was rapid GDP growth from 2000, and in 2001 an annual rate of inflation of less than 10% was recorded for the first time since independence. At the end of the year the IMF approved a new, three-year Poverty Reduction and Growth Facility (PRGF), in support of the Government's economic reforms. In November 2001 it was reported that the IMF had agreed to cancel or restructure a proportion of the country's external debt, and in March 2002 the 'Paris Club' of creditor countries agreed to reschedule, over a period of 20 years, the repayment of some US $95m., which had been due to be serviced in 2002–04. In October 2002 a conference was held in Bishkek, at which international donors pledged some $700m. for 2003–05, a significant proportion of which was to be used in support of the country's poverty reduction programme. However, in 2002 GDP registered its first decline since 1995, of some 0.5%, resulting from reduced industrial output, particularly in the mining sector, after a landslide at the Kumtor gold mine. In the medium term, growth was likely to be severely affected by the economy's reliance on the output of the mine, the closure of which was anticipated in 2010; new gold projects were not expected to be able to compensate for the decline in production. The introduction of value-added tax (VAT) on agricultural products was expected to be of substantial benefit to the economy, and additional large-scale privatization was planned for 2003. Ultimately, however, sustained growth was dependent on the greater diversification of both exports and industry.

Education

Education is officially compulsory for nine years, comprising four years of primary school (between the ages of seven and 10), followed by five years of lower secondary school (ages 11 to 15). Pupils may then continue their studies in upper secondary schools (two years' duration), specialized secondary schools (two to four years) or technical and vocational schools (from 15 years of age). In 1997 total enrolment at primary schools was equivalent to 99.5% of the relevant age group; enrolment at secondary-school level was equivalent to 77.8%. A decree signed in December 2001 abolished free schooling. Higher education, lasting between four and six years, is provided in 40 establishments in Kyrgyzstan. These include the Kyrgyz State University, which has 12 faculties, the Kyrgyz Technical University and the Kyrgyz-Russian Slavonic University, which opened in Bishkek in 1993. In 1995 enrolment at tertiary level was equivalent to 12.2% of those in the relevant age-group (males 11.6%; females 12.8%). In 1993/94 63.6% of pupils in primary and secondary schools were taught in Kyrgyz, 23.4% were taught in Russian, 12.7% in Uzbek and 0.3% in Tajik. However, Russian was the principal language of instruction in higher educational establishments: in 1993/94 64.6% of students were taught in Russian, 34.7% in Kyrgyz and 0.7% in Uzbek. Government budgetary expenditure on education in 2001 was 2,849.3m. soms (23.2% of total spending).

Public Holidays

2003: 1 January (New Year's Day), 7 January (Christmas), 12 February* (Kurban Ait, Feast of the Sacrifice), 8 March (International Women's Day), 21 March (Nooruz, Kyrgyz New Year), 1 May (International Labour Day), 5 May (Constitution Day), 9 May (Victory Day), 31 August (Independence Day), 26 November* (Orozo Ait, end of Ramadan).

2004: 1 January (New Year's Day), 7 January (Christmas), 2 February* (Kurban Ait, Feast of the Sacrifice), 8 March (International Women's Day), 21 March (Nooruz, Kyrgyz New Year), 1 May (International Labour Day), 5 May (Constitution Day), 9 May (Victory Day), 31 August (Independence Day), 14 November* (Orozo Ait, end of Ramadan).

*These holidays are dependent on the Islamic lunar calendar and may vary by one or two days from the dates given.

Weights and Measures

The metric system is in force.

Statistical Survey

Source (unless otherwise stated): National Statistical Committee, 720033 Bishkek, Frunze 374; tel. (312) 22-63-63; fax (312) 22-07-59; e-mail zkudabaev@nsc.bishkek.su; internet nsc.bishkek.su.

Area and Population

AREA, POPULATION AND DENSITY

Area (sq km)	199,900*
Population (census results)†	
12 January 1989	4,257,755
24 March 1999	
Males	2,380,465
Females	2,442,473
Total	4,822,938
Population (official estimates at 1 January)†	
1999	4,867,000
2000	4,908,000
2001	4,947,000
Density (per sq km) at 1 January 2001	24.7

* 77,182 sq miles.

† The figures refer to *de jure* population. The *de facto* total was 4,290,442 at the 1989 census and 4,850,700 at the 1999 census.

PRINCIPAL ETHNIC GROUPS
(permanent inhabitants, 1999 census)

	Number	%
Kyrgyz	3,128,147	64.9
Uzbek	664,950	13.8
Russian	603,201	12.5
Dungan	51,766	1.1
Ukrainian	50,442	1.0
Uigur	46,944	1.0
Tatar	45,438	0.9
Kazakh	42,657	0.9
Tajik	42,636	0.9
Turkish	33,327	0.7
German	21,471	0.4
Korean	19,784	0.4
Others	72,175	1.5
Total	**4,822,938**	**100.0**

ADMINISTRATIVE DIVISIONS
(1999 census)

Oblast	Area (sq km)	Population
Batken	17,000	382,426
Chui	20,200	770,811
Issyk-Kul	43,100	413,149
Jalal-Abad	33,700	869,259
Naryn	45,200	249,115
Osh	29,200	1,175,998
Talas	11,400	199,872
Bishkek City	100	762,308
Total	199,900	4,822,938

PRINCIPAL TOWNS
(estimated population at 1 January 1991)

Bishkek (capital)*	631,300	Tokmak	71,200
Osh	238,200	Karakol† . . .	64,300
Jalal-Abad . .	79,900	Kara-Balta . . .	55,000

* Known as Frunze between 1926 and 1991.
† Formerly Przhevalsk.

1 January 1999 (estimates): Bishkek 603,800; Osh 230,700 (Source: UN, *Demographic Yearbook*).

Mid-2001 (UN estimate, incl. suburbs): Bishkek 736,000 (Source: UN, *World Urbanization Prospects: The 2001 Revision*).

BIRTHS, MARRIAGES AND DEATHS*

	Registered live births		Registered marriages		Registered deaths	
	Number	Rate (per 1,000)	Number	Rate (per 1,000)	Number	Rate (per 1,000)
1993 . .	116,795	26.1	36,874	8.2	34,513	7.7
1994 . .	110,113	24.6	26,097	5.8	37,109	8.3
1995 . .	117,340	26.0	26,866	6.0	36,915	8.2
1996 . .	108,007	23.4	26,188	5.7	34,562	7.6
1997 . .	102,050	21.8	26,588	5.7	34,540	7.4
1998 . .	104,183	21.9	25,726	5.4	34,596	7.2
1999 . .	104,068	21.5	26,033	5.4	32,850	6.8
2000 . .	96,770	19.8	n.a.	n.a.	34,111	7.0

* Rates have not been revised to take account of the results of the 1999 census.

Source: UN, *Demographic Yearbook* and *Population and Vital Statistics Report*.

Expectation of life (WHO estimates, years at birth): 64.1 (males 60.1; females 68.2) in 2001 (Source: WHO, *World Health Report*).

ECONOMICALLY ACTIVE POPULATION
(annual averages, '000 persons)

	1997	1998	1999
Agriculture, hunting and forestry	815.6	835.4	923.8
Fishing	n.a.	n.a.	0.5
Mining and quarrying	8.9	8.2	9.5
Manufacturing	143.7	143.3	127.0
Electricity, gas and water supply .	19.0	20.3	22.1
Construction	57.0	50.7	45.2
Wholesale and retail trade; repair of motor vehicles, motor cycles and personal and household goods	174.7	180.2	183.7
Hotels and restaurants . . .	12.1	13.9	11.5
Transport, storage and communications	79.3	75.2	65.8
Financial intermediation . . .	7.2	8.1	7.1
Real estate, renting and business activities	41.3	38.9	28.7
Public administration and defence; compulsory social security . .	60.4	63.0	65.7
Education	139.4	139.3	140.7
Health and social work	88.6	84.5	85.2
Other services	42.1	43.9	47.8
Total employed	1,689.3	1,704.9	1,764.3
Males	907.9	918.7	971.6
Females	781.4	786.2	792.7

Registered unemployed ('000 persons): 54.6 in 1997; 55.9 in 1998; 54.7 in 1999.

Source: ILO, *Yearbook of Labour Statistics*.

Total unemployed (estimates, '000 persons, incl. unregistered): 103.0 in 1997; 106.4 in 1998; 136.8 in 1999.

2000 ('000 persons): Total employed 1,767.1; Total unemployed 144.3.

Health and Welfare

KEY INDICATORS

Total fertility rate (childrens per woman, 2001)	2.0
Under-5 mortality rate (per 1,000 live births, 2001) . . .	61
HIV/AIDS (% of persons aged 15–49, 2001)	<0.10
Physicians (per 1,000 head, 2000)	2.92
Hospital beds (per 1,000 head, 1999)	7.9
Health expenditure (2000): US $ per head (PPP)	145
Health expenditure (2000): % of GDP	6.0
Health expenditure (2000): public (% of total)	61.7
Access to water (% of persons, 2000)	77
Access to sanitation (% of persons, 2000)	100
Human Development Index (2000): ranking	102
Human Development Index (2000): value	0.712

For sources and definitions, see explanatory note on p. vi.

Agriculture

PRINCIPAL CROPS
('000 metric tons)

	1999	2000	2001
Wheat	1,109.1	1,039.1	1,190.6
Rice (paddy)	15.1	19.0	16.6
Barley	179.9	150.2	139.9
Maize	308.4	338.3	442.8
Potatoes	957.2	1,046.0	1,168.4
Sugar beet	536.1	449.8	286.6
Cabbages	89.4	100.5	119.1
Tomatoes	138.4	155.6	165.5
Cucumbers and gherkins*	117	127	187
Dry onions	175.6	147.4	149.2
Carrots	105.4	109.4	112.5
Other vegetables*	94.0	107.0	90.0
Apples	82.6	102.9*	101.0*
Apricots*	10.0	12.6	12.3
Grapes	18.1	26.5	27.4
Watermelons†	62.8	65.3	83.5
Cotton (lint)	28*	19	23*
Cottonseed	87.0	87.9	96.2
Tobacco (leaves)	29.8	34.6	24.0

* Unofficial figure(s).
† Including melons, pumpkins and squash.

Source: FAO.

LIVESTOCK
('000 head at 1 January)

	1999	2000	2001
Horses*	336	350	346
Asses*	8	8	7
Cattle	911	947	970
Camels*	47	47	46
Pigs	105	101	87
Sheep	3,620†	3,198	3,104
Goats	191†	601	640
Chickens	2,600†	3,064	3,254
Turkeys	128†	140†	125*

* FAO estimate(s).
† Unofficial figure.

Source: FAO.

LIVESTOCK PRODUCTS
('000 metric tons)

	1999	2000	2001
Beef and veal	95.1	100.6	100.1
Mutton and lamb	43.3	39.4	40.0
Goat meat	3.3	3.7	3.8
Pig meat	28.6	23.8	25.7
Horse meat	20.3	24.2	24.6*
Poultry meat	4.5	4.6	4.9
Cows' milk	1,041.8	1,078.7	1,110.4
Cheese	2.8	3.4	3.4
Butter	1.2	1.4	1.9
Hen eggs	10.8	11.4	12.7*
Honey	1.5	1.3	1.4
Wool: greasy	11.7	11.3	11.1
Wool: scoured	7.0	11.3	11.1
Cattle hides†	9.3	10.0	9.8
Sheepskins	5.9	5.9	6.2

* Unofficial figure.
† FAO estimates.

Source: FAO.

Forestry

ROUNDWOOD REMOVALS
('000 cubic metres, excl. bark)

	1997	2000*	2001*
Sawlogs, veneer logs and logs for sleepers	7	4	5
Other industrial wood	1	1	1
Fuel wood	30	20	16
Total	38	25	22

* Unofficial figures.

Source: FAO.

1998–99: All production 0 (FAO estimates).

SAWNWOOD PRODUCTION
('000 cubic metres, incl. railway sleepers, unofficial figures)

	1999	2000	2001
Coniferous (softwood)	9	2	2
Broadleaved (hardwood)	14	4	4
Total	23	6	6

Source: FAO.

Fishing

(FAO estimates, metric tons, live weight)

	1998	1999	2000
Capture	80	48	52
Freshwater bream	5	3	3
Common carp	15	9	10
Silver carp	12	7	8
Other cyprinids	18	11	12
Pike-perch	3	2	2
Whitefishes	26	15	16
Aquaculture	97	71	58
Common carp	50	31	10
Grass carp	10	5	5
Silver carp	30	35	43
Trout	5	–	–
Total catch	177	119	110

Source: FAO, *Yearbook of Fishery Statistics*.

Mining

	1999	2000	2001
Coal ('000 metric tons)	417.0	424.9	477.3
Crude petroleum ('000 metric tons)	77.0	77.1	75.5
Natural gas (million cu metres)	25.1	32.2	32.7
Cement	386.3	452.9	n.a.
Gold (metric tons)*	20.0	22.0	24.6

* Source : Gold Fields Mineral Services, *Gold Survey 2002*.
Source: US Geological Survey.

Industry

SELECTED PRODUCTS
('000 metric tons, unless otherwise indicated)

	1999	2000	2001
Vegetable oil	7.5	8.7	6.8
Refined sugar.	70.3	58.0	30.5
Vodka ('000 hectolitres) . . .	9.9	13.6	18.2
Beer ('000 hectolitres)	12.2	12.4	8.6
Cigarettes (million)	2,102.5	3,168.6	3,013.4
Textile fabrics ('000 sq metres). .	14,032.9	8,702.7	7,955.0
Carpets ('000 sq metres) . . .	1,675	2,449	n.a.
Footwear ('000 pairs)	88.0	136.9	169.7
Motor spirit (petrol)	72.5	61.9	47.9
Gas-diesel (distillate fuel) oil . .	53.7	34.0	43.4
Cement	386.3	452.9	468.9
Electric energy (million kWh) . .	13,159.2	14,931.3	13,639.6

Source: partly IMF, *Kyrgyz Republic: Statistical Appendix* (December 2001).

Finance

CURRENCY AND EXCHANGE RATES

Monetary Units
100 tiyins = 1 som

Sterling, Dollar and Euro Equivalents (31 December 2002)
£1 sterling = 74.30 soms
US $1 = 46.09 soms
€1 = 48.34 soms
1,000 soms = £13.46 = $21.69 = €20.67

Average Exchange Rate (soms per US $)
2000   47.704
2001   48.378
2002   46.937

Note: In May 1993 Kyrgyzstan introduced its own currency, the som, replacing the Russian (former Soviet) rouble at an exchange rate of 1 som = 200 roubles.

BUDGET
(million soms)*

Revenue†	1999	2000	2001
Taxation	5,954.0	7,675.5	9,187.9
Personal income taxes . . .	546.2	753.8	960.9
Profit taxes	567.6	572.8	993.7
Value-added tax	2,253.1	2,976.2	4,221.4
Excises	1,252.6	1,518.4	1,102.6
Taxes on international trade and transactions	306.6	275.1	301.4
Other current revenue . . .	1,771.3	1,581.0	2,676.5
Capital revenue	148.5	23.5	57.1
Total	7,873.7	9,280.1	11,921.6

Expenditure‡	1999	2000	2001
Administration, defence and internal security	2,683.9	3,637.1	3,839.2
Education	1,991.3	2,293.0	2,849.3
Health care	1,125.3	1,295.9	1,378.3
Social insurance and security . .	1,198.1	1,113.9	1,417.4
Housing and public utilities . .	464.7	666.5	800.2
Subsidies to economic sectors . .	1,108.7	1,342.7	1,421.4
Total (incl. others)	9,312.0	11,308.2	12,257.0

* Figures represent a consolidation of the budgetary transactions of the central Government and local governments. The operations of extra-budgetary accounts, including the Social Fund (formed in 1994 by an amalgamation of the Pension Fund, the Unemployment Fund and the Social Insurance Fund), are excluded.
† Excluding grants received (million soms): 278.8 in 1999; 608.2 in 2000; 622.0 in 2001.
‡ Including lending minus repayments.

INTERNATIONAL RESERVES
(US $ million at 31 December)

	2000	2001	2002
Gold	22.8	23.0	28.5
IMF special drawing rights. . .	0.7	1.3	0.6
Foreign exchange.	238.3	262.2	288.2
Total	261.8	286.5	317.3

Source: IMF, *International Financial Statistics*.

MONEY SUPPLY
(million soms at 31 December)

	2000	2001	2002
Currency outside banks . . .	4,102	5,016	6,866
Demand deposits at banking institutions	504	542	811
Total money	4,606	5,558	7,677

Source: IMF, *International Financial Statistics*.

COST OF LIVING
(Retail price index; base: 1992 = 100)

	1999	2000	2001
Food	10,604.7	12,679.3	13,407.1
Fuel and light	6,040.1	8,018.7	10,285.1
Clothing	4,748.3	5,121.8	5,064.4
Rent	278,485.7	255,000.0	389,892.9
All items (incl. others)	11,678.3	13,862.4	14,821.9

Source: ILO.

NATIONAL ACCOUNTS
(million soms at current prices)

Expenditure on the Gross Domestic Product

	1999	2000	2001
Government final consumption expenditure.	9,320.1	13,098.6	12,774.3
Private final consumption expenditure.	37,848.2	42,929.6	49,020.4
Increase in stocks	992.9	1,136.0	1,219.3
Gross fixed capital formation . .	7,793.8	11,942.1	10,904.6
Statistical discrepancy	—	—	69.0
Total domestic expenditure . .	55,955.0	69,106.3	73,987.6
Exports of goods and services . .	20,571.4	27,350.8	27,003.9
Less Imports of goods and services	27,782.4	31,099.2	27,101.8
GDP in purchasers' values . .	48,744.0	65,357.9	73,889.7

Gross Domestic Product by Economic Activity

	1998	1999	2000
Agriculture	12,286.2	16,965.5	22,336.0
Forestry	38.0	37.2	37.0
Industry*	5,559.2	10,573.5	15,261.0
Construction	1,537.3	1,484.7	2,492.8
Other branches of material production	366.9	391.1	553.7
Trade and catering†	4,335.3	6,317.7	7,842.5
Transport and communications .	1,535.0	2,355.9	2,495.3
Housing and communal services	1,763.7	1,381.2	1,502.4
Health care, social security, physical culture and sports . .	757.2	1,229.1	1,306.8
Education	1,388.1	1,591.7	1,891.5
Financing and insurance . . .	384.3	126.4	286.3
General administration, defence and internal security	1,035.5	2,111.7	4,070.4
Other services	457.5	635.6	942.1
Sub-total	31,444.2	45,201.3	61,017.8
Less Imputed bank service charge	269.8	76.0	215.3
GDP at basic prices	31,174.4	45,125.3	60,802.5
Taxes on products	3,219.1	3,998.9	5,001.6
Less Subsidies on products . . .	212.1	380.2	446.2
GDP in purchasers' values . .	34,181.4	48,744.0	65,357.9

2001 (million som): GDP in purchasers' values 73,889.7.

* Comprising manufacturing (except printing and publishing), mining and quarrying, electricity, gas, water, logging and fishing.

† Including material and technical supply.

BALANCE OF PAYMENTS
(US $ million)

	1999	2000	2001
Exports of goods f.o.b.	462.6	510.9	480.3
Imports of goods f.o.b.	−551.1	−506.4	−441.2
Trade balance	−88.5	4.6	39.1
Exports of services	65.0	61.8	80.5
Imports of services	−154.4	−148.8	−125.1
Balance on goods and services	−177.9	−82.4	−5.5
Other income received	10.9	17.0	11.9
Other income paid	−85.4	−100.9	−77.4
Balance on goods, services and income	−252.4	−166.3	−71.0
Current transfers received	1.2	43.0	21.6
Current transfers paid	−1.2	−2.4	−3.2
Current balance	−252.4	−125.8	−52.6
Capital account (net)	−15.2	−11.3	−32.0
Direct investment abroad	−6.1	−4.5	−6.1
Direct investment from abroad	44.4	−2.4	5.0
Portfolio investment assets	—	−1.6	1.2
Portfolio investment liabilities	0.1	0.3	—
Financial derivatives assets	26.4	25.8	17.6
Other investment assets	−0.7	−27.3	−4.3
Other investment liabilities	156.6	66.6	17.9
Net errors and omissions	−3.0	9.8	21.3
Overall balance	−49.7	−70.4	32.0

Source: IMF, *International Financial Statistics*.

External Trade

PRINCIPAL COMMODITIES
(US $ million)

Imports c.i.f.	1998	1999	2000
Industrial products	822.9	568.3	513.2
Petroleum and gas	199.0	118.7	120.8
Non-ferrous metallurgy	30.6	22.9	13.1
Chemicals	41.2	24.5	30.5
Fuel	34.3	14.2	17.7
Machinery and metalworking	219.3	202.4	150.6
Timber, wood and paper	35.3	19.1	25.6
Light industry	60.3	38.6	38.8
Food and beverages	106.6	54.2	46.9
Medical products	27.8	42.3	28.1
Agricultural products (unprocessed)	18.6	31.4	40.9
Total	841.5	599.7	554.1

Exports f.o.b.	1998	1999	2000
Industrial products	461.1	396.9	457.5
Electricity	25.6	52.0	79.8
Non-ferrous metallurgy	221.0	217.2	234.4
Machinery and metalworking	70.1	46.8	53.7
Construction materials	24.0	8.2	8.4
Light industry	40.8	32.3	43.9
Food and beverages	54.5	19.1	13.5
Agricultural products (unprocessed)	52.5	56.8	46.9
Total (incl. others)	513.6	453.8	504.5

PRINCIPAL TRADING PARTNERS
(US $ million)

Imports c.i.f.	1999	2000	2001
Belarus	5.3	3.9	6.0
Belgium	14.5	10.7	n.a.
Brazil	1.2	0.3	n.a.
Canada	25.4	11.3	10.9
China, People's Republic	36.9	36.9	48.5
Cuba	4.1	0.0	0.1
France	9.0	5.7	n.a.
Germany	47.3	25.2	24.3
India	4.7	2.9	n.a.
Iran	8.6	8.7	n.a.
Italy	11.7	3.8	n.a.
Japan	12.0	10.3	5.8
Kazakhstan	72.7	57.4	81.8
Korea, Republic	27.1	6.8	n.a.
Russia	109.4	132.6	85.1
Sweden	6.9	27.2	n.a.
Turkey	23.1	26.7	15.8
Turkmenistan	7.8	18.7	9.0
Ukraine	6.3	7.0	6.2
United Arab Emirates	9.6	7.0	n.a.
United Kingdom	7.0	5.5	n.a.
USA	54.2	53.8	26.8
Uzbekistan	50.0	75.1	66.7
Total (incl. others)	599.7	554.1	467.2

Exports f.o.b.	1999	2000	2001
Belarus	4.9	3.0	3.2
Belgium	2.4	0.1	n.a.
China, People's Republic	25.3	44.1	19.4
Czech Republic	7.0	2.7	n.a.
France	8.2	3.3	1.8
Germany	148.2	144.6	94.4
India	5.9	0.8	n.a.
Iran	7.6	6.7	n.a.
Kazakhstan	45.0	33.4	39.0
Latvia	2.2	10.5	n.a.
Lithuania	5.0	1.2	n.a.
Russia	70.7	65.1	64.5
Switzerland	18.1	34.1	124.2
Tajikistan	9.5	7.5	6.7
Turkey	4.6	7.2	13.8
United Kingdom	12.4	18.8	14.1
USA	11.2	2.8	7.1
Uzbekistan	46.6	89.4	48.0
Total (incl. others)	453.8	504.5	476.2

Transport

RAILWAYS
(traffic)

	1998	1999	2000
Passenger-km (million)	59	31	44
Freight net ton-km (million)	466	354	348

Source: UN, *Statistical Yearbook*.

ROAD TRAFFIC
(vehicles in use at 31 December)

	1997	1998	1999
Passenger cars	176,075	187,734	187,322
Motorcycles and mopeds	26,634	23,909	20,789

Source: International Road Federation, *World Road Statistics*.

CIVIL AVIATION
(traffic on scheduled services)

	1997	1998	1999
Kilometres flown (million) . . .	8	9	9
Passengers carried ('000) . . .	423	427	312
Passenger-km (million)	531	519	532
Total ton-km (million)	52	60	56

Source: UN, *Statistical Yearbook*.

Tourism

FOREIGN TOURIST ARRIVALS

Country of Residence	1998	1999
China, People's Republic.	6,088	6,237
CIS countries*	42,027	31,158
Germany	822	1,695
India	1,360	1,870
Turkey	2,467	2,882
USA	696	2,868
Total (incl. others)	59,363	68,863

* Comprising Armenia, Azerbaijan, Belarus, Georgia, Kazakhstan, Moldova, the Russian Federation, Tajikistan, Turkmenistan, Ukraine and Uzbekistan.

2000 (total arrivals): 69,000.

Tourism receipts (US $ million): 8 in 1998; 8 in 2000.

Sources: World Tourism Organization, *Yearbook of Tourism Statistics*; World Bank, *World Development Indicators*.

Communications Media

	1998	1999	2000
Television receivers ('000 in use) . . .	220	230	240
Telephones ('000 main lines in use) . .	368.4	370.6	376.1
Mobile cellular telephones ('000 subscribers)	1.4	2.6	9.0
Internet users ('000)	3.5	10.0	51.6

2001: Mobile cellular telephones ('000 subscribers) 27.0.

Radio receivers ('000 in use): 520 in 1997.

Daily newspapers: 3 (average circulation 67,000) in 1996.

Non-daily newspapers: 146 (average circulation 896,000) in 1996.

Book production: 351 titles (1,980,000 copies) in 1996.

Sources: International Telecommunication Union; UNESCO, *Statistical Yearbook*.

Education

(1999/2000)

	Institutions	Teachers	Students
Pre-primary	420	2,500	45,000
Primary	1,985	19,200	466,200
Secondary: general	n.a.	36,600	633,900
Secondary: vocational	n.a.	5,100	52,200
Higher (all institutions)	n.a.	8,400	159,200

Source: UN, *Statistical Yearbook for Asia and the Pacific*.

Adult literacy rate (1999 census): 98.7%.

Directory

The Constitution

A new Constitution was proclaimed on 5 May 1993. The following is a summary of its main provisions (including amendments endorsed in referendums held on 22 October 1994, 10 February 1996 and 17 October 1998, and other modifications approved by the Constitutional Court):

GENERAL PROVISIONS

The Kyrgyz Republic (Kyrgyzstan) is a sovereign, unitary, democratic republic founded on the principle of lawful, secular government. All state power belongs to the people, who exercise this power through the state bodies on the basis of the Constitution and laws of the republic. Matters of legislation and other issues pertaining to the state may be decided by the people by referendum. The President of the Republic, the deputies of the Zhogorku Kenesh (Supreme Council), and representatives of local administrative bodies are all elected directly by the people. Elections are held on the basis of universal, equal and direct suffrage by secret ballot. All citizens of 18 years and over are eligible to vote.

The territory of the Kyrgyz Republic is integral and inviolable. The state languages are Kyrgyz and Russian. The equality and free use of other languages are guaranteed. The rights and freedoms of citizens may not be restricted on account of ignorance of the state language.

THE PRESIDENT

The President of the Kyrgyz Republic is Head of State and Commander-in-Chief of the Armed Forces, and represents Kyrgyzstan both within the country and internationally. Any citizen of the republic between the ages of 35 and 65, who has a fluent command of the state language, may stand for election. The President's term of office is five years; he/she may not serve more than two consecutive terms. The President is directly elected by the people.

The President appoints and dismisses (subject to approval by the legislature) the Prime Minister; appoints the other members of the Government, as well as heads of administrative offices and other leading state posts; presents draft legislation to the Zhogorku Kenesh on his/her own initiative; signs legislation approved by the Zhogorku Kenesh or returns it for further scrutiny; signs international agreements; may call referendums on issues of state; may

dissolve the legislature (should a referendum demand this) and call fresh elections; announces a general or partial mobilization; and declares a state of war in the event of an invasion by a foreign power.

ZHOGORKU KENESH
(SUPREME COUNCIL)

Supreme legislative power is vested in the 105-member Zhogorku Kenesh, which comprises two chambers: the 45-member Legislative Assembly (lower chamber), which is a permanent chamber, and the 60-member People's Assembly (upper chamber), which sits twice yearly and represents regional interests. Members of both chambers are elected for a term of five years on the basis of universal, equal and direct suffrage by secret ballot.

The Zhogorku Kenesh approves amendments and additions to the Constitution; enacts legislation; confirms the republican budget and supervises its execution; determines questions pertaining to the administrative and territorial structure of the republic; designates presidential elections; approves the appointment of the Prime Minister, as nominated by the President; approves the appointment of the Procurator-General, the Chairman of the Supreme Court and the Chairman of the National Bank, as nominated by the President; ratifies or abrogates international agreements, and decides questions of war and peace; and organizes referendums on issues of state.

THE GOVERNMENT

The Government of the Kyrgyz Republic is the highest organ of executive power in Kyrgyzstan. The Prime Minister heads the Government, which also comprises Deputy Prime Ministers and Ministers. The members of the Government are appointed by the President; however, the President's appointment of the Prime Minister depends upon approval by the Zhogorku Kenesh. The President supervises the work of the Government and has the right to chair its sessions. The Prime Minister must deliver an annual report to the Zhogorku Kenesh on the work of the Government.

The Government determines all questions of state administration, other than those ascribed to the Constitution or to the competence of the President and the Zhogorku Kenesh; drafts the republican budget and submits it to the Zhogorku Kenesh for approval; co-ordinates budgetary, financial, fiscal and monetary policy; administers state property; takes measures to defend the country and state security; executes foreign policy; and strives to guarantee the rights and freedoms of the citizens and to protect property and social order.

JUDICIAL SYSTEM

The judicial system comprises the Constitutional Court, the Supreme Court, the Higher Court of Arbitration and regional courts. Judges of the Constitutional Court are appointed by the Zhogorku Kenesh, on the recommendation of the President, for a term of 15 years, while those of the Supreme Court and the Higher Court of Arbitration are appointed by the Zhogorku Kenesh, on the recommendation of the President, for ten years. The Constitutional Court is the supreme judicial body protecting constitutionality. It comprises the Chairman/woman, his/her deputies and seven judges. The Supreme Court is the highest organ of judicial power in the sphere of civil, criminal and administrative justice.

The Government

HEAD OF STATE

President of the Kyrgyz Republic: ASKAR AKAYEV (elected 28 October 1990; re-elected, by direct popular vote, 12 October 1991, 24 December 1995 and 29 October 2000).

GOVERNMENT
(April 2003)

Prime Minister: NIKOLAI TANAYEV.

First Deputy Prime Minister and Minister of Justice: KURMANBEK OSMONOV.

Deputy Prime Minister and Minister of Economic Development and Investments: DZHOOMART OTORBAYEV.

Deputy Prime Minister and Minister of Transport and Communications: KUBANYCHBEK ZHUMALIYEV.

Minister of Foreign Trade and Industry: SADRIDDIN DZHIYENBEKOV.

Minister of Agriculture, Water Resources and Processing Industry: ALEKSANDR KOSTYUK.

Minister of Foreign Affairs: ASKAR AITMATOV.

Minister of Education and Culture: ISHENKUL BOLDZHUROVA.

Minister of Health: MITALIP MAMYTOV.

Minister of Finance: BOLOT ABILDAYEV.

Minister of Labour and Social Welfare: ROZA AKNAZAROVA.

Minister of Internal Affairs: BAKIRDIN SUBANBEKOV.

Minister of Defence: Maj.-Gen. ESEN TOPOYEV.

Minister of Local Self-Government and Regional Development Affairs: TOLOBEK OMURALIYEV.

Minister of Ecology and Emergency Situations: SATYVALDY CHYRMASHEV.

Chief of Presidential Administration: BEKBOLOT TALGARBEKOV.

HEADS OF GOVERNMENT BODIES

National Bank: ULAN SARBANOV.

National Security Service: KALYK IMANKULOV.

State Secretary: OSMONAKUN IBRAIMOV.

State Committee for Management of State Property and Attraction of Direct Investment: RAVSHAN ZHEYENBEKOV.

State Agency for Registration of Real Estate Rights: TOLOBEK OMURALIYEV.

State Agency for Tourism, Sport and Youth Policy: OKMOTBEK ALMAKUCHUKOV.

State Agency for Science and Intellectual Property: ROMAN OMOROV.

State Agency for Standardization and Meteorology: BATYRBEK DAVLESOV.

State Agency for Geology and Mineral Resources: SHEISHENALY MURZAGAZIYEV.

State Agency for Power Engineering: ULARBEK MATEYEV.

State Border Service: KALMURAT SADIYEV.

State Commission for Anti-monopoly Policy: EMILBEK UZAKBAYEV.

State Commission for Architecture and Construction: ANVAR TURSONOV.

State Commission for Business Development: KAMILA KENENBAYEVA.

State Commission for Drugs Control: KURMANBEK KUBATBEKOV.

State Commission for Religious Affairs: OMURZAK MAMAYUSUPOV.

State Commission for Standards, Financial Accounts and Auditing: KANATBEK SAGYNOV.

State Securities Commission: URAN ABDYNASYROV.

State Communications Agency: ANDREI TITOV.

MINISTRIES

Office of the President: 720003 Bishkek, Govt House, Dom Pravitelstva; tel. (312) 21-24-66; fax (312) 21-86-27; e-mail office@mail.gov.kg; internet www.president.kg.

Office of the Prime Minister: 720003 Bishkek, Govt House; tel. (312) 22-56-56; fax (312) 21-86-27; internet www.gov.kg/prime.htm.

Office of the First Deputy Prime Minister: 720003 Bishkek, Govt House; tel. (312) 21-89-35 (Economic Policy Dept); tel. 21-16-52 (Social Policy Dept); fax (312) 21-86-27 (Agriculture Dept); internet www.gov.kg/vicep.htm.

Ministry of Agriculture, Water Resources and Processing Industry: 720040 Bishkek, Kievskaya 96A; tel. (312) 62-36-33; fax (312) 62-36-32; e-mail mawr@bishkek.gov.kg.

Ministry of Defence: 720001 Bishkek, Logvinenko 26; tel. (312) 22-78-79; e-mail ud@bishkek.gov.kg.

Ministry of Ecology and Emergency Situations: 720055 Bishkek, Aliyaskara Toktonaliyeva 2/1; e-mail admin@mecd.bishkek.gov.kg.

Ministry of Economic Development and Investments: Bishkek.

Ministry of Education and Culture: 720040 Bishkek, Tynystanova 257; tel. (312) 26-31-52; fax (312) 22-86-04; e-mail monk@monk.bishkek.gov.kg.

Ministry of Finance: 720040 Bishkek, pr. Erkindik 58; tel. (312) 22-89-22; fax (312) 22-74-04; e-mail postmaster@mf.bishkek.gov.kg.

Ministry of Foreign Affairs: 720050 Bishkek, Razzakova 59; tel. (312) 22-05-45; fax (312) 26-36-39; e-mail postmaster@mfa.bishkek.gov.kg.

Ministry of Foreign Trade and Industry: 720002 Bishkek, pr. Chui 106; tel. (312) 22-38-66; fax (312) 22-07-93; e-mail postmaster@mvtp.bishkek.gov.kg; internet mvtp.bishkek.gov.kg.

Ministry of Health: 720040 Bishkek, Moskovskaya 148; tel. (312) 22-86-97; fax (312) 22-84-24; e-mail minzdrav@minzdrav.bishkek.gov.kg.

Ministry of Internal Affairs: 720040 Bishkek, Frunze 469; tel. (312) 22-38-66; fax (312) 22-32-78; e-mail mail@mvd.bishkek.gov.kg.

Ministry of Justice: 720321 Bishkek, Orozbekova 37; tel. (312) 22-84-89; fax (312) 26-11-15; e-mail minjust@bishkek.gov.kg; internet www.minjust.bishkek.gov.kg.

Ministry of Labour and Social Welfare: 720041 Bishkek, Tynystanova 215; tel. (312) 26-42-50; e-mail mlsp@mlsp.kg; internet mlsp.bishkek.gov.kg.

Ministry of Local Self-Government and Regional Development Affairs: 720040 Bishkek, Orozbekova 44; e-mail gosreg@bishkek.gov.kg.

Ministry of Transport and Communications: 720017 Bishkek, Isanova 42; tel. (312) 61-04-72; fax (312) 66-47-81; e-mail mtk@mtk.bishkek.gov.kg; internet www.mtk.bishkek.gov.kg.

President and Legislature

PRESIDENT

Presidential Election, 29 October 2000

Candidates	% of votes
Askar Akayev	74.5
Omurbek Tekebayev	13.9
Almazbek Atambayev	6.0
Melis Eshimkanov	1.1
Bakir Ulu Tursunbay	1.0
Tursunbek Akunov	0.4
Blank or spoiled	3.1
Total	**100.0**

ZHOGORKU KENESH
(SUPREME COUNCIL)

The Zhogorku Kenesh is a bicameral legislative body, comprising the People's Assembly and the Legislative Assembly.

People's Assembly and Legislative Assembly: 720003 Bishkek, Kirova 205; tel. (312) 22-55-23; fax (312) 22-24-04; e-mail postmaster@kenesh.gov.kg; internet kenesh.bishkek.gov.kg.

Chairman (Speaker) of People's Assembly: ALTAI BORUBAYEV.

Chairman (Speaker) of Legislative Assembly: ABDYGANY ERKE-BAYEV. Elections were held to both chambers of the Zhogorku Kenesh on 20 February 2000, with a second round of voting ('run-off' elections) held on 12 March.

General Election, 20 February and 12 March 2000*

Parties and blocs	Party-list seats	Single-mandate constituency seats	Total seats
Union of Democratic Forces .	4	8	12
Party of Communists of Kyrgyzstan.	5	1	6
My Country Party of Action .	1	3	4
Ata-Meken Socialist Party .	1	1	2
Democratic Women's Party of Kyrgyzstan†	2	—	2
Party of Veterans of the War in Afghanistan. . . .	2	—	2
Poor and Unprotected People's Party.	—	2	2
Agrarian Labour Party of Kyrgyzstan.	—	1	1
Erkin Kyrgyzstan Progressive and Democratic Party.	—	1	1
Independents	—	73	73
Total	**15**	**90**	**105**

*Election results include both the People's Assembly (the 45-member upper chamber) and the Legislative Assembly (the 60-member lower chamber).

†In August 2000 it was reported that the two seats gained by representatives of the Democratic Women's Party of Kyrgyzstan had been withdrawn, owing to the violation of regulations during the nomination process.

Political Organizations

Adilettuuluk (Justice): Cholpon-Ata; f. 1999 to campaign for the rights of national minorities; Leader MARAT SULTANOV; Dep. Leader BOLOT KARABALAYEV.

Agrarian Labour Party of Kyrgyzstan: Bishkek, Kievskaya 120; tel. (312) 26-58-13; f. 1994; Chair. U. S. SYDYKOV.

Agrarian Party of Kyrgyzstan: Bishkek, Kievskaya 96; tel. (312) 22-68-52; f. 1993; represents farmers' interests; Chair. E. ALIYEV.

Ar-Namys (Dignity) Party: Bishkek; internet arnamys.by.ru; f. 1999; moderate opposition party; Chair. FELIKS KULOV.

Asaba (Banner) Party of National Revival: Bishkek, pr. Chui 26; tel. (312) 43-04-45; f. 1991; nationalist party; Chair. AZIMBEK BEKNAZAROV.

Ashar: Bishkek, pr. Molodoi Gvardii 132; tel. (312) 25-71-88; f. 1989; socio-political movement concerned with development of a parliamentary state and with the revival of national architecture; Chair. ZHUMAGAZY USUP-CHONAIU.

Ata-Meken (Fatherland) Socialist Party: Bishkek, bul. Erkindik 38; tel. (312) 26-22-49; f. 1992; nationalist; Leader ONURBEK TEKE-BAYEV.

Birimdik Party: 720040 Bishkek, Tynystanova 249; tel. (312) 66-38-12; fax (312) 66-29-50; e-mail birimdik_party@mail.ru; f. 1994; seeks to unite people within a democratic movement; Chair. KARYPBEK ALYMKULOV.

Communist Party of Kyrgyzstan (CPK): Bishkek; f. 1999, following split from the Party of Communists of Kyrgyzstan; Chair. KLARA ADZHIBEKOVA.

Democratic Movement of Kyrgyzstan (DMK): Bishkek, Abdymomunova 205; tel. (312) 22-50-97; f. 1990; registered as a political party in 1993; campaigns for civil liberties; Pres. DZHYPAR DZHEKSHEYEV.

Democratic Party of Economic Unity: Bishkek, Popova 4; f. 1994; Chair. A. D. TASHTANBEKOV.

Economic Revival Party: Bishkek; f. 1998; Leader VALERII KHON.

El (Beibecharalai) Partiyasy: Bishkek, Moskovskaya 172; tel. (312) 21-59-64; f. 1995; Chair. DANIYAR USENOV.

Emgekchil el Partiyasy: Bishkek, Ivanitsina 121; f. 1997; supports the democratic movement and private ownership; Chair. E. O. OMURAKUNOV.

Erkin (Free) Kyrgyzstan Progressive-Democratic Party (ERK): Bishkek, Abdymomunova 207; tel. (312) 22-49-57; fax (312) 22-60-35; f. 1991; social-democratic party; Chair. BAKIR ULU TURSUNBAY.

Erkindik (Liberty): Bishkek; f. 2000 following a split from the ERK; Chair. TOPCHUBEK TURGUNALIYEV.

Islamic Democratic Party: Bishkek; f. 2002; Leader NARKAS MULLADZHANOV.

Kayran El (Poor Nation) Party: Bishkek; nationalist; Leader DOORONBEK SADYRBAYEV.

Kok-Zhar Sociopolitical Organization: Bishkek, Mikroraion 7-34-64; f. 1992; seeks to provide housing for the underprivileged; Chair. ZH. ISAYEV.

Kyrgyz Committee for Human Rights: Bishkek, Kievskaya 96; e-mail chrights@imfiko.bishkek.su; internet www.kchr.elcat.kg; banned by the Ministry of Justice in Oct. 1998, re-registered in Aug. 1999 following international pressure; Chair. RAMAZAN DYRYLDAYEV.

Manas: Bishkek; f. 2000; electoral bloc formed prior to Feb. 2000 parliamentary election; composed of the Republican Popular Party and the Party for the Protection of the Interests of Industrial Workers, Farmers and Poor Families.

Manas El (People of Manas) Party: Bishkek, Panfilova 239; tel. (312) 22-26-73; f. 1995; promotes unity of the Kyrgyz people; Chair. CH. T. AITMATOV.

My Country Party of Action: 720040 Bishkek, Tynystanova 110; tel. (312) 22-75-81; e-mail mstrana@hotmail.com; internet www.strana.kg; f. 1998; 670 mems; Chair. DZHOOMART OTARBAYEV; Leader ALMAZBEK ISMANKULOV.

National Unity Democratic Movement: Bishkek, bul. Erkindik 41-17; tel. (312) 22-50-84; f. 1991; seeks to unite different ethnic groups; Chair. YU. RAZGULYAYEV.

Party of Communists of Kyrgyzstan (KCP): Bishkek, bul. Erkindik 31-6; tel. (312) 22-59-63; formerly known as the Communist Party; disbanded 1991, re-established 1992; 25,000 mems; Chair. ABSAMAT M. MASALIYEV.

Party for the Protection of the Interests of Industrial Workers, Farmers and Poor Families: Bishkek, pr. Mira 1; tel. (312) 21-58-42; f. 1996; promotes social and economic reforms; Chair. AKBARALY AITIKEYEV.

Party of Veterans of the War in Afghanistan and of Participants in other Local Conflicts.

Patriotic Party of Kyrgyzstan: Bishkek; f. 1998; not registered with the Ministry of Justice; Leader NAZARBEK NYSHANOV.

People's Congress: Bishkek; f. 2001 as an opposition alliance; Chair. FELIKS KULOV.

People's Mother: Bishkek; f. 2000 to encourage women from all social backgrounds to take part in politics.

People's Patriotic Movement: Bishkek; f. 2001; alliance of the Agrarian Labour Party, the Ar-Namys (Dignity) Party, the Ata-Meken (Fatherland) Socialist Party, the Communist Party of Kyrgyzstan, Erkindik, Kairan-El, the Party of Communists of Kyrgyzstan, the People's Party and the Republican Party; aims to defend democracy and human rights.

Poor and Unprotected People's Party: in opposition; Chair. MELIS ESHIMKANOV.

Republican Movement for the Union and Brotherhood of Nations: Bishkek, pr. Chui 114; tel. (312) 22-16-49; Chair. K. AJIBEKOVA.

Republican Party of Kyrgyzstan (RPK): registered in 1999; advocates parliamentary republicanism; Chair. GIYAZ TOKOMBAYEV; Leader ZAMIRA SIDIKOVA.

Republican Popular Party: Bishkek, bul. Erkindik 36; tel. (312) 25-43-73; f. 1992 by prominent scientists and academics; centrist; Chair. ZH. TENTIYEV.

Slavic Association Soglasiye (Accord): Bishkek; f. 1994 to eliminate causes of Russian emigration and to preserve Russian community in Kyrgyzstan; Vice-Pres. ANATOLII BULGAKOV.

Social Democratic Party of Kyrgyzstan: Bishkek, Sovetskaya 176; tel. (312) 22-08-05; f. 1994; Chair. ALMAZBEK ATAMBAYEV.

Union of Democratic Forces: Bishkek; f. 1999; pro-Government electoral alliance formed prior to Feb. 2000 parliamentary election; composed of the Social Democratic Party of Kyrgyzstan, the Economic Revival Party and the Birimdik Party.

Unity Party of Kyrgyzstan: Bishkek, Akhunbayeva 119A; tel. (312) 42-42-26; f. 1994; anti-nationalist; Leader E. ALYMBEKOV.

Women's Democratic Party of Kyrgyzstan: Bishkek, Sovetskaya 145; tel. (312) 28-19-47; f. 1994 to encourage the participation of women in politics; Chair. TOKON ASANOVNA SHAILIYEVA.

Youth Party of Kyrgyzstan: Bishkek; Leader AIDAR BAKIYEV.

Diplomatic Representation

EMBASSIES IN KYRGYZSTAN

Afghanistan: Bishkek; Ambassador ABDULKADYR DOSTUM.

Belarus: Bishkek, Moskovskaya 210; tel. (312) 24-29-43; Ambassador ALYAKSANDR KOZYR.

China, People's Republic: Bishkek, Toktogula 196; tel. (312) 22-24-23; Ambassador HONG JIUYIN.

Egypt: Bishkek; Ambassador MUHAMMAD NABIL ABDEL AZI FEDAUI.

France: Bishkek, Manas 43; tel. (312) 66-00-53; Ambassador SERGE SMESSOW.

Germany: 720040 Bishkek, Razzakova 28; tel. (312) 66-66-24; fax (312) 66-66-30; e-mail gerembi@elcat.kg; internet www.deutschebotschaft.bishkek.kg; Ambassador KLAUS ACHENBACH.

India: Bishkek, pr. Chui 164A , Hotel Bishkek; tel. (312) 21-08-63; fax (312) 66-07-08; e-mail india@elcat.kg; Ambassador OM PRAKASH.

Iran: Bishkek, Razzakova 36; tel. (312) 22-69-64; Ambassador JAVAD HAJ-SAYYED-JAVADI.

Japan: Bishkek; Ambassador TOSHIO TSUNOZAKI.

Kazakhstan: Bishkek, Togolok Moldo 10; tel. (312) 22-54-63; Ambassador MUKHTAR SHAKHANOV.

Myanmar: Bishkek.

Pakistan: Bishkek, Serova-Bailonova 37; tel. (312) 22-72-09; fax (312) 66-15-50; e-mail parepbishkek@exnet.kg; internet www.pakemb.com.kg.

Russia: Bishkek, Razzakova 17; tel. (312) 22-16-91; fax (312) 22-18-23; e-mail rusemb@imfiko.bishkek.su; Ambassador YEVGENII SHMAGIN.

Turkey: 720001 Bishkek, Moskovskaya 89; tel. (312) 22-78-82; fax (312) 26-88-35; Ambassador MUSTAFA EROKTEM.

Ukraine: 720000 Bishkek, bul. Pushkina 70; tel. (312) 66-55-90; e-mail emb_kg@mfa.gov.ua; Ambassador PETR SHAPOVAL.

USA: 720016 Bishkek, pr. Mira 171; tel. (312) 55-12-41; fax (312) 55-12-64; e-mail mukambaevaibx@state.gov; Ambassador JOHN MARTIN O'KEEFE.

Uzbekistan: 720040 Bishkek, Tynystanova 213; tel. (312) 66-20-65; fax (312) 66-44-03; e-mail uzbembish@infotel.kg; Ambassador ALISHER SALAHITDINOV.

Judicial System

(see under Constitution, above)

Chairman of the Constitutional Court: CHOLPON BAYEKOVA.

Chairman of the Supreme Court: NELYA BEYSHENALIYEVA.

Prosecutor-General: MYKTYBEK ABDYLDAYEV.

Religion

State Commission for Religious Affairs: 720040 Bishkek, Kievskaya 90; e-mail mail@religion.bishkek.gov.kg; Chair. OMURZAK MAMAYUSUPOV.

ISLAM

The majority of Kyrgyz are Sunni Muslims (Hanafi school), as are some other groups living in the republic, such as Uzbeks and Tajiks. Muslims in Kyrgyzstan are officially under the jurisdiction of the Muslim Board of Central Asia, based in Uzbekistan. The Board is represented in the country by a kazi.

Kazi of Muslims of Kyrgyzstan: Mullah ABDYSATAR.

Mufti of the Spiritual Directorate of Kyrgyzstan Muslims: Haji MURTALY AJI JUMANOV.

Islamic Centre of Kyrgyzstan: Osh; Pres. Haji SADYKZHAN KAMALOV.

CHRISTIANITY

Roman Catholic Church

The Church is represented in Kyrgyzstan by a Mission, established in December 1997. There were an estimated 300 adherents at 31 December 2000

Superior: Rev. Fr ALEKSANDR KAN, 720072 Bishkek, Vasilyeva 197; tel. and fax (312) 21-78-32; e-mail root@catholic.freenet.bishkek.kg.

The Press

In 1996 there were 146 non-daily newspapers published in Kyrgyzstan, and the average circulation per issue was 896,000 copies. There were three daily newspapers published in that year, with an average circulation of 67,000 copies.

PRINCIPAL NEWSPAPERS

Asaba (The Standard): Bishkek; tel. (312) 26-47-39; weekly; Kyrgyz; publication resumed in Oct. 2001, after having been suspended for seven months; Editor JUMABEK MEDERALIYEV; circ. 10,000.

Bishkek Shamy (Bishkek Evening Newspaper): Bishkek, Pravdi 24; tel. (312) 72-57-80; f. 1989; daily; official organ of the Bishkek City Council; Kyrgyz; Editor ABDIDJAPAR SOOTBEKOV; circ. 10,000.

Bishkek Observer: Bishkek; tel. (312) 29-87-26; independent; Russian and English; Editor AVTAR SINH.

Char Tarap (Echo of Events): Bishkek; tel. (312) 28-94-63; f. 1994; weekly; Kyrgyz; Editor KALEN SYDYKOVA; circ. 5,000; Parallel edition in Russian, Ekho Sobytii, Editor Mursurkul Kabylbekov.

Chui Baayni: Bishkek, Ibraimova 24; tel. (312) 42-83-31; weekly; Kyrgyz; Editor KURMANBEK RAMATOV.

Chuskye Izvestiya (Chui News): Bishkek, pr. Erkindik 45; tel. (312) 42-83-31; weekly; Russian; Editor D. PARCHUKOV.

Delo No (Case Number): Bishkek; tel. (312) 22-84-62; fax (312) 66-36-03; e-mail delo@transfer.kg; internet www.delo.elcat.kg; f. 1991; weekly; Russian; opposition; Editor VIKTOR ZAPOLSKII; circ. 50,000.

Erkin Too: Bishkek, Ibraimova 24; tel. (312) 42-03-15; 3 a week; Kyrgyz; Editor MELIS AYDAPKYLOV.

Kyrgyz Madaniyaty (Kyrgyz Culture): 720301 Bishkek, Bokonbayeva 99; tel. (312) 26-14-58; f. 1967; weekly; organ of the Union of Writers; Editor NURALY KAPAROV; circ. 15,940.

Kyrgyz Tuusu: Bishkek, Abdymomunova 193; tel. (312) 22-45-09; f. 1924; daily; organ of the Government; Kyrgyz; Editor A. MATISAKOV.

Kyrgyzstan Chronicle: Bishkek; tel. (312) 22-48-32; f. 1993; weekly; independent; English; Editor BAYAN SARYGULOV; circ. 5,000.

Limon: Bishkek, ul. Moskovskaya 189; tel. (312) 65-03-03; fax (312) 65-02-04; e-mail limon@akipress.org; internet www.akipress.org; f. 1994; Russian; independent; Dir VENERA DJAMANKULOVA.

Moya Stolitsa—Novosti (My Capital—News): Bishkek; f. 2001; independent; publication suspended in Jan. 2002.

Res Publica (Republic): Bishkek, Belinskogo 28; tel. (312) 21-97-33; e-mail repub@kyrnet.kg; internet www.respublica.elcat.kg; f. 1992; 2 a week; independent; Russian and English; publication suspended Jan.–May 2002; Editor ZAMIRA SIDIKOVA.

Slovo Kyrgyzstana (Word of Kyrgyzstan): Bishkek, Abdymomunova 193; tel. (312) 22-53-92; f. 1925; daily; organ of the Government; Russian; Editor ALEKSANDR I. MALEVANY.

Svobodniye Gori (The Free Mountains): Bishkek, Razzakova 63, POB 1450; tel. (312) 26-34-22; 3 a week; Russian; Editor L. DJOLMY-KHAMEDOVA.

The Times of Central Asia: 720000 Bishkek, pr. Chui 155; tel. (312) 68-05-67; fax (312) 68-07-69; e-mail edittimes@infotel.kg; internet www.times.kg; f. 1995; weekly; English; also distributed in Kazakhstan, Turkmenistan and Uzbekistan; subscribers in Canada, Europe, Malaysia, Turkey and the USA; Editor LYDIA SAVINA.

Vechernii Bishkek (Bishkek Evening Newspaper): Bishkek, pr. Usenbayev 2; tel. (312) 28-45-97; fax (312) 68-02-68; e-mail webmaster@vb.kg; internet vb.kyrnet.kg; f. 1974; daily; independent; Russian; Editor KHASAN YA. MUSTAFAYEV; circ. (Mon.–Thur.) 20,000, (Fri.) 50,000.

Yuzhnyi Kurier (Southern Courier): Bishkek; tel. (312) 26-10-53; f. 1993; weekly; independent; Russian; Editor ALEKSANDR KNYAZYEV; circ. 10,000.

Zaman Kyrgyzstan (Kyrgyzstan Herald): Bishkek, Frunze 390; tel. (312) 21-35-66; fax (312) 21-57-29; e-mail zamankrg@asiainfo .kg; f. 1992; weekly; independent; Kyrgyz, Turkish and English; Editor HÜSEYIN DINLEMEZ; circ. 15,000.

PRINCIPAL PERIODICALS

Monthly, unless otherwise indicated.

Ala Too (Ala Too Mountains): Bishkek; tel. (312) 26-55-12; f. 1931; organ of the Union of Writers; politics, novels, short stories, plays, poems of Kyrgyz authors and translations into Kyrgyz; Kyrgyz; Editor KENESH JUSUPOV; circ. 3,000.

Chalkan (Stinging Nettle): Bishkek; tel. (312) 42-16-38; f. 1955; satirical; Kyrgyz; Editor B. AZIZOV; circ. 7,600.

Den-sooluk (Health): Bishkek; tel. (312) 22-46-37; f. 1960; weekly; journal of the Ministry of Health; popular science; Kyrgyz; Editor MAR ALIYEV; circ. 20,000.

Korporativnyi Vestnik (Corporate Bulletin): Bishkek, pr. Chui 106; tel. (312) 22-45-07; fax (312) 66-16-64; e-mail info@cdc.kg; internet www.kv.cdc.kg; bulletin of the govt-controlled Corporate Development Centre; Dir B. KARTANBAYEV.

Kyrgyz Analytical Magazine: Bishkek, ul. Moskovskaya 189; tel. (312) 65-02-02; fax (312) 65-02-04; e-mail aki@inftel.kg; internet www.akipress.kg; f. 1993; Russian; independent; Dir MARAT TAZABEKOV.

Kyrgyzstan Ayaldary (Women of Kyrgyzstan): Bishkek; tel. (312) 42-12-26; f. 1951; popular; Kyrgyz; Editor S. AKMATBEKOVA; circ. 500.

Literaturnyi Kyrgyzstan (Literary Kyrgyzstan): 720301 Bishkek, Pushkina 70; tel. (312) 26-14-63; e-mail lk@users.kyrnet.kg; internet lk.kyrnet.kg; f. 1955; journal of the Union of Writers; fiction, literary criticism, journalism; Russian; Editor-in-Chief A. I. IVANOV; circ. 3,000.

Zdravookhraneniye Kyrgyzstana (Public Health System of Kyrgyzstan): 720005 Bishkek, Sovetskaya 34; tel. (312) 44-41-39; f. 1938; 4 a year; publ. by the Ministry of Health; experimental medical work; Russian; Editor-in-Chief N. K. KASIYEV; circ. 3,000.

NEWS AGENCIES

AKIpress: Bishkek, ul. Moskovskaya 189; tel. (312) 61-03-96; fax (312) 65-02-04; e-mail post@akipress.org; internet www.akipress .org; f. 2000; Russian and English; independent; Dir MARAT TAZABEKOV.

Belyi Parokhod: 720011 Bishkek, Pushkina 50; tel. (312) 26-45-23; e-mail parokhod@infotel.kg; internet www.kg/parokhod; f. 1997; independent.

KABAR (Kyrgyz News Agency): 720337 Bishkek, Sovetskaya 175; tel. (312) 22-67-39; fax (312) 66-14-67; e-mail mlkabar@infotel.kg; internet www.kyrgpress.org.kg; fmrly KyrgyzTag until 1992, and Kyrgyzkabar until 1995; Pres. KOUBANYCHBEK TAABALDIYEV; Editor-in-Chief DJUMAKAN SARIYEV.

Foreign Bureaux

Informatsionnoye Telegrafnoye Agentstvo Rossii– Telegrafnoye Agentstvo Suverennykh Stran (ITAR—TASS) (Russia): Bishkek, Sovetskaya 175; tel. (312) 26-59-20; Correspondent BORIS M. MAINAYEV.

Interfax (Russia): Bishkek, Toktogula 97, Rm 6; tel. and fax (312) 26-72-87; Bureau Chief BERMET MALIKOVA.

Reuters (United Kingdom): Bishkek; tel. (312) 54-52-01.

Publishers

Akyl: 720000 Bishkek, Sovetskaya 170; tel. (312) 22-47-57; f. 1994; science, politics, economics, culture, literature; Chair. AMANBEK KARYPKULOV.

Ilim (Science): 720071 Bishkek, pr. Chui 265A; tel. (312) 25-53-60; e-mail ilimph@hotmail.kg; internet ilim.aknet.kg; scientific and science fiction; Dir L. V. TARASOVA.

Kyrgyzskaya Entsiklopediya (Kyrgyz Encyclopaedia): 720040 Bishkek, bul. Erkindik 56; tel. (312) 22-77-57; dictionaries and encyclopaedias; Dir BAKTYGUL KALDYBAYEVA; Editor-in-Chief AMANBEK KARYPKULOV.

Kyrgyzstan (Kyrgyzstan Publishing House): Bishkek; tel. (312) 26-48-54; politics, science, economics, literature; Dir BERIK N. CHALAGYZOV.

Uchkun: Bishkek; state-owned.

Broadcasting and Communications

State Communications Agency: 720005 Bishkek, Sovetskaya 76; e-mail postmaster@nca.bishkek.gov.kg; Dir ANDREI TITOV.

TELECOMMUNICATIONS

Kyrgyztelekom: 720000 Bishkek, pr. Chui 96; tel. (312) 68-16-16; fax (312) 66-24-24; e-mail info@kt.kg; internet www.kt.kg; f. 1994, transformed into public co in 1997; state telecommunications co; undergoing privatization in 2002; Pres. NASIRDIN TURDALIYEV; Vice-Pres. BURKAN JUMABAYEV, ISKENDER KOLBAYEV.

BROADCASTING

Radio

State National Television and Radio Broadcasting Corpn: Chair. AMANBEK KARYPLULOV.

   Kyrgyz Radio: 720010 Bishkek, Molodoi Gvardii 59; tel. (312) 25-79-36; fax (312) 65-10-64; f. 1931; broadcasts in Kyrgyz, Russian, English, German, Ukrainian, Uzbek, Dungan and Uigur; Vice-Pres. BAYMA SUTENOVA; Pres. MOLDOSEIT MAMBETAKUNOV.

Dom Radio: 720885 Bishkek, Molodoi Gvardii 63.

Radio Azattyk: Bishkek; news broadcasts in Kyrgyz.

Radio Pyramid: 720300 Bishkek, Molodoi Gvardii 59; tel. (312) 28-28-28; fax (312) 52-61-65; e-mail pyramid@mail.elcat.kg; internet www.pyramid.elcat.kg; f. 1992; privately owned; broadcasts to Bishkek and neighbouring regions.

Sodruzhestvo: Osh; f. 1996; broadcasts to Kazakhstan, Kyrgyzstan, Tajikistan and Uzbekistan; established by ethnic Russian groups.

There are several other private radio stations operating in Kyrgyzstan.

Television

State National Television and Radio Broadcasting Corpn.

Kyrgyz Television: 720300 Bishkek, pr. Molodoi Gvardii 63; tel. (312) 25-79-36; fax (312) 25-79-30; Gen. Dir TUGELBAY KAZAKOV.

TV Pyramid: 720005 Bishkek; tel. and fax (312) 41-01-31; e-mail pyramid@ss5-22.kyrnet.kg; internet www.pyramid.elcat.kg/tv; f. 1991; privately owned; broadcasts to Bishkek and neighbouring regions.

Russian Public Television broadcasts for six hours daily in some regions of Kyrgyzstan. Relays from Kazakhstan, Turkey and Uzbekistan are also broadcast.

Finance

(cap. = capital; res = reserves; m. = million; brs = branches; amounts in soms, unless otherwise indicated)

BANKING

Central Bank

National Bank of the Kyrgyz Republic: 720040 Bishkek, Umetaliyeva 101; tel. (312) 66-90-11; fax (312) 61-07-30; e-mail mail@nbkr.kg; internet www.nbkr.kg; f. 1992; cap. 50m., res 534.4m. (Dec. 2001); Chair. ULAN K. SARBANOV.

Other Banks

In early 2001 there were 22 commercial banks in operation in Kyrgyzstan.

Amanbank: 720400 Bishkek, Tynystanova 249; tel. (312) 22-23-11; fax (312) 66-24-39; e-mail amanbank@transfer.kg; f. 1995; cap. 55m., dep. 58.9m. (Aug. 2002); Pres. SHATKUL I. KUDABAYEVA.

AsiaUniversalBank: 720033 Bishkek, Togolok Moldo 59; tel. (312) 67-01-44; fax (312) 67-04-22; e-mail reception@aub.bg; internet www .aub.kg; f. 1997 as International Business Bank, changed name as above 2000; cap. 100.0m., res 0.1m., dep. 115.1m. (Dec. 2000); Pres. and Chair. JOHN JAPARKULOV.

Bank Bakai: 720001 Bishkek, Isanov 75; tel. (312) 66-06-10; fax (312) 66-06-12; e-mail bank@bakai.kg; internet www.bakai.kg; f. 1998; cap. 38.0m., res 3.2m., dep. 111.3m. (July 2002); Chair. MARAT ALAPAYEV; Pres. MUHAMED IBRAGIMOV.

Energobank JSC: 720070 Bishkek, Jibek-Jolu 493; tel. and fax (312) 67-04-71; e-mail energykg@elcat.kg; internet www .energobank.kg; f. 1992 as Kyrgyzenergobank, changed name as above 2000; cap. US $72m., dep. $8m. (Sept. 2002); Chair. MAKSAT ISHENBAEV.

Investment Export-Import Bank: 720001 Bishkek, K. Akiyev 57; tel. (312) 65-06-10; fax (312) 62-06-54; e-mail ineximbank@infotel.kg; internet www.ineximbank.com; f. 1996 as Eridan Bank, name changed 2001; cap. 100.0m., res 4.1m., dep. 44.8m. (Aug. 2002); Chair. MURAT K. KUNAKUNOV; 1 br.

JSCB Kyrgyzavtobank: 720017 Bishkek, Isanova 42; tel. (312) 66-46-46; fax (312) 66-07-04; e-mail autobank@autobank.kg; internet www.autobank.kg; f. 1991; cap. 25m., res 1m., dep. 93m. (Dec. 2001); Chair. AKYLBEK JUMABAYEV; 6 brs.

JSCB Kyrgyzstan Bank: 720001 Bishkek, Togolok Moldo 54; tel. (312) 21-95-98; fax (312) 61-02-20; e-mail akb@bankkg.kg; internet www.bankkg.kg; f. 1991; cap. 127.0m., res 36.4m., dep. 280.7m. (Jan. 2002); Pres. SHARIPA S. SADYBAKASOVA; 29 brs.

JSCB Tolubay Bank: 720010 Bishkek, Toktogula 247; tel. (312) 25-29-13; fax (312) 24-32-82; e-mail tolubay@infotel.kg; f. 1996; cap. 26m., dep. 71.4m. (Dec. 2001); Pres. JENISHBEK S. BAIGUTTIYEV; 1 br.

Kairat Bank: 720033 Bishkek, Frunze 390; tel. (312) 21-89-32; fax (312) 21-89-55; e-mail kairat@kairatbank.kg; internet www.kairatbank.kg; f. 1999 to replace Maksat Bank (f. 1991); cap. 170.0m., res 0.0m., dep. 237.9m. Chair. MAMYTOVA KASTORU KASYMBEKOVNA; 5 brs.

OJSC Kyrgyzpromstroibank: 720040 Bishkek, pr. Chui 168; tel. (312) 61-07-43; fax (312) 21-84-45; e-mail kirgpasb@transfer.kz; f. 1991; cap. 100m. (Jan. 2001), dep. 43.3m. (Jan. 2000); Pres. MURATBEK O. MUKASHEV; 26 brs.

Foreign Banks

Demir Kyrgyz International Bank (DKIB): 720001 Bishkek, pr. Chui 245; tel. (312) 61-06-10; fax (312) 61-04-45; e-mail dkib@demirbank.kg; internet www.demirbank.kg; f. 1997; cap. 54.1m., dep. 524.1m. (Dec. 2002); Chair. HALIT CINGILLIOGLU; Gen. Man. AHMET KAMIL PARMAKSIZ.

Ecobank: 720031 Bishkek, Geologicheskii per. 17; tel. (312) 54-35-82; fax (312) 54-35-80; e-mail ecobank@totel.kg; internet www.ecobank.kg; f. 1996 as Bank Rossiiskii Kredit; name changed 1998; joint-stock commercial bank; cap. 61.0m., dep. 88.8m. (Feb. 2001); Chair. ANVAR K. ABDRAYEV; Dep. Chair. CHOLPON Z. ISAYEVA.

National Bank of Pakistan: 720017 Bishkek, pr. Manas 9; tel. (312) 66-11-32; fax (312) 66-33-32; Gen. Man. SHUJAUL MULK.

COMMODITY EXCHANGE

Kyrgyzstan Commodity and Raw Materials Exchange: 720001 Bishkek, Belinskaya 40; tel. (312) 22-13-75; fax (312) 22-27-44; f. 1990; Gen. Dir TEMIR SARIYEV.

STOCK EXCHANGE

Kyrgyz Stock Exchange: 720010 Bishkek, Moskovskaya 172; tel. (312) 66-50-59; fax (312) 66-15-95; e-mail kse@kse.kg; internet www.kse.kg; Pres. AMANGELDY M. MURALIYEV; Chair. CHINARBEK OTUNCHIYEV.

INSURANCE

Kyrgyzinstrakh: f. 1996 by the Russian joint-stock insurance company Investstrakh, Kyrgyz insurance companies and the Kyrgyz Government to insure foreign investors.

Trade and Industry

GOVERNMENT AGENCIES

State Agency for Geology and Mineral Resources: 720739 Bishkek, pr. Erkindik 2; tel. (312) 66-49-01; fax (312) 66-03-91; e-mail mail@geoagency.bishkek.gov.kg; internet www.kgs.bishkek.gov.kg; Chair. SHEISHENALY MURZAGAZIYEV.

State Agency for Power Engineering: 720055 Bishkek, Akhunbayeva 119; e-mail postmaster@gae.bishkek.gov.kg; Dir ULARBEK MATEYEV.

State Agency for Registration of Real Estate Rights: 720040 Bishkek, Orozbekova 44; e-mail gosreg@bishkek.gov.kg; Chair. TOLOBEK OMURALIYEV.

State Agency for Science and Intellectual Property: 720021 Bishkek, Moskovskaya 62; tel. (312) 68-08-19; fax (312) 68-17-03; e-mail kyrgyzpatent@infotel.kg; internet www.kyrgyzpatent.kg; Dir ROMAN OMOROV.

State Agency for Standardization and Metrology (Kyrgyzstandard): 720040 Bishkek, Panfilova 197; tel. (312) 22-78-84; fax (312) 66-13-67; e-mail gost@kmc.bishkek.gov.kg; internet www.kmc.bishkek.gov.kg; f. 1927; certification, control and testing of products and services; Dir BATYRBEK DAVLESOV.

State Commission for Anti-monopoly Policy: 720040 Bishkek, pr. Chui 114; Chair. EMILBEK UZAKBAYEV.

State Commission for Architecture and Construction: 720026 Bishkek, pr. Manasa 28; e-mail mail@gosstroy.bishkek.gov.kg; Chair. ANVAR TURSUNOV.

State Commission for Business Development: 720002 Bishkek, pr. Erkindik 57; e-mail fsmb@bishkek.gov.kg; Chair. KAMILA KENENBAYEVA.

State Commission for Drugs Control: 720010 Bishkek, Razzakova 63; e-mail gkkn@bishkek.gov.kg; Chair. KURMANBEK KUBATBEKOV.

State Commission for Standards, Financial Accounts and Auditing: 720040 Bishkek, pr. Chui 106; Chair. KANATBEK SAGYNOV.

State Committee for Management of State Property and Attraction of Direct Investment: 720002 Bishkek, pr. Erkindik 57; tel. (312) 22-77-06; fax (312) 66-02-36; e-mail spf@intranet.kg; internet spf.gov.kg; f. 1991; responsible for the privatization of state-owned enterprises and deals with bankruptcies; Chair. RAVSHAN ZHEYENBEKOV.

State Securities Commission: 720040 Bishkek, pr. Chui 114; e-mail nsc@nsc.kg; Chair. URAN ABDYNASYROV.

CHAMBER OF COMMERCE

Chamber of Commerce and Industry of the Kyrgyz Republic: 720001 Bishkek, Kievskaya 107; tel. (312) 21-05-65; fax (312) 21-05-75; e-mail cci-kr@totel.kg; internet www.chamber.kg; f. 1959; supports foreign economic relations and the development of small and medium-sized enterprises; Pres. BORIS V. PERFILIYEV.

TRADE ASSOCIATION

Kyrgyzvneshtorg Ltd: 720033 Bishkek, Abdymomunova 276; tel. (312) 21-39-78; fax (312) 66-08-36; e-mail kvt@infotel.kg; f. 1992; export-import org. Gen. Dir K. K. KALIYEV.

UTILITIES

Electricity

JSC National Electric Grid of Kyrgyzstan: 720070 Bishkek, Jibek Jolu 326; tel. (312) 66-10-00; fax (312) 66-06-56; e-mail aoke@infotel.kg; divided into seven companies in 2001; undergoing privatization in 2002; Gen. Dir BAKIRGIN SARATKAZIYEV.

Gas

Kyrgyzazmunayzat: 720000 Bishkek, L. Tolstogo 114; tel. (312) 24-53-80; fax (312) 24-53-93; state-owned joint-stock co; f. 1997 through merger; Dir-Gen. BAKIRDIN SUBANBEKOV.

Kyrgyzgaz: 720661 Bishkek, Gorkogo 22; tel. (312) 53-00-45; fax (312) 43-09-80; state-owned joint-stock co; scheduled for privatization; Dir-Gen. AVTANDIL SYDYKOV.

TRADE UNIONS

Kyrgyzstan Federation of Trade Unions: Bishkek; Chair. S. BOZBUNBAYEV.

Transport

RAILWAYS

Owing to the country's mountainous terrain, the railway network consists of only one main line (340 km) in northern Kyrgyzstan, which connects the republic, via Kazakhstan, with the railway system of Russia. Osh, Jalal-Abad and four other towns in regions of Kyrgyzstan bordering Uzbekistan are linked to that country by short lengths of railway track. In mid-1998 work began on a US $2,500m. project to construct a railway line connecting eastern Uzbekistan with southern Kyrgyzstan. In June 2001 the Governments of Kyrgyzstan and the People's Republic of China signed a memorandum on the construction of a rail link from Kashgar (China) to Bishkek.

Kyrgyz Railway Administration: 720009 Bishkek, L. Tolstogo 83; tel. (312) 25-30-54; fax (312) 24-56-11; f. 1924; Pres. I. S. OMURKULOV; Dir SADYKBEK A. ABLESOV.

ROADS

In 1999 Kyrgyzstan's road network totalled an estimated 18,500 km, including 140 km of motorway; in 1996 there were 3,200 km of main roads and 6,380 km of secondary roads. About 91% of roads were paved. Many of the best road links are with neighbouring countries —mainly with Kazakhstan in the north, with Uzbekistan in the west and with China in the south-east. A main road linking the cities of Bishkek and Osh was under reconstruction in the early 2000s. The International Development Bank allocated US $37m. towards the $60m. cost of repairing the Taras–Talas–Susamyr road by 2002.

CIVIL AVIATION

There are two international airports at Bishkek (Manas Airport) and at Osh. The approval in December 2001 of the use of Manas Airport by troops of the US-led anti-terrorism coalition formed after 11 September was expected to result in foreign funding for its reconstruction. The reconstruction of Osh airport, at a cost of some US $9.5m., was planned to take place in 2002, with International Development Bank funding. There were 13 privately owned airlines in Kyrgyzstan in early 2001.

Asian Star: 720000 Bishkek, Tynystanova 120; tel. (312) 26-34-55; fax (312) 64-04-05; regional charter passenger services; Pres. BORIS ROLNIK.

Kyrgyzstan Airlines (Kyrgyzstan Aba Zholdoru): 720044 Bishkek, pr. Mir 95; tel. (312) 54-80-66; fax (312) 54-80-66; e-mail office@ kyrgyzstanairlines.kg; internet www.kyrgyzstanairlines.kg; f. 1992;

operates scheduled and charter flights to destinations in Azerbaijan, the People's Republic of China, Germany, India, Kazakhstan, Pakistan, Russia and Uzbekistan; scheduled for privatization; Pres. OKENOV TAALAYBEK BEYSHEYEVICH.

Tourism

There was little tourism in Kyrgyzstan during the Soviet period. In the first years of independence tourist facilities remained very limited, and foreign visitors tended to be mountaineers. However, the Government hoped that the country's spectacular and largely unspoilt mountain scenery, as well as the great crater lake of Issyk-Kul, might attract foreign tourists and investment. By the late 1990s the number of tourists visiting Kyrgyzstan was increasing (there were some 69,000 tourist arrivals in 2000, compared with around 59,000 in 1998). The Government's promotion strategy centred on the country's position on the ancient 'Silk Road' trade route, and its potential as a destination for nature tourism and adventure holidays. There were also plans to develop Kyrgyzstan's ski resorts.

State Agency for Tourism, Sport and Youth Policy: 720033 Bishkek, Togolok Moldo 17; tel. (312) 22-06-57; fax (312) 21-28-45; e-mail gatiskr@bishkek.gov.kg; Chair. OKMOTBEK ALMAKUCHUKOV.

LAOS

Introductory Survey

Location, Climate, Language, Religion, Flag, Capital

The Lao People's Democratic Republic is a land-locked country in South-East Asia, bordered by the People's Republic of China to the north, by Viet Nam to the east, by Cambodia to the south, by Thailand to the west and by Myanmar (formerly Burma) to the north-west. The climate is tropical, with a rainy monsoon season lasting from May to September. The temperature in the capital ranges between 23°C and 38°C in the hottest month, April, and between 14°C and 28°C in the coolest month, January. Laos comprises 47 ethnic groups. The official language, Lao or Laotian, is spoken by about two-thirds of the population. French is also spoken, and there are numerous tribal languages, including Meo. The principal religion is Buddhism. There are also some Christians and followers of animist beliefs. The national flag (proportions 2 by 3) has three horizontal stripes, of red, blue (half the total depth) and red, with a white disc in the centre. The capital is Vientiane (Viangchan).

Recent History

Laos was formerly a part of French Indo-China and comprised the three principalities of Luang Prabang, Vientiane and Champasak. These were merged in 1946, when France recognized Sisavang Vong, ruler of Luang Prabang since 1904, as King of Laos. In May 1947 the King promulgated a democratic constitution (although women were not allowed to vote until 1957). The Kingdom of Laos became independent, within the French Union, in July 1949, and full sovereignty was recognized by France in October 1953. The leading royalist politician was Prince Souvanna Phouma, who was Prime Minister in 1951–54, 1956–58, 1960 and in 1962–75. King Sisavang Vong died in October 1959, and was succeeded by his son, Savang Vatthana.

From 1950 the Royal Government was opposed by the Neo Lao Haksat (Lao Patriotic Front—LPF), an insurgent movement formed by a group of former anti-French activists. The LPF's Chairman was Prince Souphanouvong, a half-brother of Prince Souvanna Phouma, but its dominant element was the communist People's Party of Laos (PPL), led by Kaysone Phomvihane. During the 1950s the LPF's armed forces, the Pathet Lao, gradually secured control of the north-east of the country with the assistance of the Vietnamese communists, the Viet Minh, who were engaged in war with the French (until 1954). Several agreements between the Royal Government and the LPF, attempting to end the guerrilla war and reunite the country, failed during the 1950s and early 1960s. By 1965 the de facto partition of Laos was established, with the LPF refusing to participate in national elections and consolidating its power over the north-eastern provinces.

During the 1960s, as the 'Ho Chi Minh Trail' (the communist supply route to South Viet Nam) ran through Pathet Lao-controlled areas, Laos remained closely involved with the war between communist forces and anti-communist troops (supported by the USA) in Viet Nam. In 1973 the Viet Nam peace negotiations included provisions for a cease-fire in Laos. A new Government was formed in April 1974 under Prince Souvanna Phouma, with royalist, neutralist and LPF participation; Prince Souphanouvong was appointed Chairman of the Joint National Political Council. However, the LPF increased its power and eventually gained effective control of the country. This was confirmed by election victories in October and November 1975. In November King Savang Vatthana abdicated, and Prince Souvanna Phouma resigned.

In December 1975 the National Congress of People's Representatives (264 delegates elected by local authorities) abolished the monarchy and elected a 45-member legislative body, the Supreme People's Council (now the Supreme People's Assembly). Souphanouvong was appointed President of the renamed Lao People's Democratic Republic and President of the Supreme People's Council. Kaysone Phomvihane, who had become Secretary-General of the Phak Pasason Pativat Lao (Lao People's Revolutionary Party—LPRP, a successor to the PPL), was appointed Prime Minister. The former King Savang Vatthana was designated Supreme Counsellor to the President, but he refused to co-operate with the new regime and was arrested

in March 1977. (He was subsequently stated to have died in a 're-education camp'.) The LPF was replaced in February 1979 by the Lao Front for National Construction (LFNC), under the leadership of the LPRP.

In October 1986 the ailing Souphanouvong announced his resignation from his duties as President of the Republic (while retaining the title) and of the Supreme People's Assembly. Phoumi Vongvichit, formerly a Vice-Chairman in the Council of Ministers, became acting President of the Republic, while Sisomphon Lovansai, a Vice-President of the Supreme People's Assembly and a member of the LPRP Politburo, became acting President of the Assembly. In November Kaysone Phomvihane was re-elected Secretary-General of the LPRP. In September 1987 it was announced that Phoumi Vongvichit had also replaced Souphanouvong as Chairman of the LFNC.

In June 1988 elections (the first since the formation of the Lao People's Democratic Republic) took place to determine the members of 113 district-level People's Councils. The LFNC approved 4,462 candidates to contest 2,410 seats. Provincial prefectural elections took place in November, when 898 candidates contested 651 seats. At a general election in March 1989, 121 candidates contested 79 seats in the enlarged Supreme People's Assembly. At its inaugural session in May, Nouhak Phoumsavanh (a Vice-Chairman of the Council of Ministers) was elected President of the Assembly.

Armed opposition to the Government persisted during the 1980s, particularly among hill tribes. In October 1982 Gen. Phoumi Nosavan, a 'conservative' who had been living in exile since 1965, formed the anti-communist Royal Lao Democratic Government, led by former Laotian military officers. However, many prominent exiles and resistance fighters in the United Front for the National Liberation of the Lao People (UFNLLP—formed in September 1980, and reportedly led by Gen. Phoumi since mid-1981) dissociated themselves from the Royal Government, which had established itself in southern Laos. In October 1988 the Government announced the capture of the Chief of Staff of the UFNLLP.

In December 1989 the right-wing United Lao National Liberation Front (ULNLF) proclaimed the 'Revolutionary Provisional Government' of Laos. The self-styled Government, which was headed by Outhong Souvannavong (the former President of the Royal Council of King Savang Vatthana), claimed to have used military force to 'liberate' one-third of Laotian territory. Although there were reports of attacks by insurgent guerrillas in northern Laos at this time, it was widely assumed that the ULNLF's claims were exaggerated and that its proclamation was an attempt to elicit popular support. Responsibility for defence was reportedly allocated to Gen. Vang Pao, a leader of the Hmong tribe who in the 1970s had been a commander of the Royalist army (and who had lived in exile in the USA since 1975); Somphorn Wang (also formerly a prominent Royalist) was described as secretary of state in the 'Revolutionary Provisional Government'. In late 1992 Gen. Vang Pao reportedly travelled to Singapore to direct an unsuccessful military operation from Thailand. In October Gen. Vang Pao's brother, Vang Fung, and another Hmong rebel, Moua Yee Julan (who were allegedly preparing an incursion into Laos under Gen. Vang Pao's command), were arrested in Thailand. In September 1993 Thai troops launched an offensive against Gen. Vang Pao's forces, expelling 320 rebels from Thai territory.

In June 1990 a draft constitution, enshrining free-market principles, was published in the LPRP newspaper, Pasason. Later in the same month the Supreme People's Assembly approved legislation that included provision for the ownership of property, for inheritance rights and contractual obligations. In October three former government officials were arrested in connection with what were termed 'activities aimed at overthrowing the regime'. It was reported in Thailand that they had formed part of a 'Social Democrat Group', which was actively seeking the introduction of multi-party democracy. In November 1992 all three were sentenced to 14 years' imprisonment.

In March 1991, at the Fifth Congress of the LPRP, Souphanouvong retired from all his party posts. Phoumi Vongvichit and

Sisomphon Lovansai also retired, and the three were appointed to a newly created advisory board to the LPRP Central Committee. Kaysone Phomvihane's title was altered from General Secretary to President of the LPRP, and his power was slightly enhanced following the abolition of the party Secretariat. A new Politburo and (younger) Party Central Committee were elected. Gen. Sisavat Keobounphan, the military Chief of the General Staff, was not re-elected to the Politburo. The leadership pledged a continuance of free-market economic reforms, but denied the need for political pluralism. However, the national motto ('peace, independence, unity, socialism') was changed to 'peace, independence, democracy, unity, prosperity'.

On 14 August 1991 the Supreme People's Assembly adopted a new constitution, which provided for a National Assembly, confirmed the leading role of the LPRP, enshrined the right to private ownership, and endowed the presidency with executive powers; new electoral legislation was also promulgated. Kaysone Phomvihane was appointed President of Laos. Gen. Khamtay Siphandone, a Vice-Chairman of the Council of Ministers, Minister of National Defence and Supreme Commander of the Lao People's Army, replaced Kaysone Phomvihane as Chairman of the Council of Ministers, restyled Prime Minister.

Kaysone Phomvihane died in November 1992. He was replaced as President of the LPRP by Gen. Khamtay Siphandone, and on 25 November a specially convened meeting of the Supreme People's Assembly elected Nouhak Phoumsavanh as President of State. Elections to the new National Assembly took place on 20 December; 99.33% of eligible voters participated in the election, in which 154 LFNC-approved candidates contested 85 seats. On 22 February 1993 the new National Assembly re-elected Nouhak Phoumsavanh as President, confirmed Khamtay Siphandone as Prime Minister, and implemented the most extensive reorganization of the Council of Ministers since the LPRP's accession to power in 1975. Phoumi Vongvichit died in January 1994, and Souphanouvong in January 1995.

Although the 20th anniversary of the beginning of communist rule was celebrated in 1995, the Laotian Government was gradually attempting to replace communist ideology with Lao nationalism, as Laos developed as a market economy with increasing foreign participation. In July senior Buddhist monks were assembled in Vientiane (as Buddhism was deemed central to Laotian cultural identity) and were encouraged by the Government to lead a 'cultural renaissance'. Meanwhile, the Government urged the security forces to suppress social problems, particularly corruption and prostitution, perceived as arising from increasing external influences.

The results of the elections at the LPRP congress at the end of March 1996 consolidated the country's apparent progress towards a form of military-dominated authoritarian government. The armed forces gained a majority of seats on the new nine-member Politburo; Khamtay Siphandone was elected as its President (replacing Nouhak Phoumsavanh, who retired from this post), and the Minister of National Defence and Commander-in-Chief of the armed forces, Lt-Gen. Choummali Saignason, was promoted to third position, after the Chairman of the National Assembly, Lt-Gen. Saman Vignaket. The most significant development was the failure of Khamphoui Keoboualapha, a Deputy Prime Minister responsible for many of Laos's reforms, to be re-elected either to the Politburo or to the Central Committee. Lts-Gen. Choummali Saignason and Saman Vignaket were widely reported to be opposed to rapid economic and political reform.

At the opening session of the National Assembly in April 1996 Nouhak Phoumsavanh was, despite his retirement from the Politburo, confirmed as Head of State until the end of his term of office in February 1998. Sisavat Keobounphan (who had been restored to the Politburo at the previous month's elections) was elected to the new office of Vice-President, in order to relieve Nouhak Phoumsavanh of a number of presidential duties. Boungnang Volachit was approved by the National Assembly as a Deputy Prime Minister, although, contrary to expectation, Khamphoui Keoboualapha also retained his posts as Deputy Prime Minister and Chairman of the State Committee for Planning and Co-operation. However, it was expected that the latter's influence would be diminished by his exclusion from the Politburo and also by the establishment of a new State Planning Committee, which was to assume some of the responsibilities hitherto exercised by Khamphoui's Committee.

Elections to the National Assembly took place on 21 December 1997, at which 159 LFNC-approved candidates, including 41 members of the outgoing legislature, contested 99 seats. The

three members of the LPRP Politburo and 10 Central Committee members who stood for election were all successful; one of the four 'independent' candidates without affiliation to the LPRP was elected. The level of participation by voters was officially registered to have been 99.37%. The first session of the new National Assembly was held on 23–26 February 1998, during which the Assembly elected Gen. Khamtay to succeed Phoumsavanh as President of State. The Assembly also endorsed the appointment of Sisavat Keobounphan as Prime Minister and of Oudom Khattigna in his place as Vice-President, re-elected Saman Vignaket as President of the National Assembly, and approved a redistribution of ministerial posts.

As part of another reorganization of the Council of Ministers in March 2001, Oudom was replaced as Vice-President by Lt-Gen. Choummali Saignason, who had relinquished his bid for the premiership owing to ill health. Prime Minister Sisavat Keobounphan became another scapegoat of the Asian financial crisis, when he was forced to resign after only three years in office, in order to take responsibility for the mismanagement of the economy. His successor, the former Deputy Prime Minister and Minister of Finance, Boungnang Volachit, provided a civilian balance to the entirely military executive branch. The appointment of Thongloun Sisolit to the post of Deputy Prime Minister further enhanced the greater civilian representation on the Council of Ministers.

From the mid-1990s uprisings against the Government became more frequent. In July 1995 an army unit based near Luang Prabang mutinied after its commander, a Hmong general, was passed over for promotion. Five members of the armed forces died in the rebellion, which was believed to be symptomatic of the resentment felt by hill tribes over the political and military dominance of the lowland Lao. About 2,000 troops were dispatched to Luang Prabang to restore order. In November several people were killed in an armed assault on a bus near Luang Prabang. The attack was attributed to disaffected Hmong tribesmen who had pledged to disrupt that year's 20th anniversary celebrations of the beginning of communist rule. In October a shipment of explosives, allegedly destined for Hmong insurgents, had been intercepted on the Mekong River. Several incidents in the Luang Prabang region during 1996, including, in September, an armed attack on a vehicle as a result of which five people (among them a French expatriate) were killed, were ascribed to Hmong rebels. Meanwhile, fund-raising by the Hmong community in the USA was reportedly a cause for concern within the Laotian Government. Also in September an arms cache believed to belong to Gen. Vang Pao's anti-Government forces was discovered in northern Thailand.

In October 1999 an anti-Government demonstration by students and teachers was held in Vientiane. Leaflets demanding the resignation of the Government, the release of political prisoners and the establishment of a dialogue between the authorities and opposition groups were reportedly distributed by the demonstrators. The protest, which constituted an extremely rare overt demonstration of public dissatisfaction, was reportedly swiftly dispersed by police. The Government subsequently refuted claims that about 50 people who were involved or suspected to have been involved in the protest had been arrested, and, furthermore, denied that the demonstration had taken place; in late March 2000, however, it was reported that the whereabouts of one professor and at least five students arrested during the protest remained unknown.

Civil unrest intensified throughout 2000, with a spate of bomb attacks. The first occurred in a restaurant on 30 March, immediately drawing international attention to the event, as several tourists were injured in the blast. Two further attacks took place in Vientiane in May, coinciding with the separate visits of the Thai Prime Minister, Chuan Leekpai, and his Minister of Foreign Affairs, Surin Pitsuwan. Two more strikes followed within a week of each other, bringing the total to five explosions within three months, more than 20 people having been injured and at least two killed. Under pressure, the Government, blaming the campaign on Hmong insurgents, claimed to have arrested two men (one Lao and one Hmong) carrying explosive devices in mid-June. Despite the arrests, the bombing operation continued unabated. A bomb was defused near the Vietnamese embassy in Vientiane at the end of July, lending credence to the suspicion that the action was part of an internal power struggle between pro-Chinese and pro-Vietnamese governmental factions. In total, at least nine bombs exploded between March 2000 and January 2001, with the penultimate detonation occurring on the eve of the meeting of the European Union and Association of

South East Asian Nations (EU-ASEAN summit) on 10 December 2000.

Although no group admitted responsibility for the bombings, a pre-dawn raid in July 2000 on immigration and customs offices in Vang Tao, opposite the Chong Mek checkpoint, indicated the involvement of royalist rebels. The Government claimed that the attack was merely a robbery, but during the incursion, in which six men died in an exchange of gunfire with Lao soldiers and another 28 were arrested after fleeing over the Thai border, the former royal flag was raised over the immigration office. In mid-November 2000 about 200 workers and students were reported to have staged a demonstration in the southern province of Champasak, calling for democracy. The protest was swiftly quelled, with 15 people being arrested. The timing of the demonstration, however, exacerbated the increasing sense of instability, as less than two weeks previously, Helen Clark, the Prime Minister of New Zealand, had confirmed that her Government had granted political asylum to Khamsay Souphanouvong, a minister attached to the Prime Minister's office and son of the first President of the Lao People's Democratic Republic.

In December 2000 Kerry and Kay Danes, an Australian couple, were arrested on suspicion of involvement in the theft of over US $6m. worth of sapphires. In March 2001 the Australian Minister for Foreign Affairs, Alexander Downer, stated that the continued detention of the couple without formal charge could threaten the strong diplomatic relationship between the two countries. Following the conclusion of an investigation into the case in April, a Laotian court finally convicted the couple of embezzlement, tax evasion and destruction of evidence in June 2001. They were sentenced to prison terms of seven years each. However, the couple were provisionally released in October 2001, having spent 10 months in custody. Following protracted diplomatic negotiations, and in large part due to Laos's strong ties with Australia, the pair received a formal presidential pardon in November.

In October 2001 five European activists, including Olivier Dupuis, a Belgian member of the European Parliament, were arrested for handing out pro-democracy leaflets at a peaceful protest in Vientiane. The protest was held to commemorate the second anniversary of the disappearance of five students who had participated in the demonstration of October 1999. In November 2001, following expressions of concern at the conditions the detainees were being forced to endure, Romani Prodi, President of the European Commission, warned the Laotian authorities that the continued detention of the activists would threaten diplomatic relations with the EU. In the same month, following a swift trial, the prisoners were convicted of attempting to spread unrest and ordered to be deported. They were also fined and given two-year suspended prison terms.

On 24 February 2002 elections took place from among 166 LFNC-approved candidates to the 109 seats available in the National Assembly. Only one of the elected members was not affiliated to the LPRP, ensuring that the ruling party secured a comprehensive victory. In April, at the opening session of the National Assembly, the existing Cabinet was almost wholly re-elected. The former Minister of the Interior, Maj.-Gen. Asang Laoli, became Deputy Prime Minister and Maj.-Gen. Soutchey Thammasith subsequently assumed the interior portfolio. In January 2003 a cabinet reorganization was announced in an apparent attempt to strengthen the national economy. The former Governor of the Central Bank, Chansy Phosikham, was appointed Minister of Finance, Onneua Phommachanh became Minister of Industry and Handicrafts and Soulivong Daravong was placed in charge of the Ministry of Commerce and Tourism.

In September 2002 a bomb exploded at the Si Muang temple in Vientiane, injuring two children; it was unclear whether the attack was linked to the bombings that had occurred in 2000. In January 2003, for the first time, national celebrations were held to commemorate the anniversary of the birth of King Fa Ngoum, accredited with founding the Kingdom of Lane Xang in 1353; a statue was erected and a public holiday declared. The celebrations were thought to be an attempt to encourage national unity. In the following month a group of armed men ambushed a bus near the town of Vang Vieng; the attack resulted in the deaths of 13 people, including three foreign nationals, two of whom were tourists. Several arrests were later made in connection with the ambush, which was thought to have been carried out by bandits rather than terrorists. It was feared that the incident might discourage tourists from visiting the country.

From 1975 Laos was dependent on Vietnamese economic and military assistance, permitting the stationing of Vietnamese troops (estimated in 1987 to number between 30,000 and 50,000) on its territory. In 1977 a 25-year treaty of friendship between the two countries was signed, and Laos supported the Vietnamese-led overthrow of the Khmer Rouge regime in Kampuchea (Cambodia) in January 1979. Following the outbreak of hostilities between Viet Nam and the People's Republic of China in that year, Laos allied itself with the former. Viet Nam withdrew its military presence from Laos during 1988. The two countries signed a protocol governing military co-operation in March 1994. In July 2001 Prime Minister Boungnang Volachit visited Viet Nam on his first overseas trip since assuming office in March. In May 2002 President Gen. Khamtai Siphandone paid an official friendship visit to Viet Nam, which was reciprocated in October by the Chairman of the Vietnamese National Assembly, Nguyen Van An. The visits affirmed the strength of ties between the two countries.

In February 1993 Laos, Thailand, Viet Nam and Cambodia signed a joint communiqué providing for the resumption of co-operation in the development of the Mekong River. In April 1995 in Chiang Rai, Thailand, representatives of the four countries signed an agreement on the joint exploitation and development of the lower Mekong. The accord provided for the establishment of the Mekong River Commission (see p. 341) as a successor to the Committee for Co-ordination of Investigations of the Lower Mekong Basin.

In July 1992 Laos strengthened ties with members of the Association of South East Asian Nations (ASEAN, see p. 146) by signing the ASEAN Treaty of Amity and Co-operation, which provided for wider regional co-operation and was regarded as a preliminary step to full membership of the Association. Laos attended ASEAN meetings with observer status from this time, and applied for membership of the organization in March 1996. The country was formally admitted as a full member at the organization's meeting of ministers responsible for foreign affairs in July 1997. In August 2001 Indonesian President Megawati Sukarnoputri visited Laos on the third leg of her tour of ASEAN nations.

Relations with the People's Republic of China improved in December 1986, when a Chinese delegation, led by the Deputy Minister of Foreign Affairs, made the first official Chinese visit to Laos since 1978. In December 1987, after an assurance from the People's Republic of China that support would be withdrawn from Laotian resistance groups operating from within China, the two countries agreed to restore full diplomatic relations and to encourage bilateral trade. Relations between the LPRP and the Chinese Communist Party were fully restored in August 1989. In October 1991 the Laotian and Chinese Prime Ministers signed a border treaty, which established a framework for meetings of a Laotian-Chinese joint border committee. In January 1992 the committee adopted a resolution providing for the demarcation of the common border, and in June an agreement on the delineation of boundaries was signed. In November 1994 Laos and China signed a reciprocal agreement on the transport of passengers and goods on each other's sections of the Mekong River. In February 1996 Laos and China opened a section of their border to highway traffic. In October 1997 Chinese Vice-Premier Wu Bangguo made a three-day visit to Laos, and in early 1999 Prime Minister Sisavat Keobounphan made an eight-day official visit to China. The first visit ever made by a Chinese head of state to Laos was by President Jiang Zemin in November 2000.

Relations with Thailand from 1975 were characterized by mutual suspicion. Thailand intermittently closed its border to Laotian imports and exports, causing considerable hardship. Disputed sovereignty claims in border areas were a cause of friction, and led to clashes between Laotian and Thai troops in 1984. Further hostilities began in December 1987, resulting in hundreds of casualties. In February 1988 the two sides agreed to declare a cease-fire, to withdraw their troops from the combat area, and to attempt to negotiate a peaceful solution. In March 1991 (following the recent military coup in Thailand) representatives of the two countries signed an agreement providing for the immediate withdrawal of troops from disputed areas. The Thai Government also undertook to suppress the activities of Laotian insurgents operating from Thai territory. In December Thailand and Laos signed a border co-operation agreement.

In June 1992 the Thai Crown Prince, Maha Vajiralongkorn, visited Vientiane for the first time. On the following day, however, about 300 guerrillas from a Thai-based rebel group, the Free Democratic Lao National Salvation Force, attacked three Laotian government posts, killing two people and causing significant damage. In the same month Laos refuted allegations made by a senior Thai military officer that a Laotian government unit was receiving training in chemical warfare from Cuban and Vietnamese experts, and also dismissed previous accusations by Laotian resistance fighters and Western aid agencies of its use of chemical warfare to suppress the activities of rebel groups. Bilateral relations improved in July, when the Thai authorities announced the arrest of 11 Laotian citizens accused of planning subversive activities against the Government in Vientiane. Further arrests were made in October. The first bridge (over the Mekong River) linking Laos and Thailand was opened in April 1994; construction of a second bridge began in February 1998. In September 1996 the countries' Joint Co-operation Commission agreed to establish a boundary commission, in an effort to resolve demarcation problems. In March 1997, none the less, Laotian radio reported that Thai reconnaissance aircraft had violated Laotian airspace on five occasions during the previous month. In April 1997 and February 1999 Laotian and Thai Governors of the provinces along the common border held meetings at which border issues were discussed. In March 1999 Prime Minister Sisavat Keobounphan made a three-day official visit to Thailand. Despite various diplomatic moves to stimulate co-operation between the two countries, such as the signing of an extradition treaty in January 2001, the relationship was strained by the July 2000 incursion launched from Thai territory by suspected royalist rebels. The situation deteriorated further after Laotian troops occupied two islands in the Mekong River, evicting 65 Thai farming families. Laos claimed that under a 1926 treaty it had sovereignty over all the islands in the Mekong, while Thailand merely requested the withdrawal of the troops. Nevertheless, there were plans for the building of another Mekong Friendship Bridge. Construction was scheduled to begin in 2002 and to be completed in 2005. In April 2001 the Thai Minister of Foreign Affairs, Surakiart Sathirathai, visited Laos, affirming the beginning of a new era of friendly Lao-Thai relations based on shared cultural values. In June Thai Prime Minister Thaksin Shinawatra arrived in Vientiane on a two-day official visit intended further to consolidate co-operative ties between the two countries. However, border demarcation issues, including the dispute over the Mekong islands, remained an unresolved source of tension in early 2003, although it was hoped that border demarcation would be completed by the middle of that year.

During the 1970s and 1980s thousands of Laotian refugees fled to Thailand to escape from civil war and food shortages. In January 1989 an estimated 90,000 Laotian refugees remained in border camps in Thailand. The office of the UN High Commissioner for Refugees (UNHCR) began a programme of voluntary repatriation in 1980. By late 1990 fewer than 6,000 refugees had been repatriated under UNHCR supervision, while some 15,000 had returned independently, and others had been resettled abroad. In June 1991 UNHCR, Laos and Thailand signed an agreement guaranteeing the repatriation or resettlement in a third country of the remaining 60,000 Laotian refugees in Thailand by the end of 1994. In July 1994, however, UNHCR, Laos and Thailand revised their agreement to the effect that the repatriation programme would be completed by early 1995, and this deadline was subsequently revised on several occasions. In December 1996, according to UNHCR figures, 3,293 Laotian refugees remained in Thailand. In December 1997 UNHCR announced that a final review of the status of the last remaining refugees at Ban Napho camp in Thailand would be completed by January 1998, whereupon they would be repatriated or resettled in a third country. Among the camp's 1,344 refugees were reportedly 964 Hmong, most of whom were unwilling to return to Laos.

Laos's uneasy political relationship with Thailand, in conjunction with Thailand's economic superiority in the region, is widely regarded as having prompted the Laotian Government during the 1990s to forge closer links with Myanmar and, more recently, with Cambodia. In February 1992 Khamtay Siphandone was the first foreign head of government to visit Myanmar since the military coup in that country in 1988, and in June 1994 Senior Gen. Than Shwe visited Laos, his first foreign visit as Myanmar's Head of State. Bilateral contacts continued on a frequent basis. Laos signed a treaty of friendship and assistance with Cambodia in December 1995, further to which Joint Co-operation Committees were established. In November 2001 Prince Norodom Ranariddh headed a Cambodian delegation on an official goodwill visit to Laos, confirming the continued strength of bilateral ties.

From 1989 the Laotian Government sought to improve relations with non-communist countries, in order to reduce its (especially economic) dependence on the USSR and Viet Nam. Following a visit to Japan in that year by Kaysone Phomvihane (his first official visit to a non-communist country), the Japanese Government agreed to increase grant aid to Laos. In December 1995 Japan announced that it would resume the provision of official loans to Laos in 1996. In January 2000 the Japanese Prime Minister, Keizo Obuchi, made an official visit to Laos, and in August 2000 a bridge over the Mekong, built with a 5,460m.-yen grant from the Japanese Government, was officially opened in Paksé. In mid-2001 Prince Akishino of Japan made a 10-day unofficial visit to Laos and, in September, Japan agreed a further loan to fund the construction of the second Mekong Friendship Bridge, beginning in 2002 and scheduled for completion in 2005.

In November 2002 the Prime Minister of India, Atal Bihari Vajpayee, paid the first visit to Laos by an Indian head of government in more than 45 years. During his stay the two countries signed agreements on co-operation in defence issues and control of drug-trafficking. The Indian Government also agreed to provide US $10m. of credit to Laos at low interest rates.

During the Viet Nam war US aircraft completed almost 600,000 bombing missions over Laos, leaving large amounts of undetonated explosives, which were estimated to cause 50–100 fatalities per year in the 1990s. The National Unexploded Ordnance Awareness and Clearance Programme was established in Laos in May 1995, with support from the UN.

In 1985 Laos agreed to co-operate with the USA in recovering the remains of US soldiers 'missing in action' in Laos since the war in Viet Nam. In August 1987 a US delegation visited Vientiane to discuss 'humanitarian co-operation' by Laos in tracing missing US soldiers, and agreed to provide Laos with aid. The first remains of US soldiers were passed to the US Government in February 1988. Laos postponed further searching for a short period in 1989, when the USA, alleging that Laos was failing to assist in the suppression of drugs-trafficking, suspended aid and preferential treatment. The USA restored aid to Laos in early 1990, following a visit to Vientiane by the Chairman of the US House of Representatives Committee on Narcotics and Drug Control. (In March 1992 Laos, Myanmar and Thailand signed a draft co-operation treaty on narcotics suppression.) In November 1991, in response to continued Laotian co-operation and the implementation of limited political and economic reforms, the US Government announced that diplomatic relations with Laos were to be upgraded to ambassadorial level. Further progress was achieved in tracing the remains of US soldiers during 1992, and in January 1993 a joint recovery operation was undertaken. In the same month, following 17 months of hearings, a special US Senate panel concluded that (despite considerable public speculation to the contrary) there was 'no compelling evidence' of the survival of US servicemen in the region. During 1993–98 Laos and the USA co-operated in further operations to locate the remains of US soldiers. In May 1995 the USA announced the ending of a 20-year embargo on aid to Laos. In November 1997 the US Deputy Secretary of State, Strobe Talbott, led the highest-level US delegation to Laos since the mid-1970s. During the visit further US support was pledged for a programme to clear unexploded ordnance from the Viet Nam war, which had been supported by the USA since 1996. In mid-1998 US officials agreed to extend financial and logistical support for the programme until September 1999. Further co-operation between the two nations occurred in March–April 2000, when a joint operation in search of US soldiers' remains was resumed. The search operation continued in 2001. In November 2001, during a visit by a US State Department official, the USA officially thanked the Laotian Government for its co-operation in the search for soldiers' remains and for its support against terrorism.

Government

Under the terms of the 1991 Constitution, executive power is vested in the President of State, while legislative power resides with the National Assembly. The President is elected for five years by the National Assembly. Members of the National Assembly are elected for a period of five years by universal adult suffrage. The Lao People's Revolutionary Party remains the sole legal political party. With the approval of the National Assembly, the President appoints the Prime Minister and members of the Council of Ministers, who conduct the government of the country. The President also appoints provincial governors and mayors of municipalities, who are responsible for local administration.

Defence

In August 2002, according to Western estimates, the strength of the armed forces was 29,100 (Lao People's Army 25,600, navy 600, air force 3,500). Military service is compulsory for a minimum of 18 months. There is a paramilitary self-defence force numbering more than 100,000. In 2001 defence expenditure was budgeted at an estimated 120,000m. kips.

Economic Affairs

In 2001, according to estimates by the World Bank, Laos's gross national income (GNI), measured at average 1999–2001 prices, was US $1,650m., equivalent to $310 per head (or $1,610 per head on an international purchasing-power parity basis). During 1990–2001, it was estimated, the population increased by an annual average of 2.5%, while gross domestic product (GDP) per head increased, in real terms, by an average of 3.6% per year. Overall GDP increased, in real terms, at an average annual rate of 6.2% in 1990–2001. According to the Asian Development Bank (ADB), GDP increased by 5.8% in 2000 and by 5.7% in 2001.

Agriculture (including forestry and fishing) contributed an estimated 51.3% of GDP in 2001. An estimated 76.3% of the working population were employed in the sector in the same year. Rice is the staple crop, occupying an estimated 85% of cultivated land in the mid-1990s. Other crops include sweet potatoes, maize, cassava and sugar cane; coffee is grown for export. In 1995 forest covered about 47% of the country (compared with 55% in 1991). Wood products were the third largest export commodity in 2001, accounting for an estimated 23.2% of total export revenue. During the early 1990s the Government initiated policies aimed at conserving the country's forest resources. The cultivation and illicit export of narcotic drugs is believed to be widespread. Despite having been outlawed in 1997, opium production was estimated to total 134 metric tons in 2001. According to the UN Office on Drugs and Crime (formerly the UN Office of Drug Control and Crime Prevention), Laos was the third largest source of illicit opium in the world in that year, behind Afghanistan and Myanmar. During 1990–2001, according to the ADB, agricultural GDP increased by an average of 4.5% per year. Compared with the previous year, the rate of growth was estimated at 4.9% in 2000 and at 3.8% in 2001.

Industry (including mining, manufacturing, construction and utilities) contributed an estimated 23.7% of GDP in 2001. The sector employed about 6.3% of the working population in 1990. During 1990–2001, according to the ADB, industrial GDP increased at an average annual rate of 11.0%. Growth in the sector was estimated at 8.5% in 2000 and at 9.7% in 2001.

Mining contributed only an estimated 0.5% of GDP in 2001. Laos has, however, considerable mineral resources: iron ore (the country's principal mineral resource), coal, tin and gypsum are among the minerals that are exploited. Other known mineral deposits include zinc, copper, nickel, potash, lead, limestone and small quantities of gold, silver and precious stones. During 1990–2001, according to the ADB, the GDP of the mining sector increased by an average of 18.0% per year. Growth was estimated at 1.3% in 2000 and at 1.2% in 2001.

Manufacturing contributed an estimated 17.9% of GDP in 2001, although the sector employed less than 1% of the working population in the mid-1980s. It is mainly confined to the processing of raw materials (chiefly sawmilling) and agricultural produce, the production of textiles and garments (a principal export commodity), and the manufacture of handicrafts and basic consumer goods for the domestic market. According to the ADB, manufacturing GDP increased at an average annual rate of 12.0% in 1990–2001; manufacturing GDP increased by 7.2% in 2000 and by 11.5% in 2001.

Electrical energy is principally derived from hydroelectric power. Electricity is exported to Thailand and Viet Nam, and is one of Laos's principal sources of foreign exchange. In 1998 the country's total electricity generation reached almost 2,000m. kWh. Laos's total hydroelectric power potential was estimated at 25,000 MW in 2000. A new hydroelectric project began exporting electricity to Thailand in April 1998, and two further projects were scheduled to become operational during 2001. In 2002 the Government granted a concession to the Nam Theun 2 Power Company (NTPC), enabling it to assume control of the construction of a US $1,100m. hydroelectric dam—Nam Theun 2. The dam was scheduled for completion in 2008. Later in the

same year Laos signed an agreement with Cambodia, China, Myanmar, Thailand and Viet Nam concerning the establishment of a regional power distribution system, which would form the basis for a programme of hydropower development in the Mekong region. Laos is totally dependent on imports, mainly from Thailand, for supplies of mineral fuels.

The services sector contributed an estimated 25.0% of GDP in 2001, and engaged 17.2% of the total labour force in 1980. Receipts from tourism increased from US $43.6m. in 1996 to $114m. in 2000. Tourist arrivals rose from 614,278 in 1999 to 737,208 in 2000. According to the ADB, the GDP of the services sector increased at an average annual rate of 6.6% in 1990–2001. Annual increases were estimated at 5.1% in 2000 and at 5.6% in 2001.

In 2001 Laos recorded a visible trade deficit of US $216.8m., and there was a deficit of $82.4m. on the current account of the balance of payments. Remittances from relatives residing overseas are a significant source of income for many Lao. In 2001 Thailand was the principal source of imports, supplying 52.5% of the total. Viet Nam was also an important source of imports (26.8%) in that year, along with China, Singapore and Japan. The principal destination of exports from Laos in 2001 was Viet Nam, purchasing 41.7% of the total. Other significant purchasers in that year were Thailand (14.9%), France (6.2%) and Germany (4.3%). It was estimated that the main exports in 2001 were electricity (32.6% of the total), garments (28.6%), wood products (23.2%) and motorcycles (6.7%). The principal imports in that year were consumer goods (49.4%), investment goods (29.3%), materials for the garments industry (11.8%) and motorcycle parts for assembly (5.3%).

In the financial year ending 30 September 2002 Laos projected an overall budget deficit of 1,133,000m. kips. At the end of 2000 the country's external debt totalled US $2,499m., of which $2,449m. was long-term public debt. In that year the cost of debt-servicing was equivalent to 8.1% of revenue from export of goods and services. Consumer prices increased by an annual average of 37.7% in 1995–2002. According to the IMF, the annual rate of inflation averaged 25.1% in 2000, declining to 7.8% in 2001, before increasing to an estimated 10.6% in 2002. The unemployment rate totalled 2.4% in 1995, according to the census conducted in that year.

Laos is a member of the Asian Development Bank (ADB, see p. 143), of the Association of South East Asian Nations (ASEAN, see p. 146), of the Colombo Plan (see p. 339), which promotes economic and social development in Asia and the Pacific, and of the Mekong River Commission (see p. 341).

From late 1986 the Government undertook a radical programme of economic liberalization, known as the New Economic Mechanism, with the aim of transforming the hitherto centrally planned economy into a market-orientated system. Fiscal reforms were introduced and government expenditure was restricted; the introduction of a liberal foreign investment law in 1988 and the implementation of a privatization programme encouraged revenue from external sources, thus offsetting the loss of aid and concessionary trade arising from the disintegration of the communist bloc. The banking sector and public administration were restructured and price controls ended. Laos remains extremely underdeveloped, however, and, as one of the poorest countries in Asia, is heavily reliant on external aid. A lack of modernization in the agricultural sector has impeded diversification, and although industrial output is expanding rapidly, the manufacturing base remains narrow. Laos's admission to ASEAN in July 1997 was expected to facilitate the country's closer regional economic integration. However, a decline in the value of the national currency of Laos, from early 1997, was exacerbated after July by the currency crisis in neighbouring Thailand, leading to rapid price increases. The regional economic crisis also resulted in a significant loss of foreign capital for Laos, as Thailand and other countries affected by the crisis had been among the most important investors in the country. Having reached US $160m. in 1996, foreign direct investment had declined to $72m. in 2000, according to the ADB. By early 2001 the economy had partially recovered, with the rate of inflation (according to the Government) having been drastically reduced to around 10% from a peak of 167% (according to the IMF) in March 1999. However, having stabilized somewhat during the first half of 2000, the kip subsequently began to weaken once again. The Fifth Five-Year Plan (2001–05), announced at the Seventh Congress of the Lao People's Revolutionary Party (LPRP) in March 2001, envisaged an average annual GDP growth rate of between 7.0% and 7.5%. The Plan emphasized the eradication of poverty, the restriction of opium cultivation and integrated rural development through the strengthening of basic political units. Other targets included a reduction in the annual level of inflation to a single-digit rate, the maintenance of a stable exchange rate and the restriction of the budget deficit to the equivalent of 5% of GDP. International donors, however, were disappointed at the Plan's failure to incorporate development of the private sector, while corruption among Lao officials and the lack of skilled personnel to manage the financial sector (particularly in view of a decline in the value of the currency in 2001) remained causes for concern. In April 2001 the IMF announced that it was implementing a US $40.2m. three-year arrangement under the Poverty Reduction and Growth Facility. This was intended to promote macroeconomic stability and reduce poverty in the area. Restructuring of the banking sector and enhanced promotion of the private sector were integral to the plan. In mid-2002 a significant depreciation of the kip was accompanied by a rise in inflation, which reached a high of 15%–16% in September of that year. While in late 2002 macroeconomic stability had been improved and some structural reforms implemented, further reforms remained essential if an environment were to be created in which sustained economic growth could be achieved. The reduction of state involvement in the country's commercial sector and increased access to the resources necessary to reduce the country's high level of poverty remained priorities. In 2002 GDP growth was estimated to have been 5.5%.

Education

Education, which is officially compulsory for five years between the ages of six and 15, was greatly disrupted by the civil war, causing a high illiteracy rate, but educational facilities have since improved significantly. Lao is the medium of instruction. A comprehensive education system is in force. In 1990 the Government issued a decree permitting the establishment of private schools, in an effort to accommodate the increasing number of students.

Primary education begins at six years of age and lasts for five years. Secondary education, beginning at the age of 11, lasts for six years, comprising two three-year cycles. In 1996 enrolment in primary education was equivalent to 112% of children in the primary age-group (males 123%; females 101%). In that year enrolment in secondary education was equivalent to 28% of the relevant age-group (males 34%; females 23%). The total enrolment at primary and secondary schools was equivalent to 72% of the school-age population (males 80%; females 63%). Government expenditure on education for 1997/98 was forecast at 37,400m. kips, representing 6.9% of total projected expenditure.

Public Holidays

2003: 1 January (New Year's Day), 5 January (Anniversary of Birth of King Fa Ngoum), 6 January (Pathet Lao Day), 20 January (Army Day), 8 March (Women's Day), 22 March (People's Party Day), 13–15 April (Lao New Year), 1 May (Labour Day), 1 June (Children's Day), 13 August (Free Laos Day), 23 August (Liberation Day), 12 October (Liberation from the French Day, Vientiane only), 2 December (Independence Day).

2004: 1 January (New Year's Day), 5 January (Anniversary of Birth of King Fa Ngoum), 6 January (Pathet Lao Day), 20 January (Army Day), 8 March (Women's Day), 22 March (People's Party Day), 13–15 April (Lao New Year), 1 May (Labour Day), 1 June (Children's Day), 13 August (Free Laos Day), 23 August (Liberation Day), 12 October (Liberation from the French Day, Vientiane only), 2 December (Independence Day).

Weights and Measures

The metric system is in force.

Statistical Survey

Source (unless otherwise stated): Service National de la Statistique, Vientiane.

Area and Population

AREA, POPULATION AND DENSITY

Area (sq km)	236,800*
Population (census results)	
1 March 1985.	3,584,803
1 March 1995	
Males	2,265,867
Females.	2,315,391
Total	4,581,258
Population (official estimate at mid-year)	
2000	5,218,000
Density (per sq km) at mid-2000	22.0

* 91,400 sq miles.

PROVINCES
(official estimates, mid-1995)

	Area (sq km)	Population	Density (per sq km)
Vientiane (municipality) . . .	3,920	531,800	135.6
Phongsali	16,270	153,400	9.4
Luang Namtha	9,325	115,200	12.4
Oudomxay.	15,370	211,300	13.7
Bokeo	6,196	114,900	18.5
Luang Prabang	16,875	367,200	21.8
Houaphanh	16,500	247,300	15.0
Sayabouri	16,389	293,300	17.9
Xiangkhouang	15,880	201,200	12.7
Vientiane	15,927	286,800	18.0
Bolikhamsai	14,863	164,900	11.1
Khammouane.	16,315	275,400	16.9
Savannakhet	21,774	674,900	31.0
Saravan	10,691	258,300	24.2
Sekong.	7,665	64,200	8.4
Champasak	15,415	503,300	32.7
Attopu	10,320	87,700	8.5
Special region.	7,105	54,200	7.6
Total	236,800	4,605,300	19.4

PRINCIPAL TOWNS
(population at 1995 census)

Viangchan (Vientiane—capital)	160,000	Xam Nua (Sam Neua) . . .	33,500
Savannakhet (Khanthaboury) .	58,500	Luang Prabang	25,500
Pakxe (Paksé) . . .	47,000	Thakek (Khammouan) .	22,500

Source: Stefan Helders, *World Gazetteer* (internet www.world -gazetteer.com).

Mid-2001 (UN estimate, incl. suburbs): Vientiane 663,000 (Source: UN, *World Urbanization Prospects: The 2001 Revision*).

BIRTHS AND DEATHS
(UN estimates, annual averages)

	1985–90	1990–95	1995–2000
Birth rate (per 1,000) . . .	44.6	41.3	38.2
Death rate (per 1,000) . . .	18.2	15.8	14.1

Source: UN, *World Population Prospects: The 2000 Revision*.

Birth rate (1999): 38.8 per 1,000.

Death rate (1999): 13.0 per 1,000.

Source: UN, *Statistical Yearbook for Asia and the Pacific*.

Expectation of life (WHO estimates, years at birth): 54.6 (males 53.5; females 55.6) in 2001 (Source: WHO, *World Health Report*).

ECONOMICALLY ACTIVE POPULATION
(ILO estimates, '000 persons at mid-1980)

	Males	Females	Total
Agriculture, etc.	717	675	1,393
Industry	79	51	130
Services	193	123	316
Total labour force	990	849	1,839

Source: ILO, *Economically Active Population Estimates and Projections, 1950–2025*.

Mid-2001 (estimates in '000): Agriculture, etc. 2,059; Total labour force 2,699 (Source: FAO).

Health and Welfare

KEY INDICATORS

Total fertility rate (children per woman, 2001) . . .	5.0
Under-5 mortality rate (per 1,000 live births, 2001) . . .	100
HIV/AIDS (% of persons aged 15–49, 2001)	<0.10
Physicians (per 1,000 head, 1996)	0.24
Hospital beds (per 1,000 head, 1990)	2.57
Health expenditure (2000): US $ per head (PPP) . . .	52
Health expenditure (2000): % of GDP	3.4
Health expenditure (2000): public (% of total) . . .	38.0
Access to adequate water (% of persons, 2000) . . .	90
Access to adequate sanitation (% of persons, 2000) . .	46
Human Development Index (2000): ranking	143
Human Development Index (2000): value	0.485

For sources and definitions, see explanatory note on p. vi.

Agriculture

PRINCIPAL CROPS
('000 metric tons)

	1999	2000	2001
Rice (paddy)	2,103	2,202	2,335
Maize	96	117	112
Potatoes	33†	33†	33*
Sweet potatoes	81	118	101
Cassava (Manioc)	71†	71†	71*
Sugar cane	174	297	209
Pulses*	13	14	14
Soybeans	6	5	3
Groundnuts (in shell) . . .	13	13	17
Sesame seed	5	5*	5*
Vegetables and melons* . . .	269	671	665
Bananas*	22	23	23
Oranges*	28	29	29
Pineapples*	34	35	35
Other fruit (excl. melons)* . .	89	93	93
Coffee (green)	18	24	26
Tobacco (leaves)	24	33	30

* FAO estimate(s).
† Unofficial figure.

Source: FAO.

LIVESTOCK
('000 head, year ending September)

	1999	2000	2001
Horses*	28	29	29
Cattle	1,000	1,100	1,217
Buffaloes	1,008	1,028	1,051
Pigs	1,320	1,425	1,426
Goats	200	217	240*
Chickens	12,353	13,095	14,063
Ducks	1,351	1,630*	1,700*

* FAO estimate(s).

Source: FAO.

LIVESTOCK PRODUCTS
('000 metric tons)

	1999	2000	2001
Beef and veal	19	16	26*
Buffalo meat	19	17	17*
Pig meat	32	33	35†
Poultry meat	11	13	13
Cows' milk*	6	6	6
Hen eggs	9	10	10*
Cattle and buffalo hides (fresh)* .	4	4	6

* FAO estimate(s).
† Unofficial figure.

Source: FAO.

Forestry

ROUNDWOOD REMOVALS
('000 cubic metres, excl. bark)

	1999*	2000	2001
Sawlogs, veneer logs and logs for sleepers	734	435	438
Other industrial wood* . . .	132	132	132
Fuel wood*	5,843	5,872	5,885
Total	6,709	6,439	6,455

* FAO estimates.
Source: FAO.

SAWNWOOD PRODUCTION
('000 cubic metres, incl. railway sleepers)

	1999*	2000	2001
Coniferous (softwood) . . .	150	—	—
Broadleaved (hardwood). . . .	200	208	227
Total	350	208	227

* FAO estimates.
Source: FAO.

Fishing

(FAO estimates, '000 metric tons, live weight)

	1998	1999	2000
Capture	19.6	30.0	29.3
Cyprinids	3.0	4.5	4.4
Other freshwater fishes . .	16.6	25.5	24.9
Aquaculture	21.2	30.4	42.1
Common carp	2.7	3.9	5.4
Roho labeo	2.6	3.8	5.2
Mrigal carp.	2.6	3.8	5.2
Bighead carp	2.6	3.8	5.2
Catla	2.6	3.8	5.2
Grass carp (White amur). . .	2.6	3.8	5.2
Silver carp	2.6	3.8	5.2
Nile tilapia	2.6	3.8	5.2
Total catch	40.9	60.4	71.3

Source: FAO, *Yearbook of Fishery Statistics*.

Mining

('000 metric tons, unless otherwise indicated)

	1999	2000	2001*
Coal (all grades)	78.8	121.3	125.0
Gemstones ('000 carats). . .	4,013.3	150.0*	100.0
Gypsum	134.7	147.7	150.0
Salt.	1.7	1.5	1.6
Tin (metric tons)†	404	414	400

* Estimated production.
† Figures refer to metal content.

Source: US Geological Survey.

Industry

SELECTED PRODUCTS

	1999	2000	2001*
Beer ('000 hectolitres) . . .	480	508	577
Soft drinks ('000 hectolitres) . .	123	143	142
Cigarettes (million packs) . .	38	41	41
Garments ('000 pieces) . .	21	24	32
Wood furniture (million kips) .	12,725	12,700	15,240
Plastic products (metric tons) . .	3,900	3,850	4,350
Detergent (metric tons)	879	900	700;
Agricultural tools ('000) . .	4	4	4
Nails (metric tons)	691	650	740
Bricks (million)	65	66	87
Electric energy (million kWh) .	2,436	3,678	3,590
Tobacco (metric tons)	757	1,277	358
Plywood ('000 sheets)	2,086	2,150	2,200

* Estimates.

Source: IMF, *Lao People's Democratic Republic: Selected Issues and Statistical Appendix* (September 2002).

Finance

CURRENCY AND EXCHANGE RATES

Monetary Units
100 at (cents) = 1 new kip

Sterling, Dollar and Euro Equivalents (29 November 2002)
£1 sterling = 16,715.0 new kips
US $1 = 10,770.0 new kips
€1 = 10,691.4 new kips
100,000 new kips = £5.983 = $9.285 = €9.353.

Average Exchange Rate (new kips per US $)
2000   7,887.64
2001   8,954.58
2002   10,056.33

Note: In September 1995 a policy of 'floating' exchange rates was adopted, with commercial banks permitted to set their rates.

GENERAL BUDGET
('000 million new kips, year ending 30 September)*

Revenue†	1999/2000	2000/01‡	2001/02§
Tax revenue	1,367	1,629	2,043
Profits tax	187	205	362
Income tax	117	153	190
Turnover tax	290	318	452
Taxes on foreign trade . . .	176	236	291
Import duties	135	179	229
Export duties	41	57	62
Excise tax	226	371	362
Timber royalties	273	182	165
Hydro royalties	22	51	55
Other revenue	324	372	438
Payment for depreciation or dividend transfers	42	67	89
Leasing income	15	39	57
Administrative fees	17	41	62
Overflight	123	114	153
Interest or amortization . . .	79	76	42
Total	1,691	2,000	2,481

Expenditure	1999/2000‡	2000/01‡	2001/02§
Current expenditure.	1,050	1,229	1,449
Wages and salaries	335	410	517
Transfers	130	243	292
Materials and supplies . . .	174	330	370
Interest	103	134	145
Timber royalty-financed expenditure	242	—	—
Capital expenditure and net lending	1,704	1,911	2,165
Domestically-financed. . . .	481	872	1,017
Foreign-financed	1,302	1,200	1,256
Loan-funded projects . . .	827	724	826
Grant-funded projects . . .	475	476	430
Onlending (net)	−78	−160	−108
Total (incl. others)	2,754	3,140	3,614

* Since 1992 there has been a unified budget covering the operations of the central Government, provincial administrations and state enterprises.
† Excluding grants received ('000 million new kips): 475 in 1999/2000; 476 in 2000/01‡; 549 in 2001/02§.
‡ Estimates.
§ Budget forecasts.

Source: IMF, *Lao People's Democratic Republic: Selected Issues and Statistical Appendix* (September 2002).

INTERNATIONAL RESERVES
(US $ million at 31 December)

	2000	2001	2002
Gold*	0.59	2.53	2.53
IMF special drawing rights. . .	0.10	3.42	6.07
Foreign exchange.	138.87	127.51	185.51
Total	139.56	133.46	194.14

* National valuation.

Source: IMF, *International Financial Statistics*.

MONEY SUPPLY
(million new kips at 31 December)

	2000	2001	2002
Currency outside banks . . .	67,830	113,080	237,840
Demand deposits at commercial banks . . .	272,230	256,880	358,150
Total (incl. others) . . .	344,351	371,840	596,030

Source: IMF, *International Financial Statistics*.

COST OF LIVING
(Consumer Price Index for Vientiane; base: 1995 = 100)

	2000	2001	2002
All items	786.4	847.8	937.9

Source: IMF, *International Financial Statistics*.

NATIONAL ACCOUNTS

Expenditure on the Gross Domestic Product
(million new kips at current prices)

	1989	1990	1991
Government final consumption expenditure	34,929	61,754	69,499
Private final consumption expenditure	414,639	558,437	647,826
Increase in stocks . . . } Gross fixed capital formation. }	55,560	75,572	91,435
Total domestic expenditure	505,128	695,763	808,760
Exports of goods and services .	49,421	69,411	73,359
Less Imports of goods and services	128,613	150,154	156,550
GDP in purchasers' values .	425,936	615,020	725,569
GDP at constant 1987 prices .	213,769	228,105	237,098

Source: World Bank, *Historically Planned Economies: A Guide to the Data*.

Gross Domestic Product by Economic Activity
(million new kips at current prices)

	1999	2000	2001
Agriculture, hunting, forestry and fishing	5,507,539	7,127,372	7,974,629
Mining and quarrying . . .	53,625	67,033	73,150
Manufacturing	1,744,051	2,305,848	2,772,616
Electricity, gas and water . . .	246,919	423,331	450,414
Construction	276,090	309,341	376,985
Wholesale and retail trade, restaurants and hotels . .	991,694	1,283,970	1,502,018
Transport, storage and communications . . .	590,780	794,024	929,723
Finance, insurance, real estate and business services	57,478	105,170	134,618
Public administration . . .	219,394	392,690	496,698
Other services	566,056	756,786	820,392
GDP at factor cost. . . .	10,253,626	13,565,564	15,531,241
Indirect taxes *less* subsidies .	74,990	105,728	138,747
GDP in purchasers' values . .	10,328,616	13,671,292	15,669,988

Source: Asian Development Bank, *Key Indicators of Developing Asian and Pacific Countries*.

BALANCE OF PAYMENTS
(US $ million)

	1999	2000	2001
Exports of goods f.o.b. . . .	338.2	330.3	311.1
Imports of goods f.o.b. . . .	−527.7	−535.3	−527.9
Trade balance	−189.5	−205.0	−216.8
Exports of services	130.0	175.7	166.1
Imports of services	−51.8	−43.1	−31.6
Balance on goods and services.	−111.3	−72.4	−82.3
Other income received . . .	10.5	7.3	5.8
Other income paid	−49.9	−59.7	−39.6
Balance on goods, services and income	−150.7	−124.7	−116.1
Current transfers received . .	80.2	116.3	33.7
Current transfers paid . . .	−50.6	—	—
Current balance	−121.1	−8.5	−82.4
Other investment assets . .	−43.2	18.8	25.2
Other investment liabilities . .	−3.7	73.3	86.6
Net errors and omissions . . .	−165.1	−74.2	−57.2
Overall balance	−333.1	43.4	−3.9

Source: IMF, *International Financial Statistics*.

External Trade

PRINCIPAL COMMODITIES
(US $ million)

Imports c.i.f.	1999	2000	2001†
Investment goods.	184.0	161.8	166.4
Machinery and equipment . .	21.0	16.2	—
Vehicles*	35.8	23.3	—
Fuel*	36.7	79.1	—
Construction/electrical equipment	90.5	43.2	—
Consumption goods	252.7	288.0	280.1
Materials for garments industry .	66.5	60.4	67.2
Motorcycle parts for assembly . .	38.4	22.6	30.0
Unrecorded imports	—	27.0‡	9.4
Total	554.3	569.4	567.4

* Estimates based on the assumption that 50% of total are consumption goods.
† Estimates.
‡ Estimate included due to weaknesses in customs data.

Exports f.o.b.	1999	2000	2001*
Wood products	84.9	87.1	81.0
Logs	20.0	26.0	n.a.
Timber	26.9	37.7	n.a.
Other and unrecorded. . .	38.0	23.4	n.a.
Coffee	15.2	12.1	7.8
Other agricultural products . .	8.3	15.4	12.6
Manufactures†	27.9	9.6	9.7
Garments	72.0	91.6	100.0
Motorcycles	38.4	22.1	23.4
Electricity	90.5	112.2	114.2
Total (incl. others)	342.1	351.0	349.8

* Estimates.
† Excluding garments and wood products.

Source: IMF, *Lao People's Democratic Republic: Selected Issues and Statistical Appendix* (September 2002).

PRINCIPAL TRADING PARTNERS
(US $ million)

Imports	1999	2000	2001
China, People's Republic . .	24.4	37.9	49.4
France	7.6	27.5	8.4
Germany	9.5	3.6	2.7
Hong Kong	11.0	7.9	9.8
Japan	24.9	23.6	12.6
Korea, Republic	11.9	4.9	8.4
Singapore	37.0	33.6	28.9
Thailand*	452.0	419.0	451.7
United Kingdom	8.7	6.1	3.6
Viet Nam	181.8	209.1	230.8
Total (incl. others)	807.6	816.8	859.7

Exports	1999	2000	2001
Belgium	13.5	13.6	12.4
China, People's Republic . . .	8.7	6.7	—
France	18.2	27.1	33.7
Germany	27.0	20.8	23.4
Italy	5.9	9.2	11.1
Japan	12.3	10.9	6.6
Netherlands	8.9	10.0	9.0
Thailand*	51.6	68.9	81.0
United Kingdom	12.5	7.2	8.4
USA	12.6	8.8	3.6
Viet Nam	179.4	206.4	227.0
Total (incl. others)	320.6	502.5	544.9

* Trade with Thailand may be overestimated, as it may include goods in transit to and from other countries.

Source: Asian Development Bank, *Key Indicators of Developing Asian and Pacific Countries.*

Transport

ROAD TRAFFIC
(motor vehicles in use at 31 December, estimates)

	1994	1995	1996
Passenger cars	18,240	17,280	16,320
Buses and coaches	440	n.a.	n.a.
Lorries and vans	7,920	6,020	4,200
Motorcycles and mopeds . . .	169,000	200,000	231,000

Source: International Road Federation, *World Road Statistics.*

SHIPPING

Inland Waterways
(traffic)

	1993	1994	1995
Freight ('000 metric tons) . . .	290	876	898
Freight ton-kilometres (million) .	18.7	40.8	98.8
Passengers ('000)	703	898	652
Passenger-kilometres (million) . .	110.2	60.6	24.3

Source: Ministry of Communications, Transport, Post and Construction.

Merchant Fleet
(registered at 31 December)

	1999	2000	2001
Number of vessels	1	1	1
Displacement ('000 grt)	2.4	2.4	2.4

Source: Lloyd's Register-Fairplay, *World Fleet Statistics.*

CIVIL AVIATION
(traffic on scheduled services)

	1997	1998	1999
Kilometres flown (million) . .	1	1	1
Passengers carried ('000) . .	125	124	197
Passenger-kilometres (million) . .	48	48	78
Total ton-kilometres (million) . .	5	5	8

Source: UN, *Statistical Yearbook.*

Tourism

FOREIGN VISITOR ARRIVALS
(incl. excursionists)

Country of Nationality	1998	1999	2000
China, People's Republic . . .	15,802	20,269	28,215
France	17,863	19,960	24,534
Japan	12,936	14,860	20,687
Thailand	273,095	356,105	442,564
United Kingdom	8,902	12,298	15,204
USA	20,174	24,672	32,869
Viet Nam	78,216	71,748	68,751
Total (incl. others)	500,200	614,278	737,208

Source: World Tourism Organization, *Yearbook of Tourism Statistics.*

Tourism receipts (US $ million): 80 in 1998; 97 in 1999; 114 in 2000 (Source: World Bank).

Communications Media

	1999	2000	2001
Television receivers ('000 in use) .	51	52	n.a
Telephones ('000 main lines in use)	35.1	40.9	52.6
Mobile cellular telephones ('000 subscribers)	12.1	12.7	29.5
Personal computers ('000 in use)	12	14	16
Internet users ('000)	2.0	6.0	10.0

Radio receivers ('000 in use): 730 in 1997.

Facsimile machines (estimated number in use): 500 in 1994 (Source: UN, *Statistical Yearbook*).

Book production (1995): Titles 88; copies ('000) 995.

Daily newspapers (1996): 3 (average circulation 18,000).

Non-daily newspapers (1988, estimates): 4 (average circulation 20,000).

Sources (unless otherwise specified): International Telecommunication Union; UNESCO, *Statistical Yearbook.*

Education

(1996/97)

	Institu-tions	Teachers	Students Males	Females	Total
Pre-primary . . .	695	2,173	18,502	19,349	37,851
Primary	7,896	25,831	438,241	348,094	786,335
Secondary:					
general . . .	n.a.	10,717	108,996	71,164	180,160
vocational* . .	n.a.	808	3,731	1,928	5,659
teacher training .	n.a.	197	960	780	1,740
University level . .	n.a.	456	3,509	1,764	5,273
Other higher . . .	n.a.	913	5,378	2,081	7,459

* Data for 1995/96.

Source: UNESCO, *Statistical Yearbook.*

Adult literacy rate (UNESCO estimates): 48.7% (males 64.1%; females 33.2%) in 2000 (Source: UN Development Programme, *Human Development Report*).

Directory

The Constitution

The new Constitution was unanimously endorsed by the Supreme People's Assembly on 14 August 1991. Its main provisions are summarized below:

POLITICAL SYSTEM

The Lao People's Democratic Republic (Lao PDR) is an independent, sovereign and united country and is indivisible.

The Lao PDR is a people's democratic state. The people's rights are exercised and ensured through the functioning of the political system, with the Lao People's Revolutionary Party as its leading organ. The people exercise power through the National Assembly, which functions in accordance with the principle of democratic centralism.

The State respects and protects all lawful activities of Buddhism and the followers of other religious faiths.

The Lao PDR pursues a foreign policy of peace, independence, friendship and co-operation. It adheres to the principles of peaceful co-existence with other countries, based on mutual respect for independence, sovereignty and territorial integrity.

SOCIO-ECONOMIC SYSTEM

The economy is market-orientated, with intervention by the State. The State encourages all economic sectors to compete and co-operate in the expansion of production and trade.

Private ownership of property and rights of inheritance are protected by the State.

The State authorizes the operation of private schools and medical services, while promoting the expansion of public education and health services.

FUNDAMENTAL RIGHTS AND OBLIGATIONS OF CITIZENS

Lao citizens, irrespective of their sex, social status, education, faith and ethnic group, are equal before the law.

Lao citizens aged 18 years and above have the right to vote, and those over 21 years to be candidates, in elections.

Lao citizens have freedom of religion, speech, press and assembly, and freedom to establish associations and to participate in demonstrations which do not contradict the law.

THE NATIONAL ASSEMBLY

The National Assembly is the legislative organ, which also oversees the activities of the administration and the judiciary. Members of the National Assembly are elected for a period of five years by universal adult suffrage. The National Assembly elects its own Standing Committee, which consists of the Chairman and Vice-Chairman of the National Assembly (and thus also of the National Assembly Standing Committee) and a number of other members. The National Assembly convenes its ordinary session twice annually. The National Assembly Standing Committee may convene an extraordinary session of the National Assembly if it deems this necessary. The National Assembly is empowered to amend the Constitution; to endorse, amend or abrogate laws; to elect or remove the President of State and Vice-Presidents of State, as proposed by the Standing Committee of the National Assembly; to adopt motions expressing 'no confidence' in the Government; to elect or remove the President of the People's Supreme Court, on the recommendation of the National Assembly Standing Committee.

THE PRESIDENT OF STATE

The President of State, who is also Head of the Armed Forces, is elected by the National Assembly for a five-year tenure. Laws adopted by the National Assembly must be promulgated by the President of State not later than 30 days after their enactment. The President is empowered to appoint or dismiss the Prime Minister and members of the Government, with the approval of the National Assembly; to appoint government officials at provincial and municipal levels; and to promote military personnel, on the recommendation of the Prime Minister.

THE GOVERNMENT

The Government is the administrative organ of the State. It is composed of the Prime Minister, Deputy Prime Ministers and Ministers or Chairmen of Committees (which are equivalent to Ministries), who are appointed by the President, with the approval of the National Assembly, for a term of five years. The Government implements the Constitution, laws and resolutions adopted by the National Assembly and state decrees and acts of the President of State. The Prime Minister is empowered to appoint Deputy Ministers and Vice-Chairmen of Committees, and lower-level government officials.

LOCAL ADMINISTRATION

The Lao PDR is divided into provinces, municipalities, districts and villages. Provincial governors and mayors of municipalities are appointed by the President of State. Deputy provincial governors, deputy mayors and district chiefs are appointed by the Prime Minister. Administration at village level is conducted by village heads.

THE JUDICIARY

The people's courts comprise the People's Supreme Court, the people's provincial and municipal courts, the people's district courts and military courts. The President of the People's Supreme Court and the Public Prosecutor-General are elected by the National Assembly, on the recommendation of the National Assembly Standing Committee. The Vice-President of the People's Supreme Court and the judges of the people's courts at all levels are appointed by the National Assembly Standing Committee.

The Government

HEAD OF STATE

President of State: Gen. KHAMTAY SIPHANDONE (took office February 1998).

Vice-President: Lt-Gen. CHOUMMALI SAIGNASON.

COUNCIL OF MINISTERS
(April 2003)

Prime Minister: BOUNGNANG VOLACHIT.

Deputy Prime Minister and President of the State Planning Committee: THONGLOUN SISOLIT.

Deputy Prime Minister and Minister of Foreign Affairs: SOMSAVAT LENGSAVAT.

Deputy Prime Minister: Maj.-Gen. ASANG LAOLI.

Minister of Defence: Maj.-Gen. DOUANGCHAI PHICHIT.

Minister of Finance: CHANSY PHOSIKHAM.

Minister of the Interior: Maj.-Gen. SOUDCHAI THAMMASITH.

Minister of Justice: KHAMOUANE BOUPHA.

Minister of Agriculture and Forestry: SIANE SAPHANTHONG.

Minister of Communications, Transport, Post and Construction: BOUATHONG VONGLOKHAM.

Minister of Industry and Handicrafts: ONNEUA PHOMMACHANH.

Minister of Commerce and Tourism: SOULIVONG DARAVONG.

Minister of Information and Culture: PHANDOUANGCHIT VONGSA.

Minister of Labour and Social Welfare: SOMPHAN PHENGKHAMMI.

Minister of Education: PHIMMASONE LEUANGKHAMMA.

Minister of Public Health: Dr PONEMEKH DARALOY.

Minister to the Office of the President: SOUBANH SRITHIRATH.

Ministers to the Prime Minister's Office: BOUNTIEM PHITSAMAI, SOULI NANTHAVONG, SAISENGLI TENGBIACHU, SOMPHUNG MONGKHUNVILAI.

MINISTRIES

Office of the President: rue Lane Xang, Vientiane; tel. (21) 214200; fax (21) 214208.

Office of the Prime Minister: Ban Sisavat, Vientiane; tel. (21) 213653; fax (21) 213560.

Ministry of Agriculture and Forestry: Ban Phonxay, Vientiane; tel. (21) 412359; fax (21) 412344.

Ministry of Commerce and Tourism: Ban Phonxay, Muang Saysettha, Vientiane; tel. (21) 412436; fax (21) 412434; internet www.moc.gov.la.

Ministry of Communications, Transport, Post and Construction: Ban Phonxay, Vientiane; tel. (21) 412251; fax (21) 414123.

Ministry of Education: BP 67, Vientiane; tel. (21) 216004; fax (21) 212108.

Ministry of Finance: rue That Luang, Ban Phonxay, Vientiane; tel. (21) 412401; fax (21) 412415.

Ministry of Foreign Affairs: rue That Luang 01004, Ban Phonxay, Vientiane; tel. (21) 413148; fax (21) 414009; e-mail sphimmas@laonet.net; internet www.mfa.laogov.net.

Ministry of Industry and Handicrafts: rue Nongbone, Ban Phai, BP 4708, Vientiane; tel. (21) 416718; fax (21) 413005; e-mail mihplan@laotel.com.

Ministry of Information and Culture: rue Sethathirath, Ban Xiengnheun, Vientiane; tel. (21) 210409; fax (21) 212408.

Ministry of the Interior: rue Nongbone, Ban Hatsady, Vientiane; tel. (21) 212500.

Ministry of Justice: Ban Phonxay, Vientiane; tel. (21) 414105.

Ministry of Labour and Social Welfare: rue Pangkham, Ban Sisaket, Vientiane; tel. (21) 213003.

Ministry of National Defence: rue Phone Kheng, Ban Phone Kheng, Vientiane; tel. (21) 412803.

Ministry of Public Health: Ban Simeuang, Vientiane; tel. (21) 214002; fax (21) 214001; e-mail cabinet.fr@moh.gov.la.

Legislature

At the election held on 24 February 2002 166 candidates, approved by the Lao Front for National Construction, contested the 109 seats in the National Assembly.

President of the National Assembly: Lt-Gen. SAMAN VIGNAKET.

Vice-President: PANY YATHOTU.

Political Organizations

Lao Front for National Construction (LFNC): POB 1828, Vientiane; f. 1979 to replace the Lao Patriotic Front; comprises representatives of various political and social groups, of which the LPRP (see below) is the dominant force; fosters national solidarity; Pres. PHENG LASOUKANH; Vice-Chair. SIHO BANNAVONG, KHAMPHOUI CHANTHASOUK, TONG YEUTHOR.

Phak Pasason Pativat Lao (Lao People's Revolutionary Party—LPRP): Vientiane; f. 1955 as the People's Party of Laos; reorg. under present name in 1972; Cen. Cttee of 53 full mems elected March 2001; Pres. Gen. KHAMTAY SIPHANDONE.

Political Bureau (Politburo)

Full members: Gen. KHAMTAY SIPHANDONE, Lt-Gen. SAMAN VIGNAKET, Lt-Gen. CHOUMMALI SAIGNASON, THONGSIN THAMMAVONG, Gen. OSAKAN THAMMATHEVA, BOUNGNANG VOLACHIT, Gen. SISAVAT KEOBOUNPHAN, Maj.-Gen. ASANG LAOLI, THOUNGLONG SISOLIT, Maj.-Gen. DOUANGCHAI PHICHIT, BOUSONE BOUPAVANH.

Numerous factions are in armed opposition to the Government. The principal groups are:

Ethnics' Liberation Organization of Laos: Leader PA KAO HER.

Free Democratic Lao National Salvation Force: based in Thailand.

United Front for the Liberation of Laos: Leader PHOUNGPHET PHANARETH.

United Front for the National Liberation of the Lao People: f. 1980; led by Gen. PHOUMI NOSAVAN until his death in 1985.

United Lao National Liberation Front: Sayabouri Province; comprises an estimated 8,000 members, mostly Hmong (Meo) tribesmen; Sec.-Gen. VANG SHUR.

Diplomatic Representation

EMBASSIES IN LAOS

Australia: rue Pandit J. Nehru, quartier Phonxay, BP 292, Vientiane; tel. (21) 413600; fax (21) 413601; e-mail lynne.hunt@dfat.gov.au; internet www.laos.embassy.gov.au; Ambassador MICHAEL JONATHAN THWAITES.

Brunei: Unit 12, Ban Thoungkang, rue Lao-Thai Friendship, Muang Sisattanak, Xaysettha District, Vientiane; tel. (21) 352294; fax (21) 352291; e-mail embdlaos@laonet.com; Ambassador Pengiran Haji HAMDAN BIN Haji ISMAIL.

Cambodia: rue Thadeua, Km 2, BP 34, Vientiane; tel. (21) 314952; fax (21) 314951; e-mail recamlao@laotel.com; Ambassador HUOT PHAL.

China, People's Republic: rue Wat Nak, Muang Sisattanak, BP 898, Vientiane; tel. (21) 315100; fax (21) 315104; e-mail embassyprc@laonet.net; Ambassador LIU ZHENGXIU.

Cuba: Ban Saphanthong Neua 128, BP 1017, Vientiane; tel. (21) 314902; fax (21) 314901; e-mail embacuba@laonet.net; Ambassador MARÍA AIDA NOGALES JIMÉNEZ.

France: rue Sethathirath, Vientiane; tel. (21) 215253; fax (21) 215250; e-mail contact@ambafrance-laos.org; internet www.ambafrance-laos.org; Ambassador BERNARD POTTIER.

Germany: rue Sok Paluang 26, BP 314, Vientiane; tel. (21) 312110; fax (21) 314322; e-mail germemb@laotel.com; Ambassador CHRISTIAN K. G. BERGER.

India: rue That Luang, BP 225, Vientiane; tel. (21) 412640; fax (21) 412768; e-mail indemblaos@laonet.net; internet www.indianembassylaos.com; Ambassador LAVANYA PRASAD.

Indonesia: ave Phone Keng, BP 277, Vientiane; tel. (21) 413909; fax (21) 214828; Ambassador ZAINUDDIN NASUTION.

Japan: rue Sisangvone, Vientiane; tel. (21) 414401; fax (21) 414406; Ambassador YOSHINORI MIYAMOTO.

Korea, Democratic People's Republic: quartier Wat Nak, Vientiane; tel. (21) 315261; fax (21) 315260; Ambassador CHOE PYONG KWAN.

Korea, Republic: rue Lao-Thai Friendship, Ban Watnak, Sisattanak District, BP 7567, Vientiane; tel. (21) 415833; fax (21) 415831; e-mail koramb@laotel.com; Ambassador CHANG CHUL-KYOON.

Malaysia: rue That Luang, quartier Pholxay, POB 789, Vientiane; tel. (21) 414205; fax (21) 414201; e-mail mwvntian@laonet.net; Ambassador MOHAMMED DAUD MOHAMMED YUSOF.

Mongolia: rue Wat Nak, Km 3, BP 370, Vientiane; tel. (21) 315220; fax (21) 315221; e-mail embmong@laotel.com; Ambassador N. ALIASUREN.

Myanmar: Ban Thong Kang, rue Sok Palaung, BP 11, Vientiane; tel. (21) 314910; fax (21) 314913; e-mail mev@loxinfo.co.th; Ambassador U TIN OO.

Philippines: Ban Phonsinuane, Sisattanak, BP 2415, Vientiane; tel. (21) 452490; fax (21) 452493; e-mail pelaopdr@laotel.com; Ambassador MARIO I. GALMAN.

Poland: 263 Ban Thadeua, Km 3, quartier Wat Nak, BP 1106, Vientiane; tel. (21) 312940; fax (21) 312085; e-mail vieampol@laotel.com; Chargé d'affaires Dr TOMASZ GERLACH.

Russia: Ban Thadeua, quartier Thaphalanxay, BP 490, Vientiane; tel. (21) 312222; fax (21) 312210; e-mail rusemb@laotel.com; Ambassador YURI RAIKOV.

Singapore: Unit 12, Ban Naxay, rue Nong Bong, Muang Sat Settha, Vientiane; tel. (21) 416860; fax (21) 416855; e-mail sinemvte@laotel.com; internet www.mfa.gov.sg/vientiane; Ambassador HOY CHENG SEETOH.

Sweden: rue Sok Paluang, BP 800, Vientiane; tel. (21) 313772; fax (21) 315001; e-mail embassy.vientiane@sida.se; Chargé d'affaires a.i. CHRISTER HOLTSBERG.

Thailand: ave Phone Keng, Vientiane; tel. (21) 214581; fax (21) 214580; e-mail thaivtn@mfa.go.th; Ambassador RATHAKIT MANATHAT.

USA: 19 rue Bartholonie, BP 114, Vientiane; tel. (21) 212581; fax (21) 212584; e-mail khammanpx@state.gov; internet usembassy.state.gov/laos; Ambassador DOUGLAS A. HARTWICK.

Viet Nam: 85 rue That Luang, Vientiane; tel. (21) 413409; fax (21) 413379; e-mail dsqvn@laotel.com; Ambassador HUYNH ANH DUNG.

Judicial System

President of the People's Supreme Court: KHAMMY SAYAVONG.

Vice-President: DAVON VANGVICHIT.

People's Supreme Court Judges: NOUANTHONG VONGSA, NHOTSENG LITTHIDETH, PHOUKHONG CHANTHALATH, SENGSOUVANH CHANTHALOUNNAVONG, KESON PHANLACK, KONGCHI YANGCHY, KHAMPON PHASAIGNAVONG.

Public Prosecutor-General: KHAMPANE PHILAVONG.

Religion

The 1991 Constitution guarantees freedom of religious belief. The principal religion of Laos is Buddhism.

BUDDHISM

Lao Unified Buddhists' Association: Maha Kudy, Wat That Luang, Vientiane; f. 1964; Pres. (vacant); Sec.-Gen. Rev. SIHO SIHA-VONG.

CHRISTIANITY

The Roman Catholic Church

For ecclesiastical purposes, Laos comprises four Apostolic Vicariates. At 31 December 2000 an estimated 0.7% of the population were adherents.

Episcopal Conference of Laos and Cambodia

c/o Mgr Pierre Bach, Paris Foreign Missions, 254 Silom Rd, Bangkok 10500, Thailand.

f. 1971; Pres. Mgr JEAN KHAMSÉ VITHAVONG ((Titular Bishop of Moglaena), Vicar Apostolic of Vientiane).

Vicar Apostolic of Luang Prabang: Mgr BANCHONG THOPAYONG, Evêché, BP 74, Luang Prabang.

Vicar Apostolic of Paksé: Mgr LOUIS-MARIE LING MANGKHANEKHOUN (Titular Bishop of Proconsulari), Centre Catholique, BP 77, Paksé, Champasak; tel. (31) 212879.

Vicar Apostolic of Savannakhet: Mgr JEAN SOMMENG VORACHAK (Titular Bishop of Muzuca in Proconsulari), Centre Catholique, BP 12, Thakhek, Khammouane; tel. (51) 212184; fax (51) 213070.

Vicar Apostolic of Vientiane: Mgr JEAN KHAMSÉ VITHAVONG (Titular Bishop of Moglaena), Centre Catholique, BP 113, Vientiane; tel. (21) 216219; fax (21) 215085.

The Anglican Communion

Laos is within the jurisdiction of the Anglican Bishop of Singapore.

BAHÁ'Í FAITH

National Spiritual Assembly: BP 189, Vientiane; tel. (21) 216996; fax (21) 217127; e-mail nsalaos@laotel.com.

The Press

Aloun Mai (New Dawn): Vientiane; f. 1985; theoretical and political organ of the LPRP.

Heng Ngan: 87 ave Lane Xang, BP 780, Vientiane; tel. (21) 212750; fortnightly; organ of the Federation of Lao Trade Unions; Editor BOUAPHENG BOUNSOULINH.

Lao Dong (Labour): 87 ave Lane Xang, Vientiane; f. 1986; fortnightly; organ of the Federation of Lao Trade Unions; circ. 46,000.

Laos: 80 rue Sethathirath, BP 3770, Vientiane; tel. (21) 21447; fax (21) 21445; internet www.laolink.com; quarterly; published in Lao and English; illustrated; Editor V. PHOMCHANHEUANG; English Editor O. PHRAKHAMSAY.

Meying Lao: rue Manthatoarath, BP 59, Vientiane; e-mail chansoda@hotmail.com; f. 1980; monthly; women's magazine; organ of the Lao Women's Union; Editor-in-Chief VATSADY KHUTNGOTHA; Editor CHANSODA PHONETHIP; circ. 7,000.

Noum Lao (Lao Youth): Vientiane; f. 1979; fortnightly; organ of the Lao People's Revolutionary Youth Union; Editor DOUANGDY INTHAVONG; circ. 6,000.

Pasason (The People): 80 rue Setthathirath, BP 110, Vientiane; f. 1940; daily; organ of the Cen. Cttee of the LPRP; Editor BOUABAN VOLAKHOUN; circ. 28,000.

Pathet Lao: 80 rue Setthathirath, Vientiane; tel. (21) 215402; fax (21) 212446; f. 1979; monthly; Lao and English; organ of Khao San Pathet Lao (KPL); Dep. Dir SOUNTHONE KHANTHAVONG.

Sciences and Technics: Dept of Science and Technology, Science, Technology and the Environment Agency (STEA), POB 2279, Vientiane; f. 1991 as Technical Science Magazine; quarterly; organ of the Dept of Science and Technology; scientific research and development.

Siang Khong Gnaovason Song Thanva (Voice of the 2nd December Youths): Vientiane; monthly; youth journal.

Sieng Khene Lao: Vientiane; monthly; organ of the Lao Writers' Association.

Suksa Mai: Vientiane; monthly; organ of the Ministry of Education.

Valasan Khosana (Propaganda Journal): Vientiane; f. 1987; organ of the Cen. Cttee of the LPRP.

Vientiane Mai (New Vientiane): rue Setthathirath, BP 989, Vientiane; tel. (21) 2623; fax (21) 5989; f. 1975; morning daily; organ of

the LPRP Cttee of Vientiane province and city; Editor SICHANE (acting); circ. 2,500.

Vientiane Times: BP 5723, Vientiane; tel. (21) 216364; fax (21) 216365; internet www.vientianetimes.com; f. 1994; 2 a week; English; emphasis on investment opportunities; Editor SOMSANOUK MIXAY; circ. 3,000.

Vientiane Tulakit (Vientiane Business-Social): rue Setthathirath, Vientiane; tel. (21) 2623; fax (21) 6365; weekly; circ. 2,000.

There is also a newspaper published by the Lao People's Army, and several provinces have their own newsletters.

NEWS AGENCIES

Khao San Pathet Lao (KPL): 80 rue Setthathirath, Vientiane; tel. (21) 215402; fax (21) 212446; e-mail kpl@laonet.net; internet www.kplnet.net; f. 1968; organ of the Cttee of Information, Press, Radio and Television Broadcasting; news service; daily bulletins in Lao, English and French; teletype transmission in English; Gen. Dir KHAMSÈNE PHONGSA.

Foreign Bureaux

Rossiiskoye Informatsionnoye Agentstvo—Novosti (RIA—Novosti) (Russia): Vientiane; tel. (21) 213510; f. 1963.

Viet Nam News Agency (VNA): Vientiane; Chief Do VAN PHUONG.

Reuters (UK) is also represented in Laos.

PRESS ASSOCIATION

The Journalists' Association of the Lao PDR: BP 122, Vientiane; tel. (21) 212420; fax (21) 212408; Pres. BOUABANE VORAKHOUNE; Sec.-Gen. KHAM KHONG KONGVONGSA.

Publishers

Khoualuang Kanphim: 2–6 Khoualuang Market, Vientiane.

Lao-phanit: Ministry of Education, Bureau des Manuels Scolaires, rue Lane Xang, Ban Sisavat, Vientiane; educational, cookery, art, music, fiction.

Pakpassak Kanphin: 9–11 quai Fa-Hguun, Vientiane.

State Printing: 314/C rue Samsemthai, BP 2160, Vientiane; tel. (21) 213273; fax (21) 215901; Dir NOUPHAY KOUNLAVONG.

Broadcasting and Communications

TELECOMMUNICATIONS

Entreprises des Postes et Télécommunications de Laos: ave Lane Xang, 01000 Vientiane; tel. (21) 215767; fax (21) 212779; e-mail laoposts@laotel.com; state enterprise, responsible for the postal service and telecommunications; Dir-Gen. KIENG KHAMKETH.

Lao Télécommunications Co Ltd: ave Lane Xang, BP 5607, 0100 Vientiane; tel. (21) 216465; fax (21) 213493; e-mail hpinthar@laotel.com; internet www.laotel.com; f. 1996; a joint venture between a subsidiary of the Shinawatra Group of Thailand and Entreprises des Postes et Télécommunications de Laos; awarded a 25-year contract by the Government in 1996 to undertake all telecommunications projects in the country; Dir-Gen. HOUMPHANH INTHARATH.

BROADCASTING

Radio

In addition to the national radio service, there are several local stations.

Lao National Radio: rue Phangkham, Km 6, BP 310, Vientiane; tel. (21) 212428; fax (21) 212432; e-mail lnradio@hotmail.com; f. 1960; state-owned; programmes in Lao, French, English, Thai, Khmer and Vietnamese; domestic and international services; Dir-Gen. BOUNTHANH INTHAXAY.

In 1990 resistance forces in Laos established an illegal radio station, broadcasting anti-Government propaganda: **Satthani Vithayou Kachai Siang Latthaban Potpoi Sat Lao** (Radio Station of the Government for the Liberation of the Lao Nation): programmes in Lao and Hmong languages; broadcasts four hours daily.

Television

A domestic television service began in December 1983. In May 1988 a second national television station commenced transmissions from Savannakhet. In December 1993 the Ministry of Information and Culture signed a 15-year joint-venture contract with a Thai firm on the development of broadcasting services in Laos. Under the resultant International Broadcasting Corporation Lao Co Ltd, IBC Channel 3 was inaugurated in 1994 (see below).

Lao National Television (TVNL): rue Chommany Neua, Km 6, BP 5635, Vientiane; tel. (21) 412183; fax (21) 412182; f. 1983; colour television service; Dir-Gen. BOUASONE PHONGPHAVANH.

Laos Television 3: Vientiane; operated by the International Broadcasting Corpn Lao Co Ltd; f. 1994 as IBC Channel 3; 30% govt-owned, 70% owned by the International Broadcasting Corpn Co Ltd of Thailand; programmes in Lao.

Finance

(cap. = capital; dep. = deposits; br.(s) = branch(es); m. = million)

BANKING

The banking system was reorganized in 1988–89, ending the state monopoly of banking. Some commercial banking functions were transferred from the central bank and the state commercial bank to a new network of autonomous banks. The establishment of joint ventures with foreign financial institutions was permitted. Foreign banks have been permitted to open branches in Laos since 1992. In 1998 there were nine private commercial banks in Laos, most of them Thai. In March 1999 the Government consolidated six state-owned banks into two new institutions—Lane Xang Bank Ltd and Lao May Bank Ltd; these merged in 2001.

Central Bank

Banque de la RDP Lao: rue Yonnet, BP 19, Vientiane; tel. (21) 213109; fax (21) 213108; f. 1959 as the bank of issue, became Banque Pathetlao 1968, took over the operations of Banque Nationale du Laos 1975; known as Banque d'État de la RDP Lao from 1982 until adoption of present name; Gov. PHOUMI THIPPHAVONE.

Commercial Banks

Agriculture Promotion Bank: 58 rue Hengboun, Ban Haysok, BP 5456, Vientiane; tel. (21) 212024; fax (21) 213957; e-mail apblaopdr@laonet.net; Man. Dir BOUNSONG SOMMALAVONG.

Banque pour le Commerce Extérieur Lao (BCEL): 1 rue Pangkham, BP 2925, Vientiane; tel. (21) 213200; fax (21) 213202; e-mail bcelhovt@laotel.com; f. 1975; 100% state-owned; Chair. BOUNTHONG KEOMAHAVONG; Man. Dir SOMPHAO PHAYSITH.

Joint Development Bank: 75/1–5 ave Lane Xang, BP 3187, Vientiane; e-mail jdb@jdbbank.com; internet www.jdbbank.com; f. 1989; the first joint-venture bank between Laos and a foreign partner; 30% owned by Banque de la RDP Lao, 70% owned by Thai company, Phrom Suwan Silo and Drying Co Ltd; cap. US $4m.

Lao May Bank Ltd: 39 rue Pangkam, BP 2700, Vientiane; tel. (21) 213300; fax (21) 213304; f. 1999 as a result of the consolidation by the Government of ParkTai Bank, Lao May Bank and NakornLuang Bank; merged with Lane Xang Bank Ltd in 2001.

Lao-Viet Bank (LVB): 5 ave Lane Xang, Vientiane; tel. (21) 251418; fax (21) 212197; e-mail lvb@laonet.net; internet www.laovietbank.com; f. 1999; joint venture between BCEL and the Bank for Investment and Development of Vietnam.

Vientiane Commercial Bank Ltd: 33 ave Lane Xang, Ban Hatsady, Chanthaboury, Vientiane; tel. (21) 222700; fax (21) 213513; f. 1993; privately-owned joint venture by Laotian, Thai, Taiwanese and Australian investors; Man. Dir SOP SISOMPHOU.

Foreign Banks

Bangkok Bank Public Co Ltd (Thailand): 38/13–15 rue Hatsady, BP 5400, Vientiane; tel. (21) 213560; fax (21) 213561; f. 1993; Man. TOSSATIS RODPRASERT.

Bank of Ayudhya Public Co Ltd (Thailand): 79/6 Unit 17, ave Lane Xang, BP 5072, Vientiane; tel. (21) 213521; fax (21) 213520; e-mail baylaos@laotel.com; internet www.bay.co.th; f. 1994; Man. SUWAT TANTIPATANASAKUL.

Krung Thai Bank Public Co Ltd (Thailand): Unit 21, 80 ave Lane Xang, Ban Xiengngeuanthong, Chanthaboury, Vientiane; tel. (21) 213480; fax (21) 222762; e-mail ktblao@laotel.com; internet www.ktb.co.th; f. 1993; Gen. Man. SOMCHAI KANOKPETCH.

Public Bank Berhad (Malaysia): 100/1-4 rue Talat Sao, BP 6614, Vientiane; tel. (21) 216614; fax (21) 222743; e-mail pbbvte@laotel.com; Gen. Man. TAY HONG HENG.

Siam Commercial Bank Public Co Ltd (Thailand): 117 ave Lane Xang-Samsenethai, BP 4809, Ban Sisaket Mouang, Chanthaboury, Vientiane; tel. (21) 213500; fax (21) 213502; Gen. Man. CHARANYA DISSAMARN.

Thai Military Bank Public Co Ltd: 69 rue Khoun Boulom, Chanthaboury, BP 2423, Vientiane; tel. (21) 217174; fax (21) 216486; the first foreign bank to be represented in Laos; Man. AMNAT KOSKTPON.

INSURANCE

Assurances Générales du Laos (AGL): Vientiane Commercial Bank Bldg, ave Lane Xang, BP 4223, Vientiane; tel. (21) 215903; fax (21) 215904; e-mail agl@agl-allianz.com; Dir-Gen. PHILIPPE ROBINEAU.

Trade and Industry

GOVERNMENT AGENCY

National Economic Research Institute: rue Luang Prabang, Sithanneua, Vientiane; govt policy development unit; Dir SOUPHAN KEOMISAY.

DEVELOPMENT ORGANIZATIONS

Department of Livestock and Fisheries: Ministry of Agriculture and Forestry, BP 811, Vientiane; tel. (21) 416932; fax (21) 415674; e-mail eulaodlf@laotel.com; public enterprise; imports and markets agricultural commodities; produces and distributes feed and animals.

State Committee for State Planning: Vientiane; Pres. BOUATHONG VONGLOKHAM.

CHAMBER OF COMMERCE

Lao National Chamber of Commerce and Industry: rue Sihom, Ban Haisok, BP 4596, Vientiane; tel. and fax (21) 219223; e-mail ccilcciv@laotel.com; f. 1990; executive board comprising 11 mems and five advisers; Acting Pres. CHANHPHENG BOUNNAPHOL.

INDUSTRIAL AND TRADE ASSOCIATION

Société Lao Import-Export (SOLIMPEX): 43–47 ave Lane Xang, BP 278, Vientiane; tel. (21) 213818; fax (21) 217054; Dir KANHKEO SAYCOCIE; Dep. Dir KHEMMANI PHOLSENA.

UTILITIES

Electricity

Electricité du Laos: rue Nongbone, BP 309, Vientiane; tel. (21) 451519; fax (21) 416381; e-mail edlgmo@laotel.com; responsible for production and distribution of electricity; Gen. Man. VIRAPHONH VIRAVONG.

Lao National Grid Co: Vientiane; responsible for Mekong hydro-electricity exports.

Water

Nam Papa Lao (Lao Water Supply Authority): rue Phone Kheng, Thatluang Neua Village, Sat Settha District, Vientiane; tel. (21) 412880; fax (21) 414378; f. 1962; responsible for the water supply of the entire country; Gen. Man. Dr SOMPHON DETHOUDON.

STATE ENTERPRISES

Agricultural Forestry Development Import-Export and General Service Co: trading co of the armed forces.

Bolisat Phatthana Khet Phoudoi Import-Export Co: Lak Sao; f. 1984; trading co of the armed forces.

Dao-Heuang Import-Export Co: 38/2 Ban Hatsadi, POB 384, Vientiane; tel. (21) 213790; fax (21) 216317; internet www.dao-heuang.com; imports and distributes whisky, beer, mineral water and foodstuffs.

Luen Fat Hong Lao Plywood Industry Co: BP 83, Vientiane; tel. (21) 314990; fax (21) 314992; internet www.luenfathongyada.laopdr.com; development and management of forests, logging and timber production.

CO-OPERATIVES

Central Leading Committee to Guide Agricultural Co-operatives: Vientiane; f. 1978 to help organize and plan regulations and policies for co-operatives; by the end of 1986 there were some 4,000 co-operatives, employing about 74% of the agricultural labour force; Chair. (vacant); Chief KHAMSEN VONONOKEO.

TRADE UNION ORGANIZATION

Federation of Lao Trade Unions: 87 ave Lane Xang, BP 780, Vientiane; tel. (21) 313682; e-mail kammabanlao@pan-laos.net.la; f.

1956; 21-mem. Cen. Cttee and five-mem. Control Cttee; Chair. KHAMPAN PHILAVONG; Vice-Chair. BOUNPHON SANGSOMSAK; 70,000 mems.

Transport

RAILWAYS

The construction of a 30-km rail link between Vientiane and the Thai border town of Nong Khai began in January 1996; the rail link was scheduled for completion in 1998, but was indefinitely postponed in February of that year as an indirect consequence of a severe downturn in the Thai economy. In 1997 the Government announced plans to develop a comprehensive railway network, and awarded a contract to a Thai company, although no timetable for the implementation of the scheme was announced.

ROADS

The road network provides the country's main method of transport, accounting for about 90% of freight traffic and 95% of passenger traffic in 1993 (according to the Asian Development Bank—ADB). In 1999 there were an estimated 21,716 km of roads, of which 9,664 km were paved. The main routes link Vientiane and Luang Prabang with Ho Chi Minh City in southern Viet Nam and with northern Viet Nam and the Cambodian border, Vientiane with Savannakhet, Phong Saly to the Chinese border, Vientiane with Luang Prabang and the port of Ha Tinh (northern Viet Nam), and Savannakhet with the port of Da Nang (Viet Nam). In 2002 Laos, Thailand and China agreed to a US $45m. road project intended to link the three countries; most of the road construction would be carried out in Laos. The project was to be completed by 2006.

The Friendship Bridge across the Mekong river, linking Laos and Thailand between Tha Naleng (near Vientiane) and Nong Khai, was opened in April 1994. In early 1998 construction work began in Paksé on a second bridge across the Mekong river. The project was granted substantial funding from the Japanese Government, and was completed in August 2000. An additional bridge, linking Savannakhet and Mukdahan, is also planned and is scheduled for completion by 2005.

INLAND WATERWAYS

The Mekong River, which forms the western frontier of Laos for much of its length, is the country's greatest transport artery. However, the size of river vessels is limited by rapids, and traffic is seasonal. In April 1995 Laos, Cambodia, Thailand and Viet Nam signed an agreement regarding the joint development of the lower Mekong, and established a Mekong River Commission. There are about 4,600 km of navigable waterways.

CIVIL AVIATION

Wattai airport, Vientiane, is the principal airport. Following the signing of an agreement in 1995, the airport was to be upgraded by Japan; renovation work commenced in 1997, and a new passenger terminal was opened in 1998. The development of Luang Prabang airport by Thailand, at a cost of 50m. baht, began in May 1994 and the first phase of the development programme was completed in 1996; the second phase was completed in 1998. In April 1998 Luang Prabang airport gained formal approval for international flights. The airports at Paksé and Savannakhet were also scheduled to be upgraded to enable them to accommodate wide-bodied civilian aircraft; renovation work on the airport at Savannakhet was completed in April 2000. Construction of a new airport in Oudomxay Province was completed in the late 1990s.

Lao Civil Aviation Department: BP 119, Vientiane; tel. and fax (21) 512163; e-mail laodca@laotel.com; Dir-Gen. YAKUA LOPANGKAO.

Lao Aviation (International): National Air Transport Co, 2 rue Pangkham, BP 6441, Vientiane; tel. (21) 212057; fax (21) 212056; e-mail pothong@lao-aviation.com; internet www.lao-aviation.com; f. 1975; state airline, fmrly Lao Aviation; operates internal and international passenger and cargo transport services within South-East Asia; Gen. Man. Dir POTHONG NGONPHACHANH.

Tourism

Laos boasts spectacular scenery, ancient pagodas and abundant wildlife. However, the development of tourism remains constrained by the poor infrastructure in much of the country. Western tourists were first permitted to enter Laos in 1989. In 1994, in order to stimulate the tourist industry, Vientiane ended restrictions on the movement of foreigners in Laos. Also in 1994 Laos, Viet Nam and Thailand agreed measures for the joint development of tourism. Luang Prabang was approved by UNESCO as a World Heritage site in February 1998. The number of visitors reached 614,278 in 1999, when receipts from tourism were estimated at US $97m. Tourist arrivals increased further, to 737,208, in 2000, when receipts from tourism totalled an estimated US $114m. 1999–2000 were designated as Visit Laos Years.

National Tourism Authority of Lao PDR: ave Lane Xang, BP 3556, Hadsady, Chanthaboury, Vientiane; tel. (21) 212251; fax (21) 212769; e-mail mtsc@mekongcenter.com; internet www.mekongcenter.com; 17 provincial offices; Dir CHENG SAYAVONG.

LATVIA

Introductory Survey

Location, Climate, Language, Religion, Flag, Capital

The Republic of Latvia (formerly the Latvian Soviet Socialist Republic) is situated in north-eastern Europe, on the east coast of the Baltic Sea. The country is bounded by Estonia to the north and by Lithuania to the south and south-west. To the east it borders Russia, and to the south-east Belarus. Owing to the influence of maritime factors, the climate is relatively temperate, but changeable. Average temperatures in January range from –2.8°C (26.6°F) in the western coastal town of Liepāja to –6.6°C (20.1°F) in the inland town of Daugavpils. Mean temperatures for July range from 16.7°C (62.1°F) in Liepāja to 17.6°C (63.7°F) in Daugavpils. Average annual rainfall in Rīga is 617 mm (24 ins). The official language is Latvian. The major religion is Christianity: most ethnic Latvians are traditionally Lutherans or Roman Catholics, whereas ethnic Russians are mainly adherents of the Russian Orthodox Church or Old Believers. The national flag (proportions 1 by 2) has a maroon background, with a narrow white horizontal stripe superimposed across the central part. The capital is Rīga (Riga).

Recent History

In November 1917 representatives of Latvian nationalist groups elected a provisional national council, which informed the Russian Government of its intention to establish a sovereign, independent Latvian state. On 18 November 1918 the Latvian National Council, which had been constituted on the previous day, proclaimed the independent Republic of Latvia, with Jānis Čakste as President. Independence, under the nationalist Government of Kārlis Ulmanis, was fully achieved after the expulsion of the Bolsheviks from Rīga in May 1919, with the aid of German troops, and from the eastern province of Latgale, with Polish and Estonian assistance, in January 1920. A Latvian-Soviet peace treaty was finally signed in August 1920. Latvia's first Constitution was adopted in 1922. An electoral system based on proportional representation permitted a large number of small parties to be represented in the Saeima (legislature). As a result, there was little administrative stability, with 18 changes of government in 1922–34. None the less, under the dominant party, the Latvian Farmers' Union (LFU, led by Ulmanis), agrarian reforms were successfully introduced and agricultural exports flourished. The world-wide economic decline of the early 1930s, together with domestic political fragmentation, prompted a (bloodless) *coup d'état* in May 1934, led by Ulmanis. Martial law was introduced, the Saeima was dissolved and all political parties, including the LFU, were banned. A Government of National Unity, with Ulmanis as Prime Minister, assumed the legislative functions of the Saeima. Ulmanis became President in 1936.

Under the Treaty of Non-Aggression (the 'Molotov-Ribbentrop Pact'), signed by Germany and the USSR in August 1939, the incorporation of Latvia into the USSR was agreed by the two powers. A Treaty of Mutual Aid between the USSR and Latvia allowed the establishment of Soviet military bases in Latvia, and in June 1940 it was occupied by Soviet forces. In common with the neighbouring Baltic states of Estonia and Lithuania, Latvia did not offer military resistance, being greatly outnumbered by the Soviet forces. A new 'puppet' administration, under Augusts Kirhenšteins, was installed, and the election to the Saeima of Soviet-approved candidates took place in July. In that month the legislature proclaimed the Latvian Soviet Socialist Republic, which in the following month was formally incorporated into the USSR as a constituent union republic.

In the first year of Soviet rule almost 33,000 Latvians were deported to Siberia and other areas of the Russian Federation, and a further 1,350 were killed. Latvian language, traditions and culture were also suppressed. In July 1941 Soviet rule in Latvia was interrupted by German occupation. Most German troops had withdrawn by 1944, although the Kurzeme region, in south-western Latvia, was retained by Germany until the end of the Second World War. Soviet Latvia was re-established in 1944–45 and the process of 'sovietization' was resumed. There were further mass deportations of Latvians to Russia and Central Asia. Independent political activities were prohibited and exclusive political power was exercised by the Communist Party of Latvia (CPL). A process of industrialization encouraged significant and sustained Russian and other Soviet immigration into the republic. The problem of agricultural stagnation (a consequence of Latvia's industrialization) was not addressed until the mid-1950s, when the Latvian authorities were accorded greater powers as a result of the policy of economic decentralization introduced in the USSR. This coincided with a movement within the CPL for greater cultural, especially linguistic, autonomy. However, under CPL First Secretary Arvīds Pelše (appointed in 1959) and his successor, Augusts Voss (First Secretary, 1966–84), the limited autonomy gained in the 1950s was reversed, and repression of Latvian cultural and literary life was increased.

There was a significant revival in traditional Latvian culture from the late 1970s. Political groups began to be established, including the Environmental Protection Club and Helsinki-86, established to monitor Soviet observance of the Helsinki Final Act adopted in 1975 by the Conference on (now Organization for) Security and Co-operation in Europe (CSCE—now OSCE, see p. 283). In June and August 1986 anti-Soviet demonstrations, organized by Helsinki-86, were suppressed by the police. In 1987 there were further demonstrations on the anniversaries of significant events in Latvian history. Such movements, fostered by the greater freedom of expression permitted under the new Soviet policy of *glasnost* (openness), were strongly opposed by the CPL, headed from 1984 by Boris Pugo. In 1988 opposition movements in Latvia began to unite, forging a significant political force. Prominent intellectuals, led by Jānis Peters (the Chairman of the Latvian Writers' Union), criticized the CPL for its reactionary attitude to the new Soviet policy of *perestroika* (restructuring) and advocated more radical political and economic change. In June Latvia's cultural unions issued a joint resolution demanding that Latvian be made the state language, that 'secret protocols' of the 1939 Nazi-Soviet Treaty be published and that measures be taken to address the ecological degradation resulting from forced industrialization. In October 1988 representatives of the leading opposition movements, together with CPL radicals, organized the inaugural congress of the Popular Front of Latvia (PFL), at which delegates resolved to seek sovereignty for Latvia within a renewed Soviet federation. The PFL, chaired by Dainis Ivāns, quickly became the largest and most influential political force in Latvia, with an estimated membership of 250,000 by the end of 1988.

In September 1988 Boris Pugo was transferred to the Russian and Soviet capital, Moscow, and replaced as First Secretary of the CPL by Jānis Vagris. The new CPL leadership came increasingly under the influence of members of the PFL. At the end of September Latvian was designated the state language. In March 1989 candidates supported by the PFL won 26 of the 34 contested seats in elections to the USSR's Congress of People's Deputies. On 28 July, following similar moves by Lithuania and Estonia, the Latvian Supreme Soviet (legislature) adopted a declaration of sovereignty and economic independence. However, there was growing support within the republic for full independence from the USSR. The Latvian National Independence Movement (LNIM), formed in 1988, advocated full economic and political independence. In December 1989, despite the establishment of political groups opposed to the PFL, candidates supported by the PFL won some 75% of seats contested in local elections.

In January 1990 the Latvian Supreme Soviet voted to abolish the constitutional provisions that guaranteed the CPL's political predominance. In the following month the Supreme Soviet adopted a declaration condemning the Latvian legislature's decision to request admission to the USSR in 1940 and the flag, state emblems and anthem of pre-1940 Latvia were restored to official use. At elections to the Supreme Soviet held in March and April 1990, pro-independence candidates endorsed by the PFL won 131 of the 201 seats; the CPL and the anti-independence Interfront (dominated by member of the Russian-speaking population) together won 59 seats. The CPL subsequently split into two parties: the majority of delegates at an extraordinary congress rejected a motion to leave the Communist Party of the Soviet Union (CPSU), and elected Alfrēds Rubiks, an opponent of independence, as First Secretary. Meanwhile, a pro-independence faction established the Independent Communist Party of Latvia, under the chairmanship of Ivars Kezbers.

The new Supreme Council (the former Supreme Soviet) was convened in early May 1990, and elected Anatolijs Gorbunovs, a member of the CPSU-affiliated CPL, as its Chairman (*de facto* President of the Republic). On 4 May the Supreme Council adopted a resolution that declared the incorporation of Latvia into the USSR in 1940 as unlawful, and announced the beginning of a transitional period that was to lead to full political and economic independence. Four articles of the 1922 Constitution, defining Latvia as an independent democratic state and asserting the sovereignty of the Latvian people, were restored, and were to form the basis of the newly declared Republic of Latvia's legitimacy. Ivars Godmanis, the Deputy Chairman of the PFL, was elected Prime Minister in a new, PFL-dominated Government. Meanwhile, a rival body to the Supreme Soviet had been convened at the end of April 1990. This Congress of Latvia had been elected in an unofficial poll, in which some 700,000 people were reported to have participated: only citizens of the pre-1940 republic and their descendants had been entitled to vote. The Congress, in which members of the radical LNIM predominated, declared Latvia to be an occupied country and adopted resolutions on independence and the withdrawal of Soviet troops.

The Supreme Council's resolutions, although more cautious than independence declarations adopted in Lithuania and Estonia, severely strained relations with the Soviet authorities. On 14 May 1990 the Soviet President, Mikhail Gorbachev, issued a decree that annulled the Latvian declaration of independence, condemning it as a violation of the USSR Constitution. The declaration was also opposed within the republic by some non-Latvians, who organized protest strikes and demonstrations. In subsequent months local anti-Government movements (allied with Soviet troops stationed in Latvia) conducted a campaign of propaganda and harassment against the Government. In December the Latvian Government claimed that special units (OMON) of the Soviet Ministry of Internal Affairs had been responsible for a series of explosions in Rīga, and in January 1991 OMON troops seized the Rīga Press House, previously the property of the CPL. Later in January a 'Committee of Public Salvation', headed by Alfrēds Rubiks, declared itself as a rival Government to the Godmanis administration; on the same day five people died when OMON troops attacked the Ministry of the Interior in Rīga. (In November 1999 10 former Soviet officers were convicted of attempting to overthrow the Latvian Government in 1991: seven received suspended prison sentences of up to four years' duration.)

The attempted seizure of power by Rubiks' Committee reinforced opposition in Latvia to inclusion in the new union treaty being prepared by nine Soviet republics. Latvia refused to conduct the all-Union referendum on the future of the USSR, which was scheduled for 17 March 1991 (although some 680,000 people, mostly Russians and Ukrainians, did participate on an unofficial basis). Instead, a referendum on Latvian independence took place on 3 March. Of those eligible to vote, 87.6% participated, of whom, according to official results, 73.7% endorsed proposals for 'a democratic and independent Latvian republic'.

At the time of the attempted overthrow of the Gorbachev administration in Moscow in August 1991, immediate Soviet military intervention in Latvia was widely anticipated. However, an emergency session of the Supreme Council was convened and the full independence of Latvia was proclaimed. As the coup collapsed, the Godmanis Government took prompt action to assert control in Latvia, banning the CPL and detaining Rubiks. On 6 September 1991 the USSR State Council formally recognized the independent Republic of Latvia, and the country was admitted to the UN later that month. In late 1991 the Supreme Council adopted legislation guaranteeing the right of citizenship to all citizens of the pre-1940 republic (including non-ethnic Latvians) and their descendants. Remaining residents of Latvia (mainly Russians and other Slavs) were to be required to apply for naturalization after final legislation governing citizenship was determined by a restored Saeima.

The first legislative election since the restoration of independence took place in June 1993, with the participation of about 90% of the electorate. Only citizens of pre-1940 Latvia and their descendants were entitled to vote; consequently, some 27%

of the population (mainly ethnic Russians) were excluded from the election. A total of 23 parties, movements and alliances contested the poll, of which eight secured representation in the 100-seat Saeima. The Latvian Way, a broadly-based movement established earlier in the year, emerged as the strongest party, with more than 32% of the votes and 36 seats in the assembly. Only 11 of the elected deputies were non-ethnic Latvians (six of whom were ethnic Russians). The results of the election demonstrated strong popular support for the more moderate nationalist parties, and socialist-orientated parties (including the successor of the CPL, the Latvian Socialist Party—LSP) failed to win representation. The PFL also failed to secure any seats.

The first session of the Saeima began on 6 July 1993 with the election of Anatolijs Gorbunovs as its Chairman (speaker). The Saeima also voted to restore the Constitution of 1922, and undertook to elect the President of the Republic from among three prominent deputies. At a third round of voting, on 7 July 1993, Guntis Ulmanis (the great-nephew of Kārlis Ulmanis) of the revived LFU succeeded in winning a majority of 53 votes. He was inaugurated as President the following day, whereupon he appointed Valdis Birkavs (formerly a Deputy Chairman of the Supreme Council and a leading member of the Latvian Way) as Prime Minister. Birkavs' Cabinet of Ministers represented a coalition agreement between the Latvian Way (the majority partner) and the LFU.

The requirements for naturalization proposed by the Government's draft citizenship law included a minimum of 10 years' permanent residence, a knowledge of Latvian to conversational level and an oath of loyalty to the republic. In March 1994 the Saeima approved the establishment of the new post of State Minister for Human Rights, in an attempt to counter accusations of violations of minority rights in Latvia. Final legislation on citizenship and naturalization was adopted by the Saeima in June. However, following international criticism, and amid concern that the new law would jeopardize Latvia's application for membership of the Council of Europe, the Cabinet of Ministers persuaded President Ulmanis to reject the legislation. In July the Saeima adopted an amended citizenship law. Latvia was admitted to the Council of Europe (see p. 181) in February 1995.

Meanwhile, in July 1994 the LFU announced its withdrawal from the governing coalition, following disagreements with the Latvian Way over economic and agricultural policy. A new Cabinet was appointed in September. It, too, was dominated by Latvian Way members, including the Prime Minister, Māris Gailis (hitherto Deputy Prime Minister and Minister of State Reform); Birkavs became Deputy Prime Minister and Minister of Foreign Affairs. Four opposition factions within the Saeima—including the Latvian National Conservative Party (LNCP), as the LNIM had been renamed, and the LFU—announced their union as a 'national bloc' to co-ordinate opposition activities in the legislature.

In July 1995 Alfrēds Rubiks was found guilty of having sought to 'overthrow Latvia's state authorities by force' in 1991. He was sentenced to eight years' imprisonment (four of which he had already served). Rubiks was released in November 1997 and immediately announced his intention to resume political life. In December 1995 Maj.-Gen. Alfons Noviks, who had headed the Latvian branch of the Soviet security service in 1940–53, was found guilty of genocide and was sentenced to life imprisonment; he died in prison in March 1996. Noviks was held accountable for the deportation to Siberia of more than 60,000 Latvians in 1940–41 and 1949, in addition to torture and murder.

A general election was held on 30 September–1 October 1995. Nine parties and coalitions succeeded in obtaining the 5% of the votes required for representation in the Saeima; as a result, the assembly was highly fragmented. The Latvian Way's share of the 100 seats was more than halved, to 17, while the largest number of seats (18) was won by the newly established, leftist Democratic Party Saimnieks (The Master—DPS). The most unexpected outcome of the poll was the success of the People's Movement for Latvia (Zigerists' Party—PML), which won 16 seats. The party, established by Joahims Zigerists, had campaigned on a platform of nationalist and anti-Russian policies; moreover, Zigerists was linked to an extremist right-wing organization in Germany, and in 1994 had been convicted in that country for inciting racial hatred. Negotiations among parties to form a coalition government capable of commanding a parliamentary majority proved to be protracted. In December 1995 the Saeima finally endorsed a Cabinet of Ministers led by Andris Šķēle (an entrepreneur with no party affiliation). The new Government was a broad coalition of the DPS, the Latvian Way, the Union 'For Fatherland and Freedom' (UFF), the LNCP, the LFU and the Latvian Unity Party (LUP). Zigerists' PML was, notably, excluded from the coalition. Former Prime Ministers Gailis and Birkavs were appointed to the new Cabinet, the former as Deputy Prime Minister and Minister of Environmental Protection and Regional Development, and the latter as Minister of Foreign Affairs. The stability of the coalition was tested in May 1996, when the Deputy Prime Minister and Minister of Agriculture, Albērīs Kauls, was dismissed, after criticizing the Prime Minister's agricultural policies. The LUP (of which Kauls was the leader) temporarily withdrew its support from the coalition, but shortly afterwards rejoined the Government, having nominated (and secured approval for) a new candidate as Minister of Agriculture.

On 18 June 1996 the Saeima re-elected Guntis Ulmanis as President for a second three-year term. The presidential election revealed disagreements among the coalition members over the choice of candidate, and in July Šķēle conducted a cabinet reshuffle in an attempt to create a more cohesive Government. Also in July it was announced that the LUP was to merge with the DPS, reinforcing the latter as the dominant party in the coalition. Despite this, and the adoption of a coalition co-operation agreement in September, instability in the Government and in the legislature continued. In October Aivars Kreituss tendered his resignation as Minister of Finance, having in the previous month been expelled from the DPS for his perceived failure to promote the party's interests. Meanwhile, Alfrēds Čepānis was elected to the post of Chairman of the Saeima, following the removal from office of Ilga Kreituse. Also in October the Deputy Prime Minister, Ziedonis Čevers (also leader of the DPS), submitted his resignation, citing differences of opinion with Šķēle. The collapse of the coalition appeared inevitable in January 1997, when Šķēle resigned as Prime Minister, in what was interpreted as a response to criticism from President Ulmanis over Šķēle's approval of Vasilijs Melniks as the new Minister of Finance. Negotiations began for the formation of a new Government, but Šķēle was swiftly reappointed by Ulmanis, who indicated his support for the continuation of the Prime Minister's economic and structural reforms. A new, largely unaltered, Cabinet was appointed in February; Roberts Zīle replaced Melniks as Minister of Finance. Local elections conducted in March demonstrated a considerable increase in support for the LFU, which won 168 seats, compared with 83 for the DPS and 44 for the UFF.

By July 1997 the governing coalition had begun to disintegrate, not least because a series of corruption scandals had, since May, prompted the resignation of several ministers, and at the end of the month Šķēle announced the resignation of the Government. President Ulmanis invited Guntars Krasts, the outgoing Minister of the Economy, to form a new administration. In early August the Saeima approved Krasts' proposals for a new, five-party coalition, comprising the Conservative Union 'For Fatherland and Freedom'/LNNK (his own party, formed in the previous month by the merger of the UFF and the Latvian National Independence Movement—LNNK), the DPS, the Latvian Way, the LFU and the Christian Democratic Union of Latvia (CDUL).

Krasts' leadership was tested in early 1998 following suggestions by an investigative parliamentary committee that he had been guilty of negligence with regard to a privatization proposal for the state power utility, Latvenergo, during his time as Minister of the Economy. In March Krasts formally requested that the Saeima conduct a vote of confidence in his personal integrity, in order to confirm his mandate. The refusal of any parliamentary faction to organize such a vote was interpreted by the Prime Minister as an endorsement of his leadership. In that month former Prime Minister Šķēle announced the formation of a new political party, later named the People's Party, to contest the forthcoming elections.

In April 1998 the Minister of the Economy, Atis Sausnītis, was dismissed, following a well-publicized attempt to draw attention to the possible adverse economic consequences of sustained diplomatic tensions with Russia (see below). Sensing that Krasts' Government might be on the point of collapse, the DPS announced its withdrawal from the coalition. At the end of the month, however, Krasts survived a parliamentary vote of 'no confidence' proposed by the LFU and the Latvian Way. At the same session the Saeima approved appointments to a new coalition Government, with members of the Cabinet of Ministers drawn from the LFU, the Latvian Way and an alliance of the Latvian National Reform Party and the Latvian Green Party.

The question of citizenship returned to prominence in April 1998, following the adoption, in response to long-standing recommendations made by the OSCE, of draft amendments to the strict legislation regulating rights to citizenship. The amendments, which removed the age-related system of naturalization that allocated dates for application by age-group, granted citizenship to stateless children (permanently resident in Latvia) born after the 1991 declaration of independence and relaxed the citizenship requirements for Russian-speakers, were approved by the Saeima in June. Although widely welcomed elsewhere in Europe, the amendments were deemed inadequate by the Russian authorities, and nationalist groups within the Latvian legislature rallied sufficient support inside and outside the Saeima to force a delay to the enactment of the new legislation and the organization of a referendum on the subject. The referendum was duly conducted concurrently with the 3 October general election (see below); the results demonstrated a 52.5% majority in favour of the amendments, which were promulgated later in the month.

At the general election, Šķēle's People's Party was the most successful single party, taking 21.2% of the votes (and 24 seats), ahead of the Latvian Way with 18.1% (21 seats) and the Conservative Union 'For Fatherland and Freedom'/LNNK with 14.7% (17 seats). Only six of the 21 participating political parties secured the minimum 5% of the votes necessary for representation in the Saeima. It was not until the end of November that the Saeima approved a new, three-party, minority coalition Government, to be headed by Vilis Krištopans of the Latvian Way. The coalition, comprising the Latvian Way, the Conservative Union 'For Fatherland and Freedom'/LNNK and the New Party (which held eight legislative seats), also drew support from the Latvian Social Democratic Alliance, which controlled 14 seats in the Saeima. In early February 1999 the Social Democrats formally joined the coalition with the appointment of one of their members to the agriculture portfolio in the Cabinet of Ministers.

On 17 June 1999 Vaira Viķe-Freiberga was elected President at a seventh round of voting in the Saeima, with the support of 53 deputies (compared with 20 for Valdis Birkavs of the Latvian Way and nine for Ingrīda Udre of the New Party). Born in Latvia, but resident in Canada from the end of the Second World War until 1998, Viķe-Freiberga thus became the first female President in Central and Eastern Europe. At her inauguration, on 8 July 1999, Viķe-Freiberga identified as priorities for her presidency Latvia's entry into the European Union (EU, see p. 199) and NATO (see p. 271). Three days before her inauguration, Kristopans announced his Government's resignation, apparently in response to the recent signing by the Conservative Union 'For Fatherland and Freedom'/LNNK of a co-operation accord with the opposition People's Party. President Viķe-Freiberga subsequently asked Andris Šķēle to form a new government. Šķēle thus became Prime Minister for the third time, leading a coalition of his own People's Party, the Conservative Union 'For Fatherland and Freedom'/LNNK and the Latvian Way; the coalition controlled 62 of the 100 seats in the Saeima.

Meanwhile, in early July 1999 the Saeima adopted controversial new language legislation, which, notably, required that all business (whether in state or private organizations) and all state- and municipally-organized gatherings be conducted in Latvian. Russia immediately denounced the legislation as openly discriminatory against Latvia's national minorities, and it was also condemned by the OSCE, the Council of Europe, and the European Commission. Within Latvia, the legislation attracted criticism from groups representing non-ethnic-Latvians; furthermore, business interests warned that restrictions on the use of language could deter foreign investors. President Viķe-Freiberga swiftly returned the legislation to the Saeima for further consideration, and revised legislation was approved in early December. The new law, which incorporated amendments urged by the OSCE, was said by its proponents to allow the preservation and strengthening of the Latvian language, while ensuring compliance with international standards: Latvian was to be used for all business in the state sector, and for certain private-sector activities. In August 2000 implementation regulations were adopted, concerning issues such as transliteration, and the language law came into effect at the beginning of September, prompting protests from both the parliamentary opposition and the ethnic Russian community.

Amendments to the pensions law were approved by the Saeima in early August 1999, whereby the statutory retirement age was to be increased, and payments reduced for those of pensionable age who continued to work. The changes were condemned by trade unions and groups representing the elderly, and the Pensioners' Federation successfully petitioned for a referendum (set for mid-November) on the issue. Although some 94.1% of participants at the referendum voted against the amended law, the low rate of electoral participation (25.1%) invalidated the result, and the legislation thus entered into effect.

A much-publicized paedophilia scandal assumed wider political significance in February 2000, when Jānis Ādamsons, the Chairman of a parliamentary commission established to investigate the affair, alleged that witnesses had implicated Prime Minister Šķēle, former Prime Minister Birkavs (by this time Minister of Justice) and the head of the State Revenue Service, Andrejs Sonciks; he further stated that members of the commission had been subject to blackmail attempts and intimidation. The Office of the Prosecutor-General immediately instigated slander proceedings, and Šķēle denounced the assertions as politically motivated. The charges against Birkavs and Sonciks were dismissed on 31 July, and on the following day the Prosecutor-General's office announced that it had closed the case against Šķēle.

In the mean time, Šķēle had resigned the premiership in mid-April 2000, after the Latvian Way withdrew from the governing coalition, owing to a dispute over the running of the Latvian Privatization Agency. President Viķe-Freiberga asked Andris Bērziņš, hitherto the Mayor of Rīga, to form a new government; his cabinet (a coalition of the People's Party, the Latvian Way, the Conservative Union 'For Fatherland and Freedom'/LNNK and the New Party) was approved by the Saeima in early May. In mid-January 2001 the New Party was renamed the New Christian Party; the New Faction was formed by disenchanted former New Party members. In late January the Prime Minister asked the New Faction to leave the Government, after parliamentary deputies from the party supported an opposition tax proposal. The party resigned from the Government early in the following month, and in late February it signed a co-operation agreement with the Latvian Social Democratic Workers' Party. Local elections held in March demonstrated a considerable increase in support for the latter party in the capital and in surrounding areas.

In November 2001 Einārs Repše resigned as Governor of the Bank of Latvia (one year before his term of office was due to expire), in order to found a new political party, New Era. Despite a delay in declaring its policy objectives, the rightist party attracted immediate popular support. Repše was elected Chairman of New Era at its founding congress, which was held in early February 2002. Meanwhile, following the re-election, at the end of October 2001, of Juris Bojārs as Chairman of the Latvian Social Democratic Workers' Party, five principal members left the party in January 2002, in protest at his allegedly authoritarian style of leadership. The defectors initially formed a separate faction in the Saeima, prior to the establishment of a new party, the Union of Social Democrats, in March. Further political consolidation took place in early 2002, in advance of the imminent general election: the Labour Party and the Latvian Democratic Party founded the Centre alliance, and the New Christian Party and the Christian Democratic Union of Latvia also entered into an electoral co-operation agreement. In early May Bērziņš dismissed the Minister of Welfare, Andrejs Pozarnovs; Viktors Jaksons was subsequently appointed as his successor. In the same month the Saeima adopted amendments to national electoral legislation, abolishing the controversial requirement that candidates be fluent in the Latvian language, which had been perceived as an obstacle to NATO membership; however, the Saeima had passed legislation reinforcing Latvian as the official working language of parliament at the end of the preceding month. Also in May the new Christian, centrist First Party of Latvia (LPP) was formed, and the Latvian Freedom Party was founded by former Minister of the Interior Ziedonis Cevers. Minister of the Interior Mareks Segliņš, a member of the People's Party, was dismissed from his post at the end of September; on the same day members of the Latvian Way were accused of libelling the People's Party, thus compromising relations between the coalition partners.

In the legislative election, held, as scheduled, on 5 October 2002, Repše's New Era won 23.9% of the votes cast (26 seats); the leftist, pro-Russian electoral bloc For Human Rights in a United Latvia, which included the National Harmony Party and the Latvian Socialist Party, obtained 18.9% of the votes (25 seats); and the People's Party received 16.7% (20 seats). Other parties to achieve representation in the Saeima were the

Greens' and Farmers' Union (an alliance of the Latvian Farmers' Union and the Latvian Green Party), with 12 seats, the LPP (10 seats) and the Conservative Union 'For Fatherland and Freedom'/LNNK (seven); the Latvian Way failed to secure the 5% of the votes required to obtain a seat in the Saeima. The rate of participation by the electorate was some 72.5%. Following the collapse of talks with the People's Party, Repše decided to form a coalition government with the LPP, the Greens' and Farmers' Union and the Conservative Union 'For Fatherland and Freedom'/LNNK. The new Government, led by Einars Repše, was approved by the Saeima on 7 November; New Era assumed nine posts in the Cabinet of Ministers, the LPP took responsibility for four, the Greens' and Farmers' Union took three portfolios (as well as the position of parliamentary Chairman), and the Conservative Union 'For Fatherland and Freedom'/LNNK controlled two ministries. The Minister of Defence, Ģirts Kristovskis, was the only member of the Cabinet of Ministers to have retained his previous portfolio; a new post of Deputy Prime Minister was established, to which Ainārs Šlesers was appointed. At the end of November Atis Slakteris replaced Andris Šķēle as Chairman of the People's Party; in January 2003 Šķēle announced his intention to withdraw from politics.

In early January 2003 the Cabinet of Ministers approved measures that increased ministers' salaries threefold, with the reported aim of discouraging corruption. In February the National Harmony Party withdrew from the For Human Rights in a United Latvia alliance, apparently in a desire to pursue more moderate policies. In early March the Saeima voted in favour of bringing forward the presidential election by three months, to mid-March, with a view to focusing efforts on Latvia's preparations for EU and NATO membership. However, there were opposition protests that an early election would be unconstitutional, and shortly afterwards the Saeima reversed its decision. In late March the Minister of Health, Aris Auders, was dismissed, despite having survived a parliamentary vote of 'no confidence' in January, following allegations of corruption in his former post; he was replaced by Ingrīda Circene.

Latvia's post-independence relations with its eastern neighbour, Russia, were troubled by two issues. The first concerned the citizenship and linguistic rights of Latvia's large Russian community (see above). Of comparable importance was the issue of the 100,000 former Soviet troops still stationed in Latvia (jurisdiction over whom had been transferred, following the dissolution of the USSR, to Russia). Following negotiations, which commenced in 1992, withdrawal of the troops began early in that year. The process was hampered by a series of disagreements, in particular over the issue of a Russian military radar station at Skrunda, in western Latvia, that the Russians wished to retain. However, in February 1994 Latvia and Russia accepted a US-sponsored compromise, and in April agreements were concluded on the complete withdrawal of the remaining 10,000 Russian troops by the end of August, as well as on social guarantees for the estimated 22,000 Russian military pensioners residing in Latvia. Installations at the Skrunda base were subsequently dismantled.

Negotiations regarding the demarcation of the Latvian-Russian border, and Latvia's claim to some 1,640 sq km of land transferred from Latvia to Russia during the Soviet era, commenced in April 1996. Latvia initially insisted (as Estonia had done) that any future border agreement should include a reference to the 1920 treaty, in which Russia recognized Latvia's independence. However, in February 1997 the Latvian administration abandoned this demand, and agreed that claims to property in the disputed territory should be discussed separately from the main border agreement. In March a draft treaty on the demarcation of the border was agreed by the two countries, and full agreement on a border treaty was reached in October. However, the Russian Government subsequently signalled its intention to link its acceptance of the treaty to an improvement in the civil rights of ethnic Russians in Latvia. Relations became strained in March 1998, following the use of force by the Latvian police in order to disperse a demonstration of about 1,000 protesters—mostly ethnic-Russian pensioners—who were demonstrating in Rīga against price increases. Relations deteriorated further later in the month, following the organization, in Rīga, of a rally of Latvian veterans of Nazi German *Waffen SS* units, who had fought Soviet forces during the Second World War; the participation of senior Latvian politicians and military personnel attracted particular criticism from the Russian authorities. When the rally was repeated in

March 2000 government officials and serving military officers were not permitted to take part. Meanwhile, the Government had been criticized by Russia for what it perceived as anti-Soviet bias in the pursuit of criminal cases against individuals accused of war crimes. Notably, in January 2000 Vasilii Kononov, an anti-Nazi resistance fighter during the Second World War, was sentenced to six years' imprisonment for the murder of nine Latvians in 1944; his retrial was ongoing in early 2003. In March 2000 the Supreme Court rejected a final appeal against sentence brought by Mikhail Farbtukh, who had in September 1999 been convicted of genocide against the Latvian people in 1941–49; an earlier appeal had reduced his seven-year sentence to one of five years' custody. The Russian authorities asserted that Latvia's concern to expedite the prosecution of those suspected of crimes under the Soviet occupation contrasted with its apparent tardiness in investigating and bringing to justice alleged perpetrators of war crimes during the Nazi era. Tensions arising from repeated Russian threats to impose economic sanctions against Latvia, if the Government did not promptly address the perceived infringement of minority rights, were exacerbated by Latvia's new state language law (see above). In November 1999 the Russian State Duma voted to impose economic sanctions against Latvia, although this decision was never enforced. The revised language law, as approved by the Saeima in December, was again denounced by Russia. The OSCE's announcement, in December 2001, that its mandate in Latvia had been fulfilled, and the subsequent closure of its office there, also prompted criticism from Russia, which maintained that insufficient measures had been taken to protect the ethnic Russian population in Latvia from discrimination. Economic issues threatened to raise further tensions between the two countries in early 2003, following Russia's decision to cease using the port of Ventspils for its petroleum exports, primarily owing to the opening of a new Russian petroleum terminal at Primorsk.

Latvia enjoys close political, economic and cultural relations with Estonia and Lithuania, and the three countries have established a number of institutions to promote co-operation, including the interparliamentary Baltic Assembly and the Baltic Council of Ministers (which meets twice yearly). In 1992 Latvia became a founder member, with Estonia, Lithuania and other countries of the region, of the Council of Baltic Sea States (see p. 179), a principal aim of which was to assist the political and economic development of its three former communist member states. In that year it was agreed to abolish almost all trade restrictions between the three countries and to introduce a common visa policy, and a tripartite agreement on free trade and regional security was signed in 1993. A customs agreement came into force in June 1996, which constituted the first stage towards the establishment of a unified customs system. In November 1997 the three countries undertook to remove all non-tariff customs barriers between them. At a meeting in Sigulda in July 1998, the three countries' premiers agreed further to harmonize their respective customs procedures and labour movement regulations. In January 2000 the Latvian, Lithuanian and Estonian ministers responsible for finance agreed to work towards the application of a uniform strategy for excise tax. In January 1998 the Presidents of the three states had met President Bill Clinton of the USA in Washington, DC, and signed a Charter of Partnership, which was described as a framework for the development of closer political and economic ties.

Differences arose in the mid-1990s between Latvia and its two closest Baltic neighbours, in particular concerning the demarcation of maritime borders. However, agreement on the delimitation of the sea border with Estonia was reached in May 1996, and the document was ratified by both countries' legislatures in August. A further agreement on fishing rights was concluded in early 1997. The demarcation of the land border between the two countries was completed in December 1997. Negotiations between Lithuania and Latvia on their maritime border were complicated in October 1996 by the Saeima's ratification of an agreement with two foreign petroleum companies to explore and develop offshore oilfields in disputed areas of the Baltic Sea. Although the two countries signed an agreement on the delimitation of their territorial waters in July 1999, protests from the Latvian fishing industry prevented the agreement from being ratified by the Saeima. In December 2000 a protocol was signed on the re-demarcation of the land border between the two countries.

A priority of Latvian foreign policy is full membership of the EU. Latvia became an associate member of the EU in June 1995,

and in October it applied for full membership. A number of political and economic agreements concluded between the EU and the Baltic states in 1995, with the aim of facilitating their membership of the EU, came into force on 1 February 1998. In May, in contravention of the European Convention on Human Rights and Fundamental Freedoms, the Saeima voted to retain the death penalty for certain criminal acts, frustrating the attempts of President Ulmanis to fulfil a commitment to abolish capital punishment made by Latvia on its accession to the Council of Europe in 1995. The Saeima finally abolished the death penalty in April 1999. In December the summit meeting of EU Heads of State and Government, held in Helsinki, Finland, endorsed proposals to begin accession talks with six countries, including Latvia; formal negotiations commenced in February 2000, and in December 2002 Latvia, together with nine other countries, was formally invited to become a full member of the EU from 1 May 2004. A referendum on EU membership was due to be held in Latvia on 20 September 2003. Latvia, together with its Baltic neighbours, Estonia and Lithuania, also seeks membership of NATO, as the principal guarantor of its security. In February 2002 the Secretary-General of NATO warned the Latvian Government that its existing language requirements, which demanded that candidates standing in regional and national elections be fluent in Latvian, threatened to affect adversely the likelihood of the country being admitted to the Alliance; amendments to the electoral law were duly passed in May, mitigating the language requirements. At a summit meeting held in Prague, Czech Republic, in November, Latvia was one of seven countries invited to join NATO. Latvia signed the NATO accession protocol in March 2003, and hoped to become a full member in 2004.

Government

Under the terms of the 1922 Constitution, which was restored in July 1993 (and amended in December 1997), Latvia is an independent democratic parliamentary republic. The supreme legislative body is the Saeima (Parliament), the 100 members of which are elected by universal adult suffrage for a four-year term. The President of the Republic, who is Head of State, is elected by a secret ballot of the Saeima, also for a period of four years. The President, who is also Head of the Armed Forces, may not serve for more than two consecutive terms. Executive power is held by the Cabinet of Ministers, which is headed by the Prime Minister. The Prime Minister is appointed by the President; the remaining members of the Cabinet are nominated by the Prime Minister. For administrative purposes, Latvia is divided into 26 districts and seven towns (including the capital, Rīga).

Defence

Until independence in August 1991, Latvia had no armed forces separate from those of the USSR. A Ministry of Defence was established in November, and by August 2002 Latvia's total armed forces numbered 5,500, comprising an army of 4,300, a navy of 930 and an air force of 270. In addition, there was a paramilitary force numbering 3,200. There were also reserve forces in the national guard (of an estimated 14,050). Military service is compulsory from 19 years of age and lasts for 12 months. In August 1994 the withdrawal from Latvia of all former Soviet forces was completed. In January 1998 it was announced that an additional 742-strong professional military unit (the Latvian Battalion—LATBAT) was to be created over the next four years. In 1998 the Baltic states agreed to establish a joint airspace observation system (BALTNET), a defence college (BALTDEFCOL) and a peace-keeping battalion (BALTBAT). A Baltic naval unit (BALTRON) was established in mid-1998. The defence budget for 2001 was 43.4m. LVL, and the budget for 2002 allocated some 69m. LVL to defence. It was planned to increase defence expenditure to 2.0% of GDP by 2003, in line with NATO recommendations. Latvia joined NATO's 'Partnership for Peace' (see p. 273) programme in February 1994, and was expected to become a full member of NATO in 2004.

Economic Affairs

In 2001, according to estimates by the World Bank, Latvia's gross national income (GNI), measured at average 1999–2001 prices, was US $7,719m., equivalent to $3,260 per head (or $7,870 per head on an international purchasing-power parity basis). During 1990–2001, it was estimated, the population decreased by an annual average of 1.2%, while gross domestic product (GDP) per head decreased at an average annual rate of 2.4%, in real terms. Overall GDP decreased, in real terms, by an annual average of 3.6% in 1990–2001; however, real GDP increased by 7.7% in 2001 and by 6.1% in 2002.

Agriculture (including hunting, forestry and fishing) contributed 4.7% of GDP in 2002, and provided 15.3% of employment in 2000. The principal sectors are dairy farming and pig-breeding. Cereals, sugar beet, potatoes and fodder crops are the main crops grown. As part of the process of land reform and privatization, the liquidation of collective and state farms was undertaken in the early 1990s (some 38% of all arable land had been privatized by 1995). In 2003 Latvia approved a seven-year ban on the sale of rural land to foreign purchasers. Fishing makes an important contribution to the economy (an estimated 70% of the total annual catch is exported), and there is considerable growth potential in the forestry industry (43.9% of Latvia's land area is classified as forest). Agricultural GDP decreased, in real terms, by an average of 6.0% per year in 1990–2001; however, the GDP of the agriculture sector (excluding fishing) increased by 8.2% in 2001 and by 4.2% in 2002.

Industry (including mining and quarrying, manufacturing, construction and power) contributed 24.7% of GDP in 2002, and provided 24.4% of employment in 2000. Industrial GDP declined, in real terms, at an average annual rate of 8.6% in 1990–2001. However, sectoral GDP increased by 6.9% in 2001 and by 5.8% in 2002.

The mining sector contributed only 0.2% of GDP in 2002, and employed only 0.2% of workers in 2000. Latvia has limited mineral resources, the principal resources being peat, dolomite, limestone, gypsum, amber, gravel and sand. Offshore and onshore petroleum reserves have been located. The GDP of the mining sector decreased at an average annual rate of 14.5% in 1990–98; however, mining GDP increased by 5.7% in 1999, by 8.1% in 2000, by 16.7% in 2001 and by 7.7% in 2002.

The manufacturing sector contributed 14.8% of GDP in 2002, and provided 16.2% of employment in 2000. In 2001 the principal manufacturing branches, measured by value of output, were food products (31.6%), wood products, light industry and machinery and equipment. Real manufacturing GDP decreased by an average of 7.4% per year in 1990–2001. However, the GDP of the sector increased by 10.2% in 2001 and by 7.2% in 2002.

Latvia is highly dependent on imported fuels to provide energy. In 2001 imports of mineral products represented 11.1% of the total value of Latvia's imports. Electric energy is supplied primarily by Estonia and Lithuania, and petroleum products are supplied by Russia and Lithuania. In 1999 hydroelectric plants provided some 67.1% of annual domestic electricity production in Latvia; a further 23.2% was derived from natural gas, and the remainder from petroleum and coal.

The services sector has increased in importance in recent years, and in 2002 it contributed 70.6% of GDP; the sector accounted for 60.3% of employment in 2000. The sector's GDP increased, in real terms, by an average of 2.1% annually during 1990–2001; services GDP increased by 8.3% in 2001 and by 5.9% in 2002.

In 2001 Latvia recorded a visible trade deficit of US $1,350.5m., while there was a deficit of $731.6m. on the current account of the balance of payments. The principal source of imports in 2001 was Germany, which accounted for 17.0% of total imports; other major sources were Russia, Lithuania, Finland and Sweden. The main market for exports in that year was also Germany, accounting for 16.7% of total exports; other significant purchasers were the United Kingdom, Sweden, Lithuania and Russia. The principal exports in 2001 were wood and wood products, followed by textiles, base metals and manufactures, machinery and electrical equipment, and chemicals. The principal imports in that year were machinery and electrical equipment, mineral products, chemical products, vehicles, aircraft, vessels and transport equipment, base metals and manufactures, textiles and foodstuffs, beverages and tobacco.

In 2001 the consolidated state budget recorded a deficit of 64.6m. LVL (equivalent to 1.4% of GDP). Latvia's total external debt at the end of 2000 was US $3,378.7m., of which $827.1m. was long-term public debt. In that year the cost of debt-servicing was equivalent to 15.8% of the value of exports of goods and services. Annual inflation averaged 48.9% in 1991–2001; the rate of increase in consumer prices had slowed to an average of 17.6% by 1996, and it continued to decline. Consumer prices increased by 2.5% in 2001 and by 1.9% in 2002. At the end of February 2003 there were some 93,600 registered jobseekers in Latvia, and some 7.9% of the economically active population was officially recorded as unemployed.

Latvia is a member (as a 'country of operations') of the European Bank for Reconstruction and Development (EBRD, see p. 193). An agreement on a free-trade area between Latvia, Lithuania and Estonia entered into effect in April 1994, and in July of that year Latvia signed an agreement on free trade with the European Union (EU, see p. 199); Latvia became an associate member of the EU in June 1995, and was expected to become a full member in May 2004. Latvia became a member of the World Trade Organization (WTO, see p. 323) in February 1999.

The Government's programme of stabilization, initiated in 1992, achieved considerable success, with a dramatic reduction in the average annual rate of inflation and modest growth in GDP in 1994. A crisis in the banking sector in 1995 undermined economic recovery, but, following the introduction of new legal requirements and stricter bank licensing regulations, the situation was stabilized by 1996. The rate of growth slowed to just 1.1% in 1999, largely reflecting the adverse consequences of the Russian economic crisis of 1998. Moreover, a widening deficit on the current account of the balance of payments reflected the collapse of the Russian market and Latvia's failure adequately to reorientate external trade. However, there were signs of economic recovery in 2000, and in 2001 Latvia demonstrated one of the best economic performances of all the candidate countries for EU membership, although the concomitant decline in foreign trade led to an increased current-account deficit. In October 2002 Latvia notified the IMF that it would no longer sign memoranda on economic policy with the Fund, as it had not borrowed from the organization since 1993. None the less, in the same month the World Bank approved lending of US $20m. to support structural reforms in Latvia. The rate of inflation in 2002 was the lowest since independence in 1991, and strong growth was recorded; the volume of goods exported in that year increased by 12.1%, and the volume imported by 13.4%. However, there was concern at the substantial consolidated budgetary deficit, and the IMF recommended that the Government postpone the introduction of planned reductions to corporate income tax and social tax, in the hope of avoiding another large fiscal deficit in 2003. The EU, to which Latvia hoped to accede in 2004, stipulated that the public-finance deficit of member states be restrained to less than 3% of GDP.

Education

Primary education begins at seven years of age and lasts for four years. Secondary education, beginning at the age of 11, lasts for as long as eight years, comprising a first cycle of five years and a second of three years. The first nine years of education are officially compulsory. In 1998 primary enrolment included 94% of children in the relevant age-group. The comparable ratio in secondary enrolment was 83%. In the 2000/01 academic year some 71% of school-age pupils were taught in Latvian-language schools, and some 17% were taught in Russian-language schools; 12% were taught in schools offering instruction in both Latvian and Russian. In 2000/01 there were five Polish schools, one Ukrainian school and one Lithuanian school. Latvian was due to become the main language of instruction in all secondary schools from September 2004. In 2000/01 higher education was offered at 33 institutions, with a total enrolment of 101,270 students. According to the IMF, in 2001 consolidated central Government expenditure on education amounted to 87.8m. LVL (representing 6.3% of expenditure).

Public Holidays

2003: 1 January (New Year's Day), 18–21 April (Easter), 1 May (Labour Day), 23–24 June (Midsummer Festival), 18 November (National Day, proclamation of the Republic), 25–26 December (Christmas), 31 December (New Year's Eve).

2004: 1 January (New Year's Day), 9–12 April (Easter), 1 May (Labour Day), 23–24 June (Midsummer Festival), 18 November (National Day, proclamation of the Republic), 25–26 December (Christmas), 31 December (New Year's Eve).

Weights and Measures

The metric system is in force.

Statistical Survey

Source (unless otherwise stated): Central Statistical Bureau of Latvia, Lāčplēša iela 1, Rīga 1301; tel. 736-6850; fax 783-0137; e-mail csb@csb.lv; internet www.csb.lv.

Area and Population

AREA, POPULATION AND DENSITY

Area (sq km)	64,589*
Population (census results)	
12 January 1989†	2,666,567
31 March 2000	
Males	1,093,384
Females	1,281,955
Total	2,375,339
Population (official estimates at 1 January)	
2001	2,364,300
2002	2,345,800
2003	2,328,600
Density (per sq km) at 1 January 2003	36.1

* 24,938 sq miles.

† Figure refers to the *de jure* population. The *de facto* total was 2,680,029.

POPULATION BY ETHNIC GROUP
(permanent inhabitants)

	1989 census		2000 census	
	Number	%	Number	%
Latvian	1,387,757	52.0	1,369,432	57.7
Russian	905,515	34.0	702,526	29.6
Belarusian	119,702	4.5	97,064	4.1
Ukrainian	92,101	3.5	63,558	2.7
Polish	60,416	2.3	59,461	2.5
Lithuanian	34,630	1.3	33,334	1.4
Jewish	22,897	0.9	10,376	0.4
Total (incl. others) . . .	2,666,567	100.0	2,375,339	100.0

PRINCIPAL TOWNS
(population at 2000 census)*

Rīga (Riga, the		Jelgava	63,269
capital) . . .	764,328	Jūrmala	55,671
Daugavpils . . .	114,829	Ventspils	43,891
Liepāja . . .	89,439	Rēzekne	39,462

* Figures are provisional.

BIRTHS, MARRIAGES AND DEATHS

	Registered live births		Registered marriages		Registered deaths	
	Number	Rate (per 1,000)	Number	Rate (per 1,000)	Number	Rate (per 1,000)
1995 . .	21,595	8.7	11,072	4.5	38,931	15.7
1996 . .	19,782	8.1	9,634	3.9	34,320	14.0
1997 . .	18,830	7.7	9,680	4.0	33,533	13.8
1998 . .	18,410	7.6	9,641	4.0	34,200	14.2
1999 . .	19,396	8.1	9,399	3.9	32,844	13.7
2000 . .	20,248	8.5	9,211	3.9	32,205	13.6
2001 . .	19,664	8.3	9,258	3.9	32,991	13.9
2002 . .	20,020	n.a.	9,738	n.a.	32,530	n.a.

Expectation of life (WHO estimates, years at birth): 70.7 (males 65.2; females 76.0) in 2001 (Source: WHO, *World Health Report*).

IMMIGRATION AND EMIGRATION
('000 persons)

	2000	2001	2002
Immigrants	1.6	1.4	1.9
Emigrants.	7.1	6.6	6.6

EMPLOYMENT
(annual averages, '000 persons)

	1998	1999	2000
Agriculture, hunting and forestry	178	171	153
Fishing	6	5	6
Mining and quarrying . . .	2	2	2
Manufacturing	171	164	168
Electricity, gas and water . . .	19	18	18
Construction	63	64	65
Wholesale and retail trade; repair of motor vehicles, motorcycles and personal and household goods .	169	170	174
Hotels and restaurants . . .	22	24	26
Transport, storage and communications . . .	90	88	85
Financial intermediation . . .	15	16	16
Real estate, renting and business activities	47	53	57
Public administration and defence, compulsory social security . .	64	64	64
Education	90	89	87
Health and social work . . .	62	61	59
Other community, social and personal service activities . .	45	49	58
Total	1,043	1,038	1,038
Males	537	535	n.a.
Females	506	503	n.a.

Registered unemployed (year end, '000 persons): 93.3 in 2000; 91.6 in 2001; 89.7 in 2002.

2001 (annual average): Total employment 1,037,000.

Source: partly IMF, *The Republic of Latvia: Statistical Appendix* (January 2002).

Health and Welfare

KEY INDICATORS

Total fertility rate (children per woman, 2001)	1.1
Under-5 mortality rate (per 1,000 live births, 2001) . . .	21
HIV/AIDS (% of persons aged 15–49, 2001)	0.40
Physicians (per 1,000 head, 1998)	2.82
Hospital beds (per 1,000 head, 1996)	10.3
Health expenditure (2000): US $ per head (PPP)	398
Health expenditure (2000): % of GDP	5.9
Health expenditure (2000): public (% of total)	60.0
Human Development Index (2000): ranking	53
Human Development Index (2000): value	0.800

For sources and definitions, see explanatory note on p. vi.

Agriculture

PRINCIPAL CROPS
('000 metric tons)

	1999	2000	2001
Wheat	351.9	427.4	451.7
Barley	232.6	261.1	231.1
Rye	88.7	110.7	107.2
Oats	66.1	79.6	82.4
Triticale (wheat-rye hybrid)	11.9	13.5	28.9
Other cereals*	32.4	45.4	46.7
Potatoes	795.5	747.1	615.3
Sugar beet	451.5	407.7	491.2
Dry peas	2.2	3.0	2.6
Other pulses	3.2	1.1	1.4
Rapeseed	8.4	10.0	13.0
Cabbages	65.3	50.4	61.8
Cucumbers and gherkins	10.4	10.4	17.4*
Dry onions	5.5	8.3	7.1
Carrots	20.9	21.1	42.8
Other vegetables*	27.8	15.7	35.6
Apples	34.1	35.4	36.1
Currants	4.4	3.4	4.1
Cranberries	3*	8	8†

* Unofficial figure(s).
† FAO estimate.

Source: FAO.

LIVESTOCK
('000 head at 1 January)

	1999	2000	2001
Cattle	434	378	367
Pigs	421	405	394
Sheep	27	27	29
Goats	10	8	10
Horses	19	19	20
Poultry	3,209	3,237	3,105

Source: FAO.

LIVESTOCK PRODUCTS
('000 metric tons, unless otherwise indicated)

	1999	2000	2001
Beef and veal	20.5	22.4	19.0
Pig meat	34.6	31.5	31.6
Chickenmeat	6.3	7.2	8.9
Cows' milk	797.0	823.0	845.6
Cheese	11.2	11.1	13.2
Butter	7.4	7.2	7.1
Hen eggs	23.2*	24.4*	27.1
Cattle hides†	2.8	3.5	2.7
Sheepskins†	9.4	13.9	12.6

* Unofficial figure.
† FAO estimates.

Source: FAO.

Forestry

ROUNDWOOD REMOVALS
('000 cubic metres, excl. bark)

	1999	2000	2001
Sawlogs, veneer logs and logs for sleepers	6,882	8,642	7,359
Pulpwood	2,200	3,517	3,330
Other industrial wood	2,436*	465	572
Fuel wood	2,490	1,680	1,580
Total	14,008	14,304	12,841

* FAO estimate.

Source: FAO.

SAWNWOOD PRODUCTION
('000 cubic metres, incl. railway sleepers)

	1999	2000	2001
Coniferous (softwood)	3,047	3,320	3,195
Broadleaved (hardwood)	593	580	645
Total	3,640	3,900	3,840

Source: FAO.

Fishing

('000 metric tons, live weight)

	1998	1999	2000
Capture	102.3	125.4	136.4
Atlantic cod	7.8	6.9	6.3
Jack and horse mackerels	8.7	14.3	22.6
Atlantic herring	24.4	27.2	26.8
Sardinellas	6.1	15.0	7.9
European sprat	44.9	42.8	46.2
Chub mackerel	2.6	3.1	7.2
European anchovy	2.0	4.9	10.1
Aquaculture	0.4	0.5	0.3
Total catch	102.8	125.9	136.7

Source: FAO, *Yearbook of Fishery Statistics*.

Mining

('000 metric tons)

	1997	1998	1999
Peat	554.7	171.7	956.4
for fuel	362.1	45.6	315.4
for agriculture	163.9	111.1	567.1
Gypsum	116.9	119.1	96.6
Limestone	372.7	363.3	436.8

2000 ('000 metric tons): Peat 346.7 (Source: US Geological Survey).

Industry

SELECTED PRODUCTS

('000 metric tons, unless otherwise indicated)

	1997	1998	1999*
Sausages	32.2	33.1	26.4
Preserved fish	89.9	76.6	62.8
Whole milk	61.2	67.3	14.6†
Yoghurt	5.0	4.8	4.4
Ice-cream	6.2	4.7	9.8†
Preserved milk	15.1	17.5	6.1
Chocolate and sugar confectionery containing cocoa	10.1	7.1	10.8
Mayonnaise	5.5	4.4	4.5
Refined sugar	88.5	85.6	66.5
Beer ('000 hectolitres)	714.9	721.0	953.2
Cigarettes (million)	1,775	2,018	1,916
Woven cotton fabrics (million sq metres)	3.1	7.4	11.8
Linen fabrics (million sq metres)	0.6	0.4	3.7
Leather footwear ('000 pairs)	577	620	350
Rubber footwear ('000 pairs)	499	605	186
Plywood ('000 cu metres)	121.4	150.5	202.8
Paper	4.4	3.8	2.4
Synthetic resins	31.4	39.6	25.9
Cement	246	366	301
Crude steel	465.0	471.0	483.7
Washing machines ('000)	3.0	1.5	—
Chain drives	6.3‡	6.6‡	3.6
Milking machines ('000)	0.1	0.3	0.3
Radio receivers ('000)	9.9	2.3	1.7
Buses (number)	102	—	—
Electric energy (million kWh)	4,503	5,797	4,101

* From 1999 data on industrial production are compiled according to EU classification methods.
† Million litres.
‡ Million metres.

2000: Crude steel ('000 metric tons) 500.3 (Source: US Geological Survey).

Finance

CURRENCY AND EXCHANGE RATES

Monetary Units

100 santimi = 1 lats (LVL)

Sterling, Dollar and Euro Equivalents (31 December 2002)

£1 sterling = 95.7 santimi
US $1 = 59.4 santimi
€1 = 62.3 santimi
100 LVL = £104.45 = $168.35 = €160.53

Average Exchange Rate (LVL per US $)

2000   0.607
2001   0.628
2002   0.618

Note: Between March and June 1993 Latvia reintroduced its national currency, the lats, replacing the Latvian rouble (Latvijas rublis), at a conversion rate of 1 lats = 200 Latvian roubles. The Latvian rouble had been introduced in May 1992, replacing (and initially at par with) the Russian (formerly Soviet) rouble.

BUDGET

(million LVL*)

Revenue†	1999	2000	2001
Tax revenue	1,072.9	1,096.9	1,156.5
Taxes on income, profits and capital gains	161.0	147.9	178.2
Individual	68.8	74.2	79.8
Corporate	92.2	73.7	98.4
Social security contributions	411.3	424.5	439.2
Domestic taxes on goods and services	483.8	509.9	524.2
General sales, turnover or value-added taxes	316.2	337.9	350.6
Excises	155.1	164.0	161.0
Import duties	16.1	14.4	15.3
Other current revenue	147.9	141.6	87.2
Administrative fees and charges, non-industrial and incidental sales	99.4	95.9	39.2
Capital revenue	12.0	0.4	0.5
Total	1,232.8	1,238.9	1,244.1

Expenditure‡	1999	2000	2001
General public services	77.0	74.7	77.4
Defence	34.5	36.6	43.4
Public order and safety	99.3	93.6	97.7
Education	66.9	77.1	87.8
Health	150.8	146.4	154.4
Social security and welfare	591.4	577.4	570.6
Housing and community amenities	12.2	18.9	16.8
Recreational, cultural and religious affairs and services	25.5	29.1	25.6
Economic affairs and services	190.8	165.1	161.5
Agriculture, forestry, fishing and hunting	76.7	62.4	61.3
Transport and communications	90.6	77.8	75.6
Other purposes	131.6	152.2	164.7
Interest payments	28.0	45.2	48.6
Total	1,379.9	1,371.1	1,399.8
Current	1,267.7	1,275.7	1,310.2
Capital	112.2	95.4	89.7

* Figures refer to the consolidated accounts of the central Government, comprising the operations of the general budget, the Social Security Fund, the State Property Privatization Fund and other extrabudgetary special funds. In 1997 there were changes to education and health functions within the components of central Government and between the Government and local authorities.
† Excluding grants received (million LVL): 16.7 in 1999; 25.9 in 2000; 96.8 in 2001. Data on grants provided through some foreign assistance programmes are not included.
‡ Excluding lending minus repayments (million LVL): 3.3 in 1999; 5.4 in 2000; 5.7 in 2001.

Source: IMF, *Government Finance Statistics Yearbook*.

INTERNATIONAL RESERVES

(US $ million at 31 December)

	2000	2001	2002
Gold*	68.38	69.66	85.90
IMF special drawing rights	0.01	0.09	0.07
Reserve position in IMF	0.07	0.07	0.08
Foreign exchange	850.83	1,148.59	1,241.27
Total	919.29	1,218.40	1,327.32

* Valued at market prices.

Source: IMF, *International Financial Statistics*.

MONEY SUPPLY

(million LVL at 31 December)

	2000	2001	2002
Currency outside banks	427.66	485.19	543.13
Demand deposits at banking institutions	332.97	374.97	501.36
Total money (incl. others)	764.57	863.59	1,047.50

Source: IMF, *International Financial Statistics*.

COST OF LIVING
(Consumer price index; base: 1993 = 100)

	1999	2000	2001
Food and non-alcoholic beverages	178.8	180.0	188.6
Fuel and light	194.4	202.8	206.1
Clothing (incl. footwear).	297.3	301.0	303.6
Rent	461.2	470.4	482.8
All items (incl. others)	232.1	238.2	244.2

Source: ILO.

NATIONAL ACCOUNTS
(million LVL at current prices)

Expenditure on the Gross Domestic Product

	1999	2000	2001
Government final consumption expenditure.	800.2	857.1	914.5
Private final consumption expenditure.	2,489.7	2,759.5	2,963.6
Increase in stocks	65.7	22.5	144.1
Gross fixed capital formation	980.0	1,151.5	1,297.5
Total domestic expenditure.	4,335.6	4,790.6	5,319.7
Exports of goods and services	1,708.1	1,983.8	2,138.3
Less Imports of goods and services	2,109.8	2,360.0	2,676.0
GDP in purchasers' values	3,889.7	4,348.3	4,758.6
GDP at constant 2000 prices	4,069.8	4,348.3	4,682.4

Source: IMF, *International Financial Statistics*.

Gross Domestic Product by Economic Activity

	1999	2000	2001
Agriculture and hunting	89.8	97.5	108.1
Forestry, logging and related services	52.1	62.8	66.2
Fishing	12.3	15.1	13.4
Mining and quarrying	5.0	5.2	5.6
Manufacturing	521.4	560.9	624.9
Electricity, gas and water supply	151.5	147.7	158.7
Construction	242.7	258.0	259.7
Wholesale and retail trade; repair of motor vehicles, motorcycles and personal and household goods	600.7	688.5	790.4
Hotels and restaurants	43.1	47.1	54.8
Transport, storage and communications	522.0	590.9	645.4
Financial intermediation	170.0	206.1	195.9
Real estate, renting and business activities	320.0	397.6	478.8
Public administration and defence; compulsory social security	235.0	253.9	271.1
Education	183.3	206.5	223.2
Health and social work	116.9	119.6	129.6
Other community, social and personal service activities	145.1	165.3	178.6
GDP at basic prices	3,410.8	3,822.6	4,204.2
Taxes *less* subsidies on products	486.2	513.5	536.6
GDP in purchasers' values	3,897.0	4,336.1	4,740.8

Source: partly IMF, *The Republic of Latvia: Statistical Appendix* (January 2002).

BALANCE OF PAYMENTS
(US $ million)

	1999	2000	2001
Exports of goods f.o.b.	1,889.1	2,058.1	2,215.9
Imports of goods f.o.b.	−2,916.1	−3,116.3	−3,566.4
Trade balance	−1,027.0	−1,058.2	−1,350.5
Exports of services	1,024.2	1,212.1	1,188.8
Imports of services	−688.5	−770.1	−692.7
Balance on goods and services	−691.3	−616.2	−854.4
Other income received	157.8	215.2	278.2
Other income paid	−213.6	−190.9	−233.9
Balance on goods, services and income	−747.1	−591.9	−810.1
Current transfers received	113.8	202.8	221.4
Current transfers paid	−21.0	−105.4	−142.9
Current balance	−654.3	−494.5	−731.6
Capital account (net)	12.6	29.6	44.7
Direct investment abroad	−17.0	−9.4	−12.4
Direct investment from abroad.	347.6	410.0	163.9
Portfolio investment assets	57.9	−346.4	−57.1
Portfolio investment liabilities	215.4	25.1	184.1
Financial derivatives assets	—	2.2	3.4
Financial derivatives liabilities	—	−0.3	−2.6
Other investment assets	−214.1	−360.5	−66.8
Other investment liabilities	378.6	773.3	741.4
Net errors and omissions	38.3	−26.2	47.4
Overall balance	165.0	2.9	314.3

Source: Bank of Latvia.

External Trade

PRINCIPAL COMMODITIES
(million LVL)

Imports c.i.f.	1999	2000	2001
Vegetable products	59.8	77.1	73.4
Prepared foodstuffs; beverages spirits and vinegar; tobacco and manufactured substitutes	115.7	115.2	135.6
Mineral products	195.8	249.4	245.1
Products of chemical or allied industries	206.7	205.5	230.4
Plastics, rubber and articles thereof	76.7	89.0	104.2
Paper-making material; paper and paperboard and articles thereof	72.9	82.4	92.0
Textiles and textile articles.	132.0	147.8	163.4
Base metals and articles thereof	120.3	162.7	182.4
Machinery and mechanical appliances; electrical equipment; sound and television apparatus	378.5	400.8	465.0
Vehicles, aircraft, vessels and associated transport equipment	142.9	150.2	206.6
Total (incl. others)	1,723.9	1,933.9	2,201.6

Exports f.o.b.	1999	2000	2001
Prepared foodstuffs; beverages spirits and vinegar; tobacco and manufactured substitutes	38.1	40.1	72.5
Mineral products	33.6	30.7	21.2
Products of chemical or allied industries	60.9	72.0	79.5
Wood, cork and articles thereof; wood charcoal; manufactures of straw, esparto, etc.	376.0	423.3	427.3
Textiles and textile articles.	155.4	158.7	177.5
Base metals and artices thereof	115.7	151.2	159.8
Machinery and mechanical appliances; electrical equipment; sound and television apparatus	49.7	62.2	80.0
Miscellaneous manufactured articles	54.4	60.4	71.2
Total (incl. others)	1,008.3	1,131.3	1,256.4

PRINCIPAL TRADING PARTNERS
(million LVL)*

Imports c.i.f.	1998	1999	2000
Austria	23.6	22.9	20.7
Belarus	32.0	49.3	66.5
Belgium	41.2	32.0	34.6
Czech Republic	25.6	21.0	24.3
Denmark	71.0	67.0	69.8
Estonia	124.8	110.2	120.5
Finland	179.2	156.9	167.1
France	49.4	55.3	58.7
Germany	315.5	261.3	302.6
Italy	68.0	64.3	70.5
Lithuania	118.5	126.3	146.4
Netherlands	67.0	67.7	66.6
Norway	29.0	29.6	21.6
Poland	66.2	75.6	91.9
Russia	221.3	181.0	224.5
Sweden	135.1	124.8	130.4
Switzerland	28.9	36.7	34.0
Ukraine	35.4	19.3	26.0
United Kingdom	58.6	56.1	51.3
USA	38.3	35.1	38.4
Total (incl. others)	1,881.3	1,723.9	1,933.9

Exports f.o.b.	1998	1999	2000
Belarus	21.1	17.4	13.7
Belgium	11.6	14.5	14.7
Denmark	54.5	61.7	65.9
Estonia	48.5	47.2	60.1
Finland	22.9	19.1	21.7
France	18.2	18.5	20.4
Germany	166.8	170.0	194.3
Italy	19.1	16.9	17.4
Lithuania	79.3	75.9	85.7
Netherlands	37.1	35.4	45.1
Poland	18.8	17.9	18.2
Russia	129.0	66.4	47.3
Sweden	110.0	107.6	122.5
Ukraine	30.6	29.0	26.8
United Kingdom	144.3	165.8	196.5
USA	30.7	53.0	37.7
Total (incl. others)	1,068.9	1,008.3	1,131.3

* Imports by country of origin; exports by country of destination.

Transport

RAILWAYS
(traffic)*

	1998	1999	2000
Passenger journeys (million)	30.1	24.9	18.2
Passenger-kilometres (million)	1,059	984	715
Freight transported (million metric tons)	37.9	33.2	36.4
Freight ton-kilometres (million)	12,995	12,210	13,310

* Data relating to passengers include railway personnel, and data on freight include passengers' baggage, parcel post and mail.

2001: Freight transported (million metric tons): 37.9; Freight ton-kilometres (million) 14,179.

2002: Freight transported (million metric tons): 40.1; Freight ton-kilometres (million) 15,020.

ROAD TRAFFIC
(motor vehicles in use at 31 December)

	1998	1999	2000
Passenger cars	482,670	525,572	556,771
Buses and coaches	11,508	11,556	11,501
Lorries and vans	84,942	90,220	97,081
Motorcycles and mopeds	19,409	20,057	20,732

Source: IRF, *World Road Statistics.*

SHIPPING
Merchant Fleet
(registered at 31 December)

	1999	2000	2001
Number of vessels	174	163	160
Total displacement ('000 grt)	118.1	97.9	68.3

Source: Lloyd's Register-Fairplay, *World Fleet Statistics.*

International Sea-borne Freight Traffic
('000 metric tons)

	1998	1999	2000
Goods loaded	48,575	45,145	49,278
Goods unloaded	3,717	3,887	2,567

2001 ('000 metric tons): Total loaded and unloaded: 56,918.

CIVIL AVIATION
(traffic)

	1997	1998	1999
Passengers carried ('000)	270.2	261.9	239.5
Passenger-kilometres (million)	320.9	297.5	237.7
Cargo ton-kilometres ('000)	11,591	9,138	10,329

Tourism

FOREIGN TOURIST ARRIVALS*

Country of residence	1998	1999	2000
Belarus	7,751	6,945	6,918
Denmark	8,321	10,651	10,212
Estonia	18,622	16,972	23,840
Finland	32,378	33,990	41,561
Germany	25,847	26,945	31,679
Lithuania	16,619	17,833	19,484
Norway	7,412	8,694	8,859
Russia	30,055	21,710	21,755
Sweden	26,925	24,235	22,408
United Kingdom	8,978	11,165	14,644
USA	9,363	9,527	9,965
Total (incl. others)	238,835	240,799	268,083

* Figures refer to arrivals at accommodation establishments. Including excursionists, the total number of visitor arrivals (in '000) was: 1,788 in 1998; 1,738 in 1999; 1,882 in 2000.

Tourism receipts (US $ million): 181.7 in 1998; 117.7 in 1999; 131.0 in 2000; 119.5 in 2001 (Source: Bank of Latvia).

Communications Media

	1998	1999	2000
Telephones ('000 main lines in use)	742.3	731.5	742.3
Mobile cellular telephones ('000 subscribers).	167.5	278.9	401.3
Personal computers ('000 in use)	150	200	340
Internet users ('000).	80.0	105.0	150.0
Book production: titles . . .	2,596	2,652	n.a.
Book production: copies ('000) . .	8,203	7,160	n.a.
Daily newspapers: number . . .	24	23	n.a.
Daily newspapers: average circulation ('000 copies) . . .	304	297	n.a.
Non-daily newspapers: number .	202	212	n.a.
Non-daily newspapers: average circulation ('000 copies) . . .	1,875	1,808	n.a.
Other periodicals: number . . .	266	262	n.a.
Other periodicals: average circulation ('000 copies) . . .	2,126	1,391	n.a.

Radio receivers ('000 in use): 1,760 in 1997.

Television receivers ('000 in use): 1,220 in 1997.

Facsimile machines (number in use): 900 in 1996.

2001: Telephones ('000 main lines in use) 724.8; Mobile cellular telephones ('000 subscribers) 656.8; Personal computers ('000 in use) 360; Internet users ('000) 170.

Sources: mostly UNESCO, *Statistical Yearbook*; UN, *Statistical Yearbook* and International Telecommunication Union.

Education

(2000/01)

	Institutions	Students
Schools*	973	334,572
Latvian.	687	203,012
Russian	167	93,799
Latvian-Russian†	112	36,427
Polish	5	951
Ukrainian	1	302
Belarusian.	1	64
Lithuanian	—	17
Vocational schools	120	48,625
Higher education institutions	33	101,270
Special schools (for the physically and and mentally handicapped)	64	10,250

* Including primary (Grades 1–4), basic schools (Grades 1–9) and secondary schools (Grades 1–12).

† Mixed schools with two languages of instruction.

Teachers: Pre-primary 671; Primary (including basic schools) 8,690; Secondary 17,105; Special schools 1,811; Vocational 5,439.

Institutions (1997/98): Primary and basic schools 638; Secondary schools 380 (Source: Ministry of Education and Science, Rīga).

Adult literacy rate (UNESCO estimates): 99.8% (males 99.8%; females 99.8%) in 2000 (Source: UN Development Programme, *Human Development Report*).

Directory

The Constitution

The Constitution of the Republic of Latvia, which had been adopted on 15 February 1922, was annulled at the time of the Soviet annexation in 1940. Latvia became a Union Republic of the USSR and a new Soviet-style Constitution became the legal basis for the governmental system of the republic. The constitutional authority for Latvian membership of the USSR, the Resolution on Latvian Entry into the USSR of 21 July 1940, was declared null and void on 4 May 1990. In the same declaration the Latvian Supreme Council announced the restoration of Articles 1, 2 and 3 of the 1922 Constitution, which describe Latvia as an independent and sovereign state, and Article 6, which states that the legislature (the Saeima) is elected by universal, equal, direct and secret vote, on the basis of proportional representation. On 6 July 1993 the 1922 Constitution was fully restored by the Saeima, following its election on 5 and 6 June. A summary of the Constitution's main provisions (including amendments adopted since its restoration) is given below.

BASIC PROVISIONS

Latvia is an independent, democratic republic, in which the sovereign power of the State belongs to the people. The territory of the Republic of Latvia comprises the provinces of Vidzeme, Latgale, Kurzeme and Zemgale, within the boundaries stipulated by international treaties.

THE SAEIMA

The Saeima (Parliament) comprises 100 representatives of the people and, according to a constitutional amendment adopted in December 1997, is elected by universal, equal, direct and secret vote, on the basis of proportional representation, for a period of four years. All Latvian citizens who have attained 18 years of age are entitled to vote and are eligible for election to the Saeima.

The Saeima elects a Board, which consists of the Chairperson, two Deputies, and Secretaries. The Board convenes the sessions of the Saeima and decrees regular and extraordinary sittings. The sessions of the Saeima are public (sittings in camera are held only by special request).

The right of legislation belongs to both the Saeima and the people. Draft laws may be presented to the Saeima by the President of the Republic, the Cabinet of Ministers, the Committees of the Saeima, no fewer than five members of the Saeima, or, in special cases, by one-tenth of the electorate. Before the commencement of each financial year, the Saeima approves the state budget, the draft of which is submitted by the Cabinet of Ministers. The Saeima decides on the strength of the armed forces during peacetime. The ratification of the Saeima is indispensable to all international agreements dealing with issues resolved by legislation.

THE PRESIDENT OF THE REPUBLIC

According to a constitutional amendment adopted by the Saeima in December 1997, the President of the Republic is elected by a secret ballot of the Saeima for a period of four years. A majority of no fewer than 51 votes is required for his/her election. No person of less than 40 years of age may be elected President of the Republic. The office of President is not compatible with any other office, and the President may serve for no longer than two consecutive terms.

The President represents the State in an international capacity; he/she appoints Latvian representatives abroad, and receives representatives of foreign states accredited to Latvia; implements the decisions of the Saeima concerning the ratification of international treaties; is Head of the Armed Forces; appoints a Commander-in-Chief in time of war; and has the power to declare war on the basis of a decision of the Saeima.

The President has the right to pardon criminals serving penal sentences; to convene extraordinary meetings of the Cabinet of Ministers for the discussion of an agenda prepared by him/her, and to preside over such meetings; and to propose the dissolution of the Saeima. The President may be held criminally accountable if the Saeima sanctions thus with a majority vote of no fewer than two-thirds of its members.

THE CABINET OF MINISTERS

The Cabinet comprises the Prime Minister and the ministers nominated by him/her. This task is entrusted to the Prime Minister by the President of the Republic. All state administrative institutions are subordinate to the Cabinet, which, in turn, is accountable to the Saeima. If the Saeima adopts a vote expressing 'no confidence' in the Prime Minister, the entire Cabinet must resign. The Cabinet discusses all draft laws presented by the ministries as well as issues concerning the activities of the ministries. If the State is threatened by foreign invasion or if events endangering the existing order of the State arise, the Cabinet has the right to proclaim a state of emergency.

THE JUDICIARY

All citizens are equal before the law and the courts. Judges are independent and bound only by law. The appointment of judges is confirmed by the Saeima. Judges may be dismissed from office against their will only by a decision of the Supreme Court. The retiring age for judges is stipulated by law. Judgement may be

LATVIA *Directory*

passed solely by institutions that have been so empowered by law and in such a manner as specified by law. A Constitutional Court was established in 1996 to examine the legality of legislation.

The Government

HEAD OF STATE

President: VAIRA VĪĶE-FREIBERGA (inaugurated 8 July 1999).

CABINET OF MINISTERS
(April 2003)

A coalition of New Era, the First Party of Latvia (LPP), the Greens' and Farmers' Union (Latvian Green Party/LFU) and the Conservative Union 'For Fatherland and Freedom'/LNNK.

Prime Minister: EINARS REPŠE (New Era).

Deputy Prime Minister: AINĀRS ŠLESERS (LPP).

Minister of Defence: ĢIRTS VALDIS KRISTOVSKIS (Conservative Union/LNNK).

Minister of Foreign Affairs: SANDRA KALNIETE (New Era).

Minister of Finance: VALDIS DOMBROVSKIS (New Era).

Minister of the Economy: JURIS LUJĀNS (LPP).

Minister of the Interior: MĀRIS GULBIS (New Era).

Minister of Education and Science: KĀRLIS ŠADURSKIS (New Era).

Minister of Agriculture: MĀRTIŅŠ ROZE (Latvian Green Party/LFU).

Minister of Culture: INGUNA RĪBENA (New Era).

Minister of Welfare: DAGNIJA STAĶE (Latvian Green Party/LFU).

Minister of Transport: ROBERTS ZĪLE (Conservative Union/LNNK).

Minister of Justice: AIVARS AKSENOKS (New Era).

Minister of the Environment: RAIMONDS VĒJONIS (Latvian Green Party/LFU).

Minister of Health: INGRĪDA CIRCENE (New Era).

Minister of Regional Development and Local Governments: IVARS GATERS (New Era).

Minister of Special Assignment on Children and Family Affairs: AINARS BAŠTIKS (LPP).

Minister of Special Assignment on Social Integration: NILS MUIŽNIEKS (LPP).

MINISTRIES

Chancery of the President: Pils lauk. 3, Rīga 1900; tel. 737-7548; fax 709-2106; e-mail chancery@president.lv; internet www.president.lv.

Office of the Cabinet of Ministers: Brīvības bulv. 36, Rīga 1520; tel. 708-2800; fax 728-0469; e-mail pasts@mk.gov.lv; internet www.mk.gov.lv/lv.

Ministry of Agriculture: Republikas lauk. 2, Rīga 1981; tel. 702-7107; fax 702-7250; internet www.zm.gov.lv.

Ministry of Culture: K. Valdemāra iela 11A, Rīga 1364; tel. 722-4772; fax 722-4916; e-mail culture@com.latnet.lv; internet www.culture.lv.

Ministry of Defence: K. Valdemāra iela 10–12, Rīga 1473; tel. 721-0124; fax 721-2307; e-mail kanceleja@mod.lv; internet www.mod.lv.

Ministry of the Economy: Brīvības iela 55, Rīga 1010; tel. 701-3101; fax 728-0882; e-mail em@lem.gov.lv; internet www.lem.gov.lv.

Ministry of Education and Science: Vaļņu iela 2, Rīga 1098; tel. 722-2415; fax 721-3992; internet www.izm.gov.lv.

Ministry of the Environment: Peldu iela 25, Rīga 1494; tel. 702-6400; fax 782-0442; e-mail kristine@varam.gov.lv; internet www.varam.gov.lv/.

Ministry of Finance: Smilšu iela 1, Rīga 1050; tel. 722-6672; fax 709-5503; internet www.fm.gov.lv/.

Ministry of Foreign Affairs: Brīvības bulv. 36, Rīga 1395; tel. 701-6210; fax 782-8121; e-mail info@mfa.gov.lv; internet www.am.gov.lv.

Ministry of Health: Brīvības bulv. 36, Rīga 1520.

Ministry of the Interior: Raiņa bulv. 6, Rīga 1050; tel. 721-9210; fax 722-8283; e-mail pc@iem.gov.lv; internet www.iem.gov.lv/.

Ministry of Justice: Brīvības bulv. 36, Rīga 1536; tel. 708-8220; fax 728-5575; e-mail justice@latnet.lv; internet www.jm.gov.lv/.

Ministry of Regional Development and Local Governments: Rīga.

Ministry of Social Integration: Brīvības bulv. 36, Rīga 1520.

Ministry of Transport: Gogoļa iela 3, Rīga 1743; tel. 722-6922; fax 721-7180; e-mail satmin@sam.gov.lv; internet www.sam.gov.lv/.

Ministry of Welfare: Skolas iela 28, Rīga 1331; tel. 702-1600; fax 727-6445; internet www.lm.gov.lv.

Legislature

SAEIMA

Parliament

Jekaba iela 11, Rīga 1811; tel. 708-7111; fax 708-7100; e-mail web@saeima.lv; internet www.saeima.lv.

Chairman: INGRIDA UDRE.

Deputy Chairmen: ERIKS JEKABSONS, JĀNIS STRAUME.

General Election, 5 October 2002

Parties and coalitions	% of votes	Seats
New Era	23.93	26
For Human Rights in a United Latvia*	18.94	25
People's Party	16.71	20
First Party of Latvia†	9.58	10
Greens' and Farmers' Union	9.46	12
Conservative Union 'For Fatherland and Freedom'/LNNK	5.39	7
Others	15.99	—
Total	**100.00**	**100**

* An electoral bloc composed of the Latvian Socialist Party and the National Harmony Party.
† Including the Christian Democratic Union of Latvia.
‡ Comprising the Latvian Green Party and the Latvian Farmers' Union.

Political Organizations

There were some 40 political organizations registered in Latvia in 2001; among the most influential were:

Christian Democratic Union of Latvia (CDUL) (Latvijas Kristīgi Demokrātiskā savienība): Jēkaba iela 26, Rīga 1811; tel. 732-3534; fax 783-0333; internet www.kds.lv; f. 1991; Chair. JURIS KOKINS; 600 mems.

Conservative Union 'For Fatherland and Freedom'/LNNK (Aprienība 'Tēvzemei un Brīvībai'/LNNK): Kalēju iela 10, Rīga 1050; tel. 708-7273; fax 708-7268; e-mail agulbe@saeima.lv; internet www.tb.lv; f. 1997; as a result of a merger between the Union 'For Fatherland and Freedom' and the Latvian National Independence Conservative Movement; conservative; Chair. JĀNIS STRAUME; Vice-Chair. VLADIMIRS MAKAROVS.

First Party of Latvia (LPP) (Latvijas Pirmā Partija): Rīga; f. 2002; absorbed New Christian Party in 2003; Christian, centrist; Chair. ERIKS JEKABSONS.

For Latvia's Freedom: Rīga; pro-European Union; forms part of the Centre alliance; Chair. ODISEJS KOSTANDA.

Helsinki-86: A. Čaka iela 28–19, Rīga 1011; tel. 728-0272; as human rights protection group; political status awarded in 1998.

Labour Party: f. 1996; advocates programme for the renewal and restructuring of industry; part of the Centre alliance; Chair. AIVARS KREITUSS.

Latvian Democratic Party: M. Monētu iela 3, Rīga 1050; tel. 728-7739; fax 728-8211; e-mail ldp@ldp.lv; internet www.ldp.lv; f. 1995; fmrly Democratic Party Saimnieks (the Master), name changed 1999; part of the Centre alliance; Chair. ANDRIS AMERIKS; 900 mems.

Latvian Farmers' Union (LFU) (Latvijas Zemnieku savienība): Republikas lauk. 2, Rīga 1010; tel. 702-7163; fax 702-7467; e-mail lzs@delfi.lv; internet www.lzs.lv; f. 1917; re-est. 1990; merged with Political Asscn of Economists 1996; rural, centrist; forms part of the governing Greens' and Farmers' Union; Chair. AUGUSTS BRIGMANIS; 2,850 mems.

Latvian Freedom Party: Rīga; f. 2002; social-liberal; Founder ZIEDONIS CEVERS.

Latvian Green Party (Latvijas Zaļā partija): Kalnciema iela 30, Rīga 1046; tel. 761-4272; fax 761-4927; e-mail lzp@zp.lv; internet www.zp.lv; f. 1990; environmental political party; forms part of the governing Greens' and Famers' Union; Chair. INGRIDA UDRE.

Latvian National Democratic Party (LNDP): Rīga; f. 2000; joined by the unregistered Russian National Unity Party in 2002; Leader YEVGENIY OSIPOV; 1,650 mems.

Latvian Social Democratic Welfare Party: Rīga; f. 1999; against Latvian membership of NATO; Chair. JURIS ZURAVLOVS.

Latvian Social Democratic Workers' Party (Latvijas Sociāl-demokrātiskā strādnieku partija—LSDSP): Ranka dambis 1, Rīga 1048; tel. 761-4099; fax 761-4600; e-mail lsdsp@lis.lv; internet www .lsdsp.lv; f. 1999; as a result of a merger with the Latvian Social Democratic Union; Chair. DAINIS IVANS.

Latvian Socialist Party (Latvijas Sociālistiskā Partija): Burt-nieku iela 23; tel. and fax 755-5535; internet www.vide.lv/lsp; f. 1994; forms part of the For Human Rights in a United Latvia bloc; Chair. ALFRĒDS RUBIKS.

Latvian United Republican Party: Rīga; f. 2001; Chair. AINARS STRAKIS.

Latvian Way (Latvijas ceļš): Jaunu iela 25/29, Rīga 1050; tel. 728-5539; fax 782-1121; e-mail lc@lc.lv; internet www.lc.lv; f. 1993; unites prominent political figures from Latvia and abroad; Chair. ANDRIS BĒRZIŅŠ; Dep. Chair. IVĀRS GODMANIS; 900 mems.

National Harmony Party (Tautas Saskanas Partija): Elizabetes iela 23A/15, Rīga 101; tel. 750-8552; fax 728-1619; e-mail tsp@latnet .lv; internet www.tsp.lv; f. 1993; advocates the rapid integration of non-citizens into Latvian society; withdrew from the For Human Rights in a United Latvia bloc in 2003; Chair. JĀNIS JURKĀNS; Dep. Chair. JĀNIS URBANOVICS.

New Era (Jaunais laiks): Jēkaba Kazarmās, Torna iela 4–3B, Rīga 1050; tel. 720-5472; fax 720-5473; e-mail birojs@jaunaislaiks.lv; internet www.jaunaislaiks.lv; f. 2002; right-wing; Chair. EINĀRS REPŠE.

New Faction: Rīga; f. 2001 by former members of the New Party; Chair. INGRĪDA UDRE; Dep. Chair. IMANTS STIRANS.

Our Latvia (Musu Latvija): Rīga; e-mail mz@parks.lv; internet home.parks.lv/mz; f. 2001; liberal, centrist party; advocates membership of the European Union; Chair. DAINIS TURLAIS.

People's Party (Tautas partija): Dzirnavu iela 68, Rīga; tel. 728-6441; fax 728-6405; e-mail koord1@tautas.lv; internet www .tautaspartija.lv; f. 1998; Chair. ATIS SLAKTERIS; Vice-Chair. JĀNIS LAGZDINS.

Progressive Centre Party: f. 2002; supports President Viķe-Frei-berga; Chair. INTA STAMGUTE.

Social Justice and Equal Rights Movement: f. 1996; against membership of the European Union and NATO, and supports the granting of citizenship to all permanent residents of Latvia; also know as the Equality Movement; member of the For Human Rights in a United Latvia alliance; Chair. TATJANA ZDANOKA; 224 mems.

Union of Social Democrats (SDS): Rīga; f. 2002; centre-left; splinter group from Latvian Social Democratic Workers' Party; Chair. EGILS BALDZĒNS; 958 mems.

Diplomatic Representation

EMBASSIES IN LATVIA

Austria: Elizabetes iela 21A, 4th Floor, Apt 11, Rīga 1010; tel. 721-6125; fax 721-4401; Ambassador Dr WOLFGANG JILLY.

Belarus: Jēzusbaznīcas iela 12, Rīga 1050; tel. 722-2560; fax 732-2891; e-mail latvia@belembassy.org; Ambassador VADIM LAMKAU.

Canada: Doma lauk. 4, Rīga 1977; tel. 722-6315; fax 783-0140; e-mail riga@dfait-maeci.gc.ca; internet www.dfait-maeci.gc.ca/dfait/missions/baltiks; Ambassador ROBERT ANDRIGO.

China, People's Republic: Ganību dambis 5, Rīga 1045; tel. 735-7023; fax 735-7025; Ambassador WANG KAIWEN.

Czech Republic: Elizabetes iela 29A, Rīga 1010; tel. 721-7814; fax 721-7821; e-mail zuczriga@parks.lv; internet www.mfa.cz/riga; Chargé d'Affaires a.i. IVO LOSMAN.

Denmark: L. Pils iela 11, Rīga 1863; tel. 722-6210; fax 722-9218; e-mail rixamb@um.dk; internet www.denmark.lv; Ambassador OLE HARALD LISBORG.

Estonia: Skolas iela 13, Rīga 1010; tel. 781-2020; fax 781-2029; e-mail embassy.riga@mfa.ee; Ambassador TOOMAS LUKK.

Finland: Kalpaka bulv. 1, Rīga 1605; tel. 7078800; fax 707-8814; e-mail rii.sanomat@formin.fi; internet www.finland.lv; Ambassador KIRSTI ESKELINEN-LIUKKONEN.

France: Raiņa bulv. 9, Rīga 1050; tel. 703-6600; fax 703-6616; e-mail webmastre.ambafrance-lv@diplomatie.gouv.fr; internet www .ambafrance-lv.org; Ambassador MICHEL FOUCHER.

Germany: Raiņa blvd 13, Rīga 1050; POB 183, 1047 Rīga; tel. 722-9096; fax 782-0223; e-mail mailbox@deutschebotschaft-riga.lv; internet www.deutschebotschaft-riga.lv; Ambassador ECKHART HEROLD.

Israel: Elizabetes iela 2, 3rd Floor, Rīga 1340; tel. 732-0739; fax 783-0170; e-mail press@rig.mfa.gov.il; Ambassador AVRAHAM BENJAMIN.

Italy: Teātra iela 9, 3rd/4th Floors, Rīga 1050; tel. 721-6069; fax 721-6084; e-mail ambitalia.riga@apollo.lv; internet www.ambitalia .apollo.lv; Ambassador MAURIZIO LO RE.

Japan: Kr. Valdemara iela 21, Rīga 1010; tel. 781-2001; fax 781-2004; Ambassador TOMIO UCHIDA.

Lithuania: Rupniecibas iela 24, Rīga 1010; tel. 732-1519; fax 732-1589; e-mail lithemb@ltemb.vip.lv; Ambassador PETRAS VAITIEKŪNAS.

Netherlands: Torņu iela 4, Jēkaba Kazarmas 1A, Rīga 1050; tel. 732-6147; fax 732-6151; e-mail nlgovrig@mailbox.riga.lv; internet www.netherlandsembassy.lv; Ambassador NICOLAAS BEETS.

Norway: Zirgu iela 14, Rīga 1050; POB 173, 1047 Rīga; tel. 781-4100; fax 781-4108; e-mail embassy@norway.lv; Ambassador JAN WESSEL HEG.

Poland: Mednieku iela 6B, Rīga 1010; tel. 703-1500; fax 703-1549; e-mail ambpol@apollo.lv; Ambassador TADEUSZ FISZBACH.

Russia: Antonijas iela 2, Rīga 1010; tel. 733-2579; fax 783-0209; e-mail rusembas@junik.lv; internet www.latvia.mid.ru; Ambassador IGOR STUDENNIKOV.

Slovakia: Smilšu iela 8, 1050 Rīga; tel. 781-4280; fax 781-4290; e-mail embassy@slovakia.lv; Ambassador JOSEF DRAVECKÝ.

Sweden: A. Pumpura iela 8, Rīga 1010; tel. 733-8770; fax 782-8031; e-mail ambassaden.riga@swedenemb.lv; internet www.swedenemb .lv; Ambassador TOMAS BERTELMAN.

Switzerland: Elizabetes iela 2, 3rd Floor, Rīga 1340; tel. 733-8351; fax 733-8354; e-mail vertretung@rig.rep.admin.ch; Ambassador WILLY HOLD.

Ukraine: Kalpaka bulv. 3, Rīga 1010; tel. 724-3082; fax 732-5583; e-mail emb_lv@mfa.gov.ua; Ambassador VIKTOR MYKHAYLOVSKIY.

United Kingdom: J. Alunāna iela 5, Rīga 1010; tel. 777-4700; fax 777-4707; e-mail british.embassy@apollo.lv; internet www.britain .lv; Ambassador ANDREW TESORIERE.

USA: Raiņa bulv. 7, Rīga 1510; tel. 703-6200; fax 782-0047; e-mail pas@usembassy.lv; internet www.usembassy.lv; Ambassador BRIAN E. CARLSON.

Uzbekistan: Elizabetes iela 11, 2nd Floor, Rīga 1010; tel. 732-2424; fax 732-2306; e-mail posoluz@apollo.lv; Ambassador KOBILJON NAZAROV.

Judicial System

Constitutional Court

J. Alunāna iela 1, Rīga 1010; tel. 722-1412; fax 722-0572; e-mail aivars.e@satv.tiesa.gov.lv; internet www.satv.tiesa.gov.lv.

f. 1996 to rule on constitutionality of legislation; comprises seven judges, appointed by the Saeima for a term of 10 years.

Chairman: AIVARS ENDZIŅŠ.

Deputy Chairman: ROMĀNS APSĪTIS.

Supreme Court

Brīvības bulv. 36, Rīga 1050; tel. 702-0350; fax 702-0351.

Chairman: ANDRIS GUĻĀNS.

Office of the Prosecutor-General

Kalpaka bulv. 6, Rīga 1801; tel. 704-4400; fax 704-4449; e-mail gen@ lrp.gov.lv.

Prosecutor-General: JĀNIS MAIZITIS.

Religion

From the 16th century the traditional religion of the Latvians was Lutheran Christian. Russian Orthodoxy was the religion of most of the Slav immigrants. After 1940, when Latvia was annexed by the USSR, many places of religious worship were closed and clergymen were imprisoned or exiled. In the late 1980s there was some improvement in the official attitude to religious affairs. Following the restoration of independence in 1991, religious organizations regained their legal rights, as well as property that had been confiscated during the Soviet occupation. Since 1988 more than 400 new religious organizations have been officially registered in Latvia, and at 1 July 2000 the statutes of 1,095 religious organizations were registered. The total number of congregations was 1,072, of which 308 were Lutheran, 250 Roman Catholic, 118 Pentecostal, 117 Orthodox, 85 Baptists, 66 Old Believers (Orthodox), 45 Adventist, 11 Methodist, seven Hebrew and six Muslim.

Association for Freedom of Religion (AFFOR): Ganībudambis 3–2, Rīga 1045; e-mail ringolds.balodis@apollo.lv; f. 1999 to protect religious freedom in Latvia; Vice-Pres. SINTIJA BALODE.

Board of Religious Affairs: Pils lauk. 4, Rīga 1050; tel. 722-0585; e-mail ringolds.balodis@apollo.lv; f. 2000; govt agency, attached to the Ministry of Justice; Principal Dr RINGOLDS BALODIS.

CHRISTIANITY

Protestant Churches

Consistory of the Evangelical Lutheran Church of Latvia: M. Pils iela 4, Rīga 1050; tel. 722-6057; fax 782-0041; e-mail konsistorija@parks.lv; internet www.lutheran.lv; f. 1922; Archbishop JĀNIS VANAGS.

Latvian Conference of Seventh-day Adventists in Latvia: Baznīcas iela 12A, Rīga 1010; tel. and fax 724-0013; e-mail viesturs@baznica.lv; internet www.adventistu.baznica.lv; f. 1920; Pres. of Council VIESTURS REĶIS.

Union of Baptist Churches in Latvia: Lāčplēša iela 37, Rīga 1011; tel. 722-3379; fax 722-2651; e-mail ildzjur@latnet.lv; f. 1860; Bishop ANDREJS ŠTERNS; Gen. Sec. ILMĀRS HIRŠS.

Union of Latvian Pentecostal Congregations: Laimas iela 14, Jelgava 3000; tel. 302-5011; f. 1989; Bishop JĀNIS OZOLINKEVIČS.

United Methodist Church in Latvia: Klaipēdas iela 56, Liepāja 3401; tel. 343-2161; fax 346-9848; re-est. 1991; Supt ĀRIJS VĪKSNA.

The Roman Catholic Church

Latvia comprises one archdiocese and three dioceses. At 31 December 2000 there were an estimated 408,187 adherents in the country.

Bishops' Conference
(Conferentia Episcopalis Lettoniae)

M. Pils iela 2A, Rīga 1050; tel. 722-7266; fax 722-0775.

Pres. Cardinal JĀNIS PUJATS.

Archbishop of Rīga: Cardinal JĀNIS PUJATS, Metropolijas Kurija, M. Pils iela 2A, Rīga 1050; tel. 722-7266; fax 722-0775; internet www .catholic.lv.

The Orthodox Church

Although the Orthodox Church of Latvia has close ties with the Moscow Patriarchate, it has administrative independence. The spiritual head of the Orthodox Church is elected by its Saeima (or assembly).

Synod of the Orthodox Church of Latvia: M. Pils iela 14, Rīga 1050; tel. 722-4345; f. 1850; mems are mostly ethnic Slavs; Bishop ALEKSANDRS KUDRJAŠOV.

Latvian Old Believer Pomor Church: Krasta iela 73, Rīga 1003; tel. 711-3083; fax 714-4513; e-mail oldbel@junik.lv; f. 1760; Head of Central Council IVANS MIZOĻUBOVS (Fr Ioann).

JUDAISM

Hebrew Religious Community of Rīga: Peitavas iela 6/8, Rīga 1050; tel. 722-4549; f. 1764; Rabbi NATAN BARKAN.

OTHER RELIGIOUS GROUPS

Dievturu sadraudze: Rīga; community celebrating the ancient Latvian animist religion; Leader JĀNIS SILIŅŠ.

International Society for Krishna Consciousness: K. Barona iela 56, Rīga 1011; tel. 227-2490; e-mail padasevanam@mail.delfi.lv; internet www.gauranga.lv; Co-ordinator HARIJIS SAUSS.

The Press

The joint-stock company Preses nams (Press House—q.v.) is the leading publisher of newspapers and magazines in Latvia.

The publications listed below are in Latvian, unless otherwise indicated.

DAILIES

Diena (Day): Mūkusalas iela 41, Rīga 1004; tel. 706-3100; fax 706-3190; e-mail diena@diena.lv; internet www.diena.lv; f. 1990; Latvian; social and political issues; Editor-in-Chief SARMĪTE ĒLERTE; circ. 62,000.

Neatkarīgā Rita Avize (Independent Morning Paper): Balasta dambis 3, Rīga 1081; tel. 706-2462; fax 706-2465; e-mail redakcija@ nra.lv; internet www.nra.lv; f. 1990; Editor-in-Chief ALDIS BĒRZIŅŠ; circ. 40,000.

Rīgas Balss (Voice of Rīga): Balasta dambis 3, Rīga 1081; tel. 706-4420; fax 706-2400; e-mail lita@rb.lv; f. 1957; city evening newspaper; Latvian and Russian; Editor-in-Chief ANITA DAUKSTE; circ. 56,800 (Mon.–Thurs.), 69,570 (Fri.).

Sports: Balasta dambis 3, Rīga 1081; tel. 246-4117; fax 786-0000; f. 1955; Editor DACE MILLERE; circ. 7,800.

Vakara Ziņas (Evening News): Rīga; tel. 261-7595; fax 261-2383; f. 1993; Editor-in-Chief AINIS SAULĪTIS; circ. 53,000.

WEEKLIES

The Baltic Times: Skunu iela 16, Rīga 1050; tel. 722-4073; fax 722-6041; e-mail editorial@baltictimes.com; internet www.baltictimes .com; f. 1996; news from Estonia, Latvia and Lithuania; English; Man. Dir RAISA ROLDUGINA; Editor-in-Chief ILZE ARKLINA; circ. 12,000.

Dienas Bizness (Daily Business): a/k 2, Balasta dambis 3, POB 2, Rīga 1081; tel. 706-2622; fax 706-2309; e-mail nberch@db.lv; internet www.db.lv; f. 1992; Editor-in-Chief JURIS PAIDERS; circ. 17,000.

Ieva: Balasta dambis 3, Rīga 1081; tel. 246-3667; fax 246-1438; e-mail santa@santa.lv; f. 1997; weekly; illustrated journal for women; Latvian; Editor-in-Chief INGA GORBUNOVA; circ. 76,000.

Izglītība un Kultūra (Education and Culture): Torna iela 11, Rīga 1050; tel. 722-8013; fax 722-5632; f. 1948; Editor ANDRA MANGALE; circ. 6,000.

Latvijas Vēstnesis (Latvian Herald): Brūninieku iela 36-2, Rīga 1001; tel. 229-8833; fax 229-9410; e-mail editor@mail.lv-laiks.lv; internet www.lv-laiks.lv; f. 1993; official newspaper of the Republic of Latvia; Editor-in-Chief OSKARS GERTS; circ. 5,200.

Lauku Avīze (Country Newspaper): Dzirnavu iela 21, Rīga 1010; tel. 709-6600; fax 709-6645; e-mail redakcija@laukuavize.lv; f. 1988; three a week; popular agriculture, politics and sport; Editor-in-Chief VIESTURS SERDĀNS; circ. 75,000.

PRINCIPAL PERIODICALS

Daugava: Balasta dambis 3, Rīga 1081; tel. 728-0290; e-mail ravdin@mailbox.riga.lv; f. 1977; 6 a year; literary journal; Latvian; Editor-in-Chief ZHANNA EZIT; circ. 500.

Karogs (Banner): Kurša iela 24, Rīga 1006; tel. 755-4145; f. 1940; literary monthly; Editor-in-Chief MĀRA ZĀLĪTE; circ. 2,000.

Klubs: Balasta dambis 3, Rīga 1081; tel. 246-5534; fax 246-5450; e-mail santa@parks.lv; internet www.klubs.lv; f. 1994; monthly; illustrated journal for men; Latvian; Editor-in-Chief AINĀRS ĒRGLIS; circ. 20,000.

Liesma (Flame): Balasta dambis 3, Rīga 1081; tel. 246-6480; f. 1958; monthly; for young people; Editor-in-Chief DAINIS CAUNE; circ. 20,000.

Mans Mazais: Balasta dambis 3, Rīga 1081; tel. 762-8274; fax 246-5450; e-mail mansmazais@santa.lv; f. 1994; monthly; illustrated journal for young parents; Latvian; Editor-in-Chief VITA BEĻAUNIECE; circ. 20,000.

Mūsmājas (Our Home): Meža iela 4, Rīga 1048; tel. 761-5812; fax 786-0002; e-mail dadzis@latnet.lv; f. 1993; monthly; illustrated magazine for housewives; Latvian; Editor-in-Chief ILZE STRAUTIŅA; circ. 50,000.

Rīgas Laiks (Rīga Times): Lāčplēša iela 25, Rīga 1011; tel. 728-7922; fax 783-0542; e-mail pasts@rigaslaiks.lv; internet www .rigaslaiks.lv; f. 1993; monthly; Editor-in-Chief INESE ZANDERE; circ 10,000.

Santa: Balasta dambis 3, POB 32, Rīga 1081; tel. 762-8274; fax 246-5450; e-mail santa@santa.lv; f. 1991; monthly; illustrated journal for women; Latvian; Editor-in-Chief SANTA ANCHA; circ. 42,000.

NEWS AGENCIES

Baltic News Service: Baznīcas iela 8, Rīga 1010; tel. 708-8600; fax 708-8601; e-mail bns@rb.bns.lv; internet bnsnews.bns.lv; f. 1990; news from Latvia, Lithuania, Estonia and the CIS; in English, Russian and the Baltic languages; Dir LIGA MENGELSONA.

LETA (Latvian News Agency): Palasta iela 10, Rīga 1502; tel. 722-2509; fax 722-3850; e-mail leta.marketing@leta.lv; internet www .leta.lv; f. 1919; independent news agency; Chair. MĀRTIŅŠ BARKĀNS.

Foreign Bureau

Reuters (United Kingdom): Kaļķu iela 15, Rīga 1050; tel. 722-2079; fax 724-3139; e-mail reuters@reuters.lv; Bureau Chief ALAN CROSBY.

PRESS ASSOCIATIONS

Latvian Journalists' Union (Latvijas Žurnālistu savienība): Marstaļy iela 2, Rīga 1050; tel. 721-1433; fax 782-0233; f. 1992; 700 mems; Pres. LIGITA AZOVSKA.

Publishers

Avots (Spring): Aspazijas bulv. 24, Rīga 1050; tel. 721-1394; fax 722-5824; f. 1980; fiction, dictionaries, crafts, hobbies, art, agriculture, law, reference books, etc. Pres. JĀNIS LEJA.

Elpa (Breath): Doma lauk. 1, Rīga 1914; tel. 721-1776; fax 750-3326; f. 1990; books and newspapers; Pres. MAIRITA SOLIMA.

Jumava: Dzirnavu iela 73, Rīga 1011; tel. and fax 728-0314; e-mail jumava@parks.lv; internet www.jumava.lv; f. 1994; translations, dictionaries, fiction, etc. Pres. JURIS VISOCKIS.

Kontinents: Elijas iela 17, Rīga 1050; tel. 720-4130; fax 720-4133; e-mail kontinent@parks.lv; internet www.kontinent.lv; f. 1991.

Latvijas Enciklopēdija (Latvian Encyclopaedia Publishers): Rīga; tel. 722-0150; fax 782-0113; f. 1963; encyclopaedias, dictionaries, reference books; Dir VIKTORS TĒRAUDS.

Nordik: Daugavgrīvas 36–9, Rīga 1007; tel. 760-2672; fax 760-2818; e-mail nordik@nordik.lv; internet www.nordik.lv; sister co, Tapals, at same address; Dir JĀNIS JUŠKA.

Preses nams (Press House): Balasta dambis 3, Rīga 1081; tel. 246-5732; internet www.presesnams.lv; f. 1990; printing, publishing and property management; publishes five newspapers, magazines, encyclopaedias, scientific and field literature; controlling interest owned; by Ventspils Nafta (q.v.); Dir EGONS LAPIŅŠ.

Jāņa sēta: Elizabetes iela 83–85, Rīga 1050; tel. 709-2290; fax 709-2292; e-mail janaseta@janaseta.lv; internet www.janaseta.lv; f. 1991; the Jāņa sēta cartographers became a separate co in 1999; travel and culinary books; Dir AIVARS ZVIRBULIS.

Smaile (Peak): Brīvības iela 104, Rīga 1001; tel. 731-5137; f. 1999; fiction, poetry, fine arts; Dir ANDREJS BRIMERBERGS.

Sprīdītis: Kalēju iela 51, Rīga 1050; tel. 728-6516; fax 728-6818; f. 1989; books for children and young people; Dir ANDREJS RIJNIEKS.

Zinātne (Science): Akadēmijas lauk. 1, Rīga 1050; tel. 721-2797; fax 722-7825; e-mail zinatne@navigator.lv; f. 1951; non-fiction, text books, dictionaries, reference books; Dir IEVA JANSONE.

ZVAIGZNE ABC Ltd (Star): K. Valdemāra iela 6, Rīga 1010; tel. 732-4518; fax 750-8798; e-mail info@zvaigzne.lv; internet www.zvaigzne.lv; f. 1966; privately owned since 1993; educational literature, manuals, dictionaries, non-fiction for children and adults, fiction; Pres. VIJA KILBLOKA; 173 employees.

PUBLISHERS' ASSOCIATIONS

Latvian Publishers' Association (Latvijas Grāmatizdevēju asociāciāja): K. Barona iela 36–4, Rīga 1011; tel. 728-2392; fax 728-0549; e-mail lga@gramatizdeveji.lv; internet www.gramatizdeveji.delfi.lv; f. 1993; 47 mems; Pres. ANITA ROŽKALNE.

Latvian Press Publishers' Association: Balasta dambis 3, Rīga 1081; tel. and fax 732-2489; e-mail epia@age.lv; f. 1993; 33 mems; Pres. AIVARS RUDZINSKIS.

WRITERS' UNION

Latvian Writers' Union (Latvijas Rakstnieku savienība): Kuršu iela 24, Rīga 1426; tel. 755-5180; fax 755-4034; 291 mems; Chair. VALDIS RŪMNIEKS.

Broadcasting and Communications

TELECOMMUNICATIONS

In 2001 there were 724,800 main telephone lines in use; 52% of lines were digital in 2000. The Government was preparing legislation to abolish SIA Lattelekom's monopoly by 2002.

Regulatory Organizations

Department of Communications (Ministry of Transport): Gogoļa iela 3, Rīga 1190; tel. 724-2321; fax 782-0636; e-mail diana .ainep@sam.gov.lv; f. 1991; Dir INĀRA RUDAKA.

Telecommunications Tariff Council: Meistaru iela 10, Rīga 1050; tel. 721-3109; fax 782-0519; Chair. RAIMONDS JONITIS.

Major Service Providers

Latvian Mobile Telephone (Latvijas Mobilais telefons): Unijas iela 39, POB 116, Rīga 1039; tel. 777-3200; fax 753-5353; e-mail inform@lmt.lv; internet www.lmt.lv; f. 1992; partly owned by Telia (Sweden) and Sonera (Finland); Gen. Man. JURIS BINDE; 150 employees.

Radiokom: Elizabetes iela 45–47, Rīga 1010; Dir JANA BALODE.

SIA Lattelekom: Vaļņu iela 30, Rīga 1050; tel. 705-5222; fax 705-5001; e-mail gstrautma@exchange.telekom.lv; internet www.cwcee .co.uk; f. 1992; partially privatized; 44% owned by Sonera; Pres. GUNDARS STRAUTMANIS; 6,500 employees.

Tele2: Kurzemes pr. 3, Rīga 1067; tel. 706-0069; fax 706-0176; internet www.tele2.lv; f. 1991; owned by Tele2 AB (Sweden); name changed from Baltkom GSM in 2001; Pres. BILL BUTLER; 110 employees.

Telecommunication Association of Latvia: Rm 702, Academic lauk. 1, Rīga 1050; tel. 722-6962; e-mail kaiva@mail.lv; Pres. PĒTERIS ŠMIDRE.

BROADCASTING

Amendments to the broadcasting law approved in October 1998 required greater use of the Latvian language in all programmes. Foreign programmes were restricted to 25% of daily broadcast time.

Regulatory Organization

National Broadcasting Council of Latvia: Smilšu iela 1–3, Rīga 1939; tel. 722-1848; fax 722-0448; e-mail tvcounc@mailbox.riga.lv; internet www.nrtp.lv; f. 1992; defends social interests and maintains free accessibility to information; Chair. OJĀRS RUBENIS.

Radio

Latvijas Radio (Latvian Radio): Doma lauk. 8, Rīga 1505; tel. 720-6722; fax 720-6709; internet www.radio.org.lv; f. 1925; state-operated service; broadcasts in Latvian, Russian and English; Dir-Gen. DZINTRIS KOLĀTS.

Alise Plus: Raiņa iela 28, Daugavpils 5403; e-mail alise_plus@ daugavpils.apollo.lv; 24-hour transmissions in Russian and Latvian.

European Hit Radio: Elijas iela 17, Rīga 1050; tel. 957-5757; fax 720-4407; e-mail radio@superfm.lv; internet www.europeanhitradio .com; f. 1994; 24-hour transmissions in Latvian, Russian, Estonian, Lithuanian and English; Pres. UGIS POLIS; Dir RICHARD ZAKSS.

Latvijas Kristīgais Radio: Lāčplēša iela 37, Rīga 1011; tel. 721-3704; fax 782-0633; e-mail lkz@am.lv; 24-hour transmissions in Latvian and Russian.

Radio Ef-Ei: Atbrvōsanas aleja 98, Rēzekne 4600; e-mail efei@ mailbox.riga.lv; 24-hour transmissions in Russian and Latvian.

Radio Imanta: Tērbatas iela 1, Valmiera 4201; tel. 422-4070; fax 423-1200; e-mail radio@valmiera.lanet.lv; 24-hour transmissions in Russian and Latvian; Chief Editor ANDRIS STRAUME.

Radio Mazsalaca: Avotu iela 13, Mazsalaca 4215; 15 hours daily in Latvian.

Radio Merkūrijs: Bērzpils iela 2A, Balvi 4501; e-mail merkurijs@ ridzene.lv; 24-hour transmissions in Latvian and Russian.

Radio Mix FM: L. Nometņu iela 62, Rīga 1002; 24-hour transmissions in Russian.

Radio Rīgai: Televīzijas centrs, Zaķusalas krastmala 3, Rīga 1509; 24-hour transmissions in Latvian.

Radio Saules Iela: Saules iela 8A, Cēsis 4100; 24-hour transmissions in Latvian.

Radio Sigulda: L. Paegles iela 3, Sigulda 2150; 24-hour transmissions in Latvian.

Radio SWH: Skanstes iela 13, Rīga 1013; internet www.radio.swh .lv.

Radio Trīs: Vaļņu iela 5, Cēsis 4101; tel. 412-4566; fax 412-7041; e-mail radio@radio3.lv; internet www.radio3.lv; f. 1994; 24-hour transmissions in Latvian; Dir EGILS VISKRINTS.

Radio Zemgale: Grāfa laukums 6, Lecava 3913; e-mail rz@apollo .lv; internet www.radiozemgalei.lv; f. 2000; 24 hours daily in Latvian; Dir DACE DUBKEVIČA.

Television

Latvijas Televīzija (Latvian Television): Zaķusalas krastmala 3, Rīga 1509; tel. 720-0314; fax 720-0025; e-mail ltv@ltv.lv; internet www.ltv.lv; f. 1954; state-operated service; two channels in Latvian (Channel II also includes programmes in Russian, Polish, Ukrainian, German, English and French); Dir ULDIS GRAVA.

LNT (Latvian Independent Television): Elijas iela 17, Rīga 1050; tel. 707-0200; fax 782-1128; e-mail lnt@lnt.lv; internet www.lnt.lv; f. 1996; entertainment programming, news reports; Dir-Gen. ANDREJS ĒĶIS.

Finance

(cap. = capital; res = reserves; dep. = deposits; m. = million; brs = branches; amounts in LVL)

BANKING

Following the restoration of independence in 1991, the country's central bank, the Bank of Latvia (originally founded in 1922), was re-established, and commercial banks began to proliferate. By late 1993, owing to the country's liberal regulatory system, there were 63 commercial banks operating in Latvia. In the following year the Government began to reorganize the sector, revoking the licences of 11 of the smaller and weaker banks, and declaring a further six insolvent. However, such measures were not sufficient to prevent a crisis in the banking sector in 1995, and further closures, including that of the country's largest commercial bank, Banka Baltija, ensued. The crisis was contained by early 1996. At the end of 2002 there were 22 banks in operation.

Central Bank

Bank of Latvia (Latvijas Banka): K. Valdemāra iela 2A, Rīga 1050; tel. 702-2300; fax 702-2420; e-mail info@bank.lv; internet www.bank .lv; f. 1922; cap. 10.1m., res 64.8m., dep. 211.8m. (Dec. 2001); Gov. and Chair. of Bd ILMĀRS RIMŠĒVIČS.

Commercial Banks

Aizkraukles Banka: Elizabetes iela 23, Rīga 1010; tel. 777-5555; e-mail bank@ab.lv; internet www.ab.lv; f. 1993; cap. 51,541.0 (1997); Chair. of Bd ALEKSANDRS BERGMANIS.

A/S Vereinsbank Rīga: Elizabetes iela 63, Rīga 1050; tel. 708-5500; fax 708-5507; e-mail info@vereinsbank.lv; internet www .vereinsbank.lv; f. 1997; 100% owned by Vereins- und Westbank AG (Germany); cap. 13.9m., res. –0.4m., dep. 68.0m. (Dec. 2001); Pres. THOMAS SCHÜTZE.

Baltic Transit Bank (Baltijas Tranzītu Banka): 13. Janvāra iela 3, Rīga 1050; tel. 702-4747; fax 721-1985; e-mail btb@btb.lv; internet www.btb.lv; f. 1992; joint-stock commercial bank; merged with Rīgas Naftas un Kimijas Banka in 1999; cap. 8.6m., res –1.0m., dep. 101.0m. (Dec. 2001); Pres. and Chair. of Bd EDGARS DUBRA; 30 brs.

Business Bank of Latvia (Latvijas Biznesa Banka): 3 Antonijas iela, Rīga 1010; tel. 777–5800; fax 777–5849; e-mail pstbox@lbb.lv; internet www.lbb.lv; f. 1992; 99.72% owned by Moscow Municipal Bank—Bank of Moscow (Russian Federation); cap. 3.0m., res 0.1m., dep 5.1m. (Dec. 2001); Chair. and Pres. GEORGIJS DRAGILEVS.

Credit Bank of Latvia (Latvijas Kredītbanka): Antonilas iela 7, Rīga 1920; tel. 722-6631; fax 782-1094; f. 1992; cap. 3.5m. Pres. JĀNIS SILPINS; 3 brs.

Economic Commercial Bank of Latvia—Lateko (Latvijas Ekonomiskā Komercbanka): E. Birznieka-Upiša iela 21, Rīga 1011; tel. 704-1100; fax 704-1111; e-mail latbk@lateko.lv; internet www .lateko.lv; f. 1992; cap 5.0m., res 0.0m., dep. 104.0m. (Dec. 2001); Pres. OSKARS GULĀNS.

Hansabanka: Kaļķu iela 26, Rīga 1050; tel. 702-4444; fax 702-4400; e-mail info@hansabanka.lv; internet www.hansabanka.lv; f. 1992; present name since 1999; merged with Latvijas Zemes banka 1999, merged with Ventspils ABB 2000; cap. 40.0m., res 2.3m., dep. 459.9m. (Dec. 2001); Chair. of Bd INGRIDA BLUMA.

Industrial Bank of Latvia (Latvijas Industriālā banka—Lainbanka): Rīga; tel. 721-6529; fax 722-1135; f. 1991; cap. 9,905.5 (1997); Pres. VILIS DAMBIŅŠ.

Land Bank of Latvia (Latvijas Zemes banka): Republic lauk. 2, Rīga 1924; tel. 702-9883; fax 721-1995; e-mail lzbint@mail.bkc.lv; f. 1989; cap. 6.0m., res 0.2m., dep. 36.5m. (Dec. 1997); Chair. of Bd and Chief Exec. ANDRIS RUSELIS; 16 brs.

JSC Latvian Trade Bank (Latvijas Tirdzniecības Banka): Trijadibas iela 4, Rīga 1048; tel. 761-1818; fax 786-0077; e-mail ltb@ltblv .com; internet www.ltblv.com; f. 1991; 99.4% owned by Latvian Investment Gp ApS (Denmark); cap. 3.0m., res 0.0m., dep. 85.6m. (Dec. 2001); Pres. and Chair. ARMANDS SHTEINBERGS; Vice-Chair. DZINTARS PELCBERGS.

Māras banka: Lāčplēša iela, Rīga 1011; tel. 728–6661; fax 728–2788; e-mail info@marasbanka.lv; internet www.marasbanka.lv; f. 1997; privately owned; mortgage banking; cap. 3.5m., res 0.9m., dep. 12.4m. (Dec. 2001); Chair. of Exec. Bd and Pres. NIKOLAJS SIGURDS BULMANIS; Dir-Gen. JNGA GULBE.

Merita Nordbanken Latvia: Kaļķu iela 15, Rīga 1050; tel. 709-6200; fax 782-0325; e-mail mnb@meritanordbanken.lv; internet www.meritanordbanken.lv; f. 1992; cap. 5.3m., res. 0.7m., dep. 30.3m. (Dec. 1998); Pres. and Chief Exec. AIVARS JURCĀNS.

Mortgage and Land Bank of Latvia (Latvijas Hipoteku un Zemes Banka): Doma lauk. 4, Rīga 1977; tel. 722-2945; fax 782-0143; e-mail banka@hipo.lv; internet www.hipo.lv; f. 1993; cap. 7.7m., res 1.5m., dep. 92.8m. (Dec. 2001); Pres. and Chair. of Bd INESIS FEIFERIS; 32 brs.

Multibanka: Elizabetes iela 57, Rīga 1772; tel. 728-9546; fax 782-8232; e-mail info@multibanka.com; internet www.multibanka.lv; f. 1994; cap. 4.3m., res –0.1m.., dep. 69.2m. (Dec. 2001); Pres., Chair. and Chief Exec. SVETLANA DZENE.

Ogre Commercial Bank (Ogres Komercbank): 36 Brīvības iela, Ogre 5001; f. 1993; cap. 3.3m., res 0.1m., dep. 102.2m. (Dec. 2001); Pres. and Chair. VOLDEMARS EIHE.

Parex Bank (Parekss Banka): Smilšu iela 3, Rīga 1522; tel. 701-0000; fax 701-0001; e-mail inquiry@parex.lv; internet www.parex.lv; f. 1992; 50.93% owned by Europe Holding Ltd. cap. 30.0m., res –0.2m., dep. 592.5m. (Dec. 2001); Pres. VALERY KARGIN; Chair. VICTOR KRASOVITSKY; 5 brs.

Pirmā Banka JSC (First Bank): Smilšu iela 6, Rīga 1803; tel. 701-5204; fax 732-3449; e-mail office@pirmabanka.lv; internet www .pirmabanka.lv; f. 1989; fmrly Rīgas Komercbanka PLC; operations suspended in March 1999; re-opened as Pirmā Latvijas Komercbanka in Oct. 1999; name changed as above in June 2001; 98.8% owned by Norddeutsche Landesbank Girozentrale (Germany); cap. 20.2m., res 1.4m., dep. 70.7m. (Dec. 2001); Pres. and Chair. of Bd JÜRGEN MACHALETT; 10 brs.

Rietmu Bank: Brīvības iela 54, Rīga 1011; tel. 702-5555; fax 702-5588; e-mail info@rietumu.lv; internet www.rietumu.lv; f. 1992; cap. 17.4m., res 0.02m., dep. 96.6m. (Dec. 1999); merged with Saules Banka in July 2001; Pres. and Chief Exec. MICHAEL J. BOURKE.

Trust Commercial Bank (Trasta komercbanka): Miesnieku iela 9, Rīga 1050; tel. 702-7777; fax 702-7700; e-mail info@tkb.lv; internet www.tkb.lv; f. 1989; present name adopted 1996; cap. 3.6m., res –0.4m., dep. 15,3m. (Dec. 2001); Pres. GUNDARS GRIEZE.

Unibank (Latvijas Unibanka): L. Pils iela 23, Rīga 1050; tel. 721-2808; fax 721-5335; e-mail public.relations@unibanka.lv; internet www.unibanka.lv; f. 1993; 98.2% of shares acquired by Skandinaviska Enskilda Banken (Sweden) in Nov. 2000; cap. and res 56.3m., dep. 332.3m. (May 2002); 68 brs.

Savings Bank

JSC Latvian Savings Bank (Latvijas Krājbanka): Palasta iela 1, Rīga 1954; tel. 709-2001; fax 721-2083; e-mail info@lkb.lv; internet www.krajbanka.lv; f. 1924 as Post Office Savings Bank, name changed as above 1998; 32.1% state-owned; cap. and res 10.0m., dep. 147.7m. (June 2002); Pres. and Chair. of Bd ZIGURDS JEROMANOVS; 14 brs.

Regulatory Authority

Financial and Capital Markets Commission: Kungu iela 1, Rīga 1050; tel. 702-2267; fax 702-2117; e-mail fk@fk.lv; internet www.fk .lv; f. 2000; Chair. ULDIS CERPS.

Banking Association

Association of Latvian Commercial Banks: Pērses iela 9–11, Rīga 1011; tel. 728-4528; fax 782-8170; e-mail bankas@latnet.lv; f. 1992; 21 mems; Pres. TEODORS TVERIJONS.

INSURANCE

At the end of 1999 there were 27 insurance companies in Latvia.

Balta Insurance Company Ltd: Vaļņu iela 1, Rīga 1050; tel. 722-9660; fax 782-1014; e-mail balta@balta.lv; automobile, property, freight, travel, agricultural insurance; Pres. ANDRIS LAIZĀNS.

Balva: K. Valdemāra iela 36, Rīga 1010; tel. 750-6955; fax 750-6956; e-mail balva@balva.lv; internet www.balva.lv; f. 1992; non-life insurance; Pres. VASILY RAGOZIN.

JSIC ERGO Latvija: Unijas iela 45, Rīga 1035; tel. 784-0101; fax 784-0102; e-mail info@ergo.lv; bought by Alte Leipziger (Germany) in 2000; all types of risk insurance; Pres. of Bd ILMARS VEIDE.

Estora Reinsurance Co: Elizabetes iela 14, Rīga 1010; tel. 733-3335; fax 733-3898; e-mail estora@estora.com; internet www.estora .com; f. 1992; reinsurance; Dir-Gen. JERGENIJS TOLOČKOVS.

Ezerzeme: Raiņa iela 28, Daugavpils 5403; tel. 542-2555; fax 542-2177; f. 1992; state, private firm, personal property, long- and short-term life, life, domestic animals, accident, freight, travel, funeral insurance; Chair. of Bd PĒTERIS SAVOSTJANOVS.

Helga Joint Stock Insurance Company: Elizabetes iela 20, Rīga 1050; tel. 7243-074; fax 7243-067; e-mail helga@parks.lv.

Latva: Vaļņu iela 1, Rīga 1912; tel. 721-2341; fax 721-0134; e-mail latva@latva.lv; f. 1940; state insurance co; accident, passenger, child and adult life insurance; Chair. MARGARITA PABĒRZA.

Rīga Insurance Company: Grēcinieku iela 22–24, Rīga 1050; tel. 721-1764; fax 722-3437; general liability, professional liability, health, motor, natural disasters, fire, freight insurance; Pres. AIVARS BERGERS.

Union Unlimited: tel. 221-3150; fax 222-5397; travel, property, athletes', freight, state, co-operative, joint-stock, credit, medical, accident insurance; Chair. of Bd AIVARS SALIŅŠ.

COMMODITY AND STOCK EXCHANGES

Latgale Exchange (Latgales birža): Sakņu iela 29, Daugavpils 5403; tel. 542-6044; fax 542-6351; f. 1992; Gen. Dir ANATOLII BOTUSHANSKII.

Latvian Universal Exchange (Latvijas Universālā birža): Rīga; tel. 721-2559; fax 722-4515; f. 1991; Pres. JĀNIS VALTERS.

Rīga Stock Exchange (Rīgas Fondu birža): Doma lauk. 6, Rīga 1885; tel. 721-2431; fax 722-9411; e-mail rfb@rfb.lv; internet www .rfb.lv; f. 1993; Pres. GUNTARS KOKOREVICS.

Trade and Industry

GOVERNMENT AGENCY

Latvian Privatization Agency: K. Valdemāra iela 31, Rīga 1010; tel. 702-1358; fax 783-0363; e-mail lpa@mail.bkc.lv; internet www .lpa.bkc.lv; f. 1994; Dir-Gen. ARNIS OZOLNIEKS.

DEVELOPMENT ORGANIZATIONS

Interlatvija: Kalpaka bulv. 1, Rīga 1010; tel. 733-3602; f. 1987; seeks to promote exports, imports and the establishment of joint ventures; Dir-Gen. MĀRIS FORSTS.

Latvian Development Agency: Pērses iela 2, Rīga 1442; tel. 703-9400; fax 703-9401; e-mail invest@lda.gov.lv; internet www.lda.gov .lv; f. 1993; foreign investment and export promotion; Dir-Gen. MĀRIS ELERTS.

CHAMBER OF COMMERCE

Latvian Chamber of Commerce and Industry (Latvijas Tirdzniecības un rūpniecības kamera): K. Valdemāra iela 35, Rīga; tel. 722-5595; fax 782-0092; e-mail info@chamber.lv; internet www .chamber.lv; f. 1934; re-est. 1990; mem. of International Chamber of Commerce, Baltic Chambers of Commerce Association, Eurochamber; Pres. VIKTORS KULBERGS; Dir-Gen. VOLDEMARS GAVARS.

INDUSTRIAL AND TRADE ASSOCIATIONS

Latvian Association of Business Consultants: Pērses iela 2–408, Rīga 1011; tel. and fax 722-7623; e-mail lbka@lbka.lv; f. 1995; Man. Dir DAINIS LOCANS.

Latvian Export Association (Latvijas Eksporta Asociācija): Valmieras iela 41, Rm 11, Rīga; tel. and fax 770-1213; Pres. IVAR STRAUTINSH.

Latvian Small Business Association: Akas iela 5–7, Rīga 1010; tel. and fax 727-9808; e-mail info@lbka.lv; f. 1996; Chair. DAINIS LOCANS.

UTILITIES

Regulatory Authority

Energy Regulation Council: Brīvības bulv. 55, Rīga 1010; tel. 701-3291; fax 731-2763; e-mail regulators@erp.riga.lv; internet www.erp.riga.lv; f. 1996; operated under auspices of Department of Energy at Ministry of the Economy; Chair. J. DAUSKANS.

Electricity

Major suppliers include:

Augstspriegauma tikls: Jatnieku iela 95, Daugavpils 5410.

Austrumu Electricity: A. Pumpura iela 5, Daugavpils 5404.

Centralie elektriskie tikli: Stopinu pagasts, Lici 2118.

Dienvidu Electricity Network: Elektribas iela 10, Jelgava 3001.

Latvenergo: Pulkveža brieža 12, Rīga 1230; tel. 732-8309; e-mail webadm@energo.lv; internet www.energo.lv; state-owned producer and distributor; Pres. KĀRLIS MIĶELSONS; 7,127 employees.

Northern-eastern Electricity Network (LATVENERGO): Mednieku 3, Aizkraukle 5101; tel. 518-1530; fax 518-1539.

Rigas elektrotikls: Pernavas iela 19, Rīga 1012.

Vangazu elektrikis: Gaujas iela 24, Vangazi 2136; tel. and fax 299-5535.

Vats: Talsu iela 84, Ventspils 3602.

Western Electricity Network: Rīga iela 56, Liepāja 3401; tel. 342-3532; fax 342-3105.

Ziemelu Electricity Network: Raiņa iela 14, Valmiera 4201.

Gas

Major suppliers include:

Aga: Katrinas iela 5, Rīga 1045.

Elme L: Aplokciema iela 3, Rīga 1034.

Energija-G: Maskavas iela 85, Rīga 1003.

Gazes transports: Bikernieku iela 111, Rīga 1079.

Katlinieks: Lugazu iela 14, Rīga 1045.

Lanteks: Pernavas iela 42-3, Rīga 1009.

Latvian Gas (Latvijas gaze): A. Briana iela 6, Rīga 1001; tel. 736-9132; fax 782-1406; e-mail latvijas_gaze@lg.lv; internet www.lg.lv; partially privatized in 2000–01; 8% state-owned; Chair. MĀRIS GAILIS; 2,817 employees.

Latvijas Propāna Gāze: Kurzemes prospekts 19, Rīga 1067; tel. 741-3709; fax 741-3712; e-mail lpg@lsg.lv; internet www.lsg.lv; f. 2000; purchase, sale and shipment of liquefied petroleum gas.

Remifa: Abolu iela 3, Rīga 1058.

Rīgas gaze: Vagornu iela 20, Rīga 1009.

SIIL: Pushkina iela 3, Rīga 1050.

Saullekts: Virsu iela 11, Rīga 1035.

VITEG: Bruņinieku iela 108, Rīga 1009.

Vitne: Maskavas iela 457, Rīga 1063.

Water

Major suppliers include:

Aizkraukles udens: Tornu iela 1, Aizkraukle 5101.

A/S Madonas udens: Raiņa iela 54, Madona 4801; tel. 480-7071; fax 486-0106; e-mail udens@kvarcs.lv.

Bauskas udenssaimnieciba: Birzu iela 8a, Bauska 3901; tel. 396-0565; fax 396-0566; e-mail baude@apollo.lv.

Buvenergo: Stabu iela 58, Rīga 1011.

Daugavpils Water (Municipal Ltd.): Udensvada iela 3, Daugavpils 5403.

JS & J Udenmeistars: Ramulu iela 1, Rīga 1005.

Liepajas udens: K. Valdemāra iela 12, Liepāja 3401; tel. 541-1416; fax 541-0769; e-mail dmeu@dpu.lv.

Rīgas udens (Rīga Water): Basteja bulv. l, k. 5, Rīga 1495; tel. 708-8555; fax 722-2660; e-mail office@ru.lv; internet www.rw.lv; water supply and sewage treatment.

Udens inzinieri: Gānibu dambis 26–601, Rīga 1005.

Udensvada un Kanalizacijas saimnieciba: Udensvada iela 4, Jelgava 3001.

TRADE UNIONS

Free Trade Union Confederation of Latvia (LBAS): Bruņinieku iela 29–31, Rīga 1001; tel. 727-0351; fax 727-6649; e-mail intern@latnet.lv; internet www.lbas.lv; f. 1990; Pres. JURIS RADZEVICS.

Transport

RAILWAYS

In 2000 there were 2,298 km of railways on the territory of Latvia. Latvian railways carried 18.2m. passengers in 2000 and 40.1m. metric tons of freight in 2002.

Latvian Railway (Latvijas Dzelzceļš): Gogoļa iela 3, Rīga 1547; tel. 583-4940; fax 782-0231; e-mail info@ldz.lv; internet www.ldz.lv; f. 1993; state joint-stock co; Dir-Gen. ANDRIS ZORGEVICS.

ROADS

In 2000 Latvia's total road network was 73,202 km, of which 7,011 km were main roads. In that year there were 556,771 passenger cars, 97,081 goods vehicles and 11,501 buses and coaches in use.

Latvian Road Administration: Gogoļa iela 3, Rīga 1050; tel. 702-1868; fax 702-8304; e-mail lad@lad.lv; internet www.lad.lv; Dir TĀLIS STRAUME.

SHIPPING

At 31 December 2001 the Latvian-registered merchant fleet numbered 160 vessels, with a combined total displacement of 68,253 grt. In 2001 some 56.9m. metric tons of freight were transported through the three main and seven smaller Latvian ports (Ventspils—accounting for 37.9m. metric tons, Rīga—14.9m., and Liepāja (which was used as a Russian naval port until its conversion into a trade port in the early 1990s). Ventspils is particularly important for the shipping of petroleum and fuel exports (27.3m. metric tons in 1998) and is included in a special economic zone; Rīga and Ventspils operate in a free port regime.

Maritime Department: Gogoļa iela 3, Rīga 1743; tel. 702-8198; fax 733-1406; e-mail krastins@sam.gov.lv; internet www.sam.gov.lv; Dir AIGARS KRASTIŅŠ.

Port Authorities

Liepāja Port Authority: Liepāja Special Economic Zone, Feniksa iela 4, Liepāja 3401; tel. 342-7605; fax 348-0252; e-mail authority@lsez.lv; internet www.lsez.lv; Man. Dir AIVARS BOJA.

Rīga Commercial Port: Eksporta iela 15, Rīga 1227; tel. 732-9224; fax 783-0215; e-mail rto@mail.bkc.lv; internet www.rto.lv; Pres. AIVARS TAURINS.

Rīga Fishing Seaport: Atlantijas iela 27, Rīga 1020; tel. 235-1514; fax 235-3168; Dir G. SHEVCHUK.

Rīga Port Authority: Eksporta iela 6, Rīga 1010; tel. 703-0800; fax 783-0051; e-mail rop@mail.rop.lv; internet www.rop.lv; f. 1992; Chief Exec. LEONIDS LOGINOVS.

Ventspils Free Port Authority: Jāņa iela 19, Ventspils 3601; tel. 362-2586; fax 362-1297; e-mail vbparvalde@apollo.lv; internet www.ventspils.lv; f. 1991; Chief Exec. IMANTS SARMULIS.

Ventspils Commercial Port Authority: Dzintaru iela 22, Ventspils 3602; tel. 362-2821; fax 366-8870; e-mail vcp@vcp.lv; Pres. VALERIY PASHUTA.

Shipping Companies

Latvian Shipping Co (LASCO) (Latvijas Kugniecība): Basteja bulv. 2, Rīga 1807; tel. 702-0111; fax 782-8106; e-mail lsc@lsc.riga.lv; internet www.latshipcom.lv; f. 1991; tanker, reefer, LPG and dry cargo transportation; partially privatized in 2002; Pres. ANDRIS KLAVIŅŠ.

Rīga Shipping Co: Balasta dambis 9, Rīga 1048; tel. 760-1133; fax 786-0243; e-mail riga@shipping.lv; internet www.rigashipping.lv; f. 1994; complete technical management of ships including crewing; Dir MIKS ĒKBAUMS.

CIVIL AVIATION

There are two international airports, at Rīga and at Jelgava (south-west of Rīga). The Department of Aviation of the Ministry of Transport co-ordinates the financing of air transport in Latvia, and the Civil Aviation Administration supervises the operation and safety of flights.

Civil Aviation Administration of Latvia: Rīga Airport, Rīga 1053; tel. 720-7307; fax 720-7417; internet www.caa.lv; Dir-Gen. MĀRIS GORODCOVS.

Department of Aviation: Gogoļa iela 3, Rīga 1743; tel. 702-8209; fax 721-7180; Dir ARNIS MUIŽNIEKS.

AirBaltic Corpn AS: Rīga Airport, Rīga 1053; tel. 720-7069; fax 720-7369; e-mail info@airbaltic.lv; internet www.airbaltic.com; f. 1995; 52.58% govt-controlled; operates services to Scandinavia, the Baltic states and Western Europe; Pres. and Chief Exec. BERTOLT FLICK.

Baltic Express Line: Dzirnavu iela 100, Rīga 1010; tel. 728-1037; fax 728-4806; e-mail bel@binet.lv; internet www.binet.lv/home/bel/english; f. 1993; flights to Bulgaria, Egypt, Greece, Spain and Turkey; Pres. BORIS BELOUSSOV; Dir VALERIY LITAVAR.

A/C Inversija: Rīga Airport, Rīga 1053; tel. 720-7095; fax 720-7476; f. 1988; cargo service; operates routes to destinations in Europe and the Far East; Dir-Gen. SEFIM BROOK.

RAF-AVIA: Duntes iela 34, Rīga 1005; tel. 732-4661; fax 733-9045; e-mail rafaviation@hotmail.com; internet www.rafavia.com; f. 1991; scheduled and charter flights; Pres. JURIJS HMELEVSKII.

Transeast Airlines: Rīga International Airport, Rīga 1053; tel. 720-7771; fax 720-7772; e-mail tea@mail.junik.lv; internet www.junik.lv/~tea/; f. 1992; scheduled services between Rīga and Denmark and Sweden; Man. Dir SERGEY AVVAKUMOVS.

Tourism

Among Latvia's principal tourist attractions are the historic centre of Rīga, with its medieval and art nouveau buildings, the extensive beaches of the Baltic coastline, and Gauja National Park, which stretches east of the historic town of Sigulda for nearly 100 km along the Gauja river. Sigulda also offers winter sports facilities. Revenue from tourism in 2000 was some US $131m.; however, revenue declined to some $120m. in 2001. Foreign tourist arrivals in 2000 numbered 268,083, of whom 15.5% were from Finland, 11.8% from Germany and 8.9% from Estonia.

Latvia Tours: Kaļķu iela 8, Rīga 1050; tel. 708-5001; fax 782-0020; e-mail hq@latviatours.lv; internet www.latviatours.lv; Dir GUNDEGA ZELTIŅA.

Latvian Tourism Development Agency: Pils lauk. 4, Rīga 1050; tel. and fax 722-9945; e-mail tda@latviatourism.lv; internet www.latviatourism.lv; f. 1993; Dir AIVARS KALNINSCARON.

LEBANON

Introductory Survey

Location, Climate, Language, Religion, Flag, Capital

The Republic of Lebanon lies in western Asia, bordered by Syria to the north and east, and by Israel and the Palestinian Autonomous Areas to the south. The country has a coastline of about 220 km (135 miles) on the eastern shore of the Mediterranean Sea. The climate varies widely with altitude. The coastal lowlands are hot and humid in summer, becoming mild (cool and damp) in winter. In the mountains, which occupy much of Lebanon, the weather is cool in summer, with heavy snowfalls in winter. Rainfall is generally abundant. The official language is Arabic, which is spoken by almost all of the inhabitants. French is widely used as a second language, while Kurdish and Armenian are spoken by small ethnic minorities. At December 2002 there were 389,233 Palestinian refugees registered in Lebanon. The major religions are Islam and Christianity, and there is a very small Jewish community. In the early 1980s it was estimated that 57% of Lebanon's inhabitants were Muslims, with about 43% Christians. The principal Muslim sects are Shi'a and Sunni, while there is also a significant Druze (Druse) community. By the 1980s it was generally considered that Shi'a Muslims, totalling an estimated 1.2m., constituted Lebanon's largest single community. Most Christians adhere to the Roman Catholic Church, principally the Maronite rite. There are also Armenian, Greek and Syrian sects (both Catholic and Eastern Orthodox) and small groups of Protestants. The national flag (proportions 2 by 3) has three horizontal stripes, of red, white (half the depth) and red, with a representation of a cedar tree (in green and brown) in the centre of the white stripe. The capital is Beirut.

Recent History

Lebanon, the homeland of the ancient Phoenicians, became part of Turkey's Ottoman Empire in the 16th century. When, in 1918 (at the end of the First World War), the Ottoman Empire was dissolved, a Greater Lebanese state was created by the Allied powers. The new state was a response to the nationalist aspirations of the predominant Christian population in the area, but it included territories traditionally considered to be part of Syria, with largely Muslim populations. Lebanon was administered by France, under a League of Nations mandate, from 1920 until independence was declared on 26 November 1941. A republic was established in 1943, and full autonomy was granted in January 1944.

Lebanon is characterized by great religious and cultural diversity. At the time of independence Christians formed a slight majority of the population, the largest single community (nearly 30% of the total) being the Maronite Christians, who mostly inhabited the north of the country and the capital, Beirut. Other Christian groups included Greek Orthodox communities, Greek Catholics and Armenians. The Muslim groups were the Sunnis, living mainly in the coastal towns of Sur (Tyre), Saida (Sidon) and Beirut, the Shi'as, a predominantly rural community in southern Lebanon and the northern Beka'a valley, and, in much smaller numbers, the Druzes, an ancient community in central Lebanon. The relative size of the various communities provided the basis for the unwritten 'national pact' of 1943, whereby executive and legislative posts were to be shared in the ratio of six Christians to five Muslims, and seats in the Chamber of Deputies (renamed the National Assembly in 1979) were distributed on a religious, rather than a politico-ideological, basis. The convention according to this 'confessional' arrangement was that the President was a Maronite Christian, the Prime Minister a Sunni Muslim, and the President of the National Assembly a Shi'a Muslim.

Lebanon's first President, from 1943 until 1952, was Sheikh Bishara el-Khoury. His successor was Camille Chamoun, whose reforms included the enfranchisement of women. Following elections to the Chamber of Deputies in 1957 there was considerable unrest, mainly among Muslims who mistrusted Chamoun's pro-Western foreign policy and advocated Lebanon's closer alignment with Syria and Egypt. In July 1958 Chamoun appealed to the USA for military assistance; US forces remained in Beirut until October, by which time peace had been restored.

Meanwhile, Chamoun was persuaded not to seek a further presidential term, and the Chamber elected Gen. Fouad Chehab as his successor. Chehab, who took office in September 1958, adopted a more neutralist foreign policy, and introduced state provision of health, education and other services. In 1964 he was succeeded by Charles Hélou, who continued many of Chehab's policies but was faced by increasing controversy over the status of Palestinians in Lebanon.

After the establishment of Israel in 1948, and during the subsequent Arab–Israeli wars, thousands of Palestinians fled to Lebanon, where most were housed in refugee camps in the south of the country. Following the creation of the Palestine Liberation Organization (PLO) in 1964, military training centres for Palestinian guerrilla fighters were established in the camps. From 1968 these self-styled *fedayeen* ('martyrs') began making raids into Israel, provoking retaliatory attacks by Israeli forces against targets in southern Lebanon. In 1969 there were clashes between Lebanese security forces and the *fedayeen*. Many Christians, particularly the Maronites, advocated strict government control over the Palestinians' activities, but the majority of Muslims strongly supported Palestinian operations against Israel.

Hélou's successor, Sulayman Franjiya, took office in 1970. During his presidency the Palestinian issue was exacerbated by an influx of Palestinian fighters who had been expelled from Jordan in July 1971. Conflict between Israeli forces and Palestinians based in Lebanon intensified, while Christian groups began their own armed campaign against the *fedayeen*. In July 1974 there were clashes between Palestinian forces and armed members of the Phalangist Party (the Phalanges Libanaises, or al-Kata'eb, a militant right-wing Maronite Christian group). Further conflict between Phalangists and Palestinians from April 1975 quickly descended into full-scale civil war between the Lebanese National Movement (LNM) of left-wing Muslims (including Palestinians), led by Kamal Joumblatt of the Parti Socialiste Progressiste (PSP, a mainly Druze-supported group), and conservative Christian groups, mainly the Phalangist militia. Although the initial cause of the violence was the status of Palestinians, Lebanon's constitutional order soon became the main divisive issue: the LNM advocated an end to the 'confessional' system, claiming this unduly favoured Christians (who by now were generally accepted as no longer forming a majority of the population). Despite diplomatic efforts by Arab and Western countries, no durable cease-fire was achieved until October 1976, largely as a result of intervention in the conflict (in order to prevent an outright LNM victory) by Syrian forces in mid-1976. Under the terms of the cease-fire a 30,000-strong Arab Deterrent Force (ADF), composed mainly of Syrian troops, entered Lebanon.

Franjiya was succeeded as President in September 1976 by Elias Sarkis. In December Rashid Karami, who had been Prime Minister during the 1975–76 civil war, was succeeded by Selim al-Hoss. Legislative elections, due in April 1976, were postponed for an initial period of 26 months—the term of the Chamber of Deputies was subsequently extended further. Although the constitutional forms of the State remained intact, the civil war, in which more than 30,000 people had died, had left the militias of the various warring factions in control of most of the country. In September 1976 Maronite militias united to form the Lebanese Forces (LF), which gradually took control of east Beirut and much of northern Lebanon. West Beirut was controlled by Muslim groups, while Palestinians dominated much of southwest Lebanon.

In March 1978 a raid by forces of Fatah (the Palestine National Liberation Movement), the main guerrilla group within the PLO, provoked retaliatory action by Israel, whose forces advanced into southern Lebanon. UN Security Council Resolution 425, adopted on 17 March, demanded that Israel respect Lebanon's territorial integrity, sovereignty and independence and withdraw its troops; the resolution also established a UN Interim Force in Lebanon (UNIFIL, see p. 63), initially of 4,000 troops. Israeli forces withdrew in June, but transferred control of a border strip to the pro-Israeli Christian militias of Maj. Saad Haddad. In October, following several months of renewed fighting in Beirut between Syrian troops of the ADF and right-wing Christian militias, the ADF states agreed on a peace plan (the Beiteddin Declaration), which aimed to restore the authority of the Lebanese Government and army. Attempts to implement the plan were unsuccessful, however, and Lebanon's fragmentation deepened.

Chafic al-Wazzan became Prime Minister in October 1980 in place of al-Hoss, who had resigned in June. In August 1982, in an election boycotted by most Muslim deputies, the renamed National Assembly designated Bachir Gemayel (the younger son of the founder of the Phalangist Party and commander of the LF) to succeed President Sarkis. The President-elect was assassinated in September, and his brother, Amin, was elected in his place. Following the assassination, Phalangist forces (with what subsequent evidence indicated was the complicity of occupying Israeli forces) stormed the Palestinian refugee camps of Sabra and Chatila, in west Beirut, massacring some 2,000 refugees. Israeli forces had re-entered Lebanon in June 1982, with the declared aim of finally eliminating the PLO's military threat to Israel's northern border. Israeli troops quickly defeated Palestinian forces in south-west Lebanon and surrounded the western sector of Beirut, trapping more than 6,000 Palestinian fighters there. In August US diplomatic efforts achieved an agreement allowing the dispersal of the PLO fighters from Beirut to various Arab countries and the deployment of a multinational peace-keeping force in the city. Negotiations between Lebanon and Israel began in December, culminating in May 1983 in an agreement to end all hostilities (including the theoretical state of war that had existed between the two countries since 1948) and to withdraw all foreign troops from Lebanon. However, Syria did not recognize the accord, leaving 40,000 of its own troops and 7,000 PLO fighters in the Beka'a valley and northern Lebanon. Similarly, Israel did not withdraw its forces, although these were redeployed south of Beirut, along the Awali river, in September, and were reduced from 30,000 to 10,000 by the end of 1983. Maj. Saad Haddad's South Lebanon Army (SLA) was to police southern areas as Israel's role lessened. Meanwhile, the multinational force in Beirut (comprising some 5,800 mainly French, Italian and US personnel) was drawn increasingly into the fighting, coming under frequent attack from Muslim militias who opposed its tantamount support for the Christian-led Government. In October 241 US and 58 French marines were killed in suicide bombings by Muslim groups.

In mid-1983 a struggle became evident for control of Fatah, involving the PLO Chairman, Yasser Arafat, and Syrian-backed rebels. Fighting between rival factions intensified in September, and persisted until a truce agreement, brokered by Saudi Arabia and Syria, provided for the evacuation, under UN protection, of Arafat and some 4,000 of his troops to Algeria, Tunisia and the Yemen Arab Republic.

The conflict in Beirut was punctuated by numerous short-lived cease-fires, but efforts to achieve a comprehensive peace settlement failed, and in February 1984 intense fighting erupted. Attempts to reimpose state authority through a reconstituted Lebanese army (armed and trained by the USA) largely failed, principally because the Muslim community regarded it as an instrument of the Christian President and Phalangist militia. Prime Minister al-Wazzan resigned, and shortly afterwards the USA, Italy and the United Kingdom announced their withdrawal from the peace-keeping force; French troops were withdrawn in March. By this time successive defeats had left Gemayel's forces with effective control only in the mainly Christian-populated east Beirut. In March President Gemayel abrogated the May 1983 agreement with Israel, and in April 1984, with Syrian support, he formed a Government of National Unity under former premier Rashid Karami. A Syrian-sponsored security plan, implemented in July, had only limited success. Sporadic fighting persisted between rival Christian and Muslim militias, and also between Sunni and Shi'ite Muslims of the Murabitoun and Amal militias. The Lebanese army failed to gain control of Beirut, and Gemayel's efforts to obtain approval for constitutional reform, already constrained by his fear of alienating his Christian supporters, were further undermined by divisions within the Cabinet.

The Israeli Government formed by Shimon Peres in September 1984 pledged to withdraw Israeli forces from Lebanon. However, while the Lebanese authorities demanded that UNIFIL police the Israeli–Lebanese border, by the time the Israeli withdrawal was completed, in June 1985, Israel had ensured that a narrow buffer zone, policed by the SLA (now commanded by Gen. Antoine Lahad), was in place along the border. With the Israeli presence in Lebanon reduced to a token force, Syria withdrew about one-third of its troops from the Beka'a valley in July, leaving some 25,000 in position.

Sporadic conflict persisted throughout 1985, but in December the leaders of the three main Lebanese militias (the Druze forces, Amal and the LF) signed an accord in the Syrian capital, Damascus, providing for an immediate cease-fire and for the cessation of the civil war within one year. The militias were to be disarmed and disbanded, and a new constitutional regime was to be introduced within three years. However, the militias of the Shi'ite Hezbollah and the Sunni Murabitoun were not parties to the agreement, which was also opposed by influential Christian elements. Furthermore, there were clashes later in December between supporters of the agreement within the LF and those who resented the concessions made by their leader, Elie Hobeika. In January 1986 Hobeika was forced into exile and replaced as LF leader by Samir Geagea, who, in urging renegotiation of the Damascus accord, effectively ended any prospect of its implementation.

During 1986 Palestinian guerrillas resumed rocket attacks on settlements in northern Israel, provoking retaliatory air attacks by Israel on targets in the Beka'a valley and southern Lebanon. Meanwhile, the Iranian-backed fundamentalist Hezbollah escalated its attacks on SLA positions within the Israeli buffer zone, and also clashed with UNIFIL. Fighting between Palestinian guerrillas and Shi'ite Amal militiamen for control of the refugee camps in south Beirut escalated in May, before a cease-fire was imposed around the camps in June, as part of a Syrian-sponsored peace plan for Muslim west Beirut. The deployment of Lebanese and Syrian troops in west Beirut succeeded temporarily in curbing the activities of the Amal, Druze and Sunni militias in the area, but failed to prevent fighting across the so-called 'Green Line', which had effectively divided the area from Christian east Beirut since early 1984. In October 1986 there was further conflict between Amal and Palestinian fighters around refugee camps in Tyre, Sidon and Beirut. By the time Amal and the PLO agreed in September 1987 to end hostilities, more than 2,500 people had died in the 'war of the camps'. However, differences over the withdrawal of some 5,000–8,000 Palestinian guerrillas led to renewed fighting near Sidon by October. In January 1988, avowedly as a gesture of support for the *intifada* (uprising) by Palestinians in the Israeli-occupied territories, the Amal leader, Nabih Berri, announced an end to the siege of the Palestinian refugee camps in Beirut and southern Lebanon.

Prime Minister Karami was killed in a bomb explosion in June 1987. Selim al-Hoss (Prime Minister in 1976–80) was appointed acting premier. As Gemayel's presidential term neared its end in 1988, a political crisis developed as it proved impossible to find a successor acceptable to all the warring factions. The three leading contenders for the presidency were Gen. Michel Awn (Commander-in-Chief of the Lebanese army), Raymond Eddé (leader of the Maronite Bloc National) and Sulayman Franjiya (President in 1970–76). Franjiya was Syria's preferred candidate but was notably opposed by Geagea, who apparently ensured that the National Assembly was inquorate when it convened for the election in August 1988. In September the USA and Syria agreed to support another candidate, Mikhail ad-Daher, but Christian army and LF leaders remained opposed to the imposition of any candidate by foreign powers. Gemayel's term of office expired later in the month, when a further attempt by the National Assembly to hold an election was inquorate. The outgoing President appointed an interim military administration, comprising three Christians and three Muslims, with Gen. Awn as Prime Minister. However, there was political confusion as the three nominated Muslim officers immediately refused to serve in the new administration, while two Christian members of the al-Hoss Government resigned, signalling their recognition of the interim military administration. The constitutional crisis, with two Governments claiming legitimacy, was further complicated in November, when the Minister of Defence in the al-Hoss Government dismissed Awn as Commander-in-Chief of the Lebanese army; however, Awn retained the loyalty of large sections of the military and thus remained its *de facto* leader.

In March 1989 violent clashes erupted in Beirut between, on the one hand, Awn's Lebanese army and its allies and, on the other, Syrian troops and their local militias. By August it was estimated that more than 600 people had been killed in the fighting, and that some 500,000 had fled Beirut. In September a Tripartite Arab Committee—formed in May by an emergency session of Arab leaders, and comprising King Hassan of Morocco, King Fahd of Saudi Arabia and President Chadli of Algeria—announced a peace plan whereby, most notably, the Lebanese National Assembly would meet to discuss a draft charter of national reconciliation. The Committee's charter was approved by the Syrian Government and the leaders of Lebanon's Muslim militias. Gen. Awn rejected its terms, on the grounds that it did not provide for the withdrawal of Syrian forces, but he was forced to relent, in view of support for the charter by almost every Arab country, as well as the USA, the USSR, the United Kingdom and France; a cease-fire accordingly took effect. The National Assembly subsequently met in Ta'if, Saudi Arabia, to discuss the charter, which was finally approved (with some amendments) in October by 58 of the 62 attending deputies (of the 99 deputies elected in May 1972, only 73 survived). The charter provided for the transfer of executive power from the presidency to a cabinet, with portfolios divided equally between Christian and Muslim ministers. The number of seats in the National Assembly was to be increased to 108, comprising equal numbers of Christian and Muslim deputies. Following the election of a President and the formation of a new government, all militias involved in the Lebanese conflict were to be disbanded within six months, while the internal security forces would be strengthened; the Syrian armed forces would assist the new Government in implementing the security plan for a maximum of two years.

Meeting in the northern town of Qlaiaat in early November 1989, the National Assembly elected René Mouawad, a Maronite Christian deputy and a former Minister of Education and Arts, as President. The Assembly also unanimously endorsed the Ta'if agreement. However, Awn, who denounced the agreement as a betrayal of Lebanese sovereignty, declared the presidential election unconstitutional and its result null and void, proclaiming himself President two days later. Mouawad was assassinated only 17 days after his election. The National Assembly again convened and elected Elias Hrawi (who had stood against Mouawad earlier in the month) as the new President; the legislature also voted to extend its own term until 1994. A new Cabinet was formed by Selim al-Hoss in late November 1989.

The Christian communities were divided over the Ta'if agreement. Maronite leaders had sought to avoid open conflict with Awn by minimizing their approval of the accord, but Geagea's refusal to reject the agreement precipitated violent clashes between his LF and Awn's forces in January 1990: by March more than 800 people had been killed in inter-Christian fighting. In April Geagea announced the LF's recognition of the al-Hoss Government, thus accepting the Ta'if agreement. In August the National Assembly duly approved amendments to the Constitution, in accordance with the agreement, increasing the number of seats in the National Assembly to 108, to be divided equally between Muslims and Christians. On 21 September the Second Lebanese Republic was officially inaugurated when President Hrawi formally endorsed the amendments. In October Awn and his forces (who continued to reject the Ta'if agreement) were expelled from east Beirut by Syrian forces and units of the Lebanese army loyal to Hrawi. The Lebanese army began to deploy in Beirut in December, by which time all militia forces had withdrawn from the city. In the same month al-Hoss submitted his Government's resignation, and Hrawi invited Omar Karami (Minister of Education and Arts in the outgoing administration) to form a government of national unity, as stipulated by the Ta'if agreement. By February 1991 the Lebanese army was established in most major southern Lebanese towns. In the following month the Government approved a plan for the disbandment of the militias and for the transfer to the Lebanese army of responsibility for security throughout Lebanon by September. Both were largely undertaken, although Hezbollah maintained armaments in the Beka'a valley and in southern Lebanon. In May the National Assembly approved amendments to the electoral law, and in June the Cabinet appointed 40 deputies to fill the seats that had become vacant since the 1972 election as well as the nine new seats created under the Ta'if agreement. In August 1991 the National Assembly approved a general amnesty for crimes perpetrated during the civil war, although its terms excluded several specified crimes committed during 1975–90. Under a presidential pardon, Awn was allowed to leave the French embassy compound (where he had been sheltering since his defeat in 1990) and depart for exile in France.

Meanwhile, in May 1991 Lebanon and Syria signed a bilateral treaty establishing formal relations in political, military and economic affairs, and confirming the role of the Syrian army as guarantor of the security plans enshrined in the Ta'if agreement. The treaty was immediately condemned by Israel as a further step towards the formal transformation of Lebanon into a Syrian protectorate, while its opponents within Lebanon denounced it as a threat to the country's independence. In September Lebanon and Syria concluded a mutual security agreement. Syrian forces began to withdraw from Beirut in March 1992, in preparation for their scheduled withdrawal to eastern Lebanon by September.

Israel's assertions that it had no intention of withdrawing from the buffer zone, nor of reducing support for the SLA, were reinforced by fierce attacks by Israeli forces on Palestinian bases in southern Lebanon in June 1991. Lebanese forces began to take up positions in Sidon at the beginning of July. Initial resistance from Palestinians loyal to Arafat was swiftly overcome, and an agreement was concluded with the PLO to allow the Lebanese army to assume control of the area. Israeli military activity against Hezbollah targets in southern Lebanon intensified in late 1991, and the conflict escalated further following the assassination by the Israeli air force of the Secretary-General of Hezbollah, Sheikh Abbas Moussawi, in February 1992.

Lebanon's economic situation deteriorated dramatically in early 1992, and the value of the Lebanese pound depreciated sharply. Consequent price increases provoked widespread public discontent, and the government's authority, already undermined by allegations of corruption and incompetence, was further challenged by a series of general strikes. Karami announced his Cabinet's resignation in May, and, following discussions in Damascus between President Hrawi and the Syrian leadership, Rashid Solh was appointed Prime Minister (a position that he had previously held in 1974–75). In July 1992 the National Assembly approved a new electoral law whereby the number of seats in the Assembly was raised from 108 to 128, to be divided equally between Christian and Muslim deputies. The Government's intention to conduct legislative elections in mid-1992 had prompted Christian groups to threaten a boycott of the polls, since it was not certain that Syrian forces would have withdrawn to the eastern area of the Beka'a valley by that time, in accordance with the Ta'if agreement. The Government, for its part, stated that the Lebanese army was not yet able to guarantee the country's security in the absence of Syrian troops.

Lebanon's first legislative elections for 20 years were held in three rounds, on 23 August (in the governorates of the North and the Beka'a valley), 30 August (Beirut and Mount Lebanon) and 6 September 1992 (South and An-Nabatiyah). The rate of participation in the poll was low (averaging 32%), especially in Maronite districts where leaders had urged a boycott. Hezbollah, for the first time contesting the elections as a political party, enjoyed considerable success, notably in southern constituencies. The Amal leader, Nabih Berri, was appointed President of the new National Assembly in October. Shortly afterwards Hrawi invited Rafik Hariri, a Lebanese-born Saudi Arabian business executive, to form a new government, amid hopes that he would restore some confidence in the Lebanese economy and thus facilitate the country's reconstruction. Hariri's Cabinet included many technocrats, and (unlike in previous administrations), portfolios were not distributed on an entirely 'confessional' basis. Following a meeting between Hrawi and President Hafiz al-Assad of Syria shortly after the elections, it was announced that a timetable for the withdrawal of Syrian armed forces would be compiled in October. It subsequently emerged, however, that there would be no withdrawal until a comprehensive peace treaty had been concluded between Syria and Israel.

The conflict in southern Lebanon between Hezbollah fighters and the SLA and Israeli army escalated sharply from October 1992. In December the Lebanese army took up positions in southern suburbs of Beirut for the first time in eight years; no resistance was reported from Hezbollah, which had hitherto effectively controlled the areas. In mid-1993 the Lebanese Government was said to be attempting to curtail the activities of the Damascus-based Popular Front for the Liberation of Palestine—General Command (PFLP—GC), which had begun to mount guerrilla attacks on Israeli military positions from southern Lebanon. In July Israeli armed forces launched their heaviest artillery and air attacks on targets in southern Lebanon since 1982. The declared aim of 'Operation Accountability' was to

eradicate the threat posed by Hezbollah and Palestinian guerrillas, and to create a flow of refugees so as to compel the
Lebanese and Syrian authorities to take action to curb Hezbollah and the Palestinians. According to Lebanese sources, the
week-long offensive displaced some 300,000 civilians towards
the north and resulted in 128 (mainly civilian) deaths. Although
a US-brokered cease-fire 'understanding' entered effect at the
end of July 1993, hostilities continued in subsequent months. In
August, meanwhile, apparently as part of the cease-fire, units of
the Lebanese army took up positions assigned to UNIFIL since
the late 1970s near the Israeli security zone.

An air attack by Israeli forces on a Hezbollah training camp in
the Beka'a valley in June 1994 resulted (according to Hezbollah)
in the deaths of 26 fighters. Hezbollah responded with rocket
attacks into the security zone and northern Israel. In August
Israel issued a formal apology after operations by its forces in
southern Lebanon caused eight civilian deaths. In October an
Israeli attack on the town of An-Nabatiyah at-Tahta (Naba-
tiyah), in which seven civilians died, was apparently provoked
by the deaths of 22 people in a bomb attack, attributed to
militants of the Palestinian fundamentalist Hamas, in the
Israeli city of Tel-Aviv: hitherto, Israeli operations in Lebanon
had tended to be in reprisal for terrorist activity in the security
zone. Clashes in southern Lebanon in December reportedly
resulted in the killing by Hezbollah of several members of the
Israeli military and SLA, and seemingly prompted a retaliatory
bomb attack on a suburb of southern Beirut, in which a senior
Hezbollah official was killed. Israeli attacks south of Beirut in
January 1995 targeted alleged PFLP—GC bases. In February
Israel began a blockade of southern Lebanese fishing ports,
following the imposition by the Lebanese army of stricter controls between the Israeli security zone and sovereign Lebanese
territory.

In March 1994 the National Assembly approved legislation
instituting the death penalty for what were termed 'politically
motivated' murders. Shortly afterwards the Maronite LF was
proscribed, on the grounds that the organization had promoted
the establishment of a Christian enclave and thus the country's
partition. The LF leader, Samir Geagea, was subsequently
arrested and charged, along with several of his associates, in
connection with the murder, in October 1990, of Dany Chamoun,
son of former President Camille Chamoun and the leader of the
right-wing Maronite Parti National Libéral (PNL), and with the
bombing of a Maronite church outside Beirut in January 1994.
In September it was reported that the LF had temporarily
relieved Geagea of the organization's leadership and revoked his
recognition of the Ta'if agreement; the LF command had also
reportedly countermanded Geagea's formal dissolution, under
the Ta'if agreement, of the organization's militia status. (A
successor political organization, the Lebanese Forces Party, had
been created in September 1990.) In June 1995 Geagea and a co-
defendant were convicted of instigating the murder of Chamoun,
and were (together with seven others convicted *in absentia*)
sentenced to death; the sentences were immediately commuted
to life imprisonment with hard labour.

In October 1995 the National Assembly voted to amend the
Constitution to extend President Hrawi's mandate for a further
three years. Prime Minister Hariri had sought an extension of
the presidential term in the stated interest of promoting
stability in the economic reconstruction process, and the amendment had been facilitated following intervention by Syria to
resolve a procedural dispute between Hariri and the President
of the National Assembly, Nabih Berri.

Elections to the National Assembly took place, in five rounds,
in August–September 1996. Pro-Hariri candidates enjoyed considerable success in the first three rounds of voting (in Mount
Lebanon, North Lebanon and Beirut governorates), with the
Prime Minister himself winning the largest number of votes at
the third round; there were, however, allegations of vote-buying
involving Hariri's supporters in Beirut. In the fourth and fifth
rounds (in the South and An-Nabatiyah, and in the Beka'a
valley) an electoral alliance led by Amal and Hezbollah was
reported to have won all but one of the total 46 seats. Prior to the
fifth round Syria had redeployed some 12,000 of its estimated
30,000 troops in Lebanon to the eastern part of the Beka'a
valley. (Under the terms of the Ta'if agreement, the redeployment should have been completed in 1992.) The overall rate of
participation averaged about 45%, suggesting that many voters
had disregarded demands particularly by Awn, Gemayel and
other exiled figures for a boycott of the polls. Berri was re-elected
President of the National Assembly when the new legislature

convened in October 1996. Hrawi invited Hariri to form a new
government: the distribution of portfolios in the new Cabinet
(named in early November, following consultations with Syrian
leaders) among the country's various interests remained largely
unchanged. (In May 1997 the Constitutional Court annulled the
results of voting for four seats, having found evidence of electoral malpractice. By-elections took place in June, at which all
but one of the deputies elected in 1996 were returned to office.)

A further death sentence (commuted to life imprisonment)
was imposed on Geagea in May 1996, following his conviction for
ordering the assassination of another Maronite rival in 1990. In
July 1996 he was acquitted of involvement in the Maronite
church bombing of February 1994, although he received a 10-
year prison sentence for attempting to recruit and arm militiamen after 1991 (when all militias had been banned). In August
1996 Geagea was further charged with orchestrating the death
of Prime Minister Rashid Karami in 1987; his trial in this case
began in December 1997 and ended in June 1999 with a further
sentence of life imprisonment. Meanwhile, in May 1997 Geagea
received yet another death sentence (again commuted to life
imprisonment), having been convicted of an assassination
attempt in 1991 against the then Minister of Defence, Michel
Murr.

In April 1996 Israeli armed forces began a sustained campaign of intense air and artillery attacks on alleged Hezbollah
positions in southern Lebanon and suburbs in the south of
Beirut. The declared aim of the Israeli offensive ('Operation
Grapes of Wrath') was to achieve the complete cessation of
rocket attacks by Hezbollah on settlements in northern Israel—
stated by Hezbollah to have been provoked by deliberate attacks
on Lebanese civilians by Israeli armed forces or their proxies.
(An important element of the 1993 cease-fire 'understanding'
was that Hezbollah and Israel had effectively confined their
conflict largely to the region of the security zone by agreeing to
halt unprovoked attacks on civilian targets.) Some 400,000
Lebanese were displaced northwards, after the Israeli military
warned that they would be endangered by the offensive against
Hezbollah. Moreover, the shelling by Israeli forces of a UNIFIL
base at Qana, which resulted in the deaths of more than 100
Lebanese civilians who had been sheltering there, and of four
UNIFIL soldiers, provoked international condemnation. After
more than two weeks of hostilities a cease-fire 'understanding'
took effect in late April 1996. As in 1993, this was effectively a
compromise confining the conflict to the area of the security
zone, recognizing both Hezbollah's right to resist Israeli occupation and Israel's right to self-defence; the 'understanding' also
envisaged the establishment of an Israel-Lebanon Monitoring
Group (ILMG), comprising representatives of Israel, Lebanon,
Syria, France and the USA, to supervise the cease-fire.
According to the Israeli authorities, Operation Grapes of Wrath
resulted in no Israeli death, while 170–200 Lebanese civilians,
in addition to some 50 fighters, were killed. Hezbollah claimed to
have sustained minimal casualties, and its military capacity
appeared largely undiminished. A subsequent UN report on the
killing of Lebanese civilians at Qana concluded that it was
'unlikely' that the shelling of the UNIFIL base had, as claimed
by the Israelis, been the result of 'gross technical and/or procedural errors'. Prior to the first meeting of the ILMG, in July,
Israel and Hezbollah were reported to have exchanged prisoners
and bodies of members of their armed forces for the first time
since 1991.

Despite the April 1996 cease-fire 'understanding', sporadic
clashes continued between Hezbollah and Israeli armed forces,
causing both sides to issue complaints to the ILMG. The conflict
escalated in August 1997, and, following the deaths of two
civilians in a bomb explosion in Jezzine, north of the security
zone, the SLA launched an artillery attack on Sidon, killing at
least six civilians. Hezbollah in turn violated the cease-fire
'understanding' with rocket attacks into northern Israel,
prompting Israel to direct intensive air-strikes against presumed Hezbollah and PFLP—GC targets. In late August four
Amal fighters and four members of the Israeli security forces
were killed following an ambush by the Israeli military on the
edge of the occupied zone; this followed the death of an Amal
commander by a car bomb in central Beirut. In September 12
members of an élite Israeli commando unit were killed (reportedly the highest Israeli death toll in a single operation since
1985) after Amal fighters and the Lebanese army foiled an
operation, apparently against an Amal base, south of Sidon.
Later in the month a son of the Hezbollah Secretary-General,

Sheikh Hasan Nasrallah, was killed during intense fighting in the security zone.

The extent of Israeli casualties as a result of the occupation of southern Lebanon prompted a vocal campaign within Israel for a unilateral withdrawal from the security zone. In April 1998 Israel's 'inner' Security Cabinet voted to adopt UN Security Council Resolution 425, but with the stipulation that Lebanon provide guarantees of the security of Israel's northern border. Lebanon, however, emphasized that Resolution 425 demanded an unconditional withdrawal, and stated that neither would it be able to guarantee Israel's immunity from attack, nor would it be prepared to deploy the Lebanese army in southern Lebanon for this purpose; furthermore, Lebanon could not support the continued presence there of the SLA. Concern was also expressed that a unilateral withdrawal from Lebanon in the absence of a comprehensive Middle East peace settlement might foment regional instability.

In July 1997 the USA announced an end to its ban on travel to Lebanon, in response to a commitment by Hariri to increase co-operation in combating terrorism. (The USA had halted flights following the hijacking to Beirut of a US commercial flight in 1985, and, amid fears for the safety of US nationals within Lebanon, had announced in 1987 that US passports were invalid for travel to Lebanon.) In September Madeleine Albright became the first US Secretary of State to visit Beirut since 1983. Following talks in Washington, DC, between Hariri, President Bill Clinton and Albright in June 1998, the USA ended its ban on the sale of tickets to US citizens travelling to Lebanon.

Meanwhile, in late 1996 the Government had ordered the closure of about 150 radio and 50 television stations; licences to broadcast political items had been granted to only a limited number of stations, most of which were owned by prominent political figures. In September 1997 the authorities began to close down unlicensed broadcasters, and two people died when security forces opened fire on members of the fundamentalist Tawheed Islami group who were attempting to prevent the closure of a private station in the northern city of Tarabulus (Tripoli). In December the Minister of the Interior, deputy premier Michel Murr, prohibited a televised satellite broadcast, from France, by Gen. Awn, on the grounds that such transmissions were undermining national security. The ban provoked a violent demonstration in Beirut: a number of arrests were made, and it was announced subsequently that 10 people were to be tried by military court for attacking the security forces, while civil charges were to be brought against a further 23 protesters who had defied a ban (imposed in 1993) on public demonstrations. Awn's interview was eventually broadcast in January 1998 by a private terrestrial channel. In that month the Government announced a ban on the broadcast of all news programmes by private satellite stations (including a company owned by Hariri) unless the bulletins had been prepared by the state-controlled Télé-Liban.

In March 1998 President Hrawi presented legislation to the Cabinet that would enable marriages to be conducted by civil (as opposed to religious) authorities. Supporters of the bill stated that this would facilitate inter-faith marriages and thus erode sectarian divisions. However, the legislation was strongly opposed by religious leaders and the Prime Minister. Hariri refused to sign the bill on the grounds that it would offend religious sensibilities and create divisions at a time when a consensus was vital in order to facilitate the implementation of the Government's economic programme. The National Assembly President reportedly lent his support to Hrawi's legislation after the latter sought the establishment of a parliamentary committee to consider the 'deconfessionalization' of public life—a process that, it was generally considered, would be to the advantage of the Shi'ite community.

Voting in Lebanon's first municipal elections since 1963 took place, in four rounds, in May–June 1998. At the first round (in Mount Lebanon governorate) Hezbollah won convincing victories in Beirut's southern suburbs, despite an attempt by Hariri and Berri to moderate the influence of the opposition by supporting joint lists of candidates; right-wing organizations opposed to the Government, including Dory Chamoun's PNL (which had boycotted the 1992 and 1996 National Assembly elections), also took control of several councils. At the second round, in North Lebanon, efforts failed to achieve an inter-community balance in Tripoli, where a council comprising 23 Muslims and only one Christian was elected; elsewhere in the governorate there was notable success for candidates loyal to Samir Geagea. However, a joint list of candidates supported by

Hariri and Berri won control of the Beirut council at the third round. Candidates endorsed by Hariri won seats in Sidon, while Berri's Amal gained overall control in Tyre. At the final round of voting (in the Beka'a valley) Hezbollah candidates were largely defeated by their pro-Syrian secular rivals and by members of the governorate's leading families. Other than in Beirut, the rate of voter participation was high (about 70%).

As President Hrawi's mandate neared completion in 1998, the Commander-in-Chief of the armed forces, Gen. Emile Lahoud, was increasingly suggested as a suitable successor: Lahoud's strong leadership and firm stance on corruption, in addition to his success in having reconstructed the army following the civil war, were thought likely to assist the process of political reform and economic regeneration. Despite Lahoud's reputation as a nationalist, his candidacy was fully endorsed by Syria, whose influence remained crucial in Lebanese politics. To enable Lahoud's appointment, the National Assembly overwhelmingly adopted an exceptional amendment to Article 49 of the Constitution—which requires that senior civil servants resign their post two years prior to seeking political office—and Lahoud was duly elected President on 15 October, with the approval of all 118 National Assembly deputies present (the vote was boycotted by the Druze leader, Walid Joumblatt, and his supporters). Lahoud took office on 24 November, identifying law enforcement and the elimination of official corruption as priorities for his administration. Hariri unexpectedly declined an invitation from Lahoud to form a new government. Following consultations between Lahoud and the National Assembly, at the beginning of December Selim al-Hoss (who had headed four administrations during the civil war) was designated Prime Minister. His new Cabinet, which was almost halved in size (to 16 members), included only two ministers from the previous administration—Michel Murr notably retained the post of deputy premier as well as the interior portfolio. The appointment of several 'reformists', in conjunction with the exclusion of representatives of the various 'confessional' blocs and former militia leaders whose rivalries had frequently undermined previous governments, was said to illustrate al-Hoss's declared commitment to pursuing a comprehensive programme of reconstruction. Hezbollah declined to participate in the new Government. At the Cabinet's first session, held later in December, Gen. Michel Sulayman was appointed to succeed Lahoud as head of the armed forces. The incoming Government also revoked the five-year ban on the holding of public demonstrations.

The al-Hoss Government's programme emphasized anti-corruption measures, economic liberalization and reduction of the public debt, as well as accelerated electoral reform. In accordance with the expressed aim of countering corruption and waste in public life—estimated to have cost the State some US $4,500m. since 1990—the judiciary was granted powers to investigate a number of political scandals and bring former high-ranking officials to trial. In June 1999 the state-run news agency published a strong criticism of Hariri, reportedly originating from anonymous 'ministerial sources', accusing the former Prime Minister of corruption, of seeking to undermine the Government in order to facilitate his return to power, and of collusion with Israel; al-Hoss denied that his Government had any prior knowledge of the anti-Hariri statement. Concerns were also expressed in mid-1999 at the recent prosecution of several prominent journalists in Lebanon.

Clashes persisted in southern Lebanon following Israel's 'adoption' of Resolution 425, amid continuing protests of violations of the April 1996 cease-fire 'understanding'. In May 1998 at least 10 people were killed in an Israeli air raid on a Fatah training camp in the central Beka'a valley. At the end of the month, following a week of intense fighting in which five Hezbollah fighters and four SLA militiamen had died, two Israeli soldiers were killed in an ambush on their patrol. Despite the deaths of two further Israeli soldiers in June, an exchange of bodies and prisoners of war proceeded under an arrangement brokered by the International Committee of the Red Cross. In August at least nine Israelis were injured when rockets were fired into northern Israel, in retaliation for the death of an Amal commander near Tyre. In two separate incidents in November, seven Israeli soldiers were killed as a result of attacks by Hezbollah on Israeli patrols in the occupied zone. There were further serious exchanges in December, when 13 civilians were injured by Hezbollah rocket attacks in northern Israel, launched in reprisal for an Israeli air-strike in southern Lebanon in which eight civilians were killed. (Israel subsequently issued a formal apology for the incident, and both assaults were condemned by the ILMG.) In January 1999 Israel's Security Cabinet voted to respond to future Hezbollah offensives by targeting infrastructure in central and northern Lebanon (thereby extending the conflict beyond suspected guerrilla bases in the south). Meanwhile, the Israeli army's annual report claimed that the number of Hezbollah attacks against Israeli forces in southern Lebanon had increased from 715 in 1997 to around 1,200 in 1998, resulting in the deaths of some 23 soldiers in that year. Hostilities escalated in February 1999, when Israeli forces annexed the village of Arnoun, just outside the occupied zone. At the end of the month hundreds of Lebanese students stormed Arnoun, apparently forcing its release from Israeli control; however, Israeli forces reannexed the village in April. Meanwhile, Israel launched intensive air attacks on Hezbollah targets, following an ambush in the security zone in late February that had killed Brig.-Gen. Erez Gerstein, the commander of the Israeli army's liaison unit with the SLA (together with two other Israeli soldiers and a journalist): Gerstein was the most senior member of the Israeli command to be killed in Lebanon since the 1982 occupation.

Following a grenade attack in Beirut on a hostel for Syrian migrant workers, in May 1999 eight people were arrested and reportedly admitted to having plotted several bomb attacks against Syrian and Lebanese military sites. The men, who were apparently protesting against the continued 'occupation' of Lebanon by Syrian forces, were also implicated in an attack on a Syrian military centre in Hadath in December 1998. Also in May 1999 a senior official of the Fatah faction of the PLO and his wife were killed in Sidon by unidentified gunmen, believed to be PLO activists opposed to Fatah's willingness to negotiate with Israel. A car bomb in southern Lebanon shortly afterwards seriously wounded another Fatah official and led to fears of a renewed cycle of violence between rival Palestinian factions in Lebanon. In June four judges in Sidon were killed in a gun attack on the court room in which they were conducting the trial of two Palestinians. In October a senior Fatah commander, Sultan Abu al-Aynayn (a close ally of Yasser Arafat), was sentenced to death *in absentia* by a military court in Beirut, having been found guilty of leading a militia and of encouraging anti-Government rebellion. His conviction was widely interpreted as evidence of a growing struggle between Arafat and the Lebanese and Syrian Governments for influence over Palestinian refugees in Lebanon. (In December 2000, again *in absentia*, al-Aynayn was convicted by a military court of weapons-trafficking and of plotting terrorist actions in southern Lebanon; he was sentenced to 15 years' imprisonment.) Two other Fatah leaders in southern Lebanon were detained by the Lebanese military in November 1999, on charges of murder and of plotting bomb attacks during the 1980s; five further officials of the organization were reportedly arrested in late 1999 and early 2000. Meanwhile, in December 1999 five Lebanese soldiers were killed near Tripoli in an ambush on their patrol. The perpetrators of the attack were believed to be members of an Egyptian-based Sunni Muslim fundamentalist group, Takfir wal Hijra, two of whom were about to be arrested for their alleged involvement in recent grenade attacks on Orthodox churches in the Tripoli area. The incident resulted in the largest Lebanese military operation for a decade, during which nine Lebanese soldiers and several Islamists, as well as at least two civilians, were killed. In January 2000 the Government ordered a judicial enquiry into the recent upsurge in sectarian violence.

Prior to his election in May 1999 Israel's new Prime Minister, Ehud Barak, made a campaign pledge to effect an Israeli withdrawal from southern Lebanon by July 2000. (In April 1999 the Israeli Minister of Defence had announced that 80% of Israel's army posts in southern Lebanon had been transferred to the SLA and that further transfers were imminent, thus enabling additional Israeli troops to withdraw from their 'security zone'.) In June the SLA completed a unilateral withdrawal from the enclave of Jezzine, in the north-east of the occupied zone. Two SLA soldiers were killed during the operation, while about 100 others reportedly surrendered to the Lebanese army. Following further Hezbollah attacks on northern Israel, towards the end of June the outgoing administration of Binyamin Netanyahu ordered a series of air-strikes against infrastructure targets in central and southern Lebanon—the heaviest aerial bombardment since 'Operation Grapes of Wrath' in 1996. At least nine civilians died in the assaults, which destroyed two power plants in Beirut, as well as bridges and a telecommunications centre. Also in June 1999 UNIFIL accused Hezbollah of encouraging attacks on UN positions near the occupied zone by using

UNIFIL outposts to launch attacks on Israel and the SLA. In August a senior Hezbollah official was killed by a car bomb in Sidon. Two Israeli soldiers were subsequently killed in retaliatory Hezbollah attacks, to which Israel responded with raids on several villages outside the security zone. In December the Israeli Government issued an apology to the Lebanese authorities, after at least 15 Lebanese schoolchildren were injured as a result of an assault by its forces. The incident came amid an escalation in Hezbollah operations following the resumption of Israeli-Syrian peace negotiations. In that month an 'understanding in principle' was reportedly reached between Israel and Syria in order to curb the fighting in southern Lebanon, although the informal cease-fire ended in late January 2000 when a senior SLA commander was killed; the deaths of three Israeli soldiers at the end of the month led Israel to declare that peace talks with Syria (now again postponed indefinitely) could resume only if Syria took action to restrain Hezbollah. In early February Israel conducted a series of air raids against Hezbollah targets and Lebanese infrastructure, including three power stations outside Beirut. By mid-February three further Israeli soldiers had been killed in the security zone, and Israel announced that its Prime Minister would henceforth be empowered to order immediate retaliatory raids against Hezbollah without discussion with the Security Cabinet.

Meanwhile, preparations for an Israeli withdrawal from southern Lebanon had reportedly begun in late 1999, and in March 2000 the Israeli Cabinet voted unanimously to withdraw its forces from southern Lebanon by July, even if no agreement had been reached on the Israeli-Syrian track of the Middle East peace process. In that month Israeli forces attacked two Palestinian refugee camps to the east of Beirut; the offensive was widely believed to be in response to a recent resolution adopted by the League of Arab States (the Arab League, see p. 260) warning that Palestinian militant organizations might resume attacks on Israeli targets in the event of Israel's withdrawing from Lebanon without having negotiated the resettlement of Palestinian refugees currently residing in other Arab states. In April Israel released 13 Lebanese prisoners who had been held without trial for more than a decade as 'bargaining counters' for Israeli soldiers missing in Lebanon. Israel also gave the UN official notification that it intended to withdraw its forces from southern Lebanon 'in one phase' by 7 July. Also in April the Lebanese Government stated for the first time that it would accept a UN peace-keeping force in southern Lebanon after the Israeli withdrawal. In mid-May two senior SLA fighters were killed as fighting escalated between Israeli forces and Hezbollah. On 23 May Israel's Security Cabinet voted to accelerate the withdrawal of its remaining troops from Lebanon, after Hezbollah had taken control of about one-third of southern Lebanon following the evacuation by the SLA of outposts transferred to its control by the Israeli army. Both the Israeli Government and the UN had expected the withdrawal to take place on 1 June; however, the rapid and chaotic withdrawal of Israeli forces from southern Lebanon was completed on 24 May, almost six weeks ahead of Barak's original deadline of July. As the troops were departing, Lebanese citizens stormed the notorious al-Khiam prison in Israel's former security zone, releasing its inmates.

In June 2000 the UN Security Council endorsed the verification of Secretary-General Kofi Annan that the Israeli withdrawal had been completed, although both the Lebanese Government and Hezbollah maintained that Israel was still required to depart from territory known as Shebaa Farms and to release all Lebanese prisoners. (The UN maintains that Shebaa Farms is part of territory captured by Israel from Syria, and as such must be considered under the Israeli-Syrian track of the Middle East peace process.) In July a limited contingent of UNIFIL troops began to redeploy close to the Lebanese border with Israel, to fill the vacuum created by the departure of Israeli forces. At the same time the UN Security Council voted to extend UNIFIL's mandate for a further six months. In August a Joint Security Force of some 1,000 Lebanese troops and Internal Security Forces reportedly deployed in southern Lebanon (other than in the border area), charged with the provision of general security in the territory. Responsibility for the border with Israel remained with UNIFIL (whose troops in Lebanon now numbered some 5,600).

Meanwhile, in June 2000 the Lebanese authorities initiated a military trial against more than 2,500 former SLA militiamen, who were charged with having collaborated with Israel during its occupation of southern Lebanon; some of the defendants were tried *in absentia* (many SLA members, fearing reprisals, had fled with the departing Israeli army). Human rights organizations strongly criticized the trial, which by early January 2001 had resulted in the conviction of an estimated 2,041 alleged collaborators.

Elections to the National Assembly took place on 27 August (Mount Lebanon and North Lebanon) and 3 September 2000 (Beirut, the Beka'a valley, An-Nabatiyah and the South). For the first time since 1972 Lebanese citizens in the former Israeli-occupied zone of southern Lebanon participated in the elections. Voting patterns in the first round swiftly indicated a rejection of al-Hoss's premiership, as the Druze leader, Walid Joumblatt (one of former premier Rafik Hariri's staunchest allies), secured an overwhelming victory in Mount Lebanon governorate. Furthermore, while Deputy Prime Minister Michel Murr retained his seat in the Maronite Northern Metn district, the election there of Pierre Gemayel, son of Amin Gemayel, was regarded as a considerable reverse for President Lahoud. Turn-out by voters was estimated at 51% of the registered electorate, apparently indicating that voters had largely ignored appeals by some Christian parties for a boycott of the poll. At the second round of voting, with a period of political 'cohabitation' between Lahoud and Hariri already appearing likely, the latter's Al-Karamah (Dignity) list proceeded to secure 18 of the 19 assembly seats in Beirut (the remaining seat being won by a Hezbollah candidate); al-Hoss lost his own seat in the legislature. In the south an alliance of Hezbollah and Amal candidates took all the governorate's 23 seats, while Hezbollah enjoyed similar successes in the Beka'a. Independent monitors reported numerous instances of electoral malpractice. In all, Hariri was reported to have the support of between 92–106 of the 128 seats in the new legislature. In late October President Lahoud formally appointed Rafik Hariri to the premiership. The composition of his radically altered Cabinet (newly expanded to 30 members) was announced a few days later. Issam Fares was named as Deputy Prime Minister, while Sulayman Franjiya became the Minister of Public Health. One notable appointment was that of Elias Murr, the son-in-law of President Lahoud and a non-parliamentarian, who replaced his father, Michel Murr, as Minister of the Interior and of Municipal and Rural Affairs. (Resistance and Development, the party list including Hezbollah, had declined to join the Government.) Prior to his appointment, Hariri was reported to have reached an informal 'power-sharing' agreement with President Lahoud, whereby he would be responsible for economic policy, while the President would take charge of defence and foreign affairs. However, there were reports of increasing tensions between the two men during the latter part of 2000. Hariri won a vote of confidence in the National Assembly in November, instigated by a group of pro-Syrian deputies who had questioned his past criticism of Syria's military involvement in Lebanon.

Divisions between pro- and anti-Syrian elements within Lebanon had become increasingly vocal in the aftermath of the Israeli withdrawal from southern Lebanon in May 2000 and the death of Syria's President Hafiz al-Assad in the following month. An unofficial visit to Beirut by his successor, Bashar al-Assad, for meetings with key Lebanese politicians shortly before the legislative elections appeared to indicate that the new Syrian President was likely to continue his late father's role as power-broker in Lebanon. However, the decisive rejection of the Syrian-backed Government of Selim al-Hoss prompted speculation that there might be some redefinition of Syrian influence in Lebanese politics. This was considered all the more probable given the electoral successes for Joumblatt, who appeared to make common cause with Maronite supporters of Amin Gemayel and the imprisoned Samir Geagea in demanding the withdrawal of Syrian forces. Moreover, in late September Maronite bishops issued a statement urging the departure of the Syrian military. In November mass demonstrations were held by anti-Syrian protesters in Beirut. Nabih Berri (who had been re-elected as President of the National Assembly) subsequently asserted that the Lebanese and Syrian Governments were preparing to hold discussions concerning the imminent redeployment of Syrian troops, although this was denied by Syria. While the Maronite community and other Christian groups maintained that the departure of Syrian forces was necessary in order for full Lebanese sovereignty to be attained, both President Lahoud and Prime Minister Hariri continued to defend Syria's military presence. In December Syria—which had never previously confirmed that it was holding Lebanese prisoners—freed 46 Lebanese political prisoners (including many Chris-

tians who had been detained by Syrian troops during 1975–1990), apparently as a gesture of 'goodwill'. In January 2001 the Lebanese Government established a commission to examine the issue of Lebanese prisoners held in Syria. In the same month a Jordanian newspaper reported that Gen. Michel Awn had declared himself ready to return to Lebanon from exile in France in order to appear before the Lebanese judiciary; the former Christian militia leader's announcement apparently followed discussions between Hariri and the Syrian President. In mid-March the Lebanese authorities ordered a large deployment of army and security forces to Beirut, to contain protest actions led by students demanding the complete withdrawal of Syrian troops from the country. The mass protests followed renewed calls by Awn for his supporters to hold peaceful demonstrations against Syria. It was reported in early April that President Lahoud had urged pro- and anti-Syrian elements in Lebanon to begin a national dialogue in an attempt to defuse rising tensions, while the Government banned all unlicensed protests against Syria. The situation appeared to deteriorate in that month when three relatives of a PSP deputy were injured by a parcel bomb.

In late September 2000 the Middle East entered a period of deep crisis, when Palestinians in the West Bank and Gaza resumed their *intifada* against Israel. At the same time uncertainty regarding the permanence of the Israeli withdrawal from southern Lebanon was intensified, as Hezbollah renewed its campaign against the Israeli military. In early October Hezbollah fighters captured three Israeli soldiers in Shebaa Farms, with the demand that Israel release 19 Lebanese and dozens of Palestinians from Israeli detention. Amid concerted international diplomatic efforts to prevent the Israeli–Palestinian crisis from developing into a wider regional conflict, the UN Secretary-General, Kofi Annan, visited Beirut for talks regarding the soldiers' release. In the following week, however, a senior Israeli army reservist was kidnapped in Switzerland, apparently by Hezbollah (which claimed that the officer was working for Israeli intelligence). By November Hezbollah appeared to be intensifying its attacks against Israeli military patrols in Shebaa Farms. The killing of an Israeli soldier there at the end of the month prompted Israel to launch air-strikes against suspected Hezbollah targets in southern Lebanon. The Hezbollah action also provoked harsh criticism from the UN. Meanwhile, in mid-November the UN Security Council urged the Lebanese Government to comply with international law by deploying its armed forces on the Israeli border with southern Lebanon (where Hezbollah still controlled the line of withdrawal, or 'Blue Line'). However, Lebanon rejected such a deployment until such time as Israel had signed a comprehensive peace treaty with both Lebanon and Syria. Exchanges of gunfire and mortar fire between Israeli troops and Lebanese fighters at the border were reported in late December 2000 and January 2001, in which at least one Lebanese civilian died. At the end of that month the UN Security Council voted to extend UNIFIL's mandate in Lebanon until the end of July, when its operational strength was to be reduced to about 4,500—the number of troops deployed prior to the Israeli withdrawal. The Security Council also reiterated its appeals to both Israel and Lebanon to halt the numerous violations of the Blue Line.

In mid-January 2001 the Lebanese Government ordered an inquiry into allegations that the Israeli army had employed weaponry with a depleted uranium (DU) component during its occupation of southern Lebanon. There were fears that the increased incidence of cancers among Lebanese civilians in areas targeted by Israeli forces during 'Operation Grapes of Wrath' in 1996 might be linked to the use of DU ammunition. Lebanon was said to be considering the inclusion of DU pollution in a list of claims for compensation from Israel, as part of a reparations lawsuit filed with the International Court of Justice at The Hague, Netherlands. Israel, however, denied the use of DU weaponry in Lebanon.

The Lebanese leadership was generally pessimistic as to the prospects for peace in the Middle East following the election, in February 2001, of Likud leader Ariel Sharon as Israeli Prime Minister. (Sharon is held by the vast majority of Lebanese to have been responsible for the massacre of Palestinian refugees in the Sabra and Chatila camps in September 1982—at which time he was Israel's Minister of Defence.) Also in February 2001, following criticism from the UN, Israel agreed to move a concrete security fence that it had constructed some 400 m inside Lebanese territory. In mid-February Israel launched mortar attacks close to Shebaa Farms, in reprisal for the death of an

Israeli soldier in a bomb attack there. Tensions escalated once again in mid-April: Israel responded to the killing by Hezbollah of another of its soldiers in Shebaa Farms with the first military action against Syrian troops since 1996, launching air raids on a Syrian radar base to the east of Beirut. According to Syrian sources, at least one Syrian soldier died in the attack, which Israel claimed had been provoked by Syria's sponsorship of Hezbollah.

In late April 2001 Rafik Hariri visited Washington, DC, for discussions with US President George W. Bush, during which the Lebanese premier urged the US Administration to increase its involvement in international diplomatic attempts to revive the Middle East peace process. At the same time President Lahoud requested that the European Union (EU, see p. 199), and in particular France, also assume a greater role in such efforts. During a visit by Lahoud to France in late May President Jacques Chirac urged the Lebanese Government to send its army to the southern border zone in order to prevent the Israeli–Palestinian violence from spreading to Lebanon. However, Lahoud insisted that Lebanon would not deploy its forces along the Blue Line prior to the conclusion of a comprehensive Middle East peace settlement.

During mid-June 2001 Syria withdrew an estimated 6,000–10,000 troops from the largely Christian eastern and southern suburbs of Beirut and from Mount Lebanon; a large number of the troops were redeployed in the Beka'a valley. The departure of Syrian forces from Beirut was welcomed by Christian leaders in Lebanon. However, although some commentators expected the redeployment to ease tensions between pro- and anti-Syrian groups, others regarded Syria's withdrawal from the Lebanese capital as merely symbolic, since it retained 15 military bases in strategic parts of Beirut. In early August the Maronite patriarch, Cardinal Sfeir, held highly symbolic discussions with the other principal advocate of a 'readjustment' in Syrian-Lebanese relations, Druze leader Walid Joumblatt, apparently to demonstrate a new era of 'reconciliation' between the two communities. Within days, however, the mainly pro-Syrian army intelligence service began demanding mass arrests of Maronite Christians who were again demanding a complete Syrian withdrawal from Lebanon; some 200–250 Maronites—most of whom were members of the banned LF or supporters of Gen. Awn—were arrested on charges of participation in 'illegal gatherings', of attempting to destabilize and partition the country, and of conspiring with Israel. Many Christian and Muslim deputies condemned the detentions as 'unconstitutional', while protesters demonstrating against the growing influence of the military clashed with police. Among those detained in a further series of arrests were two leading Lebanese journalists accused of having contacts with Israel. A few days later a military court began trial proceedings against more than 20 Christian activists who had participated in the anti-Syrian protests; by late August the majority of those arrested for their role in the disturbances had reportedly been released, or tried on more minor charges, although LF members and the two journalists remained in detention. (They were formally indicted in December, and were expected to be committed for military trial; their treatment was strongly criticized by human rights organizations.) Meanwhile, Hariri's political standing appeared to have been weakened by the security forces' actions, which had been undertaken when he was out of the country, as in mid-August the National Assembly approved legislation granting increased powers to President Lahoud. At the end of the month the Prime Minister held talks with the President regarding the consequences of the recent security operation; Hariri pledged to remain in office, despite reports that he was angered by the military's failure to consult him prior to its campaign of arrests. In early September Maronite bishops again issued a strong criticism of Syria's dominance of Lebanese affairs. It was reported at this time that up to seven Syrians had been killed in Lebanon during the past month.

In early September 2001 municipal elections took place in southern Lebanon for the first time since 1963; the region had been under Israeli occupation when the rest of the country elected municipal authorities in 1998.

At the end of June 2001 the UN disclosed that it was in possession of video footage, reportedly filmed by a UNIFIL peace-keeper, apparently containing important evidence regarding the abduction of the three Israeli soldiers by Hezbollah in October 2000. Israeli security forces alleged that UNIFIL had been negligent in not preventing the kidnapping, and were critical of the UN's failure to hand over the video-cassette more promptly. In early August 2001 an internal UN investigation into the incident found several 'lapses in judgment and failures in communication' by UN officials, but rejected claims that these were guilty of conspiracy. Israel launched a further air attack on a Syrian radar station in eastern Lebanon at the beginning of July (wounding up to three Syrian soldiers and a Lebanese conscript), again apparently in response to an assault by Hezbollah against the Israeli military in Shebaa Farms. At the end of July the UN Security Council voted for an extension of UNIFIL's mandate for a further six months; the peace-keeping force was to be reduced in size from 4,500 to 3,600 troops, with the possibility that its status would be downgraded to that of an observer mission (this was implemented before the expiry of the six-month mandate). In early October Hezbollah guerrillas broke what had effectively been a three-month cease-fire by launching an attack against two Israeli military positions in Shebaa Farms, to which Israeli forces responded by shelling a Hezbollah patrol in the area. A similar Israeli response was reported in late October, after Hezbollah attacked five Israeli army positions in the territory. Israel alleged, furthermore, that Hezbollah was directly involved in the Palestinian *intifada*, and was supplying weapons to Palestinians in the West Bank and Gaza. (Hezbollah's leadership initially denied this; however, in early March 2002 Sheikh Nasrallah admitted that two Lebanese militants detained in Jordan had been attempting to smuggle weapons into the West Bank.) In January 2002 Hezbollah again carried out cross-border mortar attacks against military targets in Israel, provoking Israeli air raids across southern Lebanon. In that month the UN Security Council expressed concern regarding recent Israeli violations of Lebanese airspace, and criticized Hezbollah for its frequent interference with the freedom of movement of UNIFIL. The UN again urged the Lebanese Government to deploy its army along the Blue Line. The observer mission's mandate was extended for a further six months from 31 January, and for the same period from the end of July. By the end of 2002 the strength of the force had been reduced to some 2,000 troops. A new UN resolution approved in January 2003 extended UNIFIL's mandate until 31 July.

The September 2001 suicide attacks on New York and Washington, DC, were condemned unequivocally by Lebanon's political and religious leadership. However, there were fears, especially amongst Lebanese Shi'ites, that a possible retaliatory campaign against Islamist groups deemed to be involved in terrorism might target Hezbollah. In mid-October, following the commencement of US-led military action in Afghanistan against the Taliban regime and alleged bases of the al-Qa'ida (Base) organization, the fundamentalist Islamist network held by the USA to be principally responsible for September's atrocities, Muslim clerics in Lebanon issued a ruling in support of the Afghan people and against the use of Lebanese airspace by the campaign forces. Meanwhile, a list of 22 'most wanted' terrorist suspects, published in early October by the US Federal Bureau of Investigation, included three Lebanese men—believed to be members of Hezbollah involved in the 1985 hijacking of a US commercial flight. Lebanese security forces detained two men in Tripoli in mid-October 2001, on charges of plotting terrorist actions against US targets in the Middle East. (In mid-March 2002 a military court sentenced one of the defendants to a three-year prison term, and the other to 18 months' imprisonment, both with hard labour.) Nevertheless, Lebanese officials refuted claims by Jordanian officials to have uncovered a plot by the Lebanese-based Palestinian militant group Asbat al-Ansar to attack foreign embassies in Beirut. In early November 2001 the Lebanese Government resisted US pressure to freeze the assets of Hezbollah, included on a new US list of proscribed 'terrorist' groups, insisting that it regarded Hezbollah as a legitimate organization of resistance against Israeli occupation. Amid an evident rise in anti-US sentiment in Lebanon, as a result of public anger over US foreign policy regarding the Israeli–Palestinian conflict and Iraq, in late November 2002 an American nurse and Christian missionary was killed by an unidentified gunman in Sidon; however, the exact motive for the killing was unknown.

In late January 2002 Elie Hobeika, the former leader of the Christian LF militia, was killed in a car bombing in Beirut; three of his aides and two bystanders also reportedly died in the blast. A previously unknown anti-Syrian group, styled the 'Lebanese for a Free and Independent Lebanon', claimed responsibility for the attack, alleging that Hobeika was a 'Syrian agent'. Israel denied in the strongest terms assertions made by some Lebanese sources that Israeli interests had instigated the killing, since Hobeika had declared his willingness to give evidence to an investigation being carried out by a Belgian court into alleged 'crimes against humanity' by Ariel Sharon, owing to his implication in the massacre of Palestinians in Sabra and Chatila refugee camps in 1982 (see above). Hobeika was the first prominent Lebanese politician to be assassinated since the civil war ended in 1990. (A Belgian appeals court judged the case against Sharon to be inadmissible at the end of June 2002.)

Fears were heightened during early 2002 that rising tensions between Israel and Lebanon might escalate into a 'second front' of Arab–Israeli conflict. In early February Iran denied allegations made by Israeli officials that it was supplying Hezbollah with vast consignments of *Katyusha* rockets, and that it had sent a number of its Revolutionary Guards to Lebanon. Tensions increased significantly in early March when at least six Israelis were killed close to the Lebanese border by three unidentified gunmen, two of whom were shot dead by Israeli security forces. It was unclear as to whether the militants had infiltrated Israeli territory from Lebanon or from the Palestinian West Bank; Hezbollah denied involvement in the shootings. At the end of March Hezbollah initiated cross-border mortar, missile and machine-gun attacks against Israeli military targets in Shebaa Farms, asserting that these were in retaliation for Israeli violations of Lebanese airspace. Israel responded to the escalation of Hezbollah attacks by shelling suspected militant bases in southern Lebanon. In early April, as Hezbollah again intensified its cross-border assaults, there were reports that Israel was mobilizing army reservists to be deployed along its northern border, although Hezbollah's leadership stated that there was no intention, at that time, of extending activities beyond Shebaa Farms. Also in early April Lebanese security forces arrested nine Palestinians on charges of plotting to launch rocket assaults against northern Israel. Meanwhile, the UN condemned Hezbollah for increasing the instability along the Blue Line, and also for an incident in which five members of UNIFIL allegedly came under attack by Hezbollah guerrillas near Shebaa Farms.

In late March 2002 Beirut hosted the annual summit meeting of the Council of the Arab League, at which the principal issue under discussion was a peace initiative for the Middle East proposed by Crown Prince Abdullah of Saudi Arabia. The conference was the largest international event to take place in Lebanon for decades. However, only 10 out of 22 Arab heads of state attended the summit. President Mubarak of Egypt and King Abdullah of Jordan, notably, declined to participate in the discussions, reportedly in order to demonstrate solidarity with the President of the Palestinian (National) Authority (PA), Yasser Arafat, who remained effectively under Israeli blockade in the West Bank. Furthermore, Palestinian delegates were angered by Lebanon's decision to not allow a video-link address by Arafat to proceed (the summit's hosts asserted that the broadcast was liable to be disrupted by Israel). At the conclusion of the summit, Arab leaders unanimously endorsed the Saudi peace initiative. Incorporated in the Beirut Declaration, this required from Israel a complete withdrawal from all Arab territories occupied in June 1967, and what were termed 'territories still occupied in southern Lebanon', a 'just solution' to the issue of Palestinian refugees, and acceptance of the establishment of a sovereign Palestinian state in the West Bank and Gaza Strip with East Jerusalem as its capital; in return, the Arab states undertook to consider the Arab–Israeli conflict at an end, to sign a peace agreement with Israel, and to establish normal relations with Israel within this comprehensive peace framework. The initiative was, however, rejected by Israel, which maintained that it would lead to the destruction of the State of Israel. (At least 19 Israelis had died in a suicide bomb attack perpetrated by a Hamas militant while the summit was in progress.) The US Secretary of State, Colin Powell, visited both Lebanon and Syria in mid-April 2002, as part of a wider mission to the region; the Lebanese leadership maintained its stance that its obligation to respect the Blue Line did not exclude resistance (i.e. by Hezbollah) to 'liberate' Shebaa Farms, while President al-Assad gave no indication that he would exert his influence to halt Hezbollah offensives from southern Lebanon against Israel. At the end of August Hezbollah launched its first significant assault against the Israeli military since April, killing one soldier and wounding two others in Shebaa Farms. The Israeli Government responded by targeting suspected Hezbollah bases in southern Lebanon, and issued a firm warning to Lebanon and Syria that they must take immediate action to end such attacks.

Tensions between Israel and Lebanon were heightened in September 2002, owing to a dispute regarding access to drinking water supplies in Israel's former security zone in southern Lebanon. Israel claimed that a Lebanese project to supply water from a tributary of the Hasbani river to recently repopulated villages close to the border would affect the flow of water to Israel, and issued a direct threat of military action against Lebanon should the authorities there proceed with the project. While the USA sent a team of experts to the region to attempt to negotiate a peaceful solution to the water dispute, in early October the UN issued a report stating that the construction of a new water pumping station in southern Lebanon did not contravene any international agreements. President Lahoud inaugurated the controversial project in mid-October. At the end of January 2003, and again in subsequent months, the Lebanese Government accused Israel of intentionally seeking to raise tensions in the region by ordering low-level military flights within Lebanese airspace.

In early March 2002, meanwhile, President Bashar al-Assad of Syria undertook an historic visit to Beirut for discussions with President Lahoud. This first official visit by a Syrian leader to Beirut since 1947 was welcomed by many Lebanese as a formal recognition by Syria of Lebanese sovereignty. The talks resulted in several agreements regarding closer economic co-operation, including a pledge by Syria to reduce the cost of imported natural gas. It was reported in early April 2002 that Syrian troops were soon to redeploy from central Lebanon to the Beka'a valley, thus fulfilling one of the requirements of the 1989 Ta'if agreement. The redeployment was expected to lead to an improvement in Syrian-Lebanese relations, although hundreds of Syrian intelligence officers were likely to remain in central Lebanon. In mid-February 2003 Syria was reported to have begun the redeployment of some 4,000 troops from northern Lebanon, under the terms of the Ta'if agreement.

In early September 2002 the Lebanese Government closed down a Christian opposition-controlled television station, Murr Television, and its sister radio station, Radio Mount Lebanon, claiming that they had (among other charges) undermined relations with Syria and violated electoral legislation banning party political broadcasts during a recent by-election in the Metn district, where one of the stations' owners, the nephew of interior minister Elias Murr, had won the seat. The ruling against Murr Television was upheld by a higher court at the end of December and a final appeal was rejected in late April 2003, resulting in the station's permanent closure. Meanwhile, in late November 2002 international donors attending a conference in Paris, France, reportedly agreed to provide Lebanon with an aid package worth some US $4,300m. to assist the country with its heavy burden of debt and to finance development projects.

Following weeks of reported disagreements between members of the Cabinet over economic and other domestic policies, the Prime Minister, Rafik Hariri, tendered his resignation and that of his Government in mid-April 2003. However, after his premiership was endorsed by the Lebanese parliament, Hariri was asked by President Lahoud to form a new 30-member Cabinet. Many analysts believed that the government changes were precipitated by Syria's desire to strengthen its position in Lebanon and the wider Middle East region as its relations with the US Administration under President George W. Bush deteriorated sharply at this time (see the chapter on Syria). The new Lebanese Government, announced two days after Hariri's resignation, brought in 11 new ministers, including Jean Obeid, who replaced Mahmoud Hammoud as Minister of Foreign Affairs and Emigrants. Hammoud was named as the new Minister of Defence. The new Cabinet was widely considered to be the most pro-Syrian for more than a decade; it contained no members of the Christian opposition, nor of Hezbollah (who were said to have been willing to join the new administration).

Meanwhile, in January 1999 the Lebanese authorities agreed to upgrade the status of travel documents issued to Palestinians residing in Lebanon to allow them to be treated as holders of Lebanese passports. However, in the months prior to the resumption of 'final status' talks between Israeli and Palestinian negotiators in late 1999, the issue of Palestinian refugees in Lebanon assumed particular importance. (According to the UN Relief and Works Agency for Palestine Refugees in the Near East, in December 2002 389,233 Palestinian refugees were registered in Lebanon.) The Lebanese Government had been angered by an announcement made by Ehud Barak in July 1999 that the refugees would under no circumstances be permitted to return to Israel, and that 'a solution should be found in the countries where they are now living'. President Lahoud responded by demanding that any permanent peace agreement should guarantee the right of Palestinians to return home; he subsequently initiated legislation to prevent Palestinian refugees in Lebanon from being granted Lebanese citizenship.

The head of the PFLP—GC's military operations and son of the group's leader, Jihad Jibril, was killed by a car bomb in west Beirut in late May 2002. The Lebanese security forces blamed inter-Palestinian rivalries for the assassination, although many PFLP—GC officials held the Israeli intelligence services responsible. In August two people were killed and six others injured in the worst factional fighting at the Ain al-Hilweh Palestinian refugee camp for several years. Tensions escalated following the arrest of an Islamist militant the previous month (accused of killing three Lebanese army intelligence officers) by the Lebanese army, aided by Fatah. (In early September the Israeli daily, *Ha'aretz*, alleged that the violence at Ain al-Hilweh was linked to the presence there of up to 200 al-Qa'ida militants who had returned from the war in Afghanistan.) Clashes between the Lebanese army and Palestinian militants occurred at the normally relatively calm al-Jalil refugee camp, near Ba'albak (Ba'albek), in September, which left one soldier and three Palestinians dead, and at least 11 others wounded. Lebanese soldiers had entered the camp in search of a wanted man and removed a cache of armaments from offices of the Fatah Revolutionary Council, an organization founded by the militant leader Abu Nidal, who was found dead in Baghdad, Iraq, in August. There were reports in early October that three alleged members of al-Qa'ida (two Lebanese and a Saudi Arabian) had been detained by the Lebanese authorities, on suspicion of seeking to establish a base of the militant network in Lebanon.

Government

Under the 1926 Constitution (as subsequently amended), legislative power is held by the National Assembly (called the Chamber of Deputies until March 1979), with 128 members elected by universal adult suffrage for four years (subject to dissolution), on the basis of proportional representation. Seats are allocated on a religious basis (divided equally between Christians and Muslims). The President of the Republic is elected for six years by the National Assembly. The President, in consultation with deputies and the President of the National Assembly, appoints the Prime Minister and other ministers to form the Cabinet, in which executive power is vested.

Defence

In August 2002 the Lebanese armed forces numbered 71,830 (army 70,000, air force 1,000, navy 830). Paramilitary forces included an estimated 13,000 members of the Internal Security Force. Hezbollah's active members numbered some 2,000 in August 2002. At that time there were also an estimated 18,000 Syrian troops in Lebanon. Israeli armed forces and the Israeli-backed South Lebanon Army (SLA) withdrew from Lebanon in May 2000. Government expenditure on defence was budgeted at £L812,000m. in 2002.

The UN Interim Force in Lebanon (UNIFIL, see p. 63) observer mission numbered 1,998 troops at the end of March 2003, assisted by about 50 military observers of the UN Truce Supervision Organization (UNTSO).

Economic Affairs

In 2001, according to estimates by the World Bank, Lebanon's gross national income (GNI), measured at average 1999–2001 prices, was US $17,585m., equivalent to $4,010 per head (or $4,640 per head on an international purchasing-power parity basis). During 1990–2001, it was estimated, the population increased at an average annual rate of 1.7%, while gross domestic product (GDP) per head increased, in real terms, by an average of 4.8% per year. Overall GDP increased, in real terms, at an average annual rate of 6.6% in 1990–2001; although zero growth was registered in 2000, GDP growth of some 1.3% was recorded in 2001. According to the Ministry of Finance, GDP increased by 2% in 2002.

Agriculture (including hunting, forestry and fishing) contributed an estimated 11.8% of GDP in 2000. According to FAO data, some 3.5% of the labour force were employed in the sector in 2001. The principal crops are citrus fruits, tomatoes, potatoes and grapes. Viticulture is also significant. Hashish is a notable, albeit illegal, export crop, although the Government is attempting to persuade growers to switch to other crops. The GDP of the agricultural sector was estimated to have increased by an average of 2.2% annually in 1994–2000, although agricultural GDP declined by an estimated 1.2% in 1998 and by 0.7% in

1999. According to FAO data, agricultural production increased by 7.6% in 2000, but declined by 3.9% in 2001.

The industrial sector (including manufacturing, construction and power) contributed an estimated 20.8% of GDP in 2000. Some 25.9% of the labour force were employed in industry in 1997. Lebanon's only mineral resources consist of small reserves of lignite and iron ore, and their contribution to GDP is insignificant. The GDP of the industrial sector decreased by an estimated average of 1.2% per year in 1994–2000; however, industrial GDP grew by an estimated 3.7% in 1998 and by 1.4% in 1999.

Manufacturing contributed an estimated 10.3% of GDP in 2000. The sector employed about 10% of the labour force in 1985. The most important branches have traditionally been food-processing, petroleum refining, textiles and furniture and wood-working. Manufacturing GDP was estimated to have decreased at an average annual rate of 6.5% in 1994–2000; however, the sector's GDP declined by an estimated 0.9% in 1998 and by 0.7% in 1999.

Energy is derived principally from thermal power stations, using imported petroleum (which accounted for 95.9% of total electricity production in 1999). However, in order to meet Lebanon's growing energy requirements, plans for the construction of an offshore pipeline—capable of importing 6m.–9m. cu m of natural gas per day from Syria—were in progress in 2002, with an anticipated completion date of 2003. A second pipeline was planned that would enable Lebanon to import an estimated 9m. cu m of natural gas per day from Egypt and 3m. cu m per day from Syria in 2002–05.

The services sector contributed an estimated 67.4% of GDP in 2000. In 1997 some 65.1% of the working population were employed in the sector, which has traditionally been dominated by trade and finance. Financial services, in particular, withstood many of the disruptions inflicted on the economy by the civil conflict, although the Beirut Stock Exchange did not recommence trading until 1996. Lebanon is also becoming increasingly important as a centre for telecommunications. Recent efforts to revive the tourist industry have met with considerable success, and have been a major source of growth in the construction industry. Tourist arrivals increased by 31.5% in 1997, by 13.1% in 1998, by 6.7% in 1999 and by 10.1% in 2000 (despite the regional impact of the Israeli–Palestinian crisis, which has partly undermined the revival of Lebanon's tourist industry). Numbers of tourist arrivals from Gulf and other Arab states were reported to be increasing in 2001 and 2002. The GDP of the services sector increased at an average annual rate of some 3.7% in 1994–2000; the sector's GDP was estimated to have increased by 5.9% in 1998 and by 2.0% in 1999.

In 2000 Lebanon recorded a trade deficit of US $5,510m., while there was a deficit of $5,630m. on the current account of the balance of payments. The principal markets for exports in 2001 were Saudi Arabia (which took 9.6% of Lebanese exports in that year) and the United Arab Emirates (8.2%); other significant purchasers included Iraq and Switzerland. The principal suppliers of imports in 2001 was Italy (9.7%); Germany, France and the USA were also important suppliers. The principal exports in 2001 were food products, jewellery, machinery and electrical equipment, and chemical products. The principal imports in that year were mineral products, food products, machinery and electrical equipment, and vehicles.

In 2000 Lebanon recorded an overall budget deficit of £L5,872,030m. Budget forecasts for 2002 projected a deficit of £L3,875,000m., equivalent to 41.3% of budgeted expenditure. At the end of 2000 Lebanon's total external debt was US $10,311m., of which $7,034m. was long-term public debt. The annual rate of inflation averaged 23.9% in 1990–97. However, this reflected high rates of inflation in the aftermath of the civil war; consumer prices decreased by an average of 0.9% in 2000, but increased by 1.3% in 2001. In 1997, according to official figures, 8.5% of the labour force were unemployed (representing a significant decline from a level of 35% in 1990), although youth unemployment was reported to be much higher.

Lebanon is a member of the Arab Fund for Economic and Social Development (see p. 136), the Arab Monetary Fund (see p. 138) and the Islamic Development Bank (see p. 257). A customs union with Syria entered into effect in January 1999, and in 2002 the creation of a free-trade zone was under discussion. Lebanon is also involved in efforts to finalize establishment of a Greater Arab Free Trade Area. A Euro-Mediterranean Association Agreement was signed with the European Union (EU, see p. 199) in June 2002.

By the end of the 1990s the Lebanese Government had achieved considerable success in rehabilitating and expanding basic infrastructure, as envisaged under the first phase of its Horizon 2000 investment programme, which covers the period 1995–2007. The second phase was to focus on development of social infrastructure, with investment of US $5,000m. envisaged on education, health and sanitation projects in 1998–2002. The reconstruction process was undertaken with the support of the international donor community, which in late 1996 pledged grants and concessionary loans totalling some $3,200m. However, GDP growth since 1996 has been considerably lower than the targeted annual average of 8% under Horizon 2000. The principal factors inhibiting growth have been identified as the failure to control both the budget deficit and the accumulated public debt (equivalent to 170%–180% of GDP by early 2003). In early 1999 the World Bank agreed to disburse some $600m. in concessionary loans over a three-year period, and in April 2000 the EU granted its first aid programme to Lebanon (worth around $47.9m.). However, in 1999 the Lebanese economy was in recession, owing to the decline in domestic demand and inadequate levels of job creation; no overall growth was recorded in 2000. The withdrawal of Israeli troops from southern Lebanon in May 2000 brought about an acceleration of the country's economic reconstruction, despite the high costs involved in rehabilitation projects for the south. The return of Rafik Hariri to the Lebanese premiership in October afforded further optimism, particularly in the construction sector. The new Government pledged to stimulate growth by reducing taxation and import duties, by encouraging the privatization of state-owned enterprises, and by controlling public expenditure in order to reduce the state debt. Liberalization of trade, both regionally and through association with the EU, was also identified as a priority. In April 2001 the National Assembly amended banking secrecy legislation in an effort to eliminate money-laundering. In October the IMF recommended a devaluation of the Lebanese pound as a means of easing the Government's fiscal crisis. A value-added tax of 10% was introduced in February 2002. The draft budget for 2003 projected a reduced budget deficit, an improvement in debt management and the generation of some $5,000m. in state revenues from the sale of 40% of Electricité du Liban, as well as from privatization of state-owned telecommunications and transport companies. The Lebanese economy was expected to suffer from the effects of the temporary loss of trade with Iraq, as a result of the conflict there during early 2003 (see the chapter on Iraq), and there were signs that tourism in Lebanon was likely to be seriously affected. Meanwhile, in early 2001 international donors apparently agreed to provide the Lebanese authorities with $458m., in order to assist the economic reform programme. An aid package totalling an estimated $4,300m. was agreed by international donors in late November 2002, in order to provide further assistance with Lebanon's debt restructuring and to finance development projects. Such funding, in addition to the willingness of the Lebanese to tolerate economic austerity, as well as eventual progress towards a Middle East peace settlement, will be essential to the restoration of international competitiveness and enhanced investment.

Education

There are state-controlled primary and secondary schools, but private institutions provide the main facilities for secondary and higher education. Education is not compulsory, but state education is provided free of charge. Primary education begins at six years of age and lasts for five years. Secondary education, beginning at the age of 11, lasts for a further seven years, comprising a first cycle of four years and a second of three years. In 1996 the total enrolment at primary and secondary schools was equivalent to 94% of all school-age children (93% of boys; 95% of girls); enrolment at secondary schools in that year was equivalent to 81% of the appropriate age-group (males 78%; females 84%). Some 87,957 Lebanese students were enrolled at the country's seven universities in the 1996/97 academic year. In 1998 Lebanon secured a loan of US $60m. from the World Bank, in order to restructure the country's system of technical and vocational education. Lebanon has the highest literacy rate in the Arab world. Expenditure on education by the central Government in 1999 was some £L645,000m. (7.2% of total budgetary expenditure).

Public Holidays

2003: 1 January (New Year's Day), 9 February (Feast of St Maron), 12 February* (Id al-Adha, Feast of the Sacrifice), 5 March* (Muharram, Islamic New Year), 14 March* (Ashoura), 22 March (Arab League Anniversary), 21 April (Easter, Western Church), 25–28 April (Greek Orthodox Easter), 14 May* (Mouloud/Yum an-Nabi, birth of Muhammad), 29 May (Ascension Day, Western Church), 15 August (Assumption), 24 September* (Leilat al-Meiraj, ascension of Muhammad), 1 November (All Saints' Day), 22 November (Independence Day), 26 November* (Id al-Fitr, end of Ramadan), 25 December (Christmas Day).

2004: 1 January (New Year's Day), 2 February* (Id al-Adha, Feast of the Sacrifice), 9 February (Feast of St Maron), 22 February* (Muharram, Islamic New Year), 2 March* (Ashoura), 22 March (Arab League Anniversary), 9–12 April (Greek Orthodox Easter), 12 April (Easter, Western Church), 2 May* (Mouloud/Yum an-Nabi, birth of Muhammad), 20 May (Ascension Day, Western Church), 15 August (Assumption), 12 September* (Leilat al-Meiraj, ascension of Muhammad), 1 November (All Saints' Day), 14 November* (Id al-Fitr, end of Ramadan), 22 November (Independence Day), 25 December (Christmas Day).

*These holidays are determined by the Islamic lunar calendar and may vary by one or two days from the dates given.

Weights and Measures

The metric system is in force.

Statistical Survey

Source (unless otherwise stated): Central Administration for Statistics, Beirut; internet www.cas.gov.lb; Direction Générale des Douanes, Beirut.

Area and Population

AREA, POPULATION AND DENSITY

Area (sq km)	10,452*
Population (official estimate)	
15 November 1970†	
Males	1,080,015
Females.	1,046,310
Total	2,126,325
Population (UN estimates at mid-year)‡	
1999	3,438,000
2000	3,496,000
2001	3,556,000
Density (per sq km) at mid-2001	340.2

* 4,036 sq miles.

† Figures are based on the results of a sample survey, excluding Palestinian refugees in camps. The total of registered Palestinian refugees in Lebanon was 384,918 at 31 December 2001.

‡ Source: UN, *World Population Prospects: The 2000 Revision.*

PRINCIPAL TOWNS
(population in 1998)*

Beirut (capital) . .	1,100,000	Jounieh	75,000
Tarabulus (Tripoli) .	200,000	Zahleh.	72,000
Saida (Sidon). . .	140,000	Baabda	55,000
Sur (Tyre). . . .	110,000	Ba'albak (Ba'albek) .	28,000
An-Nabatiyah at-			
Tahta (Nabatiyah)	84,000	Alayh	25,100

* Figures are rounded.

Source: Stefan Helders, *World Gazetteer* (internet www.world-gazetteer.com).

BIRTHS AND DEATHS
(UN estimates, annual averages)

	1985–90	1990–95	1995–2000
Birth rate (per 1,000)	27.9	25.6	20.3
Death rate (per 1,000)	7.8	6.8	5.4

Source: UN, *World Population Prospects: The 2000 Revision*.

2001 (official estimates, numbers registered): Live births 83,693; Marriages 32,225; Deaths 17,568.

2002 (official estimates, numbers registered): Live births 76,405; Marriages 31,653; Deaths 17,294.

Expectation of life (WHO estimates, years at birth): 69.8 (males 67.6; females 72.0) in 2001 (Source: WHO, *World Health Report*).

EMPLOYMENT
(ISIC major divisions)

	1975	1985*
Agriculture, hunting, forestry and fishing . .	147,724	103,400
Manufacturing	139,471	45,000
Electricity, gas and water	6,381	10,000
Construction	47,356	25,000
Trade, restaurants and hotels	129,716	78,000
Transport, storage and communications . .	45,529	20,500
Other services	227,921	171,000
Total	744,098	452,900

* Estimates.

1997 (provisional estimates at mid-year): Total employed 1,246,000; Unemployed 116,000; Total labour force 1,362,000.

Source: National Employment Office.

Health and Welfare

KEY INDICATORS

Total fertility rate (children per woman, 2001)	2.2
Under-5 mortality rate (per 1,000 live births, 2001) . . .	32
HIV/AIDS (% of persons aged 15–49, 1994)	0.09
Physicians (per 1,000 head, 1997)	2.10
Hospital beds (per 1,000 head, 1997)	2.7
Health expenditure (2000): US $ per head (PPP)	696
Health expenditure (2000): % of GDP	11.8
Health expenditure (2000): public (% of total)	27.8
Access to water (% of persons, 2000)	100
Access to sanitation (% of persons, 2000)	99
Human Development Index (2000): ranking	75
Human Development Index (2000): value	0.755

For sources and definitions, see explanatory note on p. vi.

Agriculture

PRINCIPAL CROPS
('000 metric tons, FAO estimates)

	1999*	2000	2001
Wheat *	58	60	61
Barley *	28	29	30
Potatoes *	250	260	260
Sugar beet	310	342†	15†
Almonds *	31	32	33
Olives	95	190	86†
Cabbages *	75	83	84
Lettuce*	75	82	83
Tomatoes *	325	335	336
Cauliflower *	40	42	43
Pumpkins, squash and gourds* . .	39	39	40
Cucumbers and gherkins* . . .	180	190	195
Aubergines (Eggplants)* . . .	39	45	46
Dry onions *	80	85	85
Garlic *	45	49	50
Green beans *	36	37	38
Green broad beans *	22	23	23
Carrots *	35	40	41
Other vegetables*	103	105	107
Bananas *	105	110	115
Oranges *	155	185	190
Tangerines, mandarins, clementines and satsumas * . .	35	35	36
Lemons and limes *	111	111	112
Grapefruit and pomelo * . . .	54	58	59
Apples *	118	120	122
Pears *	63	65	68
Apricots *	62	65	66
Cherries*	87	88	89
Peaches and nectarines * . . .	50	52	53
Plums *	35	41	42
Grapes *	245	248	250
Watermelons *	130	135	135
Cantaloupes and other melons* .	35	36	37
Other fruits and berries* . . .	159	161	163

* FAO estimates.
† Unofficial figure.

Source: FAO.

LIVESTOCK
('000 head, year ending September)

	1999	2000*	2001*
Horses*	6	6	6
Mules*	6	6	6
Asses*	25	25	25
Cattle	76	76	76
Pigs	62*	64	64
Sheep	378	380	385
Goats	436	445	450
Poultry	31,000*	32,000	32,500

* FAO estimate(s).

Source: FAO.

LIVESTOCK PRODUCTS
('000 metric tons, FAO estimates)

	1999	2000	2001
Beef and veal .	29.7	27.7	27.7
Mutton and lamb.	5.9	4.7	4.7
Goat meat .	3.2	3.2	3.2
Pig meat .	8.5	8.7	8.8
Poultry meat .	93.0	96.0	97.5
Cows' milk .	201	205	205
Sheep's milk .	33.8	34.0	35.0
Goats' milk .	37.5	39.0	39.0
Cheese .	21.1	21.5	21.5
Hen eggs .	42	43	45
Honey .	1	1	1
Cattle hides .	4.0	4.0	4.0
Sheepskins .	0.8	0.6	0.6
Goatskins .	0.5	0.5	0.5
Wool: greasy .	1.6	1.7	1.7
Wool: scoured .	0.8	0.8	0.9

Source: FAO.

Forestry

ROUNDWOOD REMOVALS
('000 cubic metres, excluding bark)

	1999	2000	2001
Industrial wood* .	7	7	7
Fuel wood .	18	19	82†
Total .	25	26	89†

* Assumed unchanged since 1992 (FAO estimates).
† FAO estimate.
Source: FAO.

SAWNWOOD PRODUCTION
('000 cubic metres, including railway sleepers)

	1999	2000	2001
Total (all broadleaved)* .	9	9	9

* Assumed to be unchanged since 1991 (FAO estimates).
Source: FAO.

Fishing

(metric tons, live weight)

	1998	1999	2000
Capture .	3,520	3,560	3,666
Groupers and seabasses .	250	250	230
Porgies and seabreams .	400	450	450
Surmullets (Red mullets) .	200	200	250
Barracudas .	200	200	200
Mullets .	300	300	—
Scorpionfishes .	100	150	150
Carangids .	400	350	450
Clupeoids .	600	500	700
Tuna-like fishes .	400	400	500
Mackerel-like fishes .	300	300	350
Marine crustaceans .	50	125	55
Aquaculture .	400	300	400
Rainbow trout .	400	300	400
Total catch .	3,920	3,860	4,066

Source: FAO, *Yearbook of Fishery Statistics*.

Mining

(estimates, '000 metric tons)

	1999	2000	2001
Salt (unrefined) .	3.5	3.5	3.5

Source: US Geological Survey.

Industry

SELECTED PRODUCTS
('000 metric tons, unless otherwise indicated)

	1999	2000	2001
Olive oil*† .	6.3	5.3	5.8
Sunflower seed oil*‡ .	6.5	1.5	2.0
Raw sugar* .	40†	34.2†	1.9‡
Wine*‡ .	18.0	18.8	19.5
Beer*‡ .	10.9	12.1	17.6
Plywood ('000 cubic metres)*‡ .	34	34	34
Paper*‡ .	42	42	42
Cement§ .	2,714	2,808	2,700

* Source: FAO.
† Unofficial figure.
‡ FAO estimate(s).
§ Source: US Geological Survey.

Electric energy (provisional, million kWh): 7,467 in 2000.

Finance

CURRENCY AND EXCHANGE RATES

Monetary Units
100 piastres = 1 Lebanese pound (£L)

Sterling, Dollar and Euro Equivalents (31 December 2002)
£1 sterling = £L2,429.8
US $1 = £L1,507.5
€1 = £L1,580.9
£L10,000 = £4.116 sterling = $6.634 = €6.325

Exchange Rate: The official exchange rate has been maintained at US $1 = £L1,507.5 since September 1999.

BUDGET
(£L '000 million)*

Revenue†	1997	1998	1999
Tax revenue .	2,894	3,303	3,507‡
Taxes on income, profits and capital gains .	340	404	531
Taxes on property .	377	377	426
Domestic taxes on goods and services .	245	372	971‡
Excises .	25	170	788‡
Import duties .	1,741	1,944	1,366‡
Other current revenue .	860	1,146	1,362
Entrepreneurial and property income .	266	486	691
Administrative fees and charges, non-industrial and incidental sales .	295	375	436
Total .	3,753	4,449	4,868‡

Expenditure	1997	1998	1999
General public services	1,222	1,116	1,046
Defence	824	810	948
Public order and safety	320	318	343
Education	723	696	645
Health	222	221	180
Social security and welfare . . .	752	536	463
Housing and community amenities	154	174	119
Recreational, cultural and religious			
affairs and services	68	66	59
Economic affairs and services . .	1,332	1,036	1,413
Fuel and energy	155	9	161
Mining and mineral resources,			
manufacturing and			
construction	502	482	466
Transport and communications	340	296	192
Other purposes	4,398	3,607	4,274
Interest payments	3,482	3,352	3,624
Total	9,728	8,385	8,910
Current	7,761	6,845	7,357
Capital	1,967	1,540	1,553

* Figures, which are rounded, represent the consolidated operations of the central Government's General Budget and the Council for Development and Reconstruction. The accounts of other central government units with individual budgets (including the general social security scheme) are excluded.

† Excluding grants received from abroad (£L million): 72,000 in 1997.

‡ Prior to 1999, excise taxes levies on imported products are included with other import duties.

Source: IMF, *Government Finance Statistics Yearbook.*

2000 (£L million): Revenue 4,552,420; Expenditure 10,424,460 (Source: Ministry of Finance).

2001 (estimates, £L million): Revenue 4,900,000; Expenditure 9,900,000 (Source: Ministry of Finance).

2002 (estimates, £L million): Revenue 5,500,000; Expenditure 9,375,000 (Source: Ministry of Finance).

INTERNATIONAL RESERVES
(US $ million at 31 December)

	2000	2001	2002
Gold*	2,524.6	2,561.1	3,216.3
IMF special drawing rights . . .	23.7	24.3	27.3
Reserve position in IMF . .	24.5	23.7	25.6
Foreign exchange	5,895.4	4,965.8	7,190.9
Total	8,468.3	7,574.9	10,460.1

* Valued at US $290.40 per troy ounce in 1999, at $273.75 per ounce in 2000 and at $277.70 per ounce in 2001.

Source: IMF, *International Financial Statistics.*

MONEY SUPPLY
(£L '000 million at 31 December)

	1999	2000	2001
Currency outside banks . .	1,369.3	1,423.4	1,381.7
Demand deposits at commercial			
banks	845.8	862.2	889.6
Total money (incl. others) . .	2,260.8	2,389.3	2,365.3

Source: IMF, *International Financial Statistics.*

COST OF LIVING
(Consumer Price Index for Beirut; base: December 1998 = 100)

	1999	2000	2001
Food and beverages	96.4	93.7	94.5
Water, electricity and gas . . .	105.7	105.5	104.9
Clothing and footwear	104.8	104.7	108.4
Transport and communications .	107.8	109.9	111.6
All items (incl. others)	100.7	99.8	101.1

NATIONAL ACCOUNTS
(UN estimates, £L '000 million at current prices)

Expenditure on the Gross Domestic Product

	1997	1998	1999
Government final consumption			
expenditure	2,544.7	2,594.3	2,581.3
Private final consumption			
expenditure	24,240.3	25,086.3	25,389.8
Increase in stocks . . . . . ⎫			
Gross fixed capital formation . ⎭	6,011.2	5,996.1	5,756.1
Total domestic expenditure .	32,796.1	33,676.7	33,727.3
Exports of goods and services .	1,632.3	1,829.5	1,993.4
Less Imports of goods and			
services	11,548.0	10,996.8	10,598.5
GDP in purchasers' values .	22,880.4	24,509.5	25,122.2
GDP at constant 1995 prices	19,230.3	19,807.2	20,005.2

Source: UN Economic and Social Commission for Western Asia, *National Accounts Studies of the ESCWA Region* (2000).

Gross Domestic Product by Economic Activity

	1997	1998	1999
Agriculture, hunting, forestry and			
fishing	2,522.8	2,601.5	2,612.9
Manufacturing	2,372.9	2,441.0	2,459.5
Electricity, gas and water . . .	1,393.1	1,487.2	1,510.7
Construction	1,248.1	1,069.9	1,040.6
Trade, restaurants and hotels . .	6,528.4	6,757.4	6,679.1
Transport, storage and			
communications	518.5	569.9	565.0
Finance, insurance, real estate and			
business services	4,323.3	5,360.7	5,972.9
Government services	2,000.9	2,063.9	2,106.5
Other community, social and			
personal services	1,972.5	2,158.1	2,175.0
GDP in purchasers' values . .	22,880.4	24,509.5	25,122.2

Source: UN Economic and Social Commission for Western Asia, *National Accounts Studies of the ESCWA Region* (2000).

2000 (estimates, % of GDP): Agriculture 11.8, Industry 20.8, Services 67.4 (Source: World Bank).

BALANCE OF PAYMENTS
(US $ million)

	1998	1999	2000
Exports of goods f.o.b.	716	678	718
Imports of goods c.i.f.	−7,060	−6,206	−6,228
Trade balance	−6,344	−5,528	−5,510
Services, income and current			
transfers (net)	481	−98	−120
Current balance	−5,863	−5,626	−5,630
Capital account (net)	5,375	5,887	5,341
Overall balance	−487	261	−289

Source: Ministry of Economy and Trade.

External Trade

PRINCIPAL COMMODITIES
(US $ million)*

Imports c.i.f.	1999	2000	2001
Live animals and animal products	349.8	336.1	359.4
Vegetable products	355.5	328.7	361.9
Prepared foodstuffs; beverages, spirits and vinegar; tobacco and manufactured substitutes	463.6	415.3	502.7
Mineral products	613.4	1,095.6	1,340.6
Products of chemical or allied industries	574.8	525.5	595.4
Plastics, rubber and articles thereof	230.6	222.0	257.8
Textiles and textile articles	386.2	352.0	464.7
Natural or cultured pearls, precious or semi-precious stones, precious metals and articles thereof; imitation jewellery; coin	461.7	423.3	363.9
Base metals and articles thereof	407.3	382.1	426.7
Machinery and mechanical appliances; electrical equipment; sound and television apparatus	910.2	800.4	999.0
Vehicles, aircraft, vessels and associated transport equipment	615.2	555.3	712.6
Total (incl. others)	6,206.5	6,227.9	7,291.1

Exports f.o.b.	1999	2000	2001
Vegetable products	52.3	48.5	49.8
Prepared foodstuffs; beverages, spirits and vinegar; tobacco and manufactured substitutes	74.0	72.5	99.7
Products of chemical or allied industries	84.9	88.4	88.1
Paper-making material; paper and paperboard and articles thereof	54.4	53.5	60.2
Textiles and textile articles	54.6	41.5	77.0
Natural or cultured pearls, precious or semi-precious stones, precious metals and articles thereof; imitation jewellery; coin	95.6	126.8	140.9
Base metals and articles thereof	78.6	63.1	65.2
Machinery and mechanical appliances; electrical equipment; sound and television apparatus	72.8	74.8	114.4
Total (incl. others)	676.8	714.3	889.3

* Figures are calculated on the basis of the official dollar rate, which is the previous month's average exchange rate of Lebanese pounds per US dollar.

Source: Ministry of Economy and Trade; Banque du Liban.

PRINCIPAL TRADING PARTNERS
(US $ million)*

Imports c.i.f.	1999	2000	2001
Belgium	116.4	108.0	135.3
China, People's Republic	261.5	287.1	410.9
France	594.8	526.5	614.9
Germany	552.7	519.6	623.1
Greece	111.7	157.2	142.1
Ireland	89.9	n.a.	n.a.
Italy	679.0	679.9	708.4
Japan	259.0	210.9	235.4
Korea, Republic	n.a.	74.7	100.7
Netherlands	114.3	124.6	129.2
Russia	n.a.	215.2	409.3
Saudi Arabia	102.6	164.9	259.5
Spain	147.7	136.3	184.4
Switzerland	443.0	431.5	333.7
Syria	223.5	283.3	327.9
Taiwan	82.6	69.9	77.4
Turkey	163.9	138.5	237.2
Ukraine	108.9	88.4	125.8
United Kingdom	271.7	243.4	284.7
USA	500.9	457.4	515.0
Total (incl. others)	6,203.9	6,227.9	7,291.1

Exports f.o.b.	1999	2000	2001
Belgium	10.9	n.a.	n.a.
Cyprus	7.4	n.a.	n.a.
Egypt	15.3	22.4	23.9
France	52.1	30.1	38.2
Germany	24.5	17.7	17.2
India	14.7	13.9	14.2
Iraq	21.8	33.4	68.0
Italy	19.0	22.0	26.2
Jordan	27.0	31.2	30.7
Kuwait	30.4	26.3	27.8
Malta	6.8	11.0	20.3
Netherlands	15.3	13.6	15.7
Saudi Arabia	70.9	77.7	85.4
Spain	12.2	18.6	18.2
Switzerland	44.6	51.0	63.2
Syria	32.3	25.8	35.2
Turkey	14.4	23.2	24.8
United Arab Emirates	53.9	74.9	72.9
United Kingdom	24.3	11.0	14.3
USA	42.0	46.4	60.8
Total (incl. others)	676.8	714.2	889.3

* Imports by country of production; exports by country of last consignment.

Source: mainly Banque du Liban.

Transport

ROAD TRAFFIC
(motor vehicles in use)

	1995	1996*	1997*
Passenger cars (incl. taxis)	1,197,521	1,217,000	1,299,398
Buses and coaches	5,514	5,640	6,833
Lorries and vans	79,222	81,000	85,242
Motorcycles and mopeds	53,317	54,450	61,471

* Estimates.

Source: International Road Federation, *World Road Statistics*.

SHIPPING

Merchant Fleet
(registered at 31 December)

	1999	2000	2001
Number of vessels	106	105	99
Total displacement ('000 grt)	322.2	362.7	301.7

Source: Lloyd's Register-Fairplay, *World Fleet Statistics*.

International Sea-borne Freight Traffic
('000 metric tons)

	1988	1989	1990
Goods loaded	148	150	152
Goods unloaded	1,120	1,140	1,150

Source: UN, *Monthly Bulletin of Statistics*.

2001 ('000 metric tons, Beirut port only): Goods loaded 330; Goods unloaded 5,134.

CIVIL AVIATION
(revenue traffic on scheduled services)

	1997	1998	1999
Kilometres flown (million)	21	20	20
Passengers carried ('000)	857	716	719
Passenger-km (million)	2,116	1,504	1,288
Total ton-km (million)	319	247	222

Source: UN, *Statistical Yearbook*.

Tourism

FOREIGN TOURIST ARRIVALS

('000)*

Country of nationality	1998	1999	2000
Australia	24.3	27.6	30.6
Canada	22.3	28.1	30.2
Egypt	39.2	34.4	35.7
France	58.5	67.0	64.8
Germany	27.1	30.0	35.4
Iran	6.0	14.0	23.2
Italy	14.7	15.8	14.7
Jordan	53.6	61.0	69.6
Kuwait	40.2	41.1	47.6
Saudi Arabia	71.1	82.6	98.3
Sri Lanka	16.6	10.3	16.5
United Kingdom	22.0	22.3	24.3
USA	31.4	40.4	43.3
Total (incl. others)	630.8	673.3	741.6

* Figures exclude arrivals of Syrian nationals, Palestinians and students.

Source: World Tourism Organization, *Yearbook of Tourism Statistics*.

Tourism receipts (US $ million): 1,221 in 1998; 673 in 1999; 742 in 2000 (Source: World Tourism Organization).

Communications Media

	1998	1999	2000
Television receivers ('000 in use)	1,120	1,150	1,170
Telephones ('000 main lines in use)	620.0	650.0	681.5
Mobile cellular telephones ('000 subscribers)	505.3	627.0	743.0
Personal computers ('000 in use)	125	150	175
Internet users ('000)	100	200	300

Personal computers ('000 in use): 200 in 2001.

Radio receivers ('000 in use): 2,850 in 1997.

Facsimile machines (number in use): 3,000 in 1992.

Daily newspapers (1996): 15 titles; average circulation (estimate, '000 copies) 435.

Non-daily newspapers (estimates, 1988): 15 titles; average circulation 240,000 copies.

Sources: UNESCO, *Statistical Yearbook*; UN, *Statistical Yearbook* and International Telecommunication Union.

Education

(1996/97, unless otherwise indicated)

	Institutions	Teachers	Students
Pre-primary	1,938		164,397*
Primary	2,160	67,935	382,309*
Secondary:			
general	n.a.		292,002*
vocational	275†	7,745	55,848*
Higher	n.a.	10,444‡	81,588‡

* Estimate.
† 1994 figure.
‡ 1995/96 figure.

Sources: UNESCO, *Statistical Yearbook*; Banque du Liban, *Annual Report*.

Adult literacy rate (UNESCO estimates): 86.0% (males 92.1%; females 80.3%) in 2000 (Source: UNDP, *Human Development Report*).

Directory

The Constitution

The Constitution was promulgated on 23 May 1926 and amended by the Constitutional Laws of 1927, 1929, 1943, 1947 and 1990.

According to the Constitution, the Republic of Lebanon is an independent and sovereign state, and no part of the territory may be alienated or ceded. Lebanon has no state religion. Arabic is the official language. Beirut is the capital.

All Lebanese are equal in the eyes of the law. Personal freedom and freedom of the press are guaranteed and protected. The religious communities are entitled to maintain their own schools, on condition that they conform to the general requirements relating to public instruction, as defined by the state. Dwellings are inviolable; rights of ownership are protected by law. Every Lebanese citizen over 21 is an elector and qualifies for the franchise.

LEGISLATIVE POWER

Legislative power is exercised by one house, the National Assembly, with 108 seats (raised, without amendment of the Constitution, to 128 in 1992), which are divided equally between Christians and Muslims. Members of the National Assembly must be over 25 years of age, in possession of their full political and civil rights, and literate. They are considered representative of the whole nation, and are not bound to follow directives from their constituencies. They can be suspended only by a two-thirds majority of their fellow-members. Secret ballot was introduced in a new election law of April 1960.

The National Assembly holds two sessions yearly, from the first Tuesday after 15 March to the end of May, and from the first Tuesday after 15 October to the end of the year. The normal term of the National Assembly is four years; general elections take place within 60 days before the end of this period. If the Assembly is dissolved before the end of its term, elections are held within three months of dissolution.

Voting in the Assembly is public—by acclamation, or by standing and sitting. A quorum of two-thirds and a majority vote is required for constitutional issues. The only exceptions to this occur when the Assembly becomes an electoral college, and chooses the President of the Republic, or Secretaries to the National Assembly, or when the President is accused of treason or of violating the Constitution. In such cases voting is secret, and a two-thirds majority is needed for a proposal to be adopted.

EXECUTIVE POWER

With the incorporation of the Ta'if agreement into the Lebanese Constitution in August 1990, executive power was effectively transferred from the presidency to the Cabinet. The President is elected for a term of six years and is not immediately re-eligible. He is responsible for the promulgation and execution of laws enacted by the National Assembly, but all presidential decisions (with the exception of those to appoint a Prime Minister or to accept the resignation of a government) require the co-signature of the Prime Minister, who is head of the Government, implementing its policies and speaking in its name. The President must receive the approval of the Cabinet before dismissing a minister or ratifying an international treaty. The ministers and the Prime Minister are chosen by the President of the Republic in consultation with the members and President of the National Assembly. They are not necessarily members of the National Assembly, although they are responsible to it and have access to its debates. The President of the Republic must be a Maronite Christian, and the Prime Minister a Sunni Muslim; the choice of the other ministers must reflect the level of representation of the communities in the Assembly.

Note: In October 1998 the National Assembly endorsed an exceptional amendment to Article 49 of the Constitution to enable the election of Gen. Emile Lahoud, then Commander-in-Chief of the armed forces, as President of the Republic: the Constitution requires that senior state officials relinquish their responsibilities two years prior to seeking public office.

The Government

HEAD OF STATE

President: Gen. EMILE LAHOUD (inaugurated 24 November 1998).

CABINET
(April 2003)

Prime Minister: RAFIK HARIRI.

Deputy Prime Minister: ISSAM FARES.

Minister of Foreign Affairs and Emigrants: JEAN OBEID.

Minister of the Interior: ELIAS MURR.

Minister of National Defence: MAHMOUD HAMMOUD.

Minister of the Displaced: ABDULLAH FARHAT.

Minister of Industry: ELIAS SKAFF.

Minister of Energy and Water: AYOUB HUMAYED.

Minister of Public Health: SULAYMAN FRANJIYA.

Minister of Social Affairs: ASSAD DIEB.

Minister of Finance: FOUAD SINIORA.

Minister of Education and Higher Education: SAMIR JISR.

Minister of the Environment: FARES BOUEIZ.

Minister of Tourism: ALI HUSSEIN ABDULLAH.

Minister of Public Works and Transport: NAJIB MIQATI.

Minister of Youth and Sports: SEBOUH HOFNANIAN.

Minister of Information: MICHEL SAMAHA.

Minister of Economy and Trade: MARWAN HAMADEH.

Minister of Justice: BAHIJ TABBARA.

Minister of Labour: ASSAD HARDAN.

Minister of Culture: GHAZI ARIDI.

Minister of Agriculture: ALI HASSAN KHALIL.

Minister of Telecommunications: JEAN-LOUIS KORDAHI.

Minister of State for Administrative Development: KARIM PAK-RADOUNI.

Ministers of State without portfolio: ASSEM QANSO, KARAM KARAM, TALAL ARSLAN, KHALIL HRAWI, MICHEL MOUSSA, ABD AR-RAHIM MRAD.

MINISTRIES

Office of the President: Presidential Palace, Baabda, Beirut; tel. (5) 920900; fax (5) 922400; e-mail president_office@presidency.gov .lb; internet www.presidency.gov.lb.

Office of the President of the Council of Ministers: Grand Sérail, place Riad es-Solh, Beirut; tel. (1) 746800; fax (1) 865630.

Ministry of Agriculture: blvd Camille Chamoun, Beirut; tel. (1) 455631; fax (1) 455475; e-mail ministry@agriculture.gov.lb; internet www.agriculture.gov.lb.

Ministry of Culture: Beirut.

Ministry of the Displaced: Damour, Beirut; tel. (1) 325726; fax (1) 503040; e-mail mod@dm.net.lb.

Ministry of Economy and Trade: rue Artois, Hamra, Beirut; tel. (1) 340503; fax (1) 354640; e-mail postmaster@economy.gov.lb; internet www.economy.gov.lb.

Ministry of Education and Higher Education: Campus de l'Unesco, Beirut; tel. (1) 866430; fax (1) 645844.

Ministry of Energy and Water: Shiah, Beirut; tel. (1) 270256.

Ministry of the Environment: POB 70-1091, Antélias, Beirut; tel. (4) 522222; fax (4) 525080; e-mail webmaster@moe.gov.lb; internet www.moe.gov.lb.

Ministry of Finance: Immeuble MOF, place Riad es-Solh, Beirut; tel. (1) 981001; fax (1) 981059; e-mail infocenter@finance.gov.lb; internet www.finance.gov.lb.

Ministry of Foreign Affairs and Emigrants: rue Sursock, Ach-rafieh, Beirut; tel. (1) 333100; responsible for.

   General Directorate of Emigrants: Beirut; e-mail info@ emigrants.gov.lb; internet www.emigrants.gov.lb.

Ministry of Industry: rue Sami Solh, Beirut; tel. (1) 427042; fax (1) 427112; e-mail ministry@industry.gov.lb; internet www.industry .gov.lb.

Ministry of Information: rue Hamra, Beirut; tel. (1) 345800.

Ministry of the Interior: Grand Sérail, place Riad es-Solh, Beirut; tel. (1) 863910.

Ministry of Justice: rue Sami Solh, Beirut; tel. (1) 422953; e-mail justice@ministry.gov.lb; internet www.justice.gov.lb.

Ministry of Labour: Shiah, Beirut; tel. (1) 274140.

Ministry of National Defence: Yarze, Beirut; tel. (5) 920400; fax (5) 951014; e-mail ministry@lebarmy.gov.lb; internet www.lebarmy .gov.lb.

Ministry of Public Health: place du Musée, Beirut; tel. (1) 615716; fax (1) 645099; e-mail minister@public-health.gov.lb; internet www .public-health.gov.lb.

Ministry of Public Works and Transport: Shiah, Beirut; tel. (1) 428980; internet www.public-works.gov.lb.

Ministry of State for Administrative Reform: Immeuble Starco, 5e étage, rue George Picot, Beirut; tel. (1) 371510; fax (1) 371599; e-mail newsletter@omsar.gov.lb; internet www.omsar.gov.lb.

Ministry of State for Affairs of the South and Reconstruction: Beirut.

Ministry of Telecommunications: rue Sami Solh, 3e étage, Beirut; tel. (1) 424400; fax (1) 888310; e-mail webmaster@mpt.gov .lb; internet www.mpt.gov.lb.

Ministry of Tourism: POB 11-5344, rue Banque du Liban 550, Beirut; tel. (1) 340940; fax (1) 340945; e-mail mot@lebanon-tourism .gov.lb; internet www.lebanon-tourism.gov.lb.

Ministry of Youth and Sports: Beirut.

Legislature

MAJLIS ALNWAB
(National Assembly)

The equal distribution of seats among Christians and Muslims is determined by law, and the Cabinet must reflect the level of representation achieved by the various religious denominations within that principal division. Deputies of the same religious denomination do not necessarily share the same political, or party allegiances. The distribution of seats is as follows: Maronite Catholics 34; Sunni Muslims 27; Shi'a Muslims 27; Greek Orthodox 14; Druzes 8; Greek-Melkite Catholics 8; Armenian Orthodox 5; Alawites 2; Armenian Catholics 1; Protestants 1; Others 1.

President: NABIH BERRI.

Vice-President: ELIE FERZLI.

General election, 27 August and 3 September 2000

Party list	Seats
Resistance and Development	23
Al-Karamah (Dignity)	18
Ba'albek-Hermel al-Ii'tilafiah (Ba'albek-Hermel Coalition)	9
Al-Jabhar an-Nidal al-Watani (National Defence Front)	8
Wahdal al-Jabal (Mountain Union)	7
Ii'tilafiah (Coalition)	6
Al-Karal (Decision)	6
Al-Kitla al-Chaabi—Elias Shaft (People's Front—Elias Shaft)	5
Al-Wifah al-Matni (Metn Accord)	5
Al-Karamah wah Tajdid (Dignity and Renewal) . . .	5
Al-Karal al-Chaabi (Popular Decision)	3
Al-Wifac at-Tajdid (Reconciliation and Renewal). . . .	3
Al-Irada al-Chaabia (Popular Will)	3
Al-Karamah al-Wataniyah (National Dignity) . . .	2
At-Tawafoc al-Watani (National Understanding) . . .	1
Al-Kitla al-Chaabi—Fouad el Turk (People's Front—Fouad el Turk)	1
Lubnan (Lebanon)	1
Al-Hurriya (Freedom)	1
Independents	20
Others	1
Total	**128**

Political Organizations

Amal (Hope): f. 1975; Shi'ite politico-military organization which in recent years has become more akin to a political party; Principal Controller of Command Council Sheikh MUHAMMAD MANDI SHAMS AD-DIN; Chair. SADR AD-DIN AS-SADR; Leader NABIH BERRI.

Armenian Revolutionary Federation (ARF): rue Spears, Beirut; f. 1890; principal Armenian party; also known as Tashnag Party, which was the dominant nationalist party in the independent Armenian Republic of Yerevan of 1917–21, prior to its becoming part of the USSR; socialist ideology; collective leadership.

Al-Baath: f. in Syria, 1940, by Michel Aflak; secular pro-Syrian party with policy of Arab union, branches in several Middle Eastern countries; Sec.-Gen. ABDULLAH AL-AMIN (Beirut).

Al-Baath: pro-Iraqi wing of Al-Baath party; Sec.-Gen. ABD AL-MAJID RAFEI.

Bloc national libanais: rue Pasteur, Gemmayze, Beirut; tel. (1) 584585; fax (1) 584591; f. 1943; right-wing Lebanese party with policy of power-sharing between Christians and Muslims and the exclusion of the military from politics; Pres. SÉLIM SALHAB; Sec.-Gen. JEAN HAWAT.

Hezbollah (Party of God): Beirut; e-mail hizbollahmedia@hizbollah .org; internet www.hizbollah.org; f. 1982 by Iranian Revolutionary Guards who were sent to Lebanon; militant Shi'ite faction which has become the leading organization of Lebanon's Shi'a community and a recognized political party; demands the withdrawal of Israeli forces from the occupied Shebaa Farms area of southern Lebanon and the release of all Lebanese prisoners from Israeli detention; Chair. MUHAMMAD RA'D; Spiritual leader MUHAMMAD HUSSEIN FADLALLAH; Leader and Sec.-Gen. Sheikh HASAN NASRALLAH.

Al-Katae'b (Phalanges Libanaises, Phalangist Party): POB 992, place Charles Hélou, Beirut; tel. (1) 584107; e-mail admin@kataeb .com; internet www.lebanese-kataeb.org; f. 1936 by the late Pierre Gemayel; nationalist, reformist, democratic social party; largest Maronite party; 100,000 mems; announced merger with Parti national libéral, May 1979; Pres. MOUNIR EL-HAJJ; Sec.-Gen. JOSEPH ABOU KHALIL.

Lebanese Democratic Movement: Beirut; Pres. JACQUES TAMER; Sec.-Gen. NAJI HATAB.

An-Najjadé (The Helpers): c/o Sawt al-Uruba, POB 3537, Beirut; f. 1936; Arab socialist unionist party; 3,000 mems; Founder and Pres. ADNANE MOUSTAFA AL-HAKIM.

National Lebanese Front: Beirut; f. 1999; Pres. ERNEST KARAM.

Parti communiste libanais (Lebanese Communist Party): Beirut; e-mail info@communistparty-lb.org; internet www .communistparty-lb.org; f. 1924; officially dissolved 1948–71; Marxist, much support among intellectuals; Pres. MAURICE NOHRA; Sec.-Gen. FARUQ DAHRUJ.

Parti national libéral (PNL) (Al-Wataniyin al-Ahrar): POB 165576, rue du Liban, Beirut; tel. (1) 338000; fax (1) 200335; e-mail ahrar@ahrar.org.lb; internet www.ahrar.org.lb; f. 1958; liberal reformist secular party, although has traditionally had a predominantly Maronite Christian membership; Pres. DORY CHAMOUN.

Parti socialiste nationaliste syrien: internet www.ssnp.com; f. 1932; banned 1962–69; advocates a 'Greater Syria', composed of Lebanon, Syria, Iraq, Jordan, Palestine and Cyprus; Leader JIBRAN ARAIJI.

Parti socialiste progressiste (At-Takadumi al-Ishteraki—PSP): POB 2893, Moussaitbé, Beirut; tel. and fax (1) 301231; e-mail secretary@psp.org.lb; internet www.psp.org.lb; f. 1949; progressive party, advocates constitutional road to socialism and democracy; over 25,000 mems; mainly Druze support; Pres. WALID JOUMBLATT; Sec.-Gen. SHARIF FAYAD.

Al-Wa'ad (National Secular Democratic Party—Pledge): Beirut; f. after 1975–90 civil war by the late Elie Hobeika; Leader (vacant).

Other parties include the **Independent Nasserite Movement** (Murabitoun; Sunni Muslim Militia; Leader IBRAHIM QULAYAT) and the **Lebanese Popular Congress** (Pres. KAMAL SHATILA). The **Nasserite Popular Organization** and the **Arab Socialist Union** merged in January 1987, retaining the name of the former (Sec.-Gen. MUSTAFA SAAD). The **Islamic Amal** is a breakaway group from Amal, based in Ba'albak (Ba'albek) (Leader HUSSEIN MOUSSAVI). **Islamic Jihad** (Islamic Holy War) is a pro-Iranian fundamentalist guerrilla group (Leader IMAAD MOUGNIEH). The **Popular Liberation Army** is a Sunni Muslim faction, active in the south of Lebanon (Leader MUSTAFA SAAD). **Tawheed Islami** (the Islamic Unification Movement; f. 1982; Sunni Muslim) and the **Arab Democratic Party** (or the Red Knights; Alawites; pro-Syrian; Leader ALI EID) are based in Tripoli.

Diplomatic Representation

EMBASSIES IN LEBANON

Algeria: POB 4794, face Hôtel Summerland, rue Jnah, Beirut; tel. (1) 826711; fax (1) 826712; Ambassador AHMAD BOUTEHRI.

Argentina: Immeuble Khaled Daouk, 2e étage, Rue Melki/Omar Daouk, Centre Ville, Mina el Hosn, Beirut; tel. (1) 987900; fax (1) 987903; e-mail embarg@cyberia.net.lb; Ambassador JOSÉ PEDRO PICO.

Armenia: POB 70607, rue Jasmin, Mtaileb, Beirut; tel. (4) 418860; fax (4) 402952; e-mail armenia@dm.net.lb; Ambassador AREG HOVHANNISSIAN.

Australia: POB 11-1860, Farra Bldg, Bliss St, Ras Beirut; tel. (1) 374701; fax (1) 374709; e-mail austemle@cyberia.net.lb; internet www.lebanon.embassy.gov.au; Ambassador STEPHANIE SHWABSKY.

Austria: Achrafieh, Beirut; tel. (1) 217360; fax (1) 217772; e-mail beirutob@bmaa.gv.at; Ambassador Dr HELMUT FREUDENSCHUSS.

Bahrain: Sheikh Ahmed ath-Thani Bldg, Raoucheh, Beirut; tel. (1) 805495; Ambassador MUHAMMAD BAHLOUL.

Belgium: POB 11–1600, Riad es-Solh, Beirut; tel. (1) 976001; fax (1) 976007; e-mail beirut@diplobel.org; Ambassador FRANÇOISE GUSTIN.

Bolivia: Dora, Beirut; tel. (1) 240711; fax (1) 240710; Chargé d'affaires a.i. GEORGES NAGIB GHOSN.

Brazil: POB 166175, rue des Antonins, Baabda, Beirut; tel. (5) 921256; fax (5) 923001; Chargé d'affaires a.i. RICARDO ALONSO BASTOS.

Bulgaria: POB 11-6544, Immeuble Hibri, rue de l'Australie 55, Raouche, Beirut; tel. (1) 861352; fax (1) 800265; e-mail bgemb_lb@ hotmail.com; Ambassador NIKOLAI ANDREEV.

Canada: POB 60163, 1e étage, Immeuble Coolrite, Autostrade Jal ed-Dib, Beirut; tel. (4) 713900; fax (4) 710595; e-mail berut@ dfait-maeci.gc.ca; internet www.canada-lb.org; Ambassador MICHEL DUVAL.

Chile: Beirut; tel. (4) 418670; fax (4) 418672; Ambassador OVID HARASICH.

China, People's Republic: POB 11-8227, Beirut 1107 2260; tel. (1) 856133; fax (1) 822492; e-mail emb.prc@dm.net.lb; Ambassador LIU ZHENTANG.

Colombia: 5th Floor, Mazda Centre, Jal ed-Dib, Beirut; tel. (4) 712646; fax (4) 712656; e-mail colombia@cyberia.net.lb; Chargé d'affaires a.i. ARMANDO ECHEVERRI JIMÉNEZ.

Cuba: Immeuble Ghazzal, rue Abd as-Sabbah, rue Sakiet el-Janzir/rue de Vienne, Beirut; tel. (1) 805025; fax (1) 810339; Ambassador ENRIQUE ROMÁN HERNANDEZ.

Czech Republic: POB 40195, Baabda, Beirut; tel. (5) 468763; fax (5) 922120; e-mail czechemb@cyberia.net.lb; Ambassador EVA FILIPIOVA.

Denmark: POB 11-5190, Immeuble 812 Tabaris, 4e étage, ave Charles Malek, Achrafieh, Beirut; tel. (1) 335860; fax (1) 335865; e-mail dk-emb@dm.net.lb; Ambassador OLE WØHLERS OLSEN.

Egypt: rue Thomas Eddison, Beirut; tel. (1) 867917; fax (1) 863751; Ambassador HATEM SEIF EL-NASR.

France: Résidence des Pins, Mar-Takla, Beirut; tel. (1) 420000; fax (1) 420007; e-mail ambafr@ciberia.net.lb; internet www .ambafrance-liban.org.lb; Ambassador PHILIPPE LECOURTIER.

Gabon: Hadath, Beirut; tel. (5) 924875; fax (5) 924643; Ambassador SIMON NTOUTOUME EMANE.

Germany: POB 11-2820, near Jesus and Mary High School, Rabieh/Mtaileb, Beirut; tel. (4) 914444; fax (4) 914450; e-mail germanemb@germanembassy.org.lb; internet www .germanembassy.org.lb; Ambassador GISELA KAEMPFFE-SIKORA.

Greece: POB 11–0309, Immeuble Boukhater, rue des Ambassades, Naccache, Beirut; tel. (4) 521700; fax (4) 418774; e-mail hellas.emb@ inco.com.lb; Ambassador GEORGES GABRIELIDES.

Holy See: POB 1061, Jounieh (Apostolic Nunciature); tel. (9) 263102; fax (9) 264488; e-mail naliban@terra.net.lb; Apostolic Nuncio Most Rev. LUIGI GATTI (Titular Archbishop of Santa Giusta).

Hungary: POB 90618, Centre Massoud, Fanar, Beirut; tel. (1) 898840; fax (1) 873391; e-mail huembbej@inco.com.lb; Ambassador PÁL JENŐ FÁBIÁN.

India: POB 113-5240, Immeuble Sahmarani, rue Kantari 31, Hamra, Beirut; tel. (1) 373539; fax (1) 373538; e-mail indembei@dm .net.lb; Ambassador NANTU SARKAR.

Indonesia: Baabda, Beirut; tel. (5) 924682; fax (5) 924678; Ambassador Maj.-Gen. SYAN SOEMANEGARA.

Iran: POB 5030, Beirut; tel. (1) 821224; fax (1) 821230; Ambassador MASSOUD IDRIS KARMANSHAHI.

Italy: Immeuble Assicurazioni Generali, Beirut; tel. (1) 985200; fax (1) 985303; e-mail amb@ambitaliabeirut.org; internet www .ambitaliabeirut.org; Ambassador FRANCO MISTRETTA.

Japan: POB 11-3360, Army St, Zkak al-Blat, Serail Hill, Beirut; tel. (1) 985751; fax (1) 989754; e-mail japanemb@japanemb.org.lb; internet www.lb.emb-japan.go.jp; Ambassador NAOTO AMAKI.

Jordan: POB 109, Baabda; tel. (5) 922500; fax (5) 922502; e-mail joremb@dm.net.lb; Ambassador ANMAR AL-HMOUD.

Korea, Republic: Baabda, Beirut; tel. (5) 922151; fax (5) 922153; e-mail koremadm@dm.net.lb; Ambassador KI-HYUN LEE.

Kuwait: Rond-point du Stade, Bir Hassan, Beirut; tel. (1) 822515; fax (1) 840613; Ambassador ALI SULEIMAN AS-SAEID.

Libya: Beirut; tel. (1) 806314; fax (1) 805349; Ambassador (vacant).

Mexico: POB 70–1150, Antélias; tel. (4) 418871; fax (4) 418873; e-mail embamex@dm.net.lb; internet www.embamex.org.lb; Ambassador ARTURO PUENTE.

Morocco: Bir Hassan, Beirut; tel. (1) 859829; fax (1) 859839; e-mail sifmar@cyberia.net.lb; Ambassador ABD AL-JALIL FENJIRO.

Netherlands: POB 167190, ABN AMRO Tower, 9e étage, ave Charles Malek, Achrafieh, Beirut; tel. (1) 204663; fax (1) 204664; e-mail nlgovbei@sodetel.net.lb; internet www.netherlandsembassy .org.lb; Ambassador JAN PIET KLEIWEG DE ZWAAN.

Norway: Immeuble Dimashki, rue Bliss, Ras Beirut, Beirut; tel. (1) 372977; fax (1) 372979; Ambassador SVEIN SEVJE.

Pakistan: POB 135506, Immeuble Shell, 11e étage, Raoucheh, Beirut; tel. (1) 863041; fax (1) 864583; e-mail pakemblb@cyberia.net .lb; Ambassador KHALID M. MIR.

Philippines: Raoucheh, Beirut; tel. (1) 791092; fax (1) 791095; Ambassador FORTUNATO OBLENA.

Poland: POB 40-215, Immeuble Khalifa, ave Président Sulayman Franjiya 52, Baabda, Beirut; tel. (5) 924881; fax (5) 924882; e-mail polamb@cyberia.net.lb; Chargé d'affaires WALDEMAR MARKIEWICZ.

Qatar: POB 6717, Beirut; tel. (1) 865271; fax (1) 810460; Ambassador ABDALLAH BIN MUHAMMAD AL-KHATER.

Romania: Route du Palais Presidentiel, Baabda, Beirut; tel. (5) 924848; fax (5) 924747; e-mail romembey@inco.com.lb; Ambassador AUREL CALIN.

Russia: rue Mar Elias et-Tineh, Wata Mseitbeh, Beirut; tel. (1) 300041; fax (1) 303837; Ambassador BORIS BOLOTINE.

Saudi Arabia: rue Bliss, Manara, Beirut; tel. (1) 860351; fax (1) 860411; Ambassador FUAD BIN SADEK MUFTI.

Spain: POB 11-3039, Riad es-Solh, Beirut; tel. (5) 464120; fax (5) 464030; e-mail embspain@cyberia.net.lb; Ambassador MIGUEL ANGEL CARRIEDO.

Sri Lanka: Baabda, Beirut; tel. (5) 924765; fax (5) 924768; Ambassador MUHAMMAD ISMAIL MUHSEN.

Sudan: POB 2504, Hamra, Beirut; tel. (1) 350057; fax (1) 353271; e-mail ; Ambassador SAYED AHMAD AL-BAKHIT.

Switzerland: Beirut; tel. (1) 324129; fax (1) 324167; Ambassador THOMAS LITSCHER.

Tunisia: Hazmieh, Mar-Takla, Beirut; tel. (5) 457431; fax (5) 950434; Ambassador FETHI HOUIDI.

Turkey: POB 70–666, zone II, rue 3, Rabieh, Beirut; tel. (4) 520929; fax (4) 407557; e-mail trbebeyr@intracom.net.lb; Ambassador CELA-LETTIN KART.

Ukraine: POB 431, Jardin al-Bacha, Jisr al-Bacha, Sin el-Fil, Beirut; tel. (1) 510527; fax (1) 510531; e-mail ukrembassy@inco.com .lb; internet www.ukremblebanon.com; Ambassador VALERII RYLACH.

United Arab Emirates: Immeuble Wafic Tanbara, Jnah, Beirut; tel. (1) 857000; fax (1) 857009; Ambassador MUHAMMAD HAMAD OMRAN.

United Kingdom: POB 11-471, Embassies Complex, Army St, Zkak al-Blat, Serail Hill, Beirut; tel. (1) 990400; fax (1) 990420; e-mail britemb@cyberia.net.lb; internet www.britishembassy.org.lb; Ambassador RICHARD KINCHEN.

USA: POB 70-840, Antélias, Aoucar, Beirut; tel. (4) 542600; fax (4) 544136; e-mail pas@inco.com.lb; internet www.usembassy.gov.lb; Ambassador VINCENT M. BATTLE.

Uruguay: POB 2051, Centre Stella Marris, 7e étage, rue Banque du Liban, Jounieh; tel. (9) 636529; fax (9) 636531; e-mail uruliban@dm .net.lb; Ambassador ALBERTO VOSS RUBIO.

Venezuela: POB 603, Immeuble Baezevale House, 5e étage, Zalka, Beirut; tel. (1) 888701; fax (1) 900757; e-mail embavene@dm.net.lb; Ambassador EFRAIN SILVA.

Yemen: Bir Hassan, Beirut; tel. (1) 852688; fax (1) 821610; e-mail yemenembassy@yemenembassy-lebanon.org; internet www .yemenembassy-lebanon.org; Ambassador AHMAD ABDULLAH AL-BASHA.

Note: Lebanon and Syria have very close relations but do not exchange formal ambassadors.

Judicial System

Law and justice in Lebanon are administered in accordance with the following codes, which are based upon modern theories of civil and criminal legislation:

Code de la Propriété (1930).

Code des Obligations et des Contrats (1932).

Code de Procédure Civile (1933).

Code Maritime (1947).

Code de Procédure Pénale (Code Ottoman Modifié).

Code Pénal (1943).

Code Pénal Militaire (1946).

Code d'Instruction Criminelle.

The following courts are now established:

(*a*) Fifty-six **'Single-Judge Courts'**, each consisting of a single judge, and dealing in the first instance with both civil and criminal cases; there are seventeen such courts at Beirut and seven at Tripoli.

(*b*) Eleven **Courts of Appeal,** each consisting of three judges, including a President and a Public Prosecutor, and dealing with civil and criminal cases; there are five such courts at Beirut.

(*c*) Four **Courts of Cassation,** three dealing with civil and commercial cases and the fourth with criminal cases. A Court of Cassation, to be properly constituted, must have at least three judges, one being the President and the other two Councillors. The First Court consists of the First President of the Court of Cassation, a President and two Councillors. The other two civil courts each consist of a President and three Councillors. If the Court of Cassation reverses the judgment of a lower court, it does not refer the case back but retries it itself.

First President of the Court of Cassation: MUNIR HONEIN.

(*d*) **The Council of State,** which deals with administrative cases. It consists of a President, Vice-President and four Councillors. A Commissioner represents the Government.

President of the Court of the Council of State: GHALEB GHANEM.

(*e*) **The Court of Justice,** which is a special court consisting of a President and four judges, deals with matters affecting the security of the State; there is no appeal against its verdicts.

In addition to the above, the Constitutional Court considers matters pertaining to the constitutionality of legislation. Military courts are competent to try crimes and misdemeanours involving the armed and security forces. Islamic (*Shari'a*), Christian and Jewish religious courts deal with affairs of personal status (marriage, death, inheritance, etc.).

Religion

Of all the regions of the Middle East, Lebanon probably presents the closest juxtaposition of sects and peoples within a small territory. Estimates for 1983 assessed the sizes of communities as: Shi'a Muslims 1.2m., Maronites 900,000, Sunni Muslims 750,000, Greek Orthodox 250,000, Druzes 250,000, Armenians 175,000. The Maronites, a uniate sect of the Roman Catholic Church, inhabited the old territory of Mount Lebanon, i.e. immediately east of Beirut. In the south, towards the Israeli frontier, Shi'a villages are most common, while between the Shi'a and the Maronites live the Druzes (divided between the Yazbakis and the Joumblatis). The Beka'a valley has many Greek Christians (both Roman Catholic and Orthodox), while the Tripoli area is mainly Sunni Muslim.

CHRISTIANITY

The Roman Catholic Church

Armenian Rite

Patriarchate of Cilicia: Patriarcat Arménien Catholique, rue de l'Hôpital Libanais, Jeitawi, 2400 Beirut; tel. (1) 585671; fax (1) 449160; e-mail patrarca@magnarama.com; f. 1742; established in Beirut since 1932; includes patriarchal diocese of Beirut, with an estimated 12,000 adherents (31 December 2000); Patriarch Most Rev. NERSES BEDROS XIX TARMOUNI; Protosyncellus Rt Rev. VARTAN ACHKARIAN (Titular Bishop of Tokat (Armenian Rite)).

Chaldean Rite

Diocese of Beirut: Evêché Chaldéen de Beyrouth, POB 373, Hazmieh, Beirut; tel. (5) 459088; fax (5) 457731; e-mail chaldepiscopus@hotmail.com; an estimated 12,500 adherents (31 December 2000); Bishop of Beirut MICHEL KASSARJI.

Latin Rite

Apostolic Vicariate of Beirut: Vicariat Apostolique, POB 11-4224, Beirut; tel. (9) 236101; fax (9) 236102; e-mail vicariatlat@hotmail.com; an estimated 20,000 adherents (31 December 2000); Vicar Apostolic PAUL DAHDAH (Titular Archbishop of Arae in Numidia).

Maronite Rite

Patriarchate of Antioch and all the East

Patriarcat Maronite, Bkerké; tel. (9) 915441; fax (9) 938844; e-mail jtawk@bkerke.org.lb.

Includes patriarchal dioceses of Jounieh, Sarba and Jobbé; Patriarch Cardinal NASRALLAH PIERRE SFEIR; The Maronite Church in Lebanon comprises four archdioceses and six dioceses. At 31 December 2000 there were an estimated 1,373,587 adherents in the country.

Archbishop of Antélias: Most Rev. JOSEPH MOHSEN BÉCHARA, Archevêché Maronite, POB 70400, Antélias; tel. (4) 410020; fax (4) 921313.

Archbishop of Beirut: Most Rev. PAUL YOUSSEF MATAR, Archevêché Maronite, 10 rue Collège de la Sagesse, Beirut; tel. (1) 561980; fax (1) 561931.

Also representative of the Holy See for Roman Catholics of the Coptic Rite in Lebanon.

Archbishop of Tripoli: Most Rev. YOUHANNA FOUAD EL-HAGE, Archevêché Maronite, POB 104, rue al-Moutran, Karm Sada, Tripoli; tel. (6) 624324; fax (6) 629393; e-mail rahmat@inco.com.lb.

Archbishop of Tyre: Most Rev. MAROUN KHOURY SADER, Archevêché Maronite, Tyre; tel. (7) 740059; fax (7) 344891.

Melkite Rite

Patriarch of Antioch

The Patriarch of Antioch and all the East, of Alexandria and of Jerusalem, Most Rev. GRÉGOIRE LAHAM III; is resident in Damascus, Syria. The Melkite Church in Lebanon comprises seven archdioceses. At 31 December 2000 there were an estimated 381,250 adherents in the country.

Archbishop of Ba'albek: Most Rev. CYRILLE SALIM BUSTROS, Archevêché Grec-Catholique, Ba'albek; tel. (8) 370200; fax (8) 373986.

Archbishop of Baniyas: Most Rev. ANTOINE HAYEK, Archevêché de Panéas, Jdeidet Marjeyoun; tel. (3) 814487.

Archbishop of Beirut and Gibail: JOSEPH KALLAS, Archevêché Grec-Melkite-Catholique, POB 901, rue de Damas, Beirut; tel. (1) 616104; fax (1) 616109; e-mail agmcb@terra.net.lb.

Archbishop of Saida (Sidon): Most Rev. GEORGES KWAÏTER, Archevêché Grec-Melkite-Catholique, POB 247, rue el-Moutran, Sidon; tel. (7) 720100; fax (7) 722055; e-mail mkwaiter@inco.com.lb.

Archbishop of Tripoli: Most Rev. GEORGE RIASHI, Archevêché Grec-Catholique, POB 72, Tripoli; tel. (6) 431602; fax (6) 441716.

Archbishop of Tyre: Most Rev. JEAN ASSAAD HADDAD, Archevêché Grec-Melkite-Catholique, POB 257, Tyre; tel. (7) 740015; fax (7) 349180; e-mail eegc@inco.com.lb.

Archbishop of Zahleh and Furzol: Most Rev. ANDRÉ HADDAD, Archevêché Grec-Melkite-Catholique, Saidat en-Najat, Zahleh; tel. (8) 820540; fax (8) 822406.

Syrian Rite

Patriarchate of Antioch: Patriarcat Syrien Catholique d'Antioche, rue de Damas, POB 116/5087, Beirut 1106-2010; tel. (1) 615892; fax (1) 616573; e-mail psc_lb@yahoo.com; jurisdiction over about 150,000 Syrian Catholics in the Middle East, including (at 31 December 2000) 20,000 in the diocese of Beirut; Patriarch: Most Rev. IGNACE PIERRE ABDEL AHAD VIII; Protosyncellus Mgr GEORGES MASRI.

The Anglican Communion

Within the Episcopal Church in Jerusalem and the Middle East, Lebanon forms part of the diocese of Jerusalem (see the chapter on Israel).

Other Christian Groups

Armenian Apostolic Orthodox: Armenian Catholicosate of Cilicia, POB 70317, Antélias, Beirut, Lebanon; tel. (4) 410001; fax (4) 419724; e-mail cathcil@cathcil.org; internet www.cathcil.org; f. 1441; in Cilicia (now in Turkey), transferred to Antélias, Lebanon, 1930; Leader His Holiness ARAM (KESHISHIAN) I (Catholicos of Cilicia); jurisdiction over an estimated 1m. adherents in Lebanon, Syria, Cyprus, Kuwait, Greece, Iran, the United Arab Emirates, the USA and Canada.

Greek Orthodox: Patriarch of Antioch and all the East, Patriarcat Grec-Orthodoxe, POB 9, Damascus, Syria; Leader His Beatitude IGNATIUS IV.

National Evangelical Synod of Syria and Lebanon: POB 70890, Antélias, Beirut; tel. (4) 525030; fax (4) 411184; e-mail nessl@minero.net; 80,000 adherents (2003); Gen. Sec. Rev. ADEEB AWAD.

Protestants: Leader Rev. Dr Salim Sahiouny, Pres. of Supreme Council of the Evangelical Community in Syria and Lebanon, POB 70/1065, rue Rabieh 34, Antélias; tel. (4) 525036; fax (4) 405490; e-mail suprcoun@minero.net.

Syrian Orthodox: Patriarch of Antioch and all the East, Patriarcat Syrien Orthodoxe, Bab Toma, POB 22260, Damascus, Syria; tel. 5432401; fax 5432400; Leader IGNATIUS ZAKKA I IWAS.

Union of the Armenian Evangelical Churches in the Near East: POB 11-377, Beirut; tel. (1) 565628; fax (1) 565629; e-mail uaecne@cyberia.net.lb; f. 1846 in Turkey; comprises about 30 Armenian Evangelical Churches in Syria, Lebanon, Egypt, Cyprus, Greece, Iran, Turkey and Australia; 7,500 mems (1990); Pres. Rev. MEGRDICH KARAGOEZIAN; Gen. Sec. SEBOUH TERZIAN.

ISLAM

Shi'a Muslims: Leader Imam Sheikh SAYED MOUSSA AS-SADR (went missing during visit to Libya in August 1978); President of the Supreme Islamic Council of the Shi'a Community of Lebanon, ABD AL-AMIR QABALAN (acting), Beirut.

Sunni Muslims: Grand Mufti of Lebanon, Dar el-Fatwa, rue Ilewi Rushed, Beirut; tel. (1) 422340; Leader SG Sheikh Dr MUHAMMAD RASHID QABBANI.

Druzes: Supreme Spiritual Leader of the Druze Community, Beirut; tel. (1) 341116; Acting leader SG Sheikh BAHJAT GHEITH.

Alawites: a schism of Shi'ite Islam; there are an estimated 50,000 Alawites in northern Lebanon, in and around Tripoli.

JUDAISM

Jews: Leader CHAHOUD CHREIM (Beirut).

The Press

DAILIES

Al-Ahrar: POB 165600, rue al-Jeitaoui al-Marsad, Beirut; tel. (1) 333899; published by Dar al-Bouhous.

Al-Amal (Hope): rue Libérateur, Beirut; tel. (1) 382992; f. 1939; Arabic; organ of the Phalangist Party; Chief Editor ELIAS RABABI; circ. 35,000.

Al-Anwar (Lights): c/o Dar Assayad, POB 11-1038, Hazmieh, Beirut; tel. (5) 456374; fax (5) 452700; e-mail info@alanwar.com; internet www.alanwar.com; f. 1959; Arabic; independent; supplement, Sunday, cultural and social; published by Dar Assayad SAL; Editors-in-Chief MICHEL RAAD, RAFIC KHOURY; circ. 25,000.

Ararat: Nor Hagin, Beirut; f. 1937; Armenian; Communist; Editor KRIKOR HAJENIAN; circ. 5,000.

Aztag: Beirut; tel. (1) 366607; f. 1927; Armenian; circ. 6,500.

Al-Bairaq (The Standard): rue Monot, Beirut; f. 1911; Arabic; published by Soc. Libanaise de Presse; Editor RAYMOND KAWASS; circ. 3,000.

Bairut: Beirut; f. 1952; Arabic.

Ach-Chaab (The People): POB 5140, Beirut; f. 1961; Arabic; Nationalist; Propr and Editor MUHAMMAD AMIN DUGHAN; circ. 7,000.

Ach-Chams (The Sun): Beirut; f. 1925; Arabic.

Ach-Charq (The East): POB 11-0838, rue Verdun, Riad es-Solh, Beirut; tel. (1) 810820; fax (1) 866105; e-mail info@elshark.com; f. 1926; Arabic; Editor AOUNI AL-KAAKI.

Daily Star: 6th Floor, Marine Tower, rue de la Sainte Famille, Achrafieh, Beirut; tel. (1) 587277; fax (1) 561333; e-mail webmaster@dailystar.com.lb; internet www.dailystar.com.lb; f.

1952; English; Publr and Editor-in-Chief JAMIL K. MROUE; circ. 10,550.

Ad-Diyar (The Homeland): an-Nahda Building, Yarze, Beirut; tel. (5) 923830; fax (5) 923773; e-mail aldiyar2002@yahoo.com; f. 1987; Arabic; Propr CHARLES AYYUB.

Ad-Dunya (The World): Beirut; f. 1943; Arabic; political; Chief Editor SULIMAN ABOU ZAID; circ. 25,000.

Al-Hakika (The Truth): Beirut; Arabic; published by Amal.

Al-Hayat (Life): POB 11–987, Immeuble Gargarian, rue Emil Eddé, Hamra, Beirut; tel. (1) 352674; fax (1) 866177; internet www.alhayat.com; f. 1946; Arabic; independent; circ. 196,800.

Al-Jarida (The (News) Paper): POB 220, place Tabaris, Beirut; f. 1953; Arabic; independent; Editor ABDULLAH SKAFF; circ. 22,600.

Al-Jumhuriya (The Republic): Beirut; f. 1924; Arabic.

Journal al-Haddis: POB 300, Jounieh; f. 1927; Arabic; political; Owner GEORGES ARÈGE-SAADÉ.

Al-Khatib (The Speaker): rue Georges Picot, Beirut; Arabic.

Al-Kifah al-Arabi (The Arab Struggle): POB 5158–14, Immeuble Rouche-Shams, Beirut; f. 1974; Arabic; political, socialist, Pan-Arab; Publr and Chief Editor WALID HUSSEINI.

Lisan ul-Hal (The Organ): rue Châteaubriand, Beirut; f. 1877; Arabic; Editor GEBRAN HAYEK; circ. 33,000.

Al-Liwa' (The Standard): POB 11-2402, Beirut; tel. (1) 735749; fax (1) 735742; f. 1963; Arabic; Propr ABD AL-GHANI SALAM; Editor SALAH SALAM; circ. 26,000.

Al-Mustuqbal: Beirut; f. 1999; Owner RAFIK HARIRI; Editor FADHL SHALAQ; circ. 20,000.

An-Nahar (The Day): Immeuble Cooperative de Presse, rue Banque du Liban, Hamra, Beirut; tel. (1) 340960; fax (1) 344567; e-mail annahar@annahar.com.lb; internet www.annahar.com.lb; f. 1933; Arabic; independent; Pres. and Gen. Man. GEBRAN TUENI; Editor-in-Chief OUNSI EL-HAJJ; circ. 50,000.

An-Nass (The People): POB 4886, ave Fouad Chehab, Beirut; tel. (1) 308695; fax (1) 376610; f. 1959; Arabic; Editor-in-Chief HASSAN YAGHI; circ. 22,000.

An-Nida (The Appeal): Beirut; f. 1959; Arabic; published by the Lebanese Communist Party; Editor KARIM MROUÉ; circ. 10,000.

Nida' al-Watan (Call of the Homeland): Beirut; f. 1937; Arabic.

An-Nidal (The Struggle): Beirut; f. 1939; Arabic.

L'Orient-Le Jour: POB 166495, rue Banque du Liban, Beirut; tel. (1) 340560; e-mail redaction@lorient-lejour.com.lb; internet www .lorient-lejour.com.lb; f. 1942; French; independent; Chair. MICHEL EDDÉ; Dir CAMILLE MENASSA; Editorial Dir AMINE ABOU-KHALED; Editor ISSA GORAÏEB; circ. 23,000.

Raqib al-Ahwal (The Observer): Beirut; f. 1937; Arabic; Editor SIMA'N FARAH SEIF.

Rayah (Banner): POB 4101, Beirut; Arabic.

Le Réveil: Beirut; tel. (1) 890700; f. 1977; French; Editor-in-Chief JEAN SHAMI; Dir RAYMOND DAOU; circ. 10,000.

Ar-Ruwwad: POB 2696, rue Mokhalsieh, Beirut; f. 1940; Arabic; Editor BESHARA MAROUN.

Sada Lubnan (Echo of Lebanon): Beirut; f. 1951; Arabic; Lebanese Pan-Arab; Editor MUHAMMAD BAALBAKI; circ. 25,000.

As-Safir: POB 113/5015, Immeuble as-Safir, rue Monimina, Hamra, Beirut 1103-2010; tel. (1) 350080; fax (1) 349431; e-mail co-ordinator@assafir.com; internet www.assafir.com; f. 1974; Arabic; political; Propr and Editor-in-Chief TALAL SALMAN; Gen. Man. YASSER NEHME; circ. 50,000.

Sawt al-Uruba (The Voice of Europe): POB 3537, Beirut; f. 1959; Arabic; organ of the An-Najjadé Party; Editor ADNANE AL-HAKIM.

Le Soir: POB 1470, rue de Syrie, Beirut; f. 1947; French; independent; Dir DIKRAN TOSBATH; Editor ANDRÉ KECATI; circ. 16,500.

Telegraf—Bairut: rue Béchara el-Khoury, Beirut; f. 1930; Arabic; political, economic and social; Editor TOUFIC ASSAD MATNI; circ. 15,500 (5,000 outside Lebanon).

Al-Yaum (Today): Beirut; f. 1937; Arabic; Editor WAFIC MUHAMMAD CHAKER AT-TIBY.

Az-Zamane: Beirut; f. 1947; Arabic.

Zartonk: POB 11-617, rue Nahr Ibrahim, Beirut; tel. and fax (1) 566709; e-mail zartonk@dm.net.lb; f. 1937; Armenian; official organ of Armenian Liberal Democratic Party; Man. Editor BAROUYR H. AGHBASHIAN.

WEEKLIES

Al-Alam al-Lubnani (The Lebanese World): POB 462, Beirut; f. 1964; Arabic, English, Spanish, French; politics, literature and social economy; Editor-in-Chief FAYEK KHOURY; Gen. Editor CHEIKH FADI GEMAYEL; circ. 45,000.

Achabaka (The Net): c/o Dar Assayad SAL, POB 11-1038, Hazmieh, Beirut; tel. (5) 456373; fax (5) 452700; f. 1956; Arabic; society and features; Founder SAID FREIHA; Editor GEORGE IBRAHIM EL-KHOURY; circ. 108,000.

Al-Ahad (Sunday): Beirut; Arabic; political; organ of Hezbollah; Editor RIAD TAHA; circ. 32,000.

Al-Akhbar (The News): Beirut; f. 1954; Arabic; published by the Lebanese Communist Party; circ. 21,000.

Al-Anwar Supplement: c/o Dar Assayad, POB 1038, Hazmieh, Beirut; cultural-social; every Sunday; supplement to daily *Al-Anwar*; Editor ISSAM FREIHA; circ. 90,000.

Argus: Bureau of Lebanese and Arab Documentation, POB 16–5403, Beirut; tel. (1) 219113; Arabic, French and English; economic bulletin; circ. 1,000.

Assayad (The Hunter): c/o Dar Assayad, POB 11-1038, Hazmieh, Beirut; tel. (5) 456373; fax (5) 452700; f. 1943; Arabic; political and social.

Le Commerce du Levant: Beirut; tel. (1) 297770; f. 1929; weekly and special issue quarterly; French; commercial and financial; publ. by Société de la Presse Economique; Pres. MAROUN AKL; circ. 15,000.

Dabbour: Place du Musée, Beirut; tel. (1) 616770; fax (1) 616771; e-mail addabbour@yahoo.com; internet www.addabbour.com; f. 1922; Arabic; Editor JOSEPH RICHARD MUKARZEL; circ. 12,000.

Ad-Dyar: Immeuble Bellevue, rue Verdun, Beirut; f. 1941; Arabic; political; circ. 46,000.

Al-Hadaf (The Target): Beirut; tel. (1) 420554; f. 1969; organ of Popular Front for the Liberation of Palestine (PFLP); Arabic; Editor-in-Chief SABER MOHI ED-DIN; circ. 40,000.

Al-Hawadess (Events): POB 1281, rue Clémenceau, Beirut; published from London (183–185 Askew Rd, W12 9AX); tel. (20) 8740-4500; fax (20) 8749-9781; f. 1911; Arabic; news; Editor-in-Chief MELHIM KAVAM; circ. 120,000.

Al-Hiwar (Dialogue): Beirut; f. 2000; Arabic; Chair. FOUAD MAKH-ZOUMI; Editor-in-Chief SAM MOUNASSA.

Al-Hurriya (Freedom): Beirut; f. 1960; Arabic; organ of the Democratic Front for the Liberation of Palestine; Editor DAOUD TALHAME; circ. 30,000.

Al-Iza'a (Broadcasting): POB 462, rue Selim Jazaerly, Beirut; f. 1938; Arabic; politics, art, literature and broadcasting; Editor FAYEK KHOURY; circ. 11,000.

Al-Jumhur (The Public): POB 1834, Moussaitbé, Beirut; f. 1936; Arabic; illustrated weekly news magazine; Editor FARID ABU SHAHLA; circ. 45,000, of which over 20,000 outside Lebanon.

Kul Shay' (Everything): POB 3250, rue Béchara el-Khoury, Beirut; Arabic.

Magazine: POB 1404, Immeuble Sayegh, rue Sursock, Beirut; tel. (1) 202070; fax (1) 202663; e-mail info@magazine.com.lb; internet www.magazine.com.lb; f. 1956; French; political, economic and social; published by Editions Orientales SAL; Pres. CHARLES ABOU ADAL; circ. 18,000.

Massis: c/o Patriarcat Arménien Catholique, rue de l'Hôpital Libanais Jeitawi, 2400 Beirut; Armenian; Catholic; Editor Fr ANTRANIK GRANIAN; circ. 2,500.

Al-Moharrir (The Liberator): Beirut; f. 1962; Arabic; circ. 87,000; Gen. Man. WALID ABOU ZAHR.

Monday Morning: POB 165612, Immeuble Dimitri Trad, rue Issa Maalouf, Sioufi, Beirut; tel. (1) 200961; fax (1) 334116; e-mail mondaymorning@mmorning.com; internet www.mmorning.com; f. 1972; news and current affairs; published by Dar Alf Leila wa Leila; circ. 11,000.

Al-Ousbou' al-Arabi (Arab Week): POB 1404, Immeuble Sayegh, rue Sursock, Beirut; tel. (1) 202070; fax (1) 202663; e-mail info@ arabweek.com.lb; internet www.arabweek.com.lb; f. 1959; Arabic; political and social; published by Editions Orientales SAL; Pres. CHARLES ABOU ADAL; circ. 88,407 (circulates throughout the Arab World).

Phoenix: POB 113222, Beirut; tel. (1) 346800; fax (1) 346359; for women; published by Al-Hasna.

Ar-Rassed: Beirut; Arabic; Editor GEORGE RAJJI.

Revue du Liban (Lebanon Review): POB 165612, rue Issa Maalouf, Beirut; tel. (1) 200961; fax (1) 334116; e-mail rdl@rdl.com.lb;

internet www.rdl.com.lb; f. 1928; French; political, social, cultural; Publr MELHEM KARAM; Gen. Man. MICHEL MISK; circ. 22,000.

Sabah al-Khair (Good Morning): Beirut; Arabic; published by the Syrian Nationalist Party.

Samar: c/o Dar Assayad, POB 11-1038, Hazmieh, Beirut; tel. (5) 452700; fax (5) 452957; Arabic; for teenagers; published by Dar Assayad SAL.

Ash-Shira' (The Sail): POB 13-5250, Beirut; tel. (1) 70300; fax (1) 866050; Arabic; Editor HASSAN SABRA; circ. 40,000.

OTHER SELECTED PERIODICALS

Alam at-Tijarat (Business World): Immeuble Strand, rue Hamra, Beirut; f. 1965; monthly; commercial; Editor NADIM MAKDISI; international circ. 17,500.

Al Computer, Communications and Electronics: c/o Dar Assayad, POB 1038, Hazmieh, Beirut; tel. (5) 456374; fax (5) 452700; f. 1984; monthly; computer technology; published by Dar Assayad Inter-national; Chief Editor ANTOINE BOUTROS.

Arab Construction World: POB 13–5121, Chouran, Beirut 1102-2802; tel. (1) 352413; fax (1) 352419; e-mail info@acwmag.com; internet www.acwmag.com; f. 1985; every two months; English and Arabic; published by Chatila Publishing House; Publr FATHI CHATILA; Editor-in-Chief RIYADH CHEHAB; circ. 10,614.

Arab Defense Journal: c/o Dar Assayad, POB 11-1038, Hazmieh, Beirut; tel. (5) 456373; fax (5) 452700; e-mail assayad@inco.com.lb; f. 1976; monthly; military; published by Dar Assayad International; Chief Editor Gen. WADIH JUBRAN; circ. 24,325 (Jan.–June 1999).

Arab Economist: POB 11–6068, Beirut; monthly; published by Centre for Economic, Financial and Social Research and Documentation SAL; Chair. HEKMAT KASSIR.

Arab Water World: POB 13–5121, Chouran, Beirut 1102-2802; tel. (1) 352413; fax (1) 352419; e-mail info@awwmag.com; internet www .awwmag.com; f. 1977; every two months; English and Arabic; published by Chatila Publishing House; Editor-in-Chief FATHI CHATILA; circ. 8,443.

The Arab World: POB 567, Jounieh; tel. and fax (9) 935096; e-mail najinaaman@yahoo.com; f. 1985; 24 a year; published by Dar Naaman lith-Thaqafa; Editor NAJI NAAMAN.

Déco: POB 1404, Immeuble Sayegh, rue Sursock, Beirut; tel. (1) 202070; fax (1) 202663; e-mail info@decomag.com.lb; internet www .ediori.com.lb; f. 2000; quarterly; French; architecture and interior design; published by Editions Orientales SAL; Pres. CHARLES ABOU ADAL; circ. 14,000.

Fairuz Lebanon: c/o Dar Assayad, POB 11-1038, Hazmieh, Beirut; tel. (5) 456374; fax (5) 452700; f. 1982; monthly; Arabic; for women; also *Fairuz International*; published by Dar Assayad International; Chief Editor ELHAM FREIHA.

Fann at-Tasswir: POB 16-5947, Beirut; tel. (1) 498950; monthly; Arabic; photography.

Al Fares: c/o Dar Assayad, POB 11-1038, Hazmieh, Beirut; tel. (5) 456374; fax (5) 452700; f. 1991; monthly; Arabic; men's interest; published by Dar Assayad International; Chief Editor ELHAM FREIHA.

Al-Idari (The Manager): c/o Dar Assayad, POB 11-1038, Hamzieh, Beirut; tel. (5) 456374; fax (5) 452700; f. 1975; monthly; Arabic; business management, economics, finance and investment; published by Dar Assayad International; Pres. and Gen. Man. BASSAM FREIHA; Chief Editor HASSAN EL-KHOURY; circ. 31,867.

Al-Intilak (Outbreak): Al-Intilak Printing and Publishing House, POB 4958, Beirut; tel. (1) 302018; e-mail tonehnme@cyberia.net.lb; f. 1960; monthly; Arabic; literary; Chief Editor MICHEL NEHME.

Al-Jeel (The Generation): Beirut; monthly; Arabic; literary.

Al-Khalij Business Magazine: POB 13-5877, Beirut; tel. (1) 345568; fax (1) 602089; e-mail massaref@dm.net.lb; f. 1981; fmrly based in Kuwait; 6 a year; Arabic; Editor-in-Chief ZULFICAR KOBEISSI; circ. 16,325.

Lebanese and Arab Economy: POB 11-1801, Sanayeh, Beirut; tel. (1) 744160; fax (1) 353395; e-mail info@.ccib.org.lb; internet www .ccib.org.lb; f. 1951; monthly; Arabic, English and French; Publr Beirut Chamber of Commerce and Industry.

Majallat al-Iza'at al-Lubnaniat (Lebanese Broadcasting Magazine): c/o Radio Lebanon, rue des Arts et Métiers, Beirut; tel. (1) 863016; f. 1959; monthly; Arabic; broadcasting affairs.

Al-Mar'a: POB 1404, Immeuble Sayegh, rue Sursock, Beirut; tel. (1) 202070; fax (1) 202663; e-mail info@almara.com.lb; internet www .ediori.com.lb; f. 2000; monthly; Arabic; for women; published by Editions Orientales SAL; Pres. CHARLES ABOU ADAL; circ. 20,000.

Middle East Food: POB 13-5121, Chouran, Beirut 1102-2802; tel. (1) 352413; fax (1) 352419; e-mail info@mefmag.com; internet www

.mefmag.com; every two months; published by Chatila Publishing House; Editor-in-Chief SAAD ED-DIN CHEHAB; circ. 9,341.

Al-Mouktataf (The Selection): Beirut; monthly; Arabic; general.

Al-Mukhtar (Reader's Digest): Beirut; monthly; general interest.

Qitāboul A'lamil A'rabi (The Arab World Book): POB 567, Jounieh; tel. and fax (9) 935096; e-mail najinaaman@yahoo.com; f. 1991; 6 a year; Arabic; published by Dar Naaman lith-Thaqafa; Editor NAJI NAAMAN.

Rijal al-Amal (Businessmen): Beirut; f. 1966; monthly; Arabic; business; Publr and Editor-in-Chief MAHIBA AL-MALKI; circ. 16,250.

Scoop: POB 55342, Beirut; tel. (1) 482185; fax (1) 490307; general interest; published by La Régie Libanaise de Publicité.

As-Sihāfa wal I'lām (Press and Information): POB 567, Jounieh; tel. and fax (9) 935096; e-mail najinaaman@yahoo.com; f. 1987; 12 a year; Arabic; published by Dar Naaman lith-Thaqafa; Editor NAJI NAAMAN.

Siyassa was Strategia (Politics and Strategy): POB 567, Jounieh; tel. and fax (9) 935096; e-mail najinaaman@yahoo.com; f. 1981; 36 a year; Arabic; published by Dar Naaman lith-Thaqafa; Editor NAJI NAAMAN.

Tabibok (Your Doctor): POB 90434, Beirut; tel. in Syria (963-11) 2212980; fax (963-11) 3738901; e-mail sskabbani@mail.sy; f. 1956; monthly; Arabic; medical, social, scientific; Editor Dr SAMI KABBANI; circ. 90,000.

Takarir Wa Khalfiyat (Background Reports): c/o Dar Assayad, POB 11-1038, Hamzieh, Beirut; tel. (5) 456374; fax (5) 452700; f. 1976; tri-monthly; Arabic; political and economic bulletin; published by Dar Assayad SAL.

At-Tarik (The Road): Beirut; monthly; Arabic; cultural and theoretical; published by the Parti communiste libanais; circ. 5,000.

Travaux et Jours (Works and Days): Rectorat de l'Université Saint-Joseph, rue de Damas, Beirut; tel. (1) 611172; fax (1) 423369; e-mail travauxetjours@usj.edu.lb; internet www.usj.edu.lb; f. 1961; publ. twice a year; French; political, social and cultural; Editor MOUNIR CHAMOUN.

Welcome to Lebanon and the Middle East: Beirut; f. 1959; monthly; English; on entertainment, touring and travel; Editor SOUHAIL TOUFIK ABOU JAMRA; circ. 6,000.

NEWS AGENCIES

National News Agency (NNA): Hamra, Beirut; tel. (1) 342290; fax (1) 746031; e-mail nna-leb@nna-leb.gov.lb; internet www.nna-leb .gov.lb; state-owned; Dir KHALIL KHOURY.

Foreign Bureaux

Agence France-Presse (AFP): POB 11-1461, Immeuble Najjar, rue de Rome, Beirut; tel. (1) 347461; fax (1) 350318; e-mail afp_bey@ inco.com.lb; internet www.afp.com; Dir PASCAL MALLET.

Agenzia Nazionale Stampa Associata (ANSA) (Italy): POB 113/6545, 2e étage, Immeuble Safieddine, rue Rashid Karame, Beirut; tel. (1) 787237; fax (1) 787236; e-mail ansa@sodetel.net.lb; Correspondent FURIO MORRONI.

Allgemeiner Deutscher Nachrichtendienst (ADN) (Germany): Beirut; Correspondent HARALD DITTMAR.

Associated Press (AP) (USA): POB 3780, Immeuble Shaker et Oueini, place Riad es-Solh, Beirut; tel. (1) 985190; fax (1) 985196; e-mail info@ap.org; internet www.ap.org; Correspondent SAM F. GHATTAS.

Kuwait News Agency (KUNA): Beirut; tel. (1) 354377; fax (1) 602088.

Kyodo Tsushin (Japan): POB 13-5060, Immeuble Makarem, rue Makdessi, Ras Beirut, Beirut; tel. (1) 863861; Correspondent IBRAHIM KHOURY.

Middle East News Agency (MENA) (Egypt): POB 2268, 72 rue al-Geish, Beirut.

Reuters (United Kingdom): POB 11-1006, Immeuble Hibat al-Maarad, place Riad es-Solh, Beirut; tel. (1) 983885; fax (1) 983889; e-mail samia.nakhoul@reuters.com; internet www.reuters.com; Bureau Chief SAMIA NAKHOUL.

Rossiiskoye Informatsionnoye Agentstvo—Novosti (RIA—Novosti) (Russia): POB 11-1086, Beirut; tel. (1) 300219; fax (1) 314168; e-mail novosti@cyberia.net.lb; Dir KONSTANTIN MAXIMOV.

United Press International (UPI) (USA): Hamra, Beirut; internet www.upi.com; Bureau Man. RIAD KAJ.

Xinhua (New China) News Agency (People's Republic of China): POB 114-5075, Beirut; tel. (1) 830359.

BTA (Bulgaria), INA (Iraq), JANA (Libya), Prensa Latina (Cuba) and Saudi Press Agency (SPA) are also represented in Lebanon.

PRESS ASSOCIATION

Lebanese Press Order: POB 3084, ave Saeb Salam, Beirut; tel. (1) 865519; fax (1) 865516; e-mail mail@pressorder.org; internet www .pressorder.org; f. 1911; 18 mems; Pres. MUHAMMAD AL-BAALBAKI; Vice-Pres. GEORGES SKAFF; Sec. MALEK MROUEH.

Publishers

Dar al-Adab: POB 11-4123, Beirut; tel. and fax (1) 861633; e-mail d_aladab@cyberia.net.lb; f. 1953; dictionaries, literary and general; Man. RANA IDRISS; Editor-in-Chief SAMAH IDRISS.

Arab Institute for Research and Publishing (Al-Mouasasah al-Arabiyah Lildirasat Walnashr): POB 1107-2190, Tour Carlton, Saqiat el-Janzeer, Beirut; tel. and fax (1) 751438; e-mail mkayyali@ jonet.com; f. 1969; Dir. MAHER KAYYALI; works in Arabic and English.

Arab Scientific Publishers BP: POB 13-5574, Immeuble Ein at-Tenah Reem, rue Sakiet al-Janzir, Beirut; tel. (1) 811385; fax (1) 860138; e-mail bchebaro@asp.com.lb; internet www.asp.com.lb; computer science, biological sciences, cookery, travel; Pres. BASSAM CHEBARO.

Dar Assayad Group (SAL and International): POB 11-1038, Hazmieh, Beirut; tel. (5) 456373; fax (5) 452700; e-mail assayad@ inco.com.lb; internet www.interlink.com.lb/acce; f. 1943; Dar Assayad International founded in 1983; publishes in Arabic *Al-Anwar* (daily, plus weekly supplement), *Assayad* (weekly), *Achabaka* (weekly), *Background Reports* (three a month), *Arab Defense Journal* (monthly), *Fairuz Lebanon* (monthly, plus international monthly edition), *Al-Idari* (monthly), *Al Computer, Communications and Electronics* (monthly), *Al-Fares* (monthly); has offices and correspondents in Arab countries and most parts of the world; Chair. ISSAM FREIHA; Pres. and Man. Dir BASSAM FREIHA.

Chatila Publishing House: POB 13-5121, Chouran, Beirut 1102-2802; tel. (1) 352413; fax (1) 352419; e-mail info@chatilapublishing .com; internet www.chatilapublishing.com; publishes *Arab Construction World* (every two months), *Arab Water World* (every two months), *Middle East Food* (every two months), *Middle East and World Food Directory* (bi-annual), *Middle East and World Water Directory* (bi-annual).

Edition Française pour le Monde Arabe (EDIFRAMO): POB 113-6140, Immeuble Élissar, rue Bliss, Beirut; tel. (1) 862437; Man. TAHSEEN S. KHAYAT.

Editions Orientales SAL: POB 1404, Immeuble Sayegh, rue Sursock, Beirut; tel. (1) 202070; fax (1) 202663; e-mail info@ediori.com .lb; internet www.ediori.com.lb; political and social newspapers and magazines; Pres. and Editor-in-Chief CHARLES ABOU ADAL.

Geoprojects SARL: POB 113–5294, Immeuble Barakat, 13 rue Jeanne d'Arc, Beirut; tel. (1) 344236; fax (1) 353000; e-mail allprint@ cyberia.net.lb; f. 1978; regional issues, travel; Man. Dir TAHSEEN KHAYAT.

Dar el-Ilm Lilmalayin: POB 1085, Centre Metco, rue Mar Elias, Beirut 2045–8402; tel. (1) 306666; fax (1) 701657; e-mail malayin@ malayin.com; internet www.malayin.com; f. 1945; dictionaries, encyclopaedias, reference books, textbooks, Islamic cultural books; CEO TAREF OSMAN.

Institute for Palestine Studies, Publishing and Research Organization (IPS): POB 11-7164, rue Anis Nsouli, off Verdun, Beirut; tel. and fax (1) 868387; e-mail ipsbrt@palestine-studies.org; f. 1963; independent non-profit Arab research organization; to promote better understanding of the Palestine problem and the Arab–Israeli conflict; publishes books, reprints, research papers, etc. Chair. Dr HISHAM NASHABE; Exec. Sec. Prof. WALID KHALIDI.

The International Documentary Center of Arab Manuscripts: POB 2668, Immeuble Hanna, Ras Beirut, Beirut; e-mail alafaq@ cyberia.net.lb; f. 1965; publishes and reproduces ancient and rare Arabic texts; Propr ZOUHAIR BAALBAKI.

Dar al-Kashaf: POB 112091, rue Assad Malhamee, Beirut; tel. (1) 296805; f. 1930; publishers of *Al-Kashaf* (Arab Youth Magazine), maps, atlases and business books; printers and distributors; Propr M. A. FATHALLAH.

Khayat Book and Publishing Co SARL: 90–94 rue Bliss, Beirut; Middle East, Islam, history, medicine, social sciences, education, fiction; Man. Dir PAUL KHAYAT.

Dar al-Kitab al-Lubnani: Beirut; tel. (1) 861563; fax (1) 351433; f. 1929; Man. Dir HASSAN EZ-ZEIN.

Librairie du Liban Publishers: POB 11-9232, Beirut; tel. (9) 217944; fax (9) 217734; e-mail psayegh@librairie-du-liban.com.lb;

internet www.librairie-du-liban.com.lb; f. 1944; publisher of children's books, dictionaries and reference books; distributor of books in English and French; Man. Dirs HABIB SAYEGH, PIERRE SAYEGH.

Dar al-Maaref Liban SARL: Beirut; tel. (1) 931243; f. 1959; children's books and textbooks in Arabic; Man. Dir Dr FOUAD IBRAHIM; Gen. Man. JOSEPH NACHOU.

Dar al-Machreq SARL: c/o Librairie orientale, POB 55206, Beirut; tel. (1) 202423; fax (1) 329348; e-mail machreq@cyberia.net.lb; internet www.darelmachreq.com; f. 1848; religion, art, Arabic and Islamic literature, history, languages, science, philosophy, school books, dictionaries and periodicals; Man. Dir CAMILLE HÉCHAIMÉ.

Dar Naamān lith-Thaqāfa: POB 567, Jounieh; tel. and fax (9) 935096; e-mail naamanculture@lynx.net.lb; f. 1979; publishes *Mawsou'atul 'Alamil 'Arabiyyil Mu'asser* (Encyclopaedia of Contemporary Arab World), *Mawsou'atul Waqa'e'il 'Arabiyya* (Encyclopaedia of Arab Events), *Qitāboul A'lamil A'rabi, Siyassa was Strategia, As-Sahafa wal I'lam*in Arabic and *The Arab World* in English; Propr NAJI NAAMAN; Exec. Man. MARCELLE AL-ASHKAR.

Dar an-Nahar SAL: POB 11-226, rue de Rome, Hamra, Beirut; tel. (1) 347176; fax (1) 738159; e-mail fadit@annahar.com.lb; f. 1967; a Pan-Arab publishing house; Pres. GHASSAN TUÉNI; Dir FADI TUÉNI.

Naufal Group SARL: POB 11-2161, Immeuble Naufal, rue Sourati, Beirut; tel. (1) 354898; fax (1) 354394; e-mail naufalgroup@terra.net .lb; f. 1970; subsidiary cos Macdonald Middle East Sarl, Les Editions Arabes; encyclopaedias, fiction, children's books, history, law and literature; Man. Dir TONY NAUFAL.

Publitec Publications: POB 166142, Beirut; tel. (1) 495401; fax (1) 493330; e-mail publitecpublications@hotmail.com; internet www .whoswhointhearabworld.info; f. 1965; publishes *Who's Who in Lebanon* and *Who's Who in the Arab World*; Pres. CHARLES GEDEON; Man. KRIKOR AYVAZIAN.

Dar ar-Raed al-Lubnani: POB 93, Immeuble Kamal al-Assad, Hazmieh, Sammouri, Beirut; tel. (5) 450757; f. 1971; CEO RAYED SAMMOURI.

Rihani Printing and Publishing House: Beirut; f. 1963; Propr ALBERT RIHANI; Man. DAOUD STEPHAN.

World Book Publishing: POB 11-3176, rue Emile Eddé, Beirut; tel. (1) 349370; fax (1) 351226; e-mail info@arabook.com; internet www.arabook.com; f. 1929; literature, education, philosophy, current affairs, self-help, children's books; Vice-Pres. TOUFIC EZ-ZEIN; Gen. Man. RAFIC EZ-ZEIN.

Broadcasting and Communications

TELECOMMUNICATIONS

Regulatory Authority

Direction Générale des Télécommunications pour l'Exploitation et la Maintenance: Ministry of Posts and Telecommunications (see above); Dir-Gen. ABDUL M. YOUSSEF.

Service Providers

France-Télécom Mobile Liban (FTML): POB 50257, Beirut; tel. (3) 391850; fax (3) 391859; internet www.ftml.com.lb; f. 1994; operates Cellis (see below); Chair. and Gen. Man. SALAH BOURAAD.

> **Cellis:** Beirut; internet www.cellis.com.lb; f. 1995; provides mobile cellular telephone services.

LibanCell SAL: POB 136406, Immeuble LibanCell, ave Charles Hélou, Beirut; tel. (1) 566111; fax (1) 564184; e-mail info@libancell .com.lb; internet www.libancell.com.lb; provides mobile cellular telephone services; Chair. HUSSEIN RIFAI.

BROADCASTING

Radio

Radio Liban: rue Arts et Métiers, Beirut; tel. (1) 346880; part of the Ministry of Information; f. 1937; Dir-Gen. QASSEM HAGE ALI.

The Home Service broadcasts in Arabic on short wave, and the Foreign Service broadcasts in Portuguese, Armenian, Arabic, Spanish, French and English.

Television

Lebanese Broadcasting Corporation (LBC) Sat Ltd: POB 111, Zouk; tel. (9) 850850; fax (9) 850916; e-mail lbcsat@lbcsat.com.lb; internet www.lbcsat.com; f. 1985 as Lebanese Broadcasting Corporation International SAL; name changed 1996; operates satellite channel on Arabsat 2A; programmes in Arabic, French and English; Chair. Sheikh PIERRE ED-DAHER.

Télé-Liban (TL) SAL: POB 11-5055, Hazmieh, 4848 Beirut; tel. and fax (1) 793000; fax (1) 950286; e-mail tl@tele-liban.com.lb; f. 1959; commercial service; programmes in Arabic, French and English on three channels; privatization pending in 2001; Chair. and Dir-Gen. IBRAHIM EL-KHOURY; Dep. Dir-Gen. MUHAMMAD S. KARIMEH.

Future Television: White House, rue Spears, Sanayeh, Beirut; tel. (1) 347121; fax (1) 602310; e-mail future@future.com.lb; internet www.future.com.lb; commercial; privately-owned; Owner RAFIK HARIRI; Gen. Man. NADIM AL-MONLA.

Al-Manar (Lighthouse): Beirut; e-mail almanar@almanar.com.lb; f. 1991; television station owned by Lebanese Communication Group (LCG) and partly controlled by Hezbollah; operates satellite channel since May 2000; Chair. of Bd NAYEF KRAYEM.

During 1996–98 the Government took measures to close down unlicensed private broadcasters, and to restrict the activities of those licensed to operate. In particular, the broadcasting of news and political programmes by private satellite television channels was banned.

Finance

(cap. = capital; dep. = deposits; res = reserves; m. = million; brs = branches; amounts in £L)

BANKING

Beirut was, for many years, the leading financial and commercial centre in the Middle East, but this role was destroyed by the civil conflict. To restore the city as a regional focus for investment banking is a key element of the Government's reconstruction plans.

Central Bank

Banque du Liban: POB 11-5544, rue Masraf Loubnane, Beirut; tel. (1) 750000; fax (1) 747600; e-mail bdlit@bdl.gov.lb; internet www.bdl .gov.lb; f. 1964 to take over the banking activities of the Banque de Syrie et du Liban in Lebanon; cap. and res £L911,900m., dep. £L9,341,400m. (Dec. 2000); Gov. RIAD SALAMEH; 9 brs.

Principal Commercial Banks

Allied Business Bank SAL: POB 113-7165, Allied House Bldg, ave Charles Malek, St Nicolas, Achrafieh, Beirut; tel. (1) 323116; fax (1) 200660; e-mail mailbox@abb.com.lb; internet www.abb.com.lb; f. 1962; cap. £L15,000m., res £L12,846m., dep. £L330,792m. (Dec. 2000); Chair. ABDULLAH S. ZAKHEM; Man. Dir HABIB F. ABU FADIL; 14 brs in Lebanon, 1 in Cyprus.

Al Mawarid Bank SAL: POB 113-6260, Immeuble Yared, 3e étage, rue Abd al-Aziz, Beirut; tel. (1) 350612; fax (1) 341340; e-mail mail@ almawarid.com.lb; internet www.almawarid.com.lb; f. 1980; cap. £L12,500m., res £L4,545m., dep. £L398,993m. (Dec. 2000); Chair. and Gen. Man. SALIM KHEIREDDINE; 10 brs.

Bank of Beirut SAL: POB 11-7354, Bank of Beirut SAL Bldg, Foch St, Beirut Central District, Beirut; tel. (1) 985418; fax (1) 985327; e-mail executive@bankofbeirut.com.lb; internet www.bankofbeirut .com.lb; f. 1973; absorbed Transorient Bank 1999; merger with Beirut Riyad Bank pending; cap. £L52,338m., res £L107,208m., dep. £2,458,020m. (Dec. 2000); Chair. and Gen. Man. SALIM G. SFEIR; 32 brs.

Bank of Beirut and the Arab Countries SAL: POB 11-1536, Immeuble de la Banque, 250 rue Clémenceau, Riad es-Solh, Beirut 1107 2080; tel. (1) 366630; fax (1) 374299; e-mail marketing@bbac .com.lb; internet www.bbac.net; f. 1956; cap. £L72,000m., res £L54,142m., dep. £L2,092,817m. (Dec. 2000); Chair. and Gen. Man. GHASSAN T. ASSAF; 30 brs.

Bank of Kuwait and the Arab World SAL: POB 113-6248, Immeuble Belle Vue, Ain at-Tineh, Verdun, Beirut; tel. (1) 866305; fax (1) 865299; e-mail bkaw@sodetel.net.lb; f. 1959; cap. £L28,000m., res £L12,493m., dep. £L374,230m. (Dec. 2002); Chair. and Gen. Man. ABDUL RAZZAK ACHOUR; 13 brs.

Bank Al-Madina SAL: POB 113-7221, Immeuble Bank Al-Madina, rue Commodore, Hamra, Beirut; tel. (1) 351296; fax (1) 343762; e-mail intdep@bankal-madina.com; f. 1982; cap. £L45,540m., dep. £L226,084m. (Dec. 2000); Hon. Chair. and Gen. Man. Dr ADNAN ABOU AYYASH; Chair. and Gen. Man. Sheikh IBRAHIM ABOU AYYASH; 18 brs.

Banque Audi SAL: POB 11-2560, Riad es-Solh, Beirut 1107 2808; tel. (1) 994000; fax (1) 990555; e-mail bkaudi@audi.com.lb; internet www.audi.com.lb; f. 1962; acquired Orient Credit Bank 1997 and Banque Nasr 1998; cap. £L45,799m., dep. £L6,386,238m. (Dec. 2002); Chair. and Gen. Man. RAYMOND W. AUDI; 65 brs.

Banque de la Beka'a SAL: POB 117, Centre Fakhoury, Zahleh, Beirut; tel. (8) 803217; fax (8) 429387; f. 1965; cap. £L2,000m., dep.

£L112,650m. (Dec. 1996); Chair. and Gen. Man. CHAOUKI W. FAKHOURY.

Banque de Crédit National SAL: POB 110-204, Centre Gefinor, Bloc B, 15e étage, rue Clémenceau, Beirut; tel. (1) 752777; fax (1) 752555; e-mail bcnsafra@dm.net.lb; f. 1920; cap. £L11,000m., res £L2,443m., dep. £L17,809m. (Dec. 1998); Chair. and Gen. Man. EDMOND J. SAFRA.

Banque de l'Industrie et du Travail SAL: POB 11-3948, Riad es-Solh, Beirut 1107 2150; tel. (4) 712539; fax (4) 712538; e-mail international@bitbank.com.lb; internet www.bitbank.com.lb; f. 1960; cap. £L4,000m., res £L2,207m., dep. £L369,080m. (Dec. 2002); Chair. and Gen. Man. Sheikh FOUAD JAMIL EL-KHAZEN; Dir and Gen. Man. NABIL N. KHAIRALLAH; 12 brs.

Banque du Liban et d'Outre-Mer SAL (BLOM Bank): POB 11-1912, Immeuble BLOM Bank, rue Rachid Karameh, Verdun, Beirut 1107 2807; tel. (1) 743300; fax (1) 738946; e-mail blommail@blom .com.lb; internet www.blom.com.lb; f. 1951; cap. £L185,000m., res £L242,447m., dep. £L8,329,126m. (Dec. 2001); Chair. and Gen. Man. Dr NAAMAN AZHARI; Vice-Chair. and Gen. Man. SAMER AZHARI; 42 brs in Lebanon.

Banque Libano-Française SAL: POB 11-0808, Tour Liberty, rue de Rome, Beirut 1107-2804; tel. (1) 791332; fax (1) 340350; e-mail info@eblf.com; internet www.eblf.com; f. 1967; cap. £L100,000m., res £L175,992m., dep. £L4,371,259m. (Dec. 2001); Pres. and Chair. FARID RAPHAEL; 23 brs.

Banque de la Méditerranée SAL: POB 11-348, 482 rue Clémenceau, Beirut 2022 9302; tel. (1) 373937; fax (1) 362706; f. 1944; cap. £L530,000m., res £L33,259m., dep. £L5,077,238m. (Dec. 2000); Chair. and Gen. Man. Dr MUSTAFA H. RAZIAN; 25 brs.

Banque Misr-Liban SAL: rue Riad es-Solh, Beirut 1107 2010; tel. (1) 980399; fax (1) 980604; e-mail mail@bml.com.lb; internet www .bml.com.lb; f. 1929; cap. £L27,000m., res £L212,296m., dep. £L615,392m. (Dec. 2002); Chair. Dr BAHAA ED-DIN HELMY; Gen. Man. MUHAMMAD ZAHRAN; 15 brs.

Banque Saradar SAL: POB 11-1121, Beirut 1107-2805; tel. (4) 416804; fax (4) 404490; e-mail saradar@saradar.com.lb; internet www.saradar.com.lb; f. 1948; cap. £L40,000m., res £L61,441m., dep. £L2,425,027m. (Dec. 2000); Chair. and Gen. Man. MARIO JOE SARADAR; 8 brs.

Beirut Riyad Bank SAL: POB 11-4668, Immeuble BRB, rue Riad es-Solh, Beirut 1107-2170; tel. (1) 980222; fax (1) 980358; e-mail beriba@cyberia.net.lb; internet www.brb.com.lb; f. 1958; merger with Bank of Beirut pending; cap. £L40,320m. (Dec. 2001); Chair. and Gen. Man. ANWAR M. EL-KHALIL; Dep. Chair. and Gen. Man. SAMIR H. MANSOUR; 11 brs in Lebanon, 1 in UK.

BEMO (Banque Européenne pour le Moyen-Orient) SAL: POB 1100–2120, Immeuble BEMO, place Sassine, Achrafieh, Beirut; tel. (1) 200505; fax (1) 330780; e-mail bemosal@dm.net.lb; internet www .bemo.com.lb; f. 1964; cap. £L44,247m., res £L7,624m., dep. £L558,312m. (Dec. 2000); Chair. HENRY Y. OBEGI; Gen. Man. RIAD B. OBEGI; 6 brs.

Byblos Bank SAL: POB 11-5605, ave Elias Sarkis, Achrafieh, Beirut; tel. (1) 335200; fax (1) 335540; e-mail byblosbk@byblosbank .com.lb; internet www.byblosbank.com; f. 1959; merged with Banque Beyrouth pour le Commerce SAL 1997; acquired Byblos Bank Europe SA 1998 and Wedge Bank Middle East SAL 2001; cap. £L245,878m., res £L202,802m., dep. £L5,354,583m. (Dec. 2000); Chair. and Gen. Man. Dr FRANÇOIS SEMAAN BASSIL; 57 brs in Lebanon, 4 abroad.

Crédit Bancaire SAL: POB 16-5795, Immeuble Crédit Bancaire SAL, blvd Bachir Gemayel, Achrafieh, Beirut; tel. (1) 218183; fax (1) 200483; e-mail info@creditbancair.com.lb; internet www .creditbancaire.com.lb; f. 1981; cap. £L10,800m., res £L12,196m., dep. £L272,445m. (Dec. 2000); Chair. and Gen. Man. PAUL A. KEBBÉ; Man. Dir TAREK KHALIFEH; 9 brs.

Crédit Libanais SAL: POB 53492, Centre Sofil, ave Charles Malek, Beirut; tel. (1) 200028; fax (1) 602615; e-mail info@ creditlibanais.com.lb; internet www.creditlibanais.com.lb; f. 1961; cap. £L80,000m., res £L147,204m., dep. £L2,694,740m. (Dec. 2001); Chair. and Gen. Man. Dr JOSEPH M. TORBEY; 47 brs.

Federal Bank of Lebanon SAL: POB 11-2209, Immeuble Renno, ave Charles Malek, St Nicolas, Beirut; tel. (1) 212300; fax (1) 215847; e-mail federal@cyberia.net.lb; f. 1952; cap. £L9,845m., res £L12,143m., dep. £L154,643m. (Dec. 2001); Chair. and Gen. Man. AYOUB FARID MICHEL SAAB; Gen. Man. BECHARA CHAKIB MATTAR; 8 brs.

Fransabank SAL: POB 11-0393, Riad es-Solh, Beirut 1107 2803; tel. (1) 340180; fax (1) 354572; e-mail fsb@fransabank.com; internet www.fransabank.com; f. 1978 as merger of Banque Sabbag and Banque Française pour le Moyen Orient SAL; acquired Banque Tohmé SAL 1993, Universal Bank SAL 1999 and United Bank of Saudi and Lebanon SAL 2002; cap. £L233,114m., res £L92,720m., dep. £L3,941,853m. (Dec. 2001); Chair. ADNAN KASSAR; Vice-Chair. ADEL KASSAR; 52 brs.

Intercontinental Bank of Lebanon SAL: POB 11-5292, Ittihadiah Bldg, Charles Malek Ave, Beirut 1107-2190; tel. (1) 200350; fax (1) 204505; e-mail ibl@ibl.com.lb; f. 1961; cap. £L14,414m., res £L13,254m., dep. £L691,340m. (Dec. 2001); Chair. and Gen. Man. SELIM HABIB; 9 brs.

Jammal Trust Bank SAL: POB 11-5640, Immeuble Jammal, rue Verdun, Beirut; tel. (1) 805702; fax (1) 864170; e-mail info@jammalbank.com.lb; internet www.jammalbank.co.lb; f. 1963 as Investment Bank, SAL; cap. £L29,692m., res £L24,527m., dep. £L217,741m. (Dec. 2000); Pres., Chair. and Gen. Man. ALI ABDULLAH JAMMAL; 20 brs in Lebanon, 4 in Egypt.

Lebanese Canadian Bank: POB 11-2520, Immeuble Ghantous, blvd Dora, Riad es-Solh, Beirut 1107-2110; tel. (1) 250222; fax (1) 250777; e-mail lebcan@lebcanbank.com; internet www.lebcanbank.com; f. 1960; cap. £L14,000m., res £L11,196m., dep. £L684,790m. (Dec. 2000); Pres., Chair. and Gen. Man. GEORGES ZARD ABOU JAOUDÉ; 16 brs.

Lebanese Swiss Bank SAL: POB 11-9552, Immeuble Hoss, 6e étage, rue Emile Eddé, Hamra, Beirut; tel. (1) 354501; fax (1) 346242; e-mail lbs@t-net.com.lb; f. 1973; cap. £L24,000m., res £L8,289m., dep. £L326,889m. (Dec. 2000); Chair. and Gen. Man. Dr TANAL SABBAH; 7 brs.

Lebanon and Gulf Bank SAL: POB 113-6404, Immeuble Rinno, 585 rue de Lyon, Hamra, Beirut; tel. (1) 340190; fax (1) 743135; internet www.lgb@lgb.com.lb; f. 1963 as Banque de Crédit Agricole, name changed 1980; cap. £L30,000m., res £L5,842m., dep. £L832,068m. (Dec. 2000); Chair. and Gen. Man. ABD AL-HAFIZ MAHMOUD ITANI; 10 brs.

Middle East and North Africa Bank SAL: POB 14-5958, Beirut 1105 2080; tel. (1) 826740; fax (1) 841190; e-mail meabho@cyberia.net.lb; internet www.meabank.com; f. 1991; cap. £L24,000m., res £L978m., dep. £L296,791m. (Dec. 2000); Pres., Chair. and Gen. Man. HASSAN HEJEIJ; 4 brs.

National Bank of Kuwait (Lebanon) SAL: POB 11-5727, BAC Bldg, Sanayeh Sq., Justinien St, Riad es-Solh, Beirut 1107 2200; tel. (1) 741111; fax (1) 747866; e-mail info@nbk.com.lb; internet www.nbk.com.lb; f. 1963 as Rifbank, name changed 1996; cap. £L40,020m., res £L4,781m., dep. £L278,617m. (Dec. 2001); Chair. IBRAHIM DABDOUB; Gen. Man. HANY SHERIF; 9 brs.

Near East Commercial Bank SAL: POB 16-5766, 6e étage, Centre Sofil, ave Charles Malek, St Nicolas, Beirut; tel. and fax (1) 200331; e-mail necb@dm.net.lb; f. 1978; cap. £L11,500m., res £L591m., dep. £L180,919m. (Dec. 2001); Chair. and Gen. Man. PAUL CALAND; 5 brs.

North Africa Commercial Bank SAL: POB 11-9575, Centre Aresco, rue Justinian, Beirut; tel. (1) 346320; fax (1) 346322; e-mail nacb@sodetel.net.lb; f. 1973; cap. £L45,687m., dep. £L482,735m. (Dec. 2001); Pres. and Chair. ABOUBAKER ALI SHERIF; Gen. Man. HADI I. ENGIM; 2 brs.

Saudi Lebanese Bank SAL: POB 11-6765, Riad es-Solh, Beirut 1107 2220; tel. (1) 868987; fax (1) 790250; e-mail slbl@t-net.com.lb; f. 1979 as Lebanese Saudi Credit SAL, name changed as above 1981; cap. £L40,000m., res £L15,244m., dep. £L675,651m. (Dec. 1997); Chair. and Gen. Man. Dr MOUSTAFA RAZIAN; 6 brs.

Société Bancaire du Liban SAL: POB 165192, place Sassine, Achrafieh, Beirut 1100 2020; tel. (1) 204826; fax (1) 200455; e-mail sbl-dg@dm.net.lb; f. 1899; cap. £L11,344m., res £L3,229m., dep. £L119,572m. (Dec. 2001); Chair. ANDRE BOULOS; Vice-Chair. SOLLY LAWI; 4 brs.

Société Générale de Banque au Liban (SGBL): POB 11-2955, rond-point Salomé, Sin el-Fil, Beirut; tel. (1) 499813; fax (1) 502820; e-mail sgleb@socgen.com.lb; internet www.sgleb.com; f. 1953 as Société Générale Libano Européenne de Banque SAL (SGLEB); absorbed Inaash Bank SAL 2000; name changed as above 2001; cap. £L106,512m., res £L6,241m., dep. £L3,390,201m. (Dec. 2000); Pres., Chair. and Gen. Man. MAURICE SEHNAOUI; 43 brs in Lebanon.

Société Nouvelle de la Banque de Syrie et du Liban SAL (SNBSL): POB 11-957, Highway, Dbayé, Beirut; tel. and fax (1) 402420; fax (1) 404561; e-mail snbsl@snbsl.com.lb; f. 1963; cap. £L27,600m., res £L6,559m., dep. £L569,463m. (Dec. 2001); Chair. RAMSAY A. EL-KHOURY; Gen. Man. HABIB KAHAWATI; 17 brs.

Standard Chartered Bank SAL: POB 70216, Antélias, Beirut; tel. (4) 542474; fax (4) 542374; e-mail metro@metrob.com; internet www.standardchartered.com.lb; f. 1979; acquired Metropolitan Bank SAL 2000; cap. £L12,000m., res £L329m., dep. £L127,440m. (Dec. 2001); Chair. ZAHID RAHIM; Gen. Man. MICHELA CHERENHI; 5 brs.

Syrian Lebanese Commercial Bank SAL: POB 113-5127, Immeuble Cinéma Hamra, rue Hamra, Hamra, Beirut; tel. (1) 341262; fax (1) 341208; e-mail hamra@slcbk.com; f. 1974; cap. £L33,000m., res

£L5,168m., dep. £L134,375m. (Dec. 2000); Pres., Chair. and Gen. Man. TAREK AS-SARRAJ; 3 brs.

United Credit Bank SAL: POB 13-5086, Beirut; tel. (1) 792795; fax (1) 795094; f. 1982 as Commercial Facilities Bank SAL; name changed 1998; cap. £L14.3m., dep. £L29.6m. (Dec. 1999); Chair. and Gen. Man. Dr ADNAN M. ABOU AYYASH; 4 brs.

Development Bank

Audi Investment Bank SAL: POB 16-5110, Centre Sofil, ave Charles Malek, St Nicolas, Achrafieh, Beirut; tel. (1) 994000; fax (1) 990555; e-mail customerhelpline@audi.com.lb; internet www.audi.com.lb; f. 1974 as Investment and Finance Bank, present name since 1996; medium- and long-term loans, 100% from Lebanese sources; owned by Banque Audi SAL (99.3%); cap. £L25,075m., res £L9,846m., dep. £L802,127m. (Dec. 2000); Chair. and Gen. Man. RAYMOND WADIH AUDI.

Principal Foreign Banks

ABN AMRO Bank Lebanon (Netherlands): POB 113-5162, ABN AMRO Tower, ave Charles Malek, St Nicolas, Achrafieh, Beirut 1103-2807; tel. (1) 219200; fax (1) 217756; e-mail abn@abnamro.com.lb; internet www.abnamro.com.lb; f. 1954; cap. £L23,485m., res £L10,714m., dep. £L955,199m. (Dec. 2000); Man. Dir ELIA NAHAS; 6 brs.

Arab Bank plc (Jordan): POB 11-1015, rue Riad es-Solh, Beirut; tel. (1) 980246; fax (1) 980803; e-mail beirut@arabbank.com.lb; f. 1930; cap. £L31,700m., res £L31,100m. dep. £L2,001,400m. (Dec. 2001); Exec. Vice-Pres. and Regional Man. Dr HISHAM BSAT.

Banque Nationale de Paris Intercontinentale SA (France): POB 11-1608, Tour el Ghazal/BNPI, ave Fouad Chehab, Beirut; tel. (1) 333717; fax (1) 200604; e-mail bnpi.liban@bnpi.com.lb; internet www.liban.bnpi.bnpgroup.com; f. 1944; total assets £L2,061,529m. (Dec. 2000); Pres. HENRI TYAN; Gen. Man. GUY LEPINARD.

Citibank NA (USA): POB 113-579, Centre Gefinor, Bloc E, rue Clémenceau, Beirut; tel. (1) 738400; fax (1) 738406; cap. £L7,943m., res £L738m., dep. £L171,860m. (Dec. 2000); CEO ELIA SAMAHA.

Habib Bank (Overseas) Ltd (Pakistan): POB 5616, Fadlallah Centre, 1st Floor, blvd esh-Shiah, Musharaffieh, Beirut; tel. (1) 558992; fax (1) 558995; e-mail habibbkbey@t-net.com.lb; Gen. Man. MUHAMMAD SHAHAB KHATTACK.

HSBC Bank Middle East (United Kingdom): POB 11-1380, HSBC Bldg, Minet el-Hosn, Riad es-Solh, Beirut 1107-2080; tel. (1) 377477; fax (1) 372362; internet www.hsbc.com; f. 1946; cap. £L10,750m. (Dec. 1999); CEO KEVIN SMORTHWAITE; 5 brs.

Jordan National Bank SA: POB 5186, Immeuble Diamond Tower, rue Verdun, Beirut; tel. (1) 797078; fax (1) 794955; e-mail jnbobs@netgate.com.lb; cap. £L7,961m., dep. £L121,964m. (Dec. 1997); Regional Gen. Man. RAFIC ARAMOUNI; 3 brs.

Saudi National Commercial Bank: POB 11-2355, Riad es-Solh, Beirut 1107 2100; tel. (1) 860863; fax (1) 867728; e-mail sncb@sncb.com.lb; cap. £L10,000m., res £L7,933m., dep. £L87,470m. (Dec. 2002); Gen. Man. HANI HOUSSAMI.

Numerous other foreign banks have representative offices in Beirut.

Banking Association

Association of Banks in Lebanon: POB 976, Association of Banks in Lebanon Bldg, Gouraud St, Saifi, Beirut; tel. (1) 970500; fax (1) 970501; e-mail abl@abl.org.lb; internet www.abl.org.lb; f. 1959; serves and promotes the interests of the banking community in Lebanon; mems: 62 banks and 8 banking rep. offices; Pres. Dr JOSEPH TORBEY; Gen. Sec. Dr MAKRAM SADER.

STOCK EXCHANGE

The Beirut Stock Exchange recommenced trading in January 1996.

Beirut Stock Exchange (BSE): POB 13-6690, Tour Soudat, 2e étage, rue Soudat, Hamra, Beirut; tel. (1) 786501; fax (1) 786499; e-mail bse@bse.com.lb; internet www.bse.com.lb; f. 1920; 10 cttee mems; Cttee Pres. Dr FADI KHALAF; Cttee Vice-Pres. Dr GHALEB MAHMASANY.

INSURANCE

About 80 insurance companies were registered in Lebanon in the late 1990s, although less than one-half of these were operational. An insurance law enacted in mid-1999 has increased the required capital base for insurance firms and provided tax incentives for mergers within the sector.

Arabia Insurance Co SAL: POB 11-2172, Arabia House, rue de Phénicie, Beirut; tel. (1) 363610; fax (1) 365139; e-mail arabia@arabia-ins.com.lb; internet www.arabiainsurance.com; f. 1944; cap. £L51,000m. Chair. Dr HISHAM BSAT; Gen. Man. FADY SHAMMAS; 20 brs.

Bankers Assurance SAL: POB 11-4293, Immeuble Capitole, rue Riad es-Solh, Beirut; tel. (1) 988777; fax (1) 984004; e-mail mail@bankers-assurance.com; internet www.bankers.com.lb; f. 1972; Chair. Saba Nader; Gen. Man. Eugène Nader.

Commercial Insurance Co (Lebanon) SAL: POB 4351, Centre Starco, Beirut; POB 84, Jounieh; tel. (1) 373070; fax (1) 373071; e-mail comins@commercialinsurance.com.lb; internet www.commercialinsurance.com.lb; f. 1962; Chair. Max R. Zaccar.

Compagnie Libanaise d'Assurances SAL: POB 3685, rue Riad es-Solh, Beirut; tel. (1) 868988; f. 1951; cap. £L3,000m. (1991); Chair. Jean F. S. Aboujaoudé; Gen. Man. Mamdouh Rahmoun.

Al-Ittihad al-Watani: POB 1270, Immeuble Al-Ittihadia, ave Fouad Chehab, St Nicolas, Beirut; tel. (1) 330840; f. 1947; cap. £L30m. Chair. Joe I. Kairouz; Exec. Dir Tannous Feghali.

Libano-Suisse Insurance Co SAL: POB 11-3821, Beirut 1107-2150; tel. (1) 374900; fax (1) 368724; e-mail insure@libano-suisse.com; internet www.libano-suisse.com.lb; f. 1959; cap. £L4,050m. (2000); Chair. Michel Pierre Pharaon; Gen. Man. Samir Nahas.

Al-Mashrek Insurance and Reinsurance SAL: POB 16-6154, Immeuble Al-Mashrek, 65 rue Aabrine, Beirut 1100 2100; tel. (1) 200541; fax (1) 337625; e-mail amirco@inco.com.lb; f. 1962; cap. £L5,000m., (1999); Chair. and Gen. Man. Abraham Matossian.

'La Phénicienne' SAL: POB 11-5652, Immeuble Hanna Haddad, rue Amine Gemayel, Sioufi, Beirut; tel. (1) 425484; fax (1) 424532; f. 1964; Chair. and Gen. Man. Tannous C. Feghali.

Société Nationale d'Assurances SAL: POB 11-4805, Immeuble SNA, Hazmieh, Beirut; tel. (1) 956600; fax (1) 956624; e-mail sna@sna.com.lb; internet www.sna.com.lb; f. 1963; Chair. Antoine Wakim.

Trade and Industry

DEVELOPMENT ORGANIZATIONS

Council for Development and Reconstruction (CDR): POB 116-5351, Tallet es-Serail, Beirut; tel. (1) 643982; fax (1) 647947; e-mail general@cdr.gov.lb; internet www.cdr.gov.lb; f. 1977; an autonomous public institution reporting to the Cabinet, the CDR is charged with the co-ordination, planning and execution of Lebanon's public reconstruction programme; it plays a major role in attracting foreign funds; Pres. Jamal Itani; Sec.-Gen. George Samaha.

Investment Development Authority of Lebanon (IDAL): POB 113-7251, Cristal Bldg 1145, Hussein el-Adhab St, Nijmeh Sq., Beirut; tel. (1) 983306; fax (1) 983302; e-mail mail@idal.com.lb; internet www.idal.com.lb; f. 1994; state-owned; Chair. and Gen. Man. Samih Barbir.

Société Libanaise pour le Développement et la Reconstruction de Beyrouth (SOLIDERE): POB 11-9493, 149 rue Saad Zagloul, Beirut; tel. (1) 980650; fax (1) 980662; e-mail solidere@solidere.com.lb; internet www.solidere.com.lb; f. 1994; real estate co responsible for reconstruction of Beirut Central District; Dir-Gen. Mounir Douaidy.

CHAMBERS OF COMMERCE AND INDUSTRY

International Chamber of Commerce in Lebanon: POB 11-1801, Immeuble Elias Abd-an Nour, Achrafieh, Beirut; tel. (1) 200437; fax (1) 321220; Chair. Adnan Kassar; Gen. Sec. Louis G. Hobeika.

Beirut Chamber of Commerce and Industry: POB 11-1801, rue Justinian, Sanayeh, Beirut; tel. (1) 744160; fax (1) 353395; e-mail info@ccib.org.lb; internet www.ccib.org.lb; f. 1898; 32,000 mems; Pres. Adnan Kassar; Dir-Gen. Dr Walid Naja.

Tripoli Chamber of Commerce and Industry: POB 27, blvd Tripoli, Tripoli; tel. (6) 432790; Pres. Hassan el-Mounla.

Chamber of Commerce and Industry in Sidon and South Lebanon: POB 41, rue Maarouf Saad, Sidon; tel. (7) 720123; fax (7) 722986; e-mail chamber@ccias.org.lb; internet www.ccias.org.lb; f. 1933; Pres. Mohamad Zaatari.

Zahleh Chamber of Commerce and Industry: POB 100, Zahleh; tel. (8) 802602; fax (8) 800050; f. 1939; 2,500 mems; Pres. Edmond Jreissati.

EMPLOYERS' ASSOCIATION

Association of Lebanese Industrialists: Chamber of Commerce and Industry Bldg, 5e étage, Sanayeh, Beirut; tel. (1) 350280; fax (1) 350282; e-mail ali@ali.org.lb; internet www.ali.org.lb; Pres. Jacques J. Sarraf; Sec.-Gen. Ghazi F. Yahya.

UTILITIES

Electricity

Electricité du Liban (EdL): POB 131, Immeuble de l'Electricité du Liban, 22 rue du Fleuve, Beirut; tel. (1) 442556; fax (1) 583084; f. 1954; state-owned; scheduled for privatization in 2003; Dir-Gen. Kamal F. Hayek.

Water

In the late 1990s the Government was in the process of establishing five new regional water authorities (in the governorates of the North, South, Beka'a, Beirut and Mount Lebanon), to replace the existing water authorities and committees. Under the reorganization the new authorities were to operate under the supervision of the Ministry of Energy and Water.

Beirut Water Supply Office: Beirut; Pres. Lucien Mobayad.

TRADE UNION FEDERATION

Confédération Générale des Travailleurs du Liban (CGTL): POB 4381, Beirut; f. 1958; 300,000 mems; only national labour centre in Lebanon and sole rep. of working classes; comprises 18 affiliated federations including all 150 unions in Lebanon; Chair. Ghneim az-Zoghbi; Pres. Elias Abu Rizq.

Transport

RAILWAYS

Office des Chemins de Fer de l'Etat Libanais et du Transport en Commun: POB 11-0109, Gare St Michel, Nahr, Beirut; tel. (1) 587211; fax (1) 447007; since 1961 all railways in Lebanon have been state-owned. The original network of some 412 km is no longer functioning. However, the Lebanese authorities have agreed a rail reconstruction project involving a section of the network between Tripoli and the Syrian border; Dir-Gen. Radwan Bou Nasser ed-Din.

ROADS

At 31 December 1996 Lebanon had an estimated 6,350 km of roads, of which 2,170 km were highways, main or national roads and 1,370 km were secondary or regional roads. The total road network was estimated at 7,300 km in 1999. The two international motorways are the north–south coastal road and the road connecting Beirut with Damascus in Syria. Among the major roads are that crossing the Beka'a and continuing south to Bent-Jbail and the Shtaura–Ba'albek road. Hard-surfaced roads connect Jezzine with Moukhtara, Bzebdine with Metn, Meyroub with Afka and Tannourine. A road construction project, costing some US $100m., was planned for Beirut in the late 1990s. A new 8-km highway, linking around 26 villages in southern Lebanon, was inaugurated in August 2000.

SHIPPING

A two-phase programme to rehabilitate and expand the port of Beirut is currently under way. In the second phase, which commenced in early 1997, the construction of an industrial free zone, a fifth basin and a major container terminal are envisaged, at an estimated cost of US $1,000m. Tripoli, the northern Mediterranean terminus of the oil pipeline from Iraq (the other is Haifa, Israel—not in use since 1948), is also a busy port, with good equipment and facilities. Jounieh, north of Beirut, is Lebanon's third most important port. A new deep-water sea port is to be constructed south of Sidon. The reconstructed port of an-Naqoura, in what was then the 'security zone' along the border with Israel, was inaugurated in June 1987.

Port Authorities

Gestion et Exploitation du Port de Beyrouth: POB 1490, Beirut; tel. (1) 580210; fax (1) 585835; e-mail pob-mis@dm.net.lb; internet www.portdebeyrouth.com; Pres., Dir-Gen. and Man. Dir Hassan Kamal Kraytem; Harbour Master Maroun Khoury.

Service d'Exploitation du Port de Tripoli: El Mina, Tripoli; tel. (6) 601225; fax (6) 220180; e-mail tport@terra.net.lb; f. 1959; Harbour Master Marwan Baroudi.

Principal Shipping Companies

Youssef A Abourahal and Hanna N Tabet: POB 11-5890, Immeuble Ghantous, autostrade Dora, Beirut; tel. (1) 263872.

Ets Paul Adem: Centre Moucarri, 6e étage, autostrade Dora, Beirut; tel. and fax (1) 582421.

Ademar Shipping Lines: POB 175-231, Beirut; tel. (1) 444100; fax (1) 444101.

Adriatica Levant Lines SARL: Immeuble Tanios Saba, rue Ibrahim Bacha, Medawar, Beirut; tel. (1) 580181.

Agence Générale Maritime (AGEMAR) SARL: POB 9255, Centre Burotec, 7e étage, rue Pasteur, Beirut; tel. (1) 583885; fax (1) 583884; Dirs S. MEDLEJ, N. MEDLEJ.

Kawar Amin & Sons: Beirut; tel. (1) 352525; fax (1) 353802; f. 1963; Chair. TAWFIQ KAWAR AMIN.

Arab Shipping and Chartering Co: POB 1084, Immeuble Ghandour, ave des Français, Beirut; tel. (1) 371044; fax (1) 373370; e-mail arabship@dm.net.lb; agents for China Ocean Shipping Co.

Associated Levant Lines SAL: POB 110371, Immeuble Mercedes, autostrade Dora, Beirut; tel. (1) 255366; fax (1) 255362; e-mail tgf-all@dm.net.lb; Dirs T. GARGOUR, N. GARGOUR, H. GARGOUR.

Wafic Begdache: Immeuble Wazi, 4e étage, rue Moussaitbé, Beirut; tel. (1) 319920; fax (1) 815002; e-mail mody@lebaneseshipping.com.

Bulk Traders International: POB 70-152, Centre St Elie, Bloc A, 6e étage, Antélias, Beirut; tel. (4) 410724; fax (4) 402842; e-mail bulk@cyberia.net.lb.

Continental Shipmanagement SARL: POB 901413, Centre Dora Moucarri, 8e étage, appt 804, Beirut; tel. (1) 583654; fax (1) 584440.

O. D. Debbas & Sons: Head Office: POB 166678, Immeuble Debbas, 530 blvd Corniche du Fleuve, Beirut; tel. (1) 585253; fax (1) 587135; e-mail oddebbas@oddebbas.com; f. 1892; Man. Dir OIDIH ELIE DEBBAS.

Dery Shipping Lines Ltd: POB 5720-113, Beirut; tel. (1) 862442; fax (1) 344146.

Diana K Shipping Co: POB 113-5125, Immeuble Ajouz, rue Kenedi, Ein Mreisseh, Beirut; tel. (1) 363314; fax (1) 369712; e-mail dianak@cyberia.net.lb; Marine Dept Man. Capt. AMIN HABBAL.

Fauzi Jemil Ghandour: POB 1084, Beirut; tel. (1) 373376; fax (1) 360048; e-mail alifgand@dm.net.lb; agents for Denizçlik Bankasi TAO (Denizvollari); Ecuadorian Line, Festival Shipping and Tourist Enterprises Ltd.

Gezairi Chartering and Shipping Co (GEZACHART): POB 11-1402, Immeuble Gezairi, place Gezairi, Ras Beirut; tel. (1) 783783; fax (1) 784784; e-mail gezachart@gezairi.com; internet www.gezairi.com; ship management, chartering, brokerage.

Gulf Agency Co (Lebanon) Ltd: POB 4392, Beirut; tel. (1) 446086; fax (1) 446097; e-mail gacleltd@dm.net.lb; f. 1969; Gen. Man. SIMON G. BEJJANI.

Lebanese Navigators Co SARL: Beirut; tel. (1) 603335; fax (1) 603334.

Medawar Shipping Co SARL: POB 8962/11, Immeuble Kanafani, rue al-Arz, Saifi, Beirut; tel. (1) 447277; fax (1) 447662.

Mediterranean Feedering Co SARL: POB 70-1187, Immeuble Akak, autostrade Dbayeh, Beirut; tel. (1) 403056; fax (1) 406444; e-mail mfcbeirut@attmail.com; Man. Dir EMILE AKEF EL-KHOURY.

Orient Shipping and Trading Co SARL: POB 11-2561, Immeuble Moumneh, no 72, rue Ain al-Mraisseh 54, Beirut; tel. (1) 644252; fax (1) 602221; Dirs ELIE ZAROUBY, EMILE ZAROUBY.

Rassem Shipping Agency: POB 11-8460, Immeuble Agha, Raoucheh, Beirut; tel. (1) 866372; fax (1) 805593.

Riga Brothers: POB 17-5134, Immeuble Mitri Haddad, rue du Port, Beirut; tel. (1) 406882.

G. Sahyouni & Co SARL: POB 17-5452, Mar Mikhael, Beirut 1104 2040; tel. (1) 257046; fax (1) 241317; e-mail lloydsbey@inco.com.lb; f. 1989; agents for Baltic Control Lebanon Ltd., SARL, and Lloyds; Man. Dir. GEORGE SHYOUNI; Financial Man. HENRY CHIDIAC.

Sinno Trading and Navigation Agency: POB 113-6977, Immeuble Rebeiz, 4e étage, rue du Port, Beirut; tel. (1) 446698; fax (1) 446707; Chair. MUHIEDDINE F. SINNO; Man. Dir AHMED JABBOURY.

A Sleiman Co & Sons: Immeuble Saroulla, 3e étage, rue Hamra, Beirut; tel. (1) 354240; fax (1) 340262.

Union Shipping and Chartering Agency SAL: POB 2856, Immeuble Ghandour, ave des Français, Beirut; tel. (1) 373376; fax (1) 360048; e-mail unichart@dm.net.lb; agents for Croatia Line, Jadroslobodna, Jugo Oceania, Atlanska Plovidba, Jadroplov and Maruba S.C.A.

CIVIL AVIATION

Services from the country's principal airport, in Beirut, were subject to frequent disruptions after 1975; its location in predominantly Muslim west Beirut made it virtually inaccessible to non-Muslims. In 1986 a new airport, based on an existing military airfield, was opened at Halat, north of Beirut, by Christian concerns, but commercial operations from the airport were not authorized by the Government. Services to and from Beirut by Middle East Airlines (MEA) were suspended, and the airport closed, at the end of January 1987, after the Christian LF militia shelled the airport and threatened to attack MEA aircraft if services from their own airport, at Halat, did not receive official authorization. Beirut airport was reopened in May, after the LF accepted government assurances that Halat would receive the necessary authorization for civil use. However, the commission concluded that Halat did not possess the facilities to cater for international air traffic. Some 2.4m. passengers used Beirut International Airport in 2001. In late 2001 a major expansion project at the airport was completed, at an estimated cost of US $600m.; facilities included a new terminal building and two new runways, increasing handling capacity to 6m. passengers a year.

MEA (Middle East Airlines, Air Liban SAL): POB 206, Headquarters MEA, blvd de l'Aéroport, Beirut; tel. (1) 628888; fax (1) 629260; e-mail mea@mea.net.lb; internet www.mea.com.lb; f. 1945; acquired Lebanese International Airways in 1969; privatization scheduled for 2003; regular services throughout Europe, the Middle East, North and West Africa, and the Far East; Chair. MUHAMMAD EL-HOUT; Commercial Man. NIZAR KHOURY.

Trans-Mediterranean Airways SAL (TMA): Beirut International Airport, POB 11–3018, Beirut; tel. (1) 629210; fax (1) 629219; e-mail cargo@tma.com.lb; internet www.tma.com.lb; f. 1953; scheduled services, charter activities and aircraft lease operations covering Europe, the Middle East, Africa and the Far East; also provides handling, storage and maintenance services; Chair. and Pres. FADI N. SAAB.

Tourism

Before the civil war, Lebanon was a major tourist centre, and its scenic beauty, sunny climate and historic sites attracted some 2m. visitors annually. In 1974 tourism contributed about 20% of the country's income. Since the end of the civil conflict, tourist facilities (in particular hotels) have begun to be reconstructed, and the Government has chosen to concentrate its efforts on the promotion of cultural as well as conference and exhibition-based tourism. In 1999 UNESCO declared Beirut as the Cultural Capital of the Arab World. Lebanon is also being promoted as an 'eco-tourism' destination. Excluding Syrian visitors, the annual total of tourist arrivals increased from 177,503 in 1992 to 741,648 in 2000. Tourism receipts reached an estimated US $1,221m. in 1998; however, receipts fell to $742m. in 2000. Of total arrivals in 2000, 38.8% were from Arab countries (excluding Syria) and 30.9% from Europe.

National Council of Tourism in Lebanon (NCTL): POB 11-5344, rue Banque du Liban 550, Beirut; tel. (1) 343196; fax (1) 343279; e-mail tourism@cyberia.net.lb; internet www.lebanon-tourism.gov.lb; government-sponsored autonomous organization responsible for the promotion of tourism; overseas offices in Paris (France) and Cairo (Egypt); Pres. FOUAD FAWAZ; Dir-Gen. NASSER SAFIEDDINE.

LESOTHO

Introductory Survey

Location, Climate, Language, Religion, Flag, Capital

The Kingdom of Lesotho is a land-locked country, entirely surrounded by South Africa. The climate is generally mild, although cooler in the highlands: lowland temperatures range from a maximum of 32°C (90°F) in summer (October to April) to a minimum of −7°C (20°F) in winter. Rainfall averages about 725 mm (29 ins) per year, mostly falling in summer. The official languages are English and Sesotho. About 90% of the population are Christians. The largest denominations are the Roman Catholic, Lesotho Evangelical and Anglican Churches. The national flag (official proportions 2 by 3) is divided diagonally from lower hoist to upper fly, with the hoist triangle of white bearing, in brown silhouette, a traditional Basotho shield with crossed knobkerrie (club), barbed assegai (spear) and a thyrsus of ostrich feathers, and the fly triangle comprising a blue diagonal stripe and a green triangle. The capital is Maseru.

Recent History

Lesotho was formerly Basutoland, a dependency of the United Kingdom. In 1868, at the request of the Basotho people's chief, the territory became a British protectorate. Basutoland was annexed to Cape Colony (now part of South Africa) in 1871, but detached in 1884. It became a separate British colony and was administered as one of the High Commission Territories in southern Africa (the others being the protectorates of Bechuanaland, now Botswana, and Swaziland). The British Act of Parliament that established the Union of South Africa in 1910 also provided for the possible inclusion in South Africa of the three High Commission Territories, subject to local consent: the native chiefs opposed requests by successive South African Governments for the transfer of the three territories.

Within Basutoland a revised Constitution, which established the colony's first Legislative Council, was introduced in 1956. A new document, granting limited powers of self-government, was adopted in September 1959. Basutoland's first general election, on the basis of universal adult suffrage, took place on 29 April 1965, and full internal self-government was achieved the following day. Moshoeshoe II, Paramount Chief since 1960, was recognized as King. The Basutoland National Party (BNP), a conservative group supporting limited co-operation with South Africa, narrowly won a majority of the seats in the new Legislative Assembly. The BNP's leader, Chief Leabua Jonathan, failed to win a seat, but won a by-election in July 1965, whereupon he became Prime Minister. Basutoland became independent, as Lesotho, on 4 October 1966. The new Constitution provided for a bicameral legislature, comprising the 60-seat National Assembly and the 33-member Senate; executive power was vested in the Cabinet, which was presided over by the Prime Minister. The King was designated Head of State.

The BNP, restyled the Basotho National Party, remained in power at independence. A constitutional crisis arose in December 1966, when King Moshoeshoe II attempted to obtain wider personal powers, but in January 1967 the King signed an undertaking to abide by the Constitution. A general election was held in January 1970, at which the opposition Basotho Congress Party (BCP), a pan-Africanist group led by Dr Ntsu Mokhehle, appeared to have won a majority of seats in the National Assembly. Chief Jonathan declared a state of emergency, suspended the Constitution and arrested several BCP organizers. The election was annulled, and the legislature prorogued. King Moshoeshoe was placed under house arrest and subsequently exiled, although he returned in December after accepting a government order banning him from participating in politics. The country was thus effectively under the Prime Minister's personal control. An interim National Assembly, comprising the former Senate (mainly chiefs) and 60 members nominated by the Cabinet, was inaugurated in April 1973. The state of emergency was revoked in July. However, following a failed coup attempt in January 1974 by alleged supporters of the BCP, Chief Jonathan introduced stringent security laws. Mokhehle and other prominent members of the BCP went into exile abroad, and the party split into two factions, internal and external. The latter, led by Mokhehle, was supported by the Lesotho Liberation Army (LLA), which was responsible for terrorist attacks in Lesotho during the late 1970s and the 1980s. (The South African Government consistently denied allegations that it supported the LLA.)

Although Lesotho was economically dependent on South Africa, and the Government's official policy during the 1970s was one of 'dialogue' with its neighbour, Chief Jonathan repeatedly criticized the apartheid regime, and supported the then banned African National Congress of South Africa (ANC). In December 1982 South African forces launched a major assault on the homes of ANC members in Maseru, killing more than 40 people. In August 1983 South Africa threatened to impose sanctions unless Lesotho expelled or repatriated 3,000 South African refugees. Two groups of refugees were subsequently reported to have left Lesotho. None the less, Lesotho's persistent refusal to sign a joint non-aggression pact led South Africa to impound consignments of armaments destined for Lesotho, and again, in August 1984, to threaten economic sanctions.

The Parliament Act of May 1983 repealed the emergency order of 1970 that had suspended the Constitution. In January 1985 the National Assembly was dissolved. Legislative elections scheduled for September were cancelled in August, when no opposition candidates were nominated: the opposition parties claimed that their prospective candidates had been denied access to the voters' rolls and had therefore been prevented from securing sufficient signatures to qualify for nomination. BNP candidates in all 60 constituencies were thus returned to office unopposed.

In December 1985 South African commando troops were held responsible by the Lesotho Government for a raid in Maseru in which nine people (including several ANC members) were killed. South Africa imposed a blockade on the border with Lesotho from the beginning of 1986. Five of Lesotho's opposition leaders were arrested on their return from talks in South Africa, and there were reports of fighting between factions of the armed forces. On 20 January Chief Jonathan's Government was overthrown in a coup led by Maj.-Gen. Justin Lekhanya, the head of the armed forces. A Military Council, chaired by Lekhanya, was established. The 1983 Parliament Act was revoked, and it was announced that executive and legislative powers were to be vested in King Moshoeshoe, assisted by the Military Council and a (mainly civilian) Council of Ministers. About 60 ANC members were subsequently deported from Lesotho, and the South African blockade was ended. In March 1986 the Military Council suspended all formal political activity. In September the Council of Ministers was restructured, giving increased responsibility to Lekhanya, and the Military Council held discussions with the leaders of the five main opposition parties.

Although the South African Government denied having any part in the coup, the Lekhanya regime proved to be more amenable to South Africa's regional security policy. In March 1986 it was announced that the two countries had reached an informal agreement whereby neither would allow its territory to be used for attacks against the other. Moreover, the Lesotho Government did not join other African states in pressing for international economic sanctions against South Africa. By August more than 200 South African refugees, believed to be ANC members, were reported to have been expelled from Lesotho (although the Lesotho Government did not permit their extradition directly to South Africa). In March 1988 Lesotho and South Africa reached final agreement on the Lesotho Highlands Water Project (LHWP), a major scheme to supply water to South Africa.

In May 1988 Mokhehle was allowed to return to Lesotho after 14 years of exile. In 1989 the LLA was said to have disbanded, and by 1990 the two factions of the BCP had apparently reunited under Mokhehle's leadership. Meanwhile, in mid-1989 elements within the Government reportedly sought the resignation of Lekhanya from the chairmanship of the Military Council, in response to widespread reports implicating him in the fatal shooting, in 1988, of a civilian: it was claimed that Lekhanya had falsely attributed responsibility for the incident to a subordinate. At a subsequent inquest Lekhanya admitted the truth of the allegations; nevertheless, a verdict of justifiable homicide was recorded.

In February 1990 Lekhanya dismissed three members of the Military Council and one member of the Council of Ministers, accusing them of 'insubordination'. When Moshoeshoe refused to approve new appointments to the Military Council, Lekhanya suspended the monarch's executive and legislative powers, which were assumed by the Military Council in March. Moshoeshoe (who remained Head of State) was exiled in the United Kingdom. Lekhanya announced that a general election would take place during 1992; however, party political activity remained outlawed. In June 1990 a National Constituent Assembly (including Lekhanya, members of the Council of Ministers, representatives of banned political parties, traditional chiefs and business leaders) was inaugurated to draft a new constitution. In October Lekhanya invited the King to return from exile. Moshoeshoe responded that his return would be conditional upon the ending of military rule and the establishment of an interim government, pending the readoption of the 1966 Constitution. On 6 November 1990 Lekhanya promulgated an order dethroning the King with immediate effect. Lesotho's 22 principal chiefs elected Moshoeshoe's elder son, Prince David Mohato Bereng Seeiso, as the new King; on 12 November he acceded to the throne, as King Letsie III, having undertaken to remain detached from politics.

On 30 April 1991 Lekhanya was deposed in a coup organized by disaffected army officers. Col (later Maj.-Gen.) Elias Phitsoane Ramaema succeeded Lekhanya as Chairman of the Military Council. Ramaema repealed the ban on party political activity, and by July the National Constituent Assembly had completed the draft Constitution. In May 1992 Lesotho and South Africa agreed to establish diplomatic relations at ambassadorial level. Following talks in the United Kingdom with Ramaema, former King Moshoeshoe returned from exile in July.

The general election was eventually held on 27 March 1993. The BCP secured all 65 seats in the new National Assembly, winning 54% of the votes cast. Although international observers pronounced the election to have been generally free and fair, the BNP—which took 16% of the votes—rejected the result, alleging that there had been widespread irregularities, and later declined the new administration's offer of two seats in the restored Senate. On 2 April Mokhehle was inaugurated as Prime Minister, and King Letsie swore allegiance to the new Constitution, under the terms of which he remained Head of State with no executive or legislative powers; executive authority was vested in the Cabinet.

A mutiny in November 1993 by about 50 junior officers in the national army, the Royal Lesotho Defence Force (RLDF), was apparently precipitated by a proposal to place the military under the command of a senior member of the LLA—as part of government efforts to integrate its former armed wing with the RLDF. Four senior army officers were subsequently reported to have resigned their posts. Skirmishes near Maseru in January 1994 escalated into more serious fighting between some 600 rebel troops and a 150-strong contingent of forces loyal to the Government, reportedly resulting in the deaths of at least five soldiers and three civilians. Following mediation efforts involving representatives of Botswana, South Africa, Zimbabwe, the Commonwealth (see p. 164), the Organization of African Unity (OAU, now the African Union, see p. 130) and the UN, a truce entered force, and at the beginning of February the rival factions surrendered their weapons and returned to barracks. In April, however, the Deputy Prime Minister, Selometsi Baholo (who also held the finance portfolio), was killed during an abduction attempt by disaffected troops. In the following month police-officers demanding increased pay and allowances briefly held hostage the acting finance minister, Mpho Malie (the Minister of Information and Broadcasting). Agreement was subsequently reached on increased allowances, and the Government announced the formation of an independent commission to review salary structures in the public sector.

A commission to investigate the armed forces unrest of January and April 1994 began work in July. In that month Mokhehle appointed a commission of inquiry into the dethronement of King Moshoeshoe II. In August King Letsie petitioned the High Court to abolish the commission on the grounds of bias on the part of its members. On 17 August Letsie announced that he had dissolved the National Assembly, dismissed the Government and suspended sections of the Constitution, citing 'popular dissatisfaction' with the BCP administration. Although several thousand people gathered outside the royal palace in Maseru in

support of the deposed Government, army and police support for Letsie's 'royal coup' was evident, and subsequent clashes between demonstrators and the security forces reportedly resulted in five deaths. A well-known human rights lawyer, Hae Phoofolo, was appointed Chairman of a transitional Council of Ministers, and the Secretary-General of the BNP, Evaristus Retselisitsoe Sekhonyana, was appointed Minister of Foreign Affairs. Phoofolo identified as a priority for his administration the amendment of the Constitution to facilitate the restoration of Moshoeshoe; in the mean time, King Letsie was to act as executive and legislative Head of State.

The suspension of constitutional government was widely condemned outside Lesotho. The Presidents of Botswana, South Africa and Zimbabwe led diplomatic efforts to restore the elected Government, supported by the OAU and the Commonwealth. The USA withdrew financial assistance, and several other countries threatened sanctions. Following negotiations in South Africa, in September 1994 King Letsie and Mokhehle signed an agreement, guaranteed by Botswana, South Africa and Zimbabwe, providing for the restoration of Moshoeshoe II as reigning monarch and for the restitution of the elected organs of government; the commission of inquiry into Moshoeshoe's dethronement was to be abandoned; all those involved in the 'royal coup' were to be immune from prosecution; the political neutrality of the armed forces and public service was to be guaranteed, and consultations were to be undertaken with the aim of broadening the democratic process. Moshoeshoe was restored to the throne on 25 January 1995, undertaking not to interfere in politics. Letsie took the title of Crown Prince.

Meanwhile, in October 1994 Sekhonyana was ordered to pay a substantial fine (or be sentenced to two years' imprisonment), after being convicted of sedition and the incitement to violence of army and police troops against former LLA members earlier in the year. The director and another senior officer of the National Security Service (NSS) were held hostage by junior officers (who were demanding improved terms and conditions of service, as well as the officers' enforced retirement and prosecution on charges of attempted murder, corruption and breach of security laws) for two weeks in March 1995, and were released only after intervention by the Commonwealth Secretary-General. In September the human rights organization Amnesty International urged the Mokhehle Government to act to eliminate abuses of human rights by the security forces, condemning what it alleged were arbitrary arrests and incommunicado detentions, as well as the ill-treatment of detainees.

In April 1995 government representatives and military officials from Lesotho met with their counterparts from Botswana, South Africa and Zimbabwe to discuss progress in the restoration of constitutional order in Lesotho. The conference examined the recommendations of the commission of inquiry into the army mutiny of 1994: these included a streamlining of existing forces, a clearer definition of their functions, and improved training. In May 1995 two people were shot dead in Maseru during rioting that had erupted while police were maintaining an indefinite 'go slow', as part of their continuing salary campaign. Apparently in an attempt to deter further indiscipline, the Government announced 15% salary increases for the armed and security forces, thus bringing their pay into line with remuneration for other public-sector employees. In August a 5,000-strong demonstration was organized in Maseru to protest against proposed legislation to debar public servants from trade union membership and Mokhehle's plans to reduce earlier salary increases that were now said to have been granted in error.

King Moshoeshoe was killed in a motor accident on 15 January 1996. The College of Chiefs subsequently elected Crown Prince David to succeed his father, and the prince was restored to the throne, resuming the title King Letsie III, on 7 February. Like his father in January 1995, King Letsie undertook not to involve the monarchy in any aspect of political life.

In February 1996 premises of the national radio service were seized by a small group that broadcast an apparently groundless statement that the Government had been overthrown. The alleged perpetrators of the 'false coup'—Makara Sekautu, the President of the opposition United Party, together with two former members of the Lesotho Defence Force (LDF, as the RLDF had been redesignated) and a former member of the NSS —were subsequently charged with high treason; in March 1997 three of the accused, including Sekautu, were given custodial sentences.

In February 1997 the LDF was mobilized to quell a rebellion at the police headquarters in Maseru. More than 100 police-officers were arrested, and 10 alleged leaders of the rebellion were remanded in custody on charges of sedition and contravention of internal security legislation. Further individuals were subsequently indicted, and charges of high treason added. Two of the instigators of the mutiny fled to South Africa, where they were subsequently granted political asylum. In July 2000 23 police-officers were convicted of sedition, two of contravention of internal security legislation and three acquitted on both counts. All of the accused were acquitted of high treason.

Meanwhile, in April 1997 the National Assembly approved legislation for a reduction in the age of eligibility to vote (from 21 to 18 years), and for the establishment of a three-member Independent Electoral Commission (IEC). In June, following a protracted struggle between rival factions for control of the party, Mokhehle resigned from the BCP and formed the Lesotho Congress for Democracy (LCD), to which he transferred executive power. Mokhehle's opponents denounced the move as a 'political coup', declaring that he should have resigned from the premiership and sought a dissolution of the National Assembly and new elections. However, some 38 members of the National Assembly joined the LCD. In July Molapo Qhobela was elected leader of the BCP. There was further controversy in August, when the Speaker of the National Assembly designated the BCP as the official opposition party. In October members of the Senate (most of whom apparently refused to recognize the legitimacy of Mokhehle's Government) voted to suspend discussion of proposed legislation, pending the King's response to appeals for the dissolution of the National Assembly. At the first annual conference of the LCD, held in January 1998, Mokhehle resigned as leader, and was made Honorary Life President of the party. In February Deputy Prime Minister Bethuel Pakalitha Mosisili was elected to succeed him as party leader. (Mokhehle died in January 1999.)

Elections to an expanded National Assembly took place on 23 May 1998. An application by the three main opposition parties —the BCP, the BNP and the Marematlou Freedom Party (MFP) —for a postponement of the poll, on the grounds that the IEC had not allowed sufficient time for parties to examine the electoral register, had been rejected by the High Court. The LCD secured an overwhelming victory, winning 78 of the Assembly's 80 seats (with some 60.7% of the votes cast); the BNP, which took one seat (with 24.5% of the votes), was the only other party to win representation. Voting for one seat was postponed, owing to the death of a candidate. The IEC and observers representing the Southern African Development Community (SADC, see p. 311) and the Commonwealth concluded that the polls had been generally free and fair. However, the opposition protested that the outcome of the poll reflected fraud on the part of the LCD, and demonstrations in Maseru to denounce the result were reportedly attended by thousands of activists. Mosisili was elected Prime Minister by the National Assembly in late May, and a new Government was appointed in June. At the end of June the BCP, the BNP and the MFP appealed to the High Court to annul the election results; in the following month the Court ordered the IEC to permit the opposition parties to inspect election documents.

In August 1998 opposition activists began a mass vigil outside the royal palace; within one week some 2,000 people were reported to have joined the protest against the outcome of the poll. Tensions escalated as LCD militants blocked access roads to the capital, in a stated attempt to prevent supplies of weapons to the protesters, while it was reported that a government official attempting to flee the country had been stoned to death after opening fire on an opposition blockade. Following consultations involving the Lesotho Government and the main opposition parties, with mediation by the Government of South Africa, Mosisili announced the establishment of an independent commission, comprising representatives of the SADC 'troika' of Botswana, South Africa and Zimbabwe, to investigate the conduct and results of the May election. The commission was to be chaired by Pius Langa, the Deputy President of South Africa's Constitutional Court. The LDF failed to disperse the protesters outside the palace, and further clashes were reported between opposition and LCD activists.

Meanwhile, revelations that state funds had been used to purchase farmland for the Commander of the LDF, Lt-Gen. Makhula Mosakeng, fuelled opposition allegations of the Commander's complicity in corruption and vote-rigging. (Mosakeng stated that the land had been acquired for army, rather than personal, use.) Rumours of political divisions within the army were apparently confirmed in September 1998, when Mosakeng

and several of his senior colleagues were detained by junior officers (who were reported to have been angered by the recent dismissal of an officer who had countermanded orders to disperse protesters by force). Mosakeng announced his resignation and stated that 26 members of the military command had been dismissed.

By mid-September 1998 frustration was evident at delays in releasing the report of the Langa Commission. Protesters marched to the government complex in Maseru (where the South African Minister of Defence was meeting with government representatives and army officers) and subsequently to the South African High Commissioner's residence. The blockade forced the closure of government offices, and essential public services were paralysed as civil servants reportedly joined the protest. The Langa Commission's report, which was finally released on 17 September, expressed serious concerns at apparent irregularities and discrepancies in the conduct of the May general election, but the Commission was 'unable to state that the invalidity of the elections had been conclusively established'. There was considerable confusion in the days following the publication of the report. Rumours that the Mosisili Government had been overthrown were denied; however, it was confirmed that Lesotho had appealed to the SADC for assistance, in view of a breakdown in security. On 22 September an SADC peace-keeping force, initially comprising 600 South African troops and 200 from Botswana, entered Lesotho. In response to criticism that he had not consulted King Letsie prior to requesting external military assistance, Mosisili stated that the monarch had, by harbouring opposition protesters in the palace grounds, contributed to the instability that had necessitated SADC intervention. (It was subsequently reported that the King had been prevented from making a broadcast to the nation.) Within Lesotho, there was widespread outrage at what was perceived as an effective 'invasion' by South Africa, and the SADC force encountered unexpectedly strong resistance. There was sustained fighting between the intervention force and rebel units of the LDF before strategic points, including military bases and the Katse Dam (part of the LHWP essential to the supply of water to South Africa), were secured, while rioting in Maseru and other towns targeted in particular South African interests and caused widespread destruction. Mosakeng and his officers, who had fled to South Africa earlier in the month, returned to resume the army command on 24 September: Mosakeng stated that his resignation had been exacted under duress and, since it had not been approved by the King, was invalid. According to figures subsequently released by the Lesotho authorities, three days of fighting resulted in the deaths of 18 members of the LDF and of 47 civilians; nine members of the South African army were killed during the operation. In addition, as many as 4,000 refugees were reported to have crossed into South Africa.

Following meetings with representatives of the SADC 'troika', in early October 1998 it was reported that the LCD and the main opposition parties had agreed in principle that fresh elections should be held within 15–18 months. In the mean time, the IEC was to be restructured, and the electoral system was to be reviewed, with the aim of ensuring wider inclusion in political affairs (many parties felt that the simple majority voting system was incompatible with the nature of Lesotho's political evolution). Tensions again escalated after shots were fired at an LCD rally east of Maseru. The opposition denied claims by the ruling party of an attempt to assassinate the Prime Minister and his deputy, who were attending the rally; further violence at the meeting reportedly resulted in the deaths of two opposition activists. None the less, inter-party talks proceeded, and in mid-October agreement was reached on a transitional structure, designated the Interim Political Authority (IPA), to comprise representatives of 12 political parties, as well as government and parliamentary delegates, to oversee preparations for fresh elections to the National Assembly.

Shortly after the conclusion of this interim settlement it was announced that some 30 members of the LDF had been arrested on suspicion of involvement in the army rebellion of September 1998. The opposition subsequently expressed considerable concern at the alleged ill-treatment of the detainees and denounced continuing operations by SADC units to locate suspected mutineers who had failed to return to barracks following the suppression of the rebellion. Multi-party talks took place in Pretoria, South Africa, during November, but progress towards the establishment of the IPA was impeded after warrants were issued for the arrest, on murder charges, of several opposition activists, including two leading members of the BCP and BNP youth wings. The opposition parties stated that they would not co-operate in arrangements for the IPA until outstanding security matters, including the release of all rebel soldiers, had been expedited. A court martial in October 1999 ruled against the discharge of a total of 38 members of the LDF accused of mutiny.

The BNP leader, Evaristus Sekhonyana, died in November 1998. The party elected Justin Lekhanya to succeed him in March 1999. The withdrawal of the SADC intervention force was completed in May. This force was immediately succeeded by a new SADC mission, comprising some 300 military personnel from South Africa, Botswana and (subsequently) Zimbabwe, which remained until May 2000, assisting in the retraining and restructuring of the LDF.

Meanwhile, the 24-member IPA was inaugurated on 9 December 1998. After protracted consultations, the IPA announced in September 1999 that the number of seats in the National Assembly was to be increased by 50, to 130, effective from the elections scheduled for April 2000, with seats to be allocated according to a combination of proportional representation and simple majority voting. However, arbitration was required to resolve divisions within the IPA as to the number of seats to be decided by each method, and it was not until December 1999 that a Commonwealth-brokered agreement was signed, providing for 80 seats to be allocated on the basis of simple majority in single-member constituencies, and 50 by proportional representation. The mandate of the IPA was to be extended until elections took place. In the mean time, the Presidents of South Africa, Botswana, Mozambique and Zimbabwe, together with the UN, OAU and Commonwealth Secretaries-General, were to act as guarantors to ensure the implementation of the accord.

In February 2000 the IPA accused the Government of reneging on the December 1999 accord, after the LCD-dominated National Assembly voted to submit the proposed electoral changes to a referendum. Further arbitration concluded in May 2000 that the elections should proceed within 10–12 months. In July the IEC identified 26 May 2001 as the provisional date for the elections; however, delays in enacting legislation concerning voter registration and the electoral model caused the abandonment of this date.

In April 2000 the establishment of a commission of inquiry to investigate political events during July–November 1998 was announced. The commission, comprising three senior judges and chaired by Nigel Leon, met for the first time in June 2000 and heard evidence from several public figures. However, a number of opposition politicians criticized the commission, expressing doubts as to its impartiality. In August three LDF members were convicted by a court martial of participation in the mutiny of September 1998 and sentenced to a combined 29 years' imprisonment; a further 33 LDF members were convicted in November. The Leon commission of inquiry, which submitted its report to Prime Minister Mosisili in October 2001, rejected demands for a general amnesty to be granted to perpetrators of violence during the period under review, recommending the indictment of a number of opposition politicians and members of the armed forces. The commission also proposed measures aimed at ensuring the political neutrality of the armed forces and the police, and the establishment of an informal body, comprising the King, traditional chiefs and representatives of the armed forces, the police, the NSS, churches, political organizations, and the industrial and agricultural sectors, to discuss issues affecting Basotho.

In January 2001 a congress of the LCD re-elected Mosisili as leader of the party, for a five-year term. Shakhane Mokhehle, the incumbent and brother of the party's founder, was defeated in the election to the post of Secretary-General of the LCD by the Minister in the Prime Minister's Office, Sephiri Motanyane. In a minor cabinet reshuffle in July Mokhehle, who had disputed the results of the LCD elections, was dismissed as Minister of Justice, Human Rights and Rehabilitation, Law and Constitutional Affairs. Deputy Prime Minister Kelebone Maope resigned from the Government in September and broke away from the LCD, together with Mokhehle, to form a new opposition party, the Lesotho People's Congress (LPC), to prepare for forthcoming elections. By mid-October a total of 27 deputies had defected from the LCD to join the LPC, which was declared the main opposition party. Mosisili made new cabinet appointments in October, in an effort to consolidate his position ahead of the elections.

In mid-January 2002 a protracted dispute over the leadership of the BCP, which had been ongoing since the late 1990s, also appeared to be resolved, when the High Court ruled in favour of Tseliso Makhakhe's leadership of the party. Qhobela subsequently formed a new party, known as the Basutoland African Congress (BAC), which had been the name of the BCP in 1952–59.

Meanwhile, divisions over the electoral model, notably regarding the number of seats to be allocated by proportional representation, had continued to impede progress towards the elections in 2001. In January 2002 Parliament finally approved amendments to the electoral legislation, providing for the expansion of the National Assembly to 120 members, with 80 to be elected on a constituency basis and 40 selected by proportional representation.

The LCD won a resounding victory at the general election, which took place on 25 May 2002, retaining 77 of the 78 contested constituency seats, with 54.9% of the valid votes cast. The BNP became the second largest legislative party, securing 21 of the 40 seats allocated by proportional representation (known as compensatory seats), with 22.4% of the votes cast; the LPC won one constituency seat and four compensatory seats. Voting in two constituencies was postponed, owing to the deaths of candidates. Of the remaining 15 compensatory seats, the National Independent Party secured five, the BAC and the BCP both won three, while four smaller parties each took one seat. Mosisili was re-elected Prime Minister by the National Assembly in early June, and a new Cabinet was subsequently appointed.

In May 2002 Masupha Sole, the former Chief Executive of the Lesotho Highlands Development Authority, who was alleged to have accepted some US $2m. in bribes over a 10-year period from companies awarded contracts to work on the LHWP, was convicted on 13 charges of bribery and fraud, and was subsequently sentenced to 57 years' imprisonment. In September a court in Lesotho found a Canadian construction company guilty of paying bribes to Sole in return for a contract to work on the LHWP, and imposed a fine of $2.5m on the company in the following month.

Meanwhile, the Government declared a state of famine in April 2002, following a period of severe weather conditions, which had damaged crop production; in December the UN World Food Programme estimated that about one-quarter of the population would require emergency food aid during 2003. The rate of infection with HIV/AIDS among people aged 15–49 stood at 31% at the end of 2001, one of the highest in the world. In January 2003 antiretroviral drugs became available to pregnant women infected with HIV in order to reduce mother-to-child transmission.

As exemplified by South Africa's prominent role in the resolution of the 1994 constitutional crisis and by its intervention in the political crisis of September 1998, Lesotho's internal affairs continue to be strongly influenced by South Africa. Long-standing problems of border security and, in particular, the issue of disputed land in South Africa's Free State (formerly Orange Free State) have periodically caused friction between the two countries. During a two-day state visit to Lesotho in July 1995, President Nelson Mandela of South Africa advocated the pursuit of mutually-beneficial policies of regional integration, and he and Prime Minister Mokhehle agreed that the issue of sovereignty in Free State should be discussed by 'appropriate' authorities. Relations between the two countries were strained in August 2000 when Lesotho withdrew its support shortly before the scheduled signing of an agreement with Botswana, Namibia and South Africa on the management of water resources from the Orange river. In September an official at the South African High Commission was killed in Maseru. Representatives of both countries met in Pretoria in November and recommended increased co-operation in areas including education and criminal justice. During a visit to Lesotho by President Thabo Mbeki of South Africa in April 2001, it was agreed to replace an intergovernmental liaison committee that had been established following SADC intervention in 1998 (see above) with a joint binational commission at ministerial level, with the aim of enhancing bilateral relations. Relations between Lesotho and South Africa were further enhanced in May 2002, when their ministers of foreign affairs signed the Joint Bilateral Commission of Co-operation programme, which aimed to raise Lesotho from its current status as a 'least developed country' by 2007.

Government

Lesotho is an hereditary monarchy. Under the terms of the Constitution, which came into effect following the March 1993 election, the King, who is Head of State, has no executive or legislative powers. The College of Chiefs is theoretically empowered, under traditional law, to elect and depose the King by a majority vote. Executive power is vested in the Cabinet, which is headed by the Prime Minister. Legislative power is exercised by the National Assembly, which is elected, at intervals of no more than five years, by universal adult suffrage in the context of a multi-party political system. A system of mixed member proportional representation was introduced at the general election of May 2002, when the National Assembly was expanded to 120 members (80 elected by simple majority in single-member constituencies and 40 selected from party lists). The upper house, the Senate, comprises traditional chiefs and 11 nominated members. Lesotho comprises 10 administrative districts, each with an appointed district co-ordinator.

Defence

Military service is voluntary. The Lesotho Defence Force (LDF) comprised 2,000 men in August 2002. The creation of a new commando force unit, the first professional unit in the LDF, was announced in October 2001, as part of ongoing efforts to restructure the armed forces. Projected budgetary expenditure on defence for 2002 was M230m.

Economic Affairs

In 2001, according to estimates by the World Bank, Lesotho's gross national income (GNI), measured at average 1999–2001 prices, was US $1,127m., equivalent to $550 per head (or $2,670 per head on an international purchasing-power parity basis). During 1990–2001, it was estimated, the population increased at an average annual rate of 1.9%, while gross domestic product (GDP) per head increased, in real terms, by an average of 1.8% per year. Overall GDP increased, in real terms, at an average annual rate of 3.7% in 1990–2001; growth in 2001 was 3.0%.

Agriculture, forestry and fishing contributed 16.3% of GDP in 2000/01, and employed some 37.6% of the labour force in mid-2001. The principal agricultural exports are wool and mohair, cereals and live animals. The main subsistence crops are maize, sorghum and wheat. Lesotho remains a net importer of staple foodstuffs, largely owing to its vulnerability to adverse climatic conditions, especially drought; it was estimated that 338,000 metric tons of cereals would have to be imported in 2002/03. During 1990–2001 agricultural GDP remained constant, on average. Agricultural GDP decreased by 0.1% in 2001.

Industry (including mining, manufacturing, construction and power) provided 42.4% of GDP in 2000/01, and engaged 27.9% of the labour force in 1990. During 1990–2001 industrial GDP increased by an average of 6.0% per year. Industrial GDP increased by 5.3% in 2001.

Mining contributed 0.1% of GDP in 2000/01. Lesotho has reserves of diamonds, which during the late 1970s provided more than 50% of visible export earnings, but large-scale exploitation of these ceased in 1982; however, it is planned to reopen the Letseng-la Terai mine, and industrial mining at other sites is envisaged. Lesotho also possesses deposits of uranium, lead and iron ore, and is believed to have petroleum deposits. The GDP of the mining sector increased by an average of 0.8% per year in 1996/97–2000/01; growth in 2000/01 was 14.3%.

Manufacturing contributed 15.6% of GDP in 2000/01. During 1990–2001 manufacturing GDP increased by an average of 5.9% per year; growth in 2001 was 1.9%.

The Lesotho Highlands Water Project (LHWP), the first phase of which was completed in 1998, provides hydroelectricity sufficient for all Lesotho's needs and for export to South Africa. The scheme is expected to be completed by about 2030. Prior to the LHWP more than 90% of Lesotho's energy requirements were imported from South Africa. Imports of fuel and energy comprised an estimated 18.5% of the total value of imports in 1995.

The services sector contributed an estimated 41.3% of GDP in 2001. During 1990–2001 the GDP of the services sector increased at an average annual rate of 4.7%. Services GDP decreased by 1.1% in 2000, but increased by 4.1% in 2001.

In 2001 Lesotho recorded a visible trade deficit of US $483.6m. and a deficit of $144.7m. on the current account of the balance of payments. In 2000 the principal source of imports (85.3%) was the Southern African Customs Union (SACU—i.e. chiefly South Africa—see below), which was also the second largest market for exports (40.7%), behind the USA (57.5%). The principal exports in 2000 were clothing and foodstuffs. The principal imports in 1981 were food and live animals, machinery and transport equipment, and petroleum products.

In the financial year ending 31 March 2001 there was an overall budgetary deficit of M143.6m. (equivalent to 2.3% of GDP in that year). Lesotho's external debt totalled US $715.9m. at the end of 2000, of which $697.8m. was long-term public debt. In that year the cost of debt-servicing was equivalent to 12.1% of revenue from exports of goods and services. The annual rate of inflation averaged 8.5% in 1990–2001; consumer prices increased by an average of 6.1% in 2000, but declined by 9.6% in 2001. It was estimated that more than 40% of the labour force were unemployed in mid-2001. In 2000 an estimated 17% of Lesotho's adult male labour force were employed in South Africa (compared with some 35% in 1996); Basotho workers are mainly employed in South Africa's gold mines, and in the education and health sectors.

Lesotho is a member of the Common Monetary Area (with Namibia, South Africa and Swaziland), and a member of SACU (with Botswana, Namibia, South Africa and Swaziland). Lesotho also belongs to the Southern African Development Community (SADC, see p. 311).

Impediments to economic development in Lesotho include vulnerability to drought and serious land shortages, combined with the country's dependence on South Africa (the Lesotho currency, the loti, is fixed at par with the South African rand, exposing Lesotho to fluctuations within the South African economy). From 1988 Lesotho undertook major economic reforms, supported by the IMF and other donors. However, by the late 1990s the strong growth that had prevailed for most of the decade was being eroded, in particular as the first phase of the LHWP was completed, while retrenchment in the South African gold-mining sector resulted in a marked decline in remittances from Basotho working abroad. The Government accelerated its programme of privatization in 2000, with, most notably, the sale of a 70% holding in the Lesotho Telecommunications Corporation. Under a utilities reform project, initiated in May 2001 and supported by the African Development Bank, the World Bank and the European Union (EU), the Lesotho Electricity Corporation began a restructuring process in preparation for transfer to private ownership in early 2003. An agreement was reached with South Africa in January 2001 to restructure bilateral economic relations and to increase mutual co-operation for economic development. In March the IMF approved a three-year loan of some US $31m., under the Poverty Reduction and Growth Facility, on condition that Lesotho encouraged private economic activity, limited the role of the public sector and strengthened fiscal stability. The Lesotho Revenue Authority, intended to improve the administration of taxation and other revenue, commenced operations in January 2003. In April 2001 Lesotho was declared eligible to benefit from the USA's African Growth and Opportunities Act (AGOA); under its terms, textiles and clothing made in Lesotho have unlimited access to the US market, and by early 2002 exports of these products to the USA had increased by nearly 40%. Lesotho's qualification for the benefits of the AGOA attracted interest from foreign investors in Lesotho, notably Taiwanese textile manufacturers, who employed 11,600 Basotho in 2001; a further 5,000 jobs were expected to be created in the textile industry by 2004. Lesotho's eligibility for tariff preferences under the AGOA was renewed in December 2002. In October of that year the EU granted aid worth €110m. to Lesotho for infrastructural development and the treatment of HIV/AIDS.

Education

All primary education is available free of charge, and is provided mainly by the three main Christian missions (Lesotho Evangelical, Roman Catholic and Anglican), under the direction of the Ministry of Education. Education at primary schools is officially compulsory for seven years between six and 13 years of age. Secondary education, beginning at the age of 13, lasts for up to five years, comprising a first cycle of three years and a second of two years. Of children in the relevant age-groups in 1999/2000, 58.5% (males 54.7%; females 62.3%) were enrolled at primary schools, while only 19.6% (males 15.1%; females 24.2%) were enrolled at secondary schools. The National University of Lesotho is at Roma; some 4,582 students were enrolled at tertiary-level institutions in 1998/99. The budget for 2000/01 allocated M600.6m. to education and community services (representing 20.7% of total government expenditure).

Public Holidays

2003: 1 January (New Year's Day), 11 March (Moshoeshoe Day), 18–21 April (Easter), 1 May (Workers' Day), 25 May (Africa Day and Heroes' Day), 29 May (Ascension Day), 17 July (King's Birthday), 4 October (National Independence Day), 25 December (Christmas Day), 26 December (Boxing Day).

2004: 1 January (New Year's Day), 11 March (Moshoeshoe Day), 9–12 April (Easter), 1 May (Workers' Day), 20 May (Ascension Day), 25 May (Africa Day and Heroes' Day), 17 July (King's Birthday), 4 October (National Independence Day), 25 December (Christmas Day), 26 December (Boxing Day).

Weights and Measures

The metric system of weights and measures is in force.

Statistical Survey

Source (unless otherwise stated): Bureau of Statistics, POB 455, Maseru 100; tel. 323852.

Area and Population

AREA, POPULATION AND DENSITY

Area (sq km)	30,355*
Population (census results)†	
12 April 1986 (provisional)	1,447,000
14 April 1996 (provisional)	1,862,275
Population (UN estimates at mid-year)†‡	
1998	1,977,000
1999	2,008,000
2000	2,035,000
Density (per sq km) at mid-2000	67.0

* 11,720 sq miles.

† Excluding absentee workers in South Africa, numbering 152,627 (males 129,088; females 23,539) in 1976.

‡ Source: UN, *World Population Prospects: The 2000 Revision.*

DISTRICTS

(*de jure* population at 1986 census, provisional)*

District	Population
Berea.	194,600
Butha-Buthe	100,600
Leribe	257,900
Mafeteng.	195,600
Maseru.	311,200
Mohale's Hoek	164,400
Mokhotlong	74,700
Qacha's Nek.	64,000
Quthing	110,400
Thaba-Tseka	104,100
Total.	1,577,500

* Including absentee workers in South Africa.

Note: Each district has the same name as its chief town.

PRINCIPAL TOWNS

(population at 1986 census)

Maseru (capital) . .	109,400	Hlotse	9,600
Maputsoa	20,000	Mohale's Hoek . .	8,500
Teyateyaneng . .	14,300	Quthing	6,000
Mafeteng	12,700		

Source: Stefan Helders, *World Gazetteer* (www.world-gazetteer.com).

Mid-2001 (UN estimate, including suburbs): Maseru, population 271,000 (Source: UN, *World Urbanization Prospects: The 2001 Revision*).

BIRTHS AND DEATHS

(UN estimates, annual averages)

	1985–90	1990–95	1995–2000
Birth rate (per 1,000)	38.5	36.6	35.0
Death rate (per 1,000)	12.6	11.5	14.6

Source: UN, *World Population Prospects: The 2000 Revision.*

Expectation of life (WHO estimates, years at birth): 40.0 (males 40.1; females 39.8) in 2001 (Source: WHO, *World Health Report*).

ECONOMICALLY ACTIVE POPULATION

(ILO estimates, '000 persons at mid-1990)

	Males	Females	Total
Agriculture, etc.	130	150	280
Industry	183	13	196
Manufacturing	8	7	15
Services	134	91	225
Total	447	254	701

Source: ILO.

Mid-2001 (estimates in '000): Agriculture, etc. 329; Total 874 (Source: FAO).

In 2000 about 17% of the total adult male labour force were in employment in South Africa.

Health and Welfare

KEY INDICATORS

Total fertility rate (children per woman, 2001)	4.5
Under-5 mortality rate (per 1,000 live births, 2001) . .	132
HIV/AIDS (% of persons aged 15–49, 2001)	31.00
Physicians (per 1,000 head, 1995)	0.05
Health expenditure (2000): US $ per head (PPP) . . .	82
Health expenditure (2000): % of GDP	6.3
Health expenditure (2000): public (% of total)	82.3
Access to water (% of persons, 2000).	91
Access to sanitation (% of persons, 2000)	92
Human Development Index (2000): ranking	132
Human Development Index (2000): value	0.535

For sources and definitions, see explanatory note on p. vi.

Agriculture

PRINCIPAL CROPS

('000 metric tons)

	1999	2000	2001*
Wheat	15	51*	51
Maize	125	297*	300
Sorghum	33	25*	46
Roots and tubers*	85	90	90
Dry beans	9	8*	8
Dry peas	3	6*	7
Vegetables*	19	18	18
Fruit*	14	13	13

* FAO estimate(s).

Source: FAO.

LIVESTOCK
('000 head, year ending September)

	1999	2000*	2001*
Cattle	510	520*	510
Sheep	936	750*	730
Goats	730	580*	570
Pigs*	63	65	60
Horses*	98	100	100
Asses*	152	154	154
Mules*	1	1	1
Poultry*	1,700	1,800	1,700

* FAO estimate(s).

Source: FAO.

LIVESTOCK PRODUCTS
(FAO estimates, '000 metric tons)

	1999	2000	2001
Cows' milk	23	24	24
Beef and veal	11	11	8
Mutton and lamb	3	3	3
Goat meat	2	2	2
Pig meat	3	3	3
Poultry meat	2	2	2
Game meat	4	4	4
Hen eggs	1	2	2
Wool (greasy)	2	3	3

Source: FAO.

Forestry

ROUNDWOOD REMOVALS
('000 cubic metres, excluding bark)

	1998	1999	2000
Total (all fuel wood)	1,594	2,004	2,022*

* FAO estimate.

Source: FAO.

Fishing

(FAO estimates, metric tons, live weight)

	1998	1999	2000
Capture	30	30	32
Common carp	18	18	20
North African catfish	2	2	2
Other freshwater fishes . . .	10	10	10
Aquaculture	8	4	8
Common carp	6	4	8
Rainbow trout	2	0	0
Total catch	38	34	40

Source: FAO, *Yearbook of Fishery Statistics*.

Finance

CURRENCY AND EXCHANGE RATES

Monetary Units
100 lisente (singular: sente) = 1 loti (plural: maloti)

Sterling, Dollar and Euro Equivalents (31 December 2002)
£1 sterling = 13.9260 maloti
US $1 = 8.6400 maloti
€1 = 9.0608 maloti
1,000 maloti = £71.81 = $115.74 = €110.37

Average Exchange Rate (maloti per US $)
2000   6.93983
2001   8.60918
2002   10.54075

Note: The loti is fixed at par with the South African rand.

BUDGET
(million maloti, year ending 31 March)

Revenue*	1998/99	1999/2000	2000/01
Tax revenue	1,694.7	1,888.8	1,941.9
Taxes on net income and profits	387.0	419.5	468.8
Company tax	65.0	58.5	126.3
Individual income tax . . .	278.0	306.5	314.7
Taxes on goods and services . .	270.9	283.2	343.6
Sales tax	233.3	238.0	279.8
Petrol levy	35.9	43.6	62.0
Taxes on international trade and transactions	1,034.4	1,183.1	1,126.1
Customs duties	1,033.4	1,183.1	1,126.1
Non-tax revenue	478.9	424.0	684.7
Administative fees, charges and non-industrial sales . . .	67.8	142.7	162.4
Total	2,173.6	2,312.8	2,626.6

Expenditure†	1998/99	1999/2000	2000/01
General public services	836.1	1,623.9	884.8
Public order, safety and defence	394.6	489.8	397.4
Health, social security and welfare	227.5	243.9	286.4
Education and community services	652.6	694.3	600.6
Economic services	542.5	517.6	303.0
Agriculture and rural development	125.4	151.7	108.2
Commerce, tourism and industry	49.4	51.3	39.5
Water, energy and mining . .	121.7	139.6	30.1
Roads	228.3	116.9	87.8
Other transport and communications	17.7	58.1	37.4
Unallocable and other purposes	179.8	293.7	823.2
Total	2,438.5	3,373.4	2,895.8
Current	1,942.7	2,318.5	2,382.6
Capital†	495.8	1,054.9	515.3

* Excluding grants received (million maloti): 120.0 in 1998/99; 130.0 in 1999/2000; 125.6 in 2000/01.

† Including lending minus repayments.

Source: IMF, *Lesotho: Statistical Annex* (May 2002).

INTERNATIONAL RESERVES
(US $ million at 31 December)

	2000	2001	2002
IMF special drawing rights . . .	0.66	0.58	0.60
Reserve position in IMF	4.61	4.45	4.82
Foreign exchange	412.62	381.46	n.a.
Total	417.89	386.49	n.a.

Source: IMF, *International Financial Statistics*.

MONEY SUPPLY
(million maloti at 31 December)

	1999	2000	2001
Currency outside banks	122.66	139.34	147.14
Demand deposits at commercial banks	821.27	873.73	939.04
Total money (incl. others) . . .	957.32	1,035.96	1,292.27

Source: IMF, *International Financial Statistics*.

COST OF LIVING
(Consumer Price Index; base: 1995 = 100)

	1999	2000	2001
All items	138.6	147.1	132.9

Source: IMF, *International Financial Statistics*.

NATIONAL ACCOUNTS
(million maloti at current prices)

Expenditure on the Gross Domestic Product
(year ending 31 March)

	1998/99	1999/2000	2000/01
Government final consumption expenditure	1,814.2	2,135.1	2,123.2
Private final consumption expenditure.	4,373.7	5,338.6	5,679.4
Increase in stocks	−84.1	−86.7	−133.7
Gross fixed capital formation . .	2,471.0	2,105.0	2,270.5
Total domestic expenditure. .	8,574.8	9,492.0	9,939.4
Exports of goods and services . } Less Imports of goods and services }	3,493.0	3.758.6	3,562.2
GDP in purchasers' values . .	5,081.8	5,733.4	6,377.2
GDP at constant 1995 prices	3,857.8	3,952.1	4,079.0

Source: IMF, *Lesotho: Statistical Annex* (May 2002).

Gross Domestic Product by Economic Activity

	1998/99	1999/2000	2000/01
Agriculture, forestry and fishing .	808.7	894.9	975.9
Mining and quarrying	4.1	5.6	8.0
Manufacturing	787.5	844.8	929.4
Electricity, gas and water . . .	249.6	321.2	327.9
Construction	766.2	1,007.1	1,264.4
Trade, restaurants, and hotels . .	470.6	515.7	606.4
Transport and communications .	166.8	185.2	195.7
Finance, insurance, real estate and business services	410.8	450.2	538.7
Government services. . . .	956.8	1,035.9	1,059.5
Other services	54.6	59.1	63.6
Sub-total	4,675.5	5,319.4	5,969.3
Less Imputed bank service charge	98.8	123.9	188.8
GDP at factor cost. . . .	4,576.7	5,195.5	5,780.5
Indirect taxes, less subsidies . .	505.1	537.9	596.8
GDP in purchasers' values . .	5,081.8	5,733.4	6,377.2

Source: IMF, *Lesotho: Statistical Annex* (May 2002).

BALANCE OF PAYMENTS
(US $ million, year ending 31 March)

	1998/99	1999/2000	2000/01
Exports of goods f.o.b.	191.5	188.4	221.6
Imports of goods f.o.b.	−781.4	−796.4	−705.2
Trade balance	−589.9	−608.0	−483.6
Exports of services	39.9	45.6	41.4
Imports of services	−51.0	−47.4	−44.4
Balance on goods and services	−601.0	−609.8	−486.6
Other income received	349.3	322.3	277.2
Other income paid	−106.7	−76.6	−63.6
Balance on goods, services and income	−358.4	−364.1	−273.0
Current transfers (net) . . .	139.5	155.9	128.3
Current balance	−218.9	−208.2	−144.7
Capital account (net) . . .	16.4	21.1	18.7
Direct investment from abroad. .	217.0	153.9	119.7
Other investment assets . .	18.3	−30.7	2.0
Other investment liabilities . .	−34.7	−12.0	−40.4
Net errors and omissions . . .	−35.1	−6.4	−34.6
Overall balance	−37.0	−82.3	−79.4

Source: IMF, *Lesotho: Statistical Annex* (May 2002).

External Trade

PRINCIPAL COMMODITIES

Imports c.i.f. ('000 maloti)	1979	1980	1981
Food and live animals	68,559	76,918	82,902
Beverages and tobacco	13,725	16,233	21,761
Clothing	31,652	34,452	36,733
Machinery and transport equipment	44,084	58,397	74,647
Petroleum products	22,848	31,633	37,766
Chemicals	16,372	18,853	28,229
Footwear	10,556	12,423	14,338
Total (incl. others)	303,612	360,757	439,375

Total imports (million maloti): 497.8 in 1982; 539.7 in 1983; 634.5 in 1984; 751.0 in 1985; 803.3 in 1986; 954.8 in 1987; 1,327.5 in 1988; 1,552 in 1989; 1,738 in 1990; 2,242 in 1991; 2,564 in 1992; 2,839 in 1993; 3,000 in 1994; 3,576 in 1995; 4,303 in 1996; 4,722 in 1997; 4,699 in 1998; 4,773 in 1999; 5,048 in 2000; 5,823.8 in 2001 (Source: IMF, *International Financial Statistics*).

Exports (million maloti)	1998	1999	2000
Foodstuffs, etc.	75.5	119.3	111.7
Cereals	23.8	36.2	28.0
Beverages and tobacco . . .	38.7	73.4	63.9
Livestock materials	18.8	15.6	37.0
Wool	16.7	14.6	32.2
Road vehicles	15.5	4.8	11.3
Clothing, etc.	415.4	612.5	953.2
Footwear	253.6	n.a.	n.a.
Total (incl. others)	1,113.6	1,057.6	1,470.0

Source: IMF, *Lesotho: Statistical Annex* (May 2002).

PRINCIPAL TRADING PARTNERS
(million maloti)

Imports*	1998	1999	2000
Africa	4,615.7	4,737.7	4,316.2
SACU†	4,614.9	4,736.4	4,309.3
Asia	370.9	372.4	526.0
Hong Kong	22.2	31.0	70.3
Taiwan	203.1	192.2	294.6
European Union	105.7	83.7	42.7
North America	70.1	50.0	104.8
Canada	45.1	41.9	97.2
Total (incl. others)	5,199.9	5,288.8	5,050.5

Exports	1998	1999	2000
Africa	691.9	556.0	592.5
SACU†	690.6	554.4	591.8
European Union	6.0	1.9	1.8
North America	371.6	494.9	858.3
Canada	3.8	5.7	22.5
USA	367.8	489.2	835.8
Total (incl. others)	1,071.1	1,054.1	1,453.3

* Valuation exclusive of import duties. Figures also exclude donated food.
† Southern African Customs Union, of which Lesotho is a member; also including Botswana, Namibia, South Africa and Swaziland.

Source: IMF, *Lesotho: Statistical Annex* (May 2002).

Transport

ROAD TRAFFIC
(estimates, motor vehicles in use at 31 December)

	1994	1995	1996
Passenger cars	9,900	11,160	12,610
Lorries and vans	20,790	22,310	25,000

Source: IRF, *World Road Statistics*.

CIVIL AVIATION
(traffic on scheduled services)

	1997	1998	1999
Kilometres flown (million) . . .	0	1	0
Passengers carried ('000) . . .	10	28	1
Passenger-km (million)	3	9	0
Total ton-km (million)	0	1	0

Source: UN, *Statistical Yearbook*.

Tourism

	1996	1997	1998
Tourist arrivals*	311,802	323,868	289,819
From South Africa. . . .	295,926	301,869	281,906
Tourism receipts (US $ million) .	19	20	n.a.

* Figures refer to arrivals at frontiers from visitors abroad and include same-day visitors.

Source: World Tourism Organization, *Yearbook of Tourism Statistics*.

1999: Tourist arrivals 186,000; Tourism receipts (US $ million) 19 (Source: World Bank).

Communications Media

	1999	2000	2001
Television receivers ('000 in use)	33	35	n.a.
Telephones ('000 main lines in use)	21.6	22.2	n.a.
Mobile cellular telephones ('000 subscribers).	n.a.	21.6	33.0
Internet users ('000)	1.0	4.0	5.0

Facsimile machines (number in use, year ending 31 March 1996): 569.

Radio receivers ('000 in use): 104 in 1997.

Daily newspapers (1996): 2 (average circulation 15,000 copies).

Non-daily newspapers (1996): 7 (average circulation 74,000 copies).

Sources: UNESCO, *Statistical Yearbook*; International Telecommunication Union.

Education

(1998)

	Institu-tions	Teachers	Students		
			Males	Females	Total
Pre-primary . .	n.a.	1,970	17,016*	19,063*	36,079
Primary . . .	1,264	14,555	178,131	191,384	369,515
Secondary:					
general . . .	n.a.	3,126*†	29,570	41,692	71,262
technical and					
vocational. .	n.a.	n.a.	494	479	973
Tertiary . . .	n.a.	436	1,822*	2,760*	4,582*

* Estimate.
† Includes figure for technical and vocational teachers.

Source: UNESCO Institute for Statistics.

Adult literacy rate (UNESCO estimates): 83.4% (males 72.5%; females 93.6%) in 2000 (Source: UN Development Programme, *Human Development Report*).

Directory

The Constitution

The Constitution of the Kingdom of Lesotho, which took effect at independence in October 1966, was suspended in January 1970. A new Constitution was promulgated following the March 1993 general election. Its main provisions, with subsequent amendments, are summarized below

Lesotho is an hereditary monarchy. The King, who is Head of State, has no executive or legislative powers. Executive authority is vested in the Cabinet, which is headed by the Prime Minister, while legislative power is exercised by the 120-member National Assembly, which comprises 80 members elected on a single-member constituency basis and 40 selected by a system of proportional representation. The National Assembly is elected, at intervals of no more than five years, by universal adult suffrage in the context of a multi-party political system. There is also a Senate, comprising 22 traditional chiefs and 11 nominated members. The Prime Minister is the official head of the armed forces.

The Government

HEAD OF STATE

King: HM King LETSIE III (acceded to the throne 7 February 1996).

CABINET
(April 2003)

Prime Minister and Minister of Defence and Public Service: BETHUEL PAKALITHA MOSISILI.

Deputy Prime Minister and Minister of Education: ARCHIBALD LESAO LEHOHLA.

Minister of Local Government: PONTS'O SUZAN MATUMELO SEKATLE.

Minister of Home Affairs: MOTSOAHAE THOMAS THABANE.

Minister of Tourism, Culture and Environment: LEBOHANG NTSINYI.

Minister of Natural Resources (Water, Lesotho Water Highlands Project, Energy, Mining and Technology): MONYANE MOLELEKI.

Minister of Foreign Affairs: MOHLABI KENNETH TSEKOA.

Minister of Industry, Trade and Marketing: MPHO MELI MALIE.

Minister of Agriculture, Co-operatives and Land Reclamation: VOVA BULANE.

Minister of Communications (Information, Broadcasting, Posts and Telecommunications): MAMPHONO KHAKETLA.

Minister of Public Works and Transport: MOFELEHETSI SALOMONE MOERANE.

Minister of Gender, Youth and Sports: MATHABISO LEPONO.

Minister of Finance and Development Planning: TIMOTHY THAHANE.

Minister of Health and Social Welfare: Dr MOTLOHELOA PHOOKO.

Minister of Employment and Labour: SELLO CLEMENT MACHAKELA.

Minister of Justice, Human Rights and Rehabilitation, Law and Constitutional Affairs: REFILOE MASEMENE.

Minister in the Prime Minister's Office: SEPHIRI ENOCH MOTANYANE.

MINISTRIES

Office of the Prime Minister: POB 527, Maseru 100; tel. 311000; fax 310102; internet www.lesotho.gov.ls.

Ministry of Agriculture, Co-operatives and Land Reclamation: POB 24, Maseru 100; tel. 316407; fax 310349.

Ministry of Communications: POB 36, Maseru 100; tel. 323864; fax 310003.

Ministry of Defence and Public Service: POB 527, Maseru 100; tel. 311000; fax 310319.

Ministry of Education: POB 47, Maseru 100; tel. 312849; fax 310206.

Ministry of Employment and Labour: Private Bag A1164, Maseru 100; tel. 322602; fax 310374.

Ministry of Finance and Development Planning: POB 395, Maseru 100; tel. 310826; fax 310157.

Ministry of Foreign Affairs: POB 1387, Maseru 100; tel. 311150; fax 310178.

Ministry of Gender, Youth and Sports: POB 10993, Maseru 100; tel. 314763; fax 310506.

Ministry of Health and Social Welfare: POB 514, Maseru 100; tel. 314404; fax 310467.

Ministry of Home Affairs: POB 174, Maseru 100; tel. 323771; fax 310319.

Ministry of Industry, Trade and Marketing: POB 747, Maseru 100; tel. 312938; fax 310644.

Ministry of Justice, Human Rights and Rehabilitation, Law and Constitutional Affairs: POB 402, Maseru 100; tel. 322683; fax 310365; e-mail ps@justice.gov.ls.

Ministry of Local Government: POB 686, Maseru 100; tel. 325331.

Ministry of Natural Resources: POB 772, Maseru 100; tel. 323163; fax 310520.

Ministry of Public Works and Transport: POB 20, Maseru 100; tel. 311362; fax 310125.

Ministry of Tourism, Culture and Environment: POB 52, Maseru 100; tel. 313034; fax 310194.

Legislature

PARLIAMENT

National Assembly

Speaker: NTLHOI MOTSAMAI.

General Election, 25 May 2002

Party	Constituency seats	Compensatory seats*	Total seats
Lesotho Congress for Democracy	77	—	77
Basotho National Party	—	21	21
Lesotho People's Congress	1	4	5
National Independent Party	—	5	5
Basotho Congress Party	—	3	3
Basutoland African Congress	—	3	3
Lesotho Workers' Party	—	1	1
Marematlou Freedom Party	—	1	1
National Progressive Party	—	1	1
Popular Front for Democracy	—	1	1
Total	78†	40	118†

* Allocated by proportional representation.
† Voting in two constituencies was postponed, owing to the deaths of candidates.

Senate

Speaker: Chief SEMPE LEJAHA.

The Senate is an advisory chamber comprising 22 traditional chiefs and 11 members appointed by the monarch.

Political Organizations

Basotho Congress Party (BCP): POB 111, Maseru 100; tel. 8737076; f. 1952; Leader TSELISO MAKHAKHE.

Basotho Democratic Alliance (BDA): Maseru; f. 1984; Pres. S. C. NKOJANE.

Basotho National Party (BNP): POB 124, Maseru 100; f. 1958; Leader JUSTIN METSING LEKHANYA; Sec.-Gen. LESETELI MALEFANE; 280,000 mems.

Basutoland African Congress (BAC): Maseru; f. 2002 following split in the BCP; Leader MOLAPO QHOBELA; Sec.-Gen. MAHOLELA MANDORO.

Khokanyana-Phiri Democratic Alliance: Maseru; f. 1999; alliance of opposition parties.

Christian Democratic Party: Maseru.

Communist Party of Lesotho (CPL): Maseru; f. 1962; banned 1970–91; supported mainly by migrant workers employed in South Africa; Sec.-Gen. MOKHAFISI KENA.

Kopanang Basotho Party (KBP): Maseru; f. 1992; campaigns for women's rights; Leader LIMAKATSO NTAKATSANE.

National Independent Party (NIP): Maseru; f. 1984; Pres. ANTHONY C. MANYELI.

National Progressive Party (NPP): Maseru; f. 1995 following split in the BNP; Leader Chief PEETE NKOEBE PEETE.

Popular Front for Democracy (PFD): Maseru; f. 1991; Leader LEKHETHO RAKUANE.

Social Democratic Party: Maseru; Leader MASITISE SELESO.

Lesotho Congress for Democracy (LCD): Maseru; f. 1997 as a result of divisions within the BCP; Chair. SELLO CLEMENT MACHAKELA; Leader BETHUEL PAKALITHA MOSISILI; Sec.-Gen. SEPHIRI ENOCH MOTANYANE; 200,000 mems.

Lesotho Labour Party (LLP): Maseru; f. 1991; Leader PATRICK SALIE.

Lesotho People's Congress (LPC): f. 2001 following split in the LCD; Interim Leader KELEBONE ALBERT MAOPE; Interim Sec.-Gen. SHAKHANE MOKHEHLE.

Lesotho Workers' Party (LWP): f. 2001; Leader BILLY MACAEFA.

Marematlou Freedom Party (MFP): POB 0443, Maseru 105; tel. 315804; f. 1962; Leader VINCENT MOEKETSE MALEBO; Dep. Leader THABO LEANYA; 300,000 mems.

Sefate Democratic Union (SDU): Maseru; Leader BOFIHLA NKUEBE.

United Democratic Party (UDP): POB 776, Maseru 100; f. 1967; Chair. BEN L. SHEA; Leader CHARLES D. MOFELI; Sec.-Gen. MOLOMO NKUEBE; 26,000 mems.

United Party (UP): Maseru; Pres. MAKARA SEKAUTU.

Diplomatic Representation

EMBASSIES AND HIGH COMMISSIONS IN LESOTHO

China, People's Republic: POB 380, Maseru 100; tel. 316521; fax 310489; Ambassador ZHANG XIANJI.

Denmark: Site 16, Industrial Area, POB 1259, Maseru 100; tel. 313630; fax 310138; Ambassador ALF JÖNSSON.

Korea, Democratic People's Republic: Maseru; Ambassador AN KYONG HYON.

South Africa: Lesotho Bank Tower, 10th Floor, Kingsway, Private Bag A266, Maseru 100; tel. 315758; fax 310128; e-mail sahcis@lesoff.co.za; High Commissioner M. JAPHET NDLOVU.

United Kingdom: Linare Rd, POB MS521, Maseru 100; tel. 313961; fax 310120; e-mail hcmaseru@bhc.org.ls; internet www.bhc.org.ls; High Commissioner FRANCIS MARTIN.

USA: 254 Kingsway, POB 333, Maseru 100; tel. 312666; fax 310116; e-mail info@embassy.org.ls; internet www.usembassy.org.ls; Ambassador ROBERT GEERS LOFTIS.

Judicial System

HIGH COURT

The High Court is a superior court of record, and in addition to any other jurisdiction conferred by statute it is vested with unlimited original jurisdiction to determine any civil or criminal matter. It also has appellate jurisdiction to hear appeals and reviews from the subordinate courts. Appeals may be made to the Court of Appeal.

Chief Justice: JOSEPH LEBONA KHEOLA.

Judges: M. L. Lehohla, W. C. M. Maqutu, B. K. Molai, T. E. Mon-apathi, K. Guni, G. Mofolo, M. Ramolibeli, S. Peete, M. Hlajoane.

COURT OF APPEAL

Judges: T. Browde, R. N. Leon, J. N. Steyn, G. Friedman, M. Ramodibedi.

SUBORDINATE COURTS

Each of the 10 districts possesses subordinate courts, presided over by magistrates.

JUDICIAL COMMISSIONERS' COURTS

These courts hear civil and criminal appeals from central and local courts. Further appeal may be made to the High Court and finally to the Court of Appeal.

CENTRAL AND LOCAL COURTS

There are 71 such courts, of which 58 are local courts and 13 are central courts which also serve as courts of appeal from the local courts. They have limited civil and criminal jurisdiction.

Religion

About 90% of the population profess Christianity.

CHRISTIANITY

African Federal Church Council: POB 70, Peka 340; f. 1927; co-ordinating org. for 48 African independent churches; Co-ordinator Rev. S. Mohono.

Christian Council of Lesotho: Maseru 100; tel. 323639; fax 310310; f. 1973; six mem. and four assoc. mem. churches; Chair. Rev. Lebohang Kheekhe; Sec. R. M. Taole.

The Anglican Communion

Anglicans in Lesotho are adherents of the Church of the Province of Southern Africa. The Metropolitan of the Province is the Archbishop of Cape Town, South Africa. Lesotho forms a single diocese, with an estimated 100,000 members.

Bishop of Lesotho: Rt Rev. Joseph Mahapu Tsubella, Bishop's House, POB 87, Maseru 100; tel. 311974; fax 310161; e-mail diocese@lesotho.com.

The Roman Catholic Church

Lesotho comprises one archdiocese and three dioceses. At 31 December 2000 there were some 894,418 adherents of the Roman Catholic Church.

Lesotho Catholic Bishops' Conference
Catholic Secretariat, POB 200, Maseru 100; tel. 312525; fax 310294. f. 1972; Pres. Most Rev. Bernard Mohlalisi (Archbishop of Maseru).

Archbishop of Maseru: Most Rev. Bernard Mohlalisi, Arch-bishop's House, 19 Orpen Rd, POB 267, Maseru 100; tel. 312565; fax 310425; e-mail archmase@lesoff.co.za.

Other Christian Churches

African Methodist Episcopal Church: POB 223, Maseru 100; tel. 322616; f. 1903; 11,295 mems.

Dutch Reformed Church in Africa: POB 454, Maseru 100; tel. 314669; f. 1957; 7,396 mems (1991).

Lesotho Evangelical Church: POB 260, Maseru 100; tel. 323942; f. 1833; independent since 1964; Moderator Rev. G. L. Sibolla; Exec. Sec. Rev. A. M. Thebe; 211,000 mems (1990).

Methodist Church of Southern Africa: POB 81, Maseru 100; tel. 322412; f. 1927; Supt Rev. D. Senkhane; c. 10,000 mems and adherents (1989).

Other denominations active in Lesotho include the Apostolic Faith Mission, the Assemblies of God, the Full Gospel Church of God and the Seventh-day Adventists. There are also numerous African independent churches.

BAHÁ'Í FAITH

National Spiritual Assembly: POB 508, Maseru 100; tel. 312346; fax 310092; e-mail bahailesotho@lesotho.com; mems resident in 443 localities.

The Press

Lentsoe la Basotho: POB 353, Maseru 100; tel. 323561; fax 310003; e-mail lbmin@lesoff.co.za; f. 1974; weekly; Sesotho; publ. by Ministry of Communications; Editor Kahliso Lebenya; circ. 14,000.

Leselinyana la Lesotho (Light of Lesotho): POB 7, Morija 190; tel. 360244; fax 360005; f. 1863; fortnightly; Sesotho, with occasional articles in English; publ. by Lesotho Evangelical Church; Editor A. B. Thoalane; circ. 10,000.

Lesotho Today: POB 36, Maseru 100; tel. 323586; fax 310003; weekly; English; publ. by Ministry of Communications; Editor T. Tsepane; circ. 7,000.

Lesotho Weekly: POB 353, Maseru 100; weekly.

Makatolle: POB 111, Maseru 100; tel. 850990; f. 1963; weekly; Sesotho; Editor M. Ramangoei; circ. 2,000.

The Mirror: POB 903, Maseru 100; tel. 315602; fax 310216; f. 1986; weekly; English; Editor Nat Molomo; circ. 4,000.

MoAfrika: POB 7234, Maseru 100; tel. 325034; f. 1990; weekly; Sesotho; Editor-in-Chief Candi Ramainoane; circ. 5,000.

Moeletsi oa Basotho: Mazenod Institute, POB 18, Mazenod 160; tel. 350465; fax 350010; f. 1933; weekly; Roman Catholic; Sesotho; Editor Fr F. S. Shopane; circ. 20,000.

Mopheme (the Survivor): POB 14184, Maseru; tel. and fax 311670; e-mail mopheme@lesoff.co.za; internet www.lesoffice.co.za/mopheme; weekly; English; Editor Lawrence Keketso; circ. 2,500.

Public Eye: POB 14129, Maseru; tel. 3201414; fax 310614; e-mail voicemed@lesoff.co.za; internet www.publiceye.co.ls; f. 1997; weekly; English; Editor Bethuel Thai; circ. 18,000.

Shoeshoe: POB 36, Maseru 100; tel. 323561; fax 310003; quarterly; women's interest; publ. by Ministry of Communications.

Southern Star: POB 7590, Maseru; tel. 312269; fax 310167; e-mail b&a-holdings@ilesotho.com; weekly; English; Editor Frank Boffoe; circ. 1,500.

The Sun: POB 1013, Maseru; weekly; English; Editor M. Ranouku; circ. 6,500.

Thebe ea Khotso: POB 15303, Maseru; Sesotho; Editor Mohapi Motba; circ. 7,000.

NEWS AGENCIES

Lesotho News Agency (LENA): POB 36, Maseru 100; tel. 315317; fax 326408; e-mail l_lenanews@hotmail.com; internet www.lena.gov.ls; f. 1986; Dir Nkoe Thakali; Editor Violet Maraisane.

Foreign Bureau

Inter Press Service (IPS) (Italy): c/o Lesotho News Agency, POB 36, Maseru 100; Correspondent Lebohang Lejakane.

Publishers

Longman Lesotho (Pty) Ltd: POB 1174, 104 Christie House, Orpen Rd, Maseru 100; tel. 314254; fax 310118; Man. Dir Seymour R. Kikine.

Macmillan Boleswa Publishers Lesotho (Pty) Ltd: POB 7545, Maseru 100; tel. 317340; fax 310047; e-mail macmillan@lesoff.co.ls.

Mazenod Institute: POB 39, Mazenod 160; tel. 350224; f. 1933; Roman Catholic; Man. Fr B. Mohlalisi.

Morija Sesuto Book Depot: POB 4, Morija 190; tel. and fax 360204; f. 1862; owned by the Lesotho Evangelical Church; religious, educational and Sesotho language and literature.

St Michael's Mission: The Social Centre, POB 25, Roma; tel. 316234; f. 1968; religious and educational; Man. Dir Fr M. Ferrange.

Government Publishing House

Government Printer: POB 268, Maseru; tel. 313023.

Broadcasting and Communications

TELECOMMUNICATIONS

Telecom Lesotho: POB 1037, Maseru 100; tel. 211100; fax 310183; internet www.telecom.co.ls; 70% holding acquired by the Mountain Kingdom Communications consortium in 2000; 30% state-owned; CEO A. Van Der Veer; Chair. Dr Daniel Phororo.

VCL Communications: Development House, Kingsway Rd, POB 7387, Maseru 100; tel. 212000; fax 311079; f. 1996; jt venture between Telecom Lesotho and Vodacom (Pty) Ltd; operates mobile cellular telephone network.

BROADCASTING

Lesotho National Broadcasting Service: POB 552, Maseru 100; tel. 323561; fax 322500; programmes in Sesotho and English; radio transmissions began in 1964 and television transmissions in 1988; Dir MOLAHLEHI LETLOTLO; Dir of Programming MAMONYANE MATSABA.

Finance

(cap. = capital; res = reserves; dep. = deposits; m. = million; brs = branches; amounts in maloti)

BANKING

Central Bank

Central Bank of Lesotho: cnr Airport and Moshoeshoe Rds, POB 1184, Maseru 100; tel. 314281; fax 310051; e-mail cbl@centralbank .org.ls; internet www.centralbank.org.ls; f. 1980; bank of issue; cap. 25.0m., res 1,021.6m., dep. 1,931.4m. (Dec. 2000); Gov. and Chair. M. S. SWARAY.

Commercial Banks

Lesotho Bank: Central Services, Lesotho Bank Towers, Kingsway, POB 1053, Maseru 100; tel. 314333; fax 310348; f. 1972; transferred to majority private ownership in Aug. 1999; 70% owned by Standard Bank Lesotho Ltd; commercial bank, also carries out development banking functions; cap. and res 70m. (2000); Exec. Dir C. ADDIS; 15 brs.

Nedbank Lesotho: Standard Bank Bldg, 1st Floor, Kingsway, POB 1001, Maseru 100; tel. 312696; fax 310025; e-mail nedles@adelfang .co.za; fmrly Standard Chartered Bank Lesotho Ltd; owned by Nedcor Bank Ltd (South Africa); cap. 20m., res 20.3m., dep. 428.3m. (Dec. 2000); Chair. W. P. FROST; 3 brs and 7 agencies.

Standard Bank Lesotho Ltd: Bank Bldg, 1st Floor, Kingsway, POB 115, Maseru 100; tel. 312423; fax 310068; e-mail horst@ilesotho .com; internet www.standardbank.co.ls; f. 1957 as Barclays Bank DCO; fmrly Stanbic Bank Lesotho Ltd, present name since 1997; owned by Standard Bank Investment Corpn Ltd; cap. 16.5m., res 15.1m., dep. 301.5m. (Dec. 1998); Chair. ROBERT E. NORVAL; Exec. Dir V. KENNEDY; 5 brs and 2 agencies.

Development Bank

Lesotho Building Finance Corpn (LBFC): Private Bag A59, Maseru 100; tel. 313514; fax 310348; state-owned; Man. Dir N. MONYANE; 3 brs.

INSURANCE

Alliance Insurance Co Ltd: POB 1118, Maseru West 105; tel. 312357; fax 310313; e-mail alliance@alliance.co.ls; Man. Dir JOHANN PIENAAR.

Lesotho National Insurance Corpn (Pty) Ltd: Private Bag A96, Lesotho Insurance House, Kingsway, Maseru 100; tel. 313031; fax 310007; e-mail inig@lesoff.co.za; f. 1977; Chair. Dr M. SENAOANA; CEO M. MOLELEKOA.

Mamoth Insurance: Christie House, 4th Floor, POB 1659, Maseru 100; e-mail mamoth@adelfng.co.za; internet www.mamoth.co.ls; f. 1998; Chair. THABO RAMOKGOPA.

Metropolitan Life Ltd: POB 645, Maseru; tel. 323970; fax 317126; Regional Man. E. L. TSHABALALA.

Minet Kingsway Lesotho (Pty) Ltd: POB 993, Maseru 100; tel. 313540; fax 310033; f. 1969; 31% holding acquired by Aon Risk Services (United Kingdom) in 2000, 20% state-owned; Chair. R. A. DAVISON; Man. Dir A. T. WHITEHORN.

Thebe Insurance Brokers (Lesotho) (Pty) Ltd: Options Bldg, 1st Floor, Pioneer Rd, Private Bag A244, Maseru 100; tel. 313018; fax 310513; Chair. C. J. SOUNES; Man. Dir D. T. MALING.

Trade and Industry

GOVERNMENT AGENCIES

Privatization Unit: c/o Ministry of Finance and Development Planning, Private Bag A249, Maseru 100; tel. 317902; fax 317551; e-mail dirpp@adelfang.co.za; Dir MOTHUSI MASHOLOGU.

Trade Promotion Unit: c/o Ministry of Industry, Trade and Marketing, POB 747, Maseru 100; tel. 322138; fax 310121.

DEVELOPMENT ORGANIZATIONS

Basotho Enterprises Development Corpn (BEDCO): POB 1216, Maseru 100; tel. 312094; fax 310455; e-mail bedco@lesoff.co .za; f. 1980; promotes and assists in the establishment and development of small-scale Basotho-owned enterprises; CEO SIMON PHAWANE.

Lesotho Highlands Development Authority: Lesotho Bank Towers, 3rd Floor, POB 7332, Maseru 100; tel. 311280; fax 310060; internet www.lhda.org.ls; f. 1986 to supervise the Highlands Water Project (internet www.lhwp.org.ls), being undertaken jtly with South Africa; Chair. H. M. MHLANGA; CEO MAKASE MARUMO.

Lesotho National Development Corpn (LNDC): Development House, 1st Floor, Kingsway Rd, Private Bag A96, Maseru 100; tel. 312012; fax 310038; e-mail lndc@ilesotho.com; internet www.lndc .org.ls; f. 1967; 90% state-owned; cap. M40m. interests include candle, carpet, tyre-retreading, explosives, fertilizer, clothing, jewellery and furniture factories, potteries, two diamond prospecting operations, an abattoir, a diamond-cutting and polishing works, a housing co, a brewery and an international hotel with a gambling casino; Chair. Minister of Industry, Trade and Marketing; CEO SOPHIA MOHAPI.

Lesotho Co-operatives Handicrafts: Maseru; f. 1978; marketing and distribution of handicrafts; Gen. Man. KHOTSO MATLA.

CHAMBER OF COMMERCE

Lesotho Chamber of Commerce and Industry: POB 79, Maseru 100; tel. 323482; fax 310414; e-mail lcci@lesoff.co.za.

INDUSTRIAL AND TRADE ASSOCIATIONS

Livestock Marketing Corpn: POB 800, Maseru 100; tel. 322444; f. 1973; sole org. for marketing livestock and livestock products; liaises closely with marketing boards in South Africa; projects include an abattoir, tannery, poultry and wool and mohair scouring plants; Gen. Man. S. R. MATLANYANE.

Produce Marketing Corpn: Maseru; f. 1974; Gen. Man. M. PHOOFOLO.

EMPLOYERS' ORGANIZATION

Association of Lesotho Employers: POB 1509, Maseru 100; tel. 315736; e-mail alemp@ilesotho.com; f. 1961; represents mems in industrial relations and on govt bodies, and advises the Govt on employers' concerns; Pres. BRIAN MCCARTHY; Exec. Dir T. MAKEKA.

UTILITIES

Lesotho Electricity Corpn: POB 423, Maseru 100; tel. 312236; fax 310093; internet www.lec.co.ls; f. 1969; transfer to the private sector scheduled for early 2003; Man. Dir S. L. MHAVILLE.

Lesotho Water and Sewerage Authority: POB 426, Maseru 100; tel. 312449; fax 312006; e-mail makhoalibe@wasa.co.ls; Chair. S. MAKHOALIBE.

TRADE UNIONS

Construction and Allied Workers Union of Lesotho (CAWULE): Private Bag A445, Maseru 100; tel. 333035.

Lesotho General Workers' Union: POB 322, Maseru 100; f. 1954; Chair. J. M. RAMAROTHOLE; Sec. T. MOTLOHI.

Lesotho Transport and Telecommunication Workers' Union: Maseru 100; f. 1959; Pres. M. BERENG; Sec. P. MOTRAMAI.

Lesotho University Teachers' and Researchers' Union (LUTARU): Maseru.

National Union of Construction and Allied Workers: Maseru; f. 1967; Pres. L. PUTSOANE; Sec. T. TLALE.

National Union of Printing, Bookbinding and Allied Workers: PO Mazenod 160; f. 1963; Pres. G. MOTEBANG; Gen. Sec. CLEMENT RATSIU.

Union of Shop Distributive and Allied Workers: Maseru 100; f. 1966; Pres. P. BERENG; Sec. J. MOLAPO.

Transport

RAILWAYS

Lesotho is linked with the South African railway system by a short line (2.6 km in length) from Maseru to Marseilles, on the Bloemfontein/Natal main line.

ROADS

In 1999 Lesotho's road network totalled 5,940 km, of which 1,084 km were main roads and 1,950 km were secondary roads. About 18.3% of roads were paved. In 1996 the International Development Association granted US $40m. towards the Government's rolling five-year road programme. From 1996/67 an extra-budgetary Road Fund was to finance road maintenance. In March 2000 a major road network was opened, linking Maseru with the Mohale Dam.

CIVIL AVIATION

King Moshoeshoe I International Airport is at Thota-Moli, some 20 km from Maseru; in January 2002 the Government announced plans for its expansion. There are 40 smaller airfields in Lesotho. International services between Maseru and Johannesburg are operated by South African Airlink.

Lesotho Airways Corpn: POB 861, Maseru 100; tel. 324507; fax 310617; domestic and international passenger services; privatized 1999; Man. Dir MICHAEL SCHRIENER.

Tourism

Spectacular mountain scenery is the principal tourist attraction, and a new ski resort was scheduled to be opened in 2003. In 1999 there were 186,000 tourist arrivals, and receipts from tourism totalled about US $19m.

Lesotho Tourist Board (Boto Ea Tsa Boeti Lesotho): POB 1378, Maseru 100; tel. 313760; fax 310108; e-mail infomsu@ltb.org.ls; f. 1983; Man. Dir MANDISA MASHOLOGU.

LIBERIA

Introductory Survey

Location, Climate, Language, Religion, Flag, Capital

The Republic of Liberia lies on the west coast of Africa, with Sierra Leone and Guinea to the north, and Côte d'Ivoire to the east. The climate is tropical, with temperatures ranging from 18°C (65°F) to 49°C (120°F). English is the official language but the 16 major ethnic groups speak their own languages and dialects. Liberia is officially a Christian state, though some Liberians hold traditional beliefs. There are about 670,000 Muslims. The national flag (proportions 10 by 19) has 11 horizontal stripes, alternately of red and white, with a dark blue square canton, containing a five-pointed white star, in the upper hoist. The capital is Monrovia.

Recent History

Founded by liberated black slaves from the southern USA, Liberia became an independent republic in 1847. The leader of the True Whig Party, William Tubman, who had been President of Liberia since 1944, died in July 1971 and was succeeded by his Vice-President, William R. Tolbert, who was re-elected in October 1975. The True Whig Party's monopoly of power was increasingly criticized, and in 1978 a major opposition group, the Progressive Alliance of Liberia, was formed.

In April 1980 Tolbert was assassinated in a military coup, led by Master Sergeant (later Commander-in-Chief) Samuel Doe, who assumed power as Chairman of the newly established People's Redemption Council (PRC), suspending the Constitution and proscribing all political parties. The new regime attracted international criticism for its summary execution of 13 former senior government officials who had been accused of corruption and mismanagement. In July 1981 all civilian ministers received commissions, thus installing total military rule.

During the early 1980s there were frequent dismissals and resignations from the PRC and the Cabinet, as Doe demonstrated his avowed determination to eliminate corruption and abuse of public office. The draft Constitution was approved by 78.3% of registered voters in a national referendum in July 1984. In the same month Doe dissolved the PRC and appointed a 58-member Interim National Assembly, comprising 36 civilians and all the members of the former PRC. The ban on political organizations was repealed in the same month, to enable parties to secure registration prior to presidential and legislative elections, which were due to take place in October 1985. In August 1984 Doe founded the National Democratic Party of Liberia (NDPL) and formally announced his candidature for the presidency. By early 1985 a total of 11 political parties had been formed; however, two influential parties, the Liberian People's Party (LPP) and the United People's Party (UPP), were proscribed, and only three parties besides the NDPL—the Liberian Action Party (LAP), the Liberia Unification Party (LUP) and the Unity Party (UP)—were eventually permitted to participate in the elections. Doe won the presidential election, receiving 50.9% of the votes. At the concurrent elections to the bicameral National Assembly, the NDPL won 22 of the 26 seats in the Senate and 51 of the 64 seats in the House of Representatives.

On 6 January 1986 Doe was inaugurated as President. He appointed a new Cabinet (which largely comprised members of the previous administration). Six members of the opposition parties continued to boycott the National Assembly, and their seats were taken by NDPL representatives at a by-election in December. Several government members were dismissed during 1987–88, in connection with allegations of financial malpractice. In March 1988 Gabriel Kpolleh, the leader of the LUP, was among several people arrested on charges of planning to overthrow the Government. In October he and nine others were sentenced to 10 years' imprisonment for treason.

In December 1989 an armed insurrection by rebel forces began in the north-eastern border region of Nimba County. In early 1990 several hundred deaths ensued in fighting between the Liberian army (the Armed Forces of Liberia—AFL) and the rebels, who claimed to be members of a hitherto unknown opposition group, the National Patriotic Front of Liberia (NPFL), led by a former government official, Charles Taylor. The fighting swiftly degenerated into a war between Doe's

ethnic group, the Krahn, and the local Gio and Mano tribes, and many thousands of people took refuge in neighbouring Guinea and Côte d'Ivoire. By April the NPFL had overcome government resistance in Nimba County, gaining control of a large part of the area. Following the advance of rebels on the capital, Monrovia, in May, most foreign residents were evacuated. NPFL forces entered Monrovia in July; Taylor's authority as self-proclaimed President of his own interim administration, known as the National Patriotic Reconstruction Assembly, was, however, challenged by a faction of the NPFL, led by Prince Yormie Johnson, whose troops rapidly gained control of parts of Monrovia. In the subsequent conflict both government and rebel forces were responsible for numerous atrocities against civilians. The Economic Community of West African States (ECOWAS, see p. 187) repeatedly failed to negotiate a cease-fire, and in late August it dispatched a military force to restore peace in the region. Doe and Johnson agreed to accept this monitoring group (ECOMOG, see p. 189), but its initial occupation of the port area of Monrovia encountered armed opposition by Taylor's forces.

On 30 August 1990 exiled representatives of Liberia's principal political parties and other influential groups met at a conference convened by ECOWAS in the Gambian capital, Banjul, where they elected Dr Amos Sawyer, the leader of the LPP, as President of an Interim Government of National Unity (IGNU). Doe was taken prisoner by Johnson's rebel Independent National Patriotic Front of Liberia (INPFL) on 9 September, and was killed on the following day. In early October, following Taylor's rejection of a proposed peace settlement, ECOMOG began an offensive aimed at establishing a neutral zone in Monrovia separating the three warring factions. By mid-October ECOMOG had gained control of central Monrovia. On 22 November Sawyer was inaugurated as Interim President, under the auspices of ECOWAS, in Monrovia. Later that month, following ECOWAS-sponsored negotiations in the Malian capital, Bamako, the AFL, the NPFL and the INPFL signed a cease-fire agreement. By January 1991 all rebel forces had withdrawn from Monrovia, and in that month Sawyer nominated ministers to the IGNU. Legislative power was vested in a 28-member Interim National Assembly, which represented the principal political factions, including the INPFL; however, the NPFL refused to participate. On 19 April a national conference re-elected Sawyer as Interim President and appointed a member of the INPFL, Peter Naigow (a former minister in Doe's administration), as Vice-President. In June Sawyer nominated a new Council of Ministers, which was subsequently approved by the Interim National Assembly. In August, however, the INPFL representatives, including Naigow, resigned from the IGNU, after Sawyer denounced the execution, apparently at Johnson's instigation, of four members of the INPFL who had reportedly complied with arrangements to relinquish weapons to ECOMOG.

During March 1991 members of the NPFL perpetrated several incursions into Sierra Leone. In April Sierra Leonean forces entered Liberian territory and launched retaliatory attacks against NPFL bases, while the NPFL reportedly advanced within Sierra Leone. It was reported that NPFL forces were supporting a Sierra Leonean resistance movement, the Revolutionary United Front (RUF), in attacks against government forces of that country (see the chapter on Sierra Leone). In September members of a newly emerged rebel movement, comprising former supporters of the late President Doe, the United Liberation Movement of Liberia for Democracy (ULIMO), initiated attacks from Sierra Leone against NPFL forces in north-western Liberia.

At the end of October 1991 a summit meeting between Sawyer and Taylor, which took place in Yamoussoukro, Côte d'Ivoire, under the aegis of an ECOWAS five-nation committee, resulted in a peace agreement whereby the troops of all warring factions were to be disarmed and restricted to camps, while the NPFL was to relinquish the territory under its control to ECOMOG. It was also agreed that all Liberian forces would be withdrawn from Sierra Leone, and that a demilitarized zone, under the control of ECOMOG, would be created along Liberia's border with Sierra Leone. However, the NPFL failed to disarm and restrict its forces to camps within the time limit that had been stipulated in the peace agreement. In January 1992 the Interim Election Commission and Supreme Court were established, in accordance with the peace accord. In April the conditions of the Yamoussoukro agreement were reaffirmed at a summit meeting in Geneva, Switzerland. At the end of that month, in response to pressure from within the NPFL, Taylor announced that NPFL troops were to withdraw from the border with Sierra Leone; ULIMO also agreed to co-operate in the implementation of the Yamoussoukro accord. In May ECOMOG began to disarm the rebel factions and to deploy troops in territory controlled by the NPFL, and, despite continued fighting between ULIMO and NPFL forces, established a demilitarized zone along the border with Sierra Leone.

In August 1992 a renewed offensive by ULIMO in western Liberia resulted in intense fighting. By the end of that month it was reported that ULIMO had gained control of Bomi and Grand Cape Mount Counties in western Liberia. In October the NPFL claimed that Nigerian aircraft under ECOMOG command had bombed NPFL bases at Kakata and Harbel (the site of the Roberts Field International Airport and the country's principal rubber plantation), near Monrovia, and at Buchanan, following an NPFL attack on ECOMOG forces stationed in the Monrovia region. The NPFL subsequently captured a number of strategic areas on the outskirts of Monrovia; more than 100,000 civilians took refuge from the conflict in central Monrovia. An ECOWAS summit meeting in Cotonou, Benin, demanded that ULIMO and the NPFL observe an immediate cease-fire, and threatened to impose economic sanctions (comprising a total land, sea and air blockade); the implementation of sanctions was referred to the UN Security Council for endorsement. Hostilities continued, however, and ECOMOG forces (who were supported by members of the AFL and militia loyal to the IGNU) began retaliatory attacks against NPFL positions around Monrovia. In late October it was reported that ECOMOG units had captured the INPFL base at Caldwell, near Monrovia, and that Johnson had surrendered. (The INPFL was subsequently disbanded.) In November the UN Security Council adopted a resolution imposing a mandatory embargo on the supply of armaments to Liberia, and authorized the UN Secretary-General to send a special representative to the country.

In December 1992 ECOMOG claimed that it had regained control of the strategic positions on the outskirts of Monrovia that had been seized by the NPFL in October. In early 1993 ECOMOG began to advance in south-eastern Liberia, recapturing Harbel, while ULIMO was reported to have gained control of Lofa County in the west. In March ULIMO accepted an invitation from Sawyer to join the IGNU; ULIMO forces in Monrovia were subsequently disarmed, in accordance with the Yamoussoukro agreement. Following a major offensive, ECOMOG announced in April that it had gained control of Buchanan (which was reopened to shipping later that year). In June some 600 refugees were found to be have been killed at the Harbel rubber plantation. Taylor denied accusations by the IGNU of NPFL involvement.

In July 1993 a conference, attended by the factions involved in the hostilities, was convened (under the auspices of the UN and ECOWAS) in Geneva. Following several days of negotiations, the IGNU, the NPFL and ULIMO agreed to a cease-fire (to be monitored by a joint committee of the three factions, pending the deployment of UN observers and a reconstituted peace-keeping force), and to the establishment of a transitional government. The peace accord was formally signed in Cotonou on 25 July. Under its terms, the IGNU was to be replaced by the Liberian National Transitional Government (LNTG), with a five-member transitional Council of State and a 35-member Transitional Legislative Assembly (comprising 13 representatives of the IGNU, 13 of the NPFL and nine of ULIMO), pending presidential and general elections. In response to demands by Taylor, the dominance in ECOMOG of the Nigerian contingent was to be considerably reduced, and the peace-keeping force was to be supplemented with additional troops from other African states.

The cease-fire came into effect at the end of July 1993; however, ECOMOG subsequently accused the NPFL of violating the Cotonou accord by repeatedly entering territory under the control of the peace-keeping force. In August the IGNU, the NPFL and ULIMO each appointed a representative to the Council of State, while a list of nine candidates, nominated by the three factions, elected the two remaining members (who

were representatives of the IGNU and ULIMO respectively) from among their number. Dr Bismark Kuyon, a member of the IGNU, was subsequently elected Chairman of the Council of State. Shortly afterwards, however, Kuyon announced that the inauguration of the Council of State (originally scheduled to take place on 24 August) was to be postponed, pending the clear implementation of the process of disarmament.

In September 1993 a report by a UN mission concluded that AFL troops had perpetrated the massacre at Harbel (which had been widely attributed to the NPFL), and implied that ECOMOG had deliberately failed to identify those responsible. In the same month the UN Security Council approved the establishment of a 300-member UN Observer Mission in Liberia (UNOMIL), which was to co-operate with ECOMOG and the Organization of African Unity (now the African Union, see p. 130) in overseeing the transitional process. In October the Transitional Legislative Assembly was established, in accordance with the peace agreement. Sawyer dismissed Kuyon (who had reportedly dissociated himself from the IGNU's refusal to relinquish power prior to disarmament) and appointed Philip Banks, hitherto Minister of Justice, in his place.

Meanwhile, it was feared that renewed hostilities in several areas of the country would jeopardize the peace accord. An armed faction styling itself the Liberia Peace Council (LPC), which reportedly comprised members of the Krahn ethnic group from Grand Gedeh County, joined by a number of disaffected AFL troops, emerged in September 1993 and subsequently entered into conflict with the NPFL in south-eastern Liberia. In December fighting between ULIMO and a newly formed movement, the Lofa Defence Force (LDF), was also reported in Lofa County. The NPFL denied involvement with the LDF, which occupied territory previously controlled by ULIMO in the northwest.

At the end of February 1994 the Council of State elected David Kpomakpor, a representative of the IGNU, as its Chairman. In early March units belonging to UNOMIL and the new ECOMOG force (which had been supplemented by contingents from Tanzania and Uganda) were deployed, and the disarmament of all factions commenced. On 7 March the Council of State was inaugurated; it was envisaged that the presidential and legislative elections (originally scheduled for February) would take place in September. However, the disarmament process was subsequently impeded by an increase in rebel activity: in addition to continuing hostilities involving the LDF and the LPC, more than 200 people were killed in clashes within ULIMO between members of the Krahn and Mandingo ethnic groups, particularly in the region of Tubmanburg (in Bomi County, where the organization was officially based). The hostilities, which followed the dispute earlier that month between the leader of ULIMO, Alhaji G. V. Kromah (a Mandingo), and the Chairman of the organization's military wing, Maj.-Gen. Roosevelt Johnson (a Krahn), were prompted by resentment among the Krahn at the predominance of the Mandingo in ULIMO's representation in the transitional institutions.

In April 1994 UNOMIL's mandate (which was due to expire that month) was extended, pending the completion of the transitional process. In May, following prolonged controversy over the allocation of principal portfolios, a 19-member Cabinet was installed, comprising seven representatives of the NPFL, seven of ULIMO and five of the former IGNU. In July, however, Kromah's faction (henceforth referred to as ULIMO—K) initiated an offensive to recapture Tubmanburg, which was under the control of Roosevelt Johnson's forces (ULIMO—J). Also in July the UN Security Council urged the LNTG to convene a meeting of the armed factions to discuss a programme for disarmament. Later that month the Minister of Labour in the LNTG, Thomas Woewiyu, accused Taylor of responsibility for atrocities perpetrated against civilians.

In early September 1994 (when the original mandate of the LNTG was due to expire) a meeting, chaired by Rawlings, of the NPFL, the AFL and ULIMO—K took place in Akosombo, Ghana. On 12 September Taylor, Kromah and the Chief of Staff of the AFL, Lt-Gen. Hezekiah Bowen, signed a peace accord providing for the immediate cessation of hostilities and for the establishment later that month of a reconstituted Council of State, in which four of the five members were to be nominated, respectively, by the three factions and a civilian Liberian National Conference (LNC—which had been convened in Monrovia at the end of August). Meanwhile, following clashes between dissident members of the NPFL and troops loyal to Taylor, the dissidents' Central Revolutionary Council (CRC) announced that Taylor had been deposed and replaced by Woewiyu, who indicated that he was not prepared to accept the Akosombo agreement. In mid-September disaffected members of the AFL, led by a former officer who had served in the Doe administration, Gen. Charles Julu, seized the presidential mansion, but were subsequently overpowered by ECOMOG forces. (Almost 80 members of the AFL, including Julu, were later arrested, and a further 2,000 troops were disarmed by ECOMOG.) Later that month the CRC, apparently in alliance with elements of the AFL, ULIMO, the LPC and the LDF, took control of Taylor's base at Gbarnga (in the central Bong County); forces loyal to Taylor had retreated to the town of Palala, to the east of Gbarnga, while Taylor was said to have taken refuge in Côte d'Ivoire.

In October 1994 both the ECOMOG and UNOMIL contingents were reduced in size, in view of the lack of progress achieved in the peace process. In November a conference, attended by Bowen, Taylor, Woewiyu, the leader of the LPC, Dr George Boley, and the leader of the LDF, François Massaquoi, together with representatives of the LNC and the LNTG, was convened in the Ghanaian capital, Accra, to discuss preparations for the installation of a reconstituted Council of State. Meanwhile, it was reported that the NPFL had regained control of much of the territory, including Gbarnga, that the CRC had captured in September. On 22 December the participants of the peace conference reached agreement for a cease-fire to enter into force later that month and reaffirmed the terms of the Akosombo agreement, including provisions for the establishment of demilitarized zones throughout Liberia and for the installation of a reconstituted Council of State—to comprise a single representative of each of the NPFL, ULIMO, the 'Coalition Forces' (a loose alliance comprising the CRC, the LPC, the LDF and elements of the AFL), and the LNC, with a fifth member elected jointly by the NPFL and ULIMO from traditional rulers. New institutions were to be installed on 1 January 1996, following multi-party elections. Later in December 1994 the UN Security Council extended the mandate of UNOMIL (now comprising 90 observers) until April 1995, while the Nigerian Government reduced its ECOMOG contingent to 6,000 (from about 10,000), in accordance with its stated aim gradually to withdraw from Liberia. The cease-fire, which entered into force on 28 December, was widely observed.

In April 1995 hostilities between the NPFL and the LPC resumed near Buchanan; renewed fighting in other parts of Liberia was also reported. At the end of April Tanzania withdrew its 800-strong ECOMOG contingent, in response to the failure of the UN to disburse funds that had been pledged to the Tanzanian Government. In May an ECOWAS summit meeting, convened in the Nigerian capital to discuss the Liberian conflict, failed to resolve the outstanding issues; it was subsequently announced that the installation of the Council of State was to be postponed until the factions demonstrated commitment to the implementation of the cease-fire and the disarmament process. Peace negotiations, which resumed in Monrovia in July, were again boycotted by Charles Taylor.

Negotiations regarding the composition of the Council of State were impeded by Taylor's persistent demands, opposed by the other factional leaders, that he be granted the chairmanship of the Council. On 19 August 1995, following a further ECOWAS summit meeting in Abuja, the armed factions (the NPFL, ULIMO—K, the LPC, the CRC, the LDF, ULIMO—J and the AFL) finally signed a compromise agreement providing for the installation of a reconstituted Council of State, which was to remain in power, pending elections, for one year. An academic with no factional affiliations, Prof. Wilton Sankawulo, was to assume the office of Chairman, while the other seats were to be allocated to Taylor, Kromah, Boley, the LNC representative, Oscar Quiah, and a traditional ruler who had been nominated by ULIMO and the NPFL, Chief Tamba Taylor. Later that month a cease-fire entered into force, in compliance with the terms of the peace accord. The new transitional Council of State was formally installed on 1 September, whereupon the UN special representative announced that the elections were to take place on 20 August 1996. The Council of State subsequently appointed a new transitional Council of Ministers, comprising members of the seven factions that had signed the Abuja agreement. Later in September the UN Security Council extended UNOMIL's mandate until the end of January 1996.

At an emergency meeting of ECOWAS in October 1995 a number of member states pledged to contribute additional troops to ECOMOG in order to implement the peace process. Meanwhile, in November a demilitarized zone was established

between NPFL and ULIMO—K forces in the region of St Paul River (between Bong and Lofa Counties). Deployment of ECOMOG forces commenced, in accordance with the Abuja peace terms, in December. Following continued clashes between the ULIMO factions, however, ULIMO—J attacked ECOMOG troops in the region of Tubmanburg. ECOMOG suspended deployment of its forces, and launched a counter-offensive in an attempt to restore order. Hostilities continued in early 1996, with large numbers of civilians killed or displaced.

In February 1996 military and executive officials within ULIMO—J issued a resolution to the effect that Johnson had been replaced as leader of the movement in the interests of the peace process. In March the Council of State announced the removal of Johnson (who had hitherto held the rural development portfolio) from the Council of Ministers. Clashes erupted between the two factions of ULIMO—J, in which forces loyal to Johnson allegedly killed a supporter of the new leadership. The Council of State subsequently ordered that Johnson be arrested on charges of murder. Johnson, however, refused to surrender to the authorities, and became effectively besieged in his private residence in Monrovia. In April government forces, led by Charles Taylor, engaged in hostilities with Johnson's supporters, in an effort to force him to surrender. The principal factions represented in the transitional authorities thus became involved in the conflict: elements of the LPC and AFL (which were predominantly Krahn) supported Johnson's forces, while the NPFL and ULIMO—K opposed them. Fighting rapidly intensified in central Monrovia, resulting in the displacement of large numbers of civilians, who fled the capital or took refuge in embassy compounds. ECOMOG (which had refrained from military intervention) deployed its forces in the region of Monrovia, with the aim of negotiating between the warring factions. Following a lull in the fighting, however, some of Johnson's supporters launched attacks in the residential area of Mamba Point (where embassies and offices of humanitarian organizations were situated) and seized a number of civilians as hostages. The US Government began to evacuate US citizens, and other foreign nationals, from the US embassy (where some 20,000 civilians had taken shelter). Johnson's supporters, together with their hostages, took to former army barracks (the Barclay Training Centre) in Monrovia; NPFL and ULIMO—K forces subsequently surrounded the barracks, where, in addition, several thousand civilians were sheltered. As the evacuation of foreign nationals continued, the US Government dispatched five warships to the region, with the stated aim of ensuring the protection of US diplomatic staff in Monrovia. Later in April 1996 a further cease-fire agreement was negotiated under the aegis of the US Government, the UN and ECOWAS. Under the terms of the accord, ECOMOG troops were subsequently deployed throughout Monrovia, while most of the remaining hostages were released by Johnson's supporters.

In May 1996, during the absence of Johnson (who had left the country under US protection, to attend a planned ECOWAS summit meeting), the NPFL launched a further attack against the Barclay Training Centre, prompting large numbers of civilians to flee to Monrovia Free Port. At the end of May the UN Security Council renewed the mandate of UNOMIL for a further three months, but warned the armed factions that international support would be withdrawn if fighting continued; UNOMIL was henceforth to comprise only the five military and 20 civilian personnel remaining in the country following the evacuation of a further 93 observers in April. In June Johnson's supporters agreed to disarm and to leave the Barclay Training Centre, while an ECOWAS arbitration mission commenced discussions with the faction leaders in an effort to restore the peace process.

In August 1996, at an ECOWAS conference in Abuja, the principal faction leaders (apart from Johnson, who remained abroad) signed a further peace agreement, whereby a reconstituted Council of State was to be installed by the end of that month, with a former senator, Ruth Perry, replacing Sankawulo as Chairman; Taylor and Boley were to remain members of the new administration. Under a revised schedule, elections were to take place at the end of May 1997, and power was to be transferred to an elected government by mid-June, while the armed factions were to have been dissolved by the end of January of that year. In order to implement the new timetable, ECOMOG (which then numbered 8,500) was to be reinforced by personnel from several west African states. At the end of August 1996 the mandate of UNOMIL was again extended. Perry was inaugurated as Chairman of the Council of State in early September; Johnson was again allocated a ministerial portfolio in a subsequent reorganization of the Cabinet.

In September 1996, following the installation of the new transitional administration, the faction leaders ordered their forces to disarm and to remove road-blocks in territory under their control. ECOMOG troops were deployed in strategic regions, including Kakata and Buchanan, and committees comprising ECOMOG and UNOMIL officials, together with representatives of the armed factions, began to visit remote areas of the country to verify the implementation of the disarmament process. Subsequent progress in disarming the members of the various factions was slow, owing, in part, to delays in the delivery of logistical equipment pledged by the international community to ECOMOG. Following the expiry of the deadline for the completion of the disarmament process, which had been extended from the end of January 1997 to early February, ECOMOG announced that about 91% of the rebel forces (who numbered 30,000–35,000, according to revised estimates) had relinquished their armaments.

In January 1997 Taylor announced that the NPFL had been officially dissolved, in accordance with the peace agreement; the movement was subsequently reconstituted as a political organization, the National Patriotic Party (NPP). In the same month Kromah declared that ULIMO—K had also ceased to exist as a military organization, and was to be reconstituted as the All Liberian Coalition Party (ALCOP). Meanwhile, former political parties, which had effectively become inactive during the civil conflict, were revived, and new groupings emerged and applied for official registration. In March Taylor, Kromah and Boley resigned from the Council of State, in compliance with stipulations in the peace agreement, to allow their candidacy in the forthcoming elections. From March a number of west African countries began to dispatch additional contingents to reinforce ECOMOG (which was expected to be enlarged to about 16,000 personnel prior to the elections), with the USA providing logistical and financial assistance. In May, however, following a request by several political parties, the elections were postponed until 19 July to allow all the newly registered organizations sufficient time for preparation.

A 10-day registration process commenced at the end of June 1997, but was extended by three days in some regions to compensate for logistical difficulties. A total of 13 presidential candidates had emerged by this time, among them Ellen Johnson-Sirleaf (a political exile who had served in the Doe administration and subsequently a UN official, who was to contest the election on behalf of the UP). Taylor conducted a large-scale electoral campaign, financed by profits accrued from unofficial exports and his private radio station, Kiss FM. Despite demands for a further postponement, the elections proceeded on 19 July. The Independent Elections Commission announced on 23 July that Taylor had been elected President, with 75.3% of votes cast; Johnson-Sirleaf (who had been widely expected to be Taylor's strongest challenger) received only 9.6% of the votes. In the concurrent elections to the bicameral legislature (at which seats were allocated on a proportionate basis), the NPP secured 49 seats in the 64-member House of Representatives and 21 seats in the 26-member Senate, the UP won seven seats in the House of Representatives and three in the Senate, while ALCOP obtained three seats in the House of Representatives and two in the Senate. Kromah (who had won only 4.0% of the votes) subsequently declared that serious irregularities had occurred, but international observers declared the conduct of the elections to have been 'free and fair'. Taylor's overwhelming victory was generally ascribed to the widely held perception that he was the candidate most likely to achieve long-term stability in the country.

Taylor was inaugurated as President on 2 August 1997, and subsequently nominated a 19-member Cabinet, which was approved by the Senate. The new Government retained several members of the previous transitional administration, including Johnson and Woewiyu. A nine-member National Security Council, comprising several government ministers, the Chief of Staff of the Armed Forces and the Commander of ECOMOG, was established with the aim of ensuring the maintenance of civil order.

At an ECOWAS summit meeting, in Abuja, at the end of August 1997 it was agreed that the ECOMOG force in Liberia was to be reconstituted and would henceforth assist in the process of national reconstruction, including the restructuring of the armed and security forces, and the maintenance of security; it was further envisaged that ECOMOG's mandate

(officially due to expire on 2 February 1998) would be extended in agreement with the Liberian Government. Following the military coup in Sierra Leone in May 1997, ECOMOG was authorized to enforce international sanctions against the new junta led by Maj. Johnny Paul Koroma (see the chapter on Sierra Leone). In October, however, Taylor announced that he opposed the use of military force to oust the Koroma regime, and that ECOMOG would no longer be permitted to launch offensives against Sierra Leone from Liberian territory. Taylor ordered the closure of Liberia's border with Sierra Leone in response to civil disorder within that country, and announced the formation of a 1,000-member security force to be deployed at the joint border. At the end of October Taylor established a National Human Rights Commission, which was empowered to investigate complaints of human rights violations.

In November 1997, following several months of rumours of the influence in Guinea of Liberian rebels (principally members of the former ULIMO), constituting a threat to security in both countries, it was reported that some 30 members of ULIMO had been arrested in southern Guinea. The alleged presence of former Liberian factions in Guinea was discussed at a meeting between Taylor and the Guinean President, Gen. Lansana Conté, in December. Taylor subsequently appointed Kromah (who had taken up residence in Guinea following his electoral defeat in July) to the post of Chairman of a National Commission on Reconciliation, which was to undertake a major programme to reconstruct public facilities in Liberia. Also in December several members of the Gbarnga security services were arrested in connection with the killing of a former member of the NPFL, Samuel Saye Dokie, and three of his relatives; it was reported that Dokie had been involved in the attempt to overthrow the NPFL leadership in August 1994. Civilian organizations subsequently demanded that the Government initiate an independent investigation into the deaths.

By early 1998 the number of ECOMOG troops had been reduced to about 5,000. Following Taylor's insistence that the Liberian authorities be accorded control of the restructuring of the armed forces, the Government had notified ECOWAS of its desire for ECOMOG to withdraw formally by 2 February, and had requested that Nigeria, Ghana, Burkina Faso and Niger continue to provide military assistance. (In January the Government removed from service some 2,400 members of the AFL, including senior officials, with the apparent aim of reducing the dominance of the Krahn ethnic group.) The publication of a national newspaper was suspended, after it criticized government policy regarding ECOMOG, compounding widespread concerns that the Taylor administration suppressed the independent media. Following the seizure of the Sierra Leonean capital, Freetown, by ECOMOG troops, Taylor protested that the arrest by ECOMOG of about 25 senior members of Sierra Leone's ousted junta at James Spriggs Payne Airport was an infringement of Liberian territory. The Liberian Government recalled its ambassador in Nigeria for consultations, and subsequently submitted a formal complaint to ECOWAS.

In March 1998 violent clashes erupted in Monrovia between the security forces and Johnson's supporters; Johnson subsequently claimed that members of Taylor's special security forces had attacked his private residence. ECOMOG troops were deployed to prevent further violence, and, in an attempt to ease tension in the capital, Johnson was removed from the Cabinet and appointed ambassador to India. In the same month Kromah, who had expressed concern regarding his own safety, was removed from his position as Chairman of the National Commission on Reconciliation, and replaced by a prominent member of the NPP. Later that month, following increasing tension between ECOMOG troops and Liberian security forces, the Government and ECOWAS signed an agreement revising ECOMOG's mandate in the country; the contingent was henceforth banned from intervening in civil disputes. Also in June the House of Representatives approved legislation providing for the creation of a further county, River Gee, in south-eastern Liberia.

In September 1998 security forces attempted to arrest Johnson (who had not yet assumed his ambassadorial post), pursuing him to the US embassy compound, where he and a number of his supporters had taken refuge; some 50 people were killed in ensuing clashes between members of the security forces and Johnson's followers. (It was reported that, following the attacks on Johnson's Krahn supporters by the security forces, a further 4,000 Krahn had fled to Sierra Leone.) The Government subsequently announced that Johnson, Kromah and 21 of their associates had been charged with treason, following an abortive coup attempt, and demanded that US embassy officials relin-quish Johnson to Liberian authority. After discussions with the Liberian authorities, however, US officials transported Johnson to Sierra Leone. In response to an incursion by Liberian security forces into the US embassy compound during the fighting, the US Government temporarily closed the embassy and deployed a naval vessel near the Liberian coast to facilitate the evacuation of US nationals in the event of an escalation of violence in Monrovia. The Liberian Government subsequently issued a formal apology to the USA and announced that an investigation would be conducted into the incident, in co-operation with the US authorities. In October 32 people (several, including Johnson, *in absentia*) were formally charged with treason; their trial commenced in November. In the same month Taylor reor-ganized the Cabinet.

By November 1998 most of the ECOMOG forces in Liberia had been redeployed in Sierra Leone, owing to increased rebel activity in that country, and to continued tension between the Liberian Government and ECOMOG officials; about 2,000 Nigerian and Ghanaian ECOMOG troops remained in Mon-rovia. In late December the Government closed Liberia's border with Sierra Leone, in response to the escalation in civil conflict in the neighbouring country, and pledged support for the admin-istration of President Ahmed Kabbah. In January 1999 it was announced that further ECOMOG troops in Liberia were to be relocated to Sierra Leone, following a major offensive by RUF forces against Freetown. A small number of ECOMOG forces remained in the country to supervise a programme for the destruction of armaments surrendered by the former armed factions. Later that month Taylor dismissed US and British allegations that the Liberian Government was providing clan-destine military support to the RUF. In April 13 of the defend-ants on trial for treason were convicted and sentenced to 10 years' imprisonment.

In April 1999 unidentified forces, who were believed to have entered the country from Guinea, attacked the northern town of Voinjama, in Lofa County, temporarily taking hostage several western European diplomats. AFL troops subsequently regained control of the town, and Taylor submitted a formal protest to the Guinean Government (which denied that the offensive had been staged from Guinean territory). In August members of a rebel movement, styled the Joint Forces for the Liberation of Liberia (JFLL—reported to comprise former mem-bers of ULIMO—K), attacked principal towns in Lofa County from Guinea. Some 80 aid workers, including six foreign nationals, were taken hostage by the JFLL during the fighting, but were released a few days later, following negotiations by humanitarian relief officials. The Guinean authorities again denied accusations by the Liberian Government of involvement in the rebel offensive. Taylor ordered the closure of the border with Guinea and declared a temporary state of emergency in Lofa County. In the same month the Liberian Government intensified diplomatic efforts to persuade the UN to end its embargo on the export of armaments to Liberia. In September the Guinean authorities claimed that unidentified Liberian rebels had launched attacks on border villages in southern Guinea, killing some 28 civilians. At an ECOWAS meeting regarding relations between Liberia and Guinea, which took place in Abuja later that month, it was agreed that a commission would be established to address the issue of security at the border between Liberia, Guinea and Sierra Leone. The border was reopened in February 2000.

Taylor effected a number of cabinet changes in September and October 1999, and again in January 2000. At the beginning of May the Government announced that it had initiated a pro-gramme to restructure the armed forces, with the aim of reducing them substantially in size and establishing an ethnic balance. In that month Taylor assisted in negotiating the release of UN personnel taken hostage by the RUF in Sierra Leone (q.v.). In June the Vice-President, Enoch Dogolea, died, apparently as a result of a deterioration in his health following a longstanding illness. He was replaced in July by a former ambassador, Moses Blah, who had been nominated by Taylor in accordance with the Constitution. The Government subse-quently established a commission to investigate the circum-stances of Dogolea's death, following rumours, strongly denied by Taylor, that he had been murdered.

Meanwhile, reports of increased activity by Liberian dis-sidents, both in Sierra Leone, where rebels had allied with Kamajor militia, and in Guinea, resulted in a further deteri-oration in relations between the Liberian authorities and the

Governments of those countries. In July 2000 rebel forces again launched an offensive from Guinean territory against Voinjama. A hitherto unknown movement, known as Liberians United for Reconciliation and Democracy (LURD), believed to be a grouping of former members of the armed factions (particularly ULIMO–K), claimed responsibility for the attacks. Taylor and Conté subsequently conducted further discussions, with medi-ation from the Malian President, Alpha Oumar Konaré.

In early August 2000 the House of Representatives estab-lished a 13-member committee of both government and opposi-tion representatives to investigate the continued allegations of the United Kingdom and the USA that the Liberian Govern-ment supplied the RUF with armaments in exchange for illicitly mined diamonds; Taylor had offered to resign from office if the claims were substantiated by the committee. Later that month Johnson-Sirleaf and a further 14 prominent opposition leaders (many of whom were abroad) were charged with alleged involve-ment with the LURD dissidents in conflict with government forces in Lofa County.

In September 2000 Conté claimed that Liberian and Sierra Leonean refugees in Guinea were supporting the activity of rebels attempting to overthrow his Government (see the chapter on Guinea), and ordered them to leave the country. Following a further rebel attack on the Guinean border town of Macenta, staged from Liberian territory, government forces bombarded the Liberian town of Zorzor, 220 km north-east of Monrovia, where dissident Liberian forces were based. In early October tripartite discussions between Liberia, Guinea and Sierra Leone commenced. In mid-November ECOWAS dispatched a six-member technical committee, comprising representatives of Mali and Nigeria, to investigate the violent clashes on the border between Liberia and Guinea. Following an ECOWAS meeting in Abuja at the end of December, it was envisaged that a contingent of peace-keeping troops, contributed by Mali, Niger, Nigeria and Senegal, would be deployed along Guinea's borders with Liberia and Sierra Leone. In January 2001 the Liberian Government withdrew its ambassador in Guinea, fol-lowing further Guinean bombardment of towns in the Foya district of northern Liberia. In the same month a committee of the UN Security Council reported that the Liberian Government actively supported the RUF and proposed the imposition of UN sanctions against Liberia. In early February the authorities announced that the Commander of the RUF, Sam Bockarie, had left the country, and that the rebels' liaison office had been closed. In early March the UN Security Council renewed the embargo on the supply of armaments to Liberia and voted in favour of a 12-month ban on diamond exports from Liberia and restrictions on the foreign travel of senior government and military officials; these latter measures were, however, deferred for a period of two months to allow the Government time to comply with demands that it expel RUF members from Liberia and end financial and military aid to the rebels. (In October 2000 the US Government had announced the imposition of diplomatic sanctions against Taylor, his relatives and close associates, prohibiting them from entering the USA until Liberia withdrew support for the RUF.) In late March 2001 Taylor expelled the ambassadors of Guinea and Sierra Leone from Liberia, claiming that they had been engaged in activity incompatible with their office, and announced the closure of the border with Sierra Leone. The Sierra Leonean authorities subsequently retaliated by ordering the Liberian chargé d'affaires to leave the country.

In April 2001 François Massaquoi, the former leader of the LDF, and Minister of Youth and Sport since 1997, was killed, after LURD forces fired on the helicopter transporting him to Voinjama. The Government subsequently intensified operations to suppress the continuing insurgency in northern Lofa County, near the border with Guinea. By May, however, the LURD claimed to have gained control of that region, and to have advanced to the neighbouring newly created Gbarpolu County, prompting the displacement of several thousand civilians. Early that month, in response to Taylor's perceived failure to comply with UN demands, the embargo on exports of diamonds from Liberia, together with the travel restrictions on senior govern-ment and military officials, entered into effect. Taylor con-demned the imposition of UN sanctions, claiming that he had ended all connections with the RUF, while a large demon-stration was staged in Monrovia in protest at the measures.

In July 2001 Taylor offered a general amnesty to active rebel supporters and to opposition members in exile who had been charged with treason or associated crimes. In August the Gov-ernment announced that its order of expulsion against the ambassadors of Guinea and Sierra Leone accredited to Liberia had been formally withdrawn, following a request by ECOWAS Heads of State. In September Johnson-Sirleaf (who had been charged with supporting anti-Government activities) returned to Monrovia under the terms of the general amnesty. In October a five-member UN commission issued a report recommending the extension of the existing sanctions against Liberia. The UN report also stated that the Liberian Government continued to use revenue generated by the timber industry and maritime activities to finance illicit trade in armaments with the RUF, and proposed the imposition of additional sanctions on timber exports. Meanwhile, the authorities continued to take repressive measures against the independent media, temporarily suspending publication of a privately owned newspaper and detaining its Chairman, purportedly owing to his failure to pay taxes. Prominent opposition leaders, including Johnson-Sirleaf, Kromah and Amos Sawyer, proposed that Taylor be excluded from seeking re-election in October 2003, on the grounds that conditions would be prejudiced in his favour.

By early 2002 LURD forces had gained considerable territory from government troops, and continued to advance southwards towards Monrovia. At the end of January it was reported that the insurgents had briefly occupied the village of Sawmill, 80 km north of Monrovia, and had gained control of much of the surrounding region. Thousands of civilians took refuge in Monrovia in early February, after LURD members attacked the town of Klay, in Bomi County, 30 km north-west of the capital. In response to the continued failure of government troops to halt the rapid approach of LURD forces towards Monrovia, Taylor declared a national state of emergency on 8 February (which was subsequently ratified by the legislature, and was to be revised after three months). Later that month the Government announced that it was to establish a permanent security presence at the country's northern border with Sierra Leone and Guinea. At that time 50,000–60,000 civilians were internally displaced, according to estimates by the office of the UN High Commissioner for Refugees; some 10,700 Liberians had fled to south-eastern Sierra Leone since the beginning of the month, while a further several thousand had also taken refuge in Côte d'Ivoire and Guinea. (Many of the 38,000 Sierra Leonean refugees hitherto resident in Liberia had decided to leave the country.) At the beginning of March the leader of LURD, Sekouh Damate Conneh, announced that his forces aimed to depose Taylor and install a transitional administration, headed by himself, in Monrovia. The rebels declared a few days later that they were prepared to enter into dialogue with government officials, but demanded that Taylor be excluded from discussions. The Government responded by insisting that it would not contemplate the negotiation of a power-sharing agreement with the movement. Later that month a meeting of representatives of the Liberian authorities and opposition was convened at Abuja, under the aegis of ECOWAS; the discussions were regarded as preparatory to a National Reconciliation Conference, which was scheduled to take place in July. (However, representatives of LURD failed to attend the negotiations, purportedly owing to the logistical difficulties in travelling to Abuja.) At the conclusion of the discussions delegates representing 29 political and civil society associations, including major opposition leaders, urged the Government and LURD forces to declare a cease-fire. Nevertheless, fighting between government and rebel forces continued, particularly at Liberia's northern border with Guinea. At the end of March the ECOWAS Council of Ministers imposed travel restrictions on the LURD leadership, on the grounds that the movement had initiated renewed hostilities against the Government.

On 6 May 2002 the UN Security Council adopted a resolution extending the armaments and diamond embargoes, and the travel ban, for a further 12 months. The resolution indicated that, if an effective certification scheme were established, Liberian diamonds proven to be legally mined would be exempted from the embargo, and also urged Liberia to introduce internationally verifiable systems to ensure that revenue derived from the maritime registry and the timber industry be used only for legitimate purposes. Also in May the Liberian legislature extended for a further six months the national state of emergency, after LURD forces gained further territory, seizing control of Gbarnga, in Bong County. In July Taylor reorganized the Government, appointing a former prominent member of the NPFL and an associate, Charles Bright, as Minister of Finance. In September 12 registered political parties attended a National Peace and Reconciliation Conference to discuss preparations for presidential and legislative elections, scheduled to take place in 2003. In the same month Taylor ended the national state of emergency and the ban on political demonstrations, announcing that government forces had regained control of much of the territory captured by the LURD, including the significant town of Bopolu, 100 km north-west of Monrovia.

In December 2002 a US newspaper published evidence resulting from an investigation into the financing of the al-Qa'ida (Base) terrorist network, which implicated the Governments of Liberia and Burkina Faso. Taylor subsequently denied that the Liberian authorities had assisted members of the al-Qa'ida movement to operate an illicit diamond trade in the country, prior to the terrorist attacks against the USA on 11 September 2001. In January 2003 the UN Security Council approved a resolution establishing a panel of experts to investigate the Liberian Government's compliance with the UN diamond embargo. In the same month the electoral commission announced that the forthcoming presidential and legislative elections were to take place on 14 October. In February LURD forces recaptured Bopolu, and resumed their advance towards Monrovia, causing large numbers of civilians to take refuge in the capital. By April Gbarnga had also been reoccupied by the rebels, and government and LURD forces were engaged in intensive fighting for control of the town of Ganta, 180 km north-east of Monrovia. At the end of that month Taylor met with the President of Côte d'Ivoire, Laurent Gbagbo, in Togo, in an effort to resolve a further escalation of fighting at the joint border. On 6 May the UN Security Council renewed the existing embargoes in force against Liberia for a further year, and imposed an additional ban on timber exports (which was to enter into effect in early July for an initial period of 10 months).

Government

Under the Constitution of January 1986, legislative power is vested in the bicameral National Assembly, comprising the 26-member Senate and the 64-member House of Representatives. Executive power is vested in the President, who holds office for a six-year term (renewable only once). The President, who appoints the Cabinet (subject to the approval of the Senate), is directly elected by universal adult suffrage, as are members of the Assembly. Members of the House of Representatives are elected for a term of six years, and senators for a term of nine years. There were 13 counties at the time of the 1997 senatorial elections; two further counties were created in 1998 and 2001, respectively.

Defence

The total strength of the Armed Forces of Liberia (AFL) at August 2002 was estimated at 11,000–15,000. In May 2000 a government programme to restructure the AFL was officially initiated. It was envisaged that the AFL was to be reorganized to comprise an army of about 4,000, a navy of 1,000 and an air force of 300. In 2001 military expenditure was estimated at US $25m.

Economic Affairs

In 2001, according to IMF estimates, Liberia's gross domestic product (GDP) was US $523m., equivalent to $188 per head. During 1988–2001, it was estimated, the population increased at an average annual rate of 2.5%, while GDP per head declined, in real terms, by an estimated average of 7.2% per year. Overall GDP declined, in real terms, at an average annual rate of 6.0% in 1988–2001; however, growth was 20.4% in 2000, slowing to an estimated 5.3% in 2001.

Agriculture (including forestry and fishing) contributed an estimated 74.2% of GDP in 2001. An estimated 67.0% of the labour force were employed in the sector in that year. The principal cash crops are rubber (which accounted for an estimated 52.9% of export earnings in 2001), cocoa and coffee. The principal food crops are rice, cassava, sweet potatoes, yams, plantains and bananas. Timber production has traditionally represented an important source of export revenue, providing an estimated 46.2% of export earnings in 2001. Agricultural GDP, according to the IMF, increased at an average annual rate of 0.6% in 1988–2001; the GDP of the sector increased by 21.9% in 2000 and by an estimated 5.5% in 2001.

Industry (including mining, manufacturing, construction and power) contributed an estimated 8.7% of GDP in 2001, and employed 8% of the labour force in 1999. Industrial GDP, according to the IMF, declined at an average annual rate of 15.4% in 1988–2001; however, the GDP of the sector increased by 16.7% in 2000 and by an estimated 9.1% in 2001.

Mining contributed an estimated 0.1% of GDP in 2001, and engaged 5.1% of the employed labour force in 1980. Gold and diamonds are mined, and Liberia possesses significant amounts of barytes and kyanite. The production and export of mineral products were severely disrupted from 1990, as a result of the civil conflict. In 1997 total mineral reserves were estimated to include more than 10m. carats of diamonds and 3m. troy oz of gold. In the late 1990s illicit mining and export of diamonds remained widespread, while official revenue from the mining sector (amounting to only about US $1m.) was mainly derived from local production of alluvial gold and diamonds. The GDP of the mining sector, according to the IMF, declined at an average annual rate of 33.9% in 1988–2001; mining GDP increased by 49.8% in 2000, but declined by an estimated 63.9% in 2001.

Manufacturing provided an estimated 6.5% of GDP in 2001, and engaged about 1.2% of the employed labour force in 1980. Manufacturing GDP, according to the IMF, declined at an average annual rate of 9.5% in 1988–2001; however, the GDP of the sector increased by 15.3% in 2000 and by an estimated 14.4% in 2001.

Energy is derived from the consumption of fossil fuels (62.2%) and from hydroelectric power (37.8%). Imports of mineral fuels and lubricants comprised an estimated 20.6% of the value of total imports in 2001.

The services sector contributed an estimated 17.1% of GDP and employed about 22% of the labour force in 1999. The GDP of the services sector, according to the IMF, declined at an average annual rate of 13.3% in 1988–2001; however, growth in the sector was 14.7% in 2000, slowing to an estimated 3.6% in 2001.

Liberia's large open-registry ('flag of convenience') merchant shipping fleet has become an increasingly significant source of foreign exchange. In 2001 revenue from Liberia's maritime programme accounted for an estimated 21.6% of total revenue.

In 1999 Liberia recorded a visible trade deficit of US $111.7m., and there was a deficit of $42.3m. on the current account of the balance of payments. In 2001 the current-account deficit was estimated at $56.2m. In 1997 the principal source of imports (38%) was the Republic of Korea; other major suppliers in that year were Japan, Italy and Singapore. The principal market for exports in 2001 was Norway (23.8%); other important purchasers were Germany, the USA, France and Singapore. The principal exports in 2001 were rubber and timber. The principal imports in that year were food (particularly rice) and live animals, mineral fuels (principally petroleum), machinery and transport equipment, and basic manufactures.

Liberia's budgetary surplus was US $7.6m. (equivalent to 1.5% of GDP) in 2001, according to IMF estimates. The country's external debt totalled $2,032m. at the end of 2000, of which $1,040m. was long-term public debt. In 1987 the cost of servicing an external debt of $1,705m. was equivalent to 3.7% of the value of exports of goods and services. Consumer prices increased by 5.2% in 2000 and by an estimated 12.4% in 2001. In early 2002 unemployment was estimated at about 87% of the labour force.

Liberia is a member of the Economic Community of West African States (ECOWAS, see p. 187) and the Mano River Union (see p. 341), both of which aim to promote closer economic co-operation in the region.

Prior to the civil conflict, which commenced at the end of 1989, exports of iron ore, rubber and forestry products accounted for a significant proportion of Liberia's gross national income. Following the occupation of significant regions by rebel forces, production of these commodities was severely disrupted, although some informal exports continued. After elections in July 1997, the new Government announced that national revenue had dwindled to a negligible amount, while external and domestic arrears had increased dramatically, and introduced measures to regain control of public expenditure. Substantial levels of growth were recorded in subsequent years (although GDP remained at about one-third of the pre-conflict level), while domestic production, particularly of timber, rubber and rice, increased steadily. In 2000 a new tax system was introduced, currency reforms were implemented, and the financial position of the Central Bank was strengthened. Most significantly, however, a progressive deterioration in Liberia's relations with donors and external creditors resulted in a suspension in the disbursement of post-conflict financial assistance. In May 2001 a UN ban on exports of diamonds from Liberia was imposed (see Recent History). In that year economic recovery slowed considerably, owing to a number of factors, including domestic conflict, deteriorating international relations, and the continued poor state of infrastructure. Progress in implementing IMF-stipulated reforms was also limited. Increasing levels of poverty were widely attributed to mismanagement and criminal activities on the part of the administration. A projected decline in rubber production, together with environmental restrictions on logging activities, were also expected to impede reconstruction efforts. In 2002 hostilities between government forces and a newly emerged rebel grouping in the north of the country intensified, resulting in the mass displacement of civilians. In March 2003 the IMF suspended Liberia's voting and related rights in the Fund, owing to the country's continued arrears. Escalated fighting in the first half of 2003 resulted in a further deterioration in the security situation.

Education

Primary and secondary education are available free of charge. Education is officially compulsory for nine years, between seven and 16 years of age. Primary education begins at seven years of age and lasts for six years. Secondary education, beginning at 13 years of age, lasts for a further six years, divided into two cycles of three years each. Following elections in July 1997, the new Government aimed to rehabilitate large numbers of children who had been recruited to fight for the armed factions during the period of civil conflict. In 1999, following a programme of rehabilitation and reconstruction, the number of primary schools in the country increased to more than 4,500 (compared with 1,500 in 1998), while the number of secondary schools rose to 461 (compared with 241 in the previous year). In 1998 395,611 pupils were enrolled at primary schools. In 1999/2000 20.3% of children in the relevant age-group were enrolled at secondary schools (23.7% of boys; 16.9% of girls). In early 2002 it was reported that only 40% of children of school age had access to educational facilities. In 1998 20,804 students were enrolled at institutes providing higher education, including the University of Monrovia, the Cuttington University College (controlled by the Protestant Episcopal Church), a college of technology and a computer science institute. The Government announced that about 10.9% of projected 1999 budget expenditure was allocated to education.

Public Holidays

2003: 1 January (New Year's Day), 11 February (Armed Forces Day), 12 March (Decoration Day), 15 March (J. J. Robert's Birthday), 11 April (Fast and Prayer Day), 18 April (Good Friday), 14 May (National Unification Day), 26 July (Independence Day), 24 August (Flag Day), 6 November (Thanksgiving Day), 12 November (National Memorial Day), 29 November (President Tubman's Birthday), 25 December (Christmas Day).

2004: 1 January (New Year's Day), 11 February (Armed Forces Day), 12 March (Decoration Day), 15 March (J. J. Robert's Birthday), 9 April (Good Friday), 11 April (Fast and Prayer Day), 14 May (National Unification Day), 26 July (Independence Day), 24 August (Flag Day), 6 November (Thanksgiving Day), 12 November (National Memorial Day), 29 November (President Tubman's Birthday), 25 December (Christmas Day).

Weights and Measures

Imperial weights and measures, modified by US usage, are in force.

Statistical Survey

Sources (unless otherwise stated): the former Ministry of Planning and Economic Affairs, POB 9016, Broad Street, Monrovia.

Area and Population

AREA, POPULATION AND DENSITY

Area (sq km)	97,754*
Population (census results)	
1 February 1974	1,503,368
1 February 1984 (provisional)	
Males	1,063,127
Females.	1,038,501
Total	2,101,628
Population (UN estimates at mid-year)†	
1998	2,502,000
1999	2,709,000
2000	2,913,000
Density (per sq km) at mid-2000	29.8

* 37,743 sq miles.
† Source: UN, *World Population Prospects: The 2000 Revision*.

ADMINISTRATIVE DIVISIONS
(population at 1984 census)

Counties:				
Bomi	66,420	Nimba . . .	313,050
Bong	255,813	Rivercess . .	37,849
Grand Bassa . .	159,648	Sinoe . . .	64,147
Grand Cape Mount	79,322	*Territories:*	
Grand Gedeh . .	102,810	Gibi . . .	66,802
Lofa	247,641	Kru Coast . .	35,267
Maryland . .	85,267	Marshall . . .	31,190
Montserrado . .	544,878	Sasstown . .	11,524
		Total	2,101,628

Note: The counties of Grand Kru and Margibi were subsequently established. Two further counties, River Gee and Gbarpolu, were created in 1998 and 2001, respectively.

PRINCIPAL TOWNS
(2003)

Monrovia (capital) .	550,200	Harbel	17,700
Zwedru . . .	35,300	Tubmanburg . . .	16,700
Buchanan . .	27,300	Gbarnga . .	14,200
Yekepa . . .	22,900	Greenville . . .	13,500
Harper . . .	20,000	Ganta	11,200
Bensonville . .	19,600		

Source: Stefan Helders, *World Gazetteer* (internet www.world-gazetteer.com).

BIRTHS AND DEATHS
(UN estimates, annual averages)

	1985–90	1990–95	1995–2000
Birth rate (per 1,000)	43.6	40.9	50.1
Death rate (per 1,000)	14.2	23.3	16.6

Source: UN, *World Population Prospects: The 2000 Revision*.

Expectation of life (WHO estimates, years at birth): 46.2 (males 44.6; females 48.0) in 2001 (Source: WHO, *World Health Report*).

ECONOMICALLY ACTIVE POPULATION

	1978	1979	1980
Agriculture, forestry, hunting and fishing	355,467	366,834	392,926
Mining	25,374	26,184	28,047
Manufacturing	6,427	6,631	7,102
Construction	4,701	4,852	5,198
Electricity, gas and water . . .	245	246	263
Commerce	18,668	19,266	20,636
Transport and communications .	7,314	7,549	8,086
Services	49,567	51,154	54,783
Others	28,555	29,477	31,571
Total	496,318	512,193	548,615

Mid-2001 (estimates in '000): Agriculture, etc. 829; Total labour force 1,237 (Source: FAO).

Health and Welfare

KEY INDICATORS

Total fertility rate (children per woman, 2001)	6.8
Under-5 mortality rate (per 1,000 live births, 2001) . . .	235
HIV/AIDS (% of persons aged 15–49, 1999)	2.80
Physicians (per 1,000 head, 1997)	0.02
Health expenditure (2000): US $ per head (PPP)	3
Health expenditure (2000): % of GDP	4
Health expenditure (2000): public (% of total)	76.2

For sources and definitions, see explanatory note on p. vi.

Agriculture

PRINCIPAL CROPS
('000 metric tons)

	1998	1999	2000
Rice (paddy)*	209.4	196.3	183.4
Sweet potatoes†	17	18	18
Cassava (Manioc)*	307.0	361.3	440.5
Taro (Coco yam)†	22	22	22
Yams†	20	20	20
Sugar cane†	250	250	250
Coconuts†	7	7	7
Oil palm fruit†	174	174	174
Vegetables and melons† . . .	76	76	76
Bananas†	90	95	95
Plantains†	36	37	37
Oranges†	7	7	7
Pineapples†	7	7	7
Natural rubber (dry weight)* . .	75	100	127

* Unofficial figures.
† FAO estimates.

Source: FAO.

LIVESTOCK
(FAO estimates, '000 head, year ending September)

	1998	1999	2000
Cattle	36	36	36
Pigs	120	120	120
Sheep	210	210	210
Goats	220	220	220
Chickens	3,500	3,500	3,500
Ducks	200	200	200

Source: FAO.

LIVESTOCK PRODUCTS
(FAO estimates, metric tons)

	1998	1999	2000
Pig meat	4,000	4,000	4,000
Poultry meat	5,800	5,800	5,800
Other meat	8,316	8,316	8,316
Cows' milk	715	715	715
Hen eggs	3,600	3,600	3,600

Source: FAO.

Forestry

ROUNDWOOD REMOVALS
('000 cubic metres, excluding bark)

	1998	1999*	2000*
Sawlogs, veneer logs and logs for sleepers	157	157	157
Other industrial wood	164*	180	180
Fuel wood	3,736*	4,202	4,725
Total	4,057	4,539	5,062

* FAO estimate(s).

Source: FAO.

SAWNWOOD PRODUCTION
('000 cubic metres, including railway sleepers)

	1999	2000	2001
Total (all broadleaved)	4	10	20

Source: FAO.

Fishing

(metric tons, live weight, capture)

	1998	1999	2000
Freshwater fishes	4,000	4,000	4,000
West African croakers	433	1,025	327
Dentex	974	936	588
Sardinellas	620	1,112	887
Other clupeoids	416	509	318
Bigeye tuna	108	112	201
Marlins, sailfishes, etc.	840	550	683
Swordfish	21	39	42
Sharks, rays, skates, etc.	656	1,135	1,132
Total catch (incl. others)	10,830	15,472	11,726

Source: FAO, *Yearbook of Fishery Statistics.*

Mining

	1999	2000	2001
Diamonds ('000 carats)	200	170	170
Gold (kilograms)*	1,000	1,000	1,000

* Figures refer to the metal content of ores.

Source: US Geological Survey.

Iron ore (metal content, '000 metric tons): 2,490 in 1990; 804 in 1991; 1,142 in 1992 (Source: UN, *Industrial Commodity Statistics Yearbook*).

Industry

SELECTED PRODUCTS

	1999	2000	2001*
Gold (ounces)	550	701	1,431
Diamonds (carats)	8,728	22,220	3,885
Beer (litres)	3,113,463	2,942,873	2,143,706

* Year to September.

Source: IMF, *Liberia: Statistical Appendix (July 2002).*

Electric energy (million kWh, estimates): 488 in 1996; 495 in 1997; 498 in 1998 (Source: UN, *Industrial Commodity Statistics Yearbook*).

Palm oil (FAO estimates, '000 metric tons): 42 in 1999; 42 in 2000; 42 in 2001 (Source: FAO).

Cement ('000 metric tons): 15 in 1999; 15 in 2000; 15 in 2001 (Source: US Geological Survey).

Finance

CURRENCY AND EXCHANGE RATES

Monetary Units
100 cents = 1 Liberian dollar (L $)

Sterling, Dollar and Euro Equivalents (31 December 2002)
£1 sterling = L $104.77
US $1 = L $65
€1 = L $68.17
L $1,000 = £9.54 = US $15.38 = €14.67

Average Exchange Rate (L $ per US $)
2000   40.9525
2001   48.5833
2002   61.7542

Note: The aforementioned data are based on market-determined rates of exchange. Prior to January 1998 the exchange rate was a fixed parity with the US dollar (L $1 = US $1).

BUDGET
(US $ million)

Revenue	1999	2000	2001*
Tax revenue	61.7	70.9	68.7
Taxes on income and profits	15.0	15.6	11.1
Companies	7.7	4.8	4.5
Individuals	5.5	9.3	5.9
Taxes on goods and services	17.7	17.3	23.1
Petroleum sales tax	6.1	7.2	5.5
Maritime revenue	15.2	14.5	16.0
Taxes on international trade	19.7	23.3	18.3
Taxes on imports	19.3	23.0	18.1
Taxes on exports	0.4	0.3	0.1
Other revenue	3.8	4.6	5.3
Total	65.5	75.5	74.0

Expenditure	1999	2000	2001*
Current expenditure	40.5	79.6	55.7
Wages and salaries	10.5	17.7	20.4
Other goods and services	17.0	36.9	30.8
Subsidies and transfers	9.2	15.5	1.2
Debt service	3.8	9.6	3.3
Capital expenditure†	18.9	7.8	17.4
Unallocable expenditure‡	4.0	1.0	—
Total	63.5	88.4	73.1

* Estimates.
† Excluding expenditure financed by grants.
‡ Including non-budgetary and unallocated expenditure.

Source: IMF, *Liberia: Statistical Appendix* (July 2002).

INTERNATIONAL RESERVES
(US $ million at 31 December)

	2000	2001	2002
Reserve position in IMF	0.03	0.03	0.04
Foreign exchange	0.23	0.44	3.26
Total	0.27	0.48	3.30

Source: IMF, *International Financial Statistics.*

MONEY SUPPLY
(L $ million at 31 December)

	2000	2001	2002
Currency outside banks*	698.3	845.1	1,045.0
Demand deposits at commercial banks	898.8	851.6	1,318.2
Total money	1,597.0	1,703.4†	2,363.2

* Figures refer only to amounts of Liberian coin in circulation. US notes and coin also circulate, but the amount of these in private holdings is unknown. The amount of Liberian coin in circulation is small in comparison to US currency.

† Including others.

Source: IMF, *International Financial Statistics*.

COST OF LIVING
(Consumer Price Index; base: May 1998 = 100)

	1999	2000
Food	103.1	101.7
Fuel and light	109.9	122.7
Clothing	104.8	104.8
Rent	109.0	126.2
All items (incl. others)	105.6	111.1

Source: IMF, *Liberia: Statistical Appendix* (July 2002).

NATIONAL ACCOUNTS
(at current prices)

Expenditure on the Gross Domestic Product
(L $ million)

	1987	1988	1989
Government final consumption expenditure	143.9	136.3	141.6
Private final consumption expenditure	713.9	733.3	656.8
Increase in stocks*	7.0	3.5	4.0
Gross fixed capital formation	120.4	115.3	96.8
Statistical discrepancy	22.9	39.1	48.2
Total domestic expenditure	1,008.1	1,027.5	947.4
Exports of goods and services	438.2	452.3	521.4
Less Imports of goods and services	356.8	321.5	275.2
GDP in purchasers' values	1,089.5	1,158.3	1,193.6
GDP at constant 1981 prices	1,015.0	1,043.7	1,072.8

* Figures refer only to stocks of iron ore and rubber.

Source: UN, *National Accounts Statistics*.

Gross Domestic Product by Economic Activity
(US $ million)

	1999	2000	2001*
Agriculture, hunting, forestry and fishing	336.6	395.5	388.2
Mining and quarrying	1.2	1.0	0.3
Manufacturing	21.4	26.9	34.1
Electricity, gas and water	2.3	3.0	3.1
Construction	6.9	7.8	7.8
Trade, restaurants and hotels	17.0	21.1	23.0
Transport, storage and communications	21.6	24.4	23.2
Finance, insurance, real estate and business services	13.3	15.1	14.7
Government services	11.2	16.9	14.1
Other services	10.3	13.9	14.5
GDP in purchasers' values*	441.8	525.6	522.9

* Estimates.

Source: IMF, *Liberia: Statistical Appendix* (July 2002).

BALANCE OF PAYMENTS
(US $ million)

	1997	1998	1999*
Exports of goods f.o.b.	25.3	42.7	55.7
Imports of goods c.i.f.	-243.2	-161.2	-167.5
Trade balance	-217.9	-118.5	-111.7
Services (net)	-4.6	1.1	3.9
Balance on goods and services	-222.5	-117.4	-107.8
Income (net)	-33.2	-38.7	-44.2
Balance on goods, services and income	-255.7	-156.1	-152.0
Current transfers (net)	175.0	114.1	109.7
Current balance	-80.7	-41.9	-42.3
Capital balance (net)	14.9	3.5	3.0
Net errors and omissions	6.5	-16.1	-12.1
Overall balance	-59.4	-54.5	-51.4

* Estimates.

Source: IMF, *Liberia: Selected Issues and Statistical Appendix* (April 2000).

External Trade

PRINCIPAL COMMODITIES
(US $ million)

Imports c.i.f.	1999	2000	2001*
Food and live animals	54.0	53.9	56.3
Rice	21.8	26.2	30.7
Beverages and tobacco	7.7	6.3	5.8
Crude materials, inedible (excl. fuel)	11.3	6.6	3.8
Mineral fuels and lubricants	50.7	44.9	37.2
Petroleum	47.3	42.9	35.2
Chemicals and related products	14.8	14.3	8.4
Basic manufactures	17.0	20.8	19.4
Machinery and transport equipment	38.9	30.0	31.9
Miscellaneous manufactured articles	11.5	9.3	4.5
Total (incl. others)	209.6	189.3	180.9

Exports f.o.b.	1999	2000	2001*
Rubber	33.1	57.1	67.4
Timber	23.4	61.0	58.9
Cocoa	1.3	0.6	0.5
Total (incl. others)	58.9	120.3	127.4

* Estimates.

Source: IMF, *Liberia: Statistical Appendix* (July 2002).

PRINCIPAL TRADING PARTNERS
(US $ million)*

Imports c.i.f.	1986	1987	1988
Belgium-Luxembourg	8.5	11.2	15.0
China, People's Repub.	7.1	14.7	4.8
Denmark	10.6	7.6	5.9
France (incl. Monaco)	6.5	6.4	4.7
Germany, Fed. Repub.	32.7	52.3	39.5
Italy	2.5	2.2	7.3
Japan	20.1	15.0	12.0
Netherlands	20.6	26.8	14.4
Spain	2.5	6.6	3.1
Sweden	2.4	0.6	4.6
United Kingdom	24.2	18.4	12.7
USA	42.5	58.0	57.7
Total (incl. others)	259.0	307.6	272.3

Exports f.o.b.		1986	1987	1988
Belgium-Luxembourg	. . .	29.2	23.2	28.2
France (incl. Monaco)	. . .	33.1	33.2	33.2
Germany, Fed. Repub.	. .	114.5	109.2	108.1
Italy	. . . . . .	70.3	63.4	63.2
Japan	. . . . . .	4.9	1.0	4.8
Netherlands	. . . .	14.4	11.5	10.5
Spain	. . . . . .	16.4	17.8	13.4
United Kingdom	. . . .	7.2	8.8	6.3
USA	. . . .	93.2	73.9	74.6
Total (incl. others)	. . . .	408.4	382.2	396.3

* Imports by country of origin; exports by country of last consignment.

Source: UN, *International Trade Statistics Yearbook.*

Transport

RAILWAYS
(estimated traffic)

		1991	1992	1993
Passenger-km (million)	. . .	406	417	421
Freight ton-km (million)	. . .	200	200	200

Source: UN Economic Commission for Africa, *African Statistical Yearbook.*

ROAD TRAFFIC
(estimates, vehicles in use at 31 December)

		1994	1995	1996
Passenger cars	. . . . .	13,720	10,340	9,400
Goods vehicles	. . . . .	26,000	28,420	32,000

Source: International Road Federation, *World Road Statistics.*

1998 ('000s of vehicles): Passenger cars: 17.4; Commercial vehicles: 10.7 (Source: UN, *Statistical Yearbook*).

SHIPPING

Merchant Fleet
(registered at 31 December)

		1999	2000	2001
Number of vessels	. . . . .	1,629	1,557	1,556
Displacement ('000 gross registered tons)	. . . . . .	54,107.2	51,450.9	51,784.0

Source: Lloyd's Register-Fairplay, *World Fleet Statistics.*

International Sea-borne Freight Traffic
(estimates, '000 metric tons)

		1991	1992	1993
Goods loaded	. . . . .	16,706	17,338	21,653
Goods unloaded	. . . .	1,570	1,597	1,608

Source: UN Economic Commission for Africa, *African Statistical Yearbook.*

CIVIL AVIATION
(traffic on scheduled services)

		1990	1991	1992
Passengers carried ('000)	. . .	32	32	32
Passenger-km (million)	. . .	7	7	7
Total ton-km (million)	. . . .	1	1	1

Source: UN, *Statistical Yearbook.*

Communications Media

	1995	1996	1997
Radio receivers ('000 in use) . .	675	715	790
Television receivers ('000 in use) .	56	60	70
Telephones ('000 main lines in use)	5	5	6
Daily newspapers:			
number	8	6	n.a.
average circulation ('000 copies, estimates)	35	35	n.a.

Sources: UNESCO, *Statistical Yearbook*; UN, *Statistical Yearbook.*

Telephones ('000 main lines in use): 6.5 in 1998; 6.6 in 1999; 6.7 in 2000 (Source: International Telecommunication Union).

Internet users ('000): 0.1 in 1998; 0.3 in 1999; 0.5 in 2000 (Source: International Telecommunication Union).

Education
(1998)

			Students		
	Teachers	Males	Females	Total
Pre-primary	. . . . .	6,158	n.a.	n.a.	111,590
Primary	. . . . .	10,047	227,953	167,658	395,611
Secondary	. . . . .	6,621	69,523	44,355	113,878
General	. . . . .	n.a.	55,759	38,367	94,126
Technical and vocational	.	n.a.	13,764	5,988	19,752
Higher	. . . . . .	633	16,817	3,987	20,804

Source: UNESCO Institute for Statistics.

Adult literacy rate (UNESCO estimates): 54.0% in 2000 (Source: UN, *Human Development Report*).

Directory

The Constitution

The Constitution of the Republic of Liberia entered into effect on 6 January 1986, following its approval by national referendum in July 1984. Its main provisions are summarized below.

PREAMBLE

The Republic of Liberia is a unitary sovereign state, which is divided into counties for administrative purposes. There are three separate branches of government: the legislative, the executive and the judiciary. No person is permitted to hold office or executive power in more than one branch of government. The fundamental human rights of the individual are guaranteed.

LEGISLATURE

Legislative power is vested in the bicameral National Assembly, comprising a Senate and a House of Representatives. Deputies of both chambers are elected by universal adult suffrage. Each county elects two members of the Senate for a term of nine years, while members of the House of Representatives are elected by legislative constituency for a term of six years. Legislation requires the approval of two-thirds of the members of both chambers, and is subsequently submitted to the President for endorsement. The Constitution may be amended by two-thirds of the members of both chambers.

EXECUTIVE

Executive power is vested in the President, who is Head of State and Commander-in-Chief of the armed forces. The President is elected by universal adult suffrage for a term of six years, and is restricted to a maximum of two terms in office. A Vice-President, who is also President of the Senate, is elected at the same time as the President. The President appoints a Cabinet, and members of the judiciary and armed forces, with the approval of the Senate. The President is empowered to declare a state of emergency.

JUDICIARY

Judicial power is vested in the Supreme Court and any subordinate courts, which apply both statutory and customary laws in accordance with standards enacted by the legislature. The judgements of the Supreme Court are final and not subject to appeal or review by any other branch of government. The Supreme Court comprises one Chief Justice and five Associate Justices. Justices are appointed by the President, with the approval of the Senate.

POLITICAL PARTIES AND ELECTIONS

Political associations are obliged to comply with the minimum registration requirements imposed by the Elections Commission. Organizations that endanger free democratic society, or that organize, train or equip groups of supporters, are to be denied registration. Prior to elections, each political party and independent candidate is required to submit statements of assets and liabilities to the Elections Commission. All elections of public officials are determined by an absolute majority of the votes cast. If no candidate obtains an absolute majority in the first ballot, a second ballot is conducted between the two candidates with the highest number of votes. Complaints by parties or candidates must be submitted to the Elections Commission within seven days of the announcement of election results. The Supreme Court has final jurisdiction over challenges to election results.

The Government

HEAD OF STATE

President: CHARLES GHANKAY TAYLOR (took office 2 August 1997).
Vice-President: MOSES ZEH BLAH.

CABINET
(April 2003)

Minister of Agriculture: OTHELLO BRANDY.
Minister of Commerce and Industry: CORA PEABODY.
Minister of Defence: DANIEL CHEA.
Minister of Education: Dr EVELYN WHITE-KANDAKAI.
Minister of Finance: CHARLES BRIGHT.

Minister of Foreign Affairs: MONIE CAPTAN.
Minister of Gender Development: DOROTHY MUSULENG COOPER.
Minister of Health and Social Welfare: Dr PETER COLEMAN.
Minister of Information, Culture and Tourism: REGINALD GOODRIDGE.
Minister of Internal Affairs: RICHARD FLOMO.
Minister of Justice: LAVELI KORBOI JOHNSON.
Minister of Labour: CHRISTIAN HERBERT.
Minister of Lands, Mines and Energy: JENKINS DUNBAR.
Minister of National Security: Brig.-Gen. PHILIP KAMMAH.
Minister of Planning and Economic Affairs: ROLAND MASSAQUOI.
Minister of Posts and Telecommunications: MELVIN SOGBANDI.
Minister of Public Works: EMMET TAYLOR.
Minister of Rural Development: Lt-Gen. (retd) HEZEKIAH BOWEN.
Minister of Transport: JOE MULBAH.
Minister of State for Presidential Affairs: JONATHAN TAYLOR.
Minister of State for Planning and Economic Affairs: WISSEH MCCLAIN.
Minister of State without Portfolio: AUGUSTINE ZAYZAY.

MINISTRIES

Office of the President: Executive Mansion, POB 10-9001, Capitol Hill, 1000 Monrovia 10; e-mail emansion@liberia.net.

Ministry of Agriculture: Tubman Blvd, POB 10-9010, 1000 Monrovia 10; tel. 226399.

Ministry of Commerce and Industry: Ashmun St, POB 10-9014, 1000 Monrovia 10; tel. 226283.

Ministry of Defence: Benson St, POB 10-9007, 1000 Monrovia 10; tel. 226077.

Ministry of Education: E. G. N. King Plaza, Broad St, POB 10-1545, 1000 Monrovia 10; tel. and fax 226216.

Ministry of Finance: Broad St, POB 10-9013, 1000 Monrovia 10; tel. 226863.

Ministry of Foreign Affairs: Mamba Point, POB 10-9002, 1000 Monrovia 10; tel. 226763.

Ministry of Gender Development: Monrovia.

Ministry of Health and Social Welfare: Sinkor, POB 10-9004, 1000 Monrovia 10; tel. 226317.

Ministry of Information, Culture and Tourism: Capitol Hill, POB 10-9021, 1000 Monrovia 10; tel. and fax 226269; e-mail webmaster@micat.gov.lr; internet www.micat.gov.lr.

Ministry of Internal Affairs: cnr Warren and Benson Sts, POB 10-9008, 1000 Monrovia 10; tel. 226346.

Ministry of Justice: Ashmun St, POB 10-9006, 1000 Monrovia 10; tel. 227872.

Ministry of Labour: Mechlin St, POB 10-9040, 1000 Monrovia 10; tel. 226291.

Ministry of Lands, Mines and Energy: Capitol Hill, POB 10-9024, 1000 Monrovia 10; tel. 226281.

Ministry of National Security: 1000 Monrovia 10.

Ministry of Planning and Economic Affairs: Broad St, POB 10-9016, 1000 Monrovia 10; tel. 226962.

Ministry of Posts and Telecommunications: Carey St, 1000 Monrovia 10; tel. 226079.

Ministry of Presidential Affairs: Executive Mansion, Capitol Hill, 1000 Monrovia 10; tel. 228026.

Ministry of Public Works: Lynch St, POB 10-9011, 1000 Monrovia 10; tel. 227972.

Ministry of Rural Development: POB 10-9030, 1000 Monrovia 10; tel. 227938.

Ministry of Transport: 1000 Monrovia 10.

President and Legislature

PRESIDENT

Presidential Election, 19 July 1997

	Votes	% of votes
Charles Taylor (NPP)	468,443	75.33
Ellen Johnson-Sirleaf (UP)	59,557	9.58
Alhaji G. V. Kromah (ALCOP)	25,059	4.03
Cletus Wotorson (Alliance of Political Parties)	15,969	2.57
Gabriel Baccus Matthews (UPP)	15,604	2.51
Dr Togba-Nah Tipoteh (LPP)	10,010	1.61
Dr George Boley (NDPL)	7,843	1.26
Dr Henry Moniba (LINU)	6,708	1.08
Fiyah Gbolie (PDPL)	3,497	0.56
Martin Sherif (NRP)	2,965	0.48
Chea Cheapoo (PPP)	2,142	0.34
Dr Henry Fahnbulleh (RAP)	2,067	0.33
Dr George T. Washington (FDP)	2,016	0.32
Total	**621,880**	**100.00**

LEGISLATURE

Senate

Speaker: Moses Zeh Blah.

Elections to the 26-member Senate took place on 19 July 1997, with each county electing two senators. The National Patriotic Party secured 21 seats, the Unity Party three seats, and the All Liberian Coalition Party two seats.

House of Representatives

Speaker: Nyudueh Morkonmana.

General Election, 19 July 1997

Party	Seats
National Patriotic Party	49
Unity Party	7
All Liberian Coalition Party	3
Alliance of Political Parties*	2
United People's Party	2
Liberian People's Party	1
Total	**64**

* Coalition of the Liberian Action Party and the Liberian Unification Party.

Political Organizations

At the end of January 1997 the armed factions in Liberia officially ceased to exist as military organizations; a number of them were reconstituted as political parties, while long-standing political organizations re-emerged. Elections in July of that year were contested by 13 political associations. A number of political associations opposing the Government continued to be based in the USA.

All Liberian Coalition Party (ALCOP): f. 1997; from elements of the fmr armed faction of Alhaji G. V. Kromah, the United Liberation Movement of Liberia for Democracy; Chair. David Kortie.

Citizens' Development Party (CDP): Monrovia; f. 2002 by mems of fmr rebel group the Independent National Front of Liberia; Prince Yormie Johnson.

Collaborating Liberian Political Parties (CLPP): Monrovia; alliance of 12 parties opposing the Govt, led by the True Whig Party.

Free Democratic Party (FDP): Monrovia; Leader Dr George T. Washington.

Liberian Action Party (LAP): Monrovia; f. 1984; Leader Cletus Wotorson.

Liberian National Union (LINU): Monrovia; Leader Henry Moniba.

Liberian People's Party (LPP): Monrovia; f. 1984 by fmr mems of the Movement for Justice in Africa; Leader Togba-Nah Tipoteh.

Liberian Unification Party (LUP): Monrovia; f. 1984; Leader Laveli Supuwood.

Movement for the Defence of Human Rights (MODHAR): 152 Carey St, Monrovia; tel. 227334; Chair. Nigba Wiaplah (acting).

Movement for Democratic Change in Liberia: Monrovia; Chair. Nohn Rebecca Kidau.

National Democratic Party of Liberia (NDPL): Monrovia; f. 1997 from the fmr armed faction the Liberia Peace Council; Leader Dr George E. Saigbe Boley.

National Patriotic Party (NPP): Monrovia; f. 1997 from the fmr armed faction the National Patriotic Front of Liberia; won the majority of seats in legislative elections in July; Chair. Cyril Allen; Sec.-Gen. John Whitfield.

National Reformation Party (NRP): Monrovia; Leader Martin Sherif.

People's Democratic Party of Liberia (PDPL): Monrovia; Leader Fiyah Gbolie.

People's Progressive Party (PPP): Monrovia; Leader Chea Cheapoo.

Reformation Alliance Party (RAP): Monrovia; Leader Henry Boimah Fahnbulleh.

True Whig Party (TWP): Monrovia; Leader Rudolph Sherman.

United People's Party (UPP): Monrovia; f. 1984 by fmr mems of the Progressive People's Party, which led opposition prior to April 1980 coup; Leader Wesley Johnson.

Unity Party (UP): Monrovia; f. 1984; Leader Ellen Johnson-Sirleaf.

In 2003 the following rebel movement remained in conflict with government forces:

Liberians United for Reconciliation and Democracy (LURD): emerged 2000, comprising mems of fmr rebel factions; Chair. Sekou Damate Konneh.

Diplomatic Representation

EMBASSIES IN LIBERIA

Algeria: Capitol By-Pass, POB 2032, Monrovia; tel. 224311; Chargé d'affaires a.i. Muhammad Azzedine Azzouz.

Cameroon: 18th St and Payne Ave, Sinkor, POB 414, Monrovia; tel. 261374; Ambassador Victor E. Ndiba.

China, People's Republic: Tubman Blvd, Congotown, POB 5970, Monrovia; tel. 228024; fax 226740; Ambassador Yeong-cho Chen.

Congo, Democratic Republic: Spriggs Payne Airport, Sinkor, POB 1038, Monrovia; tel. 261326; Ambassador (vacant).

Côte d'Ivoire: Tubman Blvd, Sinkor, POB 126, Monrovia; tel. 261123; Ambassador Clément Kaul Meledje.

Cuba: 17 Kennedy Ave, Congotown, POB 3579, Monrovia; tel. 262600; Ambassador M. Gauneano Cardoso Toledo.

Egypt: POB 462, Monrovia; tel. 226226; fax 226122; Ambassador Fathy Guergis Beshara.

Ghana: cnr 11th St and Gardiner Ave, Sinkor, POB 471, Monrovia; tel. 261477; Ambassador Ernest Amoa-Awua.

Guinea: Monrovia; Ambassador Baba Soare.

Israel: Gardiner Ave, between 11th and 12th Sts, Sinkor, Monrovia; tel. 262861; Ambassador Moshe Itan.

Korea, Republic: 10th St and Payne Ave, Sinkor, POB 2769, Monrovia; tel. 261532; Ambassador Kim Yong-Jip.

Lebanon: 12th St, Monrovia; tel. 262537; Chargé d'affaires Gabriel Geara.

Libya: Monrovia; Ambassador Muhammad Umarat-Tabi.

Morocco: Tubman Blvd, Congotown, Monrovia; tel. 262767; Chargé d'affaires a.i. Dr Moulay Abbes al-Kadiri.

Nigeria: Congotown, POB 366, Monrovia; tel. 227345; fax 226135; Ambassador Joshua Iroha.

Russia: Payne Ave, Sinkor, POB 2010, Monrovia; tel. 261304; Ambassador Vasilii S. Bebko.

Senegal: Monrovia; Ambassador Moctar Traoré.

Sierra Leone: Tubman Blvd, POB 575, Monrovia; tel. 261301; Ambassador Kemoh Salia-Bao.

USA: 111 United Nations Drive, Mamba Point, POB 10-0098, Monrovia; tel. 226370; fax 226148; e-mail montgomery@state.gov; internet www.usembassy.state.gov/monrovia; Ambassador John W. Blaney.

Judicial System

In February 1982 the People's Supreme Tribunal (which had been established following the April 1980 coup) was renamed the People's Supreme Court, and its Chairman and members became the Chief Justice and Associate Justices of the People's Supreme Court. The judicial system also comprised People's Circuit and Magistrate Courts. The five-member Supreme Court (composed of representatives of the interim Government and of the NPFL) was established in January 1992 to adjudicate in electoral disputes.

Chief Justice of the Supreme Court of Liberia: GLORIA M. MUSU-SCOTT.

Religion

Liberia is officially a Christian state, although complete religious freedom is guaranteed. Christianity and Islam are the two main religions. There are numerous religious sects, and many Liberians hold traditional beliefs.

CHRISTIANITY

Liberian Council of Churches: 16 St, Sinkor, POB 10-2191, 1000 Monrovia; tel. 226630; fax 226132; f. 1982; 11 mems, two assoc. mems, one fraternal mem. Pres. Rt Rev. Dr W. NAH DIXON; Gen. Sec. Rev. STEVEN W. MUIN.

The Anglican Communion

The diocese of Liberia forms part of the Church of the Province of West Africa, incorporating the local Protestant Episcopal Church. Anglicanism was established in Liberia in 1836, and the diocese of Liberia was admitted into full membership of the Province in 1982. In 1985 the Church had 125 congregations, 39 clergy, 26 schools and about 20,000 adherents in the country. The Metropolitan of the Province is the Bishop of Koforidua, Ghana.

Bishop of Liberia: Rt Rev. EDWARD NEUFVILLE, POB 10-0277, 1000 Monrovia 10; tel. 224760; fax 227519.

The Roman Catholic Church

Liberia comprises the archdiocese of Monrovia and the dioceses of Cape Palmas and Gbarnga. At 31 December 2000 there were an estimated 141,665 adherents in the country, equivalent to 5.4% of the total population.

Catholic Bishops' Conference of Liberia
POB 10-2078, 1000 Monrovia 10; tel. 227245; fax 226175.
f. 1998; Pres. Most Rev. MICHAEL KPAKALA FRANCIS (Archbishop of Monrovia).

Archbishop of Monrovia: Most Rev. MICHAEL KPAKALA FRANCIS, Archbishop's Office, POB 10-2078, 1000 Monrovia 10; tel. 227245; fax 226175.

Other Christian Churches

Assemblies of God in Liberia: POB 1297, Monrovia; f. 1908; 14,578 adherents, 287 churches; Gen. Supt JIMMIE K. DUGBE, Sr.

Lutheran Church in Liberia: POB 1046, Monrovia; tel. 226633; fax 226262; e-mail lwfliberia@compuserve.com; 35,600 adherents; Pres. Bishop SUMOWARD E. HARRIS.

Providence Baptist Church: cnr Broad and Center Sts, Monrovia; f. 1821; 2,500 adherents, 300 congregations, 6 ministers, 8 schools; Pastor Rev. A. MOMOLUE DIGGS.

The Liberia Baptist Missionary and Educational Convention, Inc: POB 390, Monrovia; tel. 222661; f. 1880; Pres. Rev. J. K. LEVEE MOULTON; Nat. Vice-Pres. Rev. J. GBANA HALL; Gen. Sec. CHARLES W. BLAKE.

United Methodist Church in Liberia: cnr 12th St and Tubman Blvd, POB 1010, 1000 Monrovia 10; tel. 223343; f. 1833; c. 70,000 adherents, 487 congregations, 450 ministers, 300 lay pastors, 38 schools; Resident Bishop Rev. ARTHUR F. KULAH; Sec. Rev. JULIUS SARWOLO NELSON.

Other active denominations include the National Baptist Mission, the Pentecostal Church, the Presbyterian Church in Liberia, the Prayer Band and the Church of the Lord Aladura.

ISLAM

The total community numbers about 670,000.

National Muslim Council of Liberia: Monrovia; Leader Shaykh KAFUMBA KONNAH.

The Press

NEWSPAPERS

The Inquirer: Benson St, POB 20-4209, Monrovia; tel. and fax 227105; independent; Man. Editor PHILIP WESSEH.

Monrovia Guardian: Monrovia; independent; Editor SAM O. DEAN.

The New Liberian: Monrovia; govt-owned.

News: ACDB Bldg, POB 10-3137, Carey Warren St, Monrovia; tel. 227820; e-mail imms@afrlink.com; independent; weekly; Chair. WILSON TARPEH; Editor-in-Chief JEROME DALIEH.

PERIODICALS

The Kpelle Messenger: Kpelle Literacy Center, Lutheran Church, POB 1046, Monrovia; Kpelle-English; monthly; Editor Rev. JOHN J. MANAWU.

Liberia Orbit: Voinjama; e-mail orbit@tekmail.com; internet www.liberiaorbit.org; national current affairs; Editor LLOYD SCOTT.

Liberian Post: e-mail info@Liberian.org; internet www.Liberian.tripod.com/Post0.html; independent internet magazine; tourist information; Publr WILLEM TIJSSEN.

New Democrat: Monrovia; e-mail newdemnews@yahoo.com; internet www.newdemocrat.org; national news and current affairs.

Patriot: Congotown 1000, Monrovia; internet www.allaboutliberia.com/patriot.htm.

The People Magazine: Bank of Liberia Bldg, Suite 214, Carey and Warren Sts, POB 3501, Monrovia; tel. 222743; f. 1985; monthly; Editor and Publr CHARLES A. SNETTER.

PRESS ORGANIZATIONS

Liberia Institute of Journalism: Kashour Bldg, 2nd Floor, cnr Broad and Johnson Sts, POB 2314, Monrovia; tel. 227327; e-mail lij@kabissa.org; internet www.kabissa.org/lij; Dir VINICIUS HODGES.

Press Union of Liberia: Benson St, POB 20-4209, Monrovia; tel. and fax 227105; e-mail pul@kabissa.org; internet www.kabissa.org/pul; f. 1985; Pres. JAMES G. KIAZOLU.

NEWS AGENCIES

Liberian News Agency (LINA): POB 9021, Capitol Hill, Monrovia; tel. and fax 226269; e-mail lina@afrlink.com; Dir-Gen. ERNEST KIAZOLY (acting).

Foreign Bureaux

Agence France-Presse (AFP): Monrovia; Rep. JAMES DORBOR.

United Press International (UPI) (USA): Monrovia; Correspondent T. K. SANNAH.

Xinhua (New China) News Agency (People's Republic of China): Adams St, Old Rd, Congotown, POB 3001, Monrovia; tel. 262821; Correspondent SUN BAOYU.

Reuters (United Kingdom) is also represented in Liberia.

Broadcasting and Communications

TELECOMMUNICATIONS

Liberia Telecommunications Corpn: Monrovia; tel. 227523; CEO CHARLES ROBERTS.

BROADCASTING

Radio

Liberia Communications Network: Congotown 1000, Monrovia; govt-operated; broadcasts information, education and entertainment 24 hours daily in English, French and several African languages; short-wave service.

Liberia Rural Communications Network: POB 10-02176, 1000 Monrovia 10; tel. 271368; f. 1981; govt-operated; rural development and entertainment programmes; Dir J. RUFUS KAINE (acting).

Radio Veritas: Monrovia; Catholic; independent; nation-wide shortwave broadcasts; operations suspended by the Govt early 2002.

Star Radio: Sekou Toure Ave, Mamba Point, Monrovia; tel. 226820; fax 227360; e-mail star@liberia.net; independent news and information station; f. July 1997 by Fondation Hirondelle, Switzerland, with funds from the US Agency for International Development; broadcasts in English, French and 14 African languages; operations suspended by the Govt March 2000; Dir GEORGE BENNETT.

Television

Liberia Broadcasting System: POB 594, Monrovia; tel. 224984; govt-owned; Pres. Bockarie Musa.

Finance

(cap. = capital; res = reserves; dep. = deposits; m. = million; br. = branch; amounts in Liberian dollars)

BANKING

Most banking operations in Liberia were suspended in 1990, as a result of the disruption caused by the civil conflict. A number of commercial banks subsequently resumed operations.

Central Bank

Central Bank of Liberia: Warren and Carey Sts, POB 2048, Monrovia; tel. 226144; fax 227928; f. 1974 as National Bank of Liberia; name changed March 1999; bank of issue; cap. and res 17.1m., dep. 70.7m. (1986); Gov. Eli Saleeby.

Other Banks

Agricultural and Co-operative Development Bank: Carey and Warren Sts, POB 10-3585, Monrovia; tel. 224385; fax 221500; f. 1977; 65% govt-owned; operations suspended in 1996; restructure under way in 2001; cap. 6.6m. (Dec. 1989), res 6.7m., dep. 30.6m. (Dec. 1987); Pres. and CEO Jerome M. Hodge; Gen. Man. Ethel Davis; 6 brs.

Ecobank Liberia Ltd: Ashmun and Randall Sts, POB 4825, Monrovia; tel. 226428; fax 227029; e-mail ecobanklr@ecobank.com; internet www.ecobank.com; commenced operations Aug. 1999; cap. US $2m. Chair. Eugene H. Cooper; Man. Dir Ofong Ambah.

International Bank (Liberia) Ltd: 64 Broad St, POB 10-292, Monrovia; tel. 226279; fax 226159; f. 1948 as International Trust Co of Liberia; name changed April 2000; cap. 2m. (1989), dep. 96.4m. (Dec. 1996); Pres. F. A. Guida; 1 br.

Liberian Bank for Development and Investment (LBDI): Ashmun and Randall Sts, POB 547, Monrovia; tel. 227140; fax 226359; e-mail lbdi@liberia.net; f. 1961; cap. 5.2m. (March 1997), dep. 34.1m. (Dec. 1993); Chair. Elie E. Saleeby; Gen. Man. Francis A. Dennis.

Liberian Trading and Development Bank Ltd (TRADEVCO): 57 Ashmun St, POB 10-293, Monrovia; tel. 226072; fax 226471; f. 1955; wholly-owned subsidiary of Mediobanca SpA (Italy); cap. and res 3.2m., dep. 64.7m. (June 1995); Pres. Giorgio Picotti; CEO Silvio Vigotti.

Liberia United Bank Inc: Broad and Randall Sts, POB 10-9066, Monrovia; tel. 227869; fax 226167; seized by Central Bank April 2000; under restructure 2001; Chair. Dr William Taylor Neal.

Banking Association

Liberia Bankers' Association: POB 292, Monrovia; mems include commercial and development banks; Pres. Len Maestre.

INSURANCE

American International Underwriters, Inc: Carter Bldg, 39 Broad St, POB 180, Monrovia; tel. 224921; general; Gen. Man. S. B. Mensah.

American Life Insurance Co: Carter Bldg, 39 Broad St, POB 60, Monrovia; f. 1969; life and general; Vice-Pres. Allen Brown.

Insurance Co of Africa: 64 Broad St, POB 292, Monrovia; f. 1969; life and general; Pres. Samuel Owaree Mintah.

National Insurance Corpn of Liberia (NICOL): LBDI Bldg Complex, POB 1528, Sinkor, Monrovia; tel. 262429; f. 1983; state-owned; sole insurer for Govt and parastatal bodies; also provides insurance for the Liberian-registered merchant shipping fleet; Man. Dir Miatta Edith Sherman.

Royal Exchange Assurance: Ashmun and Randall Sts, POB 666, Monrovia; all types of insurance; Man. Ronald Woods.

United Security Insurance Agencies Inc: Randall St, POB 2071, Monrovia; life, personal accident and medical; Dir Ephraim O. Okoro.

Trade and Industry

GOVERNMENT AGENCIES

Budget Bureau: Capitol Hill, POB 1518, Monrovia; tel. 226340; Dir Emmanuel Gardner.

General Services Agency (GSA): Sinkor, Monrovia; tel. 226745; Dir Timothy Thomas.

DEVELOPMENT ORGANIZATIONS

Forestry Development Authority: POB 3010, 1000 Monrovia; tel. 224940; fax 226000; f. 1976; responsible for forest management and conservation; Man. Dir Demetrious B. Taylor.

Liberia Industrial Free Zone Authority: Bushrod Island, POB 9047, Monrovia; f. 1975; 98 mems; Man. Dir Gbai M. Gbala.

National Investment Commission (NIC): Fmr Executive Mansion Bldg, POB 9043, Monrovia; tel. 226685; internet www.nic.gov.lr; f. 1979; autonomous body negotiating investment incentives agreements on behalf of Govt; promotes agro-based and industrial development; Chair. Somah Paygai.

CHAMBER OF COMMERCE

Liberia Chamber of Commerce: POB 92, Monrovia; tel. 223738; f. 1951; Pres. David A. B. Jallah; Sec.-Gen. Luesette S. Howell.

INDUSTRIAL AND TRADE ASSOCIATIONS

Liberian Produce Marketing Corpn: POB 662, Monrovia; tel. 222447; f. 1961; govt-owned; exports Liberian produce, provides industrial facilities for processing of agricultural products and participates in agricultural development programmes; Man. Dir Tijani Garba.

Liberian Resources Corpn (LIBRESCO): controls Liberia's mineral resources; 60% govt-owned; 40% owned by South African co, Amalia Gold.

EMPLOYERS' ASSOCIATION

National Enterprises Corpn: POB 518, Monrovia; tel. 261370; importer, wholesaler and distributor of foodstuffs, and wire and metal products for local industries; Pres. Emmanuel Shaw, Sr.

UTILITIES

Electricity

Liberia Electricity Corpn: Waterside, POB 165, Monrovia; tel. 226133; Man. Dir Joseph Mayar.

TRADE UNIONS

Congress of Industrial Organizations: 29 Ashmun St, POB 415, Monrovia; Pres. Gen. J. T. Pratt; Sec.-Gen. Amos N. Gray; 5 affiliated unions.

Labor Congress of Liberia: 71 Gurley St, Monrovia; Sec.-Gen. P. C. T. Sonpon; 8 affiliated unions.

Liberian Federation of Labor Unions: J. B. McGill Labor Center, Gardnersville Freeway, POB 415, Monrovia; f. 1980 by merger; Sec.-Gen. Amos Gray; 10,000 mems (1983).

Transport

RAILWAYS

Railway operations were suspended in 1990, owing to the civil conflict. Large sections of the 480-km rail network were subsequently dismantled.

Bong Mining Co Ltd: POB 538, Monrovia; tel. 225222; fax 225770; f. 1965; Gen. Man. Hans-Georg Schneider.

Liberian Mining Co: Monrovia; tel. 221190; govt-owned; assumed control of LAMCO JV Operating Co in 1989.

National Iron Ore Co Ltd: POB 548, Monrovia; f. 1951; Gen. Man. S. K. Datta Ray.

ROADS

In 1996 the road network in Liberia totalled an estimated 10,600 km, of which about 657 km were paved. The main trunk road is the Monrovia–Sanniquellie motor road, extending north-east from the capital to the border with Guinea, near Ganta, and eastward through the hinterland to the border with Côte d'Ivoire. Trunk roads run through Tapita, in Nimba County, to Grand Gedeh County and from Monrovia to Buchanan. A bridge over the Mano river connects with the Sierra Leone road network, while a main road links Monrovia and Freetown (Sierra Leone). The use of the road network was subject to considerable disruption from 1990, as a result of the armed conflict in Liberia. Following a peace agreement in August 1996, most of the principal roads were reopened to commercial traffic in early 1997.

SHIPPING

In December 2001 Liberia's open-registry fleet (1,556 vessels), the second largest in the world (after Panama) in terms of gross tonnage, had a total displacement of 51.8m. grt. Commercial port activity in Liberia was frequently suspended from 1990, as a result of the armed conflict, but resumed in late 1996.

Bureau of Maritime Affairs: Tubman Blvd, POB 10-9042, 1000 Monrovia 10; tel. and fax 226069; e-mail maritime@liberia.net; internet www.maritime.gov.lr; Commissioner BENONI UREY.

Liberia National Shipping Line (LNSL): Monrovia; f. 1987; jt venture by the Liberian Govt and private German interests; routes to Europe, incl. the United Kingdom and Scandinavia.

National Port Authority: POB 1849, Monrovia; tel. 226646; fax 226180; e-mail natport@liberia.net; f. 1967; administers Monrovia Free Port and the ports of Buchanan, Greenville and Harper; Man. Dir ALPHONSO B. GAYE.

CIVIL AVIATION

Liberia's principal airports are Roberts Field International Airport, at Harbel, 56 km east of Monrovia, and James Spriggs Payne Airport, at Monrovia. In 1999 there were about 43 other airfields and airstrips. As a result of the armed conflict in Liberia, normal air services were suspended in 1990. James Spriggs Payne Airport was reopened in mid-1996. Roberts Field International Airport was reopened at the end of 1997; it was announced that US $50m. was required for its rehabilitation.

ADC Liberia Inc: Monrovia; f. 1993; services to the United Kingdom, the USA and destinations in West Africa.

Air Liberia: POB 2076, Monrovia; f. 1974 by merger; state-owned; scheduled passenger and cargo services; Man. Dir JAMES K. KOFA.

LIBYA

Introductory Survey

Location, Climate, Language, Religion, Flag, Capital

The Great Socialist People's Libyan Arab Jamahiriya extends along the Mediterranean coast of North Africa. Its neighbours are Tunisia and Algeria to the west, Niger and Chad to the south, Egypt to the east, and Sudan to the south-east. The climate is very hot and dry. Most of the country is part of the Sahara, an arid desert, but the coastal regions are cooler. Average temperatures range from 13°C (55°F) to 38°C (100°F), but a maximum of 57.3°C (135°F) has been recorded in the interior. Arabic is the official language; English and Italian are also used in trade. Almost all of the population are Sunni Muslims. The national flag (proportions 2 by 3) is plain green. The administrative capital was formerly Tripoli (Tarabulus), but under a decentralization programme announced in September 1988 most government departments and the legislature were relocated to Sirte (Surt), while some departments were transferred to other principal towns.

Recent History

Formerly an Italian colony, Libya was occupied in 1942 by British and French troops. Cyrenaica and Tripolitania were subsequently administered by the United Kingdom, and Fezzan by France. The country attained independence as the United Kingdom of Libya on 24 December 1951. Muhammad Idris as-Sanusi, Amir of Cyrenaica, became King Idris of Libya. British and US forces maintained bases in Libya in return for economic assistance; however, the discovery of petroleum reserves in 1959 greatly increased the country's potential for financial autonomy.

King Idris was deposed in September 1969, in a bloodless revolution led by a group of young nationalist army officers. A Revolution Command Council (RCC) was established, with Col Muammar al-Qaddafi as Chairman, and a Libyan Arab Republic was proclaimed. British and US military personnel withdrew from Libya in 1970, and in 1972 British oil interests in Libya were nationalized.

The Arab Socialist Union (ASU) was established in June 1971 as the country's sole political party. People's Congresses and Popular Committees were formed, and an undertaking was made to administer the country in accordance with Islamic principles. The General National Congress of the ASU (which comprised members of the RCC, leaders of the People's Congresses and Popular Committees and of trade unions and professional organizations) held its first session in January 1976; it was subsequently restyled the General People's Congress (GPC).

In March 1977 the GPC endorsed constitutional changes, recommended by Qaddafi, whereby the official name of the country was changed to the Socialist People's Libyan Arab Jamahiriya. Power was vested in the people through the GPC and its constituent parts. The RCC was dissolved, and a General Secretariat of the GPC (with Qaddafi as Secretary-General) was established. The GPC elected Qaddafi as Revolutionary Leader of the new state. The Council of Ministers was replaced by a General People's Committee, initially with 26 members—each a secretary of a department.

In March 1979 Qaddafi resigned from the post of Secretary-General of the General Secretariat of the GPC to devote more time to 'preserving the revolution'. The creation in early 1984 of the post of Secretary for External Security and of an office, attached to the Secretariat for Foreign Liaison, to 'combat international terrorism', combined with repressive measures to curb the activity of dissidents, apparently reflected Qaddafi's increasing sensitivity to the growth of opposition groups—principally the National Front for the Salvation of Libya (NFSL), which he accused foreign governments of fostering. In early 1986 the GPC reduced the number of secretariats in the General People's Committee, transferring their responsibilities to specially created national companies such as already existed for the petroleum industry.

From 1988, in an apparent attempt to allay domestic dissatisfaction and international criticism, Qaddafi initiated a series of liberalizing economic and political reforms. In foreign policy he adopted a more pragmatic approach to his ambition of achieving Maghreb union (see below), and to his relations with other Arab and African countries. Within Libya he accused the Revolutionary Committees (young, pro-Qaddafi activists) of murdering political opponents of his regime. Qaddafi encouraged the reopening of private businesses, in recognition of the inadequacy of state-sponsored supermarkets, and declared an amnesty for all prisoners, other than those convicted of violent crimes or of conspiring with foreign powers. Libyan citizens were guaranteed freedom to travel abroad, and the powers of the Revolutionary Committees were curbed. The GPC created a People's Court and People's Prosecution Bureau to replace the revolutionary courts, and approved a charter of human rights. In August Qaddafi announced that the army was to be replaced by a force of 'Jamahiri Guards', which would be supervised by 'people's defence committees'. In September it was decided to relocate all but two of the secretariats of the GPC, mostly to the town of Sirte (Surt), 400 km east of Tripoli, and in January 1989 Qaddafi announced that all state institutions, including the state intelligence service and the official Libyan news agency, were to be abolished. Despite this process of political and economic liberalization, in February 1989 there were anti-Government disturbances in Tripoli. While the principal focus of discontent was the management of the economy, members of fundamentalist Islamist groups were also reported to have been involved in the unrest. Further clashes between Islamist militants and the security forces were reported in November.

In October 1990 the GPC implemented extensive changes to the General People's Committee, creating three new secretariats and electing a new Secretary-General, Abu Sa'id Omar Durdah, as well as 11 new secretaries. Three of the five-member General Secretariat of the GPC were replaced, and Abd ar-Raziq as-Sawsa was appointed Secretary-General of the GPC. There was a further reorganization of the General People's Committee in October–November 1992. The former Secretary for Economic Planning, Omar al-Muntasir, was named Secretary for Foreign Liaison and International Co-operation. Regarded as a moderate, al-Muntasir's appointment was viewed by some observers as a sign of Libya's willingness to resume dialogue with the West over the Lockerbie issue (see below).

Western media reported in October 1993 that elements loyal to Qaddafi had put down an attempted military *coup d'état*, and that Libya's second-in-command, Maj. Abd as-Salam Jalloud, was among many placed under house arrest. Qaddafi denied that a coup had been attempted, but the appointment of known loyalists to senior positions in the General People's Committee was announced in January 1994. Most notably, Abd al-Majid al-Aoud, a member of Qaddafi's closest personal entourage, replaced Durdah, a close associate of Jalloud, as Secretary-General.

At its annual convention in March 1997 the GPC endorsed legislation, termed a 'Charter of Honour', providing for the collective punishment of families or tribal clans for crimes including sabotage, arms-trafficking and assisting terrorists. The GPC meeting also made changes to the composition and structure of the General People's Committee. Muhammad Ahmad al-Manqush was appointed Secretary-General of the Committee in December, as part of a further reorganization. The Secretariat for Arab Unity was abolished in a restructuring of the General People's Committee in December 1998, in accordance with Qaddafi's recently stated intention to forge closer relations with African rather than Arab countries.

In January 2000 Qaddafi unexpectedly attended the opening session of the GPC, at the end of which he demanded that the budget for 2000 be redrafted, with a view to channelling petroleum revenues into education, health and public services. Furthermore, he urged that the current administrative system, based on General People's Committees, be abandoned in favour of an alternative form of government. Accordingly, a radical decentralization of the Government was announced in March, whereby almost all of the People's Committees were dissolved and their responsibilities devolved mainly to local level: only those areas described as 'sovereign' were to remain under the control of the General People's Committee, now led by Mubarak

Abdallah ash-Shamikh (hitherto responsible for housing and utilities). Most notably, Ali Abd as-Salam at-Turayki was allocated the new post of Secretary for African Unity, being replaced as Secretary for Foreign Liaison and International Co-operation by Abd ar-Rahman Muhammad Shalgam, while Muhammad Abdallah Bait al-Mal retained the post of Secretary for Finance. Qaddafi described the restructuring as representing the creation of 'a new country, a new situation and a new administration', on a model unprecedented in the world. Later in March the GPC approved a revised budget for 2000. In July it was reported that Bait al-Mal, along with the President of the Central Bank of Libya and a further 22 senior Libyan bankers, had been implicated in allegations of financial impropriety. They were suspected of having granted unsecured loans to several prominent figures, including a number of senior army officers. Al-Ujayli Abd as-Salam Burayni replaced Bait al-Mal as Secretary for Finance in October, when a further restructuring of the General People's Committees was announced.

In late September 2000 clashes took place throughout the country between Libyans and nationals of several other African countries. The confrontations were believed to reflect resentment within Libya at the increasing numbers of black African migrants entering the country. A large number of Chadians and Sudanese were reportedly killed in incidents in the town of Az-Zawiyah, some 30 km west of Tripoli, and thousands more were interned in military camps. The Nigerien embassy in Tripoli was ransacked, and Libyan youths were also held responsible for an attack on a camp which was razed to the ground. The General People's Congress announced its intention formally to investigate the incidents, and in mid-October the evacuation and deportation of migrant workers from Nigeria, Chad, Niger, Sudan and Ghana commenced. It was estimated that as a result of the clashes more than 100 Africans had been killed and as many as 30,000 migrants had left Libya. Qaddafi subsequently apportioned blame for the incidents on 'foreign hostile hands' opposed to his plans to create an African Union. In May 2001 two Libyans, four Nigerians and one Ghanaian were sentenced to death for their roles in the violence. A further 12 defendants were sentenced to life imprisonment.

In early September 2001 a minor reorganization of the General People's Committee was announced, including the creation of a new Secretariat for Infrastructure, Urban Planning and Environment to be headed by Hutaywish Faraj al-Hutaywish. In November it was announced that more than 40 government and bank officials had been sentenced to varying terms of imprisonment for corruption and embezzlement; reportedly among those convicted was Secretary for Finance Burayni, who received a one-year prison sentence for negligence, although he continued to appear on official government lists. In late December Shukri Muhammad Ghanem was appointed to replace Adb as-Salem Ahmad Jouir as Secretary for the Economy and Trade.

In mid-January 2003 Libya was elected to chair the session of the UN Human Rights Commission scheduled to be held in March. For the first time since the formation of the Commission in 1947, the decision was voted upon, with Libya securing 33 of the 53 votes, with 17 countries, including the United Kingdom, abstaining; the USA, Canada and Guatemala opposed the proposal. Libya's election was widely criticized by a number of international human rights organizations.

Various plans for Pan-Arab unity led to the formation, in January 1972, of the Federation of Arab Republics, comprising Libya, Egypt and Syria. In 1972 Libya concluded an agreement with Egypt to merge the two countries in 1973. Neither union was effective, and proposals for union with Tunisia in 1974, Syria in 1980, Chad in 1981, Morocco in 1984, Algeria in 1987 and Sudan in 1990 also proved abortive.

Relations with Egypt, already tense following the failure of the Libya-Egypt union, further deteriorated when President Anwar Sadat launched the October 1973 war against Israel without consulting Qaddafi. In common with the other members of the League of Arab States (the Arab League, see p. 260), Libya strongly objected to Sadat's peace initiative with Israel which culminated in the Camp David accords in 1978, and Libya also condemned the proposals for Middle East peace that were agreed by other Arab states in Fez, Morocco, in 1982. From the late 1980s, none the less, Egypt and Libya forged a close relationship, with Egypt acting as an intermediary between Libya and Western nations.

In 1973 Libyan forces occupied the 'Aozou strip', a reputedly mineral-rich region of 114,000 sq km in the extreme north of Chad, to which it laid claim on the basis of an unratified border treaty concluded by Italy and France in 1935. Thereafter, Libya became embroiled in the lengthy struggle for political control between rival forces in Chad (q.v.). During 1987 intense fighting took place for control of north-western Chad, and in August President Hissène Habré's forces advanced into the 'Aozou strip', occupying the town of Aozou. Libya responded by bombing towns in northern Chad, and recaptured Aozou. In September Chadian forces destroyed an airbase 100 km inside Libya (allegedly a base for Libyan raids on Chad). Later in September the two countries agreed to observe a cease-fire sponsored by the Organization of African Unity (OAU, now African Union—AU, see p. 130), and in October 1988 Libya and Chad restored diplomatic relations. In August 1989, with Algerian mediation, Chad and Libya concluded an agreement to attempt to resolve the dispute over sovereignty of the 'Aozou strip' through a political settlement. Accordingly, the issue was submitted to the International Court of Justice in The Hague, Netherlands, which in February 1994 ruled against Libya's claim. All Libyan troops remaining in the 'Aozou strip' were withdrawn in May. In June Libya and Chad concluded a treaty of friendship, neighbourly terms and co-operation. In May 1998 Qaddafi made his first visit to Chad for 17 years, and in November the two countries officially opened two of their common border posts. Chad's President Idriss Deby (who had overthrown Habré in 1990) and members of his administration made several visits to Libya after 1997 and in January 2002 Libyan mediation resulted in the brokering of a peace agreement between the Chadian Government and the rebel Mouvement pour la démocratie et la justice au Tchad, which had been in conflict since late 1998.

Libya's outspoken criticism of other Arab regimes (accused of lacking commitment to the Palestinian cause, and as a result of failed attempts at mergers), and perceived interference in the internal affairs of other countries, led to years of relative political isolation. However, in 1987 Qaddafi sought to realign Libyan policy with that of the majority of Arab states. Qaddafi was reconciled in March with Yasser Arafat's Fatah wing of the Palestine Liberation Organization (PLO—against which he had previously advocated revolt, owing to its more moderate policies) and attempted to reunite the opposing factions of the Palestinian movement. In September Libya re-established 'fraternal' links with Iraq, modifying its support for Iran in the Iran–Iraq War and urging a cease-fire. In the same month Jordan restored diplomatic relations with Libya.

A summit meeting of North African Heads of State, held in Morocco in February 1989, concluded a treaty proclaiming the Union du Maghreb arabe (UMA—Union of the Arab Maghreb, see p. 342), comprising Algeria, Libya, Mauritania, Morocco and Tunisia. The treaty envisaged the establishment of a council of heads of state; regular meetings of ministers of foreign affairs; and the eventual free movement of goods, people, services and capital throughout the countries of the region. During 1989–92 the member states formulated 15 regional co-operation conventions. In February 1993, however, it was announced that, in view of the differing economic orientations of each signatory, no convention had actually been implemented, and the UMA's activities were to be limited. UMA leaders met in April 1994 (and subsequently on an annual basis). In 1994 Libya threatened to leave the UMA unless member states ceased to comply with UN sanctions imposed on Libya (see below), and in 1995 it refused to assume the chairmanship of the organization, owing to their continuing compliance.

In February 1997, at a meeting hosted by Libya and attended by the Presidents of Sudan, Chad, Mali and Niger, and government ministers from Egypt, Burkina Faso and Tunisia, a treaty establishing the Community of Sahel-Saharan States (COMESSA, now CEN-SAD, see p. 339) was signed. CEN-SAD's general secretariat was temporarily located in Tripoli, and provisions were made for the establishment of a development bank, a council of heads of state and an executive council.

Libya's relations with the USA, which had been strained for many years, deteriorated significantly under the presidency of Ronald Reagan (1981–89) who accused the Libyan Government of sponsoring international terrorism. In January 1986 Reagan severed of all economic and commercial relations with Libya, and in March Libyan forces fired missiles at US fighter aircraft which were challenging Libya's attempts to enforce recognition of the whole of the Gulf of Sirte as its territorial waters. In two retaliatory attacks US fighters destroyed missile and radar facilities in the town of Sirte, and four Libyan patrol boats in the

Gulf. In April US military aircraft bombed military installations, airports and official buildings, as well as alleged terrorist training camps and communication centres in Tripoli and Benghazi. The US Administration claimed in justification to have irrefutable proof of Libyan involvement in terrorist attacks and plots against US targets in Europe and the Middle East. A total of 101 people, including many civilians, were reported to have died in the raids. Tensions increased in late 1988 after Reagan stated that the USA was considering military action against a factory at Rabta, outside Tripoli, where Libya was allegedly preparing to manufacture chemical weapons. In January 1989 two Libyan fighter aircraft were shot down during an encounter over the Mediterranean with US military aircraft.

In November 1991 the US and British Governments announced that they would seek to extradite two Libyan citizens, Abd al-Baset Ali Muhammad al-Megrahi (a former head of security of Libyan Arab Airlines) and Al-Amin Khalifa Fhimah (an employee of the airline), alleged to have been responsible for an explosion that destroyed a Pan American World Airways (Pan Am) passenger aircraft over Lockerbie, Scotland, in December 1988, resulting in the deaths of 270 people. The Libyan Government denied any involvement in the bombing, and recommended that the allegations be investigated by a neutral body. In January 1992 the UN Security Council adopted a resolution (No. 731) demanding Libya's compliance with requests for the extradition of its two nationals and its co-operation with a French inquiry into the bombing over Niger, in September 1989, of a UTA passenger airline, in which all 171 passengers and crew had been killed. Libya's offer to try on its own territory the two men accused of the Lockerbie bombing was rejected by the USA, the United Kingdom and France, which urged the UN to impose sanctions on Libya. On 31 March 1992 the UN Security Council adopted a resolution (No. 748) imposing economic sanctions, including the severance of international air links, the prohibition of trade in arms and the reduction of Libya's diplomatic representation abroad, against Libya if it refused to comply with Resolution 731, and commit itself to a renunciation of international terrorism, by 15 April. Sanctions were duly imposed on the specified date. In May, at Qaddafi's instigation, 1,500 People's Congresses were convened in Libya and abroad, to enable the country's citizens to decide the fate of the two Lockerbie suspects and their response to the UN sanctions. The GPC announced in the following month its decision to allow the two Lockerbie suspects to be tried abroad, provided that the proceedings were 'fair and just'.

In August 1993 the USA, the United Kingdom and France announced that they would request the UN Security Council to strengthen the sanctions in force against Libya if, by 1 October, Libya had still not complied with Resolutions 731 and 748. The Libyan Government rejected this ultimatum, but stated its willingness to commence discussions with those three countries on an appropriate venue for the trial of the two Lockerbie suspects. In October the UN Secretary-General, Dr Boutros Boutros-Ghali, met the Libyan Secretary for Foreign Liaison and International Co-operation, but failed to secure agreement on a timetable for the surrender of the two Lockerbie suspects to either the USA or the United Kingdom. In November the Security Council adopted a resolution (No. 883) providing for the strengthening of the economic sanctions in force against Libya in the event of the country's failure fully to comply with Resolutions 731 and 748 by 1 December. The sanctions, which were duly applied, included the closure of all Libyan Arab Airlines' offices abroad; a ban on the sale of equipment and services for the civil aviation sector; the sequestration of all Libyan financial resources overseas; a ban on the sale to Libya of specified items for use in the petroleum and gas industries; and a reduction in personnel levels at Libyan diplomatic missions abroad. In December Pan Am announced its intention to sue the State of Libya, Libyan Arab Airlines and the two Libyan citizens accused of the Lockerbie bombing for the destruction of its airliner and subsequent loss of business. In March 1998 a US court ruled against a contention by Libya that, as a sovereign nation, it could not be sued by US citizens, thus enabling victims' families to sue for damages.

In January 1994 the Scottish lawyer representing the two Lockerbie suspects stated that they might be willing to stand trial in The Hague; this was subsequently endorsed as an appropriate venue by Qaddafi. In February, however, US President Bill Clinton recommended that an embargo should be imposed on Libya's sales of petroleum (which accounted for some 98% of its export earnings) if the country continued to defy the international community. In January 1995 British media published a US intelligence report, compiled in March 1991, that alleged that the Lockerbie bombing had been perpetrated by Palestinian agents at the bidding of a former Iranian Minister of the Interior, in retaliation for the attack on an Iran Air passenger flight, mistakenly shot down by a US aircraft carrier in July 1988. It had been variously claimed by different sources that Iranian, Syrian and Palestinian agents—sometimes separately, sometimes in collaboration—had been responsible for the explosion. Nevertheless, both the US and the British authorities remained convinced that there was sufficient evidence to continue to seek the extradition of the two Libyan suspects who had been formally indicted for the offence in the USA and Scotland.

In mid-1996, following its repeated failure to persuade the UN to agree yet more stringent sanctions against Libya, the US Congress approved unilateral 'secondary' sanctions against Libya (and Iran). In effect, the Iran-Libya Sanctions Act (ILSA), as it was termed, sought to penalize companies operating in US markets that were investing more than US $40m. (later amended to $20m.) in Libya's oil and gas industries. In May 1997 the UN Security Council issued a statement condemning Libya's violation of Resolution 748, after Qaddafi had travelled by air to Niger and Nigeria. (Libya had defied the sanctions in respect of air travel on several previous occasions.)

In July 1997 the Arab League, which had been criticized by Qaddafi for its lack of support, formally proposed that the two Libyan suspects in the Lockerbie case be tried by Scottish judges under Scottish law in a neutral country. In September the members of the League urged a relaxation of the air embargo on Libya and voted to defy UN sanctions by permitting aircraft carrying Qaddafi, and other flights for religious or humanitarian purposes, to land on their territory. In October the United Kingdom requested that the UN send envoys to examine the Scottish legal system, and in December the UN issued a report concluding that the Libyan suspects would receive a fair trial under Scottish law.

In April 1998 the official spokesman for the families of the British victims of the Lockerbie bombing, together with an expert in Scottish law, held talks with Qaddafi in Libya, following which it was reported that Qaddafi had agreed to allow the two Libyan suspects to stand trial in the Netherlands under Scottish law. In August the United Kingdom and the USA proposed that the trial of the two Libyan suspects be held in the Netherlands under Scottish law and presided over by Scottish judges. The UN Security Council adopted a resolution (No. 1192) welcoming the initiative and providing for the suspension of sanctions upon the arrival in the Netherlands of the two suspects; additional sanctions were threatened if the Libyan authorities did not comply with the resolution.

In December 1998 the UN Secretary-General, Kofi Annan, held a meeting with Qaddafi in Libya in an attempt to expedite a trial. Shortly afterwards the GPC, which had been asked to consider the matter, endorsed the principle of a trial of the Lockerbie suspects, but requested that the USA and the United Kingdom remove 'all remaining obstacles'. In a bid to break the impasse arising from Qaddafi's demand that the trial include a panel of international judges, envoys from Saudi Arabia and South Africa were dispatched to Libya in January 1999 to negotiate with Qaddafi. In February it was reported that the envoys had reached an understanding with the Libyan leader whereby UN observers would be allowed to monitor the two Libyan suspects during the trial, to ensure that they were not questioned by US and British agents, and afterwards, if they were convicted and imprisoned in Scotland. The diplomatic initiative culminated in March with a visit by President Nelson Mandela of South Africa to Libya, during which Qaddafi undertook to surrender the suspects by 6 April. The two Libyan suspects duly arrived for trial in the Netherlands on 5 April and were transferred to Camp Zeist, a former US airbase near Utrecht designated Scottish territory for the purposes of the trial, where they were formally arrested and charged with murder, conspiracy to murder and contravention of the 1982 Aviation Security Act. The UN Security Council immediately voted to suspend sanctions against Libya indefinitely, although they were not to be permanently revoked until Libya had met with other conditions stipulated in UN Security Council Resolution 1192 (including the payment of compensation to the families of victims of the Lockerbie bombing). The Security Council was to review the sanctions issue after three months, following a report from the UN Secretary-General. The USA refused to remove 'secondary' sanctions against Libya (see above), but subsequently announced that it would allow the sale of food and medical items to Libya on a 'case-by-case' basis. In June 1999 the US and Libyan ambassadors to the UN took part in what represented the first official contact between the two countries in 18 years. During the talks the USA informed Libya that it could not support a permanent end to UN sanctions until Libya had fully complied with UN Security Council Resolution 1192; thus in July Kofi Annan reported to the Security Council that he was unable to secure support for the permanent revocation of sanctions against Libya.

The two Libyan suspects appeared before the Scottish court in the Netherlands for the first time in December 1999, at a pre-trial hearing to decide on the jurisdiction of the Scottish court. The presiding Scottish judge ruled that the two suspects could be tried on all three charges, and that they could be described as members of the Libyan intelligence services. (Defence lawyers had argued that to describe the Libyans as members of the intelligence services was irrelevant and prejudicial.) The trial of al-Megrahi and Fhimah eventually commenced on 3 May 2000; both pleaded not guilty to the charges brought against them, and defence lawyers accused a number of organizations, including militant Palestinian resistance groups, of perpetrating the bombing.

In early January 2001 prosecution lawyers unexpectedly announced that they would no longer pursue charges of conspiracy to murder and contravention of the 1982 Aviation Security Act. Accordingly, the trial proceeded on the sole charge of murder. On 31 January 2001 the judges announced that they had unanimously found al-Megrahi guilty of the murder of 270 people and sentenced him to life imprisonment, with the recommendation that he serve a minimum of 20 years. The judges accepted that al-Megrahi was a member of the Libyan intelligence services, and although they acknowledged their awareness of what they termed 'uncertainties and qualifications' in the case, they concluded that the evidence against him combined to form 'a real and convincing pattern' which left them with no reasonable doubt as to his guilt. Fhimah, however, was unanimously acquitted, owing to lack of proof, and freed to return to Libya. Despite mounting pressure from Arab League states, the British Government asserted that sanctions against Libya would not be permanently revoked until Libya accepted responsibility for the bombing and paid 'substantial' compensation. The newly inaugurated US President, George W. Bush, also indicated his support for this stance, and in July 2001 ILSA was extended for a further five–year term.

Meanwhile, demands for further investigation into the bombing, and Qaddafi's role in it, were rejected by senior Scottish legal officials, who stated that there was insufficient evidence to justify any further proceedings against those alleged to have abetted al-Megrahi, despite the fact that it was apparent that he had not acted alone. In early February 2001 protesters attempted to storm the British embassy in Tripoli, but were dispersed by security forces using tear gas. Lawyers for al-Megrahi subsequently lodged an appeal against the conviction. The appeal hearing, before five Scottish judges, began at Camp Zeist in late January 2002. Al-Megrahi's lawyers based their case on what they termed new 'strong circumstantial evidence', which raised the possibility that the bomb had been placed on the aircraft at London, United Kingdom, and not in Malta, as the trial judges had concluded. In mid-March the appeal was unanimously rejected, and al-Megrahi was transferred to a prison in Scotland to begin his sentence. The decision was, however, condemned by the Libyan authorities, while an Austrian UN observer referred to the verdict as a 'spectacular miscarriage of justice'. In late February Qaddafi's eldest son, Seif al-Islam (whose increasingly prominent role fuelled speculation that he was being prepared as an eventual successor to the Libyan leader), had indicated that Libya would pay compensation to the families of those killed in the Lockerbie bombing, regardless of the outcome of the appeal. Former South African President Nelson Mandela visited al-Megrahi in prison in June to assess the conditions of his imprisonment and concluded that al-Megrahi's detention in solitary confinement amounted to psychological persecution. Mandela requested that al-Megrahi be allowed to serve the remainder of his sentence in a Muslim country, suggesting Egypt, Morocco or Tunisia as possibilities. Nevertheless, in August the British Secretary of State for Foreign and Commonwealth Affairs pledged that al-Megrahi would serve the full term of his sentence in Scotland.

In July 1999 Libya and the United Kingdom reached agreement on the full restoration of diplomatic relations after Qaddafi issued a statement in which he accepted Libya's 'general responsibility' for the death of a British policewoman, who was shot outside the Libyan People's Bureau in London in 1984, and agreed to co-operate with the investigation into the killing. The payment by Libya, in November 1999, of compensation to the victim's family facilitated the reopening of the British embassy in Tripoli the following month. In January 2000, however, the British Government confirmed that its customs officials had, in late 1999, seized a consignment of *Scud* missile parts which had arrived in the United Kingdom from Taiwan and was bound for Libya via Malta. (It subsequently transpired that the parts had been impounded in mid-1999, prior to the full restoration of diplomatic relations between the United Kingdom and Libya.) Despite this incident and the delivery of the Lockerbie trial verdict, the normalization of relations between the United Kingdom and Libya progressed and in March 2001 Libya appointed an ambassador to the United Kingdom for the first time in 17 years. In early August 2002 a minister of the British Foreign and Commonwealth Office visited Libya for talks with Qaddafi: this was the first visit by a British government minister to Libya for some 20 years. After the meeting it was reported that Libya had given strong indications that it was ready to accept responsibility for the for the Lockerbie bombing, while the Libyan Secretary for Foreign Affairs declared that Libya was ready 'in principle' to take steps to compensate the relatives of victims. Qaddafi had also expressed his willingness to co-operate with the international community on issues such as weapons of mass destruction and the 'war against terror'.

In February 1996 the US Central Intelligence Agency repeated claims, first made in the US media three years earlier, that Libya was constructing an underground factory for the manufacture of chemical weapons at Tarhunah, south-east of Tripoli. In March the US Secretary of Defense declared that the USA would, if necessary, use force to close the plant. Libya denied the existence of the factory and alleged that the USA was using the accusation as a pretext for an attack on Libya. None the less, charges of Libyan involvement in the production of chemical weapons persisted.

In early 2002 it was revealed that several discussions had taken place between senior Libyan and US officials, although the USA maintained that there would be no change in its position regarding Libya until the latter had fully complied with UN Security Council Resolution 1192. Qaddafi had been swift to condemn the September 2001 suicide attacks on New York and Washington, DC, as 'horrifying', and claimed to have taken action against Libyan Islamists with links to Osama bin Laden and the al-Qa'ida (Base) organization, held by the USA to be principally responsible for the attacks.

In January 2000 (shortly after the revelation of the seizure of missile parts by the United Kingdom) the European Union (EU, see p. 199) withdrew an invitation to Qaddafi, issued by the Commission President, Romano Prodi, to visit the European Commission headquarters in Brussels, on the grounds that Libya had not accepted EU conditions regarding commitment to human rights, democracy, free trade and support for the Middle East peace process. Apparently in reprisal, Libya immediately announced major commercial contracts with Russia and the People's Republic of China. Qaddafi none the less attended the EU-Africa summit meeting in Cairo, Egypt, in April, at which talks with Prodi and other European officials were described as 'positive'. Relations with the EU, and particularly with France, generally improved following talks in early 1996 between Libyan and EU representatives in Belgium. In July of that year Qaddafi granted the French authorities investigating the 1989 bombing of the UTA passenger aircraft unprecedented access to Libyan evidence. This resulted in February 1998 in a judge's decision to try *in absentia* six Libyans suspected of involvement in the attack, and in March 1999 a French court sentenced the six suspects *in absentia* to life imprisonment. The French authorities issued international arrest warrants for the Libyans, and threatened to intensify sanctions against Libya if it did not impose the verdicts on the accused. In July 1999 Libya began payment of some US $31m. in compensation to the families of those killed in the bomb attack. France stated that this represented an acknowledgement by Libya of the responsibility of its citizens for the bombing. However, attempts by French lawyers on behalf of the victims' families to prosecute Qaddafi for complicity in the bombing of the aircraft were unsuccessful. In October 2001 the French Minister-delegate in charge of Co-operation and Francophone Affairs, Charles Josselin, the first government official from that country to visit Libya for almost 10 years, discussed with Qaddafi the strengthening of bilateral relations.

In October 1996, meanwhile, the German authorities announced that evidence existed to prove the Libyan Government's direct involvement in a bomb attack on a discothèque in Berlin in 1986. Arrest warrants were subsequently issued for the four Libyans suspected of involvement, but in March 1997 a German parliamentary delegation recommended that regular contact between the German Parliament and the GPC should continue. In April 1998 Libya resolved to allow the German authorities to question the Libyan suspects. In the following month the two countries signed an agreement on economic co-operation. Following a lengthy trial, in mid-November 2001 a court in Berlin sentenced four people, including a Libyan national, to between 12 and 14 years' imprisonment for their involvement in the bomb attack. Although Qaddafi's personal complicity in the incident could not be proven, the presiding judge stated that there was sufficient evidence to ascertain that the bombing had been carried out by members of the Libyan secret service and employees of the Libyan People's Bureau in the former East Germany.

In February 1998 a Spanish minister visited Tripoli, following an announcement of Spain's intention to renew political and economic ties with Libya. However, the decision by France, Spain, Italy and Portugal to create a rapid reaction force in the Mediterranean was strongly condemned by Qaddafi. In July Italy formally apologized for its colonial rule of Libya, and commitments were made to improve bilateral relations. The Italian Minister of Foreign Affairs, Lamberto Dini, visited Libya in April 1999, immediately after the suspension of international sanctions. Italy's Prime Minister, Massimo D'Alema, travelled to Libya in December, thus becoming the first EU premier to visit the country since 1992. In July 2000 Libya's ambassador to Italy accused the Italian Government of failing to honour its commitment, made in a joint declaration in May 1998, to remove from Libyan territory landmines planted during the Second World War and to compensate victims of landmine explosions; Dini visited Libya in August 2000 to discuss the implementation of the agreements. In December the Libyan Secretary for Foreign Liaison and International Co-operation attended talks with Dini in Rome, at which accords regarding political consultation, visas and the removal of landmines were signed.

In June 1995 Libya adopted legislation forbidding foreign workers without contracts to remain in Libya. The ensuing mass expulsions principally affected Sudanese workers, but in September, in an attempt to expose what Libya regarded as the inadequacies of the Declaration of Principles on Palestinian Self-Rule and subsequent agreements concluded within its framework by Israel and the PLO, Qaddafi announced that, since their land had been liberated, 30,000 Palestinians were to be expelled from Libya. The expulsion of an initial 1,500 Palestinians provoked international concern, as Egypt, Israel and Lebanon all refused them entry, leaving the refugees stranded in border areas without essential supplies. Following intensive mediation by Egypt, the programme was suspended in October, but many Palestinians remained in refugee camps on the Egyptian border. The expulsion order was formally revoked in January 1997, but many Palestinians refused to return to Libya. In April it was reported that armed security forces had forcibly returned the refugees to Libya and dismantled the camps.

In mid-1998 Qaddafi announced his intention to ally Libya more closely with African rather than Arab countries; later in the year numerous African heads of state visited Tripoli, all of whom defied UN sanctions by travelling to Libya by air (see above). In October, as further evidence of his dissatisfaction with Arab states, Qaddafi changed the name of Libya's mission to the Arab League from 'permanent' to 'resident'. In September 1999, on the occasion of the 30th anniversary of his seizure of power, Qaddafi hosted an extraordinary OAU summit in Sirte. Qaddafi presented his vision of a United States of Africa, and demanded that Africa be given veto power on the UN Security Council. The 'Sirte Declaration', a final document adopted by the 43 attending heads of state and government, called for the strengthening of the OAU, the establishment of a pan-African parliament, African monetary union and an African court of justice. At a further extraordinary summit of the OAU in Sirte in early March 2001 it was announced that the organization's member states had overwhelmingly endorsed the proposals to declare the formation of the AU. In early July 2002 Qaddafi

travelled to Durban, South Africa, for the 38th and final summit of the OAU, which saw the formal creation of the new AU, chaired by South African President Thabo Mbeki. During the summit Mbeki and numerous other African heads of state attempted to persuade Qaddafi to abandon his hostility towards the New Partnership for Africa's Development, a contract between Africa and the international community under which, in exchange for aid and investment, the African states agreed to strive towards democracy and good governance. After the summit Qaddafi visited Mozambique, Zimbabwe and Malawi. In October Libya notified the Arab League of its intention to withdraw from the organization. Although no official reason for the withdrawal was given, reports indicated that senior Libyan officials had cited the Arab League's 'inefficiency' in dealing with the crises in Iraq and the Palestinian territories as its motives. Arab League ministers of foreign affairs subsequently convened to request that Libya reconsider its decision to withdraw, although it appeared unlikely that Libya would relent. However, Qaddafi's growing influence in Africa was also somewhat checked in January 2003 following the removal of some 300 Libyan troops from the Central African Republic, where they had been providing protection to the Government of that country. In the previous month an agreement between Libya and Zimbabwe which would have resulted in the exchange of Libyan fuel for Zimbabwean beef, sugar and tobacco was abandoned.

Government

Power is vested in the people through People's Congresses, Popular Committees, Trade Unions, Vocational Syndicates, and with the General People's Congress (GPC) and its General Secretariat. The Head of State is the Revolutionary Leader, elected by the GPC. Executive power is exercised by the General People's Committee. The country is divided into three provinces, 10 governorates and 1,500 administrative communes.

Defence

Libya's active armed forces totalled 76,000 (including an estimated 38,000 conscripts) in August 2002: army 45,000; air force 23,000; navy 8,000. Military service is by selective conscription, lasting up to two years. There was additionally a People's Militia of 40,000 reserves. Libya's defence budget in 2001 was an estimated LD 650m.

Economic Affairs

In 1989, according to estimates by the World Bank, Libya's gross national income (GNI), measured at average 1987–89 prices, was US $23,333m., equivalent to $5,310 per head. (In 1994, according to unofficial estimates, GNI at current prices was $26,000m., equivalent to $5,650 per head.) During 1990–2001, it was estimated, the population increased at an average annual rate of 2.1%, while, according to the IMF, gross domestic product (GDP) per head declined, in real terms, by an average of 0.2% per year. Overall GDP increased, in real terms, at an average annual rate of 2.1% in 1990–2001.

Agriculture (including forestry and fishing) contributed an estimated 6.6% of GDP in 1996, and engaged 17.9% of the employed labour force in that year. The principal subsistence crops are barley and wheat; other crops include tomatoes, citrus fruits, watermelons, potatoes, olives, onions and dates. Output is limited by climatic conditions and irrigation problems, although cultivable land was being significantly increased by the Great Man-made River Project, whereby water was to be carried from the south of the country to the north and thence to the east and west. However, the highly ambitious nature of the scheme has provided engineers with serious difficulties and by mid-2003, after 19 years of construction work, the project remained only half completed. Agriculture is based mainly on animal husbandry; sheep are the principal livestock, but goats, cattle, camels, horses and poultry are also kept. According to FAO data, agricultural production increased at an annual average rate of 4.4% in 1990–2000; output declined by 7.1% in 1999, but increased by 6.1% in 2000.

Industry (including mining, manufacturing, construction and power) contributed 44.0% of GDP in 1996, and engaged 29.9% of the employed labour force in that year. Virtually all of the industrial sector is state-controlled.

Mining contributed 25.8% of GDP in 1996, but engaged only 2.5% of the employed labour force in that year. The petroleum and natural gas sector contributed 24.0% of GDP, and engaged 1.7% of the employed labour force. Libya's economy depends almost entirely on its petroleum and natural gas resources. The

National Oil Corporation of Libya (NOC) controls about three-quarters of the petroleum produced in Libya, largely through production-sharing agreements. At the end of 2001 proven recoverable reserves of petroleum were estimated at 29,500m. barrels, sufficient to enable production to be maintained—at that year's levels, averaging 1.43m. barrels per day (b/d)—until 2058. With effect from 1 February 2003 Libya's production quota within the Organization of the Petroleum Exporting Countries (OPEC, see p. 298) was 1,312,000 b/d. Libya's natural gas reserves are extensive (estimated at 1,310,000m. cu m at the end of 2001). Libya also has reserves of iron ore, salt, limestone, clay, sulphur and gypsum.

Manufacturing contributed 9.4% of GDP in 1996, and engaged 10.5% of the employed labour force in that year. The principal manufacturing activity is petroleum refining. There are three refineries, at Brega, Ras Lanouf and Az-Zawiyah. A petrochemicals site is located at Brega, and in the late 1990s there were plans to construct a new petrochemicals complex at Ras Lanouf. Other important manufacturing activities were the production of iron, steel and cement, and the processing of agricultural products.

Energy is derived almost exclusively from oil-fired power. Libya is a net exporter of fuels (less than 10% of petroleum production is used for domestic energy requirements), with imports of energy products comprising only an estimated 0.2% of the value of merchandise imports in 1997.

Services contributed 49.4% of GDP in 1996, and engaged 52.2% of the employed labour force in that year. Visitor arrivals declined from 1.8m. in 1995 to 858,000 in 1999. Receipts from tourism in the latter year amounted to US $28m. In an attempt to stimulate growth in the tourism sector, the Government invested heavily in 1996–2001 to expand and rehabilitate tourism infrastructure.

In 1999 Libya recorded a visible trade surplus of US $2,762m., and there was a surplus of $1,984m. on the current account of the balance of payments. In 1999 the principal sources of imports were Italy (which provided 18.3% of total imports), Germany (14.5%), the Republic of Korea, the United Kingdom and France. The principal market for exports in that year was Italy (37.8%); Germany, Spain, France and Viet Nam were also important purchasers. The petroleum sector is overwhelmingly Libya's principal generator of exports revenue: exports of mineral fuels, lubricants, etc. accounted for 94.8% of Libya's export earnings in 1997. The principal imports were machinery and transport equipment, basic manufactures and food and live animals.

Projected budgetary revenue and expenditure for 1999 were to balance at LD 4,900m. The budget deficit in 1998 was forecast at LD 650m. in December of that year. Libya's total external debt was about US $3,800m. at the end of 1999, according to estimates quoted by the *Middle East Economic Digest*. According to the same source, the rate of inflation averaged an estimated 24.0% in 1999, compared with 5.6% in 1997. The rate of unemployment was unofficially estimated to be about 30% by the end of the 1990s.

Libya is a member of the Arab Monetary Fund (see p. 138), the Council of Arab Economic Unity (see p. 178), the Islamic Development Bank (see p. 257), the Organization of Arab Petroleum Exporting Countries (see p. 292), OPEC (see p. 298) and the Union du Maghreb arabe (Union of the Arab Maghreb, see p. 342).

In recent years Libya's principal economic difficulty has been its dependence on exports of crude petroleum, with income from the sector consistently providing an estimated 95% of annual export revenue. The economy's vulnerability to fluctuations in the international price of petroleum was exacerbated by the UN's imposition of sanctions in 1992 (see Recent History). Following their suspension in April 1999, Libyan government

ministers and petroleum company officials invited foreign investors to take advantage of opportunities for overseas participation in the hydrocarbons sector. (Despite the UN's decision, in mid-2001 the USA extended unilateral 'secondary' sanctions imposed on Libya in 1996 for a further five years, thus excluding US companies from potentially lucrative contracts.) In 2000 the NOC announced that a total of 137 new petroleum exploration blocks, representing about 70% of Libya's unexplored land mass, would be put to tender. Petroleum output was scheduled to increase from 1.4m b/d in 2001 to more than 2.0m. b/d by 2003, considerably in excess of its OPEC quota. Libya also possesses considerable natural gas reserves and an underwater pipeline linking Libya with Italy, scheduled to be completed in 2004, is expected to enable some 8,000m. cu m per year of that commodity to be exported to Europe. In an attempt to compensate for the losses incurred by the country's economy as a result of UN sanctions, the Libyan Government announced plans to put to tender reconstruction projects to the value of some US $35,000m. during 2001–05 and foreign companies were expected to assume a major role in the upgrading of Libyan port facilities and roads, as well as in the construction of a rail network along the coastline. Progress has, however, been slow despite the devaluation of the dinar by more than 50% in early 2002, which was intended to increase the flow of foreign direct investment into the country, and bureaucratic delays and poor communications remained major disincentives to foreign investors. Revenues from hydrocarbons were projected to have increased by some 35% in 2002 compared with the previous year, and although Libya benefited from sustained high international oil prices in the early 2000s, any fall in the price of petroleum could have severe negative effects on the country's economy. GDP growth of 3.1% was recorded in 2002, and growth was forecast to continue into 2003. None the less, a number of socio-economic problems—notably the very high rate of unemployment—remained to be addressed through the effective deployment of the country's apparent increased revenues.

Education

Education is compulsory for children between six and 15 years of age. Primary education begins at the age of six and lasts for nine years. In 1992 primary enrolment included 96% of the relevant age-group (males 97%; females 96%). Secondary education, from the age of 15, lasts for three years. In 1992 secondary enrolment was equivalent to 98% of pupils in the relevant age-group. Libya also has institutes for agricultural, technical and vocational training. There are 13 universities. In 1992 enrolment in tertiary education was equivalent to 18.4% of the relevant age-group (males 19.2%; females 17.6%).

Public Holidays

2003: 12 February* (Id al-Adha, Feast of the Sacrifice), 5 March* (Islamic New Year), 14 March* (Ashoura), 28 March (Evacuation Day), 14 May* (Mouloud, Birth of Muhammad), 11 June (Evacuation Day), 1 September (Revolution Day), 24 September* (Leilat al-Meiraj, ascension of Muhammad), 7 October (Evacuation Day), 26 November* (Id al-Fitr, end of Ramadan).

2004: 2 February* (Id al-Adha, Feast of the Sacrifice), 22 February* (Islamic New Year), 2 March* (Ashoura), 28 March (Evacuation Day), 2 May* (Mouloud, Birth of Muhammad), 11 June (Evacuation Day), 1 September (Revolution Day), 12 September* (Leilat al-Meiraj, ascension of Muhammad), 7 October (Evacuation Day), 14 November* (Id al-Fitr, end of Ramadan).

*These holidays are dependent on the Islamic lunar calendar and may vary by one or two days from the dates given.

Weights and Measures

The metric system is in force.

Statistical Survey

Sources (unless otherwise stated): National Corporation for Information and Documentation; Census and Statistical Dept, Secretariat of Planning, Sharia Damascus 40, 2nd Floor, Tripoli; tel. (21) 3331731.

Area and Population

AREA, POPULATION AND DENSITY

Area (sq km)	1,775,500*
Population (census results)	
31 July 1984	
Males	1,953,757
Females	1,688,819
Total	3,642,576
August 1995 (provisional)	
Total	4,811,902†
Population (UN estimates at mid-year)‡	
1999	5,175,000
2000	5,290,000
2001	5,408,000
Density (per sq km) at mid-2001	3.0

* 685,524 sq miles.

† Comprising 4,404,986 Libyan nationals (males 2,236,943, females 2,168,043) and 406,916 non-Libyans.

‡ Source: UN, *World Population Prospects: The 2000 Revision*.

POPULATION BY REGION
(1995 census, provisional figures)

Al-Batnan	151,240	Misratah (Misurata)	488,573
Jebel Akhdar	381,165	Najghaza	244,553
Banghazi (Benghazi)	665,615	Tarabulus (Tripoli)	1,313,996
Al-Wosta	240,574	Az-Zawiyah (Zawia)	517,395
Al-Wahat	62,056	Jebel Gharbi	316,970
Al-Jufra	39,335	Fazzan (Fezzan)	314,029
Sofuljin	76,401	**Total**	4,811,902

PRINCIPAL TOWNS
(population at census of 31 July 1973)

Tarabulus (Tripoli, the capital)	481,295	Ajdabiyah	31,047
		Darnah (Darna)	30,241
Banghazi (Benghazi)	219,317	Sabhah (Sebha)	28,714
Misratah (Misurata)	42,815	Tubruq (Tobruk)	28,061
Az-Zawiyah (Zawia)	39,382	Al-Marj	25,166
Zawiyat al-Baida (Beida)	31,796	Zlitan (Zliten)	21,340

Mid-2000 (UN estimate, incl. suburbs): Benghazi 829,000.

Mid-2001 (UN estimate, incl. suburbs): Tripoli 1,776,000 (Source: UN, *World Urbanization Prospects: The 2001 Revision*).

BIRTHS, MARRIAGES AND DEATHS

	Registered live births		Registered marriages*		Registered deaths*	
	Number	Rate (per 1,000)	Number	Rate (per 1,000)	Number	Rate (per 1,000)
1994	98,423	20.1	19,190	3.9	14,036	2.9
1995	88,779	17.9	21,358	4.3	13,538	4.6
1996	90,428	17.8	18,743	3.7	12,281	2.4

* Registration is incomplete.

Source: UN, *Demographic Yearbook*.

Expectation of life (WHO estimates, years at birth): 70.4 (males 68.3; females 73.1) in 2001 (Source: WHO, *World Health Report*).

EMPLOYMENT
(official estimates, '000 persons)

	1994	1996*
Agriculture, forestry and fishing	213.4	219.5
Mining and quarrying	29.9	31.0
Manufacturing	124.1	128.5
Electricity, gas and water	33.7	35.5
Construction	168.3	171.0
Trade, restaurants and hotels	70.7	73.0
Transport, storage and communications	97.7	104.0
Financing, insurance, real estate and business services	18.7	22.0
Other services	434.8	439.5
Total	1,191.3	1,224.0
Libyans	1,035.2	1,092.1
Non-Libyans	156.1	131.9

* Figures for 1995 are not available.

Health and Welfare

KEY INDICATORS

Total fertility rate (children per woman, 2001)	3.5
Under-5 mortality rate (per 1,000 live births, 2001)	19
HIV/AIDS (% of persons aged 15–49, 2001)	0.24
Physicians (per 1,000 head, 1997)	1.28
Hospital beds (per 1,000 head, 1997)	4.3
Health expenditure (2000): US $ per head (PPP)	392
Health expenditure (2000): % of GDP	3.3
Health expenditure (2000): public (% of total)	48.6
Access to water (% of persons, 2000)	72
Access to sanitation (% of persons, 2000)	97
Human Development Index (2000): ranking	64
Human Development Index (2000): value	0.773

For sources and definitions, see explanatory note on p. vi.

Agriculture

PRINCIPAL CROPS

('000 metric tons)

	1999*	2000	2001*
Wheat .	130	125†	130
Barley .	75	80†	80
Potatoes	209	210*	210
Dry broad beans .	12	13*	13
Almonds .	31	31*	31
Groundnuts (in shell)	23	25*	26
Olives .	190	190*	190
Tomatoes .	245	250*	250
Pumpkins, squash and gourds .	28	29*	29
Cucumbers and gherkins	10	11*	11
Chillies and green peppers .	14	15*	15
Green onions and shallots .	50	53*	53
Dry onions .	180	180*	180
Green peas	12	12*	12
Green broad beans .	14	15*	15
Carrots .	23	24*	24
Other vegetables .	74	76*	76
Oranges .	42	43*	43
Tangerines, mandarins, etc.	10	10*	10
Lemons and limes	14	14*	14
Apples .	46	47*	47
Apricots .	16	17*	17
Peaches and nectarines .	9	10*	10
Plums .	32	33*	33
Grapes .	39	40*	40
Watermelons .	212	215*	215
Cantaloupes and other melons .	26	27*	27
Figs .	29	30*	30
Dates .	132	133*	133

* FAO estimate(s).
† Unofficial figure.

Source: FAO.

LIVESTOCK

(FAO estimates, '000 head, year ending September)

	1999	2000	2001
Horses .	45	46	46
Asses .	29	30	30
Cattle .	190	210	220
Camels .	70	71	72
Sheep .	5,000	5,100	5,200
Goats .	1,800	1,900	1,950
Poultry .	24,500	24,800	25,000

Source: FAO.

LIVESTOCK PRODUCTS

('000 metric tons)

	1999*	2000*	2001
Beef and veal .	15	8	10†
Mutton and lamb .	28	29	30*
Goat meat .	9	9	10*
Poultry meat .	98	99	100*
Cows' milk	135	135	135*
Sheeps' milk .	54	56	56*
Goats' milk	15	15	15*
Hen eggs .	58	59	59*
Wool: greasy .	9	9	9*
Wool: scoured .	2	2	2*
Cattle hides .	3	3	1*
Sheepskins	6	7	7*

* FAO estimate(s).
† Unofficial figure.

Source: FAO.

Forestry

ROUNDWOOD REMOVALS

(FAO estimates, '000 cubic metres, excl. bark)

	1999	2000	2001
Sawlogs, veneer logs and logs for sleepers*	63	63	63
Other industrial wood	53	53	53
Fuel wood*	536	536	536
Total .	652	652	652

* Annual output assumed to be unchanged since 1978.

Source: FAO.

SAWNWOOD PRODUCTION

(FAO estimates, '000 cubic metres, incl. railway sleepers)

	1998	1999	2000
Total (all broadleaved)*	31	31	31

* Annual output assumed to be unchanged since 1978.

Source: FAO.

Fishing

(FAO estimates, metric tons, live weight)

	1998	1999	2000
Capture .	32,911	32,850	33,387
Groupers	4,000	4,000	4,000
Bogue .	2,500	2,500	2,500
Porgies and seabreams	4,000	4,000	4,000
Red mullet .	4,000	4,000	4,000
Jack and horse mackerels	3,000	3,000	3,000
Sardinellas .	7,000	7,000	7,000
Northern bluefin tuna	1,331	1,195	1,550
'Scomber' mackerels	3,000	3,000	3,000
Aquaculture .	100	100	100
Total catch (incl. others) .	33,011	32,950	34,487

Source: FAO, *Yearbook of Fishery Statistics*.

Mining

(estimates, '000 metric tons, unless otherwise indicated)

	1998	1999	2000
Crude petroleum ('000 barrels) .	540,000	520,000	538,000
Natural gas (million cu m)* .	12,600	12,400	12,000
Salt .	30	30	40
Gypsum (crude) .	150	150	175

* Figures refer to gross volume. The dry equivalent (estimates, million cubic metres) was: 6,360 in 1998; 6,200 in 1999; 6,100 in 2000.

Source: US Geological Survey.

Industry

SELECTED PRODUCTS
('000 metric tons, unless otherwise indicated)

	1996	1997	1998
Olive oil (crude)	7	9	10
Paper and paperboard . . .	6	6	6
Jet fuels*	1,423	1,339	1,339
Motor spirit (petrol)	1,957	1,970	1,970*
Naphthas	1,984	1,998	1,998*
Kerosene	259	274	274*
Gas-diesel (distillate fuel) oil . .	4,244	4,272	4,272*
Residual fuel oils*	4,799	4,834	4,834
Liquefied petroleum gas:			
from natural gas plants* . .	670	682	685
from petroleum refineries . .	250*	263	263*
Petroleum bitumen (asphalt) . .	103	106	106
Cement	3	3	3
Electric energy (million kWh) . .	18,300	18,974	19,496

* Provisional or estimated figure(s).

1999 ('000 metric tons): Olive oil (crude) 10; Paper and paperboard 6; Cement 3.

Source: UN, *Industrial Commodity Statistics Yearbook.*

Finance

CURRENCY AND EXCHANGE RATES

Monetary Units
  1,000 dirhams = 1 Libyan dinar (LD)

Sterling, Dollar and Euro Equivalents (31 November 2002)
  £1 sterling = 1.926 dinars
  US $1 = 1.241 dinars
  €1 = 1.231 dinars
  100 Libyan dinars = £51.92 = $80.58 = €81.17

Average Exchange Rate (US $ per Libyan dinar)
  1995   2.8894
  1996   2.7653
  1997   2.6210

Note: In March 1986 the value of the Libyan dinar was linked to the IMF's special drawing right (SDR). Between November 1994 and November 1998 the official mid-point exchange rate was SDR1 = 525 dirhams (LD1 = SDR 1.90476). In February 1999 a rate of LD1 = SDR 1.577 (SDR1 = 634.1 dirhams) was introduced, but from September 1999 to September 2000 the value of the dinar fluctuated. In September 2000 a new rate of LD1 = SDR 1.4204 (SDR1 = 704.03 dirhams) was established, but in June 2001 the Libyan dinar was devalued to SDR 1.224 (SDR1 = 816.99 dirhams). The latter rate remained in effect until the end of December 2001. In January 2002 the value of the Libyan dinar was adjusted to SDR 0.608 (SDR 1 = LD 1.64474): a devaluation of 50.3%.

BUDGET
(projections, LD million)

	1998*	1999
Total revenue	5,311	n.a.
Petroleum revenue	3,633	3,268
Total expenditure	5,311	4,900

* In December 1998 it was reported that petroleum revenue for the year was expected to be LD2,363 million, and that there would be an overall budget deficit of LD650 million.

INTERNATIONAL RESERVES
(US $ million at 31 December)

	2000	2001	2002
Gold*	194	194	194
IMF special drawing rights . .	538	554	610
Reserve position in IMF . . .	515	497	538
Foreign exchange	11,408	13,749	13,621
Total	12,655	14,994	14,963

* Valued at US $42 per troy ounce.

Source: IMF, *International Financial Statistics.*

MONEY SUPPLY
(LD million at 31 December)

	1999	2000	2001
Currency outside banks . . .	2,657.5	2,711.0	2,577.4
Private-sector deposits at Central			
Bank	133.7	200.8	297.8
Demand deposits at commercial			
banks	4,162.8	4,363.1	4,370.1
Total money (incl. others) . . .	7,001.2	7,313.5	7,402.7

Source: IMF, *International Financial Statistics.*

COST OF LIVING
(Consumer Price Index, excluding rent, for Tripoli; base: 1979 = 100)

	1982	1983	1984
Food	134.9	152.9	169.5
Clothing	141.1	150.6	169.4
All items (incl. others) . . .	137.6	152.2	165.8

Source: ILO, *Yearbook of Labour Statistics.*

NATIONAL ACCOUNTS
(LD million at current prices)

National Income and Product

	1983	1984	1985
Compensation of employees . .	2,763.1	2,865.8	2,996.2
Operating surplus	5,282.7	4,357.8	4,572.4
Domestic factor incomes . .	8,045.8	7,223.6	7,568.6
Consumption of fixed capital . .	436.1	457.5	481.6
Gross domestic product (GDP)			
at factor cost	8,481.9	7,681.1	8,050.2
Indirect taxes	470.0	462.2	389.0
Less Subsidies	146.7	130.0	162.2
GDP in purchasers' values . .	8,805.2	8,013.3	8,277.0
Factor income from abroad . .	200.2	142.8	122.5
Less Factor income paid abroad .	989.0	727.7	397.9
Gross national product . .	8,016.4	7,428.4	8,001.6
Less Consumption of fixed capital .	436.1	457.5	481.6
National income in market			
prices	7,580.3	6,970.9	7,520.0
Other current transfers from			
abroad	8.6	2.3	2.6
Less Other current transfers paid			
abroad	25.2	27.9	16.0
National disposable income . .	7,563.7	6,945.3	7,506.6

Source: UN, *National Accounts Statistics.*

Expenditure on the Gross Domestic Product

	1998	1999	2000
Government final consumption			
expenditure	3,339	3,102	3,616
Private final consumption			
expenditure	8,072	8,514	7,962
Increase in stocks	127	46	40
Gross fixed capital formation . .	1,397	1,536	2,281
Total domestic expenditure . .	12,935	13,198	13,899
Exports of goods and services . .	2,468	3,374	6,186
Less Imports of goods and services	2,661	2,433	2,690
GDP in purchasers' values . .	12,742	14,139	17,395

Source: IMF, *International Financial Statistics.*

Gross Domestic Product by Economic Activity
(estimates)

	1994	1995	1996
Agriculture, forestry and fishing .	601.5	680.5	782.5
Mining and quarrying . . .	2,728.5	2,840.0	3,036.5
Petroleum and natural gas . .	2,559.5	2,675.0	2,822.0
Manufacturing	865.5	980.0	1,107.0
Electricity, gas and water . . .	191.0	213.5	240.5
Construction	604.5	580.5	797.0
Trade, restaurants and hotels . .	1,100.0	1,190.5	1,345.5
Transport, storage and			
communications	846.0	925.5	1,025.5
Finance, insurance and real estate*	641.5	686.5	739.5
Public services	2,048.5	2,143.0	2,247.5
Other services	286.5	352.5	461.0
Total	9,913.5	10,592.5	11,782.5

* Including imputed rents of owner-occupied dwellings.

BALANCE OF PAYMENTS
(US $ million)

	1997	1998	1999
Exports of goods f.o.b.	9,876	6,328	6,758
Imports of goods f.o.b.	−7,160	−5,857	−3,996
Trade balance	2,716	471	2,762
Exports of services	33	47	55
Imports of services	−920	−1,016	−918
Balance on goods and services.	1,829	−498	1,899
Other income received . . .	640	633	507
Other income paid	−354	−259	−218
Balance on goods, services and			
income	2,115	−124	2,187
Current transfers received . . .	4	5	6
Current transfers paid . . .	−244	−272	−210
Current balance	1,875	−391	1,984
Direct investment abroad . . .	−282	−304	−210
Direct investment from abroad. .	−82	−152	−119
Portfolio investment assets . . .	−774	−212	−3
Other investment assets . . .	−1,040	−164	−293
Other investment liabilities . .	1,294	277	−346
Net errors and omissions . . .	878	432	−372
Overall balance	1,869	−513	641

Source: IMF, *International Financial Statistics*.

External Trade

PRINCIPAL COMMODITIES
(distribution by SITC, US $ million, excl. military goods)

Imports c.i.f.	1997
Food and live animals	1,119.4
Cereals and cereal preparations	519.9
Meal and flour of wheat and meslin	185.0
Chemicals and related products	417.9
Basic manufactures	1,126.2
Textile yarn, fabrics, etc.	170.9
Iron and steel	398.2
Tubes, pipes and fittings	314.1
Machinery and transport equipment	2,012.4
Machinery specialized for particular industries . . .	251.6
General industrial machinery, equipment and parts . . .	554.8
Electrical machinery, apparatus, etc.	462.2
Road vehicles and parts*	562.4
Passenger motor cars (excl. buses)	314.8
Miscellaneous manufactured articles	658.5
Clothing and accessories (excl. footwear)	223.6
Total (incl. others)	5,592.9

* Data on parts exclude tyres, engines and electrical parts.

Exports f.o.b.	1997
Mineral fuels, lubricants, etc.	8,557.4
Petroleum, petroleum products, etc.	8,386.7
Crude petroleum oils, etc.	6,897.5
Refined petroleum products.	1,489.2
Gasoline and other light oils	282.3
Residual fuel oils	1,206.9
Chemicals and related products	294.2
Total (incl. others)	9,028.7

Source: UN, *International Trade Statistics Yearbook*.

PRINCIPAL TRADING PARTNERS
(US $ million)*

Imports c.i.f.	1997	1999†
Australia	89.0	27.6
Austria	51.2	44.9
Belgium‡	101.1	68.1
Canada	150.5	54.5
China, People's Republic	86.9	86.5
Egypt	129.0	69.2
France (incl. Monaco)	345.5	227.6
Germany	717.8	599.3
Greece	69.8	38.3
Ireland	75.7	14.7
Italy	882.2	755.9
Japan	455.3	203.3
Korea, Republic	168.6	321.9
Malta	63.9	66.4
Morocco	117.0	115.8
Netherlands	141.7	81.8
Spain	148.6	115.9
Sweden	94.0	62.7
Switzerland-Liechtenstein	219.3	170.8
Tunisia	220.5	141.6
Turkey	164.4	27.1
United Kingdom	436.3	265.9
USA	78.7	84.0
Total (incl. others)	5,592.9	4,140.4

Exports f.o.b.	1997	1999†
Austria	466.0	87.0
Egypt	84.7	94.1
France (incl. Monaco)	411.2	509.8
Germany	1,353.3	1,507.1
Greece	256.9	186.1
Italy	3,267.6	2,987.0
Netherlands	77.4	81.8
Portugal	127.2	20.6
Spain	825.6	1,084.5
Switzerland-Liechtenstein	393.6	105.2
Tunisia	384.7	320.6
Turkey	508.9	5.7
United Kingdom	202.0	104.4
Viet Nam	—	449.1
Yugoslavia	171.6	14.4
Total (incl. others)	9,028.7	7,905.1

* Imports by country of origin; exports by country of destination. Figures exclude trade in gold.

† Figures for 1998 are not available.

‡ Figures for 1997 include trade with Luxembourg.

Source: UN, *International Trade Statistics Yearbook*.

Transport

ROAD TRAFFIC
(motor vehicles in use at 31 December)

	1995	1996
Passenger cars	794,525	809,514
Buses and coaches	1,424	1,490
Goods vehicles	342,918	356,038
Motorcycles and mopeds	1,078	1,112

Source: IRF, *World Road Statistics*.

SHIPPING
Merchant Fleet
(registered at 31 December)

	1999	2000	2001
Number of vessels	142	142	140
Total displacement ('000 grt) . .	438.9	433.7	250.8

Source: Lloyd's Register-Fairplay, *World Fleet Statistics.*

International Sea-borne Freight Traffic
(estimates, '000 metric tons)

	1991	1992	1993
Goods loaded	57,243	59,894	62,491
Goods unloaded	7,630	7,710	7,808

Source: UN Economic Commission for Africa, *African Statistical Yearbook.*

CIVIL AVIATION
(traffic on scheduled services)

	1996	1997	1998
Kilometres flown (million) . . .	4	4	4
Passengers carried ('000) . . .	639	571	571
Passenger-km (million)	412	377	377
Total ton-km (million)	33	30	27

Source: UN, *Statistical Yearbook.*

Tourism
VISITOR ARRIVALS BY COUNTRY OF ORIGIN*

	1998	1999	2000
Algeria.	30,776	39,193	85,181
Egypt	336,325	374,388	372,914
Morocco	20,108	24,350	23,088
Tunisia	404,716	428,871	400,843
Total (incl. others)	850,292	965,307	962,559

* Including same-day visitors (excursionists).

Source: World Tourism Organization, *Yearbook of Tourism Statistics.*

Tourism Receipts (US $ million): 18 in 1998; 28 in 1999 (Source: World Tourism Organization).

Communications Media

	1999	2000	2001
Telephones ('000 main lines in use)	550	605	610
Mobile cellular telephones ('000 subscribers).	30	40	50
Internet users ('000).	7	10	20

1994: Book production (titles) 26.

1996: Daily newspapers 4 (estimated average circulation 71,000).

1997: Radio receivers ('000 in use) 1,350; Television receivers ('000 in use) 730.

Sources: UNESCO, *Statistical Yearbook*; International Telecommunication Union.

Education
(1995/96, unless otherwise indicated)

	Institutions	Teachers	Students
Primary and preparatory: general	2,733*	122,020	1,333,679
Primary and preparatory: vocational . . .	168	n.a.	22,490
Secondary: general . . .	n.a.	17,668	170,573
Secondary: teacher training.	n.a.	2,760†	23,919
Secondary: vocational . .	312	n.a.	109,074
Universities	13	n.a.	126,348

* 1993/94.
† 1992/93.

Source: partly UNESCO, *Statistical Yearbook.*

Adult literacy rate (UNESCO estimates): 80.0.% (Males 90.8%; Females 68.2%) in 2000 (Source: UNDP, *Human Development Report*).

Directory

The Constitution

The Libyan Arab People, meeting in the General People's Congress in Sebha from 2–28 March 1977, proclaimed its adherence to freedom and its readiness to defend it on its own land and anywhere else in the world. It also announced its adherence to socialism and its commitment to achieving total Arab Unity; its adherence to the moral human values; and confirmed the march of the revolution led by Col Muammar al-Qaddafi, the Revolutionary Leader, towards complete People's Authority.

The Libyan Arab People announced the following:

(i) The official name of Libya is henceforth The Socialist People's Libyan Arab Jamahiriya.

(ii) The Holy Koran is the social code in The Socialist People's Libyan Arab Jamahiriya.

(iii) The Direct People's Authority is the basis for the political order in The Socialist People's Libyan Arab Jamahiriya. The People shall practise its authority through People's Congresses, Popular Committees, Trade Unions, Vocational Syndicates, and The General People's Congress, in the presence of the law.

(iv) The defence of our homeland is the responsibility of every citizen. The whole people shall be trained militarily and armed by general military training, the preparation of which shall be specified by the law.

The General People's Congress in its extraordinary session held in Sebha issued four decrees:

The first decree announced the establishment of The People's Authority in compliance with the resolutions and recommendations of the People's Congresses and Trade Unions.

The second decree stipulated the choice of Col Muammar al-Qaddafi, the Revolutionary Leader, as Secretary-General of the General People's Congress.

The third decree stipulated the formation of the General Secretariat of the General People's Congress (see The Government, below).

The fourth decree stipulated the formation of the General People's Committee to carry out the tasks of the various former ministries (see The Government, below).

In 1986 it was announced that the country's official name was to be The Great Socialist People's Libyan Arab Jamahiriya.

The Government

HEAD OF STATE*

Revolutionary Leader: Col MUAMMAR AL-QADDAFI (took office as Chairman of the Revolution Command Council 8 September 1969).

Second-in-Command: Maj. ABD AS-SALAM JALLOUD.
* Qaddafi himself rejects this nomenclature and all other titles.

GENERAL SECRETARIAT OF THE GENERAL PEOPLE'S CONGRESS
(April 2003)

Secretary: MUHAMMAD AZ-ZANATI.

Assistant Secretary for Popular Congresses: AHMAD MUHAMMAD IBRAHIM.

Assistant Secretary for Popular Committees: Dr ABD AL-KADER MUHAMMAD AL-BAGHDADI.

Secretary for Culture and Mass Mobilization: ABD AL-HAMID AS-SID ZINTANI.

Secretary for Trade Unions, Leagues and Professional Unions: ABDALLAH IDRIS IBRAHIM.

Secretary for Social Affairs: SALIMA SHAIBAN ABD AL-JABAR.

Secretary for Infrastructure, Urban Planning and Environment: Dr SALIM AHMAD FUNAYT.

Secretary for Human Resources: Dr AL-BAGHDADI ALI AL-MAHMOUDI.

Secretary for Foreign Affairs: SULEIMAN SASI ASH-SHAHUMI.

Secretary for Economy: ABD AS-SALAM AHMAD NUWEIR.

Secretary for Legal Affairs and Human Rights: MUHAMMAD ABDALLAH AL-HARARI.

Secretary for Security Affairs: MUFTAH ABD AS-SALAM BUKAR.

GENERAL PEOPLE'S COMMITTEE
(April 2003)

Secretary: MOHANDIS MUBARAK ABDALLAH ASH-SHAMIKH.

Deputy Secretary: ABDALLAH SALEM AL-BADRI.

Secretary for Justice and Public Security: MUHAMMAD ALI AL-MUSRATI.

Secretary for Finance: AL-UJAYLI ABD AS-SALAM BURAYNI.

Secretary for Foreign Liaison and International Co-operation: ABD AR-RAHMAN MUHAMMAD SHALGAM.

Secretary for African Unity: Dr ALI ABD AS-SALAM AT-TURAYKI.

Secretary for the Economy and Trade: SHUKRI MUHAMMAD GHANEM.

Secretary for Infrastructure, Urban Planning and Environment: HUTAYWISH FARAJ AL-HUTAYWISH.

Deputy Secretary for Production: AL-BAGHDADI ALI AL-MAHMOUDI.

Deputy Secretary for Services: AMMAR MABRUK AL-LUTAYYIF.

Legislature

GENERAL PEOPLE'S CONGRESS

The Senate and House of Representatives were dissolved after the *coup d'état* of September 1969, and the provisional Constitution issued in December 1969 made no mention of elections or a return to parliamentary procedure. However, in January 1971 Col Qaddafi announced that a new legislature would be appointed, not elected; no date was mentioned. All political parties other than the Arab Socialist Union were banned. In November 1975 provision was made for the creation of the 1,112-member General National Congress of the Arab Socialist Union, which met officially in January 1976. This later became the General People's Congress (GPC), which met for the first time in November 1976 and in March 1977 began introducing the wide-ranging changes outlined in the Constitution (above).

Secretary-General: ABD AR-RAZIQ SAWSA.

Political Organizations

In June 1971 the Arab Socialist Union (ASU) was established as the country's sole authorized political party. The General National Congress of the ASU held its first session in January 1976 and later became the General People's Congress (see Legislature, above).

The following groups are in opposition to the Government:

Ansarollah Group: f. 1996.

Fighting Islamic Group: claimed responsibility for subversive activities in early 1996; seeks to establish an Islamic regime.

Islamic Martyrs' Movement (IMM): Spokesman ABDALLAH AHMAD.

Libyan Baathist Party.

Libyan Change and Reform Movement: breakaway group from NFSL.

Libyan Conservatives' Party: f. 1996.

Libyan Constitutional Grouping.

Libyan Democratic Movement: f. 1977; external group.

Libyan Democratic Authority: f. 1993.

Libyan Democratic Conference: f. 1992.

Libyan Movement for Change and Reform: f. 1994; based in London, United Kingdom.

Libyan National Alliance: f. 1980; in Cairo, Egypt.

Libyan National Democratic Rally.

Movement of Patriotic Libyans: f. 1997.

National Front for the Salvation of Libya (NFSL): e-mail visitor@nfsl-libya.com; internet www.nfsl-libya.com; f. 1981 in Khartoum, Sudan; aims to replace the existing regime by a democratically-elected govt; Leader MUHAMMAD MEGARIEF.

Diplomatic Representation

EMBASSIES IN LIBYA

Afghanistan: POB 4245, Sharia Mozhar al-Aftes, Tripoli; tel. (21) 75192; fax (21) 609876; Ambassador (vacant).

Algeria: Sharia Kairauan 12, Tripoli; tel. (21) 4440025; fax (21) 3334631; Ambassador MUHAMMAD KAMAL REZAG BARA.

Argentina: POB 932, Gargaresh, Madina Syahia, Tripoli; tel. (21) 4834956; fax (21) 4836399; e-mail embartrip@hotmail.com; Ambassador MANUEL A. FERNÁNDEZ SALORIO.

Armenia: Tripoli.

Austria: POB 3207, Sharia Khalid ibn al-Walid, Garden City, Tripoli; tel. (21) 4443379; fax (21) 4440838; e-mail austroamb_tripolis@hotmail.com; Ambassador Dr ROBERT KARAS.

Bangladesh: POB 5086, Hadaba al-Khadra, Villa Omran al-Wershafani, Tripoli; tel. (21) 900856; fax (21) 4906616; Ambassador M. SHAFIULLAH.

Belgium: Tower 4, Floor 5, That el-Imad, Tripoli; tel. (21) 3350117; fax (21) 3350118; Ambassador JACQUES SCAVEE.

Benin: POB 6676 254 rue Oumaween, Cité EC Analous, Tripoli; tel. (21) 830990; fax (21) 834569; Ambassador LAFIA CHABI.

Bosnia and Herzegovina: POB 84373, Sharia ben Ashour, Tripoli; tel. and fax (21) 602162; Ambassador MUHAMMAD KUPOSOVIĆ.

Brazil: POB 2270, Sharia ben Ashour, Tripoli; tel. (21) 3614894; fax (21) 3614895; e-mail brcastripoli@Ittnet.net; Ambassador JOAQUIM PALMEIRO.

Bulgaria: POB 2945, Sharia Talha ben Abdullah 5-7, Tripoli; tel. (21) 3609988; fax (21) 3609990; e-mail bulem_lib@hotmail.com; Ambassador LYUDMIL SPASOV.

Burkina Faso: POB 81902, Tripoli; tel. (21) 71221; fax (21) 72626; Ambassador YOUSSOUF SANGARE.

Burundi: POB 2817, Sharia Ras Hassan, Tripoli; tel. (21) 608848; Ambassador ZACHARIE BANYIYEZAKO.

Canada: Tripoli; Chargé d'affaires a.i. GEORGE JACOBY.

Chad: POB 1078, Sharia Muhammad Mussadeq 25, Tripoli; tel. (21) 4443955; Ambassador IBRAHIM MAHAMAT TIDEI.

China, People's Republic: POB 5329, Andalous, Gargaresh, Tripoli; tel. (21) 830860; Ambassador LUO XINGWU.

Cuba: POB 83738, Andalous, Gargaresh, Tripoli; tel. (21) 71346; Ambassador RAÚL RODRÍGUEZ RAMOS.

Cyprus: POB 3284, Sharia Ad-Dhul 60, Ben Ashour, Tripoli; tel. (21) 3600499; fax (21) 3613516; Ambassador ARGYROS ANTONIOU.

Czech Republic: POB 1097, Sharia Ahmad Lutfi Sayed, Sharia ben Ashour, Tripoli; tel. (21) 3615436; fax (21) 3615437; e-mail tripoli@embassy.mzv.cz; Ambassador PAVEL ŘEZÁČ.

Egypt: The Grand Hotel, Tripoli; tel. (21) 605500; fax (21) 4445959; Ambassador HANY KHALLAF.

Equatorial Guinea: Tripoli.

Eritrea: Tripoli; Ambassador UTHMAN MUHAMMAD UMAR.

Finland: POB 2508, Tripoli; tel. and fax (21) 4831132; Chargé d'affaires ULLA-MAIJA SUOMINEN.

France: POB 312, Sharia Beni al-Amar, Hay Andalous, Tripoli; tel. (21) 4774 891; fax (21) 4778266; internet ambafrance-ly.org; Ambassador JEAN-JACQUES BEAUSSOU.

Germany: POB 302, Sharia Hassan al-Mashai, Tripoli; tel. (21) 3330554; fax (21) 4448968; e-mail germanembassytrip@web.de; Ambassador DIETMAR GREINEDER.

Ghana: POB 4169, Andalous 21/A, nr Funduk-Shati, Tripoli; tel. (21) 4773379; fax (21) 4773557; e-mail ghaemb@bsisp.net; Ambassador GEORGE KUMI.

Greece: POB 5147, Sharia Jalal Bayar 18, Tripoli; tel. (21) 3338563; fax (21) 3336689; e-mail grembtri@hotmail.com; Ambassador Dr PANAYOTIS THEODORACOPOULOS.

Guinea: POB 10657, Andalous, Tripoli; tel. (21) 4772793; fax (21) 4773441; e-mail magatte@lttnet.net; Ambassador EL H. ABOUBACAR DIONE.

Holy See: Tripoli; Apostolic Nuncio Most Rev. LUIGI CONTI (Titular Archbishop of Gratiana (resident in Malta)).

Hungary: POB 4010, Sharia Talha ben Abdullah, Tripoli; tel. (21) 605799; Chargé d'affaires FERENC CSILLAG.

India: POB 3150, 16 Sharia Mahmud Shaltut, Tripoli; tel. (21) 4441835; fax (21) 3337560; e-mail indemtrip@mail.link.net.mt; Ambassador APPUNNI RAMESH.

Iran: Tripoli; e-mail iran_em_tripoli@hotmail.com; Ambassador MUHAMMAD MENHAJ.

Iraq: POB 974, Sharia Karji, Tripoli; tel. (21) 4778195; fax (21) 4778196; Ambassador ANWAAR MAWOLOD THEBAN.

Italy: POB 912, Sharia Vahran 1, Tripoli; tel. (21) 3334133; fax (21) 3331673; e-mail ambasciate.tripoli@esteri.it; Ambassador CLAUDIO PACIFICO.

Japan: Tower 4, That al-Imad Complex, Sharia Organization of African Unity, Tripoli; tel. (21) 607463; fax (21) 607462; Ambassador AKIRA WATANABE.

Korea, Democratic People's Republic: Tripoli; Ambassador CHOE IN SOP.

Korea, Republic: POB 4781, Gargaresh, Tripoli; tel. (21) 4831322; fax (21) 4831324; Ambassador HUH BANG-BIN.

Kuwait: POB 2225, Beit al-Mal Beach, Tripoli; tel. (21) 4440281; fax (21) 607053; Chargé d'affaires KHALED MOTLAQ AD-DUWAILA.

Lebanon: POB 927, Sharia Omar bin Yasser Hadaek 20, Tripoli; tel. (21) 3333733; Ambassador MOUNIR KHOREISH.

Malaysia: POB 6309, Hai Andalus, Tripoli; tel. (21) 4830854; fax (21) 4831496; e-mail mwtripoli@lttnet.net; Ambassador: Datuk SHAPII BIN ABU SAMAH.

Mali: Sharia Jaraba Saniet Zarrouk, Tripoli; tel. (21) 4444924; Ambassador EL BEKAYE SIDI MOCTAR KOUNTA.

Malta: POB 2534, Sharia Ubei ben Ka'ab, Tripoli; tel. (21) 3611181; fax (21) 3611180; e-mail rvellalaurenti@yahoo.com; Ambassador Dr RICHARD VELLA LAURENTI.

Mauritania: Sharia Eysa Wokwak, Tripoli; tel. (21) 4443223; Ambassador YAHIA MUHAMMAD EL-HADI.

Morocco: POB 908, Sharia ben Ashour, Tripoli; tel. (21) 600110; fax (21) 4445757; Ambassador DRISS ALAOUI.

Netherlands: POB 3801, Sharia Jalal Bayar 20, Tripoli; tel. (21) 4441549; fax (21) 4440386; Ambassador JAN-JAAP VAN DE VELDE.

Nicaragua: Tripoli; Ambassador GUILLERMO ESPINOSA.

Niger: POB 2251, Fachloun Area, Tripoli; tel. (21) 4443104; Ambassador KARIM ALIO.

Nigeria: POB 4417, Sharia Bashir al-Ibrahim, Tripoli; tel. (21) 4443038; Ambassador Prof. DANDATTI ABD AL-KADIR.

Pakistan: POB 2169, Sharia Abdul Karim al-Khattabi 16, Maidan al-Qadasia, Tripoli; tel. (21) 4440072; fax (21) 4444698; Ambassador KHAWAR RASHID PIRZADA.

Philippines: POB 12508, Andalous, Gargaresh, Tripoli; tel. and fax (21) 4833966; Ambassador MUKHTAR M. MUALLAM.

Poland: POB 519, Sharia ben Ashour 61, Tripoli; tel. (21) 3615972; fax (21) 3615199; Ambassador Dr WITOLD JURASZ.

Qatar: POB 3506, Sharia ben Ashour, Tripoli; tel. (21) 4446660; Chargé d'affaires HASAN AHMAD ABU HINDI.

Romania: POB 5085, Sharia Ahmad Lotfi Sayed, Sharia ben Ashour, Tripoli; tel. (21) 3615295; fax (21) 3607597; e-mail ambaromatrip@hotmail.com; Chargé d'affaires a.i. MIRCEA HAS.

Russia: POB 4792, Sharia Mustapha Kamel, Tripoli; tel. (21) 3330545; fax (21) 4446673; Ambassador ALEKSEI B. PODTSEROB.

Rwanda: POB 6677, Villa Ibrahim Musbah Missalati, Andalous, Tripoli; tel. (21) 72864; fax (21) 70317; Chargé d'affaires CHRISTOPHE HABIMANA.

Saudi Arabia: Sharia Kairauan 2, Tripoli; tel. (21) 30485; Chargé d'affaires MUHAMMAD HASSAN BANDAH.

Serbia and Montenegro: POB 1087, Sharia Turkia 14–16, Tripoli; tel. (21) 3330819; fax (21) 3334114; e-mail yuambtripoli@yahoo.com; Ambassador Dr VASILIJE ILIC.

Sierra Leone: Tripoli; Ambassador el Hadj MOHAMMED SAMURA.

Slovakia: POB 5721, 3km, Hay al-Andalus, Gergarsh, Tripoli; tel. (21) 4781388; fax (21) 4781387; e-mail slovembtrp@mwc.ly; Ambassador JÁN BÓRY.

Spain: POB 2302, Sharia el-Amir Abd al-Kader al-Jazairi 36, Tripoli; tel. (21) 3336797; fax (21) 4443743; Ambassador PABLO BENAVIDES ORGAZ.

Sudan: POB 1076, Sharia Gargarish, Tripoli; tel. (21) 4775387; fax (21) 4774781; e-mail sudtripoli@hotmail.com; Ambassador OSMAN M. O. DIRAR.

Switzerland: POB 439, Sharia ben Ashour, Tripoli; tel. (21) 3614118; fax (21) 3614238; Ambassador PAUL KOLLER.

Syria: POB 4219, Sharia Muhammad Rashid Reda 4, Tripoli (Relations Office); tel. (21) 3331783; Head MUNIR BORKHAN.

Togo: POB 3420, Sharia Khaled ibn al-Walid, Tripoli; tel. (21) 4447551; fax (21) 3332423; Ambassador TCHAO SOTOU BERE.

Tunisia: POB 613, Sharia Bashir al-Ibrahim, Tripoli; tel. (21) 3331051; fax (21) 4447600; High Representative MANSOUR EZZEDDINE.

Turkey: POB 947, Sharia Zaviya Dahmani, Tripoli; tel. (21) 3337717; fax (21) 3337686; e-mail trablus.be@mfa.gov.tr; Ambassador RIZA ERKMENOĞLU.

Uganda: POB 80215, Sharia ben Ashour, Tripoli; tel. (21) 604471; fax (21) 4831602; Ambassador WILLIAM N. HAKIZA.

Ukraine: POB 4555, Sharia ben Ashour, Ares, Tripoli; tel. (21) 3608665.

United Kingdom: POB 4206, Tripoli; tel. (21) 3343630; fax (21) 3343634; e-mail belibya@hotmail.com; internet www .britain-in-libya.org; Ambassador RICHARD DALTON (to January 2003).

Venezuela: POB 2584, Sharia ben Ashour, Jamaa al sagaa Bridge, Tripoli; tel. (21) 3600408; fax (21) 3600407; Ambassador JULIO CÉSAR PINEDA.

Viet Nam: POB 587, Sharia Talha ben Abdullah, Tripoli; tel. (21) 833704; fax (21) 830494; Ambassador DANG SAN.

Yemen: POB 4839, Sharia Ubei ben Ka'ab 36, Tripoli; tel. (21) 607472; Ambassador ALI AIDAROUS YAHYA.

Judicial System

The judicial system is composed, in order of seniority, of the Supreme Court, Courts of Appeal, and Courts of First Instance and Summary Courts.

All courts convene in open session, unless public morals or public order require a closed session; all judgments, however, are delivered in open session. Cases are heard in Arabic, with interpreters provided for aliens.

The courts apply the Libyan codes which include all the traditional branches of law, such as civil, commercial and penal codes, etc. Committees were formed in 1971 to examine Libyan law and ensure that it coincides with the rules of Islamic *Shari'a*. The proclamation of People's Authority in the Jamahiriya provides that the Holy Koran is the law of society.

Attorney-General: SALIM MUHAMMAD SALIM.

SUPREME COURT

The judgments of the Supreme Court are final. It is composed of the President and several Justices. Its judgments are issued by circuits of at least three Justices (the quorum is three). The Court hears appeals from the Courts of Appeal in civil, penal, administrative and civil status matters.

President: HUSSEIN MUKTAR AL-BUEISHI.

COURTS OF APPEAL

These courts settle appeals from Courts of First Instance; the quorum is three Justices. Each court of appeal has a court of assize.

COURTS OF FIRST INSTANCE AND SUMMARY COURTS

These courts are first-stage courts in the Jamahiriya, and the cases heard in them are heard by one judge. Appeals against summary judgments are heard by the appellate court attached to the court of first instance, whose quorum is three judges.

PEOPLE'S COURT

Established by order of the General People's Congress in March 1988.

President: ABD AR-RAZIQ ABU BAKR AS-SAWSA.

PEOPLE'S PROSECUTION BUREAU

Established by order of the General People's Congress in March 1988.

Secretary: MUHAMMAD ALI AL-MISURATI.

Religion

ISLAM

The vast majority of Libyan Arabs follow Sunni Muslim rites, although Col Qaddafi has rejected the Sunnah (i.e. the practice, course, way, manner or conduct of the Prophet Muhammad, as followed by Sunnis) as a basis for legislation.

Chief Mufti of Libya: Sheikh TAHIR AHMAD AZ-ZAWI.

CHRISTIANITY

The Roman Catholic Church

Libya comprises three Apostolic Vicariates and one Apostolic Prefecture. At 31 December 2000 there were an estimated 77,000 adherents in the country.

Apostolic Vicariate of Benghazi: POB 248, Benghazi; tel. (91) 9096563; fax (61) 9081599; Vicar Apostolic Mgr SYLVESTER CARMEL MAGRO (Titular Bishop of Saldae).

Apostolic Vicariate of Derna: c/o POB 248, Benghazi; Vicar Apostolic (vacant).

Apostolic Vicariate of Tripoli: POB 365, Dahra, Tripoli; tel. (21) 3331863; fax (21) 3334696; e-mail bishoptripolibya@hotmail.com; Vicar Apostolic Mgr GIOVANNI INNOCENZO MARTINELLI (Titular Bishop of Tabuda).

The Anglican Communion

Within the Episcopal Church in Jerusalem and the Middle East, Libya forms part of the diocese of Egypt (q.v.).

Other Christian Churches

The Coptic Orthodox Church is represented in Libya.

The Press

Newspapers and periodicals are published either by the Jamahiriya News Agency (JANA), by government secretariats, by the Press Service or by trade unions.

DAILIES

Ash-Shams: Tripoli; internet www.alshames.com.

Az-Zahf al-Akhdar (The Green March): POB 14373–6998, Tripoli; fax (21) 4772502; e-mail info@azzahfalakhder.com; internet www.azzahfalakhder.com; ideological journal of the Revolutionary Committees.

PERIODICALS

Al-Amal (Hope): POB 4845, Tripoli; internet alalmalmag.com; monthly; social, for children; published by the Press Service.

Ad-Daawa al-Islamia (Islamic Call): POB 2682, Sharia Sawani, km 5, Tripoli; tel. (21) 4800294; fax (21) 4800293; f. 1980; weekly (Wednesdays); Arabic, English, French; cultural; published by the World Islamic Call Society; Eds MUHAMMAD IMHEMED AL-BALOUSHI, ABDULAHI MUHAMMAD ABDUL-JALEEL.

Al-Fajr al-Jadid (The New Dawn): Press Building, Sharia al-Jamhariya, Tripoli; tel. (21) 3606393; fax (21) 3605728; internet www.alfajraljadeed.com; f. 1969; publ. by JANA; bi-monthly.

Economic Bulletin: POB 2303, Tripoli; tel. (21) 3337106; monthly; published by JANA.

Al-Jamahiriya: POB 4814, Tripoli; tel. (21) 4449294; internet www.aljamahiria.com; f. 1980; weekly; Arabic; political; published by revolutionary committees.

Al-Jarida ar-Rasmiya (The Official Newspaper): Tripoli; irregular; official state gazette.

Libyan Arab Republic Gazette: Secretariat of Justice, NA, Tripoli; weekly; English; published by the Secretariat of Justice.

Risalat al-Jihad (Holy War Letter): POB 2682, Tripoli; tel. (21) 3331021; f. 1983; monthly; Arabic, English, French; published by the World Islamic Call Society.

Scientific Bulletin: POB 2303, Tripoli; tel. (21) 3337106; monthly; published by JANA.

Ath-Thaqafa al-Arabiya (Arab Culture): POB 4587, Tripoli; f. 1973; weekly; cultural; circ. 25,000.

Al-Usbu ath-Thaqafi (The Cultural Week): POB 4845, Tripoli; weekly.

Al-Watan al-Arabi al-Kabir (The Greater Arab Homeland): Tripoli; f. 1987.

NEWS AGENCIES

Jamahiriya News Agency (JANA): POB 2303, Sharia al-Fateh, Tripoli; tel. (21) 3402606; fax (21) 3402624; e-mail mail@jamahiriyanews.com; internet www.jamahiriyanews.com; branches and correspondents throughout Libya and abroad; serves Libyan and foreign subscribers.

Foreign Bureaux

Informatsionnoye Telegrafnoye Agentstvo Rossii—Telegrafnoye Agentstvo Suverennykh Stran (ITAR—TASS) (Russia): Sharia Mustapha Kamel 10, Tripoli; Correspondent GEORG SHELENKOV.

ANSA (Italy) is also represented in Tripoli.

Publishers

Ad-Dar al-Arabia Lilkitab (Maison Arabe du Livre): POB 3185, Tripoli; tel. (21) 4447287; f. 1973 by Libya and Tunisia.

Al-Fatah University, General Administration of Libraries, Printing and Publications: POB 13543, Tripoli; tel. (21) 621988; f. 1955; academic books.

General Co for Publishing, Advertising and Distribution: POB 921, Sirte (Surt); tel. (54) 63170; fax (54) 62100; general, educational and academic books in Arabic and other languages; makes and distributes advertisements throughout Libya.

Broadcasting and Communications

TELECOMMUNICATIONS

General Directorate of Posts and Telecommunications: POB 81686, Tripoli; tel. (21) 3604101; fax (21) 3604102; Dir-Gen. ABU ZAID JUMA AL-MANSURI.

General Post and Telecommunications Co: POB 886, Sharia Zawia, Tripoli; tel. (21) 3600777; fax (21) 3609515; f. 1985; Chair. FARAJ AMARI.

BROADCASTING

Radio

Great Socialist People's Libyan Arab Jamahiriya Broadcasting Corporation: POB 9333, Tripoli; POB 119, al-Baida; tel. (21) 3332451; f. 1957; broadcasts in Arabic and English from Tripoli and Benghazi; from September 1971 special daily broadcasts to Gaza and other Israeli-occupied territories were begun.

Voice of Africa: POB 4677, Sharia al-Fateh, Tripoli; tel. (21) 4449209; fax (21) 4449875; f. 1973 as Voice of the Greater Arab Homeland; adopted current name in 1998; broadcasts in Arabic, French and English; transmissions in Swahili, Hausa, Fulani and Amharic scheduled to begin in 2000; Dir-Gen. ABDALLAH AL-MEGRI.

Television

People's Revolution Broadcasting TV: POB 333, Tripoli; f. 1968; broadcasts in Arabic; additional channels broadcast for limited hours in English, Italian and French; Dir YOUSUF DEBRI.

Finance

(cap. = capital; res = reserves; dep. = deposits; LD = Libyan dinars; m. = million; brs = branches)

BANKING

Central Bank

Central Bank of Libya: POB 1103, Sharia al-Malik Seoud, Tripoli; tel. (21) 3333591; fax (21) 4441488; internet www.cbl-ly.com; f. 1955 as National Bank of Libya, name changed to Bank of Libya 1963, to Central Bank of Libya 1977; bank of issue and central bank carrying govt accounts and operating exchange control; commercial operations transferred to National Commercial Bank 1970; Gov. and Chair. Dr TAHER E. JEHAIMI.

Other Banks

Ahli Bank: Jadu; f. 1998; private bank.

Gumhouria Bank: POB 396, Sharia Emhemed Megrief, Tripoli; tel. (21) 3333553; fax (21) 3339489; f. 1969 as successor to Barclays Bank International in Libya; known as Masraf al-Jumhuriya until March 1977; known as Jamahiriya Bank until December 2000; wholly-owned subsidiary of the Central Bank; throughout Libya; Chair. MUHAMMAD A. SHOKRI; 53 brs.

Libyan Arab Foreign Bank: POB 2542, Tower 2, Dat al-Imad Complex, Tripoli; tel. (21) 3350155; fax (21) 3350164; f. 1972; offshore bank wholly owned by Central Bank of Libya; cap. and res LD 275.2m., dep. LD 2,560.0m. (Dec. 2000); Chair. and Gen. Man. MUHAMMAD H. LAYAS.

National Commercial Bank SAL: POB 543, HO G.S.P.L.A.J., al-Baida; tel. (21) 3612267; fax (21) 3610306; f. 1970 to take over commercial banking division of Central Bank (then Bank of Libya) and brs of Aruba Bank and Istiklal Bank; wholly owned by Central Bank of Libya; cap. LD 35m., res LD 63.4m., dep. LD 1,545.6m. (Dec. 1998); Chair. and Gen. Man. BADER A. ABU AZIZA; 49 brs.

Sahara Bank SPI: POB 270, Sharia 1 September 10, Tripoli; tel. (21) 3339804; fax (21) 3337922; f. 1964 to take over br. of Banco di Sicilia; 82% owned by Central Bank of Libya; cap. LD 525,000, res LD 52.5m., dep. LD 488.4m. (March 1988); Chair. and Gen. Man. OMAR A. SHABOU; 20 brs.

Umma Bank SAL: POB 685, 1 Giaddat Omar el-Mokhtar, Tripoli; tel. (21) 3334031; fax (21) 3332505; e-mail ummabank@umma-bank.com; internet www.umma-bank.com; f. 1969 to take over brs of Banco di Roma; wholly owned by Central Bank of Libya; cap. LD 23m., res LD 25.3m., dep. LD 1,393.8m. (Dec. 2001); Chair. and Gen. Man. AYAD DAHAIM; 50 brs.

Wahda Bank: POB 452, Fadiel Abu Omar Sq., El-Berkha, Benghazi; tel. (61) 24709; fax (61) 3337592; f. 1970 to take over Bank of North Africa, Commercial Bank SAL, Nahda Arabia Bank, Société Africaine de Banque SAL, Kafila al-Ahly Bank; 87%-owned by Central Bank of Libya; cap. LD 36m., res LD 106.1m., dep. LD 1,553.3m. (Dec. 1999); Chair. and Gen. Man. Dr MUHAMMAD M. GHADBAN; 59 brs.

INSURANCE

Libya Insurance Co: POB 64, Sharia Jamal Abdul Nasser, Zawia; tel. (23) 629768; fax (23) 629490; f. 1964; merged with Al-Mukhtar Insurance Co in 1981; all classes of insurance; Man. BELAID ABU GHALIA.

Trade and Industry

There are state trade and industrial organizations responsible for the running of industries at all levels, which supervise production, distribution and sales. There are also central bodies responsible for the power generation industry, agriculture, land reclamation and transport.

GOVERNMENT AGENCY

Great Man-made River Authority (GMRA): Sharia Ben-Ghasir, Tripoli; tel. (21) 3600042; fax (21) 3619437; supervises construction of pipeline carrying water to the Libyan coast from beneath the Sahara desert, to provide irrigation for agricultural projects; Sec. for the Great Man-made River project ABD AL-MAJID AL-AOUD.

DEVELOPMENT ORGANIZATIONS

Arab Organization for Agricultural Development: POB 12898, Zohra, Tripoli; tel. and fax (21) 3619275; e-mail arabagri@lycos.com; responsible for agricultural development projects.

General National Organization for Industrialization: Sharia San'a, Tripoli; tel. (21) 3334995; f. 1970; a public org. responsible for the devt of industry.

Kufra and Sarir Authority: Council of Agricultural Development, Benghazi; f. 1972 to develop the Kufra oasis and Sarir area in southeast Libya.

CHAMBERS OF COMMERCE

Benghazi Chamber of Commerce, Trade, Industry and Agriculture: POB 208 and 1286, Benghazi; tel. (61) 95142; fax (61) 80761; f. 1956; Pres. Dr SADIQ M. BUSNAINA; Gen. Man. YOUSUF AL-JIAMI; 45,000 mems.

Tripoli Chamber of Commerce, Industry and Agriculture: POB 2321, Sharia Najed 6–8, Tripoli; tel. (21) 3336855; fax (21) 3332655; f. 1952; Pres. ABDALLAH AL-BARONE; Dir-Gen. RAMADAN A. ZEREG; 60,000 mems.

UTILITIES

Electricity

General Electricity Company of Libya: POB 668, Tripoli; Sec. of People's Cttee OMRAN IBRAHIM ABUKRAA.

STATE HYDROCARBONS COMPANIES

Until 1986 petroleum affairs in Libya were dealt with primarily by the Secretariat of the General People's Committee for Petroleum. This body was abolished in March 1986, and sole responsibility for the administration of the petroleum industry passed to the national companies which were already in existence. The Secretariat of the General People's Committee for Petroleum was re-established in March 1989 and incorporated into the new Secretariat for the General People's Committee for Energy in October 1992. This was dissolved in March 2000, and responsibility for local oil policy transferred to the National Oil Corporation, under the supervision of the General People's Committee. Since 1973 the Libyan Government has entered into participation agreements with some of the foreign oil companies (concession holders), and nationalized others. It has concluded 85%–15% production-sharing agreements with various oil companies.

National Oil Corporation (NOC): POB 2655, Tripoli; tel. (21) 4446180; fax (21) 3331390; e-mail info@noclibya.com; internet www.noclibya.com; f. 1970 to undertake joint ventures with foreign cos; to build and operate refineries, storage tanks, petrochemical facilities, pipelines and tankers; to take part in arranging specifications for local and imported petroleum products; to participate in general planning of oil installations in Libya; to market crude oil and petroleum and petrochemical products and to establish and operate oil terminals; from 2000 responsible for deciding local oil policy, under supervision of General People's Committee; Chair. Dr ABD AL-HAFID ZLITNI.

> **Oilinvest International:** Tripoli; wholly-owned subsidiary of the NOC; Chair. and Gen. Man. AHMAD ADB AL-KARIM AHMAD.

Agip North Africa and Middle East Ltd—Libyan Branch: POB 346, Tripoli; tel. and fax (21) 3335135; Sec. of People's Cttee A. M. CREUI.

Arabian Gulf Oil Co (AGOCO): POB 263, Benghazi; tel. (61) 28931; fax (21) 49031; Chair. F. SAID.

Az-Zawiyah Oil Refining Co: POB 15715, Zawia; tel. (23) 20125; fax (23) 605948; f. 1973; Gen. Man. H. LASOUD.

Brega Oil Marketing Co: POB 402, Sharia Bashir as-Saidawi, Tripoli; tel. (21) 4440830; f. 1971; Chair. Dr DOKALI B. AL-MEGHARIEF.

International Oil Investments Co: Tripoli; f. 1988, with initial capital of $500m. to acquire 'downstream' facilities abroad; Chair. MUHAMMAD AL-JAWAD.

National Drilling and Workover Co: POB 1454, 208 Sharia Omar Mukhtar, Tripoli; tel. (21) 3332411; f. 1986; Chair. IBRAHIM BAHI.

Ras Lanouf Oil and Gas Processing Co (RASCO): POB 1971, Ras Lanouf, Benghazi; tel. (21) 3605177; fax (21) 607924; f. 1978; Chair. MAHMUD ABDALLAH NAAS.

Sirte Oil Co: POB 385, Marsa el-Brega, Tripoli; tel. (21) 607261; fax (21) 601487; f. 1955 as Esso Standard Libya, taken over by Sirte Oil Co 1982; absorbed the National Petrochemicals Co in October 1990; exploration, production of crude oil, gas, and petrochemicals, liquefaction of natural gas; Chair. M. M. BENNIRAN.

Umm al-Jawaby Petroleum Co: POB 693, Tripoli; Chair. and Gen. Man. MUHAMMAD TENTTOUSH.

Waha Oil Co: POB 395, Tripoli; tel. (21) 3331116; fax (21) 3337169; Chair. SALEH M. KAABAR.

Zueitina Oil Co: POB 2134, Tripoli; tel. (21) 3338011; fax (21) 3339109; f. 1986; Chair. of Management Cttee M. Oun.

TRADE UNIONS

General Federation of Producers' Trade Unions: POB 734, Sharia Istanbul 2, Tripoli; tel. (21) 4446011; f. 1952; affiliated to ICFTU; Sec.-Gen. Bashir Ihwij; 17 trade unions with 700,000 mems.

General Union for Oil and Petrochemicals: Tripoli; Chair. Muhammad Mithnani.

Pan-African Federation of Petroleum Energy and Allied Workers: Tripoli; affiliated to the Organisation of African Trade Union Unity.

Transport

Department of Road Transport and Railways: POB 14527, Sharia Az-Zawiyah, Secretariat of Communications and Transport Bldg, Tripoli; tel. (21) 609011; fax (21) 605605; Dir-Gen. Projects and Research Muhammad Abu Zian.

RAILWAYS

There are, at present, no railways in Libya. In mid-1998, however, the Government invited bids for the construction of a 3,170 km-railway, comprising one branch, 2,178 km in length, running from north to south, and another, 992 km in length, running from east to west. The railway may eventually be linked to other North African rail networks.

ROADS

The most important road is the 1,822-km national coast road from the Tunisian to the Egyptian border, passing through Tripoli and Benghazi. It has a second link between Barce and Lamluda, 141 km long. Another national road runs from a point on the coastal road 120 km south of Misurata through Sebha to Ghat near the Algerian border (total length 1,250 km). There is a branch 247 km long running from Vaddan to Sirte (Surt). A 690-km road, connecting Tripoli and Sebha, and another 626 km long, from Ajdabiyah in the north to Kufra in the south-east, were opened in 1983. The Tripoli–Ghat section (941 km) of the third, 1,352-km-long national road was opened in September 1984. There is a road crossing the desert from Sebha to the frontiers of Chad and Niger.

In addition to the national highways, the west of Libya has about 1,200 km of paved and macadamized roads and the east about 500 km. All the towns and villages of Libya, including the desert oases, are accessible by motor vehicle. In 1996 Libya had 47,590 km of paved roads.

SHIPPING

The principal ports are Tripoli, Benghazi, Mersa Brega, Misurata and as-Sider. Zueitina, Ras Lanouf, Mersa Hariga, Mersa Brega and as-Sider are mainly oil ports. A pipeline connects the Zelten oilfields with Mersa Brega. Another pipeline joins the Sarir oilfield with Mersa Hariga, the port of Tobruk, and a pipeline from the Sarir field to Zueitina was opened in 1968. A port is being developed at Darnah. Libya also has the use of Tunisian port facilities at Sand Gabès, to alleviate congestion at Tripoli. At 31 December 2001 Libya's merchant fleet consisted of 140 vessels, with a combined displacement of 250,796 grt.

General National Maritime Transport Co: POB 80173, Sharia Ahmad Sharif 2, Tripoli; tel. (21) 3333155; fax (21) 6361664; f. 1971 to handle all projects dealing with maritime trade; Chair. Said Milud al-Ahrash.

CIVIL AVIATION

There are four international airports: Tripoli International Airport, situated at ben Gashir, 34 km (21 miles) from Tripoli; Benina Airport 19 km (12 miles) from Benghazi; Sebha Airport; and Misurata Airport. There are a further 10 regional airports. A US $800m. programme to improve the airport infrastructure and air traffic control network was approved in mid-2001.

Libyan Arab Airlines: POB 2555, ben Fernas Bldg, Sharia Haiti, Tripoli; tel. (21) 3617638; fax (21) 3614815; f. 1989 by merger of Jamahiriya Air Transport (which in 1983 took over operations of United African Airlines) and Libyan Arab Airlines (f. 1964 as Kingdom of Libya Airlines and renamed 1969); passenger and cargo services from Tripoli, Benghazi and Sebha to destinations in Europe, North Africa, the Middle East and Asia; domestic services throughout Libya; Chief Exec. Sabri Abdallah.

Tourism

The principal attractions for visitors to Libya are Tripoli, with its beaches and annual International Fair, the ancient Roman towns of Sabratha, Leptis Magna and Cyrene, and historic oases. There were 962,559 visitor arrivals in 2000; in 1999 receipts totalled some US $28m.

Department of Tourism and Fairs: POB 891, Sharia Omar Mukhtar, Tripoli; tel. (21) 3332255; fax (21) 4448385; Head of Fairs Muhammad Elgadi.

General Board of Tourism: POB 91871, Tripoli; tel. and fax (21) 503041; Chair. Muhammad Sealna.

LIECHTENSTEIN

Introductory Survey

Location, Climate, Language, Religion, Flag, Capital

The Principality of Liechtenstein is in central Europe. The country lies on the east bank of the Upper Rhine river, bordered by Switzerland to the west and south, and by Austria to the north and east. Liechtenstein has an Alpine climate, with mild winters. The average annual temperature is about 10°C, while average annual rainfall is about 1,000 mm. The official language is German, of which a dialect—Alemannish—is spoken. Almost all of the inhabitants profess Christianity, and about 78% are adherents of the Roman Catholic Church. The national flag (proportions 3 by 5) consists of two equal horizontal stripes, of royal blue and red, with a golden princely crown, outlined in black, in the upper hoist. The capital is Vaduz.

Recent History

Liechtenstein has been an independent state since 1719, except while under French domination briefly in the early 19th century. In 1919 Switzerland assumed responsibility for Liechtenstein's diplomatic representation, replacing Austria. In 1920 a postal union with Switzerland was agreed, and in 1924 a treaty was concluded with Switzerland whereby Liechtenstein was incorporated in a joint customs union. Franz Josef II succeeded as ruling Prince in 1938. In 1950 Liechtenstein became a party to the Statute of the International Court of Justice, and in 1978 it was admitted to the Council of Europe (see p. 181). Liechtenstein became a member of the UN in September 1990 (hitherto the country had been a member of some UN specialized agencies). In the following year Liechtenstein became a full member of the European Free Trade Association (EFTA, see p. 195).

After 42 years as the dominant party in government, the Fortschrittliche Bürgerpartei Liechtensteins (FBP—Progressive Citizens' Party of Liechtenstein) was defeated by the Vaterländische Union (VU—Patriotic Union) at a general election to the Landtag (parliament) in February 1970. Four years later the FBP regained its majority. At the general election to the Landtag in February 1978, the VU, led by Hans Brunhart, won eight of the 15 seats, although with a minority of the votes cast, while the remaining seats were taken by the FBP, led by Dr Walter Kieber, the Head of Government since March 1974. After protracted negotiations, Brunhart replaced Kieber in April 1978. At the general election in February 1982, the distribution of seats remained unchanged, although the VU gained a majority of votes. Following a referendum in July 1984, women were granted the right to vote on a national basis. However, women were still not permitted to vote on communal affairs in three of Liechtenstein's 11 communes until April 1986, when they were finally accorded full voting rights. (In 1992 an amendment to the Constitution took effect which declared equality between men and women.) In August 1984 Prince Franz Josef transferred executive power to his son, Prince Hans-Adam, although he remained titular Head of State until his death in November 1989, when he was succeeded by Hans-Adam (Hans-Adam II).

The composition of the Landtag remained unchanged following a general election in February 1986, when women voted for the first time in a national poll. In January 1989 the Landtag was dissolved by Prince Hans-Adam, following a dispute between the VU and the FBP regarding the construction of a new museum to accommodate the royal art collection. At the subsequent general election, which took place in March 1989, the number of seats in the Landtag was increased from 15 to 25; the VU retained its majority, securing 13 seats, while the FBP took the remaining 12 seats.

At the next general election, which took place in February 1993, the VU lost its majority, taking only 11 of the Landtag's 25 seats. The FBP again returned 12 representatives, and two seats were won by an environmentalist party, the Freie Liste (FL—Free List). Lengthy negotiations resulted in the formation of a new coalition between the FBP and the VU, in which the FBP was the dominant party, and Markus Büchel of the FBP became Head of Government. In September, however, following a unanimous vote in the Landtag expressing 'no confidence' in his leadership, Büchel was dismissed from his post, and Prince Hans-Adam dissolved the legislature. At a further general election, which was held in October, the VU regained its parliamentary majority, winning 13 seats, while the FBP took 11 seats and the FL secured one seat. The VU became the dominant party in a new coalition with the FBP, with Mario Frick of the VU as Head of Government.

In October 1992 almost 2,000 people demonstrated in Vaduz to protest against a threat by Prince Hans-Adam that he would dissolve the Landtag if deputies did not submit to his wish to hold a proposed referendum to endorse Liechtenstein's entry to the nascent European Economic Area (EEA) shortly in advance of a similar vote in Switzerland. The Prince believed that the outcome of the Swiss plebiscite might be prejudicial to that of the Liechtenstein vote, and that, in the event of voters' rejecting EEA membership at an early referendum, Liechtenstein might still be able to join other EFTA members in applying for admission to the European Community (EC—now European Union, EU, see p. 199). A compromise was reached, whereby the referendum was scheduled to take place shortly after the Swiss vote, while the Government agreed actively to promote a vote in favour of the EEA and to explore the possibility of applying to the EC should EEA membership be rejected. (The authorities subsequently decided that admission to the EU would not be beneficial to the Principality.) At the referendum in December, although Switzerland's voters had rejected accession to the EEA, Liechtenstein's membership was approved by 55.8% of those who voted (about 87% of the Principality's electorate); consequently, the two countries' joint customs union was renegotiated. In April 1995 a further national referendum was held, at which 55.9% of those who voted (around 82% of the electorate) approved the revised customs arrangements. Liechtenstein joined the EEA at the beginning of May.

In March 1996 the Landtag adopted a unanimous motion of loyalty in the hereditary monarchy, after Prince Hans-Adam offered to resign (following tension between the Prince and the legislature—see above). At the next general election, which took place in February 1997, the VU retained its majority with 13 seats, while the FBP secured 10 and the FL two seats. Frick remained Head of Government. In April the FBP withdrew from the ruling coalition, leaving a single party (the VU) to govern alone for the first time since 1938. The constitutional role of the ruling Prince came under renewed scrutiny in 1997, when, against the wishes of the Landtag, Prince Hans-Adam refused to reappoint Dr Herbert Wille, a senior judge who had advocated that constitutional issues should be decided by the Supreme Court rather than the Monarch. Dr Wille subsequently presented a formal complaint to the European Court of Human Rights, which ruled, in November 1999, that Prince Hans-Adam had restricted Wille's right to free speech; the Prince was required to pay 100,000 Swiss francs in costs.

In December 1999 Prince Hans-Adam II requested an Austrian prosecutor, Kurt Spitzer, to investigate allegations in the German press based on an unpublished report of April 1999 by the German secret service that international criminals were using financial institutions in Liechtenstein to 'launder' the proceeds of organized crime. As a result, five people were placed under investigative arrest in May 2000, including the brothers of both the Deputy Head of Government and of one of the principality's most senior judges; all five were later released without charge. In his final report, which was released at the end of August, Spitzer concluded that Liechtenstein was no more culpable of money-laundering than other countries in Europe. He blamed the current problems on the principality's over-bureaucratic and inefficient banking system and the poor application of existing legislation designed to combat economic crimes; criminal proceedings were initiated against two judges for abusing their authority. Spitzer also revealed that a money-laundering investigation was under way against Herbert Batliner, a prominent lawyer who had been implicated in the party-funding scandal involving Germany's former Chancellor, Helmut Kohl, and his party, the Christian Democratic Union, and in another case involving proceeds from drugs-trafficking in Colombia. In June the Financial Action Task Force on Money

Laundering (FATF), a commission of the Organisation for Economic Co-operation and Development (OECD, see p. 277) included Liechtenstein on a list of countries considered unco-operative in international attempts to combat money-laundering. In an effort to reverse some of the damage done to the country's international reputation, the Liechtenstein Bankers' Association announced in July that anonymous accounts would be abolished. In the same month the Government approved the establishment of a new financial investigative unit within the police force and measures to accelerate legal assistance to foreign countries in money-laundering investigations. Legislation was promulgated in December requiring financial institutions to maintain tighter controls over accounts and transactions, including the abolition of anonymous accounts. Liechtenstein was removed from the FATF's list of unco-operative countries in 2001, and, in October of that year, the Government appointed the former head of the Swiss anti-money-laundering authority, Daniel Thelesklaf, to administer a new financial surveillance unit, which was to enforce new regulations requiring banks and lawyers to be able to verify the identity of their clients. However, Liechtenstein was among seven jurisdictions identified on an OECD list as 'unco-operative tax havens' lacking financial transparency in April 2002, under its initiative to abolish 'harmful tax practices'. OECD urged these to amend their national financial legislation or face possible sanctions beginning in April 2003.

In the general election that took place on 9 and 11 February 2001 the VU lost its parliamentary majority, securing only 41.1% of the votes cast (11 of the 25 seats in the Landtag), while the FBP won 49.9% (13 seats) and the FL obtained 8.8% (one seat); voter participation was 86.7% of the electorate. The VU administration's popularity had been adversely affected by an unresolved dispute with Prince Hans-Adam over his demands for constitutional changes, notably with regard to appointments in the judiciary (the Prince advocated that judges be nominated by the reigning Monarch rather than by parliamentary deputies); the Prince claimed that these amendments would benefit the people, whilst the VU regarded them as an attempt to extend the royal prerogative. A new Government comprising solely the FBP, under the leadership of Otmar Hasler, took office on 5 April. The Prince had previously announced that if he failed to secure the support of the new Government for his proposed constitutional reforms, he would seek a national referendum; in December he also threatened to leave the Principality and take up residence in Vienna, Austria.

The issue of constitutional reform was finally resolved by a national referendum, held on 14 and 16 March 2003, in which the participation rate was 87.7%. Following an acrimonious campaign Prince Hans-Adam won an overwhelming majority of the votes cast, with 64.3% to 35.7% in favour of granting the Prince new powers. As a result of the referendum, the Prince gained the right to dismiss a government even if it retained parliamentary confidence, to appoint an interim administration pending elections, to preside over a panel to select judges, to veto laws by not signing them within a six-month period and to adopt emergency legislation. Conversely citizens could now force a referendum on any subject (including the future of the monarchy) by collecting a minimum of 1,500 signatures. A compromise proposal put forward by a cross-party group that included the former premier, Mario Frick (the Volksinitiative für Verfassungsfrieden—People's Initiative for Constitutional Peace), which suggested that a princely veto could be overruled by a referendum and sought to limit the Prince's use of emergency legislation to times of war, received the support of only 16.5% of the voters. The overwhelming support for the Prince's proposed changes was partially attributed to widespread fear that, if fulfilled, his threat of self-imposed exile as a symbolic monarch would cause economic decline and social upheaval. Prince Hans-Adam dismissed the findings of a commission established by the Council of Europe, which stated that the constitutional amendments would constitute a retrograde step for democracy and could lead to the isolation of Liechtenstein in Europe and indicated that he would begin to transfer power to his son, Alois.

Government

The Constitution of the hereditary Principality provides for a unicameral Landtag (parliament), comprising 25 members, who are elected by universal adult suffrage for a term of four years (subject to dissolution), on the basis of proportional representation. A five-member Government is nominated by the reigning Prince, on the recommendation of the Landtag, for four years. In

March 2003 constitutional changes were approved by a referendum which extended the powers of the monarch; he was empowered to dismiss governments (even if they retained parliamentary confidence), appoint an interim administration pending an election, approve judicial nominees, veto laws and invoke emergency legislation. Citizens could force an referendum on any subject, including the future of the monarchy, by collecting 1,500 signatures.

Defence

Although Liechtensteiners under the age of 60 years are liable to military service in an emergency, there has been no standing army since 1868 and there is only a small police force, with 63 members.

Economic Affairs

In 1997 Liechtenstein's gross national product (GNP) per head was estimated by the World Bank to be US $50,000, at average 1995–97 prices, ranking as the highest in the world at that time. During 1986–95 the population increased at an average annual rate of 1.4%. During 1990–99, it was estimated, GDP grew at an average annual rate of 1.6%; GDP increased by 4.5% in 1998 but declined by 0.9% in 1999.

Following the Second World War, the importance of agriculture declined in favour of industry. Within the agricultural sector the emphasis is on cattle-breeding, dairy-farming and market gardening. The principal crops are maize and potatoes. In addition, wine is produced, and forestry is a significant activity. In 1999 1.3% of those employed in Liechtenstein worked in agriculture (including forestry).

In 1999 45.2% of those employed in Liechtenstein worked in industrial activity (including mining and quarrying, processing industries, energy and water supply and construction). The metal, machinery and precision instruments industry is by far the most prominent sector. Other important areas are the pharmaceutical, textiles and ceramics industries.

In 1999 some 92.9% of energy requirements were imported from other countries. In that year natural gas supplied 24.2% of energy requirements, electricity 23.6%, fuel oil 23.5%, motor fuel (petrol) 19.2%, diesel 8.2% and firewood 1.2%.

In 1999 53.5% of those employed in Liechtenstein worked in the services sector. Financial services are of great importance. Numerous foreign corporations, holding companies and foundations (estimated to number about 75,000) have nominal offices in Liechtenstein, benefiting from the Principality's stable political situation, tradition of bank secrecy (although stricter banking legislation was introduced in 1997 and in 2000–02, partly to increase the transparency of the sector) and low fiscal charges. Such enterprises pay no tax on profit or income, contributing instead an annual levy on capital or net worth. These levies account for about 20% of the Principality's annual direct revenue. In 1980 Liechtenstein adopted legislation to increase controls on foreign firms, many of which were thereafter subject to audit and entered in the public register. Following the Principality's accession to the European Economic Area (EEA) in 1995, the registration of foreign banks was permitted. New legislation governing insurance companies was approved in 1996, and during the late 1990s the insurance sector expanded rapidly. The building and hotel trades and other service industries are also highly developed.

With a very limited domestic market, Liechtenstein's industry is export-orientated. In 1998 total exports amounted to 3,634.7m. Swiss francs (with imports totalling 1,240m. Swiss francs). Switzerland is the principal trading partner, receiving 12.7% of exports in 1998. In that year members of the European Union (EU, see p. 199) accounted for 37.8% of total exports. Specialized machinery, artificial teeth and other materials for dentistry, and frozen food are important exports. The sale of postage stamps, mainly to tourists, provided about 3.0% of the national income in 1997.

The 1998 budget envisaged a surplus of 14.7m. Swiss francs. The annual average rate of inflation increased from 1.9% in 1988 to 5.9% in 1991, decreasing again, to 0.5%, in 1997. Traditionally the unemployment rate has been negligible; in 1999 the rate of unemployment (as a percentage of those employed) was 1.2%. More than one-third of Liechtenstein's population are resident foreigners, many of whom provide the labour for industry, while in December 1999 9,741 workers crossed the borders from Austria and Switzerland each day to work in the Principality.

Liechtenstein has important economic links with neighbouring Switzerland. It is incorporated in a customs union with that country, and uses the Swiss franc as its currency. Liechtenstein became a member of the European Free Trade Association (EFTA, see p. 195) in May 1991, and the EEA in May 1995. The Principality is also a member of the European Bank for Reconstruction and Development (EBRD, see p. 193).

Education

Compulsory education begins at seven years of age. Basic instruction is given for five years at a primary school (Primarschule), after which a pupil may transfer to a lower secondary school (Oberschule) or secondary school (Realschule) for four years, or to the Liechtensteinisches Gymnasium (grammar school) for eight years. There is no university. Many Liechtensteiners continue their studies at universities in Austria and Switzerland. Liechtenstein has a further education college for the study of philosophy, a technical college (Fachhochschule), a music school, an art school, an adult education centre and a school for mentally disabled children. Government expenditure on education totalled 95m. Swiss francs in 1999 (15.1% of total expenditure).

Public Holidays

2003: 1 January (New Year's Day), 2 January (St Berchtold's Day), 6 January (Epiphany), 2 February (Candelmas), 4 March (Shrove Tuesday), 19 March (St Joseph's Day), 18 April (Good Friday), 21 April (Easter Monday), 1 May (Labour Day), 29 May (Ascension), 9 June (Whit Monday), 19 June (Corpus Christi), 15 August (Assumption and National Holiday), 8 September (Nativity of the Virgin Mary), 1 November (All Saints' Day), 8 December (Immaculate Conception), 25 December (Christmas), 26 December (St Stephen's Day).

2004: 1 January (New Year's Day), 2 January (St Berchtold's Day), 6 January (Epiphany), 2 February (Candelmas), 24 February (Shrove Tuesday), 19 March (St Joseph's Day), 9 April (Good Friday), 12 April (Easter Monday), 1 May (Labour Day), 20 May (Ascension Day), 31 May (Whit Monday), 10 June (Corpus Christi), 15 August (Assumption and National Holiday), 8 September (Nativity of the Virgin Mary), 1 November (All Saints' Day), 8 December (Immaculate Conception), 25 December (Christmas), 26 December (St Stephen's Day).

Weights and Measures

The metric system is in force.

Statistical Survey

Source: Presse- und Informationsamt, Regierungsgebäude, 9490 Vaduz; tel. (423) 2366271; fax (423) 2366460; e-mail presseamt@llv.li; internet www.presseamt.li.

AREA AND POPULATION

Area: 160.0 sq km (61.8 sq miles).

Population: 29,868 (incl. 11,432 resident aliens) at census of December 1992; 32,426 (incl. 11,112 resident aliens) at December 1999.

Density (December 1999): 202.7 per sq km.

Principal Towns (population at December 1999): Schaan 5,346; Vaduz (capital) 5,043; Triesen 4,292; Balzers 4,183; Eschen 3,661; Mauren 3,216; Triesenberg 2,505.

Births, Marriages and Deaths (1998): Live births 382 (11.9 per 1,000); Marriages 423 (13.2 per 1,000); Deaths 206 (6.4 per 1,000).

Employment (1999): Agriculture and forestry 327; Industry and skilled trades 11,450 (Mining and quarrying 51, Processing industries 9,125, Energy and water supply 174, Construction 2,100); Services 13,566 (Retail repairs etc. 2,314, Hotels and restaurants 777, Transport and communications 790, Banking and insurance 1,893, Real estate, business services etc. 1,996, Legal consultancy and trust management 1,497, Public administration 1,270, Education 722, Health and social services 1,202, Other services 1,105); Total 25,343.

HEALTH AND WELFARE

Key Indicators

Under-5 Mortality Rate (per 1,000 live births 2001): 11.

Physicians (per 1,000 head, 1997): 1.31 (Source: Statistik des Fürstentums Liechtenstein, *Statistisches Jahrbuch (1998)*).

For sources (unless specified) and definitions, see explanatory note on p. vi.

AGRICULTURE, ETC.

Principal Crops (metric tons, 1987): Wheat 460; Oats 4; Barley 416; Silo-maize 27,880; Potatoes 1,040.

Livestock (1999): Cattle 5,093; Pigs 2,122; Horses 354; Sheep 3,262; Goats 313.

Dairy Produce (1998): Total production 13,292 metric tons.

Forestry ('000 cubic metres, 1999): Roundwood removals (excl. bark) 13 (Sawlogs, veneer logs and logs for sleepers 9, Fuel wood 4). Source: FAO, *Yearbook of Forest Products*.

FINANCE

Currency and Exchange Rates: Swiss currency: 100 Rappen (centimes) = 1 Franken (Swiss franc). *Sterling, Dollar and Euro Equivalents* (31 December 2002): £1 sterling = 2.2352 Franken; US $1 = 1.3868 Franken; €1 = 1.4543 Franken; 100 Franken = £44.74 = $72.11 = €68.76. For average exchange rate, see chapter on Switzerland.

Budget (estimates, '000 Swiss francs, 1998): Revenue 615,069; Expenditure 600,332.

EXTERNAL TRADE

Total Imports (million Swiss francs, 1998): 1,240.

Exports by Destination (million Swiss francs, 1998): Switzerland 462.4; EU 1,799.0; Others 1,373.3; Total 3,634.7.

TRANSPORT

Road Traffic (registered motor vehicles, December 1999): Passenger cars 21,150; Commercial vehicles 2,428; Motorcycles 3,563.

TOURISM

Foreign Tourist Arrivals (at hotels and similar establishments): 59,228 in 1998; 59,502 in 1999; 61,550 in 2000 (Source: World Tourism Organization, *Yearbook of Tourism Statistics*).

Arrivals by Country of Residence (2000): Austria 2,724; France 1,870; Germany 23,233; Italy 2,351; Netherlands 1,488; Switzerland 13,626; United Kingdom 2,411; USA 3,817; Total (incl. others) 61,550 (Source: World Tourism Organization, *Yearbook of Tourism Statistics*).

COMMUNICATIONS MEDIA

Newspapers (1995): 3 (total circulation 10,450 copies).

Radio Receivers (1997): 12,382 in use.

Television Receivers (1997): 11,979 in use.

Telephones (2000): 20,072 main lines in use (Source: International Telecommunication Union).

Mobile Cellular Telephones (2000): 14,743 subscribers (Source: International Telecommunication Union).

EDUCATION

(1998/99)

Kindergarten: 56 schools; 60 teachers; 826 pupils.

Primary: 14 schools; 151 teachers; 2,053 pupils.

Lower secondary: 3 schools; 55 teachers; 433 pupils.

Secondary: 5 schools; 62 teachers; 705 pupils.

Grammar: 1 school; 48 teachers; 651 pupils.

Music: 1 school; 85 teachers; 2,281 pupils.

Directory

The Constitution

Under the Constitution of 5 October 1921, the monarchy is hereditary in the male line. The reigning Prince, who is constitutionally responsible for foreign affairs, exercises legislative power jointly with the Landtag (parliament). The Landtag comprises 25 members, who are elected for a term of four years (subject to dissolution) by universal adult suffrage, on a basis of proportional representation. Under the Constitution (as amended in 1969, 1984 and 2003), all citizens of over 20 years of age are eligible to vote. The voters participate directly in legislation through referendums.

In a referendum on 14 and 16 March 2003 the electorate approved constitutional amendments extending the powers of the monarch. He was awarded the right to dismiss governments (even if they retained parliamentary confidence), to appoint an interim administration pending fresh elections, to veto laws by not signing them within a six-month period, to dismiss individual ministers, subject to approval by members of the Landtag, to preside over a panel to select judges (with a casting vote) and to invoke emergency legislation. Citizens were accorded the right to force a referendum on any subject, including the future of the monarchy, by collecting 1,500 signatures.

In accordance with a treaty concluded with Switzerland in 1924, Liechtenstein is incorporated in Swiss customs territory, and uses Swiss currency, customs and postal administration.

The Government

HEAD OF STATE

Ruling Prince: Prince Hans-Adam II (Prince of Liechtenstein, Duke of Troppau and Jägerndorf, Count of Rietberg—succeeded 13 November 1989).

GOVERNMENT
(April 2003)

All members of the Government belong to the Fortschrittliche Bürgerpartei Liechtensteins (FBP).

Head of Government (also responsible for Central Government Affairs; Family and Equal Opportunities; Finance; Construction): Otmar Hasler.

Deputy Head of Government (also responsible for Education; Transport and Communications; Justice): Rita Kieber-Beck.

Government Councillors: Hansjörg Frick (Health; Social Affairs; Economy), Dr Alois Ospelt (Internal Affairs; Culture and Sports; Environment; Agriculture and Forestry), Dr Ernst Walch (Foreign Affairs).

GOVERNMENT OFFICES

Regierungsgebäude: 9490 Vaduz; tel. 2366111; fax 2366022.

Legislature

LANDTAG

President: Klaus Wanger (FBP).

Vice-President: Dr Peter Wolff (VU).

General Election, 9 and 11 February 2001

Party	% of votes	Seats
FBP (Progressive Citizens' Party of Liechtenstein)	49.9	13
VU (Patriotic Union)	41.1	11
FL (Free List)	8.8	1
Total	100.0*	25

* Including spoilt ballots.

Political Organizations

Fortschrittliche Bürgerpartei Liechtensteins (FBP) (Progressive Citizens' Party of Liechtenstein): Aeulestr. 56, Postfach 1213, 9490 Vaduz; tel. 2377940; fax 2377949; e-mail marcus.vogt@fbp.li; internet www.fbp.li; f. 1918; Chair. Johannes Matt; Sec. Marcus Vogt.

Freie Liste (FL) (Free List): Im Bretscha 4, Postfach 177, 9494 Schaan; e-mail fliste@lie-net.li; internet www.freieliste.li; f. 1985; progressive ecological party; Chair. Karin Jenni.

Vaterländische Union (VU) (Patriotic Union): Fürst-Franz-Josef-Str. 13, 9490 Vaduz; tel. 2320832; fax 2322632; internet www.vu-online.li; f. 1936 by merger of the People's Party (f. 1918) and the Heimatdienst movement; Chair. Oswald Kranz; Sec.-Gen. Jürgen Nigg.

Diplomatic Representation

According to an arrangement concluded in 1919, Switzerland has agreed to represent Liechtenstein's interests in countries where it has diplomatic missions and where Liechtenstein is not represented in its own right. In so doing, Switzerland always acts only on the basis of mandates of a general or specific nature, which it may either refuse or accept, while Liechtenstein is free to enter into direct relations with foreign states or to establish its own additional missions. Liechtenstein has an embassy in Bern (Switzerland), a non-resident ambassador to Austria and a non-resident ambassador to the Holy See, as well as a permanent representative to the Council of Europe in Strasbourg (France) and a permanent mission to the UN in New York (USA). There are 37 consular representatives accredited to Liechtenstein.

Judicial System

CIVIL COURTS

Landgericht (County Court): 9490 Vaduz; tel. 2366111; fax 2366539; Court of First Instance; one presiding judge; Presiding Judge Dr Benedikt Marxer.

Obergericht (Superior Court): 9490 Vaduz; Court of Second Instance; bench of five judges; Presiding Judge Lic. Iur. Max Bizozzero.

Oberster Gerichtshof (Supreme Court): 9490 Vaduz; Court of Third Instance; bench of five judges; Presiding Judge Dr Hansjörg Rück.

CRIMINAL COURTS

Landgericht (Petty Sessions): 9490 Vaduz; tel. 2366111; fax 2366539; for summary offences; Presiding Judge Lothar Hagen.

Schöffengericht (Court of Assizes): 9490 Vaduz; for minor misdemeanours; bench of three judges; Presiding Judge Dr Benedikt Marxer.

Kriminalgericht (Criminal Court): bench of five judges; Presiding Judge Dr Lothar Hagen.

Obergericht (Superior Court): Court of Second Instance; bench of five judges; Presiding Judge Lic. Iur. Max Bizozzero.

Oberster Gerichtshof (Supreme Court): Court of Third Instance; bench of five judges; Presiding Judge Dr Hansjörg Rück.

ADMINISTRATIVE COURTS

Verwaltungsbeschwerdeinstanz (Administrative Court of Appeal): 9490 Vaduz; appeal against decrees and decisions of the Government may be made to this court; five members; Presiding Judge Lic. Iur. Andreas Batliner.

State Court: 9490 Vaduz; five members; exists for the protection of Public Law; Presiding Judge Lic. Iur. Harry Gstöhl.

Religion

CHRISTIANITY

The Principality comprises a single archdiocese, Vaduz, created in 1997, which is directly responsible to the Holy See. At 31 December 2000 there were an estimated 24,993 adherents (some 78% of the population). The few Protestants (7.3%) belong to the parish of Vaduz.

Archdiocese of Vaduz: Erzbischöfliche Kanzlei, Fürst-Franz-Josef-Str. 112, Postfach 103, 9490 Vaduz; tel. 2332311; fax 2332324; e-mail ebv@supra.net; Archbishop: Most Rev. WOLFGANG HAAS.

The Press

Apotheke und Marketing: Fürst-Johannes-Str. 70, 9494 Schaan; tel. 2332585; fax 2332586; e-mail info@am-verlag.com; internet www.am-verlag.com; Editor RALF DOEKEN; circ. 22,000.

Liechtensteiner Vaterland: Fürst-Franz-Josef-Str. 13, 9490 Vaduz; tel. 2361616; fax 2361617; e-mail redaktion@vaterland.li; internet www.vaterland.li; f. 1913; daily (Monday to Saturday); organ of the VU; Editor GÜNTHER FRITZ; circ. 10,295.

Liechtensteiner Volksblatt: Feldkircher-Str. 5, 9494 Schaan; tel. 2375151; fax 2375155; e-mail redaktion@volksblatt.li; internet www .volksblatt.li; f. 1878; daily (Monday to Saturday); organ of the FBP; Chief Editor MARTIN FROMMELL; circ. 7,515.

Liechtensteiner Wochenzeitung: 9494 Schaan; tel. 2361692; fax 2361699; e-mail liewo@lie-net.li; f. 1993; weekly (Sunday); Dir HANS-PETER RHEINBERGER; Editors SANDRA CASALINI, JOACHIM BATLINER.

PRESS AGENCY

Presse- und Informationsamt (Press and Information Office): Regierungsgebäude, 9490 Vaduz; tel. 2366721; fax 2366460; e-mail presseamt@llv.li; internet www.presseamt.li; f. 1962; Dir DANIELA CLAVADETSCHER.

Publishers

Buch und Verlagsdruckerei: Landstr. 153, 9494 Schaan; tel. 2361836; fax 2361840; e-mail bvd@bvd.li.

Frank P. van Eck Publishers: Haldenweg 8, 9495 Triesen; tel. 3923000; fax 3922277; e-mail vaneck@datacomm.ch; f. 1982; art, local interest, juvenile, golf, crime fiction; Man. Dir ELISABETH VAN ECK-SCHAEDLER.

A. R. Gantner Verlag KG: Industriestr. 105A, Postfach 131, 9491 Ruggell; tel. 3771808; fax 3771802; e-mail bgc@adon.li; botany; Dir BRUNI GANTNER-CAPLAN.

Liechtenstein-Verlag AG: Herrengasse 21, Postfach 339, 9490 Vaduz; tel. 2396010; fax 2396019; e-mail flbooks@verlag_ag.lol.li; f. 1947; belles-lettres and legal and scientific books; agents for international literature; Man. ALBART SCHIKS.

Litag Anstalt—Literarische, Medien und Künstler Agentur: Industriestr. 105A, Postfach 131, 9491 Ruggell; tel. 3771809; fax 3771802; f. 1956; Dir BRUNI GANTNER-CAPLAN.

Sändig Reprint Verlag Wohlwend: Am Schrägen Weg 12, 9490 Vaduz; tel. 2323627; fax 2323649; e-mail saendig@adon.li; internet www.saendig.com; f. 1965; natural sciences, linguistics, free-masonry, fiction, folklore, music, history; Dir CHRISTIAN WOHLWEND.

Topos Verlag AG: Industriestr. 105A, Postfach 551, 9491 Ruggell; tel. 3771111; fax 3771119; e-mail topos@supra.net; internet www .topos.li; f. 1977; law, politics, literature, social science, periodicals; Dir GRAHAM A. P. SMITH.

Broadcasting and Communications

TELECOMMUNICATIONS

Amt für Kommunikation: Kirchstr. 10, 9490 Vaduz; tel. 2366488; fax 2366489; e-mail office@ak.liv.li; internet www.ak.li; regulatory body; Dir STEFAN BECKER.

Telecom FL AG: Austr. 77, 9490 Vaduz; tel. 2377400; fax 2377401; e-mail telecom-fl@telecom-fl.com; internet www.telecom-fl.com; f. 1999.

BROADCASTING

Radio Liechtenstein: Dorfstr. 24, 9495 Triesen; tel. 3991313; fax 3991399; e-mail redaktion@radiol.li; internet www.radiol.li; f. 1995.

Finance

(cap. = capital; res = reserves; dep. = deposits; m. = millions; brs = branches; amounts in Swiss francs)

BANKING

Anlage- und Geschäfts-Bank AG: Egertastr. 10, 9490 Vaduz; tel. 2655353; fax 2655363.

Bank von Ernst (Liechtenstein) AG: POB 112, Egertastr. 10, 9492 Vaduz; tel. 2655353; fax 2655363; e-mail info@bve.li; internet www.bve.li; wholly owned by Bank von Ernst & Cie AG (Switzerland); cap. 25m., res –1m., dep. 143m. (Dec. 2000); Gen. Mans MAX CADERAS, ERNST WEDER.

Bank Frick & Co. AG: Landstr. 8, Postfach 43, 9496 Balzers; tel. 3882121; fax 3882122; e-mail bank@bfc.li; internet www.bfc.li.

Centrum Bank AG: Heiligkreuz 8, Postfach 1168, 9490 Vaduz; tel. 2358585; fax 2358686; e-mail cbk@centrumbank.li; f. 1993; cap. 20m., res 68m., dep. 823m. (Dec. 2001); Chair. Dr PETER MARXER.

Hypo Investment Bank (Liechtenstein) AG: Austr. 59, 9490 Vaduz; tel. 2655656; fax 2655699; e-mail info@hib.li; internet www .hib.li; Chair. Dr ANDREAS INSAM.

LGT Bank in Liechtenstein Ltd: Herrengasse 12, Postfach 85, 9490 Vaduz; tel. 2351122; fax 2351522; e-mail info@lgt.com; internet www.lgt.com; f. 1920; present name adopted 1996; cap. 291m., res 678m., dep. 11,616m. (Dec. 2000); Chair. PRINCE PHILIPP OF LIECHTENSTEIN; CEO THOMAS PISKE; 2 brs.

Liechtensteinische Landesbank AG (State Bank): Städtle 44, Postfach 384, 9490 Vaduz; tel. 2368811; fax 2368822; e-mail llb@llb .li; internet www.llb.li; f. 1861; present name adopted 1955; cap. 180m., res 680m., dep. 9,564m. (Dec. 2001); Chair. KARLHEINZ HEEB; Exec. Dir Dr JOSEPH FEHR; brs in Schaan, Triesenberg, Eschen and Balzers.

Neue Bank AG: Marktgass 20, Postfach 1533, 9490 Vaduz; tel. 2360808; fax 2329260; e-mail info@neuebankag.li; internet www .neuebankag.li.

Raiffeisen Bank (Liechtenstein) AG: Landstr. 140, 9494 Schaan; tel. 2370707; fax 2370777; e-mail info@raiffeisen.li; internet www .raiffeisen.li; f. 1998; total assets 517m. (June 2002).

Swissfirst Bank (Liechtenstein) AG: Austr. 61, Postfach, 9490 Vaduz; tel. 2393333; fax 2393300; e-mail swissfirst@swissfirst.li; internet www.swissfirst.li.

Verwaltungs- und Privat-Bank AG (Private Trust Bank Corporation): Im Zentrum, Postfach 885, 9490 Vaduz; tel. 2356655; fax 2356500; e-mail info@vpbank.li; internet www.vpbank.li; f. 1956; cap. 86m., res 557m., dep. 7,130m. (Dec. 2001); Chair. HANS BRUNHART; Gen. Man. ADOLF E. REAL; 4 brs.

Vorarlberger Volksbank AG: Heiligkreuz 42, Postfach, 9490 Vaduz; tel. 2376930; fax 2376948; e-mail info@volksbank.li; internet www.volksbank.li; Man. Dirs DANIEL BECK, GERHARD HAMEL.

INSURANCE

AIG Life Insurance Co (Liechtenstein) Ltd: Landstr. 38, 9494 Schaan; tel. 2376880; fax 2376889; e-mail info@aiglife.ch; internet www.aiglife.ch; f. 1996.

Alters- und Hinterlassenen-Versicherung (AHV) (Old Age and Survivors' Insurance): 9490 Vaduz; tel. 2381616; fax 2381600; e-mail postmaster@ahv.li; internet www.ahv.li; state-owned; Dir GERHARD BIEDERMANN.

Amisia Fluss-Kasko Versicherungs-AG: Pflugstr. 20, 9490 Vaduz; tel. 2376760; fax 2333050.

AXA Nordstern Versicherungs-AG: Neugasse 15, 9490 Vaduz; tel. 2375010; fax 2375019; e-mail kundendienst@axa-nordstern.li; internet www.axa-nordstern.li; f. 1995.

CapitalLeben Versicherung AG: Landstr. 126A, 9494 Schaan; tel. 2374837; fax 2374848; e-mail office@capitalleben.li; internet www .capitalleben.li; f. 1997; life insurance; Chair. KLAUS OSTERTAG; Man. Dirs Dr MARKUS HETZER, ALEXANDER T. SKREINER.

Fortuna Lebens-Versicherungs-AG: Stadtle 35, 9490 Vaduz; tel. 2361545; fax 2361546; e-mail fl.service@fortuna.li; internet www .fortuna.li; f. 1996; Man. JÜRG BAUERTE.

Swisscom Re AG: Schmedgass 6, 9490 Vaduz; tel. 2301665; fax 2301666; Man. Dirs BERNHARD LAMPERT, URS LUGINBÜHL, MARCEL VON VIVIS, THOMAS WITTBJER.

Transmarine Insurance Co Ltd: Aeulestr. 38, 9490 Vaduz; tel. 2334488; fax 2334489; f. 1996.

Valorlife Lebensversicherungs-AG: Landstr. 114, 9495 Triesen; tel. 3992950; fax 3992959; e-mail info@valorlife.com; internet www .valorlife.com.

Trade and Industry

CHAMBER OF COMMERCE

Liechtenstein Chamber of Commerce and Industry (LCCI): Josef-Rheinberger-Str. 11, 9490 Vaduz; tel. 2375511; fax 2375512; e-mail info@lcci.li; internet www.lcci.li; f. 1947; Pres. MICHAEL HILTI; Gen. Man. JOSEF BECK; 42 mems.

INDUSTRIAL ASSOCIATION

Vereinigung Bäuerlicher Organisationen im Fürstentum Liechtenstein (VBO) (Agricultural Union): Postfach 351, 9493 Mauren; tel. 3759050; fax 3759051; e-mail vbo@kba.li; Pres. THOMAS BÜCHEL; Sec. KLAUS BÜCHEL.

UTILITY

Gas

Liechtensteinische Gasversorgung: Im Rietacker 4, 9494 Schaan; tel. 2361555; fax 2361566; Dir ANTON GERNER.

TRADE UNIONS

Gewerbe- und Wirtschaftskammer für das Fürstentum Liechtenstein (Trades' Union): Zollstr. 23, 9494 Schaan; tel. 2377788; fax 2377789; e-mail gwk@gwk.li; internet www.gwk.li; f. 1936; aims to protect the interests of Liechtenstein artisans and tradespeople; Pres. ARNOLD MATT; Sec. OLIVER GERSTGRASSER; 3,000 mems.

Liechtensteiner Arbeitnehmer-Verband (Employees' Association): 9495 Triesen; tel. 3993838; fax 3993839; e-mail lanv@supra .net; internet www.lanv.li; Pres. ALICE FEHR; Sec. ALBERT JEHLE.

Transport

RAILWAYS

Liechtenstein is traversed by some 18.5 km of railway track, which is administered by Austrian Federal Railways. There is a station at Nendeln, as well as two halts at Schaan and Schaanwald. A local service connects Feldkirch in Austria and Buchs in Switzerland via Liechtenstein, and the Arlberg express (Paris to Vienna) passes through the Principality.

ROADS

Modern roads connect the capital, Vaduz, with all the towns and villages in the Principality. The Rhine and Samina valleys are connected by a tunnel 740 m long. Public transport is provided by a well-developed network of postal buses.

INLAND WATERWAYS

A canal of 26 km, irrigating the Rhine valley, was opened in 1943.

Tourism

Liechtenstein has an Alpine setting in the Upper Rhine area. The principal tourist attractions include a renowned postal museum, a National Museum and the Liechtenstein State Art Collection at Vaduz, as well as the Prince's castle (although this is closed to the public) and two ruined medieval fortresses at Schellenberg. Annually about two-fifths of foreign tourists visit the winter sports resort at Malbun, in the south-east of the Principality. For summer visitors there are some 400 km of hiking trails and an extensive network of cycling paths. In 2000 Liechtenstein received 61,550 foreign visitors.

Liechtenstein Tourismus: Postfach 139, 9490 Vaduz; tel. 2396300; fax 2396301; e-mail touristinfo@liechtenstein.li; internet www.tourismus.li; Dir ROLAND BÜCHEL.

LITHUANIA

Introductory Survey

Location, Climate, Language, Religion, Flag, Capital

The Republic of Lithuania (formerly the Lithuanian Soviet Socialist Republic) is situated on the eastern coast of the Baltic Sea, in north-eastern Europe. It is bounded by Latvia to the north, by Belarus to the south-east, by Poland to the south-west and by Russian territory around Kaliningrad to the west. Lithuania's maritime position moderates an otherwise continental-type climate. Temperatures range from an average of −4.9°C (23.2°F) in January to a July mean of 17.0°C (62.6°F). Rainfall levels vary considerably from region to region: in the far west the annual average is 700 mm–850 mm (28 ins–33 ins), but in the central plain it is about 600 mm (24 ins). The official language is Lithuanian. The predominant religion is Christianity. Most ethnic Lithuanians are Roman Catholics by belief or tradition, but there are small communities of Lutherans and Calvinists, as well as a growing number of modern Protestant denominations. Adherents of Russian Orthodoxy are almost exclusively ethnic Slavs, while most Tatars have retained an adherence to Islam. The national flag (proportions 1 by 2) consists of three equal horizontal stripes of yellow (top), green and red (bottom). The capital is Vilnius.

Recent History

Prior to annexation by the Russian Empire in 1795, Lithuania was united in a Commonwealth with Poland. In 1915, after the outbreak of the First World War, it was occupied by German troops. A 'Lithuanian Conference' was convened in September 1917, which demanded the re-establishment of an independent Lithuanian state and elected a 'Lithuanian Council', headed by Antanas Smetona; it proceeded to declare independence on 16 February 1918. The new state survived both a Soviet attempt to create a Lithuanian-Belarusian Soviet republic and a Polish campaign aimed at reincorporating Lithuania. In October 1920 Poland annexed the region of Vilnius, but was forced to recognize the rest of Lithuania as an independent state (with its temporary capital at Kaunas). Soviet Russia had recognized Lithuanian independence in the Treaty of Moscow, signed in July. Lithuania's first Constitution, which declared Lithuania a parliamentary democracy, was adopted in August 1922. In December 1926 Antanas Smetona seized power in a military *coup d'état* and established an authoritarian regime, which endured until 1940.

According to the 'Secret Protocols' to the Treaty of Non-Aggression (the Molotov-Ribbentrop Pact), signed on 23 August 1939 by the USSR and Germany, Lithuania was to be part of the German sphere of influence. However, the Nazi-Soviet Treaty on Friendship and Existing Borders, agreed in September (following the outbreak of the Second World War), permitted the USSR to take control of Lithuania. In October Lithuania was compelled to agree to the stationing of 20,000 Soviet troops on its territory. In return, the USSR granted the city and region of Vilnius (which had been seized by Soviet troops in September) to Lithuania. In June 1940 the USSR dispatched a further 100,000 troops to Lithuania and forced the Lithuanian Government to resign. A Soviet-approved People's Government was formed. Elections to a People's Seim (parliament), which only pro-Soviet candidates were permitted to contest, took place in July. The Seim proclaimed the Lithuanian Soviet Socialist Republic on 21 July, and on 3 August Lithuania formally became a Union Republic of the USSR. The establishment of Soviet rule was followed by the arrest and imprisonment of many Lithuanian politicians and government officials.

Some 210,000 people, mainly Jews, were killed during the Nazi occupation of Lithuania (1941–44). The return of the Soviet Army, in 1944, was not welcomed by most Lithuanians, and anti-Soviet partisan warfare continued until 1952. Lithuanian agriculture was forcibly collectivized and rapid industrialization was implemented. Meanwhile, some 150,000 people were deported, and leaders and members of the Roman Catholic Church were persecuted and imprisoned. Lithuanian political parties were disbanded, and political power became the exclusive preserve of the Communist Party of Lithuania (CPL), the local branch of the Communist Party of the Soviet Union

(CPSU). The leader (First Secretary) of the CPL in 1940–74 was Antanas Sniečkus.

A significant dissident movement was established during the 1960s and 1970s. There were demonstrations in Kaunas in May 1972, in support of demands for religious and political freedom. With the introduction of the policy of *glasnost* (openness) by the Soviet leader, Mikhail Gorbachev, in the mid-1980s, a limited discussion of previously censored aspects of Lithuanian history appeared in the press. Dissident groups took advantage of a more tolerant attitude to political protests, organizing a demonstration in August 1987 to denounce the Pact. However, in February 1988 security forces were deployed to prevent the public celebration of the 70th anniversary of Lithuanian independence. This, together with frustration among the intelligentsia at the slow pace of reform in the republic, led to the establishment in June of the Lithuanian Movement for Reconstruction (Sąjūdis). Sąjūdis organized mass demonstrations to protest against environmental pollution, the suppression of national culture and 'russification', and to condemn the signing of the Molotov-Ribbentrop Pact. The movement appealed to the CPL to support a declaration of independence and the recognition of Lithuanian as the state language. The latter demand was adopted by the Lithuanian Supreme Soviet (legislature) in November, and traditional Lithuanian state symbols were restored. Other concessions made by the CPL during 1988 included the restoration of Independence Day as a public holiday and the return of buildings to the Roman Catholic Church.

Sąjūdis won 36 of the 42 popularly-elected seats at elections to the all-Union Congress of People's Deputies in March 1989. Thereafter, the CPL began to adopt a more radical position, in an attempt to retain some measure of popular support. On 18 May the CPL-dominated Supreme Soviet approved a declaration of Lithuanian sovereignty, which asserted the supremacy of Lithuania's laws over all-Union legislation. Public debate concerning the legitimacy of Soviet rule in Lithuania intensified: a commission of the Lithuanian Supreme Soviet declared the establishment of Soviet power in 1940 to have been unconstitutional and, in August, on the 50th anniversary of the signing of the Pact with Nazi Germany, more than 1m. people participated in a 'human chain' extending from Tallinn in Estonia, through Latvia, to Vilnius.

Despite denunciations of Baltic nationalism by the all-Union authorities, the Lithuanian Supreme Soviet continued to adopt reformist legislation, including the establishment of freedom of religion and the legalization of a multi-party system. In December 1989 the CPL declared itself an independent party, no longer subordinate to the CPSU, adopting a new programme that condemned communist policies of the past and declared support for multi-party democracy and independent statehood. Shortly afterwards a group of former CPL members who were opposed to independence formed a separate movement, the Lithuanian Communist Party on the CPSU Platform (LCP). Meanwhile, Algirdas Brazauskas, First Secretary of the CPL since October 1988, was elected Chairman of the Presidium of the Lithuanian Supreme Soviet, defeating three other candidates, including Romualdas Ozolas, a leading member of Sąjūdis. None the less, Sąjūdis remained the dominant political force in the republic, and its supporters won an overall majority in the elections to the Lithuanian Supreme Soviet in February–March 1990. This new, pro-independence parliament elected Vytautas Landsbergis, the Chairman of Sąjūdis, to replace Brazauskas as its Chairman (*de facto* President of Lithuania), and on 11 March declared the restoration of Lithuanian independence: Lithuania thus became the first of the Soviet republics to make such a declaration. The legislature (restyled the Supreme Council) also restored the pre-1940 name of the country (the Republic of Lithuania) and suspended the USSR Constitution on Lithuanian territory. Kazimieras Prunskienė, a member of the CPL and hitherto a Deputy Chairman of the Council of Ministers, was appointed to be the first Prime Minister of the restored republic.

The Lithuanian declarations were condemned by a special session of the all-Union Congress of People's Deputies as 'unconstitutional', and Soviet forces occupied CPL buildings in Vilnius and took control of newspaper presses. An economic embargo was imposed on Lithuania in April, and vital fuel supplies were suspended; it remained in force for more than two months, until Lithuania agreed to a six-month moratorium on the independence declaration, pending formal negotiations. However, talks, which began in August, were soon terminated by the Soviet Government, and in January 1991 Landsbergis revoked the suspension of the declaration of independence, since negotiations on Lithuania's status had not resumed. Tension increased in the republic when the Soviet authorities dispatched to Vilnius troops (led by the special OMON units) of the Soviet Ministry of Internal Affairs, who occupied former CPSU properties that had been nationalized by the Lithuanian Government. Landsbergis mobilized popular support to help to defend the parliament building, which he believed to be under threat. In mid-January 13 people were killed and about 500 injured, when Soviet troops seized the broadcasting centre in Vilnius. (In August 1999 six former officers of the LCP were convicted of complicity in attempts to overthrow the Lithuanian Government in January 1991, and sentenced to between three and 12 years' imprisonment.)

Meanwhile, policy differences had arisen within the Lithuanian leadership, and earlier in January 1991 Prunskienė and her Council of Ministers had resigned after the Supreme Council refused to sanction proposed price increases. Gediminas Vagnorius, a member of the Supreme Council, was appointed Prime Minister. The military intervention strengthened popular support for independence. A referendum on this issue took place in the republic on 9 February, at which 90.5% of voters expressed support for the re-establishment of an independent Lithuania and for the withdrawal of the USSR army from the republic. In common with five other Soviet republics, Lithuania refused to conduct the all-Union referendum on the future of the USSR, which was held in March. (Voting did take place unofficially in predominantly Russian- and Polish-populated areas of Lithuania, where the majority endorsed the preservation of the USSR.)

A series of attacks by OMON forces on members of the nascent Lithuanian defence force and on the customs posts on the border with Belarus, combined with the seizure of power in Moscow by the State Committee for the State of Emergency (SCSE) in August 1991, led to fears in Lithuania that there would be a renewed attempt to overthrow the Landsbergis administration and reimpose Soviet rule. Soviet military vehicles entered Vilnius, but did not prevent the convening of an emergency session of the Supreme Council, which condemned the SCSE and issued a statement supporting Boris Yeltsin, President of the Russian Federation. As the coup collapsed, the Lithuanian Government ordered the withdrawal of Soviet forces from the republic and banned the LCP. (The successor party to the CPL, the Lithuanian Democratic Labour Party—LDLP, was not banned.) The Government also began to assume effective control of the country's borders. The failed coup prompted the long-awaited recognition of Lithuanian independence by other states, and on 6 September the USSR State Council recognized the independence of Lithuania and the other Baltic republics (Estonia and Latvia), all three of which were admitted to the UN and the Conference on (now Organization for) Security and Co-operation in Europe (OSCE, see p. 283) later in the month. Throughout the remainder of 1991 the Government continued to assert control over former Soviet institutions and entered into negotiations with Soviet and Russian representatives on matters related to the restoration of Lithuanian independence. Foremost among these was the issue of Soviet troops remaining in Lithuania (see below).

During the first half of 1992 there was an increasing polarity within the Supreme Council between Sąjūdis deputies and those of the mainly left-wing opposition parties, most prominently the LDLP, led by Brazauskas. In April 10 members of the of Council of Ministers criticized Vagnorius's 'dictatorial' methods, and two ministers subsequently resigned. Vagnorius tendered his resignation as Prime Minister in May, but remained in the post until July, when the legislature approved a motion of 'no confidence' in his leadership. The Seimas (as the Supreme Council had been renamed) appointed Aleksandras Abišala, a close associate of Landsbergis, as Prime Minister; a new Council of Ministers was named shortly afterwards. Meanwhile, the growing division within the legislature had led to a boycott by pro-Sąjūdis deputies, rendering it frequently inquorate. In July, however, the Seimas approved a new electoral law, whereby Lithuania's first

post-Soviet legislative elections, scheduled for late 1992, would be held under a mixed system of majority voting (for 71 seats) and proportional representation on the basis of party lists (70 seats).

The LDLP emerged as the leading party in the elections to the Seimas, which took place on 25 October and 15 November 1992, winning a total of 73 of the 141 seats. The defeat of Sąjūdis (which, in alliance with the Citizens' Charter of Lithuania, secured only 30 seats) was largely attributed to popular disenchantment with its management of economic reform. The Christian Democratic Party of Lithuania (CDPL), which was closely aligned with Sąjūdis, won 16 seats. Also on 25 October a referendum approved a new Constitution, which stipulated that state powers were to be 'exercised by the Seimas, the President, the Government and the Judiciary', and which was adopted by the Seimas on 6 November. Pending an election to the new post of President of the Republic, Brazauskas was elected by the Seimas to be its Chairman and acting Head of State. In December 1992 Brazauskas appointed Bronislovas Lubys (hitherto a Deputy Prime Minister) as Prime Minister. Lubys formed a new coalition Council of Ministers, retaining six members of the previous Government and including only three representatives of the LDLP.

The presidential election, on 14 February 1993, was won by Brazauskas, with some 60% of the votes cast. His only rival was Stasys Lozoraitis, Lithuania's ambassador to the USA. Brazauskas subsequently announced his resignation from the LDLP. In March Adolfas Šleževičius, a former Deputy Minister of Agriculture, replaced Lubys as Prime Minister. In the following month Šleževičius was appointed Chairman of the LDLP. In May a new political organization, the Conservative Party of Lithuania (CP), also known as the Homeland Union (Lithuanian Conservatives), was formed. Mainly comprising former members of Sąjūdis, and chaired by Landsbergis, the CP rapidly established itself as the principal opposition party. (In December Sąjūdis announced its transformation into a 'public movement', a development that further reflected its diminishing influence.)

Persistent allegations of high-level corruption, combined with reports of ideological divisions within the LDLP, as well as several ministerial resignations or dismissals during 1993–94, suggested that the Government was increasingly unstable. The right-wing opposition, led by the CP, repeatedly questioned the Government's competence and demanded fresh legislative elections. Increasing popular support for the CP was confirmed at local elections in March 1995, when the party won some 29% of the votes, while its close ally, the CDPL, received 17%; the LDLP took only 20%.

The Minister of the Economy, Aleksandras Vasiliauskas, resigned in October 1995, following the collapse of several small commercial banks and in view of the slow progress achieved in the second stage of the privatization programme. In the same month a new State Privatization Agency was established. In November the Government survived its second vote of 'no confidence', initiated by the conservative opposition, which accused the LDLP of economic mismanagement. The banking crisis culminated in December with the suspension of the operations of the country's two largest commercial banks, the Lithuanian Joint-Stock Innovation Bank (LJIB) and Litimpex Bank, owing to insolvency; senior officials of both institutions were arrested on charges of fraud. In January 1996 it was revealed that Šleževičius had withdrawn funds from the LJIB only two days before the bank's suspension; however the Prime Minister refused to submit to opposition demands that he resign. Later in January Romasis Vaitekūnas resigned as Minister of the Interior, following intense public criticism of his handling of the crisis; it was revealed that Vaitekūnas had also withdrawn funds from the LJIB before its closure. Kazys Ratkevičius, the Chairman of the Bank of Lithuania (the central bank) also resigned. Šleževičius initially disregarded a presidential decree that he should leave office, which was upheld by the Seimas in February. He was replaced as Prime Minister by Laurynas Mindaugas Stankevičius, hitherto Minister of Government Reforms and Local Governments. Šleževičius also resigned as Chairman of the LDLP, and was succeeded by Česlovas Juršėnas, the Chairman of the Seimas. In October Šleževičius was charged with abuse of office, in connection with the collapse of the LJIB.

A general election took place in two rounds on 20 October and 10 November 1996. The results confirmed the substantial loss of popular support for the LDLP, which retained only 12 seats in the Seimas. The CP achieved a total of 70 seats, and the right-wing CDPL secured 16. The right-wing Centre Union won 13 seats and the Lithuanian Social Democratic Party (LSDP) 12. Some 53% of eligible voters participated in the first round, and about 40% took part in the second. Following the election, a coalition agreement was signed by the leaders of the CP and the CDPL. Landsbergis was elected Chairman of the Seimas at the assembly's first sitting, in late November, and shortly afterwards the Seimas approved the appointment of Vagnorius as Prime Minister. His Government was dominated by members of the CP, with three representatives of the CDPL and two of the Centre Union. In January 1997 the Minister of Finance, Rolandas Matiliauskas, resigned, amid allegations of financial impropriety; he was subsequently charged with the misappropriation of property and the violation of regulations while he had been employed at a commercial bank. The Prosecutor-General, Valdas Nikitinas, also resigned, following criticism of his handling of investigations into the financial crises of 1995. In November 1997 the Seimas approved new legislation whereby the Government's voucher scheme for privatization was to be superseded by a simplified cash system. A new Fund for State Property and the Restoration of People's Savings was to be responsible for the distribution and investment of revenue derived from the scheme, much of which was to be used to compensate individuals whose savings had depreciated as a result of the recent crises.

In July 1997 the Seimas announced that a presidential election would be conducted on 21 December. Brazauskas did not seek re-election, and in the first round of voting none of the seven candidates won the overall majority of votes needed to secure the presidency. In a second round of voting on 4 January 1998 the second-placed candidate after the first round, Valdas Adamkus (a former environmental protection executive, who had been naturalized in the USA), narrowly defeated Artūras Paulauskas (a prominent lawyer and deputy Prosecutor-General, supported by the Lithuanian Liberal Union), with 50.4% of the votes. The new President immediately endorsed the mandate of the incumbent Government, and in March Vagnorius was confirmed as Prime Minister by the Seimas. In April Paulauskas announced the formation of a new, centre-left political party, the New Union (also known as the Social Liberals), which hoped to attract the support of young voters.

A serious conflict of interests between Adamkus and Vagnorius intensified in April 1999, following the President's public criticism of what he regarded as the Government's inadequate attempts to eradicate corruption in the public sector. In mid-April the President openly criticized the Prime Minister's abilities, particularly his 'authoritarian' handling of recent privatizations, and urged the coalition parties to consider appointing a new government. Vagnorius secured the confidence of the Seimas in a non-binding vote shortly afterwards, but, none the less, at the end of the month he announced his intention to resign. In mid-May Adamkus invited the Mayor of Vilnius, Rolandas Paksas (a member of the CP), to form a new government. His Council of Ministers, announced at the beginning of June, was again formed from a coalition led by the CP and the CDPL. In October Paksas indicated that he would not endorse an agreement to sell a one-third stake in the state-owned Mažeikiai NAFTA petroleum refinery to a US oil company, Williams International, under the terms of which Lithuania would be required to provide long-term financing of some 1,400m. litai (more than twice the price paid by the US company), in order to offset the refinery's debts and shortfall in working capital. None the less, the Council of Ministers endorsed the sale, which was strongly supported by Adamkus and by the majority of the CP, prompting the resignations of the Ministers of National Economy and of Finance, and, in late October, of Paksas. The Minister of Social Security and Labour, Irena Degutienė (who had assumed the interim premiership following Vagnorius's resignation earlier in the year), was again appointed acting Prime Minister, but she declined an invitation to form a new government. At the end of October Adamkus nominated Andrius Kubilius, the First Deputy Chairman of the Seimas, as Prime Minister. Kubilius's Council of Ministers, named in early November and approved by the legislature one week later, retained largely the same membership as the previous administration. Following the appointment of the new Government, the Centre Union announced that it was to become an opposition party; the party's leader, Romualdas Ozolas, had resigned as a Deputy Chairman of the Seimas after criticizing Landsbergis (who chaired both the CP and the legislature). The

Minister of Justice, Gintaras Balčiūnas, subsequently withdrew from the party, remaining in the Government as an independent. In mid-November Paksas announced his resignation from the CP; in early December he was elected Chairman of the Lithuanian Liberal Union.

Local elections in mid-March 2000 resulted in considerable successes for parties of the left, most notably the centre-left New Union, which had campaigned against the sale of principal state properties to foreign interests. Disappointing results for the CP apparently precipitated a split in the party, as several deputies established a 'moderate' faction in the Seimas, thus depriving the CP-CDPL coalition of an automatic majority in the legislature. In late April the President announced that a legislative election was to be held on 8 October. In the following month the country's two largest left-wing parties, the LSDP and the LDLP, agreed to contest the election in alliance, reportedly in response to the perceived threat from new parties, such as the New Union. The New Democracy Party and the Lithuanian Russians' Union subsequently joined the alliance, which was known as the A. Brazauskas Social Democratic Coalition, after the former President, who had been elected Honorary Chairman.

The legislative election was held, as scheduled, on 8 October 2000, with the participation of 28 political parties and alliances; some 56.2% of eligible voters took part. The ruling CP won only nine seats, compared with 70 in 1996. The Social Democratic Coalition obtained the largest representation, with 51 seats. However, the Lithuanian Liberal Union (with 34 seats) and the New Union (with 29), which had formed an informal alliance prior to the election, subsequently signed a coalition agreement and, with the support of the Lithuanian Centre Union, the Modern Christian-Democratic Union and deputies from single-seat constituencies, secured the 71 seats necessary to obtain a parliamentary majority. On 26 October Rolandas Paksas of the Lithuanian Liberal Union was approved as Prime Minister, obtaining 79 votes in the Seimas; the leader of the New Union, Artūras Paulauskas, was elected Chairman of the Seimas. The new Council of Ministers was appointed at the end of the month. Jonas Lionginas of the Lithuanian Liberal Union, who had briefly occupied the post of Minister of Finance in 1999, was re-appointed to the Government, and Antanas Valionis of the New Union became Minister of Foreign Affairs. However, shortly after its appointment a number of ministers resigned from the cabinet; the Minister of the Economy, Eugenijus Maldeikis, resigned in early February, despite being cleared of ethical violations, following an unofficial meeting with the directors of the Russian company, Gazprom, allegedly in relation to the planned privatization of the Lithuanian gas utility. This was the second time that Maldeikis had resigned from a cabinet headed by Paksas; he was replaced by Eugenijus Gentvilas.

Meanwhile, in October 2000 Romualdas Ozolas and Egidijus Bičkauskas resigned as leaders of the Lithuanian Centre Union, owing to their party's poor result in the general election (it had obtained two seats in the Seimas). Formalizing their electoral alliance, the LDLP merged with the LSDP at a joint congress held in late January 2001; the LSDP thereby became the single party with the greatest number of seats in the Seimas, and former President Algirdas Brazauskas was elected its Chairman. Further political consolidation took place in May, when the CDPL merged with the Christian Democratic Union to form the Lithuanian Christian Democrats.

In mid-June 2001 the six New Union cabinet members resigned their portfolios, following disagreements with the Lithuanian Liberal Union over privatization of the energy sector and economic reform, and criticism of the Prime Minister's style of leadership. Paksas was subsequently unable to form an alternative coalition Government and, despite surviving a vote of 'no confidence', he resigned on 20 June; Eugenijus Gentvilas was appointed interim Prime Minister. Hopes that the previous coalition could be resurrected were short-lived; the Government had struggled for much of its brief existence, owing to the two parties' ideological differences, and the New Union sought a new alliance with the LSDP. At the end of the month President Adamkus offered the post of Prime Minister to the Chairman of the LSDP, Algirdas Brazauskas, who was confirmed in the post by the Seimas on 3 July. The LSDP did not, however, offer the New Union a formal coalition agreement, but instead agreed to an informal accord, which granted the New Union the same six cabinet positions from which it had withdrawn in June, including the foreign affairs portfolio. The Minister of Defence, Linas Linkevicius, formerly of the Lithuanian Liberal Union, was also re-appointed to the cabinet, having declared himself an independent. The Minister of Agriculture and Forestry, Kęstutis Krištinatis, a member of the New Union, submitted his resignation in mid-September; Jeronimas Kraujelis was appointed to succeed him in the following month. Also in September, Paksas resigned as Chairman of the Lithuanian Liberal Union, in compliance with demands from within the party. Gentvilas was appointed acting Chairman, and was confirmed in the post in October. In late December Paksas and 10 other deputies, including the former Minister of the Economy, Eugenijus Maldeikis, left the parliamentary faction of the Lithuanian Liberal Union, owing, in part, to its failure to nominate Paksas as First Deputy Chairman of the Seimas, and indications that he would be unable to rely on the party's support, were he to stand as a candidate in the presidential election due to take place in 2002. Paksas and the former Lithuanian Liberal Union deputies were formally expelled from the party in January 2002, and in March they founded the rightist Lithuanian Liberal Democratic Party (LLDP), with Paksas as its Chairman.

The results of the presidential election, held on 22 December 2002, were inconclusive. Adamkus failed to secure an overall majority, obtaining 35.5% of the votes cast, while Paksas was the second-placed candidate, with 19.7% of the votes; Artūras Paulauskas received just 8.3%. A second round of voting took place on 5 January 2003, in which Paksas obtained 54.7% of the votes cast, defeating Adamkus, with 45.3%, despite the fact that most major political parties had expressed support for the latter candidate. However, Paksas had pursued a populist campaign, and observers noted that Adamkus appeared to have lost popularity through his implementation of pro-market economic reforms. Paksas was inaugurated as President on 26 February. On 4 March Brazauskas was re-appointed as Prime Minister; he re-nominated the existing Council of Ministers, with the exception of the Minister of Health Care, Konstantinas Dobrovolskis of the New Union. Dobrovolskis was replaced by Juozas Olekas of the LSDP. Following the presidential election, Paksas resigned as Chairman of the LLDP, and Valentinas Mazuronis was elected as his successor in early March. Meanwhile, in mid-January the Lithuanian Centre Union, the Lithuanian Liberal Union and the Modern Christian-Democratic Union agreed to merge; Artūras Zuokas was to be the new party's leader.

Whereas Lithuania's Baltic neighbours, Estonia and Latvia, have large national minorities, ethnic Lithuanians constitute the overwhelming majority of the republic's population: in January 1997 ethnic Lithuanians represented some 81% of the total, while the two largest minority groups, Russians and Poles, represented 8% and 7%, respectively, of the total population. As a result, the requirements for naturalization of non-ethnic-Lithuanians have been less stringent than in the neighbouring Baltic republics, where national identity has been perceived in some quarters as being under threat. Under new citizenship laws adopted in late 1989, all residents, regardless of ethnic origin, were eligible to apply for naturalization; by early 1993 more than 90% of the country's non-ethnic-Lithuanian residents had been granted citizenship. None the less, the Lithuanian population declined by some 184,000 between 1989 and 2001. In an attempt to counter emigration (in particular to the USA), in September 2002 the Seimas approved legislation permitting Lithuanian citizens to hold dual citizenship, thereby facilitating the subsequent return of Lithuanian nationals to the country.

Mainly because of its citizenship laws, Lithuania's relations with Russia have been less strained than those of Estonia and Latvia. Negotiations for the withdrawal of the estimated 38,000 former Soviet troops remaining in Lithuania, which were held between the Lithuanian and Russian Governments during 1992, resulted, in September, in an agreement by Russia to repatriate all the troops by the end of August 1993. The final troops left, as scheduled, on 31 August, whereupon full state sovereignty was perceived as having been restored in Lithuania.

In November 1993 Lithuania and Russia signed several agreements, including an accord on most-favoured nation status in bilateral trade, and another concerning the transportation, via Lithuania, of Russian military equipment and troops from the Russian exclave of Kaliningrad Oblast. However, there was disagreement between the two countries during 1994, following Lithuania's decision to introduce new regulations governing military transits. A compromise appeared to have been reached in January 1995, when the Lithuanian Government extended until December the existing procedure for military transits; Russia duly indicated that the agreement on bilateral trade would enter into force immediately. In October 1997 President Brazauskas undertook the first official visit to Russia by a Baltic

head of state since the disintegration of the former USSR. During the visit a state border delimitation treaty was signed by both sides, and bilateral co-operation agreements on joint economic zones, and on the Baltic continental shelf, were also concluded. The border treaty was ratified by the Seimas in October 1999, but at early 2003 had still to be ratified by the Russian side. A source of tension with Russia until the early 2000s was Russian opposition to Lithuania's prospective membership of NATO (see p. 271); in common with Estonia and Latvia, Lithuania regarded membership of that organization as the principal guarantee of the country's security. In June 2000 President Adamkus withheld his approval of a bill claiming compensation from Russia for the damage sustained by Lithuania during its time as a constituent part of the USSR; however, the legislation was signed into law by the parliamentary Chairman, Vytautas Landsbergis, and a visit by a delegation of the State Duma was subsequently cancelled in protest. In October a commission estimated the damages owed to Lithuania from Russia at 80,000m. litai. Despite these tensions, Lithuania expressed support for an agreement between the European Union (EU, see p. 199) and Russia in late 2002, which proposed simplified visa arrangements for Russian citizens traversing Lithuania to reach the exclave of Kaliningrad. New transit arrangements were implemented in Lithuania at the beginning of February 2003.

Lithuania's relations with neighbouring Poland have largely been concerned with the status of the Polish minority in Lithuania (and likewise with the ethnic Lithuanian population in Poland). Following the failed coup attempt of August 1991 in Moscow, leaders of councils in Polish-populated regions of Lithuania were dismissed, in response to their alleged support for the coup, and direct rule was introduced. However, in January 1992 Lithuania and Poland signed a 'Declaration on Friendly Relations and Neighbourly Co-operation', which guaranteed the rights of the respective ethnic minorities and also recognized the existing border between the two countries. A full treaty of friendship and co-operation was signed by the respective Heads of State in April 1994. The treaty, notably, did not include a condemnatory reference to Poland's occupation of the region of Vilnius in 1920–39 (a provision that had originally been demanded by Lithuania). An agreement on free trade was signed by the two countries in June 1996. During 1997 the Lithuanian and Polish Governments established regular forums for inter-presidential and inter-parliamentary discussion. In September, following the organization by the two countries of a summit meeting of 12 leaders of Central and Eastern European countries in Vilnius, an inaugural session of a Polish-Lithuanian inter-governmental co-operation council was conducted.

Among the former Soviet republics, Lithuania enjoys closest relations with Estonia and Latvia, with which it shares strong cultural and historical ties. Relations between the three states are co-ordinated through the consultative inter-parliamentary Baltic Assembly, the Council of Baltic Sea States (see p. 179) and the Baltic Council (see p. 349). A series of tripartite meetings of the Baltic states during 1997 resulted in agreements to further liberalize trade, to combat 'money-laundering' and illegal immigration and to renew efforts to gain entry to NATO. In January 1998 the Presidents of the three states met President Bill Clinton of the USA in Washington, DC, and all parties signed a Charter of Partnership, described as a framework for the development of closer political and economic ties. At a meeting in Sigulda, Latvia, in July, the three countries' premiers agreed further to harmonize their respective customs procedures and labour movement regulations. In January 2000 the Latvian, Lithuanian and Estonian ministers of finance agreed to work towards the application of a uniform strategy for excise tax. Lithuania's relations with Latvia have, none the less, been strained as a result of disagreements over the demarcation of the countries' maritime border. In October 1995 the Lithuanian Government protested at Latvia's signature of a preliminary agreement with two foreign petroleum companies to explore oilfields in the disputed waters. Tension increased following the ratification of the agreement by the Latvian parliament in October 1996, although in July 1999 the two countries signed an agreement on the Delimitation of the Territorial Sea, Exclusive Economic Zone and Continental Shelf in the Baltic Sea. However, protests from the Latvian fishing industry prevented the agreement from being ratified by the Latvian parliament and, therefore, Lithuania's ratification was invalidated. In December 2000 a protocol was signed for the re-demarcation of the land border between the two countries.

Lithuania has pursued close co-operation with, and eventual integration into, the political, economic and defence systems of western Europe, notably seeking full membership of the EU. A number of political and economic agreements concluded between the EU and the Baltic states in 1995, with the aim of facilitating their membership of the EU, came into effect on 1 February 1998. In December, in accordance with the European Convention on Human Rights and Fundamental Freedoms, the Seimas voted to abolish the death penalty. In December 1999 a summit meeting of EU Heads of State and Government in Helsinki, Finland, endorsed proposals to begin accession talks with six countries, including Lithuania; formal negotiations commenced in February 2000. As a concession to achieve EU membership, the Government approved a draft national energy strategy in September 1999, which provided for the decommissioning of the first unit of the Ignalina nuclear power plant by 2005. In June 2002 Lithuania agreed to decommision the plant's remaining unit in 2009, in return for a significant contribution from the EU towards the cost of the endeavour. In December 2002 Lithuania, and nine other countries, were formally invited to join the EU in May 2004; at a national referendum, held on 10–11 May 2003, over 91% of participants voted in favour of membership. Meanwhile, in November 2002 Lithuania was one of seven countries invited to join NATO in 2004.

Government

Under the terms of the Constitution that was approved in a national referendum on 25 October 1992, supreme legislative authority resides with the Seimas (Parliament), which has 141 members, elected by universal adult suffrage for a four-year term. (In total, 71 deputies are directly elected by majority vote, with the rest being selected from party lists, on the basis of proportional representation.) The President of the Republic (who is Head of State) is elected by direct popular vote for a period of five years (and a maximum of two consecutive terms). Executive power is vested in the Council of Ministers. This is headed by the Prime Minister, who is appointed by the President with the approval of the Seimas. For administrative purposes, Lithuania is divided into 10 counties (subdivided into 56 municipalities).

Defence

Until independence Lithuania had no armed forces separate from those of the USSR. The Department of State Defence (established in April 1990) was reorganized as the Ministry of Defence in October 1991. In 1998 the Baltic states agreed to establish a joint airspace observation system (BALTNET), a defence college and a peace-keeping battalion (BALTBAT). A Baltic naval unit (BALTRON) was established in mid-1998. BALTNET's regional airspace control and co-ordination centre, outside Kaunas, became operational in June 1999. In August 2002 Lithuania's active armed forces totalled an estimated 13,510 (including 1,800 centrally controlled personnel and a 1,960-strong Voluntary National Defence Force): army 8,100 (including 3,027 conscripts), navy 650 (including 300 conscripts) and air force 1,000. There was also a paramilitary of 13,850, including a border guard of 5,000. Military service is compulsory and lasts for 12 months. The 2001 budget allocated 755.4m. litai (6.0% of total expenditure) to defence. Lithuania was expected to become a full member of NATO in 2004.

Economic Affairs

In 2001, according to estimates by the World Bank, Lithuania's gross national income (GNI), measured at average 1999–2001 prices, was US $11,401m., equivalent to $3,270 per head (or $7,610 per head on an international purchasing-power parity basis). During 1990–2001 the population decreased by an annual average of 0.5%, while gross domestic product (GDP) per head declined, in real terms, by an average of 2.0% per year. Overall GDP decreased, in real terms, by an average of 2.5% annually. However, real GDP increased by 4.0% in 2000 and by 6.5% in 2001.

Agriculture (including hunting, forestry and fishing) contributed 7.2% of GDP in 2001, and engaged 17.2% of the employed population. Principal crops are cereals, sugar beet, potatoes and vegetables. In 1991 legislation was adopted permitting the restitution of land to its former owners, and the privatization of state-owned farms and reorganization of collective farms was initiated. By the mid-1990s almost 40% of arable land was privately cultivated. Legislation approved in January 2003 authorized the sale of agricultural land to foreign owners, although its implementation was to be subject to a seven-year

transition period. Real agricultural GDP decreased, in real terms, by an annual average of 1.5% during 1990–2001. The GDP of the sector increased by 4.9% in 2000 and by 2.5% in 2001.

Industry (including mining, manufacturing, construction and power) contributed 31.5% of GDP in 2001, when the sector engaged 27.3% of the employed population. According to World Bank estimates, industrial GDP declined by an annual average of 7.0%, in real terms, during 1990–2001; the GDP of the sector increased by 1.9% in 2000 and by 2.0% in 2001.

In 2001 mining and quarrying contributed 0.7% of GDP and provided just 0.2% of employment. Lithuania has significant reserves of peat and materials used in construction (limestone, clay, dolomite, chalk, and sand and gravel), as well as small deposits of petroleum and natural gas. Real mining GDP increased by 18.9% in 2000 and by 30.6% in 2001.

The manufacturing sector provided 20.5% of GDP in 2001, when it engaged 18.0% of the employed labour force. Based on the value of output, the principal branches of manufacturing in 1996 were food products (particularly dairy products—accounting for 9.5% of the total), refined petroleum products, textiles and clothing and chemicals. The World Bank estimated that manufacturing GDP declined, in real terms, by an annual average of 7.6% during 1990–2001. However, according to official figures, sectoral GDP increased by 9.8% in 2000 and by 13.1% in 2001.

In 1999 nuclear power provided 75.4% of gross electricity production, followed by petroleum (13.8%). Lithuania has substantial petroleum-refining and electricity-generating capacities, which enable it to export refined petroleum products and electricity. In 1999 Lithuania exported an estimated 55.9% of its gross electricity production. In 2002 imports of mineral products accounted for some 17.8% of the total value of merchandise imports, according to provisional figures.

The services sector contributed 61.3% of GDP in 2001, when it provided 55.6% of total employment. The Baltic port of Klaipėda is a significant entrepôt for regional trade in minerals. The GDP of the services sector decreased, in real terms, by an annual average of 0.2% in 1990–2001. However, real services GDP increased by 4.9% in 2000 and by 4.1% in 2001.

In 2001 Lithuania recorded a visible trade deficit of US $1,108.0m., and there was a deficit of $573.6m. on the current account of the balance of payments. In 2002 the principal source of imports was Russia (accounting for an estimated 21.4% of the total); other major sources were Germany, Italy, Poland and France. The United Kingdom was the main market for exports in that year (accounting for an estimated 13.5%). Other principal markets were Russia, Germany and Latvia. In 2002 the principal exports were mineral products (representing an estimated 19.0% of total exports), followed by vehicles and transportation equipment (15.9%), textiles (15.0%), machinery and electrical equipment (9.9%), chemical products (6.5%), and wood products (5.4%). The principal imports were mineral products (representing an estimated 17.8% of total imports), machinery and electrical equipment (17.5%), vehicles and transportation equipment (16.4%), chemical products (8.7%), textiles (7.9%) and base metals (6.8%).

In 2001, according to IMF estimates, there was a budgetary deficit of 171.8m. litai (equivalent to 0.6% of GDP). Lithuania's total external debt was US $4,854.9m. at the end of 2000, of which $2,188.2m. was long-term public debt. In that year the cost of debt-servicing was equivalent to 17.1% of the value of exports of goods and services. Annual inflation averaged 70.0% in 1991–2001. The average annual rate of inflation declined from 1,021% in 1991 to 24.6% in 1996. In 2001 the rate of inflation was 1.3%, and it was 0.3% in 2002. The average rate of unemployment was 13.8% in 2002, when 224,400 people were officially registered as unemployed.

Lithuania is a member, as a 'Country of Operations', of the European Bank for Reconstruction and Development (EBRD, see p. 193), as well as of the IMF and the World Bank. An agreement on a free-trade area between Lithuania, Latvia and Estonia entered into force in April 1994. In December 2000 Lithuania became a member of the World Trade Organization (WTO, see p. 323). Lithuania became an associate member of the European Union (EU, see p. 199) in June 1995. In February 2000 it officially commenced the negotiation process towards full membership, and in December 2002 it was invited to accede in May 2004.

By the mid-1990s the Government's stabilization programme had achieved modest success: the development of the private sector was well advanced, most prices had been liberalized, and progress had been achieved in restructuring the financial sector. However, the economy contracted in 1999, largely owing to the economic crisis in Russia in 1998. Following the controversial sale of part of the Government's stake in the Mažeikiai NAFTA petroleum refinery in late 1999 (see Recent History), other major privatizations were initiated from 2000, and much was achieved in the way of recovery in that year. The last remaining state-owned bank was privatized in 2002, and energy-sector privatization was under way, with arrangements for the partial privatization of the gas utility, Lietuvos Dujos, close to completion by early 2003. In an effort to facilitate increased integration with EU economies and further reorientate foreign trade, from February 2002 the national currency's fixed rate of exchange was linked to the euro, instead of the US dollar, resulting in increased business confidence and investment, and a very low rate of inflation. In June formal agreement was reached with the EU on the closure of the Ignalina nuclear power plant; the first of the plant's reactors was to be decommissioned in 2005 and the second in 2009, in return for substantial financing from the EU to compensate for the costs incurred. Significant reforms were implemented in 2002, and there were changes to taxation legislation and the pensions system, as well as new regulations to combat 'money-laundering', and the introduction of a new labour code. Macroeconomic performance was better than anticipated in that year, owing to improved domestic demand, and GDP increased by 6.7%. The planned fiscal deficit for 2003, equivalent to some 2% of GDP, was based on the need for increased expenditure in preparation for accession to the EU in 2004.

Education

Under the terms of the 1992 Constitution, education, beginning at seven years of age, is compulsory until the age of 16. There are three principal levels of education: comprehensive (from seven to 16 years of age), vocational schools and schools of further education (16–18) and higher. There are three principal types of comprehensive school: primary (Grades 1–4), basic (Grades 5–9) and secondary (Grades 10–12). From January 2003 a uniform tuition fee was to be introduced for students of higher education, although there were to be exemptions for the highest achievers. There are three main types of comprehensive school: primary, basic and secondary. In 2000/01 94.7% of the relevant age-group was enrolled in primary education, while enrolment in secondary education was equivalent to 88.4%. In 1997/98 enrolment in basic education was equivalent to 93.4% of the relevant age-group. In the 2002/03 academic year 594,300 students were enrolled in 2,172 comprehensive schools. In that year there were 82 vocational schools, 51 schools of higher education, and 19 universities. Total enrolment at universities was 119,600 in 2002/03. In 1991 the first private schools were opened; by 1999 there were 38 private schools or colleges and one private university. Lithuanian is the main language of instruction, although in 1999/2000 7.7% of students at comprehensive schools were taught in Russian and 3.8% were taught in Polish. The state budget for 2001 allocated 925.5m. litai (7.3% of total expenditure) to education.

Public Holidays

2003: 1 January (New Year's Day), 16 February (Day of the Restoration of the Lithuanian State), 11 March (Day of the Re-establishment of Independence), 21 April (Easter Monday), 1 May (Mothers' Day), 6 July (Anniversary of the Coronation of Grand Duke Mindaugas of Lithuania), 15 August (Assumption), 1 November (All Saints' Day), 25–26 December (Christmas).

2004: 1 January (New Year's Day), 16 February (Day of the Restoration of the Lithuanian State), 11 March (Day of the Re-establishment of Independence), 12 April (Easter Monday), 1 May (Mothers' Day), 6 July (Anniversary of the Coronation of Grand Duke Mindaugas of Lithuania), 15 August (Assumption), 1 November (All Saints' Day), 25–26 December (Christmas).

Weights and Measures

The metric system is in force.

Statistical Survey

Source (unless otherwise indicated): Department of Statistics to the Government of Lithuania (Statistics Lithuania), Gedimino pr. 29, Vilnius 2600; tel. (523) 64822; fax (523) 64845; e-mail statistika@mail.std.lt; internet www.std.lt.

Area and Population

AREA, POPULATION AND DENSITY

Area (sq km)	65,301*
Population (census results)	
12 January 1989†	3,674,802
6 April 2001	
Males	1,629,148
Females	1,854,824
Total	3,483,972
Population (official estimates at 1 January)	
2001	3,486,998
2002	3,475,586
2003‡	3,462,600
Density (per sq km) at 1 January 2003	53.0

* 25,213 sq miles.
† Figure refers to the *de jure* population. The *de facto* total was 3,689,779.
‡ Provisional figure, rounded.

POPULATION BY ETHNIC GROUP
(permanent inhabitants at 2001 census)*

	'000	%
Lithuanian	2,907.3	83.5
Polish	235.0	6.7
Russian	219.8	6.3
Belarusian	42.9	1.2
Total (incl. others)	3,484.0	100.0

* Figures are provisional.

ADMINISTRATIVE DIVISIONS
(2001 census)

County	Area (sq km)	Population	Density (per sq km)
Alytus	5,425	187,769	34.6
Kaunas	8,170	701,529	85.9
Klaipėda	5,746	385,768	67.1
Marijampolė	4,463	188,634	42.3
Panevėžys	7,881	299,990	38.1
Šiauliai	8,751	370,096	42.3
Tauragė	3,874	134,275	34.7
Telšiai	4,139	179,885	43.5
Utena	7,201	185,962	25.8
Vilnius	9,650	850,064	88.1
Total	65,301	3,483,972	53.4

PRINCIPAL TOWNS
(population at 2001 census)

Vilnius (capital) . .	542,287	Šiauliai . . .	133,883
Kaunas . . .	378,943	Panevėžys . . .	119,749
Klaipėda . . .	192,954	Alytus . . .	71,491

2002 (official estimate at 1 January): Vilnius 553,373.

LITHUANIA

BIRTHS, MARRIAGES AND DEATHS

	Registered live births		Registered marriages		Registered deaths	
	Number	Rate (per 1,000)	Number	Rate (per 1,000)	Number	Rate (per 1,000)
1995 . .	41,195	11.4	22,150	6.1	45,306	12.5
1996 . .	39,066	10.8	20,433	5.7	42,896	11.9
1997 . .	37,812	10.6	18,796	5.3	41,143	11.5
1998 . .	37,019	10.4	18,486	5.2	40,757	11.5
1999 . .	36,415	10.3	17,868	5.1	40,003	11.3
2000 . .	34,149	9.8	16,906	4.8	38,919	11.1
2001 . .	31,546	9.1	15,764	4.5	40,399	11.6
2002* .	30,153	8.7	16,162	4.7	41,162	11.9

* Provisional figures.

Expectation of life (WHO estimates, years at birth): 72.9 (males 67.7; females 66.7) in 2001 (Source: WHO, *World Health Report*).

IMMIGRATION AND EMIGRATION
('000 persons)

	1999	2000	2001
Immigrants	2.7	1.5	4.7
Emigrants	1.4	2.6	7.3

EMPLOYMENT
(annual averages, '000 persons)

	1999	2000	2001
Agriculture, hunting, forestry and fishing	332.5	315.4	260.7
Mining and quarrying . . .	3.7	3.5	3.3
Manufacturing	283.2	280.3	272.5
Electricity, gas and water . .	39.5	35.8	38.5
Construction	108.6	96.4	99.4
Wholesale and retail trade; repair of motor vehicles, motorcycles and personal and household goods	236.9	232.6	233.9
Hotels and restaurants . . .	26.7	28.0	27.9
Transport, storage and communications	105.1	100.6	92.0
Financial intermediation . .	16.4	15.4	15.0
Real estate, renting and business activities	55.1	57.9	60.7
Public administration and defence; compulsory social security . .	72.4	76.9	76.7
Education	158.4	162.5	165.5
Health and social work . . .	110.8	110.5	106.8
Other community, social and personal service activities . .	94.9	67.4	64.4
Other activities not adequately defined	3.3	2.8	4.5
Total	**1,647.5**	**1,586.0**	**1,521.8**
Males	836.9	794.6	756.3
Females	810.6	791.4	765.5

Unemployed (annual averages, '000 persons): 263.3 in 1999; 275.7 in 2000; 299.3 in 2001; 224.4 in 2002.

Health and Welfare

KEY INDICATORS

Total fertility rate (children per woman, 2001)	1.3
Under-5 mortality rate (per 1,000 live births, 2001) . . .	9
HIV/AIDS (% of persons aged 15–49, 2001)	0.07
Physicians (per 1,000 head, 1998)	3.95
Hospital beds (per 1,000 head, 2000)	10.1
Health expenditure (2000): US $ per head (PPP) . . .	420
Health expenditure (2000): % of GDP	6.0
Health expenditure (2000): public (% of total) . . .	72.4
Human Development Index (2000): ranking	49
Human Development Index (2000): value	0.808

For sources and definitions, see explanatory note on p. vi.

Agriculture

PRINCIPAL CROPS
('000 metric tons)

	1999	2000	2001
Wheat	870.9	1,237.6	1,076.3
Barley	741.6	859.6	776.2
Rye	260.9	311.4	231.1
Oats	67.1	82.9	84.3
Buckwheat	8.6	14.8	12.7
Triticale (wheat-rye hybrid) .	85.1	130.9	36.7
Other cereals	14.4	20.6	19.8
Potatoes	1,708.0	1,791.6	1,054.4
Sugar beet	870.9	881.6	900.0
Dry peas	46.5	49.7	30.0
Other pulses*	16.4	23.5	22.2
Rapeseed	115.0	81.0	64.8
Cabbages	119.6	125.7	121.3
Tomatoes	6.8	5.1	4.4
Cucumbers and gherkins . .	12.0*	12.0	8.0
Dry onions	23.1	20.3	22.7
Carrots	47.4	65.3	61.6
Green peas*	5.0	6.0	5.0
Other vegetables*	111.2	98.3	99.0
Apples	100.0	98.6	151.1
Pears	9.2	3.0	4.0
Grapes†	22.0	20.0	n.a.

* Unofficial figure(s).
† FAO estimates.

Source: FAO.

LIVESTOCK
('000 head at 1 January)

	1999	2000	2001
Horses	74	75	68
Cattle	923	898	748
Pigs	1,159	936	856
Sheep	16	14	12
Goats	24	25	23
Chickens	6,749	6,372	5,576
Turkeys	377*	400†	400†
Rabbits	102	85	82

* Unofficial figure.
† FAO estimate.

Source: FAO.

LIVESTOCK PRODUCTS
('000 metric tons, unless otherwise indicated)

	1999	2000	2001
Beef and veal	77.3	75.4	63.9
Pig meat	91.0	84.5	91.6
Poultry meat	23.0	17.2*	18.5*
Cows' milk	1,714.2	1,724.7	1,794.0
Cheese	37.2	43.6	47.0
Butter	26.2	19.3	21.0
Eggs	40.1	36.4	37.4
Honey	0.8	0.8	0.8
Cattle hides (fresh)†	9.2	10.7	8.1

* Unofficial figure.
† FAO estimates.

Source: FAO.

Forestry

ROUNDWOOD REMOVALS
('000 cubic metres, excl. bark)

	1999	2000	2001
Sawlogs, veneer logs and logs for sleepers	2,535	2,900	2,850
Pulpwood	1,240	1,100	1,150
Other industrial wood . . .	25	50	50
Fuel wood	1,124	1,450	1,650
Total	4,924	5,500	5,700

Source: FAO.

SAWNWOOD PRODUCTION
('000 cubic metres, incl. railway sleepers)

	1999	2000	2001
Coniferous (softwood)	850	1,000	950
Broadleaved (hardwood). . .	300	300*	300*
Total	1,150	1,300	1,250

* FAO estimate.

Source: FAO.

Fishing

(metric tons, live weight)

	1998	1999	2000
Capture	66,578	33,594	78,987
Atlantic cod.	3,296	4,371	4,721
Atlantic redfishes	1,769	3,884	6,687
Jack and horse mackerels . .	11,902	2,641	25,464
Atlantic herring	2,368	1,313	1,198
Sardinellas	10,575	2,814	6,324
European sprat	4,460	3,117	1,682
European anchovy. . . .	3,612	1,067	16,137
Chub mackerel.	5,420	549	3,871
Atlantic mackerel	2,823	4,936	2,085
Largehead hairtail . . .	9,708	2	32
Northern prawn	3,340	4,167	6,376
Aquaculture	1,516	1,650	1,996
Common carp	1,516	1,650	1,921
Total catch	68,094	35,244	80,983

Source: FAO, *Yearbook of Fishery Statistics*.

Mining

('000 metric tons, unless otherwise indicated)

	2000	2001	2002
Crude petroleum	232	316	471
Dolomite ('000 cubic metres) . .	735	524	384
Limestone	1,060	850	894
Clay ('000 cubic metres). . .	247	177	171
Peat	380	259	259

Industry

SELECTED PRODUCTS
('000 metric tons, unless otherwise indicated)

	1999	2000	2001
Sausages and smoked meat products.	54.1	55.2	54.2
Flour	215.3	204.9	211.5
Mayonnaise	7.9	8.6	10.2
Refined sugar.	121.2	126.6	108.7
Beer ('000 hectolitres) . . .	184.8	210.5	219.3
Wine ('000 hectolitres) . . .	646	403	429
Cigarettes (million)	8,200	7,200	n.a.
Cotton fabrics (million sq m) . .	57.0	55.1	44.3
Linen fabrics (million sq m) . .	20.0	17.8	13.8
Fabrics of man-made fibres. . .	39.2	17.7	8.0
Footwear—excl. rubber and plastic ('000 pairs)	1,800	700	900
Rubber and plastic footwear ('000 pairs)	500	400	400
Plywood ('000 cubic metres) . .	14.3	21.2	27.6
Particle board ('000 cubic metres)	101.9	172.2	197.4
Paper	9.6	12.3	13.9
Paperboard	27.6	41.0	54.3
Motor spirit (petrol)	4,507	4,659	6,544
Sulphuric acid	800	809	465
Mineral and chemical fertilizers	885	924	832
Nitrogenous fertilizers . . .	557	595	611
Cement	666	570	500*
Cast iron	23.4	23.2	24.6
Television receivers ('000) . .	186.5	207.2	143.2
Refrigerators and freezers ('000)	229.2	216.3	320.4
Bicycles ('000).	188	254	323
Electric energy (million kWh) . .	13,535	11,400*	14,700*

* Figure is rounded.

Finance

CURRENCY AND EXCHANGE RATES

Monetary Units
100 centas = 1 litas (plural: litai)

Sterling, Dollar and Euro Equivalents (31 December 2002)
£1 sterling = 5.337 litai
US $1 = 3.311 litai
€1 = 3.453 litai
100 litai = £18.74 = $30.21 = €28.96

Note: In June 1993 Lithuania reintroduced its national currency, the litas, replacing a temporary coupon currency, the talonas, at a conversion rate of 1 litas = 100 talonai. The talonas had been introduced in May 1992, initially circulating alongside (and at par with) the Russian (formerly Soviet) rouble. An official mid-point exchange rate of US $1 = 4.00 litai was in operation from 1 April 1994 until 1 February 2002. From 2 February 2002 the litas was linked to the euro, with the exchange rate set at €1 = 3.4528 litai.

BUDGET
(million litai)*

Revenue†	1999	2000	2001
Tax revenue	10,452.0	10,316.8	10,697.4
Taxes on income, profits and capital gains	1,398.8	1,334.7	1,273.0
Corporate.	360.8	311.7	259.2
Individual	1,038.0	1,023.0	1,013.8
Social security contributions	3,405.5	3,597.7	3,678.0
Domestic taxes on goods and services	5,433.5	5,239.5	5,596.9
Excises	1,643.4	1,459.8	1,643.0
General sales, turnover or value-added taxes . . .	3,741.9	3,698.2	3,831.4
Taxes on international trade	192.6	142.9	133.8
Other current revenue . . .	585.6	775.8	1,032.6
Administrative fees and charges, non-industrial and incidental sales	207.9	188.2	537.7
Capital revenue	13.4	42.7	29.2
Total	11,051.0	11,135.3	11,759.2

Expenditure‡	1999	2000	2001
General public services	530.9	519.2	599.6
Defence	440.4	589.3	755.4
Public order and safety	871.6	829.7	833.0
Education	749.3	724.0	925.5
Health	1,945.0	1,956.6	2,028.9
Social security and welfare . .	4,519.8	4,574.6	4,480.1
Recreational, cultural and religious affairs and services . . .	272.4	232.7	233.4
Economic affairs and services . .	1,540.3	1,577.6	1,527.2
Agriculture, forestry, fishing and hunting	561.1	731.6	587.7
Transport and communications .	833.5	720.6	680.6
Other purposes	2,386.1	1,443.5	1,233.7
Interest payments	626.7	771.0	741.7
Total	13,260.8	12,447.3	12,616.8
Current	11,120.9	11,533.6	11,499.5
Capital	2,139.9	913.7	1,117.3

* Figures refer to the consolidated accounts of the central Government, comprising the operations of the central budget, the Guarantee Fund and Fund for Financial Support to Bankrupted Enterprises, Privatization Funds, the Road Fund, Social Security Funds and others.

† Excluding grants received (million litai): 239.9 in 2001.

‡ Excluding lending minus repayments (million litai): 796.8 in 1999; −727.3 in 2000; −445.9 in 2001.

Source: IMF, *Government Finance Statistics Yearbook*.

INTERNATIONAL RESERVES
(US $ million at 31 December)

	2000	2001	2002
Gold*	47.10	51.47	63.82
IMF special drawing rights . . .	1.32	18.43	53.44
Reserve position in IMF	0.02	0.02	0.02
Foreign exchange	1,310.21	1,599.27	2,302.78
Total	1,358.65	1,669.19	2,420.06

* National valuation.

Source: IMF, *International Financial Statistics*.

MONEY SUPPLY
(million litai at 31 December)

	2000	2001	2002
Currency outside banks	2,658.3	2,919.9	3,756.4
Demand deposits at banking institutions	3,002.6	3,808.0	4,553.0
Total money (incl. others) . . .	5,672.6	6,744.5	8,329.2

Source: IMF, *International Financial Statistics*.

COST OF LIVING
(Consumer Price Index; base: 1993 = 100)

	1999	2000	2001
Food (incl. beverages)	17,997.5	17,562.6	18,193.3
Fuel and light	783.6	914.8	933.0
Clothing	343.7	341.0	326.7
Rent	682.1	698.0	714.8
All items (incl. others)	19,750.8	19,937.4	20,195.9

Source: ILO.

2002 (base: 2001 = 100): All items 100.3.

NATIONAL ACCOUNTS
(million litai at current prices)

Expenditure on the Gross Domestic Product

	1999	2000	2001
Final consumption expenditure .	37,146.7	38,566.7	40,124.1
Households	27,441.8	28,580.7	30,407.3
Non-profit institutions serving households	71.2	132.3	119.2
General government	9,633.8	9,853.7	9,597.6
Gross capital formation	9,858.2	9,025.9	9,979.8
Gross fixed capital formation .	9,614.2	8,565.3	9,784.6
Changes in inventories . . .	229.1	448.9	186.0
Acquisitions, *less* disposals, of valuables	14.9	11.7	9.2
Total domestic expenditure . .	47,004.9	47,592.6	50,103.9
Exports of goods and services . .	16,952.9	20,436.5	24,182.3
Less Imports of goods and services	21,349.5	23,331.2	26,788.6
GDP in market prices . . .	42,608.3	44,697.9	47,497.6
GDP at constant 2000 prices	42,608.3	44,697.9	47,497.6

Gross Domestic Product by Economic Activity

	1999	2000	2001
Agriculture, hunting and forestry	3,191.8	3,174.3	3,039.8
Fishing	22.9	26.7	28.8
Mining and quarrying	178.8	279.0	317.6
Manufacturing	6,985.1	7,981.6	8,767.7
Electricity, gas and water supply	1,660.1	1,540.9	1,786.1
Construction	2,949.4	2,429.9	2,597.0
Wholesale and retail trade . . .	6,065.9	6,685.0	7,478.3
Hotels and restaurants . . .	652.1	619.0	676.7
Transport, storage and communications	4,003.7	5,013.1	5,384.6
Financial intermediation . . .	868.2	881.0	987.5
Real estate, renting and business activities	3,186.4	3,403.7	3,554.6
Public administration and defence	2,678.2	2,786.9	2,474.6
Education	2,655.2	2,595.9	2,722.6
Health and social work	1,542.6	1,466.3	1,464.7
Other community, social and personal service activities . .	1,237.7	1,302.8	1,404.1
Private households with employed persons	31.0	37.6	43.6
Sub-total	37,909.3	40,223.8	42,728.3
Less Financial intermediation services indirectly measured . .	612.7	590.5	593.4
Gross value added in basic prices	37,296.6	39,633.3	42,134.9
Taxes *less* subsidies on products	5,311.7	5,064.5	5,362.8
GDP in purchasers' values . .	42,608.3	44,697.8	47,497.7

BALANCE OF PAYMENTS
(US $ million)

	1999	2000	2001
Exports of goods f.o.b.	3,146.7	4,050.4	4,889.0
Imports of goods f.o.b.	−4,551.3	−5,154.1	−5,997.0
Trade balance	−1,404.6	−1,103.8	−1,108.0
Exports of services	1,091.5	1,058.8	1,157.0
Imports of services	−786.1	−678.7	−700.3
Balance on goods and services	−1,099.1	−723.7	−651.4
Other income received	114.8	185.5	205.7
Other income paid	−372.6	−379.3	−385.5
Balance on goods, services and income	−1,356.8	−917.5	−831.1
Current transfers received . . .	167.4	246.8	262.0
Current transfers paid	−4.6	−4.3	−4.5
Current balance	−1,194.1	−674.9	−573.6
Capital account (net)	−3.3	2.2	1.4
Direct investment abroad . . .	−8.6	−3.7	−7.1
Direct investment from abroad .	486.5	378.9	445.8
Portfolio investment assets . .	−2.0	−141.4	26.2
Portfolio investment liabilities . .	512.7	405.9	238.0
Financial derivatives assets . .	—	—	18.3
Financial derivatives liabilities . .	—	—	−19.6
Other investment assets . . .	−182.5	39.9	−225.0
Other investment liabilities . .	259.8	22.8	300.9
Net errors and omissions . . .	−42.2	128.3	153.6
Overall balance	−178.7	158.0	359.0

External Trade

PRINCIPAL COMMODITIES
(million litai)

Imports c.i.f.	2000	2001	2002*
Vegetable products	698.4	692.7	711.0
Prepared foodstuffs; beverages, spirits and vinegar; tobacco and manufactured substitutes . .	874.0	990.7	1,002.5
Mineral products	5,082.2	5,385.8	5,014.2
Products of the chemical or allied industries	1,986.2	2,338.7	2,443.5
Plastics, rubber and articles thereof	1,201.9	1,340.9	1,476.4
Textiles and textile articles . .	2,038.4	2,226.7	2,240.2
Base metals and articles thereof .	1,156.7	1,328.5	1,916.9
Machinery and mechanical appliances; electrical equipment; sound and television apparatus .	3,418.1	4,250.6	4,931.4
Vehicles, aircraft, vessels and associated transport equipment .	1,900.3	2,923.2	4,619.3
Total (incl. others)	21,826.0	25,413.2	28,220.1

Exports f.o.b.	2000	2001	2002*
Live animals and animal products	809.9	853.6	803.5
Vegetable products	309.1	497.1	413.2
Prepared foodstuffs; beverages, spirits and vinegar; tobacco and manufactured substitutes . .	650.5	886.3	914.8
Mineral products	3,234.3	4,287.9	3,856.9
Products of the chemical or allied industries	1,201.3	1,179.9	1,316.3
Plastics, rubber and articles thereof	475.8	536.5	570.7
Wood cork and articles thereof; wood charcoal; manufactures of straw, esparto, etc.	901.1	964.6	1,093.7
Textiles and textile articles. . .	2,836.3	2,994.1	3,048.9
Base metals and articles thereof .	634.3	680.9	957.3
Machinery and mechanical appliances; electrical equipment; sound and television apparatus .	1,619.7	1,960.2	2,015.7
Vehicles, aircraft, vessels and associated transport equipment .	1,034.9	1,694.0	3,219.5
Miscellaneous manufactured articles	643.0	769.8	997.6
Total (incl. others)	15,237.5	18,332.0	20,279.8

* Figures are provisional.

PRINCIPAL TRADING PARTNERS
(million litai)

Imports c.i.f.	2000	2001	2002*
Belarus	394.4	483.4	422.8
Belgium	430.8	497.9	529.2
China, People's Republic . .	336.2	500.2	671.7
Czech Republic	299.3	344.1	366.6
Denmark	675.7	742.0	834.2
Estonia	254.1	274.9	n.a.
Finland	557.1	582.3	647.2
France	922.1	956.7	1,096.2
Germany	3,285.1	4,377.7	4,850.5
Italy	788.7	1,073.0	1,381.9
Japan	406.1	482.4	608.7
Kazakhstan	90.3	37.0	399.2
Latvia	360.1	392.4	454.2
Netherlands	496.2	598.2	640.8
Norway	168.9	245.0	415.6
Poland	1,076.2	1,233.0	1,365.1
Russia	5,973.1	6,428.0	6,048.5
Spain	242.3	323.5	n.a.
Sweden	743.2	771.4	930.9
Ukraine	330.8	414.3	463.5
United Kingdom	985.3	851.8	939.4
USA	517.4	771.9	810.3
Total (incl. others)	21,826.0	25,413.2	28,220.1

Exports f.o.b.	2000	2001	2002*
Belarus	442.8	714.5	649.7
Belgium	241.3	299.5	388.4
Denmark	743.9	822.2	1,009.2
Estonia	343.0	595.2	771.7
Finland	194.1	255.1	235.0
France	667.6	601.3	831.5
Germany	2,183.5	2,303.1	2,094.1
Italy	356.4	369.3	563.0
Latvia	2,287.8	2,316.3	1,955.3
Netherlands	730.4	538.6	654.6
Norway	170.6	239.1	487.1
Poland	832.3	1,148.3	720.4
Russia	1,083.7	2,019.7	2,463.2
Spain	182.0	247.4	n.a.
Sweden	667.5	671.3	849.9
Switzerland	193.5	107.7	338.1
Turkey	266.8	260.2	352.2
Ukraine	670.8	618.9	528.3
United Kingdom	1,185.9	2,532.6	2,745.7
USA	739.2	696.8	733.5
Total (incl. others)	15,237.5	18,332.0	20,279.8

* Provisional figures.

Transport

RAILWAYS
(traffic)

	1999	2000	2001
Passenger journeys ('000) . .	11,527	8,852	7,718
Passenger-km (million) . . .	745	611	533
Freight transported ('000 metric tons)	28,347	30,712	29,174
Freight ton-km (million) . . .	7,849	8,919	7,741

ROAD TRAFFIC
(public transport and freight)

	1999	2000	2001
Passenger journeys ('000) . . .	458,328	372,684	346,401
Passenger-km (million) . . .	2,665	2,154	2,119
Freight transported ('000 metric tons)	45,651	45,013	45,075
Freight ton-km (million) . .	7,740	7,769	8,274

ROAD TRAFFIC
(motor vehicles in use at 31 December)

	1999	2000	2001
Passenger cars	1,089,334	1,172,394	1,133,477
Buses and coaches	15,590	15,069	15,171
Lorries and vans	86,824	88,346	89,373
Motorcycles and mopeds . . .	19,515	19,842	20,244

INLAND WATERWAYS

	1999	2000	2001
Passenger journeys ('000) . . .	1,728.3	1,299.9	1,323.6
Passenger-km (million) . . .	2	2	1
Freight transported ('000 metric tons)	796.7	852.4	543.3
Freight ton-km (million)	3	2	1

SHIPPING

Merchant Fleet
(registered at 31 December)

	1999	2000	2001
Number of vessels	192	185	175
Total displacement ('000 grt) . .	424.3	434.2	393.3

Source: Lloyd's Register-Fairplay, *World Fleet Statistics*.

International Sea-borne Freight Traffic
('000 metric tons)

	1999	2000	2001
Goods loaded	12,864	18,552	18,144
Goods unloaded	2,796	4,296	4,224

Source: UN, *Monthly Bulletin of Statistics.*

CIVIL AVIATION
(traffic on scheduled services)

	1996	1997	1998
Kilometres flown (million) . .	8	9	10
Passengers carried ('000) . .	214	236	259
Passenger-km (million) . . .	304	301	307
Total ton-km (million) . . .	29	30	31

Source: UN, *Statistical Yearbook.*

1999: Passengers carried 296 million; Passenger-km 387 million; Freight transported 2.0 million metric tons.

2000: Passengers carried 343 million; Passenger-km 461 million; Freight transported 3.3 million metric tons.

2001: Passengers carried 363 million; Passenger-km 484 million; Freight transported 3.3 million metric tons.

Tourism

FOREIGN VISITORS BY COUNTRY OF ORIGIN
(arrivals at accommodation establishments)

	1999	2000	2001
Belarus	12,971	14,034	19,195
Estonia	12,499	11,425	14,011
Finland	20,960	22,775	21,282
Germany	48,390	52,089	54,479
Latvia	27,354	24,750	27,252
Poland	33,288	37,477	45,820
Russia	24,890	28,282	44,859
Sweden	14,099	15,174	14,013
United Kingdom	13,332	13,383	11,138
USA	12,479	13,120	13,310
Total (incl. others)	293,247	299,938	349,662

Source: Lithuanian State Department of Tourism, Vilnius.

Receipts from tourism (US $ million): 550.4 in 1999; 391.3 in 2000; 383.0 in 2001 (Source: Bank of Lithuania).

Communications Media

	1999	2000	2001
Television receivers ('000) . . .	1,555	1,560	n.a.
Telephones ('000 main lines in use)	1,152.6	1,187.7	1,151.7
Mobile cellular telephones ('000 subscribers)	332.0	524.0	932.0
Personal computers ('000 in use) .	220	240	260
Internet users ('000)	103	225	250

1997: Radio receivers ('000 in use) 1,900; Facsimile machines (number in use) 6,200.

1999: Book titles (incl. brochures) 4,097; Newspapers 377 (number), 2,188 (average circulation, '000 copies); Other periodicals 418.

Sources: International Telecommunication Union; UNESCO, *Statistical Yearbook* ; UN, *Statistical Yearbook* and Ministry of Education and Science, Vilnius.

Education

(2002/03)

	Institutions	Teachers*	Students*
Comprehensive schools	2,172	50,200	594,300
Vocational schools	82	4,700	44,400
Schools of further education . .	51	5,300	48,600
Universities	19	8,900	119,600

* Figures are rounded.

Source: Ministry of Education and Science, Vilnius.

Teachers (1999): Pre-primary schools 12,526; Primary and general secondary schools 52,000; Vocational schools 5,032.

Adult literacy rate (UNESCO estimates): 99.6% (males 99.5%; females 99.7%) in 2000 (Source: UN Development Programme, *Human Development Report*).

Directory

The Constitution

The Constitution was approved in a national referendum on 25 October 1992 and adopted by the Seimas on 6 November. The following is a summary of its main provisions:

THE STATE

The Republic of Lithuania is an independent and democratic republic; its sovereignty is vested in the people, who exercise their supreme power either directly or through their democratically elected representatives. The powers of the State are exercised by the Seimas (Parliament), the President of the Republic, the Government and the Judiciary. The most significant issues concerning the State and the people are decided by referendum.

The territory of the republic is integral. Citizenship is acquired by birth or on other grounds determined by law. With certain exceptions established by law, no person may be a citizen of Lithuania and of another state at the same time. Lithuanian is the state language.

THE INDIVIDUAL AND THE STATE

The rights and freedoms of individuals are inviolable. Property is inviolable, and the rights of ownership are protected by law. Freedom of thought, conscience and religion are guaranteed. All persons are equal before the law. No one may be discriminated against on the basis of sex, race, nationality, language, origin, social status, religion or opinion. Citizens may choose their place of resi-

dence in Lithuania freely, and may leave the country at their own will. Citizens are guaranteed the right to form societies, political parties and associations. Citizens who belong to ethnic communities have the right to foster their language, culture and customs.

SOCIETY AND THE STATE

The family is the basis of society and the State. Education is compulsory until the age of 16. Education at state and local government institutions is free of charge at all levels. State and local government establishments of education are secular, although, at the request of parents, they may offer classes in religious instruction. The State recognizes traditional Lithuanian and other churches and religious organizations, but there is no state religion. Censorship of mass media is prohibited. Ethnic communities may independently administer the affairs of their ethnic culture, education, organizations, etc. The State supports ethnic communities.

NATIONAL ECONOMY AND LABOUR

Lithuania's economy is based on the right to private ownership and freedom of individual economic activity. Every person may freely choose an occupation, and has the right to adequate, safe and healthy working conditions, adequate compensation for work, and social security in the event of unemployment. Trade unions may be freely established and may function independently. Employees have the right to strike in order to protect their economic and social interests. The state guarantees the right of citizens to old-age and disability pensions, as well as to social assistance in the event of unemployment, sickness, widowhood, etc.

THE SEIMAS

Legislative power rests with the Seimas. It comprises 141 members, elected for a four-year term on the basis of universal, equal and direct suffrage by secret ballot. Any citizen who has attained 25 years of age may be a candidate for the Seimas. Members of the Seimas may not be found criminally responsible, may not be arrested, and may not be subjected to any other restrictions of personal freedom, without the consent of the Seimas. The Seimas convenes for two regular four-month sessions every year.

The Seimas considers and enacts amendments to the Constitution; enacts laws; adopts resolutions for the organization of referendums; announces presidential elections; approves or rejects the candidature of the Prime Minister, as proposed by the President of the Republic; establishes or abolishes government ministries, upon the recommendation of the Government; supervises the activities of the Government, with the power to express a vote of 'no confidence' in the Prime Minister or individual ministers; appoints judges to the Constitutional Court and the Supreme Court; approves the state budget and supervises the implementation thereof; establishes state taxes and other obligatory payments; ratifies or denounces international treaties whereto the republic is a party, and considers other issues of foreign policy; establishes administrative divisions of the republic; issues acts of amnesty; imposes direct administration and martial law, declares states of emergency, announces mobilization, and adopts decisions to use the armed forces.

THE PRESIDENT OF THE REPUBLIC

The President of the Republic is the Head of State. Any Lithuanian citizen by birth, who has lived in Lithuania for at least the three preceding years, who has reached 40 years of age and who is eligible for election to the Seimas, may be elected President of the Republic. The President is elected by the citizens of the republic, on the basis of universal, equal and direct suffrage by secret ballot, for a term of five years. No person may be elected to the office for more than two consecutive terms.

The President resolves basic issues of foreign policy and, in conjunction with the Government, implements foreign policy; signs international treaties and submits them to the Seimas for ratification; appoints or recalls, upon the recommendation of the Government, diplomatic representatives of Lithuania in foreign states and international organizations; appoints, upon the approval of the Seimas, the Prime Minister, and charges him/her with forming the Government, and approves its composition; removes, upon the approval of the Seimas, the Prime Minister from office; appoints or dismisses individual ministers, upon the recommendation of the Prime Minister; appoints or dismisses, upon the approval of the Seimas, the Commander-in-Chief of the armed forces and the head of the Security Service.

THE GOVERNMENT

Executive power is held by the Government of the republic (Council of Ministers), which consists of the Prime Minister and other ministers. The Prime Minister is appointed and dismissed by the President of the Republic, with the approval of the Seimas. Ministers are appointed by the President, on the nomination of the Prime Minister.

The Government administers the affairs of the country, protects the inviolability of the territory of Lithuania, and ensures state security and public order; implements laws and resolutions of the Seimas as well as presidential decrees; co-ordinates the activities of the ministries and other governmental institutions; prepares the draft state budget and submits it to the Seimas; executes the state budget and reports to the Seimas on its fulfilment; drafts legislative proposals and submits them to the Seimas for consideration; establishes and maintains diplomatic representation with foreign countries and international organizations.

JUDICIAL SYSTEM

The judicial system is independent of the authority of the legislative and executive branches of government. It consists of a Constitutional Court, a Supreme Court, a Court of Appeal, and district and local courts (for details, see section on Judicial System below).

The Government

HEAD OF STATE

President: ROLANDAS PAKSAS (elected 5 January 2003; inaugurated 26 February 2003).

COUNCIL OF MINISTERS
(April 2003)

Prime Minister: ALGIRDAS MYKOLAS BRAZAUSKAS.

Minister of the Economy: PETRAS ČĖSNA.

Minister of Finance: DALIA GRYBAUSKAITĖ.

Minister of National Defence: LINAS ANTANAS LINKEVIČIUS.

Minister of Culture: ROMA DOYDĖNIENĖ.

Minister of Social Security and Labour: VILIJA BLINKEVIČIŪTĖ.

Minister of Justice: VYTAUTAS MARKEVIČIUS.

Minister of Transport and Communications: ZIGMANTAS BALČYTIS.

Minister of Health Care: JUOZAS OLEKAS.

Minister of Foreign Affairs: ANTANAS VALIONIS.

Minister of the Interior: VIRGILIJUS BULOVAS.

Minister of Agriculture and Forestry: JERONIMAS KRAUJELIS.

Minister of Education and Science: ALGIRDAS MONKEVIČIUS.

Minister of the Environment: ARŪNAS KUNDROTAS.

MINISTRIES

Office of the President: S. Daukanto 3/8, Vilnius 2008; tel. (526) 28986; fax (521) 26210; e-mail info@president.lt; internet www .president.lt.

Office of the Prime Minister: Gedimino pr. 11, Vilnius 2039; tel. (526) 63874; fax (521) 63877; e-mail kasp@lrvk.lt; internet www.lrvk .lt.

Ministry of Agriculture and Forestry: Gedimino pr. 19, Vilnius 2025; tel. (523) 91001; fax (521) 24440; e-mail zum@zum.lt; internet www.zum.lt.

Ministry of Culture: J. Basanavičiaus 5, Vilnius 2600; tel. (526) 19486; fax (526) 23120; e-mail culture@muza.lt; internet www.muza .lt.

Ministry of the Economy: Gedimino pr. 38/2, Vilnius 2600; tel. (526) 22416; fax (526) 23974; e-mail pr@po.ekm.lt; internet www .ekm.lt.

Ministry of Education and Science: A. Volano 2/7, Vilnius 2691; tel. (527) 43126; fax (526) 12077; e-mail smmin@smm.lt; internet www.smm.lt.

Ministry of the Environment: Jakšto 4/9, Vilnius 2694; tel. (526) 16148; fax (521) 20847; e-mail kanceliarja@aplinkuma.lt; internet www.gamta.lt.

Ministry of Finance: J. Tumo-Vaižganto 8A/2, Vilnius 2600; tel. (523) 90005; fax (521) 26387; e-mail finmin@finmin.lt; internet www .finmin.lt.

Ministry of Foreign Affairs: J. Tumo-Vaižganto 2, Vilnius 2600; tel. (523) 62444; fax (523) 13090; e-mail urm@urm.lt; internet www .urm.lt.

Ministry of Health Care: Vilniaus 33, Vilnius 2001; tel. (526) 21625; fax (521) 24601; e-mail webmaster@sam.lt; internet www .sam.lt.

Ministry of the Interior: Šventaragio 2, Vilnius 2600; tel. (527) 18451; fax (527) 18551; e-mail atstovasspaudai@vrm.lt; internet www.vrm.lt.

Ministry of Justice: Gedimino pr. 30/1, Vilnius 2600; tel. (526) 24670; fax (526) 25940; e-mail tm1@utic.tm.lt.

Ministry of National Defence: Totorių 25/3, Vilnius 2001; tel. (526) 24821; fax (521) 26082; e-mail vis@kam.lt; internet www.kam .lt.

Ministry of Social Security and Labour: A. Vivulskio 11, Vilnius 2693; tel. (526) 03790; fax (526) 03813; e-mail post@socmin.lt; internet www.socmin.lt.

Ministry of Transport and Communications: Gedimino pr. 17, Vilnius 2679; tel. (523) 93911; fax (521) 24335; e-mail transp@transp .lt; internet www.transp.lt.

President and Legislature

PRESIDENT

Presidential Election, First Ballot, 22 December 2002

Candidates	Valid votes cast	% valid votes cast
Valdas Adamkus	514,154	35.53
Rolandas Paksas	284,559	19.66
Artūras Paulauskas	120,238	8.31
Vytautas Šerenas	112,215	7.75
Vytenis Povilas Andriukaitis	105,584	7.30
Kazimieras Prunskienė	72,925	5.04
Juozas Edvardas Petraitis	54,139	3.74
Eugenijus Gentvilas	44,562	3.08
Julius Veselka	32,293	2.23
Algimantas Matulevičius	32,137	2.22
Others	74,311	5.14
Total	**1,447,117**	**100.00**

Second Ballot, 5 January 2003

Candidates	Valid votes cast	% valid votes cast
Rolandas Paksas	777,769	54.71
Valdas Adamkus	643,870	45.29
Total	**1,421,639**	**100.00**

SEIMAS
(Parliament)

Gedimino pr. 53, Vilnius 2002; tel. (523) 96880; fax (523) 99607; e-mail bendrasis@lrs.lt; internet www.lrs.lt.

Chairman: ARTŪRAS PAULAUSKAS.

First Deputy Chairman: ČESLOVAS JURŠĖNAS.

Deputy Chairmen: VYTENIS ANDRIUKAITIS, ARTŪRAS SKARDŽIUS, GINTARAS STEPONAVIČIUS.

General Election, 8 October 2000

Parties	% of votes	Seats
A. Brazauskas Social Democratic Coalition*	31.1	51
Lithuanian Liberal Union	17.3	34
New Union (Social Liberals)	19.6	29
Conservative Party of Lithuania	8.6	9
Lithuanian Farmers' Party	4.1	4
Christian Democratic Party of Lithuania	3.1	2
Lithuanian Centre Union	2.9	2
Lithuanian Poles' Electoral Action	1.9	2
Christian-Democratic Union	4.2	1
Moderate Conservative Union	2.0	1
Lithuanian Freedom Union	1.3	1
Young Lithuania National Party	1.2	1
Modern Christian-Democratic Union	—	1
Independents	—	3
Others	2.6	0
Total	**100.0**	**141**

*Comprising the Lithuanian Democratic Labour Party and the Lithuanian Social Democratic Party (the two parties formally merged under the latter name in 2001), the New Democracy Party (which merged with the Lithuanian Peasants' Party to form the Peasants' and New Democracy Union in 2002) and the Lithuanian Russians' Union.

Political Organizations

In early 2003 37 political parties were registered with the Ministry of Justice.

Conservative Party of Lithuania (CP) (Homeland Union—Lithuanian Conservatives): Gedimino pr. 15, Vilnius 2001; tel. and fax (523) 96450; e-mail info@tslk.lt; internet www.tslk.lt; f. 1993; from elements of Sąjūdis; Chair. VYTAUTAS LANDSBERGIS; Exec. Sec. JURGIS RAZMA; 15,000 mems.

Lithuanian Centre Union: Literaty 8, Vilnius 2001; tel. (521) 24095; fax (521) 23790; e-mail info@lcs.lt; internet www.lcs.lt; f. 1993; agreed to merger with the Lithuanian Liberal Union and the

Modern Christian-Democratic Union in Jan. 2003; Chair. Prof. KĘSTUTIS GLAVECKAS; 3,000 mems.

Lithuanian Christian Democrats: Pylimo 36/2, Vilnius 2001; tel. (526) 26126; fax (521) 27387; e-mail lkdp@takas.lt; internet www.lkdp.lt; f. 1904; re-est. 1989; formed in 2001 by merger of the Christian Democratic Party of Lithuania and the Christian Democratic Union; Chair. KAZYS BOBELIS; 12,000 mems.

Lithuanian Citizens' Alliance: Vilnius; tel. (527) 33394; f. 1996; Chair. MEČISLAV VAŠKOVIČ.

Lithuanian Economic Party: Vilnius; tel. (526) 31564; fax (526) 51380; f. 1995; Chair. KLEMENSAS ŠEPUTIS; 1,500 mems.

Lithuanian Freedom Union: Donelaičio 6, Kaunas; tel. (372) 02594; f. 1994; Chair. VYTAUTAS ŠUSTAUSKAS.

Lithuanian Green Party: Antakalnio 46–40, Vilnius 2055; tel. (374) 25566; fax (374) 25207; e-mail zigmasvaisvila@lrs.lt; internet www.zalieji.lt; f. 1989; Chair. RŪTA GAJAUSKAITE; 400 mems.

Lithuanian Humanistic Party: Vilnius; tel. (527) 35831; f. 1990; Chair. LEOPOLDAS TARAKEVIČIUS.

Lithuanian Justice Party: Nemuno 19, Kaunas; tel. (372) 09382; f. 1995; Chair. BRONIUS SIMANAVIČIUS.

Lithuanian Liberal Democratic Party (LLDP): Pylimo 27/14, Vilnius 2000; tel. (526) 23493; e-mail sekretoriatas@ldp.lt; internet www.ldp.lt; f. 2002; right-wing; Chair. VALENTINAS MAZURONIS; 1,500 mems.

Lithuanian Liberal Union: A. Jakšto 9, Vilnius 2001; tel. (523) 13264; fax (527) 91910; e-mail lls@lls.lt; internet www.lls.lt; f. 1990; agreed to merger with the Lithuanian Centre Union and the Modern Christian-Democratic Union in Jan. 2003; Chair. EUGENIJUS GENTVILAS; 1,100 mems.

Lithuanian Life Logics Party: Vilnius; f. 1996; Chair. VYTAUTAS BERNATONIS.

Lithuanian National Union: Gedimino pr. 22, Vilnius 2600; tel. (526) 24935; fax (526) 17310; e-mail lietauta@takas.lt; internet www.lts.lt; f. 1924; refounded 1989; Chair. GEDIMINAS SAKALNIKAS; 3,000 mems.

Lithuanian People's Party: Pelesos 1/2, Vilnius; tel. (526) 30429; f. 1996; Chair. VYTAUTAS LAZINKA.

Lithuanian Poles' Electoral Action: Didžioji 40, Vilnius 2601; tel. (521) 23388; f. 1994; Chair. JAN SINKIEWICZ; 1,000 mems.

Lithuanian Polish People's Party (Polska Partia Ludowa): Vilnius; Chair. ANTONINA POLTAWIEC.

Lithuanian Political Prisoners' Party: Kipro Petrausko pr. 38, Kaunas 3005; tel. and fax (377) 95494; f. 1995; Chair. ZIGMAS MEDINECKAS.

Lithuanian Reform Party: Gedimino pr. 2, Vilnius; tel. (521) 25800; f. 1996; Chair. ALGIRDAS PILVELIS.

Lithuanian Republican Party: Pramonės pr. 3–62, Kaunas 3031; tel. (373) 51214; e-mail respublikos_varpai@takas.lt; internet respublikosvarpai.5u.com; active 1922–29; re-est. 1991; Chair. KAZIMIERAS PETRAITIS; 2,450 mems.

Lithuanian Rightist Union: A. Jakšto 9, Vilnius 2001; f. 2001; by the merger of the Lithuanian Independence Party, the Lithuanian Democratic Party, the Lithuanian Freedom League and the Homeland People's Union; Chair. ARŪNAS ZEBRIUNAS; 2,000 mems.

Lithuanian Russians' Union: Savanorių pr. 11–70, Vilnius 2015; tel. (523) 96636; fax (526) 24248; e-mail sergejus.dmitrijevas@lrs.lt; internet www.sojuzrus.visiems.lt; f. 1995; contested the 2000 legislative election as part of the A. Brazauskas Social Democratic Coalition; Chair. SERGEJ DMITRIJEV; 1,200 mems.

Lithuanian Social Democratic Party (LSDP): Barboros Radvilaites 1, Vilnius 2600; tel. (526) 13907; fax (526) 15420; e-mail info@lsdp.lt; internet www.lsdp.lt; absorbed the Lithuanian Democratic Labour Party in 2001; Chair. ALGIRDAS BRAZAUSKAS; 11,000 mems.

Lithuanian Social Justice Union: Žirmūnų 30A–42, Vilnius; tel. (527) 32055; f. 1996; Chair. KAZIMIERAS JONAS JOCIUS.

Lithuanian Socialist Party: Šeškinės 65/58, Vilnius 2010; tel. (524) 19765; f. 1994; Chair. ALBINAS VISOCKAS; 800 mems.

Lithuanian Union of Political Prisoners and Deportees: Laisvės 39, Kaunas 3000; tel. (373) 23214; fax (377) 74100; e-mail tremtinys@takas.lt; internet www.lpkts.lt; f. 1988; Pres. POVILAS JAKUČIONIS; 60,000 mems.

Moderate Conservative Union: Odminių g. 5, Vilnius 2002; tel. (521) 26876; fax (521) 26880; e-mail info@nks.lt; internet www.nks.lt; f. 2000; centre-right; Chair. GEDIMINAS VAGNORIUS.

Modern Christian-Democratic Union: Vilnius; f. 2000; from a faction of the Christian Democratic Party; agreed to merge with the

Lithuanian Centre Union and the Lithuanian Liberal Union in Jan. 2003; Leader VYTAUTAS BOGUSIS.

National Progress Party: Vilnius ; tel. (523) 96656; fax (523) 96779; e-mail egidijus.klumbys@lrs.lt; internet www.tpp.lt; active 1916–24, re-est. 1994; Chair. EGIDIJUS KLUMBYS; 1,100 mems.

New Union (Social Liberals): Gedimino pr. 10/1, Vilnius 2001; tel. (521) 07600; fax (521) 07602; e-mail centras@nsajunga.lt; internet www.nsajunga.lt; f. 1998; centre-left; Chair. ARTŪRAS PAULAUSKAS.

Peasants' and New Democracy Union: A. Jakšto 9–22, Vilnius 2001; tel. and fax (526) 15613; e-mail ndpartija@takas.lt; internet www.5ci.lt/ndmp; f. 2001; by the merger of the New Democracy Party and the Lithuanian Peasants' Party (Lithuanian Farmers' Party); Chair. KAZIMIERA PRUNSKIENĖ; 1,500 mems.

Young Lithuania National Party ('Jaunoji Lietuva'): Čiurlionio 9/2, Vilnius 2009; tel. (372) 26254; fax (527) 03217; e-mail jaunalietuviai@is.lt; internet www.is.lt/jaunalietuviai; f. 1994; Chair. STANISLOVAS BUŠKEVIČIUS; 1,000 mems.

Diplomatic Representation

EMBASSIES IN LITHUANIA

Austria: Gaono g. 6, Vilnius; tel. (526) 60580; fax (527) 91363; e-mail a80645@post.omnitel.net; Ambassador MICHAEL SCHWARZINGER.

Belarus: Mindango 13, Vilnius 2600; tel. (526) 62200; fax (526) 62212; internet www.belarus.lt; Ambassador VLADIMIR GARKUN.

China, People's Republic: Algirdo 36, Vilnius 2006; tel. (521) 62861; fax (521) 62682; e-mail chinaemb_lithuania@mfa.gov.ch; internet www.chinaembassy.lt; Ambassador CHEN YUMING.

Czech Republic: Tilto g. 1–2, Vilnius 2000; tel. (526) 61040; fax (526) 61066; e-mail cz.embassy.vilnius@post.omnitel.net; Ambassador PETR VOZNICA.

Denmark: T. Kosciuškos 36, Vilnius 2001; tel. (521) 53434; fax (523) 12300; e-mail vnoamb@um.dk; internet www.denmark.lt; Ambassador EVA JANSON.

Estonia: Mickevičiaus 4A, Vilnius 2004; tel. (527) 80200; fax (527) 80201; e-mail sekretar@estemb.lt; Ambassador REIN OIDEKIVI.

Finland: Klaipėdos 6, Vilnius 2600; tel. (521) 21621; fax (521) 22463; e-mail sanomat.vil@formin.fi; internet www.finland.lt; Ambassador TAINA KIEKKO.

France: Švarco g. 1, Vilnius 2600; tel. (521) 22979; fax (521) 24211; e-mail ambafrance.vilnius@diplomatie.gouv.fr; internet www.ambafrance-lt.org; Ambassador JEAN-BERNARD HARTH.

Germany: Z. Sierakausko 24/8, Vilnius 2600; tel. (521) 31815; fax (521) 31812; e-mail germ.emb@takas.lt; internet www.deutschebotschaft-wilna.lt; Ambassador Dr ALEXANDER VON ROM.

Holy See: Kosciuškos g. 28, Vilnius 2001; tel. (521) 23696; fax (521) 24228; e-mail nuntiusbalt@aiva.lt; Apostolic Nuncio Most Rev. PETER STEPHAN ZURBRIGGEN (Titular Archbishop of Glastonia (Glastonbury)).

Italy: Tauro 12, Vilnius 2001; tel. (521) 20620; fax (521) 20405; e-mail ambasciata@ambitvilnius.lt; Ambassador BERNARDO UGUCCIONI.

Kazakhstan: Birutes 20A/35 , Vilnius 2004; tel. (521) 22123; fax (521) 33701; e-mail kazakhstan@embassy.lt; internet kazakhstan.embassy.lt; Ambassador RASHID IBRAYEV.

Latvia: M. K. Čiurlionio 76, Vilnius 2600; tel. (521) 31260; fax (521) 31130; e-mail lietuva@latvia.balt.net; internet latvia.balt.net; Ambassador MAIRA MORA.

Norway: D. Poškos 59, Vilnius 2004; tel. (527) 26926; fax (527) 26964; e-mail emb.vilnius@mfa.no; internet www.norvegija.lt; Ambassador KÅRE HAUGE.

Poland: Smėlio 20A, Vilnius 2055; tel. (527) 09001; fax (527) 09007; internet www.polandembassy.lt; Ambassador JERZY BAHR.

Romania: Vivulskio 19, Vilnius; tel. (523) 10527; fax (523) 10652; e-mail ambromania@post.omnitel.net; internet www.romania.lt; Ambassador LUCIAN FATU.

Russia: Latviu 53/54, Vilnius 2600; tel. (527) 21763; fax (527) 23877; e-mail rusemb@rusemb.lt; Ambassador YURII A. ZUBAKOV.

Sweden: Didzioji 16, Vilnius 2600; tel. (526) 85010; fax (526) 85030; e-mail ambassaden.vilnius@foreign.ministry.se; internet www.swedishembassy.lt; Ambassador JAN PALMSTIERNA.

Turkey: Didžioji 37, Vilnius 2001; tel. (526) 49570; fax (521) 23277; e-mail turemvil@eunet.lt; Ambassador ALI NAZIM BELGER.

Ukraine: Teatro 4, Vilnius 2600; tel. (521) 21536; fax (521) 20475; e-mail ukrembassy@post.5ci.lt; internet www.5ci.lt/ukrembassy; Ambassador MYKOLA DERKACH.

United Kingdom: Antakalnio 2, Vilnius 2055; tel. (524) 62900; fax (524) 62901; e-mail be-vilnius@britain.lt; internet www.britain.lt; Ambassador JEREMY HILL.

USA: Akmenų 6, Vilnius 2600; tel. (521) 23031; fax (523) 12819; e-mail mail@usembassy.lt; internet www.usembassy.lt; Ambassador STEPHEN D. MULL.

Judicial System

The organs of justice are the Supreme Court, the Court of Appeal, district courts, local courts of administrative areas and a special court—the Commercial Court. The Seimas (Parliament) appoints and dismisses from office the judges of the Supreme Court in response to representations made by the President of the Republic (based upon the recommendation of the chairman of the Supreme Court). Judges of the Court of Appeal are appointed by the President with the approval of the Seimas (on the recommendation of the Minister of Justice), while judges of district and local courts are appointed and dismissed by the President. The Council of Judges submits recommendations to the President of the Republic concerning the appointment of judges, as well as their promotion, transfer or dismissal from office.

The Constitutional Court decides on the constitutionality of acts of the Seimas, as well as of the President and the Government. It consists of nine judges, who are appointed by the Seimas for a single term of nine years; one-third of the Court's members are replaced every three years.

The Office of the Prosecutor-General is an autonomous institution of the judiciary, comprising the Prosecutor-General and local and district prosecutors' offices which are subordinate to him. The Prosecutor-General and his deputies are appointed for terms of seven years by the President, subject to approval by the Seimas, while the prosecutors are appointed by the Prosecutor-General. The Office of the Prosecutor-General incorporates the Department for Crime Investigation. The State Arbitration decides cases of business litigation. A six-volume Civil Code, in accordance with European Union and international law, came into effect in 2001, replacing the Soviet civil legal system, which had, hitherto, remained in operation.

Constitutional Court: Gedimino pr. 36, Vilnius 2600; tel. (521) 26398; fax (521) 27975; e-mail mailbox@lrkt.lt; internet www.lrkt.lt; f. 1993; Chair. EDIGLJUS KURIS.

Court of Appeal: Gedimino pr. 40/1, Vilnius 2600; tel. (526) 26876; fax (526) 18039; Chair. VYTAUTAS MILIUS.

Supreme Court: Gynėjų 6, Vilnius 2725; tel. (526) 10560; fax (526) 27950; e-mail lat@tic.lt; internet www.lat.litlex.lt; Chair. VYTAUTAS GREIČIUS.

Office of the Prosecutor-General: A. Smetonos 4, Vilnius 2709; tel. (526) 62305; fax (526) 62317; e-mail cekelil@lrgp.lt; Prosecutor-General ANTANAS KLIMAVIČIUS.

Religion

Lithuania adopted Christianity at the end of the 14th century. However, the country's geographical position and history have long predetermined a diversity of religious communities. The restoration of independence, in 1991, stimulated the revival of religious practice, which was widely suppressed or banned during the Soviet period. Traditional religious communities were re-established and new ones came into existence. In 2001 there were 923 traditional and 176 non-traditional religious organizations registered in the country.

CHRISTIANITY

The Roman Catholic Church

Roman Catholicism has been the principal religious affiliation in Lithuania for more than 600 years (it was adopted by the Lithuanian State in 1387). The Roman Catholic Church in Lithuania comprises two archdioceses and five dioceses. There are seminaries at Vilnius, Kaunas and Telšiai. At 31 December 2000 there were an estimated 2.8m. adherents (approximately 74% of the population).

Lithuanian Bishops' Conference
(Conferentia Episcopalis Lituaniae)

Skapo 4, Vilnius 2001; tel. (521) 25455; fax (521) 20972; e-mail lvk@post.omnitel.net.

f. 1996; Pres. Cardinal Audrys Juozas Bačkis (Archbishop of Vilnius).

Archbishop of Kaunas: Most Rev. Sigitas Tamkevičius, Rotušės 14A, Kaunas 3000; tel. (374) 09026; fax (373) 20090; e-mail kurija@kn.lcn.lt; internet www.kaunas.lcn.lt.

Archbishop of Vilnius: Cardinal Audrys Juozas Bačkis, Šventaragio 4, Vilnius 2001; tel. (526) 27098; fax (521) 22807; e-mail vilncnsis@takas.lt.

The Byzantine Rite Catholic (Uniate) Church

Established in 1596 by the Lithuanian Brasta (Brest) Church Union, the Uniate Church is headed by the Metropolitan Archbishop of Lviv (Ukraine) and is under the judicial protection of the Roman Catholic Church of Lithuania. At 1 January 1996 there were five communities, with three priests, one monastic order and one church returned to the adherents in Vilnius.

Representation of the Order of St Basil the Great in Lithuania: Aušros Vartų 7B, Vilnius 2001; tel. (521) 22578; Centre of the Byzantine Rite Catholics (Uniates) in Lithuania; Superior Pavlo Jachimec.

Orthodox Churches

Russian Orthodox Church

The first communities appeared during the 12th century and the first monastery was established in Vilnius in 1597. While Lithuania formed part of the Russian Empire (1795–1915), Orthodoxy was considered the state religion. The Vilnius and Lithuanian Eparchy of the Russian Orthodox Church is under the jurisdiction of the Moscow Patriarchate. At 1 January 1996 there were 41 communities (with 30 clergymen and 41 churches). There were an estimated 180,000 adherents in 2001.

Vilnius and Lithuanian Eparchy of the Russian Orthodox Church: Aušros Vartų 10, Vilnius 2001; tel. (521) 27765; Metropolit Chryzostom (Georgii Martishkin).

Lithuanian Old Believers Pomor Church

The first communities settled in Lithuania in 1679 and the Church was established in 1709. At 1 January 1996 there were approximately 34,000 adherents (mainly ethnic Russians) in 58 communities, with 23 clergymen and 50 churches.

Supreme Council of the Old Believers (Pomor) Church in Lithuania: Naujininkų 20, Vilnius 2030; tel. (526) 95271; f. 1925; Chair. Mark Semionov (acting).

Protestant Churches

Lithuanian Evangelical Lutheran Church

The first parishes were established in 1539–69. In 1563 the Evangelical Church divided into Lutheran and Reformed Churches. Church attendance revived after 1990. The Lithuanian Evangelical Lutheran Church comprises one diocese. At 1 January 1998 there were approximately 30,000 adherents in 54 parishes (with 18 priests and 41 churches).

Consistory of the Lithuanian Evangelical Lutheran Church: Tumo-Vaizganto 50, Tauragė 5900; tel. and fax (446) 61145; e-mail konsistorija@takas.lt; Bishop Jonas Kalvanas.

Lithuanian Evangelical Reformed Church

The first parishes were established after 1563. At 1 January 1996 there were approximately 12,000 adherents in 11 parishes (with two pastors and nine churches).

Lithuanian Evangelical Reformed Church: POB 661, Vilnius 2049; tel. and fax (524) 50656; Pres. of Synodie Collegium Povilas A. Jašinskas.

Lithuanian Baptist Union and Other Churches

Parliament awarded the Baptist Union 'recognized' status in July 2001, the first religious community to be awarded this status. There has been a Baptist presence in Lithuania since the 18th century. The United Methodist Church, the New Apostolic Church, the Pentecostal Union and the Adventist Church ETH are all similarly seeking such status, beyond their current one of simply being registered.

ISLAM

Sunni Islam is the religion of the ethnic Tatars of Lithuania. The first Tatar communities settled there in the 14th century. The first mosque in Vilnius was erected in 1558. At 1 January 1996 there were five Tatar religious communities (with 10 clergymen, four mosques and one prayer house). In 2001 there were an estimated 5,000 adherents in Lithuania.

Lithuanian Muslims' Religious Community: A. Vivulskio 3, Vilnius 2009; tel. (526) 52051; Imam Mikas Chaleckas.

JUDAISM

The first Jewish communities appeared in Lithuania in the 15th century. In the 15th–17th centuries Lithuania was an important centre of Jewish culture and religion. Before the Second World War approximately 250,000 Jews lived in Lithuania; an estimated 90% were murdered during the German occupation (1941–44). At 1 January 1996 there were five Judaic religious communities, with two synagogues (in Vilnius and Kaunas). There were an estimated 5,000 adherents in Lithuania in 2001.

Jewish Community of Lithuania: Pylimo 4, Vilnius 2001; tel. (526) 13003; fax (521) 27915; e-mail jewishcom@post.5ci.lt; internet www.litjews.org; f. 1992 to replace and expand the role of the Jewish Cultural Society; Chair. Simonas Alperavičius; Chief Rabbi Samuel Kahn (London, United Kingdom).

The Press

In 1999 there were 377 newspapers and 418 periodicals published in Lithuania.

The publications listed below are in Lithuanian, except where otherwise indicated.

PRINCIPAL NEWSPAPERS

Kauno diena (Kaunas Daily): Vytauto pr. 27, Kaunas 3687; tel. (373) 41971; fax (374) 23404; e-mail redakcija@kaunodiena.lt; internet www.kaunodiena.lt; f. 1945; 6 a week; Editor-in-Chief Aušra Leka; circ. 50,000.

Klaipėda: Šauliu 21, Klaipėda 5800; tel. (463) 97701; e-mail office@klaipeda.daily.lt; internet www.klaipeda.daily.lt; Editor Antanas Stanevičius.

Kurier Wileński (Vilnius Express): Laisvės pr. 60, Vilnius 2056; tel. (524) 27901; fax (524) 27265; f. 1953; 5 a week; in Polish; Editor-in-Chief Czesław Malewski; circ. 8,000.

Lietuvos aidas (Echo of Lithuania): Maironio 1, Vilnius 2710; tel. (526) 15208; fax (521) 24876; e-mail centr@aidas.lt; internet www.aidas.lt; f. 1917; re-est 1990; 5 a week; Editor-in-Chief Roma Griniūtė-Grinbergienė; circ. 20,000.

Lietuvos rytas (Lithuania's Morning): Gedimino pr. 12A, Vilnius 2001; tel. (527) 43600; fax (527) 43700; e-mail daily@lrytas.lt; internet www.lrytas.lt; f. 1990; 6 a week in Lithuanian, with 3 supplements per week; Editor-in-Chief Gedvydas Vainauskas; circ. 65,000 (Mon.–Fri.), 200,000 (Sat.).

Lietuvos zinios: Kęstučiog. 4, Vilnius; tel. (527) 54904; fax (527) 53131; e-mail lzinios@lzinios.lt; internet www.lzinios.lt; 6 a week; Editor-in-Chief Rytas Staselis.

Respublika (Republic): A. Smetonos 2, Vilnius 2600; tel. (521) 23112; fax (521) 23538; f. 1989; 6 a week in Lithuanian, with 5 Russian editions per week; Editor-in-Chief Vitas Tomkus; circ. 55,000.

Vakarinės naujienos (Evening News): Laisvės pr. 60, Vilnius 2056; tel. (524) 28052; fax (524) 28563; e-mail info@vnaujienos.lt; internet www.vnaujienos.lt; f. 1958; 5 a week; in Lithuanian and Russian; Editor Ričardas Jarmalavičius; circ. 15,000.

Vakarų ekspresas (Western Express): H. Manto 2, Klaipėda 5800; tel. (462) 18074; fax (463) 10102; e-mail sek.ve@balt.net; internet www.vakaru-ekspresas.lt; f. 1990; 6 a week; Editor-in-Chief Gintaras Tomkus; circ. 15,000.

PRINCIPAL PERIODICALS

Apžvalga (Review): Pylimo 362, Vilnius 2001; tel. (526) 11151; fax (526) 10503; f. 1990; fortnightly; publ. by Christian Democratic Party of Lithuania; Editor-in-Chief Darius Vilimas; circ. 2,000.

Artuma: M. Daukšos 21, Kaunas 3000; tel. and fax (372) 09683; f. 1989; monthly; Editor-in-Chief Vanda Ibianska; circ. 3,000.

Dienovidis (Midday): Pilies 23A, Vilnius 2001; tel. (521) 21911; fax (521) 23101; e-mail dienovidis@takas.lt; f. 1990; weekly; Editor-in-Chief Aldona Žemaitytė; circ. 4,500.

Ekho Litvy (Echo of Lithuania): Laisvės pr. 60, Vilnius 2056; tel. (524) 28463; fax (524) 28463; e-mail echo.litvy@aunet.lt; f. 1940; daily; in Russian; Editor-in-Chief Algimantas Zhukas; circ. 5,000.

Genys (Woodpecker): Geležinio Vilko 12, Vilnius 2001; tel. (523) 13621; fax (523) 13622; f. 1940; monthly; illustrated; for 8–12-year-olds; Editor-in-Chief Vytautas Račickas; circ. 5,000.

Kultūros barai (Domains of Culture): Latako 3, Vilnius 2001; tel. (526) 16696; fax (526) 10538; e-mail kulturosbarai@takas.lt; f. 1965; monthly; Editor-in-Chief Bronys Savukynas; circ. 3,000.

Liaudies kultūra (Ethnic Culture): Barboros Radvilaitės 8, Vilnius 2600; tel. (526) 13412; fax (521) 24033; e-mail lfcc@lfcc.lt; internet neris.mii.lt/heritage/lfcc/lfcc.html; f. 1988; 6 a year; Editor-in-Chief DALIA ANTANINA RASTENIENĖ; circ. 1,100.

Lietuvos sportas (Lithuanian Sports): Odminių 3, Vilnius 2600; tel. and fax (526) 16757; f. 1922; re-est. 1992; 3 a week; Editor-in-Chief BRONIUS ČEKANAUSKAS; circ. 18,000.

Lietuvos ūkis (Lithuanian Economy): Algirdo 31, Vilnius 2600; tel. (521) 36718; fax (522) 36445; f. 1921; monthly; Editor-in-Chief ALGIRDAS JASIONIS; circ. 3,000.

Literatūra ir menas (Literature and Art): Z. Sierakausko 15, Vilnius 2009; tel. (523) 33189; fax (523) 33181; e-mail lmenas@takas.lt; internet www.culture.lt/lmenas; f. 1946; weekly; publ. by the Lithuanian Writers' Union; Editor-in-Chief KORNELIJUS PLATELIS; circ. 3,000.

Lithuania in the World: T. Vrublevskio 6, Vilnius 2600; tel. (526) 14432; fax (526) 13521; e-mail lw.magazine@post.omnitel.net; internet www.kryptis.lt/lithuania; f. 1993; 6 a year; in English; Editor-in-Chief STASYS KAŠAUSKAS; circ. 15,000.

Magazyn Wileński (Vilnius Journal): Laisvės pr. 60, Vilnius 2056; tel. (524) 27718; fax (524) 29065; e-mail magazyn@magwil.lt; internet www.magwil.lt; f. 1990; monthly; political, cultural; in Polish; Editor-in-Chief MICHAŁ MACKIEWICZ; circ. 5,000.

Metai (Year): K. Sirvydo 6, Vilnius 2600; tel. (526) 17344; f. 1991; monthly; journal of the Lithuanian Writers' Union; Editor-in-Chief DANIELIUS MUŠINSKAS; circ. 2,000.

Mokslas ir gyvenimas (Science and Life): Antakalnio 36, Vilnius 2055; tel. and fax (523) 41572; internet ausis.gf.vu.lt/mg/; f. 1957; monthly; popular science; Editor-in-Chief JUOZAS BALDAUSKAS; circ. 3,500.

Moksleivis (Schoolmate): A. Jakšto 8–10, Vilnius 2600; tel. (526) 27604; f. 1959; monthly; Editor-in-Chief ALGIMANTAS ZURBA; circ. 14,000.

Moteris (Woman): Vykinto 7, Vilnius 2004; tel. and fax (521) 24741; e-mail redakcija@moteris.lt; internet www.moteris.lt; f. 1952; monthly; popular, for women; Editor-in-Chief EGLE STRIAUKIENE; circ. 40,000.

Mūsų gamta (Our Nature): Rudens 33B, Vilnius 2600; tel. (526) 96964; f. 1964; 6 a year; Editor-in-Chief VYTAUTAS KLOVAS; circ. 2,500.

Naujasis Židinys (New Hearth): Tilto g. 8/3, Vilnius 2001; tel. (522) 20311; fax (521) 22363; f. 1991; monthly; religion and culture; Editor-in-Chief SAULIUS DRAZDAUSKAS; circ. 1,200.

Nemunas: Gedimino 45, Kaunas 3000; tel. (373) 22244; f. 1967; monthly; journal of the Lithuanian Writers' Union; Editor-in-Chief ALGIMANTAS MIKUTA; circ. 1,500.

Panele (Young Miss): Vykinto 7, Vilnius 2004; tel. (527) 15900; fax (527) 15901; e-mail magazine@panele.lt; internet www.panele.lt; f. 1994; monthly; popular, for ages 12–25; Editor-in-Chief JURGA SIMKIENE; circ. 66,000.

7 meno dienos (7 Days of Art): Bernardinų 10, Vilnius 2001; tel. (526) 13039; fax (526) 11926; e-mail 7md@culture.lt; internet www.culture.lt/7menodienos; f. 1992; weekly; Editor-in-Chief LINAS VILDŽIŪNAS; circ. 2,000.

Sandora (Covenant): Dominikonų 6, Vilnius 2001; tel. (521) 22141; fax (521) 20598; e-mail sandora@hotmail.com; f. 1989; monthly; Editor-in-Chief ELVYRA KUČINSKAITĖ; circ. 9,000.

Švyturys (Beacon): Maironio 1, Vilnius 2600; tel. (526) 10791; fax (526) 14690; f. 1949; monthly; politics, economics, history, culture, fiction; Editor-in-Chief JUOZAS BAUŠYS; circ. 10,000.

Tremtinys (Deportee): Laisvės 39, Kaunas 3000; tel. (372) 09530; f. 1988; weekly; publ. by the Lithuanian Union of Political Prisoners and Deportees; Editor-in-Chief ROMUALDAS JURGELIONIS; circ. 4,000.

Valstiečių laikraštis (Farmer's Newspaper): Laisvės pr. 60, Vilnius 2056; tel. and fax (524) 21281; e-mail redakcija@valstietis.lt; internet www.valstietis.lt; f. 1940; 2 a week; Editor-in-Chief JONAS ŠVOBA; circ. 78,000.

Vasario 16 (16 February): J. Gruodžio 9–404, Kaunas 3000; tel. (372) 25219; f. 1988; fortnightly; journal of the Lithuanian Democratic Party; Sec. PRIMAS NOREIKA; circ. 1,600.

NEWS AGENCIES

Baltic News Service (BNS): Jogailos g. 9/1, Vilnius 2001; tel. (523) 12410; fax (526) 81515; e-mail bns@bns.lt; f. 1991; Dir RIMANTAS ŠIMKUS.

ELTA (Lithuanian News Agency): Gedimino pr. 21/2, Vilnius 2600; tel. (526) 28864; fax (526) 19507; e-mail zinias@elta.lt; internet www.elta.lt; f. 1920; Dir KĘSTUTIS JANKAUSKAS.

Publishers

Alma littera: A. Juozapavičiaus 6/2, Vilnius 2600; tel. (527) 28246; fax (5) 28026; e-mail post@almali.lt; internet www.almali.lt; f. 1990; fiction, children's books, textbooks; Dir-Gen. ARVYDAS ANDRIJAUSKAS.

Baltos lankos (White Meadows): Mėsinių 4, Vilnius 2001; tel. (521) 20126; fax (521) 20152; e-mail baltos.lankos@post.omnitel.net; internet www.baltoslankos.lt; f. 1992; literature, humanities, social sciences, fiction and textbooks; Editor SAULIUS ŽUKAS.

Eugrimas: Šilutés 42A, Vilnius 2042; tel. (523) 00075; e-mail eugrimas@eugrimas.com; internet www.eugrimas.com; f. 1995; economics, education, law, politics and philosophy; Dir EUGENIJA PETRULIENĖ.

Katalikų pasaulis (Catholic World): Dominikonų 6, Vilnius 2001; tel. (521) 22422; fax (526) 26462; f. 1990; Dir KĘSTUTIS LATOŽA.

Lietuvos rašytojų sąjungos leidykla (Lithuanian Writers' Union Publishers): K. Sirvydo 6, Vilnius 2600; tel. (526) 28643; fax (526) 28945; e-mail rsleidykla@is.lt; internet www.rsleidykla.lt; f. 1990; fiction, essays, literary heritage, children's books; Dir GIEDRE SORIENE.

Mintis (Idea): Z. Sierakausko 15, Vilnius 2600; tel. (523) 32943; fax (521) 63157; f. 1949; philosophy, history, law, economics, tourist information; Dir ALEKSANDRAS KRASNOVAS.

Mokslo ir enciklopedijų leidybos institutas (Science and Encyclopaedia Publishing Institute): L. Asanavičiūtės 23, Vilnius 2050; tel. (524) 58526; fax (524) 58537; e-mail meli@meli.lt; internet www .meli.lt; f. 1992; science and reference books, dictionaries, encyclopaedias, higher education textbooks, books for the general reader; Dir RIMANTAS KARECKAS.

Presvika: Pamėnkalnio 25/11, Vilnius 2001; tel. (526) 23182; fax (526) 23110; e-mail presvika@post.5ci.lt; f. 1996; educational literature and textbooks; Dir VIOLETA BILAIŠYTĖ.

Šviesa (Light): Vytauto 25, Kaunas 3000; tel. (373) 41834; fax (373) 42032; e-mail sviesa@balt.net; internet www.sviesa.lt; f. 1945; textbooks and pedagogical literature; Dir JONAS BARCYS.

Tyto alba: J. Jasinskio 10, Vilnius 2001; tel. and fax (524) 98602; e-mail tytoalba@taide.lt; internet www.tytoalba.lt; f. 1993; literature in translation; Dir LOLITA VARANAVIČIENĖ.

Vaga (Furrow): Gedimino pr. 50, Vilnius 2600; tel. (526) 26443; fax (526) 16902; e-mail vaga@post.omnitel.net; internet www.lietus.lt/vaga; f. 1945; fiction, non-fiction, art, children's books; Dir ARTURAS MICKEVIČUS.

Vyturys (Lark): J. Tumo-Vaižganto 2, Vilnius 2600; tel. and fax (526) 29407; f. 1985; fiction and non-fiction for children and youth; Dir ALEKSAS BOČIAROVAS.

PUBLISHERS' ASSOCIATION

Lithuanian Publishers' Association: K. Sirvydo 6, Vilnius 2000; tel. and fax (526) 17740; e-mail lla@centras.lt; f. 1989; Pres. SAULIUS ZUKAS.

Broadcasting and Communications

TELECOMMUNICATIONS

Regulatory Authority

Communications Regulatory Authority (Ryšių Reguliavimo Tarnyba): Algirdo 27, Vilnius 2006; tel. (521) 05633; fax (521) 61564; e-mail rrt@rrt.lt; internet www.rrt.lt; f. 2001; Dir TOMAS BARAKAUSKAS.

Major Service Provider

Lietuvos Telekomas AB: Savanorių pr. 28, Vilnius 2001; tel. (521) 27755; fax (521) 26655; e-mail info@telecom.lt; internet www .telecom.lt; f. 1992; privatized 1998; operates public telecommunications network, repairs telecommunications equipment; Pres. and Gen. Man. TAPIO PAARMA; 5,200 employees.

BROADCASTING

Lietuvos Radijo ir televizijos komisija (Radio and Television Commission of Lithuania): Vytenio 6, Vilnius 2009; tel. (523) 30660; fax (526) 47125; e-mail lrtk@rtk.lt; internet www.rtk.lt.

Radio

Lietuvos radijas ir televizija (Lithuanian Radio and Television): S. Konarskio 49, Vilnius 2600; tel. (523) 63000; fax (523) 63208;

e-mail forel@lrtv.lt; internet www.lrtv.lt; f. 1926; govt-owned; Chair. MARCELIJUS MARTINAITIS; Gen. Dir KĘSTUTIS PETRAUSKIS.

Lietuvos radijas (Lithuanian Radio): S. Konarskio 49, Vilnius 2600; tel. (523) 63010; fax (521) 35333; internet www.lrtv.lt/lt_lr .htm; f. 1926; broadcasts in Lithuanian, Russian, Polish, Yiddish, Belarusian and Ukrainian; Dir JŪRATĖ LAUČIŪTĖ.

A2: Vilnius; tel. (526) 41229; e-mail a2@post.inet.lt; internet www .a2.lt; private, commercial.

Aukštaitijos radijas: Laisvės 1, Panevėžys 5300; tel. and fax (455) 96969; e-mail armac@laineta.lt; private, commercial; Dir ALGIRDAS ŠATAS.

Bumsas: Smiltelės 13–64, Klaipėda 5802; tel. (463) 20909; fax (463) 22020; e-mail bumsas@bumsas.lt; internet www.bumsas.lt; private, commercial; Dir DALIUS NOREIKA.

FM 99: Rotuses 2, POB 119, Alytus 4580; tel. (315) 77711; fax (315) 74646; e-mail fm99@fm99.lt; internet www.fm99.lt; private, commercial; Dir LIUDAS RAMANAUSKAS.

Kapsai: P. Armino 71, Marijampolė 4520; tel. and fax (343) 54512; e-mail kapsai@mari.omnitel.net; internet www1.omnitel.net/ kapsai; private, commercial; Dir RAIMUNDAS MARUSKEVIČIUS.

Kauno fonas 105.4: Radastu 2, Kaunas 3000; tel. (373) 30390; fax (373) 30368; e-mail reklama@kaunoradijas.lt; internet www .kaunoradijas.lt; private, commercial; Dir ORESTAS MINDERIS.

Labas FM: Naugarduko 91, Vilnius 2006; tel. (521) 63591; internet www.labasfm.lt; Dir DARIUS UZKURAITIS.

Laisvoji banga: Naugarduko 91, Vilnius 2006; tel. (521) 63836; fax (521) 63591; e-mail radio@lbanga.lt; internet www.lbanga.lt; private, commercial; Dir VYTAUTAS BARTKUS.

Laluna: M. Mazvydo 11, Klaipėda 5800; tel. and fax (463) 43232; e-mail laluna@laluna.lt; internet www.laluna.lt; private, commercial; Dir RUSLANAS ALEKSANDRAVIČIUS.

M-1: Laisvės pr. 60, Vilnius 2056; tel. (523) 60360; fax (523) 60366; e-mail m-1@m-1.lt; internet www.m-1.lt; private, commercial; Dir-Gen. HUBERTAS GRUSNYS.

Mazeikiu aidas: Sodu 13–93, Mazeikiai 5500; tel. (443) 65095; fax (443) 65600; private, commercial; Dir ALINA JONIKAITĖ.

Nevėzio radijas: Kniaudiskiu 87/84 P.d. 107, Panevėžys 5304; tel. (454) 23922; fax (455) 96888; e-mail rolka@nradijas.lt; private, commercial; Dir ALVYDAS ADUKONIS.

Pukas: Šaldytuvu 25, Kaunas 3002; tel. (373) 42424; fax (373) 42434; e-mail boss@pukas.lt; f. 1991; private, commercial; Dir KĘSTUTIS PŪKAS.

Radiocentras: Laisvės pr. 60, Vilnius 2056; tel. (521) 28706; fax (524) 29073; e-mail biuras@radiocentras.lt; internet www .radiocentras.lt; private, commercial; Dir-Gen. M. GARBERIS.

Ratekona: P.d. 3300, Vilnius 2013; tel. (685) 76840; fax (521) 52171; e-mail consult@zilionis.cjb.net; f. 1994; private, commercial; Dir SIGITAS ZILIONIS.

Saules radijas: Dvaro 88, Šiauliai 5400; tel. (414) 22431; fax (414) 32816; e-mail src@siauliai.aiva.lt; private, commercial; Editor-in-Chief VALENTINAS DIDZGALVIS.

Tau: Draugystės 19, Kaunas 3031; tel. (373) 52790; fax (373) 52128; e-mail info@tau.balt.net; internet www.tau.lt; private, commercial; Dir ALGIRDAS KEPEŽINSKAS.

Titanika: Sporto 6, Kaunas 3000; tel. (372) 03404; fax (372) 08222; e-mail titanika@kaunas.sav.lt; internet www.kaunas.sav.lt/ titanika/; private, commercial.

Ventus: Montuotoju 2, Mazeikiai 5500; tel. (443) 96225; fax (443) 96226; e-mail admin@ventus.lt; internet www.ventus.lt; private, commercial; Dir-Gen. GIEDRIUS STELMOKAS.

V. Mečkausko firma 'Versmės' radijas ir televizija: Pergalės 57–9, Elektrėnai 4061; tel. (528) 39543; fax (528) 39616; e-mail mesta@one.lt.

Všļ Kauno radijas ir televizija: S. Daukanto 28A, Kaunas 3000; tel. (373) 21010; fax (373) 22570; e-mail kaunas@lrtv.lt; Dir P. GARNYS.

Žemaitijos radijas: Mažeikių 18, Telšiai 5610; tel. (444) 74433; fax (444) 75445; e-mail zemaitijos@radijas.lt; internet www.radijas.lt; private, commercial; Dir ALGIMANTAS GINČIAUSKIS.

UAB Znad Wilii radijo stotis: Laisvės pr. 60, Vilnius 2056; tel. (524) 90870; fax (527) 84446; e-mail radio@znadwilii.lt; internet www.znadwilii.lt; f. 1992; private, commercial; Dir-Gen. MIROSLAVAS JUCHNEVIČIUS.

Television

Lietuvos radijas ir televizija: see Radio.

Lietuvos televizija: S. Konarskio 49, Vilnius 2600; tel. (523) 63100; fax (521) 63282; e-mail romas@litv.lt; programmes in Lithuanian, Russian, Polish, Ukrainian and Belarusian; Dir ROMAS JANKAUSKAS.

Aidas: Birutes 42, Trakai 4050; tel. (528) 52480; mainly relays German programmes; private, commercial; Dir ČESLOVAS RULEVIČIUS.

Baltijos televizija: Laisvės pr. 60, Vilnius 2056; tel. (524) 28917; fax (524) 26623; e-mail webmaster@btv.lt; internet www.btv.lt; broadcasts own programmes and relays German, Polish and US broadcasts; private, commercial; Dir-Gen. GINTARAS SONGAILA.

Kaunas plius: P.d. 2040, Kaunas 3000; tel. (372) 20650; fax (372) 20640; private, commercial; Pres. HENRIKAS ZUKAUSKAS.

LNK TV (Laisvas Nepriklausomas Kanalas): Šeškinės 20, Vilnius 20010; tel. (521) 24061; fax (521) 23924; e-mail lnk@lnk.lt; internet www.lnk.lt; private, commercial; Dir PAULIUS KOVAS.

PAN-TV: Laisvės 26–211, Panevėžys 5300; tel. (454) 64267; fax (454) 35889; private, commercial; Dir SAULIUS BUKELIS.

Raseiniu TV: Vytauto Didziojo 10, Raseiniai 4400; tel. (428) 53955; fax (428) 53735; e-mail mirkliai@raseiniai.omnitel.net; Dir KĘSTUTIS SKAMARAKAS.

Šiaulių TV: Aušros al. 48, Šiauliai 5400; tel. and fax (415) 23809; private; Dir STASYS SUSINSKAS.

TV3: Nemencines 4, Vilnius 2016; tel. (523) 16131; fax (527) 64253; e-mail postmaster@tv3.lt; internet www.tv3.lt; broadcasts own programmes (20% of schedule) in Lithuanian and English, and relays international satellite channels; private, commercial; Dir VILMA MARČIULEVIČIUTE.

Vilniaus TV: Vivulskio 23, Vilnius 2600; tel. (521) 35560; fax (523) 37904; e-mail vk@mail.iti.lt; internet www.vtv.lt; f. 1994; private, commercial; Dir LEONAS REMEIKA.

Finance

(cap. = capital; res = reserves; dep. = deposits; m. = million; brs = branches; amounts in litai, unless otherwise stated)

BANKING

In the early 1990s, following independence, comprehensive reforms were made in Lithuania's banking system, beginning with the establishment of a central bank, the Bank of Lithuania. During 1995 several of the smaller commercial banks became bankrupt, culminating in the collapse in December of the two largest—the Lithuanian Joint-Stock Innovation Bank (LJIB) and Litimpex Bank. The crisis resulted in the eventual closure of 16 of the 28 banks in operation at that time. As a result, the Government devised a programme, in consultation with the IMF and the World Bank, to secure and restructure the banking system. At the end of 2001 nine banks were operating under a license from the Bank of Lithuania; there were also four branches of foreign banks, and five representative offices of foreign banks in Lithuania.

Central Bank

Bank of Lithuania (Lietuvos bankas): Gedimino pr. 6, Vilnius 2001; tel. (526) 80029; fax (526) 28124; e-mail bank_of_lithuania@ lbank.lt; internet www.lbank.lt; f. 1922; re-est. 1990; central bank, responsible for bank supervision; cap. 100m., res 1,813.4m. (Feb. 2002); Chair. of Bd REINOLDIJUS ŠARKINAS.

Commercial Banks

Agricultural Bank of Lithuania (AB Lietuvos Žemės Ūkio Bankas): J. Basanavičiaus 26, Vilnius 2600; tel. (523) 93553; fax (521) 39058; e-mail lzub-info@lzub.lt; internet www.lzub.lt; f. 1924 as Žemės Bankas; re-founded in 1992 as successor to Agropramoninis Bankas; 93.08% owned by Norddeutsche Landesbank Girozentrale (Germany); cap. 102.8m., res 25.6m., dep. 1,273.1m. (Dec. 2001); Chair. of Bd THOMAS STEPHAN BUERKLE; 46 brs.

Bank of Vilnius (Vilniaus bankas AB): Gedimino pr. 12, Vilnius 2600; tel. (526) 82514; fax (526) 26557; e-mail info@vb.lt; internet www.vb.lt; f. 1990 as Spaudos Bankas; absorbed AB Bankas Hermis in 2000; 98% owned by Skandinaviska Enskilda Banken (Sweden); cap. 154.4m., res 430.8m., dep. 5,165.3m. (Dec. 2001); Chair. and Chief Exec. JULIUS NIEDVARAS; 18 brs.

AB Bankas Hansa-LTB: Savanoriu pr. 19, Vilnius 2009; tel. (526) 84444; fax (522) 32433; e-mail info@ltb.lt; internet www.hansa.lt; f. 2001 by merger of Lieutuvos Taupomasis Bankas and Hansabankas; owned by Hansapank (Estonia); cap. 370.3m., res 32.3m., dep. 3,429.4m. (Dec. 2001); Chair. of Bd ARŪNAS ŠIKŠTA.

LITIMPEKS Bank: Vilniaus 28, Vilnius 2600; tel. (523) 97497; fax (523) 97444; e-mail info@litimpeks.lt; internet www.litimpeks.lt; f.

1991; cap. 64.1m., dep. 171.1m. (Dec. 1997); Chair. and Chief Exec. GINTAUTAS PREIDYS; 10 brs.

Medical Bank (Medicinos Bankas): Pamėnkalnio 40, Vilnius 2600; tel. (521) 23321; fax (526) 24481; e-mail info@medbank.lt; internet www.medbank.lt; f. 1992; cap. 34.4m., res 2.1m., dep. 92.2m. (Dec. 2001); Chair. of Bd KĘSTUTIS OLSAUSKAS; 7 brs.

AB Parex Bankas: K. Kalinausko 13, Vilnius 2009; tel. (526) 64600; fax (526) 64601; e-mail info@parex.lt; internet www.parex.lt; f. 1996; cap. 31.0m. , res 0.9m., dep. 128.1m. (Dec. 2002); Chair. and Chief Exec. JANIS TUKANS; 6 brs.

UAB Sampo Bankas: Gelezinio Vilko 18A, Vilnius 2004; tel. (521) 09400; fax (521) 09409; f. 1994; fmrly Lithuanian Development Bank; present name adopted 2001; 99.99% owned by Samplo plc (Finland); cap. 37.1m., res 3.3m., dep. 129.9m. (Dec. 2001); Chair. of Bd GINTAUTAS GALVANAUSKAS.

Šiaulių Bank: Tilžės 149, Šiauliai 5400; tel. (415) 22117; fax (414) 30774; e-mail info@sb.lt; internet www.sb.lt; f. 1992; cap. 34.0m., res 1.8m., dep. 263.1m. (Dec. 2001); Chair. ALGIRDAS BUTKUS; 8 brs.

Snoras Bank: A. Vivulskio 7, Vilnius 2600; tel. (526) 62700; fax (523) 10155; e-mail info@snoras.com; internet www.snoras.com; f. 1992; cap. 163.5m. (Dec. 2001), dep. 655.1m., total assets 884.0m. (Dec. 2001); Chair. of Management Bd RAIMONDAS BARANAUSKAS; 10 brs.

Tauro Bank: K. Kalinausko 13, Vilnius 2600; tel. (521) 25030; fax (521) 25066; f. 1991; cap. 36.0m., dep. 152.6m. (Dec. 1996); Chair. GINTARAS TERLECKAS; 9 brs.

AB Ūkio Bankas: J. Gruodžio 9, Kaunas 3000; tel. (373) 01301; fax (373) 23188; e-mail ub@ub.lt; internet www.ub.lt; f. 1989; cap. 90.7m. (Dec. 2002), dep. 633.4m. (Dec. 2001); Chair. of Bd and Chief Exec. EDITA NAVICKAITE; 12 brs.

Lithuanian Savings Bank (AB Lietuvos Taupomasis Bankas): Savanorių pr. 19, Vilnius 2009; tel. (521) 32370; fax (521) 32431; f. 1919; 90.7% owned by Hansapank (Estonia); cap. 167.3m., res 86.4m., dep. 2,980.5m. (Dec. 2000); scheduled for privatization; Chair. of Bd ARŪNAS ŠIKŠTA.

Property Banks

Nuosavybes Bank (Property Bank): Vilnius; loan-recovery agency.

Turto Bank: Kestucio 46, Vilnius 2600; tel. (527) 80900; fax (527) 51155; e-mail info@turtas.lt; internet www.turtas.lt; f. 1996; cap. 8.9m., total assets 1,001.9m. (Dec. 2000); recovery of non-performing loans, administration of Ministry of Finance loans; Chair. of Bd STEPONAS VYTAUTAS JURNA; 6 brs.

Banking Association

Association of Lithuanian Banks: Ankštoji g. 5, Vilnius 2600; tel. (524) 96669; fax (524) 96139; e-mail info@lba.lt; f. 1991; Pres. EDUARDAS VILKELIS; 10 mems.

COMMODITY EXCHANGES

National Commodity Exchange: Laisvės 35, Kaunas 3000; tel. (372) 24498; fax (376) 20726; f. 1992; Pres. VYTAUTAS VINKLERIS; 16 mems.

Baltic Exchange: Pylimo 2/6, Vilnius 2001; tel. (521) 61195; fax (521) 26842; f. 1991; Pres. VYTAUTAS JAKELIS; 16 mems.

STOCK EXCHANGE

National Stock Exchange: Ukmergės 41, Vilnius 2600; tel. (527) 23871; fax (527) 24894; e-mail office@nse.lt; internet www.nse.lt; f. 1993; Pres. RIMANTAS BUSILA.

Trade and Industry

GOVERNMENT AGENCIES

Fund for State Property and Restoration of People's Savings: Vilnius; f. 1997; supervises distribution and uses of revenues derived from privatization.

Lithuanian State Enterprise State Property Fund: Vilnius 16, Vilnius 2600; tel. (526) 84902; fax (526) 84997; e-mail info@vtf.lt; internet www.vtf.lt; f. 1995; privatization and management of state-owned and municipal property; Dir POVILAS MILAŠAUSKAS.

CHAMBERS OF COMMERCE

Association of Lithuanian Chambers of Commerce, Industry and Crafts: J-Tumo-Vaižganto 9/1–63A, Vilnius 2001; tel. (526) 12102; fax (526) 12112; e-mail lppra@post.omnitel.net; internet www.lithuaniachambers.lt; f. 1992; mem. of International Chamber of Commerce and of Asscn of European Chambers of Commerce and Industry; Dir-Gen. RIMAS VARKULEVIČIUS.

Kaunas Chamber of Commerce, Industry and Crafts: K. Donelaičio 8, Kaunas 3000; POB 2111, Kaunas; tel. (372) 01491; fax (372) 08330; e-mail chamber@chamber.lt; internet www .chamber.lt; f. 1925; re-est. 1991; Pres. M. RONDOMANSKAS.

Klaipėda Chamber of Commerce, Industry and Crafts: POB 148, Klaipėda 5800; tel. (464) 10628; fax (464) 10626; e-mail krppr@klaipeda.omnitel.net; Pres. SIGITAS PAULAUSKAS; Dir VIKTORAS KROLIS.

Marijampolė Chamber of Commerce and Industry: Kęstučio 9/20, Marijampolė 4520; tel. (343) 55568; fax (343) 56346; Pres. VYGANDAS MATULIS.

Panevėžys Chamber of Commerce, Industry and Crafts: Respublikos 34, Panevėžys 5319; tel. (454) 63687; fax (454) 62227; e-mail panevezys@chambers.lt; internet www.ccic.lt; f. 1991; Pres. VYTAUTAS ŠIDLAUSKAS; Gen. Dir VYTAUTAS KAZAKEVIČIUS.

Šiauliai Chamber of Commerce, Industry and Crafts: Vilniaus 88, Šiauliai 5400; tel. (414) 27709; fax (414) 39973; e-mail siauliai-cci@siauliai.omnitel.net; Dir-Gen. DAILIS BARAKAUSKAS.

Vilnius Chamber of Commerce, Industry and Crafts: Algirdo 31, Vilnius 2600; tel. (521) 35550; fax (521) 35542; e-mail vilnius@cci.lt; internet www.cci.lt; f. 1991; Pres. VYTAS NAVICKAS; 427 mems.

INDUSTRIAL ASSOCIATION

Lithuanian Industrialists' Confederation: A. Vienuolio 8, Vilnius 2001; tel. (521) 25217; fax (527) 23320; f. 1989; Pres. BRONISLOVAS LUBYS.

EMPLOYERS' ORGANIZATION

Lithuanian Business Employers' Confederation: A. Rotundo 5, Vilnius 2600; tel. (526) 29729; fax (521) 20448; e-mail lvdk@post .omnitel.net; internet 195.182.80.20/lvdk; f. 1999; Pres. VIKTOR USPASKICH.

UTILITIES

Energy System of Lithuania: Zveju 14, Vilnius 2600; tel. (527) 34638; fax (521) 26736; Gen. Dir ANZELMAS BACIALISKAS.

Electricity

Lietuvos energija AB (Lithuanian Power): Zveju 14, Vilnius 2600; tel. (527) 82406; fax (521) 26736; e-mail lietuvos.energija@lpc.lt; internet www.lpc.lt; f. 1995; restructured in 2000; Man. Dir RYMANTAS JUOZAITIS; 11,500 employees.

Alytus Electric Utility: Pramonės 7, Alytus 4580; tel. (315) 25745; fax (315) 34827; e-mail aet@lpc.lt; f. 1962; transmission and distribution; 127,000 customers (Dec. 1996); Dir VITAS BLAZAUSKAS.

Klaipėda Electric Utility: Liepu 64A, Klaipėda 5799; tel. (463) 15064; fax (463) 15056; f. 1957; transmission and distribution; 218,000 customers (Dec. 1996); Dir VYTAUTAS GIRDVAINIS.

Rytu Skirstomieji Tinklai AB: Senamiesčio 102B, Panevėžys 5319; tel. (455) 04459; fax (454) 81394; e-mail pet@pet.lt; internet rytis.rst.lt; f. 1957; distribution of electricity; 156,000 customers (Dec. 2002); Dir LEONAS MIKALAJŪNAS.

Šiauliai Electric Utility: Tilžės 68, Šiauliai 5409; tel. (415) 94459; fax (415) 53041; e-mail info@set.lpc.lt; f. 1957; transmission and distribution; 190,000 customers (Jan. 2002); Dir VINCAS PONELIS.

Utena Electric Utility: Uzpaliu 87, Utena 4910; tel. (389) 62150; fax (389) 62196; e-mail utenoset@uet.lpc.lt; f. 1964; transmission and distribution; 113,900 customers (Jan. 2001); Dir JURGIS DUMBRAVA.

JSC Vakaru skirstomieji tinklai: Kestučio 36, Kaunas 3000; tel. (373) 09259; fax (373) 09269; e-mail vest@vest.lt; internet www.vest .lt; f. 2001; distribution in central and western Lithuania; 263,000 customers (Dec. 1996); Chief Exec. ARŪNAS KESERAUSKAS; 3,000 employees.

Vilnius Electric Utility: Motoru 2, Vilnius 2038; tel. (521) 67465; fax (521) 67467; f. 1957; transmission and distribution; 268,000 customers (Dec. 1996); Dir RIMANTAS MILISAUSKAS.

Gas

Lietuvos Dujos (Lithuanian Gas): Aguonų 24, Vilnius 2600; tel. (523) 60210; fax (523) 60200; e-mail lt@lietuvosdujos.lt; internet www.dujos.lt; f. 1995; natural gas transmission and distribution; scheduled for privatization; Gen. Man. VIKORAS VALENTUKEVIČIUS; 4,300 employees.

TRADE UNIONS

Christian Farmers' Union of Lithuania: V. Mykolaičio-Putino 5, Vilnius 2009; tel. and fax (523) 12029; f. 1919; re-est. 1995; 10 regional brs; 6,000 mems; Chair. JUOZAS ALEKNAVIČIUS.

Lithuanian Labour Federation: V. Mykolaičio-Putino 5/140, Vilnius 2600; tel. and fax (523) 12029; e-mail ldforg@ldf.lt; internet www.ldf.lt; f. 1919; re-est. 1991; 20,000 mems; Chair. KAZIMIERAS KUZMINSKAS; Sec.-Gen. REGINA REKESIENĖ.

Lithuanian Trade Unions Centre: Basanavičiaus 29A, Vilnius 2600; tel. (526) 14888; fax (526) 60217; f. 1993; 13 affiliated unions with 140,000 mems; Chair. ALGIRDAS KVEDARAVIČIUS.

Lithuanian Union of Free Trade Unions: J. Jasinskio 9, Vilnius 2600; tel. (526) 10921; fax (526) 19078; f. 1992; 8 affiliated unions with 50,000 mems; Chair. ALGIRDAS SYSAS.

Lithuanian Workers' Union: V. Mykolaičio-Putino 5, Vilnius 2009; tel. (526) 21743; fax (521) 33295; e-mail ltds@takas.lt; internet www.darbininkas.lt; f. 1989; 28 regional brs; 7 federations; 52,000 mems; Pres. ALDONA BALSIENĖ.

Transport

RAILWAYS

In 2001 there were 1,696 km of railway track in use in Lithuania; in the same year some 122 km of track were electrified. Main lines link Vilnius with Rīga (Latvia), Minsk (Belarus), Kaliningrad (Russia) and Warsaw (Poland), via the Belarusian town of Grodno.

Lithuanian Railways (Lietuvos geležinkeliai AB): Mindaugo 12–14, Vilnius 2600; tel. (526) 93300; fax (526) 18323; e-mail 24@litrail.lt; internet www.litrail.lt; f. 1991; Gen. Dir K. DIRGELA; 15,500 employees.

ROADS

In 2001 the total length of the road network was 76,573 km. The motorway network totalled 417 km and some 91% of roads were paved.

Lithuanian Road Administration (Lietuvos automobilių kelių direkcija): J. Basanavicius 36/2, Vilnius 2009; tel. (521) 31361; fax (521) 31362; e-mail info@lra.lt; internet www.lra.lt; Gen. Dir VIRGAUDAS PUODZIUKAS.

SHIPPING

The main port is at Klaipėda. During the Soviet period the port was used as an important transit facility, with some 90% of its total traffic being transit trade to and from the republics of the USSR. This role diminished with the establishment of Lithuanian independence in 1991 and the disruption of traditional trading patterns following the dissolution of the USSR. The Lithuanian Shipping Company was formerly part of the Soviet merchant shipping system.

In the early 1990s it was restructured as an independent enterprise, although it was adversely affected by declining trade and a largely obsolete fleet. In 2000 the World Bank funded an investment project for the reconstruction of the port gate and protection measures for the environment.

Port Authority

Klaipėda State Seaport Authority: J. Janonio 24, Klaipėda 5800; tel. (464) 99799; fax (464) 99777; e-mail info@port.lt; internet www.port.lt.

Shipowning Company

Public Company Lithuanian Shipping Company (AB Lietuvos Jūrų Laivininkystė): Malunininku 3, Klaipėda 5813; tel. (463) 93105; fax (463) 93119; e-mail gp@ljl.lt; internet www.ljl.lt; f. 1969; partially privatized in June 2001; 73.24% state-owned; transportation of cargo; Gen. Dir VYTAUTAS VISMANTAS.

CIVIL AVIATION

Lithuania has air links with Western European destinations and with cities in the former USSR. The state airline, Lietuvos avialinijos, is based at the international airports at Vilnius and Kaunas. An airport at Šiauliai opened for international flights at the end of 1993.

Directorate of Civil Aviation (Oro Navigacija): Rodūnės kelias 2, Vilnius 2023; tel. (527) 39102; fax (527) 39161; e-mail info@ans.lt; internet www.ans.lt; Gen. Dir ALGIMANTAS RAŠČIUS.

Lithuanian Airlines (Lietuvos avialinijos): A. Gustaičio 4, Vilnius 2038; tel. (523) 06017; fax (521) 66828; e-mail info@lal.lt; internet www.lal.lt; f. 1991; state-owned; scheduled for privatization in 2002; operates passenger and cargo flights to regional and European destinations; Dir-Gen. STASYS JARMALAVIČIUS.

Aviakompanija Lietuva (Air Lithuania): Veiverių 132, Karmelava Airport, Kaunas 3018; tel. (373) 91420; fax (372) 26030; e-mail hdoffice@airlithuania.lt; internet www.airlithuania.lt; f. 1991; state-owned; operates passenger and cargo services to Europe; became subsidiary of Lithuanian Airlines in August 1997; Chair. and Dir-Gen. TOMAS LAURINAITIS.

Tourism

Tourist attractions in Lithuania include the historic cities of Vilnius, Kaunas, Kėdainiai, Trakai and Klaipėda, coastal resorts, such as Palanga and Kuršių Nerija, and picturesque countryside. There were some 350 private travel agencies in operation in 1999 and some 349,662 tourists visited the country in 2001; tourist receipts in that year totalled US $383.0m.

Lithuanian State Department of Tourism: Vilniaus 4/35, Vilnius 2600; tel. (526) 22610; fax (521) 26819; e-mail tb@tourism.lt; internet www.tourism.lt; Dir ALVITIS LUKOSEVICIUS.

LUXEMBOURG

Introductory Survey

Location, Climate, Language, Religion, Flag, Capital

The Grand Duchy of Luxembourg is a land-locked country in Western Europe. It is bordered by Belgium to the west and north, by France to the south, and by Germany to the east. The climate is temperate, with cool summers and mild winters. In Luxembourg-Ville the average temperature ranges from 1°C (33°F) in January to 18°C (64°F) in July, while annual rainfall averages 782 mm. Letzeburgish (Luxembourgish), a German-Moselle-Frankish dialect, is the spoken language and became the official language in 1985. French is generally used for administrative purposes, while German is the principal written language of commerce and the press. Almost all of the inhabitants profess Christianity: about 88% are Roman Catholics and a small minority are Protestants. The national flag (proportions 3 by 5) consists of three equal horizontal stripes, of red, white and blue. The capital is Luxembourg-Ville (Lützelburg).

Recent History

As a founder member of the European Community (EC—now European Union—EU, see p. 199), of which Luxembourg-Ville is one of the main bases, Luxembourg has played a significant role in progress towards European integration since the Second World War. Luxembourg's commitment to such integration was exemplified by its status as one of the original signatories to the June 1990 Schengen Agreement (named after the town in Luxembourg where the accord was signed), which binds signatories to the abolition of internal border controls.

The Belgo-Luxembourg Economic Union (BLEU) has existed since 1921, except for the period from 1940–1944, when the Grand Duchy was subject to wartime occupation by Germany. In 1948 the Benelux Economic Union (see p. 339) was inaugurated between Belgium, Luxembourg and the Netherlands, becoming effective in 1960, and establishing the three countries as a single customs area in 1970.

In November 1964 Grand Duchess Charlotte abdicated, after a reign of 45 years, and was succeeded by her son, Prince Jean.

Pierre Werner, leader of the Parti Chrétien Social (PCS), became Prime Minister in February 1959. After the fall of the Government in October 1968, Werner headed a coalition of the PCS and the Parti Démocratique ('Liberals') from January 1969 until May 1974. At a general election in May 1974, the PCS lost its political dominance for the first time since 1919, and in June a centre-left coalition between the Parti Ouvrier Socialiste Luxembourgeois (POSL) and the Parti Démocratique Luxembourgeois (PDL) was formed under the premiership of Gaston Thorn, the Minister of Foreign Affairs since 1969. At the next general election, which took place in June 1979, the PCS increased its strength in the 59-member Chambre des Députés from 18 to 24 seats. In July Werner again formed a coalition Government, comprising his party and the PDL, which held 15 seats.

At a general election in June 1984 the PCS again secured the largest number of seats (25) in the enlarged 64-member legislature. However, the success of the POSL, which took 21 seats (compared with 14 in the previous election), was widely attributed to general dissatisfaction with an economic austerity programme, which had been introduced during the early 1980s, and with the rising level of unemployment. A centre-left coalition was formed in July 1984 between the PCS and the POSL, with Jacques Santer of the PCS (hitherto Minister of Finance, Labour and Social Security) as Prime Minister. New elections to the Chambre des Députés (whose membership had been reduced to 60 in January 1989) took place in June 1989. The PCS, the POSL and the PDL each lost three seats (returning, respectively, 22, 18 and 11 deputies). In the following month Santer was again sworn in as the head of a coalition Government, which comprised equal numbers of representatives from the PCS and the POSL. At the next general election, in June 1994, the PCS and the POSL each lost one representative in the Chambre des Députés, winning 21 and 17 seats respectively; the PDL secured 12 seats. The PCS-POSL coalition was renewed, and Santer was reappointed Prime Minister. In January 1995 Santer took office as President of the Commission of the EU. He was succeeded as

Prime Minister by Jean-Claude Juncker, hitherto Minister of the Budget, of Finance and of Labour.

In January 1998 the Minister of the Environment and of Health, Johny Lahure, resigned from his posts following the disclosure of a financial scandal within the Ministry of Health, and in May 1999 the President of the National Audit Office, Gérard Reuter, was suspended from office, pending investigation into allegations of mismanagement and fraud.

The two governing parties both recorded losses at the general election held concurrently with elections to the European Parliament on 13 June 1999, the PCS emerging with 19 seats and the POSL with 13. The main opposition party, the PDL, increased its representation from 12 to 15 seats, while the Comité d'Action pour la Démocratie et la Justice took seven seats (an increase of two). The environmentalist party, Déi Gréng, retained its five seats in the Chambre des Députés. Juncker, who remained as Prime Minister, subsequently formed a new centre-right coalition of his PCS and the PDL, which took office in early August; the POSL thus returned to opposition for the first time in 15 years.

In March 1998 Grand Duke Jean conferred broad constitutional powers upon his son and heir, Prince Henri, permitting him to deputize for the Grand Duke in all official capacities, including the signing of legislation, and in late December 1999 Grand Duke Jean announced his intention to abdicate the following year. On 7 October 2000 the Grand Duke's eldest son, Prince Henri, succeeded him as Head of State.

Luxembourg's banking secrecy laws have for many years been a cause of concern regarding the activities of banks and individual depositors benefiting from such legislation. Attempts by the EC, in the early 1990s, to impose more uniform regulations on the conduct of financial services in its member countries, in conjunction with the world-wide liquidation, in July 1991, of the Bank of Credit and Commerce International, the holding company and a subsidiary of which were incorporated in Luxembourg, focused renewed attention on Luxembourg's regulatory procedures. In April 1993 legislation was introduced which permitted the confiscation of deposits in Luxembourg banks accruing from suspected illegal drugs-related activities. Further legislation was introduced in 1997 which extended the State's powers of confiscation to include funds believed to be derived from other illegal sources, including arms-smuggling. During 1997 Luxembourg's financial sector came under renewed scrutiny when the Belgian authorities conducted an investigation into alleged widespread tax evasion by Belgian citizens and companies based in the Grand Duchy. The German authorities also launched a similar investigation. Luxembourg was further criticized for refusing, as did Switzerland, to endorse the code of conduct with respect to tax 'havens' drafted by the Organisation for Economic Co-operation and Development (OECD, see p. 277) in April 1998. During 1998 Luxembourg also opposed European Commission moves towards European taxation harmonization, which would oblige Luxembourg to impose tax on non-residents' interest and dividend income for the first time, thereby reducing the attraction of Luxembourg as a financial centre. In May 2000, however, Luxembourg for the first time endorsed reforms, proposed by a report by the OECD, aimed at limiting the use of bank secrecy laws in order to evade paying taxes; the report did, however, acknowledge the legitimacy of bank secrecy. In October the Chambre des Députés approved a relaxation of bank secrecy laws to facilitate co-operation with the US Internal Revenue Service in its attempts to halt tax evasion.

In December 2000 the Government was very active during negotiations regarding the Treaty of Nice, which aimed to reform the institutions of the EU in light of its forthcoming enlargements. The terms of the Treaty substantially safeguarded Luxembourg's privileged position in the EU: Luxembourg was to continue to have a European Commissioner, to maintain its six seats in the European Parliament and to continue to enjoy a voting weight in the Council of the European Union out of proportion to its size. Consequently it was no surprise that, in July 2001, the Chambre des Députés ratified the Treaty by a large majority, making the Grand Duchy the third EU member state to do so. At the same time, Luxembourg continued, much to the frustration of most of its EU partners, to oppose the removal from Luxembourg-Ville of the Secretariat of the European Parliament, together with its 1,500 staff, whose continued presence in the Grand Duchy was considered by the Luxembourg Government to be vital to the local economy.

The leaders and ministers responsible for foreign affairs from seven of the EU's smaller states (Luxembourg, Austria, Belgium, Finland, the Netherlands and Portugal) met in Luxembourg in early April 2003 to prepare a unified position against the potential diminution of their powers by the Convention on the Future of Europe, which aims to draft the EU's first constitution. Notably, they were opposed to a French and German initiative to install an elected President for the European Council, to replace the current system whereby the presidency is rotated among the members every six months on the grounds that the latter effectively guaranteed smaller countries a role in EU policy formation. Moreover, four EU countries, Luxembourg, Belgium, France and Germany, all of which were opposed to the US-led military campaign to remove the regime of Saddam Hussein in Iraq, agreed to hold a special summit to discuss defence matters at the end of April.

In June 2002 new legislation was enacted which enabled women who had never worked and therefore not contributed to a pension fund to be entitled to receive a pension in their own right from the age of 60 years. The following month laws to assist first-time house buyers were introduced. Also in July controversial new legislation allowing for the expansion of Findel Airport was approved.

In November 2002 a Luxair commuter aircraft travelling from Berlin crashed shortly before it was due to land at Findel Airport; 20 of the 22 passengers were killed. In February 2003 the preliminary results of a government inquiry indicated that both engines on the aircraft had failed.

Government

Luxembourg is an hereditary and constitutional monarchy. Legislative power is exercised by the unicameral Chambre des Députés, with 60 members elected by universal adult suffrage for five years (subject to dissolution) on the basis of proportional representation. Some legislative functions are also entrusted to the advisory Conseil de l'Etat, with 21 members appointed for life by the Grand Duke, but decisions made by this body can be overruled by the legislature.

Executive power is vested in the Grand Duke, but is normally exercised by the Council of Ministers, led by the President of the Government (Prime Minister). The Grand Duke appoints ministers, but they are responsible to the legislature. Luxembourg is divided into three districts (Luxembourg, Diekirch, Grevenmacher), 12 cantons and 118 municipalities.

Defence

Luxembourg was a founder member of NATO in 1949. Compulsory military service was abolished in 1967, but Luxembourg maintains an army of volunteers, totalling 900, and a gendarmerie numbering 612 (August 2002). Defence expenditure in the budget for 2002 was about €177m. In March 1987 the country became a signatory of the Benelux military convention, together with Belgium and the Netherlands. This aimed at the standardization of training methods and of military equipment in the three countries. Luxembourg committed 100 troops to the proposed joint EU rapid reaction force, which was to be ready to be deployed by 2003.

Economic Affairs

In 2001, according to estimates by the World Bank, Luxembourg's gross national income (GNI), measured at average 1999–2001 prices, was US $18,550m., equivalent to $41,770 per head (or $48,080 per head on an international purchasing-power parity basis). During 1990–2001, it was estimated, the population increased at an average rate of 1.4% per year, while gross domestic product (GDP) per head increased, in real terms, by an average of 4.3% per year. Overall GDP increased, in real terms, at an average annual rate of 5.8% in 1990–2001; growth in 2001 was 5.1%.

Agriculture (including forestry and fishing) contributed 0.7% of GDP in 2001. In the same year an estimated 1.3% of the employed labour force were engaged in the agricultural sector. The principal crops are cereals, potatoes and wine grapes. Livestock-rearing and dairy farming are also of some importance. According to the IMF, agricultural GDP declined at an

average annual rate of 0.4% in 1990–95 and, according to the World Bank, it decreased by 1.5% per year during 1995–2000. However, in 2000, real agricultural GDP grew by 8.2%.

Industry (including mining, manufacturing, construction and power) provided 19.2% of GDP in 2001, and in the same year engaged an estimated 22.7% of the employed labour force. Industrial GDP increased, in real terms, at an average annual rate of 0.3% in 1990–95 and by 8.4% per year in 1995–2000; it rose by 0.6% in 1999 and by 7.2% in 2000.

Manufacturing activities, excluding power and water, constitute the most important industrial sector, contributing 11.6% of GDP and engaged 12.2% of the employed workforce in 2001. Although the country's deposits of iron ore are no longer exploited, the iron and steel industry remains one of the most important sectors of the Luxembourg economy; metal manufactures accounted for an estimated 28.1% of total exports in 2001. The Luxembourg steel industry is dominated by Arcelor, which was formed in June 2001 by the merger of the Luxembourg-based Aciéries Réunies de Burbach-Eich-Dudelange SA—ARBED and the steel companies Usinor, of France, and Aceralia, of Spain, to form the world's largest steel group. Machinery and equipment provided 24.0% of total exports in 2001. Other important branches of manufacturing are basic manufactures and chemicals and related products. According to the IMF, real manufacturing GDP increased by an average of 1.5% per year in 1990–95 and, according to the World Bank, by 3.3% per year in 1995–2000; it grew by 5.5%% in 1999 and but declined by 0.01% in 2000.

In 1997 43.6% of electricity was derived from natural gas, 20.7% from coal, 20.4% from hydroelectric installations and 3.2% from petroleum. Fuel imports comprised 7.1% of the value of total imports in 2000.

The services sector contributed 80.1% of GDP in and engaged 76.0% of the employed labour force in 2001. Favourable laws governing banking secrecy and taxation have encouraged the development of Luxembourg as a major international financial centre. Financial services contributed 21.9% of GDP in 2001. In December 2001 there were 184 banks in Luxembourg, and 23,651 people were employed in banking activities. At 1 January 1999 23,651 holding companies were registered in Luxembourg. Stock exchange activities (notably the 'Eurobond' market and investment portfolio management) are also prominent; Luxembourg's investment fund sector was the biggest in Europe, with assets of €848,000m., at April 2000. At the end of 2000 there were 94 approved insurance companies in Luxembourg, as well as 264 reinsurance companies. Net profits in the banking sector increased at an average annual rate of 21.9% in 1990–97. According to the IMF, the GDP of the services sector increased, in real terms, at an average annual rate of 6.8% in 1990–95 and, according to World Bank figures, by 6.5% per year in 1995–2000; it rose by 9.1% in both 1999 and 2000.

In 2001, according to IMF figures, Luxembourg recorded a visible trade deficit of US $2,399m.; however, there was a surplus on the current account of the balance of payments of $1,674m. Other members of the European Union (EU—formerly the European Community, EC, see p. 199) account for much of Luxembourg's foreign trade (supplying 86.7% of imports and purchasing 84.7% of exports, according to provisional figures for 2001). In 2001 the principal source of imports (34.3%) was Belgium; other major providers were Germany (25.1%), France (12.8%) and the Netherlands (5.1%). The principal market for exports in that year was Germany (24.5%); other major purchasers were France (19.6%), Belgium (12.3%), the United Kingdom (8.2%) and Italy (6.2%). The principal exports in 2001 were metal manufactures, machinery and transport equipment and other basic manufactures. The principal imports were machinery and transport equipment, metal manufactures, chemicals and related products, and mineral fuels and lubricants.

In 1999 there was an overall budgetary surplus equivalent to 2.3% of GDP. Government debt was equivalent to 6.2% of GDP in that year. The annual rate of inflation averaged 2.2% in 1990–2001; consumer prices rose by 2.7% in 2001 and by 2.1% in 2002. According to the IMF, the unemployment rate averaged 2.6% in 2001, the lowest rate in the EU. Cross-border commuters from neighbouring states totalled 70,300 in 1999, constituting over one-quarter of the total employed in Luxembourg.

Luxembourg was a founder member of the EU and of the Benelux Economic Union (see p. 339). Luxembourg is also a member of the European Bank for Reconstruction and Development (see p. 193), and the European System of Central Banks (ESCB), inaugurated in 1998 (see European Central Bank).

Luxembourg's economy expanded at an average annual rate of more than 5% during 1985–2000, recording increases in GDP even in the early 1990s when neighbouring countries were in recession. The country's economic success was based on its development as an international financial centre, following the decline in the importance of the country's previously dominant iron and steel industry. In recent years significant growth has also taken place in the media and communications sector. This economic growth, which has ensured buoyant public finances, has been achieved with virtually no inflationary effect, although inflation rose slightly in 2000 and 2001, owing to the increase in international petroleum prices and subsequent wage rises, it declined in 2002. However, rapid economic expansion in Luxembourg has attracted an increasing number of cross-border workers from neighbouring countries, who already accounted for well over one-quarter of the work-force in 1999. Of the 11,500 new jobs created in 1999, 7,800 were taken by cross-border commuters. These workers pay social security contributions in Luxembourg but retire to their native countries to spend their pensions, which are financed by Luxembourg. The solution advanced by the Government is to eschew further job creation in favour of the development of high-technology industries (with a substantial value added), which do not require a larger work-force. This plan would also help to diversify the economy away from too great a dependence on the financial sector, the future profitability of which was likely to be eroded by the effects of EU integration, including the harmonization of taxation and regulatory structures (such as the adoption of rules on taxing non-residents' savings and the removal of banking secrecy). In January 1999 Luxembourg participated in the adoption of the euro as the single unit of currency for transactions throughout the euro zone and as an internationally traded currency in the 11 EU countries participating in economic and monetary union. In order to promote the country's long-term prospects, the IMF recommended tax reform, the restructuring of the pension system, the introduction of measures to improve the flexibility of the labour market and continuing support to the financial sector through effective supervision. (Government proposals to reduce corporate and personal taxes, and to promote private pension savings took effect from the budget of 2002.) The IMF also warned that the rapid growth of the late 1990s was unlikely to be replicated in the future and that the sharp rise in expenditure at central government level might become unsustainable. However, the European Commission predicted that Luxembourg would be relatively unaffected by the development of short-term international economic problems and forecast growth of 6.6% in 2003.

Education

Education in Luxembourg is compulsory from the age of four to 15 years. Primary education begins at six years of age and lasts for six years. German is the initial language of instruction at primary level. French is added to the programme in the second year, and replaces German as the language of instruction at higher secondary level.

At the age of 12, children can choose between secondary school (lycée) and technical education (lycée technique). The first year of secondary school is a general orientation course on comprehensive lines, which is then followed by a choice between two sections: the Classical Section, with an emphasis on Latin, and the Modern Section, which stresses English and other modern languages. The completed secondary course lasts seven years, and leads to the Certificat de Fin d'Etudes Secondaires, which qualifies for university entrance. The technical education course (six to eight years) leads either to a vocational diploma, a technician's diploma (diplôme de technicien) or a technical baccalaureate diploma (bac technique) and is devised in three parts: an orientation and observation course, an intermediate course and an upper course.

The Centre Universitaire was established in 1969, offering one-year or two-year courses in the humanities, sciences and law and economics, as well as training courses for lawyers and teachers, following which the students generally attend other European universities. The Institut Supérieur de Technologies (IST) is an institute for higher education at university level in civil engineering, electrical engineering, applied computer sciences and mechanical engineering.

Central government expenditure on primary, secondary and vocational education in 2001 was projected at €559m.

Public Holidays

2003: 1 January (New Year's Day), 3 March (Carnival), 21 April (Easter Monday), 1 May (Labour Day), 29 May (Ascension Day), 9 June (Whit Monday), 23 June (National Day), 15 August (Assumption), 1 September (Luxembourg City Fête, Luxembourg City only), 1 November (All Saints' Day), 25 December (Christmas), 26 December (St Stephen's Day).

2004: 1 January (New Year's Day), 23 February (Carnival), 12 April (Easter Monday), 1 May (Labour Day), 20 May (Ascension Day), 31 May (Whit Monday), 23 June (National Day), 15 August (Assumption), 6 September (Luxembourg City Fête, Luxembourg City only), 1 November (All Saints' Day), 25 December (Christmas), 26 December (St Stephen's Day).

Weights and Measures

The metric system is in force.

Statistical Survey

Source (unless otherwise stated): Service Central de la Statistique et des Etudes Economiques (STATEC), Ministère de l'Economie, 6 blvd Royal, BP 304, 2013 Luxembourg; tel. 478-42-52; fax 46-42-89; e-mail statec.post@statec.etat.lu; internet www.statec.lu.

AREA AND POPULATION

Area: 2,586 sq km (999 sq miles).

Population: 384,634 at census of 1 March 1991; 439,539 (males 216,540, females 222,999) at census of 15 February 2001; 441,000 (official estimate) at mid-2001. Source: partly UN, *Population and Vital Statistics Report*.

Density (February 2001): 170.0 per sq km.

Principal Towns (population at 2001 census): Luxembourg-Ville (capital) 76,688; Esch-sur-Alzette 27,146; Differdange 18,172; Dudelange 17,320; Pétange 13,491; Sanem 13,041; Hesperange 10,400.

Births, Marriages and Deaths (2001): Live births 5,459 (birth rate 12.4 per 1,000); Marriages 1,983 (marriage rate 4.5 per 1,000); Deaths 3,719 (death rate 8.4 per 1,000).

Expectation of Life (WHO estimates, years at birth): 78.5 (males 74.9; females 81.4 in 2001. Source: WHO, *World Health Report*.

Immigration and Emigration (2001): Arrivals 12,135; Departures 8,824.

Employment (estimates, '000 persons, incl. armed forces, 2001): Agriculture, hunting, forestry and fishing 3.6; Mining and quarrying 0.3; Manufacturing 33.9; Electricity, gas and water supply 1.6; Construction 27.1; Wholesale and retail trade, repair of motor vehicles, motorcycles and personal and household goods 39.0; Hotels and restaurants 12.5; Transport, storage and communications 23.0; Financial intermediation 32.4; Real estate, renting and business activities 43.9; Public administration and defence; compulsory social security 15.2; Education 11.8; Health and social work 16.4; Other community, social and personal service activities 9.9; Private households with employed persons 6.3; Total employed 277.0; Total unemployed 4.9.

HEALTH AND WELFARE

Key Indicators

Total Fertility Rate (children per woman, 2001): 1.7.

Under-5 Mortality Rate (per 1,000 live births, 2001): 5.

HIV/AIDS (% of persons aged 15–49, 2000): 0.16.

Physicians (per 1,000 head, 2001): 2.5.

Hospital Beds (per 1,000 head, 2001): 6.9.

Health Expenditure (2000): US $ per head (PPP): 2,740.

Health Expenditure (2000): % of GDP: 5.8.

Health Expenditure (2000): public (% of total): 91.1.

Human Development Index (2000): ranking: 16.

Human Development Index (2000): value: 0.925.
For sources and definitions, see explanatory note on p. vi.

AGRICULTURE, ETC.

Principal Crops (provisional figures, '000 metric tons, 1998): Wheat 60.1; Rye 4.1; Barley 63.2; Oats 11.7; Potatoes 22.7 (2001); Wine grapes 15.0 (1995).

Livestock (May 2001): Cattle 205,193; Horses 3,126; Pigs 78,540; Sheep 8,476; Poultry 68,364 (1998).

Livestock Products ('000 metric tons, 2001): Meat (bovine and pig meat, without calf and piglet meat) 27.2; Milk 269.5; Butter 3.1 (1996); Cheese 3.0 (1996).

Forestry (FAO estimates, '000 cubic metres, 2000): Roundwood removals (excl. bark) 259 (Sawlogs, veneer logs and logs for sleepers 113, Pulpwood 72, Other industrial wood 56, Fuel wood 1); Sawnwood production (incl. railway sleepers) 133 (Coniferous 113, Broadleaved 20). Source: FAO.

INDUSTRY

Selected Products ('000 metric tons, unless otherwise indicated, 2001): Crude steel 2,725; Rolled steel products 3,990; Wine ('000 hl) 134.8.

FINANCE

Currency and Exchange Rates: 100 cent = 1 euro (€). *Sterling and Dollar Equivalents* (31 December 2002): £1 sterling = 1.536951 euros; US $1 = 0.953562 euros; 100 euros = £65.06 = $104.87. *Average Exchange Rate* (euros per US dollar): 1.0854 in 2000; 1.1175 in 2001; 1.0625 in 2002. Note: The national currency was formerly the Luxembourg franc. From the introduction of the euro, with Luxembourg's participation, on 1 January 1999, a fixed exchange rate of €1 = 40.3399 Luxembourg francs was in operation. Euro notes and coins were introduced on 1 January 2002. The euro and local currency circulated alongside each other until 28 February, after which the euro became the sole legal tender. Some of the figures in this Survey are still in terms of Luxembourg francs.

Budget (provisional, '000 million Luxembourg francs, 1999)* *Revenue:* Direct taxes 119.9; Indirect taxes 103.1; Social security contributions 86.4; Interest revenue 8.1; Other revenue 21.0; Total 338.6. *Expenditure:* Intermediate input 25.2; Wages and salaries 63.6; Social transfers 146.3; Subsidies 12.6; Public investment 34.9; Other expenditures 39.0; Total 321.7.
* Figures refer to a consolidation of the operations of the central Government, local authorities and social security funds. Source: IMF, *Luxembourg: Selected Issues and Statistical Appendix* (May 2000).

General Budget (million euros): *Revenue* 7,645 in 1998; 8,433 in 1999; 9,475 in 2000. *Expenditure* 6,736 in 1998; 7,450 in 1999; 7,883 in 2000. (Source: IMF, *Supplement to the 2002 Government Finance Statistics Yearbook*).

International Reserves (US $ million at 31 December 2002): Gold 26.00; IMF special drawing rights 9.14, Reserve position in IMF 142.406; Total 151.54. Source: IMF, *International Financial Statistics*.

Money Supply (million euros at 31 December 2002): Currency issued 677.0*; Demand deposits at banking institutions 48,161.1.
* Currency put into circulation by the Banque Centrale du Luxembourg was 9,932 million euros. Source: IMF, *International Financial Statistics*.

Cost of Living (Consumer Price Index; base: 1995 = 100): All items 104.8 in 1999; 108.1 in 2000; 111.0 in 2001. Source: IMF, *International Financial Statistics*.

Expenditure on the Gross Domestic Product (million euros at current prices, 2001): Government final consumption expenditure 3,701.2; Private final consumption expenditure 8,759.0; Increase in stocks 73.7; Gross fixed capital formation 4,653.9; *Total domestic expenditure* 17,187.9; Exports of goods and services 32,256.8; *Less* Imports of goods and services 28,221.1; *GDP in purchasers' values* 21,223.5.

Gross Domestic Product by Economic Activity (million euros at current prices, 2001): Agriculture, hunting, forestry and fishing 144.9; Mining and quarrying 30.5; Manufacturing 2,415.9; Electricity, gas and water supply 227.1; Construction 1,332.2; Wholesale and retail trade, repair of motor vehicles, motorcycles and personal and household goods 2,145.7; Hotels and restaurants 426.8; Transport and communications 2,333.1; Financial services 4,553.2; Real estate, renting and business activities 3,746.1; Public administration and defence; compulsory social security 1,230.2; Education 783.1; Health and social work 822.7; Other community, social and personal service activities 553.9; Private households with employed persons 89.1; *Sub-total* 20,834.3; *Less* Imputed financial services 1,974.3; *GDP at basic prices* 18,860.3; Taxes on products 2,576.6; *Less* subsidies on products 213.4; *GDP in purchasers' values* 21,223.5.

Balance of Payments (US $ million, 2001): Exports of goods f.o.b. 8,996; Imports of goods f.o.b. –11,395; *Trade balance* –2,399; Exports of services 19,945; Imports of services –13,708; *Balance on goods and services* 3,838; Other income received 52,302; Other income paid –53,941; *Balance on goods, services and income* 2,199; Current transfers received 2,269; Current transfers paid –2,794; *Current balance* 1,674. Source: IMF, *International Financial Statistics*.

EXTERNAL TRADE

Principal Commodities (million euros, provisional 2001): *Imports:* Food and live animals 826.0; Beverages and tobacco 398.6; Crude materials (inedible) except fuels 665.9; Mineral fuels, lubricants, etc. 932.3; Chemicals and related products 1,244.5; Metal manufactures 1,396.1; Other basic manufactures 934.2; Machinery and other equipment 2,657.8; Transport equipment 1,876.6; Miscellaneous manufactured articles 1,403.0; Total (incl. others) 12,335.0. *Exports:* Food and live animals 382.0; Chemicals and related products 576.7; Metal manufactures 2,548.3; Other basic manufactures 1,440.1; Machinery and other equipment 2,183.5; Transport equipment 390.1; Miscellaneous manufactured articles 1,219.5; Total (incl. others) 9,081.5.

Principal Trading Partners (million euros, provisional, 2001): *Imports:* Belgium 4,232.8; France 1,574.8; Germany 3,099.5; Japan 133.2; Italy 210.3; Netherlands 630.4; United Kingdom 516.5; USA 711.5; Total (incl. others) 12,335.0. *Exports:* Austria 111.0; Belgium 1,114.9; France 1,781.4; Germany 2,223.1; Ireland 115.3; Italy 565.6; Netherlands 407.4; Spain 273.7; Sweden 93.1; United Kingdom 744.5; USA 319.0; Total (incl. others) 9,081.9.

TRANSPORT

Railways (traffic, million, 2001): Passenger-kilometres 346; Freight ton-kilometres 634.

Road Traffic (motor vehicles in use at 1 January 2002): Private cars 280,713; Buses and coaches 1,123; Goods vehicles 21,782; Tractors 13,692; Total (incl. others) 341,351.

River Traffic (Port of Mertert, '000 metric tons, 2001): Goods loaded 450, Goods unloaded 1,141.

Civil Aviation (traffic on scheduled services, 2001): Passengers carried 1,625,000; Freight (metric tons) 510,965.

TOURISM

Foreign Tourist Arrivals (at accommodation establishments): 862,822 in 1999; 835,256 in 2000; 811,615 in 2001. Source: Office National de Tourisme.

Arrivals by Country (2001): Belgium 199,637; France 68,085; Germany 100,006; Italy 18,270; Netherlands 225,002; United Kingdom 52,542; USA 24,735; Total (incl. others) 811,615. Source: Office National du Tourisme.

COMMUNICATIONS MEDIA

Facsimilie Machines: 20,000 in use (1998).

Mobile Cellular Telephones: 432,400 subscribers (2001).

Telephones: 350,000 main lines in use (2001).

Personal Computers ('000 in use): 230 (2001).

Internet Users ('000): 100 (2001).

Daily Newspapers: 5 (1998).

Book Production: 513 titles (1997).

Radio Receivers: 285,000 in use (1997).

Television Receivers: 260,000 in use (2000).
Sources: partly UNESCO, *Statistical Yearbook;* International Telecommunication Union.

EDUCATION
(2000/01)

Nursery: 751 teachers; 10,706 pupils.

Primary: 2,135 teachers; 31,278 pupils.

Secondary, Middle, Vocational and Technical: 3,125 teachers (State sector only); 9,859 pupils (Secondary), 21,359 pupils (Middle, vocational and technical).

Higher Institute of Technology: 283 students.

Teacher Training: 393 students.

Other University-level: 6,874 students, incl. 5,017 studying abroad.

Directory

The Constitution

The Constitution now in force dates back to 17 October 1868, but in 1919 a constituent assembly introduced some important changes, declaring that the sovereign power resided in the nation, that all secret treaties were denounced and that deputies were to be elected by a list system by means of proportional representation, on the basis of universal adult suffrage. Electors must be citizens of Luxembourg and must have attained 18 years of age. Candidates for election must have attained 21 years of age. The Grand Duke, who is Sovereign, chooses government ministers, may intervene in legislative questions and has certain judicial powers. There is a single-chamber legislature, the Chamber of Deputies (Chambre des Députés), with 60 members elected for five years. There are four electoral districts, the North, the Centre, the South and East. By the law of 9 October 1956 the Constitution was further revised to the effect that: 'The exercise of prerogatives granted by the Constitution to the legislative, executive and judiciary powers, can, by treaty, be temporarily vested in institutions of international law.' The Constitution was further amended on 12 December 1994, 12 July 1996 (introducing a Constitutional Court) and 12 January 1998. In addition to the Council of Ministers, which consists of the President of the Government (Prime Minister) and at least three other ministers, the State Council (which is the supreme administrative tribunal and which also fulfils certain legislative functions) comprises 21 members nominated for life by the Sovereign.

The Government

HEAD OF STATE

Grand Duke: HRH HENRI ALBERT FÉLIX MARIE GUILLAUME (succeeded to the throne 7 October 2000).

Marshal of the Court: HENRI AHLBORN.

COUNCIL OF MINISTERS
(April 2003)

A coalition of the Parti Chrétien Social (PCS) and the Parti Démocratique Luxembourgeois (PDL).

Prime Minister and Minister of State and of Finance: JEAN-CLAUDE JUNCKER (PCS).

Deputy Prime Minister and Minister of Foreign Affairs and Trade, and of the Civil Service and Administrative Reform: LYDIE POLFER (PDL).

Minister of Agriculture, Viticulture and Rural Development, and of Small Business, Tourism and Housing: FERNAND BODEN (PCS).

Minister of Family Affairs, Social Solidarity and Youth, and of Women's Affairs: MARIE-JOSÉE JACOBS (PCS).

Minister of Culture, Further Education and Research, and of Public Works: ERNA HENNICOT-SCHOEPGES (PCS).

Minister of the Interior: MICHEL WOLTER (PCS).

Minister of Justice, and of the Treasury and Budget: LUC FRIEDEN (PCS).

Minister of National Education, Vocational Training and Sport: ANNE BRASSEUR (PDL).

Minister of the Economy and of Transport: HENRI GRETHEN (PDL).

Minister of Co-operation, Humanitarian Action and Defence, and of the Environment: CHARLES GOERENS (PDL).

Minister of Health and of Social Security: CARLO WAGNER (PDL).

Minister of Labour and Employment, of Parliamentary Relations, of Religious Affairs, and Minister delegate of Communications: FRANÇOIS BILTGEN (PDL).

Secretary of State for the Civil Service and Administrative Reform: JOSEPH SCHAAK (PDL).

Secretary of State for the Environment: EUGÈNE BERGER (PDL).

MINISTRIES

Office of the Prime Minister: Hôtel de Bourgogne, 4 rue de la Congrégation, 2910 Luxembourg; tel. 478-21-06; fax 46-17-20.

Ministry of Agriculture, Viticulture and Rural Development: 1 rue de la Congrégation, 1352 Luxembourg; tel. 478-25-00; fax 46-40-27; internet www.etat.lu/MA.

Ministry of the Civil Service and Administrative Reform: 63 ave de la Liberté, BP 1087; 1018 Luxembourg; tel. 478-31-06; fax 478-31-22; e-mail Ministere-FonctionPublique@mfp.etat.lu; internet www.etat.lu.

Ministry of Communications: 18 montée de la Pétrusse, 2945 Luxembourg; tel. 478-67-10; fax 40-89-40; e-mail officielle.boite@mz.etat.lu; internet www.etat.lu/mss.

Ministry of Co-operation, Humanitarian Action and Defence: 6 rue de la Congrégation, 1352 Luxembourg; tel. 478-23-00; fax 22-20-48.

Ministry of Culture, Further Education and Research: 20 montée de la Pétrusse, 2273 Luxembourg; tel. 478-6619; fax 40-24-27; internet www.ltam.lu/culture.

Ministry of the Economy: 19–21 blvd Royal, 2449 Luxembourg; tel. 478-41-37; fax 46-04-48; e-mail Luc.Rischard@eco.etat.lu; internet www.etat.lu/ECO.

Ministry of the Environment: 18 montée de la Pétrusse, 2918 Luxembourg; tel. 478-68-24; fax 40-04-10; e-mail patrick.grivet@mev.etat.lu; internet www.mev.etat.lu.

Ministry of Family Affairs, Social Solidarity and Youth: 12–14 ave Emile Reuter, 2919 Luxembourg; tel. 478-1; fax 478-65-71.

Ministry of Finance: 3 rue de la Congrégation, 2931 Luxembourg; tel. 478-1; fax 47-52-41; internet www.etat.lu/FI.

Ministry of Foreign Affairs and Trade: 5 rue Notre Dame, 2240 Luxembourg; tel. 478-1; fax 22-31-44.

Ministry of Health: Villa Louvigny, allée Marconi, 2120, Luxembourg; tel. 478-1; fax 46-79-63; e-mail ministere-sante@ms.etat.lu; internet www.etat.lu/MS.

Ministry of the Interior: 19 rue Beaumont, 1219 Luxembourg; tel. 478-46-06; fax 22-11-25; internet www.etat.lu/MI.

Ministry of Justice: 16 blvd Royal, 2934 Luxembourg; tel. 478-45-06; fax 22-76-61.

Ministry of Labour and Employment: 26 rue Zithe, 2939 Luxembourg; tel. 478-61-22; fax 48-03-85-; e-mail Jean.Zahlen@mt.etat.lu; internet www.etat.lu/MT.

Ministry of National Education, Vocational Training and Sport: BP 180, 2011 Luxembourg; tel. 478-34-00; fax 478-34-40; e-mail pisa@men.lu; internet www.men.lu.

Ministry of Public Works: 4 blvd F. D. Roosevelt, 2450 Luxembourg; tel. 478-33-00; fax 22-31-60; e-mail webmaster@tp.etat.lu; internet www.etat.lu/MTP.

Ministry of Religious Affairs: 4 rue de la Congrégation, 2910 Luxembourg; tel. 478-1; fax 46-17-20.

Ministry of Small Business, Tourism and Housing: 6 ave E. Reuter, 2937 Luxembourg; tel. 478-47-15; fax 478-47-40; internet www.etat.lu/MCMT.

Ministry of Social Security: 26 rue Zithe, 2763 Luxembourg; tel. 478-63-11; fax 478-63-28; e-mail Romain.Fehr@mss.etat.lu; internet www.etat.lu/MSS.

Ministry of State: 4 rue de la Congrégation, 1352 Luxembourg; tel. 478-21-00; fax 46-17-20; e-mail ministere.etat@me.etat.lu; internet www.etat.lu.

Ministry of Transport: 19–21 blvd Royal, 2449 Luxembourg; tel. 478-44-11; fax 46-43-15.

Ministry of Women's Affairs: 12–14 ave E. Reuter, 2921 Luxembourg; tel. 478-58-14; fax 24-18-86; e-mail promotionfeminine@ mpf.etat.lu; internet www.mpf.lu.

Legislature

CHAMBRE DES DÉPUTÉS
(Chamber of Deputies)

President: JEAN SPAUTZ (Parti Chrétien Social).

General Election, 13 June 1999

Party	Seats
Parti Chrétien Social	19
Parti Démocratique Luxembourgeois	15
Parti Ouvrier Socialiste Luxembourgeois	13
Comité d'Action pour la Démocratie et la Justice	7
Déi Gréng	5
Déi Lénk	1
Total	**60**

Advisory Councils

Conseil Economique et Social: 31 blvd Konrad Adenauer, BP 1306, 1013 Luxembourg; tel. 43-58-51; fax 42-27-29; e-mail ces@ces .etat.lu; internet www.etat.lu/CES; f. 1966; consultative body on economics and social affairs; 35 mems; Pres. GASTON REINESCH; Sec.-Gen. MARIANNE NATI-STOFFEL.

Conseil d'Etat: 5 rue Sigefroi, 2536 Luxembourg; tel. 47-30-71; fax 46-43-22; e-mail conseil@ce.smtp.etat.lu; internet www.etat.lu/CE; 21 mems nominated for life by the Sovereign; Pres. PAUL BEGHIN; Vice-Pres RAYMOND KIRSCH, PAUL-HENRI MEYERS.

Political Organizations

Comité d'Action pour la Démocratie et la Justice: 9 rue de la Loge, 1945 Luxembourg; tel. 46-37-42; fax 46-37-45; e-mail adr@chd .lu; internet www.adr.lu; f. 1989; present name adopted 1994; conservative; campaigns to secure improved pension rights for private-sector employees; Pres. ROBERT MEHLEN; Sec.-Gen. FERNAND GREISEN.

Déi Gréng (Greens): BP 454, 2014 Luxembourg; tel. 46-37-40-1; fax 46-37-43; e-mail greng@greng.lu; internet www.greng.lu; f. 1983; fmrly Déi Gréng Alternativ (Green Alternative Party); merged with the Gréng Lëscht Ekologesch Initiativ (Green List Ecological Initiative) in 1995; advocates 'grass-roots' democracy, environmental protection, social concern and increased aid to developing countries; Secs ABBES JACOBY, NADINE ENTRINGER.

Déi Lénk (The Left): BP 817, 2018 Luxembourg; tel. 26-20-20-72; fax 46-69-66-960; e-mail sekretariat@dei-lenk.lu; internet www .dei-lenk.lu; f. 1999; individual membership; no formal leadership.

Parti Chrétien Social (PCS) (Christian Social Party): 4 rue de l'Eau, BP 826, 2018 Luxembourg; tel. 22-57-31-1; fax 47-27-16; e-mail csv@csv.lu; internet www.csv.lu; f. 1914; advocates political stability, sustained economic expansion, ecological and social progress; 9,500 mems; Pres. ERNA HENNICOT-SCHOEPGES; Sec.-Gen. JEAN-LOUIS SCHILTZ.

Parti Communiste Luxembourgeois (Communist Party): 2 rue Astrid, 1143 Luxembourg; tel. 44-60-66; e-mail zeiluvol@pt.lu; f. 1921; Pres. ALI RUCKERT.

Parti Démocratique Luxembourgeois (PDL) (Democratic Party): 46 Grand'rue, BP 794, 2017 Luxembourg; tel. 22-10-21; fax 22-10-13; e-mail groupdp@dp.lu; internet www.dp.lu; liberal; Leader LYDIE POLFER; Sec.-Gen. HENRI GRETHEN.

Parti Ouvrier Socialiste Luxembourgeois (POSL) (Socialist Workers' Party): 16 rue de Crécy, 1364 Luxembourg; tel. 45-59-91; fax 45-65-75; e-mail info@lsap.lu; internet www.lsap.lu; f. 1902; social democrat; 6,000 mems; Pres. JEAN ASSELBORN; Sec.-Gen. PAUL BACH.

Diplomatic Representation

EMBASSIES IN LUXEMBOURG

Austria: 3 rue des Bains, 1212 Luxembourg; tel. 47-11-88; fax 46-39-74; e-mail luxemburg-ob@bmaa.gv.at; Ambassador CHRISTIAN STROHAL.

Belgium: 4 rue des Girondins, 1626 Luxembourg; tel. 44-27-46-1; fax 45-42-82; e-mail luxembourg@diplobel.org; Ambassador PATRICK VERCAUTEREN DRUBBEL.

Cape Verde: 46 rue Goethe, 1637 Luxembourg; tel. 26-48-09-48; fax 26-48-09-49; Chargé d'affaires a.i. OCTAVIO BENTO GOMES.

China, People's Republic: 2 rue Van der Meulen, 2152 Luxembourg; tel. 43-69-91-1; fax 42-24-23; Ambassador SUN RONGMIN.

Denmark: 4 bvld Royal, 2449 Luxembourg; tel. 22-21-22-1; fax 22-21-24; e-mail luxamb@um.dk; Ambassador IB RITTO ANDREASEN.

Finland: 2 rue Heine, 1720 Luxembourg; tel. 49-55-51-1; fax 49-46-40; e-mail sanomat.lux@formin.fi; Ambassador SAULI FEODOROW.

France: 8B blvd Joseph 11, BP 359, 2013 Luxembourg; tel. 45-72-71-1; fax 45-72-71-227; Ambassador PIERRE CARRIGUE-GUYONNAUD.

Germany: 20–22 ave Emile Reuter, BP 95, 2010 Luxembourg; tel. 45-34-45-1; fax 45-56-04; internet webplaza.pt.lu/public/dtbotlux; Ambassador ROLAND LOHKAMP.

Greece: 117 val Ste Croix, 1371 Luxembourg; tel. 44-51-93; fax 45-01-64; Ambassador PANAYOTIS MACRIS.

Ireland: 28 route d'Arlon, 1140 Luxembourg; tel. 45-06-10; fax 45-88-20; e-mail luxembourg@iveagh.irlgov.ie; Ambassador MICHAEL HOEY.

Italy: 5–7 rue Marie-Adélaïde, 2128 Luxembourg; tel. 44-36-44-1; fax 45-55-23; e-mail italamb@ambitalialux.lu; Ambassador RAFFAELE CAMPANELLA.

Japan: 62 ave de la Faïencerie, BP 92, 2010 Luxembourg; tel. 46-41-51-1; fax 46-41-76; Ambassador MASAHIRO ANDO.

Netherlands: 5 rue C. M. Spoo, 2546 Luxembourg; tel. 22-75-70; fax 40-30-16; e-mail nlgovlux@pt.lu; Ambassador JOHAN S. L. GUALTHÉRIE VAN WEEZEL.

Portugal: 24 rue Guiliaame Schneider, 2522 Luxembourg; tel. 46-61-90-1; fax 46-51-69; e-mail embport@pt.lu; Ambassador PAULO COUTO BARBOSA.

Romania: 94 ave du Dix Septembre, 2550 Luxembourg; tel. 45-51-59; fax 45-51-63; Ambassador LIVIU-PETRU ZAPÎRTAN.

Russia: Château de Beggen, 1719 Luxembourg; tel. 42-23-33; fax 42-23-34; Ambassador OLEG KRIVONOGOV.

Spain: 4–6 blvd E. Servais, 2535 Luxembourg; tel. 46-02-55; fax 47-48-50; Ambassador RAMIRO PÉREZ-MAURA DE HERRERA.

Sweden: 2 rue Heine, 1720 Luxembourg; tel. 29-68-34; fax 29-69-09; e-mail ambassaden.luxemburg@foreign.ministry.se; internet www .ambsuede-lux.com; Ambassador ANN WILKENS.

Switzerland: 25A blvd Royal, BP 469, 2014 Luxembourg; tel. 22-74-74-1; fax 22-74-74-20; e-mail vertretung@lux.rep.admin.ch; Ambassador INGRID APELBAUM-PIDOUX.

Turkey: 20 rue Marie-Adélaïde, 2128 Luxembourg; tel. 44-32-81; fax 44-32-81-34; e-mail ambturq@pt.lu; Ambassador YALÇIN ORAL.

United Kingdom: 14 blvd Roosevelt, 2450 Luxembourg; tel. 22-98-64; fax 22-98-67; e-mail britemb@pt.lu; internet webplaza.pt.lu/ public/britemb; Ambassador GORDON WETHERELL.

USA: 22 blvd E. Servais, 2535 Luxembourg; tel. 46-01-23; fax 46-14-01; internet www.amembassy.lu; Ambassador PETER TERPELUK, Jr.

Judicial System

The lowest courts in Luxembourg are those of the Justices of the Peace, of which there are three, at Luxembourg-Ville, Esch-sur-Alzette and Diekirch. These are competent to deal with civil, commercial and criminal cases of minor importance. Above these are the two District Courts, Luxembourg being divided into the judicial districts of Luxembourg and Diekirch. These are competent to deal with civil, commercial and criminal cases. The Superior Court of Justice includes both a court of appeal, hearing decisions made by District Courts, and the Cour de Cassation. As the judicial system of the Grand Duchy does not employ the jury system, a defendant is acquitted if a minority of the presiding judges find him or her guilty. The highest administrative court is the Comité du Contentieux du Conseil d'Etat. Special tribunals exist to adjudicate upon various matters of social administration such as social insurance. The department of the Procureur Général (Attorney-General) is responsible for the administration of the judiciary and the supervision of judicial police investigations. In July 1996 an amendment to the Constitution introduced a Constitutional Court.

Judges are appointed for life by the Grand Duke, and are not removable except by judicial sentence.

President of the Superior Court of Justice: PAUL KAYSER.

Attorney-General: CAMILLE WAMPACH.

Religion

CHRISTIANITY

The Roman Catholic Church

For ecclesiastical purposes, Luxembourg comprises a single archdiocese, directly responsible to the Holy See. At 31 December 2000 there were an estimated 378,000 adherents in the country, representing about 87% of the total population.

Archbishop of Luxembourg: Most Rev. FERNAND FRANCK, Archevêché, 4 rue Génistre, BP 419, 2014 Luxembourg; tel. 46-20-23; fax 47-53-81; e-mail archeveche@cathol.lu.

The Anglican Communion

Within the Church of England, Luxembourg forms part of the diocese of Gibraltar in Europe.

Chaplain: Rev. CHRISTOPHER LYON, 89 rue de Muehlenbach, 2168 Luxembourg; tel. and fax 43-95-93; e-mail christopher.lyon@ci.educ .lu; English-speaking church (Anglican Chaplaincy).

Protestant Church

The Evangelical Church in the Grand Duchy of Luxembourg: rue de la Congrégation, 1352 Luxembourg; tel. 22-96-70; fax 46-71-88; e-mail mail@protestant.lu; internet www.protestant.lu; f. 1818 as Protestant Garnison Church, 1868 as community for the Grand Duchy; there are about 1,500 Evangelicals; Pres. Pasteur MICHEL FAULLIMMEL.

JUDAISM

Chief Rabbi: JOSEPH SAYAGH, 34 rue Alphouse Munchen, 2172 Luxembourg; tel. 45-23-66; fax 25-04-30.

The Press

DAILIES

Lëtzebuerger Journal: Résidence de Beauvoir, 51 rue de Strasbourg, BP 2101, 1021 Luxembourg; tel. 49-30-33; fax 49-20-65; f. 1948; organ of the Democratic Party; Editor ROB ROEMEN; circ. 13,500 (1993).

Luxemburger Wort/La Voix du Luxembourg: 2 rue Christophe Plantin, 2988 Luxembourg; tel. 49-93-1; fax 49-93-38-4; e-mail wort@wort.lu; internet www.wort.lu; f. 1848; German and French; Catholic; Christian Democrat; Chief Editor LÉON ZECHES; circ. 87,126 (2000).

Le Républicain Lorrain: 7 rue d'Esch, BP 2211, 1022 Luxembourg; tel. and fax 44-77-44-37-01; f. 1963; French; Head of Publicity MARC TURMES; circ. 16,200 (1999).

Tageblatt/Zeitung fir Letzebuerg: 44 rue du Canal, 4050 Esch-sur-Alzette; tel. 54-71-31-1; fax 54-71-30; e-mail tageblatt@tageblatt .lu; internet www.tageblatt.lu; f. 1913; French and German; Dir ALVIN SOLD; circ. 29,601 (1998).

Zeitung vum Lëtzeburger Vollek: 16 rue Christophe Plantin, 2339 Luxembourg, BP 2106, 1021 Luxembourg; tel. 49-21-01; fax 44-25-25; f. 1946; organ of the Communist Party; Dir FRANÇOIS HOFFMANN; circ. 8,000 (1992).

PERIODICALS

Ardenner Zeitung: 7 rue Robert Stümper, 2557 Luxembourg; tel. 29-04-35; fax 29-04-36; f. 1991; regional magazine for northern Luxembourg and German-speaking Belgium; monthly; German; Editor CLAUDE PRUD'HOMMES.

AutoRevue: BP 231, 2012 Luxembourg; tel. 22-99-3; f. 1948; monthly; illustrated; Publr PAUL NEYENS; circ. 12,000.

Carrière: BP 2535, 1025 Luxembourg; tel. 85-89-19; fax 85-89-19; e-mail carriere@logic.lu; internet www.logic.lu/carriere; f. 1988; women's interest; French and German; Editor MONIQUE MATHIEU; circ. 5,000.

Echo de l'Industrie: 7 rue Alcide de Gasperi, BP 1304, 1013 Luxembourg; tel. 43-53-66-1; fax 43-23-28; e-mail echo@fedil.lu; f.

1920; monthly; industry, commerce; publ. by Fédération des Industriels Luxembourgeois; Dir NICOLAS SOISSON; circ. 2,100.

d'Eechternoacher nei Zeidung: POB 48, 6401 Echternach; tel. 73-04-36; fax 73-04-35; internet www.neizeidung.lu; f. 1974; regional magazine; monthly; German; Editor ROB KÖLLER-JOCHIMS; circ. 15,000.

Handelsblad/Le Journal du Commerce: 31 blvd Konrad Adenauer, BP 482, 2014 Luxembourg; tel. 43-94-44; fax 43-94-50; f. 1945; 6 a year; journal of the Confédération du Commerce Luxembourgeois; circ. 2,100.

D'Handwierk: BP 1604, 1016 Luxembourg; tel. 42-45-11-1; fax 42-45-25; e-mail contact@federation-des-artisans.lu; internet www .federation-des-artisans.lu; monthly; organ of the Fédération des Artisans and the Chambre des Métiers; circ. 7,000.

Horesca—Informations: 7 rue Alcide de Gasperi, BP 2524, 1025 Luxembourg; tel. 42-13-55-1; fax 42-13-55-299; e-mail info@horesca .lu; monthly; hotel trade, tourism, gastronomy; Editor DAVE GIANNANDREA; circ. 6,000.

Le Jeudi: 32 rue du Curé, 1368 Luxembourg; tel. 22-05-50; fax 22-05-44; e-mail redaction@le-jeudi.lu; internet www.lejeudi.lu; f. 1997; weekly; French; Dir DANIÈLE FONCK; circ. 10,854 (1998).

De Konsument: 55 rue des Bruyères, 1274 Howald; tel. 49-60-22-1; fax 49-49-57; e-mail ulcegc@pt.lu; internet www.ulc.lu; 12 a year; consumer affairs.

De Lëtzeburger Bauer: 16 blvd d'Avranches, 2980 Luxembourg; tel. 48-81-61-1; fax 40-03-75; e-mail letzeburger.bauer@netline.lu; f. 1944; weekly; journal of Luxembourg farming; circ. 7,500.

D'Lëtzeburger Land: 59 rue Glesener, BP 2083, 1020 Luxembourg; tel. 48-57-57; fax 49-63-09; e-mail land@land.lu; internet www.land.lu; f. 1954; weekly; political, economic, cultural affairs; Man. Editor MARIO HIRSCH; circ. 6,500.

Lëtzeburger Sonndesblad: 2 rue Christophe Plantin, 2988 Luxembourg; weekly; Catholic; Dir LÉON ZECHES; circ. 8,000.

Lux-Post: Editions Saphir, 23 rue des Gênets, 1621 Luxembourg; tel. 49-53-63; fax 48-53-70; local news; four regional edns; French and German.

Muselzeidung: 30 rue de Trèves, POB 36, 6701 Grevenmacher; tel. 75-87-47; fax 75-84-32; f. 1981; regional magazine; monthly; German; Editor TANIA USELDINGER.

OGB-L Aktuell/Actualités: 4002 Esch-sur-Alzette; tel. 54-05-45-1; fax 54-16-20; e-mail ogbl@first-luxembourg.lu; internet www.ogb-l .lu; f. 1919; monthly; journal of the Confederation of Independent Trade Unions of Luxembourg; circ. 43,000.

Revue/D'Letzebuerger Illustréiert: 2 rue Dicks, BP 2755, 1027 Luxembourg; tel. 49-81-81-1; fax 48-77-22; e-mail revue@revue.lu; internet www.revue.lu; f. 1945; weekly; illustrated; Man. Dir GUY LUDIG; Editor-in-Chief CLAUDE WOLF; circ. 31,000.

Revue Technique Luxembourgeoise: 4 blvd Grande-Duchesse Charlotte, Luxembourg; tel. 45-13-54; fax 45-09-32; internet www .aliai.lu; f. 1908; quarterly; technology.

Sauerzeidung: 30 rue de Trèves, BP 36, 6701 Grevenmacher; tel. 75-87-47; fax 75-84-32; f. 1988; regional newspaper; monthly; German; Publr EUGENE BURTON; circ. 10,000.

Soziale Fortschrett (LCGB): 11 rue du Commerce, BP 1208, Luxembourg; tel. 49-94-24-1; fax 49-94-24-49; internet www.lcgb.lu; f. 1921; monthly; journal of the Confederation of Christian Trade Unions of Luxembourg; Pres. ROBERT WEBER; circ. 36,000.

Télécran: 2 rue Christophe Plantin, BP 1008, 1010 Luxembourg; tel. 49-93-50-0; fax 49-93-59-0; e-mail telecran@telecran.lu; internet www.telecran.lu; f. 1978; TV and family weekly; illustrated; Man. Editor FERN MORBACH; circ. 46,500.

Transport: 13 rue du Commerce, BP 2615, 1026 Luxembourg; tel. 22-67-86-1; fax 22-67-09; e-mail syprolux@pt.lu; fortnightly; circ. 3,800.

Woxx: 51 ave de la Liberté, BP 684, 2016 Luxembourg; tel. 29-79-99-0; fax 29-79-79; e-mail woxx@woxx.lu; internet www.woxx.lu; f. 1988 as GréngeSpoun; weekly; social, ecological, environmental and general issues; Secs ROBERT GARCIA, RICHARD GRAF, RENÉE WAGENER; circ. 3,000.

NEWS AGENCIES

Among the foreign bureaux in Luxembourg are:

Agence Europe SA: BP 428, 2014 Luxembourg; tel. 22-00-32; fax 46-22-77; internet www.agenceurope.com.

Reuters Ltd (United Kingdom): 25c blvd Royal, 2449 Luxembourg; Bureau Chief JEAN-MARC PAUFIQUE.

Agence France-Presse, Associated Press (USA), and United Press International (USA) are also represented in Luxembourg.

PRESS ASSOCIATIONS

Association Luxembourgeoise des Editeurs de Journaux: 2 rue Christophe Plantin, 2988 Luxembourg; tel. 49-93-200; fax 49-93-38-6; e-mail paul.zimmer@saint.paul.lu; Pres. ALVIN SOLD; Sec. PAUL ZIMMER.

Association Luxembourgeoise des Journalistes: BP 1732, 1027 Luxembourg; tel. 46-09-52; fax 51-82-36; Pres. JEAN-CLAUDE WOLFF.

Publishers

Editions François Mersch: BP 231, 2012 Luxembourg; tel. 22-99-3; history, photography.

Editions Phi: BP 321, 4004 Esch-sur-Alzette; tel. 54-13-82-220; fax 54-13-87; e-mail editions.phi@editpress.lu; internet www.phi.lu; f. 1980; fmrly Editions Francis van Maele; literature, art; Dir A. THOME.

Editions Schortgen: 121 rue de l'Alzette, BP 367, 4004 Esch-sur-Alzette; tel. 54-64-87; fax 53-05-34; art, literature, factual, cuisine, comics; Dir JEAN-PAUL SCHORTGEN.

Editpress Luxembourg SA: 44 rue du Canal, BP 147, 4050 Esch-sur-Alzette; tel. 54-71-31-1; fax 54-71-30; e-mail tageblatt@tageblatt.lu; internet www.tageblatt.lu; Dir ALVIN SOLD.

Edouard Kutter: BP 319, 2013 Luxembourg; tel. 22-35-71; fax 47-18-84; e-mail edouard.kutter@kutter.lu; internet www.kutter.lu; art, photography, facsimile edns on Luxembourg.

Imprimerie Joseph Beffort: 5 rue Pletzer, 8080 Luxembourg; tel. 25-44-55-1; fax 25-44-19; f. 1869; scientific, economic reviews.

St-Paul Luxembourg SA: 2 rue Christophe Plantin, 2988 Luxembourg; tel. 49-93-1; fax 49-93-38-6; e-mail direction@saint-paul.lu; internet www.saint-paul.lu; f. 1887; Man. Dir PAUL ZIMMER.

PUBLISHERS' ASSOCIATIONS

Fédération Luxembourgeoise des Editeurs de Livres: 31 blvd Konrad Adenauer, BP 482, 2014 Luxembourg; tel. 43-94-44-1; fax 43-94-50; e-mail info@clc.lu; internet www.clc.lu; Pres. ALBERT DAMING.

Fédération Luxembourgeoise des Travailleurs du Livre: 26A rue de Pulvermühl, 2356 Luxembourg; tel. 42-24-18; fax 42-24-19; e-mail fltl@pt.lu; f. 1864; Pres. GUST STEFANETTI; Sec. LOUIS PINTO.

Broadcasting and Communications

TELECOMMUNICATIONS

Regulatory Authority

Institut Luxembourgeois de Régulation (ILR): 45A ave de Monterey, 2922 Luxembourg; tel. 45-88-45-1; fax 45-88-45-88; e-mail ilr@ilr.etat.lu; internet www.ilr.lu; Dir ODETTE WAGENER.

Major Service Providers

Cegecom SA: 3 rue Jean Piret, BP 2708, 1027 Luxembourg; tel. 26-49-91; fax 26-49-96-99; e-mail info@cegecom.lu; internet www.cegecom.lu; Man. Dir FRANÇOIS THYS.

Entreprise des Postes et Télécommunications (EPT): 8A ave Monterey, 2020 Luxembourg; tel. 47-65-1; fax 47-51-10; e-mail registry@pt.lu; internet www.telecom.lu; f. 1992; post, telecommunications and internet service provider; Pres. MARCEL GROSS.

Equant (Global One Communications SA): 201 rte de Thionville, 5885 Howald; tel. 27-30-11; fax 27-30-13-01; e-mail info.luxembourg@equant.com; internet www.equant.com; telecommunications operator; Dir (Sales) VIRGINIE LÉGER.

LUXGSM: 8A ave Monterey, 2020 Luxembourg; tel. 47-65-1; fax 47-51-10; internet www.luxgsm.lu; f. 1993; mobile cellular telephone operator; subsidiary of Entreprise des Postes et Télécommunications.

GTS Bénélux: 8 rue Henri Snadt, 2530 Luxembourg; tel. 26-48-18-48; fax 26-48-18-58; internet www.gtsgroup.lu.

KPN Luxembourg: 3 rue Jean Piret, 2350 Luxembourg; tel. 48-75-63; fax 48-75-38; internet www.kpnluxembourg.lu.

Millicom Luxembourg SA (Tango): 177 rue de Luxembourg, 8080 Bertrange; tel. 45-77-44-1; fax 45-77-44-222; e-mail info@tango.lu; internet www.tango.lu; subsidiary of Société Européenne de Communication SA.

Télé 2 Luxembourg SA: 75 rte de Longwy, 8080 Bertrange; tel. 45-77-44-1; fax 47-76-44; internet www.tele2.lu; f. 1999; subsidiary of Société Européenne de Communication SA.

BROADCASTING

Regulatory Authority

Commission Indépendante de la Radiodiffusion Luxembourgeoise: Luxembourg.

Radio

Eldoradio: 47 Mühlenweg, BP 1344, 1013 Luxembourg; tel. 40-95-09-1; fax 40-95-09-509; e-mail eldoradio@eldoradio.lu; internet www.eldoradio.lu; music station.

Honnert, 7 (de soziokulturelle radio): 459 route de Longwy, BP 1833, 1018 Luxembourg; tel. 44-00-44-1; fax 44-66-60; e-mail dweyler@100komma7.lu; internet www.100komma7.lu; f. 1993; non-commercial cultural broadcaster.

Radio Ara: 2 rue de la Boucherie, BP 266, 2012 Luxembourg; tel. 22-22-89; fax 22-22-66; e-mail radioara@pt.lu; internet www.ara.lu; music broadcaster.

Radio DNR: 2 rue Christophe Plantin, BP 1522, 1015 Luxembourg; tel. 40-70-601; fax 40-79-98; internet www.dnr.lu; e-mail dnr@dnr.lu.

Radio Latina: 2 rue Astrid, BP 1915, 1019 Luxembourg; tel. 29-95-96-1; fax 40-24-76; programmes for foreign communities in Luxembourg.

Radio LRB: BP 8, 3201 Bettembourg; tel. 52-44-88; fax 52-44-88; e-mail info@lrb.lu; internet www.lrb.lu.

Radio WAKY Power FM 107: POB 70, 5801 Hesperange; tel. 48-20-85; fax 48-21-13; internet www.radio.lu; English and Letzeburgish.

RTL Group: 45 blvd Pierre Frieden, 2850 Luxembourg; tel. 42-14-21; fax 42-142-27-60; internet www.rtlgroup.com; f. 2000 by merger of CLT-UFA and Pearson TV; 90.2% owned by Bertelsmann AG (Germany); 9.8% public ownership; 37 radio stations and television channels in 8 countries; CEO DIDIER BELLENS; Chair. JUAN ABELLÓ.

RTL Radio Lëtzeburg: 45 blvd Pierre Frieden, 2850 Luxembourg; tel. 42-14-23; fax 42-14-22-737; internet www.rtl.lu; broadcasts in English, German and Letzeburgish; Head of Radio PHILIPPE LABRO; Chief Editor ROBY RAUCHS.

SES Global: Château de Betzdorf, 6815 Betzdorf; tel. 710-725-1; fax 710-725-227; internet www.ses-global.com; f. 1985; partly government owned, 30% owned by General Electric (USA); operates 13 satellites (broadcasting 1,100 digital and analogue television and radio channels) including the ASTRA 1A television satellite (launched in 1988), ASTRA 1B (1991), ASTRA 1C (1993), ASTRA 1D (1994), ASTRA 1E (1995), ASTRA 1F (1996), ASTRA 1G (1997), ASTRA 2A (1998), ASTRA 1K (1999); Chair. RENÉ STEICHEN; CEO ROMAIN BAUSCH.

Sunshine Radio: 40 rue de Bragrance, 1255 Luxembourg; tel. 22-57-92; fax 22-57-92; English and Letzeburgish.

Television

RTL Télé Lëtzeburg: 177 rue de Luxembourg, 8077 Bertrange; tel. 52-72-51; fax 72-54-31; internet www.rtl.lu; subsidiary of RTL Group.

Société Européenne des Satellites (SES): (see Radio).

Finance

(cap. = capital; res = reserves; dep. = deposits; m. = million; brs = branches; amounts in euros unless otherwise indicated)

BANKING

In December 2001 there were 189 banks in Luxembourg, most of which were subsidiaries or branches of foreign banks; a selection of the principal banks operating internationally is given below.

Central Bank

Banque Centrale du Luxembourg: 2 blvd Royal, 2983 Luxembourg; tel. 47-74-1; fax 47-74-49-01; e-mail sg@bcl.lu; internet www.bcl.lu; f. 1998 to replace the Institut Monétaire Luxembourgeois; represents Luxembourg within the European System of Central Banks (ESCB); issues bank notes and coins and is responsible for the introduction of the euro; cap. 25.0m., res 134.9m., dep. 5,547.8m. (Dec. 2000); Pres. YVES MERSCH; Exec. Dirs ANDRÉE BILLON, SERGE KOLB.

Principal Banks

ABN Amro Bank (Luxembourg) SA: 4 rue Jean Monnet, BP 581, 2015 Luxembourg; tel. 42-49-49-42; fax 42-49-49-499; internet www.abnamro.com; f. 1991 by merger; cap. 372.0m. res 38.5m. dep. 4,642.8m. (Dec. 2001); Chair. M. H. REUCHLIN; Man. Dir F. B. DEITERS.

Banca di Roma International SA: 26 blvd Royal, BP 692, 2016 Luxembourg; tel. 47-79-06-1; fax 47-79-06-228; e-mail info@bancaroma.lu; internet www.bancaroma.lu; f. 1992 by merger; cap. 120.0m., res 69.8m., dep. 4,288.7m. (Dec. 2000); Chair. GIANFRANCO IMPERATORI; Gen. Man. ALESSANDRO AGNOLUCCI.

Banca Nazionale del Lavoro International SA: 51 rue des Glacis, BP 286, 2012 Luxembourg; tel. 22-50-31; fax 22-36-08; e-mail info@bnli.lu; f. 1977; cap. 25.0m., res 4.4m., dep. 2,984.1m. (Dec. 2000); Pres. RODOLFO RINALDI; Gen. Man. FABIO DI VINCENZO.

Banco di Sicilia International SA: 14 ave Marie-Thérèse, BP 903, 2019 Luxembourg; tel. 45-40-40-1; fax 45-40-40-22; e-mail bdsintlux@cmdnet.lu; f. 1986; cap. 20.0m., res 1.7m., dep. 1,985.1m. (Dec. 2000); Chair. ALESSANDRO PIOZZI; Gen. Man. LUCIANO COLLOT.

Bank Sarasin Benelux SA: 287–289 route d'Arlon, 1014 Luxembourg; tel. 45-78-80-1; fax 45-23-96; e-mail infolux@sarasin.com; internet www.sarasin.lu; f. 1988; cap. 16.3m., res 14.1m., dep. 1,472.0m. (Dec. 1999); Chair. GUIDO VAN BERKEL; Man. Dir VICTOR DEN HOEDT.

Bankgesellschaft Berlin International SA: 30 blvd Royal, 2449 Luxembourg; tel. 47-78-1; fax 47-78-20-29; e-mail contact@bankgesellschaft.lu; internet www.bankgesellschaft.lu; f. 1995 by merger; cap. 57.0m., res 130.4m., dep. 8,257.0m. (Dec. 2000); Chair. SERGE DEMOLIERE; Man. Dirs HORST-DIETER HOCHSTETTER, UWE JUNGERWIRTH.

Banque et Caisse d'Epargne de l'Etat, Luxembourg: 1 place de Metz, 1930 Luxembourg; tel. 40-15-1; fax 40-15-20-99; internet www.bcee.lu; f. 1856 as Caisse de l'Epargne de l'Etat du Grand-Duché de Luxembourg, name changed as above 1989; govt-owned; cap. 173.5m., res 632.4m., dep. 32,662.9m. (Dec. 2001); Chair. VICTOR ROD; Pres. and CEO RAYMOND KIRSCH; 96 brs.

Banque Degroof Luxembourg SA: 7 blvd Joseph II, BP 902, 2019 Luxembourg; tel. 45-35-45-1; fax 25-07-21; e-mail degroof@tcp.ip.lu; cap. 37.0m., res 49.8m., dep. 1,116.3m. (Sep. 2000); Chair. ALAIN PHILIPPSON; Man. Dir FERNAND DE JAMBLINNE DE MEUX.

Banque Générale du Luxembourg SA: 50 ave John F. Kennedy, 2951 Luxembourg; tel. 42-42-1; fax 42-42-25-79; e-mail info@bgl.lu; internet www.bgl.lu; f. 1919; Fortis Bank Luxembourg SA merged into the above in Nov. 2001; cap. 12,467m. Luxembourg francs, res 17,741m. Luxembourg francs, dep. 1,244,262m. Luxembourg francs (Dec. 2000); Chair. MARCEL MART; 40 brs.

Banque Ippa et Associés SA: 34 ave de la Liberté, BP 1134, 1011 Luxembourg; tel. 26-29-26-29; fax 26-29-26-26; e-mail customer@bia.lu; internet www.bia.lu; f. 1989 as Banque Ippa et Associés; current name adopted in 2000 following merger with Bank Anhyp Luxembourg SA; cap. 28.9m., res 4.3m., dep. 1,029.1m. (2000); Chair. PIERRE BULTEZ; Man. Dir YVES LAHAYE.

Banque de Luxembourg SA: 14 blvd Royal, BP 466, 2014 Luxembourg; tel. 49-92-41; fax 47-26-65; e-mail bllux@pt.lu; internet www.banquedeluxembourg.com; f. 1937; 71% owned by Crédit Industriel d'Alsace et de Lorraine; cap. 100.0m., res 173.0m., dep. 9,844.8m. (Dec. 2001); Chair. ROBERT RECKINGER; 4 brs.

Banque Raiffeisen SC: 28 blvd Royal, BP 111, 2011 Luxembourg; tel. 46-21-51; fax 47-14-69; internet www.raiffessen.lu; f. 1926 as Caisse Centrale Raiffeisen SC, name changed as above July 2001; res 51.4m., dep. 1,745.2m. (Dec. 2000); Pres. PAUL LAUTERBOUR; Chair. and Gen. Man. ALPHONSE SINNES.

Banque Safra Luxembourg SA: 10A blvd Joseph II, BP 887, 2018 Luxembourg; tel. 45-47-73; fax 45-47-86; internet www.safra.lu; cap. Swiss francs 24.2m., res Swiss francs 106.5m., dep. Swiss francs 3,979.5m. (Dec. 2000); Chair. JOSEPH SAFRA; Man. Dir. JORGE ALBERTO KININSBERG.

BHF-BANK International SA: 283 route d'Arlon, BP 258, 2012 Luxembourg; tel. 45-76-76-1; fax 45-83-20; f. 1972; cap. 26.0m., res 40.2m., dep. 3,687.0m. (Dec. 2000); Chair. ROLAND SCHARFF; Man. Dirs Dr HARTMUT ROTHACKER, FRANK RYBKA.

BNP Paribas Luxembourg: 10A blvd Royal, 2093 Luxembourg; tel. 46-46-1; fax 46-46-41-41; cap. 100.0m., res 160.0m., dep. 17,000.0m. (Dec. 2001); Chair. VIVIEN LEVY-GARBOUA; Gen. Mans ALAIN BAILLY, PATRICE CROCHET.

Clearstream Banking SA: 1 rue Hoehenhof, 1736 Senningerberg, Luxembourg; tel. 44-99-21; fax 44-99-28-210; e-mail marketing@clearstream.com; internet www.clearstream.com; f. 1970 as Cedelbank, name changed as above Jan. 2000; private bank; acts as the central bank's securities depository; cap. 56.8m., res 16.8m., dep.

4,325.1m. (Dec. 2000); Chair. ROBERT R. DOUGLASS; CEO ANDRÉ ROELANTS.

Commerzbank International SA: 11 rue Notre Dame, BP 303, 2013 Luxembourg; tel. 47-79-11-1; fax 47-79-11-270; e-mail cisal@commerzbank.com; internet www.commerzbank.lu; f. 1969; cap. DM 1,115m., res DM 2,381.2m., dep. DM 16,273.6m. (Dec. 2000); Pres. and Chair. KLAUS-PETER MULLER; Man. Dir BERND HOLZENTHAL; Gen. Man. ADRIEN NEY.

Crédit Agricole Indosuez Luxembourg SA: 39 allée Scheffer, BP 1104, 1011 Luxembourg; tel. 47-67-1; fax 46-24-42; internet www.e-private.com; f. 1969; present name adopted 1997; cap. 3,000.0m. Luxembourg francs; res 539.7m. Luxembourg francs, dep. 286,240.1m. Luxembourg francs (Dec. 2000); Chair. ARIBERTO FASSATI; Man. Dir PATRICK ZURSTRASSEN.

Crédit Européen SA: 52 route d'Esch, 1470 Luxembourg; tel. 44-99-11; fax 44-99-12-31; internet www.cebank.lu; f. 1960; owned by Bank Brussels Lambert, Belgium; cap. 73.0m., res 183.0m., dep. 8,013.3m. (Dec. 2001); Chair PHILLIPE DALMAS; Man. Dir BRUNO COLMANT; 20 brs.

Crédit Lyonnais Luxembourg SA: 26A blvd Royal, BP 32, 2094 Luxembourg; tel. 47-68-31-1; fax 42-68-31-501; e-mail info@creditlyonnais.lu; internet www.creditlyonnais.lu; cap. 55m., res 23,170m. (Dec. 2001); Pres. PATRICE DURAND; Gen. Man. PIERRE-PAUL COCHET.

Crédit Suisse (Luxembourg) SA: 56 Grand'rue, BP 40, 2010 Luxembourg; tel. 46-00-11-1; fax 46-32-70; cap. Swiss francs 25.0m., res Swiss francs 36.9m., dep. Swiss francs 2,429.0m. (Dec. 2000); Pres. ALEXANDRE ZELLER; Man. Dir HANS-ULRICH HÜGLI.

Danske Bank International SA: 2 rue du Fossé, 1536 Luxembourg; tel. 46-12-75-1; fax 47-30-78; e-mail 4959@lu.danskebank.com; internet www.danskebank.com/lu; f. 1976; cap. 90.6m., res 17.9m., dep. 492.9m. (Dec. 2000); Chair. SVEN ERIK LYSTBØK; Man. Dir PETER PREISLER.

DekaBank Deutsche Girozentrale Luxembourg SA: 16 blvd Royal, 2449 Luxembourg; tel. 46-24-71-1; fax 46-24-77; e-mail mail@dgzbank.lu; f. 1971 as Deutsche Girozentrale International SA, name changed as above after merger with DekaBank Luxembourg SA in Jan. 2002; cap. 25.6m., res 83.6m., dep. 5,739.5m. (Dec. 2000); Chair. HANS-JOACHIM REICHERT; Man. Dir BRUNO STUCKENBROEKER.

Deutsche Bank Luxembourg SA: 2 blvd Konrad Adenauer, 1115 Luxembourg; tel. 42-12-21; fax 42-12-24-49; internet www.deutsche-bank.lu; f. 1970 as Deutsche Bank Compagnie Financière Luxembourg; cap. 215.0m., res 411.1m., dep. 46,180.0m. (Dec. 2001); CEO ERNST WILHELM CONTZEN.

Deutsche Postbank International SA: Airport Centre, 2 route des Trèves, 2633 Senningerberg; tel. 34-95-31-1; fax 34-62-06; e-mail deutsche.postbank@postbank.lu; internet www.postbank.de; f. 1993; cap. 145.0m., res 18.3m., dep. 7,907.9m. (Dec. 2000); Chair. LOUKAS RIZOS; Gen. Mans CHRISTOPH SCHMITZ, JOCHEN BEGAS.

Dexia Banque Internationale à Luxembourg (Dexia BIL): 69 route d'Esch, 2953 Luxembourg; tel. 45-90-1; fax 45-90-20-10; e-mail contact@dexia-bil.lu; internet www.dexia-bil.lu; f. 1856 as Banque Internationale à Luxembourg, name changed as above in 2000; 66% owned by Dexia Bank SA; share cap. 131.8m., total assets 44,700m. (Dec. 2001); Chair. FRANÇOIS NARMON; CEO MARC HOFFMANN; 44 brs.

Dexia Nordic Private Bank Luxembourg SA: 18–20 ave Marie Thérèse, BP 594, 2015 Luxembourg; tel. 45-78-68-1; fax 45-78-60; e-mail contact@dexia-nordic.lu; f. 1990; cap. 37.5m., res 2.9m., dep. 1,260.0m. (Dec. 2000); Chair. MARC HOFFMANN; Man. Dir JENS KRISTIAN ANDERSEN.

Dresdner Bank Luxembourg SA: 26 rue de Marché-aux-Herbes, 2097 Luxembourg; tel. 47-60-1; fax 47-60-33-1; e-mail info@Dresdner-Bank.lu; internet www.dresdner-bank.lu; f. 1967; cap. 125.0m., res 764.0m., dep. 14,572.7m. (Dec. 2001); Chair. Dr BERND FAHRHOLZ; Pres. WOLFGANG A. BAERTZ; Man. Dirs Dr WALTER H. DRAISBACH, REINHARD H. KRAFFT.

DZ Bank International SA: 4 rue Thomas Edison, BP 661, 2016 Luxembourg; tel. 44-90-31; fax 44-90-32-00-1; e-mail info@dglux.lu; internet www.dglux.lu; f. 1978; previously called DG Bank Luxembourg SA, name changed as above in November 2001 after merger with GZ Bank International SA; 70.15% owned by DG International Beteiligungsgesellschaft, 27.27% owned by Finanzverbund Beteiligungsgesellschaft; cap. 80.7m., res 198.4m., dep. 13,725.3m. (Dec. 2001); Chair. HEINZ HILGERT; Man. Dirs HANS-PETER SÄTTELE, BERNHARD SINGER, FRANZ SCHULZ, RAINER STEGMANN.

EFG Private Bank (Luxembourg) SA: 5 rue Jean Monnet, BP 897, 2018 Luxembourg; tel. 42-07-24-1; fax 42-07-24-650; f. 1986; cap. 70.0m., res 4.5m., dep. 1,321.8m. (Dec. 2000); Chair. PAUL MUNCHEN; Man. Dir FRANÇOIS RIES.

HSBC Republic Bank (Luxembourg) SA: 32 blvd Royal, BP 733, 2017 Luxembourg; tel. 47-93-31-1; fax 47-93-31-337; e-mail hrlu@

hsbcrepublic.com; internet www.hsbcrepublic.com; f. 1985; cap. 30.1m., res 24.5m., dep. 2,677.0m. (Dec. 2001); Chair. MICHAEL S. ELIA; Man. Dir and CEO DAVID LEVY.

HSBC Trinkhaus & Burkhardt (International) SA: 1–7 rue Nina et Julien Lefèvre, BP 579, 2015 Luxembourg; tel. 47-18-47-1; fax 47-18-47-64-1; f. 1977; cap. 15.3m., res 52.3m., dep. 1,317.4m. (Dec. 2000); Pres. Dr S. ROMETSCH; Man. Dirs HANS-JOACHIM ROSTECK, JÖRG MEIER.

HVB Banque Luxembourg SA: 4 rue Alphonse Weicker, 2721 Luxembourg; tel. 42-72-1; fax 42-72-45-00; e-mail contact@ hypovereinsbank.lu; internet www.hypovereinsbank.lu; f. 1998 by merger of Hypobank International SA and Vereinsbank International SA Luxembourg, name changed as above in Oct. 2001; cap. 188.0m., res 432.5m., dep. 27,634.0m. (Dec. 1999); Pres. and Chair. Dr WOLFGANG SPRISSLER; Man. Dirs ERNST-DIETER WIESNER, GUNNAR HOMANN, BERND JANIETZ.

IKB International SA: 2 rue Jean Monnet, BP 771, 2017 Luxembourg; tel. 42-41-11; fax 42-06-03; e-mail ikb.luxembourg@ikb.de; internet www.ikb.de; f. 1979; cap. 222.5m., res 54.8m., dep. 5,109.0m. (March 2001); Chair. STEFAN ORTSEIFEN.

IMI Bank (Lux) SA: 8 ave de la Liberté, BP 1022, 1010 Luxembourg; tel. 40-45-75-1; fax 49-36-22; e-mail postmaster@imi.lu; internet www.imi.lu; f. 1990; cap. 68.3m., res 7.8m., dep. 2,062.1m. (Dec. 2000); Chair. GIANFRANCO MATTEI; Gen. Mans CARLO ALBERTO MONTAGNA, GABRIELE DALLA TORRE.

Kredietbank SA Luxembourgeoise: 43 blvd Royal, 2955 Luxembourg; tel. 47-97-1; fax 47-26-67; internet www.kbl.lu; f. 1949; cap. 189.0m., res 779.0m., dep. 21,178.5m. (Dec. 2000); Pres. ETIENNE VERWILGHEN; 5 brs.

Landesbank Rheinland-Pfalz International SA: 10–12 blvd Roosevelt, BP 84, 2010 Luxembourg; tel. 47-59-21-1; fax 47-59-21-314; e-mail info@lri.lu; internet www.lri.lu; f. 1978; cap. 216.0m., res 113.2m., dep. 5,157.8m. (Dec. 2001); Chair. PAUL K. SCHMINKE; Man. Dirs ALAIN BAUSTERT, ROBY HAAS, ANDREAS HAUCK.

Landesbank Schleswig-Holstein International SA: 2 rue Jean Monnet, BP 612, 2016 Luxembourg; tel. 42-41-41-1; fax 42-41-97; e-mail info@lbsh-int.com; internet www.lbsh-int.com; f. 1977; cap. 43.0m., res 112.1m., dep. 7,146.8m. (Dec. 2000); Chair. Dr DIETRICH RÜMKER; CEO Dr HANS-ALBRECHT SASSE.

LBLux SA: 3 rue Jean Monnet, BP 602, 2016 Luxembourg; tel. 42-43-41; fax 42-43-45-099; e-mail bank@lblux.lu; internet www.lblux .lu; f. 1973; cap. 100.0m., res 208.6m., dep. 11,850.5m. (Dec. 2000); Chair. Dr PETER KAHN; Man. Dirs HENRI STOFFEL, ALEX MEYER.

Norddeutsche Landesbank Luxembourg SA: 26 route d'Arlon, BP 121, 2011 Luxembourg; tel. 45-22-11-1; fax 45-22-11-31-9; f. 1972; cap. 145.0m., res 199.0m., dep. 18,883.8m. (Dec. 2000); Man. Dir JOCHEN PETERMANN.

Nordea Bank SA: 672 rue de Neudorf-Findel, BP 562, 2015 Luxembourg; tel. 43-88-71; fax 43-93-52; e-mail nordea@nordea.lu; internet www.nordea.lu; f. 1976 as Privatbanken International (Denmark) SA, Luxembourg, changed name to Unibank SA in 1990, present name adopted Feb. 2001; cap. 25.0m., res 140.5m., dep. 2,075.3m. (Dec. 2001); Chair. CHRISTIAN CLAUSEN; Man. Dir JHON MORTENSEN.

Sanpaolo Bank SA: 12 ave de la Liberté, BP 2062, 1020 Luxembourg; tel. 40-37-60-1; fax 49-53-91; f. 1981 as Sanpaolo-Lariano Bank SA, name changed as above 1995; cap. 70.0m., res 1.9m., dep. 3,199.2m. (Dec. 2000); Chair. MARCO MAZZUCCHELLI; Man. Dir DORIANO DEMI.

SEB Private Bank SA: 6A Circuit de la Foire Internationale, BP 487, 2014 Luxembourg; tel. 26-23-1; fax 26-23-20-01; internet www .sebprivatebank.com; f. 1977 as Skandinaviska Enskilda Banken (Luxembourg) SA, merged with sister bank and name changed to S-E-Banken Luxembourg SA in 1994, present name adopted in 1999; merged with BfG Bank Luxembourg SA March 2001; cap. 118.0m., res 79.8m., dep. 1,590.5m. (Dec. 2001); Chair. MARIANA BURENSTAM LINDER; Man. Dir LARS BJERREK.

Société Européenne de Banque SA: 19–21 blvd du Prince Henri, BP 21, 2010 Luxembourg; tel. 46-14-11; fax 22-37-55; e-mail seb@pt .lu; f. 1976; cap. 45.0m., res 32.3m., dep. 3,502.6m. (Dec. 2000); Chair. and CEO CLAUDE DESCHENAUX; Man. Dir ARNALDO LANTERI.

Société Générale Bank & Trust: 11 ave Emile Reuter, BP 1271, 1012 Luxembourg; tel. 22-88-51; fax 22-88-59; e-mail sgbt.lu@socgen .com; internet www.sgbt.lu; f. 1956 as International and General Finance Trust; cap. 7,200m. Luxembourg francs, res 3,355m. Luxembourg francs, dep. 415,701m. Luxembourg francs (Dec. 2000); Chair. PIERRE MATHE; Man. Dir ALBERT LE DIRAC'H.

UBS (Luxembourg) SA: 36–38 Grand'rue, BP 2, 2010 Luxembourg; tel. 45-12-11; fax 45-12-12-700; f. 1998 by merger of Swiss Bank Corporation (Luxembourg) SA and Union de Banques Suisses (Luxembourg) SA; cap. Swiss francs 150m., res Swiss francs 282m.,

dep. Swiss francs 12,885m. (Dec. 2000); Chair. RAOUL WEIL; Man. Dir ROGER HARTMANN.

WestLB International SA: 32–34 blvd Grande-Duchesse Charlotte, BP 420, 2014 Luxembourg; tel. 44-74-11; fax 44-74-12-10; e-mail info@westlb.lu; internet www.westlb.lu; f. 1972; subsidiary of WestLB AG (Germany); cap. 65.0m., res 167.9m., dep. 15,198.3m. (Dec. 2000); Pres. GERHARD ROGGEMANN; Man. Dirs Dr GEORG BISSEN, FRANZ RUF.

Banking Association

Association des Banques et Banquiers Luxembourg (ABBL): 20 rue de la Poste, BP 13, 2010 Luxembourg; tel. 46-36-60-1; fax 46-09-21; e-mail mail@abbl.lu; internet www.abbl.lu; f. 1939; Dir LUCIEN THIEL.

STOCK EXCHANGE

Société de la Bourse de Luxembourg SA: 11 ave de la Porte-Neuve, BP 165, 2011 Luxembourg; tel. 47-79-36-1; fax 47-32-98; e-mail info@bourse.lu; internet www.bourse.lu; f. 1928; Chair. JEAN KRIER; CEO MICHEL MAQUIL.

INSURANCE

At the end of 2000 there were 94 approved insurance companies and, in addition, 264 reinsurance companies. A selection of insurance companies is given below:

Aon Insurance Managers (Luxembourg) SA: 19 rue de Bitbourg, BP 593, 2015 Luxembourg; tel. 22-34-221; fax 31-71-74; e-mail lambert_schroeder@aon.com; f. 1994; Man. Dir. LAMBERT SCHROEDER.

Assurances Européennes SA: 47 blvd Joseph II, BP 787, 2017 Luxembourg; tel. 44-96-96-55; fax 44-96-96-29.

AXA Assurances Luxembourg: 7 rue de la Chapelle, 1325 Luxembourg; tel. 45-30-20-1; fax 45-83-39; e-mail info@axa-assurances .lu; internet www.axa-assurances.lu; f. 1977; all branches and life; Chair. PIERRE BULTEZ.

Fortis Luxembourg Assurances: 16 blvd Royal, 2449 Luxembourg; tel. 24-18-58-1; fax 24-18-58-905; e-mail info@fortis.lu; internet www.fortis.lu; life and non-life insurance.

Le Foyer, Groupe d'Assurances: 6 rue Albert Borschette, 1246 Luxembourg; tel. 43-74-37; fax 43-83-22; e-mail contact@lefoyer.lu; internet www.lefoyer.lu; f. 1922; all branches and life.

La Luxembourgeoise SA d'Assurances: 10 rue Aldringen, 1118 Luxembourg; tel. 47-61-1; fax 47-61-30-0; e-mail groupell@lalux.lu; internet www.lalux.lu; f. 1989; all branches of non-life; Chair. GABRIEL DEIBENER; Dir-Gen. PIT HENTGEN.

West of England Shipowners' Mutual Insurance Assen (Luxembourg): 33 blvd du Prince Henri, BP 841, 2018 Luxembourg; tel. 47-00-67; fax 22-52-53; f. 1970; marine mutual insurance; Gen. Man. P. A. ASPDEN.

Trade and Industry

GOVERNMENT AGENCY

Société Nationale de Crédit et d'Investissement (SNCI): 7 rue du St-Esprit, BP 1207, 1012 Luxembourg; tel. 46-19-71-1; fax 46-19-79; e-mail snci@snci.lu; internet www.snci.lu; f. 1978; cap. and res €401m. (Dec. 2000), dep. €275.5m., assets €722.8m. (1998); SNCI finances participations in certain cos, provides loans for investment and research and development projects, provides export credit; Chair. GEORGES SCHMIT; Gen. Man. GEORGES BOLLIG.

CHAMBER OF COMMERCE

Chambre de Commerce du Grand-Duché de Luxembourg: 31 blvd Konrad Adenauer, 2981 Luxembourg-Kirchberg; tel. 42-39-39-1; fax 43-83-26; e-mail chamcom@cc.lu; internet www.cc.lu; f. 1841; Pres. JOSEPH KINSCH; Dir PAUL HIPPERT; 35,000 mems.

INDUSTRIAL AND TRADE ASSOCIATIONS

Centrale Paysanne Luxembourgeoise: 16 blvd d'Avranches, 2980 Luxembourg; tel. 48-81-61-1; fax 40-03-75; f. 1945; Pres. CARLO RAUS; Sec. LUCIEN HALLER; groups all agricultural organizations.

Chambre d'Agriculture: 261 route d'Arlon, BP 81, 8001 Strassen; tel. 31-38-76; fax 31-38-75; e-mail chaagri@pt.lu; Pres. MARCO GAASCH; Sec.-Gen. ROBERT LEY.

Confédération Luxembourgeoise du Commerce (CLC): 7 rue Alcide de Gasperi, BP 482, 2014 Luxembourg; tel. 43-94-44; fax 43-94-50; e-mail info@clc.lu; internet www.clc.lu; f. 1909; Pres. NORBERT FRIOB; Sec.-Gen. THIERRY NOTHUM; 3,500 mems.

Fédération des Artisans du Grand-Duché de Luxembourg: BP 1604, 1016 Luxembourg; tel. 42-45-11-1; fax 42-45-25; e-mail contact@federation-des-artisans.lu; internet www .federation-des-artisans.lu; f. 1905; Chair. NORBERT GEISEN; Dir ROMAIN SCHMIT; 4,000 mems.

Fédération des Industriels Luxembourgeois (FEDIL): 1st Floor, 31 blvd Konrad Adenauer, BP 1304, 1013 Luxembourg; tel. 43-53-66-1; fax 43-23-28; e-mail fedil@fedil.lu; internet www.fedil.lu; f. 1918; Pres. CHARLES KROMBACH; Administrative Dir NICOLAS SOISSON; c. 420 mems.

Groupement des Industries Sidérurgiques Luxembourgeoises (Federation of Iron and Steel Industries in Luxembourg): BP 1704, 1017 Luxembourg; tel. 48-00-01; fax 48-35-32; f. 1927; Pres. FERNAND WAGNER (Arcelor); Dir PIERRE REITER.

UTILITIES

Regulatory Authority

Service de l'Energie de l'Etat (SEE): 34 ave de la Porte-Neuve, 2227 Luxembourg, BP 10, 2010 Luxembourg; tel. 46-97-46-1; fax 22-25-24; e-mail see.administration@eg.etat.lu; internet www.etat.lu/SEE; f. 1967; civil service department with responsiblity for testing, standardization and certification; Dir JEAN-PAUL HOFFMANN.

Electricity

Compagnie Grand-Ducale d'Electricité de Luxembourg (CEGEDEL): 2089 Luxembourg; tel. 26-24-1; fax 26-24-6100; e-mail mail@cegedel.lu; internet www.cegedel.lu; f. 1928; produces and distributes electricity; 33% state-owned; Chair. ROLAND MICHEL; Gen. Man. ROMAIN BECKER.

Gas

SUDGAZ SA: BP 383, 4004 Esch-sur-Alzette; tel. 55-66-55-1; fax 57-20-44; e-mail contact@sudgaz.lu; internet www.sudgaz.lu; f. 1899; gas distribution co; Dir JO SIMON.

TRADE UNIONS

Confédération Générale du Travail du Luxembourg (CGT)/Onofhaengege Gewerkschaftbond-Letzeburg (OGB-L) (Luxembourg General Confederation of Labour): 60 blvd J. F. Kennedy, BP 149, 4002 Esch-sur-Alzette; tel. 54-05-45-1; fax 54-16-20; e-mail ogb-l@ogb-l.lu; internet www.ogb-l.lu; f. 1921; Pres. JOHN CASTEGNARO; Sec.-Gen. JEAN-CLAUDE REDING; 52,000 mems (1998).

Landesverband Luxemburger Eisenbahner, Transportarbeiter, Beamten und Angestellten (National Union of Luxembourg Railway and Transport Workers and Employees): 63 rue de Bonnevoie, 1260 Luxembourg; tel. 48-70-44-1; fax 48-85-25; e-mail secretariat@fncttfel.lu; internet www.fncttfel.lu; f. 1909; affiliated to CGT and International Transport Workers' Federation; Pres. NICO WENNMACHER; Gen. Sec. GUY GREIVELDING; 8,000 mems.

Lëtzebuerger Chrëschtleche Gewerkschaftsbond (LCGB) (Confederation of Christian Trade Unions): 11 rue du Commerce, BP 1208, 1012 Luxembourg; tel. 49-94-24-1; fax 49-94-24-49; e-mail lcgb@euromail.lu; internet www.lcgb.lu; f. 1921; affiliated to European Trade Union Confederation and World Confederation of Labour; Pres. ROBERT WEBER; Gen. Sec. MARC SPAUTZ; 37,000 mems.

Transport

RAILWAYS

At 1 January 2001 there were 274 km of electrified railway track.

Société Nationale des Chemins de Fer Luxembourgeois: 9 place de la Gare, BP 1803, 1018 Luxembourg; tel. 49-90-1; fax 49-90-44-70; e-mail av.clients@cfl.lu; internet www.cfl.lu; Pres. J. WARINGO; Dir and CEO ALEX KREMER.

ROADS

At 1 January 2002 there were 2,873 km of roads, of which motorways comprised 125 km.

Ministry of Public Works: (see Ministries).

INLAND WATERWAYS AND SHIPPING

Rhine shipping has direct access to the Luxembourg inland port of Mertert as a result of the canalization of the Moselle River. An 'offshore' shipping register was established in 1991.

CIVIL AVIATION

There is an international airport near Luxembourg-Ville.

Luxair (Société Luxembourgeoise de Navigation Aérienne): Aéroport de Luxembourg, 2987 Luxembourg; tel. 47-98-42-81; fax 47-98-42-89; e-mail info@luxair.lu; internet www.luxair.lu; f. 1962; regular services to destinations in Europe and North Africa; Pres. and CEO CHRISTIAN HEINZMANN.

Cargolux Airlines International SA: Aéroport de Luxembourg, 2990 Luxembourg; tel. 42-11-1; fax 43-54-46; internet www.cargolux .com; f. 1970; regular international all-freighter services; technological development; owned by Luxair, a consortium of Luxembourg banks and Swissair; Dir and CEO ROGER SIETZEN (acting).

Tourism

Many tourist resorts have developed around the ruins of medieval castles such as Clerf, Esch/Sauer, Vianden and Wiltz. The Benedictine Abbey at Echternach is also much visited. There is a thermal centre at Mondorf-les-Bains, supplied by three mineralized springs. In addition, there are numerous footpaths and hiking trails. Luxembourg-Ville, with its many cultural events and historical monuments, is an important centre for congresses. In 2001 there were 811,615 tourist arrivals at hotels and similar establishments.

Office National du Tourisme (ONT): 68–70 blvd de la Pétrusse, BP 1001, 1010 Luxembourg; tel. 42-82-82-1; fax 42-82-82-38; e-mail info@ont.lu; internet www.ont.lu; f. 1931; 189 mems; Chair. M. SCHANK; Dir ROBERT L. PHILIPPART.

THE FORMER YUGOSLAV REPUBLIC OF MACEDONIA

Introductory Survey

Location, Climate, Language, Religion, Flag, Capital

The former Yugoslav republic of Macedonia (FYRM) is situated in south-eastern Europe. The FYRM is a land-locked state and is bounded by Serbia to the north, Albania to the west, Greece to the south and Bulgaria to the east. The republic is predominantly mountainous with a continental climate, although the Vardar (Axiós) river valley, which bisects the country from north-west to south-east, across the centre of the republic and into Greece, has a mild Mediterranean climate with an average summer-time temperature of 27°C (80°F). The official language of the republic, under the Constitution of November 1991, was originally stipulated as Macedonian, which is written in the Cyrillic script. Constitutional amendments adopted in November 2001 accorded minority languages, such as Albanian, the status of official languages in communities where speakers constitute 20% of the population. Most of the population is nominally Christian and of the Eastern Orthodox faith. The ethnic Macedonians (who accounted for 66.6% of the total population according to the 1994 census) are adherents of the Macedonian Orthodox Church, which is autocephalous but not recognized by other Orthodox churches. Most of the ethnic Albanians (officially recorded as 22.7% of the population) are Muslims, as are the majority of the remaining minority groups. The national flag (proportions 1 by 2) comprises, in the centre of a red field, a yellow disc, tangential to which eight yellow rays extend to the edges of the flag. The capital is Skopje.

Recent History

After the First World War, during which Macedonia was occupied by the Bulgarians and the Central Powers, Vardar Macedonia, the area now known as the former Yugoslav republic of Macedonia (FYRM), became part of the new Kingdom of Serbs, Croats and Slovenes (formally named Yugoslavia in 1929). In the Second World War, however, the Bulgarian occupation of 1941–44 disillusioned many Yugoslav Macedonians. From 1943 Tito's Partisans (Josip Broz—alias Tito—was the General Secretary of the banned Communist Party of Yugoslavia) began to increase their support in the region, and after the war the new Federal People's Republic of Yugoslavia and its communist rulers resolved to include a Macedonian nation as a federal partner (having rejected the idea of a united Macedonia under Bulgaria). A distinct Macedonian identity was promoted, and a linguistic policy that encouraged the establishment of a Macedonian literary language distinct from Bulgarian and Serbian, together with the consolidation of an historical and cultural tradition, increased Macedonian self-awareness. In 1967 the Orthodox Church in Macedonia declared itself autocephalous, a move strongly contested by the Serbian Orthodox Church.

The presence of a large ethnic Albanian minority (22.7% of the population, according to the 1994 census) in western Macedonia added to Macedonian insecurities. The proximity of neighbouring Kosovo (a province of Serbia with a majority ethnic Albanian population) and demands, from the late 1960s, for the creation of a Yugoslav Albanian republic alarmed the Macedonian authorities, who became particularly active against Albanian nationalism from 1981. In 1989 the ruling communists amended the republican Constitution to allow for the introduction of a multi-party system; however, Macedonia was declared to be a 'nation-state' of the ethnic Macedonians, and mention of the 'Albanian and Turkish minorities' was excluded. Tension continued into the early 1990s, with the new Constitution of 1991 also refusing to specify the republic (with its new sovereign status) as a 'homeland' of the Albanians as well as the Macedonians, although it was enacted only by avoiding reference to official languages—a move designed to satisfy one of the requirements stipulated by the European Community (EC, now European Union, EU, see p. 199) for recognition of the new independent state. In January 1992 an unofficial referendum (declared illegal by the Macedonian authorities) resulted in a 99.9% vote in favour of territorial and political autonomy for the ethnic Albanian population.

In February 1990 the newly established Movement for All-Macedonian Action (MAMA) organized several large demonstrations to protest against the oppression of fellow nationals in Albania, Bulgaria and Greece. In June a more fundamentalist nationalist party, the Internal Macedonian Revolutionary Organization—Democratic Party for Macedonian National Unity (IMRO—DPMNU), led by Ljubčo Georgievski, declared its support for the return of territories then within Serbia. The republican communist leader, Petar Gosev, President of the renamed League of Communists of Macedonia—Party for Democratic Reform (LCM—PDR), also condemned the threat of Serbian nationalism.

In November and December 1990 the first multi-party elections to a unicameral republican Sobranje (Assembly) were held in Macedonia. The MAMA and the IMRO—DPMNU, which had formed an electoral alliance, the Front for Macedonian National Unity, to counter the strong support for the ruling LCM—PDR, alleged irregularities after failing to win any seats at the first round. Following two further rounds of voting, however, the IMRO—DPMNU unexpectedly emerged as the single party with the most seats (a total of 37) in the 120-member Sobranje. The LCM—PDR won 31 seats and the two predominantly Albanian parties (the Party for Democratic Prosperity—PDP and the People's Democratic Party) a total of 25. The republican branch of the federal Alliance of Reform Forces (ARF, subsequently the Liberal Party—LP) won 19 seats. Since no party or alliance controlled an overall majority of the seats, negotiations began for a coalition administration; finally, in January 1991 Kiro Gligorov of the LCM—PDR was elected President of the Republic, with Georgievski as Vice-President, and Stojan Andov of the ARF was elected President of the Sobranje. After some dispute over the allocation of portfolios, the three parties agreed to support a government largely comprising members without political affiliation. In March the Sobranje approved a new administration, headed by Nikola Kljušev. The LCM—PDR was renamed the Social Democratic Alliance of Macedonia (SDAM) in April.

On 25 January 1991 the Sobranje unanimously adopted a motion declaring the republic a sovereign territory. The Macedonian administration was, none the less, active in subsequent attempts to mediate in the growing crisis in Yugoslavia. After the June declarations of Croatian and Slovenian 'dissociation' and the later descent into civil war, Macedonia became wary of Serbian domination of the remaining federal institutions, declaring its neutrality and emphasizing its sovereign status. On 8 September a republican referendum (boycotted by the ethnic Albanian population) overwhelmingly supported the sovereignty of Macedonia.

Georgievski resigned the vice-presidency in October 1991, and the IMRO—DPMNU announced that it had joined the opposition, on the grounds that, despite having the largest representation in the Sobranje, it had been excluded from the decision-making process. The preparation of the new Constitution was delayed by the IMRO—DPMNU's proposal for an introductory nationalist statement, which was strongly opposed by the predominantly ethnic Albanian parties. Although the final version did not declare Macedonia to be the 'motherland' of the Macedonian people, it failed to grant the Albanian language official equality with Macedonian. On 17 November the Constitution was endorsed by 96 of the 120 Assembly members: the majority of ethnic Albanian deputies and three IMRO—DPMNU deputies did not support its enactment.

The complete withdrawal of federal troops from Macedonia in March 1992, in conjunction with the adoption in April of a new Constitution in the Federal Republic of Yugoslavia (FRY), referring only to Serbia and Montenegro, effectively signalled Yugoslav acceptance of Macedonian secession from the federation.

Macedonia established diplomatic relations with Slovenia in March, and with Croatia in April.

Macedonian affairs were now dominated by the question of wider international recognition. The republic, while no longer part of Yugoslavia, was unable to act as an independent nation in the international community. Bulgaria recognized the state of Macedonia (although not the existence of a distinct Macedonian nationality or language) in January 1992, closely followed by Turkey in February, thus provoking mass protests in Thessaloníki, the capital of the Greek region of Macedonia. The Greek authorities insisted that 'Macedonia' was a purely geographical term (delineating an area that included a large part of northern Greece), and expressed fears that the republic's independence under the name 'Macedonia' might foster a false claim to future territorial expansion. Greece was instrumental in the formulation of an EC policy, adopted in early 1992, that the republic should be awarded no formal recognition of independence until stringent constitutional requirements had been fulfilled. In May Gligorov rejected a statement by the EC that it was 'willing to recognize Macedonia as a sovereign and independent state within its existing borders under a name that can be accepted by all concerned'. Negotiations with Greece ended in failure in June (prompting the resignation of the Macedonian Minister of Foreign Relations). In July a motion expressing 'no confidence' in the Government received overwhelming support in the Sobranje, and large demonstrations were staged in Skopje in protest at the EC declaration and the Government's failure to gain international recognition for an independent Macedonia. The Government resigned later in the month. The IMRO—DPMNU failed to form a new coalition and, eventually, in September Branko Crvenkovski, the Chairman of the SDAM, was installed as Prime Minister of a coalition Government.

The adoption of a new flag in August 1992 attracted particular opposition from Greece, which objected to the depiction outside Greece of the 'Vergina Star' (regarded as an ancient Greek symbol of Philip of Macedon and Alexander the Great). As a result of a blockade of petroleum deliveries imposed on Macedonia by Greece, by September reserves at the Skopje petroleum refinery were exhausted. In February 1993 Greece agreed to international arbitration over the issue of Macedonia's name, undertaking to abide by its final outcome. On 8 April the republic was admitted to the UN under the temporary name of 'the former Yugoslav republic of Macedonia', pending settlement of the issue of a permanent name by international mediators. However, Greece continued to assert, and the FYRM to deny, that the use of the 'Vergina Star' emblem and the name 'Macedonia' implied territorial claims on the northern Greek province of Macedonia; international mediation efforts achieved little, and in October the Greek Government announced that Greece was to withdraw from UN-sponsored negotiations on the issue of a permanent name. In January 1994 Greece requested that the other nations of the EU prevail upon the FYRM (which was by this time recognized by all the other EU member states) to make concessions concerning its name, flag and Constitution, and threatened to ban trade with the FYRM if these preconditions were not fulfilled. From February (shortly after Russia and the USA had formally recognized the FYRM) Greece blocked all non-humanitarian shipments to the FYRM from the port of Thessaloníki, and also road and rail transport links with the FYRM; the Greek consulate in Skopje was subsequently closed. In April the European Commission, which contested that the Greek embargo was in violation of EU trade legislation, initiated legal proceedings against Greece at the Court of Justice of the European Communities. In April 1995, however, the Court issued a preliminary opinion that the embargo was not in breach of Greece's obligations under the Treaty of Rome. Meanwhile, Greece agreed to resume negotiations in April with the FYRM, under the auspices of the UN; in May the Organization for Security and Co-operation in Europe (OSCE, see p. 283) announced that it was to join the mediation efforts. In September an interim accord was signed at the UN headquarters in New York, the USA, by the FYRM Minister of Foreign Affairs and his Greek counterpart. The agreement provided for the mutual recognition of existing frontiers and respect for the sovereignty and political independence of each state, and for the free movement of goods and people between the two countries. Greece was to end its trade embargo and veto on the FYRM's entry into international organizations, while the FYRM undertook to abandon its use of the Vergina emblem in any form, and to amend parts of its Constitution that had been regarded by Greece as 'irredentist'. (The issue of a permanent name for the FYRM was to be the subject of further negotiations.) In early October the Sobranje approved a new state flag, depicting an eight-rayed sun in place of the Vergina emblem. The interim accord was ratified by the Sobranje on 9 October, and was formally signed in Skopje by representatives of the FYRM and Greece on 13 October. The border between the two countries was subsequently reopened.

The Albanian Government formally recognized the FYRM in April 1993. However, relations between the Macedonian authorities and the country's ethnic Albanian minority continued to deteriorate. In November several ethnic Albanians were arrested in the western towns of Gostivar and Tetovo (both of which had predominantly Albanian populations) and in Skopje. The Government stated that the arrests had been made following the discovery of a conspiracy to form paramilitary groups, with the eventual aim of establishing an Albanian republic in the west of the country. Further arrests followed, and in June 1994 Mithat Emini, the former General Secretary of the PDP, was sentenced to eight years' imprisonment, after being convicted of conspiring to engage in hostile activity; nine others received custodial sentences of between five and eight years. (In February 1995 all the sentences were reduced by two years.)

In February 1994, after several months of disunity, the PDP split when a group of delegates withdrew from the party's congress. This faction, led by Xheladin Murati (the Deputy President of the Sobranje), included the PDP's representatives in the Government and in the legislature, and claimed to have retained the party's original programme. The other grouping, led by Arben Xhaferi, made more radical demands regarding the status of ethnic Albanians in the FYRM. Organizations representing ethnic Albanians protested that inadequate preparations for a national census, conducted in mid-1994, effectively prevented the full enumeration of the ethnic Albanian community. It was reported that many ethnic Albanians boycotted the census, despite appeals by their political leaders for full participation. Following the publication of the census results, ethnic Albanian groups continued to assert that their community was considerably larger than officially indicated. The sentencing of Emini and his co-defendants prompted ethnic Albanian deputies to boycott the Sobranje in July (although they resumed their seats to defeat a motion, proposed by the IMRO—DPMNU, expressing 'no confidence' in the Government). Murati resigned from the leadership of his PDP faction (and from the office of Deputy President of the Sobranje) later in July, reportedly in protest at the sentences; he was succeeded as party leader by Abdurahman Aliti.

Gligorov, representing the Alliance for Macedonia (an electoral coalition of the SDAM, the LP and the Socialist Party of Macedonia—SPM) was re-elected to the presidency on 16 October 1994, winning 78.4% of the valid votes cast; his only challenger was Ljubiša Georgievski of the IMRO—DPMNU. A first round of voting to the new Sobranje took place on the same day. The IMRO—DPMNU, which failed to secure any seats, alleged widespread electoral fraud in both the presidential and parliamentary elections, and boycotted the second round of legislative voting, which took place on 30 October (a third round was necessary in 10 constituencies on 13 November, owing to irregularities in earlier rounds). The final results confirmed that the Alliance for Macedonia had won the majority of seats in the Sobranje (with the SDAM taking 58, the LP 29 and the SPM eight seats). Aliti's 'moderate' PDP, which had been legally recognized as the successor to the original party, secured 10 seats; members of the 'radical' PDP had been obliged to stand as independent candidates (Xhaferi was among the independent candidates to be elected). Gligorov subsequently requested that Branko Crvenkovski form a new government, and the SDAM-led administration, which also included members of the LP, Aliti's PDP and the SPM, was approved by the Sobranje in December.

Tensions were exacerbated by efforts by the ethnic Albanian community to establish an Albanian-language university in Tetovo, following continued claims by ethnic Albanian groups that the education system of the FYRM disadvantaged ethnic minorities. Despite government objections that to establish such an institution would be unconstitutional, the university was formally established in December 1994. The opening of the Tetovo university in February 1995 provoked considerable unrest, however; an ethnic Albanian was killed in clashes with security forces, and several people were arrested, including the rector of the university, who was charged with incitement to resistance. Following negotiations with the PDP, the authorities agreed to withdraw police reinforcements from Tetovo (while continuing to assert that the university was illegal). In July 1996 five of the university's founders, including its rector, received custodial sentences for inciting the riots, prompting protests by ethnic Albanians in Tetovo and other parts of the country.

In October 1995 Gligorov was injured in a car-bomb attack in Skopje, which was condemned by all political parties; he resumed full presidential duties in January 1996. Meanwhile, divisions had emerged within the Alliance for Macedonia. Despite appeals for unity by Gligorov, the alliance that had supported his election to the presidency collapsed, and the LP was excluded from the Government following a reallocation of portfolios in February. Andov resigned as President of the Sobranje in early March, stating that Crvenkovski had acted unconstitutionally in expelling the LP from the Government. In April the IMRO—DPMNU and the Democratic Party (DP) submitted to the Sobranje a petition of 200,000 signatures, appealing for a referendum to be held on the issue of early elections (warranted, it was claimed, by the Government's lack of popularity). Although the petition was submitted in accordance with the Constitution, it was rejected by the Sobranje, and the IMRO—DPMNU and the DP appealed unsuccessfully to the Constitutional Court to overturn the legislature's decision. A new penal code, under which the death penalty was abolished, entered into force in November.

In September 1996, prior to local elections scheduled for 17 November, the Sobranje approved legislation reorganizing the territorial division of the FYRM into 123 municipalities. In October three opposition parties, the IMRO—DPMNU, the DP and the newly established Movement for All-Macedonian Action (MAAK)—Conservative Party, formed a coalition to contest the elections. Xhaferi's faction, which had been reconstituted as the Party of Democratic Prosperity of Albanians in Macedonia (PDPAM), and the (also ethnic Albanian) National Democratic Party (NDP) agreed to present joint candidates in some parts of the country. Following the first round of the local elections, opposition parties claimed that the electoral lists had been falsified by the Government to ensure favourable results for the SDAM. The SDAM received the greatest number of votes, followed by the coalition led by the IMRO—DPMNU, and the PDP. Observers from the Council of Europe (see p. 181) declared that, overall, the elections had been conducted fairly.

In January 1997, following a campaign by ethnic Albanian students, legislation was adopted to permit Albanian to become the language of instruction at the teacher-training faculty of the university at Skopje. This provoked outrage among Macedonian students at the faculty, and a series of protests by university and secondary school students ensued. In the same month the Sobranje rejected demands by ethnic Albanian deputies for provision for the use of the Albanian language in new regulations on parliamentary procedure. Ethnic tensions were further compounded by the civil conflict that erupted in Albania in early 1997.

A financial scandal emerged in March 1997, involving the embezzlement of funds invested in 'pyramid' savings schemes. Crvenkovski pledged an investigation to identify those responsible for the losses sustained by large numbers of investors, and several officials, including the Deputy Governor of the central bank, were subsequently arrested on suspicion of involvement in the fraudulent schemes. Although the Government won a vote of confidence in its management of the affair, the LP deputies withdrew from the parliamentary chamber to register their disapproval of the measures undertaken. In April the Government announced plans to reimburse losses incurred by investors, following the failure of a major savings institution in the south-western town of Bitola; in the following month the Sobranje approved the replacement of the Governor of the central bank, who was believed to have been involved in the failure of the investment scheme. Earlier in the month the IMRO—DPMNU had organized a demonstration in Skopje to demand the resignation of the Government, and Crvenkovski subsequently reorganized the Cabinet. (In early June 1998 the owner of the institution in Bitola was sentenced to eight years' imprisonment, and four government financial officials also received custodial terms.)

In May 1997 ethnic Albanians in Gostivar took part in protests against a ruling by the Constitutional Court that prohibited the use of the Albanian flag in the FYRM. A number of municipalities with a predominantly ethnic Albanian population refused to comply with the order of the Court, and in June the President of the Constitutional Court issued a statement

demanding that the Government enforce the Court's ruling. In early July the Sobranje adopted legislation stipulating that the use of the Albanian flag, and flags of other ethnic minorities, would only be permitted on national holidays, with the Macedonian flag being displayed at the same time. None the less, the mayors of Gostivar and Tetovo continued to refuse to comply with the order of the Constitutional Court, and government officials forcibly removed Albanian flags that had been displayed at municipal buildings. Ensuing protests in Gostivar resulted in violent clashes between security forces and demonstrators, as a result of which three ethnic Albanians were killed; some 500 protesters were arrested. Security forces were finally withdrawn from Gostivar and Tetovo later in July. A report on the violence submitted to the Sobranje by the Ministry of the Interior was rejected by ethnic Albanian deputies, who condemned the actions of the security forces. In September the mayor of Gostivar, Rufi Osmani, received a custodial sentence of some 13 years (reduced to seven years in February 1998), after being convicted on charges of inciting ethnic tension and rebellion, while the Chairman of the municipal council was sentenced to three years' imprisonment for failing to adopt the ruling of the Constitutional Court. In April the Democratic Party of Albanians (DPA—which had been formed in July 1997 by the amalgamation of the PDPAM and the NDP) announced that it was to withdraw its representatives from all government bodies, in protest at Osmani's continuing imprisonment.

In early August 1998 the Government announced that the forthcoming election to the Sobranje would take place on 18 October. At the end of August the DPA and PDP established an electoral alliance. In early September the IMRO—DPMNU and the newly formed Democratic Alternative (DA) formed an electoral coalition, styled For Changes. Later that month, following clashes between ethnic Albanian activists and security forces, a number of ethnic Albanians were arrested on suspicion of involvement in a series of bomb attacks in principal towns earlier that year, for which the Kosovo Liberation Army (KLA—Ushtria Clirimtare e Kosoves, see below) had claimed responsibility.

After the first round of the legislative election on 18 October 1998, a second round of voting proceeded on 1 November; the For Changes alliance secured an absolute majority in the Sobranje, with 58 seats, while the SDAM obtained 29, and the alliance of the PDP and DPA 24 seats. Owing to irregularities, a further round of voting took place in two electoral districts, at which one seat was won by the For Changes alliance, and the other by the PDP–DPA alliance. Later in November the leader of the IMRO—DPMNU, Ljubčo Georgievski, was nominated to the office of Prime Minister. The DPA was subsequently invited to join the governing coalition of the IMRO—DPMNU and the DA. In early December the Cabinet, comprising 14 representatives of the IMRO—DPMNU, eight of the DA and five of the DPA, was formed. Georgievski pledged to end government corruption, and to support the FYRM's aim of membership of the EU and NATO. In early December the DPA leadership formally reversed its decision to withdraw its representatives from government bodies, in view of its participation in the new Cabinet. At the end of December the Sobranje approved legislation (supported by the new Government) providing for the release of some 8,000 prisoners, among them Osmani. In January 1999, however, Gligorov refused to approve the amnesty, which he claimed to be unconstitutional. In February the amnesty legislation was resubmitted to the Sobranje (in accordance with the Constitution) and subsequently adopted by the government parties. At the end of June Georgievski was re-elected President of the IMRO—DPMNU at a party congress. In August the Speaker of the Sobranje announced that the first round of the forthcoming presidential election would take place on 31 October (followed by a second round on 14 November if no candidate achieved an outright majority of the votes).

The first round of the presidential election, on 31 October 1999, was contested by six candidates: Tito Petkovski, representing the SDAM, secured 33.2% of the votes cast, and Boris Trajkovski, the IMRO—DPMNU candidate (who had hitherto served as Deputy Foreign Minister), won 20.6%; Vasil Tupurkovski, the DA leader, took 16.0%, and Muharem Nexipi, the DPA candidate, 14.8%. At a second round, which was contested between Petkovski and Trajkovski on 14 November, Trajkovski was elected to the presidency with about 52.8% of votes cast (after DPA and DA voters transferred support to his candidacy). The SDAM disputed the results of the election, claiming that widespread malpractice had been perpetrated, particularly in the west of the country. On 27 November the Supreme Court upheld a legal appeal by the SDAM against the results, and ruled that a further ballot take place in some western regions. A partial round, affecting about 10% of the total electorate, consequently took place on 5 December. However, the overall results were virtually unchanged after the ballot, with Trajkovski receiving some 52.9% of the votes cast. Although the SDAM again claimed that irregularities had taken place, Petkovski finally accepted Trajkovski's election to the presidency. Trajkovski, who was formally inaugurated as President on 15 December, pledged to aim for greater democracy and stability in the country. Following negotiations between the two leaders of the For Changes coalition, Georgievski and Tupurkovski, the IMRO—DPMNU, DA and DPA reached agreement on the formation of a new Government later that month. The coalition Cabinet, which contained seven new ministers (including Tupurkovski, who became a Deputy Prime Minister), was formally approved by the Sobranje on 27 December.

In January 2000 the Government announced that amendments to the Constitution, which would allow higher education to be conducted in the language of ethnic minorities, would be submitted for approval by the Sobranje. In April legislation obliging the authorities to return property expropriated under the communist regime was adopted. In the same month disaffected members of IMRO—DPMNU, headed by a former Minister of Finance, Boris Zmejkovski, established a breakaway faction, which became known as 'Real' IMRO. In early May the SDAM, the reconstituted LP (now the Liberal-Democratic Party —LDP) and the Democratic League—Liberal Party established an electoral alliance. In July Georgievski reorganized the Cabinet, reducing the number of ministries from 21 to 14. In the same month the Sobranje approved legislation granting the university at Tetovo legal status as a private foundation, but failed to meet demands by the DPA that it be government-funded, with equal status to Macedonian-language institutions. Local government elections took place in two rounds on 10 and 24 September, amid reports of numerous violent incidents. After a further round of voting took place, owing to electoral irregularities, it was announced at the end of the month that the parties of the government coalition had secured 75 of the 123 municipalities. Following prolonged dissent between Georgievski and Tupurkovski, the DA withdrew from the coalition Government and from the Sobranje at the end of November. Georgievski subsequently formed a new Cabinet, which, for the first time, included members of the LDP.

In early 2001 ethnic Albanian militants, members of the self-styled National Liberation Army (NLA—which had emerged as the successor movement to the KLA), began to infiltrate northern parts of the FYRM from Kosovo, clashing with Macedonian security forces. In early March NLA forces seized the border village of Tanusevci, north of Skopje, prompting counter-attacks from government troops. The border with Kosovo was officially closed, after senior government officials visiting the border region were attacked and temporarily besieged by the NLA. Although the authorities succeeded in regaining control of Tanusevci, in mid-March NLA forces (reported to number about 200) attempted to occupy Tetovo. The Government imposed curfew regulations in Tetovo, but rejected the demands of Macedonian nationalists, who demonstrated in Skopje in favour of the introduction of martial law. Following an appeal by the Government to the international community for military assistance, NATO announced that a further 1,000 troops were to be deployed at the border with Kosovo to prevent the NLA from receiving supplies from the province. (The NATO troops stationed in the FYRM had only a mandate to provide logistical support to KFOR.) On 21 March the UN Security Council adopted Resolution 1345, condemning the nationalist violence in the FYRM as constituting a threat to the stability of the region. Despite reports that the ethnic Albanian rebels aimed to establish a 'greater Albania' (to comprise Kosovo, northern and western FYRM and the Presevo Valley), the NLA insisted that the conflict had been initiated to pressurize the Macedonian Government to institute constitutional changes guaranteeing equal rights for ethnic Albanians. Government forces staged a major counter-offensive against the rebels, who had refused to comply with an ultimatum to cease hostilities. The prolonged bombardment of rebel positions resulted in a withdrawal by the NLA from the Tetovo region, and hostilities temporarily subsided in early April. However, at the end of the month eight members of the Macedonian security forces were killed in an NLA attack near the border with Kosovo. Their funeral pre-

cipitated rioting and attacks by Macedonians on Albanian-owned property in the southern town of Bitola. Government troops subsequently launched an offensive against rebel ethnic Albanian positions at the border villages of Vakcince and Slupcane, near Kumanovo, after two further members of the armed forces were killed.

Meanwhile, in early April 2001, following the temporary suppression of the insurgency, inter-party discussions regarding the ethnic Albanian demands commenced. After signing a Stabilization and Association Agreement with the EU, the Government pledged to initiate political, social and economic reforms by mid-2001. Ethnic Albanian proposals included the postponement of the national census, due to take place in May, until October, to allow the return of refugees who had fled the conflict; state funding for the university at Tetovo; and the conversion of the state television's third service into an Albanian-language channel. However, the Government continued to oppose principal demands that the Constitution be amended to grant the ethnic Albanian population (hitherto officially categorized as a minority) equal rights with the Macedonian population, and Albanian the status of a second official language.

In early May 2001, following the resumption of intensive hostilities in the north of the country, the Government announced that the declaration of a state of war (which would allow the authorities to adopt emergency powers and Trajkovski to rule by decree) was under debate; the declaration, which required the approval of a two-thirds' majority in the Sobranje, was strongly opposed by ethnic Albanian deputies. Intensive discussions ensued between the principal political parties, attended by the EU High Representative responsible for foreign and security policy, Javier Solana Madariaga, and the NATO Secretary-General, Lord Robertson of Port Ellen, who visited Skopje to urge the Government to continue dialogue with the ethnic Albanian minority; it was agreed that the SDAM, the DPA and the PDP would join a government of national unity, and the parliamentary debate on the declaration of a state of war was suspended. The PDP subsequently demanded that the Government declare a cease-fire in the conflict in the north, as a precondition to the ethnic Albanian party's participation in the new Cabinet. After the government offensive against the rebels was temporarily suspended, the Government of national unity (which was again headed by Georgievski) was approved by the Sobranje on 13 May. NLA leaders stated that the rebel movement (which still held several villages) would continue hostilities until the Government agreed to enter into political dialogue with them.

On 8 June 2001 Trajkovski announced proposals for a comprehensive peace plan, which provided for the proportional representation of ethnic Albanians in all levels of government, the increased official use of the Albanian language, and a partial amnesty for NLA combatants. Solana subsequently announced his support for the plan; however, the NLA demanded that the Government end hostilities and enter into negotiations on constitutional reforms, and rebel forces seized the town of Aracinovo, only some 6 km east of Skopje. Later in June the Government announced the suspension of its offensive against the NLA, following pressure from international envoys. However, violent protests were staged by Macedonian nationalists at the parliament building in Skopje, in response to the NATO-mediated cease-fire arrangement at Aracinovo, which was perceived to be lenient towards the ethnic Albanian rebels. On 29 June NATO formally approved an operation to deploy a 3,500-member multinational force in the FYRM to assist in the disarmament of the NLA, which was, however, conditional on the imposition of a lasting cease-fire. On 5 July the Government announced that an official cease-fire agreement had been signed by both sides, and negotiations resumed between leaders of the principal Macedonian and ethnic Albanian parties regarding a permanent peace settlement. However, Georgievski and his nationalist cabinet supporters strongly opposed proposals, detailed by EU and US special envoys, for the extension of the use of the Albanian language, and accused international mediators of sympathizing with the rebels. After minor violations, the cease-fire collapsed after 17 days, when the NLA launched further attacks on government forces deployed at villages near Tetovo. (By that time some 60,000 ethnic Albanians had fled to Kosovo, while a further 30,000 had become internally displaced.) International diplomatic efforts subsequently intensified, following renewed fears of widespread civil conflict. On 26 July, following discussions between Trajkovski, Solana and Robertson, it was announced that an accord had been reached to restore the cease-fire between government forces and the ethnic Albanian rebels, who had agreed to withdraw from newly captured territory near Tetovo. On the same day, however, the extreme nationalist Minister of Internal Affairs, Ljube Boshkovski, announced that 11 prominent members of the NLA, including the movement's leader, Ali Ahmeti, were to be charged with war crimes. At the end of July further negotiations on the peace proposals, between Macedonian and ethnic Albanian representatives, commenced at the western town of Ohrid. Progress in the discussions was reported in early August, following the resolution of the two main issues of contention (the extension of the official use of the Albanian language and the right to proportional representation of the ethnic Albanian community in the security forces). In response to increasing pressure from the EU and the USA, the Government announced a unilateral cease-fire, and on 13 August the Macedonian and ethnic Albanian leaders at Ohrid signed a framework peace agreement, providing for the amendment of the Constitution to grant greater rights to the ethnic Albanian community. On the following day Ahmeti agreed that the NLA, numbering an estimated 2,500–3,000, would relinquish its armaments to NATO troops. Following an assessment of the security situation, NATO announced that the cease-fire was generally being observed, and on 22 August the activation order for a NATO mission, Operation Essential Harvest, was released. The force, which finally comprised 4,500 troops (of whom the United Kingdom contributed about 1,900), had a mandate to disarm the ethnic Albanian combatants and destroy their weapons within 30 days of its deployment. Contention ensued, after the Ministry of Internal Affairs claimed the NLA to be in possession of some 85,000 armaments; however, NATO estimated the number of weapons to be collected at 3,000–4,000.

In early September 2001 parliamentary debate on constitutional reform was delayed by mass nationalist protests against the peace plan. Macedonian nationalist parties in the legislature continued to dispute the extent of a number of the proposed amendments, while ethnic Albanian representatives insisted that attempts to limit the proposals, or to submit them to a referendum, would provoke renewed conflict. Meanwhile, investigators from the International Criminal Tribunal for the former Yugoslavia (ICTY, see p. 15) at the Hague, Netherlands, had been dispatched to the FYRM to conduct preliminary inquiries into the killing of six ethnic Albanian civilians in the village of Ljuboten in early August; Boshkovski was suspected of responsibility for the massacre. On 26 September NATO's 30-day disarmament programme was declared to have been successful, with the collection of some 3,875 armaments. On the same day the establishment of a further, reduced NATO mission, Operation Amber Fox, was authorized. (In response to international pressure, the Government had invited NATO to retain a military presence in the country, despite domestic opposition.) The new mission, comprising 700 troops, together with 300 forces already stationed in the FYRM, was deployed under German leadership, with a three-month renewable mandate to protect EU and OSCE monitors supervising the implementation of the peace agreement. On 27 September Ahmeti announced that the NLA had been formally dissolved, following the completion of the disarmament process. In early October the EU criticized delays in implementing constitutional reforms, after Macedonian parties announced that the legislative process would be suspended pending the release of 14 Macedonian civilians allegedly seized by the NLA earlier that year. Following pressure from Trajkovski, and further diplomatic visits by Solana and Robertson, who urged acceptance of the plan, discussion on the measures resumed in the Sobranje. Later that month Trajkovski approved plans for the deployment of ethnically-mixed security units in regions formerly held by the NLA. Cease-fire violations, which included the killing of three members of the security forces and the temporary abduction of civilians by dissident former NLA combatants, were reported in the northwest of the country in early November.

On 16 November 2001 the Sobranje finally adopted 15 main amendments to the existing Constitution (although the extent of some provisions had been reduced at the insistence of the Macedonian parties). The principal reforms were: the revision of the Constitution's preamble to include a reference to members of non-ethnic Macedonian communities as citizens of the country; the introduction in the Sobranje of a 'double majority' system, whereby certain legislation would require the approval of a minority group; the establishment of Albanian as the second official language in communities where ethnic Albanians com-

prised more than 20% of the population; and the right to proportional representation for ethnic Albanians in the Constitutional Court, all areas of government administration, and the security forces. The adoption of the reforms was received with approval by the international community. Later in November the SDAM and the allied LDP withdrew from the coalition Government (which was subsequently reorganized), on the grounds that their participation was no longer necessary.

In early December 2001 NATO again extended the mandate of Operation Amber Fox, until 26 March 2002. An EU-sponsored international donor conference on economic assistance for the FYRM, originally scheduled to take place in October 2001, was further postponed in December, pending the implementation of additional reforms. In January 2002 new legislation providing for the devolution of greater authority to local government (thereby granting a measure of self-rule to predominantly ethnic Albanian regions) was approved by the Sobranje, and the donor conference duly took place in March (see Economic Affairs). Also in January a Deputy Prime Minister, Dosta Dimovska (who was considered to be a moderate), resigned from the Government, following disagreement with Georgievski over issues relating to the deployment of security units in previously NLA-controlled villages. In February, following a formal request by Georgievski, NATO again extended the mandate of Operation Amber Fox, until 26 June. Later that month the three principal ethnic Albanian political parties (the DPA, the PDP and the NDP) and the former NLA leadership officially established a co-ordinating council, confirming speculation that Ahmeti would enter domestic politics. In March the Sobranje adopted legislation granting immunity from prosecution to several thousand former NLA insurgents (excluding those indictable by the ICTY), in accordance with the peace settlement. It was announced in early April that the national census (the organization of which had been repeatedly postponed, owing to the uncertain security situation) would be conducted in April 2003. In May 2002 the mandate of Operation Amber Fox was further extended, to 26 October. In accordance with the peace agreement, the Sobranje was dissolved on 18 July, prior to legislative elections, which were scheduled for 15 September and were to be monitored by the OSCE.

In May 2002 Ahmeti established a new political party, the Democratic Union for Integration (DUI), which was believed to comprise mainly former NLA combatants. Later that month two ministers belonging to 'Real' IMRO resigned from the Government, on the grounds that former NLA members had become dominant within the principal ethnic Albanian parties. In the same month the Sobranje approved legislation whereby Albanian became an official language in accordance with the Ohrid peace accord. At the end of August fears of a resurgence in violence emerged, after ethnic Albanians took hostage five Macedonian civilians at Gostivar; large numbers of security forces surrounded an ethnic Albanian base and killed two of the kidnappers. However, the elections to the legislature took place peacefully on 15 September, attracting commendation from the international community, after an OSCE mission of 800 observers declared them to have been conducted democratically. Georgievski's Government was removed from power by a 10-party alliance (led by the SDAM and the LDP), known as Together for Macedonia, which secured 60 of the 120 seats in the Sobranje. (IMRO—DPMNU won 33 seats and the newly established DUI 16 seats.) Allegations of malpractice by the outgoing Government were rejected by the electoral commission. The Together for Macedonia alliance and the DUI subsequently signed an agreement for the establishment of a coalition Government (which was, however, to exclude former NLA combatants). The new 18-member administration, comprising members of the SDAM, the LDP and the DUI, headed by Crvenkovski, was officially approved by the Sobranje on 1 November.

In October 2002 NATO agreed to extend the mandate of Operation Amber Fox until December (following controversy within the Government over plans for the contingent to be replaced by EU forces). On 14 December Operation Amber Fox was succeeded by a 450-member mission, Allied Harmony, with a mandate to protect international monitors and advise Macedonian security forces. On 31 March 2003 this contingent was replaced by an EU-led mission, known as Operation Concordia, comprising 350 military personnel; 13 EU member states and 14 non-EU nations were to participate in the force, which was expected to remain in the country for a minimum of six months. The purpose of the operation, which was deployed at the official

request of Trajkovski, was to maintain security in order to facilitate the implementation of the Ohrid peace agreement.

In early 2003 a newly emerged ethnic Albanian extremist group, the Albanian National Army (ANA), threatened to launch a military offensive against the Government. The ANA, which had claimed responsibility for a number of bomb attacks, including one against the regional court at Struga, supported the creation of a 'greater Albania'. In April the Government announced a new anti-corruption strategy, whereby constitutional amendments would provide a legal basis for penalizing malpractice in public administration.

Both the September 1995 interim agreement with Greece and the November Dayton peace accord (for further details, see the chapter on Bosnia and Herzegovina) were of great significance in promoting diplomatic and external economic links for the FYRM, despite the still unresolved issue of a permanent name for the country. The FYRM was admitted to the Council of Europe in late September, and to the OSCE in mid-October; in the following month the FYRM joined NATO's 'Partnership for Peace' (see p. 273) programme. The agreement with Greece facilitated the establishment of full diplomatic relations with the EU from January 1996, and negotiations subsequently began for a co-operation accord; a declaration on co-operation was, furthermore, signed with the European Free Trade Association (see p. 195) in early April. By the end of 1996 more than 75 countries had recognized the FYRM, with about two-thirds using the country's constitutional name, the Republic of Macedonia.

In July 1995 the FYRM and Turkey signed a 20-year co-operation agreement and a mutual security accord. Turkey, together with Albania, Bulgaria and Italy, was involved (between February 1994 and October 1995) in providing trading routes whereby the FYRM could bypass the Greek blockade. None the less, the issue of ethnic Albanians' rights in the FYRM was a frequent source of tension with Albania, and relations with Bulgaria continued to be impeded, specifically, by the question of its recognition of a distinct Macedonian language and nationality.

Although the FYRM formally supported the UN embargo on the FRY, there was frequent evidence that the FYRM Government permitted violations of the blockade. Regular trade with both Greece and the FRY resumed in late 1995, while discussions continued between Macedonian, Greek and UN officials regarding the issue of a permanent name for the FYRM. By 1999 the FYRM's relations with Greece had improved significantly, and in December the two countries signed an agreement on military co-operation. At the end of 2000 the principal border crossing between the FYRM and Greece was reopened.

An agreement signed by the FYRM and the FRY in early April 1996, regulating bilateral relations and promoting mutual co-operation, was regarded as particularly significant in formalizing the FRY's recognition of the FYRM as a sovereign state. Although criticized by most opposition groups within the FYRM, the agreement, since it took into account the position of ethnic Serbs in the FYRM, was welcomed by representatives of the ethnic-Serb community—which constituted about 2% of the total population in 1994, according to census results—who were campaigning for constitutional recognition as a distinct ethnic group of the FYRM. Meanwhile, the FYRM, Croatia, Slovenia and Bosnia and Herzegovina were co-operating in efforts to secure international recognition for all the former republics as successor states to the SFRY, and thereby win access to a share of the assets of the former Yugoslavia. In September the FRY Prime Minister, Radoje Kontić, on his first official visit to the FYRM, signed seven bilateral agreements, including a trade agreement zone designed to be the first stage in the creation of a free-trade zone linking the two countries.

In late 1992 the UN Security Council approved the deployment of members of the UN Protection Force along the FYRM's border with the FRY and Albania, in an effort to protect the FYRM from any external threat to its security; in March 1995 the operation in the FYRM was renamed the UN Preventive Deployment Force (UNPREDEP). In June 1996 the USA and the FYRM exchanged diplomatic notes regulating the status of US troops participating in UNPREDEP. Following a reduction in UNPREDEP's authorized strength by the Security Council, the US contingent of military personnel was placed under direct US administration. In April 1997 the mandate of UNPREDEP was extended to the end of May, in view of the civil disorder in Albania (q.v.); it was further extended in June and December. Following the civil unrest in Albania, a number of border incur-

sions by armed groups of Albanian rebels were reported, and in September two members of the FYRM's security forces were killed in a clash with Albanians who had entered the country illegally. In October the Ministers of Defence of the FYRM and Albania signed an agreement providing for increased security along the joint border between the two countries.

In the first months of 1998 increasing clashes were reported in Kosovo between members of the Serbian security forces and the KLA, a paramilitary movement established by ethnic Albanians. In late July the UN Security Council extended the mandate of UNPREDEP until 28 February 1999 and agreed to increase the size of the contingent from 750 to about 1,100, with the aim of reinforcing border control. In early December 1998, following discussions between President Gligorov and NATO officials, it was announced that a NATO 'extraction force' was to be deployed in the FYRM to effect the evacuation of OSCE monitors in Kosovo in the event of large-scale conflict. In late February 1999 the People's Republic of China vetoed a UN Security Council resolution to extend the mandate of UNPREDEP for a further six months, following a decision by the FYRM Government to extend diplomatic recognition to Taiwan, which also prompted the People's Republic of China to suspend diplomatic relations with the FYRM. In the same month additional NATO troops began to assemble near the FYRM border with Kosovo (where the 2,300-member 'extraction force', principally comprising French and British troops, was already stationed). Diplomatic efforts failed, however, and NATO forces commenced an intensive aerial bombardment of strategic targets in the FRY in late March. Ethnic Serbs in the FYRM subsequently increased demonstrations against the presence of NATO forces in the country. The NATO air offensive precipitated increased reprisals by Serbian security forces against the ethnic Albanian population in Kosovo and by early April some 140,000 refugees had fled to the FYRM. The FYRM Government denied foreign allegations of the maltreatment by its security forces of the Kosovar refugees, and complained of delays in assistance from the EU. By mid-April about 14,000 NATO troops were deployed near the FYRM border with Kosovo, and were involved in assisting the refugees. Owing to concern over internal destabilization, the FYRM authorities repeatedly closed the border with Kosovo to prevent the continued arrival of large numbers of ethnic Albanians, and demanded that the international community fulfil pledges to accept a proportion of the refugees. By late May some 60,000 refugees had been transported from the FYRM for provisional resettlement abroad, while an estimated 250,000 remained in the country. In early June the strength of NATO forces stationed in the FYRM was increased to 16,000. Shortly afterwards the Yugoslav Government accepted a peace plan which provided for the withdrawal of Serbian forces from Kosovo, the return of ethnic Albanian refugees and the deployment of a NATO-led Kosovo Peace Implementation Force (KFOR). NATO troops, which were to be deployed under the KFOR mandate, entered Kosovo from the FYRM. On 20 June NATO announced that the air campaign had officially ended, following the withdrawal of Serbian forces from Kosovo. Large numbers of ethnic Albanian refugees subsequently began to return to Kosovo from the FYRM. Some 4,000 NATO troops remained in the FYRM, with a mandate to provide logistical support to KFOR.

In early 2001 an ethnic Albanian insurgency spread into the FYRM from Kosovo (see above). In June the FYRM and the People's Republic of China agreed to restore diplomatic relations (thereby ensuring Chinese support in the UN Security Council for the deployment of a NATO peace-keeping operation from August); Taiwan subsequently announced the severance of relations with the FYRM. In March 2002 Trajkovski and the head of the UN Interim Administration Mission in Kosovo agreed to establish a joint committee to discuss border issues.

Government

According to the 1991 Constitution, which was amended in November 2001, legislative power is vested in the Sobranje (Assembly), with 120 members, elected for a four-year term by universal adult suffrage (85 in single-seat constituencies and 35 members by proportional representation). The President is directly elected for a five-year term, and appoints a Prime Minister to head the Government. The Ministers are elected by the Sobranje. The FYRM is divided into 123 municipalities for the purposes of local government.

Defence

In August 2002 the armed forces of the FYRM totalled 12,300 in active service (including 7,600 conscripts); the air force numbered about 800. Paramilitary forces comprised a police force of 7,600, of which some 5,000 were armed. Conscription was introduced in April 1992, and military service lasts for nine months. On 31 March 2003 the existing NATO contingent in the FYRM was replaced by an EU mission, known as Operation Concordia, comprising 350 military personnel; 13 EU member states and 14 non-EU nations were to participate in the operation, which was to remain in the country for a minimum of six months. Expenditure on defence was budgeted at 7,620m. new denars (equivalent to 3.0% of GDP) in 2002.

Economic Affairs

In 2001, according to World Bank estimates, the FYRM's gross national income (GNI), measured at average 1999–2001 prices, was US $3,445m., equivalent to $1,690 per head (or $4,860 per head on an international purchasing-power parity basis). During 1990–2001, it was estimated, the population increased by an average of 0.7% per year, while gross domestic product (GDP) per head declined, in real terms, at an average annual rate of 1.1%. Overall GDP declined, in real terms, at an average annual rate of 0.5% in 1990–2001; real GDP increased by 4.5% in 2000, but declined by 4.1% in 2001.

Agriculture contributed an estimated 11.8% of GDP in 2002. About 12.1% of the employed labour force were engaged in the agricultural sector in that year. Dairy farming is significant, and the principal agricultural exports are tobacco, vegetables and fruit. The wine industry is of considerable importance, and the FYRM is also a producer of wheat, maize and barley. During 1990–2001, according to the World Bank, the GDP of the agricultural sector declined, in real terms, at an average annual rate of 0.4%; real agricultural GDP increased by 1.1% in 2000, but declined by 14.2% in 2001.

Industry contributed an estimated 28.9% of GDP in 2002, and engaged 33.5% of the employed labour force in 2000. During 1990–2001, according to the World Bank, the GDP of the industrial sector declined, in real terms, at an average annual rate of 4.1%; real industrial GDP increased by 2.8% in 2000, but declined by 7.4% in 2001.

Mining contributed an estimated 0.6% of GDP in 2002, and engaged 1.9% of all employees in 1997. The only major mining activity is the production of lignite (brown coal), although there are also deposits of iron, zinc, lead, copper, chromium, manganese, antimony, silver, gold and nickel. Production in the mining and quarrying sector increased at an average annual rate of 5.9% in 1996–2000.

The manufacturing sector contributed an estimated 18.1% of GDP in 2002, and engaged 32.3% of all employees in 1997. In 1996 the principal branches of the sector, measured by gross value of output, were food products (accounting for 19.1% of the total), textiles and clothing (11.9%), machinery (11.0%), chemicals, and iron and steel. The GDP of the manufacturing sector decreased, in real terms, at an average annual rate of 6.1% in 1990–2001; real manufacturing GDP increased by 3.8% in 2000, but declined by 8.6% in 2001.

Energy is derived principally from coal and lignite, which provided 79.8% of the electricity generated in 2000. The first stage of a pipeline from the Bulgarian border to carry natural gas to the FYRM from Russia became operational in late 1995. A 214-km pipeline, which was to transport petroleum from the Greek port of Thessaloníki to Skopje, was inaugurated in July 2002. Imports of mineral fuels accounted for 13.9% of the value of total imports in 2001.

Services (including handicrafts) accounted for an estimated 59.3% of GDP in 2002, and engaged 44.2% of the employed labour force, in 2001. Regional instability, notably ethnic hostilities in the north of the FYRM in 2001, has had an adverse impact on tourist activity. During 1990–2001, according to the World Bank, the GDP of the services sector increased at an average annual rate of 1.0%; services GDP increased by 5.6% in 2000, but declined by 0.8% in 2001.

In 2001 the FYRM recorded a visible trade deficit of US $421.4m., while there was a deficit of $324.3m. on the current account of the balance of payments. In 2001 the principal source of imports (12.6%) was Germany; other major sources were Greece, the FRY, Russia, Slovenia, Italy, Bulgaria and Ukraine. The principal market for exports in that year was the FRY (15.8%); other important purchasers were Germany, Greece, the USA and Italy. The principal exports in 2001 were miscellaneous manufactured articles (notably clothing and accessories), basic manufactures (particularly iron and steel), beverages and tobacco, machinery and transport equipment, and food and live animals. The main imports in that year were machinery and transport equipment (particularly road vehicles and parts), mineral fuels and lubricants (notably petroleum and petroleum products), basic manufactures, food and live animals, and chemical products.

The FYRM recorded an overall budgetary surplus of 5,861m. new denars in 2000, but an estimated budgetary deficit of 13,978m. new denars in 2001. At the end of 2000 the FYRM's total external debt was estimated at US $1,465m., of which $1,165m. was long-term public debt. In that year the cost of debt-servicing was equivalent to 9.3% of the value of exports of goods and services. The annual rate of inflation averaged 72.8% in 1990–2001. Consumer prices increased by 5.5% in 2001, and by 0.1% in 2002. The rate of unemployment was estimated at some 31.9% in 2002.

The FYRM is a member of the IMF and the European Bank for Reconstruction and Development (EBRD, see p. 193). It become a member of the World Trade Organization (WTO, see p. 323) in April 2003.

The FYRM's economic prospects were significantly improved by the removal, in late 1995, of what had been major impediments to growth: the Greek embargo on trade with the FYRM and the UN sanctions against the FRY, which had severely disrupted the FYRM's trading links. Progress was achieved through mass privatization, particularly the restructuring of the banking sector; a stock exchange was opened in Skopje in March 1996. In October of that year the FYRM reached agreement with the 'London Club' of commercial banks on the FYRM's liability for the former Yugoslavia's commercial debt, which was to allow the FYRM access to international capital markets for the first time. In April 1997 the IMF approved a three-year loan to support the Government's economic reform programme. The NATO aerial bombardment of the FRY in March–June 1999, resulting in a mass influx of refugees from Kosovo, adversely affected the FYRM economy. Following the end of the conflict, however, Macedonian enterprises profited from involvement in the reconstruction of infrastructural damage in Kosovo, and from Serbia's economic regeneration. A significant improvement in relations between Greece and the FYRM also provided for substantial Greek investment in the FYRM's petroleum refinery, banking sector and other assets. The introduction of value-added tax in 2000 proved highly successful, and in November the IMF approved a further three-year loan to support the Government's economic reforms. However, border clashes between ethnic Albanian rebels and Macedonian security forces escalated into severe fighting in the north of the country in early 2001 (see Recent History), prompting renewed fears of widespread civil conflict. The poor security situation contributed to a substantial deterioration of the fiscal position in that year. Following the negotiation of a peace agreement in August, the authorities requested considerable donor assistance to finance the reconstruction of damaged infrastructure and housing, and the relocation of displaced civilians. A Stabilization and Association Agreement was signed with the European Union (EU) in April. A major donor aid conference, sponsored by the EU and the World Bank, finally took place in March 2002; international donors pledged a total of US $515m. (more than twice the amount initially envisaged) to support reconstruction. In September the Government, which had been widely regarded as responsible for mismanagement and widespread corruption, was replaced. At that time illicit trade remained endemic, about one-half of the population suffered from poverty, and the economy was sustained by continued bilateral and multilateral credit. Measures to investigate suspected embezzlement in public institutions and to combat further malpractice were immediately introduced. Other priorities of the new Government were to reduce the exceptionally high rate of unemployment, increase productivity and attract foreign investment. In October the WTO formally approved the FYRM's accession, and it became a full member in April 2003. A further stand-by credit agreement with the IMF, signed in early 2003, was conditional on the imposition of certain measures, including tax increases. Plans for a rise in the prices of essential commodities, also stipulated by the IMF, prompted general concern and threats of strike action.

Education

Elementary education is provided free of charge, and is officially compulsory for all children between the ages of seven and 15.

Various types of secondary education, beginning at 15 years of age and lasting for four years, are available to those who qualify. In 1999/2000 primary enrolment included 93.6% of children in the relevant age-group (males 94.0%, females 93.1%), while the comparable ratio for secondary education was equivalent to 83.6% (males 85.0%; females 82.2%). The Constitution guarantees nationals the right to elementary and secondary education in their mother tongue. In 2000/01 Albanian was the language of education in 273 primary schools and 23 secondary schools, Turkish in 56 primary schools and five secondary schools, and Serbian in 14 primary schools. There are universities at Skopje and at Bitola. In July 2000 new legislation permitted the use of Albanian and other languages in private tertiary institutions, and an Albanian-language university at Tetovo was granted legal status as a private foundation. In 2001/02 some 44,710 students were enrolled in higher education. Expenditure on education by the central Government in 2002 was budgeted at 7,591m. denars (11.4% of total expenditure).

Public Holidays

2003: 1 January (New Year), 7 January (Christmas), 27–28 April (Orthodox Easter), 1–2 May (Labour Days), 2 August (National Day), 8 September (Independence Day), 11 October (Rebellion Day).

2004: 1 January (New Year), 7 January (Christmas), 11–12 April (Orthodox Easter), 1–2 May (Labour Days), 2 August (National Day), 8 September (Independence Day), 11 October (Rebellion Day).

Weights and Measures

The metric system is in force.

Statistical Survey

Source (unless otherwise indicated): State Statistical Office of the Republic of Macedonia, 91000 Skopje, Dame Gruev 4, POB 506; tel. (2) 114904; fax (2) 111336; e-mail info@stat.gov.mk; internet www.stat.gov.mk.

Area and Population

AREA, POPULATION AND DENSITY

Area (sq km)	25,713*
Population (census results)	
31 March 1991†	2,033,964
20 June 1994‡	
Males	974,255
Females	971,677
Total	1,945,932
Population (official estimates at mid-year)‡	
1999	2,017,142
2000	2,026,350
2001§	2,031,112
Density (per sq km) at 31 December 2001	79.0

* 9,928 sq miles.

† The total refers to the *de jure* population, i.e. persons with a permanent residence in the country, including residents temporarily abroad (regardless of the duration of their absence). Other persons present in Macedonia were excluded.

‡ Figures from the 1994 census and mid-year estimates for subsequent years refer to persons with an official place of residence in the country (including those temporarily abroad for less than a year) and persons from other countries who have been granted a residence permit in Macedonia and have been present there for at least a year.

§ At 31 December.

PRINCIPAL ETHNIC GROUPS
(census results)

	1991	1994
Macedonian	1,328,187	1,295,964
Albanian	441,987	441,104
Turkish	77,080	78,019
Roma (Gypsy)	52,103	43,707
Serbian	42,775	40,228
Muslim	31,356	15,418
Vlach	7,764	8,601
Total (incl. others)	2,033,964	1,945,932

PRINCIPAL TOWNS
(population at 1994 census)

Skopje (capital) . .	444,299		Veles	46,798
Bitola	77,464		Štip	41,730
Kumanovo . . .	71,853		Ohrid	41,146
Prilep	68,148		Strumica	34,067
Tetovo	50,344			

BIRTHS, MARRIAGES AND DEATHS*

		Registered live births		Registered marriages		Registered deaths	
		Number	Rate (per 1,000)	Number	Rate (per 1,000)	Number	Rate (per 1,000)
1994	. .	33,487	17.2	15,736	8.1	15,771	8.1
1995	. .	32,154	16.3	15,823	8.0	16,338	8.3
1996	. .	31,403	15.8	14,089	7.1	16,063	8.1
1997	. .	29,478	14.8	14,072	7.0	16,596	8.3
1998	. .	29,244	14.6	13,993	7.0	16,870	8.4
1999	. .	27,309	13.5	14,172	7.0	16,789	8.3
2000	. .	29,308	14.5	14,255	7.0	17,253	8.5
2001	. .	27,010	13.3	13,267	6.5	16,919	8.3

* Prior to 1994, rates per 1,000 are not comparable with figures for later years.

Expectation of life (WHO estimates, years at birth): 71.8 (males 68.9; females 74.9) in 2001 (Source: WHO, *World Health Report*).

ECONOMICALLY ACTIVE POPULATION
(sample surveys, '000 persons aged 15 years and over, at April)

	1998	1999	2000
Agriculture and fishing	102.2	111.7	116.5
Forestry	5.0	3.7	3.5
Water management	2.8	2.9	2.7
Industry*	152.1	151.1	148.6
Construction	35.8	31.3	35.7
Wholesale and retail trade . . .	53.6	55.3	53.0
Catering and tourism	14.8	14.6	15.7
Transport and communications	26.8	27.5	27.5
Crafts and trades	18.6	15.8	13.9
Housing and municipal services .	8.8	9.6	10.6
Financial, technical and business services	14.6	17.0	15.7
Education, science, culture and information	41.6	40.5	40.3
Health care and social security	31.9	31.2	31.7
Administration and social organizations	30.4	32.2	32.5
Total employed†	539.8	545.2	549.8
Unemployed	284.1	261.5	261.7
Total labour force	823.8	806.7	811.6
Males	506.8	496.1	488.5
Females	317.0	310.5	323.0

* Including mining, manufacturing and electricity. Figures exclude crafts and trades, listed separately.

† Including others.

Source: IMF, *Former Yugoslav Republic of Macedonia: Selected Issues and Statistical Appendix* (March 2002).

Health and Welfare

KEY INDICATORS

Total fertility rate (children per woman, 2001)	1.6
Under-5 mortality rate (per 1,000 live births, 2001) . . .	26
HIV/AIDS (% of persons aged 15–49, 2001)	<0.10
Physicians (per 1,000 head, 2001)	4.4
Hospital beds (per 1,000 head, 2001)	10.0
Health expenditure (2000): US $ per head (PPP)	300
Health expenditure (2000): % of GDP	6.0
Health expenditure (2000): public (% of total)	84.5
Human Development Index (2000): ranking	65
Human Development Index (2000): value	0.772

For sources and definitions, see explanatory note on p. vi.

Agriculture

PRINCIPAL CROPS
('000 metric tons)

	1999	2000	2001
Wheat	377.8	299.0	246.0
Rice (paddy)*	21.3	19.0	19.0
Barley	126.0	110.0	91.5
Maize	200.2	127.0	118.3
Rye	11.0	7.0†	7.0*
Potatoes	165.0	164.0	176.0
Sugar beet	67.0	56.0	38.0
Dry beans*	13.7	13.6	13.5
Sunflower seed	14.0	10.0*	12.0†
Cabbages	69.5	70.4	75.3
Tomatoes	128.4	134.7	126.3
Cucumbers and gherkins* . .	22	22	22
Chillies and green peppers* . .	109.0	110.0	110.0
Dry onions	38.3	36.3	30.6
Green beans*	17.8	17.7	17.5
Other vegetables	23.0	22.5	23.1
Apples	73.0	84.3	38.4
Pears	9.8	8.9	6.5
Peaches and nectarines . . .	9.0	9.5	4.6
Plums	28.1	23.4	13.3
Cherries (incl. sour)	9.5	9.8*	11.1*
Grapes	230.1	264.3	229.8
Watermelons and melons . .	121.3	122.0*	122.0*
Other fruits	10.9	10.6	7.4
Tobacco (leaves)	32.0	28.0†	28.0*

* FAO estimate(s).
† Unofficial figure.

Source: FAO.

LIVESTOCK
('000 head, year ending September)

	1999	2000	2001
Horses	60	57	57*
Cattle	267	270	265†
Pigs	197	226	204
Sheep	1,315	1,289	1,251
Poultry	3,339	3,350*	3,350*

* FAO estimate.
† Unofficial figure.

Source: FAO.

LIVESTOCK PRODUCTS
('000 metric tons)

	1999	2000	2001
Beef and veal	7.7	7.0*	9.0*
Mutton and lamb	4.4	4.5†	5.9†
Pig meat	9.2	9.0†	8.8†
Poultry meat†	12	12	12
Cows' milk	208.7	200.0*	200.0†
Sheep's milk	39.1	40.0†	40.0†
Butter†	9.3	9.5	9.5
Cheese	1.4	1.4†	1.4†
Poultry eggs	20.7†	20.5	20.6†
Honey	1.6	1.5†	1.6†
Wool: greasy	2.0	2.0†	2.0†
Cattle hides†	1.4	1.3	1.3
Sheepskins†	0.9	0.9	0.9

* Unofficial figure.
† FAO estimate(s).

Source: FAO.

Forestry

ROUNDWOOD REMOVALS
('000 cubic metres, excl. bark)

	1999	2000	2001
Sawlogs, veneer logs and logs for sleepers . . .	113	164	125
Pulpwood*	5	5	5
Other industrial wood	5	8	10
Fuel wood	699	875	605
Total	822	1,052	745

* FAO estimates.

Source: FAO.

SAWNWOOD PRODUCTION
('000 cubic metres, incl. railway sleepers)

	1998	1999	2000
Coniferous (softwood)	6	10	8
Broadleaved (hardwood)	21	27	28
Total	27	37	36

Source: FAO.

Fishing

(metric tons, live weight)

	1998	1999	2000
Capture	131	135	208
Freshwater fishes	113	113	77
Trouts	18	22	131
Aquaculture	1,257	1,669	1,626
Common carp	135	215	238
Bleak	236	130	110
Other freshwater fishes . . .	258	210	330
European eel	72	60	50
Trouts	324	788	705
Huchen	214	244	173
White fishes	18	22	20
Total catch	1,388	1,804	1,834

Source: FAO, *Yearbook of Fishery Statistics*.

Mining

('000 metric tons)

	1997	1998	1999
Lignite.	7,442.9	8,144.7	7,277.6
Copper concentrates*	46.8	39.1	37.8
Lead concentrates*	19.5	16.8	12.3
Zinc concentrates*	15.5	14.3	10.2
Chromium concentrates*	1.5	—	—
Gypsum (crude)	51.4	55.0	76.2

* Figures refer to the metal content of concentrates.

2000 ('000 metric tons): Zinc concentrates (metal content) 12.2 (Source: US Geological Survey).

Industry

SELECTED PRODUCTS
('000 metric tons, unless otherwise indicated)

	1997	1998	1999
Vegetable oils: refined	21.0	18.8	11.3
Flour	164.4	154.2	140.4
Refined sugar.	35.2	40.4	43.0
Wine ('000 hectolitres)	957.6	1,227.1	911.9
Beer ('000 hectolitres)	600.1	578.2	651.9
Soft drinks ('000 hectolitres)	941.9	816.5	685.2
Cigarettes (million)	9,678	7,009	17,758
Wool yarn: pure and mixed.	4.4	3.3	0.5
Cotton yarn: pure and mixed	4.0	4.1	2.3
Woven cotton fabric (million sq metres)	9.8	13.7	6.1
Woven woollen fabrics (million sq metres)	5.4	5.2	0.8
Leather footwear ('000)	1,138	1,382	1,837
Sulphuric acid	105.0	100.8	87.8
Caustic soda (Sodium hydroxide)	3.4	24.1	0.6
Motor spirit (petrol)	97.3	152.8	266.8
Gas-diesel (distillate fuel) oil	122.7	272.1	203.6
Residual fuel oils (Mazout)	128.9	289.6	248.2
Cement	610.8	461.2	563.3
Ferro-alloys	85.9	106.7	77.5
Lead: unwrought.	56.6	57.7	46.8
Zinc: unwrought	3.1	8.6	4.0
Refrigerators ('000)	11.7	4.0	—
Electric energy (million kWh)	6,718.8	7,036.5	6,821.7

Finance

CURRENCY AND EXCHANGE RATES

Monetary Units
100 deni = 1 new Macedonian denar

Sterling, Dollar and Euro Equivalents (31 December 2002)
£1 sterling = 94.86 new denars
US $1 = 58.86 new denars
€1 = 61.72 new denars
1,000 new denars = £10.54 = $17.00 = €16.20

Average Exchange Rate (new denars per US $)
2000   65.904
2001   68.037
2002   64.354

Note: The Macedonian denar was introduced in April 1992, replacing (initially at par) the Yugoslav dinar. In May 1993 a new Macedonian denar, equivalent to 100 of the former units, was established as the sole legal tender.

BUDGET
(million new denars)*

Revenue†	1999	2000	2001‡
Tax revenue	41,850	51,115	47,566
Personal income tax	10,230	10,793	7,248
Profit tax	2,560	2,793	3,006
Sales tax	9,959	17,452	17,132
Excises	10,674	12,281	10,680
Import duties	8,302	7,733	6,111
Non-tax revenue	2,724	3,028	3,425
Capital revenue	153	424	499
Total	44,574	54,142	50,991

Expenditure	1999	2000	2001‡
Current expenditure.	43,127	45,027	56,686
Wage, salaries and allowances	17,757	16,285	16,407
Other purchases of goods and services	5,224	6,137	19,825
Refugees and poverty-related expenditure	2,456	1,482	582
Transfers	14,671	17,174	15,672
Interest payments	3,019	3,949	4,200
Capital expenditure	2,957	5,751	7,178
Change in arrears	−494	—	—
Enterprise sector reform	—	344	239
Public administration reform	—	60	944
Statistical discrepancy	−84	184	171
Total§	45,613	51,520	65,384

* Figures refer to transactions of the central Government, excluding the operations of extrabudgetary funds.

† Excluding foreign grants received (million new denars): 2,477 in 1999; 3,239 in 2000; 415 (estimate) in 2001.

‡ Estimates.

§ Including transfers to reserves (million new denars): 107 in 1999; 154 in 2000; 166 (estimate) in 2001.

Source: IMF, *Former Yugoslav Republic of Macedonia: Selected Issues and Statistical Appendix* (March 2002).

INTERNATIONAL RESERVES
(US $ million at 31 December)

	2000	2001	2002
Gold*	30.7	53.7	63.1
IMF special drawing rights.	0.7	2.2	6.1
Foreign exchange.	428.7	742.9	714.4
Total	460.1	798.8	783.6

* National valuation.

Source: IMF, *International Financial Statistics*.

MONEY SUPPLY
(million new denars at 31 December)

	1999	2000	2001
Currency outside banks.	8,271	9,522	14,134
Demand deposits at deposit money banks	10,458	11,896	11,168
Total (incl. others)	19,795	22,392	25,302

Source: IMF, *International Financial Statistics*.

COST OF LIVING
(Consumer price index; base: 1990=100)

	1999	2000	2001
Food (incl. beverages)	38,216	38,061	40,685
Fuel and light	33,051	42,107	43,753
Clothing (incl. footwear).	38,492	37,607	38,094
Rent and water	99,307	108,046	120,253
All items (incl. others)	43,154	45,665	48,176

Source: ILO.

NATIONAL ACCOUNTS
(million new denars at current prices)

National Income and Product

	1994	1995	1996
Compensation of employees. . .	95,546	104,503	109,183
Operating surplus	9,218	17,337	18,587
Domestic factor incomes. . .	104,764	121,840	127,770
Consumption of fixed capital . .	20,558	23,290	23,628
Gross domestic product (GDP)			
at factor cost	125,322	145,130	151,398
Indirect taxes	25,315	27,781	28,235
Less Subsidies	4,228	3,390	3,190
GDP in purchasers' values . .	146,409	169,521	176,444
Factor income from abroad . . .	432	1,206	1,778
Less Factor income paid abroad .	2,462	2,283	2,966
Gross national product (GNP) .	144,379	168,445	175,256
Less Consumption of fixed capital .	20,558	23,290	23,628
National income in market			
prices	123,821	145,155	151,628
Other current transfers from			
abroad	17,711	16,320	18,997
Less Other current transfers paid			
abroad	7,819	7,494	10,518
National disposable income. .	133,713	153,981	160,106

Expenditure on the Gross Domestic Product

	1998	1999	2000
Government final consumption			
expenditure.	39,504	43,009	43,021
Private final consumption			
expenditure.	141,078	145,693	175,965
Increase in stocks	9,426	6,461	12,351
Gross fixed capital formation . .	33,982	34,710	38,332
Total domestic expenditure. .	223,990	229,873	269,669
Exports of goods and services . .	80,343	88,143	114,209
Less Imports of goods and services	109,355	109,007	147,489
GDP in purchasers' values . .	194,979	209,010	236,389
GDP at constant 1995 prices .	179,879	187,684	196,223

Gross Domestic Product by Economic Activity

	2000	2001	2002*
Agriculture, hunting and forestry .	23,756	22,933	24,398
Fishing	14	24	25
Industry†	53,163	50,940	48,423
Construction	13,361	11,801	11,462
Wholesale and retail trade . .	25,402	26,076	29,077
Hotels and restaurants . . .	3,463	3,410	3,788
Transport and communications. .	21,261	21,694	24,213
Financial services	7,342	7,420	8,445
Real estate and business			
services‡	17,931	18,935	18,804
Public administration and			
defence	14,333	14,445	15,249
Education	8,266	8,048	8,353
Health care and social work . .	8,987	8,690	9,119
Other community, social and			
personal services	5,217	5,552	5,699
Sub-total	202,496	199,968	207,055
Less Imputed bank service charge	5,153	4,738	5,393
GDP at basic prices. . . .	197,344	195,230	201,660
Taxes on products . . . . }			
Less Subsidies on products . . }	39,045	38,611	37,230
GDP in purchasers' values .	236,389	233,841	238,890

* Estimates.

† Including mining, manufacturing and electricity. Figures exclude crafts and trades, listed separately.

‡ Including imputed rents of owner-occupied dwellings.

BALANCE OF PAYMENTS
(US $ million)

	1999	2000	2001
Exports of goods f.o.b. . . .	1,192.1	1,317.1	1,153.5
Imports of goods f.o.b. . . .	−1,602.2	−1,875.2	−1,574.9
Trade balance	−410.1	−558.0	−421.4
Exports of services	248.4	303.1	233.8
Imports of services	−323.8	−357.8	−336.7
Balance on goods and services.	−485.5	−612.7	−524.3
Other income received . . .	22.5	42.2	48.1
Other income paid	−66.3	−87.3	−88.6
Balance on goods, services and			
income	−529.4	−657.8	−564.8
Current transfers received . .	750.3	923.1	872.5
Current transfers paid . . .	−330.2	−372.4	−632.0
Current balance	−109.3	−107.2	−324.3
Capital account (net) . . .	4.4	0.3	1.3
Direct investment abroad . .	—	0.6	−0.9
Direct investment from abroad. .	30.1	175.6	443.2
Portfolio investment assets . . .	−0.4	—	3.2
Portfolio investment liabilities . .	0.5	−0.1	—
Other investment assets . .	−81.0	−81.1	8.8
Other investment liabilities . .	240.4	290.2	−66.1
Net errors and omissions . . .	34.5	−46.0	25.9
Overall balance	119.2	232.3	91.1

Source: IMF, *International Financial Statistics*.

External Trade

PRINCIPAL COMMODITIES
(distribution by SITC, US $ million)

Imports c.i.f.	1999	2000	2001
Food and live animals . . .	212.1	211.6	194.1
Meat and meat preparations . .	69.2	63.3	61.8
Cereals and cereal preparations .	31.7	40.1	31.3
Crude materials (inedible)			
except fuels	56.5	54.5	47.1
Mineral fuels, lubricants, etc. .	162.4	289.8	233.9
Petroleum, petroleum products etc.	135.1	255.7	192.4
Chemicals and related			
products	184.4	188.5	171.4
Basic manufactures	272.7	270.2	206.3
Iron and steel.	46.9	57.2	34.8
Machinery and transport			
equipment.	355.4	409.8	283.0
Machinery specialized for			
particular industries . . .	62.6	63.6	51.4
General industrial machinery			
equipment and parts . . .	53.4	51.7	44.0
Electrical machinery, apparatus			
etc. (excl. telecommunications			
and sound equipment) . . .	48.5	61.7	47.6
Road vehicles and parts* . . .	113.3	137.8	62.2
Miscellaneous manufactured			
articles.	97.5	103.3	105.0
Total (incl. others)	1,776.2	2,093.9	1,687.6

* Data on parts exclude tyres, engines and electrical parts.

Exports f.o.b.	1999	2000	2001
Food and live animals . . .	67.0	65.8	65.3
Vegetables and fruit . . .	37.4	30.5	30.1
Beverages and tobacco . . .	159.9	129.4	121.5
Beverages	46.9	44.3	46.5
Tobacco and tobacco manufactures	113.0	85.1	75.0
Crude materials (inedible)			
except fuels	50.8	49.0	37.4
Chemicals and related			
products	55.1	59.8	60.4
Basic manufactures . . .	354.2	487.3	372.2
Textile yarn, fabrics, etc. . . .	40.4	36.9	37.2
Iron and steel	182.4	289.4	195.4
Non-ferrous metals	73.5	90.4	73.4
Machinery and transport			
equipment	83.1	83.2	76.0
Electrical machinery, apparatus			
etc. (excl. telecommunications			
and sound equipment) . .	45.4	46.5	46.4
Miscellaneous manufactured			
articles	372.3	378.2	374.2
Clothing and accessories (excl.			
footwear)	320.3	317.9	319.4
Footwear	34.1	38.4	36.9
Total (incl. others)	1,191.3	1,322.6	1,155.1

PRINCIPAL TRADING PARTNERS
(US $ million)

Imports c.i.f.	1999	2000	2001
Argentina	3.3	8.0	7.5
Austria	44.5	41.7	43.9
Bulgaria	91.6	97.6	103.4
Croatia	62.2	57.9	46.4
France	40.4	38.6	30.3
Germany	245.8	253.3	213.4
Greece	164.5	201.6	184.4
Hungary	20.0	31.4	17.5
Italy	92.7	111.1	107.7
Japan	17.9	22.0	16.7
Netherlands	39.5	45.3	45.8
Poland	22.6	20.9	15.2
Russia	91.2	191.9	139.3
Slovenia	156.7	144.2	118.9
Sweden	25.1	31.7	18.8
Switzerland-Liechtenstein . . .	22.7	28.2	24.0
Turkey	53.7	52.4	46.4
Ukraine	114.8	205.8	86.0
United Kingdom	33.6	32.0	26.2
USA	54.7	83.1	51.5
Yugoslavia	183.9	190.4	157.2
Total (incl. others)	1,776.2	2,093.9	1,687.6

Exports f.o.b.	1999	2000	2001
Albania	15.0	12.8	10.1
Belgium	17.2	23.9	7.4
Bosnia and Herzegovina . . .	19.4	23.2	16.2
Bulgaria	26.1	26.9	20.7
Croatia	49.0	47.7	58.4
Cyprus	15.4	20.9	1.6
France	12.7	14.9	16.0
Germany	254.3	257.5	237.5
Greece	85.9	84.1	101.4
Italy	77.6	90.8	88.7
Netherlands	40.5	36.0	45.3
Russia	15.1	10.4	13.9
Slovenia	34.0	26.4	20.9
Spain	8.8	13.2	21.4
Switzerland-Liechtenstein . . .	23.0	35.7	40.5
United Kingdom	27.5	27.2	26.6
USA	136.1	165.7	99.7
Yugoslavia	254.5	335.1	266.8
Total (incl. others)	1,191.3	1,322.6	1,687.6

Transport

RAILWAYS
(traffic)

	1999	2000	2001
Passenger journeys ('000) . . .	1,662	1,862	1,344
Passenger-km (million)	150	176	133
Freight carried ('000 metric tons).	2,166	3,231	2,799
Freight net ton-km (million) . .	380	527	462

ROAD TRAFFIC
(motor vehicles in use at 31 December)

	1999	2000	2001
Motorcycles	3,506	3,729	4,483
Passenger cars	289,860	299,588	309,562
Buses	2,479	2,498	2,620
Commercial vehicles	20,011	20,763	21,727
Special vehicles	7,610	8,552	9,554
Tractors and working vehicles . .	1,777	1,417	1,560

INLAND WATERS
(lake transport)

	1998	1999	2000
Passengers carried ('000) . . .	15.0	9.5	10.3
Passenger-km ('000)	375	265	321

CIVIL AVIATION
(traffic on scheduled services)

	1997	1998	1999
Kilometres flown (million) . . .	5	5	7
Passengers carried ('000) . . .	250	295	488
Passenger-kilometres (million) . .	285	328	599
Total ton-kilometres (million) . .	27	31	57

Source: UN, *Statistical Yearbook*.

Tourism

TOURISTS BY COUNTRY OF ORIGIN*

	1999	2000	2001
Albania	21,248	24,747	6,419
Bulgaria	18,770	27,623	8,484
Croatia	3,260	4,651	2,609
France	4,735	4,768	2,313
Germany	12,370	10,349	4,860
Greece	10,152	21,304	10,637
Italy	6,259	4,410	2,511
Netherlands	5,953	6,809	1,564
Russia	3,366	3,078	1,647
Slovenia	4,606	5,288	2,658
Turkey	5,038	6,700	3,101
Ukraine	622	6,347	3,405
United Kingdom	9,126	6,693	4,357
USA	13,900	15,312	7,099
Yugoslavia	29,346	35,522	16,429
Total (incl. others)	180,788	224,016	98,946

* Figures refer to arrivals from abroad at accommodation establishments.

Tourism receipts (US $ million): 15 in 1998; 40 in 1999; 37 (preliminary) in 2000 (Source: World Tourism Organization).

Communications Media

	1998	1999	2000
Television receivers ('000 in use) .	500	550	570
Telephones ('000 main lines in use)	439.2	471.0	516.0
Mobile cellular telephones ('000 subscribers).	30.1	47.7	115.7
Internet users ('000)	20.0	30.0	n.a.
Book production: titles*	738	733	727
Book production: copies ('000)*. .	2,101	1,858	968
Daily newspapers: titles. . .	4	5	6
Daily newspapers: average circulation ('000 copies) . .	32,060	32,988	32,640
Non-daily newspapers: titles . .	26	29	33
Non-daily newspapers: average circulation ('000 copies) . . .	2,818	3,139	2,619

* Including pamphlets.

2001: Telephones ('000 main lines in use) 538.5; Mobile cellular telephones ('000 subscribers) 223.3; Internet users ('000) 70.0.

Radio receivers ('000 in use): 410 in 1997.

Facsimile machines (number in use): 3,000 in 1997.

Sources: mainly International Telecommunication Union; UNESCO, *Statistical Yearbook* and UN, *Statistical Yearbook*.

Education

(2000/01, unless otherwise indicated)

	Institutions	Teachers	Students
Primary	1,010	13,329	246,490
Secondary	95	5,467	90,990
University level*	29	1,501	43,587
Other higher*	1	60	1,123

* 2001/02 figures.

Adult literacy rate (latest available): Males 97%; Females 91% (Source: UNICEF, *The State of the World's Children*).

Directory

The Constitution

The Constitution of the former Yugoslav republic of Macedonia was promulgated on 17 November 1991. The September 1995 interim agreement with Greece required guarantees that the Macedonian Constitution enshrined or implied no claim to territory beyond the country's existing borders. Some amendment of the 1991 document was thus necessitated. Following the framework agreement between the principal Macedonian and ethnic Albanian parties, reached in August 2001 (see Recent History), the Constitution was revised on 16 November to include 15 principal amendments. The following is a summary of the main provisions of the Constitution, which describes the country as the Republic of Macedonia:

GENERAL PROVISIONS

The Republic of Macedonia is a sovereign, independent, democratic state, where sovereignty derives from democratically elected citizens, referendums and other forms of expression. The citizens of the Republic of Macedonia are defined as the Macedonian people, as well as citizens living within its borders who are, *inter alia*, ethnic Albanians, ethnic Turks, ethnic Serbs and Vlach. The fundamental values defined by the Constitution are: basic human rights, free expression of nationality, the rule of law, a policy of pluralism and the free market, local self-government, entrepreneurship, social justice and solidarity, and respect for international law. State power is divided into legislative, executive and judicial power.

BASIC RIGHTS

The following rights and freedoms are guaranteed and protected in the Republic: the right to life, the inviolability of each person's physical and moral integrity, the right to freedom of speech, public appearance, public information, belief, conscience and religion, and the freedom to organize and belong to a trade union or a political party. All forms of communication and personal data are secret, and the home is inviolable.

The Macedonian language is the official language in use throughout the Republic of Macedonia. Any other language spoken by at least 20% of the population (such as Albanian) is also an official language. The official personal documentation of citizens speaking an official language other than Macedonian will also be issued in that language.

Military and semi-military associations, which do not belong to the Armed Forces of the Republic, are prohibited.

Any citizen who has reached the age of 18 years has the right to vote and to be elected to organs of government. The right to vote is equal, general and direct, and is realized in free elections by secret ballot. The proportional representation of each community must be assured in the public services and in all areas of public life. Citizens enjoy equal freedoms and rights without distinction as to sex, race, colour, national and social origin, political and religious conviction, material and social position. All religious creeds are separate from the State and are equal under the law. They are identified, *inter alia*, as the Macedonian Orthodox Church, the Islamic Community of Macedonia, the Roman Catholic Church, the Evangelic Methodist Church and the Jewish Community. The members of all such communities are free to establish schools and other charitable institutions in the fields of culture, art and education.

GOVERNMENT

Legislature

Legislative power resides with the Sobranje (assembly), which consists of between 120 and 140 deputies elected for four years. The Sobranje adopts and amends the Constitution, enacts laws and gives interpretations thereof, adopts the budget of the Republic, decides on war and peace, chooses the Government, elects judges and releases them from duty. The Sobranje may decide, by a majority vote, to call a referendum on issues within its competence. A decision is adopted at a referendum if the majority of voters taking part in the ballot votes in favour of it and if more than one-half of the electorate participates in the vote. The Sobranje forms a Council for Inter-Ethnic Relations, comprising seven representatives from each of the ethnic Macedonian and Albanian communities, and five representatives of other nationalities living in the state. Parliamentary legislation on issues of culture and identity, particularly in the areas of language and education, can only be adopted if a majority of the deputies representing these communities votes in favour, in addition to the overall majority. Three of the nine judges of the Constitutional Court and three of the seven members of the Republican Judicial Council must also be elected by a double majority vote.

President

The President of the Republic represents the country and is responsible for ensuring respect for the Constitution and laws. He is Commander of the Armed Forces and appoints the Prime Minister. He appoints three members of the Security Council of the Republic (of which he is President) and ensures that the Council reflects the composition of the country's population.

Ministers

Executive power in the Republic resides with the Prime Minister and Ministers, who are not permitted concurrently to be deputies in the Sobranje. The Ministers are elected by the majority vote of all the deputies in the Sobranje. The Ministers implement laws and the state budget, and are responsible for foreign and diplomatic relations.

Judiciary

Judicial power is vested in the courts, and is autonomous and independent. The Supreme Court is the highest court. The election and dismissal of judges is proposed by the Republican Judicial Council.

Local Government

Legislation at local and municipal level is adopted by a two-thirds' majority vote of the total number of representatives. Legislation regulating such areas as local finance, elections and municipal boundaries must be adopted by a majority of the representatives representing the minority communities, as well as by an overall majority. In units of local self-government, citizens participate in decision-making on issues of local relevance directly, and through representatives.

OTHER PROVISIONS

The Sobranje elects an Ombudsman to ensure that constitutional rights are upheld, particularly the principles of non-discrimination and fair representation of the respective communities in public life. Revision of the Constitution must be approved by a two-thirds' majority in the Sobranje. Certain articles, such as the Preamble and those relating to local councils and minority rights, also require a majority of the vote by deputies from the minority communities.

The Government

President of the Republic: BORIS TRAJKOVSKI (inaugurated 15 December 1999).

GOVERNMENT
(April 2003)

A coalition of the Social Democratic Alliance of Macedonia (SDAM), the Liberal-Democratic Party (LDP) and the Democratic Union for Integration (DUI).

Prime Minister: BRANKO CRVENKOVSKI (SDAM).

Deputy Prime Ministers and Minister of Finance: PETAR GOSEV (LDP).

Deputy Prime Minister, with responsibility for Political Systems: MUSA XHAFERI (DUI).

Deputy Prime Minister, with responsibility for European Integration: RADMILA SEKERINSKA (SDAM).

Minister of Defence: VLADO BUCHKOVSKI (SDAM).

Minister of Internal Affairs: HARI KOSTOVI (SDAM).

Minister of Justice: ISMAIL DARDHISHTA (DUI).

Minister of Foreign Affairs: ILINKA MITREVA (SDAM).

Minister of the Economy: ILIJA FILIPOVSKI (SDAM).

Minister of Transport and Communications: MILAIM AJDINI (DUI).

Minister of Agriculture, Forestry and Water Resources: SLAVKO PETROV (LDP).

Minister of Labour and Social Welfare: JOVAN MANASIEVSKI (LDP).

Minister of Education and Science: AZIZ POLLOZHANI (DUI).

Minister of Culture: BLAGOJA STEFANOVSKI (SDAM).

Minister of Health: REXHEP SELMANI (DUI).

Minister of Local Self-Government: ALEKSANDAR GESTAKOVSKI (SDAM).

Minister of the Environment and Urban Planning: LJUBOMIR JANEVI (SDAM).

Minister without Portfolio: VLADO POPOVSKI (LDP).

MINISTRIES

Office of the President: 1000 Skopje, 11 Oktomvri bb; tel. (2) 113318; fax (2) 112147; internet www.president.gov.mk.

Office of the Prime Minister: 1000 Skopje, Ilindenska bb; tel. (2) 115389; fax (2) 112561; e-mail office@primeminister.gov.mk; internet www.primeminister.gov.mk.

Ministry of Agriculture, Forestry and Water Resources: 1000 Skopje, Leninova 2; tel. (2) 134477; fax (2) 239429.

Ministry of Culture: 1000 Skopje, Ilindenska bb; tel. (2) 118022; fax (2) 127112; internet www.gov.mk/kultura.

Ministry of Defence: 1000 Skopje, Orce Nikolov bb; tel. and fax (2) 230928; e-mail info@morm.gov.mk; internet www.morm.gov.mk.

Ministry of the Economy: 1000 Skopje, Bote Bocevski 9; tel. (2) 113705; fax (2) 111541; e-mail ms@mt.net.mk; internet www.ms.gov.mk.

Ministry of Education and Science: 1000 Skopje, Dimitrija Čupovski 9; tel. (2) 117836; fax (2) 118414; e-mail mofk@mofk.gov.mk; internet www.mofk.gov.mk.

Ministry of the Environment and Urban Planning: 1000 Skopje, ul. Drezdenska 52; tel. (2) 366595; fax (2) 366931; e-mail info@moe.gov.mk; internet www.moe.gov.mk.

Ministry of Finance: 1000 Skopje, Dame Gruev 14; tel. (2) 117288; fax (2) 117280; internet www.finance.gov.mk.

Ministry of Foreign Affairs: 1000 Skopje, Dame Gruev 6; tel. (2) 115266; fax (2) 115790; e-mail mailmnr@mnr.gov.mk; internet www.mnr.gov.mk.

Ministry of Health: 1000 Skopje, Vodnjanska bb; tel. (2) 147147; fax (2) 113014; internet www.zdravstvo.com.mk.

Ministry of Internal Affairs: 1000 Skopje, Dimitar Mirchev bb; tel. (2) 117222; fax (2) 112468.

Ministry of Justice: 1000 Skopje, Dimitrija Čupovski 9; tel. (2) 117277; fax (2) 226975; internet www.covekovi-prava.gov.mk.

Ministry of Labour and Social Welfare: 1000 Skopje, Dame Gruev 14; tel. (2) 117787; fax (2) 118242; e-mail mtsp@mt.net.mk; internet www.mtsp.gov.mk.

Ministry of Local Self-Government: 1000 Skopje, Dimitrija Čupovski 9; tel. (2) 117288; fax (2) 211764.

Ministry of Sports and Youth: 1000 Skopje, Jurij Gagarin 15; tel. (2) 393408; fax (2) 384472.

Ministry of Transport and Communications: 1000 Skopje, plostad Crvena skopska opstina 4; tel. (2) 126228; fax (2) 123292.

President and Legislature

PRESIDENT

Presidential Election, First Ballot, 31 October 1999

Candidate	% of votes
Tito Petkovski (SDAM)	33.2
Boris Trajkovski (IMRO—DPMNU)*	20.6
Vasil Tupurkovski (DA)*	16.0
Muharem Nexipi (DPA)*	14.8
Stojan Andov (LDP)	11.2
Muhamet Halili (PDP)	4.2
Total	100.0†

* The IMRO—DPMNU, the DPA and the DA constituted the 'For Changes' alliance.
† Including invalid and spoilt votes.

Second Ballot, 14 November 1999*

Candidate	% of votes†
Boris Trajkovski (IMRO—DPMNU)	52.9
Tito Petkovski (SDAM)	45.9
Total	100.0

* A further partial round was conducted on 5 December 1999.
† Including invalid and spoilt votes.

SOBRANJE
(Assembly)

President: NIKOLA POPOVSKI, 1000 Skopje, 11 Oktomvri bb; tel. (2) 112255; fax (2) 237947; e-mail sgjorgiøsembly.gov.mk; internet www.assembly.gov.mk/sobranje.

General Election, 15 September 2002*

Party	Votes	% of votes	Seats
Together for Macedonia†	494,744	40.46	60
IMRO—DPMNU‡	298,404	24.41	33
DUI	114,913	11.85	16
DPA	63,695	5.21	7
PDP	28,397	2.32	2
NDP	26,237	2.15	1
SPM	25,976	2.12	1
Others	140,345	11.48	—
Total	1,222,711	100.00	120

* Of the 120 members of the Assembly, 85 were elected in single-member constituencies. The remaining 35 were elected by a national system of proportional representation, in which voters chose from lists of candidates submitted by individual parties or by groups of parties.
† Electoral coalition of 10 parties, led by the SDAM.
‡ The IMRO—DPMNU contested the elections in alliance with the LPM.

Political Organizations

Democratic Alliance: Skopje; f. 2000; Chair. ASLLAN SELMANI.

Democratic Alliance of Serbs in Macedonia (Demokratski Savez Srba u Makedoniji—DSSM): Skopje; f. 1994; Chair. BORIVOJE RISTIĆ.

Democratic Alternative (DA) (Demokratska Alternativa): c/o Sobranje, 1000 Skopje, 11 Oktomvri bb; tel. (2) 362713; fax (2) 363089; internet www.da.org.mk; f. 1998; formed an electoral alliance with the IMRO—DPMNU; Chair. VASIL TUPURKOVSKI.

Democratic League—Liberal Party: Skopje, Gale Hristov k. 3-6; tel. (2) 263523; Leader XHEMIL IDRIZI.

Democratic Muslim Party: Skopje; f. 2001; Leader TEFIK KADRI.

Democratic Party of Albanians (DPA): Tetovo, Maršal Tito 2; tel. (44) 31534; f. July 1997 by a merger of the Party of Democratic Prosperity of Albanians in Macedonia (f. 1994) and the National Democratic Party (f. 1990); officially registered in July 2002; Chair. ARBEN XHAFERI.

Democratic Party of Serbs in Macedonia (DPSM): Skopje, 27 Mart 11; tel. (2) 254274; f. 1996; Pres. DRAGISA MILETIĆ.

Democratic Party of Turks in Macedonia (DPTM) (Demokratska Partija na Turcite va Makedonija): Skopje, bul. Krste Misirkova 67; tel. (2) 114696; Leader ERDOGAN SARACH.

Democratic Party of Yugoslavs of Macedonia (DPYM) (Demokratska Partija Jugoslovena Makedonije—DPJM): Skopje; f. 1993; Chair. ZIVKO LEKOSKI; Gen. Sec. BOGDAN MICKOSKI.

Democratic Union for Integration (DUI) (Demokratska Unija za Integracija): Tetovo; f. 2002; ethnic Albanian, dominated by former mems of rebel National Liberation Army; Chair. ALI AHMETI.

Front for Albanian National Unification (FANU): emerged in 2003 as political wing of rebel Albanian National Army; supports creation of 'greater Albania'; Sec.-Gen. ALBAN VJOSA.

Internal Macedonian Revolutionary Organization ('Real') ('Real' IMRO) (Vnatrešno-Makedonska Revolucionerna Organizacija—VMRO): Skopje; f. 2000 by fmr mems of the IMRO—DPMNU; centre-right; Chair. BORIS ZMEJKOVSKI.

Internal Macedonian Revolutionary Organization—Democratic Party for Macedonian National Unity (IMRO—DPMNU) (Vnatrešno-Makedonska Revolucionerna Organizacija—Demokratska Partija za Makedonsko Nacionalno Edinstvo—VMRO—DPMNE): 1000 Skopje, Petar Drapshin br. 36; tel. (2) 111441; fax (2) 211586; e-mail info@vmro-dpmne.org.mk; internet www.vmro-dpmne.org.mk; nationalist; formed an electoral alliance with the Democratic Alternative; Pres. LJUBČO GEORGIEVSKI.

Liberal-Democratic Party (LDP) (Liberalno-Demokratska Partija): Skopje, Ilindenska bb; tel. and fax (2) 116106; internet www.ldp.org.mk; f. 1996 by a merger of the Liberal Party and the Democratic Party; Leader RISTO GUSTEROV.

Liberal Party of Macedonia (LPM) (Liberalna Partija na Makedonije): Skopje; Leader STOJAN ANDOV.

Macedonian Democratic Party: Tetovo, Bazaar 3; tel. (44) 20826; fax (44) 24860; Leader TOMISLAV STOJANOVSKI.

Movement for all-Macedonian Action (MAAK)—Conservative Party: Skopje, Maksim Gorki 18/111; tel. (2) 116540; f. 1996; right-wing nationalist; Leader STRASO ANGELOVSKI.

National Democratic Party (NDP): Skopje; f. 2001; ethnic Albanian; Leader KASTRIOT HAXLEXHA.

Party of Democratic Action—Islamic Way (Stranka Demokratske Akcije—Islamski Put): Tetovo, Ilindenska 191; tel. (44) 32113; Leader MAZLAM KENAN.

Party for Democratic Prosperity (PDP) (Partija za Demokratski Prosperitet): Tetovo, Karaorman 62; tel. (44) 25709; f. 1990; split 1994; predominantly ethnic Albanian and Muslim party; Chair. ABDURAHMAN ALITI; Sec.-Gen. NASER ZYBERI.

Party for the Full Emancipation of Romanies in Macedonia (Demokratska Progresivna Partija na Romite od Makedonija): Skopje, Shuto Orizari bb; tel. (2) 612726; Leader FAIK ABDIĆ.

Republican Party of Albanians: Skopje; f. May 2002; Leader MEVLAN TAHIRI.

Social Democratic Alliance of Macedonia (SDAM) (Socijaldemokratski Sojuz na Makedonije—SDSM): 1000 Skopje, Bihačka 8; tel. (2) 135380; fax (2) 120462; e-mail contact@sdsm.org.mk; internet www.sdsm.org.mk; f. 1943; name changed from League of Communists of Macedonia—Party of Democratic Reform in 1991; led alliance, Together for Macedonia, which was elected to govt in Sept. 2002; Chair. BRANKO CRVENKOVSKI; Gen. Sec. GEORGI SPASOV.

Social Democratic Party of Macedonia (Socijaldemokratska Partija na Makedonije): Skopje, bul. Kliment Ohridski 54; tel. and fax (2) 223681; Leader BRANKO JANEVSKI.

Socialist Party of Macedonia (SPM) (Socijalistiska Partija na Makedonije): 1000 Skopje, 11 Oktomvri 17; tel. (2) 228015; fax (2) 220075; f. 1990; left-wing; Chair. LJUBISAV IVANOV; Vice-Chair. BLAGOJE FILIPOVSKI.

Union of Ethnic Croats: Skopje; f. 1996; Pres. MARIJA DAMJANOVSKA.

Union of Roma in Macedonia (Sojuz na Romite od Makedonija): Skopje.

Diplomatic Representation

EMBASSIES IN THE FORMER YUGOSLAV REPUBLIC OF MACEDONIA

Albania: 1000 Skopje, Hristijan Todorovski-Karposh 94; tel. (2) 614636; fax (2) 614200; e-mail ambshquip@lotus.mpt.com.mk; Ambassador VLADIMIR PRELJA.

Austria: 1000 Skopje, Vasil Stefanovski 7; tel. (2) 109550; fax (2) 130237; e-mail austramb@unet.com.mk; Ambassador HARALD W. KOTSCHY.

Bulgaria: 1000 Skopje, Zlatko Shnaider 3; tel. (2) 229444; fax (2) 116139; e-mail bgemb@unet.com.mk; Ambassador ALEKSANDAR YORDANOV.

Canada: 1000 Skopje, Mitropolit Teodosie Gologanov 104, POB 68; tel. (2) 125228; fax (2) 122681; e-mail dfaitmk@unet.com.mk; Ambassador RAPHAEL GIRARD.

China, People's Republic: 1000 Skopje; tel. (2) 134392; fax (2) 133405; Ambassador ZHANG WANXUE.

Croatia: 1000 Skopje, Mitropolit Teodosij Gologanov 59; tel. (2) 127350; fax (2) 127417; e-mail velhrskp@mpt.com.mk; Ambassador VITOMIR MIRO LASIĆ.

France: 1000 Skopje, Salvador Aljende 73; tel. (2) 118749; fax (2) 117760; e-mail franamba@nic.mpt.com.mk; Ambassador JEAN-FRANÇOIS TERRAL.

Germany: 1000 Skopje, Dimitrija Čupovski 26; tel. (2) 110507; fax (2) 117713; e-mail dtboskop@unet.com.mk; internet www.deutschebotschaft-skopje.com.mk; Ambassador Dr IRENE HINRICHSEN.

Hungary: 1000 Skopje, Mirka Ginova 27; tel. (2) 363423; fax (2) 363070; Ambassador JÓZSEF SZÁSZ.

Iran: 1000 Skopje, Gjorgji Peskov 6; tel. (2) 118020; fax (2) 118502; e-mail iri-emb@unet.cpm.mk; Chargé d'affaires a.i. MOSLEM SABERI.

Italy: 1000 Skopje, 8 Udarna brig. 22; tel. (2) 117430; fax (2) 117087; internet www.ambasciata.org.mk; Ambassador Dr ANTONIO TARELLI.

Netherlands: 1000 Skopje, Leninova 69–71; tel. (2) 129319; fax (2) 129309; Ambassador JOHANNES HENDRICUS MARIA WOLFS.

Norway: 1000 Skopje, Mitropolit Teodosie Gologanov 59/2A; tel. (2) 129165; fax (2) 111138; Chargé d'affaires a.i. VIBEKE LILLOE.

Poland: 1000 Skopje, Djuro Djakovic 50; tel. and fax (2) 119744; e-mail ambpol@unet.com.mk; Chargé d'affaires a.i. ANDRZEJ DOBRZYŃSKI.

Romania: 1000 Skopje, Londonska 11A; tel. (2) 370144; fax (2) 361130; e-mail romanamb@rsc.com.mk; Chargé d'affaires NICOLAE MARES.

Russia: 1000 Skopje, Pirinska 44; tel. (2) 117160; fax (2) 117808; e-mail rusembas@mol.com.mk; f. 1994; Ambassador AGARON ASATUR.

Serbia and Montenegro: 1000 Skopje, Pitu Guli 8; tel. (2) 129298; fax (2) 129427; Ambassador BISERKA MATIĆ SPASOJEVIĆ.

Slovenia: 1000 Skopje, Vodnjanska 42; tel. (2) 178730; fax (2) 176631; Ambassador MITJA ŠTRUKELJ.

Switzerland: Skopje 1000, Naroden Front 19; tel. (2) 128300; fax (2) 116205; Ambassador STEFAN MELLEN.

Turkey: 1000 Skopje, Slavej Planina bb; tel. (2) 113270; fax (2) 117024; e-mail turkish@mol.com.mk; Ambassador MEHMET TASER.

United Kingdom: 1000 Skopje, Dimitrija Čupovski 26, 4th Floor; tel. (2) 299299; fax (2) 299236; e-mail beskopje@mt.net.com; internet www.britishembassy.org.mk; Ambassador GEORGE EDGAR.

USA: 1000 Skopje, Ilindenska bb; tel. (2) 116180; fax (2) 118105; e-mail usis@usemb-skopje.mpt.com.mk; internet usembassy.mpt .com.mk; Ambassador LAWRENCE BUTLER.

Judicial System

The FYRM has 27 Courts of First Instance and three Courts of Appeal. The Republican Judicial Council, which comprises seven members elected by the Sobranje for a term of six years, proposes the election or dismissal of judges to the Sobranje. The Constitutional Court, comprising nine judges elected by the Sobranje with a mandate of nine years, is responsible for the protection of constitutional and legal rights, and ensures that there is no conflict in the exercise of legislative, executive and judicial powers. The Supreme Court is the highest court in the country, and guarantees the equal administration of legislation by all courts

Constitutional Court of the Republic of Macedonia: 1000 Skopje, 12 Udarna brig. 2; tel. (2) 165153; fax (2) 119355; e-mail usud@usud.gov.mk; Pres. Dr TODOR DŽUNOV.

Supreme Court: 1000 Skopje, Krste Misirkova bb; tel. (2) 234064; fax (2) 237538; Pres. SIMEON GELEVSKI.

Republican Judicial Council: 1000 Skopje, Lazar Lichenoski 13; tel. (2) 213084; fax (2) 116458; Pres. TIHOMIR VELKOVSKI.

Office of the Public Prosecutor: 1000 Skopje, Krste Misirkova bb; tel. (2) 229314; Public Prosecutor ALEKSANDR PRCEVSKI.

Religion

Most ethnic Macedonians are adherents of the Eastern Orthodox Church, and since 1967 there has been an autocephalous Macedonian Orthodox Church. However, the Serbian Orthodox Church refuses to recognize it, and has persuaded the Ecumenical Patriarch and other Orthodox Churches not to do so either. There are some adherents of other Orthodox rites in the country. Those Macedonian (and Bulgarian) Slavs who converted to Islam during the Ottoman era are known as Pomaks and are included as an ethnic group of Muslims. The substantial Albanian population is mostly Muslim (mainly Sunni, but some adherents of a Dervish sect); there are a few Roman Catholic Christians and a small Jewish community.

CHRISTIANITY

Macedonian Orthodox Church: Skopje, Betovenova bb, POB 69; tel. (2) 230697; fax (2) 230685; Metropolitan See of Ohrid revived in 1958; autocephaly declared 1967; 1.5m. mems; comprises seven bishoprics in Macedonia and three abroad; Head of Church and Archbishop of Ohrid and Macedonia Metropolitan Archbishop MIHAIL RIĆ (of Skopje).

The Roman Catholic Church

The diocese of Skopje, suffragan to the archdiocese of Vrhbosna (Bosnia and Herzegovina), covers most of the FYRM. The Bishop is also Apostolic Exarch for Catholics of the Byzantine Rite in the FYRM. At 31 December 2000 there were an estimated 4,000 adherents of the Latin Rite in the diocese, and the country had 6,320 adherents of the Byzantine Rite.

Bishop of Skopje: Rt Rev. JOAKIM HERBUT, Biskupski Ordinarijat, 1000 Skopje, Risto Šiškov 31; tel. and fax (2) 164123.

ISLAM

Islamic Community of Macedonia: Skopje, Chairska 52; tel. (2) 117530; fax (2) 117883; e-mail bim@bim.org.mk; internet www.bim .org.mk; formerly headquarters of the Skopje Region, one of the four

administrative divisions of the Yugoslav Muslims; Leader Hadži ARIF EMINI.

JUDAISM

Jewish Community: 1000 Skopje, Borka Taleski 24.

The Press

In 2000 a total of 39 newspapers and 116 magazines were published in the FYRM.

PRINCIPAL DAILY NEWSPAPERS

Bechuk: 1000 Skopje, MOST Ltd, Dame Gruev 5; tel. (2) 117377; fax (2) 118638; e-mail vesnik@utrinski.com.mk; internet www.int .utrinskivesnik.com.mk; Dir EROL RIZAOV; Editor-in-Chief BRANKO TRICKOVSKI.

Denes: 1000 Skopje, M.°H. Jasmin 50; tel. (2) 110239; fax (2) 110150; e-mail denes@unet.com.mk; internet www.denes.com.mk; Dir GEORGI AJANOVSKI; Editor NIK DENES.

Dnevnik: 1000 Skopje, Teodosij Gologanov 28; tel. (2) 297555; fax (2) 297554; e-mail dnevnik@dnevnik.com.mk; internet www .dnevnik.com.mk; independent; Editor-in-Chief BRANKO GEROSKI.

Flaka e vëllazërimit (Flame of Brotherhood): 1000 Skopje, Mito Hadživasilev bb; tel. (2) 112025; fax (2) 224829; f. 1945; relaunched 1994; Albanian-language newspaper; Editor-in-Chief ABDULHADI ZUL-FIQARI; circ. 4,000.

Nova Makedonija: 1000 Skopje, Mito Hadživasilev bb; tel. (2) 237455; fax (2) 118238; internet www.novamakedonija.com.mk; f. 1944; morning; in Macedonian; Editor-in-Chief GEORGI AJANOVSKI; circ. 25,000.

Večer: 1000 Skopje, Mito Hadživasilev bb; tel. (2) 111537; fax (2) 238327; internet www.vecer.com.mk; f. 1963; evening; in Macedonian; Editor-in-Chief STOJAN NASEV; circ. 29,200.

PERIODICALS

Delo: Skopje, Petar Drapshin 26; tel. (2) 231949; fax (2) 115748; f. 1993; weekly; nationalist; Editor-in-Chief BRATISLAV TASKOVSKI.

Fokus: Skopje, Zheležniča 53; tel. (2) 111327; fax (2) 111685; weekly; independent; Editor-in-Chief NIKOLA MLADENOV.

Macedonian Times: 1000 Skopje, Vasil Gorgov 39; tel. and fax (2) 121182; e-mail mian@mian.com.mk; internet www.unet.com.mk/ mian; f. 1994; monthly; politics and current affairs; English; Editor-in-Chief JOVAN PAVLOSKI.

Puls: 1000 Skopje, Mito Hadživasilev bb; tel. (2) 117124; fax (2) 118024; weekly; Editor-in-Chief VASIL MICKOVSKI.

Roma Times: Skopje; e-mail mail@dostae.net.mk; internet www .dostae.net.mk/mk/press_mk_roma.htm; f. 2001; 3 a week; circ. 3,000.

Sport Magazine: 1000 Skopje, Mito Hadživasilev Jasmin bb; tel. and fax (2) 116254; e-mail lav@unet.com.mk; f. 1991; weekly; circ. 6,000.

Trudbenik: Skopje, Udarna brigada 12; weekly; organ of Macedonian Trade Unions; Editor SIMO IVANOVSKI.

NEWS AGENCIES

Macedonian Information Agency: 1000 Skopje, Bojmija K/2; tel. (2) 461600; fax (2) 464048; e-mail mia@mia.com.mk; internet www .mia.com.mk; f. 1992; 24-hr news service in Macedonian, Albanian and English; Exec. Dir ZIVKO GEORGIEVSKI.

Makfax: 1000 Skopje, 11 Oktomvri 36/3, POB 738; tel. (2) 110125; fax (2) 1101184; e-mail makfax@unet.com.mk; internet www .makfax.com.mk; f. 1993; independent; provides daily regional news service; Macedonian, Albanian and English.

PRESS ASSOCIATION

Journalists' Association of Macedonia: 1000 Skopje, Gradskizid 13, POB 498; tel. and fax (2) 116447; Pres. STOJAN NASEV.

Publishers

Detska radost/Nova Makedonija: 1000 Skopje, Mito Hadživasilev Jasmin bb; tel. (2) 213059; fax (2) 225830; f. 1944; children's books; Dir KIRIL DONEV.

Kultura: 1000 Skopje, Sv. Kliment Ohridski 68A; tel. (2) 111332; fax (2) 228608; e-mail ipkultura@simt.com.mk; f. 1945; history, philosophy, art, poetry, children's literature and fiction; in Macedonian; Dir DIMITAR BAŠEVSKI.

Kulturen Život: 1000 Skopje, Ruzveltova 6; tel. (2) 239134; f. 1971; Editor LJUBICA ARSOVSKA.

Makedonska kniga: 1000 Skopje, 11 Oktomvri; tel. (2) 224055; fax (2) 236951; f. 1947; arts, non-fiction, novels, children's books; Dir SANDE STOJČEVSKI.

Matica Makedonska: 1000 Skopje, ul. Maršal Tito br. 43/1-6; tel. (2) 230358; fax (2) 229244; f. 1991; Dir RADE SILJAN.

Metaforum: 1000 Skopje, Goce Delčev 6; tel. (2) 114890; fax (2) 115634; f. 1993; Dir RUŽICA BILKO.

Misla: 1000 Skopje, Partizanski odredi 1; tel. (2) 221844; fax (2) 118439; f. 1966; modern and classic Macedonian and translated literature; Pres. ZLATA BUNTESLEA.

Naša kniga: 1000 Skopje, Maksim Gorki 21, POB 132; tel. (2) 228066; fax (2) 116872; f. 1948; Dir STOJAN LEKOVSKI.

Nova Makedonija: 1000 Skopje, Mito Hadživasilev Jasmin bb; tel. (2) 116366; fax (2) 118238; newspapers, general publishing; Chief Exec. SLOBODAN CASULE; Editor-in-Chief NOVE CVETANOVSKI.

Prosvetno delo: 1000 Skopje, Dimitrija Čupovski 15; tel. (2) 117255; fax (2) 225434; f. 1945; works of domestic writers and textbooks in Macedonian for elementary, professional and high schools; fiction and scientific works; Dir Dr KRSTE ANGELOVSKI.

Tabernakul: 1000 Skopje, POB 251, Mihail Cokov; tel. and fax (2) 115329; e-mail tabervt@mol.com.mk; internet www.tabernakul .com; f. 1989; Dir CVETAN VRAŽIVIRSKI.

Radio and Television

TELECOMMUNICATIONS

Makedonski Telekomunikacii (MT): 1000 Skopje, Direkcija, Orce Nikolov bb; tel. (2) 141141; fax (2) 126244; e-mail info@mpt.com .mk; internet www.mt.com.mk; 51% of shares divested to the Matáv Hungarian Telecommunications Co in Jan. 2001; Chief Exec. DAN DONCEV.

BROADCASTING

Radio

Makedonska Radio-Televizija (MRT): 1000 Skopje, Goce Delčev bb; tel. (2) 236839; fax (2) 111821; e-mail info@mr.com.mk; internet www.mkrtv.com.mk; f. 1944; fmrly Radiotelevizija Skopje, name changed 1991; 6 radio services; broadcasts in Macedonian, Albanian, Turkish, Serb, Roma and Vlach; Dir-Gen. GORDANA SIOSIE; Dir of Radio ANTON SEREČI.

Antenna 5 Radio: 1000 Skopje, Tetovska 35; tel. (2) 111911; fax (2) 113281; e-mail mail@antenna5.com.mk; internet www.antenna5 .com.mk; 12 transmitters broadcast to 80% of the country.

Television

Makedonska Radio-Televizija (MRT): 1000 Skopje, Goce Delčev bb; tel. (2) 112200; fax (2) 111821; e-mail gstosic@unet.com.mk; internet www.mkrtv.com.mk; f. 1964; fmrly Radiotelevizija Skopje, name changed 1991; state broadcasting co; 3 television services; broadcasts in Macedonian, Albanian, Turkish, Serb, Roma and Vlach; Dir-Gen. GORDANA SIOSIE; Dir of Television LJUPCO TOZIJA.

A1 Television: 1000 Skopje, Pero Nakov bb; tel. (2) 551919; fax (2) 551970; e-mail altv@al.com.mk; internet www.al.com.mk.

SITEL Television: Skopje; tel. (2) 116566; fax (2) 114898; internet www.sitel.com.mk.

Finance

(cap. = capital; res = reserves; dep. = deposits; m. = million; amounts in new Macedonian denars, unless otherwise indicated; brs = branches)

BANKS

At the end of September 2001 there were 20 commercial banks in the FYRM; of these, the two largest banks (Stopanska Banka and Komercijalna Banka) accounted for more than one-half of the banking system assets and about two-thirds of the deposits. At that time a total of six banks had majority foreign shareholders. The privatization of the banking sector was completed in early 2000.

National Bank

Narodna Banka na Makedonija (National Bank of the Republic of Macedonia): 1000 Skopje, POB 401, Kompleks banki bb; tel. (2) 112177; fax (2) 113481; e-mail nbmdevre@nlc.mpt.com.mk; internet www.nbrm.gov.mk; central bank and bank of issue; total assets 112.1m. (Dec. 1999); Gov. LJUBE TRPEVSKI.

Selected Banks

Balkanska Banka: 1000 Skopje, Maksim Gorki 6; tel. (2) 286100; fax (2) 130448; e-mail balkbank@mt.net.mk; internet www.bbs.com .mk.

Eksport-Import Banka a.d.—Skopje: 91000 Skopje, DTC Paloma Bjanka, Dame Gruev 16; tel. (2) 133411; fax (2) 112744; e-mail info@ eximb.com.mk; internet www.eximb.com.mk; f. 1994; cap. 455.3m., res 178.6m., dep. 2,576.9m. (Dec. 1999); Pres. METODIJA SMILENSKI.

Izvozna I. Kreditna Banka a.d.: 1000 Skopje, Partizanski odredi 3, POB 421; tel. (2) 129147; fax (2) 122393; e-mail ikbanka@ikbanka .com.mk; f. 1993; cap. 671.0m., res 25.1m., dep. 822.4m. (Dec. 2000); Pres. PANCE MANCEVSKI.

Komercijalna Banka a.d.—Skopje: 1000 Skopje, Kej Dimitar Vlahov 4; tel. (2) 107107; fax (2) 111780; e-mail contact@kb.com.mk; internet www.kb.com.mk; f. 1955 as Komunalna Banka; name changed as above in 1991; cap. 1,925.7m., res 800.0m., dep. 12,242.3m. (Dec. 1999); Pres. TRAJKO DAVITKOVSKI; 33 brs.

Kreditna Banka a.d.—Skopje: 1000 Skopje, Dame Gruev 1, POB 564; tel. (2) 116433; fax (2) 116830; e-mail kreditnabank@mt.net.mk; f. 1993; cap. 185.8m., res 379.1m., dep. 612.7m. (Dec. 2000); Chair. SPYROS FILARETOS; 3 brs.

Makedonska Banka a.d.—Skopje: 91000 Skopje, Blok 12/2, bul. VMRO br. 3, POB 505; tel. (2) 117111; fax (2) 117191; e-mail info@ makbanka.com; internet www.makbanka.com; f. 1972; name changed in 1994; cap. 230.1m., res 519.8m., dep. 1,601.8m. (Dec. 1999); Pres. ALEKSANDAR NIKOLOVSKI.

Ohridska Banka a.d.—Ohrid: 6000 Ohrid, Makedonski Prosveti-teli 19; tel. (46) 206600; fax (46) 254130; internet www.ob.com.mk; cap. 636.8m., res 136.7m., dep. 2,929.4m. (Dec. 2002); Pres. NAUM HADZILEGA; Chair. VANGEL NIKOLOSKI.

Stopanska Banka a.d.—Bitola: 97000 Bitola, Dobrivoe Rado-savljević 21; tel. (47) 37048; fax (47) 223876; e-mail stbbt@mt.net .mk; f. 1948 as Komunalna Banka Bitola; name changed as above in 1995; cap. 664.1m., res 10.3m., dep. 1,169.4m. (Dec. 1998); Pres. VANGEL TORKOV.

Stopanska Banka a.d.—Skopje: 1000 Skopje, 11 Oktomvri 7; tel. (2) 295295; fax (2) 114503; e-mail sbank@stb.com.mk; internet www .stb.com.mk; f. 1944; cap. 3,602.2m., res 1.1m., dep. 18,116.7m. (Dec. 2002); privatized in April 2000; Chair. THEODOROS KARATZAS; 23 brs.

Teteks Bank a.d.: 1000 Skopje, POB 198; tel. (2) 119206; fax (2) 222370; e-mail tebank@mol.com.mk; f. 1993; cap. 272.9m., res 2.2m., dep. 784.4m. (Dec. 1995); Pres. GLIGORIE GOGOVSKI.

Tutunska Banka: 1000 Skopje, 12-ta Udarna brigada bb, POB 702; tel. (2) 105600; fax (2) 231114; e-mail tutban@mpt.com.mk; internet www.tb.com.mk; f. 1985; cap. 506.3m., res 811.2m., dep. 2,751.1m. (Dec. 2000); Pres. MARKO VOLJC.

STOCK EXCHANGE

Skopje Stock Exchange: 1000 Skopje, Mito Hadživasilev Jasmin 20; tel. (2) 122055; fax (2) 122069; e-mail mse@unet.com.mk; internet www.mse.org.mk; f. 1996; Chair. EVGENI ZOGRAFSKI.

INSURANCE

Stock Co for Insurance and Reinsurance 'Makedonija'—Skopje: 1000 Skopje, 11 Oktomvri 25; tel. (2) 115188; fax (2) 115374; internet www.qbe.com; f. 1945; stock company for insurance and reinsurance.

Trade and Industry

GOVERNMENT AGENCY

Agency of Information: 1000 Skopje, Guro Gakovik 64; tel. (2) 214723; fax (2) 115659; e-mail sinf@sinf.gov.mk; internet www.sinf .gov.mk; Dir VEBI BEXHETI.

Privatization Agency of the Republic of Macedonia: 1000 Skopje, Nikola Vapcarov 7, POB 410; tel. (2) 117564; fax (2) 126022; e-mail agency@mpa.org.mk; internet www.mpa.org.mk; Dir MARINA NAKEVA-KAVRAKOVA.

Securities and Exchange Commission: 1000 Skopje, Kuzman Josifovski Pitu 1, POB 859; tel. and fax (2) 114199; e-mail khv@sec .gov.mk; internet www.sec.gov.mk; Pres. NIKOLA GRUEVSKI.

CHAMBERS OF COMMERCE

Economic Chamber of Macedonia: 1000 Skopje, Dimitrija Čupovski 13; tel. (2) 118088; fax (2) 116210; e-mail ic@ic.mchamber .org.mk; internet www.mchamber.org.mk; f. 1962; Pres. DUŠAN PET-RESKI.

Regional Chamber of Commerce of Skopje: 1000 Skopje, Partizanski odredi 2, POB 509; tel. (2) 112511; fax (2) 116419; e-mail regkomsk@regkom.org.mk; Pres. BORIS DIMOVSKI.

UTILITIES

Electricity

Electric Power Industry of Macedonia (Elektrostopanstvo na Makedonija): 1000 Skopje, Bate Bacevski br. 9; tel. (2) 111077; fax (2) 227827; production, transfer and distribution of electric power.

TRADE UNIONS

Federation of Trade Unions of Macedonia: 1000 Skopje; tel. (2) 231374; fax (2) 115787; Pres. VANCO MURATOVSKI; 320,000 mems.

Transport

RAILWAYS

In 2001 the rail network totalled 699 km, of which 233 km were electrified. From 2000 the European Investment Bank made a series of loans to finance the modernization of the railways.

Makedonski Železnici (MZ) (Macedonian Railways): 1000 Skopje, železnička 50; tel. (2) 227903; fax (2) 462330; e-mail mzdir@mt.net .mk; f. 1992; Dir-Gen. RATKO STEFANOVSKI.

ROADS

The FYRM's road network totalled 12,927 km in 2001, of which about 6,710 km were paved. The principal road links Tabanovtse, at the border with Serbia and Montenegro, and Bogoroditsa, at the border with Greece. In July 1998 the European Investment Bank

granted the FYRM a ECU 70m. loan to construct two motorways, between Skopje and Tetovo and Stobi and Demir Kapija.

Fund for National and Regional Roads: 1000 Skopje, Dame Gruev 14; tel. (2) 118044; fax (2) 220535; e-mail tanjam@mpt.net .mk.

CIVIL AVIATION

The FYRM has two international airports, at Petrovets, 25 km from Skopje, and at Ohrid.

Adria Airways: 1000 Skopje, Gradski zid, blok 11; tel. (2) 117009; fax (2) 235531.

Avioimpex: 1000 Skopje, Oktomvri K14 11; tel. (2) 239933; fax (2) 119348; e-mail axx@lotus.mpt.com.mk; internet www.avioimpex .com; f. 1992; flights within Europe; Pres. ILIJA SMILEV.

Macedonian Airlines (MAT): 1000 Skopje, Vasil Glavinov 3; tel. (2) 292333; fax (2) 229576; e-mail mathq@mat.com.mk; internet www.mat.com.mk; f. 1994; domestic services and flights within Europe; Man. Dir DUSKO GRUEVSKI.

Palair Macedonian Airlines: 1000 Skopje, Kuzman Jusifovski Pitu bb; tel. (2) 115868; fax (2) 238238; f. 1991; domestic services and flights within Europe and to the USA, Canada and Australia; Chair. BITOLJANA VANJA.

Tourism

Following independence in 1991, the FYRM's tourist industry (formerly a major source of foreign exchange) experienced a decline, largely owing to the country's proximity to the conflict in other republics of the former Yugoslavia, domestic instability and the sanctions imposed by Greece. Receipts from tourism were estimated at US $37m. in 2000. However, continuing regional instability, including fighting in the north of the country in 2001, has adversely affected tourism. Tourist arrivals declined dramatically, from 224,016 in 2000 to 98,946 in 2001.

Tourist Association of Macedonia: 1000 Skopje, Dame Gruev 28/5; tel. (2) 290862; e-mail tarm@mt.net.mk; internet www.tarm .org.mk.

Tourist Association of Skopje: 1000 Skopje, POB 399, Dame Gruev, blok 3; tel. (2) 118498; fax (2) 230803.

MADAGASCAR

Introductory Survey

Location, Climate, Language, Religion, Flag, Capital

The Republic of Madagascar comprises the island of Madagascar, the fourth largest in the world, and several much smaller offshore islands, in the western Indian Ocean, about 500 km (300 miles) east of Mozambique, in southern Africa. The inland climate is temperate; in Antananarivo temperatures are generally between 8°C (48°F) and 27°C (81°F), with cooler, dryer weather between May and October. The coastal region is tropical, with an average daily maximum temperature of 32°C (90°F). The rainy season extends from November to April in the highlands (average annual rainfall is 1,000 mm–1,500 mm) but is more prolonged on the coast, where average annual rainfall can reach 3,500 mm. The official language is Malagasy, and government acts are published in both Malagasy and French. Hova and other dialects are also widely spoken. More than 50% of the population follow animist beliefs, while about 43% are Christians and the remainder are Muslims. The national flag (proportions 2 by 3) has a vertical white stripe (one-third of the length) at the hoist and two equal horizontal stripes, of red and green, in the fly. The capital is Antananarivo (formerly Tananarive).

Recent History

A French possession since 1896, Madagascar became an autonomous state within the French Community in October 1958, as the Malagasy Republic. In May 1959 Philibert Tsiranana, leader of the Parti social démocrate (PSD), was elected President. The country achieved full independence on 26 June 1960. Prior to independence France supported the PSD, which was identified with the majority coastal tribes (côtiers), as an alternative to the more nationalistic highland people, the Merina, who were the traditional ruling group in the island.

After 1967 the economy deteriorated, and there was growing opposition to the Government's alleged authoritarianism and subservience to French interests. In May 1972, following civil unrest, President Tsiranana transferred full powers to the Army Chief of Staff, Gen. Gabriel Ramanantsoa. In October 1973 pro-Government parties secured a decisive victory in legislative elections. A prolonged crisis followed an attempted military coup in December 1974, and in early February 1975 Ramanantsoa transferred power to Col Richard Ratsimandrava, hitherto Minister of the Interior; however, Ratsimandrava was assassinated shortly afterwards. On 12 February Brig.-Gen. Gilles Andriamahazo assumed power and imposed martial law. All political parties were suspended. In June Andriamahazo was succeeded as Head of State by Lt-Commdr (later Adm.) Didier Ratsiraka, a côtier and a former Minister of Foreign Affairs, who became Chairman of the Supreme Revolutionary Council (SRC).

In a referendum in December 1975 more than 94% of voters approved a new Constitution, which provided for radical administrative and agrarian reforms, and the appointment of Ratsiraka as President of the Republic for a term of seven years. The country's name was changed to the Democratic Republic of Madagascar, and a 'Second Republic' was proclaimed. In January 1976 the civilian element in the Government was increased, and representatives of different regions and parties were included. In March the Avant-garde de la révolution malgache (AREMA—Antoky Ny Revolosiona Malagasy) was founded as the nucleus of the Front national pour la défense de la révolution socialiste malgache (FNDR), the only political organization permitted by the Constitution.

At local government elections in March–June 1977 AREMA secured the majority of votes, resulting in division within the FNDR. The left-wing Mouvement national pour l'indépendance de Madagascar (Monima Ka Miviombio, known as Monima), led by Monja Jaona, withdrew from the FNDR and was subsequently proscribed. At legislative elections in June AREMA secured 112 of the 137 seats in the National People's Assembly. A new Council of Ministers was formed in August, and the membership of the SRC was extended to include leaders of the former political parties and additional côtiers, in an effort to restore political equilibrium.

In October 1980 the arrest of Jaona (who was accused of inciting resentment against the Government) prompted demonstrations. Civil unrest continued in 1981, despite Monima's decision, in March, to rejoin the FNDR and Jaona's subsequent appointment to the SRC. In November 1982 Ratsiraka was re-elected President, receiving 80.2% of the votes cast. Jaona was removed from the SRC in December, following his appeal for a general strike in protest against the election results. At elections to the National People's Assembly in August 1983 AREMA won 117 of the 137 seats. Open dissatisfaction with the Government's policies persisted, however.

In February 1988 the Prime Minister, Col Désiré Rakotoarijaona, resigned, owing to poor health, and was replaced by Lt-Col Victor Ramahatra, formerly Minister of Public Works. Ratsiraka was re-elected to the presidency in March 1989 for a further seven-year term, with 62.7% of the total votes cast. In April rioting followed opposition allegations of electoral irregularities. At legislative elections in May AREMA won 120 seats. The Mouvement pour le pouvoir prolétarien (Mpitolona ho amin'ny Fonjakan'ny Madinika—MFM), which obtained only seven seats, rejected the official results, alleging electoral misconduct. The Élan populaire pour l'unité nationale (Vonjy Iray Tsy Mivaky, known as Vonjy) secured four seats, AKFM/Fanavaozana (a newly formed group, comprising former members of the Parti du congrès de l'indépendance de Madagascar—AKFM), won three seats, the original AKFM two seats, and Monima only one seat.

In August 1989 Ratsiraka assented to opposition demands for discussions about the future role and structure of the FNDR. In September AREMA secured the majority of votes in local government elections. In December the National People's Assembly adopted a constitutional amendment abolishing the requirement for political parties to be members of the FNDR (thereby effectively dissolving the FNDR), despite opposition from MFM deputies.

In March 1990 the Government formally permitted the resumption of multi-party politics. Numerous new organizations emerged, while other parties that had hitherto operated within the FNDR became official opposition movements. Several pro-Government political associations joined AREMA to form a new coalition, the Mouvement militant pour le socialisme malgasy (MMSM). The principal opposition movements included the Union nationale pour le développement et la démocratie (UNDD) and the MFM (restyled the Mouvement pour le progrès de Madagascar, or Mpitolona ho amin'ny Fandrosoan'ny Madagasikara). An informal alliance, the Comité des forces vives—subsequently known as Forces vives (FV, Hery Velona)—was formed by 16 opposition factions, and trade unions and other groups.

In December 1990 the National People's Assembly approved the abolition of press censorship and the establishment (in partnership with the Government) of private broadcasting stations. In May 1991 legislation providing for extensive constitutional amendments was submitted to the National People's Assembly. Opposition parties criticized the proposals, on the grounds that the revised Constitution would retain references to socialism. In June opposition leaders applied to the Constitutional High Court to effect Ratsiraka's removal from office, while the FV organized demonstrations in support of its demands for the resignation of the President and the convening of a national conference to draft a new constitution. Ratsiraka refused to resign. Later in June the FV formed a 'parallel' administration, which it termed the 'Provisional Government'.

In July 1991 the FV organized a general strike, warning that it would continue until the Government acceded to its demands for constitutional reform. Subsequent negotiations between the MMSM and the FV achieved little. The FV appointed Jean Rakotoharison, a retired army general, as President of the 'Provisional Government', and Albert Zafy, the leader of the UNDD, as its Prime Minister. However, Manandafy Rakotonirina, the leader of the MFM, rejected the formation of the 'Provisional Government', favouring further negotiations, and withdrew his party from the FV. Members of the 'Provisional

Government' subsequently occupied the premises of six official government ministries. Later in July Ratsiraka ordered the detention of several members of the 'Provisional Government' and imposed a state of emergency in Antananarivo. The FV withdrew from negotiations with the MMSM, in protest against the arrests, while the French Government appealed to Ratsiraka to release the opposition leaders. In response to increasing public pressure, Ratsiraka dissolved the Council of Ministers and pledged to organize a constitutional referendum before the end of 1991. Members of the 'Provisional Government' were released from custody, and Ratsiraka repealed legislation that authorized the detention of opponents of the Government.

In August 1991 Ratsiraka appointed Guy Razanamasy, the mayor of Antananarivo, as Prime Minister. In the same month a number of demonstrators were killed when an anti-Government rally was violently suppressed by the presidential guard. Negotiations between the MMSM and the FV were again suspended, and the armed forces withdrew their support for Ratsiraka. Later that month Ratsiraka declared Madagascar to be a federation of six states, with himself as President, and claimed to command the support of five provinces where AREMA continued to hold the majority of seats in regional councils. However, the FV disregarded the proclamation and continued to demand that Ratsiraka relinquish the presidency. At the end of August Razanamasy formed an interim Government, not including members of the FV or the MFM, which was condemned by opposition leaders.

On 31 October 1991 representatives of the Government, the FV, the MFM, church leaders and the armed forces signed an agreement providing for the suspension of the Constitution and the creation of a transitional Government, which was to remain in office for a maximum period of 18 months, pending presidential and legislative elections. The SRC and the National People's Assembly were to be replaced by interim bodies, respectively the High State Authority for Transition to the Third Republic and the National Committee for Economic and Social Regeneration. On an interim basis, Ratsiraka was to remain as President of the Republic and Razanamasy as Prime Minister. Zafy was designated President of the High State Authority, which was to comprise 18 representatives of the FV, seven of the MFM and six of the MMSM. Rakotonirina and Pastor Richard Andriamanjato, the leader of AKFM/Fanavaozana, were appointed as joint Presidents of the 131-member National Committee for Economic and Social Regeneration. The power to appoint or to dismiss government ministers, hitherto vested in the President, was granted to Razanamasy. A new constitution was to be submitted to a national referendum by the end of 1991. Zafy subsequently rejected the agreement, on the grounds that Ratsiraka was to retain the nominal post of Commander-in-Chief of the Armed Forces. In November Razanamasy formed a new interim Government, which included three representatives of the MFM and one MMSM member. Francisque Ravony, of the MFM, was appointed to the new post of Deputy Prime Minister. Owing to Zafy's refusal to participate in the Government, 10 portfolios that had been allocated to the FV remained vacant. Later in November, however, Zafy agreed to accept the presidency of the High State Authority.

In December 1991 Razanamasy announced that the formation of the coalition Government had proved unsuccessful, and 11 ministers, including Ravony, resigned. Razanamasy appointed a larger Government of national consensus, in which 14 (of 36) portfolios were allocated to the FV. In January 1992 it was announced that all political factions had now accepted the terms of the October 1991 agreement. The institutions that had been established by the accord were to prepare for the constitutional referendum, now scheduled for June 1992, and for local, presidential and legislative elections, which were to take place by the end of the year. In February regional debates took place to compile proposals for the new constitution, which was to be drafted (together with an electoral code) by a National Forum. Also in February the High State Authority for Transition to the Third Republic announced the dissolution of the SRC and the National People's Assembly, in accordance with the October 1991 agreement, and indicated that a new body was to be created to supervise local elections, replacing the existing system of government, based on village assemblies (*fokontany*). However, the MMSM claimed that the High State Authority was not empowered to dissolve the local government structure. The Government subsequently announced that control of local government was to be transferred from elected councils to special

delegations, and that security commissions were to be established to organize the *fokontany*.

At the National Forum, which was convened in March 1992, the MMSM agreed to abandon its proposals for the creation of a federal republic, but continued to profess adherence to a decentralized system of government. At the end of March, following a decision by the Forum to restrict the President to two terms of office (thereby debarring Ratsiraka from contesting the presidential election), supporters of the MMSM attacked the conference hall during a session of the Forum.

The draft Constitution of the Third Republic, as submitted to the Government in April 1992, envisaged a unitary state and provided for a bicameral legislature, comprising a Senate and a National Assembly. Two-thirds of the members of the Senate were to be selected by an electoral college, with the remaining one-third to be appointed by the President, while the 184-member National Assembly was to be elected by universal suffrage, under a system of proportional representation, for a four-year term. The authority of the President was reduced, and executive power was vested in the Prime Minister, who was to be appointed by the National Assembly. (The stipulation in the draft Constitution that the President be restricted to two terms of office had, however, been withdrawn.) Ratsiraka reiterated his intention to contest the presidential election and demanded that a draft providing for a federal system of government also be submitted to the forthcoming referendum, as an alternative to the National Forum's proposals.

In August 1992 supporters of a federal system of government took control of the airport and the radio and television stations at Antsiranana, and announced the establishment of a federal directorate in the town; similar incidents followed at Toamasina, in the east, and Toliary, in the south-west of the country. The new Constitution was approved by 72.2% of votes cast in a national referendum on 19 August. Federalists forcibly prevented the electorate from voting in a number of regions, and several people were killed in clashes between supporters of the MMSM and members of the FV at Toamasina. Later that month the armed forces regained control of the towns that had been occupied by the federalists.

In September 1992 several prominent political figures, including Zafy and Rakotonirina, announced that they were to contest the forthcoming presidential election. Divisions emerged within the FV after a number of constituent parties presented alternative candidates to Zafy, the alliance's official candidate. Later in September the National Forum's electoral code was submitted to a committee of government officials and church leaders, which proposed that the stipulation restricting the President to two terms of office be incorporated in the code. Shortly afterwards MMSM supporters unilaterally declared Antsiranana, Toliary, Toamasina and Fianarantsoa (in central Madagascar) to be federal states, and suspended infrastructural links between these provinces and Antananarivo. In October federalists in Antsiranana, apparently supported by members of the presidential guard, took hostage members of the FV and seized control of the radio and television stations. Razanamasy declared the unilateral proclamation of independence of the four provinces to be illegal, but initiated negotiations with the federalists, in an effort to prevent disruption of the presidential election. Later that month there were further clashes in Toliary between supporters of the FV and federalists, led by Monja Jaona, who had declared himself to be Governor of the province. At the end of October, however, the federalists agreed to participate in the presidential election, although the MMSM continued officially to reject the new Constitution.

The presidential election took place on 25 November 1992, contested by eight candidates. Zafy secured 45.1% of votes cast, and Ratsiraka 29.2%. Prior to a second round of voting, on 10 February 1993, the remaining six candidates withdrew in favour of Zafy, who thus secured 66.7% of the votes cast. Zafy's inauguration, on 27 March, was accompanied by violent clashes between security forces and federalists in the north. In accordance with the Constitution, Zafy resigned as President of the UNDD at a party congress in May; Emmanuel Rakotovahiny, the Minister of State for Agriculture and Rural Development, was elected as his successor.

Several constituent parties of the FV that had not supported Zafy in the first round of the presidential election subsequently presented independent lists of candidates for the forthcoming legislative elections; the remaining parties in the alliance became known as Forces vives Rasalama (Hery Velona Rasalama—HVR). Violence intensified prior to polling: two people were killed, and 40 (including Jaona) arrested, after security forces attacked federalists who had occupied the prefecture at Toliary. The elections, to a reduced 138-member National Assembly, took place on 16 June 1993, and were contested by 121 political associations. The HVR secured 46 seats, the MFM 15, and a new alliance of pro-Ratsiraka parties 11 seats. The official results indicated that parties supporting Zafy had won 75 seats in the National Assembly. In August Francisque Ravony was elected Prime Minister and formed a new Council of Ministers. Richard Andriamanjato was elected President of the National Assembly.

By early 1994, owing to frequent party realignments, Ravony no longer commanded a majority in the legislature. In June government proposals for economic reforms were rejected by the National Assembly. Nevertheless, in July a motion of censure against Ravony's Government was rejected. In the same month scheduled elections to establish new regional authorities (already postponed from October 1993) were further delayed, owing to lack of agreement regarding proposals for decentralization. In August 1994, following negotiations with the HVR, Ravony formed a new Council of Ministers.

In October 1994 controversy over a local subsidiary enterprise, Flamco Madagascar, which had failed to reimburse funds advanced by the Government, prompted increased division between Ravony and Andriamanjato regarding economic policy. Meanwhile, opposition leaders demanded the removal of Zafy, Ravony and Andriamanjato, amid general resentment towards the Government, which had been precipitated by an increase in the rate of inflation resulting from the flotation of the Malagasy franc. At a regional congress of AREMA, which took place at the end of October, Ratsiraka urged the resignation of Ravony and dissolution of the Government. In the same month pro-Andriamanjato sections of the HVR demanded the dismissal of three government ministers, including the Minister of Finance and the Budget, José Yvon Raserijaona, on the grounds of incompetence, subsequently joining the opposition in urging Ravony's resignation, after he failed to replace the three ministers concerned. In January 1995 Ravony dismissed the Governor of the central bank, who had approved the financial transaction with Flamco Madagascar, at the insistence of the IMF and World Bank, and (apparently as a concession to Andriamanjato) also dismissed Raserijaona, assuming the finance and budget portfolio himself.

In July 1995, apparently at Zafy's instigation, deputies belonging to the HVR, the UNDD and AKFM/Fanavaozana proposed a motion of censure against Ravony in the National Assembly (which was, however, rejected by a large majority). Zafy subsequently announced that he was unable to co-operate with Ravony and decreed that a constitutional amendment empowering the President, rather than the National Assembly, to select the Prime Minister, be submitted for approval in a national referendum. Ravony indicated that he would resign after the referendum, regardless of the outcome. In August Ravony formed a new Council of Ministers, comprising representatives of the parliamentary majority that had supported him in the previous month. The referendum proceeded in September, at which the constitutional amendment was approved by 63.6% of votes cast. Ravony duly resigned in October, and Zafy appointed Rakotovahiny as Prime Minister. Rakotovahiny's Council of Ministers included several members of the outgoing administration, although the leader of the HVR, Alain Ramaroson (the only member of the HVR to be allocated a portfolio), refused to join the Government. In accordance with government plans to restructure local government, elections to 1,400 new communes took place on 5 November. An abstention rate of 60% was recorded, and a decline in support for the HVR was apparent.

Following the installation of the new Government, disagreement between Rakotovahiny and the Minister of the Budget, Finance and Planning, Jean Claude Raherimanjato, delayed the adoption of the budget for 1996. In addition, dissension emerged between the parties that supported Zafy over the composition of the Council of Ministers; in December 1995 associates of Andriamanjato demanded that an alternative cabinet be appointed. In April 1996 an attempt by Raherimanjato to dismiss senior ministry officials (which Rakotovahiny refused to endorse) prompted industrial action by civil servants at the Ministry of the Budget, Finance and Planning. In the same month opposition members took part in further demonstrations to demand Zafy's resignation. In May a motion of censure against Rakotovahiny's Government, apparently instigated by Raherimanjato,

was approved by a large majority in the National Assembly. Rakotovahiny's subsequently resigned, and Zafy appointed Norbert Ratsirahonana, hitherto President of the Constitutional High Court, as Prime Minister.

Zafy refused to approve the new Government initially proposed by Ratsirahonana, insisting on the inclusion of five UNDD members who had served in the previous Council of Ministers. In protest, most of the opposition deputies consequently left the legislative chamber when the Prime Minister presented the new Government to the National Assembly in June 1996. Ratsirahonana, however, won a vote of confidence in the legislature in July, by associating the vote with legislation providing for the implementation of economic reforms stipulated by the IMF and the World Bank. On 26 July a motion in the National Assembly to remove Zafy from office for numerous contraventions of the Constitution was supported by 99 of 131 votes cast. (Meanwhile, local elections, which had been scheduled for August, and were to replace the existing six provinces with 28 regions, were postponed as a result of the presidential crisis.) The Constitutional High Court endorsed the President's impeachment in September, upholding the majority of the charges against him; Zafy maintained that his impeachment was illegal, but resigned the same day. Ratsirahonana was appointed interim President by the Constitutional High Court, pending an election; he formed a new interim Government that represented the majority in the National Assembly and excluded members of the UNDD. Zafy announced his intention to contest the forthcoming election, as did Ratsiraka, Ratsirahonana and Ravony. In October Ravony withdrew from the presidential election and, unexpectedly, declared his support for Zafy.

In all, 15 candidates stood in the first round of the presidential election, which proceeded peacefully on 3 November 1996; Ratsiraka (with 36.6% of the votes cast) and Zafy (with 23.4%) qualified to contest the second round. The head of LEADER/Fanilo, Herizo Razafimahaleo, obtained 15.1%, and Ratsirahonana 10.1%, of the votes. Razafimahaleo urged his supporters to vote for Ratsiraka. None of the unsuccessful candidates chose to support Zafy, who declared his intention, if elected, to retain Ratsirahonana (who had successfully concluded an agreement with the IMF in August) as Prime Minister; Ratsirahonana, however, refused to endorse either candidate. At the second round, which took place on 29 December, Ratsiraka narrowly won, with 50.71% of the valid votes cast, although more than 50% of the registered electorate abstained from voting. Ratsiraka was inaugurated as President on 9 February. He appointed Pascal Rakotomavo (a former Minister of Finance) as Prime Minister. Rakotomavo's Government included Razafimahaleo as Deputy Prime Minister in charge of Foreign Affairs. During a visit to France in March, Ratsiraka discussed plans to effect constitutional change by referendum.

In May 1997 legislative elections, which had been scheduled for August, were postponed, officially to allow time for identity cards to be issued to voters. The opposition, led by Zafy, denounced the delay as a violation of the Constitution and, in early August, demanded the resignation of the Government and of the Constitutional High Court (which had endorsed the extension of the existing legislature's mandate), as well as the dissolution of the National Assembly. In August a commission that had been appointed by the Prime Minister to draft constitutional amendments presented its proposals. However, apparently following intervention from Andriamanjato, who was said to have insisted that the National Assembly alone was responsible for constitutional revision, regional forums, attended by local officials and representatives of non-governmental organizations, were held in September to put forward proposals for one constitutional project. (Ratsiraka had originally favoured submitting two alternatives to a referendum, one for a federal state, the other for a decentralized, unitary state.) A new constitution was then to be drafted by a 15-member National Consultative Commission, nominated by Ratsiraka, Rakotomavo and Andriamanjato. Meanwhile, in October the Government condemned declarations apparently made by Zafy and his supporters that Antsiranana had become a 'liberated territory'.

In January 1998 Ratsiraka invited political leaders to attend discussions on constitutional reform, although Hery Miara-dia, an opposition grouping led by Zafy, and members of the Panorama Group, a more moderate alliance led by Ravony and Ratsirahonana, refused to participate. None the less, Ratsiraka subsequently announced that a constitutional referendum would take place on 15 March 1998, to be followed by legislative elections. The draft amendments to the Constitution envisaged a 'federal-style' state, composed of six autonomous provinces, and also provided for increased presidential powers.

In February 1998 a motion of impeachment against Ratsiraka failed to gain the requisite two-thirds' majority in the National Assembly. Later that month the principal opposition parties urged voters to boycott the forthcoming referendum, claiming that the Government had ignored the views presented at the regional forums and the proposals of the National Consultative Commission, and had deliberately delayed discussion on legislation proposed by Rakotonirina (who had chaired the Commission) whereby any draft constitution would require the approval of more than 50% of all registered voters in order to become law. The referendum proceeded on 15 March 1998, when extensive revisions to the Constitution were narrowly endorsed by 50.96% of votes cast. Rakotonirina's proposed legislation was approved by the National Assembly later that month. However, Ratsiraka referred the legislation back to the National Assembly, and in April it was rejected after further deliberation.

Elections to an expanded National Assembly followed on 17 May 1998, under a new electoral law. Of the 150 seats, 82 were to be filled from single-member constituencies, with the remaining deputies to be elected by a system of proportional representation in 34 two-member constituencies. Ratsiraka's party, AREMA, performed well in the elections, winning 63 seats, while the pro-presidential LEADER/Fanilo and the Rassemblement pour le socialisme et la démocratie (RPSD) secured 16 and 11 seats, respectively. Ratsirahonana's party, Ny asa vita no ifampitsara (AVI), emerged as the strongest opposition party, with 14 seats, while Zafy's new party—Asa, Faharaminana, Fampandrasoana, Arinda (AFFA)—won six seats; independent candidates took 32 seats. Several leading political figures failed to secure re-election, notably Andriamanjato, and Rakotonirina and Germain Rakotonirainy, the leaders of the MFM (which won only three seats). The AVI and 24 independent deputies were subsequently reported to have joined the AREMA majority, leaving the AFFA and the remaining independents as the only significant parliamentary opposition. In July Tantely Andrianarivo, hitherto Deputy Prime Minister, was appointed as Prime Minister, retaining responsibility for finance and the economy. The 31-member Council of Ministers was dominated by AREMA, with the key portfolios largely unchanged; 12 new ministers were appointed.

The first local government elections—communal voting for 20,000 councillors and 1,392 mayors—since the reintroduction of the three-tier system of local government (provinces, regions and communes), under the amended Constitution of 1998, took place on 14 November 1999. The greatest successes were recorded by independent (or nominally independent) candidates. Most notably, Marc Ravalomanana, the head of the country's largest agro-industrial processor, Tiko, was elected mayor of Antananarivo; Ravalomanana had been a principal donor of electoral funds to the AVI, but had stood as an independent. Roland Ratsiraka, a nephew of the President, was elected independent mayor of Toamasina, while Zafy failed to secure election to the post of mayor of Diego Garcia. Following the party's poor performance in the elections, Pierrot Rajaonarivelo, the Deputy Prime Minister, resigned as Secretary-General of AREMA. Regional elections were postponed.

Provincial elections took place on 3 December 2000 to elect 336 councillors, as a preliminary step to the decentralization of certain powers to six autonomous provinces (legislation on the organization of which had been approved by the National Assembly in August). Voter participation in the capital was reported to have been very low, at about 30%, following calls by various organizations, including opposition parties and the Christian Council of Churches in Madagascar, for a boycott of the elections. It was reported that AREMA had secured control of most of the major towns, although the AVI won a majority of seats in Antananarivo.

On 18 March 2001 a 1,727-member electoral college, which included mayors and local councillors, elected 60 members of the new Senate. AREMA won 49 of the 60 seats, while LEADER/Fanilo secured five seats and opposition parties a total of six, including two for the AVI. President Ratsiraka subsequently named the remaining 30 senators who would constitute the 90-seat upper house.

A presidential election took place on 16 December 2001, contested by six candidates, including Ratsiraka, Zafy, Razafimahaleo and Marc Ravalomanana. According to the official results, Ravalomanana, whose candidacy was supported by a number of opposition parties, most notably the AVI, the RPSD

and the MFM, secured 46.21% of the votes cast and Didier Ratsiraka 40.89%, thereby necessitating a second round of voting. However, Ravalomanana's own electoral observers disputed this result, claiming that he had won an outright victory, with 52.15% of the votes, and demanded a public comparison of voting records. The opposition was supported in these demands by international electoral observers. A re-count was subsequently conducted, and on 25 January 2002 the Constitutional High Court endorsed the official results and ruled that a second round of voting should take place within 30 days. Ravalomanana rejected this verdict and called for a national strike in protest. Some 500,000 people responded by gathering in Antananarivo; government offices, public utilities and banks ceased operations, and air traffic was suspended. Ravalomanana's supporters also closed the central bank in order to prevent Ratsiraka from withdrawing special funds from the treasury. Strike action continued, in varying forms, for eight weeks. Following a meeting between Ravalomanana and Ratsiraka in mid-February, negotiations were conducted between their representatives, with mediation by the Organization of African Unity (OAU); Ratsiraka's delegates rejected Ravalomanana's proposals for the formation of an interim government and new appointments to the Constitutional High Court and electoral committee. Meanwhile, the Minister of the Armed Forces, Gen. Marcel Ranjeva, declared that the army would remain neutral in the electoral dispute.

On 22 February 2002 Ravalomanana accelerated events by unilaterally declaring himself President in an inaugural ceremony in Antananarivo attended by 100,000 supporters. The President of the Senate immediately declared Ravalomanana's proclamation to be illegal, and it was widely condemned by the international community. In response, President Ratsiraka declared a three-month 'state of national necessity', according himself broad powers, including the right to pass laws by decree. On 26 February Ravalomanana named Jacques Sylla, a former Minister of Foreign Affairs under Zafy's presidency, as his Prime Minister. On the following day Ratsiraka's Minister of Foreign Affairs and Minister of Posts and Telecommunications both resigned. Meanwhile, after weeks of largely peaceful protests, violent clashes erupted between supporters of Ratsiraka and Ravalomanana in Antananarivo, prompting Ratsiraka to decree martial law and appoint a military governor, Gen. Léon-Claude Raveloarison, in the capital. None the less, Ravalomanana proceeded with the formation of his rival Government in early March, while opposition supporters erected barricades against the army and set fire to the military headquarters; 17 of those appointed to Ravalomanana's administration were successfully installed in government offices, accompanied by large crowds of supporters and unopposed by the military. On the same day the governors of the five remaining provinces of the country declared their allegiance to Ratsiraka, recognizing his hometown, Toamasina (where Ratsiraka and his ministers had relocated) as a temporary 'alternative capital'. A few days later Gen. Ranjeva resigned as Minister of the Armed Forces, shortly after Ravalomanana's rival Government had taken control of his offices in Antananarivo. Gen. Raveloarison resigned as military governor of Antananarivo some three weeks after his appointment, having failed to apply martial law and order troops to end protests, on the grounds that this would have incurred deaths. Later in March 58 of Madagascar's 150 deputies attended a parliamentary session called by Ravalomanana and elected an interim President of the National Assembly.

An OAU mission held talks with Ravalomanana and Ratsiraka in March 2002, in an attempt to resolve the ongoing political crisis, but its proposal for a 'government of national reconciliation' was rejected by both sides. In late March four supporters of Ravalomanana were killed, and a further 28 injured, during clashes with the security forces in Fianarantsoa, bringing the estimated number of deaths in the protests since January to 25. At the beginning of April, supporters of Ratsiraka, who had erected roadblocks to isolate Antananarivo in February, destroyed two of the bridges located on its supply routes to the rest of the island, in an effort to intensify the effective siege of the capital, which was already suffering from severe fuel shortages. The situation fostered fears of ethnic conflict, with Ravalomanana supported by the predominantly Merina population of Antananarivo and the central highlands, and Ratsiraka by the *côtiers*. This concern was exacerbated by Ravalomanana's appeal for his supporters to overthrow the roadblocks around the capital, declaring the country to be in a state of war and listing the names of those considered to be enemies. The OAU condemned Ravalomanana's statements as incitement to violence.

On 10 April 2002 the Supreme Court ruled that there had been irregularities in the appointment, shortly before the presidential election, of six of the nine judges of the Constitutional High Court, which had endorsed the official results; one week later the Supreme Court annulled the disputed results and ordered a re-count of the votes. On the following day Ratsiraka and Ravalomanana signed a peace accord in Dakar, Senegal, where they had been holding talks under the auspices of the OAU and the UN, and with mediation by the Presidents of Senegal, Benin, Côte d'Ivoire and Mozambique. Following the completion of the re-count, in late April, the Constitutional High Court ruled that Ravalomanana had secured the presidency, with 51.46% of the votes cast, while Ratsiraka had won 35.90%. Ratsiraka, who had failed to remove the blockade of Antananarivo (in contravention of the Dakar accord), refused to accept the Court's decision. Nevertheless, Ravalomanana was inaugurated as President on 6 May, largely without international recognition, and appointed a new Council of Ministers later that month. Four of the country's six provincial governors, who were loyal to Ratsiraka, subsequently threatened to secede. Ravalomanana and Ratsiraka failed to reach agreement at further talks in Dakar in early June. Heavy fighting ensued, as troops loyal to Ravalomanana conducted a military offensive against areas controlled by Ratsiraka, securing two provincial capitals, Mahajanga and Toliary, in mid-June.

In mid-June 2002 Ravalomanana dissolved the Government that he had formed in May, immediately reappointing Sylla as Prime Minister; however, despite nominating six new members of the Council of Ministers, he failed to appoint a government of national unity. At the end of June the USA recognized Ravalomanana as the legitimate leader of Madagascar; endorsement soon followed from France and, in contravention of the policy of the OAU, Senegal. Meanwhile, the OAU suspended Madagascar from its meetings, pending the staging of free and fair elections leading to the establishment of a legitimate government; this decision was upheld by the African Union (AU, see p. 130), which replaced the OAU in July. In early July Ravalomanana's government troops took control of Antsiranana and Toamasina, and Ratsiraka sought exile in France; this apparent admission of defeat allowed for an international conference to take place in Paris, France, on the donation of aid for the reconstruction of Madagascar. The new Government was in full control of the island by the middle of the month. Ravalomanana replaced the 30 presidentially appointed members of the Senate, with the approval of the Constitutional High Court, despite the fact that those appointed by Ratsiraka had been appointed for a tenure of six years. In August six of the nine members of the Constitutional High Court were also replaced. In early October Ravalomanana dismissed Narisoa Rajaonarivony as Deputy Prime Minister and Minister of Finance and Development and altered the portfolio of Benjamin Andriamparany Radavidson from Minister of Economy and Planning to that of Minister of the Economy, Finance and the Budget.

In mid-October 2002 the National Assembly was dissolved in preparation for legislative elections, brought forward from May 2003, in response to pressure from aid donors, in order to finalize the legitimacy of Ravalomanana's mandate. At the elections, which took place on 15 December 2002, Ravalomanana's party, Tiako i Madagasikara (I Love Madagascar), won 102 of the 160 seats and the pro-Ravalomanana Firaisankinam-Pirenena (National Union) secured a further 22 seats; the formerly incumbent AREMA party won only three seats. (Foreign observers were permitted to be present at the elections for the first time in Malagasy electoral history.) In mid-January a new Government was appointed, which included 10 new ministers; former Minister of Public Works, Jean Lahiniriako, was elected President of the National Assembly. In early 2003 the only significant authority not to have recognized the new Government remained the AU, although there was some hope that it would readmit the country to its meetings at its General Assembly in July. Meanwhile, various members of the former Ratsiraka administration were arrested and tried in court, including the former Governors of Fianarantsoa and Toamasina.

Madagascar's foreign policy is officially non-aligned: while it formerly maintained close links with communist countries (particularly the People's Republic of China, the Democratic People's Republic of Korea and the former USSR), the Zafy Government established relations with Israel, South Africa and the Republic of Korea. Relations with France have been affected by disputes

over compensation for nationalized French assets and over the continuing French claim to the Iles Glorieuses, north of Madagascar, and three other islets in the Mozambique Channel. In 1980 the UN voted in favour of restoring all the disputed islets to Madagascar. In early 1986 the Government announced the extension of Madagascar's exclusive economic zone to include the Iles Glorieuses and the three islets. In 1997 government announcements regarding future privatization plans in Madagascar prompted renewed appeals from France for compensation for nationalized French assets. In response, the Government allocated some 50,000m. francs MG as initial compensation in the budget for 1998. In February 2000 it was agreed that the Iles Glorieuses would be co-administered by France, Madagascar and Mauritius, without prejudice to the question of sovereignty.

Relations with the People's Republic of China were strengthened in January 1999, during a visit by Vice-President Hu Jintao; agreements were signed on the expansion of bilateral economic relations and China's provision of preferential loans to Madagascar. In September 2000 the representative office for Taiwan in Madagascar was closed down, following an official visit by the Malagasy Minister of Foreign Affairs to China. (It was claimed that this was carried out by the Government in support of the 'one China' policy; however, the Taiwanese claimed that the office had never functioned effectively.)

Government

The Constitution of the Third Republic was endorsed by national referendum on 19 August 1992, but was extensively revised by amendments that were endorsed by national referendum on 15 March 1998. The amended Constitution enshrines a 'federal-style' state, composed of six autonomous provinces, each with a provincial council (holding legislative power) elected by universal suffrage for a term of five years. Each provincial council elects a governor, who appoints up to 12 general commissioners to exercise executive power in the province. The first local elections (for communal councillors and mayors) under the restored three-tier system of provinces, regions and communes, as envisaged in the Constitution, took place in November 1999. Provincial elections were held in December 2000. The Constitution provides for a bicameral legislature, comprising a Senate (established in March 2001) and a National Assembly. Two-thirds of the members of the Senate are elected by the autonomous provinces, and the remaining one-third of the members are appointed by the President, while the National Assembly is elected by universal suffrage for a five-year term of office. The constitutional Head of State is the President, who is elected for a term of five years, and can be re-elected for two further terms. The President appoints the Prime Minister and, on the latter's recommendation, the other members of the Council of Ministers.

Defence

At 1 August 2002 total armed forces numbered about 13,500 men: army 12,500, navy 500 and air force 500. There is a paramilitary gendarmerie of 8,100. The 2001 budget allocated 428,400m. francs MG (8.1% of total expenditure) to defence.

Economic Affairs

In 2001, according to estimates by the World Bank, Madagascar's gross national income (GNI), measured at average 1999–2001 prices, was US $4,170m., equivalent to about $260 per head (or $870 per head on an international purchasing-power parity basis). During 1990–2001, it was estimated, the population increased at an average annual rate of 2.9%, while gross domestic product (GDP) per head decreased, in real terms, by an average of 0.7% per year. Overall GDP increased, in real terms, at an average annual rate of 2.2% in 1990–2001; growth in 2001 was 6.7%.

In 2001 the agricultural sector (including forestry and fishing) accounted for 24.6% of GDP and employed an estimated 73.8% of the labour force. Rice, the staple food crop, is produced on some 50% of cultivated land. Since 1972, however, imports of rice have been necessary to supplement domestic production: net imports of 158,000 metric tons of rice were recorded in 2001. The most important cash crops are coffee, cloves and vanilla. Coffee remained Madagascar's principal export in 1998, accounting for 17.2% of total export revenue. Sugar, coconuts, tropical fruits, cotton and sisal are also cultivated. Cattle-farming is important. Sea fishing by coastal fishermen (particularly for crustaceans) is being expanded, while vessels from the European Union fish for tuna and prawns in Madagascar's exclusive maritime zone, within 200 nautical miles (370 km) of the coast, in return for compensation. According to the World Bank, agricultural GDP increased by an average of 1.7% per year in 1990–2001; growth in 2001 was 5.2%.

Industry (including mining, manufacturing, construction and power) contributed 12.0% of Madagascar's GDP in 2001, and employed about 5.5% of the labour force in 1999. According to the World Bank, industrial GDP increased at an average annual rate of 3.1% in 1990–2001; growth in 2001 was 10.0%.

The mining sector contributed only 0.3% of GDP in 1991 and, together with manufacturing, engaged about 1.5% of the labour force in 1993. However, Madagascar has sizeable deposits of a wide range of minerals, principally chromite (chromium ore), which, with graphite and mica, is exported, together with small quantities of semi-precious stones. A proposed major project to resume the mining of ilmenite (titanium ore) in south-eastern Madagascar, which would generate US $550m. over a 30-year period, but had prompted considerable controversy on environmental grounds, received approval from the Government in 2001, pending the completion of further studies. Other potential mineral projects included the exploitation of an estimated 100m. metric tons of bauxite in the south-east of the country, and of nickel and cobalt deposits in central Madagascar. Following exploratory drilling for petroleum at three offshore areas in the early 1990s, it was announced that only non-commercial deposits of oil and gas had been discovered, although contracts for further exploration were granted in 1997 and 1999. The mining of sapphires commenced in southern Madagascar in 1998, but in March 1999 the Government ordered the suspension of sapphire mining pending the results of studies into the effects of exploitation on the environment; however, unauthorized mining continued on a wide scale.

Manufacturing contributed 11.1% of GDP in 1997. The petroleum refinery at Toamasina, using imported petroleum, provides a significant share of export revenue. Other important branches of manufacturing are textiles and clothing, food products, beverages and chemical products. The introduction of a new investment code in 1990 and the creation of a number of export processing zones achieved some success in attracting foreign private investment, particularly in the manufacturing branches of textiles, cement, fertilizers and pharmaceuticals. According to the World Bank, manufacturing GDP increased at an average annual rate of 0.6% in 1990–2000.

Energy generation depends on imports of crude petroleum (which accounted for 15.0% of the value of total imports in 2001, according to IMF figures) to fuel thermal installations, although hydroelectric resources have also been developed, and accounted for an estimated 67.6% of electricity production in 2001.

The services sector accounted for 63.4% of GDP in 2001, and engaged some 10.9% of the labour force in 1993. According to the World Bank, the GDP of the services sector increased by an average of 2.7% per year in 1990–2001; growth in 2001 was 6.8%.

In 2001 Madagascar recorded a visible trade deficit of US $3.2m., and there was a deficit of $20.3m. on the current account of the balance of payments. The principal source of imports in 2001 was France (21.5%); other major suppliers were the People's Republic of China and South Africa. France was also the principal market for exports (accounting for 29.7% of exports in that year); the USA was also an important purchaser. The principal exports in 1998 were cotton fabrics, coffee and shrimps and prawns. The principal imports in that year included chemicals, transport equipment, minerals (chiefly crude petroleum), base metals (chiefly iron and steel), machinery and mechanical appliances and vegetable products.

Madagascar's overall budget deficit for 2001 was estimated at 1,322,000m. francs MG (equivalent to 4.4% of GDP). Madagascar's external debt totalled US $4,701m. at the end of 2000, of which $4,295m. was long-term public debt. In the same year the cost of debt-servicing was estimated to be equivalent to 7.7% of the value of exports of goods and services. The annual rate of inflation averaged 15.7% in 1990–2001; consumer prices increased by 6.9% in 2001 and by 15.9% in 2002. About 6% of the labour force was estimated to be unemployed in 1995.

Madagascar is a member of the Indian Ocean Commission (see p. 340) and of the Common Market for Eastern and Southern Africa (COMESA, see p. 162).

Madagascar's dominant agricultural sector is vulnerable to adverse climatic conditions, including cyclones, and to fluctuations in the market prices of the country's principal exports. In December 2000 the IMF and the World Bank agreed to support

a comprehensive debt reduction package under the enhanced Heavily Indebted Poor Countries (HIPC) initiative. Following progress in trade liberalization and further privatization in the petroleum sector, the IMF approved a loan, of US $103m., in March 2001 under the Poverty Reduction and Growth Facility (PRGF). Also in March Madagascar was declared eligible to benefit from the USA's African Growth and Opportunity Act, allowing duty free access to the US market, and both exports to the USA and foreign investment in Madagascar increased dramatically as a result. In December the IMF reported that economic performance had been favourable in 2001, with strong GDP growth, necessary reforms, a reduction in inflation and increased exports, but expressed concern at the persistently high level of poverty in the country. Economic activity was paralysed from the beginning of 2002—amid political uncertainty caused by the disputed presidential election (see Recent History)—by the strikes called by Marc Ravalomanana and the blockades ordered by Didier Ratsiraka. Neither raw materials could be delivered, nor export produce transported, and both the textiles and tourism sectors, the country's two main sources of income, were severely affected. In February the World Bank estimated that the strike was costing Madagascar up to $14m. per day (the entire annual savings from debt relief) and that 50,000 jobs were threatened. The closure of the central bank from the end of January also resulted in the freezing of the nation's assets, rendering Madagascar unable to service its debts and at risk of default; the decline in real GDP for the year was estimated at 12%. Companies in the export processing zone, specializing in textiles for export, and the agricultural sector were severely affected by the political crisis, being highly dependent on foreign purchasers and the transportation network; tourism also was drastically curtailed. In July international donors pledged some $2,300m. (one-half of which was to be supplied by the Bretton Woods institutions) over a period of four years towards the reconstruction and development of the country, which subsequently enabled the authorities to repay the arrears on all external payments. From August the foreign-exchange markets reopened and the currency remained broadly stable after an initial decline. In October the IMF fully disbursed a structural adjustment credit of $100m., and in November it approved an Emergency Economic Recovery Credit and other loans aimed at public-sector management and private-sector development; in December the Fund granted $15m. under the PRGF and extended the arrangement until November 2004, in addition to allotting $4m. in interim assistance under the HIPC initiative. The IMF also encouraged the Government to incorporate the precious-stone mining industry into the formal economy in order to increase fiscal revenues; preliminary measures were taken towards achieving this in early 2003. The budget for 2003 relied heavily on public investment and focused on infrastructural and social needs.

Education

Six years' education, to be undertaken usually between six and 13 years of age, is officially compulsory. Madagascar has both public and private schools, although legislation that was enacted in 1978 envisaged the progressive elimination of private education. Primary education generally begins at the age of six and lasts for five years. Secondary education, beginning at 11 years of age, lasts for a further seven years, comprising a first cycle of four years and a second of three years. In 1999/2000 primary enrolment included 66.4% of children in the relevant age-group (males 66.1%; females 66.7%). In 1998/99, according to UNESCO estimates, secondary enrolment included 11.5% of children in the relevant age-group (males 11.3%; females 11.6%). In 1999 the OPEC Fund granted a loan worth US $10m. to support a government programme to improve literacy standards and to increase access to education. In 2001 the Arab Bank for Economic Development in Africa granted a loan of $8m. to finance a project in support of general education. Following the political crisis of 2002, the Government abolished attendance fees for primary schools for a period of six months. The budget for 2001 allocated 736,600m. francs MG (14.0% of total expenditure) to education.

Public Holidays

2003: 1 January (New Year), 29 March (Martyr's Day, Commemoration of 1947 Rebellion), 21 April (Easter Monday), 1 May (Labour Day), 25 May (Organization of African Unity Day), 29 May (Ascension Day), 9 June (Whitsun), 26 June (Independence Day), 15 August (Assumption), 1 November (All Saints' Day), 25

December (Christmas), 30 December (Anniversary of the Demo-cratic Republic of Madagascar).
2004: 1 January (New Year), 29 March (Martyr's Day, Com-memoration of 1947 Rebellion), 12 April (Easter Monday), 1 May (Labour Day), 9 May (Ascension Day), 25 May (Organization of African Unity Day), 31 May (Whitsun), 26 June (Independence Day), 15 August (Assumption), 1 November (All Saints' Day), 25 December (Christmas), 30 December (Anniversary of the Dem-ocratic Republic of Madagascar).

Weights and Measures
The metric system is in force.

Statistical Survey

Source (unless otherwise stated): Institut National de la Statistique de Madagascar, BP 485, Anosy Tana, 101 Antananarivo; e-mail dginstat@dts.mg; internet rova.cite.mg/instat; tel. (20) 2227418.

Area and Population

AREA, POPULATION AND DENSITY

Area (sq km)	587,041*
Population (census results)	
1974–75†	7,603,790
1–19 August 1993	
Males	5,991,171
Females.	6,100,986
Total	12,092,157
Population (official estimates at mid-year)‡	
1999	14,650,000
2000	15,085,000
2001	15,529,000
Density (per sq km) at mid-2000	26.4

* 226,658 sq miles.

† The census took place in three stages: in provincial capitals on 1 December 1974; in Antananarivo and remaining urban areas on 17 February 1975; and in rural areas on 1 June 1975.

‡ Source: IMF, *Madagascar: Selected Issues and Statistical Appendix* (January 2003).

PRINCIPAL ETHNIC GROUPS
(estimated population, 1974)

Merina (Hova) . .	1,993,000	Sakalava . . .	470,156*
Betsimisaraka . .	1,134,000	Antandroy . . .	412,500
Betsileo . . .	920,600	Antaisaka. . .	406,468*
Tsimihety . . .	558,100		

* 1972 figure.

PRINCIPAL TOWNS
(population at 1993 census)

Antananarivo		Mahajanga	
(capital). . .	1,103,304	(Majunga) . . .	106,780
Toamasina		Toliary	
(Tamatave). . .	137,782	(Tuléar). . .	80,826
Antsirabé . . .	126,062	Antsiranana	
Fianarantsoa . .	109,248	(Diégo-Suarez). .	59,040

2001 (estimated population, incl. Renivohitra and Avaradrano): Antana-narivo 1,111,392.

BIRTHS AND DEATHS

	1998	1999	2000
Birth rate (per 1,000)	43.5	43.0	42.5
Death rate (per 1,000)	14.4	14.1	13.8

Source: African Development Bank.

Expectation of life (WHO estimates, years at birth): 54.8 (males 53.3; females 56.4) in 2001 (Source: WHO, *World Health Report*).

ECONOMICALLY ACTIVE POPULATION
('000 persons)

	1991	1992	1993
Agriculture	4,926	5,057	5,100
Manufacturing and mining . . .	82	84	86
Construction	44	45	46
Trade, banking and insurance . .	141	145	149
Transport and telecommunications	40	41	42
Administration	180	193	208
Other activities*	240	246	243
Total labour force	**5,653**	**5,811**	**5,874**

* Including artisans and domestic servants.

Labour force ('000 persons): 6,165 in 1994; 6,350 in 1995; 6,540 in 1996; 6,737 in 1997.

Source: IMF, *Madagascar: Recent Economic Developments and Selected Issues* (August 2000).

1993 census (persons aged 10 years and over): Total labour force 5,299,563 (males 3,181,509; females 2,118,054) (Source: ILO, *Yearbook of Labour Statistics*).

Mid-2001 (estimates in '000): Agriculture, etc. 5,803; Total labour force 7,861 (Source: FAO).

Health and Welfare

KEY INDICATORS

Total fertility rate (children per woman, 2001).	5.8
Under-5 mortality rate (per 1,000 live births, 2001) . . .	136
HIV/AIDS (% of persons aged 15–49, 2001).	0.29
Physicians (per 1,000 head, 1996)	10.7
Hospital beds (per 1,000 head, 1990)	0.94
Health expenditure (2000): US $ per head (PPP) . . .	33
Health expenditure (2000): % of GDP	3.5
Health expenditure (2000): public (% of total)	71.8
Access to water (% of persons, 2000).	47
Access to sanitation (% of persons, 2000)	42
Human Development Index (2000): ranking	147
Human Development Index (2000): value	0.469

For sources and definitions, see explanatory note on p. vi.

Agriculture

PRINCIPAL CROPS

('000 metric tons)

	1998	1999	2000
Rice (paddy)	2,447	2,637	2,300
Maize	152	181	150
Potatoes	280	285	293
Sweet potatoes . .	510	520	476
Cassava (Manioc) . .	2,412	2,435	2,228
Taro (Coco yam)† . .	155	160	190
Sugar cane	2,180	2,180	2,200
Dry beans	80	82*	84*
Other pulses† . .	16	15	15
Groundnuts (in shell) . . .	34	34	35
Coconuts†	84	85	84
Oil palm fruit† . .	21	22	21
Cottonseed . . .	23	20*	17*
Tomatoes†	23	23	22
Other vegetables† . .	327	333	322
Bananas†	260	265	290
Oranges†	84	85	83
Mangoes†	204	206	210
Avocados†	23	24	23
Pineapples†	51	52	51
Cashewapple† . . .	68	69	68
Other fruits† . . .	158	167	165
Coffee (green) . . .	60	65	64
Vanilla	2	2	2
Cinnamon (Canella)† . .	2	2	2
Cloves	14	15	16*
Cotton (lint)* . . .	15	14	11
Sisal	18	17	15
Tobacco (leaves) . . .	4	4	2

* Unofficial figure(s).
† FAO estimates.

Source: FAO.

LIVESTOCK

('000 head, year ending September)

	1999	2000	2001
Cattle	10,353	10,364	10,300
Pigs*	1,500	1,450	850
Sheep*	790	800	790
Goats*	1,360	1,370	1,350
Chickens*	19,000	20,000	19,000
Ducks*	3,700	3,900	3,800
Geese*	2,900	3,100	3,000
Turkeys*	1,900	2,000	1,900

* FAO estimates.

Source: FAO.

LIVESTOCK PRODUCTS

('000 metric tons)

	1998	1999	2000
Cows' milk*	525	530	535
Beef and veal . . .	148	148	148
Pig meat	72	74	44
Poultry meat . . .	57	60	63
Hen eggs*	13	14	15
Honey*	4	4	4
Cattle hides . . .	21	21	21

* FAO estimates.

Source: FAO.

Forestry

ROUNDWOOD REMOVALS

('000 cubic metres, excl. bark)

	1999	2000	2001
Sawlogs, veneer logs and logs for sleepers	80	70	70*
Pulpwood	35	23	23*
Fuel wood	9,357	9,637	9,919
Total	9,472	9,730	10,012

* FAO estimate.

Source: FAO.

SAWNWOOD PRODUCTION

(FAO estimates, '000 cubic metres, incl. railway sleepers)

	1999	2000	2001
Coniferous (softwood) . . .	3	4	4*
Broadleaved (hardwood) . . .	99	481	396
Total	102	485	400

* FAO estimate.

Source: FAO.

Fishing

('000 metric tons, live weight)

	1998	1999	2000
Capture	118.5	131.6	132.1
Cyprinids	4.0	4.0	4.0
Cichlids	21.5	21.5	21.5
Other freshwater fishes . .	4.5	4.5	4.5
Narrow-barred Spanish mackerel	12.0	12.0	12.0
Other marine fishes . .	69.7	74.4	75.1
Shrimps and prawns . .	11.5	10.5	12.1
Aquaculture	8.5*	9.5*	7.3
Brine shrimp	2.5	3.5	4.8
Total catch	127.0*	141.1*	139.4

Note: Figures exclude aquatic plants ('000 metric tons, capture only): 2.5 in 1998; 1.9 in 1999; 5.8 in 2000. Also excluded are crocodiles, recorded by number rather than weight, and shells. The number of Nile crocodiles caught was: 6,520 in 1998; 4,302 in 1999; 3,900 in 2000. The catch of marine shells (in metric tons) was: 10 in 1998; 8 in 1999; 74 in 2000.
* FAO estimate.

Source: FAO, *Yearbook of Fishery Statistics*.

Mining

(metric tons)

	1999	2000	2001
Chromite*	144	131,293	23,637
Salt	26,131	25,530	25,928
Graphite (natural) . . .	16,137	40,328	2,013
Mica	54	66	90

* Figures refer to gross weight. The estimated chromium content is 27%.

Industry

SELECTED PRODUCTS
(metric tons, unless otherwise indicated)

	1999	2000	2001
Raw sugar.	61,370	62,487	67,917
Beer ('000 hectolitres)	610.1	645.5	691.7
Cigarettes.	3,839	4,139	4,441
Woven cotton fabrics (million metres)	20.4	23.3	29.6
Leather footwear ('000 pairs)	460	570	n.a.
Plastic footwear ('000 pairs)	375	303	291
Paints	1,918	1,487	1,554
Soap	15,884	15,385	15,915
Motor spirit—petrol ('000 cu metres)	98.0	122.6	128.3
Kerosene ('000 cu metres)	65.0	65.2	75.1
Gas-diesel (distillate fuel) oil ('000 cu metres)	119.0	150.4	150.2
Residual fuel oils ('000 cu metres).	198.8	225.7	247.2
Cement	45,701	50,938	51,882
Electric energy (million kWh)*.	721.3	779.8	833.9

* Production by the state-owned utility only, excluding electricity generated by industries for their own use.

Finance

CURRENCY AND EXCHANGE RATES

Monetary Units
100 centimes = 1 franc malgache (franc MG—Malagasy franc)

Sterling, Dollar and Euro Equivalents (31 December 2002)
£1 sterling = 10,371.6 francs MG
US $1 = 6,434.8 francs MG
€1 = 6,748.81 francs MG
100,000 francs MG = £9.642 = $15.541 = €14.819

Average Exchange Rate (Malagasy francs per US $)
2000   6,767.5
2001   6,588.5
2002   6,832.0

GENERAL BUDGET
('000 million francs MG)*

Revenue†	1999	2000	2001
Budgetary revenue	2,667	3,068	3,029
Tax revenue	2,580	2,972	2,906
Taxes on income, profits and capital gains	398	467	595
Corporate	207	236	301
Individual	190	231	293
Domestic taxes on goods and services	661	865	804
General sales, turnover or value-added tax	389	513	536
Excises	128	160	110
Fiscal monoply profits	111	179	146
Taxes on international trade and transactions	1,481	1,591	1,452
Import duties	1,481	1,591	1,452
Other revenue	87	96	123
Non-budgetary revenue	—	—	—
Total	2,667	3,068	3,029

Expenditure‡	1999	2000	2001
Current expenditure.	2,175.0	2,402.6	3,081.7
General services	695.0	880.0	1,067.5
Defence	382.8	319.7	428.4
Education	392.0	555.5	736.6
Health	150.3	182.6	265.4
Social and community services	34.1	46.3	48.0
Economic services	143.2	160.9	163.2
Agriculture	55.9	83.2	72.4
Public works.	41.7	18.8	25.3
Other purposes.	760.4	577.3	801.0
Interest on government debt	492.8	612.3	591.9
Operations financed by counterpart funds	n.a.	2.0	1.4
Capital expenditure	1,615.9	1,766.1	2,180.9
Total	3,790.9	4,168.7	5,262.6

* Figures exclude the net cost of structural reforms ('000 million francs MG): 369.7 in 1999; 582.7 in 2000; 223.1 in 2001.
† Excluding grants received ('000 million francs MG): 842.5 in 1999; 946.7 in 2000; 1,161.6 in 2001. Also excluded is divestment revenue ('000 million francs MG): 51.8 in 1999; 46.3 in 2000; 104.1 in 2001.
‡ Excluding adjustment for changes in payment arrears.

Source: IMF, *Madagascar: Selected Issues and Statistical Appendix* (January 2003).

INTERNATIONAL RESERVES
(US $ million at 31 December)

	2000	2001	2002
IMF special drawing rights.	0.0	0.1	0.0
Foreign exchange.	285.1	398.2	363.2
Total	285.2	398.4	363.2

Source: IMF, *International Financial Statistics.*

MONEY SUPPLY
('000 million francs MG at 31 December)

	2000	2001	2002
Currency outside banks.	1,789.1	2,159.6	2,325.1
Demand deposits at deposit money banks	2,228.9	3,074.1	3,297.8
Total money.	4,018.0	5,233.7	5,623.0

Source: IMF, *International Financial Statistics.*

COST OF LIVING
(Consumer Price Index for Madagascans in Antananarivo; base: 1990 = 100)

	1998	1999	2000
Food	381.7	428.4	489.4
All items*	376.6	414.0	463.1

* Excluding rent.
Source: UN, *Monthly Bulletin of Statistics.*

NATIONAL ACCOUNTS
('000 million francs MG at current prices)

Expenditure on the Gross Domestic Product

	1998	1999	2000
Government final consumption expenditure	1,234.8	1,420.6	2,063.8
Private final consumption expenditure	17,712.7	20,232.9	23,437.6
Increase in stocks	3,007.0	3,485.0	3,480.0
Gross fixed capital formation.			
Total domestic expenditure	21,954.5	25,138.5	28,981.4
Exports of goods and services	4,358.1	5,702.6	7,420.4
Less Imports of goods and services	5,969.2	7,462.0	9,519.1
GDP in purchasers' values	20,343.4	23,379.1	26,882.8
GDP at constant 1984 prices	2,126.1	2,225.1	2,332.3

Source: IMF, *International Financial Statistics.*

Gross Domestic Product by Economic Activity

	1998	1999	2000
Agriculture, hunting, forestry and fishing	5,719.4	6,366.1	6,858
Mining and quarrying. . . .			
Manufacturing	2,549.3	2,916.7	3,412
Electricity, gas and water. . .			
Construction	296.4	355.0	396
Trade, restaurants and hotels .	2,386.3	2,624.2	2,927
Transport, storage and communications	3,654.5	4,034.7	4,501
Government services	1,051.4	1,266.0	1,412
Other services	3,285.7	3,948.5	4,404
Sub-total	18,943.1	21,511.2	23,912
Less imputed bank charges . .	237.6	308.6	329
GDP at factor cost . .	18,705.5	21,202.6	23,583
Indirect taxes, *less* subsidies .	1,637.9	2,176.5	2,659
GDP in purchasers' values .	20,343.4	23,379.1	26,242

Source: IMF, *Madagascar: Selected Issues and Statistical Appendix* (December 2001).

BALANCE OF PAYMENTS

(US $ million)

	1999	2000	2001
Exports of goods f.o.b.	584.0	823.7	110.7
Imports of goods f.o.b.	−742.5	−997.5	−113.9
Trade balance	−158.5	−173.7	−3.2
Exports of services	326.1	364.1	41.8
Imports of services	−456.2	−522.1	−60.9
Balance on goods and services	−288.6	−331.7	−22.3
Other income received	20.6	22.4	2.8
Other income paid	−63.1	−64.1	−12.7
Balance on goods, services and income	−331.0	−373.4	−32.2
Current transfers received . . .	110.9	121.9	13.6
Current transfers paid	−31.8	−31.3	−1.8
Current balance	−252.0	−282.8	−20.3
Capital account (net)	128.8	115.0	13.4
Direct investment from abroad. .	58.4	83.0	11.1
Other investment assets . . .	−73.1	−87.3	−15.3
Other investment liabilities . .	1.1	−26.3	−12.3
Net errors and omissions . . .	32.4	38.6	−30.7
Overall balance	−104.3	−160.0	−54.0

Source: IMF, *International Financial Statistics*.

External Trade

PRINCIPAL COMMODITIES

(million francs MG)

Imports c.i.f.	1996	1997	1998
Animal products	41,489	31,054	23,060
Vegetable products	123,160	179,366	209,037
Wheat and meslin	58,202	17,408	84,893
Rice	34,684	85,063	89,287
Animal or vegetable fats, oils and waxes	65,520	127,199	73,645
Food oils	40,623	98,020	55,712
Prepared foodstuffs	37,167	85,129	114,500
Mineral products	295,782	109,032	306,716
Crude petroleum	178,453	47,156	195,014
Chemical products	305,971	420,279	411,362
Pharmaceutical products . .	61,669	115,176	95,348
Plastic materials	56,947	86,868	93,555
Rubber manufactures	67,439	63,080	62,056
Rubber tyres	49,576	44,322	41,029
Paper, paperboard, etc.	79,716	94,341	117,323
Base metals and articles thereof .	162,796	196,607	266,712
Iron and steel	75,202	89,955	145,903
Machinery and mechanical appliances (non-electric) . . .	210,186	227,423	254,895
Electrical machinery and appliances	193,262	202,450	228,883
Radio and television equipment .	104,791	96,258	112,291
Transport equipment	214,846	316,391	313,012
Passenger cars and buses . .	73,180	115,774	140,689
Lorries	80,749	101,922	106,639
Total (incl. others)	2,056,108	2,392,164	2,748,989

2001: Food 7.5%; Energy (petroleum) 15.0%; Equipment goods 14.7%; Raw materials and spare parts 11.7%; Consumer goods 11.8%; Other imports (including EPZ) 39.3% (Source: IMF, *Madagascar: Selected Issues and Statistical Appendix*, January 2003).

Exports f.o.b.	1996	1997	1998
Animal products	233,919	87,679	123,654
Shrimps and prawns . . .	178,627	41,423	81,732
Vegetable products	471,104	437,564	436,199
Coffee (green)	232,242	168,397	218,922
Vanilla	47,988	49,196	38,718
Cloves	22,814	62,764	49,969
Litchis	25,052	16,996	14,804
Prepared foodstuffs	30,730	15,066	9,966
Mineral products	227,557	134,424	143,858
Graphite	33,061	35,716	36,382
Chromium ores	151,610	45,712	49,540
Petroleum products	39,414	40,851	53,772
Chemical products	24,920	30,894	35,039
Wood, cork and articles thereof .	25,277	38,860	57,245
Textiles and textile articles . . .	117,400	286,922	268,083
Cotton fabrics	43,612	89,865	179,416
Total (incl. others)	1,215,702	1,139,067	1,273,767

Source: Ministère du commerce et de la consommation.

PRINCIPAL TRADING PARTNERS
(million francs MG)

Imports	1996	1997	1998
Belgium-Luxembourg . . .	35,539	44,147	39,960
China, People's Repub. . . .	94,410	128,287	131,531
France	638,339	388,689	660,021
Germany	12,193	126,282	198,242
India	35,339	51,062	59,742
Iran	187,198	50,785	197,992
Italy	40,578	71,606	61,028
Japan	118,265	176,887	163,037
Malaysia	33,632	29,531	32,108
Netherlands	23,261	34,932	30,771
Pakistan	2,432	58,965	49,452
Romania	17,440	4,684	40,500
Singapore	47,497	36,435	19,328
SACU*	169,140	161,028	165,787
United Kingdom	47,459	67,491	69,161
USA	102,889	130,160	108,151
Total (incl. others)	2,056,108	2,392,164	2,748,989

* Southern African Customs Union, comprising Botswana, Lesotho, Namibia, South Africa and Swaziland.

2001: France 21.5%; People's Republic of China 9.1%; South Africa 5.5%; Japan 4.4%; USA 4.2%; Mauritius 2.9% (Source: IMF, *Madagascar: Selected Issues and Statistical Appendix*).

Exports	1996	1997	1998
Belgium-Luxembourg . . .	53,179	44,329	597
France	385,865	388,689	500,841
Germany	77,513	69,015	57,557
Italy	53,896	42,261	46,858
Japan	192,659	36,885	24,773
Mauritius	47,691	55,592	87,180
Netherlands	19,333	14,651	8,059
Portugal	16,570	3,360	16,055
Réunion	69,184	63,194	48,550
Singapore	19,124	43,134	34,907
Spain	27,563	32,963	18,674
United Kingdom	36,956	45,414	35,933
USA	50,797	53,571	76,589
Total (incl. others)	1,215,702	1,139,067	1,273,767

Source: Ministère du commerce et de la consommation.

2001: France 29.7%; USA 13.9%; Mauritius 2.6% (Source: IMF, *Madagascar: Selected Issues and Statistical Appendix*).

Transport

RAILWAYS
(traffic)

	1997	1998	1999
Passengers carried ('000) . . .	359	293	273
Passenger-km (millions) . . .	37	35	31
Freight carried ('000 metric tons) .	227	213	141
Ton-km (millions)	81	71	46

Source: Réseau National des Chemins de Fer Malagasy.

ROAD TRAFFIC
(vehicles in use)

	1994	1995	1996*
Passenger cars	54,821	58,097	60,480
Buses and coaches	3,797	4,332	4,850
Lorries and vans	35,931	37,232	37,972
Road tractors	488	560	619

* Estimates.

Source: IRF, *World Road Statistics*.

SHIPPING

Merchant Fleet
(registered at 31 December)

	1999	2000	2001
Number of vessels	101	105	104
Displacement ('000 gross registered tons)	42.6	43.7	43.4

Source: Lloyd's Register-Fairplay, *World Fleet Statistics*.

International Sea-borne Freight Traffic
('000 metric tons)

	1987	1988	1989
Goods loaded:			
Mahajanga	17	18	29.4
Toamasina	252	350	360.6
other ports	79	100	137.4
Total	348	468	527.4
Goods unloaded:			
Mahajanga	37	32	30.8
Toamasina	748	778	708.9
other ports	48	53	52.0
Total	833	863	791.7

1990 ('000 metric tons): Goods loaded 540; Goods unloaded 984 (Source: UN, *Monthly Bulletin of Statistics*).

CIVIL AVIATION
(traffic on scheduled services)

	1996	1997	1998
Kilometres flown (million) . . .	8	9	9
Passengers carried ('000) . . .	542	575	318
Passenger-km (million)	659	758	718
Total ton-km (million)	85	98	94

Source: UN, *Statistical Yearbook*.

Tourism

TOURIST ARRIVALS BY NATIONALITY

	1998	1999	2000
Canada and USA	2,424	6,913	6,402
France	61,815	74,657	88,039
Germany	4,850	5,530	6,403
Italy	7,273	8,295	8,004
Japan	1,454	2,489	2,055
Mauritius	3,394	3,871	4,526
Réunion	12,121	11,060	14,406
Switzerland	4,847	2,765	3,201
United Kingdom	3,636	4,148	4,802
Total (incl. others)	121,207	138,253	160,071

2001: 170,208 tourist arrivals.

Tourism receipts (US $ million): 91 in 1998; 100 in 1999; 116 in 2000.

Source: World Tourism Organization, mainly *Yearbook of Tourism Statistics*.

Communications Media

	1999	2000	2001
Television receivers ('000 in use)	360	375	n.a.
Telephones ('000 main lines in use)	50.2	56.7	58.4
Mobile cellular telephones ('000 subscribers).	35.8	63.1	147.5
Personal computers ('000 in use)	30	n.a.	40
Internet users ('000)	25	30	35

Source: International Telecommunication Union.

1995: Radio receivers ('000 in use) 2,850; Book production (incl. pamphlets): titles 131, copies ('000) 292; Daily newspapers: number 6, circulation ('000 copies) 59 (Source: UNESCO, *Statistical Yearbook*).

1996: Radio receivers ('000 in use) 2,950; Book production (incl. pamphlets): titles 119, copies ('000) 296; Daily newspapers: number 5, circulation ('000 copies) 66 (Source: UNESCO, *Statistical Yearbook*).

1997: Radio receivers ('000 in use) 3,050 (Source: UNESCO, *Statistical Yearbook*).

Education

(1998, unless otherwise indicated)

	Institu-tions	Teachers	Pupils		
			Males	Females	Total
Pre-primary* . . .	n.a.	n.a.	28,657	29,186	57,843
Primary	14,438	42,678	1,024,286	988,130	2,012,416
Secondary: general .	n.a.	18,987†	168,634	165,616	334,250
Secondary: teacher training‡ . .	n.a.	58	199	142	341
Secondary: vocational§ . .	n.a.	1,092	5,708	2,430	8,138
Tertiary	6	1,471	16,826	14,187	31,013

* 1994/95 figures.
† UNESCO estimate.
‡ 1993/94 figures.
§ 1995/96 figures, public education only.

Source: UNESCO, Institute for Statistics.

Adult literacy rate (UNESCO estimates): 66.5% (males 73.6%; females 59.7%) in 2000 (Source: UN Development Programme, *Human Development Report*).

Directory

The Constitution

The Constitution of the Third Republic of Madagascar was endorsed by national referendum on 19 August 1992, but was substantially altered by amendments that were endorsed in a national referendum on 15 March 1998. The amended Constitution enshrines a 'federal-style' state, composed of six autonomous provinces—each with a governor and up to 12 general commissioners (holding executive power) and a provincial council (holding legislative power). It provides for a government delegate to each province, who is charged with supervising the division of functions between the state and the province. The bicameral legislature consists of the National Assembly (the lower house), which is elected by universal adult suffrage, under a mixed system of single-seat constituencies and a form of proportional representation, for a five-year term of office. The Constitution also provides for a Senate (the upper house), of which one-third of the members are presidential nominees and two-thirds are elected in equal numbers by the provincial councillors and mayors of each of the six autonomous provinces, for a term of six years. The constitutional Head of State is the President. If no candidate obtains an overall majority in the presidential election, a second round of voting is to take place a maximum of 30 days after the publication of the results of the first ballot. Any one candidate can be elected for a maximum of three five-year terms. The powers of the President were greatly increased by constitutional amendments of March 1998: he has the power to determine general state policy in the Council of Ministers, to call referendums on all matters of national importance, and to dissolve the National Assembly not less than one year after a general election. Executive power is vested in a Prime Minister, who is appointed by the President. The President appoints the Council of Ministers, on the recommendation of the Prime Minister.

The Government

HEAD OF STATE

President: MARC RAVALOMANANA (inaugurated 6 May 2002, following a disputed presidential election—see Recent History).

COUNCIL OF MINISTERS
(April 2003)

Prime Minister: JACQUES SYLLA.

Deputy Prime Minister in charge of Economic Programmes and Minister of Transport, Public Works and Regional Planning: ZAZA MANITRANJA RAMANDIMBIARISON.

Minister of the Economy, Finance and the Budget: BENJAMIN ANDRIAMPARANY RADAVIDSON.

Minister of Justice and Keeper of the Seals: ALICE RAJAONAH.

Minister of Foreign Affairs: Gen. MARCEL RANJEVA.

Minister of the Interior and Administrative Reform: JEAN SETH RAMBELOALIJAONA.

Minister of Defence: Maj.-Gen. JULES MAMIZARA.

Minister of Public Security: Gen. AUGUSTIN AMADY.

Minister of Higher Education and Scientific Research: JEAN THÉODORE RANJIVASON.

Minister of Secondary and Basic Education: MICHEL RAZAFINDRANDRIATSIMANIRY.

Minister of Health: ANDRY RASAMINDRAKOTROKA.

Minister of the Population: JACOB FÉLICIEN ANDRIAMPANJAVA.

Minister of Industry, Trade and the Development of the Private Sector: MEJAMIRADO RAZAFIMIHARY.

Minister of the Civil Service: Dr VOLA DIEUDONNÉ RAZAFINDRALAMBO.

Minister of Labour and Social Legislation: JEAN JACQUES RABENIRINA.

Minister of the Environment, Water and Forests: Maj.-Gen. CHARLES SYLVAIN RABOTOARISON.

Minister of Energy and Mining: JACQUIS H. RABARISON.

Minister of Agriculture and Livestock: YVAN RANDRIASANDRATRINIONY.

Minister of Telecommunications, Post and Communications: HAJANIRINA RAZAFINJATOVO.

Minister of Youth, Sports and Leisure: RENÉ NDALANA.

Minister of Tourism: ROGER F. MAHAZOASY.

Minister of Culture: ODETTE RAHAINGOSOA.

Minister at the Presidency for Decentralization and the Development of the Autonomous Provinces: MONIQUE ANDREAS ESOAVELOMANDROSO.

MINISTRIES

Office of the Prime Minister: BP 248, Mahazoarivo, 101 Antananarivo; tel. (20) 2225258; fax (20) 2235258.

Ministry of Agriculture and Livestock: BP 301, Ampandrianomby, 101 Antananarivo; tel. (20) 2227227; fax (20) 2226561.

Ministry of the Civil Service: BP 270, Cité des 67 Hectares, Tsaralalana, 101 Antananarivo; tel. (20) 2223082; fax (20) 2233856.

Ministry of Culture: BP 305, Antaninarenina, 101 Antananarivo; tel. (20) 2227477; fax (20) 2229848.

Ministry of Decentralization and the Development of the Autonomous Provinces: BP 24 bis, 101 Antananarivo; tel. (20) 2235881; fax (20) 2237516.

Ministry of Defence: BP 08, Ampahibe, 101 Antananarivo; tel. (20) 2222211; fax (20) 2235420.

Ministry of the Economy, Finance and the Budget: BP 61, Antaninarenina, 101 Antananarivo; tel. (20) 2264681; fax (22) 2234530; e-mail cabmefb@dts.mg; internet www.mefb.gov.mg.

Ministry of Energy and Mining: BP 527, Immeuble de l'Industrie, Antaninarenina, 101 Antananarivo; tel. (20) 2228928; fax (20) 2232554; internet www.cite.mg/mine.

Ministry of the Environment, Water and Forests: rue Farafaty, BP 571 Ampandrianomby, 101 Antananarivo; tel. (20) 2240908; fax (20) 2241919.

Ministry of Foreign Affairs: BP 836, Anosy, 101 Antananarivo; tel. (20) 2221198; fax (20) 2234484.

Ministry of Health: BP 88, Ambohidahy, 101 Antananarivo; tel. (20) 2263121; fax (20) 2264228.

Ministry of Higher Education and Scientific Research: BP 4163, Tsimbazaza, 101 Antananarivo; tel. (20) 2229423; fax (20) 2234508; internet www.refer.mg/edu/minesup.

Ministry of Industry, Trade and the Development of the Private Sector: BP 527, Immeuble de l'Industrie, Antaninarenina, 101 Antananarivo; tel. (20) 2232251; fax (20) 2228024; e-mail celenv-mind@dts.mg; internet www.industrie.gov.mg.

Ministry of the Interior and Administrative Reform: BP 833, Anosy, 101 Antananarivo; tel. (20) 2223084; fax (20) 2235579.

Ministry of Justice: rue Joel Rakotomalala, BP 231, Faravohitra, 101 Antananarivo; tel. (20) 2237684; fax (20) 2264458; e-mail minjust.roger@simicro.mg; internet www.justice.gov.mg.

Ministry of Labour and Social Legislation: Immeuble FOP, 67 Ha, 101 Antananarivo; tel. (20) 2233859; fax (20) 2221309.

Ministry of the Population: BP 723, Ambohijatovo, 101 Antananarivo; tel. (20) 2227691; fax (20) 2264823; internet www .madapopulation.net.

Ministry of Public Security: BP 23 bis, 101 Antananarivo; tel. (20) 2221029; fax (20) 2231861.

Ministry of Secondary and Basic Education: BP 267, Anosy, 101 Antananarivo; tel. (20) 2221325; fax (20) 2224765.

Ministry of Telecommunications, Post and Communications: Antaninarenina, 101 Antananarivo; tel. (20) 2223267; fax (20) 2235894.

Ministry of Tourism: BP 610, Tsimbazaza, 101 Antananarivo; tel. (20) 2226298; fax (20) 2278953; e-mail mintour@dts.mg; internet www.madagascar-contacts.com/mintourcomfr.

Ministry of Transport, Public Works and Regional Planning: BP 3378, 101 Antananarivo; tel. (20) 2235612.

Ministry of Youth, Sports and Leisure: Ambohijatovo, Place Goulette, BP 681, 101 Antananarivo; tel. (20) 2227780; fax (20) 2234275.

President and Legislature

PRESIDENT

Presidential Election, 16 December 2001

Candidate	% of votes
Marc Ravalomanana	51.46
Adm. (retd) Didier Ratsiraka	35.90
Others	12.64
Total	100.00

LEGISLATURE

Senate

President: GUY RAJEMISON RAKOTOMAHARO.

Senatorial Election, 18 March 2001

Party	Seats
AREMA	49
LEADER/Fanilo	5
Independents	3
AVI	2
AFFA	1
Total	60*

* Elected by a 1,727-member electoral college of provincial councillors and mayors. An additional 30 seats were appointed by the President.

National Assembly

President: JEAN LAHINIRIAKO.

General Election, 15 December 2002

Party	Seats
TIM	103
FP	22
RPSD	5
AREMA	3
LEADER/Fanilo	2
MFM	2
HBM	1
Independents	22
Total	160

Political Organizations

Following the restoration of multi-party politics in March 1990, more than 120 political associations emerged, of which nine secured representation in the National Assembly in 1998. The following were among the more influential political organizations in mid-2003:

AKFM/Fanavaozana (AKFM/Renouveau): f. 1989 by fmr mems of the Marxist Parti du congrès de l'indépendance de Madagascar (AKFM); liberal orientation; Leader Pastor RICHARD ANDRIAMANJATO.

Asa, fahamarinana, fampandrosoana, arinda (AFFA—Action, Truth, Development and Harmony): f. 1998; opposition party; Leader Prof. ALBERT ZAFY.

Association pour la renaissance de Madagascar (Andry sy riana enti-manavotra an'i Madigasikara) (AREMA): f. 1975 as Avant-garde de la révolution malgache; adopted present name 1997; party of Pres. DIDIER RATSIRAKA; Sec.-Gen. (vacant).

Firaisankinam-Pirenena (FP—National Union): f. 2002; a pro-Ravalomanana alliance, consisting of TIM, AVI and RPSD mems.

Herim-Bahoaka Mitambatra (HBM): supports Pres. Ravalomanana; Leader TOVONANAHARY RABERSITONTA.

LEADER/Fanilo (Torch): f. 1993 as a party of 'non-politicians'; Leader Prof. MANASSE ESOAVELOMANDROSO.

Mouvement pour le progrès de Madagascar (Mpitolona ho amin'ny fandrosoan'ny Madagasikara) (MFM): 101 Antananarivo; f. 1972 as Mouvement pour le pouvoir prolétarien (MFM), adopted present name in 1990; advocates liberal and market-orientated policies; Leader MANANDAFY RAKOTONIRINA; Sec.-Gen. GERMAIN RAKOTONIRAINY.

Ny asa vita no ifampitsara (AVI—People are judged by the work they do): f. 1997 to promote human rights, hard work and development; Leader NORBERT RATSIRAHONANA.

Parti sociale démocrate (PSD): f. 1957; party of fmr Pres. Tsiranana; ruling party 1958–72; relaunched 1990; Leader RUFFINE TSIRANANA.

Rassemblement pour le socialisme et la démocratie (RPSD): f. 1993 by fmr mems of PSD; also known as Renaissance du parti social-démocratique; Leader EVARISTE MARSON; Sec.-Gen. JEAN EUGÈNE VONINAHITSY.

Tiako i Madagasikara (TIM—I Love Madagascar): internet www.tim-madagascar.org; f. 2002; supports Pres. Ravalomanana; Leader GUY RAJEMISON RAKOTOMAHARO; Sec.-Gen. JACQUES SYLLA.

Toamasina Tonga Saina (TTS): pro-AREMA party.

Diplomatic Representation

EMBASSIES IN MADAGASCAR

China, People's Republic: Ancien Hôtel Panorama, BP 1658, 101 Antananarivo; tel. (20) 2240129; fax (20) 2240215; Ambassador Xu Jinghu.

Egypt: LOT MD 378 Ambalatokana Mandrosoa Ivato, BP 4082, 101 Antananarivo; tel. (20) 2245497; fax (20) 2245379; Ambassador Azzah Abd al-Fatah Nassir.

France: 3 rue Jean Jaurès, BP 204, 101 Antananarivo; tel. (20) 2239898; fax 2239927; e-mail ambatana@dts.mg; Ambassador Catherine Boivineau.

Germany: 101 rue du Pasteur Rabeony Hans, BP 516, Ambodirotra, 101 Antananarivo; tel. (20) 2223802; fax (20) 2226627; e-mail amballem@dts.mg; Ambassador Dr Heinz-Peter Behr.

Holy See: Amboniloha Ivandry, BP 650, 101 Antananarivo; tel. (20) 2242376; fax (20) 2242384; e-mail noncapmg@dts.mg; Apostolic Nuncio Most Rev. Bruno Musarò (Titular Archbishop of Abari).

India: 4 làlana Emile Rajaonson, Tsaralalana, BP 1787, 101 Antananarivo; tel. (20) 2223334; fax (20) 2233790; e-mail indembmd@bow.dts.mg; Ambassador Sibabrata Tripathi.

Indonesia: 26–28 rue Patrice Lumumba, BP 3969, 101 Antananarivo; tel. (20) 2224915; fax (20) 2232857; Chargé d'affaires a.i. Slamet Suyata Sastramihardza.

Iran: route Circulaire, Lot II L43 ter, 101 Antananarivo; tel. (20) 2228639; fax (20) 2222298; Ambassador Ali Amoui.

Italy: 22 rue Pasteur Rabary, BP 16, Ankadivato, 101 Antananarivo; tel. (20) 2221217; fax (20) 2223814; e-mail ambanta@simicro.mg; Ambassador Renato Volpini.

Japan: 8 rue du Dr Villette, BP 3863, Isoraka, 101 Antananarivo; tel. (20) 2226102; fax (20) 2221769; Ambassador Toshio Watanabe.

Korea, Democratic People's Republic: 101 Antananarivo; tel. (20) 2244442; Ambassador Ri Hyong Yon.

Libya: Lot IIb, 37a route Circulaire Ampandrana-Ouest, 101 Antananarivo; tel. (20) 2221892; Chargé d'affaires Dr Mohamed Ali Sharfedin al Fituri.

Mauritius: Anjaharay, route Circulaire, BP 6040, Ambanidia 101, Antananarivo; tel. (20) 2221864; fax (20) 2221939; Ambassador Ghislaine Henry.

Russia: BP 4006, Ivandry-Ambohijatovo, 101 Antananarivo; tel. (20) 2242827; fax (20) 2242642; Ambassador Yurii N. Merzliakov.

Switzerland: BP 118, 101 Antananarivo; tel. (20) 2262997; fax (20) 2228940; Chargé d'affaires Rosmarie Schelling.

United Kingdom: Lot II I164 ter, Alarobia, Amboniloha, BP 167, 101 Antananarivo; tel. (20) 2249378; fax (20) 2249381; e-mail ukembant@simicro.mg; Ambassador Brian Donaldson.

USA: 14–16 rue Rainitovo, Antsahavola, BP 620, 101 Antananarivo; tel. (20) 2221257; fax (20) 2234539; Ambassador Wanda L. Nesbitt.

Judicial System

HIGH CONSTITUTIONAL COURT

Haute Cour Constitutionnelle: POB 835, Ambohidahy, 101 Antananarivo; tel. 2266061; e-mail hcc@simicro.mg; internet www .simicro.mg/hcc; interprets the Constitution and rules on constitutional issues; nine mems; Pres. Jean-Michel Rajaonarivony.

HIGH COURT OF JUSTICE

Haute Cour de Justice: 101 Antananarivo; nine mems.

SUPREME COURT

Cour Suprême: Palais de Justice, Anosy, 101 Antananarivo; Pres. Alice Rajaonah (acting); Attorney-General Colombe Ramanantsoa (acting); Chamber Pres Yolande Ramangasoavina, François Ramanandraibe.

COURT OF APPEAL

Cour d'Appel: Palais de Justice, Anosy, 101 Antananarivo; Pres. Aimée Rakotonirina; Pres of Chamber Charles Rabetokotany, Pétronille Andriamihaja, Bakolalao Ranaivoharivony, Bertholier Ravelontsalama, Lucien Rabarijhon, Nelly Rakotobe, Arlette Ramaroson, Clémentine Ravandison, Gisèle Rabotovao, Jean-Jacques Rajaona.

OTHER COURTS

Tribunaux de Première Instance: at Antananarivo, Toamasina, Antsiranana, Mahajanga, Fianarantsoa, Toliary, Antsirabé, Ambatondrazaka, Antalaha, Farafangana and Maintirano; for civil, commercial and social matters, and for registration.

Cours Criminelles Ordinaires: tries crimes of common law; attached to the Cour d'Appel in Antananarivo but may sit in any other large town. There are also 31 Cours Criminelles Spéciales dealing with cases concerning cattle.

Tribunaux Spéciaux Economiques: at Antananarivo, Toamasina, Mahajanga, Fianarantsoa, Antsiranana and Toliary; tries crimes specifically relating to economic matters.

Tribunaux Criminels Spéciaux: judges cases of banditry and looting; 31 courts.

Religion

It is estimated that more than 50% of the population follow traditional animist beliefs, some 43% are Christians (about one-half of whom are Roman Catholics) and the remainder are Muslims.

CHRISTIANITY

Fiombonan'ny Fiangonana Kristiana eto Madagasikara (FFKM)/Conseil Chrétien des Eglises de Madagascar/Christian Council of Churches in Madagascar: Vohipiraisama, Ambohijatovo-Atsimo, BP 798, 101 Antananarivo; tel. (20) 2229052; f. 1980; four mems and one assoc. mem. Pres. Pastor Edmond Razafimahaleo; Gen. Sec. Rev. Lala Andriamiharisoa.

Fiombonan'ny Fiangonana Protestanta eto Madagasikara (FFPM)/Fédération des Eglises Protestantes à Madagascar/Federation of the Protestant Churches in Madagascar: VK 3 Vohipiraisana, Ambohijatovo-Atsimo, BP 4226, 101 Antananarivo; tel. (20) 2220144; f. 1958; two mem churches; Pres. Pastor Edmond Razafimahefa; Gen. Sec. Rev. Dr Roger Andriatsiratahina.

The Anglican Communion

Anglicans are adherents of the Church of the Province of the Indian Ocean, comprising six dioceses (four in Madagascar, one in Mauritius and one in Seychelles). The Archbishop of the Province is the Bishop of Antananarivo. The Church has about 160,000 adherents in Madagascar, including the membership of the Eklesia Episkopaly Malagasy (Malagasy Episcopal Church), founded in 1874.

Bishop of Antananarivo (also Archbishop of the Province of the Indian Ocean): Most Rev. Rémi Joseph Rabenirina, Evêché Anglican, Lot VK57 ter, Ambohimanoro, 101 Antananarivo; tel. (20) 2220827; fax (20) 2261331; e-mail eemdanta@dts.mg.

Bishop of Antsiranana: (vacant), Evêché Anglican, BP 278, 201 Antsiranana; tel. (20) 8222650; e-mail eemdants@dts.mg.

Bishop of Mahajanga: Rt Rev. Jean-Claude Andrianjafimanana, BP 169, 401 Mahajanga; e-mail eemdmaha@dts.mg.

Bishop of Toamasina: Rt Rev. Donald Westwood Smith, Evêché Anglican, rue de la Fraternité, BP 531, 501 Toamasina; tel. (20) 5332163.

The Roman Catholic Church

Madagascar comprises three archdioceses and 17 dioceses. At 31 December 2000 the number of adherents in the country represented about 22.9% of the total population.

Bishops' Conference

Conférence Episcopale de Madagascar, 102 bis, rue Cardinal Jerôme Rakotomalala, BP 667, 101 Antananarivo; tel. (20) 2220478; fax (20) 2224854; e-mail ecar@vitelcom.mg.

f. 1969; Pres. Rt Rev. Fulgence Rabeony (Bishop of Toliary).

Archbishop of Antananarivo: Cardinal Armand Razafindratandra, Archevêché, Andohalo, BP 3030, 101 Antananarivo; tel. (20) 2220726; fax (20) 2264181; e-mail ecar-andolaho@simicro.org.

Archbishop of Antsiranana: Most Rev. Michel Malo, Archevêché, BP 415, 201 Antsiranana; tel. (82) 21605.

Archbishop of Fianarantsoa: Most Rev. Philibert Randriambololona, Archevêché, place Mgr Givelet, BP 1440, Ambozontany, 301 Fianarantsoa; tel. (20) 7550027; fax (20) 7551436; e-mail ecarfianar@vitelcom.mg.

Other Christian Churches

Fiangonan' i Jesoa Kristy eto Madagasikara/Eglise de Jésus-Christ à Madagascar: Lot 11 B18, Tohatohabato Ranavalona 1, Trano 'Ifanomezantsoa', BP 623, 101 Antananarivo; tel. (20)

2226845; fax (20) 2226372; e-mail fjkm@dts.mg; f. 1968; Pres. Rev. EDMOND RAZAFIMAHEFA; Gen. Sec. Rev. CHARLES RAKOTONIRINA; 2m. mems.

Fiangonana Loterana Malagasy (Malagasy Lutheran Church): BP 1741, 101 Antananarivo; tel. (20) 2222347; Pres. Rev. BENJAMIN RABENOROLAHY; 600,000 mems.

The Press

In December 1990 the National People's Assembly adopted legislation guaranteeing the freedom of the press and the right of newspapers to be established without prior authorization.

PRINCIPAL DAILIES

Bulletin de l'Agence Nationale d'Information 'Taratra' (ANTA): 3 rue du R. P. Callet, Behoririka, BP 386, 101 Antananarivo; tel. (20) 2221171; f. 1977; French; Man. Dir JEANNOT FENO.

L'Express de Madagascar: BP 3893, 101 Antananarivo; tel. (20) 2221934; fax (20) 2262894; e-mail lexpress@malagasy.com; internet www.lexpressmada.com; f. 1995; French and Malagasy; Editor CHRISTIAN CHADEFAUX; circ. 10,000.

Gazetiko: BP 1414 Ankorondrano, 101 Antananarivo; tel. (20) 2269779; fax (20) 2227351; e-mail gazetikom@yahoo.fr; Malagasy.

Imongo Vaovao: 11K 4 bis Andravoahangy, BP 7014, 101 Antananarivo; tel. (20) 2221053; f. 1955; Malagasy; Dir CLÉMENT RAMAMONJISOA; circ. 10,000.

Madagascar Tribune: Immeuble SME, rue Ravoninahitriniarivo, BP 659, Ankorondrano, 101 Antananarivo; tel. (20) 2222635; fax (20) 2222254; e-mail tribune@bow.dts.mg; internet www .madagascar-tribune.com; f. 1988; independent; French and Malagasy; Editor RAHAGA RAMAHOLIMIHASO; circ. 12,000.

Maresaka: 12 làlana Ratsimba John, Isotry, 101 Antananarivo; tel. (20) 2223568; f. 1953; independent; Malagasy; Editor M. RALAIARI-JAONA; circ. 5,000.

Midi Madagasikara: làlana Ravoninahitriniarivo, BP 1414, Ankorondrano, 101 Antananarivo; tel. (20) 2269779; fax (20) 2227351; e-mail midi@dts.mg; internet www.dts.mg/midi; f. 1983; French and Malagasy; Dir MAMY RAKOTOARIVELO; circ. 25,500.

PRINCIPAL PERIODICALS

Basy Vava: Lot III E 96, Mahamasina Atsimo, 101 Antananarivo; tel. (20) 2220448; f. 1959; Malagasy; Dir GABRIEL RAMANANJATO; circ. 3,000.

Bulletin de la Société du Corps Médical Malgache: Imprimerie Volamahitsy, 101 Antananarivo; Malagasy; monthly; Dir Dr RAKOTO-MALALA.

Dans les Médias Demain (DMD): Immeuble Jeune Afrique, 58 rue Tsiombikibo, BP 1734, Ambatovinaky, 101 Antananarivo; tel. (20) 2263615; fax (20) 2230629; e-mail dmd@dts.mg; internet www.dmd .mg; f. 1986; independent; economic information and analysis; weekly; Dir HONORÉ RAZAFINTSALAMA; circ. 4,000.

Feon'ny Mpiasa: Lot M8, Isotry, 101 Antananarivo; trade union affairs; Malagasy; monthly; Dir M. RAZAKANAIVO; circ. 2,000.

Fiaraha-Miasa: BP 1216, 101 Antananarivo; Malagasy; weekly; Dir SOLO NORBERT ANDRIAMORASATA; circ. 5,000.

Gazetinao: Lot IPA 37, BP 1758, Anosimasina, 101 Antananarivo; tel. (20) 2261979; e-mail jamesdigne@caramail.com; f. 1976; French and Malagasy; monthly; Editors-in-Chief ANDRIANIAINA RAKOTOMAHA-NINA, JAMES FRRANKLIN; circ. 3,000.

La Gazette d'Antsirabé: 110 Antsirabé; f. 1989; Dir VOLOLOHARIMA-NANA RAZAFIMANDIMBY; circ. 7,000.

Gazety Medikaly: 101 Antananarivo; tel. (20) 2227898; f. 1965; medical; monthly; Dir PAUL RATSIMISETA; circ. 2,000.

Isika Mianakavy: Ambatomena, 301 Fianarantsoa; f. 1958; Roman Catholic; Malagasy; monthly; Dir J. RANAIVOMANANA; circ. 21,000.

Journal Officiel de la République de Madagascar: BP 248, 101 Antananarivo; tel. (20) 2265010; fax 2225319; e-mail segma.gvt@dts .mg; f. 1883; official announcements; Malagasy and French; weekly; Dir HONORÉE ELIANNE RALALAHARISON; circ. 1,545.

Journal Scientifique de Madagascar: BP 3855, Antananarivo; f. 1985; Dir Prof. MANAMBELONA; circ. 3,000.

Jureco: BP 6318, Lot IVD 48 bis, rue Razanamaniraka, Behoririka, 101 Antananarivo; tel. (20) 2255271; e-mail jureco@malagasy.com; internet www.jureco.com; law and economics; monthly; French; Dir MBOARA ANDRIANARIMANANA.

Lakroan'i Madagasikara: BP 1169, Maison Jean XXIII, Mahama-sina Sud, 101 Antananarivo; tel. (20) 2221158; fax (20) 224020;

e-mail lakroa@dts.mg; internet lakroa.free.fr; f. 1927; Roman Catholic; French and Malagasy; weekly; Dir LOUIS RASOLO; circ. 25,000.

Mada—Economie: 15 rue Ratsimilaho, BP 3464, 101 Antananarivo; tel. (20) 2225634; f. 1977; reports events in south-east Africa; monthly; Editor RICHARD-CLAUDE RATOVONARIVO; circ. 5,000.

Mpanolotsaina: BP 623, 101 Antananarivo; tel. (20) 2226845; fax (20) 2226372; e-mail fjkm@dts.mg; religious, educational; Malagasy; quarterly; Dir RAYMOND RAJOELISOL.

New Magazine: BP 7581, Newprint, Route des Hydrocarbures, 101 Antananarivo; tel. (20) 2233335; fax (20) 2236471; e-mail newmag@ dts.mg; internet www.dts.mg/newmag; 2 a month; in French; Dir CLARA RAVOAVAHY.

Ny Mpamangy-FLM: 9 rue Grandidier Isoraka, BP 538, Antsahamanitra, 101 Antananarivo; tel. (20) 2232446; f. 1882; monthly; Dir Pastor JEAN RABENANDRASANA; circ. 3,000.

Ny Sakaizan'ny Tanora: BP 538, Antsahaminitra, 101 Antananarivo; tel. (20) 2232446; f. 1878; monthly; Editor-in-Chief DANIEL PROSPER ANDRIAMANJAKA; circ. 5,000.

PME Madagascar: rue Hugues Rabesahala, BP 953, Antsakaviro, 101 Antananarivo; tel. (20) 2222536; fax (20) 2234534; f. 1989; French; monthly; economic review; Dir ROMAIN ANDRIANARISOA; circ. 3,500.

Recherche et Culture: BP 907, 101 Antananarivo; tel. (20) 2226600; f. 1985; publ. by French dept of the University of Antananarivo; 2 a year; Dir GINETTE RAMAROSON; circ. 1,000.

Revue Ita: BP 681, 101 Antananarivo; tel. (20) 2230507; f. 1985; controlled by the Ministry of Population, Women's Affairs and Children; monthly; Dir FILS RAMALANJAONA; circ. 1,000.

Revue de l'Océan Indien: Communication et Médias Océan Indien, rue H. Rabesahala, BP 46, Antsakaviro, 101 Antananarivo; tel. (20) 2222536; fax (20) 2234534; e-mail roi@dts.mg; internet www .madatours.com/roi; f. 1980; monthly; French; Man. Dir GEORGES RANAIVOSOA; Sec.-Gen. HERY M. A. RANAIVOSOA; circ. 5,000.

Sahy: Lot VD 42, Ambanidia, 101 Antananarivo; tel. (20) 2222715; f. 1957; political; Malagasy; weekly; Editor ALINE RAKOTO; circ. 9,000.

Sosialisma Mpiasa: BP 1128, 101 Antananarivo; tel. (20) 2221989; f. 1979; trade union affairs; Malagasy; monthly; Dir PAUL RABEMA-NANJARA; circ. 5,000.

Valeurs—L'Hebdomadaire de Madagascar: Antananarivo; f. 1995; weekly; Dir RIJA RASENDRATSIROFO.

Vaovao: BP 271, 101 Antananarivo; tel. (20) 2221193; f. 1985; French and Malagasy; weekly; Dir MARC RAKOTONOELY; circ. 5,000.

NEWS AGENCIES

Agence Nationale d'Information 'TARATRA' (ANTA): 7 rue Jean Ralaimongo, Ambohiday, BP 386, 101 Antananarivo; tel. and fax (20) 2236047; e-mail anta@blanbir.mg; f. 1977; Man. Dir JOÉ ANACLET RAKOTOARISON.

Foreign Bureaux

Associated Press (AP) (USA): BP 73, 101 Antananarivo; tel. (20) 2241944; e-mail zadefo@malagasy.com; Correspondent CHRISTIAN CHADEFAUX.

Korean Central News Agency (KCNA) (Democratic People's Republic of Korea): 101 Antananarivo; tel. (20) 2244795; Dir KIM YEUNG KYEUN.

Xinhua (New China) News Agency (People's Republic of China): BP 1656, 101 Antananarivo; tel. (20) 2229927; Chief of Bureau WU HAIYUN.

Reuters (United Kingdom) is also represented in Madagascar.

Publishers

Edisiona Salohy: BP 4226, 101 Antananarivo; Dir MIRANA VOLO-LOARISOA RANDRIANARISON.

Editions Ambozontany: BP 40, 301 Fianarantsoa; tel. (20) 7550603; f. 1962; religious and school textbooks; Dir R. F. GIAMBRONE.

Foibe Filankevitry Ny Mpampianatra (FOFIPA): BP 202, 101 Antananarivo; tel. (20) 2227500; f. 1971; textbooks; Dir Frère RAZA-FINDRAKOTO.

Imprimerie Nouvelle: PK 2, Andranomahery, route de Majunga, BP 4330, 101 Antananarivo; tel. (20) 2221036; fax (20) 2269225; e-mail nouvelle@wanadoo.mg; Dir EUGÈNE RAHARIFIDY.

Imprimerie Takariva: 4 rue Radley, BP 1029, Antanimena, 101 Antananarivo; tel. (20) 2222128; f. 1933; fiction, languages, school textbooks; Man. Dir PAUL RAPATSALAHY.

Madagascar Print and Press Co (MADPRINT): rue Rabesahala, Antsakaviro, BP 953, 101 Antananarivo; tel. (20) 2222536; fax (20) 2234534; f. 1969; literary, technical and historical; Dir GEORGES RANAIVOSOA.

Maison d'Edition Protestante Antso: 19 rue Venance Manifatra, Imarivolanitra, BP 660, 101 Antananarivo; tel. (20) 2220886; fax (20) 2226372; e-mail fjkm@dts.mg; f. 1972; religious, school, social, political and general; Dir HANS ANDRIAMAMPIANINA.

Nouvelle Société de Presse et d'Edition (NSPE): Immeuble Jeune Afrique, 58 rue Tsiombikibo, BP 1734, Ambatorinaky, 101 Antananarivo; tel. (20) 2227788; fax (20) 2230629.

Office du Livre Malgache: Lot 111 H29, Andrefan' Ambohijanahary, BP 617, 101 Antananarivo; tel. (20) 2224449; f. 1970; children's and general; Sec.-Gen. JULIETTE RATSIMANDRAVA.

Société Malgache d'Edition (SME): BP 659, Ankorondrano, 101 Antananarivo; tel. (20) 2222635; fax (20) 2222254; e-mail tribune@bow.dts.mg; f. 1943; general fiction, university and secondary textbooks; Man. Dir RAHAGA RAMAHOLIMIHASO.

Société Nouvelle de l'Imprimerie Centrale (SNIC): làlana Ravoninahitriniarivo, BP 1414, 101 Antananarivo; tel. (20) 2221118; e-mail mrakotoa@dts.mg; f. 1959; science, school textbooks; Man. Dir MAMY RAKOTOARIVELO.

Société de Presse et d'Edition de Madagascar: Antananarivo; non-fiction, reference, science, university textbooks; Man. Dir RAJAOFERA ANDRIAMBELO.

Trano Printy Fiangonana Loterana Malagasy (TPFLM): BP 538, 9 ave Général Gabriel Ramanantsoa, 101 Antananarivo; tel. (20) 2223340; fax (20) 2262643; e-mail impluth@dts.mg; f. 1877; religious, educational and fiction; Man. RAYMOND RANDRIANATOANDRO.

Government Publishing House

Imprimerie Nationale: BP 38, 101 Antananarivo; tel. (20) 2223675; all official publs; Dir JEAN DENIS RANDRIANIRINA.

Broadcasting and Communications

TELECOMMUNICATIONS

Mobile cellular telephone networks are operated by Antaris, Sacel and Telecel.

Office Malagasy d'Etudes et de Régulation des Télécommunications (OMERT): BP 99991, Route des Hydrocarbures-Alarobia, 101 Antananarivo; tel. (20) 2242119; fax (20) 2221516; e-mail omert@dts.mg; internet www.omert.mg; f. 1997; Gen. Man. GILBERT ANDRIANIRINA RAJAONASY.

Société Anonyme Télécom Malagasy (TELMA): BP 763, 101 Antananarivo; tel. (20) 2242705; fax (20) 2242654; e-mail rakotoar@bow.dts.mg; internet www.telma.net; 66% state-owned, 34% owned by France Câbles et Radio; transfer to private sector pending in early 2003, with Distacom (Hong Kong) selected provisionally as purchaser; Chair. MAMIHARILALA RASOLOJAONA; Dir-Gen. BRUNO ANTRIATAVISON.

BROADCASTING

Radio

Radio Nationale Malagasy: BP 442, Anosy, 101 Antananarivo; tel. (20) 2226120; fax (20) 2232715; e-mail radmad@dts.mg; internet www.takelaka.dts.mg/radmad; state-controlled; broadcasts in French, Malagasy and English; Dir FÉLIX MALAZARIVO.

Le Messager Radio Evangélique: BP 1374, 101 Antananarivo; tel. (20) 2234495; broadcasts in French, English and Malagasy; Dir JOCELYN RANJARISON.

Radio Antsiva: Lot VA, BP 6323, 21 Ambohitantely, 101 Antananarivo; tel. (20) 2265789; internet www.antsiva.mg; broadcasts in French, English and Malagasy; Dir ISMAËL RAZAFINARIVO.

Radio Feon'ny Vahoaka (RFV): 103 Immeuble Ramaroson, 8e étage, 101 Antananarivo; tel. (20) 2233820; broadcasts in French and Malagasy; Dir ALAIN RAMAROSON.

Radio Korail: 101 Antananarivo; tel. and fax (20) 2224494; f. 1993; broadcasts in French and Malagasy; Dir ALAIN RAJAONA.

Radio Lazan'iarivo (RLI): Lot V A49, Andafiavaratra, 101 Antananarivo; tel. (20) 2229016; fax (20) 2267559; e-mail rli@simicro.mg; broadcasts in French, English and Malagasy; Dir IHOBY RABARIJOHN.

Radio Tsioka Vao (RTV): BP 315, Tana; tel. (20) 2221749; f. 1992; broadcasts in French, English and Malagasy; Dir DETKOU DEDONNAIS.

Television

MA TV: BP 1414 Ankorondrano, 101 Antananarivo; tel. (20) 2220897; fax (20) 2234421; e-mail matv@dts.mg; internet www.matvonline.tv.

Radio Télévision Analamanga: Immeuble Fiaro, 101 Antananarivo; e-mail rta@rta.mg; internet www.rta.mg; including four provincial radio stations; Dir-Gen. J. C. AUCHAN.

Télévision Nasionaly Malagasy: BP 1202, 101 Antananarivo; tel. (20) 2222381; state-controlled; broadcasts in French and Malagasy; Dir-Gen. RAZAFIMAHEFA HERINIRINA LALA.

Finance

(cap. = capital; res = reserves; dep. = deposits; m. = million; brs = branches; amounts in Malagasy francs)

BANKING

Central Bank

Banque Centrale de Madagascar: ave de la Révolution Socialiste Malgache, BP 550, 101 Antananarivo; tel. (20) 2221751; fax (20) 2234532; e-mail banque-centrale@banque-centrale-madagascar.mg; f. 1973; bank of issue; cap. 1,000m., res 17,616.2m. (Dec. 2001), dep. 2,475,613m. (Dec. 2000); Gov. GASTON RAVELOJAONA.

Other Banks

Bank of Africa (BOA)—Madagascar: 2 place de l'Indépendance, BP 183, 101 Antananarivo; tel. (20) 2239100; fax (20) 2229408; e-mail boadgle@dts.mg; internet www.bkoafrica.net; f. 1976 as Bankin'ny Tantsaha Mpamokatra, name changed as above 1999; 15% state-owned; commercial bank, specializes in micro-finance; cap. 40,000m., res 3,295m., dep. 946,979m. (Dec. 2000); Pres. PAUL DERREUMAUX; Dir-Gen. BERNARD HAIZET; 48 brs.

Banque Malgache de l'Océan Indien (BMOI) (Indian Ocean Malagasy Bank): place Philibert Tsiranana, BP 25 Bis, Antaninarenina, Antananarivo 101; tel. (20) 2234609; fax (20) 2234610; e-mail bmoi.st@simicro.mg; internet www.bmoi.mg; f. 1990; 37.5% owned by Banque Nationale de Paris; cap. and res 118,800m., total assets 916,504m. (Dec. 1998); Pres. GASTON RAMENASON; Dir-Gen. JEAN-CLAUDE HERIDE; 8 brs.

Banque de Solidarité Malgache (SBM): rue Andrianary Ratianarivo Antsahavola 1, 101 Antananarivo; tel. (20) 2266607; fax (20) 2266608; e-mail sbmm@dts.mg; f. 1996; cap. 14,502.6m., res 2,272.1m., dep. 125,439.3m. (Dec. 2000); Chair. CHAITLALL GUNNESS; Gen. Man. KRISHNADUTT RAMBOJUN.

BFV—Société Générale: Làlana Jeneraly Rabetevitra 14, BP 196, Antananarivo 101; tel. (20) 2220691; fax (20) 2234554; f. 1977 as Banky Fampandrosoana ny Varotra; changed name in 1998; 70% owned by Société Générale (France) and 30% state-owned; cap. 70,000m., res 6,572m., dep. 754,126m. (Dec. 2000); Chief Exec. JEAN-PIERRE DUCROQUET; 24 brs.

BNI—Crédit Lyonnais Madagascar: 74 rue du 26 Juin 1960, BP 174, 101 Antananarivo; tel. (20) 2223951; fax (20) 2233749; e-mail stdg@bni.mg; internet www.bni.mg; f. 1976 as Bankin 'ny Indostria; 32.58% state-owned; cap. 13,500m., res 97,196.8m., dep. 1,276,694.6m. (Dec. 2001); Pres. and Chair. EVARISTO MARSON; Dir-Gen. DOMINIQUE TISSIER; 22 brs.

Union Commercial Bank SA (UCB): 77 rue Solombavambahoaka Frantsay, Antsahavola, BP 197, 101 Antananarivo; tel. (20) 2227262; fax (20) 2228740; e-mail ucb.int@dts.mg; f. 1992; 70% owned by Mauritius Commercial Bank Ltd; cap. 6,000m., res 37,397.2m., dep. 250,894.0m. (Dec. 2000); Pres. RAYMOND HEIN; Gen. Man. PAUL GIBLIN; 3 brs.

INSURANCE

ARO (Assurances Réassurances Omnibranches): Antsahavola, BP 42, 101 Antananarivo; tel. (20) 2220154; fax (20) 2234464; e-mail arol@dts.mg; Pres. FRANCIS RAKOTO; Dir-Gen. JEAN-BAPTISTE GUERRA.

Assurance France-Madagascar: 7 rue Rainitovo, BP 710, 101 Antananarivo; tel. (20) 2223024; fax (20) 2269201; e-mail l.afm@wanadoo.mg; f. 1951; Dir RAKOUTH ZAFIARISOA.

Compagnie Malgache d'Assurances et de Réassurances: Immeuble 'Ny Havana', Zone des 67 Ha, BP 3881, 101 Antananarivo; tel. (20) 2226760; fax (20) 2224303; f. 1968; cap. 16,050m. (1996); Dir-Gen. ROLAND RASAMOELY.

Mutuelle d'Assurances Malagasy (MAMA): Lot 1F, 12 bis, rue Rainibetsimisaraka, Ambalavao-Isotry, BP 185, 101 Antananarivo; tel. (20) 2222508; Pres. FRÉDÉRIC RABARISON.

Ny Havana: BP 3881, Antananarivo 101; tel. (20) 2226760; fax (20) 2224303; Dir-Gen. ROLAND RASAMOELY.

Société Malgache d'Assurances, Faugère, Jutheau et Cie: 13 rue Patrice Lumumba, BP 673, 101 Antananarivo; tel. (20) 2223162; f. 1952; Dir ANDRIANJAKA RAVELONAHIANA.

Trade and Industry

DEVELOPMENT ORGANIZATIONS

Office des mines nationales et des industries stratégiques (OMNIS): 21 làlana Razanakombana, BP 1 bis, 101 Antananarivo; tel. (20) 2224439; fax (20) 2222985; e-mail omnis@simicro.mg; f. 1976; promotes the exploration and exploitation of mining resources, in particular oil resources; Dir-Gen. Gen. RANDRIANAFIDISOA.

Société d'Etude et de Réalisation pour le Développement Industriel (SERDI): 78 bis, ave Lénine Ankaditapaka, BP 3180, 101 Antananarivo; tel. (20) 2221335; fax (20) 2229669; f. 1966; Dir-Gen. RAOILISON RAJAONARY.

CHAMBER OF COMMERCE

Fédération des Chambres de Commerce, d'Industrie et d'Agriculture de Madagascar: 20 rue Paul Dussac, BP 166, 101 Antananarivo; tel. (20) 2221567; 12 mem. chambers; Pres. JEAN RAMAROMISA; Chair. HENRI RAZANATSEHENO; Sec.-Gen. HUBERT RATSIANDAVANA.

TRADE ASSOCIATION

Société d'Intérêt National des Produits Agricoles (SINPA): BP 754, rue Fernand-Kasanga, Tsimbazaza, Antananarivo; tel. (20) 2220558; fax (20) 2220665; f. 1973; monopoly purchaser and distributor of agricultural produce; Chair. GUALBERT RAZANAJATOVO; Gen. Man. JEAN CLOVIS RALIJESY.

EMPLOYERS' ORGANIZATIONS

Groupement des Entreprises de Madagascar (GEM): Kianja MDRM sy Tia Tanindrazana, BP 1338, 101 Antananarivo; tel. (20) 23841; e-mail gem@simicro.mg; f. 1973; eight nat. syndicates and five regional syndicates comprising 725 cos and 49 directly affiliated cos; Pres. GASTON RAMENASON; Sec.-Gen. ZINAH RASAMUEL RAVALOSON.

Groupement National des Exportateurs de Vanille de Madagascar (GNEV): BP 21, Antalaha; tel. (13) 20714532; fax (13) 20816017; e-mail rama.anta@wanadoo.mg; 18 mems; Pres. JEAN GEORGES RANDRIAMIHARISOA.

Syndicat des Importateurs et Exportateurs de Madagascar: 2 rue Georges Mandel, BP 188, 101 Antananarivo; Pres. M. FONTANA.

Syndicat des Industries de Madagascar: Immeuble Kobana Soanierana; BP 1695, 101 Antananarivo; tel. (20) 2223608; fax (20) 2233043; f. 1958; Chair. NAINA ANDRIANTSITOHAINA.

Syndicat des Planteurs de Café: 37 làlana Razafimahandry, BP 173, 101 Antananarivo.

Syndicat Professionnel des Agents Généraux d'Assurances: Antananarivo; f. 1949; Pres. SOLO RATSIMBAZAFY; Sec. IHANTA RANDRIAMANDRANTO.

UTILITIES

Electricity and Water

Jiro sy Rano Malagasy (JIRAMA): BP 200, 149 rue Rainandriamampandry, Faravohitra, 101 Antananarivo; tel. (20) 2220031; fax (20) 2233806; f. 1975; state-owned; controls production and distribution of electricity and water; Chair. GÉRARD ANDRIAMILEROVASON; Dir-Gen. DESIRÉ RASIDY.

TRADE UNIONS

Cartel National des Organisations Syndicales de Madagascar (CARNOSYAMA): BP 1035, 101 Antananarivo.

Confédération des Travailleurs Malagasy Révolutionnaires (FISEMARE): Lot IV N 76-A, Ankadifotsy, BP 1128, Befelatanana-Antananarivo 101; tel. (20) 2221989; fax (20) 2267712; f. 1985; Pres. PAUL RABEMANANJARA.

Confédération des Travailleurs Malgaches (Fivomdronamben'ny Mpiasa Malagasy—FMM): Lot IVM 133 A Antetezanafovoany I, BP 846, 101 Antananarivo; tel. (20) 2224565; f. 1957; Sec.-Gen. JEANNOT RAMANJARA; 30,000 mems.

Fédération des Syndicats des Travailleurs de Madagascar (Firaisan'ny Sendika eran'i Madagaskara—FISEMA): Lot III, rue Pasteur Isotry, 101 Antananarivo; f. 1956; Pres. DESIRÉ RALAMBOTA-

HINA; Sec.-Gen. M. RAZAKANAIVO; 8 affiliated unions representing 60,000 mems.

Sendika Kristianina Malagasy (SEKRIMA) (Christian Confederation of Malagasy Trade Unions): Soarano, route de Mahajanga, BP 1035, 101 Antananarivo; tel. (20) 2223174; f. 1937; Pres. MARIE RAKOTOANOSY; Gen. Sec. RAYMOND RAKOTOARISAONA; 158 affiliated unions representing 40,000 mems.

Sendika Revolisakionera Malagasy (SEREMA): 101 Antananarivo.

Union des Syndicats Autonomes de Madagascar (USAM): Ampasadratsarahoby, Lot 11 H67, Faravohitra, BP 1038, 101 Antananarivo; Pres. NORBERT RAKOTOMANANA; Sec.-Gen. VICTOR RAHAGA; 46 affiliated unions representing 30,000 mems.

Transport

RAILWAYS

In 2001 there were 893 km of railway, including four railway lines, all 1-m gauge track. The northern system, which comprised 720 km of track, links the east coast with Antsirabé, in the interior, via Moramanga and Antananarivo, with a branch line from Moramanga to Lake Alaotra and was privatized in 2001. The southern system, which comprised 163 km of track, links the east coast with Fianarantsoa.

Réseau National des Chemins de Fer Malagasy: 1 ave de l'Indépendance, BP 259, Soarano, 101 Antananarivo; tel. (20) 2220521; fax (20) 2222288; f. 1909; transfer to private sector pending; Administrator DANIEL RAZAFINDRABE.

ROADS

In 2001 there were an estimated 49,837 km of classified roads; about 11.6% of the road network was paved. In 1987 there were 39,500 km of unclassified roads, used only in favourable weather. A road and motorway redevelopment programme, funded by the World Bank (€300m.) and the European Union (EU—€61m.), began in June 2000. In August 2002 the EU pledged to disburse US $10m. for the reconstruction of 11 bridges destroyed during the political crisis in that year.

INLAND WATERWAYS

The Pangalanes Canal runs for 600 km near the east coast from Toamasina to Farafangana. In 1984 the Government initiated a project to rehabilitate more than 200 km of the canal by 1988, at a cost of 18.5m. Malagasy francs. In early 1990 432 km of the canal between Toamasina and Mananjary were navigable.

SHIPPING

There are 18 ports, the largest being at Toamasina, which handles about 70% of total traffic, and Mahajanga. In 1987 Madagascar received foreign loans totalling US $34.8m., including a credit of $16m. from the World Bank, to finance a project to rehabilitate 10 ports.

Compagnie Générale Maritime (CGM): BP 69, 501 Toamasina; tel. (20) 5332312; fax (20) 5331037; f. 1976 by merger; Dir-Gen. GILLES-LOUIS TROIANO.

Compagnie Malgache de Navigation (CMN): rue Toto Radona, BP 1621, 101 Antananarivo; tel. (20) 2225516; f. 1960; coasters; 13,784 grt; 97.5% state-owned; privatization pending; Pres. ELINAH BAKOLY RAJAONSON; Dir-Gen. ARISTIDE EMMANUEL.

Navale et Commerciale Havraise Peninsulaire (NCHP): rue Rabearivelo Antsahavola, BP 1021, 101 Antananarivo; tel. (20) 2222502; Rep. JEAN-PIERRE NOCKIN.

Société Nationale Malgache des Transports Maritimes (SMTM): 6 rue Indira Gandhi, BP 4077, 101 Antananarivo; tel. (20) 2227342; fax (20) 2233327; f. 1963; 59% state-owned; privatization pending; services to Europe; Chair. ALEXIS RAZAFINDRATSIRA; Dir-Gen. ANDRIONORO RAMANANTSOA.

CIVIL AVIATION

The Ivato international airport is at Antananarivo, while the airports at Mahajanga, Toamasina and Nossi-Bé can also accommodate large jet aircraft. There are 211 airfields, two-thirds of which are privately owned. In 1996 the Government invited tenders for a rehabilitation project, which was to include nine of the major airports. Later that year the Government authorized private French airlines to operate scheduled and charter flights between Madagascar and Western Europe.

Aviation Civile de Madagascar (ACM): BP 4414, 101 Tsimbazaza-Antananarivo; tel. (20) 2222162; fax (20) 2224726; e-mail acm@acm.mg; Pres. NARIFERA RAOBANITRA; Dir-Gen. TOVON RABEMANANTSOA.

Société Nationale Malgache des Transports Aériens (Air Madagascar): 31 ave de l'Indépendance, BP 437, 101 Antananarivo; tel. (20) 2222222; fax (20) 2225728; e-mail airmad@dts.mg; internet www.air-mad.com; f. 1962; 89.58% state-owned; transfer to the private sector pending; extensive internal routes connecting all the principal towns; external services to France, Germany, Italy, Singapore, the Comoros, Kenya, Mauritius, Réunion, Seychelles and South Africa; Pres. NIRINA ANDRIAMANERASOA; Gen. Dirs ROLLAND BESOA RAZAFIMAHARO, JAMES ANDRIANALISOA.

Transports et Travaux Aériens de Madagascar: 17 ave de l'Indépendance, Analakely, Antananarivo; tel. (20) 2222222; fax (20) 2224340; e-mail tamdg@dts.mg; f. 1951; provides airline services; Pres. and Dir-Gen. JACQUES ANDRIANOMANANA.

Tourism

Madagascar's attractions include unspoiled scenery, many unusual varieties of flora and fauna, and the rich cultural diversity of Malagasy life. In 2000 a total of 160,071 tourists visited Madagascar. Revenue from tourism in that year was estimated at US $116m. The number of hotel rooms increased from some 3,040 in 1991 to an estimated 7,207 in 1999.

Direction du Tourisme de Madagascar: Ministry of Tourism, Tsimbazaza, BP 610, 101 Antananarivo; tel. (20) 2226298; fax (20) 2278953; e-mail mintour@dts.mg; internet www .madagascar-contacts.com/mintourcomfr.

La Maison du Tourisme de Madagascar: place de l'Indépendance, BP 3224, 101 Antananarivo; tel. (20) 2235178; fax (20) 2269522; e-mail mtm@simicro.mg; internet www.tourisme .madagascar.com; Exec. Dir ANDRÉ ANDRIAMBOAVONJY.

MALAWI

Introductory Survey

Location, Climate, Language, Religion, Flag, Capital

The Republic of Malawi is a land-locked country in southern central Africa, with Zambia to the west, Mozambique to the south and east, and Tanzania to the north. Lake Malawi forms most of the eastern boundary. The climate is tropical, but much of the country is sufficiently high above sea-level to modify the heat. Temperatures range from 14°C (57°F) to 18°C (64°F) in mountain areas, but can reach 38°C (100°F) in low-lying regions. There is a rainy season between November and April. The official language is English, although Chichewa is being promoted as the basis for a 'Malawi Language'. Some 80% of the population profess Christianity, while a further 13%, largely Asians, are Muslims. Most of the remaining Malawians follow traditional beliefs, although there is also a Hindu minority. The national flag (proportions 2 by 3) has three equal horizontal stripes, of black, red and green, with a rising sun, in red, in the centre of the black stripe. The capital is Lilongwe.

Recent History

Malawi was formerly the British protectorate of Nyasaland. In 1953 it was linked with two other British dependencies, Northern and Southern Rhodesia (now Zambia and Zimbabwe), to form the Federation of Rhodesia and Nyasaland. Elections in August 1961 gave the Malawi Congress Party (MCP), led by Dr Hastings Kamuzu Banda, a majority of seats in the Legislative Council. Dr Banda became Prime Minister in February 1963, and the Federation was dissolved in December. Nyasaland gained independence, as Malawi, on 6 July 1964. The country became a republic and a one-party state, with Banda as its first President, on 6 July 1966. In 1967 Malawi created a major controversy among African states by officially recognizing the Republic of South Africa. Banda, named Life President in 1971, in that year became the first African head of state to visit South Africa. In 1976, however, Malawi recognized the communist-backed Government in Angola in preference to the South African-supported forces. Malawi did not recognize the 'independence' granted by South Africa to four of its African 'homelands'.

Until 1993 all Malawian citizens were obliged to be members of the MCP; no political opposition was tolerated, and only candidates who had been approved by Banda were allowed to contest elections to the National Assembly. In 1979 Banda openly admitted that a letter bomb that injured the exiled leader of the Socialist League of Malawi (LESOMA), Dr Attati Mpakati, had been sent on his instructions. In March 1983 Mpakati was assassinated in Zimbabwe, although the Malawi Government denied any responsibility for his death. In May of that year Orton Chirwa and his wife, Vera, the leaders of the Malawi Freedom Movement (MAFREMO), were sentenced to death for treason, although Banda subsequently commuted the sentences to life imprisonment. (Orton Chirwa died in prison in October 1992; Vera Chirwa was pardoned and released in January 1993.)

Frequent reorganizations of the Cabinet effectively prevented the emergence of any political rival to Banda. However, it was reported in 1983 that a conflict had developed between Dick Matenje, the Minister without Portfolio in the Cabinet and Secretary-General of the MCP, and John Tembo, the Governor of the Reserve Bank of Malawi, concerning the eventual succession to Banda. In May the authorities reported that Matenje and three other senior politicians had died in a road accident; Malawian exiles claimed that the four men had been shot while attempting to flee the country. (In January 1994 a former police-officer claimed to have taken part in the shootings, under official orders; the Banda Government, however, rejected calls for an official inquiry.) In August 1984 Banda reorganized the MCP Executive Committee; the important post of party Secretary-General remained vacant, however, until the appointment of Gwandaguluwe Chakuamba in October 1993 (see below).

At elections to the National Assembly in May 1987 213 members of the MCP contested 69 of the 112 elective seats in the Assembly. Some 33 candidates were elected unopposed, and several elective seats were not filled. Banda subsequently nom-

inated further members to the Assembly, bringing its total membership to 116 in 1989. In January 1992 Tembo (now widely regarded as Banda's probable successor) was appointed Minister of State in the President's Office. Legislative elections took place in June: 96 of the elective seats (by then numbering 141) were contested by 630 members of the MCP, while 45 candidates were returned unopposed. Five seats remained vacant, after some candidates were disqualified. An additional 10 members of the Assembly were subsequently nominated by Banda.

Political opposition by Malawian dissidents in exile continued throughout the 1980s and into the 1990s, and international human rights organizations accused the Government of using detention without trial, torture and assassination to suppress political opposition.

Opposition to the Government intensified during 1992: in March Malawi's Roman Catholic bishops published an open letter criticizing the Government's alleged abuses of human rights. In April Chakufwa Chihana, a prominent trade union leader who had demanded multi-party elections, was arrested. In May industrial unrest in the southern city of Blantyre escalated into violent anti-Government riots, which spread to the capital, Lilongwe, and reportedly resulted in 38 deaths. Later in the month Western creditors suspended all but urgent humanitarian aid to Malawi, pending improvements in the Government's human rights record. In July Chihana was charged with sedition, and in August the police detained 11 church leaders and prohibited a planned rally by pro-democracy supporters. In September opposition activists formed the Alliance for Democracy (AFORD), a pressure group operating within Malawi, under the chairmanship of Chihana, which aimed to campaign for democratic political reform. Another opposition grouping, the United Democratic Front (UDF), was formed in October. In that month Banda conceded that a referendum on the introduction of a multi-party system would take place. However, in November the Government banned AFORD. In the following month Chihana was found guilty of sedition and sentenced to two years' hard labour (reduced to nine months' in March 1993). In January 1993 LESOMA merged with the Malawi Democratic Union to form the United Front for Multi-party Democracy. In March MAFREMO dissolved itself, and its membership joined AFORD.

The referendum on the introduction of a multi-party system was held on 14 June 1993, monitored by UN representatives. Despite evidence of MCP attempts to disrupt the opposition's activities prior to the poll, 63.2% of those who participated (some 63.5% of the electorate) voted for an end to single-party rule. Banda rejected opposition demands for the immediate installation of an interim government of national unity. He agreed, however, to the establishment of a National Executive Council to oversee the transition to a multi-party system and the holding of free elections, and of a National Consultative Council to implement the necessary amendments to the Constitution. Both councils were to include members of the Government and the opposition. Banda announced an amnesty for thousands of political exiles, and stated that a general election would be held, on a multi-party basis, within a year. In late June the Constitution was amended to allow the registration of political parties other than the MCP: by mid-August five organizations, including AFORD and the UDF, had been accorded official status.

In September 1993 Banda carried out an extensive cabinet reshuffle, relinquishing the post of Minister of External Affairs, which he had held since 1964. In October 1993 Banda underwent neurological surgery in South Africa. Interim executive power was assumed by a three-member Presidential Council, chaired by the new Secretary-General of the MCP, Chakuamba. (Chakuamba, a former government minister, had been released in July from a 22-year prison sentence, imposed for sedition in 1981.) The two other members, Tembo and the Minister of Transport and Communications, Robson Chirwa, were also senior MCP officials. In November 1993 a further cabinet reshuffle relieved Banda of all ministerial responsibilities. Later in November the National Assembly approved a Constitutional Amendment Bill, which, *inter alia*, abolished the institution of life presidency, ended the requirement that election candidates be members of the MCP, repealed the right of the President to nominate members of the legislature exclusively from the MCP, and lowered the minimum voting age from 21 to 18 years. The Assembly also amended the Public Security Act to outlaw detention without trial.

Having made a rapid and unexpected recovery, Banda resumed full presidential powers in December 1993. Shortly afterwards, in response to increasing pressure from the opposition, the Government amended the Constitution to provide for the appointment of an acting President in the event of the incumbent's being incapacitated. In February 1994 the MCP announced that Banda was to be the party's presidential candidate in the forthcoming general election (scheduled for May); Chakuamba was named as the MCP's candidate for the vice-presidency. Also in February the National Assembly approved an increase in the number of elective seats in the legislature from 141 to 177.

Meanwhile, the MCP announced in September 1993 that members of the Malawi Young Pioneers (MYP), a notorious paramilitary section of the ruling party, were to be gradually disarmed. In December, following the murder of three soldiers by MYP members, the regular army acted to close MYP offices and camps. In the ensuing violence, exacerbated by long-standing tensions between the army and the MYP, 32 people were reported to have been killed. Banda appointed a Minister of Defence (having hitherto held personal responsibility for defence) to oversee the MYP disarmament process and investigate army grievances. By early 1994 the authorities stated that the disarmament had been satisfactorily completed; it was known, however, that several thousand MYP members had crossed the border into Mozambique to take refuge in rebel bases. In January the Governments of Malawi and Mozambique agreed to a programme for the repatriation of MYP members. In the following month the MYP was officially disbanded, although it was subsequently reported that many armed MYP members remained in hiding in Mozambique (see below).

On 16 May 1994 the National Assembly adopted a provisional Constitution, which provided for the appointment of a Constitutional Committee and of a human rights commission, and abolished the system of 'traditional' courts. Malawi's first multi-party parliamentary and presidential elections took place on 17 May. In the presidential election the Secretary-General of the UDF, (Elson) Bakili Muluzi (a former government minister and MCP Secretary-General), took 47.3% of the votes cast, defeating Banda (who won 33.6% of the votes). Eight parties contested the legislative elections: of these, the UDF won 84 seats in the National Assembly, the MCP 55 and AFORD 36. (Voting was repeated in two constituencies where irregularities had been found, as a result of which the UDF and MCP each won a further seat.) The distribution of seats was strongly influenced by regional affiliations, with AFORD winning all of the Northern Region's seats, and the MCP and UDF particularly successful in the Central and Southern Regions, respectively. The Constitution was introduced for a one-year period on 18 May; it was to be subject to further review prior to official ratification one year later.

President Muluzi and his Vice-President, Justin Malewezi, were inaugurated on 21 May 1994. The stated aims of the new administration were to alleviate poverty and ensure food security, and to combat corruption and the mismanagement of resources. Three prisons where abuses of human rights were known to have taken place were closed. The new UDF-dominated Government also proclaimed an amnesty for the country's remaining political prisoners, and commuted all death sentences to terms of life imprisonment. Attempts to recruit members of AFORD into a coalition administration failed, owing to disagreements regarding the allocation of senior portfolios, and in June AFORD and the MCP agreed to function as an opposition front. The Muluzi Government was thus deprived of a majority in the National Assembly, which was inaugurated at the end of June. In August it was announced that Banda, while remaining honorary Life President of the MCP, was to retire from active involvement in politics. Chakuamba, as Vice-President of the party, effectively became the leader of the MCP.

In September 1994 a number of AFORD members were appointed to the Government, including Chihana as Second Vice-President and Minister of Irrigation and Water Development. In January 1995 AFORD announced an end to its co-operation with the MCP. Meanwhile, the creation of the post of Second Vice-President had necessitated a constitutional amendment, and

provoked severe criticism from the MCP. Moreover, the National Constitutional Conference recommended that the post be abolished. In March, however, the National Assembly (in the absence of MCP deputies, who boycotted the vote) approved the retention of the second vice-presidency; the Assembly also endorsed recommendations for the establishment—although not before May 1999—of a second chamber of parliament, as well as a constitutional clause requiring that senior state officials declare all personal assets within two months of assuming their post. The Constitution took effect on 18 May 1995.

In June 1994 Muluzi established an independent commission of inquiry to investigate the deaths of Matenje and his associates in May 1983. In January 1995, in accordance with the findings of the commission, Banda was placed under house arrest and Tembo and two former police-officers were detained; the four were charged with murder and conspiracy to murder. A former inspector-general of police was charged later in the month. Cecilia Kadzamira, Tembo's niece and the former President's 'Official Hostess', was charged, in April, with conspiracy to murder and was subsequently released on bail. The trial opened later that month, but was immediately adjourned, owing to Banda's failure to appear in court (his defence counsel asserted that he was too ill to stand trial) and to the failure of the state prosecution to submit certain evidence to the defence. Hearings resumed, in Banda's absence, in July. In September Tembo and the two former police-officers were granted bail, and most restrictions on Banda's movements were ended. The case against Kadzamira was abandoned in December, owing to lack of evidence, and later in the month Banda, Tembo and the other defendants were found not guilty of conspiracy to murder and conspiracy to defeat justice. The Director of Public Prosecutions subsequently appealed against the verdict, complaining that the presiding judge had effectively instructed the jury to acquit the defendants. In January 1996 an MCP-owned newspaper printed a statement by Banda in which he admitted that he might unknowingly have been responsible for brutalities perpetrated under his regime and apologized to Malawians for 'pain and suffering' inflicted during his presidency. Meanwhile, in July 1995 Tembo and four other members of the Banda regime were charged with conspiring to murder the bishops who had published criticisms of the former administration in 1992. (The charges were withdrawn 'in the interests of national reconciliation' in October 2000.)

In July 1995 lawyers acting for Banda demanded that Muluzi explain the apparent payment of a substantial sum to a witness in the trial of Banda and his associates. Meanwhile, there were further allegations that the Muluzi administration had been involved in dubious financial transactions. It emerged, in mid-1995, that the President had authorized the payment of some 6.2m. kwacha from the state poverty alleviation account to UDF deputies (to enable the payment of loans to their constituents); there was also evidence of the involvement of government ministers in the smuggling of maize to neighbouring countries. Moreover, it was claimed that few ministers had complied with the constitutional requirement regarding the declaration of assets. An investigation of Banda's financial interests was initiated in September. In February 1996 Muluzi announced that an independent Anti-Corruption Bureau was to be established to investigate allegations of corruption.

In July 1995 the UDF and AFORD signed a formal co-operation agreement. In December, however, Chihana warned that AFORD might withdraw from the coalition Government, alleging that the UDF was using public funds to secure political influence, and complaining of a lack of openness in the Muluzi administration. Chihana resigned from the Government in May 1996, expressing his intention to devote himself more fully to the work of his party. The post of Second Vice-President remained vacant following a subsequent reorganization of the Cabinet. In late May another AFORD minister resigned. In June AFORD withdrew from its coalition with the UDF, declared that remaining AFORD ministers should resign, and appointed a 'shadow cabinet'. Five members were dismissed from AFORD's National Executive, and another was suspended, having refused to relinquish their ministerial posts. AFORD and the MCP insisted that AFORD ministers should be regarded as members of the UDF. The rejection of this demand resulted in a parliamentary boycott by both opposition parties. At the beginning of December the AFORD ministers remaining in the Cabinet asserted that they were independent and had not joined the UDF. In March 1997 AFORD stated that the party would continue its boycott until the ministers resigned both their government posts and parliamentary seats. In April the MCP and AFORD ended their parliamentary boycott, following a meeting with Muluzi at which he had allegedly promised to amend the Constitution to prevent parliamentary delegates from changing their political affiliation without standing for re-election. In July 1997 and March 1998 further cabinet reorganizations took place, reducing the number of ministries, as part of the Government's reform of the civil service.

In January 1997 it was announced that Banda was to be charged with embezzling state funds for the establishment of a private school; however, in May he was discharged as unfit to attend court. In July the Supreme Court dismissed an appeal against the acquittal, in December 1995, of Banda and Tembo on murder charges, shortly after Muluzi reportedly requested that all criminal cases against Banda be discontinued. Also in July 1997 Banda announced his intention to resign as President of the MCP. In November Banda died in South Africa, where he had been undergoing emergency medical treatment. He was accorded a state funeral, with full military honours, which was attended by some 100,000 Malawians.

In June 1998 the National Assembly approved legislation providing for the introduction of a single-ballot electoral system to replace the existing multiple-ballot system and for a strengthening of the authority and independence of the Electoral Commission. In November legislation was adopted to allow presidential and parliamentary elections to run concurrently (as Muluzi's term was due to end several weeks earlier than that of the National Assembly), and the elections were subsequently scheduled for 18 May 1999. An electoral alliance between the MCP and AFORD, which was officially announced in February 1999, created serious divisions within the MCP, when the party's leader and presidential candidate, Chakuamba, chose Chihana, the leader of AFORD, as the candidate for the vice-presidency, in preference to Tembo. Thousands of Tembo's supporters were reported to have mounted protests to demand Chakuamba's resignation. The Chakuamba-Chihana partnership also provoked a wider dispute with the UDF and the Electoral Commission, which claimed that the arrangement was unconstitutional. In February the National Assembly adopted a controversial report by the Electoral Commission that recommended the creation of a further 72 parliamentary seats, including an additional 42 in the Southern Region, a UDF stronghold. In response to widespread opposition to the proposals, however, only 16 of the 72 seats were approved.

Having been postponed twice, the presidential and legislative elections were held on 15 June 1999. Muluzi was re-elected to the presidency, securing 51.37% of the votes cast, while Chakuamba obtained 43.30%. Turn-out was high, with some 93.8% of registered voters reported to have participated. At the elections to the expanded National Assembly the ruling UDF won 93 seats, while the MCP secured 66 seats, AFORD 29 and independent candidates four. (Owing to the death of a candidate, voting in the remaining constituency was postponed until October, when the seat was won by the UDF.) The opposition disputed the results, and violent clashes ensued in the northern districts. Despite declarations from international observers that the elections were largely free and fair, the MCP-AFORD alliance filed two petitions with the High Court, challenging Muluzi's victory and the results in 16 districts. The opposition alleged irregularities in the voter registration process and claimed that Muluzi's victory was unconstitutional, as he had failed to gain the support of 50% of all registered voters. None the less, Muluzi was inaugurated later in June, and a new Cabinet was appointed. In mid-August the UDF regained a parliamentary majority when the four independent deputies decided to ally themselves with the UDF, of which they had previously been members.

Chakuamba, who had maintained a boycott of the new parliament pending the result of his party's challenge to the outcome of the elections, was suspended from the chamber in June 2000. Tembo assumed the leadership of the opposition and appointed his supporters to prominent posts within the MCP. Chakuamba was reinstated in September, and a dispute between the two factions ensued. In October the opposition's petitions against the election results were dismissed by the High Court.

Muluzi reorganized the Cabinet in March 2000 and again in August, following the resignation of a deputy minister who had been charged with manslaughter. In October a report was published criticizing the Malawian Government for the purchase of a new fleet of cars for the use of government officials, allegedly with money donated in aid by the United Kingdom. In

November, following these and other allegations of corruption made against several ministers, Muluzi dismissed the entire Cabinet and announced direct presidential rule, before appointing a new administration some days later. Brown Mpinganjira, the Minister of Transport and Public Works, Cassim Chilumpha, the Minister of Education, Science and Technology, and Peter Chupa, the Minister of Labour and Vocational Training, were not reappointed. They were subsequently investigated for their alleged involvement in the corrupt awarding of a number of construction contracts. Mpinganjira, who claimed the accusations were politically motivated, was charged with receiving illegal payments in December.

The country's first multi-party local elections were held in November 2000. The MCP was disqualified from contesting a number of wards where both factions of the party had submitted nominations. Amid allegations of electoral malpractice, the UDF secured victory in 610 of the 860 contested wards, AFORD winning 120 seats and the MCP 84.

Mpinganjira was acquitted of the corruption charges in January 2001 and subsequently formed a new political movement, the National Democratic Alliance (NDA). It was reported that five members of the National Assembly had joined the NDA by February. Meanwhile, in January 2001 deputies from the Tembo faction of the MCP ensured the approval by the National Assembly of a UDF proposal to abandon plans (ostensibly for financial reasons) for the creation of a second legislative chamber, the Senate, which would have had powers to impeach the President; AFORD boycotted the vote. In February Chilumpha was arrested on charges of corruption connected with campaigning for the June 1999 elections. In March 2001 six people were arrested and charged with treason for allegedly planning a coup against Muluzi; the leader of the plot was said to be Sudi Sulaimana, a political activist who had previously been arrested in 1993 for attempting to overthrow Banda. However, Chakuamba claimed that the Government had fabricated the plot in order to curb the activities of its political opponents. In October Mpinganjira was arrested and charged with treason for alleged involvement in the March coup attempt, but was released after a court ruled that his detention was unconstitutional. Meanwhile, in June, at a rally in Lilongwe, 37 of the 41 MCP district chairmen publicly endorsed Tembo as their new leader, declaring that they had lost confidence in Chakuamba; however, the latter dismissed the significance of the endorsement. In November seven deputies who had joined the NDA, including Mpinganjira and Makhumula, were excluded from the National Assembly for abandoning the political parties for which they had been elected, an action proscribed by law since May, when the UDF acted to prevent defections to the NDA; Sam Mpasu, the Speaker, defied an order of the High Court restraining him from expelling the deputies. Also in November the UDF-dominated National Assembly approved a motion to commence impeachment proceedings against three High Court judges for allegedly favouring the opposition, despite objections from the International Commission of Jurists, religious leaders and civil rights group.

In January 2002 Muluzi effected a minor cabinet reshuffle, notably dismissing Mathews Chikaonda as Minister of Finance and Economic Planning. In the mean time, negotiations between Chihana and Muluzi on the possible formation of a government of national unity had created divisions within AFORD. The minister responsible for poverty alleviation, Leonard Mangulama, was dismissed in August after a report was published implicating him in the sale of emergency maize reserves to Kenya when Minister of Agriculture and Irrigation Development. A minor reorganization of ministerial portfolios took place in September. In the same month it was reported that Mpinganjira had fled the country following the murder of a supporter of the UDF in late August. In October Tembo was convicted of contempt of court for organizing a convention of the MCP in June, in defiance of a court injunction.

Proposed legislation to change the Constitution to allow Muluzi to seek a third presidential term failed to gain the requisite support of two-thirds of the members of the National Assembly in July 2002. A further attempt to introduce a constitutional amendment also failed in January 2003, when the bill was withdrawn; the Minister of Commerce and Industry, Peter Kaleso, was dismissed in that month in a minor cabinet reshuffle, as he had been expected to vote against the amendment. The UDF declared that it would hold a referendum on the issue later in the year. However, in late March Muluzi declared that he would not seek a third presidential term, and proposed

Dr Bingu wa Mutharika, recently appointed Minister of Economic Planning and Development, as his successor, to contest the presidential election scheduled for May 2004. (Mutharika had represented the United Party at the 1999 presidential election, but subsequently defected to the UDF.) Two days later, in early April 2003, Muluzi dismissed his entire Cabinet, apparently without explanation. However, several ministers reported that Muluzi had imposed the appointment of Mutharika on the party without sufficient consultation, and suggested that they had been dismissed for expressing opposition to the President's decision; Muluzi appointed a new administration later that month.

Despite being the only African country to have maintained full diplomatic relations with South Africa during the apartheid era, Malawi joined the Southern African Development Co-ordination Conference (subsequently the Southern African Development Community, see p. 311), which originally aimed to reduce the dependence of southern African countries on South Africa.

Relations with Mozambique were frequently strained during the early and mid-1980s by the widely held belief that the Banda regime was supporting the Resistência Nacional Moçambicana (Renamo—see the chapter on Mozambique). Following the death of President Machel of Mozambique in an air crash in South Africa in October 1986, the South African Government claimed that documents discovered in the wreckage revealed a plot by Mozambique and Zimbabwe to overthrow the Banda Government. Angry protests from Malawi were answered by denials of the accusations from the Mozambican and Zimbabwean Governments. In December, however, Malawi and Mozambique signed an agreement on defence and security matters, which was believed to include co-operation in eliminating Renamo operations. Malawian troops were subsequently stationed in Mozambique to protect the strategic railway line linking Malawi to the Mozambican port of Nacala. In July 1988, during an official visit to Malawi, President Chissano of Mozambique stated that he did not believe Malawi to be supporting Renamo and expressed gratitude for Malawi's military presence in his country. In December of that year Malawi, Mozambique and the office of the UN High Commissioner for Refugees (UNHCR) signed an agreement to promote the voluntary repatriation of an estimated 650,000 Mozambican refugees who had fled into Malawi during the previous two years. However, by mid-1992 the number of Mozambican refugees in Malawi had reportedly reached 1m. Under the provisions of the General Peace Agreement signed in Mozambique in October 1992, all Malawian troops were withdrawn from Mozambique by June 1993. Large numbers of refugees returned to Mozambique in 1993–94, but in May 1995 Malawi demanded the repatriation of the remainder—estimated to total some 39,000—stating that food aid and other assistance to those who failed to leave would be reduced. The programme of the Malawi-Mozambique-UNHCR commission officially ended in November: it was estimated that a total of 1m. refugees had been repatriated, although a small number remained in Malawi. Meanwhile, during a visit by Chissano to Malawi in March 1995, the two countries agreed to review their joint defence and security co-operation accords to reflect current issues such as drugs-trafficking and arms-smuggling. None the less, the continued presence of more than 2,000 MYP members in Mozambique (many of whom were said to have been harboured in Renamo bases) remained a cause of concern. In October it was announced that the two countries were to establish a commission to locate renegade MYP members and persuade them to return to Malawi. Following a meeting of the joint defence and security commission in mid-1996, a sub-committee to regulate border issues and joint committees on security and police matters were to be established. At the commission's eighth session, in early 1998, the Malawian Government expressed concern over uncertainty regarding the whereabouts of remaining MYP members. (In September 1997 10 Malawians had been detained in Mozambique on suspicion of destabilizing border areas.)

In October 2001 the Danish Government was forced to recall its ambassador to Lilongwe after the Malawian Ministry of Foreign Affairs and International Co-operation alleged that the ambassador had made derogatory comments about Muluzi; the ambassador had recently commissioned an audit report on aid from the Danish Government, following suspicions that funds may have been misused. In January 2002 Denmark announced that it was to withdraw all financial assistance to Malawi, owing to negative political developments in the country, and subsequently closed its embassy in Lilongwe.

Government

The Head of State is the President, who is elected by universal adult suffrage, in the context of a multi-party political system, for a term of five years. Executive power is vested in the President, and legislative power in the National Assembly, which has 193 elective seats. Members of the Assembly are elected for five years, by universal adult suffrage, in the context of a multi-party system. Cabinet ministers are appointed by the President. The country is divided into three administrative regions (Northern, Central and Southern), sub-divided into 24 districts.

Defence

Malawi's active defence forces at 1 August 2002 comprised a land army of 5,300, a marine force of 220 and an air force of 80; all form part of the army. There was also a paramilitary police force of 1,500. Expenditure on defence in the 2000/01 budget was 989m. kwacha (equivalent to 2.8% of total expenditure).

Economic Affairs

In 2001, according to estimates by the World Bank, Malawi's gross national income (GNI), measured at average 1999–2001 prices, was US $1,778m., equivalent to $170 per head (or $620 per head on an international purchasing-power parity basis). During 1990–2001, it was estimated, the population increased at an average annual rate of 2.0%, while gross domestic product (GDP) per head increased, in real terms, by an average of 1.5% per year. Overall GDP increased, in real terms, at an average annual rate of 3.4% in 1990–2001; growth in 2001 was 2.8%.

Measured at constant 1994 prices, agriculture (including forestry and fishing) contributed 37.7% of GDP and engaged an estimated 82.4% of the labour force in 2001. The principal cash crops are tobacco (which accounted for an estimated 65.9% of domestic export earnings in 1999), tea and sugar cane. The principal food crops are maize, potatoes, cassava, plantains, groundnuts and pulses. Periods of severe drought and flooding have necessitated imports of basic foods in recent years: Malawi's maize deficit was estimated at 180,000 metric tons in mid-2001. During 1990–2001, according to the World Bank, agricultural GDP increased at an average annual rate of 6.5%. Growth in agricultural GDP was 5.4% in 2000 and 1.8% in 2001.

Industry (including manufacturing, mining, construction and power) contributed 17.0% of GDP in 2001, and engaged 4.5% of the employed labour force in 1998. During 1990–2001, according to the World Bank, industrial GDP increased by an average of 1.6% per year. Industrial GDP decreased by 0.1% in 2000, but increased by 0.1% in 2001.

Mining and quarrying contributed 1.5% of GDP in 2001, and engaged less than 0.1% of the employed labour force in 1998. Limestone, coal and gemstones are mined, and there are plans to develop deposits of bauxite, high-calcium marble and graphite. There are also reserves of phosphates, uranium, glass sands, asbestos and vermiculite. In August 2000 an Australian company announced it had begun work on the establishment of a uranium mine in northern Malawi, near the frontier with Tanzania. In 2001 environmental concerns delayed plans to exploit an estimated 30m. metric tons of bauxite deposits at Mount Mulanje. The GDP of the mining sector declined at an average annual rate of 2.3% in 1996–2001, according to the IMF, but increased by 9.6% in 2001.

Manufacturing contributed 12.2% of GDP in 2001, and engaged 2.7% of the employed labour force in 1998. During 1990–2001, according to the World Bank, manufacturing GDP increased by an average of 0.4% per year. Manufacturing GDP decreased by 2.5% in 2000, but increased by 0.1% in 2001.

Production of electrical energy is by hydroelectric (principally) and thermal installations. Some 90% of energy for domestic use is derived from fuel wood, although the Muluzi administration has announced that it intends to reduce dependence on this source for ecological reasons. In October 1997 an agreement was signed regarding the connection of Malawi's electricity system to the Cahora Bassa hydroelectric dam in Mozambique. In October 2000 a hydroelectric power plant, with a generation capacity of 64 MW, was opened at Kapichira. In January 2001 the Government introduced a campaign to widen access to electricity, especially in rural areas; in 2001 only 4% of Malawians had access to electricity. Imports of fuel comprised an estimated 9.6% of the value of total imports in 1998.

The services sector contributed 45.3% of GDP in 2001, and engaged 11.0% of the employed labour force in 1998. The GDP of the services sector increased by an average of 2.3% per year in

1990–2001, according to the World Bank. Services GDP remained constant in 2000 and increased by 4.5% in 2001.

In 2001 Malawi recorded a visible trade surplus of 3,907.8m. kwacha, while there was a deficit of 4,202.1m. kwacha on the current account of the balance of payments. In 2001 the principal source of imports was South Africa (39.7%); Zimbabwe and Zambia were also notable suppliers. South Africa was also the principal market for exports (19.1%) in that year; other important markets were the USA, Germany, Japan and the Netherlands. The principal exports in 1998 were tobacco, tea and sugar. The principal imports in that year were machinery and transport equipment (particularly road vehicles and parts), basic manufactures, food and live animals (notably cereals and cereal preparations), chemicals and related products, and mineral fuels.

In the financial year ending 30 June 2002 Malawi's overall budget deficit was an estimated 10,959m. kwacha (equivalent to 8.1% of GDP). The country's external debt totalled US $2,716m. at the end of 2000, of which $2,555m. was long-term public debt. In that year the cost of debt-servicing was equivalent to 11.7% of exports of goods and services. The annual rate of inflation averaged 29.6% in 1990–2001; consumer prices increased by an average of 29.6% in 2000 and by 17.6% in 2001. Some 1.1% of the labour force were unemployed in 1998.

Malawi is a member of the Southern African Development Community (see p. 311) and also of the Common Market for Eastern and Southern Africa (COMESA, see p. 162). Nine members of COMESA, including Malawi, became inaugural members of the COMESA Free Trade Area in October 2000. The country belongs to the International Tea Promotion Association (see p. 337) and to the International Tobacco Growers' Association (see p. 337).

Upon assuming office in May 1994, the Muluzi administration inherited an economy weakened not only by natural impediments to growth (including Malawi's land-locked position, the vulnerability of the dominant agricultural sector to drought, and a high rate of population growth), but also by the severe mismanagement of economic affairs by the Banda regime. The Muluzi Government continued policies of economic liberalization and diversification initiated in the last years under Banda, including privatization of many state concerns and the ending of most agricultural monopolies and subsidies, and also undertook to combat corruption and inefficiency. However, by 1997, as adherence to the programme slackened, the budget deficit widened and GDP growth slowed, leading to the suspension of IMF disbursements. In October 1999 the IMF approved a loan worth US $10.6m. in support of the Government's economic programme for 1999–2000. However, a significant decline in revenue from tobacco exports adversely affected the economy in 2000, and GDP growth failed to meet expected targets. The devaluation of the kwacha continued throughout 2000–01. (From May 2000 the central bank discontinued its policy of quoting an exchange rate for the kwacha and allowed the markets to determine the currency's relative value.) In November 2000 Malawi was granted debt relief equating to $1,000m. under the World Bank's Heavily Indebted Poor Countries (HIPC) initiative, and in December the IMF approved a loan of some $58m. in support of the agreed poverty reduction strategy. In March 2001 the African Development Bank (ADB) agreed to grant Malawi debt relief worth $71.2m. Structural reforms planned for 2001 included the continuing restructuring of the civil service and of the tax system, in addition to progress with the privatization of state-owned enterprises. The privatization programme was suspended for review by the Cabinet in July 2001, but was resumed in October after the IMF and other donors threatened to withhold loan disbursements. In November, none the less, it was reported that the European Union, the USA and the United Kingdom had suspended aid to Malawi, in response to concerns regarding corruption and economic mismanagement. Furthermore, in January 2002 Denmark announced that it was to withdraw all assistance to the country, and in March the ADB withheld some $250m. in development aid. In April Malawi was suspended from the HIPC initiative over allegations of corruption concerning the sale of its grain reserves. Meanwhile, in February President Muluzi declared a state of national disaster and appealed for $21.6m. in international aid, as an estimated 70% of the population were seriously affected by food shortages, following severe flooding in 2001. In response, the USA provided some $29m. of aid in August 2002; in the following months the IMF and the International Development Association provided emergency financial aid packages, and the World Bank approved grants and loans worth around $100m. to improve agricultural production and disaster management. The UN World Food Programme reportedly distributed food to some 3.6m. Malawians in February 2003.

Education

During the Banda regime a large number of Malawians were denied basic education. Primary education is now officially compulsory, however, beginning at six years of age and lasting for eight years. Secondary education, which begins at 14 years of age, lasts for four years, comprising two cycles of two years. In 1995 the total enrolment at primary and secondary schools was equivalent to 100% of the school-age population (males 106%; females 94%). According to UNESCO estimates, in 1999/2000 primary enrolment included 68.5% of children in the relevant age-group (males 65.7%; females 71.4%), while in 1998/99 secondary enrolment was equivalent to 45.2% (males 50.3%; females 40.0%). A programme to expand education at all levels has been undertaken; however, the introduction of free primary education in September 1994 led to the influx of more than 1m. additional pupils, resulting in severe overcrowding in schools. In January 1996 the International Development Association granted US $22.5m. for the training of 20,000 newly recruited teachers, appointed in response to the influx. In mid-1997 additional funding was provided by the African Development Bank for the construction of primary and secondary schools. The University of Malawi had 3,872 students in 1995/96. Some students attend institutions in the United Kingdom and the USA. Estimated expenditure on education in the 2001/02 budget was 6,790m. kwacha (equivalent to 15.8% of total expenditure).

Public Holidays

2003: 1 January (New Year's Day), 15 January (John Chilembwe Day), 3 March (Martyrs' Day), 18–21 April (Easter), 1 May (Labour Day), 14 June (Freedom Day), 6 July (Republic Day), 13 October (Mothers' Day), 25–26 December (Christmas).

2004: 1 January (New Year's Day), 15 January (John Chilembwe Day), 3 March (Martyrs' Day), 9–12 April (Easter), 1 May (Labour Day), 14 June (Freedom Day), 6 July (Republic Day), 11 October (Mothers' Day), 25–26 December (Christmas).

Weights and Measures

The metric system is in use.

Statistical Survey

Sources (unless otherwise indicated): National Statistical Office of Malawi, POB 333, Zomba; tel. 524377; fax 525130; e-mail enquiries@statistics.gov.mw; internet www.nso.malawi.net; Reserve Bank of Malawi, POB 30063, Capital City, Lilongwe 3; tel. 780600; fax 782752; internet www.rbm.malawi.net.

Area and Population

AREA, POPULATION AND DENSITY

Area (sq km)	118,484*
Population (census results)	
1–21 September 1987	7,988,507
1–21 September 1998	
Males	4,867,563
Females.	5,066,305
Total	9,933,868
Density (per sq km) at September 1998.	83.8

* 45,747 sq miles. The area includes 24,208 sq km (9,347 sq miles) of inland water.

Ethnic groups (1977 census): Africans 5,532,298; Europeans 6,377; Asians 5,682; others 3,103.

REGIONS
(census of September 1998)

Region	Area (sq km)*	Population	Density (per sq km)	Regional capital
Southern	31,753	4,633,968	145.9	Blantyre
Central	35,592	4,066,340	114.2	Lilongwe
Northern	26,931	1,233,560	45.8	Mzuzu
Total	94,276	9,933,868	105.4	

* Excluding inland waters, totalling 24,208 sq km.

PRINCIPAL TOWNS
(population at census of September 1998)

Blantyre . . .	502,053	Karonga . . .	.	27,811
Lilongwe (capital)	440,471*	Kasungu . . .	.	27,754
Mzuzu.	86890	Mangochi . . .	.	26,570
Zomba.	65915			

* Including Limbe.
Source: Thomas Brinkoff, *City Population* (internet www.citypopulation.de).

BIRTHS AND DEATHS
(UN estimates, annual averages)

	1985–90	1990–95	1995–2000
Birth rate (per 1,000)	51.9	50.2	47.2
Death rate (per 1,000)	20.5	21.1	22.2

Source: UN, *World Population Prospects: The 2000 Revision.*

Expectation of life (WHO estimates, years at birth): 36.3 (males 35.7; females 36.9) in 2001 (Source: WHO, *World Health Report*).

ECONOMICALLY ACTIVE POPULATION*
(persons aged 10 years and over, 1998 census)

	Males	Females	Total
Agriculture, hunting, forestry and fishing	1,683,006	2,082,821	3,765,827
Mining and quarrying	2,206	293	2,499
Manufacturing	94,545	23,938	118,483
Electricity, gas and water . . .	6,656	663	7,319
Construction	70,196	3,206	73,402
Trade, restaurants and hotels . .	176,466	80,923	257,389
Transport, storage and communications	29,438	3,185	32,623
Financing, insurance, real estate and business services	10,473	3,484	13,957
Public administration	82,973	18,460	101,433
Community, social and personal services	52,980	33,016	85,996
Total employed	2,208,940	2,249,989	4,458,929
Unemployed	34,697	15,664	50,361
Total labour force	2,243,637	2,265,653	4,509,290

* Excluding armed forces.

Mid-2001 (estimates in '000): Agriculture, etc. 4,587; Total 5,564 (Source: FAO).

Health and Welfare

KEY INDICATORS

Total fertility rate (children per woman, 2001)	6.5
Under-5 mortality rate (per 1,000 live births, 2001) . . .	183
HIV/AIDS (% of persons aged 15–49, 2001).	15.00
Hospital beds (per 1,000 head, 1998)	1.34
Health expenditure (2000): US $ per head (PPP)	38
Health expenditure (2000): % of GDP	7.6
Health expenditure (2000): public (% of total)	47.8
Access to water (% of persons, 2000).	57
Access to sanitation (% of persons, 2000)	77
Human Development Index (2000): ranking	163
Human Development Index (2000): value	0.400

For sources and definitions, see explanatory note on p. vi.

Agriculture

PRINCIPAL CROPS
('000 metric tons)

	1999	2000	2001
Rice (paddy)	93	72	93
Maize	2,479	2,501	1,589
Millet	20	20	20
Sorghum	41	37	37
Potatoes	1,840	2,037	2,852
Cassava (Manioc)	895	2,757*	3,313
Dry beans	52	58	60*
Chick-peas*	36	35	35
Cow peas (dry)*	55	54	54
Pigeon peas*	80	79	79
Groundnuts (in shell) . . .	125	117	148
Sunflower seed	2	3	4
Cabbages*	29	28	28
Tomatoes*	36	35	35
Onions (dry)*	19	18	18
Other vegetables*	176	175	175
Mangoes*	34	33	33
Bananas*	95	93	93
Plantains*	205	200	200
Other fruits*	187	185	150
Sugar cane*	1,700	2,000	1,900
Coffee (green)	4†	4†	4
Tea	48	45	37
Tobacco (leaves)	85	99	83
Cotton (lint)*	10	10	10

* FAO estimate(s).
† Unofficial figure.

Source: FAO.

LIVESTOCK
(FAO estimates, '000 head, year ending September)

	1999	2000	2001
Cattle	712	763	749
Pigs	444	468	436
Sheep	103	112	115
Goats	1,427	1,689	1,670
Poultry*	14,800	15,000	15,200

* FAO estimates.

Source: FAO.

LIVESTOCK PRODUCTS
(FAO estimates, '000 metric tons)

	1999	2000	2001
Beef and veal	15	16	16
Goat meat	5	6	6
Pig meat	20	22	20
Poultry meat	15	15	15
Cows' milk	34	35	35
Hen eggs	19	20	20

Source: FAO.

Forestry

ROUNDWOOD REMOVALS
(FAO estimates, '000 cubic metres, excluding bark)

	1999	2000	2001
Sawlogs, veneer logs and logs for sleepers*	130	130	130
Other industrial wood	390	390	390
Fuel wood	4,922	4,964	4,996
Total	5,442	5,484	5,516

* Output assumed to be unchanged since 1993.

Source: FAO.

SAWNWOOD PRODUCTION
('000 cubic metres, including railway sleepers)

	1991*	1992†	1993
Coniferous (softwood) . . .	28	28	30
Broadleaved (hardwood) . . .	15	15	15†
Total	43	43	45

* Unofficial figures.
† FAO estimate(s).

1994–2001: Annual production as in 1993 (FAO estimates).

Source: FAO.

Fishing

('000 metric tons, live weight)

	1998	1999	2000
Capture	41.1	45.4	45.0
Tilapias	5.1	6.8	6.8
Torpedo-shaped catfishes . .	3.9	8.5	8.4
Other freshwater fishes . .	32.1	30.1	29.8
Aquaculture	0.2*	0.6	0.5
Total catch	41.3	46.0	45.5

* FAO estimate.

Source: FAO, *Yearbook of Fishery Statistics*.

Mining

('000 metric tons, unless otherwise indicated)

	1998	1999	2000*
Coal	54.2	43.8	44.9
Limestone	171.9	171.9	183.0
Lime	2.6	2.9	3.1
Gemstones (kilograms) . . .	934	649	665
Aggregate ('000 cubic metres) . .	182.6	71.7	76.2

* Estimates.

Source: US Geological Survey.

Industry

SELECTED PRODUCTS
('000 metric tons, unless otherwise indicated)

	1997	1998	1999
Raw sugar	105	107	113
Beer ('000 hectolitres) . . .	292	206	684
Cigarettes (million)	731	501	n.a.
Blankets ('000)	838	799	478
Cement	70	83	204
Electric energy (million kWh) . .	878	n.a.	n.a.

Source: UN, *Industrial Commodity Statistics Yearbook*.

Finance

CURRENCY AND EXCHANGE RATES

Monetary Units
100 tambala = 1 Malawi kwacha (K)

Sterling, Dollar and Euro Equivalents (31 December 2002)
£1 sterling = 140.45 kwacha
US $1 = 87.14 kwacha
€1 = 91.38 kwacha
1,000 Malawi kwacha = £7.120 = $11.476 = €10.943

Average Exchange Rate (kwacha per US $)
2000   59.5438
2001   72.1973
2002   76.6866

BUDGET
(K million, year ending 30 June)

Revenue*	1999/2000	2000/01	2001/02†
Tax revenue‡	14,353.3	19,285	20,168
Taxes on income and profits . .	6,590.5	8,740	9,338
Companies	2,569.8	3,140	2,987
Individuals	4,020.7	5,601	6,350
Taxes on goods and services . .	5,833.7	8,169	8,772
Surtax	5,189.3	6,091	6,472
Excise duties.	644.4	2,078	2,250
Taxes on international trade. .	2,242.0	2,905	2,540
Import duties	2,200.6	2,385	2,396
Non-tax revenue . . .	1,454.9	1,595	2,495
Departmental receipts . .	1,050.0	1,036	1,202
Total	15,808.1	20,880	22,663

Expenditure	1999/2000	2000/01	2001/02†
General public services	5,805	14,609	14,729
Defence	698	989	1,032
Public order and safety . . .	881	1,164	1,633
Education	3,395	4,337	6,790
Health	1,975	2,275	4,334
Social security and welfare . . .	1,680	1,392	307
Housing and community amenities	1,946	2,015	113
Recreational, cultural and other social services	61	74	61
Economic affairs and services . .	4,935	6,914	6,489
Agriculture and natural resources	2,058	1,541	2,356
Transport and communications .	2,523	3,540	2,940
Unallocable expenditure . . .	3,251	4,114	10,119
Total	23,189	35,822	43,051

* Excluding grants received (K million): 6,296 in 1999/2000; 10,353 in 2000/01; 9,429 in 2001/02.

† Estimates.

‡ After deduction of tax refunds (K million): 432 in 1999/2000; 460 in 2000/01; 373 in 2001/02.

Source: IMF, *Malawi: Selected Issues and Statistical Appendix* (August 2002).

INTERNATIONAL RESERVES
(US $ million at 31 December)

	2000	2001	2002
Gold*	0.54	0.54	0.51
IMF special drawing rights . . .	0.47	0.84	0.90
Reserve position in IMF	2.91	2.85	3.11
Foreign exchange	243.52	203.05	161.98
Total	247.45	207.28	166.50

* National valuation.

Source: IMF, *International Financial Statistics*.

MONEY SUPPLY
(K million at 31 December)

	1999	2000	2001
Currency outside banks . . .	2,992.02	4,144.86	4,208.47
Demand deposits at commercial banks	3,641.75	4,934.39	5,473.00
Total money (incl. others) . . .	6,651.15	9,096.63	9,828.85

Source: IMF, *International Financial Statistics*.

COST OF LIVING
(National Consumer Price Index; base: 1990 = 100)

	1999	2000	2001
Food (incl. beverages) . . .	1,346.3	1,611.7	2,111.3
Clothing (incl. footwear). . . .	417.9	764.2	999.3
All items (incl. others)	1,140.5	1,478.0	1,738.1

Source: ILO, *Yearbook of Labour Statistics*.

NATIONAL ACCOUNTS

Expenditure on the Gross Domestic Product
(K million at current prices)

	1999	2000	2001
Government final consumption expenditure	9,676.3	12,933.2	18,906.8
Private final consumption expenditure	69,869.8	88,007.3	117,857.3
Increase in stocks	1,600.0	1,290.0	1,360.0
Gross fixed capital formation . .	9,870.5	12,792.2	15,740.8
Total domestic expenditure . .	91,016.5	115,022.6	153,865.0
Exports of goods and services . .	21,941.6	26,622.1	31,741.6
Less Imports of goods and services	33,898.3	37,845.7	43,876.8
GDP in purchasers' values . .	79,059.8	103,799.1	141,729.7
GDP at constant 1994 prices .	13,022.6	13,295.8	13,690.3

Source: IMF, *International Financial Statistics*.

Gross Domestic Product by Economic Activity
(K million at constant 1994 prices)

	1999	2000	2001
Agriculture, forestry and fishing .	4,944	5,210	5,305
Mining and quarrying	170	188	206
Manufacturing	1,749	1,705	1,716
Electricity and water	172	189	182
Construction	293	288	294
Distribution	2,765	2,759	2,939
Transport and communications .	576	552	576
Finance, insurance and business services	1,032	1,055	1,091
Ownership of dwellings . . .	180	185	190
Private social services	264	271	279
Government services	1,257	1,282	1,305
Sub-total	13,401	13,786	14,084
Less Imputed bank service charges	378	388	394
GDP at factor cost	13,023	13,296	13,690

BALANCE OF PAYMENTS
(K million)

	1999	2000	2001
Exports of goods f.o.b.	19,712.5	23,925.2	30,122.0
Imports of goods f.o.b.	−25,240.8	−27,414.2	−26,214.2
Trade balance	−5,528.2	−3,489.0	3,907.8
Services and other income (net) .	−7,614.0	−8,959.4	−9,225.9
Balance on goods, services and income	−13,142.2	−12,448.4	−5,318.1
Private transfers (net)	391.0	467.0	1,116.1
Current balance	−12,751.2	−11,981.4	−4,202.1
Capital account (net)	10,651.7	14,469.4	4,034.6
Net errors and omissions . . .	3,262.0	2,896.1	689.8
Overall balance	1,162.5	5,384.1	522.3

External Trade

PRINCIPAL COMMODITIES
(distribution by SITC, US $ million)

Imports c.i.f.	1996	1997	1998
Food and live animals	56.5	67.5	97.9
Cereals and cereal preparations	41.5	45.7	78.4
Maize (unmilled)	11.2	14.5	55.1
Flour of wheat or of meslin	19.8	22.7	13.6
Mineral fuels, lubricants, etc.	72.0	94.0	57.4
Petroleum, petroleum products,			
etc.	70.8	93.4	56.9
Refined petroleum products	67.1	89.8	55.1
Chemicals and related			
products	118.6	125.8	79.0
Medicinal and pharmaceutical			
products	16.6	23.7	11.2
Manufactured fertilizers	56.7	37.6	29.9
Nitrogenous fertilizers (mineral			
or chemical)	35.0	21.4	13.7
Artificial resins, plastic materials,			
etc.	13.5	23.9	10.9
Basic manufactures	128.5	148.2	131.4
Paper, paperboard, etc.	21.4	25.3	18.6
Textile yarn, fabrics, etc.	42.9	45.5	39.4
Iron and steel	23.5	19.8	24.3
Machinery and transport			
equipment	206.4	272.8	161.2
Machinery specialized for			
particular industries	25.2	90.6	24.1
General industrial machinery,			
equipment and parts	19.5	18.7	24.1
Telecommunications and sound			
equipment	33.6	13.1	7.7
Road vehicles and parts*	93.0	111.3	69.5
Passenger motor cars (excl.			
buses)	19.9	20.0	13.2
Motor vehicles for goods			
transport, etc.	33.4	47.6	32.1
Goods vehicles (lorries and			
trucks)	32.1	45.9	26.9
Miscellaneous manufactured			
articles	32.9	48.4	38.1
Total (incl. others)	644.8	800.3	598.7

* Excluding tyres, engines and electrical parts.

Exports f.o.b.	1994	1995
Food and live animals	79.9	79.6
Sugar, sugar preparation and honey	24.8	19.7
Sugar and honey	24.8	19.7
Raw beet and cane sugars	17.6	16.2
Coffee, tea, cocoa and spices	45.3	44.2
Unroasted coffee, husks and skins	14.8	15.5
Tea	30.0	26.6
Beverages and tobacco	198.7	300.0
Tobacco and tobacco manufactures	198.2	295.7
Unmanufactured tobacco; tobacco refuse	196.7	293.8
Unstripped tobacco	67.9	70.8
Stripped or partly stripped tobacco	128.9	223.1
Crude materials (inedible) except fuels	10.5	11.3
Basic manufactures	20.0	17.0
Textile yarn, fabrics, etc.	15.1	11.1
Woven cotton fabrics (excl. narrow or special		
fabrics)	12.0	7.1
Unbleached fabrics (not mercerized)	10.8	6.5
Machinery and transport equipment	13.3	8.6
Miscellaneous manufactured articles	12.6	15.0
Clothing and accessories (excl. footwear)	11.2	13.4
Total (incl. others)	337.1	433.4

Source: UN, *International Trade Statistics Yearbook*.

1996 (K million): Total imports c.i.f. 9,544.9; Total exports f.o.b. 7,214.1 (Tobacco 4,408.0, Sugar 522.8, Tea 400.3, Cotton 227.6).

1997 (K million): Total imports c.i.f. 12,847.7; Total exports f.o.b. 8,827.4 (Tobacco 5,426.6, Tea 673.3, Cotton 477.9, Sugar 467.3).

1998 (K million): Total imports c.i.f. 17,998; Total exports f.o.b. 16,533 (Tobacco 9,678.7, Tea 1,249.0, Sugar 1,178.7, Cotton 155.9).

1999 (K million): Total imports c.i.f. 30,758; Total exports f.o.b. 19,425.

2000 (K million): Total imports c.i.f. 31,159; Total exports f.o.b. 22,499.

Sources (for 1996–2000): Malawi Government, *Economic Report*; IMF, *International Financial Statistics*; Reserve Bank of Malawi.

PRINCIPAL TRADING PARTNERS
(US $ million)

Imports	1999	2000	2001
France	10.0	5.1	6.1
Germany	30.1	13.0	17.3
Japan	16.6	12.7	12.4
Mozambique	5.3	12.1	13.3
Netherlands	4.0	7.4	3.6
South Africa	258.2	260.2	252.3
United Kingdom	31.2	18.1	13.0
USA	9.5	14.4	16.3
Zambia	66.1	62.8	69.3
Zimbabwe	80.3	92.3	101.5
Total (incl. others)	631.6	621.6	636.0

Exports	1999	2000	2001
France	8.6	8.8	11.3
Germany	72.1	29.3	55.9
Japan	21.1	46.5	37.6
Mozambique	2.5	0.6	0.7
Netherlands	43.0	28.6	26.8
South Africa	74.7	85.9	94.8
United Kingdom	16.0	15.3	19.6
USA	69.1	53.8	76.5
Zambia	2.6	2.2	2.4
Zimbabwe	7.0	8.1	8.9
Total (incl. others)	482.4	441.6	497.2

Transport

RAILWAYS
(traffic)

	1996	1997	1998
Passengers carried ('000)	339,000	452,000	349,000
Freight ('000 metric tons)	132,000	167,000	197,000

Source: Ministry of Finance and Economic Planning, *Economic Report 1999*.

ROAD TRAFFIC
(estimates, motor vehicles in use at 31 December)

	1994	1995	1996
Passenger cars	23,520	25,480	27,000
Lorries and vans	26,000	29,000	29,700

Source: International Road Federation, *World Road Statistics*.

SHIPPING

Inland waterways
(lake transport)

	1996	1997	1998
Freight ('000 metric tons)	13,000	10,000	14,000
Passengers carried ('000)	191,000	133,000	115,000

Source: Ministry of Finance and Economic Planning, *Economic Report 1999*.

CIVIL AVIATION
(traffic on scheduled services)

	1997	1998	1999
Kilometres flown (million)	3	3	2
Passengers carried ('000)	158	158	112
Passenger-kilometres (million)	336	337	224
Total ton-kilometres (million)	33	33	21

Source: UN, *Statistical Yearbook*.

Tourism

FOREIGN TOURIST ARRIVALS BY COUNTRY OF RESIDENCE

	1998	1999	2000
Mozambique	24,617	20,924	18,300
North America	6,038	6,995	3,000
South Africa*	19,623	16,680	15,000
United Kingdom and Ireland. . .	19,322	22,383	17,200
Zambia	44,935	38,195	34,200
Zimbabwe	23,941	20,350	18,700
Total (incl. others).	219,570	254,352	228,106

* Includes South Africa, Botswana, Lesotho and Swaziland.

Source: World Tourism Organization, *Yearbook of Tourism Statistics*.

Tourism receipts (US $ million): 15 in 1998; 20 in 1999; 27 in 2000 (Source: World Bank).

Communications Media

	1999	2000	2001
Telephones ('000 main lines in use)	41.4	45.0	54.1
Mobile cellular telephones ('000 subscribers).	22.5	49.5	55.7
Internet users ('000)	10.0	15.0	20.0

Radio receivers ('000 in use): 4,929 in 1998.

Television receivers ('000 in use): 27 in 1999.

Facsimile machines (number in use): 1,250 in 1997.

Book production: 117 titles in 1996.

Daily newspapers: 5 in 1996; estimated average circulation 25,000 copies in 1995.

Non-daily newspapers: 4 in 1996 (estimated average circulation 120,000 copies).

Sources: UNESCO, *Statistical Yearbook*; UN, *Statistical Yearbook*; International Telecommunication Union.

Education

(1998)

	Institu-tions	Teachers	Students Males	Students Females	Students Total
Primary*† . . .	3,160	340,375	1,057,273	1,045,151	2,102,424
Secondary† . . .	n.a.	18,197	531,771	414,358	946,309
Tertiary	n.a.	509	8,303	3,176	11,479

* 1997 figures.
† UNESCO estimates.

Source: UNESCO Institute for Statistics.

Adult literacy rate (UNESCO estimates): 60.1% (males 74.5%; females 46.5%) in 2000 (Source: UN Development Programme, *Human Development Report*).

Directory

The Constitution

A new Constitution, replacing the (amended) 1966 Constitution, was approved by the National Assembly on 16 May 1994, and took provisional effect for one year from 18 May. During this time the Constitution was to be subject to review, and the final document was promulgated on 18 May 1995. The main provisions (with subsequent amendments) are summarized below:

THE PRESIDENT

The President is both Head of State and Head of Government. The President is elected for five years, by universal adult suffrage, in the context of a multi-party political system. The Constitution provides for up to two Vice-Presidents.

PARLIAMENT

Parliament comprises the President, the Vice-President(s) and the National Assembly. The National Assembly has 193 elective seats, elections being by universal adult suffrage, in the context of a multi-party system. Cabinet ministers who are not elected members of parliament also sit in the National Assembly. The Speaker is appointed from among the ordinary members of the Assembly. The parliamentary term is normally five years. The President has power to prorogue or dissolve Parliament.

In 1995 the National Assembly approved proposals for the establishment of a second chamber, the Senate, to be implemented in 1999. The chamber was not established by that date, however, and in January 2001 the National Assembly approved a proposal to abandon plans for its creation.

EXECUTIVE POWER

Executive power is exercised by the President, who appoints members of the Cabinet.

The Government

HEAD OF STATE

President: Dr (ELSON) BAKILI MULUZI (took office 21 May 1994; re-elected 15 June 1999).

Vice-President: JUSTIN MALEWEZI.

CABINET
(April 2003)

President and Head of Government: Dr BAKILI MULUZI.

Vice-President and Minister responsible for Privatization: JUSTIN MALEWEZI.

Vice-President and Minister of Agriculture and Irrigation Development: CHAKUFWA CHIHANA.

Minister of Natural Resources and Environmental Affairs: ULADI MUSSA.

Minister of Foreign Affairs and International Co-operation: LILIAN PATEL.

Attorney-General and Minister of Justice: PAUL MAULUDI.

Minister of Finance: FRIDAY JUMBE.

Minister of Economic Planning and Development: Dr BINGU WA MUTHARIKA.

Minister of Home Affairs and Internal Security: MANGEZA MALOZA.

Minister of State for Presidential Affairs: KEN LIPENGA.

Minister of Tourism: WALLACE CHIUME.

Minister of Youth, Sports and Culture: HENDERSON MABETI.

Minister of Commerce and Industry: SAMUEL LEMMOTH MPASU.

Minister of Health and Population: YUSUF MWAWA.

Minister of HIV/AIDS Programmes: MARY BANDA.

Minister of State in the President's Office, responsible for People with Disabilities: SUSAN CHITIMBE.

Minister of Transport and Public Works: CLEMENT STAMBULI.

Minister of Lands, Physical Planning and Surveys: THENGO MALOYA.

Minister of Housing: KALIYOMA PHUMISA.

Minister of State in the President's Office, responsible for Districts and Local Government Administration: SALIM BAGUS.

Minister of Education, Science and Technology: GEORGE MTAFU.

Minister of State in the President's Office, responsible for Statutory Corporations: BOB KHAMISA.

Minister of Water Development: DUMBO LEMANI.

Minister of Defence: RODWELL MUNYENYEMBE.

Minister of Information: BERNARD CHISALE.

Minister of Women, Youth and Community Services: ALICE SUMANI.

Minister of Labour and Vocational Training: LEE MLANGA.

Minister of State, responsible for Poverty Alleviation Programmes and Disaster Management: LUDOVIKO SHATI.

Minister without Portfolio: CHIPIMPHA MUGHOGHO.

There were also 10 Deputy Ministers.

MINISTRIES

Office of the President and Cabinet: Private Bag 301, Capital City, Lilongwe 3; tel. 782655; fax 783654.

Ministry of Agriculture and Irrigation Development: POB 30144, Capital City, Lilongwe 3; tel. 783450; fax 784299.

Ministry of Commerce and Industry: POB 30366, Capital City, Lilongwe 3; tel. 780244; fax 780680.

Ministry of Defence: Private Bag 339, Lilongwe 3; tel. 782200; fax 781282.

Ministry of District and Local Government Administration: POB 30312, Lilongwe 3; tel. 784500; fax 782130.

Ministry of Economic Planning and Development: Lilongwe.

Ministry of Education, Science and Technology: Private Bag 328, Capital City, Lilongwe 3; tel. 784800; fax 782873.

Ministry of Finance: POB 30049, Capital City, Lilongwe 3; tel. 782199; fax 781679.

Ministry of Foreign Affairs and International Co-operation: POB 30315, Capital City, Lilongwe 3; tel. 731788; fax 781516.

Ministry of Health and Population: POB 30377, Capital City, Lilongwe 3; tel. 783044; fax 783109.

Ministry of HIV/AIDS Programmes: Lilongwe.

Ministry of Housing: Lilongwe.

Ministry of Information: Private Bag 310, Lilongwe 3; tel. 783233; fax 784568.

Ministry of Justice: Private Bag 333, Capital City, Lilongwe 3; tel. 788411; fax 788332; e-mail justice@sdnp.org.mw; internet www.sdnp.org.mw/ruleoflaw.

Ministry of Labour and Vocational Training: Private Bag 344, Capital City, Lilongwe 3; tel. 783277; fax 783805; e-mail labour@eo.wn.apc.org.

Ministry of Lands Physical Planning and Surveys: Private Bag 311, Lilongwe 3; tel. 784766; fax 781389.

Ministry of Natural Resources and Environmental Affairs: Private Bag 350, Lilongwe 3; tel. 782600; fax 780260.

Ministry of Statutory Corporations: POB 30061, Lilongwe 3; tel. 784266; fax 784110.

Ministry of Tourism: Private Bag 326, Lilongwe 3; tel. 775499; fax 770650; e-mail tourism@malawi.net.

Ministry of Transport and Public Works: Private Bag 322, Capital City, Lilongwe 3; tel. 80344; fax 784678.

Ministry of Water Development: Tikwere House, Private Bag 390, Capital City, Lilongwe 3; tel. 782600; fax 780260.

Ministry of Women, Youth and Community Services: Private Bag 330, Capital City, Lilongwe 3; tel. 780411; fax 780826.

Ministry of Youth, Sports and Culture: POB 30387, Lilongwe 3.

President and Legislature

PRESIDENT

Presidential Election, 15 June 1999

Candidate	Votes	% of votes
Bakili Muluzi (UDF)	2,442,685	51.37
Gwandaguluwe Chakuamba (MCP—AFORD)	2,106,790	44.30
Kamulepo Kalua (MDP) . . .	67,856	1.43
Rev. Daniel Nkhumbwe (CNU) .	24,347	0.51
Bingu wa Mutharika (UP). . .	22,073	0.46
Invalid votes	91,671	1.93
Total	4,755,422	100.00

NATIONAL ASSEMBLY

Speaker: SAMUEL LEMMOTH MPASU.

General Election, 15 June 1999

Party	Seats
UDF.	93
MCP	66
AFORD.	29
Independents	4
Total*	192

* Voting in the remaining constituency was postponed, owing to the death of a candidate. The seat was won by a candidate of the UDF at a by-election in October.

Political Organizations

Alliance for Democracy (AFORD): Private Bag 28, Lilongwe; f. 1992; in March 1993 absorbed membership of fmr Malawi Freedom Movement; Pres. CHAKUFWA CHIHANA; First Vice-Pres. KALUNDI CHIRWA; Sec.-Gen. WALLACE CHIUME.

Congress for the Second Republic (CSR): Leader KANYAMA CHIUME.

Forum Party (FP): f. 1997; Leader KALONGA STAMBULI.

Malawi Congress Party (MCP): Private Bag 388, Lilongwe 3; tel. 730388; f. 1959; sole legal party 1966–93; Leader GWANDAGULUWE CHAKUAMBA.

Malawi Democratic Party (MDP): Pres. KAMULEPO KALUA.

Malawi Democratic Union (MDU): Pres. JAMES TABUNA DISENTIKUBA.

Malawi Forum for Unity and Development: f. 2002; aims to combat corruption and food shortages.

Mass Movement for the Young Generation (MM): Lilongwe; f. 1998; Interim Pres. CHAIMA BANDA.

National Democratic Alliance (NDA): POB 994, Blantyre; tel. 842593; e-mail nda-mw@yahoo.com; internet www.geocities.com/nda_mw; f. 2001; Pres. BROWN MPINGANJIRA; Chair. JAMES MAKHUMULA.

Pamodzi Freedom Party (PFP): Lilongwe; f. 2002; Interim Pres. RAINSFORD CHIGADULA NDIWO.

Social Democratic Party (SDP): Pres. ISON KAKOME.

United Democratic Front (UDF): POB 5446, Limbe; internet www.udf.malawi.net; f. 1992; Pres. Dr BAKILI MULUZI; Vice-Pres. JUSTIN MALEWEZI; Sec.-Gen. WILLIE KATENGA KAUNDA.

United Front for Multi-party Democracy (UFMD): f. 1992 by three exiled political groups: the Socialist League of Malawi, the Malawi Freedom Party and the Malawi Democratic Union; Pres. EDMOND JIKA.

United Party (UP): f. 1997.

The Movement for the Restoration of Democracy in Malawi (f. 1996) is based in Mozambique and consists of fmr Malawi Young Pioneers; it conducts occasional acts of insurgency.

Diplomatic Representation

EMBASSIES AND HIGH COMMISSIONS IN MALAWI

China (Taiwan): Area 40, Plot No. 9, POB 30221, Capital City, Lilongwe 3; tel. 773611; fax 774812; e-mail rocemml@malawi.net; Ambassador CHEN HSI-TSAN.

Egypt: POB 30451, Lilongwe 3; tel. 780668; fax 780691; e-mail egy_emb_Malawi@yahoo.com; Ambassador ADEL EL MELIGUI.

Germany: POB 30046, Lilongwe 3; tel. 772555; fax 770250; e-mail germanemb@malawi.net; Ambassador Dr FRANZ RING.

Mozambique: POB 30579, Lilongwe 3; tel. 784100; fax 781342; e-mail mozambique@malawi.net; High Commissioner JORGE DE SOUSA MATEUS.

Norway: Private Bag B323, Lilongwe 3; tel. 774211; fax 772845; e-mail emb.lilongwe@mfa.no; Ambassador ASBJØRN EIDHAMMER.

South Africa: Kang'ombe House, 3rd Floor, City Centre, POB 30043, Lilongwe 3; tel. 773722; fax 772571; High Commissioner N. M. C. SELEKA.

United Kingdom: British High Commission Bldg, Capital Hill, POB 30042, Lilongwe 3; tel. 782400; fax 772657; e-mail britcom@malawi.net; High Commissioner NORMAN LING.

USA: Area 40, Plot 18, POB 30016, Lilongwe 3; tel. 773166; fax 770471; Ambassador ROGER MEECE.

Zambia: POB 30138, Lilongwe 3; tel. 782635; fax 784349; High Commissioner Col (retd) LAWRENCE M. H. HAAMAUNDU.

Zimbabwe: POB 30187, Lilongwe 3; tel. 784988; fax 782382; e-mail zimhighcomllw@malawi.net; High Commissioner E. T. MANYIKA.

Judicial System

The courts administering justice are the Supreme Court of Appeal, High Court and Magistrates' Courts.

The High Court, which has unlimited jurisdiction in civil and criminal matters, consists of the Chief Justice and five puisne judges. Traditional Courts were abolished under the 1994 Constitution. Appeals from the High Court are heard by the Supreme Court of Appeal in Blantyre.

High Court of Malawi

POB 30244, Chichiri, Blantyre 3; tel. 670255; fax 670213.

Registrar W. W. QOTO.

Chief Justice: RICHARD A. BANDA.

Justices of Appeal: L. A. UNYOLO, H. M. MTEGHA, J. B. KALAILE, D. G. TAMBALA, A. S. E. MSOSA.

High Court Judges: M. P. MKANDAWIRE, I. J. MTAMBO, D. F. MWAUNGULU, A. K. C. NYIRENDA, D. S. L. KUMANGE, G. M. CHIMASULA PHIRI, E. B. Z. KUMITSONYO, CHIUDZA BANDA, L. B. T. NDOVIE, W. M. HANJA HANJA, E. B. TWEA, R. R. MZIKAMANDO, J. M. ANSAH, R. R. CHINANGWA, A. CHIPETA.

Religion

About 75% of the population profess Christianity. The Asian community includes Muslims and Hindus, and there is a small number of African Muslims. Traditional beliefs are followed by about 10% of the population.

CHRISTIANITY

Malawi Council of Churches: POB 30068, Capital City, Lilongwe 3; tel. 783499; fax 783106; f. 1939; 19 mems and 12 associates; Chair. Rt Rev. JAMES TENGATENGA; Gen. Sec. Rev. Dr A.C. MUSOPOLE.

The Anglican Communion

Anglicans are adherents of the Church of the Province of Central Africa, covering Botswana, Malawi, Zambia and Zimbabwe. The Church comprises 12 dioceses, including three in Malawi. The Archbishop of the Province is the Bishop of Botswana. There are about 80,000 adherents in Malawi.

Bishop of Lake Malawi: Rt Rev. PETER NATHANIEL NYANJA, POB 30349, Capital City, Lilongwe 3; tel. and fax 731966.

Bishop of North Malawi: Rt Rev. JACKSON BIGGERS, POB 120, Mzuzu; tel. 335085; e-mail biggers@malawi.net.

Bishop of Southern Malawi: Rt Rev. JAMES TENGATENGA, POB 30220, Chichiri, Blantyre 3; tel. and fax 641235; e-mail angsoma@clcom.net; internet www.clcom.net/angsoma.

Protestant Churches

Church of Central Africa (Presbyterian): Blantyre Synod: POB 413, Blantyre; tel. and fax 633942; comprises three synods in Malawi (Blantyre, Livingstonia and Nkhoma); Co-ordinator Rev. J. J. MPHATSE; more than 1m. adherents in Malawi.

Evangelical Association of Malawi: Lilongwe; tel. and fax 730373; e-mail evangelicalassmw@malawi.net; Chair. Rev. MVULA J. MVULA; Gen. Sec. FRANCIS MKANDAWIRE.

The Indigenous Baptist Convention of Malawi: POB 51083, Limbe; tel. 643224; Chair. Rev. S. L. MALABWANYA; Gen. Sec. Rev. M. T. KACHASO GAMA.

The Lutheran Church of Central Africa: POB 748, Blantyre; tel. 630821; fax 630821; f. 1963; evangelical and medical work; Co-ordinator J. M. JANOSEK; 35,000 mems. in Malawi.

Seventh-day Adventists: POB 951, Blantyre; tel. 620264; fax 620528; e-mail 1016631763@malawi.net; Pres. B. E. MALOPA; Exec. Sec. R. R. MZUMARA.

The African Methodist Episcopal Church, the Churches of Christ, the Free Methodist Church, the Pentecostal Assemblies of God and the United Evangelical Church in Malawi are also active.

The Roman Catholic Church

Malawi comprises one archdiocese and six dioceses. At 31 December 2000 some 19.8% of the total population were adherents of the Roman Catholic Church.

Episcopal Conference of Malawi

Catholic Secretariat of Malawi, Chimutu Rd, POB 30384, Capital City, Lilongwe 3; tel. 782066; fax 782019; e-mail ecm@malawi.net. f. 1969; Pres. Most Rev. TARCISIUS GERVAZIO ZIYAYE (Archbishop of Blantyre).

Archbishop of Blantyre: Most Rev. TARCISIUS GERVAZIO ZIYAYE, Archbishop's House, POB 385, Blantyre; tel. 633905; fax 636107.

BAHÁ'Í FAITH

National Spiritual Assembly: POB 5849, Limbe; tel. 771713; e-mail malawinsa@africa-online.net; f. 1970; mems resident in over 1,500 localities.

The Press

ABA Today: POB 5861, Limbe; f. 1982; monthly; publ. by African Businessmen's Association of Malawi.

Blantyre Handbook: Centraf Associates, POB 30462, Chichiri, Blantyre; f. 1978; quarterly.

Boma Lathu: POB 494, Blantyre; tel. 620266; fax 620039; e-mail manabt@Malawi.net; internet www.mafor.malawi.net; f. 1973; monthly; Chichewa; publ. by the Ministry of Information; circ. 100,000.

Business and Development News: POB 829, Development House, Victoria Avenue, Blantyre; f. 1973; monthly.

Business Monthly: POB 906646, Blantyre 9; tel. 6301114; fax 620039; e-mail aluviza@miw.healthnet.org; f. 1995; 6 a year; English; economic, financial and business news; Editor ANTHONY LIVUZA; circ. 10,000.

The Daily Times: Private Bag 39, Blantyre; tel. 671566; fax 671114; e-mail dailytimes@malawi.net; f. 1895; Mon.–Fri. English; Editor-in-Chief VELS MACHOA; circ. 11,500.

Kuunika: POB 17, Nkhoma, Lilongwe; f. 1909; monthly; Chichewa; Presbyterian; Editor Rev. M. C. NKHALAMBAYAUSI; circ. 6,000.

Malawi Life: Private Bag 39, Ginnery Corner, Blantyre; tel. 671566; f. 1991; monthly magazine; English.

Malawi Government Gazette: Government Printer, POB 37, Zomba; tel. 523155; f. 1894; weekly.

Malawi News: Private Bag 39, Blantyre; tel. 671566; fax 671114; e-mail dailytimes@malawi.net; f. 1959; weekly; English, Chichewa; Editor HORACE SOMANJE; circ. 40,000.

Medical Quarterly: Centraf Associates, POB 30462, Chichiri, Blantyre; f. 1980; quarterly; English; journal of the Medical Association of Malawi.

The Mirror: POB 30721, Blantyre; tel. 675043; f. 1994; weekly; English; Editor-in-Chief GEORGE TUKHUWA; circ. 10,000.

Moni: POB 5592, Limbe; tel. 651139; fax 641126; e-mail mpp@clcom.net; f. 1964; monthly; Chichewa and English; circ. 40,000.

The Monitor: POB 2521, Blantyre; tel. 673901; f. 1993; daily; English; Publisher CLEMENT STANBULI; circ. 7,000.

Moyo: Health Education Unit, POB 30377, Lilongwe 3; bi-monthly; English; publ. by Ministry of Health and Population; Editor-in-Chief W. G. BOMBA.

Nation: POB 30408, Chichiri, Blantyre; tel. 673703; fax 674343; internet www.nation.malawi.net; f. 1993; weekly; English; independent; Editor ALFRED NTONGA; circ. 10,000.

National Magazine: Blantyre Newspapers Ltd, Blantyre; tel. 671566; fax 6711114; f. 1991; monthly.

Odini: POB 133, Lilongwe; tel. 721135; fax 721141; f. 1949; fortnightly; Chichewa and English; Roman Catholic; Dir P. I. AKOMENJI; circ. 12,000.

This is Malawi: POB 494, Blantyre; tel. 620266; fax 620807; e-mail alivuza@malawi.net; internet www.maform.malawi.net; f. 1964; monthly; English and Chichewa edns; publ. by the Dept of Information; Editor ANTHONY LIVUZA; circ. 12,000.

The Weekly Chronicle: POB 40521, Lilongwe; f. 1993; weekly; English, independent; Editor WILLIE ZINGANI; circ. 5,000.

NEWS AGENCIES

Malawi News Agency (MANA): Mzuza; tel. 636122; f. 1966.

Foreign Bureau

Newslink Africa (UK): POB 2688, Blantyre; Correspondent HOBBS GAMA.

Publishers

Christian Literature Association in Malawi: POB 503, Blantyre; tel. 620839; f. 1968; general and religious publs in Chichewa and English; Gen. Man. J. T. MATENJE.

Likuni Press and Publishing House: POB 133, Lilongwe; tel. 721388; fax 721141; f. 1949; publs in English and Chichewa; Gen. Man. (vacant).

Mzuzu Publishing Co: POB 225, Nkhata Bay; tel. 352353; f. 1977; Exec. Chair. M. W. KANYAMA CHIUME.

Popular Publications: POB 5592, Limbe; tel. 651833; fax 641126; e-mail mpp@clcom.net; f. 1961; general and religious; Gen. Man. VALES MACHILA.

Government Publishing House

Government Printer: POB 37, Zomba; tel. 523155.

Broadcasting and Communications

TELECOMMUNICATIONS

Malawi Telecommunications Ltd (MTL): Lamya House, Masauko Chipembere Highway, POB 537, Blantyre; tel. 620977; fax 624445; e-mail mtlceo@malawi.net; f. 2000 following division of Malawi Posts and Telecommunications Corpn into two separate entities; partial privatization projected for 2003; CEO EMMANUEL MAHUKA.

Mobile Systems International (MSI): f. 1998; operates the Celtel mobile cellular telephone network; Man. Dir DAVID BAMFORD.

Telekom Networks Malawi (TNM): tel. 641088; fax 642805; e-mail nasirbah@malawi.net; operates mobile cellular telephone network; CEO NASIR BAHARONI.

BROADCASTING

Radio

Malawi Broadcasting Corpn: POB 30133, Chichiri, Blantyre 3; tel. 671222; fax 671257; e-mail dgmbc@malawi.net; f. 1964; statutory body; semi-commercial, partly state-financed; two channels; programmes in English, Chichewa, Chitumbuka, Lomwe and Yao; Chair. Maj. Gen. B. NAMWAL; Dir-Gen. WILSON PANKUKU (acting); Dir of News and Current Affairs MOLLAND NKHATA.

Television

Television Malawi (TVM): f. 1999; broadcasts 55 hours per week, of which 10 hours are produced locally; relays programmes from France, Germany, South Africa and the United Kingdom; Chair. MOHAMMED KULESI.

Finance

(cap. = capital; res = reserves; dep. = deposits; m. = million; brs = branches; amounts in kwacha)

BANKING

Central Bank

Reserve Bank of Malawi: POB 30063, Capital City, Lilongwe 3; tel. 770600; fax 772752; e-mail reservebank@malawi.net; internet www.rbm.malawi.net; f. 1965; bank of issue; cap. 306.0m., res 6,447.7m., dep. 2,834.3m. (Dec. 2000); Gov. Dr ELIAS E. NGALANDE BANDA; Gen. Mans E. J. KAMBALAME, C. S. R. CHUKA; br. in Blantyre.

Commercial Banks

Commercial Bank of Malawi Ltd: POB 1111, Blantyre; tel. 620144; fax 620360; e-mail combank@malawi.net; internet www.combank-mw.malawi.net; f. 1970; 22% state-owned; cap. and res 1,239.0m., dep. 6,895.0m. (Dec. 2000); Chair. TIMON SAM MANGWAZU; CEO VICTOR MBEWE; 13 brs.

Finance Bank of Malawi: Finance House, Victoria Ave, POB 421, Blantyre; tel. 624799; fax 622957; e-mail makhan@malawi.net; cap. 23.0m, total assets 1,005.6m. (Dec. 1999); Chair. Dr R. L. MAHTANI; Man. Dir N. A. QURESHI (acting).

Loita Investment Bank: Loita House, Victoria Ave, Private Bag 389, Chichiri, Blantyre 3; tel. 620099; fax 622683; e-mail lib@loita.malawi.net; internet www.loita.com; Chair. N. JUSTIN CHINYATA; Gen. Man. JEROME BISSAY.

National Bank of Malawi: Victoria Ave, POB 945, Blantyre; tel. 620622; fax 620606; e-mail natbank@malawi.net; internet www.natbank.malawi.net; f. 1971; cap. 450m., res 452m., dep. 8,052m. (Dec. 2000); CEO T. J. O. BARNES; 13 brs; agencies throughout Malawi.

Development Bank

Investment and Development Bank of Malawi Ltd (INDEBANK): Indebank House, Kaushong Rd, Top Mandala, POB 358, Blantyre; tel. 620055; fax 623353; e-mail indebank@malawi.net; f. 1972; cap. 35.0m., total assets 417.0m. (Dec. 1999); provides loans to statutory corpns and to private enterprises in the agricultural, industrial, tourism, transport and commercial sectors; Chair. CHRISTOPHER BARROW; Gen. Man. M. J. M. PHIRI.

Merchant Banks

First Merchant Bank Ltd: First House, Glyn Jones Road, POB 122, Blantyre; tel. 622787; fax 621978; e-mail fmbhq@malawi.net; cap. 30.0m., dep. 997.9m., total assets 1,970.5m. (Dec. 2000); Chair. RASIKBHAI C. KANTARIA; Gen. Man. S. SRINIVASAN.

Leasing and Finance Co of Malawi Ltd: Indebank House, 1st Floor, Top Mandala, POB 1963, Blantyre; tel. 620233; fax 620275; e-mail lfc@malawi.net; f. 1986; cap. 8.0m., dep. 265.8m. (Aug. 1999); Chair. AGNES VALERA; Gen. Man. J. N. WHITEHEAD.

National Finance Co Ltd: Plantation House, POB 821, Blantyre; tel. 623670; fax 620549; e-mail natfin@malawi.net; f. 1958; cap. and res 87.0m., total assets 243.0m. (Dec. 2001); Chair. T. J. O. BARNES; Gen. Man. M. T. BAMFORD.

Savings Bank

Malawi Savings Bank: Unloyo House, Victoria Ave, POB 521, Blantyre; tel. 625111; fax 621929; e-mail msb@msb.mw.net; state-owned; total assets 777.5m. (2001); Chair. P. CHILAMBE; Gen. Man. IAN BONONGWE.

STOCK EXCHANGE

Malawi Stock Exchange: Able House, Ground Floor, cnr Hannover Ave and Chilembwe Rd, POB 2598, Blantyre; tel. 821783; fax 624353; f. 1995; Chair. C. MPANDE; CEO THOM MPINGANJIRA.

INSURANCE

National Insurance Co Ltd: NICO House, POB 501, Blantyre; tel. 622699; fax 622364; e-mail nico@nico.malawi.net; f. 1971; transferred to private sector in 1998; cap. and res 104.7m. (Sept. 1997); offices at Blantyre, Lilongwe, Mzuzu and Zomba; agencies countrywide; CEO and Man. Dir FELIX L. MLUSU.

Old Mutual Malawi: POB 393, Blantyre; tel. 620677; fax 622649; e-mail oldmutual@malawi.net; f. 1845; Gen. Man. MARIUS WALTERS.

Royal Insurance Co of Malawi Ltd: POB 442, Blantyre; tel. 624044; fax 623862; Gen. Man. ROBERT G. NDUNGU.

United General Insurance Co Ltd: POB 383, Blantyre; tel. 621577; fax 621980; e-mail ugi@malawi.net; Gen. Man. I. KUMWENDA.

Trade and Industry

GOVERNMENT AGENCIES

Malawi Export Promotion Council: Delamere House, POB 1299, Blantyre; tel. 620499; fax 635429; e-mail mepco@malawi.net; f. 1974; Gen. Man. G. I. L. MANGOCHI.

Malawi Investment Promotion Agency (MIPA): Aquarius House, Private Bag 302, Lilongwe 3; tel. 770800; fax 771781; e-mail mipall@malawi.net; internet www.mipa.malawi.net; f. 1993; promotes and facilitates local and foreign investment; CEO TED A. KALEBE.

Privatization Commission: POB 937, Blantyre; tel. 623655; fax 621248; f. 1996; to oversee privatization programme.

DEVELOPMENT ORGANIZATIONS

Agricultural Development and Marketing Corpn (ADMARC): POB 5052, Limbe; tel. 640500; fax 640486; f. 1971; govt agency; markets agricultural crops produced by smallholder farmers; exports confectionery-grade groundnut kernels, maize, cassava and sunflower seed; primary marketing of tobacco, wheat and beans, peas and other seeds; co-operates with commercial cos in the cultivation and processing of agricultural produce; in process of privatization in 2003; Chair. J. STEVENS.

Malawi Development Corpn (MDC): MDC House, Glyn Jones Rd, POB 566, Blantyre; tel. 620100; fax 620584; e-mail mdcgm@malawi.net; internet www.mdc.co.mw; f. 1964; state-owned; provides finance and management advice to commerce and industry; 23 subsidiary and assoc. cos; Chair. Dr JERRY A. A. JANA; Gen. Man. PATRICK A. MAKINA.

Small Enterprise Development Organization of Malawi (SEDOM): POB 525, Blantyre; tel. 622555; fax 622781; e-mail sedom@sdnp.org.mw; f. 1982; financial services and accommodation for indigenous small- and medium-scale businesses.

CHAMBER OF COMMERCE

Malawi Chamber of Commerce and Industry: Chichiri Trade Fair Grounds, POB 258, Blantyre; tel. 671988; fax 671147; e-mail mcci@eo.wn.apc.org; f. 1892; 400 mems; Chair. MARK KATSONGO PHIRI.

INDUSTRIAL AND TRADE ASSOCIATIONS

Smallholder Coffee Farmers Trust: POB 20133, Luwinga, Mzuzu 2; tel. 332899; fax 332902; e-mail mzuzucoffee@malawi.net; producers and exporters of arabica coffee.

Smallholder Sugar Authority: Blantyre.

Smallholder Tea Authority: POB 80, Thyolo.

Tea Association of Malawi Ltd: POB 930, Blantyre; tel. 671355; fax 671427; f. 1936; 20 mems; Man. Dir G. D. BANDA.

Tobacco Association of Malawi: POB 31360, Lilongwe 3; tel. 783099; fax 783493; e-mail tama@eo.wn.apc.org; f. 1929; 60,000 mems; Pres. ALBERT W. KAMULAGA; Exec. Sec. Dr G. THYANGATHYANGA.

Tobacco Exporters' Association of Malawi Ltd: Private Bag 403, Kanengo, Lilongwe 4; tel. 710663; fax 710668; e-mail tobacco-exporters@sndp.org.mw; f. 1930; 9 mems; Chair. CHARLES A. M. GRAHAM; Exec. Sec. H. M. MBALE.

EMPLOYERS' ORGANIZATIONS

Employers' Consultative Association of Malawi (ECAM): POB 2134, Blantyre; tel. and fax 670715; e-mail ecam@malawi.net; f. 1963; 250 mems; Chair. H. C. MVULA; Exec. Dir V. F. SINJANI.

Master Builders', Civil Engineering Contractors' and Allied Trades' Association: POB 311, Blantyre; tel. and fax 624754; e-mail bes@malawi.net; f. 1955; 41 mems (2003); Chair. E. BIZZARO.

Master Printers' Association of Malawi: POB 2460, Blantyre; tel. 670608; f. 1962; 21 mems; Chair. PAUL FREDERICK.

Motor Traders' Association: POB 311, Blantyre; tel. and fax 624754; e-mail bes@malawi.net; f. 1954; 24 mems (2003); Chair. A. R. OSMAN.

UTILITY

Electricity

Electricity Supply Commission of Malawi (ESCOM): ESCOM House, Haile Selassie Rd, POB 2047, Blantyre; tel. and fax 622008; f. 1966; controls electricity distribution; Chair. FRANK JIYA; CEO REYNOLD DUNCAN.

TRADE UNIONS

Trades Union Congress of Malawi (TUCM): POB 5094, Limbe; f. 1964; 6,500 mems; Chair. KEN WILLIAM MHANGO; Gen. Sec. EATON V. LAITA; the following are among the principal affiliated unions:

> **Building Construction, Civil Engineering and Allied Workers' Union:** Limbe; tel. 650598; f. 1961; 6,000 mems; Chair. W. I. SOKO; Gen. Sec. G. SITIMA.

> **Railway Workers' Union of Malawi:** POB 5393, Limbe; tel. 640844; f. 1954; 3,000 mems; Pres. THOMAS CHISAKANIZA; Gen. Sec. MACDONALD LUWANJA.

Other unions affiliated to the TUCM are the Commercial and Allied Workers' Union, the Civil Servants' Trade Union, the Hotels, Food and Catering Workers' Union, the Local Government Employees' Union, the Plantation and Agricultural Workers' Union, the Teachers' Union of Malawi, the Textile, Garment, Guards and Leather Workers' Union, the Transport and General Workers' Union and the Sugar Plantation and Allied Workers' Union. The TUCM and its affiliated unions had a total membership of 450,000 in 1995.

Transport

RAILWAYS

The Central East African Railways Co (fmrly Malawi Railways) operates between Nsanje (near the southern border with Mozambique) and Mchinji (near the border with Zambia) via Blantyre, Salima and Lilongwe, and between Nkaya and Nayuchi on the eastern border with Mozambique, covering a total of 797 km. The Central East African Railways Co and Mozambique State Railways connect Malawi with the Mozambican ports of Beira and Nacala. These links, which traditionally form Malawi's principal trade routes, were effectively closed during 1983–85, owing to insurgent activity in Mozambique. The rail link to Nacala was reopened in October 1989; however, continued unrest and flooding in Mozambique prevented full use of the route until the completion of a programme of improvements in September 2000; the service was temporarily suspended in 2002 while safety was improved. There is a rail/lake interchange station at Chipoka on Lake Malawi, from where vessels operate services to other lake ports in Malawi.

Central East African Railways Co Ltd: POB 5144, Limbe; tel. 640844; fax 643262; f. 1994 as Malawi Railways Ltd; sold to a consortium owned by Mozambique's Empresa Nacional dos Portos e Caminhos de Ferro de Moçambique and the USA's Railroad Corpn in mid-1999 and subsequently renamed as above; CEO ROBERT MORTENSEN; Gen. Man. BRANDLEY KNAPP.

ROADS

In 1997 Malawi had a total road network of some 16,451 km, of which 4,520 km were main roads and 2,768 km were secondary roads; about 19.0% of the road network was paved. In 1999 the total road network was estimated at 28,400 km. In addition, unclassified community roads total an estimated 10,000 km. All main roads, and most secondary roads, are all-weather roads. Major routes link Lilongwe and Blantyre with Harare (Zimbabwe), Lusaka (Zambia) and Mbeya and Dar es Salaam (Tanzania). A 480-km highway along the western shore of Lake Malawi links the remote Northern Region with the Central and Southern Regions. A project to create a new trade route, or 'Northern Corridor', through Tanzania, involving road construction and improvements in Malawi, was completed in 1992.

Road Transport Operators' Association: Makata Industrial Site, POB 30740, Chichiri, Blantyre 3; tel. 670422; fax 671423; f. 1956; 254 mems (1995); Chair. E. MUHOMED.

CIVIL AVIATION

Lilongwe (formerly Kamuzu) International Airport was opened in 1982. There is another main airport, at Blantyre, which serves a number of regional airlines, and three domestic airports.

Air Malawi Ltd: 4 Robins Rd, POB 84, Blantyre; tel. 620811; fax 620042; e-mail it@airmalawi.malawi.net; internet www.africaonline.co.ke/airmalawi; f. 1967; restructuring in preparation for privatization began in 1999; scheduled domestic and regional services, scheduled services to the United Kingdom suspended in June 1999; Chair. B. G. BOWLER; CEO FRANCIS PELEKAMOYO.

Tourism

Fine scenery, beaches on Lake Malawi, big game and an excellent climate form the basis of the country's tourist potential. The number of foreign visitor arrivals increased from 219,570 in 1998 to 254,352 in 1999, before declining to 228,106 in 2000; receipts from tourism totalled US $27m. in 2000.

Department of Tourism: POB 402, Blantyre; tel. 620300; fax 620947; f. 1969; responsible for tourist policy; inspects and licenses tourist facilities, sponsors training of hotel staff and publishes tourist literature; Dir of Tourism Services F. MASIMBE.

Tourism Development and Investment Co (TDIC): Blantyre; f. 1988 by Malawi Development Corpn to operate hotels and tours; Chief Exec. FRANCIS MBILIZI.

MALAYSIA

Introductory Survey

Location, Climate, Language, Religion, Flag, Capital

The Federation of Malaysia, situated in South-East Asia, consists of 13 states. Eleven of these are in Peninsular Malaysia, in the southern part of the Kra peninsula (with Thailand to the north and the island of Singapore to the south), and two, Sabah and Sarawak, are on the north coast of the island of Borneo, two-thirds of which comprises the Indonesian territory of Kalimantan. Sarawak also borders Brunei, a coastal enclave in the north-east of the state. The climate is tropical, there is rain in all seasons and temperatures are generally between 22°C (72°F) and 33°C (92°F), with little variation throughout the year. The official language is Bahasa Malaysia, based on Malay, but English is also widely used. Chinese, Tamil and Iban are spoken by minorities. Islam is the established religion, practised by about 53% of the population (including virtually all Malays), while about 19%, including most of the Chinese community, follow Buddhism. The Indians are predominantly Hindus. There is a minority of Christians among all races, and traditional beliefs are practised, particularly in Sabah and Sarawak. Malaysia's national flag (proportions 1 by 2) has 14 horizontal stripes, alternating red and white, with a blue rectangular canton, containing a yellow crescent and a 14-pointed yellow star, in the upper hoist. The capital is Kuala Lumpur. A new administrative capital, Putrajaya, has been developed south of Kuala Lumpur.

Recent History

The 11 states of Malaya, under British protection, were united as the Malayan Union in April 1946 and became the Federation of Malaya in February 1948. An armed communist offensive began in 1948, and was not effectively suppressed until the mid-1950s. After 1960 the remainder of the banned Communist Party of Malaya (CPM) took refuge in southern Thailand. Meanwhile, Malaya was granted independence, within the Commonwealth, on 31 August 1957.

Malaysia was established on 16 September 1963, through the union of the independent Federation of Malaya (renamed the States of Malaya), the internally self-governing state of Singapore, and the former British colonies of Sarawak and Sabah (North Borneo). Singapore left the federation in August 1965, reducing the number of Malaysia's component states from 14 to 13. The States of Malaya were designated West Malaysia in 1966 and later styled Peninsular Malaysia.

In 1970 serious inter-communal rioting, engendered by Malay resentment of the Chinese community's economic dominance and of certain pro-Chinese electoral results, precipitated the resignation of Tunku Abdul Rahman, who had been Prime Minister of Malaya (and subsequently of Malaysia) since independence. The new Prime Minister, Tun Abdul Razak, widened the Government coalition, dominated by the United Malays National Organization (UMNO), to create a national front, Barisan Nasional (BN). The BN originally comprised 10 parties, absorbing most of the former opposition parties. In January 1976 the Prime Minister died and was succeeded by the Deputy Prime Minister, Dato' Hussein bin Onn.

Political stability was subsequently threatened by the resurgence of the communist guerrilla movement, which conducted a series of terrorist attacks in Peninsular Malaysia during 1976–78. However, CPM activity subsequently declined, owing to co-operation between Malaysia and Thailand in military operations along their common border. In 1987, in a Thai-sponsored amnesty, about 700 Malaysian communists surrendered to the Thai authorities. In December 1989, following a year of negotiations with the Thai Government, the remaining 1,188 rebels (including recruits from Thailand and Singapore) agreed to terminate all armed activities. The peace agreements, signed by the leader of the CPM and representatives of the Malaysian and Thai Governments, made provision for the resettlement of the insurgents in either Malaysia or Thailand and their eventual participation in legitimate political activity in Malaysia.

In October 1977 the expulsion of the Chief Minister (Menteri Besar) of Kelantan from the dominant Parti Islam se Malaysia (PAS—Islamic Party of Malaysia) resulted in violent political disturbances in Kelantan and the declaration of a state of emergency by the federal Government. Direct rule was imposed in Kelantan, and the PAS was expelled from the BN coalition in December. In the federal and state elections of July 1978 Hussein consolidated the position of the BN, while the PAS, in opposition, suffered a serious reversal. In 1978, following the federal Government's rejection of proposals for a Chinese university, racial and religious tensions re-emerged.

In July 1981 Hussein was succeeded as Prime Minister by Dato' Seri Dr Mahathir Mohamad, Deputy Prime Minister since 1976. Mahathir called a general election in April 1982; the BN coalition won convincingly in all states and increased its overall strength in the House of Representatives.

At an election for the Sabah State Legislative Assembly in April 1985, a new political party, the Parti Bersatu Sabah (PBS—Sabah United Party) obtained more than one-half of the seats; Sabah thus became the only state that was not controlled by the BN. The legality of the new PBS Government was challenged by Muslim opponents, and in February 1986 the Chief Minister (Ketua Menteri) called a further election. In the May election the PBS won an increased majority of seats in the Assembly, and in June the BN agreed to admit the PBS into its ruling coalition, together with the United Sabah National Organization (USNO), which had been expelled in 1984.

In February 1986 Mahathir's leadership of the federal Government and of UMNO was challenged when Datuk Musa Hitam, the Deputy Prime Minister, resigned from the Government, owing to 'irreconcilable differences' with Mahathir. However, Musa retained his position as Deputy President of UMNO. During the following months Musa's supporters became increasingly critical of Mahathir, and divisions within the party widened. At an early general election in August, the BN coalition took 148 of the 177 seats in an enlarged House of Representatives: UMNO secured 83 seats, while the Malaysian Chinese Association (MCA) won 17. Of the opposition parties, the Democratic Action Party (DAP) won 24 seats, having gained support from ethnic Chinese voters who were disillusioned with the MCA. In state elections held simultaneously, the BN retained control of all the State Legislative Assemblies in Peninsular Malaysia. Several ministers who had supported Musa were subsequently demoted or removed from the Government.

In early 1987 there was a serious challenge for the presidency of UMNO from Tengku Razaleigh Hamzah, the Minister of Trade and Industry. At the UMNO General Assembly in April, none the less, Mahathir was elected UMNO President for the third time (and thus retained the position of Prime Minister at the head of the BN coalition), albeit with a greatly reduced majority. The General Assembly also narrowly elected Abdul Ghafar Baba (who had replaced Musa as Deputy Prime Minister in February 1986) as UMNO Deputy President, a position that Musa had previously occupied. Mahathir subsequently announced the resignation of Razaleigh and of Datuk Rais Yatim, the Minister of Foreign Affairs, from the Cabinet, and the dismissal of several other pro-Razaleigh ministers.

Criticism of Mahathir's leadership persisted during 1987, both from within UMNO and from other political parties. At the same time, racial tensions intensified in various parts of the country over Chinese-language education, religion and other issues. In October–November, allegedly to prevent violent racially-motivated riots between Chinese and Malays over politically sensitive issues, 106 people were detained under the provisions of the Internal Security Act (ISA), which allows detention without trial on grounds of national security. Those detained included politicians from all parties (most notably the leader of the DAP, Lim Kit Siang), lawyers, journalists and leaders of pressure groups. Three newspapers were closed by the Government, and political rallies were prohibited. In November the Government introduced legislation to impose stringent penalties on editors and publishers disseminating what the Government regarded as 'false' news. From December the Minister of Information was empowered to monitor all radio and television broadcasts, and to revoke the licence of any private broadcasting company not conforming with 'Malaysian values'. By April 1989 all the detainees under the ISA had been released (although often under restrictive conditions).

In February 1988 the High Court gave a ruling on a suit filed in the previous June by dissatisfied members of UMNO, who claimed that, since some of the delegations taking part in the UMNO elections of April 1987 had not been legally registered, the elections should be declared null and void. On account of the irregularities, the Court ruled that UMNO was an 'unlawful society' and that there had been 'no election at all'. Mahathir maintained that the ruling did not affect the legal status of the Government, and the Head of State, Tunku Mahmood Iskandar, expressed support for Mahathir. Later in February 1988 Mahathir announced that UMNO Baru (New UMNO) had been formed and that members of the original party would have to re-register in order to join. In March it was stated that Razaleigh and his supporters were to be excluded from the new party. The assets of UMNO Baru (hereafter referred to as UMNO) were 'frozen' and placed under judicial control until the party's legal status had been resolved; they were finally returned in September 1994.

Tension between the executive and the judiciary was intensified by Parliament's approval in March 1988 of constitutional amendments limiting the power of the judiciary to interpret laws. The Lord President of the Supreme Court, Tun Mohammed Salleh bin Abas, wrote to the Head of State to complain about government attempts to reduce the independence of the judiciary, and was subsequently dismissed from office. In June 1989 the Government further limited the powers of the judiciary when it introduced a security law, removing the right of persons being detained under provisions of the ISA to have recourse to the courts.

In September 1988 Razaleigh and 12 others followed two earlier dissidents and left the BN coalition to join the opposition in the House of Representatives as independents. They were joined in October by Musa. In December Musa and his supporters drafted a six-point resolution (the Johore Declaration), specifying the terms under which they would consent to join UMNO. These terms were accepted by UMNO in January 1989 but were binding only in the state of Johore. Following the defeat at a by-election in that month of an opposition representative by an MCA candidate with UMNO support, Musa announced his membership of UMNO, prompting a further eight dissident representatives in Johore to join the party.

In March 1989 Razaleigh's movement established an alliance with the fundamentalist PAS. In May Razaleigh's party registered as Semangat '46 (Spirit of 1946, a reference to the year of foundation of the original UMNO). The DAP, whose followers were largely urban Chinese, agreed to co-operate with Semangat '46 and the PAS, but refused to join a formal alliance, owing to their opposition to the PAS's proclaimed policy of forming an Islamic state in Malaysia. In June a former breakaway faction from the PAS, Barisan Jama'ah Islamiah Sa-Malaysia, left the BN coalition to join Semangat '46, the PAS and the Parti Hisbul Muslimin Malaysia in an opposition coalition, Angkatan Perpaduan Ummah (APU—Muslim Unity Movement). APU subsequently won a by-election by a small margin in Trengganu. In May and August, however, the BN won three by-elections. In December Mahathir held a cordial but unproductive meeting with Razaleigh, in an attempt to heal the rift in the ethnic Malay community.

A general election took place in October 1990. The opposition parties formed an informal electoral alliance, Gagasan Rakyat (People's Might). (Gagasan Rakyat was formally registered in April 1992, and Razaleigh was elected as Chairman in July.) Prior to the election the PBS withdrew from the BN and aligned itself with the opposition. Despite the defection of the PBS (which won the 14 seats that it contested), the BN controlled 127 of the 180 seats in the enlarged House of Representatives, thus retaining the two-thirds' majority necessary to amend the Constitution. The opposition's share of the seats increased from 37 to 53. However, Semangat '46 won only eight seats (compared with the 12 that it had held previously) of a total of 61 that it contested. Elections to 11 of the 13 State Legislative Assemblies (excluding Sabah and Sarawak) took place simultaneously. The BN obtained a majority of seats in every state except Kelantan, where APU won every seat in both the federal and state elections. Mahathir subsequently declared that it would be difficult for the federal Government to co-operate with the opposition state administrations in Sabah and Kelantan.

In November 1990, at a meeting of the UMNO General Assembly, Mahathir and Abdul Ghafar Baba were unanimously re-elected, respectively, as President and Deputy President of the party. Two incumbent Vice-Presidents of UMNO, Dato' Anwar Ibrahim, the Minister of Education, and Datuk Abdullah Ahmad Badawi, a former Minister of Defence (who had been dismissed in 1987 for supporting Razaleigh's leadership challenge), were re-elected; Datuk Seri Sanusi Junid, the Minister of Agriculture, was also elected a Vice-President. In February 1991 Mahathir announced cabinet changes, appointing Anwar, widely regarded as the probable future leader of UMNO, as Minister of Finance and Abdullah, his long-standing rival, as Minister of Foreign Affairs.

In January 1991 the Chief Minister of Sabah and President of the PBS, Datuk Seri Joseph Pairin Kitingan, was arrested and charged with corruption. It was widely conjectured that his arrest and his press adviser's detention, under the ISA, were politically motivated. In May UMNO secured its first seat in Sabah, in a by-election necessitated by the defection to UMNO of USNO's founder and President, Tun Mustapha Harun. Shortly afterwards Jeffrey Kitingan (the brother of the Chief Minister) was detained under the ISA, accused of plotting Sabah's secession from Malaysia.

At the UMNO General Assembly in November 1991, Mahathir made reference to the nine hereditary rulers' supposed abuse of privilege for personal gain. In February 1992 a delegation of senior UMNO representatives (excluding Mahathir) presented the Sultans with a memorandum that alleged interference by the rulers in both political and commercial spheres. UMNO criticism of the Sultans was widely suspected to be due, in part, to the Sultan of Kelantan's open support for Razaleigh (a prince of Kelantan) in the 1990 general election. In July 1992 four of the nine Sultans approved a Proclamation of Constitutional Principles, drafted in consultation with UMNO, establishing a code of conduct for the Sultans. There was further controversy in November when the Sultan of Johore assaulted a sports official. (In 1977, before he became Sultan, Mahmood Iskandar was convicted of 'culpable homicide' but was pardoned by his father, the Sultan.) Mahathir, who in 1983 had successfully forced the Sultans to surrender their right to refuse assent to laws passed by Parliament, proposed to remove the rulers' constitutional immunity from prosecution. In January 1993 Parliament approved amendments ending the Sultans' legal immunity, curtailing their power to pardon the offences of family members, and allowing parliamentary criticism of their misdeeds. Under the terms of the Constitution, however, the Sultans' privileges could not be restricted without the consent of the Conference of Rulers, comprising the nine Sultans. The Sultans indicated initially that they would approve the amendments, but, two hours before Parliament met, the rulers rejected the changes entirely. Mahathir responded by withdrawing from the Sultans various customary royal privileges (many of them financial) not stipulated in the Constitution. A constitutional crisis was averted when, in February, the Conference of Rulers agreed to the amendments with the inclusion of slight modifications; they were thus finally adopted with royal consent in March.

In August 1993, despite earlier assertions that he would not challenge the incumbent Ghafar, Anwar announced his decision to contest the post of UMNO Deputy President in the party's divisional elections which Mahathir had postponed until November. The post was particularly significant as the Deputy President of UMNO was traditionally also accorded the position of Deputy Prime Minister and would be regarded as Mahathir's probable successor. In October Mahathir was returned unopposed as President of UMNO. Ghafar submitted his resignation as Deputy Prime Minister, seemingly in protest against Mahathir's failure actively to support his candidacy for the party post. By November Anwar, representing the *Malayu baru* (new Malays—younger, urban, mainly professional Malays who had prospered as a result of economic expansion), had secured overwhelming support for his candidacy, prompting the more traditional Ghafar to withdraw from the contest (the latter also resigned from UMNO). Anwar was duly elected Deputy President of UMNO, and all three vice-presidential posts were won by his self-styled 'Vision Team', which comprised Tan Sri Haji Muhyiddin Yassim (the Chief Minister—Menteri Besar—of Johore), Datuk Seri Najib Razak (the Minister of Defence) and Tan Sri Dato' Mohammed Haji Mohammed Taib (the Chief Minister—Menteri Besar—of Selangor). Anwar was appointed Deputy Prime Minister in December.

In April 1993 USNO, now led by Tun Mustapha Amirkahar (the son of Tun Mustapha Harun), left the opposition in the

Sabah State Legislative Assembly to form a coalition with the ruling PBS. Prior to the announcement six of the 11 elected representatives of USNO joined UMNO. USNO's defection prompted the federal Government successfully to seek the party's deregistration in August, on the grounds that it had breached its own statutes. In the same month Tun Mustapha Harun was appointed to the federal post of Minister of Sabah Affairs.

In January 1994 Pairin Kitingan dissolved the Sabah State Legislative Assembly in preparation for elections, although the Assembly's mandate did not expire until 1995. Shortly afterwards Pairin Kitingan was convicted on charges of corruption by the High Court. (Hearings had begun in January 1992.) He was, however, fined less than the minimum RM 2,000 that was required to disqualify him from office. Although Pairin Kitingan gained popular sympathy owing both to his perceived victimization in the corruption case and to his resistance to federal encroachment on Sabahan authority, a faction emerged in the PBS that favoured more harmonious relations with the federal Government. Former members of the deregistered USNO joined the PBS for the election, and the party also gained the support of Tun Mustapha Harun, who had resigned from his federal position of Minister of Sabah Affairs and as a member of UMNO in January. (Tun Mustapha Harun died in January 1995.) At the election, which took place on 18–19 February 1994, the PBS won a narrow majority, securing 25 of the 48 elective seats. Shortly before his inauguration as Chief Minister, however, Pairin Kitingan was informed that the state ruler, Tan Sri Mohamad Said Keruak, was too ill to carry out the ceremony. PBS leaders accused Said of allowing the BN time to persuade the PBS legislators to defect. Pairin Kitingan was finally sworn in as Chief Minister two days later. In March, however, several PBS members did defect to the opposition; among these was Jeffrey Kitingan, who announced the formation of a breakaway party, the Parti Demokratik Sabah Bersatu (PDSB—United Sabah Democratic Party). Jeffrey Kitingan had been released from detention under the ISA in December 1993: although he was initially confined to Seremban town in Negri Sembilan for two years, all restrictions on him were swiftly revoked, encouraging suspicions of an agreement with the federal authorities. Pairin Kitingan tried to call new elections, but Said refused to sign the order of dissolution of the Assembly. On 17 March 1994 Pairin Kitingan resigned as Chief Minister, and on the following day Tan Sri Sakaran Dandai, a leader of the Sabah wing of UMNO, was sworn in at the head of a new administration.

In June 1994 the BN coalition agreed to admit two breakaway parties from the PBS, the Parti Demokratik Sabah (Sabah Democratic Party), led by Datuk Bernard Dompok, and the Parti Bersatu Rakyat Sabah (PBRS—United Sabah People's Party), led by Joseph Kurup, but refused to accept the application for membership of a third, Setia (Sabah People's United Democratic Party). In the same month it was announced that Dompok and Jeffrey Kitingan were to be appointed to the federal Government: in August Dompok became Minister in the Prime Minister's Department and Jeffrey Kitingan Deputy Minister for Housing and Local Government. Also in June Jeffrey Kitingan was cleared of corruption in the High Court.

In May 1994 the House of Representatives approved the 1994 Constitution (Amendment) Act, which further restricted the powers of the monarchy and provided for the restructuring of the judiciary. Hitherto the Yang di-Pertuan Agong (Head of State) had been competent to withhold assent from and return legislation, within 30 days, to Parliament for further consideration. The amendment required the Yang di-Pertuan Agong to give his assent to a bill within 30 days; if he failed to do so, the bill would, none the less, become law. The changes to the judiciary in the amendment included the creation of a Court of Appeal, the restyling of the Supreme Court as the Federal Court and of the Lord President as the Chief Justice.

From June 1994 the Government took action to suppress the activities of Al-Arqam, an Islamic sect which had been founded by Ashaari Muhammad in 1968. Al-Arqam was believed to have about 10,000 members in Malaysia, many of whom were public servants, and was alleged to control considerable assets. Although Al-Arqam had traditionally eschewed politics, the Government asserted that the group was a threat to national security and denounced its Islamic teachings as 'deviationist'; moreover, the Malaysian authorities accused it of training a military force in Thailand, although this was denied by both Al-Arqam and the Thai Government. In July UMNO threatened to expel party members who refused to leave Al-Arqam, and in

early August the National Fatwa (Islamic Advisory) Council banned the sect on the grounds that its doctrine contravened Islamic principles.

During the second half of 1994 there was considerable controversy surrounding the Chief Minister of Malacca, Tan Sri Datuk Rahim Thamby Chik. In August Rahim (the leader of the powerful UMNO youth wing and a close associate of Anwar) was accused of having sexual relations with a minor, an offence constituting statutory rape. Rahim was also accused of having made large profits from dubious property deals. In September he resigned as Chief Minister of Malacca, and was obliged to take indefinite leave from his other party and administrative posts pending investigations into his alleged misdeeds. Although the authorities decided in October that there was insufficient evidence to proceed with a prosecution against Rahim on the charge of statutory rape, in December he was charged on two counts of corruption (to which he pleaded not guilty).

Mahathir announced that general elections would take place on 24–25 April 1995. Following an often acrimonious election campaign, in which opposition parties complained of biased coverage by the media and undemocratic practices by the Mahathir Government (including the manipulation of electoral boundaries to its own advantage), the BN won an overwhelming majority, taking 162 of the 192 seats in the House of Representatives (with some 64% of the total votes cast). The PBS won eight of Sabah's federal seats, including those held by Jeffrey Kitingan and Dompok. Although this constituted a loss of six seats, it was an indication that, despite the BN's assumption of power at state level through the defection of former PBS members of the legislature, the PBS remained a significant political force in Sabah. The BN also retained control of 10 of the 11 State Legislative Assemblies for which voting took place, in most cases securing a two-thirds' majority. In Kelantan, which remained the only state under opposition control, a coalition of the PAS and Semangat '46 took 35 of the 43 state seats.

Despite his overwhelming election victory, Mahathir's position appeared vulnerable during the divisional elections of UMNO in 1995. The defeat of several Mahathir supporters was widely attributed to the influence of Anwar's associates, and prompted speculation that Anwar might challenge Mahathir for the leadership. In November, however, UMNO's General Assembly adopted an unprecedented resolution to avoid any contest for the two senior party positions in 1996; Anwar finally declared that he would not challenge Mahathir, and Mahathir for the first time said that he would retire in the near future and again named Anwar as his successor. The day after the closure of the General Assembly corruption charges against Rahim were dismissed. In January 1996 Mahathir's renewed security within UMNO was demonstrated by his success in bringing about Rahim's reinstatement as leader of the youth wing, despite Anwar's disapproval and the opposition of many local youth wing leaders.

Semangat '46 was formally dissolved in October 1996, and its members were admitted to UMNO. At that month's UMNO General Assembly Mahathir and Anwar were, as anticipated, returned unopposed to their posts. In contrast to the 1993 party elections, in which Anwar's supporters had been particularly successful, a large proportion of Mahathir loyalists were now elected. Notably, in the elections for the vice-presidencies, Muhyiddin Yassim, the only member of Anwar's 'Vision Team' who had remained loyal to the Deputy President, was defeated by Dato' Abdullah Ahmad Badawi (the Minister of Foreign Affairs, who had been a vice-president prior to 1993); Najib Razak and Mohammad Taib were re-elected. However, the Minister of International Trade and Industry, Dato' Seri Paduka Rafidah Aziz, a Mahathir loyalist, who had been investigated in 1994 by the Anti-Corruption Agency for corrupt sharedealing, was defeated as head of the women's wing by an Anwar-backed candidate, while Rahim was ousted from the youth-wing leadership by another supporter of Anwar. No former member of Semangat '46, including Razaleigh, secured a position on the UMNO Supreme Council.

In October 1996 the PAS announced that it was to abandon its attempt (of some six years' standing) to replace secular criminal laws with *hudud*, the Islamic criminal code, in Kelantan, unless this was approved by the federal Government: Mahathir was known to be strongly opposed to such a policy. The PAS won a by-election for the State Legislative Assembly in Kelantan in January 1997. Although the PAS took the seat by only a narrow margin (the seat had been won convincingly at the previous election by a Semangat '46 candidate), the results were nevertheless indicative of Razaleigh's weakened position in the state.

In May 1997 Mahathir appointed Anwar as Acting Prime Minister while he took two months' leave of absence from the post. On his return, Mahathir's response to the currency crisis affecting the region, following Thailand's effective devaluation of the baht in early July, was widely perceived to have exacerbated Malaysia's economic position. His criticism of international investors, particularly the US currency speculator, George Soros, resulted in further losses to the value of both the currency and shares on the stock exchange. Meanwhile Anwar benefited politically from the situation, appearing to act responsibly in reassuring investors and rescinding the newly imposed financial restrictions. Political opponents, however, attempted to undermine Anwar through the circulation of a series of letters accusing him of sexual indiscretions. International criticism of Mahathir's outspokenness prompted popular demonstrations of support for the premier within Malaysia and near unanimous support for a vote of confidence in his leadership, which was held in the House of Representatives during November. In the same month Mahathir announced the formation of an executive authority to address the economic crisis, the National Economic Action Council. The composition of the Council, including the appointment of the former Minister of Finance, Dato' Paduka Daim Zainuddin, as Executive Director of the Council, was approved by the Cabinet in January 1998. At the UMNO annual convention in September 1997 Mahathir criticized the increasing tendency of Malaysian Muslims to attach excessive importance to external symbols of Islam (such as beards and headscarves) and warned of the dangers of extremism. Mahathir's speech, which was resented by many Muslims, followed the widely publicized arrest, in June, of three Muslim women for taking part in a beauty contest in Selangor. The arrests prompted debate concerning the position of women in Malaysian society and resulted in demands for the reform of the Islamic Syariah (Shariah) courts; a fatwa (religious edict) had the force of law in the state in which it was issued, which arguably violated the liberties of Malaysians as guaranteed under the federal Constitution. In November 10 men were detained under the ISA for disseminating Shia Muslim teachings (Malaysian Muslims belong predominantly to the Sunni sect) which were perceived as militant and a threat to national security. Many non-governmental organizations (NGOs) and political parties called for the detainees to be released or allowed to stand trial under the Sedition Act.

At internal elections for divisional committee members in UMNO, which took place in March 1998, most of Mahathir's supporters retained their positions. However, evidence of a growing divide between Mahathir and Anwar became apparent at the UMNO annual party congress held in June, where Ahmad Zahid Hamidi, the head of the youth wing of UMNO and one of Anwar's supporters, made a speech attacking what he termed the debilitating impact of corruption in the party. Zahid's speech, which was reminiscent of Anwar's recent condemnation of corruption and political restrictions, was perceived as an attack on the party's leadership; Mahathir responded by publishing a list of hundreds of people and companies who had received privatization contracts in recent years, which included close associates of Anwar and members of his family. During the following weeks Mahathir acted to counter the influence of Anwar. He promoted Daim Zainuddin (a close personal ally) to the position of Minister of Special Functions in charge of economic development, thus undermining Anwar's position as Minister of Finance. It was suggested that the rift between Mahathir and Anwar was a result of economic policy divisions. (Mahathir's solution to the economic crisis lay in protectionism and continued expansion in contrast to Anwar's support for austerity measures.) These allegations were, however, formally denied by Mahathir. Mahathir also dismissed newspaper editors close to Anwar and ordered the arrest of an associate of Anwar on firearms charges, which carried the death penalty under Malaysian law. The resignation on 28 August of the Governor (a close ally of Anwar) and Deputy Governor of the central bank, reportedly owing to a disagreement over policy with Mahathir, served as an indication of the intensification of the rift within the Government. Supporters loyal to the Prime Minister responded to the perceived threat to Mahathir's leadership by circulating a brochure entitled 'Fifty Reasons Why Anwar Cannot Become Prime Minister', in which Anwar was accused of sexual offences and corruption.

Allegations of Anwar's supposed sexual misconduct increased throughout the months following the UMNO congress, and, following Anwar's refusal to resign, culminated in Mahathir's dismissal of Anwar as Deputy Prime Minister and Minister of Finance on 2 September 1998, on the grounds that he was morally unfit to hold office. On the following day Anwar was expelled from UMNO, and affidavits accusing him of sexual impropriety were filed with the High Court. The allegations were denied by Anwar, who asserted that they constituted part of a high-level political conspiracy to discredit him. Anwar began a tour of the country, drawing extensive support for his calls for the wide-ranging reform of the political system from the many thousands who attended his public appearances. His supporters adopted the slogan '*reformasi*' (reform), which had united the popular forces that ousted President Suharto in Indonesia. In mid-September Anwar's adoptive brother, Sukma Darmawan Samitaat Madja, and a former speech-writer for Anwar, Munawar Ahmad Anees, were each sentenced to six months' imprisonment after they confessed to illegal homosexual activity with Anwar. The following day, at a meeting attended by at least 40,000 people in Kuala Lumpur, Anwar called directly for Mahathir's resignation; he was arrested shortly afterwards and detained under the ISA. A further 17 people, including a number of close associates of Anwar, were also detained under the same act. Anwar's arrest provoked demonstrations of protest, which erupted into violence, when demonstrations involving up to 60,000 people were violently dispersed by the security forces; 132 people were arrested.

Following Anwar's arrest, his wife, Wan Azizah Wan Ismail, emerged as the *de facto* leader of the opposition movement, making appearances at rallies attended by Anwar's supporters and condemning her husband's detention. Despite a restriction order issued against Wan Azizah, barring her from holding rallies at her residence, demonstrations in protest at Anwar's detention continued to be held throughout September 1998 and became the forum for demands for widespread political reform and the removal of the restrictions on freedom of speech and assembly imposed under the ISA. Anwar finally appeared in court in Petaling Jaya at the end of September, where he pleaded not guilty to five charges of corruption and five charges of sexual impropriety. Allegations made by Anwar, who appeared in court with visible bruising to his face, that he had been severely beaten while in police custody and had subsequently been denied medical attention for a number of days, provoked expressions of extreme concern from foreign Governments—in particular from the Presidents of the Philippines and Indonesia —and prompted the UN Secretary-General, Kofi Annan, to urge the Malaysian Government to ensure humane treatment for Anwar. The Malaysian Government initially dismissed Anwar's claims of assault; however, it was subsequently announced that a special investigation would be established. In December the Inspector-General of the Malaysian police force, Tan Sri Abdul Rahim Noor, resigned after an initial inquiry blamed the police for the injuries Anwar had received. Malaysia's Attorney-General publicly admitted in January 1999 that Anwar had been assaulted by the police while in custody, and a Royal Commission of Inquiry into Anwar's injuries, which was completed in March, found Rahim Noor to be personally responsible for the beating. In accordance with the recommendations of the inquiry, in April Rahim Noor was charged with assaulting Anwar. In March 2000 Rahim Noor was sentenced to two months' imprisonment and fined RM 2,000 after pleading guilty to a lesser charge of assault against Anwar.

Anwar's trial on four charges of corruption (which referred to efforts allegedly made by him in 1997 to obtain through the police written denials that he was guilty of sexual misconduct and sodomy) began in November 1998. The presiding judge ruled that official foreign observers were not to be allowed at the trial. The credibility of the prosecution was undermined by the professed willingness of a principal witness to lie under oath, the withdrawal by a witness for the prosecution of his claims to have engaged in illegal homosexual activity with Anwar and the retraction by Anwar's adoptive brother and his speech-writer of their confessions, which they claimed had been obtained through police coercion. The defence suffered a number of reverses during the trial: in November the judge sentenced one of Anwar's lawyers to three months' imprisonment for contempt of court, because of a motion he had filed on behalf of Anwar to have two of the prosecutors dismissed from the case; the charges against Anwar were unexpectedly amended in January 1999, with the emphasis being shifted from sexual misconduct to abuse of power (the amendment meant that the prosecution would no longer have to prove that Anwar had committed sexual offences, but only that he had attempted to use his position to influence the police to quash the investigation into the allegations, effectively making it far easier for the prosecution to obtain a conviction). In addition, the judge ruled that all evidence given by several witnesses was inadmissible, despite requests from Anwar's lawyers that some parts of the testimony be retained as evidence for the defence. Following a disagreement between the defence and the presiding judge over the judge's refusal to hear a motion tabled by the defence that he be dismissed, the defence team refused to sum up its case, and the trial was ended abruptly in late March. The verdict was delivered in mid-April; Anwar was found guilty on each of the four charges of corruption and a sentence of six years' imprisonment was imposed (under Malaysian law, this would be followed by a five-year period of disqualification from political office). Following the delivery of the verdict, supporters of the former Deputy Prime Minister clashed with security forces outside the court. Violent protests continued for the next three days, resulting in the arrest of 18 demonstrators. Following the trial, the three prosecution witnesses who had withdrawn their testimony against Anwar were charged with perjury. In late April Anwar was further charged with one count of illegal homosexual activity, to which he pleaded not guilty; it was announced that four other similar charges and one additional corruption charge against him had been suspended.

On the first day of Anwar's second trial in early June 1999 the prosecution amended the wording of its charge, changing the month and year (for the second time) in which the alleged crimes were supposedly committed. The trial was adjourned in September and Anwar was sent for medical examination following claims by the defence that Anwar had proven high levels of arsenic in his blood and was quite possibly the victim of deliberate poisoning. In the same month, some 10,000 Anwar supporters gathered to demonstrate against the Government's treatment of the former Deputy Prime Minister and Minister of Finance; following the protests, several prominent allies of Anwar were reported to have been arrested. Anwar's trial resumed in late September, however, after medical tests found that Anwar showed no clinical signs of arsenic poisoning, although concerns over Anwar's health continued to be expressed in October. Also in September Anwar lost a defamation suit he had filed against Mahathir following his arrest. In his testimony in court in October and November, Anwar made potentially damaging allegations of corruption against members of the Government (including the Minister of Finance, Daim, and the Minister of Domestic Trade and Consumer Affairs, Dato' Seri Megat Junid bin Megat Ayob) whom he alleged had conspired to remove him from office. In mid-November the trial of Anwar was adjourned indefinitely without explanation; supporters of Anwar claimed that the adjournment was a government attempt to silence him in the approach to the general election, which was to be held in late November. The trial resumed on 25 January 2000, but was adjourned again in late February at the request of the defence. Meanwhile, the appeal hearing began against Anwar's conviction and sentencing in April 1999 on four charges of corruption. The Court of Appeal upheld the conviction in April 2000.

Anwar suffered a further set-back in early June 2000, after the Court of Appeal rejected his plea for a stay of proceedings, ordering the trial on charges of sodomy to continue. In July the presiding judge ordered Anwar's defence lawyers to conclude their case, although they protested that they had intended to call further witnesses. Despite an indefinite postponement of the verdict, initially scheduled for early August, by the judge, and several police warnings, some 200 protesters gathered outside the High Court in a pro-Anwar rally. Seven people were subsequently arrested for illegal assembly and distribution of anti-government literature, before the announcement of the verdict. The High Court found Anwar guilty of sodomy, sentencing him to a further nine years' imprisonment, thus bringing his term to a total of 15 years. His adopted brother, Sukma Darmawan, was sentenced to six years' imprisonment and four strokes of the cane for the same offence. Although the verdict of guilty had been widely expected, observers were surprised by the severity of the sentence and by the judge's ruling that the punishments should be served consecutively rather than concurrently.

Although Anwar had been effectively removed from public office for 15 years, the affair continued to receive prominence in the media. In mid-October 2000 the former Deputy Prime Minister went on a three-day fast before authorities allowed him to visit his ailing mother in hospital. Anwar was himself hospitalized in November, suffering from an acute back problem that required critical surgery. The Government refused a request for Anwar to travel abroad for surgery and, after becoming exasperated at Anwar's indecision, in April 2001 issued an ultimatum to Anwar either to accept treatment in a state hospital or return to his cell. He returned to his cell in May. In the same month public prosecutors announced that the remaining charges of corruption and sodomy against him were to be abandoned and, in July, Anwar lodged an appeal against his sodomy conviction. Meanwhile, in June 2001 the contempt verdict passed against one of Anwar's lawyers was overturned after the High Court ruled that the lawyer had been acting only in the interests of his client. In October Anwar filed a defamation lawsuit against the Government and the state television channel over the broadcast in September of two programmes, which he claimed had portrayed him as an Islamist extremist. In July 2002 Anwar lost his final appeal against his corruption conviction. In October of the same year Mahathir launched bankruptcy proceedings against Anwar, following his refusal to pay the costs of the defamation lawsuit he had brought against the Prime Minister in 1999.

In January 1999, meanwhile, prior to the closure of the first trial of Anwar, Mahathir effected a major cabinet reorganization, in which Abdullah Badawi was appointed as Deputy Prime Minister and Minister for Home Affairs (a post relinquished by Mahathir) and Daim Zainuddin was allocated the finance portfolio, which had been assumed by Mahathir following the dismissal of Anwar in September 1998. Also in January 1999 the UMNO Supreme Council announced its decision to postpone for 18 months elections for senior posts within the party, previously scheduled to be held in June, effectively preventing any potential challenge to Mahathir's leadership from within the party. The BN won a significant victory in the elections to the State Legislative Assembly in Sabah on 12–13 March, securing 31 of the 48 seats; Mahathir indicated, however, that the result would not induce him to call an early general election. In early April a new opposition party, the Parti Keadilan Nasional (PKN—National Justice Party) was launched by Wan Azizah in anticipation of the general election; the new party reportedly aimed to establish itself as a multi-ethnic and multi-religious party and declared that its first act, should it come to power, would be to seek a royal pardon for Anwar. Anwar himself, however, did not join the new party. Despite its stated aspirations to multi-ethnicity, the initial membership of the party appeared to be predominantly Muslim.

In November 1999 the Government unexpectedly announced that a general election was to be held later the same month. The opposition expressed dissatisfaction at the limited period of time allowed by the Government for campaigning in advance of the election, and the DAP mounted an unsuccessful legal challenge against the Government in protest at the effective exclusion from the early election of about 650,000 young voters (thought likely to favour political change) who were scheduled to join the electoral roll in mid-January 2000. At the election, which was held on 29 November, a decisive victory was won by the governing BN coalition, which gained 148 of a total of 193 seats in the House of Representatives, thereby retaining the two-thirds' majority required to allow the Government to amend the Constitution. The opposition coalition, the Barisan Alternatif (Alternative Front—which had been formed by the PAS, the PKN, the DAP and the Parti Rakyat Malaysia (PRM—Malaysian People's Party) in June 1999 and which subsequently selected Anwar as its prime ministerial candidate) won a total of 42 seats, while the opposition PBS (which remained outside the Barisan Alternatif) secured three seats. Despite the BN's victory in the general election, UMNO experienced a significant loss of support amongst Malay voters (mainly to the PAS which secured 27 seats) and lost 23 seats, including those of four cabinet ministers. The party also performed poorly in the assembly elections held simultaneously in 11 Malaysian states: the PAS secured control of the state legislature in Trengganu, retained power in Kelantan and made significant gains in Mahathir's home state of Kedah. This erosion of confidence in UMNO was widely believed to be a result of the Government's treatment of Anwar and the concomitant decline of public confidence in the country's institutions, including the police and the judicial system. While there were a number of new appointments to the Cabinet, which was announced in early December, many of the key portfolios remained unchanged. In an unexpected move, however, Mahathir promoted the unelected academic, Musa Mohamad, neither an existing government minister nor a member of UMNO, to the influential post of Minister of Education; Musa replaced Dato' Seri Najib Abdul Razak, a former potential successor to Mahathir, who was transferred to the less powerful Ministry of Defence in what was perceived by many as an effective demotion. Also in December Mahathir announced that he intended this (his fifth) term of office to be his last, and for the first time formally identified the Deputy Prime Minister, Abdullah Ahmad Badawi, as his preferred successor. In the same month the opposition Barisan Alternatif nominated Fadzil Nor, President of the PAS, as the new parliamentary leader of the opposition. He replaced Lim Kit Siang, who had lost his seat in the general election in November 1999 and who in early December resigned as the Secretary-General of the DAP in acknowledgement of the party's poor performance in the elections, which was largely attributed to ethnic Chinese alarm at the prospect of an Islamic state as envisaged by the DAP's electoral partner, the PAS.

In late March 2000 Mahathir secured nomination as the sole candidate for the UMNO party presidency after Razaleigh, who had presented himself as a potential candidate for the party leadership, failed to attain the required level of support from the party's 165 divisions; Abdullah was also the sole nominee for the deputy-presidency. At the UMNO party elections, held in May, Mahathir and Abdullah were formally elected President and Deputy President of the party, respectively. Despite consolidating his own position within UMNO, Mahathir came under increasing pressure from both the opposition and the BN.

Recognizing the need for change in order to improve the increasingly unfavourable public image of the Government, in November 2000 the Prime Minister appointed Mohamed Dzaiddin Abdullah as the new Chief Justice, in a bid to enhance the credibility of the judiciary, tarnished by the Anwar trials. Later that month UMNO held a special general assembly, at which measures were approved to revitalize the image of the party and to attract more young professionals, including women. These developments failed to prevent the opposition PKN from taking a seat from the BN coalition at a by-election in the Lunas constituency of Kedah. The loss, thought to be due to the thousands of ethnic Chinese and young voters who had joined the electorate since the 1999 election, was unexpected, as the BN had held the Lunas seat since independence in 1957.

In April 2001 the Minister of Finance, Daim Zainuddin, decided to take a two-month leave of absence. The leave was seen as having been enforced by Mahathir, who wanted to distance himself from criticism arising from two controversial nationalization agreements involving the heavily-indebted Malaysia Airlines and Time dotCom (the telecommunications unit of the Renong Group) in late 2000, both companies being connected to protégés of Daim. In June 2001 Daim formally resigned from his post, following widespread allegations that he had taken advantage of public funds to help business associates. Mahathir assumed the finance portfolio on an interim basis.

Possibly fearing a split in the Malay vote over the Anwar affair, Mahathir attempted to strengthen support by using the race issue in August 2000, when he criticized Suqiu, the Malaysian Chinese Organizations' Election Appeals Committee, branding some of its members extremists and likening them to communists for urging the abolition of the New Vision Policy. The policy had for 30 years ensured favouritism for the Malay majority in education and commerce, in an attempt to reduce the inequality of wealth between Malays and Chinese. The effect of the criticism may have been merely to alienate Chinese supporters, integral to the BN's 1999 victory, although Suqiu did withdraw its demands after a series of meetings with UMNO in January 2001. In early March Mahathir confirmed that the New Vision Policy, due to end in 2001, was to be extended for a further 10 years.

In January 2000, meanwhile, government suppression of dissent increased significantly. Three prominent members of the opposition were arrested; the deputy leader of the DAP and Anwar's legal representative, Karpal Singh, and the Vice-President of the PKN, Marina Yusoff, were charged under the Sedition Act, while Mohamad Ezam Mohamad Noor was charged under the Official Secrets Act. In the same month the editor and the printer of the popular PAS newspaper, *Harakah*, were also charged with sedition in connection with an article concerning the trial of Anwar that reportedly included a quote accusing the authorities of conspiring against him. The arrests

were perceived by observers to constitute an attempt by the Government to curb the influence of the PAS following the party's strong performance in the general election. In early March 2000, the Government acted to restrict sales of *Harakah*, ordering that the newspaper be published just twice a month instead of twice weekly and restricting sales of the publication to members of the PAS only. In an apparent further attempt by the Government to stifle the expression of dissent in the national press, the group editor of the New Straits Times, Kadir Jasin, was forced to resign in January following the publication of an editorial which questioned the decision by the UMNO Supreme Council to reject demands that the party's two most senior positions be contested from within the party in the forthcoming UMNO internal elections (the Supreme Council proposed instead that Mahathir and Abdullah Ahmad Badawi be renominated for the party presidency and vice-presidency unopposed). In January 2002 public prosecutors abandoned the sedition charges against Karpal Singh. No explanation was given for the decision.

The Anwar issue continued to incite public unrest, and in April 2000 a protest to mark the anniversary of Anwar's conviction for corruption was broken up by riot police, 48 PKN activists being arrested. Public criticism of the Government, and subsequent detentions, became more frequent after Anwar's second conviction, as confidence in Mahathir's leadership continued to decline. Mohamad Ezam Mohamad Noor was arrested in March 2001 as a result of allegedly seditious comments, despite already being on trial for releasing a secret report on corruption. A month later he was detained again, along with six other opposition leaders, including Tian Chua and the PKN youth Vice-Chairman, N. Gobala Krishnan, under the ISA (which allows for detention without trial for up to two years). The aim of these arrests seemed to be to dissuade protesters from gathering for the second anniversary of Anwar's conviction. The effect was significant as only 2,000 demonstrators defied the authorities' ban to attend the peaceful 'Black 14' rally, named after and coinciding with the date of Anwar's first conviction, 14 April. The seven detainees were not immediately released after the rally, however, and three more arrests were made under the ISA. During late April the PKN youth leaders, Dr Badrul Amin Baharom and Loman Noor Adam, were arrested, as was the human rights activist, Badarudiin Ismail, thus bringing the total of recent detainees under the provisions of the ISA to 10. In August 2002 Mohamad Ezam Mohamad Noor was sentenced to a two-year prison term, having been convicted of 'leaking' state secrets.

In July 2001 the PKN announced that it was to merge with the smaller PRM in the hope of strengthening its opposition to the BN and furthering Anwar's cause. The planned merger was expected to take effect in time for the general election scheduled for 2004.

In early August 2001 an extraordinary session of the Court of Final Appeal heard arguments against the detention of five people under the ISA. Significantly, the judges ruled that the onus was on the State to produce evidence that those arrested posed a real threat to national security. Meanwhile, Nik Adli Nik Abdul Aziz, son of PAS spiritual leader Datuk Haji Nik Abdul Aziz Nik Mat, became one of 10 men detained under the Act on suspicion of membership of the Kumpulan Mujahidin Malaysia (KMM), an Islamist fundamentalist group believed to be engaged in a long-term plot to overthrow the Government. Seven of those taken into custody were also members of the PAS. Soon afterwards 25 supporters of Anwar Ibrahim were freed from prison and promptly rearrested on new charges, before being granted bail. In September the Government announced that Nik Adli Nik Abdul Aziz was to be detained for two years without trial under the provisions of the ISA. Eight of the nine men arrested with him were also imprisoned. Human rights activists accused the Government of exploiting the aftermath of the terrorist attacks on the USA in the same month (see the chapter on the USA) to suppress national opposition groups. Further arrests continued to be made under the ISA, as the Government tightened its control of national security.

In September 2001 the opposition was destabilized by the withdrawal of the DAP from the Barisan Alternatif. The party accused the PAS of alienating Chinese voters through its support for an Islamic state. In the same month an election in Malaysia's largest state, Sarawak, confirmed the strength of the ruling coalition. The BN won 60 out of 62 available seats in the state legislature. The DAP secured one seat; an independent candidate the other. Neither the PAS—contesting an election in the region for the first time—nor the PKN achieved any success. In November the PBS decided to rejoin the Government following more than a decade of absence from power; the party was formally readmitted to the BN in January 2002. Also in January, at a by-election in the Perlis district of Indera Kayangan, the PKN, supporting the cause of Anwar Ibrahim, was heavily defeated by Mahathir's BN. The PAS accused the Government of using devious methods to exploit popular fear of Islamist militancy in the aftermath of the September terrorist attacks and thus secure a resounding victory in the election.

On 21 November 2001 Sultan Salahuddin Abdul Aziz Shah Al-Haj ibni Al-Marhum Sultan Hisamuddin Alam Shah Al-Haj died at the age of 75. On 13 December the Raja of Perlis, Tuanku Syed Sirajuddin Syed Putra Jamalullail, was sworn in as the new monarch, following his election by secret ballot from amongst the remaining eight Malay rulers. The Sultan of Trengganu continued as his deputy.

In December 2001 a court convicted 19 members of the Islamist cult al-Ma'unah of treason for plotting to overthrow the Government. The men had been arrested following the murder of two hostages during a confrontation with security forces after a weapons robbery in July 2000. Ten other cult members had pleaded guilty to lesser charges and received 10-year prison terms. Three of the sect's ringleaders were sentenced to death for their part in the armed rebellion. The remaining men were given life terms. In the same month *The Sun* published a story claiming the existence of a plot to assassinate Prime Minister Mahathir. The story was later proved to be false and more than one-half of the editorial staff were dismissed, leading to allegations that the authorities had plotted to discredit the newspaper and thus more easily subject it to Malaysia's rigorous censorship laws. In January 2002 the Government announced further measures intended to stifle potential sources of dissent, stating that, with effect from May 2002, students and staff at public universities would be required to sign a pledge declaring allegiance to their king, country and government. Students had played a leading role in the protests that had followed the dismissal of Anwar Ibrahim in 1998.

In June 2002, during a speech to the annual congress of UMNO, Prime Minister Mahathir made the dramatic announcement that he intended to resign from the Government, with immediate effect. However, he was persuaded to withdraw his resignation shortly afterwards and, following some discussion, it was decided that he would remain in power until October 2003, when he would be succeeded by the Deputy Prime Minister, Abdullah Ahmad Badawi. During the transition period Abdullah would assume increased responsibility for the running of the Government. Meanwhile, Fadzil Nor, President of the PAS, died following complications arising from heart surgery; Abdul Hadi Awang assumed the party leadership on an interim basis.

In July 2002 Abdul Hadi Awang announced the imposition of Islamic law in Terengganu state, of which he was the Chief Minister. The Government continued to oppose efforts to enforce the new law code, however. In the same month, at a by-election to the Kedah seat of Pendang, which had become vacant upon the death of Fadzil Nor, the BN secured a narrow victory.

In October 2002 police arrested five men, believed to be members of the regional terrorist organization Jemaah Islamiah, under the ISA. The arrests brought the total number of ISA detainees to approximately 70. Members of Jemaah Islamiah were believed to be responsible for the recent terrorist attack on the Indonesian island of Bali (see the chapter on Indonesia), which had resulted in the deaths of an estimated 200 people, including many tourists. In November the ISA attracted renewed criticism when a court ordered the release of Nasharuddin Nasir, who had been detained under its provisions since April of that year, on the grounds that no evidence had been provided to substantiate claims that he had engaged in terrorist activities. The Government, in contravention of the judicial order, rearrested him almost immediately after his release. It was announced subsequently that the ISA was to be strengthened in order to prevent further challenges by the courts. Meanwhile, Prime Minister Mahathir announced the appointment of Datuk Dr Jamaluddin Jarjis as Minister of Finance II; Mahathir himself continued to hold the other finance portfolio.

Malaysia's foreign policy was dominated by its membership of the regional grouping, the Association of South East Asian Nations (ASEAN, see p. 146), founded in 1967. Mahathir was instrumental in bringing Myanmar into ASEAN in 1997 under the Policy of Constructive Engagement. Malaysia also played an integral role in bringing together the military junta and Aung San Suu Kyi for negotiations in late 2000, although it was thought that financial considerations might have been significant, with a promise of direct investment in Myanmar by PETRONAS in return for a semblance of progress on the part of the junta. Mahathir's visit to Myanmar in January 2001 confirmed Malaysia's interest in Myanmar, a possible alternative source of natural gas. In September 2001 the Myanma leader, Gen. Than Shwe, paid an official visit to Malaysia during which a number of bilateral agreements were signed. In August 2002 Mahathir visited Myanmar again; during his visit he met with Aung San Suu Kyi and, it was thought, attempted to encourage the junta to engage in further dialogue with the opposition.

Relations with Singapore had always been characterized by mistrust, after the city-state left the Federation of Malaya in 1965. Resentment increased as Singapore advanced more swiftly than Malaysia economically, creating a certain acrimonious competition between the two countries. As Malaysia also developed, however, bilateral relations became more cordial, and co-operation increased. The visit in August 2000 by Singapore's Senior Minister and figurehead, Lee Kuan Yew, to Mahathir in Kuala Lumpur demonstrated the growing convergence of the two countries' viewpoints. In September 2001 Lee Kuan Yew travelled to Kuala Lumpur again, on a visit intended to further enhance ties between the two countries. Relations threatened to deteriorate from early 2002, however, as tensions arose over the renegotiation of a 1961 agreement by which Malaysia supplied Singapore with water. The problems were exacerbated when reclamation work being carried out by Singapore near the joint border was alleged to be disrupting entry into Malaysian ports. Negotiations took place in July and October 2002 in an attempt to resolve the problems arising from the water dispute, but without success. It was feared that the issue would have to be referred to an international court of arbitration to secure its resolution. In February 2003 Prime Minister Mahathir stated that, while Malaysia would cease to supply Singapore with untreated water in 2011, it would continue to supply filtered water, at a reasonable price, for as long as necessary. The dispute continued to constitute the primary source of tension in bilateral relations in early 2003.

In January 1993 Gen. Fidel Ramos visited Malaysia, the first Philippine President to do so since 1968, owing to strained relations over the Philippines' claim to Sabah. Mahathir and Ramos agreed to establish a joint commission to address bilateral problems. In February 1994 Mahathir made the first official visit by a Malaysian head of government to the Philippines. Relations with the Philippines, however, were strained in April 2000, when Muslim separatists from the southern Philippines abducted a group of tourists from the Malaysian resort of Sipadan, off the coast of Sabah. Following a similar kidnapping incident in September, the Malaysian Government dispatched an additional 600 troops to the region.

Relations with Indonesia generally improved from the mid-1990s. In June 1996 the two countries agreed on joint measures to limit the flow of illegal workers into Malaysia. Wide-ranging amendments to the Immigration Act in Malaysia in October 1996 failed to halt the flow of illegal immigrants, which was blamed for rising social tensions. The regional economic crisis, which began in mid-1997, led to an increase in illegal immigrants arriving in Malaysia and prompted Malaysia to begin a repatriation programme to Indonesia and elsewhere. Violent protests against deportation took place in detention centres in March 1998. In addition, groups of illegal Indonesian immigrants entered the compounds of several foreign embassies and the office of the United Nations High Commissioner for Refugees in March and April and requested political asylum to prevent their repatriation to the Indonesian province of Aceh, where they claimed that as members of secessionist groupings, they would be subject to persecution. Some of the immigrants were subsequently granted asylum by Denmark and Norway. In November 2000 Malaysia and Indonesia agreed to intensify border patrols, after four Malaysians were detained by Indonesian police in June of that year for allegedly stealing logs.

Relations with both Indonesia and the Philippines, meanwhile, were strained in 1998 following the arrest in September of the former Malaysian Deputy Prime Minister and Minister of Finance, Anwar Ibrahim: both the President of Indonesia and the President of the Philippines made explicit criticisms of the Malaysian Government regarding its treatment of Anwar. Although the controversy surrounding Anwar's treatment receded as an international issue in 1999, bilateral relations with the Philippines were adversely affected by President Estrada's granting of an audience to Anwar's wife, Wan Azizah Wan Ismail, when she visited the Philippines in April. The new President of Indonesia, Abdurrahman Wahid, demonstrated the close relations between Indonesia and Malaysia by visiting Kuala Lumpur immediately after his election in October 1999.

In August 2001 President Wahid's successor, Megawati Sukarnoputri, visited Malaysia on the final stage of her tour of ASEAN nations. In the same month the new President of the Philippines, Gloria Macapagal Arroyo, also paid her first official visit to the country. However, relations with Indonesia soon threatened to deteriorate again. In 2001 the Government announced that it would deport 10,000 Indonesian illegal immigrants each month in an attempt to tighten controls on foreign labour in the country at a time of economic slowdown. In December 2001 and January 2002 a series of riots by Indonesian labourers led Prime Minister Mahathir to comment that Malaysia might give workers of different nationalities preference in the labour market owing to the problems caused by the illegal immigrants. In late January the Deputy Prime Minister, Abdullah Ahmad Badawi, announced the imposition of a temporary ban on new workers arriving from Indonesia. Soon afterwards the Indonesian Government issued a formal apology for the behaviour of its workers and stated that it hoped the trouble caused would not affect an otherwise harmonious relationship. Relations with the Philippines were also threatened in November 2001 when the authorities arrested the fugitive Philippine rebel leader, Nur Misuari, on charges of attempting to enter Malaysia illegally. After much indecision, he was finally deported in January 2002 to face trial in Manila (see the chapter on the Philippines). In May 2002 Malaysia, Indonesia and the Philippines signed an anti-terrorism pact enabling them to exchange intelligence and to launch joint police operations, in an effort to combat regional terrorist organizations; Thailand and Cambodia also acceded to the pact later in the year. In August the implementation of new legislation requiring that all illegal immigrants leave the country, or face penalties including fines, imprisonment and caning, strained relations with both the Philippines and Indonesia, as the majority of the workers affected were citizens of those countries. In September the Malaysian Government announced that, owing to diplomatic pressure, exacerbated by public protests being held in Indonesia and the Philippines over the apparently inhumane nature of the expulsions, deportations were being temporarily halted.

In 1994 Malaysian and Indonesian officials commenced discussions to resolve their conflicting claims to the sovereignty of two small islands off the coast of Borneo, Sipadan and Ligitan. In October 1996 an agreement was reached by both countries to refer the issue to the International Court of Justice (ICJ, see p. 17). In December 2002 the ICJ ruled that Malaysia would be awarded sovereignty of the islands, thus bringing an end to the dispute. Another territorial claim being pursued through negotiations was the dispute with Singapore over the island of Batu Putih (Pedra Branca). In February 2003 the two countries finally signed a formal agreement referring the dispute to the ICJ. Malaysia is also involved with Brunei, Viet Nam, the People's Republic of China, the Philippines and Taiwan in disputed sovereignty claims over the Spratly Islands in the South China Sea. In November 2002 the ASEAN member states approved a Code of Conduct for the islands; the agreement was also sanctioned by China.

Relations with Thailand were strained at the end of 1995 following the killing by the Malaysian navy of two Thai citizens fishing illegally in Malaysian waters. In December the two countries agreed to establish a committee to resolve a long-standing dispute over fishing rights. In February 1996 relations deteriorated, owing to Thailand's opposition to Malaysia's construction of a 27-km wall (completed in 1997) along its border with Thailand, intended to deter illegal immigration from that country. However, in January 1997 the two countries agreed to co-operate in preventing Bangladeshi migrant workers from entering Malaysia and in expediting the return of illegal Thai workers from Malaysia. The arrest in January 1998 of three Thai Muslim separatists by the Malaysian authorities and their deportation to Thailand demonstrated continued co-operation between the two countries since Malaysia was often regarded as a place of sanctuary for Muslim separatists in southern Thailand. Relations between Malaysia and Thailand were further enhanced in April when the two countries signed an agreement to share equally the natural gas produced in an offshore area to which both countries had made territorial claims. However, the

Thai Minister of Foreign Affairs, Surin Pitsuwan, was amongst a number of international political figures who expressed concern at the arrest and detention of the former Deputy Prime Minister and Minister of Finance, Anwar Ibrahim, in September. In April 2001 the Thai Prime Minister, Thaksin Shinawatra, made his first official visit to the country on a trip intended to enhance co-operative ties. Bilateral talks were also held in January 2002 in an attempt to resolve problems arising from a planned project to build a gas pipeline between the two countries.

Malaysia's relations with the People's Republic of China remained extremely cordial, with Malaysia frequently offering public support to China, particularly in response to US criticism. Mahathir paid another of a long series of official visits to China in November 2000, and the Chinese Premier, Zhu Rongji, made an official visit to Malaysia in November 1999. In May 2001 the Yang di-Pertuan Agong paid an official state visit to China at the invitation of the Chinese President, Jiang Zemin.

Mahathir's proposal to establish an East Asian Economic Caucus (EAEC), a trade group intended to exclude the USA, met with considerable resistance from the US Government (which continued to promote the US-dominated Asia-Pacific Economic Co-operation forum—APEC, see p. 139) and Australia. In July 1993 ASEAN agreed, despite the continuing reluctance of Japan to participate, that the EAEC should operate as an East Asian interest group within APEC. In November 1999 (although Mahathir was absent owing to the Malaysian general election) the third informal summit meeting of the 10 ASEAN countries and the Republic of China, Japan and the Republic of Korea took place. At the meeting it was agreed to hold annual East Asian summits of all 13 nations and to strengthen present economic co-operation with the distant aim of forming an East Asian bloc with a common market and monetary union. This ambition was brought closer in April 2001 when, at a meeting of ASEAN countries which China, Japan and the Republic of Korea also attended, plans were agreed for a network of currency 'swap' arrangements to prevent a repetition of the regional financial crisis of 1997.

In 1999 Mahathir objected to Australia's leadership of the UN-mandated peace-keeping mission in East Timor (now Timor-Leste, following the territory's accession to independence in May 2002), the UN Transitional Administration in East Timor (UNTAET), claiming that an ASEAN-led mission would be more appropriate. Other ASEAN members were, however, reluctant to assume responsibility for the peace-keeping body and Australia and East Timor both objected to the notion of Malaysia leading transitional arrangements, owing to its close relations with Indonesia. Only after the intervention of the UN Secretary-General did Malaysia finally contribute limited personnel to UNTAET. In February 2001 Malaysia announced that it would open a liaison office in Dili, East Timor, which became an embassy upon the declaration of East Timor as a fully independent state in May 2002.

In July 1997 Mahathir (who was often regarded as the international spokesperson for developing countries) indicated that he might submit a proposal to the UN to review its 1948 Universal Declaration of Human Rights, with regard to the specific priorities of less developed countries. While this sentiment was supported by many Asian countries, the USA reacted angrily to any suggestion of compromise on the issue of human rights. Relations with the USA were also strained by the involvement of Malaysia's national petroleum corporation, PETRONAS, in a consortium that signed an agreement during September to invest in Iran, in contravention of US sanctions against Iran. In October Mahathir paid a formal visit to Cuba, the first such visit by a Malaysian leader, and urged Malaysian firms to invest in the country, in defiance of US legislation which threatened reprisals against firms conducting business with Cuba. Bilateral relations deteriorated further in the same month following Mahathir's suggestion that the economic crisis in the South-East Asian region was due to hostile Jewish currency speculation aimed at preventing progress among Muslim nations. A resolution tabled by 34 members of the US Congress calling for the withdrawal of the remarks or Mahathir's resignation was condemned by Mahathir and the Malaysian press. Relations with the USA were further strained in 1998 following US condemnation of the detention and treatment of the former Deputy Prime Minister and Minister of Finance, Anwar Ibrahim; the Malaysian Government was particularly angered by a speech delivered at the APEC summit meeting in Kuala Lumpur in November by the US Vice-President, Albert

Gore, in which Gore expressed support for the movement for political reform in Malaysia. During a speech to UMNO members in June 1999, Mahathir criticized the influence on the country of non-Malaysians (and, in particular, ethnic Europeans) whom Mahathir claimed were attempting to 're-colonize' Malaysia. Relations with the USA were improved with a visit by Adm. Dennis Blair, the Commander-in-Chief of the US Pacific Command, to Kuala Lumpur in January 2001. At his meeting with Mahathir, the first between the Prime Minister and a US Pacific commander, the two countries agreed to extend military co-operation. However, the new US President, George W. Bush, insisted that any further improvement in relations would depend on better treatment for Anwar Ibrahim and other detained members of the Malaysian opposition.

In September 2001 bilateral ties with the USA were greatly strengthened when Mahathir moved quickly to condemn attacks on the US mainland thought to have been carried out by the al-Qa'ida terrorist network. However, during a meeting with the US President at an APEC summit meeting in Shanghai that month, Mahathir refused to lend his Government's support to the US-led retaliatory attacks on Afghanistan that began in October, voicing his concerns at the large numbers of civilian casualties resulting from the raids. At a meeting of ASEAN leaders in November, Malaysia agreed to co-operate with other member nations in the fight against terrorism. In January 2002 the USA congratulated the Malaysian Government on its demonstration of support for the international coalition against terrorism, following the detention of at least 15 suspected terrorists. However, it demanded assurances that the suspects would receive a fair trial under the ISA. In October it was reported that the US Government had requested that Malaysia be the host for a regional anti-terrorism training centre.

While the Malaysian Government continued to take action against suspected terrorists and, thus, to support the US-led global anti-terrorism campaign throughout 2002 and into 2003, bilateral relations experienced increasing strain from late 2002, as speculation intensified that there would be a US-led war in the Middle East. Several domestic anti-war protests took place and, during a speech at a summit meeting of the Non-aligned Movement (see p. 350) held in Kuala Lumpur in February 2003, Mahathir criticized the USA strongly for its belligerence, claiming that any war would be perceived to be a war against Muslims.

In June 1997 the inauguration took place of a group that aimed to foster economic co-operation among Muslim developing countries, the Developing-Eight (D-8), comprising Malaysia, Bangladesh, Egypt, Indonesia, Iran, Nigeria, Pakistan and Turkey. Malaysia continued to express its close relationship with Arab countries after it denounced US and British air strikes against Iraq in February 2001, while demanding the removal of UN sanctions.

Government

Malaysia is a federation of 13 states. The capital, Kuala Lumpur, is a separate Federal Territory, as is the island of Labuan and the newly developed administrative capital of Putrajaya. The Head of State, or Supreme Head of Malaysia, is a monarch (Yang di-Pertuan Agong), elected for a five-year term (with a Deputy Head of State) by and from the hereditary rulers of nine of the states. The monarch acts on the advice of Parliament and the Cabinet. Parliament consists of the Dewan Negara (Senate) and the Dewan Rakyat (House of Representatives). The Senate has 70 members, including 40 appointed by the Head of State and 30 elected members, two chosen by each of the 13 State Legislative Assemblies and four from the Federal Territories. The House of Representatives consists of 193 members, elected for five years by universal adult suffrage: 144 from Peninsular Malaysia, 28 from Sarawak, 20 from Sabah and one from Labuan. The Head of State appoints the Prime Minister and, on the latter's recommendation, other ministers. The Cabinet is responsible to Parliament. The country is divided into 130 administrative districts, and the Federal Territories of Kuala Lumpur, Labuan and Putrajaya.

Defence

Malaysia participates in the Five-Power Defence Arrangements with Australia, New Zealand, Singapore and the United Kingdom. In August 2002 the active armed forces totalled 100,000 men: army 80,000, navy 12,000 and air force 8,000. Military service is voluntary. Reserve forces numbered 41,600 (army 40,000, navy 1,000, air force 600). Paramilitary forces in 2002 included a General Operations Force (formerly the Police Field Force) of 18,000 men and a People's Volunteer Corps with about 240,000 members. Federal budget plans for 2002 allocated RM 11,000m. to defence.

Economic Affairs

In 2001, according to estimates by the World Bank, Malaysia's gross national income (GNI), measured at average 1999–2001 prices, was US $86,510m., equivalent to $3,640 per head (or $8,340 per head on an international purchasing-power parity basis). During 1990–2001, it was estimated, the population increased at an annual average of 2.5%, while gross domestic product (GDP) per head increased, in real terms, by an average of 3.9% per year. Overall GDP increased, in real terms, at an average annual rate of 6.4% in 1990–2001. According to the Bank Negara Malaysia (BNM), GDP increased by 0.4% in 2001 and by 4.2% in 2002.

Agriculture (including forestry and fishing) contributed 8.8% of GDP in 2002, according to the BNM. The sector engaged 15.2% of the employed labour force in 2000. The principal subsistence crop is rice. Malaysia is the world's leading producer of palm oil, exports of which contributed an estimated 5.0% of the value of total merchandise exports in 2002. It was also formerly the world's leading producer of natural rubber, but by 1992 both Thailand and Indonesia had surpassed Malaysian production levels. Production of rubber continued to decline, and in 2002 it accounted for less than an estimated 0.8% of total exports. Other important cash crops include cocoa, coconuts, bananas, tea and pineapples. Sawlogs accounted for only an estimated 0.6% of total exports in 2002, owing to a government policy of sustainable management which led to the imposition of restrictions on exports of logs in 1993. During 1990–2001, according to the Asian Development Bank (ADB), agricultural GDP increased, in real terms, at an average annual rate of 0.4%. According to the BNM, agricultural GDP increased by 1.8% in 2001 and by 0.3% in 2002.

Industry (including mining, manufacturing, construction and utilities) contributed 46.5% of GDP in 2002. The sector engaged 37.0% of the employed labour force in 2000. During 1990–2001, according to the ADB, industrial GDP increased, in real terms, at an average annual rate of 7.7%. According to the BNM, industrial GDP declined by 3.2% in 2001 but grew by 4.3% in 2002.

Mining contributed 9.8% of GDP in 2002. However, it engaged only 0.4% of the employed labour force in 2000. At the end of 2001 estimated proven gas reserves stood at 2,120,000m. cu m, and petroleum reserves at 3,000m. barrels. Petroleum production in 2001 averaged 788,000 barrels per day from Malaysia's 33 oilfields, enough to sustain production for less than 12 years. At that year's level, natural gas production could be sustained for less than 45 years. Exports of crude petroleum provided an estimated 3.9% of total export earnings in 2002. Malaysia is one of the world's leading producers of tin, although in 2002 sales of this commodity accounted for only 0.1% of total export revenue. Bauxite, copper, iron, gold and coal are also mined. The GDP of the mining sector increased at an average annual rate of 3.4% in 1990–2001. Mining GDP increased by 1.6% in 2001 and by 4.5% in 2002.

Manufacturing (the largest export sector) contributed 29.5% of GDP in 2002. The manufacturing sector engaged 27.6% of the employed labour force in 2000. The most important branches of manufacturing, measured by gross value of output, in 1997 were electrical machinery and appliances (accounting for 33.1% of the total), food products (13.1%), metals and metal products, non-electrical machinery, transport equipment, rubber and plastic products, chemical products, wood products and furniture. During 1990–2001 manufacturing GDP increased, in real terms, at an average annual rate of 8.9%. Manufacturing GDP declined by 6.2% in 2001, but increased by 4.1% in 2002.

Energy is derived principally from Malaysia's own reserves of hydrocarbons. The country's dependence on petroleum as a source of electric energy declined from 55.9% in 1990 to 8.3% in 1999. The share contributed by natural gas increased from 22.0% to 77.6% over the same period. In 1999 hydropower and coal accounted for 11.5% and 2.5%, respectively, of the country's electricity production, which reached 72,313m. kWh in 2001. By 1994 five independent power plants had been licensed to supplement the production capacity of the partially-privatized state supplier, Tenaga Nasional. Construction of a controversial 2,400-MW hydroelectric dam at Bakun in Sarawak, at an estimated cost of RM 15,000m., was postponed in 1997, owing to the financial crisis, although preparatory work such as river diversion and resettling of the area's population continued. In February 2001 the Government gave its final approval for the project to recommence, but on a smaller scale, the revised cost being an estimated RM 9,000m., with the dam's 2,400-MW capacity confined to the eastern states. In early 2003 construction of the dam had yet to commence. None the less, total electricity capacity in 1997 was 10,110 MW, while peak demand reached only 7,063 MW. Imports of mineral fuels comprised 5.2% of the value of merchandise imports in 2001.

The services sector contributed 44.7% of GDP in 2002. It engaged 47.8% of the employed labour force in 2000. Tourism makes a significant contribution to the economy. Tourist arrivals rose from almost 12.8m. in 2001 to 13.3m. in 2002; receipts from the sector reached RM 24,221.5m. in 2001. However, it was feared that, in the aftermath of the terrorist attack in Bali in October 2002 (see the chapter on Indonesia), Malaysia's tourism sector might be adversely affected; following the attack, warnings were issued by several foreign governments against travel to Malaysia. In 2002 the financial and real estate sector, along with business services, contributed an estimated 10.6% of GDP. The banking system in Malaysia was severely damaged by the regional financial crisis in 1997; a series of mergers was planned in order to consolidate the sector. The Kuala Lumpur Stock Exchange was also adversely affected by the crisis, with some shares losing up to 80% of their value between July 1997 and January 1998 alone. The GDP of the services sector increased by an average of 8.0% per year in 1990–2001. Services GDP grew by 5.6% in 2001 and by 4.3% in 2002.

In 2001 Malaysia recorded a visible trade surplus of US $18,383m., with a surplus of $7,287m. on the current account of the balance of payments. In 2002 the principal source of imports (providing 17.8% of the total) was Japan; other major suppliers were the USA (16.4%), Singapore (12.0%), the People's Republic of China and Taiwan. The principal market for exports (20.2%) was the USA; other significant purchasers were Singapore (17.1%) and Japan (11.2%). The principal imports in 2001 were machinery and transport equipment, basic manufactures and chemicals. The principal exports in 2002 were electrical machinery and parts (particularly semiconductors and electronic equipment), chemicals, textiles, palm oil and products, crude petroleum and liquefied natural gas.

In 2001 there was a federal budgetary deficit of approximately RM 18,422m. The 2003 budget envisaged expenditure of RM 109,800m. (the substantial allocation to infrastructural spending being expected to result in a deficit equivalent to 3.9% of GDP). At the end of 2000 Malaysia's external debt totalled US $41,797m., of which $19,090m. was long-term public debt. The cost of debt-servicing in that year was equivalent to 5.3% of the value of exports of goods and services. The annual rate of inflation averaged 3.7% in 1990–2000. Consumer prices increased by an average of 1.4% in 2001 and by 1.8% in 2002. In 2001 3.7% of the labour force were unemployed.

Malaysia is a member of the Asian Development Bank (ADB, see p. 143), the Association of South East Asian Nations (ASEAN, see p. 146), the Colombo Plan (see p. 339) and Asia-Pacific Economic Co-operation (APEC, see p. 139), all of which aim to accelerate economic progress in the region. In January 1992 the member states of ASEAN agreed to establish a free-trade zone, the ASEAN Free Trade Area (AFTA). The original target for the reduction of tariffs to between 0% and 5% was 2008, but this was subsequently advanced to 2003 and then 2002, when AFTA was formally established. Malaysia itself, however, was granted a three-year delay in January 2001 for the opening of its politically-sensitive automotive industry to the free-trade agreements, fearing competition from Thailand.

In September 1998 the Malaysian Government introduced controversial capital controls to limit the repercussions of regional developments and ensure stability in domestic prices and exchange rates. The ringgit was fixed at 3.80 to the US dollar and from 1 October became non-convertible overseas, trading of Malaysian shares in Singapore was halted and foreign portfolio investment in the Malaysian stock market had to remain in the country for one year to prevent stock manipulation. These measures enabled Malaysia to reduce interest rates and raise domestic demand without destabilizing the currency. The economy therefore made a rapid recovery from the regional economic crisis of 1997/98, and the last of the capital controls for non-residents were removed in May 2001, although the ringgit 'peg' remained in place. In 1999, meanwhile, the Government intensified its efforts towards the restructuring of the financial sector with the announcement in late July of its intention forcibly to consolidate the country's 58 domestic commercial banks, merchant banks and finance companies into just six major financial institutions. However, in February 2000, having abandoned its original plan in November 1999, the Government announced that it had instead approved plans for the creation of up to 10 banking groups from the merging financial institutions; under the terms of the new plan, which was scheduled to be enacted by the end of December 2000, banks were to be permitted to choose their merger partners. By August 2001 51 banks had merged under the terms of the plan, highlighting the substantial progress made in financial sector reforms. In April 2001 the Government announced the Eighth Malaysia Plan (EMP), which gave economic projections for 2001–05. According to the EMP, the economy was to grow at an average annual rate of 7.5% over the next five years, with the manufacturing sector attaining growth of 8.9% a year. The services sector was expected to expand by 7.7% a year, with private consumption increasing by an average of 7.4% annually. The Government also expected to achieve a substantial reduction in levels of poverty. In March 2001 additional budgetary spending for 2002 was announced and, in October, the Prime Minister stated that budget expenditure was to be increased further, to just over RM 100,000m. The increases were part of a range of measures intended to stimulate growth and combat the onset of recession during the global economic downturn. Following the economic recovery of 1999–2000, foreign investment in Malaysia decreased from 2001 onwards. This could partially be attributed to the increasing attractiveness of the People's Republic of China as an alternative destination for foreign investment in the region, following its accession to the World Trade Organization (WTO, see p. 323) in 2001. The decline in world demand for manufactured goods, in particular information technology products, led to a protracted deceleration in the global economy, which was compounded by the effects of the terrorist attacks on the USA—a major export market—in September 2001. GDP growth rate in 2001 was severely curtailed, reaching only 0.4%. In 2002, while global demand for Malaysia's principal export commodities, such as electrical and electronic goods, remained slow, an increase in the prices of palm oil, crude petroleum and chemicals, amongst others, contributed to a recovery in exports. Domestic demand was also strengthened by the Government's introduction of further measures intended to encourage economic growth. GDP expanded by 4.2% in 2002 and, in the same year, the fiscal deficit was equivalent to 4.7% of GDP. In early 2003 speculation as to the effects of a possible US-led war in the Middle East prompted the Government to announce further measures intended to counter any possible downturn in the economy. A GDP growth rate of 4.7% was predicted for the year.

Education

Under the Malaysian education system, free schooling is provided at government-assisted schools for children between the ages of six and 18 years. There are also private schools, which receive no government financial aid. Education is compulsory for 11 years between the ages of six and 16 years. Bahasa Malaysia is the main medium of instruction, while English is taught as a second language; Chinese and Tamil are used for instruction only in primary institutions. In January 2003 new legislation came into effect, requiring that all mathematics and science classes in schools be taught in English. Primary education begins at six years of age and lasts for six years. In 1997 the number of pupils attending primary schools was equivalent to 101% of children in the relevant age-group (males 101%; females 101%). Secondary education, beginning at the age of 12, lasts for seven years, comprising a first cycle of three years and a second of four. Pupils may attend vocational and technical secondary schools instead of the final four years of academic education. In 1997 the total enrolment at secondary schools was equivalent to 64% of the school-age population (males 59%; females 69%). In 1997 Malaysia had 11 state universities and three private universities; in 1995 total enrolment at tertiary level was equivalent to 12% of the relevant age-group. In October 1994 the Government introduced a bill that would allow foreign universities to establish branch campuses in Malaysia. From the end of that year the Government permitted the use of English as a medium of instruction in science and engineering subjects at tertiary level. At the seventh ASEAN summit meeting in November 2001 it was decided that the town of Bandar Nusajaya in Johor would be the location for the first ASEAN university. It would be Malaysia's second international university.

Preliminary federal budget expenditure for 2001 allocated RM 14,422m. (22.6% of total expenditure) to education.

Public Holidays

Each state has its own public holidays, and the following federal holidays are also observed:

2003: 1–2 February* (Chinese New Year), 12 February† (Hari Raya Haji, Feast of the Sacrifice), 5 March† (Muharram, Islamic New Year), 1 May (Labour Day), 14 May† (Mouloud, Prophet Muhammad's Birthday), 15 May (Vesak Day), 7 June (Official Birthday of HM the Yang di-Pertuan Agong), 31 August (National Day), 24 October‡ (Deepavali), 26 November† (Hari Raya Puasa, end of Ramadan), 25 December (Christmas Day).

2004: 22–23 January* (Chinese New Year), 2 February† (Hari Raya Haji, Feast of the Sacrifice), 22 February† (Muharram, Islamic New Year), 1 May (Labour Day), 2 May† (Mouloud, Prophet Muhammad's Birthday), 2 June (Vesak Day), 5 June (Official Birthday of HM the Yang di-Pertuan Agong), 31 August (National Day), 12 November‡ (Deepavali), 14 November† (Hari Raya Puasa, end of Ramadan), 25 December (Christmas Day).

*The first two days of the first moon of the lunar calendar.

†These holidays are dependent on the Islamic lunar calendar and may vary by one or two days from the dates given.

‡Except Sabah and Sarawak.

Weights and Measures

The metric system is in force. There is also a local system of weights and measures:

1 cupak = 1 quart (1.1365 litres);

1 gantang = 1 gallon (4.5461 litres);

1 tahil = 11/3 ounces (37.8 grams);

16 tahils = 1 kati = 11/3 lb (604.8 grams);

100 katis = 1 picul = 1331/3 lb (60.48 kg);

40 piculs = 1 koyan = 5,3331/3 lb (2,419.2 kg).

Statistical Survey

Sources (unless otherwise stated): Department of Statistics, Blok C6, Parcel C, Pusat Pentadbiran Kerajaan Persekutuan, 62514 Putrajaya; tel. (3) 88857000; fax (3) 88889248; e-mail jpbpo@stats.gov.my; internet www.statistics.gov.my; Departments of Statistics, Kuching and Kota Kinabalu. Note: Unless otherwise indicated, statistics refer to all states of Malaysia.

Area and Population

AREA, POPULATION AND DENSITY

Area (sq km)	
Peninsular Malaysia.	131,686
Sabah (incl. Labuan)	73,711
Sarawak	124,450
Total	329,847*
Population (census results)	
14 August 1991	18,379,655
5–20 July 2000	
Males	11,853,432
Females.	11,421,258
Total	23,274,690
Density (per sq km) at mid-2000 .	70.6

* 127,355 sq miles.

PRINCIPAL ETHNIC GROUPS

(at census of August 1991)*

	Peninsular Malaysia	Sabah†	Sarawak	Total
Malays and other indigenous groups .	8,433,826	1,003,540	1,209,118	10,646,484
Chinese.	4,250,969	218,233	475,752	4,944,954
Indians .	1,380,048	9,310	4,608	1,393,966
Others	410,544	167,790	10,541	588,875
Non-Malaysians .	322,229	464,786	18,361	805,376
Total	14,797,616	1,863,659	1,718,380	18,379,655

* Including adjustment for underenumeration.
† Including the Federal Territory of Labuan.

Mid-1997 (estimates, '000 persons): Malays 10,233.2; Other indigenous groups 2,290.9; Chinese 5,445.1; Indian 1,541.7; Others 685.7; Non-Malaysians 1,468.9; Total 21,665.5.

STATES

(census of 5–20 July 2000)

	Area (sq km)	Population*	Density (per sq km)	Capital
Johor (Johore) .	18,987	2,740,625	144.3	Johore Bahru
Kedah .	9,425	1,649,756	175.0	Alor Star
Kelantan .	15,024	1,313,014	87.4	Kota Bahru
Melaka (Malacca) .	1,652	635,791	384.9	Malacca
Negeri Sembilan (Negri Sembilan) .	6,644	859,924	129.4	Seremban
Pahang .	35,965	1,288,376	35.8	Kuantan
Perak .	21,005	2,051,236	97.7	Ipoh
Perlis .	795	204,450	257.2	Kangar
Pulau Pinang (Penang) .	1,031	1,313,449	1,274.0	George Town
Sabah .	73,619	2,603,485	35.4	Kota Kinabalu
Sarawak .	124,450	2,071,506	16.6	Kuching
Selangor .	7,960	4,188,876	526.2	Shah Alam
Terengganu (Trengganu) .	12,955	898,825	69.4	Kuala Trengganu
Federal Territory of Kuala Lumpur.	243	1,379,310	5,676.2	—
Federal Territory of Labuan.	92	76,067	826.8	Victoria
Total .	329,847	23,274,690	70.6	

* Including adjustment for underenumeration.

PRINCIPAL TOWNS

(population at 2000 census)

Kuala Lumpur (capital)* .	1,297,526	Kuala Terengganu (Kuala Trengganu) .	250,528
Ipoh .	566,211	Seremban .	246,441
Kelang (Klang) .	563,173	Kota Baharu (Kota Bahru).	233,673
Petaling Jaya .	438,084	Sandakan .	220,000†
Shah Alam .	319,612	Taiping‡.	183,320
Kuantan.	283,041	George Town (Penang)	180,573

* The new town of Putrajaya is now the administrative capital.
† Provisional.
‡ Excluding a part of Pondok Tanjong, which is in the District of Kerian.
Source: Thomas Brinkhoff, *City Population* (internet www.citypopulation.de).

Mid-2001 (UN estimate, incl. suburbs): Kuala Lumpur 1,410,000 (Source: UN, *World Urbanization Prospects: The 2001 Revision*).

BIRTHS AND DEATHS

	Registered live births		Registered deaths	
	Number	Rate (per 1,000)	Number	Rate (per 1,000)
1993	541,760	27.7	87,594	4.5
1994	537,611	26.7	90,051	4.5
1995	539,234	24.9	95,025	4.4
1996	540,866	25.5	95,520	4.5
1997	537,104	24.8	97,042	4.5
1998	554,573	25.0	97,906	4.4

Source: UN, mainly *Demographic Yearbook*.

1999 (rates per 1,000): Births 25.4; Deaths 4.6 (Source: Ministry of Health, Kuala Lumpur).

2000 (provisional, rates per 1,000): Births 24.5; Deaths 4.4 (Source: Ministry of Health, Kuala Lumpur).

2001 (provisional, rates per 1,000): Births 22.3; Deaths 4.4 (Source: Ministry of Health, Kuala Lumpur).

2002 (provisional, rates per 1,000): Births 21.8; Deaths 4.4 (Source: Ministry of Health, Kuala Lumpur).

Expectation of life (WHO estimates, years at birth): 71.7 (males 69.2; females 74.4) in 2001 (Source: WHO, *World Health Report*).

ECONOMICALLY ACTIVE POPULATION*
(sample surveys, ISIC major divisions, '000 persons aged 15 to 64 years)

	1998	1999	2000
Agriculture, forestry and fishing	1,401	1,389	1,408
Mining and quarrying	42	42	41
Manufacturing	2,277	2,379	2,559
Electricity, gas and water	70	72	75
Construction	810	804	755
Trade, restaurants and hotels	1,437	1,449	1,584
Transport, storage and communications	435	442	462
Finance, insurance, real estate and business services	418	420	509
Government services	875	877	981
Other services	832	867	899
Total employed	8,597	8,741	9,271
Unemployed	284	269	302
Total labour force	8,881	9,010	9,573

* Excluding members of the armed forces.

Source: IMF, *Malaysia: Statistical Appendix* (October 2001).

Health and Welfare

KEY INDICATORS

Total fertility rate (children per woman, 2001)	3.0
Under-5 mortality rate (per 1,000 live births, 2001)	8
HIV/AIDS (% of persons aged 15–49, 2001)	0.35
Physicians (per 1,000 head, 1996)	2.01
Health expenditure (2000): US $ per head (PPP)	234
Health expenditure (2000): % of GDP	2.5
Health expenditure (2000): public (% of total)	58.8
Human Development Index (2000): ranking	59
Human Development Index (2000): value	0.782

For sources and definitions, see explanatory note on p. vi.

Agriculture

PRINCIPAL CROPS
('000 metric tons)

	1999	2000	2001
Rice (paddy)	2,037	2,195†	2,277†
Maize†	57	65	67
Sweet potatoes*	41	41	41
Cassava (Manioc)*	380	380	370
Other roots and tubers*	48	45	45
Sugar cane*	1,600	1,600	1,600
Groundnuts (in shell)*	6	6	6
Coconuts†	792	721	713
Oil palm fruit*	55,000	56,600	66,200
Cabbages*	47	47	47
Tomatoes*	10	10	10
Pumpkins, squash and gourds*	14	14	14
Cucumbers and gherkins*	52	40	50
Other vegetables and melons*	235	250	245
Watermelons*	130	100	100
Mangoes*	19	30	30
Pineapples*	134	130	130
Papayas*	56	50	60
Bananas*	545	550	560
Oranges*	12	12	12
Other fruit (excl. melons)*	300	302	302
Coffee (green)*	13	14	14
Cocoa beans	84	70	58
Tea (made)	5*	5	5*
Tobacco (leaves)	8	7†	10†
Natural rubber	769	615	547

* FAO estimate(s).
† Unofficial figure(s).

Source: FAO.

LIVESTOCK
('000 head, year ending September)

	1999	2000*	2001*
Cattle	723	750	760
Buffaloes	155	150	145
Goats	232	225	220
Sheep	175	160	165
Pigs	1,829	2,000	2,000
Chickens*	118,000	120,000	125,000
Ducks*	13,000	13,000	13,000

* FAO estimates.

Source: FAO.

LIVESTOCK PRODUCTS
('000 metric tons)

	1999	2000	2001
Beef and veal*	20	21	21
Buffalo meat*	4	4	4
Pig meat*	250	252	250
Poultry meat*	810	821	831
Cows' milk†	41	37	37
Buffaloes' milk*	7	7	7
Hen eggs*	398	413	420
Other poultry eggs*	14	14	14
Cattle and buffalo hides*	4	4	4

* FAO estimates.
† Unofficial figures.

Source: FAO.

Forestry

ROUNDWOOD REMOVALS
('000 cubic metres, excl. bark)

	1999	2000	2001
Sawlogs, veneer logs and logs for sleepers	21,687	15,095	13,061
Pulpwood	703	—	—
Other industrial wood	847	—	—
Fuel wood*	3,382	3,346	3,286
Total	26,619	18,441	16,347

* FAO estimates.

Source: FAO.

SAWNWOOD PRODUCTION
('000 cubic metres, incl. railway sleepers)

	1999	2000	2001
Total (all broadleaved)	5,237	5,590	4,700

Source: FAO.

Fishing

('000 metric tons, live weight)

	1998	1999	2000
Capture	1,153.7	1,251.8	1,289.2
Threadfin breams	40.3	39.7	32.5
Indian scad	53.4	70.2	84.2
Marine clupeoids	46.3	45.5	33.6
Kawakawa	49.4	57.3	56.5
Yellowstripe scad	32.7	41.3	44.3
Indian mackerels	102.1	111.4	98.1
Prawns and shrimps	47.2	90.5	96.0
Squids	38.7	40.3	54.4
Aquaculture	133.6	155.1	151.8
Blood cockle	81.7	79.9	64.4
Total catch	1,287.3	1,406.9	1,441.0

Note: Figures exclude crocodiles, recorded by number rather than by weight. The number of estuarine crocodiles caught was: 320 in 1998; 120 in 1999; 559 in 2000. Also excluded are shells and corals. Catches of turban shells (FAO estimates, metric tons) were: 80 in 1998; 80 in 1999; 80 in 2000. Catches of hard corals (FAO estimates, metric tons) were: 4,000 in 1998; 4,000 in 1999; 4,000 in 2000.

Source: FAO, *Yearbook of Fishery Statistics*.

Mining

PRODUCTION
(metric tons, unless otherwise indicated)

	1999	2000	2001*
Tin-in-concentrates	7,340	6,307	4,973
Copper concentrates	4,600	n.a.	n.a.
Bauxite	222,724	123,000	64,000
Iron ore†	337,462	259,000	376,000
Kaolin	213,973	233,885	286,648
Gold (kg)	3,449	4,026	3,965
Silver (kg)§	2,744	4	3
Barytes	13,506	7,274	649
Hard coal	308,502	382,942	545,845
Crude petroleum ('000 barrels)	252,115	249,159	243,696
Natural gas (million cu m)‡	51,376	56,929	58,751
Ilmenite†	127,695	124,801	122,462
Zirconium†	1,763	3,642	3,768

* Data are preliminary.

† Figures refer to the gross weight of ores and concentrates.

‡ Including amount reinjected, flared and lost.

§ Includes by-product from a copper mine in Sabah, tin mines in Peninsular Malaysia and gold mines in Peninsular Malaysia and Sarawak.

Sources: Minerals and Geoscience Dept; US Geological Survey; UN, *Statistical Yearbook for Asia and the Pacific*.

Industry

SELECTED PRODUCTS
('000 metric tons, unless otherwise indicated)

	2000	2001	2002
Canned fish, frozen shrimps/prawns	35.8	40.1	40.3
Palm oil (crude)	10,842	11,804	11,908
Refined sugar	1,234.1	1,210.4	1,404.8
Soft drinks ('000 litres)	403.1	501.6	439.9
Cigarettes (metric tons)	27,271	25,618	23,079
Woven cotton fabrics (million metres)	187.5	177.4	166.2
Veneer sheets ('000 cu metres)	1,468.0	1,173.2	1,100.0
Plywood ('000 cu metres)	3,739.8	3,937.5	4,000.3
Gasoline (motor spirit)*	2,612	n.a.	n.a.
Kerosene and jet fuel	2,533.1	3,293.1	3,170.7
Gas-diesel (distillate fuel) oil*	7,716	n.a.	n.a.
Residual fuel oil*	1,864	n.a.	n.a.
Liquefied petroleum gas	1,918.8	2,308.0	2,945.4
Inner tubes and pneumatic tyres ('000)	26,208	26,391	27,181
Rubber gloves (million pairs)	11,598.0	12,256.3	12,171.9
Earthen brick and cement roofing tiles (million)	1,036.3	1,196.1	1,317.1
Cement	11,445	13,820	14,370
Iron and steel bars and rods	2,583.6	2,691.3	3,222.6
Refrigerators for household use ('000)	215.3	186.0	172.1
Television receivers ('000)	10,550.5	9,501.2	10,492.6
Radio receivers ('000)	36,348	28,839	21,884
Semiconductors (million)	16,373	13,524	15,047
Electronic transistors (million)	17,519	19,989	20,345
Integrated circuits (million)	21,424	17,457	19,826
Passenger motor cars ('000)†	300.8	383.6	418.8
Commercial vehicles('000)†	55.7	62.7	72.0
Motorcycles and scooters ('000)	273.6	235.9	242.4

* Source: UN, *Monthly Bulletin of Statistics*.

† Vehicles assembled from imported parts.

Tin (smelter production of primary metal, metric tons): 28,913 in 1999; 26,228 in 2000; 32,566 (preliminary figure) in 2001 (Source: US Geological Survey).

Source (unless otherwise indicated): Bank Negara Malaysia, Kuala Lumpur.

Finance

CURRENCY AND EXCHANGE RATES

Monetary Units
100 sen = 1 ringgit Malaysia (RM—also formerly Malaysian dollar)

Sterling, US Dollar and Euro Equivalents (31 December 2002)
£1 sterling = RM 6.1248
US $1 = RM 3.8000
€1 = RM 3.9851
RM 100 = £16.33 = US $26.32 = €25.09

Exchange Rate
A fixed exchange rate of US $1 = RM 3.8000 has been in effect since September 1998

FEDERAL BUDGET
(RM million)

Revenue	1999	2000	2001*
Tax revenue	45,346	47,173	61,492
Taxes on income and profits	27,246	29,156	42,097
Companies (excl. petroleum)	15,742	13,905	20,770
Individuals	6,419	7,015	9,436
Petroleum	2,856	6,010	9,858
Export duties	670	1,032	867
Import duties	4,720	3,599	3,193
Excises on goods	4,723	3,803	4,130
Sales tax	4,488	5,968	7,356
Service tax	1,459	1,701	1,927
Other revenue	13,329	14,692	18,076
Total	58,675	61,864	79,567

Expenditure	1999	2000	2001*
Defence and security.	6,108	6,958	8,310
Economic Services	4,213	6,637	5,150
Agriculture and rural development	1,222	1,323	1,366
Trade and industry	1,596	3,761	1,870
Transport	1,156	1,286	1,672
Social services	16,612	18,784	21,757
Education	11,458	12,923	14,422
Health	3,626	4,131	4,680
Transfer payments	2,542	2,524	5,561
Debt service charges	7,941	9,055	9,634
Pensions and gratuities	3,793	4,187	4,711
General administration	5,490	8,401	8,636
Total	46,699	56,547	63,757

* Preliminary figures.

Source: Bank Negara Malaysia, Kuala Lumpur.

FEDERAL DEVELOPMENT EXPENDITURE
(RM million)

	1999	2000	2001*
Defence and security.	3,122	2,332	3,287
Social services	6,936	11,077	15,384
Education	3,865	7,099	10,363
Health	836	1,272	1,570
Housing	1,081	1,195	1,268
Economic services	8,969	10,412	12,724
Agriculture and rural development	1,088	1,183	1,395
Public utilities	1,850	1,517	1,092
Trade and industry	2,798	3,667	4,829
Transport	2,893	3,636	5,042
General administration	3,587	4,122	3,839
Total	22,614	27,942	35,235

* Estimates.

Source: Bank Negara Malaysia, Kuala Lumpur.

INTERNATIONAL RESERVES
(US $ million at 31 December)

	2000	2001	2002
Gold*	53	51	56
IMF special drawing rights	105	125	151
Reserve position in IMF.	792	764	790
Foreign exchange.	28,625	29,585	33,280
Total	29,576	30,526	34,277

* Valued at SDR 35 per troy ounce.

Source: IMF, *International Financial Statistics.*

MONEY SUPPLY
(RM million at 31 December)

	2000	2001	2002
Currency outside banks	22,263	22,148	23,896
Demand deposits at commercial banks	54,520	57,791	63,892
Total money (incl. others)	80,656	83,882	91,931

Source: IMF, *International Financial Statistics.*

COST OF LIVING
(Consumer Price Index; base 2000 = 100)

	1999	2001	2002
Food	98.1	100.7	101.4
Beverages and tobacco	97.2	104.8	109.2
Clothing and footwear	101.8	97.4	95.2
Rent and other housing costs, heating and lighting	98.6	101.4	102.1
Furniture, domestic appliances, tools and maintenance	100.0	100.1	99.7
Medical care	98.0	102.9	105.4
Transport and communications	98.0	103.6	110.4
Education and leisure	99.5	99.9	100.1
Other goods and services	99.1	100.7	101.8
All items	98.5	101.4	103.2

Source: Bank Negara Malaysia, Kuala Lumpur.

NATIONAL ACCOUNTS
(RM million at current prices)

Expenditure on the Gross Domestic Product

	2000	2001	2002*
Government final consumption expenditure.	36,231	42,859	51,410
Private final consumption expenditure.	144,726	150,555	159,071
Change in stocks	4,998	−3,661	4,536
Gross fixed capital formation	87,729	83,345	83,632
Total domestic expenditure.	273,684	273,099	298,649
Exports of goods and services	427,003	389,256	411,391
Less Imports of goods and services	358,529	327,765	348,443
GDP in purchasers' values	342,157	334,589	361,597
GDP at constant 1987 prices	209,538	210,480	219,342

* Preliminary figures.

Source: Bank Negara Malaysia, Kuala Lumpur.

Gross Domestic Product by Economic Activity

	2000	2001	2002
Agriculture, forestry and fishing	29,730	28,461	33,070
Mining and quarrying	37,428	35,969	36,685
Manufacturing	112,755	102,276	110,868
Electricity, gas and water	10,928	11,794	12,396
Construction	14,080	14,273	14,710
Trade, restaurants and hotels	47,113	47,914	50,604
Transport, storage and communications	22,880	24,296	25,892
Finance, insurance, real estate and business services	39,085	39,187	39,671
Government services.	22,695	24,157	27,844
Other services	21,644	22,568	23,854
Sub-total	358,337	350,895	375,591
Import duties	5,826	5,841	6,815
Less Imputed bank service charges	22,006	22,147	20,809
GDP in purchasers' values	342,157	334,589	361,597

Source: Bank Negara Malaysia, Kuala Lumpur.

BALANCE OF PAYMENTS
(US $ million)

	1999	2000	2001
Exports of goods f.o.b.	84,097	98,429	87,981
Imports of goods f.o.b.	−61,453	−77,602	−69,597
Trade balance	22,644	20,827	18,383
Exports of services	11,919	13,941	14,455
Imports of services	−14,735	−16,747	−16,657
Balance on goods and services	19,828	18,020	16,182
Other income received	2,003	1,986	1,847
Other income paid	−7,499	−9,594	−8,590
Balance on goods, services and income	14,332	10,412	9,439
Current transfers received	801	756	537
Current transfers paid	−2,529	−2,680	−2,689
Current balance	12,604	8,488	7,287
Direct investment abroad	−1,422	−2,026	−267
Direct investment from abroad	3,895	3,788	554
Portfolio investment liabilities	−892	−2,145	−724
Other investment assets	−7,936	−5,565	−2,702
Other investment liabilities	—	—	−830
Net errors and omissions	−1,273	−3,221	−2,394
Overall balance	4,711	−1,009	−1,000

Source: IMF, *International Financial Statistics*.

External Trade

PRINCIPAL COMMODITIES
(RM million)

Imports c.i.f.	1999	2000	2001
Food and live animals	10,873	11,393	12,310
Beverages and tobacco	682	709	925
Crude materials (inedible) except fuels	6,225	7,096	6,911
Mineral fuels, lubricants, etc.	7,489	14,973	14,697
Animal and vegetable oils and fats	1,056	604	794
Chemicals	18,790	22,371	20,725
Basic manufactures	28,467	32,596	29,642
Machinery and transport equipment	153,971	195,728	169,964
Miscellaneous manufactured articles	12,873	17,659	16,075
Other commodities and transactions	8,050	8,330	8,649
Total	248,477	311,459	280,691

Exports f.o.b.	1999	2000	2001
Food and live animals	6,229	6,470	6,596
Beverages and tobacco	1,047	1,215	1,307
Crude materials (inedible) except fuels	9,910	10,288	7,563
Mineral fuels, lubricants, etc.	22,480	35,903	32,505
Animal and vegetable oils and fats	18,280	12,937	12,323
Chemicals	10,353	14,278	14,376
Basic manufactures	24,243	25,788	24,194
Machinery and transport equipment	200,072	233,379	202,734
Miscellaneous manufactured articles	26,188	29,925	29,263
Other commodities and transactions	2,758	3,088	3,559
Total	321,560	373,270	334,420

Source: Asian Development Bank, *Key Indicators of Developing Asian and Pacific Countries*.

PRINCIPAL TRADING PARTNERS
(RM million)

Imports c.i.f.	2000	2001	2002
Australia	6,052	5,944	5,411
China, People's Republic	12,321	14,473	23,472
France	5,139	4,349	4,255
Germany	9,282	10,451	11,163
Hong Kong	8,557	7,064	8,837
India	2,748	2,934	2,445
Indonesia	8,623	8,536	9,689
Ireland	2,611	3,811	2,656
Italy	2,092	2,865	2,519
Japan	65,513	53,750	53,912
Korea, Republic	13,926	11,249	16,079
Philippines	7,562	6,987	9,863
Singapore	44,696	35,352	36,317
Taiwan	17,511	15,930	16,863
Thailand	11,987	11,120	12,017
United Kingdom	6,080	6,846	5,970
USA	51,744	44,881	49,692
Total (incl. others)	311,459	280,229	303,506

Exports f.o.b.	2000	2001	2002
Australia	9,210	7,795	8,013
Belgium	3,526	2,536	2,039
China, People's Republic	11,507	14,683	19,966
France	2,752	3,569	5,172
Germany	9,336	7,766	7,963
Hong Kong	16,854	15,437	20,128
India	7,312	5,992	6,692
Indonesia	6,484	5,930	6,846
Japan	48,770	44,393	39,778
Korea, Republic	12,464	11,108	11,823
Netherlands	15,616	15,438	13,146
Philippines	6,558	4,892	5,073
Singapore	68,574	56,643	60,660
Taiwan	14,188	12,167	13,224
Thailand	13,485	12,756	15,096
United Kingdom	11,566	8,759	8,353
USA	76,579	67,618	71,502
Total (incl. others)	373,270	334,284	354,430

Source: Bank Negara Malaysia, Kuala Lumpur.

Transport

RAILWAYS
(traffic, Peninsular Malaysia and Singapore)

	1998	1999	2000
Passenger-km (million)	1,397	1,313	1,220
Freight ton-km (million)	992	908	917

Source: UN, *Statistical Yearbook*.

ROAD TRAFFIC
(registered motor vehicles at 31 December)

	1998*	1999*	2000
Passenger cars	3,517,484	3,852,693	4,212,567
Buses and coaches	45,643	47,674	48,662
Lorries and vans	599,149	642,976	665,284
Road tractors	286,898	304,135	315,687
Motorcycles and mopeds	4,692,183	5,082,473	5,356,604

* Source: International Road Federation, *World Road Statistics*; data for 1999 are estimates.

SHIPPING

Merchant Fleet
(registered at 31 December)

	1999	2000	2001
Number of vessels	828	865	882
Total displacement ('000 grt)	5,244.7	5,328.1	5,207.1

Source: Lloyd's Register-Fairplay, *World Fleet Statistics*.

Sea-borne Freight Traffic*
(Peninsular Malaysia, international and coastwise, '000 metric tons)

	1998	1999	2000
Goods loaded	35,206	39,755	42,547
Goods unloaded	48,314	54,854	56,537

* Including transhipments.

Source: UN, *Monthly Bulletin of Statistics*.

CIVIL AVIATION
(traffic on scheduled services)

	1997	1998	1999
Kilometres flown (million) . . .	183	189	207
Passengers carried ('000) . . .	15,592	13,654	14,985
Passenger-km (million)	28,698	29,372	33,708
Total ton-km (million)	3,777	3,777	4,431

Source: UN, *Statistical Yearbook*.

Tourism

TOURIST ARRIVALS BY COUNTRY OF RESIDENCE*

	2000	2001	2002
Australia	236,775	222,340	193,794
Brunei	195,059	309,529	256,952
China, People's Republic . .	425,246	453,246	557,647
Indonesia	545,051	777,449	769,128
Japan	455,981	397,639	354,563
Singapore	5,420,200	6,951,594	7,547,761
Taiwan	213,016	249,811	209,706
Thailand	940,215	1,018,797	1,166,937
United Kingdom	237,757	262,423	239,294
Total (incl. others)	10,221,582	12,775,073	13,292,010

* Including Singapore residents crossing the frontier by road through the Johore Causeway.

Tourism receipts (RM million): 12,321 in 1999; 17,335.4 in 2000; 24,221.5 in 2001.

Source: Malaysia Tourism Promotion Board.

Communications Media

	1999	2000	2001
Television receivers ('000 in use)* .	3,800	3,900	n.a.
Telephones ('000 main lines in use)	4,430.8	4,634.3	4,738.0
Mobile cellular telephones ('000 subscribers)	2,990.0	4,960.8	7,128.0
Personal computers ('000 in use)*	1,500	2,400	3,000
Internet users ('000)*	2,500	3,700	5,700

Radio receivers ('000 in use, 1997): 9,100.

Facsimile machines ('000 in use): 175.0* in 1998.

Book production (1999): 5,084 titles (29,040,000 copies in 1996)†.

Newspapers (1996): 42 dailies (average circulation 3,345,000 copies); 44 non-dailies (average circulation 1,424,000 copies).

Periodicals (1992): 25 titles (average circulation 996,000 copies).
* Estimate(s).
† Including pamphlets (106 titles and 646,000 copies in 1994).

Sources: International Telecommunication Union; UNESCO, *Statistical Yearbook*; UN, *Statistical Yearbook*.

Education

(January 2001, unless otherwise indicated)

	Institutions	Teachers	Students
Primary	7,305	157,985	2,916,841
Secondary	1,713	115,098	2,015,579
Regular	1,534	103,711	1,919,974
Fully residential	39	2,584	23,979
Vocational	4	156	648
Technical	80	5,772	34,672
Religious	53	2,730	35,816
Special	3	145	490
Tertiary*	48	14,960	210,724
Universities	9	7,823	97,103
Teacher training	31	3,220	46,019
MARA Institute of Technology .	1	2,574	42,174

* 1995 figures.

Source: Ministry of Education.

Pre-primary: 9,743 schools (1994); 20,352 teachers (1994); 459,015 pupils (1995) (Source: UNESCO, *Statistical Yearbook*).

Adult literacy rate (UNESCO estimates): 87.5% (males 91.4%; females 83.4%) in 2000 (Source: UN Development Programme, *Human Development Report*).

Directory

The Constitution

The Constitution of the Federation of Malaya became effective at independence on 31 August 1957. As subsequently amended, it is now the Constitution of Malaysia. The main provisions are summarized below.

SUPREME HEAD OF STATE

The Yang di-Pertuan Agong (King or Supreme Sovereign) is the Supreme Head of Malaysia.

Every act of government is derived from his authority, although he acts on the advice of Parliament and the Cabinet. The appointment of a Prime Minister lies within his discretion, and he has the right to refuse to dissolve Parliament even against the advice of the Prime Minister. He appoints the Judges of the Federal Court and the High Courts on the advice of the Prime Minister. He is the Supreme Commander of the Armed Forces. The Yang di-Pertuan Agong is elected by the Conference of Rulers, and to qualify for election he must be one of the nine hereditary Rulers. He holds office for five years or until his earlier resignation or death. Election is by secret ballot on each Ruler in turn, starting with the Ruler next in precedence after the late or former Yang di-Pertuan Agong. The first Ruler to obtain not fewer than five votes is declared elected. The Deputy Supreme Head of State (the Timbalan Yang di-Pertuan Agong) is elected by a similar process. On election the Yang di-Pertuan Agong relinquishes, for his tenure of office, all his functions as Ruler of his own state and may appoint a Regent. The Timbalan Yang di-Pertuan Agong exercises no powers in the ordinary course, but is immediately available to fill the post of Yang di-Pertuan Agong and carry out his functions in the latter's absence or disability. In the event of the Yang di-Pertuan Agong's death or resignation he takes over the exercise of sovereignty until the Conference of Rulers has elected a successor.

CONFERENCE OF RULERS

The Conference of Rulers consists of the Rulers and the heads of the other states. Its prime duty is the election by the Rulers only of the Yang di-Pertuan Agong and his deputy. The Conference must be consulted in the appointment of judges, the Auditor-General, the Election Commission and the Services Commissions. It must also be consulted and concur in the alteration of state boundaries, the extension to the federation as a whole, of Islamic religious acts and observances, and in any bill to amend the Constitution. Consultation is mandatory in matters affecting public policy or the special position of the Malays and natives of Sabah and Sarawak. The Conference also considers matters affecting the rights, prerogatives and privileges of the Rulers themselves.

FEDERAL PARLIAMENT

Parliament has two Houses—the Dewan Negara (Senate) and the Dewan Rakyat (House of Representatives). The Senate has a membership of 70, comprising 30 elected and 40 appointed members. Each state legislature, acting as an electoral college, elects two Senators; these may be members of the State Legislative Assembly or otherwise. The remaining four Senators represent the two Federal Territories, Kuala Lumpur and the island of Labuan. The Yang di-Pertuan Agong appoints the other 40 members of the Senate. Members of the Senate must be at least 30 years old. The Senate elects its President and Deputy President from among its members. It may initiate legislation, but all proposed legislation for the granting of funds must be introduced in the first instance in the House of Representatives. All legislative measures require approval by both Houses of Parliament before being presented to the Yang di-Pertuan Agong for the Royal Assent in order to become law. A bill originating in the Senate cannot receive Royal Assent until it has been approved by the House of Representatives, but the Senate has delaying powers only over a bill originating from and approved by the House of Representatives. Senators serve for a period of three years, but the Senate is not subject to dissolution. Parliament can, by statute, increase the number of Senators elected from each state to three. The House of Representatives consists of 193 elected members (see Amendments). Of these, 144 are from Peninsular Malaysia (including seven from Kuala Lumpur), 28 from Sarawak and 21 from Sabah (including one from Labuan). Members are returned from single-member constituencies on the basis of universal adult franchise. The term of the House of Representatives is limited to five years, after which time a fresh general election must be held. The Yang di-Pertuan Agong may dissolve Parliament before then if the Prime Minister so advises.

THE CABINET

To advise him in the exercise of his functions, the Yang di-Pertuan Agong appoints the Cabinet, consisting of the Prime Minister and an unspecified number of Ministers (who must all be Members of Parliament). The Prime Minister must be a citizen born in Malaysia and a member of the House of Representatives who, in the opinion of the Yang di-Pertuan Agong, commands the confidence of that House. Ministers are appointed on the advice of the Prime Minister. A number of Deputy Ministers (who are not members of the Cabinet) are also appointed from among Members of Parliament. The Cabinet meets regularly under the chairmanship of the Prime Minister to formulate policy.

PUBLIC SERVICES

The Public Services, civilian and military, are non-political and owe their loyalty not to the party in power but to the Yang di-Pertuan Agong and the Rulers. They serve whichever government may be in power, irrespective of the latter's political affiliation. To ensure the impartiality of the service, and its protection from political interference, the Constitution provides for a number of Services Commissions to select and appoint officers, to place them on the pensionable establishment, to determine promotion and to maintain discipline.

THE STATES

The heads of nine of the 13 states are hereditary Rulers. The Ruler of Perlis has the title of Raja, and the Ruler of Negeri Sembilan that of Yang di-Pertuan Besar. The rest of the Rulers are Sultans. The heads of the States of Melaka (Malacca), Pinang (Penang), Sabah and Sarawak are each designated Yang di-Pertua Negeri and do not participate in the election of the Yang di-Pertuan Agong. Each of the 13 states has its own written Constitution and a single Legislative Assembly. Every state legislature has powers to legislate on matters not reserved for the Federal Parliament. Each State Legislative Assembly has the right to order its own procedure, and the members enjoy parliamentary privilege. All members of the Legislative Assemblies are directly elected from single-member constituencies. The head of the state acts on the advice of the State Government. This advice is tendered by the State Executive Council or Cabinet in precisely the same manner in which the Federal Cabinet tenders advice to the Yang di-Pertuan Agong.

The legislative authority of the state is vested in the head of the state in the State Legislative Assembly. The executive authority of the state is vested in the head of the state, but executive functions may be conferred on other persons by law. Every state has its own Executive Council or Cabinet to advise the head of the state, headed by its Chief Minister (Ketua Menteri in Melaka, Pinang, Sabah and Sarawak and Menteri Besar in other states), and collectively responsible to the state legislature. Each state in Peninsular Malaysia is divided into administrative districts, each with its District Officer. Sabah is divided into four residencies: West Coast, Interior, Sandakan and Tawau, with headquarters at Kota Kinabalu, Keningua, Sandakan and Tawau, respectively. Sarawak is divided into five Divisions, each in charge of a Resident—the First Division, with headquarters at Kuching; the Second Division, with headquarters at Simanggang; the Third Division, with headquarters at Sibu; the Fourth Division, with headquarters at Miri; the Fifth Division, with headquarters at Limbang.

AMENDMENTS

From 1 February 1974, the city of Kuala Lumpur, formerly the seat of the Federal Government and capital of Selangor State, is designated the Federal Territory of Kuala Lumpur. It is administered directly by the Federal Government and returns five members to the House of Representatives.

In April 1981 the legislature approved an amendment empowering the Yang di-Pertuan Agong to declare a state of emergency on the grounds of imminent danger of a breakdown in law and order or a threat to national security.

In August 1983 the legislature approved an amendment empowering the Prime Minister, instead of the Yang di-Pertuan Agong, to declare a state of emergency.

The island of Labuan, formerly part of Sabah State, was designated a Federal Territory as from 16 April 1984.

The legislature approved an amendment increasing the number of parliamentary constituencies in Sarawak from 24 to 27. The amendment took effect at the general election of 20–21 October 1990. The total number of seats in the House of Representatives, which had increased to 177 following an amendment in August 1983, was thus expanded to 180.

In March 1988 the legislature approved two amendments relating to the judiciary (see Judicial System).

In October 1992 the legislature adopted an amendment increasing the number of parliamentary constituencies from 180 to 192. The Kuala Lumpur Federal Territory and Selangor each gained three seats, Johor two, and Perlis, Kedah, Kelantan and Pahang one. The amendment took effect at the next general election (in April 1995).

In March 1993 an amendment was approved which removed the immunity from prosecution of the hereditary Rulers.

In May 1994 the House of Representatives approved an amendment which ended the right of the Yang di-Pertuan Agong to delay legislation by withholding his assent from legislation and returning it to Parliament for further consideration. Under the amendment, the Yang di-Pertuan Agong was obliged to give his assent to a bill within 30 days; if he failed to do so, the bill would, none the less, become law. An amendment was simultaneously approved restructuring the judiciary and introducing a mandatory code of ethics for judges, to be drawn up by the Government.

In 1996 an amendment was approved, increasing the number of parliamentary constituencies from 192 to 193.

In 2001 an amendment was approved banning all discrimination on grounds of gender.

From 1 February 2001 the city of Putrajaya, formerly part of Selangor State, was designated a Federal Territory.

The Government

SUPREME HEAD OF STATE

Yang di-Pertuan Agong: HM Tuanku SYED SIRAJUDDIN IBNI AL-MARHUM SYED PUTRA JAMALULLAIL (Raja of Perlis) (took office 13 December 2001).

Deputy Supreme Head of State (Timbalan Yang di-Pertuan Agong): HRH Sultan MIZAN ZAINAL ABIDIN (Sultan of Terengganu).

THE CABINET
(April 2003)

Prime Minister and Minister of Finance and of Special Functions: Dato' Seri Dr MAHATHIR BIN MOHAMAD.

Deputy Prime Minister and Minister of Home Affairs: Dato' Seri ABDULLAH BIN Haji AHMAD BADAWI.

Minister of Housing and Local Government: Dato' ONG KAH TING.

Minister of Foreign Affairs: Datuk Seri SYED HAMID BIN SYED JAAFAR ALBAR.

Minister of International Trade and Industry: Dato' Seri Paduka RAFIDAH BINTI AZIZ.

Minister of Domestic Trade and Consumer Affairs: Tan Sri Dato' Haji MUHYIDDIN BIN Haji MOHD YASSIN.

Minister of Defence: Dato' Seri NAJIB BIN Tun ABDUL RAZAK.

Minister of Transport: Dato' Seri Dr LING LIONG SIK.

Minister of National Unity and Social Development: Dato' Dr SITI ZAHARAH BINTI SULAIMAN.

Minister of Primary Industries: Dato' Seri Dr LIM KENG YAIK.

Minister of Energy, Communications and Multimedia: Datuk LEO MOGGIE ANAK IROK.

Minister of Works: Dato' Seri S. SAMY VELLU.

Minister of Youth and Sports: Dato' HISHAMUDDIN BIN Tun HUSSEIN.

Minister of Education: Tan Sri MUSA BIN MOHAMAD.

Minister of Information: Tan Sri MOHD KHALIL BIN YAACOB.

Minister of Human Resources: Datuk Dr FONG CHAN ONN.

Minister of Land and Co-operative Development: Tan Sri Datuk KASITAH BIN GADDAM.

Minister of Culture, Arts and Tourism: Datuk ABDUL KADIR BIN Haji Sheikh FADZIR.

Minister of Science, Technology and the Environment: Datuk LAW HIENG DING.

Minister of Health: Dato' CHUA JUI MENG.

Minister of Agriculture: Datuk MOHAMED EFFENDI BIN NORWAWI.

Minister of Rural Development: Dato' AMZI BIN KHALID.

Minister of Entrepreneur Development: Datuk MOHAMED NAZRI BIN Tan Sri Dato' ABDUL AZIZ.

Minister of Women's Affairs: Datuk SHAHRIZAT BTE ABDUL JALIL.

Minister of Finance II: Datuk Dr JAMALUDDIN JARJIS.

Ministers in the Prime Minister's Department: Brig.-Gen. Senator Datuk ABDUL HAMID BIN ZAINAL ABIDIN, Tan Sri Datuk Seri Panglima BERNARD GILUK DOMPOK, Dato' RAIS BIN YATIM, Datuk Tengku ADNAN Tengku MANSOR.

Note: in 2003 the telephone and fax numbers of Malaysia remained in the process of change. See www.telekom.com.my for further details.

MINISTRIES

Prime Minister's Department (Jabatan Perdana Menteri): Blok Utama, Tingkat 1–5, Pusat Pentadbiran Kerajaan Persekutuan, 62502 Putrajaya; tel. (3) 88888000; fax (3) 88883424; e-mail ppm@smpke.jpm.my; internet www.smpke.jpm.my.

Ministry of Agriculture (Kementerian Pertanian): Tingkat 4, Wisma Tani, Jalan Sultan Salahuddin, 50624 Kuala Lumpur; tel. (3) 26982011; fax (3) 26913758; e-mail admin@moa.my; internet www.agrolink.moa.my.

Ministry of Culture, Arts and Tourism (Kementerian Kebudayaan, Kesenian dan Pelancongan): Menara Dato' Onn, 34th–36th Floors, POB 5–7, Putra World Trade Centre, 45 Jalan Tun Ismail, 50694 Kuala Lumpur; tel. (3) 26937111; fax (3) 26941146; e-mail mocat@tourism.gov.my; internet www.mocat.gov.my.

Ministry of Defence (Kementerian Pertahanan): Wisma Pertahanan, Jalan Padang Tembak, 50634 Kuala Lumpur; tel. (3) 26921333; fax (3) 26914163; e-mail cpa@mod.gov.my; internet www.mod.gov.my.

Ministry of Domestic Trade and Consumer Affairs (Kementerian Perdagangan Dalam Negeri Dan Hal Ehwal Pengguna): Tingkat 33, Menara Dayabumi, Jalan Sultan Hishamuddin, 50632 Kuala Lumpur; tel. (3) 22742100; fax (3) 22745260; e-mail menteri@kpdnhq.gov.my; internet www.kpdnhq.gov.my.

Ministry of Education (Kementerian Pendidikan): Blok J, Tingkat 7, Pusat Bandar Damansara, 50604 Kuala Lumpur; tel. (3) 2586900; fax (3) 2543107; e-mail webmaster@moe.gov.my; internet www.moe.gov.my.

Ministry of Energy, Communications and Multimedia (Kementerian Tenaga, Telekom dan Pos): Wisma Damansara, 3rd Floor, Jalan Semantan, 50668 Kuala Lumpur; tel. (3) 20875000; fax (3) 20957901; e-mail ZainalAbidin@ktkm.gov.my; internet www.ktkm.gov.my.

Ministry of Entrepreneur Development (Kementerian Pembangunan Usahawan): Tingkat 22–26, Medan MARA, Jalan Raja Laut, 50652 Kuala Lumpur; tel. (3) 26985022; fax (3) 26917623; e-mail nazri@kpun.gov.my; internet www.kpun.gov.my.

Ministry of Finance (Kementerian Kewangan): Kompleks Kementerian Kewangan, Precinct 2, Pusat Pentadbiran Kerajaan Persekutuan, 62592 Putrajaya; tel. (3) 88823000; fax (3) 88823892; e-mail mk1@treasury.gov.my; internet www.treasury.gov.my.

Ministry of Foreign Affairs (Kementerian Luar Negeri): Wisma Putra, 1 Jalan Wisma Putra, 62602 Putrajaya; tel. (3) 88874000; fax (3) 88891717; e-mail webmaster@kln.gov.my; internet www.kln.gov.my.

Ministry of Health (Kementerian Kesihatan): Jalan Cenderasari, 50590 Kuala Lumpur; tel. (3) 26985077; fax (3) 26985964; e-mail CJM@moh.gov.my; internet www.moh.gov.my.

Ministry of Home Affairs (Kementerian Dalam Negeri): Blok D1, Parcel D, Pusat Pentadbiran Kerajaan Persekutuan, 62546 Putrajaya; tel. (3) 88868000; e-mail irg@kdn.gov.my; internet www.kdn.gov.my.

Ministry of Housing and Local Government (Kementerian Perumahan dan Kerajaan Tempatan): Paras 4 and 5, Blok K, Pusat Bandar Damansara, 50782 Kuala Lumpur; tel. (3) 2547033; fax (3) 2547380; e-mail menteri@kpkt.gov.my; internet www.kpkt.gov.my.

Ministry of Human Resources (Kementerian Sumber Manusia): Level 6–9, Blok D3, Parcel D, Pusat Pentadbiran Kerajaan Persekutuan, 62502 Putrajaya; tel. (3) 88865000; fax (3) 88893381; e-mail mhr@po.jaring.my; internet www.jaring.my/ksm.

Ministry of Information (Kementerian Penerangan): 5th Floor, Wisma TV, Angkasapuri, 50610 Kuala Lumpur; tel. (3) 2825333; fax (3) 2821255; e-mail webmaster@kempen.gov.my; internet www.kempen.gov.my.

Ministry of International Trade and Industry (Kementerian Perdagangan Antarabangsa dan Industri): Blok 10, Kompleks Pejabat Kerajaan, Jalan Duta, 50622 Kuala Lumpur; tel. (3) 62033022; fax (3) 62031303; e-mail mitiweb@miti.gov.my; internet www.miti.gov.my/.

Ministry of Land and Co-operative Development (Kementerian Tanah dan Pembangunan Koperasi): Wisma Tanah, 11th Floor, Jalan Semarak, 50574 Kuala Lumpur; tel. (3) 26921566; fax (3) 26919426; e-mail kasitah@ktpk.gov.my; internet www.ktpk.gov.my.

Ministry of National Unity and Social Development (Kementerian Perpaduan Negara dan Pembangunan Masyarakat): Tingkat 19–21, Wisma Bumi Raya, Jalan Raja Laut, 50562 Kuala Lumpur; tel. (3) 26925022; fax (3) 26937353; e-mail adminkpn@kempadu.gov.my; internet www.kempadu.gov.my.

Ministry of Primary Industries (Kementerian Perusahaan Utama): Menara Dayabumi, 6th–8th Floors, Jalan Sultan Hishamuddin, 50654 Kuala Lumpur; tel. (3) 22747511; fax (3) 22745014; e-mail webeditor@kpu.gov.my; internet www.kpu.gov.my.

Ministry of Rural Development (Kementerian Pembangunan Luar Bandar): Aras 5–9, Blok D9, Parcel D, Pusat Pentadbiran Kerajaan Persekutuan, 62606 Putrajaya; tel. (3) 88863500; fax (3) 88892096; e-mail info@kplb.gov.my; internet www.kplb.gov.my.

Ministry of Science, Technology and Environment (Kementerian Sains, Teknologi dan Alam Sekitar): Level 4, Blok C5, Parcel C, Federal Government Administrative Centre, 62662 Putrajaya; tel. (3) 88858000; fax (3) 88892980; e-mail mastic@mastic.gov.my; internet www.moste.gov.my.

Ministry of Transport (Kementerian Pengangkutan): Wisma Perdana, Level 5–7, Blok D5, Parcel D, Federal Government Administrative Centre, 62502 Putrajaya; tel. (3) 88866000; fax (3) 88892537; e-mail LeeLC@mot.gov.my; internet www.mot.gov.my.

Ministry of Works (Kementerian Kerja Raya): Ground Floor, Blok A, Kompleks Kerja Raya, Jalan Sultan Salahuddin, 50580 Kuala Lumpur; tel. (3) 27111100; fax (3) 27116612; e-mail menteri@kkr.gov.my; internet www.kkr.gov.my.

Ministry of Youth and Sports (Kementerian Belia dan Sukan): Blok G, Jalan Dato' Onn, 50570 Kuala Lumpur; tel. (3) 26932255; fax (3) 26932231; e-mail webmaster@kbs.gov.my; internet www.kbs.gov.my.

Legislature

PARLIAMENT

Dewan Negara
(Senate)

The Senate has 70 members, of whom 30 are elected. Each State Legislative Assembly and Federal Territory elects two members. The Supreme Head of State appoints the remaining 40 members.

President: Tan Sri MICHAEL CHEN WING SUM.

Dewan Rakyat
(House of Representatives)

The House of Representatives has a total of 193 members: 144 from Peninsular Malaysia (including seven from Kuala Lumpur), 28 from Sarawak and 21 from Sabah (including one from the Federal Territory of Labuan).

Speaker: Tan Sri MUHAMMAD ZAHIR ISMAIL.

Deputy Speaker: Datuk LIM SI CHENG.

General Election, 29 November 1999

Party	Seats
Barisan Nasional (National Front)	148
United Malays National Organization	72
Malaysian Chinese Association	28
Parti Pesaka Bumiputera Bersatu	10
Sarawak United People's Party	7
Malaysian Indian Congress	7
Parti Gerakan Rakyat Malaysia	7
Parti Bansa Dayak Sarawak	6
Sarawak National Action Party	4
UPKO	3
Sabah Progressive Party	2
Liberal Democratic Party	1
Direct BN	1
Barisan Alternatif (Alternative Front)	42
Parti Islam se Malaysia	27
Democratic Action Party	10
Parti Keadilan Nasional	5
Parti Bersatu Sabah	3
Total	**193**

The States

JOHOR
(Capital: Johor Bahru)

Sultan: HRH Tuanku MAHMOOD ISKANDAR IBNI AL-MARHUM Sultan ISMAIL.

Menteri Besar: Datuk Haji ABDUL GHANI OTHMAN.

State Legislative Assembly: 40 seats: Barisan Nasional 40; elected November 1999.

KEDAH
(Capital: Alor Star)

Sultan: HRH Tuanku Haji ABDUL HALIM MU'ADZAM SHAH IBNI AL-MARHUM Sultan BADLISHAH.

Menteri Besar: Datuk SYED RAZAK SYED ZAIN BARAKBAH.

State Legislative Assembly: 36 seats: Barisan Nasional 24; Parti Islam se Malaysia 12; elected November 1999.

KELANTAN
(Capital: Kota Baharu)

Sultan: HRH Tuanku ISMAIL PETRA IBNI AL-MARHUM Sultan YAHAYA PETRA.

Menteri Besar: Tuan Guru Haji Nik ABDUL AZIZ BIN Nik MAT.

State Legislative Assembly: 43 seats: Parti Islam se Malaysia 41; Barisan Nasional 2; elected November 1999.

MELAKA (MALACCA)
(Capital: Melaka)

Yang di-Pertua Negeri: HE Tun Datuk Sri UTAMA SYED AHMAD Al-Haj BIN SYED MAHMUD SHAHABUDIN.

Ketua Menteri: Datuk WIRA MOHAMED ALI RUSTAM.

State Legislative Assembly: 25 seats: Barisan Nasional 21; Democratic Action Party 4; elected November 1999.

NEGERI SEMBILAN
(Capital: Seremban)

Yang di-Pertuan Besar: Tuanku JA'AFAR IBNI AL-MARHUM Tuanku ABDUL RAHMAN.

Menteri Besar: Tan Sri MOHAMMED ISA BIN Datuk Haji ABDUL SAMAD.

State Legislative Assembly: 32 seats: Barisan Nasional 32; elected November 1999.

PAHANG
(Capital: Kuantan)

Sultan: HRH Haji AHMAD SHAH AL-MUSTA'IN BILLAH IBNI AL-MARHUM Sultan ABU BAKAR RI'AYATUDDIN AL-MU'ADZAM SHAH.

Menteri Besar: Dato' ADNAN BIN YAAKOB.

State Legislative Assembly: 38 seats: Barisan Nasional 30; Parti Islam se Malaysia 6; Democratic Action Party 1; Parti Keadilan Nasional 1; elected November 1999.

PERAK
(Capital: Ipoh)

Sultan: HRH Sultan AZLAN SHAH.

Menteri Besar: Dato' Seri DiRaja MOHAMAD TAJOL ROSLI.

State Legislative Assembly: Pejabat Setiausaha Kerajaan Negeri, Perak Darul Ridzuan, Bahagian Majlis, Jalan Panglima Bukit Gantang Wahab, 30000 Ipoh; tel. (05) 2410451; fax (05) 2552890; e-mail master@perak.gov.my; internet www.perak.gov.my; 52 seats: Barisan Nasional 44; Democratic Action Party 4; Parti Islam se Malaysia 3; Parti Keadilan Nasional 1; elected November 1999.

PERLIS
(Capital: Kangar)

Regent: Tuanku SYED FAIZUDDIN PUTRA IBNI Tuanku SYED SIRAJUDDIN PUTRA JAMALULAIL.

Menteri Besar: Dato' Seri SHAHIDAN KASSIM.

State Legislative Assembly: internet www.perlis.gov.my; 15 seats: Barisan Nasional 12; Parti Islam se Malaysia 3; elected November 1999.

PINANG (PENANG)
(Capital: George Town)

Yang di-Pertua Negeri: HE Datuk ABDUL RAHMAN Haji ABBAS.

Ketua Menteri: Tan Sri Dr KOH TSU KOON.

State Legislative Assembly: 33 seats: Barisan Nasional 30; Democratic Action Party 1; Parti Islam se Malaysia 1; Parti Keadilan Nasional 1; elected November 1999.

SABAH
(Capital: Kota Kinabalu)

Yang di-Pertua Negeri: HE Tan Sri SAKARAN DANDAI.

Ketua Menteri: Datuk MUSA AMAN.

State Legislative Assembly: Dewan Undangan Negeri Sabah, Aras 4, Bangunan Dewan Undangan Negeri Sabah, Peti Surat 11247, 88813 Kota Kinabalu; tel. (88) 427533; fax (88) 427333; e-mail pejduns@sabah.gov.my; internet www.sabah.gov.my; 48 seats: Barisan Nasional 31, Parti Bersatu Sabah 17; elected March 1999.

SARAWAK
(Capital: Kuching)

Yang di-Pertua Negeri: HE Tun Datuk Patinggi Abang Haji MUHAMMED SALAHUDDIN.

Ketua Menteri: Datuk Patinggi Tan Sri Haji ABDUL TAIB BIN MAHMUD.

State Legislative Assembly: Bangunan Dewan Undangan Negeri, 93502 Petra Jaya, Kuching, Sarawak; tel. (82) 441955; fax (82) 440790; e-mail mastapaj@sarawaknet.gov.my; internet www.dun.sarawak.gov.my; 62 seats: Barisan Nasional 60; Democratic Action Party 1; Independents 1; elected September 2001.

SELANGOR
(Capital: Shah Alam)

Sultan: Tuanku IDRIS SALAHUDDIN ABDUL AZIZ SHAH.

Menteri Besar: MOHAMAD KHIR TOYO.

State Legislative Assembly: 48 seats: Barisan Nasional 42; Parti Islam se Malaysia 4; Democratic Action Party 1; Parti Keadilan Nasional 1; elected December 1999.

TERENGGANU
(Capital: Kuala Terengganu)

Sultan: HRH Sultan MIZAN ZAINAL ABIDIN.

Menteri Besar: ABDUL HADI AWANG.

State Legislative Assembly: 32 seats: Parti Islam se Malaysia 28; Barisan Nasional 4; elected November 1999.

Political Organizations

Barisan Nasional (BN) (National Front): Suite 1–2, 8th Floor, Menara Dato' Onn, Pusat Dagangan Dunia Putra, Jalan Tun Ismail 50480 Kuala Lumpur; tel. (3) 2920384; fax (3) 2934743; e-mail info@bn.org.my; internet www.bn.org.my; f. 1973; the governing multiracial coalition of 15 parties; Sec.-Gen. Dato' Datuk Sri MOHAMMED RAHMAT; Comprises:

Angkatan Keadilan Rakyat (AKAR) (People's Justice Movement): Tingkat 2, No. 16, Lot 8, Blok B, Nountun Light Industrial Estate, Lorong Perindustrian Nountun, Kota Kinabalu, 88450 Sabah; tel. (88) 437485; fax (88) 434716; Dusun-based breakaway faction of the PBS; Leaders Dato' MARK KODING, KALAKAU UNTOL, PANDIKAR AMIN MULIA.

Liberal Democratic Party: Tingkat 2, Lot 1, Wisma Jasaga, POB 1125, Sandakan, 90712 Sabah; tel. (89) 271888; fax (89) 288278; e-mail ldpkk@tm.net.my; Chinese-dominated; Pres. Datuk CHONG KAH KIAT; Sec.-Gen. Datuk ANTHONY LAI VAI MING.

Malaysian Chinese Association (MCA): Wisma MCA, 8th Floor, 163 Jalan Ampang, POB 10626, 50720 Kuala Lumpur; tel. (3) 21618044; fax (3) 21619772; e-mail info@mca.org.my; internet www.mca.org.my; f. 1949; c. 1,033,686 mems; Pres. Dato' Seri Dr LING LIONG SIK; Sec.-Gen. Dato' Seri Dr TING CHEW PEH.

Malaysian Indian Congress (MIC): Menara Manickavasagam, 6th Floor, 1 Jalan Rahmat, 50350 Kuala Lumpur; tel. (3) 4424377; fax (3) 4427236; internet www.mic.malaysia.org; f. 1946; 401,000 mems (1992); Pres. Dato' Seri S. SAMY VELLU; Sec.-Gen. Dato' G. VADIVELOO.

Parti Bansa Dayak Sarawak (PBDS) (Sarawak Native People's Party): 622 Jalan Kedandi, Tabuan Jaya, POB 2148, Kuching, Sarawak; tel. (82) 365240; fax (82) 363734; f. 1983 by fmr mems of Sarawak National Party; Pres. Datuk LEO MOGGIE ANAK IROK; Vice-Pres. Datuk DANIEL TAJEM.

Parti Bersatu Rakyat Sabah (PBRS) (United Sabah People's Party): POB 20148, Luyang, Kota Kinabalu, 88761 Sabah; tel. and fax (88) 269282; f. 1994; breakaway faction of PBS; mostly Christian Kadazans; Leader Datuk JOSEPH KURUP.

Parti Bersatu Sabah (PBS) (Sabah United Party): Block M, Lot 4, 2nd and 3rd Floors, Donggongon New Township, Penampang, Kota Kinabalu, Sabah; POB 13066, 88834 Kota Kinabalu, Sabah; tel. (88) 714891; fax (88) 718067; internet www.pbs-sabah.org; f. 1985; multiracial party, left the BN in 1990 and rejoined in January 2002; Pres. Datuk Seri JOSEPH PAIRIN KITINGAN; Sec.-Gen. RADIN MALLEH.

Parti Gerakan Rakyat Malaysia (GERAKAN) (Malaysian People's Movement): Tingkat 5, Menara PGRM, 8 Jalan Pudu Ulu Cheras, 56100 Kuala Lumpur; tel. (3) 92876868; fax (3) 92878866; e-mail gerakan@gerakan.org.my; internet www.gerakan.org.my; f. 1968; 300,000 mems; Pres. Dato' Seri Dr LIM KENG YAIK; Sec.-Gen. CHIA KWANG CHYE.

Parti Pesaka Bumiputera Bersatu (PBB) (United Traditional Bumiputra Party): Lot 401, Jalan Bako, POB 1953, 93400 Kuching, Sarawak; tel. (82) 448299; fax (82) 448294; f. 1983; Pres. Tan Sri Datuk Patinggi Amar Haji ABDUL TAIB MAHMUD; Dep. Pres. Datuk ALFRED JABU AK NUMPANG.

Parti Progresif Penduduk Malaysia (PPP) (People's Progressive Party): 27–29A Jalan Maharajalela, 50150 Kuala Lumpur; tel. (3) 2441922; fax (3) 2442041; e-mail info@ppp.com.my; internet www.jaring.my/ppp; f. 1953 as Perak Progressive Party; joined the BN in 1972; Pres. Datuk M. KAYVEAS.

Sabah Progressive Party (SAPP) (Parti Maju Sabah): Lot 23, 2nd Floor, Bornion Centre, 88300 Kota Kinabalu, Sabah; tel. (88) 242107; fax (88) 254799; e-mail sapp@po.jaring.my; internet www.jaring.my/sapp/; f. 1994; non-racial; Pres. Datuk YONG TECK LEE.

Sarawak National Action Party (SNAP): 304–305 Bangunan Mei Jun, 1 Jalan Rubber, POB 2960, 93758 Kuching, Sarawak; tel. (82) 254244; fax (82) 253562; internet www.snap.org.my; f. 1961; Pres. Datuk Amar JAMES WONG KIM MIN; Sec.-Gen. PETER GANI AK KIAI.

Sarawak United People's Party (SUPP): 7 Jalan Tan Sri Ong Kee Hui, POB 454, 93710 Kuching, Sarawak; tel. (82) 246999; fax (82) 256510; e-mail supp@po.jaring.my; internet www.sarawak.com.my/supp/; f. 1959; Sarawak Chinese minority party; Pres. Datuk Dr GEORGE CHAN HONG NAM; Sec.-Gen. SIM KHENG HUI.

United Kadazan People's Organization (UPKO): Penampang Service Centre, Km 11, Jalan Tambunan, Peti Surat 420, 89507 Penampang, Sabah; tel. (88) 718182; fax (88) 718180; f. 1994 as the Parti Demokratik Sabah (PDS—Sabah Democratic Party); formed after collapse of PBS Govt by fmr leaders of the party; represents mostly Kadazandusun, Rungus and Murut communities; Pres. Tan Sri BERNARD GILUK DOMPOK.

United Malays National Organization (Pertubuhan Kebangsaan Melayu Bersatu—UMNO Baru) (New UMNO): Menara Dato' Onn, 38th Floor, Jalan Tun Dr Ismail, 50480 Kuala Lumpur; tel. (3) 40429511; fax (3) 40412358; e-mail email@umno.net.my; internet www.umno.org.my; f. 1988 to replace the original UMNO (f. 1946) which had been declared an illegal organization, owing to the participation of unregistered branches in party elections in April 1987; Supreme Council of 45 mems; 2.5m. mems; Pres. Dato'

Seri Dr MAHATHIR BIN MOHAMAD; Dep. Pres. Dato' Seri ABDULLAH BIN Haji AHMAD BADAWI; Sec.-Gen. Tan Sri MOHD KHALIL BIN YAACOB.

Angkatan Democratic Liberal Sabah (Adil): Sabah; intended primarily to attract Malay Muslims.

Angkatan Keadilan Insan Malaysia (AKIM) (Malaysian Justice Movement): f. 1995 by fmr members of PAS and Semangat '46; Pres. CHE GU MUSA SALIH.

Barisan Alternatif (Alternative Front): Kuala Lumpur; f. June 1999 to contest the general election; opposition electoral alliance originally comprising the PAS, the DAP, the PKN and the PRM; the DAP left in Sept. 2001.

Barisan Jama'ah Islamiah Sa-Malaysia (Berjasa) (Front Malaysian Islamic Council—FMIC): Kelantan; f. 1977; pro-Islamic; 50,000 mems; Pres. Dato' Haji WAN HASHIM bin Haji WAN ACHMED; Sec.-Gen. MAHMUD ZUHDI BIN Haji ABDUL MAJID.

Bersatu Rakyat Jelata Sabah (Berjaya) (Sabah People's Union): Natikar Bldg, 1st Floor, POB 2130, Kota Kinabalu, Sabah; f. 1975; 400,000 mems; Pres. Haji MOHAMMED NOOR MANSOOR.

Democratic Action Party (DAP): 24 Jalan 20/9, 46300 Petaling Jaya, Selangor; tel. (3) 7578022; fax (3) 7575718; e-mail dap.Malaysia@pobox.com; internet www.malaysia.net/dap; f. 1966; main opposition party; advocates multiracial society based on democratic socialism; 12,000 mems; Chair. LIM KIT SIANG; Sec.-Gen. KERK KIM HOCK.

Democratic Malaysia Indian Party (DMIP): f. 1985; Leader V. GOVINDARAJ.

Kongres Indian Muslim Malaysia (KIMMA): Kuala Lumpur; tel. (3) 2324759; f. 1977; aims to unite Malaysian Indian Muslims politically; 25,000 mems; Pres. AHAMED ELIAS; Sec.-Gen. MOHAMMED ALI BIN Haji NAINA MOHAMMED.

Malaysian Solidarity Party: Kuala Lumpur.

Parti Hisbul Muslimin Malaysia (Hamim) (Islamic Front of Malaysia): Kota Bahru, Kelantan; f. 1983 as an alternative party to PAS; Pres. Datuk ASRI MUDA.

Parti Ikatan Masyarakat Islam (Islamic Alliance Party): Terengganu.

Parti Islam se Malaysia (PAS) (Islamic Party of Malaysia): Pejabat Agung PAS Pusat, Lorong Haji Hassan, off Jalan Batu Geliga, Taman Melewar, 68100 Batu Caves, Selangor Darul Ehsan; tel. (3) 61895612; fax (3) 61889520; e-mail pas@po.jaring.my; internet www.parti-pas.org; f. 1951; seeks to establish an Islamic state; 700,000 mems; Pres. ABDUL HADI AWANG (acting); Sec.-Gen. NASHARUDIN MAT ISA.

Parti Keadilan Masyarakat (PEKEMAS) (Social Justice Party): Kuala Lumpur; f. 1971 by fmr mems of GERAKAN; Chair. SHAHARYDDIN DAHALAN.

Parti Keadilan Nasional (PKN) (National Justice Party): Kuala Lumpur; internet www.partikeadilan.org; f. 1999 to unite the supporters of Anwar Ibrahim's *reformasi* movement; due to merge with the PRM before 2004; Pres. WAN AZIZAH WAN ISMAIL; Dep. Pres. ABDUL RAHMAN OTHMAN; Sec.-Gen. ANUAR TAHIR.

Parti Nasionalis Malaysia (NasMa): f. 1985; multiracial; Leader ZAINAB YANG.

Parti Rakyat Jati Sarawak (PAJAR) (Sarawak Native People's Party): 22A Jalan Bampeylde, 93200 Kuching, Sarawak; f. 1978; Leader ALI KAWI.

Parti Rakyat Malaysia (PRM) (Malaysian People's Party): 42 Jalan Masjid, 46000 Petaling Jaya, Selangor; tel. (3) 77812151; fax (3) 77818704; e-mail p_rakyat@hotmail.com; internet www.partirakyat.org; f. 1955; named Parti Sosialis Rakyat Malaya from 1970–90; due to merge with the PKN before 2004; Pres. Prof. SYED HUSIN ALI; Sec.-Gen. SANUSI OSMAN.

Persatuan Rakyat Malaysian Sarawak (PERMAS) (Malaysian Sarawak Party): Kuching, Sarawak; f. March 1987 by fmr mems of PBB; Leader Haji BUJANG ULIS.

Pertubuhan Bumiputera Bersatu Sarawak (PBBS) (United Sarawak National Association): Kuala Lumpur; f. 1986; Chair. Haji WAN HABIB SYED MAHMUD.

Pertubuhan Rakyat Sabah Bersatu (United Sabah People's Organization—USPO): Kota Kinabalu, Sabah.

Sabah Chinese Party (PCS): Kota Kinabalu, Sabah; f. 1986; Pres. Encik FRANCIS LEONG.

Sabah Chinese Consolidated Party (SCCP): POB 704, Kota Kinabalu, Sabah; f. 1964; 14,000 mems; Pres. JOHNNY SOON; Sec.-Gen. CHAN TET ON.

Setia (Sabah People's United Democratic Party): Sabah; f. 1994.

United Malaysian Indian Party: aims to promote unity and economic and social advancement of the Indian community; Sec. KUMAR MANOHARAN.

Diplomatic Representation

EMBASSIES AND HIGH COMMISSIONS IN MALAYSIA

Afghanistan: Suite 606, 6th Floor, North Block, The Amp Walk, 218 Jalan Ampang, 50450 Kuala Lumpur; tel. (3) 21628897; fax (3) 21628924; e-mail murad1@tm.net.my; Chargé d'affaires a.i. ABDUL SATTAR MURAD.

Albania: 2952 Jalan Bukit Ledang, off Jalan Duta, 50480 Kuala Lumpur; tel. (3) 2537808; fax (3) 2537359; Chargé d'affaires a.i. AHMET LALA.

Algeria: 5 Jalan Mesra, off Jalan Damai, 55000 Kuala Lumpur; tel. (3) 21488159; fax (3) 21488154; Ambassador RACHID BLADEHANE.

Argentina: 3 Jalan Semantan Dua, Damansara Heights, 50490 Kuala Lumpur; tel. (3) 2550176; fax (3) 2552706; e-mail emsia@po .jaring.my; Ambassador ALFREDO MORELLI.

Australia: 6 Jalan Yap Kwan Seng, 50450 Kuala Lumpur; tel. (3) 21465555; fax (3) 21415773; e-mail info@australia.org.my; internet www.australia.org.my; High Commissioner JAMES WISE.

Austria: MUI Plaza, 7th Floor, Jalan P. Ramlee, POB 10154, 50704 Kuala Lumpur; tel. (3) 21484277; fax (3) 21489813; e-mail kuala-lumpur-ob@bmaa.gv.at; Ambassador Dr OSWALD SOUKOP.

Bangladesh: Block 1, Lorong Damai 7, Jalan Damai, 55000 Kuala Lumpur; tel. (3) 21487490; fax (3) 21413381; e-mail bddoot@pc .jaring.my; High Commissioner MUHAMMAD KAMALUDDIN.

Belgium: 8A Jalan Ampang Hilir, 55000 Kuala Lumpur; tel. (3) 42525733; fax (3) 42527922; e-mail kualalumpur@diplobel.org; Ambassador ROLAND VAN REMOORTELE.

Bosnia and Herzegovina: JKR 854, Jalan Bellamy, 50460 Kuala Lumpur; tel. (3) 21440353; fax (3) 21426025; e-mail hsomun@ hotmail.com; Ambassador HAJRUDIN SOMUN.

Brazil: 22 Pesiaran Damansara Endah, Damansara Heights, 50490 Kuala Lumpur; tel. (3) 2548607; fax (3) 2555086; e-mail brazil@po .jaring.my; Ambassador GERALDO AFFONSO MUZZI.

Brunei: Tingkat 19, Menara Tan & Tan, Jalan Tun Razak, 50400 Kuala Lumpur; tel. (3) 21612800; fax (3) 2631302; e-mail bhckl@ brucomkul.com.my; High Commissioner Dato' Paduka Haji ABDULLAH bin Haji MOHAMMAD JAAFAR.

Cambodia: 46 Jalan U Thant, 55000 Kuala Lumpur; tel. (3) 42537711; fax (3) 42571157; e-mail reckl@tm.net.my; Ambassador KEO PUTH REASMEY.

Canada: POB 10990, 50732 Kuala Lumpur; tel. (3) 27183333; fax (3) 27183399; e-mail klmpr-td@dfait-maeci.gc.ca; internet www .dfait-maeci.gc.ca/kualalumpur; High Commissioner JEAN C. MCCLOSKEY.

Chile: 8th Floor, West Block 142-C, Jalan Ampang, Peti Surat 27, 50450 Kuala Lumpur; tel. (3) 21616203; fax (3) 21622219; e-mail eochile@ppp.nasionet.net; internet www.chileembassy-malaysia .com.my; Ambassador ROBERTO IBARRA GARCÍA.

China, People's Republic: 229 Jalan Ampang, 50450 Kuala Lumpur; tel. (3) 2428495; fax (3) 2414552; e-mail cn@tm.net.my; Ambassador HU ZHENGYUE.

Colombia: Level 26, UOA Centre, 19 Jalan Pinang, 50450 Kuala Lumpur; tel. (3) 21645488; fax (3) 21645487; e-mail ekualalumpur@ minrelext.gov.co; Ambassador FERNANDO MARIN VALENCIA.

Croatia: 3 Jalan Menkuang, off Jalan Ru Ampang, 55000 Kuala Lumpur; tel. (3) 42535340; fax (3) 42535217; e-mail croemb@tm.net .my; Ambassador DAMIR PERINČIĆ.

Cuba: 20 Lingkungan U Thant, off Jalan U Thant, 55000 Kuala Lumpur; tel. (3) 42516808; fax (3) 42520428; e-mail malacub@po .jaring.my; Ambassador PEDRO MONZÓN BARATA.

Czech Republic: 32 Jalan Mesra, off Jalan Damai, 55000 Kuala Lumpur; tel. (3) 21427185; fax (3) 21412727; e-mail kualalumpur@ embassy.mzv.cz; internet www.mzv.cz/kualalumpur; Ambassador Dr VÍTĚZSLAV GREPL.

Denmark: POB 10908, 50728 Kuala Lumpur; tel. (3) 20322001; fax (3) 20322012; e-mail denmark@denmark.com.my; internet www .denmark.com.my; Ambassador LASSE REIMANN.

Ecuador: 8th Floor, West Block, Wisma Selangor Dredging, 142-C Jalan Ampang, 50450 Kuala Lumpur; tel. (3) 2635078; fax (3) 2635096; e-mail embecua@po.jaring.my; Chargé d'affaires a.i. Dr MARCO TULIO CORDERO ZAMORA.

Egypt: 28 Lingkungan U Thant, POB 12004, 55000 Kuala Lumpur; tel. (3) 4568184; fax (3) 4573515; e-mail egyembkl@tm.net.my; Ambassador MOHAMED AFIFI.

Fiji: Level 2, Menara Chan, 138 Jalan Ampang, 50450 Kuala Lumpur; tel. (3) 27323335; fax (3) 27327555; e-mail fhckl@pd.jaring .my; High Commissioner Adi SAMANUNU Q. TALAKULI CAKOBAU.

Finland: Wisma Chinese Chamber, 258 Jalan Ampang, POB 10909, 50728 Kuala Lumpur; tel. (3) 42577746; fax (3) 42577793; e-mail sanomat.kul@formin.fi; Ambassador UNTO JUHANI TURUNEN.

France: 196 Jalan Ampang, 50450 Kuala Lumpur; tel. (3) 20535500; fax (3) 20535501; e-mail ambassade .kuala-lumpur-amba@diplomatie.gouv.fr; internet www.france.org .my; Ambassador JACQUES LAPOUGE.

Germany: 3 Jalan U Thant, POB 10023, 50700 Kuala Lumpur; tel. (3) 21169666; fax (3) 21413943; e-mail contact@german-embassy.org .my; internet www.german-embassy.org.my; Ambassador JUERGEN A. R. STAKS.

Ghana: 14 Ampang Hilir, off Jalan Ampang, 55000 Kuala Lumpur; tel. (3) 42526995; fax (3) 42578698; e-mail ghcomkl@tm.net.my; High Commissioner JOHN BENTUM-WILLIAMS.

Guinea: 5 Jalan Kedondong, off Jalan Ampang Hilir, Kuala Lumpur; tel. (3) 42576500; fax (3) 42511500; Ambassador MAMADOU TOURÉ.

Hungary: City Square Centre, 30th Floor, Empire Tower, Jalan Tun Razak, 50400 Kuala Lumpur; tel. (3) 21637914; fax (3) 21637918; e-mail huembkl@tm.net.my; Ambassador LÁSZLÓ VÁRKONYI.

India: 2 Jalan Taman Duta, off Jalan Duta, 50480 Kuala Lumpur; tel. (3) 2533510; fax (3) 2533507; e-mail information@po.jaring.my; High Commissioner VEENA SIKRI.

Indonesia: 233 Jalan Tun Razak, POB 10889, 50400 Kuala Lumpur; tel. (3) 2452011; fax (3) 2417908; internet www.kbrikl.org .my; Ambassador HADI A. WARAYABI ALHADAR.

Iran: 1 Lorong U Thant Satu, off Jalan U Thant, 55000 Kuala Lumpur; tel. (3) 42514824; fax (3) 42562904; e-mail ir_emb@tm.net .my; Ambassador MOHAMMAD GHASEM MOHEB ALI.

Iraq: 2 Jalan Langgak Golf, off Jalan Tun Razak, 55000 Kuala Lumpur; tel. (3) 2480555; fax (3) 2414331; Ambassador ADNAN MALIK AL-GHAZALI.

Ireland: Ireland House, The Amp Walk, 218 Jalan Ampang, POB 10372, 50450 Kuala Lumpur; tel. (3) 21612963; fax (3) 21613427; e-mail ireland@po.jaring.my; Ambassador DANIEL MULHALL.

Italy: 99 Jalan U Thant, 55000 Kuala Lumpur; tel. (3) 42565122; fax (3) 42573199; e-mail embassyit@italy-embassy.org.my; internet www.italy-embassy.org.my; Ambassador ANACLETO FELICANI.

Japan: 11 Pesiaran Stonor, off Jalan Tun Razak, 50450 Kuala Lumpur; tel. (3) 21427044; fax (3) 21672314; internet www.my .emb-japan.go.jp; Ambassador MASAKI KONISHI.

Jordan: 2 Jalan Kedondong, off Jalan Ampang Hilir, 55000 Kuala Lumpur; tel. (3) 4653318; fax (3) 4653353; e-mail jorembk1@ streamyx.com; Ambassador MAZEN JUMA.

Kazakhstan: Suite 607, 6th Floor, North Block, The Amp Walk, 218 Jalan Ampang, 50540 Kuala Lumpur; tel. (3) 21664144; fax (3) 21668553; e-mail klkazemb@po.jaring.my; Ambassador BOLATKHAN K. TAIZHAN.

Kenya: Kuala Lumpur Empire Tower Unit, 38C, 38th Floor, 182 Jalan Tun Razak, 50400 Kuala Lumpur; tel. (3) 21645015; fax (3) 21645017; e-mail kenya@po.jaring.my; High Commissioner JAMES K. KARUGA.

Korea, Democratic People's Republic: 9 Jalan Madge, off Jalan U Thant, 55000 Kuala Lumpur; tel. (3) 4569913; fax (3) 4569933; Ambassador KIM WON HO.

Korea, Republic: Lot 9 and 11, Jalan Nipah, off Jalan Ampang, 55000 Kuala Lumpur; tel. (3) 4512336; fax (3) 4521425; e-mail korem-my@mofat.go.kr; Ambassador RHEE YOUNG-MIN.

Kuwait: 229 Jalan Tun Razak, 50400 Kuala Lumpur; tel. (3) 21410033; fax (3) 21426126; Ambassador SHAMLAN ABDUL AZIZ MOHAMMAD SHAMLAN AL-ROOMI.

Kyrgyzstan: 1 Lorong Damai 10, 55000 Kuala Lumpur; tel. (3) 21649862; fax (3) 21632024; e-mail kyrgyz@tm.net.my; Ambassador MAMBETJUNUS ABYLOV.

Laos: 12A Pesiaran Madge, off Jalan Ampang Hilir, 55000 Kuala Lumpur; tel. (3) 42511118; fax (3) 42510080; Ambassador CHALEUNE WARINTHRASAK.

Libya: 6 Jalan Madge, off Jalan U Thant, 55000 Kuala Lumpur; tel. (3) 21411035; fax (3) 21413549; Chargé d'affaires a.i. (vacant).

Luxembourg: Menara Keck Seng Bldg, 16th Floor, 203 Jalan Bukit Bintang, 55100 Kuala Lumpur; tel. (3) 21433134; fax (3) 21433157;

e-mail emluxem@po.jaring.my; Chargé d'affaires a.i. CHARLES SCHMIT.

Mauritius: Lot W17-B1 and C1, 17th Floor, West Block, Wisma Selangor Dredging, Jalan Ampang, 50450 Kuala Lumpur; tel. (3) 21636306; fax (3) 21636294; e-mail maur@tm.net.my; High Commissioner S. K. S. DUSOWOTH.

Mexico: Menara Tan & Tan, 22nd Floor, 207 Jalan Tun Razak, 50400 Kuala Lumpur; tel. (3) 21646362; fax (3) 21640964; e-mail embamex@po.jaring.my; internet www.embamex.org.my; Ambassador ALFREDO PÉREZ BRAVO.

Morocco: Wisma Selangor Dredging, 3rd Floor, East Block, 142B Jalan Ampang, 50450 Kuala Lumpur; tel. (3) 21610701; fax (3) 21623081; e-mail sifmakl@po.jaring.my; Ambassador BADR EDDINE ALLALI.

Myanmar: 10 Jalan Mengkuang, off Jalan Ru, 55000 Kuala Lumpur; tel. (3) 4560280; fax (3) 4568320; e-mail mekl@tm.net.my; Ambassador U HLA MAUNG.

Namibia: 11 Jalan Mesra, off Jalan Damai, 55000 Kuala Lumpur; tel. (3) 2433595; fax (3) 2417803; e-mail namhckl@po.jaring.my; High Commissioner NDEUTAPO AMAGULU.

Netherlands: The Amp Walk, 7th Floor, 218 Jalan Ampang, POB 10543, 50450 Kuala Lumpur; tel. (3) 21686200; fax (3) 21686240; e-mail nlgovkl@netherlands.org.my; internet www.netherlands.org.my; Ambassador J. C. F. VON MÜHLEN.

New Zealand: Menara IMC, 21st Floor, 8 Jalan Sultan Ismail, 50250 Kuala Lumpur; tel. (3) 20782533; fax (3) 20780387; e-mail nzhckl@po.jaring.my; High Commissioner DAVID PINE; (acting).

Nigeria: 85 Jalan Ampang Hilir, 55000 Kuala Lumpur; tel. (3) 42517843; e-mail nighcomm@tm.net.my; High Commissioner IBRAHIM YARIMA ABDULLAH.

Norway: Suite CD, 53rd Floor, Empire Tower, Jalan Tun Razak, 50400 Kuala Lumpur; tel. (3) 21637100; fax (3) 21637108; e-mail emb.kualalumpur@mfa.no; Ambassador ARILD EIK.

Oman: 6 Jalan Langgak Golf, off Jalan Tun Razak, 55000 Kuala Lumpur; tel. (3) 21452827; fax (3) 21452826; e-mail omanemb@jaring.my; Ambassador Sheikh GHAZI BIN SAID BIN ABDULLAH AL BAHR AL RAWAS.

Pakistan: 132 Jalan Ampang, 50450 Kuala Lumpur; tel. (3) 21618877; fax (3) 21645958; e-mail parepklumpur@po.jaring.my; internet www3.jaring.my/pakistanhc/; High Commissioner Gen. (retd) NASIM RANA.

Papua New Guinea: 46 Jalan U Thant, 55000 Kuala Lumpur; tel. (3) 42532400; fax (3) 42532411; e-mail pnghckl@tm.net.my; High Commissioner EMILY DAVID (acting).

Peru: Wisma Selangor Dredging, 6th Floor, South Block 142-A, Jalan Ampang, 50450 Kuala Lumpur; tel. (3) 21633034; fax (3) 21633039; e-mail info@embperu.com.my; internet www.embperu.com.my; Ambassador JAVIER GONZALES.

Philippines: 1 Changkat Kia Peng, 50450 Kuala Lumpur; tel. (3) 21484233; fax (3) 21483576; e-mail philgov@tm.net.my; internet www.philembassykl.org.my; Chargé d'affaires a.i. NORBERTO R. BASILIO.

Poland: 495 Bt 4½ Jalan Ampang, 68000 Ampang; tel. (3) 42576733; fax (3) 42570123; e-mail polamba@tm.net.my; Ambassador MAREK PASZUCHA.

Romania: 114 Jalan Damai, off Jalan Ampang, 55000 Kuala Lumpur; tel. (3) 21423172; fax (3) 21448713; e-mail romemb@tm.net.my; Chargé d'affaires a.i. DRAGOS SERBANESCU.

Russia: 263 Jalan Ampang, 50450 Kuala Lumpur; tel. (3) 42567252; fax (3) 42576091; e-mail consulrf@tm.net.my; Ambassador VLADIMIR NIKOLAEVICH MOROZOV.

Saudi Arabia: 7 Jalan Kedondong, off Jalan Ampang, POB 12002, 55000 Kuala Lumpur; tel. (3) 42579433; fax (3) 42578751; e-mail myemb@mofa.gov.sa; Ambassador HAMED MOHAMMED YAHYA.

Seychelles: 2nd Floor, 50 Jalan SS 19/1D, Subang Jaya, 47500 Petaling Jaya, Selangor Darul Ehsan; tel. (3) 7389881; fax (3) 7380108; e-mail seyhicom@po.jaring.my; High Commissioner LOUIS SYLVESTRE RADEGONDE.

Singapore: 209 Jalan Tun Razak, 50400 Kuala Lumpur; tel. (3) 21616277; fax (3) 21616343; e-mail shckl@po.jaring.my; internet www.mfa.gov.sg/kl; High Commissioner ASHOK KUMAR MIRPURI.

South Africa: 12 Lorong Titiwangsa, Taman Tasik Titiwangsa, Setapak, 53200 Kuala Lumpur; tel. (3) 40244456; fax (3) 40249896; e-mail sahcpol@tm.net.my; internet www.afrikaselatan.com; High Commissioner Dr ABRAHAM SOKHAYA NKOMO.

Spain: 200 Jalan Ampang, 50450 Kuala Lumpur; tel. (3) 21484868; fax (3) 21424582; e-mail embespmy@mail.mae.es; Ambassador ALVARO IRANZO GUTIÉRREZ.

Sri Lanka: 116 Jalan Damai, off Jalan Ampang, 55000 Kuala Lumpur; tel. (3) 21612199; fax (3) 21612219; e-mail slhicom@putra.net.my; internet www.kuala-lumpur.mission.gov.lk; High Commissioner DAYACHANDRA YASASIRI LIYANAGE.

Sudan: 2A Persiaran Ampang, off Jalan Ru, 55000 Kuala Lumpur; tel. (3) 42569104; fax (3) 42568107; e-mail sudanikuala@hotmail.com; Ambassador MOHAMED ADAM ISMAIL.

Swaziland: Suite 22.03 and 03 (A), Menara Citibank, 165 Jalan Ampang, 50450 Kuala Lumpur; tel. (3) 21632511; fax (3) 21633326; e-mail swazi@tm.net.my; High Commissioner MABILI D. DLAMIMI.

Sweden: Wisma Angkasa Raya, 6th Floor, 123 Jalan Ampang, POB 10239, 50708 Kuala Lumpur; tel. (3) 21485433; fax (3) 21486325; e-mail ambassaden.kuala-lumpur@foreign.ministry.se; internet www.embassyofswedenmy.org; Ambassador BRUNO BEIJER.

Switzerland: 16 Persiaran Madge, 55000 Kuala Lumpur; tel. (3) 21480622; fax (3) 21480935; e-mail vertretung@kua.rep.admin.ch; Ambassador Dr PETER A. SCHWEIZER.

Thailand: 206 Jalan Ampang, 50450 Kuala Lumpur; tel. (3) 21488222; fax (3) 21486527; e-mail thaikul@mfa.go.th; Ambassador CHAISIRI ANAMARN.

Turkey: 118 Jalan U Thant, 55000 Kuala Lumpur; tel. (3) 42572225; fax (3) 42572227; e-mail turkbe@tmnet.my; Ambassador KORAY TARGAY.

United Arab Emirates: 1 Gerbang Ampang Hilir, off Persiaran Ampang Hilir, 55000 Kuala Lumpur; tel. (3) 42535221; fax (3) 42535220; Ambassador MOHAMMED ALI AL-OSAIMI.

United Kingdom: 185 Jalan Ampang, 50450 Kuala Lumpur; POB 11030, 50732 Kuala Lumpur; tel. (3) 21702200; fax (3) 21442370; e-mail political.kualalumpur@fco.gov.uk; internet www.britain.org.my; High Commissioner BRUCE CLEGHORN.

USA: 376 Jalan Tun Razak, POB 10035, 50700 Kuala Lumpur; tel. (3) 21685000; fax (3) 21422207; internet www.usembassymalaysia.org.my; Ambassador MARIE T. HUHTALA.

Uruguay: 6 Jalan 3, Taman Tun Abdul Razak, 68000 Ampang, Selangor Darul Bhsan; tel. (3) 42518831; fax (3) 42517878; e-mail urukual@po.jaring.my; Ambassador ROBERTO PABLO TOURINO TURNES.

Uzbekistan: Suite 6.03, 6th Floor, North Block, The Amp Walk, 218 Jalan Ampang, 50450 Kuala Lumpur; tel. (3) 21618100; fax (3) 21618102.

Venezuela: Suite 603, 6th Floor, Wisma MCA, 163 Jalan Ampang, 50450 Kuala Lumpur; tel. (3) 21633444; fax (3) 21636819; e-mail venezuela@po.jaring.my; internet www.venezuela.org.my; Ambassador Maj.-Gen. (retd) NOEL ENRIQUE MARTÍNEZ OCHOA.

Viet Nam: 4 Pesiaran Stonor, 50450 Kuala Lumpur; tel. (3) 2484036; fax (3) 2483270; e-mail daisevn@putra.net.my; Ambassador TRAN TRONG TOAN.

Yemen: 6 Jalan Kedondong, off Jalan Ampang Hilir, 55000 Kuala Lumpur; tel. (3) 42511793; fax (3) 42511794; Ambassador MOHAMED TAHA MUSTAFA.

Zimbabwe: 124 Jalan Sembilan, Taman Ampang Utama, 68000 Ampang, Selangor Darul Ehsan; tel. (3) 4516779; fax (3) 4516782; High Commissioner CHITSAKA CHIPAZIWA.

Judicial System

The two High Courts, one in Peninsular Malaysia and the other in Sabah and Sarawak, have original, appellate and revisional jurisdiction as the federal law provides. Above these two High Courts is the Court of Appeal, which was established in 1994; it is an intermediary court between the Federal Court and the High Court. When appeals to the Privy Council in the United Kingdom were abolished in 1985 the former Supreme Court became the final court of appeal. Therefore, at that stage only one appeal was available to a party aggrieved by the decision of the High Court. Hence, the establishment of the Court of Appeal. The Federal Court (formerly the Supreme Court) has, to the exclusion of any other court, jurisdiction in any dispute between states or between the Federation and any state; and has special jurisdiction as to the interpretation of the Constitution. The Federal Court is headed by the Chief Justice (formerly the Lord President); the other members of the Federal Court are the President of the Court of Appeal, the two Chief Judges of the High Courts and the Federal Court Judges. Members of the Court of Appeal are the President and the Court of Appeal judges, and members of the High Courts are the two Chief Judges and their respective High Court judges. All judges are appointed by the Yang di-Pertuan Agong on the advice of the Prime Minister, after consulting the Conference of Rulers. In 1993 a Special Court was established to hear cases brought by or against the Yang di-Pertuan Agong or a Ruler of State (Sultans).

The Sessions Courts, which are situated in the principal urban and rural centres, are presided over by a Sessions Judge, who is a member of the Judicial and Legal Service of the Federation and is a qualified barrister or a Bachelor of Law from any of the recognized universities. Their criminal jurisdiction covers the less serious indictable offences, excluding those that carry the death penalty. Civil jurisdiction of a Sessions Court is up to RM 250,000. The Sessions Judges are appointed by the Yang di-Pertuan Agong.

The Magistrates' Courts are also found in the main urban and rural centres and have both civil and criminal jurisdiction, although of a more restricted nature than that of the Sessions Courts. The Magistrates consist of officers from the Judicial and Legal Service of the Federation. They are appointed by the State Authority in which they officiate on the recommendation of the Chief Judge.

There are also Syariah (Shariah) courts for rulings under Islamic law. In July 1996 the Cabinet announced that the Syariah courts were to be restructured with the appointment of a Syariah Chief Judge and four Court of Appeal justices, whose rulings would set precedents for the whole country.

Prior to February 1995 trials for murder and kidnapping in the High Courts were heard with jury and assessors, respectively. The amendment to the Criminal Procedure Code abolished both the jury and the assessors systems, and all criminal trials in the High Courts are heard by a judge sitting alone. In 1988 an amendment to the Constitution empowered any federal lawyer to confer with the Attorney-General to determine the courts in which any proceedings, excluding those before a Syariah court, a native court or a court martial, be instituted, or to which such proceedings be transferred.

Federal Court of Malaysia

Bangunan Sultan Abdul Samad, Jalan Raja, 50506 Kuala Lumpur; tel. (3) 26939011; fax (3) 26932582; internet www.kehakiman.gov.my.

Chief Justice of the Federal Court: Tan Sri Dato' Sri AHMAD FAIRUZ BIN Dato' Sheikh ABDUL HALIM.

President of the Court of Appeal: (vacant).

Chief Judge of the High Court in Peninsular Malaysia: Dato' HAIDAR BIN MOHAMED NOOR.

Chief Judge of the High Court in Sabah and Sarawak: Datuk STEVE SHIP LIM KIONG.

Attorney-General: ABDUL GANI PATAIL.

Religion

Islam is the established religion but freedom of religious practice is guaranteed. Almost all ethnic Malays are Muslims, representing 53% of the total population in 1985. In Peninsular Malaysia 19% followed Buddhism (19% in Sarawak and 8% in Sabah), 7% were Christians (29% in Sarawak and 24% in Sabah), and Chinese faiths, including Confucianism and Daoism, were followed by 11.6%. Sikhs and other religions accounted for 0.5%, while 2%, mostly in Sabah and Sarawak, were animists.

Malaysian Consultative Council of Buddhism, Christianity, Hinduism and Sikhism (MCCBCHS): 8 Jalan Duku, off Jalan Kasipillai, 51200 Kuala Lumpur; tel. (3) 40414669; fax (3) 40444304; e-mail hsangam@po.jaring.my; f. 1981; a non-Muslim group.

ISLAM

President of the Majlis Islam: Datuk Haji MOHD FAUZI BIN Haji ABDUL HAMID (Kuching, Sarawak).

Jabatan Kemajuan Islam Malaysia (JAKIM) (Department of Islamic Development Malaysia): Aras 4–9, Block D7, Pusat Pentadbiran Persekutuan, 62502 Putrajaya; tel. (3) 88864000; e-mail faizal@islam.gov.my; internet www.islam.gov.my.

Istitut Kefahaman Islam Malaysia (IKIM) (Institute of Islamic Understanding Malaysia): 2 Langgak Tunku, off Jalan Duta, 50480 Kuala Lumpur; tel. (3) 62010889; fax (3) 62014189; internet www.ikim.gov.my.

BUDDHISM

Malaysian Buddhist Association (MBA): MBA Building, 113, 3¼ Miles, Jalan Klang, 58000 Kuala Lumpur; tel. (3) 7815595; e-mail mbapg@po.jaring.my; internet www.jaring.my/mba; f. 1959; the national body for Chinese-speaking monks and nuns and temples from the Mahayana tradition; Pres. Venerable CHEK HUANG.

Young Buddhist Association of Malaysia (YBAM): 10 Jalan SS2/75, 47300 Petaling Jaya, Selangor; tel. (3) 78764591; fax (3) 78762770; e-mail ybamhq@po.jaring.my; internet www.ybam.org.my; f. 1970.

Buddhist Missionary Society Malaysia (BMSM): 123 Jalan Berhala, off Jalan Tun Sambanthan, 50470 Brickfields, Kuala Lumpur; tel. (3) 22730150; fax (3) 22740245; e-mail president@bmsm.org.my; internet www.bmsm.org.my; f. 1962 as Buddhist Missionary Society; Pres. ANG CHOO HONG.

Malaysian Fo Kuang Buddhist Association: 2 Jalan SS3/33, Taman University, 47300 Petaling Jaya, Selangor.

Buddhist Tzu-Chi Merit Society (Malaysia): 24 Jesselton Ave, 10450 Pinang; e-mail mtzuchi@po.jaring.my; internet www.tzuchi.org.my.

Sasana Abhiwurdhi Wardhana Society: 123 Jalan Berhala, off Jalan Tun Sambanthan, 50490 Kuala Lumpur; f. 1894; the national body for Sri Lankan Buddhists belonging to the Theravada tradition.

CHRISTIANITY

Majlis Gereja-Gereja Malaysia (Council of Churches of Malaysia): 26 Jalan Universiti, 46200 Petaling Jaya, Selangor; tel. (3) 7567092; fax (3) 7560353; e-mail cchurchm@tm.net.my; internet www.ccmalaysia.org; f. 1947; 16 mem. churches; 8 associate mems; Pres. Most Rev. Datuk YONG PING CHUNG (Anglican Bishop of Sabah); Gen. Sec. Rev. Dr HERMEN SHASTRI.

The Anglican Communion
Malaysia comprises three Anglican dioceses, within the Church of the Province of South East Asia.

Primate: Most Rev. Datuk YONG PING CHUNG (Bishop of Sabah).

Bishop of Kuching: Rt Rev. MADE KATIB, Bishop's House, POB 347, 93704 Kuching, Sarawak; tel. (82) 240187; fax (82) 426488; e-mail bkg@pc.jaring.my; has jurisdiction over Sarawak, Brunei and part of Indonesian Kalimantan (Borneo).

Bishop of Sabah: Most Rev. Datuk YONG PING CHUNG, Rumah Bishop, Jalan Tangki, POB 10811, 88809 Kota Kinabalu, Sabah; tel. (88) 247008; fax (88) 245942; e-mail pcyong@pc.jaring.my.

Bishop of West Malaysia: Rt. Rev. Tan Sri Dr LIM CHENG EAN, Bishop's House, 14 Pesiaran Stonor, 50450 Kuala Lumpur; tel. (3) 20312728; fax (3) 20313225; e-mail diocese@tm.net.my.

The Baptist Church

Malaysia Baptist Convention: 2 Jalan 2/38, 46000 Petaling Jaya, Selangor; tel. (3) 77823564; fax (3) 77833603; e-mail mbcpj@tm.net.my; Chair. Dr TAN ENG LEE.

The Methodist Church

Methodist Church in Malaysia: 69 Jalan 5/31, 46000 Petaling Jaya, Selangor; tel. (3) 79541811; fax (3) 79541788; e-mail methmas@tm.net; 140,000 mems; Bishop Dr PETER CHIO SING CHING.

The Presbyterian Church

Presbyterian Church in Malaysia: Joyful Grace Church, Jalan Alsagoff, 82000 Pontian, Johor; tel. (7) 711390; fax (7) 324384; Pastor TITUS KIM KAH TECK.

The Roman Catholic Church
Malaysia comprises two archdioceses and six dioceses. At 31 December 2000 approximately 3.3% of the population were adherents.

Catholic Bishops' Conference of Malaysia, Singapore and Brunei
Xavier Hall, 133 Jalan Gasing, 46000 Petaling Jaya, Selangor; tel. and fax (3) 79581371; e-mail cbcmsb@pc.jaring.my.

Pres. Most Rev. A. SOTER FERNANDEZ (Archbishop of Kuala Lumpur).

Archbishop of Kuala Lumpur: Most Rev. ANTHONY SOTER FERNANDEZ, Archbishop's House, 528 Jalan Bukit Nanas, 50250 Kuala Lumpur; tel. (3) 2388828; fax (3) 2013815; e-mail archbishop@archway.org.my.

Archbishop of Kuching: Most Rev. PETER CHUNG HOAN TING, Archbishop's Office, 118 Jalan Tun Abang Haji Openg, POB 940, 93718 Kuching, Sarawak; tel. (82) 242634; fax (82) 425724.

BAHÁ'Í FAITH

Spiritual Assembly of the Bahá'ís of Malaysia: 4 Lorong Titiwangsa 5, off Jalan Pahang, 53200 Kuala Lumpur; tel. (3) 40235183; fax (3) 40226277; e-mail nsa-sec@bahai.org.my; internet www.bahai.org.my; mems resident in 800 localities.

The Press

PENINSULAR MALAYSIA DAILIES

English Language

Business Times: Balai Berita 31, Jalan Riong, 59100 Kuala Lumpur; tel. (3) 2822628; fax (3) 2825424; e-mail bt@nstp.com.my; internet www.btimes.com.my; f. 1976; morning; Editor HARDEV KAUR; circ. 15,000.

Malay Mail: Balai Berita 31, Jalan Riong, 59100 Kuala Lumpur; tel. (3) 2822829; fax (3) 2821434; e-mail malaymail@nstp.com.my; internet www.malaymail.com.my; f. 1896; afternoon; Editor FAUZI OMAR; circ. 75,000.

Malaysiakini: 2–4 Jalan Bangsa-Utang 9, 59000 Kuala Lumpur; tel. (3) 22835567; fax (3) 22892579; e-mail editor@malaysiakini.com; internet www.malaysiakini.com; Malaysia's first on-line newspaper; English and Malay; Editor STEVEN GAN.

New Straits Times: Balai Berita 31, Jalan Riong, 59100 Kuala Lumpur; tel. (3) 2823322; fax (3) 2821434; e-mail mishar@nstp.com.my; internet www.nstpi.com.my; f. 1845; morning; Exec. Dir ABDULLAH AHMAD; Group Editor (vacant); circ. 190,000.

The Edge: G501–G801, Levels 5–8, Block G, Phileo Damansara I, Jalan 16/11, off Jalan Damansara, 46350 Petaling Jaya, Selangor; tel. (3) 76603838; fax (3) 76608638; e-mail eeditor@bizedge.com; internet www.theedgedaily.com; f. 1996; weekly, with daily internet edition; business and investment news.

The Star: 13 Jalan 13/6, 46200 Petaling Jaya, POB 12474, Selangor; tel. (3) 7581188; fax (3) 7551280; e-mail msd@thestar.com.my; internet www.thestar.com.my; f. 1971; morning; Group Chief Editor NG POH TIP; circ. 192,059.

The Sun: Sun Media Corpn Sdn Bhd, Lot 6, Jalan 51/217, Section 51, 46050 Petaling Jaya, Selangor Darul Ehsan; tel. (3) 7946688; fax (3) 7952624; e-mail editor@sunmg.po.my; f. 1993; Editor-in-Chief HO KAY TAT; Man. Dir TAN BOON KEAN; circ. 82,474.

Chinese Language

China Press: 80 Jalan Riong, 59100 Kuala Lumpur; tel. (3) 2828208; fax (3) 2825327; circ. 206,000.

Chung Kuo Pao (China Press): 80 Jalan Riong, 59100 Kuala Lumpur; tel. (3) 2828208; fax (3) 2825327; f. 1946; Editor POON CHAU HUAY; Gen. Man. NG BENG LYE; circ. 210,000.

Guang Ming Daily: 19 Jalan Semangat, 46200 Petaling Jaya, Selangor; tel. (3) 7582888; fax (3) 7575135; circ. 87,144.

Kwong Wah Yit Poh: 19 Jalan Presgrave, 10300 Pinang; tel. (4) 2612312; fax (4) 2615407; e-mail editor@kwongwah.com.my; internet www.kwongwah.com.my; f. 1910; morning; Chief Editor TAN AYE CHOO; circ. 72,158.

Nanyang Siang Pau (Malaysia): 1 Jalan SS7/2, 47301 Petaling Jaya, Selangor; tel. (3) 78776000; fax (3) 78776855; e-mail editor@nanyang.com.my; internet www.nanyang.com.my; f. 1923; morning and evening; Editor-in-Chief WONG KAM HOR; circ. 185,000 (daily), 223,000 (Sunday).

Shin Min Daily News: 31 Jalan Riong, Bangsar, 59100 Kuala Lumpur; tel. (3) 2826363; fax (3) 2821812; f. 1966; morning; Editor-in-Chief CHENG SONG HUAT; circ. 82,000.

Sin Chew Jit Poh (Malaysia): 19 Jalan Semangat, POB 367, Jalan Sultan, 46200 Petaling Jaya, Selangor; tel. (3) 7582888; fax (3) 7570527; internet www.sinchew-i.com; f. 1929; morning; Chief Editor LIEW CHEN CHUAN; circ. 227,067 (daily), 230,000 (Sunday).

Malay Language

Berita Harian: Balai Berita 31, Jalan Riong, 59100 Kuala Lumpur; tel. (3) 2822323; fax (3) 2822425; e-mail bharian@bharian.com.my; internet www.bharian.com.my; f. 1957; morning; Group Editor AHMAD REJAL ARBEE; circ. 350,000.

Metro Ahad: Balai Berita 31, Jalan Riong, 59100 Kuala Lumpur; tel. (3) 2822328; fax (3) 2824482; e-mail metahad@nstp.com.my; internet www.metroahad.com.my; circ. 132,195.

Mingguan Perdana: 48 Jalan Siput Akek, Taman Billion, Kuala Lumpur; tel. (3) 619133; Group Chief Editor KHALID JAFRI.

Utusan Malaysia: 46M Jalan Lima, off Jalan Chan Sow Lin, 55200 Kuala Lumpur; tel. (3) 2217055; fax (3) 2220911; e-mail corpcomm@utusan.com.my; internet www.utusan.com.my; Editor-in-Chief (vacant).

Watan: 23–1 Jalan 9A/55A, Taman Setiawangsa, 54200 Kuala Lumpur; tel. (3) 4523040; fax (3) 4523043; circ. 80,000.

Tamil Language

Malaysia Nanban: 11 Jalan Murai Dua, Batu Kompleks, off Jalan Ipoh, 51200 Kuala Lumpur; tel. (3) 6212251; fax (3) 6235981; circ. 45,000.

Tamil Nesan: 28 Jalan Yew, Pudu, 55100 Kuala Lumpur; tel. (3) 2216411; fax (3) 2210448; f. 1924; morning; Editor V. VIVEKANANTHAN; circ. 35,000 (daily), 60,000 (Sunday).

Tamil Osai: 19 Jalan Murai Dua, Batu Kompleks, Jalan Ipoh, Kuala Lumpur; tel. (3) 671644; circ. 21,000 (daily), 40,000 (Sunday).

Tamil Thinamani: 9 Jalan Murai Dua, Batu Kompleks, Jalan Ipoh, Kuala Lumpur; tel. (3) 66719; Editor S. NACHIAPPAN; circ. 18,000 (daily), 39,000 (Sunday).

SUNDAY PAPERS

English Language

New Sunday Times: Balai Berita 31, Jalan Riong, 59100 Kuala Lumpur; tel. (3) 2822328; fax (3) 2824482; e-mail news@nstp.com.my; f. 1932; morning; Group Editor (vacant); circ. 191,562.

Sunday Mail: Balai Berita 31, Jalan Riong, 59100 Kuala Lumpur; tel. (3) 2822328; fax (3) 2824482; e-mail smail@nstp.com.my; f. 1896; morning; Editor JOACHIM S. P. NG; circ. 75,641.

Sunday Star: 13 Jalan 13/6, 46200 Petaling Jaya, POB 12474, Selangor Darul Ehsan; tel. (3) 7581188; fax (3) 7551280; f. 1971; Editor DAVID YEOH; circ. 232,790.

Malay Language

Berita Minggu: Balai Berita 31, Jalan Riong, 59100 Kuala Lumpur; tel. (3) 2822328; fax (3) 2824482; e-mail bharian@bharian.com.my; f. 1957; morning; Editor Dato' AHMAD NAZRI ABDULLAH; circ. 421,127.

Mingguan Malaysia: 11A The Right Angle, Jalan 14/22, 46100 Petaling Jaya; tel. (3) 7563355; fax (3) 7577755; f. 1964; Editor-in-Chief JOHAN JAAFAR; circ. 493,523.

Utusan Zaman: 11A The Right Angle, Jalan 14/22, 46100 Petaling Jaya; tel. (3) 7563355; fax (3) 7577755; f. 1939; Editor MUSTAFA FADULA SUHAIMI; circ. 11,782.

Tamil Language

Makkal Osai: 11 Jalan Murai Dua, Batu Kompleks, off Jalan Ipoh, 51200 Kuala Lumpur; tel. (3) 6212251; fax (3) 6235981; circ. 28,000.

PERIODICALS

English Language

Her World: Berita Publishing Sdn Bhd, Balai Berita, 31 Jalan Riong, 59100 Kuala Lumpur; tel. (3) 2824322; fax (3) 2828489; monthly; Editor ALICE CHEE LAN NEO; circ. 35,000.

Malaysia Warta Kerajaan Seri Paduka Baginda (HM Government Gazette): Percetakan Nasional Malaysia Berhad, Jalan Chan Sow Lin, 50554 Kuala Lumpur; tel. (3) 92212022; fax (3) 92220690; e-mail pnmb@po.jaring.my; fortnightly.

Malaysian Agricultural Journal: Ministry of Agriculture, Publications Unit, Wisma Tani, Jalan Sultan Salahuddin, 50624 Kuala Lumpur; tel. (3) 2982011; fax (3) 2913758; f. 1901; 2 a year.

Malaysian Forester: Forestry Department Headquarters, Jalan Sultan Salahuddin, 50660 Kuala Lumpur; tel. (3) 26988244; fax (3) 26925657; e-mail skthai@forestry.gov.my; f. 1931; quarterly; Editor THAI SEE KIAM.

The Planter: Wisma ISP, 29–33 Jalan Taman U Thant, POB 10262, 50708 Kuala Lumpur; tel. (3) 21425561; fax (3) 21426898; e-mail isphq@tm.net.my; internet www.isp.org.my; f. 1919; publ. by Isp Management (M); monthly; Editor W. T. PERERA; circ. 4,000.

Young Generation: 11A The Right Angle, Jalan 14/22, 46100 Petaling Jaya, Selangor; tel. (3) 7563355; fax (3) 7577755; monthly; circ. 50,000.

Chinese Language

Mister Weekly: 2A Jalan 19/1, 46300 Petaling Jaya, Selangor; tel. (3) 7562400; fax (3) 7553826; f. 1976; weekly; Editor WONG AH TAI; circ. 25,000.

Mun Sang Poh: 472 Jalan Pasir Puteh, 31650 Ipoh; tel. (5) 3212919; fax (5) 3214006; bi-weekly; circ. 77,958.

New Life Post: 80M Jalan SS21/39, Damansara Utama, 47400 Petaling Jaya, Selangor; tel. (3) 7571833; fax (3) 7181809; f. 1972; bi-weekly; Editor LOW BENG CHEE; circ. 231,000.

New Tide Magazine: Nanyang Siang Pau Bldg, 2nd Floor, Jalan 7/2, 47301 Petaling Jaya, Selangor; tel. (3) 76202118; fax (3)

76202131; e-mail newtidemag@hotmail.com; f. 1974; monthly; Editor NELLIE OOI; circ. 39,000.

Malay Language

Dewan Masyarakat: Dewan Bahasa dan Pustaka, POB 10803, 50926 Kuala Lumpur; tel. (3) 2481011; fax (3) 2484211; f. 1963; monthly; current affairs; Editor ZULKIFLI SALLEH; circ. 48,500.

Dewan Pelajar: Dewan Bahasa dan Pustaka, Jalan Wisma Putra, POB 10803, 50926 Kuala Lumpur; tel. (3) 2481011; fax (3) 2484211; f. 1967; monthly; children's; Editor ZALEHA HASHIM; circ. 100,000.

Dewan Siswa: POB 10803, 50926 Kuala Lumpur; tel. (3) 2481011; fax (3) 2484208; monthly; circ. 140,000.

Gila-Gila: 38-1, Jalan Bangsar Utama Satu, Bangsar Utama, 59000 Kuala Lumpur; tel. (3) 22824970; fax (3) 22824967; fortnightly; circ. 70,000.

Harakah: Jabatan Penerangan dan Penyelidikan PAS, 28A Jalan Pahang Barat, Off Jalan Pahang, 53000 Kuala Lumpur; tel. (3) 40213343; fax (3) 40212422; e-mail hrkh@pc.jaring.my; internet www.harakahdaily.com; two a month; Malay; organ of the Parti Islam se Malaysia (PAS—Islamic Party of Malaysia); Editor ZULKIFLI SULONG.

Jelita: Berita Publishing Sdn Bhd, 16–20 Jalan 4/109E, Desa Business Park, Taman Desa, off Jalan Klang Lama, 58100 Kuala Lumpur; tel. (3) 7620811; fax (3) 76208015; e-mail jelita@com.my; internet www.jelita.com.my; monthly; fashion and beauty magazine; Editor ROHANI PA' WAN CHIK; circ. 80,000.

Mangga: 11A The Right Angle, Jalan 14/22, 46100 Petaling Jaya, Selangor; tel. (3) 7563355; fax (3) 7577755; monthly; circ. 205,000.

Mastika: 11A The Right Angle, Jalan 14/22, 46100 Petaling Jaya, Selangor; tel. (3) 7363355; fax (3) 7577755; monthly; Malayan illustrated magazine; Editor AZIZAH ALI; circ. 15,000.

Utusan Radio dan TV: 11A The Right Angle, Jalan 14/22, 46100 Petaling Jaya, Selangor; tel. (3) 7363355; fax (3) 7577755; fortnightly; Editor NORSHAH TAMBY; circ. 115,000.

Wanita: 11A The Right Angle, Jalan 14/22, 46100 Petaling Jaya, Selangor; tel. (3) 7563355; fax (3) 7577755; monthly; women; Editor NIK RAHIMAH HASSAN; circ. 85,000.

Punjabi Language

Navjiwan Punjabi News: 52 Jalan 8/18, Jalan Toman, Petaling Jaya, 46050 Selangor; tel. (3) 7565725; f. 1950; weekly; Assoc. Editor TARA SINGH; circ. 9,000.

SABAH DAILIES

Api Siang Pau (Kota Kinabalu Commercial Press): 24 Lorong Dewan, POB 170, Kota Kinabalu; f. 1954; morning; Chinese; Editor Datuk LO KWOCK CHUEN; circ. 3,000.

Borneo Mail (Nountan Press Sdn Bhd): 1 Jalan Bakau, 1st Floor, off Jalan Gaya, 88999 Kota Kinabulu; tel. (88) 238001; fax (88) 238002; English; circ. 14,610.

Daily Express: News House, 16 Jalan Pasar Baru, POB 10139, 88801 Kota Kinabalu; tel. (88) 256422; fax (88) 238611; e-mail sph@tm.net.my; internet www.dailyexpress.com.my; f. 1963; morning; English, Bahasa Malaysia and Kadazan; Editor-in-Chief SARDATHISA JAMES; circ. 30,000.

Hwa Chiaw Jit Pao (Overseas Chinese Daily News): News House, 16 Jalan Pasar Baru, POB 10139, 88801 Kota Kinabalu; tel. (88) 256422; e-mail sph@tm.net.my; internet www.dailyexpress.com.my; f. 1936; morning; Chinese; Editor HII YUK SENG; circ. 30,000.

Merdeka Daily News: Lot 56, BDC Estate, Mile 1½ North Road, POB 332, 90703 Sandakan; tel. (89) 214517; fax (89) 275537; e-mail merkk@tm.net.my; f. 1968; morning; Chinese; Editor-in-Chief FUNG KON SHING; circ. 8,000.

New Sabah Times: Jalan Pusat Pembangunan Masyarakat, off Jalan Mat Salleh, 88100 Kota Kinabalu; POB 20119, 88758 Kota Kinabalu; tel. (88) 230055; fax (88) 241155; internet www.newsabahtimes.com.my; English, Malay and Kadazan; Editor-in-Chief EDDY LOK; circ. 30,000.

Syarikat Sabah Times: Kota Kinabalu; tel. (88) 52217; f. 1952; English, Malay and Kadazan; circ. 25,000.

Tawau Jih Pao: POB 464, 1072 Jalan Kuhara, Tawau; tel. (89) 72576; Chinese; Editor-in-Chief STEPHEN LAI KIM YEAN.

SARAWAK DAILIES

Berita Petang Sarawak: Lot 8322, Lorong 7, Jalan Tun Abdul Razak, 93450 Kuching; POB 1315, 93726 Kuching; tel. (82) 480771; fax (82) 489006; f. 1972; evening; Chinese; Chief Editor HWANG YU CHAI; circ. 12,000.

Borneo Post: 40 Jalan Tuanku Osman, POB 20, 96000 Sibu; tel. (84) 332055; fax (84) 321255; internet www.borneopost.com.my; morning; English; Man. Dir LAU HUI SIONG; Editor NGUOI HOW YIENG; circ. 60,000.

Chinese Daily News: Lot 164–165, Jalan Sungei Padungan, Kuching; tel. (82) 233888; fax (82) 233399; internet www.chinesedaily.com.my; f. 1945; Chinese; Editor T. T. CHOW; circ. 10,406.

International Times: Lot 2215, Jalan Bengkel, Pending Industrial Estate, POB 1158, 93724 Kuching; tel. (82) 482215; fax (82) 480996; e-mail news@intimes.com; internet www.intimes.com.my; f. 1968; morning; Chinese; Editor LEE FOOK ONN; circ. 37,000.

Malaysia Daily News: 7 Island Rd, POB 237, 96009 Sibu; tel. (84) 330211; tel. (84) 320540; f. 1968; morning; Chinese; Editor WONG SENG KWONG; circ. 22,735.

Miri Daily News: Lot 88, Piasau Industrial Estate, POB 377, 98007 Miri; tel. (85) 656666; fax (85) 655655; internet www.miridaily.com.my; f. 1957; morning; Chinese; Editor KU KIANG FAH; Man. HWANG JUN HIEN; circ. 22,431.

Sarawak Tribune and Sunday Tribune: Lot 231, Jalan Nipah, off Jalan Abell, 93100 Kuching; tel. (82) 424411; fax (82) 420358; internet www.jaring.my/tribune; f. 1945; English; Editor FRANCIS SIAH; circ. 29,598.

See Hua Daily News: 40 Jalan Tuanku Osman, POB 20, 96000 Sibu; tel. (84) 332055; fax (84) 321255; f. 1952; morning; Chinese; Man. Editor LAU HUI SIONG; circ. 80,000.

PERIODICALS

Pedoman Rakyat: Malaysian Information Dept, Mosque Rd, 93612 Kuching; tel. (82) 240141; f. 1956; monthly; Malay; Editor SAIT BIN HAJI YAMAN; circ. 30,000.

Pembrita: Malaysian Information Services, Mosque Rd, 93612 Kuching; tel. (82) 247231; f. 1950; monthly; Iban; Editor ALBAN JAWA; circ. 20,000.

Sarawak Gazette: Sarawak Museum, Jalan Tun Abang Haji Openg, 93566 Kuching; tel. (82) 244232; fax (82) 246680; e-mail museum@po.jaring.my; f. 1870; 2 a year; English; Chief Editor Datu Haji SALLEH SULAIMAN.

Utusan Sarawak: Lot 231, Jalan Nipah, off Jalan Abell, POB 138, 93100 Kuching; tel. (82) 424411; fax (82) 420358; internet www.tribune.com.my/tribune; f. 1949; Malay; Editor Haji ABDUL AZIZ Haji MALIM; circ. 32,292.

NEWS AGENCIES

Bernama (Malaysian National News Agency): Wisma Bernama, 28 Jalan 1/65A, off Jalan Tun Razak, POB 10024, 50700 Kuala Lumpur; tel. (3) 2945233; fax (3) 2941020; e-mail sjamil@bernama.com; internet www.bernama.com; f. 1968; general and foreign news, economic features and photo services, public relations wire, screen information and data services, stock market on-line equities service, real-time commodity and monetary information services; daily output in Malay and English; in June 1990 Bernama was given the exclusive right to receive and distribute news in Malaysia; Gen. Man. SYED JAMIL JAAFAR.

Foreign Bureaux

Agence France-Presse (AFP): 26 Hotel Equatorial, 1st Floor, Jalan Treacher, 2610520 Kuala Lumpur; tel. (3) 2691906; fax (3) 2615606; Correspondent MERVIN NAMBIAR.

Associated Press (AP) (USA): Wisma Bernama, 28 Jalan 1/65A, off Jalan Tun Razak, POB 12219, Kuala Lumpur; tel. (3) 2926155; Correspondent HARI SUBRAMANIAM.

Inter Press Service (IPS) (Italy): 32 Jalan Mudah Barat, Taman Midah, 56000 Kuala Lumpur; tel. (3) 9716830; fax (3) 2612872; Correspondent (vacant).

Press Trust of India: 114 Jalan Limau Manis, Bangsar Park, Kuala Lumpur; tel. (3) 940673; Correspondent T. V. VENKITACHALAM.

United Press International (UPI) (USA): Room 1, Ground Floor, Wisma Bernama, Jalan 1/65A, 50400 Kuala Lumpur; tel. (3) 2933393; fax (3) 2913876; Rep. MARY LEIGH.

Reuters (UK) and Xinhua (People's Republic of China) are also represented in Malaysia.

PRESS ASSOCIATION

Persatuan Penerbit-Penerbit Akhbar Malaysia (Malaysian Newspaper Publishers' Asscn): Unit 706, Block B, Phileo Damansara 1, 9 Jalan 16/11, off Jalan Damansara, 46350 Petaling Jaya; tel. (3) 76608535; fax (3) 76608532; e-mail mnpa@macomm.com.my; Chair. ROSELINA JOHARI.

Publishers

KUALA LUMPUR

Arus Intelek Sdn Bhd: Plaza Mont Kiara, Suite E-06-06, Mont Kiara, 50480 Kuala Lumpur; tel. (3) 62011558; fax (3) 62018698; e-mail arusintelek@po.jaring.my; Man. Datin AZIZAH MOKHZANI.

Berita Publishing Sdn Bhd: Balai Berita, 31 Jalan Riong, 59100 Kuala Lumpur; tel. (3) 2824322; fax (3) 2821605; internet www.jelita .com.my; education, business, fiction, cookery; Man. ABDUL MANAF SAAD.

Dewan Bahasa dan Pustaka (DBP) (Institute of Language and Literature): POB 10803, 50926 Kuala Lumpur; tel. (3) 21481011; fax (3) 21444460; e-mail aziz@dbp.gov.my; internet www.dbp.gov.my; f. 1956; textbooks, magazines and general; Chair. Tan Sri KAMARUL ARIFFIN MOHAMED YASSIN; Dir-Gen. Dato' Haji A. AZIZ DERAMAN.

International Law Book Services: Lot 4.1, Wisma Shen, 4th Floor, 149 Jalan Masjid India, 50100 Kuala Lumpur; tel. (3) 2939864; fax (3) 2928035; e-mail gbc@pc.jaring.my; Man. Dr SYED IBRAHIM.

Jabatan Penerbitan Universiti Malaya (University of Malaya Press): University of Malaya, Lembah Pantai, 50603 Kuala Lumpur; tel. (3) 79574361; fax (3) 79574473; e-mail hamedi@um.edu.my; internet www.um.edu.my/umpress; f. 1954; general fiction, literature, economics, history, medicine, politics, science, social science, law, Islam, engineering, dictionaries; Chief Editor Dr HAMEDI MOHD ADNAN.

Malaya Press Sdn Bhd: Kuala Lumpur; tel. (3) 5754650; fax (3) 5751464; f. 1958; education; Man. Dir LAI WING CHUN.

Pustaka Antara Sdn Bhd: Lot UG 10–13, Upper Ground Floor, Kompleks Wilayah, 2 Jalan Munshi Abdullah, 50100 Kuala Lumpur; tel. (3) 26980044; fax (3) 26917997; e-mail pantara@tm.net .my; textbooks, children's, languages, fiction; Man. Dir Datuk ABDUL AZIZ BIN AHMAD.

Utusan Publications and Distributors Sdn Bhd: 1 and 3 Jalan 3/91A, Taman Shamelin Perkasa, Cheras, 56100 Kuala Lumpur; tel. (3) 9856577; fax (3) 9846554; e-mail rose@utusan.com.my; internet www.upnd.com.my; school textbooks, children's, languages, fiction, general; Exec. Dir ROSELINA JOHARI.

JOHOR

Penerbitan Pelangi Sdn Bhd: 66 Jalan Pingai, Taman Pelangi, 80400 Johor Bahru; tel. (7) 3316288; fax (7) 3329201; e-mail ppsb@ po.jaring.my; internet www.pelangibooks.com; children's books, guidebooks and reference; Man. Dir SAMUEL SUM KOWN CHEEK.

Textbooks Malaysia Sdn Bhd: 49 Jalan Tengku Ahmad, POB 30, 85000 Segamat, Johor; tel. (7) 9318323; fax (7) 9313323; school textbooks, children's fiction, guidebooks and reference; Man. Dir FREDDIE KHOO.

NEGERI SEMBILAN

Bharathi Press: 166 Taman AST, POB 74, 70700 Seremban, Negeri Sembilan Darul Khusus; tel. (6) 7622911; f. 1939; Mans M. SUBRAMANIA BHARATHI, BHARATHI THASAN.

Minerva Publications: 96 Jalan Dato, Bandar Tunggal, 70000 Seremban, Negeri Sembilan; tel. and fax (6) 7634439; f. 1964; English, business, religion; Man. Dir TAJUDDIN MUHAMMED.

PINANG

Syarikat United Book Sdn Bhd: 187–189 Lebuh Carnarvon, 10100 Pulau Pinang; tel. (4) 61635; fax (4) 615063; textbooks, children's, reference, fiction, guidebooks; Man. Dir CHEW SING GUAN.

SELANGOR

SNP Panpac (Malaysia) Sdn Bhd: Lot 3, Jalan Saham 23/3, Kawasan MIEL Phase 8, Section 23, 40300 Shah Alam, Selangor Darul Ehsam; tel. (3) 55481088; fax (3) 55481080; e-mail eastview@ snpo.com.my; f. 1980; fmrly SNP Eastview Publications Sdn Bhd; school textbooks, children's, fiction, reference, general; Dir CHIA YAN HENG.

Federal Publications Sdn Bhd: Lot 46, Subang Hi-Tech Industrial Park, Batu Tiga, 40000 Shah Alam, Selangor; tel. (3) 56286888; fax (3) 56364620; e-mail fpsb@tpg.com.my; f. 1957; computer, children's magazines; Gen. Man. STEPHEN K. S. LIM.

FEP International Sdn Bhd: 6 Jalan SS 4c/5, POB 1091, 47301 Petaling Jaya, Selangor; tel. (3) 7036150; fax (3) 7036989; f. 1969; children's, languages, fiction, dictionaries, textbooks and reference; Man. Dir LIM MOK HAI.

Mahir Publications Sdn Bhd: 39 Jalan Nilam 1/2, Subang Sq., Subang Hi-Tech Industrial Park, Batu Tiga, 40000 Shah Alam, Selangor; tel. (3) 7379044; fax (3) 7379043; e-mail mahirpub@tm.net .my; Gen. Man. ZAINORA BINTI MUHAMAD.

Pearson Education Malaysia Sdn Bhd: Lot 2, Jalan 215, off Jalan Templer, 46050 Petaling Jaya, Selangor; tel. (3) 77820466; fax (3) 77818005; e-mail inquiry@pearsoned.com.my; internet www .pearsoned.com.my; textbooks, mathematics, physics, science, general, educational materials; Dir WONG WEE WOON; Man. WONG MEI MEI.

Pelanduk Publications (M) Sdn Bhd: 12 Jalan SS 13/3E, Subang Jaya Industrial Estate, 47500 Subang Jaya, Selangor; tel. (3) 7386885; fax (3) 7386575; e-mail pelpub@tm.net.my; internet www .pelanduk.com; Man. JACKSON TAN.

Penerbit Fajar Bakti Sdn Bhd: 4 Jalan U1/15, Sekseyen U1, Hicom-Glenmarie Industrial Park, 40150 Shah Alam, Selangor; tel. (3) 7047011; fax (3) 7047024; e-mail edes@pfb.po.my; school, college and university textbooks, children's, fiction, general; Man. Dir EDDA DE SILVA.

Penerbit Pan Earth Sdn Bhd: 11 Jalan SS 26/6, Taman Mayang Jaya, 47301 Petaling Jaya, Selangor; tel. (3) 7031258; fax (3) 7031262; Man. STEPHEN CHENG.

Penerbit Universiti Kebangsaan Malaysia: Universiti Kebangsaan Malaysia, 43600 UKM, Selangor; tel. (3) 8292840; fax (3) 8254375; Man. HASROM BIN HARON.

Pustaka Delta Pelajaran Sdn Bhd: Wisma Delta, Lot 18, Jalan 51A/22A, 46100 Petaling Jaya, Selangor; tel. (3) 7570000; fax (3) 7576688; e-mail dpsb@po.jaring.my; economics, language, environment, geography, geology, history, religion, science; Man. Dir LIM KIM WAH.

Pustaka Sistem Pelajaran Sdn Bhd: Lot 17–22 and 17–23, Jalan Satu, Bersatu Industrial Park, Cheras Jaya, 43200 Cheras, Selangor; tel. (3) 9047558; fax (3) 9047573; Man. T. THIRU.

Sasbadi Sdn Bhd: 103A Jalan SS 21/1A, Damansara Utama, 47400 Petaling Jaya, Selangor; tel. (3) 7182550; fax (3) 7186709; Man. LAW KING HUI.

Times Educational Sdn Bhd: 22 Jalan 19/3, 46300 Petaling Jaya, Selangor; tel. (3) 7571766; fax (3) 7573607; textbooks, general and reference; Man. FOONG CHUI LIN.

GOVERNMENT PUBLISHING HOUSE

Percetakan Nasional Malaysia Bhd (Malaysia National Printing Ltd): Jalan Chan Sow Lin, 50554 Kuala Lumpur; tel. (3) 2212022; fax (3) 2220690; fmrly the National Printing Department, incorporated as a company under govt control in January 1993.

PUBLISHERS' ASSOCIATION

Malaysian Book Publishers' Association: 306 Block C, Glomac Business Centre, 10 Jalan SS 6/1 Kelana Jaya, 47301 Petaling Jaya, Selangor; tel. (3) 7046628; fax (3) 7046629; e-mail mabopa@po.jaring .my; internet www.mabopa.com.my; f. 1968; Pres. NG TIEH CHUAN; Hon. Sec. KOW CHING CHUAN; 95 mems.

Broadcasting and Communications

TELECOMMUNICATIONS

Celcom (Malaysia) Sdn Bhd: Menara TR, 161B Jalan Ampang, 50450 Kuala Lumpur; tel. (3) 2623900; fax (3) 2625900; internet www.celcom.com.my; private co licensed to operate mobile cellular telephone service; Pres. ROSLI BIN MAN; Group Exec. Vice-Pres. WAN AISHA WAN HAMID.

DiGi Telecommunications Sdn Bhd: Lot 30, Jalan Delima 1/3, Subang Hi-Tech Industrial Park, 40000 Shah Alam, Selangor; tel. (3) 57211800; fax (3) 57211857; internet www.digi.com.my; private co licensed to operate mobile telephone service; Chair. Tan Sri Dato' Seri VINCENT TAN CHEE YIOUN.

Jabatan Telekomunikasi Malaysia (JTM): c/o Ministry of Energy, Communications and Multimedia, Wisma Damansara, 3rd Floor, Jalan Semantan, 50668 Kuala Lumpur; tel. (3) 2575000; fax (3) 2557901; internet www.ktkm.gov.my.

Maxis Communications Bhd: Menara Maxis, Kuala Lumpur City Centre, 50088 Kuala Lumpur; tel. (3) 3807802; fax (3) 3807010; internet www.maxis.com.my; provides mobile, fixed line and multimedia services; 800,000 subscribers in 1999; CEO JAMALUDIN IBRAHIM.

Telekom Malaysia Bhd: Ibu Pejabat Telekom Malaysia, 1st Floor, Jalan Pantai Baru, 50672 Kuala Lumpur; tel. (3) 2082103; fax (3) 7574747; internet www.telekom.com.my; public listed co responsible for operation of basic telecommunications services; 74% govt-owned; 4.22m. fixed lines (95% of total); Chair Haji MUHAMMAD RADZI BIN Haji MANSOR; Chief Exec. Dr MD KHIR ABDUL RAHMAN.

Technology Resources Industries Bhd (TRI): Menara TR, 23rd Floor, 161B Jalan Ampang, 50450 Kuala Lumpur; tel. (3) 2619555; fax (3) 2632018; operates mobile cellular telephone service; Chair. and Chief Exec. Tan Sri Dato' TAJUDIN RAMLI.

Time dotCom Bhd: Wisma Time, 1st Floor, 249 Jalan Tun Razak, 50400 Kuala Lumpur; tel. (3) 27208000; fax (3) 27200199; internet www.time.com.my; f. 1996 as Time Telecommunications Holdings Bhd; name changed as above in Jan. 2000; state-controlled co licensed to operate trunk network and mobile cellular telephone service; Exec. Chair. Dato' Prof. ZAIDIN Haji OTHMAN.

BROADCASTING

Regulatory Authority

Under the Broadcasting Act (approved in December 1987), the Minister of Information is empowered to control and monitor all radio and television broadcasting, and to revoke the licence of any private company violating the Act by broadcasting material 'conflicting with Malaysian values'.

Radio Televisyen Malaysia (RTM): Dept of Broadcasting, Angkasapuri, Bukit Putra, 50614 Kuala Lumpur; tel. (3) 22825333; fax (3) 2824735; e-mail helpdesk@rtm.net.my; internet www.rtm.net.my; f. 1946; television introduced 1963; supervises radio and television broadcasting; Dir-Gen. JAAFAR KAMIN; Dep. Dir-Gen. TAMIMUDDIN ABDUL KARIM.

Radio

Radio Malaysia: Radio Televisyen Malaysia (see Regulatory Authority), POB 11272, 50740 Kuala Lumpur; tel. (3) 2823991; fax (3) 2825859; f. 1946; domestic service; operates six networks; broadcasts in Bahasa Malaysia, English, Chinese (Mandarin and other dialects), Tamil and Aborigine (Temiar and Semai dialects); Dir of Radio MADZHI JOHARI.

Suara Islam (Voice of Islam): Islamic Affairs Division, Prime Minister's Department, Blok Utama, Tingkat 1–5, Pusat Pentadbiran Kerajaan Persekutuan, 62502 Putrajaya; internet www.smpke.jpm .my; f. 1995; Asia-Pacific region; broadcasts in Bahasa Malaysia on Islam.

Suara Malaysia (Voice of Malaysia): Wisma Radio, Angkasapuri, POB 11272, 50740 Kuala Lumpur; tel. (3) 22887824; fax (3) 22847594; f. 1963; overseas service in Bahasa Malaysia, Arabic, Myanmar (Burmese), English, Bahasa Indonesia, Chinese (Mandarin/Cantonese), Tagalog and Thai; Controller of Overseas Service STEPHEN SIPAUN.

Radio Televisyen Malaysia—Sabah: Jalan Tuaran, 88614 Kota Kinabalu; tel. (88) 213444; fax (88) 223493; f. 1955; television introduced 1971; a dept of RTM; broadcasts programmes over two networks for 280 hours a week in Bahasa Malaysia, English, Chinese (two dialects), Kadazan, Murut, Dusun and Bajau; Dir of Broadcasting JUMAT ENGSON.

Radio Televisyen Malaysia—Sarawak: Broadcasting House, Jalan P. Ramlee, 93614 Kuching; tel. (82) 248422; fax (82) 241914; e-mail pvgrtmsw@tm.net.my; f. 1954; a dept of RTM; broadcasts 445 hours per week in Bahasa Malaysia, English, Chinese, Iban, Bidayuh, Melanau, Kayan/Kenyah, Bisayah and Murut; Dir of Broadcasting NORHYATI ISMAIL.

Rediffusion Sdn Bhd: Rediffusion House, 17 Jalan Pahang, 53000 Kuala Lumpur; tel. (3) 4424544; fax (3) 4424614; f. 1949; two programmes; 44,720 subscribers in Kuala Lumpur; 11,405 subscribers in Pinang; 6,006 subscribers in Province Wellesley; 20,471 subscribers in Ipoh; Gen. Man. ROSNI B. RAHMAT.

Time Highway Radio: Wisma Time, 10th Floor, Jalan Tun Razak, 50400 Kuala Lumpur; tel. (3) 27202993; fax (3) 27200993; e-mail chief@thr.fm; internet www.thr.fm; f. 1994; serves Kuala Lumpur region; broadcasts in English; CEO ABDUL AZIZ HAMDAN.

Television

Measat Broadcast Network Systems Sdn Bhd: Kuala Lumpur; internet www.astro.com.my; nation-wide subscription service; Malaysia's first satellite, Measat 1, was launched in January 1996; a second satellite was launched in October of that year; Chair. T. ANANDA KRISHNAN.

Mega TV: Kuala Lumpur; internet www.megatv.com.my; subscription service; began broadcasting in November 1995; 5 foreign channels; initially available only in Klang Valley; 40%-owned by the Govt.

MetroVision: 33 Jalan Delima, 1/3 Subang Hi-Tech Industrial Park, 40000 Shah Alam, Selangor; tel. (3) 7328000; fax (3) 7328932;

e-mail norlin@metrovision.com.my; internet www.metrovision.com .my; began broadcasting in July 1995; commercial station; operates only in Klang Valley; 44%-owned by Senandung Sesuria Sdn Bhd, 56%-owned by Metropolitan Media Sdn Bhd; Man. Dr SABRI ABDUL RAHMAN.

Radio Televisyen Malaysia—Sabah: see Radio.

Radio Televisyen Malaysia—Sarawak: see Radio.

Sistem Televisyen Malaysia Bhd (TV 3): 3 Persiaran Bandar Utama, Bandar Utama, 47800 Petaling, Selangor Darul Ehsan; tel. (3) 77266333; fax (3) 77261333; internet www.tv3.com.my; f. 1983; Malaysia's first private television network, began broadcasting in 1984; Chair. Dato' MOHD NOOR YUSOF; Man. Dir Hisham Dato' ABD. RAHMAN.

Televisyen Malaysia: Radio Televisyen Malaysia (see Regulatory Authority); f. 1963; operates two national networks, TV1 and TV2; Controller of Programmes ISMAIL MOHAMED JAH.

Under a regulatory framework devised by the Government, the ban on privately-owned satellite dishes was ended in 1996.

Finance

(cap. = capital; auth. = authorized; res = reserves; dep. = deposits; m. = million; brs = branches; amounts in ringgit Malaysia)

BANKING

In July 2002 there were 47 domestic commercial banks, merchant banks and finance companies. In February 2000 the Government announced that it had approved plans for the creation of up to 10 banking groups to be formed through the merger of existing institutions. By August 2001 51 banks had merged under the terms of these plans. In February 1998 59 banks held offshore licences in Labuan.

Central Bank

Bank Negara Malaysia: Jalan Dato' Onn, 50480 Kuala Lumpur; tel. (3) 26988044; fax (3) 2912990; e-mail info@bnm.gov.my; internet www.bnm.gov.my; f. 1959; bank of issue; financial regulatory authority; cap. 100m., res 23,904.5m., dep. 76,772.0m. (April 2001); Gov. Datuk Dr ZETI AKHTAR AZIZ; 12 brs.

Regulatory Authority

Labuan Offshore Financial Services Authority (LOFSA): Level 17, Main Office Tower, Financial Park Labuan, Jalan Merdeka, 87000 Labuan; tel. (87) 408188; fax (87) 413328; e-mail communication@lofsa.gov.my; internet www.lofsa.gov.my; regulatory body for the International Offshore Financial Centre of Labuan established in October 1990; Chair. (vacant) (Gov. of Bank Negara Malaysia); Dir-Gen. NOORAZMAN AZIZ.

Commercial Banks

Peninsular Malaysia

ABN Amro Bank Bhd: Level 1, 25–27 MNI Twins Tower II, 11 Jalan Pinang, 50450 Kuala Lumpur; tel. (3) 21627888; fax (3) 21625692; internet www.abnamromalaysia.com; f. 1963.

Affin Bank Bhd: Menara AFFIN, 17th Floor, Jalan Raja Chulan, 50200 Kuala Lumpur; tel. (3) 20559000; fax (3) 2061415; e-mail head .ccd@affinbank.com.my; internet www.affinbank.com.my; f. 1975 as Perwira Habib Bank Malaysia Bhd; name changed to Perwira Affin Bank Bhd 1994; merged with BSN Commercial Bank (Malaysia) Bhd Jan. 2001, and name changed as above; cap. 650.0m., res 424.6m., dep. 12,350.0m. (Dec. 1999); Chair. Tan Sri Dato' ZAIN HASHIM; Deputy Chair. and CEO Raja Dato' AMAN AHMAD; 110 brs.

Alliance Bank Malaysia Bhd: Menara Multi-Purpose, Ground Floor, Capital Square, 8 Jalan Munshi Abdullah, 50100 Kuala Lumpur; POB 10069, 50704 Kuala Lumpur; tel. (3) 26948800; fax (3) 26946727; e-mail multilink@alliancebg.com.my; internet www .alliancebank.com.my; f. 1982 as Malaysian French Bank Berhad; name changed to Multi-Purpose Bank Bhd 1996; name changed as above Jan. 2001, following acquisition of six merger partners; cap. 230.0m., res 183.7m., dep. 7,907.2m. (Dec. 1999); Chair. Tan Sri ABU TALIB OTHMAN; Chief Exec. Dir NG SIEK CHUAN; 73 brs.

AmBank Bhd: Level 18, Menara Dion, Jalan Sultan Ismail, 50250 Kuala Lumpur; POB 10980, 50732 Kuala Lumpur; tel. (3) 2063939; fax (3) 2066855; internet www.ambg.com.my; f. 1994; fmrly Arab-Malaysian Bank Bhd; cap. 348.0m., res 337.9m., dep. 9,902.2m. (March 1999); Chair. Tan Sri Dato' AZMAN HASHIM; Man. Dir AZLAN ZAINOL.

Bangkok Bank Bhd (Thailand): 105 Jalan Tun H. S. Lee, 50000 Kuala Lumpur; POB 10734, 50923 Kuala Lumpur; tel. (3) 2324555; fax (3) 2388569; e-mail bbb@tm.net.my; f. 1958; cap. 88.5m., res

41.2m., dep. 508.7m. (Dec. 2000); Chair. ALBERT CHEOK SAYCHUAN; CEO CHALIT TAYJASANANT; 1 br.

Bank of Tokyo-Mitsubishi (Malaysia) Bhd (Japan): 1 Leboh Ampang, 50100 Kuala Lumpur; POB 10959, 50931 Kuala Lumpur; tel. (3) 2389100; fax (3) 2308340; f. 1996 following merger of the Bank of Tokyo and Mitsubishi Bank; cap. 200m., res 300m., dep. 1,718m. (1998); Chair. AKIRA OKUHATA.

Bank Pembangunan & Infrastruktur Malaysia Bhd: Menara Bank Pembangunan, POB 12352, Jalan Sultan Ismail, 50774 Kuala Lumpur; tel. (3) 26152020; fax (3) 26928520; e-mail bpimb-pr@bpimb.com.my; internet www.bpimb.com.my; f. 1973; cap. 1,000m. (Dec. 1999); dep. 2,190m. (Dec. 2000); Exec. Chair. Tan Sri Datuk Dr ARIS OTHMAN; Man. Dir Datuk NIK IBRAHIM ABDULLAH; 13 brs.

Bumiputra Commerce Bank Bhd: 6 Jalan Tun Perak, 50050 Kuala Lumpur; POB 10753, 50724 Kuala Lumpur; tel. (3) 2931722; fax (3) 2986628; internet www.bcb.com.my; f. 1999, following merger of Bank Bumiputra Malaysia Bhd with Bank of Commerce Bhd; cap. 1,708.3m., res 1,773.2m., dep. 48,969.3m. (Dec. 2000); Chair. Tan Sri RADIN SOENARNO AL-HAJ; Man. Dir and CEO Dr ROZALI MOHAMED ALI; 249 brs.

Citibank Bhd (USA): 165 Jalan Ampang, POB 10112, 50904 Kuala Lumpur; tel. (3) 2325334; fax (3) 2328763; internet www.citibank .com.my; f. 1959; cap. 121.7m., res 519.2m., dep. 10,683.3m. (1998); CEO ROBERT MATTHEWS; 3 brs.

Deutsche Bank (Malaysia) Bhd (Germany): 18–20 Menara IMC, 8 Jalan Sultan Ismail, 50250 Kuala Lumpur; tel. (3) 2021163; fax (3) 2019822; f. 1994; cap. 124.0m., res 144.1m., dep. 1,328.4m. (Dec. 2000); Man. Dir ERDMANN R. G. VOGT.

EON Bank Bhd: Wisma Cyclecarri, 11th Floor, 288 Jalan Raja Laut, 50350 Kuala Lumpur; POB 12996, 50796 Kuala Lumpur; tel. (3) 26941188; fax (3) 26949588; e-mail eontsy@tm.net.my; internet www.eonbank.com.my; f. 1963; fmrly Kong Ming Bank Bhd; merged with Oriental Bank Bhd, Jan. 2001; cap. 1,168.2m., res 137.1m., dep. 6,906.2m. (Dec. 2000); Chair. Tan Sri Dato' Seri MOHAMED SALEH BIN SULONG; Dir and CEO KOK NAM SOON; 46 brs.

Hong Leong Bank Bhd: Wisma Hong Leong, Level 3, 18 Jalan Perak, 50450 Kuala Lumpur; POB 12372, 50776 Kuala Lumpur; tel. (3) 21642828; fax (3) 27156365; internet www.hlb.hongleong.com .my; f. 1905; fmrly MUI Bank Bhd; merged with Wah Tat Bank Bhd, Jan. 2001; cap. 577.2m., res 1,152.4m., dep. 15,568.6m. (June 2000); Chair. Tan Sri QUEK LENG CHAN; Man. Dir JAMES LIM CHENG POH; 72 brs.

HSBC Bank Malaysia Bhd (Hong Kong): 2 Leboh Ampang, POB 10244, 50912 Kuala Lumpur; tel. (3) 2300744; fax (3) 2302678; e-mail manager.public.affairs@hsbc.com.my; internet www.hsbc .com.my; f. 1860; fmrly Hongkong Bank Malaysia Bhd; adopted present name in 1999; cap. 304.5m., res 828.4m., dep. 20,502.8m. (Dec. 1999); Chair. ARMAN MEHTA.

Malayan Banking Bhd (Maybank): Menara Maybank, 100 Jalan Tun Perak, 50050 Kuala Lumpur; POB 12010, 50936 Kuala Lumpur; tel. (3) 2308833; fax (3) 2302611; e-mail maybank@po .jaring.my; internet www.maybank.com.my/maybank; f. 1960; acquired Pacific Bank Bhd, Jan. 2001; merged with PhileoAllied Bank (Malaysia) Bhd, March 2001; cap. 2,308m., res 5,588m., dep. 57,581m. (Dec. 1999); Chair. Tan Sri MOHAMED BASIR BIN AHMAD; Man. Dir Datuk AMIRSHAM A. AZIZ; 264 domestic brs, 30 overseas brs.

OCBC Bank (Malaysia) Bhd: Tingkat 1–8, Wisma Lee Rubber, Jalan Melaka, 50100 Kuala Lumpur; POB 10197, 50100 Kuala Lumpur; tel. (3) 26920344; fax (3) 26926518; f. 1932; cap. 287.5m., res 1,438.5m., dep. 17,108.8m. (Dec. 2000); Chair. Tan Sri Dato' NASRUDDIN BAHARI; CEO ALBERT YEOH BEOW TIT; 25 brs.

Public Bank Bhd: Menara Public Bank, 146 Jalan Ampang, 50450 Kuala Lumpur; POB 12542, 50947 Kuala Lumpur; tel. (3) 21638888; fax (3) 21639917; internet www.publicbank.com.my; f. 1965; merged with Hock Hua Bank Bhd, March 2001; cap. 1,195.1m., res 2,429.6m., dep. 27,777.3m. (Dec. 2000); Chair. Tan Sri Dato' THONG YAW HONG; Pres. and CEO Tan Sri Dato' Dr TEH HONG PIOW; 213 domestic brs, 3 overseas brs.

RHB Bank Bhd: Towers Two and Three, RHB Centre, 426 Jalan Tun Razak, 50400 Kuala Lumpur; tel. (3) 9878888; fax (3) 9879000; e-mail md_ceo@rhbbank.com; internet www.rhbbank.com; formed in 1997 by a merger between DCB Bank Bhd and Kwong Yik Bank Bhd; officially took over Sime Bank Bhd in mid-1999; cap. 3,318.1m., res 1,218.6m., dep. 38,854.9m. (June 2000); Chair. Dato' ALI HASSAN; CEO YVONNE CHIA; 148 brs.

Southern Bank Bhd: 83 Medan Setia 1, Plaza Damansara, Bukit Damansara, 50490 Kuala Lumpur; POB 12281, 50772 Kuala Lumpur; tel. (3) 2637000; fax (3) 2017305; e-mail info@sbbgroup.com .my; internet www.sbbgroup.com.my; f. 1963; merged with Ban Hin Lee Bank Bhd, July 2000; cap. 1,122.8m., res 765.7m., dep. 19,149.6m. (Dec. 2000); Chair. Tan Sri OSMAN S. CASSIM; CEO Dato' TAN TEONG HEAN; 105 domestic brs, 1 overseas br.

Standard Chartered Bank Malaysia Bhd: 1st Floor, 2 Jalan Ampang, 50450 Kuala Lumpur; tel. (3) 20726555; fax (3) 2010621; internet www.standardchartered.com.my.

United Overseas Bank (Malaysia) Bhd: Menara UOB, Jalan Raja Laut, POB 11212, 50738 Kuala Lumpur; tel. (3) 26927722; fax (3) 26981228; e-mail uobmtre@uobgrp.po.my; f. 1920; merged with Chung Khiaw Bank (Malaysia) Bhd in 1997; cap. 470m., res 785.4m., dep. 7,239.5m. (Dec. 1999); Chair. WEE EE CHEONG; Dir and CEO FRANCIS LEE CHIN YONG; 25 brs.

Sarawak

Bank Utama (Malaysia) Bhd: Lot 363, Jalan Kulas, POB 2049, 93400 Kuching; tel. (82) 419294; fax (82) 424954; e-mail utamab@tm .net.my; internet www.cmsb.com.my/ubg; f. 1976; cap. 800.0m., res 142.9m., dep. 4,657.5m. (Dec. 1999); Chair. Tan Sri Datuk AMAR MOHD JEMURI BIN SERJAN; Pres. and CEO ABDULLAH MAT NOH; 35 brs.

Merchant Banks

Affin Merchant Bank Bhd: Menara Boustead, 27th Floor, 69 Jalan Raja Chulan, POB 1124, 50200 Kuala Lumpur; tel. (3) 2423700; fax (3) 2424982; f. 1970 as Permata Chartered Merchant Bank Bhd; name changed as above March 2001; cap. 187.5m., res 168.9m., dep. 1,732.1m. (Dec. 2000); Chair. Tan Sri YAACOB MOHAMED ZAIN; CEO HASSAN HUSSEIN.

Alliance Merchant Bank Bhd: Menara Multi-Purpose, 20th Floor, Capital Sq., 8 Jalan Munshi Abdullah, 50100 Kuala Lumpur; tel. (3) 26927788; fax (3) 26928787; e-mail amanah@amanahb.po .my; f. 1974 as Amanah-Chase Merchant Bank Bhd; name changed as above Jan. 2001, following merger with Bumiputra Merchant Bankers Bhd; cap. 125.0m., res 42.5m., dep. 1,685.1m. (Dec. 1997); Chair. Dato' ABDUL KHALID BIN IBRAHIM; CEO AZMAN BIN YAHYA.

AmMerchant Bank Bhd: Bangunan Arab-Malaysian, 22nd Floor, 55 Jalan Raja Chulan, 50200 Kuala Lumpur; POB 10233, 50708 Kuala Lumpur; tel. (3) 2382633; fax (3) 2382842; e-mail jida@ammb .com.my; internet www.ambg.com.my; f. 1975; fmrly Arab-Malaysian Merchant Bank Bhd; cap. 292.5m., res 333.0m., dep. 13,423.9m. (March 2000); Chair. Tan Sri Dato' AZMAN HASHIM; Man. Dir CHEAH TEK KUANG; 4 brs.

Aseambankers Malaysia Bhd: Menara Maybank, 33rd Floor, 100 Jalan Tun Perak, 50050 Kuala Lumpur; POB 11057, 50734 Kuala Lumpur; tel. (3) 20591888; fax (3) 2384194; e-mail faudziah@aseam .com.my; f. 1973; cap. 50.1m., res 236.0m., dep. 2,616.6m. (June 2000); Man. Dir Encik AGIL NATT; Snr Gen. Mans ROZIDIN MASARI, WONG YOKE NYEN; 2 brs.

Commerce International Merchant Bankers Bhd: Commerce Sq., 10th–12th Floors, Jalan Semantan, Damansara Heights, 50490 Kuala Lumpur; tel. (3) 2536688; fax (3) 2535522; f. 1974; cap. 250.2m., res 544.3m., dep. 4,492.2m. (Dec. 2000); Chair. Dato' MOHAMED NOR BIN MOHAMED YOUSOF.

Malaysian International Merchant Bankers Bhd: Wisma Cyclecarri, 21st Floor, 288 Jalan Raja Laut, 50350 Kuala Lumpur; POB 12250, 50772 Kuala Lumpur; tel. (3) 26910200; fax (3) 26948388; f. 1970; cap. 75.0m., res 163.3m., dep. 1,887.0m. (March 2000); Chair. Tan Sri Dato' Ir WAN A. RAHMAN YAACOB; CEO YANG SHU-YIN; 2 brs.

RHB Sakura Merchant Bankers Bhd: 9th–13th Floors, RHB Centre, 426 Jalan Tun Razak, 50400 Kuala Lumpur; tel. (3) 9873888; fax (3) 9878000; f. 1974; cap. 60.0m., res 81.0m., dep. 4,045.4m. (Dec. 1996); Chair. Tan Sri Dato' ABDUL RASHID HUSSAIN; Man. Dir GEORGE RATILAL.

Southern Investment Bank Bhd: POB 10491, 50714 Kuala Lumpur; tel. (3) 20594188; fax (3) 20722964; e-mail sibb@sibb.com .my; internet www.sibb.com.my; f. 1988; fmrly Perdana Merchant Bankers Bhd; cap. 77.9m., res 47.7m., dep. 449.3m. (Dec. 1998); Chair. Dato' Nik IBRAHIM KAMIL; CEO YAP FAT (acting).

Utama Merchant Bank Bhd: Central Plaza, 27th Floor, Jalan Sultan Ismail, 50250 Kuala Lumpur; POB 12406, 50776 Kuala Lumpur; tel. (3) 2438888; fax (3) 2430357; e-mail umbb@umbb.po .my; internet www.cmsb.com.my; f. 1975 as Utama Wardley Bhd, name changed 1996; cap. 223.0m., res 63.6m., dep. 992.6m. (Dec. 1999); Chair. Nik HASHIM BIN NIK YUSOFF; CEO DONNY KWA SOO CHUAN; 1 br.

Co-operative Bank

Bank Kerjasama Rakyat Malaysia Berhad: Bangunan Bank Rakyat, Jalan Tangsi, Peti Surat 11024, 50732 Kuala Lumpur; tel. (3) 2985011; fax (3) 2985981; f. 1954; 83,095 mems. of which 823 were co-operatives (Dec. 1996); Chair. Dr YUSUF YACOB; Man. Dir Dato' ANUAR JAAFAR; 67 brs.

Development Banks

Bank Industri & Teknologi Malaysia Bhd (Industrial Development Bank of Malaysia): Level 28, Bangunan Bank Industri, Bandar Wawasan, 1016 Jalan Sultan Ismail, POB 10788, 50724 Kuala Lumpur; tel. (3) 26929088; fax (3) 26985701; e-mail pru@bankindustri.com.my; internet www.bankindustri.com.my; f. 1979; govt-owned; finances long-term, high-technology projects, shipping and shipyards and engineering (plastic, electrical and electronic); cap. 320.5m., res 10.1m., dep. 3,368.4m. (Dec. 1998); Chair. Tan Sri Datuk WIRA ABDUL RAHMAN ARSHAD; Man. Dir Encik MD NOOR YUSOFF.

Sabah Development Bank Bhd: SDB Tower, Wisma Tun Fuad Stephens, POB 12172, 88824 Kota Kinabalu, Sabah; tel. (88) 232177; fax (88) 261852; e-mail sdbank@po.jaring.my; internet www.borneo-online.com.my/sdb; f. 1977; wholly owned by State Government of Sabah; cap. 350m., res 152.1m., dep. 607.3m. (Dec. 2000); Chair. PETER SIAU; Man. Dir and CEO PETER LIM.

Islamic Banks

Bank Islam Malaysia Bhd: Darul Takaful, 10th Floor, Jalan Sultan Ismail, 50250 Kuala Lumpur; POB 11080, 50734 Kuala Lumpur; tel. (3) 26935842; fax (3) 26922153; e-mail bislam@po.jaring.my; internet www.bankislam.com.my; f. 1983; cap. 500m., res 478.5m., dep. 7,350.5m. (June 2000); Chair. Dato' MOHAMED YUSOFF BIN MOHAMED NASIR; Man. Dir Dato' Haji AHMAD TAJUDIN ABDUL RAHMAN; 82 brs.

Bank Muamalat Malaysia Bhd: 21 Jalan Melaka, 50100 Kuala Lumpur; tel. (3) 26988787; e-mail webmaster@muamalat.com.my; internet www.muamalat.com.my; f. 1999; CEO Tuan Haji MOHD SHUKRI HUSSIN; 40 brs.

'Offshore' Banks

ABN Amro Bank, Labuan Branch: Level 9 (A), Main Office Tower, Financial Park Labuan, Jalan Merdeka, 87000 Labuan; tel. (87) 423008; fax (87) 421078; Man. WILLIAM YAP KIM SEONG.

AMInternational (L) Ltd: Level 12 (B), Block 4, Office Tower, Financial Park Labuan, Jalan Merdeka, 87000 Labuan; tel. (87) 413133; fax (87) 425211; e-mail felix-leong@ambg.com.my; internet www.ambg.com.my; CEO PAUL ONG WHEE SEN.

Asahi Bank Ltd, Labuan Branch: Level 12 (D), Main Office Tower, Financial Park Labuan, Jalan Merdeka, 87000 Labuan; tel. (87) 422516; fax (87) 422517; Gen. Man. SHINICHI HAYASHI.

Bank Islam (L) Ltd: Level 15, Block 4, Financial Park Labuan, Jalan Merdeka, 87000 Labuan; tel. (87) 451802; fax (87) 451800; e-mail bislamln@tm.net.my; CEO Y. M. Raja ZAINAL ALAM SHAH BIN Raja ABDULLAH OMAR.

Bank of America, National Trust and Savings Association, Labuan Branch: Level 13 (D), Main Office Tower, Financial Park Labuan, Jalan Merdeka, 87000 Labuan; tel. (87) 411778; fax (87) 424778; Man. IBRAHIM BIN NASIR.

Bank of Commerce (L) Ltd: Level 13 (A), Main Office Tower, Financial Park Labuan, Jalan Merdeka, 87000 Labuan; tel. (87) 410305; fax (87) 410313; Gen. Man. HARI PRASAD.

Bank of East Asia Ltd, Labuan Offshore Branch: Level 10 (C), Main Office Tower, Financial Park Labuan, Jalan Merdeka, 87000 Labuan; tel. (87) 451145; fax (87) 451148; e-mail bealbu@hkbea.com.my; Gen. Man. THOMAS WONG WAI YIP.

Bank of Nova Scotia, Labuan Branch: Level 10 (C2), Main Office Tower, Financial Park Labuan, Jalan Merdeka, 87000 Labuan; tel. (87) 451101; fax (87) 451099; Man. M. S. SEVILLA.

Bank of Tokyo-Mitsubishi Ltd, Labuan Branch: Level 12 (A & F), Main Office Tower, Financial Park Labuan, Jalan Merdeka, 87000 Labuan; tel. (87) 410487; fax (87) 410476; Gen. Man. SEITA TSUSHIMA.

Banque Nationale de Paris, Labuan Branch: Level 13 (C2), Main Office Tower, Financial Park Labuan, Jalan Merdeka, 87000 Labuan; tel. (87) 419103; fax (87) 419105; Gen. Man. CHUA PIN.

Barclays Bank PLC: Level 5(A), Main Office Tower, Financial Park Labuan, Jalan Merdeka, 87000 Labuan; tel. (87) 425571; fax (87) 425575; e-mail barclay@tm.net.my; Man. MIAW SIAW LOONG.

Bayerische Landesbank Girozentrale, Labuan Branch: Level 14 (C), Block 4, Office Tower, Financial Park Labuan, Jalan Merdeka, 87000 Labuan; tel. (87) 422170; fax (87) 422175; e-mail blblab@tm.net.my; Exec. Vice-Pres., CEO and Gen. Man. LOUISE PAUL.

BNP Paribas, Labuan Branch: Level 9 (E), Main Office Tower, Financial Park Labuan, Jalan Merdeka, 87000 Labuan; tel. (3) 2458068; fax (3) 2458066; e-mail bnpkul@tm.net.my; Gen. Man. YAP SIEW YING.

Bumiputra Commerce International Trust: Level 14(B), Main Office Tower, Financial Park Labuan, Jalan Merdeka, 87000 Labuan; tel. (87) 414252; fax (87) 411855; e-mail bumitrst@tm.net.my; Trust Officer NOR AZLI MOHD NOOR.

Chase Manhattan Bank, Labuan Branch: Level 5 (F), Main Office Tower, Financial Park Labuan, Jalan Merdeka, 87000 Labuan; tel. (87) 424384; fax (87) 424390; e-mail fauziah.hisham@chase.com; Gen. Man. PUAN FAUZIAH HISHAM.

Citibank Malaysia (L) Ltd: Level 11 (F), Main Office Tower, Financial Park Labuan, Jalan Merdeka, 87000 Labuan; tel. (87) 421181; fax (87) 419671; Gen. Man. CLARA LIM AI CHENG.

Commerzbank AG, Labuan Branch: Level 6 (E), Main Office Tower, Financial Park Labuan, Jalan Merdeka, 87000 Labuan; tel. (87) 416953; fax (87) 413542; Gen. Man. DENIS POO.

Crédit Agricole Indosuez, Labuan Branch: Level 11 (C), Main Office Tower, Financial Park Labuan, Jalan Merdeka, 87000 Labuan; tel. (87) 425118; fax (87) 424998; Gen. Man. BOON EONG TAN.

Crédit Lyonnais, Labuan Branch: Level 6 (B), Main Office Tower, Financial Park Labuan, Jalan Merdeka, 87000 Labuan; tel. (87) 408331; fax (87) 439133; Man. CLEMENT WONG.

Crédit Suisse First Boston, Labuan Branch: Level 10 (B), Main Office Tower, Financial Park Labuan, Jalan Merdeka, 87000 Labuan; tel. (87) 425381; fax (87) 425384; Gen. Man. TAN BOON EONG.

Dai-Ichi Kangyo Bank Ltd, Labuan Branch: Level 9 (B and C), Main Office Tower, Financial Park Labuan, Jalan Merdeka, 87000 Labuan; tel. (87) 419418; fax (87) 419424; Gen. Man. RYOICHI SHIMIZU.

Deutsche Bank AG, Labuan Branch: Level 14 (C), Main Office Tower, Financial Park Labuan, Jalan Merdeka, 87000 Labuan; tel. (87) 439811; fax (87) 439866; Gen. Man. GRACE WONG.

Development Bank of Singapore Ltd, Labuan Branch: Level 12 (E), Main Office Tower, Financial Park Labuan, Jalan Merdeka, 87000 Labuan; tel. (87) 423375; fax (87) 423376; Gen. Man. TAN CHEE CHEONG (acting).

Dresdner Bank AG, Labuan Branch: Level 13 (C), Main Office Tower, Financial Park Labuan, Jalan Merdeka, 87000 Labuan; tel. (87) 419271; fax (87) 419272; Gen. Man. JAMALUDIN NASIR.

First Commercial Bank, Labuan Branch: Main Office Tower, 6th Floor, Financial Park Labuan, Jalan Merdeka, 87000 Labuan; tel. (87) 451699; fax (87) 451366; Gen. Man. JAN REN-WEN.

Fuji Bank Ltd, Labuan Branch: Level 10 (A), Main Office Tower, Financial Park Labuan, Jalan Merdeka, 87000 Labuan; tel. (87) 417766; fax (87) 419766; Gen. Man. KEN UEDA.

Hongkong & Shanghai Banking Corporation, Offshore Banking Unit: Level 11 (D), Main Office Tower, Financial Park Labuan, Jalan Merdeka, 87000 Labuan; tel. (87) 417168; fax (87) 417169; Man. ROSLI RAHMAT.

Industrial Bank of Japan Ltd, Labuan Branch: Level 11 (A), Main Office Tower, Financial Park Labuan, Jalan Merdeka, 87000 Labuan; tel. (87) 419115; fax (87) 419121; Gen. Man. KOHEI OHGAKI.

ING Bank N.V.: Level 8 (B2), Main Office Tower, Financial Park Labuan, Jalan Merdeka, 87000 Labuan; tel. (87) 425733; fax (87) 425734; e-mail Jean-Francois.Gillard@Asia.ING.com; Gen. Man. JEAN-FRANCOIS GILLARD.

International Commercial Bank of China: Level 7 (E2), Main Office Tower, Financial Park Labuan, Jalan Merdeka, 87000 Labuan; tel. (87) 581688; fax (87) 581668; Gen. Man. YU CHENG HSIUNG.

J. P. Morgan Malaysia Ltd: Level 9 (G2), Main Office Tower, Financial Park Labuan, Jalan Merdeka, 87000 Labuan; tel. (87) 459000; fax (87) 451328; Gen. Man. RAMESH RAMANKUTTY NAIR.

KBC Bank N.V., Labuan Branch: Main Office Tower, 3rd Floor, Financial Park Labuan, Jalan Merdeka, 87000 Labuan; tel. (87) 581778; fax (87) 583787; Gen. Man. KONG KOK CHEE.

Lloyds TSB Bank PLC: Lot B, 11th Floor, Wisma Oceanic, Jalan OKK Awang Besar, 87007 Labuan; tel. (87) 418918; fax (87) 411928; e-mail labuan@lloydstsb; Dir and Gen. Man. BARRY FRANCIS LEA.

Maybank International (L) Ltd: Level 16 (B), Main Office Tower, Financial Park Labuan, Jalan Merdeka, 87000 Labuan; tel. (87) 414406; fax (87) 414806; e-mail millmit@tm.net.my; Gen. Man. RIDZUAN SALLEH.

Merrill Lynch Capital Markets Bank Ltd, Labuan Branch: Unit 4G, Level 4, Main Office Tower, Financial Park Labuan, Jalan Merdeka, 87000 Labuan; tel. (87) 453800; fax (87) 453808; Gen. Man. Dato' KAMARUDIN ABU.

Morgan Guaranty Trust Co of New York, Labuan Branch: Level 9 (G2), Main Office Tower, Financial Park Labuan, Jalan Merdeka, 87000 Labuan; tel. (87) 459000; fax (87) 451328; Gen. Man. RAMESH RAMANKUTTY NAIR.

Natexis Banque Populaires: Level 9 (G), Main Office Tower, Financial Park Labuan, Jalan Merdeka, 87000 Labuan; tel. (87) 581009; fax (87) 583009; Gen. Man. RIZAL ABDULLAH.

National Australia Bank, Labuan Branch: Level 12 (C2), Main Office Tower, Financial Park Complex, Jalan Merdeka, 87008 Labuan; tel. (87) 443286; fax (87) 443288; e-mail natausm@po.jaring .my; Gen. Man. GREG WARD.

Oversea-Chinese Banking Corporation Ltd: Level 8 (C), Main Office Tower, Financial Park Labuan, Jalan Merdeka, 87000 Labuan; tel. (87) 423381; fax (87) 423390; Gen. Man. BRYAN LO.

Overseas Union Bank Ltd, Labuan Branch: Level 13 (B), Main Office Tower, Financial Park Labuan, Jalan Merdeka, 87000 Labuan; tel. (87) 418909; fax (87) 411909; Gen. Man. DANIEL LOW THIEN SU.

Public Bank (L) Ltd: Level 8 (A and B), Main Office Tower, Financial Park Labuan, Jalan Merdeka, 87000 Labuan; tel. (87) 411898; fax (87) 413220; Man. ALEXANDER WONG.

Rabobank Nederland, Labuan Branch: Lot C, Level 7, Wisma Oceanic, Jalan OKK Awang Besar, 87007 Labuan; tel. (87) 423603; fax (87) 423607; Man. RICARDO BABA.

RHB Bank (L) Ltd: Level 15 (B), Main Office Tower, Financial Park Labuan, Jalan Merdeka, 87000 Labuan; tel. (87) 417480; fax (87) 417484; Gen. Man. TOH AY LENG.

Sanwa Bank Ltd, Labuan Branch: Level 10 (D), Main Office Tower, Financial Park Labuan, Jalan Merdeka, 87000 Labuan; tel. (87) 419200; fax (87) 419202; Gen. Man. YASUSHI ONUKI.

Sime International Bank (L) Ltd: Level 16 (A), Main Office Tower, Financial Park Labuan, Jalan Merdeka, 87000 Labuan; tel. (87) 417475; fax (87) 417470; CEO TEO KENG LEE.

Société Générale, Labuan Branch: Level 11 (B), Main Office Tower, Financial Park Labuan, Jalan Merdeka, 87000 Labuan; tel. (87) 421676; fax (87) 421669; Man. CHOW YING HOONG.

Standard Chartered Bank Offshore Labuan: Level 10 (F), Main Office Tower, Financial Park Labuan, Jalan Merdeka, 87000 Labuan; tel. (87) 417200; fax (87) 417202; Gen. Man. THOMAS LEE OY BENG.

Sumitomo Mitsui Banking Corpn, Labuan Branch: Level 12 (B and C), Main Office Tower, Financial Park Labuan, Jalan Merdeka, 87000 Labuan; tel. (87) 410955; fax (87) 410959; Gen. Man. TAKAYA LIDA.

Tat Lee Bank Ltd: Level 8 (D), Main Office Tower, Financial Park Labuan, Jalan Merdeka, 87000 Labuan; tel. (87) 451292; fax (87) 442292; Gen. Man. LIM TENG HO.

Tokai Bank Ltd, Labuan Branch: Level 7 (D), Main Office Tower, Financial Park Labuan, Jalan Merdeka, 87000 Labuan; tel. (87) 408025; fax (87) 419193; Gen. Man. SUSUMU ARAKI.

Union Bank of Switzerland, Labuan Branch: Level 5 (E), Main Office Tower, Financial Park Labuan Complex, Jalan Merdeka, 87000 Labuan; tel. (87) 421743; fax (87) 421746; Man. ZELIE HO SWEE LUM.

Union Européenne de CIC, Labuan Branch: Level 11 (C2), Main Office Tower, Financial Park Labuan, Jalan Merdeka, 87000 Labuan; tel. (87) 452008; fax (87) 452009; Gen. Man. YEOW TIANG HUI.

United Overseas Bank Ltd, Labuan Branch: Level 6 (A), Main Office Tower, Financial Park Labuan, Jalan Merdeka, 87000 Labuan; tel. (87) 424388; fax (87) 424389; Gen. Man. NG KEOK HU.

United World Chinese Commercial Bank: Level 3 (C), Main Office Tower, Financial Park Labuan, Jalan Merdeka, 87000 Labuan; tel. (87) 452168; fax (87) 453678; Gen. Man. THOMAS TANG TOR-TSAI.

Banking Associations

Association of Banks in Malaysia: UBN Tower, 17th Floor, 10 Jalan P. Ramlee, 50250 Kuala Lumpur; tel. (3) 2388041; fax (3) 2388004; Chair. AMIRSHAM A. AZIZ; Exec. Dir WONG SUAN LYE.

Institute of Bankers Malaysia: Wisma IBI, 5 Jalan Semantan, Damansara Heights, 50490 Kuala Lumpur; tel. (3) 20956833; fax (3) 20952322; e-mail ibbm@ibbm.org.my; internet www.ibbm.org.my; Chair. Tan Sri Dato' Dr ZETI AKHTAR AZIZ.

Malayan Commercial Banks' Association: POB 12001, 50764 Kuala Lumpur; tel. (3) 2983991.

Persatuan Institusi Perbankan Tanpa Faedah Malaysia (Association of Islamic Banking Institutions Malaysia—AIBIM): Tingkat 9, Menara Tun Razak, Jalan Raja Laut, 50350 Kuala Lumpur; tel. (3) 26932936; fax (3) 26910453; e-mail secretariat@ aibim.com.my; internet www.aibim.com.my.

STOCK EXCHANGES

Commodity and Monetary Exchange of Malaysia: Citypoint, Dayabumi Complex, 5th Floor, Jalan Sultan Hishamuddin, 50050 Kuala Lumpur; tel. (3) 2936822; fax (3) 2738057; e-mail inquiry@ commex.com.my; internet www.commex.com.my; f. 1998 as a result of the merger of the Kuala Lumpur Commodity Exchange and the Malaysia Monetary Exchange Bhd; multi-product futures exchange trading mainly in palm oil (crude palm oil futures); Exec. Chair. Dato' SYED ABDUL JABBAR SHAHABUDIN; Gen. Man. RAGHBIR SINGH BHART.

Kuala Lumpur Stock Exchange (KLSE): Exchange Sq., Bukit Kewangan, 50200 Kuala Lumpur; tel. (3) 2067099; fax (3) 2063684; internet www.klse.com.my; f. 1973; in 1988 KLSE authorized the ownership of up to 49% of Malaysian stockbroking companies by foreign interests; 112 mems; 727 listed cos (June 1998); merged with Malaysian Exchange for Securities Dealing and Automated Quotation Bhd (MESDAQ) in March 2002; Chair. MOHAMAD AZLAN HASHIM; Pres. Dato' MOHD SALLEH BIN ABDUL MAJID.

Regulatory Authority

Securities Commission (SC): 3 Sri Semantan Satu, 50490 Kuala Lumpur; tel. (3) 2539988; fax (3) 2536184; e-mail cau@seccom.com .my; internet www.sc.com.my; f. 1993; Chair. Datuk ALI ABDUL KADIR.

INSURANCE

From 1988 onwards, all insurance companies were placed under the authority of the Central Bank, Bank Negara Malaysia. In 1997 there were 69 insurance companies operating in Malaysia; nine reinsurance companies, 11 composite, 40 general and life and two takaful insurance companies.

Principal Insurance Companies

Allianz Life Insurance Malaysia Bhd: Wisma UOA II, Floors 23 and 23A, 21 Jalan Pinang, 50450 Kuala Lumpur; tel. (3) 27166848; fax (3) 21633596; fmrly MBA Life Assurance Sdn Bhd; Chief Financial Officer CHARLES ONG ENG CHOW.

Asia Insurance Co Ltd: Bangunan Asia Insurance, 2 Jalan Raja Chulan, 50200 Kuala Lumpur; tel. (3) 2302511; fax (3) 2323606; f. 1923; general.

Capital Insurance Bhd: 38 Jalan Ampang, POB 12338, 50774 Kuala Lumpur; tel. (3) 2308033; fax (3) 2303657; Gen. Man. MOHD YUSOF IDRIS.

John Hancock Life Insurance (Malaysia) Bhd: Bangunan John Hancock, 6th Floor, Jalan Semantan, Damansara Heights, 50490 Kuala Lumpur; tel. (3) 2548055; fax (3) 2556291; life and non-life insurance; fmrly British American Life and General Insurance Bhd; Chair. Tun AZMI BIN Haji MOHAMED; Man. Dir ALEX FOONG SOO HAH.

Hong Leong Assurance Sdn Bhd: Wisma Hla, 18th Floor, Jalan Raja Chulan, 50200 Kuala Lumpur; tel. (3) 2421267; fax (3) 2414022; Man. CHIA AH KOW.

Jerneh Insurance Corpn Sdn Bhd: Wisma Jerneh, 12th Floor, 38 Jalan Sultan Ismail, POB 12420, 50788 Kuala Lumpur; tel. (3) 2427066; fax (3) 2426672; f. 1970; general; Gen. Man. GOH CHIN ENG.

Malaysia National Insurance Sdn Bhd: Tower 1, 26th Floor, MNI Twins, 11 Jalan Pinang, 50450 Kuala Lumpur; tel. (3) 2645000; fax (3) 2641010; internet www.mni.com.my; f. 1970; life and general; CEO SULAIMAN SALLEH.

Malaysian Co-operative Insurance Society Ltd: Wisma MCIS, Jalan Barat, 46200 Petaling Jaya, Selangor; tel. (3) 7552577; fax (3) 7571563; e-mail info@mcis.po.my; internet www.mcis.com.my/mcis; f. 1954; CEO L. MEYYAPPAN.

Mayban Assurance Bhd: 27 Lorong Medan Tuanku Satu, 50300 Kuala Lumpur; tel. (3) 2918777; fax (3) 2914930; e-mail mayassur@ tm.net.my; internet www.maybangen.com.my; Man. KASSIM ZAKARIA.

MBf Insurans Sdn Bhd: Plaza MBf, 5th Floor, Jalan Ampang, POB 10345, 50710 Kuala Lumpur; tel. (3) 2613466; fax (3) 2613466; Man. MARC HOOI TUCK KOK.

Multi-Purpose Insurans Bhd: Menara Multi-Purpose, 9th Floor, Capital Square, 8 Jalan Munshi Abdullah, 50100 Kuala Lumpur; tel. (3) 26919888; fax (3) 26945758; e-mail info@mpib.com.my; fmrly Kompas Insurans Bhd; Man. LIUNG CHEONG POH.

Overseas Assurance Corpn Ltd: Wisma Lee Rubber, 21st Floor, Jalan Melata, 50100 Kuala Lumpur; tel. (3) 2022939; fax (3) 2912288; Gen. Man. A. K. WONG.

Progressive Insurance Sdn Bhd: Plaza Berjaya, 9th, 10th and 15th Floors, 12 Jalan Imbi, POB 10028, 50700 Kuala Lumpur; tel. (3) 2410044; fax (3) 2418257; Man. JERRY PAUT.

RHB Insurance Bhd: Tower 1, 4th Floor, RHB Centre, Jalan Tun Razak, 50450 Kuala Lumpur; tel. (3) 9812731; fax (3) 9812729; Man. MOHAMMAD ABDULLAH.

Sime AXA Assurance Bhd: Wisma Sime Darby, 15th Floor, Jalan Raja Laut, 50350 Kuala Lumpur; tel. (3) 2937888; fax (3) 2914672; e-mail hkkang@simenet.com; Gen. Man. HAK KOON KANG.

South-East Asia Insurance Bhd: Tingkat 9, Menara SEA Insurance, 1008 Jalan Sultan Ismail, 50250 Kuala Lumpur; POB 6120 Pudu, 55916 Kuala Lumpur; tel. (3) 2938111; fax (3) 2930111; internet www.sea.com.my; CEO HASHIM HARUN.

UMBC Insurans Sdn Bhd: Bangunan Sime Bank, 16th Floor, Jalan Sultan Sulaiman, 50000 Kuala Lumpur; tel. (3) 2328733; fax (3) 2322181; f. 1961; CEO ABDULLAH ABDUL SAMAD.

United Oriental Assurance Sdn Bhd: Wisma UOA, 36 Jalan Ampang, 50450 Kuala Lumpur; tel. (3) 2302828; fax (3) 2324250; e-mail uoa@uoa.po.my; f. 1976; CEO R. NESARETNAM.

Zürich Insurance (Malaysia) Bhd: Wisma Selangor Dredging, 4th Floor, South Block, 142A Jalan Ampang, 50450 Kuala Lumpur; tel. (3) 27133838; fax (3) 27133833; CEO MICHAEL WONG TECK KAT.

Trade and Industry

GOVERNMENT AGENCIES

Corporate Debt Restructuring Committee (CDRC): Kuala Lumpur; f. 1998 to restructure corporate and financial debt; Chair. C. RAJANDRAM.

Danamodal Nasional Bhd (Danamodal): Level 11and 12, Blok C, Bank Negara Malaysia, Jalan Dato' Onn, POB 10922, 50929 Kuala Lumpur; tel. (3) 2943954; fax (3) 2948632; e-mail dmodal2@tm.net .my; internet www.bnm.gov.my/danamodal/main2bck.htm; f. 1998 to recapitalize banks and restructure financial institutions, incl. arranging mergers and consolidations; Man. Dir MARIANUS VONG SHIN TZOI.

Federal Agricultural Marketing Authority (FAMA): Fama Point Bldg, Lot 17304, Jalan Persiaran 1, Bandar Baru Selayang, 68100 Batu Caves, Selangor Darul Ehsan; tel. (3) 61389622; fax (3) 61365597; f. 1965 to supervise, co-ordinate and improve existing markets and methods of marketing agricultural produce, and to seek and promote new markets and outlets for agricultural produce; Chair. SHAHIDAN KASSIM; Dir-Gen. Dr ABDUL AZIZ MOHAMED YAACOB.

Federal Land Development Authority (FELDA): Jalan Maktab, 54000 Kuala Lumpur; tel. (3) 2935066; fax (3) 2920087; f. 1956; govt statutory body formed to develop land into agricultural smallholdings to eradicate rural poverty; 893,150 ha of land developed (1994); involved in rubber, oil palm and sugar-cane cultivation; Chair. Raja Tan Sri MUHAMMAD ALIAS; Dir-Gen. MOHAMED FADZIL YUNUS.

Khazanah Nasional: 21 Putra Place 100, Ilu Putra, 50350 Kuala Lumpur; e-mail knb@po.jaring.my; f. 1994; state-controlled investment co; assumed responsibility for certain assets fmrly under control of the Minister of Finance Inc. holds 40% of Telekom Malaysia Bhd, 40% of Tenaga Nasional Bhd, 6.6% of HICOM Bhd and 17.8% of PROTON; Chair. Datuk Seri Dr MAHATHIR MOHAMAD.

Malaysia Export Credit Insurance Bhd: Bangunan Bank Industri, 17th Floor, Bandar Wawsan, 1016 Jalan Sultan Ismail, POB 11048, 50734 Kuala Lumpur; tel. (3) 26910677; fax (3) 26910353; e-mail mecib@mecib.com.my; internet www.mecib.com .my; f. 1977; wholly-owned subsidiary of Bank Industri Malaysia Technologi Bhd; provides insurance, financial guarantee and other trade-related services for exporters of locally manufactured products and for banking community; cap. RM 150m., exports declared RM 740m. (2001); Gen. Man. EN. AMINURRASHID ZULKIFLY; 67 employees.

Malaysia External Trade Development Corpn (MATRADE): Wisma Sime Darby, Jalan Raja Laut, 50350 Kuala Lumpur; tel. (3) 26947259; fax (3) 26947362; e-mail info@hq.matrade.gov.my; internet www.matrade.gov.my; f. 1993; responsibility for external trade development and promotion; CEO MERLYN KASIMIR.

Malaysian Institute of Economic Research: Menara Dayabumi, 9th Floor, Jalan Sultan Hishamuddin, POB 12160, 50768 Kuala Lumpur; tel. (3) 22725897; fax (3) 22730197; e-mail Admin@mier.po .my; internet www.mier.org.my; Exec. Dir MOHAMED ARIFF.

Malaysian Palm Oil Board (MPOB): Lot 6, SS6, Jalan Perbandaran, 47301 Kelana Jaya, Selangor; tel. (3) 7035544; fax (3) 7033533; internet porla.gov.my; f. 2000 by merger of Palm Oil Registration and Licensing Authority and Palm Oil Research Institute of Malaysia; Dir-Gen. Dato' MOHD YUSOF BASIR.

Malaysian Timber Industry Board (Lembaga Perindustrian Kayu Malaysia): 13–17 Menara PGRM, Jalan Pudu Ulu, POB 10887, 50728 Kuala Lumpur; tel. (3) 9822235; fax (3) 9851477;

e-mail mtib@po.jaring.my; internet www.gov.my; f. 1968 to promote and regulate the export of timber and timber products from Peninsular Malaysia; Chair. Dato' Dr Haji ABDULLAH BIN MOHD TAHIR; Dir-Gen. Dato' Haji ABDUL RASHID MAT AMIN.

Muda Agricultural Development Authority (MADA): MADA HQ, Ampang Jajar, 05990 Alor Setar, Kedah; tel. (4) 7728255; fax (4) 7722667; internet www.mada.gov.my; Chair. Dato' Seri SYED RAZAK BIN SYED ZAIN.

National Economic Action Council: NEAC-MTEN, Office of the Minister of Special Functions, Level 2, Block B5, Federal Government Administrative Centre, 62502 Putrajaya, Selangor Darul Ehsan; tel. (88) 883333; internet www.neac.gov.my/; Exec. Dir Dato' MUSTAPA MOHAMED.

National Information Technology Council (NITC): Kuala Lumpur; Sec. Datuk Tengku Dr MOHD AZZMAN SHARIFFADEEN.

National Timber Certification Council: Kuala Lumpur; Chair. CHEW LYE TENG.

Pengurusan Danaharta Nasional Bhd (Danaharta): Tingkat 10, Bangunan Setia 1, 15 Lorong Dungun, Bukit Damansara, 50490 Kuala Lumpur; tel. (3) 2531122; fax (3) 2537482; internet www .danaharta.com.my; f. 1998 to acquire non-performing loans from the banking sector and to maximize the recovery value of those assets; Man. Dir Dato' AZMAN YAHYA.

Perbadanan Nasional Bhd (PERNAS): Kuala Lumpur; tel. (3) 2935177; f. 1969; govt-sponsored; promotes trade, banking, property and plantation development, construction, mineral exploration, steel manufacturing, inland container transportation, mining, insurance, industrial development, engineering services, telecommunication equipment, hotels and shipping; cap. p.u. RM 116.25m. 10 wholly-owned subsidiaries, over 60 jointly-owned subsidiaries and 18 assoc. cos; Chair. Tunku Dato' SHAHRIMAN BIN Tunku SULAIMAN; Man. Dir Dato' A. RAHMAN BIN HAMIDON.

DEVELOPMENT ORGANIZATIONS

Fisheries Development Authority of Malaysia: Tingkat 7, Wisma PKNS, Jalan Raja Laut, Peti Surat 12630, 50784 Kuala Lumpur; tel. (3) 2924044; fax (3) 2911931; e-mail info@kim.moa.my.

Johor Corporation: 13th Floor, Menara Johor Corporation, Kotaraya, 80000 Johor Bahru; tel. (7) 2232692; fax (7) 2233175; e-mail pdnjohor@jcorp.com.my; internet www.jcorp.com.my; development agency of the Johor state govt; Chief Exec. Dato' H. MUHAMMAD ALI.

Kumpulan FIMA Bhd (Food Industries of Malaysia): Kompleks FIMA, International Airport, Subang, Selangor; tel. (3) 7462199; f. 1972; fmrly govt corpn, transferred to private sector in 1991; promotes food and related industry through investment on its own or by co-ventures with local or foreign entrepreneurs; oil palm, cocoa and fruit plantation developments; manufacturing and packaging, trading, supermarkets and restaurants; Man. Dir Dato' MOHD NOOR BIN ISMAIL; 1,189 employees.

Majlis Amanah Rakyat (MARA) (Trust Council for the People): MEDAN MARA Bldg, 13th Floor, Jalan Raja Laut, 50609 Kuala Lumpur; tel. (3) 2915111; fax (3) 2913620; f. 1966 to promote, stimulate, facilitate and undertake economic and social development; to participate in industrial and commercial undertakings and jt ventures; Chair. Tan Sri NAZRI AZIZ.

Malaysian Industrial Development Authority (MIDA): Wisma Damansara, 6th Floor, Jalan Semantan, POB 10618, 50720 Kuala Lumpur; tel. (3) 2553633; fax (3) 2557970; e-mail promotion@mida .gov.my; internet www.mida.gov.my; f. 1967; Chair. Tan Sri Datuk ZAINAL ABIDIN BIN SULONG; Dir-Gen. Dato' ZAINUN AISHAH AHMAD.

Malaysian Industrial Development Finance Bhd: 195A Jalan Tun Razak, POB 12110, 50939 Kuala Lumpur; tel. (3) 2610066; fax (3) 2615973; f. 1960 by the Govt, banks, insurance cos; industrial financing, advisory services, project development, merchant and commercial banking services; Chair. Tan Sri Dato' Seri AHMAD SARJI BIN ABDUL HAMID; CEO and Dir DARWIS BIN MOHD DAEK.

Malaysian Pepper Marketing Board: Tanah Putih, POB 1653, 93916 Kuching; tel. (82) 331811; fax (82) 336877; e-mail pmb@ pepper.po.my; internet www.sarawakpepper.gov.my/ sarawakpepper; f. 1972; responsible for the statutory grading of all Sarawak pepper for export, licensing of pepper dealers and exporters, trading and the development and promotion of pepper grading, storage and processing facilities; Gen. Man. GRUNSIN AYOM.

Pinang Development Corporation: Pinang; development agency of the Pinang state government; Gen. Man. SITI BALKISH BIN SHARIFF.

Sarawak Economic Development Corpn: Menara SEDC, 6th–11th Floors, Sarawak Plaza, Jalan Tunku Abdul Rahman, POB 400, 93902 Kuching; tel. (82) 416777; fax (82) 424330; f. 1972; statutory org. responsible for commercial and industrial development in Sarawak either solely or jtly with foreign and local entrepreneurs;

responsible for the development of tourism infrastructure; Chair. Haji Talib Zulpilip.

Selangor State Development Corporation (PKNS): f. 1964; partially govt-owned; Corporate Man. Yusof Othman.

CHAMBERS OF COMMERCE

The Associated Chinese Chamber of Commerce: Wisma Chamber, 4th Floor, Lot 214, Jalan Bukit Mata, 93100 Kuching; tel. (82) 428815; fax (82) 429950; e-mail kcjong@pc.jaring.my; f. 1965; Pres. Tiong Su Kouk; Sec. Gen. Lee Khim Sin.

Associated Chinese Chambers of Commerce and Industry of Malaysia: 8th Floor, Office Tower, Plaza Berjaya, 12 Jalan Imbi, 55100 Kuala Lumpur; tel. (3) 2452503; fax (3) 2452562; e-mail acccim@mol.net.my; internet www.acccim.org.my; Pres. Dato' Lim Guan Teik; Exec. Sec. Ong Kim Seng.

Malay Chamber of Commerce and Industry of Malaysia: Plaza Pekeliling, 17th Floor, Jalan Tun Razak, 50400 Kuala Lumpur; tel. (3) 4418522; fax (3) 4414502; Pres. Tan Sri Dato' Tajudin Ramli; Sec.-Gen. Zaki Said.

Malaysian Associated Indian Chambers of Commerce and Industry: 116 Jalan Tuanku Abdul Rahman, 2nd Floor, 50100 Kuala Lumpur; tel. (3) 26931033; fax (3) 26911670; e-mail klsicci@po .jaring.my; internet www.maicci.com; f. 1950; Pres. Dato' K. Kenneth Eswaran; Hon. Sec.-Gen. Muthusamy V. V. M. Samy; 8 brs.

> **Malaysian International Chamber of Commerce and Industry (MICCI)** (Dewan Perniagaan dan Perindustrian Antarabangsa Malaysia): C-8-8, 8th Floor, Block C, Plaza Mont' Kiara, 50480 Kuala Lumpur; tel. (3) 62017708; fax (3) 62017705; e-mail micci@micci.com; internet www.micci.com; f. 1837; brs in Pinang, Perak, Johor, Melaka and Sabah; 1,100 corporate mems; Pres. P. J. Dingle; Exec. Dir Stewart J. Forbes.

National Chamber of Commerce and Industry of Malaysia: 37 Jalan Kia Peng, 50450 Kuala Lumpur; tel. (3) 2419600; fax (3) 2413775; e-mail nccim@po.jaring.my; internet www.nccim.org.my/ nccim; f. 1962; Pres. Tan Sri Tajudin Ramli; Sec.-Gen. Dato' Abdul Halim Abdullah.

Sabah Chamber of Commerce and Industry: Jalan Tiga, Sandakan; tel. (89) 2141; Pres. T. H. Wong.

Sarawak Chamber of Commerce and Industry (SCCI): POB A-841, Kenyalang Park Post Office, 93806 Kuching; tel. (82) 237148; fax (82) 237186; e-mail phtay@pc.jaring.my; internet www.cmsb .com.my/scci; f. 1950; Chair. Datuk Haji Mohamed Amin Haji Satem; Dep. Chair. Datuk Abang Haji Abdul Karim Tun Abang Haji Openg.

South Indian Chamber of Commerce of Sarawak: 37c India St, Kuching; f. 1952; Pres. Haja Nazimuddin bin Abdul Majid; Vice-Pres. Syed Ahmad.

INDUSTRIAL AND TRADE ASSOCIATIONS

Federation of Malaysian Manufacturers: Wisma FMM, 3 Persiaran Dagang, PJU 9 Bandar Sri Damansara, 52200 Kuala Lumpur; tel. (3) 6361211; fax (3) 6341266; e-mail webmaster@fmm .org.my; internet www.fmm.org.my; f. 1968; 2,036 mems (Feb. 2000); Pres. Jen (B.) Tan Sri Dato' Zain Hashim; CEO Lee Cheng Suan.

Federation of Rubber Trade Associations of Malaysia: 138 Jalan Bandar, 50000 Kuala Lumpur; tel. (3) 2384006.

Malayan Agricultural Producers' Association: Kuala Lumpur; tel. (3) 42573988; fax (3) 42573113; f. 1997; 464 mem. estates and 115 factories; Pres. Tan Sri Dato' Haji Basir bin Ismail; Dir Mohamad bin Audong.

Malaysian Iron & Steel Industry Federation: 28e, 30e, 5th Floor, Block 2, Worldwide Business Park, Jalan Tinju 13/50, Section 13, 40675 Shah Alam, Selangor; tel. (3) 55133970; fax (3) 55133891; e-mail misif@po-jaring.my; Chair. Tan Sri Dato' Soong Siew Hoong; 150 mems.

Malaysian Oil Palm Growers' Council: Bangunan Getah Asli I, 3rd Floor, 148 Jalan Ampang, POB 10747, 50724 Kuala Lumpur; tel. (3) 2615088; fax (3) 2612504; f. 1953.

The Malaysian Pineapple Industry Board: Wisma Nanas, 5 Jalan Padi Mahsuri, Bandar Baru UDA, 81200 Johor Bahru; tel. (7) 2361211; fax (7) 2365694; e-mail mpib@tm.net.my; Dir-Gen. Tuan Haji Ismail bin Abd Jamal.

The Malaysian Rubber Products Manufacturers' Association: 1 Jalan USJ 11/1j, Subang Jaya, 47620 Petaling Jaya, Selangor; tel. (3) 56316150; fax (3) 56316152; e-mail mrpma@po .jaring.my; internet www.mrpma.com; f. 1952; Pres. Tan Sri Datuk Arshad Ayub; 144 mems.

Malaysian Rubber Board: 148 Jalan Ampang, 50450 Kuala Lumpur; tel. (3) 92062000; fax (3) 21634492; e-mail dg@lgm.gov.my; internet www.lgm.gov.my; f. 1998; implements policies and develop-

ment programmes to ensure the viability of the Malaysian rubber industry; regulates the industry (in particular, the packing, grading, shipping and export of rubber); Dir-Gen. Dato' Abdul Hamid bin Sawal.

Malaysian Wood Industries Association: 19b, 19th Floor, Menara PGRM, 8 Jalan Pudu Ulu, Cheras, 56100 Kuala Lumpur; tel. (3) 92821778; fax (3) 92821779; e-mail mwia@tm.net.my; f. 1957.

National Tobacco Board Malaysia (Ibu Pejabat Lembaga Tembakau Negara): Kubang Kerian, POB 198, 15720 Kota Bharu, Kelantan; tel. (9) 7652933; fax (9) 7655640; e-mail ltnm@ltn.gov.my; Dir-Gen. Teo Hui Bek.

Northern Malaya Rubber Millers and Packers Association: 22 Pitt St, 3rd Floor, Suites 301–303, 10200 Pinang; tel. (4) 620037; f. 1919; 153 mems; Pres. Hwang Sing Lue; Hon. Sec. Lee Seng Keok.

Palm Oil Refiners' Association of Malaysia (PORAM): Kuala Lumpur; tel. (3) 2488893; f. 1975 to promote the palm oil refining industry; Chair. Datuk Robert W. K. Chan; 27 mems.

Rubber Industry Smallholders' Development Authority (RISDA): 4½ Miles, Jalan Ampang, 50450 Kuala Lumpur; tel. (3) 4564022; Dir-Gen. Mohd Zain bin Haji Yahya.

Tin Industry Research and Development Board: West Block, 8th Floor, Wisma Selangor Dredging, Jalan Ampang, POB 12560, 50782 Kuala Lumpur; tel. (3) 21616171; fax (3) 21616179; e-mail mcom@po.jaring.my; Chair. Mohamed Ajib Anuar; Sec. Muhamad Nor Muhamad.

EMPLOYERS' ORGANIZATIONS

Malaysian Employers' Federation: 3A06–3A07, Block A, Pusat Dagangan Phileo Damansara II, 15 Jalan 16/11, off Jalan Damansara, 46350 Petaling Jaya, Selangor; tel. (3) 79557778; fax (3) 79559008; e-mail mef-hq@mef.po.my; internet www.mef.org.my; f. 1959; Pres. Jafar Abdul Carrim; private-sector org. incorporating 10 employer organizations and 3,447 individual enterprises, including:

> **Association of Insurance Employers:** c/o Royal Insurance (M) Sdn Bhd, Menara Boustead, 5th Floor, 69 Jalan Raja Chulan, 50200 Kuala Lumpur; tel. (3) 2410233; fax (3) 2442762; Pres. Ng Kim Hoong.

> **Commercial Employers' Association of Peninsular Malaysia:** c/o The East Asiatic Co (M) Bhd, 1 Jalan 205, 46050 Petaling Jaya, Selangor; tel. (3) 7913322; fax (3) 7913561; Pres. Hamzah Haji Ghulam.

> **Malayan Commercial Banks' Association:** see Banking Associations, above.

> **Malaysian Chamber of Mines:** West Block, Wisma Selangor Dredging, 8th Floor, Jalan Ampang, 50350 Kuala Lumpur; tel. and fax (3) 21616171; e-mail mcom@po.jaring.my; internet www .mcom.com.my; f. 1914; promotes and protects interests of Malaysian mining industry; Pres. Ir Abdul Rahman Dahan; Exec. Dir Muhamad nor Muhamad.

> **Malaysian Textile Manufacturers' Association:** Wisma Selangor Dredging, 9th Floor, West Block, 142c Jalan Ampang, 50450 Kuala Lumpur; tel. (3) 21621587; fax (3) 21623953; e-mail textile@po.jaring.my; internet www.fashion-asia.com; Pres. Bahar Ahmad; Exec. Dir Choy Ming Bil; 230 mems.

> **Pan Malaysian Bus Operators' Association:** 88 Jalan Sultan Idris Shah, 30300 Ipoh, Perak; tel. (5) 2549421; fax (5) 2550858; Sec. Datin Teoh Phaik Lean.

> **Sabah Employers' Consultative Association:** Dewan SECA, No. 4, Block A, 1st Floor, Bandar Ramai-Ramai, 90000 Sandakan, Sabah; tel. and fax (89) 272846; Pres. E. M. Khoo.

> **Stevedore Employers' Association:** 5 Pengkalan Weld, POB 288, 10300 Pinang; tel. (4) 2615091; Pres. Abdul Rahman Maidin.

UTILITIES

Electricity

Electricity Supply Department: Kuala Lumpur; regulatory body supervising electricity supply.

Tenaga Nasional Bhd: 129 Jalan Bangsar, POB 11003, 50732 Kuala Lumpur; tel. (3) 2825566; fax (3) 2823274; e-mail webadmin@ tnb.com.my; internet www.tnb.com.my; f. 1990 through the corporatization and privatization of the National Electricity Board; 53% govt-controlled; generation, transmission and distribution of electricity in Peninsular Malaysia; generating capacity of 7,573 MW (65% of total power generation); also purchases power from 12 licensed independent power producers; Chair. Jamaluddin Jaris; CEO Dato' Fuad B. Jaafar (acting).

Sabah Electricity Board (SEB): Wisma Lembaga Letrik Sabah, 88673 Kota Kinabalu; tel. (88) 211699; generation, transmission and distribution of electricity in Sabah.

Sarawak Electricity Supply Corpn (SESCO): POB 149, Kuching, Sarawak; tel. (82) 441188; fax (82) 444434; generation, transmission and distribution of electricity in Sarawak.

Gas

Gas Malaysia Sdn Bhd: West Block, Wisma Selangor Dredging, 1st Floor, 142c Jalan Ampang, POB 12968, 50794 Kuala Lumpur; tel. (3) 2632333; fax (3) 2633208; f. 1992; Chair. Tan Sri Dato' IBRAHIM MENUDIN; CEO AHMAD DAMANHURI ABDUL RAHIM.

Water

Under the federal Constitution, water supply is the responsibility of the state Governments. In 1998, owing to water shortages, the National Water Resources Council was established to co-ordinate management of water resources at national level. Malaysia's sewerage system is operated by Indah Water Konsortium, owned by Prime Utilities.

National Water Resources Council: c/o Ministry of Works, Jalan Sultan Salahuddin, 50580 Kuala Lumpur; tel. (3) 2919011; fax (3) 2986612; f. 1998 to co-ordinate management of water resources at national level through co-operation with state water boards; Chair. Dato' Seri Dr MAHATHIR BIN MOHAMAD.

Regulatory Authorities

Johor State Regulatory Body: c/o Pejabat Setiausaha Kerajaan Negeri Johor, Aras 1, Bangunan Sultan Ibrahim, Jalan Bukit Timbalan, 80000 Johor Bahru; tel. (7) 223850; Dir Tuan Haji OMAR BIN AWAB.

Kelantan Water Department: Tingkat Bawah Blok 6, Kota Darul Naim, 15503 Kota Bahru, Kelantan; tel. (9) 7475240; Dir Tuan Haji WAN ABDUL AZIZ BIN WAN JAAFAR.

Water Supply Authorities

Kedah Public Works Department: Bangunan Sultan Abdul Halim, Jalan Sultan Badlishah, 05582 Alor Setar, Kedah; tel. (4) 7334041; fax (4) 7341616; Dir Dr NORDIN BIN YUNUS.

Kelantan Water Sdn Bhd: 14 Beg Berkunci, Jalan Kuala Krai, 15990 Kota Bahru, Kelantan; tel. (10) 9022222; fax (10) 9022236; Dir PETER NEW BERKLEY.

Kuching Water Board: Jalan Batu Lintang, 93200 Kuching, Sarawak; tel. (82) 240371; fax (82) 244546; Dir DAVID YEU BIN TONG.

Labuan Public Works Department: Jalan Kg. Jawa, POB 2, 87008 Labuan; tel. (87) 414040; fax (87) 412370; Dir Ir ZULKIFLY BIN MADON.

LAKU Management Sdn Bhd: Soon Hup Tower, 6th Floor, Lot 907, Jalan Merbau, 98000 Miri; tel. (85) 442000; fax (85) 442005; e-mail chuilin@pd.jaring.my; serves Miri, Limbang and Bintulu; CEO YONG CHIONG VAN.

Melaka Water Corpn: Tingkat Bawah, 1 10–13, Graha Maju, Jalan Graha Maju, 75300 Melaka; tel. (6) 2825233; fax (6) 2837266; Ir ABDUL RAHIM SHAMSUDI.

Negeri Sembilan Water Department: Wisma Negeri, 70990 Seremban; tel. (6) 7622314; fax (6) 7620753; Ir Dr MOHD AKBAR.

Pahang Water Supply Department (Jabatan Bekalan Air Pahang): 9–10 Kompleks Tun Razak, Bandar Indera Mahkota, 25582 Kuantan, Pahang; tel. (9) 5721222; fax (9) 5721221; e-mail p-jba@pahang.gov.my; Dir Ir Haji ISMAIL BIN Haji MAT NOOR.

Pinang Water Supply Department: Level 29, KOMTAR, 10000 Pinang; tel. (4) 6505462; fax (4) 2645282; e-mail lyc@sukpp.gov.my; f. 1973; Gen. Man. Datuk Ir LEE YOW CHING.

Perak Water Board: Jalan St John, Peti Surat 589, 30760 Ipoh, Perak; tel. (5) 2551155; fax (5) 2556397; Dir Ir SANI BIN SIDIK.

Sabah Water Department: Wisma MUIS, Blok A, Tingkat 6, Beg Berkunci 210, 88825 Kota Kinabalu; tel. (88) 232364; fax (88) 232396; Man. Ir BENNY WANG.

SAJ Holdings Sdn Bhd: Bangunan Ibu Pejabat SAJ Holdings, Jalan Garuda, Larkin, POB 262, 80350 Johor Bahru; tel. (7) 2244040; fax (7) 2236155; e-mail support@saj.com.my; internet www.saj.com.my; f. 1999; Exec. Chair. Dir Dato' Haji HAMDAN BIN MOHAMED.

Sarawak Public Works Department: Wisma Seberkas, Jalan Tun Haji Openg, 93582 Kuching; tel. (82) 244041; fax (82) 429679; Dir MICHAEL TING KUOK NG.

Selangor Water Department: POB 5001, Jalan Pantai Baru, 59990 Kuala Lumpur; tel. (3) 2826244; fax (3) 2827535; f. 1972; Dir Ir LIEW WAI KIAT.

Sibu Water Board: Km 5, Jalan Salim, POB 405, 96007 Sibu, Sarawak; tel. (84) 211001; fax (84) 211543; e-mail pengurus@swb.po.my; Man. DANIEL WONG PARK ING.

Terengganu Water Department: Tkt 3, Wisma Negeri, Jalan Pejabat, 20200 Kuala Terengganu; tel. (9) 6222444; fax (9) 6221510; Ir Haji WAN NGAH BIN WAN.

TRADE UNIONS

In 1995 there were 502 trade unions, 56% of which were from the private sector. About 8.2% of the Malaysian work-force of 7.9m. belonged to unions.

Congress of Unions of Employees in the Public Administrative and Civil Services (CUEPACS): a nat. fed. with 53 affiliates, representing 120,150 govt workers (1994).

Malaysian Trades Union Congress: Wisma MTUC, 10–5, Jalan USJ 9/5T, 47620 Subang Jaya, Selangor; POB 3073, 46000 Petaling Jaya, Selangor; tel. (3) 80242953; fax (3) 80243224; e-mail mtuc@tm.net.my; internet www.mtuc.org.my; f. 1949; 230 affiliated unions; Pres. ZAINAL RAMPAK; Sec.-Gen. G. RAJASEKARAN.

Principal affiliated unions:

All Malayan Estates Staff Union: POB 12, 46700 Petaling Jaya, Selangor Darul Ehsan; tel. (3) 7249533; e-mail mes@po.jaring.my; 2,654 mems; Pres. TITUS GLADWIN; Gen. Sec. D. P. S. THAMOTHARAM.

Amalgamated Union of Employees in Government Clerical and Allied Services: 32A Jalan Gajah, off Jalan Yew, Pudu, 55100 Kuala Lumpur; tel. (3) 9859613; fax (3) 9838632; 6,703 mems; Pres. IBRAHIM BIN ABDUL WAHAB; Gen. Sec. MOHAMED IBRAHIM BIN ABDUL WAHAB.

Chemical Workers' Union: Petaling Jaya, Selangor; 1,886 mems; Pres. RUSIAN HITAM; Gen. Sec. JOHN MATHEWS.

Electricity Industry Workers' Union: 55-2 Jalan SS 15/8A, Subang Jaya, 47500 Petaling Jaya, Selangor; tel. (3) 7335243; 22,000 mems; Pres. ABDUL RASHID; Gen. Sec. P. ARUNASALAM.

Federation of Unions in the Textile, Garment and Leather Industry: c/o Selangor Textile and Garment Manufacturing Employees Union, 9D Jalan Travers, 50470 Kuala Lumpur; tel. (3) 2742578; f. 1989; four affiliates; Pres. ABDUL RAZAK HAMID; Gen. Sec. ABU BAKAR IBRAHIM.

Harbour Workers' Union, Port Kelang: 106 Persiaran Raja Muda Musa, Port Kelang; 2,426 mems; Pres. MOHAMED SHARIFF BIN YAMIN; Gen. Sec. MOHAMED HAYAT BIN AWANG.

Kesatuan Pekerja Tenaga Nasional Bhd: 30 Jalan Liku Bangsar, POB 10400, 59100 Kuala Lumpur; tel. (3) 2745657; 10,456 mems; Pres. MOHAMED ABU BAKAR; Gen. Sec. IDRIS BIN ISMAIL.

Kesatuan Pekerja-Pekerja FELDA: 2 Jalan Maktab Enam, Melalui Jalan Perumahan Gurney, 54000 Kuala Lumpur; tel. (3) 26929972; fax (3) 26913409; 3,111 mems; Pres. INDERA PUTRA Haji ISMAIL; Gen. Sec. JAMALLUDIN BIN LIMUN.

Kesatuan Pekerja-Pekerja Perusahaan Membuat Tekstil dan Pakaian Pulau Pinang dan Seberang Prai: 23 Lorong Talang Satu, Prai Gardens, 13600 Prai; tel. (4) 301397; 3,900 mems; Pres. ABDUL RAZAK HAMID; Gen. Sec. KENNETH STEPHEN PERKINS.

Malayan Technical Services Union: 3A Jalan Menteri, off Jalan Cochrane, 55100 Kuala Lumpur; tel. (3) 92851778; fax (3) 92811875; 6,500 mems; Pres. Haji MOHAMED YUSOP Haji HARMAIN SHAH; Gen. Sec. SAMUEL DEVADASAN.

Malaysian Rubber Board Staff Union: POB 10150, 50908 Kuala Lumpur; tel. (3) 4565102; 1,108 mems; Pres. JUDE MICHAEL; Gen. Sec. NG SIEW LAN.

Metal Industry Employees' Union: Metalworkers' House, 5 Lorong Utara Kecil, 46200 Petaling Jaya, Selangor; tel. (3) 79567214; fax (3) 79550854; e-mail mieum@tm.net.my; 15,491 mems; Pres. KAMARUSZAMAN BIN MANSOR; Gen. Sec. JACOB ENGKATESU.

National Union of Commercial Workers: Bangunan NUCW, 98A–D Jalan Masjid India, 50100 Kuala Lumpur; POB 12059, 50780 Kuala Lumpur; tel. (3) 2927385; fax (3) 2925930; f. 1959; 11,937 mems; Pres. TAIB SHARIF; Gen. Sec. C. KRISHNAN.

National Union of Plantation Workers: 428 A, B, Jalan 5/46, Gasing Indah, POB 73, 46700 Petaling Jaya, Selangor; tel. (3) 77827622; fax (3) 77815321; e-mail sangkara@mail.tm.net.my; f. 1990; 41,000 mems; Pres. AWI BIN AWANG; Gen. Sec. G. SANKARAN.

National Union of PWD Employees: 32B Jalan Gajah, off Jalan Yew, 55100 Kuala Lumpur; tel. (3) 9850149; 5,869 mems; Pres. KULOP IBRAHIM; Gen. Sec. S. SANTHANASAMY.

National Union of Telecoms Employees: Wisma NUTE, 17A Jalan Bangsar, 59200 Kuala Lumpur; tel. (3) 2821599; fax (3) 2821015; 15,874 mems; Pres. MOHAMED SHAFIE B. P. MAMMAL; Gen. Sec. MOHD JAFAR BIN ABDUL MAJID.

Non-Metallic Mineral Products Manufacturing Employees' Union: 99A Jalan SS 14/1, Subang Jaya, 47500 Petaling Jaya, Selangor; tel. (3) 56352245; fax (3) 56333863; e-mail nonmet@tm.net.my; 10,000 mems; Pres. ABDULLAH ABU BAKAR; Sec. S. SOMAHSUNDRAM.

Railwaymen's Union of Malaya: Bangunan Tong Nam, 1st Floor, Jalan Tun Sambathan (Travers), 50470 Kuala Lumpur; tel. (3) 2741107; fax (3) 2731805; 5,500 mems; Pres. ABDUL GAFFOR BIN IBRAHIM; Gen. Sec. S. VEERASINGAM.

Technical Services Union—Tenaga Nasional Bhd: Bangunan Keselamatan, POB 11003, Bangsar, Kuala Lumpur; tel. (3) 2823581; 3,690 mems; Pres. RAMLY YATIM; Gen. Sec. CLIFFORD SEN.

Timber Employees' Union: 10 Jalan AU 5c/14, Ampang, Ulu Kelang, Selangor; 7,174 mems; Pres. ABDULLAH METON; Gen. Sec. MINHAT SULAIMAN.

Transport Workers' Union: 21 Jalan Barat, Petaling Jaya, 46200 Selangor; tel. (3) 7566567; 10,447 mems; Pres. NORASHIKIN; Gen. Sec. ZAINAL RAMPAK.

Independent Federations and Unions

Kongres Kesatuan Guru-Guru Dalam Perkhidmatan Pelajaran (Congress of Unions of Employees in the Teaching Services): Johor; seven affiliates; Pres. RAMLI BIN MOHD JOHAN; Sec.-Gen. KASSIM BIN Haji HARON.

Malaysian Medical Association: MMA House, 4th Floor, 124 Jalan Pahang, 53000 Kuala Lumpur; tel. (3) 40420617; fax (3) 40418187; e-mail mma@tm.net.my; internet www.mma.org.my; 10 affiliates; Pres. Datuk Dr N. ATHIMULAM.

National Union of Bank Employees: NUBE Bldg, 61 Jalan Ampang, POB 12488, 50780 Kuala Lumpur; tel. (3) 20789800; fax (3) 20703800; e-mail nubehq@pd.jaring.my; internet www.nube.org.my; 27,000 mems; Gen. Sec. J. SOLOMON.

National Union of Journalists: 30B Jalan Padang Belia, 50470 Kuala Lumpur; tel. (3) 2742867; fax (3) 2744776; f. 1962; 1,700 mems; Gen. Sec. ONN EE SENG.

National Union of Newspaper Workers: 11B Jalan 20/14, Paramount Garden, 46300 Petaling Jaya, Selangor; tel. (3) 78768118; fax (3) 78751490; e-mail nunwl@tm.net.my; 3,000 mems; Pres. GAN HOE JIAN; Gen. Sec. R. CHANDRASEKARAN.

Sabah

Sabah Banking Employees' Union: POB 11649, 88818 Kota Kinabalu; internet sbeukk@tm.net.my; 729 mems; Gen. Sec. LEE CHI HONG.

Sabah Civil Service Union: Kota Kinabalu; f. 1952; 1,356 mems; Pres. J. K. K. VOON; Sec. STEPHEN WONG.

Sabah Commercial Employees' Union: Sinsuran Shopping Complex, Lot 3, Block N, 2nd Floor, POB 10357, 88803 Kota Kinabalu; tel. (88) 225971; fax (88) 213815; e-mail sceu-kk@tm.net.my; f. 1957; 980 mems; Gen. Sec. REBECCA CHIN.

Sabah Medical Services Union: POB 11257, 88813 Kota Kinabalu; tel. (88) 242126; fax (88) 242127; e-mail smsu65@hotmail.com; 4,000 mems; Pres. KATHY LO NYUK CHIN; Gen. Sec. LAURENCE VUN.

Sabah Petroleum Industry Workers' Union: POB 1087, Kota Kinabalu; 168 mems; Gen. Sec. THIEN FOOK SHIN.

Sabah Teachers' Union: POB 10912, 88810 Kota Kinabalu; tel. (88) 420034; fax (88) 431633; f. 1962; 3,001 mems; Pres. KWAN PING SIN; Sec.-Gen. PATRICK Y. C. CHOK.

Sarawak

Kepak Sarawak (Kesatuan Pegawai-Pegawai Bank, Sarawak): POB 62, Bukit Permata, 93100 Kuching, Sarawak; tel. (19) 8549372; e-mail kepaksar@tm.net.my; bank officers' union; 1,430 mems; Gen. Sec. DOMINIC CH'NG YUNG TED.

Sarawak Commercial Employees' Union: POB 807, Kuching; 1,636 mems; Gen. Sec. SONG SWEE LIAP.

Sarawak Teachers' Union: 139A Jalan Rock, 1st Floor, 93200 Kuching; tel. (82) 245727; fax (82) 245757; e-mail swktu@po.jaring.my; internet www.geocities.com/swktu; f. 1965; 12,832 mems; Pres. WILLIAM GHANI BINA; Sec.-Gen. THOMAS HUO KOK SEN.

Transport

RAILWAYS

Peninsular Malaysia

The state-owned Malayan Railways had a total length of 1,672 km in Peninsular Malaysia in 1996. The main railway line follows the west coast and extends 782 km from Singapore, south of Peninsular Malaysia, to Butterworth (opposite Pinang Island) in the north. From Bukit Mertajam, close to Butterworth, the Kedah line runs north to the Thai border at Padang Besar where connection is made with the State Railway of Thailand. The East Coast Line, 526 km long, runs from Gemas to Tumpat (in Kelantan). A 21-km branch line from Pasir Mas (27 km south of Tumpat) connects with the State Railway of Thailand at the border station of Sungei Golok. Branch lines serve railway-operated ports at Port Dickson and Telok Anson as well as Port Klang and Jurong (Singapore). An express rail link connecting central Kuala Lumpur and the new Kuala Lumpur International Airport (KLIA) opened in 2001.

Keretapi Tanah Melayu Bhd (KTMB) (Malayan Railways): KTMB Corporate Headquarters, Jalan Sultan Hishamuddin, 50621 Kuala Lumpur; tel. (3) 22757142; fax (3) 27105706; e-mail pro@ktmb.com.my; internet www.ktmb.com.my; f. 1885; incorporated as a co under govt control in Aug. 1992; privatized in Aug. 1997; managed by the consortium Marak Unggal (Renong, DRB & Bolton); Chair. Tan Sri Dato' THONG YAW HONG.

Sabah

Sabah State Railway: Karung Berkunci 2047, 88999 Kota Kinabalu; tel. (88) 254611; fax (88) 236395; 134 track-km of 1-m gauge (1995); goods and passenger services from Tanjong Aru to Tenom, serving part of the west coast and the interior; diesel trains are used; Gen. Man. Ir BENNY WANG.

ROADS

Peninsular Malaysia

Peninsular Malaysia's road system is extensive, in contrast to those of Sabah and Sarawak. In 1999 the road network in Malaysia totalled an estimated 65,877 km, of which 16,206 km were highways and 31,777 km secondary roads; 75.8% of the network was paved.

Sabah

Jabatan Kerja Raya (Public Works Department): 88582 Kota Kinabalu, Sabah; tel. (88) 244333; fax (88) 237234; e-mail pos@jkr.sabah.gov.my; maintains a network totalling 10,878 km, of which 1,230 km were trunk roads in 1997; the total included 4,007 km of sealed roads; Dir DAVID CHIU SIONG SENG.

Sarawak

Jabatan Kerja Raya (Public Works Department): 88582 Kota Kinabalu, Sabah; tel. (88) 244333; fax (88) 237234; e-mail pos@jkr.sabah.gov.my; road network totalling 10,979 km, of which 3,986 km were sealed roads; Dir DAVID CHIU SIONG SENG.

SHIPPING

The ports in Malaysia are classified as federal ports, under the jurisdiction of the federal Ministry of Transport, or state ports, responsible to the state ministries of Sabah and Sarawak.

Peninsular Malaysia

The federal ports in Peninsular Malaysia are Klang (the principal port), Pinang, Johor and Kuantan.

Johor Port Authority: POB 66, 81707 Pasir Gudang, Johor; tel. (7) 2517721; fax (7) 2517684; e-mail jport@lpj.com.my; internet www.lpj.gov.my; f. 1973; Gen. Man. MOHD ROZALI BIN MOHD ALI.

Johor Port Bhd: POB 151, 81707 Pasir Gudang, Johor; tel. (7) 2525888; fax (7) 2522507; e-mail joport@silicon.net.my; internet www.joport.com.my; Exec. Chair. Dato' MOHD TAUFIK ABDULLAH.

Klang Port Authority: POB 202, Jalan Pelabuhan, 42005 Port Klang, Selangor; tel. (3) 31688211; fax (3) 31670211; e-mail pka_admin@pka.gov.my; f. 1963; Gen. Man. Datin Paduka O. C. PHANG.

Kuantan Port Authority: Tanjung Gelang, POB 161, 25720 Kuantan, Pahang; tel. (9) 5833201; fax (9) 5833866; e-mail lpk@po.jaring.my; internet www.lpktn.gov.my; f. 1974; Gen. Man. KHAIRUL ANUAR BIN ABDUL RAHMAN.

Penang Port Commission: POB 143, 10710 Pinang; tel. (4) 2633211; fax (4) 2626211; e-mail sppp@po.jaring.my; internet www.penangport.gov.my; f. 1956; Gen. Man. Dato' Capt. Haji ABDUL RAHIM ABDUL AZIZ.

Sabah

The chief ports are Kota Kinabalu, Sandakan, Tawau, Lahad Datu, Kudat, Semporna and Kunak and are administered by the Sabah Ports Authority. Many international shipping lines serve Sabah. Local services are operated by smaller vessels. The Sapangar Bay oil terminal, 25 km from Kota Kinabalu wharf, can accommodate oil tankers of up to 30,000 dwt.

Sabah Ports Authority: Bangunan Ibu Pejabat LPS, Jalan Tun Fuad, Tanjung Lipat, 88617 Kota Kinabalu, Sabah; tel. (88) 256155; fax (88) 223036; e-mail sabport@po.jaring.my; internet www .infosabah.com.my/spa.

Sarawak

There are four port authorities in Sarawak: Kuching, Rajang, Miri and Bintulu. Kuching, Rajang and Miri are statutory ports, while Bintulu is a federal port. Kuching port serves the southern region of Sarawak, Rajang port the central region, and Miri port the northern region.

Kuching Port Authority: Jalan Pelabuhan, Pending, POB 530, 93710 Kuching, Sarawak; tel. (82) 482144; fax (82) 481696; e-mail kuport@po.jaring.my; f. 1961; Gen. Man. CHOU CHII MING.

Rajang Port Authority: 96000 Sibu, Sarawak; tel. (84) 319004; fax (84) 318754; e-mail rajang@po.jaring.my; f. 1970; Gen. Man. Haji BAHRIN Haji ADENG.

Principal Shipping Companies

Achipelego Shipping (Sarawak) Sdn Bhd: Lot 267/270, Jalan Chan Chin Ann, POB 2998, 93758 Kuching; tel. (82) 412581; fax (82) 416249; Gen. Man. MICHAEL M. AMAN.

Malaysia Shipping Corpn Sdn Bhd: Office Tower, Plaza Berjaya, Suite 14c, 14th Floor, 12 Jalan Imbi, 55100 Kuala Lumpur; tel. (3) 2418788; fax (3) 2429214; e-mail mscsb@po.jaring.my; Chair. Y. C. CHANG.

Malaysian International Shipping Corpn Bhd (National Shipping Line of Malaysia): Suite 3–8, Tingkat 3, Wisma MISC, 2 Jalan Conlay, 50450 Kuala Lumpur; tel. (3) 2428088; fax (3) 2486602; e-mail zzainala@miscnote1.miscbhd.com; internet www.misc-bhd .com; f. 1968; regular sailings between the Far East, South-East Asia, Australia, Japan and Europe; also operates chartering, tanker, haulage and warehousing and agency services; major shareholder, Petroliam Nasional Bhd (PETRONAS); Chair. Tan Sri Dato' MOHD HASSAN BIN MARICAN; Man. Dir Dato' Haji MOHD ALI BIN Haji YASIN.

Perbadanan Nasional Shipping Line Bhd (PNSL): Kuala Lumpur; tel. (3) 2932211; fax (3) 2930493; f. 1982; specializes in bulk cargoes; Chair. Tunku Dato' SHAHRIMAN BIN Tunku SULAIMAN; Exec. Dep. Chair. Dato' SULAIMAN ABDULLAH.

Persha Shipping Agencies Sdn Bhd: Bangunan Mayban Trust, Penthouse Suite, Jalan Pinang, 10200 Pinang; tel. (4) 2612400; fax (4) 2623122; Man. Dir MOHD NOOR MOHD KAMALUDIN.

Syarikat Perkapalan Kris Sdn Bhd (The Kris Shipping Co Ltd): 3AO7 Block A, Kelana Centre Point, 3 Jalan SS7/19, Kelana Jaya; POB 8428, 46789 Petaling Jaya, Selangor; tel. (3) 7046477; fax (3) 7048007; domestic services; Chair. Dato' Seri SYED NAHAR SHAHABUDIN; Gen. Man. ROHANY TALIB; Dep. Gen. Man. THO TEIT CHANG.

Trans-Asia Shipping Corpn Sdn Bhd: Unit 715–718, Block A, Kelana Business Centre, 97 Jalan SS7/2, Kelana Jaya, 47301 Petaling Jaya, Selangor; tel. (3) 78802020; fax (4) 78802200; e-mail ahmad@tasco.com.my; internet www.tasco.com.my; Man. Dir LEE CHECK POH.

CIVIL AVIATION

The new Kuala Lumpur International Airport (KLIA), situated in Sepang, Selangor (50 km south of Kuala Lumpur) began operations in June 1998, with an initial capacity of 25m.–30m. passengers a year, rising to 45m. by 2020. It replaced Subang Airport in Kuala Lumpur (which was renamed the Sultan Abdul Aziz Shah Airport in 1996). An express rail link between central Kuala Lumpur and KLIA opened in early 2001. There are regional airports at Kota Kinabalu, Pinang, Johor Bahru, Kuching and Pulau Langkawi. In addition, there are airports catering for domestic services at Alor Star, Ipoh, Kota Bahru, Kuala Terengganu, Kuantan and Melaka in Peninsular Malaysia, Sibu, Bintulu and Miri in Sarawak and Sandakan, Tawau, Lahad Datu and Labuan in Sabah. There are also numerous smaller airstrips.

Department of Civil Aviation (Jabatan Penerbangan Awam Malaysia): Aras B1, 1, 2 and 3, Block D5, Parcel D, Pusat Pentadbiran Kerajaan Persekutuan, 62502 Putrajaya; tel. (3) 88866000; fax (3) 88891541; Dir-Gen. (vacant).

Air Asia Sdn Bhd: Wisma HICOM, 6th Floor, 2 Jalan Usahawan, U1/8, Seksyen Ul, 40150 Shah Alam, Selangor; tel. (3) 2028007; fax (3) 2028137; internet www.airasia.com; f. 1993; f. 1993; a second national airline, with a licence to operate domestic, regional and international flights; 85%-owned by HICOM.

Berjaya Air: Apprentice Training Bldg, 1st Floor, Mas Complex B (Hangar 1), Lapangan Terbang Sultan Abdul Aziz Shah, Shah Alam, Selangor, 47200 Kuala Lumpur; tel. (3) 7476828; fax (3) 7476228; e-mail berjayaa@tm.net.my; f. 1989; scheduled and charter domestic services; Pres. Dato TENGKU ADNAN MANSOR.

Malaysia Airlines: 32nd Floor, Bangunan MAS, Jalan Sultan Ismail, 50250 Kuala Lumpur; tel. (3) 21655140; fax (3) 21633178; e-mail grpcomm@malaysiaairlines.com.my; internet www .malaysiaairlines.com.my; f. 1971 as the Malaysian successor to the Malaysia Singapore Airlines (MSA); known as Malaysian Airline System (MAS) until Oct. 1987; services to 33 domestic points and to 79 international destinations; Chair. Tan Sri Datuk Seri AZIZAN ZAINUL ABIDIN.

Pelangi Air: Kuala Lumpur; tel. (3) 2624453; fax (3) 2624515; internet www.asia123.com/pelangi/home.htm; f. 1988; domestic scheduled passenger services; Chair. Tan Sri SAW HWAT LYE.

Transmile Air: Wisma Semantan, Mezzanine 2, Block B, 12 Jalan Gelenggang, Bukit Damansara, 50490 Kuala Lumpur; tel. (3) 2537718; fax (3) 2537719; f. 1992; scheduled and charter regional and domestic services for pasengers and cargo; Chair. Tan Sri ZAINOL MAHMOOD.

Tourism

Malaysia has a rapidly-growing tourist industry, and tourism remains an important source of foreign-exchange earnings. In 2002 some 13.3m. tourists visited Malaysia. In 2001 tourist receipts totalled RM 24,221.5m.

Malaysia Tourism Promotion Board: Menara Dato' Onn, 17th, 24th–27th, 30th Floors, Putra World Trade Centre, Jalan Tun Ismail, 50480 Kuala Lumpur; tel. (3) 26935188; fax (3) 26935884; e-mail tourism@tourism.gov.my; internet www.tourism.gov.my; f. 1972 to co-ordinate and promote activities relating to tourism; Chair. Datuk Paduka ABDUL KADIR Haji Sheikh FADZIR; Dir-Gen. Datuk ABDULLAH JONID.

Sabah Tourist Association: Kota Kinabalu; tel. (88) 211484; f. 1962; 55 mems; parastatal promotional org. Chair. THOMAS MORE WILLIE; Exec. Sec. CHRISTINE NGUI.

Sarawak Tourist Association: Sarawak Tourist Information Centre, Main Bazaar, 93000 Kuching; POB 887, 93718 Kuching; tel. (82) 240620; fax (82) 427151; f. 1963; Chair. PHILIP YONG KHI LIANG; Hon. Sec. AUDRY WAN ULLOK.

THE MALDIVES

Introductory Survey

Location, Climate, Language, Religion, Flag, Capital

The Republic of Maldives (commonly referred to as 'the Maldives') is in southern Asia. The country, lying about 675 km (420 miles) south-west of Sri Lanka, consists of 1,190 small coral islands (of which 200 are inhabited), grouped in 26 natural atolls (but divided, for administrative purposes, into 20 atolls), in the Indian Ocean. The climate is hot and humid. The average annual temperature is 27°C (80°F), with little daily or seasonal variation, while annual rainfall is generally between 2,540 mm and 3,800 mm (100 ins to 150 ins). The national language is Dhivehi (Maldivian), which is related to Sinhala. Islam is the state religion, and most Maldivians are Sunni Muslims. The national flag (proportions 2 by 3) is red, with a green rectangle, containing a white crescent, in the centre. The capital is Malé.

Recent History

The Maldives, called the Maldive Islands until April 1969, formerly had an elected Sultan as head of state. The islands were placed under British protection, with internal self-government, in 1887. They became a republic in January 1953, but the sultanate was restored in February 1954. The Maldives became fully independent, outside the Commonwealth, on 26 July 1965. Following a referendum, the country became a republic again in November 1968, with Amir Ibrahim Nasir, Prime Minister since 1957, as President.

In 1956 the Maldivian and British Governments agreed to the establishment of a Royal Air Force staging post on Gan, an island in the southernmost atoll, Addu. In 1975 the British Government's decision to close the base and to evacuate British forces created a large commercial and military vacuum. In October 1977 President Nasir rejected an offer of an annual payment of US $1m. from the USSR to lease the former base on Gan, announcing that he would not lease the island for military purposes, nor lease it to a superpower. In 1981 the President announced plans to establish an industrial zone on Gan. By 1990 there were two factories (producing ready-made garments) operating on Gan. The airport on Gan, which links the capital, Malé, with the south, is now fully operational and is due to become an international airport in the near future.

A new Constitution, promulgated in 1968, vested considerable powers in the President, including the right to appoint and dismiss the Prime Minister and the Cabinet of Ministers.

In March 1975, following rumours of a coup conspiracy, President Nasir dismissed the Prime Minister, Ahmed Zaki, and the premiership was abolished. Unexpectedly, President Nasir announced that he would not seek re-election at the end of his second term in 1978. To succeed him, the Majlis (legislature) chose Maumoon Abdul Gayoom, Minister of Transport under Nasir, who was approved by referendum in July 1978 and took office in November. President Gayoom announced that his main priority would be the development of the poor rural regions, while in foreign affairs the existing policy of non-alignment would be continued.

Ex-President Nasir left the country after his resignation, but the authorities subsequently sought his return to the Maldives, where he was required to answer charges of misappropriating government funds. In 1980 President Gayoom confirmed an attempted coup against the Government and implicated Nasir in the alleged plot. Nasir was to stand trial, in his absence, on these and other charges. In April 1981 Ahmed Naseem, former Deputy Minister of Fisheries and brother-in-law of Nasir, was sentenced to life imprisonment for plotting to overthrow President Gayoom. Nasir himself denied any involvement in the coup, and attempts to extradite him from Singapore were unsuccessful. (In July 1990, however, President Gayoom officially pardoned Nasir *in absentia*, in recognition of the role that he had played in winning national independence.) In 1983 another unsuccessful plot against President Gayoom was reported. In September he was re-elected as President, for a further five years, by a national referendum (with 95.6% of the popular vote). In September 1988 Gayoom was again re-elected unopposed, for a third five-year term, obtaining a record 96.4% of the popular vote.

A third, and more serious, attempt to depose President Gayoom took place in November 1988, when a sea-borne mercenary force, which was composed of around 80 alleged Sri Lankan Tamil separatists (led by a disaffected Maldivian businessman, Abdullah Luthufi), landed in Malé and endeavoured to seize control of important government installations. At the request of President Gayoom, however, the Indian Government dispatched an emergency contingent of 1,600 troops, which rapidly and successfully suppressed the attempted coup. Nineteen people were reported to have been killed in the fighting. In September 1989 the President commuted to life imprisonment the death sentences imposed on 12 Sri Lankans and four Maldivians, who took part in the aborted coup. The Indian Government withdrew its remaining 160 troops from the Maldives in November.

In February 1990, despite alleged opposition from powerful members of the privileged élite, President Gayoom announced that, as part of proposals for a broad new policy of liberalization and democratic reform, he was planning to introduce legislation, in the near future, enabling him to distribute powers, currently enjoyed by the President alone, amongst other official bodies. A further sign of growing democratization in the Maldives was the holding of discussions by the President's Consultative Council, in early 1990, concerning freedom of speech (particularly in the local press). In April, however, it became apparent that some Maldivians opposed political change, when three pro-reform members of the Majlis received anonymous death threats. A few months later, following the emergence of several politically outspoken magazines, including *Sangu* (The Conchshell), there was an abrupt reversal of the Government's policy regarding the liberalization of the press. All publications not sanctioned by the Government were banned, and a number of leading writers and publishers were arrested.

As part of a major cabinet reshuffle in May 1990, President Gayoom dismissed the Minister of State for Defence and National Security, Ilyas Ibrahim (who also held the Trade and Industries portfolio and headed the State Trading Corporation), from his post, following the latter's abrupt and unannounced departure from the country. The Government later disclosed that Ibrahim (Gayoom's brother-in-law) was to have appeared before a presidential special commission investigating alleged embezzlement and misappropriation of government funds. On his return to the Maldives in August, Ibrahim was placed under house arrest. In March 1991, however, the special commission concluded that there was no evidence of involvement, either direct or indirect, by Ibrahim in the alleged financial misdeeds; in the same month the President appointed Ilyas Ibrahim as Minister of Atolls Administration. In April the President established an anti-corruption board, which was to investigate allegations of corruption, bribery, fraud, misappropriation of government funds and property, and misuse of government office.

In early August 1993, a few weeks before the Majlis vote on the presidential candidate, Gayoom was informed that Ilyas Ibrahim, whose position as Minister of Atolls Administration had afforded him the opportunity to build a political base outside Malé (where he already enjoyed considerable popularity), was seeking the presidency and attempting to influence members of the Majlis (at that time, the Majlis nominated and elected by secret ballot a single candidate, who was presented to the country in a referendum). In the Majlis vote, held in late August, the incumbent President, who had previously been unanimously nominated for the presidency by the legislature, obtained 28 votes, against 18 for his brother-in-law. For his allegedly unconstitutional behaviour, however, Ibrahim was charged with attempting to 'influence the members of the Majlis' and he promptly left the country. Ibrahim was subsequently tried *in absentia* and sentenced to 15 years' imprisonment. In addition, his brother, Abbas Ibrahim, was removed from his post as Minister of Fisheries and Agriculture. (Ilyas Ibrahim returned to the Maldives in 1996 when he was placed under house arrest; this restriction was lifted in 1997.)

In October 1993 Gayoom was re-elected as President, for a further five years, by a national referendum in which he obtained 92.8% of the popular vote. Following his re-election, the President carried out an extensive cabinet reshuffle and a far-reaching reorganization of government bodies, including the establishment of two new ministries (that of Youth, Women's Affairs and Sports and that of Information and Culture), in order to increase efficiency and to further democratic reform.

In November 1994, at an official ceremony marking Republic Day, President Gayoom outlined various measures intended to strengthen the political system and to advance the process of democratization. These included the granting of greater autonomy and responsibilities to members of the Cabinet of Ministers, the introduction of regulations governing the conduct of civil servants (in order to increase their accountability), the introduction of democratic elections to island development committees and atoll committees, and the establishment of a Law Commission to carry out reforms to the judicial system.

In November 1996 President Gayoom effected an extensive cabinet reshuffle and a reorganization of government bodies, including the establishment of a Supreme Council for Islamic Affairs, which was to be under direct presidential control and was to advise the Government on matters relating to Islam. In early 1997 President Gayoom announced that the Citizens' Special Majlis (which was established in 1980 with the specific task of amending the Constitution) had resolved to complete the revision of the Constitution during that year and to implement the amended version by 1 January 1998. The Citizens' Special Majlis finished its 17-year-long task in early November 1997 (passing the amendments by 88 votes to two votes). The revised Constitution was ratified by the President on 27 November and came into effect, as planned, on 1 January 1998. Under the new 156-article Constitution, a formal, multi-candidate contest was permitted for the legislature's nomination for the presidency; no restriction was placed on the number of terms a president may serve; for administrative purposes, the number of atolls was increased from 19 to 20; the Majlis, which was henceforth known as the People's Majlis, was enlarged from 48 to 50 seats; the Citizens' Special Majlis was renamed the People's Special Majlis; the rights of the people were expanded; parliamentary immunity was introduced; the office of auditor-general was created; the post of commissioner of elections was constitutionalized; ministers were afforded greater power; public officers were made more accountable; parliamentary questions were allowed; and judges and magistrates were obliged to take special oaths of loyalty.

In September 1998 five individuals declared their candidacy for the presidency; the People's Majlis unanimously voted by secret ballot for the incumbent President Gayoom to go forward to the national referendum. In the referendum, which was held in mid-October, Gayoom was re-elected as President for a fifth term in office, obtaining 90.9% of the popular vote. Following his re-election, the President carried out a cabinet reorganization, including the establishment of two new ministries (that of Communications, Science and Technology and that of Human Resources, Employment and Labour). In an unexpected move, Ilyas Ibrahim was appointed to hold the new portfolio of transport and civil aviation.

In November 1999 elections for 42 members of the 50-seat People's Majlis were conducted (on a non-partisan basis). In an attempt to strengthen and develop the Maldivian system of public administration, the President established an Advisory Committee on Public-Sector Reform and Modernization and a Network of Senior Government Officials in November 1999 and February 2000, respectively. At the end of May 2000 the Minister of State for Finance and Treasury, Arif Hilmy, resigned owing to ill health, and was replaced by Mohamed Jaleel. In September the Comprehensive Nuclear Test Ban Treaty was ratified by the Maldives. As part of a government initiative to promote the advancement of women in public life, President Gayoom appointed a woman as the new Island Chief of Himmafushi in June 2001. In December a woman was appointed as Atoll Chief of Vaavu atoll (the first woman to be assigned a senior executive position of an atoll). In October the President announced his support for the US-led military campaign against the al-Qa'ida (Base) organization, held principally responsible for the suicide attacks in New York and Washington, DC, USA in September.

In early September 2002 an armed passenger attempted to hijack an Air Seychelles aircraft en route from Mumbai (India) to the Seychelles, via Malé. Airline staff managed to overpower the hijacker, who was arrested in Malé; no other passengers were injured. It was reported that the suspect, an Indian

national, and his assistant, an Indian citizen also on the flight, wanted to divert the aeroplane to another destination.

In October 2002 the President carried out a partial government reorganization. Meanwhile, in July three journalists and their assistant were sentenced to 10 years' imprisonment for writing articles criticizing the President and the Government. In early 2003 international activists demanded the release of the detainees, claiming that the journalists had not advocated violent opposition to President Gayoom or the Government, and that they had only been exercising their right to freedom of speech.

In November 1989, meanwhile, the Maldives hosted an international conference, with delegates from other small island nations, to discuss the threat posed to low-lying island countries by the predicted rise in sea-level caused by heating of the earth's atmosphere as a result of pollution (the 'greenhouse effect'). In June 1990 an Environmental Research Unit, which was to operate under the Ministry of Planning and the Environment, was established in the Maldives. The Maldives again expressed its serious concern with regard to problems of world-wide environmental pollution when it hosted the 13th conference of the UN's Intergovernmental Panel on Climate Change (IPCC, see p. 123) in September 1997. In September 1999 a special session of the UN General Assembly was convened in New York to address the specific problems faced by the 43-member Alliance of Small Island States (including the Maldives), notably climate change, rising sea levels and globalization. At the UN Millennium Summit meeting in September 2000 the President of the Maldives again took the opportunity to urge leaders to address environmental issues. The Government expressed its grave disappointment and concern at the USA's decision in April 2001 to reject the Kyoto Protocol to the UN's Framework Convention on Climate Change. The rest of the international community adopted the protocol in July after many of the targets had been reduced. The USA proposed an alternative initiative in February 2002; however, most states dismissed it as ineffective. In early March the Maldives, Kiribati and Tuvalu announced their decision to take legal action against the USA for refusing to sign the Kyoto Protocol (thus contributing to global warming which has produced the rising sea levels that threaten to submerge the islands). President Gayoom attended the South Asian Regional Conference on Ecotourism in India in January 2002. At the World Summit on Sustainable Development held in September 2002 in Johannesburg, South Africa, President Gayoom warned the international community that low-lying islands were at greater risk than ever before. He called for urgent action, including the universal ratification and implementation of the Kyoto Protocol, to prevent a global environmental catastrophe. On his return to the Maldives, the President stated that some progress had been made in certain areas, although the decisions were not as far-reaching as desired by small island nations.

The Maldives is a founder member of the South Asian Association for Regional Co-operation (SAARC, see p. 310), which was formally constituted in December 1985, and the country became a full member of the Commonwealth in June 1985. The Maldives' international standing was enhanced in November 1990, when it successfully hosted the fifth SAARC summit meeting, which was held in Malé. In October 1995 the Maldives opened its third resident diplomatic mission (in addition to those in Sri Lanka and at the UN headquarters in New York, USA) in London, in the United Kingdom. The 11th SAARC Summit Conference of heads of state and government took place in early January 2002 in Kathmandu, Nepal, despite rising tensions between India and Pakistan. The member countries signed two conventions on the promotion of child welfare in South Asia (proposed by President Gayoom) and the prevention and combat of the trafficking of women and children for prostitution. In December 2002 the number of countries with which the Maldives had established diplomatic relations stood at 135.

Government

Legislative power is held by the unicameral People's Majlis, with 50 members, including 42 elected for five years by universal adult suffrage (two by the National Capital Island and two from each of the 20 atolls) and eight appointed by the President. Executive power is vested in the President, who is elected by secret ballot by the People's Majlis (under the 1998 constitutional revisions, more than one candidate may be nominated for election) and endorsed in office for five years by a national referendum. He governs with the assistance of an appointed Cabinet of Ministers, which is responsible to the People's Majlis. The country has 21 administrative districts: the capital is under direct central administration while the 20 atolls are each under an atoll chief (verin) who is appointed by the President, under the general guidance of the Minister of Atolls Administration. There are no political parties.

Economic Affairs

In 2001, according to estimates by the World Bank, the Maldives' gross national income (GNI), measured at average 1999–2001 prices, was US $578m., equivalent to $2,040 per head (or $4,520 per head on an international purchasing-power parity basis). During 1990–2001, it was estimated, the population increased at an average annual rate of 2.6%, while gross domestic product (GDP) per head increased, in real terms, by an average of 4.6% per year. Overall GDP increased, in real terms, at an average annual rate of 7.3% in 1990–2001; growth in 2001 was 3.5%.

Agriculture and fishing contributed an estimated 7.6% of GDP (at constant 1995 prices) in 2001. About 14% of the total working population were employed in the sector (more than 10% in fishing) in 2000. In 2001 revenue from exports of marine products totalled 538.3m. rufiyaa, thus accounting for 57.4% of total export earnings. In February 1999 the Kooddoo Fisheries Complex in the South Huvadhu atoll, the largest fisheries project ever implemented in the Maldives, was officially opened. The project incorporated the construction of a refrigeration complex with a capacity of 1,900 metric tons, a quay for collector vessels (four of which were purchased as part of the project) and an ice plant. In January 2001 the fresh fish export market was opened to the private sector. Small quantities of various fruits, vegetables and cereals are produced, but virtually all of the principal staple foods have to be imported. The dominant agricultural activity (not including fishing) in the Maldives is coconut production. In early 1996, in an attempt to combat deforestation, the Government instituted a three-year afforestation programme, which aimed to plant 1m. trees (the target was later increased to 2m. trees, owing to the rapid success of the programme). Agricultural GDP increased, in real terms, by an annual average of 1.7% in 1990–2000. Real agricultural GDP grew by 1.2% in 1997 and by 3.4% in 1998.

Industry (including mining, manufacturing and construction) employed about 19% of the working population in 2000, and provided an estimated 14.7% of GDP in 2001.

Mining and quarrying contributed an estimated 0.5% of GDP in 2001, and employed 0.5% of the working population in 2000. No reserves of petroleum or natural gas have, as yet, been discovered in Maldivian waters.

The manufacturing sector employed 13% of the working population in 2000. Including electricity, gas and water, the manufacturing sector contributed 11.8% of GDP in 2001. There are only a small number of 'modern' manufacturing enterprises in the Maldives, including fish-canning, garment-making and soft-drink bottling. In early 1998 there were eight garment factories operating in the Maldives, and later that year the Foreign Investment Services Bureau announced that seven new garment factories were to be built over the next two years (creating about 7,000 new jobs). In mid-1999 the opening of a cement-packing factory on Thilafushi Island in Malé atoll was expected to bring considerable economic benefits to the Maldives. Although cottage industries (such as the weaving of coir yarn and boat-building) employ nearly one-quarter of the total labour force, there is little scope for expansion, owing to the limited size of the domestic market. Because of its lack of manufacturing industries, the Maldives has to import most essential consumer and capital goods. In the late 1980s and 1990s traditional handicrafts, such as lacquer work and shell craft, revived as a result of the expansion of the tourism sector. Manufacturing GDP increased, in real terms, by an annual average of 6.8% in 1990–2001. Real manufacturing GDP grew by 9.8% in 1997 and by 5.0% in 1998.

Energy is derived principally from petroleum, imports of which comprised 11.1% of the cost of imports in 1997. Owing to a surge in commercial activities and a significant increase in construction projects in Malé, demand for electricity in the capital grew rapidly in the late 1980s and early 1990s. Accordingly, plans were formulated in late 1991 to augment the generating capacity of the power station in Malé and to improve the distribution network. By early 1998 20 islands had been provided with electricity (equivalent to about 60% of the total population). In early 2001 the third phase of the Malé power project, further to increase the capital's power supply, was under way. In December the Asian Development Bank (ADB)

agreed to provide a loan to improve the supply of electricity to some 40 outer islands.

Following the decline of the shipping industry in the 1980s, tourism gained in importance as an economic sector, and by 1989 it had overtaken the fishing industry as the Maldives' largest source of foreign exchange. In 1999 the tourism sector provided 18.5% of GDP. Revenue from tourism totalled about US $344m. in 2000. In 2001 tourist arrivals decreased by 1.3%, compared with the previous year, to reach 460,984, owing to the global economic slowdown and concerns over travel safety and stability in the South Asian region after the terrorist attacks on the USA in September. In 2002 tourist arrivals increased by 5.1% to reach 484,680. In late 2001 a four-year plan was under way to convert 12 islands into holiday resorts and to increase the number of hotel beds by 4,000.

In 2001 the Maldives recorded a visible trade deficit of US $237.8m., and there was a deficit of $61.0m. on the current account of the balance of payments. In 2000 the principal source of imports was Singapore (accounting for 25.4% of the total); other major sources were Sri Lanka, India and Malaysia. The principal market for exports was the USA (accounting for 40.7% of the total); other major purchasers were Sri Lanka, the United Kingdom and Thailand. The principal exports were marine products (tuna being the largest export commodity) and clothing. The principal imports were machinery and mechanical appliances and electrical equipment, mineral products and textile and textile articles.

Foreign grant aid in 2000 totalled an estimated US $17.7m.; Japan is the Maldives' largest aid donor (disbursing $11.9m. in 1997). Reflecting an improvement in the country's general economic condition (aided by the fact that the Maldives was not significantly affected by the Asian financial crisis of 1997), the overall budgetary deficit, including grants, was reduced from 5% of GDP in 1997 to about 3% in 1998. However, the country's fiscal deficit grew from 4.9% in 2000 to 5.3% in 2001. Budgetary deficit was expected to reach 7% in 2002. The Maldives' total external debt was US $206.7m. at the end of 2000, of which $185.3m. was long-term public debt. In that year the cost of debt-servicing was equivalent to 4.3% of revenue from exports of goods and services. During 1990–2001 the average annual rate of inflation was 6.6%. Consumer prices rose by 7.6% in 1997. In 1998, however, consumer prices declined sharply, the rate of deflation reaching 1.4%. An inflation rate of 3.0% was recorded in 1999, but there was deflation averaging 1.1% in 2000. Consumer prices increased by an estimated 0.7% in 2001.

The Maldives is a member of the Asian Development Bank (ADB, see p. 143), the Colombo Plan (see p. 339), and the South Asian Association for Regional Co-operation (SAARC, see p. 310).

One result of the rapid growth and increasing importance of the tourism sector in the Maldives in the late 1990s was the Government's efforts to improve the infrastructure (including development of communication systems, sanitation and water supply). By 1999 the Maldivian telecommunications company, DHIRAAGU, had provided telephone facilities to all of the inhabited islands. In mid-1999 DHIRAAGU signed a 47m.-rufiyaa contract with a French telecommunications company for the supply and implementation of a mobile cellular telephone system for the Maldives and by March 2002 22,800 inhabitants had subscribed to mobile cellular telephones. In early 2003 mobile cellular telephone coverage reached 54% of the population; in March DHIRAAGU announced its aim to expand its services to 73% of the population by the end of the year. In mid-2000 DHIRAAGU launched its 'Instant Internet Access'. Overall economic performance in 1999 was favourable, with greater private-sector participation in the economy, a rise in foreign investment, and continued expansion in the tourism sector. However, the islands experienced a shortage of domestic labour: in 2001 about 29,201 expatriate workers (mainly from India, Sri Lanka and Bangladesh) were employed in the Maldives, and it was estimated that in 1999 almost 20% of the country's GDP went to non-Maldivians. Despite a recovery in fish exports and buoyant tourism receipts in the latter half of the 1990s, the current-account deficit persisted and the trade deficit continued to grow. In 2000 the Maldives was still confronted with the problem of serious macroeconomic imbalances, which have resulted in rising debt, low levels of foreign-exchange reserves and an overvalued nominal exchange rate. In April 2000 Air Maldives, a joint venture between the Government and a Malaysian company, Naluri Bhd, permanently ceased operating international flights, owing to estimated losses of US $50–$70m. This outcome adversely affected the tourist industry and business confidence in 2000. The tourist industry suffered further in 2001, owing to the suicide attacks on the USA and the subsequent military action in Afghanistan. The fisheries sector, however, fared better. In early 2001 the Government opened up the export of fresh and canned fish to the private sector, and in that year the Maldives Industrial Fisheries Company recorded a 13% increase in sales of fish, compared with the previous year. In 2002 the fisheries sector continued to expand (earnings from fish exports increased by 35%, compared with the previous year) and tourism gradually began to recover. Real GDP growth was estimated to have reached 4.3% in that year. The current-account deficit, however, remained high and fiscal deficit continued to grow, largely owing to an increase in government expenditure. The Government pledged to continue to implement necessary structural reforms and to open up of the highly-regulated public sector to private investment in 2003. In January President Gayoom announced that the 2003 budget would focus on accelerating social and economic progress and the development of atolls. Reforms are required in the banking and financial sectors. In June 2000 the Maldives was one of more than 30 countries and territories named by the Organisation for Economic Co-operation and Development (OECD, see p. 277) as unfair tax havens. Moreover, public expenditure needs to be further curtailed for the Government to make any significant progress in strengthening the economy. The high average annual rate of population growth (estimated at 2.7% in 1990–95), which has placed a heavy burden on the economy in general and on the congested capital island of Malé in particular, is an issue that is effectively being addressed (according to the results of the March 2000 census, the rate of increase had fallen to 1.9% in 1995–2000). From 2000, in an attempt to solve the problem of overcrowding in Malé, a nearby island was being developed as a suburb to relieve congestion in the capital. In March 2002 the Maldives and the ADB signed a partnership agreement to reduce poverty. Some of the aims were to reduce absolute poverty from 43% in 1998 to 25% by 2015 and to promote involvement of local communities in public sector decision-making. Two other key issues that require prompt attention are: the protection of the fragile environment to ensure sustainable economic growth; and an improvement in Maldivian teaching standards in order to upgrade the national skills base.

Education

Education is not compulsory. There are three types of formal education: traditional Koranic schools (Makthab), Dhivehi-language primary schools (Madhrasa) and English-language primary and secondary schools. Schools of the third category are the only ones equipped to teach a standard curriculum. In 1984 a national curriculum was introduced in all schools. In 1989 the Government established a National Council on Education to oversee the development of education in the Maldives. Primary education begins at six years of age and lasts for five years. Secondary education, beginning at the age of 11, lasts for up to seven years, comprising a first cycle of five years and a second of two years. In 1997 the total enrolment at primary and secondary schools was equivalent to 96% of the school-age population. In 1997 primary enrolment was equivalent to 128% of children in the relevant age-group (boys 130%; girls 127%); the comparable ratio for secondary enrolment was 69% (boys 67%; girls 71%). The construction of the first secondary school outside Malé was completed, on Hithadoo Island in Addu Atoll, in 1992. There is a full-time vocational training centre, a teacher-training institute, an institute of hotel and catering services (opened in 1987), an Institute of Management and Administration, a Science Education Centre, an Islamic education centre, and a Non-formal Education Centre (renamed as Centre for Continuing Education in October 2002). The Maldives Institute of Technical Education, which was completed in late 1996, was expected to alleviate the problem of the lack of local skilled labour. The Maldives College of Higher Education, which was established to provide a uniform framework and policies for post-secondary education institutes, was opened in late 1998. Projected budgetary expenditure on education by the central Government in 2002 was 597.2m. rufiyaa, representing 18% of total spending.

Public Holidays

2003: 12 February* (Id al-Adha, feast of the Sacrifice), 5 March* (Islamic New Year), 3 May* (National Day), 14 May* (Birth of the Prophet Muhammad), 26–27 July (Independence Days), 27 October* (Ramadan begins), 3 November (Victory Day), 11–12 November (Republic Days), 26 November* (Id al-Fitr, end of Ramadan), 10 December (Fishermen's Day).

2004: 2 February* (Id al-Adha, feast of the Sacrifice), 22 February* (Islamic New Year), 21 April* (National Day), 2 May* (Birth of the Prophet Muhammad), 26–27 July (Independence Days), 15 October* (Ramadan begins), 3 November (Victory Day), 11–12 November (Republic Days), 14 November* (Id al-Fitr, end of Ramadan), 10 December (Fishermen's Day).

*These holidays are dependent on the Islamic lunar calendar and may vary by one or two days from the dates given.

Statistical Survey

Sources (unless otherwise stated): Ministry of Planning and National Development, Ghaazee Bldg, 4th Floor, Ameer Ahmed Magu, Malé 20-05; tel. 322919; fax 327351; internet www.planning.gov.mv.

AREA AND POPULATION

Area: 298 sq km (115 sq miles).

Population: 244,814 at census of 25 March 1995; 270,101 (males 137,200, females 132,901) at census of 31 March–7 April 2000; 276,000 (official estimate) at mid-2001.

Density (mid-2001): 926 per sq km.

Principal Town (population, 2000 census): Malé (capital) 74,069.

Births and Deaths (provisional, 2001): Registered live births 4,882 (birth rate 17.7 per 1,000); Registered deaths 1,079 (death rate 3.9 per 1,000).

Expectation of Life (WHO estimates, years at birth): 64.0 (males 63.9; females 64.4) in 2001. Source: WHO, *World Health Report*.

Economically Active Population (persons aged 12 years and over, census of April 2000): Agriculture, hunting and forestry 2,495; Fishing 9,294; Mining and quarrying 473; Manufacturing 11,081; Electricity, gas and water 1,132; Construction 3,691; Trade, restaurants and hotels 15,606; Transport, storage and communications 7,873; Financing, insurance, real estate and business services 1,690; Community, social and personal services 18,089; Activities not adequately defined 14,821; Total employed 86,245 (males 57,351; females 28,894); Unemployed 1,742 (males 928, females 814); Total labour force 87,987 (males 58,279; females 29,708).

HEALTH AND WELFARE

Key Indicators

Total Fertility Rate (children per woman, 2001): 5.5.

Under-5 Mortality Rate (per 1,000 live births, 2001): 77.

HIV/AIDS (% of persons aged 15–49, 2001): 0.06.

Physicians (per 1,000 head, 1996): 0.40.

Hospital Beds (per 1,000 head, 1996): 0.76.

Health Expenditure (2000): US $ per head (PPP): 254.

Health Expenditure (2000): % of GDP: 7.6.

Health Expenditure (2000): public (% of total): 83.4.

Access to Water (% of persons, 2000): 100.

Access to Sanitation (% of persons, 2000): 56.

Human Development Index (2000): ranking: 84.

Human Development Index (2000): value: 0.743.

For sources and definitions, see explanatory note on p. vi.

AGRICULTURE, ETC.

Principal Crops (metric tons, 1992): Coconuts (number of nuts) 13,442,737, Finger millet 5.7, Maize 1.6, Cassava 31.6, Sweet potatoes 13.8, Taro (Colocasia) 141.7, Alocasia 522.3, Onions 0.1, Chillies 40.3, Sorghum 2.0.

Coconuts (number): 13.2m in 1999; 18.9m. in 2000; 27.2m. in 2001.

Sea Fishing ('000 metric tons, 2000): Total catch 132.4 (Skipjack tuna—Oceanic skipjack 79.7; Yellowfin tuna 11.7; Sharks, rays, skates, etc. 13.5) (Source: FAO, *Yearbook of Fishery Statistics*). *2001* ('000 metric tons): Total catch 127.2 (Skipjack tuna—Ocean skipjack 88.0; Yellowfin tuna 15.2).

INDUSTRY

Selected Products ('000 metric tons, unless otherwise indicated, 1999): Frozen fish 9.5; Salted, dried or smoked fish 6.5; Canned fish 4.6. Source: UN, *Industrial Commodity Statistics Yearbook*.

Electric Energy (million kWh): 107 in 1999; 117 in 2000 (Source: Asian Development Bank, *Key Indicators of Developing Asian and Pacific Countries*). *2001:* 130.

FINANCE

Currency and Exchange Rates: 100 laari (larees) = 1 rufiyaa (Maldivian rupee). *Sterling, Dollar and Euro Equivalents* (31 December 2002): £1 sterling = 20.631 rufiyaa; US $1 = 12.800 rufiyaa; €1 = 13.423 rufiyaa; 1,000 rufiyaa = £48.47 = $78.13 = €74.50. *Average Exchange Rate* (rufiyaa per US dollar): 11.770 in 2000; 12.242 in 2001; 12.800 in 2002. Note: Between October 1994 and July 2001 the mid-point rate of exchange was maintained at US $1 = 11.77 rufiyaa. In July 2001 a new rate of $1 = 12.80 rufiyaa was introduced.

Budget (forecasts, million rufiyaa, 2002): *Revenue:* Tax revenue 1,100.3; Other current revenue 1,528.2; Capital revenue 12.3; Total 2,640.8, excl. grant received (99.5). *Expenditure:* General public services 785.0, Defence 449.2, Education 597.2, Health 314.6, Social security and welfare 80.2, Community programmes 500.0, Economic services 467.7 (Agriculture 31.0, Trade and industry 5.6, Electricity, gas and water 61.7, Transport and communications 339.5, Tourism 29.9); Total (incl. others) 3,320.8 (Current 2,113.0, Capital 1,207.8), excl. net lending (–41.5).

International Reserves (US $ million at 31 December 2002): IMF special drawing rights 0.38; Reserve position in IMF 2.11; Foreign exchange 130.65; Total 133.14. Source: IMF, *International Financial Statistics*.

Money Supply (million rufiyaa at 31 December 2002): Currency outside banks 569.88; Demand deposits at commercial banks 1,252.96; Total money (incl. others) 1,886.71. Source: IMF, *International Financial Statistics*.

Cost of Living (Consumer price index; base: 1995 = 100): All items 116.0 in 1999; 114.7 in 2000; 115.4 in 2001. Source: IMF, *International Financial Statistics*.

Gross Domestic Product by Economic Activity (revised estimates, million rufiyaa at constant 1995 prices, 2001): Agriculture 181.4; Fishing 383.6; Coral and sand mining 36.6; Manufacturing, electricity and water supply 772.6; Construction 176.4; Wholesale and retail trade, tourism 2,366.7; Transport and communications 1,048.6; Finance, real estate and business services 897.7; Public administration 814.7; Education, health and social services 138.6; *Sub-total* 6,816.9; *Less* Financial intermediation services indirectly measured 422.9; *Total* 6,393.9.

Balance of Payments (US $ million, 2001): Exports of goods f.o.b. 110.2; Imports of goods f.o.b. –348.0; *Trade balance* –237.8; Exports of services 354.1; Imports of services –109.3; *Balance on goods and services* 7.0; Other income received 6.9; Other income paid –45.4; *Balance on goods, services and income* –31.5; Current transfers received 20.1; Current transfers paid –49.6; *Current balance* –61.0; Direct investment from abroad 11.7; Other investment assets 21.3; Other investment liabilities 2.1; Net errors and omissions –3.8; *Overall balance* –29.7. Source: IMF, *International Financial Statistics*.

Official Development Assistance (US $ million, 2000): Bilateral 12.1, Multilateral 7.2; Total 19.3 (Grants 17.7, Loans 1.6); Per caput assistance (US $) 71.1. Source: UN, *Statistical Yearbook for Asia and the Pacific*.

EXTERNAL TRADE

Principal Commodities (million rufiyaa, 2001): *Imports*: Live animals; animal products 272.7 (Dairy produce, eggs, honey and edible products 158.2); Vegetable products 375.5 (Edible vegetables 130.2, Edible fruits and nuts, peel of citrus or melons 98.2); Prepared food, beverages, spirits and tobacco 411.8 (Beverages, spirits and vinegar 111.7); Mineral products 704.0 (Salt, sulphur, earth and stone, lime and cement 142.9; Mineral fuels, oils, waxes, bituminous substances 559.5); Chemicals and allied industries 262.8; Plastics, rubber and articles thereof 112.6 (Plastics and articles thereof 99.7); Wood, wood charcoal, cork, straw, plaiting materials and articles thereof 163.5 (Wood and articles of wood; wood charcoal 161.9); Paper-making material, paper and paperboard and articles thereof 118.9; Textile and textile articles 506.6 (Cotton incl. yarns and woven fabrics thereof 175.9); Articles of stone, plaster, cement, asbestos, mica or similar materials, glass and glassware 80.0; Base metal and articles of base metal 260.3; Machinery and mechanical appliances; electrical equipment, parts and accessories 884.6 (Nuclear reactors, boilers, machinery and mechanical appliances, computers 447.9; Electrical machinery and equipment and parts thereof, telecommunications equipment, sound recorders, television recorders 436.7); Vehicles, aircraft, vessels and associated transport equipment 293.1 (Vehicles other than railway or tramway rolling stock 105.4; Aircraft, spacecraft and parts thereof 81.3); Miscellaneous manufactured articles 151.8 (Furniture, bedding, cushions, lamps and light fittings, illuminated signs, nameplates, prefabricated buildings 105.7); Total (incl. others) 4,741.0. *Exports*: Marine products 538.3 (Fresh or chilled tuna 64.8; Fresh or chilled reef fish 23.1; Frozen tuna 88.9; Dried tuna 136.3; Sea cucumber 34.3; Canned fish 120.2; Live reef fish 37.1; Other marine products 12.8); (Apparel and clothing accessories 396.7); Total (incl. others) 937.3.

Principal Trading Partners (million rufiyaa, 2001): *Imports*: Australia 106.1, Canada 68.1, Denmark 141.7, France 58.1, Germany 63.6, Hong Kong 53.9, India 502.4, Indonesia 176.1, Italy 52.9, Japan 107.7, Malaysia 421.2, Netherlands 96.7, New Zealand 67.9, Singapore 1,204.3, Sri Lanka 619.7, Thailand 148.8, United Arab Emirates 397.5, United Kingdom 129.2, USA 99.8; Total (incl. others) 4,741.0. *Exports*: Canada 11.9, Germany 56.8, Hong Kong 38.7, Japan 43.0, Singapore 25.0, Sri Lanka 180.9, Thailand 80.3, United Kingdom 84.7, USA 381.4; Total (incl. others) 937.3.

TRANSPORT

Road Traffic (estimates, 1996): Passenger cars 1,080, Buses and coaches 200, Lorries and vans 1,060, Road tractors 320, Motorcycles and mopeds 5,640, Bicycles 49,026 (1994) (Source: mainly International Road Federation, *World Road Statistics*). *1999:* Passenger cars 3,037, Commercial vehicles 1,003 (Source: UN, *Statistical Yearbook for Asia and the Pacific*).

Merchant Shipping Fleet (displacement, '000 gross registered tons at 31 December): 89.9 in 1999; 78.4 in 2000; 66.6 in 2001. Source: Lloyd's Register-Fairplay, *World Fleet Statistics*.

International Shipping (freight traffic, '000 metric tons, 1990): Goods loaded 27; Goods unloaded 78. Source: UN, *Monthly Bulletin of Statistics*.

Civil Aviation (traffic on scheduled services, 1999): Passengers carried 344,000; Passenger-km (million) 501. Source: UN, *Statistical Yearbook*.

TOURISM

Foreign Visitors by Country of Nationality (2001): Austria 10,476, France 30,542, Germany 65,956, Italy 115,327, Japan 41,895, Switzerland 28,313, United Kingdom 77,151; Total (incl. others) 460,984. Source: Ministry of Tourism, Malé.

Tourism Receipts (US $ million): 303 in 1998; 325 in 1999; 344 in 2000 (estimate). Source: World Tourism Organization.

COMMUNICATIONS MEDIA

Radio Receivers (July 2000): 29,724 registered.

Television Receivers (July 2000): 10,701 registered.

Telephones (main lines in use): 22,179 in 1999; 24,432 in 2000; 27,242 in 2001.

Mobile Cellular Telephones (March 2002): 22,800 subscribers.

Personal Computers (2001): 6,000 in use.

Internet Users (2001): 10,000.

Sources: Ministry of Planning and National Development, Malé; International Telecommunication Union.

EDUCATION

Pre-primary: 148 schools (2000); 12,809 pupils (2001); 411 teachers (2000).

Primary (2000): 230 schools; 46,229 pupils; 2,221 teachers.

Middle (2000): 222 schools; 27,293 pupils; 1,025 teachers.

Lower Secondary: 74 schools (2000); 21,644 pupils (2001); 1,134 teachers (2000).

Higher Secondary: 2 schools (2000); 824 pupils (2001); 53 teachers (2000).

Teacher training (1999): 171 students.

Vocational: 11 schools (1986); 151 students (2000); 54 teachers (1986).
Source: mainly Ministry of Education, Malé.

Adult Literacy Rate (UNESCO estimates): 96.7% (males 96.6%; females 96.8%) in 2000 (Source: UN Development Programme, *Human Development Report*).

Directory

The Constitution

Following a referendum in March 1968, the Maldive Islands (renamed the Maldives in April 1969) became a republic on 11 November 1968. On 27 November 1997 the President ratified a new 156-article Constitution, which was to replace the 1968 Constitution; the new Constitution came into effect on 1 January 1998. The main constitutional provisions are summarized below:

STATE, SOVEREIGNTY AND CITIZENS

The Maldives shall be a sovereign, independent, democratic republic based on the principles of Islam, and shall be a unitary State, to be known as the Republic of Maldives. In this Constitution, the Republic of Maldives shall hereinafter be referred to as 'the Maldives'.

The powers of the State of the Maldives shall be vested in the citizens. Executive power shall be vested in the President and the Cabinet of Ministers, legislative power shall be vested in the People's Majlis (People's Council) and the People's Special Majlis, and the power of administering justice shall be vested in the President and the courts of the Maldives.

The religion of the State of the Maldives shall be Islam. The national language of the Maldives shall be Dhivehi.

FUNDAMENTAL RIGHTS AND DUTIES OF CITIZENS

Maldivian citizens are equal before and under the law and are entitled to the equal protection of the law. No Maldivian shall be deprived of citizenship, except as may be provided by law. No person shall be arrested or detained, except as provided by law. Any Maldivian citizen subjected to oppressive treatment shall have the right to appeal against such treatment to the concerned authorities and to the President.

The following are guaranteed: inviolability of residential dwellings and premises; freedom of education; inviolability of letters, messages and other means of communication; freedom of movement; the right to acquire and hold property; protection of property rights; the right to work; and freedom of expression, assembly and association.

Loyalty to the State and obedience to the Constitution and to the law of the Maldives shall be the duty of every Maldivian citizen, irrespective of where he may be.

THE PRESIDENT

The President shall be the Head of State, Head of Government and the Commander-in-Chief of the Armed Forces and of the Police.

The President shall be elected by secret ballot by the People's Majlis (more than one candidate may be nominated for election) and endorsed in office for five years by a national referendum.

In addition to the powers and functions expressly conferred on or assigned to the President by the Constitution and law, the President shall have the power to execute the following: appointment to and removal from office of the Vice-President, Chief Justice, Speaker and Deputy Speaker of the People's Majlis, Ministers, Attorney-General, Atoll Chiefs, judges, Auditor-General and Commissioner of Elections; appointment and dissolution of the Cabinet of Ministers; presiding over meetings of the Cabinet of Ministers; making a statement declaring the policies of the Government at the opening session of the People's Majlis every year; promulgating decrees, directives and regulations, as may be required from time to time for the purposes of ensuring propriety of the affairs of the Government and compliance with the provisions of the Constitution and law; holding public referendums on major issues; the declaration of war and peace.

While any person holds office as President, no proceedings shall be instituted or continued against him in any court or tribunal in respect of anything done or omitted to be done by him either in his official or private capacity.

A motion to remove the President from office may be considered in the People's Majlis only when one-third of the members of the Majlis

have proposed it and two-thirds of the Majlis have resolved to consider it.

In the event that the presidency becomes vacant by reason of death, resignation or removal from office, the Speaker of the People's Majlis shall discharge the functions as Acting President from the time of occurrence of such vacancy. He shall continue to discharge these functions until a three-member Council is elected by a secret ballot of the People's Majlis to administer the State.

The President shall have the right to appoint at his discretion a Vice-President to discharge the duties and responsibilities assigned by the President.

THE CABINET OF MINISTERS

There shall be a Cabinet of Ministers appointed by the President, and the Cabinet shall be presided over by the President. The Cabinet of Ministers shall consist of the Vice-President (if any), Ministers charged with responsibility for Ministries and the Attorney-General.

The Cabinet of Ministers shall discharge the functions assigned to it by the President. The following shall be included in the said functions: to assist the President in formulating government policy on important national and international matters and issues; to advise the President on developing the Maldives economically and socially; to assist the President in the formulation of the annual state budget and government bills to be submitted to the People's Majlis; and to advise the President on the ratification of international treaties and agreements signed by the Maldivian Government with foreign administrations that require ratification by the State.

The President may, at his discretion, remove any Minister or the Attorney-General from office.

In the event of a vote of no confidence by the People's Majlis in a member of the Cabinet of Ministers, such member shall resign from office.

The President may dissolve the Cabinet of Ministers if, in his opinion, the Cabinet of Ministers is unable effectively to discharge its functions. Upon dissolution of the Cabinet of Ministers, the President shall inform the People's Majlis of the fact, specifying the reasons thereof, and shall appoint a new Cabinet of Ministers as soon as expedient.

THE PEOPLE'S MAJLIS

Legislative power, except the enactment of the Constitution, shall be vested in the People's Majlis. The People's Majlis shall consist of 50 members, of whom eight members shall be appointed by the President, two members elected from Malé and two members elected from each of the atolls. The duration of the People's Majlis shall be five years from the date on which the first meeting of the People's Majlis is held after its election. The Speaker and Deputy Speaker of the People's Majlis shall be appointed to and removed from office by the President. The Speaker shall not be a member of the People's Majlis, whereas the Deputy Speaker shall be appointed from among the members of the People's Majlis.

There shall be three regular sessions of the People's Majlis every year. The dates for the commencement and conclusion of these sessions shall be determined by the Speaker. An extraordinary sitting of the People's Majlis shall only be held when directed by the President. With the exception of the matters that, in accordance with the Constitution, require a two-thirds' majority for passage in the People's Majlis, all matters proposed for passage in the People's Majlis shall be passed by a simple majority.

Prior to the commencement of each financial year, the Minister of Finance shall submit the proposed state budget for approval by the People's Majlis.

A bill passed by the People's Majlis shall become law and enter into force upon being assented to by the President.

A motion expressing want of confidence in a member of the Cabinet of Ministers may be moved in the People's Majlis.

THE PEOPLE'S SPECIAL MAJLIS

The power to draw up and amend the Constitution of the Maldives shall be vested in the People's Special Majlis. The People's Special

Majlis shall consist of: members of the Cabinet of Ministers, members of the People's Majlis, 42 members elected from Malé and the atolls, and eight members appointed by the President.

Any article or provision of the Constitution may be amended only by a law passed by a majority of votes in the People's Special Majlis and assented to by the President.

THE JUDICIARY

The High Court shall consist of the Chief Justice and such number of Judges as may be determined by the President. The Chief Justice and the Judges of the High Court shall be appointed by the President.

All appeals from the courts of the Maldives shall, in accordance with regulations promulgated by the President, be heard by the High Court. The High Court shall hear cases determined by the President to be filed with the High Court from among the proceedings instituted by the State.

There shall be in the Maldives such number of courts at such places as may be determined by the President. The judges of the courts shall be appointed by the President.

PROCLAMATION OF EMERGENCY

Where the President has determined that the security of the Maldives or part thereof is threatened by war, foreign aggression or civil unrest, the President shall have the right to issue a Proclamation of Emergency. While the Proclamation is in force, the President shall have the power to take and order all measures expedient to protect national security and public order. Such measures may include the suspension of fundamental rights and laws. A Proclamation of Emergency shall initially be valid for a period of three months. The Proclamation may be extended, if approved by the People's Majlis, for a period determined by the People's Majlis.

GENERAL PROVISIONS

No bilateral agreement between the Government of the Maldives and the government of a foreign country and no multilateral agreement shall be signed or accepted by the Government of the Maldives unless the President has authorized in writing such signature or acceptance. In the event that such agreement requires ratification by the Maldives, such agreement shall not come into effect unless the President has ratified the same on the advice of the Cabinet of Ministers.

The Government

HEAD OF STATE

President: MAUMOON ABDUL GAYOOM (took office 11 November 1978; re-elected 30 September 1983, 1 October 1993 and 16 October 1998).

THE CABINET OF MINISTERS
(April 2003)

President, Minister of Defence and National Security, and of Finance and Treasury: MAUMOON ABDUL GAYOOM.

Minister of Fisheries, Agriculture and Marine Resources: ABDUL RASHEED HUSSAIN.

Minister of Foreign Affairs: FATHULLA JAMEEL.

Minister of Women's Affairs and Social Security: ANEESA AHMED.

Minister of Education: Dr ISMAIL SHAFEEU.

Minister of Trade and Industries: ABDULLA YAMEEN.

Minister of Health: AHMED ABDULLA.

Minister of Justice: AHMED ZAHIR.

Minister of Tourism: HASSAN SOBIR.

Minister of Transport and Civil Aviation: ILYAS IBRAHIM.

Minister of Planning and National Development: IBRAHIM HUSSAIN ZAKI.

Minister of Home Affairs, Housing and Environment: (vacant).

Minister of Communication, Science and Technology: MIDHATH HILMY.

Minister of Construction and Public Works: UMAR ZAHIR.

Minister of Atolls Administration: ABDULLA HAMEED.

Minister of Youth and Sports: MOHAMED ZAHIR HUSSAIN.

Minister of Information, Arts and Culture: IBRAHIM MANIK.

Minister of Human Resources, Employment and Labour: ABDULLA KAMALUDDEEN.

Minister at the President's Office: ABDULLA JAMEEL.

Deputy Minister of Home Affairs, Housing and Environment: ABDUL AZIZ YOOSUF .

Minister of State for Presidential Affairs: MOHAMED HUSSAIN.

Minister of State for Defence and National Security: Maj.-Gen. ANBAREE ABDUL SATTAR.

Minister of State for Finance and Treasury: MOHAMED JALEEL.

Minister of State and Auditor-General: ISMAIL FATHY.

Attorney-General: Dr MOHAMED MUNAVVAR.

MINISTRIES

The President's Office: Boduthakurufaanu Magu, Malé 20-05; tel. 323701; fax 325500; internet www.presidencymaldives.gov.mv.

The Attorney-General's Office: Huravee Bldg, Malé 20-05; tel. 323809; fax 314109.

Ministry of Atolls Administration: Faashana Bldg, Boduthakurufaanu Magu (North), Malé 20-05; tel. 323070; fax 327750.

Ministry of Communication, Science and Technology: 5th Floor, Bank of Maldives Bldg, Boduthakurufaanu Magu, Malé 20-05; tel. 331695; fax 331694; e-mail secretariat@mcst.gov.mv; internet www.mcst.gov.mv.

Ministry of Construction and Public Works: Izzuddeen Magu, Malé 20-01; tel. 323234; fax 328300; e-mail mcpw@dhivehinet.net.mv.

Ministry of Defence and National Security: Bandaara Koshi, Ameer Ahmed Magu, Malé 20-05; tel. 322607; fax 332689; e-mail admin@defence.gov.mv.

Ministry of Education: Ghaazee Bldg, 2nd Floor, Ameer Ahmed Magu, Malé 20-05; tel. 323262; fax 321201; e-mail educator@dhivehinet.net.mv; internet www.moe.gov.mv.

Ministry of Finance and Treasury: Block 379, Ameenee Magu, Malé 20-03; tel. 317590; fax 324432; e-mail minfin@dhivehinet.net.mv.

Ministry of Fisheries, Agriculture and Marine Resources: Ghaazee Bldg, Ground Floor, Ameer Ahmed Magu, Malé 20-05; tel. 322625; fax 326558; internet www.fishagri.gov.mv.

Ministry of Foreign Affairs: Boduthakurufaanu Magu, Malé 20-05; tel. 323400; fax 323841; e-mail admin@foreign.gov.mv.

Ministry of Health: Ameenee Magu, Malé 20-03; tel. 328887; fax 328889; e-mail moh@dhivehinet.net.mv; internet www.health.gov.mv.

Ministry of Home Affairs, Housing and Environment: Huravee Bldg, 3rd Floor, Ameer Ahmed Magu, Malé 20-05; tel. 323820; fax 324739; e-mail env@environment.gov.mv; internet www.environment.gov.mv.

Ministry of Human Resources, Employment and Labour: Ghaazee Bldg, 4th Floor, Ameer Ahmed Magu, Malé 20-05; e-mail info@manpowermaldives.org; internet www.manpowermaldives.org.

Ministry of Information, Arts and Culture: Buruzu Magu, Malé 20-04; tel. 323836; fax 326211; e-mail informat@dhivehinet.net.mv; internet www.maldivesinfo.gov.mv.

Ministry of Justice: Justice Bldg, Orchid Magu, Malé 20-05; tel. 322303; fax 325447.

Ministry of Planning and National Development: Ghaazee Bldg, 4th Floor, Ameer Ahmed Magu, Malé 20-05; tel. 322919; fax 327351; internet www.planning.gov.mv.

Ministry of Trade and Industries: Ghaazee Bldg, 1st Floor, Ameer Ahmed Magu, Malé 20-05; tel. 323668; fax 323840; e-mail trademin@dhivehinet.net.mv; internet www.investmaldives.com.

Ministry of Transport and Civil Aviation: Huravee Bldg, Ameer Ahmed Magu, Malé 20-05; tel. 323992; fax 323994; e-mail admin@transport.gov.mv; internet www.transport.gov.mv.

Ministry of Women's Affairs and Social Security: Umar Shopping Arcade, 2nd and 4th Floors, Chaandhanee Magu, Malé 20-02; tel. 323687; fax 316237.

Ministry of Youth and Sports: Ghaazee Bldg, Ameer Ahmed Magu, Malé 20-05; tel. 326986; fax 327162.

Legislature

PEOPLE'S MAJLIS

The People's Majlis (People's Council) comprises 50 members, of whom eight are appointed by the President, two elected by the people of Malé and two elected from each of the 20 atolls (for a five-year term). The most recent election was held on 19 November 1999.

Speaker: ABDULLA HAMEED.

Deputy Speaker: ABDUL RASHEED HUSSAIN.

Political Organizations

There are no political parties in the Maldives.

Diplomatic Representation

HIGH COMMISSIONS IN THE MALDIVES

Bangladesh: H. High Grove, 6, Hithaffinivaa Magu, Malé; tel. 315541; fax 315543; e-mail bdootmal@dhivehinet.net.mv; High Commissioner ABDUL LATIF (acting).

India: H. Athireege-Aage, Ameeru Ahmed Magu, Malé; tel. 323015; fax 324778; High Commissioner S. M. GAVAI.

Pakistan: G. Penta Green, Majeedhee Magu, Malé; tel. 322024; fax 321832; High Commissioner SAID AKBAR AFRIDI.

Sri Lanka: H. Sakeena Manzil, Medhuziyaaraiyh Magu, Malé 20-05; tel. 322845; fax 321652; e-mail highcom@dhivehinet.net.mv; High Commissioner ZAROOK SAMSUDEEN.

Judicial System

The administration of justice is undertaken in accordance with Islamic (*Shari'a*) law. In 1980 the Maldives High Court was established. There are four courts in Malé, and 200 island courts, one in every inhabited island. All courts, with the exception of the High Court, are under the control of the Ministry of Justice.

In January 1999 the Government declared that the island court of each atoll capital would thenceforth oversee the administration of justice in that atoll. At the same time it was announced that arrangements were being made to appoint a senior magistrate in each atoll capital.

HIGH COURT

Chief Justice: MOHAMED RASHEED IBRAHIM.

Judges: IBRAHIM NASEER, AHMED HAMEED FAHMY, ALI HAMEED MOHAMED.

In February 1995 the President established a five-member Advisory Council on Judicial Affairs. The Council was to function under the President's Office (equivalent, in this respect, to a Supreme Court) and was to study and offer counsel to the President on appeals made to the President by either the appellant or the respondent in cases adjudicated by the High Court. The Council was also to offer such counsel as and when requested by the President on other judicial matters.

ADVISORY COUNCIL ON JUDICIAL AFFAIRS

Members: MOOSA FATHY, ABDULLA HAMEED, DR MOHAMED MUNAWWAR, Prof. MOHAMED RASHEED IBRAHIM, AL-SHEIKH HASSAN YOOSUF.

Religion

Islam is the state religion, and the Maldivians are Sunni Muslims. In mid-1991 there were 724 mosques and 266 women's mosques throughout the country.

In late 1996 a Supreme Council for Islamic Affairs was established, under the authority of the President's Office. The new body was to authorize state policies with regard to Islam and to advise the Government on Islamic affairs.

Musthashaaru of the Supreme Council for Islamic Affairs: MOOSA FATHY.

President of the Supreme Council for Islamic Affairs: MOHAMED RASHEED IBRAHIM.

Deputy President of the Supreme Council for Islamic Affairs: AHMED FAROOG MOHAMED.

The Press

In 1993 the Government established a National Press Council to review, monitor and further develop journalism in the Maldives.

DAILIES

Aafathis Daily News: Feerpaz Magu, Maafannu, Malé 20-02; tel. 318609; fax 312425; e-mail aafathis@dhivehinet.net.mv; internet www.aafathisnews.com.mv; f. 1979; daily; Dhivehi and English; Editor AHMED ZAAHIR; circ. 3,000.

Haveeru Daily: Ameenee Magu, POB 20103, Malé; tel. 325671; fax 323103; e-mail haveeru@haveeru.com.mv; internet www.haveeru.com.mv; f. 1979; Dhivehi and English; Chair. MOHAMED ZAHIR HUSSAIN; Editor ALI RAFEEQ; circ. 4,500.

Miadhu News: G. Mascot, Koimalaa Hingun, Malé 20-02; tel. 320700; fax 320500; e-mail miadhu@dhivehinet.net.mv; internet www.miadhu.com; daily newspaper; Propr IBRAHIM RASHEED MOOSA; Chair. AHMED ABDULLA.

PERIODICALS

Adduvas: Malé; f. 2000; weekly; news, entertainment, health issues and social affairs.

Dheenuge Magu (The Path of Religion): The President's Office, (Mulee-aage) Boduthakurufaanu Magu, Malé 20-05; tel. 325500; e-mail info@presidencymaldives.gov.mv; f. 1986; weekly; Dhivehi; religious; publ. by the President's Office; Editor President MAUMOON ABDUL GAYOOM; Dep. Editor MOHAMED RASHEED IBRAHIM; circ. 7,500.

Dhivehingetharika (Maldivian Heritage): National Centre for Linguistic and Historical Research, Soasun Magu, Malé 20-05; tel. 323206; fax 326796; e-mail nclhr@dhivehinet.net.mv; f. 1998; Dhivehi; Maldivian archaeology, history and language.

Faiythoora: National Centre for Linguistic and Historical Research, Soasun Magu, Malé 20-05; tel. 323206; fax 326796; e-mail nclhr@dhivehinet.net.mv; f. 1979; monthly magazine; Dhivehi; Maldivian history, culture and language; Editor Uz ABDULLA HAMEED; circ. 800.

Furadhaana: Ministry of Information, Arts and Culture, Buruzu Magu, Malé 20-04; tel. 321749; fax 326211; e-mail informat@dhivehinet.net.mv; internet www.maldives-info.com; f. 1990; monthly; Dhivehi; Editor IBRAHIM MANIK; circ. 1,000.

Jamaathuge Khabaru (Community News): Centre for Continuing Education, Salahudeen Bldg, Malé 20-04; tel. 328772; fax 322223; monthly; Dhivehi; Editor AHMED ZAHIR; circ. 1,500.

Maldives Marine Research Bulletin: Marine Research Centre, Ministry of Fisheries, Agriculture and Marine Resources, H. White Waves, Malé 20-06; tel. 322328; fax 322509; e-mail marine@fishagri.gov.mv; f. 1995; biannual; fisheries and marine research; Asst Dir-Gen. AHMED HAFIZ.

Maldives News Bulletin: Maldives News Bureau, Ministry of Information, Arts and Culture, Buruzu Magu, Malé 20-04; tel. 323838; fax 326211; e-mail informat@dhivehinet.net.mv; internet www.maldives-info.com; weekly; English; Editor ALI SHAREEF; circ. 350.

Monday Times: H. Neel Villa, Boduthakunufaanu Magu, Malé; tel. and fax 315084; e-mail info@mondaytimes.com.mv; internet www.mondaytimes.com.mv; f. 2000; weekly; Editor MOHAMED BUSHRY.

Our Environment: Forum of Writers on the Environment, c/o Ministry of Planning and National Development, Ghaazee Bldg, Ameer Ahmed Magu, Malé 20-05; tel. 324861; fax 327351; f. 1990; monthly; Dhivehi; Editor FAROUQ AHMED.

Rasain: Ministry of Fisheries, Agriculture and Marine Resources, Ghaazee Bldg, Ameer Ahmed Magu, Malé 20-05; tel. 322625; fax 326558; e-mail fishagri@dhivehinet.net.mv; f. 1980; annual; fisheries development.

Samugaa: Malé; f. 1995; publ. by the Government Employees' Club.

NEWS AGENCIES

Haveeru News Service (HNS): POB 20103, Malé; tel. 313825; fax 323103; e-mail haveeru@dhivehinet.net.mv; internet www.haveeru.com; f. 1979; Chair. MOHAMED ZAHIR HUSSAIN; Man. Editor AHMED ZAHIR.

Hiyama News Agency: H. Navaagan, Malé 20-05; tel. 322588.

Maldives News Bureau (MNB): Ministry of Information, Arts and Culture, Buruzu Magu, Malé 20-04; tel. 323836; fax 326211; e-mail informat@dhivehinet.net.mv; internet www.maldives-info.com.

PUBLISHERS

Corona Press: Faamudheyri Magu, Malé; tel. 314741.

Cyprea Print: Raiydhebai Magu, Malé 20-03; tel. 328381; fax 328380; f. 1984; Man. Dir ABDULLA SAEED.

Loamaafaanu Print: POB 20103, Malé 20-04; tel. 317209; fax 313815; e-mail haveeru@netlink.net.mv.

Novelty Printers and Publishers: Malé 20-01; tel. 318844; fax 327039; e-mail novelty@dhivehinet.net.mv; general and reference books; Man. Dir ASAD ALI.

Ummeedhee Press: M. Aasthaanaa Javaahirumagu, Malé 20-02; tel. 325110; fax 326412; e-mail ummpress@dhivehinet.net.mv; f. 1986; printing and publishing; Principal Officers ABDUL SHAKOOR ALI, MOHAMED SHAKOOR.

Broadcasting and Communications

TELECOMMUNICATIONS

Ministry of Communication, Science and Technology: Post and Telecommunication Section, Telecom Bldg, Husnuheena Magu, Malé 20-04; tel. 323344; fax 320000; e-mail telecom@dhivehinet.net.mv; regulatory authority; Dir-Gen. (Post and Telecommunication Section) HUSSAIN SHAREEF; Dir MOHAMED AMIR.

Dhivehi Raajjeyge Gulhun Ltd (DHIRAAGU): Medhuziyaaraiy Magu, Malé 20-03; tel. 322802; fax 322800; e-mail info@dhiraagu.com.mv; internet www.dhiraagu.com.mv; f. 1988; jointly-owned by the Maldivian Government (55%) and by Cable and Wireless PLC of the UK (45%); functions under Ministry of Communication, Science and Technology; operates all national and international telecommunications services in the Maldives (incl. internet service–Dhivehinet); Chair. ISMAIL SHAFEEU; CEO and Gen. Man. ISMAIL WAHEED.

RADIO

Radio Eke: Malé.

Voice of Islam: Malé.

Voice of Maldives (VOM) (Dhivehi Raajjeyge Adu): Moonlight Higun, Malé 20-06; tel. 325577; fax 328357; radio broadcasting began in 1962 under name of Malé Radio; name changed as above in 1980; three channels; home service in Dhivehi (0530 hrs–2245 hrs daily) and English (1700 hrs–1900 hrs daily); Dir-Gen. IBRAHIM MANIK.

TELEVISION

Television Maldives: Buruzu Magu, Malé 20-04; tel. 323105; fax 325083; television broadcasting began in 1978; two channels: TVM broadcasts for an average of 6–7 hrs daily and TVM Plus (f. 1998) broadcasts for 10 hrs daily; covers a 40-km radius around Malé; Dir-Gen. HUSSAIN MOHAMED; Dep. Dirs MOHAMED NASHID, ABDUL MUHUSIN.

Finance

(cap. = capital; brs = branches; amounts in US dollars unless otherwise stated)

BANKING

Central Bank

Maldives Monetary Authority (MMA): Umar Shopping Arcade, 3rd Floor, Chandhanee Magu, Maafannu, Malé 20-01; tel. 323783; fax 323862; e-mail mail@mma.gov.mv; internet www.mma.gov.mv; f. 1981; bank of issue; supervises and regulates commercial bank and foreign exchange dealings and advises the Govt on banking and monetary matters; authorized cap. 4m. rufiyaa (2001); Gov. President MAUMOON ABDUL GAYOOM; Vice-Gov. MOHAMED JALEEL; Gen. Man. ABDUL GHAFOOR.

Commercial Bank

Bank of Maldives (PLC) Ltd (BML): 11 Boduthakurufaanu Magu, Malé 20-05; tel. 322948; fax 328233; e-mail info@bml.com.mv; internet www.bankofmaldives.com.mv; f. 1982; 75% state-owned, 25% privately-owned; cap. 36.5m., res 147m., dep. 1,378m. (2001); Chair. ABDULLA HAMEED; Gen. Man. KEITH L. BROWN; 15 brs.

Foreign Banks

Bank of Ceylon (Sri Lanka): 'Meedhufaru', 2 Orchid Magu, Malé; tel. 323045; fax 320575; e-mail bcmale@dhivehinet.net.mv; internet www.bankofceylon.net; Country Man. ROY JAYASUNDARA; 1 br.

Habib Bank Ltd (Pakistan): Ground Floor, Ship Plaza, 1/6 Orchid Magu, POB 20121, Malé; tel. 322051; fax 326791; e-mail hblmale@dhivehinet.net.mv; Vice-Pres. and Chief Man. MUHAMMAD ASAF SHAIKH.

Hong Kong and Shanghai Banking Corpn Ltd (Hong Kong): MTCC Bldg, 1st Floor, Boduthakurufaanu Magu, Malé; CEO MARK HUMBLE.

State Bank of India: Boduthakurufaanu Magu, Malé; tel. 320860; fax 323053; e-mail sbimale@dhivehinet.net.mv; CEO G. N. DASH.

INSURANCE

Allied Insurance Co of the Maldives (Pte) Ltd: 04–06 STO Trade Centre, Orchid Magu, Malé; tel. 324612; fax 325035; e-mail allied@dhivehinet.net.mv; internet www.alliedmaldives.com; f. 1985; all classes of non-life insurance; operated by State Trading Organisation (see below); Chief Exec. MOHAMED MANIKU; Gen. Man. ISMAIL RIZA.

Trade and Industry

GOVERNMENT AGENCIES

Foreign Investment Services Bureau (FISB): Malé; tel. 323890; fax 323756; e-mail trademin@dhivehinet.net.mv; internet www.investmaldives.com; under administration of Ministry of Trade and Industries; Dir-Gen. AHMED NASEEM.

Maldives Housing and Urban Development Board: Malé; Dir ABDUL AZEEZ; Dep. Dir ABDULLAH SODIQ.

CHAMBER OF COMMERCE AND INDUSTRY

Maldives National Chamber of Commerce and Industry (MNCCI): G. Viyafaari Hiyaa, Ameenee Magu, POB 92, Malé 20-04; tel. 310234; fax 310233; e-mail mncci@dhivehinet.net.mv; f. 1994; merged with the Maldivian Traders' Association in 2000; Pres. AHMED MUJUTHABA; Chair. GASIM IBRAHIM.

INDUSTRIAL AND TRADE ASSOCIATIONS

Sri Lanka Trade Centre: 3rd Floor, Girithereyege Bldg, Hithaffinivaa Magu, Malé; tel. 315183; fax 315184; e-mail dirsltc@avasmail.com.mv; f. 1993 to facilitate and promote trade, tourism, investment and services between Sri Lanka and the Maldives; Dir G. V. CHANDRASENA.

State Trading Organisation (STO): STO Bldg, 7 Haveeree Higun, Malé 20-02; tel. 323279; fax 325218; e-mail sto@dhivehinet.net.mv; internet www.stomaldives.com; f. 1964 as Athirimaafannue Trading Account, renamed as above in 1976; became private limited company in 2001; state-controlled commercial organization; under administration of independent Board of Directors; imports and distributes staple foods, fuels, pharmaceuticals and general consumer items; acts as purchaser for govt requirements; undertakes long-term development projects; Man. Dir MOHAMED MANIKU; Dir ISMAIL IBRAHIM.

UTILITIES

Electricity

Maldives Electricity Bureau: Malé; tel. 328753; fax 323840; e-mail trademin@dhivehinet.net.mv; f. 1998; under administration of Ministry of Trade and Industries; regulatory authority.

State Electric Co (STELCO) Ltd: Malé; e-mail admin@stelco.com.mv; internet www.stelco.com.mv; f. 1997 to replace Maldives Electricity Board; under administration of Ministry of Trade and Industries; provides electricity, consultancy services, electrical spare parts service, etc. operates 22 power stations; installed capacity 32,921 kW (Dec. 2000); Chair. ABDULLAH YAMEEN; Man. Dir ABDUL SHAKOOR.

Gas

Maldive Gas Pvt Ltd: Thilafushi, Malé Atoll; f. 1999; as a jt venture between State Trading Organisation and Champa Gas and Oil Co; Chair. MOHAMED MANIK.

Water

Maldives Water and Sanitation Authority (MWSA): Malé; f. 1973; Dir FAROOQ MOHAMED HASSAN.

Malé Water and Sewerage Co: Ameenee Magu, Machangolhi, POB 20148, Malé 20–375; tel. 323209; fax 324306; e-mail mwsc@dhivehinet.net.mv; f. 1995; 70% govt-owned; produces approximately 5,000 cubic metric tons of fresh, desalinated water daily; provides water and sewerage services to the islands of Malé, Hulhumalé and Villingili; Chair. HASSAN SOBIR; Gen. Man. MOHAMED AHMED DIDI.

Transport

Maldives Transport and Contracting Co Ltd (MTCC): MTCC Bldg, 4th Floor, Boduthakurufaanu Magu, POB 2063, Malé 20-02; tel. 326822; fax 323221; e-mail mtcc@dhivehinet.net.mv; internet www.mtccmaldives.com; f. 1980; 60% state-owned, 40% privately-owned; marine transport, civil and technical contracting, harbour development, shipping agents for general cargo, passenger liners and oil tankers; Man. Dir BANDHU IBRAHIM SALEEM; Dirs UMAR ZAHIR, ABDULLAH MAJEED, MOHAMED NAZEER.

SHIPPING

Vessels operate from the Maldives to Sri Lanka and Singapore at frequent intervals, also calling at points in India, Pakistan, Myanmar (formerly Burma), Malaysia, Bangladesh, Thailand, Indonesia and the Middle East. In 1998 the merchant shipping fleet of the Maldives numbered 68 vessels. Smaller vessels provide services between the islands on an irregular basis. Malé is the only port handling international traffic. In 1986 a new commercial harbour was opened in Malé. The Malé Harbour Development Project was implemented during 1991–97, and improved and increased the capacity and efficiency of Malé Port.

Maldives Ports Authority (MPA): Commercial Harbour, Malé 20-02; tel. 329339; fax 325293; e-mail maldport@dhivehinet.net.mv; f. 1986; under administration of Ministry of Transport and Civil Aviation; Man. Dir ISMAIL SHAFEEQ.

Island Enterprises Pvt Ltd: Maaram, 1st Floor, Ameeru Ahmed Magu, Henveiru, POB 20169, Malé 20-05; tel. 323531; fax 325645; e-mail info@ielmaldives.com; internet www.iemaldives.com; f. 1978; fleet of eight vessels; exporters of frozen fish, owners of processing plant, shipping agents, chandlers, cruising agents, surveyors and repairs; Man. Dir OMAR MANIK.

Precision Marine Pvt Ltd: Maaram, 1st Floor, Ameeru Ahmed Magu, Henveiru, POB 20169, Malé 20-05; tel. 323531; fax 325645; e-mail fiberbot@dhivehinet.net.mv; internet www.pmlboatyard.com .mv; subsidiary of Island Enterprises Pvt Ltd; mfrs and repairers of fibreglass boats, launches, yachts, marine sports equipment, etc. Dir OMAR MANIK.

Madihaa Co (Pvt) Ltd: 1/40 Shaheed Ali Higun, Malé; tel. 327812; fax 322251; e-mail madicom@dhivehinet.net.mv; f. 1985; imports and exports fresh fruit and vegetables, construction raw materials, confectionary items and soft drinks; Man. Dir MOOSA AHMED.

Maldives National Shipping Ltd: Ship Plaza, 2nd Floor, 1/6 Orchid Magu, POB 2022, Malé 20-02; tel. 323871; fax 324323; e-mail mns@dhivehinet.net.mv; f. 1965; 100% state-owned; fleet of seven general cargo vessels and one container vessel; br. in Mumbai (India); Gen. Man. MOHAMED HILMY; Man. Dir ALI UMAR MANIK.

Matrana Enterprises (Pvt) Ltd: 97 Majeedhee Magu, Malé; tel. 321733; fax 322832; Sr Exec. MOHAMED ABDULLA.

Villa Shipping and Trading Co (Pvt) Ltd: Villa Bldg, POB 2073, Malé; tel. 325195; fax 325177; e-mail villa@dhivehinet.net.mv; Man. Dir QASIM IBRAHIM.

CIVIL AVIATION

The existing airport on Hululé Island near Malé, which was first opened in 1966, was expanded and improved to international standard with financial assistance from abroad and, as Malé International Airport, was officially opened in 1981. Charter flights from Europe subsequently began. In addition, there are four domestic airports covering different regions of the country: one on Gan Island, another on Kadhdhoo Island, Hadhdhummathi Atoll, another on Hanimaadhoo Island, South Thiladhummathi Atoll, and another on Kaadedhdhoo Island, South Huvadhu Atoll. The airport on Gan Island was expected to be capable of servicing international flights in the near future. Construction of a fifth domestic airport, in Raa Atoll Dhuvaafaru, was scheduled to begin in 1994. In early 1995 there were 10 helipads in use in the Maldives.

Maldives Airport Co Ltd: Malé International Airport, Hulhule; tel. 323506; fax 325034; e-mail enquiry@airports.com.mv; internet www.airports.com.mv; f. 2000; 100% govt-owned; under administration of Ministry of Transport and Civil Aviation; Man. Dir AHMED ALI MANIKU.

Air Maldives Ltd: 26 Ameer Ahmed Magu, Henveyru, POB 2049, Malé 20-05; tel. 328454; fax 318757; e-mail airmldvs@dhivehinet.net .mv; f. 1974; 51% govt-owned, 49% owned by Naluri Bhd (Malaysia); under administration of Ministry of Transport and Civil Aviation; domestic flights; operated international flights until March 2000; national carrier.

Island Aviation Services Ltd: Malé; e-mail info@island.com.mv; internet www.island.com.mv; f. 2000; 100% govt-owned; operates domestic flights (suspended by Air Maldives Ltd in April 2000); Chair. ABDULLA YAMEEN; Man. Dir BANDHU IBRAHIM SALEEM.

Maldivian Air Taxi: Malé International Airport, POB 2023, Malé; tel. 315201; fax 315203; e-mail mat@mat.com.mv; internet www .mataxi.com; f. 1993; seaplane services between Malé and outer islands; operates 15 aircraft; Chair. LARS ERIK NIELSEN; Gen. Man. AUM FAWZY.

Ocean Air (Pvt) Ltd: Malé; scheduled domestic flights between Malé and Gan.

Trans Maldivian Airways (Pvt) Ltd: POB 2079, Malé; tel. 325708; fax 323161; e-mail mail@tma.com.mv; internet www.tma .com.mv; f. 1989 as Hummingbird Island Airways Pvt Ltd, name changed as above in 2000; operates 12 floatplanes; Man. Dir Capt. ERNST-ULRICH MAAS.

Tourism

The tourism industry brings considerable foreign exchange to the Maldives, and receipts from tourism amounted to an estimated US $344m. in 2000. The islands' attractions include white sandy beaches, excellent diving conditions and multi-coloured coral formations. By April 2001 there were 87 island resorts in operation, and 16,428 hotel beds were available. The annual total of foreign visitors increased from only 29,325 in 1978 to 467,154 in 2000. Tourist arrivals decreased to 460,984 in 2001, before rising to 484,680 in 2002. A plan was implemented in late 2001 to convert 12 islands into resorts and to increase the number of hotel beds by some 4,000 by 2005.

Maldives Association of Tourism Industry (MATI): Gadhamoo Bldg, 3rd Floor, Henveyru, Malé; tel. 326640; fax 326641; e-mail mati@dhivehinet.net.mv; f. 1984; promotes and develops tourism; Chair. M. U. MANIKU; Sec.-Gen. S. I. MOHAMED.

Maldives Tourism Promotion Board: Bank of Maldives Bldg, 4th Floor, Boduthakurufaanu Magu, Malé 20-05; tel. 323228; fax 323229; e-mail mtpb@visitmaldives.com.mv; internet www .visitmaldives.com; f. 1998.

Air Maldives Travel Bureau/Tourist Information: Arrival Hall, Malé International Airport, Hululé Island; tel. 325511 (Ext. 8240); fax 325056; f. 1997.

MALI

Introductory Survey

Location, Climate, Language, Religion, Flag, Capital

The Republic of Mali is a land-locked country in West Africa, with Algeria to the north, Mauritania and Senegal to the west, Guinea and Côte d'Ivoire to the south, and Burkina Faso and Niger to the east. The climate is hot throughout the country. The northern region of Mali is part of the Sahara, an arid desert. It is wetter in the south, where the rainy season is from June to October. Temperatures in Bamako are generally between 16°C (61°F) and 39°C (103°F). The official language is French but a number of other languages, including Bambara, Fulfulde, Sonrai, Tamashek, Soninke and Dogon, are widely spoken. It is estimated that about 80% of the population are Muslims and 18% follow traditional animist beliefs; under 2% are Christians. The national flag (proportions 2 by 3) has three equal vertical stripes, of green, gold and red. The capital is Bamako.

Recent History

Mali, as the former French West African colony of Soudan, merged in April 1959 with Senegal to form the Federation of Mali, which became independent on 20 June 1960. Senegal seceded two months later, and the remnant of the Federation was proclaimed the Republic of Mali on 22 September 1960. Its first President was Modibo Keita, the leader of the Union soudanaise—Rassemblement démocratique africain (US—RDA), who pursued authoritarian socialist policies and severed Mali's links with the French political and financial sphere. Mali withdrew from the Franc Zone (see p. 237) in 1962, and developed close relations with the communist bloc. Economic difficulties caused Mali to return to the Franc Zone in 1968, although the country was not fully reintegrated into the Zone's monetary union until 1984.

Keita dissolved the elected legislature in January 1968. Following a series of purges of US—RDA and public officials, Keita was overthrown in November of that year by a group of junior army officers, who assumed power as the Comité militaire pour la libération nationale (CMLN). The Constitution was abrogated, and all political activity was banned. Lt (later Gen.) Moussa Traoré became Head of State and President of the CMLN, while Capt. Yoro Diakité became President of the Government (Prime Minister). In September 1969 Traoré assumed the presidency of the Government, demoting Diakité to a lesser ministerial post.

A draft Constitution, providing for the establishment of a one-party state at the end of a five-year transitional period of military rule, was approved by a national referendum in June 1974. Proposals for the single party, the Union démocratique du peuple malien (UDPM), which were announced in September 1976, were denounced by supporters of multi-party democracy, and anti-Government demonstrations followed Keita's death in custody in 1977.

The UDPM was officially constituted in March 1979, and presidential and legislative elections took place in June. Traoré, the sole candidate for the presidency, was elected for a five-year term; a single list of UDPM candidates for the 82-member Assemblée nationale was elected for a four-year term.

A constitutional amendment in September 1981 increased the presidential term of office to six years and reduced that of the legislature to three years. Elections to the Assemblée nationale were thus held in June 1982 and June 1985, with UDPM candidates being elected unopposed on both occasions. In June 1985 Traoré was re-elected President, reportedly obtaining 99.9% of the votes cast. He relinquished the defence portfolio to a close associate, Gen. Sékou Ly, in June 1986, and appointed Dr Mamadou Dembélé to the restored office of Prime Minister.

A long-standing territorial dispute between Mali and Burkina Faso, concerning the Agacher strip (a reputedly mineral-rich area of their common border), escalated into armed conflict in December 1985, resulting in some 50 deaths. The International Court of Justice (ICJ), to which the issue had been referred in 1983, urged both countries to withdraw their troops from the disputed zone, and in January 1986, following regional mediation, troops were withdrawn from the area. The two states resumed full diplomatic relations in June, and in December

accepted the ICJ's ruling that each be awarded sovereignty over one-half of the territory.

The office of Prime Minister was again abolished in June 1988, and Traoré resumed responsibility for defence. At legislative elections later in June only about one-half of the incumbent deputies were returned to office, after provision was made for as many as three UDPM-nominated candidates to contest each seat.

In March 1990 Traoré initiated a nation-wide series of conferences to consider the exercise of democracy within and by the UDPM. Mali's first cohesive opposition movements began to emerge in that year, among them the Comité national d'initiative démocratique (CNID) and the Alliance pour la démocratie au Mali (ADEMA), which together organized mass pro-democracy demonstrations in December.

In January 1991 Traoré assigned the defence portfolio to Brig.-Gen. Mamadou Coulibaly. The security forces harshly repressed violent pro-democracy demonstrations in Bamako in March 1991: official figures later revealed that 106 people were killed, and 708 injured, in three days of unrest. On 26 March it was announced that Traoré had been arrested. A military Conseil national de réconciliation (CNR), led by Lt-Col (later Gen.) Amadou Toumani Touré (the commander of the army's parachute regiment), assumed power, and the Constitution and its institutions were abrogated. The CNR was succeeded by a 25-member Comité de transition pour le salut du peuple (CTSP), chaired by Touré. It was announced that a national conference would be convened, and that the armed forces would relinquish power to democratic institutions on 20 January 1992. Soumana Sacko (who had briefly been Minister of Finance and Trade in 1987) returned to Mali from the Central African Republic to head a transitional, civilian-dominated government.

The transitional regime affirmed its commitment to the economic adjustment efforts of recent years, and undertook the reform of Malian political life. Among those arrested in subsequent months were Gen. Ly (Minister of the Interior and Basic Development at the time of the violently repressed demonstrations in early 1991), Mamadou Coulibaly and the former army Chief of Staff, Ousmane Coulibaly. The new administration also promised to recover Traoré's personal fortune, rumoured to total some US $2,000m., which had reputedly been deposited in overseas bank accounts. In July 1991 an amnesty for most political prisoners detained under Traoré was proclaimed, and provision made for the legalization of political parties. The CNID was registered as the Congrès national d'initiative démocratique, and ADEMA adopted the additional title of Parti pan-africain pour la liberté, la solidarité et la justice. Pre-independence parties, banned for many years, re-emerged, most notably the US—RDA.

The National Conference began in July 1991. Over a period of two weeks its 1,800 delegates adopted a draft Constitution (of what was designated the Third Republic of Mali), an electoral code and a charter governing the activities of political parties. In August seven government ministers and about one-half of the members of the CTSP were replaced, following reports implicating them in acts of repression earlier in the year. In November the period of transition to democratic rule was extended until 26 March 1992. The delay was attributed principally to the CTSP's desire to conclude a peace agreement with Tuareg rebels in the north of the country (see below); however, it was also stated that foreign assistance hitherto received was insufficient to finance the electoral programme. The draft Constitution was finally submitted to a national referendum on 12 January 1992, when it was endorsed by 99.8% of those who voted (about 43% of the registered electorate).

Municipal elections proceeded on 19 January 1992, at which 23 of the 48 authorized parties presented candidates, and in which ADEMA enjoyed the greatest success, winning 214 of 751 municipal seats. At the elections to the Assemblée nationale, on 23 February and 8 March, ADEMA won 76 of the 129 seats, the CNID took nine seats, and the US—RDA eight. The date for the transition to civilian rule was again postponed, and the first round of the presidential election eventually proceeded on 12

April, contested by nine candidates. The leader of ADEMA, Alpha Oumar Konaré, won the largest share of the votes cast (some 45%). He and his nearest rival, Tiéoulé Mamadou Konaté (of the US—RDA), proceeded to a second round, on 26 April, at which Konaré secured 69% of the votes. Overall, only about 20% of the electorate were reported to have voted in the presidential election; a similar turn-out was reported in the legislative polls. Konaré was inaugurated as President on 8 June. He appointed Younoussi Touré (hitherto the national director of the Banque centrale des états de l'Afrique de l'ouest) as Prime Minister. Touré's first Council of Ministers was dominated by members of ADEMA, although a small number of portfolios were allocated to representatives of the US—RDA and of the Parti pour la démocratie et le progrès (PDP).

The trial of Traoré and his associates began, after considerable delay, in November 1992. In February 1993 Traoré, Ly, Mamadou Coulibaly and Ousmane Coulibaly were sentenced to death, having been convicted of 'premeditated murder, battery and voluntary manslaughter' at the time of the March 1991 unrest. The Supreme Court rejected appeal proceedings in May 1993; however, Konaré subsequently indicated that no death penalty would be exacted under his presidency. Charges remained against Traoré, his wife and several others in connection with the 'economic crimes' of the former administration.

Touré resigned in April 1993, following violent disturbances in Bamako, involving students and school pupils disaffected by the adverse effects of economic austerity measures. The new Prime Minister, Abdoulaye Sekou Sow (hitherto Minister of State, responsible for Defence), implemented an extensive reorganization of the Government. The Council of Ministers remained dominated by ADEMA, but also included representatives of other parties, including the CNID; Sow was not himself a member of any political party. Later in the year members of ADEMA, the CNID and the US—RDA expressed dissatisfaction at their exclusion from the decision-making process. Following the resignation of ADEMA's Vice-President, Mohamed Lamine Traoré, from a senior government post, a governmental reorganization, in November, included the appointment of new ministers responsible for finance and for foreign affairs. ADEMA remained the most prominent party in the new Council of Ministers, which also incorporated members of the CNID, the PDP, the Rassemblement pour la démocratie et le progrès (RDP) and, for a brief period, prior to their withdrawal from government, representatives of the US—RDA.

Meanwhile, a programme of austerity measures, announced in September 1993, provoked considerable political controversy and failed to prevent the suspension of assistance by the IMF and the World Bank. The 50% devaluation of the CFA franc, in January 1994, exacerbated differences regarding economic policy within the Government. Sow resigned in February, and was replaced by Ibrahim Boubacar Keita, since November 1993 the Minister of Foreign Affairs, Malians Abroad and African Integration, a member of ADEMA 'radical' wing, opposed to Sow's economic policies. The subsequent withdrawal from the coalition of the CNID and the RDP, protesting that they had not been consulted about the recent changes, prompted the appointment of a new Government, again dominated by ADEMA; the PDP in turn withdrew (although its representative in the Council of Ministers resigned from the party in order to retain his portfolio).

Mali's first national forum took place in December 1994; the Prime Minister and other government members answered questions submitted by members of the public on any matter of national concern. The forum was broadcast nationally, and was held on an annual basis thereafter.

The election of Keita as President of ADEMA in September 1994, and the subsequent resignation from the party of Mohamed Lamine Traoré and other prominent figures, apparently confirmed rumours of internal party divisions. Defectors from ADEMA subsequently formed the Mouvement pour l'indépendance, la renaissance et l'intégration africaine (MIRIA). In January 1995 a party established by supporters of the UDPM, the Mouvement patriotique pour le renouveau (MPR), was granted official status; a previous attempt to reconstitute the UDPM had been prohibited by the Supreme Court. In October the Parti pour la renaissance nationale (PARENA), comprising several leading members of the CNID, who alleged excessive dominance by the party Chairman, Mountaga Tall, was registered. PARENA and ADEMA established a political alliance in February 1996, and PARENA's leaders, Yoro Diakité and Tiébilé Dramé, were appointed to the Government in July.

In October 1996 it was announced that a prominent member of the MPR and former minister under Traoré, Mady Diallo, had been arrested, together with several armed forces officers, following the discovery of a plot to assassinate Konaré, Keita and other government ministers. Diallo was later released, but was rearrested in April 1997. The trial of Diallo and six army officers accused of plotting to overthrow President Konaré, began in March 1998, and in March 1999 the seven were sentenced to prison terms of 15–18 months.

Meanwhile, the Government adopted a new electoral code in August 1996, introducing elements of proportional representation in municipal and legislative elections and opposition representation on the Commission électorale nationale indépendante (CENI). The code was approved by the Assemblée nationale in September, although opposition deputies boycotted the vote, regarding the provisions of the code as being unduly favourable to ADEMA. Moreover, the Constitutional Court subsequently deemed certain clauses to be unacceptable. A revised code, which restored the two-round system of majority voting in legislative elections that had been employed in 1992, was approved by the legislature in January 1997 (although opposition deputies again declined to vote on the amended code).

In early 1997 the first round of legislative elections was postponed from 9 March until 13 April, when, despite opposition demands for further delay, voting proceeded accordingly. More than 1,500 candidates, mainly representing 36 of the country's 61 registered political parties, sought election to the enlarged (147-seat) Assemblée nationale. As early results indicated that ADEMA was the only party to have won seats outright at this round, the main opposition parties denounced the results as fraudulent and announced their intention to withdraw from the second round. Although independent monitors described the poll as flawed, but not fraudulent, the opposition parties also withdrew their candidates from the forthcoming presidential and municipal elections. On 24 April the Constitutional Court invalidated the results of the first round of voting, citing irregularities in the conduct of the poll.

The presidential election was postponed, by one week, until 11 May 1997. Konaré stated that he did not wish to be the sole candidate and appealed to the opposition to participate in the interests of democracy. In early May the leader of the Parti pour l'unité, la démocratie et le progrès, Mamadou Maribatou Diaby, announced that he was prepared to contest the presidency. The Constitutional Court rejected an opposition petition for the cancellation of the poll, and the presidential election proceeded in generally peaceful conditions. According to the final results, Konaré was re-elected to the presidency, securing 95.9% of the valid votes cast. What had become known as the radical opposition collective expressed satisfaction at the success of its campaign for a boycott by voters, stating that the low rate of participation (28.4% of the registered electorate) effectively invalidated Konaré's victory, although the turn-out was higher than that recorded at the 1992 presidential election. International observers expressed satisfaction at the conduct of the poll. At the end of the month the municipal elections were postponed indefinitely.

Violent protests occurred in Bamako on 8 June 1997, as Konaré was sworn in for a second term of office. Five opposition leaders, among them Tall (the CNID Chairman), Almamy Sylla (the RDP President and leader of the radical opposition collective) and Sogal Maïga (the MPR Secretary-General), were subsequently arrested and charged with 'non-recognition of the results of the presidential election', opposition to state authority, and arson and incitement to violence. They were released on bail in mid-June, shortly after the first round of the legislative elections (due on 6 July) had been postponed by two weeks. Meanwhile, several opposition activists had been sentenced to three months' imprisonment for their part in recent disturbances.

A small number of opposition parties announced their intention to present candidates for the Assemblée nationale, but the radical collective, known as the Collectif des partis politiques de l'opposition (COPPO), at this time numbering 18 parties of varying political tendencies, reiterated its refusal to re-enter the electoral process unless its demands were met in full. Violent disturbances, in which two deaths were reported, preceded the first round of legislative voting on 20 July 1997, which was contested by 17 parties (including five 'moderate' opposition parties) and a number of independent candidates. COPPO again asserted that its appeal for a boycott had been heeded, and that the low rate of participation by voters (at about 12% of the registered electorate in Bamako, and 22% outside the capital) would render the new parliament illegitimate. The official results confirmed the outright success of ADEMA. A second round of voting was necessary for eight seats on 3 August. The final results allocated 130 of the 147 seats to ADEMA, eight to PARENA, four to the Convention démocratique et sociale (CDS), three to the Union pour la démocratie et le développement (UDD) and two to the PDP. International monitors stated that both rounds of legislative voting had been conducted fairly.

Although Konaré undertook a series of consultations with representatives of the political majority and opposition, the opposition persisted in its refusal to recognize the legislature. However, by September 1997 there were indications that ADEMA was willing to consider a degree of compromise in order to defuse tensions. Konaré held a meeting with some 20 opposition leaders, including representatives of COPPO, at which he presented proposals for a broadly based coalition government. A new Council of Ministers, under Keita, was appointed in mid-September. Although it was emphasized that this was not a transitional government, the new administration included, in addition to members of ADEMA and its allies, a small number of representatives of the moderate opposition parties (among them the UDD and PDP), although close associates of the President held several important portfolios. Further measures intended to promote national reconciliation were implemented, and in December Konaré formally commuted a total of 21 death sentences, including, most notably, those imposed on ex-President Traoré and his associates.

Meanwhile, although several parties had withdrawn from COPPO, little progress was made towards a full political reconciliation. In February 1998 13 radical opposition parties confirmed their intention to boycott the municipal elections (scheduled for 19 April), stating that the voters' register remained unreliable, and denouncing the Government for planning the elections in the absence of a wider political settlement. The municipal elections were subsequently postponed.

In April 1998 former US President Jimmy Carter visited Bamako to mediate between the Government and opposition. He recommended that the opposition recognize Konaré's legitimacy as elected President, that a new electoral commission be formed to replace the CENI, and that new electoral lists be prepared prior to municipal elections. The radical opposition accepted the principle of mediation, but reiterated their demands for Konaré's resignation; furthermore, COPPO announced its intention to organize a campaign of civil disobedience throughout the country in pursuit of its objectives. The cohesion of the opposition was undermined in May, when Daba Diawara, the leader of a 'moderate' faction of the US—RDA, announced his willingness to recognize Konaré as President and urged the party to participate in the municipal elections. Although the Chairman of the US—RDA, Mamadou Bamou Touré, subsequently suspended 29 'moderates' from the party's political bureau, Diawara was elected as party Chairman, at an extraordinary congress of the party in July, at which 'dissident' members who opposed political reconciliation were expelled. Meanwhile, in May leaders of the MPR, increasingly regarded as the principal opposition party, met ADEMA officials, with the aim of defusing the political situation.

The municipal elections finally commenced on 21 June 1998, with voting in 19 communes, amid sporadic violence, in which one death was reported, while several members of the CNID were arrested on attempted sabotage charges. The remaining COPPO parties boycotted the elections, in which turn-out was estimated at 25.5% overall. Elections in the majority of communes (some 682) were scheduled to take place in November 1998; however, in September it was announced that voting was to be postponed until April 1999, to allow for the resolution of outstanding administrative problems and, furthermore, for negotiations on participation by all political tendencies.

In October 1998 the trial for 'economic crimes' began in Bamako of ex-President Traoré, his wife Mariam, her brother, Abraham Douah Cissoko (the former head of customs), a former Minister of Finance and Trade, Tiénan Coulibaly, and the former representative in France of the Banque de développement du Mali, Moussa Koné. In January 1999 Traoré, his wife and brother-in-law were sentenced to death, having been convicted of 'economic crimes' to the value of some US $350,000 (the original charges had cited embezzled funds amounting to $4m.). Coulibaly and Koné were acquitted. In September Konaré commuted the death sentences to terms of life imprisonment.

Only four of the 19 radical opposition parties took part in the national forum held in January 1999. On the eve of the forum Bamou Touré (whose faction of the US—RDA was to boycott the talks) indicated willingness to recognize the legitimacy of Konaré's presidency, in return for opposition participation in government and the holding of early legislative elections. In February, prior to an announcement by the Parti progressiste soudanais that it would contest the forthcoming municipal elections, it was reported that the party had been expelled from COPPO. Several other members of the radical opposition subsequently announced their intention to participate. In municipal voting, held in May and June 1999, ADEMA won more than one-half of the contested seats; more than 30 parties contested the elections, although significant elements of the radical opposition maintained their boycott.

Clashes were reported in July 1999 in Gao and Kidal between members of the Arab and Kounta communities, apparently provoked by disagreements between the two groups following the municipal elections in Tarkint. Ten people were reportedly killed in the violence, and security forces were deployed in the area to prevent further disturbances. Meanwhile, ethnic violence was also reported in the Kayes region, where eight people were killed in a dispute between Soninké farmers and Fulani (Peul) herders. Numerous disputes between the two groups had been reported in the area since early 1999, but at the end of July a government-brokered peace agreement was signed by representatives of both communities and by the President of the Assemblée nationale. In August further clashes between the Arab and Kounta communities resulted in nine deaths. The Minister of the Interior subsequently visited the area in an attempt to restore order; in October, however, renewed clashes between the two groups were reported to have killed up to 40 people.

In September 1999 President Konaré launched an anti-corruption campaign, in which a number of senior public officials and directors of state-owned companies were dismissed. Konaré emphasized that he expected legal proceedings to be pursued against any official criticized in the report of a commission established to investigate public-sector fraud. In January 2000 the commission's report detailed widespread irregularities in the management of state-owned companies and a lack of transparency in local government.

In February 2000 Keita submitted his Government's resignation. Observers suggested that the resignation had been prompted by widespread discontent with Keita's leadership within ADEMA, and also by Keita's desire to promote his candidature in the presidential election, scheduled for 2002. An extensively reorganized Council of Ministers was subsequently appointed. The new Prime Minister, Mandé Sidibé, was widely regarded as a supporter of economic reform and of the President's anti-corruption campaign. In June Choguel Kokala Maïga, the leader of the MPR, was among opposition leaders who announced their intention to participate fully in the elections to be held in 2002, stating that conditions for electoral fairness and transparency seemed likely to be achieved.

In July 2000 the Assemblée nationale approved legislation providing for state funding of political parties. Other new legislation sought to increase press freedom. The Assemblée also adopted a revision of the Constitution proposed by Konaré, according to which some 50 articles of the 1992 document would be amended, subject to approval by referendum. Significant proposed changes to the Constitution included authorization for people of dual nationality to stand in presidential elections, the abolition of the Supreme Court and the creation of a new press regulatory body.

Also in July 2000 speculation regarding internal tensions within ADEMA appeared to be confirmed, as some 69 of the party's 130 deputies sought, unsuccessfully, to convene an extraordinary congress of the party, apparently in order to undermine Keita's prospects of securing the party's candidacy for the next presidential election. Meanwhile, COPPO, which now comprised 15 parties and was led by Almamy Sylla of the RDP, announced that it would henceforth participate in the electoral process.

In October 2000 the Constitutional Court rejected new electoral legislation that had been adopted by the Assemblée nationale in August, claiming that eligibility criteria for candidates were unequal. (The proposed legislation had reportedly envisaged an Assemblée nationale comprising 150 members, 40 of whom would have been elected by a system of proportional representation.) Also in October it was reported that Sékou Ly, having been acquitted of economic crimes in September, had additionally been pardoned by President Konaré for his involvement in anti-Government actions in 1991.

Keita resigned from the leadership of ADEMA in October 2000, following the announcement that his opponents within the party had finally succeeded in calling an extraordinary congress of the party, to be held in late November. Prominent members of this reformist grouping within ADEMA included the Minister of the Armed Forces and Former Combatants, Soumeylou Boubèye Maïga, and the Minister of Facilities, National Development, the Environment and Town Planning, Soumaïla Cissé. At the congress, several new members were appointed to the ADEMA's executive committee, and Dioncounda Traoré was elected as the new Chairman of the party. None the less, Keita insisted that he would continue to seek election as President of Mali in 2002. In February 2001 a number of leading members of ADEMA, loyal to Keita and led by Issa N'Diaye, including some 21 deputies and four former ministers, formed a new movement, 'Alternative-2002', in an attempt to distance themselves from the leadership and policies of the party. A further 12 ADEMA deputies announced that they had joined the movement in late March. Meanwhile, opposition leaders claimed that the recently completed electoral census had been conducted fraudulently.

In May 2001 the head of the Office de Radiodiffusion-Télévision Malienne, Sidiki Konate, was imprisoned on charges of criminal defamation, after the television channel broadcast a programme alleging the corruption and inefficiency of Malian magistrates. A minor ministerial reshuffle was effected in June; notably Adama Koné, hitherto Minister of Youth and Sports, and Ascofaré Oulématou Tamboura, the erstwhile Minister of Communications, left the Government; Koné and Tamboura had both been implicated in cases of alleged corruption, reportedly in connection with the trafficking of visas and mismanagement within the state telecommunications company, respectively. In July a new party led by Keita, the Rassemblement pour le Mali (RPM), was officially registered; the formation of the RPM was widely regarded as a measure to assist Keita's anticipated candidature for the presidential election.

In November 2001 Konaré indefinitely postponed a referendum (due to take place in December) on the constitutional amendments adopted by the legislature in July 2000, following pressure from opposition parties and the judiciary. Meanwhile, ADEMA remained divided, with four candidates seeking to represent the party at the forthcoming presidential election, which was scheduled for 28 April and 5 May 2002. In January 2002 Soumaïla Cissé was elected as the party's candidate. In March Modibo Keita, hitherto Secretary-General at the presidency, was appointed as Prime Minister, after Sidibé resigned to contest the presidency as an independent candidate. Ahmed El Madani Diallo, the Minister of Rural Development, also resigned from the Government later that month and announced his presidential candidacy. In early April it was reported that 16 opposition parties, including the CNID, the RPM and the MPR, had formed an electoral alliance, Espoir 2002, agreeing to support a single opposition candidate (generally expected to be Ibrahim Boubacar Keita, who was to contest the election on behalf of the RPM) in the event of a second round of voting. Twenty-four candidates registered to contest the election to determine Konaré's successor, notably including Gen. (retd) Amadou Toumani Touré, the leader of the 1991 coup and subsequent transitional regime, who was supported by an alliance of 23 political parties, including MIRIA, PARENA and the US—RDA.

At the first round of the presidential election, which was held, as scheduled, on 28 April 2002, Touré secured the largest share of the votes cast, with 28.7%, followed by Cissé, with 21.3%, and Keita, with 21.0%. Of the remaining 21 candidates, none received more than 4% of the votes cast. As no candidate had secured an overall majority, Touré and Cissé contested a second round of voting on 12 May. Touré, supported by more than 40 parties (including those of Espoir 2002), won 65.0% of the votes cast, thus defeating Cissé. The electoral process was marred by allegations of fraud and incompetence, which led the Constitutional Court to annul 25% of the votes cast in the first ballot. None the less, international observers described the elections as generally free, fair and open. Touré was inaugurated as President on 8 June, and subsequently formed a new, interim, Government, comprising 21 ministers. The new Prime Minister and Minister of African Integration, Ahmed Mohamed Ag Hamani, was regarded as a technocrat; in addition to having previously held various ministerial posts under Traoré, he had, more recently, served as ambassador to Belgium and to Morocco and

as High Commissioner of the Organisation pour la mise en valeur du fleuve Sénégal (see p. 340). Despite the support that Touré had received from the parties of the Espoir 2002 grouping in the presidential election, it was emphasized that the newly elected President was not affiliated to any particular political party, and would be prepared to govern with any future parliamentary majority. Meanwhile, in late May, in the stated interests of national reconciliation, Konaré announced that Traoré and his wife were to be pardoned. However, Traoré denounced the gesture as politically motivated, and only left prison in mid-July, after Konaré's term of office had ended.

The elections to the Assemblée nationale further demonstrated the clear lack of any one dominant political grouping in Mali, while the rate of participation, at 25.7% nation-wide, in the second round, was low. The first round of polls, which was held on 14 July 2002, was largely inconclusive. According to provisional results, issued by the Ministry of Territorial Administration and Local Government after the second round, held on 28 July, ADEMA had won the largest number of seats (57) in the new Assemblée, although remaining short of the overall majority that the party had held in the outgoing legislature. However, as a result of various irregularities in the conduct of the polls, several thousand votes were invalidated; following the publication, in early August, of revised results by the Constitutional Court, the RPM emerged as the single largest party, with 46 of the 147 seats (although 20 of its seats had been won in local electoral alliances with other parties of the Espoir 2002 grouping), while ADEMA secured 45 seats. Other parties of Espoir 2002 obtained a further 21 seats, giving a total of 66 to supporters of the RPM, while the pro-ADEMA Alliance pour la République et la démocratie won an additional six seats, giving a total of 51. The CNID received 13 seats, while parties belonging to an informal alliance supportive of President Touré, the Alliance pour l'alternance et le changement (ACC), including PARENA and the US—RDA, won a total of 10 seats. A recently formed party led by a former student activist, Cheick Oumar Sissoko, the Parti de la solidarité africaine pour la démocratie et l'indépendance, won six seats, and six independent candidates were elected. The Constitutional Court declared void the results of voting in eight constituencies in Sikasso, in the south, and Tin-Essako, in the north, owing to administrative flaws; by-elections were scheduled to be held in October. In early September 19 deputies, comprising those of the ACC parties, several independent deputies and other declared supporters of Touré, formed a grouping, the Bloc présidentiel, within the legislature, with the declared intention of forming a stable presidential majority. Later in the month Ibrahim Boubakar Keita was elected President of the Assemblée nationale. Meanwhile, in mid-August Mamadou Bamou Touré resigned as Secretary-General of the US—RDA.

In mid-October 2002 Touré announced the formation of a Government of National Unity, comprising 21 ministers and seven minister-delegates. Although many of the principal posts remained unchanged from the interim administration appointed in June, one notable appointment was that of Bassari Touré, a former official of the World Bank, as Minister of the Economy and Finance, who was expected to institute an expedited process of reform. The new Government stated that improvements to the health and education systems were among its priorities, as was the introduction of measures to alleviate the consequences of recent price rises in foodstuffs, electricity and water. Notably, value-added tax was to be suspended on rice and salt in September–December 2002, while water and electricity rates were to be reduced by 2.85%. Meanwhile, ADEMA increased its representation in the Assemblée nationale to 53 deputies, becoming the largest party grouping, following its victory in by-elections in all eight constituencies where elections were rerun on 20 October. A minor government reorganization was announced in mid-November.

A predominant concern in the first half of the 1990s was the rebellion in the north of Mali, which began as large numbers of light-skinned Tuareg nomads, who had migrated to Algeria and Libya at times of drought, began to return to West Africa (see also the Recent History of Niger). A Tuareg attack in June 1990 on Menaka (in north-eastern Mali, near the border with Niger) precipitated a state of emergency in the Gao and Tombouctou regions, and the armed forces began a campaign against the nomads. A peace accord signed in January 1991 in Tamanrasset, Algeria, by representatives of the Traoré Government and delegates from two Tuareg groups, the Mouvement populaire de l'Azaouad (MPA) and the Front islamique-arabe de l'Azaouad

(FIAA), failed to provide a lasting solution to the conflict. Following the overthrow of the Traoré regime, the transitional administration affirmed its commitment to the Tamanrasset accord, and Tuareg groups were represented in the CTSP. However, unrest continued. At the time of the National Conference it was reported that at least 150 members of the armed forces had been killed since 1990; meanwhile, thousands of Tuaregs, Moors and Bella (the descendants of the Tuaregs' black slaves, some of whom remained with the nomads) had fled to neighbouring countries.

In February 1992, following negotiations between representatives of the Malian Government and of the Mouvements et fronts unifiés de l'Azaouad (MFUA), comprising the MPA, the FIAA and the Armée révolutionnaire de l'Azaouad (ARLA), with Algerian mediation, a truce entered into force, and a commission of inquiry was inaugurated to examine acts of violence perpetrated and losses suffered during the conflict; the more militant Front populaire de libération de l'Azaouad (FPLA) was not reported to have attended the talks. Following further discussions, the Malian authorities and the MFUA signed a draft 'National Pact' in April. Meanwhile, an exchange of prisoners was undertaken, and measures were initiated to facilitate the repatriation of refugees. Although sporadic attacks continued, particularly against members of the northern majority Songhaï, provisions of the National Pact were implemented: joint patrols were established, and in November President Konaré visited the north to inaugurate new administrative structures. In February 1993 the Malian Government and the MFUA signed an accord facilitating the integration of an initial 600 Tuaregs into the national army. In May Rhissa Ag Sidi Mohamed, the leader of the FPLA, expressed satisfaction at the success of early efforts to repatriate refugees, and he and his supporters subsequently returned from their base in Burkina to Mali.

In February 1993 an agreement was signed with the Algerian Government regarding the proposed repatriation of Malian refugees from southern Algeria. In May it was announced that the office of the UN High Commissioner for Refugees (UNHCR) was to oversee a two-year voluntary repatriation programme, whereby 12,000 refugees would be resettled in Mali by the end of 1993. However, the assassination, in February 1994, of the MPA's military leader—now, in accordance with the Pact, a senior officer in the Malian army—resulted in several weeks of clashes between the MPA and the ARLA, which was blamed for his death.

In May 1994 the Malian authorities and Tuareg leaders reached agreement regarding the integration of 1,500 former rebels into the Malian army and of a further 4,860 Tuaregs into civilian sectors. The success of the agreement was, however, undermined by an intensification of disorder in northern Mali. Tensions, periodically escalating into violence, were also reported between the integrated Tuareg fighters and regular members of the Malian armed forces. Meanwhile, a Songhaï-dominated black resistance movement, the Mouvement patriotique malien Ghanda Koy ('Masters of the Land'), emerged, amid rumours of official complicity in its offensives against the Tuaregs. In June one of the leaders of the FIAA died as a result of a clash with members of the armed forces. Meeting in Tamanrasset shortly afterwards, the Malian authorities and the MFUA endorsed a reinforcement of the army presence in areas affected by the violence, and agreed procedures for the more effective integration of Tuareg fighters.

Despite a serious escalation of violence in July 1994, the ministers responsible for foreign affairs of Mali, Algeria, Burkina Faso, Libya, Mauritania and Niger met in Bamako in August to discuss the Tuareg issue. Mali, Algeria, UNHCR and the International Fund for Agricultural Development reached a new agreement for the voluntary repatriation from Algeria of Malian refugees: Mali undertook to protect the fundamental rights and dignity of the Tuaregs, and international protection for the refugees was guaranteed. A meeting of MFUA leaders in Tamanrasset welcomed the agreement, pledged the reconciliation of the Tuareg movements, and reiterated its commitment to the National Pact. However, representatives of the 'dissident' Tuaregs did not attend the talks, and hostilities continued.

In October 1994 both the Government and the MFUA appealed for an end to the violence, following an attack on Gao (for which the FIAA claimed responsibility) and retaliatory action, as a result of which 66 deaths were officially reported. A new Minister of the Armed Forces and Veterans was appointed shortly afterwards, and the authorities subsequently appeared to adopt a less conciliatory approach to the rebels, with the army

claiming to have captured several bases. The FIAA was increasingly marginalized in the peace process, with its Algerian-based leader, Zahabi Ould Sidi Mohamed, identified by Keita as being personally responsible for endangering the National Pact. In January 1995 representatives of the FPLA and Ghanda Koy, meeting in Bourem, issued a joint statement appealing for an end to hostilities in the north, and for the implementation of the Pact. Further discussions involving Tuareg groups, Ghanda Koy and representatives of local communities resulted in the signing, in April, of an agreement providing for co-operation in resolving hitherto contentious issues. In May representatives of the organs of state, the MFUA and Ghanda Koy toured the north, as well as refugee areas in Algeria, Burkina and Mauritania, in order to promote awareness of the peace process; Konaré also visited those countries, appealing to refugees to return and participate in the process of reconstruction. In June the FIAA announced an end to its armed struggle, and expressed its willingness to join national reconciliation efforts.

In July 1995 a meeting, in Tombouctou, of representatives of the Government and of Mali's creditors agreed development strategies for the northern regions, incorporating the restoration of civilian local government, education and health-care facilities and basic utilities. A programme for the encampment of former rebels, in preparation for their eventual integration into the national army or civilian structures, began in November and ended in February 1996, by which time some 3,000 MFUA fighters and Ghanda Koy militiamen had registered and surrendered their weapons. The MFUA and Ghanda Koy subsequently issued a joint statement affirming their adherence to Mali's Constitution, national unity and territorial integrity, urging the full implementation of the National Pact and associated accords and proclaiming the 'irreversible dissolution' of their respective movements.

In September 1997 the graduation of MFUA and Ghanda Koy contingents in the gendarmerie was reported as marking the accomplishment of the integration of all fighters within the national armed and security forces. In October the former FPLA leader, Rhissa Ag Sidi Mohamed, who had not previously been regarded as a party to the peace process, returned to Mali and expressed willingness to join efforts to consolidate peace and promote the development of the north. None the less the Ministers of Justice and of the Armed Forces and Veterans expressed concern that the continued proliferation of weapons, as well as the inadequacy of military and administrative structures in the north, could result in renewed clashes. In November 2000 it was reported that Malian government forces had been dispatched to end widespread banditry by an armed group, led by Ibrahim Bahanga, a former Tuareg rebel, in the Kidal area, near to the border with Algeria. In September 2001 Bahanga reportedly announced that his forces were to cease hostilities, following talks with a state official.

The presence of large numbers of refugees from the conflict in northern Mali dominated Mali's relations with its neighbours during the 1990s, and even after the completion of the process of repatriation in mid-1998 (and the conclusion of a UNHCR programme in June 1999) the north of the country remained vulnerable to cross-border banditry. In May 1998 the ministers responsible for the interior of Mali, Mauritania and Senegal met with a view to strengthening co-operation and border controls, and in December Mali and Senegal agreed to improve border security. In February 1999 Mali and Algeria agreed to revive their joint border committee to promote development and stability in the region. In March Konaré visited Mauritania to discuss border stability; however, in June a dispute over watering rights escalated into an armed conflict between neighbouring Malian and Mauritanian communities, in which 13 people were killed. The two Governments responded to the disturbances by increasing border controls and by sending a joint delegation to the villages involved. In August 1999 at a meeting in Dakar, Senegal, the Malian, Mauritanian and Senegalese ministers responsible for the interior agreed to establish an operational unit drawn from the police forces of the three countries in order to ensure security in the area of their joint border.

France remains an important trading partner and the principal donor of bilateral aid. From mid-1996 a series of expulsions from France of illegal immigrants, including many Malians, was generally criticized in Mali. The issue of immigration was a principal focus of discussions during a visit by the French Prime Minister, Lionel Jospin, in December 1997 (the first visit by a French premier to independent Mali). Progress was achieved in

September 1998, with the establishment of a Franco-Malian joint committee on immigration, intended to promote co-operation on the repatriation of migrants and their reintegration into Malian society. The new Government formed in October 2002 included a Minister-delegate for Malians Abroad and African Integration, and the issue of immigration was, again, a principal topic of discussion when the French Minister of the Interior, Internal Security and Local Freedoms, Nicolas Sarkozy, visited Mali later that month.

President Konaré regarded the development of a wider international role for Mali as a priority in foreign policy, and Mali has contributed actively to UN peace-keeping forces. Following an official visit by Konaré to Washington, DC, in November 1997, when he met US President Bill Clinton, US military instructors were dispatched to Mali to train Malian troops for peace-keeping missions. Mali contributed troops to a regional surveillance mission, and the UN peace-keeping force that succeeded it, in the Central African Republic between February 1997 and February 2000, and to an enlarged peace-keeping force of the Economic Community of West African States (ECOWAS)—ECOMOG (see p. 189)—prior to elections in Liberia in 1997.

In February 1999 some 488 Malian troops joined ECOMOG forces in Sierra Leone, although the Malian authorities emphasized that these troops would take on a purely peace-keeping role. However, following widespread demands in Mali for a withdrawal, during August the majority of the force departed Sierra Leone; it was later announced that seven Malian soldiers had been killed and 10 seriously injured while serving in Sierra Leone. As Chairman of ECOWAS, in March 2001 Konaré hosted a mini-summit, attended by the leaders of the three countries of the Mano River Union (see p. 341), Sierra Leone, Liberia and Guinea, in Bamako on the subject of the peace process in Sierra Leone. Konaré sought to emphasize the role of Mali in ECOWAS, and in November 2000 a 120-member ECOWAS parliament, which was to promote regional co-operation, was inaugurated in Bamako.

Mali has in recent years forged closer relations with Libya, and was a founder member of the Community of Sahel-Saharan States (see p. 339), established in Tripoli in 1997.

Government

The Constitution of the Third Republic, which was approved in a national referendum on 12 January 1992, provides for the separation of the powers of the executive, legislative and judicial organs of state. Executive power is vested in the President of the Republic, who is elected for five years by universal suffrage. The President appoints a Prime Minister, who, in turn, appoints a Council of Ministers. Legislative power is vested in the 147-seat unicameral Assemblée nationale, elected for five years by universal suffrage. Elections take place in the context of a multi-party political system.

Mali has eight administrative regions, each presided over by a governor, and a district government in Bamako. Following a significant revision of local government structures in 1999, the number of elected mayors across Mali increased from 19 to 701. The Constitution makes provision for the establishment of a High Council of Local Communities.

Defence

In August 2002 the active Malian army numbered about 7,350 men, including a naval force of about 50 men (with patrol boats on the River Niger) and an air force of 400. Paramilitary forces comprised the gendarmerie (1,800), republican guard (2,000), militia (3,000) and national police (1,000). Military service is by selective conscription and lasts for two years. The defence budget for 2002 was estimated at 50,000m. francs CFA.

Economic Affairs

In 2001, according to estimates by the World Bank, Mali's gross national income (GNI), measured at average 1999–2001 prices, was US $2,280m., equivalent to $210 per head (or $810 on an international purchasing-power parity basis). During 1990–2001, it was estimated, the population increased at an average annual rate of 2.5%, while gross domestic product (GDP) per head increased, in real terms, by an average of 1.3% per year. Overall GDP increased, in real terms, at an average annual rate of 3.8% in 1990–2001. Real GDP increased by 1.5% in 2001 and by some 9.6% in 2002, according to preliminary figures, largely as a result of a significant increase in the cotton crop.

Agriculture (including livestock-rearing, forestry and fishing) contributed 50.7% of GDP in 2001. An estimated 80.4% of the labour force were employed in the sector in that year. Mali is among Africa's foremost producers and exporters of raw cotton (exports of which contributed an estimated 38.1% of the value of merchandise exports in 1999). Cotton production increased significantly in 2001/02, to a record 571,000 metric tons, compared with the 243,000 tons recorded in 2000/01. Shea-nuts (karité nuts), groundnuts, vegetables and mangoes are also cultivated for export. The principal subsistence crops are millet, sorghum, fonio, rice and maize. Cereal imports remain necessary in most years, although a crop of 2,300m. tons was forecast for 2002/03, some 22% more than in the previous year. The livestock-rearing and fishing sectors make an important contribution to the domestic food supply and (in the case of the former) to export revenue, although both are highly vulnerable to drought. According to the World Bank, agricultural GDP increased by an average of 1.8% per year in 1990–2001. Agricultural GDP increased by 6.7% in 2000, but declined by 13.0% in 2001.

Industry (including mining, manufacturing, construction and power) contributed 20.7% of GDP in 2001. According to the World Bank, industrial GDP increased at an average annual rate of 8.7% in 1990–2001. Industrial GDP increased by 7.6% in 2000 and by 31.0% in 2001.

Mining contributed 8.7% of GDP in 2001. The importance of the sector has increased with the successful exploitation of the country's gold reserves: exports of gold contributed 42.1% of the value of total exports in 1999. Gold exports increased steadily during the late 1990s; in 2000 annual gold exports stood at 26,000 kg. In early 2001 Mali became the third largest gold producer in Africa and was expected to be producing 50,000 kg per year by 2006. Salt, diamonds, marble and phosphate rock are also mined. The future exploitation of deposits of iron ore and uranium is envisaged. According to the IMF, the GDP of the mining sector increased at an average annual rate of 30.9% in 1995–2000; growth in mining GDP reached 140.8% in 1997, before slowing to 11.1% by 2000.

The manufacturing sector, including electricity and water, contributed 4.6% of GDP in 2001. The main areas of activity are agro-industrial (chiefly the processing of cotton, sugar and rice). Brewing and tobacco industries are represented, and some construction materials are produced for the domestic market. According to the World Bank, manufacturing GDP increased at an average annual rate of 2.7% in 1990–2001. Manufacturing GDP increased by 5.8% in 2000, but declined by 1.5% in 2001.

Of total electric energy generated in 1995, about 80% was derived from hydroelectric installations. Mali began to receive power supplies from the Manantali hydroelectric project (constructed and operated under the auspices of the Organisation pour la mise en valeur du fleuve Sénégal—OMVS) from December 2001, and there were also plans to link the Malian network with those of Côte d'Ivoire, Burkina Faso and Ghana. An agreement on energy supply was also reached with Algeria in February 1998. In July 2000 Belgium provided a loan of 2,600m. francs CFA for the construction of two high-voltage power stations in Bamako. Imports of petroleum products comprised 22.2% of the value of merchandise imports in 2000.

The services sector contributed 28.6% of GDP in 2001. In preparation for the African Nations Cup football tournament, which Mali hosted in early 2002, the Government began to implement a social development programme, 'Mali 2002', which was also intended to develop the tourism industry. Under the programme, the construction of two new international airports was envisaged, as well as other infrastructural improvements. According to the World Bank, the GDP of the services sector increased at an average annual rate of 2.9% in 1990–2001. Services GDP increased by 6.2% in 2000 and by 1.1% in 2001.

In 2001 Mali recorded a visible trade surplus of an estimated 82,900m. francs CFA, while there was a deficit of 208,700m. francs CFA on the current account of the balance of payments. In 2000, based on data from selected countries only, the principal sources of imports were Côte d'Ivoire and France (which supplied, respectively, 17.4% and 12.7% of total imports). The largest market for exports, according to figures from selected countries, was Germany (which accounted for 6.8% of total exports). The three principal exports in 1999 were gold, raw cotton and live animals chiefly for food, together comprising 89.5% of total exports. The principal imports in 2000 were machinery and transport equipment, refined petroleum products, chemicals and related products, and food and live animals. In 2001 an overall budget deficit of 112,200m. francs CFA was recorded, equivalent to 5.4% of GDP. In 2002, according to IMF estimates, Mali recorded an overall budget deficit of 123,100m. francs CFA. Mali's total external debt was US $2,956m. at the end of 2000, of which \$2,645m. was long-term public debt. In that year the cost of debt-servicing was equivalent to 12.1% of the value of exports of goods and services. The annual rate of inflation averaged 3.9% in 1990–2001. Consumer prices increased by 5.2% in 2001, and by 5.1% in 2002.

Mali is a member of numerous international and regional organizations, including the Economic Community of West African States (ECOWAS, see p. 187), the West African organs of the Franc Zone (see p. 238), the African Groundnut Council (see p. 335), the Liptako-Gourma Integrated Development Authority (see p. 341), the Niger Basin Authority (see p. 341) and the OMVS (see p. 340).

Mali's economic development is hindered by its vulnerability to drought, its dependence on imports and its narrow range of exports. The country also lacks facilities for the processing of its important cotton crop; it was reported in 2002 that only 1% of Mali's cotton crop was processed in the country. In August 1999 the IMF approved a four-year loan for Mali under the Enhanced Structural Adjustment Facility (ESAF), equivalent to about US \$633m., in support of the Government's programme of economic reform. The decline in world prices for cotton and gold, Mali's principal exports, and also the increasing cost of petroleum, a major import, adversely affected the country's economy in the late 1990s. Mali's external debt remains at a high level, despite a rescheduling of commitments along concessionary lines by official creditors in 1996, the granting of some \$870m. in debt-service relief under the Heavily Indebted Poor Countries initiative of the IMF and the World Bank in 2000, and the cancellation by France, in September 2002, of €80m. of bilateral debt. During the early 2000s the cotton sector was undergoing restructuring and a partial transfer to private ownership. Additionally, the transfer of the state oilseed-processing plant to private ownership was scheduled to take place in 2003. Mali's strong economic performance in 2002 was largely attributable to favourable climatic conditions, resulting in large cotton and cereal crops, and an unexpected increase in gold production. However, GDP was forecast to decline by 0.4% in 2003, partially as a consequence of the ongoing political crisis in Côte d'Ivoire (through which more than 70% of Mali's external trade, excluding gold, was previously shipped, and where some 800,000 Malians reside), and also as a result of inadequate rainfall in the second half of 2002. In particular, delays to the export of cotton and livestock caused by the closure of the Bamako–Abidjan road in late 2002 had an adverse short-term effect on the Malian economy. The new Government of Prime Minister Ahmed Mohamed Ag Hamani, appointed in October 2002, announced its commitment to the IMF-supported programme of reforms, and to a Poverty Reduction Strategy Paper agreed by the previous administration and the Fund in May 2002. None the less, in the absence of a more diversified economic base, Mali's economy remains vulnerable both to external shocks and to fluctuations in the terms of trade of its principal import and export commodities.

Education

Education is provided free of charge and is officially compulsory for nine years between seven and 16 years of age. Primary education begins at the age of seven and lasts for six years. Secondary education, from 13 years of age, lasts for a further six years, generally comprising two cycles of three years. The rate of school enrolment in Mali is among the lowest in the world: in 1997 total enrolment at primary and secondary schools excluding Medersas (Islamic schools) was equivalent to only 32% of the school-age population (males 39%; females 25%). In 1998/99 primary enrolment included 43.3% of the appropriate age-group (males 50.7%; females 35.9%), according to UNESCO estimates, while secondary enrolment was equivalent to only 15.0% (males 19.8%; females 10.3%). Tertiary education facilities include the national university, developed in the mid-1990s. Hitherto many students have received higher education abroad, mainly in France and Senegal. Estimated budgetary expenditure on education in 2000 was 64,930m. francs CFA, equivalent to 15.6% of total government expenditure in that year.

Public Holidays

2003: 1 January (New Year's Day), 20 January (Armed Forces Day), 12 February* (Tabaski, Feast of the Sacrifice), 25 March (Commemoration of the overthrow of Moussa Traoré), 21 April (Easter Monday), 1 May (Labour Day), 14 May* (Mouloud, Birth of the Prophet), 25 May (Africa Day, anniversary of the OAU's foundation), 13 June* (Baptism of the Prophet), 22 September (Independence Day), 26 November* (Korité, end of Ramadan), 25 December (Christmas).

2004: 1 January (New Year's Day), 20 January (Armed Forces Day), 2 February* (Tabaski, Feast of the Sacrifice), 25 March (Commemoration of the overthrow of Moussa Traoré), 12 April (Easter Monday), 1 May (Labour Day), 2 May* (Mouloud, Birth of the Prophet), 25 May (Africa Day, anniversary of the OAU's foundation), 1 June* (Baptism of the Prophet), 22 September (Independence Day), 14 November* (Korité, end of Ramadan), 25 December (Christmas).

*These holidays are determined by the Islamic lunar calendar and may vary by one or two days from the dates given.

Weights and Measures

The metric system is in force.

Statistical Survey

Source (unless otherwise stated): Direction Nationale de la Statistique et de l'Informatique, BP 12, Bamako; tel. 22-24-55; fax 22-71-45.

Area and Population

AREA, POPULATION AND DENSITY

Area (sq km)	1,240,192*
Population (census results)†	
1–30 April 1987	7,696,348
17 April 1998	
Males	4,847,436
Females.	4,943,056
Total	9,790,492
Population (UN estimates at mid-year)‡	
1998	10,741,000
1999	11,039,000
2000	11,351,000
Density (per sq km) at mid-2000	9.2

* 478,841 sq miles.

† Figures are provisional and refer to the *de jure* population.

‡ Source: UN, *World Population Prospects: The 2000 Revision*; Figures have not been revised to take account of the 1998 census result.

ETHNIC GROUPS (percentage of total, 1995): Bambara 36.5; Peul 13.9; Sénoufo 9.0; Soninké 8.8; Dogon 8.0; Songhaï 7.2; Malinké 6.6; Diola 2.9; Bobo and Oulé 2.4; Tuareg 1.7; Moor 1.2; Others 1.8 (Source: La Francophonie).

ADMINISTRATIVE DIVISIONS

(*de jure* population at 1998 census, provisional figures)

District		Mopti	1,475,274
Bamako . . .	1,016,167	Kayes	1,372,019
Regions		Tombouctou . .	461,956
Sikasso	1,780,042	Gao	397,516
Ségou	1,679,201	Kidal	42,479
Koulikoro	1,565,838		

PRINCIPAL TOWNS*

(*de jure* population at 1998 census, provisional figures)

Bamako (capital). .	1,016,167	Koutiala	74,153
Sikasso	113,813	Kayes	67,262
Ségou	90,898	Gao	54,903
Mopti	79,840	Kati	49,756

* With the exception of Bamako, figures refer to the population of communes (municipalities).

BIRTHS AND DEATHS
(UN estimates, annual averages)

	1985–90	1990–95	1995–2000
Birth rate (per 1,000)	50.1	50.1	49.9
Death rate (per 1,000) . . .	19.5	19.1	18.5

Source: UN, *World Population Prospects: The 2000 Revision.*

Expectation of life (WHO estimates, years at birth): 45.2 (males 44.2; females 46.2) in 2001 (Source: WHO, *World Health Report*).

ECONOMICALLY ACTIVE POPULATION
('000 persons, ILO estimates, 1990)

	Males	Females	Total
Agriculture, hunting, forestry and fishing	1,990	1,846	3,837
Industry	55	33	88
Manufacturing	40	32	72
Services	352	195	547
Total	2,437	2,106	4,544

Source: ILO.

2001 ('000 persons, estimates): Agriculture, etc. 4,580; Total labour force 5,695 (Source: FAO).

Health and Welfare

KEY INDICATORS

Total fertility rate (children per woman, 2001)	7.0
Under-5 mortality rate (per 1,000 live births, 2001) . . .	231
HIV/AIDS (% of persons aged 15–49, 2001)	1.65
Physicians (per 1,000 head, 1994)	0.05
Hospital beds (per 1,000 head, 1998)	0.24
Health expenditure (2000): US $ per head (PPP)	32
Health expenditure (2000): % of GDP	4.9
Health expenditure (2000): public (% of total)	45.5
Access to water (% of persons, 2000)	65
Access to sanitation (% of persons, 2000)	69
Human Development Index (2000): ranking	164
Human Development Index (2000): value	0.386

For sources and definitions, see explanatory note on p. vi.

Agriculture

PRINCIPAL CROPS
('000 metric tons)

	1999	2000	2001
Wheat	7.5	6.1	9.1
Rice (paddy)	727.1	742.6	932.6
Maize	619.9	214.5	299.4
Millet	818.9	759.1	792.5
Sorghum	688.8	564.7	516.7
Fonio	31.2	22.7	21.4
Sweet potatoes	46.8	47.1	68.9
Cassava (Manioc)	11.9	14.8	17.7
Yams	48.8	15.4	36.8
Sugar cane	291.3	313.0	285.2
Pulses	151.7	152.9*	156.3*
Groundnuts (in shell) . . .	190.9	193.1	196.0
Karité nuts (Sheanuts)* . . .	85	85	85
Cottonseed*	197	100	229
Tomatoes	23.7	36.5	35.1
Dry onions	25.7	20.3	30.2
Other vegetables*	241.5	242.1	242.5
Mangoes	30.8	25.9	33.1
Cotton (lint)†	197.0†	100.8†	230.0*

* FAO estimate(s).
† Unofficial figures.

Source: FAO.

LIVESTOCK
('000 head, year ending September)

	1999	2000	2001
Cattle	6,428	6,620	6,735
Sheep	6,607	6,200*	6,040†
Goats	9,379	9,849	8,691†
Pigs	66	66	83†
Horses	165	165*	165*
Asses	680	680*	680*
Camels	467	467*	467*
Chickens	25,000*	25,000*	23,364†

* FAO estimate.
† Unofficial figure.

Source: FAO.

LIVESTOCK PRODUCTS
(FAO estimates, '000 metric tons)

	1999	2000	2001
Beef and veal	88.7	91.0	97.5
Mutton and lamb	25.0	26.3	25.6
Goat meat	35.0	36.4	33.6
Chicken meat	29.2	29.2	27.2
Camel meat	7.4	7.4	7.4
Game meat	17.0	17.0	17.0
Other meat	4.6	4.6	5.2
Cows' milk	156.8	161.7	164.2
Sheeps' milk	93.0	96.0	90.0
Goats' milk	195.6	195.9	180.0
Camels' milk	54.6	54.6	54.6
Cattle hides (fresh)	13.7	14.0	15.0
Sheepskins (fresh)	5.8	6.1	5.9
Goatskins (fresh)	5.0	5.2	4.8

Source: FAO.

Forestry

ROUNDWOOD REMOVALS
(FAO estimates, '000 cubic metres, excl. bark)

	1999	2000	2001
Sawlogs, veneer logs and logs for sleepers	4	4	4
Other industrial wood	409	409	409
Fuel wood	4,671	4,731	4,788
Total	5,084	5,143	5,200

Source: FAO.

SAWNWOOD PRODUCTION
('000 cubic metres, incl. railway sleepers)

	1987	1988	1989
Total (all broadleaved)	11	13	13*

* FAO estimate.

1990–2001: Annual production as in 1989 (FAO estimates).

Source: FAO.

Fishing

('000 metric tons, live weight)

	1998	1999	2000
Capture	98.0	98.5	109.9
Nile tilapia	26.7	26.8	33.0
Bottlenose fishes	n.a.	n.a.	7.7
Characins	8.3	8.4	5.5
Black catfishes	3.7	3.7	4.4
North African catfish	15.0	15.1	27.5
Upsidedown catfishes	4.1	4.1	3.3
Nile perch	5.0	5.1	6.6
Other freshwater fishes	35.3	35.4	22.0
Aquaculture	0.1*	0.1	0.0
Total catch	98.1	98.6	109.9

* FAO estimate.

Source: FAO, *Yearbook of Fishery Statistics*.

Mining

(estimates, metric tons, unless otherwise indicated)

	1998	1999	2000
Gold (kg)	21,156	25,265	28,278
Silver (kg)	900	1,000	1,000
Gypsum	500	500	500
Salt	6,000	6,000	6,000

Gold (kg): 53,658 in 2001; 63,000 in 2002.

Sources: mainly Banque centrale des états de l'Afrique de l'ouest, US Geological Survey.

Industry

SELECTED PRODUCTS
('000 metric tons, unless otherwise indicated)

	1997	1998	1999
Raw sugar	25.5	28.5	31.2*
Cigarettes ('000 packets)	81.9	50.9	51.4
Electric energy (million kWh)	384.6	423.0	372.7

* Unofficial figure.

Salted, dried or smoked fish ('000 metric tons): 12.1 in 1996.

Cement ('000 metric tons): 21 in 1996.

Raw sugar ('000 metric tons): 29.1 in 2000; 28.0 in 2001.

Source: partly FAO; UN, *Industrial Commodity Statistics Yearbook*.

Finance

CURRENCY AND EXCHANGE RATES

Monetary Units
100 centimes = 1 franc de la Communauté financière africaine (CFA)

Sterling, Dollar and Euro Equivalents (31 December 2002)
£1 sterling = 1,008.17 francs CFA
US $1 = 625.50 francs CFA
€1 = 655.96 francs CFA
10,000 francs CFA = £9.992 = $15.987 = €15.245

Average Exchange Rate (francs CFA per US $)
2000   711.98
2001   733.04
2002   696.99

Note: An exchange rate of 1 French franc = 50 francs CFA, established in 1948, remained in force until January 1994, when the CFA franc was devalued by 50%, with the exchange rate adjusted to 1 French franc = 100 francs CFA. This relationship to French currency remained in effect with the introduction of the euro on 1 January 1999. From that date, accordingly, a fixed exchange rate of €1 = 655.957 francs CFA has been in operation.

BUDGET
('000 million francs CFA)*

Revenue†	1998	1999	2000
Budgetary revenue	231.7	247.8	245.5
Tax revenue	221.3	235.3	233.3
Taxes on net income and profits	42.8	34.7	45.4
Payroll tax	4.6	4.7	4.8
Property taxes	3.2	4.8	6.9
Domestic taxes on goods and services	30.9	39.7	42.1
Value-added tax	24.3	30.3	35.1
Taxes on international trade	127.8	135.4	123.1
Value-added tax on imports	35.3	45.1	46.5
Petroleum import duties	33.4	48.3	37.0
Other tax revenue	12.0	16.0	11.1
Stamp duties	5.8	6.8	4.6
Payment of tax arrears	2.3	5.0	3.4
Other current revenue	10.4	12.6	12.2
Special funds and annexed budgets	23.2	24.8	24.4
Social security fund	21.5	22.9	22.5
Total	254.9	272.6	269.9

2001 (estimates, '000 million francs CFA)† Total revenue 320.1 (Budgetary revenue 292.6; Tax revenue 281.6; Other current revenue 11.0; Special funds and annexed budgets 27.5).

2002 (estimates, '000 million francs CFA)† Total revenue 379.4 (Budgetary revenue 343.2; Tax revenue 313.6; Other current revenue 29.6; Special funds and annexed budgets 36.2).

Expenditure‡	2000	2001§	2002§
Budgetary expenditure	417.3	515.7	565.2
Current expenditure	199.3	243.7	280.7
Personnel	73.1	81.9	89.5
Supplies	28.5	32.1	29.7
Scholarships	6.2	4.7	5.6
Communications, transport and energy	28.9	33.0	n.a.
Interest payments (scheduled)	16.0	14.6	20.8
Externally financed	n.a.	13.8	18.7
Capital expenditure	217.1	235.9	246.6
Externally financed	157.1	174.0	178.4
HIPC expenditures‖	—	16.8	31.8
Restructuring of public enterprises	n.a.	19.3	6.1
Special funds and annexed budgets	24.4	27.5	36.2
Sub-total	441.7	543.2	601.5
Adjustment for payments arrears	—	—	—
Adjustment to cash basis	−1.6	—	—
Total	440.1	543.2	601.5

* Figures represent a consolidation of the central government budget, special funds and annexed budgets.
† Excluding grants received ('000 million francs CFA): 89.9 in 1998; 83.4 in 1999; 101.2 in 2000; 100.3 in 2001; 94.9 in 2002.
‡ Excluding net lending ('000 million francs CFA): −2.2 in 1999; −2.5 in 2000; −10.6 in 2001; −4.1 in 2002.
§ Estimated figures.
‖ Including expenditures from World Bank credit.

Sources: IMF, *Mali: Selected Issues and Statistical Annex* (January 2002), *Mali: Fourth Review Under the Poverty Reduction and Growth Facility Arrangement and Request for Waiver of Performance Criteria—Staff Report; Staff Statement; and News Brief on the Executive Board Discussion* (August 2002) and *Mali: Fifth Review Under the Poverty Reducation and Growth Facility—Staff Report; Staff Statement; and Press Release on the Executive Board Discussion* (March 2003).

INTERNATIONAL RESERVES
(excluding gold, US $ million at 31 December)

	1999	2000	2001
IMF special drawing rights	0.6	0.1	0.4
Reserve position in IMF	12.1	11.4	11.1
Foreign exchange	337.1	369.7	337.4
Total	349.8	381.2	348.9

2002 (US $ million at 31 December): Reserve position in IMF 12.0.

Source: IMF, *International Financial Statistics*.

MONEY SUPPLY
(million francs CFA at 31 December)

	1999	2000	2001
Currency outside banks	123,392	146,911	179,046
Demand deposits	142,266	143,630	197,808
Total money (incl. others) . . .	266,025	291,151	377,204

Source: IMF, *International Financial Statistics.*

COST OF LIVING
(Consumer Price Index for Bamako: base: 1996 = 100)

	2000	2001	2002
Food, beverages and tobacco . .	95.7	103.3	110.9
Clothing	104.4	109.5	109.3
Housing, water, electricity and gas	104.8	110.0	117.5
All items (incl. others)	101.4	106.6	112.0

Source: Banque centrale des états de l'Afrique de l'ouest.

NATIONAL ACCOUNTS
('000 million francs CFA at current prices)

Expenditure on the Gross Domestic Product

	1999	2000	2001
Government final consumption expenditure	232.5	199.3	243.7
Private final consumption expenditure	1,271.3	1,356.2	1,525.0
Increase in stocks	21.8	18.1	8.8
Gross fixed capital formation . .	313.0	369.2	508.6
Total domestic expenditure . .	1,838.6	1,942.8	2,286.1
Exports of goods and services . .	376.4	458.6	606.0
Less Imports of goods and services	544.3	659.9	818.5
GDP in purchasers' values . .	1,670.7	1,741.6	2,073.6

Source: Banque centrale des états de l'Afrique de l'ouest.

Gross Domestic Product by Economic Activity

	1999	2000	2001
Agriculture, livestock-rearing, forestry and fishing	682.2	667.5	986.8
Mining	85.5	113.3	169.9
Manufacturing	95.4	99.7	88.9
Electricity, gas and water . . .	23.2	28.6	29.8
Construction and public works .	88.7	104.1	114.1
Transport and telecommunications	91.1	96.0	85.7
Trade	275.5	306.6	268.9
Other marketable services . .	79.0	82.7	71.6
Public administration . . .	136.8	119.6	129.5
GDP at factor cost	1,557.4	1,618.1	1,945.2
Import duties	113.3	123.5	128.4
GDP in purchasers' values . .	1,670.7	1,741.6	2,073.6

Source: Banque centrale des états de l'Afrique de l'ouest.

BALANCE OF PAYMENTS
('000 million francs CFA)

	2000	2001	2002*
Exports of goods f.o.b.	388.0	531.1	635.5
Imports of goods f.o.b.	−421.5	−533.1	−552.7
Trade balance	−33.4	−2.0	82.9
Services and other income (net)	−237.8	−310.4	−346.7
Balance on goods, services and income	−271.2	−312.4	−263.8
Private transfers (net) . . .	44.3	39.5	27.0
Official transfers (net) . . .	45.7	42.7	28.1
Current balance	−181.2	−230.2	−208.7
Capital account (net)	72.3	72.8	78.0
Private finance (net)	72.3	31.0	82.2
Official finance (net)	61.8	83.0	89.1
Net errors and omissions . . .	2.7	10.9	—
Overall balance	27.8	−32.5	40.6

* Estimated figures.

Source: IMF, *Mali: Fourth Review under the Poverty Reduction and Growth Facility Arrangement and Request for Waiver of Performance Criteria—Staff Report; Staff Statement; and News Brief on the Executive Board Discussion* (August 2002) and *Mali: Enhanced Initiative for Heavily Indebted Poor Countries—Completion Point Document* (March 2003).

External Trade

PRINCIPAL COMMODITIES
(distribution by SITC, US $ million)

Imports c.i.f.	1998	1999	2000
Food and live animals . . .	145.4	136.9	93.4
Dairy products and birds' eggs . .	24.7	25.1	15.9
Milk and cream	24.3	24.8	15.9
Milk and cream, preserved, concentrated or sweetened .	24.0	24.2	15.7
Cereals and cereal preparations .	43.1	38.1	25.6
Rice, semi-milled or wholly milled	22.4	20.3	9.3
Sugar, sugar preparations and honey	30.1	27.5	17.2
Sugar and honey	29.8	27.1	16.9
Refined sugar, etc . . .	29.3	26.4	16.5
Mineral fuels, lubricants, etc .	113.7	115.5	169.9
Petroleum, petroleum products, etc	112.3	113.9	168.6
Petroleum products, refined .	110.7	112.0	167.2
Chemicals and related products	127.5	127.6	101.0
Medicinal and pharaceutical products	23.5	27.5	24.3
Fertilizers, manufactured . .	50.1	37.8	29.4
Nitrogen-phosphorus-potassium fertilizer	36.7	21.5	17.8
Basic manufactures . . .	110.5	142.2	108.5
Non-metallic mineral manufactures	31.8	32.5	38.6
Lime, cement and fabricated construction materials . .	26.8	24.0	33.6
Cement	25.3	22.5	30.5
Iron and steel	32.4	45.5	18.5
Machinery and transport equipment	193.9	248.0	237.9
Power generating machinery and equipment	15.2	26.3	27.9
Machinery specialized for particular industries . .	47.1	44.8	58.1
Civil engineering, contractors' plant, equipment and parts .	22.2	23.0	39.3
Construction and mining machinery	14.1	12.9	28.7
General industrial machinery, equipment and parts . .	23.5	26.1	18.7
Electrical machinery, apparatus, appliances and parts . . .	23.0	25.3	24.1
Road vehicles	72.6	96.1	82.7
Passenger motor vehicles (excl. buses)	23.2	27.3	22.4
Lorries and motor vehicles for special purposes . . .	26.3	31.3	38.3
Motor vehicles for the transport of goods or materials	26.3	31.3	38.3
Miscellaneous manufactured articles	23.7	30.0	29.6
Total (incl. others)	736.6	823.8	759.1

Exports f.o.b.	1997	1998	1999
Food and live animals . .	14.7	61.7	59.3
Live animals chiefly for food . .	9.3	50.0	53.3
Crude materials (inedible) except fuels	264.6	286.6	227.2
Textile fibres (not wool tops) and their wastes (not in yarn) .	263.1	284.4	226.5
Raw cotton, excl. linters, not carded or combed	254.5	284.1	217.6
Basic manufactures	1.9	5.9	17.3
Gold, non-monetary (excl. gold ores and concentrates) . .	16.1	236.8	240.2
Total (incl. others)	302.4	619.7	571.0

Source: UN, *Industrial Trade Statistics Yearbook.*

2000 ('000 million francs CFA): Total imports c.i.f. 589.40; Total exports f.o.b. 388.13 (Source: IMF, *International Financial Statistics*).

2001 ('000 million francs CFA): Total imports c.i.f. 741.90; Total exports f.o.b. 530.50 (Source: IMF, *International Financial Statistics*).

SELECTED TRADING PARTNERS
(US $ million)*

Imports	1998	1999	2000
Belgium-Luxembourg	52.0	33.3	33.8
China, People's Repub.† . . .	54.2	54.7	67.5
Côte d'Ivoire	233.6	222.7	227.7
France (incl. Monaco) . . .	226.8	222.2	167.0
Germany	28.1	34.8	50.6
Spain	22.1	22.8	15.2
United Kingdom	29.3	28.4	29.8
Total (incl. others)	1,239.4	1,264.7	1,312.1

Exports	1998	1999	2000
Belgium-Luxembourg	5.6	9.1	7.7
China, People's Repub.† . . .	5.2	1.7	0.5
Côte d'Ivoire	1.9	0.9	3.1
France (incl. Monaco) . . .	4.6	4.7	4.2
Germany	4.7	4.3	13.2
Spain	7.6	4.3	3.9
United Kingdom	0.7	4.1	9.2
Total (incl. others)	293.9	239.3	194.7

* Data are compiled on the basis of reporting by Mali's trading partners.
† Including Hong Kong and Macau.

Source: IMF, *Mali: Selected Issues and Statistical Annex* (January 2002).

Transport

RAILWAYS
(traffic)

	1997	1998	1999
Passengers ('000)	862	790	778
Freight carried ('000 metric tons) .	565	566	536
Passenger-km (million)	223	218	210
Freight ton-km (million) . . .	258	256	241

ROAD TRAFFIC
(estimates, motor vehicles in use)

	1994	1995	1996
Passenger cars	24,250	24,750	26,190
Lorries and vans	16,000	17,100	18,240

Source: IRF, *World Road Statistics.*

CIVIL AVIATION
(traffic on scheduled services)*

	1997	1998	1999
Kilometres flown (million) . . .	3	3	3
Passengers carried ('000) . . .	86	91	84
Passenger-km (million) . . .	242	258	235
Total ton-km (million)	38	38	36

* Including an apportionment of the traffic of Air Afrique.

Source: UN, *Statistical Yearbook.*

Communications Media

	1999	2000	2001
Television receivers ('000 in use)	140	160	n.a.
Telephones ('000 main lines in use)	33.8	39.2	49.9
Mobile cellular telephones ('000			
subscribers).	6.4	10.4	45.3
Personal computers ('000 in use)	11	13	14
Internet users ('000).	7.0	18.8	30.0

Source: International Telecommunication Union.

Book production (first editions, excluding pamphlets): 14 titles (28,000 copies) in 1995 (Source: UNESCO, *Statistical Yearbook*).

Daily newspapers (1996): Number 3; Estimated average circulation ('000 copies) 12 (Source: UNESCO, *Statistical Yearbook*).

Radio receivers ('000 in use): 570 in 1997 (Source: UNESCO, *Statistical Yearbook*).

Tourism

	1998	1999	2000*
Tourist arrivals ('000)	83	87	91
Tourism receipts (US $ million)	50	50	50

* Estimates.

Sources: World Tourism Organization.

Education

(1998/99, unless otherwise indicated)

	Institu- tions	Teachers	Students		
			Males	Females	Total
Pre-primary	212	1,050	10,056	15,085	25,141
Primary*	2,871	15,447†	565,743	393,192	958,935
Secondary:					
general	n.a.	}	127,214	63,702	190,916
technical and		7,663 {			
vocational.	n.a.		16,070	10,714	26,784
teacher training‡	n.a.	77§	1,052	494	1,596
Tertiary	n.a.	960	n.a.	n.a.	18,662

* Data exclude Medersas (Islamic schools).
† National estimate.
‡ 1997/98 figures, unless otherwise indicated.
§ 1996/97 figure.

1999/2000: *Primary*: 1,235,605 students; *Secondary*: 245,000 students.

2000/01: *Pre-primary*: 27,263 students; *Primary*: 14,692 teachers; 1,115,563 students; *Secondary General* 257,564 students; *Technical and vocational* 41,873 students; *Teacher training* 6,010 students; *Tertiary and higher* 1,312 teachers; 28,000 students.

Adult literacy rate (UNESCO estimates): 41.5% (males 48.9%; females 34.4%) in 2000 (Source: UN Development Programme, *Human Development Report*).

Source: mainly UNESCO Institute for Statistics and Ministry of Education, Bamako.

Directory

The Constitution

The Constitution of the Third Republic of Mali was approved in a national referendum on 12 January 1992. The document upholds the principles of national sovereignty and the rule of law in a secular, multi-party state, and provides for the separation of the powers of the executive, legislative and judicial organs of state.

Executive power is vested in the President of the Republic, who is Head of State and is elected for five years by universal adult suffrage. The President appoints the Prime Minister, who, in turn, appoints other members of the Council of Ministers.

Legislative authority is exercised by the unicameral 147-member Assemblée nationale, which is elected for five years by universal adult suffrage.

The Constitution guarantees the independence of the judiciary. Final jurisdiction in constitutional matters is vested in a Constitutional Court.

The rights, freedoms and obligations of Malian citizens are enshrined in the Constitution. Freedom of the press and of association are guaranteed.

The Government

HEAD OF STATE

President: Gen. (retd) AMADOU TOUMANI TOURÉ (took office 8 June 2002).

COUNCIL OF MINISTERS
(April 2003)

Prime Minister, Minister of African Integration: AHMED MOHAMED AG HAMANI.

Minister of Health: KÉITA ROKIATOU N'DIAYE.

Minister of the Economy and Finance: BASSARI TOURÉ.

Minister of Crafts and Tourism: BAH N'DIAYE.

Minister of State-Administered Estates and Housing Affairs: BOUBACAR SIDIKI TOURÉ.

Minister of Industry and Trade: CHOGUEL KOKALA MAÏGA.

Minister of Agriculture, Livestock and Fisheries: SEYDOU TRAORÉ.

Minister of National Education: MAMADOU LAMINE TRAORÉ.

Minister of Equipment and Transport: OUSMANE ISSOUFI MAÏGA.

Minister of Foreign Affairs and International Co-operation: LASSINE TRAORÉ.

Minister of the Armed Forces and War Veterans: MAHAMANE KALIL MAÏGA.

Minister of Territorial Administration and Local Communities: Gen. KAFOUGOUNA KONÉ.

Minister of Mining, Energy and Water Resources: AHMED DIANA SEMEGA.

Minister of the Environment and Town Planning: NANCOUMA KÉITA.

Minister of Internal Security and Civil Protection: Col SOULEYMANE SIDIBÉ.

Minister of Communication and New Information Technologies: GAOUSSOU DRABO.

Minister of Social Development, Solidarity and the Elderly: N'DIAYE FATOUMATA COULIBALY.

Minister of Labour and the Civil Service: MODIBO DIAKITÉ.

Minister for the Promotion of Women, Children and the Family: BERTHÉ AÏSSATA BENGALY.

Minister of Culture: CHEICK OUMAR SISSOKO.

Minister of Justice, Keeper of the Seals: ABDOULAYE GARBO TAPO.

Minister of Youth and Sports: DJIBRIL TANGARA.

There are also seven Minister-delegates, responsible for the Reform of the State and Relations with the Institutions; Planning; the Promotion of Investment and the Private Sector; Food Security; Transport; Malians Abroad and African Integration; and Employment and Professional Training.

MINISTRIES

Office of the President: BP 1463, Koulouba, Bamako; tel. 222-25-72; fax 223-00-26.

Office of the Prime Minister and Ministry of African Integration: quartier du Fleuve, BP 790, Bamako; tel. 223-06-80; fax 222-85-83.

Ministry of Agriculture, Livestock and Fisheries: BP 1676, Bamako; tel. 222-27-85.

Ministry of the Armed Forces and War Veterans: route de Koulouba, BP 2083, Bamako; tel. 222-50-21; fax 223-23-18.

Ministry of Communication and New Information Technologies: quartier du Fleuve, BP 116, Bamako; tel. 222-26-47; fax 223-20-54.

Ministry of Crafts and Tourism: quartier du Fleuve, BP 1759, Bamako; tel. 222-80-58; fax 223-02-67.

Ministry of Culture: Korofina, BP 4075, Bamako; tel. 224-66-63; fax 224-57-27; e-mail info@culture.gov.ml; internet w3.culture.gov.ml.

Ministry of the Economy and Finance: BP 234, Koulouba, Bamako; tel. 222-51-56; fax 222-01-92.

Ministry of Equipment and Transport: Bamako; tel. 222-39-37.

Ministry of the Environment and Town Planning: Bamako; tel. 223-05-39.

Ministry of Foreign Affairs and International Co-operation: Koulouba, Bamako; tel. 222-83-14; fax 222-52-26.

Ministry of Health: BP 232, Koulouba, Bamako; tel. 222-53-02; fax 223-02-03.

Ministry of Industry and Trade: quartier du Fleuve, BP 234, Koulouba, Bamako; tel. 222-43-87; fax 222-88-53.

Ministry of Internal Security and Civil Protection: Bamako; tel. 222-34-31.

Ministry of Justice: quartier du Fleuve, BP 97, Bamako; tel. 222-26-42; fax 223-00-63.

Ministry of Labour and the Civil Service: route de Koulouba, Bamako; tel. 222-34-31; fax 222-34-31.

Ministry of Mining, Energy and Water Resources: BP 238, Bamako; tel. 222-41-84; fax 222-21-60.

Ministry of National Education: BP 71, Bamako; tel. 222-57-80; fax 222-21-26.

Ministry for the Promotion of Women, Children and the Family: Torokorobougou, BP 2688, Bamako; tel. 228-74-42; fax 228-75-04; e-mail mpfef@fib.com.

Ministry of Social Development, Solidarity and the Elderly: Bamako; tel. 223-23-01.

Ministry of State-Administered Estates and Housing Affairs: Bamako; tel. 223-63-44.

Ministry of Territorial Administration and Local Communities: face Direction de la RCFM, BP 78, Bamako; tel. 222-42-12; fax 223-02-47; internet w3.matcl.gov.ml.

Ministry of Youth and Sports: route de Koulouba, BP 91, Bamako; tel. 222-31-53; fax 223-10-87.

President and Legislature

PRESIDENT

Presidential Election, First Ballot, 28 April 2002

Candidates	Votes	% of votes
Gen. (retd) Amadou Toumani Touré (Independent)	449,176	28.71
Soumaïla Cissé (ADEMA)	333,525	21.31
Ibrahim Boubacar Keita (RPM)	329,143	21.03
Tiébilé Dramé (PARENA)	62,493	3.99
Mountaga Tall (CNID)	58,695	3.75
Moussa Balla Coulibaly (UDD)	50,211	3.21
Choguel Kokala Maïga (MPR)	42,469	2.71
Mamadou Bakary Sangaré (CDS)	34,603	2.21
Mandé Sidibé (Independent)	31,389	2.01
Ahmed El Madani Diallo (Independent)	25,584	1.63
Daba Diawara (PIDS)	17,156	1.10
Others	130,332	8.33
Total	**1,564,776**	**100.00**

Second Ballot, 12 May 2002

Candidates	Votes	% of votes
Gen. (retd) Amadou Toumani Touré (Independent)	926,243	65.01
Soumaïla Cissé (ADEMA)	498,503	34.99
Total	**1,424,746**	**100.00**

ASSEMBLÉE NATIONALE

President: IBRAHIM BOUBACAR KEITA.

General Election, 14 and 28 July 2002*

Parties and alliances	Seats
Alliance pour la démocratie au Mali—Parti pan-africain pour la liberté, la solidarité et la justice (ADEMA)	53
Rassemblement pour le Mali (RPM)	46†
Congrès national d'initiative démocratique—Faso Yiriwa Ton (CNID)	13
Rassemblement pour la démocratie et le travail (RDT)	7
Parti de la solidarité africaine pour la démocratie et l'indépendance (SADI)	6
Convention démocratique et sociale (CDS)	4
Bloc pour la démocratie et l'intégration africaine—Faso Jigi (BDIA)	3
Union soudanaise—Rassemblement démocratique africaine (US—RDA)/Rassemblement national pour la démocratie (RND)	3
Mouvement patriotique pour le renouveau (MPR)	2
Rassemblement malien pour le travail (RAMAT)	2
Parti pour la démocratie et le renouveau—Dounkafa Ton (PDR)	1
Parti pour la renaissance nationale (PARENA)	1
Independents	6
Total	**147**

* These figures include the results of voting in eight constituencies where the elections were rerun on 20 October 2002.

† Including 20 seats won in coalitions with other parties.

Advisory Councils

Constitutional Court: BP 213, Bamako; tel. 222-56-32; fax 223-42-41; f. 1994; Pres. ABDARAHMAN BABA TOURÉ; Sec.-Gen. BOUBACAR TAHOUATI.

Economic, Social and Cultural Council: Bamako; tel. 222-43-68; fax 222-84-52; e-mail cesc@cefib.com; f. 1987; Pres. MOUSSA BALLA COULIBALY.

Political Organizations

In mid-2002, when there were some 87 functioning political groups, the most active parties and political groupings included:

Alliance pour l'alternance et le changement (ACC): Bamako; f. 2002 prior to legislative elections by supporters of Pres. Touré; 28 constituent parties in May 2002; Pres. IBRAHIM BOUBACAR BÂH.

Bloc pour la démocratie et l'intégration africaine—Faso Jigi (BDIA): rue du RDA, Missira, porte 41, BP E 1413, Bamako; tel. 221-45-22; fax 220-82-93; f. 1993; liberal and democratic; Leader YOUSSOUF TRAORÉ.

Mouvement pour l'indépendance, la renaissance et l'intégration africaine (MIRIA): Dravéla Bolibana, rue 417, porte 66, Bamako; tel. 229-29-81; e-mail lemiria@iquebec.com; internet quebec.ifrance.com/miria; f. 1994 following split in ADEMA; Pres. MOHAMED LAMINE TRAORÉ.

Parti pour la démocratie et le renouveau—Dounkafa Ton (PDR): Niaréla, rue 428, porte 94, près Carré des Martyrs, Bamako; f. 1998; Pres. ADAMA KONÉ; Leader KALILOU SAMAKE.

Parti pour la renaissance nationale (PARENA): rue Soundiata, porte 1397, Ouolofobougou, Bamako; tel. 223-49-54; fax 222-29-08; e-mail parena@cefib.com; f. 1995 following split in CNID; Pres. TIÉBILÉ DRAMÉ; Sec.-Gen. AMIDOU DIABATÉ.

Rassemblement malien pour le travail (RAMAT): Marché, Hippodrome, rue 224, porte 1393, BP E 2281, Bamako; f. 1991; Leader ABDOULAYE MACKO.

Rassemblement national pour la démocratie (RND): Niaréla, route Sotuba, porte 1892, Hamdallaye, Bamako; tel. 229-73-88; fax 221-73-88; f. 1997 by 'moderate' breakaway group from RDP; Pres. ABDOULAYE GARBA TAPO.

Union des forces démocratiques pour le progrès—Samaton (UFDP): Djicoroni Para, carré Son Président, Bamako; tel. 223-17-66; f. 1991; Sec.-Gen. Col YOUSSOUF TRAORÉ.

Union soudanaise—Rassemblement démocratique africain (US—RDA): Missira, porte 41, BP E 1413, Bamako; tel. and fax 221-45-22; f. 1946; sole party 1960–68, banned 1968–1991; 'moderate' faction split from party in 1998; Hon. Pres. Dr MAMADOU EL-BÉCHIR GOLOGO; Sec.-Gen. (vacant).

Alliance pour la République et la démocratie: Bamako; f. 2001; Pres. MOUSSA BABA COULIBALY.

Alliance pour la démocratie au Mali—Parti pan-africain pour la liberté, la solidarité et la justice (ADEMA): rue Fankélé, porte 145, BP 1791, Bamako-Coura; tel. 222-03-68; f. 1990 as Alliance pour la démocratie au Mali; Pres. DIONCOUNDA TRAORÉ; Sec.-Gen. MARIMATIA DIARRA.

Union pour la démocratie et le développement (UDD): ave OUA, porte 3626, Sogoniko, BP 3275, Bamako; tel. 222-46-94; f. 1991 by supporters of ex-Pres. Traoré; Leader MOUSSA BABA COULIBALY.

Convention démocratique et sociale (CDS): N'Tomikorobougou, rue 673, porte 108, Bamako; tel. 222-62-76; f. 1996; Chair. MAMADOU BAKARY SANGARÉ.

Convention parti du peuple (COPP): Hippodrome, BP 9012, Bamako; f. 1996; Pres. Me MAMADOU GACKOU.

Espoir 2002: Bamako; f. 2001; 16 constituent parties in March 2002.

Congrès national d'initiative démocratique—Faso Yiriwa Ton (CNID): 58 rue 429, Niarela, BP 2572, Bamako; tel. 221-42-75; fax 222-83-21; e-mail cnid@cefib.com; internet www.cnid.org.ml; f. 1991; Chair. Me MOUNTAGA TALL; Sec.-Gen. N'DIAYE BA.

Mouvement patriotique pour le renouveau (MPR): chez Choguel Maïga, Baco-Djicoroni ACI, Bamako; tel. 222-40-23; f. 1995; Pres. Dr CHOGUEL KOKALA MAÏGA.

Parti pour l'indépendance, la démocratie et la solidarité (PIDS): Hippodrome, rue 300, porte 426, Bamako; f. 2001 by dissidents from US—RDA; Pres. DABA DIAWARA.

Rassemblement pour la démocratie et le progrès (RDP): Niarela, rue 485, porte 11, BP 2110, Bamako; tel. 221-30-92; fax 222-67-95; f. 1991; Pres. ALMAMY SYLLA.

Rassemblement pour la démocratie et le travail (RDT): Immeuble El-hadj Balla Camara, place du Souvenir, Bamako; tel. 222-25-58; f. 1991; Leader AMADOU ALI NIANGADOU.

Rassemblement pour le Mali (RPM): Hippodrome, rue 228, porte 1164, Bamako; tel. 221-69-40; f. 2001; Leader IBRAHIM BOUBACAR KEITA.

Parti de la solidarité africaine pour la démocratie et l'indépendance (SADI): Djélibougou, rue 246, porte 559, BP 3140, Bamako; tel. 224-87-82; f. 2002; Leader CHEICK OUMAR SISSOKO.

Parti pour la démocratie et le progrès (PDP): Niarela, rue 428, porte 94, BP 2351, Bamako; tel. 224-16-75; f. 1991; Leader MADY KONATÉ.

Parti malien pour le développement et le renouveau (PMDR): Sema I, rue 76, porte 62, BP 553, Badalabougou, Bamako; tel. 222-25-58; f. 1991; social democratic; Pres. Me ABDOUL WAHAB BERTHE.

Diplomatic Representation

EMBASSIES IN MALI

Algeria: Sogoninko BP 02, Bamako; tel. 220-51-76; fax 222-93-74; Ambassador MOHAMED ANTAR DAOUD.

Burkina Faso: route INRSP, Hippodrome, Bamako; tel. 223-31-71; fax 221-92-66; e-mail ambafaso@datatech.toolnet.org; Ambassador Prof. SANNÉ MOHAMED TOPAN.

Canada: route de Koulikoro, immeuble Séméga, BP 198, Hippodrome, Bamako; tel. 221-22-36; fax 221-43-62; e-mail bamako@dfait-macci.gc.ca; Ambassador LOUISE OUIMET.

China, People's Republic: route de Koulikoro, Hippodrome, BP 112, Bamako; tel. 221-35-97; fax 222-34-43; e-mail amchimali@spider.toolnet.org; Ambassador MA ZHIXUE.

Côte d'Ivoire: square Patrice Lumumba, immeuble CNAR, BP E 3644, Bamako; tel. 222-03-89; fax 222-13-76; Ambassador ABOUBACAR SIRIKI DIABATÉ.

Cuba: Niarela, Bamako; tel. 221-02-89; fax 221-02-93; Ambassador GARCÍA ARMANDO.

Egypt: BP 44, Badalabougou-est, Bamako; tel. 222-35-65; fax 222-08-91; e-mail mostafa@datatech.net.ml; Ambassador MOHAMED EL-GHOBARI.

France: square Patrice Lumumba, BP 17, Bamako; tel. 222-29-51; fax 222-31-36; e-mail ambassade@france-mali.org.ml; Ambassador NICOLAS NORMAND.

Germany: Badalabougou-est, rue 14, porte 334, BP 100, Bamako; tel. 222-32-99; fax 222-96-50; e-mail allemagne.presse@afribone.net.ml; Ambassador INGMAR BRENTLE.

Ghana: Bamako; Ambassador KWADKO AFOAKWA SARPONG.

Guinea: Immeuble Saybou Maïga, quartier du Fleuve, BP 118, Bamako; tel. 222-30-07; fax 221-08-06; Ambassador MOHAMED LAMINE JO SOUMAH.

Iran: Hippodrome, ave al-Quds, BP 2136, Bamako; tel. 221-76-38; fax 221-07-31; Ambassador HEDAYATOLAH GHAREDAGHI.

Iraq: BP 2512, Badalabougou-est, Bamako; tel. 222-38-06; fax 222-24-16; Ambassador MOWAFLAQ M. JASSIN.

Libya: Badala Ouest, face Palais de la Culture, BP 1670, Bamako; tel. 222-34-96; fax 222-66-97; Ambassador Dr SALAHEDDIN AHMED ZAREM.

Mauritania: route de Koulikoro, Hippodrome, BP 135, Bamako; tel. 221-48-15; fax 222-49-08; Ambassador MOHAMED SIE'AHMED OULD LECKHALE.

Morocco: rue 25, porte 80, BP 2013, Badalabougou-est, Bamako; tel. 222-21-23; fax 222-77-87; e-mail sifamali@afribone.net.ml; Ambassador MOHAMED RCHOUK.

Netherlands: rue 437, BP 2220, Hippodrome, Bamako; tel. 221-56-11; fax 221-36-17; e-mail bam@minbuza.nl; Ambassador SASKIA ELIZABETH DE LANG.

Nigeria: BP 57, Badala-est; tel. 221-53-28; fax 222-39-74; e-mail ngrbko@malinet.ml; Ambassador MOHAMMED SANI KANGIWA.

Russia: BP 300, Niarela, Bamako; tel. 221-55-92; fax 221-99-26; e-mail ambrusse_mali@datatech.toolnet.org; Ambassador ANATOLII I. KLIMENKO.

Saudi Arabia: Villa Bal Harbour, 28 Cité du Niger, BP 81, Bamako; tel. 221-25-28; fax 221-50-64; e-mail mlemb@mofa.gov.sa; Chargé d'affaires KHALED OMAR ABDRABUH.

Senegal: quartier du Fleuve, BP 42, Bamako; tel. 222-82-74; fax 221-17-80; Ambassador AMADOU DEME.

South Africa: Résidence Kome, Room 016, Hamdallaye, ACI-2000, Bamako; tel. 229-00-00; fax 229-00-00; e-mail bamako@foreign.gov.za; Chargé d'affaires a.i. L. S. L. LEKANA.

Tunisia: quartier du Fleuve, Bamako; tel. 223-28-91; fax 222-17-55; Ambassador BÉCHIR MSAKNI.

United Kingdom: rue 132, porte 902, BP 2069, Badalabougou-ouest, Bamako; tel. and fax 223-34-12; e-mail info@britembmali.org; scheduled to close in mid-2003; Ambassador GRAEME LOTEN.

USA: angle rue Rochester NY, ave Mohamed V, BP 34, Bamako; tel. 222-54-70; fax 222-37-12; e-mail webmaster@usa.org.ml; internet w3.usa.org.ml; Ambassador VICKI HUDDLESTON.

Judicial System

The 1992 Constitution guarantees the independence of the judiciary.

Supreme Court: BP 7, Bamako; tel. 222-24-06; e-mail c.supreme@spider.toolnet.org; f. 1969; judicial section comprises two civil chambers, one commercial chamber, one social chamber and one criminal chamber; in addition, there are administrative and financial regulatory sections; Pres. ASKIA M'BARAKOU TOURÉ; Sec.-Gen. ALKAÏDY SANIBIÉ TOURÉ.

President of the Bar: Me MAGATTÉ SÈYE.

There are three Courts of Appeal, seven Tribunaux de première instance (Magistrates' Courts) and also courts for labour disputes.

Religion

According to the UN Development Programme's *Human Development Report*, around 80% of the population are Muslims, while 18% follow traditional animist beliefs and under 2% are Christians.

ISLAM

Association Malienne pour l'Unité et le Progrès de l'Islam (AMUPI): Bamako; state-endorsed Islamic governing body.

Chief Mosque: place de la République, Bagadadji, Bamako; tel. 221-21-90.

In late 2000 the Government announced proposals to create a Haut Conseil Islamique. Among the functions of this council would be the management of relations between the Muslim communities and the State.

CHRISTIANITY

The Roman Catholic Church

Mali comprises one archdiocese and five dioceses. At 31 December 2000 there were an estimated 210,601 Roman Catholics, comprising about 1.6% of the total population.

Bishops' Conference

Conférence Episcopale du Mali, Archevêché, BP 298, Bamako; tel. 222-54-99; fax 222-52-14.

f. 1973; Pres. Rt Rev. Jean-Gabriel Diarra (Bishop of San).

Archbishop of Bamako: Jean Zerbo, Archevêché, BP 298, Bamako; tel. 222-54-99; fax 222-52-14.

Other Christian Churches

There are several Protestant mission centres, mainly administered by US societies.

BAHÁ'Í FAITH

National Spiritual Assembly: BP 1657, Bamako; e-mail ntirandaz@aol.com.

The Press

The 1992 Constitution guarantees the freedom of the press. In 2000 there were six daily newspapers, 18 weekly or twice-weekly publications and six monthly or twice-monthly publications.

DAILY NEWSPAPERS

Les Echos: Hamdallaye, ave Cheick Zayed, porte 2694, BP 2043, Bamako; tel. 229-62-89; fax 226-76-39; e-mail jamana@malinet.ml; f. 1989; publ. by Jamana cultural co-operative; circ. 30,000; Dir-Gen. Hamidou Konaté; Editor-in-Chief Aboubacar Saliph Diarra.

L'Essor: square Patrice Lumumba, BP 141, Bamako; tel. 222-36-83; fax 222-47-74; e-mail info@essor.gov.ml; internet www.essor.gov.ml; f. 1949; pro-Govt newspaper; Editor Souleymane Drabo; circ. 3,500.

Info Matin: rue 56/350, Bamako Coura, BP E 4020, Bamako; tel. 223-82-09; fax 223-82-27; e-mail redaction@info-matin.com; internet www.info-matin.com; independent; Dir Sambi Touré; Editor-in-Chief Mohamed Sacko.

Nouvel Horizon: rue 223, porte 145, Sogoniko, BP 942, Bamako; tel. 220-06-91; independent; Dir Chouaidou Traoré.

Le Républicain: Dravela-Bolibana, BP 1484, Bamako; tel. 229-09-00; f. 1992; independent; Dir Salif Koné.

PERIODICALS

26 Mars: Bamako; f. 1998; weekly; independent; Editor Boubacar Sanghare.

L'Aurore: rue 438 P 298, BP 3150, Bamako; tel. and fax 221-69-22; f. 1990; 2 a week; independent; Dir Karamoko N'Diaye.

Le Canard Libéré: rue 56/350, Bamako Coura, BP E 4020, Bamako; tel. 223-82-09; fax 223-82-27; e-mail redaction@info-matin.com; weekly; Dir Sambi Touré.

Le Carrefour: Bamako; tel. 222-49-01; Dir Mahamane Imrane Coulibaly.

Citoyen: Bamako; f. 1992; fortnightly; independent.

Le Continent: BP E 4338, Bamako; tel. 229-57-39; weekly; Dir Ibrahima Traoré.

Le Courrier: rue 42, Hamdallaye Marché, BP E 2882, Bamako; tel. 229-18-62; e-mail syattara@yahoo.fr; weekly; Dir Sadou A. Yattara.

　Le Courrier Magazine: BP 1258, Bamako; tel. 229-98-35; monthly; Dir Mahamane Hameye Cissé.

L'Indépendant: Immeuble Sossoh, 2ème étage, BP E 1040, Bamako; tel. and fax 223-27-27; 2 a week; Dir Saouti Haïdara.

L'Inspecteur: BP 2725, Bamako; tel. 222-49-55; weekly; Dir Aly Diarra.

Jamana—Revue Culturelle Malienne: BP 2043, Bamako; BP E 1040; e-mail jamana@malinet.ml; f. 1983; quarterly; organ of Jamana cultural co-operative.

Journal Officiel de la République du Mali: Koulouba, BP 14, Bamako; tel. 222-59-86; fax 222-70-50; official gazette.

Kabaaru: Mopti; monthly; Fulbé language; rural interest; Editor Badama Doucouré; circ. 5,000.

Kabako: rue 228, porte 474, Hippodrome, BP 9005, Bamako; tel. 221-29-12; weekly; Dir Macoro Camara.

Kibaru: BP 1463, Bamako; monthly; Bambara and three other languages; rural interest; Editor Nianzé Samaké; circ. 5,000.

Liberté: Hamdallaye Marché, BP E 241, Bamako; tel. 228-18-98; weekly; Dir Abdoulaye Ladji Guindo.

Le Malien: rue 497, porte 277, Badialan III, BP E 1558, Bamako; tel. 223-57-29; weekly; Dir Sidi Keita.

Match: Hamadallaye, BP 100, Bamako; tel. 229-18-82; weekly; Dir Baba Cissouma.

Musow: Bamako; e-mail musow@musow.com; internet www.musow.com; women's interest.

Nyeleni Magazine: rue 42, Hamdallaye Marché, BP 3381, Bamako; tel. 229-24-01; monthly; Dir Bintou Traoré.

L'Observateur: Galérie Djigué, rue du 18 juin, BP E 1002, Bamako; tel. and fax 223-06-89; 2 a week; Dir Belco Tamboura.

Le Reflet: BP E 1688, Bamako; tel. 224-39-52; e-mail tan@malinet.ml; weekly; fmrly *Le Carcan*; present name adopted Jan. 2001; Dir Abdoul Karim Dramé.

Le Scorpion: rue 42, Hamdallaye Marché, BP 1258, Bamako; tel. 222-98-35; fax 222-69-22; weekly; Dir Mahamane Haméye Cissé.

Le Soudanais: Hamdallaye, BP E 535, Bamako; tel. 229-10-55; weekly; Dir Kissima Gakou.

Le Tambour: rue 497, porte 295, Badialan III, BP E 289, Bamako; tel. and fax 222-75-68; 2 a week; Dir Yéro Diallo.

Tatou Sports: BP 98, Sikasso; tel. 262-02-46; Dir Saïd Diarrassouba.

NEWS AGENCIES

Agence Malienne de Presse et Publicité (AMAPP): Ministry of Culture, Korofina, BP 4075, Bamako; tel. 224-66-63; fax 224-57-27; f. 1977; Dir Gaoussou Darbo.

Foreign Bureau

Agence France-Presse (AFP): BP 778, Bamako; tel. 222-07-77.

IPS (Italy) and Xinhua (New China) News Agency (People's Republic of China) are also represented in Mali.

PRESS ASSOCIATIONS

Association des Editeurs de la Presse Privée (ASSEP): BP E 2882, Bamako; tel. 229-18-62; e-mail syattara@yahoo.fr; Pres. Sadou A. Yattara.

Association des Femmes de la Presse Privée: Porte 474, rue 428, BP E 731, Bamako; tel. 221-29-12; Pres. Fanta Diallo.

Association des Journalistes Professionels des Médias Privés du Mali (AJPM): BP E 2456, Bamako; tel. 222-19-15; fax 223-54-78; Pres. Momadou Fofana.

Association des Professionnelles Africaines de la Communication (APAC MALI): Porte 474, rue 428, BP E 731, Bamako; tel. 221-29-12; Pres. Macoro Camara Diaby.

Maison de la Presse de Mali: BP E 2456, Bamako; tel. 222-19-15; fax 223-54-78; e-mail maison-presse@cefib.com; internet www.cefib.com/presse; independent media association; Pres. Sadou A. Yattara.

Union Interprofessionnelle des Journalistes et de la Presse de Langue Française (UIJPLF): rue 42, Hamdallaye Marché, BP 1258, Bamako; tel. 229-98-35; Pres. Mahamane Haméye Cissé.

Union Nationale des Journalistes Maliens (UNAJOM): BP 141, Bamako; tel. 222-36-83; fax 223-43-13; e-mail amap@djata.malinet.ml; Pres. Ousmane Maïga.

Publishers

EDIM SA: ave Kassé Keïta, BP 21, Bamako; tel. 222-40-41; f. 1972 as Editions Imprimeries du Mali, reorg. 1987; general fiction and non-fiction, textbooks; Chair. and Man. Dir Alou Tomota.

Editions Donniya: Cité du Niger, BP 1273, Bamako; tel. 221-46-46; fax 221-90-31; e-mail donniya@malinet.ml; internet www.cefib.com/impcolor/donniya.htm; f. 1996; general fiction, history, reference and children's books in French and Bambara.

Le Figuier: 151 rue 56, Semal, BP 2605, Bamako; tel. and fax 223-32-11; e-mail lefiguier@afribone.net.ml; f. 1997; fiction and non-fiction.

Editions Jamana: BP 2043, Bamako; tel. 229-62-89; fax 229-76-39; e-mail jamana@malinet.ml; f. 1988; literary fiction, poetry, reference; Dir Ba Maïra Sow.

Editions Teriya: BP 1677, Bamako; tel. 224-11-42; theatre, literary fiction; Dir Gaoussou Diawara.

Broadcasting and Communications

TELECOMMUNICATIONS

Ikatel: Bamako; f. 2003; fixed-line and mobile cellular telecommunications; jtly owned by France Telecom and Société Nationale des Télécommunications du Sénégal; Dir-Gen. ALIOUNE N'DIAYE.

Malitel: Bamako; tel. 222-47-31; fax 222-47-30; e-mail malitel@cefib .com; internet www.malitel.com; f. 1999; operates fixed-line telephone services, also mobile and cellular telecommunications in Bamako, Kayes, Mopti, Ségou and Sikasso.

Société des Télécommunications du Mali (SOTELMA): route de Koulikoro, BP 740, Bamako; tel. 222-77-38; fax 221-30-22; e-mail segal@sotelma.ml; f. 1990; state-owned; 49% privatization pending in 2003; Pres. and Dir-Gen. M. SOW.

BROADCASTING

Radio

Office de Radiodiffusion-Télévision Malienne (ORTM): BP 171, Bamako; tel. 222-47-29; fax 222-42-05; e-mail ortm@spider .toolnet.org; Man. Dir ABDOULAYE SIDIBÉ; Dir of Radio OUMAR TOURÉ.

Radio Mali–Chaîne Nationale: BP 171, Bamako; tel. 221-20-19; fax 221-42-05; e-mail ortm@spider.toolnet.org; f. 1957; state-owned; radio programmes in French, Bambara, Peulh, Sarakolé, Tamachek, Sonrai, Moorish, Wolof, English.

Chaîne 2: Bamako; f. 1993; radio broadcasts to Bamako.

In early 2003 there were an estimated 100 private radio stations broadcasting in Mali, including:

Fréquence 3: Bamako; f. 1992; commercial.

Radio Balanzan: BP 419, Ségou; tel. 232-02-88.

Radio Bamakan: Marché de Médine, BP E 100, Bamako; tel. and fax 221-27-60; e-mail radio.bamakan@ifrance.com; f. 1991; community station; 104 hours of FM broadcasts weekly; Man. MODIBO DIALLO.

Radio Espoir: BP 1399, Bamako; tel. 220-67-08; Dir PHILIPPE DOUMBIA.

Radio Foko de Ségou Jamana: BP 2043, Bamako; tel. 232-00-48; fax 222-76-39; e-mail radiofoko@cefib.com.

Radio Guintan: BP 2546, Bamako; tel. 220-09-38; Dir RAMATA DIA.

Radio Jamana: BP 2043, Bamako; tel. 229-62-89; fax 229-76-39; e-mail jamana@malinet.net.

Radio Kayira: BP 3140, Bamako; tel. 224-22-43; fax 222-75-68; f. 1992; supports the CNID; Dir CHEICK O. SISSOKO.

Radio Klédu: BP 2322, Bamako; tel. 221-00-18; f. 1992; commercial; Propr MAMADOU COULIBALY.

Radio Liberté: BP 5015, Bamako; tel. 223-05-81; f. 1991; commercial station broadcasting 24 hours daily; Dir ALMANY TOURÉ.

Radio Patriote: BP E 1406, Bamako; Dir MOUSSA KEITA.

Radio Rurale: BP 94, Kayes; tel. 252-14-76; e-mail rrk@afribone .net.ml; community stations established by the Agence de coopération culturelle et technique (ACTT); transmitters in Niono, Kadiolo, Bandiagara and Kidal.

Sahel FM: BP 392, Kayes; tel. 252-21-87; f. 1995; broadcasts began 1997; Man. Dir MOUCTAR THIAM.

Radio Tabalé: BP 697, Bamako; tel. and fax 222-78-70; f. 1992; independent public-service station; broadcasting 57 hours weekly; Dir TIÉMOKO KONÉ.

La Voix du Coran et du Hadit: Bamako; tel. 221-63-44; Islamic station broadcasting on FM in Bamako; Dir El Hadj M. DICKO.

Radio Wassoulou: BP 61, Koutiala; tel. 264-01-34; fax 64-01-34.

Radio France International, the Voix de l'Islam, and the Gabonese-based Africa No. 1 began FM broadcasts in Mali in 1993; broadcasts by Voice of America and the World Service of the British Broadcasting Corpn are also transmitted via private radio stations.

Television

Office de Radiodiffusion-Télévision Malienne (ORTM): see Radio; Dir of Television BALY IDRISSA SISSOKO.

Multicanal SA: Quinzambougou, BP E 1506, Bamako; tel. 221-49-64; e-mail sandrine@multi-canal.com; internet www.multi-canal .com; private subscription broadcaster; relays international broadcasts; Pres. ISMAÏLA SIDIBÉ.

TV Klédu: 600 ave Modibo Keïta, BP E 1172, Bamako; tel. 223-90-00; fax 223-70-50; e-mail info@tvkledu.com; internet www.cefib.com/tvkledu; private cable TV operator; relays international broadcasts; Pres. MAMADOU COULIBALY.

Finance

(cap. = capital; res = reserves; dep. = deposits; m. = million; brs = branches; amounts in francs CFA)

BANKING

Central Bank

Banque Centrale des Etats de l'Afrique de l'Ouest (BCEAO): BP 206, Bamako; tel. 222-37-56; fax 222-47-86; internet www.bceao .int; f. 1962; HQ in Dakar, Senegal; bank of issue for the mem. states of Union économique et monétaire ouest-africaine (UEMOA, comprising Benin, Burkina Faso, Côte d'Ivoire, Guinea-Bissau, Mali, Niger, Senegal and Togo); cap. and res 850,500m., total assets 45,157,700m. (Dec. 2001); Gov. CHARLES KONAN BANNY; Dir in Mali IDRISSA TRAORÉ; brs at Mopti and Sikasso.

Commercial Banks

Bank of Africa—Mali (BOA): 418 ave de la Marné, Bozola, BP 2249, Bamako; tel. 221-47-61; fax 221-46-53; e-mail boamali@ datatech.toolnet.org; internet www.pelnet.com/boa; f. 1982; cap. 2,000m., total assets 53,654m. (Dec. 2000); Pres. BOUREIMA SYLLA; Dir-Gen. MICHEL LE BLANC; 5 brs.

Banque Commerciale du Sahel SA (BCS–SA): rue 127, angle rue 122, Boyola, BP 2372, Bamako; tel. 221-01-95; fax 221-05-35; f. 1980; fmrly Banque Arabe Libyo-Malienne pour le Commerce Extérieur et le Développement; 50.0% owned by Libyan-Arab Foreign Bank, 49.5% state-owned; cap. and res 2,096m., total assets. 15,243m. (Dec. 1999); Pres. FANGATIGUI DOUMBIA; Dir-Gen. MOHAMED SAED EL ATRACH; 1 br.

Banque de l'Habitat du Mali (BHM): rue de Métal Soudan, quartier du Fleuve, BP 2614, Bamako; tel. 222-91-90; fax 222-93-50; f. 1990; fmrly Société des Chèques Postaux et de la Caisse d'Epargne; 37.1% owned by Institut National de Prévoyance Social; 14.8% state-owned; cap. 4,000m, dep. 16,423m. (Dec. 1999); Pres. BAKARY KONIBA TRAORÉ; Dir-Gen. MAMADOU SAMBA DIARRA; 1 br.

Banque International pour le Commerce et l'Industrie au Mali (BICI–Mali): Immeuble Nimagala, blvd du Peuple, BP B72, Bamako; tel. 223-33-70; fax 223-33-73; e-mail bicim-sa@cefib.com; f. 1999; 50% owned by SFOM Interafrica, 20% by BNP Paribas (France), 15% by Banque Mauritanienne pour le Commerce International; cap. and res 1,808m., total assets 19,061m. (Dec. 1999); Pres. and Dir-Gen. LUC VIDAL; 1br.

Banque Internationale pour le Mali (BIM): blvd de l'Indépendance, BP 15, Bamako; tel. 222-51-11; fax 222-45-66; e-mail bim@ malinet.ml; internet www.malinet.ml/pratique/bim/index.html; f. 1981; fmrly BIAO—Mali, present name since 1995; 61.5% state-owned; privatization pending; cap. 4,255m., dep. 53,378m. (Dec. 1999); Administrator DIAKARIDIA KEITA (acting); 6 brs.

Banque Malienne de Crédit et de Dépôts: ave Mobido Keita, BP 45, Bamako; tel. 222-53-36; fax 222-79-50; e-mail bmcd@malinet.ml; 100% state-owned; transfer to private-sector ownership proposed in 2003.

Banque Nationale de Développement Agricole—Mali (BNDA): Immeuble BNDA, ave du Mali, ACI 2000, BP 2424, Bamako; tel. 229-64-64; fax 229-25-75; e-mail bnda@bndamali.com; f. 1981; 38.5% state-owned; cap. 10,510m., total assets 75,820m. (Dec. 2001); Pres. and Dir-Gen. MOUSSA KALIFA TRAORÉ; 21 brs.

Ecobank Mali: place de la Nation, quartier du Fleuve, BP E 1272, Bamako; tel. 223-33-00; fax 223-33-05; e-mail ecobank@cefib.com; f. 1998; 50% owned by Ecobank Transnational Inc., 18% by Ecobank Bénin, 15% by Ecobank Togo; cap. 2,525m., dep. 25,175m., total assets 37,318m. (Dec. 2001); Pres. SEYDOU DJIM SYLLA; Dir-Gen. KASSIM ABOU KABASSI; 1 br.

Development Banks

Banque de Développement du Mali (BDM) SA: ave Modibo Keita, quartier du Fleuve, BP 94, Bamako; tel. 222-20-50; fax 222-50-85; e-mail info@bdm-sa.com; f. 1968; absorbed Banque Malienne de Crédit et de Dépôts in 2001; 20% state-owned, 20% owned by BCEAO, 20% by Banque ouest-africaine de développement; cap. 3,860m. (Nov. 2001), dep. 112,975m. (Dec. 1999); Pres. and Dir-Gen. ABDOULAYE DAFFÉ; 14 brs.

Banque Nationale de Développement Agricole—Mali (BNDA—Mali): Immeuble Dette Publique, quartier du Fleuve, BP 2424,

Bamako; tel. 222-64-64; fax 222-29-61; e-mail bnda@malinet.ml; f. 1981; 40.6% state-owned; cap. 10,133m., dep. 33,351m., total assets 68,700m. (Dec. 2000); Chair. and Man. Dir MOUSSA KALIFA TRAORÉ; 21 brs.

Financial Institutions

Direction Générale de la Dette Publique: Immeuble ex-Caisse Autonome d'Amortissement, quartier du Fleuve, BP 1617, Bamako; tel. 222-29-35; fax 222-07-93; management of the public debt; Dir NAMALA KONÉ.

Société Malienne de Financement (SOMAFI): blvd du 22 octobre 1946, BP E3643, Bamako; tel. 222-18-66; fax 222-18-69; e-mail somafi@malinet.ml; f. 1997; cap. and res 137m., total assets 1,217m. (Dec. 1999); Pres. M. SYLLA; Man. Dir ERIC LECLÈRE.

STOCK EXCHANGE

Bourse Régionale des Valeurs Mobilières (BRVM): Chambre de Commerce et de l'Industrie du Mali, place de la Liberté, BP E 1398, Bamako; tel. 223-23-54; fax 223-23-59; e-mail abocoum@brvm .org; f. 1998; national branch of BRVM (regional stock exchange based in Abidjan, Côte d'Ivoire, serving the mem. states of UEMOA); Man. AMADOU DJÉRI BOCOUM.

INSURANCE

Les Assurances Générales de France (AGF): ave du Fleuve, BP 190, Bamako; tel. 222-58-18.

Assurance Colina Mali SA: BP E 154, Bamako; tel. 222-57-75; fax 223-24-23; e-mail c-mali@colina-sa.com; f. 1990; cap. 1,000m. Dir-Gen. MARYUONNE SIDIRE.

Caisse Nationale d'Assurance et de Réassurance du Mali (CNAR): BP 568, Bamako; tel. 222-64-54; fax 222-23-29; f. 1969; state-owned; cap. 50m. Dir-Gen. F. KEITA; 10 brs.

Compagnie d'Assurance Privée—La Soutra: BP 52, Bamako; tel. 222-36-81; fax 222-55-23; f. 1979; cap. 150m. Chair. AMADOU NIONO.

Compagnie d'Assurance et de Réassurance de Mali: BP 1822, Bamako; tel. 222-60-29.

Compagnie d'Assurance Sabu Nyuman: Bamako Coura 135–136, BP 1822, Bamako; tel. 222-60-29; fax 222-57-50; f. 1984; cap. 250m. Dir-Gen. MOMADOU SANOGO.

Lafía Assurances: ave de la Nation, BP 1542, Bamako; tel. 222-35-51; fax 222-52-24; f. 1983; cap. 50m. Dir-Gen. ABDOULAYE TOURÉ.

Trade and Industry

GOVERNMENT AGENCIES

Centre d'Etudes et de Promotion Industrielle (CEPI): BP 1980, Bamako; tel. 222-22-79; fax 222-80-85.

Direction Nationale des Affaires Économiques (DNAE): rue de Sotuba, BP 210, Bamako; tel. 222-23-14; fax 222-22-56; involved in economic and social affairs.

Direction Nationale des Travaux Publics (DNTP): ave de la Liberté, BP 1758, Bamako; tel. and fax 222-29-02; administers public works.

Guichet Unique–Direction Nationale des Industries: rue Titi Niare, Quinzambougou, BP 96, Bamako; tel. and fax 222-31-66.

Office du Niger: BP 106, Ségou; tel. 232-02-92; fax 232-01-43; f. 1932; taken over from the French authorities in 1958; restructured in mid-1990s; cap. 7,139m. francs CFA; principally involved in cultivation of food crops; Pres. and Man. Dir NANCOMA KEÏTA.

Office des Produits Agricoles du Mali (OPAM): BP 132, Bamako; tel. 222-37-55; fax 221-04-06; e-mail opam@datatech .toolnet.org; f. 1965; cap. 5,800m. francs CFA; state-owned; manages National (Cereals) Security Stock, administers food aid, responsible for sales of cereals and distribution to deficit areas; Pres. and Dir-Gen. ABDOULAYE KOITA.

DEVELOPMENT ORGANIZATIONS

Agence Française de Développement (AFD): Quinzambougou, Route de Sotuba, BP 32, Bamako; tel. 221-28-42; fax 221-86-46; internet www.afd.fr; fmrly Caisse Française de Développement; Dir in Mali DOMINIQUE DORDAIN.

Office de Développement Intégré du Mali-Ouest (ODIMO): square Patrice Lumumba, Bamako; tel. 222-57-59; f. 1991 to succeed Office de Développement Intégré des Productions Arachidières et Céréalières; development of diversified forms of agricultural production; Man. Dir ZANA SANOGO.

Service de Coopération et d'Action Culturelle: square Patrice Lumumba, BP 84, Bamako; tel. 221-83-38; fax 221-83-39; e-mail scac@cefib.com; administers bilateral aid from France; Dir MICHEL COLIN DE VERDIÈRE.

CHAMBER OF COMMERCE

Chambre de Commerce et d'Industrie du Mali: place de la Liberté, BP 46, Bamako; tel. 222-50-36; fax 222-21-20; f. 1906; Pres. MAMADOU LAMINE TOUNKARA; Sec.-Gen. DABA TRAORÉ.

EMPLOYERS' ASSOCIATIONS

Association Malienne des Exportateurs de Légumes (AMELEF): BP 1996, Bamako; f. 1984; Pres. BADARA FAGANDA TRAORÉ; Sec.-Gen. BIRAMA TRAORÉ.

Association Malienne des Exportateurs de Ressources Animales (AMERA): Centre Malien de Commerce Extérieur, BP 1996, Bamako; tel. 222-56-83; f. 1985; Pres. AMBARKÉ YERMANGORE; Admin. Sec. ALI HACKO.

Fédération Nationale des Employeurs du Mali (FNEM): BP 2445, Bamako; tel. 221-63-11; fax 221-90-77; f. 1980; Pres. MOUSSA MARY BALLA COULIBALY; Permanent Sec. LASSINA TRAORÉ.

UTILITIES

Electricity

Energie du Mali (EDM): square Patrice Lumumba, BP 69, Bamako; tel. 222-30-20; fax 222-84-30; e-mail sekou.edm@cefib.com; f. 1960; 60% owned by Saur International (France); planning, construction and operation of power-sector facilities; cap. 7,880m. Pres. YORO DIAKITE; Dir-Gen. HAROUNA DIAKITE; 1,401 employees (2001).

Enertech GSA: marché de Lafiabougou, BP 1949, Bamako; tel. 222-37-63; fax 222-51-36; f. 1994; cap. 20m. solar energy producer; Dir MOCTAR DIAKITE.

Société de Gestion de l'Energie de Manantali (SOGEM): Immeuble 790, Hippodrome, rue 335 x 336, BP 4015, Bamako; tel. 221-03-92; fax 221-11-22; to generate and distribute electricity from the Manantali HEP project, under the auspices of the Organisation pour la mise en valeur du fleuve Sénégal.

Gas

Maligaz: route de Sotuba, BP 5, Bamako; tel. 222-23-94; gas distribution.

TRADE UNION FEDERATION

Union nationale des travailleurs du Mali (UNTM): Bourse du Travail, blvd de l'Indépendance, BP 169, Bamako; tel. 222-36-99; fax 223-59-45; f. 1963; Sec.-Gen. ISSA DOUCOURÉ.

There are, in addition, several non-affiliated trade unions.

Transport

RAILWAYS

Mali's only railway runs from Koulikoro, via Bamako, to the Senegal border. The line continues to Dakar, a total distance of 1,286 km, of which 729 km is in Mali. The track is in very poor condition, and is frequently closed during the rainy season. In 1995 the Governments of Mali and Senegal agreed to establish, with a view to privatization, a joint company to operate the Bamako–Dakar line. Some 536,000 metric tons of freight were handled on the Malian railway in 1999. Plans exist for the construction of a new rail line linking Bamako with Kouroussa and Kankan, in Guinea.

Régie du Chemin de Fer du Mali (RCFM): BP 260, Bamako; tel. 222-59-68; fax 222-83-88; e-mail rcfm@cefib.com; f. 1960; privatization proposed in 2003; Pres. DIAKARIDIA SIDIBÉ; Man. Dir LASSANA KONÉ.

ROADS

The Malian road network in 1999 comprised 17,107 km, of which about 1,500 km were main roads. About 2,760 km of the network were paved. A bituminized road between Bamako and Abidjan (Côte d'Ivoire) provides Mali's main economic link to the coast; construction of a road linking Bamako and Dakar (Senegal) is to be financed by the European Development Fund. The African Development Bank also awarded a US $31.66m. loan to fund the Kankan–Kouremale–Bamako road between Mali and Guinea. A road across the Sahara to link Mali with Algeria is also planned.

Compagnie Malienne de Transports Routiers (CMTR): BP 208, Bamako; tel. 222-33-64; f. 1970; state-owned; Man. Dir MAMADOU TOURÉ.

INLAND WATERWAYS

The River Niger is navigable in parts of its course through Mali (1,693 km) during the rainy season from July to late December. The River Senegal was, until the early 1990s, navigable from Kayes to Saint-Louis (Senegal) only between August and November, but its navigability was expected to improve following the inauguration, in 1992, of the Manantali dam, and the completion of works to deepen the river-bed.

Compagnie Malienne de Navigation (COMANAV): BP 10, Koulikoro; tel. 226-20-94; fax 226-20-09; f. 1968; state-owned; partial privatization pending; river transport; Pres. and Man. Dir YACOUBA DIALLO.

Société Navale Malienne (SONAM): rue Achkhabad Niaréla, BP 10, Bamako; tel. 222-60-52; fax 222-60-66; f. 1981; transferred to private ownership in 1986; Chair. ALIOUNE KEÏTA.

Société Ouest-Africaine d'Entreprise Maritime (SOAEM): rue Mohamed V, BP 2428, Bamako; tel. 222-58-32; fax 222-40-24; maritime transport co.

CIVIL AVIATION

The principal airport is at Bamako-Senou. The other major airports are at Bourem, Gao, Goundam, Kayes, Kita, Mopti, Nioro, Ségou, Tessalit and Tombouctou. There are about 40 small airfields. Mali's airports are being modernized with external financial assistance.

Direction Nationale de l'Aéronautique Civile: Bamako; tel. 222-55-24.

Air Affaires Mali: BP E 3759, Badalabougou, Bamako; tel. 222-61-36.

Air Mali: BP 2690, Bamako; tel. 222-59-52; fax 222-94-03; f. 1993 to succeed Mali Tombouctou Air Service (MALITAS); 45% owned by Air Maintenance Corpn (Egypt); domestic, regional and international services; Pres. and Dir-Gen. CHEIKH AMADOU KANTÉ.

Société des Transports Aériens (STA): BP 1809, Bamako; f. 1984; privately-owned; local services; Man. Dir MELHEM ELIE SABBAGUE.

Tourism

Mali's rich cultural heritage is promoted as a tourist attraction. In 1999 the Government launched a three-year cultural and tourism development programme centred on Tombouctou, Gao and Kidal. An estimated 91,000 tourists visited Mali in 2000, when receipts from tourism totalled some US $50m.

Office Malien du Tourisme et de l'Hôtellerie (OMATHO): BP 191, Bamako; tel. 222-56-73; fax 222-55-41; e-mail tombouctou2000@tourisme.gov.ml; internet w3.tourisme.gov.ml; f. 1995; Dir AGUIBOU GUISSÉ.

MALTA

Introductory Survey

Location, Climate, Language, Religion, Flag, Capital

The Republic of Malta is in southern Europe. The country comprises an archipelago in the central Mediterranean Sea, consisting of the inhabited islands of Malta, Gozo and Comino, and the uninhabited islets of Cominotto, Filfla and St Paul's. The main island, Malta, lies 93 km (58 miles) south of the Italian island of Sicily and 288 km (179 miles) east of the Tunisian coast, the nearest point on the North African mainland. The climate is warm, with average temperatures of 22.6°C (72.7°F) in summer and 13.7°C (56.6°F) in winter. Average annual rainfall is 578 mm (22.8 ins). Maltese and English are the official languages, although Italian is widely spoken. About 91% of the inhabitants are Christians belonging to the Roman Catholic Church. The national flag (proportions 2 by 3) consists of two equal vertical stripes, white at the hoist and red at the fly, with a representation of the George Cross, edged with red, in the upper hoist. The capital is Valletta, on the island of Malta.

Recent History

Malta, which had been a Crown Colony of the United Kingdom since 1814, became an independent sovereign state, within the Commonwealth, on 21 September 1964. The Government, led by Dr Giorgio Borg-Olivier of the Nationalist Party (Partit Nazzjonalista—PN), negotiated defence and financial aid agreements, effective over a 10-year period, with the United Kingdom.

In June 1971 the Malta Labour Party (Partit Laburista—MLP), led by Dom Mintoff, assumed power after winning a general election. Pursuing a policy of non-alignment, the Government concluded agreements for cultural, economic and commercial co-operation with Italy, Libya, Tunisia, the USSR, several East European countries, the USA, the People's Republic of China and others, and received technical assistance, notably from Libya. The MLP Government abrogated the 1964 Mutual Defence and Assistance Agreement with the United Kingdom. This agreement was replaced in 1972 by a new seven-year agreement, under which Malta was to receive substantially increased rental payments for the use of military facilities by the United Kingdom and other members of the North Atlantic Treaty Organization (NATO, see p. 271). British troops were finally withdrawn in March 1979.

Malta became a republic in December 1974. The MLP retained power at general elections held in September 1976 and in December 1981, when it secured a majority of three seats in the House of Representatives, although obtaining only 49.1% of the votes cast. The PN, which had received 50.9% of the votes cast, contested the result, refused to take its seats in the House of Representatives, and organized a campaign of civil disobedience. In March 1983 the PN terminated its legislative boycott, but immediately withdrew again, in protest against a government resolution to loosen ties with the European Community (EC, now the European Union—EU, see p. 199). Although Mintoff promised constitutional amendments and weekly consultations with the opposition, these arrangements collapsed in June, when the Government blamed the PN for a bomb attack on government offices. In November a police raid on the PN headquarters was alleged to have discovered a cache of arms and ammunition.

In June 1983 the House of Representatives approved controversial legislation, under which about 75% of church property was to be expropriated to provide finance for a programme of universal free education and the abolition of fee-paying church schools. Opponents of the measure denounced it as both unconstitutional and a violation of religious liberty, and in September 1984 the courts disallowed the legislation. In April 1984 the House approved legislation forbidding any school to accept fees (including voluntary gifts and donations). The Roman Catholic Archbishop of Malta rejected the government conditions, and closed all church schools, in response to growing tensions and public unrest. A strike by state school teachers in October and November further polarized opinion, but an agreement was reached in November, when the schools were re-opened.

Mintoff retired in December 1984 and was replaced as Prime Minister by the new leader of the MLP, Dr Carmelo Mifsud

Bonnici. In April 1985 the Government reached agreement with the Roman Catholic Church, providing for the phased introduction of free education in church secondary schools, and guaranteeing the autonomy of church schools. However, in July 1988 the enforced introduction of new licensing procedures for church schools led to demands by the Roman Catholic Church that the State should reduce its supervisory powers over church education.

At a general election held in May 1987 the PN obtained 50.9% of the votes cast but won only 31 of the 65 seats in the House of Representatives, while the MLP, with 48.9% of the votes cast, won the remaining 34 seats. However, in accordance with a constitutional amendment that had been adopted in January (see Government, below), the PN was allocated four additional seats, giving it a majority of one in the legislature, thus ending the MLP's 16-year tenure in office. The leader of the PN, Dr Eddie Fenech Adami, became Prime Minister. The PN secured an increased majority of three seats over the MLP at a general election held in February 1992. This result was widely interpreted as an endorsement of the PN's pro-EC policies.

Malta has maintained a policy of non-alignment in its international relations, and has negotiated economic co-operation agreements with many countries. In 1984 the Governments of Malta and Libya signed a five-year treaty of co-operation, which included an undertaking by Libya to provide military training. The treaty signified a return to the previously close relations between the two countries, which had deteriorated in 1980, owing to a dispute over a maritime boundary (eventually resolved by the International Court of Justice in 1985). Malta has an association agreement with the EU, originally signed in 1970 and periodically renewed. On becoming Prime Minister in May 1987, Fenech Adami declared that the Government, while retaining Malta's non-aligned status and its links with Libya, would seek closer relations with the USA and other Western countries, and would apply for full membership of the EC.

A formal application for full membership of the EC was submitted by the Maltese Government in July 1990. In June 1993 the EC Commission recommended that, subject to the Government of Malta's satisfying EC requirements for regulatory reforms in financial services, competition and consumer protection, favourable consideration should be given to the future accession of Malta to the EU. In June 1994 the Council of the EU affirmed that the next phase of enlargement, following the (then) expected accession to the EU in January 1995 of Austria, Finland, Norway and Sweden, would involve Malta and Cyprus. In June 1995 the EU affirmed that full negotiations on Malta's accession were to begin six months after the conclusion of the 1996 Intergovernmental Conference.

Domestic opposition to Maltese accession to the EU had been led by the MLP, on the grounds that EU agricultural policies would increase the cost of living, and that integration into the EU would conflict with the Republic's traditional neutrality in its foreign relations. In September 1996 the PN Government, seeking to confirm its mandate to pursue the goal of full membership of the EU, called a general election for the following month. Although the PN contested the election on its record of economic success, the Government's introduction of value-added tax (VAT), as a precondition of Malta's admission to the EU, had proved unpopular with the electorate, and its proposed abolition by the MLP (which would concurrently disqualify Malta from EU membership), was widely regarded as the decisive factor in the election. With a participation rate of 97.1% of eligible voters, the MLP secured 50.7% of the votes cast, as against 47.8% for the PN. The MLP obtained 35 seats in the House of Representatives, with the PN receiving 34 seats. (As the MLP actually won three seats less than the PN in the election, four seats were added to its final total, giving it a one-seat majority in the House.) Dr Alfred Sant, the leader of the MLP, formed a new Government with the declared intention of replacing the 1970 association agreement (see above) with new arrangements providing for an eventual 'free-trade zone' between Malta and the EU. The MLP also emphasized its commitment to the advancement of Malta's financial services sector.

In February 1997 the Government announced the initiation of a 'national discussion' of proposals to legalize divorce. However, the imposition of tax increases and levies on public utilities substantially diminished the Government's popularity. Sant called a general election for September, three years earlier than constitutionally required, and in the poll, for which there was a participation rate of 95.4%, the PN, led by Fenech Adami, obtained a five-seat majority, having obtained 51.8% of votes cast, with the MLP receiving 48.0%. Immediately following the election, Fenech Adami reactivated Malta's application for full membership of the EU. In December 1999 the European Commission agreed that accession negotiations could begin in February 2000, and in the following month the President of the Commission paid an official visit to the island. In November 2000 the Commission published a report which stated that Malta was among the best-equipped economically of those countries seeking to join the EU. Further action was required in Malta to reduce state aid (notably the politically sensitive LM 15m. annual subsidy to the island's dry docks), to implement privatization plans and to strengthen tax and customs administrations. There were also some environmental issues that required attention, notably the inadequate sewerage system.

Accession talks for the EU were formally concluded on 13 December 2002 in Copenhagen. Malta had obtained 77 exemptions in the discussions aimed largely at protecting its industrial and agricultural sectors but also including cultural issues such as the right to maintain the predominantly Roman Catholic country's ban on divorce. A non-binding referendum was called for 8 March 2003 to determine whether the country would join the EU. Support for membership of the EU was led by the ruling PN of Fenech Adami and opposition to it by Sant's MLP, who told voters to abstain, vote against the motion to join or spoil their ballots. Following an acrimonious campaign, 53.65% of the votes were cast in favour of joining with 46.35% against. Sant refused to concede defeat arguing that since the turnout had been 91% the vote in support of membership of the EU did not amount to more than one-half of the electorate. Fenech Adami, whose mandate expired in 2004, called a general election for April 12 2003, four days before the proposed signing of the EU accession treaty by 10 applicant countries, including Malta.

At the general election that took place on 12 April 2003 96% of the electorate participated; the PN won 51.8% of the votes, while the MLP received 47.5% and the environmentalist Alternattiva Demokratika (Green Party) 0.7%. Fenech Adami was sworn in as Prime Minister on 14 April, announced the new Cabinet the following day (which included two new ministries with responsibility for environmental and rural affairs and youth and the arts) and signed the EU accession treaty in Athens, Greece on 16 April. Sant declared that he would not seek re-election to the leadership of the MLP at a party congress to be held to discuss the electoral defeat.

Malta is a member of the Council of Europe (see p. 181) and the Organization for Security and Co-operation in Europe (see p. 283). Participation by Malta in the NATO 'Partnership for Peace' programme formally commenced in 1995, but was suspended by the MLP Government during 1996–98.

Government

Under the 1974 Constitution, legislative power is held by the unicameral House of Representatives, whose 65 members are elected by universal adult suffrage for five years (subject to dissolution) on the basis of proportional representation. The Constitution was amended in January 1987 to ensure that a party that received more than 50% of the total votes cast in a general election would obtain a majority of seats in the legislature (by the allocation—if necessary—of extra seats to that party). The President is the constitutional Head of State, elected for a five-year term by the House, and executive power is exercised by the Cabinet. The President appoints the Prime Minister and, on the latter's recommendation, other Ministers. The Cabinet is responsible to the House.

Defence

In August 2002 the armed forces of Malta comprised a regular army of 2,140. Military service is voluntary. Budgetary expenditure on defence in 2001 was estimated at LM 11.5m.

Economic Affairs

In 2000, according to estimates by the World Bank, Malta's gross national income (GNI), measured at average 1998–2000 prices, was US $3,559m., equivalent to $9,120 per head (or $16,530 per head on an international purchasing-power parity basis). During 1990–2001, it was estimated, the population increased at an average annual rate of 0.8%, while during 1990–2000 gross domestic product (GDP) per head increased, in real terms, at an average annual rate of 4.0%. Overall GDP increased, in real terms, at an average annual rate of 4.8% in 1990–2000; growth in 2000 was 4.7%.

Agriculture (including hunting, forestry and fishing) contributed an estimated 2.4% of GDP in 2001. Some 1.7% of the working population were employed in the sector in 2000. The principal export crop is potatoes. Tomatoes and other vegetables, cereals (principally wheat and barley) and fruit are also cultivated. Livestock and livestock products are also important, and efforts are being made to develop the fishing industry. Exports of food and live animals accounted for 6.9% of total exports in 2000. According to FAO, Malta's agricultural production increased at an average rate of 2.6% per year in 1990–2001. Output rose by 1.0% in 2000 and declined by 1.2% in 2001.

Industry (including mining, manufacturing and construction) provided an estimated 25.8% of GDP in 2001, and engaged 33.0% of the employed labour force in 2000. Industrial production (including also electricity and water, but excluding construction) increased at an average rate of 12.2% per year in 1990–96. It rose by 11.0% in 1995, but declined by 4.7% in 1996.

Mining and quarrying, together with construction, contributed 3.0% of GDP in 2001, and engaged 7.5% of the employed labour force in 2000 (mining and quarrying alone engaged just 0.6% of the employed labour force). The mining sector's output expanded at an average annual rate of 18.3% in 1990–96. Production rose by 26.6% in 1995 and by 11.0% in 1996. The principal activities are stone and sand quarrying. There are reserves of petroleum in Maltese offshore waters, and petroleum and gas exploration is proceeding.

Manufacturing (excluding government enterprises) contributed an estimated 22.9% of GDP in 2001. Some 23.2% of the working population were employed in the manufacturing sector in 2000. Based on the gross value of output, the principal branches of manufacturing, excluding ship-repairing, in 1999 were transport equipment and machinery (accounting for 54.7% of the total), food products and beverages (12.4%) and textiles, footwear and clothing (8.4%). Manufacturing production increased at an average rate of 7.6% per year in 1990–96. It advanced by 8.1% in 1995, but declined by 6.2% in 1996.

Energy is derived principally from imports of crude petroleum (the majority of which is purchased, at preferential rates, from Libya) and coal. Imports of mineral fuels comprised 7.1% of the value of total imports in 2000.

Services (including public utilities and other government enterprises) provided 71.8% of GDP in 2001, and engaged 65.2% of the employed labour force in 2000. Tourism is a major source of foreign exchange earnings. In 2000 Malta received 1,215,713 foreign visitors, and revenue from the sector reached an estimated LM 261m. in 2001. In 2000 some 7.3% of the employed labour force were engaged in hotels and catering establishments.

In 2000 Malta recorded a visible trade deficit of US $621.7m., and there was a deficit of $521.0m. on the current account of the balance of payments. More than two-thirds of Malta's trade is with the countries of the European Union (EU, see p. 199). In 2000 the principal source of imports (accounting for 18.9% of the total) was France; other major suppliers were Italy (16.7%), the USA (10.7%), Germany (8.2%) and the United Kingdom (8.1%). The USA was the principal market for exports (taking 27.4% of the total); other significant purchasers of domestic exports were Germany (9.9%), France (8.6%), the United Kingdom (7.2%) and Switzerland (7.0%). The principal domestic exports in 2000 were machinery and transport equipment (mainly telecommunications components), accounting for 75.3% of the total, and miscellaneous manufactured articles (including clothing), accounting for 15.5%. The principal imports were machinery and transport equipment, accounting for 57.1%, miscellaneous manufactured articles, accounting for 9.8%, and basic manufactures (including textile yarn and fabrics), accounting for 9.7%.

In 2000 Malta recorded a budgetary deficit of LM 73.2m. (equivalent to 4.7% of GDP in that year). At the end of 1997 Malta's external debt totalled US $1,034m., of which $125m. was long-term public debt. In that year the cost of debt-servicing was equivalent to 2.1% of the value of exports of goods and services. The annual rate of inflation averaged 2.9% in 1990–2001; consumer prices increased by 2.4% in 2000 and 2.9% in 2001. In 2000 5.3% of the labour force were unemployed.

Malta is a member of the World Trade Organization (WTO, see p. 323) and of the European Bank for Reconstruction and Development (EBRD, see p. 193).

Malta signed an association agreement with the European Community (EC, now EU) in 1970, allowing favourable trading conditions for Malta, together with economic assistance from that organization. In July 1990 Malta formally applied for full membership of the EC, and in June 1993 the European Commission confirmed Malta's eligibility for eventual accession to the EU. However, following the transfer of power to the Malta Labour Party in October 1996, the new Government announced that EU membership would not be sought, although it was proposed eventually to replace the 1970 association agreement with the formation of a 'free-trade zone' affording Malta certain commercial and social links with the EU. On resuming office in September 1998, the Nationalist Party resumed negotiations for full membership of the EU. Accession talks formally ended on 13 December 2002 and in a non-binding referendum on 8 March 2003 53.6% voted in favour of membership of the EU compared with 46.3% against. The decision to proceed with accession to the EU was confirmed by the victory of the Nationalist Party (Partit Nazzjonalista) in a general election on the 12 April. On 16 April Malta signed the EU accession treaty in Athens, Greece, with nine other applicant countries, all of whom were expected to join the EU in May 2004.

Following the closure, in 1979, of the British military base and naval docks, on which Malta's economy had been largely dependent, successive Governments have pursued a policy of restructuring and diversification. The domestic market is limited, owing to the small population. There are few natural resources, and almost all raw materials have to be imported. Malta's development has therefore been based on the promotion of the island as an international financial centre and on manufacturing for export (notably in non-traditional fields, such as electronics, information technology and pharmaceuticals), together with the continuing development of tourism. Following its accession to power in 1998 the Nationalist Government attempted to address the budget deficit. A budget reduction programme, which included limits on public-sector expenditure (particularly wage increases), a privatization programme and more stringent efforts to combat the country's high level of tax evasion and the large 'parallel' economy, aimed to reduce the deficit to 3% of GDP by 2004. It was also hoped that privatization would increase investment in Malta's inadequate infrastructure. In late 2001 there was a deceleration in growth in the tourism and manufacturing sectors, partly as a result of the terrorist attacks in the USA on 11 September, which prompted the Government to revise growth forecasts for the year down to 3% in real terms—low for a small island economy. However, this was offset by success in government efforts to consolidate public finances by reducing spending and rationalizing tax collection. Malta's main prospect for continuing economic prosperity remained, however, its forthcoming entry into the EU, and the increased trade flows and foreign investment that would accompany it.

Education

Education is compulsory between the ages of five and 16 years, and is available free of charge in government schools and institutions, from kindergarten to university. Kindergarten education is provided for three- and four-year-old children. Primary education begins at five years of age and lasts for six years. Secondary education, beginning at 11 years of age, lasts for a maximum of seven years, but this period is extended in the case of technology and vocational courses. After completing five years of secondary-level education, students having the necessary qualifications may opt to follow a higher academic or technical or vocational course. In October 1999 there were 80 state primary schools, 22 state secondary schools and 11 junior lyceums, which offer a more challenging curriculum. The junior college, administrated by the University, prepares students specifically for a university course. About 30% of the student population attend schools administered by the Roman Catholic Church, from kindergarten to higher secondary level. The Government subsidizes the provision of free education for students in church schools. In 1999 enrolment at primary and secondary schools was equivalent to 98% of the school-age population. Enrolment at primary schools in that year included 100% of both boys and girls in the relevant age-group, while the comparable ratio for secondary enrolment was 84% (males 84%; females 83%). Higher education is available at the University of Malta, at which approximately 7,500 students were enrolled in 1999. There are also a number of technical institutes, specialist schools and an extended skill-training scheme for trade-school leavers. The Government also provides adult education courses. Of total recurrent budgetary expenditure in 2000 LM 40.0m. (5.7%) was allocated to education.

Public Holidays

2003: 1 January (New Year's Day), 10 February (St Paul's Shipwreck), 19 March (St Joseph), 31 March (Freedom Day), 18 April (Good Friday), 1 May (St Joseph the Worker), 7 June (Memorial of 1919 Riot), 29 June (St Peter and St Paul), 15 August (Assumption), 8 September (Our Lady of Victories), 21 September (Independence Day), 8 December (Immaculate Conception), 14 December (Republic Day), 25 December (Christmas Day).

2004: 1 January (New Year's Day), 10 February (St Paul's Shipwreck), 19 March (St Joseph), 31 March (Freedom Day), 9 April (Good Friday), 1 May (St Joseph the Worker), 7 June (Memorial of 1919 Riot), 29 June (St Peter and St Paul), 15 August (Assumption), 8 September (Our Lady of Victories), 21 September (Independence Day), 8 December (Immaculate Conception), 14 December (Republic Day), 25 December (Christmas).

Carnival is also celebrated each year on the Saturday to Tuesday before Ash Wednesday. This will be 1–4 March in 2003; 21–24 February in 2004.

Weights and Measures

The metric system is in force.

Statistical Survey

Source (unless otherwise stated): National Statistics Office, Lascaris, Valletta; tel. 21223221; fax 21249841; e-mail nso@magnet.mt; internet www.nso.gov.mt.

AREA AND POPULATION

Area: 316 sq km (122 sq miles).

Population: 378,132 (males 186,836, females 191,296) at census of 26 November 1995 (figures refer to *de jure* population); 394,641 (males 195,363, females 199,278) at 31 December 2001 (incl. 9,564 foreigners).

Density (Maltese only, 31 December 2001): 1,249 per sq km.

Principal Towns (estimated population at 31 December 1998): Birkirkara 21,350; Qormi 17,881; Mosta 17,051; Zabbar 14,427; Sliema 12,308; Valletta (capital) 7,100.

Births, Marriages and Deaths (2001): Registered live births 3,935 (birth rate 10.0 per 1,000); Marriages 2,545 (marriage rate 6.7 per 1,000)*; Registered deaths 3,007 (death rate 7.6 per 1,000).
* 2000 figures.

Expectation of Life (WHO estimates, years at birth): 78.1 (males 75.8; females 80.3) in 2001. Source: WHO, *World Health Report*.

Economically Active Population (2000): Agriculture, hunting and forestry 2,213; Fishing 317; Mining and quarrying 845; Manufacturing 33,749; Electricity, gas and water supply 3,308; Construction 10,076; Wholesale and retail trade; repair of motor vehicles, motorcycles and personal and household goods 20,589; Hotels and restaurants 10,627; Transport, storage and communications 11,197; Financial intermediation 5,250; Real estate, renting and business activities 5,964; Public administration and defence; compulsory social security 12,457; Education 11,797; Health and social work 10,396; Other community, social and personal service activities 5,892; Private households with employed persons 360; Extra-territorial organizations and bodies 166; Total employed 145,203; Unemployed 10,151; Total labour force 155,354 (males 109,059, females 46,295).

HEALTH AND WELFARE

Key Indicators

Total Fertility Rate (children per woman, 2001): 1.8.

Under-5 Mortality Rate (per 1,000 live births, 2001): 5.

HIV/AIDS (% of persons aged 15–49, 2001): 0.13.

Physicians (per 1,000 head, 1998): 0.1.

Hospital Beds (per 1,000 head, 1995): 5.43.

Health Expenditure (2000): US $ per head (PPP): 803.

Health Expenditure (2000): % of GDP: 8.8.

Health Expenditure (2000): public (% of total): 68.5.

Access to Water (% of persons, 2000): 100.

Access to Sanitation (% of persons, 2000): 100.

Human Development Index (2000): ranking: 30.

Human Development Index (2000): value: 0.875.
For sources and definitions, see explanatory note on p. vi.

AGRICULTURE, ETC

Principal Crops ('000 metric tons, 2001): Wheat 9.6*; Barley 2.2*; Potatoes 26.9; Cabbages 4.3; Tomatoes 20.5; Cauliflowers 7.4; Pumpkins, squash and gourds 1.3*; Dry onions 7.6; Garlic 0.8; Green broad beans 1.2; Other vegetables 7.4*; Melons 13.9*; Citrus fruit 1.0*; Grapes 1.1; Other fruits and berries 3.8*.
*FAO estimate. Source: FAO.

Livestock ('000 head, year ending September 2001): Cattle 19; Pigs 80; Sheep 16*; Goats 9*; Rabbits 0.2*; Chickens 0.8*; Horses 1*; Asses 0.5*; Mules 0.3*.
*FAO estimate. Source: FAO.

Livestock Products ('000 metric tons, 2001): Beef and veal 1.6; Pig meat 9.9; Rabbit meat 1.4*; Poultry meat 5.7; Cows' milk 47.2; Sheep's milk 1.5*; Poultry eggs 8.0.
*FAO estimate. Source: FAO.

Fishing (metric tons, live weight 2000): Capture 1,039 (Common dolphinfish 234, Northern bluefin tuna 376, Swordfish 140); Aquaculture 1,746 (European seabass 234, Gilthead seabream 1,512); Total catch 2,785. Source: FAO, *Yearbook of Fishery Statistics*.

INDUSTRY

Production (gross output, excl. ship-repairing, LM '000, 1999): Stone quarrying and sand pits 3,825; Food and beverages 125,442; Tobacco products 24,226; Textiles, footwear and clothing (incl.leather products) 85,174; Wood and wood products (excl. furniture) 1,346; Printing, publishing and allied trades 51,249; Rubber, chemicals, and non-metallic products 89,375; Metals 23,562; Transport equipment and machinery 554,863; Construction 56,341; Furniture 57,784; Miscellaneous industries 715; Total 1,074,402.

FINANCE

Currency and Exchange rates: 1,000 mils = 100 cents = 1 Maltese lira (LM; plural: liri). *Sterling, Dollar and Euro Equivalents* (31 December 2002): £1 sterling = 642.3 mils; US $1 = 398.8 mils; €1 = 418.2 mils; LM 100 = £155.57 = $250.74 = €230.10. *Average Exchange Rate* (US $ per Maltese lira): 2.2851 in 2000; 2.2226 in 2001; 2.3102 in 2002.

Budget (LM million, 2001): *Revenue:* Income tax 166.3; Customs and excise 60.9; Value-added tax 114.7; Social security 179.1; Grants and loans 108.2; Total (incl. others) 797.4. *Expenditure:* Recurrent expenditure 614.6 (of which Social security 184.4; Health, incl. care of the elderly n.a.; Education 46.7; Defence n.a.); Public debt servicing 71.4; Capital expenditure 80.6; Total 766.7.

International Reserves (US $ million at 31 December 2002): Gold 1.2; IMF special drawing rights 39.3; Reserve position in IMF 54.7; Foreign exchange 2,115.2; Total 2,210.4. Source: IMF, *International Financial Statistics*.

Money Supply (LM million at 31 December 2002): Currency outside banks 436.8; Demand deposits at commercial banks 241.8; Total money (incl. others) 680.1. Source: IMF, *International Financial Statistics*.

Cost of Living (Retail Price Index; base: 1995 = 100): All items 110.5 in 1999; 113.1 in 2000; 116.4 in 2001. Source: IMF, *International Financial Statistics*.

Gross Domestic Product (LM million at current market prices, provisional): 1,456.1 in 1999; 1,558.4 in 2000; 1,618.4 in 2001.

Gross Domestic Product by Economic Activity (provisional, LM million at current prices, 2001): Agriculture, hunting, forestry and fishing 33.2; Mining and quarrying (incl. construction) 40.7; Manufacturing 314.6; Government enterprises 83.9; Wholesale and retail trade 1524; Transport, storage and communications 92.3; Insurance, banking and real estate 126.4; Property income 148.2; Other private services 158.2; Public administration 226.7; *GDP at factor cost* 1,376.6; Indirect taxes 253.9 *Less* Subsidies 12.1; *GDP in purchasers' values* 1,618.4.

Balance of Payments (US $ million, 2001): Exports of goods f.o.b. 2,002.8; Imports of goods f.o.b. –2,492.4; *Trade balance* –489.6; Exports of services 1,106.8; Imports of services –791.1; *Balance on goods and services* –173.8; Other income received 815.2; Other income paid –821.2; *Balance on goods, services and income* –179.9; Current transfers received 190.2; Current transfers paid –182.7; *Current balance* –172.4; Capital account (net) 1.6; Direct investment abroad –6.5; Direct investment from abroad 293.3; Portfolio investment assets –445.8; Portfolio investment liabilities –6.7; Other investment assets 1,823.3; Other investment liabilities –1,405.7; Net errors and omissions 173.9; *Overall balance* 225.1. Source: IMF, *International Financial Statistics*.

EXTERNAL TRADE

Principal Commodities (LM million, 2000): *Imports c.i.f.:* Food and live animals 103.6; Mineral fuels, lubricants, etc. 106.5; Chemicals 92.5; Basic manufactures 145.0; Machinery and transport equipment 852.6; Miscellaneous manufactured articles 146.8; Total (incl. others) 1,492.4. *Exports f.o.b.:* Basic manufactures 53.9; Machinery and transport equipment 736.1; Miscellaneous manufactured articles 151.3; Total (incl. others) 977.5. Data for exports exclude re-exports, totalling LM 94.9 million.

Selected Trading Partners (LM '000, 1999): *Imports:* Belgium 16,705; France 281,876; Germany 122,113; Italy 249,743; Netherlands 29,662; Sweden 26,970; Switzerland 22,790; United Kingdom 119,673; Total (incl. others) 1,492,377. *Exports* (excl. re-exports): Belgium 20,306; France 84,081; Germany 96,687; Italy 33,070; Netherlands 11,006; Switzerland 68,433; United Kingdom 69,980; Total (incl. others) 977,536. Note: According to the Central Bank of Malta, imports from the USA in 2000 totalled LM 159,192,000, while exports to the USA (incl. re-exports) were LM 293,857,000.

TRANSPORT

Road Traffic (motor vehicles in use, September 2000): Private cars 182,105, Commercial vehicles 43,165, Buses and minibuses 1,132 (1999), Motorcycles 12,167; Total (incl. others) 248,825.

Shipping: *Merchant Fleet* (31 December 2001): Vessels 1,421; Total displacement 27,052,579 grt (Source: Lloyds Register-Fairplay, World Fleet Statistics). *International Freight Traffic* (metric tons, 1994): Goods loaded 309,124; Goods unloaded 1,780,629.

Civil Aviation (traffic on scheduled services, 1999): Kilometres flown (million) 24; Passengers carried ('000) 1,421; Passenger-km (million) 2,320; Total ton-km (million) 214. Source: UN, *Statistical Yearbook*.

TOURISM

Tourist Arrivals: 1,182,240 in 1998; 1,214,230 in 1999; 1,215,713 in 2000. Figures exclude cruise passengers ('000): 144.0 in 1998; 187.8 in 1999.

Arrivals by Country of Origin (excluding cruise passengers, 2000): Austria 28,119; Belgium 26,713; France 75,814; Germany 204,747; Italy 92,522; Libya 43,267; Netherlands 64,166; United Kingdom 428,779; Total (incl. others) 1,215,713.

Tourism Receipts (LM million): 254.6 in 1998; 271.4 in 1999; 268.2 in 2000; 260.7 in 2001.

COMMUNICATIONS MEDIA

Radio Receivers (1997): 255,000 in use*.

Television Receivers (1999): 212,000 in use*.

Telephones (main lines, 2001): 207,700 in use†.

Facsimile Machines (1996): 6,000 in use (estimate)‡.

Mobile Cellular Telephones (2001): 138,800 subscribers†.

Personal Computers (2001): 90,000 in use†.

Internet Users (2001): 99,000†.

Book Production (1995): 404 titles*.

Daily Newspapers (1999): 4 titles (combined average circulation 54,000 copies per issue).

Non-daily Newspapers (1999): 10 titles.

Other Periodicals (1992): 359 titles*.

*Source: UN, *Statistical Yearbook*.

†Source: International Telecommunication Union.

‡Source: UNESCO, *Statistical Yearbook*.

EDUCATION

Pre-primary (1995/96): 111 schools; 934 teachers; 10,378 students.

Primary (1995/96): 106 schools; 1,990 teachers; 35,479 students.

Secondary (1995/96): *General:* 59 schools; 2,679 teachers; 29,907 students; *Vocational:* 22 schools; 541 teachers; 4,539 students; *Junior College:* 1 school; 1,800 students.

Universities, etc. (1996/97): 709 teachers; 8,260 students.

Students (1996/97): Pre-primary 11,171; Primary 35,374; Secondary 34,216.

Adult Literacy Rate (UNESCO estimates): 92.0% in 2000 (Source: UN Development Programme, *Human Development Report*).

Source: UNESCO, *Statistical Yearbook*.

Directory

The Constitution

On 13 December 1974 the Independence Constitution of 1964 was substantially amended to bring into effect a Republican Constitution, under the terms of which Malta became a democratic republic within the Commonwealth, founded on work and on respect for the fundamental rights and freedoms of the individual. The new Constitution provided for the creation of the office of President of Malta to replace that of Governor-General.

The religion of the Maltese people is recognized to be the Roman Catholic Apostolic Religion, and the Church Authorities have the constitutional right and duty to teach according to its principles. The religious teaching of the Roman Catholic Church is provided in all state schools as part of compulsory education.

The Constitution provides that the national language and the language of the Courts is Maltese but that both Maltese and English are official languages.

An independent Public Services Commission, consisting of three to five members, is appointed by the President, on the advice of the Prime Minister, to make recommendations to the Prime Minister concerning appointments to public office and the dismissal and disciplinary control of persons holding public office.

The Constitution also provides for an Employment Commission, consisting of a chairman and four other members, the function of which is to ensure that, in respect of employment, no distinction, exclusion or preference that is not justifiable is made or given in favour of or against any person by reason of his or her political opinion.

The Judicature is independent.

Radio and television broadcasting is controlled by an independent authority.

DECLARATION OF PRINCIPLES

The Constitution upholds the right to work and to reasonable hours of work, the safeguarding of rights of women workers, the encouragement of private economic enterprise, the encouragement of co-operatives, the provision of free and compulsory primary education, and the provision of social assistance and insurance.

FUNDAMENTAL RIGHTS AND FREEDOMS OF THE INDIVIDUAL

The Constitution provides for the protection of the right to life, freedom from arbitrary arrest or detention, protection of freedom of conscience, protection from discrimination on the grounds of race, etc.

THE PRESIDENT

Under the Constitution, the office of President becomes vacant after five years from the date of appointment made by resolution of the House of Representatives. The President appoints the Prime Minister, choosing the member of the House of Representatives who is judged to be ablest to command the confidence of a majority of the members. On the advice of the Prime Minister, the President appoints the other ministers, the Chief Justice, the Judges and the Attorney-General.

THE CABINET

The Cabinet consists of the Prime Minister and such number of other ministers as recommended by the Prime Minister.

PARLIAMENT

The House of Representatives consists of such number of members, being an odd number and divisible by the number of divisions, as Parliament by law determines from time to time. In future the electoral divisions are not to be fewer than nine and not more than 15, as Parliament may from time to time determine. The normal life of the House of Representatives is five years, after which a general election is held. Election is by universal adult suffrage on the basis of proportional representation. The age of majority is 18 years. Under a constitutional amendment adopted in January 1987, it was ensured that a party receiving more than 50% of the total votes cast in a general election would obtain a majority of seats in the House of Representatives, by the allocation (if necessary) of extra seats to that party.

NEUTRALITY AND NON-ALIGNMENT

In January 1987 a constitutional amendment was adopted, aiming to entrench in the Constitution Malta's status of neutrality and adherence to a policy of non-alignment, and stipulating that no foreign military base was to be permitted on Maltese territory.

The Government

HEAD OF STATE

President: Prof. GUIDO DE MARCO (took office 4 April 1999).

THE CABINET
(May 2003)

Prime Minister: Dr EDWARD (EDDIE) FENECH ADAMI.

Deputy Prime Minister and Minister for Social Policy: Dr LAWRENCE GONZI.

Minister of Education: Dr LOUIS GALEA.

Minister for Finance and Economic Affairs: JOHN DALLI.

Minister for Tourism: Dr FRANCIS ZAMMIT DIMECH.

Minister for Justice and Home Affairs: Dr TONIO BORG.

Minister for Resources and Infrastructure: NINU ZAMMIT.

Minister for Gozo: GIOVANNA DEBONO.

Minister of Health: Dr LOUIS DEGUARA.

Minister for Information Technology and Investment: Dr AUSTIN GATT.

Minister of Foreign Affairs: Dr JOE BORG.

Minister for Rural Affairs and the Environment: GEORGE PULLICINO.

Minister for Youth and the Arts: JESMOND MUGLIETT.

PARLIAMENTARY SECRETARIES (ATTACHED TO MINISTRIES)

Ministry for Social Policy: DELORES CRISTINA.

Ministry for Finance and Economic Affairs: EDWIN VASSALLO.

Ministry for Justice and Home Affairs: CARMELLO MIFSUD BONNICI.

MINISTRIES

Office of the President: The Palace, Valletta CMR 02; tel. 21221221; fax 21241241.

Office of the Prime Minister: Auberge de Castille, Valletta CMR 02; tel. 21242560; fax 21249888; internet www.opm.gov.mt.

Ministry for Education: Great Siege Rd, Floriana CMR 02; tel. 21250909; fax 21221634; e-mail communications.moed@magnet.mt; internet www.education.gov.mt.

Ministry of Finance and Economic Affairs: Auberge d'Aragon, Independence Sq., Valletta CMR 02; tel. 21226263; fax 21250965; e-mail info.mof@gov.mt; internet www.mes.gov.mt.

Ministry of Foreign Affairs: Palazzo Parisio, Merchants St, Valletta CMR 02; tel. 21242853; fax 21237822; internet www.foreign .gov.mt.

Ministry for Gozo: St Francis Sq., Victoria VCT 112, Gozo; tel. 21561482; fax 21559360; internet www.gozo.gov.mt.

Ministry of Health: Palazzo Castellania, 15 Merchants St, Valletta CMR 02; tel. 21224071; fax 22992655; internet www.health.gov.mt.

Ministry for Information Technology and Investment: 168 Triq id-Dejqa, Valletta CMR 02; tel. 21226808; fax 21250700.

Ministry for Justice and Home Affairs: Casa Leoni, 476 St Joseph High Rd, St Venera HMR 18; tel. 21485100; fax 21493744; internet www.justice.gov.mt.

Ministry for Resources and Infrastructure: Block B, Floriana CMR 02; tel. 21222378; fax 21243306; internet www.mri.gov.mt.

Ministry for Rural Affairs and the Environment: Barriera Wharf, Valletta CMR 02; tel. 21252005; fax 21231294; internet www .maf.gov.mt.

Ministry for Social Policy: Palazzo Ferreria, Republic St, Valletta CMR 02; tel. 21243166; fax 21243017; e-mail info@msp.gov.mt; internet www.msp.gov.mt.

Ministry of Tourism: Auberge d'Italie, Merchants St., Valletta CMR 02; tel. 22981306; fax 22981301; e-mail marisa.delorenzo@gov .mt; internet www.tourism.gov.mt.

Ministry for Transport and Communications: House of Four Winds, Hastings Gdns, Valletta CMR 02; tel. 21225200; fax 21248937; e-mail raj.cutajar@gov.mt; internet www.mtc.gov.mt.

Ministry for Youth and the Arts: Cavalier House, 158 Old Mint Sq., Valletta CMR 02; tel. 21243275; fax 21241032.

Legislature

HOUSE OF REPRESENTATIVES

Speaker: ANTON TABONE.

General Election, 12 April 2003

Party	Votes	%	Seats
Partit Nazzjonalista (Nationalist Party)	146,172	51.8	35
Malta Labour Party (Partit Laburista)	134,092	47.5	30
Alternattiva Demokratika (Green Party)	1,929	0.7	—
Others	20	0.0	—
Total	282,213	100.0	65

Political Organizations

Alternattiva Demokratika (Green Party): 149 Archbishop St, Valletta; tel. 21240334; fax 21224745; e-mail alternattiva@usa.net; internet www.alternattiva.org.mt; f. 1989; emphasizes social and environmental issues; Chair. Dr HARRY VASSALLO; Sec.-Gen. MARIO MALLIA.

Malta Labour Party (MLP) (Partit Laburista): National Labour Centre, Mile End Rd, Hamrun HMR 02; tel. 21249900; fax 21244204; e-mail mlp@mlp.org.mt; internet www.mlp.org.mt; f. 1921; democratic socialist; Leader Dr ALFRED SANT; Pres. EMMLE CUSCHIERI; Gen. Sec. JIMMY MAGRO; 39,000 mems.

Partit Nazzjonalista (Nationalist Party—PN): Herbert Ganado St, Pietà HMR 08; tel. 21243641; fax 21243640; e-mail pn@pn.org.mt; internet www.pn.org.mt; f. 1880; Christian democratic; advocates full membership of the EU; Leader Dr EDWARD (EDDIE) FENECH ADAMI; Sec.-Gen. JOE SALIBA; 31,000 mems.

Diplomatic Representation

EMBASSIES AND HIGH COMMISSIONS IN MALTA

Australia: Villa Fiorentina, Ta'Xbiex Terrace, Ta'Xbiex MSD 11; tel. 21338201; fax 21344059; High Commissioner IAIN DICKIE.

China, People's Republic: Karmnu Court, Lapsi St, St Julian's; tel. 21384695; fax 21344730; Ambassador ZU QINSHUN.

Egypt: Villa Mon Rêve, 10 Sir Temi Zammit St, Ta'Xbiex MSD 11; tel. 21333259; fax 21319230; Ambassador YEHYA IBRAHIM EL-RAM-LAWY.

France: POB 408, Valletta CMR 01; 130 Melita St, Valletta CMR 01; tel. 21232430; fax 21233528; e-mail france@global.net.mt; Ambassador DIDIER DESTREMAU.

Germany: 'Il-Piazzetta', Entrance B, 1st Floor, Tower Rd, Sliema, SLM 16; POB 48, Marsa, GPO 01; tel. 21336531; fax 21333976; e-mail germanembassy@waldonet.net.mt; Ambassador GEORG MERTEN.

Holy See: Villa Cor Jesù, Tal-Virtù Rd, Tal-Virtù, Rabat (Apostolic Nunciature); tel. 21453422; fax 21453423; e-mail apost@mail .keyworld.net; Apostolic Nuncio Most Rev. LUIGI CONTI (Titular Archbishop of Gratiana).

India: Regional Rd, St Julian's SGN 02; tel. 21344302; fax 21344259; internet www.incore.com/india/traveli.embassy.html; High Commissioner SURENDRA KUMAR.

Italy: 5 Vilhena St, Floriana; tel. 21233157; fax 21235339; e-mail ambitalia@waldonet.net.mt; Ambassador Dr GIANCARLO RICCIO.

Libya: Dar Jamahariya, Notabile Rd, Balzan; tel. 21486347; fax 21483939; Ambassador ALI SALEH MOHAMED NAGEM.

Russia: Ariel House, Anthony Schembri St, Kappara, San Gwann; tel. 21371905; fax 21372131; e-mail rusemb@keyworld.net; Ambassador SERGEI S. ZOTOV.

Tunisia: 144 Tower Rd, Flat 2, Sliema SLM 08; tel. 21345866; fax 21331345; e-mail ambtunismalta@waldonet.net.mt; Ambassador ABDESSALEM HETIRA.

United Kingdom: 7 St Anne St, Floriana VLT 15; tel. 21233134; fax 21242001; e-mail bhc@vol.net.mt; internet www.britain.com.mt; High Commissioner HOWARD J. S. PEARCE.

USA: Development House, 3rd Floor, St Anne St, Floriana; tel. 21235960; fax 21243229; Ambassador ANTHONY GIOIA.

Judicial System

The legal system consists of enactments of the Parliament of Malta, and those of the British Parliament not repealed by enactments of the Maltese legislature. Maltese Civil Law derives largely from Roman Law, while British Law has significantly influenced Maltese public law.

The Courts are: Constitutional Court, Court of Appeal, Court of Criminal Appeal, Civil Court, Criminal Court, Commercial Court, Court of Magistrates, Juvenile Court and Small Claims Tribunal.

Chief Justice and President of the Court of Appeal and the Constitutional Court: Dr VINCENT A. DE GAETANO.

Judges: CARMEL A. AGIUS, JOSEPH D. CAMILLERI, JOSEPH A. FILLETTI, FRANCO DEPASQUALE, ANTON DEPASQUALE, FRANK G. CAMILLERI, ALBERTO J. MAGRI, NOEL ARRIGO, GEOFFREY VALENZIA, GIANNINO CARUANA DEMAJO, GINO CAMILLERI, CARMELO FARRUGIA SACCO, RAYMOND PACE, DAVID P. SCICLUNA.

Attorney-General: ANTHONY BORG BARTHET.

Religion

CHRISTIANITY

The Roman Catholic Church

Malta comprises one archdiocese and one diocese. At 31 December 2000 there were 364,208 adherents in the country, representing about 96% of the total population.

Bishops' Conference

Conferenza Episcopale Maltese, Archbishop's Curia, Floriana; tel. 21234317; fax 21223307; e-mail info@maltachurch.org.mt.
f. 1971; Pres. Most Rev. JOSEPH MERCIECA (Archbishop of Malta).

Archbishop of Malta: Most Rev. JOSEPH MERCIECA, Archbishop's Curia, Floriana; POB 29, Valletta; tel. 21234317; fax 21223307; e-mail info@maltachurch.org.mt.

Bishop of Gozo: Rt Rev. Nikol Joseph Cauchi, Chancery Office, POB 1, Republic St, Victoria VCT 103, Gozo; tel. 21556661; fax 21551278; e-mail diocese@gozodiocese.org.

The Anglican Communion

Malta forms part of the diocese of Gibraltar in Europe.

Church of England: Pro-Cathedral of St Paul, Independence Sq., Valletta VLT 12; tel. 21225714; fax 21225867; e-mail anglican@onvol.net; internet www.vol.net.mt/anglicansmalta; Bishop of Gibraltar in Europe Rt Rev. Geoffrey Rowell (resident in England); Suffragan Bishop Rt Rev. David Hamid (resident in England); Archdeacon of Italy and Malta Ven. Gordon Reid (resident in Italy); Senior Chaplain and Chancellor of the Pro-Cathedral Rev. Canon Alan Woods.

The Press

DAILIES

The Malta Independent: Standard House, Birkirkara Hill, St Julian's STJ 09; tel. 21345888; fax 21344860; e-mail tmi@maltanet .net; English; Editor Fr Noel Grima.

In-Nazzjon: Herbert Ganado St, POB 37, Pietà HMR 08; tel. 21243641; fax 21242886; e-mail nazzjon@vol.net.mt; internet www .media.link.com.mt; f. 1970; Maltese; publ. by Media.link Communications; Editor John Zammit; circ. 20,000.

L-Orizzont: Union Print Co, A-41 Industrial Estate, Valletta Rd, Marsa HMR 15; tel. 21244557; fax 21238484; e-mail unionprint@kemmunet.net.mt; f. 1962; Maltese; Editor Frans Ghirxi; circ. 25,000.

The Times: Allied Newspapers Ltd, 341 St Paul St, Valletta VLT 07; tel. 21241464; fax 21247901; e-mail daily@timesofmalta.com; internet www.timesofmalta.com; f. 1935; English; Editor Victor Aquilina; circ. 23,000.

WEEKLIES

Business Times: Network Publications Ltd, Vjal ir-Rihan, San Gwann SGN 07; tel. 21382741; fax 21385075; e-mail editorial@networkpublications.com.mt; internet www.businesstimes.com.mt; f. 1999; Editor Saviour Balzan.

Il-Gens: Media Centre, National Rd, Blata il-Bajda HMR 02; tel. 25699119; fax 25699123; e-mail gens@mediacentre.org.mt; internet www.rtk.org.mt; f. 1988; Maltese; Editor Nicholas Baldacchino; circ. 13,000.

Il-Gwida: Mercury Publicity Services, POB 83, Valletta CMR 01; tel. and fax 21220932; Maltese and English; radio, television and entertainment guide; Editor Joe Calleja; circ. 12,000.

Kulhadd: Centru Nazzjonali Laburista, Mile End Rd, Hamrun, HMR 02; tel. 21235313; fax 21240717; e-mail kulhadd@keyworld .net; f. 1993; Maltese; Editor Felix Agius.

Lehen Is-Sewwa: Catholic Institute, Floriana VLT 16; tel. and fax 21225847; internet www.lehenissewwa.com.mt; f. 1928; Roman Catholic; Editor Paul Saliba; circ. 10,000.

The Malta Business Weekly: Standard House, Birkirkara Hill, St Julian's STJ 09; tel. 21345888; fax 21346062; e-mail tmbw@mail .independent.com.mt; internet www.maltabusinessweekly.com; f. 1994; English; Editor David John Kelleher.

The Malta Independent on Sunday: Standard House, Birkirkara Hill, St Julian's STJ 09; tel. 21345888; fax 21344884; e-mail amanduca@independent.com.mt; internet www.independent.com .mt; English; Editor Anthony Manduca.

Il-Mument: Herbert Ganado St, POB 37, Pietà HMR 08; tel. 21243641; fax 21240839; e-mail nazzjon@mbox.vol.net.mt; f. 1972; Maltese; Editor Victor Camilleri; circ. 25,000.

The Sunday Times: Allied Newspapers Ltd, POB 328, Valletta CMR 01; tel. 21241464; fax 21240806; e-mail Sunday@timesofmalta .com; internet www.timesofmalta.com; f. 1922; English; Editor Laurence Grech; circ. 40,000.

It-Tórca (The Torch): Union Press, A 41, Marsa Industrial Estate, Marsa HMR 15; tel. 21244557; fax 21238484; e-mail unionprint@kemmunet.net.mt; f. 1944; Maltese; Editor Alfred Briffa; circ. 30,000.

SELECTED PERIODICALS

BASE: Valletta; tel. 21245779; fax 21245778; quarterly; Editor Jacqueline Fenech.

Commercial Courier: Malta Chamber of Commerce, Exchange Bldgs, Republic St, Valletta VLT 05; tel. 21247233; fax 21245223;

e-mail admin@chamber.org.mt; monthly; Editor Kevin J. Borg; circ. 1,500.

The Employer: Malta Employers' Asscn, 35/1 South St, Valletta VLT 11; tel. 21222992; fax 21230227; e-mail mea@maltanet.net; internet www.maltanet.net/mea; Editor Joseph Farrugia.

Industry Today: Floriana VLT 01; tel. 21234428; fax 21240702; e-mail info@foi.org.mt; internet www.foi.org.mt; journal of the Malta Fed. of Industry; quarterly; Editor Edwin Calleja; circ. 1,000.

Malta Business Online: 33/4 St. Nicholas Bldgs, Abate Rigord St, Ta'Xbiex MSD 12; tel. 21342704; fax 21316694; e-mail mbo@tcin .com; internet www.mbo.com.mt; f. 1986 as Business Review; monthly; publ. by E-business Ltd; Editor Stephen P. D'Alessandro.

Malta Government Gazette: Department of Information, 3 Castille Pl., Valletta CMR 02; tel. 223410; fax 250580; e-mail info@gov .mt; internet www.doi.gov.mt; f. 1813; official notices; Maltese and English; 2 a week; circ. 3,000.

Malta In Figures: National Statistics Office, Lascaris, Valetta CMR 02; tel. 21223221; fax 21249841; e-mail nso@gov.mt; internet www.nso.gov.mt; official statistics; annual.

Malta This Month: Advantage Advertising Ltd, 3rd Floor, Regency House, Republic St, Valletta VLT 04; tel. 21249924; fax 21249927; e-mail advantage@onvol.net; publ. by Air Malta; monthly; Editor Peter Darmanin.

The Retailer: Association of General Retailers and Traders, Exchange Bldgs, Republic St, Valletta VLT 05; tel. 21230459; fax 21246925; monthly; Editor Vincent Farrugia.

The Teacher: Teachers' Institute, 213 Republic St, Valletta VLT 03; tel. 21237815; fax 21244074; e-mail info@mut.org.mt; internet www.mut.org.mt; journal of the Malta Union of Teachers; quarterly; Editor Joseph P. DeGiovanni.

XPRESS: 149 Archbishop St, Valletta; tel. 21240334; fax 21224745; publ. of the Alternattiva Demokratika; Maltese; monthly; Editor Neil Spiteri.

NEWS AGENCIES

Agence France-Presse (AFP): 370 Zabbar Rd, Fgura PLA 16; tel. 21693210; Correspondent Maria Inguanez.

Agenzia Nazionale Stampa Associata (ANSA) (Italy): c/o The Sunday Times, Allied Newspapers Ltd, 341 St Paul St, POB 328, Valletta CMR 01; tel. 21224406; fax 21240806; e-mail lgrech@timesofmalta.com; Correspondent Laurence Grech.

Associated Press (AP) (USA): c/o The Times, Allied Newspapers Ltd, 341 St Paul St, Valletta VLT 07; tel. 21241464; fax 21247901; e-mail daily@timesofmalta.com; Correspondents Victor Aquilina, George Ciri.

Jamahiriya News Agency (JANA) (Libya): 239 St Paul's St, POB 270, Valletta; tel. 21239392; fax 21239405; Correspondent F. M. Hewat.

Reuters (United Kingdom): 119 Censu Busuttid St, Halin 11; tel. 21415171; fax 21247901; e-mail cscicluna@timesofmalta.com; Correspondent Cristopher Scicluna.

United Press International (USA): 1 The Elms, Dahlet Ic-Cipress, Attard; tel. 21423068; fax 21247901; Correspondent Victor Aquilina.

Publishers

Gozo Press: Mgarr Rd, Ghajnsielem, Gozo; tel. 21551534; e-mail gozopress@onvol.net; popular and academic; Dir John Sultana.

Progress Press Co Ltd: Strickland House, 341 St Paul St, POB 328, Valletta VLT 07; tel. 21241464; fax 21237150; e-mail agius@timesofmalta.com; f. 1957; educational and textbooks, fiction, guidebooks; Chair. Ronald Agius; Man. Dir Wilfrid B. Asciak.

Publishers Enterprises Group (PEG) Ltd: PEG Bldg, UB7 Industrial Estate, San Gwann SGN 09; tel. 21440083; fax 21488908; e-mail contact@peg.com.mt; internet www.peg.com.mt; f. 1983; educational, children's, cookery, technical, tourism, leisure; Man. Dir Emanuel Debattista.

University of Malta Press: University Campus, Msida MSD 06; tel. 21313416; fax 21344879; e-mail mupl@mus.com.mt; f. 1953; Maltese folklore, history, law, bibliography and language.

Broadcasting and Communications

All broadcasting services are under the overall supervision of the Broadcasting Authority. In early 1999 there were 13 radio stations, four television stations and a cable television service.

TELECOMMUNICATIONS

Maltacom PLC: Spencer Hill, Marsa CMR 01; POB 40, Qormi QMR 01; tel. 21212121; fax 25945895; e-mail info@maltacom.com; internet www.maltacom.com; f. 1975; operates all telecommunications services; 60% govt-owned, 40% held by private-sector investors; Chair. MAURICE ZARB ADAMI.

Go Mobile: mobile cellular subsidiary; CEO Prof. JUANITO CAMILLERI.

BROADCASTING

Regulatory Authority

Malta Broadcasting Authority: Mile End Rd, Hamrun HMR 02; tel. 21247908; fax 21240855; e-mail info@ba-malta.org; internet www.ba-malta.org; f. 1961; statutory body responsible for the supervision and regulation of sound and television broadcasting; Chair. Prof. JOSEPH M. PIROTTA; CEO Dr KEVIN AQUILINA.

Radio and Television

Bay Radio: St George's Bay, St Julian's STJ 02; tel. 21373813; fax 21376113; e-mail 897@bay.com.mt; Station Man. TERRY FARRUGIA.

Campus FM: Old Humanities Bldg, University of Malta, Msida MSD 06; tel. 21333313; fax 21314485; e-mail campusfm@um.edu.mt; internet www.campusfm.um.edu.mt.

Capital Radio: MEDIA Co-op Ltd, 149 Archbishop St, Valletta; tel. 21233078; fax 21239701; e-mail capital@maltanet.net; internet www.capitalradio.com.mt; Station Man. JOHN MALLIA.

Island Sound Radio: 46 Robert Samut Sq., Floriana VLT 14; tel. 21249141; fax 21343770; News Co-ordinator BERNIE LYNCH.

Media.link Communications Co Ltd: Dar Centrali, Herbert Ganado St, Pietà HMR 08; tel. 21243641; fax 21243640; e-mail antona@vol.net.mt; internet www.media.link.com.mt.

Net TV: Dar Centrali, Herbert Ganado St, Pietà HMR 08; tel. 21243641; fax 21226645; CEO ANTON ATTARD.

Radio 101: Independence Point, Herbert Ganado St, Pietà HMR 08; tel. 21241164; fax 21564111; Head of News PIERRE PORTELLI.

Mediapact Ltd: Centrepoint, B'Kara By-pass, B'Kara; tel. 21443131; fax 21443232; internet www.maxplus.com.mt; operates television channel Max Plus.

Melita Cable PLC: 109 William Reid St, Gzira GZR 04; tel. 21345434; fax 21345435; e-mail info@melitacable.com; internet www.melitacable.com; CEO FRANK LEITER.

Multi Media Education and Broadcasting Centre: Maria Regina School, Mile End Rd, Hamrun HMR 02; tel. 21239274; fax 21240701; operates television channel Education 22.

One Productions Ltd: A28B, Industrial Estate, Marsa LQA 06; tel. 21226634; fax 21248249; e-mail livetv@super1.com; internet www.super1.com; f. 1999; owned by Malta Labour Party; Chair RENALD DALLI; CEO ALBERT MARSHALL.

Super One Radio: tel. 21244905; fax 21231472; e-mail radio@super1.com; broadcasts 24 hours daily.

Super One Television: Centru Nazzjonali Laburista, 4th Floor, Mile End Rd, Hamrun HMR 02; tel. 21234574; fax 21235474; e-mail kullhadd@keyworld.net; broadcasts 126 hours weekly; Head of News GINO CAUCHI.

Public Broadcasting Services Ltd: St Luke's Rd, G'Mangia MSD 09; tel. 21225051; fax 21244601; e-mail info@pbs.com.mt; f. 1991; govt-owned; operates national radio and television services: Radio 'Radju Malta', 'FM Bronja' and 'Radju Parlament'; Television Malta and Channel 12; Chair. A. J. TABONE; CEO ANDREW PSAILA.

Radio Calypso: Oasis, Mons. P. Pace St, Victoria VCT 111, Gozo; tel. 21563000; fax 21563565; News Editor SIMON LUMSDEN.

Radju MAS: 15 Old Mint St, Valletta VLT 12; tel. 21237755; fax 21247246; Editor Mgr FORTUNATO MIZZI.

RTK Radio: Media Centre, National Rd, Blata il-Bajda HMR 02; tel. 25699100; fax 25699151; e-mail ncachia@mediacentre.org.mt; internet www.rtk.org.mt; f. 1992; radio station of the Catholic Church of Malta; Chair. Fr NICHOLAS CACHIA; Man. Dir JEFFREY CALFATO.

Smash TV and Radio: Smash Communications, Thistle Lane, Paola PLA 19; tel. 21697829; fax 21697830; f. 1992; Man. Dir JOSEPH BALDACCHINO.

Voice of the Mediterranean (VOM): Chircop Bldgs, Floor 2, Msida Valley Rd, Birkirkara BKR 14; POB 143, Valletta; tel. 22797000; fax 22797111; e-mail info@vomradio.com; internet www.vomradio.com; f. 1988; programmes in English, Arabic, French, Italian, German, Maltese and Japanese; Man. Dir RICHARD MUSCAT.

Finance

(cap. = capital; res = reserves; dep. = deposits; m. = million; br. = branch; amounts in Maltese liri, unless otherwise stated)

BANKING

Central Bank

Central Bank of Malta: Castille Place, POB 378, Valletta CMR 01; tel. 21247480; fax 21243051; e-mail info@centralbankmalta.com; internet www.centralbankmalta.com; f. 1968; bank of issue; cap. 5m., res 90m., dep. 224m. (Dec. 2001); Gov. MICHAEL C. BONELLO.

Commercial Banks

APS Bank Ltd: APS House, 24 St Anne Sq., Floriana VLT 16; tel. 21226644; fax 21226202; e-mail headoffice@apsbank.com.mt; internet www.apsbank.com.mt; f. 1910; cap. 2m., res 3m., dep. 124m. (Dec. 2001); Chair. Prof. EMMANUEL P. DELIA; CEO EDWARD CACHIA; 4 brs.

Bank of Valletta PLC: BOV Centre, High St, Sliema SLM 16; tel. 21333084; fax 21333279; e-mail customercare@bov.com; internet www.bov.com; f. 1974; cap. 12m., res 8m., dep. 1,565m. (Sept. 2001); merged with Valletta Investment Bank Ltd in Oct. 2000; Chair. JOSEPH F. X. ZAHRA; 50 brs.

HSBC Bank Malta PLC: 233 Republic St, Valletta VLT 05; tel. 21245281; fax 21485857; e-mail info@hsbcmalta.com; internet www.hsbcmalta.com; f. 1975 as Mid-Med Bank; Maltese Govt's 67% interest acquired by Midland Bank International Financial Services Ltd 1999; cap. and res 110m., dep. 1,289m. (June 2002); Chair. ALBERT MIZZI; CEO THOMAS ROBSON; 45 brs and agencies.

Lohombus Bank Ltd: Spencer Gardens, Blata l-Bajda HMR 12; tel. 21226030; fax 21242669; e-mail info@lohombus@kemmunet.net.mt; internet www.lohombus.com; cap. and res 13.3m., dep. 5.5m. (Sept. 1998); Chair. DENNIS DE GEORGIO; Gen. Man. JOHN A. GAUCI.

Lombard Bank Malta PLC: 67 Republic St, Valletta VLT 05; tel. 21240442; fax 21247442; e-mail mail@lombardmalta.com; f. 1969; cap. 2m., res 4m., dep. 110m. (Dec. 2000); Chair. CHRISTIAN LEMMERICH; CEO JOSEPH SAID; 5 brs.

Principal 'Offshore' Banks

First International Merchant Bank PLC: Plaza Commercial Centre, 7th Floor, Bisazza St, Sliema SLM 15; tel. 21322100; fax 21322122; e-mail info@fimbank.com; internet www.fimbank.com; f. 1994; cap. and res US $38m., dep. US $62m. (Dec. 2001); Chair. NAJEEB H. M. AL-SALEH; Pres. CLAUDE L. ROY.

Izola Bank Ltd: 53/58 East St, Valletta VLT 06; tel. 21241258; fax 21241250; Gen. Man. ANDREW MIFSUD.

Volksbank Malta Ltd: 53 Dingli St, Sliema SLM 09; tel. 21336100; fax 21336090; e-mail info@volksbank.com.mt; f. 1995; Chair. MAURICE MIZZI; Man. Dir THOMAS HAVLIK.

STOCK EXCHANGE

Malta Stock Exchange: Garrison Chapel, Castille Pl., Valletta CMR 01; tel. 21244051; fax 21244071; e-mail borza@maltanet.net; f. 1992; Chair. ALFRED MALLIA.

INSURANCE

Aon Malta Ltd: 53 Mediterranean Bldg, Abate Rigord St, Ta'Xbiex MSD 12; tel. 23433234; fax 21341597; e-mail info@aon.com.mt; internet www.aon.com.mt; f. 1976; Chair. MART JAN VAN DER KNOOP; Man. Dir JOSEPH CUTAJAR.

Middle Sea Insurance PLC: Middle Sea House, Floriana VLT 16; tel. 21246262; fax 21248195; e-mail middlesea@middlesea.com; internet www.middlesea.com; f. 1981; Chair. MARIO C. GRECH; Gen. Man. JOSEPH M. RIZZO.

Numerous foreign insurance companies, principally British, Canadian and Italian, are represented in Malta by local agents.

Trade and Industry

GOVERNMENT AGENCIES

Malta External Trade Corporation Ltd (METCO): Trade Centre, Industrial Estate, San Gwann SGN 09; POB 8, San Gwann SGN 01; tel. 21446186; fax 21496687; e-mail info@metco.net; internet www.metco.net; f. 1989; promotes exports and external trade; Chair. ANTHONY S. DIACONO; Gen. Man. STEPHEN SULTANA.

MALTA *Directory*

Malta Financial Services Centre: Attard; tel. 21441155; fax 21441188; e-mail communications@mfsc.com.mt; internet www .mfsc.com.mt; promotes and supervises the financial services sector, incl. banking and investments; Chair. Prof. JOSEPH BANNISTER; CEO EDWARD CARBONE.

Malta Freeport Terminals Ltd: Freeport Centre, Port of Marsaxlokk, Kalafrana BBG 05; tel. 21650200; fax 21654814; e-mail marketing@maltafreeport.com.mt; internet www.maltafreeport .com.mt; f. 1988; container terminals and distribution centre; also operates petroleum products terminal and general warehousing facilities; Chair. MARK PORTELLI.

Malta Investment Management Co Ltd (MIMCOL): Trade Centre, San Gwann Industrial Estate, B'Kara SGN 09; tel. 21497970; fax 21499568; e-mail mimcol@maltanet.net; f. 1988; manages govt investments in domestic commercial enterprises and encourages their transfer to private-sector ownership; Chair. IVAN FALZON.

DEVELOPMENT ORGANIZATION

Malta Development Corporation (MDC): POB 141, Marsa GPO 01; tel. 21441888; fax 21441887; e-mail info@mdc.com.mt; internet www.investinmalta.com; f. 1967; administers govt programme of investment incentives; liaises between industry and the Govt and assists foreign cos; maintains offices in Italy, Germany and the USA; Chair. LAWRENCE ZAMMIT.

CHAMBER OF COMMERCE

Malta Chamber of Commerce: Exchange Bldgs, Republic St, Valletta VLT 05; tel. 21233873; fax 21245223; e-mail admin@ chamber.org.mt; internet www.chamber.org.mt; f. 1848; Pres. REGINALD FAUA; 1,000 mems.

EMPLOYERS' ORGANIZATIONS

Malta Employers' Association: 35/1 South St, Valletta VLT 11; tel. 21222992; fax 21230227; e-mail mea@maltanet.net; internet www.maltanet.net/mea; f. 1965; Pres. JOSEPH DELIA; Dir-Gen. JOSEPH FARRUGIA.

Malta Federation of Industry: Development House, St Anne St, Floriana VLT 01; tel. 21234428; fax 21240702; e-mail info@foi.org .mt; internet www.foi.org.mt; f. 1946; nat. org. for industry; 300 corporate mems; Pres. JOSEPH ZAMMIT TABONA; Dir-Gen. EDWIN CALLEJA.

UTILITIES

Electricity

Enemalta Corporation: Church Wharf, Marsa; POB 6, Hamrun HMR 01; tel. 21223601; fax 21243055; e-mail chairman@enemalta .com.mt; f. 1977; state energy corpn; purchases and distributes petroleum products and operates two oil-fired power stations for electricity generation; distributes electricity, petroleum products and LPG; Chair. Prof. ROBERT GHIRLANDO.

Water

Water Services Corporation: Qormi Rd, Luqa LQA 05; tel. 21249851; fax 21223016; e-mail water@wsc.com.mt; internet www .wsc.com.mt; f. 1991; govt agency responsible for supply, distribution and production of water; Chair. MICHAEL FALZON; CEO ANTHONY RIZZO.

TRADE UNIONS

In June 1998 there were 34 registered trade unions (with a combined membership of 81,700).

Confederation of Malta Trade Unions (CMTU): 9c M. A. Vassalli St, Valletta VLT 13; tel. 21237313; fax 21250146; e-mail cmtu@ maltanet.net; f. 1958; affiliated to the World Confed. of Labour, to the Commonwealth Trade Union Council and to the European Trade Union Confed. Pres. ALFRED BUHAGIAR; Gen. Sec. CHARLES MAGRO; 32,400 mems.

The principal affiliated unions include:

Association of General Retailers & Traders Union (GRTU): Exchange Bldgs, Republic St, Valletta VLT 05; tel. 21230459; fax 21246925; f. 1948; Pres. CHARLES J. BUSUTTIL; Sec. PHILIP FRENCH; 6,400 mems.

Malta Union of Teachers: Teachers' Institute, 213 Republic St, Valletta VLT 03; tel. 21237815; fax 21244074; e-mail info@mut .org.mt; internet www.mut.org.mt; f. 1919; Pres. J. BENCINI; Gen. Sec. JOSEPH P. DEGIOVANNI; 5,770 mems.

Union Haddiema Maghqudin (UHM): 'Dar Reggie Miller', St Thomas St, Floriana VLT 15; tel. 21220847; fax 21246091; e-mail uhm@maltanet.net; internet www.uhm.org.mt; f. 1966; Pres. G. TANTI; Sec.-Gen. G. VELLA; 25,793 mems.

The General Workers' Union (GWU): Workers' Memorial Bldg, South St, Valletta VLT 11; tel. 21244300; fax 21242975; e-mail info@ gwu.org.mt; internet www.gwu.org.mt; f. 1943; affiliated to the Int. Confed. of Free Trade Unions, to the European Trade Union Confed. and to the Commonwealth Trade Union Confed. Pres. SALV SAMMUT; CEO and Gen. Sec. TONY ZARB; 48,758 mems.

Transport

RAILWAYS

There are no railways in Malta.

ROADS

In 1999 there were 1,742 km of roads. About 96.2% of roads are paved. Bus services serve all parts of the main island and most parts of Gozo.

Public Transport Directorate: Sa Maison Rd, Pietà MSD 08; tel. 21255168; fax 21255175; e-mail pta@maltanet.net; internet www .maltatransport.com; f. 1989; regulatory body for public transport in Malta, part of Malta Transport Authority; Chair. (vacant).

Roads Department: Sa Maison Hill, Floriana CMR 02; tel. 21234686; fax 21243753; e-mail carmel.zammit@magnet.mt; Chair. C. DEMICOLI; CEO M. FALZON.

SHIPPING

Malta's national shipping register is open to ships of all countries. At 31 December 2001 Malta's merchant fleet comprised 1,421 vessels, with a total displacement of 27,052,579 gross registered tons. The island's dry dock facilities are also an important source of revenue.

Malta Maritime Authority: Ports Directorate, Marina Pinto, Valletta VLT 01; tel. 21222203; fax 21250365; e-mail info@mma.gov.at; internet www.mma.gov.mt; f. 1991; govt agency supervising the administration and operation of ports and yachting centres, and of vessel registrations under the Maltese flag; Chair. Dr MARC BONELLO.

Bianchi & Co (1916) Ltd: Palazzo Marina, 143 St Christopher St, Valletta VLT 02; tel. 21232241; fax 21232991; e-mail info@bianchi .com.mt; Man. Dir R. BIANCHI.

Cassar & Cooper Ltd: Valletta Bldgs, 54 South St, POB 311, Valletta, VLT 11; tel. 21232221; fax 21237864; e-mail info@ cassar-cooper.com; internet www.cassar-cooper.com; Dir MICHAEL COOPER.

O. F. Gollcher & Sons Ltd: 19 Zachary St, POB 268, Valletta VLT 10; tel. 25691100; fax 21234195; e-mail contact@gollcher.com; internet www.gollcher.com; Dir MARK GOLLCHER.

Medserv Ltd: Manoel Island, Gzira GZA 03; tel. 21336408; fax 21339511; Dir ANTHONY J. DUNCAN.

Mifsud Brothers Ltd: 27 South St, Valletta VLT 11; tel. 21232157; fax 21221331; e-mail info@mbl.com.mt; internet www.mbl.com.mt; f. 1860; shipping and travel agents; Man. Dir IVAN MIFSUD.

S. Mifsud & Sons Ltd (SMS): 131 East St, Valletta VLT 06; tel. 21233127; fax 21234180; cargo and ferry services between Malta/Catania, Reggio di Calabria; Dir ADRIAN S. MIFSUD.

Ripard, Larvan & Ripard Ltd: 156 Ta'Xbiex Seafront, Gzira GZR 03; tel. 21335591; fax 21343419; e-mail chandlery@rlryachting.com; Man. Dir CHRISTIAN RIPARD.

Sea Malta Co Ltd: Flagstone Wharf, Marsa HMR 12; tel. 21232230; fax 21225776; e-mail info@seamalta.com.mt; internet www .seamalta.com.mt; f. 1973; govt-owned national shipping line; operates roll-on/roll-off services between Malta, France, Italy, Northern Europe, Sicily, Spain and Tunisia; represents shipping line that operates passenger service between Malta and Libya; agency and insurance services, ship management, freight forwarding, shipbroking, bunkering, warehouse and passenger services; Chair. MARLENE MIZZI; Gen. Man. JOSEPH BUJEGA.

Sullivan Shipping Agencies Ltd: Exchange Bldgs, Republic St, Valletta VLT 05; tel. 21245127; fax 21233417; e-mail bsullivan@ sullivanshipping.com.mt; internet www.sullivanshipping.com.mt; Man. Dir BERNARD SULLIVAN.

Thomas Smith & Co Ltd: 12 St Christopher St, Valletta VLT 06; tel. 21245071; fax 21242056; e-mail info@tcsmith.com; internet www .tcsmith.com; Man. Dir JOE GERADA.

Virtu Steamship Co Ltd: 3 Princess Elizabeth Terrace, Ta'Xbiex MSD 11; tel. 21345220; fax 21314533; f. 1945; ship-owners; ship agents; shipbrokers; Malta–Sicily express passenger ferry service; Man. Dir F. A. PORTELLI.

CIVIL AVIATION

Malta International Airport is situated at Gudja (8 km from Valletta). In 1998 a total of 2.74m. passengers (excluding passengers in transit) passed through the airport.

Air Malta PLC: Luqa LQA 01; tel. 21690890; fax 21673241; e-mail info@airmalta.com.mt; internet www.airmalta.com; f. 1973; national airline with a 96.4% state shareholding; scheduled passenger and cargo services to mainland Europe, the United Kingdom, Sicily, North Africa and the Middle East; charter services to the United Kingdom and mainland Europe; CEO ERNST FUNK.

Tourism

Malta offers climatic, scenic and historical attractions, including fine beaches. Tourism forms a major sector of Malta's economy, generating foreign exchange earnings estimated at LM 261m. in 2001; in 2000 tourist arrivals totalled 1,215,713.

Malta Tourism Authority: Auberge d'Italie, 229 Merchant St., Valletta CMR 02; tel. 21224444; fax 21220401; e-mail info@visitmalta.com; internet www.maltatourismauthority.com; Chair. Dr JOHN C. GRECH; CEO LESLIE VELLA.

THE MARSHALL ISLANDS

Introductory Survey

Location, Climate, Language, Religion, Flag, Capital

The Republic of the Marshall Islands consists of two groups of islands, the Ratak ('sunrise') and Ralik ('sunset') chains, comprising 29 atolls (some 1,225 islets) and five islands, and covering about 180 sq km (70 sq miles) of land. The territory lies within the area of the Pacific Ocean known as Micronesia (which includes Kiribati, Tuvalu and other territories). The islands lie about 3,200 km (2,000 miles) south-west of Hawaii and about 2,100 km (1,300 miles) south-east of Guam. Rainfall decreases from south to north, with January, February and March being the driest months, although seasonal variations in rainfall and temperature are generally small. The native population comprises various ethno-linguistic groups, but English is widely understood. The principal religion is Christianity. The national flag (proportions 100 by 190) is dark blue, with a representation of a white star (with 20 short and four long rays) in the upper hoist; superimposed across the field are two progressively-wider stripes (orange above white), running from near the lower hoist corner to near the upper fly corner. The capital is the Dalap-Uliga-Darrit Municipality, on Majuro Atoll.

Recent History

The first European contact with the Marshall and Caroline Islands was by Spanish expeditions in the 16th century, including those led by Alvaro de Saavedra and Fernão de Magalhães (Ferdinand Magellan), the Portuguese navigator. The islands received their name from the British explorer, John Marshall, who visited them at the end of the 18th century. Spanish sovereignty over the Marshall Islands was recognized in 1886 by the Papal Bull of Pope Leo XIII, which also gave Germany trading rights there (German trading companies had been active in the islands from the 1850s). In 1899 Germany bought from Spain the Caroline Islands and the Northern Mariana Islands (except Guam, which had been ceded to the USA after the Spanish–American War of 1898). In 1914, at the beginning of the First World War, Japan occupied the islands, and received a mandate for its administration from the League of Nations in 1920. After the capture of the islands by US military forces in 1944 and 1945, most of the Japanese settlers were repatriated, and in 1947 the UN established the Trust Territory of the Pacific Islands (comprising the Caroline Islands, the Marshall Islands and the Northern Mariana Islands), to allow the USA to administer the region. The territory was governed by the US Navy from 1947 until 1951, when control passed to a civil administration—although the Northern Mariana Islands remained under military control until 1962.

From 1965 onwards there were increasing demands for local autonomy. In that year the Congress of Micronesia was formed; in 1967 a commission was established to examine the future political status of the islands. In 1970 it declared Micronesians' rights to sovereignty over their own lands, of self-determination, to their own constitution and to revoke any form of free association with the USA. In 1977, after eight years of negotiations, President Jimmy Carter announced that his administration intended to adopt measures to terminate the trusteeship agreement by 1981.

On 9 January 1978 the Marianas District achieved separate status as the Commonwealth of the Northern Mariana Islands (q.v.), but remained legally a part of the Trusteeship until 1986. The Marshall Islands District drafted its own Constitution, which came into effect on 1 May 1979, and the four districts of Yap, Truk (now Chuuk), Ponape (now Pohnpei) and Kosrae ratified a new Constitution, to become the Federated States of Micronesia (q.v.), on 10 May 1979. In the Palau District a referendum in July 1979 approved a proposed local constitution, which came into effect on 1 January 1981, when the district became the Republic of Palau (q.v.).

The USA signed the Compact of Free Association with the Republic of Palau in August 1982, and with the Marshall Islands and the Federated States of Micronesia in October. The trusteeship of the islands was due to end after the principle and terms of the Compacts had been approved by the respective peoples and legislatures of the new countries, by the US Congress and by the UN Security Council. Under the Compacts, the four countries (including the Northern Mariana Islands) would be independent of each other and would manage their internal and foreign affairs separately, while the USA would be responsible for defence and security. The Compacts with the Federated States of Micronesia and the Marshall Islands were approved in plebiscites in June and September 1983 respectively. The Congress of the Federated States of Micronesia ratified the country's decision in September. Under the Compact with the Marshall Islands, the USA was to retain its military bases in the Marshall Islands for at least 15 years and, over the same period, was to provide annual aid of US $30m.

The Compact between the Marshall Islands and the USA came into effect on 21 October 1986, following its approval by the islands' Government. In November President Ronald Reagan issued a proclamation formally ending US administration of Micronesia. The first President of the Republic of the Marshall Islands was Iroijlaplap (paramount chief) Amata Kabua, who was re-elected in 1984, 1988, 1992 and 1995. In December 1990 the UN Security Council finally ratified the termination of the trusteeship agreement; the Marshall Islands became a member of the UN in 1991. Renegotiation of the terms of the Compact began in October 1999.

The Marshall Islands' atolls of Bikini and Enewetak were used by the US Government for experiments with nuclear weapons: Bikini in 1946–58 and Enewetak in 1948–58. A total of 67 such tests were carried out during this period. The native inhabitants of Enewetak were evacuated before tests began, and were allowed to return to the atoll in 1980, after much of the contaminated area had supposedly been rendered safe. The inhabitants of Bikini Atoll campaigned for similar treatment, and in 1985 the US administration agreed to decontaminate Bikini Atoll over a period of 10–15 years (see below). Under the terms of the Compact, the US administration consented to establish a US $150m. trust fund to settle claims against the USA resulting from nuclear testing in the Marshall Islands during the 1940s and 1950s. In 1989 the US Supreme Court ruled that the Compact of 1983 and subsequent US legislation in 1986 prevented the islanders from suing the USA for any additional compensation, but in January 1990 a panel of judges approved further compensation for the islanders. In 1992 more than 400 Marshall Islanders received the first nuclear test compensation for personal injury, from a fund of $45m., to be paid over 15 years. In 1995 islanders from Enewetak began campaigning for compensation from the fund for the loss of their land, resulting from the complete or partial vaporization of five islands in the atoll by the tests. A concrete dome on the atoll in which nuclear debris had been stored since 1977 was reported at this time to be leaking.

Another atoll in the Marshall Islands, Kwajalein, has been used since 1947 as a target for the testing of missiles fired from California, USA. The Compact committed the US Government to provide an estimated US $170m. in rent, over a period of 30 years, for land used as the site of a missile-tracking station, and a further $80m. for development projects. The inhabitants of Kwajalein Atoll were concentrated on the small island of Ebeye, adjacent to the US base on Kwajalein Island, before a new programme of weapons-testing began in 1961. Consequent overcrowding reportedly led to numerous social problems on Ebeye. In 1985 the entire population of Rongelap Atoll (which had been engulfed in nuclear fall-out from the tests at Bikini in 1954) was forced to resettle on Mejato Atoll, after surveys suggested that levels of radiation there remained dangerous. Tests carried out by US scientists in 1992 found that Bikini Atoll also remained contaminated. In 1989 the Marshall Islands Government agreed that the USA could lease a further four islands in the atoll, for five years, for the purpose of military tests. A further lease agreement was signed in 1995 for the use of Biken Island (in Aur Atoll) and Wake Island in the missile-testing programme. In early 1999 the Marshall Islands Government announced plans to increase the rental charges for Kwajalein. (The islands received US $12.76m. in payment from the USA for use of the base in 1998.) In 2001 the Kwajalein Missile Range changed its name to the Ronald Reagan Ballistic Missile Defense Test Site, and in July the USA tested an intercontinental missile in the Pacific as part of its plans to develop a missile defence shield. The missile, fired from California, successfully shot down a target launched from Kwajalein Atoll. A Greenpeace activist who had been camping on a nearby island to witness the test was arrested, and the USA unsuccessfully put pressure on the Marshall Islands Government to deport him. A total of six missile tests were scheduled to take place in 2002 (in December an attempt to intercept a missile fired from California was unsuccessful). In mid-January 2003 it was announced that the USA and the Marshall Islands Government had reached agreement on new terms for the lease of the Kwajalein site. The pact replaced the previous arrangement (scheduled to end in 2016) and envisaged the payment of some $3,100m. for use of the site until 2066, with an option to extend the lease by a further 20 years. Moreover, it was also confirmed that the USA would continue to provide an annual $1.9m. in social funding for the residents of Ebeye. However, in late January a group of some 70 Kwajalein landowners rejected the agreement, claiming that the planned increase in annual payments (from the present $11.3m. to $18m. in 2014) constituted insufficient compensation, and demanded an annual rental of $19.1m. with immediate effect.

In January 1994 several senior members of the Marshall Islands' legislature, the Nitijela, demanded that the US Government release detailed information on the effects of its nuclear-testing programme in the islands. In July documentation released by the US Department of Energy gave conclusive evidence that Marshall Islanders had been deliberately exposed to high levels of radiation in order that its effects on their health could be studied by US medical researchers. Further evidence emerged during 1995 that the US Government had withheld the medical records of islanders involved in radiation experiments (which included tritium and chromium-51 injections and genetic and bone-marrow transplant experiments). Japanese scientists reported in that year that some 40% of the former inhabitants of Rongelap Atoll were suffering from cancer. In 1997 the islands' Nuclear Claims Tribunal ruled that compensation from the US Government was not sufficient to meet the health requirements of Marshall Islanders affected by the tests, reiterating that the full extent of the problems caused by the tests had not been known when the terms of compensation were agreed in the early 1980s. In late 1998 representatives of the islanders appealed to the US Congress for the immediate payment of compensation to seriously ill victims of the tests. Officials claimed that about one-third of islanders eligible for compensation had died before receiving any payment; subsequently it was claimed that the total number of people and extent of territory exposed to fall-out as a result of nuclear testing at Bikini Atoll was far greater than had been acknowledged by the USA. A further study by US scientists concluded in early 1999 that rates of cancer in the Marshall Islands associated with nuclear testing had reached what were termed extreme levels. In October the Nuclear Claims Tribunal announced that an overall annual compensation payment of US $2.3m. was to be made to victims of nuclear testing, bringing total payments made by the Tribunal to US $39.4m. In late 1999 the US Congress confirmed an agreement regarding compensation for the resettled inhabitants of Rongelap Atoll. In May 2000 the Nuclear Claims Tribunal awarded some US $578m. in compensation to the inhabitants of Enewetak Atoll. However, it was reported that the Tribunal did not possess sufficient funds to pay the compensation in full; it subsequently requested that the shortfall be provided by the USA. In 2002 islanders affected by radiation continued to put pressure on the US Congress to increase compensation levels, and requested a full apology for the tests.

In February 1997, meanwhile, a group of Bikini Islanders returned to the atoll for the first time since 1946 to assist in the rehabilitation of the atoll for resettlement. The operation was to involve the removal of radioactive topsoil (although the matter of its disposal presented a serious problem) and the saturation of the remaining soil with potassium, which is believed to inhibit the absorption of radioactive material by root crops. In early 1999 the Nuclear Claims Tribunal demanded the adoption of US Environmental Protection Agency standards in the rehabilitation of contaminated islands, claiming that Marshall Islanders deserved to receive the same treatment as US citizens would in similar circumstances. The US Department of Energy, however, expressed strong resistance to the suggestion.

In late February 2001 a report published by an eminent Japanese scientist stated that radiation levels on Rongelap

Island, according to research conducted in 1999, had now declined to such a level that human habitation of the island was again possible. (However, in October 2000 another scientific report had concluded that islanders had been exposed to more than 20 times as much radiation as had been previously stated.) In March 2001 the Marshall Islands Nuclear Claims Tribunal awarded US $563m. in compensation to former inhabitants of Bikini Atoll, although, as the tribunal had insufficient funds to pay the award, it was unclear what compensation islanders would in fact receive. (In late 2000 the Government had petitioned the US Congress for an additional US $270m. in compensation, although the outcome of this petition remained uncertain, subject to further renegotiation of the Compact of Free Association.) In April, following the adoption by the USA of a new standard of radioactivity considered to be acceptable, some six times lower than the previous level, the Tribunal announced that Ailuk Atoll was to be evacuated and environmental studies conducted. In mid-May two members of the environmentalist organization, Greenpeace, were arrested following a demonstration outside Kwajalein. In July 2002 the Government retained a former US Attorney-General in order to restore momentum to the outstanding $200m. claim for compensation against the US Government; claims for Rongelap and Utrik were still pending despite the absence of tribunal funds. In 2002 a working group of representatives from the US Department of Energy and the Marshall Islands Government was established; this was to meet henceforth several times a year.

In 1989 it was announced that up to 3,000 Marshall Islands passports were to be offered for sale at a price of US $250,000 (subsequently reduced to $100,000), in an attempt to stimulate Asian investment. The passport scheme (which earned an estimated US $10m. between 1995 and 1997) was officially suspended in 1997, following a sudden influx of Chinese nationals to the islands. In March 2003 the USA expressed a wish to renegotiate the terms for immigration into the USA established under the Compact of Free Association, prompted by the comparative ease of access afforded by Marshall Islands passports and by concerns over an apparent rise in alleged illegal adoptions of Marshallese babies by US citizens. (In December 2002 controversy relating to illegal adoption had increased following allegations by the former Chief Justice of the Marshall Islands, Charles N. Henry, that the Government's charges against him of 'cheating' (with regard to his travel expenses and other costs) were related to his efforts to eradicate the practice.)

Following legislative elections in November 1995, at which eight incumbent members of the 33-seat Nitijela were defeated, Kabua was re-elected for a fifth term. The President died in December 1996. Iroijlaplap Imata Kabua, a cousin of the late President, was elected as his successor on 13 January 1997.

In 1996 the Nitijela approved legislation allowing for the introduction of gambling in the islands, in order to provide an additional source of revenue. However, income earned from the venture did not fulfil expectations. Moreover, a vociferous campaign by local church leaders to revoke the legislation led to fierce debate in the Nitijela in early 1998. Divisions within the Cabinet ensued, with three members supporting the President's pro-gambling stance and four others opposing. In April the Nitijela voted to repeal the law legalizing gambling: several influential politicians (including Imata Kabua) known to have major gambling interests were disqualified from voting. A second bill containing further measures to ensure the prohibition of all gambling activity in the islands was narrowly approved. Three ministers who had supported the anti-gambling legislation were dismissed in a cabinet reorganization in August. In the following month one of the dismissed ministers proposed a motion of 'no confidence' in Kabua. The President and his supporters boycotted subsequent sessions of the Nitijela, thereby rendering the legislature inquorate and effectively precluding the vote, as well as delaying the approval of the budget for the impending financial year. Despite opposition claims that Kabua's continued absence from the Nitijela violated the terms of the Constitution, the motion of 'no confidence' in Kabua was eventually defeated by a margin of one vote in October.

At legislative elections held on 15 November 1999 the opposition United Democratic Party (UDP) secured a convincing victory over the incumbent administration, winning 18 of the 33 seats in the Nitijela. Five senior members of the outgoing Government were defeated, including the Ministers of Finance and of Foreign Affairs and Trade—both of whom had played a prominent role in the establishment of diplomatic relations with Taiwan in 1998 (see below). The former Nitijela Speaker, Kessai

Note, was elected President on 3 January 2000 (the islands' first non-traditional leader to assume the post). The UDP Chairman, Litokwa Tomeing, became Speaker of the legislature. Note subsequently appointed a 10-member Cabinet, and reiterated his administration's intention to pursue anti-corruption policies. In May a task-force was established by the Government for the purposes of investigating misconduct and corruption; it was hoped that the task-force would help to render Government more accountable.

In September 2000 a Marshall Islands High Court judge ruled that a case brought by the Government against US tobacco companies could be heard on the Islands; the tobacco companies had claimed that they would be unable to receive a fair trial. The Government was seeking more than US $ 14,000m. in damages for health-care costs faced by smokers on the islands. In late February 2001 10 of the 11 charges against the tobacco companies were dismissed by the High Court judge for lack of evidence. The US Government had reportedly warned that its overseas aid flows might be threatened if the trial were to proceed; however, in early April a US judge had ruled that the companies would receive a fair trial in the Marshall Islands. However, following a series of reversals, which included questions on the legal status of the Marshall Islands High Court, the case was finally dismissed by the Islands' cabinet-appointed Supreme Court in May 2002.

In November 2000, it was reported that finance officials had discovered that Imata Kabua had used funds granted to the Marshall Islands under the terms of the Compact of Free Association to pay off a personal loan, although the former President denied any wrongdoing. In mid-January 2001 Imata Kabua and former ministers in his Government, including the former Minister of Education, Justin DeBrum, presented a 'no confidence' motion against President Note to the Nitijela. Although it was suggested that the vote had been intended to delay the publication of a report into mismanagement and corruption on the part of the former Government, DeBrum stated that the motion resulted from a number of failings by the Note Government, including its unwillingness to renegotiate land rental payments with the USA for the use of the military base on Kwajalein Atoll and also the development of an economic relationship between the Note Government and Rev. Sun Myung Moon, the founder of the Unification Church (known as the 'Moonies'). However, the Government was successful in defeating the vote by a margin of 19 to 14. In mid–2001 Note announced a cabinet reshuffle.

Meanwhile, in June 2000 the Marshall Islands was one of more than 30 countries and territories criticized by the Organisation for Economic Co-operation and Development (OECD, see p. 277) for the provision of inappropriate 'offshore' financial establishments. The OECD threatened to implement sanctions against 'unco-operative tax havens' unless reforms were introduced before July 2001. In May 2000, meanwhile, the Group of Seven industrialized nations (G-7) alleged that the Marshall Islands had become a significant centre for the 'laundering' of money generated by international criminal activity. In September the Nitijela passed legislation to ensure the closer regulation of the banking and financial sector, although in October the Marshall Islands was again included in a list of countries judged to be unhelpful in the combating of international financial crime, which was issued by the Financial Action Task Force (FATF), based in Paris, France. However, following a commendation from the IMF on a series of new measures to combat fraud, including specific legislation and the establishment of a Domestic Financial Intelligence Unit, the FATF removed the Marshall Islands from the list in October 2002.

In mid-1999 the Government of the Marshall Islands accused the USA of failing to honour its obligations under the terms of the Compact of Free Association, and that a shortfall of some US $18m., which had been promised in 1983, was undermining efforts to promote economic development. Negotiations began between the US and Marshall Islands Governments in July 2001 to renew the 15-year provisions of the Compact, which was due to expire at the end of September 2001. An extension of up to two years was permitted whilst negotiations were under way, during which time assistance to the Marshall Islands was to increase by some US $5.5m. An agreement was originally scheduled for early 2002 in order to allow adequate time for the US Congress to review it and to pass the requisite legislation (by 1 October 2003), but the procedure was postponed until early May 2002 after the Marshall Islands Government submitted a proposal seeking financing of more than $1,000m. over 15 years.

The Government had also objected to being allocated 25%–30% less in US grant assistance per caput than that apportioned to the Federated States of Micronesia since the year 2000. In a further attempt to increase the national income, the Government sought to raise significantly both the level of rental payments charged for the Kwajalein base as well as the level of taxes levied on the employees of the US facility. In early November 2002 the USA and the Marshall Islands Government announced a programme of direct funding of $822m., to be disbursed over 20 years, in addition to the expansion of many US government services in the islands. The new funding structure was described as an 'important milestone' towards the final agreement of the new Compact of Free Association, although the question of taxes on employees of the US base remained unresolved.

In 1989 a UN report on the 'greenhouse effect' (heating of the earth's atmosphere) predicted a possible resultant rise in sea-level of some 3.7 m by 2030, which would completely submerge the Marshall Islands. The islands' Government strongly criticized the Australian Government's refusal, at the conference on climate change in Kyoto, Japan, in December 1997, to reduce its emission of pollutant gases known to contribute to the 'greenhouse effect'. Furthermore, in early 2002 the Intergovernmental Panel on Climate Change (IPCC) projected that during the 21st century global sea-level rises would submerge over 80% of Majuro atoll. However, the Marshall Islands Government has itself caused regional concerns regarding pollution, notably with regard to the possible establishment of large-scale facilities for the storage of nuclear waste. Criticism by the US Government of the plans, announced in 1994, was strongly denounced by the Marshall Islands authorities, which claimed that the project constituted the only opportunity for the country to generate sufficient income for the rehabilitation of contaminated islands and the provision of treatment for illnesses caused by the US nuclear-test programme. In mid-1997 President Imata Kabua announced the indefinite suspension of the project (despite the initiation of a feasibility study into the development of a nuclear waste storage facility). None the less, the Government approved plans for a new feasibility study on the subject in April 1998. The new Minister of Foreign Affairs appointed by President Note in January 2000 was known to be strongly opposed to the scheme.

In November 1998 the Marshall Islands established full diplomatic relations with Taiwan. The action was immediately condemned by the People's Republic of China, which in December severed diplomatic ties with the islands, closing its embassy in Majuro and suspending all intergovernmental agreements. The Marshall Islands Government insisted that it wished to maintain cordial relations with both governments. The Note administration, which took office in January 2000, emphasized its commitment to the maintenance of diplomatic relations with Taiwan. In February 2001 a proposed visit by a flotilla of Taiwanese naval vessels to the Marshall Islands was vetoed by the USA, on the grounds that the defence protocol of the Compact of Free Association prohibited such a visit.

Government

The Constitution of the Republic of the Marshall Islands, which became effective on 1 May 1979, provides for a parliamentary form of government, with legislative authority vested in the 33-member Nitijela. The Nitijela (members of which are elected, by popular vote, for a four-year term) elects the President of the Marshall Islands (also a four-year mandate) from among its own members. Under the terms of the Compact of Free Association (which was signed by the Governments of the Marshall Islands and the USA on 25 June 1983, and which was effectively ratified by the US Congress on 14 January 1986) the Republic of the Marshall Islands is a sovereign, self-governing state.

Local governmental units are the municipalities and villages. Elected Magistrates and Councils govern the municipalities. Village government is largely traditional.

Defence

The defence of the Marshall Islands is the responsibility of the USA, which maintains a military presence on Kwajalein Atoll.

Economic Affairs

In 2001, according to estimates by the World Bank, the Marshall Islands' gross national income (GNI), measured at average 1999–2001 prices, was US $115m., equivalent to $2,190 per head. During 1990–2001, it was estimated, the population increased at an average annual rate of 2.0%, while gross domestic product (GDP) declined, in real terms, at an average rate of 1.5% per year. According to the Asian Development Bank (ADB), GDP grew by only 0.1% in 1999, decreased by 0.9% in 2000, but increased by 1.7% in 2001.

Agriculture is mainly on a subsistence level. The sector (including fishing and livestock-rearing) contributed an estimated 13.7% of GDP in 1999/2000. According to FAO, the sector engaged 6,000 people in 2001. The principal crops are coconuts, cassava and sweet potatoes. In 2000 some 2,706 short tons of copra were produced (a decrease of 19.2% compared with the previous year); in that year exports of copra and coconut oil comprised 31.0% of the value of total exports. Copra production suffered a severe decline in the late 1990s, following sustained low prices, an ageing tree stock and a reduction in the number of government-owned vessels used for transport purposes. The fishing sector incorporates a commercial tuna-fishing industry, including a tuna-canning factory and transhipment base on Majuro. The cultivation of seaweed was developed extensively in 1992, and in 1994 a project to cultivate blacklip pearl oysters on Arno Atoll was undertaken with US funding. The sale of fishing licences is an important source of revenue and earned the islands an estimated US $3m. in 2000/01. The Marshall Islands expected to receive annual revenues of some $21m. following the renewal of a treaty between the USA and the Forum Fisheries Agency (FFA) group of Pacific island nations in 2003. In 2001 the Japanese Government funded the construction of a commercial fishing base at Jaluit Atoll. According to initial estimates by the Asian Development Bank (ADB), compared with the previous year the GDP of the agricultural sector declined by 13.9% in 1998, but increased by 1.7% in 1999 and by 3.7% in 2000.

Industrial activities (including mining, manufacturing, construction and power) contributed an estimated 15.1% of GDP in 1999/2000, and engaged 9.4% of the employed labour force in 1988. Between 1990 and 1999 industrial GDP declined at an average annual rate of 1.5%. According to provisional estimates by the ADB, compared with the previous year the GDP of the industrial sector rose by 1.3% in 1999 and by 3.7% in 2000. The islands have few mineral resources, although there are high-grade phosphate deposits on Ailinglaplap Atoll.

Manufacturing activity, which provided 1.8% of GDP in 1999/2000, consists mainly of the processing of agricultural products and of fish. According to the ADB, the manufacturing sector engaged a total of 800 workers in 2000. Tolobar, the Marshall Islands' leading copra-processing company, was unable to process any further supplies of the commodity in 2001, owing to the size of its stockpile of oil and the lack of any additional storage capacity. In April 2002 the Taiwanese Government invested US $1.2m., enabling Tobolar to sell its stockpile, to begin processing again, and to open a new oil refinery (hitherto, the Marshall Islands had produced only unrefined oil).

The services sector provided an estimated 71.3% of GDP in 1999/2000. The international shipping registry experienced considerable expansion following the political troubles in Panama in 1989, and continued to expand in the mid-1990s (largely as a result of US ships' re-flagging in the islands). The shipping industry also benefited from the construction of a floating dry-dock on Majuro in 1995. Tourist receipts reached US $4m. in 1999. The number of tourist arrivals rose from 5,246 in 2000 to 5,399 in 2001. According to initial estimates by the ADB, compared with the previous year the GDP of the services sector expanded by only 0.2% in 1998, before contracting by 0.5% in 1999 and by 0.8% in 2000.

In the financial year ending 30 September 2000 the Marshall Islands recorded an estimated trade deficit of US $50.9m., but a surplus of $4.9m. on the current account of the balance of payments. The only significant domestic exports in 2000 were coconut products and fish. The principal imports included mineral fuels and lubricants (which accounted for 43.6% of total expenditure on merchandise imports), food and live animals, and machinery and transport equipment. In that year the principal sources of imports were the USA (which provided 61.4% of total imports) and Japan (5.1%). The USA was also the principal export destination, receiving 71.2% of total exports.

A budgetary surplus equivalent to 17.5% of GDP was forecast for 2000/01. Financial assistance from the USA, in accordance with the terms stipulated in the Compact of Free Association, contributes a large part of the islands' revenue. Aided by an increase in this support, estimates for 2001/02 envisaged a rise in budgetary expenditure to US $74m. (compared with $66m. in the previous year). Recurrent expenditure was projected to increase from $55m. in 2000/01 to $59m. in 2001/02. The islands' external debt was estimated at $67.0m. in 2000/01. In that year

the cost of debt-servicing (including repayments) was equivalent to 168.7% of the value of exports of goods and services. The Marshall Islands received $499 of aid per caput in 2000, which increased to $551 budgeted for 2003. In 2000/01 budgeted aid from the USA amounted to $20.7m. (35% of which was to be provided under the Compact agreement). The US aid budget for 2002 included a grant of $2.5m. to the Marshall Islands for an extension of the Military Use and Operating Rights Agreement (in addition to its mandatory annual payments of support for Enewetak Atoll and the Compact of Free Association). Aid is also provided by Japan and Taiwan. According to the ADB, annual inflation in Majuro averaged 5.3% in 1990–2000. Consumer prices were estimated to have increased by an annual average of 1.7% in 1999 and by 1.6% in 2000. The unemployment rate stood at 31.5% of the economically active population in 2000.

The Marshall Islands is a member of the Pacific Community (see p. 304), the Pacific Islands Forum (see p. 306), the South Pacific Regional Trade and Economic Co-operation Agreement (SPARTECA, see p. 308), the UN Economic and Social Commission for Asia and the Pacific (ESCAP, see p. 28) and the Asian Development Bank (ADB, see p. 143). In early 1996 the Marshall Islands and other countries and territories of Micronesia established the Council of Micronesian Government Executives. The new body aimed to facilitate discussion of economic developments in the region, and to examine possibilities for reducing the considerable cost of shipping essential goods between the islands.

The introduction, from the mid-1990s, of retrenchment measures in the public sector was welcomed by several international financial organizations and supported by the ADB. However, it was subsequently observed that reform of the public sector, which until the recession of the mid-1990s had employed up to one-half of the economically-active population, had been accompanied by a decline in employment in the private sector, leading to a very high rate of unemployment and suggesting that the private sector in the Marshall Islands existed largely as a secondary sector. In 1999 the Kabua Government reduced import duties by more than 50% on many items, in an attempt to revitalize the local economy. Reforms to promote the private sector were also announced. A major priority for the administration of Kessai Note, which took office in January 2000, was to be the renegotiation of assistance under the Compact of Free Association with the USA, which was due to expire in 2001, although there would be a two-year transitional period until 2003. During the 1990s the Marshall Islands sought to diversify its international economic relations. This policy achieved considerable initial success with the People's Republic of China, prior to the Marshall Islands' decision in 1998 to recognize Taiwan (see Recent History). Consequently, the People's Republic of China suspended diplomatic relations and withdrew all economic support for the islands later in the year. The Marshall Islands have since benefited from numerous economic agreements with Taiwan, worth an estimated US $20m., which have financed many projects including the construction of roads, the acquisition of boats, and the development of the agricultural sector. However, concern was expressed by the ADB in 1999 that reliance on external aid was hampering economic reform in the Marshall Islands (in 2000 bilateral and multilateral aid to the Marshall Islands totalled $57.2m.) In June 2001 the ADB itself approved a programme of low-interest loans totalling $12m., urging the Government to use it to improve budgeting and accounting practices. In September 2002 the Marshallese Government's audit of its own 2001 accounts identified a possible misallocation of some $4.4m. in US aid funds, and criticized accounting practices prior to the Note Government's period in office. In December 2002 the ADB approved a further total of $7.25m. in loans and grants in order to improve the country's infrastructure. The lack of internationally-marketable natural resources and the remote location of the islands present major challenges for the Marshall Islands Government in its efforts to revitalize and expand the economy. Attempts to circumvent these difficulties, including efforts to introduce gambling and 'offshore' financial services (see Recent History) have generated political controversy, both domestically and internationally. Allegations of 'money-laundering' activities continued in 2002, although in October the Marshall Islands was removed from the Financial Action Task Force (FATF) list of Non Co-operative Countries and Territories (NCCT) following the successful implementation of a series of regulatory measures (see above). External debt-repayment obligations were expected to decline sharply in 2002, leading to the release of substantial resources which the Government planned to channel into the Marshall Islands Intergenerational Trust Fund. In 2001 the Government had transferred a total of $14m. to the Fund, to which it was envisaged future contributions from the USA and financial assistance from other donors would be allocated. It was hoped that within 20 years the Fund might total $750m. and in due course provide an annual income of $30m.–$40m. However, the subsequent downturn in the US financial markets was believed to have significantly affected the value of the Fund.

Education

Education is compulsory between the ages of six and 14. In 1999 a total of 12,421 children attended the 103 primary schools of the Marshall Islands. A total of 2,667 pupils were enrolled at 16 secondary schools in 1999. The College of the Marshall Islands (which became independent from the College of Micronesia in 1993) is based on Majuro. In 1995 the University of the South Pacific opened an extension centre on Majuro. The Fisheries and Nautical Center offers vocational courses for Marshall islanders seeking employment in the fishing industry or on passenger liners, cargo ships and tankers. Government expenditure on education in the 1997/98 budget was estimated at $10.0m., equivalent to 23.5% of total recurrent budgetary spending.

Public Holidays

2003: 1 January (New Year), 1 March (Nuclear Victims' Remembrance Day), 18 April (Good Friday), 1 May (Constitution Day), 4 July (Fishermen's Day), 5 September (Ri-Jerbal—Labour Day), 26 September (Manit—Culture Day), 14 November (President's Day), 7 December (Kamolol—Gospel Day), 25 December (Christmas).

2004 (provisional): 1 January (New Year), 1 March (Nuclear Victims' Remembrance Day), 9 April (Good Friday), 1 May (Constitution Day), 4 July (Fishermen's Day), 5 September (Ri-Jerbal—Labour Day), 26 September (Manit—Culture Day), 14 November (President's Day), 7 December (Kamolol—Gospel Day), 25 December (Christmas).

Weights and Measures

With certain exceptions, the imperial system is in force. One US cwt equals 100 lb; one long ton equals 2,240 lb; one short ton equals 2,000 lb. A policy of gradual voluntary conversion to the metric system is being undertaken.

Statistical Survey

AREA AND POPULATION

Area: 181.4 sq km (70.0 sq miles) (land only); two island groups, the Ratak Chain (88.1 sq km) and the Ralik Chain (93.3 sq km).

Population: 43,380 at census of 13 November 1988; 50,848 (males 26,034, females 24,814) at census of June 1999. *By island group* (1999): Ratak Chain 30,932 (Majuro Atoll 23,682); Ralik Chain 19,916 (Kwajalein Atoll 10,903).

Density (1999 census): 280.3 per sq km.

Births and Deaths (estimates, 1999): Birth rate 41.8 per 1,000; Death rate 4.9 per 1,000.

Expectation of Life (WHO estimates, years at birth): 62.4 (males 60.7; females 64.3) in 2001. Source: WHO, *World Health Report.*

Economically Active Population (2000): Agriculture, forestry and fishing 2,100; Manufacturing 800; Activities not adequately defined 7,400; Total employed 10,300; Unemployed 4,500; Total labour force 15,000. Source: Asian Development Bank, *Key Indicators of Developing Asian and Pacific Countries.*

HEALTH AND WELFARE

Key Indicators

Total Fertility Rate (children per woman, 2000): 5.9.

Under-5 Mortality Rate (per 1,000 live births, 2001): 66.

Physicians (per 1,000 head, 1996): 0.42.

Health Expenditure (2000): US $ per head (PPP): 312.

Health Expenditure (2000): % of GDP: 9.4.

Health Expenditure (2000): public (% of total): 61.4.
For sources and definitions, see explanatory note on p. vi.

AGRICULTURE, ETC.

Principal Crops, Livestock and Livestock Products: see chapter on the Federated States of Micronesia.

Fishing (metric tons, live weight): Total catch 7,960 in 2000. Source: FAO, *Yearbook of Fishery Statistics.*

INDUSTRY

Electric Energy (million kWh)* 64.1 in 1998; 62.9 in 1999; 63.0 in 2000. Source: Asian Development Bank, *Key Indicators of Developing Asian and Pacific Countries.*
*Figures refer to Majuro only.

FINANCE

Currency and Exchange Rates: United States currency is used: 100 cents = 1 United States dollar (US $). *Sterling and Euro Equivalents* (31 December 2002): £1 sterling = US $1.6118; €1 = US $1.05; US $100 = £62.04 = €95.36.

Budget (estimates, US $ million, year ending 30 September 2001): *Revenue:* Recurrent 23.0 (Tax 17.7, Non-tax 5.3); Grants 60.9; Total 83.9. *Expenditure:* Recurrent 54.8; Capital (incl. net lending) 11.5; Total 66.3. Source: Asian Development Bank, *Key Indicators of Developing Asian and Pacific Countries.*

Cost of Living (Consumer Price Index for Majuro; base: Oct.–Dec. 1982 = 100): All items 190.8 in 1998; 194.0 in 1999, 197.1 in 2000. Source: Asian Development Bank, *Key Indicators of Developing Asian and Pacific Countries.*

Gross Domestic Product by Economic Activity (estimates, US $ million at current prices, year ending 30 September 2000): Agriculture 13.2; Mining 0.3; Manufacturing 1.7; Electricity, gas and water 2.2; Construction 10.4; Trade 17.1; Transport and communications 5.2; Finance 15.7; Other 30.9; *Sub-total* 96.7; Import duties 7.0; *Less* Imputed bank service charges 6.2; *GDP in purchasers' values* 97.5. Source: Asian Development Bank, *Key Indicators of Developing Asian and Pacific Countries.*

Balance of Payments (estimates, US $ million, year ending 30 September 2001): Merchandise exports f.o.b. 7.3; Merchandise imports c.i.f. –68.2; *Trade balance* –61.0; Exports of services 35.0; Imports of services –13.2; *Balance on goods and services* –21.8; Private unrequited transfers (net) 0.7; Official unrequited transfers (net) 44.1; *Current balance* 14.3; Capital account (net) –22.0; Net errors and omissions 9.3; *Overall balance* 1.6. Source: Asian Development Bank, *Key Indicators of Developing Asian and Pacific Countries.*

EXTERNAL TRADE

Principal Commodities (estimates, US $ million, 2000): *Imports:* Food, live animals, beverages and tobacco 7.4; Crude materials, inedible, except fuels 2.9; Mineral fuels, lubricants and related materials 29.7; Animal and vegetable oils and fats 2.9; Chemicals 0.2; Basic manufactures 4.0; Machinery and transport equipment 11.5; Miscellaneous manufactured articles 1.9; Goods not classified by kind 7.7; Total 68.2. *Exports:* Coconut oil (crude) 1.1; Copra cake 1.2; Pet fish 0.5; Total (incl. others) 7.3. Source: mainly Asian Development Bank, *Key Indicators of Developing Asian and Pacific Countries.*

Principal Trading Partners (estimates, US $ million, 2000): *Imports:* Australia 1.4; Hong Kong 1.3; Japan 3.5; New Zealand 0.9; USA 41.9; Total (incl. others) 68.2. *Exports:* USA 5.2; Total (incl. others) 7.3. Source: mainly Asian Development Bank, *Key Indicators of Developing Asian and Pacific Countries.*

TRANSPORT

Road Traffic (vehicles registered, 1999): Trucks 64; Pick-ups 587; Sedans 1,404; Jeeps 79; Buses 75; Vans 66; Scooters 47; Other motor vehicles 253.

Shipping: *Merchant Fleet* (at 31 December 2001): Vessels 360; Displacement ('000 grt) 11,719 (Source: Lloyd's Register-Fairplay, *World Fleet Statistics*). *International Sea-borne Freight Traffic* (estimates, '000 metric tons, 1990)*: Goods loaded 29; Goods unloaded 123 (Source: UN, *Monthly Bulletin of Statistics*).
* Including the Northern Mariana Islands, the Federated States of Micronesia and Palau.

Civil Aviation (traffic on scheduled services, 1998): Passengers carried 32,000; Passenger-km 20 million. Total ton-km 2 million. Source: UN, *Statistical Yearbook*.

TOURISM

Tourist Arrivals: 4,622 in 1999; 5,246 in 2000; 5,399 in 2001.

Arrivals by Country (2001): Australia 134; Fiji 147; Japan 933; Kiribati 275; Federated States of Micronesia 239; Philippines 180; USA 1,922; Total (incl. others) 5,399.

Tourism Receipts (US $ million): 3 in 1997; 3 in 1998; 4 in 1999. Sources: World Tourism Organization, *Yearbook of Tourism Statistics*, and Marshall Islands Visitor Authority.

COMMUNICATIONS MEDIA

Telephones (main lines in use): 4,200 in 2001*.

Mobile Cellular Telephones (subscriptions): 500 in 2001*.

Facsimile Machines (number): 160 in 1996†.

Personal Computers: 4,000 in 2001*.

Internet Users: 900 in 2001*.

Non-daily Newspapers: 1 (average circulation 10,000 copies) in 1996‡.
* Source: International Telecommunication Union.
† Source: UN, *Statistical Yearbook*.
‡ Source: UNESCO, *Statistical Yearbook*.

EDUCATION

Primary (1998): 103 schools; 548 teachers; 12,421 pupils enrolled.

Secondary (1998): 16 schools; 162 teachers; 2,667 pupils enrolled.

Higher (1994): 1 college; 25 teachers; 1,149 students enrolled.

Directory

The Constitution

On 1 May 1979 the locally-drafted Constitution of the Republic of the Marshall Islands became effective. The Constitution provides for a parliamentary form of government, with legislative authority vested in the 33-member Nitijela. Members of the Nitijela are elected by a popular vote, from 25 districts, for a four-year term. There is an advisory council of 12 high chiefs, or Iroij. The Nitijela elects the President of the Marshall Islands (who also has a four-year mandate) from among its own members. The President then selects members of the Cabinet from among the members of the Nitijela. On 25 June 1983 the final draft of the Compact of Free Association was signed by the Governments of the Marshall Islands and the USA, and the Compact was effectively ratified by the US Congress on 14 January 1986. By the terms of the Compact, free association recognizes the Republic of the Marshall Islands as an internally sovereign, self-governing state, whose policy concerning foreign affairs must be consistent with guide-lines laid down in the Compact. Full responsibility for defence lies with the USA, which undertakes to provide regular economic assistance. The economic and defence provisions of the Compact are renewable after 15 years, but the status of free association continues indefinitely.

The Government

HEAD OF STATE

President: KESSAI H. NOTE (took office 10 January 2000).

THE CABINET
(April 2003)

Minister in Assistance to the President: TADASHI LOMETO.

Minister of Education: WILFRED I. KENDALL.

Minister of Finance: MICHAEL M. KONELIOS.

Minister of Transportation and Communication: BRENSON S. WASE.

Minister of Health and Environment: ALVIN JACKLICK.

Minister of Public Works: RIEN R. MORRIS.

Minister of Internal Affairs: NIDEL L. LORA.

Minister of Justice: WITTEN T. PHILIPPO.

Minister of Resources and Development: JOHN M. SILK.

Minister of Foreign Affairs and Trade: GERALD ZACKIOS.

MINISTRIES

Office of the President: Govt of the Republic of the Marshall Islands, POB 2, Majuro, MH 96960; tel. (625) 3445; fax (625) 4021; e-mail presoff@ntamar.com.

Ministry of Education: POB 3, Majuro, MH 96960; tel. (625) 5261; fax (625) 7735/3861; e-mail secmoe@ntamar.com.

Ministry of Finance: POB D, Majuro, MH 96960; tel. (625) 7420; fax (625) 3607; e-mail minfin@ntamar.com.

Ministry of Foreign Affairs: POB 1349, Majuro, MH 96960; tel. (625) 3012; fax (623) 4979; e-mail mofatadm@ntamar.com.

Ministry of Health and Environment: POB 16, Majuro, MH 96960; tel. (625) 5660; fax (625) 3432; e-mail mipamohe@ntamar.com.

Ministry of Internal Affairs: POB 18, Majuro, MH 96960; tel. (625) 8240/8718; fax (625) 5353; e-mail rmihpo@ntamar.com.

Ministry of Justice: c/o Office of the Attorney General, Majuro, MH 96960; tel. (625) 3244/8245; fax (625) 5218; e-mail agoffice@ntamar.com.

Ministry of Public Works: POB 1727, Majuro, MH 96960; tel. (625) 8911; fax (625) 3005; e-mail rndadm@ntamar.com.

Ministry of Resources and Development: POB 1727, Majuro, MH 96960; tel. (625) 3206/3277; fax (625) 3821; e-mail rndsec@ntamar.com.

Ministry of Transportation and Communication: POB 1079, Majuro, MH 96960; tel. (625) 3129/8869; fax (625) 3486; e-mail rmimotc@ntamar.com.

Legislature

THE NITIJELA

The Nitijela (lower house) consists of 33 elected members, known as Senators. The most recent election was held on 15 November 1999.

Speaker: Sen. LITOKWA TOMEING.

THE COUNCIL OF IROIJ

The Council of Iroij is the upper house of the bicameral legislature, comprising 12 tribal chiefs who advise the Presidential Cabinet and review legislation affecting customary law or any traditional practice.

Chairman: Iroij KOTAK LOEAK.

Political Organizations

Ralik Ratak Democratic Party: f. 1991; inactive; opposed the late Amata Kabua; Founder TONY DEBRUM.

United Democratic Party: Majuro; inactive; Chair. LITOKWA TOMEING.

Diplomatic Representation

EMBASSIES IN THE MARSHALL ISLANDS

China (Taiwan): POB 1229, Majuro, MH 96960; tel. (625) 4051; fax (625) 4056; Ambassador GARY LIN.

Japan: POB 300, Majuro, MH 96960; Ambassador ATSUO SAEGUSA.

USA: POB 1379, Majuro, MH 96960; tel. (625) 4011; fax (625) 4012; e-mail usembmaj@ntamar.com; internet www.usembassy.state.gov/majuro/; Ambassador GRETA N. MORRIS (designate).

Judicial System

The judicial system consists of the Supreme Court and the High Court, which preside over District and Community Courts, and the Traditional Rights Court.

Supreme Court of the Republic of the Marshall Islands: POB 378, Majuro, MH 96960; tel. (625) 3201; fax (625) 3323; e-mail jutrep@ntamar.com; Chief Justice CARL INGRAM.

District Court of the Republic of the Marshall Islands: Majuro, MH 96960; tel. (625) 3201; fax (625) 3323; Presiding Judge BOKEPOK HELAI.

Traditional Rights Court of the Marshall Islands: Majuro, MH 96960; customary law only; Chief Judge RAILEY ALBERILTAR.

Religion

The population is predominantly Christian, mainly belonging to the Protestant United Church of Christ. The Roman Catholic Church, Assembly of God, Bukot Nan Jesus, Seventh-day Adventists, the Church of Jesus Christ of Latter-day Saints (Mormons), the Full Gospel and the Bahá'í Faith are also represented.

CHRISTIANITY

The Roman Catholic Church

The Apostolic Prefecture of the Marshall Islands included 4,576 adherents at 31 December 2000.

Prefect Apostolic of the Marshall Islands: Rev. Fr JAMES C. GOULD, POB 8, Majuro, MH 96960; tel. (625) 6675; fax (625) 5520; e-mail catholic@ntamar.com.

Protestant Churches

The Marshall Islands come under the auspices of the United Church Board for World Ministries (475 Riverside Drive, New York, NY 10115, USA); Sec. for Latin America, Caribbean and Oceania Dr Patricia Rumer.

BAHÁ'Í FAITH

National Spiritual Assembly: POB 1017, Majuro, MH 96960; e-mail nsabaimh@ntamar.com; internet www.mh.bahai.org; mems resident in 50 localities; Sec. Dr IRENE J. TAAFAKI.

The Press

Kwajalein Hourglass: POB 23, Kwajalein, MH 96555; tel. (355) 3539; e-mail jbennett@kls.usaka.smdc.army.mil; internet www.smdc.army.mil/KWAJ/Hourglass/Hourglass.html; f. 1954; 2 a week; Editor JIM BENNETT; circ. 2,300.

Marshall Islands Journal: POB 14, Majuro, MH 96960; tel. (625) 8143; fax (625) 3136; e-mail journal@ntamar.com; f. 1970; weekly; Editor GIFF JOHNSON; circ. 3,700.

Broadcasting and Communications

TELECOMMUNICATIONS

National Telecommunications Authority (NTA): POB 1169, Majuro, MH 96960; tel. (625) 3852; fax (625) 3952; e-mail aefowler@ntamar.com; internet www.ntamar.com; privatized in 1991; sole provider of local and long-distance services in the Marshall Islands; Chair. ALEX C. BING; Pres. and Gen. Man. ALAN FOWLER.

BROADCASTING

Radio

Radio Marshalls V7AB: POB 3250, Majuro, MH 96960; tel. (625) 8411; fax (625) 5353; govt-owned; commercial; programmes in English and Marshallese; Station Man. ANTARI ELBON.

Marshall Islands Broadcasting Co: POB 19, Majuro, MH 96960; tel. (625) 3250; fax (625) 3505; privately-owned; Chief Information Officer PETER FUCHS.

Television

Alele Museum Foundation: POB 629, Majuro, MH 96960; tel. and fax (625) 3226; broadcasts educational programmes.

Marshall Broadcasting Co Television: POB 19, Majuro, MH 96960; tel. (625) 3413; privately-owned; Chief Information Officer PETER FUCHS.

The US Dept of Defense operates a radio station and a television station (24 hours a day) for the military base on Kwajalein Atoll.

Finance

(cap. = capital; res = reserves; dep. = deposits; amounts in US dollars)

BANKING

Bank of Guam (USA): POB C, Majuro, MH 96960; tel. (625) 3322; fax (625) 3444; internet www.bankofguam.com; Man. ROMY ANGEL; brs in Ebeye, Kwajalein and Majuro.

Bank of the Marshall Islands: POB 116, Majuro, MH 96960; tel. (625) 3636; fax (625) 3661; e-mail bankmar@ntamar.com; internet www.angelfire.com/ms/bankofMI; f. 1982; 40% govt-owned; dep. 39,202.9m., total assets 48,968.1m. (Dec. 2001); Chair. GRANT LABAUN; Gen. Man. PATRICK CHEN; brs in Majuro and Ebeye.

Marshall Islands Development Bank: POB 1048, Majuro, MH 96960; tel. (625) 3230; fax (625) 3309; f. 1989; total assets 19.5m. (Dec. 1992); Man. Dir AMON TIBON.

INSURANCE

Marshalls Insurance Agency: POB 113, Majuro, MH 96960; tel. (625) 3366; fax (625) 3189; Man. TOM LIKOVICH.

Moylan's Insurance Underwriters (Marshall) Inc: POB 727, Majuro, MH 96960; tel. (625) 3220; fax (625) 3361; e-mail marshalls@moylansinsurance.com; internet www.moylansinsurance.com; Pres. JOEL PHILIP.

Trade and Industry

DEVELOPMENT ORGANIZATIONS AND STATE AUTHORITIES

Marshall Islands Environmental Protection Agency: Majuro, MH 96960; Dir ABRAHAM HICKIN (acting).

Marshall Islands Development Authority: Majuro, MH 96960; Gen. Man. DAVID KABUA.

Marshall Islands Marine Resources Authority: Majuro, MH 96960; Dir DANNY WASE.

Kwajalein Atoll Development Authority (KADA): POB 5159, Ebeye Island, Kwajalein, MH 96970; Dir JEBAN RIKLON.

Tobolar Copra Processing Authority: POB G, Majuro, MH 96960; tel. (625) 3494; fax (625) 7206; e-mail tobolar@ntamar.com; Gen. Man. MIKE SLINGER.

CHAMBER OF COMMERCE

Majuro Chamber of Commerce: Majuro, MH 96960; Pres. KIRTLEY PINHO.

UTILITIES

Electricity

Marshalls Energy Company: POB 1439, Majuro, MH 96960; tel. (625) 3829; fax (625) 3397; Gen. Man. WILLIAM F. ROBERTS.

Kwajalein Atoll Joint Utility Resource (KAJUR): POB 5819, Ebeye Island, Kwajalein, MH 96970; tel. (329) 3799; fax (329) 3722.

Water

Majuro Water and Sewage Services: POB 1751, Majuro, MH 96960; e-mail htakju@ntamar.com; internet www.omip.org/majuro.html; Man. HACKNEY TAKJU.

CO-OPERATIVES

These include the Ebeye Co-op, Farmers' Market Co-operative, Kwajalein Employees' Credit Union, Marshall Is Credit Union, Marshall Is Fishermen's Co-operative, Marshall Is Handicraft Co-operative.

Transport

ROADS

Macadam and concrete roads are found in the more important islands. In 1996 there were 152 km of paved roads in the Marshall Islands, mostly on Majuro and Ebeye. Other islands have stone and coral-surfaced roads and tracks. In early 1997 the Marshall Islands received a grant of some US $0.5m. from Japan for a road-improvement project on Majuro. The project was to form part of an extensive programme costing US $15m., which was due to be completed by 1999.

SHIPPING

The Marshall Islands operates an 'offshore' shipping register. At the end of 2001 the merchant fleet comprised 360 vessels, with a combined displacement of some 11.7m. grt.

Vessel Registry:

Marshall Islands Maritime and Corporate Administrators Inc: 11495 Commerce Park Drive, Reston, VA 20191-1507, USA; tel. (703) 620-4880; fax (703) 476-8522; e-mail info@register-iri.com; internet www.register-iri.com; Senior Deputy Commissioner DAVID J. F. BRUCE; Local Office.

The Trust Company of the Marshall Islands Inc: Trust Company Complex, Ajeltake Island, POB 1405, Majuro, MH 96960; tel. (247) 3018; fax (247) 3017; e-mail tcmi@ntamar.com; Pres. GUY EDISON CLAY MAITLAND.

CIVIL AVIATION

In June 1995 the Marshall Islands, Kiribati, Nauru and Tuvalu agreed to begin discussions on the establishment of a joint regional airline. In May 1997 the Marshall Islands signed a bilateral agreement on international air transport with the Federated States of Micronesia. Continental Micronesia operates three flights a week from Honolulu and Guam, Air Marshall Islands provides a daily domestic service and Aloha Airlines provides a weekly service from Honolulu to Kwajalein and to Majuro.

Air Marshall Islands (AMI): POB 1319, Majuro, MH 96960; tel. (625) 3731; fax (625) 3730; e-mail amisales@ntamar.com; f. 1980; internal services for the Marshall Islands; international operations ceased in early 1999; also charter, air ambulance and maritime surveillance operations; Chair. KUNIO LAMARI; CFO NEIL ESCHERRA.

Tourism

Tourism, which has been hindered by the difficulty of gaining access to the islands and a lack of transport facilities, was expected to develop significantly in the late 1990s, owing to the establishment of major resort complexes on Majuro and on Mili Atoll, funded at an estimated cost of US $1,000m. by South Korean investors. In 1997 the Marshall Islands Visitor Authority was established as a private-sector agency (it had previously existed as a small division within the Ministry of Resources and Development). There were 5,399 tourist arrivals in 2001. In that year some 35.6% of visitors came from the USA and 17.3% from Japan. The islands' attractions include excellent opportunities for diving, game-fishing and the exploration of sites and relics of Second World War battles. The Marshall Islands Visitor Authority has implemented a short-term tourism development programme focusing on special-interest tourism markets. In the long term the Visitor Authority hopes to promote the development of small-island resorts throughout the country.

Marshall Islands Visitor Authority: POB 5, Majuro, MH 96960; tel. (625) 6482/5581; fax (625) 6771; e-mail tourism@ntamar.com; internet www.visitmarshallislands.com; Gen. Man. MARK STEGE.

MAURITANIA
Introductory Survey

Location, Climate, Language, Religion, Flag, Capital

The Islamic Republic of Mauritania lies in north-west Africa, with the Atlantic Ocean to the west, Algeria and the disputed territory of Western Sahara (occupied by Morocco) to the north, Mali to the east and south, and Senegal to the south. The climate is hot and dry, particularly in the north, which is mainly desert. Average annual rainfall in the capital in the 1990s was 131 mm (5.1 ins). The 1991 Constitution designates Arabic (which is spoken by the Moorish majority) as the official language, and Arabic, Poular, Wolof and Solinke as the national languages. The black population in the south is largely French-speaking, and French is widely used in commercial and business circles. Islam is the state religion, and the inhabitants are almost all Muslims. The national flag (proportions 2 by 3) comprises a green field, bearing, on the vertical median, a yellow five-pointed star between the upward-pointing horns of a yellow crescent. The capital is Nouakchott.

Recent History

Mauritania, formerly part of French West Africa, achieved full independence on 28 November 1960 (having become a self-governing member of the French Community two years earlier). Moktar Ould Daddah, leader of the Mauritanian Assembly Party (MAP) and Prime Minister since June 1959, became Head of State at independence, and was elected President in August 1961. All parties subsequently merged with the MAP to form the Mauritanian People's Party (MPP), with Ould Daddah as Secretary-General, and Mauritania became a one-party state in 1964. In 1973 Mauritania joined the League of Arab States (see p. 260), and withdrew from the Franc Zone in the following year, as part of a general trend towards the establishment of closer relations with Arab nations.

Under a tripartite agreement of November 1975, Spain ceded Spanish (now Western) Sahara to Mauritania and Morocco, to be apportioned between them. The agreement took effect in February 1976, when Mauritania occupied the southern portion of the territory. Fighting ensued between Moroccan and Mauritanian troops and the guerrilla forces of the Frente Popular para la Liberación de Saguia el-Hamra y Río de Oro (the Polisario Front), which sought independence for Western Sahara. Attacks within Mauritania by Polisario forces proved highly damaging to the economy. Diplomatic links with Algeria, which supported Polisario bases within its borders, were severed in March 1976. Meanwhile, relations with Morocco improved, following that country's renunciation of territorial claims that included Mauritania, and in mid-1977 a joint defence pact was formed.

By 1977 Mauritania was spending two-thirds of its budget on defending territory that promised no economic benefits. The disruption of iron-ore exports, combined with the effects of drought, had brought the country almost to bankruptcy. In July 1978 Ould Daddah was deposed in a bloodless coup, led by the armed forces Chief of Staff, Lt-Col (later Col) Moustapha Ould Mohamed Salek, who took power as Chairman of a Military Committee for National Recovery (MCNR). The Constitution was suspended, and the Government, National Assembly and MPP were dissolved: a 'constitutional charter' vested executive authority in the Chairman of the MCNR. Polisario immediately declared a cease-fire with Mauritania, but the continuing presence of several thousand Moroccan troops in Mauritania impeded a full settlement. The deadlock led to internal political instability, and in April 1979 the MCNR was replaced by a Military Committee for National Salvation (MCNS). Salek continued to head the MCNS, but relinquished the post of Prime Minister to Lt-Col Ahmed Ould Bouceif. The MCNS adopted a new charter, assuming legislative power for itself and separating the roles of Head of State and Head of Government. Bouceif died in an air crash in May, and the MCNS appointed Lt-Col Mohamed Khouna Ould Haidalla in his place. Salek resigned in June, and was replaced as titular Head of State by Lt-Col Mohamed Mahmoud Ould Ahmed Louly. In July Polisario announced a resumption of hostilities against Mauritania. Later that month the Organization of African Unity (OAU, now the African Union, see p. 130) recommended that a referendum

be held to determine the future of the disputed region. These events provided the impetus for Mauritania's withdrawal from the war: Haidalla renounced Mauritania's territorial claims in Western Sahara, and a peace treaty was signed with Polisario in August. Morocco announced its annexation of the entire territory, and diplomatic relations between Mauritania and Algeria were re-established.

Haidalla succeeded Louly as Head of State in January 1980; he retained the posts of Prime Minister and Minister of Defence until December, when Sid'Ahmed Ould Bneijara was appointed premier in a largely civilian Council of Ministers. A draft Constitution, envisaging a multi-party system, was prepared, pending approval in a national referendum. However, an attempted coup in March 1981 prompted Haidalla to end civilian participation in the Government. The new Prime Minister, Lt-Col (later Col) Maawiya Ould Sid'Ahmed Taya (a prominent member of the MCNS and the army Chief of Staff) assumed the defence portfolio in April, and the draft Constitution was abandoned. Another coup plot was discovered in February 1982, resulting in the arrest and imprisonment of its leaders, Salek and Bneijara.

In March 1984 widespread student unrest was denounced by the Government as a Libyan-backed 'destabilization plot'. Haidalla again assumed the positions of Prime Minister and Minister of Defence, reappointing Col Taya as army Chief of Staff. On 12 December, while Haidalla was temporarily absent from the country, Taya assumed the presidency in a bloodless coup and also took the defence portfolio in the new Government. An amnesty was proclaimed for all political prisoners and exiles, including Ould Daddah (then in exile in Tunisia), Salek and Bneijara. Haidalla was detained upon his return to Mauritania, but was released, with five of his associates, in December 1988.

Although the Taya administration gained international financial support for a major programme of economic adjustment, an escalation of ethnic tensions threatened internal stability. In late 1986 the conviction of 20 prominent black activists, on charges of 'undermining national unity', led to civil disturbances and to increased activity by organizations opposed to what they claimed to be the oppression of black Mauritanians by the light-skinned Moorish community. Following the discovery of a coup plot in October 1987, three military officers of the black Toucouleur ethnic group were sentenced to death, and 41 others were imprisoned. Allegations that some detainees had been tortured were subsequently made by a Senegalese-based opposition movement, the Mauritanian African Liberation Forces (MALF), which conducted a sporadic campaign of attacks on official targets during the late 1980s and early 1990s. In January 1988 it was reported that more than 500 black personnel had been expelled from the armed forces, as a result of disturbances following the executions of the convicted officers.

In late 1990 many arrests followed the disclosure of an alleged coup plot, in which the Senegalese Government denied any involvement (see below). As part of clemency measures, announced from March 1991, the Government stated that almost all Mauritania's political prisoners had been freed, although other sources disputed this statement.

A draft Constitution, providing for the introduction of a multi-party political system, was submitted to a national referendum on 12 July 1991. Official reports stated that 97.9% of those who voted (85.3% of the registered electorate) endorsed the proposals, which accorded extensive powers to the President of the Republic, although opposition groups contested this result. Pending the installation of the organs of State provided for in the new document, Taya and the MCNS were to remain in power. Following the adoption of the Constitution, legislation permitting the registration of political parties was promulgated: among the first organizations to be accorded official status was the Democratic and Social Republican Party (DSRP), which was closely linked with Taya and was criticized by opposition movements for its privileged access to the state apparatus.

Four candidates contested the presidential election on 17 January 1992. Taya was elected President by 62.7% of the poll (51.7% of the registered electorate voted); his nearest rival was

Ahmed Ould Daddah, with 32.8% of votes cast. The defeated candidates alleged electoral fraud and appealed unsuccessfully to the Supreme Court to declare the election invalid. Independent observers reported that they did not regard the poll as fraudulent. Unrest in the aftermath of the election resulted in at least two deaths and about 160 arrests.

Six opposition parties withdrew their candidates prior to legislative elections, which were held on 6 and 13 March 1992, protesting that certain electoral procedures were unduly favourable to the DSRP. Taya's party took 67 of the 79 seats in the National Assembly, and independent candidates won 10 of the remaining twelve seats; a low rate of participation by voters was reported. Following elections to the Senate, on 3 and 10 April, the new, 56-member upper house (which was elected by municipal leaders) included 36 DSRP members and 17 independents (one other party had, unsuccessfully, presented candidates for election); three seats were reserved for representatives of Mauritanians resident abroad. Taya was inaugurated as President on 18 April. He named the hitherto Minister of Finance, Sidi Mohamed Ould Boubacar, a civilian, as Prime Minister, to lead a Government that included three black ministers, one opposition representative, and only one member of the military.

In May 1993 the National Assembly approved legislation pardoning all those convicted of offences perpetrated in connection with 'armed operations and acts of violence and terrorism' in the three years preceding Taya's inauguration as elected President. Opponents of the measure protested that it exonerated members of the armed forces for crimes committed during a period of severe repression of the black community.

At Mauritania's first multi-party municipal elections, in January and February 1994, the DSRP won control of 172 of the country's 208 administrative districts. Ahmed Ould Daddah's Union of Democratic Forces—New Era (UDF—NE) secured control of 17 districts, the remainder being taken by independent candidates. Shortly before the first round of voting the President of the unauthorized Mauritanian Human Rights Association (MHRA), Cheikh Sadibou Camara (who was also a member of a prominent opposition party, the Union for Democracy and Progress—UDP), had been detained for several days, reportedly on charges of incitement to agitation. Camara had apparently reported to a visiting delegation of international human rights organizations that children of Harratin (mainly dark-skinned Moors who had formerly been slaves) had been abducted and sold into slavery: Mauritanian law regards any reference to a return to slavery (which had been prohibited by law on several occasions, most recently in 1980) as injurious to national unity.

In September 1994 more than 90 alleged members of illicit Islamist organizations were arrested, although in October an amnesty was granted to the detainees following the broadcast of 'confessions', in which several detainees, including prominent members of the UDF—NE, had admitted their membership of reputedly extremist groups. The Taya Government subsequently prohibited the delivery of political speeches in places of worship and outlawed several Islamist organizations.

Government changes in February 1995 included the appointment of new Ministers of Finance and of Defence. Internal tensions within the UDF—NE threatened to undermine the influence of the party, as dissident groups complained of excessive centralization around Ould Daddah's leadership. In March the Movement of Independent Democrats, which until 1994 had been a member of the UDF—NE, announced that it was to join the DSRP. In July several UDF—NE members were reported to have defected to the UDP. In mid-1995, none the less, six opposition parties (including the UDF—NE and the UDP) announced that they had agreed a series of joint demands regarding future elections, including the compilation of an accurate voters' register, the formulation of a new electoral code, and guarantees of judicial independence.

In October 1995 the Taya administration declared the Iraqi Ambassador *persona non grata* and demanded his departure from Mauritania. The expulsion coincided with reports of a foiled coup in Mauritania, allegedly sponsored by the Iraqi Government, which, it was claimed, had funded 'secret organizations' to conduct espionage in Mauritania, and a series of arrests ensued; among those detained were two parliamentarians (one from the DSRP, the other from the UDP), the Secretary-General of the National Assembly and army officers. In December 52 defendants stood trial on charges of forming an illegal organization; all 52 were discharged on appeal in January 1996.

In January 1996 Taya appointed Cheikh el Avia Ould Mohamed Khouna (hitherto Minister of Fisheries and Marine Economy) as Prime Minister, and a new Council of Ministers was formed. In March the UDP announced its intention to boycott elections to renew one-third of the Senate, scheduled for April, in protest at the Government's failure to address the opposition's demands. The DSRP won 17 of the 18 seats contested; an independent candidate took the remaining seat.

At legislative elections, held on 11 and 18 October 1996, the DSRP won 71 of the 79 seats in the National Assembly. The Rally for Democracy and Unity (RDU), closely allied with the administration, also secured a seat. Action for Change (AC), which sought to represent the interests of Harratin, was the only opposition party to win a seat in the Assembly; six independent candidates also secured election. Several opposition parties disputed the validity of the results, and denounced censorship measures imposed in the period preceding the elections. Moreover, the UDP, which had participated in the first round of the elections, withdrew from the second round in protest at what it alleged were unfair electoral procedures. Later in October the Prime Minister named a new Council of Ministers.

In January 1997 several opposition leaders, including Messaoud Ould Boulkheir, the AC Chairman, and Mohamed Hassaoud Ould Ismael, the Secretary-General of the People's Progressive Party (PPP), were arrested on charges of maintaining 'suspicious relations' with Libya. Although Ould Boulkheir, Ould Ismael and several others had been freed by February, five PPP members received prison sentences for conspiring to break the law; in April the court of appeal acquitted four of the five convicted. In February five prominent opposition parties, including the AC and the UDF—NE, formed a coalition, the Forum of Opposition Parties (FOP), which subsequently announced that it would boycott the forthcoming presidential election.

At the presidential election, held on 12 December 1997, and contested by four candidates, Taya was returned to office with 90.9% of the valid votes cast; his nearest rival, Mohamed Lemine Ch'Bih Ould Cheikh Melainine (who had resigned from the DSRP in 1996), obtained 7.0% of the vote. Opposition parties alleged that there had been widespread electoral fraud and disputed the official rate of voter participation, of 73.8%. Taya subsequently appointed Mohamed Lemine Ould Guig, a university academic, as Prime Minister, and a new Council of Ministers, which included three women, was installed. In April 1998 the DSRP won 17 seats in elections to renew 18 seats in the Senate; an independent candidate took the remaining seat. In November Cheikh el Avia Ould Mohamed Khouna (who had previously held the post in 1996) was appointed as Prime Minister.

Meanwhile, in March 1998 internal divisions in the UDF—NE resulted in a split in the party, with two rival factions, led by Ahmed Ould Daddah and Moustapha Ould Bedreddine, both claiming leadership of the party. In December Ould Daddah and two other members of his faction were placed under house arrest after they demanded that a public inquiry be held into allegations that Mauritania had agreed to allow Israeli nuclear waste to be stored underground in its territory. They were acquitted in March 1999 of charges of threatening public order.

Municipal elections, held in early 1999 were boycotted by the principal opposition parties. In November the Government banned the pro-Iraqi Baathist National Vanguard Party (Taliaa), a constituent member of the FOP, following its criticism of the Mauritanian Government's decision to establish full diplomatic relations with Israel in the previous month. Partial elections to the Senate took place on 7 and 14 April 2000. The DSRP secured 13 of the 18 contested seats, the UDP and the National Union for Democracy and Development each won one seat, and independent candidates won three seats. Later that month Ould Daddah was detained two days prior to a meeting of the UDF—NE, at which he was expected to address the acquisition of wealth by associates of President Taya. Ould Daddah was released after five days, although a ban on public gatherings implemented following his arrest remained in force.

In June 2000 security forces used tear gas to disperse a meeting of at least 4,000 UDF—NE members in Nouadhibou. In August concerns regarding increasing press censorship were heightened by the Government's seizure of copies of four weekly news publications; according to an international press freedom group, Reporters sans frontières, seven publications had been subject to such seizures since the beginning of 2000, in accordance with press legislation that permitted the Government to suppress the distribution of any publication it regarded as likely to 'undermine the principles of Islam or the credibility of the State'.

A government reshuffle took place in September 2000. From October, following the onset of the second Palestinian *intifada* (uprising) in Israel and the Palestinian Autonomous Areas (q.v.), the Mauritanian Government experienced increasing pressure from a number of opposition groups, including the UDF —NE, to break off diplomatic relations with Israel. In October several pro-Palestinian demonstrations in Nouakchott and Nouadhibou led to violent anti-Israeli protests. Arrests of members of clandestine Islamist groups and of militants of the UDF —NE were reported. In late October the Council of Ministers held an extraordinary session in which the UDF—NE was officially dissolved, on the grounds that the party had incited violence and sought to damage Mauritanian national interests. Several members of the party's executive committee were detained in November. A demonstration in Nouadhibou by supporters of the UDF—NE reportedly attracted 15,000 protesters (the party was believed to have around 100,000 members). Ould Daddah refused to recognize the dissolution of the party, and the UDF—NE's partners in the FOP condemned the Government's action as unconstitutional. Six detained officials of the party began a hunger strike, although four of these were released by the end of November. Meanwhile, the faction of the UDF—NE led by Moustapha Ould Bedreddine, which remained authorized, restyled itself as the Union of Progressive Forces (UPF).

In December 2000 President Taya announced that an element of proportional representation would be introduced in subsequent elections to the National Assembly, and that the State would seek to facilitate funding and equal access to the media for all parties. The National Assembly approved these measures in January 2001, although the radical opposition, including the FOP, continued to demand the establishment of an independent electoral commission and the reregistration of the banned Taliaa and the UDF—NE. (In January the Supreme Court rejected an appeal filed by Ould Daddah against the dissolution of the UDF—NE.)

In January 2001 a government reshuffle included the appointment of a new Minister of Foreign Affairs and Co-operation, Dah Ould Abdi. In April it was announced that six new political groupings had been officially recognized, including a breakaway group from the AC, the Alliance for Justice and Democracy, led by Kabeh Abdoulaye. A further minor government reshuffle was effected in mid-May. Meanwhile, in early April Mohamed Lemine Ch'Bih Ould Cheikh Melainine, now the leader of the Popular Front (PF—a constituent party of the FOP), was arrested on charges of conspiring with Libya to commit acts of sabotage and terrorism. Human rights groups criticized the conduct of his trial, including its relocation from Nouakchott to the remote location of Aïoun and the refusal to grant visas to prominent legal observers from overseas. In mid-June Melainine was sentenced to five years' imprisonment; in protest at this decision, the Mauritanian Renewal Party, one of the new parties officially registered in April, announced its withdrawal from the governing coalition.

Some 15 political parties contested legislative and municipal elections, held on 19 and 26 October 2001, although independent candidacies were prohibited. An electoral turn-out of some 55% was reported. The DSRP won 64 of the 81 seats in the enlarged National Assembly, and the RDU and the UDP, both allied with the ruling party, each secured three seats. The AC was the most successful of the opposition parties, winning four seats, while the UPF and the newly formed Rally of Democratic Forces (RDF), which replaced the banned UDF—NE, also each took three seats, and the PF secured the remaining seat; the People's Progressive Alliance (PPA, as the PPP was now known) boycotted the elections, having previously demanded the postponement of polling. The DSRP secured control of more than four-fifths of Mauritania's districts at the concurrent municipal elections, although opposition parties had their greatest success in Nouakchott, securing control of six of the capital's nine districts. In November President Taya reappointed Cheikh el Avia Ould Mohamed Khouna as Prime Minister, and the Council of Ministers was reshuffled; 14 ministers from the previous administration were retained.

In January 2002 Ould Daddah was elected President of the RDF; four former vice-presidents of the UDF—NE were also appointed to the 12-member executive committee of the RDF. In

that month the Government officially dissolved the AC. The Minister of Communication and Relations with Parliament, Cheyakh Ould Ely, accused the party of promoting racism and extremism, and of attempting to undermine national unity and good relations with Senegal. In February the Supreme Court rejected an appeal by the AC against its dissolution.

At partial senatorial elections, held on 12 and 19 April 2002, the DSRP won 17 of the 18 contested seats. The remaining seat was won by the RDF, the first time part of the radical opposition had gained representation in the Senate. In August the Convention for Change (CC), an organization including many former members of the AC, and led by Ould Boulkheir, was denied the right to register as a political party; it was reported that a government spokesman had declared that the CC was simply a renamed form of the AC and, as such, a continued threat to national unity.

In October 2002 the UFP announced that it was to organize a series of meetings intended to promote a 'national dialogue' between the authorities and the opposition parties; the first such meeting was scheduled to occur at the end of October. However, later that month seven other opposition parties, including the CC (which remained banned), the PF, the PPA and the RDF, formed a new grouping, the United Opposition Framework (UOF), which also stated as its purpose the co-ordination of dialogue between the opposition and the Government pertaining to democratic reform; the UFP was, notably, excluded from the UOF, reportedly at the initiative of the RFD. Consequently, the initial meeting proposed by the UFP was postponed indefinitely, and, expressing discontent at the situation, in mid-November the UFP announced its withdrawal from the National Assembly. As a result of the withdrawal of the three UFP deputies from the Assembly, the group of opposition deputies was dissolved, as it was now reduced to eight members, less than the 10 required for the formation of a parliamentary group. None the less, the UFP emphasized that it remained prepared to participate in any dialogue on democratic reform together with other opposition groups.

On 27 October 2002 a government reorganization was effected. Notably, Dah Ould Abdi was replaced as Minister of Foreign Affairs and Co-operation by Mohamed Ould Tobar; new Ministers of Rural Development and the Environment and of Health were also appointed.

A long-standing border dispute with Senegal was exacerbated by the deaths, in April 1989, of two Senegalese farmers, who had been involved in a dispute regarding grazing rights with Mauritanian livestock-breeders. The ensuing crisis served to illustrate the persistence of mutual ethnic and economic rivalries. Mauritanian nationals resident in Senegal were attacked, and their businesses (primarily those of the retail trade) looted, while Senegalese nationals in Mauritania and black Mauritanians suffered similar aggression. By early May it was believed that several hundred people, mostly Senegalese, had been killed. Operations to repatriate nationals of both countries commenced, with international assistance. Amid allegations that the Mauritanian authorities had begun to instigate expulsions of the indigenous black population to Senegal or to Mali, a prominent human rights organization, Amnesty International, expressed concern at the reported violation of black Mauritanians' rights. Mauritania and Senegal suspended diplomatic relations in August 1989, and sporadic outbreaks of violence were reported later that year. OAU mediation efforts in early 1990 were thwarted by military skirmishes in the border region, resulting in several deaths.

In late 1990 the Senegalese Government denied accusations made by the Mauritanian authorities that it was implicated in an alleged attempt to overthrow Taya. In December the arrests of large numbers of black Mauritanians were reported. In early 1991 Mauritanian naval vessels were reported to have opened fire on Senegalese fishing boats, apparently in Senegal's territorial waters; in March several deaths were reported to have resulted from a military engagement on Senegalese territory, following an incursion by Senegalese troops into Mauritania.

Following renewed diplomatic activity, diplomatic relations with Senegal were resumed in April 1992, and the process of reopening the border began in May. However, Mauritanian refugees in Senegal insisted that, as long as the Taya Government refused to recognize their national identity (*mauritanité*) and land and property rights, they would not return to Mauritania. In September 1993 the Mauritanian authorities announced that Senegalese nationals would henceforth be required to fulfil certain criteria, including currency-exchange requirements, before being allowed to remain in (or to enter) Mauritania. In January 1996 several hundred Mauritanian refugees staged demonstrations in northern Senegal, protesting at the Mauritanian Government's proposed repatriation programme, and insisting that their earlier demands be met and that the repatriation process be organized by the office of the UN High Commissioner for Refugees in co-operation with the two Governments. By late 2000 the number of Mauritanian refugees in Senegal had declined to 19,800 (compared with 65,500 in mid-1995). Meanwhile, in early June 2000 relations between Mauritania and Senegal deteriorated after Mauritania accused the new Senegalese administration of relaunching an irrigation project, which involved the use of joint waters from the Senegal river, in contravention of the Organisation pour la mise en valeur du fleuve Sénégal project (see p. 341). The dispute escalated when the Mauritanian authorities requested that all of its citizens living in Senegal return home and issued the estimated 100,000 Senegalese nationals living in Mauritania with a 15-day deadline by which to leave the country. In mid-June, following mediation by King Muhammad VI of Morocco and the Presidents of The Gambia and Mali, the Mauritanian Minister of the Interior announced that the decision to expel Senegalese citizens had been withdrawn and that Mauritanians living in Senegal could remain there. President Wade of Senegal visited Mauritania later that month and announced that the irrigation project had been abandoned. In April 2001 President Taya's presence as guest of honour at a ceremony in Dakar to commemorate the 41st anniversary of the independence of Senegal was widely regarded as indicating an improvement in relations between the countries.

Meanwhile, in April 1994 Mauritania, Mali and Senegal agreed to strengthen military co-operation in order to improve joint border security. In mid-1996, at the conclusion of a meeting in Nouakchott of their ministers responsible for the interior, the three countries established joint security measures on their common borders. In August 1999 representatives of the Malian, Senegalese and Mauritanian Governments signed an agreement, which provided for the establishment of a special operational unit drawn from the police forces of the three countries to combat border crime.

Diplomatic relations between Mauritania and Morocco were severed in 1981, following accusations, denied by both countries, of involvement in mutual destabilization attempts. In 1983 Mauritania sought to improve relations between the Maghreb countries (Algeria, Morocco, Mauritania, Tunisia and Libya) and was a signatory of the Maghreb Fraternity and Co-operation Treaty, drafted by Algeria and Tunisia. Relations with Morocco again deteriorated from February 1984, when Mauritania announced its recognition of the Sahrawi Arab Democratic Republic (the Western Saharan state proclaimed by Polisario in 1976), although Taya restored diplomatic relations with Morocco in April 1985. In February 1989 Mauritania was a founder member, with Algeria, Libya, Morocco and Tunisia, of the Union of the Arab Maghreb (UMA, see p. 342). In September 2001 King Muhammad of Morocco paid a three-day official visit to Mauritania, aimed at improving bilateral relations between the two countries.

Mauritania's relations with France improved significantly from the early 1990s, following the introduction of multi-party institutions. Bilateral relations were consolidated in September 1997 and in February 1998 as a result of reciprocal official visits made by President Jacques Chirac of France and Taya, respectively. However, relations deteriorated abruptly in 1999, following the arrest by the French authorities in July of Ali Ould Dah, a captain in the Mauritanian army, who was attending a training course in France. Ould Dah was charged with the torture, in 1991, of fellow Mauritanian soldiers suspected of participating in the unsuccessful attempt to overthrow the Taya administration in 1990. The Mauritanian Government responded by suspending military co-operation with France and introducing visas for French nationals visiting Mauritania. In late September a court in Montpellier, France, ordered Ould Dah's release from custody, although he was required to remain in France until the end of legal proceedings. By April 2000, however, Ould Dah had illicitly returned to Mauritania. Relations with France appeared to improve following the election of a new, centre-right, Government there in 2002, and in September of that year the French Minister of Defence, Michèle Alliot-Marie, met Taya in Nouakchott, and affirmed that co-operation between the two countries was to be strengthened.

In November 1995 Mauritania signed an agreement to recognize and establish relations with Israel. The Libyan Government denounced these measures, promptly closed its embassy in Mauritania and severed all economic assistance to the country. Diplomatic relations between the two countries were, however, restored in March 1997. In October 1998 Mauritania's Minister of Foreign Affairs and Co-operation visited Israel, where he held talks with the Prime Minister, Binyamin Netanyahu. The Arab League strongly criticized the visit, claiming that it contravened the League's resolutions on the suspension of the normalization of relations with Israel, and threatened to impose sanctions on Mauritania. Widespread controversy was provoked both domestically, and in Arab countries, by the establishment of full diplomatic relations between Mauritania and Israel in October 1999. (Of Arab countries, only Egypt and Jordan had taken such a step, under the terms of their respective peace treaties with Israel.) In November Mauritania broke off diplomatic relations with Iraq, following allegations that Iraq was planning acts of subversion in Mauritania, with the assistance of the Taliaa political party, which Mauritania banned. Following the resumption of the Palestinian uprising in Israel and the Palestinian Autonomous Areas in September 2000, the Mauritanian Government came under renewed pressure, both domestically and internationally, to suspend diplomatic relations with Israel, although Taya's Government refused to accede to these demands. In protest against Mauritanian policy towards Israel, Iraq refused admittance to a Mauritanian aircraft that was to bring humanitarian aid to Iraq in early November 2000, and in March 2001 Syria reduced its diplomatic representation in Nouakchott to the level of a chargé d'affaires, and closed its cultural centre in Mauritania. A visit by the Mauritanian Minister of Foreign Affairs and Co-operation, Dah Ould Abdi, to Israel in May 2001, when he met Israeli Prime Minister Ariel Sharon and President Moshe Katsav, and entered into negotiations with the Minister of Foreign Affairs, Shimon Peres, provoked further controversy, particularly as a result of an escalation in the Israeli–Palestinian conflict and an appeal by the Arab League, issued earlier that month, for all member countries to cease political contacts with Israel. A further meeting between Peres, Taya and Ould Abdi, in Nouakchott, in early October 2002, provoked further controversy.

Mauritania withdrew from the Economic Community of West African States (see p. 187), with effect from 31 December 2000, owing to decisions adopted by the organization at its summit in December 1999, including the integration of the armed forces of member states and the removal of internal border controls and tariffs.

Government

The Constitution that was approved in a national referendum on 12 July 1991 vests executive power in the President of the Republic (who is elected by universal adult suffrage for a period of six years). The bicameral legislature comprises an 81-member National Assembly (elected by universal suffrage for five years, with 20% of its membership being elected by a form of proportional representation, with effect from the elections held in October 2001) and a 56-member Senate (elected by municipal leaders with a six-year mandate—part of its membership being elected every two years). All elections are conducted in the context of a multi-party political system. The President of the Republic is empowered to appoint a Prime Minister, who is designated Head of Government.

For the purpose of local administration, Mauritania is divided into 12 provinces and the capital city of Nouakchott, together comprising a total of 216 districts.

Defence

In August 2002 the total armed forces were estimated to number 15,750 men: army 15,000, navy about 500, air force 250. Full-time membership of paramilitary forces totalled about 5,000. Military service is by authorized conscription, and lasts for two years. The defence budget for 2002 was estimated at UM 7,100m.

Economic Affairs

In 2001, according to estimates by the World Bank, Mauritania's gross national income (GNI), measured at average 1999–2001 prices, was US $974m., equivalent to $350 per head (or $1,680 on an international purchasing-power parity basis). During 1990–2001, it was estimated, the population increased at an average annual rate of 2.8%, while gross domestic product (GDP) per head increased, in real terms, by an average of 1.1%

per year. Overall GDP increased, in real terms, at an average annual rate of 4.1% in 1990–2001; GDP increased by 4.5% in 2001 and by an estimated 4.2% in 2002.

Agriculture (including forestry and fishing) contributed 21.0% of GDP in 2001. In that year about 52.6% of the labour force were employed in the sector. Owing to the unsuitability of much of the land for crop cultivation, output of staple foods (millet, sorghum, rice and pulses) is insufficient for the country's needs. Livestock-rearing is the principal occupation of the rural population. Fishing, which in 1999 provided 41.4% of export earnings, supplies 5%–10% of annual GDP and up to 30% of budgetary revenue, and also makes a significant contribution to domestic food requirements. During 1990–2001, according to the World Bank, agricultural GDP increased by an average of 4.7% per year. Agricultural GDP increased by 2.9% in 2000, but declined by 0.3% in 2001.

Industry (including mining, manufacturing, construction and power) provided 30.4% of GDP in 2001. An estimated 11.6% of the labour force were employed in the industrial sector in 1994. During 1990–2001, according to the World Bank, industrial GDP increased at an average annual rate of 2.4%. Industrial GDP increased by 6.7% in 2000 and by 1.3% in 2001.

Mining contributed 14.3% of GDP in 2001. The principal activity in this sector is the extraction of iron ore, exports of which contributed 54.6% of total merchandise export earnings in 2001. Gypsum, salt, gold and copper are also mined. Other exploitable mineral resources include diamonds, phosphates, sulphur, peat, manganese and uranium. In October 1999 highly valuable blue granite deposits were discovered in the north of the country. Many international companies were involved in offshore petroleum exploration in Mauritania in the early 2000s, with reserves at the offshore Shafr el Khanjar and Chinguetti fields estimated at 450m.–1,000m. barrels. In September 2000 a five-year programme intended to accelerate the growth of the mining sector commenced, with a US $16.5m. loan from the World Bank. The GDP of the mining sector declined by an average of 2.7% per year in 1997–2001, according to the IMF. Mining GDP increased by 9.1% in 2000, but declined by 7.4% in 2001.

The manufacturing sector contributed 9.3% of GDP in 2001. Fish-processing (which contributed 4.6% of GDP in 2001) is the most important activity. The processing of minerals (including imported petroleum) is also of some significance. According to the World Bank, manufacturing GDP increased at an average annual rate of 1.4% in 1990–2001; it increased by 2.7% in 2000 and by 4.4% in 2001.

Mauritania began to utilize electricity generated at hydro-electric installations constructed under the Organisation pour la mise en valeur du fleuve Sénégal (OMVS, see p. 341) project in late 2002, thus reducing the country's dependence on power generated at thermal stations. Imports of petroleum products comprised an estimated 13.6% of the value of merchandise imports in 1999.

The services sector contributed 48.6% of GDP in 2001, and engaged an estimated 25.8% of the labour force in 1994. According to the World Bank, the combined GDP of the services sector increased by an average rate of 5.2% per year during 1990–2001. Services GDP increased by 6.3% in 2000 and by 11.4% in 2001.

In 2001 Mauritania recorded a visible trade deficit of US $11.5m., and a deficit of $21.3m. on the current account of the balance of payments. In 2001 the principal source of imports (23.3%) was France; other major suppliers were the Belgo-Luxembourg Economic Union, Spain and Italy. The principal markets for exports in that year were Italy (15.4%), France (15.1%), Spain and Japan. The principal exports in 1999 were iron ore and fish, crustaceans and molluscs. The principal imports were foodstuffs, capital goods, petroleum products and vehicles and components.

Mauritania's overall budget deficit for 2001 was UM 9,800m., equivalent to 4.0% of GDP. Mauritania's total external debt was US $2,500m. at the end of 2000, of which $2,150m. was long-term public debt. In that year the cost of debt-servicing was equivalent to 25.9% of the value of exports of goods and services. The annual rate of inflation averaged 5.9% in 1990–2001; consumer prices increased by an average of 3.3% in 2000 and by 4.7% in 2001.

Mauritania is a member of the Islamic Development Bank (see p. 257), of the OMVS (see p. 341) and of the Union of the Arab Maghreb (see p. 342).

Mauritania's economy is largely dependent on fishing and on the exploitation of iron ore. Economic adjustment programmes have been undertaken since the late 1980s, including agreements with the IMF and the World Bank, resulting in the liberalization and restructuring of the economy. In 1998 an agreement was signed with the World Bank to reduce the country's multilateral debt substantially, and in July 1999 the IMF approved a three-year loan worth US $56.53m. to support the Government's 1999–2002 economic programme. In February 2000 Mauritania became one of the first countries to receive assistance under the joint IMF/World Bank Heavily Indebted Poor Countries initiative, which would amount to a reduction of Mauritania's debt by $622m., representing savings of an estimated 40% of yearly debt-service obligations; in June 2002 Mauritania became the sixth country to reach 'completion point' under the initiative. By late 2000 the share of the state's holding in the national airline had been reduced from 72% to 11%. A majority share in the state telecommunications company was sold in 2001. From the late 1980s government revenue has been bolstered by the sale of fishing licences to foreign fleets, although over-fishing in the mid 1990s led Mauritania to impose an annual moratorium (for a period of one–two months) in order to allow the replenishment of stocks. In July 2001 the European Union (EU) renewed its fishing agreement with Mauritania. In return for increased financial aid (of some €430m. during 2001–06), EU vessels were granted improved fishing rights in Mauritania's waters. In the early 2000s the services sector has been a major source of economic growth, in particular in the areas of trade, transport and telecommunications, while considerable potential exists for the expansion of activities related to tourism. Although a severe drought in late 2002, which resulted in a much depleted cereals harvest, and a lower than average fish catch, ensured that growth in that year, at 4.2%, was lower than anticipated, economic indicators in the early 2000s were generally favourable, and considerable progress was made in the implementation of structural reforms. A substantial reorganization and simplification of the taxation system was to be implemented in 2003, and, following initial difficulties, the transfer to majority private ownership of the state electricity company was expected to be completed by mid-2004. Meanwhile, further economic progress remained largely dependent on the diversification of Mauritania's production base. GDP growth of 5.3% was projected for 2003.

Education

Primary education, which is officially compulsory, begins at six years of age and lasts for six years. In 1999/2000 total enrolment at primary schools was equivalent to 84.3% of children in the relevant age-group (86.8% of boys; 81.8% of girls). Secondary education begins at 12 years of age and lasts for six years, comprising two cycles of three years each. The total enrolment at secondary schools in that year was equivalent to only 18.4% of children in the appropriate age-group (21.4% of boys; 15.4% of girls). In 1998/99 a total of 12,912 students were enrolled at Mauritania's four higher education institutions (including the Université de Nouakchott, which was founded in 1981). In 2001 a UN project was initiated to address sexual inequality in the Mauritanian education system, which was particularly evident at higher education institutions, where only 16.6% of students were female in 1998. Total expenditure on education in 1998 was UM 6,197.8m. (equivalent to 27.5% of total government expenditure). In 1999 total expenditure on education amounted to UM 6,557.6m.

Public Holidays

2003: 1 January (New Year's Day), 12 February* (Tabaski—Id al-Adha, Feast of the Sacrifice), 5 March* (Islamic New Year), 1 May (Labour Day), 14 May* (Mouloud, Birth of Muhammad), 25 May (African Liberation Day, anniversary of the OAU's foundation), 10 July (Armed Forces Day), 24 September* (Leilat al-Meiraj, Ascension of Muhammad), 26 November* (Korité—Id al-Fitr, end of Ramadan), 28 November (Independence Day).

2004: 1 January (New Year's Day), 2 February* (Tabaski—Id al-Adha, Feast of the Sacrifice), 22 February* (Islamic New Year), 1 May (Labour Day), 2 May* (Mouloud, Birth of Muhammad), 25 May (African Liberation Day, anniversary of the OAU's foundation), 10 July (Armed Forces Day), 12 September* (Leilat al-Meiraj, Ascension of Muhammad), 14 November* (Korité—Id al-Fitr, end of Ramadan), 28 November (Independence Day).

*These holidays are determined by the Islamic lunar calendar and may vary by one or two days from the dates given.

Weights and Measures
The metric system is in force.

Statistical Survey

Figures exclude Mauritania's section of Western Sahara, annexed in 1976 and relinquished in 1979.

Source (unless otherwise stated): Office National de la Statistique, BP 240, Nouakchott; tel. 525-28-80; fax 525-51-70; e-mail webmaster@ons.mr; internet www.ons.mr.

Area and Population

AREA, POPULATION AND DENSITY

Area (sq km)	1,030,700*
Population (census results)	
5–20 April 1988	1,864,236†
1–15 November 2000‡	
Males	1,240,414
Females.	1,307,743
Total	2,548,157
Density (per sq km) at November 2000	2.5

* 397,950 sq miles.
† Including an estimate of 224,095 for the nomad population.
‡ Figures are provisional and include nomads, totalling 123,009 (males 62,947, females 60,062), enumerated during 10 March–20 April 2001.

ETHNIC GROUPS (percentage of total, 1995): Moor 81.5; Wolof 6.8; Toucouleur 5.3; Sarakholé 2.8; Peul 1.1; Others 2.5 (Source: La Francophonie).

REGIONS
(census of November 2000, provisional figures)

Region	Area ('000 sq km)	Population*	Chief town
Hodh Ech Chargui . .	183	275,288	Néma
Hodh el Gharbi . . .	53	219,167	Aïoun el Atrous
Assaba	37	249,596	Kiffa
Gorgol	14	248,980	Kaédi
Brakna	33	240,167	Aleg
Trarza	68	252,664	Rosso
Adrar	215	60,847	Atâr
Dakhlet-Nouadhibou .	22	75,976	Nouadhibou
Tagant	95	61,984	Tidjikja
Guidimaka	10	186,697	Sélibaby
Tiris Zemmour . . .	253	53,586	Zouïrât
Inchiri	47	11,322	Akjoujt
Nouakchott (district) .	1	611,883	Nouakchott
Total	1,030	2,548,157	

* Including nomad population, enumerated during 10 March–20 April 2001.

PRINCIPAL TOWNS
(population at census of 1988)

Nouakchott (capital).	393,325		Rosso	27,783
Nouadhibou . . .	59,198		Zouïrât	25,892
Kaédi	30,515		Atâr	21,366
Kiffa	29,292			

2000 (census, provisional figures): Nouakchott 611,883; Nouadhibou 75,976; Zouïrât 44,718.

Source: Thomas Brinkhoff, *City Population* (internet www.citypopulation.de).

BIRTHS AND DEATHS
(UN estimates, annual averages)

	1985–90	1990–95	1995–2000
Birth rate (per 1,000)	44.3	43.9	43.5
Death rate (per 1,000)	16.9	16.2	15.4

Source: UN, *World Population Prospects: The 2000 Revision*.

Expectation of life (WHO estimates, years at birth): 52.0 (males 50.9; females 53.1) in 2001 (Source: WHO, *World Health Report*).

ECONOMICALLY ACTIVE POPULATION
(estimates, '000 persons, 1994)

	Males	Females	Total
Agriculture, etc.	332	98	430
Industry	69	11	80
Services	155	22	177
Total	556	131	687

Source: UN Economic Commission for Africa, *African Statistical Yearbook*.

Mid-2001 (estimates in '000): Agriculture, etc. 638; Total labour force 1,213 (Source: FAO).

Health and Welfare

KEY INDICATORS

Total fertility rate (children per woman, 2001).	6.0
Under-5 mortality rate (per 1,000 live births, 2001) . . .	183
HIV/AIDS (% of persons aged 15–49, 1999).	0.52
Physicians (per 1,000 head, 1995)	0.14
Hospital beds (per 1,000 head, 1990)	0.67
Health expenditure (2000): US $ per head (PPP) . . .	52
Health expenditure (2000): % of GDP	4.3
Health expenditure (2000): public (% of total)	79.3
Access to water (% of persons, 2000).	37
Access to sanitation (% of persons, 2000)	33
Human Development Index (2000): ranking	152
Human Development Index (2000): value	0.438

For sources and definitions, see explanatory note on p. vi.

Agriculture

PRINCIPAL CROPS
('000 metric tons)

	1999	2000	2001
Rice (paddy)	51.9	76.2	67.2*
Maize	8.3	5.5*	7.8*
Millet	10.4	7.3*	3.1*
Sorghum	74.8	95.3*	83.7*
Roots and tubers†	5.5	5.5	5.5
Cow peas†	22	22	22
Other pulses†	16	16	16
Oilseeds†	5.0	5.0	5.0
Vegetables†	3.5	3.5	3.5
Dates	20.0	22.0†	22.0†
Watermelons†	10.0	10.0	10.0

* Unofficial figure.
† FAO estimate(s).

Source: FAO.

LIVESTOCK
('000 head, year ending September)

	1999	2000	2001*
Cattle	1,433	1,476	1,500
Goats	4,784†	5,023†	5,100
Sheep	7,176†	7,535†	7,600
Asses*	157	157	158
Horses*	20	20	20
Camels	1,206	1,230†	1,230
Chickens*	4,100	4,100	4,100

* FAO estimates.
† Unofficial figure.

Source: FAO.

LIVESTOCK PRODUCTS
('000 metric tons)

	1999	2000	2001
Beef and veal*	10.3	10.4	10.5
Mutton and lamb†	17.1	18.0	18.0
Goat meat†	11.4	12.0	12.0
Camel meat†	18.5	19.0	19.0
Chicken meat†	4.0	4.0	4.0
Camel milk†	21.3	21.5	21.5
Cows' milk†	112.0	113.8	115.5
Sheep's milk†	84.2	84.2	84.2
Goats' milk†	101.3	101.3	101.3
Cheese†	2.0	2.0	2.1
Hen eggs†	4.9	4.9	4.9
Cattle hides†	1.5	1.6	1.6
Sheepskins†	2.3	2.4	2.4
Goatskins†	1.4	1.4	1.4

* Unofficial figures.
† FAO estimates.

Source: FAO.

Forestry

ROUNDWOOD REMOVALS
(FAO estimates, '000 cubic metres, excluding bark)

	1999	2000	2001
Sawlogs, veneer logs and logs for sleepers	1	1	1
Other industrial wood . . .	5	5	5
Fuel wood	1,393	1,428	1,464
Total	1,399	1,434	1,470

Source: FAO.

Fishing

('000 metric tons, live weight)

	1998	1999	2000
Freshwater fishes*	5.0	5.0	5.0
Hakes	0.8	0.6	1.6
Cuttlefishes and bobtail squids .	3.0	3.4	4.4
Octopuses	10.4	11.3	14.1
Total catch (incl. others) . . .	37.9	37.8	38.1

* FAO estimates.

Source: FAO, *Yearbook of Fishery Statistics*.

Mining

('000 metric tons)

	1998	1999	2000
Gypsum*	100	100	100
Iron ore: gross weight . . .	11,373	10,401	11,345
Iron ore: metal content . . .	7,410	7,475	n.a.
Salt*	5.5	5.5	5.5

* Estimated production.

Source: mostly US Geological Survey.

Iron ore (gross weight, '000 metric tons): 10,301 in 2001 (Source: IMF, *Islamic Republic of Mauritania: Statistical Appendix—*January 2003).

Industry

SELECTED PRODUCTS
('000 metric tons, unless otherwise indicated)

	1995	1996	1997
Frozen fish*	16.0	17.5	13.6
Salted, dried and smoked fish*. .	11.5	12.5	5.8
Electric energy (net production, million kWh)	168.0	185.7	199.4

* Data from FAO.

Source: partly UN, *Industrial Commodity Statistics Yearbook*.

Electric energy (million kWh): 215.7 in 1998; 226.7 in 1999; 227.2 in 2000.

Finance

CURRENCY AND EXCHANGE RATES

Monetary Units
5 khoums = 1 ouguiya (UM)

Sterling, Dollar and Euro Equivalents (31 July 2002)
£1 sterling = 429.70 ouguiyas
US $1 = 274.50 ouguiyas
€1 = 268.54
1,000 ouguiyas = £2.327 = $3.643 = €3.724

Average Exchange Rate (ouguiyas per US $)
1999   209.514
2000   238.923
2001   255.629

BUDGET
('000 million ouguiyas)

Revenue*	1999	2000	2001
Budgetary revenue	55.6	57.9	51.8
Tax revenue	31.6	33.3	36.4
Taxes on income and profits . .	9.9	10.6	11.3
Taxes on goods and services . .	15.8	16.5	18.2
Value-added tax	6.9	7.8	9.3
Turnover taxes	4.3	4.8	4.3
Tax on petroleum products . .	2.6	2.1	2.6
Taxes on international trade. .	5.4	5.5	6.1
Other current revenue	23.4	23.0	13.0
Fishing royalties and penalties	16.1	16.4	5.3
Revenue from public enterprises	5.0	4.1	3.6
Capital revenue	0.5	1.6	2.4
Special accounts	0.4	0.1	0.0
Total	56.0	58.0	51.8

Expenditure	1999	2000	2001
Current expenditure	36.0	39.2	42.2
Wages and salaries	9.6	11.0	12.2
Goods and services	11.6	13.0	14.3
Transfers and subsidies . . .	3.0	3.6	4.0
Military expenditure . . .	4.1	4.2	4.4
Interest on public debt . . .	7.2	7.4	7.2
Other (incl. unclassified) . .	0.4	0.0	0.0
Capital expenditure and net lending	15.2	28.7	23.1
Fixed capital formation . .	11.6	16.9	20.5
Restructuring and net lending	3.5	11.8	2.6
Total†	51.7	68.0	65.6

* Excluding grants received ('000 million ouguiyas): 5.2 in 1999; 2.7. in 2000; 4.0 in 2001.

† Including adjustments.

Source: IMF, *Islamic Republic of Mauritania: Statistical Appendix* (January 2003).

INTERNATIONAL RESERVES
(US $ million at 31 December)

	1997	1998	1999
Gold*	3.3	3.3	3.3
IMF special drawing rights . . .	0.4	—	—
Foreign exchange	200.4	202.8	224.3
Total	204.1	206.2	227.6

2000 (US $ million at 31 December): IMF special drawing rights 0.4; Gold* 3.1.

2001 (US $ million at 31 December): IMF special drawing rights 0.2; Gold* 3.1.

2002 (US $ million at 31 December): IMF special drawing rights 0.2.

* Valued at market-related prices.

Source: IMF, *International Financial Statistics*.

MONEY SUPPLY
(million ouguiyas at 31 December)

	1999	2000	2001
Currency outside banks . . .	5,963	6,402	6,688
Demand deposits at deposit money banks	13,697	17,749	21,033
Total money (incl. others) . .	19,675	24,151	27,721

Source: IMF, *International Financial Statistics*.

COST OF LIVING
(Consumer Price Index in Nouakchott; base: July 1985 = 100)

	1999	2000	2001
Food (incl. beverages) . . .	261.0	271.1	288.8
Clothing (incl. footwear) . . .	210.6	220.1	225.0
Rent	257.1	262.5	271.0
All items (incl. others) . . .	245.9	253.9	265.9

NATIONAL ACCOUNTS
Expenditure on the Gross Domestic Product
('000 million ouguiyas at current prices)

	1999	2000	2001
Government final consumption expenditure	30.5	38.7	38.4
Private final consumption expenditure*	157.8	143.7	172.4
Increase in stocks . . . . }			
Gross fixed capital formation . }	35.2	67.7	65.9
Total domestic expenditure . .	223.4	250.1	276.6
Exports of goods and services .	76.1	90.9	98.1
Less Imports of goods and services	98.7	117.4	129.2
GDP in purchasers' values .	200.9	223.7	245.6
GDP at constant 1985 prices .	84.1	88.3	92.3

* Including public enterprises.

Source: IMF, *Islamic Republic of Mauritania: Statistical Appendix* (January 2003).

Gross Domestic Product by Economic Activity
(million ouguiyas at current prices)

	1999	2000	2001
Agriculture, hunting, forestry and fishing	42,473	44,422	46,492
Mining and quarrying	24,188	31,224	31,524
Manufacturing	16,861	18,529	20,530
Electricity, gas and water . . }			
Construction . . . . . }	11,229	12,592	15,137
Trade, restaurants and hotels .	36,513	39,616	43,519
Transport, storage and communications	16,172	19,800	24,298
Public administration	20,992	23,381	26,389
Other services	11,123	12,111	13,255
GDP at factor cost . . .	179,552	201,675	221,144
Indirect taxes, *less* subsidies . .	21,314	21,981	24,453
GDP in purchasers' values .	200,866	223,657	245,596

Source: IMF, *Islamic Republic of Mauritania: Statistical Appendix* (January 2003).

BALANCE OF PAYMENTS
(US $ million)

	1999	2000	2001
Exports of goods f.o.b. . . .	333.1	344.7	345.1
Imports of goods f.o.b. . . .	−304.7	−329.5	−356.7
Trade balance	28.4	15.2	−11.5
Services (net)	−112.2	−106.4	−133.3
Balance on goods and services .	−83.8	−91.2	−144.8
Private unrequited transfers (net) .	42.4	35.4	47.9
Official transfers	81.4	63.4	75.6
Current balance	40.0	7.6	−21.3
Direct investment	0.0	40.1	14.4
Official medium- and long-term loans.	−38.2	−8.0	−29.8
Other capital and errors and omissions	−20.6	−26.9	−27.3
Overall balance	−18.8	12.8	−64.1

Source: IMF, *Islamic Republic of Mauritania: Sixth Review Under the Poverty Reduction and Growth Facility and Request for Waiver of Performance Criterion—Staff Report; News Brief on the Executive Board Discussion; and Statement by the Executive Director for the Islamic Republic of Mauritania* (January 2003).

External Trade

PRINCIPAL COMMODITIES
(million ouguiyas)

Imports c.i.f.	1997	1998	1999
Capital goods	18,400	16,400	13,100
Petroleum products	10,200	12,900	8,700
Food products.	18,200	23,700	23,100
Vehicles and components . . .	4,800	5,900	7,300
Construction materials	3,800	2,900	2,800
Total (incl. others)	66,500	67,600	64,000

Exports f.o.b.	1997	1998	1999
Iron ore	32,100	39,500	45,600
Fish, crustaceans and molluscs .	28,000	26,100	32,400
Total (incl. others)	61,600	65,900	78,200

PRINCIPAL TRADING PARTNERS
(million SDR)*

Imports c.i.f.	1999	2000	2001
Algeria.	44.0	18.2	18.8
Belgium-Luxembourg . . .	36.1	43.9	49.3
Brazil.	5.3	2.6	3.6
China, People's Republic . . .	14.3	20.6	24.5
Côte d'Ivoire	3.6	5.3	6.1
France	104.5	125.3	122.2
Germany	28.4	22.8	25.8
Hong Kong	7.4	4.4	4.0
Indonesia	6.4	15.6	16.0
Italy	11.7	29.1	27.3
Japan	16.1	12.1	13.4
Netherlands	10.5	13.2	13.7
Senegal	16.9	12.7	14.5
Spain	29.5	28.9	31.4
United Kingdom	6.4	11.3	10.2
USA	20.8	12.8	22.0
Total (incl. others)	437.5	481.4	525.4

Exports c.i.f.	1999	2000	2001
Belgium-Luxembourg . . .	25.7	32.1	29.1
Cameroon	5.6	5.8	6.0
Congo, Republic	3.7	4.8	5.0
Côte d'Ivoire	9.1	14.0	15.9
France	60.4	66.4	57.8
Germany	15.6	13.8	17.0
Italy	47.0	49.5	59.2
Japan	75.3	55.3	35.5
Liberia.	6.9	8.2	9.4
Spain	34.3	39.8	45.1
Togo	6.3	7.5	8.5
United Kingdom	22.4	5.6	6.2
Total (incl. others)	373.7	363.1	383.9

* Data are compiled on the basis of reporting by Mauritania's trading partners.

The average annual exchange rate was as follows: 1999: 1 SDR=\$1.373; 2000: 1 SDR=\$1.303; 2001: 1 SDR=\$1.257.

Source: IMF, *Islamic Republic of Mauritania: Statistical Appendix* (January 2003).

Transport

RAILWAYS

1984: Passengers carried 19,353; Passenger-km 7m.; Freight carried 9.1m. metric tons; Freight ton-km 6,142m.

Freight ton-km (million): 6,365 in 1985; 6,411 in 1986; 6,473 in 1987; 6,535 in 1988; 6,610 in 1989; 6,690 in 1990; 6,720 in 1991; 6,810 in 1992; 6,890 in 1993 (figures for 1988–93 are estimates) (Source: UN Economic Commission for Africa, *African Statistical Yearbook*).

ROAD TRAFFIC
(estimates, '000 motor vehicles in use)

	1994	1995	1996
Passenger cars	16.8	17.5	18.8
Commercial vehicles	9.0	9.3	10.5

Source: IRF, *World Road Statistics*.

SHIPPING

Merchant Fleet
(registered at 31 December)

	1999	2000	2001
Number of vessels	143	144	141
Total displacement ('000 grt) . .	48.6	49.2	47.4

Source: Lloyd's Register-Fairplay, *World Fleet Statistics*.

International Sea-borne Freight Traffic
(Port of Nouadhibou, '000 metric tons)

	1996	1997	1998
Goods loaded	11,623	11,906	11,450
Goods unloaded	139	119	119

Source: Port Autonome de Nouadhibou.

CIVIL AVIATION
(traffic on scheduled services)*

	1997	1998	1999
Kilometres flown (million) . .	4	4	4
Passengers carried ('000) . . .	245	250	187
Passenger-km (million)	324	340	290
Total ton-km (million)	46	46	41

* Including an apportionment of the traffic of Air Afrique.

Source: UN, *Statistical Yearbook*.

Tourism

Tourist arrivals (estimates, '000): 24 in 1999.

Receipts from tourism (US \$ million): 20 in 1998; 28 in 1999 (Source: World Tourism Organization).

Communications Media

	1998	1999	2000
Television receivers ('000 in use) .	231	247	n.a.
Telephones ('000 main lines in use)	15.0	16.5	19.0
Facsimile machines (number in use)	2,600	3,300	n.a.
Mobile cellular telephones ('000 subscribers).	n.a.	n.a.	7.1
Personal computers ('000 in use)*	15	20	25
Internet users ('000)*	1	3	5

2001: Personal computers ('000 in use) 27*; Internet users ('000) 7*.

Daily newspapers (1996): Number 2; Estimated average circulation ('000 copies) 12.

Radio receivers ('000 in use, 1997): 570.

* Estimate(s).

Sources: UNESCO, *Statistical Yearbook*; UN, *Statistical Yearbook*; International Telecommunication Union.

Education

(1998/99, unless otherwise indicated)

	Institu-tions	Teach-ers	Students		
			Males	Females	Total
Pre-primary*	36	108	n.a.	n.a.	800
Primary	2,676	7,366	178,672	167,550	346,222
Secondary:†					
general	n.a.	2,185	35,192	24,837	60,029
technical and vocational . .	3‡		1,148	534	1,682
teacher training . .	2‡	43§	803§	327§	1,130§
Tertiary	4§	270§	n.a.	n.a.	12,912

* 1992/93 figures.
† Data refer to public education only.
‡ 1991/92 figure.
§ 1995/96 figure.

1999/2000: Primary: 355,922 students; Secondary: 63,735 students.

Adult literacy rate (UNESCO estimates): 40.2% (males 50.7%; females 30.1%) in 2000 (Source: UN Development Programme, *Human Development Report*).

Sources: mainly UNESCO Institute for Statistics and Ministry of National Education, Nouakchott.

Directory

While no longer an official language under the terms of the 1991 Constitution (see below), French is still widely used in Mauritania, especially in the commercial sector. Many organizations are therefore listed under their French names, by which they are generally known.

The Constitution

The Constitution of the Arab and African Islamic Republic of Mauritania was approved in a national referendum on 12 July 1991.

The Constitution provides for the establishment of a multi-party political system. The President of the Republic is elected, by universal adult suffrage (the minimum age for voters being 18 years), for a period of six years: no limitations regarding the renewal of the presidential mandate are stipulated. Legislative power is vested in a National Assembly (al Jamiya al-Wataniyah—elected by universal suffrage for a period of five years) and in a Senate (Majlis al-Shuyukh—elected by municipal leaders with a six-year mandate, part of its membership being elected every two years). The President of the Republic is empowered to appoint a Head of Government. Provision is also made for the establishment of a Constitutional Council and a High Council of Islam (both of which were inaugurated in 1992), as well as an Economic and Social Council.

The Constitution states that the official language is Arabic, and that the national languages are Arabic, Pular, Wolof and Solinké.

The Government

HEAD OF STATE

President: Col MAAWIYA OULD SID'AHMED TAYA (took office 12 December 1984; elected President 17 January 1992; re-elected 12 December 1997).

COUNCIL OF MINISTERS
(May 2003)

Prime Minister: CHEIKH EL-AVIA OULD MOHAMED KHOUNA.

Minister Counsellor to the Presidency: NAHA MINT MEKNES.

Minister of Foreign Affairs and Co-operation: MOHAMED OULD TOLBA.

Minister of Defence: KABA OULD ELEWA.

Minister of Justice: SGHAIR OULD M'BAREK.

Minister of the Interior, Posts and Telecommunications: LEMRABOTT SIDI MOHAMED CHEIKH OULD AHMED.

Minister of Finance: BIODIEL OULD HOUMEID.

Minister of Fisheries and Marine Economy: AHMADOU OULD AHMADOU.

Minister of Economic and Development Affairs: ABDELLAHI OULD SOULEIMANE OULD CHEIKH SIDYA.

Minister of Trade, Handicrafts and Tourism: ISSELMOU OULD ABDUL KADER.

Minister of National Education: ABOUBEKRINE OULD AHMED.

Minister of Industry and Mines: ZIDANE OULD HAMIDA.

Minister of Equipment and Transport: DJABIRA BAKARY.

Minister of Culture and Islamic Orientation: LEMRABET OULD LEMINE.

Minister of the Civil Service, Labour, Youth and Sports: BABA OULD SIDI.

Minister of Water and Energy: KANE MOUSTAPHA.

Minister of Rural Development and the Environment: BA BOCAR SOULÉ.

Minister of Health and Social Affairs: MOHAMED MAHOUD JAAFAR.

Minister of Communication and Relations with Parliament: HAMMOUD OULD M'HAMED.

Minister, Director of the Office of the President: SIDI MOHAMED OULD BOUBACAR.

Minister, Secretary-General of the Presidency: MOHAMED HADIYA OULD MOKTAR HASAN.

Minister, Secretary-General of the Government: DIALLOU ABOU-MOUSSA.

President of the Court of Audit: MOHAMED LEMINE OULD GUIG.

Secretary of State, in charge of Civil Status: KHADIJETOU MINT BOUBOU.

Secretary of State for Literacy and Basic Education: SIDI MOHAMED.

Secretary of State, in charge of Women's Issues: MINTATA MINT HEDEID.

Secretary of State, in charge of Union of the Arab Maghreb Affairs: HAMA OULD SOUILEM.

Secretary of State to the Prime Minister, in charge of the Development and Promotion of Information Technology: FATIMETOU MINT MOHAMED OULD SALECK.

MINISTRIES

Office of the President: Présidence de la République, BP 184, Nouakchott; tel. 525-26-36; internet www.mauritania.mr.

Office of the Prime Minister: Nouakchott.

Ministry of the Civil Service, Labour, Youth and Sports: BP 193, Nouakchott; tel. and fax 525-84-10.

Ministry of Communication and Relations with Parliament: Nouakchott.

Ministry of Culture and Islamic Orientation: BP 223, Nouakchott; tel. 525-11-30.

Ministry of Defence: BP 184, Nouakchott; tel. 525-20-20.

Ministry of Economic and Development Affairs: 303 Ilot C, BP 5150, Nouakchott; tel. 529-06-93; fax 529-06-01; e-mail cdhlcpi@opt .mr.

Ministry of Equipment and Transport: BP 237, Nouakchott; tel. 525-33-37.

Ministry of Finance: BP 181, Nouakchott; tel. 525-20-20.

Ministry of Fisheries and Marine Economy: BP 137, Nouakchott; tel. 525-24-76; fax 525-31-46.

Ministry of Foreign Affairs and Co-operation: BP 230, Nouakchott; tel. 525-26-82; fax 525-28-60.

Ministry of Health and Social Affairs: BP 177, Nouakchott; tel. 525-20-52; fax 525-22-68.

Ministry of Industry and Mines: BP 199, Nouakchott; tel. 525-30-83; fax 525-69-37; e-mail mmi@mauritania.mr.

Ministry of the Interior, Posts and Telecommunications: BP 195, Nouakchott; tel. 525-36-61; fax 525-36-40; e-mail paddec@ mauritania.mr.

Ministry of Justice: BP 350, Nouakchott; tel. 525-10-83.

Ministry of National Education: BP 387, Nouakchott; tel. 525-12-37; fax 525-12-22.

Ministry of Rural Development and the Environment: BP 366, Nouakchott; tel. 525-15-00; fax 525-74-75.

Ministry of Trade, Handicrafts and Tourism: BP 182, Nouakchott; tel. 525-35-72; fax 525-76-71.

Ministry of Water and Energy: BP 4913, Nouakchott; tel. 525-71-44; fax 529-42-87; e-mail saadouebih@yahoo.fr.

Office of the Secretary-General of the Government: BP 184, Nouakchott.

President and Legislature

PRESIDENT

Election, 12 December 1997

	Votes	% of votes
Maawiya Ould Sid'Ahmed Taya	801,190	90.94
Mohamed Lemine Ch'Bih Ould Cheikh Melainine	61,869	7.02
Others	17,950	2.04
Total	881,009	100.00

NATIONAL ASSEMBLY
(al Jamiya al-Wataniyah)

National Assembly (al Jamiya al-Wataniyah): ave de l'Indépendance, BP 185, Nouakchott; tel. 525-11-30; fax 525-70-78; internet www.mauritania.mr/assemble.

President: RACHID OULD SALEH.

General Election, 19 and 26 October 2001

	Seats
Democratic and Social Republican Party (DSRP)	64
Action for Change (AC)	4
Rally for Democracy and Unity (RDU)	3
Rally of Democratic Forces (RDF)	3
Union for Democracy and Progress (UDP)	3
Union of Progressive Forces (UPF)	3
Popular Front (PF)	1
Total	81

SENATE
(Majlis al-Shuyukh)

Senate (Majlis al-Shuyukh): ave de l'Indépendance, BP 5838, Nouakchott; tel. 525-68-77; fax 525-73-73.

President: BOUBOU FARBA DIENG.

The 54 members of the Senate are indirectly elected for a term of six years, with one-third of the seats renewable every two years.

After the most recent election, held on 12 and 19 April 2002, the strength of the parties was as follows:

	Seats
Democratic and Social Republican Party (DSRP)	47
National Union for Democracy and Development (NUDD)	1
Rally of Democratic Forces (RDF)	1
Union for Democracy and Progress (UDP)	1
Non-attached	4
Total	54

Advisory Councils

Constitutional Council: f. 1992; includes six mems, three nominated by the Head of State and three designated by the Presidents of the Senate and National Assembly; Pres. ABDOULLAH OULD ELY SALEM; Sec.-Gen. MOHAMED OULD M'REIZIG.

Economic and Social Council: Nouakchott.

Political Organizations

In early 2003 there were about 20 officially registered parties and, in addition, several influential political groups that were not recognized as legitimate by the Government. The organizations listed below are among the most significant officially registered parties, unless otherwise stated.

Democratic Alliance: Nouakchott; f. 2001; Leader MOHAMED OULD TALEB OTHMAN.

Democratic and Social Republican Party (DSRP): Nouakchott; tel. 525-58-55; e-mail prds@prds.mr; internet www.prds.mr; f. 1991; absorbed Movement of Independent Democrats in 1995; Pres. Col MAAWIYA OULD SID'AHMED TAYA; Sec.-Gen. Dr LOULEÏD OULD WEDDAD; 451,333 mems (2000).

Mauritanian Labour Party: Nouakchott; f. 2001; Leader MOHAMED HAFID OULD DENNA.

Mauritanian Liberal Democrats: Nouakchott; f. 2001; Leader MUSTAPHA OULD LEMRABET.

Mauritanian Renewal Party: Nouakchott; f. 2001; Leader MOULAY al-HASSAN OULD JEYDID.

National Renaissance Party (PRN): f. 2001; Leader MOHAMED OULD ABDELLAHI OULD EYYE.

National Union for Democracy and Development (NUDD): f. 1997; Leader TIDJANE KOITA.

Rally for Democracy and Unity (RDU): f. 1991; supports Govt of Pres. Taya; Chair. AHMED OULD SIDI BABA.

Third Generation: Nouakchott; f. 2001; Leader LEBAT OULD JEH.

Union for Democracy and Progress (UDP): Nouakchott; f. 1993; Pres. NAHA MINT MOUKNASS; Sec.-Gen. SIDI OULD AHMED DEYA.

Union of Progressive Forces (UPF) (Ittihad Quwa al-Taqaddum): Nouakchott; e-mail ufpweb2@yahoo.fr; internet www .ufpweb.org; f. 1998 within the fmr Union of Democratic Forces—New Era; f. 2000 as separate party; Pres. MOHAMED OULD MAOULOUD; Sec.-Gen. MOHAMED EL MOUSTAPHA OULD BEDREDDINE.

United Opposition Framework (UOF) (al-Itar al-Muwahhad li-al-Mu'aradah): f. 2002 to replace Forum of Opposition Parties; coalition of radical opposition parties; mems include:

Alliance for Justice and Democracy: Nouakchott; f. 2000 as breakaway group from Action for Change; Leader KABEH ABDOULAYE.

Convention for Change (CC): Nouakchott; f. 2002 to replace the banned Action for Change, to represent the interests of Harratin (black Moors who had fmrly been slaves); refused registration by Govt in Aug. 2002; Chair. MESSAOULD OULD BOULKHEIR; Sec.-Gen. IBRAHIM ASSAR.

Popular Front (PF): Nouakchott; f. 1998; social-liberal; Leader MOHAMED LEMINE CH'BIH OULD CHEIKH MELAININE (sentenced to five years' imprisonment in June 2001).

Popular Progressive Alliance (PPA): Nouakchott; f. 1991; Sec.-Gen. MOHAMED HASSAOUD OULD ISMAËL.

Rally of Democratic Forces (RDF): f. 2001 by fmr mems of the officially dissolved Union of Democratic Forces—New Era (f. 1991); Pres. AHMED OULD DADDAH.

Unauthorized, but influential, is the Islamic **Ummah Party** (the Constitution prohibits the operation of religious political organizations), founded in 1991 and led by Iman SIDI YAHYA, and the Baathist **National Vanguard Party (Taliaa)**, which was officially dissolved by the Government in 1999 and is led by AHMEDOU OULD BABANA. The clandestine **Mauritanian African Liberation Forces (MALF)** was founded in 1983 in Senegal to represent Afro-Mauritanians; internet flamnet.fr.fm; Pres. SAMBA THIAM. A further group based in exile is the **Arab-African Salvation Front Against Slavery, Racism and Tribalism (AASF)**; e-mail faas@caramail.com; internet membres.lycos.fr/faas.

Diplomatic Representation

EMBASSIES IN MAURITANIA

Algeria: Tevragh Zeina, BP 625, Nouakchott; tel. 525-35-69; fax 525-47-77; Ambassador ABDELKRIM BEN HOCINE.

China, People's Republic: Tevragh Zeina, BP 257, Nouakchott; tel. 525-20-70; fax 525-24-62; e-mail www.ambchine@opt.mr; Ambassador LI GUOXUE.

Congo, Democratic Republic: Tevragh Zeina, BP 5714, Nouakchott; tel. 525-46-12; fax 525-50-53; e-mail ambardc.rim@caramail.com; Chargé d'affaires a.i. TSHIBASU MFUAD.

Egypt: Villa no. 167, Tevragh-Zeina, BP 176, Nouakchott; tel. 525-21-92; fax 525-33-84; Ambassador AHMED NABAWI.

France: rue Ahmed Ould M'Hamed, BP 231, Nouakchott; tel. 525-17-40; fax 525-69-38; e-mail ambafrance.nouakchott-amba@diplomatie.gouv.fr; internet www.france-mauritanie.mr; Ambassador JEAN-FRANÇOIS THIBAULT.

Germany: Tevragh Zeina, BP 372, Nouakchott; tel. 525-17-29; fax 525-17-22; e-mail amb-allemagne@toptechnology.mr; Ambassador Dr BERND MORAST.

Israel: Ilot A516, Tevragh Zeina, BP 5714, Nouakchott; tel. 525-82-35; fax 525-46-12; e-mail nouakchott@israel.org; Ambassador FREDDY EYTAN.

Korea, Republic: Tevragh Zeina, BP 324, Nouakchott; tel. 525-32-38; fax 525-44-43; Ambassador PAK HO-IL.

Kuwait: Tevragh Zeina, BP 345, Nouakchott; tel. 525-33-05; fax 525-41-45.

Libya: BP 673, Nouakchott; tel. 525-52-02; fax 525-50-53.

Mali: Tevragh Zeina, BP 5371, Nouakchott; tel. 525-40-81.

Morocco: 569, Ilot C, BP 5303, Nouakchott; tel. 529-43-61; fax 529-46-44; Ambassador ABDERRAHMANE BENOMAR.

Nigeria: Ilot P9, BP 367, Nouakchott; tel. 525-23-04; fax 525-23-14; Ambassador Alhaji BALA MOHAMED SANI.

Qatar: BP 609, Nouakchott; tel. 525-23-99; fax 525-68-87; e-mail nouakchoti@mofa.gov.qa; Ambassador MOHAMMED MOUBARAK AL-MOHANNADI.

Russia: BP 221, Nouakchott; tel. 525-19-73; fax 525-52-96; e-mail ambruss@opt.mr; Ambassador VASILII G. SUKHIN.

Saudi Arabia: Las Balmas, Zinat, BP 498, Nouakchott; tel. 525-26-33; fax 525-29-49; e-mail mremb@mofa.gov.sa; Ambassador MOHAMED AL FADH EL ISSA.

Senegal: BP 2511, Nouakchott; tel. 525-72-90; fax 525-72-91.

Spain: BP 232, Nouakchott; tel. 525-20-80; fax 525-40-88; e-mail ambespmr@correo.mae.es; Ambassador ENRIQUE RUIZ MOLERO.

Syria: Tevragh Zeina, BP 288, Nouakchott; tel. 525-27-54; fax 525-45-00.

Tunisia: BP 681, Nouakchott; tel. 525-28-71; fax 525-18-27; Ambassador ABDEL WEHAB JEMAL.

United Arab Emirates: BP 6824, Nouakchott; tel. 525-10-98; fax 525-09-92.

USA: rue Abdallaye, BP 222, Nouakchott; tel. 525-26-60; fax 525-15-92; e-mail aemnouak@opt.mr; Ambassador JOHN W. LIMBERT.

Yemen: Tevragh Zeina, BP 4689, Nouakchott; tel. 525-55-91; fax 525-56-39.

Judicial System

The Code of Law was promulgated in 1961 and subsequently modified to incorporate Islamic institutions and practices. The main courts comprise three courts of appeal, 10 regional tribunals, two labour tribunals and 53 departmental civil courts. A revenue court has jurisdiction in financial matters. The members of the High Court of Justice are elected by the National Assembly and the Senate.

Shari'a (Islamic) law was introduced in February 1980. A special Islamic court was established in March of that year, presided over by a magistrate of Islamic law, assisted by two counsellors and two *ulemas* (Muslim jurists and interpreters of the Koran). A five-member High Council of Islam, appointed by the President, advises upon the conformity of national legislation to religious precepts, at the request of the President.

Audit Court (Cour des Comptes): Nouakchott; audits all govt institutions; Pres. SOW ADAMA SAMBA.

High Council of Islam (al-Majlis al-Islamiya al-A'la'): Nouakchott; f. 1992; Pres. AHMED OULD NEINI.

High Court of Justice: BP 201, Palais de Justice, Nouakchott; tel. 525-21-63; f. 1961; comprises an equal number of appointees elected from their membership by the National Assembly and the Senate, following each partial or general renewal of those legislative bodies; intended to ensure the independence of the judiciary; the court is competent in juridical, administrative and electoral matters; Pres. MAHFODH OULD LEMRABOTT.

Religion

ISLAM

Islam is the official religion, and the population are almost entirely Muslims of the Malekite rite. The major religious groups are the Tijaniya and the Qadiriya. Chinguetti, in the region of Adrar, is the seventh Holy Place in Islam.

CHRISTIANITY

Roman Catholic Church

Mauritania comprises the single diocese of Nouakchott, directly responsible to the Holy See. The Bishop participates in the Bishops' Conference of Senegal, Mauritania, Cape Verde and Guinea-Bissau, based in Dakar, Senegal. At 31 December 2000 there were an estimated 4,500 adherents, mainly non-nationals, in the country.

Bishop of Nouakchott: Rt Rev. MARTIN ALBERT HAPPE, Evêché, BP 5377, Nouakchott; tel. 525-04-27; fax 525-37-51; e-mail diocesenouakchott@yahoo.com.

The Press

Of some 400 journals officially registered in Mauritania in mid-2000, less than 20 were regular, widely available publications. In early 2003 the regularly circulating press included the following:

Al-Akhbar: BP 5346, Nouakchott; tel. 525-08-94; fax 525-37-57; f. 1995; weekly; Arabic.

Al-Qalam/Le Calame: BP 1059, Nouakchott; tel. 529-02-34; fax 525-75-55; e-mail calame@compunet.mr; internet www.calame.8k.com; f. 1994; weekly; Arabic and French; independent; Editors-in-Chief RIYAD OULD AHMED EL-HADI (Arabic edn), HINDOU MINT AININA (French edn).

Le Carrefour: Nouakchott; Dir MOUSSA OULD SAMBA SY.

Châab: BP 371, Nouakchott; tel. 525-29-40; fax 525-85-47; daily; Arabic; also publ. in French **Horizons**; publ. by Agence Mauritanienne de l'Information; Dir-Gen. MOHAMED EL-HAFED OULD MAHAM.

Challenge: BP 1346, Nouakchott; tel. and fax 529-06-26.

Ech-tary: BP 1059, Nouakchott; tel. 525-50-65; fortnightly; Arabic; satirical.

L'Essor: BP 5310. Nouakchott; tel. 529-19-83; fax 525-04-07; e-mail sidel@caramail.com; monthly; economics; Dir SIDI EL-MOCTAR CHEÏGUER.

El-Anba: BP 3901, Nouakchott; tel. and fax 525-99-27.

L'Eveil-Hebdo: BP 587, Nouakchott; tel. 525-67-14; fax 525-87-54; e-mail eveil@caramail.com; f. 1991; weekly; independent; Publr MAMADOU SY.

Inimich al-Watan: Nouakchott; independent; Arabic; Dir of Publication MOHAMED OULD ELKORY.

Journal Officel: BP 188, Nouakchott; tel. 525-33-37; fax 525-34-74; fortnightly.

Maghreb Hebdo: BP 5266, Nouakchott; tel. 525-98-10; fax 525-98-11; f. 1994; weekly; Dir KHATTRI OULD DIÈ.

Nouakchott-Info: BP 1905, Nouakchott; tel. 525-02-71; fax 525-54-84; e-mail nouakinfo@toptechnology.mr; f. 1995; daily; independent; Arabic and French; Dir CHEIKHNA OULD NENNI; Editor ISSELMAI OULD MOUSTAPHA.

L'Opinion Libre: Nouakchott; weekly; Editor ELY OULD NAFA.

Rajoul Echarée: Nouakchott; e-mail rajoul_echaree@ toptechnology.mr; weekly; independent; Arabic; Dir SIDI MOHAMED OULD YOUNÈS.

Le Rénovateur: Nouakchott; every 2 months; f. 2001; Editor Chiekh TIDIANE DIA.

La Tribune: BP 6227, Nouakchott; tel. 525-44-92; fax 525-02-09; Editor-in-Chief MOHAMMED FALL OULD OUMÈRE.

NEWS AGENCIES

Agence Mauritanienne de l'Information (AMI): BP 371, Nouakchott; tel. 525-29-40; fax 525-45-87; e-mail ami@mauritania.mr; internet www.mauritania.mr/ami; fmrly Agence Mauritanienne de Presse; state-controlled; news and information services in Arabic and French; Dir MOHAMED OULD HAMADY.

Foreign Bureaux

Foreign bureaux represented in Mauritania include Agence France-Presse, Reuters (UK) and Xinhua (New China) News Agency (People's Republic of China).

Publishers

Imprimerie Commerciale et Administrative de Mauritanie: BP 164, Nouakchott; textbooks, educational.

Imprimerie Nationale: BP 618, Nouakchott; tel. 525-44-38; fax 525-44-37; f. 1978; state-owned; Pres. RACHID OULD SALEH; Man. Dir ISSIMOU MAHJOUB.

Government Publishing House

Société Nationale d'Impression: BP 618, Nouakchott; Pres. MOUSTAPHA SALECK OULD AHMED BRIHIM.

Broadcasting and Communications

TELECOMMUNICATIONS

Mauritel: BP 7000, Nouakchott; tel. 525-23-40; fax 525-17-00; e-mail webmaster@mauritel.mr; internet www.mauritel.mr; fmrly Société Mauritanienne des Télécommunications ; 54% owned by Maroc Télécom (Morocco); Dir Col AHMEDOUL OULD MOHAMED EL KORY.

El-Jawel Mauritel Mobiles: ave du Roi Fayçal, Nouakchott; tel. 29-63-36; fax 29-53-16; e-mail infos@mauritelmobiles.mr; internet www.mauritel.mr; f. 2000; operates a mobile cellular telephone network (El Jawal) in Nouakchott and more than 20 other locations nation-wide.

Société Mauritano-Tunisienne de Télécommunications (Mattel): Nouakchott; f. 2000; privately owned Mauritanian-Tunisian co; operates mobile cellular communications network in Nouakchott and more than 10 other locations nation-wide.

BROADCASTING

Radio

Radio de Mauritanie (RM): ave Nasser, BP 200, Nouakchott; tel. and fax 525-21-64; e-mail rm@mauritania.mr; f. 1958; state-con-

trolled; five transmitters; radio broadcasts in Arabic, French, Sarakolé, Toucouleur and Wolof; Dir SID BRAHIM OULD HAMDINOU.

Television

Télévision de Mauritanie (TVM): BP 5522, Nouakchott; tel. 525-40-67; fax 525-40-69; Dir YESLEM OULD EBNOU ABDEM.

Finance

(cap. = capital; res = reserves; dep. = deposits; m. = million; brs= branches; amounts in ouguiyas)

BANKING

Central Bank

Banque Centrale de Mauritanie (BCM): ave de l'Indépendance, BP 623, Nouakchott; tel. 525-22-06; fax 525-27-59; e-mail anima@ bnm.mr; f. 1973; bank of issue; cap. 200m. Gov. BA SAIDOU SAMBA; Dir MOHAMED OULD NANY; 4 brs.

Commercial Banks

Banque al-Amana pour le développement et l'Habitat (BADH): BP 5559, Nouakchott; tel. 525-34-90; fax 525-34-95; e-mail badh@opt.mr; f. 1996 as Banque de l'Habitat de Mauritanie; 50% privately owned; cap. 1,500m. (Dec. 2001), dep. 406m., total assets 2,565m. (Dec. 1999); Pres. AHAMED SALEM OULD BOUNA MOKHTAR; Dir-Gen. MOUSSA FALL; 4 brs.

Banque pour le Commerce et l'Industrie (BCI): ave Nasser, BP 5050, Nouakchott; tel. 529-28-76; fax 529-28-79; e-mail bci@opt.mr; f. 1999; cap. 1,000m. (Dec. 1999); Pres. and Dir-Gen. ISSELMOU OULD DIDI OULD TAJEDINE; 5 brs.

Banque pour le Commerce et l'Investissement en Mauritanie (Bacim-Bank): Nouakchott; f. 2002; privately-owned; cap. US $4m. (Feb. 2002); Pres. and Dir-Gen. AHMED OULD EL WAFI.

Banque Mauritanienne pour le Commerce International (BMCI): Immeuble Afarco, ave Nasser, BP 622, Nouakchott; tel. 525-28-26; fax 525-20-45; e-mail info@bmci.mr; internet www.bmci .mr; f. 1974; privately-owned; cap. 3,000m. (Dec. 2001), dep. 8,000m., total assets 17,892m. (Dec. 1999); Pres. and Dir-Gen. MOULAY OULD HACEN OULD ABASS; 10 brs.

Banque Nationale de Mauritanie (BNM): ave Nasser, BP 614, Nouakchott; tel. 525-26-02; fax 525-33-97; e-mail BNM10@opt.mr; f. 1989; privately-owned; cap. 2,500m. (Dec. 2001), total assets 15,900m. (Dec. 1999); Pres. and Dir-Gen. MOHAMED ABDELLAHI OULD NOUEIGUED; 7 brs.

Chinguitty Bank: ave Nasser, BP 626, Nouakchott; tel. 525-21-42; fax 525-23-82; f. 1972; 50% owned by Libyan Arab Foreign Bank; 50% state-owned; cap. 3,500m. (Dec. 2001), total assets 11,852m. (Dec. 1999); Pres. M. EL HASSEN OULD SALEH; Gen. Man. DAW AMAR ABDALLA; 2 brs.

Générale de Banque de Mauritanie pour l'Investissement et le Commerce SA (GBM): ave de l'Indépendance, BP 5558, Nouakchott; tel. 525-36-36; fax 525-46-47; e-mail gbm@infotel.opt.mr; f. 1995; 65% privately-owned, 30% owned by Banque Belgolaise (Belgium); cap. 1,500m, res. 4,143.8m., dep. 13,092.0m. (Dec. 2001); Pres. and Dir-Gen. MOHAMED HMAYEN OULD BOUAMATOU; 2 brs.

Islamic Banks

Banque al-Baraka Mauritanienne Islamique (BAMIS): BP 650, Nouakchott; tel. 525-14-24; fax 525-16-21; e-mail bamis@sig .mr; f. 1985; Pres. Dr HASSAN ABDULLAH KAMEL; Dir-Gen. MOHAMMED OULD MEMOUNE.

Banque al-Wava Mauritanienne Islamique (BAMIS): ave du Roi Fayçal, BP 650, Nouakchott; tel. 525-14-24; fax 525-16-21; e-mail bamis@bamis.mr; internet www.bamis.mr; f. 1985; 15.2% owned by Groupe El Baraka; cap. 2,000m., total assets 16,000m. (Dec. 2001); Pres. MOHAMED ABDELLAHI OULD ABDELLAHI; Dir-Gen. MOHAMED ABDELLAHI OULD SIDI; Exec. Dir MOHAMED OULD TAYA; 2 brs.

INSURANCE

Assurances Générales de Mauritanie: BP 2141, avenue Charles de Gaulle TZA Ilot A 667, Nouakchott; tel. 529-29-00; fax 529-29-11; Man. MOULAYE ELY BOUAMATOU.

Cie Nationale d'Assurance et de Réassurance (NASR): 12 ave Gamal-Abdel-Nasser, BP 163, Nouakchott; tel. 525-26-50; fax 525-18-18; f. 1994; state-owned; Pres. ABDELLAHI OULD MOCTAR; Dir-Gen. ABDERRAHMANE OULD BOUBOU.

Société Anonyme d'Assurances de Mauritanie (SAAR): rue J. F. Kennedy, BP 2841, Nouakchott; tel. 525-30-56.

TAAMIN: BP 5164, Nouakchott; tel. 529-40-00; fax 529-40-02; e-mail taamin@toptechnology.mr; Dir-Gen. MOULAYE EL HASSEN OULD MOCTAR EL HASSEN.

Trade and Industry

DEVELOPMENT ORGANIZATIONS

Agence Française de Développement (AFD): quartier des Ambassades, BP 211, Nouakchott; tel. 525-23-09; internet www.afd .fr; operations in Mauritania temporarily suspended from 2001.

Mission Française de Coopération et d'Action Culturelle: BP 203, Nouakchott; tel. 525-21-21; fax 525-20-50; e-mail mcap.coop .france@opt.mr; administers bilateral aid from France; Dir MAURICE DADOUCHE.

Société Nationale pour le Développement Rural (SONADER): BP 321, Nouakchott; tel. 521-18-00; fax 525-32-86; e-mail sonader@ toptechnology.mr; f. 1975; Dir AHMED OULD BAH OULD CHEIKH SIDIA.

CHAMBER OF COMMERCE

Chambre de Commerce, d'Industrie et d'Agriculture de Mauritanie: BP 215, Nouakchott; tel. 525-22-14; fax 525-38-95; f. 1954; Pres. MAHMOUD OULD AHMEDOU; Dir HABIB OULD ELY.

INDUSTRIAL AND TRADE ASSOCIATIONS

NAFTEC, SA: BP 679, Nouakchott; tel. 525-26-51; fax 525-25-42; e-mail naftec@toptechnology.mr; f. 1980; cap. UM 120m. majority-owned by Naftec (Algeria), Mauritanian Govt is a minority share-holder; import and distribution of petroleum products; fmrly Société Mauritanienne de Commercialisation des Produits Pétroliers; Dir-Gen. A. GHIMOOZ.

Société Mauritanienne de Commercialisation de Poissons, SA (SMCP): Avenida Media, BP 259, Nouadhibou; tel. 524-53-90; fax 524-55-66; f. 1984; cap. UM 500m. Govt is a minority share-holder; until 1992 monopoly exporter of demersal fish and crusta-ceans; Pres. MOHAMED SALEM OULD LEKHAL; Dir-Gen. BOIJEL OULD HEMEID.

Société Nationale d'Importation et d'Exportation (SONI-MEX): BP 290, Nouakchott; tel. 525-14-72; fax 525-30-14; f. 1966; cap. UM 914m.; 74% state-owned; import of foodstuffs and textiles, distribution of essential consumer goods, export of gum arabic; Pres. HAMOUD OULD AHMEDOU; Dir-Gen. BEBAHA OULD AHMED YOURA.

EMPLOYERS' ORGANIZATION

Confédération Générale des Employeurs de Mauritanie (CGEM): BP 383, Nouakchott; tel. 525-21-60; fax 525-33-01; e-mail germe@opt.mr; f. 1960; professional asscn for all employers active in Mauritania; Pres. MOHAMED BOUAMATOU.

UTILITIES

Electricity

Société Mauritanienne d'Electricité (SOMELEC): BP 355, Nouakchott; tel. 525-23-08; fax 525-39-95; f. 2001; state-owned; privatization planned for 2004; production and distribution of elec-tricity; Dir-Gen. Col SIDI OULD RIHA.

Gas

Société Mauritanienne des Gaz (SOMAGAZ): POB 5089, Nouakchott; tel. 525-18-71; fax 529-47-86; e-mail somagaz@ compunet.mr; production and distribution of butane gas; Dir-Gen. MOHAMED YAHYA OULD MOHAMED EL-MOCTAR.

Water

Société Nationale d'Eau (SNDE): ave 42-096, no. 106, Tevragh-Zeina, BP 796, Nouakchott; tel. 525-52-73; fax 525-19-52; e-mail mfoudail@infotel.mr; f. 2001; Dir-Gen. Col SIDI OULD RIHA; Assistant Dir-Gen. BÂ FARBA.

TRADE UNIONS

Confédération Générale des Travailleurs de Mauritanie: Nouakchott; f. 1992; obtained official recognition in 1994.

Confédération Libre des Travailleurs de Mauritanie: Nouak-chott; f. 1995; Sec.-Gen. SAMORI OULD BEYI.

Union des Travailleurs de Mauritanie (UTM): Bourse du Travail, BP 630, Nouakchott; f. 1961; Sec.-Gen. MOHAMED ELY BRAHIM DIT DINA; 45,000 mems.

Transport

RAILWAYS

A 670-km railway connects the iron-ore deposits at Zouérate with Nouadhibou; a 40-km extension services the reserves at El Rhein, and a 30-km extension those at M'Haoudat. Motive power is diesel-electric. The Société Nationale Industrielle et Minière (SNIM) oper-ates one of the longest (2.4 km) and heaviest (22,000 metric tons) trains in the world.

SNIM—Direction du Chemin de Fer et du Port: BP 42, Nouad-hibou; tel. 574-51-74; fax 574-53-96; e-mail m.khalifa.beyah@snim .com; internet www.snim.fr; f. 1963; Gen. Man. MOHAMED SALECK OULD HEYINE; Dir KHALIFA OULD BEYAH.

ROADS

In 1999 there were about 7,891 km of roads and tracks, of which only 2,090 km were paved. The 1,100-km TransMauritania highway, completed in 1985, links Nouakchott with Néma in the east of the country. Plans exist for the construction of a 7,400-km highway, linking Nouakchott with the Libyan port of Tubruq (Tobruk). In August 1999 the Islamic Development Bank granted Mauritania a loan worth US $9.4m. to help finance the rebuilding of the Chouk–Kiffa road. The construction of a 470 km highway between Nouak-chott and Nouadhibou was expected to commence in 2002.

Société Mauritanienne des Transports (SOMATRA): Nouak-chott; tel. 525-29-53; f. 1975; Pres. CHEIKH MALAININE ROBERT; Dir-Gen. MAMADOU SOULEYMANE KANE.

INLAND WATERWAYS

The River Senegal is navigable in the wet season by small coastal vessels as far as Kayes (Mali) and by river vessels as far as Kaédi; in the dry season as far as Rosso and Boghé, respectively. The major river ports are at Rosso, Kaédi and Gouraye.

SHIPPING

The principal port, at Point-Central, 10 km south of Nouadhibou, is almost wholly occupied with mineral exports. In 1998 the port handled 11.6m. metric tons of cargo, and cleared 3,804 vessels. There is also a commercial and fishing port at Nouadhibou. The deep-water Port de l'Amitié at Nouakchott, built and maintained with assistance from the People's Republic of China, was inaugur-ated in 1986. The port, which has a total capacity of about 1.5m. tons annually, handled 843,000 tons in 1998 (compared with 479,791 tons in 1990); the port cleared 453 vessels in 1998 (compared with 244 in 1990). In 2001 Mauritania's merchant fleet consisted of 141 vessels and had a total displacement of 47,394 grt.

Port Autonome de Nouakchott (Port de l'Amitié): BP 267/5103, El Mina, Nouakchott; tel. 525-14-53; fax 525-16-15; f. 1986; deep-water port; Dir-Gen. MOHAMED MAHMOUD OULD DEH.

Port Autonome de Nouadhibou: BP 236, Nouadhibou; tel. 574-51-34; f. 1973; state-owned; Pres. HABIB ELY; Dir-Gen. BÂ MAMADOU DIT M'BARÉ.

Shipping Companies

Cie Mauritanienne de Navigation Maritime (COMAUNAM): 119 ave Gamal-Abdel-Nasser, BP 799, Nouakchott; tel. 525-36-34; fax 525-25-04; f. 1973; 51% state-owned, 49% owned by Govt of Algeria; nat. shipping co; forwarding agent, stevedoring; Chair. MOHAND TIGHILT; Dir-Gen. KAMIL ABDELKADER.

Société d'Acconage et de Manutention en Mauritanie (SAMMA): BP 258, Nouadhibou; tel. 574-52-63; fax 574-52-37; f. 1960; freight and handling, shipping agent, forwarding agent, stevedoring; Dir-Gen. DIDI OULD BIHA.

Société Générale de Consignation et d'Entreprises Mari-times (SOGECO): BP 351, Nouakchott; tel. 525-22-02; fax 525-39-03; f. 1973; shipping agent, forwarding, stevedoring; Man. Dir SID' AHMED ABEIDNA.

Société Mauritanienne pour la Pêche et la Navigation (SMPN): BP 40254, Nouakchott; tel. 525-36-38; fax 525-37-87; e-mail smpn@toptechnology.mr; Dir-Gen. ABDALLAHI OULD ISMAIL.

VOTRA: BP 454, Nouakchott; tel. 525-24-10; fax 525-31-41; Dir-Gen. ABDERRAHMANE OULD CHOUAÏB.

CIVIL AVIATION

There are international airports at Nouakchott, Nouadhibou and at Néma, and 23 smaller airstrips. Facilities at Nouakchott were expanded considerably in the late 1980s and early 1990s.

Air Mauritanie (Société Mixte Air Mauritanie): BP 41, Nouak-chott; tel. 525-22-11; fax 525-38-15; e-mail reservation@

airmauritanie.mr; internet www.airmauritanie.mr; f. 1974; 11% state-owned; domestic, regional and international passenger and cargo services; Dir-Gen. SIDI ZEIN.

Tourism

Mauritania's principal tourist attractions are its historical sites, several of which have been listed by UNESCO under its World Heritage Programme, and its game reserves and national parks. Some 24,000 tourists visited Mauritania in 1999. Receipts from tourism in 1999 totalled an estimated US $28m.

Office National du Tourisme: BP 246, Nouakchott; tel. 525-35-72; f. 2002; Dir Prof. CHEIKH AHMED OULD ZAHAF.

SOMASERT: BP 42, Nouadhibou; tel. 574-90-42; fax 574-90-43; subsidiary of SNIM; responsible for promoting tourism, managing hotels and organizing tours; Dir-Gen. ABDERRAHMANE OULD DOUA.

MAURITIUS

Introductory Survey

Location, Climate, Language, Religion, Flag, Capital

The Republic of Mauritius lies in the Indian Ocean. The principal island, from which the country takes its name, lies about 800 km (500 miles) east of Madagascar. The other main islands are Rodrigues, the Agalega Islands and the Cargados Carajos Shoals (St Brandon Islands). The climate is maritime subtropical and generally humid. The average annual temperature is 23°C (73°F) at sea-level, falling to 19°C (66°F) at an altitude of 600 m (about 2,000 ft). Average annual rainfall varies from 890 mm (35 ins) at sea-level to 5,080 mm (200 ins) on the highest parts. Tropical cyclones, which may be severe, occur between September and May. Most of the population are of Indian descent. The most widely spoken languages in 1990 were Creole (35.9%), and Bhojpuri (32.5%). English is the country's official language, and Creole (derived from French) the lingua franca. The principal religious group are Hindus, who comprise more than 50% of the population. About 30% are Christians and 17% are Muslims. The national flag (proportions 2 by 3) has four equal horizontal stripes, of red, blue, yellow and green. The capital is Port Louis.

Recent History

The islands of Mauritius and Rodrigues, formerly French possessions, passed into British control in 1810. Subsequent settlement came mainly from East Africa and India, and the European population has remained largely French-speaking.

A ministerial form of government was introduced in 1957. The first elections under universal adult suffrage, held in 1959, were won by the Mauritius Labour Party (MLP), led by Dr (later Sir) Seewoosagur Ramgoolam. Mauritius became independent, within the Commonwealth, on 12 March 1968, with Ramgoolam as Prime Minister.

In November 1965 the United Kingdom transferred the Chagos Archipelago (including the atoll of Diego Garcia), a Mauritian dependency about 2,000 km (1,250 miles) north-east of the main island, to the newly created British Indian Ocean Territory (BIOT, q.v.). Mauritius has subsequently campaigned for the return of the islands, which have been developed as a major US military base. Mauritius also claims sovereignty of the French-held island of Tromelin, about 550 km (340 miles) to the north-west.

During the 1970s political opposition to successive coalition governments formed by Ramgoolam was led by a radical left-wing group, the Mouvement Militant Mauricien (MMM), founded by Paul Bérenger. Although the MMM became the largest single party in the Legislative Assembly following a general election in December 1976, Ramgoolam was able to form a new coalition Government with the support of the Parti Mauricien Social Démocrate (PMSD), which represented traditional Franco-Mauritian and Creole interests. However, social unrest and rising unemployment undermined popular support for the Government, and at a general election in June 1982 the MMM, in alliance with the Parti Socialiste Mauricien (PSM), won all 60 contested seats on the main island. Aneerood (later Sir Anerood) Jugnauth, the leader of the MMM, became Prime Minister, and Bérenger Minister of Finance.

The MMM/PSM coalition collapsed in March 1983, when Bérenger and his supporters resigned, following differences concerning economic policy and the status of Creole (which the MMM had sought to make the official language). Jugnauth formed a new Government and a new party, the Mouvement Socialiste Militant (MSM), which subsequently merged with the PSM. A general election took place in August, at which an electoral alliance of the MSM, the MLP and the PMSD, led by Sir Gaëtan Duval, gained a legislative majority. Jugnauth formed a new coalition Government, in which Duval became Deputy Prime Minister. The MLP, however, withdrew from the coalition in February 1984.

In December 1985 four members of the Legislative Assembly were arrested in the Netherlands on charges of drugs-smuggling. Four ministers resigned after Jugnauth refused to comment on allegations that other deputies were involved in the affair. In July 1986 three ministers resigned, citing lack of confidence in Jugnauth's leadership, although in the following month the MLP agreed to rejoin the government coalition.

In late 1986 a government commission of inquiry into the drugs scandal implicated three members of the Legislative Assembly, all of whom supported the government alliance, and in early 1987 a further six coalition deputies were accused by the commission of involvement in the affair. A general election followed in August. The MSM again formed an electoral alliance with the PMSD and the MLP, the three parties obtaining 39 of the 62 elective seats (although they received only 49.8% of total votes cast). Bérenger, who failed to secure a seat, transferred his functions as leader of the opposition in the Legislative Assembly to Dr Paramhansa Nababsingh (while Bérenger himself replaced Nababsingh as Secretary-General of the MMM). A new coalition, led by Jugnauth, took office in September, and the Government subsequently announced plans to make Mauritius a republic within the Commonwealth. In August 1988, following a disagreement over employment policies, the PMSD withdrew from the coalition. Two attempts on Jugnauth's life (in November 1988 and March 1989) were ascribed by him to criminals involved in drugs-trafficking.

In July 1990 the MSM and the MMM agreed to form an alliance to contest the next general election, and to promote constitutional measures allowing Mauritius to become a republic within the Commonwealth. This proposal, however, was jointly opposed by the MLP and the PMSD, prompting Jugnauth to dismiss the MLP leader, Sir Satcam Boolell, from the Government, together with two dissident ministers from the MSM. A further three ministers representing the MLP resigned, leaving only one MLP member in the Government. Boolell subsequently relinquished the leadership of the MLP to Dr Navinchandra Ramgoolam (the son of the late Sir Seewoosagur Ramgoolam). In September Jugnauth formed a new coalition Government, in which Nababsingh was appointed a Deputy Prime Minister.

Jugnauth dissolved the Legislative Assembly in August 1991. At the subsequent general election, which took place on 15 September, an alliance of the MSM, the MMM and the small Mouvement des Travaillistes Démocrates (MTD), won 57 of the 62 directly elected seats, while the MLP/PMSD alliance obtained three seats. The two remaining seats were secured by the Organisation du Peuple Rodriguais (OPR). Four 'additional' seats were subsequently allocated to members of the MLP/PMSD alliance. Jugnauth formed a new government coalition, to which nine representatives of the MMM (including Bérenger, who became Minister of External Affairs) and one representative of the MTD were appointed. Shortly afterwards Duval resigned from the Legislative Assembly.

In December 1991 the Legislative Assembly approved the constitutional framework for the country's transition to a republic within the Commonwealth. Following the proclamation of the Republic of Mauritius on 12 March 1992, the Legislative Assembly was redesignated as the National Assembly, and the incumbent Governor-General, Sir Veerasamy Ringadoo, became interim President. Later in March the Government announced its choice of Cassam Uteem, the Minister of Industry and Industrial Technology and a member of the MMM, to assume the presidency in June. Uteem was duly elected President by the National Assembly; Sir Rabindrah Ghurburrun, a member of the MMM, took office as Vice-President.

Controversial political manoeuvres in the National Assembly by the government coalition followed the announcement in October 1992 by Ramgoolam that he was to return to the United Kingdom to complete legal studies (while retaining the leadership of the MLP), despite a constitutional stipulation that the mandate of a parliamentary deputy who failed to attend sessions of the National Assembly for a period of more than three months would be suspended. Plans by Ramgoolam to return to Mauritius to attend subsequent parliamentary meetings were thwarted by Jugnauth, who, in December, unexpectedly curtailed a session of the National Assembly, and, in January 1993, convened a further session without prior notice (contrary to usual practice). Legal proceedings, initiated by the MSM, to exclude Ramgoolam from the National Assembly were subsequently dismissed by the Supreme Court.

The government coalition came under increasing pressure during 1993, amid intensifying disputes between the MSM and the MMM. In August, following an unexpected success by the PMSD in municipal by-elections in a constituency that traditionally supported the MMM, a meeting between Bérenger and Ramgoolam prompted speculation that an MMM/MLP alliance was contemplated. Shortly afterwards Jugnauth dismissed Bérenger from the Council of Ministers, on the grounds that he had repeatedly criticized government policy.

The removal of Bérenger precipitated a serious crisis within the MMM, whose political bureau decided that the other nine members of the party who held ministerial portfolios should remain in the coalition Government. Led by Nababsingh, the Deputy Prime Minister, and Jean-Claude de l'Estrac, the Minister of Industry and Industrial Technology, supporters of the pro-coalition faction announced in October 1993 that Bérenger had been suspended as Secretary-General of the MMM. Bérenger and his supporters responded by expelling 11 MMM officials from the party, and seeking a legal ban on Nababsingh and de l'Estrac from using the party name. The split in the MMM led in November to a government reshuffle, in which the remaining two MMM ministers supporting Bérenger were replaced by members of the party's pro-coalition faction.

In April 1994 the MLP and the MMM announced that they had agreed terms for an alliance to contest the next general elections. Under its provisions, Ramgoolam was to be Prime Minister and Bérenger the Deputy Prime Minister, with ministerial portfolios allocated on the basis of 12 ministries to the MLP and nine to the MMM. In the same month, three deputies from the MSM, who had been close associates of a former Minister of Agriculture dismissed two months earlier, withdrew their support from the Government.

Nababsingh and the dissident faction of the MMM, having lost Bérenger's legal challenge for the use of the party name, formed a new party, the Renouveau Militant Mauricien (RMM), which formally commenced political activity in June 1994. In the same month Jugnauth declared that the Government, which retained a cohesive parliamentary majority, would remain in office to the conclusion of its mandate in September 1996.

During the course of a parliamentary debate in November 1994, Bérenger and de l'Estrac accepted a mutual challenge to resign their seats in the National Assembly and to contest by-elections. In the following month the MSM indicated that it would not oppose RMM candidates in the two polls. In January 1995, however, Jugnauth unsuccessfully sought to undermine the MLP/MMM alliance by offering electoral support to the MLP. The by-elections, held in February, were both won by MLP/MMM candidates, and Bérenger was returned to the National Assembly. Following these results, Jugnauth opened political negotiations with the PMSD, whose leader, Xavier-Luc Duval (the son of Sir Gaëtan Duval), entered the coalition as Minister of Industry and Industrial Technology and Minister of Tourism. The post of Attorney-General and Minister of Justice was also allocated to the PMSD, and Sir Gaëtan Duval agreed to act as an economic adviser to the Prime Minister. As a result, however, of widespread opposition within the PMSD to participation in the coalition, Xavier-Luc Duval left the Government in October, and Sir Gaëtan Duval subsequently resumed the leadership of the party. The Minister for Rodrigues, representing the OPR, also left the Government.

In November 1995 the Government was defeated in a parliamentary vote, requiring a two-thirds' majority, to introduce a constitutional requirement for instruction in oriental languages to be provided in primary schools. Jugnauth dissolved the National Assembly, and at the subsequent general election in December the MLP/MMM alliance won a decisive victory: of the 62 elected seats, the MLP secured 35 seats, the MMM obtained 25 seats and the OPR two seats. Under constitutional arrangements providing representation for unsuccessful candidates attracting the largest number of votes, Sir Gaëtan Duval re-entered the National Assembly, together with two members of the Mouvement Rodriguais and a representative of Hizbullah, an Islamic fundamentalist group. Ramgoolam became Prime Minister of the new MLP/MMM coalition, with Bérenger as Deputy Prime Minister with responsibility for foreign and regional relations. The more equitable distribution of the country's recent prosperity was identified as a primary aim of the new Government. Sir Gaëtan Duval died in May 1996 and was succeeded in the National Assembly and as leader of the PMSD by his brother, Hervé Duval, although Xavier-Luc Duval continued to command a significant following within the party.

The MLP/MMM coalition began to experience strain in June 1996, when austerity proposals, put forward in the budget, aroused considerable opposition from Bérenger and the MMM. The Minister of Finance, Rundheersing Bheenick, subsequently resigned, and the finance portfolio remained under the supervision of Ramgoolam until November, when an extensive reallocation of ministerial responsibilities was carried out.

More serious divisions began to emerge within the coalition Government in late 1996, when differences were reported between Ramgoolam and Bérenger over the allocation of ministerial responsibilities and the perception by the MMM of delays in the implementation of social and economic reforms. In January 1997 rumours had begun to circulate of a possible political alliance between the MMM and the MSM, and in March it was reported that Ramgoolam intended to seek support from certain members of the PMSD should the MMM decide to withdraw from the Government. Bérenger's criticism of the coalition's performance intensified in the following months, and culminated in June in his dismissal from the Government and the consequent withdrawal of the MMM from the coalition. Following unsuccessful efforts by Ramgoolam to draw the PMSD into a new administration, an MLP Council of Ministers was formed by Ramgoolam, who additionally assumed Bérenger's former responsibilities for foreign affairs. Bheenick returned to the Government as Minister of Economic Development and Regional Co-operation. Ahmed Rashid Beebeejaun, Minister of Land Transport, Shipping and Public Safety in the former coalition, left the MMM and retained his former portfolio as an independent. Ramgoolam emphasized his determination to remain in office for the full legislative term to December 2000. On 28 June 1997 the National Assembly re-elected Cassam Uteem to a second five-year term as President. A prominent supporter of the MLP, Angidi Verriah Chettiar, was elected Vice-President.

Following the dissolution of the MLP/MMM alliance, Bérenger sought to assume the leadership of a consolidated political opposition to the Government. In August 1997 two small parties, the Mouvement Militant Socialiste Mauricien (MMSM) and the Rassemblement pour la Réforme (RPR), agreed to support Bérenger in this aim. The alliance was extended to include a breakaway faction of the PMSD, known as the 'Vrais Bleus', under the leadership of Hervé Duval, who had been replaced as party leader by his nephew, Xavier-Luc Duval, an opponent of co-operation with the MMM.

In April 1998 the MMM, the MMSM, the RPR and the 'Vrais Bleus' formed an electoral coalition, the Alliance Nationale, to contest a by-election for a vacant seat in the National Assembly. The seat, which was retained by the MLP, had also been sought by Jugnauth on behalf of the MSM, which remained unrepresented in the National Assembly. Jugnauth, seeking to revitalize his party's prospects in preparation for the next general election (which was constitutionally required to take place by December 2000), subsequently entered negotiations with Bérenger for an electoral alliance, and in December 1998 both parties agreed terms for a joint list of candidates. Ramgoolam, following a reshuffle of the Council of Ministers in October, announced proposals in the following month for an all-party review of the electoral system, with a view to considering the adoption of proportional representation.

In February 1999 Mauritius experienced three days of serious rioting, following the death in police custody of a popular Creole musician. The public disorders, during which three deaths and damage estimated at £20m. were caused, were widely interpreted as an indication of the resentment felt by the Creole community, which has remained at the margin of the Republic's economic prosperity. Lesser disturbances took place on Rodrigues, whose population is predominantly Creole, in early May. During the following months escalating social tensions in Mauritius were evidenced by a number of violent confrontations involving members of several of the island's various ethnic and religious communities, and in December the Government enacted legislation granting it wide powers to suppress public disorder.

The MLP announced in mid-1999 its endorsement of the candidature of Xavier-Luc Duval for a legislative by-election to be held in September. Duval, after obtaining the vacant seat, joined the Government as Minister of Industry, Commerce, Corporate Affairs and Financial Services, following an extensive government reshuffle completed at the end of the month. The selection in October of Pravind Jugnauth, the son of Sir Anerood Jugnauth, as Deputy Leader of the MSM gave rise to speculation that Sir Anerood was contemplating retirement from politics and intended his son to be his successor. It also provoked divisions within the informal alliance that had been formed between the MMM and the MSM in February 1999.

None the less, in August 2000 the MSM/MMM alliance was made official, in advance of the imminent general election, on the basis that Jugnauth would lead as Prime Minister for three years in the event of victory, before assuming the more honorary role of President, thus allowing Bérenger to become Prime Minister for the remaining two years. In the same month both the Minister of Social Security and National Unity, Prakash Bundhun, and the Minister of Health, Nundhkeshwarsingh Deerpalsingh, resigned, following separate allegations of fraud and investigations by the Economic Crime Office; Deerpalsingh was subsequently arrested.

A general election was held on 11 September 2000. There was a high rate of participation, with 81% of the 790,000 registered electors casting their ballots. The MSM/MMM alliance achieved a significant victory, winning 54 of the 62 directly elected seats in the National Assembly, while the MLP/PMSD alliance gained only six seats and the OPR two seats. As agreed, Sir Anerood Jugnauth became Prime Minister again, while Paul Bérenger was appointed Deputy Prime Minister and Minister of Finance. A new Council of Ministers was appointed one week later.

In November 2000 the British High Court of Justice ruled that the eviction of several thousand inhabitants of the Chagos Archipelago between 1967 and 1973, to allow the construction of a US military base on the atoll of Diego Garcia, had been unlawful, and overturned a 1971 ordinance preventing the islanders from returning to the Archipelago. (The majority of the displaced islanders had been resettled in Mauritius, which had administered the Chagos Archipelago until its transfer to BIOT in 1965.) Following the ruling, the Mauritian Government declared its right to sovereignty over the islands to be indisputable and sought international recognition as such. Jugnauth stated that he would be prepared to negotiate with the USA over the continued presence of the military base. The United Kingdom responded that it would return the islands if, as had been maintained for many years, the USA was prepared to move out of the base on Diego Garcia. India declared its support for the Mauritian Government's claim to sovereignty, as part of the close relationship being encouraged between the two countries.

Municipal elections were held on 7 October 2001; the ruling MSM/MMM alliance won 115 of the country's 226 council seats and secured control of all five municipalities.

In November 2001 exiled Chagos islanders demonstrated outside the British High Commission in Port Louis, in support of their demands for compensation from the British Government. In February 2002 legislation allowing the displaced islanders to apply for British citizenship received royal assent in the United Kingdom. At that time the British Government was also examining the feasibility of a return to the Chagos Archipelago for the islanders, who continued to seek compensation.

In January 2002 a commission on constitutional and electoral reform presented its proposals at a series of public forums, before submitting them to the Government for consideration. Recommendations included the introduction of a system of proportional representation in legislative elections and a reinforcement of presidential powers. In mid-February controversial legislation on the prevention of terrorism was finally promulgated by the Chief Justice of the Supreme Court, Arianga Pillay, acting as interim President, following the resignations of both President Uteem and his successor, Vice-President Chettiar, over the issue. The legislation had been rejected by opposition parties and proved unpopular with many sections of society for arrogating excessive powers to the authorities and infringing on citizens' rights. On 25 February Karl Offman was elected as President by an extraordinary session of the National Assembly, which was boycotted by opposition deputies. Although formally elected for five years, Offman was to relinquish the presidency to Jugnauth in September 2003; in preparation for this, in April 2003 Jugnauth announced his resignation from the leadership of the MSM, to be succeeded by his son, Pravind. In January of that year the Minister of Housing and Land, Mookhesswur Choonee, resigned from his post, following his arrest on suspicion of illegally having sold state-owned land to a private investor. His duties were subsequently appended to those of the Minister of Local Government and Rodrigues, Georges Lesjongard. Further corruption was revealed by the Independent Commission Against Corruption in March, when the former Director of Mauritius' oldest bank, Mauritius Commercial Bank, was brought to trial for the alleged theft of up to Rs 800m. from the National Pension Fund over the preceding six months.

Government

Constitutional amendments, which were approved by the Legislative Assembly (henceforth known as the National Assembly) in December 1991 and came into effect on 12 March 1992, provided for the establishment of a republic. The constitutional Head of State is the President of the Republic, who is elected by a simple majority of the National Assembly for a five-year term of office. Legislative power is vested in the unicameral National Assembly, which comprises the Speaker, 62 members elected by universal adult suffrage for a term of five years, up to eight 'additional' members (unsuccessful candidates who receive the largest number of votes at a legislative election, to whom seats are allocated by the Electoral Supervisory Commission to ensure a balance in representation of the different ethnic groups), and the Attorney-General (if not an elected member). Executive power is vested in the Prime Minister, who is appointed by the President and is the member of the National Assembly best able to command a majority in the Assembly. The President appoints other ministers, on the recommendation of the Prime Minister.

Defence

The country has no standing defence forces, although at 1 August 2002 paramilitary forces were estimated to number 2,000, comprising a special mobile force of 1,500, to ensure internal security, and a coastguard of 500. Projected budgetary expenditure on defence for 2002 was Rs 260m.

Economic Affairs

In 2001, according to estimates by the World Bank, Mauritius' gross national income (GNI), measured at average 1999–2001 prices, was US $4,592m., equivalent to $3,830 per head (or $10,410 per head on an international purchasing-power parity basis). During 1990–2001, it was estimated, the population increased at an average annual rate of 1.1%, while gross domestic product (GDP) per head increased, in real terms, by an average of 4.1% per year. Overall GDP increased, in real terms, at an average annual rate of 5.2% in 1990–2001; growth in 2001 was 7.2%.

Agriculture (including hunting, forestry and fishing) contributed an estimated 6.0% of GDP in 2002, according to provisional figures, and engaged 9.6% of the employed labour force in that year. The principal cash crops are sugar cane (sugar accounted for 19.2% of total export earnings in 2001, according to provisional figures), tea and tobacco. Food crops include potatoes and vegetables. Poultry farming is also practised. During 1990–2001, according to the World Bank, the GDP of the agricultural sector increased, in real terms, at an average rate of 0.5% per year; growth in 2001 was 25.9%.

Industry (including mining, manufacturing, construction and utilities) contributed an estimated 29.2% of GDP in 2002, according to provisional figures, and engaged 38.4% of the employed labour force in that year. During 1990–2001, according to the World Bank, industrial GDP increased, in real terms, at an average annual rate of 5.7%; growth in 2001 was 7.0%. Mining is negligible, accounting for only 0.3% of employment and 0.1% of GDP in 2002.

Manufacturing contributed an estimated 21.3% of GDP in 2002, according to provisional figures, and engaged 28.5% of the employed labour force in that year. The principal branches of manufacturing are textiles and clothing and food products, mainly sugar. Clothing (excluding footwear) provided 59.1% of total export earnings in 2001. Factories in the Export Processing Zone (EPZ) process imported raw materials to produce goods for the export market. Textile firms accounted for 88.4% of total EPZ employment in 1998 and 84.4% of EPZ exports (mainly in the form of clothing) in 1997. Other important products include fish preparations, watches and clocks, and precious stones. Export receipts by the EPZ represented almost 76.4% of total export earnings in 1999. During 1990–2001, according to the World Bank, the GDP of the manufacturing sector increased, in real terms, at an average annual rate of 5.4%; growth in 2001 was 6.6%.

Electric energy is derived principally from hydroelectric and thermal (oil-fired) power stations; bagasse (a by-product of sugar cane) is also used as fuel for generating electricity: in 1992 a programme was initiated to enable Mauritius eventually to derive 15% of its energy requirements from bagasse. Imports of refined petroleum products comprised 9.5% of the value of merchandise imports in 2001, according to provisional figures. Thermal energy accounted for 97.9% of electricity generated in 1999.

The services sector contributed an estimated 64.8% of GDP in 2002, according to provisional figures, and engaged 52.0% of the employed labour force in that year. Tourism is the third most important source of revenue, after agriculture and manufacturing. The number of foreign tourist arrivals increased to 681,648 in 2002 from 422,000 in 1995. Receipts from tourism were estimated to total Rs 18,328m. in 2002. An 'offshore' banking sector and a stock exchange have operated since 1989. According to the World Bank, the real GDP of the services sector increased at an average annual rate of 6.3% in 1990–2001; growth in 2001 was 6.7%.

In 2001 Mauritius recorded a visible trade deficit of US $255.9m., and there was a surplus of $246.6m. on the current account of the balance of payments. In 2001 the principal source of imports (13.8%) was South Africa; other major suppliers were France, India and the People's Republic of China. The principal market for exports (taking 31.1% of exports in that year) was the United Kingdom; other significant purchasers were the USA and France. The principal exports in 2001 were clothing and sugar. The principal imports in that year were textile yarn and fabrics, machinery, food products and mineral fuels.

In 2000/01 there was an estimated budgetary deficit of Rs 6,826.4m. (equivalent to 6.5% of GDP). Mauritius' external debt totalled US $2,374m. at the end of 2000, of which $889m. was long-term public debt. In that year the cost of debt-servicing was equivalent to 20.8% of the value of exports of goods and services. The annual rate of inflation averaged 6.6% in 1990–2001. Consumer prices increased by an average of 4.2% in 2000 and 5.4% in 2001. About 9.8% of the labour force were unemployed in 2002.

Mauritius is a member of the Common Market for Eastern and Southern Africa (COMESA, see p. 162), the Southern African Development Community (SADC, see p. 311) and the Indian Ocean Commission (IOC, see p. 340), which aims to promote regional economic co-operation. Mauritius was among the founder members of the Indian Ocean Rim Association for Regional Co-operation (IOR—ARC, see p. 340) in 1997.

Mauritius' economy was traditionally dependent on sugar production, and economic growth was therefore vulnerable to adverse climatic conditions and changes in international prices for sugar. However, since the 1980s the Government has pursued a successful policy of diversification, encouraging labour-intensive manufacturing (particularly of clothing) in the EPZ, and extensive reforms have been implemented with IMF support. Port Louis has been established as a free port. Since the mid-1990s the Government has continued to promote further measures to achieve economic diversification and liberalization, aimed at encouraging foreign investment and increasing export revenue. The expansion of tourism has also been actively promoted. The geographical location of Mauritius has contributed to its successful establishment as an international financial centre. By the late 1990s the island had become a significant provider of 'offshore' banking and investment services for a number of south Asian countries (particularly India), as well as for members of the SADC and IOR—ARC groupings. Since 1999 the Prime Minister has also promoted the country as a future hub of communications and information technology, as a means of encouraging the next stage of economic development and transferring the emphasis towards services. The construction of a free zone 'cybercity' was initiated, with an investment of US $110m. from India, and in 2000 a South Africa–Far East underwater fibre optic cable was laid, linking Port Louis to both regions. However, a review of the economy published by the new Government at the end of 2000 examined a number of issues of concern, including growing unemployment, high inflation, excessive public debt, inadequate labour-force skills and an ageing population. These negative factors may have been exacerbated by record drought in 1998–2000, which caused an estimated Rs 2,000m. of damage and reduced the sugar harvest

by an estimated 40%. However, a programme was initiated in 2000 to convert a large proportion of tea plantations to the production of sugar cane in order to meet quotas from the European Union (EU) and generate more income. In August 2001 the Prime Minister announced a restructuring and centralization plan for the sugar industry, whereby 7,000 workers were to be invited to retire over three years and several factories were closed, in order to reduce costs and improve international competitiveness. The textile industry, the country's second largest foreign-exchange earner, was eroded by the transfer, in 2000, of the operations of more than 20 major Mauritian manufacturers to Madagascar, owing to lower costs in that country. Furthermore, in January 2002 more than 1,000 textile workers in the EPZ were made redundant, owing to a decline in trade following the suicide attacks on the USA in September 2001; exports to the USA had previously been expected to increase, as a result of the USA's African Growth and Opportunity Act (AGOA), which granted duty-free access to the US market for textile products from Mauritius. The expiry of the preferential Multi-Fibre Agreement with the EU in December 2004 will pose a further threat to the textiles industry, exposing it to direct competition from countries with lower labour costs, particularly those in Asia. Similarly, the possibility of the liberalization of the EU's trade arrangements for sugar, following enquiries by several countries in 2002 as to its legality under World Trade Organization legislation, would seriously undermine Mauritius' position, owing to its high production costs. However, in January 2003 Mauritius hosted the second AGOA forum, at which President George W. Bush of the USA suggested extending the Act beyond 2008; it was hoped that the country's developed transport and communications infrastructure could help it to become a major container hub for East Africa as a result of AGOA trade.

Education

Education is officially compulsory for seven years between the ages of five and 12. Primary education begins at five years of age and lasts for six years. Secondary education, beginning at the age of 11, lasts for up to seven years, comprising a first cycle of three years and a second of four years. Primary and secondary education are available free of charge. In 1999/2000 primary enrolment included 94.2% of children in the appropriate age-group (males 94.1%; females 94.3%), while the comparable ratio for secondary enrolment was 72.5% (males 71.1%; females 73.9%). The education system provides for instruction in seven Asian languages (65% of primary school children were studying at least one of these in 2001). The Government exercises indirect control of the large private sector in secondary education. Some 22 new colleges were to be constructed for use by early 2003. The University of Mauritius had 3,667 students in 1997/98; in addition, many students receive further education abroad. Of total forecast expenditure by the central Government in 2002/03, Rs 4,574m. (14.8%) was for education.

Public Holidays

2003: 1–2 January (New Year), 19 January (Thaipoosam Cavadee), 1 February (Chinese New Year), 1 March (Maha Shivaratree), 12 March (National Day), 2 April (Ougadi), 18 April (Good Friday), 1 May (Labour Day), 1 September (Ganesh Chathurti), 25 October (Divali), 1 November (All Saints' Day), 26 November (Id al-Fitr, end of Ramadan), 25 December (Christmas Day).

2004: 1–2 January (New Year), 22 January (Chinese New Year), February (Thaipoosam Cavadee), 18 February (Maha Shivaratree), 12 March (National Day), 9 April (Good Friday), 13 April (Ougadi), 1 May (Labour Day), 18 September (Ganesh Chathurti), 1 November (All Saints' Day), 12 November (Divali), 14 November (Id al-Fitr, end of Ramadan), 25 December (Christmas Day).

*This holiday is dependent on the Islamic lunar calendar and may vary by one or two days from the dates given.

Weights and Measures

The metric system is in standard use.

Statistical Survey

Source (unless otherwise stated): Central Statistical Office, LIC Centre, President John F. Kennedy St, Port Louis; tel. 212-2316; fax 211-4150; e-mail cso@intnet.mu; internet ncb.intnet.mu/cso.

Area and Population

AREA, POPULATION AND DENSITY

Area (sq km)	2,040
Population (census results)	
1 July 1990	1,058,942
2 July 2000	
Males	583,949
Females.	595,188
Total	1,179,137
Population (official estimates at mid-year)	
2000	1,186,873
2001	1,199,881
2002	1,210,196
Density (per sq km) at mid-2002	593.2

* 788 sq miles.
† Including an adjustment of 2,115 for underenumeration.
‡ Excluding an adjustment for underenumeration.
§ Islands of Mauritius and Rodrigues only (area 1,969 sq km).

ISLANDS

		Population	
	Area (sq km)	1990 census	2000 census
Mauritius	1,865	1,024,571	1,143,069
Rodrigues	104	34,204	35,779
Other islands . .	71	167	289

* Including adjustment for underenumeration.

ETHNIC GROUPS: Island of Mauritius, mid-1982: 664,480 Indo-Mauritians (507,985 Hindus, 156,495 Muslims), 264,537 general population (incl. Creole and Franco-Mauritian communities), 20,669 Chinese.

LANGUAGE GROUPS
(census of 2 July 2000)

Arabic	806	Marathi	16,587
Bhojpuri	361,250	Tamil	44,731
Chinese	16,972	Telegu	18,802
Creole	454,763	Urdu	34,120
English	1,075	Other languages . .	169,619
French	21,171	Not stated . . .	3,170
Hindi	35,782	**Total**	1,178,848

* Figures refer to the languages of cultural origin of the population of the islands of Mauritius and Rodrigues only. The data exclude an adjustment for underenumeration.

POPULATION BY DISTRICT
(2001)

Plaine Wilhems . .	364,000	Riv du Rempart . .	100,800
Flacq	129,500	Moka	76,700
Port Louis	129,400	Savanne . . .	67,300
Pamplemousses . .	124,900	Black River . .	62,600
Grand Port . . .	108,700	Rodrigues	36,000

PRINCIPAL TOWNS
(census of 2 July 2000)

Port Louis (capital) .	144,303	Curepipe	78,920
Beau Bassin/Rose Hill	103,872	Quatre Bornes . .	75,884
Vacoas/Phoenix . .	100,066		

Source: Thomas Brinkhoff, *City Population* (internet www.citypopulation.de).

BIRTHS, MARRIAGES AND DEATHS

	Registered live births		Registered marriages		Registered deaths	
	Number	Rate (per 1,000)	Number	Rate (per 1,000)	Number	Rate (per 1,000)
1995 . .	20,549	18.3	10,624	9.5	7,465	6.7
1996 . .	20,763	18.3	10,700	9.4	7,670	6.8
1997 . .	20,012	17.4	10,887	9.5	7,986	7.0
1998 . .	19,434	16.7	10,898	9.4	7,839	6.8
1999 . .	20,311	17.3	11,295	9.6	7,944	6.8
2000 . .	20,205	17.0	10,963	9.2	7,982	6.7
2001 . .	19,696	16.4	10,635	8.9	7,983	6.7
2002 . .	19,995	16.5	10,464	8.6	8,330	6.9

* Figures refer to the islands of Mauritius and Rodrigues only. The data are tabulated by year of registration, rather than by year of occurrence.

Expectation of life (WHO estimates, years at birth): 71.1 (males 67.5; females 74.9) in 2001 (Source: WHO, *World Health Report*).

ECONOMICALLY ACTIVE POPULATION
(persons aged 12 years and over)

	2000	2001	2002
Agriculture, forestry and fishing .	55,800	54,300	47,300
Sugar cane	29,400	28,100	21,600
Mining and quarrying	1,300	1,300	1,300
Manufacturing	142,000	143,500	139,600
EPZ	89,800	91,000	85,700
Electricity and water	2,900	3,000	3,100
Construction	42,800	43,500	44,100
Wholesale and retail trade, repair of motor vehicles and household goods	63,700	65,100	67,100
Hotels and restaurants . . .	22,700	24,200	25,300
Transport, storage and communications	30,800	31,600	33,400
Financial intermediation . . .	7,300	7,500	7,500
Real estate, renting and business activities	14,100	14,300	14,200
Public administration and defence .	35,100	36,200	38,200
Education	22,700	23,300	24,300
Health and social work	12,600	12,300	12,600
Other services	29,800	30,700	32,000
Total employed	483,600	490,800	490,000
Males	318,700	321,600	324,100
Females	164,900	169,200	165,900
Unemployed	45,000	47,700	51,100
Total labour force	528,600	538,500	541,100

* Includes foreign workers.

Health and Welfare

KEY INDICATORS

Total fertility rate (children per woman, 2001)	1.9
Under-5 mortality rate (per 1,000 live births, 2001) . . .	19
HIV/AIDS (% of persons aged 15–49, 2001)	0.10
Physicians (per 1,000 head, 1995)	0.85
Hospital beds (per 1,000 head, 1994)	3.07
Health expenditure (2000): US $ per head (PPP)	330
Health expenditure (2000): % of GDP	3.4
Health expenditure (2000): public (% of total)	56.3
Access to water (% of persons, 2000)	100
Access to sanitation (% of persons, 2000)	99
Human Development Index (2000): ranking	67
Human Development Index (2000): value	0.772

For sources and definitions, see explanatory note on p. vi.

Agriculture

PRINCIPAL CROPS
('000 metric tons)

	1999	2000	2001
Potatoes	15.3	14.3	15.0
Sugar cane	3,882.6	5,109.0	5,500.0
Coconuts	1.8	1.9	1.9
Cabbages	8.2	10.8	11.0
Lettuce	1.2	1.7	1.7
Tomatoes	8.0	9.7	9.7
Cauliflower	1.3	2.0	2.0
Pumpkins, squash and gourds	11.5	13.0	13.0
Cucumbers and gherkins	8.7	9.0	9.0
Aubergines (Eggplants)	1.7	1.6	1.6
Dry onions	9.1	11.1	10.5
Carrots	6.1	11.5	11.0
Other vegetables	32.8	36.6	36.7
Bananas	7.6	6.5	6.5
Pineapples	1.0	3.4	3.5
Other fruit	1.1	1.2	1.1
Tea (made)	1.5	1.3	1.4
Tobacco (leaves)	0.7	0.6	0.6

* FAO estimate(s).

Source: FAO.

LIVESTOCK
(FAO estimates, '000 head, year ending September)

	1999	2000	2001
Cattle	25	27	28
Pigs	10	12	14
Sheep	14	10	7
Goats	93	94	95
Chickens	7,000	7,700	7,700

Source: FAO.

LIVESTOCK PRODUCTS
('000 metric tons)

	1999	2000	2001
Beef and veal	3	3	3
Poultry meat	21	21	22
Cows' milk	5	5	5
Hen eggs	5	5	5

* FAO estimates.

Source: FAO.

Forestry

ROUNDWOOD REMOVALS
('000 cubic metres, excl. bark)

	1998	1999	2000
Sawlogs, veneer logs and logs for sleepers	8	7	5
Other industrial wood	4	6	3
Fuel wood	10	12	10
Total	22	25	18

SAWNWOOD PRODUCTION
('000 cubic metres, incl. railway sleepers)

	1998	1999	2000
Coniferous (softwood)	4	4	2
Broadleaved (hardwood)	1	1	1
Total	5	5	3

2001: Production as in 2000 (FAO estimates).

Source: FAO.

Fishing

(metric tons, live weight)

	1998	1999	2000
Capture	12,026	12,004	9,299
Unicorn cod	336	285	347
Groupers and seabasses	931	826	863
Emperors (Scavengers)	4,981	4,598	4,698
Goatfishes	436	509	541
Spinefeet (Rabbitfishes)	494	461	448
Skipjack tuna	1,685	2,361	298
Yellowfin tuna	1,443	751	214
Octopuses	299	299	303
Aquaculture	83	85	87
Total catch	12,109	12,089	9,386

Source: FAO, *Yearbook of Fishery Statistics*.

Industry

SELECTED PRODUCTS
(metric tons, unless otherwise indicated)

	1999	2000	2001
Frozen fish	3,922	4,700	n.a.
Canned fish	18,992	20,173	n.a.
Raw sugar	373,294	569,289	645,598
Molasses	132,000	146,430	175,700
Beer and stout (hectolitres)	358,450	374,970	328,100
Cigarettes (million)	979	976	n.a.
Iron bars and steel tubes	45,000	46,125	48,000
Fertilizers	85,300	87,400	83,000
Electric energy (million kWh)	1,559	1,600	1,659

* Rounded figure.

Finance

CURRENCY AND EXCHANGE RATES

Monetary Units
100 cents = 1 Mauritian rupee

Sterling, Dollar and Euro Equivalents (31 December 2002)
£1 sterling = 47.06 rupees
US $1 = 29.21 rupees
€1 = 30.62 rupees
1,000 Mauritian rupees = £21.25 = $34.25 = €32.66

Average Exchange Rate (Mauritian rupees per US $)
2000   26.250
2001   29.129
2002   29.962

BUDGET
(million rupees, year ending 30 June)

Revenue	1998/99	1999/2000	2000/01
Direct taxes	4,023.1	4,206.7	4,494.5
Individual income taxes	1,362.8	1,539.7	1,540.0
Corporate tax	1,337.0	1,340.9	1,515.0
Taxes on properties, capital and financial transactions	1,209.2	1,206.0	1,316.5
Indirect taxes	13,848.4	16,526.3	15,605.5
Domestic taxes on goods and services	8,772.5	9,579.1	9,268.0
Excises	2,685.8	2,159.5	2,100.0
Sales tax, value-added tax	4,638.6	5,604.4	5,880.0
Taxes on gambling	607.6	892.1	870.0
Taxes on international trade and transactions	5,063.1	6,935.2	6,325.0
Receipts from public utilities	496.9	245.5	275.9
Receipts from public services	564.9	647.9	690.3
Other current receipts	2,393.4	978.3	2,968.8
Total	21,326.7	22,604.8	24,035.0

* Revised estimates.

Source: Bank of Mauritius, Port Louis.

Expenditure	1999/2000	2000/01
Current expenditure	23,379.2	26,203.7
Expenditure on goods and services. . . .	10,117.3	10,812.0
Wages and salaries. . . .	7,763.1	8,157.1
Other goods and services	2,354.2	2,654.9
Interest payments	3,856.1	5,032.2
Current transfers and subsidies . . .	9,405.8	10,359.5
Capital expenditure	3,380.5	3,767.1
Acquisition of fixed capital assets . .	1,924.8	1,927.4
Capital transfers	1,397.8	1,744.7
To non-financial public enterprises . . .	1,198.7	1,510.4
Expenditure through privatization fund . . .	883.0	600.0
Total derived expenditure	27,642.7	30,570.8
Lending minus repayments	167.3	290.6
Total	27,810.0	30,861.4

* Revised estimates.

INTERNATIONAL RESERVES
(US $ million at 31 December)

	2000	2001	2002
Gold	12.3	12.3	12.3
IMF special drawing rights . . .	21.4	21.1	23.2
Reserve position in IMF	18.9	18.2	19.7
Foreign exchange	857.1	796.3	1,184.5
Total	909.8	847.9	1,239.7

* Valued at market-related prices.

Source: IMF, *International Financial Statistics*.

MONEY SUPPLY
(million rupees at 31 December)

	2000	2001	2002
Currency outside banks	6,647.6	7,329.0	8,286.0
Demand deposits at deposit money banks	6,563.6	7,974.9	9,759.0
Total money (incl. others) . . .	13,297.1	15,451.7	18,156.6

Source: IMF, *International Financial Statistics*.

COST OF LIVING
(Consumer Price Index; base: July 1996–June 1997 = 100)

	1999	2000	2001
Food and non-alcoholic beverages .	117.1	118.6	123.4
Alcoholic beverages and tobacco .	144.0	156.4	168.1
Clothing and footwear	112.0	114.9	116.3
Fuel and electricity	100.5	106.3	122.4
Housing and household operations .	110.2	118.9	122.2
All items (incl. others)	117.1	122.0	128.6

NATIONAL ACCOUNTS
(million rupees in current prices)

Components of the Gross National Product

	2000	2001	2002
Compensation of employees . .	46,531	50,180	53,419
Operating surplus . . . . } Consumption of fixed capital . . }	57,024	66,132	70,745
Gross domestic product (GDP) at factor cost . . .	103,555	116,312	124,164
Indirect taxes	16,745	16,425	19,262
Less Subsidies	771	848	1,124
GDP in purchasers' values .	119,529	131,889	142,302
Factor income received from abroad . . . . } *Less* Factor income paid abroad . }	−783	393	295
Gross national product (GNP) at market prices . . .	118,746	132,282	142,597

* Figures are provisional.

Expenditure on the Gross Domestic Product
(estimates)

	2000	2001	2002
Government final consumption expenditure	15,582	16,752	18,125
Private final consumption expenditure	73,939	80,112	88,025
Increase in stocks	2,611	−2,600	109
Gross fixed capital formation . .	28,069	29,798	31,238
Total domestic expenditure . .	120,201	124,062	137,497
Exports of goods and services . .	73,841	90,463	88,757
Less Imports of goods and services	74,513	82,636	83,952
GDP in purchasers' values . .	119,529	131,889	142,302

* Including statistical discrepancies.

† Revised estimates.

‡ Preliminary estimates.

Gross Domestic Product by Economic Activity

	2000	2001	2002
Agriculture, hunting, forestry, and fishing	7,144	8,493	7,989
Mining and quarrying	142	150	75
Manufacturing	24,702	27,015	28,190
Electricity, gas and water . . .	1,820	2,634	3,040
Construction	6,225	6,540	7,284
Wholesale and retail trade, repair of motor vehicles and personal goods	13,009	13,780	14,715
Hotels and restaurants	5,860	7,509	7,580
Transport, storage and communications	13,577	15,251	17,325
Financial intermediation . . .	9,556	11,473	11,901
Real estate, renting and business activities	9,372	10,534	11,856
Public administration and defence; compulsory social security . .	6,867	7,291	7,892
Education	4,833	5,200	5,648
Health and social work	3,032	3,311	3,724
Other services	4,085	4,500	5,100
Sub-total	110,224	123,681	132,319
Less Imputed bank service charges	5,707	6,200	6,968
GDP at basic prices . . .	104,517	117,391	125,351
Taxes on products, *less* subsidies	15,012	14,498	16,951
GDP in purchasers' values . .	119,529	131,889	142,302

* Revised estimates.

† Provisional estimates.

BALANCE OF PAYMENTS
(US $ million)

	1999	2000	2001
Exports of goods f.o.b.	1,589.2	1,552.2	1,615.4
Imports of goods f.o.b.	−2,107.9	−1,944.4	−1,871.2
Trade balance	−518.7	−392.1	−255.9
Exports of services	1,035.6	1,071.2	1,222.0
Imports of services	−728.1	−762.5	−803.3
Balance on goods and services .	−211.2	−84.5	162.8
Other income received	35.1	48.7	75.2
Other income paid	−58.6	−64.9	−60.9
Balance on goods, services and income	−234.8	−100.7	177.1
Current transfers received . . .	196.4	167.6	195.5
Current transfers paid	−92.7	−103.8	−126.0
Current balance	−131.1	−36.9	246.6
Capital account (net)	−0.5	−0.6	−1.4
Direct investment abroad . . .	−6.4	−13.0	−2.4
Direct investment from abroad . .	49.4	265.6	−47.5
Portfolio investment assets . . .	59.1	-17.9	−25.3
Portfolio investment liabilities . .	−61.4	−117.81	−8.7
Other investment assets . . .	−245.9	−193.4	−448.2
Other investment liabilities . .	339.4	194.9	156.7
Net errors and omissions . . .	187.3	6.6	−15.9
Overall balance	189.7	87.6	−146.0

Source: IMF, *International Financial Statistics*.

External Trade

PRINCIPAL COMMODITIES
(million rupees)

Imports c.i.f.	1999	2000	2001
Food and live animals . . .	6,761	6,948	8,235
Fish and fish preparations .	n.a.	1,058	1,754
Crude materials (inedible) except			
fuels	1,667	1,654	1,787
Mineral fuels, lubricants, etc. .	4,046	6,450	6,504
Refined petroleum products .	3,506	5,634	5,532
Chemicals . . .	3,882	4,260	4,777
Basic manufactures . . .	17,036	17,570	17,694
Textile yarn, fabrics, etc . .	10,382	10,843	10,738
Textile yarn and thread . .	4,412	4,431	n.a.
Textile fabrics, etc. . . .	5,970	6,375	n.a.
Cotton fabrics . .	2,813	3,222	n.a.
Machinery and transport			
equipment . . .	17,145	12,427	13,132
Machinery specialized for			
particular industries . . .	2,488	2,251 }	3,631
General industrial machinery,			
equipment and parts . .	1,803	1,729	
Telecommunications and sound			
equipment . . .	1,700	1,641	n.a.
Other electrical machinery,			
apparatus, etc. . . .	1,898	1,757	n.a.
Road motor vehicles. . .	4,092	2,916	2,755
Aircraft, marine vessels and			
parts	2,876	135	1,967
Miscellaneous manufactured			
articles . . .	4,842	4,710	5,015
Total (incl. others). . . .	56,629	54,928	58,115

Exports f.o.b.	1999	2000	2001
Food and live animals . . .	9,142	7,154	10,909
Sugar . . .	7,602	5,544	8,138
Basic manufactures . . .	2,767	3,046	3,535
Textile yarn, fabrics, etc. . .	1,732	1,823	2,225
Miscellaneous manufactured			
articles . . .	25,114	26,718	27,219
Clothing and accessories (excl.			
footwear) . . .	23,210	24,961	25,094
Total (incl. others)	37,705	37,609	42,474

* Provisional.

† Excluding re-exports (million rupees): 1,455 in 1999; 1,463 in 2000; 1,944 (provisional) in 2001. Also excluded are stores and bunkers for ships and aircraft (million rupees): 865 in 1999; 1,810 in 2000; 1,937 (provisional) in 2001.

PRINCIPAL TRADING PARTNERS
(million rupees)

Imports c.i.f.	1999	2000	2001
Argentina	674	604	n.a.
Australia	1,836	1,897	2,383
Bahrain	881	1,348	n.a.
Belgium	1,187	965	796
China, People's Repub. . . .	3,231	4,152	4,154
France	8,345	5,248	5,431
Germany	2,155	2,113	3,137
Hong Kong	2,131	1,881	1,381
India	4,715	4,821	4,656
Indonesia	839	1,200	n.a.
Italy	2,001	1,815	1,911
Japan	3,411	2,255	2,139
Korea, Repub..	873	911	n.a.
Madagascar	596	874	n.a.
Malaysia	1,914	1,681	1,711
Pakistan	711	740	n.a.
Saudi Arabia	1,273	876	n.a.
Singapore	1,062	1,080	1,223
South Africa	6,165	8,198	8,031
Spain	822	1,001	n.a.
Switzerland	941	875	1,267
Taiwan.	1,183	1,060	1,040
Thailand	782	821	n.a.
United Arab Emirates . . .	382	578	n.a.
United Kingdom	2,587	2,378	2,108
USA	1,882	1,601	1,827
Total (incl. others)	56,629	54,928	58,115

Exports f.o.b.	1999	2000	2001
Belgium	949	897	732
France	7,262	7,743	7,938
Germany	1,725	1,414	1,584
Italy	1,249	1,515	1,605
Madagascar	1,894	1,580	2,012
Netherlands	943	652	777
Portugal	460	381	742
Réunion	595	509	532
Spain	994	869	701
Switzerland	556	452	n.a.
United Kingdom	12,798	11,276	13,822
USA	7,030	7,873	8,774
Total (incl. others)	39,160	39,072	44,418

* Imports by country of origin; exports by country of destination.

† Provisional.

‡ Including re-exports, but excluding stores and bunkers for ships and aircraft (million rupees): 865 in 1999; 1,810 in 2000; 1,937 (provisional) in 2001.

Transport

ROAD TRAFFIC
(motor vehicles registered at 31 December)

	2000	2001	2002
Private vehicles: cars . . .	84,784	89,748	95,635
Private vehicles: motorcycles and			
mopeds	116,478	119,953	122,801
Commercial vehicles: buses. . .	2,394	2,408	2,450
Commercial vehicles: taxis . .	5,039	5,318	5,801
Commercial vehicles: goods			
vehicles	29,292	31,582	32,986

SHIPPING

Merchant Fleet
(registered at 31 December)

	1999	2000	2001
Number of vessels	42	40	42
Total displacement ('000 grt) . .	149.9	91.2	96.9

Source: Lloyd's Register-Fairplay, *World Fleet Statistics*.

Sea-borne Freight Traffic
('000 metric tons)

	1999	2000	2001
Goods unloaded	3,355	3,677	4,362
Goods loaded	1,198	1,514	1,365

* Excluding ships' bunkers.

CIVIL AVIATION
(traffic)

	1998	1999	2000
Aircraft landings	7,320	7,612	8,349
Freight unloaded (metric tons) . .	17,516	20,290	20,113
Freight loaded (metric tons) . .	19,559	20,695	21,156

* Commercial aircraft only.

Tourism

FOREIGN TOURIST ARRIVALS

Country of Residence	2000	2001	2002
France	198,423	197,595	202,869
Germany	52,869	50,866	53,762
India	17,241	18,890	20,898
Italy	39,000	37,343	38,263
Réunion	86,945	91,140	96,375
South Africa	48,683	47,882	42,685
Switzerland	20,743	18,427	17,371
United Kingdom	74,488	77,888	80,667
Total (incl. others)	656,453	660,318	681,648

Tourism earnings (million rupees): 14,234 in 2000; 18,166 in 2001; 18,328 in 2002.

Communications Media

	1999	2000	2001
Telephones ('000 main lines in use)	257.1	280.9	306.8
Mobile cellular telephones ('000 subscribers)	102.1	180.0	300
Personal computers ('000 in use)	110	120	130
Internet users ('000)	55	87	158
Television sets licensed ('000) . .	220.0	223.9	235.4
Daily newspapers	6	6	6
Non-daily newspapers	35	35	35

1995: Facsimile machines (number in use) 20,000; Book production: titles 64, copies ('000) 116.

1996: Facsimile machines (number in use) 25,000; Book production: titles 80, copies ('000) 163.

1997: Facsimile machines (number in use) 28,000.

Sources: partly UNESCO, *Statistical Yearbook*; UN, *Statistical Yearbook*; International Telecommunication Union.

Education

(March 2002)

	Institutions	Teachers	Students
Pre-primary	1,071	2,421	36,982
Primary	290	5,256	132,432
Secondary	143	5,553	99,687
Technical and vocational . .	70	380	6,354

* By enrolment.

Adult literacy rate (UNESCO estimates): 84.5% (males 87.8%; females 81.3%) in 2000 (Source: UN Development Programme, *Human Development Report*).

Directory

The Constitution

The Mauritius Independence Order, which established a self-governing state, came into force on 12 March 1968, and was subsequently amended. Constitutional amendments providing for the adoption of republican status were approved by the Legislative Assembly (henceforth known as the National Assembly) on 10 December 1991, and came into effect on 12 March 1992. The main provisions of the revised Constitution are listed below:

HEAD OF STATE

The Head of State is the President of the Republic, who is elected by a simple majority of the National Assembly for a five-year term of office. The President appoints the Prime Minister (in whom executive power is vested) and, on the latter's recommendation, other ministers.

COUNCIL OF MINISTERS

The Council of Ministers, which is headed by the Prime Minister, is appointed by the President and is responsible to the National Assembly.

THE NATIONAL ASSEMBLY

The National Assembly, which has a term of five years, comprises the Speaker, 62 members elected by universal adult suffrage, a maximum of eight additional members and the Attorney-General (if not an elected member). The island of Mauritius is divided into 20 three-member constituencies for legislative elections. Rodrigues returns two members to the National Assembly. The official language of the National Assembly is English, but any member may address the Speaker in French.

The Government

HEAD OF STATE

President: KARL OFFMAN (took office 25 February 2002).
Vice-President: RAOUF BUNDHUN.

COUNCIL OF MINISTERS
(April 2003)

Prime Minister, Minister of Defence and Home Affairs, and Minister of External Communications: Sir ANEROOD JUGNAUTH.

Deputy Prime Minister and Minister of Finance: PAUL BÉRENGER.

Minister of Industry and International Trade: JAYA KRISHNA CUTTAREE.

Minister of Agriculture, Food Technology and Natural Resources: PRAVIND KUMAR JUGNAUTH.

Minister of Social Security, National Solidarity and Senior Citizens' Welfare and Reform Institutions: SAMIOULLAH LAUTHAN.

Minister of Local Government, Rodrigues and Minister of Housing and Land: GEORGES PIERRE LESJONGARD.

Minister of Public Utilities: ALAN GANOO.

Minister of Tourism and Leisure: NANDCOOMAR BODHA.

Minister of the Environment: RAJESH ANAND BHAGWAN.

Minister of Public Infrastructure, Land Transport and Shipping: ANIL KUMAR BACHOO.

Minister of Civil Service Affairs and Administrative Reform: AHMAD SULLIMAN JEEWAH.

Minister of Labour and Industrial Relations: SHOWKUTALLY SOODHUN.

Minister of Women's Rights, Child Development and Family Welfare: MARIA ARIANNE NAVARRE-MARIE.

Minister of Foreign Affairs and Regional Co-operation: ANIL KUMARSINGH GAYAN.

Minister of Education and Scientific Research: LOUIS STEVEN OBEEGADOO.

Minister of Health and Quality of Life: ASHOCK KUMAR JUGNAUTH.

Minister of Arts and Culture: MOTEE RAMDASS.

Minister of Fisheries: LOUIS SYLVIO MICHEL.

Minister of Economic Development, Financial Services and Corporate Affairs: KHUSHHAL CHAND KHUSHIRAM.

Minister of Commerce and Co-operatives: PREMDUT KOONJOO.

Minister of Information Technology and Telecommunications: DEELCHAND JEEHA.

Attorney-General and Minister of Justice and Human Rights: EMMANUEL JEAN LEUNG SHING.

Minister of Training, Skills Development and Productivity: SANGEET FOWDAR.

Minister of Youth and Sports: RAVI RAJ YERRIGADOO.

MINISTRIES

President's Office: Clarisse House, Vacoas, Port Louis; tel. 697-0077; fax 697-2347; e-mail statepas@intnet.mu; internet ncb.intnet.mu/president.htm.

Prime Minister's Office: Government Centre, Port Louis; tel. 202-9010; fax 208-8619; internet primeminister.gov.mu.

Ministry of Agriculture, Food Technology and Natural Resources: Renganaden Seeneevassan Bldg, 9th Floor, Port Louis; tel. 212-0814; fax 212-4427; internet agriculture.gov.mu.

Ministry of Arts and Culture: Renganaden Seeneevassen Bldg, 7th Floor, cnr Pope Hennessy and Maillard Sts, Port Louis; tel. 212-9993; fax 212-9366; e-mail minoac@intnet.mu; internet culture.gov.mu.

Ministry of Civil Service Affairs and Administrative Reform: New Government Centre, 7th Floor, Port Louis; tel. 201-1886; fax 212-9528; e-mail civser@intnet.mu; internet civilservice.gov.mu.

Ministry of Commerce and Co-operatives: Life Insurance Corpn of India Bldg, 3rd Floor, John F. Kennedy St, Port Louis; tel. 208-4812; fax 208-9263; e-mail pscoop@intnet.mu; internet cooperatives.gov.mu.

Ministry of Defence and Home Affairs: Government Centre, 4th Floor, Port Louis; internet ncb.intnet.mu/dha/ministry.

Ministry of Economic Development, Financial Services and Corporate Affairs: Emmanuel Anquetil Bldg, Level 9, Sir Seewoosagur Ramgoolam St, Port Louis; tel. 201-1260; fax 212-4124; e-mail medrc@intnet.mu; internet economicdevelopment.gov.mu.

Ministry of Education and Scientific Research: IVTB House, Pont Fer, Phoenix; tel. 698-0464; fax 698-2550; e-mail meduhrd@bow.intnet.mu; internet ministry-education.gov.mu.

Ministry of the Environment: Ken Lee Tower, Barracks St, Port Louis; tel. 212-3363; fax 212-8324; e-mail admenv@internet.mu; internet environment.gov.mu.

Ministry of External Communications: Air Mauritius Bldg, 5th Floor, Port Louis; tel. 210-3537; fax 211-7708; internet externalcom.gov.mu.

Ministry of Finance: Government House, Ground Floor, Port Louis; tel. 201-1146; fax 211-0096; e-mail finance@mof.intnet.mu; internet mof.gov.mu.

Ministry of Fisheries: Life Insurance Corpn of India Bldg, 4th Floor, John F. Kennedy St, Port Louis; tel. 211-2470; fax 208-1929; internet fisheries.gov.mu.

Ministry of Foreign Affairs and Regional Co-operation: New Government Centre, 5th Floor, Port Louis; tel. 201-1648; fax 208-8087; e-mail mfa@mail.gov.mu; internet foreign.gov.mu.

Ministry of Health and Quality of Life: Emmanuel Anquetil Bldg, Sir Seewoosagur Ramgoolam St, Port Louis; tel. 201-1912; fax 208-0376; e-mail mohql@intnet.mu; internet health.gov.mu.

Ministry of Housing and Land: Moorgate House, Port Louis; tel. 212-6022; fax 212-7482; internet housing.gov.mu.

Ministry of Industry and International Trade: Air Mauritius Centre, 7th Floor, John F. Kennedy St, Port Louis; tel. 201-7100; fax 212-8201; e-mail minic@intnet.mu; internet industry.gov.mu.

Ministry of Information Technology and Telecommunications: Air Mauritius Centre, Level 9, John F. Kennedy St, Port Louis; tel. 210-0201; fax 212-1673; e-mail mtel@mail.gov.mu; internet telecomit.gov.mu.

Ministry of Justice and Human Rights: Renganaden Seeneevassen Bldg, 2nd Floor, Port Louis; tel. 212-2139; fax 212-6742; e-mail sgo@intnet.mu; internet attorneygeneral.gov.mu.

Ministry of Labour and Industrial Relations: Victoria House, cnr St Louis and Barracks Sts, Port Louis; tel. 207-2600; fax 212-3070; e-mail mol@mail.gov.mu; internet labour.gov.mu.

Ministry of Local Government, Rodrigues and Rural and Urban Development: Emmanuel Anquetil Bldg, 3rd Floor, cnr Sir Seewoosagur Ramgoolam and Jules Koenig Sts, Port Louis; tel. 201-1216; fax 208-1450; e-mail minlogov@intnet.mu; internet localgovernment.gov.mu.

Ministry of Public Infrastructure, Land Transport and Shipping: Moorgate House, 4th Floor, Sir W. Newton St, Port Louis; tel. 208-3063; fax 208-7149; internet publicinfrastructure.gov.mu.

Ministry of Public Utilities: Medcor Bldg, 10th Floor, John F. Kennedy St, Port Louis; tel. 210-3994; fax 208-6497; e-mail minpuuti@intnet.mu; internet publicutilities.gov.mu.

Ministry of Social Security, National Solidarity and Senior Citizens' Welfare and Reform Institutions: Renganaden Seeneevassen Bldg, Jules Koenig St, Port Louis; tel. 212-9813; fax 212-8190; e-mail mssns@intnet.mu; internet socialsecurity.gov.mu.

Ministry of Tourism and Leisure: Air Mauritius Centre, Level 12, John F. Kennedy St, Port Louis; tel. 210-1329; fax 208-6776; e-mail mot@intnet.mu; internet tourism.gov.mu.

Ministry of Training, Skills Development and Productivity: NPF Bldg, 6th Floor, cnr Jules Koenig and Maillard Sts, Port Louis; tel. 212-5051; fax 212-5820; e-mail mhrd@intnet.mu; internet training.gov.mu.

Ministry of Women's Rights, Child Development and Family Welfare: CSK Bldg, cnr Remy Ollier and Emmanuel Anquetil Sts, Port Louis; tel. 240-1377; fax 240-7717; e-mail mwfwcd@bow.intnet.mu; internet women.gov.mu.

Ministry of Youth and Sports: Emmanuel Anquetil Bldg, 3rd Floor, Sir Seewoosagur Ramgoolam St, Port Louis; tel. 201-2543; fax 211-2986; e-mail mys@mail.gov.mu; internet youthsport.gov.mu.

Legislature

NATIONAL ASSEMBLY

Speaker: PREMNATH RAMNAH.

General Election, 11 September 2000

Party	Seats
Mouvement Socialiste Militant (MSM)/Mouvement Militant Mauricien (MMM)	54
Mauritius Labour Party (MLP)/Parti Mauricien Social Démocrate (PMSD)	6
Organisation du Peuple Rodriguais (OPR)	2

*Additional members were to be appointed from the unsuccessful candidates who attracted the largest number of votes.

Political Organizations

Comité d'Action Musulman (CAM): Port Louis; f. 1958; Muslim support; Pres. YOUSSUF MOHAMMED.

Hizbullah: Port Louis; Islamist; Leader CEHL MEEAH.

Mauritius Labour Party (MLP): 7 Guy Rozemont Sq., Port Louis; tel. 212-6691; e-mail labour@intnet.mu; internet www.labour.intnet.mu; f. 1936; formed an alliance with the Parti Mauricien Social Démocrate for the 2000 election; Leader Dr NAVINCHANDRA RAMGOOLAM; Chair. JEAN-FRANÇOIS CHAUMIÈRE; Sec.-Gen. SARAT DUTT LALLAH.

Mouvement Militant Mauricien (MMM): 21 Poudrière St, Port Louis; tel. 212-6553; fax 208-9939; internet mmm.intnet.mu; f. 1969; socialist; formed an alliance with the Mouvement Socialiste Militant for the 2000 election and subsequently a coalition govt; Chair. AHMAD JEEWAH; Leader PAUL BÉRENGER; Sec.-Gen. IVAN COLLENDAVELLOO.

Mouvement Rodriguais: Port Mathurin, Rodrigues; tel. 831-1876 (Port Mathurin); tel. and fax 686-8859 (Port Louis); f. 1992; represents the interests of Rodrigues; Leader JOSEPH (NICHOLAS) VON-MALLY.

Mouvement Socialiste Militant (MSM): Sun Trust Bldg, 31 Edith Cavell St, Port Louis; tel. 212-8787; fax 208-9517; e-mail request@msmsun.com; internet www.msmsun.com; f. 1983 by fmr mems of the MMM; dominant party in subsequent coalition govts until Dec. 1995 and again in 2000; Leader Sir PRAVIND JUGNAUTH; Chair. JOE LESJONGARD; Sec.-Gen. VISHWANATH SAJADAH.

Organisation du Peuple Rodriguais (OPR): Port Mathurin, Rodrigues; represents the interests of Rodrigues; Leader LOUIS SERGE CLAIR.

Parti Mauricien Social Démocrate (PMSD): Melville, Grand Gaube; also known as the Parti Mauricien Xavier-Luc Duval (PMXD); centre-right; formed an alliance with the Mauritius Labour Party for the 2000 election; Leader CHARLES GAËTAN XAVIER-LUC DUVAL; Sec.-Gen. JACQUES PANGLOSE.

Minor parties include the **Mouvement Militant Socialiste Mauricien** (Leader MADUN DULLOO), the **Rassemblement pour la Réforme** (Leader SHEILA BAPPOO), the **Renouveau Militant Mauricien** (Leader Dr PARAMHANSA (PREM) NABABSINGH), the **'Vrais Bleus'** (Leader HERVÉ DUVAL), the **Parti Socialiste Ouvrier** (Sec.-Gen. DIDIER EDMOND), the **Rassemblement pour l'Organisation des Créoles, Lalit** and the **Mouvement Républicain**.

Diplomatic Representation

EMBASSIES AND HIGH COMMISSIONS IN MAURITIUS

Australia: Rogers House, 2nd Floor, John F. Kennedy St, POB 541, Port Louis; tel. 208-1700; fax 208-8878; e-mail austhc@intnet.mu; internet www.ahcmauritius.org; High Commissioner JEFFREY SCOUGALL.

China, People's Republic: Royal Rd, Belle Rose, Rose Hill; tel. 454-9111; fax 464-6012; Ambassador WANG FUYUAN.

Egypt: Forest Lane, Floreal, POB 8, Port Louis; tel. 696-5012; fax 686-5575; Ambassador MAGDA HOSNI NASR AHMED.

France: 14 St George St, Port Louis; tel. 202-0100; fax 202-0110; e-mail ambafr@intnet.mu; internet www.ambafrance-mu.org; Ambassador HENRI VIGNAL.

India: Life Insurance Corpn of India Bldg, 6th Floor, John F. Kennedy St, POB 162, Port Louis; tel. 208-3775; fax 208-6859; High Commissioner VIJAY KUMAR (recalled April 2003).

Madagascar: Guiot Pasceau St, Floreal, POB 3, Port Louis; tel. 686-5015; fax 686-7040; Ambassador PAUL A. TSILANIZARA.

Pakistan: 9A Queen Mary Ave, Floreal, Port Louis; tel. 698-8501; fax 698-8465; High Commissioner G. R. BALUCH.

Russia: Queen Mary Ave, POB 10, Floreal, Port Louis; tel. 696-1545; fax 696-5027; e-mail rusemb.mu@intnet.mu; Ambassador V. M. NESTERUSHKIN.

South Africa: BAI Bldg, 4th Floor, 25 Pope Hennessy St, POB 908, Port Louis; tel. 212-6925; fax 212-6936; High Commissioner LOUIS L. A. MNGUNI.

United Kingdom: Les Cascades Bldg, 7th Floor, Edith Cavell St, POB 1063, Port Louis; tel. 202-9400; fax 202-9408; e-mail bhc@intnet.mu; High Commissioner DAVID SNOXELL.

USA: Rogers House, 4th Floor, John F. Kennedy St, Port Louis; tel. 208-4400; fax 208-9534; e-mail usembass@intnet.mu; internet mauritius.usembassy.gov; Ambassador JOHN PRICE.

Judicial System

The laws of Mauritius are derived both from the French Code Napoléon and from English Law. The Judicial Department consists of the Supreme Court, presided over by the Chief Justice and eight other Judges who are also Judges of the Court of Criminal Appeal and the Court of Civil Appeal. These courts hear appeals from the Intermediate Court, the Industrial Court and 10 District Courts. The Industrial Court has special jurisdiction to protect the constitutional rights of the citizen. There is a right of appeal in certain cases from the Supreme Court to the Judicial Committee of the Privy Council in the United Kingdom.

Chief Justice: ARIANGA PILLAY.

Senior Puisne Judge: B. SIK YUEN.

Puisne Judges: V. BOOLELL, K. P. MATADEEN, R. N. NARAYEN, E. BALANCY, P. LAM SHANG LEEN.

Religion

Hindus are estimated to comprise more than 50% of the population, with Christians accounting for some 30% and Muslims 17%. There is also a small Buddhist community.

CHRISTIANITY

The Anglican Communion

Anglicans in Mauritius are within the Church of the Province of the Indian Ocean, comprising six dioceses (four in Madagascar, one in Mauritius and one in Seychelles). The Archbishop of the Province is the Bishop of Antananarivo, Madagascar. In 1983 the Church had 5,438 members in Mauritius.

Bishop of Mauritius: Rt Rev. IAN ERNEST, Bishop's House, Phoenix; tel. 686-5158; fax 697-1096; e-mail dioang@intnet.mu.

Presbyterian Church of Mauritius

Minister: Pasteur ANDRÉ DE RÉLAND, 11 Poudrière St, Port Louis; tel. 208-2386; f. 1814.

The Roman Catholic Church

Mauritius comprises a single diocese, directly responsible to the Holy See. At 31 December 2000 there were an estimated 287,726 adherents in the country, representing about 24.4% of the total population.

Bishop of Port Louis: Rt Rev. MAURICE PIAT, Evêché, 13 Mgr Gonin St, Port Louis; tel. 208-3068; fax 208-6607; e-mail eveche@intnet.mu.

BAHÁ'Í FAITH

National Spiritual Assembly: POB 538, Port Louis; tel. 212-2179; mems resident in 190 localities.

ISLAM

Mauritius Islamic Mission: Noor-e-Islam Mosque, Port Louis; Imam S. M. BEEHARRY.

The Press

DAILIES

China Times: 24 Emmanuel Anquetil St, POB 325, Port Louis; tel. 240-3067; f. 1953; Chinese; Editor-in-Chief LONG SIONG AH KENG; circ. 3,000.

Chinese Daily News: 32 Rémy Ollier St, POB 316, Port Louis; tel. 240-0472; f. 1932; Chinese; Editor-in-Chief WONG YUEN MOY; circ. 5,000.

L'Express: 3 Brown Sequard St, POB 247, Port Louis; tel. 202-8200; fax 208-8174; e-mail sentinelle@bow.intnet.mu; internet www.lexpress-net.com; f. 1963; English and French; Editor-in-Chief JEAN-CLAUDE DE L'ESTRAC; circ. 35,000.

Maurice Soir: Port Louis; f. 1996; Editor SYDNEY SELVON; circ. 2,000.

Le Mauricien: 8 St George St, POB 7, Port Louis; tel. 208-3251; fax 208-7059; e-mail redaction@lemauricien.com; internet www.lemauricien.com; f. 1907; English and French; Editor-in-Chief GILBERT AHNEE; circ. 35,000.

L'Observateur: Port Louis; f. 1997; French.

Le Quotidien: Port Louis; tel. 211-4800; fax 211-7479; e-mail quotidie@bow.intnet.mu; f. 1996; English and French; Dirs JACQUES DAVID, PATRICK MICHEL; circ. 30,000.

Le Socialiste: Manilall Bldg, 3rd Floor, Brabant St, Port Louis; tel. 208-8003; fax 211-3890; English and French; Editor-in-Chief VEDI BALLAH; circ. 7,000.

The Sun: 31 Edith Cavell St, Port Louis; tel. 212-4820; fax 208-9517; English and French; Editor-in-Chief SUBASH GOBIN; circ. 4,000.

The Tribune: Port Louis; f. 1999; Publr HARISH CHUNDUNSING.

WEEKLIES AND FORTNIGHTLIES

5-Plus Dimanche: Résidence des Palmiers, 198 Royal Rd, Beau Bassin; tel. 454-3353; fax 454-3420; f. 1994; English and French; Editor-in-Chief FINLAY SALESSE; circ. 30,000.

5-Plus Magazine: Résidence des Palmiers, 198 Royal Rd, Beau Bassin; tel. 454-3353; fax 454-3420; f. 1990; English and French; Editor-in-Chief PIERRE BENOÎT; circ. 10,000.

Business Magazine: TN Tower, 1st Floor, 13 St George St, Port Louis; tel. 211-1925; fax 211-1926; f. 1993; English and French; Editor-in-Chief LYNDSAY RIVIÈRE; circ. 6,000.

Le Croissant: cnr Velore and Noor Essan Mosque Sts, Port Louis; tel. 240-7105; English and French; Editor-in-Chief RAYMOND RICHARD NAUVEL; circ. 25,000.

Le Dimanche: 5 Jemmapes St, Port Louis; tel. 212-5887; fax 212-1177; e-mail ledmer@intnet.mu; f. 1961; English and French; Editor RAYMOND RICHARD NAUVEL; circ. 25,000.

La Gazette des Iles: Port Louis; historical journal.

L'Hebdo-Militant: Port Louis.

Impact News: 6 Grandcourt, Port Louis; tel. 240-8567; English and French; Editor-in-Chief CADER SAIB.

Lalit de Klas: 153B Royal Rd, G.R.N.W., Port Louis; tel. 208-2132; English, French and Creole; Editor ASHOK SUBRON.

Le Lotus: 73 Prince of Wales St, Rose Hill; tel. 208-4068; English and French; Editor-in-Chief MOGANADEN PILLAY.

Le Mag: Industrial Zone, Tombeay Bay; tel. 247-1005; fax 247-1061; f. 1993; English and French; Editor (vacant); circ. 8,000.

Mauritius Times: 23 Bourbon St, Port Louis; tel. and fax 212-1313; e-mail mtimes@intnet.mu; f. 1954; English and French; Editor-in-Chief MADHUKAR RAMLALLAH; circ. 15,000.

Le Militant Magazine: 7 Lord Kitchener St, Port Louis; tel. 212-6050; fax 208-2291; f. 1989; English and French; Editor-in-Chief MITRADEV PEERTHUM; circ. 2,000.

Mirror: 39 Emmanuel Anquetil St, Port Louis; tel. 240-3298; Chinese; Editor-in-Chief NG KEE SIONG; circ. 4,000.

News on Sunday: Port Louis; tel. 211-5902; fax 211-7302; e-mail newsonsunday@hotmail.com; internet www.newsonsunday.com; f. 1996; weekly; Editor MICHAEL LYNCH; circ. 15,000.

Le Nouveau Militant: 21 Poudrière St, Port Louis; tel. 212-6553; fax 208-2291; f. 1979; publ. by the Mouvement Militant Mauricien; English and French; Editor-in-Chief J. RAUMIAH.

Le Rodriguais: Saint Gabriel, Rodrigues; tel. 831-1613; fax 831-1484; f. 1989; Creole, English and French; Editor JACQUES EDOUARD; circ. 2,000.

Star: Port Louis; tel. 212-2736; e-mail starpress@intnet.mu; internet www.mauriweb.com/star; English and French; Editor-in-Chief Dr HASSAM RUHOMALLY.

Style: Port Louis; women's interest; weekly.

Sunday: Port Louis; tel. 208-9516; fax 208-7059; f. 1966; English and French; Editor-in-Chief SUBASH GOBIN.

La Vie Catholique: 28 Nicolay Rd, Port Louis; tel. 242-0975; fax 242-3114; e-mail viecatho@intnet.mu; internet pages.intnet.mu/lavie; f. 1930; weekly; English, French and Creole; Editor-in-Chief Fr GEORGES CHEUNG; circ. 8,000.

Week-End: 8 St George St, Port Louis; tel. 208-3252; fax 208-7059; internet www.lemauricien.com/weekend; f. 1966; French and English; Editor-in-Chief GÉRARD CATEAU; circ. 80,000.

Week-End Scope: 8 St George St, Port Louis; tel. 208-3251; fax 208-7059; internet www.lemauricien.com/wes; English and French; Editor-in-Chief AHMAD SALARBUX.

OTHER SELECTED PERIODICALS

CCI-INFO: 3 Royal St, Port Louis; tel. 208-3301; fax 208-0076; e-mail mcci@intnet.mu; internet www.mcci.org; English and French; f. 1995; publ. of the Mauritius Chamber of Commerce and Industry.

Ciné Star Magazine: 64 Sir Seewoosagur Ramgoolam St, Port Louis; tel. 240-1447; English and French; Editor-in-Chief ABDOOL RAWOOF SOOBRATTY.

Education News: Edith Cavell St, Port Louis; tel. 212-1303; English and French; monthly; Editor-in-Chief GIAN AUBEELUCK.

Le Message de L'Ahmadiyyat: c/o Ahmadiyya Muslim Asscn, POB 6, Rose Hill; tel. 464-1747; fax 454-2223; e-mail jamaatmu@bow.intnet.mu; French; monthly; Editor-in-Chief ZAFRULLAH DOMUN; circ. 3,000.

Le Progrès Islamique: 51B Solferino St, Rose Hill; tel. 467-1697; fax 467-1696; f. 1948; English and French; monthly; Editor DEVINA SOOKIA.

La Voix d'Islam: Parisot Rd, Mesnil, Phoenix; f. 1951; English and French; monthly.

Publishers

Boukié Banané (The Flame Tree): 5 Edwin Ythier St, Rose Hill; tel. 454-2327; fax 465-4312; e-mail limem@intnet.mu; internet pages .intnet.mu/develog; f. 1979; Morisien literature, poetry and drama; Man. Dir DEV VIRAHSAWMY.

Business Publications Ltd: TN Tower, 1st Floor, St George St, Port Louis; tel. 211-1925; fax 211-1926; f. 1993; English and French; Dir LYNDSAY RIVIÈRE.

Editions du Dattier: 82 Goyavier Ave, Quatre Bornes; tel. 466-4854; fax 446-3105; e-mail dattier@intnet.mu; English and French; Dir JEAN-PHILIPPE LAGESSE.

Editions de l'Océan Indien: Stanley, Rose Hill; tel. 464-6761; fax 464-3445; e-mail eoibooks@intnet.mu; f. 1977; textbooks, literature; English, French and Asian languages; Gen. Man. (vacant).

Editions Le Printemps: 4 Club Rd, Vacoas; tel. 696-1017; fax 686-7302; e-mail elp@bow.intnet.mu; Man. Dir A. I. SULLIMAN.

Broadcasting and Communications

TELECOMMUNICATIONS

Mauritius Telecommunications Authority (MTA): Port Louis; f. 1999; regulatory authority; Chair. RAJESKUMAR UNNUTH.

Mauritius Telecom: Telecom Tower, Edith Cavell St, Port Louis; tel. 203-7000; fax 208-1070; e-mail mtelecom@intnet.mu; internet mt.intnet.mu; f. 1992; 40% owned by France Telecom; privatized in 2000; provides all telecommunications services; Chair. Dr PREM NABABSING; Chief Exec. MEGHANATHAN PILLAY.

BROADCASTING

In 1997 the Supreme Court invalidated the broadcasting monopoly held by the Mauritius Broadcasting Corporation.

Radio

Mauritius Broadcasting Corpn: Broadcasting House, Louis Pasteur St, Forest Side; tel. 675-5001; fax 676-7332; e-mail mbc@intnet .mu; internet mbc.intnet.mu; f. 1964; independent corpn operating five national radio services and three television channels; Chair. SHIRIN ARUMEERUDDY-CZIFFRA; Dir-Gen. HOOTESH RAMBURN.

Radio One: Port Louis; f. 2002; owned by Sentinelle media group; news and entertainment; Dir-Gen. JEAN-MICHEL FONTAINE.

A further two private stations, Radio Plus and Sunrise Radio, were issued licences in early 2002.

Television

Independent television stations were to commence broadcasting from 2002, as part of the liberalization of the sector.

Mauritius Broadcasting Corpn: see Radio.

Finance

(cap. = capital; res = reserves; dep. = deposits; m. = million; brs = branches; amounts in Mauritian rupees, unless otherwise stated)

BANKING

Central Bank

Bank of Mauritius: Sir William Newton St, POB 29, Port Louis; tel. 202-3800; fax 208-9204; e-mail bomrd@bow.intnet.mu; internet bom.intnet.mu; f. 1967; bank of issue; cap. 10.0m., res 13,100.1m., dep. 4,098.0m. (June 2001); Gov. RAMESWURLALL BASANT ROI; Man. Dir BABOO RAJENDRANATHSING GUJADHUR.

Principal Commercial Banks

Bank of Baroda: Sir William Newton St, POB 553, Port Louis; tel. 208-1504; fax 208-3892; e-mail bobgen@intnet.mu; cap. and res 19.9m., dep. 396m. (March 1998); Pres. R. A. ALMEIDA; 6 brs.

Barclays Bank PLC, Mauritius: Sir William Newton St, POB 165, Port Louis; tel. 208-2685; fax 208-2720; f. 1919; absorbed Banque Nationale de Paris Intercontinentale in 2002; cap. 100.0m., res 616.1m., dep. 6,886.7m. (Dec. 2001); Dir JACQUES DE NAVACELLE; 16 brs.

The First City Bank: 16 Sir William Newton St, POB 485, Port Louis; tel. 208-5061; fax 208-5388; f. 1991 as the Delphis Bank Ltd; merged with Union International Bank in 1997; private bank; taken over by consortium in 2002; 51.6% owned by the Development Bank of Mauritius; cap. 300m., dep. 4,673m. (Dec. 2000); Chair. PIERO SOTERIOU; Man. Dir ROHIT AUKLE.

Hongkong and Shanghai Banking Corpn Ltd (HSBC): place d'Armes, POB 50, Port Louis; tel. 208-1801; fax 210-0400; e-mail hsbcmauritius@hsbc.co.mu; internet www.hsbc.co.mu; f. 1916; CEO SANJIV BHASIN.

Indian Ocean International Bank Ltd: 34 Sir William Newton St, POB 863, Port Louis; tel. 208-0121; fax 208-0127; f. 1978; cap. 100.5m., res 252.8m., dep. 2,661.3m. (June 2001); Chair. and Man. Dir S. M. CUNDEN; 8 brs.

Mauritius Commercial Bank Ltd: MCB Centre, 9–15 Sir William Newton St, Port Louis; tel. 202-5000; fax 208-7054; e-mail publicrelations@mcb.co.mu; internet www.mcbgroup.com; f. 1838; cap. 582.6m., res 7,303.0m., dep. 74,646.3m. (June 2002); Pres. JACQUES HAREL; Gen. Man. PIERRE GUY NOËL; 41 brs.

South East Asian Bank Ltd: Max City Bldg, 2nd Floor, cnr Rémy Ollier and Louis Pasteur Sts, POB 13, Port Louis; tel. 216-8826; fax 241-7379; e-mail seab@intnet.mu; f. 1989; cap. and res 114.7m., dep. 1,001.3m. (Dec. 2000); Chief Exec. VINCENT LEE; Chair. Tan Sri Dato' ABDUL KHALID BIN SAHAN; 5 brs.

State Bank of Mauritius Ltd: State Bank Tower, 1 Queen Elizabeth II Ave, POB 152, Port Louis; tel. 202-1111; fax 202-1234; e-mail sbm@sbm.intnet.mu; internet www.sbm-online.com; f. 1973; cap. 382.5m., res 4,504.4m., dep. 24,765.2m. (June 2002); Chair. Sir DEWOONARAIN DOOKUN; Chief Exec. MUNI KRISHNA T. REDDY; 45 brs.

Development Bank

Development Bank of Mauritius Ltd: La Chaussée, POB 157, Port Louis; tel. 208-0241; fax 208-8498; e-mail dbm@intnet.mu; internet www.dbm-ltd.com; f. 1964; 65% govt-owned; cap. 125m., res 1,130.0m., total assets 3,981.3m. (June 2001); Chair. A. HOSSEN; Man. Dir B. CHOORAMUN.

Principal 'Offshore' Banks

Banque Internationale des Mascareignes Ltd: Le Caudan Waterfront, 4th Floor, Barkly Wharf, POB 489, Port Louis; tel. 212-4978; fax 212-4983; e-mail bim@intnet.mu; internet www.bim.intnet .mu; f. 1991; jt venture of Banque de la Réunion (50.5%), Mauritius Commercial Bank Ltd (35%) and Crédit Lyonnais de France (14.5%); cap. US $6.0m., res $1.5m., dep. $106.5m. (Dec. 2001); Chair. SERGE ROBERT; Gen. Man. YVES NAMY.

SBI International (Mauritius) Ltd: Harbour Front Bldg, 7th Floor, John F. Kennedy St, POB 376, Port Louis; tel. 212-2054; fax 212-2050; e-mail sbilmaur@intnet.mu; f. 1989; subsidiary of the State Bank of India; cap. US $10.0m., res $8.6m., dep. $135.1m. (Dec. 2001); Chair. JANKI BALLABH; Man. Dir S. K. BHATTACHARYA.

Bank of Baroda, Banque Nationale de Paris Intercontinentale, Barclays Bank PLC, African Asian Bank, PT Bank International Indonesia, Investec Bank (Mauritius) and HSBC Bank PLC also operate 'offshore' banking units.

STOCK EXCHANGE

Financial Services Commission: Harbour Front Bldg, 4th Floor, John F. Kennedy St, Port Louis; tel. 210-7000; fax 208-7172; e-mail fscmauritius@intnet.mu; f. 1993; regulatory authority for securities, insurance and global business activities; Chief Exec. IQBAL RAJAHBALEE.

Stock Exchange of Mauritius: Cascades Bldg, 2nd Floor, Edith Cavell St, Port Louis; tel. 212-9541; fax 208-8409; e-mail stockex@ bow.intnet.mu; internet www.semdex.com; f. 1989; 11 mems; Chair. JEAN DE FONDAUMIÈRE; CEO SUNIL BENIMADHU.

INSURANCE

Albatross Insurance Co Ltd: 22 St George St, POB 116, Port Louis; tel. 207-9007; fax 208-4800; e-mail headoffice@albatross.mu; internet www.albatross-insurance.com; f. 1975; Chair. TIMOTHY TAYLOR; Man. Dir JEAN DE LA HOGUE.

Anglo-Mauritius Assurance Society Ltd: Swan Group Centre, 10 Intendance St, POB 837, Port Louis; tel. 202-8600; fax 208-8956; e-mail anglomtius@intnet.mu; internet www.groupswan.com; f. 1951; Chair. J. CYRIL LAGESSE; CEO JEAN DE FONDAUMIÈRE.

British American Insurance Co (Mauritius) Ltd: BAI Bldg, 25 Pope Hennessy St, POB 331, Port Louis; tel. 202-3600; fax 208-3713; e-mail bai@intnet.mu; f. 1920; Chair. DAWOOD RAWAT; Man. Dir HEINRICH K. DE KOCK.

Ceylinco Stella Insurance Co Ltd: 36 Sir Seewoosagur Ramgoolam St, POB 852, Port Louis; tel. 208-0056; fax 208-1639; e-mail stellain@intnet.mu; internet www.stellain.com; f. 1977; Chair. and Man. Dir R. KRESHAN JHOBOO.

Indian Ocean General Assurance Ltd: 35 Corderie St, POB 865, Port Louis; tel. 212-4125; fax 212-5850; e-mail iogaltd@intnet.mu; f. 1971; Chair. SAM M. CUNDEN; Man. Dir D. A. CUNDEN.

Island Insurance Co Ltd: Labourdonnais Court, 5th Floor, cnr Labourdonnais and St George Sts, Port Louis; tel. 212-4860; fax 208-8762; e-mail island.ins@intnet.mu; f. 1998; Chair. CARRIM A. CURRIMJEE; Man. Dir OLIVIER LAGESSE.

Jubilee Insurance (Mauritius) Ltd: PCL Bldg, 4th Floor, 43 Sir William Newton St, POB 301, Port Louis; tel. 210-3678; fax 212-7970; e-mail jubilee@intnet.mu; f. 1998; Chair. and CEO AUGUSTINE J. HATCH.

Lamco International Insurance Ltd: 12 Barracks St, Port Louis; tel. 212-0233; fax 208-0630; e-mail lamco@intnet.mu; internet www .lamcoinsurance.com; f. 1978; Chair. A. B. ATCHIA.

Life Insurance Corpn of India: LIC Centre, John F. Kennedy St, Port Louis; tel. 212-5316; fax 208-6392; e-mail liccmm@intnet.mu; f. 1956; Chief Man. HEMANT BHARGAVA.

Mauritian Eagle Insurance Co Ltd: 1st Floor, IBL House, Caudan Waterfront, POB 854, Port Louis; tel. 203-2200; fax 208-8608; e-mail meagle@meagle.intnet.mu; internet www.iblgroup .com/mauritianeagle; f. 1973; Chair. P. D'HOTMAN DE VILLIERS; Exec. Dir G. LAN HUN KUEN.

Mauritius Union Assurance Co Ltd: 4 L'Homme St, POB 233, Port Louis; tel. 208-4185; fax 212-2962; e-mail mua@bow.intnet.mu; internet www.muaco.com; f. 1948; Chair. Sir MAURICE LATOUR-ADRIEN; Gen. Man. JOHN NOËL LAM CHUN.

The New India Assurance Co Ltd: Bank of Baroda Bldg, 3rd Floor, 15 Sir William Newton St, POB 398, Port Louis; tel. 208-1442; fax 208-2160; e-mail niassurance@intnet.mu; f. 1935; Chief Man. V. K. GOYAL.

La Préservatrice Foncière: 6 Dumas St, Port Louis; tel. 212-1352; fax 208-3604; Dirs MAURICE MARTIN, FRANÇOIS MARTIN.

La Prudence Mauricienne Assurances Ltée: Le Caudan Waterfront, 2nd Floor, Barkly Wharf, POB 882, Port Louis; tel. 207-2500; fax 208-8936; e-mail prudence@intnet.mu; Chair. ROBERT DE FROBERVILLE; Man. Dir FÉLIX MAUREL.

Rainbow Insurance Co Ltd: 23 Edith Cavell St, POB 389, Port Louis; tel. 212-5767; fax 208-8750; f. 1976; Chair. B. GOKULSING; Man. Dir PREVIN RENBURG.

State Insurance Co of Mauritius Ltd (SICOM): SICOM Bldg, Sir Célicourt Antelme St, Port Louis; tel. 208-5406; fax 208-7662; e-mail email@sicom.intnet.mu; internet sicom.intnet.mu; f. 1975; Chair. A. F. HO CHAN FONG; Man. Dir K. BHOOJEDHUR-OBEEGADOO.

Sun Insurance Co Ltd: 2 St George St, Port Louis; tel. 208-0769; fax 208-2052; f. 1981; Chair. Sir KAILASH RAMDANEE; Man. Dir A. MUSBALLY.

Swan Insurance Co Ltd: Swan Group Centre, 10 Intendance St, POB 364, Port Louis; tel. 211-2001; fax 208-6898; e-mail swan@ intnet.mu; f. 1955; Chair. J. M. ANTOINE HAREL; CEO JEAN DE FONDAUMIÈRE.

L. and H. Vigier de Latour Ltd: Les Jamalacs Bldg, Old Council St, Port Louis; tel. 212-2034; fax 212-6056; Chair. and Man. Dir L. J. D. HENRI VIGIER DE LATOUR.

Trade and Industry

GOVERNMENT AGENCIES

Agricultural Marketing Board (AMB): Dr G. Leclézio Ave, Moka; tel. 433-4025; fax 433-4837; e-mail agbd@intnet.mu; markets certain locally produced and imported food crops; also collects and distributes milk and provides cold store facilities.

Mauritius Meat Authority: Abattoir Rd, Roche Bois, POB 612, Port Louis; tel. 242-5884; fax 242-4695; e-mail msa@bow.intnet.mu; licensing authority; controls and regulates sale of meat and meat products; also purchases and imports livestock and markets meat products.

Mauritius Sugar Authority: Ken Lee Bldg, 2nd Floor, Edith Cavell St, Port Louis; tel. 208-7466; fax 208-7470; e-mail msa@bow .intnet.mu; internet www.mns.intnet.mu/msa.htm; Chair. S. SEEBALUCK; Exec. Dir G. RAJPATI.

Mauritius Tea Board: Wooton St, Curepipe Rd, Curepipe; tel. 675-3497; fax 676-1445; regulates and controls the activities of the tea industry; Gen. Man. A. SEEPERGAUTH.

DEVELOPMENT ORGANIZATIONS

Financial Services Commission (FSC): Barkly Wharf, 5th Floor, le Caudan Waterfront, Old Pavilion St, Port Louis; tel. 210-7000; fax

212-9459; e-mail mobaa@bow.intnet.mu; internet www.mobaa.net; f. 1992; regulates and supervises commercial activities; Dir SATYADEV DEONARAIN BIKOO.

Mauritius Freeport Authority: Trade and Marketing Centre, Freeport Zone 6, Mer Rouge; tel. 206-2500; fax 206-2600; e-mail mfa@freeport.intnet.mu; internet www.efreeport.com; f. 1990; Chair. KAVYDASS ROMANO; Dir-Gen. GÉRARD SANSPEUR.

Mauritius Industrial Development Authority (MIDA): BAI Bldg, 2nd Floor, 25 Pope Hennessy St, POB 1184, Port Louis; tel. 208-7750; fax 208-5965; e-mail media@intnet.mu; internet ncb .intnet.mu/mida; f. 1985 to promote the export of goods and services and to encourage export-orientated investment; Chair. MARDAY VENKATASAMY; CEO ELIZABETH AH CHONG.

Mauritius Infocom Development Authority: Port Louis; f. 2001; responsible for both the Mauritius Telecommunications Authority and the National Computer Board.

Mauritius Investment Board: Port Louis; f. 2000 to promote international investment, business and services.

State Investment Corpn Ltd (SIC): Air Mauritius Centre, 15th Floor, John F. Kennedy St, Port Louis; tel. 212-2978; fax 208-8948; e-mail sicadmin@intnet.mu; provides support for new investment and transfer of technology, in agriculture, industry and tourism; Man. Dir SEILENDRA GOKHOOL; CEO RAJIV BEEHARRY.

CHAMBERS OF COMMERCE

Chinese Chamber of Commerce: Port Louis; tel. 208-0946; fax 242-1193; Pres. JEAN KOK SHUN.

Mauritius Chamber of Commerce and Industry: 3 Royal St, Port Louis; tel. 208-3301; fax 208-0076; e-mail mcci@intnet.mu; internet www.mcci.org; f. 1850; 416 mems; Pres. TIM TAYLOR; Sec.-Gen. MAHMOOD CHEEROO.

INDUSTRIAL ASSOCIATION

Mauritius Sugar Producers' Association: Plantation House, Duke of Edinburgh Ave, Port Louis; tel. 212-0295; fax 212-5727; e-mail mspa@intnet.mu; Chair. GEORGES LEUNGSHING; Dir P. DE LABAUVE D'ARIFAT.

EMPLOYERS' ORGANIZATION

Mauritius Employers' Federation: Cerné House, 1st Floor, Chaussée St, Port Louis; tel. 212-1599; fax 212-6725; e-mail mef@ intnet.mu; f. 1962; Pres. DAN BUNDHOO; Dir Dr AZAD JEETUN.

UTILITIES

Electricity

Central Electricity Board: Royal Rd, POB 40, Curepipe; tel. 675-5010; fax 675-7958; e-mail ceb@intnet.mu; internet ceb.intnet.mu; f. 1952; state-operated; scheduled for privatization; Chair. Prof. A. SWALEY KASENALLY; Gen. Man. PAUL VAN NIEKERK.

Water

Central Water Authority: Royal Rd, St Paul-Phoenix; tel. 601-5000; fax 686-6264; e-mail cwa@bow.intnet.mu; internet www.ncb .intnet.mu/putil/cwa; state-operated; scheduled for privatization; f. 1971; Gen. Man. ROHIT MUNGRA; Exec. Chair. H. K. BOOLUCK.

TRADE UNIONS

Federations

Federation of Civil Service Unions (FCSU): Jade Court, Rm 308, 3rd Floor, Jummah Mosque St, Port Louis; tel. 216-1977; fax 216-1475; e-mail f.c.s.u.@intnet.mu; f. 1957; 67 affiliated unions with 25,000 mems (2000); Pres. RASHID IMRITH; Sec. SOONDRESS SAWMYNADEN.

General Workers' Federation: 13 Brabant St, Port Louis; tel. 212-3338; Pres. FAROOK AUCHOYBUR; Sec.-Gen. DEVANAND RAMJUTTUN.

Mauritius Federation of Trade Unions: Arc Bldg, 3rd Floor, cnr Sir William Newton and Sir Seewoosagur Ramgoolam Sts, Port Louis; tel. 208-9426; f. 1958; four affiliated unions; Pres. FAROOK HOSSENBUX; Sec.-Gen. R. MAREEMOOTOO.

Mauritius Labour Congress: 8 Louis Victor de la Faye St, Port Louis; tel. 212-4343; fax 208-8945; f. 1963; 55 affiliated unions with 70,000 mems (1992); Pres. NURDEO LUCHMUN ROY; Gen. Sec. JUGDISH LOLLBEEHARRY.

Principal Unions

Government Servants' Association: 107A Royal Rd, Beau Bassin; tel. 464-4242; f. 1945; Pres. A. H. MALLECK-AMODE; Sec.-Gen. S. P. TORUL; 14,000 mems (1984).

Government Teachers' Union: 3 Mgr Gonin St, POB 1111, Port Louis; tel. 208-0047; fax 208-4943; f. 1945; Pres. JUGDISH LOLLBEEHARRY; Sec. SHEIKH NASHIR RAMJAN; 4,358 mems (1998).

Nursing Association: Royal Rd, Beau Bassin; tel. 464-5850; f. 1955; Pres. CASSAM KUREEMAN; Sec.-Gen. FRANCIS SUPPARAYEN; 2,040 mems (1980).

Organization of Artisans' Unity: 42 Sir William Newton St, Port Louis; tel. 212-4557; fax 212-4557; f. 1973; Pres. AUGUSTE FOLLET; Sec. ROY RAMCHURN; 2,874 mems (1994).

Plantation Workers' Union: 8 Louis Victor de la Faye St, Port Louis; tel. 212-1735; f. 1955; Pres. C. BHAGIRUTTY; Sec. N. L. ROY; 13,726 mems (1990).

Port Louis Harbour and Docks Workers' Union: 19B Poudrière St, Port Louis; tel. 208-2276; Pres. M. VEERABADREN; Sec.-Gen. GERARD BERTRAND; 2,198 mems (1980).

Sugar Industry Staff Employees' Association: 1 Rémy Ollier St, Port Louis; tel. 212-1947; f. 1947; Chair. T. BELLEROSE; Sec.-Gen. G. CHUNG KWAN FANG; 1,450 mems (1997).

Textile, Clothes and Other Manufactures Workers' Union: Thomy d'Arifat St, Curepipe; tel. 676-5280; Pres. PADMATEE TEELUCK; Sec.-Gen. DÉSIRÉ GUILDAREE.

Union of Bus Industry Workers: 19B Poudrière St, Port Louis; tel. 212-3338; Pres. BABOOA; Sec.-Gen. F. AUCHOYBUR; 1,783 mems (1980).

Union of Employees of the Ministry of Agriculture and other Ministries: Royal Rd, Curepipe; tel. 686-1847; f. 1989; Sec. P. JAGARNATH; 2,131 mems (1988).

Union of Labourers of the Sugar and Tea Industry: Royal Rd, Curepipe; f. 1969; Sec. P. RAMCHURN; 2,150 mems (1980).

Transport

RAILWAYS
There are no operational railways in Mauritius.

ROADS
In 2001 there were 2,000 km of classified roads, of which 60km were motorways, 950 km were other main roads, and 592 km were secondary roads. About 98% of the road network is paved. An urban highway links the motorways approaching Port Louis. A motorway connects Port Louis with Plaisance airport.

SHIPPING
Mauritius is served by numerous foreign shipping lines. In 1990 Port Louis was established as a free port to expedite the development of Mauritius as an entrepôt centre. In 1995 the World Bank approved a loan of US $30.5m. for a programme to develop the port. At 31 December 2001 Mauritius had a merchant fleet of 42 vessels, with a combined displacement of 96,945 grt.

Mauritius Ports Authority: Port Administration Bldg, POB 379, Mer Rouge, Port Louis; tel. 206-5400; fax 240-0856; e-mail mauport@intnet.mu; internet www.mauport.com; f. 1976; Chair. R. MAUNTHROOA; Dir-Gen. Capt. JEAN WONG CHUNG TOI.

Ireland Blyth Ltd: IBL House, Caudan, Port Louis; tel. 203-2000; fax 208-1014; e-mail iblinfo@ibl.intnet.mu; internet www.iblgroup .com; Chair. ARNAUD DALAIS; CEO P. D'HOTMAN DE VILLIERS; 2 vessels.

Islands Services Ltd: Rogers House, 5 John F. Kennedy St, POB 60, Port Louis; tel. 208-6801; fax 208-5045; services to Indian Ocean islands; Chair. Sir RENÉ MAINGARD; Exec. Dir Capt. RENÉ SANSON.

Mauritius Shipping Corpn Ltd: St James Court, Suite 417/418, St Denis St, Port Louis; tel. 210-6120; fax 210-5176; e-mail mauriship@intnet.mu; internet www.mrushipping.com; f. 1985; state-owned; Pres. B. P. DAUMOO.

Société Mauricienne de Navigation Ltée: 1 rue de la Reine, POB 53, Port Louis; tel. 208-3241; fax 208-8931; e-mail iblsh@bow.intnet .mu; Man. Dir Capt. FRANÇOIS DE GERSIGNY.

CIVIL AVIATION
Sir Seewoosagur Ramgoolam international airport is at Plaisance, 4 km from Mahébourg. Proposals are being considered for the construction of a second airport, at Plaine-les-Roches, in the north of the island.

Air Mauritius: Air Mauritius Centre, John F. Kennedy St, POB 441, Port Louis; tel. 207-7070; fax 208-8331; e-mail mkcare@

airmauritius.intnet.mu; internet www.airmauritius.com; f. 1967; 51% state-owned; services to 28 destinations in Europe, Asia, Australia and Africa; CEO ARJOON SUDDHOO; Chair. and Man. Dir VINOD CHIDAMBARAM.

Tourism

Tourists are attracted to Mauritius by its scenery and beaches, the pleasant climate and the blend of cultures. Accommodation capacity totalled 17,776 beds in 2000. The number of visitors increased from 300,670 in 1990 to 681,648 in 2002, when the greatest numbers of visitors were from France (29.8%), Réunion (14.1%) and the United Kingdom (11.8%). Gross revenue from tourism in 2002 was estimated at Rs 18,328m.

Mauritius Tourism Promotion Authority: Air Mauritius Centre, 11th Floor, John F. Kennedy St, Port Louis; tel. 210-1545; fax 212-5142; e-mail mtpa@intnet.mu; internet www.mauritius.net; Chair. GUY HUGNIN; Dir Dr KARL A. MOOTOOSAMY.

MEXICO

Introductory Survey

Location, Climate, Language, Religion, Flag, Capital

The United Mexican States is bordered to the north by the USA, and to the south by Guatemala and Belize. The Gulf of Mexico and the Caribbean Sea lie to the east, and the Pacific Ocean and Gulf of California to the west. The climate varies with altitude. The tropical southern region and the coastal lowlands are hot and wet, with an average annual temperature of 18°C (64°F), while the highlands of the central plateau are temperate. Much of the north and west is arid desert. In Mexico City, which lies at about 2,250 m (nearly 7,400 ft) above sea-level, temperatures are generally between 5°C (42°F) and 25°C (78°F). The country's highest recorded temperature is 58°C (136°F). The principal language is Spanish, spoken by more than 90% of the population in 1990, while about 8% speak indigenous languages, of which Náhuatl is the most widely spoken. Almost all of Mexico's inhabitants profess Christianity, and about 90% are adherents of the Roman Catholic Church. The national flag (proportions 4 by 7) has three equal vertical stripes from hoist to fly, of green, white and red, with the state emblem (a brown eagle, holding a snake in its beak, on a green cactus, with a wreath of oak and laurel beneath) in the centre of the white stripe. The capital is Mexico City.

Recent History

Conquered by Hernán Cortés in the 16th century, Mexico was ruled by Spain until the wars of independence of 1810–21. After the war of 1846, Mexico ceded about one-half of its territory to the USA. Attempts at political and social reform by the anti-clerical Benito Juárez precipitated civil war in 1857–60, and the repudiation of Mexico's external debts by Juárez in 1860 led to war with the United Kingdom, the USA and France. The Austrian Archduke Maximilian, whom France tried to install as Emperor of Mexico, was executed, on the orders of Juárez, in 1867. Order was restored during the dictatorship of Porfirio Díaz, which lasted from 1876 until the Revolution of 1910. The Constitution of 1917 embodied the aims of the Revolution by revising land ownership, by drafting a labour code and by curtailing the power of the Roman Catholic Church. From 1929–2000 the country was dominated by the Partido Revolucionario Institucional (PRI), for much of that time in an effective one-party system, although a democratic form of election was maintained. However, allegations of widespread electoral malpractice persistently arose in connection with PRI victories.

In presidential elections held in July 1976, the PRI candidate, José López Portillo, was elected with almost 95% of the votes cast. In 1977 López Portillo initiated reforms to increase minority party representation in the legislature and to widen democratic participation. The high level of political participation in the presidential election of July 1982 (held amid a financial crisis) was without precedent, with left-wing groups taking part for the first time; however, the PRI's candidate, Miguel de la Madrid Hurtado, was successful. The concurrent elections to the Cámara Federal de Diputados (Federal Chamber of Deputies) resulted in another overwhelming victory for the PRI, which performed strongly in the single-member constituencies. On taking office in December, the new President embarked on a programme of major economic reform, giving precedence to the repayment of Mexico's debts, a policy which imposed severe financial constraints upon the middle and lower classes and which led to growing disaffection among traditional PRI supporters. Notably, the Partido Acción Nacional (PAN), an opposition party, made important gains at municipal elections in two state capitals in mid-1983. The PRI's effective response ensured success at the remaining elections, but provoked opposition allegations of widespread electoral fraud. Contrary to expectations, at gubernatorial and congressional elections conducted in July 1985, the PRI secured all seven of the available state governorships and won 288 of the 300 directly elective seats in the Cámara.

The formation of a major left-wing alliance, the Partido Mexicano Socialista—PMS (comprising six parties), in 1987 and, in particular, the emergence of a dissident faction, the Corriente Democrática (CD), within the PRI in 1986 were disturbing political developments for the ruling party. In early 1988 the CD and four left-wing parties (including the PMS coalition) formed an electoral alliance, the Frente Democrático Nacional (FDN), headed by CD leader Cuauhtémoc Cárdenas Solórzano. The legitimacy of the PRI victory at the presidential and congressional elections, conducted in July, was fiercely challenged by the opposition groups, following a delay in the publication of official results, reports of widespread electoral fraud and the failure of the Federal Electoral Commission to release details of results from almost 50% of polling stations. Moreover, Cárdenas claimed victory on behalf of the broad-left coalition; for the first time ever, the opposition secured seats in the Senado (Senate), while the PRI suffered defeats in the Distrito Federal and at least three other states.

In August 1988 the new Congreso de la Unión (Congress) was installed and immediately assumed the function of an electoral college, in order to investigate the claims of both sides. In September the allocation of 200 seats in the Cámara by proportional representation afforded the PRI a congressional majority and effective control of the electoral college. Opposition members withdrew from the Cámara in protest at the PRI's obstruction of the investigation, enabling the ruling party to ratify Carlos Salinas de Gortari (hitherto the Secretary of Planning and Financial Budget) as the new President with 50.7% of the votes cast. Cárdenas was credited with 31.1% of the ballot. The results, although widely regarded as having been manipulated by the PRI, nevertheless revealed a considerable erosion in support for the party, particularly among the traditional bastions of the trade unions, peasant groups and bureaucracy.

President Salinas took office in December 1988, declaring that his administration's priorities would include renegotiating the foreign debt and combating poverty, fraud and corruption. During 1989, despite the Government's active reinforcement of its commitment to the elimination of corruption, the initiative was undermined by the implication of police and security forces in a succession of abuses of human rights.

Agreements on rescheduling Mexico's vast foreign debts were reached with the 'Paris Club' of official creditors in 1989, and with some 450 commercial banks in early 1990. Success for the Government in financial negotiations with creditors was largely dependent upon its ability to provide evidence of a stable and developing domestic economy. In January 1989 a Pact for Economic Stability and Growth was implemented, with the agreement of employers' organizations and trade unions, and was subsequently extended until the end of 1994. None the less, the country experienced severe labour unrest in 1989 in support of greater pay increases and in protest at the Government's divestment programme.

In May 1989, following the dissolution of the FDN earlier in the year, supporters of the CD, together with the PMS, formed the Partido de la Revolución Democrática (PRD), under the leadership of Cárdenas. During the year political opposition to the PRI was strengthened by success in gubernatorial and municipal elections, and by further accusations against the PRI of electoral fraud. In October proposed constitutional amendments, drafted in order to facilitate the future adoption of the PRI's Federal Electoral Code, were approved with the unexpected support of the PAN. A 'governability clause', whereby an absolute majority of seats in the Cámara would be awarded to the leading party, should it receive at least 35% of the votes at a general election, was criticized by the PRD.

In July 1991 the Federal Electoral Code was approved by the Cámara with support from all represented parties, except the PRD. The legislation contained provisions for the compilation of a new electoral roll, the issue of more detailed identification cards for voters, the modification of the Federal Electoral Institute (IFE), and the creation of a Federal Electoral Tribunal. Although the PRI insisted that the overall emphasis of the reform was to allow greater public access to the electoral process, the PRD was highly critical of many of the provisions, including alleged procedural obstacles to the formation of political alliances, and the power given to the President to appoint the head of the IFE (the Secretary of the Interior) and to nominate six 'independent' lawyers to its executive.

In June 1990, in response to continuing allegations of federal police complicity in abuses of human rights, President Salinas announced the creation of the National Commission for Human Rights (CNDH). Opposition groups and independent human rights organizations were critical of the Government's stipulation that the Commission should be excluded from addressing cases relating to political campaigns or electoral processes. In October the Government proposed legislation transferring responsibility for the interrogation of suspected criminals from the federal judicial police to the public magistrate's office. The proposed legislation also sought to undermine the validity of confession alone (often allegedly extracted under torture) as sufficient grounds for conviction.

The PRI continued to secure disputed electoral success at municipal and state level in 1991. At mid-term congressional elections in August, the party received 61.5% of the votes cast, winning 290 of the 300 directly elective seats in the Cámara (plus 30 of the 200 seats awarded by proportional representation) and 31 of the 32 contested seats in the Senado. The return to the level of support that the PRI had enjoyed prior to the 1988 elections was largely attributed to the success of the Government's programme of economic reform. The election results were less encouraging for the opposition; the PAN secured 10 directly elective seats in the Cámara and its first seat in the Senado, but the PRD failed to win a directly elective seat in either congressional house.

In November 1991 President Salinas announced proposals for constitutional reform with regard to agriculture, education and religion. Concern was expressed by PRI traditionalists that the agricultural reform programme (which envisaged the liberalization and development of the sector through the abolition of the land-distribution programme and by the effective 'privatization' of the inefficient *ejido* system of rural worker tenants) and the proposals for the devolution of federal responsibility for education might jeopardize the PRI's broad base of support from the rural community and from the 1.2m.-strong teachers' union. Legislation to enact the agrarian reform was adopted in March 1992. Reform proposals to grant legal recognition to the Roman Catholic Church received congressional approval in December 1991, and constitutional restrictions on the Church were ended by a new law, promulgated by the President in January 1992. A National Agreement for the Modernization of Basic Education was agreed between the federal Government, state governments and the national teachers' union in May 1992.

In late April 1992 the Governor of Jalisco, Guillermo Cosío Vidaurri, resigned after he had provoked public outrage by attempting to exonerate state and local officials of responsibility (through negligence) for a series of explosions earlier in the month that had severely damaged the state capital, Guadalajara, and resulted in the deaths of more than 200 inhabitants.

PRI victories at gubernatorial and legislative elections in several states during 1993 were denounced by the opposition as fraudulent. In July, in response to persistent criticism of the country's electoral system, President Salinas presented an electoral reform proposal (approved by the Congreso in September), which included provisions for greater access to the media for all parties, restrictions on party funding, and improved impartiality of supervision. Other measures sought to increase the representation of minority parties in the Senado, and to end over-representation of larger parties in the Cámara. The 'governability clause' introduced in 1989 was to be removed. Meanwhile, divisions within the PRI emerged in November, following the selection of Luis Donaldo Colosio, the Secretary of Social Development, as the party's candidate in the presidential elections that were scheduled to be held in August 1994. The Regent (*Regente*—see Government section below) of the Distrito Federal, Manuel Camacho Solís, who had been widely expected to secure the candidacy, immediately resigned his post, but subsequently accepted the foreign affairs portfolio in a reorganized Cabinet. Additional electoral reforms, which claimed to end PRI control of the IFE, received congressional approval in March 1994, but failed to appease PRD leaders, who demanded that the incumbent head of the IFE should be replaced by an impartial president elected by the IFE's newly created six-member commission.

On 1 January 1994 armed Indian groups numbering 1,000–3,000 took control of four municipalities of the southern state of Chiapas. The rebels issued the Declaration of the Lacandona Jungle, identifying themselves as the Ejército Zapatista de Liberación Nacional—EZLN (after Emiliano Zapata, who championed the land rights of Mexican peasants during the 1910–17 Revolution), and detailed a series of demands for economic and social change in the region, culminating in a declaration of war against the Government and a statement of intent to depose the 'dictator', President Salinas. A charismatic rebel spokesman, identified as 'subcomandante Marcos', stated that the insurgency had been timed to coincide with the implementation of the North American Free Trade Agreement (NAFTA—see below), which the rebels considered to be the latest in a series of segregative government initiatives adopted at the expense of indigenous groups. During the first day of the uprising the insurgents killed several police officials and abducted some prominent local figures, including a former Chiapas state governor. On 10 January the Government announced a unilateral cease-fire and an amnesty (effective from 22 January) for those EZLN members prepared to surrender arms. Camacho Solís was also appointed head of a peace and reconciliation commission in Chiapas on the same day. He enlisted the help of Samuel Ruiz, Bishop of San Cristóbal de las Casas, one of Chiapas' largest towns, in an attempt to foster a peaceful dialogue with the EZLN, although sporadic fighting continued throughout January. Negotiations between Camacho Solís and the rebels began in February, mediated by Ruiz, and were concluded in March with the publication of a document detailing 34 demands of the EZLN, and the Government's response to them. A preliminary accord was reached following the Government's broad acceptance of many of the rebels' stipulations, including an acceleration of the wide-ranging anti-poverty programme in the region, the incorporation of traditional Indian structures of justice and political organization, and a commitment from the Government to investigate the impact of NAFTA and recent land-reform legislation on Indian communities. Official figures suggested that 100–150 guerrillas, soldiers and civilians had been killed during the conflict, while the Roman Catholic Church estimated that there had been as many as 400 casualties. In June the EZLN announced that, following lengthy consultation, the Government's peace proposal had been rejected by an overwhelming majority of the movement's supporters. However, a similar majority had rejected the resumption of hostilities with the security forces, and had endorsed the extension of the cease-fire pending renewed bilateral discussions. In response, Salinas was critical of the work of the peace and reconciliation commission, prompting the resignation of Camacho Solís, who was replaced by Jorge Madrazo Cuéllar, the head of the CNDH.

Meanwhile, in March 1994 the PRI's presidential candidate, Colosio, was assassinated at a campaign rally. Mario Aburto Martínez, arrested at the scene of the murder, was later identified as the apparently motiveless assassin. However, speculation that Colosio had been the victim of a conspiracy within the PRI establishment increased following the arrest, in connection with the incident, of a number of party members associated with police and intelligence agencies. The PRI subsequently named Ernesto Zedillo Ponce de León, a former cabinet minister who had most recently been acting as Colosio's campaign manager, as the party's presidential candidate. Zedillo was elected President on 21 August, with 48.8% of the votes, ahead of the PAN candidate, Diego Fernández de Cevallos (25.9%), and the PRD candidate, Cuauhtémoc Cárdenas (16.6%). The PRI also achieved considerable success at the concurrent congressional elections, securing all of the directly elected seats in the Senado and all but 23 of the directly elected seats in the Cámara. Zedillo was considered to have conducted an unremarkable electoral campaign (during which he had promised to suspend the privilege of the *dedazo*—the presidential right to nominate PRI officials), and he was the first PRI presidential candidate to receive less than 50% of the votes. Despite the participation of some 70,000 impartial monitors and the attendance of a UN advisory technical team, numerous incidents of electoral malpractice were reported.

Zedillo identified the immediate aims of his administration as the promotion of the independence of the judiciary, the separation of party political activity from the functions of federal government and the further reform of the electoral system. Public confidence in the impartiality and ability of the judiciary had been seriously undermined by the inconsistency and confusion surrounding recent investigations into the deaths of Colosio and José Francisco Ruiz Massieu (see below). Zedillo's appointment of a senior member of the PAN to the post of Attorney-General in a new Cabinet announced in November

1994, together with the disclosure, in December, of more detailed plans for judicial reform (including proposals to prevent politicians from securing judicial office), sought to restore the prestige of the judiciary. In late December a sudden financial crisis prompted the replacement of the Secretary of Finance and Public Credit.

The report of a special investigation into Colosio's murder, published in July 1994, concluded that Aburto Martínez had acted alone in the assassination, reversing the findings of a preliminary investigation which had suggested the existence of a number of conspirators. The report provoked public incredulity, and President Salinas immediately commissioned a further independent investigation to be conducted by a newly appointed special prosecutor. Speculation that Colosio had been the first victim of a politically motivated campaign of violence, conducted by a cabal of senior PRI traditionalists in order to check the advance of the party's reformist wing, intensified following the murder, in September, of the PRI Secretary-General, José Francisco Ruiz Massieu, although responsibility for Ruiz Massieu's death was initially attributed to the powerful Golfo drugs cartel (allegedly based in the north-eastern state of Tamaulipas, and responsible for the bulk of cross-border trafficking of cocaine to the USA). In October Aburto Martínez was sentenced to 42 years' imprisonment for Colosio's murder. In February 1995, however, a report issued by the Attorney-General, Fernando Antonio Lozano Gracia, was highly critical of all previous investigations of the incident, concluding that the assassination had involved at least two gunmen. (An alleged second gunman was acquitted in August 1996.) Meanwhile, in November 1994 Ruiz Massieu's brother, Mario, resigned his post as Deputy Attorney-General, claiming that senior PRI officials, including the party's President and Secretary-General, had impeded his investigation into his brother's death, in an attempt to protect the identities of those responsible for the assassination. In February 1995 Raúl Salinas de Gortari, brother of former President Salinas, was arrested on charges of complicity in Ruiz Massieu's murder, and in April Fernando Rodríguez González (a former employee at the Cámara, who was charged with hiring the assassins) implicated several new conspirators, including five state Governors. Mario Ruiz Massieu was subsequently detained in the USA on charges of corruption and of obstructing the investigation. Repeated attempts by the Mexican Government to secure his extradition were frustrated. In October two men were each sentenced to 18 years' imprisonment for perpetrating the murder of the PRI Secretary-General. In October 1996 the case against Raúl Salinas was prejudiced further by the discovery of a body buried in the grounds of his property in Mexico City. The deceased was initially assumed to be Manuel Muñoz Rocha, a former federal congressman who was alleged to have been Salinas's accomplice in the assassination of Ruiz Massieu and who had disappeared shortly after the incident. In December Jorge Madrazo Cuéllar was appointed Attorney-General to replace Lozano Gracia, who had failed to reveal that scientific evidence proved that the body exhumed was not that of Muñoz Rocha.

In March 1995, following the arrest of his brother, former President Salinas began a solitary public campaign to discredit the new administration and to defend himself from accusations of responsibility for the country's economic crisis and from allegations that he had obstructed attempts to bring to justice those responsible for Colosio's death. Salinas's efforts culminated in a highly-publicized but brief hunger strike which prompted the Attorney-General to issue a statement confirming that there was no evidence that Salinas had impeded the Colosio murder inquiry. Some days later, allegedly at the suggestion of Zedillo, Salinas left the country, accompanied by his family. Raúl Salinas was convicted of murder and sentenced to 50 years' imprisonment in January 1999; the sentence was reduced, on appeal, to almost 28 years in July. (However, in August 2002, following investigation by prosecutors in Switzerland, he was additionally charged with the embezzlement of up to 209m. new pesos from a secret presidential fund under his brother's control.) In September 1999 Mario Ruiz Massieu committed suicide in the USA while awaiting trial on charges of 'laundering' money gained from drugs-trafficking; he left a note repeating his earlier accusations against the PRI and blaming Zedillo and other senior officials for his own death and the assassination of Colosio.

By October 1994 tensions in Chiapas had increased (partly as a result of a conflict of interests between evangelical Christian Indian groups and Indian traditionalists) and the EZLN announced its withdrawal from negotiations with the Government, citing an increase in the military presence in the area and the controversial victory of the PRI candidate, Eduardo Robledo Rincón, in gubernatorial elections to the state, as reasons for the escalation in civil unrest. Violent confrontations between left- and right-wing groups, peasants and landowners and EZLN supporters and security forces increased in the weeks preceding Robledo Rincón's inauguration. A second national democratic convention in November endorsed a campaign of civil disorder to disrupt the Governor's inauguration, but voted to resume negotiations with the Government. Fears that the Government might again seek a military solution to the crisis were aroused following the installation by opposition groups of a parallel state administration for Chiapas in December. Such concerns were initially dispelled by both sides' adoption of a more conciliatory approach to negotiations during December 1994 and January 1995, and by the establishment of a national mediation commission, the Comisión Nacional de Intermediación (CONAI), led by Bishop Ruiz. However, in February President Zedillo announced the resumption of a military offensive against EZLN positions in Chiapas, following the discovery of a number of illegal arsenals in Mexico City and Veracruz, allegedly amassed by the EZLN in preparation for a nation-wide offensive. Zedillo also issued warrants for the arrest of several EZLN leaders, including subcomandante Marcos, who was identified as Rafael Sebastián Guillén Vicente. Some days later the Government appeared to adjust this stance: military operations in the region were suspended while Robledo Rincón announced a temporary leave of absence from the post of Governor of Chiapas. The warrants for the arrest of EZLN leaders were subsequently suspended, and in March the Law for Dialogue, Conciliation and Honourable Peace in Chiapas was enacted by the Government, with the support of all major political parties. The Law, which sought to facilitate future negotiations and to establish commissions to instigate and monitor the peace process, was welcomed by EZLN spokesmen, who conveyed their willingness to renew a dialogue with the authorities. Formal discussions between the two sides began in San Andrés Larraínzar in April.

Existing tensions between peasant groups and the authorities were exacerbated in July 1995 by the arrest of a number of police officials implicated in the shooting of 17 members of a local peasant workers' organization in the state of Guerrero in June. A CNDH report contradicted Governor Rubén Figueroa's assertion that the security forces had been acting in self-defence, and recommended that senior state officials should be dismissed for attempting to manipulate evidence relating to the deaths. In January 1996 it was announced that four former state officials and a number of police officers had been arrested on charges (including murder) in connection with the incident; Figueroa resigned in March. In April the Supreme Court ruled that Figueroa and several others had deliberately suppressed information regarding the massacre.

In August 1995 an unofficial plebiscite organized by the EZLN in Mexico City and the state of Chiapas recorded an almost equal division of support from around 1.2m. voters for the guerrilla movement's evolution into an independent political force and for its alignment with an existing political body. A preparatory accord between the Government and the EZLN was signed in September, establishing procedures and a broad agenda for formal discussion; in February 1996 the two sides signed an agreement in San Andrés Larraínzar on the guarantee of cultural, linguistic and local government rights for indigenous groups, although the issue of land reform was not addressed. However, the EZLN announced its withdrawal from the peace negotiations in September as the agreement had not been implemented. In December the Comisión de Concordia y Pacificación (COCOPA), a multi-party congressional committee charged with finding a peace settlement, presented draft legislation on indigenous rights based on the San Andrés Larraínzar agreement. Although the bill was supported by the EZLN, it was rejected by the Government on the grounds that it threatened national sovereignty. In January 1997, in an apparent attempt to renew dialogue with the Zapatistas, the authorities released seven alleged EZLN members from prison.

In June 1996 some 100 members of a previously unknown guerrilla group, the Ejército Popular Revolucionario (EPR), apparently formed in mid-1994, commemorated the first anniversary of the Guerrero shootings (see above) by staging a rally in the village of Aguas Blancas, Guerrero. The Government responded by launching a major military offensive in the state, resulting in the capture, in July, of eight alleged EPR members. In August the EPR announced its allegiance to a new political grouping, the Partido Popular Revolucionario Democrático, and launched armed attacks, claiming self-defence, on government installations in the states of Guerrero, México and Oaxaca; 17 people were killed and at least 21 were injured during the assaults. Concurrently, subcomandante Marcos sent an open letter to the EPR, distancing the EZLN from the new guerrilla group. Although the military intensified its counter-insurgency campaign in September, at the end of the month the EPR announced a temporary unilateral cease-fire in Guerrero in order not to impede mayoral and legislative elections (scheduled for October). The EPR also declared a unilateral cease-fire in México state in the weeks preceding the municipal elections due in November. In January 1997 the authorities arrested Benigno Guzmán Martínez, said to be the EPR leader, bringing to 85 the total number of supposed EPR members arrested since mid-1996. (During 1997 the EPR continued to launch sporadic attacks. In June 1998 the armed forces killed 11 EPR members and arrested 21 others during a military offensive in Guerrero state.)

The Government's ongoing attempts to effect political reform were reactivated in January 1996 at a meeting of some 50 civil and political groups. However, subsequent discussion of the 60-point document issued by the convention was regularly interrupted during early 1996 by the demands of opposition parties for the annulment of a number of disputed election results. In July the PRI, the PAN, the PRD and the Partido del Trabajo (PT, a labour party) reached consensus on reforms that would include introducing a directly elected Governor of the Distrito Federal (a Regent had hitherto been appointed by the President), increasing and regulating public financing for political parties, employing proportional representation in elections to the Senado, granting a right of vote to Mexican citizens resident abroad, and allowing the IFE greater independence. The reforms received congressional approval in August. However, in November, in apparent response to their diminishing share of the vote in recent municipal elections, PRI traditionalists secured the adoption by the Cámara of a series of amendments to the electoral-reform bill, increasing public funding in 1997 for political parties by some 476%, pronouncing that to exceed campaign finance limits would no longer be a criminal or electoral offence, expanding the Government's access to the media, and restricting the right of opposition parties to form coalitions.

Internal tensions in the PRI became increasingly apparent during 1996. At the party's 15th National Assembly, convened in September, PRI traditionalists retaliated against the progressive faction by voting to alter the prerequisites for senior government positions. Candidates would thenceforth be required to have held previous elected office, and to have been PRI members for a minimum of 10 years. Notably, the new conditions would have prevented the selection of President Zedillo and of most of his Cabinet. Nevertheless, in December one of Zedillo's close allies, Humberto Roque Villanueva, replaced Oñate as party president.

In May 1996 Zedillo dismissed Mexico City's chief of police following public outcry at the violent tactics employed by his officers to disperse a group of striking teachers in the capital. In the following months hundreds of police employees throughout the country were dismissed for incompetence or corruption, while army officers were increasingly appointed to positions within the police force. In March 1997 some 2,500 members of Mexico City's police force were replaced by army personnel, and in October an élite police unit was disbanded after accusations that as many as 35 of its members were implicated in the torture and murder of three youths in September. Several officers at the anti-abduction unit in the state of Morelos were also accused of torture and murder in early 1998, precipitating the resignation of the state's PRI Governor in May.

At elections held on 6 July 1997 for all 500 members of the Cámara the PRI lost its overall majority for the first time, while the PRD and the PAN made substantial gains. At concurrent elections held for one-quarter of the seats in the Senado the PRI retained its overall majority, albeit significantly reduced, while the PAN and the PRD increased their representation. In addition, the PRI was defeated by the PAN in two of six gubernatorial elections conducted at the same time. Most significant, however, was the election of Cárdenas, the PRD candidate, as Governor of the Distrito Federal, who secured 47.8% of the votes cast, compared with 25.6% by Alfredo del Mazo, a PRI traditionalist. The electoral defeats suffered by the PRI exacerbated tensions within the party and prompted the resignation of its president, Roque Villanueva, in September. Several PRI mem-

bers had defected to the PRD, some of whom were selected as PRD candidates in gubernatorial elections. The PRI remained divided on the issue of the selection of candidates for senior government positions as the prerequisites agreed at the 15th National Assembly (see above) reduced significantly the number of eligible party members.

The first opposition-dominated Cámara convened in September 1997. The PAN, the PRD, the Partido Verde Ecologista de México (PVEM) and the PT agreed an informal alliance, as a result of which opposition parties succeeded in taking control of important legislative committees, including those concerning the budget, the interior and anti-corruption. It was anticipated that this would lead to the closer scrutiny of government expenditure and to the possible removal of the largely discretionary funds controlled by Zedillo.

Despite attempts by the COCOPA to resume peace negotiations, clashes between EZLN supporters and the security forces in the state of Chiapas continued during 1997. The Government came under criticism for increasing its military presence in the state and for expelling foreign human rights activists from the region. In September, in an attempt to rally support for their cause, several thousand Zapatistas and their sympathizers staged a peaceful demonstration in Mexico City, during which the EZLN inaugurated the Frente Zapatista de Liberación Nacional, a political force created in 1996 to embody the Zapatistas' ideology. The prospect of reaching a peaceful solution in Chiapas was undermined in November 1997 by an apparent assassination attempt on Bishop Ruiz, allegedly by members of Paz y Justicia, a paramilitary group financed by anti-EZLN landowners. In December, moreover, there was widespread disquiet at the killing of 45 Indians (primarily women and children) in a church in the village of Acteal, in the municipality of Chenalhó, Chiapas. President Zedillo promptly announced that the Attorney-General would launch an investigation into the incident. Some 58 residents of Chenalhó were arrested subsequently, including the mayor, Jacinto Arias. In January 1998 demonstrations were held across Mexico to condemn the massacre and to demand the resumption of peace negotiations. Meanwhile, Chuayffet, the Secretary of the Interior, and Julio César Ruiz Ferro, the Governor of Chiapas, were forced to resign, following criticism of their roles in the events leading to the Acteal massacre. Both Francisco Labastida Ochoa and Roberto Albores Guillén, who succeeded Chuayffet and Ruiz Ferro, respectively, made conciliatory gestures towards the EZLN. In February Zedillo announced the appointment of a new government peace negotiator; nevertheless, the military presence in Chiapas increased, purportedly to disarm paramilitary groups in the region. In April 1998 Gen. Julio César Santiago Díaz, who had been acting chief of staff of Chiapas state police at the time of the massacre, was arrested and charged with failing to intervene to prevent the bloodshed. Trials of those implicated in the killings were held in 1998–99; in September 1999 Jacinto Arias was convicted on charges of supplying the weapons used in the massacre and sentenced to 35 years' imprisonment. In November 2002 18 people were each sentenced to 36 years' imprisonment for their involvement in the deaths as part of a paramilitary group with links to the PRI; they joined 70 others previously convicted.

In March 1998, following President Zedillo's unsuccessful attempt to persuade the COCOPA to revise the draft law that it had presented in December 1996, Labastida announced draft legislation on indigenous rights and culture. The COCOPA, the PAN and the EZLN rejected the proposals on the grounds that they failed to comply with the San Andrés Larraínzar agreement. The EZLN, angered by the Government's failure to consult with the Zapatistas, demanded that certain preconditions be met before it resumed dialogue with the authorities. In June Bishop Ruiz resigned from the CONAI, accusing the Government of behaving in an increasingly aggressive manner towards the Commission, and of weakening reconciliation efforts. Concurrently, the CONAI announced its dissolution. During May and June eight Zapatista sympathizers were killed and more than 100 were arrested when the security forces attempted to dismantle two 'autonomous municipalities' (villages which, with EZLN support, had declared themselves outside federal and state control) in Chiapas.

In October 1998 the EZLN declared its willingness to renew dialogue with the COCOPA, and in the following month bilateral talks were held in San Cristóbal de las Casas, during which the EZLN expressed regret at the dissolution of the CONAI, and reiterated its preconditions for entering into dialogue with the

Government. In March 1999 some 5,000 Zapatistas conducted a nation-wide unofficial plebiscite to determine, *inter alia*, the level of support for the recognition of Indian rights, the San Andrés Larraínzar agreement and the demilitarization of Chiapas. According to the EZLN, 2.5m. people participated in the poll, of whom 97% concurred with Zapatista demands.

The Government made efforts to initiate negotiations with the EZLN in September 1999, when, in an open letter to the Zapatistas, the Secretary of the Interior, Diódoro Carrasco, proposed independent (although not international) mediation and the establishment of a special judicial authority to investigate paramilitary activities in Chiapas. Furthermore, a number of Zapatista sympathizers were released from prison. Meanwhile, Samuel Ruiz retired as Bishop of San Cristóbal de las Casas in January 2000. Despite appeals from Ruiz and Indian groups, the Vatican declined to appoint Ruiz's coadjutor, Raúl Vera López (who had in December been named Bishop of Saltillo), as his successor.

The popularity of the PRI appeared to recover during 1998, with the ruling party winning seven of the 10 governorships contested that year, and performing well in municipal and local elections. Notably, a PRI candidate won the gubernatorial election in Chihuahua, a stronghold of the PAN. However, the PAN won the governorship of Aguascalientes (hitherto held by the PRI), while PRI defectors claimed victory for the PRD in Zacatecas, and for an alliance of the PRD, the PT and the PVEM in Tlaxcala. (In early 1999 the PRI also lost the governorship of Baja California Sur to the PRD-PT-PVEM alliance, led by a former PRI member.) The PRI later acknowledged that the holding of open primaries might have prevented the costly defections to the opposition, and Zedillo again pledged to end the practice of the *dedazo*. In March 1999 José Antonio González Fernández, hitherto Secretary of Labour, became the first elected President of the PRI.

In May 1998, at the culmination of a three-year counternarcotics operation, the US authorities made more than 160 arrests in Mexico and indicted three Mexican financial groups on charges of laundering the profits from cocaine cartels; a further nine banks were implicated in the scandal. (It was estimated that drugs cartels in Mexico and Colombia laundered some US $8,000m. annually through Mexican financial institutions.) The Zedillo administration, which in March had admitted that a small financial group had been purchased by drugs-traffickers in 1995, protested that it had not been informed about the operation, despite bilateral agreements on drugs-trafficking intelligence. The Government maintained that it was pursuing its own investigations into irregularities at financial institutions, and in June succeeded in extraditing from Spain a fugitive Mexican banker, who had allegedly stolen $2,000m. from one of the country's principal banks.

Meanwhile, in mid-1998 the PRI encountered strong opposition in the Congreso to its proposals to convert into public debt liabilities to the value of some $65,000m. assumed by the bank rescue agency, the Fondo Bancario de Protección al Ahorro (FOBAPROA), after the financial crisis of late 1994. Frustrated by the Government's refusal to release full details about the rescue programme, in August the PRD issued a list of more than 300 business executives (including many PRI associates) who were alleged to have benefited from the scheme, and conducted a nation-wide survey to determine the level of support for the PRI's proposal. The PRD claimed that 3m. people participated in the poll, of whom 94% opposed the Government's plans. In December, after protracted negotiations, a revised bill establishing a successor to the FOBAPROA was approved by the Cámara. The PAN abandoned demands for the resignation of the Governor of the central bank, Guillermo Ortiz, who had held the finance portfolio at the time of the rescue programme, while the Government was forced to concede that FOBAPROA's liabilities would not automatically become public debt. Congressional approval would thenceforth be required annually for part of the budget for bonds issued to refinance FOBAPROA's liabilities. FOBAPROA's successor, the Instituto de Protección al Ahorro Bancario was created in May 1999.

In April 1999 a warrant was issued for the arrest of the outgoing Governor of the state of Quintana Roo, Mario Villanueva, only hours after the end of his term. Villanueva, who had already fled the state to escape what he claimed was political persecution, was alleged to have been involved in drugs-trafficking and to have links with the Juárez cartel. Villanueva was arrested in Cancún in late May 2001, and in January 2002 a federal court in New York, USA, presented a formal request for

his extradition to the Mexican Secretariat of State for Foreign Affairs; he was alleged to have assisted two cartel leaders, also threatened with extradition, in the smuggling of 200 tons of cocaine from Colombia to the USA via the state of Quintana Roo.

In May 1999 the PRI announced that, for the first time ever, nation-wide open primaries would be held to select its candidate for the presidential election, scheduled to be held in July 2000. Roberto Madrazo Pintado, the Governor of Tabasco, declared his intention to stand for election, as did Francisco Labastida Ochoa, who resigned as Secretary of the Interior. Following a bitterly fought contest in November, Labastida secured the PRI nomination. Meanwhile, in May, the PRD and the PAN commenced negotiations on the possibility of forming an opposition coalition to contest the forthcoming elections. The results of gubernatorial elections held in the states of Nayarit and México in July seemed to support the view that only a joint PAN-PRD candidate could present a serious threat to the PRI in the presidential election. In the state of México the PRI candidate had easily defeated a divided opposition, while in Nayarit a coalition candidate representing the four main opposition parties had secured victory.

In September 1999 a guerrilla group known as the Ejército Revolucionario Popular Insurgente (ERPI) reportedly attacked an army convoy, killing four soldiers. Jacobo Silva Nogales (also known as 'comandante Antonio'), a former EPR (see above) member and the apparent founder and leader of the ERPI, was arrested in October, together with three other senior members of the group. Also in September, the PAN's only presidential aspirant, Vicente Fox Quesada, who had recently resigned as Governor of Guanajuato state, was approved as the party's candidate for the election. In October Cárdenas, who had resigned as Governor of the Distrito Federal in the previous month, was formally nominated as the PRD's candidate. By the close of registration in January 2000 six presidential candidates had emerged: Labastida, Cárdenas (standing for the PRD-dominated Alianza por México—AM), Fox (representing a PAN-PVEM alliance styled the Alianza por el Cambio—AC), Manuel Camacho Solís, the leader of the Partido de Centro Democrático, Gilberto Rincón Gallardo, the President of Democracia Social, and Porfirio Muñoz Ledo, representing the Partido Auténtico de la Revolución Mexicana.

In the presidential election held on 2 July 2000, Fox secured 43.5% of the votes cast, while Labastida won 36.9% and Cárdenas 17.0%. Fox was thus elected President, ending the PRI's 71-year hegemony in Mexican government. In the concurrent elections to the Congreso the AC secured 223 of the 500 seats (208 of them won by the PAN, 15 by the PVEM), compared with 209 won by the PRI and 68 by the parties of the AM. The PRI remained the largest grouping in the Senado, however, with 60 seats, compared with 51 held by the AC and 17 by the AM. Fox immediately announced that, upon taking office, he would establish a commission to investigate 'past events', while stating that his primary motive in doing so was 'national reconciliation', rather than retribution. To the same end, he announced he would invite members of the PRI and the PRD to join his first cabinet. The governorship of the Distrito Federal, contested on the same day as the federal elections, was won by López Obrador of the PRD, who secured some 34.5% of the votes cast, compared with his nearest rival, Santiago Creel Miranda of the PAN, who obtained some 33.4% of the ballot. In August Pablo Salazar of the Alliance for Chiapas movement (which united several national and local parties and movements in opposition to the PRI), defeated Sami David of the PRI in the Chiapas state gubernatorial election.

Meanwhile, in August 2000, the Secretary of Tourism in the outgoing Zedillo administration, Oscar Espinosa Villareal, suddenly resigned his position and disappeared. Espinosa had been under investigation on allegations of embezzlement relating to his term, in 1994–97, as the last appointed Regent of the Distrito Federal. He was not subsequently seen in public until November when, upon his arrival in Nicaragua, he claimed political asylum, stating that the investigation into his activities was politically motivated. In December the Mexican authorities petitioned Nicaragua for his extradition and Espinosa was detained in the Nicaraguan capital, Managua. Extradition hearings began in January 2001, following the rejection of Espinosa's asylum request; in August, after being extradited from Nicaragua, he was committed to stand trial on charges of embezzling US $45m. from Distrito Federal state funds.

The gubernatorial election held in the state of Tabasco in October 2000 resulted in a narrow victory for the PRI candidate,

Manuel Andrade, although the PAN and the PRD both disputed the result, alleging electoral malpractice. The case was subsequently referred to the Federal Election Tribunal, which annulled the result and empowered the state legislature to appoint an interim Governor, pending a new election within 18 months. The PAN and the PRD objected to the outgoing legislature's appointee, Enrique Priego Oropeza of the PRI, on the grounds that he held a seat in the federal Congreso. The new state legislature then nominated a different PRI official, Adán Augusto López, to the position. Following intensive negotiations and intervention by the Secretary of the Interior, Priego agreed to take leave of absence from his seat in the Congreso and López allowed him to assume the interim governorship. Andrade stood as a candidate at a new election in August 2001, and won with 51% of the votes cast, defeating the PRD candidate, Raúl Ojeda, who secured 46% of the valid ballot.

Fox took office as President on 1 December 2000, stating that his priorities were a reduction in poverty, improved relations with the USA and peace and reconciliation within Mexico. His first cabinet contained members of the PAN, PRI and other parties, in addition to a number of prominent figures from commerce and academia. The PRD declined an offer of three cabinet portfolios, however, stating that it did not support Fox's economic or social policies. The finance portfolio was granted to Francisco Gil Díaz, who had been a junior minister responsible for taxation issues during Salinas' presidency.

Upon taking office President Fox announced that 53 military checkpoints in Chiapas were to be abandoned and that proposed legislation based on the San Andrés Larraínzar peace accords, rejected in 1996, would be reintroduced to the Congreso. In response, subcomandante Marcos issued a statement stating that negotiations could be reopened on three conditions: that seven military bases in the state be abandoned, that EZLN prisoners be released and that the proposed legislation be enacted. Four of the seven bases were subsequently closed and a number of EZLN activists released. The remaining three bases were designated for closure during 2001. In January 2001 the Government announced a series of new proposals aimed at the restoration of peace in Chiapas, including the establishment of offices in the state's major towns to facilitate liaison among the parties involved. In February subcomandante Marcos, other Zapatista leaders and numerous other campaigners for indigenous rights began a tour of Mexico, visiting several major cities. The tour culminated in Mexico City in early March, where a rally in the capital's main square, attended by an estimated 150,000 people, was held in support of congressional approval of the proposed indigenous-rights legislation, which would open the way for the reopening of peace negotiations. The rebels rejected a government proposal to meet with the Senado's peace commission, insisting that they wanted to address both legislative chambers. The Congreso approved the demand by a margin of 10 votes and, following the historic address by four EZLN leaders, on 28 March, the EZLN announced that formal dialogue with the Government would recommence, even though its other demands had not been met. Subcomandante Marcos successfully negotiated the dismantling of all seven garrisons in Chiapas, and in April the Congreso approved amendments to six articles of the Constitution, which recognized and guaranteed indigenous political, legal, social and economic rights, and prohibited discrimination against Indians based on race and tribal affiliation. However, the legislation, which came into force in August, fell short of granting indigenous peoples the right to autonomy over land and natural resources; in response, the EZLN suspended all contact with the Government.

Controversy arose in the state of Yucatán in February 2001, when the PRI-led state government defied an order by the Federal Electoral Commission to dissolve the state electoral commission by the end of that month, following allegations of a pro-PRI bias within its ranks in the months preceding the gubernatorial election, scheduled to be held in May. PRI activists subsequently barricaded themselves in the commission's headquarters in protest and refused to allow federal officers to enter the building; the election was eventually won in May by Patricio Patrón Laviada, representing a PAN-led alliance. Furthermore, in July Eugenio Elorduy of the PAN defeated the PRI candidate in the gubernatorial election in Baja California, while in November the PRD candidate Lazaro Cárdenas (grandson of President Cárdenas—1934–40), defeated the PRI incumbent to become governor of the southern state of Michoacán, further evidence that the PRI was continuing to lose support in its traditional strongholds.

In October 2001 the Government announced that eight parties, including the PRI and the PRD, had signed the Acuerdo Político para el Desarrollo Nacional (Political Agreement for National Development), designed to facilitate law-making. Under the terms of the Agreement, the parties promised to support government measures to improve public finances and to deregulate the energy and telecommunications sectors. Nevertheless, the Government continued to encounter congressional opposition to its proposed fiscal reforms.

Although the elimination of corruption and an improvement in human rights were priorities in Fox's electoral campaign, little was done to address these issues in the President's first year in office. The country's poor human rights record was highlighted in late 2001 by the assassination in October of the leading civil liberties lawyer, Digna Ochoa, and by the publication, in December, of an Amnesty International report, which alleged that Mexican security forces were involved in widespread human rights violations. In response, President Fox announced an official inquiry into the 'disappearance' of 532 people detained by security forces in the 1970s and 1980s. In February 2002 Fox ordered the immediate release of Gen. José Francisco Gallardo, who had been sentenced to 28 years' imprisonment in 1993 after being convicted of misappropriating military property. Human rights groups and supporters of Gallardo had maintained that the charges were fabricated and that he had been incarcerated after demanding a reform of the military justice system.

In January 2002 the Government announced that an investigation was to be held into allegations that the state petroleum company, PEMEX, had covertly funded the election campaign of the PRI presidential candidate, Francisco Labastida, in 2000. The affair, the ramifications of which continued throughout 2002, centred on the alleged diversion of 1,580m. new pesos in PEMEX funds into PRI accounts by two leaders of the petroleum workers' union, the Sindicato de Trabajadores Petroleros de la República Mexicana (STPRM), Carlos Romero Deschamps and Ricardo Aldana. In May a former director of PEMEX, Manuel Gómez-Peralta, was detained in connection with the allegations; furthermore, a former PEMEX President, Rogelio Montemayor, was arrested in Houston, Texas (USA) in October. In September the Attorney-General requested that Deschamps and Aldana be stripped of their right (as deputy and senator, respectively) to immunity from prosecution. The affair resulted in a deterioration in relations between the Government and the STPRM, which led to a narrowly averted strike in October. In early 2003 the PRI was fined 1,000m. new pesos by the IFE. Meanwhile, in October 2002 opposition parties demanded that President Fox allow the re-opening of investigations into allegations that the PAN organization Amigos de Fox, responsible for Fox's presidential campaign, had received substantial illegal foreign funding. (The investigation had been suspended on grounds of banking secrecy, but had been ordered to recommence by the electoral tribunal in May.) The PRI threatened to initiate a congressional investigation unless the Amigos de Fox's accounts were made public.

In March 2002 Roberto Madrazo Pintado, the former Governor of Tabasco, defeated Beatrix Paredes, the former Governor of Tlaxcala, to win the PRI leadership, although there were subsequent allegations of electoral fraud from Paredes' supporters. In March Luis Felipe Bravo Mena was elected President of the PAN and, in the same month, Rosario Robles Berlanga was elected President of the PRD. In April, following President Fox's support for a UN investigation into human rights abuses in Cuba, with whom Mexico had a traditionally strong relationship, the Congreso refused to grant Fox permission to travel to the USA and Canada.

In May 2002 27 Zapotec Indians were killed in suspicious circumstances at Agua Fría, in Santiago Textitlán, Oaxaca; state authorities arrested 17 villagers, blaming the deaths on narcotics-trafficking or land issues, but local Indian organizations claimed that paramilitary groups had been involved in the attacks. Following the incident, an Amnesty International official denounced the state Attorney-General's office for abuses. In July protests by farmers and Zapatistas over the proposed construction of a new international airport for Mexico City near the village of San Salvador Atenco descended into violence; in subsequent clashes with the police one person was killed and 31 injured. In response, the protestors, who were opposed to proposed legislation expropriating their land, threatened to kill 12 hostages (a further three hostages were later taken). A reversal in government policy on the project was announced by the

Minister for Transport, Pedro Cerisola, on 2 August; the announcement was hailed by the PAN as proof of its willingness to negotiate, but decried by the opposition as weakness on the part of the Government.

In his annual 'Informe' address in September 2002, President Fox urged the Congreso to support legislation for structural reform, particularly of the electricity sector, and stressed the need for partnership between President and legislature. This, however, proved difficult to achieve, particularly in the midst of allegations and counter-allegations of electoral financial malpractice between the PRI and the PAN. In November there was conflict over both a proposed delay in the extension of value-added tax (VAT), and the introduction of a so-called 'luxuries tax', proposed by the PRD. Furthermore, in December the PRD obstructed legislation proposing the reduction in the number of lower-house seats elected by proportional representation (from 200 to 100).

The Fox administration had pledged to address the problem of drugs-trafficking. A subsequent increased fight against drugs had led to an average of 23 arrests per day during 2002 (including the leaders of the Tijuana and Gulf cocaine cartels in March and May, respectively). However, the anti-narcotics programme was itself the subject of an anti-corruption drive in the same year that led to a number of specialized army units being dismantled. Meanwhile, in November the investigation into the 'guerra sucia' (dirty war) of the late 1970s resulted in the conviction of Brigadier-Gen. Mario Acosta and Gen. Francisco Quirós on charges of protecting the operations of the Juárez cartel; they also faced charges over the disappearance of 143 activists. In the same month a special investigation by the Office of the Public Prosecutor accused Elba Ester Gordillo Morales, the PRI Secretary-General, of involvement in the deaths of several teachers while she was head of the Sindicato Nacional de Trabajadores de la Educación (SNTE) teachers' union; the accusations were supported by the dissident Coordinadora Nacional de Trabajadores de la Educación (CNTE), which additionally claimed that Gordillo had illegally transferred SNTE funds to the presidential campaign of Labastida in 2000. In December the CNTE, supported by farmers and Zapatistas, forced their way into the Congreso building on horseback to demand that more funding be given to rural areas, education and poverty reduction. Also in December the Government succeeded in gaining congressional approval for a conservative budget for 2003, despite obstruction by the PRI and PRD (see Economic Affairs).

In January 2003 the Secretary of Foreign Affairs, Jorge Castañeda, resigned, prompting President Fox to carry out a cabinet reshuffle. Castañeda was replaced by the Secretary of the Economy, Luis Ernesto Derbez Bautista, who in turn was succeeded by Fernando Canales Barragán, the Governor of Nuevo León. In April the Comptroller-General, Francisco Barrio Terrazas, resigned in order to stand in the mid-term elections that were scheduled to be held in July. He was replaced by his deputy, Eduardo Ramero Ramos.

The removal of tariffs on the import of a number of agricultural products from January 2003, under the aegis of NAFTA, prompted a demonstration by 100,000 farmers in Mexico City on 1 February. Following negotiations with the protesters, the Government committed itself to a revision, but not renegotiation, of the NAFTA import tariffs. In February conflicts within the PRD led to the cancellation of internal elections for candidates to stand in the July mid-term elections. Instead, candidates were picked by the national committee, and included a number of recent PRI converts, who had left the party following the electoral funding scandal of 2002. In March Eduardo Fernández, a former head of the Comisión Nacional Bancaria y de Valores, was arrested on charges of money-laundering; Fernández had earlier accused the Government of concealing the illegal financing of the Fox election campaign in 2000. When the case against him was dismissed for lack of evidence, it was largely perceived as a defeat for the Government.

Municipal elections were held in the state of México in March 2003. The results, which were interpreted as an indication of the outcome of the July national mid-term elections, saw the PAN lose its majority in the state legislature to the PRI, which contested the ballot in conjunction with the PVEM. President Fox's negative reaction to the US-led military campaign against the regime of Saddam Hussein in Iraq in March–April (see below), as well as the consequent deterioration in relations with the USA, resulted in an increase in public support for his

Government, however, which was likely to help the PAN in the mid-term elections.

Mexico's foreign policy has been determined largely by relations with the USA. The rapid expansion of petroleum production from the mid-1970s onwards gave Mexico a new independence, empowering it to favour the left-wing regimes in Cuba and Nicaragua, opposed by the USA, during the 1980s. In February 1985 relations between Mexico and the USA deteriorated following the murder of an agent of the US Drug Enforcement Administration (DEA) by Mexican drugs-traffickers. The situation worsened in April 1990, when a Mexican physician was abducted, in Mexico, by agents employed by the DEA, and transported to the USA to be arrested on charges relating to the murder. The Mexican authorities considered this action to be in violation of the existing US-Mexican extradition treaty, and refused to recognize the legality of the trial (which was dismissed in December 1992, owing to lack of evidence). Meanwhile, relations between Mexico and the USA remained tense, largely because of disagreement over the problem of illegal immigration from Mexico into the USA and Mexico's failure to take effective action against the illegal drugs trade. This situation improved in 1996 following the deportation to the USA of Juan García Abrego, the alleged head of the Golfo drugs cartel, to face charges of organizing the transport of illicit drugs into the USA, and of concealing the origin of money acquired through drugs-related activities. In February 1997 Mexico's credibility in combating drugs-trafficking was seriously undermined when Gen. Jesús Gutiérrez Rebollo, the head of the counter-narcotics agency, was dismissed and charged with receiving payment from Amado Carrillo Fuentes, the head of the Juárez drugs cartel. (In March 1998 Gutiérrez Rebollo was sentenced to nearly 14 years' imprisonment for storing and transporting weapons and for abuse of authority; in June an appeals tribunal increased the sentence to more than 30 years' detention.) However, later in February 1997 the new head of the Golfo drugs cartel was arrested, and in March the USA 'certified' Mexico as a country co-operating in its campaign against drugs-trafficking. In May, shortly before the first official visit to the country by the US President, Bill Clinton, Mexico's discredited counter-narcotics agency was disbanded and replaced with a specially trained (and better-paid) anti-drugs unit under the auspices of the Attorney-General. (In September, nevertheless, 18 agents of the new unit were arrested on charges of drugs-smuggling.) During his visit, Clinton concluded agreements on border co-operation (further to accords signed during 1996) and on measures to combat the illegal trade in drugs and weapons. In March 1998 Mexico was 'certified' again; however, bilateral relations were strained in May, when a major US counter-narcotics operation was conducted in Mexico, without Mexican authorization. None the less, additional co-operation agreements were signed by the two countries in early 1999 (during a further visit by Clinton), and Mexico was duly 'certified' again. In November 1999 more than 600 Mexican soldiers, aided by agents of the USA's Federal Bureau of Investigation, began the excavation of four suspected mass graves near Ciudad Juárez on the US–Mexican border. It was estimated that the graves contained the remains of at least 100 people believed to have been victims of the Juárez drugs cartel. In March 2000 Mexico was again 'certified' by the USA for its co-operation in the campaign against drugs-trafficking. Upon taking office in late 2000, Fox criticized the practice of 'certification', declaring it unilateral, and advocated its abolition. Despite the new President's hostility, and ongoing concerns regarding corruption in the army and law enforcement agencies (two senior army officers were arrested on suspicion of drugs-trafficking in August 2000), the 'certification' was reaffirmed in March 2001. In 2002 the US Congress suspended its 'certification' process for one year; however, in November 2001 Mexico appeared in a list of countries deemed to be major illicit drug-producing countries by the USA. In August 2002 Fox cancelled a scheduled visit to the USA in protest at the execution of a Mexican national in Texas. In early 2003 a ruling by the International Court of Justice prevented the execution of Mexican prisoners in the USA, pending the legal resolution of the issue.

In December 1992 Mexico, the USA and Canada formally approved NAFTA, which duly took effect from 1 January 1994. Among NAFTA's provisions are the gradual reduction of tariffs on 50% of products over a period of 10–15 years (some 57% of tariffs on agricultural trade between the USA and Mexico was removed immediately), and the establishment, by Mexico and the USA, of a North American Development Bank (NADBank) charged with the funding of initiatives for the rehabilitation of the two countries' common border. From January 2003 tariffs on a number of agricultural products were reduced or removed entirely, provoking widespread discontent among Mexico's 25m.-strong rural community. In particular, they pointed to the greater subsidies received by US farmers (US \$200,000m. in 2003, over US \$10,000m. in Mexico), and to a poor transport infrastructure, which resulted in higher costs. A pledge by President Fox in May 2002 to repay Mexico's 'water debt' to the USA had also angered Mexican farmers.

The Fox Government sought to persuade the US Administration of George W. Bush (2001–) to adopt a more liberal position on Mexican immigrants to the USA. In July 2001 President Bush proposed a possible amnesty for all illegal Mexican immigrants in the USA (estimated to number 3m. in 2001). US trade unions, once opposed to such an idea on the grounds that it would undermine the interests of US workers, indicated their support for the proposal. In August the US Senate voted to ban Mexican trucks operating outside a 32 km zone north of the US–Mexican border. In response, the Mexican Government threatened to impose trade sanctions, claiming that the ban contravened NAFTA regulations. However, in December President Bush, who had opposed the ban, approved legislation allowing Mexican trucks unrestricted access to US highways, although more rigorous safety inspections were to be introduced. In early September President Fox visited Washington, DC, where he addressed the US Congress, in an attempt to regularize the flow of Mexican immigrants to the USA by the end of 2001. However, progress on immigration policy was suspended following the terrorist attacks in the USA on 11 September, and proposals to tighten security on the US-Mexican border were included in the budget presented to the US Congress in February 2002. In the following month, nevertheless, following a summit meeting in Monterrey, the two Presidents announced a 'smart border' partnership agreement, intended to facilitate the legal entry of Mexican people and goods into the USA while, at the same time, securing the frontier against possible acts of terrorism. Attempts to regularize the status of illegal Mexican immigrants in the USA led to the preliminary introduction of identity cards in Texas in May.

In September 2002, however, Fox requested that the emphasis in US-Mexican relations be shifted back to bilateral issues, which had been neglected in favour of border security. Also in September, Mexico unilaterally withdrew from the Inter-American Treaty of Reciprocal Assistance (the Rio Treaty), the defence pact linking Mexico to the USA, resulting in a downturn in relations with the USA. In March 2003, with Mexican public opinion strongly against armed intervention to remove the regime of Saddam Hussein in Iraq, President Fox risked a further deterioration of relations with both the USA and Spain by stating his opposition to war. His opposition was all the more significant owing to Mexico's place as one of the five non-permanent members of the UN Security Council. Although US sources maintained this would not affect bilateral relations, it was likely that recent progress made on immigration issues would be, at least temporarily, halted, while US-Mexico border trade decreased significantly following the commencement of the US-led military campaign in Iraq.

In January 1991 a preliminary free-trade agreement was signed with Honduras, Guatemala, El Salvador, Nicaragua and Costa Rica, in order to facilitate the negotiation of bilateral agreements between Mexico and each of the five countries, leading to free trade in an increasing range of products over a six-year period. During the 1990s Mexico concluded agreements for greater economic co-operation and increased bilateral trade with Colombia and Venezuela (as the Group of Three—G-3 (see p. 340), established in 1994), with Bolivia, Costa Rica and with the European Union (EU, see p. 199). A free-trade accord with Nicaragua was signed in 1992, and came into force in 1998; a similar accord with Chile was signed in 1998 and came into force in the following year. A further trade agreement with Guatemala, Honduras and El Salvador (the Northern Triangle) was concluded in 2000. In March 2000 Mexico and the EU signed a free-trade agreement, the first to be signed between the EU and a Latin American country. The accord provided for the gradual elimination of tariffs on industrial and agricultural products, the progressive liberalization of trade in services, and preferential access to public procurement; it also obliged the signatories to respect democratic principles and human rights.

Government

Mexico is a federal republic comprising 31 states and a Distrito Federal—Federal District (around the capital). Under the 1917 Constitution, legislative power is vested in the bicameral Congreso de la Unión, elected by universal adult suffrage. The Senado has 128 members (four from each state and the Distrito Federal), serving a six-year term. The Cámara Federal de Diputados, directly elected for three years, has 500 seats, of which 300 are filled from single-member constituencies. The remaining 200 seats, allocated so as to achieve proportional representation, are filled from parties' lists of candidates. Executive power is held by the President, directly elected for six years at the same time as the Senado. He governs with the assistance of an appointed Cabinet. Each state has its own constitution and is administered by a Governor (elected for six years) and an elected chamber of deputies. The Distrito Federal is also administered by a Governor.

Defence

Military service, on a part-time basis (four hours per week), is compulsory for conscripts selected by lottery, for one year. In August 2002 the active armed forces totalled 192,770: 144,000 in the army (including 60,000 conscripts), 37,000 in the navy (including naval air force and marines) and 11,770 in the air force. There is a rural defence militia numbering 14,000. The reserve numbered 300,000. Defence expenditure for 2002 was budgeted at 31,200m. new pesos.

Economic Affairs

In 2001, according to estimates by the World Bank, Mexico's gross national income (GNI), measured at average 1999–2001 prices, was US \$550,456m., equivalent to \$5,540 per head (or \$8,770 per head on an international purchasing-power parity basis). During 1990–2001, it was estimated, the population increased at an average annual rate of 1.6%, while gross domestic product (GDP) per head increased, in real terms, by an average of 1.5% per year. Overall GDP increased, in real terms, at an average annual rate of 3.1% in 1990–2001; GDP decreased by 0.3% in 2001.

Agriculture (including forestry and fishing) contributed an estimated 4.1% of GDP in 2001, according to government figures, and engaged about 18.1% of the employed labour force in the same year. The staple food crops are maize, wheat, sorghum, barley, rice, beans and potatoes. The principal cash crops are coffee, cotton, sugar cane, and fruit and vegetables (particularly tomatoes). Livestock-raising and fisheries are also important. During 1990–2001, according to government sources, agricultural GDP increased at an average annual rate of 1.9%; agricultural GDP rose by 0.4% in 2000 and by 6.1% in 2001. The reduction and eventual removal of import tariffs proposed under NAFTA was a significant blow to Mexico's agriculture sector, which had lower subsidies and higher overhead costs than in the USA; the elimination of tariffs on 21 products in January 2003 was to be offset by a US \$10,000m. aid programme, announced in November 2002.

Industry (including mining, manufacturing, construction and power) engaged an estimated 22.9% of the employed labour force in 2001, and provided an estimated 26.7% of GDP in that year, according to government figures. During 1990–2001 industrial GDP increased by an average of 3.3% per year; industrial GDP increased by 6.0% in 2000, but decreased by 3.5% in 2001.

Mining contributed an estimated 1.3% of GDP in 2001, according to government figures, and engaged an estimated 0.3% of the employed labour force in that year. During 1990–2001 the GDP of the mining sector increased by an average of 1.9% per year; mining GDP increased by 3.8% in 2000 and by 0.8% in 2001. Mexico has large reserves of petroleum (which accounted for 9.6% of total export earnings in 2000) and natural gas. Zinc, salt, silver, copper, celestite and fluorite are also major mineral exports. In addition, mercury, bismuth, antimony, cadmium, manganese and phosphates are mined, and there are significant reserves of uranium.

Manufacturing provided an estimated 19.3% of GDP in 2001, according to government figures, and engaged an estimated 18.9% of the employed labour force in that year. Manufacturing GDP increased by an annual average of 3.7% in 1990–2001; the sector increased by 6.9% in 2000, but decreased by 3.7% in 2001. In 1999 the most important branches of manufacturing (based on value of output) were motor vehicles, chemicals, beverages, iron and steel, food products, and electrical machinery. Petroleum refineries also contribute significantly to the sector. By December 2000 Mexico had 3,703 *maquiladora* export plants (where intermediate materials produced on US territory are processed or assembled on the Mexican side of the border), providing an estimated 1.3m. jobs and making an increasingly significant contribution to the sector (accounting for 54.7% of total revenue from manufacturing exports in 2000).

Energy is derived principally from mineral fuels and lubricants and hydroelectric power. In 1999 some 47.2% of total output of electricity production was derived from petroleum, 17.1% was derived from hydroelectric plants, 17.9% came from natural gas and 9.4% came from coal-powered plants. During the late 1990s the Government initiated a programme to deregulate the energy sector; in 1997 private consortia were awarded concessions to build and lease power-stations in Mexico. In 2000 fuel imports accounted for 2.9% of total merchandise imports. In late 2001 the Governments of Mexico and Guatemala reached agreement, under the regional 'Plan Puebla-Panamá' (a series of joint transport, industry and tourism projects intended to integrate the Central American region), to link their electricity grids. In 2002 the Government planned to reform the energy sector in an attempt to improve efficiency and attract investment; however, the proposals faced congressional opposition throughout the year.

The services sector contributed an estimated 69.3% of GDP in 2001, according to government figures, and engaged an estimated 55.6% of the employed labour force in that year. According to government figures, the GDP of the sector increased by an average of 3.7% per year in 1990–2001; the sector experienced growth of 7.4% in 2000 and of 1.0% in 2001. Tourism is one of Mexico's principal sources of foreign exchange. In 2001 there were an estimated 19.8m. foreign visitors to Mexico (mostly from the USA and Canada), providing revenue of US $8,401m.

In 2001 Mexico recorded a visible trade deficit of US $9,955m., and there was a deficit of $17,708m. on the current account of the balance of payments. In 2002 the principal source of imports (63.4%) was the USA, which was also the principal market for exports (89.0%). The principal exports in 2000 were machinery and transport equipment (particularly spare parts for road vehicles, electrical machinery and apparatus), petroleum and petroleum products, and basic manufactures. The principal imports in 2000 were machinery and transport equipment (particularly electrical machinery and apparatus), basic manufactures, and chemicals and related products. In 2002 the Fox Goverment aimed to increase Mexico's trade with the countries of Mercosur (Mercado Común del Sur, or Southern Common Market, see p. 316).

In 2001 there was an estimated budgetary deficit of 57,836.1m. new pesos, equivalent to 1.0% of GDP. Mexico's external debt totalled an estimated US $164,600m. at the end of 2001, of which $94,800m. was long-term public debt. In that year the cost of debt-servicing was equivalent to 39.4% of the value of exports of goods and services. The average annual rate of inflation was 17.2% in 1990–2001. Consumer prices increased by an average of 3.4% in 2001. Some 1.7% of the total labour force were officially recorded as unemployed in 2001, according to ILO figures.

Mexico is a member of the Inter-American Development Bank (IDB, see p. 239), and of the Latin American Integration Association (see p. 259). Mexico was admitted to the Asia-Pacific Economic Co-operation group (APEC, see p. 139) in 1993, and joined the Organisation for Economic Co-operation and Development (OECD, see p. 277) in 1994. Mexico is also a signatory nation to the North American Free Trade Agreement (NAFTA, see p. 270).

Mexico's economic development, centred on the expansion of the petroleum industry, was impeded from the mid-1980s by the decrease in international petroleum prices, in addition to the persistent problems of the flight of capital, the depreciation of the peso, a shortage of foreign exchange and vast foreign debt. A programme of tax reform and economic liberalization was undertaken from the late 1980s, but in late 1994 and early 1995 a sharp devaluation of the peso provoked a financial crisis, necessitating a stringent policy of economic adjustment and the procurement of substantial international credit facilities. During 1995–97 a state agency, FOBAPROA, assumed some US $65,000m. in bank liabilities as a result of the crisis. In 1998, despite a dramatic decline in the price of petroleum and the adverse effects of a fall in the value of the peso against the US dollar, GDP growth of 5.0% was recorded, not least because of the strength of the manufacturing sector. A reform of the banking sector was undertaken in May 1999, creating the Instituto para la Protección al Ahorro Bancario to manage the assets previously assumed by FOBAPROA and removing all restrictions on foreign ownership of banks. In 1999 economic performance was again favourable, with GDP growth of 3.8% exceeding the forecast rate of 3%, mainly owing to strong export growth. In 2000 GDP growth accelerated to 6.6%, reflecting continuing strong export growth, particularly in the *maquiladora* industries; foreign direct investment grew from $10,700m. in 1999 to $12,400m, although the deficit on the current account widened as petrol prices fell. President Fox took office in December 2000, having made electoral commitments to achieve an annual GDP growth rate of 7.0% by 2006, and to reduce inflation to 3% by 2003. However, GDP actually declined by 0.3% in 2001, with contractions in the manufacturing and construction sectors responsible for the reverse. Furthermore, public revenue was estimated to be 15% lower than previously projected, cancelling out the fiscal surplus. The *maquiladora* sector was particularly badly affected by the economic slowdown, contracting by 8.9% in 2001; employment in the sector fell by 11.3% in 2000–01, following the closure of 57 plants. President Fox dismissed a relaxation in monetary policy as a way of encouraging economic growth, and blamed average salary increases of 9%–10% over the previous year for rising unemployment. Economic forecasts for 2002 put GDP growth at 1.4% (though the budget claimed 1.7%). The Government's failure to gain congressional approval for an ambitious fiscal reform programme in late 2001 contributed to the modest growth predictions for 2002. The 2002 budget included tax increases amounting to a 1.2% rise in GDP. In April, however, a reduction in public expenditure of US $1,100m. was deemed necessary to keep the budget deficit under the target of 0.65% of GDP, following lower than expected tax revenues; however, above-average petroleum revenues and a recovery in the US market during 2002 were expected to help reduce the budget deficit for the year as a whole. The Government's National Development Plan (NDP) for 2002–06 envisaged reform of the labour market and the energy and telecommunications sectors. These proposals, however, met with congressional opposition in 2002, and were likely to be further delayed by the mid-term legislative elections that were scheduled to be held in July 2003. The 2003 budget, passed in December 2002, set a strict fiscal deficit of 0.5% of GDP; finances were boosted in early 2003 by a massive increase in crude petroleum export prices, as a result of uncertain supplies from Venezuela and the US-led military campaign in Iraq, as well as by a weak new peso (oil revenues were paid in US dollars).

In September 2000 the outgoing Zedillo administration repaid, ahead of schedule, its outstanding debt to the IMF, totalling some $3,000m. The Fund subsequently noted Mexico's strong economic performance in 1999 and 2000, while warning that continued high consumer demand could cause inflationary pressures. In January 2002 the IDB approved a loan of US $1,000m. for poverty reduction in Mexico. An IMF report published in October 2002 commended the Fox Government's short- and medium-term fiscal strategy and Mexico's resilience to external economic instability.

Education

Education in state schools is provided free of charge and is officially compulsory. It covers six years of primary education, beginning at six years of age, and three years of secondary education, either general or technical, from the age of 12 . This can then be followed by another three-year cycle of higher or specialized secondary education. In 1996 the total enrolment at primary and secondary schools was equivalent to 90% of the school-age population (males 90%; females 89%). In that year an estimated 101% of children in the relevant age-group were enrolled in primary education (males 101%; females 102%), while the equivalent of 64% of children in the relevant age-group were enrolled in secondary schools (males 64%; females 64%). In 2001/02 there were an estimated 4,183 institutes of higher education, attended by 2,147,100 students. In 2002 there were 56 universities in Mexico. In 2001/02 nursery schools for the indigenous population numbered 8,487, while there were 9,065 primary schools for the indigenous population. However, in spite of the existence of more than 80 indigenous languages in Mexico, there were few bilingual secondary schools. Total enrolment at primary school was 14,843,400 students in 2001/02; in that year 6,112,900 students were enrolled at all levels of secondary education. The National Agreement for the Modernization of Basic Education (agreed between the Federal Government, state governments and the national teachers' union in 1992) envisaged the future devolution of federal responsibility for education, to state and municipal bodies. Federal expenditure on education in 2000 was an estimated 216,548m. new pesos (equivalent to 24.7% of total central government expenditure). In November 2002 the Congreso Nacional approved legislation establishing a lower limit on education expenditure equivalent to 8% of GDP.

Public Holidays

2003: 1 January (New Year's Day), 5 February (Constitution Day), 21 March (Birthday of Benito Juárez), 17 April (Maundy Thursday)*, 18 April (Good Friday)*, 1 May (Labour Day), 5 May (Anniversary of the Battle of Puebla)*, 16 September (Independence Day), 12 October (Discovery of America), 1 November (All Saints' Day)*, 2 November (All Souls' Day)*, 20 November (Anniversary of the Revolution), 12 December (Day of Our Lady of Guadalupe)*, 25 December (Christmas).

2004: 1 January (New Year's Day), 5 February (Constitution Day), 22 March (for Birthday of Benito Juárez), 8 April (Maundy Thursday)*, 9 April (Good Friday)*, 3 May (for Labour Day), 5 May (Anniversary of the Battle of Puebla)*, 16 September (Independence Day), 12 October (Discovery of America), 1 November (All Saints' Day)*, 2 November (All Souls' Day)*, 22 November (for Anniversary of the Revolution), 12 December (Day of Our Lady of Guadalupe)*, 25 December (Christmas).

* Widely-celebrated unofficial holidays.

Weights and Measures

The metric system is in force.

Statistical Survey

Sources (unless otherwise stated): Dirección General de Estadística, Instituto Nacional de Estadística, Geografía e Informática (INEGI), Edif. Sede, Avda Prolongación Héroe de Nacozari 2301 Sur, 20270 Aguascalientes, Ags; tel. (14) 918-1948; fax (14) 918-0739; internet www.inegi.gob.mx ; Banco de México, Avda 5 de Mayo 2, Apdo 98 bis, 06059 México, DF; tel. (5) 237-2000; fax (5) 237-2370; internet www.banxico.org.mx ; Banco Nacional de Comercio Exterior, SNC, Avda Camino Santa Teresa 1679, Col. Jardines del Pedregal, Del. Alvaro Obregón, 01900 México, DF; tel. (5) 568-2122; fax (5) 652-6662; internet www.bancomext.com.

Area and Population

AREA, POPULATION AND DENSITY

Area (sq km)	1,953,162*
Population (census results)	
5 November 1995	91,158,290
14 February 2000	
Males	47,592,253
Females	49,891,159
Total	97,483,412
Density (per sq km) at February 2000 census	49.9

* 754,120 sq miles.

ADMINISTRATIVE DIVISIONS
(at census of 14 February 2000)

States	Area (sq km)*	Population	Density (per sq km)	Capital
Aguascalientes (Ags) . .	5,197	944,285	181.7	Aguascalientes
Baja California (BC) . .	71,576	2,487,367	34.8	Mexicali
Baja California Sur (BCS) . .	71,428	424,041	5.9	La Paz
Campeche (Camp.) . . .	56,798	690,689	12.2	Campeche
Chiapas (Chis) .	73,724	3,920,892	53.2	Tuxtla Gutiérrez
Chihuahua (Chih.) . . .	245,945	3,052,907	12.4	Chihuahua
Coahuila(Coah.) .	149,511	2,298,070	15.4	Saltillo
Colima (Col.) . .	5,433	542,627	99.9	Colima
Distrito Federal (DF)	1,547	8,605,239	5,562.5	Mexico City
Durango (Dgo) .	121,776	1,448,661	11.9	Victoria de Durango
Guanajuato (Gto) .	30,768	4,663,032	151.6	Guanajuato
Guerrero (Gro) .	64,586	3,079,649	47.7	Chilpancingo de los Bravos
Hidalgo (Hgo) .	20,502	2,235,591	109.0	Pachuca de Soto
Jalisco (Jal.) . .	78,389	6,322,002	80.6	Guadalajara
México (Méx.) .	21,196	13,096,686	617.9	Toluca de Lerdo
Michoacán (Mich.) .	58,200	3,985,667	68.4	Morelia
Morelos (Mor.) .	4,968	1,555,296	313.1	Cuernavaca
Nayarit (Nay.) .	26,908	920,185	34.2	Tepic
Nuevo León (NL) .	64,210	3,834,141	59.7	Monterrey
Oaxaca (Oax.) .	93,136	3,438,765	36.9	Oaxaca de Juárez
Puebla (Pue.) . .	33,995	5,076,686	149.3	Heroica Puebla de Zaragoza
Querétaro (Qro) .	11,978	1,404,306	117.2	Querétaro
Quintana Roo (Q.Roo) . .	39,376	874,963	22.2	Ciudad Chetumal
San Luis Potosí (SLP) . .	63,038	2,299,360	36.5	San Luis Potosí
Sinaloa (Sin.) . .	56,496	2,536,844	44.9	Culiacán Rosales
Sonora (Son.) . .	180,833	2,216,969	12.3	Hermosillo
Tabasco (Tab.) .	24,578	1,891,829	77.0	Villahermosa
Tamaulipas (Tam.) . .	78,932	2,753,222	34.9	Ciudad Victoria
Tlaxcala (Tlax.) .	4,037	962,646	238.5	Tlaxcala de Xicohténcatl
Veracruz (Ver.) .	71,735	6,908,975	96.3	Jalapa Enríquez
Yucatán (Yuc.) .	43,257	1,658,210	38.3	Mérida
Zacatecas (Zac.) .	73,103	1,353,610	18.5	Zacatecas
Total	1,947,156	97,483,412	50.1	—

* Excluding islands.

PRINCIPAL TOWNS

(population at census of 14 February 2000)

Ciudad de México (Mexico City, capital)	8,605,239	Querétaro		536,463
Guadalajara	1,646,183	Torreón		502,964
Ecatepec de Morelos (Ecatepec)	1,621,827	San Nicolás de los Garzas		496,879
Heroica Puebla de Zaragoza (Puebla)	1,271,673	Santa María Chimalhuacán (Chimalhuacán)		482,530
Nezahualcóyotl	1,225,083	Atizapán de Zaragoza		467,544
Ciudad Juárez	1,187,275	Tlaquepaque		458,674
Tijuana	1,148,681	Toluca de Lerdo (Toluca)		435,125
Monterrey	1,110,909	Cuautitlán Izcalli		433,830
León	1,020,818	Victoria de Durango (Durango)		427,135
Zapopan	910,690	Tuxtla Gutiérrez		424,579
Naucalpan de Juárez (Naucalpan)	835,053	Veracruz Llave (Veracruz)		411,582
Tlalnepantla de Baz (Tlalnepantla)	714,735	Reynosa		403,718
Guadalupe	669,842	Benito Juárez (Cancún)		397,191
Mérida	662,530	Matamoros		376,279
Chihuahua	657,876	Jalapa Enríquez (Xalapa)		373,076
San Luis Potosí	629,208	Villahermosa		330,846
Acapulco de Juárez (Acapulco)	620,656	Mazatlán		327,989
Aguascalientes	594,092	Cuernavaca		327,162
Saltillo	562,587	Valle de Chalco (Xico)		322,784
Morelia	549,996	Irapuato		319,148
Mexicali	549,873	Tonalá		315,278
Hermosillo	545,928	Nuevo Laredo		308,828
Culiacán Rosales (Culiacán)	540,823			

BIRTHS, MARRIAGES AND DEATHS*

	Registered live births		Registered marriages		Registered deaths	
	Number	Rate (per 1,000)	Number	Rate (per 1,000)	Number	Rate (per 1,000)
1990	2,735,312	31.7	642,201	7.5	422,803	4.9
1991	2,756,447	31.4	652,172	7.4	411,131	4.7
1992	2,797,397	31.2	667,598	7.5	409,814	4.6
1993	2,765,580	30.3	679,911	7.5	413,756	4.5
1994	2,904,389	31.2	671,640	7.2	419,074	4.5
1995	2,750,444	30.4	658,114	7.3	430,278	4.6
1996	2,707,718	28.0	670,523	6.9	436,321	4.5
1997	2,698,425	28.6	707,840	7.5	440,437	4.7

1998: Registered live births 2,668,429; Registered deaths 444,665.

1999: Registered live births 2,769,089; Registered marriages 743,856; Registered deaths 443,950.

2000: Registered live births 2,798,339; Registered marriages 707,422; Registered deaths 437,667.

2001: Registered live births 2,767,610; Registered marriages 665,434; Registered deaths 443,127.

* Data are tabulated by year of registration rather than by year of occurrence. Rates are calculated on the basis of unrevised population estimates. However, birth registration is incomplete. According to UN estimates, the average annual rates in 1990–1995, were: births 27.0 per 1,000; deaths 5.2 per 1,000 and in 1995–2000: births 24.6 per 1,000; deaths 5.1 per 1,000 (Source: UN, *World Population Prospects: The 2000 Revision*).

Expectation of life (UN estimates, years at birth): 74.2 (males 71.6; females 76.7) in 2001 (Source: WHO *World Health Report*).

ECONOMICALLY ACTIVE POPULATION

(sample surveys, '000 persons aged 12 years and over, April–June)

	1999	2000	2001
Agriculture, hunting and forestry	8,048.6	6,901.8	6,920.7
Fishing	160.1	158.9	153.7
Mining and quarrying	133.4	155.6	127.2
Manufacturing	7,344.8	7,546.7	7,373.0
Electricity, gas and water supply	193.1	188.5	194.9
Construction	2,158.0	2,527.6	2,396.9
Wholesale and retail trade; repair of motor vehicles, motorcycles and personal and household goods	6,582.4	8,524.5	8,839.2
Hotels and restaurants	1,807.5	1,844.4	1,982.2
Transport, storage and communications	1,738.5	1,730.6	1,776.7
Financial intermediation	302.7	293.0	280.2
Real estate, renting and business activities	1,156.7	1,177.9	1,224.4
Public administration and defence, compulsory social security	1,728.3	1,739.4	1,682.1
Education	1,722.9	1,877.5	1,971.6
Health and social work	1,024.8	1,062.6	1,039.1
Other community, social and personal services activities	3,094.5	1,322.6	1,226.4
Private households with employed persons	1,707.4	1,770.9	1,673.1
Extra-territorial organizations and bodies	151.0	159.8	0.9
Activities not adequately defined	14.5	1.7	142.0
Total employed	39,069.1	38,983.8	39,004.3
Unemployed	682.3	650.0	678.5
Total labour force	39,751.4	39,633.8	39,682.8
Males	26,436.9	26,073.5	26,165.3
Females	13,314.5	13,560.3	13,517.5

Source: ILO.

Health and Welfare

KEY INDICATORS

Total fertility rate (children per woman, 2001)	2.6
Under-5 mortality rate (per 1,000 live births, 2001)	29
HIV/AIDS (% of persons aged 15–49, 2000)	0.28
Physicians (per 1,000 head, 2000)	1.20
Hospital beds (per 1,000 head, 2000)	0.8
Health expenditure (2000): US $ per head (PPP)	483
Health expenditure (2000): % of GDP	5.4
Health expenditure (2000): public (% of total)	46.4
Access to water (% of persons, 2000)	86
Access to sanitation (% of persons, 2000)	73
Human Development Index (2000): ranking	54
Human Development Index (2000): value	0.796

For sources and definitions, see explanatory note on p. vi.

Agriculture

PRINCIPAL CROPS
('000 metric tons)

	1999	2000	2001
Wheat	3,021	3,399	3,275
Rice (paddy)	394	392	227
Barley	454	718	762
Maize	17,706	18,028	20,134
Oats	121	19	89
Sorghum	5,720	6,003	6,567
Potatoes	1,477	1,627	1,628
Sugar cane	46,880*	49,275	47,275*
Dry beans	1,059	883	1,063
Chick-peas	198	237	326
Soybeans (Soya beans)	133	102	122
Groundnuts (in shell)	132	142	120
Coconuts*	1,100	1,113	1,100
Safflower seed	263	103	111
Cottonseed	237	126	277
Cabbages	256	176	216
Lettuce	216	225	213
Tomatoes	2,411	2,134	2,183
Cauliflower*	210	200	200
Pumpkins, squash and gourds*	440	440	450
Cucumbers and gherkins	420	410	410*
Chillies and green peppers	1,797	1,734	1,871
Green onions and shallots	1,227	901	1,029
Dry onions*	100	100	102
Carrots	363	384	356
Green corn*	190	190	191
Bananas	1,738	1,883	1,983
Oranges	3,520	3,795	4,035
Tangerines, mandarins, clementines and satsumas	271	312	365
Lemons and limes	1,368	1,620	1,594
Grapefruit and pomelos	211	256	320
Apples	450	327	443
Peaches and nectarines	126	138	176
Strawberries	138	113	131
Grapes	482	425	436
Watermelons	913	1,048	970
Cantaloupes and other melons*	500	500	510
Mangoes	1,508	1,560	1,577
Avocados	879	903	940
Pineapples	504	519	626
Papayas	569	676	873
Coffee (green)	302	328	303
Cocoa beans	41	28	47
Pimento and allspice*	55	55	55
Cotton (lint)	148	79	97
Tobacco (leaves)	51	45	41

* FAO estimate(s).

Source: FAO.

LIVESTOCK
('000 head, year ending September)

	1999	2000	2001
Horses*	6,250	6,250	6,255
Mules*	3,280	3,280	3,280
Asses*	3,250	3,250	3,260
Cattle	30,193	30,492	30,600*
Pigs	15,748	16,088	16,500*
Sheep	5,949	6,046	6,150*
Goats	9,068	8,704	9,100*
Chickens*	450,000	476,000	495,700
Ducks*	8,000	8,000	8,100
Turkeys*	3,000	3,000	3,000

* Estimate(s).

Source: FAO.

LIVESTOCK PRODUCTS
('000 metric tons)

	1999	2000	2001
Beef and veal	1,400	1,409	1,445
Mutton and lamb	31	33	36
Goat meat	37	39	39
Pig meat	994	1,030	1,058
Horse meat*	79	79	79
Poultry meat	1,767	1,861	1,976
Cows' milk	8,877	9,311	9,472
Goats' milk	131	131	140
Butter	15	15	15
Cheese	139	148	154
Evaporated and condensed milk*	137	153	157
Hen eggs	1,635	1,788	1,892
Cattle hides	170†	175†	176*
Honey	55	59	59

* FAO estimate(s).
† Unofficial figure.

Source: FAO.

Forestry

ROUNDWOOD REMOVALS
('000 cubic metres, excl. bark)

	1999	2000	2001
Sawlogs, veneer logs and logs for sleepers	6,551*	6,651*	6,176
Pulpwood	1,234*	1,234*	1,028
Other industrial wood	220*	220*	216
Fuel wood	37,333	37,561*	37,736*
Total	45,338	45,666	45,156

* FAO estimate.

Source: FAO.

SAWNWOOD PRODUCTION
('000 cubic metres, incl. railway sleepers)

	1997	1998	1999*
Coniferous (softwood)	2,751	3,044	3,110
Broadleaved (hardwood)	210	216	206
Total	2,961	3,260	3,316

2000–01: Production assumed to be unchanged from 1999.

* FAO estimates.

Source: FAO.

Fishing

('000 metric tons, live weight)

	1998	1999	2000
Capture	1,174.7	1,202.2	1,314.2
Tilapias	65.2	59.3	68.8
California pilchard (sardine)	323.2	314.4	459.8
Yellowfin tuna	117.8	121.9	102.3
Chub mackerel	23.0	69.4	45.2
Marine shrimps and prawns	66.6	66.5	61.6
American cupped oyster	30.7	39.3	48.1
Jumbo flying squid	26.6	58.0	56.2
Aquaculture	41.0	48.4	53.8
Total catch (incl. others)	1,215.7	1,250.6	1,368.0

Note: Figures exclude aquatic plants ('000 metric tons, capture only): 12.5 in 1998; 32.1 in 1999; 33.6 in 2000. Also excluded are aquatic mammals and crocodiles (recorded by number rather than by weight), shells and corals. The number of Morelet's crocodiles caught was: 193 in 1998; 2 in 1999; 410 in 2000. The catch of marine shells (metric tons) was: 970 in 1998; 965 in 1999; 464 in 2000.

Source: FAO, *Yearbook of Fishery Statistics*.

Mining

(metric tons, unless otherwise indicated)

	1999	2000	2001
Antimony*	273	52	81
Arsenic*	2,419	2,522	2,381
Barytes	157,953	127,668	142,017
Bismuth*	548	1,112	1,390
Cadmium*	1,311	1,297	1,434
Coal	8,767,000	8,230,115	6,986,027
Coke	2,227,531	2,235,032	2,065,483
Copper*	340,147	338,999	5,518
Crude petroleum ('000 barrels per day)	2,906	3,012	3,127
Celestite	164,682	157,420	145,789
Dolomite	415,284	403,664	670,797
Feldspar	262,241	334,439	329,591
Flourite	557,106	635,230	619,468
Gas (million cu ft per day)	4,791	4,679	4,511
Gold (kg)*	23,476	25,822	28,749
Graphite	27,781	30,330	21,442
Iron*	6,885,217	6,795,406	5,269,820
Lead*	131,402	160,607	148,625
Manganese*	169,107	156,117	99,751
Molybdenum*	7,691	6,886	5,518
Phosphate rock	950,649	1,052,464	787,283
Silica	1,700,527	1,802,545	1,720,211
Silver*	2,455,986	2,746,852	3,030,437
Sulphur	855,483	851,427	878,180
Wollastonite	44,126	30,836	39,830
Zinc*	339,758	358,576	427,273

* Figures for metallic minerals refer to metal content of ores.

2002: Crude petroleum ('000 barrels per day) 3,177; Gas (million cu ft per day) 4,423.

Industry

SELECTED PRODUCTS

('000 metric tons, unless otherwise indicated)

	1997	1998	1999
Wheat flour	2,603	2,581	2,457
Other cereal flour	2,235	2,235	1,878
Raw sugar	2,719	2,907	2,804
Beer ('000 hectolitres)	51,315	54,569	57,905
Cigarettes (million units)	57,618	60,407	59,492
Lubricating oils	407	n.a.	n.a.
Tyres ('000 units)*	13,450	16,646	17,386
Cement	29,685	30,915	31,958
Gas stoves—household ('000 units)	3,008	3,000	3,165
Refrigerators—household ('000 units)	1,942	1,986	2,083
Lorries, buses, tractors, etc. ('000 units)	118	129	154
Passenger cars ('000 units)	263	355	316
Washing machines—household ('000 units)	1,448	1,512	1,593
Cotton yarn (pure)	24	24	21
Electric energy (million kWh)	170,520	180,493	192,235

* Tyres for road motor vehicles.

Source: mainly UN, *Industrial Commodity Statistics Yearbook*.

2000: Steel ('000 metric tons) 15,631; Passenger cars ('000 units) 348; Lorries, buses, tractors etc. ('000 units) 153; Electric energy (million kWh) 204,336.

2001: Steel ('000 metric tons) 13,300; Passenger cars ('000 units) 353; Lorries ('000 units) 119; Electric energy (million kWh) 209,642.

Finance

CURRENCY AND EXCHANGE RATES

Monetary Units
100 centavos = 1 Mexican nuevo peso

Sterling, Dollar and Euro Equivalents (31 December 2002)
£1 sterling = 16.622 nuevos pesos
US $1 = 10.313 nuevos pesos
€1 = 10.815 nuevos pesos
1,000 Mexican nuevos pesos = £60.16 = $96.97 = €92.47

Average Exchange Rate (nuevos pesos per US $)
2000   9.4556
2001   9.3423
2002   9.6560

Note: Figures are given in terms of the nuevo (new) peso, introduced on 1 January 1993 and equivalent to 1,000 former pesos.

BUDGET*

(million new pesos)

Revenue	1999	2000	2001
Taxation	521,682.4	581,703.4	654,870.3
Income taxes	216,123.4	258,754.2	285,523.1
Value-added tax	151,183.5	189,606.0	208,408.1
Excise tax	106,703.7	81,544.1	110,688.8
Import duties	27,302.8	32,861.4	28,902.1
Other revenue	152,665.7	286,564.3	284,244.2
Royalties	106,373.1	210,955.2	203,751.6
Total revenue	674,348.1	868,267.7	939,114.5

Expenditure	1999	2000	2001
Programmable expenditure	469,239.7	589,402.2	631,773.7
Current expenditure	399,255.2	507,609.8	539,425.7
Consumption	87,460.6	120,437.1	123,092.3
Personal services	67,536.1	86,479.9	93,132.1
Transfers	311,794.5	387,799.3	416,333.4
Capital expenditure	69,984.5	81,792.4	92,348.0
Transfers	49,451.4	62,346.2	76,044.3
Non-programmable expenditure	291,994.8	362,680.9	365,176.9
Interest and fees	144,834.0	176,461.0	166,826.4
Revenue sharing	140,670.9	178,136.2	196,931.2
Total expenditure	761,234.4	952,083.1	996,950.6

* Figures refer to the consolidated accounts of the central Government, including government agencies and the national social security system. The budgets of state and local governments are excluded.

Source: Dirección General de Planeación Hacendaria.

INTERNATIONAL RESERVES*

(US $ million at 31 December)

	2000	2001	2002
IMF special drawing rights	366	356	392
Reserve position in the Fund	—	—	308
Foreign exchange	35,142	44,384	49,895
Total	35,509	44,741	50,594

* Excluding gold reserves ($357 million at 30 September 1989).

Source: IMF, *International Financial Statistics*.

MONEY SUPPLY

(million new pesos at 31 December)

	2000	2001	2002
Currency outside banks	182,237	199,177	232,467
Demand deposits at deposit money banks	266,975	317,377	358,547
Total money (incl. others)	450,738	527,672	618,419

Source: IMF, *International Financial Statistics*.

COST OF LIVING
(Consumer Price Index; base: 1990 = 100)

	1999	2000	2001
Food, beverages and tobacco . .	473.6	503.4	530.5
Electricity, gas and water . . .	654.4	819.1	891.7
Clothing and footwear	425.7	470.1	497.2
Rent	493.8	549.9	586.1
All items (incl. others)	491.9	538.6	572.9

Source: ILO.

NATIONAL ACCOUNTS
(million new pesos at current prices)

National Income and Product

	1998	1999	2000
Compensation of employees . .	1,176,936	1,434,759	1,714,421
Operating surplus	1,943,622	2,309,085	2,736,485
Domestic factor incomes . .	3,120,558	3,743,844	4,450,906
Consumption of fixed capital .	397,224	461,860	523,557
Gross domestic product at			
factor cost	3,517,782	4,205,704	4,974,463
Indirect taxes	346,901	404,370	527,891
Less Subsidies	18,333	16,388	16,982
GDP in purchasers' values .	3,846,350	4,593,686	5,485,372

Source: ECLAC, *Statistical Yearbook for Latin America and the Caribbean.*

Expenditure on the Gross Domestic Product*

	1999	2000	2001
Government final consumption			
expenditure	506,460	607,480	667,010
Private final consumption			
expenditure	3,084,140	3,696,140	4,044,830
Increase in stocks	109,270	128,230	64,020
Gross fixed capital formation . .	973,800	1,166,100	1,132,080
Total domestic expenditure .	4,673,670	5,597,950	5,907,940
Exports of goods and services .	1,414,340	1,703,800	1,593,690
Less Imports of goods and services	1,488,560	1,810,730	1,729,770
GDP in purchasers' values .	4,599,450	5,491,020	5,771,860
GDP at constant 1993 prices .	1,503,500	1,603,260	1,598,830

* Figures are rounded to the nearest 10 million new pesos.

Source: IMF, *International Financial Statistics.*

Gross Domestic Product by Economic Activity

	1999	2000	2001*
Agriculture, forestry and fishing .	193,803	202,010	218,770
Mining and quarrying . . .	60,140	70,178	72,144
Manufacturing	884,331	1,013,598	1,037,134
Electricity, gas and water . .	55,515	54,941	62,526
Construction	207,277	257,906	262,631
Trade, restaurants and hotels .	840,650	1,065,694	1,105,047
Transport, storage and			
communications	468,657	556,840	595,607
Finance, insurance, real estate and			
business services	555,142	605,499	642,115
Community, social and personal			
services	997,200	1,215,204	1,380,406
Sub-total	4,262,715	5,041,870	5,376,380
Less Imputed bank service charge	57,010	61,084	90,770
GDP at factor cost . . .	4,205,705	4,980,786	5,285,606
Indirect taxes, *less* subsidies .	387,981	510,909	542,984
GDP in purchasers' values . .	4,593,685	5,491,373	5,828,591

* Preliminary.
Note: Totals may not be equal to the sum of component parts, owing to rounding.

BALANCE OF PAYMENTS
(US $ million)

	1999	2000	2001
Exports of goods f.o.b.	136,392	166,456	158,443
Imports of goods f.o.b.	−141,975	−174,457	−168,398
Trade balance	−5,583	−8,001	−9,955
Exports of services	11,737	13,752	12,699
Imports of services	−14,473	−17,363	−17,194
Balance on goods and services	−8,319	−11,612	−14,150
Other income received . . .	4,476	6,049	5,098
Other income paid	−16,462	−19,173	−17,672
Balance on goods, services and			
income	−20,305	−24,736	−27,024
Current transfers received . .	6,315	7,001	9,338
Current transfers paid . . .	−27	−29	−22
Current balance	−14,017	−17,764	−17,708
Direct investment abroad . . .	—	—	−3,708
Direct investment from abroad .	12,478	14,192	24,731
Portfolio investment assets . .	−836	1,290	3,857
Portfolio investment liabilities . .	6,285	4,269	986
Other investment assets . . .	−3,170	5,808	−3,588
Other investment liabilities . .	−312	−12	−11
Net errors and omissions . .	735	3,673	2,317
Overall balance	1,163	11,456	6,876

Source: IMF, *International Financial Statistics.*

External Trade

PRINCIPAL COMMODITIES
(distribution by SITC, US $ million)

Imports f.o.b.	1998	1999	2000
Food and live animals . . .	5,285.3	5,664.1	7,050.7
Crude materials (inedible)			
except fuels	4,262.9	3,958.8	4,902.1
Chemicals and related			
products	10,718.1	11,904.0	14,892.5
Basic manufactures	21,537.2	24,781.9	33,422.8
Textile yarn, fabrics, etc. . .	3,462.4	4,867.1	6,252.6
Machinery and transport			
equipment	59,849.7	70,337.8	95,897.0
Power-generating machinery and			
equipment	4,311.0	5,345.2	6,890.4
Machinery specialized for			
particular industries . . .	4,687.3	4,766.8	5,386.7
General industrial machinery and			
equipment and parts . . .	6,966.6	8,017.3	10,281.1
Office machines and automatic			
data-processing equipment . .	3,185.7	4,323.2	5,774.9
Telecommunications and sound			
equipment	5,819.9	6,817.7	9,771.8
Other electrical machinery,			
apparatus, etc.	22,405.9	26,705.2	36,388.3
Switchgear, resistors, printed			
circuits, switchboards, etc. .	5,310.4	6,362.9	8,486.5
Thermionic valves, tubes, etc. .	7,891.6	10,093.1	14,279.5
Electronic microcircuits . .	3,946.5	5,600.3	8,937.7
Road vehicles and parts* . .	9,993.0	11,784.6	18,964.4
Parts and accessories for cars,			
buses, lorries, etc.* . . .	6,623.9	7,908.1	12,054.8
Miscellaneous manufactured			
articles	15,772.6	17,434.3	12,924.9
Articles of plastic materials, etc. .	4,582.4	5,427.8	7,265.2
Total (incl. others)	125,193.2	141,955.6	190,790.5

* Data on parts exclude tyres, engines and electrical parts.

Exports f.o.b.	1998	1999	2000
Food and live animals . .	6,134.7	5,999.6	6,472.1
Mineral fuels, lubricants, etc. .	6,979.6	9,731.0	16,052.8
Petroleum, petroleum products, etc.	6,926.5	9,604.8	15,964.1
Crude petroleum oils, etc. . .	6,398.8	8,858.8	14,878.5
Chemicals and related products . . .	4,230.8	4,402.5	5,253.1
Basic manufactures . . .	11,975.8	12,120.2	13,848.2
Machinery and transport equipment. . .	68,010.8	81,258.9	98,281.3
Power-generating machinery and equipment	5,043.1	5,731.6	6,222.4
General industrial machinery equipment and parts . .	3,571.5	4,475.4	5,171.9
Office machines and automatic data-processing equipment . .	7,535.5	9,760.3	11,756.7
Automatic data-processing machines and units . .	4,428.0	6,398.9	8,137.8
Telecommunications and sound equipment	12,075.3	14,379.5	19,221.1
Colour television receivers . .	4,908.5	5,156.1	5,727.4
Other electrical machinery apparatus, etc. . . .	18,225.6	21,756.8	26,063.9
Equipment for distributing electricity	5,223.1	6,008.2	6,719.8
Insulated electric wire, cable etc.	5,200.1	5,977.2	6,673.9
Road vehicles and parts* . . .	19,509.9	23,383.4	27,898.1
Passenger motor cars (excl. buses).	10,974.2	12,407.5	16,296.7
Goods vehicles (lorries and trucks)	3,579.0	4,101.5	4,815.7
Parts and accessories for cars, buses, lorries, etc.* . . .	4,173.7	5,107.9	5,791.0
Miscellaneous manufactured articles. . . .	16,976.0	19,379.9	22,607.6
Clothing and accessories (excl. footwear)	6,603.6	7,772.9	8,631.3
Total (incl. others)	117,325.4	136,262.8	166,191.7

* Data on parts exclude tyres, engines and electrical parts.

Source: UN, *International Trade Statistics Yearbook.*

2001 (US $ million): *Imports f.o.b.*: Agricultural products 4,655.0; Manufactured goods 159,408.5; Total (incl. others) 158,442.9; *Exports f.o.b.*: Agricultural products 3,325.8; Mineral products 12,055.1; Manufactured goods 142,115.4; Total (incl. others) 168,396.5.

PRINCIPAL TRADING PARTNERS*
(US $ million)

Imports c.i.f.	2000	2001	2002†
Brazil	1,802.9	2,101.3	2,565.0
Canada	4,016.6	4,234.9	4,480.3
China, People's Republic . .	2,879.6	4,027.3	6,274.4
China (Taiwan)	1,994.3	3,015.3	4,250.1
France	1,466.6	1,577.0	1,806.8
Germany	5,758.4	6,079.6	6,065.8
Italy	1,849.4	2,100.3	2,171.1
Japan	6,479.6	8,085.7	9,348.6
Korea, Republic	2,879.6	3,531.7	3,910.0
Malaysia	1,353.7	2,006.2	1,993.2
Spain	1,430.0	1,827.4	2,223.9
USA	127,817.7	114,061.6	106,921.9
Total (incl. others)	174,457.8	168,396.5	168,678.9

Exports f.o.b.	2000	2001	2002†
Canada	3,353.7	3,069.5	2,808.9
USA	147,639.9	140,483.95	143,162.9
Total (incl. others)	166,424.0	158,442.9	160,682.0

* Imports by country of origin; exports by country of destination.
† Preliminary data.

Transport

RAILWAYS
(traffic, million)

	1999	2000	2001
Passenger-kilometres . . .	218	n.a.	n.a.
Passengers carried ('000) . .	n.a.	334	242
Freight ton-kilometres . .	49,955	48,333	47,336

ROAD TRAFFIC
(estimates, vehicles in use at 31 December)

	1998	1999	2000
Passenger cars	9,378,587	9,842,006	10,443,489
Buses and coaches . . .	108,690	109,929	111,756
Lorries and vans	4,403,953	4,639,860	7,931,590

Source: International Road Federation, *World Road Statistics.*

SHIPPING

Merchant Fleet
(registered at 31 December)

	1999	2000	2001
Number of vessels	621	631	633
Total displacement ('000 grt) . .	917.9	883.2	908.1

Source: Lloyd's Register-Fairplay, *World Fleet Statistics.*

Sea-borne Shipping
(domestic and international freight traffic, '000 metric tons)

	1993	1994	1995
Goods loaded	129,091	130,884	135,957
Goods unloaded	53,121	56,308	53,300

CIVIL AVIATION
(traffic on scheduled services)

	1996	1997	1998
Kilometres flown (million) . . .	245	308	308
Passengers carried ('000) . .	14,678	17,752	18,685
Passenger-km (million) . . .	19,636	24,065	25,976
Total ton-km (million) . . .	1,861	2,333	2,556

Source: UN, *Statistical Yearbook.*

1999: Passengers carried ('000) 37,461 (Source: Instituto Mexicano del Transporte).

2000: Passengers carried ('000) 36,439 (Source: Instituto Mexicano del Transporte).

Tourism

	1999	2000	2001
Tourist arrivals ('000)	19,043	20,643	19,810
Border tourists ('000) . . .	8,829	10,050	9,659
Total expenditure (US $ million) .	7,223	8,295	8,401

Source: Secretaría de Turismo de México.

Communications Media

	1999	2000	2001
Television receivers ('000 in use)	26,500	28,000	n.a.
Telephone ('000 main lines in use)	10,927.4	12,332.6	13,533.0
Mobile cellular telephones ('000 subscribers)	7,731.6	14,073.7	20,136.0
Personal computers ('000 in use)	4,300	5,000	6,900
Internet users ('000)	1,822.2	2,712.4	3,500.0

Radio receivers ('000 in use): 31,000 in 1997.

Facsimile machines ('000 in use): 285 in 1997.

Daily newspapers (1996): Number 295; Average circulation 9,030,000.

Non-daily newspapers (1996): Number 23; Average circulation 620,000.

Sources: International Telecommunication Union; UNESCO, *Statistical Yearbook*; UN, *Statistical Yearbook*.

Education

(estimates, 2001/02)

	Institutions	Teachers	Students*
Pre-primary	73,384	179,985	3,432.3
Primary	99,230	609,654	14,843.4
Secondary (incl. technical) . .	29,104	317,111	5,480.2
Intermediate: professional/technical	1,592	30,914	356.3
Intermediate: Baccalaureate . .	8,995	188,554	2,764.2
Higher (incl. post-graduate) . .	4,183	216,804	2,147.1

* Figures are in thousands.

Source: Secretaría de Educación Pública.

Adult literacy rate (UNESCO estimates): 91.4% (males 93.4%; females 89.5%) in 2000 (Source: UN Development Programme, *Human Development Report*).

Directory

The Constitution

The present Mexican Constitution was proclaimed on 5 February 1917, at the end of the revolution, which began in 1910, against the regime of Porfirio Díaz. Its provisions regarding religion, education and the ownership and exploitation of mineral wealth reflect the long revolutionary struggle against the concentration of power in the hands of the Roman Catholic Church and the large landowners, and the struggle which culminated, in the 1930s, in the expropriation of the properties of the foreign petroleum companies. It has been amended from time to time.

GOVERNMENT

The President and Congress

The President of the Republic, in agreement with the Cabinet and with the approval of the Congreso de la Unión (Congress) or of the Permanent Committee when the Congreso is not in session, may suspend constitutional guarantees in case of foreign invasion, serious disturbance, or any other emergency endangering the people.

The exercise of supreme executive authority is vested in the President, who is elected for six years and enters office on 1 December of the year of election. The presidential powers include the right to appoint and remove members of the Cabinet and the Attorney-General; to appoint, with the approval of the Senado (Senate), diplomatic officials, the higher officers of the army, and ministers of the supreme and higher courts of justice. The President is also empowered to dispose of the armed forces for the internal and external security of the federation.

The Congreso is composed of the Cámara Federal de Diputados (Federal Chamber of Deputies) elected every three years, and the Senado whose members hold office for six years. There is one deputy for every 250,000 people and for every fraction of over 125,000 people. The Senado is composed of two members for each state and two for the Distrito Federal. Regular sessions of the Congreso begin on 1 September and may not continue beyond 31 December of the same year. Extraordinary sessions may be convened by the Permanent Committee.

The powers of the Congreso include the right to: pass laws and regulations; impose taxes; specify the criteria on which the Executive may negotiate loans; declare war; raise, maintain and regulate the organization of the armed forces; establish and maintain schools of various types throughout the country; approve or reject the budget; sanction appointments submitted by the President of the Supreme Court and magistrates of the superior court of the Distrito Federal; approve or reject treaties and conventions made with foreign powers; and ratify diplomatic appointments.

The Permanent Committee, consisting of 29 members of the Congreso (15 of whom are deputies and 14 senators), officiates when the Congreso is in recess, and is responsible for the convening of extraordinary sessions of the Congreso.

The States

Governors are elected by popular vote in a general election every six years. The local legislature is formed by deputies, who are changed every three years. The judicature is specially appointed under the Constitution by the competent authority (it is never subject to the popular vote).

Each state is a separate unit, with the right to levy taxes and to legislate in certain matters. The states are not allowed to levy inter-state customs duties.

The Federal District

The Distrito Federal consists of Mexico City and several neighbouring small towns and villages. The first direct elections for the Governor of the Distrito Federal were held in July 1997; hitherto a Regent had been appointed by the President.

EDUCATION

According to the Constitution, the provision of educational facilities is the joint responsibility of the federation, the states and the municipalities. Education shall be democratic, and shall be directed to developing all the faculties of the individual students, while imbuing them with love of their country and a consciousness of international solidarity and justice. Religious bodies may not provide education, except training for the priesthood. Private educational institutions must conform to the requirements of the Constitution with regard to the nature of the teaching given. The education provided by the states shall be free of charge.

RELIGION

Religious bodies of whatever denomination shall not have the capacity to possess or administer real estate or capital invested therein. Churches are the property of the nation; the headquarters of bishops, seminaries, convents and other property used for the propagation of a religious creed shall pass into the hands of the state, to be dedicated to the public service of the federation or of the respective state. Institutions of charity, provided they are not connected with a religious body, may hold real property. The establishment of monastic orders is prohibited. Ministers of religion must be Mexican; they may not criticize the fundamental laws of the country in a public or private meeting; they may not vote or form associations for political purposes. Political meetings may not be held in places of worship.

A reform proposal, whereby constitutional restrictions on the Catholic Church were formally ended, received congressional approval in December 1991 and was promulgated as law in January 1992.

LAND AND MINERAL OWNERSHIP

Article 27 of the Constitution vests direct ownership of minerals and other products of the subsoil, including petroleum and water, in the nation, and reserves to the Federal Government alone the right to grant concessions in accordance with the laws to individuals and companies, on the condition that they establish regular work for the exploitation of the materials. At the same time, the right to acquire ownership of lands and waters belonging to the nation, or concessions for their exploitation, is limited to Mexican individuals and companies, although the State may concede similar rights to foreigners who agree not to invoke the protection of their governments to enforce such rights.

The same article declares null all alienations of lands, waters and forests belonging to towns or communities made by political chiefs or other local authorities in violation of the provisions of the law of 25

June 1856,* and all concessions or sales of communally-held lands, waters and forests made by the federal authorities after 1 December 1876. The population settlements which lack ejidos (state-owned smallholdings), or cannot obtain restitution of lands previously held, shall be granted lands in proportion to the needs of the population. The area of land granted to the individual may not be less than 10 hectares of irrigated or watered land, or the equivalent in other kinds of land.

The owners affected by decisions to divide and redistribute land (with the exception of the owners of farming or cattle-rearing properties) shall not have any right of redress, nor may they invoke the right of amparo† in protection of their interests. They may, however, apply to the Government for indemnification. Small properties, the areas of which are defined in the Constitution, will not be subject to expropriation. The Constitution leaves to the Congreso the duty of determining the maximum size of rural properties.

In March 1992 an agrarian reform amendment, whereby the programme of land-distribution established by the 1917 Constitution was abolished and the terms of the ejido system of tenant farmers were relaxed, was formally adopted.

Monopolies and measures to restrict competition in industry, commerce or public services are prohibited.

A section of the Constitution deals with work and social security.

On 30 December 1977 a Federal Law on Political Organizations and Electoral Procedure was promulgated. It includes the following provisions:

Legislative power is vested in the Congreso de la Unión which comprises the Cámara Federal de Diputados and the Senado. The Cámara shall comprise 300 deputies elected by majority vote within single-member electoral districts and up to 100 deputies (increased to 200 from July 1988) elected by a system of proportional representation from regional lists within multi-member constituencies. The Senado comprises two members for each state and two for the Distrito Federal, elected by majority vote.

Executive power is exercised by the President of the Republic of the United Mexican States, elected by majority vote.

Ordinary elections will be held every three years for the federal deputies and every six years for the senators and the President of the Republic on the first Sunday of July of the year in question. When a vacancy occurs among members of the Congreso elected by majority vote, the house in question shall call extraordinary elections, and when a vacancy occurs among members of the Cámara elected by proportional representation it shall be filled by the candidate of the same party who received the next highest number of votes at the last ordinary election.

Voting is the right and duty of every citizen, male or female, over the age of 18 years.

A political party shall be registered if it has at least 3,000 members in each one of at least half the states in Mexico or at least 300 members in each one of at least half of the single-member constituencies. In either case the total number of members must be no less than 65,000. A party can also obtain conditional registration if it has been active for at least four years. Registration is confirmed if the party obtains at least 1.5% of the popular vote. All political parties shall have free access to the media.

In September 1993 an amendment to the Law on Electoral Procedure provided for the expansion of the Senado to 128 seats, representing four members for each state and the Distrito Federal, three to be elected by majority vote and one by proportional representation.

* The Lerdo Law against ecclesiastical privilege, which became the basis of the Liberal Constitution of 1857.

† The Constitution provides for the procedure known as juicio de amparo, a wider form of habeas corpus, which the individual may invoke in protection of his constitutional rights.

The Government

HEAD OF STATE

President: VICENTE FOX QUESADA (took office 1 December 2000).

CABINET
(April 2003)

Secretary of the Interior: SANTIAGO CREEL MIRANDA.

Secretary of Foreign Affairs: LUIS ERNESTO DERBEZ BAUTISTA.

Secretary of National Defence: Gen. RICARDO VEGA GARCÍA.

Secretary of the Navy: Adm. MARCO ANTONIO PEYROT GONZÁLEZ.

Secretary of Public Security and Judicial Services: ALEJANDRO GERTZ MANERO.

Secretary of Finance and Public Credit: FRANCISCO GIL DÍAZ.

Secretary of Social Development: JOSEFINA VÁZQUEZ MOTA.

Secretary of the Environment and Natural Resources: VÍCTOR LICHTINGER.

Secretary of Energy: ERNESTO MARTENS REBOLLEDO.

Secretary of Economy: FERNANDO CANALES.

Secretary of Agriculture, Livestock, Rural Development, Fisheries and Food: JAVIER USABIAGA ARROYO.

Secretary of Communications and Transport: PEDRO CERISOLA Y WEBER.

Secretary of Public Function: EDUARDO RAMERO RAMOS.

Secretary of Public Education: REYES TAMEZ GUERRA.

Secretary of Health: JULIO FRENK MORA.

Secretary of Labour and Social Welfare: CARLOS MARÍA ABASCAL CARRANZA.

Secretary of Agrarian Reform: FLORENCIO SALAZAR.

Secretary of Tourism: LETICIA NAVARRO.

Attorney-General: Gen. RAFAEL MARCIAL MACEDO DE LA CONCHA.

SECRETARIATS OF STATE

Office of the President: Los Pinos, Puerta 1, Col. San Miguel Chapultepec, 11850 México, DF; tel. (55) 5515-3717; fax (55) 5510-8713; internet www.presidencia.gob.mx.

Secretariat of State for Agrarian Reform: Avda Dr Vertiz 800, 1°, Col. Narvarte, 03020 México, DF; tel. (55) 273-9180; fax (55) 273-2481; internet www.sra.gob.mx.

Secretariat of State for Agriculture, Livestock, Rural Development, Fisheries and Food: Insurgentes Sur 476, 13°, Col. Roma Sur, 06760 México, DF; tel. (55) 5584-0096; fax (55) 5584-0268; e-mail c.informacion@sagar.gob.mx; internet www.sagarpa.gob.mx.

Secretariat of State for Communications and Transport: Avda Universidad y Xola, Cuerpo C, 1°, Col. Narvarte, 03028 México, DF; tel. (55) 5519-1319; fax (55) 5519-9748; internet www.sct.gob.mx.

Secretariat of State for the Economy: México, DF; fax (55) 5229-6134; internet www.economia.gob.mx.

Secretariat of State for Energy: Insurgentes Sur 552, 3°, Col. Roma Sur, 06769 México, DF; tel. (55) 5448-6033; fax (55) 5448-6055; e-mail energia1@energia.gob.mx; internet www.energia.gob.mx.

Secretariat of State for the Environment and Natural Resources: Blvd Adolfo Ruíz Cortines, 4209, 3°, Col. Jardines en la Montaña, Tlalpan, 14210 México, DF; tel. (55) 5628-0600; fax (55) 5628-0644; internet www.semarnat.gob.mx.

Secretariat of State for Finance and Public Credit: Palacio Nacional, primer patio Mariano, 3°, Col. Centro, 06066 México, DF; tel. (55) 5518-5420; fax (55) 5542-2821; internet www.shcp.gob.mx.

Secretariat of State for Foreign Affairs: Avda Ricardo Flores Magón 2, 4°, Col. Nonoalco Tlatelolco, 09600 México, DF; tel. (55) 5782-3982; fax (55) 5782-4109; e-mail comment@sre.gob.mx; internet www.sre.gob.mx.

Secretariat of State for Health: Lieja 7, 1° Col. Juárez, 06600 México, DF; tel. (55) 5553-0758; fax (55) 5553-7917; e-mail ssa@mail.ssa.gob.mx; internet www.ssa.gob.mx.

Secretariat of State for the Interior: Bucareli 99, 1°, Col. Juárez, 06069 México, DF; tel. (55) 5592-1141; fax (55) 5546-5350; internet www.gobernacion.gob.mx.

Secretariat of State for Labour and Social Welfare: Edif. A, 4°, Anillo Periférico Sur 4271, 4°, Col. Fuentes del Pedregal, 14149 México, DF; tel. (55) 5645-3965; fax (55) 5645-5594; e-mail correo@stps.gob.mx; internet www.stps.gob.mx.

Secretariat of State for National Defence: Manuel Avila Camacho, esq. Avda Industria Militar, 3°, Col. Lomas de Sotelo, 11600 México, DF; tel. (55) 5395-5936; fax (55) 5557-1370; internet www.sedena.gob.mx.

Secretariat of State for the Navy: Eje 2 Ote, Tramo Heroica, Escuela Naval Militar 861, Col. Los Cipreses, 04830 México, DF; tel. (55) 5684-8188; fax (55) 5679-6411; internet www.semar.gob.mx.

Secretariat of State for Public Education: República de Argentina 28, 2°, Col. Centro, 06029 México, DF; tel. (55) 5510-2557; fax (55) 5329-6873; e-mail educa@sep.gob.mx; internet www.sep.gob.mx.

Secretariat of State for Public Function: Insurgentes Sur 1735, 10°, Col. Guadalupe Inn, 01020 México DF; tel. (55) 3003-4090; fax (55) 5662-4763; e-mail ltacher@secodam.gob.mx; internet www.secodam.gob.mx.

Secretariat of State for Public Security and Judicial Services: Londres 102, 7°, Col. Juaréz, 06600 México, DF; e-mail ssp@snsp.gob.mx; internet www.ssp.gob.mx.

Secretariat of State for Social Development: Edif. B, planta alta, Constituyentes 947, Col. Belén de las Flores, 01110 México, DF; tel. (55) 5271-2650; fax (55) 5271-8862; e-mail cc@sedesol.gob.mx; internet www.sedesol.gob.mx.

Secretariat of State for Tourism: Presidente Masarik 172, Col. Polanco, 11587 México, DF; tel. (55) 5250-8555; fax (55) 5255-3112; internet www.mexico-travel.com.

Office of the Attorney-General: Paseo de la Reforma y Violeta 75, 2°, Col. Guerrero, 06300 México, DF; tel. (55) 5626-9600; fax (55) 5626-4447; internet www.pgr.gob.mx.

State Governors

(April 2003)

Aguascalientes: FELIPE GONZÁLEZ GONZALES (PAN).

Baja California: EUGENIO ELORDUY WALTHER (PAN).

Baja California Sur: LEONEL COTA MONTAÑO (PRD-PT-PVEM).

Campeche: Lic. JOSÉ ANTONIO GONZÁLEZ CURI (PRI).

Chiapas: PABLO SALAZAR MENDIGUCHÍA (Ind.).

Chihuahua: Lic. PATRICIO MARTÍNEZ GARCÍA (PRI).

Coahuila: ENRIQUE MARTÍNEZ Y MARTÍNEZ (PRI).

Colima: Lic. FERNANDO MORENO PEÑA (PRI).

Distrito Federal: ANDRÉS MANUEL LÓPEZ OBRADOR (PRD).

Durango: Lic. ANGEL SERGIO GUERRERO MIER (PRI).

Guanajuato: JUAN CARLOS ROMERO HICKS (PAN).

Guerrero: RENÉ JUÁREZ CISNEROS (PRI).

Hidalgo: MANUEL ANGEL NÚÑEZ SOTO (PRI).

Jalisco: Lic. FRANCISCO RAMIREZ ACUÑA (PAN).

México: Lic. ARTURO MONTIEL ROJAS (PRI).

Michoacán: LAZARO CÁRDENAS (PRD).

Morelos: Lic. SERGIO ESTRADA CAJIGAL RAMÍREZ (PAN).

Nayarit: ANTONIO ECHEVARRÍA (PAN-PRD-PT-PVEM).

Nuevo León: Lic. FERNANDO ELIZONDO BARRAGÁN (PAN).

Oaxaca: JOSÉ MURAT CASAB (PRI).

Puebla: MELQUIADES MORALES FLORES (PRI).

Querétaro: Ing. IGNACIO LOYOLA VERA (PAN).

Quintana Roo: JOAQUÍN HENDRICKS DÍAZ (PRI).

San Luis Potosí: FERNANDO SILVA NIETO (PRI).

Sinaloa: JUAN S. MILLÁN LIZARRAGA (PRI).

Sonora: Lic. ARMANDO LÓPEZ NOGALES (PRI).

Tabasco: MANUEL ANDRADE DÍAZ (PRI).

Tamaulipas: TOMÁS YARRINGTON RUVALCABA (PRI).

Tlaxcala: ALFONSO SÁNCHEZ ANAYA (PRD-PT-PVEM).

Veracruz: MIGUEL ALEMÁN VELAZCO (PRI).

Yucatán: PATRICIO PATRÓN LAVIADA (PAN-PRD-PT-PVEM).

Zacatecas: Lic. RICARDO MONREAL AVILA (PRD).

President and Legislature

PRESIDENT

Election, 2 July 2000

Candidate	Number of votes	% of votes
Vicente Fox Quesada (Alianza por el Cambio)	15,988,740	43.47
Francisco Labastida Ochoa (PRI)	13,576,385	36.91
Cuauhtémoc Cárdenas Solórzano (Alianza por México)	6,259,048	17.02
Others	957,455	2.60
Total	36,781,628	100.00

CONGRESO DE LA UNIÓN

Senado
(Senate)

President: ENRIQUE JACKSON RAMÍREZ.

Elections, 2 July 2000

Party	Seats
Partido Revolucionario Institucional (PRI)	60
Partido Acción Nacional (PAN)*	46
Partido de la Revolución Democrática (PRD)†	15
Partido Verde Ecologista de México (PVEM)*	5
Convergencia por la Democracia (CD)†	1
Partido del Trabajo (PT)†	1
Total	128

* Contested the elections jointly as the Alianza por el Cambio.
† Contested the elections as part of the Alianza por México.

Cámara Federal de Diputados
(Federal Chamber of Deputies)

President: ARMANDO SALINAS TORRE.

Elections, 2 July 2000

Party	Seats
Partido Revolucionario Institucional (PRI)	209
Partido Acción Nacional (PAN)*	208
Partido de la Revolución Democrática (PRD)†	52
Partido Verde Ecologista de México (PVEM)*	15
Partido del Trabajo (PT)†	8
Convergencia por la Democracia (CD)†	3
Partido de la Sociedad Nacionalista (PSN)†	3
Partido Alianza Social (PAS)†	2
Total	500

* Contested the elections jointly as the Alianza por el Cambio.
† Contested the elections as part of the Alianza por México.

Political Organizations

To retain legal political registration, parties must secure at least 1.5% of total votes at two consecutive federal elections. Several of the parties listed below are no longer officially registered but continue to be politically active.

Convergencia: Louisiana 113, Col. Nápoles 03810, México, DF; tel. (55) 5543-8513; internet www.convergencia.org.mx; f. 1995 as Convergencia por la Democracia; Pres. DANTE DELGADO RANNAURO.

Democracia Social: San Borja 416, Col. del Valle, 03100 México, DF; tel. (55) 5559-2875; f. 1999; Pres. GILBERTO RINCÓN GALLARDO.

Fuerza Ciudadana: Rochester 94, Col. Napoles 03810, México, DF; tel. (55) 5523-9512; e-mail info@fuerzaciudadana.org.mx; internet www.fuerzaciudadana.org.mx; f. 2002; Pres. JORGE ALCOCER VILLA-NUEVA; Sec.-Gen. EMILIO CABALLERO URDIALES.

Partido Acción Nacional (PAN): Avda Coyoacán 1546, Col. del Valle, México, DF; tel. (55) 5200-4000; e-mail correo@cen.pan.org.mx; internet www.pan.org.mx; f. 1939; democratic party; 150,000 mems; Pres. LUIS FELIPE BRAVO MENA; Sec.-Gen. MANUEL ESPINO BARRIENTOS.

Partido Alianza Social (PAS): Édison 89, Col. Tabacalera, 06030 México, DF; tel. (55) 5592-5688; fax (55) 5566-1665; internet www.pas.org.mx; Pres. GUILLERMO CALDERÓN DOMÍNGUEZ; Sec.-Gen. ADALBERTO ROSAS LÓPEZ.

Partido Auténtico de la Revolución Mexicana (PARM): Pueblo 286, 1°, Col. Roma, 06700 México, DF; tel. (55) 5514-9676; f. 1954 to sustain the ideology of the Mexican Political Constitution of 1917; 191,500 mems; Pres. CARLOS GUZMÁN PÉREZ.

Partido de Centro Democrático (PCD): Amores 923, Col. del Valle, Deleg. Benito Juárez, 03100 México, DF; tel. (55) 5575-3101; fax (55) 5575-8888; e-mail pcdcen@pcd2000.org.mx; centrist party; f. 1997; Leader MANUEL CAMACHO SOLÍS.

Partido del Frente Cardenista de Reconstrucción Nacional (PFCRN): Avda México 199, Col. Hipódromo Condesa, 06170 México, DF; f. 1972; Marxist-Leninist; fmrly Partido Socialista de los Trabajadores; 132,000 mems; Pres. RAFAEL AGUILAR TALAMANTES; Sec.-Gen. GRACO RAMÍREZ ABREU.

Partido Liberal México (PLM): Nuevo Leon 80, Col. Condesa 06180, México, DF; tel. (55) 5211-32958; e-mail plm@plm.org.mx; internet www.plm.org.mx; f. 2002; Pres. C. SALVADOR ORDAZ MONTES DE OCA.

Partido México Posible—La Nueva Política: Abasolo 8, Col. El Carmen 04100, México, DF; tel. (55) 5659-0807; fax (55) 5659-0778; e-mail correo@mexicoposible.org.mx; internet www.mexicoposible .org.mx; f. 2002; focus on the rights of women and indigenous peoples, and ecological issues; Pres. Patricia Mercado Castro; Sec.-Gen. Wilfrido Isamí Salzar Rule.

Partido Popular Socialista (PPS): Avda Alvaro Obregón 185, Col. Roma, 06797 México, DF; tel. (55) 5533-0816; fax (55) 5525-7131; internet www.pps.org.mx; f. 1948; left-wing party; Sec.-Gen. Manuel Fernández Flores.

Partido de la Revolución Democrática (PRD): Monterrey 50, Col. Roma, 06700 México, DF; tel. (55) 5525-6059; fax (55) 5208-7833; internet www.prd.org.mx; f. 1989 by the Corriente Democrática (CD) and elements of the Partido Mexicano Socialista (PMS); centre-left; Pres. Rosario Robles Berlanga; Sec.-Gen. Carlos Navarrete Ruiz.

Partido Revolucionario Institucional (PRI): Insurgentes Norte 59, Edif. 2, subsótano, Col. Buenavista, 06359 México, DF; tel. (55) 5591-1595; fax (55) 5546-3552; internet www.pri.org.mx; f. 1929 as the Partido Nacional Revolucionario, but is regarded as the natural successor to the victorious parties of the revolutionary period; broadly based and centre govt party; Pres. Roberto Madrazo Pintado; Sec.-Gen. Elba Ester Gordillo Morales; opinion groups within the PRI include: the Corriente Crítica Progresista, the Corriente Crítica del Partido, the Corriente Constitucionalista Democratizadora, Corriente Nuevo PRI XIV Asamblea, Democracia 2000, México Nuevo and Galileo.

Partido Social Demócrata Mexicano (PSDM): Edisón 89, Col. Revolución, 06030 México, DF; tel. (55) 5592-5688; fax (55) 5535-0031; f. 1975 as Partido Demócrata Mexicano; adopted current name in 1998; Christian Democrat party; 450,000 mems; Pres. Baltasar Ignacio Valadez Montoya.

Partido de la Sociedad Nacionalista (PSN): Magdalena 117, Col. del Valle 03100, México, DF; tel. (55) 5682-5960; e-mail psn@psn.org.mx; internet www.psn.org.mx; Pres. Gustavo Riojas Santana.

Partido del Trabajo (PT): Avda Cuauhtémoc 47, Col. Roma, 06700 México, DF; tel. and fax (55) 5525-8419; internet www.pt.org.mx; f. 1991; labour party; Leader Alberto Anaya Gutiérrez.

Partido Verde Ecologista de México (PVEM): San Luis Potosí 118, Col. Roma, 06700 México, DF; tel. and fax (55) 5574-1516; e-mail pve@infosel.net.mx; internet www.pvem.org.mx; f. 1987; ecologist party; Leader Bernardo de la Garza Herrera.

The following parties are not legally recognized:

Frente Zapatista de Liberación Nacional: Zapotecos 7, Col. Obrera, 06800 México, DF; tel. and fax (55) 5761-4236; e-mail fzln@org.mx; internet www.fzln.org.mx; f. 1996; political force embodying the ideology of the EZLN; Leader Javier Elorriaga.

Partido Social Demócrata (PSD): México, DF; lost its registration after the 1982 elections; Leader Manuel Moreno Sánchez.

Illegal organizations active in Mexico include the following:

Ejército Popular Revolucionario (EPR): internet www.pengo.it/PDPR-EPR/; f. 1994; left-wing guerrilla group active in southern states.

Ejército Revolucionario Popular Insurgente (ERPI): f. 1996; left-wing guerrilla group active in Guerrero, Morelos and Oaxaca; Leader Jacobo Silva Nogales.

Ejército Zapatista de Liberación Nacional (EZLN): internet www.ezln.org; f. 1993; left-wing guerrilla group active in the Chiapas region.

Frente Democrático Oriental de México Emiliano Zapata (FDOMEZ): peasant org.

Partido Popular Revolucionario Democrático: internet www .pengo.it/PDPR-EPR; f. 1996; political grouping representing the causes of 14 armed peasant orgs, including the EPR and the PROCUP.

Partido Revolucionario Obrerista y Clandestino de Unión Popular (PROCUP): internet www.pengo.it/PDPR-EPR/; peasant org.

Los Tecos: Guadalajara, Jal. based at the University of Guadalajara; extreme right-wing group.

Diplomatic Representation

EMBASSIES IN MEXICO

Algeria: Sierra Madre 540, Col. Lomas de Chapultepec, 11000 México, DF; tel. (55) 5520-6950; fax (55) 5540-7579; e-mail embjargl@iwm.com.mx; Ambassador Abdelkader Taffar.

Angola: Schiller 503, Col. Polanco, 11560 México, DF; tel. (55) 5545-5883; fax (55) 5545-2733; e-mail info@palanca-negra.org; Ambassador Jaime Furtado.

Argentina: Manuel Avila Camacho 1, 7°, Col. Lomas de Chapultepec, 11000 México, DF; tel. (55) 5520-9430; fax (55) 5540-5011; e-mail embajadaargentina@prodigy.net.mx; Ambassador Oscar Guillermo Galie.

Australia: Rubén Darío 55, Col. Polanco, 11580 México, DF; tel. (55) 5531-5225; fax (55) 5203-8431; e-mail dima-mexico.city@dsat.gov .au; internet www.mexico.embassy.gov.au; Ambassador Graeme John Wilson.

Austria: Sierra Tarahumara 420, Col. Lomas de Chapultepec, Del. Miguel Hidalgo, 11000 México, DF; tel. (55) 5251-1606; fax (55) 5245-0198; e-mail obmexico@data.net.mx; internet www .embajadadeaustria.com.mx; Ambassador Dr Rudolf Lennkh.

Belgium: Musset 41, Col. Polanco, 11550 México, DF; tel. (55) 5280-0758; fax (55) 5280-0208; e-mail ambelmex@adete.com; internet www.diplobel.org/mexico; Ambassador Willy Stevens.

Belize: Bernardo de Gálvez 215, Col. Lomas de Chapultepec, 11000 México, DF; tel. (55) 5520-1274; fax (55) 5520-6089; e-mail embelize@prodigy.net.mx; Ambassador Salvador Amín Figueroa.

Bolivia: Insurgentes Sur 263, 6°, esq. Alvaro Obregón, Col. Roma Sur, 06760 México, DF; tel. (55) 5564-5415; fax (55) 5564-5298; e-mail embajada@embol.org.mx; Chargé d'affaires a.i. José Gabino Villanueva Gutiérrez.

Brazil: Lope de Armendariz 130, Col. Lomas Virreyes, 11000 México, DF; tel. (55) 5202-7500; fax (55) 5520-4929; e-mail embrasil@enlaces.com.mx; Chargé d'affaires a.i. Mário Ernani Saade.

Bulgaria: Paseo de la Reforma 1990, Col. Lomas de Chapultepec, 11000 México, DF; tel. (55) 5596-3283; fax (55) 5596-1012; e-mail ebulgaria@yahoo.com; Chargé d'affaires Ivan Christov.

Canada: Schiller 529, Col. Polanco, 11560 México, DF; tel. (55) 5724-7900; fax (55) 5724-7980; e-mail embajada@canada.org.mx; internet www.canada.org.mx; Ambassador Keith H. Christie.

Chile: Andrés Bello 10, 18°, Col. Polanco, 11560 México, DF; tel. (55) 5280-9681; fax (55) 5280-9703; e-mail echilmex@prodigy.net.mx; Ambassador Luis Maira Aguirre.

China, People's Republic: Avda San Jerónimo 217B, Del. Alvaro Obregón 01090, México, DF; tel. (55) 5616-0609; fax (55) 5616-0460; e-mail embchina@data.net.mx; internet www.embajadachina.com .mx; Ambassador Li Jinzhang.

Colombia: Paseo de la Reforma 1620, Col. Lomas de Chapultepec, 11000 México, DF; tel. (55) 5202-7299; fax (55) 5520-9669; e-mail emcolmex@prodigy.net.mx; internet www.colombiaenmexico.org; Ambassador Luis Ignacio Guzmán Ramírez.

Costa Rica: Río Po 113, Col. Cuauhtémoc, 06500 México, DF; tel. (55) 5525-7764; fax (55) 5511-9240; e-mail embcrica@ri.redint.com; Ambassador Rafael Sequeira Ramírez.

Cuba: Presidente Masaryk 554, Col. Polanco, 11560 México, DF; tel. and fax (55) 5280-8039; e-mail cancilleria@embacuba.com.mx; Ambassador Jorge Bolaños Suárez.

Cyprus: Sierra Gorda 370, Col. Lomas de Chapultepec, 11000 México, DF; tel. (55) 5202-7600; fax (55) 5520-2693; e-mail chipre@data.net.mx; Ambassador Antonis Toumazis.

Czech Republic: Cuvier 22, esq. Kepler, Col. Nueva Anzures, 11590 México, DF; tel. (55) 5531-2777; fax (55) 5531-1837; e-mail mexico@embassy.mzv.cz; internet www.mzv.cz/mexico; Ambassador Vera Zemanová.

Denmark: Tres Picos 43, Apdo 105-105, Col. Chapultepec Morales, 11580 México, DF; tel. (55) 5255-3405; fax (55) 5545-5797; e-mail mexamb@um.dk; internet www.danmex.org; Ambassador Søren Haslund.

Dominican Republic: República de Guatemala 84, Centro Histórico, Del. Cuauhtémoc, 06020, México, DF; tel. (55) 5542–3593; fax (55) 5542–3553; e-mail embadomi@data.net.mx; internet www .embajadadominicana.com.mx; Ambassador Cándido Géron Araujo.

Ecuador: Tennyson 217, Col. Polanco, 11560 México, DF; tel. (55) 5545-3141; fax (55) 5254-2442; e-mail mecuamex@adetel.net.mx; Chargé d'affaires a.i. Ana Guadalupe Moreno Loayza.

Egypt: Alejandro Dumas 131, Col. Polanco, 11560 México, DF; tel. (55) 5281-0823; fax (55) 5282-1294; e-mail embofegypt@prodigy.net.mx; Ambassador REDA BEIBARS.

El Salvador: Temistocles 88, Col. Polanco, 11560 México, DF; tel. (55) 5281-5725; fax (55) 5281-5725; e-mail embesmex@webtelmex.net.mx; Ambassador EDUARDO CÁLIX LÓPEZ.

Finland: Monte Pelvoux 111, 4°, Col. Lomas de Chapultepec, Del. Miguel Hidalgo, 11000 México, DF; tel. (55) 5540-6036; fax (55) 5540-0114; e-mail finmex@prodigy.net.mx; internet www.finlandia.org.mx; Ambassador ILKKA HEISKANEN.

France: Campos Elíseos 339, Col. Polanco, 11560 México, DF; tel. (55) 5282-9700; fax (55) 5282-9703; internet www.francia.org.mx; Ambassador PHILIPPE FAURE.

Germany: Lord Byron 737, Col. Polanco, 11560 México, DF, Apdo 107-92, 06000 México, DF; tel. (55) 5283-2200; fax (55) 5281-2588; e-mail info@embajada-alemana.org.mx; internet www.embajada-alemana.org.mx; Ambassador WOLF-RUTHART BORN.

Greece: Sierra Gorda 505, Col. Lomas de Chapultepec, 11000 México, DF; tel. (55) 5520-2070; fax (55) 5202-4080; e-mail grecemb@prodigy.net.mx; Ambassador DIONYSSIUS KODELLAS.

Guatemala: Esplanada 1025, Col. Lomas de Chapultepec, 11000 México, DF; tel. (55) 5540-7520; fax (55) 5202-1142; e-mail embaguate@mexis.com; Ambassador JORGÉ R. ESCOTO MARROQUÍN.

Haiti: Pres. Don Martín 53, Del. Miguel Hidalgo 11500, México, DF; tel. (55) 5557-2065; fax (55)5395-1654; e-mail ambadh@mail.internet.com.mx; Ambassador PIERRE-JEAN IDALBERT.

Holy See: Calle Juan Pablo II 118, Col. Guadalupe Inn, Del. Alvaro Obregón, 01020 México, DF; tel. (55) 5663-3999; fax (55) 5663-5308; e-mail nuntiusmex@infosel.net.mx; Apostolic Nuncio Most Rev. GIUSEPPE BERTELLO (Titular Archbishop of Urbisaglia).

Honduras: Alfonso Reyes 220, Col. Hipódromo Condesa, 06170 México, DF; tel. (55) 5211-5747; fax (55) 5211-5425; e-mail emhonmex@mail.internet.com.mx; Ambassador RENÉ BECERRA ZELAYA.

Hungary: Paseo de las Palmas 2005, Col. Lomas de Chapultepec, 11000 México, DF; tel. (55) 5596-0523; fax (55) 5596-2378; e-mail hungria@avantel.net; Ambassador GYULA NÉMETH.

India: Musset 325, Col. Polanco, 11560 México, DF; tel. (55) 5531-1050; fax (55) 5254-2349; e-mail inembmex@prodigy.net.mx; internet www.indembassy.org; Ambassador SURINDER SINGH GILL.

Indonesia: Julio Verne 27, Col. Polanco, 11560 México, DF; tel. (55) 5280-6363; fax (55) 280-7062; e-mail kbrimex@prodigy.net.mx; Ambassador AHWIL LUTHAN.

Iran: Paseo de la Reforma 2350, Col. Lomas Altas, 11950 México, DF; tel. (55) 5596-5399; fax (55) 5251-0731; e-mail iranembmex@attglobal.net; Ambassador MOHAMMAD RUHI SEFAT.

Iraq: Paseo de la Reforma 1875, Col. Lomas de Chapultepec, 11000 México, DF; tel. (55) 5596-09833; fax (55) 5596-0254; Chargé d'affaires SUFIAN ELYAS KHIDER AL-HADITHI.

Ireland: Cerrada Blvd M. Avila Camacho 76, Third Floor, Col. Lomas de Chapultepec, 11000 México, DF; tel. (55) 5520-5803; fax (55) 5520-5892; e-mail embajada@irlanda.org.mx; Ambassador ART AGNEW.

Israel: Sierra Madre 215, Col. Lomas de Chapultepec, 11000 México, DF; tel. (55) 5201-1500; fax (55) 5201-1555; e-mail embisrael@prodigy.net.mx; Ambassador JOSEPH AMIHUD.

Italy: Paseo de las Palmas 1994, Col. Lomas de Chapultepec, 11000 México, DF; tel. (55) 5596-3655; fax (55) 5596-2472; e-mail embitalia@adetel.com.mx; internet www.embitalia.org.mx; Ambassador FRANCO TEMPESTA.

Jamaica: Schiller 326, Piso 8, Col. Chapultepec Morales, Delegación Miguel Hidalgo, 11570 México, DF; e-mail embjamaicamex@infosel.net.mx; Ambassador VILMA MCNISH.

Japan: Paseo de la Reforma 395, Col. Cuauhtémoc, Apdo 5-101, 06500 México, DF; tel. (55) 5211-0028; fax (55) 5207-7743; internet www.embjapon.com; Ambassador TAKAHIKO HORIMURA.

Korea, Democratic People's Republic: Eugenio Sue 332, Col. Polanco, 11550 México, DF; tel. (55) 5545-1871; fax (55) 5203-0019; e-mail dpkoreaemb@prodigy.net.mx; Ambassador RI KANG SE.

Korea, Republic: Lope de Armendariz 110, Col. Lomas Virreyes, 11000 México, DF; tel. (55) 5202-9866; fax (55) 5540-7446; e-mail coremex@prodigy.net; Ambassador KANG WUNG-SIK.

Lebanon: Julio Verne 8, Col. Polanco, 11560 México, DF; tel. (55) 5280-5614; fax (55) 5280-8870; e-mail embalib@prodigy.net.mx; Ambassador NOUHAD MAHMOUD.

Malaysia: Calderón de la Barca 215, Col. Polanco, 11560 México, DF; tel. (55) 5254-1118; fax (55) 5254-1295; e-mail mwmexico@ infosel.net.mx; Ambassador MOHAMMED ABDUL HALIM BIN ABDUL RAHMAN.

Morocco: Paseo de las Palmas 2020, Col. Lomas de Chapultepec, 11020 México, DF; tel. (55) 5245-1786; fax (55) 5245-1791; e-mail sifamex@infosel.net.mx; internet www.marruecos.org.mx; Ambassador YOUSSEF AMRANI.

Netherlands: Edif. Calakmul, Avda Vasco de Quiroga 3000, 7°, Col. Santa Fe, 01210 México, DF; tel. (55) 5258-9921; fax (55) 5258-8138; e-mail nlgovmex@nlgovmex.com; internet www.paisesnbajos.com.mx; Ambassador ROBERT ARTHUR VORNIS.

New Zealand: J. L. Lagrange 103, 10°, Col. Polanco, 11510 México, DF; tel. (55) 5283-9460; fax (55) 5283-9480; e-mail kiwimexico@compuserve.com.mx; Ambassador PAUL TIPPING.

Nicaragua: Prado Norte 470, Col. Lomas de Chapultepec 11000, México, DF; tel. (55) 5540-5625; fax (55) 5520-6961; e-mail embanic@prodigy.net.mx; Ambassador ALVARO JOSÉ SEVILLA SIERO.

Nigeria: Paseo de las Palmas 1875, Col. Lomas de Chapultepec 11000, México, DF; tel. (55) 5596-1274; fax (55) 5245-0105; e-mail nigembmx@att.net.mx; Ambassador ADENIKE EBUN OYAGBOLA.

Norway: Avda de los Virreyes 1460, Col. Lomas Virreyes, 11000 México, DF; tel. (55) 5540-3486; fax (55) 5202-3019; e-mail emb.mexico@mfa.no; internet www.noruega.org.mx; Ambassador HELGE SKAARA.

Pakistan: Hegel 512, Col. Chapultepec Morales, 11570 México, DF; tel. (55) 5203-3636; fax (55) 5203-9907; Ambassador Agha JEHANGIR ALI KHAN.

Panama: Horacio 1501, Col. Polanco 115600, México, DF; tel. (55) 5557-6159; fax (55) 5395-4269; e-mail embpanmx@avantel.net; Ambassador DIONISO DE GRACIA GUILLÉN.

Paraguay: Homero 415, 1°, esq. Hegel, Col. Polanco, 11570 México, DF; tel. (55) 5545-0405; fax (55) 5531-9905; e-mail embapar@prodigy.net.mx; Ambassador JOSÉ FÉLIX FERNÁNDEZ ESTIGARRIBIA.

Peru: Paseo de la Reforma 2601, Col. Lomas Reforma, 11000 México, DF; tel. (55) 5570-2443; fax (55) 5259-0530; e-mail embaperu@prodigy.net.mx; Ambassador ALFREDO AROSEMENA FERREYROS.

Philippines: Sierra Gorda 175, Col. Lomas de Chapultepec, 11000 México, DF; tel. (55) 5202-8456; fax (55) 5202-8403; e-mail ambamexi@mx.inter.net; Ambassador H. E. JUSTO O. OROS, Jr.

Poland: Cracovia 40, Col. San Ángel, 01000 México, DF; tel. (55) 5550-4700; fax (55) 5616-0822; Ambassador GABRIEL BESZŁEJ.

Portugal: Avda Alpes 1370, Lomas de Chapultepec, 11000 México, DF; tel. (55) 5520-7897; fax (55) 5520-4688; e-mail embpomex@prodigy.net.mx; Ambassador MANUEL MARCELO CURTO.

Romania: Sófocles 311, Col. Polanco, 11560 México, DF; tel. (55) 5280-0197; fax (55) 5280-0343; e-mail ambromaniei@prodigy.net.mx; Ambassador VASILE DAN.

Russia: José Vasconcelos 204, Col. Hipódromo Condesa, 06140 México, DF; tel. (55) 5273-1305; fax (55) 5273-1545; e-mail embrumex@mail.internet.com.mx; Ambassador KONSTANTIN MOZEL.

Saudi Arabia: Paseo de las Palmas 2075, Col. Lomas de Chapultepec, 11000 México, DF; tel. (55) 5596-8845; fax (55) 5251-8587; e-mail saudiemb@prodigy.net.mx; Ambassador HASSAN TALAT NAZER.

Serbia and Montenegro: Montañas Rocallosas Ote 515, Col. Lomas de Chapultepec, 11000 México, DF; tel. (55) 5520-0524; fax (55) 5520-9927; e-mail ambayumex@att.met.mx; Ambassador VESNA PESIĆ.

Slovakia: Julio Verne 35, Col. Polanco, 11560 México, DF; tel. (55) 5280-6669; fax (55) 5280-6294; e-mail embslovakia@mexis.com; Chargé d'affaires BRANISLAV HITKA.

South Africa: Andrés Bello 10, 9°, Edif. Forum, Col. Polanco, 11560 México, DF; tel. (55) 5282-9260; fax (55) 5282-9260; e-mail safrica@prodigy.net.mx; Ambassador MALCOLM GRANT FERGUSON.

Spain: Galileo 114, esq. Horacio, Col. Polanco, 11550 México, DF; tel. (55) 5282-2271; fax (55) 5282-1302; e-mail embae@prodigy.net.mx; Chargé d'affaires a.i. MUÑIZ LOVELACE.

Suriname: Calle Cicerón 609, Col. Polanco ZP5, 11510 México, DF; tel. (55) 5540-4371; Ambassador HARVEY NAARENDORP.

Sweden: Paseo de las Palmas 1375, 11000 México, DF; tel. (55) 5540-6393; fax (55) 5540-3253; e-mail info@suecia.com.mx; internet www.suecia.com.mx; Ambassador EWA POLANO.

Switzerland: Paseo de las Palmas 405, 11°, Torre Optima, Col. Lomas de Chapultepec, 11000 México, DF; tel. (55) 5520-3003; fax (55) 5520-8685; e-mail vertretung@mex.rep.admin.ch; Ambassador Dr MARCUS KAISER.

Thailand: Paseo de la Reforma 930, Col. Lomas de Chapultepec 11000, México, DF; tel. (55) 5540-4551; fax (55) 5540-4817; e-mail thaimex@infosel.net.mx; Ambassador PLERNPIT POTIGANOND.

Turkey: Monte Libano 885, Col. Lomas de Chapultepec 11000, México, DF; tel. (55) 5282-5446; fax (55) 5282-4894; e-mail turkem@mail.internet.com.mx; Ambassador MEHMET NURI EZEN.

Ukraine: Sierra Paracaima 396, Col. Lomas de Chapultepec 11000, México, DF; tel. (55) 5282-4789; fax (55) 5540-3606; e-mail ukrainembasy@mexis.com; Chargé d'affaires a.i. VALERIY SAYENKO.

United Kingdom: Río Lerma 71, Col. Cuauhtémoc, 06500 México, DF; tel. (55) 5242-8500; fax (55) 5242-8517; e-mail infogen@mail.embajadabritanica.com.mx; internet www.embajadabritanica.com.mx; Ambassador DENISE HOLT.

USA: Paseo de la Reforma 305, Col. Cuauhtémoc, 06500 México, DF; tel. (55) 5209-9100; fax (55) 5511-9980; internet www.usembassy-mexico.gov; Ambassador ANTONIO O. GARZA, Jr.

Uruguay: Hegel 149, 1°, Col. Chapultepec Morales, 11560 México, DF; tel. (55) 5531-0880; fax (55) 5531-4029; e-mail uruazte@ort.org.mx; Ambassador SAMUEL LICHTENSZTEJN TEZLER.

Venezuela: Schiller 326, Col. Chapultepec Morales, 11570 México, DF; tel. (55) 5203-4233; fax (55) 5203-8614; Ambassador LINO MARTÍNEZ SALAZAR.

Viet Nam: Sierra Ventana 255, Col. Lomas de Chapultepec, 11000 México, DF; tel. (55) 5540-1632; fax (55) 5540-1612; e-mail embviet@dsqun.spin.com.mx; Ambassador NGUYEN VAN SANH.

Judicial System

The principle of the separation of the judiciary from the legislative and executive powers is embodied in the 1917 Constitution. The judicial system is divided into two areas: the federal, dealing with federal law, and the local, dealing only with state law within each state.

The federal judicial system has both ordinary and constitutional jurisdiction and judicial power is exercised by the Supreme Court of Justice, the Electoral Court, Collegiate and Unitary Circuit Courts and District Courts. The Supreme Court comprises two separate chambers: Civil and Criminal Affairs, and Administrative and Labour Affairs. The Federal Judicature Council is responsible for the administration, surveillance and discipline of the federal judiciary, except for the Supreme Court of Justice.

In March 2002 there were 146 Collegiate Circuit Courts (Tribunales Colegiados), 58 Unitary Circuit Courts (Tribunales Unitarios) and 219 District Courts (Juzgados de Distrito). Mexico is divided into 26 judicial circuits. The Circuit Courts may be collegiate, when dealing with the derecho de amparo (protection of constitutional rights of an individual), or unitary, when dealing with appeal cases. The Collegiate Circuit Courts comprise three magistrates with residence in the cities of México, Toluca, Guadalajara, Monterrey, Hermosillo, Puebla, Boca del Río, Xalapa, Torreón, San Luis Potosí, Villahermosa, Morelia, Mazatlán, Oaxaca, Mérida, Mexicali, Guanajuato, Chihuahua, Cuernavaca, Ciudad Victoria, Tuxtla Gutiérrez, Chilpancingo, Querétaro, Pachuca, Zacatecas, Aguascalientes, Tepic and Durango. The Unitary Circuit Courts comprise one magistrate with residence mostly in the same cities as given above.

SUPREME COURT OF JUSTICE

Supreme Court of Justice, Pino Suárez 2, Col. Centro, Deleg. Cuauhtémoc, 06065 México, DF; tel. (55) 5522-0096; fax (55) 5522-0152; internet www.scjn.gob.mx

Chief Justice: MARIANO AZUELA GÜITRÓN.

First Chamber—Civil and Criminal Affairs

President: JOSÉ DE JESÚS GUDIÑO PELAYO.

Second Chamber—Administrative and Labour Affairs

President: GUILLERMO I. ORTIZ MAYAGOITIA.

Religion

CHRISTIANITY

The Roman Catholic Church

The prevailing religion is Roman Catholicism, but the Church, disestablished in 1857, was for many years, under the Constitution of 1917, subject to state control. A constitutional amendment, promulgated in January 1992, officially removed all restrictions on the Church. For ecclesiastical purposes, Mexico comprises 14 archdioceses, 64 dioceses and five territorial prelatures. An estimated 90% of the population are adherents.

Bishops' Conference

Conferencia del Episcopado Mexicano (CEM), 54760 Cuautitlán Izcalli, Prolongación Rio Acatlán, Lago de Guadalupe; tel. (55) 5877-2663; fax (55) 5877-2603.

Pres. LUIS MORALES REYES (Archbishop of San Luis Potosí).

Archbishop of Acapulco: FELIPE AGUIRRE FRANCO, Arzobispado, Quebrada 16, Apdo 201, 39300 Acapulco, Gro; tel. and fax (744) 482-0763; e-mail buenpastor@acabtu.com.mx.

Archbishop of Antequera/Oaxaca: HÉCTOR GONZÁLEZ MARTÍNEZ, Independencia 700, Apdo 31, 68000 Oaxaca, Oax. tel. (951) 64822; fax (951) 65580; e-mail antequera@oax1.telmex.net.mx.

Archbishop of Chihuahua: JOSÉ FERNÁNDEZ ARTEAGA, Arzobispado, Avda Cuauhtémoc 1828, Apdo 7, 31020 Chihuahua, Chih. tel. (614) 10-3202; fax (614) 10-5621; e-mail curiao1@chih1.telmex.net.mx.

Archbishop of Durango: HÉCTOR GONZÁLEZ MARTÍNEZ, Arzobispado, 20 de Noviembre 306 Poniente, Apdo 116, 34000 Durango, Dgo; tel. (618) 114242; fax (618) 128881; e-mail arqdgo@logicnet.com.mx.

Archbishop of Guadalajara: Cardinal JUAN SANDOVAL IÑIGUEZ, Arzobispado, Liceo 17, Apdo 1-331, 44100 Guadalajara, Jal. tel. (33) 614-5504; fax (33) 658-2300; e-mail arzgdl@arquinet.com.mx.

Archbishop of Hermosillo/Sonora: JOSÉ ULISES MACÍAS SALCEDO, Arzobispado, Dr Paliza 81, Apdo 1, 83260 Hermosillo, Son. tel. (658) 13-2138; fax (658) 13-1327; e-mail obispo@rtn.uson.mx.

Archbishop of Jalapa: SERGIO OBESO RIVERA, Arzobispado, Avda Manuel Avila Camacho 73, Apdo 359, 91000 Jalapa, Ver. tel. (932) 12-0579; e-mail arzobispadoal_xal@infosel.net.mx.

Archbishop of Mexico City: Cardinal NORBERTO RIVERA CARRERA, Curia del Arzobispado de México, Durango 90, 5°, Col. Roma, Apdo 24433, 06700 México, DF; tel. (55) 5208-3200; fax (55) 5208-5350; e-mail armexico@proyect.com.

Archbishop of Monterrey: FRANCISCO ROBLES, Zuazua 1100 con Ocampo, Apdo 7, 64000 Monterrey, NL; tel. (81) 345-2466; fax (81) 345-3557; e-mail curia@sdm.net.mx.

Archbishop of Morelia: ALBERTO SUÁREZ INDA, Arzobispado, Apdo 17, 58000 Morelia, Mich; tel. (443) 120523; fax (443) 123744; e-mail suarezi@prodigy.net.mx.

Archbishop of Puebla de los Angeles: ROSENDO HUESCA PACHECO, Avda 2 Sur 305, Apdo 235, 72000 Puebla, Pue. tel. (222) 32-4591; fax (222) 46-2277; e-mail rhuesca@mail.cem.org.mx.

Archbishop of San Luis Potosí: LUIS MORALES REYES, Arzobispado, Francisco Madero 300, Apdo 1, 78000 San Luis Potosí, SLP; tel. (444) 12-4555; fax (444) 12-7979; e-mail adiosclp@mail.cem.org.mx.

Archbishop of Tlalnepantla: RICARDO GUÍZAR DÍAZ, Arzobispado, Avda Juárez 42, Apdo 268, 54000 Tlalnepantla, Méx. tel. (55) 5565-3944; fax (55) 5565-2751; e-mail rguizar@mail.cem.org.mx.

Archbishop of Yucatán: EMILIO CARLOS BERLIE BELAUNZARÁN, Arzobispado, Calle 58 501, 97000 Mérida, Yuc. tel. (999) 28-5720; fax (999) 23-7983; e-mail acm@sureste.com.

The Anglican Communion

Mexico is divided into five dioceses, which form the Province of the Anglican Church in Mexico, established in 1995.

Bishop of Cuernavaca: MARTINIANO GARCÍA MONTIEL, Minerva 1, Las Delicias, 62330 Cuernavaca, Mor. tel. and fax (777) 15-2870; e-mail diovca@giga.com.mx.

Bishop of Mexico City: SERGIO CARRANZA GÓMEZ, Avda San Jerónimo 117, Col. San Ángel, 01000 México, DF; tel. and fax (55) 5616-2205; e-mail diomex@avantel.net.

Bishop of Northern Mexico: GERMÁN MARTÍNEZ MÁRQUEZ (currently suspended), Simón Bolívar 2005 Nte, Col. Mitras Centro, 64460 Monterrey, NL; tel. and fax (81) 48-7362; e-mail dionte@infosel.com.mx.

Bishop of South-Eastern Mexico: BENITO JUÁREZ MARTÍNEZ, Avda Las Américas 73, Col. Aguacatl, 91130 Jalapa, Ver. tel. and fax (932) 144387; e-mail dioste@prodigy.net.mx.

Bishop of Western Mexico: SAMUEL ESPINOZA VENEGAS (currently suspended), Javier Gamboa 255, Col. Sector Juarez 44100, Guadalajara, Jal. tel. (33) 3615-5070; fax (33) 615-4413; e-mail diocte@vianet.com.mx.

Other Protestant Churches

Federación Evangélica de México: Motolinia 8, Of. 107, Del. Cuauhtémoc, 1830, 06002, México, DF; tel. (55) 5585-0594; f. 1926; Pres. Prof. MOISES MÉNDEZ; Exec. Sec. Rev. ISRAEL ORTIZ MURRIETA.

Iglesia Evangélica Luterana de México: Mina Pte 5808, Nuevo Larado, Tamps; Pres. ENCARNACIÓN ESTRADA; 3,000 mems.

Iglesia Metodista de México, Asociación Religiosa: Miravelle 209, Col. Albert 03570, México, DF; tel. (55) 5539-3674; internet www.iglesia-metodista.org.mx; f. 1930; 55,000 mems; 370 congregations; comprises seven episcopal areas; Bishop (Mexico) GRACIELA ALVAREZ DELGADO; Bishop (North-East) ANTONI AGUIÑA MARQUÉZ; Bishop (North-Central) GABRIEL LOZADA VALDEZ, Bishop (East) RAÚL ROSAS GONZÁLEZ; Bishop (North) ISAÍAS RÁMOS CORONA, Bishop (South-East) ENRIQUE FLORES BARRERA.

National Baptist Convention of Mexico: Vizcaínas Ote 16, Altos, 06080 México, DF; tel. (55) 5518-2691; fax (55) 5521-0118; internet www.bautistas.org.mx/cnbm; f. 1903; Pres. ROLANDO GUTIÉRREZ CORTÉS.

BAHÁ'Í FAITH

National Spiritual Assembly of the Bahá'ís of Mexico: Emerson 421, Col. Chapultepec Morales, Del. Miguel Hidalgo, 11570 México, DF; tel. (55) 5545-2155; fax (55) 5255-5972; mems resident in 1,009 localities.

The Press

DAILY NEWSPAPERS

México, DF

La Afición: Ignacio Mariscal 23, Apdo 64 bis, Col. Tabacalera, 06030 México, DF; tel. (55) 5546-4780; fax (55) 5546-5852; e-mail opino@aguila.el-universal.com.mx; f. 1930; sport, entertainment, news; Pres. Lic. JUAN FRANCISCO EALY ORTIZ; Gen. Man. ANTONIO GARCÍA SERRANO; circ. 85,000.

La Crónica de Hoy: Grupo Editorial Convergencia, SA de CV, Balderas 333, 6°, Col. Centro, 06040 México, DF; tel. (52) 5512-4412; internet www.cronica.com.mx; Pres. JORGE KAHWAGI GASTINE.

Cuestión: Laguna de Mayrán 410, Col. Anáhuac, 11320 México, DF; tel. (55) 5260-0499; fax (55) 5260-3645; e-mail cuestion@compuserve .com; internet www.cuestion.com.mx; f. 1980; midday; Dir-Gen. Lic. ALBERTO GONZÁLEZ PARRA; circ. 48,000.

El Día: Insurgentes Norte 1210, Col. Capultitlán, 07370 México, DF; tel. (55) 5729-2155; fax (55) 5537-6629; e-mail cduran@servidor .unam.mx; f. 1962; morning; Dir-Gen. JOSÉ LUIS CAMACHO LÓPEZ; circ. 50,000.

Diario de México: Chimalpopoca 38, Col. Obrera, 06800 México, DF; tel. (55) 5588-3831; fax (55) 5578-7650; e-mail diamex@rtn.net .mx; f. 1948; morning; Dir-Gen. FEDERICO BRACAMONTES GÁLVEZ; Dir RAFAEL LIZARDI DURÁN; circ. 76,000.

Esto: Guillermo Prieto 7, 1°, 06470 México, DF; tel. and fax (55) 5591-0866; e-mail esto@oem.com.mx; internet www.oem.com.mx; f. 1941; morning; sport; Pres. Lic. MARIO VÁZQUEZ RAÑA; Dir CARLOS TRAPAGA BARRIENTOS; circ. 400,000, Mondays 450,000.

Excélsior: Reforma 18, Apdo 120 bis, Col. Centro, 06600 México, DF; tel. (55) 5566-2200; fax (55) 5566-0223; e-mail foro@excelsior .com.mx; internet www.excelsior.com.mx; f. 1917; morning; independent; Dir REGINO DÍAZ REDONDO; Gen. Man. JUVENTINO OLIVERA LÓPEZ; circ. 200,000.

El Financiero: Lago Bolsena 176, Col. Anáhuac entre Lago Peypus y Lago Onega, 11320 México, DF; tel. (55) 5227-7600; fax (55) 5227-7620; e-mail sistemas@elfinanciero.com.mx; internet www .elfinanciero.com.mx; f. 1981; financial; Dir Lic. ALEJANDRO RAMOS ESQUIVEL; circ. 135,000.

El Heraldo de México: Dr Lucio, esq. Dr Velasco, Col. Doctores, 06720 México, DF; tel. (55) 5578-7022; fax (55) 5578-9824; e-mail heraldo@iwm.com.mx; internet www.heraldo.com.mx; f. 1965; morning; Dir-Gen. GABRIEL ALARCÓN VELÁZQUEZ; circ. 209,600.

La Jornada: Francisco Petrarca 118, Col. Chapultepec Morales, 11570 México, DF; tel. (55) 5262-4300; fax (55) 5262-4354; e-mail jornada@condor.dqsca.unam.mx; internet http://unam.netgate.net/ jornada; f. 1984; morning; Dir-Gen. Lic. CARMEN LIRA SAADE; Gen. Man. Lic. JORGE MARTÍNEZ JIMÉNEZ; circ. 106,471, Sundays 100,924.

Novedades: Balderas 87, esq. Morelos, Col. Centro, 06040 México, DF; tel. (55) 5518-5481; fax (55) 5521-4505; internet www.unam .netgate.net/novedades; f. 1936; morning; independent; Pres. and Editor-in-Chief ROMULO O'FARRILL, Jr; Vice-Pres. JOSÉ ANTONIO O'FARRILL AVILA; circ. 42,990, Sundays 43,536.

Ovaciones: Lago Zirahuén 279, 20°, Col. Anáhuac, 11320 México, DF; tel. (55) 5328-0700; fax (55) 5260-2219; e-mail ovaciones@ televisa.com.mx; f. 1947; morning and evening editions; Pres. and

Dir-Gen. Lic. ALBERTO VENTOSA AGUILERA; circ. 130,000; evening circ. 100,000.

La Prensa: Basilio Badillo 40, Col. Tabacalera, 06030 México, DF; tel. (55) 5228-9947; fax (55) 5521-8209; e-mail prensa@oem.com.mx; internet www.oem.com.mx; f. 1928; morning; Pres. and Dir-Gen. Lic. MARIO VÁZQUEZ RAÑA; circ. 270,000.

Reforma: Avda México Coyoacán 40, Col. Sta Cruz Atoyac, 03310 México, DF; tel. (55) 5628-7100; fax (55) 5628-7188; internet www .reforma.infosel.com; f. 1993; morning; Pres. and Dir-Gen. ALEJANDRO JUNCO DE LA VEGA; circ. 94,000.

El Sol de México: Guillermo Prieto 7, 20°, Col. San Rafael, 06470 México, DF; tel. (55) 5566-1511; fax (55) 5535-5560; e-mail info@oem .com.mx; internet www.elsoldemexico.com.mx; f. 1965; morning and midday; Pres. and Dir-Gen. Lic. MARIO VÁZQUEZ RAÑA; Dir PILAR FERREIRA GARCÍA; circ. 76,000.

El Universal: Bucareli 8, Apdo 909, Col. Centro, 06040 México, DF; tel. (55) 5709-1313; fax (55) 5510-1269; e-mail redaccio@servidor .unam.mx; internet www.el-universal.com.mx; f. 1916; morning; independent; centre-left; Pres. and Dir-Gen. Lic. JUAN FRANCISCO EALY ORTIZ; circ. 165,629, Sundays 181,615.

Unomásuno: Retorno de Correggio 12, Col. Nochebuena, 03720 México, DF; tel. (55) 5563-9911; fax (55) 5598-8821; e-mail cduran@ servidor.unam.mx; f. 1977; morning; left-wing; Pres. MANUEL ALONSO MUÑOZ; Dir RAFAEL CARDONA S; circ. 40,000.

PROVINCIAL DAILY NEWSPAPERS

Baja California

El Mexicano: Carretera al Aeropuerto s/n, Fracc. Alamar, Apdo 2333, 22540 Tijuana, BC; tel. (664) 21-3400; fax (664) 21-2944; f. 1959; morning; Dir and Gen. Man. ELIGIO VALENCIA ROQUE; circ. 80,000.

El Sol de Tijuana: Rufino Tamayo 4, Zona Río, 22320 Tijuana, BC; tel. (664) 34-3232; fax (664) 34-2234; e-mail soltij@oem.com.mx; internet www.oem.com.mx; f. 1989; morning; Pres. and Dir-Gen. Lic. MARIO VÁZQUEZ RAÑA; circ. 50,000.

La Voz de la Frontera: Avda Madero 1545, Col. Nueva, Apdo 946, 21100 Mexicali, BC; tel. (686) 53-4545; fax (686) 53-6912; e-mail lavoz@oem.com.mx; internet www.oem.com.mx; f. 1964; morning; independent; Pres. and Dir-Gen. MARIO VÁZQUEZ RAÑA; Gen. Man. Lic. MARIO VALDÉS HERNÁNDEZ; circ. 65,000.

Chihuahua

El Diario: Publicaciones del Chuviscar, SA de CV, Avda Universidad 1900, Col. San Felipe, Chihuahua, Chih. tel. (614) 429-0700; internet www.diario.com.mx; www.eldiariodechihuahua.com .mx; f. 1976; Pres. OSVALDO RODRÍGUEZ BORUNDA.

El Heraldo de Chihuahua: Avda Universidad 2507, Apdo 1515, 31240 Chihuahua, Chih. tel. (614) 13-9339; fax (614) 13-5625; e-mail elheraldo@buzon.online.com.mx; f. 1927; morning; Pres. and Dir-Gen. Lic. MARIO VÁZQUEZ RAÑA; Dir. Lic. JAVIER H. CONTRERAS; circ. 27,520, Sundays 31,223.

Coahuila

La Opinión: Blvd Independencia 1492 Ote, Apdo 86, 27010 Torreón, Coah. tel. (871) 13-8777; fax (871) 13-8164; internet www .editoriallaopinion.com.mx; f. 1917; morning; Pres. FRANCISCO A. GONZÁLEZ; circ. 40,000.

El Siglo de Torreón: Avda Matamoros 1056 Pte, Apdo 19, 27000 Torreón, Coah. tel. (871) 12-8600; fax (871) 16-5909; internet www .elsiglodetorreon.com.mx; f. 1922; morning; Pres. OLGA DE JUAMBELZ Y HORCASITAS; circ. 38,611, Sundays 38,526.

Vanguardia: Blvd Venustiano Carranza 1918, República Oriente, 25280 Saltillo, Coah. tel. (844) 411-0835; e-mail hola@vanguardia .com.mx; internet www.vanguardia.com.mx.

Guanajuato

El Nacional: Carretera Guanajuato–Juventino Rosas, km 9.5, Apdo 32, 36000 Guanajuato, Gto; tel. (477) 33-1286; fax (477) 33-1288; f. 1987; morning; Dir-Gen. ARNOLDO CUÉLLAR ORNELAS; circ. 60,000.

Jalisco

El Diario de Guadalajara: Calle 14 2550, Zona Industrial, 44940, Guadalajara, Jal. tel. (33) 612-0043; fax (33) 612-0818; f. 1969; morning; Pres. and Dir-Gen. LUIS A. GONZÁLEZ BECERRA; circ. 78,000.

El Informador: Independencia 300, Apdo 3 bis, 44100 Guadalajara, Jal. tel. (33) 614-6340; fax (33) 614-4653; internet www.informador .com.mx; f. 1917; morning; Editor JORGE ÁLVAREZ DEL CASTILLO; circ. 50,000.

El Occidental: Calzada Independencia Sur 324, Apdo 1-699, 44100 Guadalajara, Jal. tel. (33) 613-0690; fax (33) 613-6796; f. 1942; morning; Dir Lic. RICARDO DEL VALLE DEL PERAL; circ. 49,400.

México

ABC: Avda Hidalgo Ote 1339, Centro Comercial, 50000 Toluca, Méx. tel. (722) 179880; fax (722) 179646; e-mail miled1@mail.miled.com; internet www.miled.com; f. 1984; morning; Pres. and Editor MILED LIBIEN KAUI; circ. 65,000.

Diario de Toluca: Allende Sur 209, 50000 Toluca, Méx. tel. (722) 142403; fax (722) 141523; f. 1980; morning; Editor ANUAR MACCISE DIB; circ. 22,200.

El Heraldo de Toluca: Salvador Díaz Mirón 700, Col. Sánchez Colín, 50150 Toluca, Méx. tel. (722) 173453; fax (722) 122535; f. 1955; morning; Editor ALBERTO BARRAZA SÁNCHEZ A; circ. 90,000.

El Mañana: Avda Hidalgo Ote 1339, Toluca, Méx. tel. (722) 179880; fax (722) 178402; e-mail miled1@mail.miled.com; internet www .miled.com; f. 1986; morning; Pres. and Editor MILED LIBIEN KAUI; circ. 65,000.

Rumbo: Allende Sur 205, Toluca, Méx. tel. (722) 142403; fax (722) 141523; f. 1968; morning; Editor ANUAR MACCISE DIB; circ. 10,800.

El Sol de Toluca: Santos Degollado 105, Apdo 54, 50050 Toluca, Méx. tel. (722) 150340; fax (722) 147441; f. 1947; morning; Pres. and Dir-Gen. Lic. MARIO VÁZQUEZ RAÑA; circ. 42,000.

Michoacán

La Voz de Michoacán: Blvd del Periodismo 1270, Col. Arriaga Rivera, Apdo 121, 58190 Morelia, Mich. tel. (443) 327-3712; fax (443) 327-3728; e-mail lavoz@mail.giga.com; internet www.voznet.com .mx; f. 1948; morning; Dir-Gen. Lic. MIGUEL MEDINA ROBLES; circ. 50,000.

Morelos

El Diario de Morelos: Morelos Sur 817, Col. Las Palmas, 62000 Cuernavaca, Mor. tel. (777) 14-2660; fax (777) 14-1253; internet www.diariodemorelos.com.mx; morning; Dir-Gen. FEDERICO BRACA-MONTES; circ. 47,000.

Nayarit

Meridiano de Nayarit: E. Zapata 73 Pte, Apdo 65, 63000 Tepic, Nay. tel. (321) 20145; fax (321) 26630; internet www.meridiano.com .mx; f. 1942; morning; Dir Dr DAVID ALFARO; circ. 60,000.

El Observador: Allende 110 Ote, Despachos 203-204, 63000 Tepic, Nay. tel. (321) 24309; fax (321) 24309; morning; Pres. and Dir-Gen. Lic. LUIS A. GONZÁLEZ BECERRA; circ. 55,000.

Nuevo León

ABC: Platón Sánchez Sur 411, 64000 Monterrey, NL; tel. (81) 344-4480; fax (81) 344-5990; e-mail abc2000@mexis.com; f. 1985; morning; Pres. GONZALO ESTRADA CRUZ; Dir-Gen. GONZALO ESTRADO TORRES; circ. 40,000, Sundays 45,000.

El Diario de Monterrey: Eugenio Garza Sada 2245 Sur, Col. Roma, Apdo 3128, 647000 Monterrey, NL; tel. (81) 359-2525; fax (81) 359-1414; internet www.diariodemonterrey.com; f. 1974; morning; Dir-Gen. Lic. FEDERICO ARREOLA; circ. 80,000.

El Norte: Washington 629 Ote, Apdo 186, 64000 Monterrey, NL; tel. (81) 345-3388; fax (81) 343-2476; internet www.elnorte.com.mx; f. 1938; morning; Man. Dir Lic. ALEJANDRO JUNCO DE LA VEGA; circ. 133,872, Sundays 154,951.

El Porvenir: Galeana Sur 344, Apdo 218, 64000 Monterrey, NL; tel. (81) 345-4080; fax (81) 345-7795; internet www.elporvenir.com.mx; f. 1919; morning; Dir-Gen. JOSÉ GERARDO CANTÚ ESCALANTE; circ. 75,000.

El Sol: Washington 629 Ote, Apdo 186, 64000 Monterrey, NL; tel. (81) 345-3388; fax (81) 343-2476; internet www.infosel.com.mx; f. 1922; evening (except Sundays); Man. Dir Lic. ALEJANDRO JUNCO DE LA VEGA; circ. 45,300.

Oaxaca

El Imparcial: Armenta y López 312, Apdo 322, 68000 Oaxaca, Oax. tel. (951) 516-2812; fax (951) 516-0050; internet www.imparoax.com .mx; f. 1951; morning; Dir-Gen. Lic. BENJAMÍN FERNÁNDEZ PICHARDO; circ. 17,000, Sundays 20,000.

Puebla

El Sol de Puebla: Avda 3 Ote 201, Apdo 190, 72000 Puebla, Pue. tel. (222) 42-4560; fax (222) 46-0869; internet www.oem.com.mx; f. 1944; morning; Pres. and Dir-Gen. Lic. MARIO VÁZQUEZ RAÑA; circ. 67,000.

San Luis Potosí

El Heraldo: Villerías 305, 78000 San Luis Potosí, SLP; tel. (444) 812-3312; fax (444) 812-2081; e-mail diario_heraldo@hotmail.com; internet www.elheraldodesanluis.com.mx; f. 1954; morning; Dir-Gen. ALEJANDRO VILLASANA MENA; circ. 60,620.

Momento: Zenón Fernández y Leandro Valle, Col. Jardines del Estadio, 78280 San Luis Potosí, SLP; tel. (444) 814-4444; fax (444) 812-2020; f. 1975; morning; Dir-Gen. Lic. EMILIO MANUEL TRINIDAD ZALDÍVAR; circ. 60,000.

Pulso: Galeana 485, 78000 San Luis Potosí, SLP; tel. (444) 812-7575; fax (444) 812-3525; internet www.pulsoslp.com.mx; morning; Dir-Gen. MIGUEL VALLADARES GARCÍA; circ. 60,000.

El Sol de San Luis: Avda Universidad 565, Apdo 342, 78000 San Luis Potosí, SLP; tel. and fax (444) 812-4412; f. 1952; morning; Pres. and Dir-Gen. Lic. MARIO VÁZQUEZ RAÑA; Dir JOSÉ ANGEL MARTÍNEZ LIMÓN; circ. 60,000.

Sinaloa

El Debate de Culiacán: Madero 556 Pte, 80000 Culiacán, Sin. tel. (667) 16-6353; fax (667) 15-7131; e-mail redaccion@debate.com.mx; internet www.debate.com.mx; f. 1972; morning; Dir ROSARIO I. ORO-PEZA; circ. 23,603, Sundays 23,838.

Noroeste Culiacán: Grupo Periodicos Noroeste, Angel Flores 282 Ote, Apdo 90, 80000 Culiacán, Sin. tel. (667) 713-2100; fax (667) 712-8006; e-mail cschmidt@noroeste.com.mx; internet www.noroeste .com.mx; f. 1973; morning; Pres. MANUEL J. CLOUTHIER; Editor RODOLFO DIAZ; circ. 35,000.

El Sol de Sinaloa: Blvd G. Leyva Lozano y Corona 320, Apdo 412, 80000 Culiacán, Sin. tel. (667) 13-1621; f. 1956; morning; Pres. Lic. MARIO VÁZQUEZ RAÑA; Dir JORGE LUIS TÉLLEZ SALAZAR; circ. 30,000.

Sonora

El Imparcial: Sufragio Efectivo y Mina 71, Col. Centro, Apdo 66, 83000 Hermosillo, Son. tel. (658) 59-4700; fax (658) 17-4483; e-mail impar@imparcial.com.mx; internet www.imparcial.com.mx; f. 1937; morning; Pres. and Dir-Gen. JOSÉ SANTIAGO HEALY LOERA; circ. 32,083, Sundays 32,444.

Tabasco

Tabasco Hoy: Avda de los Ríos 206, 86035 Villahermosa, Tab. tel. (993) 16-3333; fax (993) 16-2135; internet www.tabascohoy.com.mx; f. 1987; morning; Dir-Gen. MIGUEL CANTÓN ZETINA; circ. 52,302.

Tamaulipas

El Bravo: Morelos y Primera 129, Apdo 483, 87300 Matamoros, Tamps; tel. (871) 160100; fax (871) 162007; e-mail elbravo@ riogrande.net.mx; f. 1951; morning; Pres. and Dir-Gen. JOSÉ CARRE-TERO BALBOA; circ. 60,000.

El Diario de Nuevo Laredo: González 2409, Apdo 101, 88000 Nuevo Laredo, Tamps; tel. (867) 128444; fax (867) 128221; internet www.diario.net; f. 1948; morning; Editor RUPERTO VILLARREAL MON-TEMAYOR; circ. 68,130, Sundays 73,495.

Expresión: Calle 3a y Novedades 1, Col. Periodistas, 87300 Mata-moros, Tamps; tel. (871) 174330; fax (871) 173307; morning; circ. 50,000.

El Mañana de Reynosa: Prof. Lauro Aguirre con Matías Canales, Apdo 14, 88620 Ciudad Reynosa, Tamps; tel. (899) 251469; fax (899) 230198; internet www.elmananarey.com.mx; f. 1949; morning; Dir-Gen. HERIBERTO DEANDAR MARTÍNEZ; circ. 65,000.

El Mundo: Ejército Nacional 201, Col. Guadalupe, 89120 Tampico, Tamps; tel. (833) 134084; fax (833) 134136; f. 1918; morning; Dir-Gen. ANTONIO MANZUR MARÓN; circ. 54,000.

La Opinión de Matamoros: Blvd Lauro Villar 200, Apdo 486, 87400 Matamoros, Tamps; tel. (871) 123141; fax (871) 122132; e-mail opinion1@tamps1.telmex.net.mx; f. 1971; Pres. and Dir-Gen. JUAN B. GARCÍA GÓMEZ; circ. 50,000.

Prensa de Reynosa: Matamoros y González Ortega, 88500 Rey-nosa, Tamps; tel. (899) 23515; fax (899) 223823; f. 1963; morning; Dir-Gen. FÉLIX GARZA ELIZONDO; circ. 60,000.

El Sol de Tampico: Altamira 311 Pte, Apdo 434, 89000 Tampico, Tamps; tel. (833) 12-3566; fax (833) 12-6986; internet www.oem.com .mx; f. 1950; morning; Dir-Gen. Lic. RUBÉN DÍAZ DE LA GARZA; circ. 77,000.

Veracruz

Diario del Istmo: Avda Hidalgo 1115, 96400 Coatzacoalcos, Ver. tel. (921) 48302; fax (921) 48514; e-mail info@istmo.com.mx; internet www.diariodelistmo.com; f. 1979; morning; Dir-Gen. JAÍR BENJAMÍN ROBLES BARAJAS; circ. 64,600.

El Dictamen: 16 de Septiembre y Arista, 91700 Veracruz, Ver. tel. (229) 311745; fax (229) 315804; f. 1898; morning; Pres. CARLOS ANTONIO MALPICA MARTÍNEZ; circ. 38,000, Sundays 39,000.

Yucatán

Diario de Yucatán: Calle 60, No 521, 97000 Mérida, Yuc. tel. (999) 23-8444; fax (999) 42-2204; internet www.yucatan.com.mx; f. 1925; morning; Dir-Gen. CARLOS R. MENÉNDEZ NAVARRETE; circ. 54,639, Sundays 65,399.

El Mundo al Día: Calle 62, No 514A, 97000 Mérida Yuc. tel. (999) 23-9933; fax (999) 24-9629; e-mail nmerida@cancun.novenet.com.mx; f. 1964; morning; Pres. ROMULO O'FARRILL, Jr; Gen. Man. Lic. GERARDO GARCÍA GAMBOA; circ. 25,000.

Por Esto!: Calle 60, No 576 entre 73 y 71, 97000 Mérida, Yuc. tel. (999) 24-7613; fax (999) 28-6514; internet www.poresto.net; f. 1991; morning; Dir-Gen. MARIO R. MENÉNDEZ RODRÍGUEZ; circ. 26,985, Sundays 28,727.

Zacatecas

Imagen: Avda Revolución 24, Col. Tierra y Libertad, Guadalupe, Zac. tel. and fax (492) 923-4412; internet www.imagenzac.com.mx; Dir-Gen. EUGENIO MERCADO.

SELECTED WEEKLY NEWSPAPERS

Bolsa de Trabajo: San Francisco 657, 9A, Col. del Valle, 03100 México, DF; tel. (55) 5536-8387; f. 1988; employment; Pres. and Dir-Gen. MÓNICA ELÍAS CALLES; circ. 30,000.

El Heraldo de León: Hermanos Aldama 222, Apdo 299, 37000 León, Gto; tel. (477) 713-1194; fax (477) 714-3464; e-mail heraldo@el-heraldo-bajio.com; internet www.el-heraldo-bajio.com; f. 1957; Pres. and Dir-Gen. MAURICIO BERCÚN LÓPEZ; circ. 85,000.

Segundamano: Insurgentes Sur 813-501, Col. Nápoles, 03810 México, DF; tel. (55) 5729-3737; fax (55) 5687-9635; f. 1986; Dir-Gen. LUIS MAGAÑA MAGAÑA; circ. 105,000.

GENERAL INTEREST PERIODICALS

Car and Driver: Alabama 113, Col. Nápoles, 03810 México, DF; tel. (55) 5523-5201; fax (55) 5536-6399; f. 1999; monthly; Pres. PEDRO VARGAS G; circ. 80,000.

Casas & Gente: Ediarte, SA de CV, Amsterdam 112, 06100 México, DF; tel. (55) 5286-7794; fax (55) 5211-7112; e-mail informac@casasgente.com; internet www.casasgente.com; 10 a year; interior design; Dir-Gen. NICOLÁS H. SÁNCHEZ-OSORIO.

Conozca Más: Vasco de Quiroga 2000, Col. Santa Fe, 01210 México, DF; tel. (55) 5261-2600; fax (55) 5261-2704; f. 1990; monthly; scientific; Dir EUGENIO MENDOZA; circ. 90,000.

Contenido: Buffon 46, 9°, Col. Anzures, 11590 México, DF; tel. (55) 5531-3162; fax (55) 5545-7478; f. 1963; monthly; popular appeal; Dir ARMANDO AYALA A; circ. 124,190.

Cosmopolitan (México): Vasco de Quiroga 2000, Col. Santa Fe, 01210 México, DF; tel. (55) 5261-2600; fax (55) 5261-2704; f. 1973; monthly; women's magazine; Dir SARA MARÍA CASTANY; circ. 260,000.

Fama: Avda Eugenio Garza Sada 2245 Sur, Col. Roma, Apdo 3128, 64700 Monterrey, NL; tel. (81) 359-2525; fortnightly; show business; Pres. JESÚS D. GONZÁLEZ; Dir RAÚL MARTÍNEZ; circ. 350,000.

Impacto: Avda Ceylán 517, Col. Industrial Vallejo, Apdo 2986, 02300 México, DF; tel. (55) 5587-3855; fax (55) 5567-7781; f. 1949; weekly; politics; Man. and Dir-Gen. JUAN BUSTILLOS OROZCO; circ. 115,000.

Kena Especiales: Romero de Terreros 832, Col. del Valle, 03100 México, DF; tel. (55) 5543-1032; fax (55) 5669-3465; e-mail armonia@netsevice.com.mx; f. 1977; fortnightly; women's interest; Dir-Gen. Lic. LILIANA MORENO G; circ. 100,000.

Letras Libres: Presidente Carranza 210, Col. Coyoacán, 04000 México, DF; tel. (55) 5554-8810; fax (55) 5658-0074; e-mail correo@letraslibres.com; internet www.letraslibres.com; monthly; culture; Chief Editor JULIO TRUJILLO.

Marie Claire: Editorial Televisa, SA de CV, Vasco de Quiroga 2000, Col. Santa Fe, 01210 México, DF; tel. (55) 5261-2600; fax (55) 5261-2704; f. 1990; monthly; women's interest; Editor LOUISE MERELES; circ. 80,000.

Mecánica Popular: Vasco de Quiroga 2000, Edif. E, Col. Santa Fe, Deleg. Alvaro Obregón, 01210 Mexico, DF; tel. (55) 5261-2600; fax (55) 5261-2705; e-mail mecanica.popular@siedi.spin.com.mx; f. 1947; monthly; crafts and home improvements; Dir ANDRÉS JORGE; circ. 247,850.

Men's Health: Vasco de Quiroga 2000, Col. Santa Fe, 01210 México, DF; tel. (55) 5261-2645; fax (55) 5261-2733; e-mail mens.health@editorial.televisa.com.mx; f. 1994; monthly; health; Editor JUAN ANTONIO SEMPERE; circ. 130,000.

Muy Interesante: Vasco de Quiroga 2000, Col. Santa Fe, 01210 México, DF; tel. (55) 5261-2600; fax (55) 5261-2704; f. 1984; monthly; scientific devt; Dir PILAR S. HOYOS; circ. 250,000.

Proceso: Fresas 7, Col. del Valle, 03100 México, DF; tel. (55) 5629-2090; fax (55) 5629-2092; f. 1976; weekly; news analysis; Pres. JULIO SCHERER GARCÍA; circ. 98,784.

La Revista Peninsular: Calle 35, 489 x 52 y 54, Centro, Mérida, Yuc. e-mail revista@sureste.com; internet www.larevista.com.mx; weekly; news and politics; Dir-Gen. RODRIGO MENÉNDEZ CÁMARA.

Selecciones del Reader's Digest: Avda Lomas de Sotelo 1102, Col. Loma Hermosa, Apdo 552, Naucalpan, 11200 México, DF; tel. (55) 5395-7444; fax (55) 5395-3835; f. 1940; monthly; Dir AVDON CORIA; circ. 611,660.

Siempre!: Vallarta 20, Apdo 32-010, Col. Revolución, 06030 México, DF; tel. (55) 5566-9355; fax (55) 566-9355; e-mail siempre@data.net.mx; f. 1953; weekly; left of centre; Dir Lic. BEATRIZ PAGÉS REBOLLAR DE NIETO; circ. 100,000.

Tele-Guía: Vasco de Quiroga 2000, Col. Santa Fe, 01210 México, DF; tel. (55) 5261-2600; fax (55) 5261-2704; f. 1952; weekly; television guide; Editor MARÍA EUGENIA HERNÁNDEZ; circ. 375,000.

Tiempo Libre: Holbein 75 bis, Col. Nochebuena, 03720 México, DF; tel. (55) 5611-7332; fax (55) 5611-3874; e-mail info@tiempolibre.com.mx; internet www.tiempolibre.com.mx; f. 1980; weekly; entertainment guide; Dir-Gen. ANGELES AGUILAR ZINSER; circ. 95,000.

Tú: Vasco de Quiroga 2000, Col. Santa Fe, 01210 México, DF; tel. (55) 5261-2600; fax (55) 5261-2730; f. 1980; monthly; Editor MARÍA ANTONIETA SALAMANCA; circ. 275,000.

TV y Novelas: Vasco de Quiroga 2000, Col. Santa Fe, 01210 México, DF; tel. (55) 5261-2600; fax (55) 5261-2704; f. 1982; weekly; television guide and short stories; Dir JESÚS GALLEGOS; circ. 460,000.

Ultima Moda: Morelos 16, 6°, Col. Centro, 06040 México, DF; tel. (55) 5518-5481; fax (55) 5512-8902; f. 1966; monthly; fashion; Pres. ROMULO O'FARRILL, Jr; Gen. Man. Lic. SAMUEL PODOLSKY RAPOPORT; circ. 110,548.

Vanidades: Vasco de Quiroga 2000, Col. Santa Fe, 01210 México, DF; tel. (55) 5261-2600; fax (55) 5261-2704; f. 1961; fortnightly; women's magazine; Dir SARA MARÍA BARCELÓ DE CASTANY; circ. 290,000.

Visión: Homero 411, 5°, Col. Polanco, 11570 México, DF; tel. (55) 5531-4914; fax (55) 5531-4915; e-mail 74174.3111@compuserve.com; offices in Santafé de Bogotá, Buenos Aires and Santiago de Chile; f. 1950; fortnightly; politics and economics; Gen. Man. ROBERTO BELLO; circ. 27,215.

Vogue (México): Grupo Idéas de México, SA de CV, México, DF; tel. (55) 5095-8066; fax (55) 5530-2828; internet www.vogue.com.mx; f. 1999; monthly; women's fashion; circ. 208,180.

SPECIALIST PERIODICALS

Boletín Industrial: Goldsmith 37-403, Col. Polanco, 11550 México, DF; tel. (55) 5280-6463; fax (55) 5280-3194; e-mail bolind@Viernes.iwm.com.mx; internet www.bolind.com.mx; f. 1983; monthly; Dir-Gen. HUMBERTO VALADÉS DÍAZ; circ. 36,000.

Comercio: Río Tíber 87, 06500 México, DF; tel. (55) 5514-0873; fax (55) 5514-1008; f. 1960; monthly; business review; Dir RAÚL HORTA; circ. 40,000.

Gaceta Médica de México: Academia Nacional de Medicina, Unidad de Congresos del Centro Médico Nacional Siglo XXI, Bloque B, Avda Cuauhtémoc 330, Col. Doctores, 06725 México, DF; tel. (55) 5578-2044; fax (55) 5578-4271; e-mail gacetamx@starnet.net.mx; f. 1864; every 2 months; medicine; Editor Dr LUIS BENÍTEZ; circ. 20,000.

Manufactura: Sinaloa 149, 1°, Col. Roma, 06700 México, DF; tel. (55) 5511-1537; fax (55) 5208-1265; e-mail publicidad@expansion.com.mx; internet www.expansion.com.mx; f. 1994; monthly; industrial; Dir-Gen. ALEJANDRO SERNA BARRERA; circ. 29,751.

Negobancos (Negocios y Bancos): Bolívar 8-103, Apdo 1907, Col. Centro, 06000 México, DF; tel. (55) 5510-1884; fax (55) 5512-9411; e-mail nego_bancos@mexico.com; f. 1951; fortnightly; business, economics; Dir ALFREDO FARRUGIA REED; circ. 10,000.

ASSOCIATIONS

Asociación Nacional de Periodistas A.C.: Luis G. Obregón 17, Desp. 209, Col. Centro, 06020 México, DF; tel. (55) 5702-1546.

Federación Latinoamericana de Periodistas (FELAP): Nuevo Leon 144, 1°, Col. Hipódromo Condesa, 06170 México, DF; tel. (55) 5286-6055; fax (5) 286-6085.

NEWS AGENCIES

Agencia de Información Integral Periodística, SA (AIIP): Tabasco 263, Col. Roma, Delegación Cuauhtémoc, 06700 México, DF; tel. (55) 5235-3469; fax (55) 5235-3468; e-mail aiipsa@axtel.net; internet www.aiip.com.mx; f. 1987; Dir-Gen. MIGUEL HERRERA LÓPEZ.

Agencia Mexicana de Información (AMI): Avda Cuauhtémoc 16, Col. Doctores, 06720 México, DF; tel. (55) 5761-9933; e-mail info@red-ami.com; internet www.ami.com.mx; Dir-Gen. JOSÉ LUIS BECERRA LÓPEZ; Gen.-Man. EVA VÁZQUEZ LÓPEZ.

Notimex, SA de CV: Morena 110, 3°, Col. del Valle, 03100 México, DF; tel. (55) 5420-1100; fax (55) 5682-0005; e-mail comercial@notimex.com.mx; internet www.notimex.com.mx; f. 1968; services to press, radio and TV in Mexico and throughout the world; Dir-Gen. Dr JORGE MEDINA VIEDAS.

Foreign Bureaux

Agence France-Presse (AFP): Torre Latinoamericana, 9°, Eje Central y Madero 1, Torre Latinoamericana 15°, Col. Centro, 06007 México, DF; tel. (55) 5518-5494; fax (55) 5510-4564; e-mail redaccion.mexico@afp.com; Bureau Chief PAUL RUTLER.

Agenzia Nazionale Stampa Associata (ANSA) (Italy): Emerson 150, 2°, Col. Chapultepec Morales, 11570 México, DF; tel. (55) 5255-3696; fax (55) 5255-3018; e-mail ansamexico@prodigy.net.mx; Bureau Chief MARCO BRANCACCIA.

Associated Press (AP) (USA): Paseo de la Reforma 350, Col. Juárez 06600, México, DF; tel. (55) 5080-3400; fax (55) 5208-2684; e-mail apmexico@ap.org; Bureau Chief ELOY O. AGUILAR.

Deutsche Presse-Agentur (dpa) (Germany): Avda Cuauhtémoc 16-301, Col. Doctores, 06720 México, DF; tel. (55) 5578-4829; fax (55) 7561-0762; e-mail info@dpa.com.mx; Bureau Chief KLAUS BLUME.

EFE (Spain): Lafayette 69, Col. Anzures, 11590 México, DF; tel. (55) 5545-8256; fax (55) 5254-1412; e-mail jeferedaccion@efecom.mx; Bureau Chief MANUEL FUENTES GARCÍA.

Informatsionnoye Telegrafnoye Agentstvo Rossii—Telegrafnoye Agentsvo Suverennykh Stran (ITAR—TASS) (Russia): Monte Líbano 965, Col. Lomas de Chapultepec 11000, México, DF; tel. (55) 5202-4831; fax (55) 5202-4879; e-mail itartass@prodigy.net; Bureau Chief IGOR VARLAMOV.

Inter Press Service (IPS) (Italy): Avda Cuauhtémoc 16-403, Col. Doctores, Del. Cuauhtémoc, 06720 México, DF; tel. (55) 5578-0417; fax (55) 5578-2094; e-mail mex@ipservespanol.org; Chief Correspondent DIEGO CEVALLOS ROJAS.

Jiji Tsushin-Sha (Japan): Sevilla 9, 2°, Col. Juárez, Del. Cuauhtémoc, 06600 México, DF; tel. (55) 5528-9651; fax (55) 5511-0062; Bureau Chief FUJIO IKEDA.

Kyodo Tsushin (Japan): Cerro Dios de Hacha 66, Col. Romero de Terreros 04310, México, DF; tel. (55) 5554-7199; fax (55) 5658-2957; e-mail kyodonews@mexis.com; Bureau Chief MASAHARU NANAMI.

Maghreb Arabe Presse (Morocco): Miguel de Cervantes Saavedra 448, 4°, Col. Irrigación 11500, México, DF; tel. (55) 1997-2558; fax (55) 1997-6198; e-mail mohammedtanji@hotmail.com; Correspondent MOHAMMED TANJI.

Prensa Latina (Cuba): Edif. B, Dpto 504, Insurgentes Centro 125, Col. San Rafael, Del. Cuauhtémoc, 06470 México, DF; tel. (55) 5546-6015; fax (55) 5592-0570; e-mail plenmex@mail.internet.com.mx; Chief Correspondent Lic. AISSA GARCÍA GOREIA.

Reuters Ltd (United Kingdom): Manuel Ávila Camacho 36, Edif. Torre Esmeralda 11, 19°, Col. Lomas de Chapultepec 11000, México, DF; tel. (55) 5282-7000; fax (55) 5282-7171; internet about.reuters.com/latam; e-mail mexicocity.newsroom@reuters.com; Bureau Chief KIERAN MICHAEL MURRAY.

Viet Nam News Agency (VNA) (Viet Nam): Río Pánuco 180, Col. Cuauhtemoc 06500, México, DF; tel. (55) 5514-9013; fax (55) 5514-1015; e-mail vnamex@prodigy.net.mx; Correspondent PHAM PHOI.

Xinhua (New China) News Agency (People's Republic of China): Francisco I. Madero 17, Col. Tlacopac, 01040 México, DF; tel. (55) 5662-8548; fax (55) 5662-9028; e-mail xinhuamx@xinhuanet.com; Bureau Chief SONG XINDE.

ASSOCIATION

Asociación de Corresponsales Extranjeros en México (ACEM): Avda Cuauhtémoc 16, 1°, Col. Doctores, Del. Cuauhtémoc, 06720 México, DF; tel. (55) 5588-3241; fax (55) 5588-6382.

Publishers

México, DF

Aguilar, Altea, Taurus, Alfaguara, SA de CV: Avda Universidad 767, Col. del Valle, 03100 México, DF; tel. (55) 5688-8966; fax (55) 5604-2304; e-mail sealtiel@santillana.com.mx; f. 1965; general literature; Dir SEALTIEL ALATRISTE.

Arbol Editorial, SA de CV: Avda Cuauhtémoc 1430, Col. Sta Cruz Atoyac, 03310 México, DF; tel. (55) 5688-4828; fax (55) 5605-7600; e-mail editorialpax@maxis.com; f. 1979; health, philosophy, theatre; Man. Dir GERARDO GALLY TEOMONFORD.

Artes de México y del Mundo, SA de CV: Plaza Río de Janeiro, Col. Roma, 06700 México, DF; tel. (55) 5525-5905; fax (55) 5525-5925; e-mail artesdemexico@artesdemexico.com; internet www.artesdemexico.com; f. 1988; art, design, poetry.

Editorial Avante, SA de CV: Luis G. Obregón 9, 1°, Apdo 45-796, Col. Centro, 06020 México, DF; tel. (55) 5510-8804; fax (55) 5521-5245; e-mail editorialavante@editorialavante.com.mx; internet www.editorialavante.com.mx; f. 1948; educational, drama, linguistics; Man. Dir Lic. MARIO A. HINOJOSA SAENZ.

Editorial Azteca, SA: Calle de la Luna 225–227, Col. Guerrero, 06300 México, DF; tel. (55) 5526-1157; fax (55) 5526-2557; f. 1956; religion, literature and technical; Man. Dir ALFONSO ALEMÓN JALOMO.

Librería y Ediciones Botas, SA de CV: Justo Sierra 52, Apdo 941, 06020 México, DF; tel. (55) 5702-4083; fax (55) 5702-5403; e-mail botas@mail.nextgeninter.net.mx; internet members.nbci.com/botas; f. 1910; history, law, philosophy, literature, fine arts, science, language, economics, medicine; Dir ANDRÉS BOTAS HERNÁNDEZ.

Cía Editorial Continental, SA de CV (CECSA): Renacimiento 180, Col. San Juan Tlihuaca, Azcapotzalco, 02400 México, DF; tel. (55) 5561-8333; fax (55) 5561-5231; e-mail info@patriacultural.com.mx; f. 1954; business, technology, general textbooks; Pres. CARLOS FRIGOLET LERMA.

Ediciones de Cultura Popular, SA: Odontología 76, Copilco Universidad, México, DF; f. 1969; history, politics, social sciences; Man. Dir URIEL JARQUÍN GALVEZ.

Ediciones CUPSA: Centro de Comunicación Cultural CUPSA, Apdo 97 bis, 06000 México, DF; tel. (55) 5546-2100; f. 1958; biblical studies, theology, church history, devotional materials, hymn-books; Dir ELISA TOSTADO.

Editorial Diana, SA de CV: Arenal No 24, Edif. Norte, Ex-Hacienda Guadalupe, Chimalistac, Del. Álvaro Obregón, 01050 México, DF; tel. (55) 5089-1220; fax (55) 5089–1230; e-mail jlr@diana.com.mx; internet www.editorialdiana.com.mx; f. 1946; general trade and technical books; Pres. and CEO JOSÉ LUIS RAMÍREZ.

Edamex, SA de CV: Heriberto Frias 1104, Col. del Valle, 03100 México, DF; tel. (55) 5559-8588; fax (55) 5575-0555; e-mail info@edamex.com; internet www.edamex.com; arts and literature, sport, journalism, education, philosophy, food, history, children's, health, sociology; Dir-Gen. MONICA COLMENARES.

Ediciones Era, SA de CV: Calle del Trabajo 31, Col. La Fama, Tlalpan, 14269 México, DF; tel. (55) 5528-1221; fax (55) 5606-2904; e-mail edicionesera@laneta.apc.org; internet www.edicionesera.com.mx; f. 1960; general and social science, art and literature; Gen. Man. NIEVES ESPRESATE XIRAU.

Editorial Everest Mexicana, SA: Calzada Ermita Iztapalapa 1631, Col. Barrio San Miguel del Iztapalapa, 09360 México, DF; tel. (55) 5685-1966; fax (55) 5685-3433; f. 1980; general textbooks; Gen. Man. JOSÉ LUIS HUIDOBRO LEÓN.

Espasa Calpe Mexicana, SA: Pitágoras 1139, Col. del Valle, 03100 México, DF; tel. (55) 5575-5022; f. 1948; literature, music, economics, philosophy, encyclopaedia; Man. FRANCISCO CRUZ RUBIO.

Fernández Editores, SA de CV: Eje 1 Pte México-Coyoacán 321, Col. Xoco, 03330 México, DF; tel. (55) 5605-6557; fax (55) 5688-9173; f. 1943; children's literature, textbooks, educational toys, didactic material; Man. Dir LUIS GERARDO FERNÁNDEZ PÉREZ.

Editorial Fondo de Cultura Económica, SA de CV: Carretera Picacho-Ajusco 227, Col. Bosques del Pedregal, 14200 México, DF; tel. (55) 5227-4672; fax (55) 5227-4640; e-mail editorial@fce.com.mx; f. 1934; economics, history, philosophy, children's books, science, politics, psychology, sociology, literature; Dir Lic. MIGUEL DE LA MADRID.

Editorial Grijalbo, SA de CV: Calzada San Bartolo-Naucalpan 282, Col. Argentina, Apdo 17-568, 11230 México, DF; tel. (55) 5358-4355; fax (55) 5576-3586; e-mail diredit@grijalbo.com.mx; internet www.randomhousemondadori.com.mx; f. 1954; owned by Mondadori (Italy); general fiction, history, sciences, philosophy, children's books; Man. Dir AGUSTÍN CENTENO RÍOS.

Nueva Editorial Interamericana, SA de CV: Cedro 512, Col. Atlampa, Apdo 4-140, 06450 México, DF; tel. (55) 5541-6789; fax (55) 5541-1603; f. 1944; medical publishing; Man. Dir Rafael Sáinz.

Distribuidora Intermex, SA de CV: Lucio Blanco 435, Azcapotzalco, 02400 México, DF; tel. (55) 5230-9500; fax (55) 5230-9516; e-mail pmuhechi@televisa.com.mx; f. 1969; romantic fiction; Gen. Dir Lic. Alejandro Paillés.

McGraw-Hill Interamericana de México, SA de CV: Cedro 512, Col. Atlampa Cuauhtémoc, 06450 México, DF; tel. (55) 5576-7304; fax (55) 5628-5367; e-mail mcgraw-hill@infosel.net.mx; internet www.mcgraw-hill.com.mx; education, business, science; Man. Dir Carlos Rios.

Editorial Joaquín Mortiz, SA de CV: Insurgentes Sur 1162, 3°, Col. del Valle, 03100 México, DF; tel. (55) 5575-8585; fax (55) 5559-3483; f. 1962; general literature; Man. Dir Ing. Homero Gayoso Animas.

Editorial Jus, SA de CV: Plaza de Abasolo 14, Col. Guerrero, 06300 México, DF; tel. (55) 526-0616; fax (55) 5529-0951; f. 1938; history of Mexico, law, philosophy, economy, religion; Man. Tomás G. Reynoso.

Ediciones Larousse, SA de CV: Dinamarca 81, Col. Juárez, 06600 México, DF; tel. (55) 5208-2005; fax (55) 5208-6225; f. 1965; Man. Dir Dominique Bertín García.

Editora Latino Americana, SA: Guatemala 10-220, México, DF; popular literature; Dir Jorge H. Yépez.

Editorial Limusa, SA de CV: Balderas 95, 1°, Col. Centro, 06040 México, DF; tel. (55) 5521-2105; fax (55) 5512-2903; e-mail limusa@noriega.com.mx; internet www.noriega.com.mx; f. 1962; science, general, textbooks; Pres. Carlos Noriega Milera.

Editorial Nuestro Tiempo, SA: Avda Universidad 771, Desp. 103-104, Col. del Valle, 03100 México, DF; tel. (55) 5688-8768; fax (55) 5688-6868; f. 1966; social sciences; Man. Dir Esperanza Nacif Barquet.

Editorial Oasis, SA: Avda Oaxaca 28, 06700 México, DF; tel. (55) 5528-8293; f. 1954; literature, pedagogy, poetry; Man. María Teresa Estrada de Fernández del Busto.

Editorial Orión: Sierra Mojada 325, 11000 México, DF; tel. (55) 5520-0224; f. 1942; archaeology, philosophy, psychology, literature, fiction; Man. Dir Silva Hernández Baltazar.

Editorial Patria, SA de CV: Renacimiento 180, Col. San Juan Tlihuaca, Azcapotzalco, 02400 México, DF; tel. (55) 5561-6042; fax (55) 5561-5231; e-mail info@patriacultural.com.mx; f. 1933; fiction, general trade, children's books; Pres. Carlos Frigolet Lerma.

Editorial Planeta Mexicana, SA de CV: Clavijero 70, Col. Esperanza, México, DF; tel. (55) 5533-1250; internet www .editorialplaneta.com.mx; general literature, non-fiction; part of Grupo Planeta (Spain); Man. Dir Joaquin Diez-Canedo.

Editorial Porrúa Hnos, SA: Argentina 15, 5°, 06020 México, DF; tel. (55) 5702-4574; fax (55) 5702-6529; e-mail servicios@porrua.com; internet www.porrua.com; f. 1944; general literature; Dir José Antonio Pérez Porrúa.

Editorial Posada, SA de CV: Eugenia 13, Desp. 501, Col. Nápoles, 03510 México, DF; tel. (55) 5682-0660; f. 1968; general; Dir-Gen. Carlos Vigil Zubieta.

Editorial Quetzacoatl, SA: Medicina 37, Local 1 y 2, México, DF; tel. (55) 5548-6180; Man. Dir Alberto Rodríguez Valdés.

Medios Publicitarios Mexicanos, SA de CV: Avda México 99-103, Col. Hipódromo Condesa, 06170 México, DF; tel. (55) 5574-2858; fax (55) 5574-2668; e-mail editorial@mpm.com.mx; internet www.mpm.com.mx; f. 1958; advertising media rates and data; Man. Fernando Villamil Avila.

Reverté Ediciones, SA de CV: Río Pánuco 141A, 06500 México, DF; tel. (55) 5533-5658; fax (55) 5514-6799; e-mail 101545.2361@compuserve.com; f. 1955; science, technical, architecture; Man. Ramón Reverté Mascó.

Salvat Mexicana de Ediciones, SA de CV: Presidente Masarik 101, 5°, 11570 México, DF; tel. (55) 5250-6041; fax (55) 5250-6861; medicine, encyclopaedic works; Dir Guillermo Hernández Pérez.

Siglo XXI Editores, SA de CV: Avda Cerro del Agua 248, Col. Romero de Terreros, Del. Coyoacán, 04310 México, DF; tel. (55) 5658-7999; fax (55) 5658-7599; e-mail informes@sigloxxieditores .com.mx; internet www.sigloxxieditores.com.mx; f. 1966; art, economics, education, history, social sciences, literature, philology and linguistics, philosophy and political science; Dir-Gen. Lic. Jaime Labastida Ochoa; Gen. Man. Ing. José Maria Castro Mussot.

Editorial Trillas, SA: Avda Río Churubusco 385 Pte, Col. Xoco, Apdo 10534, 03330 México, DF; tel. (55) 5688-4233; fax (55) 5601-1858; e-mail trillas@ovinet.com; internet www.trillas.mx; f.

1954; science, technical, textbooks, children's books; Man. Dir Francisco Trillas Mercader.

Universidad Nacional Autónoma de México: Dirección General de Fomento Editorial, Avda del Iman 5, Ciudad Universitaria, 04510 México, DF; tel. (55) 5622-6581; fax (55) 5665-2778; f. 1935; publications in all fields; Dir-Gen. Arturo Velázquez Jiménez.

Estado de México

Pearson Educación de México, SA de CV: Calle 4, 25, Fraccionamiento Industrial Alce Blanco, Naucalpan de Juárez 53370, Méx. tel. (55) 5387-0700; fax (55) 5358-6445; internet www.pearson.com .mx; f. 1984; educational books under the imprints Addison-Wesley, Prentice Hall, Allyn and Bacon, Longman and Scott Foresman; Pres. Steve Marban.

ASSOCIATIONS

Cámara Nacional de la Industria Editorial Mexicana: Holanda 13, Col. San Diego Churubusco, 04120 México, DF; tel. (55) 5688-2011; fax (55) 5604-3147; e-mail cepromex@caniem.com; internet www.caniem.com; f. 1964; Pres. Antonio Ruano Fernández; Gen. Man. Claudia Domínguez Mejía.

Instituto Mexicano del Libro, AC: México, DF; tel. (55) 5535-2061; Pres. Klaus Thiele; Sec.-Gen. Isabel Ruiz González.

Organización Editorial Mexicana, SA: Guillermo Prieto 7, 06470 México, DF; tel. (55) 5566-1511; fax (55) 5566-0694; e-mail info@oem .com.mx; internet www.oem.com.mx; Pres. Lic. Mario Vázquez Raña.

Prensa Nacional Asociada, SA (PRENASA): Insurgentes Centro 114-411, 06030 México, DF; tel. (55) 5546-7389.

Broadcasting and Communications

TELECOMMUNICATIONS

Regulatory Authorities

Comisión Federal de Telecomunicaciones (CFT): Bosque de Radiatas 44, 4°, Col. Bosques de las Lomas, 05120 México, DF; tel. (5) 261-4000; fax (55) 5261-4125; e-mail buzon@cft.gob.mx; internet www.cft.gob.mx; Pres. Jorge Nicolín Fischer.

Dirección General de Concesiones y Permisos de Telecomunicaciones: Unidad Contel Sga, Avda de las Telecomunicaciones s/n, Ixtapalapa, 09310 México, DF; tel. (55) 5692-0077; Dir Ing. Sergio Cervantes.

Dirección General de Telecomunicaciones: Lázaro Cárdenas 567, 11°, Ala Norte, Col. Narvarte, 03020 México, DF; tel. (55) 5519-9161; Dir-Gen. Ing. Enrique Luengas H.

Principal Operators

Alestra: Paseo de las Palmas 405, Col. Lomas de Chapultepec, 11000 México, DF; internet www.alestra.com.mx; 49% owned by AT&T; Dir-Gen. Rolando Zubirán Shetler.

America Movil, SA de CV: Lago Alberto, 366 Col. Anáhuac, 11320 México, DF; internet www.americamovil.com; CEO Daniel Hajj.

Avantel: Liverpool 88, Col. Juárez, 06600 México, DF; e-mail webmaster@avantel.com.mx; internet www.avantel.net.mx; Dir-Gen. Oscar Rodríguez Martínez.

Carso Global Telecom, SA de CV: Insurgentientes Sur 3500, Col. Peña Pobre, 14060 México DF; tel. (55) 5726-3686; fax (55) 5238-0601; internet www.cgtelecom.com.mx; Chair. Carlos Slim Helu.

Iusacell, SA de CV: Avda Prolongación Paseo de la Reforma 1236, Col. Santa Fe, 05438 México, DF; internet www.iusacell.com.mx; operates mobile cellular telephone network; Pres. and Dir-Gen. Fúlvio V. Del Valle.

Telecomunicaciones de México (TELECOM): Lázaro Cárdenas 567, 11°, Ala Norte, Col. Narvarte, 03020 México, DF; tel. (55) 5629-1166; fax (55) 5559-9812; Dir-Gen. Ing. Carlos Mier y Terán Ordiales.

Telefónica México: Avda Gómez Morín 350, Col. Valle del Campestre, 66265 San Pedro Garsa García, NL; tel. (81) 368-1900; internet www.telefonica.com.mx ; operates mobile telephone service Telefónica Móviles (MoviStar), telecommunications co Telefónica Data;; controls Pegaso, Cedetel, Norcel, Movitel and Baja Celular; owned by Telefónica, SA (Spain).

Teléfonos de México, SA de CV (Telmex): Parque Via 198, Of. 701, Col. Cuauhtémoc, 06599 México, DF; tel. (55) 5222-5462; fax (55) 5545-5500; internet www.telmex.com.mx; CEO Jaime Chico Pardo.

BROADCASTING

Regulatory Authorities

Cámara Nacional de la Industria de Radio y Televisión (CIRT): Horacio 1013, Col. Polanco, 11550 México, DF; tel. (55) 5726-9909; fax (55) 5545-6767; e-mail cirt@data.net.mx; internet www.cirt.com.mx; f. 1942; Pres. JOAQUÍN VARGAS GUAJARDO; Gen. Man. Lic. CÉSAR HERNÁNDEZ ESPEJO.

Dirección General de Radio, Televisión y Cine (RTC): Secretaria de Gobernación, Bucareli 99, Col. Juaréz, Del. Cuahtémoc, 06600;, México, DF; internet www.rtc.gob.mx; tel. (55) 5566-0262.

Dirección de Normas de Radiodifusión: Eugenia 197, 1°, Col. Narvarte, 03020 México, DF; tel. (55) 5590-4372; e-mail amilpg@sct .gob.mx; internet www.sct.gob.mx; licence-issuing authority; Dir Dr ALFONSO AMILPAS.

Instituto Mexicano de Televisión: Anillo Periférico Sur 4121, Col. Fuentes del Pedregal, 14141 México, DF; tel. (55) 5568-5684; Dir-Gen. Lic. JOSÉ ANTONIO ALVAREZ LIMA.

Radio

In 2002 there were 1,142 commercial radio stations in Mexico. Among the most important commercial networks are:

ARTSA: Avda de Los Virreyes 1030, Col. Lomas de Chapultepec, 11000 México, DF; tel. (55) 5202-3344; fax (55) 5202-6940; Dir-Gen. Lic. GUSTAVO ECHEVARRÍA ARCE.

Corporación Mexicana de Radiodifusión: Tetitla 23, esq. Calle Coapa, Col. Toriello Guerra, 14050 México, DF; tel. (55) 5666-8405; fax (55) 5666-5422; e-mail comentarios@cmr.com.mx; internet www .cmr.com.mx; Pres. ENRIQUE BERNAL SERVÍN; Dir-Gen. OSCAR BELTRÁN.

Firme, SA: Gauss 10, Col. Nueva Anzures, 11590 México, DF; tel. (55) 55250-7788; fax (55) 5250-7788; Dir-Gen. LUIS IGNACIO SANTIBÁÑEZ.

Grupo Acir, SA: Monte Pirineos 770, Col. Lomas de Chapultepec, 11000 México, DF; tel. (55) 5540-4291; fax (55) 5540-4106; f. 1965; comprises 140 stations; Pres. FRANCISCO IBARRA LÓPEZ.

Grupo Radio Centro, SA de CV: Constituyentes 1154, Col. Lomas Atlas, Del. Miguel Hidalgo, 11950 México, DF; tel. (55) 5728-4947; fax (55) 5259-2915; f. 1965; comprises 100 radio stations; Pres. ADRIÁN AGUIRRE GÓMEZ; Dir-Gen. Ing. GILBERTO SOLIS SILVA.

Grupo Siete Comunicácion: Montecito 38, 31°, Of. 33, México, DF; tel. (55) 5488-0887; e-mail jch@gruposiete.com.mx; internet www.gruposiete.com.mx; f. 1997; Pres. Lic. FRANCISCO JAVIER SÁNCHEZ CAMPUZANO.

Instituto Mexicano de la Radio (IMER): Mayorazgo 83, 2°, Col. Xoco, 03350 México, DF; tel. (55) 5628-1730; f. 1983; Dir-Gen. CARLOS LARA SUMANO.

MVS Radio Stereorey y FM Globo: Mariano Escobedo 532, Col. Anzures, 11590 México, DF; tel. (55) 5203-4574; fax (55) 5255-1425; e-mail vargas@data.net.mx; f. 1968; Pres. Lic. JOAQUÍN VARGAS G; Vice-Pres. Lic. ADRIÁN VARGAS G.

Núcleo Radio Mil: Insurgentes Sur 1870, 01030 México, DF; tel. (55) 5662-6060; f. 1960; comprises seven radio stations in Mexico City and three provincial radio stations; Pres. and Dir-Gen. Lic. E. GUILLERMO SALAS PEYRÓ.

Organización Radio Centro: Artículo 123, No 90, Col. Centro, 06050 México, DF; tel. (55) 5709-2220; fax (55) 512-8588; nine stations in Mexico City; Pres. MARÍA ESTHER GÓMEZ DE AGUIRRE.

Organización Radiofónica de México, SA: Tuxpan 39, 8°, Col. Roma Sur, 06760 México, DF; tel. (55) 5264-2025; fax (55) 5264-5720; Pres. JAIME FERNÁNDEZ ARMENDÁRIZ.

Radio Cadena Nacional, SA (RCN): Lago Victoria 78, Col. Granada, 11520 México, DF; tel. (55) 2624-0401; e-mail loregonzalez@rcn.com.mx; internet www.rcn.com.mx; f. 1948; Pres. RAFAEL C. NAVARRO ARRONTE; Dir-Gen. SERGIO FAJARDO ORTIZ.

Radio Comerciales, SA de CV: Avda México y López Mateos, 44680 Guadalajara, Jal. tel. (33) 615-0852; fax (33) 630-3487; 7 major commercial stations.

Radio Educación: Angel Urraza 622, Col. del Valle, 03100 México, DF; tel. (55) 5559-6169; fax (55) 5575-6566; f. 1924; Gen. Dir LUIS ERNESTO PI OROZCO.

Radio Fórmula, SA: Privada de Horacio 10, Col. Polanco, 11560 México, DF; tel. (55) 282-1016; Dir Lic. ROGERIO AZCARRAGA.

Radiodifusoras Asociadas, SA de CV (RASA): Durango 331, 2°, Col. Roma, 06700 México, DF; tel. (55) 5553-6620; fax (55) 5286-2774; f. 1956; Pres. JOSÉ LARIS ITURBIDE; Dir-Gen. JOSÉ LARIS RODRÍGUEZ.

Radiodifusores Asociados de Innovación y Organización, SA: Emerson 408, Col. Chapultepec Morales, 11570 México, DF; tel. (55) 5203-5577; fax (55) 5545-2078; Dir-Gen. Lic. CARLOS QUIÑONES ARMENDÁRIZ.

Radiorama, SA de CV: Reforma 56, 5°, 06600 México, DF; tel. (55) 5566-1515; fax (55) 5566-1454; Dir JOSÉ LUIS C. RESÉNDIZ.

Representaciones Comerciales Integrales: Avda Chapultepec 431, Col. Juárez, 06600 México, DF; tel. (55) 5533-6185; Dir-Gen. ALFONSO PALMA V.

Sistema Radio Juventud: Pablo Casals 567, Prados Providencia, 44670 Guadalajara, Jal. tel. (33) 641-6677; fax (33) 641-3413; f. 1975; network of several stations including Estereo Soul 89.9 FM; Dirs ALBERTO LEAL A, J. JESÚS OROZCO G, GABRIEL ARREGUI V.

Sistema Radiofónico Nacional, SA: Baja California 163, Of. 602, 06760 México, DF; tel. (55) 5574-0298; f. 1971; represents commercial radio networks; Dir-Gen. RENÉ C. DE LA ROSA.

Sociedad Mexicana de Radio, SA de CV (SOMER): Gutenberg 89, Col. Anzures, 11590 México, DF; tel. (55) 5255-5297; fax (55) 5545-0310; Dir-Gen. EDILBERTO HUESCA PERROTIN.

Television

In 2002 there were 468 television stations. Among the most important are:

Asesoramiento y Servicios Técnicos Industriales, SA (ASTISA): México, DF; tel. (55) 5585-3333; commercial; Dir ROBERTO CHÁVEZ TINAJERO.

MVS (Multivisión): Blvd Puerto Aéreo 486, Col. Moctezuma, 15500 México, DF; tel. (55) 5764-8100; internet www.mvs.com; subscriber-funded.

Once TV: Carpio 475, Col. Casco de Santo Tomás, 11340 México, DF; tel. (55) 5356-1111; fax (55) 5396-8001; e-mail canal11@ vmredipn.ipn.mx; f. 1959; Dir-Gen. ALEJANDRA LAJOUS VARGAS.

Tele Cadena Mexicana, SA: Avda Chapultepec 18, 06724 México, DF; tel. (55) 5535-1679; commercial, comprises about 80 stations; Dir Lic. JORGE ARMANDO PIÑA MEDINA.

Televisa, SA de CV: Edif. Televicentro, Avda Chapultepec 28, Col. Doctores, 06724 México, DF; tel. (55) 5709-3333; fax (55) 5709-3021; e-mail webmaster@televisa.com.mx; internet www.televisa.com; f. 1973; commercial; began broadcasts to Europe via satellite in Dec. 1988 through its subsidiary, Galavisión; 406 affiliated stations; Chair. and CEO EMILIO AZCÁRRAGA JEAN; Vice-Pres. ALEJANDRO BURILLO AZCÁRRAGA.

Televisión Azteca, SA de CV: Anillo Periférico Sur 4121, Col. Fuentes del Pedregal, 14141 México, DF; tel. (55) 5420-1313; fax (55) 5645-4258; e-mail webtva@tvazteca.com; internet tvazteca.todito .com; f. 1992; to assume responsibility for former state-owned channels 7 and 13; Pres. RICARDO B. SALINAS PLIEGO.

Televisión de la República Mexicana: Mina 24, Col. Guerrero, México, DF; tel. (55) 5510-8590; cultural; Dir EDUARDO LIZALDE.

As a member of the Intelsat international consortium, Mexico has received communications via satellite since the 1960s. The launch of the Morelos I and Morelos II satellites, in 1985, provided Mexico with its own satellite communications system. The Morelos satellites were superseded by a new satellite network, Solidaridad, which was inaugurated in early 1994. In late 1997 Mexico's three satellites (grouped in a newly-formed company, SatMex) were transferred to private ownership.

Finance

(cap. = capital; dep. = deposits; m. = million; res = reserves; amounts in new pesos unless otherwise stated)

BANKING

The Mexican banking system is comprised of the Banco de México (the central bank of issue), multiple or commercial banking institutions and development banking institutions. Banking activity is regulated by the Federal Government.

Commercial banking institutions are constituted as *Sociedades Anónimas*, with wholly private social capital. Development banking institutions exist as *Sociedades Nacionales de Crédito*, participation in their capital is exclusive to the Federal Government, notwithstanding the possibility of accepting limited amounts of private capital. In 2000 there were 34 commercial banks operating in Mexico.

All private banks were nationalized in September 1982. By July 1992, however, the banking system had been completely returned to the private sector. Legislation removing all restrictions on foreign ownership of banks received congressional approval in 1999.

Supervisory Authority

Comisión Nacional Bancaria y de Valores (National Banking and Securities Commission): Insurgentes Sur 1971, Torre Norte, Sur y III, Col. Guadalupe Inn, Del. Álvaro Obregón, 01020, México, DF; tel. and fax (55) 5724-6000; e-mail info@cnbv.gob.mx; internet www.cnbv.gob.mx; f. 1924; govt commission controlling all credit institutions in Mexico; Pres. JONATHAN DAVIS ARZAC.

Central Bank

Banco de México (BANXICO): Avda 5 de Mayo 2, Apdo 98 bis, 06059 México, DF; tel. (55) 5237-2000; fax (55) 5237-2370; e-mail comsoc@banxico.org.mx; internet www.banxico.org.mx; f. 1925; currency issuing authority; became autonomous on 1 April 1994; res US $7,854m. (March 1995); Gov. GUILLERMO ORTIZ MARTÍNEZ; 9 brs.

Commercial Banks

Banamex: Avda Isabel la Católica 44, 1°, 06089 México, DF; tel. (55) 5720-7091; fax (55) 5920-7323; internet www.banamex.com; f. 1884; transferred to private ownership in 1991; merged with Citibank México, SA in 2001; cap. 41,790.8m., res −17,382.8m., dep. 243,630.6m. (Dec. 1998); Dir-Gen. ROBERTO HERNÁNDEZ RAMÍREZ; 1,260 brs.

Banca Serfín, SA: Paseo de la Reforma 500, Mod. 409, 4°, Col. Lomas de Santa Fe, 01219 México, DF; tel. (55) 5259-8860; fax (55) 5257-8387; internet www.serfin.com.mx; f. 1864; merged with Banco Continental Ganadero in 1985; transferred to private ownership in Jan. 1992; acquired by Banco Santander Central Hispano (Spain) in Dec. 2000; cap. 14,746.5m., res −167.4m., dep. 181,182.0m. (Dec. 2000); CEO ADOLFO LAGO ESPINOSA; 571 brs.

Banco del Bajío, SA: Avda Manuel J. Clouthier 508, Col. Jardines del Campestre, 37128 León, Gto; tel. (477) 710-4600; fax (477) 710-4603; e-mail info@bajionet.com.mx; internet www.bajionet.com.mx; f. 1994; cap. 711.9m., res −76.4m., dep. 5,010.0m. (Dec. 2001); Gen. Man. CARLOS DE LA CERDA SERRANO.

Banco Internacional, SA (BITAL): Paseo de la Reforma 156, Col. Juarez, 06600 México, DF; tel. (55) 5721-2983; fax (55) 5721-2393; internet www.bital.com.mx; f. 1941; owned by HSBC (UK); cap. 2,858.8m., res 1,915.8m., dep. 122,207.5m. Pres. and CEO ANTONIO DEL VALLE; Dir-Gen. JAIME RUIZ.

Banco Mercantil del Norte, SA (BANORTE): Hidalgo 250, Pte Col. Centro, 64000 Monterrey, NL; tel. (81) 3319-7200; fax (81) 3319-5216; internet www.banorte.com; f. 1899; merged with Banco Regional del Norte in 1985; cap. 4,349.4m., res 489.3m., dep. 90,860.8m. (Dec. 2000); Chair. ROBERTO GONZÁLEZ BARRERA; 457 brs.

Banpaís, SNC: Paseo de la Reforma 359, Col. Cuauhtémoc, 06500 México, DF; tel. (55) 5208-2044; fax (55) 5533-1223; f. 1892 as Banco de Nuevo León, present name 1978; merged with Banco Latino in 1985; transferred to private ownership in 1991; cap. 636,000m. old pesos, res 28,000m. old pesos, dep. 8,390,000m. old pesos (Dec. 1992); Chair. Lic. CARLOS SALES GUTIÉRREZ; 160 brs.

Scotiabank Inverlat, SA: Plaza Inverlat, Miguel Avila Camacho 1, Col. Chapultepec Polanco, 11560 México, DF; tel. (55) 5229-2929; fax (55) 5229-2114; internet www.inverlat.com.mx; f. 1977 as Multibanco Comermex, SA; changed name to Banco Inverlat, SA 1995; 55% holding acquired by Scotiabank Group (Canada) and name changed as above 2001; cap. 2,801.4m., res 509.7m., dep. 77,305.0m. (Dec. 2001); Pres. XAVIER AUDREY; 336 brs.

Development Banks

Banco Nacional de Comercio Exterior, SNC (BANCOMEXT): Periférico Sur 433, Col. Jardines en la Montaña, 14210 México, DF; tel. (55) 5449-9020; fax (55) 5449-9028; internet www.bancomext.com; f. 1937; cap. 17,613.8m., res −10,524.2.3m., dep. 45,201.0m. (Dec. 2001); Dir-Gen. JOSÉ LUIS ROMERO HICKS.

Banco Nacional de Crédito Rural, SNC (BANRURAL): Agrarismo 227, Col. Escandón, 11800 México, DF; tel. (55) 5273-1465; fax (55) 5584-2664; internet www.banrural.gob.mx; f. 1975; provides financing for agriculture and normal banking services; cap. 1,791,569m., res −155,439m. old pesos, dep. 623,402m. old pesos (Sept. 1992); Dir-Gen. Ing. JAIME DE LA MORA GÓMEZ; 187 brs.

Banco Nacional del Ejército, Fuerza Aérea y Armada, SNC (BANJERCITO): Avda Industria Militar 1055, 2°, Col. Lomas de Sotelo, 11200 México, DF; tel. (55) 5557-5728; fax (55) 5395-0909; internet www.banjercito.com.mx; f. 1947; cap. 11,035m. old pesos, res 1,780.7m. old pesos, dep. 139,184.5m. old pesos (Sept. 1990); Dir-Gen. Gral. RAFAEL PAZ DEL CAMPO; 17 brs.

Banco Nacional de Obras y Servicios Públicos, SNC (BANOBRAS): Tecoyotitla 100, 4°, esq. Francia, Col. Florida, 01030 México, DF; tel. (55) 5723-6000; fax (55) 5723-6177; e-mail bneumann@banobras.gob.mx; internet www.banobras.gob.mx; f.

1933; cap. 255.6m., res 5,297.4m, dep. 65,049.3m. (Dec. 1996); Chair. FELIPE CALDERÓN HINOJOSA.

BBVA Bancomer, SA: Centro Bancomer, Avda Universidad 1200, Apdo 9 bis, 03339 México, DF; tel. (55) 5534-0034; fax (55) 5621-3230; internet www.bancomer.com.mx; f. 2000 by merger of Bancomer (f. 1864) and Mexican operations of Banco Bilbao Vizcaya Argentaria (Spain); privatized 2002; cap. 63,446,7m., res 7,511.0m., dep. 362,096.2m. (Dec. 2001); Chair. EUGENIO GARZA LAGÜERA.

Financiera Nacional Azucarera, SNC (FINA, SNC): Insurgentes Sur 716, Col. del Valle, Apdo 10764, 03100 México, DF; tel. (55) 5325-6000; fax (55) 5325-7383; f. 1953; cap. 159,662m. old pesos, res 52,724m. old pesos, dep. 2,252,660m. old pesos (Sept. 1992); Dir-Gen. Lic. OSCAR ESPINOSA VILLARREAL.

Nacional Financiera, SNC: Insurgentes Sur 1971, Torre IV, 13°, Col. Guadalupe Inn, 01020 México, DF; tel. (55) 5325-6700; fax (55) 5661-8418; internet www.nafin.com.mx; f. 1943; Dir-Gen. MARIO LABORIN GÓMEZ; 37 brs.

Foreign Bank

Dresdner Bank Mexico, SA: Bosque de Alisos 47B, 4°, Col. Bosques de las Lomas, 05120 México, DF; tel. (55) 5258-3000; fax (55) 5258-3100; e-mail Mexico@dbla.com; f. 1995; Man. Dir LUIS NIÑO DE RIVERA.

BANKERS' ASSOCIATION

Asociación de Banqueros de México: 16 de Setiembre 27, Col. Centro Histórico, 06000 México, DF; tel. (55) 5752-4305; internet www.abm.org.mx; f. 1928; fmrly Asosición Mexicano de Bancos; Pres. OTHÓN RUIZ MONTEMAYOR; Dir-Gen. Lic. ADOLFO RIVAS MARTIN DEL CAMPO; 52 mems.

STOCK EXCHANGE

Bolsa Mexicana de Valores, SA de CV: Paseo de la Reforma 255, Col. Cuauhtémoc, 06500 México, DF; tel. (55) 5726-6600; fax (55) 5591-0642; e-mail cinforma@bmv.com.mx; internet www.bmv.com.mw; f. 1894; Pres. Lic. MANUEL ROBELDA GONZALES DE CASTILLA; Dir-Gen. Ing. GERARDO FLORES DEUCHLER.

INSURANCE

México, DF

ACE Seguros: Bosques de Alisos, 47–A, 1°, Col. Bosques de las Lomas, 5120 México, DF; tel. (5) 258-5800; fax (5) 258-5899; e-mail info@acelatinamerica.com; f. 1990; fmrly Seguros Cigna.

Aseguradora Cuauhtémoc, SA: Manuel Avila Camacho 164, 11570 México, DF; tel. (55) 5250-9800; fax (55) 5540-3204; f. 1944; general; Exec. Pres. JUAN B. RIVEROLL; Dir-Gen. JAVIER COMPEÁN AMEZCUA.

Aseguradora Hidalgo, SA: Presidente Masarik 111, Col. Polanco, Del. Miguel Hidalgo, 11570 México, DF; f. 1931; life; Dir-Gen. JOSÉ GÓMEZ GORDOA; Man. Dir HUMBERTO ROQUE VILLANUEVA.

La Continental Seguros, SA: Francisco I. Madero, 1, 10°, 06007 México, DF; tel. (55) 5518-1670; fax (55) 5510-3259; f. 1936; general; Pres. Ing. TEODORO AMERLINCK Y ZIRIÓN; Vice-Pres. Ing. RODRIGO AMERLINCK Y ASSERETO.

ING Comercial América—Seguros: Insurgentes Sur 3900, Col. Tlalpan, 14000 México, DF; tel. (55) 5727-2500; internet www.seguros.ing-comercialamerica.com; f. 1936 as La Comercial; acquired by ING Group in 2000; life, etc. Pres. GLENN HILLIARS; Dir-Gen. Ing. ADRIÁN PÁEZ.

La Nacional, Cía de Seguros, SA: México, DF; f. 1901; life, etc. Pres. CLEMENTE CABELLO; Chair. Lic. ALBERTO BAILLERES.

Pan American de México, Cía de Seguros, SA: México, DF; f. 1940; Pres. Lic. JESS N. DALTON; Dir-Gen. GILBERTO ESCOBEDA PAZ.

Previsión Obrera, Sociedad Mutualista de Seguros sobre la Vida: Avda Ricardo Flores Magón 206, México, DF; f. 1934; life; Man. ANTONIO CASTELLANOS TOVAR.

Royal & SunAlliance Mexico: Blvd Adolfo López Mateos 2448, Col. Altavista, 01060 México, DF; tel. (55) 5723-7900; fax (55) 5512-4091; e-mail omar.antonio@mx.royalsun.com; internet www.royalsun.com.mx; f. 1941; acquired Seguros BBV-Probursa in 2001; general, except life.

Seguros América Banamex, SA: Avda Revolución 1508, Col. Guadalupe Inn, 01020 México, DF; f. 1933; Pres. AGUSTÍN F. LEGORRETA; Dir-Gen. JUAN OROZCO GÓMEZ PORTUGAL.

Seguros Azteca, SA: Insurgentes 102, México, DF; f. 1933; general including life; Pres. JUAN CAMPO RODRÍGUEZ.

Seguros Constitución, SA: Avda Revolución 2042, Col. La Otra Banda, 01090 México, DF; tel. (55) 5550-7910; f. 1937; life, accident; Pres. Isidoro Rodríguez Ruiz; Dir-Gen. Alfonso de Orduña y Pérez.

Seguros el Fénix, SA: México, DF; f. 1937; Pres. Victoriano Olazábal E; Dir-Gen. Jaime Matute Labrador.

Seguros Internacional, SA: Abraham González 67, México, DF; f. 1945; general; Pres. Lic. Gustavo Romero Kolbeck.

Seguros de México, SA: Insurgentes Sur 3496, Col. Peña Pobre, 14060 México, DF; tel. (55) 5679-3855; f. 1957; life, etc. Dir-Gen. Lic. Antonio Mijares Ricci.

Seguros La Provincial, SA: México, DF; f. 1936; general; Pres. Clemente Cabello; Chair. Alberto Bailleres.

Seguros La República, SA: Paseo de la Reforma 383, México, DF; f. 1966; general; 43% owned by Commercial Union (UK); Pres. Luciano Arechederra Quintana; Gen. Man. Juan Antonio de Arrieta Mendizábal.

Guadalajara, Jal.

Nueva Galicia, Compañía de Seguros Generales, SA: Guadalajara, Jal. f. 1946; fire; Pres. Salvador Veytia y Veytia.

Monterrey, NL

Seguros Monterrey Aetna, SA: Avda Diagonal Sta Engracia 221 Ote, Col. Lomas de San Francisco, 64710 Monterrey, NL; tel. (81) 319-1111; fax (81) 363-0428; f. 1940; casualty, life, etc. Dir-Gen. Federico Reyes García.

Seguros Monterrey del Círculo Mercantil, SA, Sociedad General de Seguros: Padre Mier Pte 276, Monterrey, NL; f. 1941; life; Gen. Man. Carmen G. Masso de Navarro.

Insurance Association

Asociación Mexicana de Instituciones de Seguros, AC: Ejército Nacional 904, 6°, México, DF; internet www.amis.com.mx; f. 1946; all insurance cos operating in Mexico are members; Pres. Kurt Vogt Sartorius.

Trade and Industry

GOVERNMENT AGENCIES

Comisión Nacional de Precios: Avda Juárez 101, 17°, México 1, DF; tel. (55) 510-0436; f. 1977; national prices commission; Dir-Gen. Jesús Sánchez Jiménez.

Comisión Nacional de los Salarios Mínimos: Avda Cuauhtémoc 14, 2°, Col. Doctores, 06720 México 7, DF; tel. (55) 5578-9021; fax (55) 5578-5775; f. 1962, in accordance with Section VI of Article 123 of the Constitution; national commission on minimum salaries; Pres. Lic. Basilio González-Nuñez; Tech. Dir Alida Bernal Cosio.

Consejo Mexicano de Comercio Exterior (CONCE): Eugenio Sue 94, Polanco, 11560 México, DF; tel. (52) 5281-0595; e-mail comce@comce.org.mx; internet www.comce.org.mx; f. 1999 to promote international trade; Chair. Federico Sada González.

Consejo Nacional de Comercio Exterior, AC (CONACEX): Avda Parque Fundidora 501, Of. 95E, Edif. CINTERMEX, Col. Obrera, 64010 Monterrey, NL; tel. (81) 369-0284; fax (81) 369-0293; e-mail conacex@technet.net.mx; internet www.technet.net.mx/conacex; f. 1962 to promote national exports; Chair. Ing. Javier Prieto de la Fuente; Pres. Lic. Juan Manuel Quiroga Lam.

Consejo de Recursos Minerales: Felipe Ángeles s/n Carr. México-Pachuca, km 93.5, Col. Venta Prieta, 42080 Pachuca, HI; tel. (771) 771-4016; fax (771) 771-3252; e-mail geoinfo@coremisgm.gob.mx; internet www.coremisgm.gob.mx; f. 1957; govt agency for the devt of mineral resources; Dir-Gen. Ing. Francisco José Escandón Valle.

Dirección General de Política e Inversiones Industriales: México, DF; govt body established to direct industrial policy; took over the functions of the Comisión Coordinadora para el Desarrollo de la Industria de Maquinaria y Equipo, Comisión Nacional Coordinadora para el Desarrollo Industrial; Dir-Gen. Lic. Vladimiro Brailovsky F.

Instituto Nacional del Consumidor: Insurgentes Sur 1228, 10°, Col. del Valle Tlacoquemecatl, 03210 México, DF; tel. (55) 5559-2478; fax (55) 5559-0123; f. 1976; national institute for consumer protection; Dir-Gen. Margarita Ortega Villa.

Instituto Nacional de Investigaciones Nucleares (ININ): Centro Nuclear de México, km 36.5, Carretera México–Toluca, 52045 Ocoyoacac, Méx. tel. (55) 5329-7219; fax (55) 5329-7298; e-mail osg@nuclear.inin.mx; internet www.inin.mx; f. 1979 to plan research and devt of nuclear science and technology, as well as the peaceful uses of nuclear energy, for the social, scientific and techno-

logical devt of the country; administers the Secondary Standard Dosimetry Laboratory, the Nuclear Information and Documentation Centre , which serves Mexico's entire scientific community; the 1 MW research reactor which came into operation, in 1967, supplies part of Mexico's requirements for radioactive isotopes; also operates a 12 MV Tandem van de Graaff. Mexico has two nuclear reactors, each with a generating capacity of 654 MW; the first, at Laguna Verde, became operational in 1989 and is administered by the Comisión Federal de Electricidad (CFE); Dir-Gen. M. en C. José Raúl Ortíz Magaña.

Instituto Nacional de Pesca (National Fishery Institute): Pitágoras 1320, Col. Sta Cruz Atoyac, 03310 México, DF; tel. (55) 5688-1469; fax (55) 5604-9169; e-mail compean@inp.semarnat.gob.mx; internet http://inp.semarnat.gob.mx/; f. 1962; Dir Guillermo Compean Jiménez.

Laboratorios Nacionales de Fomento Industrial: México, DF; tel. (55) 5589-0199; fax (55) 5589-7162; f. 1948; conducts scientific research for industrial devt; Dir Dr Manuel Ruiz de Chávez.

Procuraduría Federal del Consumidor: Dr Carmona y Valle 11, Col. Doctores, 06720 México, DF; tel. (55) 5761-3021; f. 1975; consumer protection; Dir Ignacio Pichardo Pagaza.

Uranio Mexicano (URAMEX): Insurgentes Sur 1079, 3°, México, DF; tel. (5) 563-7100; supervises the use of uranium; Dir-Gen. Alberto Escoget Artigas.

DEVELOPMENT ORGANIZATIONS

Comisión Coordinadora de la Industria Siderúrgica: México, DF; f. 1972; co-ordinating commission for the devt of the iron and steel industries; Dir-Gen. Lic. Alfredo Ade Tomasini.

Comisión Nacional de las Zonas Aridas: México, DF; tel. (55) 5525-9360; internet www.conaza.gob.mx; f. 1970; commission to co-ordinate the devt and use of arid areas; Dir Ing. Manuel Agustín Reed Segovia.

Fideicomisos Instituídos en Relación con la Agricultura (FIRA): México, DF; tel. (55) 5550-7011; internet www.fira.gob.mx; Dir Ing. Antonio Baca Díaz; a group of devt funds to aid agricultural financing, under the Banco de México, comprising:

Fondo de Garantía y Fomento para la Agricultura, Ganadería y Avicultura (FOGAGA): f. 1954.

Fondo Especial para Financiamientos Agropecuarios (FEFA): f. 1965.

Fondo Especial de Asistencia Técnica y Garantía para Créditos Agropecuarios (FEGA): f. 1972.

Instituto Mexicano del Petróleo (IMP): Avda Eje Central Lázaro Cárdenas 152, Apdo 14-805, 07730 México, DF; tel. (55) 5567-6600; fax (55) 5567-6047; internet www.imp.mx; f. 1965 to foster devt of the petroleum, chemical and petrochemical industries; Dir Gustavo Chapela Castañares.

CHAMBERS OF COMMERCE

Confederación de Cámaras Nacionales de Comercio, Servicios y Turismo (CONCANACO) (Confederation of National Chambers of Commerce): Balderas 144, 3°, Col. Centro, 06079 México, DF; tel. (55) 5709-1559; fax (55) 5709-1152; f. 1917; Pres. José Yamil Hallal Zepeda; Dir-Gen. Ing. Alejandro Aguilera Gómez; comprises 283 regional Chambers.

Cámara Nacional de Comercio de la Ciudad de México (CANACO) (National Chamber of Commerce of Mexico City): Paseo de la Reforma 42, 3°, Col. Centro, Apdo 32005, 06048 México, DF; tel. (55) 5592-2677; fax (55) 5592-2279; f. 1874; 50,000 mems; Pres. Vicente Mayo García; Dir-Gen. Ing. Marcos Pérez Arenas.

Cámara Nacional de la Industria y de la Transformación (CANACINTRA): Calle Vallarta 21, 3°, México, DF; tel. (55) 5566-9333; represents majority of smaller manufacturing businesses; Pres. Víctor Manuel Terrones López.

Chambers of Commerce exist in the chief town of each State as well as in the larger centres of commercial activity.

CHAMBERS OF INDUSTRY

The 64 Industrial Chambers and 32 Associations, many of which are located in the Federal District, are representative of the major industries of the country.

Central Confederation

Confederación de Cámaras Industriales de los Estados Unidos Mexicanos (CONCAMIN) (Confed. of Industrial Chambers): Manuel María Contreras 133, 8°, Col. Cuauhtémoc, 06500 México, DF; tel. (55) 5566-7822; fax (55) 5535-6871; e-mail cetin@solar.sar.net; internet www.concamin.org.mx; f. 1918; represents and promotes the activities of the entire industrial sector; Pres.

ALEJANDRO MARTÍNEZ GALLARDO; Dir-Gen. RENÉ ESPINOSA Y TORRES ESTRADA.

INDUSTRIAL AND TRADE ASSOCIATIONS

Asociación Nacional de Importadores y Exportadores de la República Mexicana (ANIERM) (National Association of Importers and Exporters): Monterrey 130, Col. Roma-Cuauhtémoc, 06700 México, DF; tel. (55) 5564-8618; fax (55) 5584-5317; f. 1944; Pres. RODRIGO GUERRA B; Vice-Pres. Lic. HUMBERTO SIMONEEN ARDILA.

Azúcar, SA de CV: Insurgentes Sur 1079, Col. Nochebuena, 03910 México, DF; tel. (5) 563-7100; f. 1983 to develop the sugar industry; Dir Ing. EDUARDO A. MACGREGOR BELTRÁN.

Comisión de Fomento Minero: Puente de Tecamachalco 26, Lomas de Chapultepec, 11000 México, DF; tel. (55) 5540-2906; f. 1934 to promote the devt of the mining sector; Dir Lic. LUIS DE PABLO SERNA.

Comisión Nacional del Cacao (Conadeca): México, DF; tel. (55) 5286-9495; f. 1973 to promote the cultivation, industrialization and the marketing of cocoa; Dir-Gen. Lic. JULIO DERBEZ DEL PINO.

Comisión Nacional de Fruticultura (Conafrut): Querétaro, Qro; tel. (463) 570-2499; f. 1961 to develop the production, industrialization and marketing of fruits; Dir Lic. FRANCISCO MERINO RÁBAGO.

Comisión Nacional de Inversiones Extranjeras: Blvd Avila Camacho 1, 11°, 11000 México, DF; tel. (55) 5540-1426; fax (55) 5286-1551; f. 1973; commission to co-ordinate foreign investment; Exec. Sec. Dr CARLOS CAMACHO GAOS.

Comisión Nacional de Seguridad Nuclear y Salvaguardias (CNSNS): Dr Barragán 779, Col. Narvarte, 03020 México, DF; tel. (55) 5095-3240; fax (55) 095-3295; e-mail swaller@cnsns.gob.mx; f. 1979; nuclear regulatory agency; Dir-Gen. JUAN EIBENSCHUTZ HARTMAN.

Comisión Petroquímica Mexicana: México, DF; to promote the devt of the petrochemical industry; Tech. Sec. Ing. JUAN ANTONIO BARGÉS MESTRES.

Compañía Nacional de Subsistencias Populares (CONASUPO): Avda Insurgentes Sur 489, 4°, Col. Hipódromo Condesa, 06100 México, DF; tel. (55) 5272-0472; fax (55) 5272-0607; f. 1965 to protect the income of small farmers, improve the marketing of basic farm commodities and supervise the operation of rural co-operative stores; Dir Lic. JAVIER BONILLA GARCÍA.

Consejo Empresarial Mexicano para Asuntos Internacionales (CEMAI): Homero 517, 7°, Col. Polanco, 11570 México, DF; tel. (55) 5250-7033; fax (55) 5531-1590.

Consejo Mexicano del Café: Lope de Vega 125, 1°, Col. Chapultepec Morales, 115700 México, DF; tel. and fax (55) 5254-2334; e-mail cmc@sagar.gob.mx; internet www.sagarpa.gob.mx/cmc.

Fondo de Operación y Financiamiento Bancario a la Vivienda: Ejército Nacional 180, 7°, 8° y 11°, Col. Anzures, 11590 México, DF; tel. (55) 5255-4199; fax (55) 5203-7304; f. 1963 to promote the construction of low-cost housing through savings and credit schemes; devt fund under the Banco de México; Dir-Gen. Lic. MANUEL ZEPEDA PAYERAS.

Instituto del Fondo Nacional de la Vivienda para los Trabajadores (INFONAVIT): Barranca del Muerto 280, 4°, Col. Guadalupe Inn., Del. Alvaro Obregón, 01029 México, DF; tel. (55) 5660-2423; f. 1972 to finance the construction of low-cost housing for the working classes; Dir JOSÉ JUAN DE OLLOQUI Y LABASTIDA.

Instituto Mexicano del Café (Inmecafé): Carretera Jalapa-Veracruz km 4, Campo Experimental Garnica, Jalapa, Ver. Lago Merú 32, Col. Granada, México, DF; tel. (55) 5250-5543; f. 1958; sponsors cultivation to increase domestic and foreign sales of coffee; Dir-Gen. JESÚS SALAZAR TOLEDANO.

Instituto Nacional de Investigaciones Forestales y Agropecuarios (INIFAP) (National Forestry and Agricultural Research Institute): Apdo 6-882, 06600 México, DF; tel. (55) 5687-7451; f. 1985; conducts research into plant genetics, management of species and conservation; Exec. Dir Dr MANUEL R. VILLA ISSA.

Tabacos Mexicanos, SA de CV (TABAMEX): México, DF; tel. (55) 5395-5477; fax (55) 5395-6836; f. 1972 to foster the cultivation, industrialization and marketing of tobacco; Dir-Gen. GUSTAVO CARVAJAL MORENO.

EMPLOYERS' ORGANIZATIONS

Consejo Coordinador Empresarial (CCE): Paseo de la Reforma 255, 11°, Col. Cuauhtémoc, 06500 México, DF; tel. (55) 592-3910; fax (55) 592-3857; internet www.cce.org.mx; f. 1974; co-ordinating body of private sector; Pres. LUIS GERMÁN CÁRCOBA; Dir FRANCISCO CALDERÓN.

Consejo Mexicano de Hombres de Negocios (CMHN): México, DF; represents leading businesspeople; affiliated to CCE; Pres. EUGENIO CLARIOND REYES.

STATE HYDROCARBONS COMPANY

Petróleos Mexicanos (PEMEX): Avda Marina Nacional 329, 44°, Col. Huasteca, 11300 México, DF; tel. (55) 5254-2044; fax (55) 5531-6354; internet www.pemex.com; f. 1938; govt agency for the exploitation of Mexico's petroleum and natural gas resources; Dir-Gen. RAÚL MUÑOZ LEOS; 106,900 employees.

UTILITIES

Regulatory Authorities

Comisión Nacional del Agua: Avda Insurgentes Sur 2140, 2°, Col. Chimalistac, Del. Alvaro Obregón, 01070 México, DF; tel. (55) 5661-3806; e-mail webmaster@cna.gob.mx; internet www.cna.gob.mx; commission to administer national water resources; Dir CRISTOBAL JAIME JAQUEZ.

Comisión Reguladora de Energía: Horacio 1750, Col. Los Morales, 11510 México, DF; tel. (55) 5283-1500; internet www.cre.gob.mx; f. 1994; commission to control energy policy and planning; Pres. DIONISIO PÉREZ-JÁCOME.

Secretariat of State for Energy: see section on The Government (Secretariats of State).

Electricity

Comisión Federal de Electricidad (CFE): Río Ródano 14, 7°, Col. Cuauhtémoc, 06598 México, DF; tel. (55) 5207-3704; fax (55) 5553-6424; internet www.cfe.gob.mx; state-owned power utility; Dir-Gen. ALFREDO ELÍAS AYUB.

Luz y Fuerza del Centro: Melchor Ocampo 171, 7°, Col. Tlaxpana, 11379 México, DF; tel. (55) 629-7100; fax (55) 5518-0083; internet www.lfc.gob.mx; operates electricity network in the centre of the country; Dir-Gen. ALFONSO CASO AGUILAR.

Gas

Gas Natural México (GNM): Monterrey, NL; natural gas distributor; subsidiary of Spanish co Gas Natural.

Petróleos Mexicanos (PEMEX): see State Hydrocarbons Company, above: distributes natural gas.

TRADE UNIONS

Congreso del Trabajo (CT): Avda Ricardo Flores Magón 44, Col. Guerrero, 06300 México 37, DF; tel. (55) 5583-3817; f. 1966; trade union congress comprising trade union federations, confederations, etc. Pres. Lic. HÉCTOR VALDÉS ROMO.

Confederación Regional Obrera Mexicana (CROM) (Regional Confederation of Mexican Workers): República de Cuba 60, México, DF; f. 1918; Sec.-Gen. IGNACIO CUAUHTÉMOC PALETA; 120,000 mems, 900 affiliated syndicates.

Confederación Revolucionaria de Obreros y Campesinos (CROC) (Revolutionary Confederation of Workers and Farmers): Hamburgo 250, Col. Juárez, 06600 México, DF; f. 1952; Sec.-Gen. ALBERTO JUÁREZ BLANCAS; 120,000 mems in 22 state federations and 8 national unions.

Confederación Revolucionaria de Trabajadores (CRT) (Revolutionary Confederation of Workers): Dr Jiménez 218, Col. Doctores, México, DF; f. 1954; Sec.-Gen. MARIO SUÁREZ GARCÍA; 10,000 mems; 10 federations and 192 syndicates.

Confederación de Trabajadores de México (CTM) (Confederation of Mexican Workers): Vallarta 8, México, DF; f. 1936; admitted to ICFTU; Sec.-Gen. LEONARDO RODRÍGUEZ ALCAINE; 5.5m. mems.

Federación Obrera de Organizaciones Femeniles (FOOF) (Workers' Federation of Women's Organizations): Vallarta 8, México, DF; f. 1950; a women workers' union within CTM; Sec.-Gen. HILDA ANDERSON NEVÁREZ; 400,000 mems.

Federación Nacional de Sindicatos Independientes (National Federation of Independent Trade Unions): Isaac Garza 311 Ote, 64000 Monterrey, NL; tel. (8) 375-6677; internet www.fnsi.org.mx; f. 1936; Sec.-Gen. JACINTO PADILLA VALDEZ; 230,000 mems.

Federación de Sindicatos de Trabajadores al Servicio del Estado (FSTSE) (Federation of Unions of Govt Workers): Gómez Farías 40, Col. San Rafael, 06470 México, DF; f. 1938; Sec.-Gen. Lic. JOEL AYALA; 2.5m. mems; 80 unions.

Frente Unida Sindical por la Defensa de los Trabajadores y la Constitución (United Union Front in Defence of the Workers and the Constitution): f. 1990 by more than 120 trade orgs to support the implementation of workers' constitutional rights.

Unión General de Obreros y Campesinos de México, Jacinto López (UGOCM-JL) (General Union of Workers and Farmers of Mexico, Jacinto López): José María Marroquí 8, 2°, 06050 México, DF; tel. (55) 5518-3015; f. 1949; admitted to WFTU/CSTAL; Sec.-Gen. José Luis González Aguilera; 7,500 mems, over 2,500 syndicates.

Unión Nacional de Trabajadores (UNT) (National Union of Workers): México, DF; internet www.unt.org.mx; f. 1998; Leader Francisco Hernández Juárez.

A number of major unions are non-affiliated; they include:

Frente Auténtico de los Trabajadores (FAT).

Pacto de Unidad Sindical Solidaridad (PAUSS): comprises 10 independent trade unions.

Sindicato Nacional de Trabajadores Mineros, Metalúrgicos y Similares de la República Mexicana (Industrial Union of Mine, Metallurgical and Related Workers of the Republic of Mexico): Avda Dr Vertiz 668, Col. Narvarte, 03020 México, DF; tel. (55) 5519-5690; f. 1933; Sec.-Gen. Napoleon Gómez Urrutia; 86,000 mems.

Sindicato Nacional de Trabajadores de la Educación (SNTE): Venezuela 44, Col. Centro, México, DF; tel. (55) 5702-0005; fax (55) 5702-6303; teachers' union; Sec.-Gen. Tomás Vázquez Vigil; 1.2m. mems.

Coordinadora Nacional de Trabajadores de la Educación (CNTE): dissident faction; Leader Teodoro Palomino.

Sindicato de Trabajadores Petroleros de la República Mexicana (STPRM) (Union of Petroleum Workers of the Republic of Mexico): Zaragoza 15, Col. Guerrero, 06300 México, DF; tel. (55) 5546-0912; close links with PEMEX; Sec.-Gen. Carlos Romero Deschamps; 110,000 mems; includes:

Movimiento Nacional Petrolero: reformist faction; Leader Hebraícaz Vásquez.

Sindicato de Trabajadores Ferrocarrileros de la República Mexicana (STFRM) (Union of Railroad Workers of the Republic of Mexico): Avda Ricardo Flores Magón 206, Col. Guerrero, México 3, DF; tel. (55) 5597-1011; f. 1933; Sec.-Gen. Víctor F. Flores Morales; 100,000 mems.

Sindicato Unico de Trabajadores Electricistas de la República Mexicana (SUTERM) (Sole Union of Electricity Workers of the Republic of Mexico): Río Guadalquivir 106, Col. Cuauhtémoc, 06500 México, DF; tel. (55) 5207-0578; Sec.-Gen. Leonardo Rodríguez Alcaine.

Sindicato Unico de Trabajadores de la Industria Nuclear (SUTIN): Viaducto Río Becerra 139, Col. Nápoles, 03810 México, DF; tel. (55) 5523-8048; fax (55) 5687-6353; e-mail sutin@nuclear .inin.mx; internet www.prodigyweb.net.mx/sutin; Sec.-Gen. Ricardo Flores Bello.

Unión Obrera Independiente (UOI): non-aligned.

The major agricultural unions are:

Central Campesina Independiente: Dr E. González Martínez 101, México, DF; Leader Alfonso Garzón Santibáñez.

Confederación Nacional Campesina (CNC): Mariano Azuela 121, Col. Santa María de la Ribera, México, DF; Sec.-Gen. Lic. Beatriz Paredes Rangel.

Confederación Nacional Ganadera: Calzada Mariano Escobedo 714, Col. Anzures, México, DF; tel. (55) 5203-3506; Pres. Ing. César González Quiroga; 300,000 mems.

Consejo Agrarista Mexicano: México, DF; Sec.-Gen. Humberto Serrano.

Unión Nacional de Trabajadores Agriculturas (UNTA).

Transport

Road transport accounts for about 98% of all public passenger traffic and for about 80% of freight traffic. Mexico's terrain is difficult for overland travel. As a result, there has been an expansion of air transport and there were 83 international and national airports, plus 2,418 landing fields and feeder airports, in 1992. In 2002 plans to build a new airport in the capital were underway. International flights are provided by a large number of national and foreign airlines. Mexico has 140 seaports, 29 river docks and a further 29 lake shelters. More than 85% of Mexico's foreign trade is conducted through maritime transport. In the 1980s the Government developed the main industrial ports of Tampico, Coatzacoalcos, Lázaro Cárdenas, Altamira, Laguna de Ostión and Salina Cruz in an attempt to redirect growth and to facilitate exports. The port at Dos Bocas, on the Gulf of Mexico, was one of the largest in Latin America when it opened in 1999. A 300-km railway link across the isthmus of Tehuantepec connects the Caribbean port of Coatzacoalcos with the Pacific port of Salina Cruz.

In 1992, as part of an ambitious divestment programme, the Government announced that concessions would be offered for sale to the private sector, in 1993, to operate nine ports and 61 of the country's airports. The national ports authority was to be disbanded, responsibility for each port being transferred to Administraciones Portuarias Integrales (APIs). In 1998 plans were announced for public share offerings in 35 airports.

Secretaría de Transportes y Comunicaciones: see section on The Government (Secretariats of State).

Aeropuertos y Servicios Auxiliares (ASA): Dir Alfredo Elias.

Caminos y Puentes Federales de Ingresos (CPFI): Dir Gustavo Petricioli.

STATE RAILWAYS

In 2000 there were 26,662 km of main line track. In 1999 the railway system carried 80.4m. metric tons of freight and an estimated 0.7m. passengers.

Ferrocarriles Nacionales de México (National Railways of Mexico): Centro Administrativo, Avda Jesús García Corona 140, 13°, Ala 'A', Col. Buenavista, 06358 México, DF; tel. (55) 5547-6857; fax (55) 5541-6054; f. 1873; govt-owned since 1937; restructuring and privatization of national railways commenced in 1996 (see below); responsibility for signalling to be held by the Ferrocarril Terminal Valle de México; construction work on new railway links in the state of Guanajuato (at an estimated cost of US $830m.) was scheduled to begin in the late 1990s; Gen. Dir Luis de Pablos.

Ferrocarril del Noreste: Avda Manuel L. Barragán 4850, 64420 Monterrey, NL; tel. (81) 51-1204; concession awarded to TFM Kansas City Southern in 1996; links Mexico City with the ports of Lázaro Cárdenas, Veracruz and Tampico, and the US border at Laredo; transports more than 40% of Mexico's rail freight; Pres. M. Mohar.

Ferrocarril Pacifico-Norte: Avda Enrique Díaz de Leon 336, Col. Moderna, 44100 Guadalajara, Jal. tel. (33) 825-6664; 50-year concession awarded to Grupo Ferroviario Mexicano, SA, commencing in 1998.

Ferrocarril del Sureste: Montesino 1 altos, Col. Centro, 91700 Veracruz, Ver. tel. (229) 32-6144; 50-year concession awarded to Triturados Basálticos y Derivados, SA in 1998.

Servicio de Transportes Eléctricos del Distrito Federal (STE): Avda Municipio Libre 402, Col. San Andrés Tetepilco, México, DF; tel. (55) 5539-6500; fax (55) 5672-4758; suburban tram route with 17 stops upgraded to light rail standard to act as a feeder to the metro; also operates bus and trolleybus networks; Dir-Gen. J. Ortega Cuevas.

Sistema de Transporte Colectivo (Metro): Delicias 67, 06070 México, DF; tel. (55) 5709-1133; fax (55) 5512-3601; internet www .metro.df.gob.mx; f. 1967; the first stage of a combined underground and surface railway system in Mexico City was opened in 1969; 10 lines, covering 158 km, were operating, in 1998, and five new lines, bringing the total distance to 315 km, are to be completed by 2010; the system is wholly state-owned and the fares are partially subsidized; Dir-Gen. Dr Javier González Garza.

ROADS

In 2000 there were an estimated 442,553 km of roads, of which 33.4% were paved. The construction of some 4,000 km of new four-lane toll highways, through the granting of govt concessions to the private sector, was undertaken during 1989–93. In mid-1997 the Govt announced that it would repurchase almost one-half of the road concessions granted in an attempt to stimulate road construction.

Long-distance buses form one of the principal methods of transport in Mexico, and there are some 600 lines operating services throughout the country.

Dirección General de Autotransporte Federal: Calzada de las Bombas 411, 11°, Col. San Bartolo Coapa, 04800 México, DF; tel. (55) 5684-0757; co-ordinates long distance bus services.

SHIPPING

At the end of 2001 Mexico's registered merchant fleet numbered 633 vessels, with a total displacement of 908,098 grt. The Government operates the facilities of seaports. In 1989–94 US $700m. was spent on port development, much of it from the private sector. In 1994–95 management of several ports were transferred to the private sector.

Coordinadora General de Puertos y Marina Mercante: Avda Municipio Libre 377, 12°, Ala 'B', Col. Santa Cruz Atoyac, Del. Cuauhtémoc, 03310 México, DF; tel. (55) 5688-5047; fax (55) 5688-7520; Dir Pedro Pablo Zepeda.

Port of Acapulco: Puertos Mexicanos, Malecón Fiscal s/n, Acapulco, Gro. tel. (744) 22067; fax (744) 31648; Harbour Master Capt. RENÉ F. NOVALES BETANZOS.

Port of Coatzacoalcos: Administración Portuaria Integral de Coatzacoalcos, SA de CV, Interior recinto portuario s/n Coatzacoalcos, 96400 Ver. tel. (921) 2147443; fax (921) 2146758; e-mail apicoa@apicoatza.com; Dir-Gen. Ing. GILBERTO ANTÓNIO RIOS RUÍZ.

Port of Dos Bocas: Administración Portuaria Integral de Dos Bocas, SA de CV, Carretera Federal Puerto Ceiba-Paraíso 414, Col. Quintín Arzuz Paraíso, 86600 Tabasco, Tab. tel. (933) 353-2744; e-mail dosbocas@apidosbocas.com; internet www.apidosbocas.com.

Port of Manzanillo: Administración Portuaria Integral de Manzanillo, SA de CV, Avda Tte Azueta 9, Fracc. Playa Azul, 28250 Manzanillo, Col. tel. (333) 21254; fax (333) 21005; e-mail apiman@bay.net.mx; Port Supt CARLOS CABANILLAS TIRADO.

Port of Tampico: Administración Portuaria Integral de Tampico, SA de CV, Edif. API de Tampico, 1°, Recinto Portuario, 89000 Tampico, Tamps. tel. (833) 212-4660; fax (833) 212-5744; e-mail apitam@puertodetampico.com.mx; internet www.puertodetampico.com.mx; Gen. Dir Ing. RAFAEL MESEGUER LIMA.

Port of Veracruz: Administración Porturia Integral de Veracruz, SA de CV, Marina Mercante 210, 7°, 91700 Veracruz, Ver. tel. (229) 32-1319; fax (229) 32-3040; e-mail portverc@infosel.net.mx; privatized in 1994; Port Dir JUAN JOSÉ SÁNCHEZ ESQUEDA.

Petróleos Mexicanos (PEMEX): Edif. 1917, 2°, Avda Marina Nacional 329, 44°, Col. Anáhuac, 11300 México, DF; tel. (55) 5531-6053; Dir-Gen. J. R. MOCTEZUMA.

Transportación Marítima Mexicana, SA de CV: Avda de la Cúspide 4755, Col. Parques del Pedregal, Del. Tlalpan, 14010 México, DF; tel. (55) 5652-4111; fax (55) 5665-3566; internet www.tmm.com.mx; f. 1955; cargo services to Europe, the Mediterranean, Scandinavia, the USA, South and Central America, the Caribbean and the Far East; Pres. JUAN CARLOS MERODIO; Dir-Gen. JAVIER SEGOVIA.

CIVIL AVIATION

There were 55 international airports in Mexico in 2000.

Aerocalifornia: Aquiles Serdán 1955, 23000 La Paz, BCS; tel. (612) 26655; fax (612) 53993; e-mail aeroll@aerocalifornia.uabcs.mx; f. 1960; regional carrier with scheduled passenger and cargo services in Mexico and the USA; Chair. PAUL A. ARECHIGA.

Aerocancún: Edif. Oasis 29, Avda Kukulcan, esq. Cenzontle, Zona Hotelera, 77500 Cancún, Q. Roo; tel. (988) 32475; fax (988) 32558; charter services to the USA, South America, the Caribbean and Europe; Dir-Gen. JAVIER MARANON.

Aerocaribe: Aeropuerto Internacional, Zona Hangares, 97291 Mérida, Yuc. tel. (999) 46-1307; fax (999) 46-1330; e-mail qamsc@mail.interaccess.mx.com; internet www.aerocaribe.com; f. 1975; operates a network of domestic passenger flights from Cancún and Mérida; subsidiary of Mexicana; Pres. JAIME VALENZUELA TAMARIZ.

Aerocozumel: Aeropuerto Internacional, Apdo 322, Cozumel, 77600 Q. Roo; tel. (987) 23456; fax (987) 20877; f. 1978; charter airline; subsidiary of Mexicana; Dir JAIME VALENZUELA TAMARIZ.

Aeromar, Transportes Aeromar: Aeropuerto Internacional, Zona E, Hangar 7, 15620 México, DF; tel. (55) 5756-0282; fax (55) 5756-0174; e-mail dirplan@netmex.com; f. 1987; scheduled domestic passenger and cargo services; Dir-Gen. JUAN I. STETA.

Aerovías de México (Aeroméxico): Paseo de la Reforma 445, 3°, Torre B, Col. Cuauhtémoc, 06500 México, DF; tel. (55) 5133-4000; fax (55) 5133-4619; internet www.aeromexico.com; f. 1934 as Aeronaves de México, nationalized 1959; fmrly Aeroméxico until 1988, when, following bankruptcy, the Govt sold a 75% stake to private investors and a 25% stake to the Asociación Sindical de Pilotos de México; services between most principal cities of Mexico and the USA, Brazil, Peru, France and Spain; CEO ARTURO BARAHONA; Pres. and Chair. ALFONSO PASQUEL.

Mexicana (Compañía Mexicana de Aviación, SA de CV): Xola 535, 30°, Col. del Valle, Apdo 12813, 03100 México, DF; tel. (55) 5448-3000; tel. 01771247; fax (55) 5687-8786; e-mail dirgenmx@mexicana.com.mx; internet www.mexicana.com; f. 1921; operated as private co, until July 1982, when the Govt took a 58% stake; in 1989 it was returned to private ownership; international services between Mexico City and the USA, Central America and the Caribbean; domestic services; Pres. and CEO FERNANDO P. FLORES.

Tourism

Tourism remains one of Mexico's principal sources of foreign exchange. Mexico received an estimated 19.8m. foreign visitors in 2001, and receipts from tourists in that year were estimated at US $8,401m. More than 90% of visitors come from the USA and Canada. The country is famous for volcanoes, coastal scenery and the great Sierra Nevada (Sierra Madre) mountain range. The relics of the Mayan and Aztec civilizations and of Spanish Colonial Mexico are of historic and artistic interest. Zihuatanejo, on the Pacific coast, and Cancún, on the Caribbean, were developed as tourist resorts by the Government. In 1998 there were 392,402 hotel rooms in Mexico. The government tourism agency, FONATUR, encourages the renovation and expansion of old hotels and provides attractive incentives for the industry. FONATUR is also the main developer of major resorts in Mexico.

Secretariat of State for Tourism: see section on The Government (Secretariats of State).

Fondo Nacional de Fomento al Turismo (FONATUR): Insurgentes Sur 800, 17°, Col. del Valle, 03100 México, DF; tel. (55) 5687-2697; f. 1956 to finance and promote the devt of tourism; Dir-Gen. Dr KEMIL A. RIZK.

THE FEDERATED STATES OF MICRONESIA

Introductory Survey

Location, Climate, Language, Religion, Flag, Capital

The Federated States of Micronesia forms (with Palau, q.v.) the archipelago of the Caroline Islands, about 800 km east of the Philippines. The Federated States of Micronesia comprises 607 islands and includes (from west to east) the states of Yap, Chuuk (formerly Truk), Pohnpei (formerly Ponape) and Kosrae. The islands are subject to heavy rainfall, although precipitation decreases from east to west. January, February and March are the driest months, although seasonal variations in rainfall and temperature are generally small. Average annual temperature is 27°C (81°F). The native population consists of various ethno-linguistic groups, but English is widely understood. The principal religion is Christianity, much of the population being Roman Catholic. The national flag (proportions 10 by 19) consists of four five-pointed white stars, arranged as a circle, situated centrally on a light blue field. The capital is Kolonia, on Pohnpei.

Recent History

The Federated States of Micronesia was formerly part of the US-administered Trust Territory of the Pacific Islands (for history up to 1965, see the chapter on the Marshall Islands).

From 1965 there were increasing demands for local autonomy within the Trust Territory of the Pacific Islands. In that year the Congress of Micronesia was formed, and in 1967 a commission was established to examine the future political status of the islands. In 1970 it declared Micronesians' rights to sovereignty over their own lands, to self-determination, to devise their own constitution and to revoke any form of free association with the USA. In May 1977, after eight years of negotiations, US President Jimmy Carter announced that his administration intended to adopt measures to terminate the trusteeship agreement by 1981. Until 1979 the four districts of Yap, Truk (Chuuk since 1990), Ponape (Pohnpei since 1984) and Kosrae were governed by a local Administrator, appointed by the President of the USA. However, on 10 May 1979 the four districts ratified a new Constitution to become the Federated States of Micronesia. The Constitution was promulgated in 1980.

The USA signed the Compact of Free Association with the Republic of Palau in August 1982, and with the Marshall Islands and the Federated States of Micronesia in October. Under the Compacts, the four countries (including the Northern Mariana Islands) became independent of each other and took charge of both their internal and foreign affairs separately, while the USA remained responsible for defence and security. The Compact was approved by plebiscite in the Federated States of Micronesia in June 1983, and was ratified by the islands' Congress in September.

In May 1986 the UN Trusteeship Council endorsed the US Government's request for the termination of the existing trusteeship agreement with the islands. US administration of the Federated States of Micronesia was formally ended in November of that year. The UN Security Council ratified the termination of the trusteeship agreement in December 1990. Ponape was renamed Pohnpei in November 1984, when its Constitution came into effect. Truk was renamed Chuuk in January 1990, when its new Constitution was proposed (being later adopted). The Federated States of Micronesia was admitted to the UN in September 1991.

The incumbent President (since 1987), John Haglelgam, was replaced by Bailey Olter, a former Vice-President, in May 1991. At congressional elections in March 1995 Olter was re-elected to the Pohnpei Senator-at-Large seat, and in early May he was re-elected to the presidency unopposed. Similarly, Jacob Nena was re-elected as Vice-President. Allegations that financial misman-agement by the Governor of Chuuk, Sasao Gouland, had resulted in state debts of some US $20m. led to his resignation in June 1996, in order to avoid impeachment proceedings. In July Olter suffered a stroke. Jacob Nena served as acting

President during Olter's absence from office, and in May 1997 was sworn in as President of the country. (Olter died in February 1999.)

Congressional elections took place in early March 1997 for the 10 Senators elected on a two-yearly basis, at which all of the incumbents were returned to office. A referendum held concurrently on a proposed amendment to the Constitution (which envisaged increasing the allocation of national revenue to the state legislatures from 50% to 80% of the total budget) was approved in Chuuk and Yap, but rejected in Pohnpei and Kosrae.

Allegations of government interference in the media became widespread when the editor of the country's principal news-paper, *FSM News*, was refused permission to re-enter the islands in June 1997. The Government had sought to deport the editor (who was a Canadian national) following publication in the periodical of reports on government spending, which the authorities claimed were false and malicious. It was also thought that by enforcing the exclusion order, the Government hoped to suppress the publication in the newspaper of information relating to alleged corruption among public officials. The newspaper ceased publication in late 1997.

In February 1998 Congress approved proposals to restructure and reorganize the Cabinet. Several ministerial portfolios were consequently merged or abolished, with the aim of reducing government expenditure. Congressional elections took place on 2 March 1999, at which President Nena was re-elected to the Kosrae Senator-at-Large seat and Vice-President Leo Falcam to the Pohnpei Senator-at-Large seat. On 11 May Congress elected Falcam as President and the Chuuk Senator-at-Large, Redley Killion, as Vice-President.

A first round of renegotiation of the Compact of Free Association (certain terms of which were due to expire in 2001) was completed in late 1999. The USA and the Federated States of Micronesia pledged to maintain defence and security relations. It was also agreed that the USA would continue to provide economic aid to the islands and assist in the development of the private sector, as well as in promoting greater economic self-sufficiency. The Federated States of Micronesia undertook to ensure greater accountability with regard to US funding provided under the Compact. Financial terms allowing the USA exclusive access to the waters of the Federated States of Micronesia were under discussion in April 2000, when Micronesia proposed that the USA grant annual assistance of US $84m. for 20 years, as well as finance a trust fund of $20m. over the same period. In July 2001 the USA agreed to grant annual assistance of $61m. and a trust fund of $13m., which was to be paid over a period of 15 years, expressing concern that the $2,600m. of funds it had given to Micronesia and the Marshall Islands had been mismanaged. The provision of the Compact for the funding needs for Micronesia was originally due to expire on 3 November 2001, but negotiations continued during 2002 and into 2003. Provisions guaranteed a funding extension of two years for such an eventuality, during which period US assistance to Micronesia would increase by some $17m, or the 15-year average of annual US payments, known as 'bump-up' funding. Following the proposal by the USA in April 2002 to extend economic assistance for a period of 20 years, commencing with $72m. in 2004, and decreasing gradually each year thereafter, a new funding structure was agreed between the two countries in early November. Despite Micronesia's stated 'reservations', the terms included the establishment of a trust fund of $19m., to increase each year, in order to offset the agreed $800,000 decline in the annual US grant to Micronesia from 2007 and the termination of direct financial assistance after 2023. Under the terms of the new Compact, Micronesia would also be obliged to provide frequent, strictly-monitored audit information on all US funding. Furthermore, in March 2003 a provision was made under the 2004 US budget granting citizens of Micronesia access to private healthcare resources in the USA. The implementation of the new Compact of Free Association measures required the approval of the US Congress prior to October 2003.

In December 1996 a state of emergency was declared after a typhoon wreaked devastation on the islands of Yap. Flooding and mudslides in Pohnpei in April 1997, as a result of heavy rain, caused the deaths of more than 20 people; another typhoon in mid-1997 left several people dead. Furthermore, in early 1998 a state of emergency was declared, owing to severe drought throughout the islands, believed to have been caused by El Niño (a periodic warming of the tropical Pacific Ocean). In late 2000 marine biologists issued a warning regarding the erosion of the islands' coastlines, caused by the destruction of the coral reefs by pollution, overfishing and increasing sea temperatures.

In May 2000 a state of emergency was declared on Pohnpei, following an outbreak of cholera. In August the Government announced a vaccination scheme for the entire population over two years of age. Import restrictions were introduced on the surrounding islands. Pohnpei was officially declared free of cholera on 16 February 2001. During the epidemic some 20 people had died and a further 3,525 were estimated to have been infected.

Congressional elections took place on 6 March 2001 for the 10 Senators elected on a two-yearly basis and for the representatives to the Third Constitutional Convention. All the incumbents were returned to office, with the exception of the late Senator Nishima Yleizah, whose seat was occupied by Marcellino Umwech. In early April the new Cabinet was confirmed. On 9 April Senator Wagner Moses Lawrence, a member of Congress and the representative of Pohnpei's 2nd Congressional District, Madolenihmw and Kitti, died. His cousin, Onlino Lawrence, won the special election for the vacant seat, held on 30 June, and was accredited in July.

In early July 2002 at least 49 people died and extensive damage was caused to crops and buildings on Chuuk during a severe tropical storm. In early December the islands suffered further damage (albeit without loss of life) when a typhoon struck. President George W. Bush of the USA declared Micronesia a federal disaster area and ordered emergency US funding and resources to be allocated to the relief effort.

In September 2002 unrest occurred on the Faichuk islands, part of Chuuk, where the Faichuk Commission for Statehood continued its campaign to secede from Chuuk and gain equal status within the Federation. Local dissatisfaction worsened following allegations of electoral manipulation against the village mayor of Udot island, with a large crowd appearing to support attempts by local security forces to prevent the mayor's arrest by National Police. The issue of Faichuk's status remained unresolved in early 2003.

Also in September 2002 a referendum was held on a number of proposed amendments to the Constitution. The prospective changes included a provision for the direct election of presidential candidates, the extension of the right of islanders to hold dual citizenship and changes to the distribution formula for Compact of Free Association funds. However, amid widespread voter apathy, the proposals failed to achieve the required three-quarters' majority of votes and were thus rejected.

Prior to congressional elections in early March 2003, some controversy was created by the arrest in late December 2002 of the Speaker of Congress and Chuuk gubernatorial candidate, Jack Fritz, on charges of embezzlement of government funds. Notably, however, the result of the elections included the unexpected failure of President Leo Falcam to achieve re-election to a further four-year term as Senator-at-Large for Pohnpei. In mid-May 2003 Joseph J. Urusemal, Senator-at-Large for Yap, was confirmed as the country's President. The elections themselves were also the subject of some controversy, as it appeared that elected officials had disbursed a portion of the 2002 'bump-up' US funding for Micronesia (see above) in order to enhance their electoral prospects. The misallocation of funds was reportedly a significant factor in the deterioration of the financial positions of Chuuk state, Pohnpei and Kosrae during 2002 and 2003. Furthermore, in November 2002, the decision of the Bank of Hawaii (BoH) to close its office in the islands, which considerably reduced local access to banking facilities, prompted the Government to remove the BoH from its position as the principal manager of official funds and to withdraw Micronesia's deposits with the bank.

In November 2002, following a conference in Manila, the Philippines, attended by Pacific nations and those industrialized countries with significant fishing interests in the region,

Micronesia was awarded the bid to establish a headquarters for a new body to manage migratory fish stocks in the Central and Western Pacific, to be known as the Tuna Commission. The remit for the organization included the management of waters outside each nation's 200-mile exclusive economic zone, in line with the framework established under the 1995 UN Fish Stocks Agreement. Despite some doubt over the finality of Micronesia's nomination, in February 2003 a Tuna Commission Task Force was created to establish a location for the organization's headquarters on Pohnpei. In the same month Pohnpei hosted the first Summit of Micronesian Leaders.

Government

On 10 May 1979 the locally drafted Constitution of the Federated States of Micronesia, incorporating the four states of Kosrae, Yap, Ponape (later Pohnpei) and Truk (later Chuuk), became effective. The federal legislature, the Congress, comprises 14 members (Senators). The four states each elect one 'Senator-at-Large', for a four-year term. The remaining 10 Senators are elected for two-year terms: their seats are distributed in proportion to the population of each state. Each of the four states also has its own Constitution, Governor and legislature. The federal President and Vice-President are elected by the Congress from among the four Senators-at-Large; the offices rotate among the four states. (By-elections are then held for the seats to which the President and Vice-President had been elected.) In November 1986 the Compact of Free Association was signed by the Governments of the Federated States of Micronesia and the USA. Certain of its terms, due to expire in 2001, were renegotiated in late 1999. By the terms of the Compact, the Federated States of Micronesia is a sovereign, self-governing state.

Local government units are the municipalities and villages. Elected Magistrates and Councils govern the municipalities. Village government is largely traditional.

Defence

The USA is responsible for the defence of the Federated States of Micronesia.

Economic Affairs

In 2001, according to estimates by the World Bank, gross national income (GNI) in the Federated States of Micronesia, measured at average 1999–2001 prices, was US $258m., equivalent to $2,150 per head. During 1990–2001, it was estimated, the population increased at an average annual rate of 2.0%, while gross domestic product (GDP) per head decreased, in real terms, by an average of 0.5% per year. Overall GDP increased, in real terms, at an average annual rate of 1.5% in 1990–2001; growth in 2001 was 0.9%.

Agriculture is mainly on a subsistence level, although its importance is diminishing. The principal crops are coconuts (from which some 500 short tons of copra were produced in 2001), bananas, betel-nuts, cassava and sweet potatoes. White peppercorns are produced on Pohnpei. The sector (including forestry and fishing) contributed 19.1% to GDP in 1996 and engaged 55.3% of the employed labour force in 2000. Exports of bananas accounted for 1.2% of export earnings in 1999, while exports of marine products accounted for 91.9% of total export revenue in that year. Fees earned from fisheries licensing agreements, mainly with Japan, account for a substantial percentage of domestic budgetary revenue. In 1999/2000 fishing access fees totalled $16.8m. In November 2002 Micronesia was announced as the location of the headquarters for a new multilateral agency to manage migratory fish stocks in the region, to be known as the Tuna Commission.

Industry (including mining, manufacturing, utilities and construction) provided 3.9% of GDP in 1996. There is little manufacturing, other than garment production (in Yap) and the manufacture of buttons using trochus shells. The sector provided 1.4% of GDP in 1996 and engaged 3.5% of the employed labour force in 1994. The islands are dependent on imported fuels (which accounted for 20.3% of the value of total imports in 1999).

The services sector provided an estimated 77.0% of GDP in 1996 (with government services alone contributing 42.1%). A total of 6,015 people were employed by the national and state Governments in 1996/97. Tourism is an increasingly important industry; it was hoped that several projects to improve communications would further stimulate tourism, hitherto hindered by the territory's remote situation. The industry was identified in a report by the Asian Development Bank (ADB) in mid-1995 as having the greatest potential for development and thus contribution to the islands' economic growth. In 2001, however, the number of visitor arrivals, according to the ADB, declined to 15,250, compared with 16,500 in the previous year.

In the financial year ending September 2001 there was a visible trade deficit of an estimated US $130.8m., but an estimated surplus of $3.3m. on the current account of the balance of payments. The principal sources of imports in 1999 were the USA (which supplied 43.9% of the total) and Australia (19.8%). Japan was the principal market for exports in 1999, purchasing 83.9% of the total. In 1999 the main imports were food and live animals (24.8% of the total), mineral fuels and lubricants (20.3%), machines and transport equipment (19.5%) and basic manufactures (18.9%). The dominant exports were fish and fish products, mainly in the form of re-exports to Japan by foreign vessels (accounting for 91.9% of total export earnings in 1999).

In 1999/2000 there was an estimated budget surplus of US $0.4m. However, the fiscal surpluses reported for 2002 and 2003 were estimated to have been resulted primarily from increased US aid payments. The Federated States of Micronesia relies heavily on financial assistance, particularly from the USA, which according to the IMF provided an estimated $97.7m. (equivalent to 42.1% of GDP) in 2002. At the end of the 2000/01 financial year the islands' total external debt was estimated at US $58m., and in that year the cost of debt-servicing was forecast by the ADB to be equivalent to 22.0% of the value of exports of goods and services. However, by the end of 2002 the Government had successfully repaid its outstanding commercial debt; the public debt-service ratio, meanwhile, declined sharply to 6.0% of the value of exports. According to the ADB, the inflation rate steadily decreased from an estimated annual average of 6.0% in 1993 to 1.5% in 1998, before rising to 2.6% in 1999 and to 3.2% in 2000, then declining to 2.6% in 2001. According to the ADB, some 2.6% of the labour force were unemployed in 2000.

The Federated States of Micronesia is a member of the Pacific Community (see p. 304), the Pacific Islands Forum (see p. 306), the South Pacific Regional Trade and Economic Co-operation Agreement (SPARTECA, see p. 308), and the UN Economic and Social Commission for Asia and the Pacific (ESCAP, see p. 28) and the Asian Development Bank (ADB, see p. 143). The Council of Micronesian Government Executives, of which the Federated States of Micronesia was a founder member in 1996, aims to facilitate discussion of economic developments in the region and to examine possibilities for reducing the considerable cost of shipping essential goods between the islands.

The islands are vulnerable to adverse climatic conditions, as was illustrated in late 1997 and early 1998, when a prolonged drought caused problems throughout the islands, and in 2002 following a series of tropical storms. An extremely high rate of natural increase in the population has exacerbated certain economic problems, but is, however, partially offset by an annual emigration rate of more than 2%. With the renegotiation of several terms of the Compact of Free Association in late 1999 (see Recent History), the USA emphasized its continued commitment to the economic development of the islands, including the promotion of greater self-sufficiency, in return for improved accountability regarding US funding by the Micronesia Government. In December 2000 the ADB approved a US $8m. loan to fund a six-year reform programme of the health and education sectors, and followed this in December 2001 with a further loan of $13m., targeted at job creation, increasing production for both domestic and export markets, and the development of a competitive services sector. However, the private sector continued to be constrained by the disproportionately high cost of domestic labour, rates of pay in the public sector having risen substantially in recent years as a result of the large external inflows (although public sector salaries were 'frozen' under the 2004 budget). Moreover, an IMF report released in February 2003 noted that infrastructure for the private sector remained underdeveloped, notwithstanding the authorities' largely positive oversight of the banking sector. Further criticism was attached to the private sector's role as an effective provider of services to the public sector, and the public sector's tendency to operate in unequal competition with private-sector interests. Concerns also continued as to the relative lack of progress in restructuring the economy in preparation for the potentially dramatic impact of the decline and eventual withdrawal of direct US aid in 2023. (According to the UN, bilateral and multilateral aid to Micronesia totalled $101.6m. in 2000, the latter accounting for only $5.0m. of the total.) The trust fund for Micronesia established to alleviate such pressures was expected to remain vulnerable to international economic performance, the majority of this capital being invested in US stock markets. The 2002 fiscal deficit, excluding the increase in US aid payments in the year, of approximately $11m.–$12m. (equivalent to some 5% of GDP) remained a cause for concern, although the difficulties were judged to be largely due to the ongoing financial problems of the National Government and Chuuk state. None the less, a number of apparently positive measures were adopted in 2002, including an agreement in June between the Micronesian Government and the ADB to prepare a National Poverty Reduction Strategy. The repayment of substantial portions of Micronesia's external debt during 2001, and consequently reduced debt-servicing obligations from 2002, was expected to improve long-term economic prospects. However, the islands' comparatively remote position remained a factor in the development of future sources of earnings such as tourism, and while the fishing sector continued to decline. Economic growth was reported to have reached 1.5% in 2001. The IMF, however, estimated GDP growth of only 0.8% for the year ending September 2002.

Education

Primary education, which begins at six years of age and lasts for eight years, is compulsory. Secondary education, beginning at 14 years of age, comprises two cycles, each of two years. The Micronesia Maritime and Fisheries Academy, which was opened in Yap in 1990, provides education and training in fisheries technology at secondary and tertiary levels. The College of Micronesia offers two- and three-year programmes leading to a degree qualification. A summit meeting was held in September 2000 to discuss the improvement and reform of the education sector. In 1997 Micronesia had a student-teacher ratio of 17. An average of 37% of students remained in education from first grade to graduation.

Public Holidays

2003: 1 January (New Year's Day), 18 April (Good Friday, Pohnpei only), 10 May (Constitution Day), 24 October (United Nations Day), 3 November (Independence Day), 25 December (Christmas Day).

2004: 1 January (New Year's Day), 9 April (Good Friday, Pohnpei only), 10 May (Constitution Day), 24 October (United Nations Day), 3 November (Independence Day), 25 December (Christmas Day).

Weights and Measures

With certain exceptions, the imperial system is in force. One US cwt equals 100 lb; one long ton equals 2,240 lb; one short ton equals 2,000 lb. A policy of gradual voluntary conversion to the metric system is being undertaken.

Statistical Survey

Note: Further statistics relating to the Federated States of Micronesia are to be found in the chapter on the Marshall Islands

AREA AND POPULATION

Area: 700 sq km (270.3 sq miles): Chuuk (294 islands) 127 sq km; Kosrae (5 islands) 110 sq km; Pohnpei (163 islands) 344 sq km; Yap (145 islands) 119 sq km.

Population: 105,506 (53,923 males, 51,583 females) at census of 18 September 1994; 107,008 (males 54,191, females 52,817) at 2000 census (provisional). *By State* (2000): Chuuk 53,595; Kosrae 7,686; Pohnpei 34,486; Yap 11,241.

Density (2000): 153 per sq km. *By State* (per sq km): Chuuk 422.0; Kosrae 70.0; Pohnpei 100.3; Yap 94.5.

Births and Deaths (2000, official estimates): Birth rate 27.1 per 1,000; Death rate 6.0 per 1,000.

Expectation of Life (WHO estimates, years at birth): 66.1 (males 64.6; females 67.8) in 2001. Source: WHO, *World Health Report*.

Economically Active Population ('000 persons, 2000): Agriculture, forestry and fishing 17.25; Total employed (incl. others) 31.21; Unemployed 0.82; Total labour force 32.02. Source: Asian Development Bank, *Key Indicators of Developing Asian and Pacific Countries*.

HEALTH AND WELFARE

Key Indicators

Total Fertility Rate (children per woman, 2001): 5.1.

Under-5 Mortality Rate (per 1,000 live births, 2001): 24.

Physicians (per 1,000 head, 1999): 0.57.

Hospital Beds (per 1,000 head, 1989): 3.47.

Health Expenditure (2000): US $ per head (PPP): 343.

Health Expenditure (2000): % of GDP: 10.5.

Health Expenditure (2000): public (% of total): 53.7 . For sources and definitions, see explanatory note on p. vi.

AGRICULTURE, ETC.

Principal Crops* (FAO estimates, '000 metric tons, 2001): Coconuts 140; Cassava 12; Bananas 2; Sweet potatoes 3. Source: FAO.

Livestock* (FAO estimates, '000 head, year ending September 2001): Pigs 32; Cattle 14; Goats 4; Poultry 185. Source: FAO.

Livestock Products* ('000 metric tons, 2001): Beef and veal 245; Pig meat 873; Poultry meat 135; Hen eggs 175; Cattle hides 45. Source: FAO.
* Including the Northern Mariana Islands, the Marshall Islands and Palau.

Fishing ('000 metric tons, live weight, 2000): Skipjack tuna 19.2; Yellowfin tuna 6.4; Bigeye tuna 1.0; Total (incl. others) 28.0 (FAO estimate). Source: FAO, *Yearbook of Fishery Statistics*.

FINANCE

Currency and Exchange Rates: United States currency is used: 100 cents = 1 United States dollar (US $). *Sterling and Euro Equivalents* (31 December 2002): £1 sterling = US $1.6118; €1 = 1.05 US cents; US $100 = £62.04 = €95.36.

Budget (estimates, US $ million, year ending 30 September 2000): *Revenue:* Domestic 56.6 (Tax 26.3, Non-tax 30.3); Grants 96.2; Total 152.8. *Expenditure:* Recurrent 124.4; Capital 28.0; Total 152.4. Source: Asian Development Bank, *Key Indicators of Developing Asian and Pacific Countries*.

Gross Domestic Product by Economic Activity (US $ million at current prices, 1996): Agriculture, forestry and fishing 34.7; Mining and quarrying 0.7; Manufacturing 2.6; Electricity, gas and water 1.9; Construction 1.9; Wholesale and retail trade 39.5; Hotels and restaurants 4.1; Transport, storage and communications 8.5; Finance, real estate and business services 5.5; Government services 76.5; Other services 5.6; GDP in purchasers' values 181.5. Source: IMF, *Federated States of Micronesia: Recent Economic Developments* (August 1998).

Balance of Payments (estimates, US $ million, year ending 30 September 2001): Merchandise exports (incl. re-exports) f.o.b. 23.8; Merchandise imports f.o.b. −154.6; *Trade balance* −130.8; Exports of services 57.9; Imports of services −42.0; *Balance on goods and services* −114.9; Private unrequited transfers 4.2; Official unrequited transfers 107.4; *Current balance* −3.3; Long-term capital (net) −8.9; Short-term capital (net) −2.8; Net errors and omissions 11.0; *Overall balance* −4.0. Source: Asian Development Bank, *Key Indicators of Developing Asian and Pacific Countries*.

EXTERNAL TRADE

Principal Commodities (estimates, US $'000, 1999): *Imports:* Food and live animals 3,053; Beverages and tobacco 738; Crude materials (inedible) except fuel 52; Mineral fuels, lubricants, etc. 2,503; Chemicals 534; Basic manufactures 2,326; Machinery and transport equipment 2,406; Miscellaneous manufactured articles 701; Total (incl. others) 12,328. *Exports:* Fish 1,956; Bananas 25; Total (incl. others) 2,128. Source: Asian Development Bank, *Key Indicators of Developing Asian and Pacific Countries*.

Principal Trading Partners (US $'000, 1999): *Imports:* Australia 2,440; Japan 1,536; USA 5,409; Total (incl. others) 12,328. *Exports:* Japan 1,785; Marshall Islands 23; Total (incl. others) 2,128. Source: Asian Development Bank, *Key Indicators of Developing Asian and Pacific Countries*.

TRANSPORT

Shipping: *Merchant Fleet* (registered at 31 December 2001): Vessels 18; Total displacement ('000 grt) 9.2. Source: Lloyd's Register-Fairplay, *World Fleet Statistics*.

TOURISM

Foreign Tourist Arrivals: 27,222 in 1998; 27,853 in 1999; 32,530 in 2000. Source: World Tourism Organization, *Yearbook of Tourism Statistics*.

Tourist Arrivals by Country of Residence (2000): Australia 895; China, People's Republic 3,639; Japan 6,044; Korea, Republic 2,386; Philippines 2,893; Taiwan 1,197; USA 8,789; Total (incl. others) 32,530. Source: World Tourism Organization, *Yearbook of Tourism Statistics*.

COMMUNICATIONS MEDIA

Telephones ('000 main lines in use, 2001): 10.0*.

Facsimile Machines (number in use, 1998): 539*.

Radio Receivers (1996): 22,000 in use.

Internet Users ('000, 2000): 4.0*.

Television Receivers (1996): 19,800 in use.

* Source: International Telecommunication Union.

EDUCATION

Primary (1995): 174 schools; 1,051 teachers (1984); 27,281 pupils.

Secondary (1995): 24 schools; 314 teachers (1984); 6,898 pupils.

Tertiary (1994): 1,461 students.
Source: UN, *Statistical Yearbook for Asia and the Pacific*.

Directory

The Constitution

On 10 May 1979 the locally-drafted Constitution of the Federated States of Micronesia, incorporating the four states of Kosrae, Yap, Ponape (formally renamed Pohnpei in November 1984) and Truk (renamed Chuuk in January 1990), became effective. Each of the four states has its own Constitution, elected legislature and Governor. The Constitution guarantees fundamental human rights and establishes a separation of the judicial, executive and legislative powers. The federal legislature, the Congress of the Federated States of Micronesia, is a unicameral parliament with 14 members, popularly elected. The executive consists of the President, elected by the Congress, and a Cabinet. The Constitution provides for a review of the governmental and federal system every 10 years.

In November 1986 the Compact of Free Association was signed by the Governments of the Federated States of Micronesia and the USA. By the terms of the Compact, the Federated States of Micronesia is an internally sovereign, self-governing state, whose policy concerning foreign affairs must be consistent with guidelines laid down in the Compact. Full responsibility for defence lies with the USA, which also undertakes to provide regular economic assistance. The security arrangements may be terminated only by mutual agreement. The economic and defence provisions of the Compact are renewable after 15 years (a first round of negotiations was completed in 1999), but the status of free association continues indefinitely.

The Government

HEAD OF STATE

President: JOSEPH J. URUSEMAL (elected 11 May 2003).
Vice-President: REDLEY KILLION.

THE CABINET
(May 2003)

Secretary of the Department of Finance and Administration: JOHN EHSA.

Secretary of the Department of Foreign Affairs: IESKE K. IEHSI.

Secretary of the Department of Economic Affairs: SEBASTIAN ANEFAL.

Secretary of the Department of Health, Education and Social Services: Dr ELIUEL K. PRETRICK.

Secretary of the Department of Justice: PAUL McILRATH.

Secretary of the Department of Transportation, Communications and Infrastructure: AKALINO H. SUSAIA.

Public Defender: BEAUTEAN C. WORSWICK.

GOVERNMENT OFFICES

Office of the President: POB PS-53, Palikir, Pohnpei, FM 96941; tel. 320-2228; fax 320-2785.

Department of Economic Affairs: POB PS-12, Palikir, Pohnpei, FM 96941; tel. 320-2646; fax 320-5854; e-mail fsmrd@mail.fm; internet www.fsminvest.fm.

Department of Finance and Administration: POB PS-158, Palikir, Pohnpei, FM 96941; tel. 320-2640; fax 320-2380.

Department of Foreign Affairs: POB PS-123, Palikir, Pohnpei, FM 96941; tel. 320-2641; fax 320-2933; e-mail foreignaffairs@mail.fm.

Department of Health, Education and Social Services: POB PS-70, Palikir, Pohnpei, FM 96941; tel. 320-2872; fax 320-5263.

Department of Justice: POB PS-105, Palikir, Pohnpei, FM 96941; tel. 320-2644; fax 320-2234.

Department of Transportation, Communications and Infrastructure: POB PS-2, Palikir, Pohnpei, FM 96941; tel. 320-2865; fax 320-5853.

Office of the Public Defender: POB PS-174, Palikir, Pohnpei, FM 96941; tel. 320-2648; fax 320-5775.

Public Information Office: POB PS-34, Palikir, Pohnpei, FM 96941; tel. 320-2548; fax 320-4356; internet www.fsmgov.org.

The Legislature

CONGRESS OF THE FEDERATED STATES OF MICRONESIA

The Congress comprises 14 members (Senators), of whom four are elected for a four-year term and 10 for a two-year term.
Speaker: PETER CHRISTIAN.

STATE LEGISLATURES

Chuuk State Legislature: POB 189, Weno, Chuuk, FM 96942; tel. 330-2234; fax 330-2233; Senate of 10 mems and House of Representatives of 28 mems elected for four years; Gov. ANSITO WALTER.

Kosrae State Legislature: POB 187, Tofol, Kosrae, FM 96944; tel. 370-3002; fax 370-3162; e-mail kosraelc@mail.fm; unicameral body of 14 mems serving for four years; Gov. RENSLEY A. SIGRAH.

Pohnpei State Legislature: POB 39, Kolonia, Pohnpei, FM 96941; tel. 320-2235; fax 320-2505; internet www.fm/pohnpeileg/; 27 representatives elected for four years (terms staggered); Gov. JOHNNY P. DAVID.

Yap State Legislature: POB 39, Colonia, Yap, FM 96943; tel. 350-2108; fax 350-4113; 10 mems, six elected from the Yap Islands proper and four elected from the Outer Islands of Ulithi and Woleai, for a four-year term; Gov. VINCENT A. FIGIR.

Diplomatic Representation

EMBASSIES IN MICRONESIA

Australia: POB S, Kolonia, Pohnpei, FM 96941; tel. 320-5448; fax 320-5449; e-mail australia@mail.fm; internet www.australianembassy.fm; Ambassador BRENDAN DORAN.

China, People's Republic: Kolonia, Pohnpei, FM 96941; Ambassador XU JUN.

Japan: Pami Bldg, 3rd Floor, POB 1847, Kolonia, Pohnpei, FM 96941; tel. 320-5465; fax 320–5470; Chargé d'affaires a.i. SHIGEATSU NAKAJIMA.

USA: POB 1286, Kolonia, Pohnpei, FM 96941; tel. 320-2187; fax 320-2186; e-mail usembassy@mail.fm; internet www.fm/usembassy/index.htm; Ambassador LARRY DINGER.

Judicial System

Supreme Court of the Federated States of Micronesia: POB PS-J, Palikir Station, Pohnpei, FM 96941; tel. 320-2357; fax 320-2756; Chief Justice ANDON L. AMARAICH.

State Courts and Appellate Courts have been established in Yap, Chuuk, Kosrae and Pohnpei.

Religion

The population is predominantly Christian, mainly Roman Catholic. The Assembly of God, Jehovah's Witnesses, Seventh-day Adventists, the Church of Jesus Christ of Latter-day Saints (Mormons), the United Church of Christ, Baptists and the Bahá'í Faith are also represented.

CHRISTIANITY

The Roman Catholic Church

The Federated States of Micronesia forms a part of the diocese of the Caroline Islands, suffragan to the archdiocese of Agaña (Guam). The Bishop participates in the Catholic Bishops' Conference of the Pacific, based in Fiji. At 31 December 2000 there were 70,185 adherents in the diocese.

Bishop of the Caroline Islands: Most Rev. AMANDO SAMO, Bishop's House, POB 939, Weno, Chuuk, FM 96942; tel. 330-2399; fax 330-4585; e-mail diocese@mail.fm; internet www.diocesecarolines.org.

Other Churches

United Church of Christ in Pohnpei: Kolonia, Pohnpei, FM 96941.

Liebenzell Mission: Rev. Roland Rauchholz, POB 9, Weno, Chuuk, FM 96942; tel. 330-3869.

The Press

Chuuk News Chronicle: POB 244, Wenn, Chuuk, FM 96942; f. 1983; Editor MARCIANA AKASY.

FSM—Job Training Partnership Act News: Pohnpei, FM 96941; f. 1994; monthly; US-funded.

The Island Tribune: Pohnpei, FM 96941; f. 1997; 2 a week.

Micronesia Focus: Pohnpei, FM 96941; f. 1994; Editor KETSON JOHNSON.

The National Union: FSM Public Information Office, POB 490, Kolonia, Pohnpei, FM 96941; tel. 320-2548; f. 1980; 2 a month; Public Information Officer KETSON JOHNSON; circ. 5,000.

Broadcasting and Communications

TELECOMMUNICATIONS

FSM Telecommunication Corporation: POB 1210, Kolonia, Pohnpei, FM 96941; tel. 320-2740; fax 320-2745; e-mail takinaga@ mail.fm; internet www.telecom.fm; provides domestic and international services; Gen. Man. TAKURO AKINAGA.

BROADCASTING

Radio

Federated States of Micronesia Public Information Office: POB PS-34, Palikir, Pohnpei, FM 96941; tel. 320-2548; fax 320-4356; e-mail fsmpio@mail.fm; internet www.fsmpio.fm; govt-operated; four regional stations, each broadcasting 18 hours daily; Information Officer TERRY G. THINOM.

Station V6AH: POB 1086, Kolonia, Pohnpei, FM 96941; programmes in English and Ponapean; Man. DUSTY FREDERICK.

Station V6AI: POB 117, Colonia, Yap, FM 96943; tel. 350-2174; fax 350-4426; programmes in English, Yapese, Ulithian and Satawalese; Man. PETER GARAMFEL.

Station V6AJ: POB 147, Tofol, Kosrae, FM 96944; tel. 370-3040; fax 370-3880; e-mail v6aj.@mail.fm; programmes in English and Kosraean; Man. NENA TOLENNA.

Station V6AK: Wenn, Chuuk, FM 96942; programmes in Chuukese and English; Man. P. J. MAIPI.

Television

Island Cable TV—Pohnpei: POB 1628, Pohnpei, FM 96941; tel. 320-2671; fax 320-2670; e-mail ictv@mail.fm; f. 1991; Pres. BERNARD HELGENBERGER; Gen. Man. DAVID O. CLIFFE.

TV Station Chuuk (TTKK): Wenn, Chuuk, FM 96942; commercial.

TV Station Pohnpei (KPON): Central Micronesia Communications, POB 460, Kolonia, Pohnpei, FM 96941; f. 1977; commercial; Pres. BERNARD HELGENBERGER; Tech. Dir DAVID CLIFFE.

TV Station Yap (WAAB): Colonia, Yap, FM 96943; tel. 350-2160; fax 350-4113; govt-owned; Man. LOU DEFNGIN.

Finance

BANKING

Federated States of Micronesian Banking Board: POB 1887, Kolonia, Pohnpei, FM 96941; e-mail fmbb@mail.fm; f. 1980; Chair. LARRY RAIGETAL; Commissioner WILSON F. WAGUK.

Commercial Banks

Bank of the Federated States of Micronesia: POB 98, Kolonia, Pohnpei, FM 96941; tel. 320-2724; fax 370-5359; e-mail bofsmhq@ mail.fm; internet www.fm/BoFSM; brs in Kosrae, Yap, Pohnpei and Chuuk.

Bank of Guam (USA): POB 367, Kolonia, Pohnpei, FM 96941; tel. 320-2550; fax 320-2562; e-mail bogpohn@mail.fm; Man. VIDA RICA-FRENTE; brs in Chuuk and Pohnpei.

Bank of Hawaii (USA): POB 280, Kolonia, Pohnpei, FM 96941; POB 309, Yap, Western Caroline Islands FM 96943; tel. 320-2543; fax 320-2547; tel. 350-2129; Man. AREN PALIK; Man. CHRISTINA MICHELSON; brs in Kosrae.

Development Bank

Federated States of Micronesia Development Bank: POB M, Kolonia, Pohnpei, FM 96941; tel. 320-2480; fax 320-2842; e-mail fsmdb@mail.fm; f. 1979; total assets US $54m. (Dec. 1994); Chair. WILLIAM IRIARTE; Pres. MANNY MORI; 4 brs.

Banking services for the rest of the islands are available in Guam, Hawaii and on the US mainland.

INSURANCE

Actouka Executive Insurance: POB Q, Kolonia, Pohnpei; tel. 320-5331; fax 320-2331; e-mail mlamar@mail.fm.

Caroline Insurance Underwriters: POB 37, Chuuk; tel. 330-2651; fax 330-2207.

FSM Insurance Group: Kosrae; tel. 370-2294; fax 370-2120.

Moylan's Insurance Underwriters: POB 1448, Kolonia, Pohnpei; tel. 320-2118; fax 320-2519; e-mail moylan90@mail.fm.

Oceania Insurance Co.: POB 1202, Weno, Chuuk, FM 96942; tel. 330-3036; fax 330-3764/5274; owns Pacific Basin Insurance.

Pacific Basin Insurance: e-mail oceanpac@mail.fm.

Yap Insurance Agency: Yap; tel. 350-2340; fax 350-2341; e-mail tachelioyap@mail.fm.

Trade and Industry

GOVERNMENT AGENCIES

Coconut Development Authority: POB 297, Kolonia, Pohnpei, FM 96941; tel. 320-2892; fax 320-5383; e-mail fsmcda@mail.fm; responsible for all purchasing, processing and exporting of copra and copra by-products in the islands; Gen. Man. NAMIO NANPEI.

Economic Development Authority: Kolonia, Pohnpei, FM 96941; Chair. (vacant); President of the Federated States of Micronesia.

FSM National Fisheries Corporation: POB R, Kolonia, Pohnpei, FM 96941; tel. 320-2529; fax 320-2239; e-mail nfcairfreight@mail .fm; internet www.fsmgov.org/nfc/; f. 1984; in 1990 it set up, with the Economic Devt Authority and an Australian co, the Caroline Fishing Co (three vessels); exists to promote fisheries development; Pres. PETER SITAN; Chair. SEBASTIAN ANEFAL.

Micronesian Fisheries Authority: POB PS-122, Palikir, Pohnpei, FM 96941; tel. 320-2700; fax 320-2383; e-mail fsmfish@mail.fm; fmrly Micronesian Maritime Authority; responsible for conservation, management and development of tuna resources and for issue of fishing licences; Chair. JESSE RAGLMAR-SUBOLMAR; Vice-Chair. GERSON JACKSON; Exec. Dir BERNARD THOULAG.

UTILITIES

Chuuk Public Works (CPW): POB 248, Weno, Chuuk, FM 96942; tel. 330-2242; fax 320-4815; e-mail chkpublicworks@mail.fm.

Kosrae Utility Authority: POB 277, Tofol, Kosrae, FM 96944; tel. 370-3799; fax 370-3798; e-mail KUA@mail.fm; corporatized in 1994.

Pohnpei Utility Corporation: POB C, Kolonia, Pohnpei, FM 96941; tel. 320-5606; fax 320-2505; f. 1992; provides electricity, water and sewerage services.

Yap Public Services Corporation: POB 621, Colonia, Yap, FM 96943; tel. 350-2175; fax 350-2331; f. 1996; provides electricity, water and sewerage services.

CO-OPERATIVES

Chuuk: Chuuk Co-operative, Faichuk Cacao and Copra Co-operative Asscn, Pis Fishermen's Co-operative, Fefan Women's Co-operative.

Pohnpei: Pohnpei Federation of Co-operative Asscns (POB 100, Pohnpei, FM 96941), Pohnpei Handicraft Co-operative, Pohnpei Fishermen's Co-operative, Uh Soumwet Co-operative Asscn, Kolonia Consumers' and Producers' Co-operative Asscn, Kitti Minimum Co-operative Asscn, Kapingamarangi Copra Producers' Asscn, Metalanim Copra Co-operative Asscn, PICS Co-operative Asscn, Mokil Island Co-operative Asscn, Ngatik Island Co-operative Asscn, Nukuoro Island Co-operative Asscn, Kosrae Island Co-operative Asscn, Pingelap Consumers' Co-operative Asscn.

Yap: Yap Co-operative Asscn, POB 159, Colonia, Yap, FM 96943; tel. 350-2209; fax 350-4114; e-mail yca@mail.fm; f. 1952; Pres. JAMES GILMAR; Gen. Man. TONY GANNGIYAN; 1,200 mems.

Transport

ROADS

Macadam and concrete roads are found in the more important islands. Other islands have stone and coral-surfaced roads and tracks.

SHIPPING

Pohnpei, Chuuk, Yap and Kosrae have deep-draught harbours for commercial shipping. The ports provide warehousing and transhipment facilities.

Truk Shipping Company: POB 669, Weno, Chuuk, FM 96942; tel. 330-2455.

CIVIL AVIATION

The Federated States of Micronesia is served by Continental Micronesia, Air Nauru and Continental Airlines (USA). Pacific Missionary Aviation, based in Pohnpei and Yap, provides domestic air services. There are international airports on Pohnpei, Chuuk, Yap and Kosrae, and airstrips on the outer islands of Onoun and Ta in Chuuk.

Tourism

The tourist industry is a significant source of revenue, although it has been hampered by the lack of infrastructure. Visitor attractions include excellent conditions for scuba-diving (notably in Chuuk Lagoon), Second World War battle sites and relics (many underwater) and the ancient ruined city of Nan Madol on Pohnpei. In 1990 there was a total of 362 hotel rooms. The number of tourist arrivals totalled 32,530 in 2000.

Federated States of Micronesia Visitors Board: Dept of Economic Affairs, National Government, Palikir, Pohnpei, FM 96941; tel. 320-2646; fax 320-5854; internet www.visit-micronesia.fm.

Chuuk Visitors Bureau: POB FQ, Weno, Chuuk, FM 96942; tel. 330-4133; fax 330-4194; e-mail cvb@mail.fm.

Kosrae Visitors Bureau: POB 659, Tofol, Kosrae, FM 96944; tel. 370-2228; fax 370-2187; e-mail kosrae@mail.fm; internet www.kosrae.com.

Pohnpei Department of Tourism and Parks: POB 66, Kolonia, Pohnpei, FM 96941; tel. 320-2421; fax 320-6019; e-mail tourismparks@mail.fm; Deputy Chief BUMIO SILBANUZ.

Pohnpei Visitors Bureau: POB 1949, Kolonia, Pohnpei, FM 96941; tel. 320-4851; fax 320-4868; e-mail pohnpeiVB@mail.fm; internet www.visit-pohnpei.fm.

Yap Visitors Bureau: POB 36, Colonia, Yap, FM 96943; tel. 350-2298; fax 350-2571; e-mail yvb@mail.fm; internet www.visityap.com.

MOLDOVA

Introductory Survey

Location, Climate, Language, Religion, Flag, Capital

The Republic of Moldova is a small, land-locked country situated in south-eastern Europe. It includes only a small proportion of the historical territories of Moldova (or Moldavia, in its Russian form), most of which are in Romania, while others (southern Bessarabia and northern Bucovina) are in Ukraine. The republic is bounded to the north, east and south by Ukraine. To the west it borders Romania. The climate is very favourable for agriculture, with long, warm summers and relatively mild winters. Average temperatures in Chișinău range from 21°C (70°F) in July to −4°C (24°F) in January. The Constitution of July 1994 describes the official language as Moldovan (although this is widely considered to be identical to Romanian). Most of the inhabitants of Moldova profess Christianity, the largest denomination being the Eastern Orthodox Church. The national flag (proportions 1 by 2) consists of three equal vertical stripes, of light blue, yellow and red; the yellow stripe has at its centre the arms of Moldova (a shield bearing a stylized bull's head in yellow, set between an eight-pointed yellow star, a five-petalled yellow flower, and a yellow crescent, the shield being set on the breast of an eagle, in gold and red, which holds a green olive branch in its dexter talons, a yellow sceptre in its sinister talons, and a yellow cross in its beak). The capital is Chișinău (Kishinev).

Recent History

The area of the present-day Republic of Moldova corresponds to only part of the medieval principality of Moldova (also known as Moldavia), which emerged as an important regional power in the 15th century. In the following century, however, the principality came under Ottoman domination. Following a period of conflict between the Ottoman and Russian Empires in the late 18th century, Moldova was divided into two parts under the Treaty of Bucharest of 1812: the eastern territory of Bessarabia, situated between the Prut and Dniester (Dnestr or Nistru) rivers (which roughly corresponds to modern Moldova), was ceded to Russia, while the Ottomans retained control of western Moldova. A Romanian nationalist movement evolved in western Moldova and the neighbouring region of Wallachia during the 19th century, culminating in the proclamation of a sovereign Romanian state in 1877, independent of the Ottoman Empire. In 1881 Romania became a kingdom. In June 1918, after the collapse of the Russian Empire, Bessarabia was proclaimed an independent republic, although in November it voted to become part of Romania. This union was recognized in the Treaty of Paris (1920). However, the USSR (established in 1922) refused to recognize Romania's claims to the territory, and in October 1924 formed a Moldovan Autonomous Soviet Socialist Republic (ASSR) on the eastern side of the Dniester, in the Ukrainian Soviet Socialist Republic (SSR). In June 1940 Romania was forced to cede Bessarabia and northern Bucovina to the USSR, under the terms of the Treaty of Non-Aggression (the 'Molotov-Ribbentrop Pact'), concluded with Germany in August 1939. Northern Bucovina, southern Bessarabia and the Kotovsk-Balta region of the Moldovan ASSR were incorporated into the Ukrainian SSR. The remaining parts of the Moldovan ASSR and of Bessarabia were merged to form the Moldovan SSR, which formally joined the USSR on 2 August 1940. Political power in the republic was vested in the Communist Party of Moldova (CPM), a subsidiary of the Communist Party of the Soviet Union (CPSU).

Between July 1941 and August 1944 the Moldovan SSR was reunited with Romania. However, the Soviet Army reannexed the region in 1944, and the Moldovan SSR was re-established. Soviet policy in Moldova concentrated on isolating the region from its historical links with Romania: cross-border traffic virtually ceased, the Cyrillic script was imposed on the Romanian language (which was referred to as Moldovan) and Russian and Ukrainian immigration was encouraged. In the 1950s thousands of ethnic Romanians were deported to Central Asia. Moldova remained among the more conservative republics of the USSR. Two future Soviet leaders, Leonid Brezhnev and Konstantin Chernenko, held prominent positions in the CPM during their early years of CPSU service: Brezhnev as First Secretary (leader) of the CPM in 1950–52, and Chernenko as head of party propaganda in 1948–56.

The policy of *glasnost* (openness), introduced by Soviet leader Mikhail Gorbachev in 1986, allowed the expression within Moldova of opposition to the process of 'russification'. In May 1987 the CPM issued a decree increasing provision for the teaching of Romanian in schools, but this did little to satisfy public opinion. In 1988 there were demands for an immediate halt to immigration, for the restoration of the Latin alphabet and for Romanian to be declared the official language of the republic. In May 1989 a number of independent cultural and political groups, which had recently emerged but were denied legal status by the authorities, allied to form the Popular Front (PF). In June some 70,000 people attended a protest demonstration, organized by the PF, on the anniversary of the Soviet annexation of Bessarabia in 1940. This was followed, in August 1989, by mass demonstrations in the capital, Chișinău (Kishinev), in support of proposals by the Moldovan Supreme Soviet (legislature) to declare Romanian the official language of the republic. Following protests by non-ethnic Romanians, the proposals were amended: legislation was enacted providing for Russian to be retained as a language of inter-ethnic communication, but the official language was to be Romanian, written in the Latin script. Following disturbances, and subsequent riots, during the Revolution Day celebrations in Chișinău in November, the First Secretary of the CPM, Semion Grossu, was dismissed. He was replaced by Petru Lucinschi, an ethnic Romanian considered to be more supportive of Gorbachev's reforms.

The increasing influence of the Romanian-speaking population was strongly opposed by other inhabitants of the republic (who, at the 1989 census, comprised some 35% of the total population). In the areas east of the Dniester, where Russians and Ukrainians predominated, the local authorities refused to implement the language law. Opposition to growing Moldovan nationalism was led by the Yedinstvo (Unity) Movement, a group dominated by leading CPM members, and the United Work Collectives, a Slav-dominated organization based among the towns east of the Dniester. Both organizations had strong links with Gagauz Halky (Gagauz People), the most prominent of the political groups representing the 150,000-strong Gagauz minority (a Turkic people). In January 1990 a referendum took place in the eastern town of Tiraspol, in which the predominantly Russian-speaking population voted overwhelmingly to seek greater autonomy for the region beyond the Dniester (Transnistria or Transdnestria).

None of the independent political groups was officially allowed to endorse candidates in elections to the Moldovan Supreme Soviet in February 1990, but individual candidates made clear where their sympathies lay. About 80% of the 380 deputies elected were members of the CPM, but many were also sympathetic to the aims of the PF. The new Supreme Soviet convened in April, whereupon Mircea Snegur, a CPM member supported by the PF, was elected Chairman. In the following month the Government resigned after losing a vote of 'no confidence'. A new Council of Ministers, chaired by a leading economist, Mircea Druc, implemented far-reaching political changes. The CPM's constitutional right to power was revoked, and media organizations belonging to the CPM were transferred to state control. On 23 June the Supreme Soviet adopted a declaration of sovereignty asserting the supremacy of Moldova's Constitution and laws throughout the republic, which was to be known as the Soviet Socialist Republic of Moldova (as opposed to the russified 'Moldavia'). The Supreme Soviet also declared the 1940 annexation of Bessarabia to have been illegal. In September Snegur was elected to the newly instituted post of President of the Republic, and the role of Chairman of the Supreme Soviet became that of a parliamentary speaker.

The actions of the increasingly radical Romanian majority in the legislature provoked further anxiety among the country's ethnic minorities during 1990. In August the Gagauz proclaimed a separate 'Gagauz SSR' in the southern region around Comrat. In the following month east-bank Slavs proclaimed their secession from Moldova and the establishment of the 'Transdnestrian SSR', comprising Moldovan territory east of the Dniester, with its self-styled capital at Tiraspol. Both declarations were immediately annulled by the Moldovan Supreme Soviet. In October Moldovan nationalists sought to thwart elections to a Gagauz Supreme Soviet by sending some 50,000 armed volunteers to the area. Violence was prevented only by the dispatch of Soviet troops to the region. The new Gagauz Supreme Soviet convened in Comrat and elected Stepan Topal as its President. Further inter-ethnic violence occurred east of the Dniester in November, when elections were announced to a Transdnestrian Supreme Soviet. Negotiations in Moscow involving the Moldovan Government, the east-bank Slavs and the Gagauz failed to resolve the crisis, but the elections proceeded without further violence.

In mid-December 1990 an estimated 800,000 people, attending a 'Grand National Assembly', voted by acclamation to reject any new union treaty (which was being negotiated by other Soviet republics). Furthermore, in February 1991 the Moldovan Supreme Soviet resolved not to conduct the all-Union referendum on the future of the USSR, which was scheduled for March, and endorsed proposals for a confederation of states without central control as the preferred replacement for the USSR. Despite the official boycott, some 650,000 people (mostly Russians, Ukrainians and Gagauz) participated in the referendum, voting almost unanimously for the preservation of the USSR. Nevertheless, the ethnic-Romanian-dominated Government and legislature continued the process of *de facto* secession from the USSR. All-Union enterprises were placed under republican jurisdiction, a Moldovan state bank was established (independent of the USSR Gosbank), the CPM was prohibited from activities in state and government organs, and conscription to the USSR armed forces was not implemented. In May the designation 'Soviet Socialist' was removed from the republic's name and the Supreme Soviet was renamed the Moldovan Parliament. In the same month, following a vote of 'no confidence' by the legislature, Mircea Druc was removed from the post of Prime Minister.

Following the coup attempt in Moscow in August 1991, the commanders of the USSR's South-Western Military District sought to impose a state of emergency in Moldova. However, the republican leadership immediately announced its support for the Russian President, Boris Yeltsin, in his opposition to the coup, and demanded the reinstatement of Gorbachev as President of the USSR. On 27 August, after the coup had collapsed, the Moldovan Parliament and the 'Grand National Assembly' proclaimed Moldova's independence from the USSR. The Government asserted its jurisdiction over the border with Romania and introduced customs posts on the border with Ukraine. In September President Snegur ordered the creation of national armed forces, and assumed control of the republican KGB (state security service), transforming it into a Ministry of National Security. The Government announced that it would no longer participate in any Soviet structures or in negotiations for a new political union. However, in November the leadership did sign a treaty to establish an economic community.

At elections to the republican presidency on 8 December 1991 Snegur, the sole candidate, received 98.2% of the votes cast. On 21 December Moldova was among the 11 signatories to the Alma-Ata (Almaty) Declaration establishing the Commonwealth of Independent States (CIS, see p. 172). The establishment of the CIS led to wider international recognition of Moldova's independence, which had been somewhat delayed by concerns at inter-ethnic tension within the republic. Moldovan affairs during the first half of 1992 were, none the less, dominated by the armed conflict in Transnistria (see below) and by the question of possible unification with Romania, strongly advocated by the ruling PF (which in February was re-formed as the Christian Democratic Popular Front—CDPF). Moreover, a National Council for Reintegration had been established in December 1991, comprising legislators from both Moldova and Romania who were committed to the idea of a unified Romanian state. Within Moldova, however, popular support for unification remained insubstantial. In June 1992 the CDPF-dominated Government announced its resignation: this was attributed largely to popular opposition to the Government's pro-unification policies, compounded by the severe decline in the standard of living and the Government's inability to curb the increase in corruption and lawlessness. Andrei Sangheli, a Deputy Prime Minister in the outgoing administration, was appointed Prime Minister, and a new Government 'of national accord' was formed, led by the Agrarian Democratic Party (ADP), which largely comprised members of the former communist leadership —in particular collective farm managers. Several portfolios that had been reserved for representatives from Transnistria and Gagauzia were refused. The CDPF became the main opposition party. The ADP declared its commitment to consolidating Moldovan statehood, rejecting any future union with Romania in favour of a closer alignment with Russia and the CIS. The ADP's anti-unification policies were strongly supported by President Snegur, who in January 1993 proposed that the issue be resolved in a referendum, confident that it would be rejected. Snegur's proposal was, however, narrowly defeated by Parliament. The ensuing political crisis led to the resignations of both supporters and opponents of union with Romania, including the pro-unification Chairman of Parliament, Alexandru Moşanu. Moşanu was replaced in February by Petru Lucinschi, the former leader of the CPM (which had been banned following the attempted coup in Moscow in 1991).

The ADP made substantial progress with the drafting of the new Moldovan Constitution during 1993, although the document could only be ratified by the new Parliament that was due to be elected in early 1994. The draft Constitution provided, *inter alia*, for a reduced, 104-member legislature. Moldova's first multi-party election was held on 27 February 1994, with the participation of more than 73% of the electorate. On the eve of the election, the authorities in Gagauzia rescinded their decision to boycott the poll, and the rate of participation in the region was reported to be high. In Transnistria the local leadership did not permit polling stations to open; however, residents were able to vote on the left bank of the Dniester. In all, 13 parties and blocs contested the election, the result of which demonstrated widespread popular support for parties advocating continued Moldovan independence. The ADP obtained an overall majority in Parliament (56 seats). The successor party to the CPM, the Socialist Party (SP), in alliance with the Slav-based Yedinstvo Movement, won 28 seats. Two pro-unification groups shared the remaining 20 seats: the Peasants' Party of Moldova/Congress of Intelligentsia alliance (11) and the CDPF alliance (nine). The overwhelming lack of support for the pro-unification parties was confirmed in a national referendum on Moldova's statehood on 6 March. Of the 75% of the participating electorate, more than 95% were in favour of continued independence. In late March Andrei Sangheli was re-elected Prime Minister, while Petru Lucinschi was re-elected Chairman of Parliament. A new, smaller Council of Ministers, comprising solely members of the ADP, was appointed in April. In May the CPM was permitted to re-form, as the Moldovan Party of Communists (MPC).

The new Constitution was adopted by Parliament in July 1994 and entered into force in August. As well as establishing the country's permanent neutrality, the Constitution also provided for a 'special autonomous status' for Transnistria and Gagauzia within Moldova (the exact terms of which were to be determined at a later date). The official state language was specified as Moldovan (rather than Romanian), although the two languages were acknowledged to be identical. In March–April 1995 thousands of students participated in rallies in Chişinău, demanding that Romanian be redesignated the official state language. In response, Snegur decreed a six-month moratorium on the language issue; meanwhile, a special committee was to examine the matter. In June following the rejection by the ADP and its allies in Parliament of the proposal that Romanian replace Moldovan in the Constitution as the state language, Snegur resigned his membership of the ADP (which he had joined following the party's electoral victory in 1994). In August 1995 he established the Party of Rebirth and Conciliation (PRC), with the support of 11 rebel deputies from the ADP, as well as one of the Deputy Chairmen of Parliament, Nicolae Andronic, and two chairmen of parliamentary standing committees. Parliament responded by removing Andronic and the two committee chairmen from their posts. There were renewed student rallies in October; in February 1996, none the less, Parliament again rejected the proposed redesignation of the state language.

Some 68% of the registered electorate participated in the presidential election held on 17 November 1996, which was contested by nine candidates. Although Snegur received the largest share of the votes cast (39%), his failure to win an absolute majority necessitated a second round of voting, contested by the incumbent and his closest rival, the ADP-supported Petru Lucinschi (who had secured 28%). The rate of participation was slightly higher (72%) in the second round, held on 1 December, when Lucinschi emerged with a decisive 54% of the votes. The authorities in Transnistria again boycotted the poll, and there were reports that residents were prevented from leaving the region to vote on the left bank of the Dniester. Lucinschi was inaugurated as President on 15 January 1997, and a new Government was announced later that month. It retained approximately one-half of the members of the outgoing administration, and was headed by Ion Ciubuc, a non-party economist with extensive government experience. In March the leader of the ADP, Dumitru Moţpan, was elected as Lucinschi's successor as Chairman of Parliament (he had hitherto served as a Deputy Chairman).

Relations between Lucinschi and Parliament were strained during 1997, in particular over the progress of economic reforms. Parliamentary elections took place on 22 March 1998. In an apparent rejection of Lucinschi's economic reform programme, the election was won by the MPC, led by Vladimir Voronin, which took 30.1% of the votes cast (40 of the total seats). The Democratic Convention of Moldova (CDM), an alliance of right-wing parties that included the PRC, under the leadership of Snegur, achieved 19.2% (26 seats), while the Movement for a Democratic and Prosperous Moldova (MDPM) received 18.2% (24 seats) and the Moldovan Party of Democratic Forces 8.8% (11 seats). The remaining 11 parties (including the ADP) failed to secure the minimum 4% of the total votes required for representation. Three independent candidates won seats; the rate of participation was 67%, according to preliminary results. The election was, once again, boycotted in Transnistria, but voters from the region were permitted to cross the Dniester to vote.

At the first session of the new legislature, convened in late April 1998, Dumitru Diacov was elected Chairman. The Government resigned shortly afterwards. Since none of the political parties had secured an overall parliamentary majority, the new Government, appointed in late May (with Ciubuc retaining his post as Prime Minister), comprised a coalition of members of the MDPM, the CDM and the Party of Democratic Forces. Within Parliament, the coalition, called the Alliance for Democracy and Reforms, was led by Snegur. The efficacy of the new Government was swiftly undermined by differences between coalition members, although a motion of 'no confidence' in the Government, proposed by the MPC, was defeated in November.

By early 1999 it was estimated that wage and pension arrears had accumulated to the value of some 1,000m. lei, and there were protests in Chişinău by workers in the education and transport sectors. Ciubuc resigned as Prime Minister in early February, citing internal divisions. Snegur resigned as parliamentary leader of the government coalition the following day, after his nominee for the premiership, Deputy Prime Minister Nicolae Andronic, was rejected. Shortly afterwards Lucinschi nominated the Mayor of Chişinău, Serafim Urecheanu, as Prime Minister. However, Urecheanu resigned in mid-February, having failed to reach agreement with the parliamentary majority, notably on the issue of strengthening executive powers: Lucinschi had, in the mean time, submitted a presidential bill to Parliament providing for a substantial expansion of the executive's authority over the next two years, which, he maintained, was essential in order to address the economic crisis. Following Urecheanu's resignation, Lucinschi nominated Sturza, the Deputy Prime Minister and Minister of the Economy and Reforms, as Prime Minister. Although Parliament twice failed to endorse his proposed government, Lucinschi nominated Sturza a third time. Faced with a choice between acceptance or an early general election (the Constitution permits the President to dissolve the legislature if a candidate for the premiership is twice rejected), Parliament approved Sturza's Government in mid-March, with the requisite 52 votes.

Local elections were held in Moldova on 23 May 1999, after which the country was to be reorganized into nine provinces and two autonomous entities—Gagauzia and Transnistria. A referendum was held on the same day, on the issue of increasing presidential powers. Although initially invalidated because of the low rate of electoral participation, in June the Constitutional Court ruled the referendum, which had approved the President's proposals, to be valid; however, it was to have no judicial effect. In August a controversial draft law on amending the Constitution was published, whereby the President would appoint the prime minister and members of the government and adopt their programme of activity; it was also proposed that the presidential term of office be extended from four to five years and that the number of deputies be reduced from 101 to 70, elected solely on the basis of single-mandate constituencies. In

September Lucinschi announced his willingness to cancel a proposed referendum on the issue if parliamentary representatives, together with experts from the Council of Europe (see p. 181), succeeded in proposing revisions to the draft law. In the following month a group of deputies advanced a reform plan for debate in Parliament, which included a proposal that the President be appointed by the legislature. Moreover, in November the Constitutional Court ruled the May referendum to have been illegal, as it had not been announced and prepared by Parliament; in future the President would not have the right to call plebiscites.

The creation, in October 1999, of a new, independent, political bloc, by members of the MDPM and a former deputy of the Party of Democratic Forces, weakened the Government's support in Parliament. In the following month Ion Sturza lost a vote of confidence in the legislature, after the defeat of a controversial bill on the privatization of the wine and tobacco industries; the IMF and the World Bank subsequently suspended credits to Moldova (the bill was finally approved in October 2000). In mid-November 1999 Lucinschi nominated the former ambassador to Russia, Valeriu Bobutac, as Prime Minister. Bobutac resigned 10 days later, having failed to secure the necessary support in the legislature. Following the failure of a second candidate, Vladimir Voronin, the President decided to propose a third, rather than dissolve the legislature. After negotiations on the composition of a new government to be led by the former Minister of Communications, Ion Casian, failed, the President nominated Dumitru Braghiş, hitherto Deputy Minister of Economy and Reform. Braghiş was approved as Prime Minister in late December, narrowly avoiding the dissolution of Parliament and a new legislative election.

In early July 2000 Parliament voted, by 92 votes to five, in favour of amending the Constitution to permit the legislature to elect the Head of State. Although President Lucinschi vetoed the proposed constitutional change, Parliament swiftly overturned his decision, and legislation transforming Moldova into a parliamentary state was enacted in late July; the President declared the new law to be in contravention of the invalidated referendum of May 1999. In September 2000 Parliament approved an amendment to the law on presidential electoral procedure and an alteration to the electoral code, further exacerbating the conflict between the President and the legislature. In mid-October Parliament announced that a presidential election would be held at the beginning of December; in response, Lucinschi, who insisted that the Moldovan public should retain the right to elect the president, announced that he would not contest the election. In November the MPC selected its First Secretary, Vladimir Voronin, to stand as the party's candidate in the presidential election. Also contesting the election was the Chairman of the Constitutional Court, Pavel Barbalat, who had been proposed by a coalition of the Democratic Party of Moldova (PDM—as the MDPM had been renamed in April), the CDM, the Christian Democratic People's Party (CDPP, formerly the CDPF) and the Moldovan Party of Democratic Forces.

Three rounds of voting in the presidential election proved inconclusive in early December 2000, with neither of the two candidates obtaining the requisite number of votes to secure an overall victory. Dumitru Diacov, the leader of the PDM and the parliamentary Chairman, subsequently attempted to persuade Voronin to withdraw his candidacy in favour of a compromise candidate. After Voronin refused to withdraw from the election, the PDM, the CDM, the CDPP and the Moldovan Party of Democratic Forces boycotted a fourth round of voting on 21 December, preventing it from taking place (as only 48 out of the necessary quorum of 61 deputies were present), and thereby permitting the President to dissolve the legislature and schedule an early parliamentary election; Lucinschi emphasized the right of the new Parliament to overturn measures introduced by the previous legislature. Parliament was duly dissolved on 12 January 2001, and a general election was scheduled for 25 February. Lucinschi remained in office after the official expiry of his term in mid-January, until a successor could be elected.

In the legislative election, held as scheduled on 25 February 2001, the MPC won an overall majority in Parliament, securing 49.9% of the votes cast and 71 seats. The Braghiş Alliance, formed by the Prime Minister, Dumitru Braghiş, obtained 13.4% of the votes and 19 seats, while the CDPP obtained 8.3% of the votes and 11 seats. The election, which represented the first communist return to power in the former USSR since its collapse, was described as free and fair by Organization for

Security and Co-operation in Europe (OSCE, see p. 283) observers. The rate of voter participation was some 70%. In early March the MPC, which pledged to maintain a multi-party system, again nominated Vladimir Voronin to stand in the presidential election. In the election, which took place on 4 April, Voronin secured 71 votes. Dumitru Braghiş obtained 15 votes and another communist candidate, Valerian Cristea, obtained 3 votes; the 11 deputies of the CDPP abstained from voting, in order to express their lack of support for any candidate. Following his inauguration on 7 April, Voronin nominated Vasile Tarlev, a former businessman without party affiliation, to head a new government. A new Minister of Energy, Iacob Timciuc, was appointed in early August, and in early September Nicolae Dudau was appointed as Minister of Foreign Affairs.

Proposals put forward in August 2001 by the Minister of Education, Ilie Vancea, according to which the compulsory teaching of Russian language and history was to be introduced to the national curriculum from 2002, were confirmed in December 2001. A demonstration, organized by the CDPP and involving an estimated 3,000 people, took place in Chişinău on 9 January 2002 to protest against the changes to the education system and what was perceived as an attempt by the Government to bring about the 'russification' of Moldova; daily protests continued throughout the month, prompting fears of destabilization and demands for CDPP members to be deprived of their parliamentary immunity. In late January the Ministry of Justice suspended the CDPP from participation in political activities for a period of one month, thus preventing it from organizing further protests. However, in February, following intervention from the Council of Europe, the suspension of the CDPP was annulled, in order to allow the party to campaign for local elections, due to be held in April. In mid-February, however, the Constitutional Court ruled the scheduling of early local elections for April, before the expiry of the four-year mandate of the local government officials elected in 1999, to be unconstitutional.

On 29 January 2002 a communist member of Parliament, Vasile Iovv, was appointed to the hitherto vacant position of First Deputy Prime Minister; he was to share responsibility for the implementation of new legislation on local government, approved by Parliament in December 2001. The new law replaced the existing nine provinces and two autonomous regions, which had been introduced in 1999, with an administrative structure based on the Soviet system and comprising 31 districts, two autonomous territories (Transnistria and Gagauzia), and three municipalities (Chişinău, Bălţi and Tighina). Meanwhile, the protests against the reform of the education system intensified throughout February, prompting Vancea to announce that the controversial legislation would be retracted, and to apologize publicly for his actions. None the less, the domestic crisis prompted Vancea's dismissal; he was replaced by Gheorghe Sima, and Zinaida Grecîanii was appointed Minister of Finance. At the end of the month the Minister of the Interior, Vasile Draganel, resigned, amid reports that he had been unwilling to use force to dispel the protesters. Gheorghe Papuc, a long-standing member of the security forces, was nominated to replace him.

Despite a ruling by the Supreme Court declaring the ongoing protests to be illegal and demanding that they be halted, in late February 2002 demonstrators began to protest outside the headquarters of the national television company against state censorship and misinformation. On 22 March the Deputy Chairman of the CDPP, Vlad Cubreacov, who had been involved in organizing the anti-Government protests, was declared missing; thousands of demonstrators subsequently gathered to protest at Cubreacov's disappearance, which members of the CDPP attributed to the Government. In early April the Braghiş Alliance announced that it was to boycott Parliament until the Government agreed to negotiate with the protesters. At the end of the month the CDPP announced that it had discontinued its anti-Government protests, in compliance with Council of Europe recommendations, but declared that the Government's failure to comply with Council resolutions on, *inter alia*, the granting of independence to the state-owned media and the judiciary would lead to the resumption of demonstrations. In late May Cubreacov was discovered alive near the Transnistrian border. However, his kidnappers remained unidentified.

In mid-May 2002 Ştefan Odagiu was appointed Deputy Prime Minister and Minister of the Economy. In early June, at the request of the IMF, a new Civil Code (replacing that of 1964) was approved by Parliament, which incorporated the principles of a market economy, thereby allowing for the resumption of inter-

national assistance. In the same month judicial proceedings against members of the opposition (including Cubreacov) involved in the organization of public protests were suspended indefinitely. In November President Voronin dismissed the Minister of Transport and Telecommunications, Anatol Cupţov, following accusations of the embezzlement of state property. In December Vasile Sova was appointed to the new post of Minister of Reintegration, with responsibility for the resolution of the issue of Transnistria and the co-ordination of government structures, and Ion Pacuraru was replaced as Minister of Culture by Veaceslav Madan. In the same month the Social Liberal Party merged with the Party of Democratic Forces, retaining its name and its Chairman, Oleg Serebrean. In January 2003 public protests were resumed in response to the Government's blocking of a proposed referendum, which aimed to seek support for eventual Moldovan membership of NATO and the European Union (EU). The following month, however, the Braghiş Alliance ceased its boycott of Parliament, after the Government agreed to grant the party airtime on state television and to end its harassment of those in support of a referendum on the electoral system. Despite concerns about the progress of democratic reform in Moldova, the country was to take over the presidency of the Committee of Ministers of the Council of Europe in May, for a period of six month. Local elections took place in Moldova on 25 May.

Following the proclamation of Transnistria's secession in September 1990, relations between the region and the central Government in Chişinău remained tense. Armed conflict broke out in December 1991, as the leadership of the self-proclaimed republic, opposed to the Government's objective of reunification with Romania, launched a campaign to gain control of Transnistria (with the ultimate aim of unity with the Russian Federation). More than six months of military conflict ensued, as Moldovan government troops were dispatched to combat the local Slav militia. The Moldovan Government claimed that the east-bank forces were actively supported by the Russian Government, while the Moldovans were, in turn, accused of receiving military and other assistance from Romania. The situation was complicated by the presence (and alleged involvement in support of the east-bank Slavs) of the former Soviet 14th Army, which was still stationed in the region and jurisdiction over which had been transferred to the Russian Federation. Peace negotiations were held at regular intervals, with the participation of Moldova, Russia, Ukraine and Romania; however, none of the agreed cease-fires was observed. By June 1992 some 700 people were believed to have been killed in the conflict, with a further estimated 50,000 people forced to take refuge in neighbouring Ukraine. On 21 July, however, a peace agreement was finally negotiated by Presidents Snegur and Yeltsin, whereby Transnistria was accorded 'special status' within Moldova (the terms of which were to be formulated later). Later in July Russian, Moldovan and Transnistrian peace-keeping troops were deployed in the region to monitor the cease-fire. However, Moldova's relations with the Russian Federation remained strained during the remainder of 1992.

Transnistria continued to demand full statehood, and in January 1994 the Moldovan Government accepted proposals by the Conference on Security and Co-operation in Europe (CSCE—later OSCE) for greater autonomy, including economic independence, for Transnistria, within a Moldovan confederation. The Transnistrian leadership expressed its approval of the proposals, and the result of the Moldovan parliamentary election of the following month (which eliminated the possibility of Moldova's future unification with Romania) further enhanced the prospects for peace in the region. In April President Snegur and the Transnistrian leader, Igor Smirnov, pledged their commitment to holding negotiations for a peaceful resolution of the conflict, based on the CSCE recommendations.

In July 1994, following the adoption of the new Moldovan Constitution, which provided for a 'special autonomous status' for Transnistria, negotiations duly commenced on the details of the region's future status within Moldova. Progress was obstructed, in particular, by disagreement over the future of the 15,000-strong 14th Army, since the Transnistrian leadership demanded the continued presence of the Army in the region as a guarantor of security. In October, however, the Moldovan and Russian Governments reached an agreement, under which Russia was to withdraw the 14th Army within a period of three years, whereupon Transnistria's negotiated 'special autonomous status' would take effect. A referendum (declared illegal by President Snegur) was held in Transnistria in March 1995, in which some 91% of participants voted against the agreed withdrawal of the 14th Army. In late June, however, the withdrawal of weapons and ammunition of the 14th Army was begun. In December a new bicameral legislature was elected in Transnistria. On the same occasion two further referendums were held: 82.7% of the electorate endorsed a new constitution (which proclaimed the region's independence), while 89.7% voted for Transnistria to join the CIS as a sovereign state. In February 1996, however, the CIS ruled out admittance for Transnistria on such terms.

In July 1996 the executive and legislative authorities of both Moldova and Transnistria initialled a memorandum, drafted with the aid of Russian, Ukrainian and OSCE mediators, on normalizing relations; this was viewed as an important stage towards defining the 'special status' of Transnistria within a future Moldovan confederation. However, Snegur subsequently declared his opposition to the memorandum, claiming that it effectively formalized Moldova's 'disintegration into two states', and announced that any decision on the issue should be postponed until after the presidential election. Following his election as Moldova's new President in December, Petru Lucinschi announced his intention to sign the memorandum. In that month Igor Smirnov was re-elected 'President' of Transnistria, with more than 70% of the votes cast.

Meanwhile, the withdrawal of contingents of the 14th Army continued, and by early 1997 its strength had reportedly been reduced to some 5,000–6,000 men. None the less, the withdrawal agreement, although signed by the respective Governments, still awaited ratification by the Russian State Duma, and Moldova continued to press for the issue to be resolved. In April it was announced that substantial progress had been achieved in the negotiations concerning the status of Transnistria. A new article was added to the memorandum initialled in mid-1996, stating that the two sides would develop relations within the framework of one state, the borders of which would correspond to those of the former Soviet republic of Moldova. The memorandum was signed in Moscow, in early May, by Lucinschi and Smirnov, with Russia and Ukraine acting as guarantors of the document. It was agreed to resume negotiations on the defining of Transnistria's 'special status', and commissions were constituted for that purpose. Representatives of the two sides, meeting in Moscow in October, reached agreement on a number of 'confidence-building measures', and in the following month a document on economic co-operation was signed by Smirnov and Prime Minister Ciubuc. The agreement on 'confidence-building measures' was signed in Odessa, Ukraine, by Lucinschi, Smirnov, Russian Prime Minister Viktor Chernomyrdin and President Leonid Kuchma of Ukraine on 20 March 1998. A reduction in Moldovan and Transnistrian peace-keeping forces was envisaged, while Russian troops were to remain in Transnistria until a final political settlement was reached.

The success of Snegur's CDM at the March 1998 legislative election raised concerns among the Transnistrian leadership regarding the future of relations with the Moldovan Government. In June, however, Russian and Moldovan delegations to the joint commission monitoring the Odessa Accords agreed proposals for the composition of peace-keeping forces in the Transnistrian security zone. In late August the joint monitoring commission approved the deployment of Ukrainian peace-keeping forces in the security zone: at this time, there were some 700 troops from each of Moldova, Transnistria and Russia. Meanwhile Moldova's peace-keeping troops were gradually reduced in number (to about 500), and Moldova continued to urge Russia to accelerate the withdrawal of its troops and weaponry from the area. Lucinschi and Smirnov met in January 1999, and agreed to continue discussions. From late May, following local elections in Moldova (in which the region refused to participate), Transnistria was to be designated an autonomous entity, responsible for supporting itself financially.

At an OSCE summit in Istanbul, Turkey, in November 1999, Russia agreed to withdraw from Transnistria in three stages, with all hardware to be removed by the end of 2001, and all troops by the end of 2002. Meanwhile, in July Lucinschi met Smirnov, along with then Russian Prime Minister Sergei Stepashin and an OSCE representative in Kiev, Ukraine. Although the negotiations concluded with the signature of a joint declaration on the normalization of relations between Moldova and Transnistria, Smirnov declared that differences remained. The Transnistrian leadership announced in September that the region was prepared to become part of Moldova, but that since Moldova was unwilling to grant the region economic independ-

ence and did not consider Transnistria when dealing with its international affairs, the region intended to strengthen its statehood and rely solely on its internal resources. In August 2000 Smirnov signed an agreement with the Moldovan premier, Dumitru Braghiş, according to which Transnistria was to pay customs duties for the export of goods through Moldova. In mid-March, however, an agreement was signed by the Chairmen of the Moldovan Parliament and the 'Transdnestrian Supreme Soviet' to the effect that Transnistrian deputies would, henceforth, participate in the work of international parliamentary organizations as part of Moldovan delegations.

In June 2000 the 'Transdnestrian Supreme Soviet' was converted to a reduced, unicameral legislature. Smirnov introduced a form of presidential rule in the following month, although a new cabinet was installed to act as a consultative body; a legislative election was held in December. Meanwhile, in July President Lucinschi established a commission for the settlement of the regional conflict, which was to co-operate with the OSCE and with the Russian and Ukrainian commissions on Transnistria. In August, in Moscow, the Moldovan and 'Transdnestrian' delegations held separate tripartite discussions with the Russian and Ukrainian commissions, but, although new proposals for the resolution of the issue were advanced by the head of the Russian commission, the former Russian Prime Minister, Yevgenii Primakov, no agreement was reached. The new Moldovan President elected in April 2001, Vladimir Vorodin, declared the pursuit of a final political settlement for Transnistria to be a priority but, although a number of bilateral agreements were signed in Tiraspol in May, no substantive progress was made. In June the OSCE welcomed the Moldovan Government's announcement that it was to reduce the strength of its peace-keeping forces in the security zone. A deterioration in Transnistria's relations with the Moldovan Government took place in September, however, following the Government's introduction of new customs procedures, in accordance with World Trade Organization specifications; the withholding of new customs seals from the Transnistrian authorities, thereby preventing the region from conducting its own external economic activities, led to claims that the Moldovan Government was attempting to impose an 'economic blockade' on the region, and the curtailment of negotiations. Igor Smirnov was re-elected as 'President' of the region in elections held on 9 December, receiving almost 82% of the votes cast; the election result was recognized by neither the Moldovan Government nor the international community. A new Transnistrian Government was appointed in February 2002. The agreed withdrawal of all Russian military hardware from the region was subject to delays, partly owing to the obstruction of railway lines by Transnistrians who hoped to gain compensation for the equipment withdrawn. In December the OSCE amended the deadline agreed in 1999 for the removal of Russian forces from Moldova, extending it for a further year, until 31 December 2003; however, Russia indicated that even once the evacuation of its arsenal was complete, military forces would remain, with a possible mandate for maintaining peace and stability in the event of agreement on reunification. Meanwhile, in July 2002 mediators from Russia, Ukraine and the OSCE submitted a new draft agreement, whereby Moldova would become a federal state, in which autonomous territories would maintain their own legislature and constitution; Smirnov permitted participation in talks on the agreement, but insisted that recognition of Transnistria's 'independence' was a fundamental prerequisite to negotiations on a confederation of two equal states. In February 2003, in what was regarded as a concession, President Voronin proposed the joint drafting of a new constitution, which would be subject to a referendum by February 2004; preliminary agreement was reached on the matter. Further concessions granted in early 2003 included an easing in customs restrictions and the passing of legislation allowing dual citizenship, which would benefit the many Russian citizens in Transnistria. On 27 February the EU and the USA, and subsequently other countries, imposed a travel ban on those Transnistrian officials considered to be 'primarily responsible for a lack of co-operation in promoting a political settlement'; in retaliation certain Moldovan officials were deemed *persona non grata* in the region. In the same month the Transnistrian authorities sanctioned unconditionally the withdrawal of Russian military equipment.

During the period of the Transnistrian conflict, in 1991–92, the situation in Gagauzia remained peaceful, although the region continued to demand full statehood. The new Moldovan Constitution, adopted in July 1994, provided for a 'special autonomous status' for Gagauzia, as for Transnistria, and negotiations duly commenced on the details of this status. Agreement was quickly reached between the Government and the Gagauz authorities, and in December the Moldovan Parliament adopted legislation on the 'special status of Gagauz-Eri' (or Gagauzia). The regions of southern Moldova populated by the Gagauz were to enjoy broad self-administrative powers, and Gagauz was to be one of three official languages (with Moldovan and Russian). Legislative power was to be vested in a regional assembly, and a directly elected 'baskan' was to hold a quasi-presidential position. The law on the status of Gagauz-Eri entered into force in February 1995, and in the following month a referendum was held in the region to determine which settlements would form part of the region. Elections to the 35-seat regional assembly ('halk toplusu') took place in late May–early June. Elections, held simultaneously, to the post of baskan were won by Gheorghe Tabunscic, the First Secretary of the Comrat branch of the MPC. Under the new Constitution, Tabunscic, as Gagauz leader, became a member of the Council of Ministers. At the first session of the assembly, the self-proclaimed 'Gagauz Republic' was declared defunct. Following scheduled local elections in Moldova in late May 1999, Gagauzia, like Transnistria, was to be designated an autonomous entity, and was to support itself financially. Elections to the regional assembly and to the post of baskan were held in late August. Following a second round of voting in early September, Dumitru Croitor was elected as Baskan, with 61.5% of the votes cast. In mid-February 2002 the regional assembly passed a vote of 'no confidence' in Croitor, and scheduled a referendum in the hope of securing his dismissal, following allegations of the misuse of budgetary funds. However, as the confidence vote had been passed without the required majority, it was declared to be unconstitutional by supporters of Croitor. On 24 February, the date that the referendum was scheduled to take place, the security forces were reported to have seized the offices of the regional Election Commission on Croitor's orders, declaring its mandate to have expired following municipal elections held in February, and the referendum to be illegal. President Voronin subsequently visited the region and demanded the resignations of both Croitor and the Chairman of the regional assembly. In mid-April the region's Government, with the exception of Croitor, announced its resignation, in an attempt to end the conflict with the regional legislature. In mid-June, however, the Gagauz Government reversed its decision. Dumitru Croitor resigned from the position of Baskan at the end of June, and was eventually replaced in the interim by Gheorghe Molla. At the second round of the election, held on 11 October, Gheorghe Tabunscic, a representative of the MPC, secured the highest proportion of votes cast; Croitor had failed to qualify for registration in the poll owing to a legal technicality. On 29 November a new Government was approved.

Owing to the changing domestic situation, Moldova's membership of the CIS was equivocal from its signature of the Alma-Ata Declaration in December 1991 until early 1994. The republic did not become a party to the treaty on collective security (the Tashkent Agreement of May 1992), and in January 1993 Moldova was one of three CIS member states that did not sign a charter on closer political and economic integration. In August of that year the Moldovan Parliament failed by four votes to ratify the Alma-Ata Declaration, largely owing to the influence of deputies favouring unification with Romania, thus technically removing Moldova from the CIS. However, it was increasingly recognized that Moldova's economic survival depended on the CIS, and in September President Snegur signed a treaty to join the new CIS economic union. Following Moldova's parliamentary election of February 1994 and the referendum in March, which strongly endorsed continued independence, Parliament reversed its earlier decision, and in late April it finally ratified membership of the CIS. However, the legislature indicated that Moldova would participate neither in CIS military structures nor in monetary union.

The communist Government elected in 2001 undertook a policy of rapprochement with Russia, and on 27 December Parliament ratified a treaty on friendship and co-operation, which had been signed by the two countries' respective Presidents in the previous month. The treaty was ratified by the Russian State Duma in April 2002. Since gaining independence Moldova has also sought to develop good relations with the neighbouring countries of Ukraine and Romania. Agreement on the delimitation of the Moldovan–Ukrainian border, apart from the Transnistrian section, was reached in November 1997, and the two countries finally defined their border in May 1999.

Moldova and Romania finally overcame their differences on a basic political treaty in May 1999 and the document, which had been in preparation for six years, was to be signed at the next meeting between their Presidents. In February 2000 many Moldovans applied to obtain Romanian citizenship as formal negotiations on Romania's accession to the EU commenced, which meant that, if successful, its borders would be closed to Moldova. The Romanian Government introduced measures to simplify the application process, angering the Moldovan authorities, since the Constitution did not permit dual citizenship. The situation was resolved when President Lucinschi drafted a new law, allowing Moldovans to hold dual citizenship with Israel, Romania and Russia; the law was enacted in August. Moldova and Romania signed several co-operation agreements in July 2001. However, in October the Romanian Prime Minister, Adrian Năstase, cancelled a planned visit to Moldova, in response to accusations by the Moldovan Government of Romanian 'expansionism'. Meanwhile, from August Romania also expressed concern at the apparent 'russification' of Moldova, in particular following the Government's decision to introduce compulsory Russian-language teaching from 2002 (see above). Although Romania denied that it was interfering in the internal affairs of Moldova, in March 2002 a Romanian diplomat was expelled from Moldova, after having reportedly met organizers of the opposition protests; Romania responded by expelling a Moldovan diplomat from that country's embassy in Romania. However, following a meeting in September between the Presidents of the two countries, held in Beirut, Lebanon, it was agreed to establish working groups to resolve the problems in diplomatic relations. From April 2003 ministerial co-operation between Moldova and Romania was resumed, as were discussions on the updating of the basic political treaty between the two countries and the initiation of negotiations regarding a border agreement; it was confirmed that Romania would not require Moldovan citizens to possess visas until its anticipated accession to the EU in 2007. The passing of legislation in early 2003, which permitted dual citizenship for Romanians in Moldova, also served to improve relations between the two countries.

Government

Under the Constitution of 1994, supreme legislative power is held by the unicameral Moldovan Parliament, which is directly elected every four years. Parliament comprises 101 members. The President is Head of State and holds executive power in conjunction with the Council of Ministers, led by the Prime Minister. According to constitutional amendments introduced in July 2000, the President is elected by the legislature for a four-year term. Following local elections in May 1999 the country was reorganized into nine provinces and two autonomous entities—Gagauzia and Transnistria. However, new legislation approved by Parliament in December 2001 reintroduced a Soviet-style administrative structure, comprising 31 districts, the autonomous regions of Gagauzia and Transnistria, and three municipalities (Chişinău, Bălţi and Tighina).

Defence

Following independence from the USSR (declared in August 1991), the Moldovan Government initiated the creation of national armed forces. By August 2002 these were estimated to number 7,210, including an army of 5,560 and an air force of 1,400. There are an estimated 3,400 paramilitary forces, attached to the Ministry of the Interior. Military service is compulsory and lasts for up to 18 months. However, in mid-1998 it was announced that military service would no longer be required of students, and in April 2002 the Government approved plans for military reform in 2002–14, according to which there was to be a reduction in army manpower, and a reduced term of military service, of one year. Under an agreement concluded by the Moldovan and Russian Governments in late 1994, the former Soviet 14th Army (under Russian jurisdiction) was to have been withdrawn from Transnistria within three years, but in March 1998 it was agreed that Russian forces would remain in the region until a final political settlement had been reached. In July 2000 it was agreed to withdraw the Russian military presence from Transnistria in three stages, with all hardware to be removed by the end of 2001 and all troops by the end of 2002; the deadline was subsequently extended until December 2003. In early 1994 Moldova joined NATO's 'Partnership for Peace' (see p. 273) programme. The 2001 budget allocated 76.8m. Moldovan lei to defence.

Economic Affairs

In 2001, according to estimates by the World Bank, Moldova's gross national income (GNI), measured at average 1999–2001 prices, was US $1,399m., equivalent to $380 per head (or $2,420 on an international purchasing-power parity basis). During 1990–2001, it was estimated, the population decreased by an annual average of 0.2%, while gross domestic product (GDP) per head declined, in real terms, at an average rate of 8.4% per year. Overall GDP declined, in real terms, at an average annual rate of 8.5% in 1990–2001; however, GDP increased by 2.1% in 2000 and by 6.1% in 2001.

As a result of its extremely fertile land and temperate climate, Moldova's economy is dominated by agriculture and related industries. Some 85% of the country's terrain is cultivated. In 2001 agriculture (including forestry and fishing) contributed some 27.7% of GDP; if agricultural processing is included, the sector contributed some 60% of GDP in 1996. In 2001 the sector provided 51.0% of employment (excluding Transnistria). Principal crops include wine grapes and other fruit, tobacco, vegetables and grain. The wine industry has traditionally occupied a central role in the economy, and was revived after the Soviet Government's anti-alcohol campaign of the mid-1980s. The private ownership of land was legalized in 1991, although the sale of agricultural land was not to be permitted until 2001. Private farmers accounted for an estimated 67% of Moldova's agricultural output in 1999. Amendments to the Land Code in April 2002 attracted opposition from farmers, on the grounds that they constituted a return to the process of collectivization. According to the World Bank, the GDP of the sector declined, in real terms, at an average rate of 10.7% per year during 1990–2001. Agricultural GDP increased by 0.3% in 2000 and by 3.0% in 2001.

In 2001 industry (including mining, manufacturing, power and construction) contributed some 20.8% of GDP; in the same year the sector provided 13.9% of employment. In 1995, according to the IMF, the food-processing industry accounted for 50.3% of the value of total manufacturing and power output (excluding the Transnistria region). Heavy industry contributed 37.1% of the total in that year, and light industry accounted for only 4.8%. Between 1990 and 2001, according to the World Bank, industrial GDP declined at an average rate of 14.9% per year. However, real industrial GDP increased by 0.2% in 2000 and by 8.2% in 2001.

Mining and quarrying employed just 0.1% of the working population in 2001. Moldova has extremely limited mineral resources, and there is no domestic production of fuel or non-ferrous metals. Activity is focused primarily on the extraction and processing of industrial minerals such as gypsum, limestone, sand and gravel. Deposits of petroleum and natural gas were discovered in southern Moldova in the early 1990s; total reserves of natural gas have been estimated at 22,000m. cu m.

The manufacturing sector provided 9.1% of employment in 2001 and 12.8% of GDP in 2001. The sector is dominated by food-processing, wine and tobacco production, machine-building and metalworking, and light industry. In 1994 the principal branches, measured by gross value of output, were food-processing and beverages (57.8%), tobacco (4.9%), non-metallic mineral products (4.6%) and textiles (4.0%). Manufacturing GDP increased by 15.9% in 2000 and by 17.8% in 2001.

Moldova relies heavily on imported energy—primarily natural gas and petroleum products—from the Russian Federation, Romania and Ukraine. Moldova is seeking to become self-sufficient in natural gas, following the discovery of gas reserves in the south of the country. A large proportion of natural gas imports supply the Moldoveneasca power station, which contributed some 85% of the country's electrical generating capacity in 1996. (Located in the secessionist region of Transnistria, Moldoveneasca's supplies to the rest of Moldova were severed in the late 1980s; however, an integrated network was restored in 1992.) In 1999 natural gas accounted for 82.7% of electricity production, and coal accounted for 5.5%. In 1996 agreement was reached with Russia to form a joint Russian-Moldovan electric-power generation venture. Imports of mineral products comprised an estimated 27.0% of the value of total imports in 2001.

Excluding the Transnistria region, in 2001 services accounted for 35.1% of total employment and the sector contributed some 51.5% of GDP. In real terms, the GDP of the services sector declined by an annual average of 0.6% in 1991–2001. Services GDP increased, in real terms, by 0.1% in 2000 and by 5.6% in 2001.

In 2001 Moldova recorded a visible trade deficit of US $313.6m., while there was a deficit of $102.0m. on the current account of the balance of payments. In 2000 the principal source of imports was the Russian Federation (accounting for 15.4% of the value of total imports). Other major suppliers were Romania, Ukraine and Germany. The main market for exports in that year was Russia (44.4% of the value of total exports). Other important purchasers were Romania, Italy, Germany and Ukraine. In 2001 the principal imports were mineral products, machinery and mechanical appliances, textiles, and chemicals and related products. The main exports in that year were food products, beverages and tobacco (accounting for some 44.1% of the value of total exports), textiles, vegetable products and machinery and mechanical appliances.

In 2001 the state budget (excluding Transnistria) showed a deficit of 251m. Moldovan lei (equivalent to 1.3% of GDP). Moldova's total external debt at the end of 2000 was US $1,233m., of which $854m. was long-term public debt. In that year the cost of debt-servicing was equivalent to 16.7% of the value of exports of goods and services. Consumer prices increased by an annual average of 136.6% during 1991–2001. The average rate of inflation rose to 39.3% in 1999, before decreasing to 31.3% in 2000 and to 9.8% in 2001. The average rate of unemployment was 6.8% in 2002.

Moldova became a member of the IMF and the World Bank in 1992. It also joined the European Bank for Reconstruction and Development (EBRD, see p. 193). Moldova subsequently became a member of the Organization of the Black Sea Economic Co-operation (see p. 293), and it became a full member of the World Trade Organization (see p. 323) in July 2001.

In common with other former Soviet republics following independence, Moldova's planned transition to a market economic system was hampered by the serious disruptions in inter-republican trade. Another factor that adversely affected economic performance was the armed conflict in Transnistria (the main industrial centre) in the first half of 1992 and the region's subsequent attempts to secede from Moldova (see Recent History). Moldova introduced its own national currency, the Moldovan leu, in November 1993. Although by mid-1999 the IMF declared itself satisfied with Moldova's accelerated structural reforms, later that year a loan to cover the country's budgetary deficit was not disbursed, owing to Moldova's failure to complete the legislative framework for privatization of the winery and tobacco sectors; the World Bank also suspended the release of funds. Parliament finally approved the privatization programme in October 2000 and, following the approval of the budget for 2001 at the end of November, the international lending institutions agreed to resume financing. However, the communist successes in the legislative election of February 2001 and the presidential election in April resulted in a decrease in the pace of reform and a subsequent suspension of lending by the IMF. In April 2002 an agreement was signed with the World Bank supporting Moldova's request for the restructuring of its significant level of external debt (equivalent to over 150% of GDP). By mid-2002 agreement had been reached with Russia, Germany and the USA on the rescheduling of debt. IMF assistance, which resumed in June, following the adoption of a new Civil Code (see Recent History), was suspended once again at the end of the year, owing to Moldova's failure to fulfil certain criteria on the adoption of the state and social-fund budgets and the promulgation of legislation on pre-shipment inspections of imported goods (which had been annulled by the Constitutional Court earlier in the year). The legislation was finally passed in March 2003; budgetary concerns remained, however, over the financing of proposed salary increases and administrative territorial reforms. The planned completion date, of December 2002, for the country's privatization programme was extended until 2005; in 2003 there were plans for renewed efforts to sell a stake in the national fixed-line operator, Moldtelecom, as well as two power-distribution networks (a further three had been sold in 2002 to the Spanish utility, Unión Eléctrica Fenosa, SA). According to government figures the average annual rate of inflation in Moldova was significantly reduced in 2002, to 4.4%.

Education

In 1990–91 there were extensive changes to the education system, with Romanian literature and history being added to the curriculum. Many Russian-language schools were closed in the early 1990s. Education is officially compulsory in Moldova between seven and 16 years of age. Primary education begins at seven years of age and lasts for four years. Secondary education, beginning at 11, lasts for a maximum of seven years, comprising a first cycle of five years and a second of two years. Primary enrolment in 2002 was equivalent to 95% of children in the relevant age-group, and the comparable ratio for secondary enrolment was 88% in the same year. In 1997 total enrolment at primary, secondary and tertiary levels was equivalent to 71% of females and 69% of males. In 1999 measures were taken to reduce costs in the education sector. In 2001 budgetary expenditure on education was 924m. lei (representing 16.13 of total spending).

Public Holidays

2003: 1 January (New Year's Day), 7–8 January (Christmas), 8 March (International Women's Day), 27–28 April (Orthodox Easter), 1 May (Labour Day), 9 May (Victory and Commemoration Day), 27 August (Independence Day), 31 August ('Limbă Noastră', National Language Day).

2004: 1 January (New Year's Day), 7–8 January (Christmas), 8 March (International Women's Day), 11–12 April (Orthodox Easter), 1 May (Labour Day), 9 May (Victory and Commemoration Day), 27 August (Independence Day), 31 August ('Limbă Noastră', National Language Day).

Weights and Measures

The metric system is in force.

Statistical Survey

Principal sources (unless otherwise indicated): State Department for Statistics and Sociology, 2028 Chişinău, şos. Hînceşti 53D; tel. (2) 73-37-74; fax (2) 22-61-46; e-mail dass@statistica.md; internet www.statistica.md.

Note: Most of the figures for 1993–2001 exclude the Transnistria (Transdnestr) region of eastern Moldova, i.e. the area on the left bank of the Dniester (Dnestr or Nistru) river.

Area and Population

AREA, POPULATION AND DENSITY

Area (sq km)	33,800*
Population (census results)†	
17 January 1979	3,949,756
12 January 1989	
Males	2,063,192
Females	2,272,168
Total	4,335,360
Population (official estimates at 1 January)	
2000	4,281,500
2001	4,264,300
2002	3,627,812
Density (per sq km) at January 2002	107.3

* 13,050 sq miles.

† Figures refer to the *de jure* population. The *de facto* total at the 1989 census was 4,337,592 (males 2,058,160; females 2,279,432).

POPULATION BY ETHNIC GROUP

(permanent inhabitants, 1989 census)

	Number	%
Moldovan	2,794,749	64.5
Ukrainian	600,366	13.8
Russian	562,069	13.0
Gagauz	153,458	3.5
Bulgarian	88,419	2.0
Jewish	65,672	1.5
Others and unknown	70,627	1.7
Total	4,335,360	100.0

PRINCIPAL TOWNS

(estimated population at 1 January 1996)

Chişinău (Kishinev) (capital) . . .	655,000	Tighina (Bender) . .	128,000
Tiraspol . . .	187,000	Râbnita (Rybnitsa) .	62,900
Bălţi (Beltsy) . . .	153,500		

2003 (estimate, 1 January): Chişinău 662,400; Bălţi 150,600.

ADMINISTRATIVE DIVISIONS

(estimated population at 1 January 2003)

Bălţi	500,900	Taraclia	465,600
Cahul	190,800	Tighina	169,000
Chişinău	1,161,800	Ungheni	260,300
Edinet	279,100	*Autonomous territory*	
		of Gagauzia . .	158,900
Lapusna	2776,300	*Transnistria and*	
		Tighina (Bender)* .	629,800
Orhei	300,400	**Total**	3,617,700
Soroco	274,600		

* 2001 figure.

BIRTHS, MARRIAGES AND DEATHS

	Registered live births		Registered marriages		Registered deaths	
	Number	Rate (per 1,000)	Number	Rate (per 1,000)	Number	Rate (per 1,000)
1994 . .	62,085	14.3	33,742	7.8	51,514	11.8
1995 . .	56,411	13.0	32,775	7.5	52,969	12.2
1996 . .	51,865	12.0	26,089	6.0	49,748	11.5
1997 . .	51,286	11.9	26,305	6.1*	51,138	11.9
1998 . .	46,755	10.9	25,793	6.0*	47,691	11.1
1999† . .	38,501	9.0	23,524	5.5	41,315	9.6
2000† . .	36,939	8.7	21,684	5.1	41,224	9.7
2001 . .	36,448	10.0	21,200‡	5.8	40,100‡	11.0

* Estimate.

† Numbers exclude, but rates include, Transnistria.

‡ Rounded figures.

Sources: partly UN, *Population and Vital Statistics Report; Moldovan Economic Trends.*

Expectation of life (WHO estimates, years at birth): 68.0 (males 64.2; females 71.7) in 2001 (Source: WHO, *World Health Report*).

ECONOMICALLY ACTIVE POPULATION

('000 persons)

	1999	2000	2001
Agriculture, hunting and forestry	730	769.0	763.4
Fishing	1	1.4	1.4
Mining and quarrying	3	1.7	2.0
Manufacturing	135	135.8	136.8
Electricity, gas and water supply .	22	28.5	26.4
Construction	44	44.4	43.2
Wholesale and retail trade; repair of motor vehicles, motorcycles and personal and household goods	135	147.3	144.5
Hotels and restaurants . . .	15	18.0	19.3
Transport, storage and communications	70	63.9	64.3
Financial intermediation . . .	10	8.1	9.2
Real estate, renting and business activities	35	19.5	19.5
Public administration and defence; compulsory social security . .	49	64.5	65.8
Education	137	101.5	100.9
Health and social work . . .	80	74.2	70.7
Other community, social and personal service activities . .	29	28.2	28.2
Private households with employed persons	—	8.6	3.1
Total employed	1,495	1,514.6	1,499.0
Unemployed	187	140.1	117.7
Total labour force	1,682	1,654.6	1,616.7
Males	853	828.0	806.6
Females	829	826.6	810.1

Source: ILO.

Health and Welfare

KEY INDICATORS

Total fertility rate (children per woman, 2001)	1.5
Under-5 mortality rate (per 1,000 live births, 2001) . . .	32
HIV/AIDS (% of persons aged 15–49, 2001)	0.24
Physicians (per 1,000 head, 1998)	3.5
Hospital beds (per 1,000 head, 1996)	12.12
Health expenditure (2000): US $ per head (PPP)	64
Health expenditure (2000): % of GDP	3.5
Health expenditure (2000): public (% of total)	82.4
Access to water (% of persons, 2000)	100
Human Development Index (2000): ranking	105
Human Development Index (2000): value	0.701

For sources and definitions, see explanatory note on p. vi.

Agriculture

PRINCIPAL CROPS

('000 metric tons)

	1999	2000	2001
Wheat	800.4	725.0	1,180.0
Barley	182.6	133.0	232.8
Maize	1,140.3	1,031.0	1,116.5
Potatoes	329.5	330.0	384.0
Sugar beet	1,008.8	943.4	1,193.6
Dry peas	34.3	15.0	37.8
Sunflower seed	285.6	268.4	278.0
Cabbages	50.3	45.0	51.5
Tomatoes	167.2	104.0	105.0
Cucumbers and gherkins . .	32.1	26.0*	32.0*
Chillies and green peppers* . .	38	33	38
Dry onions	69.3	62.0	74.4
Carrots	19.8	20.0	20.7
Other vegetables*	50.7	50.0	51.2
Apples	56.1	162.4	186.9
Plums	38.1	41.2	59.2
Grapes	464.9	700.1	503.0
Watermelons	22.0†	28.0	27.0
Other fruits*	41.7	62.3	71.0
Tobacco (leaves)	22.4	23.5	15.1

* Unofficial figure(s).
† FAO estimate.

Source: FAO.

LIVESTOCK

('000 head at 1 January)

	1999	2000	2001
Horses*	68	68	68
Cattle	452	416	402
Pigs	807	683	447
Sheep†	1,008	830	819
Goats	97†	100	109
Chickens	13,800†	12,575	13,041

* FAO estimates.
† Unofficial figure(s).

Source: FAO.

LIVESTOCK PRODUCTS

('000 metric tons)

	1999	2000	2001
Beef and veal	23.5	21.0*	12.1
Mutton and lamb	3.6	3.4*	3.1*
Pig meat	60.8	59.8	57.2
Poultry meat	15.8	21.5	26.3
Cows' milk	569.0	554.8	560.6
Sheep's milk	16.1	14.3*	14.4*
Goats' milk	4.3	4.7*	4.5*
Butter	1.9	2.5	3.0
Cheese	5.1	4.6	4.9
Hen eggs	19.1	32.1*	34.5
Honey	2.0	1.8†	2.0†
Wool: greasy	2.3	2.1	2.1
Cattle hides (fresh)†	3.1	1.5	1.6

* Unofficial figure.
† FAO estimate(s).

Source: partly FAO.

Forestry

ROUNDWOOD REMOVALS
('000 cubic metres, excl. bark)

	1998	1999	2000
Sawlogs, veneer logs and logs for sleepers .	10	3	5
Other industrial wood . . .	7	9	24
Fuel wood	356	36	30
Total	373	49	58

Source: FAO.

SAWNWOOD PRODUCTION
('000 cubic metres, incl. railway sleepers)

	1998	1999	2000
Coniferous (softwood) . . .	25	—	—
Broadleaved (hardwood). . .	5	6	5
Total	30	6	5

Source: FAO.

Fishing

(metric tons, live weight)

	1998	1999	2000
Capture	491	129	151
Common carp	280	n.a.	n.a.
Crucian carp	159	104	132
Aquaculture	1,129	1,007	1,168
Common carp	91	299	351
Crucian carp	139	105	110
Grass carp (White amur) .	87	92	99
Silver carp	812	511	608
Total catch	1,620	1,136	1,319

Source: FAO, *Yearbook of Fishery Statistics*.

Mining

('000 metric tons)

	1998	1999	2000
Gypsum	19.8	18.5	32.1
Peat*	475	475	475

* Estimated production.

Source: US Geological Survey.

Industry

SELECTED PRODUCTS
('000 metric tons, unless otherwise indicated)

	1997	1998	1999
Vegetable oil	19	18	17
Flour	252	229	150
Raw sugar.	204	187	99
Wine from grapes (million litres) .	190.9	119.6	65.2
Mineral water (million litres) .	9.3	17.6	23.8
Soft drinks (million litres) . .	13.9	29.5	33.7
Cigarettes (million)	9,539	7,512	8,731
Carpets (million sq m) . . .	0.7	0.7	0.5
Footwear ('000 pairs) . . .	1,032	739	704
Cement	122	74	50
Refrigerators and freezers ('000 units) .	2	0	n.a.
Washing machines ('000 units). .	46	43	18
Television receivers ('000 units) .	19	10	3
Tractors ('000 units)	0.9	0.7	0.0
Electric energy (million kWh) .	5,274	4,584	n.a.

Source: UN, *Industrial Commodity Statistics Yearbook*.

Finance

CURRENCY AND EXCHANGE RATES

Monetary Units
100 bani (singular: ban) = 1 Moldovan leu (plural: lei)

Sterling, Dollar and Euro Equivalents (31 December 2002)
£1 sterling = 22.278 lei
US $1 = 13.822 lei
€1 = 14.495 lei
1,000 Moldovan lei = £44.89 = $72.35 = €68.99

Average Exchange Rate (Moldovan lei per US$)
2000   12.4342
2001   12.8651
2002   13.5705

Note: The Moldovan leu was introduced (except in the Transnistria region) on 29 November 1993, replacing the Moldovan rouble at a rate of 1 leu = 1,000 roubles. The Moldovan rouble had been introduced in June 1992, as a temporary coupon currency, and was initially at par with the Russian (formerly Soviet) rouble.

STATE BUDGET
(million lei)*

Revenue†	1999	2000	2001
Tax revenue	3,050	3,973	4,644
Taxes on profits	233	275	350
Taxes on personal incomes . .	220	265	348
Value-added tax	940	1,333	1,498
Excises	444	658	681
Taxes on international trade. .	231	222	234
Social Fund contributions . .	783	994	1,304
Other taxes	199	227	231
Non-tax revenue	535	806	749
Total	3,745	4,780	5,393

Expenditure‡	1999	2000	2001
Current budgetary expenditure .	3,176	2,922	2,890
National economy	287	331	298
Social sphere	1,340	1,570	1,795
Education	575	719	924
Health care	335	464	542
Interest payments	906	1,021	797
Capital budgetary expenditure. .	103	175	206
Social Fund expenditure . .	889	1,328	1,373
Project loan spending . . .	368	212	245
Other expenditure	643	776	946
Total	4,535	5,413	5,661

* Figures refer to a consolidation of the operations of central (republican) and local governments, including the Social Fund.
† Excluding grants received (million lei): 132 in 1999; 147 in 2000.
‡ Excluding net lending (million lei): −44 in 1999; −32 in 2000; −17 in 2001.

Source: IMF, *Republic of Moldova: 2002 Article IV Consultation* (August 2002).

INTERNATIONAL RESERVES
(US $ million at 31 December)

	2000	2001	2002
IMF special drawing rights . .	0.34	0.74	0.27
Reserve position in IMF. . .	0.01	0.01	0.01
Foreign exchange. . . .	229.80	228.29	268.46
Total (excl. gold).	230.15	229.04	268.74

Source: IMF, *International Financial Statistics*.

MONEY SUPPLY
(million lei at 31 December)

	2000	2001	2002
Currency outside banks . . .	1,469.26	1,834.20	2,288.56
Demand deposits at commercial banks	553.75	665.76	1,271.14
Total money (incl. others). . .	2,032.22	2,500.00	3,559.80

Source: IMF, *International Financial Statistics*.

COST OF LIVING
(Consumer Price Index; base: 1992 = 100)

	1999	2000	2001
Food (incl. beverages)	17,954.3	24,486.6	27,108
All items	27,046.2	35,511.6	38,979

Source: ILO.

2001 (base: 2000 = 100): All items 109.8 (Source: IMF, *International Financial Statistics*).

NATIONAL ACCOUNTS
(million lei at current prices, excl. Transnistria)

Expenditure on the Gross Domestic Product

	1999	2000	2001
Government final consumption expenditure	1,953.6*	2,471.8	2,811.9
Private final consumption expenditure	9,136.8	14,030.9	17,037.1
Changes in inventories . .	547.7	1,363.7	1,241.4
Gross fixed capital formation. .	2,272.0	2,472.5	2,574.9
Total domestic expenditure .	13,910.1	20,338.9	23,665.3
Exports of goods and services .	6,446.4		
Less Imports of goods and services	8,034.8	−4,319.3	−4,645.9
GDP in purchasers' values .	12,321.6	16,019.6	19,019.3

* Including non-profit institutions.

Sources: *Moldovan Economic Trends*, and IMF, *International Financial Statistics*.

Gross Domestic Product by Economic Activity

	1998	1999	2000
Agriculture, hunting, forestry and fishing	2,351	3,066	3,919
Mining and quarrying . . .	17	24	23
Manufacturing	1,276	1,613	2,423
Electricity, gas and water supply	229	456	358
Construction	289	409	423
Wholesale and retail trade; repair of motor vehicles, motorcycles and personal and household goods	941	1,885	2,135
Transport, storage and communications	671	1,013	1,434
Other services	2,381	3,226	4,248
Sub-total	8,155	11,692	14,963
Taxes (less subsidies) on products and imports	1,403	1,323	1,976
Less Financial intermediation services indirectly measured . .	436	693	959
GDP in purchasers' values .	9,122	12,322	15,980

BALANCE OF PAYMENTS
(US $ million)

	1999	2000	2001
Exports of goods f.o.b.	474.2	476.8	569.2
Imports of goods f.o.b.	−611.4	−770.5	−882.8
Trade balance	−137.2	−293.6	−313.6
Exports of services	134.6	165.4	171.6
Imports of services	−174.1	−2032.3	−219.1
Balance on goods and services	−176.8	−330.5	−361.0
Other income received . . .	120.4	172.1	235.2
Other income paid	−94.2	−105.0	−124.0
Balance on goods, services and income	−150.5	−263.4	−249.8
Current transfers received . .	115.8	163.6	166.0
Current transfers paid . . .	−39.7	−15.1	−18.2
Current balance	−74.5	−114.9	−102.0
Capital account (net)	1.1	1.9	−2.0
Direct investment abroad . .	−0.1	−0.1	−0.1
Direct investment from abroad	40.6	143.0	104.0
Portfolio investment assets . .	—	—	−3.2
Portfolio investment liabilities . .	−7.1	2.5	3.6
Other investment assets . .	−107.4	−35.4	−26.2
Other investment liabilities . .	40.3	44.9	−15.5
Net errors and omissions . . .	−9.1	−17.9	15.7
Overall balance	−116.1	23.9	−25.6

Source: IMF, *International Financial Statistics*.

External Trade

PRINCIPAL COMMODITIES
(US $ million)

Imports	1999	2000	2001
Mineral products	232.0	255.7	242.3
Products of chemical or allied industries	45.8	74.9	80.5
Textiles and textile articles . . .	66.4	77.5	93.6
Base metals and articles thereof .	24.9	31.5	38.1
Machinery and mechanical appliances; electrical equipment; sound and television apparatus .	69.4	98.6	124.0
Total (incl. others)	586.7	776.6	896.9

Exports f.o.b.	1999	2000	2001
Live animals and animal products	29.3	22.8	18.3
Vegetable products	68.0	65.9	79.2
Prepared foodstuffs; beverages, spirits and vinegar; tobacco and manufactured substitutes . .	196.9	197.6	251.8
Textiles and textile articles . . .	64.7	83.6	105.7
Base metals and articles thereof .	16.5	11.7	n.a.
Machinery and mechanical appliances; electrical equipment; sound and television apparatus .	27.3	24.3	31.8
Total (incl. others)	464.2	471.4	570.4

PRINCIPAL TRADING PARTNERS
(US $ million)

Imports c.i.f.	1998	1999	2000
Belarus	50.6	22.7	31.9
Bulgaria	29.3	9.4	13.6
France	22.1	12.6	20.0
Germany	91.9	61.4	87.7
Greece	6.7	8.4	15.1
Hungary	29.0	6.9	13.0
Italy	65.0	38.2	48.9
Netherlands	10.4	9.4	8.7
Poland	9.9	8.3	15.5
Romania	112.9	81.6	119.3
Russia	233.0	138.7	119.6
Turkey	10.6	11.8	18.2
Ukraine	151.5	79.2	104.8
United Kingdom	9.4	8.2	9.7
USA	33.5	22.2	48.2
Total (incl. others)	1,023.6	586.7	776.6

Exports f.o.b.	1998	1999	2000
Austria	9.5	10.0	5.6
Belarus	31.9	21.8	21.8
Bulgaria	2.8	5.3	3.6
Canada	9.5	3.3	2.1
France	8.3	6.4	7.9
Germany	23.9	33.5	36.3
Greece	4.6	5.8	2.4
Hungary	3.4	16.3	4.6
Italy	22.3	25.6	36.4
Poland	2.0	5.0	2.0
Romania	60.8	41.3	37.6
Russia	336.8	191.2	209.5
Ukraine	48.7	32.9	35.5
United Kingdom	2.6	3.9	5.4
USA	18.1	14.5	15.6
Total (incl. others)	631.8	464.2	471.4

Transport

RAILWAYS
(traffic)

	1998	1999	2000
Passenger journeys (million)	9.4	5.4	4.8
Passenger-km (million)	656	343	315
Freight transported (million metric tons)	11.1	6.6	8.2
Freight ton-km (million)	2,575	1,191	1,513

ROAD TRAFFIC
(motor vehicles in use)

	1997	1998	1999
Passenger cars	205,973	222,769	232,278
Buses and coaches	11,169	12,917	13,582
Lorries and vans	56,924	57,404	52,430

Source: IRF, *World Road Statistics*.

INLAND WATERWAYS
(traffic)

	1998	1999	2000
Freight transported ('000 metric tons)	13.1	15.9	8.7

CIVIL AVIATION
(traffic)

	1996	1997	1998
Kilometres flown (million)	5	2	4
Passengers carried ('000)	190	46	118
Passenger-km (million)	240	61	146
Total ton-km (million)	23	6	14

Source: UN, *Statistical Yearbook*.

1999: Passengers carried ('000) 200; Passenger-km (million) 240; Freight transported ('000 metric tons) 1.3; Freight ton-km (million) 3.3.

2000: Passengers carried ('000) 220; Passenger-km (million) 253; Freight transported ('000 metric tons) 1.4; Freight ton-km (million) 4.1.

Tourism

FOREIGN VISITOR ARRIVALS
(incl. excursionists)

Country of origin	1998	1999	2000
Belarus	469	550	546
Bulgaria	657	458	528
Germany	833	277	537
Italy	578	409	594
Romania	2,846	2,087	2,341
Russia	5,964	2,595	5,146
Turkey	807	1,612	2,548
Ukraine	3,323	1,944	1,969
United Kingdom	124	615	327
USA	847	889	1,030
Total (incl. others)	19,896	14,088	18,964

2002: 20,161 tourist arrivals.

Receipts from tourism (US $ million): 4 in 1998; 2 in 1999; 4 in 2000.

Source: World Tourism Organization, *Yearbook of Tourism Statistics*; and World Bank, *World Development Indicators*.

Communications Media

	1999	2000	2001
Television receivers ('000 in use)	1,300	1,300	n.a.
Telephones ('000 main lines in use)	555.3	583.8	676.1
Facsimile machines (number in use)	716	n.a.	n.a.
Mobile cellular telephones ('000 subscribers)	18.0	132.3	210.0
Personal computers ('000 in use)	35	64	70
Internet users ('000)	25	53	60

Radio receivers ('000 in use): 3,220 in 1997.

Book production (including pamphlets): 921 titles (2,779,000 copies) in 1996.

Daily newspapers: 4 (average circulation 261,000) in 1996.

Non-daily newspapers: 206 (estimated average circulation 1,350,000) in 1996.

Other periodicals: 76 (average circulation 196,000) in 1994.

Sources: UNESCO, *Statistical Yearbook*; International Telecommunication Union.

Education

(2002/03)

	Institutions	Teachers*	Students
Primary	120 ⎫	42,300	19,200
Secondary: general	1,460 ⎭		523,400
Secondary: vocational	83	2,300	22,600
Higher: colleges*	60	1,900	19,900
Higher: universities	45	5,300	95,039

* 2000/01 figures.

Adult literacy rate (UNESCO estimates): 98.9% (males 99.5%; females 98.3%) in 2000 (Source: UN Development Programme, *Human Development Report*).

Directory

The Constitution

The Constitution of the Republic of Moldova, summarized below, was adopted by the Moldovan Parliament on 28 July 1994 and entered into force on 27 August. On 28 July 2000 amendments to the Constitution were enacted, which transformed Moldova into a parliamentary republic. Following alterations to the law on presidential election procedure, approved on 22 September, the President of the Republic was, henceforth, to be elected by the legislature, rather than directly.

GENERAL PRINCIPLES

The Republic of Moldova is a sovereign, independent, unitary and indivisible state. The rule of law, the dignity, rights and freedoms of the people, and the development of human personality, justice and political pluralism are guaranteed. The Constitution is the supreme law. The Constitution upholds principles such as human rights and freedoms, democracy and political pluralism, the separation and co-operation of the legislative, executive and judicial powers of the State, respect for international law and treaties, fundamental principles regarding property, free economic initiative and the right to national identity. The national language of the republic is Moldovan and its writing is based on the Latin alphabet, although the State acknowledges the right to use other languages spoken within the country.

FUNDAMENTAL RIGHTS, FREEDOMS AND DUTIES

The Constitution grants Moldovan citizens their rights and freedoms and lays down their duties. All citizens are equal before the law; they should have free access to justice, are presumed innocent until proven guilty and have a right to an acknowledged legal status.

The State guarantees fundamental human rights, such as the right to life and to physical and mental integrity, the freedoms of movement, conscience, expression, assembly and political association, and the enfranchisement of Moldovan citizens aged over 18 years. Moldovan citizens have the right of access to information and education, of health security, of establishing and joining a trade union, of working and of striking. The family, orphaned children and the disabled enjoy the protection of the State. Obligations of the citizenry include the payment of taxes and the defence of the motherland.

PARLIAMENT

Parliament is the supreme legislative body and sole legislative authority of Moldova. It consists of 101 members, directly elected for a four-year term. The Chairman of Parliament is elected by members, also for a four-year term. Parliament holds two ordinary sessions per year. The Parliament's basic powers include: the enactment of laws, the holding of referendums, the provision of legislative unity throughout the country, the approval of state policy, the approval or suspension of international treaties, the election of state officials, the mobilization of the armed forces and the declaration of the states of national emergency, martial law and war.

THE PRESIDENT OF THE REPUBLIC

The President of the Republic is the Head of State and is elected by the legislature for a four-year term. A candidate must be aged no less than 40 years, be a Moldovan citizen and a speaker of the official language. The candidate must be in good health and, with his or her application, must submit the written support of a minimum of 15 parliamentarians. A decision on the holding of a presidential election is taken by parliamentary resolution, and the election must be held no fewer than 45 days before the expiry of the outgoing President's term of office. To be elected President, a candidate must obtain the support of three-fifths of the parliamentary quorum. If necessary, further ballots must then be conducted, contested by the two candidates who received the most votes. The candidate who receives more votes becomes President. The post of President may be held by the same person for not more than two consecutive terms.

The President's main responsibilities include the promulgation of laws, the issue of decrees, the scheduling of referendums, the conclusion of international treaties and the dissolution of the Parliament. The President is allowed to participate in parliamentary proceedings. The President, after consultation with the parliamentary majority, is responsible for nominating a Prime Minister-designate and a Government. The President can preside over government meetings and can consult the Government on matters of special importance and urgency. On proposals submitted by the Prime Minister, the President may revoke or renominate members of the Government in cases of vacancies or the reallocation of portfolios. The President is Commander-in-Chief of the armed forces.

If the President has committed a criminal or constitutional offence, the votes of two-thirds of the members of Parliament are required to remove the President from office; the removal must be confirmed by the Supreme Court of Justice, for a criminal offence, and by a national referendum, for a constitutional offence.

THE COUNCIL OF MINISTERS

The principal organ of executive government is the Council of Ministers, which supervises state policy and public administration of the country. The Council of Ministers is headed by a Prime Minister, who co-ordinates the activities of the Government. The Council of Ministers must resign if the Parliament votes in favour of a motion of 'no confidence' in the Council.

LOCAL ADMINISTRATION

For administrative purposes, the Republic of Moldova is divided into districts, towns and villages, in which local self-government is practised. At village and town level, elected local councils and mayors operate as autonomous administrative authorities. At district level, an elected council co-ordinates the activities of village and town councils.

The area on the left bank of the Dniester (Dnestr or Nistru) river, as well as certain other places in the south of the republic (i.e. Gagauzia) may be granted special autonomous status, according to special statutory provisions of organic law.

JUDICIAL AUTHORITY

Every citizen has the right to free access to justice. Justice shall be administered by the Supreme Court of Justice, the Court of Appeal, tribunals and the courts of law. Judges sitting in the courts of law and the Supreme Court of Justice are appointed by the President following proposals by the Higher Magistrates' Council. They are elected for a five-year term, and subsequently for a 10-year term, after which their term of office expires on reaching the age limit. The Higher Magistrates' Council is composed of 11 magistrates, who are appointed for a five-year term. It is responsible for the appointment, transfer and promotion of judges, as well as disciplinary action against them.

The Prosecutor-General, who is appointed by Parliament, exercises control over the enactment of law, as well as defending the legal order and the rights and freedoms of citizens.

THE CONSTITUTIONAL COURT

The Constitutional Court is the sole authority of constitutional judicature in Moldova. It is composed of six judges, who are appointed for a six-year term. The Constitutional Court's powers include: the enforcement of constitutionality control over laws, decrees and governmental decisions, as well as international treaties endorsed by the republic; the confirmation of the results of elections and referendums; the explanation and clarification of the Constitution; and decisions over matters of the constitutionality of parties. The decisions of the Constitutional Court are final and are not subject to appeal.

CONSTITUTIONAL REVISIONS

A revision of the Constitution may be initiated by one of the following: a petition signed by at least 200,000 citizens from at least one-half of the country's districts and municipalities; no less than one-third of the members of Parliament; the President of the Republic; the Government. Provisions regarding the sovereignty, independence, unity and neutrality of the State may be revised only by referendum.

The Government

HEAD OF STATE

President: VLADIMIR VORONIN (elected 4 April 2001).

COUNCIL OF MINISTERS
(April 2003)

Prime Minister: VASILE TARLEV.
First Deputy Prime Minister: VASILE IOVV.

Deputy Prime Ministers: VALERIAN CRISTEA.

Deputy Prime Minister and Minister of the Economy: ŞTEFAN ODAGIU.

Deputy Prime Minister and Minister of Agriculture and the Food Industry: DUMITRU TODOROGLO.

Minister of Foreign Affairs: NICOLAE DUDĂU.

Minister of Finance: ZINAIDA GRECÎANII.

Minister of Internal Affairs: GHEORGHE PAPUC.

Minister of Defence: Brig.-Gen. VICTOR GAICIUC.

Minister of Energy: IACOB TIMCIUC.

Minister of Industry and Trade: MIHAI GARŞTEA.

Minister of Justice: VASILE DOLGHIERU.

Minister of Labour and Social Protection: VALERIAN REVENCO.

Minister of Transport and Telecommunications: VASILE ZGARDAN.

Minister of Education and Science: GHEORGHE SIMA.

Minister of Health: ANDREI GHERMAN.

Minister of Culture: VEACESLAV MADAN.

Minister of Ecology, Construction and Territorial Development: GHEORGHE DUCA.

Minister of Reintegration: VASILE SOVA.

Baskan (Leader) of Gagauzia: GHEORGHE TABUNSCIC.

CHAIRMEN OF STATE DEPARTMENTS

Chairman of the State Department for Civil Defence and Emergencies: (vacant).

Chairman of the State Department for Fuel and Energy: VALERIU ICONNICOV.

Chairman of the State Department for Inter-Ethnic Relations and Languages: (vacant).

Chairman of the State Department for Privatization and State Property Administration: NICOLAE GUMENII.

Chairman of the State Department for Statistical and Sociological Analysis: ANA CUCUREAVI.

Chairman of the State Department for Technical Supervision, Standardization and Metrology: (vacant).

MINISTRIES

Office of the President: Chişinău, bd Ştefan cel Mare 154; tel. (2) 23-47-93.

Office of the Council of Ministers: 2033 Chişinău, Piaţa Marii Adunări Naţionale 1; tel. (2) 23-30-92.

Ministry of Agriculture and the Food Industry: 2012 Chişinău, bd Ştefan cel Mare 162; tel. (2) 23-34-27; fax (2) 23-23-68.

Ministry of Culture: 2033 Chişinău, Piaţa Marii Adunări Naţionale 1; tel. (2) 23-39-56; fax (2) 23-23-88.

Ministry of Defence: 2028 Chişinău, şos. Hînceşti 84; tel. (2) 79-94-89; fax (2) 23-45-35.

Ministry of Ecology, Construction and Territorial Development: 2005 Chişinău, str. Cosmonauţilor 9; tel. (2) 22-16-68; fax (2) 22-07-48; e-mail capcelea@moldova.md.

Ministry of the Economy: 2033 Chişinău, Piaţa Marii Adunări Naţionale 1; tel. (2) 23-74-48; fax (2) 23-40-64; e-mail minecon@moldova.md.

Ministry of Education: 2033 Chişinău, Piaţa Marii Adunări Naţionale 1; tel. (2) 23-35-15; fax (2) 23-34-74; e-mail tiron@minedu.moldnet.md.

Ministry of Energy: 2012 Chişinău, str. V. Alecsandri 78; tel. (2) 22-22-64; fax (2) 25-33-42; e-mail mdepen@rambler.ru.

Ministry of Finance: 2005 Chişinău, str. Cosmonauţilor 7; tel. (2) 23-35-75; fax (2) 22-13-07; e-mail protocol@minfin.moldova.md; internet www.moldova.md.

Ministry of Foreign Affairs: 2012 Chişinău, str. 31 August 1989 80; tel. (2) 23-39-40; fax (2) 23-23-02; e-mail massmedi@mfa.un.md; internet www.moldova.md/ro/government/oll/FOREIGN/en/index_en.html.

Ministry of Health: 2009 Chişinău, str. V. Alecsandri 1; tel. (2) 72-98-60; fax (2) 73-87-81; e-mail sdomente@mednet.md.

Ministry of Industry: 2012 Chişinău, bd Ştefan cel Mare 69; tel. (2) 27-80-59; fax (2) 27-80-00.

Ministry of Internal Affairs: 2012 Chişinău, bd Ştefan cel Mare 75; tel. (2) 22-45-47; fax (2) 22-27-43; e-mail mai@mai.md; internet www.mai.md.

Ministry of Justice: 2012 Chişinău, str. 31 August 1989 82; tel. (2) 23-47-95; fax (2) 23-47-97; e-mail dagri@cni.md.

Ministry of Labour and Social Protection: 2009 Chişinău, str. V. Alecsandri 1; tel. (2) 73-75-72; fax (2) 72-30-00; e-mail mmpsf@cni.md.

Ministry of Transport and Communications: 2012 Chişinău, bd Ştefan cel Mare 134; tel. (2) 22-10-01; fax (2) 24-15-53; e-mail secretary@mci.gov.md; internet mci.gov.md.

STATE DEPARTMENTS

State Department for Civil Defence and Emergencies: Chişinău, str. Gh. Asachi 69; tel. (2) 73-85-01; fax (2) 23-34-30.

State Department for Fuel and Energy: see Ministry of Energy.

State Department for Inter-Ethnic Relations and Languages: Chişinău.

State Department of Privatization and State Property Administration: 2012 Chişinău, str. Puşkin 26; tel. (2) 23-43-50; fax (2) 23-43-36; e-mail dep.priv@moldtelecom.md.

State Department for Statistics and Sociology: 2028 Chişinău, şos. Hînceşti 53D; tel. (2) 73-37-74; fax (2) 22-61-46; e-mail dass@statistica.md; internet www.statistica.md.

State Department for Technical Supervision, Standardization and Metrology: 2069 Chişinău, str. E. Coca 28; tel. (2) 74-85-88; fax (2) 75-05-81; e-mail moldovastandard@standart.mldnet.com.

President and Legislature

PRESIDENT

The Moldovan Parliament failed to elect a President in four rounds of voting in December 2000. Therefore, under the terms of the Constitution, Parliament had to be dissolved and legislative elections held before a fresh presidential election could take place. Three candidates contested the presidential election of 4 April 2001. Vladimir Voronin was elected President with 71 votes; Dumitru Braghiş received 15 votes and Valerian Cristea received three votes. The 11 deputies of the Christian Democratic People's Party abstained from voting.

PARLIAMENT

Parlamentul
(Parliament)

2073 Chişinău, bd Ştefan cel Mare 105; tel. (2) 23-33-52; fax (2) 23-30-12; e-mail info@parlament.md; internet www.parlament.md.

Chairman: EUGENIA OSTAPCIUC.

Deputy Chairmen: VADIM MISIN, MIHAIL CAMERZAN.

General Election, 25 February 2001

Parties and alliances	% of votes	Seats
Moldovan Party of Communists	49.93	71
Braghiş Alliance	13.40	19
Christian Democratic People's Party	8.31	11
Other parties, alliances and independents*	28.36	—
Total	100.00	101

* Including the Party of Revival and Conciliation, the Democratic Party of Moldova, the National Liberal Party, the Social Democratic Party of the Republic of Moldova and the National Peasants' Christian Democratic Party.

Political Organizations

At March 2003 26 political parties were registered with the Ministry of Justice.

Agrarian Democratic Party (ADP) (Partidul Democrat Agrar din Moldova): Chişinău; tel. (2) 22-42-74; fax (2) 22-23-63; f. 1991 by moderates from both the Popular Front of Moldova and the Communist Party of Moldova; supports Moldovan independence, and economic and agricultural reform; Chair. ANATOL POPUŞOI.

Alliance for Independent Moldova (Alianţa Indepenţilor din Republica Moldova): Chişinău, str. Maria Cebotari 4/1; tel. (2) 22-12-81; fax (2) 54-22-36; e-mail suairm@yahoo.com; f. 2001 by mayors and municipal councillors; formed the 'Moldova Noastră' Social

Liberal Alliance in 2003 with the Social Democratic Alliance of Moldova and the Moldovan Liberal Party; Leader SERAFIM URECHEAN.

Christian Democratic People's Party (CDPP) (Partidul Popular Creştin Democrat—PPCD): 2009 Chişinău, str. Nicolae Iorga 5; tel. (2) 23-33-56; fax (2) 23-86-66; e-mail magic@cni.md; internet inima .dnt.md; f. 1989 as the Popular Front of Moldova, renamed 1992, and as above 1999; advocates Moldova's entry into the European Union and NATO; Chair. IURIE ROŞCA.

Civic Dignity Party of Moldova (Particul Demnităţii Civice din Moldova—PDCM): Chişinău, str. M. Costin 7; tel. (2) 49-84-73; f. 1999; Pres. ION LIPCIU.

Democratic Labour Party of Moldova: Chişinău; f. 1993; Pres. ALECSANDRU ARSENI.

Democratic Party of Moldova (PDM) (Partidul Democrat din Moldova): 2001 Chişinău, str. Tighina 32; tel. (2) 27-82-89; fax (2) 27-82-30; e-mail mpmdp@moldova.md; internet www.pdm.md; f. 1997; centrist; formerly Movement for a Democratic and Prosperous Moldova, name changed in April 2000; formed bloc with the Party of Progressive Forces in Sept. 2001; Chair. DUMITRU DIACOV.

Democratic Unity Party: Chişinău; f. 2001; pro-European, concerned with social issues; Leader SERGIU MOCIANU.

'Green Alliance' Ecological Party of Moldova (Alianţa Verde—PEM–AVE): 2012 Chişinău, str. Şciusev 63; tel. and fax (2) 72-16-43; e-mail iondediu@yahoo.com; f. 1992; represents political ecology and sustainable development; Pres. Prof. ION DEDIU; 10,000 mems.

Moldovan Liberal Party: Chişinău, str. Puşkin 62A; tel. (2) 54-85-27; fax (2) 54-85-128; e-mail vitlaia@ch.moldpac.md; f. 2002 by the merger of the National Liberal Party, the National Peasant Christian-Democratic Party and the Party of Social Order and Justice; formed the 'Moldova Noastra' Social Liberal Alliance in 2003 with the Alliance for Independent Moldova and the Social Democratic Alliance of Moldova; Pres. VEACESLAV UNTILĂ.

Moldovan Centrist Union: Chişinău; f. 2000; splinter group of former Movement for a Democratic and Prosperous Moldova; Chair. MIHAI PETRACHE.

Moldovan Democratic Forum: Chişinău; f. 2001 by the merger of six right-wing parties: the National Liberal Party, the Moldovan Party of Democratic Forces, the National Peasants' Christian Democratic Party, the Party of Social Justice and Order, the New National Moldovan Party and the Party of Civil Dignity.

Moldovan Party of Communists (MPC) (Partidul Comunistilor din Republica Moldova): 2012 Chişinău, str. N. Iorga 11; tel. (2) 23-46-14; fax (2) 23-36-73; e-mail info@pcrm.md; internet www.pcrm .md; fmrly the Communist Party of Moldova (banned Aug. 1991); revived as above 1994; formed a ten-party Left–Centre Union for the 2003 local election; First Sec. VLADIMIR VORONIN.

National Salvation Movement (NSM): Chişinău; f. 2000; breakaway faction from the National Liberal Party.

Popular Democratic Party of Moldova (PDPM): Chişinău, str. Kogălniceanu 87; tel. (2) 24-91-10; Pres. MIHAI CEBAN.

Reform Party (PRM): Chişinău, str. Bucureşti 87; tel. (2) 23-26-89; fax (2) 22-80-97; f. 1993; centre-right Christian-Democratic party, which seeks to represent middle-class interests; Leader MIHAI GIMPU; Chair. ŞTEFAN GORDA; 12,000 mems.

Republican Party of Moldova (PRM): Chişinău, str. A. Vlahuţă 11/4; tel. (2) 22-83-18; f. 1999; Pres. VALERI EFREMOV.

Social Democratic Alliance of Moldova (Alianţa Social-Democrată din Moldova—ASDM): Chişinău, str. Columna 61; tel. (2) 54-63-17; fax (2) 54-90-19; e-mail dbragish@moldova.md; founded by members of the Braghiş Alliance (f. 1999) and the 'Furnica' Social Democratic Party of the Republic of Moldova (f. 1990); formed the 'Moldova Noastra' Social Liberal Alliance in 2003 with the Alliance for Independent Moldova and the Moldovan Liberal Party; Leader DUMITRU BRAGHIŞ.

Social Liberal Party: Chişinău, str. Bulgară 24B; tel. (2) 27-66-20; fax (2) 22-25-03; e-mail secretariat@psl.md; internet www.psl.md; f. 1999; absorbed the Christian Democratic League of Women and the National Youth League of Moldova; merged with the Party of Democratic Forces in December 2002; Leader OLEG SEREBREAN; Deputy Chair. VALERIU MATEI.

Socialist Party of Moldova (Partidul Socialist din Moldova): Chişinău, str. Calea Ieşilor 61/1, ap. 15; tel. (2) 75-87-62; successor to the former Communist Party of Moldova; favours socialist economic and social policies, defends the rights of Russian and other minorities and advocates CIS membership; Pres. VICTOR MOREV.

Yedinstvo (Unity) Movement: 2009 Chişinău, str. Hînceşti 35; tel. (2) 23-79-52; f. 1989; represents interests of ethnic minorities in Moldova; 35,000 mems; Pres. PETR SHORNIKOV.

Parties and organizations in Transnistria include: the Union of Patriotic Forces (Tiraspol; radical socialist; Leader VASILII YAKOVLEV); the Movement for the Development of Dnestr (Tiraspol; moderate); the United Council of Workers' Collectives (Tiraspol; radical); 'For Accord and Stability' (Tiraspol; moderate); and 'Position' (Tiraspol; moderate; Leader SVETLANA MIGULEA); Russia's Unity —Yedinstvo Party established a branch in Tiraspol in 2000 (founded by the local Union of Industrialists, Agriculturalists and Entrepreneurs).

Parties and organizations in Gagauzia include: the Vatan (Motherland) Party (Comrat; Leader ANDREI CHESHMEJI) and Gagauz Halky (Gagauz People—Comrat; Leader KONSTANTIN TAUSHANDJI).

Diplomatic Representation

EMBASSIES IN MOLDOVA

Belarus: 2009 Chişinău, str. Mateevici 35; tel. (2) 23-83-02; fax (2) 23-83-00; Ambassador VASILY SAKOVICH.

Bulgaria: Chişinău, str. 31 August 1989 125, Hotel Codru; tel. (2) 23-79-83; fax (2) 23-79-08; e-mail amb_bg@mdl.net; Ambassador EVGENII EKHOV.

China, People's Republic: Chişinău, str. Mitropolit Dosoftei 124; tel. (2) 24-85-51; fax (2) 24-75-46; e-mail root@chinam.mldnet.com; Ambassador XU ZHONGKAI.

France: Chişinău, str. 31 August 1989 101A; tel. (2) 22-82-04; fax (2) 22-82-24; e-mail amb-fr@cni.md; internet www.ambafrance.md; Ambassador DOMINIQUE GAZUY.

Germany: 2012 Chişinău, str. Maria Cibotari 35, Hotel Jolly Alon; tel. (2) 20-06-00; fax (2) 23-46-80; e-mail de-botschaft@riscom.md; internet ambasada-germana.org.md; Ambassador Dr MICHAEL ZICKERICK.

Hungary: 2004 Chişinău, bd Ştefan cel Mare 131; tel. (2) 22-34-04; fax (2) 22-45-13; e-mail hu.emb@cni.md; Ambassador TAMAS MIKECZ.

Poland: Chişinău, str. Plamadeala 3; tel. (2) 23-85-51; fax (2) 23-85-52; e-mail ambpolsk@ch.moldpac.md; f. 1994; Ambassador PIOTR MARCINIAK.

Romania: Chişinău, str. Bucureşti 66/1; tel. (2) 22-30-37; fax (2) 22-81-29; e-mail ambrom@ch.moldpac.md; Ambassador FILIP TEODORESCU.

Russian Federation: 2004 Chişinău, bd Ştefan cel Mare 153; tel. (2) 23-49-40; fax (2) 54-77-51; e-mail domino@mdl.net; internet www .moldova.mid.ru; Ambassador PAVEL PETROVSKII.

Turkey: Chişinău, str. Mateevici 57; tel. (2) 24-26-08; fax (2) 22-55-28; e-mail tremb@moldova.md; Ambassador OGUZ OZGE.

Ukraine: 2004 Chişinău, str. Sfatul Ţării 55; tel. (2) 58-21-51; fax (2) 58-51-08; e-mail emb_md@mfa.gov.ua; Ambassador PETRO CHALYI.

USA: 2009 Chişinău, str. Mateevici 103; tel. (2) 23-37-72; fax (2) 23-30-44; e-mail rosenquist@chisinaub.us-state.gov; internet www .usembassy.md; Ambassador HEATHER HODGES (desig.).

Judicial System

Supreme Court: Chişinău; Chair. VALERIA STERBET.

Constitutional Court

2004 Chişinău, str. A. Lapusneanu 28; tel. (2) 24-05-49; fax (2) 24-52-23; e-mail curtea@constit.mldnet.com; internet www.ccrm.rol.md.
Chair. VICTOR PUSCAS.

Prosecutor-General: VASILE RUSU.

Religion

The majority of the inhabitants of Moldova profess Christianity, the largest denomination being the Eastern Orthodox Church. The Gagauz, although of Turkic descent, are also adherents of Orthodox Christianity. The Russian Orthodox Church (Moscow Patriarchy) has jurisdiction in Moldova, but there are Romanian and Turkish liturgies.

Eastern Orthodox Church

In December 1992 the Patriarch of Moscow and All Russia issued a decree altering the status of the Eparchy of Chişinău and Moldova to that of a Metropolitan See. The Government accepted this decree, thus tacitly rejecting the claims of the Metropolitan of Bessarabia (based in Romania). However, at the end of July 2002 the Government agreed to register the Bessarabian Metropolitan Church, following international pressure.

Archbishop of Chişinău and Moldova: VLADIMIR, Chişinău, Piaţa Marii Adunări 1; tel. (2) 22-85-91.

Roman Catholic Church

In October 2001 the diocese of Chişinău, covering the whole country, was established. At 31 December 2000 there were an estimated 20,000 Catholics in Moldova.

Bishop of Chişinău: Rt Rev. ANTON COŞA, 2012 Chişinău, str. Mitropo lit Dosoftei 85; tel. (2) 22-34-70; fax (2) 22-52-10; e-mail administ@apost.moldpac.md; internet catholic.dnt.md.

The Press

In 1990 the number of Romanian-language newspapers and periodicals increased, and most publications began using the Latin script. In 1996 there were four daily newspapers published in Moldova (with a combined circulation averaging 261,000 copies). In that year 206 non-daily newspapers were published (with an estimated circulation of 1,350,000). In 1994 there were 76 other periodicals (31 for the general public and 45 for specific readership, with a total circulation of 196,000).

The publications listed below are in Romanian (or Moldovan, as it is officially termed), except where otherwise indicated.

PRINCIPAL NEWSPAPERS

Accente: Chişinău, str. Vlaicu Pîrcălab 45, 405; internet www .accente.com.md; weekly; Editor-in-Chief SERGIU AFANASIU.

Dnestrovskaya Pravda (Dnestr Truth): Tiraspol, str. 25 October 101; tel. and fax (33) 3-46-86; f. 1941; 3 a week; Russian; Editor TATYANA M. RUDENKO; circ. 7,000.

Ekonomicheskoye Obozrenie (Economic Review): Chişinău, bd Ştefan cel Mare 180; tel. (2) 24-69-52; fax (2) 24-69-50; e-mail red@ logos.press.md; internet logos.press.md; f. 1990; weekly; Editor-in-Chief SERGEI MIŞIN.

GP Flux: Chişinău, str. Corobceanu 17; tel. (2) 23-22-14; fax (2) 24-75-29; e-mail secretar@flux.press.md; internet flux.press.md; daily; Editor-in-Chief IGOR BURCIU.

Glasul Naţiunii (Voice of the Nation): Chişinău, str. 31 August 15; tel. and fax (2) 54-31-37; 2 a month; Editors VASILE NESTASE, LEONID LARI.

Jurnal de Chişinău: Chişinău, str. Puşkin 22, 446; tel. (2) 23-40-41; fax (2) 23-42-30; e-mail jurnal@chisinau.moldline.net; internet jurnal.press.md; Editor-in-Chief VAL BUTNARU.

Kishinevskiye Obozrevatel (Chişinău Correspondent): Chişinău, bd Ştefan cel Mare 162, 604/7; tel. (2) 21-02-34; fax (2) 21-02-64; e-mail oboz@molodvacc.md; internet www.ko.md; weekly; Russian; Editor-in-Chief IRINA ASTAHOVA.

Kishinevskiye Novosti (Chişinău News): Chişinău, str. Puşkin 22; tel. (2) 23-39-18; fax (2) 23-42-40; e-mail kn@mdl.net; weekly; Russian; Editor-in-Chief SERGEI DROBOT.

Kommersant Moldovy: Chişinău, str. Puşkin 22, 601; tel. (2) 23-36-94; e-mail vartem@commert.press.md; internet www.km.riscom .net; weekly; Russian; Editor-in-Chief ARTEM VARENIŢA.

Komsomolskaye Pravda Moldova: Chişinău, str. Vlaicu Pîrcălab 45; tel. (2) 22-07-13; fax (2) 22-12-74; e-mail ser@kp.md; internet www.kp.md; daily; Russian; Editor-in-Chief SERGEI CIURICOV.

Moldavskie Vedomosti (Moldovan Gazette): Chişinău, str. Banulescu-Bodoni 21; tel. and fax (2) 23-86-18; e-mail editor@mv.net.md; internet vedomosti.md; weekly; Russian; Editor-in-Chief DMITRII CIUBASENKO.

Moldova Suverană (Sovereign Moldova): 2012 Chişinău, str. Puşkin 22, et. 3; tel. (2) 23-35-38; fax (2) 23-31-96; e-mail cotidian@ suverana.press.md; internet www.moldova-suverana.md; f. 1924; daily; organ of the Govt; Editor ION BERLINSCHI; circ. 105,000.

Nezavisimaya Moldova (Independent Moldova): 2012 Chişinău, str. Puşkin 22, 303; tel. (2) 23-36-05; fax (2) 23-31-41; e-mail admin@ nm.mldnet.com; internet www.nmmd; f. 1925; daily; organ of the Govt; Russian; Editor IURII TISCENCO; circ. 60,692.

Ţara (Homeland): 2004 Chişinău, str. A. Corobceanu 15; tel. (2) 24-79-84; fax (2) 23-44-80; e-mail secretar@tara.press.md; internet tara .press.md; f. 1989; publication suspended for financial reasons in January 2003; 3 a week; Editor-in-Chief PETRU BOGATU; circ. 18,000.

Tinerimya Moldovei/Molodezh Moldovy (Youth of Moldova): Chişinău; f. 1928; 3 a week; editions in Romanian (circ. 12,212) and Russian (circ. 4,274); Editor V. BOTNARU.

Trudovoi Tiraspol (Working Tiraspol): Tiraspol, str. 25 October 101; tel. (33) 3-04-12; f. 1989; main newspaper of the east-bank Slavs; Russian; Editor DIMA KONDRATOVICH.

Viaţă Satului (Life of the Village): 2612 Chişinău, str. Puşkin 22, Casa presei, 4th Floor; tel. (2) 23-03-68; f. 1945; weekly; govt publ. Editor V. S. SPINEY.

PRINCIPAL PERIODICALS

Basarabia (Bessarabia): Chişinău; f. 1931; fmrly *Nistru*; monthly; journal of the Union of Writers of Moldova; fiction; Editor-in-Chief D. MATKOVSKY.

Chipăruş (Peppercorn): 2612 Chişinău, str. Puşkin 22; tel. (2) 23-38-16; f. 1958; fortnightly; satirical; Editor-in-Chief ION VIKOL.

Femeia Moldovei (Moldovan Woman): 2470 Chişinău, str. 28 June 45; tel. (2) 23-31-64; f. 1951; monthly; popular, for women.

Lanterna Magică (Magic Lantern): Chişinău, str. Puşkin 24, 49; tel. (2) 74-86-43; fax (2) 23-23-88; e-mail lung_ro@yahoo.com; internet www.iatp.md/lanternamagica/; f. 1990; publ. by the Ministry of Culture; 6 a year; art, culture.

Literatură şi Artă: 2009 Chişinău, str. Sfatul Ţării 2; tel. (2) 23-82-12; fax (2) 23-82-17; e-mail literatura@moldnet.md; f. 1954; weekly; organ of the Union of Writers of Moldova; literary; Editor NICOLAE DABIJA.

Moldova si Lumea (Moldova and the World): 2012 Chişinău, str. Puşkin 22, 510; tel. (2) 23-75-81; fax (2) 23-40-32; f. 1991; monthly; state-owned; international socio-political review; Editor BORIS STRATULAT.

Noi (Us): Chişinău; tel. (2) 23-31-10; f. 1930; fmrly *Scînteia Leninista*; monthly; fiction; for 10–15-year-olds; Man. VALERIU VOLONTIR.

Pămint şi Oameni (Land and People): Chişinău; tel. (2) 22-33-87; organ of the Agrarian Democratic Party; weekly.

Politica: 2033 Chişinău, bd Ştefan cel Mare 105; tel. (2) 23-74-03; fax (2) 23-32-10; e-mail vppm@cni.md; f. 1991; monthly; political issues.

Săptămína: Chişinău, str. 31 August 107; tel. (2) 22-44-61; fax (2) 21-37-07; e-mail saptamin@mom.mldnet.com; internet www.net .md/saptamina/; weekly magazine; Editor-in-Chief VIOREL MIHAIL.

Sud-Est (South-East): Chişinău, str. Maria Cibotaru 16; tel. (2) 23-26-05; fax (2) 23-22-42; internet www.sud-est.md; f. 1990; publ. by the Ministry of Culture; quarterly; art, culture; Editor-in-Chief VALENTINA TASLAUANA.

NEWS AGENCIES

AP Flux Press Agency: Chişinău, str. Corobceanu 17; tel. (2) 24-92-72; fax (2) 24-91-51; e-mail flux@cni.md; internet flux.press.md; f. 1995; Dir NADINE GOGU.

BASA-press—Moldovan Information and Advertising Agency: 2012 Chişinău, str. Vasile Alecsandri 72; tel. (2) 22-03-90; fax (2) 22-13-96; e-mail basa@basa.md; internet www.basa.md; f. 1992; independent; co-operates with Deutsche Presse-Agentur (Germany); Gen. Dir VALERIU RENITA.

DECA Press Agency: Bălti, str. Independentei 33; tel. (31) 61-385; fax (31) 607-44; e-mail info@deca-press.net; internet www .deca-press.net; f. 1996; local news; non-profit; Dir VITALIE CAZACU.

InfoMarket.MD (Denimax Grup): tel. (2) 27-76-26; e-mail editor@ infomarket.md; internet www.infomarket.md; on-line business news; Editor ALECSANDRU BURDEINII.

Infotag News Agency: 2014 Chişinău, str. Kogâlniceanu 76; tel. (2) 23-49-30; fax (2) 23-49-33; e-mail office@infotag.net.md; internet www.infotag.md; f. 1993; leading private news agency; Dir ALEXANDRU TANAS.

Interlic News Agency: 2012 Chişinău, str. M. Cibotari 37, Of. 306; tel. and fax and fax (2) 23-20-67; e-mail vox@interlic.mldnet.com; internet www.interlic.md; f. 1995; independent; Dir IVAN SVEATCENKO.

State Information Agency—Moldpres: 2012 Chişinău, str. Puşkin 22; tel. (2) 23-26-69; fax (2) 23-43-71; e-mail director@ moldpres.md; internet www.moldpres.md; f. 1990 as Moldovapres, reorganized 1994; Dir BORIS MARIAN.

PRESS ASSOCIATION

Independent Journalism Centre (IJC): 2012 Chişinău, str. Sciusev 53; tel. (2) 21-36-52; fax (2) 22-66-81; e-mail ijcnews@ijc.iatp .md; internet ijc.iatp.md; f. 1994; non-governmental org.

Independent Press Association (API): Chişinău, bd Ştefan cel Mare 123A, 14; tel. (2) 24-72-39; fax (2) 24-72-81; e-mail api@ moldtelecom.md; internet www.iatp.md/api; f. 1997; Pres. ION CUMEICA.

Mass Media Association of Moldova: Chişinău; internet www .media.ist.md; f. 2000.

Union of Journalists of Moldova: 2012 Chişinău, str. Puşkin 22; tel. and fax (2) 23-34-19; e-mail ujm@moldnet.md; internet www .iatp.md/ujm; f. 1957; Chair. VALERIU SAHARNEANU.

Publishers

In 1996 there were 921 titles (books and pamphlets) published in Moldova (2.8m. copies).

Editura Cartea Moldovei: 2004 Chişinău, bd Ştefan cel Mare 180; tel. (2) 24-65-10; fax (2) 24-64-11; f. 1977; fiction, non-fiction, poetry, art books; Dir DUMITRU FURDUI; Editor-in-Chief RAISA SUVEICA.

Editura Hyperion: 2004 Chişinău, bd Ştefan cel Mare 180; tel. (2) 24-40-22; f. 1976; fiction, literature, arts; Dir VALERIU MATEI.

Editura Lumina (Light): 2004 Chişinău, bd Ştefan cel Mare 180; tel. (2) 24-63-95; f. 1966; educational textbooks; Dir VICTOR STRATAN; Editor-in-Chief ANATOL MALEV.

Editura Ştiinţa (Science): 2028 Chişinău, str. Academiei 3; tel. (2) 73-96-16; fax (2) 73-96-27; e-mail prini@stiinta.asm.md; f. 1959; textbooks, encyclopaedias, dictionaries, children's books and fiction in various languages; Dir GHEORGHE PRINI.

Izdatelstvo Kartia Moldoveniaske: 2004 Chişinău, bd Ştefan cel Mare; tel. (2) 24-40-22; f. 1924; political and literature; Dir N. N. MUMZHI; Editor-in-Chief I. A. TSURKANU.

Broadcasting and Communications

TELECOMMUNICATIONS

Regulatory Authority

Ministry of Transport and Communications: see section on the Government.

Telecommunications Company

Moldcell SA: 2060 Chişinău, str. Belgrad 3; tel. (2) 20-62-06; fax (2) 20-62-07; e-mail moldcell@moldcell.md; internet www.moldcell.md; f. 1999; mobile-telecommunications; owned by Fintur Holdings b.v. (Netherlands).

Moldtelecom SA: 2001 Chişinău, bd Ştefan cel Mare 10; tel. (2) 54-87-97; fax (2) 54-64-19; e-mail office@moldtelecom.md; internet www .moldtelecom.md; f. 1993; telephone communication and internet service provider; 51% scheduled for divestment to Moscow City Telephone Network (Russia) in 2002; Gen. Dir STELA SÇOLA.

BROADCASTING

Regulatory Authorities

National Regulatory Agency in Telecommunications and Informatics (ANRTI): 2012 Chişinău, bd Ştefan cel Mare 134; tel. (2) 25-13-17; fax (2) 22-28-85; e-mail office@anrti.md; internet www .anrti.md; Dir (vacant).

Radio and Television Co-ordinating Council (Consiliul Coor-donator al Audiovizualului): 2001 Chişinău, bd Ştefan cel Mare 73; tel. (2) 27-75-53; fax (2) 27-74-71; e-mail cna_moldova@mdl.net; internet www.cca.md; regulatory and licensing body; Chair. ION MIHAILO.

State Communication Inspectorate (Inspectoratul de Stat al Comunicatiilor): 2021 Chişinău, str. Drumul Viilor 28-2; tel. (2) 73-53-64; fax (2) 73-39-41; e-mail ciclicci@isc.net.md; f. 1993; responsible for frequency allocations and monitoring, certification of post and communications equipment and services; Dir TEODOR CICLICCI.

Radio

State Radio and Television Company of Moldova (Teleradio) (Televiziunea de Stat a Republicii Moldova): 2028 Chişinău, str. Mioriţa 1; tel. (2) 72-10-77; fax (2) 72-33-52; e-mail info@trm.md; internet www.trm.md; f. 1994; Chair. ION GONTA.

Radio Moldova: 2028 Chişinău, str. Mioriţa 1; tel. (2) 72-13-88; fax (2) 72-35-37; f. 1930; broadcasts in Romanian, Russian, Ukrainian, Gagauz and Yiddish; Dir-Gen. CONSTANTIN VULPE.

Television

State Radio and Television Company of Moldova (Teleradio) (Televiziunea de Stat a Republicii Moldova): see Radio.

TV Moldova (Televiziunea Nationala Moldova): f. 1958; Dir-Gen. ALECSANDRU GROSU.

Chişinău Television: 2028 Chişinău, str. Hîncesti 64; tel. (2) 73-91-94; fax (2) 72-35-37; f. 1958; Dir-Gen. ARCADIE GHERASIM.

Finance

(cap. = capital; res = reserves; dep. = deposits; m. = million; brs = branches; amounts in Moldovan lei, unless otherwise stated)

BANKING

Restructuring of Moldova's banking system was begun in 1991 with the establishment of a central bank, the National Bank of Moldova (NBM), which was formerly a branch of the USSR Gosbank (state bank). The NBM is independent of the Government (but responsible to Parliament) and has the power to regulate monetary policy and the financial system. The lack of a stringent regulatory framework and the consequent proliferation of small commercial banks led the Government to introduce, in January 1996, new legislation on financial institutions. All commercial banks were subsequently inspected and a more effective banking supervision was implemented. At mid-2000 there were 21 commercial banks in operation.

Central Bank

National Bank of Moldova (Banca Naţională a Moldovei): 2006 Chişinău, bd Renaşterii 7; tel. (2) 22-50-52; fax (2) 22-05-91; e-mail official@bnm.org; internet www.bnm.org; f. 1991; cap. 100.0m., res 257.0m. (June 2002), dep. 807.1m. (Dec. 2000); Gov. LEONID TALMACI; Dep. Gov. DUMITRU URSU.

Commercial Banks

Banca de Finanţe şi Comerţ (FinComBank—Bank of Finance and Commerce): 2012 Chişinău, str. Puşkin 26; tel. (2) 22-74-35; fax (2) 22-82-53; e-mail fincom@fcb.mldnet.com; internet www .fincombank.com; f. 1993; cap 77.0m., dep. 184.2m., total assets 302.5m. (Dec. 2002); Chair. VICTOR HVOROSTOVSCHI; 5 brs.

Banca Socială: 2006 Chişinău, str. Bănulescu-Bodoni 61; tel. (2) 22-14-94; fax (2) 22-42-30; e-mail office@socbank.md; internet www .socbank.md; f. 1991; joint-stock commercial bank; cap. 57.6m., res 8.6m., dep. 451.0m. (Feb. 2002); Pres. VLADIMIR SUETNOV; Chair. VALENTIN KUNEV; 18 brs.

BC 'Eximbank' SA (Eximbank Joint-Stock Commercial Bank): 2001 Chişinău, bd Ştefan cel Mare 6; tel. (2) 27-25-83; fax (2) 54-62-34; e-mail info@eximbank.com; internet www.eximbank.com; Chair. MARCEL CHIRCĂ.

BC Unibank SA: 2012 Chişinău, str. G. Bănulescu Bodoni 45; tel. (2) 22-55-86; fax (2) 22-05-30; e-mail welcome@unibank.md; internet www.unibank.md; f. 1993; joint-stock commercial bank; cap. 78.3m., res 4.7m., dep. 177.3m. (Jan. 2003); Pres. CLAUDIA MELNIC; 5 brs.

BTR Moldova SA (Banca Commerciala BTR Moldova SA): 2005 Chişinău, bd Renaşterii 18, POB 2005; tel. (2) 20-11-00; fax (2) 22-11-03; e-mail office@btr.md; internet www.btr.md; f. 2000; joint-stock commercial bank; 99% owned by Banca Turco-Română SA (Romania); Pres. MEHMET ZAFER BAYSAL; Chair. OSMAN BINATLI.

CB Businessbank SA: 2012 Chişinău, str. Alecsandru cel Bun 97; tel. (2) 20-56-10; fax (2) 22-23-70; e-mail bank@busbank.mldnet.com; internet www.businessbank.md; f. 1997; cap. 72.1m., res 1.1m., dep. 81.1m. (Jan. 2003); Chair. of Bd SERGIU N. BRINZILA.

CB Comertbank JSC: 2001 Chişinău, str. Hîncesti 38A; tel. (2) 73-99-91; fax (2) 73-99-81; e-mail comertbank@mdl.net; internet www .comertbank.md; f. 1991; cap. 96.0m., total assets 149.9m. (Jan. 2003); Chair. NATALIA ULIYANOVA.

Energbank: 2012 Chişinău, str. Vasile Alecsandri 78; tel. (2) 54-43-77; fax (2) 25-34-09; e-mail office@energbank.com; internet www .energbank.com; f. 1997; cap. 58.3m. (2002), dep. 146.3m., total assets 239.4m. (Jan. 2003); Chair. MIHAIL OGORODNICOV; 31 brs.

EuroCreditBank JSC: 2001 Chişinău, str. Ismail 33; tel. (2) 50-01-01; fax (2) 54-88-27; e-mail info@ecb.md; internet www.ecb.md; f. 2002 to replace Petrolbank; commercial investment bank; Pres. ALEKSANDR ZHOLONDKOVSKII; Pres. DUMITRU LUPAN; 2 brs.

Guinea: 2068 Chişinău, str. Alecu Russo 1; tel. (2) 43-05-11; fax (2) 44-41-40; cap. 10.4m., total assets 59.1m. (Jan. 1998); Chair. IURII STASIEV.

IBID-MB (International Bank for Investment and Development): 2067 Chişinău, bd Moscow 21; tel. (2) 34-62-49; fax (2) 34-62-31; cap. 9.6m., total assets 24.7m. (Jan. 1998); Chair. GHEORGHE NECHIT.

Investprivatbank SA: 2001 Chişinău, str. Şciusev 34; tel. (2) 27-43-86; fax (2) 54-05-10; e-mail ipb.md@ipb.md; f. 1994; cap. 67.9m., total assets 171.4m. (Dec. 2002); Chair. IVAN CHIRPALOV.

CB Mobiasbanca JSC: 2012 Chişinău, bd Ştefan cel Mare 81; tel. and fax (2) 54-19-74; e-mail info@mobiasbank.com; internet www .mobiasbank.com; f. 1990; acquired Bank-coop in 2001; commercial bank; cap. US $8.9m., res US $0.8m., dep. US $14.8m. (Jan. 2003); Pres. VICTOR POPUSOI; Chair. of Bd NICOLAE DORIN; 8 brs.

Moldindconbank SA (Moldovan Bank for Industry and Construction): 2012 Chişinău, str. Armeneasca 38; tel. (2) 22-55-21; fax (2) 24-91-95; e-mail info@micb.net.md; internet www.moldindconbank .com; f. 1991; joint-stock commercial bank; cap. 30.1m., res 7.2m., dep. 540.1m. (Dec. 2001); Chair.of Bd VALERIAN MIRZAC; 23 brs.

Moldova-Agroindbank SA: 2006 Chişinău, str. Cosmonauţilor 9; tel. (2) 21-28-28; fax (2) 22-80-58; e-mail aib@maib.md; internet www.maib.md; f. 1991; joint-stock commercial bank; cap. 51.9m., res 31.0 m., dep. 1,056.2m. (Dec. 2001); Chair. VICTOR MICULET; Chair. of the Bd Council NATALIA VRABIE; 42 brs.

Oguzbank: 2004 Chişinău, str. Toma Ciorba 24/1; tel. (2) 24-98-40; fax (2) 24-91-00; f. 1991; cap. 17.5m., total assets 53.5m. (Jan. 1998); Chair. DUMITRU SAROV.

Universalbank: 2004 Chişinău, bd Ştefan cel Mare 180, et. 4; tel. (2) 24-64-06; fax (2) 24-64-89; e-mail ub@mail.universalbank.md; internet www.universalbank.md; f. 1994; cap. 67.4m., res 6.8m., dep. 92.7m., total assets 205.5m. (Jan. 2002); Chair. IRINA DROZD; Gen. Man. VICTORIA TOFAN.

Vias: 2002 Chişinău; tel. (2) 54-14-10; fax (2) 54-14-20; cap. 10.3m., total assets 18.1m. (Jan. 1998); Chair. NICOLAE DEDE.

Victoriabank: 2004 Chişinău, str. 31 August 141; tel. (2) 23-30-65; fax (2) 23-39-33; e-mail mail@victoriabank.md; internet www .victoriabank.md; f. 1989; cap. 146.0m., total assets 767.5m. (Dec. 2001); Chair. VICTOR ŢURCANU; 12 brs.

Savings Bank

Banca de Economii a Moldovei: 2012 Chişinău, str. Columna 115; tel. (2) 24-47-22; fax (2) 24-47-31; e-mail bem@bem.md; internet www.bem.md; f. 1992; cap. 100.0m., dep. 396.0m.. (Dec. 2001); Pres. RAISA CANTEMIR; 30 brs.

STOCK EXCHANGE

Moldovan Stock Exchange (Bursa de Valori a Moldovei SA): 2001 Chişinău, bd Ştefan cel Mare 73; tel. (2) 27-75-94; fax (2) 27-73-56; e-mail dodu@moldse.md; internet www.moldse.md; f. 1994; Chair. Dr CORNELIU DODU.

INSURANCE

QBE Asito SA: 2005 Chişinău, str. Mitropolit Banulescu-Bodoni 57/1; tel. and fax (2) 22-62-12; fax (2) 22-11-79; e-mail asito@moldova .md; internet www.qbe.com; f. 1991; 70% owned by QBE Insurance Group (based in Australia); leading insurance co, covering 80% of the market; Gen. Man. EUGENIU SHLOPAK; 1,200 employees.

Trade and Industry

GOVERNMENT AGENCY

State Department of Privatization and State Property Administration: 2012 Chişinău, str. Pushkin 26; tel. (2) 22-54-78; fax (2) 23-43-50; e-mail privatization@mop.mldnet.com; internet www .privatization.md/; Gen. Dir NICOLAE GUMENII.

Moldovan Export Promotion Organization (MEPO): 2012 Chişinău, str. Mateevici 65; tel. (2) 22-32-26; fax (2) 24-44-36; e-mail mepo@mepo.net; internet www.mepo.net; f. 1991; assists enterprises in increasing exports and improving business environment; Gen. Dir ANDREI G. MORARI.

CHAMBER OF COMMERCE

Chamber of Commerce and Industry of the Republic of Moldova: 2012 Chişinău, str. M. Eminescu 28; tel. (2) 22-15-52; fax (2) 24-14-53; e-mail inform@chamber.md; internet www.chamber.md; f. 1969; Chair. GHEORGHE CUCU.

UTILITIES

Regulatory Authority

National Energy Regulatory Agency (ANRE): 2012 Chişinău, str. Columna 90; tel. (2) 54-13-84; fax (2) 22-46-98; e-mail anre@ moldova.md; internet www.anre.moldpac.md; f. 1997; autonomous public institution; Dirs MARIN PROFIR, VASILE CARAFIZI; Gen. Dir NICOLAE TRIBOI.

Electricity

IS Moldtranselectro: 2012 Chişinău, str. Vasile Alecsandri 78; tel. (2) 25-33-50; fax (2) 25-31-41; e-mail disp@mtenerg.mldnet.com; f. 2000; state-owned operator of electricity transmission system; in 2000 plans to reorganize the co into four independent state-owned enterprises were announced; Dir-Gen. VASILE PLESHCAN.

Retelele Electrice de Distributie Nord SA: 3121 Bălţi, bd Ştefan cel Mare 180A; tel. (31) 2-20-00; fax (31) 2-33-12; e-mail red-nord@ mdl.net; f. 1997; state-owned; electricity distribution and transmission.

Retelele Electrice ale Raoinul Rîbnîta: 5501 Rîbnîta, str. Gvardeiskaia 25; tel. (55) 4-12-80; f. 1980; state-owned; electricity transmission and distribution.

Retelele Electrice Sud-Est IS: 3300 Tiraspol, str. Ukrainskaia 5; tel. (33) 3-44-23; fax (33) 3-55-87; f. 1974; state-owned; electricity transmission and distribution.

Gas

MoldovaGaz SA: 2005 Chişinău, str. Albisoara 38; tel. (2) 22-32-70; fax (2) 24-00-14; f. May 1999; national gas pipeline and distribution networks; 51% owned by Gazprom (Russia), 35% owned by Moldova and 14% held by Transnistria. In Aug. 1999 Moldova announced that it was to sell its stake in 2000; Gen. Dir GHENADII ABASCIN (acting).

Moldovatransgas SRL: 5233 Drochia, şos. Tarigrad, POB 24; tel. (52) 24-452; fax (52) 26-238; f. 1986; natural gas transportation, supply and equipment service.

TRADE UNIONS

Confederation of Trade Unions of Moldova: 2012 Chişinău, str. 31 August 129; tel. (2) 23-76-74; fax (2) 23-76-98; e-mail cfsind@cni .md; internet www.csrm.md; f. 1990; Pres. PETRU CHIRIAC.

CONSUMER ORGANIZATION

Central Union of Consumers' Co-operatives of Moldova (Uniunea Centrală a Cooperativelor de Consum din Republica Moldova —MOLDCOOP): 2001 Chişinău, bd Ştefan cel Mare 67; tel. (2) 27-15-95; fax (2) 27-41-50; f. 1925; Chair. PAVEL G. DUBALARI.

Transport

RAILWAYS

Plans for the construction of a new rail link, connecting Chişinău wth Iaşi, Romania, were announced in mid-2002.

Moldovan Railways: 2012 Chişinău, str. Vlaicu Pîrcălab 48; tel. (2) 25-44-08; fax (2) 22-13-80; e-mail secr@railway.md; internet www .railway.md; f. 1992 following the dissolution of the former Soviet Railways (SZhD) organization; total network 1,326 km; Dir-Gen. MIRON GAGAUZ.

ROADS

At 1 January 1999 Moldova's network of roads totalled 12,657 km (87.0% of which was hard-surfaced), including 2,813 km of main roads and 6,588 km of regional roads. In 1999 there was a total of 298,290 passenger cars, buses and goods vehicles in use.

INLAND WATERWAYS

In 1997 the total length of navigable waterways in Moldova was 424 km. The main river ports are at Tighina (Bender, Bendery), Rîbnîţa and Reni. The construction of a maritime port (petroleum terminal) on the River Danube was under way.

SHIPPING

Neptun-M SA: 2064 Chişinău, str. V. Belinski 101; tel. (2) 74-95-51; fax (2) 74-09-01; f. 1992; Gen. Dir VICTOR ANDRUŞCA.

CIVIL AVIATION

Chişinău International Airport and the air-traffic-control operator, Moldatsa, were re-opened in June 2000, after refurbishment funded by the European Bank for Reconstruction and Development (EBRD).

Civil Aviation Administration: 2026 Chişinău, Aeroportul Chişinău; tel. (2) 52-40-64; fax (2) 52-91-18; e-mail info@caa.md; internet www.caa.md; f. 1993; Dir VLADIMIR PETRAŞ.

Compania Aeriana Moldova Ltd: 2026 Chişinău, Aeroportul Chişinău; tel. (2) 52-51-62; fax (2) 52-40-40; formerly Air Moldova; Unistar Ventures GmbH (Germany) purchased a stake in June 2000; 51% retained by the state; scheduled and charter passenger and cargo flights to destinations in Europe and the CIS; Dir-Gen. PETER CHEBAN.

Air Moldova International: 2026 Chişinău, Aeroportul Chişinău, 4th Floor; tel. (2) 52-97-91; fax (2) 52-64-14; e-mail info@ami.md; internet www.ami.md; scheduled and charter flights to destinations in Europe and the CIS; Dir-Gen. DORIN TIMCIUC.

Moldavian Airlines SA: 2026 Chişinău, Aeroportul Chişinău; tel. (2) 52-93-56; fax (2) 52-50-64; e-mail sales@mdv.md; internet www .mdv.md; f. 1994; scheduled and charter passenger and cargo flights to destinations in Europe, the Middle East and North Africa; Pres. and Chief Exec. NICOLAE PETROV.

Moldtransavia SRL: 2026 Chişinău, Aeroportul Chişinău; tel. (2) 52-59-71; fax (2) 52-63-99; e-mail mold@travia.mldnet.com; air freight and passenger transportation.

Tourism

In 2000 18,964 tourists visited Moldova, 27% of whom were from Russia.

Federation of Sport and Tourism of the Republic of Moldova: Chişinău; tel. (2) 44-51-81; e-mail ftsmd@narod.ru; internet www .ftsmd.narod.ru; Pres. IVAN D. ZABUNOV.

Moldova-Tur SA: 2001 Chişinău, bd Ştefan cel Mare 4; tel. (2) 54-03-01; fax (2) 54-04-94; e-mail moldovatur@travers.md; internet www.jpm.md/mtur; f. 1959.

MONACO

Introductory Survey

Location, Climate, Language, Religion, Flag

The Principality of Monaco lies in western Europe. The country is a small enclave in south-eastern France, about 15 km east of Nice. It has a coastline on the Mediterranean Sea but is otherwise surrounded by French territory. The climate is Mediterranean, with warm summers and very mild winters. The official language is French, but Monégasque (a mixture of the French Provençal and Italian Ligurian dialects), Italian and English are also spoken. Most of the population profess Christianity, with about 91% belonging to the Roman Catholic Church. The national flag (proportions 4 by 5) has two equal horizontal stripes, of red and white. The state flag (proportions 4 by 5) displays the princely arms of Monaco (a white shield, held by two monks and superimposed on a pavilion of ermine) on a white background.

History

The Principality of Monaco is an hereditary monarchy, which has been ruled by the Grimaldi dynasty since 1297. It was abolished during the French Revolution but re-established in 1814. In 1861 Monaco became an independent state under the protection of France. The Constitution, promulgated in January 1911, vested legislative power jointly in the Prince and an 18-member Conseil National, selected for a term of five years by a panel comprising nine delegates of the municipality and 21 members elected by universal suffrage. Agreements in 1918 and 1919 between France and Monaco provided for Monaco's incorporation into France should the reigning prince die without leaving a male heir. Prince Louis II, the ruler of Monaco since 1922, died in May 1949, and was succeeded by his grandson, Prince Rainier III. A new Constitution, introduced in December 1962, abolished the formerly-held principle of the divine right of the ruler, and stipulated that the Conseil National be elected by universal adult suffrage.

Supporters of Prince Rainier, grouped in the Union Nationale et Démocratique dominated at five-yearly elections in 1963–88, on all but two occasions taking all 18 seats on the Conseil National. In January 1993, however, two lists of candidates, the Liste Campora (led by Jean-Louis Campora, the President of the football team, AS Monaco) and the Liste Médecin, secured 15 and two seats respectively, while an independent candidate won the remaining seat. At legislative elections in February 1998 UND candidates secured all 18 seats.

Controversy surrounding the use of Monaco's financial sector for the transfer of funds derived from criminal activities intensified in 1998 with the culmination of an investigation into the deposit of US $5.5m. in cash, suspected of originating from the illegal drugs trade, at a bank in Monaco in 1995. The affair led to a crisis in relations between France and the Principality, with the French Government overruling Prince Rainier by refusing to extend the mandate of Monaco's Chief Prosecutor, whom it suspected of not conducting a sufficiently thorough investigation of the scandal. Following further criticisms of Monégasque banking practice by a report by the Organisation for Economic Co-operation and Development (OECD, see p. 277) in April 2000, the French Government published two reports in October, which recommended a rapid revision of the bilateral treaties between Monaco and France, proposing that Monégasque institutions be brought into greater conformity with French excise, fiscal and banking regulations. A further report issued by OECD in April 2002 stated that the fiscal legislation and banking secrecy permitted in Monaco remained in breach of international conventions; consequently, the Principality, along with six other sovereign territories, could be subject to financial sanctions from April 2003.

In late March 2002 the electoral law was amended, and in early April the Conseil National approved a number of significant constitutional amendments, both moves in part with the intention of progressing Monaco's application for full membership of the Council of Europe (see p. 181), which had been submitted in October 1998. Notably, the age of majority was lowered from 21 years to 18 years, and several executive powers of the Prince were transferred to the Conseil National, the size of which was to be increased to 24 members (of whom eight were to be elected on the basis of a form of proportional representation, in accordance with the revised electoral legislation) following the elections in 2003. Additionally, the law of succession was modified, to permit succession through the female line. Further controversy regarding the banking system in Monaco was provoked in June 2002 by the publication of a book by a former judge in the Principality, Charles Duchaine, which alleged governmental interference in the operations of the Monégasque judicial system.

In late 2002 discontent was reported at a proposal, supported by Campora, to sell AS Monaco to a Ukrainian investment company, Fedcominvest, which was also the football club's principal sponsor. Following a report in Le Monde, in December 2002, which alleged that Fedcominvest was involved in 'money laundering', Prince Rainier, who on behalf of the Principality, retained ultimate control over the club, prohibited the sale of the club to Fedcominvest. which reportedly had connections with organized crime. The ensuing scandal appeared to be a significant factor in appreciably reducing support for Campora's UND at the legislative elections, held on 9 February 2003, when the UND secured only three seats on the enlarged Conseil National; the remaining 21 seats were awarded to the Union pour Monaco list, led by a former member of the UND, Stéphane Valéri. A further significant factor that was regarded as contibuting to the precipitous decline in support for the UND was the continuing delay in progressing Monaco's application for full membership of the Council of Europe, in spite of the constitutional changes approved in 2002.

Monaco participates in the work of a number of international organizations, and in 1993 became a member of the UN.

Government

Legislative power is vested jointly in the Prince, an hereditary ruler, and the 24-member Conseil National, which is elected by universal adult suffrage, partly under a system of proportional representation, for a term of five years. The electorate comprises only Monégasque citizens aged 18 years or over. Executive power is exercised, under the authority of the Prince, by the four-member Council of Government, headed by the Minister of State (a French civil servant selected by the Prince from a list of three candidates presented by the French Government). The Prince represents the Principality in its relations with foreign powers, and signs and ratifies treaties. There is, additionally, a consultative Conseil Communal, elected for a term of four years, headed by a mayor.

Economic Affairs

In 2000, according to World Bank estimates, Monaco's gross national product (GNP), measured at average 1998–2000 prices, was equivalent to approximately US $25,200 per head (or approximately $25,700 on an international purchasing-power parity basis) According to UN estimates, Monaco's gross domestic product (GDP) was $847m. in 1995 (equivalent to $26,470 per head). During 1990–95 GDP increased, in real terms, at an average annual rate of 1.1%. GDP increased by 2.2% in 1995. The annual rate of population increase averaged 0.6% in 1990–2000. Monaco has the highest population density of all the independent states in the world.

There is no agricultural land in Monaco. In 1990 a Belgian enterprise established an offshore fish farm for sea bass and sea bream.

Industry (excluding construction and public works) accounted for 11.6% of economic activity in 1993, and engaged some 11% of the employed labour force in the late 1990s. Industry is mainly light in Monaco. The principal sectors, measured by gross value of output, are chemicals, pharmaceuticals and cosmetics (which together accounted for 49% of all industrial revenue in 2000), plastics, micro-electronics and electrical goods, paper and card manufacture, and clothing and textiles.

Service industries represent the most significant sector of the economy in Monaco, contributing 49.1% of total revenue in 1993. Banking and finance accounted for more than 38% of the services sector and employed some 1,400 people in the late 1990s. At mid-1998 the total value of deposits in Monaco's private banking sector was estimated at 90,000m. French francs. Real estate accounted for 26% of the sector in 1991. By 2000 it was estimated that the share of national revenue provided by the casino had declined to some 5%, while trade accounted for 37.5% of revenue in that year, and banking and financial activities accounted for some 20.8%.

Tourism is also an important source of income, providing an estimated 25% of total government revenue in 1991 and engaging some 20% of the employed labour force in the late 1990s. In 2000 300,185 tourists (excluding excursionists) visited Monaco, representing an increase of some 7.8%, compared with 1999. Including excursionists, some 4m. people visited the Principality in 1992, and in that year revenue from tourism totalled US $1,300m. The greatest number of visitors in 2000 were from Italy (23.6%), France (16.1%), the USA (12.1%) and the United Kingdom (11.0%). In that year the conference industry accounted for about one-third of the nights spent at Monaco's foreign hotels.

Monaco's external trade is included in the figures for France. Revenue is derived principally from real estate, light and medium industry, indirect taxation and tourism.

In 2000 there was a budgetary surplus of 256m. French francs: expenditure amounted to 3,740m. francs. In the same year value-added tax (VAT) contributed 52.8% of total government revenue. In 2001 budgetary revenue amounted to €624.3 million. In the late 1990s it was estimated that less than 3% of the population were unemployed in the Principality.

Monaco is largely dependent on imports from France, owing to its lack of natural resources. There is a severe labour shortage in the Principality, and the economy is reliant on migrant workers (many of whom are from France and Italy). Following the establishment of a casino in the 1860s, tourism became the dominant sector in the economy. In particular, the Principality has sought to establish itself as a major centre of the conference industry; about one-third of the visitors to Monaco in 1994 were connected with this sector, compared with one-10th in the early 1970s. From the 1980s, however, the industry and real estate sectors expanded, as a series of land reclamation projects increased Monaco's area by 20%, and the relocation of the Principality's railway station underground. A number of foreign companies and banks are registered in Monaco in order to take advantage of the low rates of taxation on company profits. Since the removal of French restrictions on foreign exchange in 1987, Monaco's banking industry (which includes an 'offshore' sector) has expanded. In the early 1990s the Government continued its policy of promoting economic diversification with the implementation of a programme of public works, designed to encourage the establishment of small industrial enterprises. The opening of a new conference and cultural centre in mid-2000 was expected to result in the further expansion of Monaco's business conference industry. The role of tourism in the economy was expected to grow further, following the construction of a new pier for luxury vessels, completed in August 2002. The shipping and telecommunications industries were also a focus of expansion in the Principality in the early 2000s.

Education

Education follows the French system, and is compulsory for 10 years for children aged six to 16 years. Primary education begins at six years of age and lasts for five years. Secondary education begins at 11 years of age and lasts for seven years. In 1996/97 some 1,919 pupils attended the Principality's seven primary schools, while 2,358 pupils were enrolled in secondary education. Total expenditure on education amounted to 221m. French francs in 1996, equivalent to 6.3% of total budgetary expenditure.

Public Holidays

2003: 1 January (New Year's Day), 27 January (Feast of St Dévote, Patron Saint of the Principality), 21 April (Easter Monday), 1 May (Labour Day), 29 May (Ascension Day), 9 June (Whit Monday), 15 August (Assumption), 1 November (All Saints' Day), 19 November (National Day/Fête du Prince), 8 December (Immaculate Conception), 25–26 December (Christmas).

2004: 1 January (New Year's Day), 27 January (Feast of St Dévote, Patron Saint of the Principality), 12 April (Easter Monday), 1 May (Labour Day), 20 May (Ascension Day), 31 May (Whit Monday), 15 August (Assumption), 1 November (All Saints' Day), 19 November (National Day/Fête du Prince), 8 December (Immaculate Conception), 25–26 December (Christmas).

Weights and Measures

The metric system is in force.

Statistical Survey

Source: (unless otherwise stated): Direction de l'expansion économique, division des statistiques et des études économiques, 9 rue du Gabian, 98000 Monte-Carlo; tel. 93-15-41-59; fax 93-15-87-59.

AREA AND POPULATION

Area: 1.95 sq km.

Population: 29,972 at census of 23 July 1990; 32,020 (males 15,544; females 16,476) at census of July 2000.

Density (July 2000): 16,435 per sq km.

Population by nationality (2000): French 10,229; Italian 6,410; Monégasque 6,089; Other 9,292.

Districts (population at 2000 census): Monte-Carlo 15,507; Condamine 12,187; Fontvieille 3,292; Monaco-Ville (capital) 1,034.

Births, Marriages and Deaths (2002): Live births 771; Marriages 175; Deaths 564. Source: Monaco–La Mairie.

Expectation of Life (WHO estimates, years at birth): 80.3 (males 76.5; females 84.0) in 2001. Source: WHO, *World Health Report*.

Economically Active Population (incl. non-residents, September 2000): 36,519.

HEALTH AND WELFARE

Key Indicators

Total fertility rate (children per woman, 2001): 1.8.

Under-5 Mortality Rate (per 1,000 live births, 2001): 5.

Physicians (per 1,000 head, 1998): 6.64.

Health Expenditure (2000): US $ per head (PPP): 1,877.

Health Expenditure (2000): % of GDP: 7.4.

Health Expenditure (2000): public (% of total): 48.1.

Access to Water (% of persons, 2000): 100.

Access to Sanitation (% of persons, 2000): 100.
For sources and definitions, see explanatory note on p. vi.

FINANCE

Currency and Exchange Rates: French currency: 100 cent = 1 euro (€). *Sterling and Dollar Equivalents* (31 December 2002): £1 sterling = 1.5370 euros; US $1 = 1.0487 euros; 100 euros = £65.06 = $104.87. *Average Exchange Rate* (euros per US dollar): 1.0854 in 2000; 1.1175 in 2001; 1.0626 in 2002*Note:* The local currency was formerly the French franc, although some Monégasque currency, at par with the French franc, also circulated. From the introduction of the euro, with French participation, on 1 January 1999, a fixed exchange rate of €1 = 6.55957 French francs was in operation. Euro notes and coins were introduced on 1 January 2002. The euro and local currency circulated alongside each other until 17 February, after which the euro became the sole legal tender. Some of the figures in this survey are still in terms of French francs.

Budget (million francs, 2000): Revenue 3,996; Expenditure 3,740. *2001* (million euros): Revenue 624.3.

EXTERNAL TRADE

Monaco's imports and exports are included in the figures for France.

TRANSPORT

Road Traffic (vehicles in use at 31 December 1996, estimates): Passenger cars 21,120; Buses and coaches 70; Lorries and vans 2,700; Road tractors 80; Motorcycles and mopeds 5,400. Source: IRF, *World Road Statistics*.

TOURISM

Tourist Arrivals (excluding excursionists): 278,474 in 1998; 278,448 in 1999; 300,185 in 2000. Figures refer to arrivals of foreign visitors at hotels and similar establishments.

Tourist Arrivals by Country (2000): France 48,335; Germany 15,566; Italy 70,795; Japan 14,752; Netherlands 6,015; Spain 6,768; Switzerland 9,019; United Kingdom 32,993; USA 36,459; Total (incl. others) 300,185.

COMMUNICATIONS MEDIA

Radio Receivers (1997): 34,000 in use*.

Television Receivers (1997): 25,000 in use*.

Daily Newspapers (1996): 1 title (estimated circulation 8,000 copies — 1995)*.

Non-daily Newspapers (1996): 5 titles (estimated circulation 50,000 copies)*.

Telephones (2000): 30,000 main lines in use†.

Facsimile Machines (1992): 1,880 in use‡.

Mobile Cellular Telephones (2000): 18,700 subscribers†.
* Source: UNESCO, *Statistical Yearbook*.
† Source: International Telecommunication Union.
‡ Source: UN, *Statistical Yearbook*.

EDUCATION

(1996/97)

Pre-primary: 9 schools; 46 teachers (1995/96); 996 pupils (males 526; females 470).

Primary: 7 schools; 102 teachers (1995/96); 1,919 pupils (males 1,011; females 908).

General Secondary: 192 teachers; 2,358 pupils (males 1,141; females 1,217).

Vocational: 89 teachers; 528 pupils (males 287; females 241). Source: UNESCO, *Statistical Yearbook*.

Directory

The Constitution

The Constitution of 17 December 1962, as amended on 2 April 2002, vests legislative power jointly in the Prince and the 24-member National Council (Conseil National), which is elected by universal adult suffrage, partly under a system of proportional representation, for a term of five years. Executive power is exercised, under the authority of the Prince, by the four-member Council of Government, headed by the Minister of State. The Constitution maintains the traditional hereditary monarchy, although the principle of the divine right of the ruler is renounced. The law of succession was modified to permit succession through the female line in April 2002. The right of association, trade union freedom and the right to strike are guaranteed. The Supreme Tribunal safeguards fundamental liberties. Constitutional amendments have to be submitted for approval by the Conseil National. Several executive powers of the Prince were transferred to the Conseil National in April 2002.

The Government

HEAD OF STATE

Ruling Prince: HSH Prince RAINIER III (succeeded 9 May 1949).

COUNCIL OF GOVERNMENT
(April 2003)

Minister of State: PATRICK LECLERCQ.

Government Councillor for Finance and Economic Affairs: FRANCK BIANCHERI.

Government Councillor for Public Works and Social Affairs: JOSÉ BADIA.

Government Councillor for the Interior: PHILIPPE DESLANDES. There is also a Chef de Cabinet (Georges Grinda).

MINISTRIES

The postal address for all Ministries is: BP 522, MC 98015; tel. 93-15-80-00; fax 93-15-82-17; internet www.gouv.mc; tel.

Ministry of State: place de la Visitation, MC98000; e-mail cabminetat@gouv.mc.

Legislature

CONSEIL NATIONAL

The Conseil National (National Council) has 24 members. At the most recent elections, which took place on 9 February 2003, the Union pour Monaco (UPM) list secured 21 seats, with the Union Nationale et Démocratique (UND) controlling the remaining three.

Conseil National: 12 rue Bellano de Castro, MC; tel. 93–30–41–15; fax 93–25–31–90.

President: STÉPHANE VALÉRI.

Vice-President: CLAUDE BOISSON.

Political Organizations

There are no political parties as such in Monaco; however, candidates are generally grouped into lists to contest elections to the Conseil National. Between 1963 and 1992, and 1998 and 2003 the Conseil National was dominated by representatives of the **Union Nationale et Démocratique (UND).** At the 1993 elections, however, the two main groupings were the **Liste Campora,** led by Jean-Louis Campora, and the **Liste Médecin,** led by Jean-Louis Médecin. The majority of seats at the 2003 elections were secured by the **Union pour Monaco** list.

Diplomatic Representation

There are no embassies in Monaco, but diplomatic relations are maintained at consular level with 48 countries.

Judicial System

The organization of the legal system is similar to that of France. There is one Justice of the Peace, a Tribunal de Première Instance (Court of First Instance), a Cour d'Appel (Court of Appeal), a Cour de Révision (High Court of Appeal), a Tribunal Criminel (Crown Court) and finally the Tribunal Suprême (Supreme Tribunal), which deals with infringements of the rights and liberties provided by the Constitution, and also with legal actions aiming at the annulment of administrative decisions for abusive exercise of power.

Palais de Justice
5 rue Col Bellando de Castro, MC 98000; tel. 93-15-84-11; fax 93-15-85-89.

Director of Judicial Services: PATRICE DAVOST.

President of the Supreme Tribunal: ROLAND DRAGO.

President of the High Court of Appeal: YVES JOUHAUD.

President of the Court of Appeal: JEAN-FRANÇOIS LANDWERLIN.

President of the Court of First Instance: PHILIPPE NARMINO.

Religion

CHRISTIANITY

The Roman Catholic Church

Monaco comprises a single archdiocese, directly responsible to the Holy See. At 31 December 2000 there were an estimated 29,000 adherents in the Principality, representing about 91% of the total population.

Archbishop of Monaco: Most Rev. BERNARD BARSI, Archevêché, 1 rue de l'Abbaye, BP 517, MC 98015; tel. 93-30-88-10; fax 92-16-73-88; e-mail monacochan@aol.com.

The Anglican Communion

Within the Church of England, Monaco forms part of the diocese of Gibraltar in Europe.

Chaplain: (vacant), St Paul's Church House, 22 ave de Grande Bretagne, MC 98000; tel. 93-30-71-06; fax 93-30-50-39; e-mail stpauls@monaco.mc; internet www.stpauls.monaco.mc.

The Principality also has two Protestant churches and a synagogue.

The Press

Gazette Monaco—Côte d'Azur: 1, ave Princesse Alice, MC 98000; tel. 97-97-61-20; fax 93-50-68-27; e-mail lagazette@monte-carlo.mc; f. 1976; monthly; regional information; Dir-Gen. MAX POGGI; Chief Editor NOËLLE BINE-MULLER; circ. 10,000.

Journal de Monaco: Ministère d'Etat, BP 522, MC 98015; tel. 93-15-83-15; fax 93-15-82-17; internet www.gouv.mc/DataWeb/jourmon .nsf/(VDate)?OpenView&Start=1&Count=15; f. 1858; edited at the Ministry of State; official weekly; contains texts of laws and decrees; Man. Editor GILLES TONELLI.

Monaco Actualité: 2 rue du Gabian, MC 98000; tel. 92-05-75-36; fax 92-05-75-34; e-mail actualite@monaco.mc; Dir-Gen. MAURICE RICCOBONO; circ. 15,000.

Monaco Hebdo: 27 blvd d'Italie, MC 98000; tel. 93-50-56-52; fax 93-50-19-22; Man. Editor ROBERTO TESTA.

Monte-Carlo Méditerranée: tel. 92-05-67-67; fax 92-05-37-01; Dir-Gen. GÉRARD COMMAN; Chief Editor CAROLE CHABRIER.

French newspapers are widely read, and a special Monaco edition of *Nice-Matin* is published in Nice, France.

NEWS AGENCIES

Monte-Carlo Press: Monte-Carlo; e-mail mcpress@monaco.net; internet mcpress.free.fr; f. 1987.

SPORTEL Organisation: 4 blvd du Jardin Exotique, MC 98000; tel. 93-30-20-32; fax 93-30-20-33; e-mail info@sportelmonaco.com; internet www.sportelmonaco.com; Exec. Vice-Pres. DAVID TOMATIS.

Publishers

EDIPROM: Monte-Carlo; tel. 92-05-67-67; fax 92-05-37-01; advertising material, official publications; Pres. GÉRARD COMMAN.

Editions Alphée: 28 rue Comte Félix Gastaldi, MC 98015 Monaco Cédex; tel. 99-99-67-17; fax 99-99-67-18.

Editions EGC: 9 ave du Prince Héréditaire Albert, BP 438, MC 98011 Monaco Cédex; e-mail multiprint@multiprintmc.com; economics, history, literature; Gen. Man. GÉRARD COMMAN.

Editions Victor Gadoury: 57 rue Grimaldi, MC 98000; tel. 93-25-12-96; fax 93-50-13-39; e-mail contact@gadoury.com; internet www .gadoury.com; f. 1967; numismatics.

Editions de l'Oiseau-Lyre SAM: Les Remparts, BP 515, MC 98015 Monaco Cédex; tel. 93-30-09-44; fax 93-30-19-15; e-mail oiseau_lyre@compuserve.com; internet www.oiseaulyre.com; f. 1932; music publishers; Dir KENNETH GILBERT.

Editions de Radio Monte Carlo SAM: Monte-Carlo; tel. 93-15-17-57; general; Pres. JEAN PASTORELLI.

Editions Regain S.N.C. Boy et Cie: Monte-Carlo; tel. 93-50-62-04; f. 1946; fiction, essays, autobiography, travel, religion, philosophy, poetry; Dir-Gen. MICHÈLE G. BOY.

Editions du Rocher: 28 rue Comte Félix Gastaldi, MC 98015; tel. 93-30-33-41; fax 93-50-73-71; f. 1943; scientific, medical, detective and general; Dir JEAN PAUL BERTRAND.

Les Editions André Sauret SAM: Monte-Carlo; tel. 93-50-67-94; fax 93-30-71-04; art, fiction; Dir RAYMOND LEVY.

Marsu Productions: 9 ave des Castelans, MC 98000; tel. 92-05-61-11; fax 92-05-76-60; e-mail marsuproductions@compuserve.com; internet www.marsupilami.com; comic-strips, children's entertainment.

Monaco Télématique (MCTEL): 25 blvd d'Italie, MC 98004; tel. 92-16-88-88; fax 93-30-45-45; e-mail mctel@mctel.mc; internet www .mctel.mc; scientific and technical.

Broadcasting and Communications

TELECOMMUNICATIONS

Direction des Télécommunications: 23 ave Prince Héréditaire Albert, MC 98030; tel. 97-98-56-56; fax 97-98-56-57; Dir LOUIS BIANCHERI.

Monaco Telecom: 25 blvd de Suisse, MC 98000; tel. 99-66-63-00; fax 99-66-63-01; e-mail monaco-telecom@monaco-telecom.mc; f. 1997; 51% owned by Vivendi; incorporates the wholly-owned subsidiaries Monaco Telecom International, Monaco Interactive and Société Monégasque de Services de Telecoms; CEO ANTOINE VERAN.

BROADCASTING

Radio

Radio Monte Carlo SAM (RMC): Monte-Carlo; tel. 93-15-16-17; fax 93-15-16-30; the official programme of RMC is broadcast in French on 1,400 metres (216 kHz); programmes in French are broadcast on 216 metres (1,467 kHz); programmes on RMC may be backed by commercials or by sponsors; 83% owned by the French Government (Société financière de la radiodiffusion); Pres. C. C. SOLAMITO; Dir-Gen. JEAN NOEL TASSEZ.

Riviera Radio: 10–12 quai Antoine 1er, MC 98000; tel. 7-97-94-94; fax 7-97-94-95; e-mail info@rivieraradio.mc; internet www .rivieraradio.mc; broadcasts in English; Man. Dir MARC DUGIMONT.

Société Monégasque d'Exploitation et d'Études de Radio-diffusion (SOMERA): Monte-Carlo; tel. 93-15-16-17; fax 93-15-16-60; fmr subsidiary of RMC, transferred to Radio-France Internationale in 1996; in French and Arabic; Pres. JEAN-PAUL CLUZEL; Dir-Gen. CHRISTIAN CHARPY.

Trans World Radio SC: BP 349, MC 98007; tel. 92-16-56-00; fax 92-16-56-01; f. 1955; broadcasts evangelical Christian programmes in 30 languages; Pres. THOMAS J. LOWELL; Station Man. CURTISS DETWILER.

Television

TVI Monte-Carlo: 8 quai Antoine 1er, MC 98000; tel. 92-16-88-20; fax 93-25-46-39; e-mail tvimc@frateschi.mc; programmes in Italian; CEO LUIGI FRATESCHI.

Société Spéciale d'Entreprises Télé Monte-Carlo: 16 blvd Princesse Charlotte, BP 279, MC 98090; tel. 93-50-59-40; fax 93-25-01-09; internet www.cecchigori.com; f. 1954; Pres. JEAN-LOUIS MÉDECIN.

Finance

(cap. = capital, res = reserves, dep. = deposits, brs = branches, m. = million, amounts in euros—€)

BANKS

In 2001 a total of 44 banks, including major British, French, Italian and US banks, were represented in the Principality.

Banco Atlantico (Monaco), SAM: Sporting d'Hiver, 2 ave Princesse Alice, BP 147, MC 98003; tel. 92-16-57-57; fax 92-16-57-50; e-mail abcmc@webstore.mc; internet www.batlantico.es; f. 1980; 100% owned by Banco Atlántico (Spain); fmrly 49% owned by Arab Banking Corporation, Bahrain, as ABC Banque Internationale de Monaco; cap. 11.4m., res 7.9m., dep. 316.7m. (Dec. 2000); Chair. OLIMPIO FERNANDEZ; Exec. Dir and Dir-Gen. ANTONIO SALVADOR.

Banque Centrale Monégasque de Crédit: Monte-Carlo; tel. 92-16-52-00; fax 93-30-91-93; f. 1969; Pres. JEAN DEFLASSIEUX; Gen. Man. MARC LANZERINI.

Banque de Gestion Edmond de Rothschild: BP 317, Les Terrasses, 2 ave de Monte-Carlo, MC 98000; tel. 93-10-47-47; fax 93-25-75-57; e-mail banque@lcf-rothschild.mc; internet www.lcf-rothschild .com; f. 1986; present name adopted 1993; cap. 12.0m., res 9.9m., dep. 417.7m. (Dec 2001); Chair. LEONARDO P. A. POGGI; Gen. Man. GIAMPAOLO BERNINI.

Banque du Gothard (Monaco): La Belle Epoque, 15–17 bis ave d'Ostende, MC 98000; tel. 93-10-66-66; fax 93-50-60-71; e-mail philippe.tronlozai@gottardo.com; internet www.gottardo.com; f. 1994; 100% owned by Banca del Gottardo (Switzerland); cap. 40.0m., res 18.4m., dep. 1,674.6m. (Dec. 2001); Pres. NICOLA MORDASINI.

Banque Sudameris: 47–49 blvd d'Italie, MC 98000; tel. 92-16-51-00; fax 92-16-51-13; e-mail monaco@sudameris.fr; Man. MICHEL DE GIRONDE.

Barclays Bank: 31 ave de la Costa, BP 339, MC 98007; tel. 93-15-35-35; fax 93-25-15-68; Gen. Man. J. B. BUISSON; 3 brs.

Compagnie Monégasque de Banque: 23 ave de la Costa, BP 149, MC 98007; tel. 93-15-77-77; fax 93-25-08-69; e-mail cmb@cmb.mc; internet www.cmb.mc; f. 1976; cap. 111.1m., res 57.0m., dep. 1,520.9m. (Dec. 2001); Chair. ENRICO BRAGGIOTTI.

Crédit Foncier de Monaco (CFM Monaco): 11 blvd Albert 1er, BP 499, MC 98000; tel. 93-10-20-00; fax 93-10-23-50; e-mail info@cfm.mc; internet www.cfm.mc; f. 1922; 77.1% owned by Crédit Agricole Indosuez; cap. 35.0.m., res 67.7m., dep. 2,122.3m. (Dec. 2001); Chair. YVES BARSALOU; Gen. Man. HERVÉ CATALA.

Crédit Suisse (Monaco): 27 ave de la Costa, BP 155, MC 98003; tel. 93-15-27-27; fax 93-25-27-59; e-mail alexandre.zeller@cspb.com; f. 1987; cap. 12.0m., res 1.6m., dep. 564.5m. (Dec. 2001); Chair. ALEXANDRE ZELLER.

HSBC Republic Bank (Monaco): 17 ave d'Ostende, MC 98000; tel. 93-15-25-25; fax 93-15-25-00; f. 1997 as Republic National Bank of New York (Monaco) SA, present name adopted 2000; owned by HSBC Private Banking Holdings (Suisse—Switzerland); merged with Crédit Commercial de France (Monaco) in 2001; cap. 55.8m., res 1.3m., dep. 3,182.2m. (Dec. 2001); Chief Exec. and Dir-Gen. GÉRARD COHEN.

KB Luxembourg (Monaco): 8 ave de Grande Bretagne, BP 262, MC 98005; tel. 92-16-55-55; fax 92-16-55-99; e-mail contact@kblmonaco.com; f. 1996; cap. 7.2m., res 0.9m., dep. 305.7m. (Dec. 2001); Chair. of Bd ETIENNE VERWILGHEN; Dir-Gen. PAUL-MARIE JACQUES.

Société Monégasque de Banque Privée: 9 blvd d'Italie, MC 98000; tel. 93-15-23-23; fax 93-15-23-30; f. 1953; present name adopted 1996; cap. 29.6m., res. 0.9m., dep. 219.9m. (Dec. 2001); Chair. JUAN ANTONIO SAMARANCH; Dir-Gen. JOSEP TRIAS.

UBS (Monaco): 2 ave de Grande Bretagne, BP 189, MC 98007; tel. 93-15-58-15; fax 93-15-58-00; e-mail gisele.verheyden@ubs.com; internet www.ubs.com/monaco; f. 1956; present name adopted 1998; 100% owned by UBS AG (Switzerland); cap. 9.2m., res 21.82m., dep. 2,277.9m. (Dec. 2001); CEO NIKLAUS PEAU.

United European Bank—Monaco: 26 blvd d'Italie, BP 319, MC 98007; tel. 93-15-74-74; fax 93-50-15-37; e-mail ueb.mc@meditnet .com; f. 1956 as Société de Banque et d'Investissements SAM; private bank; Pres.and Chair. GÉRARD LOHIER; Dir-Gen. ERIC GEORGES.

INSURANCE COMPANIES

Eric Blair Insurance: 33 blvd Princesse Charlotte, MC 98000; tel. 93-50-99-66; fax 93-50-14-47; e-mail insure@monaco.mc; internet www.monaco.mc/co/ericblair.

Gramaglia AGF: 14 blvd des Moulins, BP 153, MC 98003; tel. 92-16-59-00; fax 92-16-59-16; e-mail info@gramaglia.mc; internet www .gramaglia.mc; Dir ANTOINE GRAMAGLIA.

Monaco Insurance Services: 3 ave Saint-Charles, BP 113, MC 98008; tel. 93-25-38-58; fax 93-25-74-37; Dir PIERRE AOUN.

Mourenon et Giannotti: 22 blvd Princesse Charlotte, MC 98000; tel. 97-97-08-88; fax 97-97-08-80; f. 1975; Dirs JEAN-PHILIPPE MOURENON, JOSÉ GIANNOTTI.

J.P. Sassi-Drouot Assurances: Monte-Carlo; tel. 93-30-45-88; Dir JEAN-PIERRE SASSI.

Silvain Assurances: 33 blvd Princesse Charlotte, BP 267, MC 98005; tel. 93-25-54-45; fax 93-50-39-05; Dir FRANÇOIS SILVAIN.

Société Française de Recours Cie d'Assurances: 28 blvd Princesse Charlotte, MC 98000; tel. 93-50-52-63; fax 93-50-54-49; Dir FLORIANO CONTE.

Trade and Industry

GOVERNMENT AGENCIES

Conseil Economique et Social: 8 rue Louis Notari, Monte-Carlo; tel. 97-97-77-90; fax 93-50-05-96; consultative org. in six sections dealing with all aspects of Monaco's economy; comprises 30 members who represent, in equal proportions, employers, workers and the Government; named by the Head of State every three years from all

nationalities; President must be Monégasque national; Pres. ANDRÉ GARINO; Vice-Pres ANDRÉ THIBAULT, JACQUES WOLZOK.

Direction de l'Action Sanitaire et Sociale: 13 rue Emile de Loth; tel. 93-15-84-20; fax 93-15-81-59; Dir Dr ANNE NEGRE.

Direction des Affaires Culturelles: 4 blvd des Moulins; tel. 93-15-85-15; fax 93-50-66-94; Dir RAINIER ROCCHI.

Direction des Affaires Maritimes: La Capitainerie, quai Jean-Charles Rey, MC 98000; tel. 93-15-86-78; fax 93-15-37-15; Dir PHILIPPE REMY.

Direction du Budget et du Trésor: 13 rue Emile de Loth; tel. 93-15-87-73; fax 93-15-84-26; Dir SOPHIE THEVENOUX.

Direction des Contentieux et des Etudes Législatives: Stade Louis II, Entrée H, 1 ave des Castelans, MC 98013; Dir ISABELLE ROUONET-PASSERON.

Direction du Contrôle des Concessions et des Télécommunications: 23 ave Prince Héréditaire Albert; tel. 93-15-88-00; fax 93-15-85-50; Dir RAOUL VIORA.

Direction de l'Education Nationale, de la Jeunesse et des Sports: Lycée Technique, ave de l'Annonciade; tel. 93-15-80-05; fax 93-15-85-74; e-mail denjs@gouv.mc; internet www.monaco.gouv.mc/Educ/EducMc.nsf/FormFr?OpenForm&1; Dir YVETTE LAMBIN DE COMBREMONT.

Direction de l'Environnement, de l'Urbanisme et de la Construction: 23 ave Prince Héréditaire Albert; tel. 93-15-22-99; fax 93-15-88-02; Dir MAUD COLLE-GAMERDINGER.

Direction de l'Expansion Economique: 9 rue du Gabian; tel. 93-15-21-74; fax 92-05-75-20; Dir CATHERINE ORECCHIA-MATTHYSSENS.

Direction de la Fonction Publique et des Ressources Humaines: Stade Louis II, entrée H, 1 ave des Castelans; tel. 93-15-81-13; fax 93-15-42-91; Dir CLAUDE COTTALORDA.

Direction de l'Habitat: 24 rue du Gabian; tel. 93-15-80-08; fax 93-15-20-06; Dir MARIE-JOSÉ CALENCO.

Direction de la Prospective et des Etudes d'Urbanisme: 3 ave de Fontvieille; tel. 93–15–80–00; fax 93–15–46–60; e-mail prospective@gouv.mc; Dir PATRICE CELLARIO.

Direction des Relations Extérieures: Ministère d'État, Place de la Visitation, MC 98000; tel. 93-15-41-66; fax 93-15-85-54; e-mail relext@gouv.mc; Dir PATRICK LECLERCQ; Sec.-Gen. CLAUDE GIORDAN.

Direction des Services Fiscaux: 57 rue Grimaldi, BP 475, 98012 Monaco Cédex; tel. 93-15-40-54; fax 93-15-81-55; Dir GÉRARD EMMEL.

Direction de la Sûreté Publique: 3–4 rue Louis Notari, BP 465, MC 98012; tel. 93-15-30-15; fax 93-50-65-47; Dir MAURICE ALBERTIN.

Direction du Travail et des Affaires Sociales: 2 rue Princesse Antoinette; tel. 93-15-88-14; fax 92-16-70-05; Dir THIERRY PICCO.

Trésorerie Générale des Finances: Cour de la Trésorie, Palais de Monaco; tel. 93-15-88-19; fax 93-15-85-75; Treas. YVON BERTRAND.

CHAMBER OF COMMERCE

Jeune Chambre Economique de Monaco: MC 98000; tel. 92-05-20-19; fax 92-05-31-29; e-mail jcemonaco@jcemonaco.mc; internet www.jcemonaco.mc; f. 1963; 102 mems; Pres. PHILIPPE VERDIER.

EMPLOYERS' ASSOCIATION

Fédération Patronale Monégasque (FPM) (Employers' Federation of Monaco): 'Le Coronado', 20 ave de Fontvielle, MC 98000; tel. 92-05-38-92; fax 92-05-20-04; e-mail info@federation-patronale.mc; internet www.federation-patronale.mc; f. 1944; Pres. F. E. GRIFFIN; 23 member orgs, with 1,500 individual mems.

UTILITIES

Electricity and Gas

Société Monégasque de l'Electricité et du Gaz (SMEG): 10 ave de Fontvieille, BP 633, MC 98013 Monaco Cédex; tel. 92-05-05-00; fax 92-05-05-92; e-mail smeg@smeg.mc; internet www.smeg.mc; f. 1890.

Water

Société Monégasque des Eaux (SME): 29 ave Princesse Grace, MC 98000; tel. 93-30-83-67; fax 92-05-05-00.

TRADE UNION

Union des Syndicats de Monaco (USM): 28 blvd Rainier III, 98000 Monaco; tel. 93-30-19-30; fax 93-25-06-73; e-mail syndicats_mc@monaco377.com; f. 1944; Pres. (vacant); Sec.-Gen. ANGÈLE BRAQUETTI; 35 mem. unions with 5,000 individual mems.

Transport

RAILWAYS

There is 1.7 km of railway track in Monaco running from France to Monte-Carlo. It is operated by the French state railway, the Société Nationale des Chemins de fer Français (SNCF). As part of the Government's policy of land reclamation an underground railway station was opened in 1999, at a cost of 1,930m. francs.

ROADS

In 1999 there were an estimated 50 km of major roads in the Principality.

SHIPPING

Monaco has an estimated docking capacity of 100 cruise ships.

Service de la Marine: 7 ave J.F. Kennedy; tel. 93-15-80-00.

Shipping Companies

Compagnie pour la Géstion des Affaires Maritimes et Industrielles SAM (COGEMA SAM): 20 blvd de Suisse, MC 98000 Cédex; tel. 93-10-52-70; fax 93-50-03-81; e-mail secretary@damicoint.com; internet www.cogema-sam.com; CEO Marco Fiori.

MC Shipping Inc.: Aigue Marine, 24 ave de Fontvieille, BP 658, MC 98013 Cédex; tel. 92-05-94-04; fax 92-05-94-16; Pres. and CEO Guy Morel.

Olympic Shipping and Management: Monte-Carlo; tel. 93-25-41-41; fax 93-30-07-10.

Société Anonyme Monégasque d'Administration Maritime et Aérienne (SAMAMA): L'Estoril, Bloc B 1er étage, 31 ave Princesse Grace, MC 98000 Cédex; tel. 99-99-51-00; fax 99-99-51-09; e-mail general@samama-monaco.com.

V. Ships Inc: Aigue Marine, 24 ave de Fontvieille, BP 639, MC 98013 Cédex; tel. 92-05-10-10; fax 92-05-94-10; internet www.vships .com; Pres. Tullio Biggi; Man. Dir Hermann Messner.

CIVIL AVIATION

There is a helicopter shuttle service between the international airport at Nice, France, and Monaco's heliport at Fontvieille.

Heli-Air Monaco SAM: Héliport de Monaco, MC 98000; tel. 92-05-00-50; fax 92-05-00-51; e-mail helico@heliairmonaco.com; internet www.heliairmonaco.com; Pres. Jacques Crovetto.

Tourism

Tourists are attracted to Monaco by the Mediterranean climate, dramatic scenery and numerous entertainment facilities, including a casino. In 2000 300,185 tourists (excluding excursionists) visited Monaco. In 1992, when (including excursionists) an estimated 4m. people visited the Principality, revenue from tourism totalled US $1,300m. In that year there were 18 hotels in the Principality.

Direction du Tourisme et des Congrès: 2A blvd des Moulins, MC 98030 Cédex; tel. 92-16-61-16; fax 92-16-60-00; e-mail dtc@monaco-congres.com; internet www.monaco-congres.com; there are also international conference centres in Monte-Carlo at: Centre de Congrès Auditorium de Monte-Carlo, blvd Louis II, at Centre de Rencontres Internationales, ave d'Ostende, and at Grimaldi Forum, ave Princesse Grace; Dir-Gen. Dario Dell'Antonia; Dir Régine May.

Société des Bains de Mer (SBM): place du Casino, BP 139, MC 98007; tel. 92-16-20-00; fax 92-16-38-60; e-mail dva@sbm.mc; internet www.sbm.mc; f. 1863; corpn in which the Government holds a 69.6% interest; controls the entertainment facilities of Monaco, including the casino and numerous hotels, clubs, restaurants and sporting facilities; Chair. Jean-Luc Biamonti; Gen. Man. Michel Novatin.

MONGOLIA

Introductory Survey

Location, Climate, Language, Religion, Flag, Capital

Mongolia is a land-locked country in central Asia, with the Russian Federation to the north and the People's Republic of China to the south, east and west. The climate is dry, with generally mild summers but very cold winters. Temperatures in Ulan Bator range between –32°C (–26°F) and 22°C (71°F). The principal language is Khalkha Mongolian. Kazakh is spoken in the province of Bayan-Ölgii. There is no state religion, but Buddhist Lamaism is being encouraged once again. The national flag (proportions 1 by 2) has three equal vertical stripes, of red, blue and red, with the 'soyombo' symbol (a combination of abstract devices) in gold on the red stripe at the hoist. The capital is Ulan Bator (Ulaanbaatar).

Recent History

The country was formerly the Manchu province of Outer Mongolia. In 1911, following the republican revolution in China, Mongolian princes declared the province's independence. With support from Tsarist Russia, Outer Mongolia gained autonomy, as a feudal Buddhist monarchy, but Russia accepted Chinese suzerainty over the province in 1915. Following the Russian revolution of 1917, China began to re-establish control in Mongolia in 1919. In 1920 Mongol nationalists appealed to the new Soviet regime for assistance, and in March 1921 they met on Soviet territory to found the Mongolian People's Party (called the Mongolian People's Revolutionary Party (MPRP) since 1924) and established a Provisional People's Government. After nationalist forces, with Soviet help, drove anti-Bolshevik troops from the Mongolian capital, independence was proclaimed on 11 July 1921. Soviet Russia recognized the People's Government in November of that year. In November 1924, after the death of Bogd Khan (King) Javzandamba Khutagt VIII, the Mongolian People's Republic (MPR) was proclaimed.

The MPR became increasingly dependent on the USSR's support. The Government conducted campaigns to collectivize the economy and to destroy the power of the nobility and Buddhist priests. In 1932 an armed uprising was suppressed with Soviet assistance. Following a purge of the MPRP and army leadership in 1936–39, power was held by Marshal Khorloogiin Choibalsan as Prime Minister and MPRP leader. The dictatorship of Choibalsan closely followed the pattern of Stalin's regime in the USSR, and its thousands of victims included eminent politicians, military officers, religious leaders and intellectuals. In 1939 a Japanese invasion from Manchuria was repelled by Soviet and Mongolian forces at Khalkhyn Gol (Nomonhan). In keeping with the Yalta agreement, war was declared on Japan in August 1945, four days before the Japanese surrender, and northern China was invaded. In a Mongolian plebiscite in October 1945, it was reported that 100% of the votes were cast in favour of independence, and this was recognized by China in January 1946.

Choibalsan died in January 1952 and was succeeded as Prime Minister by Yumjaagiin Tsedenbal, who had been the Party's First Secretary since 1940. Dashiin Damba became First Secretary of the MPRP in April 1954. In 1955 India became the first non-communist country to recognize Mongolia. Tsedenbal replaced Damba as First Secretary of the MPRP in November 1958, and a new Constitution was adopted in July 1960. Mongolia became a member of the UN in October 1961 and was subsequently accorded diplomatic recognition by the United Kingdom (1963), other Western European and developing countries. By January 1987, when Mongolia was finally granted diplomatic recognition by the USA, it maintained diplomatic relations with more than 100 states.

Jamsrangiin Sambuu, Head of State since July 1954, died in May 1972. He was replaced in June 1974 by Tsedenbal, who remained First Secretary of the MPRP (restyled General Secretary in 1981) but relinquished the post of Chairman of the Council of Ministers to Jambyn Batmönkh. In August 1984 Tsedenbal was removed from the party leadership and state presidency, apparently owing to ill health, and Batmönkh replaced him as General Secretary of the MPRP. In December Batmönkh also became Head of State, while Dumaagiin Sodnom, hitherto a Deputy Chairman of the Council of Ministers and the Chairman of the State Planning Commission, was appointed Chairman of the Council of Ministers.

By the end of 1988 the MPRP Political Bureau was obliged to admit that economic renewal was not succeeding because of the need for social reforms. Batmönkh advocated greater openness and offered the prospect of multi-candidate elections. He criticized Tsedenbal for the country's 'stagnation', also stating that the former leader had belittled collective leadership.

Between December 1989 and March 1990 there was a great upsurge in public political activity, as several newly-formed opposition movements organized a series of peaceful demonstrations in Ulan Bator, demanding political and economic reforms. The most prominent of the new opposition groups was the Mongolian Democratic Union (MDU), founded in December 1989. In January 1990 dialogue was initiated between MPRP officials and representatives of the MDU, including its chief co-ordinator, Sanjaasürengiin Zorig (a lecturer at the Mongolian State University). The emergence of further opposition groups, together with escalating public demonstrations (involving as many as 20,000 people), led to a crisis of confidence within the MPRP. At a party plenum in mid-March 1990 Batmönkh announced the resignation of the entire Political Bureau as well as of the Secretariat of the Central Committee. Gombojavyn Ochirbat, a former head of the Ideological Department of the Central Committee and a former Chairman of the Central Council of Mongolian Trade Unions, was elected the new General Secretary of the party, replacing Batmönkh. A new five-member Political Bureau was formed. The plenum voted to expel the former MPRP General Secretary, Yumjaagiin Tsedenbal, from the party and to rehabilitate several prominent victims of Tsedenbal's purges of the 1960s.

At a session of the People's Great Khural (legislature), held shortly after the MPRP plenum, Punsalmaagiin Ochirbat, hitherto the Minister of Foreign Economic Relations and Supply, was elected Chairman of the Presidium (Head of State), replacing Batmönkh, and other senior positions in the Presidium were reorganized. Dumaagiin Sodnom was dismissed from his post as Chairman of the Council of Ministers and was replaced by Sharavyn Gungaadorj, a Deputy Chairman and Minister of Agriculture and the Food Industry. The Khural also adopted amendments to the Constitution, including the deletion of references to the MPRP as the 'guiding force' in Mongolian society, and approved a new electoral law. It was decided that the next elections to the Khural would be held in mid-1990, and not in 1991 as originally planned. Meanwhile, all limits on personal livestock holdings were removed, and new regulations were introduced to encourage foreign investment in Mongolia. However, in late March 1990 an estimated 13,000 people, dissatisfied with the results of the Khural's session, demonstrated in Ulan Bator to demand the dissolution of the Khural. Opposition leaders declared that the changes introduced by the legislature were insufficient, and demanded the introduction of a multi-party electoral law.

In April 1990 the MPRP held an extraordinary congress, at which more than three-quarters of the membership of the Central Committee was renewed. General Secretary Gombojavyn Ochirbat was elected to the restyled post of Chairman of the party. The Political Bureau was renamed the Presidium, and a new, four-member Secretariat of the Central Committee was appointed. In May the People's Great Khural adopted a law on political parties, which legalized the new 'informal' parties through official registration, and also adopted further amendments to the Constitution, introducing a presidential system with a standing legislature called the State Little Khural, elected by proportional representation of parties.

At the July 1990 general election and consequent re-elections, 430 deputies were elected to serve a five-year term: 357 from the MPRP (in some instances unopposed), 16 from the Mongolian Democratic Party (MDP, the political wing of the MDU), 19 shared among the Mongolian Revolutionary Youth League, the Mongolian National Progress Party (MNPP), and the Mongolian Social-Democratic Party (MSDP), and 39 without party affiliation. Under constitutional amendments adopted in May, the People's Great Khural was required to convene at least four times in the five years of its term.

In September 1990 the People's Great Khural elected Punsalmaagiin Ochirbat to be the country's first President, with a five-year term of office; the post of Chairman of the Presidium was abolished. Dashiin Byambasüren was appointed Prime Minister (equivalent to the former post of Chairman of the Council of Ministers) and began consultations on the formation of a multi-party government. The newly-restyled Cabinet was elected by the State Little Khural in September and October. Under the amended Constitution, the President, Vice-President and Ministers were not permitted to remain concurrently deputies of the People's Great Khural; therefore, re-elections of deputies to the legislature were held in November.

The 20th Congress of the MPRP, held in February 1991, elected a new 99-member Central Committee, which, in turn, appointed a new Presidium. The Central Committee also elected a new Chairman, Büdragchaagiin Dash-Yondon, the Chairman of the Ulan Bator City Party Committee, who had become a Presidium member in November 1990.

A new Constitution was adopted by an almost unanimous vote of the Great Khural in January 1992, and entered into force in the following month. It provided for a unicameral Mongolian Great Khural, comprising 76 members, to replace the People's Great Khural, following elections to be held in June. (The State Little Khural was abolished.) The country's official name was changed from the Mongolian People's Republic to Mongolia, and the communist gold star was removed from the national flag.

At the elections to the Mongolian Great Khural in June 1992, contested by the MPRP, an alliance of the MDP, the MNPP and the United Party (UP), the MSDP, and six other parties and another alliance, a total of 293 candidates stood for 76 seats in 26 constituencies, comprising the 18 *aimag* (provinces), the towns of Darkhan and Erdenet, and Ulan Bator City (six). A total of 95.6% of the electorate participated in the elections. Candidates were elected by a simple majority, provided that they obtained the support of at least 50% of the electorate in their constituency. The MPRP candidates received some 57% of the total votes, while the candidates of the other parties (excluding independents) achieved a combined total of 40%. The outcome of the election was disproportionate, however, with the MPRP taking 70 seats (71 including a pro-MPRP independent). The remaining seats went to the MDP (two, including an independent), the MSDP, MNPP and UP (one each).

The first session of the Mongolian Great Khural opened in July 1992 with the election of officers, the nomination of Puntsagiin Jasrai (who had served as a Deputy Chairman of the Council of Ministers in the late 1980s) to the post of Prime Minister, and the approval of his Cabinet. Natsagiin Bagabandi, a Vice-Chairman of the MPRP Central Committee, was elected Chairman of the Great Khural. Jambyn Gombojav (Chairman of the People's Great Khural from late 1990 to late 1991) was elected Vice-Chairman of the new Khural. Meanwhile, a National Security Council was established, with the country's President as its Chairman, and the Prime Minister and Chairman of the Great Khural as its members.

In October 1992 the MDP, MNPP, UP and the Mongolian Renewal Party amalgamated to form the Mongolian National Democratic Party (MNDP), with a General Council headed by the MNPP leader, Davaadorjiin Ganbold, and including Sanjaasürengiin Zorig and other prominent opposition politicians. In the same month the MPRP Central Committee was renamed the MPRP Little Khural, and its membership was increased to 169 (and subsequently to 198). The Presidium was replaced by a nine-member Party Leadership Council, headed by Büdragchaagiin Dash-Yondon as its General Secretary.

The Great Khural adopted a Presidential Election Law in March 1993, and direct elections to the presidency were scheduled for 6 June. Lodongiin Tüdev, a member of the Party Leadership Council and Editor-in-Chief of the MPRP organ, *Ünen*, was chosen as the MPRP's candidate, while President Ochirbat was nominated by a coalition of the MNDP and the MSDP. The result of the election was a convincing popular victory for Ochirbat: he received 57.8% of the votes cast, compared with 38.7% for Tüdev.

The MPRP in early 1996 forced through the Great Khural amendments that increased the number of constituencies from 26 to 76, making them all single-seat constituencies, while preserving the majority vote system. To be declared elected, a candidate would have to receive only 25% of the constituency

votes. In response, opposition parties formed an election coalition, the Democratic Alliance, which received support from the Mongolian Green Party and the MDU.

At the general election, held on 30 June 1996, a resounding victory was achieved by the Democratic Alliance, which won 50 of the 76 seats in the Great Khural, receiving some 46.7% of the total votes cast. The MPRP took only 25 seats (40.6%), while one seat went to a candidate of the United Heritage Party (UHP). Electoral turn-out was 92.2%. At the legislature's inaugural session, in mid-July, the leader of the MSDP, Radnaasümbereliin Gonchigdorj, was elected to the post of Chairman of the Great Khural. Mendsaikhany Enkhsaikhan, the leader of the Democratic Alliance and the group's choice for Prime Minister, was nominated by President Ochirbat and voted into office. Following the rejection of MPRP demands concerning the allocation of positions in the Great Khural, MPRP members staged a three-day boycott of the legislature, leaving it inquorate and unable to function. After the boycott ended, the MNDP leader, Tsakhiagiin Elbegdorj, was elected Vice-Chairman of the Great Khural; a new Government was formed at the end of July.

Following their election defeat, and amid growing evidence of a rift between supporters of tradition and advocates of the reform process, in July 1996 the MPRP Little Khural elected a new Leadership Council and General Secretary of the party, Nambaryn Enkhbayar. Indications of a split in the party increased in February 1997, when the leaders of the MPRP sought to enforce their uncompromising policies on the party congress. Several prominent dissenting members resigned from the party, and Natsagiin Bagabandi, who had been Chairman of the Great Khural in 1992–96, was elected Chairman of the party.

With 18 May 1997 set by the Great Khural as the date for the presidential election, the MNDP and the MSDP proposed a joint candidate for the post of President—the incumbent, Ochirbat. The MPRP nominated the party Chairman, Bagabandi, while the UHP adopted Jambyn Gombojav, a former Vice-Chairman of the Great Khural. The election was won convincingly by Bagabandi, with some 60.8% of the total votes cast. In a severe setback to the democratic movement, Ochirbat received only 29.8%, a reflection of popular dissatisfaction at the rigorous economic reform policies implemented by the ruling Democratic Alliance. Gombojav obtained 6.6% of the votes.

Following Bagabandi's success in the presidential election, Enkhbayar was elected Chairman of the MPRP in his place. In August 1997 he won a by-election for Bagabandi's former seat in the Great Khural. Almost immediately after assuming his seat in the legislature, Enkhbayar initiated a motion of censure against the Democratic Alliance Government for its performance, but the contentious motion was defeated by the ruling Alliance after two weeks of debate.

In April 1998 the Democratic Alliance decided that, henceforth, the Cabinet was to comprise members of the Great Khural, headed by the leader of the Alliance. Tsakhiagiin Elbegdorj, leader of the MNDP, was thus appointed Prime Minister, and a new Cabinet was formed in May. The Government became embroiled in a dispute over the amalgamation of the state-owned Reconstruction Bank, declared bankrupt after over-extending its credit, with the private Golomt Bank. Amid accusations that Democratic Alliance leaders had obtained loans from the bank shortly before its failure, the MPRP effected a boycott of the Great Khural. The party rejected the Government's reinstatement of Reconstruction Bank and returned to the Great Khural in late July to pursue a vote of 'no confidence' in the Government. The vote was carried by 42 votes to 33, with the support of 15 members of the Democratic Alliance.

In August 1998 the Democratic Alliance nominated as its candidate for Prime Minister Davaadorjiin Ganbold, Chairman of the Economic Standing Committee of the Great Khural (who had been chief Deputy Prime Minister in 1990–92 and President of the MNDP in 1992–96). President Bagabandi rejected Ganbold's nomination, on the grounds of his failure to act to resolve the bank merger crisis in his capacity as Chairman of the Committee. Ganbold was nominated a second time, and again rejected by Bagabandi, who proposed Great Khural member Dogsomyn Ganbold. The Democratic Alliance persisted, and by the end of the month Davaadorjiin Ganbold had been nominated and rejected five times. The Democratic Alliance then proposed Rinchinnyamyn Amarjargal, acting Minister of External Relations and a member of the MNDP General Council. President Bagabandi accepted the nomination, but it was rejected by one vote in the Great Khural in September. Two other candidates were subsequently rejected by Bagabandi.

In October 1998 Sanjaasürengiin Zorig, the Minister of Infrastructure Development, was murdered. Zorig, the founder of the Mongolian Democratic Movement, had not been nominated, but was widely seen as a potential prime ministerial candidate. Following Zorig's state funeral, Bagabandi named six more candidates of his own, including Dogsomyn Ganbold and the Mayor of Ulan Bator, Janlavyn Narantsatsralt. The Democratic Alliance disregarded the presidential list and for the sixth time nominated Davaadorjiin Ganbold. Although the nomination was supported by all 48 Democratic Alliance members of the Great Khural, Bagabandi once again rejected him. The political crisis was then deepened by a new Constitutional Court ruling that members of the Great Khural could not serve concurrently in the Government. Two months later the Democratic Alliance finally nominated Bagabandi's candidate, Janlavyn Narantsatsralt, who was appointed Prime Minister in December. The formation of his Government was completed with the appointment of the last four ministers in January 1999.

Narantsatsralt's Government remained in power for just over six months. In July 1999 the Prime Minister was challenged in the Great Khural over a letter that he had written in January to Yurii Maslyukov, First Deputy Chairman of the Russian Government, in which he seemingly acknowledged Russia's right to privatize its share in the Erdenet joint venture without reference to the Mongolians. Unable to offer a satisfactory explanation, in late July Narantsatsralt lost a vote of confidence, in which MSDP members of the Great Khural voted with the opposition MPRP. The Democratic Alliance nominated Rinchinnyamyn Amarjargal for the post of Prime Minister, but the proposal was immediately challenged by Bagabandi. The President insisted that, following the Constitutional Court ruling of late 1998, he could consider Amarjargal's suitability for nomination in the Great Khural only after the candidate had resigned his seat. After several days of arguments, representatives of the Democratic Alliance and the President adopted a formula that allowed the Great Khural's approval of the prime ministerial nomination and the nominee's resignation of his Great Khural seat to take place simultaneously. Amarjargal was elected Prime Minister at the end of July. The ministers of Narantsatsralt's Government remained in office in an acting capacity until early September, when all but one (the Minister of Law) were reappointed. The formation of the Government was completed in late October with the appointment of Dashpuntsagiin Ganbold as Minister of Law. In November 1999 Amarjargal assumed the presidency of the MNDP, replacing Narantsatsralt.

The 1992 Constitution was amended for the first time in December 1999 by a Great Khural decree supported by all three parliamentary parties, which simplified the procedure for the appointment of the Prime Minister and allowed members of the Great Khural to serve as government ministers while retaining their seats in the legislature. An attempt by the President to veto the decree was defeated by the Great Khural in January 2000, but the Constitutional Court ruled in March that the decree had been illegal. When the Great Khural opened its spring session in April, members rejected the ruling and refused to discuss it. The Constitutional Court's demand for a statement on the issue was disregarded by the Great Khural.

As the general election approached, party political activity increased dramatically. A breakaway grouping of the MNDP reformed the Mongolian Democratic Party, and a faction of the MSDP founded the Mongolian New Social Democratic Party. Sanjaasürengiin Oyuun, the sister of the murdered minister, Zorig, established the Civil Courage Party (CCP, or Irgenii Zorig Nam) drawing away from the MNDP several more members of the Great Khural, and formed an electoral alliance with the Green Party. The MNDP, unable to reconstitute the previously-successful Democratic Alliance with the MSDP, therefore formed a new Democratic Alliance with the Mongolian Believers' Democratic Party.

At the election, held on 2 July 2000, three coalitions and 13 parties were represented by a total of 603 candidates, including 27 independents. The MPRP took 72 of the 76 seats in the Great Khural. Prime Minister Rinchinnyamyn Amarjargal and his entire cabinet lost their seats. The MPRP received 50.2% of the votes cast. The level of participation was 82.4% of the electorate. The party's victory was attributed to widespread popular support for its manifesto of social welfare and poverty reduction, and to the disintegration of the MNDP-MSDP coalition. The MPRP's main support lay in rural constituencies, where it was widely seen as willing and able to halt the economic and social stagnation of the countryside. The Democratic Alliance received

13% of the votes cast, while the MDNSP achieved 10.7% of the votes; each of them won one seat. The MSDP received 8.9% of the votes cast but won no seats.

When the Great Khural opened, Lkhamsürengiin Enebish, the MPRP General Secretary, was elected Chairman (Speaker). The nomination of the MPRP Chairman, Nambaryn Enkhbayar, for the post of Prime Minister was, however, rejected by President Bagabandi, on the grounds that priority be given to the constitutional amendments. After a week of discussions a compromise was reached whereby Enkhbayar's nomination was presented to the Great Khural, while the amendments remained in force pending a Great Khural debate and a full nine-member session of the Constitutional Court. In July 2000 the Great Khural approved Enkhbayar's appointment as Prime Minister by 67 MPRP members' votes to three. Enkhbayar's cabinet was approved in August.

Reflecting the MPRP's emphasis on social issues, Enkhbayar divided the former Ministry of Health and Social Welfare into two separate ministries, the Ministry of Health and the Ministry of Social Protection and Welfare. The Ministry of Law was renamed the Ministry of Justice and Internal Affairs and assumed control of the border troops. However, the MSDP alleged that the new Government was acting in violation of the Constitution, by dismissing large numbers of civil servants because of their party affiliation. In late September 2000 the leaders of the MNDP and the MSDP signed a joint declaration announcing that a conference of the parties would be held in early December, to formalize the merging of the two parties. This was done with a view to ensuring the necessary parliamentary basis for the nomination of Radnaasümbereliin Gonchigdorj, the leader of the MSDP, in the presidential election scheduled for 2001.

At the conference on 6 December 2000 five parties—the MNDP, MSDP, the Mongolian Democratic Party, the Believers' Democratic Party and the Democratic Renewal Party—resolved to dissolve themselves and form a new Democratic Party (DP). Dambyn Dorligjav, a former Minister of Defence and director of the Erdenet copper enterprise, was elected Chairman, while Janlavyn Narantsatsralt and the former Minister of the Environment, Sonomtserengiin Mendsaikhan, were elected as vice-chairmen. At its registration in late December the DP claimed a membership of 160,000. The party's National Advisory Committee was formed in February 2001 and comprised two members from each of the Great Khural's 76 constituencies. Members included many of the former leaders of the MNDP and the MSDP who had failed to win seats in the elections of July 2000.

In mid-December 2000 the Great Khural readopted, unchanged and for immediate implementation, the decree of December 1999 amending the 1992 Constitution. The decree was vetoed by the President, and this veto was rejected. The Constitutional Court, however, was unable to meet in full session because the election of replacements for time-expired members was delayed in the Great Khural. President Bagabandi finally approved the amendments in May 2001.

In February 2001 the 23rd congress of the ruling MPRP re-elected Prime Minister Nambaryn Enkhbayar as its Chairman, approved a new Little Khural of 244 members and enlarged the Party Leadership Council from 11 to 15 members. At the end of September Lkhamsürengiin Enebish, Chairman of the Great Khural and recently re-elected as General Secretary of the MPRP, died; he was succeeded in the latter post by Doloonjingiin Idevkhten and as Chairman of the Great Khural by Sanjbegziin Tömör-Ochir, Secretary of the MPRP.

The presidential election of 20 May 2001 was won by the MPRP's candidate, Natsagiin Bagabandi, who received 57.95% of the votes cast. Radnaasümbereliin Gonchigdorj of the Democratic Party won 36.58% of votes, and Luvsandambyn Dashnyam of the Civil Courage Party received 3.54%.

In January 2001, meanwhile, during one of Mongolia's most severe winters ever, a helicopter carrying 23 people, who were investigating the *zud* (livestock starvation owing to frozen fodder) in the Uvs *aimag* in western Mongolia, crashed, killing eight. The dead included several UN staff and Shagdaryn Otgonbileg, a member of the Great Khural and former director of the Erdenet copper enterprise, who was given a state funeral. Later that month the UN appealed for humanitarian aid to help Mongolian herders, whose animals were dying in huge numbers. In May Otgonbileg's widow Tuyaa was elected Great Khural MPRP member for his Zavkhan 22 constituency unopposed.

In March 2002 Sanjaasürengiin Oyuun's Civil Courage Party merged with Bazarsadyn Jargalsaikhan's Mongolian Republican Party to form the Civil Courage Republican Party, under Oyuun's leadership. In June 2002 the Great Khural approved the Law on Land and the Law on Land Privatization, scheduled to enter into force in 2003. Although less than 1% of the country's total territory was to be available for privatization, the laws generated much controversy. From November 2002 there were several demonstrations by tractor-driving farmers who were arrested for parking on Sükhbaatar Square in Ulan Bator. The demonstrators, led by Democratic Party leader Erdeniin Bat-Üül, protested that the poor would be denied land by the 'oligarchy'.

An effective protest against the Government's silencing of the opposition was made by Lamjavyn Gündalai, a Democratic Party member of the Great Khural, who interrupted the Prime Minister's televised address and disrupted the opening ceremony of the autumn 2002 session of the Great Khural by displaying to television cameras a series of placards on which he demanded the right to speak, condemned the imprisonment of journalists and criticized the land privatization programme.

Following the dissolution of the USSR in 1991, co-operation with the Russian Federation, the largest of the successor states, continued. During an official visit to Russia in January 1993, President Ochirbat and the Russian President, Boris Yeltsin, issued a joint statement expressing regret at the execution and imprisonment of Mongolian citizens in the USSR during the Stalinist purges. Ochirbat and Yeltsin also signed a new 20-year Mongolian-Russian Treaty of Friendship and Co-operation to replace the defunct Mongolian-Soviet treaty of 1986. A similar treaty had been signed with Ukraine in November 1992, during the official visit to Mongolia by Ukrainian President Leonid Kravchuk. In November 2000 the Russian President, Vladimir Putin, stayed overnight in Ulan Bator en route to an Asia-Pacific Economic Co-operation (APEC) conference in Brunei. He was the most senior Russian or Soviet visitor to Mongolia since 1974. Presidents Bagabandi and Putin issued a joint declaration on bilateral co-operation and the protection of each other's national interests. Russia affirmed its commitment to guaranteeing Mongolia's security in connection with its nuclear weapons-free status. In March Russia sent food aid to relieve starvation resulting from the severe Mongolian winter during which much livestock had perished (see above). Russian Prime Minister Mikhail Kasyanov officially visited Mongolia in late March 2002, to discuss economic and military co-operation, and also the issue of the latter's outstanding debt of 11,000m. transferable roubles that Moscow claimed it was owed for Soviet aid granted to Mongolia during 1947–91. Mongolia disagreed with Russia's position that the debt should be paid in full at par value with the US dollar. The disagreement disrupted Mongolian-Russian discussions in early 2003 on a new contract for the Erdenet copper-mining joint venture.

Relations with the People's Republic of China were good until the onset of the Sino-Soviet dispute in the 1960s. In 1986, however, Sino-Mongolian relations improved significantly when the Chinese Vice-Minister of Foreign Affairs visited Ulan Bator, and the two countries signed agreements on consular relations and trade. In June 1987 a delegation from the Chinese National People's Congress visited Ulan Bator, and in the same month a treaty concerning the resolution of border disputes was initialled by representatives of the two Governments.

Relations between Mongolia and China improved in April 1994, when a new Treaty of Friendship and Co-operation was concluded during a visit to Ulan Bator by the Chinese Premier, Li Peng. An agreement on cultural, economic and technical co-operation was also signed.

Mongolia continued to protest in 1995 at the ongoing series of nuclear tests carried out in China (in the Xinjiang Autonomous Region). Mongolian human rights groups and the Ulan Bator press supported protests in Inner Mongolia against the arrest by the Chinese authorities of Inner Mongolian human rights activists in December. Prime Minister Jasrai's official visit to China in March 1996, focusing on trade and co-operation, appeared not to have been affected by these events. Relations with China were further consolidated in 1997 by the visits to Ulan Bator of Qiao Shi, the Chairman of the National People's Congress Standing Committee, in April, and of Qian Qichen, the Chinese Deputy Premier and Minister of Foreign Affairs, in August.

Two important documents outlining Mongolian foreign policy objectives were published in July 1994. Advocating 'political realism', *The Mongolian National Security Concept* emphasized the importance of maintaining a 'balanced relationship' with Russia and China, while 'strengthening trust and developing all-round good-neighbourly relations and mutually beneficial co-operation with both'. *The Mongolian Foreign Policy Concept* also described as the 'foremost objective' of the country's foreign policy the pursuit of 'friendly relations with Russia and China, and without favouring one or the other to develop co-operation with them in complete equality'. Traditional features and specific aspects of economic co-operation were to be safeguarded. Other priorities listed were: good relations with the USA, Japan, Germany and other highly developed nations of West and East; consolidation of political and economic integration in the Asian region; co-operation with the UN and its various bodies; and sound relations with the newly independent states of eastern Europe and the CIS, as well as with developing countries.

Mongolia received three important foreign visitors in mid-1999: President Kim Dae-Jung of the Republic of Korea visited in May, and in July official visits were paid by Prime Minister Keizo Obuchi of Japan and President Jiang Zemin of China; in the same month the Democratic People's Republic of Korea closed its embassy in Ulan Bator for financial reasons. In November Prime Minister Amarjargal visited both North and South Korea and also China. In March 2000 he paid an official visit to the United Kingdom. Later that month a delegation from the Great Khural also visited the country. President Bagabandi travelled widely in 2000 and early 2001, visiting Germany, Italy, the Philippines, the USA, India and South Korea. Nambaryn Enkhbayar's first overseas trip as Prime Minister was to the World Economic Forum in Davos, Switzerland, in January 2001. He subsequently travelled to Japan. During an official visit to the USA in November, Prime Minister Enkhbayar addressed the UN General Assembly in New York and also had a meeting with President George W. Bush. Enkhbayar reaffirmed the strategic partnership with the USA and urged greater investment in Mongolia. Having condemned the terrorist attacks of 11 September against the USA, he informed President Bush of Mongolia's readiness to allow the use of its air space to help combat terrorism.

The seventh British-Mongolian 'Round-Table' Conference in Ulan Bator in September 2002 was attended by a parliamentary secretary of the United Kingdom's Foreign Office. The Dalai Lama visited Ulan Bator in November 2002, travelling via Japan after Russia refused him a visa and Korean Air, the national carrier of South Korea, banned him on the grounds that he posed a security threat. Although his visit was at the invitation of Mongolia's Buddhist leaders rather than the Government, the Chinese authorities indicated their displeasure by halting rail traffic on their mutual border for 36 hours.

The Secretary-General of the United Nations, Kofi Annan, paid a brief visit to Mongolia in October 2002. Pope John Paul II was scheduled to visit Mongolia in late August 2003.

Government

Supreme legislative power is vested in the 76-member Mongolian Great Khural (Assembly), elected by universal adult suffrage for four years. The Great Khural recognizes the President on his election and appoints the Prime Minister and members of the Cabinet, which is the highest executive body. The President, who is directly elected for a term of four years, is Head of State and Commander-in-Chief of the Armed Forces.

In August 2002 the Great Khural approved the reorganization of government agencies, reducing the number of regulatory agencies to eight and executive agencies to 33. Those subordinated to the Prime Minister included the Chief Directorate of Intelligence, State Property Committee, National Radio and Television, and the Monstame News Agency.

Mongolia is divided into 21 provinces (*aimag*) and one municipality (Ulan Bator), with appointed governors and elected local assemblies.

Defence

Under the 1992 Constitution, the President of Mongolia is, *ex officio*, Commander-in-Chief of the Armed Forces. The defence roles of the President, the Mongolian Great Khural, the Government and local administrations are defined by the Mongolian Law on Defence (November 1993). Mongolia's *Military Doctrine*, a summary of which was issued by the Great Khural in July 1994, defines the armed forces as comprising general purpose troops, air defence troops, construction troops and civil defence troops. The border troops and internal troops, which are not part of the armed forces, are responsible for protection of the borders and of strategic installations, respectively. In August 2002, according to the International Institute for Strategic Studies, Mongolia's defence forces numbered 9,100, comprising an army of 7,500 (of whom 4,000 were thought to be conscripts), 800 air defence personnel, 500 civil defence troops and 300 construction troops. There was a paramilitary force of about 7,200, comprising 1,200 internal security troops and 6,000 border guards. Military service is for 12 months (for males aged 18–28 years), but a system of alternative service is being introduced. Defence spending for 2003 was projected at 18,186.7m. tögrög, about 3.3% of planned government expenditure.

Economic Affairs

In 2001, according to estimates by the World Bank, Mongolia's gross national income (GNI), measured at average 1999–2001 prices, was US $962m., equivalent to $400 per head (or $1,800 per head on an international purchasing-power parity basis). During 1990–2001, it was estimated, the population increased by an average annual rate of 1.3%, while gross domestic product (GDP) per head decreased, in real terms, by an average of 1.2% per year. Overall GDP increased, in real terms, by an average annual rate of less than 0.1% in 1990–2001. According to the Asian Development Bank (ADB), GDP increased by 1.1% in 2001. Government figures stated that GDP increased by 1.6% in 2002.

According to the World Bank, agriculture (including forestry) contributed an estimated 30.5% of Mongolian GDP in 2001. The sector engaged 48.6% of the employed labour force in 2000. Animal herding is the main economic activity and is practised throughout the country. By mid-1995 more than 90% of all livestock was privately owned. Livestock numbers (sheep, goats, horses, cattle and camels) reached a new record of 33.6m. at the end of 1999, but declined to 30.0m. in 2000 and to 26.2m. in 2001. The principal crops are cereals, potatoes and vegetables. During 1990–2001 the GDP of the agricultural sector increased, in real terms, at an average annual rate of 1.9%. According to the ADB, agricultural GDP increased by 4.2% in 1999, but decreased by 14.4% in 2000 and by 16.0% in 2001.

Industry (comprising manufacturing, mining, construction and utilities) provided 16.9% of GDP in 2001, and engaged 14.1% of the employed labour force in 2000. In 1997 state-owned enterprises, employing 28.7% of the industrial labour force, produced 19.9% of gross industrial output. Joint enterprises, with 17.3% of the industrial labour force, produced 41.4%, while private companies (38.5% of the sector's labour force) contributed 32.6% of industrial output. During 1990–2001 industrial GDP declined, in real terms, at an average rate of 1.8% per year. According to the ADB, the industrial sector's GDP increased by 1.1% in 1999, by 1.3% in 2000 and by 13.0% in 2001. In the late 1990s the principal branches of industry (excluding construction), were metallic ore extraction, electric power and heat, food and beverages and textiles.

Mining contributed 11.7% of GDP in 2001, according to Mongolian sources. Mongolia has significant, largely unexplored, mineral resources and is a leading producer and exporter of copper, gold, molybdenum and fluorspar concentrates. The copper-molybdenum works at Erdenet, a Mongolian-Russian joint venture, is the most important mining operation in the country. The share of copper concentrate in Mongolia's total exports, however, decreased from 53.0% in 1995 to 27.6% in 2002. In 2000–01 the Erdenet concern operated at a loss. Other mineral resources include coal, tungsten, tin, uranium and lead. In May 2000 Mongolia's coal reserves were estimated at 150,000m. metric tons. Gold production rose from 4.5 tons in 1995 to 13.7 tons in 2001, before declining to 12.1 tons in 2002. Extraction of crude petroleum, from the Tamsag basin, commenced in 1997. According to the ADB, compared with the previous year the GDP of the mining sector expanded by 10.5% in 2001.Official figures stated that the output of the mining sector decreased by 7.4% in 2002, with exports of copper concentrate 0.4% lower by volume than in 2001 and 6.7% lower by value.

The manufacturing sector accounted for 5.1% of GDP in 2001. Manufacturing industries are based largely on the products of the agricultural and animal husbandry sector. Mongolia is one of the world's foremost producers of cashmere, and also manufactures garments, leather goods and carpets. In the late 1990s the principal branches of manufacturing were food products, textiles and non-metallic mineral products. According to the ADB, manufacturing GDP increased by 20.0% in 2001.

Energy is derived principally from thermal power stations, fuelled by coal. Most provincial centres have thermal power stations or diesel generators, while smaller rural centres generally rely on small diesel generators. In more isolated areas wood, roots, bushes and dried animal dung are used for domestic fuel. The Ulan Bator No. 4 power station, the largest in the country, went into operation in 1985. Its capacity of 380 MW doubled Mongolia's generating capacity. In 1998 imports of energy products comprised 15.7% of the total value of merchandise imports. Mongolia imports electricity and petroleum products from Russia. However, the discovery of petroleum reserves in late 1994 raised the possibility that Mongolia might become increasingly self-sufficient in energy requirements. Production of crude petroleum increased from 44,791 barrels in 1998 to 71,914 barrels in 1999, then decreased slightly to 65,522 barrels in 2000. The SOCO oil company suffered a severe fire at its Tamsag base in eastern Mongolia, and in mid-2001 had not restarted extraction at its three production wells for export to China. Mongolia's hopes of benefiting from the oil and gas pipelines to be built from Russia to China faded in mid-2001 when it emerged that the pipelines would bypass Mongolia on the way to refineries at Daqing in Heilongjiang Province, China.

The services sector contributed an estimated 52.6% of GDP in 2001 and engaged 37.2% of the employed labour force in 2000. During 1990–2001 the GDP of the sector decreased, in real terms, by an average of 0.3% annually. According to the ADB, the GDP of the services sector increased by 3.5% in 1999, by 18.3% in 2000 and by 8.2% in 2001.

In 2001 Mongolia recorded a visible trade deficit of US $89.3m., and there was a deficit of $150.6m. on the current account of the balance of payments. In 2002 the principal source of imports was Russia, supplying 34.1% of the total. Other major suppliers were the People's Republic of China (24.4%), the Republic of Korea (12.2%) and Japan (6.1%). China was the principal market for exports in that year, purchasing 42.4% of the total. Other important purchasers were the USA (31.6%) and Russia (8.6%). The principal imports in 2002 were machinery (19.5%) and mineral products (18.6%). The principal exports in 2002 were minerals (33.0% of the total), textiles and textile products (27.2%) and precious metals and jewellery (23.8%).

The budget for 2003 envisaged a deficit of 102,460.8m. tögrög. Mongolia's total external debt was US $858.8m. at the end of 2000, of which $794.8m. was long-term public debt. In that year the cost of debt-servicing was equivalent to 4.7% of the value of exports of goods and services. The annual rate of inflation averaged 97.5% during 1991–97. According to IMF figures, during 1998–2001 the average annual inflation rate was 9.0%. However, annual inflation declined to 3.1% in 2002, according to an official source. The number of registered unemployed persons decreased to 38,600 (4.6% of the labour force) at the end of 2000, and to 30,900 by the end of 2002. The number of unregistered unemployed persons was believed to be far greater, with unemployment reaching some 17% of the labour force in 2002.

In 1989 Mongolia joined the Group of 77 (an organization of developing countries, founded under the auspices of UNCTAD (see p. 43), to promote economic co-operation). In February 1991 Mongolia became a member of the Asian Development Bank (ADB, see p. 143) as well as of the IMF and World Bank. In 1994 the European Union (EU, see p. 199) announced the inclusion of Mongolia in TACIS, the EU's programme of technical assistance to the Commonwealth of Independent States. In 1997 Mongolia became a member of the World Trade Organization (WTO, see p. 323). In July 1998 Mongolia was admitted to the ASEAN Regional Forum (ARF, see p. 149), and in May 2000 the country became a member of the European Bank for Reconstruction and Development (EBRD, see p. 193).

The Democratic Alliance coalition Government, elected in June 1996, initiated a wide-ranging programme of economic reforms. At the end of that year the Government announced a four-year economic programme, and a much-needed restructuring of the banking system was initiated. Reform of the taxation system was approved in July 1997, and in August it was reported that all government-owned commercial assets and public enterprises, including the copper mine at Erdenet, were to be privatized, except for those considered essential for the country's economic security. However, by 2000 this privatization programme had hardly begun. The aid donors at the seventh Mongolia Assistance Group meeting, convened in Ulan Bator for the first time, in June 1999 pledged a record US $320m. for banking-sector reform, poverty relief and privatization. The Assistance Group urged the Mongolian Government to strengthen the financial sector by increasing transparency and improving conditions for private enterprise, including the privatization of state-owned banks and the formation of a legal framework for other financial institutions. The aid programme was approved just one week after the IMF agreed its delayed second annual arrangement under the Enhanced Structural Adjustment Facility for Mongolia. The arrangement had lapsed in mid-1998 after a sharp decline in export revenue and the lengthy delay in the formation of the new Government. Severe drought in late 1999 was followed in early 2000 by several months of acutely cold weather. In consequence, by mid-2000 an estimated 3m. head of livestock had died. International donors offered financial aid, in response to government appeals, and Red Cross relief teams were mobilized to take food and medicine to isolated herding families suffering extreme hardship. Almost 2,500 families were believed to have lost all of their animals by late June. By the end of 2000 livestock numbers had declined by some 10% compared with 1999, and in early 2001 the weakened animals faced even more severe conditions, with deep snow and exceptionally low temperatures. It was estimated that a further 1m. animals had perished by the end of February. Mongolia was offered substantial humanitarian aid from the international community, in an attempt to relieve the increasing suffering of the agricultural population. The annual livestock census in December 2001 revealed that numbers had decreased by more than 7m. head during the previous three years, owing to cold, starvation and disease. A further loss of 2.4m. head, to fewer than 23.7m., was recorded at the end of 2002. Prime Minister Enkhbayar had expressed concern about the state of the nomadic herding economy, declaring that it was important to improve the quality of stock and raise yields to meet the growing needs of large towns, especially Ulan Bator. He therefore advocated a gradual replacement of traditional nomadic family herding by livestock farming settlements with adequate provision of winter care for animals, and community facilities for herders. The national development plan announced in 2001 aimed to end Mongolia's traditional dependency on nomadic herding and envisaged the building of new towns and urbanizing 90% of the population during the next 30 years. The towns would be linked by a 2,400-km east–west highway, which would serve as a development corridor across the country, as well as fostering new trade zones on the Russian and Chinese borders. The Great Khural also approved legislation allowing for the privatization of state industries in the period to 2004; companies scheduled for transfer to the private sector in 2001 included

Gobi (cashmere processing), Neft Import Concern (petroleum import and distribution), the Trade and Development Bank and APU (distillery and soft drinks). In June 2002 the Great Khural passed a land privatization law (see History), which proved to be controversial. Meanwhile, the renamed international Consultative Group on aid to Mongolia convened in Ulan Bator in July 2002 and promised an aid programme of US $333m. for the coming year. Mongolia remained dependent on external aid, with public debt having risen to the equivalent of 80% of GDP, the majority of which was owed to foreign institutions. The were signs of an improvement in economic conditions in 2002. Foreign investment had increased to US $125,280 in 2001, from $90,586 in 2000—an increase of 38.2%—mainly owing to renewed interest in Mongolia's copper and gold resources, especially from China, which had accounted for 37% of foreign investment during the preceding three years. Light industry also experienced a revival in 2002, and increased construction activity took place in the capital.

Education

Ten-year general education is compulsory, beginning at six years of age. Pupils may attend vocational-technical schools from the ages of 16 to 18 years. In 2000/01 703 general schools, with a total enrolment of 494,500 pupils, employed 19,200 teachers. The 36 vocational training schools employed 865 teachers, and had a total enrolment of 12,177 in that year. Many Mongolian students continue their academic careers at universities and technical schools in Russia and Germany. Government expenditure on education in 2001 amounted to 97,552.7m. tögrög (20.7% of budgetary expenditure). The state budget allocation to the Ministry of Education, Culture and Science for 2003 was 126,863.4m. tögrög (22.7% of planned budgetary expenditure).

Public Holidays

2003: 1 January (New Year), 2–4 February (Tsagaan Sar, lunar new year), 11–13 July (National Days), 26 November (Republic Day).

2004: 1 January (New Year), 21–23 February (Tsagaan Sar, lunar new year), 11–13 July (National Days), 26 November (Republic Day).

Weights and Measures

The metric system is in force.

Statistical Survey

Unless otherwise indicated, revised by Alan J. K. Sanders

Area and Population

AREA, POPULATION AND DENSITY

Area (sq km)	1,564,116*
Population (census results)	
5 January 1989	2,043,400
5 January 2000	
Males	1,177,981
Females.	1,195,512
Total	2,373,493
Population (official estimates at mid-year)	
2000	2,390,000
2001	2,425,000
2002	2,510,000
Density (per sq km) at mid-2002	1.6

* 603,909 sq miles.

ADMINISTRATIVE DIVISIONS
(January 2000 census)

Province (Aimag)	Area ('000 sq km)	Estimated population ('000)	Provincial Centre
Arkhangai	55.3	97.1	Tsetserleg
Bayankhongor	116.0	84.8	Bayankhongor
Bayan-Ölgii.	45.7	91.1	Ölgii
Bulgan	48.7	61.8	Bulgan
Darkhan-Uul	3.3	83.3	Darkhan
Dornod (Eastern) . . .	123.6	75.4	Choibalsan
Dornogobi (East Gobi) . .	109.5	50.6	Sainshand
Dundgobi (Central Gobi) . .	74.7	51.5	Mandalgobi
Gobi-Altai	141.4	63.7	Altai
Gobi-Sümber	5.5	12.2	Choir
Khentii	80.3	70.9	Öndörkhaan
Khovd	76.1	86.8	Khovd
Khövsgöl	100.6	119.1	Mörön
Orkhon	0.8	71.5	Erdenet
Ömnögobi (South Gobi) . .	165.4	46.9	Dalanzadgad
Övörkhangai	62.9	111.4	Arvaikheer
Selenge	41.2	100.0	Sükhbaatar
Sükhbaatar.	82.3	56.2	Baruun Urt
Töv (Central)	74.0	99.3	Zuun mod
Ulaanbaatar (Ulan Bator)*	4.7	760.1	(capital city)
Uvs	69.6	90.0	Ulaangom
Zavkhan	82.5	90.0	Uliastai
Total	**1,564.1**	**2,373.5**	

* Ulaanbaatar, including Nalaikh, and Bagakhangai and Baganuur districts beyond the urban boundary, has special status as the capital city.

ETHNIC GROUPS
(January 2000 census)

	Number	%
Khalh (Khalkha)	1,934,700	81.5
Kazakh (Khasag)	103,000	4.3
Dörvöd (Durbet)	66,700	2.8
Bayad (Bayat)	50,800	2.1
Buryat (Buriat)	40,600	1.7
Dariganga	31,900	1.3
Zakhchin	29,800	1.3
Uriankhai	25,200	1.1
Other ethnic groups	82,600	3.5
Foreign citizens	8,100	0.3
Total	**2,373,500**	**100.0**

PRINCIPAL TOWNS
(estimated population, December 1999)

Ulan Bator (capital)	813,500*	Erdenet	65,700
Darkhan	72,600	Choibalsan	40,900†

* March 2002.
† January 2000 census.

BIRTHS, MARRIAGES AND DEATHS

	Registered live births		Registered marriages		Registered deaths	
	Number	Rate (per 1,000)	Number	Rate (per 1,000)	Number	Rate (per 1,000)
1995	54,293	24.3	15,106	6.8	16,794	7.5
1996	51,806	22.9	14,188	6.3	17,550	7.7
1997	49,488	21.5	14,421	6.3	16,980	7.4
1998	49,256	21.2	13,908	6.0	15,799	6.8
1999	49,461	21.0	13,722	5.8	16,105	6.8
2000	48,721	20.4	12,601	5.3	15,472	6.5
2001	49,685	20.5	12,393	5.1	15,999	6.6
2002	45,700	18.5	n.a.	n.a.	n.a.	6.0

Source: mainly *Mongolian Statistical Yearbook*.

Expectation of life (WHO estimates, years at birth): 64.6 (males 61.2; females 68.3) in 2001 (Source: WHO, *World Health Report*).

EMPLOYMENT
('000 employees at 31 December)

	1998	1999	2000
Agriculture and forestry	394.1	402.6	393.5
Industry*	97.9	98.8	91.0
Transport and communications	33.4	34.9	34.1
Construction	27.5	27.6	23.4
Trade	n.a.	83.1	83.9
Public administration	n.a.	31.5	34.7
Education	42.5	43.2	54.4
Science, research and development			
Health	35.6	34.8	33.5
Total (incl. others)	**809.5**	**813.6**	**809.0**

* Comprising manufacturing (except printing and publishing), mining and quarrying, electricity, water, logging and fishing.

Unemployed ('000 registered at 31 December): 49.8 in 1998; 39.8 in 1999; 38.6 in 2000.

Source: *Mongolian Statistical Yearbook*.

2001 ('000 persons at 31 December): Registered unemployed 40.2.

2002 ('000 persons at 31 December): Registered unemployed 30.9.

Health and Welfare

KEY INDICATORS

Total fertility rate (children per woman, 2001)	2.4
Under-5 mortality rate (per 1,000 live births, 2001)	76
HIV/AIDS (% of persons aged 15–49, 2001)	<0.10
Physicians (per 1,000 head, 2001)	2.7
Hospital beds (per 1,000 head, 2001)	7.4
Health expenditure (2000): US $ per head (PPP)	120
Health expenditure (2000): % of GDP	6.6
Health expenditure (2000): public (% of total)	70.3
Access to water (% of persons, 2000)	60
Access to sanitation (% of persons, 2000)	30
Human Development Index (2000): ranking	113
Human Development Index (2000): value	0.655

For sources and definitions, see explanatory note on p. vi.

Agriculture

PRINCIPAL CROPS
(metric tons)

	2000	2001	2002
Cereals*	142,200	150,900	125,860
Potatoes	58,900	58,000	51,890
Other vegetables	44,000	44,500	39,720
Hay	689,400	831,490	753,750

* Mostly wheat, but also small quantities of barley and oats.

LIVESTOCK
(at 31 December)

	2000	2001	2002
Sheep	13,876,400	11,938,100	10,536,600
Goats	10,077,500	9,683,700	9,055,900
Horses	2,660,700	2,190,800	1,970,300
Cattle	3,097,600	2,069,600	1,869,500
Camels	322,900	285,500	252,200
Pigs	14,684	n.a.	n.a.
Poultry	89,122	n.a.	n.a.

LIVESTOCK PRODUCTS
('000 metric tons, unless otherwise indicated)

	1998	1999	2000
Meat	268.3	289.0	310.6
Beef and veal	99.3	104.6	113.4
Mutton, lamb and goat meat	120.2	128.9	120.0
Sheep's wool: greasy	20.1	20.9	21.7
Raw cashmere	n.a.	3.3	3.3
Milk	430.8	467.0	375.6
Eggs (million)	8.5	9.6	6.7

Source: Mongolian Statistical Directorate.

Forestry

ROUNDWOOD REMOVALS
('000 cubic metres, excl. bark)

	1999	2000	2001
Total	631	631	631

Source: FAO.

SAWNWOOD PRODUCTION
('000 cubic metres, incl. railway sleepers)

	2000	2001	2002
Total	30.5	39.7	28.3

Source: National Statistical Office, *Monthly Bulletin of Statistics*.

Fishing

(metric tons, live weight)

	1998	1999	2000
Total catch (freshwater fishes) .	311	524	425

Source: FAO, *Yearbook of Fishery Statistics.*

Mining

(metric tons, unless otherwise indicated)

	2000	2001	2002
Coal	5,019,300	5,134,200	5,307,400
Fluorspar concentrate . . .	210,000	209,000	159,800
Copper concentrate*	357,800	381,400	376,300
Molybdenum concentrate* . .	2,843	3,028	3,384
Gold (kilograms)	11,808	13,674	12,097
Crude petroleum (barrels) . .	65,522	73,700	139,200

* Figures refer to the gross weight of concentrates. Copper concentrate has an estimated copper content of 25%, while the metal content of molybdenum concentrate is 47%.

Source: National Statistical Office, *Monthly Bulletin of Statistics.*

Industry

SELECTED PRODUCTS

	2000	2001	2002
Flour ('000 metric tons)	40.2	37.7	49.6
Bread ('000 metric tons)	20.2	23.3	21.7
Confectionery ('000 metric tons) . .	6.0	6.0	6.1
Vodka ('000 litres)	6,595.7	8,626.5	9,436.2
Beer ('000 litres)	3,247.2	4,267.8	3,375.3
Soft drinks ('000 litres)	8,644.7	11,082.7	12,907.3
Cashmere (combed) (metric tons)	450.9	608.4	622.1
Wool; scoured (metric tons) . .	1,420.0	2,089.7	1,179.6
Felt ('000 metres)	113.9	110.5	112.9
Camelhair blankets ('000). . .	28.5	43.1	38.2
Spun thread (metric tons). . .	40.8	45.6	55.9
Knitwear ('000 garments) . . .	1,233.5	2,315.7	5,563.6
Carpets ('000 sq metres) . . .	704.8	614.8	533.9
Leather footwear ('000) . . .	5.6	16.7	9.5
Felt footwear ('000 pairs) . . .	34.0	33.4	16.1
Surgical syringes (million) . . .	16.3	17.7	22.8
Bricks (million)	17.3	21.0	13.2
Lime ('000 metric tons) . . .	37.0	30.1	42.5
Cement ('000 metric tons). . .	91.7	67.7	147.6
Ferroconcrete ('000 cu metres) . .	14.8	17.0	11.9
Steel sheet and blanks ('000 metric tons)	20.4	17.2	26.3
Copper (metric tons)	641.1	1,475.9	1,500.0
Electricity (million kWh) . . .	2,239.1	2,367.0	2,463.9

Sources: *Mongolian Statistical Yearbook* (2000), and *Monthly Bulletin of Statistics.*

Finance

CURRENCY AND EXCHANGE RATES

Monetary Units
100 möngö = 1 tögrög (tughrik)

Sterling, Dollar and Euro Equivalents (31 December 2002)
£1 sterling = 1,813.3 tögrög
US $1 = 1,125.0 tögrög
€1 = 1,179.8 tögrög
10,000 tögrög = £5.515 = $8.889 = €8.476

Average Exchange Rate (tögrög per US $)
2000   1,076.67
2001   1,097.70
2002   1,110.31

BUDGET
(million tögrög)

Revenue	2000	2001	2002
Tax revenue	274,109.2	319,419.2	356,501.1
Income tax	74,088.8	64,965.2	70,921.0
Customs duty	35,741.3	49,648.5	52,344.7
Taxes on goods and services . .	117,562.3	179,199.1	204,168.5
Value-added tax. . . .	74,974.5	106,151.7	117,363.6
Social insurance	38,691.7	46,144.7	53,343.5
Other current revenue	65,555.7	95,657.5	102,932.6
Foreign aid (grants)	3,067.6	9,140.5	6,615.6
Capital revenue (privatization). .	7,469.8	327.1	477.7
Total	350,202.2	424,544.3	466,527.0

Expenditure		2001	2002
Goods and services		247,586.4	280,403.9
Wages and salaries		91,622.9	105,262.7
Interest payments		16,190.8	17,703.5
Subsidies and transfers. . . .		95,206.1	109,668.1
Capital expenditure		50,335.9	63,738.9
Lending (net).		60,745.5	65,034.8
Total (incl. others)		470,064.7	536,549.3

Source: National Statistical Office.

2000 (million tögrög): Total expenditure 412,926.6.

2003 (forecasts, million tögrög): Total revenue 455,737.8; Total expenditure 558,198.7 (Source: *Töriin Medeelel*).

INTERNATIONAL RESERVES
(US $ million at 31 December)

	2000	2001	2002
Gold*	23.31	50.91	49.79
IMF special drawing rights. . .	0.01	0.02	0.04
Reserve position in IMF. . . .	0.05	0.08	0.12
Foreign exchange.	178.70	205.60	349.50
Total	202.08	256.61	399.44

* Valued at 4,300 tögrög per gram.

Source: IMF, *International Financial Statistics.*

MONEY SUPPLY
(million tögrög at 31 December)

	2000	2001	2002
Currency outside banks . . .	100,910	109,131	120,755
Demand deposits at deposit money banks	29,842	46,995	66,944
Total money	130,751	156,126	187,699

Source: IMF, *International Financial Statistics.*

COST OF LIVING
(Consumer Price Index for Ulan Bator at December; base: December 1995 = 100)

	1996	1997	1998
Food and beverages	133.7	148.8	150.1
Clothing and footwear . . .	146.0	193.4	213.8
Rent and utilities	172.7	260.1	284.2
All items (incl. others) . . .	144.6	174.2	184.7

Source: National Statistical Office.

All items: 203.1 in 1999; 219.6 in 2000 (Source: Mongolbank, *Monthly Bulletin*).

December 2001 (base: December 2000 = 100): All items 108.0 (Source: Mongolbank, *Monthly Bulletin*).

NATIONAL ACCOUNTS
(million tögrög at current prices)

Expenditure on the Gross Domestic Product

	1996	1997	1998
Government final consumption expenditure	96,406.8	132,867.3	153,515.0
Private final consumption expenditure	373,466.0	459,922.8	486,201.8
Increase in stocks	12,281.0	17,055.3	18,078.6
Gross fixed capital formation	135,250.9	180,300.0	208,017.5
Total domestic expenditure	617,404.7	790,145.4	865,812.9
Exports of goods and services ⎫ *Less* Imports of goods and services ⎭	−11,616.6	−19,764.4	−50,568.2
Sub-total	605,788.1	770,381.0	815,244.7
Statistical discrepancy*	−19,259.2	−11,454.3	60,614.3
GDP in purchasers' values	586,528.9	758,926.7	875,859.0
GDP at constant 1993 prices	185,047.9	192,508.3	199,205.2

* Referring to the difference between the sum of the expenditure components and official estimates of GDP, compiled from the production approach.

Source: Asian Development Bank, *Key Indicators of Developing Asian and Pacific Countries*.

Gross Domestic Product by Economic Activity

	1999	2000	2001
Agriculture	342,127.6	322,876.8	300,644.7
Mining	79,780.0	117,161.0	135,418.1
Manufacturing	54,970.8	62,507.3	83,484.7
Electricity, heating and water supply	33,711.1	24,631.7	27,386.1
Construction	22,984.1	19,310.8	23,702.3
Trade	191,672.1	243,883.5	284,465.7
Transport and communications	84,690.5	112,195.8	135,759.8
Finance	4,121.7	25,414.0	40,459.3
Public administration	33,621.7	47,044.0	52,244.2
Other services	77,666.1	94,375.0	107,627.5
GDP in purchasers' values	925,345.8	1,044,577.6	1,158,208.1

Source: *Mongolian Statistical Yearbook* (2001).

BALANCE OF PAYMENTS
(US $ million)

	1999	2000	2001
Exports of goods f.o.b.	454.3	535.8	460.0
Imports of goods f.o.b.	−510.7	−608.4	−549.3
Trade balance	−56.4	−72.6	−89.3
Exports of services	75.8	77.7	86.4
Imports of services	−145.7	−162.8	−173.8
Balance on goods and services	−126.2	−157.7	−176.7
Other income received	6.7	13.0	20.8
Other income paid	−6.6	−19.5	−16.5
Balance on goods, services and income	−126.2	−164.2	−172.4
Current transfers received	17.6	25.0	41.2
Current transfers paid	−3.6	−16.9	−19.4
Current balance	−112.2	−156.1	−150.6
Direct investment from abroad	30.4	53.7	63.0
Other investment assets	−51.8	−44.3	−14.4
Other investment liabilities	91.0	80.5	72.7
Net errors and omissions	23.6	−19.3	−53.9
Overall balance	−19.0	−85.5	−83.2

Source: IMF, *International Financial Statistics*.

External Trade

PRINICIPAL COMMODITIES
(US $ million)

Imports c.i.f.	2000	2001	2002
Vegetable products	46.4	51.2	56.3
Prepared foodstuffs; beverages, spirits and vinegar; tobacco and manufactured substitutes	47.2	53.2	54.5
Mineral products	120.3	145.4	122.9
Products of chemical or allied industries	28.1	33.8	33.3
Textiles and textile articles	79.9	63.2	83.7
Base metals and articles thereof	22.7	29.7	29.7
Machinery and mechanical appliances; electrical equipment; sound and television apparatus	133.3	113.4	128.3
Vehicles, aircraft, vessels and associated transport equipment	67.0	69.1	69.8
Optical, photographic, measuring, precision and medical apparatus; clocks and watches; musical instruments	21.1	17.4	8.9
Total (incl. others)	614.5	637.7	659.0

Exports f.o.b.	2000	2001	2002
Live animals and animal products	n.a.	26.4	25.6
Mineral products	n.a.	175.2	165.5
Copper concentrate	160.3	147.9	138.0
Fluorite concentrate	19.3	19.7	13.9
Hides, skins and furs	n.a.	59.0	43.3
Hides and skins	33.8	17.3	9.7
Cashmere (dehaired)	54.5	54.9	30.1
Textiles and textile articles	192.3	171.5	136.6
Knitwear	25.9	18.9	17.5
Prescious metals and jewellery	n.a.	75.4	119.2
Gold	n.a.	74.7	117.6
Total (incl. others)	432.3	521.5	500.9

Sources: IMF, *Mongolia: Statistical Annex* (March 2000); National Statistical Office, *Monthly Bulletin of Statistics*.

PRINCIPAL TRADING PARTNERS
(US $ million)

Imports c.i.f.	2000	2001	2002
China, People's Republic	125.7	136.1	160.8
Germany	29.7	30.3	29.6
Japan	73.3	55.9	40.5
Korea, Republic	55.5	58.3	80.3
Russia	206.2	225.9	224.6
Singapore	10.6	10.4	10.9
USA	28.4	14.9	22.9
Total (incl. others)	614.5	637.7	659.0

Exports f.o.b.	2000	2001	2002
Australia	12.5	10.0	17.7
China, People's Republic	274.3	238.3	212.2
Japan	8.1	15.7	6.3
Republic of Korea	12.3	20.2	22.3
Russia	45.1	44.9	43.1
United Kingdom	17.5	12.4	17.5
USA	130.3	144.5	158.4
Total (incl. others)	535.8	521.5	500.9

Source: National Statistical Office, *Monthly Bulletin of Statistics*.

Transport

FREIGHT CARRIED
('000 metric tons)

	2000	2001	2002
Rail.	9,158.5	10,147.7	11,637.0
Road	1,480.4	1,658.2	1,888.7
Air .	2.9	2.9	2.4
Water	1.6	1.7	1.8
Total	10,643.4	11,810.5	13,529.9

Source: Mongolian Statistical Directorate.

PASSENGERS CARRIED
(million)

	2000	2001	2002
Rail.	4.3	4.1	4.0
Road	88.4	94.1	101.4
Air*	0.3	0.3	0.3
Total	93.0	98.5	105.7

* MIAT only.

Source: Mongolian Statistical Directorate.

RAILWAYS
(traffic)

	2000	2001	2002
Passengers carried ('000)	4,282.5	4,556.1	4,000.0
Freight carried ('000 metric tons)	9,158.5	10,147.7	11,637.0
Freight ton-km (million)	4,282.5	5,287.9	6,461.3

Source: Mongolian Statistical Directorate.

ROAD TRAFFIC
(motor vehicles in use)

	1998	1999	2000
Passenger cars	37,795	39,921	44,100
Buses and coaches	4,579	6,012	8,500
Lorries, special vehicles and tankers	29,116	28,907	29,100

Source: mainly Mongolian Statistical Directorate.

CIVIL AVIATION
(traffic on scheduled services)

	2000	2001	2002
Passengers carried ('000)	252.4	254.5	269.5
Freight carried (tons)	2,877.0	2,970.0	2,400.0

Source: Mongolian Statistical Directorate.

Tourism

FOREIGN ARRIVALS BY NATIONALITY

Country	1998	1999*	2000
China, People's Republic	92,789	58,346	57,546
France	1,819	1,983	1,841
Germany	3,388	3,506	4,206
Japan	11,846	11,775	11,392
Korea, Republic	3,073	5,171	8,039
Russia	63,532	55,782	49,456
United Kingdom	2,251	2,221	2,800
USA	4,622	5,381	6,451
Total (incl. others)	197,424	158,734	158,205

* Figures are provisional. The revised total is 159,745.

Source: *Mongolian Statistical Yearbook*.

2001: Total arrivals 192,051 (Source: National Statistical Office, *Monthly Bulletin of Statistics*).

Tourism receipts (US $ million): 33 in 1998; 28 in 1999 (Source: World Bank).

Communications Media

	1999	2000	2001
Television receivers ('000 in use)	168.8	169.1	n.a.
Telephones ('000 main lines in use)	104.1	112.2	119.7
Mobile cellular telephones ('000 subscribers)	48.2	75.1	195.0
Personal computers ('000 in use)	24	n.a.	35
Internet users ('000)	12.0	30.0	40.0
Newspapers printed (million copies)	22.2	18.0	19.2

Radio receivers ('000 in use): 360 in 1997.

Facsimile machines (number in use): 7,963 in 1999.

Book production (1994): 128 titles; 640,000 copies.

Non-daily newspapers (titles): 80 in 1998.

Other periodicals (titles): 24 in 1998.

2002 (telephones, '000 main lines in use): 126.7.

Sources: UNESCO, *Statistical Yearbook*; UN, *Statistical Yearbook*; International Telecommunication Union; Mongolian Statistical Directorate.

Education

(2000/01)

	Institutions	Teachers	Students
General education schools:			
Primary (grades 1–3)	133		
Incomplete secondary (grades 4–8)	219	19,200	494,500
Complete secondary (grades 9–10)	351		
Vocational schools	36	865	97,100
Higher education:			
Universities and colleges			
State-owned	38	3,455	56,906
Private	134	1,465	28,064

* Excluding those studying abroad (152 in 1999/2000).

Pre-school institutions (2000): 27 crèches (1,900 pupils) and 653 kindergartens (79,300 pupils).

Source: Mongolian Statistical Directorate.

2002: Schools 700; General education students 515,200; Vocational school students 105,700 (Source: National Statistical Office, *Monthly Bulletin of Statistics*).

Adult literacy rate (UNESCO estimates): 98.9% (males 99.1%; females 98.8%) in 2000 (Source: UN Development Programme, *Human Development Report*).

Directory

The Constitution

The Constitution was adopted on 13 January 1992 and came into force on 12 February of that year. It proclaims Mongolia (*Mongol Uls*), with its capital at Ulan Bator (Ulaanbaatar), to be an independent sovereign republic which ensures for its people democracy, justice, freedom, equality and national unity. It recognizes all forms of ownership of property, including land, and affirms that a 'multi-structured economy' will take account of 'universal trends of world economic development and national conditions'.

The 'citizen's right to life' is qualified by the death penalty for serious crimes, and the law provides for the imposition of forced labour. Freedom of residence and travel within the country and abroad may be limited for security reasons. The citizens' duties are to respect the Constitution and the rights and interests of others, pay taxes, and serve in the armed forces, as well as the 'sacred duty' to work, safeguard one's health, bring up one's children and protect the environment.

Supreme legislative power is vested in the Mongolian Great Khural (Assembly), a single chamber with 76 members elected by universal adult suffrage for a four-year term, with a Chairman and Vice-Chairman elected from amongst the members. The Great Khural recognizes the President on his election and appoints the Prime Minister and members of the Cabinet. A presidential veto of a decision of the Great Khural can be overruled by a two-thirds majority of the Khural. Decisions are taken by a simple majority.

The President is Head of State and Commander-in-Chief of the Armed Forces. He must be an indigenous citizen at least 45 years old who has resided continuously in Mongolia for the five years before election. Presidential candidates are nominated by parties with seats in the Great Khural; the winning candidate in general presidential elections is President for a four-year term.

The Cabinet is the highest executive body and drafts economic, social and financial policy, takes environmental protection measures, strengthens defence and security, protects human rights and implements foreign policy for a four-year term.

The Supreme Court, headed by the Chief Justice, is the highest judicial organ. Judicial independence is protected by the General Council of Courts. The Procurator General, nominated by the President, serves a six-year term.

Local administration in the 21 *aimag* (provinces) and Ulan Bator is effected on the basis of 'self-government and central guidance', comprising local khurals of representatives elected by citizens and governors (*zasag darga*), nominated by the Prime Minister to serve four-year terms.

The Constitutional Court, which guarantees 'strict observance' of the Constitution, consists of nine members nominated for a six-year term, three each by the Great Khural, the President and the Supreme Court.

The first amendments to the Constitution, adopted by the Mongolian Great Khural in December 2000, despite opposition over procedure from the Constitutional Court, were finally approved by President Bagabandi in May 2001. The main effects of the amendments were to clarify the method of appointment of Prime Ministers, enable decision-making by a simple majority vote, and shorten the minimum length of sessions of the Khural from 75 days to 50.

The Government

PRESIDENCY

President and Commander-in-Chief of the Armed Forces: NATSAGIIN BAGABANDI (elected President of Mongolia 18 May 1997; re-elected 20 May 2001).

Head of Presidential Secretariat: BADAMDORJIIN BATKHISHIG.

Director of the Presidential Information Service: DALANTAIN KHALIUN.

NATIONAL SECURITY COUNCIL

The President heads the National Security Council; the Prime Minister and the Chairman of the Mongolian Great Khural are its members (the Secretary is the President's national security adviser).

Chairman: NATSAGIIN BAGABANDI.

Members: NAMBARYN ENKHBAYAR, SANJBEGZIIN TÖMÖR-OCHIR.

Secretary: DÜGERJAVYN GOTOV.

CABINET
(April 2003)

Prime Minister: NAMBARYN ENKHBAYAR.

General Ministries

Minister of Foreign Affairs: LUVSANGIIN ERDENECHULUUN.

Minister of Finance and Economics: CHÜLTEMIIN ULAAN.

Minister of Justice and Home Affairs: TSENDIIN NYAMDORJ.

Sectoral Ministries

Minister of Nature and Environment: ULAMBAYARYN BARSBOLD.

Minister of Defence: JÜGDERDEMIDIIN GÜRRAGCHAA.

Minister of Education, Culture and Science: AYUURZANYN TSANJID.

Minister of Infrastructure: BYAMBYN JIGJID.

Minister of Social Protection and Labour: SHIILEGIIN BATBAYAR.

Minister of Industry and Trade: CHIMIDZORIGIIN GANZORIG.

Minister of Food and Agriculture: DARJAAGHIN NASANJARGAL.

Minister of Health: PAGVAJAVYN NYAMDAVAA.

Head of Government Affairs Directorate: ÖLZIISAIKHANY ENKHTÜVSHIN.

MINISTRIES AND GOVERNMENT DEPARTMENTS

All Ministries and Government Departments are in Ulan Bator. Some were in the process of restructuring in 2001–02.

Prime Minister's Office: State Palace, Sükhbaataryn Talbai 1, Ulan Bator 12; fax 328329; internet www.pmis.gov.mn/primeminister.

Ministry of Defence: Government Bldg 7, Dandaryn Gudamj, Bayanzürkh District, Ulan Bator 61; tel. 458495; fax 451727; e-mail mef@mongolnet.mn; internet www.pmis.gov.mn/mdef/mongolian.

Ministry of Education, Culture and Science: Government Bldg 3, Baga Toiruu 44, Sükhbaatar District, Ulan Bator 210620; tel. 322480; fax 323158; internet www.med.pmis.gov.mn.

Ministry of Finance and Economy: Government Bldg 2, Negdsen Ündestnii Gudamj 5/1, Chingeltei District, Ulan Bator 210646; tel. 320247; fax 322712; internet www.mof.pmis.gov.mn.

Ministry of Food and Agriculture: Government Bldg 9, Enkh Taivny Örgön Chölöö 16A, Bayanzürkh District, Ulan Bator 210349; tel. 450258; fax 452554; e-mail mofa@mofa.pmis.gov.mn; internet www.pmis.gov.mn/food&agriculture.

Ministry of Foreign Affairs: Enkh Taivny Örgön Chölöö 7A, Sükhbaatar District, Ulan Bator 210648; tel. 311311; fax 322127; e-mail mongmer@magicnet.mn; internet www.extmin.mn.

Ministry of Health: Government Bldg 8, Olimpiin Gudamj 2, Sükhbaatar District, Ulan Bator; tel. 323381; fax 320916; e-mail moh@moh.mng.net; internet www.pmis.gov.mn/health/index.

Ministry of Industry and Trade: Block A, Government Bldg 2, Negdsen Ündestnii Gudamj 5/1, Chingeltei District, Ulan Bator 210646; tel. 329222; fax 322595; e-mail mit@mit.pmis.gov.mn; internet www.mit.pmis.gov.mn.

Ministry of Infrastructure: Government Bldg 2, Negdsen Ündestnii Gudamj 5/1, Chingeltei District, Ulan Bator 210646; tel. 326222; fax 310612; e-mail webmaster@mid.pmis.gov.mn; internet www.mid.pmis.gov.mn.

Ministry of Justice and Home Affairs: Government Bldg 5, Khudaldaany Gudamj 6/1, Chingeltei District, Ulan Bator 210646; tel. 322383; fax 325225; e-mail forel@moj.pmis.gov.mn; internet www.pmis.gov.mn/mjus.

Ministry of Nature and the Environment: Government Bldg 3, Baga Toiruu 44, Sükhbaatar District, Ulan Bator 210620; tel. 320943; fax 321401; e-mail mtt@magicnet.mn; internet www.pmis.gov.mn/men.

Ministry of Social Protection and Labour: Government Bldg 2, Negdsen Ündestnii Gudamj 5/1, Chingeltei District, Ulan Bator 210646; tel. 328559; fax 328634; e-mail mswl@mongolnet.mn.

Government Affairs Directorate (Cabinet Secretariat): State Palace, Sükhbaataryn Talbai 1, Ulan Bator 12; tel. 323501; fax 310011; internet www.pmis.gov.mn/cabinet.

National Statistical Office: Government Bldg 3, Baga Toiruu 44, Sükhbaatar District, Ulan Bator 210620; tel. 322424; fax 324518; e-mail info@nso.mn; internet www.nso.mn.

President and Legislature

PRESIDENT

Office of the President: Ulan Bator; fax 311121; internet www.pmis.gov.mn/president.

Election, 20 May 2001

Candidate	Votes	%
Natsagiin Bagabandi (MPRP)	574,553	57.95
Radnaasümbereliin Gonchigdorj (Democratic Party)	362,684	36.58
Luvsandambyn Dashnyam (Civil Courage Party)	35,139	3.54

MONGOLIAN GREAT KHURAL

Under the fourth Constitution, which came into force in February 1992, the single-chamber Mongolian Great Khural is the State's supreme legislative body. With 76 members elected for a four-year term, the Great Khural must meet for at least 50 working days in every six months. Its Chairman may act as President of Mongolia when the President is indisposed.

Chairman: SANJBEGZIIN TÖMÖR-OCHIR.

Vice-Chairman: JAMSRANGIIN BYAMBADORJ.

General Secretary: NAMSRAIJAVYN LUVSANJAV.

General Election, 2 July 2000

Party	Seats
Mongolian People's Revolutionary Party (MPRP) . .	72
Civil Courage Party*	1
Mongolian Democratic New Socialist Party (MDNSP) .	1
Mongolian National Democratic Party (MNDP)† . .	1
Independent	1
Total	**76**

* In coalition with the Mongolian Green Party.
† In coalition with the Mongolian Believers' Democratic Party.

Political Organizations

Civil Courage Republican Party: Rm 1, Altai College, Sükhbaatar District, Ulan Bator (CPO 13, Box 37); tel. and fax 319006; e-mail oyun@mail.parl.gov.mn; f. 2002 by merger of the Civil Courage Party and Mongolian Republican Party; also known as the Citizen's Will (Republican Party); c. 150,000 mems. (Feb. 2003); Chair. SANJAASÜRENGIIN OYUUN; First Deputy Chair. BAZARSADYN JARGALSAIKHAN.

Democratic Party: f. 2000 by amalgamation of the Mongolian National Democratic Party, Mongolian Social-Democratic Party, Mongolian Democratic Party, Mongolian Democratic Renewal Party and the Mongolian Believers' Democratic Party; c. 170,000 mems. (May 2002); Chair. MENDSAIKHANY ENKHSAIKHAN; Sec.-Gen. LÜIMEDIIN GANSÜKH.

Mongolian Civil Democratic New Liberal Party: f. 1999; ruling body Little Khural of 90 mems with Leadership Council of nine; Chair (vacant); Sec.-Gen. DARIIN DANZAN.

Mongolian Communist Party: f. 1999; Chair. L. SHIITER.

Mongolian Democratic New Socialist Party (MDNSP): Erel Co, Bayanzürkh District, Ulan Bator; internet www.mongol.net/mdnsp; f. 1998; amalgamated with Mongolian Workers' Party 1999; 110,000 mems (May 2002); Chair. BADARCHIIN ERDENEBAT.

Mongolian Democratic Party: Ulan Bator; f. 1990; merged in Oct. 1992 with other parties to form the Mongolian National Democratic Party (MNDP); reconstituted in Jan. 2000, the party won no seats in the 2000 elections, and in Dec. 2000 most members merged with the MDNP and other parties to form the Democratic Party; a splinter group opposed to the merger tried unsuccessfully to challenge the legal status of the DP and then elected a new MDP leadership; Chair. DAMINDORJIIN NINJ.

Mongolian Democratic Socialist Party: State Property Bldg No. 5, Ulan Bator; 947 mems (1998); Chair. DASHDORJIIN MANDAKH.

Mongolian Green Party: POB 51, Erkh Chölöönii Gudamj 11, Ulan Bator 38; tel. 323871; fax 458859; f. 1990; political wing of the Alliance of Greens; 5,000 mems (March 1997); Chair. DAVAAGIIN BASANDORJ.

Mongolian Liberal Democratic Party: POB 470, Ulan Bator 44; tel. 151030; fax 310076; e-mail mldp@magicnet.mn; internet www.mldp.mn; f. 1998 as Mongolian Socialist Democratic (Labour) Party; ruling body Political Council; 848 mems (1998); Chair. TÜVSHINBATYN TÖMÖRMÖNKH.

Mongolian New Social Democratic Party: f. 2000 by MSDP dissidents; Chair. LANTUUGIIN DAMDINSÜREN.

Mongolian Party of Tradition and Justice: f. 1999; fmrly Mongolian National Democratic Socialist Party; Sec.-Gen. GANTÖMÖRIIN GALINA.

Mongolian People's Party: Ulan Bator; tel. 311083; f. 1991; forestalled any MPRP plans to revert to its original name, MPP; 2,000 mems (June 1995); in March 2000 some mems (led by Chairman Dembereliin Ölziibaatar) claimed to have merged the MPP with the MPRP; others reaffirmed the MPP's independence at a party congress in April; Chair. Lama DORLIGJAVYN BAASAN.

Mongolian People's Revolutionary Party (MPRP): Baga Toiruu 37/1, Ulan Bator 11; tel. 322745; fax 320368; f. 1921 as Mongolian People's Party; c. 122,000 mems (May 2002); ruling body Party Little Khural (183 mems in March 2000), which elects the Leadership Council; Chair. NAMBARYN ENKHBAYAR; Gen. Sec. DOLOONJINGIIN IDEVKHTEN.

Mongolian Rural Development Party: f. 1995 as the Mongolian Countryside Development Party, reorganized in December 1999; Pres. L. CHULUUNBAATAR.

Mongolian National Solidarity Party: 'Ikh Zasag' Institute Bldg, 4th Horoo, Bayanzürkh district, Ulan Bator; tel. and fax 455736; f. 1994 as Mongolian Solidarity Party; 15,480 mems (March 2002); Chair. NAMSRAIN NYAM-OSOR.

Mongolian Traditional United Party: Huvisgalchdyn Örgön Chölöö 26, Ulan Bator; tel. 325745; fax 342692; also known as the United Heritage (conservative) Party; f. 1993 as an amalgamation of the United Private Owners' Party and the Independence Party; 14,000 mems (1998); ruling body General Political Council; Chair. ÜRJINGIIN KHÜRELBAATAR.

Society of Russian Citizens: Ulan Bator; represents local Russian long-term residents; Chair (vacant); Chair. LYUDMILA G. MASLOVA.

United Socialist Party of Mongols: Ulan Bator; f. 2000; nationalist party; Chair. (vacant).

Diplomatic Representation

EMBASSIES IN MONGOLIA

Bulgaria: Olimpiin Gudamj 8, Ulan Bator (CPO Box 702); tel. and fax 322841; e-mail posolstvobg@magicnet.mn; Ambassador NIKOLAI MARIN.

China, People's Republic: Zaluuchuudyn Örgön Chölöö 5, Ulan Bator (CPO Box 672); tel. 320955; fax 311943; Ambassador HUANG JIAKUI.

Cuba: Negdsen Ündestnii Gudamj 18, Ulan Bator (CPOB 710); tel. 323778; fax 327709; e-mail embacuba@mongol.net; Ambassador PEDRO ARNALDO MORÁN TÁPANES.

Czech Republic: POB 665, Olimpiin Gudamj 14, Ulan Bator; tel. 321886; fax 323791; e-mail czechemb@mongol.net; Chargé d'affaires ADAM PIŇOS.

France: Diplomatic Corps Bldg, Apartment 48, Ulan Bator 6 (CPO Box 687); tel. 324519; fax 329633; e-mail ambafrance@magicnet.mn; Ambassador JACQUES-OLIVIER MANENT.

Germany: Negdsen Ündestnii Gudamj 7, Ulan Bator (CPO Box 708); tel. 323325; fax 323905; e-mail germanemb_ulanbator@mongol.net; Ambassador MICHAEL VORWERK.

Hungary: Enkh Taivny Gudamj 1, Ulan Bator (CPO Box 668); tel. 323973; fax 311793; e-mail huembuln@mongol.net; Ambassador ISTVÁN BALOGH.

India: Zaluuchuudyn Örgön Chölöö 10, Ulan Bator (CPO Box 691); tel. 329522; fax 329532; e-mail indembmongolia@magicnet.mn; Ambassador KARMA TOPDEN.

Japan: Zaluuchuudyn Gudamj 12, Ulan Bator 13 (CPO Box 1011); tel. 320777; fax 313332; e-mail eojmongol@magicnet.mn; internet www.eojmongolia.mn; Ambassador TATSUO TODA.

Kazakhstan: Diplomatic Corps Bldg, Apartment 11, Chingeltei District, Ulan Bator (CPO Box 291); tel. 312240; fax 312204; e-mail kzemby@magicnet.mn; Chargé d'affaires KAYRAT ISAGALIYEV.

Korea, Republic: Olimpiin Gudamj 10, Ulan Bator (CPO Box 1039); tel. 321548; fax 311157; Ambassador KIM WON-TAE.

Laos: Ikh Toiruu 59, Ulan Bator (CPO Box 1030); tel. 322834; fax 321048; e-mail laoemb@mongol.net; Ambassador VANHEUANG VONGVI-CHIT.

Poland: Diplomatic Corps Bldg, 95, Apartment 66–67, Ulan Bator 13; tel. 320641; fax 320576; Ambassador KRZYSZTOF DEBNICKE.

Russia: Enkh Taivny Gudamj A-6, Ulan Bator (CPO Box 661); tel. 327071; fax 324425; Ambassador OLEG DERKOVSKII.

Turkey: Enkh Taivny Örgön Chölöö 5, Ulan Bator (CPO Box 1009); tel. 313992; fax 313992; e-mail turkemb@mongol.net; Ambassador TANER KARAKAŞ.

United Kingdom: Enkh Taivny Gudamj 30, Ulan Bator 13 (CPO Box 703); tel. 458133; fax 458036; e-mail britemb@magicnet.mn; Ambassador PHILIP ROUSE.

USA: Ikh Toiruu 59/1, Ulan Bator (CPO Box 1021); tel. 329606; fax 320776; e-mail webmaster@us-mongolia.com; Ambassador JOHN R. DINGER.

Viet Nam: Enkh Taivny Örgön Chölöö 47, Ulan Bator (CPO Box 670); tel. 458917; fax 458923; Ambassador CHAN NGUYEN TICH.

Judicial System

Under the fourth Constitution, judicial independence is protected by the General Council of Courts, consisting of the Chief Justice (Chairman of the Supreme Court), the Chairman of the Constitutional Court, Procurator General, Minister of Law and others. The Council nominates the members of the Supreme Court for approval by the Great Khural. The Chief Justice is chosen from among the members of the Supreme Court and approved by the President for a six-year term. Civil, criminal and administrative cases are handled by Ulan Bator City court, the 21 *aimag* (provincial) courts, *sum* (rural district) and urban district courts, while the system of special courts (military, railway, etc.) is still in place. The Procurator General and his deputies, who play an investigatory role, are nominated by the President and approved by the Great Khural for six-year terms. The Constitutional Court safeguards the constitutional legality of legislation. It consists of nine members, three nominated each by the President, Great Khural and Supreme Court, and elects a Chairman from among its number.

Chief Justice: CHIMEDLKHAMYN GANBAT.

Procurator General: MONGOLYN ALTANKHUYAG.

Chairman of Constitutional Court: NAVAANPERENLEIN JANTSAN.

Religion

The 1992 Constitution maintains the separation of Church and State but forbids any discrimination, declaring that 'the State shall respect religion and religion shall honour the State'. During the early years of communist rule Mongolia's traditional Mahayana Buddhism was virtually destroyed, then exploited as a 'show-piece' for visiting dignitaries (although the Dalai Lama himself was not permitted to visit Mongolia until the early 1980s). The national Buddhist centre is Gandantegchinlen Khiid (monastery) in Ulan Bator, with about 100 lamas and a seminary; it is the headquarters of the Asian Buddhist Conference for Peace. In the early 1990s some 2,000 lamas established small communities at the sites of 120 former monasteries, temples and religious schools, some of which were being restored. These included two other important monasteries, Erdene Zuu and Amarbayasgalant. The Kazakhs of western Mongolia are nominally Sunni Muslims, but their mosques, also destroyed in the 1930s or closed subsequently, are only now being rebuilt or reopened. Traces of shamanism from the pre-Buddhist period still survive. In recent years there has been a new upsurge in Christian missionary activity in Mongolia. However, the Law on State-Church Relations (of November 1993) sought to make Buddhism the predominant religion and restricted the dissemination of beliefs other than Buddhism, Islam and shamanism. The law was challenged by human rights campaigners and Mongolian Christians as unconstitutional.

BUDDHISM

Living Buddha: The Ninth Javzandamba Khutagt (Ninth Bogd), Jambalnamdolchoijinjaltsan (resident in Dharamsala, India).

Buddhist Believers' Association: Pres. S. BAYANTSAGAAN.

Gandantegchinlen Monastery: Ulan Bator 58; tel. 360023; Centre of Mongolian Buddhists; Khamba Lama (Abbot) DEMBERELIIN CHOIJAMTS.

Mongolian Buddhist Association: Pres. G. ENKHSAIKHAN.

CHRISTIANITY

Roman Catholic Church

The Church is represented in Mongolia by a single mission. At 31 December 2001 there were 94 Catholic Christians in the country.

Catholic Mission: POB 694, Ulan Bator; tel. 458825; fax 458027; e-mail ccmvatican@magicnet.mn; f. 1992; Superior Rev. Fr WENS PADILLA.

Protestant Church

Association of Mongolian Protestants: f. 1990; Pastor M. BOLDBAATAR.

Russian Orthodox Church

Holy Trinity Church: Jukovyn Gudamj 55, Ulan Bator; opened in 1870, closed in 1930; services recommenced 1997 for Russian community; Father ANATOLII FESECHKO.

ISLAM

Muslim Society: f. 1990; Hon. Pres. K. SAIRAAN; Chair. of Central Council M. AZATKHAN.

BAHÁ'Í FAITH

Bahá'í Community: Ulan Bator; tel. 321867; f. 1989; Leader A. ARIUNAA.

The Press

PRINCIPAL NATIONAL NEWSPAPERS

State-owned publications in Mongolia were denationalized with effect from 1 January 1999, although proper privatization could not proceed immediately.

MN-Önöödör (Today): Mongol News Co, Ikh Toiruu 20, Ulan Bator; tel. 352504; fax 352501; e-mail mntoday@mobinet.mn; f. 1996; 304 a year; Editor-in-Chief Ts. BALDORJ; circ. 5,500.

Mongolyn Medee (Mongolian News): Erel Group, 13th District, Bayanzürkh Düüreg, Ulan Bator; tel. 453169; fax 453816; e-mail news-of-mon@magicnet.mn; 256 a year; Editor-in-Chief D. SANDAGSÜREN; circ. 2,900.

Ödriin Sonin (Daily News): Ikh Toiruu, Ulan Bator 20; tel. 99263536; fax 352499; e-mail daily_news@mbox.mn; f. 1924; restored 1990; fmrly Ardyn Erkh, Ardyn Ündesnii Erkh, Ündesnii Erkh and Ödriin Toli; 312 a year; Editor-in-Chief JAMBALYN MYAGMARSÜREN; circ. 14,200.

Ünen (Truth): Baga Toiruu 11, Ulan Bator; tel. 323847; fax 321287; e-mail unen@magicnet.mn; internet www.unen.mn; f. 1920; publ. by MPRP; 256 a year; Editor-in-Chief TSERENSODNOMYN GANBAT; circ. 8,330.

Zuuny Medee (Century's News): Amaryn Gudamj 1, Ulan Bator 20; tel. 320940; fax 321279; e-mail zuunii_medee@yahoo.com; internet www.zm.mongolmedia.com; f. 1991 as *Zasgiin Gazryn Medee*; 312 a year; Editor-in-Chief TSERENDORJIIN TSETSEGCHULUUN; circ 8,000.

PRINCIPAL PERIODICALS

81–r Suvag (Channel 81): POB 367/13, Ulan Bator; tel. 99118359; e-mail channel81@mongolmedia.com; internet www.channel81.mongolmedia.com; publishes views of the Mongolian Newspaper Assocn; 40 a year; Editor-in-Chief JAMSRANGIIN BAYARJARGAL.

Anagaakh Arga Bilig (Health Yin and Yang): POB 1053/13, Ulan Bator; tel. 321367; e-mail arslny7144@magicnet.mn; monthly; Editor YA. ARSLAN.

Ardyn Elch (People's Envoy): St. Petersburgh Centre, 2nd Floor, Rm 36, Sükhbaataryn Örgön Chölöö; tel. 95252346; fax 314580; monthly; Editor-in-Chief B. TSEDEN.

Bagsh (Teacher): Rm 106, Teachers' College, Ulan Bator; tel. 99183398; f. 1989 by Ministry of Education; 24 a year.

Business Times: Chamber of Commerce and Industry, Government Bldg 1, Rm 806, Erkh Chölöönii Talbai, Ulan Bator; tel. 325374; fax 324620; e-mail bis_times@usa.net; 48 a year; Editor B. SARANTUYAA.

Deedsiin Amidral (Elite's Life): Bldg 6, Rm 207, A. Amaryn Gudamj, POB 536/13, Ulan Bator; tel. 91189399; fax 323847; e-mail elitslife@mongolmedia.com; internet www.elitslife.mongolmedia.com; Editor-in-Chief TSEGMIDIIN CHIMIDDONDOG.

Deedsiin Khüreelen (Elite's Forum): CPO Box 1114, Ulan Bator; tel. 325687; 48 a year; Editor NYAMBUUGIIN BILGÜÜN; circ. 12,000.

Dorno-Örnö (East-West): POB 17/48, Ulan Bator; fax 322613; f. 1978; publ. by Institute of Oriental and International Studies of Acad. of Sciences; scientific and socio-political journal; history, culture, foreign relations; articles in Mongolian; two a year; Editor-in-Chief Dr N. ALTANTSETSEG.

Erüül Mend (Health): Ulan Bator; fax 321278; publ. by Ministry of Health; monthly; Editor-in-Chief SH. JIGJIDSÜREN; circ. 5,600.

Il Tovchoo (Openness): Mongol Nom Co Bldg, Rm 8, Ulan Bator; POB 234, Ulan Bator 46; tel. 325517; e-mail iltovchoo@magicnet.mn; f. 1990; current affairs and cultural news; 36 a year; Editor-in-Chief G. AKIM.

Khani (Spouse): POB 600/49, National Agricultural Co-operative Members' Association Bldg, Rm 103, Enkh Taivny Gudamj 18A-1, Bayanzürkh Düüreg, Ulan Bator; women and family issues; 36 a year; Editor-in-Chief D. OTGONTUYAA; circ. 64,920.

Khöldömör (Labour): Sükhbaataryn Talbai 3, Ulan Bator 210664; tel. 323026; f. 1928; publ. by the Confederation of Mongolian Trade Unions; 36 a year; Editor-in-Chief TSOODOLYN KHULAN; circ. 64,920.

Khökh Tolbo (Blue Spot): POB 306/24, Mon-Azi Co Bldg, Ulan Bator; tel. and fax 313405; 48 a year; Editor-in-Chief BATYN ERDENE-BAATAR; circ. 3,500.

Khuuli Züin Medeelel (Legal Information): Ministry of Justice and Home Affairs, Ulan Bator; f. 1990; 24 a year.

Khuviin Amidral (Private Life): POB 429/44, Ulan Bator 44; tel. 329926; fax 310181; 36 a year; Editor-in-Chief T. AMARDAVAA; circ. 2,900.

Khuviin Soyol (Personal Culture): CPOB 1254, Rm 2, Block 39, behind No. 5 School, Baga Toiruu, Ulan Bator; Editor BEKHBAZARYN BEKHSÜREN.

Khümüün Bichig (People and Script): Montsame, Ulan Bator; tel. 329486; fax 327857; e-mail montsame@pop.mn; current affairs in Mongolian classical script; 36 a year; Editor T. GALDAN; circ. 15,000.

Khümüüs (People): POB 411, Ulan Bator 46; tel. 328732; fax 318363; e-mail khumuus@mongol.net; 48 a year; Editor O. MÖNKH-ERDENE; circ. 21,500.

Khümüüsiin Amidral (People's Life): POB 411, Ulan Bator 46; tel. 328732; fax 318363; e-mail khumuus@mongol.net; 48 a year; Editor B. KHULAN.

Mash Nuuts (Top Secret): POB 113/49, Ulan Bator 49; 24 a year; Editors N. BATDELGER, TS. MÖNKHTUYAA.

Mongol Taims (Mongol Times): Jamyangiin Gudamj 9, Ulan Bator; tel. and fax 458802; 48 a year; Editor CHONOIN KULANDA.

Mongol Törkh (Mongolian Style): POB 418/46, MPRP Bldg, Rm 102, Sükhbaatar Düüreg, Ulan Bator; tel. and fax 311406; 36 a year; Editor D. BADAMGARAV.

Mongoljin Goo (Mongolian Beauty): POB 717/44, Mongolian Women's Federation, Ulan Bator; tel. 320790; fax 367406; e-mail monwofed@magicnet.mn; f. 1990; monthly; Editor J. ERDENECHIMEG; circ. 3,000.

Mongolyn Anagaakh Ukhaan (Mongolian Medicine): CPOB 696/13, Ulan Bator 13; tel. 112306; fax 451807; e-mail nymadawa@hotmail.com; publ. by Scientific Society of Mongolian Physicians, Sub-assembly of Medical Sciences and Mongolian Academy of Sciences; quarterly; Editor-in-Chief Prof. PAGVAJAVYN NYAMDAVAA.

Mongolyn Khödöö (Mongolian Countryside): Ulan Bator; tel. 455577; publ. by Ministry of Agriculture and Industry, and Academy of Agricultural Sciences; monthly; Editor-in-Chief TS. MÖNKHBAATAR.

Montsame—giin Medee (Montsame News): CPOB 1514, Montsame, Ulan Bator; tel. 314507; fax 314511; daily news digest primarily for government departments; 264 a year; Editor B. NAMIN-CHIMED.

Notstoi Medee (Important News): POB 359/20, Maximum Press Co, Ulan Bator; tel. 99133270; Editor B. MONKHZUL.

Oroin Medee (Evening News): Bayangol Düüreg, Ulan Bator; tel. 90151080; e-mail e_news@hotmail.com; Editor-in-Chief S. BADAM-RAGCHAA.

Sain Baina Uu? (Hello!): CPOB 1085, Chingisiin Örgön Chölöö 1, Ulan Bator; tel. 310757; fax 372810; internet sain.mongolmedia .com; publ. by the Democratic Party; 48 a year; Editor CH. CHU-LUUNBAATAR.

Serüüleg (Alarm Clock): POB 1094/13, Flat 2, Entrance 1, Block A4, 1-40 Myangat, Ulan Bator; tel. and fax 318006; 40 a year; Editor-in-Chief SENGEEGIIN BAYARMÖNKH; circ. 28,600.

Setgüülch (Journalist): POB 600/46, Ulan Bator; tel. 325388; fax 313912; f. 1982; publ. by Union of Journalists; journalism, politics, literature, art, economy; quarterly; Editor TSENDIIN ENKHBAT.

Shar Sonin (Yellow Newspaper): POB 76/20A, Ulan Bator; tel. 313984; 48 a year; Editor B. ODGEREL.

Shinjlekh Ukhaany Akademiin Medee (Academy of Sciences News): Sükhbaataryn Talbai 3, Ulan Bator; f. 1961; publ. by Academy of Sciences; quarterly; Editor-in-Chief T. GALBAATAR.

Shuurkhai Zar (Quick Advertisement): POB 151/46A, Ulan Bator Bank Bldg, Rm 104, 1st Floor, Ulan Bator; tel. 313778; e-mail shirevger@mobinet.mn; Editor E. TSEYENKHORLOO.

Tavan Tsagarig (Five Rings): National Olympic Committee, Ikh Toiruu 20, Ulan Bator; tel. 352487; fax 352462; e-mail t_ts_sport@yahoo.com; Editor-in-Chief SODNOMDARJAAGIIN BATBAATAR.

Töriin Medeelel (State Information): Secretariat of the Mongolian Great Khural, State Palace, Ulan Bator 12; tel. 329612; fax 322866; e-mail elbegsaihan@maild.parl.gov.mn; internet www.parl.gov.mn; f. 1990; presidential and governmental decrees, state laws; 48 a year; Editor R. ENKHTAIVAN; circ. 5,000.

Tsenkher Delgets (Light Blue Screen): Ulan Bator; tel. 312010; fax 311850; e-mail bsnews@magicnet.mn; weekly guide to TV and radio programmes; Editor-in-Chief GALIGAAGIIN BAYARSAIKHAN.

Tsonkh (Window): CPOB 1085, Chingisiin Örgön Chölöö 1, Ulan Bator; tel. 310717; publ. by the Democratic Party's Political Department; monthly.

Üg (Word): CPOB 680, Rm 2, Block 8B, 1 Döchin Myangat, Ulan Bator; tel. 321165; fax 329795; e-mail ugsonin@mol.mn; fmrly the journal of the Mongolian Social Democratic Party (until 2000); Editor B. KHANDOLGOR.

Ulaanbaatar Times (Ulan Bator Times): A. Amaryn Gudamj 1, Ulan Bator 20; tel. and fax 311187; f. 1990 as *Ulaanbaatar*; publ. by Ulan Bator City Govt; weekly; Editor-in-Chief JÜMPERELIIN SAR-UULBUYAN; circ. 2,000.

Utga Zokhiol Urlag (Literature and Art): Union of Writers, Sükhbaataryn Gudamj 11, Ulan Bator 46; tel. 321863; f. 1955; monthly; Editor-in-Chief Ü. KHÜRELBAATAR; circ. 3,000.

Zar Medee (Advertisement News): State Property Bldg 5, 1st Floor, Rm 130, Chingeltei Düüreg, Ulan Bator; tel. and fax 324885; e-mail advertisement-news@yahoo.com; personal and company advertisements; 102 a year; Editor D. BAYASGALAN.

Zindaa (Ranking): Kyoküshyuzan Development Fund Bldg, Chingeltei Düüreg, Ulan Bator; tel. 312008; internet www.zindaa .mongolmedia.com; wrestling news; 36 a year; Editor-in-Chief KH. MANDAKHBAYAR.

FOREIGN LANGUAGE PUBLICATIONS

Email Daily News: Ulan Bator; e-mail ganbold@magicnet.mn; press and media summaries in English; Mon.–Fri. Editor CHULUUNY GANBOLD.

Menggu Xiaoxi Bao (News of Mongolia): Montsame News Agency, CPOB 1514, Ulan Bator; e-mail mgxxbao@yahoo.com; f. 1929 as Ajilchny Zam; closed 1991, reopened 1998; 48 a year; in Chinese; Sec. B. MÖNKHTUUL.

Mongolia This Week: Ulan Bator; tel. and fax 318339; e-mail mongoliathisweek@mobinet.mn; internet www.mongoliathisweek .mn; weekly in English, online daily; Editor-in-Chief D. NARANTUYAA; English Editor ERIC MUSTAFA.

Mongoliya Segodnya (Mongolia Today): Box 609, PO 46, Ulan Bator; tel. and fax 324141; e-mail MNSegodnia@mongol.net; weekly; Editor-in-Chief DÜNGER-YAICHILIIN SOLONGO.

The Mongol Messenger: Montsame News Agency, CPOB 1514, Ulan Bator; tel. 325512; fax 327857; e-mail monmessenger@mongolnet.mn; internet www.mongolmessenger.mn; f. 1991; weekly newspaper in English; Exec. Editor B. INDRA; circ. 2,000.

Montsame Daily News: CPOB 1514, Montsame, Ulan Bator; tel. 314574; fax 327857; daily English news digest for embassies, etc.

Novosti Mongolii (News of Mongolia): CPOB 1514, Montsame, Ulan Bator; tel. 310157; fax 327857; e-mail montsame@pop .magicnet.mn; f. 1942; weekly; in Russian; Editor-in-Chief ENKH-BAYARYN RAVDAN.

The UB Post: Mongol News Co, Ikh Toiruu 20, Ulan Bator; tel. 352480; fax 352495; e-mail info@theubpost.mn; internet www .theubpost.mn; f. 1996; weekly; in English; Editor-in-Chief NAMSRAIN OYUUNBAYAR; circ. 1,700.

NEWS AGENCIES

Montsame (Mongol Tsakhilgaan Medeenii Agentlag) (Mongolian News Agency): Jigjidjavyn Gudamj 8, Ulan Bator 13 (CPO Box 1514); tel. 314502; fax 327857; e-mail montsame@magicnet.mn; internet www.montsame.mn; f. 1921; govt-controlled; Gen. Dir DOR-JIIN ARIUNBOLD (acting); Editor-in-Chief GIVAANDONDOGIIN PÜRE-VSAMBUU.

Mongolyn Medee (Mongolian News): operated by Mongolteleviz; Dir D. SANDAGSÜREN.

Foreign Bureaux

Informatsionnoye Telegrafnoye Agentstvo Rossii—Telegrafnoye Agentstvo Suverennykh Stran (ITAR—TASS) (Russia): October 4, Rm 323, Ulan Bator; Bureau Chief V. B. IONOV; Correspondent N. A. KERZHENTSEV.

Rossiiskoye Informatsionnoye Agentstvo—Novosti (RIA-Novosti) (Russia): POB 686, Ulan Bator; tel. 327384; Correspondent ALEKSANDR ALTMAN.

Xinhua (New China) News Agency (People's Republic of China): Ulan Bator; tel. 322718; Correspondent LI REN.

Publishers

Mongolian Book Publishers' Association: Ulan Bator; Exec. Dir S. TSERENDORJ.

Mongolian Free Press Publishers' Asociation: POB 306, Ulan Bator 24; tel. and fax 313405; Pres. BATYN ERDENEBAATAR.

The Government remains the largest publisher, but the ending of the state monopoly has led to the establishment of several small commercial publishers, including Shuvuun Saaral (Ministry of Defence), Mongol Khevlel and Soyombo Co, Mongolpress (Montsame), Erdem (Academy of Sciences), Süülenkhüü children's publishers, Sudaryn Chuulgan, Interpress, Sükhbaatar Co, Öngöt Khevlel, Admon, Odsar, Khee Khas Co, etc. Newspaper publishing fell from 134.1m. copies in 1990 to 21.1m. copies in 1999. Book printing likewise declined, from 96.3m. printer's sheets (each of 16 pages) in 1990 to 19.2m. in 1993. In 1994 128 book titles appeared, with a total of 640,000 copies. The two main press, periodical and book subscription agencies are Mongol Shuudan and Gurvan Badrakh Co.

Broadcasting and Communications

TELECOMMUNICATIONS

Digital exchanges have been installed in Ulan Bator, Darkhan, Erdenet, Sükhbaatar, Bulgan and Arvaikheer, while radio-relay lines have been digitalized between: Ulan Bator– Darkhan–Sükhbaatar; Ulan Bator–Darkhan–Erdenet; and Dashinchilen–Arvaikheer. Mobile telephone companies operate in Ulan Bator and other central towns, in addition to Arvaikheer, Sainshand and Zamyn-Üüd.

Datakom: Negdsen Ündestnii Gudamj 49, Ulan Bator 46; tel. 315544; fax 320210; e-mail sales@datacom.mn; internet www.web.mn; service provider for Magicnet connection to internet; Dir DANGAASÜRENGIIN ENKHBAT.

Micom: Mongol Tsakhilgaan Kholboo Co Bldg, 3rd Floor, Sükhbaataryn Talbai 1, Ulan Bator 210611; tel. 313229; fax 322473; e-mail info@micom.mng.net; internet www.micom.mng.net; Dir R. BATMEND.

MobiCom: Amryn Gudamj 2, Ulan Bator 210620 (CPO Box 20A); tel. 312222; fax 310411; e-mail mobicom@mobicom-corp.com; mobile telephone service provider.

Moncom: 51 Post Office, Box 207, Ulan Bator; tel. 329409; e-mail ch.enkhmend@hotmail.com; pager services.

Mongolia Telecom: Sükhbaataryn Talbai 1, Ulan Bator 210611 (CPO Box 1166); tel. 320597; fax 325412; e-mail mt@mtcone.net; internet www.mongol.net; 54.6% state-owned, 40.0% owned by Korea Telecom; Pres. and CEO OONOI SHAALUU.

Railcom: Business Services, Ulan Bator Railway Directorate, Ulan Bator; tel. 942600; internet www.railcom.mn; telephone, TV and internet service provider.

Skytel: Montel Co Bldg, 4th Floor, 1st Khoroo, Chingeltei District, Ulan Bator 13; tel. 318488; fax 318487; e-mail skytel@mtcone.net; mobile telephone and voice mail service provider; Mongolia-Republic of Korea joint venture; Marketing Man. G. TÜVSHINTÖGS.

BROADCASTING

A 1,900-km radio relay line from Ulan Bator to Altai and Ölgii provides direct-dialling telephone links as well as television services for western Mongolia. New radio relay lines have been built from Ulan Bator to Choibalsan, and from Ulan Bator to Sükhbaatar and Sainshand. Most of the population is in the zone of television reception, following the inauguration of relays via satellites operated by the International Telecommunications Satellite Organization (INTELSAT).

All provincial centres receive two channels of Mongolian national television; and all district centres can receive television, although only a third can receive Mongolian television.

Head of Mongolian Radio and Television Affairs Directorate: BAASANJAVYN GANBOLD.

Radio

Mongolradio: Khuvisgalyn Zam 3, Ulan Bator 11; tel. 323096; f. 1934; operates for 17 hours daily on three long wave and one medium-wave frequency, and VHF; programmes in Mongolian (two) and Kazakh; Dir BAARANGIIN PÜREVDASH.

Voice of Mongolia: Ulan Bator; e-mail radiomongolia@magicnet.mn; external service of Mongolradio; broadcasts in Russian, Chinese, English and Japanese on short wave; Dir B. NARANTUYAA.

Khökh Tenger (Blue Sky Radio): broadcasts for 12 hours Monday to Saturday and for shorter hours on Sundays on 100.9 MHz and 4850 kHz; Dir L. Amarzayaa.

The BBC World Service is relayed on 103.1 MHz in Ulan Bator.

AE and JAAG Studio: Amryn Gudamj 2, Ulan Bator 210620, POB 126, Ulan Bator; tel. 310631; fax 326545; e-mail aejaag@magicnet.mn; f. 1996; broadcasts for 4.5–5 hours daily; CEO Z. ALTAI.

FM 106.6: Ulan Bator; f. 2001; Voice of America news and information in Mongolian; English lessons and music.

FM 107 (New Century Radio): Ulan Bator; local entertainment; also relays Voice of America broadcasts in English and Russian; Dir M. BUYANBADRAKH.

Info Radio: Youth Palace, Ulan Bator; tel. 329353; e-mail inforadio@mongol.net; broadcasts on 105.5 MHz.

Puls-Misheel: Ulan Bator; f. 2001 by Mongolradio and Buryat Puls radio; Russian-language broadcaster on 102.5 MHz, 24 hours; hourly news in Russian and Mongolian.

Radio Ulaanbaatar: Ulan Bator; f. 1995; fmrly *Dörvön Uul* (Four Mountains); broadcasts on 101.6 MHz; Dir U. BULGAN.

There are seven long and shortwave radio transmitters and 49 FM stations in 23 towns (13 in Ulan Bator).

Television

Mongolteleviz: Khuvisgalyn Zam 3, Ulan Bator 11 (CPO Box 365); tel. 326663; fax 327234; e-mail mrtv@magicnet.mn; f. 1967; daily morning and evening transmissions of locally-originated material relayed by land-line and via INTELSAT satellites; Dir TSENDIIN ENKHBAT.

MN Channel 25: AE and JAAG Studio, Ulan Bator; broadcasts entertainment in the evening from Tuesday to Sunday; CEO Z. ALTAI.

Eagle (Bürged) TV: Ulan Bator; tel. 458657; fax 458505; e-mail eagle@eagletvmongolia.com; broadcasts for nine hours daily, carrying Mongolian news, cartoons, films, educational programmes, sports and relays of CNN; News Editor TSAGAANY OYUUNDARI; Gen. Man. PAUL SWARTZENDRUBER; services suspended in April 2003.

Sansar: Ikh Toiruu 46, Ulan Bator; tel. 313752; fax 313770; cable television equipment and services; Dir-Gen. TS. ELBEGZAYAA.

UBS: Ulaanbaatar Broadcasting System (operated by Ulan Bator City Government); evening broadcasts repeated the following morning except Mondays; Dir-Gen. L. BALKHJAV.

Cable TV companies (29 in total) operate in 19 towns. There are local TV stations in Ulan Bator (three), Darkhan, Sükhbaatar and Baganuur. ORT and RTR may be received via Russian satellites, and Kazakh television is received in Bayan-Ölgii. NHK, Deutsche Welle, RTF and Inner Mongolia (China) Television programmes are relayed in Ulan Bator on Channel 10.

Finance

(cap. = capital; res = reserves; dep. = deposits; m. = million; brs = branches; amounts in tögrög)

BANKING

Before 1990 the State Bank was the only bank in Mongolia, responsible for issuing currency, controlling foreign exchange and allocating credit. With the inauguration of market reforms in Mongolia in the early 1990s, the central and commercial functions of the State Bank were transferred to the newly-created specialized commercial banks: the Bank of Capital Investment and Technological Innovation and the State Bank International. In May 1991 the State Bank became an independent central bank, and the operation of private, commercial banks was permitted. By the end of 1996 there were 15 commercial banks. The performance of these banks was poor, owing to high levels of non-performing loans, inexperienced management and weak supervision. Loss of confidence in the sector resulted in the implementation of extensive restructuring: in November 1996 amendments were made to banking legislation to improve the regulation and supervision of commercial banks, and two major insolvent banks were liquidated. Restructuring continued in the late 1990s.

Central Bank

Bank of Mongolia (Mongolbank): Baga Toiruu 9, Ulan Bator 46; tel. 322169; fax 311471; e-mail ad@mongolbank.mn; internet www .mongolbank.mn; f. 1924 as the State Bank of the Mongolian People's Republic; cap. 1,000m., res. 132,932m. (Dec. 2000), dep. 176,043m. (Dec. 1999); Gov. OCHIRBATYN CHULUUNBAT.

Other Banks

AG Bank—Agricultural Bank (KhAAN Bank): Enkh Taivny Gudamj 51, Ulan Bator 240149 (POB 185, Ulan Bator 51); tel. and fax 458670; e-mail www.haanbank@magicnet.mn; f. 1991; purchased by H and S Securities (Japan) in Feb. 2003; cap. 4,945m. (Dec. 1999); CEO PETER MORROW; 352 brs.

Anod Bank: Khudaldaany Gudamj 18, Ulan Bator 211238 (POB 361, Ulan Bator 13); tel. 315315; fax 313070; e-mail anod@magicnet .mn; internet www.anod.mn; cap. 3,000m., dep. 37,588m. (Dec. 2002); Dir-Gen. D. ENKHTÖR.

Avtozam Bank (Motor Roads Bank): Bridge-Building Office, Ulan Bator; tel. 381744; fax 368094; f. 1990; cap. 95m. Dir-Gen. TS. SANGIDORJ.

Aziin Khöröngö Oruulaltyn Bank (Asian Capital Investment Bank): Khölög Group Bldg, Eastern entrance, 2nd Floor, Bayangol District, Ulan Bator; tel. 367386; Dir-Gen. TSEDENGIIN BATBOLD.

Bayanbogd Bank: Sambuugiin Gudamj 11, Ulan Bator; tel. and fax 329942; privately owned; cap. 423.7m., dep. 795.5m. (June 1999); Owner D. ADYAA.

Capitron Bank: Enkh Taivny Örgön Chölöö, Ulan Bator 210648; tel. 327550; fax 315635; e-mail info@capitronbank.mn; internet www.capitronbank.mn; f. 2001; cap. 4,000m., res 5,000m., dep 12,000m. (2002); Exec. Dir A. MÖNKHBAT.

Chingis Khan Bank: Ulan Bator; f. 2001 by Millennium Securities Management Ltd (British Virgin Islands); cap. US $4.5m.

Ediin Tenger Bank: Barilgachdyn Talbai 13, Ulan Bator; tel. 458601; Dir-Gen. D. DANZAN; licence withdrawn, Oct. 1998.

Erel Bank: 'Erel' Co No 2 Bldg, Chingisiin Örgön Chölöö, 3rd Khoroo, Ulan Bator (POB 500, Ulan Bator 36); tel. and fax 343567; e-mail erelbank@mongol.net; f. 1997; cap. 2,600m., res 34.0m., dep. 849.2m. (Aug. 2002); Owner BADARCHIIN ERDENEBAT; CEO GOMBOJAVYN DORJ.

Export Import Bank: Zamchny Gudamj 1, Bayangol District, Ulan Bator (CPO Box 28/52); tel. 311693; fax 311323; f. 1993 as Ulaanbaatar Bank; cap. 506.8m. CEO L. SARANGEREL.

Golomt Bank of Mongolia: Bodi Tower, Sükhbaataryn Talbai 3, 4th Floor, Ulan Bator 210620; tel. 311530; fax 312307; e-mail psdc@ golomtbank.com; f. 1995 by Mongolian-Portuguese IBH Bodi International Co Ltd; cap. 2,716m. dep. 25,851m. (Dec. 2001); Chair. of Bd LUVSANVANDANGIIN BOLD; Dir-Gen. D. BAYASGALAN; 10 brs.

Interbank Mongolia: Ulan Bator; tel. 327403; fax 328372; e-mail interbank@mongol.net.

Khadgalamjiin Bank (Savings Bank): Khudaldaany Gudamj 6, Ulan Bator 11; tel. 312043; fax 310621; e-mail savbank@magicnet .mn; internet www.savingsbank.mn; f. 1996 as Ardyn Bank; cap. 2,536.8m. (Dec. 2001); Dir-Gen. G. TSERENPÜREV; 37 brs.

Khöröngö Oruulalt Tekhnologiin Shinechleltiin Bank (Bank of Capital Investment and Technological Innovation, ITIBank of Mongolia): Khudaldaany Gudamj 11, Ulan Bator 46; tel. 381933; fax 381115; e-mail itibank2@magicnet.mn; f. 1991; licence withdrawn 2000; cap. 3,306m., res 2,108m., dep. 2,694m. Pres. N. CHULUUN-BAATAR; 32 brs.

Kredit Bank: State Palace Bldg (east side), Sükhbaataryn Talbai, Ulan Bator; tel. 310853; cap. 1,117m. (March 2000).

Mongol Khorshoo Bank (Mongolian Co-operative Bank): Olimpiin Gudamj 4, Ulan Bator 48; tel. 325239; f. 1990; cap. 95.8m. Chair. of Board MIJIDIIN TERBISH; 5 brs.

Mongol Shuudan Bank (Post Bank): Kholboochdyn Gudamj 4, Ulan Bator 13 (POB 874); tel. 311270; fax 328501; e-mail post_bank@mongol.net; internet www.postbank.mn; f. 1993; cap. 2,002.3m., res 582.4m., dep. 14,899.7m., equity 18,566.5m. (Dec. 2001); 100% in private ownership; Exec. Dir D. OYUUNJARGAL.

Shinechlel Bank (Innovation Bank of Mongolia): Erkh Chölöönii Örgön Chölöö, Ulan Bator 211238; tel. 312539; fax 312531; e-mail innbk@mongol.net; internet www.innovationbank.com; cap.

2,000m., res 200m., dep. 5,000m. (Jan. 2003); Chair. of the Bd AGVAANJAMYN ARIUNBOLD; Exec. Dir MEGZEMIIN MYAGMARSÜREN; 6 brs.

Teever Khögjliin Bank (Transport and Development Bank): Amarsanaagiin Gudamj 2, Bayanzürkh District, Ulan Bator; tel. 458617; Exec. Dir D. ENKHTUYAA; cap. 1,072m.

Trade and Development Bank of Mongolia (Khudaldaa Khögjliin Bank): Khudaldaany Gudamj 6, Ulan Bator 11; tel. 326289; fax 311618; e-mail tdbank@tdbm.mn; internet www.tdbm.mn; f. 1991; carries out Mongolbank's foreign operations; cap. 1,500m., res. 3,153m., dep. 83,031m. (Dec. 2000); 76% equity bought by Banca Commerciale (Lugano) and Gerald Metals (Stanford, CT), May 2002; Exec. Dir SIILEGMAAGIIN MÖNKHBAT.

Tülsh-Erchim Bank (Fuel and Power Bank): Baga Toiruu, Ulan Bator; tel. 310605; fax 310981; f. 1992; Dir M. MYAGMARSÜREN.

Ulaanbaatar Bank: Baga Toiruu 15, Ulan Bator (PO 370, Ulan Bator 46); tel. 312155; fax 311067; e-mail ubbank@magicnet.mn; f. 1998 by Capital City with assistance from the Bank of Taipei (Taiwan); cap. 4,800m; Dir-Gen. G. BUYANBAT.

Üildveriin Huvi Niilüülsen Bank (Industrial Shares Bank, 'Shinechlel' Innovation Bank): Ulan Bator 120646; tel. 310833; f. 1990; cap. 418m. Dir-Gen. SÜKHRAGCHAAGIIN MÖNKHTÖR.

XacBank: Yörönkhii said Amaryn Gudamj, Sükhbaatar District, Ulan Bator 210646 (POB 46/721); tel. 318185; fax 328701; e-mail bank@xacbank.org; internet www.xacbank.org; f. 2001; cap. 2.8m., res 7.0m., dep. 2.8m. (2002); Exec. Dir GANKHUYAGIIN CHULUUN.

Zoos Bank: 'Oi Mod' Co Bldg, Choimbolyn Gudamj 6, 2nd Khoroo, Chingeltei District, Ulan Bator (POB 314, Ulan Bator 44); tel. 312107; fax 324450; e-mail zoosbank@mongol.net; f. 1999; cap. 1,073m. Exec. Dir SH. CHUDANJII.

Banking Associations

Bankers' Association: Ulan Bator; Pres. D. NYAMTSEREN; Chair. of Bd S. ORGODOL.

Mongolian Bankers Association: Ulan Bator; e-mail monba@ mongolnet.mn; Pres. LUVSANVANDANGIIN BOLD; Exec. Dir JIGJIDIIN ÜNENBAT.

STOCK EXCHANGE

Stock Exchange: Sükhbaataryn Talbai 2, Ulan Bator; tel. 310501; fax 325170; e-mail mse@magicnet.mn; internet www.mse.com.mn; f. 1991; Dir DULAMSÜRENGIIN DORLIGSÜREN.

INSURANCE

Agricultural Insurance Co: Nairamdal District, Ulan Bator; f. 1992; insurance of farm stock, equipment and buildings.

Mongol Daatgal (National Insurance and Reinsurance Co): Ikh Toiruu 11, Ulan Bator 28; tel. 313647; fax 313901; e-mail daatgal@ magicnet.mn; internet www.mongoldaatgal.mn; f. 1934; Chair. and CEO B. JARGALSAIKHAN; Snr Vice-Pres. J. BAT-ORSHIKH; Gen. Man. U. BYAMBASÜREN.

Trade and Industry

GOVERNMENT AGENCIES

Labour Co-ordination Directorate: Khuvisgalchdyn Gudamj 14, Ulan Bator; tel. and fax 327906; Dir D. GANKHÜÜ.

Mineral Resources Authority: Government Bldg 5, Barilgachdyn Talbai 13, Ulan Bator 211238; tel. and fax 310370; e-mail mram@ magicnet.mn; Dir D. JARGALSAIKHAN.

Mongol Gazryn Tos: Üildverchnii Gudamj, Ulan Bator 37; tel. 61584; e-mail petromon@magicnet.mn; supervises petroleum exploration and development; Dir O. DAVAASAMBUU.

State Industry and Trade Control Service: POB 38/66, Barilgachdyn Talbai, Ulan Bator 38; tel. and fax 328049; e-mail chalkhaajavd@mongolnet.mn; f. 2000; enforces laws and regulations relating to trade and industry, services, consumer rights, and geology and mining; Dir DAMBADARJAAGIIN CHALKHAAJAV.

State Property Committee: Government House 4, Ulan Bator 12; tel. 312460; fax 312798; internet odmaa@spc.gov.mn; supervision and privatization of state property; Chair. LKHANAASÜRENGIIN PÜR-EVDORJ.

State Resources Agency: Ulan Bator; management of reserves of agricultural produce; Dir (vacant).

DEVELOPMENT ORGANIZATIONS

Economics and Market Research Center: Government Bldg 11, J. Sambuugiin Gudamj 11, Ulan Bator 38; tel. 324258; fax 324620; e-mail emrc@mongolchamber.mm; internet www.mongolchamber .mn; Dir J. BOZKHÜÜKHEN.

Foreign Investment and Foreign Trade Agency (FIFTA): Government Bldg 1, J. Sambuugiin Gudamj 11, Ulan Bator; tel. 326040; fax 324076; e-mail fifta@investnet.mn; internet www.investnet.mn; Chair. BAASANKHÜÜGIIN GANZORIG.

Mongolian Business Development Agency: Yörönkhii said Amaryn Gudamj, Ulan Bator; CPO Box 458, Ulan Bator 13; tel. 311094; fax 311092; e-mail mbda@mongol.net; internet www .mbda-mongolia.org; f. 1994; Gen. Man. D. BAYARBAT.

CHAMBERS OF COMMERCE

Central Asian Chamber of Commerce: PO Box 470, Ulan Bator 44; tel. 38970; fax 311757; Chair. G. TÖMÖRMÖNKH.

Junior Chamber of Commerce: Youth Union Bldg, Ulan Bator; tel. 328694; Chair NATSAGDORJ.

Mongolian National Chamber of Commerce and Industry: Sambuugiin gudamj 11, Ulan Bator 38; tel. 312501; fax 324620; e-mail chamber@mongolchamber.mn; internet www .mongolchamber.mn; f. 1960; responsible for establishing economic and trading relations, contacts between trade and industrial organizations, both at home and abroad, and for generating foreign trade; organizes commodity inspection, press information, and international exhbns and fairs at home and abroad; registration of trademarks and patents; issues certificates of origin and of quality; Chair. SAMBUUGIIN DEMBEREL.

INDUSTRIAL AND TRADE ASSOCIATIONS

Association of Private Herders' Co-operatives: POB 21/787, Ulan Bator 211121; tel. 633601; fax 325935; e-mail mongolherder@ magicnet.mn; f. 1991; Pres. R. ERDENE.

Mongolian Farmers and Flour Producers' Association: AgroPro Business Centre, 19th Khoroo, Bayangol District, Ulan Bator 24; tel. 300114; fax 362875; e-mail agropro@magicnet.mn; f. 1997; research and quality inspection services in domestic farming and flour industry; Pres. SHARAVYN GUNGAADORJ.

Mongolian Franchising Council of the Mongolian National Chamber of Commerce and Industry: Ulan Bator; tel. 327178; fax 324620; e-mail tecd@mongolchamber.mn; Pres. BAATARYN CHADRAA.

Mongolian Marketing Association: Ulan Bator; Pres. D. DAGVADORJ.

Mongolian National Mining Association: Sky Plaza Centre, Olimpiin Gudamj 14, PO Box 46/910, Ulan Bator 210646; tel. 314877; fax 314877; e-mail mongma@mobinet.mn; internet www .owc.org.mn/monnma; f. 1994; provides members of the mining sector with legal protection, and reflects their views in Government mining policy and mineral sector development; Pres. DUGARYN JARGALSAIKHAN; Exec. Dir NAMGARYN ALGAA.

Mongolian Printing Works Association: Ulan Bator; Pres. G. KHAVCHUUR.

Mongolian Wool and Cashmere Federation: Khan-Uul District, Ulan Bator; tel. 341871; fax 342814; Pres. G. YONDONSAMBUU.

EMPLOYERS' ORGANIZATIONS

Employers' and Owners' United Association: Ulan Bator; Exec. Dir. B. SEMBEEJAV.

Federation of Business Professional Women of Mongolia: Ulan Bator 20; tel. and fax 315638; e-mail mbpw@mongolnet.mn; f. 1992; provides education, training, and opportunities for women to achieve economic independence, and the running of businesses; Pres. OCHIRBATYN ZAYAA; 7,000 mems, 14 brs.

Free Labour Managers' Association: Ulan Bator; Pres. N. PÜREVDORJ.

Immovable Property (Real Estate) Business Managers' Association: Ulan Bator; Pres. J. BYAMBADORJ.

Mongolian Management Association: Ulan Bator; Chair. Exec. Council DAGVADORJIIN TSERENDORJ.

Private Business Owners' Association: Ulan Bator; Pres. T. NYAMDORJ.

Private Employers' Association: Ulan Bator; Pres. O. NATSAGDORJ.

Private Industry Owners' Association: Ulan Bator; f. 1990; with 39 mems; Pres. LUVSANBALDANGIIN NYAMSAMBUU.

UTILITIES

Electricity

TsShSG: Ulan Bator; tel. 41294; supervision of electric power network in Ulan Bator; Dir D. BASSAIKHAN.

Water

DShSG: Ulan Bator; tel. 343047; supervision of hot water district heating network in Ulan Bator; Dir SHARAVYN BAASANJAV.

USAG: Khökh Tengeriin Gudamj 5, Ulan Bator 49; tel. 455055; fax 450120; e-mail usag@magicnet.mn; supervision of water supply network in Ulan Bator; Chair. OSORYN ERDENEBAATAR.

IMPORT AND EXPORT ORGANIZATIONS

Agrotekhimpeks: Ulan Bator 32; imports agricultural machinery and implements, seed, fertilizer, veterinary medicines and irrigation equipment.

Arisimpex: Ulan Bator 52; tel. 343007; fax 343008; exports hides and skins, fur and leather goods; imports machinery, chemicals and accessories for leather, fur and shoe industries; Pres. A. TSERENBALJID.

Avtoimpeks: Sonsgolon-2, Ulan Bator (POB 37, Ulan Bator 211137); tel. 331860; fax 331383; f. 1934; privatization pending 1999; imports of vehicles and spare parts, vehicle servicing; Exec. Dir Ts. TOGTMOL.

Barter and Border: Khuvisgalchdyn Örgön Chölöö, Ulan Bator 11; tel. 324848; barter and border trade operations.

Böönii Khudaldaa: Songinokhairkhan District, Ulan Bator; wholesale trader; privately-owned; Dir-Gen. OCHBADRAKHYN BALJINNYAM.

Khorshoololimpeks: Tolgoit 37, Ulan Bator (PO Box 262); tel. 332926; fax 331128; f. 1964; exports sub-standard skins, hides, wool and furs, handicrafts and finished products; imports equipment and materials for housing, and for clothing and leather goods; Dir L. ÖLZIIBUYAN.

Kompleksimport: Enkh Taivny Gudamj 7, Ulan Bator; tel. and fax 382718; f. 1963; imports consumer goods, foodstuffs, sets of equipment and turnkey projects; training of Mongolians abroad; state-owned pending privatization in 1999; cap. 3,500m. tögrög.

Makhimpeks: 4th Khoroo, Songinokhairkhan District, Ulan Bator; tel. 63247; fax 632517; e-mail makhimpex@mongol.net; f. 1946; abattoir, meat processing, canning, meat imports and exports; 51% share privatized in 1999; cap. 7,800m. tögrög; Dir H. BATTULGA.

Materialimpex: Teeverchdiin Gudamj 35, Ulan Bator 35; tel. 365125; fax 367904; e-mail miehnco@magicnet.mn; f. 1957; exports cashmere, wool products, animal skins; imports glass, roofing material, dyes, sanitary ware, metals and metalware, wallpaper, bitumen, wall and floor tiles; privatized Feb. 1999 (most shares state-owned); Gen. Dir B. ZORIG; 126 employees.

Mongoleksport Co Ltd: Government Bldg 7, 8th Floor, Erkh Chölöönii Talbai, Ulan Bator 11; tel. 329234; fax 324848; exports wool, hair, cashmere, mining products, antler, skins and hides; Dir-Gen. D. CHIMEDDAMBAA.

Mongolemimpex: Ikh Toiruu 39, Ulan Bator 28; tel. 323961; fax 323877; e-mail moemim@magicnet.mn; procurement and distribution to hospitals and pharmacies of drugs and surgical appliances; Dir-Gen. R. BYAMBAA.

Mongolimpeks: Khuvisgalchdyn Örgön Chölöö, Ulan Bator 11; tel. 326081; exports cashmere, camels' wool, hair, fur, casings, powdered blood and horn, antler, wheat gluten, alcoholic drinks, cashmere and camels' wool knitwear, blankets, copper concentrate, souvenirs, stamps and coins; imports light and mining industry machinery, scientific instruments, chemicals, pharmaceuticals and consumer goods; state-owned; Dir-Gen. DORJPALAMYN DÖKHÖMBAYAR.

Mongol Safari Co: Ulan Bator 38; tel. 360267; fax 360067; e-mail monsafari@magicnet.mn; exports hunting products; imports hunting equipment and technology; organizes hunting and trekking tours; Dir-Gen. U. BUYANDELGER.

Monnoos: POB 450, Ulan Bator 36; tel. 343201; fax 342591; e-mail monnoos@mongolnet.mn; wool trade enterprise; Dir SANJIIN BATOYUUN.

Monos Cosmetics: Sonsgolon Toiruu 5, Songinokhairkhan District 20, POB 62, Ulan Bator 211137; tel. 633257; fax 633117; e-mail monospharma@mongol.net; f. 1994; production, export and import of cosmetics.

Monospharma Co Ltd: Chingünjavyn gudamj 9, Bayangol District 2, Ulan Bator 210526; tel. and fax 361419; e-mail monospharma@ mongol.net; f. 1990; production, export and import of medicine, medical equipment and health food; Dir-Gen. L. KHÜRELBAATAR.

MTT (Mongol Transport Team): POB 582, Ulan Bator 21; tel. 689000; fax 684953; e-mail mtt@mtteam.mn; internet www.mtteam .mn; international freight forwarders by air, sea, rail and road; offices in Beijing, Berlin, Moscow and Prague.

NIK: Yörönkhii said Amaryn Gudamj, Ulan Bator 210620; POB B20 'A', Ulan Bator; tel. 321277; fax 327288; e-mail otgongerel@nic.com .mn; imports oil and oil products; Dir-Gen. P. TÜVSHINBAATAR.

Noosimpeks: Ulan Bator 52; tel. 342611; fax 343057; exports scoured sheep's wool, yarn, carpets, fabrics, blankets, mohair and felt boots; imports machinery and chemicals for wool industry.

Nüürs: Ulan Bator 21; tel. 327428; exports and imports in coal-mining field; Man. D. DÜGERJAV.

Packaging: Tolgoit, Ulan Bator; tel. 31053; exports raw materials of agricultural origin, sawn timber, consumer goods, unused spare parts and equipment, and non-ferrous scrap; imports machinery and materials for packaging industry, and consumer goods.

Raznoimpeks: 3rd Khoroo, Bayangol District, Ulan Bator 36; tel. 329465; fax 329901; f. 1933; exports wool, cashmere, hides, canned meat, powdered bone, alcoholic drinks, macaroni and confectionery; imports cotton and woollen fabrics, silk, knitwear, shoes, fresh and canned fruit, vegetables, tea, milk powder, acids, paints, safety equipment, protective clothing, printing and packaging paper; state-owned pending planned privatization of 51% share in 1999; cap. 6,100m. tögrög; Exec. Dir TS. BAT-ENKH.

Tekhnikimport: Ulan Bator; tel. 32336; imports machinery, instruments and spare parts for light, food, wood, building, power and mining industries, road-building and communications; state-owned; Dir-Gen. ERDENIIN GANBOLD.

Tushig Trade Co Ltd: Peace Ave, Ulan Bator 44, PO Box 481; tel. 314062; fax 314052; e-mail d.ganbaatar@mongol.net; exports sheep and camel wool, and cashmere goods; imports machinery for small enterprises, foodstuffs and consumer goods; Dir-Gen. D. GANBAATAR.

Tuushin Co Ltd: Yörönkhii said Amaryn Gudamj 2, Ulan Bator 210620; tel. and fax 325909; e-mail tuushin@magicnet.mn; f. 1990; international freight forwarders; transport and forwarding policy and services, warehousing, customs agent; tourism; offices in Beijing, Moscow and Prague; Dir-Gen. N. ZORIGT.

CO-OPERATIVES

Central Association of Consumer Co-operatives: Ulan Bator 20; tel. and fax 329025; f. 1990; wholesale and retail trade; exports animal raw materials; imports foodstuffs and consumer goods; Chair. G. MYANGANBAYAR.

Individual Herdsmen's Co-operatives Association: Ulan Bator; Pres. R. ERDENE.

Mongolian Co-operatives Development Centre: Ulan Bator; Dir DANZANGIIN RADNAARAGCHAA.

Mongolian Producer Co-operatives Central Association: Ulan Bator; Pres. CHOGSOMJAVYN BURIAD.

Mongolian United Association of Savings and Credit Co-operatives: Ulan Bator; Pres. TSERENDORJIIN GANKHUYAG.

National Association of Mongolian Agricultural Co-operatives: Enkh Taivny Gudamj 11, Ulan Bator; tel. and fax 358671; Pres. N. NADMID.

Union of Mongolian Production and Services Co-operatives: POB 470, Ulan Bator 210646; tel. 328446; fax 329669; f. 1990; Pres. of Supreme Council (vacant).

TRADE UNIONS

Confederation of Mongolian Trade Unions: Sükhbaataryn Talbai 3, Ulan Bator 11; tel. 327253; fax 322128; brs throughout the country; Chair. GORCHINSÜRENGIIN ADYAA; International Relations Adviser TS. NATSAGDORJ; 450,000 mems (1994).

'Khökh Mongol' (Blue Mongolia) Free Trade Unions: Ulan Bator; f. 1991 by Mongolian Democratic Union; Leader SH. TÖMÖR-BAATAR.

United Association of Free Trade Unions: f. 1990; Pres. SH. DORJPAGMA.

Transport

RAILWAYS

In 1999 the Mongolian Railway had a total track length of 1,815 km. In 1990 it carried 2.6m. passengers and 14.5m. tons of freight (about 70% of total freight traffic). However, traffic by rail later declined, owing to fuel shortages; in 1991 rail freight carriage was 10.3m. tons, falling to 8.6m. tons in 1992. In 2001 the railway carried 4.5m.

passengers, and 10.1m. tons of freight (about 86% of total freight traffic) was transported by rail.

Ulan Bator Railway: POB 376, Ulan Bator 13; tel. 944401; fax 328360; e-mail slc-mr@magicnet.mn; internet www.mtz.mn; joint-stock co with Russian Federation; Dir RADNAABAZARYN RAASH; First Dep. Dir N. BATMÖNKH.

External Lines: from the Russian frontier at Naushki/Sükhbaatar (connecting with the Trans-Siberian Railway) to Ulan Bator and on to the Chinese frontier at Zamyn-Üüd/Erenhot, connecting with Beijing (total length 1,110 km).

Branches: from Darkhan to Sharyn Gol coalfield (length 63 km); branch from Salkhit near Darkhan, westwards to Erdenet (Erdenet-iin-ovoo open-cast copper mine) in Bulgan Province (164 km); from Bagakhangai to Baganuur coal-mine, south-east of Ulan Bator (96 km); from Khar Airag to Bor-Öndör fluorspar mines (60 km); from Sainshand to Züünbayan oilfield (63 km).

Eastern Railway, linking Mongolia with the Trans-Siberian and Chita via Borzya; from the Russian frontier at Solovyevsk to Choibalsan (238 km), with branch from Chingis Dalan to Mardai uranium mine near Dashbalbar (110 km).

IFFC (International Freight-forwarding Centre)): 2/F Ulan Bator Railway Building, Ulan Bator, CPO Box 376; tel. 312509; fax 313165; e-mail iffc@magicnet.mn; international freight forwarding.

Mongoltrans: Khan-Uul District, Ulan Bator; POB 373, Ulan Bator 211121; tel. 312281; fax 320185; e-mail montrans@magicnet.mn; internet www.magicnet.mn/montrans; rail freight forwarding; offices in Beijing and Moscow; Dir-Gen. B. MYAGMAR.

ROADS

Main roads link Ulan Bator with the Chinese frontier at Zamyn üüd/Erenhot and with the Russian frontier at Altanbulag/Kyakhta. A road from Chita in Russia crosses the frontier in the east at Mangut/Onon (Ölzii) and branches for Choibalsan and Öndörkhaan. In the west and north-west, roads from Biisk and Irkutsk in Russia go to Tsagaannuur, Bayan-Ölgii aimag, and Khankh, on Lake Khövsgöl, respectively. The total length of 'improved' roads was 3,453.5 km in 2000, and the total length of asphalted roads was 1,567.4 km. The first section of a hard-surfaced road between Ulan Bator and Bayankhongor was completed in 1975. The road from Darkhan to Erdenet was also to be surfaced. Mongolia divides its road system into state-grade and country-grade roads. State-grade roads run from Ulan Bator to provincial centres and from provincial centres to the border. There are 11,200 km of state-grade roads, of which 10% are hard-surfaced and a further 13% gravel-surfaced. Country-grade roads (also 13% gravel-surfaced) account for the remaining 38,000 km, but they are mostly rough cross-country tracks.

To mark the millennium, the Government decided to construct a new east–west road, linking the Chinese and Russian border regions via Ölgii, Lake Khar Us, Zavkhan and Arkhangai provinces, Dashinchilen, Lün, Ulan Bator, Nailakh, Baganuur, and Öndörkhaan and Sümber. Construction was expected to take about 10 years, but because of the cost, the road was not expected to be surfaced for the whole length.

According to a vehicle census reported in December 2000, Mongolia had 81,693 motor vehicles, including 24,671 goods vehicles, 1,683 tankers, 2,740 specialized vehicles (such as ambulances and fire engines), 8,548 buses and trolleybuses, and 44,051 cars. Of these vehicles, 57,814 were privately owned.

There are bus services in Ulan Bator and other large towns, and road haulage services throughout the country on the basis of motor transport depots, mostly situated in provincial centres. However, in some years services have been truncated, owing to fuel shortages.

INLAND WATERWAYS

Water transport plies Lake Khövsgöl and the River Selenge (397 km navigable) in the northern part of the country. Tugs and barges on Lake Khövsgöl transport goods brought in by road to Khankh from Russia to Khatgal on the southern shore.

CIVIL AVIATION

Civil aviation in Mongolia, including the provision of air traffic control and airport management, is the responsibility of the Civil Aviation Directorate of the Ministry of Infrastructure Development. It supervises the Mongolian national airline (MIAT) and smaller operators such as Khangarid and Tengeriin Ulaach, which operate local flights. There are scheduled services to Ulan Bator (Buyant-Ukhaa) by Aeroflot (Russia) and Air China.

Director-General of Civil Aviation: MANJIIN DAGVA.

Blue Sky Aviation: POB 932, Ulan Bator 13; tel. 312085; fax 322857; e-mail bsa@whizzmail.com; Jt venture of Mission Aviation Fellowship and Exodus International; operates charter flights and medical emergency services; Dir PAAVO KILPI; Operations Man. JAVKHLANTÖGSIIN GANBAATAR.

Khangarid: Room 210, MPRP Bldg, Baga Toiruu 37/1, Ulan Bator; tel. 379935; fax 379973; domestic and international passenger and freight services; Dir L. SERGELEN.

Mongolian Civil Air Transport (MIAT): Buyant-Ukhaa, Ulan Bator; tel. 379935; fax 379919; internet www.miat.com; f. 1956; scheduled services to Moscow, Irkutsk, Beijing, Seoul, Osaka, Berlin, Höhhot, and to some Mongolian provincial centres; in 2000 MIAT carried some 250,000 passengers and 3,000 tons of freight, and operated 10 aircraft on scheduled services; Dir LUTYN SANDAG.

Tengeriin Ulaach Shine: Buyant-Ukhaa 34-17, Khan-Uul District, Ulan Bator; tel. 983043; fax 379765; internal transport for tourists and businesspeople; Dir L. TÖMÖR.

Tourism

A foreign tourist service bureau was established in 1954, but tourism is not very developed. There are 12 hotels for foreign tourists in Ulan Bator, with some 1,500 beds, and the outlying tourist centres (Terelj, South Gobi, Öndör-Dov and Khujirt) have basic facilities. The country's main attractions are its scenery, wildlife and historical relics. There were 192,051 foreign visitors to Mongolia in 2001, of whom 31,978 had tourist visas. Tourist receipts totalled US $28m. in 1999. Tourism profits in 2002 amounted to US $102.9m., or 10.2% of GDP.

Juulchin Tourism Corporation of Mongolia: Chingis Khaan Avenue 5B, Ulan Bator 210543; tel. 328428; fax 320246; e-mail juulchin@Mongol.net; internet www.mongoljuulchin.mn; f. 1954; offices in Berlin, New Jersey, Beijing, Tokyo, Osaka and Seoul; Exec. Dir S. NERGÜI; Chair. B. DELGERSÜREN.

National Centre for Tourism: Ulan Bator; supervises 57 camps in the main tourist areas; Dir D. KHALIUN.

National Travel and Tourism Agency: Ministry of Infrastructure, Ulan Bator; internet www.mongoliatourism.gov.mn; Dir (vacant).

MOROCCO

Introductory Survey

Location, Climate, Language, Religion, Flag, Capital

The Kingdom of Morocco is situated in the extreme north-west of Africa. It has a long coastline on the shores of the Atlantic Ocean and, east of the Strait of Gibraltar, on the Mediterranean Sea, facing southern Spain. Morocco's eastern frontier is with Algeria, while to the south lies the disputed territory of Western Sahara (under Moroccan occupation), which has a lengthy Atlantic coastline and borders Mauritania to the east and south. Morocco's climate is semi-tropical. It is warm and sunny on the coast, while the plains of the interior are intensely hot in summer. Average temperatures are 27°C (81°F) in summer and 7°C (45°F) in winter for Rabat, and 38°C (101°F) and 4°C (40°F) respectively for Marrakesh. The rainy season in the north is from November to April. The official language is Arabic, but a large minority speak Berber. Spanish is widely spoken in the northern regions, and French in the rest of Morocco. The established religion is Islam, and most of the country's inhabitants are Muslims. There are Christian and Jewish minorities. The national flag (proportions 2 by 3) is red, with a green pentagram (intersecting lines in the form of a five-pointed star), known as 'Solomon's Seal', in the centre. The capital is Rabat.

Recent History

In 1912, under the terms of the Treaty of Fez, most of Morocco became a French protectorate, while a smaller Spanish protectorate was instituted in the north and far south of the country. Spain also retained control of Spanish Sahara (now Western Sahara), and Tangier became an international zone in 1923. A nationalist movement developed in Morocco during the 1930s and 1940s, led by the Istiqlal (Independence) grouping, and on 2 March 1956 the French protectorate achieved independence as the Sultanate of Morocco. Sultan Muhammad V, who had reigned since 1927 (although he had been temporarily removed from office by the French authorities between 1953 and 1955), became the first Head of State. The northern zone of the Spanish protectorate joined the new state in April 1956, and Tangier's international status was abolished in October. The southern zone of the Spanish protectorate was ceded to Morocco in 1958, but no agreement was reached on the enclaves of Ceuta and Melilla, in the north, the Ifni region in the south, or the Saharan territories to the south of Morocco, which all remained under Spanish control. The Sultan was restyled King of Morocco in August 1957, and became Prime Minister in May 1960. He died in February 1961, and was succeeded by his son, Moulay Hassan, who took the title of Hassan II.

For the first 13 years of his reign King Hassan's position was unstable. Successive Constitutions attempted to balance royal power with demands for greater political freedom. Elections to Morocco's first House of Representatives took place in May 1963, and six months later the King relinquished the post of Prime Minister. In June 1965, however, increasing political fragmentation prompted Hassan to declare a 'state of exception', and to resume full legislative and executive powers. The emergency provisions remained in force until July 1970, when a new Constitution was approved. Elections in the following month resulted in a pro-Government majority in the new Chamber of Representatives.

In July 1971 an attempted *coup d'état* was suppressed by forces loyal to the King. Among those subsequently arrested were numerous members of the left-wing Union nationale des forces populaires (UNFP), five of whom were sentenced to death. In August 1972 air force personnel attempted to shoot down an aircraft in which Hassan was travelling. Among those implicated in the plot was Gen. Muhammad Oufkir, the Minister of National Defence and head of the armed forces, who committed suicide soon afterwards.

Although a revised Constitution had been approved in March 1972 by popular referendum, a general election did not take place until June 1977. Two-thirds of the deputies in the Chamber of Representatives were directly elected, the remainder being elected by local government councils, professional associations and labour organizations. Supporters of the King's policies won a majority of seats in the new legislature.

A Government of national unity was formed, including opposition representatives from Istiqlal and the Mouvement populaire (MP) in addition to the pro-monarchist independents.

In October 1981, when it was announced that the term of office of the Chamber of Representatives was to be extended from four to six years, all 14 deputies belonging to the Union socialiste des forces populaires (USFP) withdrew from the assembly. Elections to the legislature were postponed further in November 1983, owing to the Western Sahara dispute (see below). Meanwhile, an interim Government of national unity was appointed, headed by Muhammad Karim Lamrani (Prime Minister in 1971–72). The new Government included members of the six main political parties: Istiqlal, the MP, the Parti national démocrate (PND), the Rassemblement national des indépendants (RNI), the Union constitutionnelle (UC) and the USFP. The postponed legislative elections took place in September and October 1984. Despite significant gains by the USFP, the Chamber of Representatives was again dominated by the centre-right parties. A new Cabinet, appointed in April 1985, included members of the MP, the PND, the RNI and the UC. Lamrani resigned in September 1986, on grounds of ill health, and was replaced by Az ad-Dine Laraki (hitherto Deputy Prime Minister and Minister of National Education).

In March 1992 King Hassan announced that the Constitution was to be revised and submitted for approval in a national referendum, in preparation for legislative elections (which had been postponed since 1990, pending settlement of the Western Sahara dispute). The King indicated in July that the legislative elections would take place in November, and that voting would be extended to include Western Sahara—irrespective of the UN's progress in organizing a referendum on the territory's status (see below). In August the King dissolved the Government, and named Lamrani as Prime Minister in an interim, non-partisan Government. According to official results, the revised Constitution was overwhelmingly endorsed by 99.96% of those who voted (97.29% of the electorate) in the national referendum, which was held in September; approval was officially reported to be unanimous in major cities and in three of the four provinces of Western Sahara. Under the terms of the new Constitution, the King would retain strong executive powers, including the right to appoint the Prime Minister, although the nomination of government members would henceforth be the prerogative of the premier. The Government would be required to reflect the composition of the Chamber of Representatives, and was obliged to submit its legislative programme for the Chamber's approval; new legislation would automatically be promulgated one month after having been endorsed by parliament, regardless of whether royal assent had been received. Provision was also made for the establishment of a Constitutional Council and of an Economic and Social Council, and guarantees of human rights were enshrined in the document.

Legislative elections eventually took place on 25 June 1993. Parties of the Bloc démocratique—grouping Istiqlal, the USFP, the Parti du progrès et du socialisme (PPS), the Organisation de l'action démocratique et populaire (OADP) and the UNFP—won a combined total of 99 of the 222 directly elective seats in the enlarged chamber. (Within the Bloc, the USFP won 48 seats, and Istiqlal 43.) The MP won 33 seats, the RNI 28, and the UC 27. The indirect election (by an electoral college) of the remaining 111 members of the Chamber, which followed on 17 September, was less favourable to the Bloc démocratique, which won only 21 further seats. Of the 333 seats in the Chamber, the USFP now controlled 56, the UC 54, Istiqlal 52, the MP 51, and the RNI 41. The USFP and Istiqlal protested against irregularities in the procedure of the electoral college voting, and demanded the annulment of the indirect election results. Abd ar-Rahman el-Youssoufi subsequently resigned as First Secretary of the USFP, purportedly in protest at the conduct of the electoral college. In October the USFP and Istiqlal rejected an invitation to participate in a coalition government with the loyalist, centre-right parties of the Entente nationale (which controlled the largest number of seats in the Chamber of Representatives), objecting to King Hassan's insistence that the post of Prime Minister and responsibility for foreign affairs, justice and the interior should not be conferred upon opposition groups since they lacked experience of government. In November the King reappointed Lamrani as premier. The new Government comprised technocrats and independents, and did not include any representatives of the parties that had contested the legislative elections. (By-elections took place in April 1994 in 14 constituencies—in all but one of which the Constitutional Council had annulled results of the previous year's legislative elections.)

In December 1993 the Conseil Consultatif des Droits de l'Homme (CCDH), established by the King in April 1990, substantiated allegations made by human rights organizations of the 'disappearance' and detention of political activists; however, it denied the existence of secret detention centres. King Hassan granted an amnesty for 424 (mostly political) prisoners in July 1994: among those released were Morocco's longest serving political detainee and about 100 members of the proscribed Islamist movement Al Adl wa-'l Ihsan (Justice and Charity).

In May 1994 Hassan replaced Lamrani with Abd al-Latif Filali, hitherto Minister of State for Foreign Affairs and Co-operation. Although the new Prime Minister held consultations with the political groupings represented in parliament, the composition of the new Government (in which he retained the foreign affairs portfolio) was effectively unchanged. In July the King appealed to all political parties to participate in a government of national unity, and in October he announced his intention to select a premier from the ranks of the opposition. However, negotiations on the formation of a coalition government failed, apparently owing to the Bloc démocratique's refusal to join an administration in which Driss Basri (a long-serving government member and close associate of the King) remained as Minister of the Interior and Information, and in January 1995 Hassan instructed Filali to form a new cabinet. The interior and information portfolios were, notably, separated in the new Government: Basri remained Minister of the Interior, while Driss Alaoui M'Daghri, regarded as a 'liberal' technocrat, took responsibility for the restyled Ministry of Communications.

Muhammad Basri, a prominent opposition figure (sentenced to death *in absentia* in 1974) and founder member of both the UNFP and the USFP, returned to Morocco from France in June 1995, after 28 years in exile. It was widely believed that his rehabilitation had been precipitated by the royal amnesty of July 1994 and by the return to Morocco (also from France) in May 1995 of el-Youssoufi, both of which seemed to indicate a greater level of political tolerance on the part of the Moroccan authorities. In December Abd as-Salam Yassin, the leader of Al Adl wa-'l Ihsan, was briefly released after six years of house arrest, but restrictions on his movement were reinstated after Yassin criticized the Government. Despite the King's assertion that there were no longer any political detainees in Morocco, a report published by the Association marocaine des droits de l'homme (AMDH) in February 1996 claimed that 58 political prisoners (primarily radical Islamists, supporters of independence for Western Sahara and left-wing activists) remained in detention.

In August 1996 the King presented further constitutional amendments, including the creation of an indirectly elected second parliamentary assembly, the Chamber of Advisers, and the introduction of direct elections for all members of the Chamber of Representatives. Most political parties supported the reforms; however, an appeal by the OADP leadership for a boycott of a planned referendum on the amendments led to a split in the party and the subsequent creation of the Parti socialiste démocratique (PSD). According to official results, 83.0% of the electorate participated in the referendum, held in September, with the reforms being approved by 99.6% of voters. Legislation regarding the new bicameral parliament was promulgated in August 1997: the Chamber of Representatives was to comprise 325 members, directly elected for a five-year term; the 270 members of the Chamber of Advisers would be indirectly elected, for a nine-year term, by local councils (which would chose 162 members), chambers of commerce (81) and trade unions (27). Earlier that month a new Cabinet had been named, following the resignation, at the King's behest, of numerous ministers with formal party affiliation in preparation for the forthcoming legislative elections.

At elections to the Chamber of Representatives, held on 14 November 1997, the Bloc démocratique won a combined total of 102 seats (of which the USFP took 57 and Istiqlal 32); the

Entente nationale took 100 (50 secured by the UC, 40 by the MP), and centrist parties 97 (including 46 obtained by the RNI). The Mouvement populaire constitutionnel et démocratique (MPCD), which earlier in the year had formally absorbed members of the Islamist Al Islah wa Attajdid, won nine seats, securing parliamentary representation for the first time. (In October 1998 the MPCD changed its name to the Parti de la justice et du développement—PJD.) According to official results, 58.3% of the eligible electorate participated in the poll. At indirect elections to the Chamber of Advisers, which followed on 5 December, centrist parties won 90 of the seats (42 secured by the RNI, 33 by the Mouvement démocratique et social), the Entente nationale 76 (28 obtained by the UC, 27 by the MP) and the Bloc démocratique 44 (21 won by Istiqlal). In February 1998 the King appointed Abd ar-Rahman el-Youssoufi, of the USFP, as the new Prime Minister, in an apparent attempt to appease opposition parties dissatisfied with the outcome of the legislative elections. This was the first time since independence that a socialist had been appointed to the Moroccan premiership. In March a new Cabinet was formed, including members of the USFP, the RNI, Istiqlal, the PPS, the Mouvement nationale populaire (MNP), the Front des forces démocratiques and the PSD. Driss Basri remained Minister of State for the Interior, while former Prime Minister Filali retained the foreign affairs portfolio: Filali was removed from the Government (after 14 years in this post) in April 1999, when he was replaced by Muhammad Benaissa of the RNI.

King Hassan died on 23 July 1999, after several years of ill health. His eldest son, Crown Prince Sidi Muhammad, succeeded as King Muhammad VI. At the end of July the new King decreed an amnesty whereby some 8,000 prisoners were freed and more than 38,000 had their sentences reduced. In August the King ordered the creation within the CCDH of an independent commission to determine levels of compensation for families of missing people and for those subjected to arbitrary detention. In April the CCDH had announced that it had been agreed to compensate the families of 112 people who were now officially acknowledged as having 'disappeared' between 1960 and 1990. Independent Moroccan human rights organizations asserted that the number of missing people amounted to almost 600.

In September 1999 King Muhammad approved the return to Morocco of Abraham Serfaty, a left-wing dissident who had been deported to France in 1991; Serfaty had been granted a passport by the el-Youssoufi administration in 1998, but his return had not been authorized. The family of former opposition leader Mehdi Ben Barka, who had been abducted and subsequently murdered in Paris, France, in 1965, was also permitted to return to Morocco in November. In January 2000 the location was apparently revealed of Ben Barka's burial site, beneath the Courcouronnes mosque in Paris—which was constructed in the mid-1980s with finance from King Hassan II. The French Prime Minister, Lionel Jospin, announced an end to the ban on access to archives where documents relating to the abduction and murder were kept, and later that month a French judge reopened an inquiry into the disappearance of four men who had been convicted *in absentia* in 1967 of the kidnap of Ben Barka and were believed to have fled to Morocco.

Meanwhile, in November 1999 King Muhammad dismissed the long-serving Minister of State for the Interior, Driss Basri. Basri's removal from office, apparently in response to the violent suppression of protests in Western Sahara in September (see below) was interpreted as a particularly important step towards the modernization of Moroccan society. The new Minister of the Interior, Ahmed Midaoui (a former Director of National Security), immediately pledged to work towards the strengthening of democracy and the reconciliation of the administration and the people of Morocco. Victims of repression and their families, together with left wing political parties and non-governmental organizations, subsequently formed a 'Justice and Trust' organization, which aimed to investigate human rights abuses in Morocco since independence. In April 2000 the Government commenced payments, reportedly totalling 40m. dirhams, in respect of the cases of an initial 40 victims of arbitrary detention, from the fund established in the previous year. Abd as-Salam Yassin—who earlier in the year had published a letter addressed to King Muhammad in which he vehemently criticized the reign of Hassan II and appealed to the new King to relinquish his father's assets abroad in order to pay off the national debt—was released from house arrest in May.

In early 2000, at the behest of the King, the Government introduced a programme of social reforms, a principal outcome of which would be vastly to improve the social status and legal rights of Moroccan women. Under the 'national action plan', the minimum age of marriage for a woman was to be raised from 15 to 18, polygamy would only be allowed with the permission of the first wife, and women would have equal judicial rights to divorce and to receive a fair division of marital assets. The plan provoked outrage among Islamists, who claimed it would lead to the disintegration of the traditional family and the destruction of Islamic values.

None the less, the Moroccan authorities continued to deal harshly with dissent. In June 2000 more than 40 people were injured, and over 100 arrested, as a result of clashes when security forces used violent methods to disperse an unauthorized protest by unemployed university graduates in Rabat. Some 13 members of Al Adl wa-'l Ihsan were sentenced in November to two years detention for their part in the riots. Meanwhile, in July 49 members of Al Adl wa-'l Ihsan were arrested after security forces broke up a beach camp organized by the movement north of the capital at Mahdia; in subsequent months further planned camps were either dispersed or prevented, and arrests of Al Adl wa-'l Ihsan members continued in large numbers. In December, on the occasion of UN Human Rights Day, security forces used violence to break up numerous protests nation-wide, including demonstrations in the capital organized by the AMDH and Al Adl wa-'l Ihsan. Among some 800 people reportedly arrested were Yassin's wife and daughter. More than 300 people subsequently appeared in court on charges of disturbing public order, and during early 2001 over 100 were sentenced to terms of imprisonment ranging from three months to two years.

Meanwhile, in September 2000 King Muhammad effected a cabinet reorganization, reducing the number of ministerial portfolios from 43 to 33. Notably, the leader of Istiqlal, Abbas el-Fassi, was appointed Minister of Social Development, Solidarity, Employment and Vocational Training. Shortly afterwards indirect elections were held to renew one-third of the seats in the Chamber of Advisers. The RNI won 14 of the 90 seats available, the MNP 12 and the PND 10, with the remaining 54 seats divided among smaller parties.

In March 2001 King Muhammad announced the establishment of a royal commission to revise the country's laws on personal rights and responsibilities; the commission was to be chaired by the First President of the Supreme Court, Driss Dahak, and included leading Islamic scholars and jurists. Meanwhile, the King continued to demonstrate a commitment to greater rights for Moroccan women by appointing women to posts of royal advisers, ambassadors and other senior public offices. In July King Muhammad announced his intention to create a royal institute charged with preserving the language and culture of the country's Berber population, which would also work towards the integration of the Berber language into the education system; the institute was duly established in October. In September Muhammad appointed Driss Jettou, a former Minister of Finance and Industry, as Minister of the Interior; Ahmed Midaoui became an adviser to the King.

In June 2001 the Moroccan authorities granted Jean-Baptiste Parlos, the French judge leading the inquiry into the Ben Barka affair (see above), permission to visit Morocco as part of his investigation. Later that month Ahmed Boukhari, a former member of the Moroccan special services, alleged in an article published in *Le Journal* and in the French daily *Le Monde* that Ben Barka had been kidnapped in Paris by French police-officers in the employ of the Moroccan secret service and taken to a chateau in the south of the city where he died after being tortured by Morocco's then Minister of the Interior, Gen. Muhammad Oufkir; Ben Barka's body was subsequently smuggled out of France in a Moroccan military aircraft and was dissolved in a tank of acid at a torture and detention centre in Rabat. According to Boukhari the bodies of many opponents of King Hassan's regime had been disposed of in this way during the 1960s. The USFP's political bureau demanded that legal proceedings be commenced against Boukhari and the other special services operatives named in his confession, while the Organisation marocaine des droits de l'homme (OMDH) and the AMDH demanded that the Moroccan Government establish an inquiry into the affair. In mid-July 2001 Boukhari received a summons to appear before the French investigation into Ben Barka's disappearance; however, the Moroccan authorities refused to grant Boukhari a passport, and in the following

month Boukhari was arrested on charges of cashing cheques for which he had insufficient funds. Boukhari's detention was condemned by human rights organizations, which claimed that the Moroccan Government was attempting to prevent Boukhari from testifying at the Parlos inquiry. In late August Boukhari was sentenced to one year's imprisonment, although in mid-October the sentence was reduced on appeal to three months and he was released the following month. Three former Moroccan secret service agents cited in Boukhari's revelations announced their intention to sue him for defamation, and in mid-December, after he was found guilty of the charges by a court in Casablanca, he was again imprisoned for three months and ordered to pay compensation of 300,000 dirhams. In December 2002 the Moroccan authorities announced that they would co-operate fully with the French investigation into the Ben Barka affair, and in January 2003 a French judge travelled to Rabat where he interviewed Boukhari about the disappearance of Ben Barka.

In late January 2002, el-Youssoufi stated that he would stand down as Prime Minister after the legislative elections scheduled for September, but would remain Secretary-General of the USFP. In March the Government agreed a number of changes to the electoral system, including the abandonment of the simple majority system in favour of proportional representation. The Government insisted that the new system would reduce fraudulent practices and increase public confidence in the electoral process; at least 10% of the 325 seats in the lower house were to be reserved for women. The general election took place on 27 September 2002. According to official figures, the USFP won the largest number of seats, although its representation in the Chamber of Representatives was reduced from 57 to 50 seats. Istiqlal increased its parliamentary representation to 48 members, while the PJD took 42 seats, the RNI 41, the MP 27, the MNP 18 and the UC 16. The rate of voter participation was recorded at just 51.6% of the electorate. In early October King Muhammad appointed Jettou as the new Prime Minister, and a new Government was announced the following month. Despite securing the third highest number of seats in the Chamber of Representatives, the PJD was not allocated any ministerial portfolios. The new Cabinet comprised members of the USFD, Istiqlal, the RNI, the MNP, the MP and the PPS, as well as a number of non-affiliated technocrats—one of whom, Al Mustapha Sahel, replaced Jettou as Minister of the Interior. Three women were appointed to the Government.

In mid-May 2003 up to 30 bystanders were killed, and some 100 others injured, in a series of suicide bombings launched against Western targets in Casablanca. At least 30 suspected Islamists were arrested in the days following the attacks and King Muhammad pledged to carry out a full and transparent investigation into the incidents.

Following the cession of the Spanish enclave of Ifni to Morocco in 1969, political opinion in Morocco was united in opposing the continued occupation by Spain of areas considered to be historically parts of Moroccan territory: namely Spanish Sahara and Spanish North Africa (q.v.)—a number of small enclaves on Morocco's Mediterranean coast. A campaign to annex Spanish Sahara, initiated in 1974, received active support from all Moroccan political parties. In October 1975 King Hassan ordered a 'green march' by more than 300,000 unarmed Moroccans to occupy the territory. The marchers were stopped by the Spanish authorities when they had barely crossed the border, but in November Spain agreed to cede the territory to Morocco and Mauritania, to be apportioned equally between them. Spain formally relinquished sovereignty of Spanish Sahara in February 1976. Moroccan troops moved into the territory to confront a guerrilla uprising led by the Frente Popular para la Liberación de Saguia el-Hamra y Río de Oro (the Polisario Front), a national liberation movement supported by Algeria and (later) Libya which aimed to achieve an independent Western Saharan state. On 27 February the Polisario Front declared the 'Sahrawi Arab Democratic Republic' (SADR), and shortly afterwards established a 'Government-in-exile' in Algeria. In protest, Morocco severed diplomatic relations with Algeria.

Moroccan troops inflicted heavy casualties on the insurgents, and ensured the security of Western Sahara's main population centres, but they failed to prevent constant infiltration, harassment and sabotage by Polisario forces. Moreover, Polisario had considerable success against Mauritanian troops, and in August 1979 Mauritania renounced its claim to Saharan territory and signed a peace treaty with the Polisario Front. Morocco immediately asserted its claim to the whole of Western Sahara and annexed the region.

In July 1980 the SADR applied to join the Organization of African Unity (OAU—now African Union, see p. 130) as a sovereign state. Although 26 of the 50 members then recognized the Polisario Front as the rightful government of Western Sahara, Morocco insisted that a two-thirds' majority was needed to confer membership. Morocco rejected an OAU proposal for a cease-fire and a referendum on the territory, and in 1981 heavy fighting resumed in the region. The SADR was accepted as the OAU's 51st member in early 1982, but a threat by 18 members to leave the organization in protest necessitated a compromise whereby the SADR, while remaining a member, agreed not to attend OAU meetings. In late 1984 an SADR delegation did attend a summit meeting of the OAU with little opposition from other states, causing Morocco to resign from the organization. Meanwhile, fighting continued in Western Sahara; decisive victories for Polisario proved impossible, however, as Morocco constructed a 2,500-km defensive wall of sand, equipped with electronic detectors, to surround Western Sahara.

In October 1985 Morocco announced a unilateral cease-fire in Western Sahara, and invited the UN to supervise a referendum to be held there the following January. The Moroccan Government refused to accede to the Polisario Front's demand for direct negotiations with Morocco before a referendum could proceed. A series of indirect talks between the two sides, arranged by the UN and the OAU in 1986–87, failed to achieve a solution, and in January 1988 Polisario forces renewed their offensive against Moroccan positions in Western Sahara. In August, however, it was announced that the Polisario Front and Morocco had provisionally accepted a peace plan proposed by the UN Secretary-General, Javier Pérez de Cuéllar, which envisaged the conclusion of a formal cease-fire, a reduction in Moroccan military forces in Western Sahara and the withdrawal of Polisario forces to their bases, to be followed by a referendum on self-determination in Western Sahara. A list of eligible voters was to be based on the Spanish census of 1974. Implementation of the peace process was impeded by a renewed Polisario offensive in September 1988, and Muhammad Abd al-Aziz, President of the SADR, reiterated that the peace plan was accepted in principle only and that direct negotiations with Morocco were still necessary. A meeting in Marrakesh in January 1989 between King Hassan and officials of the Polisario Front and the SADR—the first direct contact for 13 years—was apparently limited to exchanges of goodwill, but was followed, in February, by the announcement of a unilateral cease-fire by Polisario. A further meeting was postponed by Hassan, who in September rejected the possibility of official negotiations with the SADR; later that month Polisario renewed its military attacks on Moroccan positions.

UN Security Council Resolution No. 690 of April 1991 established a peace-keeping force, the UN Mission for the Referendum in Western Sahara (MINURSO, see p. 64), which was to implement the 1988 plan for a referendum on self-determination. In June 1991 Polisario agreed to a formal cease-fire, with effect from 6 September, from which date the 2,000-strong MINURSO delegation would undertake its duties in the region. The cease-fire came into effect as scheduled, and the MINURSO deployment began. Reports at this time suggested that some 30,000 people had entered Western Sahara from Morocco, prompting claims that the Moroccan authorities were attempting to alter the region's demography in advance of the referendum. It was also reported that more than 170,000 Sahrawi who had fled the region since 1976 were being repatriated in order that they might participate in the referendum. By November 1991 only 200 MINURSO personnel had been deployed in Western Sahara, and the peace process was undermined further by Morocco's failure to withdraw any of its forces from the region (under the terms of the cease-fire agreement, Morocco was to have withdrawn one-half of its 130,000 troops from Western Sahara by mid-September). In December Johannes Manz, the Secretary-General's Special Representative (appointed to oversee MINURSO) resigned stating that the timetable for the referendum and the funding allocated to the peace process were inadequate. A Pakistani diplomatist, Lt-Gen. (retd) Sahabzada Yaqub Khan, was appointed to succeed Manz in March 1992. In May Pérez de Cuéllar's successor as UN Secretary-General, Dr Boutros Boutros-Ghali, announced that Morocco and Polisario representatives were to begin indirect talks under his auspices. In the same month, however, Morocco appeared to prejudge the result of the proposed referendum by

including the population of Western Sahara in the voting lists for its own regional and local elections. In June the SADR Government, which by this time was recognized by 75 countries, appealed to the international community and the UN to condemn alleged Moroccan violations of the cease-fire and to exert pressure for the implementation of the UN peace plan. UN-sponsored negotiations in the USA in September failed to formulate acceptable criteria for the drafting of lists of eligible voters at an eventual referendum.

In March 1993 the UN Security Council approved plans for the holding of the referendum on Western Sahara by the end of the year. In July the first direct negotiations took place between the Moroccan Government and Polisario, although little progress was achieved. In September, in a reorganization of the SADR Government, Bouchraya Hammoudi Bayoune replaced Mahfoud Ali Beïba as Prime Minister.

In March 1994 Boutros-Ghali submitted a report to the UN Security Council detailing possible procedures for overcoming the impasse on the Western Saharan issue, including the effective withdrawal of the UN from the peace process. (It had been reported in September 1993 that only 360 of the proposed 2,000 UN military personnel were in place.) The Security Council subsequently agreed to a continuation of negotiations for a further three months, and undertook to review the future of MINURSO if a referendum was not organized before the end of the year. In April Polisario accepted the UN programme for the registration of voters. However, the work of a UN voter identification commission, which had been due to commence in June, was delayed by the Moroccan Government's objection to the inclusion of OAU observers in the process.

In May 1995 the Moroccan security forces arrested more than 100 pro-independence Sahrawi who were demonstrating in the Western Sahara capital, el-Aaiún; in the following month a military court sentenced eight student demonstrators to terms of imprisonment ranging from 15 to 20 years, although the sentences were reduced in July to one year's custody. Polisario had, in the mean time, withdrawn from the voter identification process, in protest at the severity of the sentences and at alleged Moroccan violations of the cease-fire. In September the SADR announced the formation of a new 14-member Government, again headed by Beïba, and in October the first elected Sahrawi National Assembly was inaugurated in a refugee camp in Tindouf, Algeria.

The UN Security Council voted periodically to extend MINURSO's mandate on a short-term basis, noting in January 1996 that it was improbable that the referendum would take place during that year. In May the Security Council voted to suspend the registration of voters in Western Sahara until 'convincing proof' was offered by the Moroccan Government and the Sahrawi leadership that they would not further obstruct preparations for the referendum. The mandate of MINURSO was extended, but its personnel was to be reduced by 20%.

In April 1996 Amnesty International, a prominent human rights organization, issued a report asserting that Moroccan security forces in Western Sahara were consistently violating human rights. The report suggested that the protection of human rights should become the priority of MINURSO, while it also expressed concern at the abuse of human rights in refugee camps run by Polisario in southern Algeria. (In November 1995 Polisario had released 186 Moroccan prisoners of war; Polisario claimed that they were released originally in 1989, but were refused entry by Morocco on the grounds that no such detainees existed.) In October 1996 the Moroccan authorities released 66 Sahrawi, some of whom had been held in detention since 1977. According to the International Committee of the Red Cross, some 1,920 Moroccans remained incarcerated by the Polisario Front.

In March 1997 the new UN Secretary-General, Kofi Annan, appointed James Baker (a former US Secretary of State) as his Personal Envoy to Western Sahara. Baker visited the region in April, and in June he mediated in talks in Portugal between representatives of Morocco and the SADR. Direct talks, under the auspices of the UN Special Representative, continued in Portugal in August and in the USA in September. The process of voter identification resumed in December for a referendum scheduled to be held one year later. However, disagreement between Morocco and Polisario regarding the eligibility of voters (notably concerning 65,000 people grouped in three contested tribes, whom the Moroccan authorities insisted should be enfranchised) delayed the identification process and led the UN to revise the proposed date for the referendum on several occasions. By September 1998 a total of 147,350 voters had been identified since the commencement of the identification process in August 1994, but the issue of the disputed tribes remained unresolved. In June 1998, meanwhile, as Morocco intensified its efforts to rejoin the OAU, several OAU member states engaged in debate as to whether to expel the SADR from the organization. Support for the SADR within the OAU had declined markedly, with only a minority of member countries continuing to recognize its independent status.

In November 1998, during talks with Moroccan and SADR officials, the UN Secretary-General warned that the UN would withdraw from Western Sahara if the two parties failed to show political will towards resolving the conflict. Annan presented proposals regarding the disputed tribes, the publication of a list of voters not contested by either party, and the repatriation of refugees under the auspices of the UN High Commissioner for Refugees. Although the proposals were accepted by Polisario, the Moroccan authorities expressed reservations. Morocco delayed the signing of a technical agreement with the UN (defining the legal status of MINURSO troops in Western Sahara) until February 1999: Algeria and Mauritania had signed similar accords with the UN in November 1998. In May 1999 William Eagleton, of the USA, was appointed as the UN Secretary-General's Special Representative to the region; he replaced Charles Dunbar, who had resigned in March 1999 apparently in frustration at the impasse regarding voter identification and at Morocco's refusal to accept Annan's proposals. In July MINURSO published a list of 84,251 people provisionally entitled to vote in the referendum, which was scheduled to be held on 31 July 2000.

In February 1999, meanwhile, the SADR announced the formation of a new Government, led by Beïba's predecessor, Bouchraya Hammoudi Bayoune. In September the Polisario Front congress re-elected Muhammad Abd al-Aziz secretary-general of the organization. Abd al-Aziz subsequently effected a reshuffle of the SADR Government; Bayoune retained the premiership and also assumed the interior portfolio. In late September it was reported that Moroccan security forces had violently suppressed demonstrations in el-Aaiún. In October a delegation comprising several ministers of the Moroccan Government was dispatched to el-Aaiún for consultations with the Sahrawi population at the behest of King Muhammad—who had in September established a royal commission to monitor affairs in Western Sahara.

In November 1999 UN officials indicated that the referendum was likely to be subject to a further postponement. In response, Polisario stated that it could not rule out a return to an armed struggle if the referendum did not take place as scheduled. Nevertheless, in late November Polisario released 191 Moroccan prisoners. In December the mandate of MINURSO was once again extended to enable it to complete its work on the identification of possible voters in the referendum. However, the UN Secretary-General subsequently announced it would be impossible to organize the referendum before 2002, owing to the large number of appeals (totalling some 79,000) lodged by those deemed ineligible to vote. In January 2000 it was announced that 86,381 out of a total of 198,481 people identified in Western Sahara would be eligible to vote in the referendum. (This included 2,130 eligible members of the disputed tribes—of a total of 51,220 who had presented themselves for identification.) In February, however, Annan postponed the referendum indefinitely, and warned, furthermore, of the possibility that it might never take place, owing to the persistent differences regarding criteria for eligibility to vote. The mandate of MINURSO was further extended in February. Later that month Polisario released a further 200 Moroccan prisoners. By March the number of appeals lodged had reached over 130,000, and Abd al-Aziz reiterated the threat of the resumption of armed hostilities if Morocco continued to obstruct the UN peace plan.

In April 2000 James Baker toured Morocco and Western Sahara, and in London, United Kingdom, in May he chaired the first direct talks between representatives of Morocco and Polisario for three years. Algeria and Mauritania also sent delegations, but the meeting failed to make any substantive progress. MINURSO's mandate was further extended until the end of July, and in late June Baker chaired another meeting of representatives of the four parties in London in an attempt to revive plans for a referendum; however, the talks again ended in failure. In October Annan urged Morocco partially to devolve authority in Western Sahara, stating that if no such concessions were granted, the UN would reactivate plans to hold a refer-

endum in the territory. Concurrently, MINURSO's mandate was extended until the end of February 2001.

In December 2000, to mark the beginning of Ramadan, Polisario released 201 Moroccan prisoners, urging Morocco to release some 150 Sahrawi from detention in Morocco. The Moroccan authorities denied the detention of any Sahrawi in Morocco, and in turn demanded the release of a further 1,500 Moroccans who they claimed were being held by Polisario. In late February 2001, on the 25th anniversary of the beginning of the Polisario Front's struggle for independence, the Moroccan Minister of the Interior, Ahmed Midaoui, asserted that there remained only one solution to the dispute—that Morocco retain control over its entire territory. Annan had recently issued a report in which he lamented the climate of increased mistrust and bitterness between the two sides, maintaining that this undermined the cease-fire. At the end of February, as MINURSO's mandate was extended for a further two months, Annan announced that if Morocco failed to offer or support some devolution of governmental authority, MINURSO would be directed to begin the process of hearing appeals regarding eligibility to vote in the referendum. A further two-month extension was approved by the UN Security Council in late April, in accordance with recommendations made by the Secretary-General: although Annan had been unable, in his latest report, to report progress towards overcoming the obstacles to implementation of the settlement plan, he expressed his view that 'substantial progress' had been made towards determining whether the Government of Morocco was 'prepared to offer or support some devolution of authority for all the inhabitants and former inhabitants of the Territory'.

In late June 2001 the UN Security Council unanimously approved a compromise resolution (No. 1359), formulated by Baker, which encouraged Polisario and Morocco to discuss an autonomy plan for Western Sahara without abandoning the delayed referendum. The resolution also extended MINURSO's mandate until the end of November. Under the terms of the autonomy proposal the inhabitants of Western Sahara would have the right to elect their own legislative and executive bodies and have control over areas of local government (including budget and taxation, law enforcement, internal security, social welfare, education, commerce, transportation, agriculture, mining, fisheries, environmental policy, urban development, utilities, roads and basic infrastructure) for a period of at least five years, during which Morocco would retain control over defence and foreign affairs. A referendum on the final status of the territory would take place within this five-year period. In late August Baker hosted three days of talks in Wyoming, USA, attended by representatives from Polisario, Mauritania and Algeria, however Polisario subsequently accused the UN of bowing to Moroccan pressure and in mid-September Polisario announced its formal rejection of Baker's proposal. In late October King Muhammad visited Western Sahara for the first time since his accession to throne, and in early November he granted an amnesty to 56 prisoners in Western Sahara. Later that month the UN Security Council approved Annan's request for an extension of MINURSO's mandate until February 2002, and in early December 2001 William Lacy Swing, a former US ambassador, succeeded Eagleton as the UN Secretary-General's Special Representative for Western Sahara. Tensions between Polisario and Morocco were further exacerbated when, in December, President Jacques Chirac of France (which lends Morocco considerable support on the Western Sahara issue) referred to the territory as part of Morocco. Polisario none the less released a further 115 Moroccan prisoners of war in early January 2002.

In early February 2002 UN legal counsel advised the Secretary-General that the Moroccan Government could not issue exploration licences for petroleum in Western Sahara without the consent of the Sahrawi people; the advice followed a request made by the SADR in late 2001 for clarification on the legality of reconnaissance licences signed by Morocco and two oil companies. Later in February 2002 Annan again expressed disappointment at the continued lack of progress and described the prospects for a settlement as 'rather bleak'. Nevertheless, he outlined four possible measures to be considered by the UN Security Council in order to attempt to resolve the continuing impasse over Western Sahara: to resume attempts to implement the 1988 settlement plan, with or without the agreement of Polisario and the Moroccan Government; to charge Baker with revising his earlier draft framework agreement; to commence discussions regarding the division of the territory; or to terminate MINURSO's mandate. Later that month the UN Security Council approved an extension of the mandate of the peace-keeping force until the end of April. Meanwhile, in early March King Muhammad again visited Western Sahara, vowing not to relinquish any part of the disputed territory. Upon its expiry at the end of April, MINURSO's mandate was renewed for a further three-months; during this period consideration would be given to the UN Secretary-General's proposals for resolving the impasse regarding the disputed territory. At the same time UN officials denied reports that James Baker had announced his intention to resign should the Security Council not accord him a mandate to revise the draft framework agreement.

In July 2002 a further 101 Moroccan prisoners of war were released by Polisario. Later that month the UN Security Council admitted that it had been unable to agree on the resolution of the Western Sahara issue (as none of the four proposals had secured the required support), but had voted unanimously to allow Baker to pursue efforts to find a political solution which would provide for self-determination. MINURSO's mandate was extended until the end of January 2003. In that month Baker visited government officials in Mauritania and Algeria, as well as Polisario leader Abd al-Aziz and Morocco's King Muhammad, to present them with the UN's most recent proposal for the settlement of the ongoing dispute. Although no details of the plan were officially disclosed, Baker asked all parties to present their comments on the proposal to him by early March. Just days later, however, it was reported that Polisario had rejected the plan. In an attempt to give the parties more time in which to consider Baker's proposals, the UN Security Council extended MINURSO's mandate until the end of March; it was subsequently extended for a further two months in order to give Baker sufficient time to evaluate the parties' responses to his proposal. In February Polisario had released another 100 Moroccan prisoners of war, although more than 1,100 reportedly remained in detention; the Security Council again urged the release of all prisoners of war.

Relations with other North African states improved significantly in the late 1980s. In May 1988 Algeria and Morocco agreed to re-establish diplomatic relations. (Relations with Mauritania had been suspended in 1981 and resumed in April 1985.) In February 1989 North African heads of state, meeting in Marrakesh, signed a treaty establishing the Union du Maghreb arabe (UMA—Union of the Arab Maghreb, see p. 342). The new body, grouping Morocco, Algeria, Libya, Mauritania and Tunisia, aimed to promote trade by allowing the free movement of goods, services and workers. During 1990 bilateral agreements on economic co-operation were concluded by Morocco with Algeria and Libya, and there were further discussions within the UMA on the formation of a North African free-trade area. However, there were political disagreements particularly over Algeria's continued support for the Polisario Front, and over Moroccan condemnation of Iraq's invasion of Kuwait in August 1990. In early 1993 it was announced that the five UMA members had decided there should be a 'pause' in the development of a closer union; of 15 conventions signed since the inauguration of the UMA, none had as yet been fully applied. However, the organization continued to hold meetings on an annual basis. In December 1995 King Hassan expressed disapproval at Algeria's continued support for the independence of Western Sahara, and demanded that UMA activities be suspended. An impending UMA summit was subsequently postponed. In March 1999 President Ben Ali of Tunisia made his first official visit to Morocco, during which he pledged to improve bilateral relations and to reactivate the UMA. At bilateral meetings during 2000 with other Maghreb Heads of State King Muhammad pledged to take measures to revive the UMA. A summit meeting of ministers responsible for foreign affairs of the five UMA states proceeded in the Algerian capital in mid-March 2001. However, the meeting, which was to have made preparations for the first summit meeting of UMA heads of state since 1995, quickly broke down following disagreements between Moroccan and Algerian representatives.

Relations with Algeria had been further undermined in mid-1994, by the murder, apparently by radical Islamists, of two Spanish tourists in Marrakesh, which the Moroccan authorities attributed in part to Algerian nationals. The imposition by Morocco of entry restrictions on Algerian citizens prompted the Algerian Government to introduce reciprocal visa restrictions and to close its border with Morocco. Tensions eased somewhat in September, when Algeria announced the appointment of a new ambassador to Morocco, and in October a Moroccan min-

ister attended ceremonies in Algeria to mark the commencement of work on a Maghreb–Europe gas pipeline. In January 1995 three people, including one Algerian, were sentenced to death for their part in acts of terrorism including the murders in Marrakesh; three others were sentenced to life imprisonment. The French security forces made further arrests in connection with the murder of the two Spaniards during 1995–96, and in early 1997 a French court sentenced another 29 alleged conspirators (two Moroccans, the remainder French citizens of Maghreb origin) to terms of imprisonment ranging from one to eight years. The Western Sahara issue remained a source of tension between Morocco and Algeria, but in mid-1998 the Moroccan authorities indicated their desire to normalize relations with Algeria and to reopen the common border. In September 1999, however, Algeria's new President, Abdelaziz Bouteflika, claimed that radical Islamist rebels were launching attacks on Algeria from Morocco, and accused Morocco of ignoring the increasing trade in illicit drugs between the two countries. Bouteflika also criticized Morocco for negotiating a separate trade agreement with the European Union (EU, see p. 199), claiming this was not in the interests of the UMA. Both Morocco and Algeria none the less subsequently reiterated their commitment to reviving the activities of the UMA. Although relations remained generally co-operative, Bouteflika was vocal in opposing the UN proposals for Western Sahara in mid-2001, which he claimed merely favoured Morocco. In late February 2002, furthermore, Morocco asserted that Algerian support for the partition of Western Sahara risked destabilizing the region; for its part, Algeria accused Morocco of blocking a UN-sponsored solution to the Western Sahara issue.

From the late 1990s Morocco was actively involved in wider regional integration efforts, as a member of the Community of Sahel-Saharan States (CEN-SAD, see p. 339), and also through bilateral and multilateral free-trade arrangements; in May 2001, notably, the Governments of Morocco, Iraq, Jordan and Tunisia agreed, at a meeting in Agadir, to establish a free-trade zone. In October Morocco and Mauritania took steps to improve bilateral relations after King Muhammad visited that country.

A visit to Rabat by the Israeli Prime Minister, Itzhak Rabin, in September 1993 was regarded as an indication of improved relations between Morocco and Israel, and of the role played by King Hassan in the Middle East peace process. In September 1994 Morocco became only the second Arab country (after Egypt) to establish direct links with Israel; liaison offices were subsequently opened in Rabat and Tel-Aviv. In March 1997, however, in condemnation of recent Israeli settlement policy, ministers of foreign affairs of the League of Arab States (the Arab League, see p. 260) recommended a number of sanctions against Israel, including the closure of representative missions. In common with most other Arab League members, Morocco did not attend the Middle East and North Africa economic conference in Qatar in November 1997: the boycott was in protest at the presence of a delegation from Israel, which was regarded as failing to fulfil its obligations under the Middle East peace process. Commercial links between Morocco and Israel were not affected. In January 2000 Morocco and Israel agreed in principle to upgrade diplomatic relations to ambassadorial level, although no indication was given as to when embassies would be established. In October, however, as the crisis in Israeli–Palestinian relations deepened, Morocco announced that it had closed down Israel's liaison office in Rabat and its own representative office in Tel-Aviv. There was widespread outrage in Morocco in response to the Israeli military offensive in Palestinian-controlled areas of the West Bank from the end of March 2002. A national march in solidarity with the Palestinian people took place in Rabat in early April, attracting more than 1m. people—the biggest demonstration in the Arab world.

Morocco has generally maintained close relations with France. However, the French Government expressed considerable concern following the imposition of death sentences on three defendants in January 1995 (see above), all of whom had been resident in France prior to their arrest. As the development of a Maghreb union slowed, Morocco attempted to improve relations with the EU, which had been critical of Morocco's human rights record. In February 1996, after two years of negotiations, Morocco signed an association agreement with the EU, which provided for greater political and economic co-operation, financial aid and the eventual establishment of a free-trade zone. In March 2000 King Muhammad made his first state visit abroad since acceding to the throne when he attended talks with President Chirac in France. During the visit Muhammad expressed his hope that Morocco would be accorded partnership status with the EU and, ultimately, full membership of the union.

In February 1995, following the approval by the Spanish parliament of statutes of autonomy for the enclaves of Ceuta and Melilla, Morocco intensified its diplomatic campaign to obtain sovereignty over the territories. Relations between Morocco and Spain deteriorated further in April, when responsibility for two bomb explosions in Ceuta was claimed by a guerrilla group suspected by the Spanish authorities of receiving clandestine support from Morocco. Tensions were exacerbated by protracted negotiations between Morocco and the EU to renew fishing licences: the failure to reach a prompt settlement had the effect of denying Spanish fishermen access to Moroccan waters for seven months, leading to protests and the blockading of Moroccan goods at several Spanish ports. Bilateral relations improved after Morocco initialled the fisheries agreement with the EU in November. In February 1996 the Spanish Prime Minister, Felipe González, attended a meeting in Rabat with Prime Minister Filali to discuss ways of increasing contacts in order to avoid similar commercial disputes. Filali made an official visit to Spain in mid-1997, and in January 1998 the two countries established a joint commission to examine security issues including illegal immigration (to Spain) and drugs-trafficking. Bilateral relations were consolidated further in April, with a visit to Morocco by the Spanish premier, José María Aznar López. In August 1999 Prime Minister el-Youssoufi urged a review of the statutes of Ceuta and Melilla; however, Spain's ruling Partido Popular asserted that no Moroccan sovereignty claims with regard to this issue would be considered. In January 2000 large amounts of Moroccan produce were destroyed during a demonstration at the port of Algeciras, in southern Spain, organized to protest against the sale of goods from Morocco in European markets. Aznar again visited Morocco in May, and in September, during King Muhammad's first visit to Spain since his accession, two economic co-operation agreements were signed. Nevertheless, relations remained strained owing to lack of progress in negotiations with the EU regarding a new fisheries accord and attacks by Spanish fishermen on lorries carrying Moroccan products through Spanish ports. In April 2001 Aznar denounced Morocco's position on the fisheries accord as 'absolutely unacceptable', warning of the serious negative consequences for relations with Spain and the EU of Morocco's refusal to renew the accord. In July, in an attempt to limit the increasing number of Moroccans entering Spain illegally, the two countries signed an agreement that would allow as many as 20,000 Moroccans to enter Spain each year in search of employment. In September, however, the Spanish Minister of Foreign Affairs, Josep Piqué i Camps, refuted allegations made by King Muhammad that Spanish criminal associations were responsible for the large increase in numbers of Moroccan economic migrants attempting illegally to cross the Straits of Gibraltar, asserting that collusion between Moroccan police and the smugglers was ongoing. Piqué visited Morocco in October, but relations between the two countries deteriorated further later that month after Morocco recalled its ambassador from Spain. The Moroccan Government was critical of border controls introduced by the Spanish authorities for Moroccans entering the Spanish enclaves of Ceuta and Melilla, and the breakdown, in April 2002, of talks on renewing the EU fisheries accord also contributed to strained relations between the two countries. A new disagreement erupted at the end of December over maritime boundaries between the Spanish Canary Islands and Morocco's Atlantic coast, following the Spanish Government's decision to grant oil exploration rights around the Canary Islands to a Spanish company, Repsol. Moroccan–Spanish relations were further strained in mid-July when a small detachment of Moroccan troops occupied the uninhabited rocky islet of Perejil (known as Leila to Morocco), west of the Spanish enclave of Ceuta and close to the Moroccan coastline. Morocco claimed that it was establishing a surveillance post on the island as part of its campaign against illegal emigration and drugs-smuggling. However, Spain insisted that there had been since 1990 an agreement that neither Morocco nor Spain would occupy Perejil, and, with the support of the EU and NATO, demanded the immediate evacuation of Moroccan troops from the island. A few days later Spain's ambassador to Morocco was recalled, and Spanish special forces intervened and forcibly removed Moroccan troops from Perejil. Spanish officials insisted that their troops would be withdrawn if King Muhammad gave assurances that Moroccan forces would not reoccupy the island, and the Spanish Minister of Foreign

Affairs, Ana de Palacio, stated that Spain had no interest in maintaining a permanent military presence on the island. Both sides stressed their desire to end the dispute through diplomatic means, and, following mediation by the US Secretary of State, Colin Powell, Spanish forces withdrew from the island. Talks held later in July in Rabat between the Palacio and her Moroccan counterpart Muhammad Benaissa (the first at this level since October 2001) resulted in an accord whereby both states agreed to return to the *status quo ante*. However, a further meeting between Palacio and Benaissa scheduled for September was cancelled by Morocco, which claimed that a Spanish aircraft had landed on the disputed islet. The two sides met again in December when they agreed to establish a number of working groups to address the main issues dividing the countries. By early 2003 relations had improved somewhat: in January Muhammad temporarily allowed Spanish boats to fish in Moroccan waters, and in the following month the two countries agreed to the return of their respective ambassadors.

The Moroccan Government was swift to condemn the September 2001 attacks on New York and Washington, DC, for which the al-Qa'ida (Base) organization of the fugitive Saudi Arabian-born militant Islamist Osama bin Laden was believed to be responsible. In early June 2002 the Moroccan authorities announced that they had arrested three Saudi nationals who were alleged to be members of an Islamist cell linked to al-Qa'ida that was preparing terrorist attacks on US and British warships in the Strait of Gibraltar. Two of the suspects' wives, both of Moroccan origin, had also been arrested, along with five other Moroccans, for allegedly acting as couriers between the Saudis in Morocco and al-Qa'ida, which had provided them with funds and logistical support. In February 2003 the three Saudis were sentenced to 10 years' imprisonment by a court in Casablanca; six of the Moroccans received sentences ranging from four months to one year for their roles in the plot. Also in February a Moroccan student who was alleged to have been a member of the cell that had planned and executed the September 2001 attacks was convicted by a court in Hamburg, Germany, of belonging to a terrorist group and of aiding and abetting the murder of 3,066 people. He was sentenced to 15 years' imprisonment.

Government

The 1992 Constitution (amended by referendum in 1996) provides for a modified constitutional monarchy, with an hereditary King as Head of State. Legislative power is vested in the Chamber of Representatives, with 325 members directly elected, on the basis of universal adult suffrage, for five years, and in the Chamber of Advisers, with 270 members chosen by electoral colleges (representing mainly local councils, with the remainder selected from professional associations and trade unions) for a nine-year term. Executive power is vested in the King, who appoints (and may dismiss) the Prime Minister and (on the latter's recommendation) other members of the Cabinet. The King may also dissolve the legislature.

Defence

In August 2002 Morocco's active armed forces numbered 196,300, consisting of an army of 175,000 (including an estimated 100,000 conscripts), a navy of 7,800 and an air force of 13,500. In addition, there was a paramilitary 'gendarmerie royale' of 20,000, and a paramilitary 'force auxiliaire' of 30,000 men (including a mobile intervention corps of 5,000). Army reserve forces totalled 150,000. Military service of 18 months is by authorized conscription. Under the 2000 budget, government expenditure on defence was projected at 18,000m. dirhams.

Economic Affairs

In 2001, according to estimates by the World Bank, Morocco's gross national income (GNI), measured at average 1999–2001 prices, was US $34,555m., equivalent to $1,180 per head (or $3,690 per head on an international purchasing-power parity basis). During 1990–2001, it was estimated, the population increased at an average annual rate of 1.8%, while gross domestic product (GDP) per head increased, in real terms, by an average of 2.6% per year. Overall GDP increased, in real terms, ay an average annual rate of 0.8% in 1990–2001; it declined by 0.7% in 1999 and was estimated to have increased by just 0.3% in 2000.

Agriculture (including forestry and fishing) contributed an estimated 15.8% of GDP in 2001, and engaged 43.6% of the employed labour force in that year. The principal crops are cereals (mainly wheat and barley), sugar beet, citrus fruit, sugar cane, tomatoes and potatoes. Almost all of Morocco's meat requirements are produced within the country. The sale of licences to foreign fishing fleets is an important source of revenue. In 2000 seafoods and seafood products accounted for an estimated 12.6% of total exports. During 1990–2001 agricultural GDP was estimated to have declined at an average annual rate of 0.4%. Agricultural GDP declined by 29.48% in 1999, and by 16.2% in 2000, as a result of severe drought, although in 2001 it increased by 23.0%.

Industry (including mining, manufacturing, construction and power) engaged 19.7% of the employed labour force in 2001, and provided an estimated 30.9% of GDP in that year. During 1990–2001 industrial GDP increased by an estimated average of 2.8% per year. Industrial GDP rose by 2.5% in 2000 and by 3.0% in 2001.

Excluding hydrocarbons, mining and quarrying contributed an estimated 1.9% of GDP in 2001; the sector engaged 0.6% of the labour force in 2000. The major mineral exports are phosphate rock and phosphoric acid, which together earned 12.7% of export revenues in 2000. Morocco is the world's largest exporter of phosphate rock. Petroleum exploration activity was revived at the end of the 1990s, and in August 2000 the discovery of major oil and natural gas reserves in the Talsinnt region of eastern Morocco was announced. Coal, salt, iron ore, barytes, lead, copper, zinc, silver, gold and manganese are mined. Deposits of nickel, cobalt and bauxite have been discovered. Mining GDP decreased by 2.2% in 1999 and by an estimated 2.0% in 2000.

Manufacturing employed 12.3% of the labour force in 2000, and contributed an estimated 16.9% of GDP in 2001. The most important branches, measured by gross value of output, are food-processing, textiles, and chemicals. During 1990–2001 manufacturing GDP was estimated to have increased at an average annual rate of 2.8%. Manufacturing GDP rose by 3.5% in 2000 and by 4.0% in 2001.

Electric energy is derived principally from thermal power stations (which accounted for an estimated 77.3% of production in 2000) using coal and imported petroleum and gas. Facilities for generating hydroelectric and wind power have also been developed. Imports of fuel and energy products comprised an estimated 17.7% of the value of total merchandise imports in 2000.

The services sector contributed an estimated 53.3% of GDP in 2001, and engaged 36.7% of the employed labour force in that year. The tourist industry is generally a major source of revenue, and tourist arrivals reached 2.5m. in 2001. The GDP of the services sector increased by an estimated average of 3.4% per year during 1990–2001. The GDP of the services sector rose by 4.1% in 2000 and by 5.2% in 2001.

In 2000 Morocco recorded a visible trade deficit of US $3,022m., but there was a surplus of $1,606m. on the current account of the balance of payments. In 2001 the principal source of imports was France (which provided an estimated 24.1% of merchandise imports); other major suppliers in that year included Spain, the United Kingdom, and Germany. France was also the principal market for exports (32.8%) in 2001; Spain, the United Kingdom and Italy were also important purchasers of Moroccan exports. The principal exports in 2001 were phosphates and phosphoric acid, hosiery, manufactured garments, seafoods and seafood products and electrical components. The principal imports in that year were crude petroleum and textiles.

In the financial year ending 30 June 2000 there was a budget deficit of 2,261m. dirhams, equivalent to 0.7% of GDP. Morocco's total external debt in 1999 was US $17,944m., of which $15,793m. was long-term public debt. The cost of debt-servicing in that year was equivalent to 25.9% of exports of goods and services. The annual rate of inflation averaged 3.9% in 1989–2001. Annual inflation slowed to an average of 1.9% in 2000 and just 0.6% in 2001. Some 12.5% of the labour force were unemployed in 2001.

Morocco is a member of the African Development Bank (see p. 128), the Islamic Development Bank (see p. 257) and of the Arab Fund for Economic and Social Development (see p. 136). It is a founder member of the Union du Maghreb arabe (Union of the Arab Maghreb, see p. 342).

Since 1980 the Moroccan authorities have undertaken a series of economic reforms (under the auspices of the IMF), including the reduction of taxes, tariffs and subsidies and the introduction of a more efficient tax system. Efforts to stimulate foreign investment have had considerable success, while a programme of privatization bolstered government revenue during 1993–98. In March 2000 a trade and co-operation agreement with the European Union (EU) came into effect, which provided for the establishment of a free-trade zone with the EU within 10 years. Meanwhile, concern regarding the depletion of fishing stocks in Moroccan waters meant that the Government refused to renew its fisheries accord with the EU; this expired in November 1999, and in April 2001 negotiations between the two parties concluded without agreement. The Government was, however, able to compensate for the loss of revenue from the fisheries accord with the sale, for US $1,100m., of Morocco's second mobile cellular telephone operating licence and the partial privatization of Maroc Télécom—35% of which was sold to the French telecommunications company Vivendi for $2,330m. The Government's five-year social and economic plan for 2000–04 aims to reduce the rate of unemployment to 12% by 2004 as well as to narrow the overall budget deficit. There are also plans substantially to increase revenues from tourism by 2010, although this sector was adversely affected by the volatile situation in the Middle East in 2002 and early 2003. Nevertheless, Morocco continued to reduce its trade balance, and, with GDP growth of 5.5% forecast in 2003, there were a number of reasons for optimism regarding the country's economic prospects. The ongoing privatization programme was also expected to contribute to continued growth, and the award of a second fixed-line telephone licence, which had initially been scheduled to take place in November 2002, was expected to take place in 2003, with privatization receipts in that year budgeted to reach some $1,200m.

Education

Morocco has state-controlled primary, secondary and technical schools, and there are also private schools. Education is compulsory for six years, to be undertaken between the ages of seven and 13 years. Primary education begins at seven years of age and lasts for six years. Secondary education, beginning at the age of 13, lasts for up to six years (comprising two cycles of three years). Primary enrolment in 1999 included 79% of children in the relevant age-group (83% of boys; 74% of girls), while secondary enrolment included 38% of the relevant age-group (boys 43%; girls 33%). In 1988 the secondary school graduation examination, the *baccalauréat*, was replaced by a system of continuous assessment. There were an estimated 260,806 students enrolled at state universities and equivalent-level institutions in 2001/02. Under the 1999/2000 budget, expenditure on education by the central Government was 17,385m. dirhams (16.2% of total spending).

Public Holidays

2003: 1 January (New Year), 11 January (Independence Manifesto), 12 February* (Eid el-Kebir—Id al-Adha, Feast of the Sacrifice), 3 March (Festival of the Throne, anniversary of King Hassan's accession), 5 March* (Islamic New Year), 14 March* (Ashoura), 1 May (Labour Day), 14 May* (Mouloud, Birth of the Prophet), 23 May (National Day), 14 August (Oued ed-Dahab Day, anniversary of 1979 annexation), 27 October* (Beginning of Ramadan), 6 November (Anniversary of the Green March), 18 November (Independence Day), 26 November* (Eid es-Seghir—Id al-Fitr, end of Ramadan).

2004: 1 January (New Year), 11 January (Independence Manifesto), 2 February* (Eid el-Kebir—Id al-Adha, Feast of the Sacrifice), 22 February* (Islamic New Year), 2 March* (Ashoura), 3 March (Festival of the Throne, anniversary of King Hassan's accession), 1 May (Labour Day), 2 May* (Mouloud, Birth of the Prophet), 23 May (National Day), 14 August (Oued ed-Dahab Day, anniversary of 1979 annexation), 15 October (Beginning of Ramadan), 6 November (Anniversary of the Green March*), 14 November* (Eid es-Seghir—Id al-Fitr, end of Ramadan), 18 November (Independence Day).

*These holidays are dependent on the Islamic lunar calendar and may vary by one or two days from the dates given.

Weights and Measures

The metric system is in force.

Statistical Survey

Sources (unless otherwise stated): Direction de la Statistique, BP 178, Rabat 10001; tel. (3) 7773606; fax (3) 7773042; e-mail webmaster@statistic.gov.ma; internet www.statistic.gov.ma; Bank Al-Maghrib, 277 ave Muhammad V, BP 445, Rabat; tel. (3) 7702626; fax (3) 7706677; e-mail dai@bkam.gov.ma; internet www.bkam.ma.
Note: Unless otherwise indicated, the data exclude Western (formerly Spanish) Sahara, a disputed territory under Moroccan occupation.

Area and Population

AREA, POPULATION AND DENSITY

Area (sq km)	710,850*
Population (census results)†	
3 September 1982	
Males	10,205,859
Females.	10,182,358
Total	20,388,217
2 September 1994	26,073,717
Population (official estimates at mid-year)†	
1999	28,238,000
2000	28,705,000
2001	29,170,000
Density (per sq km) at mid-2001	41.0

* 274,461 sq miles. This area includes the disputed territory of Western Sahara, which covers 252,120 sq km (97,344 sq miles).
† Including Western Sahara, with a population of 163,868 (provisional) at the 1982 census and 252,146 at the 1994 census.

REGIONS
(population at 1994 census)

	Area (sq km)	Population	Density (per sq km)
Sud*	394,970	3,234,024	8.2
Tensift	38,445	3,546,768	92.3
Centre.	41,500	6,931,418	167.0
Nord-Ouest	29,955	5,646,716	188.5
Centre-Nord . . .	43,950	3,042,310	69.2
Oriental	82,820	1,768,691	21.4
Centre-Sud	79,210	1,903,790	24.0
Total	710,850	26,073,717	36.7

* Including the prefectures of Boujdour, el-Aaiún, es-Smara and Oued ed-Dahab, which comprise the disputed territory of Western Sahara (area 252,120 sq km; population 252,146).

PRINCIPAL TOWNS
(population at 1994 census)

Casablanca . . .	2,770,560	Kénitra	292,627
Rabat (capital)* . .	1,335,996	Tétouan	277,516
Fès (Fez)	769,014	Safi	262,276
Marrakech		Mohammedia. . .	170,063
(Marrakesh) . .	672,506	Khouribga . . .	152,090
Agadir	524,564	El-Jadida . . .	119,083
Tanger (Tangier). .	497,147	Nador	112,450
Meknès	443,214	Ksar-el-Kebir . . .	107,065
Oujda	351,878		

* Including Salé and Temara.

Source: Thomas Brinkhoff, *City Population* (internet www.citypopulation.de).

BIRTHS AND DEATHS
(UN estimates, annual averages)

	1985–90	1990–95	1995–2000
Birth rate (per 1,000) . . .	32.8	29.1	26.8
Death rate (per 1,000) . . .	8.9	7.6	6.6

Source: UN, *World Population Prospects: The 2000 Revision.*

Expectation of life (WHO estimates, years at birth): 69.4 (males 67.5; females 71.3) in 2001 (Source: WHO, *World Health Report*).

ECONOMICALLY ACTIVE POPULATION
(sample surveys, '000 persons aged 15 years and over)

	1999	2000	2001
Agriculture, hunting, forestry and fishing	4,048	4,010	3,900
Mining and quarrying. . .	58	55 }	
Manufacturing	1,153	1,098 }	1,169
Electricity, gas and water. .	40	34 }	
Construction	560	555	598
Wholesale and retail trade . .	991	1,118	1,155
Transport, storage and communications	279	297	317
Repairing	155	158 }	
Restaurants and hotels . .	140	155 }	
Financing, insurance, real estate and business services . . .	104	105 }	835
Personal and domestic services	359	372 }	
General administration . .	500	482 }	
Other community services . .	440	443 }	976
Activities not adequately defined	17	10	5
Total employed	8,845	8,891	8,955
Unemployed	1,433	1,394	1,275
Total labour force	10,278	10,285	10,230

Health and Welfare

KEY INDICATORS

Total fertility rate (children per woman, 2001).	3.1
Under-5 mortality rate (per 1,000 live births, 2001) . . .	44
HIV/AIDS (% of persons aged 15–49, 2001).	0.08
Physicians (per 1,000 head, 1997)	0.46
Hospital beds (per 1,000 head, 1997)	0.46
Health expenditure (2000): US $ per head (PPP)	142
Health expenditure (2000): % of GDP	4.5
Health expenditure (2000): public (% of total)	29.6
Access to water (% of persons, 2000).	82
Access to sanitation (% of persons, 2000)	75
Human Development Index (2000): ranking	123
Human Development Index (2000): value	0.602

For sources and definitions, see explanatory note on p. vi.

Agriculture

PRINCIPAL CROPS
('000 metric tons)

	1999	2000	2001
Wheat	2,154	1,381	3,316
Rice (paddy)	35	25	40
Barley	1,474	467	1,155
Maize	136	95	54
Oats	27	15	15
Sorghum	19	10	10
Other cereals	15	17	17
Potatoes	1,141	1,090	1,155
Sweet potatoes	7	13	6
Sugar cane	1,369	1,318	1,321
Sugar beet	3,236	2,883	3,106
Dry beans	11	12	12*
Dry broad beans	55	33	82
Dry peas	11	6	13
Chick-peas	28	32	32
Lentils	13	13	13
Other pulses	47	45	49
Almonds	81	65	82
Groundnuts (in shell)	42	45	45*
Olives	476	400	420
Sunflower seed	49	19	25
Cabbages	37	38	35
Artichokes	28	41	45
Asparagus*	36	36	36
Tomatoes	1,116	1,165	881
Cauliflowers	40	24	38
Pumpkins, squash and gourds	89	130	130
Cucumbers and gherkins	26	24	25*
Aubergines (Eggplants)	38	34	35*
Chillies and green peppers	181	180	180*
Dry onions	523	348	53
Green beans	31	33	33*
Green peas	47	65	79
Green broad beans	119	99	96
String beans	35	37	40
Carrots	221	210	199
Carobs*	23	23	24
Other vegetables	361	367	373
Watermelons	230	219	300*
Cantaloupes and other melons	419	374	380*
Figs	82	68	68
Avacados	13	13	14
Grapes	335	262	253
Dates	73	74	32
Apples	292	300	228
Pears	50	30	36
Quinces	30	31	20
Peaches and nectarines	45	48	46
Plums	41	51	63
Strawberries	58	105	90
Oranges	874	870	708
Tangerines, mandarins, clementines and satsumas	424	531	263
Lemons and limes	9	14	6
Apricots	117	106	120
Bananas	1021	111	119
Other fruits and berries	53	48	47
Tobacco (leaves)	4	5	6

* FAO estimate(s).

Source: FAO.

LIVESTOCK
('000 head, year ending September)

	1999	2000	2001
Cattle	2,566	2,675	2,663
Sheep	16,576	17,300	17,300*
Goats	4,704	4,931	5,200
Camels*	36	36	36
Horses	149	154	155*
Mules	527	518	520*
Asses	1,001	1,099	1,000*
Poultry	140,000	135,000	137,000

* FAO estimate(s).

Source: FAO.

LIVESTOCK PRODUCTS
('000 metric tons)

	1999	2000	2001
Beef and veal	130	140	150
Mutton and lamb	126	125	125
Goat meat	35	35*	35*
Poultry meat	260	250	255
Other meat	38	38	38*
Cows' milk	1,164	1,185	1,200*
Sheep's milk	27	27*	27*
Goats' milk	35	35*	35*
Butter*	18	18	19
Cheese*	8	8	8
Poultry eggs*	245	235	235
Honey	3	2	3
Wool: greasy	38	40†	40*
Wool: scoured*	17	17	17
Cattle hides (fresh)	18	18*	20*
Sheepskins (fresh)*	13	13	13
Goatskins (fresh)*	3	3	3

* FAO estimate(s).
† Unofficial figure.

Source: FAO.

Forestry

ROUNDWOOD REMOVALS
('000 cubic metres, excl. bark)

	1999	2000	2001
Sawlogs, veneer logs and logs for sleepers	176	207	201
Pulpwood	394	362	374
Fuel wood	553	487	396
Total	1,123	1,056	971

Source: FAO.

SAWNWOOD PRODUCTION
('000 cubic metres, incl. railway sleepers)

	1987	1988	1989
Coniferous (softwood)	40	26	43
Broadleaved (hardwood)	40	27	40
Total	80	53	83

1990–2000: Annual production as in 1989.

Source: FAO.

Fishing

('000 metric tons, live weight)

	1998	1999	2000
Capture	710.4	745.4	896.6
European pilchard (sardine)	435.8	429.7	539.8
European anchovy	41.0	40.2	22.1
Chub mackerel	11.6	17.4	63.4
Cuttlefish, bobtails and squids	14.7	20.2	32.9
Octopuses	42.5	84.6	99.4
Aquaculture	2.1	2.8	1.8
Total catch (incl. others)	712.5	748.2	898.4

Note: Figures exclude aquatic plants ('000 metric tons, capture only): 7.0 in 1998; 5.9 in 1999; 6.1 in 2000.

Mining

('000 metric tons)

	1999	2000	2001*
Hard coal	129.2	30.8	1.9
Crude petroleum	11.3	13.0	10.1
Iron ore†	6.6	6.5	5.0
Copper concentrates† . . .	25.3	23.1	26.6
Lead concentrates† . . .	114.2	117.4	110.9
Manganese ore†	29.1	25.8	13.2
Zinc concentrates†	216.2	201.7	174.8
Phosphate rock‡	22,767	19,658	20,736
Fluorspar (acid grade)	83.1	77.0	96.5
Barytes	328.9	343.6	445.8
Salt (unrefined)	156.2	162.4	231.3
Clay	22.0	30.7	40.7

* Preliminary figures.
† Figures refer to the gross weight of ores and concentrates.
‡ Including production in Western Sahara.

Industry

SELECTED PRODUCTS*
('000 metric tons, unless otherwise indicated)

	1998	1999	2000†
Cement	7,155	7,194	7,497
Electric energy (million kWh) . .	12,453	13,264	13,942
Phosphate fertilizers‡	542	481	n.a.
Carpets and rugs ('000 sq m) . .	618	638	n.a.
Wine§	30	49	35
Olive oil (crude)	50	65	n.a.
Motor spirit—petrol	354	391	383
Naphthas	385	507	492
Kerosene	79	96	98
Distillate fuel oils	2,236	2,539	2,322
Residual fuel oils	1,918	2,508	2,365
Jet fuel	272	279	282
Petroleum bitumen—asphalt . .	118	116	129
Liquefied petroleum gas	252	266	239

* Major industrial establishments only.
† Preliminary figures.
‡ Estimated production in terms of phosphoric acid.
§ Source: FAO.

Source: partly UN, *Industrial Commodity Statistics Yearbook.*

Finance

CURRENCY AND EXCHANGE RATES

Monetary Units
100 centimes (santimat) = 1 Moroccan dirham

Sterling, Dollar and Euro Equivalents (31 December 2002)
£1 sterling = 16.39 dirhams
US $1 = 10.17 dirhams
€1 = 10.66 dirhams
1,000 Moroccan dirhams = £61.02 = $98.36 = €93.79

Average Exchange Rate (dirhams per US $)
2000   10.626
2001   11.303
2002   11.021

GENERAL BUDGET
(million dirhams)

Revenue	1998/99*	1999/2000*	2000†
Tax revenue	79,681	80,813	38,807
Direct taxes	25,010	26,938	12,067
Customs receipts	12,744	12,746	6,357
Indirect taxes	34,412	36,999	18,697
Registration and stamps . . .	3,892	4,130	1,686
Exceptional receipts	3,623	—	—
Non-tax revenue	9,835	19,103	2,482
Monopolies, etc.	5,759	16,519	1,352
Revenue from special accounts . .	4,685	5,383	2,053
Total	94,201	105,299	43,342

Expenditure	1998/99*	1999/2000*	2000†
Ordinary expenditure . . .	80,664	85,029	42,969
Operating expenditure . .	56,789	59,405	29,936
Personnel . . .	40,286	42,683	21,222
Interest on public debt . .	17,731	18,735	9,643
Domestic	11,088	12,540	6,250
Foreign	6,643	6,195	3,393
Price subsidies	6,144	6,889	3,390
Investment expenditure . . .	17,428	17,235	11,996
Special treasury accounts (net) . .	4,170	5,046	2,384
Expenditure from Hassan II Fund for Economic and Social Development	—	250	1,652
Total	102,262	107,560	59,001

* Figures for 1998/99 and 1999/2000 refer to the financial year ending 30 June. With effect from January 2001 the financial year was to correspond with the calendar year.
† Figures refer to the period 1 July–31 December 2000.

INTERNATIONAL RESERVES
(US $ million at 31 December)

	2000	2001	2002
Gold*	184	169	193
IMF special drawing rights . .	119	123	122
Reserve position in IMF . . .	92	89	96
Foreign exchange	4,612	8,262	9,915
Total	5,007	8,643	10,326

* National valuation of gold reserves (706,000 in 2000; 707,000 in 2001; 708,000 in 2002).

Source: IMF, *International Financial Statistics.*

MONEY SUPPLY
(million dirhams at 31 December)

	2000	2001	2002
Currency outside banks	58,169	66,025	69,565
Demand deposits at deposit money banks	156,545	181,099	199,276
Total money (incl. others) . .	216,503	249,693	272,086

Source: IMF, *International Financial Statistics.*

COST OF LIVING
(Consumer Price Index for urban areas; base: 1989 = 100)

	1999	2000	2001
Food	156.7	159.1	157.5
Clothing	157.6	161.3	163.5
Shelter	156.6	159.2	162.5
Household equipment	137.9	138.2	138.4
All items (incl. others) . . .	154.4	157.3	158.3

NATIONAL ACCOUNTS
(million dirhams at current prices)

Expenditure on the Gross Domestic Product

	1999	2000*	2001†
Government final consumption expenditure	66,146	67,689	74,619
Private final consumption expenditure	214,416	224,883	235,008
Increase in stocks	-1,984	-1,629	2,131
Gross fixed capital formation . .	81,896	85,312	85,264
Total domestic expenditure . .	360,474	376,256	397,022
Exports of goods and services . .	84,663	93,504	105,435
Less Imports of goods and services	99,543	115,693	119,560
GDP in purchasers' values . .	345,594	354,068	382,897
GDP at constant 1980 prices .	133,622	134,927	143,648

* Semi-definitive figures.
† Provisional figures.

Gross Domestic Product by Economic Activity

	1999	2000*	2001†
Agriculture, hunting, forestry and fishing	52,905.2	49,570.1	60,546.4
Energy and water	27,158.9	25,263.9	26,588.9
Other mining and quarrying	7,463.5	7,035.6	7,446.2
Other manufacturing	59,581.8	62,267.3	64,851.4
Construction	16,471.5	18,300.1	19,351.8
Wholesale and retail trade	66,339.3	70,682.7	72,894.8
Transport and communications	21,678.1	24,700.1	26,366.8
Public administration	49,424.0	50,489.2	58,138.0
Other services	44,695.4	45,758.9	46,712.8
GDP in purchasers' values	345,593.6	354,067.9	382,897.0

* Semi-definitive figures.
† Provisional figures.

BALANCE OF PAYMENTS
(US $ million)

	1999	2000	2001
Exports of goods f.o.b.	7,509	7,419	7,142
Imports of goods f.o.b.	−9,957	−10,654	−10,164
Trade balance	−2,448	−3,235	−3,022
Exports of services	3,115	3,034	4,029
Imports of services	−2,003	−1,884	−2,119
Balance on goods and services	−1,335	−2,085	−1,111
Other income received	187	276	326
Other income paid	−1,172	−1,149	−1,159
Balance on goods, services and income	−2,321	−2,958	−1,944
Current transfers received	2,246	2,574	3,670
Current transfers paid	−96	−118	−120
Current balance	−171	−501	1,606
Capital account (net)	−9	−6	−9
Direct investment abroad	−18	−59	−97
Direct investment from abroad	3	10	144
Portfolio investment liabilities	6	18	−8
Other investment liabilities	−4	−954	−1,006
Net errors and omissions	123	114	230
Overall balance	−69	−1,167	860

Source: IMF, *International Financial Statistics*.

External Trade

PRINCIPAL COMMODITIES
(million dirhams)

Imports c.i.f.	1999	2000	2001*
Foodstuffs, beverages and tobacco	11,540	14,210	15,348
Wheat	3,817	5,484	6,164
Energy and lubricants	13,000	21,657	21,874
Crude petroleum	8,941	14,710	14,488
Refined petroleum products	2,507	4,802	4,744
Crude animal and vegetable products	5,583	5,803	5,763
Semi-finished products	21,828	24,365	26,387
Chemical products	3,247	3,441	3,686
Metallurgical products	4,679	5,403	5,533
Finished industrial capital goods	27,026	24,694	22,019
Aircraft, boats and industrial vehicles	3,454	4,000	1,958
Finished consumer products	24,323	28,822	29,919
Textile products	10,479	10,740	12,190
Telecommunications receiving equipment	995	4,501	2,398
Total (incl. others)	105,931	122,527	124,081

Exports f.o.b.	1999	2000	2001*
Foodstuffs, beverages and tobacco	14,853	16,751	16,185
Citrus fruit	2,613	2,050	2,026
Crustaceans and molluscs	4,422	6,742	4,954
Prepared and preserved fish	1,961	2,141	2,543
Energy and lubricants	1,990	2,882	3,098
Crude mineral products	5,979	5,766	6,179
Phosphates	4,462	4,129	4,687
Semi-finished products	13,711	17,063	17,763
Phosphoric acid	5,777	5,365	5,380
Natural and chemical fertilizers	3,107	3,430	4,017
Electronic components (transistors)	1,826	4,253	4,302
Finished industrial capital goods	6,776	4,798	4,449
Electric wire and cable	1,633	2,074	2,512
Finished consumer products	28,456	29,753	31,392
Manufactured garments	16,172	16,195	17,164
Hosiery	8,070	8,935	8,861
Total (incl. others)	73,617	78,827	80,440

* Provisional figures.

Source: partly Office des Changes, Rabat.

PRINCIPAL TRADING PARTNERS
(million dirhams)*

Imports c.i.f.	1999	2000	2001†
Algeria	1,364.2	2,023.7	2,179.0
Argentina	704.2	1,066.8	1,651.3
Belgium-Luxembourg	1,866.5	1,952.2	1,762.6
Brazil	2,044.0	1,820.6	3,025.0
Canada	1,355.1	2,404.0	2,534.2
China, People's Republic	2,419.9	2,846.4	3,151.5
France	27,275.4	29,438.9	29,854.4
Germany	6,400.9	5,978.4	6,251.0
Iran	2,346.1	3,795.9	3,185.0
Iraq	2,481.3	5,047.6	4,640.3
Italy	5,634.1	5,809.8	6,262.0
Japan	2,359.7	2,069.4	1,889.4
Korea, Republic	918.0	1,261.9	1,452.4
Netherlands	1,892.7	2,067.8	1,948.1
Russia	2,750.2	2,663.2	4,095.2
Saudi Arabia	3,433.3	6,087.8	5,854.2
South Africa	837.9	938.4	1,619.0
Spain	11,771.2	12,092.6	12,806.9
Sweden	1,475.1	2,718.9	1,563.2
Switzerland	1,109.2	1,209.2	1,333.6
Turkey	1,202.6	1,059.7	1,261.8
Ukraine	906.1	1,056.5	1,584.6
United Kingdom	5,722.2	7,559.3	7,699.4
USA	6,929.6	6,836.1	4,557.7
Total (incl. others)	105,931.0	122,526.8	124,080.7

Exports f.o.b.	1999	2000	2001†
Belgium-Luxembourg	1,979.8	2,222.8	2,036.0
Brazil	473.6	730.2	915.5
France	26,309.4	26,392.1	26,391.7
Germany	4,186.8	3,916.8	3,361.0
India	3,550.4	3,297.9	2,894.3
Italy	3,728.0	5,616.3	4,599.5
Japan	2,679.8	3,009.8	2,041.3
Libya	1,130.3	668.7	660.5
Netherlands	1,420.1	1,316.4	2,184.5
Spain	7,867.3	10,220.2	12,274.2
United Kingdom	6,526.6	7,560.0	6,908.8
USA	2,511.8	2,693.5	3,246.0
Total (incl. others)	73,616.7	78,826.7	80,439.6

* Imports by country of production; exports by country of last consignment.
† Provisional figures.

Source: Office des Changes, Rabat.

Transport

RAILWAYS
(traffic)*

	1999	2000	2001
Passenger-km (million) . . .	1,875	1,956	2,019
Freight ton-km (million) . . .	4,828	4,650	4,699

* Figures refer to principal railways only.

ROAD TRAFFIC
(motor vehicles in use at 31 December)

	1996	1997	1998
Passenger cars	1,021,515	1,059,241	1,111,846
Goods vehicles	363,533	379,504	392,602
Motorcycles and scooters . . .	19,417	19,704	19,891

Source: Ministère du Transport et de la Marine Marchande.

SHIPPING
Merchant Fleet
(registered at 31 December)

	1999	2000	2001
Number of vessels	496	493	485
Total displacement ('000 grt) . .	448.5	466.9	461.5

Source: Lloyd's Register-Fairplay, *World Fleet Statistics*.

International Sea-borne Freight Traffic
('000 metric tons)

	1999	2000	2001
Goods loaded	24,128	23,384	24,973
Goods unloaded	28,524	29,831	32,542

CIVIL AVIATION
(traffic on Royal Air Maroc scheduled services)

	1998	1999	2000
Kilometres flown (million) . . .	58.8	65.0	67.9
Passengers carried ('000) . . .	3,046	3,460	3,676
Passenger-km (million) . . .	6,124	6,880	7,442
Total ton-km (million) . . .	562.9	678.4	718.5

Tourism

FOREIGN TOURIST ARRIVALS BY COUNTRY OF NATIONALITY*

	1999	2000	2001†
France	759,174	813,865	840,230
Germany	229,830	211,039	196,700
Italy	125,687	142,426	123,628
Maghreb countries	60,368	63,989	71,454
Spain	241,742	232,245	200,519
United Kingdom	143,689	137,232	135,642
USA	129,707	121,068	97,072
Total (incl. others)	2,274,814	2,325,505	2,249,662

* Excluding Moroccans resident abroad (1,541,827 in 1999; 1,787,532 in 2000; 1,973,653 in 2001).
† Provisional figures.

Cruise-ship passengers: 271,274 in 1999; 180,203 in 2000; 207,260 in 2001.

Receipts from tourism (provisional, US $ million): 1,850 in 1999; 2,040 in 2000.

Communications Media

	1999	2000	2001
Television receivers ('000 in use)	4,600	4,700	n.a.
Telephones ('000 main lines in use)	1,471.0	1,425.0	1,191.3
Mobile cellular telephones ('000 subscribers)	369.2	2,342.0	4,771.7
Personal computers ('000 in use)	300	350	400
Internet users ('000)	50	100	400

1996: Book production (titles) 918, ('000 copies) 1,836; Daily newspapers 22 (average circulation 704,000 copies); Other newspapers and periodicals 699 (average circulation 3,671,000 copies).

1997: Radio receivers ('000 in use) 6,640; Telefax stations (number in use) 18,000 (estimate).

Sources: UNESCO, *Statistical Yearbook*; UN, *Statistical Yearbook*; and International Telecommunication Union.

Education

(1999/2000, unless otherwise indicated)

	Institu-tions	Tea-chers	Pupils/Students		
			Males	Females	Total
Pre-primary . . .	33,577*	43,952	532,076	284,978	817,054
Primary: public . .	5,940	121,763	1,932,806	1,565,120	3,497,926
Primary: private . .	625	5,819	92,595	79,084	171,679
Secondary: general (public) . .	1,446	84,024‡	785,550	610,346	1,393,896
Secondary: general (private)	218	4,277	26,834	18,258	45,092
Secondary: vocational	69	n.a.	12,810	9,981	22,791
University level* † .	68	9,667	154,314	112,193	266,507

* 1997/98 figure(s).
† Provisional; state institutions only.
‡ Including vocational teachers.

2000/01: Primary 3,842,000 (public 3,644,404; private 177,596); Secondary 1,504,367 (public 1,457,388; private 46,979); University level 265,905.

2001/02: Primary 4,029,112 (public 3,832,356; private 196,756); Secondary 1,610,753 (public 1,561,686; private 49,067); University level 260,806.

Source: mainly Ministère de l'Education Nationale.

Adult literacy rate (UNESCO estimates): 48.9% (males 61.1%; females 35.1%) in 2000 (Source: UNDP, *Human Development Report*).

Directory

The Constitution

The following is a summary of the main provisions of the Constitution, as approved in a national referendum on 4 September 1992, and as amended by referendum on 13 September 1996.

PREAMBLE

The Kingdom of Morocco, a sovereign Islamic State whose official language is Arabic, constitutes a part of the Great Arab Maghreb. As an African State, one of its aims is the realization of African unity. It adheres to the principles, rights and obligations of those international organizations of which it is a member and works for the preservation of peace and security in the world.

GENERAL PRINCIPLES

Morocco is a constitutional, democratic and social monarchy. Sovereignty pertains to the nation and is exercised directly by means of the referendum and indirectly by the constitutional institutions. All Moroccans are equal before the law, and all adults enjoy equal political rights including the franchise. Freedoms of movement, opinion and speech and the right of assembly are guaranteed. Islam is the state religion. All Moroccans have equal rights in seeking education and employment. The right to strike, and to private property, is guaranteed. All Moroccans contribute to the defence of the Kingdom and to public costs. There shall be no one-party system.

THE MONARCHY

The Crown of Morocco and its attendant constitutional rights shall be hereditary in the line of HM King Hassan II, and shall be transmitted to the oldest son, unless during his lifetime the King has appointed as his successor another of his sons. The King is the symbol of unity, guarantees the continuity of the state, and safeguards respect for Islam and the Constitution. The King appoints, and may dismiss, the Prime Minister and other Cabinet Ministers (appointed upon the Prime Minister's recommendation), and presides over the Cabinet. He shall promulgate adopted legislation within a 30-day period, and has the power to dissolve the Chamber of Representatives and or the Chamber of Advisers. The Sovereign is the Commander-in-Chief of the Armed Forces; makes appointments to civil and military posts; appoints Ambassadors; signs and ratifies treaties; presides over the Supreme Council of the Magistracy, the Supreme Council of Education and the Supreme Council for National Reconstruction and Planning; and exercises the right of pardon. In cases of threat to the national territory or to the action of constitutional institutions, the King, having consulted the President of the Chamber of Representatives, the President of the Chamber of Advisers and the Chairman of the Constitutional Council, and after addressing the nation, has the right to declare a State of Emergency by royal decree. The State of Emergency shall not entail the dissolution of Parliament and shall be terminated by the same procedure followed in its proclamation.

LEGISLATURE

This consists of a bicameral parliament: the Chamber of Representatives and the Chamber of Advisers. Members of the Chamber of Representatives are elected by direct universal suffrage for a five-year term. Three-fifths of the members of the Chamber of Advisers are elected by electoral colleges of local councils; the remainder are elected by electoral colleges representing chambers of commerce and trade unions. Members of the Chamber of Advisers are elected for a nine-year term, with one-third renewable every three years. Deputies in both chambers enjoy parliamentary immunity. Parliament shall adopt legislation, which may be initiated by members of either chamber or by the Prime Minister. Draft legislation shall be examined consecutively by both parliamentary chambers. If the two chambers fail to agree on the draft legislation the Government may request that a bilateral commission propose a final draft for approval by the chambers. If the chambers do not then adopt the draft, the Government may submit the draft (modified, if need be) to the Chamber of Representatives. Henceforth the draft submitted can be definitively adopted only by absolute majority of the members of the Chamber of Representatives. Parliament holds its meetings during two sessions each year, commencing on the second Friday in October and the second Friday in April.

GOVERNMENT

The Government, composed of the Prime Minister and his Ministers, is responsible to the King and Parliament and ensures the execution of laws. The Prime Minister is empowered to initiate legislation and to exercise statutory powers except where these are reserved to the King. He presents to both parliamentary chambers the Government's intended programme and is responsible for co-ordinating ministerial work.

RELATIONS BETWEEN THE AUTHORITIES

The King may request a second reading, by both Chambers of Parliament, of any draft bill or proposed law. In addition, he may submit proposed legislation to a referendum by decree; and dissolve either Chamber or both if a proposal that has been rejected is approved by referendum. He may also dissolve either Chamber by decree after consulting the Chairman of the Constitutional Council, and addressing the nation, but the succeeding Chamber may not be dissolved within a year of its election. The Chamber of Representatives may force the collective resignation of the Government either by refusing a vote of confidence or by adopting a censure motion. The election of the new Parliament or Chamber shall take place within three months of its dissolution. In the interim period the King shall exercise the legislative powers of Parliament, in addition to those conferred upon him by the Constitution. A censure motion must be signed by at least one-quarter of the Chamber's members, and shall be approved by the Chamber only by an absolute majority vote of its members. The Chamber of Advisers is competent to issue 'warning' motions to the Government and, by a two-thirds' majority, force its resignation.

THE CONSTITUTIONAL COUNCIL

The Constitutional Council consists of six members appointed by the King (including the Chairman) for a period of nine years, and six members appointed for the same period—three selected by the President of the Chamber of Representatives and three by the President of the Chamber of Advisers. One-third of each category of the Council are renewed every three years. The Council is empowered to judge the validity of legislative elections and referendums, as well as that of organic laws and the rules of procedure of both parliamentary chambers, submitted to it.

JUDICIARY

The Judiciary is independent. Judges are appointed on the recommendation of the Supreme Council of the Magistracy presided over by the King.

THE ECONOMIC AND SOCIAL COUNCIL

An Economic and Social Council shall be established to give its opinion on all matters of an economic or social nature. Its constitution, organization, prerogatives and rules of procedure shall be determined by an organic law.

THE HIGH AUDIT COUNCIL

The High Audit Council exercises the general supervision of the implementation of fiscal laws. It ensures the regularity of revenues and expenditure operations of the departments legally under its jurisdiction, as it assesses the management of the affairs thereof. It is competent to penalize any breach of the rules governing such operations. Regional audit councils exercise the supervision of the accounts of local assemblies and bodies, and the management of the affairs thereof.

LOCAL GOVERNMENT

Local government in the Kingdom consists of establishing regions, governorships, provinces and communes.

REVISING THE CONSTITUTION

The King, the Chamber of Representatives and the Chamber of Advisers are competent to initiate a revision of the Constitution. The King has the right to submit the revision project he initiates to a national referendum. A proposal for a revision by either parliamentary chamber shall be adopted only if it receives a two-thirds' majority vote by the chamber's members. Revision projects and proposals shall be submitted to the nation for referendum by royal decree; a revision of the Constitution shall be definitive after approval by referendum. Neither the state, system of monarchy nor the prescriptions related to the religion of Islam may be subject to a constitutional revision.

The Government

HEAD OF STATE

Monarch: HM King MUHAMMAD VI (acceded 23 July 1999).

CABINET
(April 2003)

A coalition of the Union socialiste des forces populaires (USFP); Rassemblement national des indépendants (RNI); Istiqlal; Parti du progrès et du socialisme (PPS); Mouvement national populaire (MNP); Parti socialiste démocratique (PSD); and non-affiliates.

Prime Minister: DRISS JETTOU.

Minister of State: ABBAS EL-FASSI (Istiqlal).

Minister of Foreign Affairs and Co-operation: MUHAMMAD BENAISSA (RNI).

Minister of the Interior: AL MUSTAPHA SAHEL.

Minister of Justice: MUHAMMAD BOUZOUBAA (USFP).

Minister of Habous (Religious Endowments) and Islamic Affairs: AHMED TOUFIQ.

Minister of Territorial Planning, Water Resources and the Environment: MUHAMMAD EL-YAZGHI (USFP).

Minister of the Finance and Privatization: FATHALLAH OUALALOU (USFP).

Secretary-General of the Government: ABDESSADEK RABIAA.

Minister of Agriculture and Rural Development: MOHAND LAENSER (MP).

Minister of Employment, Social Development and Solidarity: MUSTAPHA MANSOURI.

Minister of National Education and Youth: HABIB EL-MALKI (USFP).

Minister of Higher Education and Scientific Research: KHALID ALIOUA (USFP).

Minister in charge of the Modernization of the Public Sector: NAJIB ZEROUALI (RNI).

Minister of Cultural Affairs: MUHAMMAD ACHAARI (USFP).

Minister in charge of Human Rights: MUHAMMAD AUJJAR (RNI).

Minister of Handicrafts and Social Economy: MUHAMMAD EL-KHALIFA (Istiqlal).

Minister of Equipment and Transport: KARIM GHELLAB (Istiqlal).

Minister of Industry, Commerce and Telecommunications: RACHID TALBI EL-ALAMI (RNI).

Minister of Tourism: ADIL DOURI (Istiqlal).

Minister of Health: MUHAMMAD CHEIKH BIADILLAH.

Minister of Maritime Fishing: MUHAMMAD TAIEB RHAFES (RNI).

Minister in charge of Relations with Parliament: MUHAMMAD SAAD EL-ALAMI (Istiqlal).

Minister of Energy and Mining: MUHAMMAD BOUTALEB (RNI).

Minister of Communication and Government Spokesperson: NABIL BENABDALLAH (PPS).

Minister of Foreign Trade: MUSTAPHA MECHAHOURI (MP).

Minister-delegate to the Prime Minister, in charge of the Administration of National Defence: ABD AR-RAHMAN SBAI.

Minister-delegate to the Minister of Foreign Affairs and Co-operation: TAIEB FASSI FIHRI.

Minister-delegate to the Minister of Foreign Affairs and Co-operation, in charge of Moroccans Resident Abroad: NEZHA CHEKROUNI (USFP).

Minister-delegate to the Minister of the Interior: FOUAD ALI EL-HIMMA.

Minister-delegate to the Minister of Higher Education and Scientific Research, in charge of Scientific Research: OMAR FASSI FIHRI (PPS).

Minister-delegate to the Prime Minister, in charge of Economic and General Affairs and the Balancing of the Economy: ABDERAZZAK EL-MOSSADEQ.

Minister-delegate to the Prime Minister, in charge of Housing and Town Planning: AHMED TOUFIQ HJIRA (Istiqlal).

There are also six Secretaries of State.

MINISTRIES

Office of the Prime Minister: Palais Royal, Le Méchouar, Rabat; tel. (3) 7762709; fax (3) 7769995; e-mail aughar@pm.gov.ma; internet www.pm.gov.ma.

Ministry of Agriculture and Rural Development: Quartier Administratif, Place Abdellah Chefchaouni, BP 607, Rabat; tel. (3) 7760933; fax (3) 7763378; e-mail webmaster@mardrpm.gov.ma; internet www.madrpm.gov.ma.

Ministry of Communications: 10 rue Beni Mellal, Rabat; tel. (3) 7762507; fax (3) 7760828; e-mail webmaster@minicom.gov.ma; internet www.minicom.gov.ma.

Ministry of Cultural Affairs: 10 rue Beni Mellal, Rabat; tel. (3) 7762507; fax (3) 7760828; e-mail webmaster@mincom.gov.ma; internet www.mincom.gov.ma.

Ministry of Economic Planning: ave Al Haj Ahmed Cherkaoui, BP 826, 10004 Rabat; e-mail idoubba@cnd.mpep.gov.ma; internet www.mpep.gov.ma.

Ministry of the Economy, Finance, Privatization and Tourism.

Ministry of Employment, Social Development and Solidarity: Rabat; e-mail dfp@dfp.ac.ma; internet ww.dfp.ac.ma.

Ministry of Energy and Mining: rue Abou Marouane Essaadi, Agdal, Rabat; tel. (3) 7688830; fax (3) 7688831; e-mail webmaster@mem.gov.ma; internet www.mem.gov.ma.

Ministry of Equipment and Transport: Quartier Administratif, Rabat; tel. (3) 7762811; fax (3) 7765505; internet www.mtpnet.gov.ma.

Ministry of Finance and Privatization: Quartier Administratif, Chella, Rabat; tel. (3) 7760147; fax (3) 7760509; internet www.finances.gov.ma.

Ministry of Foreign Affairs and Co-operation: ave Franklin Roosevelt, Rabat; tel. (3) 7761583; fax (3) 7765508; e-mail mail@maec.gov.ma; internet www.maec.gov.ma.

Ministry of Habous (Religious Endowments) and Islamic Affairs: Al-Mechouar Essaid, Rabat; tel. (3) 7766801; fax (3) 7765282; e-mail webmaster@habous.gov.ma; internet www.habous.gov.ma.

Ministry of Health: 335 rue Larache, blvd Muhammad V, Rabat; tel. (3) 7761121; fax (3) 7768401; e-mail inas@sante.gov.ma; internet www.sante.gov.ma.

Ministry of Higher Education and Scientific Research: 35 ave Ibn Sina, BP 707, Rabat; tel. (3) 7774733; fax (3) 7778028; e-mail dfc@dfc.gov.ma; internet www.dfc.gov.ma.

Ministry in charge of Human Rights: Rabat; tel. (3) 7673131; fax (3) 7671967.

Ministry of Industry, Commerce and Telecommunications: Rabat; tel. (3) 7761868; fax (3) 7766265; e-mail webmaster@mcinet.gov.ma; internet www.mcinet.gov.ma.

Ministry of the Interior: Quartier Administratif, Rabat; tel. (3) 7761868; fax (3) 7762056.

Ministry of Justice: Place Mamounia, Rabat; tel. (3) 7732941; fax (3) 7730772; e-mail kourout@justice.gov.ma; internet www.justice.gov.ma.

Ministry of Maritime Fishing: Rabat; e-mail webmaster@.mp3m.gov.ma; internet www.mp3m.gov.ma.

Ministry of National Education and Youth: Bab Rouah, Rabat; tel. (3) 7771822; fax (3) 7779029.

Ministry of Civil Service and Administrative Reform.

Ministry in charge of Relations with Parliament: Nouveau Quartier Administratif, Rabat; tel. (3) 7775124; e-mail mirepa@mcrp.gov.ma; internet www.mcrp.gov.ma.

Ministry of Social Development, Solidarity, Employment and Professional Training.

Ministry of Territorial Administration, Water Resources and the Environment: 36 ave el-Abtal, Agdal, Rabat; tel. (3) 7772634; fax (3) 7772756; e-mail info@minenv.gov.ma; internet www.minenv.gov.ma.

Ministry of Transport and Merchant Navy: rue Maa al-Ainane, Casier Officiel, BP 759, Rabat; tel. (3) 7774266; fax (3) 7779525.

Ministry of Youth and Sports: blvd lbn Sina, Rabat; tel. (3) 7680028; fax (3) 7680145; internet www.mjs.gov.ma.

Legislature

MAJLIS AN-NUAB
(Chamber of Representatives)

President: ABDELWAHED RADHI (USFP).

General Election, 27 September 2002

Party	% of votes	Seats
Union socialiste des forces populaires (USFP)	15.38	50
Istiqlal	14.77	48
Parti de la justice et du développement (PJD) . . .	12.92	42
Rassemblement national des indépendants (RNI) . . .	12.62	41
Mouvement populaire (MP) . .	8.31	27
Mouvement national populaire (MNP)	4.92	16
Front des forces démocratiques (FFD)	3.69	12
Parti national démocrate (PND)	3.69	12
Parti du progrès et du socialisme (PPS)	3.38	11
Union démocratique (UD) . .	3.08	10
Mouvement démocratique social (MDS)	2.15	7
Parti socialiste démocratique (PSD)	1.85	6
Parti Al Ahd	1.54	5
Alliance des libertés (ADL) . .	1.23	4
Parti de la gauche socialist unifiée (PGSU)	0.92	3
Parti de la réforme et du développement (PRD) . .	0.92	3
Parti marocain libéral (PML) .	0.92	3
Parti des forces citoyennes (PFC)	0.62	2
Parti de l'environnement et du développement (PED) . .	0.62	2
Parti démocratique et de l'indépendance (PDI) . .	0.62	2
Congrès national ittihadi (CNI)	0.31	1
Total	100.00	325*

* 30 of the 325 seats were reserved for women. Of these 30 seats five were won by the USFP; Istiqlal, the PJD and the RNI each took four seats; the MP, the MNP, the UC, the PND, the FFD and PPS all secured two seats; and the UD received one seat.

MAJLIS AL-MUSTASHARIN
(Chamber of Advisers)

President: MUSTAPHA OKACHA.

Election, 5 December 1997*

	Seats
Rassemblement national des indépendants (RNI) . .	42
Mouvement démocratique et social (MDS).	33
Union constitutionnelle (UC)	28
Mouvement populaire (MP)	27
Parti national démocrate (PND)	21
Istiqlal	21
Union socialiste des forces populaires (USFP) . . .	16
Mouvement national populaire (MNP)	15
Parti de l'action (PA)	13
Front des forces démocratiques (FFD)	12
Parti du progrès et du socialisme (PPS)	7
Parti social et démocratique (PSD)	4
Parti démocratique pour l'indépendance (PDI) . .	4
Trade unions	
Confédération Démocratique du Travail (CDT) .	11
Union Marocaine du Travail (UMT)	8
Union Générale des Travailleurs Marocains (UGMT)	3
Others	5
Total	270

* Of the Chamber of Advisers' 270 members, 162 were elected by local councils, 81 by chambers of commerce and 27 by trade unions.
Note: On 8 September 2000 elections were held to renew one-third of the seats in the Chamber of Advisers. 54 members were elected by local councils and 27 by chambers of commerce. The seats were allocated accordingly: RNI 14 seats; MNP 12; PND 10; MP 9; UC 8; Istiqlal 7; MDS 6; FFD 5; USFP 3; PPS 2; PA 2; PSD two; PDI one.

Of the nine seats elected by trade unions the CDT won 4; the UMT 2; the UGTM 2; and the l'Union Nationale des Travailleurs du Maroc (UNMT) won one seat.

Political Organizations

Congrès national ittihadi (CNI): f. 2001; Sec.-Gen. ABDELMAJID BOUZOUBAA.

Front des forces démocratiques (FFD): 13 blvd Tariq ibn Ziad, Rabat; tel. (3) 7661625; fax (3) 7661626; f. 1997 after split from PPS; Sec.-Gen. THAMI EL-KHIARI.

Istiqlal: 4 ave Ibn Toumert, Bab el Had, Rabat; tel. (3) 7730951; fax (3) 7725354; f. 1944; aims to raise living standards and to confer equal rights on all; stresses the Moroccan claim to Western Sahara; Sec.-Gen. ABBAS EL-FASSI.

Mouvement démocratique et social (MDS): 471 ave Muhammad V, Rabat; tel. (3) 7709110; f. 1996 as Mouvement national démocratique et social after split from MNP; adopted current name in Nov. 1996; Leader MAHMOUD ARCHANE.

Mouvement national populaire (MNP): Souissi, Rabat; tel. (3) 7753623; fax (3) 7759761; f. 1991; centre party; Leader MAHJOUBI AHERDANE.

Mouvement populaire (MP): 66 rue Patrice Lumumba, Rabat; tel. (3) 7767320; fax (3) 7767537; f. 1958; liberal; Sec.-Gen. MOHAND LAENSER.

Mouvement populaire pour la démocratie (MPD): Leader M. EL-KHATIB.

Organisation de l'action démocratique et populaire (OADP): Casablanca; tel. (2) 2262433; fax (2) 2278442; e-mail organisation .oadp@caramail.com; f. 1983; Sec.-Gen. MUHAMMAD BEN SAÏD AÏT IDDER.

Parti de l'action (PA): 113 ave Allal ben Abdallah, Rabat; tel. (3) 7206661; f. 1974; advocates democracy and progress; Sec.-Gen. MUHAMMAD EL IDRISSI.

Parti Al Ahd: f. 2002; Pres. BOUAZZA IKKEN.

Parti de l'avant-garde démocratique socialiste (PADS): BP 2091, 54 ave de la Résistance Océan, Rabat; tel. (3) 7200559; fax (3) 7708491; internet membres.tripod.fr/PADSMAROC/; an offshoot of the USFP; legalized in April 1992; Sec.-Gen. AHMAD BENJELLOUNE.

Parti du congrès national unioniste: Rabat; f. 2001 by dissident members of the USFP; Sec.-Gen. ABDELMAJID BOUZOUBAÂ.

Parti démocratique et de l'indépendance (PDI): Casablanca; tel. (2) 2223359; f. 1946; Sec.-Gen. ABDELWAHED MAACH.

Parti de l'environnement et du développement (PED): f. 2002; Sec.-Gen. AHMAD AL-ALAMI.

Parti des forces citoyennes (PFC): f. 2001; Sec.-Gen. ABDERRAHIM LAHJOUJI.

Parti de la gauche socialiste unifiée (PGSU): Rabat; f. 2001; left-wing coalition comprising the OADP, the MPD, the Activistes de gauche and the Démocrates indépendants; Pres. MUHAMMAD BEN SAID AIT IDDER.

Parti de la justice et du développement (PJD): 5 rue Maati Bakhay, Rabat; tel. (3) 7208862; fax (3) 7208854; e-mail pjd@ maktoub.com; f. 1967 as the Mouvement populaire constitutionnel et démocratique (MPCD); breakaway party from MP; formally absorbed members of the Islamic asscn Al Islah wa Attajdid in June 1996 and adopted current name in Oct. 1998; Sec.-Gen. ABDELKRIM KHATIB.

Parti marocain libéral (PML): f. 2002; Nat. Co-ordinator MUHAMMAD ZIANE.

Parti national démocrate (PND): 18 rue de Tunis, Rabat; tel. (3) 7732127; fax (3) 7720170; f. 1981 from split within RNI; Sec.-Gen. ABDELLAH KADIRI.

Parti de la reforme et du developpement (PRD): Rabat; f. 2001 by fmr members of the RNI; Leader ABD AR-RAHMANE KOHEN.

Parti du progrès et du socialisme (PPS): 29 ave John Kennedy, Youssoufia, Rabat; tel. (3) 7759464; fax (3) 7759476; f. 1974; successor to the Parti communiste marocain (banned in 1952), and the Parti de la libération et du socialisme (banned in 1969); left-wing; advocates modernization, social progress, nationalization and democracy; 35,000 mems; Sec.-Gen. ISMAIL ALAOUI.

Parti socialiste démocratique (PSD): 1 rue Ibn Moqla, angle les Orangers, Rabat; tel. and fax (3) 7208576; e-mail dsp1@iam.net.ma; f. 1996; breakaway party from OADP; Leader ISSA OUARDIGHI.

Rassemblement national des indépendants (RNI): 6 rue Laos, ave Hassan II, Rabat; tel. (3) 7721420; fax (3) 7733824; f. 1978 from the pro-govt independents' group that formed the majority in the Chamber of Representatives; Leader AHMAD OUSMAN.

Union constitutionnelle (UC): 158 ave des Forces Armées Royales, Casablanca; tel. (2) 2441144; fax (2) 2441141; e-mail uc@marocnet.net.ma; internet www.mincom.gov.ma/partis/uc; f. 1983; 25-member Political Bureau; Leader (vacant).

Union démocratique (UD): f. 2001; Pres. BOUAZZA IKKEN.

Union nationale des forces populaires (UNFP): 28–30 rue Magellan, BP 747, Casablanca; tel. (2) 2302023; fax (2) 2319301; f. 1959 by Mehdi ben Barka from a group within Istiqlal; left-wing; in 1972 a split occurred between the Casablanca and Rabat sections of the party; Leader MOULAY ABDALLAH IBRAHIM.

Union socialiste des forces populaires (USFP): 17 rue Oued Souss, Agdal, Rabat; tel. (3) 7773905; fax (3) 7773901; e-mail usfp@mtds.com; internet www.mtds.com/~usfp; f. 1959 as UNFP, became USFP in 1974; left-wing progressive party; 100,000 mems; First Sec. ABD AR-RAHMAN EL-YOUSSOUFI.

The following group is active in the disputed territory of Western Sahara:

Frente Popular para la Liberación de Saguia el-Hamra y Río de Oro (Frente Polisario) (Polisario Front): BP 10, el-Mouradia, Algiers; tel. (2) 747907; fax (2) 747206; e-mail dgmae@mail.wissal.dz; f. 1973 to gain independence for Western Sahara, first from Spain and then from Morocco and Mauritania; signed peace treaty with Mauritanian Govt in 1979; supported by Algerian Govt; in February 1976 proclaimed the Sahrawi Arab Democratic Republic (SADR); admitted as the 51st member of the OAU in Feb. 1982 and currently recognized by more than 75 countries worldwide; its main organs are a 33-member National Secretariat, a 101-member Sahrawi National Assembly (Parliament) and a 13-member Govt; Sec.-Gen. of the Polisario Front and Pres. of the SADR MUHAMMAD ABD AL-AZIZ; Prime Minister of the SADR BOUCHRAYA HAMMOUDI BAYOUNE.

Diplomatic Representation

EMBASSIES IN MOROCCO

Algeria: 46–48 blvd Tariq Ibn Ziad, BP 448, 10001 Rabat; tel. (3) 7765591; fax (3) 7762237; e-mail algerabat@iam.net.ma; Ambassador MUHAMMAD LAKHDAR HADJAZI.

Angola: km 4.5, route des Zaêrs, BP 1318, Soussi, Rabat; tel. (3) 7659239; fax (3) 7653703; e-mail amb.angola@iam.net.ma; Ambassador Dr LUIS JOSÉ DE ALMEIDA.

Argentina: 12 rue Mekki Bitaouri, Souissi, 10000 Rabat; tel. (3) 7755120; fax (3) 7755410; e-mail embarat@maghrebnet.net.ma; Ambassador EDGARDO RENÉ PIUZZI.

Austria: 2 rue de Tiddas, BP 135, 10001 Rabat; tel. (3) 7764003; fax (3) 7765425; e-mail autrich@mtds.com; Ambassador Dr MICHAEL FITZ.

Bangladesh: 25 ave Tarek Ibn Ziad, Rabat; tel. (3) 7766731; fax (3) 7766729; e-mail bdoot@mtds.com; internet www.bangladeshembassy-morocco.org; Ambassador Maj.-Gen. MOHAMMAD ANWAR HOSSAIN.

Belgium: 6 ave de Marrakech, BP 163, 10001 Rabat; tel. (3) 7764746; fax (3) 7767003; e-mail info@ambel-rabat.org.ma; Ambassador MICHEL CARLIER.

Benin: 30 ave Mehdi Ben Barka, BP 5187, Souissi, 10105 Rabat; tel. (3) 7754158; fax (3) 77754156; Ambassador IBRAHIM ISSIRADJOU GOMINA.

Brazil: 3 rue Cadi Benjelloun, La Pinède, BP 414, 10000 Rabat; tel. (3) 7755151; fax (3) 7755291; Ambassador LAURO BARBOSA DA SILVA MOREIRA.

Bulgaria: 4 ave Ahmed El Yazidi, BP 1301, 10000 Rabat; tel. (3) 7765477; fax (3) 7763201; Ambassador Dr GEORGE B. KAREV.

Burkina Faso: 7 rue al Bouziri, BP 6484, Agdal, 10101 Rabat; tel. (3) 7675512; fax (3) 7675517; e-mail ambfrba@smirt.net.ma; Ambassador ASSIMI KOUANDA.

Cameroon: 20 rue du Rif, BP 1790, Souissi, Rabat; tel. (3) 7754194; fax (3) 7750540; e-mail ambacamrabat@ifrance.com; Ambassador MAHAMAT PABA SALÉ.

Canada: 13 bis rue Jaafar as-Sadik, BP 709, Agdal, Rabat; tel. (3) 7687400; fax (3) 7687430; Ambassador YVES GAGNON.

Central African Republic: 42 rue Pasteur, BP 770, Agdal, 10000 Rabat; tel. (3) 7734198; Ambassador MARTIN KOYOU KOMBELE.

Chile: 35 ave Ahmed Balafrej, Souissi, Rabat; tel. (3) 7636065; fax (3) 7636067; e-mail echilema@maghrebnet.net.ma; Ambassador ALEJANDRO CARVAJAL.

China, People's Republic: 16 ave Ahmed Balafrej, 10000 Rabat; tel. (3) 7754056; fax (3) 7757519; Ambassador XIONG ZHANQI.

Colombia: Residence place Otman Ibnou Affane, 3eme étage, App. no 12, angle ave 16 Novembre et rue Honaine, Agdal, 10000 Rabat; tel. (3) 7670804; fax (3) 7670802; e-mail emcora@smirt.net.ma; Ambassador GUILLERMO SALAH ZULETTA.

Congo, Democratic Republic: 34 ave de la Victoire, BP 553, 10000 Rabat; tel. (3) 7262280; fax (3) 7262280; Chargé d'affaires a.i. WAWA BAMIALY.

Côte d'Ivoire: 21 rue de Tiddas, BP 192, 10001 Rabat; tel. (3) 7763151; fax (3) 7762792; e-mail ambcim@dial.net.ma; Ambassador AMADOU THIAM.

Croatia: 73 rue Marnissa, Souissi, Rabat; tel. (3) 7638824; fax (3) 7638827; e-mail croamb@acdim.net.ma.

Czech Republic: rue Ait Melloul, BP 410, Souissi, 10001 Rabat; tel. (3) 7755421; fax (3) 7755493; e-mail rabat@embassy.mzv.cz; internet www.mzv.cz/rabat; Ambassador PAVEL JAJTNER.

Egypt: 31 rue al-Jazair, 10000 Rabat; tel. (3) 7731833; fax (3) 7706821; Ambassador ACHRAF YUSSUF ABDELHALIM ZAÂZAÂ.

Equatorial Guinea: ave President Roosevelt, angle rue d'Agadir 9, Rabat; tel. (3) 7764793; fax (3) 7764704; Ambassador (vacant).

Finland: 145 rue Soufiane Ben Wahb, OLM, Rabat; tel. (3) 7762312; fax (3) 7762352; e-mail admin@ambafinrab.org.ma; Ambassador ESKO KIURU.

France: 3 rue Sahnoun, 10000 Rabat; tel. (3) 7689706; fax (3) 7689720; e-mail michel.de-bonnecorse@diplomatie.fr; internet www.ambafrance-ma.org; Ambassador FREDERIC GRASSET.

Gabon: ave Imam Malik, km 3.5, BP 1239, 10100 Rabat; tel. (3) 7751968; fax (3) 7757550; Ambassador VICTOR AFOUNOUNA.

Germany: 7 Zankat Madnine, BP 235, 10000 Rabat; tel. (3) 7709662; fax (3) 7706851; e-mail amballma@mtds.com; internet www.amballemagne-rabat.com; Ambassador ROLAND MAUCH.

Greece: km 5 route des Zaiers, Villa Chems, Soussi, 10000 Rabat; tel. (3) 7638964; fax (3) 7638990; e-mail ambagrec@iam.net.ma; Ambassador MICHEL CAMBANIS.

Guinea: 15 rue Hamzah, Agdal, 10000 Rabat; tel. (3) 7674148; fax (3) 7672513; Ambassador MAHMADOU SALIOU SYLA.

Holy See: rue Béni M'tir, BP 1303, Souissi, Rabat (Apostolic Nunciature); tel. (3) 7772277; fax (3) 7756213; e-mail nuntius@iam.net.ma; Apostolic Nuncio Most Rev. DOMENICO DE LUCA (Titular Archbishop of Teglata in Numidia).

Hungary: 17 Zankat Aït Melloul, Souissi, BP 5026, Rabat; tel. (3) 7750757; fax (3) 7754123; e-mail huembrba@mtds.com; Ambassador KÁROLY GEDAI.

India: 13 ave de Michlifen, 10000 Rabat; tel. (3) 7671339; fax (3) 7671269; e-mail india@maghrebnet.net.ma; Ambassador INDRAJIT SINGH RATHORE.

Indonesia: 63 rue Béni Boufrah, km 5.9 route des Zaêrs, BP 5076, 10105 Rabat; tel. (3) 7757860; fax (3) 7757859; e-mail kbrirabat@iam.net.ma; Ambassador SOEKAMTO WIENARDI.

Iran: ave Imam Malik, BP 490, 10001 Rabat; tel. (3) 7752167; fax (3) 7659118; Ambassador MUHAMMAD REDA BAKHTIARI.

Iraq: 39 blvd Mehdi Ben Barka, 10100 Rabat; tel. (3) 7754466; fax (3) 7759749; Ambassador ABD AL-JABBAR OMAR GHANI AD-DURI.

Italy: 2 rue Idriss al-Azhar, BP 111, 10001 Rabat; tel. (3) 7720852; fax (3) 7706882; e-mail ambraba@iam.net.ma; Ambassador GUIDO MARTINI.

Japan: 39 ave Ahmed Balafrej, Souissi, 10100 Rabat; tel. (3) 7631782; fax (3) 7750078; e-mail amb-japon@fusion.net.ma; Ambassador HIROMI SATO.

Jordan: Villa al-Wafae, Lot 5, Souissi II, 10000 Rabat; tel. (3) 7751125; fax (3) 7758722; Ambassador MUHAMMAD HASSAN SOLEIMANE AD-DAOUDIA.

Korea, Republic: 41 ave Mehdi Ben Barka, Souissi, 10100 Rabat; tel. (3) 7751767; fax (3) 7750189; e-mail adambco@iam.net.ma; Ambassador JU CHUL-KU.

Kuwait: ave Imam Malik, km 4.3, BP 11, 10001 Rabat; tel. (3) 7751775; fax (3) 7753591; Ambassador SALAH MUHAMMAD AL-BIJAN.

Lebanon: 19 ave Adb al-Karim Ben Jalloun, 10000 Rabat; tel. (3) 7760728; fax (3) 7760949; Ambassador MOUSTAPHA HASSAN MOUSTAPHA.

Liberia: Lotissement no 7, Napabia, rue Ouled Frej, Souissi, Rabat; tel. (3) 7638426.

Libya: 1 rue Chouaïb Doukkali, BP 225, 10000 Rabat; tel. (3) 7769566; fax (3) 7705200; Ambassador EMBAREK ABDALLAH TURKI.

Malaysia: ave Bir Kacem, Soussi, Rabat; tel. (3) 7658324; fax (3) 7658363; e-mail mwrabat@maghrebnet.net; Ambassador SIDDIQ FIRDAUSE BIN MOHD ALI.

Mali: 7 rue Thami Lamadour, Souissi, Rabat; tel. (3) 7759125; fax (3) 7754742; Ambassador Foussein Sy.

Mauritania: 6 rue Thami Lamdour, BP 207, Souissi, 10000 Rabat; tel. (3) 7656678; fax (3) 7656680; e-mail ambassadeur@mauritanie .org.ma; Ambassador Dah Ould Abdi.

Mexico: 6 rue Cadi Mohamed Brebi, BP 1789, Souissi, Rabat; tel. (3) 7631969; fax (3) 7768583; e-mail embamexmar@smirt.net.ma; Ambassador Antonio de Icaza.

Netherlands: 40 rue de Tunis, BP 329, 10001 Rabat; tel. (3) 7726780; fax (3) 7733333; e-mail nlgovrab@mtds.com; internet www .mtds.com/nlgovrab; Ambassador Johannes A. F. M. Revis.

Niger: 14 Bis, rue Jabal al-Ayachi, Agdal, Rabat; tel. (3) 7674615; fax (3) 7674629; Ambassador Ramatou Diori Hamani.

Nigeria: 70 ave Omar ibn al-Khattab, BP 347, Agdal, 10001 Rabat; tel. (3) 7673856; fax (3) 7672739; e-mail nigembassy@maghrebnet .net.ma; Ambassador Ladan Adbullahi Shuni.

Norway: 9 rue Khenifra, Agdal, Rabat; tel. (3) 7764085; fax (3) 7764088; e-mail emb.rabat@mfa.no; Ambassador Ole Kristian Holthe.

Oman: 21 rue Hamza, Agdal, 10000 Rabat; tel. (3) 7673788; fax (3) 7674567; Ambassador Mahmoud bin Ali Muhammad ar-Rahman.

Pakistan: 11 Zankat Azrou, 10000 Rabat; tel. (3) 7762402; fax (3) 7766742; e-mail parerabat@maghrebnet.net.ma; Ambassador Maj. Gen. (Retd) Shujaat Ali Khan.

Peru: 16 rue d'Ifrane, 10000 Rabat; tel. (3) 7723236; fax (3) 7702803; e-mail lepruab@netpartners.net.ma; Ambassador Juan Enrique Arevalo.

Poland: 23 rue Oqbah, Agdal, BP 425, 10000 Rabat; tel. (3) 7771173; fax (3) 7775320; e-mail apologne@iam.net.ma; internet www.ambpologne.ma; Ambassador Mieczysław Jacek Stepiński.

Portugal: 5 rue Thami Lamdour, Souissi, 10100 Rabat; tel. (3) 7756446; fax (3) 7756445; e-mail embport_rabat@hotmail.com; Ambassador Rui Gonçalo de Brito e Cunha.

Qatar: 4 ave Tarik ibn Ziad, BP 1220, 10001 Rabat; tel. (3) 7765681; fax (3) 7765774; e-mail qe-rabat@mtds.com; Ambassador Saqr Mubarak al-Mansouri.

Romania: 10 rue d'Ouezzane, 10000 Rabat; tel. (3) 7738611; fax (3) 7700196; e-mail amb.roumanie@smirt.net.ma; Ambassador Gelu Voican Voiculescu.

Russia: km 4 route des Zaiers, 10100 Rabat; tel. (3) 7753509; fax (3) 7753590; e-mail consruss@mtds.com; Ambassador Yurii Kotov.

Saudi Arabia: 43 place de l'Unité Africaine, 10000 Rabat; tel. (3) 7730171; fax (3) 7768587; e-mail ambassd@goodinfo.net.ma; Ambassador Abd al-Aziz Khodja.

Senegal: 17 rue Cadi ben Hamadi Senhaji, Souissi, 10000 Rabat; tel. (3) 7754171; fax (3) 7754149; Ambassador Doudou Diop.

Serbia and Montenegro: 23 ave Mehdi Ben Barka, Souissi, BP 5014, 10105 Rabat; tel. (3) 7752201; fax (3) 7753258; e-mail youg@ iam.net.ma; Chargé d'affaires Golub Lazović.

South Africa: 34 rue Saadiens, Rabat; tel. (3) 7706760; fax (3) 7706756; e-mail sudaf@mtds.com; Ambassador M. Mtutuzeli Mpehle.

Spain: 3 rue Madnine, BP 1354, 10000 Rabat; tel. (3) 7707600; fax (3) 7707387; e-mail infembsp@mtds.com; Ambassador Fernando Arias-Salgado y Montalvo.

Sudan: 5 ave Ghomara, Souissi, 10000 Rabat; tel. (3) 7752863; fax (3) 7752865; e-mail soudanirab@maghrebnet.net.ma; Ambassador Ahmed Mekki Ahmed Yahia.

Sweden: 159 ave John Kennedy, BP 428, 10000 Rabat; tel. (3) 7759303; fax (3) 7758048; e-mail swedrab@mtds.com; Ambassador Nils Anders Peter Bruce.

Switzerland: Square de Berkane, BP 169, 1001 Rabat; tel. (3) 7706974; fax (3) 7705749; e-mail vertretung@rab.rep.admin.ch; Ambassador Daniel von Muralt.

Syria: km 5.2, route des Zaêrs, BP 5158, Souissi, Rabat; tel. (3) 7755551; fax (3) 7757522; Ambassador Ali Hassan.

Thailand: 11 rue de Tiddas, BP 4436, Rabat; tel. (3) 7763328; fax (3) 7763920; e-mail thairab@wanadoo.net.ma; Ambassador Siriwat Suthigasame.

Tunisia: 6 ave de Fès et 1 rue d'Ifrane, 10000 Rabat; tel. (3) 7730636; fax (3) 7730637; Ambassador Salah Bekkari.

Turkey: 7 ave Abdelkrim Benjelloun, 10000 Rabat; tel. (3) 7762605; fax (3) 7660476; e-mail amb-tur-rabat@iam.net.ma; Ambassador Huseyin Naci Akinci.

Ukraine: Cite OLM Soussi II, Villa 212, Rabat; tel. (3) 7657840; fax (3) 7754679; e-mail ukremb@iam.net.ma; Ambassador Youri F. Malko.

United Arab Emirates: 11 ave des Alaouines, 10000 Rabat; tel. (3) 7702085; fax (3) 7724145; e-mail uaerabat@mtds.com; Ambassador Issaa Hamad Bushahab.

United Kingdom: 17 blvd de la Tour Hassan, BP 45, 10001 Rabat; tel. (3) 77238600; fax (3) 7704531; e-mail britemb@mtds.com; internet www.britain.org.ma; Ambassador Haydon Warren-Gash.

USA: 2 ave de Muhammad el-Fassi, Rabat; tel. (3) 7762265; fax (3) 7765661; internet www.usembassy-morocco.org.ma; Ambassador Margaret DeB. Tutwiler.

Venezuela: 173 ave John Kennedy, Soussi, Rabat; tel. (3) 7650315; fax (3) 7650372; Ambassador Horacio Arteaga Acosta.

Yemen: 11 rue Abou-Hanifa, Agdal, 10000 Rabat; tel. (3) 7674306; fax (3) 7674769; e-mail yemenembassy@iam.net.ma; Ambassador Dr Ali Mtena Hassan.

Judicial System

SUPREME COURT

Al-Majlis al-Aala

Hay Ryad, blvd An-Nakhil, Rabat; tel. (3) 7714932; e-mail coursupreme@maghrebnet.net.ma; internet www.maghrebnet.net .ma/cour-supreme/.

Is responsible for the interpretation of the law and regulates the jurisprudence of the courts and tribunals of the Kingdom. The Supreme Court sits at Rabat and is divided into six Chambers.

First President: Driss Dahak.

Attorney-General: Muhammad Abdelmounim el-Mejboud.

The 21 **Courts of Appeal** hear appeals from lower courts and also comprise a criminal division

The 65 **Courts of First Instance** pass judgment on offences punishable by up to five years' imprisonment. These courts also pass judgment, without possibility of appeal, in personal and civil cases involving up to 3,000 dirhams

The **Communal and District Courts** are composed of one judge, who is assisted by a clerk or secretary, and hear only civil and criminal cases

The seven **Administrative Courts** pass judgement, subject to appeal before the Supreme Court pending the establishment of administrative appeal courts, on litigation with Government departments

The nine **Commercial Courts** pass judgement, without the possibility of appeal, on all commercial litigations involving up to 9,000 dirhams. They also pass judgement on claims involving more than 9,000 dirhams, which can be appealed against in the commercial appeal courts

The **Special Court of Justice** presides over crimes and felonies allegedly committed by Government officials or judges involving 25,000 dirhams or more

The **Permanent Royal Armed Forces' Court** tries offences committed by the armed forces and military officers

Religion

ISLAM

About 99% of Moroccans are Muslims (of whom about 90% are of the Sunni sect), and Islam is the state religion.

CHRISTIANITY

There are about 69,000 Christians, mostly Roman Catholics.

The Roman Catholic Church

Morocco (excluding the disputed territory of Western Sahara) comprises two archdioceses, directly responsible to the Holy See. At 31 December 2000 there were an estimated 24,000 adherents in the country, representing less than 0.1% of the population. The Moroccan archbishops participate in the Conférence Episcopale Régionale du Nord de l'Afrique (f. 1985), based in Algiers (Algeria).

Archbishop of Rabat: Most Rev. Vincent Landel, Archevêché, 1 rue Hadj Muhammad Riffaï, BP 258, 10001 Rabat; tel. (3) 7709239; fax (3) 7706282; e-mail landel@wanadoo.net.ma.

Archbishop of Tangier: Most Rev. José Antonio Peiteiro Freire, Archevêché, 55 rue Sidi Bouabid, BP 2116, 9000 Tangier; tel. (3) 9932762; fax (3) 9949117; e-mail igletanger@wanadoo.net.ma.

Western Sahara comprises a single Apostolic Prefecture, with an estimated 150 Catholics (2000).

Prefect Apostolic of Western Sahara: Fr Acacio Valbuena Rodríguez, Misión Católica, BP 31, 70001 el-Aaiún; tel. 893270.

The Anglican Communion

Within the Church of England, Morocco forms part of the diocese of Gibraltar in Europe. There are Anglican churches in Casablanca and Tangier.

Protestant Church

Evangelical Church: 33 rue d'Azilal, 20000 Casablanca; tel. (2) 2302151; fax (2) 2444768; e-mail eeam@lesblancs.com; f. 1920; established in eight towns; Pres. Pastor Jean-Luc Blanc; 1,000 mems.

JUDAISM

There is a Jewish community of some 8,000. In March 1999 the Moroccan authorities reopened the synagogue in Fez, established in the 17th century.

Grand Rabbi of Casablanca: Chalom Messas (President of the Rabbinical Court of Casablanca, Palais de Justice, place des Nations Unies).

The Press

DAILIES

Casablanca

Assahra Al-Maghribia: 88 blvd Muhammad V, Casablanca; tel. (2) 2268860; fax (2) 2203935; f. 1989; Arabic; Dir Abd al-Hafid Rouissi.

Al-Bayane (The Manifesto): 62 blvd de la Gironde, BP 13152, Casablanca; tel. (2) 2307882; internet www.casanet.ma/albayane; Arabic and French; organ of the Parti du progrès et du socialisme; Dir Ismail Alaoui; circ. 5,000.

Al-Ittihad al-Ichtiraki (Socialist Unity): 33 rue Emir Abdelkader, BP 2165, Casablanca; tel. (2) 2619400; fax (2) 2619405; Arabic; organ of the Union socialiste des forces populaires; Dir Abdallah Bouhlal; Editor Abd ar-Rahman el-Youssoufi; circ. 110,000.

L'Economiste: 201 blvd Bordeaux, Casablanca; tel. (2) 2271650; fax (2) 2297285; e-mail info@leconomiste.com; internet www.leconomiste.com; f. 1991; weekly; French; Dir Abdelmounaïm Dilami; Editor Nadia Salah; circ. 24,000.

Libération: 33 rue Emir Abdelkader, Casablanca; tel. (2) 2310062; internet www.liberation.press.ma; f. 1964; French; organ of the Union socialiste des forces populaires; Dir Muhammad al-Yazghi.

Maroc Soir: 88 blvd Muhammad V, Casablanca; tel. (2) 2268860; fax (2) 2262969; f. 1971; French; Dir Drissi el-Alami; circ. 50,000.

Le Matin du Sahara et du Maghreb: 88 blvd Muhammad V, Casablanca; tel. (2) 2268860; fax (2) 2317535; e-mail contact@lematin.press.ma; internet www.lematin.press.ma; f. 1971; French; Dir Abd al-Hafid Rouissi; circ. 100,000.

Rissalat al-Oumma (The Message of the Nation): 158 ave des Forces Armées Royales, Casablanca; tel. (2) 2901925; Arabic; weekly edition in French; organ of the Union constitutionnelle; Dir Muhammad Alaoui Muhammadi.

Rabat

Al-Alam (The Flag): 11 ave Allal ben Abdallah, BP 141, Rabat; tel. (3) 7732419; fax (3) 7733896; f. 1946; organ of the Istiqlal party; Arabic; literary supplement on Fridays; weekly edition on Mondays; monthly edition on foreign policy; Dir Abd al-Krim Ghallab; circ. 100,000.

Al-Anba'a (Information): ave Allal el-Fassi, Rabat; tel. (3) 7683967; fax (3) 7683970; internet www.alanbaa.press.ma; f. 2000; daily; Arabic; publ. by Ministry of Communication; Dir (Editorial) Muhammad Belghazi.

Assyassa al-Jadida: 43 rue Abou Fares al-Marini, BP 1385, Rabat; tel. (3) 7208571; fax (3) 7208573; e-mail assassjdid@maghrebnet.net.ma; f. 1997; Arabic; organ of the Parti socialiste démocratique; Dir Abd al-Latif Aouad; Editor Talaa Assoud Alatlassi.

Al-Maghrib: 6 rue Laos, BP 469, Rabat; tel. (3) 7722708; fax (3) 7722765; f. 1977; French; organ of the Rassemblement national des indépendants (RNI); Dir Mustapha Iznasni; circ. 15,000.

Al-Mithaq al-Watani (The National Charter): 6 rue Laos, BP 469, Rabat; tel. (3) 7722708; fax (3) 7722765; f. 1977; Arabic; organ of the RNI; Dir Med Auajjar; circ. 25,000.

An-Nidal ad-Dimokrati (The Democratic Struggle): 18 rue de Tunis, Rabat; tel. (3) 7730754; fax (3) 7731255; Arabic; organ of the Parti national démocrate; Dir Muhammad Arsalane al-Jadidi.

L'Opinion: 11 ave Allal ben Abdallah, Rabat; tel. (3) 7727812; fax (3) 7732181; f. 1965; French; organ of the Istiqlal party; Dir Muhammad Idrissi Kaïtouni; Ed. Jamal Hajjam; circ. 60,000.

SELECTED PERIODICALS

Casablanca

Achamal: Casablanca; weekly; Arabic; Ed. in Chief Khalid Mechbal.

Bulletin Mensuel de la Chambre de Commerce et d'Industrie de la Wilaya du Grand Casablanca: 98 blvd Muhammad V, BP 423, Casablanca; tel. (2) 2264327; monthly; French; Pres. Lahcen el-Wafi.

CGEM Infos: angle ave des Forces Armées Royales et rue Muhammad Arrachid, 20100 Casablanca; tel. (2) 2986932; fax (2) 2253845; e-mail cgem@iam.net.ma; weekly; French; Admin. Mouhcine Ayouche.

Construire: 25 rue d'Azilal, Immeuble Ortiba, Casablanca; tel. (2) 2305721; fax (2) 2317577; f. 1940; weekly; French; Dir Talal Bouchaib.

Demain: Casablanca; f. 1997; weekly, French; Dir Ali Lamrabet.

Les Echos Africains: Immeuble SONIR, angle blvd Smiha, rue d'Anjou, BP 13140, Casablanca; tel. (2) 2307271; fax (2) 2319680; f. 1972; monthly; French; news, economics; Dir Muhammad Chouffani el-Fassi; Editor Mme Soodia Faridi; circ. 5,000.

La Gazette du Maroc: ave des Forces Armées Royales, Tour de Habous, 13eme étage, Casablanca; tel. (2) 2313925; fax (2) 2318094; e-mail info@gazette.press.ma; internet www.gazette.press.ma; weekly; French; Dir Kamal Lahlou.

Al-Ittihad al-Watani Lilkouate ach-Chaabia (National Union of Popular Forces): 28–30 rue Magellan, Casablanca; tel. (2) 2302023; fax (2) 2319301; weekly; Arabic; organ of the Union nationale des forces populaires; Dir Moulay Abdallah Ibrahim.

Le Journal: Media Trust, Iman Centre, Casablanca; tel. (2) 2548700; fax (2) 2542073; e-mail media@marocnet.net.ma; internet www.lejournal.press.ma; weekly; French; news, economics; Dir Aboubakr Jamai.

Lamalif: 6 bis rue Defly Dieude, Casablanca; tel. (2) 2220032; f. 1966; monthly; French; economic, social and cultural magazine; Dir Muhammad Loghlam.

La Mañana: 88 blvd Muhammad V, Casablanca; tel. (2) 2268860; fax (2) 2203935; f. 1990; Spanish; Dir Abd al-Hafid Rouissi.

Maroc Fruits: 22 rue Al-Messaoudi, Casablanca; tel. (2) 2363946; fax (2) 2364041; f. 1958; fortnightly; Arabic and French; organ of the Association des Producteurs d'Agrumes du Maroc; Dir Nejjai Ahmad Mansour; circ. 6,000.

Maroc Soir: 34 rue Muhammad Smiha, Casablanca; tel. (2) 2301271; fax (2) 2317535; f. 1971; French; Dir Abd al-Hafid Rouissi; circ. 30,000.

Matin Hebdo: 34 rue Muhammad Smiha, Casablanca; tel. (2) 2301271; weekly; Dir Ahmad al-Alami.

Matin Magazine: 88 blvd Muhammad V, Casablanca; tel. (2) 2268860; fax (2) 2262969; f. 1971; weekly; French; Dir Abd al-Hafid Rouissi.

An-Nidal (The Struggle): 10 rue Cols Bleus, Sidi Bousmara, Médina Kédima, Casablanca; f. 1973; weekly; Arabic; organ of the Parti national démocrate; Dir Ibrahimi Ahmad.

La Nouvelle Tribune: 1 blvd Abd al-Latif Ben Kaddour, angle blvd Zerktouni, Casablanca; tel. (2) 2940911; fax (2) 2940914; e-mail nouvelle-tribune@techno.net.ma; internet www.lanouvelletribune.press.ma; f. 1996; weekly; French; Dir Fahd Yata; circ. 25,000.

Les Nouvelles du Maroc: 28 ave des Forces Armées Royales, Casablanca; tel. (2) 2203031; fax (2) 2277181; weekly; French; Dir Khadija S. Idrissi.

Al-Ousbouaa al-Maghribia: 158 ave des Forces Armées Royales, Casablanca; f. 1984; organ of the Union constitutionnelle; Editor Mustafa Alaoui.

La Quinzaine du Maroc: 53 rue Dumont d'Urville, Casablanca; tel. (2) 2302482; fax (2) 2440426; e-mail mauro@marocnet.net.ma; f. 1951; monthly; English and French; Dir Hubert Mauro; circ. 20,000.

Revue Marocaine de Droit: 24 rue Nolly, Casablanca; tel. (2) 2273673; quarterly; French and Arabic; Dirs J. P. Razon, A. Kettani.

As-Sahifa: Casablanca; weekly; Arabic; Dir Aboubakr Jamai.

Les Temps du Maroc: 88 blvd Muhammad V, Casablanca; tel. (2) 2268860; fax (2) 2262969; e-mail contact@lematin.press.ma; internet www.tempsdumaroc.press.ma; f. 1995; weekly; French; Dir ABD AL-HAFID ROUISSI.

La Vie Economique: 5 blvd ben Yacine, 20300 Casablanca; tel. (2) 2443868; fax (2) 2304542; e-mail vieeco@marocnet.net.ma; internet www.marocnet.net.ma/vieeco; f. 1921; weekly; French; Pres. and Dir JEAN LOUIS SERVAN-SCHREIBER.

La Vie Industrielle et Agricole: 142 blvd Muhammad V, Casablanca; tel. (2) 2274407; 2 a month; French; Dir AHMAD ZAGHARI.

La Vie Touristique Africaine: 142 blvd Muhammad V, Casablanca; tel. (2) 2274407; fortnightly; French; tourist information; Dir AHMAD ZAGHARI.

Rabat

Al-Aklam (The Pens): Rabat; monthly; Arabic; Dir ABD AR-RAHMAN BEN AMAR.

Al-Anba'a (Information): ave Allal el-Fassi, Rabat; tel. (3) 7683967; fax (3) 7683970; internet www.alanbaa.press.ma; f. 2000; weekly; Arabic; publ. by Ministry of Communication; Dir (Editorial) MUHAMMAD BELGHAZI.

Assiassa Al-Jadida: 8 rue Sanaa, BP 1385, Rabat; tel. (3) 7208571; fax (3) 7208573; e-mail aouad@nsimail.com; f. 1996; weekly; Arabic; organ of the Partie socialiste démocratique; Dir ABDELLATIF AOUAD.

Ach-Chorta (The Police): BP 437, Rabat; tel. (3) 7723194; monthly; Arabic; Dir MUHAMMAD AD-DRIF.

Da'ouat Al-Haqq (Call of the Truth): al-Michwar as-Said, Rabat; tel. (3) 7760810; publ. by Ministry of Habous (Religious Endowments) and Islamic Affairs; f. 1957; monthly; Arabic.

Al-Haraka: 66 rue Patrice Lumumba, BP 1317, Rabat; tel. (3) 7768667; fax (3) 7768677; weekly; Arabic; organ of the Mouvement populaire; Dir ALI ALAOUI.

Al-Imane: rue Akenssous, BP 356, Rabat; f. 1963; monthly; Arabic; Dir ABOU BAKER AL-KADIRI.

Al-Irchad (Spiritual Guidance): al-Michwar as-Said, Rabat; tel. (3) 7760810; publ. by Ministry of Religious Endowments (Awqaf) and Islamic Affairs; f. 1967; monthly; Arabic.

Al-Khansa: 154 ave Souss Mohammadia, Rabat; monthly; Arabic; Dir ABOUZAL AICHA.

Al-Maghribi: Rabat; tel. (3) 7768139; weekly; Arabic; organ of the Parti de l'action; Dir ABDALLAH AL-HANANI.

At-Tadamoun: Rabat; monthly; Arabic; Dir ABD AL-MAJID SEMLALI EL-HASANI.

La Verité: Rabat; weekly; French; Chief Ed. ALLAL EL-MALEH.

La Voix du Centre: Rabat; weekly; French; Ed.-in-chief MUSTAPHA SHIMI.

Tangier

Actualités Touristiques: 80 rue de la Liberté, Tangier; monthly; French; Dir TAYEB ALAMI.

Le Journal de Tanger: 11 ave Moulay Abd al-Aziz, BP 420, Tangier; tel. (3) 7946051; fax (3) 7945709; e-mail redact@journaldetanger.com; internet www.journaldetanger.com; f. 1904; weekly; French, English, Spanish and Arabic; Dir BAKHAT ABD AL-HAQ; circ. 10,000.

NEWS AGENCIES

Maghreb Arabe Presse (MAP): 122 ave Allal ben Abdallah, BP 1049, 10000 Rabat; tel. (3) 7764083; fax (3) 7702734; e-mail direction@map.co.ma; internet www.map.co.ma; f. 1959; Arabic, French, English and Spanish; state-owned; Dir-Gen. MUHAMMAD YASSINE MANSOURI.

Foreign Bureaux

Agence France-Presse (AFP): 2 bis rue du Caire, BP 118, Rabat; tel. (3) 7768943; fax (3) 7700357; f. 1920; Dir IGNACE DALLE.

Agencia EFE (Spain): 14 ave du Kairouane, Rabat; tel. (3) 7723218; fax (3) 7732195; Bureau Chief ALBERTO MASEGOSA GARCÍA-CALAMARTE.

Informatsionnoye Telegrafnoye Agentstvo Rossii—Telegrafnoye Agentstvo Suverennykh Stran (ITAR—TASS) (Russia): 32 rue de la Somme, Rabat; tel. (3) 7750315; Dir OLEG CHIROKOV.

Inter Press Service (IPS) (Italy): Rabat; tel. (3) 7756869; fax (3) 7727183; e-mail ipseumed@hotmail.com; internet www.ips.org; Dir BOULOUIZ BOUCHRA.

Reuters (United Kingdom): 509 Immeuble es-Saada, ave Hassan II, Rabat; tel. (3) 7726518; fax (3) 7722499; Chief Correspondent (North Africa) JOHN BAGGALEY.

Xinhua (New China) News Agency (People's Republic of China): 4 rue Kadi Mekki el-Bitaouri, Souissi, Rabat; tel. (3) 7755320; fax (3) 7754319; Dir ZHUGE CANGLIN.

Publishers

Dar el-Kitab: place de la Mosquée, Quartier des Habous, BP 4018, Casablanca; tel. (2) 2305419; fax (2) 2304581; f. 1948; philosophy, history, Africana, general and social science; Arabic and French; Dir BOUTALEB ABDOU ABD AL-HAY; Gen. Man. KHADIJA EL KASSIMI.

Editions La Porte: 281 blvd Muhammad V, BP 331, Rabat; tel. (3) 7709958; fax (3) 7706476; e-mail la_porte@meganet.net.ma; law, guides, economics, educational books.

Les Editions Maghrébines: Quartier Industrial, blvd E, N 15, Sin Sebaa, Casablanca; tel. (2) 2351797; fax (2) 2355541; f. 1962; general non-fiction.

Government Publishing House

Imprimerie Officielle: ave Yacoub El Mansour, Rabat-Chellah; tel. (3) 7765024; fax (3) 7765179.

Broadcasting and Communications

TELECOMMUNICATIONS

Regulatory Authority

Agence Nationale de Réglementation des Télécommunications (ANRT): Centre d'Affaires, blvd Ar-Ryad; Hay Ryad, BP 2939,10100 Rabat; tel. (3) 7718400; fax (3) 7716489; e-mail webmaster@anrt.net.ma; internet www.anrt.net.ma; f. 1998; Dir-Gen. OTHMANE DEMNATI.

Principal Operators

Itissalat al-Maghrib—Maroc Télécom: ave Annakhil Hay Riad, Rabat; tel. (3) 7712626; fax (3) 7714860; internet www.iam.ma; f. 1998 to take over telephone services from the ONPT; partially privatized in 2002; Dir ABDESSALEM AHIZOUNE.

BROADCASTING

Morocco can receive broadcasts from Spanish radio stations, and the main Spanish television channels can also be received in northern Morocco.

Radio

Radiodiffusion-Télévision Marocaine: 1 rue el-Brihi, BP 1042, 1000 Rabat; tel. (3) 7709613; fax (3) 7703208; internet www.maroc.net/rc; govt station; Network A in Arabic, Network B in French, English and Spanish, Network C in Berber and Arabic; Foreign Service in Arabic, French and English; Dir-Gen. MUHAMMAD TRICHA; Dir Radio ABD AR-RAHMAN ACHOUR.

Radio Méditerranée Internationale: 3–5 rue Emsallah, BP 2055, Tangier; tel. and fax (3) 9936363; e-mail medi1@medi1.com; internet www.medi1.com; Arabic and French; Man. Dir PIERRE CASALTA.

Voice of America Radio Station in Tangier: c/o US Consulate-General, chemin des Amoureux, Tangier.

Television

Radiodiffusion-Télévision Marocaine: 1 rue el-Brihi, BP 1042, 1000 Rabat; tel. (3) 7709613; fax (3) 7703208; internet www.maroc.net/rc; govt station; transmission commenced 1962; 45 hours weekly; French and Arabic; carries commercial advertising; Dir-Gen. MUHAMMAD TRICHA; Dir Television FAICAL LAARAICHI.

SOREAD 2M: Société d'études et de réalisations audiovisuelles, km 7.3 route de Rabat, Aïn-Sebaâ, Casablanca; tel. (2) 2667373; fax (2) 2667392; internet www.2m.tv; f. 1988; transmission commenced 1989; public television channel, owned by Moroccan Government (72%) and by private national foreign concerns; broadcasting in French and Arabic; Man. Dir NOUR EDDINE SAIL.

Finance

(cap. = capital; res = reserves; dep. = deposits; m. = million;
brs = branches; amounts in dirhams unless otherwise indicated)

BANKING

Central Bank

Bank Al-Maghrib: 277 ave Muhammad V, BP 445, Rabat; tel. (3)
7702626; fax (3) 7706677; e-mail dai@bkam.gov.ma; internet www
.bkam.ma; f. 1959 as Banque du Maroc; bank of issue; cap. 500m.,
res 4,521.0m., dep. 17,063.1m. (Dec. 1999); Gov. MUHAMMAD SEQAT.

Other Banks

Banque Centrale Populaire (Crédit Populaire du Maroc): 101
blvd Muhammad Zerktouni, BP 10622, 21100 Casablanca; tel. (2)
2202533; fax (2) 2222699; e-mail bcpinternational@
banquepopulairemorocco.ma; internet www.chaabinet.com; f. 1961;
51% state-owned, 49% privately-owned; scheduled for complete privatization in 2002; cap. 1,297.7m., res 4,749.5m., total assets
68,157.8m. (Dec. 1999); Pres. and Gen. Man. NOUREDDINE OMARY; 342
brs.

Banque Commerciale du Maroc SA (BCM): 2 blvd Moulay
Youssef, BP 11141, 20000 Casablanca; tel. (2) 2298888; fax (2)
2268852; internet www.attijari.com; f. 1911; 20.3% owned by Banco
Central Hispano; cap. 1,325.0m., res 2,901.1m., dep. 35,403.5m.
(Dec. 1999); Chair. ABD AL-AZIZ ALAMI; Gen. Mans ALI IBN MANSOUR,
OMAR BENIDER; 112 brs.

Banque Marocaine du Commerce Extérieur SA (BMCE): 140
ave Hassan II, BP 13425, 20000 Casablanca; tel. (2) 2200496; fax (2)
2200512; internet www.moroccoweb.com/bmce; f. 1959; transferred
to majority private ownership in 1995; cap. 1,587.5m., res 2,899.9m.,
total assets 46,269.1m. (Dec. 2000); Chair. and CEO OTHMAN BEN
JELLOUN; 198 brs.

Banque Marocaine pour l'Afrique et l'Orient: 1 place Ban-
doeng, BP 11183, 20000 Casablanca; tel. (2) 2307070; fax (2)
2301673; f. 1975 to take over British Bank of the Middle East
(Morocco); cap. 200.0m., res 1.4m., dep. 2,042.0m. (Dec. 1996); Chair.
FARID DELLERO; Gen. Man. SAID IBRAHIMI; 29 brs.

Banque Marocaine pour le Commerce et l'Industrie SA: 26
place des Nations Unies, BP 15573, Casablanca; tel. (2) 2224101; fax
(2) 2299402; e-mail bmcisg@casanet.net.ma; internet www.bmcinet
.com; f. 1964; transferred to majority private ownership in 1995; cap.
763.0m., res 643.6m., dep. 22,568.4m. (Dec. 2001); Chair. MUSTAPHA
FARIS; Gen. Man. JEAN-JACQUES SANTINI; 125 brs.

**Banque Nationale pour le Développement Economique
(BNDE):** 12 place des Alaouites, BP 407, 10000 Rabat; tel. (3)
7706040; fax (3) 7703706; internet www.bnde.co.ma; f. 1959; 34.2%
state-owned, 65.8% privately-owned; cap. 600.0m., res 475.8m., dep.
5,200.6m. (Dec. 1999); Chair. and Man. Dir KHALID KADIRI; 14 brs.

Citibank (Maghreb): 52 ave Hassan II, Casablanca; tel. (2)
2224168; fax (2) 2205723; f. 1967; cap. 100m., res 2.5m., dep. 612.6m.
(Dec. 1996); Pres. ERIC STOCLET.

Crédit Immobilier et Hôtelier: 187 ave Hassan II, Casablanca;
tel. (2) 2479000; fax (2) 2479999; e-mail cih@cih.co.ma; f. 1920;
transferred to majority private ownership in 1995; cap. 1,326.7m.,
res 432.0m., dep. 14,406.8m. (Dec. 1999); Pres. and Gen. Man.
ABDELOUAHED SOUHAÏL; 91 brs.

Crédit du Maroc SA: 48–58 blvd Muhammad V, BP 13579, 20000
Casablanca; tel. (2) 2477000; fax (2) 2477071; e-mail cdmdai@
atlasnet.net.ma; internet www.creditdumaroc.co.ma; f. 1963; cap.
833.8m., res 648.1m., dep. 14,002.8m. (Dec. 2001); Chair. and CEO
FRANCIS SAVOYE; 122 brs.

Société Générale Marocaine de Banques SA: 55 blvd Abd al-
Moumen, BP 13090, 21100 Casablanca; tel. (2) 2438844; fax (2)
2298809; f. 1962; cap. 1,170.0m., res 621.6m. (Dec. 1999); Pres. ABD
AL-AZIZ TAZI; 180 brs.

Société Marocaine de Dépôt et Crédit: 79 ave Hassan II, BP 296,
20000 Casablanca; tel. (2) 2224114; fax (2) 2264498; f. 1974; cap.
625.9m., res 717.8m., total assets 4,811.0m. (Dec. 1998); Chair and
Gen. Man. ABD AL-LATIF IDMAHAMMA; 21 brs.

Wafabank: 163 ave Hassan II, 21000 Casablanca; tel. (2) 2200200;
fax (2) 2470398; f. 1964 as Cie Marocaine de Crédit et de Banque;
cap. 639.5m., res 2,250.9m., total assets 29,039.9m. (Dec. 1999);
Pres. and CEO ABDELHAK BENNANI; 162 brs.

Bank Organizations

**Association Professionnelle des Intermédiaires de Bourse du
Maroc:** 71 ave des Forces Armées Royales, Casablanca; tel. (2)
2314824; fax (2) 2314903; f. 1967; groups all banks and brokers in
the stock exchange of Casablanca, for studies, inquiries of general

interest and contacts with official authorities; 11 mems; Pres. ABD
AL-LATIF JOUAHRI.

Groupement Professionnel des Banques du Maroc: 71 ave des
Forces Armées Royales, Casablanca; tel. (2) 2314824; fax (2)
2314903; f. 1967; groups all commercial banks for studies, inquiries
of general interest, and contacts with official authorities; 18 mems;
Pres. ABD AL-LATIF JOUAHRI.

STOCK EXCHANGE

Bourse des Valeurs de Casablanca: ave de l'Armée Royale, Casablanca; tel. (2) 2452626; fax (2) 2452625; internet www
.casablanca-bourse.com; f. 1929; Chair. DRISS BENCHEIKH.

INSURANCE

Al-Wataniya: 83 ave des FAR, 20000 Casablanca; tel. (2) 2314850;
fax (2) 2313137; internet www.alwataniya.com; Dir-Gen. ABD AL-AZIZ
GUESSONS.

Alliance Africaine: 63 blvd Moulay Youssef, 20000 Casablanca;
tel. (2) 2200690; fax (2) 2200694; f. 1975; cap. 20m. Pres. ABD AR-
RAHIM CHERKAOUI; Dir-Gen. KHALID CHEDDADI.

Assurances Al-Amane: 122 ave Hassan II, 20000 Casablanca; tel.
(2) 2267272; fax (2) 2265664; f. 1975; cap. 120m. Pres. and Dir-Gen.
MUHAMMAD BOUGHALEB.

Atlanta Assurances: BP 13685, 20001 Casablanca; tel. (2)
2491448; fax (2) 2203011; e-mail atlanta@mbox.azur.net; f. 1947;
cap. 40m. Dirs-Gen. MUHAMMAD REYAD, OMAR BENNANI.

Cie Africaine d'Assurances: 120 ave Hassan II, 20000 Casablanca; tel. (2) 2224185; fax (2) 2260150; internet www.caa.co.ma; f.
1950; Dir-Gen. JAMAL HAROUCHI.

Cie d'Assurances et de Réassurances SANAD: 3 blvd
Muhammad V, BP 13438, 20000 Casablanca; tel. (2) 2260591; fax (2)
2293813; e-mail contact@sanad.ma; internet www.sanad.ma; f.
1975; Chair. MUHAMMAD HASSAN BENSALAH; Dir-Gen. ABDELTIF TAHIRI.

CNIA Assurance: 216 blvd Muhammad Zerktouni, 20000 Casablanca; tel. (2) 2474040; fax (2) 2206081; internet www.cnia.ma; f.
1949; cap. 30m. Pres. ABDELLATIF AL-RAYES; Dir-Gen. SAID AHMIDOUCH.

La Marocaine Vie: 37 blvd Moulay Youssef, Casablanca; tel. (2)
2206320; fax (2) 2261971; f. 1978; cap. 12m. Pres. HAMZA KETTANI.

Mutuelle Centrale Marocaine d'Assurances: 16 rue Abou Inane,
BP 27, Rabat; tel. (3) 7766960; Pres. ABD AS-SALAM CHERIF D'OUEZZANE;
Dir-Gen. YACOUBI SOUSSANE.

Mutuelle d'Assurances des Transporteurs Unis (MATU): 215
blvd Muhammad Zerktouni, Casablanca; tel. (2) 2367097; Dir-Gen.
M. BENYAMNA MUHAMMAD.

La Royale Marocaine d'Assurances (RMA): 67–69 ave de
l'Armée Royale, BP 13779, 20000 Casablanca; tel. (2) 2312163; fax
(2) 2313884; internet www.rma.co.ma; f. 1949; cap. 1,108.0m. Chair.
OTHMAN BEN JELLOUN; Dir-Gen. SÉBASTIEN CASTRO.

Es-Saada, Cie d'Assurances et de Réassurances: 123 ave
Hassan II, BP 13860, 20000 Casablanca; tel. (2) 2222525; fax (2)
2262655; e-mail es-saada@techno.net.ma; f. 1961; cap. 50m. Pres.
MEHDI OUAZZANI; Man. Dir SAÏD OUAZZANI.

Société Centrale de Réassurance: Tour Atlas, place Zallaqa, BP
13183, Casablanca; tel. (2) 2308585; fax (2) 2308672; e-mail scr@elan
.net.ma; internet www.scr.co.ma; f. 1960; cap. 30m. Chair. MUSTAPHA
BAKKOURY; Man. Dir AHMAD ZINOUN.

Société Marocaine d'Assurances à l'Exportation: 24 rue Ali
Abderrazak, BP 15953, Casablanca; tel. (2) 2982000; fax (2)
2252070; e-mail smaex@wanadoo.net.ma; internet www.smaex.com;
f. 1988; insurance for exporters in the public and private sectors;
assistance for export promotion; Pres., Dir-Gen. MUHAMMAD TAZI;
Asst Dir-Gen. ABDELKADER DRIOUACHE.

WAFA Assurance: 1–3 blvd Abd al-Moumen, BP 13420, 20001
Casablanca; tel. (2) 2224575; fax (2) 2209103; e-mail webmaster@
wafaassurance.com; internet www.wafaassurance.com; Pres. SAÂD
KETTANI; Dir-Gen. JAOUAD KETTANI.

Zurich Cie Marocaine d'Assurances: City Park Centre, 106 rue
Abderrahmane Sahraoui, 20000 Casablanca; tel. (2) 2279015; fax (2)
2491729; Pres. and Dir-Gen. HERVÉ GIRAUDON.

INSURANCE ASSOCIATION

**Fédération Marocaine des Sociétés d'Assurances et de Ré-
assurances:** 154 blvd d'Anfa, Casablanca; tel. (2) 2391850; fax (2)
2391854; f. 1958; 17 mem. cos; Pres. HAMZA KETTANI.

Trade and Industry

GOVERNMENT AGENCIES

Bureau de Recherches et de Participations Minières (BRPM): 5 ave Moulay Hassan, BP 99, 10001 Rabat; tel. (3) 7705005; fax (3) 7709411; f. 1928; state agency conducting exploration, valorization and exploitation of mineral resources; Dir-Gen. MELLE AMINA BENKHADRA.

Centre Marocain de Promotion des Exportations (CMPE): 23 blvd Bnou Majid el-Bahar, BP 10937, Casablanca; tel. (2) 2302210; fax (2) 2301793; e-mail cmpe@cmpe.org.ma; internet www.cmpe.org.ma; f. 1980; state org. for promotion of exports; Dir-Gen. MOUNIR M. BENSAID.

Direction de la Privatisation: 1 angle ave Ibn Sina et Oued al-Makhazine, Agdal, Rabat; tel. (3) 7689614; fax (3) 7673299; e-mail minpriv@mtds.com; internet www.minpriv.gov.ma; privatization agency integrated with Ministry of the Economy, Finance, Privatization and Tourism; Dir NAJIB HAJOUI.

Société de Gestion des Terres Agricoles (SOGETA): 35 rue Daïet-Erroumi, BP 731, Agdal, Rabat; tel. (3) 7772834; fax (3) 7772765; e-mail sogeta@acdim.net.ma; f. 1973; oversees use of agricultural land; Man. Dir BACHIR SAOUD.

DEVELOPMENT ORGANIZATIONS

Caisse de Dépôt et de Gestion: place Moulay El-Hassan, BP 408, 10001 Rabat; tel. (3) 7765520; fax (3) 7763849; e-mail cdg@cdg.org.ma; internet www.cdg.org.ma; f. 1959; finances small-scale projects; cap. and res 2,058.1m. dirhams (Dec. 1998); Dir-Gen. MUSTAPHA BAKKOURI; Sec.-Gen. MUSTAPHA MECHAHOURI.

Caisse Marocaine des Marchés (Marketing Fund): Résidence El Manar, blvd Abd al-Moumen, Casablanca; tel. (2) 2259118; fax (2) 2259120; f. 1950; cap. 10m. dirhams; Man. HASSAN KISSI.

Caisse Nationale de Crédit Agricole (Agricultural Credit Fund): 2 ave d'Alger, BP 49, 10001 Rabat; tel. (3) 7725920; fax (3) 7732580; f. 1961; cap. 1,573.5m. dirhams, dep. 3,471.9m. dirhams; Dir-Gen. SAID IBRAHIMI.

Office pour le Développement Industriel (ODI): 10 rue Gandhi, BP 211, 10001 Rabat; tel. (3) 7708460; fax (3) 7707695; e-mail odi@odi.gov.ma; internet www.odi.gov.ma; f. 1973; a state agency to develop industry; Dir-Gen. MURAD BACHIR BOUHALI.

Société de Développement Agricole (SODEA): ave Hadj Ahmed Cherkaoui, BP 6280, Rabat; tel. (3) 7770825; fax (3) 7774798; f. 1972; state agricultural devt org; Man. Dir M. SABBARI HASSANI LARBI.

Société Nationale d'Investissement (SNI): 60 rue d'Alger, BP 38, 20000 Casablanca; tel. (2) 2484288; fax (2) 2484303; f. 1966; transferred to majority private ownership in 1994; cap. 10,900m. dirhams; Pres. MOURAD CHERIF; Sec.-Gen. KAMAL EL-AYOUBI.

CHAMBERS OF COMMERCE

La Fédération des Chambres de Commerce et d'Industrie du Maroc: 6 rue d'Erfoud, Rabat-Agdal; tel. (3) 7767078; fax (3) 7767076; f. 1962; groups the 26 Chambers of Commerce and Industry; Pres. AHMAD M'RABET; Dir-Gen. MUHAMMAD LARBI EL HARRAS.

Chambre de Commerce, d'Industrie et de Services de la Wilaya de Rabat-Salé: 1 rue Gandhi, BP 131, Rabat; tel. (3) 7706444; fax (3) 7706768; e-mail ccisrs@ccisrs.org.ma; internet www.ccisrs.org.ma; Pres. OMAR DERRAJI; Dir ZINE EL-ABIDINE AFIA.

Chambre de Commerce et d'Industrie de la Wilaya du Grand Casablanca: 98 blvd Muhammad V, BP 423, Casablanca; tel. (2) 2264327; Pres. LAHCEN EL-WAFI.

INDUSTRIAL AND TRADE ASSOCIATIONS

Office National Interprofessionnel des Céréales et des Légumineuses: 25 ave Moulay Hassan, BP 154, Rabat; tel. (3) 7701735; fax (3) 7709626; f. 1937; Dir-Gen. ABD AL-HAI BOUZOUBAA.

Office National des Pêches: 13 rue Lieutenant Mahroud, BP 16243, 20300 Casablanca; tel. (2) 2240551; fax (2) 2242305; e-mail onp@onp.co.ma; internet www.onp.co.ma; f. 1969; state fishing org. Man. Dir MAJID KAISSAR EL-GHAIB.

EMPLOYERS' ORGANIZATIONS

Association Marocaine des Industries Textiles et de l'Habillement (AMITH): 92 blvd Moulay Rachid, Casablanca; tel. (2) 2942085; fax (2) 2940587; e-mail amith@mail.winner.net.ma; f. 1958; mems 700 textile, knitwear and ready-made garment factories; Pres. SALAH-EDDINE MEZOUAR; Dir-Gen. ABDE LALI BERRADA.

Association des Producteurs d'Agrumes du Maroc (ASPAM): 22 rue al-Messaoudi, Casablanca; tel. (2) 2363946; fax (2) 2364041; f. 1958; links Moroccan citrus growers; has its own processing plants; Pres AHMED MANSOUR NEJJAI.

Association Professionelle des Agents Maritimes, Consignataires de Naivres, et Courtiers d'Affretement du Maroc: Iman Centre No 1, 5ème Etage, rue Arrachid Muhammad (ex rue de la Plage), Casablanca; tel. (2) 2541112; fax (2) 2541415; e-mail apram@abnet.net.ma; internet www.apram.ma; Pres. A. MANTRANCH.

Association Professionnelle des Cimentiers: Casablanca; tel. (2) 2401342; fax (2) 2248208; cement manufacturers.

Confédération Générale des Entreprises du Maroc (CGEM): angle ave des Forces Armées Royales et rue Muhammad Arrachid, 20100 Casablanca; tel. (2) 2252696; fax (2) 2253839; e-mail cgem@iam.net.ma; Pres. HASSAN CHAMI.

Union Marocaine de l'Agriculture (UMA): 12 place des Alaouites, Rabat; Pres. M. NEJJAI.

UTILITIES

Electricity and Water

Office National de l'Eau Potable (ONEP): 6 bis rue Patrice Lumumba, Rabat; tel. (3) 7650695; fax (3) 7650640; e-mail onepigi@mtds.com; internet www.onep.org; f. 1972; responsible for drinking-water supply; Dir ALI FASSI-FIHRI.

Office National de l'Electricité (ONE): 65 rue Othman Ben Affan, BP 13498, 20001 Casablanca; tel. (2) 2668080; fax (2) 2220038; e-mail offelec@one.org.ma; internet www.one.org.ma; f. 1963; state electricity authority; Chair. AHMAD NAKKOUCHE.

Régie Autonome Intercommunale de Distribution d'Eau et d'Electricité de la Wilaya de Chaouia (RADEEC): industrial and commercial public body providing water and power supplies in the Chaouia region.

Régie Autonome Intercommunale de Distribution d'Eau et d'Electricité de la Wilaya de Tanger (RAID): 5 rue Oqba ibn Naffiy, BP 286, Tangier; tel. (3) 7321414; fax (3) 7322156; water, sewerage and electricity network for Tangier; a concession to manage the services was scheduled to be awarded in 1999.

Régie d'Eau et d'Electricité (RED): Rabat; in 1998 a 30-year concession to manage Rabat's water and power grids was awarded to a consortium of Electricidade de Portugal (Portugal), Urbaser (Spain) and Alborada (Morocco).

Gas

Afriquia Gaz: rue Ibnou el-Ouennanae Ain Sebaa; Casablanca; tel. (2) 2352144; fax (2) 2352239; f. 1992; Morocco's leading gas distributor; transfer to private ownership pending; Dir-Gen. RACHID, IDRISSI KAITOUNI.

TRADE UNIONS

Confédération Démocratique du Travail (CDT): 64 rue al-Mourtada, Quartier Palmier, BP 13576, Casablanca; tel. (2) 2994470; fax (2) 2258162; f. 1978; 400,000 mems; Sec.-Gen. MUHAMMAD NOUBIR AMAOUI.

Union Démocratique de l'Agriculture: f. 1997; Sec.-Gen. ABD AR-RAHMAN FILALI.

Union Générale des Travailleurs Marocains (UGTM): 9 rue du Rif, angle Route de Médiouna, Casablanca; tel. (2) 2282144; f. 1960; associated with Istiqlal; supported by unions not affiliated to UMT; 673,000 mems; Sec.-Gen. ABD AR-RAZZAQ AFILAL.

Union Marocaine du Travail (UMT): Bourse du Travail, 232 ave des Forces Armées Royales, Casablanca; tel. (2) 2302292; left-wing and associated with the UNFP; most unions are affiliated; 700,000 mems; Sec. MAHJOUB BEN SEDDIQ.

Union Syndicale Agricole (USA): agricultural section of UMT.

Union Marocaine du Travail Autonome: Rabat; breakaway union from UMT.

Transport

Office National des Transports (ONT): rue al-Fadila, Quartier Industriel, BP 596, Rabat-Chellah; tel. (3) 7797842; fax (3) 7797850; f. 1958; Man. Dir MUHAMMAD LAHBIB EL-GUEDDARI.

RAILWAYS

In 2001 there were 1,907 km of railways, of which 370 km were double track; 1,003 km of lines were electrified and diesel locomotives were used on the rest. In that year the network carried some 13.6m. passengers and 27.5m. metric tons of freight. All services are nationalized. A feasibility study was begun in early 1998 into the construction of a 28-km metro system in Casablanca.

Office National des Chemins de Fer (ONCF): 8 bis rue Abderrahmane El Ghafiki, Rabat-Agdal; tel. (3) 7774747; fax (3) 7774480; e-mail meziane@oncf.org.ma; internet www.oncf.org.ma; f. 1963; administers all Morocco's railways; Dir-Gen. KARIM GHELLAB.

ROADS

In 2001 there were 57,226 km of classified roads, of which 56.1% were paved.

Cie de Transports au Maroc (CTM—SA): 23 rue Léon l'Africain, Casablanca; tel. (2) 2753677; fax (2) 2765428; internet www.ctm.co.ma; agencies in Tangier, Rabat, Meknès, Oujda, Marrakesh, Agadir, El Jadida, Safi, Casablanca, es-Saouira, Fez and Ouarzazate; privatized in mid-1993 with 40% of shares reserved for Moroccan citizens; Pres. and Dir-Gen. ABDALLAH LAHLOU.

SHIPPING

According to the Ministry of Equipment, Morocco's 21 ports handled 53.2m. tons of goods in 2000. The most important ports, in terms of the volume of goods handled, are Casablanca, Mohammadia, Jorf Lasfar and Safi. Tangier is the principal port for passenger services. Construction work on new ports at Tangier (to handle merchandise traffic) and Agadir commenced in 2000.

Office d'Exploitation des Ports (ODEP): 175 blvd Muhammad Zerktouni, 20100 Casablanca; tel. (2) 2232324; fax (2) 2232325; e-mail administrateur@odep.org.ma; internet www.odep.org.ma; f. 1985; port management and handling of port equipment; Gen. Man. MUSTAPHA BARROUG.

Principal Shipping Companies

Agence Gibmar SA: 3 rue Henri Regnault, Tangier; tel. (3) 7935875; fax (3) 7933239; e-mail agemcemed@mamnet.net.ma; also at Casablanca; regular services from Tangier to Gibraltar; Chair. JAMES PETER GAGGERO; Dir YOUSSEF BENYAHIA.

Cie Chérifienne d'Armement: 5 blvd Abdallah ben Yacine, 21700 Casablanca; tel. (2) 2309455; fax (2) 2301186; f. 1929; regular services to Europe; Man. Dir MAX KADOCH.

Cie Marocaine d'Agences Maritimes (COMARINE): 45 ave de l'Armée Royale, BP 60, 20000 Casablanca; tel. (2) 2311941; fax (2) 2312570; e-mail comarine@marocnet.net.ma.

Cie Marocaine de Navigation (COMANAV): 7 blvd de la Résistance, BP 628, Casablanca 20300; tel. (2) 2303012; fax (2) 2308455; e-mail comanav@comanav.co.ma; internet www.comanav.co.ma; f. 1946; regular services to Mediterranean, North-west European, Middle Eastern and West African ports; tramping; Chair. MUHAMMAD BENHAROUGA.

Intercona SA: 31 ave de la Résistance, Tangier; tel. (3) 9322253; fax (3) 9943863; e-mail intercona@wanadoo.net.ma; f. 1943; daily services from Algeciras (Spain) to Tangier and Ceuta (Spanish North Africa); Dir-Gen. ANDRES VAZQUEZ ESPINOSA.

Limadet-ferry: 3 rue Ibn Rochd, Tangier; tel. (3) 933639; fax (3) 937173; f. 1966; operates between Algeciras (Spain) and Tangier, six daily; Dir-Gen. RACHID BEN MANSOUR.

Société Marocaine de Navigation Atlas: 81 ave Houmane el-Fatouaki, 21000 Casablanca; tel. (2) 2224190; fax (2) 2274401; f. 1976; Chair. HASSAN CHAMI; Man. Dir M. SLAOUI.

Union Maritime Maroc-Scandinave (UNIMAR): 12 rue de Foucauld, BP 746, Casablanca; tel. (2) 2279590; fax (2) 2223883; f. 1974; chemicals; Dir-Gen. ABD AL-WAHAB BEN KIRANE.

Voyages Paquet: Hôtel Royal Mansour, rue Sidi Belyout, 20000 Casablanca; tel. (2) 2311065; fax (2) 2442108; f. 1970; Pres. MUHAMMAD ELOUALI ELALAMI; Dir-Gen. NAÏMA BAKALI ELOUALI ELALAMI.

CIVIL AVIATION

The main international airports are at Casablanca (King Muhammad V), Rabat, Tangier, Marrakesh, Agadir Inezgane, Fez, Oujda, Al-Hocima, el-Aaiún, Ouarzazate and Agadir al-Massira. Construction of a new international airport at al-Aroui, located 25 km south of Nador, began in late 1998. In November 1999 the Arab Fund for Economic and Social Development granted a loan worth US $32.7m. to finance a project to extend and modernise King Muhammad V airport. The project, which includes the construction of a second runway and new terminal buildings, is expected to be completed by 2005.

Office Nationale des Aéroports: Casa-Oasis, BP 8101, Casablanca; tel. (2) 2339040; fax (2) 2339051; e-mail onda@mtds.com; internet www.onda.org.ma.

Regional Airlines: Aéroport de Muhammad V, BP 12518, Casablanca; tel. (2) 2538020; fax (2) 2538411; f. 1997; privately-owned; domestic flights and services to southern Spain, Portugal and the Canary Islands; Pres. and CEO MEHDI ALAOUI.

Royal Air Maroc (RAM): Aéroport de Casablanca-Anfa; tel. (2) 2912000; fax (2) 2912087; internet www.royalairmaroc.com; f. 1953; 94.4% state-owned; scheduled for partial privatization; domestic flights and services to 35 countries in Western Europe, Scandinavia, the Americas, North and West Africa, the Canary Islands and the Middle East; CEO MUHAMMAD BERRADA.

Tourism

Tourism is Morocco's second main source of convertible currency. The country's attractions for tourists include its sunny climate, ancient sites (notably the cities of Fez, Marrakesh, Meknès and Rabat) and spectacular scenery. There are popular holiday resorts on the Atlantic and Mediterranean coasts. In 2001 foreign tourist arrivals totalled 2.25m., compared with 1.63m. in 1996. Tourist receipts in 2000 totalled an estimated US $2,040m.

Office National Marocain du Tourisme: 31 angle ave al-Abtal et rue Oued Fes, Agdal, Rabat; tel. (3) 7681531; fax (3) 7777437; e-mail visitmorocco@onmt.org.ma; internet www.moroccotourism.org.ma; f. 1918; Dir-Gen. FATHIA BENNIS.

MOZAMBIQUE
Introductory Survey

Location, Climate, Language, Religion, Flag, Capital

The Republic of Mozambique lies on the east coast of Africa, bordered to the north by Tanzania, to the west by Malawi, Zambia and Zimbabwe, and to the south by South Africa and Swaziland. The country has a coastline of about 2,470 km (1,535 miles) on the shores of the Indian Ocean, and is separated from Madagascar, to the east, by the Mozambique Channel. Except in a few upland areas, the climate varies from tropical to sub-tropical. Rainfall is irregular, but the rainy season is usually from November to March, when average temperatures in Maputo are between 26°C (79°F) and 30°C (86°F). In the cooler dry season the average temperatures are 18°C (64°F) to 20°C (68°F) in June and July. Portuguese is the official language, while there are 39 indigenous languages, the most widely spoken being Makhuwa, Tsonga, Sema and Lomwe. Many of the inhabitants follow traditional beliefs. There are about 5m. Christians, the majority of whom are Roman Catholics, and 4m. Muslims. The national flag (proportions 2 by 3) has three equal horizontal stripes, of green, black and yellow, separated by narrow white stripes. At the hoist is a red triangle containing a five-pointed yellow star, on which are superimposed an open book, a hoe and a rifle. The capital is Maputo (formerly Lourenço Marques).

Recent History

Mozambique became a Portuguese colony in the 19th century and an overseas province in 1951. Nationalist groups began to form in the 1960s. The Frente de Libertação de Moçambique (Frelimo—Mozambique Liberation Front) was formed in 1962 and launched a military campaign for independence in 1964. After the coup in Portugal (q.v.) in April 1974, negotiations between Frelimo and the new Portuguese Government resulted in a period of rule in Mozambique by a transitional Government, followed by full independence on 25 June 1975. Samora Machel, leader of Frelimo since the murder of its founder, Eduardo Mondlane, in 1969, became the first President of Mozambique. In February 1977 Frelimo was reconstituted as the Frelimo Party, a 'Marxist-Leninist vanguard party', with restricted membership. Between September and December elections took place to local, district and provincial assemblies and, at national level, to the Assembléia Popular (People's Assembly).

In March 1976 Mozambique closed its border with Rhodesia (now Zimbabwe) and applied economic sanctions against that country. Mozambique was the principal base for Rhodesian nationalist guerrillas, and consequently suffered considerable devastation as a result of offensives launched by Rhodesian government forces against guerrilla camps. The border was reopened in January 1980.

After Zimbabwean independence in April 1980, South Africa adopted Rhodesia's role as supporter of the Mozambican opposition guerrilla group, Resistência Nacional Moçambicana (Renamo), also known as the Movimento Nacional da Resistência de Moçambique. The activities of Renamo subsequently increased, causing persistent disruption to road, rail and petroleum pipeline links from Mozambican ports, which were vital to the economic independence of southern African nations from South Africa. In March 1984 Mozambique and South Africa signed a formal joint non-aggression pact, known as the Nkomati accord, whereby each Government undertook to prevent opposition forces on its territory from launching attacks against the other, and a Joint Security Commission was established. The accord effectively implied that South Africa would withdraw its covert support for Renamo in return for a guarantee by Mozambique that it would prevent any further use of its territory by the then banned African National Congress of South Africa (ANC). However, following an intensification of Renamo activity, in 1985 the Frelimo Government appealed to foreign powers for increased military assistance, and in June it was agreed that Zimbabwe would augment its military presence in Mozambique. A major military offensive against Renamo in July resulted in the capture, in August, of the rebels' national operational command centre and of other major rebel bases in the area. Mozambique subsequently alleged that documents dis-

covered at one of the captured Renamo bases revealed that South Africa had repeatedly violated the Nkomati accord by providing material support for the rebels. The Joint Security Commission ceased to meet in 1985.

General elections were scheduled to take place in 1982, but were postponed several times because of the security situation. Legislative elections eventually began in August 1986, but were delayed, owing to the internal conflict. The post of Prime Minister was created in July and allocated to Mário Machungo.

President Machel died in an air crash in South Africa in October 1986. The causes of the incident were unclear, and the Mozambican Ministry of Information declared that it did not exclude the possibility of South African sabotage. In May 1998 it was announced that South Africa's Truth and Reconciliation Commission (TRC) was to examine evidence relating to the crash. The TRC final report stated that the evidence was inconclusive, but a number of questions merited further investigation. In November 1986 the Central Committee of Frelimo appointed Joaquim Alberto Chissano, hitherto Minister for Foreign Affairs, as President. The elections were then resumed. In contrast to the 1977 elections, the voters were given a choice of candidates, with 299 Frelimo nominees for the 250 seats in the Assembléia Popular; nevertheless, all government and party leaders had been re-elected when the poll was completed in December 1986.

In September 1987, amid renewed Renamo activity, talks began with South Africa in an attempt to revive the Nkomati accord. In June 1988, following six months of negotiations, Mozambique, South Africa and Portugal signed an agreement to rehabilitate the Cahora Bassa hydroelectric plant in Mozambique (potentially one of the greatest sources of electricity in southern Africa). In May Mozambican and South African officials had agreed to reactivate the Nkomati accord and to re-establish the Joint Security Commission, and in September Chissano met the South African President, P. W. Botha, in Mozambique. As a result of this meeting, Mozambique and South Africa established a joint commission for co-operation and development.

At Frelimo's fifth congress, held in July 1989, the party's exclusively Marxist-Leninist orientation was renounced, more pragmatic policies were approved, and party membership was opened to Mozambicans from all sectors of society. In January 1990 Chissano announced the drafting of a new constitution, to be presented to the Assembléia Popular for approval later in the year.

In mid-1989 Presidents Daniel arap Moi of Kenya and Robert Mugabe of Zimbabwe agreed to mediate between the Mozambique Government and Renamo. In August Renamo rejected the Government's peace proposals, and demanded recognition as a political entity, the introduction of multi-party elections and the withdrawal of Zimbabwean troops from Mozambique as preconditions for peace. Mediation by Mugabe and Moi came to an end after Renamo refused to attend a meeting between the protagonists that had been arranged to take place in Malawi in June 1990. However, direct talks were held in July in Rome, Italy. In August the Frelimo Central Committee voted unanimously in favour of introducing a multi-party system, with a view to elections planned for 1991. Further talks between the Government and the rebels resulted in an agreement, in December 1990, for a partial cease-fire. Under the terms of the agreement, all Zimbabwean troops present in Mozambique were required to retire to the Beira and Limpopo transport 'corridors' linking Zimbabwe to the Mozambican ports of Beira and Maputo. The cease-fire was confined to these areas.

The agreement in Rome followed the introduction, on 30 November 1990, of a new Mozambican Constitution, formally ending Frelimo's single-party rule and committing the State to political pluralism and a free-market economy, and enshrining private property rights and guarantees of press freedom. The official name of the country was changed from the People's Republic of Mozambique to the Republic of Mozambique. Renamo refused to recognize the new Constitution, declaring that it had been drafted without democratic consultation. The

President was henceforth to be elected by direct universal suffrage, and the legislature was renamed the Assembléia da República (Assembly of the Republic). A new law concerning the formation, structure and function of political parties came into effect in February 1991. In accordance with the Constitution, Renamo would not be recognized as a legitimate political party until it had renounced violence completely.

In December 1990 negotiations between the Government and Renamo resumed in Rome, and a Joint Verification Commission, comprising independent representatives from 10 nations, in addition to those of the Mozambican Government and Renamo, was established to monitor the partial cease-fire. Further talks took place in Rome in January 1991, but collapsed following the presentation of a report by the Joint Verification Commission containing accusations that Renamo had violated the cease-fire agreement, and did not resume until May.

In June 1991 the Government announced that it had uncovered a plot, involving several members of the armed forces, to overthrow Chissano. The leaders of the coup were believed to be opposed to the introduction of a multi-party system and to negotiations with Renamo. In August the Minister of the Interior, Col Manuel José António Mucananda, was detained in connection with the attempted coup. He was, however, exonerated in February 1992, on the grounds that he had been instrumental in bringing the coup attempt to the attention of the authorities, and resumed his ministerial post in April.

In August 1991 a Frelimo party congress undertook further structural changes. The Political Bureau was restyled the Political Commission; Chissano was re-elected as President of the party, while Feliciano Salomão Gundana, Minister of the Presidency, was appointed to the new position of Secretary-General. As part of the democratization of the party, members of the Central Committee were for the first time elected by secret ballot.

In October 1991 Renamo and the Government signed a protocol agreeing fundamental principles and containing a set of mutual guarantees as a basis for a peace accord. Throughout the discussions Renamo continued guerrilla attacks, many of which were launched (despite the Nkomati accord) from South Africa. Under the terms of the protocol, Renamo effectively recognized the legitimacy of the Government and agreed to enter the multi-party political framework. In return, the Government pledged not to legislate on any of the points under negotiation in Rome until a general peace accord had been signed. In November a second protocol, concerning party law, was signed by both parties, enabling Renamo to begin functioning as a political party immediately after the signing of a general peace accord.

In March 1992, following protracted discussions conducted in Rome, a third protocol was signed establishing the principles for the country's future electoral system. Under its terms, the elections, to be held (one year after the signing of the general peace accord) under a system of proportional representation, were to be supervised by international observers. An electoral commission was to be established, with one-third of its members to be appointed by Renamo. Discussions, which resumed in June, reached an impasse over constitutional issues. In July, following meetings with Mugabe and President F. W. de Klerk of South Africa, Chissano announced that he was prepared to meet the Renamo leader, Afonso Macacho Marceta Dhlakama, for direct talks. On 7 August, following three days of discussions in Rome, Chissano and Dhlakama signed a joint declaration committing the two sides to a total cease-fire by 1 October, as part of a General Peace Agreement (Acordo Geral de Paz—AGP). Dhlakama rejected Chissano's offer of an immediate armistice, on the grounds that the mechanisms necessary to guarantee such a truce had first to be implemented.

In September 1992 Chissano and Dhlakama met in Gaborone, Botswana, to attempt to resolve the deadlocked military and security issues. Chissano offered to establish an independent commission to monitor and guarantee the impartiality of the Serviço de Informação e Segurança do Estado (SISE—State Information and Security Service), which Renamo claimed to be merely a continuation of the disbanded political police, the Serviço Nacional de Segurança Popular (National Service of People's Security). In addition, the figure of 30,000 was agreed upon as the number of troops to comprise the joint national defence force.

The AGP was finally signed on 4 October 1992. Under the terms of the agreement, a general cease-fire was to come into force immediately after ratification of the treaty by the legislature. Both the Renamo troops and the government forces were

to withdraw to assembly points within seven days of ratification. The new national defence force, the Forças Armadas de Defesa de Moçambique (FADM), would then be created, drawing on equal numbers from each side, with the remaining troops surrendering their weapons to a UN peace-keeping force within six months. A Cease-fire Commission, incorporating representatives from the Government, Renamo and the UN, was to be established to assume responsibility for supervising the implementation of the truce regulations. Overall political control of the peace process was to be vested in a Comissão de Supervisão e Controle (CSC—Supervision and Control Commission), comprising representatives of the Government, Renamo and the UN; its remit was to include supervision of the Cease-fire Commission and other commissions charged with establishing the joint armed forces, reintegrating demobilized soldiers into civilian society, and verifying the withdrawal of foreign troops from Mozambique. In addition, Chissano was to appoint a National Information Commission (COMINFO), with responsibilities including supervision of the SISE. Presidential and legislative elections were to take place, under UN supervision, one year after the signing of the AGP, provided that it had been fully implemented and the demobilization process completed. The AGP was duly ratified by the Assembléia da República and came into force on 15 October. On that day UN observers arrived in Maputo to supervise the first phase of the cease-fire. However, shortly afterwards the Government accused Renamo of systematically violating the accord. Dhlakama subsequently claimed that Renamo's actions had been defensive manoeuvres and, in turn, accused government forces of violating the accord by advancing into Renamo territory.

In November 1992, owing to considerable delays in the formation of the various peace commissions envisaged in the AGP, the timetable for the cease-fire operations was redrafted. In December the UN Security Council finally approved a plan for the establishment of the UN Operation in Mozambique (ONUMOZ), providing for the deployment of some 7,500 troops, police and civilian observers to oversee the process of demobilization and formation of the FADM, and to supervise the forthcoming elections. However, there were continued delays in the deployment of ONUMOZ, since the UN was experiencing difficulty in persuading its member nations to contribute troops. Renamo, moreover, refused to begin confining its forces to assembly points until 65% of the UN force was in place. The location of the 49 assembly points was not agreed until February 1993. In March the peace process was effectively halted when Renamo withdrew from the CSC and the Cease-fire Commission, protesting that proper provisions had not been made to accommodate its officials, and in April Dhlakama announced that his forces would begin to report to assembly points only when Renamo received US $15m. to finance its transition into a political party. Meanwhile, the first UN troops became operational on 1 April, and in mid-April the Zimbabwean troops guarding the Beira and Limpopo 'corridors' were replaced by UN forces, six months behind schedule.

In June 1993 Renamo rejoined the CSC. The commission subsequently agreed to a formal postponement of the election date to October 1994. A meeting in Maputo of international aid donors, also in June 1993, revealed growing impatience among the international community at the repeated delays in the peace process and with Renamo's escalating demands for logistical and financial support. The meeting produced promises of additional support for the peace process, bringing the total pledged by donors to US $520m., including support for the repatriation of 1.5m. refugees from neighbouring countries, the resettlement of 4m.–5m. displaced people and the reintegration of some 80,000 former combatants into civilian life. The UN also agreed to establish a trust fund of $10m. to finance Renamo's transformation into a political party, with the disbursement of funds dependent on UN approval.

Renamo announced new preconditions to the advancement of the peace process in July 1993, insisting initially on the recognition of its own administration, to operate parallel to that of the Government, and later on the appointment of its members to five of the country's 11 provincial governorships. Under the terms of an agreement signed in September, Renamo was to appoint three advisers to each of the incumbent provincial governors to make recommendations relating to the reintegration of areas under Renamo control into a single state administration. It was also agreed that a request be made to the UN to send a police corps to supervise the activities of the national police and ensure neutrality in areas under Renamo control. In

October 1993 the CSC approved a new timetable covering all aspects of the peace process, including the elections in October 1994. In November 1993 the UN Security Council adopted a resolution renewing the mandate of ONUMOZ for a further six months. In addition, it acceded to the joint request by the Government and Renamo for a UN police corps. In the same month consensus was finally reached on the text of the electoral law, which was promulgated at the end of December.

At a meeting of the CSC in mid-November 1993 an agreement was signed providing for the confinement of troops to begin on 30 November. The process was to have been concluded by the end of the year. However, less than 15% of the total number of troops for confinement entered assembly points. In January 1994 military instructors (comprising government and Renamo troops who had been trained by British instructors in Zimbabwe) arrived in Mozambique to begin training the FADM. However, owing to logistical problems, formal training was repeatedly postponed, and eventually far fewer soldiers than originally planned were trained.

The National Electoral Commission, which was inaugurated in February 1994, comprised 10 members from the Government, seven from Renamo, three from the other opposition parties and an independent chairman. Later in February the UN Security Council announced that, in response to demands made by Renamo, it would be increasing the membership of the UN police corps monitoring the confinement areas from 128 to 1,144. By the end of February only 50% of troops had entered assembly points, and none had officially been demobilized. In March, in an effort to expedite the confinement process, the Government announced that it was to commence the unilateral demobilization of its troops. Renamo began the demobilization of its troops shortly afterwards. In April Lt-Gen. Lagos Lidimo, the nominee of the Government, and the former Renamo guerrilla commander, Lt-Gen. Mateus Ngonhamo, were inaugurated as the high command of the FADM. In the same month Chissano issued a decree scheduling the presidential and legislative elections for 27–28 October, and in May the UN Security Council renewed the mandate of ONUMOZ for the final period, ending on 15 November.

The confinement and demobilization processes continued to make slow progress, and the deadline for the completion of confinement was consequently extended to 8 July 1994, with demobilization to be completed by 15 August. By that date only 7,375 troops from both sides had enlisted in the FADM; the deadline for registration at confinement points was subsequently extended to 31 August, after which date it was to continue at three centres in the north, centre and south of the country. On 16 August, in accordance with the provisions of the AGP, the government Forças Armadas de Moçambique were formally dissolved and their assets transferred to the FADM, which was inaugurated as the country's official armed forces on the same day.

In August 1994 Renamo formally registered as a political party. In the same month the Partido Liberal e Democrático de Moçambique, the Partido Nacional Democrático and the Partido Nacional de Moçambique formed an electoral coalition, the União Democrática (UD). The presidential and legislative elections took place on 27–29 October. The extension of voting to a third day had become necessary following the withdrawal of Renamo from the elections only hours before the beginning of the poll, claiming that conditions were not in place to ensure free and fair elections. However, following concerted international pressure, Renamo abandoned its boycott after the first day. In the presidential election Chissano secured an outright majority (53.3%) of the votes. His closest rival was Dhlakama, who received 33.7% of the votes. In the legislative elections Frelimo also secured an overall majority, winning 129 of the 250 seats in the Assembléia da República; Renamo obtained 112 seats, and the UD the remaining nine. Dhlakama accepted the results of the elections, although he maintained that there had been irregularities. The UN asserted that the irregularities were insufficient to have affected the overall credibility of the poll, which it declared to have been free and fair—a view endorsed by international observers. Later in November the UN Security Council extended the mandate of ONUMOZ until the end of January 1995. In December 1994 the Cease-fire Commission issued its final report, according to which ONUMOZ had registered a combined total of 91,691 government and Renamo troops during the confinement process, of whom 11,579 had enlisted in the FADM (compared with the 30,000 envisaged in the AGP).

Chissano was inaugurated as President on 9 December 1994, and the new Government, in which all portfolios were assigned to members of Frelimo, was sworn in on 23 December. Demands by Renamo that it be awarded governorships in the five provinces where it won a majority of the votes in the legislative elections were rejected by Chissano. At the first session of the new legislature, which began on 8 December, a dispute concerning the voting procedure employed to elect its Chairman resulted in the withdrawal of the Renamo and UD deputies, who had unsuccessfully demanded a secret ballot; both parties had abandoned their boycott by the end of December, although not before the conclusion of the first session.

In March 1995 the Minister of National Defence announced that, once legislation had been enacted allowing for the reintroduction of compulsory military service, a further 4,500 troops would be drafted into the FADM. By the end of March all ONUMOZ troops and police had left Mozambique, two months later than originally envisaged, and only a small unit of ONUMOZ officials remained in the country. In February 1996 the Government proposed that municipal elections, which the Constitution stipulated must be conducted no later than October 1996, be held in 1997. Delays in the election process had resulted from a dispute between the parliamentary opposition, which demanded simultaneous local elections throughout Mozambique, and the Government, which sought to hold elections only in those areas that had attained municipal status. In October 1996 parliament approved a constitutional amendment differentiating between municipalities and administrative posts. In August 1997 the Government postponed the elections until 1998, owing to delays in the disbursement by international donors of funding for the voter registration process. In January 1998 Renamo alleged that the voter registration process, which had taken place in November 1997, had been fraudulent, and threatened to boycott the elections unless a further registration of voters was conducted. While the National Electoral Commission conceded that there had been certain material errors in the registration process, it insisted that attempts had been made to correct them and that the registration remained valid. In April 1998 Renamo was among 16 opposition parties that officially withdrew from the elections. Renamo subsequently campaigned vigorously to dissuade the electorate from participating in the ballot. At the elections, which took place on 30 June 1998, Frelimo secured all the mayoral posts and won control of all the municipal authorities contested. However, since very few opposition parties contested the election, Frelimo's main competition came from independent candidates. Moreover, the voter turnout was only 14.6%, prompting Renamo to demand the annulment of the elections on the grounds that the low level of participation greatly reduced the legitimacy of the newly elected representatives.

In October 1998 the Government published draft constitutional amendments that envisaged substantial changes to the country's political system, including a reduction in presidential powers and concomitant increase in those of the Prime Minister and the legislature. If approved, the amendments would confer the status of 'Head of Government' on the Prime Minister, transferring this from the President—who would remain 'Head of State'. In addition, a Council of State would be formed as a consultative body to advise the President. In the same month the Government presented draft electoral legislation governing the conduct of presidential and legislative elections scheduled for 1999.

Under the Constitution, presidential and legislative elections were to take place by November 1999. However, political disputes and administrative delays threatened to force a postponement of the elections. A principal cause of the delay was Renamo's insistence on the need to reregister the entire electorate. In June Frelimo announced that Chissano would stand as its presidential candidate. In the following month 11 opposition parties, led by Renamo, signed an agreement to contest the forthcoming elections as a coalition, styled Renamo—União Eleitoral (Renamo—UE). The coalition was to present a single list of legislative candidates, with Dhlakama as its presidential candidate.

Presidential and legislative elections took place on 3–5 December 1999. In the presidential contest, Chissano defeated Dhlakama (his sole challenger), taking 52.3% of the valid votes cast. Frelimo secured an outright majority in the legislative elections, winning 133 of the 250 seats in the Assembléia da República; Renamo—UE obtained the remaining seats. Renamo rejected the outcome, claiming that the vote had been fraudulent, and threatened to petition the Constitutional Council to overturn the result. However, international monitors declared that, despite some logistical problems, the vote had been free and fair. In January 2000 the Supreme Court—exercising the functions of the Constitutional Council, which had yet to be established—rejected the appeal by Renamo against the results of the elections. Later that month it was reported that, in contravention of legislation requiring political parties to be based in the capital, Renamo had moved its headquarters to Beira, leaving only a small delegation in Maputo. On 15 January Chissano was sworn in for a further five-year presidential term. However, Dhlakama refused to attend the investiture, and Renamo continued to dispute the legitimacy of the newly elected Government. In February Dhlakama issued an ultimatum to the Government, giving it 10 days in which to conduct a recount of the votes or agree to new elections, failing which it announced that it would unilaterally declare the establishment of a parallel government in the central and northern regions of the country. However, the deadline of a similar ultimatum issued in January had passed without incident.

In February 2000 massive flooding in southern and central areas caused widespread devastation to the country's social and economic infrastructure. The flooding was the worst ever on record, seriously affecting an estimated 2m. people. Some 10% of Mozambique's cultivated land was destroyed, and most of its livestock was lost. Much of the country's transport infrastructure was destroyed, as were many villages. The World Bank estimated the cost of losses at between US $270m. and $430m.

In May 2000 thousands of people took part in a march to mark Workers' Day, demanding the establishment of labour tribunals, which, despite their creation by the Government in 1992, had not yet been put into existence; workers were also seeking an increase in the minimum wage and the return of price controls. Earlier that month the Prime Minister, Pascoal Mocumbi, condemned comments by Dhlakama, in which he had threatened to regroup demobilized Renamo soldiers and seize control of the country. The Renamo political delegate for Nampula province was later arrested. It was subsequently revealed that negotiations were taking place between Chissano and Renamo. In July a senior member of Renamo, Raul Domingos, was suspended from the party, pending an investigation into negotiations conducted in June between himself and the Minister for Transport and Communications, Tomás Salomão, during which Domingos was alleged to have demanded an estimated US $500,000 to assist in personal loan repayments, up to $1m. per month for Renamo, and a $10,000 per month salary for Dhlakama. Domingos was officially expelled from the party in September.

Renamo boycotted the election of the new National Elections Commission (NEC), officially inaugurated in July 2000, on the grounds that it did not recognise the legitimacy of the current Government, and that a review of the current electoral law was needed. Frelimo appointed eight representatives to the 15-member NEC. Demonstrations held by Renamo in November, in protest at the results of the December 1999 elections, resulted in the deaths of some 41 people, following clashes between Renamo and Frelimo supporters. (In June 2001 several Renamo members were found guilty of armed rebellion in relation to the riots, while several police-officers were also prosecuted; a further 14 Renamo members and supporters were imprisoned in January 2002 for their part in the violence.) Moreover, later in November 2000 one of the country's most influential journalists, Carlos Cardoso, was killed in Maputo. It was alleged by Dhlakama that Cardoso had been murdered as a result of an article, published in the newspaper *Metical*, in which he had criticized the Government's involvement in the protests earlier in November. (It was announced in March 2001 that three people, including the former manager of a branch of the Banco Comercial de Moçambique—BCM, had been arrested in connection with Cardoso's murder; shortly before his death Cardoso had apparently uncovered details relating to the theft of some 144,000m. meticais from a branch of the BCM in 1996.) Furthermore, Renamo accused the Government of being responsible for the death of some 83 prisoners (principally Renamo supporters arrested during the protests) in late November; the Government denied the allegations, claiming that the prisoners had died of suffocation due to overcrowding. A subsequent report by the Mozambican Human Rights Association suggested that the prisoners had, in fact, died of suffocation and starvation.

In late December 2000 Dhlakama and Chissano held talks (the first since the disputed election in December 1999) in an attempt to resolve the growing political tension between their two parties. The two leaders agreed to hold further talks in 2001, and to establish inquiries into the violence in November. Moreover, Dhlakama stated that he was prepared to accept the results of the 1999 elections, and Chissano pledged to consult Renamo about future state appointments (notably in the appointment of state governors). However, comments by Dhlakama, accusing Frelimo of violence and intimidation towards Renamo, subsequently jeopardized the future of talks between the two parties. Following a second meeting between the two leaders in January 2001, the two parties appeared to be no closer to achieving a consensus; Chissano maintained his refusal to accept Dhlakama's demand that Renamo supporters be appointed as governors to those parts of the country where Renamo had gained a majority of votes in the 1999 election. Chissano also rejected Dhlakama's request for an early election. Nevertheless, it was agreed that a number of working groups (including groups on defence and security, constitutional and parliamentary affairs, and the media) would be established in February. At a further meeting, in March, Chissano referred Dhlakama's demand for the appointment of Renamo governors to the Assembléia da República, whose Frelimo representatives were strongly opposed to accommodating Renamo demands. In protest, Dhlakama ceased negotiations in April.

Floods in central Mozambique in February and March 2001 resulted in some 100 deaths and left an estimated 230,000 people homeless and displaced. In July the Government requested some US $132m. in international aid to assist in the reconstruction of damaged infrastructure, and for the development of measures to prevent a recurrence of the floods in 2002.

President Chissano announced in May 2001 that he would not stand for re-election on the expiry of his term in 2004, prompting speculation about potential successors, ahead of the eighth Frelimo party congress, to be held in June 2002. At the long-postponed Renamo congress, held in October 2001, Dhlakama was re-elected party President, obtaining over 95% of votes cast; Joaquim Vaz was elected Secretary-General. The holding of a party congress by Renamo for the first time since the end of the civil war, as well as the establishment of a 10-member Political Committee, were regarded as confirmation of the movement's decision to establish itself as a full political party, and to decentralize the party leadership and structure.

In August 2001 Siba-Siba Macuacua, the interim Chairman of Banco Austral, was murdered while investigating corruption allegations at the bank. Macuacua had published a list of more than 1,000 people, including some government officials, who had failed to repay loans to the bank. There had been little apparent progress on the investigation of the case by early 2003.

In November 2001 the Assembléia da República approved legislation prohibiting the process of money 'laundering'. The new measures imposed restrictions on banking and other local financial activities, in an attempt to render them more accountable. Also in that month a former member of the UD, António Palange, founded a new political party, the Congresso dos Democratas Unidos, aimed at promoting national reconciliation and a policy of understanding between the different ethnic and racial groups; Palange also stated that economic freedom in Mozambique was the party's principal objective.

In June 2002, at the party's eighth party congress, Frelimo elected Armando Guebuza as its Secretary-General, and thus also its candidate for the 2004 presidential election. During July Renamo's attempt to establish itself as a legitimate opposition party was threatened after Dhlakama dismissed Vaz as Secretary-General, assuming the position himself, and dissolved the party's Political Committee. In September long-standing Renamo opposition to new electoral laws (regarding the composition of a National Elections Commission) was suddenly withdrawn, and a 19-member Commission approved. In October Renamo announced its intention to contest municipal elections (due in 2003) alone, rather than in coalition, while in November 2002 the party regained some stability with the appointment of Viana Magalhaes as Secretary-General. In December, however, further controversy arose when Renamo demanded the exclusion from the Assembléia da República of five deputies who had resigned or been expelled from the party, including Domingos, who had announced his intention to present himself as an independent candidate for the 2004 presidential election. The police were called to the Assembléia to disperse Renamo protesters, who caused an estimated US $11,000 of damage to the building. The former Renamo deputies retained their right to participate in the Assembléia.

In early December 2002 legislation was passed creating a Constitutional Council, which, although enshrined in the Constitution, had not yet been established. The Council was to consist of a presidentially appointed chairperson, ratified by the Assembléia, five judges elected by the Assembléia on a proportional basis, and a seventh judge co-opted by the other six. Hermenegildo Gamito was appointed as the first Chairman, and debate on a new draft constitution commenced, with Renamo in favour of abolishing the post of Prime Minister.

Meanwhile, in November 2002, during the trial of six men for Cardoso's murder in 2000, the President's eldest son, Nyimpine Chissano, was accused by three of the defendants of having ordered or paid for the assassination; Nyimpine Chissano denied any involvement in the murder. It was additionally claimed that one of the accused, Aníbal António dos Santos, who had escaped from custody in suspicious circumstances at the beginning of September, was making secret threats against key figures in the trial. In January 2003 all six accused were found guilty of Cardoso's murder; dos Santos, who had been tried *in absentia*, was arrested in South Africa at the end of January, and extradited to Mozambique to serve a prison term of 28 years and six months.

In February 2003, in response to Renamo's decision to run alone in the municipal elections, now scheduled for 28 October, 10 opposition parties announced the formation of a new coalition, the União Eleitoral, led by Domingos. Renamo deputies subsequently threatened to disrupt legislative proceedings again unless Domingos was expelled from the Assembléia.

During 1995 the activities, principally in the border province of Manica, of a group of mainly Zimbabwean dissidents, known as Chimwenje, came under increasing scrutiny. The group, which was alleged to have links with Renamo, was believed to be preparing for military incursions into Zimbabwe, where it sought the overthrow of President Mugabe. In early 1996, following a series of armed confrontations between Chimwenje and the Mozambican security forces, the Chissano Government announced its intention to expel the dissidents from Mozambique. In June, following a series of armed attacks on both sides of the Mozambique–Zimbabwe border, which were believed to have been perpetrated by Chimwenje, bilateral discussions between the Governments of Mozambique and Zimbabwe resulted in an agreement to combine and intensify efforts to combat the activities of the dissidents. The group was eventually suppressed in late 1996, through joint military action by both countries. During late 2002 and early 2003 Mozambique accepted and resettled a number of white Zimbabwean farmers whose land had been appropriated by the Mugabe regime.

After independence, Mozambique developed strong international links with the USSR and other countries of the communist bloc, and with neighbouring African states: it is a member of the Southern African Development Community (SADC, see p. 311), founded in 1979, as the Southern African Development Co-ordination Conference, then with the aim of reducing the region's economic dependence on South Africa, principally by developing trade routes through Mozambique. In December 1996 Mozambique, Malawi, Zambia and Zimbabwe (also SADC members) formally agreed to establish the Beira Development Corridor as a trading route avoiding South Africa's ports. In 1993 full diplomatic relations were established with South Africa. In July 1994 Mozambique and South Africa established a new Joint Defence and Security Commission, replacing the Joint Security Commission originally established in 1984. In November 1995 Mozambique was admitted, by special dispensation, as a full member of the Commonwealth (see p. 164).

Government

The Constitution of 30 November 1990 provides for a multi-party political system. Legislative power is vested in the Assembléia da República, with 250 members, who are elected for a five-year term. Members are elected by universal, direct adult suffrage in a secret ballot, according to a system of proportional representation. The President of the Republic, who is Head of State, is directly elected for a five-year term; the President holds executive power and governs with the assistance of an appointed Council of Ministers. Provincial governors, appointed by the President, have overall responsibility for the functions of government within each of the 11 provinces. For the purposes of local government, Mozambique is divided into 139 municipalities and 394 administrative posts.

Defence

According to the final report, issued in December 1994, of the Cease-fire Commission, which had been established under the General Peace Agreement (Acordo Geral de Paz—AGP) to supervise the implementation of truce regulations (see Recent History), a combined total of only 11,579 government and Renamo troops (from a total of 91,691 troops registered at assembly points) had enlisted in the new Forças Armadas de Defesa de Moçambique (FADM). By the end of March 1995 all troops and police belonging to the UN Operation in Mozambique (ONUMOZ), stationed in the country to facilitate the pacification and electoral processes, had withdrawn. After that date only a small unit of ONUMOZ officials remained in the country. In November 1997 legislation was approved providing for the reintroduction of compulsory military service, which had been suspended under the AGP. It was envisaged that the strength of the FADM, which stood at less than 11,000 in late 1996, would be increased to 15,000. In late 1998 the Ministry of National Defence announced plans to recruit an additional 3,000 conscripts into the armed forces in 1999 (however, only 1,000 recruits were conscripted in that year). The total strength of the FADM was to be defined by government policy, and the figure of 30,000 envisaged in the AGP would not necessarily be observed. In August 2002 total active armed forces were estimated at 10,150–11,150 (army 9,000–10,000, navy 150, air force 1,000). Expenditure on defence and security was budgeted at an estimated 1,600,000m. meticais in 2002.

Economic Affairs

In 2001, according to estimates by the World Bank, Mozambique's gross national income (GNI), measured at average 1999–2001 prices, was US $3,747m., equivalent to $210 per head (or $1,000 per head on an international purchasing-power parity basis). During 1990–2001, it was estimated, the population increased at an average annual rate of 2.2%, while gross domestic product (GDP) per head increased, in real terms, by an average of 4.8% per year. Overall GDP increased, in real terms, at an average annual rate of 7.2% in 1990–2001; growth in 2001 was 9.0%.

Agriculture (including forestry and fishing) contributed 23.4% of GDP in 2001. In mid-2001 an estimated 80.3% of the economically active population were employed in the sector. Fishing is the principal export activity: fish, crustaceans and molluscs accounted for 27.6% of total export earnings in 1999. The principal cash crops are fruit and nuts (providing 14.8% of export earnings in 1999), cotton (accounting for 7.4% of export earnings in 1999), sugar cane (sugar and honey provided 2.0% of total 1999 exports) and copra. The main subsistence crop is cassava. During 1990–2001, according to the World Bank agricultural GDP increased by an average of 4.8% per year; growth in 2001 was 15.1%.

Industry (including mining, manufacturing, construction and power) employed 5.6% of the economically active population in 1997, and provided 25.8% of GDP in 2001. During 1990–2001, according to the World Bank, industrial GDP increased at an average annual rate of 12.8%; growth in 2001 was 21.6%.

Mining and quarrying contributed 0.4% of GDP in 2001, and employed 0.5% of the economically active population in 1997. Only coal, bentonite and salt are exploited in significant quantities, although bauxite, gravel and crushed rocks are also mined; the exploitation of commercially viable levels of graphite began in 1994, but production ceased in 2000. There are reserves of other minerals, including high-grade iron ore, gold, precious and semi-precious stones, marble and natural gas. Plans began in 1994 to develop a natural gas field at Pande, in the province of Inhambane, where reserves were estimated at 55,000m. cu m. Sales of the gas to South Africa, which was expected to be the principal consumer, were due to begin by 2000, following the construction of a 900-km pipeline. The project was subsequently delayed, following a dispute between the US-based energy conglomerate, Enron, which was involved in the project, and the Mozambique Government. However, an agreement to develop the gas fields was signed in October 2000. Construction of the pipeline to South Africa was scheduled for completion in 2004. In 1998 the Government signed a production-sharing agreement with an international consortium, led by South African and US interests, under the terms of which the consortium was to invest US $30m., over a seven-year period, in the exploration of natural gas in the Temane region of Inhambane province. In 1999 the largest reserve of titanium in the world (estimated at 100m. metric tons) was discovered in the district of Chibuto, in the province of Gaza; production from the Limpopo Corridor Sands Project in Chibuto was expected to begin in 2005, providing 1m. tons of titanium per year for 35 years. According to government targets, minerals were to account for 10% of exports and 6% of GDP by 2005, as a result of increased expenditure on mining exploration. According to official figures, mining GDP increased at an average annual rate of 18.6% in 1996–2001; growth in 2001 was 12.6%.

Manufacturing contributed 14.3% of GDP in 2001, and employed 3.0% of the economically active population in 1997. A large aluminium smelter, Mozal, was opened in June 2000; the smelter was expected to produce some 250,000 metric tons of aluminium ingots per year, increasing Mozambique's GDP by an estimated 7%. In June 2001 it was announced that Mozal was to expand, doubling production to 500,000 tons per year; Mozal 2 commenced operations in April 2003. During 1994–2001, according to the World Bank, manufacturing GDP increased at an average annual rate of 18.8%; growth in 2001 was 32.6%.

Electrical energy is derived principally from hydroelectric power, which provided some 99.6% of total electricity production in 1999. In 1988 about one-third of the electricity supply was imported from South Africa. In that year Mozambique, Portugal and South Africa signed an agreement to rehabilitate Mozambique's important Cahora Bassa hydroelectric plant on the Zambezi River. Upon completion of the project, Mozambique was to export hydroelectric power to South Africa. However, work was continually delayed as a result of the security situation. Following the signing of the General Peace Agreement (Acordo Geral de Paz—AGP) in 1992, rehabilitation of the plant and transmission lines resumed in 1995 and was completed in 1997. From 1999 a consortium involving Mozambican, French and German companies financed a feasibility study for the construction of a hydroelectric power plant at Mepanda-Ncua, some 70 km downstream of Cahora Bassa, which would help to support the 900-MW energy requirement of the Mozal smelter. Construction of the plant, which would have a generating capacity of 2,500 MW, was projected to cost some US $1,500m. It was envisaged that power from the plant, which would not be completed before 2007, would also be exported to South Africa. Mozambique currently imports all of its petroleum requirements. Imports of mineral fuels and lubricants comprised 10.8% of the value of total imports in 1999.

The services sector engaged 12.3% of the economically active population in 1997, and contributed 50.7% of GDP in 2001. By the end of the 1990s tourism was the fastest growing sector of the economy, and was estimated to contribute some US $32m. annually to the budget. Assisted by funding from the European Union, a firm of Danish consultants was preparing a comprehensive tourism development plan for Mozambique. Moreover, it was hoped that the formal opening, in April 2002, of the Great Limpopo Transfrontier Park, comprising South Africa's Kruger National Park, Zimbabwe's Gonarezhou National Park and Mozambique's Limpopo National Park, would attract additional tourists. The GDP of the services sector increased by an average of 2.3% per year in 1990–2001, according to the World Bank; growth in 2001 was 6.7%.

In 2001 Mozambique recorded a trade deficit of US $413.9m., and there was a deficit of $380.2m. on the current account of the balance of payments. In 1998 the principal source of imports (42.2%) was the Southern African Customs Union (SACU); other major suppliers were Portugal and the USA. In 1999 SACU was the principal market for exports (receiving 28.0%); other significant purchasers were Zimbabwe, Spain, India and Portugal. The principal exports in 2000 were prawns, aluminium, electricity and cotton. The principal imports in 1999 were machinery and transport equipment, food and live animals (principally cereals and cereal preparations), basic manufactures, mineral fuels and lubricants, and chemicals. Production from the Mozal aluminium smelter was expected to double the value of total exports, to about $700m., in 2001; it was announced in July 2001 that exports had increased by 172% compared with the same period in 2000, principally as a result of aluminium exports from Mozal.

In 2001 there was an overall budgetary deficit of 3,968,000m. meticais (equivalent to 5.4% of GDP). Mozambique's total external debt was estimated at US $7,135m. at the end of 2000, of which $4,599m. was long-term public debt. In that year the cost of debt-servicing was equivalent to 11.4% of the total value of exports of goods and services. The average annual rate of inflation was 27.3% in 1990–2001; consumer prices increased by an average of 9.0% in 2001 and by 16.8% in 2002. According to

official figures, the number of unemployed was 118,000 at the end of 1996.

Mozambique is a member of the Southern African Development Community (SADC, see p. 311). In November 2000 Mozambique was invited by the Common Market for Eastern and Southern Africa (COMESA, see p. 162) to rejoin the organization (Mozambique left COMESA in 1993, when it joined SADC).

In terms of average income, Mozambique is one of the poorest countries in the world. During the 1980s economic development was severely frustrated by the effects of the civil war. Since 1990 there has been considerable progress in liberalizing the economy. Increased production in rural areas, continued structural reform and the partial restoration of the infrastructure contributed to significant GDP growth from 1993, and in 1994–98 Mozambique's economy was one of the fastest growing in the world. In June 1999 the Bretton Woods institutions reduced Mozambique's public debt by almost two-thirds, significantly decreasing the country's annual servicing obligations for the period 1999–2005, and the IMF approved a loan for Mozambique, equivalent to some US $78.5m., under the Enhanced Structural Adjustment Facility (later renamed the Poverty Reduction and Growth Facility—PRGF), in support of the Government's 1999–2002 economic reform programme. In March 2000 the 'Paris Club' of official creditors deferred all payments due on the country's external debt for one year, following severe flooding in southern and central Mozambique, and the IMF increased the PRGF arrangement to some $113m. In April the IMF agreed to grant Mozambique a further $600m. in debt relief under the enhanced terms of the Heavily Indebted Poor Countries initiative. In October the Minister of Planning and Finance estimated the total cost of the floods on the country's economy at some $600m., and claimed that a large part of financial aid pledged by international donors in June had yet to be disbursed. Furthermore, following the collapse of a local bank, Banco Austral, in 2000, disbursements of IMF funds (arranged under the Poverty Reduction and Growth Facility) were temporarily suspended. None the less, at a meeting of the World Bank's Consultative Group in October 2001, donors pledged some $722m. in aid for 2002. A decline in prices for cashew nuts in 2000–01 (principally as a result of a collapse in demand in India, but also partly owing to the liberalization of Mozambique's cashew-processing industry, as requested by the World Bank) led to economic uncertainty and an increase in the country's trade deficit. Moreover, the economic decline in South Africa and Zimbabwe in 2001 adversely affected the Mozambican economy, in particular the transport sector. None the less, strong economic growth was recorded in 2001, owing to the increased output of the Mozal smelter and a recovery in the agricultural sector, following the floods in 2000. The Government's targets under its Economic and Social Plan for 2002 were met, with estimated GDP growth of 10% and cumulative inflation of 8%. The collapse and subsequent recapitalization of Banco Austral and of the Banco Comercial de Moçambique caused a significant increase in levels of domestic debt, which was expected to affect the budget for the foreseeable future. During 2002 Mozambique's foreign debt was drastically reduced by the cancellation of its obligations to Russia, Italy, Germany and the United Kingdom. In June the IMF commended Mozambique's rapid post-flood recovery, later forecasting GDP growth and an inflation rate of 7% for 2003. The 2003 state budget, which was approved without debate during a Renamo protest (see Recent History), set expenditure at 30,515,600m. meticais, around one-half of which was to be covered by foreign aid, but maintained a commitment to the country's Action Plan for the Reduction of Absolute Poverty.

Education

Education is officially compulsory for seven years from the age of seven. Primary schooling begins at seven years of age and lasts for seven years. It is divided into two cycles, of five and two years. Secondary schooling, from 13 years of age, lasts for six years and comprises two cycles, each lasting three years. As a proportion of the school-age population, the total enrolment at primary and secondary schools increased from 30% in 1972 to 52% in 1979, but declined to the equivalent of 32% in 1995 (males 38%; females 27%). In 1999/2000 50.1% of children in the relevant age-group were enrolled at primary schools (males 54.7%; females 45.6%), while secondary enrolment included 7.3% of children in the relevant age-group (males 8.5%; females 6.2%). There were 7,156 students in public higher education in 1997. Two privately owned higher education institutions, the

Catholic University and the Higher Polytechnic Institute, were inaugurated in 1996. In 1997 there were six higher education institutions in total. Education was allocated 20.3% of total current government expenditure in 1999.

Public Holidays

2003: 1 January (New Year's Day), 3 February (Heroes' Day, anniversary of the assassination of Eduardo Mondlane), 7 April (Day of the Mozambican Woman), 1 May (Workers' Day), 25 June (Independence Day), 7 September (Victory Day—anniversary of the end of the Armed Struggle), 25 September (Anniversary of the launching of the Armed Struggle for National Liberation, and Day of the Armed Forces of Mozambique), 25 December (National Family Day).

2004: 1 January (New Year's Day), 3 February (Heroes' Day, anniversary of the assassination of Eduardo Mondlane), 7 April (Day of the Mozambican Woman), 1 May (Workers' Day), 25 June (Independence Day), 7 September (Victory Day—anniversary of the end of the Armed Struggle), 25 September (Anniversary of the launching of the Armed Struggle for National Liberation, and Day of the Armed Forces of Mozambique), 25 December (National Family Day).

Weights and Measures

The metric system is in force.

Statistical Survey

Source (unless otherwise stated): Instituto Nacional de Estatística, Comissão Nacional do Plano, Avda Ahmed Sekou Touré 21, CP 493, Maputo; tel. (1) 491054; fax (1) 493547; internet www.ine.gov.mz.

Area and Population

AREA, POPULATION AND DENSITY

Area (sq km)	799,380
Population (census results)	
1 August 1980	11,673,725
1 August 1997	
Males	7,714,306
Females	8,384,940
Total	16,099,246
Population (official estimates at mid-year)	
2000	17,242,240
2001	17,656,153
2002	18,082,523
Density (per sq km) at mid-2002	22.6

* 308,641 sq miles. The area includes 13,000 sq km (5,019 sq miles) of inland water.

† Excluding an adjustment for underenumeration. This was estimated to have been 3.8%, and the adjusted total was 12,130,000.

PROVINCES

(at 1 July 2002)

Province	Area (sq km)	Population	Density (per sq km)
Cabo Delgado	82,625	1,525,634	18.5
Gaza	75,709	1,266,431	16.7
Inhambane	68,615	1,326,848	19.3
Manica	61,661	1,207,332	19.6
City of Maputo	300	1,044,618	3,482.1
Maputo province	26,058	1,003,992	38.5
Nampula	81,606	3,410,141	41.8
Niassa	129,056	916,672	7.1
Sofala	68,018	1,516,166	22.3
Tete	100,724	1,388,205	13.7
Zambézia	105,008	3,476,484	33.1
Total	799,380	18,082,523	22.6

PRINCIPAL TOWNS

(population at 1997 census)

Maputo (capital)	989,386	Nacala-Porto	164,309
Matola	440,927	Quelimane	153,187
Beira	412,588	Tete	104,832
Nampula	314,965	Xai-Xai	103,251
Chimoio	177,608	Gurue	101,367

Mid-2001 (UN estimate, incl. suburbs): Maputo 1,134,000 (Source: UN, *World Urbanization Prospects: The 2001 Revision*).

BIRTHS AND DEATHS

	1998	1999	2000
Birth rate (per 1,000)	44.1	43.5	42.9
Death rate (per 1,000)	22.7	23.0	23.3

Source: African Development Bank.

2000 (official figures): Registered live births 743,239 (birth rate 43.1 per 1,000); Registered deaths 333,468 (death rate 19.3 per 1,000).

2001 (UN estimates): Registered live births 753,252 (birth rate 41.7 in 1,000); Registered deaths 331,162 (death rate 18.8 in 1,000) (Source: UN, *Population and Vital Statistics Report*).

2002 (official figures): Birth rate (per 1,000) 42.2; Death rate (per 1,000) 18.2.

Expectation of life (WHO estimates, years at birth): 44.8 (males 43.7; females 45.9) in 2001 (Source: WHO, *World Health Report*).

ECONOMICALLY ACTIVE POPULATION

(persons aged 12 years and over, 1980 census)

	Males	Females	Total
Agriculture, forestry, hunting and fishing	1,887,779	2,867,052	4,754,831
Mining and quarrying			
Manufacturing	323,730	23,064	346,794
Construction	41,611	510	42,121
Commerce	90,654	21,590	112,244
Transport, storage and communications	74,817	2,208	77,025
Other services	203,629	39,820	243,449
Total employed	2,622,220	2,954,244	5,576,464
Unemployed	75,505	19,321	94,826
Total labour force	2,697,725	2,973,565	5,671,290

* Including electricity, gas and water.

Source: ILO, *Yearbook of Labour Statistics*.

1991 (estimates, '000 persons): Agriculture 6,870; Industry 766; Services 798; Total labour force 8,434 (Source: UN Economic Commission for Africa, *African Statistical Yearbook*).

1997 (percentage distribution of economically active population at census of 1 August): Agriculture, forestry and hunting: 91.3% of females, 69.6% of males; Mining: 0.0% of females, 1.0% of males; Manufacturing: 0.8% of females, 5.5% of males; Energy: 0.0% of females, 0.3% of males; Construction: 0.3% of females, 3.9% of males; Transport and Communications: 0.1% of females, 2.3% of males; Commerce and Finance: 4.3% of females, 9.7% of males; Services: 2.2% of females, 3.4% of males; Unknown: 0.9% of females, 1.4% of males.

Mid-2001 (estimates in '000): Agriculture, etc. 7,844; Total labour force 9,766 (Source: FAO).

Health and Welfare

KEY INDICATORS

Total fertility rate (children per woman, 2001)	6.0
Under-5 mortality rate (per 1,000 live births, 2001) . . .	197
HIV/AIDS (% of persons aged 15–49, 2001).	13.00
Hospital beds (per 1,000 head, 1990)	0.87
Health expenditure (2000): US $ per head (PPP)	30
Health expenditure (2000): % of GDP	4.3
Health expenditure (2000): public (% of total)	63.4
Access to water (% of persons, 2000).	60
Access to sanitation (% of persons, 2000)	43
Human Development Index (2000): ranking	170
Human Development Index (2000): value	0.322

For sources and definitions, see explanatory note on p. vi.

Agriculture

PRINCIPAL CROPS
('000 metric tons)

	1999	2000	2001
Rice (paddy)	186	151	167
Maize	1,246	1,019	1,143
Millet	61	49	49
Sorghum	326	252	314
Potatoes	76	50	80
Sweet potatoes	61	45	66
Cassava (Manioc)	5,353	5,362	5,362
Sugar cane	496	397	397
Pulses	195	130	205
Cashew nuts	59	58	58
Groundnuts (in shell)	147	115	109
Coconuts	435	300	265
Sunflower seed	16	11	11
Cottonseed	60	23	50
Other oil seeds	50	33	20
Tomatoes	22	7	9
Other vegetables and melons . .	165	108	117
Bananas	88	59	90
Oranges	19	13	14
Grapefruits and pomelos . . .	19	13	13
Mangoes	36	24	24
Pineapples	19	13	13
Papayas	46	31	31
Other fruits	159	107	103
Cotton (lint)	30	11	11

* FAO estimate(s).
† Unofficial figure.

Source: FAO.

LIVESTOCK
(FAO estimates, '000 head, year ending September)

	1998	1999	2000
Asses	22	23	23
Cattle	1,300	1,310	1,320
Pigs	176	178	180
Sheep	123	124	125
Goats	388	390	392
Chickens	26,000	27,000	28,000

2001: Figures assumed to be unchanged from 2000.

Source: FAO.

LIVESTOCK PRODUCTS
(FAO estimates, '000 metric tons)

	1999	2000	2001
Beef and veal	38	38	38
Goat meat	2	2	2
Pig meat	13	13	13
Poultry meat	36	36	36
Cows' milk	60	60	60
Goats' milk	8	8	8
Hen eggs	14	14	14
Cattle hides	5	5	5

Source: FAO.

Forestry

ROUNDWOOD REMOVALS
('000 cubic metres, excl. bark)

	1997	1998	1999
Sawlogs, veneer logs and logs for sleepers	129	128	128
Other industrial wood	1,139	1,166	1,191
Fuel wood	16,724	16,724	16,724
Total	17,992	18,018	18,043

2000–01: Production as in 1999 (FAO estimates).

Source: FAO.

SAWNWOOD PRODUCTION
('000 cubic metres, incl. railway sleepers)

	1997	1998	1999
Total	33	28	28

2000–01: Production as in 1999 (FAO estimates).

Source: FAO.

Fishing

(metric tons, live weight)

	1998	1999	2000
Freshwater fishes	1,681	1,191	1,275
Dagaas.	7,313	9,052	11,813
Tuna-like fishes	7,140	2,635	5,081
Penaeus shrimps	8,559	8,846	9,460
Knife shrimp	1,882	1,611	1,766
Total catch (incl. others) . . .	36,677	33,989	39,065

Note: Figures exclude crocodiles, recorded by number rather than by weight. The number of Nile crocodiles caught was: 810 in 1998; 585 in 1999; 718 in 2000.

Source: FAO, *Yearbook of Fishery Statistics*.

Mining

('000 metric tons, unless otherwise indicated)

	1999	2000	2001
Bauxite	7.9	8.1	8.6
Bentonite	10.8	16.1	17.7
Coal	8.6	16.1	17.7
Gold (kilograms)	19.0	23.0	25.0
Graphite-concentrates	4.0	—	—
Gravel and crushed rock ('000 cubic metres)	265.0	187.0	209.0
Marble (slab) ('000 square metres)	2.6	1.8	2.0
Salt (marine)	82.0	7.0	10.0
Natural gas (million cu m)	60.0	60.0	60.0

* Estimate(s).
† Figures exclude artisanal gold production; total gold output is estimated at 360 kg–480 kg per year.
‡ Reported figure.

Source: US Geological Survey.

Industry

SELECTED PRODUCTS

('000 metric tons, unless otherwise indicated)

	1997	1998	1999
Flour (cereals other than wheat)	13	11	9
Wheat flour	82	115	125
Raw sugar	42	39	46
Beer ('000 hl)	631	75	95
Soft drinks ('000 hl)	419	50	100
Cigarettes (million)	250	950	1,084
Footwear ('000 pairs)	12	10	7
Cement	217	264	266
Electric energy (million kWh)	1,485	7,345	n.a.

* Estimates.

Source: UN, *Industrial Commodity Statistics Yearbook*.

2000 ('000 metric tons): Groundnut oil 17.3; Beer of barley 48.0; Cement 270 (Sources: FAO and US Geological Survey).

2001 ('000 metric tons, reported figure): Groundnut oil 16.3; Beer of barley 48.0; Cement 265 (Sources: FAO and US Geological Survey).

Finance

CURRENCY AND EXCHANGE RATES

Monetary Units
  100 centavos = 1 metical (plural: meticais)

Sterling, Dollar and Euro Equivalents (31 December 2002)
  £1 sterling = 38,448.4 meticais
  US $1 = 23,854.3 meticais
  €1 = 25,016.0 meticais
  100,000 meticais = £2.601 = $4.192 = €3.997

Average Exchange Rate (meticais per US $)
  2000   15,447.1
  2001   20,703.6
  2002   23,678.0

Note: Between April 1992 and October 2000 the market exchange rate was the rate at which commercial banks purchased from and sold to the public. Beginning in October 2000 it is the weighted average of buying and selling rates of all transactions of commercial banks and stock exchanges with the public.

BUDGET

('000 million meticais)

Revenue	1999	2000	2001
Taxation	5,734	6,857	8,589
Taxes on income	867	1,008	1,498
Domestic taxes on goods and services	3,638	4,331	5,379
Customs duties	1,046	1,297	1,477
Other taxes	183	221	235
Non-tax revenue	474	606	1,027
Total	6,208	7,463	9,616

Expenditure	1999	2000	2001
Current expenditure	6,332	7,836	10,489
Compensation of employees	2,995	3,844	4,898
Other goods and services	1,928	1,976	2,400
Interest on public debt	324	118	478
Transfer payments	1,085	1,664	2,230
Capital expenditure	6,001	7,826	10,428
Total	12,333	15,662	20,917

* Excluding net unallocated revenue and expenditure ('000 million meticais): −220 in 1999; 443 in 2000.
† Excluding grants received ('000 million meticais): 6,073 in 1999; 6,855 in 2000; 9,637 in 2001.
‡ Excluding net lending ('000 million meticais): 482 in 1999; 1,073 in 2000; 2,304 in 2001.

Source: IMF, *Republic of Mozambique: Statistical Appendix* (July 2002).

INTERNATIONAL RESERVES

(US $ million at 31 December)

	2000	2001	2002
IMF special drawing rights	0.06	0.06	0.07
Reserve position in IMF	0.01	0.01	0.01
Foreign exchange	725.04	715.50	n.a.
Total	725.11	715.57	n.a.

Source: IMF, *International Financial Statistics*.

MONEY SUPPLY

('000 million meticais at 31 December)

	1999	2000	2001
Currency outside banks	2,174.2	2,425.3	2,970.4
Demand deposits at commercial banks	4,693.0	5,992,9	6,912.7
Total money (incl. others)	6,994.4	8,557.2	10,066.0

Source: IMF, *International Financial Statistics*.

COST OF LIVING

(Consumer Price Index for Maputo; base: 1998=100)

	2000	2001	2002
All items	187.6	204.6	238.9

Source: IMF, *International Financial Statistics*.

NATIONAL ACCOUNTS

('000 million meticais at current prices)

National Income and Product

	1998	1999	2000
Compensation of employees	8,921.6	11,173.4	13,489.6
Net operating surplus	6,602.7	7,364.1	10,158.0
Net mixed income	23,103.3	24,859.8	24,606.0
Domestic primary incomes	38,627.6	43,397.3	48,253.6
Consumption of fixed capital	4,420.9	5,096.1	6,625.3
Gross domestic product (GDP) at factor cost	39,068.5	48,493.4	54,878.9
Taxes on production and imports	3,863.2	3,472.8	2,330.0
Less Subsidies	89.3	53.0	55.7
GDP in market prices	46,911.8	51,913.2	56,917.4

Expenditure on the Gross Domestic Product

	1999	2000	2001
Government final consumption expenditure }	47,224	52,408	64,178
Private final consumption expenditure			
Increase in stock }	19,041	19,323	21,746
Gross capital formation			
Total domestic expenditure	66,265	71,731	85,924
Exports of goods and services	5,256	7,326	16,053
Less Imports of goods and services	19,607	22,139	28,087
GDP in purchasers' values	51,913	56,917	73,890

Gross Domestic Product by Economic Activity

	1999	2000	2001
Agriculture and livestock . . .	12,231	12,346	15,556
Fishing	1,310	1,378	1,627
Mining	73	206	261
Manufacturing	5,993	6,830	10,492
Electricity and water	1,447	1,281	1,430
Construction	4,021	5,308	6,737
Wholesale and retail trade . .	11,401	12,353	14,745
Restaurants and hotels . . .	626	798	785
Transport and communications .	4,924	5,298	8,334
Financial services	1,045	2,240	3,148
Real estate and business services	1,597	1,533	1,719
Public administration and defence	1,858	2,118	2,618
Education	1,290	1,564	1,979
Health	436	539	781
Other Services	2,246	2,797	3,079
Sub-Total	51,499	56,585	73,292
Less Financial services indirectly measured	594	965	987
Gross value added in basic prices	50,905	55,620	72,305
Taxes on products . . . ⎱			
Less Subsidies on products . . ⎰	1,009	1,298	1,585
GDP in market prices . . .	51,913	56,917	73,890

BALANCE OF PAYMENTS
(US $ million)

	1999	2000	2001
Exports of goods f.o.b.	283.7	364.0	703.6
Imports of goods c.i.f.	−1,199.8	−1,162.3	−1,117.5
Trade balance	−916.1	−798.3	−413.9
Exports of services and other income	355.6	405.1	347.9
Imports of services and other income	−591.6	−648.4	−783.6
Balance on goods, services and income	−1,152.1	−1,041.6	−849.5
Current transfers received . .	434.1	563.9	469.3
Current balance	−718.0	−477.7	−380.2
Direct investment from abroad (net)	381.7	139.1	182.5
Other long-term capital (net) . .	231.7	139.8	−182.6
Short-term capital (net) . . ⎱			
Net errors and omissions . . ⎰	−131.3	−152.5	−38.4
Overall balance	−235.9	−351.3	−418.7

Source: IMF, *Republic of Mozambique Statistical Appendix* (July 2002).

External Trade

PRINCIPAL COMMODITIES
(distribution by SITC, US $ million)

Imports c.i.f.	1997	1998	1999
Food and live animals . . .	152.4	173.3	113.5
Cereals and cereal preparations	91.8	104.2	76.1
Wheat and meslin (unmilled)	42.3	n.a.	n.a.
Rice (unmilled)	40.0	n.a.	n.a.
Sugar, sugar preparations and honey	31.1	25.3	14.6
Raw sugars	30.5	n.a.	n.a.
Crude materials (inedible) except fuels	24.5	24.6	15.8
Mineral fuels, lubricants etc.	90.0	66.0	73.9
Petroleum, petroleum products, etc.	73.1	n.a.	n.a.
Refined petroleum products . .	71.4	n.a.	n.a.
Animal and vegetable oils, fats and waxes	13.6	15.8	21.6
Chemicals and related products	56.6	62.6	47.7
Basic manufactures	107.6	123.4	79.4
Textile yarn, fabrics, etc. . . .	23.3	26.5	15.3
Machinery and transport equipment	254.1	286.2	287.6
Machinery specialized for particular industries	36.7	n.a.	n.a.
General industrial machinery, equipment and parts	26.3	n.a.	n.a.
Electrical machinery, apparatus, etc.	60.9	n.a.	n.a.
Road vehicles and parts . . .	101.8	n.a.	n.a.
Motor vehicles for transport of goods	47.4	n.a.	n.a.
Miscellaneous manufactured articles	47.6	51.6	38.2
Total (incl. others)	760.2	817.3	685.2

Exports f.o.b.	1997	1998	1999
Food and live animals . . .	152.4	129.2	127.9
Fish, crustaceans, molluscs and preparations	84.4	66.4	74.8
Cereals and cereal preparations	21.4	6.5	1.8
Maize (unmilled)	12.5	n.a.	n.a.
Wheat meal and flour	8.8	n.a.	n.a.
Vegetables and fruit	30.3	49.8	42.6
Fresh or dried fruit and nuts	29.8	49.5	40.2
Sugar, sugar preparations and honey	12.8	2.9	5.5
Crude materials (inedible) except fuels	38.2	17.0	28.6
Cork and wood	8.9	n.a.	n.a.
Cotton	22.2	11.0	20.0
Raw cotton (excl. linters) . . .	12.1	n.a.	n.a.
Carded or combed cotton . . .	10.0	n.a.	n.a.
Mineral fuels, lubricants, etc.	1.3	37.6	67.8
Basic manufactures	10.5	16.7	15.6
Cork and wood manufactures . .	1.3	5.2	9.2
Machinery and transport equipment	10.4	22.4	14.2
Miscellaneous manufactured articles	7.3	9.7	7.8
Total (incl. others)	230.1	244.6	270.9

Source: UN, *International Trade Statistics Yearbook*.

2000 (US $ million): Exports: Aluminium 60.2; Prawns 91.5; Electricity 67.0; Cotton 25.5; Timber 14.2; Cashew nuts (unprocessed) 11.9; Total (incl. others) 364.0 (Source: IMF, *Republic of Mozambique: Statistical Appendix* (July 2002)).

PRINCIPAL TRADING PARTNERS
(US $ million)

Imports c.i.f.	1996	1997	1998
Australia	10.3	11.2	3.1
Belgium-Luxembourg	7.8	3.2	4.1
Brazil	13.6	8.8	2.9
Canada	10.6	15.8	17.3
China, People's Repub.	4.5	7.7	12.7
Denmark	11.9	8.4	7.5
France-Monaco	34.7	19.8	17.2
Germany	20.7	17.5	8.9
India	35.8	23.2	35.2
Italy-San Marino-Vatican	32.7	13.1	8.2
Japan	31.0	33.9	32.3
Malawi	10.7	2.9	2.8
Netherlands	15.9	9.6	6.7
Norway	12.0	10.1	4.5
Pakistan	1.9	12.5	17.6
Portugal	49.3	44.7	64.2
Saudi Arabia	—	0.1	32.8
Southern African Customs Union	270.3	271.5	344.7
Spain	9.9	9.5	6.5
Sweden	8.1	16.6	5.5
Thailand	5.8	8.2	10.4
United Arab Emirates	11.4	13.4	12.1
United Kingdom	18.2	14.9	16.3
USA	32.6	38.3	43.6
Viet Nam	—	11.6	0.9
Zimbabwe	30.6	9.7	19.0
Total (incl. others)	782.6	760.2	817.3

Exports f.o.b.	1997	1998	1999
Belgium-Luxembourg	8.1	1.7	—
France-Monaco	0.4	0.6	2.7
Hong Kong	4.4	1.7	8.1
India	13.3	19.4	32.1
Japan	19.3	11.8	11.5
Malawi	17.7	10.7	4.7
Netherlands	6.9	5.6	4.5
Portugal	20.6	18.5	24.5
Southern African Customs Union	40.4	56.3	75.8
Spain	42.6	31.7	34.4
Tanzania	0.4	4.3	—
United Kingdom	1.7	3.3	2.7
USA	26.5	13.9	12.8
Zimbabwe	9.4	47.7	40.1
Total (incl. others)	230.1	244.6	270.6

* Comprises Botswana, Lesotho, Namibia, South Africa and Swaziland.

Source: UN, *International Trade Statistics Yearbook*.

Transport

RAILWAYS
(traffic)

	1999	2000	2001
Freight ton-km (million)	721.2	604.8	774.5
Passenger-km (million)	144.7	129.8	142.0

Source: IMF, *Republic of Mozambique: Statistical Appendix* (July 2002).

ROAD TRAFFIC
(motor vehicles in use at 31 December)

	1994	1995	1996
Passenger cars	30,977	25,740	4,900
Lorries and vans	10,035	7,520	7,520

* Estimates.

Source: International Road Federation, *World Road Statistics*.

SHIPPING

Merchant Fleet
(registered at 31 December)

	1999	2000	2001
Number of vessels	123	127	131
Total displacement ('000 grt)	36.3	37.4	38.0

Source: Lloyd's Register-Fairplay, *World Fleet Statistics*.

Freight Handled
('000 shipping tons)

	1999	2000	2001
Goods loaded and unloaded	6,118	6,097	7,312

Source: IMF, *Republic of Mozambique: Statistical Appendix* (July 2002).

International Sea-borne Freight Traffic ('000 metric tons, 1990): Goods loaded 2,578; Goods unloaded 3,379 (Source: *UN, Monthly Bulletin of Statistics*).

CIVIL AVIATION
(traffic on scheduled services)

	1996	1997	1998
Kilometres flown (million)	3	3	4
Passengers carried ('000)	163	188	201
Passenger-km (million)	260	292	312
Total ton-km (million)	27	32	33

Source: mainly UN, *Statistical Yearbook*.

Passenger-km (million): 330 in 1999; 378 in 2000; 272 in 2001.

Freight ton-km (million): 6.1 in 1999; 7.2 in 2000; 6.7 in 2001.

Source: IMF, *Republic of Mozambique: Statistical Appendix* (July 2002).

Communications Media

	1999	2000	2001
Television receivers ('000 in use)	100	105	n.a.
Telephones ('000 main lines in use)	78.1	85.7	89.4
Mobile cellular telephones ('000 subscribers).	12.2	51.1	169.9
Personal computers ('000 in use) .	50	60	70
Internet users ('000)	15	30	15

Source: International Telecommunication Union.

Radio receivers (1997): 730,000 in use.

Facsimile machines (1996): 7,200 in use.

Daily newspapers (1996): 2 (average circulation 49,000).

Non-daily newspapers (1996): 4 (estimated average circulation 160,000).

Periodicals (1988): 5 (average circulation 2,263,000).

Book production (1984): 66 titles (including 37 pamphlets); 3,490,000 copies (including 360,000 pamphlets).

Sources: UNESCO, *Statistical Yearbook*; UN, *Statistical Yearbook*.

Education

(1998)

	Institu-tions	Teachers	Students		
			Males	Females	Total
Pre-primary . .	5,689	28,705	n.a.	n.a.	1,745,049
Primary . . .	6,263	31,512	1,111,011	807,389	1,918,400
Secondary . .	75	8,073	149,902	104,638	254,540
Higher . . .	3	954	n.a.	n.a.	7,156

* Public education only.

† 1997 figure(s).

Source: partly UNESCO Institute for Statistics.

2001: 8,165 primary institutions.

Adult literacy rate (UNESCO estimates): 44.0% (males 60.1%; females 28.7%) in 2000 (Source: UN Development Programme, *Human Development Report*).

Directory

The Constitution

The Constitution came into force on 30 November 1990, replacing the previous version, introduced at independence on 25 June 1975 and revised in 1978. Its main provisions, as amended in 1996, are summarized below.

GENERAL PRINCIPLES

The Republic of Mozambique is an independent, sovereign, unitary and democratic state of social justice. Sovereignty resides in the people, who exercise it according to the forms laid down in the Constitution. The fundamental objectives of the Republic include:

The defence of independence and sovereignty;

the defence and promotion of human rights and of the equality of citizens before the law; and

the strengthening of democracy, of freedom and of social and individual stability.

POLITICAL PARTICIPATION

The people exercise power through universal, direct, equal, secret, personal and periodic suffrage to elect their representatives, by referenda and through permanent democratic participation. Political parties are prohibited from advocating or resorting to violence.

FUNDAMENTAL RIGHTS AND DUTIES OF CITIZENS

All citizens enjoy the same rights and are subject to the same duties, irrespective of colour, race, sex, ethnic origin, place of birth, religion, level of education, social position or occupation. In realizing the objectives of the Constitution, all citizens enjoy freedom of opinion, assembly and association. All citizens over 18 years of age are entitled to vote and be elected. Active participation in the defence of the country is the duty of every citizen. Individual freedoms are guaranteed by the State, including freedom of expression, of the press, of assembly, of association and of religion. The State guarantees accused persons the right to a legal defence. No Court or Tribunal has the power to impose a sentence of death upon any person.

STATE ORGANS

Public elective officers are chosen by elections through universal, direct, secret, personal and periodic vote. Legally-recognized political parties may participate in elections.

THE PRESIDENT

The President is the Head of State and of the Government, and Commander-in-Chief of the armed forces. The President is elected by direct, equal, secret and personal universal suffrage on a majority vote, and must be proposed by at least 10,000 voters, of whom at least 200 must reside in each province. The term of office is five years. A candidate may be re-elected on only two consecutive occasions, or again after an interval of five years between terms.

THE ASSEMBLY OF THE REPUBLIC

Legislative power is vested in the Assembléia da República (Assembly of the Republic). The Assembléia is elected by universal direct adult suffrage on a secret ballot, and is composed of 250 Deputies. The Assembléia is elected for a maximum term of five years, but may be dissolved by the President before the expiry of its term. The Assembléia holds two ordinary sessions each year.

THE COUNCIL OF MINISTERS

The Council of Ministers is the Government of the Republic. The Prime Minister assists and advises the President in the leadership of the Government and presents the Government's programme, budget and policies to the Assembléia da República, assisted by other ministers.

LOCAL STATE ORGANS

The Republic is administered in provinces, municipalities and administrative posts. The highest state organ in a province is the provincial government, presided over by a governor, who is answerable to the central Government. There shall be assemblies at each administrative level.

THE JUDICIARY

Judicial functions shall be exercised through the Supreme Court and other courts provided for in the law on the judiciary, which also subordinates them to the Assembléia da República. Courts must safeguard the principles of the Constitution and defend the rights and legitimate interests of citizens. Judges are independent, subject only to the law.

The Government

HEAD OF STATE

President of the Republic and Commander-in-Chief of the Armed Forces: Joaquim Alberto Chissano (took office 6 November 1986; elected President 27–29 October 1994; re-elected 3–5 December 1999).

COUNCIL OF MINISTERS
(April 2003)

Prime Minister: Dr Pascoal Manuel Mocumbi.

Minister of Foreign Affairs and Co-operation: Dr Leonardo dos Santos Simão.

Minister of National Defence: Gen. (retd) Tobias Dai.

Minister of Planning and Finance: Luísa Diogo.

Minister of Justice: José Ibraimo Abudo.

Minister of the Interior and Minister in the President's Office, with responsibility for Defence and Security Affairs: Almerino da Cruz Marcos Manhenje.

Minister of State Administration: José Chichava.

Minister of Agricultural and Rural Development: Hélder Monteiro Muteia.

Minister of Fisheries: Cadmiel Mutemba.

Minister of Industry and Trade: Carlos Alberto Morgado.

Minister of Mineral Resources and Energy: Castigo José Correia Langa.

Minister of Transport and Communications: Tomás Augusto Salomão.

Minister of Education: Alcido Eduardo Nguenha.

Minister of Health: Francisco Ferreira Songane.

Minister of Culture: Miguel Costa Mkaíma.

Minister of Environmental Co-ordination: John William Kachamila.

Minister of Labour: Mário Lampião Sevene.

Minister of Public Works and Housing: Roberto Costley-White.

Minister of Youth and Sport: Joel Matias Libombo.

Minister of Women's Affairs and Social Welfare Co-ordination: Virgília Santos Matabele.

Minister in the Presidency with responsibility for Parliamentary and Diplomatic Affairs: Francisco Caetano Madeira.

Minister of Tourism: Fernando Sumbane (Júnior).

Minister of Veterans' Affairs: António Hama Thay.

Minister of Higher Education, Science and Technology: Lídia Maria Ribeiro Arthur Brito.

MINISTRIES

Office of the President: Avda Julius Nyerere 1780, Maputo; tel. (1) 491121; fax (1) 492065.

Office of the Prime Minster: Praça da Marinha Popular, Maputo; tel. (1) 426861; fax (1) 426881; e-mail dgpm.gov@teledata.mz.

Ministry of Agricultural and Rural Development: Praça dos Heróis Moçambicanos, CP 1406, Maputo; tel. (1) 460011; fax (1) 460055; internet www.map.gov.mz.

Ministry of Culture: Avda Patrice Lumumba 1217, CP 1742, Maputo; tel. (1) 420086; fax (1) 429700.

Ministry of Education: Avda 24 de Julho 167, 9° andar, CP 34, Maputo; tel. (1) 492006; fax (1) 492196; internet www.mined.gov.mz.

Ministry of Environmental Co-ordination: Avda Acordos de Lusaka 2115, CP 2020, Maputo; tel. (1) 466245; fax (1) 465849; e-mail jwkacha@virconn.com; internet www.sdnp.mz/ambiente.

Ministry of Fisheries: Rua Consiglieri Pedroso 347, CP 1723, Maputo; tel. (1) 431266; fax (1) 425087; e-mail alfredo@mozpesca .org; internet www.mozpesca.org.

Ministry of Foreign Affairs and Co-operation: Avda Julius Nyerere 4, CP 2787, Maputo; tel. (1) 490222; fax (1) 494070; e-mail minec@zebra.uem.mz; internet www.minec.gov.mz.

Ministry of Health: Avdas Eduardo Mondlane e Salvador Allende 1008, CP 264, Maputo; tel. (1) 427131; fax (1) 427133.

Ministry of Higher Education, Science and Technology: Avda Julius Nyerere 1586, 1° andar, Maputo; tel. (1) 499491; fax (1) 490446; e-mail mesct@teledata.mz; internet www.mesct.gov.mz.

Ministry of Industry and Trade: Praça 25 de Junho 300, CP 1831, Maputo; tel. (1) 426093.

Ministry of the Interior: Avda Olaf Palme 46/48, CP 290, Maputo; tel. (1) 420131; fax (1) 420084.

Ministry of Justice: Avda Julius Nyerere 33, Maputo; tel. (1) 491613; fax (1) 494264.

Ministry of Labour: Avda 24 de Julho 2351–2365, CP 258, Maputo; tel. (1) 427051; fax (1) 421881.

Ministry of Mineral Resources and Energy: Avda Fernão de Magalhães 34, CP 294, Maputo; tel. (1) 429615; fax (1) 427103; e-mail minas@minas.co.mz; internet www.minas.co.mz.

Ministry of National Defence: Avda Mártires de Mueda 280, CP 3216, Maputo; tel. (1) 492081; fax (1) 491619.

Ministry of Planning and Finance: Praça da Marinha Popular, CP 272, Maputo; tel. (1) 425071; fax (1) 420137; e-mail dnpo@dnpo .uem.mz; internet www.mozambique.mz/governo/mpf/dnpo.

Ministry of Public Works and Housing: Avda Karl Marx 268, CP 268, Maputo; tel. (1) 420543; fax (1) 421369.

Ministry of State Administration: Rua da Rádio Moçambique 112, CP 4116, Maputo; tel. (1) 426666; fax (1) 428565; internet www .sdnp.org.mz/mae.

Ministry of Tourism: Avda 25 de Setembro 1018, CP 4101, Maputo; tel. (1) 306210; fax (1) 306212; internet www.mozambique .mz/turismo/index.htm.

Ministry of Transport and Communications: Avda Mártires de Inhaminga 336, Maputo; tel. (1) 420223; fax (1) 431028; e-mail celular@zebra.uem.mz; internet www.mtc.gov.mz.

Ministry of Veterans' Affairs: Rua General Pereira d'Eça 35, CP 3697, Maputo; tel. (1) 490601.

Ministry of Women's Affairs and Social Welfare Co-ordination: Rua de Tchamba 86, CP 516, Maputo; tel. (1) 490921; fax (1) 492757; e-mail vmatabele@mimucas.org.mz; internet www .mimucas.org.mz.

Ministry of Youth and Sport: Avda 25 de Setembro 529, CP 2080, Maputo; tel. (1) 431177.

PROVINCIAL GOVERNORS
(April 2003)

Cabo Delgado Province: José Pacheco.

Gaza Province: Rosário Mualeia.

Inhambane Province: Aires Aly.

Manica Province: Soares Nhaca.

Maputo Province: Alfredo Namitete.

Nampula Province: Abdul Razak.

Niassa Province: David Simango.

Sofala Province: Felício Zacarias.

Tete Province: Tomás Mandlate.

Zambézia Province: Lucas Chomera.

City of Maputo: Artur Canana.

President and Legislature

PRESIDENT

Presidential Election, 3–5 December 1999

	Votes	% of votes
Joaquim Alberto Chissano (Frelimo)	2,338,333	52.29
Afonso Macacho Marceta Dhlakama (Renamo—União Eleitoral)	2,133,655	47.71
Total	4,471,988	100.00

* Excluding 320,795 blank votes and 141,569 spoilt votes.

ASSEMBLÉIA DA REPÚBLICA

Chairman: Eduardo Mulembue.

General Election, 3–5 December 1999

	Votes	% of votes	Seats
Frente de Libertação de Moçambique (Frelimo)	2,005,713	48.54	133
Resistência Nacional Moçambicana—União Eleitoral (Renamo—UE)	1,603,811	38.81	117
Partido do Trabalho (PT)	111,139	2.69	—
Partido Liberal e Democrático de Moçambique (Palmo)	101,970	2.47	—
Partido Social, Liberal e Democrático (Sol)	83,440	2.02	—
União Moçambicana de Oposição (UMO)	64,117	1.55	—
União Democrática (UD)	61,122	1.48	—
Total (incl. others)	4,132,323	100.00	250

* Excluding 462,666 blank votes and 238,772 spoilt votes.

Political Organizations

Aliança Democrática de Moçambique (ADM): Maputo; f. 1994; Co-ordinator José Pereira Branquinho.

Aliança Independente de Moçambique (Alimo): Maputo; f. 1998; mem. of União Eleitoral; Sec.-Gen. Ernesto Sergio.

Confederação Democrática de Moçambique (Codemo): Maputo; f. 1991; Leader Domingos Cardoso.

Congresso dos Democratas Unidos (CDU): Maputo; f. 2001; Leader ANTÓNIO PALANGE.

Congresso Independente de Moçambique (Coinmo): Pres. VÍTOR MARCOS SAENE; Sec.-Gen. HILDA RABECA TSININE.

Frente de Ação Patriótica (FAP): Maputo; f. 1991; mem. of União Eleitoral; Pres. JOSÉ CARLOS PALAÇO; Sec.-Gen. RAUL DA CONCEIÇÃO.

Frente Democrática Unida—United Democratic Front (UDF): Maputo; mem. of União Eleitoral.

Frente de Libertação de Moçambique (Frelimo): Rua Pereira do Lago 10, Bairro de Sommerschield, Maputo; tel. (1) 490181; fax (1) 490008; e-mail info@frelimo.org.mz; internet www.frelimo.org.mz; f. 1962 by merger of three nationalist parties; reorg. 1977 as a 'Marxist-Leninist vanguard movement'; in July 1989 abandoned its exclusive Marxist-Leninist orientation; Pres. JOAQUIM ALBERTO CHISSANO; Sec.-Gen. ARMANDO GUEBUZA.

Frente Unida de Moçambique—Partido de Convergência Democrática (Fumo—PCD): Avda Mao Tse Tung 230, 1° andar, Maputo; tel. (1) 494044; Sec.-Gen. JOSÉ SAMO GUDO.

Movimento Nacionalista Moçambicana—Partido Moçambicano da Social Democracia (Monamo—PMSD): mem. of União Eleitoral; Sec.-Gen. Dr MÁXIMO DIOGO JOSÉ DIAS.

Partido Agrário de Moçambique (PAM): f. 1991.

Partido Comunista de Moçambique (Pacomo): f. 1995.

Partido do Congresso Democrático (Pacode): Leader VASCO CAMPIRA MAMBOYA ALFAZEMA.

Partido de Convenção Nacional (PCN): Avda 25 Setembro 1123, 3° andar, Maputo; tel. (1) 426891; obtained legal status in 1992; mem. of União Eleitoral; Chair. LUTERO CHIMBIRIMBIRI SIMANGO; Sec.-Gen. Dr GABRIEL MABUNDA.

Partido Democrático de Libertação de Moçambique (Padelimo): based in Kenya; Pres. JOAQUIM JOSÉ NIOTA.

Partido Democrático de Moçambique (Pademo): f. 1991; obtained legal status in 1993; Co-ordinator WEHIA MONAKACHO RIPUA; Gen. Sec. GIMO GUINDILA.

Partido Democrático para a Reconciliação de Moçambique (PAMOMO): mem. of União Eleitoral; Leader ALBERTO MAIOPUE.

Partido Ecologista de Moçambique (PEMO): Maputo; mem. of União Eleitoral.

Partido Independente de Moçambique (Pimo): f. 1993; Leader YAQUB SABINDY; Sec.-Gen. MAGALHÃES BRAMUGY.

Partido Internacionalista Democrático de Moçambique (Pidemo): f. 1993; Leader JOÃO KAMACHO.

Partido Liberal e Democrático de Moçambique (Palmo): obtained legal status 1993; Chair. MARTINS BILAL; Sec.-Gen. ANTONIO MUEDO.

Partido Nacional de Obreiros e Camponêses (Panaoc): Leader ARMANDO SIUEIA.

Partido Patriótico Independente de Moçambique: f. 1995; breakaway faction of Pimo.

Partido Popular de Moçambique (PPM).

Partido Progressivo e Liberal de Moçambique (PPLM): f. 1992; Pres. NEVES SERRANO.

Partido do Progresso do Povo de Moçambique (PPPM): Avda 25 Setembro, 1123, 4° andar, Maputo; tel. (1) 426925; f. 1991; obtained legal status 1992; Pres. Dr PADIMBE MAHOSE KAMATI ANDREA; Sec.-Gen. CHE ABDALA.

Partido Renovador Democrático (PRD): obtained legal status 1994; mem. of União Eleitoral; Pres. MANECA DANIEL.

Partido Revolucionário do Povo Socialista Unido de Moçambique (Prepsumo): f. 1992.

Partido Social Democrático (PSD): Leader CARLOS MACHEL.

Partido de Todos os Nativos Moçambicanos (Partonamo): f. 1996; Leader MUSSAGY ABDUL REMANE.

Partido do Trabalho (PT): f. 1993; breakaway faction of PPPM; Pres. MIGUEL MABOTE; Sec.-Gen. LUÍS MUCHANGA.

Partido Social, Liberal e Democrático (Sol): breakaway faction of Palmo; Leader CASIMIRO MIGUEL NHAMITHAMBO.

Partido de Unidade Nacional (PUN): TV Sado 9, Maputo; tel. (1) 419204; mem. of União Eleitoral.

Partido Verde de Moçambique (PVM): Leader BRUNO SAPEMBA.

Regedores e Camponeses de Moçambique (Recamo): f. by ARONE SIJAMO.

Resistência Nacional Moçambicana (Renamo): Avda Julius Nyerere 2541, Maputo; tel. (1) 493107; also known as Movimento Nacional da Resistência de Moçambique (MNR); f. 1976; fmr guerrilla group, in conflict with the Govt between 1976 and Oct. 1992; obtained legal status in 1994; Pres. AFONSO MACACHO MARCETA DHLAKAMA; Sec.-Gen. VIANA MAGALHAES.

União Democrática (UD): f. 1994; Gen. Sec. JOSÉ CHICUARRA MASSINGA; coalition comprising:

> **Partido Nacional Democrático (Panade):** Avda Trabalho 1412, 3° andar, Maputo; tel. (1) 401937; obtained legal status 1993; Leader JOSÉ CHICUARRA MASSINGA.

> **Partido Nacional de Moçambique (Panamo):** Pres. MARCOS JUMA.

União Democrática de Moçambique (Udemo): f. 1987 as the mil. wing of Unamo, from which it broke away in 1991; adopted present name in 1992; Leader GIMO PHIRI.

União Nacional Moçambicana (Unamo): f. 1987; breakaway faction of Renamo; social democratic; obtained legal status 1992; mem. of União Eleitoral; Pres. CARLOS ALEXANDRE DOS REIS; Sec.-Gen. FLORENCIA JOÃO DA SILVA.

In February 2003 10 opposition parties formed the **União Eleitoral**, a coalition to contest the municipal elections of 2003 and the presidential and legislative elections of 2004.

Diplomatic Representation

EMBASSIES AND HIGH COMMISSIONS IN MOZAMBIQUE

Algeria: Rua de Mukumbura 121–125, CP 1709, Maputo; tel. (1) 492070; fax (1) 490582; Ambassador ABDELHAMID BOUBAZINE.

Angola: Avda Kenneth Kaunda 783, Maputo; tel. (1) 493691; fax (1) 493930; Ambassador ANTÓNIO JOSÉ CONDESSE DE CARVALHO.

Brazil: Avda Kenneth Kaunda 296, CP 1167, Maputo; tel. (1) 492388; fax (1) 490986; Ambassador HÉLDER MARTINS DE MORAIS.

Canada: Avda Julius Nyerere 1128, CP 1578, Maputo; tel. (1) 492623; fax (1) 492667; e-mail canembas@ecanada.uem.mz; High Commissioner JOHN SCHRAM.

China, People's Republic: Avda dos Mártires da Machava 1309, 4° andar, Maputo; tel. (1) 491462; fax (1) 491196; e-mail chiemb@teledata.mz; Ambassador MI SHIHENG.

Congo, Democratic Republic: Rua A.W. Bayly 2, Maputo; tel. (1) 491854; Ambassador W'EBER M. B. ANGELO.

Congo, Republic: Avda dos Mártires de Machava 385, Maputo; tel. and fax (1) 493779; Chargé d'affaires a.i. MONSEGNO BASHA OSHEFWA.

Cuba: Avda Kenneth Kaunda 492, CP 387, Maputo; tel. (1) 492444; fax (1) 493673; Ambassador EVELINO DORTA GONZÁLEZ.

Denmark: Avda Julius Nyerere 1162, CP 4588, Maputo; tel. (1) 480000; fax (1) 480010; e-mail mpmamb@um.dk; Ambassador THOMAS SCHJERBECK.

Egypt: Avda Mao Tse Tung 851, CP 4662, Maputo; tel. (1) 491118; fax (1) 491489; Ambassador MOHAMED EL-ASHMAWI.

Finland: Avda Julius Nyerere 1128, CP 1663, Maputo; tel. (1) 490578; fax (1) 491661; e-mail maputo.sanomat@formin.fi; Ambassador MARKKU KAUPPINEN.

France: Avda Julius Nyerere 2361, CP 4781, Maputo; tel. (1) 490444; fax (1) 491727; e-mail ambfrmoz@virconn.com; internet www.ambafrance-mz.org; Ambassador LOUISE AVON.

Germany: Rua Damião de Góis 506, CP 1595, Maputo; tel. (1) 492714; fax (1) 492888; e-mail germaemb@tvcabo.co.mz; Ambassador Dr ULF-DIETER KLEMM.

Holy See: Avda Julius Nyerere 882, CP 2738, Maputo; tel. (1) 491144; fax (1) 492217; e-mail namoz@teledata.mz; Apostolic Nuncio Most Rev. JULIUSZ JANUSZ (Titular Archbishop of Caorle).

Iceland: Avda Julius Nyerere 1162, Maputo; tel. (1) 480030; fax (1) 480035; e-mail icemb.maputo@utn.stjr.is; internet www.iceland.org/mo; Ambassador BJØRN DAGBARTSSON.

India: Avda Kenneth Kaunda 167, CP 4751, Maputo; tel. (1) 492437; fax (1) 492364; e-mail hicomind@virconn.com; High Commissioner AVINASH C. GUPTA.

Iran: Avda dos Mártires da Machava 1630, Maputo; tel. (1) 490700; fax (1) 492005; Ambassador ABDUL ALI TAUAKALI.

Ireland: Rua Dom João IV 213, Maputo; tel. (1) 491440; fax (1) 493023; e-mail ireland@vircom.com; Chargé d'affaires a.i. TOM WRIGHT.

Italy: Avda Kenneth Kaunda 387, CP 976, Maputo; tel. (1) 491605; fax (1) 400503; e-mail ambasciata@italia.gov.mz; internet www.italia.gov.mz; Ambassador ROBERTO MARIA DI LEO.

Japan: c/o Polana Hotel, Room 417, Avda Julius Nyerere 1380, CP 2494, Maputo; tel. (1) 499819; fax (1) 498957; Ambassador KANJI TSUSHIMA.

Korea, Democratic People's Republic: Rua da Kaswende 167, Maputo; tel. (1) 491482; Ambassador RYANG GUI RAK.

Libya: Rua Pereira Marinho 274, CP 4434, Maputo; tel. (1) 490662; fax (1) 492450; Ambassador AIAD SALAH ASHAWISH.

Malawi: Avda Kenneth Kaunda 75, CP 4148, Maputo; tel. (1) 491468; fax (1) 490224; High Commissioner OWEN B. BINAULI.

Mauritius: Rua Dom Carlos 42, Maputo; tel. (1) 494182; fax (1) 494729; e-mail mhcmoz@virconn.com; High Commissioner M. THAN-CANAMOOTOO.

Netherlands: Rua de Mukumbura 285, CP 1163, Maputo; tel. (1) 490031; fax (1) 490429; e-mail map@minbuza.nl; Ambassador A. P. REMMELZWAAL.

Nigeria: Avda Kenneth Kaunda 821, CP 4693, Maputo; tel. (1) 490105; fax (1) 490991; High Commissioner ISAIAH JACKSON UDOYEN.

Norway: Avda Julius Nyerere 1162, CP 828, Maputo; tel. (1) 480100; fax (1) 480107; e-mail emb.maputo@norad.no; internet www .norway.org.mz; Ambassador HENNING STIRØ.

Portugal: Avda Julius Nyerere 720, CP 4696, Maputo; tel. (1) 490431; fax (1) 491172; e-mail cculmapa@mail.tropical.co.mz; Ambassador ANTÓNIO LUÍS DA SILVA SENNFELT.

Russia: Avda V. Lenine 2445, Maputo; tel. (1) 417707; fax (1) 417515; e-mail embrus@teledatamz; Ambassador VLADIMIR VASLIE-VICH ZEMSKIY.

Saudi Arabia: Rua João de Barros 124, Maputo; tel. (1) 490098; fax (1) 494705; Ambassador ALI MAHMOUD EMBAREK.

South Africa: Avda Eduardo Mondlane 41, CP 1120, Maputo; tel. (1) 493030; fax (1) 493029; e-mail sahc@tropical.co.mz; High Commissioner T. LUJABE-RANKOE.

Spain: Rua Damião de Góis 347, CP 1331, Maputo; tel. (1) 492025; fax (1) 492055; e-mail embespmz@correo.mae.es; Ambassador LUIS ANTONIO CALVO.

Swaziland: Avda do Zimbabwe 608, CP 4711, Maputo; tel. (1) 492451; fax (1) 492117; High Commissioner JOHN MSHWESHWE DUBE.

Sweden: Avda Julius Nyerere 1128, CP 338, Maputo; tel. (1) 490091; fax (1) 490056; e-mail ambassaden.maputo@sida.se; Ambassador MAJ-INGE KLINGVALL.

Switzerland: Avda Julius Nyerere 1213, CP 135, Maputo; tel. (1) 492432; fax (1) 492474; e-mail swiemmap@bilene.virconn.com; Ambassador RUDOLF BAERFUSS.

Tanzania: Avda dos Mártires da Machava 852, Maputo; tel. (1) 491001; fax (1) 491228; e-mail ujamaa@zebra.uem.mz; High Commissioner ISSA MOHAMED ISSA.

United Kingdom: Avda Vladimir I. Lénine 310, CP 55, Maputo; tel. (1) 420111; fax (1) 421666; e-mail bhc@virconn.com; High Commissioner B. DEWAR.

USA: Avda Kenneth Kaunda 193, CP 783, Maputo; tel. (1) 492797; fax (1) 490114; internet www.usembassy-maputo.gov.mz; Ambassador SHARON P. WILKINSON.

Zambia: Avda Kenneth Kaunda 1286, CP 4655, Maputo; tel. (1) 492452; fax (1) 491893; High Commissioner Maj.-Gen. BELLON BEST-INGS CHISUTA.

Zimbabwe: Avda dos Mártires da Machava 1623, CP 743, Maputo; tel. (1) 490404; fax (1) 492237; e-mail maro@isl.co.mz; High Commissioner DAVID HAMADZIRIDI.

Judicial System

The Constitution of November 1990 provides for a Supreme Court and other judicial courts, an Administrative Court, courts-martial, customs courts, maritime courts and labour courts. The Supreme Court consists of professional judges, appointed by the President of the Republic, and judges elected by the Assembléia da República. It acts in sections, as a trial court of primary and appellate jurisdiction, and in plenary session, as a court of final appeal. The Administrative Court controls the legality of administrative acts and supervises public expenditure.

President of the Supreme Court: MÁRIO MANGAZE.

Attorney-General: JOAQUIM MADEIRA.

Religion

There are an estimated 5m. Christians and 4m. Muslims, as well as a small Hindu community. Many inhabitants follow traditional beliefs.

CHRISTIANITY

In 1975 educational and medical facilities that had hitherto been administered by churches were acquired by the State. In June 1988 the Government announced that these facilities were to be returned.

Conselho Cristão de Moçambique (Christian Council of Mozambique): Avda Agostino Neto 1584, CP 108, Maputo; tel. (1) 322836; fax (1) 321968; e-mail com-ccmhq@isl.co.mz; internet swan.isl.co.mz/ccm; f. 1948; 22 mems; Pres. Rt Rev. BERNARDINO MANDLATE; Gen. Sec. Rev. DINIS MATSOLO.

The Roman Catholic Church

Mozambique comprises three archdioceses and nine dioceses. At 31 December 2000 adherents represented some 18.4% of the total population.

Bishops' Conference

Conferência Episcopal de Moçambique (CEM), Secretariado Geral da CEM, Avda Paulo Samuel Kankhomba 188/RC, CP 286, Maputo; tel. (1) 490766; fax (1) 492174.

f. 1982; Pres. Rt Rev. FRANCISCO JOÃO SILOTA (Bishop of Chimoio).

Archbishop of Beira: Most Rev. JAIME PEDRO GONÇALVES, Cúria Arquiepiscopal, Rua Correia de Brito 613, CP 544, Beira; tel. (3) 322313; fax (3) 327639; e-mail arquidbeira@teledata.mz.

Archbishop of Maputo: Cardinal ALEXANDRE JOSÉ MARIA DOS SANTOS, Paço Arquiepiscopal, Avda Eduardo Mondlane 1448, CP 258, Maputo; tel. (1) 426240; fax (1) 421873.

Archbishop of Nampula: Most Rev. TOMÉ MAKHWELIHA, Paço Arquiepiscopal, CP 84, 70100 Nampula; tel. (6) 213025; fax (6) 214194; e-mail arquidioce.npl@teledata.mz.

The Anglican Communion

Anglicans in Mozambique are adherents of the Church of the Province of Southern Africa. There are two dioceses in Mozambique. The Metropolitan of the Province is the Archbishop of Cape Town, South Africa.

Bishop of Lebombo: Rt Rev. DINIS SALOMÃO SENGULANE, CP 120, Maputo; tel. (1) 405364; fax (1) 401093; e-mail libombo@zebra.uem .mz.

Bishop of Niassa: Rt Rev. PAULINO TOMÁS MANHIQUE, Missão Anglicana de Messumba, Metangula, CP 264, Lichinga, Niassa.

Other Churches

Baptist Convention of Mozambique: Avda Maguiguane 386, CP 852, Maputo; tel. (1) 26852; Pres. Rev. BENTO BARTOLOMEU MATUSSE; 17,443 adherents.

Free Methodist Church: Pres. Rev. LUÍS WANELA.

Igreja Maná: Rua Francisco Orlando Magumbwe 528, Maputo; tel. (1) 490876; fax (1) 490896; e-mail adm_mocambique@igrejamana .com.

Igreja Reformada em Moçambique (Reformed Church in Mozambique): CP3, Vila Ulongue, Anogonia-Tete; internet www2 .gospelcom.net/rec/mozamb.html; f. 1908; Gen. Sec. Dr WALLACE E. CHIKAKUDA; 33,000 mems.

Presbyterian Church of Mozambique: Avda Ahmed Sekou Touré 1822, CP 21, Maputo; tel. (1) 421790; fax (1) 428623; e-mail ipmoc@zebra.uem.mz; 100,000 adherents; Pres. of Synodal Council Rev. MÁRIO NYAMUXWE.

Other denominations active in Mozambique include the Church of Christ, the Church of the Nazarene, the United Congregational Church of Mozambique, the United Methodist Church of Mozambique, and the Wesleyan Methodist Church.

ISLAM

Comunidade Mahometana: Avda Albert Luthuli 291, Maputo; tel. (1) 425181; fax (1) 300880; e-mail toranias@zebra.uem.mz; internet www.paginaislamica.8m.com/pg1.htm; Pres. ABDUL ASSIZ OSMAN LATIF.

Islamic Congress of Mozambique: represents Sunni Muslims; Chair. ASSANE ISMAEL MAQBUL.

Islamic Council of Mozambique: Leader Sheikh ABOOBACAR ISMAEL MANGIRÁ.

The Press

DAILIES

Correio da Manha: Avda Filipe Samuel Magaia 528, CP 1756, Maputo; tel. (1) 305322; fax (1) 305321; Dir REFINALDO CHILENGUE.

Diário de Moçambique: Avda 25 de Setembro 1509, 2° andar, CP 2491, Beira; tel. and fax (3) 427312; f. 1981; under state management since 1991; Dir EZEQUIEL AMBRÓSIO; Editor FARUCO SADIQUE; circ. 16,000.

Expresso da Tarde: Avda Patrice Lumumba 511, 1° andar, Maputo; tel. (1) 314912; e-mail expresso@teledata.mz; subscription only; distribution by fax; Dir SALVADOR RAIMUNDO HONWANA.

Imparcial Fax: Avda Emilia Daússe 389, CP 2517, Maputo; tel. (1) 308797; fax (1) 308796; e-mail imparcial@emilmoz.com; news-sheet by subscription only, distribution by fax; Dir MIGÉIS LOPES JUNIOR.

Mediafax: Avda Amílcar Cabral 1049, CP 73, Maputo; tel. (1) 429180; fax (1) 428799; e-mail mediafax@virconn.com; internet www .sadirectory.co.za/mediacoop; by co-operative of independent journalists Mediacoop; news-sheet by subscription only, distribution by fax and internet; Editor LOURENÇO JOSSIAS.

Metical: Avda dos Mártires da Machava 1002, CP 4371, Maputo; tel. (1) 497385; fax (1) 497387; e-mail metical@zebra.uem.mz; internet www.tropical.co.mz/~metical; f. 1997 by subscription only; distribution by fax.

Notícias: Rua Joaquim Lapa 55, CP 327, Maputo; tel. (1) 420119; fax (1) 420575; f. 1926; morning; under state management since 1991; Dir BERNARDO MAVANGA; Editor HILÁRIO COSSA; circ. 33,000.

WEEKLIES

Campeão: Avda 24 de Julho 3706, CP 2610, Maputo; tel. and fax (1) 401810; sports newspaper; Dir RENATO CALDÉIRA; Editor ALEXANDRE ZANDAMELA.

Correio Semanal: Avda Filipe Samuel Magaia 528, CP 1756, Maputo; tel. (1) 305322; fax (1) 305312; Dir REFINALDO CHILENGUE.

Demos: Avda Mohamed Siad Barre, CP 2457, Maputo; tel. (1) 401420; fax (1) 401420; Dir VIRGÍLIO MABOTA; Editor PALMIRA VELASCO.

Desafio: Rua Joaquim Lapa 55, Maputo; tel. (1) 305437; fax (1) 305431; Dir ALMIRO SANTOS; Editor BOAVIDA FUNJUA.

Domingo: Rua Joaquim Lapa 55, CP 327, Maputo; tel. (1) 431026; fax (1) 431027; f. 1981; Sun. Dir JORGE MATINE; Editor MOISES MABUNDA; circ. 25,000.

Fim de Semana: Rua da Resistência 1642, 1° andar, Maputo; tel. (1) 417012; fax (1) 416059; e-mail fsemana@teledata.mz; internet www.fimdesemana.co.mz; f. 1997; independent.

Savana: c/o Mediacoop, Avda Amílcar Cabral 1049, CP 73, Maputo; tel. (1) 429180; fax (1) 428799; e-mail mediafax@virconn.com; internet www.sadirectory.co.za/mediacoop; f. 1994; Dir KOK NAM; Editor SALOMÃO MOYOANA.

Tempo: Avda Ahmed Sekou Touré 1078, CP 2917, Maputo; tel. (1) 26191; f. 1970; magazine; under state management since 1991; Dir ROBERTO UAENE; Editor ARLINDO LANGA; circ. 40,000.

Zambeze: Rua José Sidumo, Maputo; tel. (1) 302019; Dir SALOMÃO MOYANE.

PERIODICALS

Agora: Maputo; tel. (1) 494147; fax (1) 494204; e-mail agora@agora .co.mz; internet www.agora.co.mz; f. 2000; monthly; economics, politics, society; Pres. MARIA DE LOURDES TORCATO; Dir JOVITO NUNES; circ. 5,000.

Agricultura: Instituto Nacional de Investigação Agronómica, CP 3658, Maputo; tel. (1) 30091; f. 1982; quarterly; publ. by Centro de Documentação de Agricultura, Silvicultura, Pecuária e Pescas.

Aro: Avda 24 de Julho 1420, CP 4187, Maputo; f. 1995; monthly; Dir POLICARTO TAMELE; Editor BRUNO MACAME, Jr.

Arquivo Histórico: CP 2033, Maputo; tel. (1) 421177; fax (1) 423428; f. 1987; Editor MARIA INÊS NOGUEIRA DA COSTA.

Boletim da República: Avda Vladimir I. Lénine, CP 275, Maputo; govt and official notices; publ. by Imprensa Nacional da Moçambique.

Maderazinco: Maputo; e-mail maderazinco@yahoo.com; internet www.maderazinco.tropical.co.mz; f. 2002; quarterly; literature.

Moçambique–Novos Tempos: Avda Ahmed Sekou Touré 657, Maputo; tel. (1) 493564; fax (1) 493590; f. 1992; Dir J. MASCARENHAS.

Mozambiquefile: c/o AIM, Rua da Radio Moçambique, CP 896, Maputo; tel. (1) 430723; fax (1) 421906; e-mail aim@aimmpto.uem

.mz; internet www.sortmoz.com/aimnews; monthly; Dir RICARDO MALATE; Editor PAUL FAUVET.

Mozambique Inview: c/o Mediacoop, Avda Amílcar Cabral 1049, CP 73, Maputo; tel. (1) 430106; fax (1) 302402; e-mail moz-inview@ medcoop.uem.mz; internet www.sadirectory.co.za/mediacoop; f. 1994; 2 a month; Editor WILBERT ZIVISAI.

Portos e Caminhos de Ferro: CP 276, Maputo; English and Portuguese; ports and railways; quarterly.

Revista Médica de Moçambique: Instituto Nacional de Saúde, Ministério da Saúde e Faculdade de Medicina, Universidade Eduardo Mondlane, CP 264, Maputo; tel. (1) 420368; fax (1) 431103; e-mail mdgedge@malarins.uem.mz; f. 1982; 4 a year; medical journal; Editor MARTINHO DGEDGE.

NEWS AGENCIES

Agência de Informação de Moçambique (AIM): Rua da Rádio Moçambique, CP 896, Maputo; tel. (1) 430723; fax (1) 421906; e-mail aim@aimmpto.uem.mz; internet www.sortmoz.com/aimnews; f. 1975; daily reports in Portuguese and English; Dir GUSTAVO LISSE-TIANE MAVIE.

Foreign Bureaux

Agence France-Presse (AFP): CP 4650, Maputo; tel. (1) 422940; fax (1) 422940; Correspondent RACHEL WATERHOUSE.

Agência Lusa de Informação (Portugal): Avda Ho Chi Minh 111, Maputo; tel. (1) 427591; fax (1) 421690; Bureau Chief CARLOS LOBATO.

Agenzia Nazionale Stampa Associata (ANSA) (Italy): Maputo; tel. (1) 430723; fax (1) 421906; Correspondent PAUL FAUVET.

Xinhua (New China) News Agency (China): Rua Coimbra 258,, Maputo; tel. (1) 414445.

Reuters (UK) is also represented in Mozambique.

Publishers

Arquivo Histórico: CP 2033, Maputo; tel. (1) 421177; fax (1) 423428; e-mail jneves@zebra.uem.mz; Dir JOEL DAS NEVES TEMBE.

Central Impressora: c/o Ministério de Saúde, Avdas Eduardo Mondlane e Salvador Allende 1008, CP 264, Maputo; owned by the Ministry of Health.

Centro de Estudos Africanos: Universidade Eduardo Mondlane, CP 1993, Maputo; tel. (1) 490828; fax (1) 491896; f. 1976; social and political science, regional history, economics; Dir Col SERGIO VIEIRA.

Editora Minerva Central: Rua Consiglieri Pedroso 84, CP 212, Maputo; tel. (1) 22092; f. 1908; stationers and printers, educational, technical and medical textbooks; Man. Dir J. F. CARVALHO.

Editorial Ndjira, Lda: Avda Ho Chi Minh 85, Maputo; tel. (1) 300180; fax (1) 308745.

Empresa Moderna Lda: Avda 25 de Setembro, CP 473, Maputo; tel. (1) 424594; f. 1937; fiction, history, textbooks; Man. Dir LOUIS GALLOTI.

Fundo Bibliográfico de Língua Portuguesa: Avda 25 Setembro 1230, 7° andar, Maputo; tel. (1) 429531; fax (1) 429530.

Instituto Nacional do Livro e do Disco: Avda 24 de Julho 1921, CP 4030, Maputo; tel. (1) 34870; govt publishing and purchasing agency; Dir ARMÉNIO CORREIA.

Moçambique Editora: Rua Armando Tivane 1430, Bairro de Polana, Maputo; tel. (1) 495017; fax (1) 499071; e-mail info@me.co .mz; internet www.me.co.mz; f. 1996; educational textbooks, dictionaries.

Government Publishing House

Imprensa Nacional de Moçambique: Rua da Imprensa, CP 275, Maputo; tel. (1) 423383.

Broadcasting and Communications

TELECOMMUNICATIONS

Empresa Nacional de Telecomunicações de Moçambique (TDM): Rua da Sé 2, CP 25, Maputo; tel. (1) 431921; fax (1) 431944; e-mail rfernandes@tdm.mz; internet www.tdm.mz; f. 1993; Chair. and Man. Dir RUI JORGE LOURENÇO FERNANDES.

Telecomunicações Moveis de Moçambique (TMM): Avda 25 de Setembro, Prédio do BCI, Maputo; tel. (1) 307870; subsidiary of TDM; mobile cellular telephone provider.

Vodacom Moçambique: Rua Fereira Maia 74, Maputo; tel. (1) 409272; f. 2002; owned by Vodacom (South Africa); mobile cellular telephone services to commence operations during 2003; Chair. HERMENGILDO GAMITO.

Regulatory Authority

Instituto Nacional das Comunicações de Moçambique (INCM): Avda Eduardo Mondlane 123–127, CP 1937, Maputo; tel. (1) 490131; fax (1) 492728; internet www.incm.gov.mz.

BROADCASTING

Radio

Rádio Encontro: Avda Francisco Manyanga, CP 366, Nampula; tel. (6) 215588.

Rádio Feba Moçambique: Avda Julius Nyerere 441, Maputo; tel. (1) 440002.

Rádio Maria: Rua Igreja 156, Machava; tel. (1) 750483.

Rádio Miramar: Avda Zimbabwe 1726, Maputo; tel. (1) 491772; owned by Brazilian religious sect, the Universal Church of the Kingdom of God.

Rádio Moçambique: Rua da Rádio 2, CP 2000, Maputo; tel. (1) 431679; fax (1) 421816; e-mail informação@teledata.mz; internet www.teledata.mz/radiomocambique; f. 1975; programmes in Portuguese, English and vernacular languages; Chair. MANUEL FERNANDO VETERANO.

Rádio Terra Verde: fmrly Voz da Renamo; owned by former rebel movement Renamo; transmitters in Maputo and Gorongosa, Sofala province.

Rádio Trans Mundial Moçambique: Avda Eduardo Mondlane 2998, Maputo; tel. (1) 407358; fax (1) 407357.

Television

Rádio Televisão Klint (RTK): Avda Agostinho Neto 946, Maputo; tel. (1) 422956; fax (1) 493306; Dir CARLOS KLINT.

Televisão Miramar: owned by Brazilian religious sect, the Universal Church of the Kingdom of God.

Televisão de Moçambique (TVM): Avda 25 de Setembro 154, CP 2675, Maputo; tel. (1) 308117; fax (1) 308122; internet www.tvm.co.mz; f. 1981; Pres. ANTÓNIO JÚLIO BOTELHO MONIZ; Dir ANABELA ANDRIANO POULOS.

TV Cabo Moçambique: Avda dos Presidentes 68, CP 1750, Maputo; tel. (1) 480500; fax (1) 499015; e-mail tvcabo@tvcabo.co.mz; internet www.tvcabo.co.mz; cable television and internet services in Maputo.

Finance

(cap. = capital; res = reserves; dep. = deposits; m. = million; brs = branches; amounts in meticais, unless otherwise stated)

BANKING

Central Bank

Banco de Moçambique: Avda 25 de Setembro 1679, CP 423, Maputo; tel. (1) 428151; fax (1) 429721; e-mail info@bancomoc.uem.mz; internet www.bancomoc.mz; f. 1975; bank of issue; cap. 248,952m., res 382,168m., dep. 7,443,656m. (Dec. 2001); Gov. ADRIANO AFONSO MALEIANE; 4 brs.

Commercial Banks

Banco Austral: Avda 25 de Setembro 1184, CP 757, Maputo; tel. (1) 427685; fax (1) 301094; e-mail jane.grob@teledata.mz; f. 1977; fmrly Banco Popular de Desenvolvimento (BPD); 60% transferred to private ownership in 1997; renationalized in 2001; 80% of ownership transferred to the Amalgamated Banks of South Africa in Jan. 2002; total assets 3,230,850m. (Dec. 2001); 52 brs and agencies.

Banco Comercial e de Investimentos (BCI): Edif. John Orr's, Avda 25 de Setembro 1465, CP 4745, Maputo; tel. (1) 307777; fax (1) 307152; e-mail bci@bci.co.mz; f. 1996; 60% owned by Caixa Geral de Depósitos (Portugal); total assets US $42.3m. (Dec. 1998); Chair. ABDUL MAGID OSMAN; Man. Dir MANUAL JORGE MENDES FIGUEREIRA; 5 brs.

Banco de Desenvolvimento e de Comércio de Moçambique, SARL: Apto 420–425, Avda 25 de Setembro 1230, 4° andar, Maputo; tel. (1) 301020; fax (1) 300940; f. 2000; 42% owned by Montepie Geral (Portugal).

Banco de Fomento, SARL: Avda Julius Nyerere 1016, CP 4233, Maputo; tel. (1) 494010; fax (1) 494401; e-mail bfe.moc@teledata.mz; fmrly Banco de Fomento e Exterior SA, name changed as above 1998; cap. 100,000m., res 49,642m., dep. 1,074,209m. (Dec. 2000); Pres. ARTUR SANTOS SILVA; Man. Dir JOÃO SILVA BENTO.

Banco Internacional de Comercio, SARL: Edif. INSS, Avda 24 de Julho 3549, 2° andar, Maputo; tel. (1) 404080; fax (1) 400745; e-mail icbm@isl.co.mz; f. 1998; total assets 26.7m. (Dec. 1998); Dirs JOSEPHINE SIVARETNAM, LUTFIAH ISMAIL.

Banco Internacional de Moçambique, SARL (BIM): Avda 25 de Setembro 1800, CP 865, Maputo; tel. (1) 307481; fax (1) 307546; e-mail ecassola@bim.co.mz; internet www.mundobim.co.mz; f. 1995; merged with Banco Comercial de Moçambique in 2001; 50.4% owned by Banco Comercial Português, 23.1% by the state, 16.1% by International Finance Corpn; cap. 500,000m., dep. 12,359,990m. (Dec. 2001); Chair. Dr MÁRIO FERNANDES DA GRAÇA MACHUNGO; 88 brs.

Banco Internacional de Moçambique—Investimento: Avda Kim Il Sung 961, Maputo; tel. (1) 490085; fax (1) 490212; e-mail biminvestimento@bim.co.mz; f. 1998; 50% owned by Banco Internacional de Moçambique, 25% by BCP Investimento and 15% by International Finance Corpn; total assets 102,754m. (Dec. 2000); Chair. Dr MÁRIO FERNANDES DA GRAÇA MACHUNGO; Man. Dir Dr NUNO SALGADO SANTOS.

Banco Standard Totta de Moçambique, SARL: Praça 25 de Junho 1, CP 2086, Maputo; tel. (1) 423041; fax (1) 426967; e-mail admin1@bstm.co.mz; internet www.bstm.co.mz; f. 1966; 60% owned by Banco Totta e Açores, SA; total assets 4,961,388m. (Dec. 2001); Man. Dir JOÃO FILIPE DE LIMA MAYER; 24 brs.

Cooperativa de Poupança e Crédito, SARL: Avda 25 de Setembro 1679, 3° andar, Maputo; tel. (1) 307753; fax (1) 307754; e-mail cpc-sc@teledata.mz.

Novo Banco, SARL: Avda do Trabalho 750, Maputo; tel. and fax (1) 407705; e-mail novobanco@teledata.mz; f. 2000.

Foreign Banks

BNP Nedbank (Moçambique), SARL: Avda 25 de Setembro 1230, 1° andar, CP 1445, Maputo; tel. (1) 306700; fax (1) 306305; e-mail bnpnedbank@bnpnedbank.co.mz; internet www.nedbank.com; f. 1999; 50% owned by BNP Paribas, 50% by Nedcor Bank Ltd; Chair. VINCENT DE ROUX.

ULC Moçambique, SARL: Rua da Imprensa 256, 7° andar, CP 4447, Maputo; tel. (1) 300451; fax (1) 431290; e-mail ulc@ulcmoz.uem.mz; 44.3% owned by ULC Holdings Ltd, 27.8% by EDFUND; total assets US $1.8m. (Dec. 1998); Chair. ANTÓNIO BRANCO; Gen. Man. VICTOR VISEU.

União Comercial de Bancos (Moçambique), SARL: Avda Friedrich Engels 400, Maputo; tel. (1) 495221; fax (1) 498675; e-mail banque_fc@teledata.mz; f. 1999; 62.5% owned by Mauritius Commercial Bank Group; total assets US $8.3m. (Dec. 1999); Chair. PHILIPPE ALAIN FORGET; Gen. Man. DENIS MOTET.

DEVELOPMENT FUND

Fundo de Desenvolvimento Agrícola e Rural: CP 1406, Maputo; tel. (1) 460349; fax (1) 460157; f. 1987 to provide credit for small farmers and rural co-operatives; promotes agricultural and rural development; Sec. EDUARDO OLIVEIRA.

STOCK EXCHANGE

Bolsa de Valores de Moçambique: Avda 25 de Setembro 1230, Prédio 33, 5° andar, Maputo; tel. (1) 308826; fax (1) 310559; e-mail jussub@bvm.com; Chair. Dr JUSSUB NURMAMAD.

INSURANCE

In December 1991 the Assembléia da República approved legislation terminating the state monopoly of insurance and reinsurance activities.

Companhia de Seguros de Moçambique, IMPAR: Avda 25 de Setembro 1800–17, CP 616, Maputo; tel. (1) 429696; fax (1) 430020; e-mail impar@zebra.uem.mz; f. 1992; Pres. INOCÊNCIO A. MATAVEL; Gen. Man. MANUEL BALANCHO.

Empresa Moçambicana de Seguros, EE (EMOSE): Avda 25 de Setembro 1383, CP 1165, Maputo; tel. (1) 422095; fax (1) 424526; f. 1977 as state insurance monopoly; took over business of 24 fmr cos; privatization pending; cap. 150m. Gen. Dir VENÂNCIO MONDLANE.

Seguradora Internacional de Moçambique: Maputo; tel. (1) 430959; fax (1) 430241; e-mail simseg@zebra.uem.mz; Pres. MÁRIO FERNANDES DA GRAÇA MACHUNGO.

Trade and Industry

GOVERNMENT AGENCIES

Centro de Promoção de Investimentos (CPI): Rua da Imprensa 332, CP 4635, Maputo; tel. (1) 313295; fax (1) 313325; e-mail cpi@cpi .co.mz; internet www.mozbusiness.gov.mz; encourages foreign investment and jt ventures with foreign firms; evaluates and negotiates investment proposals.

Empresa Nacional de Hidrocarbonetos de Moçambique (ENHM): Avda Fernão de Magalhães 34, CP 2904, Maputo; tel. (1) 460083; controls concessions for petroleum exploration and production; Dir MÁRIO MARQUES.

Instituto para a Promoção de Exportações (IPEX): Avda 25 de Setembro 1008, 3° andar, CP 4487, Maputo; tel. (1) 307257; fax (1) 307256; e-mail ipex@teledata.mz; internet www.ipex.gov.mz; f. 1990 for the promotion and co-ordination of national exports abroad; Pres. Dr FELISBERTO FERRÃO.

Unidade Técnica para a Reestruturação de Empresas (UTRE): Rua da Imprensa 256, 7° andar, CP 4350, Maputo; tel. (1) 426514; fax (1) 421541; e-mail utre@teledata.mz; internet www .tropical.co.mz/~parafric; implements restructuring of state enterprises; Dir MOMADE JUMAS.

CHAMBERS OF COMMERCE

Câmara de Comércio de Moçambique: Rua Mateus Sansão Muthemba 452, CP 1836, Maputo; tel. (1) 491970; fax (1) 492211; f. 1980; Pres. CARLOS KLINT; Sec.-Gen. MANUEL NOTIÇO.

Mozambique-USA Chamber of Commerce: Rua Mateus Sansão Mutemba 425, Maputo; tel. (1) 492904; fax (1) 492739; e-mail mail@ mail.ccmusa.co.mz; internet www.ccmusa.co.mz.

INDUSTRIAL AND TRADE ASSOCIATIONS

Companhia de Desenvolvimento Mineiro (CDM): Avda 24 de Julho 1895, 1°–2° andares, CP 1152, Maputo; tel. (1) 429170; fax (1) 428921; exports marble, tantalite, asbestos anthophylite, beryl, bentonite, agates, precious and semi-precious stones; Dir LUÍS JOSSENE.

Empresa Distribuidora de Equipamento Eléctrico e Electrónico e Componentes (INTERELECTRA): Maputo; tel. (1) 427091; fax (1) 420723; electrical equipment and components; Dir FRANCISCO PAULO CUCHE.

Empresa Estatal de Importação e Exportação de Medicamentos (MEDIMOC): Avda Julius Nyerere 500, 1° andar, CP 600, Maputo; tel. (1) 491211; fax (1) 490168; e-mail medimoc@zebra.uem .mz; f. 1977; pharmaceuticals, medical equipment and supplies; Gen. Dir RENATO RONDA; 230 employees.

Empresa Moçambicana de Importação e Exportação de Produtos Químicos e Plásticos (INTERQUIMICA): Maputo; tel. (1) 423168; fax (1) 21229; chemicals, fertilizers, pesticides, plastics, paper; Dir AURÉLIO RICARDO CHIZIANE.

Empresa Nacional de Carvão de Moçambique (CARBOMOC): Rua Joaquim Lapa 108, CP 1773, Maputo; tel. (1) 427625; fax (1) 424714; f. 1948; mineral extraction and export; transfer to private ownership pending; Dir JAIME RIBEIRO.

Empresa Nacional de Petróleos de Moçambique (PETROMOC): Praça dos Trabalhadores 9, CP 417, Maputo; tel. (1) 427191; fax (1) 430181; f. 1977 to take over the Sonarep oil refinery and its associated distribution co; state directorate for liquid fuels within Mozambique, incl. petroleum products passing through Mozambique to inland countries; Dir MANUEL PATRÍCIO DA CRUZ VIOLA.

ENACOMO, SARL (Empresa Nacional de Comércio): Avda Samora Machel 285, 1° andar, CP 698, Maputo; tel. (1) 430172; fax (1) 427754; f. 1976; imports, exports, acquisition, investment; Man. Dir CARLOS PACHECO FARIA.

Lojas Francas de Moçambique (INTERFRANCA): Rua Timor Leste 106, CP 1206, Maputo; tel. (1) 425199; fax (1) 431044; music equipment, motor cars, handicrafts, furniture; Gen. Dir CARLOS E. N. RIBEIRO.

Riopele Têxteis de Moçambique, SARL: Rua Joaquim Lapa 21, CP 1658, Maputo; tel. (1) 31331; fax (1) 422902; textiles; Dir CARLOS RIBEIRO.

UTILITIES

Electricity

Electricidade de Moçambique (EDM): Avda Agostinho Neto 70, CP 2447, Maputo; tel. (1) 490636; fax (1) 491048; internet www .mozambique.mz/electricity/index.htm; f. 1977; 100% state-owned; production and distribution of electric energy; Pres. VICENTE VELOSA; Dir FERNANDO RAMOS JULIÃO; 2,700 employees.

Water

Direcção Nacional de Águas: Avda 25 de Setembro 942, 9° andar, CP 1611, Maputo; tel. (1) 420469; fax (1) 421403; e-mail watco@ zebra.uem.mz; internet www.dna.mz; Dir AMÉRICO MUIANGA.

TRADE UNIONS

Freedom to form trade unions, and the right to strike, are guaranteed under the 1990 Constitution.

Confederação de Sindicatos Livres e Independentes de Moçambique (CONSILMO): Sec.-Gen. JEREMIAS TIMANE.

Organização dos Trabalhadores de Moçambique—Central Sindical (OTM—CS) (Mozambique Workers' Organization—Trade Union Headquarters): Rua Manuel António de Sousa 36, Maputo; tel. (1) 426786; fax (1) 421671; e-mail otmcs@teledata.mz; f. 1983 as trade union fed. to replace fmr production councils; officially recognized in 1990; 200,000 mems (1993); Pres. AMOS JUNIOR MATSIUHE; Sec.-Gen. JOAQUIM FANHEIRO.

Sindicato Nacional dos Trabalhadores Agro-Pecuários e Florestais (SINTAF): Avda 25 de Setembro 1676, 1° andar, Maputo; tel. (1) 312119; Sec.-Gen. EUSÉBIO LUÍS CHIVULELE.

Sindicato Nacional dos Trabalhadores da Aviação Civil, Correios e Comunicações (SINTAC): Rua de Silves 24, Maputo; tel. (1) 415926; Sec.-Gen. MANUEL SANTOS DOS REIS.

Sindicato Nacional dos Trabalhadores do Comércio, Banca e Seguros (SINTCOBASE): Avda Ho Chi Minh 365, 1° andar, CP 2142, Maputo; tel. (1) 426271; Sec.-Gen. AMÓS JÚNIOR MATSINHE.

Sindicato Nacional dos Trabalhadores da Indústria do Açúcar (SINTIA): Avda das FPLM 1912, Maputo; tel. (1) 460108; f. 1989; Sec.-Gen. ALEXANDRE CÂNDIDO MUNGUAMBE.

Sindicato Nacional dos Trabalhadores da Indústria Alimentar e Bebidas (SINTIAB): Avda Eduardo Mondlane 1267, CP 394, Maputo; tel. (1) 424709; fax (1) 424123; Gen. Sec. SAMUEL FENIAS MATSINHE.

Sindicato Nacional dos Trabalhadores da Indústria de Cajú (SINTIC): Rua do Jardim 574, 1° andar, Maputo; tel. (1) 475300; Sec.-Gen. BOAVENTURA MONDLANE.

Sindicato Nacional dos Trabalhadores da Indústria de Construção Civil, Madeira e Minas (SINTICIM): Rua Joaquim Lapa 22, 4° andar, Maputo; tel. (1) 321159; Sec.-Gen. JEREMIAS TIMANA.

Sindicato Nacional dos Trabalhadores da Indústria Hoteleira, Turismo e Similares (SINTHOTS): Avda Eduardo Mondlane 1267, CP 394, Maputo; tel. (1) 420409; Sec.-Gen. ALBERTO MANUEL NHAPOSSE.

Sindicato Nacional dos Trabalhadores da Indústria Metalúrgica, Metalomecânica e Energia (SINTIME): Avda Olof Palme 245, 1° andar, Maputo; tel. (1) 428588; fax (1) 310508; Sec.-Gen. RUI BENJAMIM COSTA.

Sindicato Nacional dos Trabalhadores da Indústria Química, Borracha, Papel e Gráfica (SINTIQUIGRA): Avda Karl Marx 414, 1° andar, CP 4433, Maputo; tel. (1) 421553; Sec.-Gen. JOAQUIM M. FANHEIRO.

Sindicato Nacional dos Trabalhadores da Indústria Têxtil Vestuário, Couro e Calçado (SINTEVEC): Avda do Trabalho 1276, 1° andar, CP 2613, Maputo; tel. (1) 426753; fax (1) 421671; Sec.-Gen. PEDRO JOAQUIM MANDJAZE.

Sindicato Nacional dos Trabalhadores da Marinha Mercante e Pesca (SINTMAP): Rua Joaquim Lapa 22, 5° andar, No 6, Maputo; tel. (1) 305593; Sec.-Gen. DANIEL MANUEL NGOQUE.

Sindicato Nacional dos Trabalhadores dos Portos e Caminhos de Ferro (SINPOCAF): Avda Guerra Popular, CP 2158, Maputo; tel. (1) 420531; Sec.-Gen. DINIS EFRAIME FRANCISCO NHANGUMBE.

Sindicato Nacional dos Trabalhadores dos Transportes Rodoviários e Assistência Técnica (SINTRAT): Avda Paulo Samuel Kankhomba 1568, 1° andar, 14, Maputo; tel. (1) 402390; Sec.-Gen. ALCANO HORÁCIO MULA.

Sindicato Nacional de Jornalistas (SNJ): Rua Gen. Pereira d'Eça 12, 1° andar, Maputo; tel. (1) 4998577; fax (1) 492031; f. 1978; Sec.-Gen. HILÁRIO M. E. MATUSSE.

Transport

The 'Beira Corridor', where rail and road links and a petroleum pipeline run from Manica, on the Zimbabwean border, to the Mozambican port of Beira, forms a vital outlet for the land-locked southern African countries, particularly Zimbabwe. Rail and road links also run from Ressano Garcia in South Africa to the port at Maputo, and from Malawi to the port of Nacala. Following the Acordo Geral de Paz (General Peace Agreement) in 1992, rehabilitation of the transport network began. In September 2000 the Nacala Corridor was officially launched; controlled by the Nacala Corridor Development Company, some US $900m. were expected to be invested in rehabilitating the transport and communications infrastructure, notably Nacala port and the railway line linking Mozambique and Malawi. Negotiations concerning the granting of similar concessions for the Maputo and Beira transport corridors, as well as for other principal railway lines, were proceeding with private contractors in 2000. In February 2000 much of the country's infrastructure in the southern and central provinces was devastated as the result of massive flooding. Railway lines, roads and bridges suffered considerable damage.

RAILWAYS

In 1999 the total length of track was 3,114 km. The railways are all state-owned. There are both internal routes and rail links between Mozambican ports and South Africa, Swaziland, Zimbabwe and Malawi. During the hostilities many lines and services were disrupted. Improvement work on most of the principal railway lines began in the early 1980s. In 1999 the World Bank approved a loan of US $100m. to help finance the reconstruction of the line linking the port of Beira with the coal-mining centre of Moatize; the total cost was estimated at some $300m. In 2000 it was announced that funding worth some $55m. was to be made available for the rehabilitation of the Limpopo railway line, which had been damaged by the floods earlier that year. The cost of repairing the damage to the railways caused by the floods was estimated at $7.3m.

Empresa Portos e Caminhos de Ferro de Moçambique (CFM-EP): Praça dos Trabalhadores, CP 2158, Maputo; tel. (1) 427173; fax (1) 427746; e-mail cfmnet@cfmnet.co.mz; internet www.cfmnet.co.mz; fmrly Empresa Nacional dos Portos e Caminhos de Ferro de Moçambique; privatized and restructured in 2002; Chair. RUI FONSECA; comprises four separate systems linking Mozambican ports with the country's hinterland, and with other southern African countries, including South Africa, Swaziland, Zimbabwe and Malawi:

CFM—Sul: Praça dos Trabalhadores, CP 2158, Maputo; tel. (1) 427173; fax (1) 427746; lines totalling 1,070 km linking Maputo with South Africa, Swaziland and Zimbabwe, as well as Inhambane–Inharrime and Xai–Xai systems; Exec. Dir CARLOS BAMBA NANGHOU.

CFM—Norte: CP 16, Nampula; tel. (6) 212927; fax (6) 214320; lines totalling 872 km, including link between port of Nacala with Malawi; management concession awarded to Nacala Corridor Development Company (a consortium 67% owned by South African, Portuguese and US companies) in January 2000; Dir FILIPE NHUSSI.

CFM—Zambézia: CP 73, Quelimane; tel. (4) 212502; fax (4) 213123; 145-km line linking Quelimane and Mocuba; Dir ORLANDO J. JAIME.

CFM—Central: CP 472, Beira; tel. (3) 326997; fax (3) 325200; lines totalling 994 km linking Beira with Zimbabwe and Malawi, as well as link to Moatize (undergoing rehabilitation); Exec. Dir JOAQUIM VERÍSSIMO.

ROADS

In 1999 there were an estimated 30,400 km of roads in Mozambique, of which 5,685 km were paved. In 1994 the Government announced a five-year road rehabilitation programme to reopen 11,000 km of roads closed during the hostilities, and to upgrade 3,000 km of paved roads and 13,000 km of secondary and tertiary roads. The programme, which was to cost an estimated US $24,000m., was to be financed mainly by international donors and the World Bank. In 1998 the Government announced a further programme, again financed by international donors, to be implemented from 1999. The programme aimed to increase the percentage of roads in 'good' or 'reasonable' condition from 39% to 70%. However, owing to the widespread destruction caused by the February 2000 flooding, much of this reconstruction work would have to be repeated.

Administraçao Nacional de Estradas (ANE): Avda de Moçambique 1225, CP 1294, Maputo; tel. (1) 475157; fax (1) 475290; e-mail pce.ane@teledata.mz; internet www.dnep.gov.mz; f. 1999 to replace the Direcção Nacional de Estradas e Pontes; implements government road policy through the Direcção de Estradas Nacionais (DEN) and the Direcção de Estradas Regionais (DER); Pres. Eng. CARLOS FRAGOSO; Dir (DEN) Eng. TIAGO MASSINGUE.

SHIPPING

The principal ports are Maputo, Beira, Nacala and Quelimane, handling an estimated 6.1m. metric tons of cargo in 1999. In mid-1999 plans were announced for the construction of a new deep-water port at Ponta Dobela, 70 km south of Maputo. The port, which was to form part of a special economic zone, was to receive a minimum investment of US $515m., and was expected eventually to handle 30m. tons of goods, principally minerals, per year. In January 2000 management of the port facilities at Nacala was awarded to a private consortium, the Nacala Corridor Development Company. In mid-2000 it was announced that the port of Maputo was to be managed by a British-led consortium, over a period of 15 years. In early 2003 it was announced that the construction of a deep-water mineral port at Ponta Dobela would begin within 18 months.

Empresa Portos e Caminhos de Ferro de Moçambique (CFM-EP): Praça dos Trabalhadores, CP 2158, Maputo; tel. (1) 427173; fax (1) 427746; e-mail cfmnet@cfmnet.co.mz; internet www.cfmnet.co.mz; fmrly Empresa Nacional dos Portos e Caminhos de Ferro de Moçambique; privatized and restructured in 2002; Port Dir ALBERTO ELIAS.

Agência Nacional de Frete e Navegação (ANFRENA): Rua Consiglieri Pedroso 396, CP 492, Maputo; tel. (1) 427064; fax (1) 427822; Dir FERDINAND WILSON.

Companhia Nacional de Navegação: CP 2064, Maputo.

Companhia Portuguesa de Transportes Marítimos: Maputo; tel. (1) 426912.

Empresa Moçambicana de Cargas (MOCARGO): Rua Consiglieri Pedroso 430, 1°–4° andares, CP 888, Maputo; tel. (1) 421440; fax (1) 302067; e-mail mocargo1@teledata.mz; f. 1984; shipping, chartering and road transport; Man. Dir MANUEL DE SOUSA AMARAL.

Manica Freight Services, SARL: Praça dos Trabalhadores 51, CP 557, Maputo; tel. (1) 426024; fax (1) 424595; e-mail achothia@manica.co.mz; international shipping agents; Man. Dir A. Y. CHOTHIA.

Maputo Port Development Company, SARL (MPDC): Avda 25 de Setembro 420, Edificio JAT, 5° andar, CP 2841, Maputo; tel. (1) 313920; fax (1) 313921; e-mail info@portmaputo.com; internet www.portmaputo.com; f. 2002; private-sector international consortium with concession (awarded 2003) to develop and run port of Maputo until 2018; CEO ALEC DON.

Mozline, SARL: Avda Karl Marx 478, 2° andar, Maputo; tel. (1) 303078; fax (1) 303073; e-mail mozline1@virconn.com; shipping and road freight services.

Navique, SARL: Avda Mártires de Inhaminga 4, CP 145, Maputo; tel. (1) 312706; fax (1) 426310; e-mail navique_adm@mail.garp.co.mz; Chair. J. A. CARVALHO; Man. Dir PEDRO VIRTUOSO.

CIVIL AVIATION

There are 16 airports, of which three are international airports.

Empresa Nacional de Transporte e Trabalho Aéreo, EE (TTA): Aeroporto Internacional de Maputo, CP 2054, Maputo; tel. (1) 465292; fax (1) 465484; scheduled services to 35 domestic points; also operates air taxi services, agricultural and special aviation services; privatized in 1997; Dir ESTEVÃO ALBERTO JUNIOR.

Linhas Aéreas de Moçambique (LAM): Aeroporto Internacional de Maputo, CP 2060, Maputo; tel. (1) 465137; fax (1) 422936; e-mail flamingoclub@lam.co.mz; internet www.lam.co.mz; f. 1980; operates domestic services and international services within Africa and to Europe and Dubai (the United Arab Emirates); privatization of 20% share pending; Chair. and Dir-Gen. JOSÉ RICARDO ZUZARTE VIEGAS.

Sociedade de Transportes Aéreos, SARL: CP 665, Maputo; tel. (1) 742366; fax (1) 491763; e-mail dido@mail.tropical.co.mz; f. 1991; airline and aircraft charter transport services; Chair. ROGÉRIO WALTER CARREIRA; Man. Dir JOSÉ CARVALHEIRA.

Tourism

Tourism, formerly a significant source of foreign exchange, ceased completely following independence, and was resumed on a limited scale in 1980. There were 1,000 visitors in 1981 (compared with 292,000 in 1972 and 69,000 in 1974). With the successful conduct of multi-party elections in 1994 and the prospect of continued peace, there was considerable scope for development of this sector. By mid-1998 some 138 tourism projects, involving investment totalling US $900m., had been approved. In July 1997 there were some 1,200 hotel beds in Mozambique. By the late 1990s tourism was the fastest growing sector of the Mozambique economy, and in 2000 it was announced that a comprehensive tourism development plan was to be devised, assisted by funding from the European Union. The opening of the Great Limpopo Transfrontier Park in April 2002, with

South Africa and Zimbabwe, was expected to attract additional tourists.

Empresa Nacional de Turismo (ENT): Avda 25 de Setembro 1203, CP 2446, Maputo; tel. (1) 421794; fax (1) 421795; e-mail entur@virconn.com; internet www.entur.imoz.com; f. 1985; hotels and tourism; Man. Dir GILDO NEVES.

Sociedade do Desenvolvimento do Turismo do Indico (INTUR): Maputo; f. 2001; promotion of tourism in the northern Nacala Development Corridor.

MYANMAR

Introductory Survey

Location, Climate, Language, Religion, Flag, Capital

The Union of Myanmar (Myanma Naing-ngan—formerly Burma) lies in the north-west region of South-East Asia, between the Tibetan plateau and the Malay peninsula. The country is bordered by Bangladesh and India to the north-west, by the People's Republic of China and Laos to the north-east and by Thailand to the south-east. The climate is tropical, with an average temperature of 27°C (80°F) and monsoon rains from May to October. Average annual rainfall is between 2,500 mm and 5,000 mm in the coastal and mountainous regions of the north and east, but reaches a maximum of only 1,000 mm in the lowlands of the interior. Temperatures in Yangon (Rangoon) are generally between 18°C (65°F) and 36°C (97°F). The official language is Myanmar (Burmese), and there are also a number of tribal languages. About 87% of the population are Buddhists. There are animist, Muslim, Hindu and Christian minorities. The national flag (proportions 5 by 9) is red, with a blue canton, in the upper hoist, bearing two ears of rice within a cog-wheel and a ring of 14 five-pointed stars (one for each state), all in white. The capital is Yangon.

Recent History

Burma (now Myanmar) was annexed to British India during the 19th century, and became a separate British dependency, with a limited measure of self-government, in 1937. Japanese forces invaded and occupied the country in 1942, and Japan granted nominal independence under a Government of anti-British nationalists. The Burmese nationalists later turned against Japan and aided Allied forces to reoccupy the country in 1945. They formed a resistance movement, the Anti-Fascist People's Freedom League (AFPFL), led by Gen. Aung San, which became the main political force after the defeat of Japan. Aung San was assassinated in July 1947 and was succeeded by U Nu. On 4 January 1948 the Union of Burma became independent, outside the Commonwealth, with U Nu as the first Prime Minister.

During the first decade of independence Burma was a parliamentary democracy, and the Government successfully resisted revolts by communists and other insurgent groups. In 1958 the ruling AFPFL split into two wings, the 'Clean' AFPFL and the 'Stable' AFPFL, and U Nu invited the Army Chief of Staff, Gen. Ne Win, to head a caretaker Government. Elections to the Chamber of Deputies in February 1960 gave an overwhelming majority to U Nu, leading the 'Clean' AFPFL (which was re-named the Union Party in March), and he resumed office in April. Despite its popularity, however, the U Nu administration proved ineffective, and in March 1962 Gen. Ne Win intervened again, staging a coup to depose U Nu (who was subsequently detained until 1966). The new Revolutionary Council suspended the Constitution and instituted authoritarian control through the government-sponsored Burma Socialist Programme Party (BSPP). All other political parties were outlawed in March 1964.

During the next decade a more centralized system of government was created, in an attempt to win popular support and to nationalize important sectors of the economy. A new Constitution, aiming to transform Burma into a democratic socialist state, was approved in a national referendum in December 1973. The Constitution of the renamed Socialist Republic of the Union of Burma, which came into force in January 1974, confirmed the BSPP as the sole authorized political party, and provided for the establishment of new organs of state. Elections to a legislative People's Assembly took place in January 1974, and in March the Revolutionary Council was dissolved. U Ne Win (who, together with other senior army officers, had become a civilian in 1972) was elected President by the newly created State Council. Burma's economic problems increased, however, and in 1974 there were riots over food shortages and social injustices. Student demonstrations took place in 1976, as social problems increased. Following an attempted coup by members of the armed forces in July, the BSPP reviewed its economic policies, and in 1977 a new economic programme was adopted in an attempt to quell unrest.

An election in January 1978 gave U Ne Win a mandate to rule for a further four years, and in March he was re-elected Chairman of the State Council. In May 1980 a general amnesty was declared for political dissidents, including exiles (as a result of which U Nu, who had been living abroad since 1969, returned to Burma in July). Gen. San Yu, formerly the Army Chief of Staff, was elected Chairman of the State Council in November 1981; U Ne Win, however, remained Chairman of the BSPP. At the fifth Congress of the BSPP, in August 1985, U Ne Win was re-elected for a further four-year term as Chairman. Elections for a new People's Assembly were held in November.

In August 1987, owing to the country's increasing economic problems, an unprecedented extraordinary meeting, comprising the BSPP Central Committee, the organs of the State Council and other state bodies, was convened. U Ne Win proposed a review of the policies of the past 25 years, and acknowledged the need to correct any shortcomings. In September the announcement of the withdrawal from circulation of high-denomination banknotes, coupled with rice shortages following a poor harvest, provoked student riots (the first civil disturbances since 1976). Owing to continued economic deprivation, further student unrest in Rangoon (now Yangon) in March 1988 culminated in major protests, which were violently suppressed by riot police under the direct command of U Sein Lwin, the BSPP Joint General Secretary. Further demonstrations, to demand the release of rioters detained in March, started in June. The Government's response was again extremely brutal, and many demonstrators were killed. In July vain attempts were made to counter the growing unpopularity of the Government, including the removal from office of Maj.-Gen. Min Gaung, the Minister of Home and Religious Affairs, and U Thien Aung, the head of the People's Police Force in Rangoon. (The Prime Minister, also, was subsequently dismissed.) Finally, at an extraordinary meeting of the BSPP Congress in July, U Ne Win resigned as party Chairman and asked the Congress to approve the holding of a national referendum on the issue of a multi-party political system. The Congress rejected the referendum proposal and the resignation of four other senior members of the BSPP, including that of U Sein Lwin, but accepted the resignation of U San Yu, the BSPP Vice-Chairman.

The subsequent election of U Sein Lwin to the chairmanship of the BSPP by the party's Central Executive Committee, and his appointment as Chairman of the State Council and as state President, increased popular discontent and provoked further student-led riots. Martial law was imposed on Rangoon, and thousands of unarmed demonstrators were reportedly massacred by the armed forces throughout the country. In August 1988 students appealed for a general strike, and U Sein Lwin was forced to resign after only 17 days in office. He was replaced by the more moderate Dr Maung Maung, hitherto the Attorney-General, whose response to the continued rioting was conciliatory. Martial law was revoked; Brig.-Gen. Aung Gyi (formerly a close colleague of U Ne Win, now an outspoken critic of the regime), who had been detained under U Sein Lwin, was released; and permission was given for the formation of the All Burma Students' Union. Demonstrations continued, however, and by September students and Buddhist monks had assumed control of the municipal government of many towns. In that month U Nu requested foreign support for his formation of an 'alternative government'. The emerging opposition leaders, Aung Gyi, Aung San Suu Kyi (daughter of Gen. Aung San) and Gen. (retd) Tin Oo (a former Chief of Staff and Minister of Defence), then formed the National United Front for Democracy, which was subsequently renamed the League for Democracy and later the National League for Democracy (NLD).

At an emergency meeting of the BSPP Congress in September 1988 it was decided that free elections would be held within three months and that members of the armed forces, police and civil service could no longer be affiliated to a political party. Now distanced from the BSPP, the armed forces, led by Gen. (later Senior Gen.) Saw Maung, seized power on 18 September, ostensibly to maintain order until multi-party elections could be arranged. A State Law and Order Restoration Council (SLORC) was formed, all state organs (including the People's Assembly, the State Council and the Council of Ministers) were abolished, demonstrations were banned and a night-time curfew was imposed nation-wide. Despite these measures, opposition movements demonstrated in favour of an interim civilian government, and it was estimated that more than 1,000 demonstrators were killed in the first few days following the coup. The SLORC announced the formation of a nine-member Government, with Saw Maung as Minister of Defence and of Foreign Affairs and subsequently also Prime Minister. Although ostensibly in retirement, it was widely believed that U Ne Win retained a controlling influence over the new leaders. The new Government changed the official name of the country to the Union of Burma (as it had been before 1973). The law maintaining the BSPP as the sole party was abrogated, and new parties were encouraged to register for the forthcoming elections. The BSPP registered as the National Unity Party (NUP), with U Tha Kyaw, the former Minister of Transport, as its Chairman. In December 1988, owing to disagreements with Suu Kyi, Aung Gyi was expelled from the NLD after he had founded the Union National Democracy Party. Tin Oo was elected as the new NLD Chairman. U Nu returned to prominence as the leader of a new party, the League for Democracy and Peace (LDP), and also commanded the support of the new Democracy Party.

From October 1988 to January 1989 Suu Kyi campaigned in townships and rural areas across the nation, and elicited much popular support, despite martial law regulations banning public gatherings of five or more people. In March 1989 there were anti-Government demonstrations in many cities, in protest at the increasing harassment of Suu Kyi and the arrest of many NLD supporters and activists. In July Suu Kyi cancelled a rally to commemorate the anniversary of the assassination of her father, owing to the threat of government violence; two days later, both she and Tin Oo were placed under house arrest, accused of 'endangering the State'.

In May 1989 electoral legislation was ratified, providing for multi-party elections to be held on 27 May 1990, and permitting campaigning only in the three months prior to the election date. In June 1989 the SLORC changed the official name of the country to the Union of Myanmar (Myanma Naing-ngan), on the grounds that the previous title conveyed the impression that the population consisted solely of ethnic Burmans. The transliteration to the Roman alphabet of many other place-names was changed, to correspond more closely with pronunciation.

In December 1989 Tin Oo was sentenced by a military tribunal to three years' imprisonment, with hard labour, for his part in the anti-Government uprising in 1988. In the same month U Nu was disqualified from contesting the forthcoming general election, owing to his refusal to dissolve the 'alternative government' that he had proclaimed in September 1988. In January 1990 U Nu and 13 members of the 'alternative government' were placed under house arrest. Five members subsequently resigned and were released. Later in January, Suu Kyi was barred from contesting the election, owing to her 'entitlement to the privileges of a foreigner' (a reference to her marriage to a British citizen) and her alleged involvement with insurgents.

Martial law was revoked in eight townships in November 1989, and in a further 10 in February 1990. It was reported that during 1989 tens of thousands of residents had been forcibly evicted from densely populated areas in major cities, where anti-Government demonstrations had received much support, and resettled in rural areas. In January and April 1989 a prominent human rights organization, Amnesty International, published information regarding violations of human rights in Myanmar, including the torture and summary execution of dissident students. This was followed by criticism from the UN later in the year.

In May 1990 93 parties presented a total of 2,296 candidates to contest 492 seats at the general election for the new assembly; there were also 87 independent candidates. Despite previous efforts to weaken the influence of known leaders and to eliminate dissidents, the voting was reported to be free and orderly. The NLD received 59.9% of the total votes and won 396 of the 485 seats that were, in the event, contested; the NUP obtained 21.2% of the votes, but won only 10 seats. The NLD demanded the immediate opening of negotiations with the SLORC, and progress towards popular rule. However, the SLORC announced that the election had been intended to provide not a legislature but a Constituent Assembly, which was to draft a constitution establishing a 'strong government', and was to be under the direction of a national convention to be established by the SLORC. The resulting draft constitution would have to be

endorsed by referendum, and subsequently approved by the SLORC. In July the SLORC announced Order 1/90, stating that the SLORC would continue as the *de facto* Government until a new constitution was drafted. Elected members of the NLD responded (independently of their leadership) with the 'Gandhi Hall Declaration', urging that an assembly of all elected representatives be convened by September.

In August 1990, at an anti-Government protest held in Mandalay to commemorate the killing of thousands of demonstrators in 1988, troops killed four protesters, including two Buddhist monks. In September the SLORC arrested six members of the NLD, including the acting Chairman, Kyi Maung, and acting Secretary-General, Chit Hlaing, on charges of passing state secrets to unauthorized persons. Kyi Maung was replaced as acting NLD Chairman by U Aung Shwe, a former ambassador to Australia and an original member of the NLD Central Executive Committee. Also in September NLD representatives discussed plans to declare a provisional government in Mandalay, without the support of the party's Central Executive Committee. Influential monks agreed to support the declaration, which was to be made in October, but the plan was abandoned after government troops surrounded monasteries. The SLORC subsequently ordered the dissolution of all Buddhist organizations involved in anti-Government activities (all except nine sects) and empowered military commanders to impose death sentences on rebellious monks. More than 50 senior members of the NLD were arrested, and members of all political parties were required to endorse Order 1/90: in acquiescing, the NLD effectively nullified its demand for an immediate transfer of power.

In December 1990 a group of candidates who had been elected to the Constituent Assembly fled to Manerplaw, on the Thai border, and announced a 'parallel government', the National Coalition Government of the Union of Burma (NCGUB), with the support of the Democratic Alliance of Burma (DAB), a broadly based organization uniting ethnic rebel forces with student dissidents and monks. The self-styled Prime Minister of the NCGUB was Sein Win, the leader of the Party for National Democracy (PND) and a cousin of Suu Kyi. The NLD leadership expelled members who had taken part in the formation of the 'parallel government', despite broad support for the move in the NLD. The SLORC annulled the PND's registration as a political party and, subsequently, the elected status of the eight members of the NCGUB. In February 1991 the SLORC annulled the registration of the LDP. Two other parties were similarly banned in early 1991. In April Gen. (later Senior Gen.) Than Shwe, the Vice-Chairman of the SLORC and the Deputy Chief of Staff of the armed forces, officially announced that the SLORC would not transfer power to the Constituent Assembly, as the political parties involved were 'subversive' and 'unfit to rule'. In response to continued pressure from the SLORC, the NLD effected a complete reorganization of the party's Central Executive Committee, replacing Suu Kyi as General Secretary with the previously unknown U Lwin, and Tin Oo with the former acting Chairman, U Aung Shwe.

In July 1991 the SLORC retroactively amended electoral legislation adopted in May 1989, extending the grounds on which representatives of the Assembly could be disqualified or debarred from contesting future elections to include convictions for breaches of law and order. More than 80 elected representatives had already died, been imprisoned or been forced into exile since the election in May 1990. In September 1991 the SLORC declared its intention to remain in charge of state administration for a further five to 10 years. In that month U Ohn Gyaw was appointed Minister for Foreign Affairs in place of Saw Maung, becoming the first civilian in the Cabinet.

In October 1991 Suu Kyi was awarded the Nobel Peace Prize. Sein Win attended the presentation of the award to Suu Kyi's family in Oslo, Norway, in December, gaining the Norwegian Government's *de facto* recognition of the NCGUB. In Myanmar students who staged demonstrations (the first since 1989) to coincide with the ceremony, protesting against Suu Kyi's continued detention and demanding progress towards democracy, were dispersed by security forces. Universities and colleges, which had reopened in May 1991, were closed, and thousands of teaching staff were dismissed or sent for re-education. It was subsequently announced that Suu Kyi had been expelled from the NLD. Also in December Amnesty International issued a report detailing the arrests of 200 political prisoners in the first seven months of 1991, bringing the total detained since 1988 to 1,500. In January 1992 Tin Oo's expulsion from the NLD was announced in a broadcast.

Three additional members were appointed to the SLORC in January 1992, and the Cabinet was expanded to include seven new ministers, four of whom were civilians. The changes, together with a reorganization of senior ministers in February, were widely perceived to benefit the Chief of Military Intelligence, Maj.-Gen. (later Lt-Gen.) Khin Nyunt (First Secretary of the SLORC). Khin Nyunt was widely regarded as the most powerful member of the SLORC, owing to U Ne Win's continued patronage. Divisions within the ruling junta between Khin Nyunt and the more senior officers were becoming increasingly evident. In March Than Shwe replaced Saw Maung as Minister of Defence, and in April Saw Maung retired as Chairman of the SLORC and Prime Minister for reasons of ill health. Than Shwe was subsequently appointed to both these posts. The SLORC promptly ordered the release of several political prisoners, including U Nu, and announced that Suu Kyi could receive a visit from her family. Than Shwe indicated that he was prepared to meet Suu Kyi personally to discuss her future. In June the first meeting took place between members of the SLORC and opposition representatives from the remaining 10 legal parties, in preparation for the holding of a national convention to draft a new constitution.

In January 1993 the National Convention finally assembled, but was adjourned several times during the year, owing to the objections of the opposition members to SLORC demands for a leading role in government for the armed forces. The SLORC reacted to what it regarded as opposition intransigence by suspending any conciliatory gestures (which had included the revocation of two martial law decrees and amnesties for a total of 534 political prisoners), and many arrests were reported. Towards the end of the year the Chairman of the National Convention's Convening Committee, U Aung Toe (the Chief Justice), announced (seemingly without grounds) that a consensus existed in favour of the SLORC's demands, which comprised: the inclusion, in both the lower and upper chambers of a proposed parliament, of military personnel (to be appointed by the Commander-in-Chief of the Armed Forces); the election of the President by an electoral college; the independent self-administration of the armed forces; and the right of the Commander-in-Chief to exercise state power in an emergency (effectively granting legitimate status to a future coup).

In September 1993 an alternative mass movement to the NUP (which had lost credibility through its election defeat) was formed to establish a civilian front through which the armed forces could exercise control. The Union Solidarity and Development Association (USDA), the aims of which were indistinguishable from those of the SLORC, was not officially registered as a political party, thus enabling civil servants to join the organization, with the incentive of considerable privileges. In January 1994 large numbers of people were apparently coerced into joining USDA rallies to demonstrate support for the constitutional proposals presented by the SLORC.

In January 1994 the National Convention reconvened, and in April it was adjourned, having adopted guidelines for three significant chapters of the future Constitution. Accordingly, Myanmar was to be renamed the Republic of the Union of Myanmar, comprising seven states (associated with some of the country's minority ethnic groups) and seven divisions in central and southern Myanmar (largely representing the areas populated by the ethnic Bamars—Burmans). The Republic would be headed by an executive President, elected by the legislature for five years; proposals for the disqualification of any candidate with a foreign spouse or children would prevent Suu Kyi from entering any future presidential election. Reconvening in September, the Convention again stressed that the central role of the military (as 'permanent representatives of the people') be enshrined in the new Constitution. It was proposed that legislative power be shared between a bicameral Pyidaungsu Hluttaw (Union Parliament) and divisional and state assemblies, all of which were to include representatives of the military. The Pyidaungsu Hluttaw was to comprise the Pyithu Hluttaw and the Amyotha Hluttaw (House of Nationalities): the former would comprise 330 elected deputies and 110 members of the armed forces, and would be elected for five years. The latter would be constituted with equal numbers of representatives from the proposed seven regions and seven states of the Republic, as well as members of the military, and was to comprise a maximum of 224 deputies. A general election was provisionally scheduled for 2 September 1997 (although it was not actually held). The session was adjourned in April 1995.

Meanwhile, in July 1994 Khin Nyunt announced what appeared to be a major change of policy: that the SLORC was prepared to hold talks with Suu Kyi. In February a delegation led by a member of the US Congress had been granted permission to visit Suu Kyi, who had expressed her willingness to negotiate with the SLORC on all issues except her release. In August a second US Congressman led a delegation to Yangon, meeting with Khin Nyunt. In September, following mediation by a senior Buddhist monk between Suu Kyi and leading members of the SLORC, Suu Kyi was permitted to leave her home for the first time to meet Than Shwe and Khin Nyunt. In October Suu Kyi held a second meeting with senior SLORC members. In November, however, a further US delegation was not permitted to visit Suu Kyi. It was reported, none the less, that she had met other detained members of the NLD, including Tin Oo. In January 1995 the SLORC announced that Suu Kyi would be freed only when the new Constitution had been completed; Suu Kyi simultaneously rejected suggestions that she might reach a compromise with the SLORC on the terms for her release. In February leading members of the SLORC held talks in Yangon with an envoy of the UN Secretary-General. In March the Government released 31 political prisoners, including Tin Oo and Kyi Maung.

In July 1995 Suu Kyi was unexpectedly granted an unconditional release from house arrest. The SLORC, which thus hoped to attract greater foreign investment, was in a powerful position: the armed forces were united; political dissent had been effectively suppressed; and cease-fire accords had been reached with nearly all the ethnic insurgent groups. On her release Suu Kyi made a conciliatory speech, urging negotiations with the SLORC and a spirit of compromise. Suu Kyi swiftly reconciled the early leaders of the NLD, including Kyi Maung and Tin Oo, with the new leadership which had compromised with the SLORC. Hundreds of supporters gathered daily to hear Suu Kyi speak outside her house in Yangon without being dispersed by security forces. Suu Kyi was reinstated as General Secretary of the NLD in October, in a reorganization of the party's executive committee; Tin Oo and Kyi Maung were named Vice-Chairmen. Aung Shwe, who had led the 'legal' NLD and represented the party at the National Convention, was retained as party Chairman. The NLD ignored the announcement by the SLORC's Election Commission that the appointments of Suu Kyi, Tin Oo and Kyi Maung were illegal under rules requiring the Commission's approval of leadership changes.

In November 1995 a report was published by the UN investigator into human rights in Myanmar, claiming that the SLORC was using forced labour for infrastructural and historical projects. The SLORC denied the allegations, insisting that donating one's labour was a Buddhist tradition in the country. The UN report also described complaints of summary executions and rape by the armed forces. In April 1996 a further UN report claimed that forced labour, torture and arbitrary executions were still widespread in Myanmar.

In November 1995 the National Convention reconvened. The NLD was becoming increasingly frustrated by the SLORC's relative success in marginalizing Suu Kyi through its failure to open talks with the NLD and its insistence that the National Convention was the proper forum for discussions. (Suu Kyi was, of course, not a member of the National Convention.) The NLD attended the opening session of the Convention, in the hope that the SLORC would respond positively to its requests to expand the Convention to make it truly representative. However, its proposals were ignored and the NLD withdrew from the Convention, denouncing it as illegitimate and undemocratic, and for the first time appealed for international support for its cause. The SLORC, which had already begun to imprison NLD supporters for petty crimes, reacted strongly to the NLD boycott, officially expelling the NLD from the Convention and threatening to 'annihilate' anyone threatening national interests. In December Suu Kyi appealed for the revival of proscribed political parties and the release of imprisoned pro-democracy activists.

During 1996 and 1997 NLD meetings and publications were prohibited, and arrests of its members were frequent. In May 1996 more than 260 members of the NLD (mostly delegates elected to the Constituent Assembly in 1990) were arrested prior to the opening of the party's first congress. The majority were detained for the duration of the congress, which only 18 NLD members were able to attend; at least nine of those arrested subsequently had charges brought against them. The congress, meanwhile, resolved to draft an alternative constitution. In

June the SLORC intensified its action against the NLD with an order banning any organization that held illegal gatherings or obstructed the drafting of the new Constitution by the National Convention; members of a proscribed party could be liable to between five and 20 years' imprisonment. Between May and September some 70 NLD members, including Suu Kyi's personal assistant, Win Htein, received prison sentences for various offences. In September police erected road-blocks around Suu Kyi's house, and again detained NLD activists, in order to prevent the holding of a further congress. Suu Kyi's telephone line was disconnected, and she was unable to deliver her weekly speech for the first time since her release from house arrest. From October the road-block was resumed each week with the purpose of preventing access to Suu Kyi's speech. The SLORC recommended talks with NLD officials later that month. However, relations quickly deteriorated following an attack on vehicles in which Suu Kyi and other NLD leaders were travelling.

In late October 1996 student action in Yangon, in protest against the detention and brutal treatment of fellow students, prompted further repression and numerous arrests (among those detained was Kyi Maung). This was followed in early December by the largest pro-democracy demonstration since 1988, involving more than 2,000 students. (The students also voiced educational, in addition to political, concerns.) The gathering was dispersed peacefully, although some 600 demonstrators were temporarily detained. Smaller student demonstrations continued sporadically until mid-December, when Suu Kyi (although she denied involvement) was briefly confined to her home, and tanks were deployed in Yangon; university establishments were closed indefinitely. At the end of December some 50 members of the Communist Party of Burma (CPB) and of the NLD were arrested in connection with the student protests. In late January 1997 14 people, including at least five NLD members, were convicted of involvement in the unrest and sentenced to seven years' imprisonment.

In early January 1997 Suu Kyi was allowed to deliver her weekly speech for the first time in three months. However, the SLORC imposed new restrictions on media access to Suu Kyi, and barricades remained outside her home. In March there were further arrests of NLD members across the country, together with an increased army presence in several towns. Also in March a series of attacks on Muslim targets by Buddhist monks took place across the country. These attacks were ru- moured to have been organized by opponents within the regime of Myanmar's application to join the Association of South East Asian Nations (ASEAN, see p. 146), in an attempt to alienate Muslim-dominated members of the grouping. Schools were closed, but reopened in August, while universities (which had been shut in December 1996 for the third time since 1988) remained closed.

In early April 1997 a bomb attack at the home of the Second Secretary of the SLORC, Tin Oo, resulted in the death of his daughter. The Government attributed the bombing to anti-Government groups based in Japan; however, major opposition groups in exile denied involvement in the attack, which was denounced by the NLD. The attack was rumoured to be related to a power struggle between Khin Nyunt, who was increasingly regarded as a moderate, and the more conservative Commander-in-Chief of the Army and Vice-Chair of the SLORC, Gen. Maung Aye, who commanded the support of Tin Oo. The arrest and detention of NLD members increased during 1997, while government propaganda vilifying the opposition grew more frequent and Suu Kyi's freedom of movement and association remained restricted. In December the SLORC announced that Kyi Maung had resigned as Vice-Chairman of the NLD as a result of conflict between himself and Suu Kyi, a claim dismissed as false by the NLD. In July 1997, however, Khin Nyunt invited the NLD Chairman, Aung Shwe, to a meeting, which constituted the first high-level contact between the SLORC and the NLD since the release of Suu Kyi from house arrest in July 1995. A further meeting between the SLORC leadership and the NLD was due to take place in mid-September, but was cancelled by the opposition, who insisted that future discussions required the participation of Suu Kyi in her capacity as Secretary-General of the NLD. The SLORC granted permission for an NLD congress to be held in September.

On 15 November 1997 the ruling junta unexpectedly announced the dissolution of the SLORC and the creation of its immediate replacement, the State Peace and Development Council (SPDC). The 19-member SPDC comprised exclusively military personnel; younger regional military commanders were included (largely to prevent them from developing local power bases), whilst the four most senior members of the SLORC retained their positions at the head of the new junta: Than Shwe was appointed Chairman, Maung Aye Vice-Chairman, Khin Nyunt First Secretary and Tin Oo Second Secretary. A number of former members of the SLORC were ostensibly promoted to an 'Advisory Group', which was, however, subsequently abolished; five members of this group, who had also held positions in the Cabinet, were placed under house arrest in December, pending investigations into allegations of corruption. The SPDC immediately implemented a reorganization of the Cabinet. The new 40-member Cabinet included 25 former ministers, but, in contrast to the SLORC (the members of which had virtually all held cabinet portfolios), only one member of the SPDC, Than Shwe, was appointed to serve concurrently as a cabinet minister. Among the more junior members of the Cabinet were an increased number of civilian appointees, largely selected from the USDA. The restructuring of the junta and the Cabinet appeared to benefit Khin Nyunt, as several supporters of Maung Aye were removed from power. In December the SPDC announced a further cabinet reorganization (which included the finance and national planning portfolios), and the SPDC announced the appointment of a new Chairman (the Minister of Hotels and Tourism, Maj.-Gen. Saw Lwin) and Vice-Chairmen of the National Convention Convening Commission; however, the Convention, which had adjourned in March 1996, remained in recess in early 2003.

Harassment and persecution of members and leaders of the NLD and other opposition movements continued throughout 1998. In March 40 people were arrested on charges of complicity in a conspiracy allegedly led by the exiled All-Burma Students Democratic Front (ABSDF, an armed movement formed in 1988 by students within the DAB, which had officially renounced its armed struggle in 1997) to assassinate leaders of the military junta and initiate terrorist attacks on government offices and foreign embassies. The ABSDF, which rejected the allegations, was accused of complicity with the NLD. Six of the accused were sentenced to death at the end of April. However, the SPDC unexpectedly authorized an NLD party congress, attended by 400 delegates, at the end of May to celebrate the eighth anniversary of the general election. In June the NLD demanded that the SPDC reconvene the Pyithu Hluttaw, in accordance with the results of the 1990 election, by 21 August. Some 40 elected NLD representatives were detained at the end of June, and others were forced to sign pledges restricting their freedom of movement. In July the SPDC ordered NLD elected representatives to report to their local police station twice a day and confined them to their townships. During July and August Suu Kyi attempted to visit NLD members outside the city, in an effort to exert pressure on the SPDC to comply with the NLD's demands. On four separate occasions the opposition leader was prevented from continuing her journey by road-blocks set up by the ruling junta. On one such occasion in July Suu Kyi was forcibly returned to her home by security forces after a six-day protest in her car, following government refusals to comply with her demands for the release of detained opposition members and the commencement of substantive dialogue with the NLD. In a further incident in August, she was returned to her home by ambulance after spending 13 days in her car, prompting considerable international criticism of the SPDC regime, particularly from the US Government. During Suu Kyi's protest in August Khin Nyunt held a reportedly cordial meeting with the NLD Chairman, Aung Shwe.

Shortly before the NLD's prescribed deadline for convening the Pyithu Hluttaw, the SPDC published an official rejection of the NLD's demands. The NLD responded by declaring its intention unilaterally to convene a 'People's Parliament', which would include elected representatives of all the ethnic minority groups. On the day that Suu Kyi abandoned her protest at the road-block, student demonstrations took place in Yangon (for the first time since December 1996), in support of the NLD's demand for the convening of the legislature. In September thousands of students staged anti-Government demonstrations, which were dispersed by security forces. Arrests of opposition activists increased dramatically, and by early September 193 elected NLD members of the Pyithu Hluttaw and hundreds of party supporters had been detained. In the same month a 10-member Representative Committee, led by Suu Kyi and Aung Shwe, was established by the NLD to act on behalf of the 'People's Parliament' until a legislature could be convened under the 1990 election law. The Committee (which claimed a mandate based on the authorization of more than one-half of the representatives of the Pyithu Hluttaw elected in 1990, many of whom were in detention) asserted that all laws passed by the military junta over the previous 10 years had no legal authority, and also demanded the immediate and unconditional release of all political prisoners. Four parties representing Shan, Mon, Arakanese and Zomi ethnic groups expressed their support for the 'People's Parliament', together with the ABSDF. In the same month 15 senior military officers were reportedly arrested for allegedly planning to meet with Suu Kyi, and a number of large pro-Government rallies were held in Yangon. The NLD condemned the alleged use of coercion, intimidation and threats by government military intelligence units to secure the involuntary resignations of vast numbers of NLD members and the closure of a number of regional party headquarters. Following the death in custody in October of a member of the NLD, detained by the SPDC since early the previous month, the NLD also formally condemned the junta's treatment of detained opposition party members in a letter to Than Shwe. (In August of the same year an elected representative of the NLD, Saw Win, had died in prison while serving an 11-year term of imprisonment, the third NLD member of the Pyithu Hluttaw to die in custody.) In October UN Assistant Secretary-General Alvaro de Soto met with SPDC leaders and also with Suu Kyi during a visit to Myanmar. He reportedly offered large-scale financial and humanitarian aid to the junta in exchange for the initiation of substantive dialogue with the NLD. During October and November about 300 opposition members were released by the Government; however, a further 500 were believed to remain in detention.

The ruling junta effected a cabinet reorganization in November 1998, in which Ohn Gyaw was replaced as Minister of Foreign Affairs by Win Aung, hitherto the Myanma ambassador to the United Kingdom and reportedly a close ally of Khin Nyunt. In the previous month a new government body, the Political Affairs Committee, had been formed by Khin Nyunt in an apparent attempt to consolidate his position within the SPDC.

In March 1999, despite requests from several foreign Governments, the ruling junta refused to grant a visa to Suu Kyi's terminally ill husband, Michael Aris. The junta instead encouraged Suu Kyi to visit Aris in the United Kingdom; however, Suu Kyi declined to leave the country for fear that she would not be permitted to return. Following Aris's death later the same month, more than 1,000 supporters of Suu Kyi were permitted to attend a Buddhist ceremony held at Suu Kyi's home in Yangon marking her husband's demise.

In April 1999 the UN adopted a unanimous resolution deploring the escalation in the persecution of the democratic opposition in Myanmar. Nevertheless, the harassment and intimidation of NLD members continued, with the resignations from the party of nearly 300 members reported in July 1999; further resignations were reported in November and in January 2000. In December 1999 it was reported that an elected representative of the People's Assembly, U Maung Maung Myint, had been forced to resign by the ruling SPDC. The lack of political progress by the NLD in 1999 led to the formation of a breakaway faction of the party by a prominent party member, Than Tun, who was subsequently expelled from the NLD.

In August 1999 a series of protests was staged by supporters of the democratic opposition to mark the anniversary of the massacre of thousands of pro-democracy demonstrators by the military Government in 1988. In September government forces blocked the roads to the NLD headquarters in preparation for the party's 11th anniversary. In October Myanmar's Supreme Court issued a declaration rejecting a claim by the NLD that its activities had been 'continuously disrupted, prevented and destroyed' and that hundreds of its members had been illegally detained. In April 2000 Suu Kyi alleged that more than 40 youth members of the NLD had been arrested by the SPDC for their involvement in party activities. In a statement issued in May the NLD called upon the military Government to end the use of forced labour and to recognize the results of the 1990 election.

Opposition radio sources continued to give details of small-scale protests throughout 2000. In May 29 monks were arrested for refusing to attend religious festivals outside their own monasteries in an act of defiance. In October it was claimed that Dagon University had been closed owing to the discovery of anti-SPDC posters on the walls. In the same month four high school students were arrested by Military Intelligence after demonstrating in the school following their expulsion. In mid-January

2001 farmers in Shan State protested over the Government's rice-purchasing policy, leading to an unknown number of arrests. A rare bomb explosion in May 2001 reportedly killed 12 people, and left eight others injured in a market in Mandalay. In the same month it was reported that religious riots in Toungoo, Pegu province, had led to the deaths of 24 Buddhist monks. The disturbances spread to other towns, prompting allegations that the SPDC had instigated the riots in an attempt to divert public attention from political and economic problems.

Aung San Suu Kyi also continued her persistent opposition to the SPDC. In August 2000 Suu Kyi and 14 NLD colleagues attempted to visit members of the party in Kunyangon, a town just outside Yangon. The group was stopped by a military roadblock, but refused to return home until allowed to pass. A nine-day stand-off then occurred, finally ending with Suu Kyi and the NLD members being forcibly returned to Yangon. Suu Kyi and eight others were kept under house arrest for the next two weeks. In early September the SPDC raided the NLD headquarters, and detained a number of other party leaders in their homes. Undeterred, the NLD announced that it was to draft a new constitution for the country, an act declared illegal in 1996 and punishable by 20 years' imprisonment. Later in the month Suu Kyi attempted to leave Yangon again, this time by train to Mandalay, only to be told that all trains were full. The NLD leader was once again returned home and placed under house arrest, while NLD Vice-Chairman Tin Oo and eight other party workers were taken to a government 'guest house'. Pressure on the NLD increased in late October 2000, when a deadline for an eviction order for the party to vacate its premises expired. The landladies responsible for the eviction order had been incarcerated by the SPDC for allowing the NLD to use loudspeakers, but claimed that their decision to evict had not been influenced by external coercion.

Despite the sustained suppression of the opposition party and the prevention of protest, the SPDC's treatment of its political rivals became markedly more liberal from mid-2000. In July the SPDC reportedly allowed 60,000 university students to resume their education. The undergraduate universities, however, were relocated in the suburbs, in order to avoid demonstrations in the city centres that might draw in other civilians. Razali Ismail, a Malaysian diplomat newly appointed as the UN Secretary-General's Special Envoy to Myanmar, was allowed access to Suu Kyi during a four-day visit in October 2000, and in the same month James Mawdsley, a British human rights activist sentenced to 17 years' imprisonment in Myanmar in September 1999, was released (see below).

Conciliation between the SPDC and the NLD was confirmed in early January 2001, when it was announced that the two parties had been holding secret talks since October, the first high-level discussions between the opponents since 1994. Lt-Gen. Khin Nyunt met with Suu Kyi several times, although the details of the talks remained closely guarded. Some analysts feared that the resumption of discussions was merely a cynical ploy by the Government to attract foreign investment and curb economic sanctions, a view supported by the fact there was little initial evidence of progress.

In January 2001, in a further placatory gesture, the SPDC ordered the media to stop the regular acrimonious attacks on Suu Kyi and the NLD. In the same month the government-controlled Yangon division court dismissed a lawsuit brought by Suu Kyi's US-based brother, Aung San Oo, who claimed ownership of half of Suu Kyi's house. Although foreigners cannot buy or transfer property in Myanmar, San Oo had been granted an exemption from the Government in July 2000, and thus requested half the family property according to Myanma inheritance law. In October 2001, however, the court rejected Suu Kyi's application to have her brother's claim dismissed. The hearing was adjourned until November. The Government denied that the decision was intended to put pressure on Suu Kyi as her talks with the NLD continued. At the end of January 2001 the SPDC released NLD Vice-Chairman Tin Oo and 84 other party supporters, who had been detained since Suu Kyi's attempted train journey in September 2000. A few days later a delegation of the European Union (EU, see p. 199) was permitted to meet with Suu Kyi, as was Dr Paulo Sérgio Pinheiro, UN human rights envoy to Myanmar, in April 2001.

In early August 2000 the Deputy Minister for National Planning and Economic Development, Brig.-Gen. Zaw Tun, was forced to resign from the SPDC. In July Zaw Tun had publicly criticized the Government's economic policy, revealing that the figure for gross domestic product (GDP) growth for the previous year had been deliberately fabricated. While the Government's figure was officially given as 10.9%, Zaw Tun claimed that the true growth rate was closer to 6%. Later in the same month the Commander-in-Chief of the Navy, Vice-Adm. Nyunt Thein, was also obliged to resign. The resignation was seen as a reflection of a power struggle in the higher echelons of the military between Gen. Maung Aye, SPDC Vice-Chairman, and Lt-Gen. Khin Nyunt, head of Military Intelligence. Two weeks later another 17 senior naval officers were removed from their posts.

In February 2001 Lt-Gen. Tin Oo, the army chief of staff and, as the Council's Second Secretary, the SPDC's fourth most powerful member, was killed in a helicopter crash. While the accident was officially attributed to bad weather and mechanical failure, there were rumours of an assassination, as Lt-Gen. Tin Oo had survived two previous attempts on his life, in 1996 and 1997.

In June 2001, as discussions continued, UN envoy Razali Ismail presented the SPDC with a priority release list of approximately 200 political prisoners that had been prepared by Suu Kyi. In the same month the Government ordered the release of a number of NLD members from prison and permitted the reopening of the NLD headquarters and several branch offices, although those outside Yangon remained closed. In July Aye Win, an imprisoned cousin of Suu Kyi, was released, together with several other NLD detainees. However, in the same month Suu Kyi failed to attend Martyrs' Day ceremonies held in Yangon to commemorate the assassination of her father in 1947. Her non-attendance prompted speculation that talks with the Government were foundering, a rumour denied by the SPDC. In August the release of Aung Shwe, Chairman of the NLD, and Tin Oo, Vice-Chairman, was hailed as an indication of progress. Shortly afterwards Ismail held further discussions with Suu Kyi during a visit to Yangon and voiced cautious optimism that she might come to an agreement with the Government.

In November 2001 two senior army generals—Lt-Gen. Win Myint (widely regarded as the fourth most powerful individual in the country) and Deputy Prime Minister Tin Hla—were dismissed. While no official explanation was given, the dismissals were thought to be connected to the fact that the two men were under investigation for corruption. As both had expressed only muted support for the ongoing talks with Suu Kyi, there was also speculation that their replacement would be more conducive to the attainment of a political settlement. Two days later the SPDC announced that five government ministers were to retire. While two Deputy Prime Ministers, Rear Adm. Maung Maung Khin and Lt-Gen. Tin Tun, had been expected to step down, the departure of Win Sein, Minister of Culture, Aung San, Minister of Co-operatives, and Saw Tun, Minister of Immigration and Population, had not been foreseen. No official explanation was given for the changes. However, it was thought that their removal constituted an attempt to improve the Government's corrupt and anti-democratic image. In the same month Razali Ismail visited the country again. It was hoped that he would be able to revitalize the ongoing negotiations between the SPDC and Suu Kyi and accelerate the release of political prisoners, using the prospect of international aid as an incentive. Upon his departure, Ismail expressed satisfaction with the progress that had been made.

In December 2001 Nobel Prize laureates attending a gathering in Oslo issued the Government with a manifesto demanding the release of Suu Kyi and the remaining political prisoners. In response, the Government issued a statement stressing that both parties were working together to reach a satisfactory political settlement. Suu Kyi, however, commented that negotiations had yet to move beyond the confidence-building stage. In late January 2002 it was reported that Suu Kyi had met privately with Gen. Than Shwe for the first time since 1994, raising hopes that the two sides might be close to reaching a breakthrough. However, in February 2002 international pressure on the SPDC to release all remaining political prisoners (an estimated 1,500, according to Amnesty International) and begin a more substantive dialogue with the NLD increased, prompted by the release of a critical report by the US Government (see below). The Myanma Government responded by releasing five further detainees and expressing its confidence that a successful conclusion to the negotiation process was imminent.

In March 2002 the son-in-law of U Ne Win, Aye Zaw Win, and three of U Ne Win's grandsons were arrested on charges of plotting to overthrow the Government. It was alleged that they had intended to abduct three government leaders and force

them to form a figurehead government under U Ne Win's influence. Four senior military officials—the Commander-in-Chief of the Air Force, Maj.-Gen. Myint Swe, the Chief of Police, Maj.-Gen. Soe Win, and two regional commanders, Brig.-Gen. Chit Than and Maj.-Gen. Aye Kwye—were dismissed and questioned in connection with the attempted coup. Ne Win and his daughter, Sandar Win, were placed under house arrest. Despite suspicions that the coup allegations were linked to internal conflicts within the military, owing to the insubstantial nature of the evidence gathered to support the charges, it was announced in April that those arrested would stand trial for high treason. In September, following their trial, U Ne Win's four relatives were convicted of the treason charges against them and sentenced to death. They entered appeals against the sentences. In December U Ne Win himself died while under house arrest.

In May 2002 Aung San Suu Kyi was finally released from house arrest. The SPDC stated that her release was unconditional and that it would not attempt to impose any restrictions upon her travel. Shortly afterwards Suu Kyi urged the immediate resumption of dialogue with the junta, which had ceased following her liberation. In June she travelled to Mandalay on her first political trip since she was freed; the journey passed without incident. In August Razali Ismail returned to the country with the intention of promoting further political dialogue between the NLD and the SPDC. Meanwhile, Suu Kyi challenged the SPDC to prove its commitment to the achievement of democracy in the country by ordering the swift and unconditional release of all political prisoners. In the following month a delegation from the EU also visited Myanmar and met with Suu Kyi. It failed, however, to secure a meeting with any members of the SPDC. In November the junta announced the release of 115 prisoners, the largest number to have been freed since negotiations began. However, the releases were dismissed by both the USA and human rights groups as inadequate. Razali Ismail returned to the country, but made little progress towards encouraging political reconciliation.

In September 2002 the SPDC announced a minor cabinet reorganization. Minister of Hotels and Tourism, Maj.-Gen. Saw Lwin, and Minister at the Office of the Prime Minister, Tin Ngwe, retired. The Minister of Communications, Posts and Telegraphs, Brig.-Gen. Thein Saw, was also assigned the hotels and tourism portfolio, while Maj.-Gen. Kyi Aung became Minister of Culture and Brig.-Gen. Kyaw Hsan Minister of Information. In February 2003 it was announced that Lt-Gen. Soe Win would assume the previously vacant post of Second Secretary of the SPDC. Meanwhile, the Minister of Health, Maj.-Gen. Ket Sein, and the Minister of Finance and Revenue, U Khin Maung Thein, were permitted to retire. They were replaced, respectively, by Dr Kyaw Myint and Maj.-Gen. Hla Tun. U Pan Aung, Minister of Rail Transportation, was reassigned to the Office of the Prime Minister; Maj.-Gen. Aung Min subsequently assumed the rail portfolio.

In early 2003 representatives from Amnesty International were permitted to enter Myanmar for the first time and to hold talks with Aung San Suu Kyi. Following the visit, the human rights organization condemned Myanmar's judicial system. Meanwhile, 12 political activists in the country were arrested on suspicion of planning anti-Government activities. In February it was reported that Suu Kyi wished for economic sanctions to be maintained against the Myanma Government until it began a meaningful dialogue with the opposition.

After Burma gained independence in 1948, various groups conducted armed insurgency campaigns against government forces. The most effective of the ethnic-based insurgency groups was the Karen (Kayin) National Union (KNU), founded in 1948, which led a protracted campaign for the establishment of an independent state for the Karen ethnic group (restyled Kayin in the transliteration changes of 1989), partly through the activities of its military wing, the Karen (Kayin) National Liberation Army (KNLA). The KNU was a member of the National Democratic Front (NDF), an organization which at one time comprised 11 ethnic minority groups—including Kachin, Karenni (Kayinni), Mon, Shan, Pa-O, Palaung, Wa, Arakanese (Rakhine) and Lahu parties—formed in 1975 (by five groups, originally) with the aim of making Burma a federal union and opposing both the Government and, initially, the CPB. The CPB was one of the most well-organized insurgent movements, in military terms, and gained control of significant areas in northern Burma. By May 1986 the various minority groups in the NDF had agreed to relinquish their individual demands for autonomy, in favour of a unified demand for a federal system of government. At the same time, the CPB withdrew its demand for a 'one-party' government and entered into an alliance with the NDF. At the second NDF Congress in June 1987, Maj.-Gen. Bo Mya, the President of the KNU and Chief of Staff of the KNLA, was replaced as NDF President by Saw Maw Reh, a former Chairman of the Karenni (Kayinni) National Progressive Party (KNPP), and further leadership changes removed all KNU representatives from senior NDF positions. The new NDF leaders advocated the establishment of autonomous, ethnic-based states within a Burmese union.

The insurgent groups were sympathetic to anti-Government movements in the major cities. Continued attacks throughout 1988 engaged the government forces in the border areas, leaving fewer of them to impose order in the towns. In September the Karens announced plans to co-operate with protesting students and Buddhist monks to work towards the achievement of democracy. After the armed forces seized power, insurgents intensified operations, aided by at least 3,000 students whom the Karen rebels agreed to train and arm. In November 22 anti-Government groups, led by members of the NDF, formed the DAB. Bo Mya was elected President, while Brang Seng (Chairman of the Kachin Independence Organization) and Nai Shwe Kyin (a Mon) were elected Vice-Presidents.

In April 1989 dissatisfaction with the leadership of the CPB led to a mutiny by Wa tribesmen, who constituted an estimated 80%–90% of the CPB's membership. Rebellious Wa soldiers captured the CPB headquarters, and the party's leaders were forced into exile in the People's Republic of China. The leaders of the mutiny subsequently accepted SLORC proposals for the former forces of the CPB army to become government-controlled militia forces in exchange for supplies of rice, financial support and development aid. The former CPB troops agreed to use their main forces against the 25,000-strong rebel separatist Mong Tai (Shan State) Army (formerly the Shan United Army), whose leader, Khun Sa, controlled much of the drug trade in the 'Golden Triangle', the world's major opium-producing area, where the borders of Myanmar, Laos and Thailand meet. The SLORC also approached members of the NDF, and was successful in securing agreements with the Shan State Progressive Party in September 1989, the Pa-O National Organization in March 1991 and the Palaung State Liberation Organization in May of that year. In July, at the third NDF Congress, these three movements were expelled, reducing the NDF's membership to eight organizations, and Nai Shwe Kyin was elected as the NDF's new President.

In December 1988, following a visit by the Prime Minister of Thailand, the SLORC granted licences to Thai business interests to exploit raw materials in Burma, in return for much-needed foreign exchange. Although there was no announcement of any official Thai-Burmese agreement, subsequent offensives by government forces against rebel groups achieved unprecedented success, with troops frequently attacking insurgent bases from Thai territory. By December 1989 six KNU bases along the Thai border had been captured, and in January 1990 two more camps, harbouring a large number of student dissidents, were seized. In January 1990 the armed forces launched an offensive against Mon separatists. In February they succeeded in capturing Three Pagodas Pass, a principal 'black market' trade route between Thailand and Myanmar, and the headquarters of the New Mon State Party.

Intense fighting between government and rebel forces continued as the KNLA advanced into the lower central Ayeyarwady (Irrawaddy) Delta in October and November 1991. This potentially diversionary tactic failed to prevent a concerted attempt by government troops to seize control of the KNU and DAB headquarters, which was also the seat of the NCGUB. However, despite the use of sophisticated weaponry purchased from the People's Republic of China, government troops failed to capture the camp at Manerplaw. In March 1992 the Thai Government fulfilled prior threats of strong retaliation, forcing hundreds of Myanma troops out of entrenched positions taken up in order to attack the KNU headquarters from the rear. In April the SLORC officially suspended its offensive against the KNU, 'in the interests of national unity'. In October, however, government troops resumed hostilities, making several incursions into Thai territory. In December the Thai and Myanma Governments agreed to 'relocate' the Myanma armed forces, and in February 1993 they resolved to demarcate their common border.

In February and March 1993 the Kachin Independence Organization (KIO) attended peace talks with the Government in the Kachin state capital of Myitkyina. The Kachins were in a vulnerable position, since they were no longer able to obtain arms from the practically defunct CPB or through Thailand (as the Mong Tai Army controlled the territory between Kachin encampments and the Thai border). The SLORC was anxious to reach an accommodation with the Kachins, as the NCGUB would be severely weakened by the loss of their support (although a *de facto* national cease-fire had been in effect since October 1992). The KIO appeared to have signed a peace agreement in April but, owing to attempts by the Kachins to persuade other members of the DAB to enter discussions with the SLORC, the cease-fire was not announced until October. The agreement was ratified in Yangon in February 1994. The KIO was suspended from the DAB in October 1993 for negotiating separately with the SLORC, and the DAB reiterated its conditions for discussions with the SLORC in a series of open letters. Its stipulations included: the recognition of the DAB as a single negotiating body (the SLORC insisted on meeting each ethnic group separately); the location of the negotiating process in a neutral country; an immediate end to the forcible mass relocation of villagers; a new body to draft a constitution; and the release of all political detainees, beginning with Suu Kyi. Under Thai pressure, however, the DAB policy of negotiating as a front was unofficially abandoned. In February 2001 there were rumours of a coup within the KIO, as Chairman Lt-Gen. Zau Mai was replaced by his deputy, Maj.-Gen. Tu Jai. The rumours were swiftly denied, the reason for the replacement being given as Zau Nai's ill health.

In May 1994 the Karenni (Kayinni) National People's Liberation Front concluded a cease-fire agreement with the SLORC, reportedly the 11th insurgent group to do so. This was followed in July by the declaration of a cease-fire by the Kayan New Land Party, and in October by the declaration of a cease-fire by the Shan State Nationalities Liberation Organization. In December government forces launched a new offensive against the KNU, recapturing its headquarters at Manerplaw in January 1995 (and forcing many hundreds of KNU fighters across the border into Thailand). The virtual defeat of the KNU forces was attributed to their reportedly severe lack of ammunition and funds and also to the recent defection from the Christian-led KNU of a mainly Buddhist faction, which established itself as the Democratic Karen (Kayin) Buddhist Army (DKBA). The DKBA, which had comprised about one-tenth of the strength of the KNLA, allegedly supported the government forces in their offensive. In February 1995 the Myanma army captured the KNU's last stronghold, and in the following month Bo Mya resigned as the Commander-in-Chief of the KNLA (although he remained the leader of the KNU). In March the KNU declared a unilateral cease-fire, with the aim of initiating negotiations with the SLORC. Earlier in the month the KNPP reportedly became the 14th ethnic insurgent group to abandon its armed struggle against the SLORC. This agreement collapsed in June, however, as government troops entered areas designated in the accord to be under KNPP control. In August 5,000 troops were dispatched to suppress the KNPP rebellion. Clashes continued throughout the year, and in January 1996 government forces captured a major Kayinni stronghold. The KNPP continued fighting, however, with support from the ABSDF. In February 1996 talks between the KNU and the SLORC in Mawlamyine (Moulmein), calling for tripartite negotiations between the NLD, the NCGUB (which had re-elected Sein Win as its head in Sweden in July 1995) and the SLORC, were inconclusive.

Further talks between the SLORC and the KNU began in November 1996, but had collapsed by December. In January 1997 the DKBA, allegedly supported by government forces, attacked Kayin refugee camps in Thailand. The KNU claimed that requests in late January for further peace negotiations were rejected by the SLORC, which then initiated a new offensive against the KNU. Fighting between the KNU and government forces continued in early March, forcing several thousand Kayins across the border into Thailand. As a result of the forcible relocation of tens of thousands of Kayins away from KNU bases in Myanmar during 1997, further refugees fled to Thailand. The Thai armed forces denied collusion with the Myanma troops in the process of forced repatriations of Kayin refugees, who were believed to number more than 100,000 in mid-1997. In March 1998 the DKBA, supported by government troops, launched two further attacks on Kayin refugee camps in Thailand, prompting a retaliatory attack by the KNU on DKBA forces. In April 1999 the KNU issued a statement confirming the deaths of seven members of a group of 13 government officials whom they had abducted in February; the remaining six were said to have been released unharmed.

In January 2000 it was reported that 800–1,000 Kayins had fled across the border into Thailand, following clashes between government forces and the KNU. In the same month Gen. Bo Mya was succeeded as the leader of the KNU by the former Secretary-General of the organization, Saw Ba Thin. Following his appointment as leader, Ba Thin announced that, while the KNU intended to continue its struggle against the ruling SPDC, the movement was prepared to negotiate a political settlement with the military regime. It was subsequently reported by both government and independent sources that an initial but inconclusive round of talks between the KNU and the SPDC was held in February, followed by further discussions in March. However, in late 2000 the Government began to use 'scorched-earth' tactics to deprive the KNU of its support base, displacing up to 30,000 people in eastern Myanmar.

In January 2001 Johnny and Luther Htoo, teenage leaders of the Karen rebel group, God's Army, surrendered with 12 of their followers to the Thai authorities. While much smaller than the KNU or the KNLA, God's Army had gained international notoriety owing to the leadership of the twin boys, thought to be aged 13 or 14. Two of the 12 members who surrendered were believed to have been involved in a raid on a Thai village that had left six civilians dead in December 2000.

Meanwhile, in December 1993 the SLORC initiated a major offensive against Khun Sa's Mong Tai Army encampments on the Thai border. During that month Khun Sa convened a Shan 'parliament' in his base of Homong, which was attended by hundreds of delegates. This was followed, in May 1994, by Khun Sa's declaration of an independent Shan State, of which he declared himself 'President'. In the same month fighting intensified between government forces and the Mong Tai Army near the Thai border, with heavy losses reported on both sides. However, Khun Sa claimed that his army retained control of two-thirds of the Shan State. In July he was reported to have offered to end opium cultivation and to surrender to the government forces, in exchange for their withdrawal from the Shan State and a guarantee of Shan independence. In March 1995 government forces launched an intensive campaign, lasting several months, against the Mong Tai Army. In August a faction calling itself the Shan State National Army broke away from the Mong Tai Army, accusing Khun Sa of using Shan nationalism as a 'front' for drugs-trafficking. Khun Sa subsequently offered to relinquish areas under his control to an international force that could ensure the safety of the Shan whilst eradicating illicit drugs. Khun Sa's position was considerably weakened in September, as improving relations between Thailand and Myanmar led to a Thai pledge to close the common border, thus obstructing his supply routes, and cease-fires with neighbouring ethnic groups allowed the Government to deploy troops in hitherto inaccessible areas. Certain ethnic groups, notably the Wa, were also actively engaged in fighting the Mong Tai Army to gain control of the opium trade. In November Khun Sa announced his retirement from all political and military positions, citing his betrayal by the breakaway group. In January 1996 government troops entered Homong without resistance, and thousands of his former supporters surrendered. Although no formal agreement with the SLORC was announced, it was widely believed that Khun Sa had previously negotiated a settlement with the authorities since he was not detained and it was officially announced that he would not be extradited to the USA on drugs-trafficking charges. (Khun Sa was, moreover, later accorded the status of an honoured elder.) The Mong Tai Army was subsequently transformed into a militia volunteer unit under the command of the armed forces.

Between November 1996 and February 1997 there were reports of clashes between the Shan United Revolutionary Party (a faction of the Mong Tai Army that had not surrendered in January 1996) and government forces. In September 1997 the alliance between three of the major Shan groups who continued their resistance—including the Shan State National Army (SSNA), remnants of the MTA, and the Shan State Peace-keeping Council (SSPC) and its military wing, the Shan State Army (SSA)—was formalized, and the groups joined together in an enlarged SSA. In November it was reported that Shan separatist groups had launched a further offensive against government troops. In May 1999 it was reported that at least 300,000 Shan had been forced from their villages into resettle-

ment camps by government troops. Clashes between SSA units and government forces were reported in December. In March 2000, following the group's announcement that it wished to seek a peaceful settlement with the ruling junta, the SSA issued a statement outlining cease-fire terms. It was later claimed by the SSA that these terms had been misinterpreted by the Government. In May several senior army officers died in an SSA ambush. In the following month more than 60 Shan and hill tribespeople, who had been forcibly relocated and had then attempted to return to their village, were reportedly killed by the Myanma military in a retaliatory attack. In similar incidents in the region in June, as many as 50 other villagers were believed to have been murdered. In 2001 the Government launched several offensives against SSA border camps, causing hundreds more Shan to flee the area. In September 2001 the leader of the SSA, Col Yodsuek, stated that the group would be willing to enter into peace talks with the SPDC.

In late 1996 Gen. Maung Aye ordered that the forces of the United Wa State Army (UWSA—who reached an accommodation with the SLORC in 1989) should withdraw from its principal base or surrender to the Government by the end of 1997. As the deadline approached, tension between the two sides increased until the UWSA was given permission to remain at the base for a further year. In January 2000 it was reported that the SPDC was to launch an operation to relocate 50,000 people from UWSA-controlled opium-growing areas with the alleged intention of eradicating the production of drugs in the areas by 2005. The relocation programme began to cause ethnic tension early in 2001, as the Shan complained that the Wa tribespeople were occupying land that they had previously owned. It was also claimed that the Wa were still growing opium, in spite of the fact that the scheme had been introduced supposedly to prevent heroin production. In February 2001 the office of the UN High Commissioner for Refugees (UNHCR) investigated reports that 300,000 Shan had fled over the border to Thailand as a result of the Wa influx.

In late 1989 the SLORC began resettling Bamar (Burman) Buddhists in the predominantly Muslim areas of Arakan (renamed Rakhine), displacing the local Rohingya Muslims. In April 1991 Rohingya refugees were forced over the border into Bangladesh, as a result of the brutal operations of the Myanma armed forces, including the destruction of villages, widespread killings and pillaging. The Rohingyas had been similarly persecuted in 1976–78, when more than 200,000 of them had sought refuge in Bangladesh. The Rohingyas had finally been repatriated, only to lose their citizenship following the introduction of new nationality legislation in 1982. In November 1991 the SLORC pledged to repatriate genuine Myanma citizens, but claimed that many of the refugees were illegal Bengali immigrants. In April 1992 the Myanma and Bangladeshi Governments signed an agreement providing for the repatriation of those Rohingya refugees in possession of official documentation. The repatriation programme was delayed, however, owing to the continuing flow of refugees to Bangladesh (reaching an estimated 270,000 by the end of June). The first Rohingya refugees were returned to Myanmar in September, without the supervision of UNHCR. Despite demonstrations by Rohingyas in Bangladesh against forced repatriation, refugees continued to be returned to Myanmar. The SLORC's agreement, in November 1993, to allow UNHCR access to repatriated Rohingyas was expected to accelerate the programme. In April 1994 guerrillas of the Rohingya Solidarity Organization carried out attacks in the Maungdaw area of Rakhine. By May 1995 more than 216,000 refugees had been repatriated. In July 1999, however, about 20,000 Rohingya refugees remained in camps in Bangladesh, despite the expiry of the official deadline for their repatriation in August 1997. In April 2000 the International Federation of Human Rights Leagues (FIDH) issued a report condemning the treatment of Rohingya Muslims by the Myanma Government, including forced labour, punitive taxes and extra-judicial killings. The FIDH claimed that the regime was attempting to force the exodus of Rohingyas from their native Rakhine and criticized UNHCR for its effective complicity with the Myanma regime in designating the more recent refugees as economic migrants. In February 2001 violence between Buddhist and Muslim communities in the state capital, Sittwe, was reported to have resulted in at least 12 deaths, prompting the Government to regulate further the movement of Rohingya and other Muslims in and out of Rakhine. In 2002 UNHCR continued to maintain a presence in the region.

The People's Republic of China restored diplomatic relations with Burma in 1978. From 1988, as Burma's international isolation deepened, China assumed an increasingly important role. It became Myanmar's principal aid donor, arms supplier and source of consumer goods, and delayed the passage of UN resolutions that were strongly critical of the SLORC's violations of human rights. In May 1997 an agreement was reached to establish a trade route through Myanmar to provide the Chinese province of Yunnan with access to the Indian Ocean. In the same year the Chinese Government signed a 30-year agreement with Myanmar that allowed for more than 200 Chinese fishing boats to operate in Myanma waters; the agreement was widely perceived as an indication of increasing Chinese influence in Myanmar. Furthermore, China announced the construction in Myanmar of two liquefied petroleum gas plants in October 2000 and also of a dry dock in February 2001. In December 2001 the Chinese President, Jiang Zemin, travelled to Myanmar, becoming the first Chinese Head of State to visit the country since 1985. Before his arrival the Government announced that it had ordered the release of more than 200 Chinese prisoners as a gesture of goodwill. Following successful discussions, the two Governments signed a series of bilateral agreements intended to enhance co-operative ties. It was reported that China had offered Myanmar US $100m. in aid and investment, although this was thought to be linked to Chinese demands that the ruling junta increase its efforts to eradicate the drug trade between the two countries.

Japan and the member states of ASEAN were anxious to halt Myanmar's excessive dependence on China for aid and trade. Myanmar, in its turn, applied to join ASEAN (which maintained a policy of 'constructive engagement' in relation to Myanmar) in an attempt to end its isolation, accelerate economic growth and gain protection from Western criticism of its internal affairs. In July 1994 Myanmar was invited to attend the annual meeting of ASEAN ministers responsible for foreign affairs, and in July 1995 it signed the organization's founding Treaty of Amity and Co-operation, a precursor to full membership. In July 1996 Myanmar was granted observer status, and in July 1997 the country was admitted as a full member of the organization. In May 1996 Myanmar joined the ASEAN Regional Forum (ARF, see p. 149) and in May 2000 the country hosted a high-level meeting of the economic ministers of the ASEAN member countries; the meeting, which was also attended by ministers from the People's Republic of China, Japan and the Republic of Korea, attracted strong criticism from the NLD. Myanmar enjoyed particularly cordial relations with Indonesia, and the military regime aspired to Indonesia's internationally accepted political system, in which the dominant role of the armed forces was enshrined in the Constitution. In September 1997 the former leader, U Ne Win, was seen in public for the first time since 1989 during a visit to Indonesia, where he was received by the Indonesian President, Gen. Suharto, who had visited Myanmar in February. The meeting prompted further speculation concerning the extent of U Ne Win's continued influence on the Myanma regime. ASEAN links were strengthened by official visits from the Prime Minister of Cambodia, Hun Sen, in February 2000, and the Vietnamese Minister of Foreign Affairs, Nguyen Dy Nien, in October of the same year. In January 2001 Dr Mahathir Mohamad, Prime Minister of Malaysia and an integral figure in gaining entry for Myanmar into ASEAN, visited Yangon. Gen. Than Shwe and Gen. Khin Nyunt paid a reciprocal visit in September. Mahathir visited the country again in August 2002.

In the late 1990s bilateral relations between Myanmar and Thailand were rather less cordial than previously, with the Thai Government advocating a more limited 'flexible engagement' with Myanmar, in place of the ASEAN policy of 'constructive engagement' formerly endorsed by the country. Relations between the two countries were placed under some strain in late 1999 when a group of armed Myanma student activists, styled the Vigorous Burmese Student Warriors, seized control of the Myanma embassy in Bangkok in early October, demanding the release of all political prisoners in Myanmar and the opening of a dialogue between the military Goverment and the opposition. All 89 hostages were released by the activists within 24 hours, in exchange for the Thai Government's provision of helicopter transport to the Thai–Myanma border. The Thai Government's release of the perpetrators angered the ruling junta in Myanmar, and Myanmar closed its border with Thailand immediately after the incident. In early November Myanmar government troops threatened to shoot at least one group of Myanma illegal labourers whom Thai officials were attempting to deport from Thailand. The border was re-opened to commerce in late November, although relations between the two countries remained strained. In January 2000 Thai troops shot dead 10 armed Myanma rebels who had taken control of a hospital in Ratchaburi, holding hundreds of people hostage. The rebels, who were reported by some sources to be linked to the Kayin insurgent group, God's Army (a small breakaway faction of the KNU—the KNU itself denied any connection with the rebels), had issued several demands, including that the shelling of their base on the Thai–Myanma border by the Thai military be halted, that co-operation between the Thai and Myanma armies against the Kayins should cease, and that Kayin tribespeople be allowed to seek refuge in Thailand. Whilst the Thai Government denied reports that the perpetrators had been summarily executed after handing over their weapons, the brutal resolution of the incident was praised by the military Government in Myanmar.

There was renewed tension on the Thai–Myanma border in October 2000 when a Thai soldier was killed and two others were injured. It was unclear whether the clash was with Myanma troops or a faction allied to the Government. Tension was further heightened in November as 2,000 Myanma troops were deployed along the border, in preparation for an offensive against the KNU. In January 2001 it was reported that a Thai F-16 fighter aircraft had intruded into Myanma airspace, prompting the Government to announce the building of air defence systems along the border. Another border transgression occurred in February, when five Myanma soldiers were arrested by the Thai Border Patrol Police (BPP). The soldiers claimed that they were searching for food, whereas the BPP believed them to be gathering intelligence on Thai positions. On the previous day an offensive had been launched against the KNU, involving 300 Myanma troops, of whom five were killed. In mid-February there was a major incursion into Thai territory by some 200 Myanma troops, in pursuit of 100 SSA rebels. The troops clashed with Thai soldiers and occupied a hill that was within Thai territory for two days. At least two Thai villagers were killed, and officially 14 Myanma soldiers and two civilians also died. A cease-fire was signed, but this did not prevent Myanmar from ordering all SPDC troops on the border to be placed on full combat-ready status. By the end of February Thailand had detained 40 Myanma nationals for spying, according to Myanma figures, while the SPDC accused Thailand of providing support to the SSA. The border skirmishes continued in March.

In May 2001 Thai-Myanma relations deteriorated further when the Thai Government lodged a formal protest over an incident in which members of the DKBA had allegedly attacked a military unit situated in a Thai border village, causing the deaths of three civilians. A further protest was made several days later when the UWSA captured a hill believed to lie within Thai territory; the hill was later recaptured by Thai troops. In response, the Myanma Government demanded the withdrawal of Thai troops from 35 border outposts and claimed that the Thai army had launched air strikes into its territory, an accusation denied by the Thai authorities. The situation was further exacerbated by the publication of an article in a Myanma newspaper which Thailand claimed was insulting to its monarchy. In June Thai Prime Minister Thaksin Shinawatra arrived in Yangon for discussions which defused the tensions, although the two sides failed to reach any firm agreement as to how they would overcome the problems affecting their relations. In the following month the Thai Minister of Defence, Chavalit Yongchaiyudh, visited Myanmar and agreed to work with the SPDC to aid the forced repatriation of refugees on the Thai–Myanma border. In September Gen. Khin Nyunt made a three-day trip to Thailand, which was seen by many to constitute a starting point for a new era of improved bilateral relations. In January 2002 a joint Thai-Myanma commission (meeting for the first time since 1999) agreed to establish a task force to assist in the repatriation of illegal workers. In February the Thai Minister of Foreign Affairs, Surakiart Sathirathai, visited Yangon. During his stay both countries agreed to co-operate in controlling the cross-border drugs trade.

In mid-2002 relations with Thailand deteriorated sharply when fighting broke out on the border between government troops, allied with the UWSA, and the SSA. It was alleged that Thai troops had fired shells into the country, in the belief that the fighting had encroached upon Thai territory. In response, the Myanma Government accused Thailand of lending its support to the SSA. The joint border was closed shortly afterwards as tensions escalated. Border incursions continued as the bilateral relationship worsened. In June masked gunmen, thought to be members of the KNU, fired shots at a Thai school bus travelling near to the border, resulting in the deaths of three children. The KNU denied responsibility for the attack and Thai Prime Minister Thaksin Shinawatra stated later that he did not believe either the KNU or Myanma soldiers to have been responsible. In August Surakiart Sathirathai met with leaders of the SPDC in an attempt to defuse the tensions; the border subsequently reopened in October. Relations continued to improve, owing in large part to the adaptation of a policy of 'soft engagement' by the Thai Government and, in early 2003, the two countries signed an unprecedented agreement pledging that future military exercises would be conducted at a suitable distance from the border.

In October 2002 the Australian Minister of Foreign Affairs, Alexander Downer, arrived in Myanmar; he was the most senior Australian politician to have visited the country for 20 years. During his stay he met with senior members of the SPDC and with Aung San Suu Kyi. However, following his departure Suu Kyi reportedly claimed that she would prefer Australia to lend its support to the international sanctions against the country rather than attempt to engage with its leaders.

Despite the killing of three Indian soldiers in a clash with Myanma troops in October 2000, relations between the two countries subsequently improved. Gen. Maung Aye paid a seven-day visit to India in November 2000, meeting both the country's President and Prime Minister. In mid-February 2001 India's Minister of External Affairs, Jaswant Singh, visited Myanmar, the first Indian cabinet minister to do so since the SLORC's assumption of power in 1988. While there, Singh officially opened the Tamu–Kalewa highway, a road built by India at a cost of US $22m. in order to increase bilateral trade with Myanmar. In January 2003 Minister of Foreign Affairs U Win Aung paid a visit to India, during which he met with the Prime Minister and several cabinet ministers. The two Governments agreed to hold regular consultations and to co-operate in counter-terrorism activities.

Following the release of Suu Kyi from house arrest in July 1995, Japan resumed substantial economic aid to Myanmar, which had been halted in 1988. In November 1999 the Japanese Prime Minister met with Senior Gen. Than Shwe during an ASEAN summit meeting in Manila; the meeting was the first between the leader of a major world power and a senior member of the military Government since the junta's suppression of the democratic opposition in 1988. In April 2001 Japan accelerated its policy of engagement, promising a US $28m. aid programme intended to facilitate the upgrading of a hydroelectric power plant in Kayah (see Economic Affairs). The renewal of aid to the country was widely perceived to be a political gesture intended to reward the SPDC for its efforts to reach a settlement with the NLD. However, by late 2001 the Japanese Cabinet had yet to approve the disbursement of the promised funds. The international community criticized Japan's decision to resume aid as being premature in the light of Myanmar's failure to end forced labour and other human rights abuses in the country.

In July 1996, as repression increased, Suu Kyi for the first time urged the imposition of international economic sanctions against Myanmar. From March 1997 the EU withdrew Myanmar's special trading status, in response to concerns over Myanmar's human rights record; later that year a meeting scheduled to take place in November between the EU and ASEAN was cancelled by the EU, owing to its objection to the representation of Myanmar at the talks. In early 1999 a further meeting between the EU and ASEAN, scheduled to be held in February, was postponed indefinitely as a result of continued disagreement between the two organizations regarding the proposed representation of Myanmar. However, an agreement was subsequently reached by the two sides to allow Myanmar to take a 'passive role' in the Joint Co-operation Committee meeting between the EU and ASEAN scheduled to take place in May. The SPDC became more open to the development of external relations when it allowed an EU delegation to visit Myanmar and hold talks with Suu Kyi in January 2001. Despite this, the EU extended its sanctions against Myanmar for a further six months in April 2001, owing to the human rights situation. However, in October the EU announced that it had decided to ease its sanctions. After Razali Ismail's fourth visit to Myanmar in November 2001, plans for a US $16m. HIV/AIDS prevention programme were mooted. Several countries, particularly Japan

and the EU, indicated that they would be willing to support a carefully monitored international aid programme, and it was hoped that the prospect of the resumption of limited aid would encourage the Government to release more political prisoners. In January 2003 the Myanma Deputy Minister of Foreign Affairs, Khin Maung Win, was permitted to attend an EU-ASEAN summit meeting for the first time since Myanmar's suspension from the meetings in 1997. In September 1999, meanwhile, a diplomatic dispute began between Myanmar and the United Kingdom after British consular staff were refused permission to visit two Britons in detention in Myanmar for their separate involvement in pro-democracy protest action. The British Government expressed its grave concern over their treatment. One of the two Britons was released in November. The second detainee, James Mawdsley, who had received a prison sentence of 17 years for entering the country illegally and carrying pro-democracy leaflets, was released in October 2000, following international pressure; he confirmed that he had been beaten heavily while in captivity.

In May 1997 the USA imposed trade sanctions in protest at persistent and large-scale repression by the SLORC. The sanctions prohibited further investment in Myanmar, but did not affect existing US interests in the country. In July 1997, at a ministerial meeting that followed the ASEAN conference, the US Secretary of State, Madeleine Albright, denounced Myanmar publicly for its poor human rights record and the country's lack of progress towards democracy. During 1998 the USA criticized the military junta in Myanmar for its treatment of Suu Kyi and also demanded the release of hundreds of political prisoners. In March 1999 Albright publicly criticized the regime for taking insufficient action to combat the production of and trade in narcotics within Myanmar. The USA showed its support for the SPDC-NLD talks with a visit by a senior State Department official to Suu Kyi in February 2001. However, whilst welcoming the discussions, the US Government renewed its sanctions later in the year. In December pro-democracy activists in Myanmar accused the USA of neglecting their cause after a reappraisal of its foreign policy in the wake of the terrorist attacks on the country in September 2001 (see the chapter on the USA). They claimed that the US Government had moderated its criticism of the ruling military junta on the grounds that it suspected the international terrorist network, al-Qa'ida, had a presence in the country. In February 2002 a report issued by the US Government offered the prospect of an easing of sanctions, but only if the military junta released all remaining political prisoners and made further tangible progress towards democracy.

In November 1998 the SPDC strongly denied claims made by the UN that the Myanma Government was responsible for the widespread abuse of human rights within the country. However, a report published in August by the International Labour Organization (ILO, see p. 94), following an investigation into the alleged use of forced labour and the suppression of trade unions in Myanmar, found the use of forced labour to be 'pervasive' throughout the whole country, and accused the military regime of using beatings, torture, rape and murder in the exaction of its forced labour policy, constituting a 'gross denial of human rights'. In June 1999 a resolution condemning Myanmar for its widespread use of forced labour was adopted by the member countries of the ILO, and the country was barred from participating in any ILO activities. (In the same month the ruling junta was accused by the human rights organization, Amnesty International, of perpetrating widespread abuses against ethnic minority groups.) Following the failure of the military Government to carry out the recommendations made by the ILO Commission of Inquiry in 1998 after the organization's initial investigation, in March 2000 the governing body of the ILO recommended that at its meeting in June the International Labour Conference take action to secure compliance by the ruling junta with the ILO's recommendations. In a statement issued in late March, the SPDC categorically rejected the governing body's decision and recommendations. Despite the Government's assurance in November 2000 that it would accept ILO monitors to verify the cessation of forced labour practices, the UN labour body voted to proceed with sanctions against Myanmar. This was the first time such action, the strongest available to the ILO, had been undertaken in the organization's 81-year history. The ILO subsequently requested its members to review their relations with Myanmar and to adopt sanctions. China, India, Malaysia and Russia voted against the action.

In September 2001 an ILO contingent arrived in Myanmar for a three-week visit intended to ascertain whether the military junta had honoured its promise to bring about the abolition of forced labour. In November the ILO issued a report concluding that, while some progress had been made, the practice was still endemic in many parts of the country. It recommended that a permanent ILO presence be established in Myanmar to monitor continued efforts to end forced labour in the region; discussions as to how this could be implemented headed the agenda during a further visit by the ILO in February 2002. The ILO delegation, however, was not permitted to see the NLD leader, Suu Kyi, during its visit and, upon departure, the head of the delegation expressed disappointment at the lack of co-operation it had received from the Myanma authorities. The Government claimed that it had attempted to be flexible. The ILO, however, claimed that the restrictions that had been imposed upon it meant that there was little basis for a dialogue. Despite this, in March the ILO agreed to establish a liaison office in the country and, in October, an ILO mission visited the country to assist further in the development of good labour practices. In early 2003 talks were under way regarding the establishment of a plan of action for the elimination of forced labour from the country.

In October 1999 the UN Secretary-General's Special Envoy for Myanmar, Alvaro de Soto, arrived in the country to attempt, for the fifth time, to promote a dialogue between the military Government and the NLD; de Soto's efforts were, however, fruitless. In April 2000 de Soto was replaced as Special Envoy for Myanmar by a Malaysian diplomat, Razali Ismail, who subsequently arranged the secret dialogue between Suu Kyi and Lt-Gen. Khin Nyunt in October. In November the UN human rights envoy to Myanmar, Rajsoomer Lallah, resigned from his position, citing lack of financial and administrative assistance. Lallah had previously produced a damning report of Myanmar's human rights situation, but had not been granted a visa throughout his four-year term. His successor, Dr Paulo Sérgio Pinheiro, was able to visit Myanmar in April 2001, within six months of taking office. He returned for a further visit in October, but was criticized by the NLD for his failure to spend enough time consulting with local communities. His visit had to be curtailed for reasons of ill health. In February 2002 Pinheiro visited the country for a third time and held further discussions with senior members of the SPDC and with Suu Kyi and other political prisoners. The Government released 11 political prisoners during his stay and, upon leaving, he declared his visit to have been a success. In October Pinheiro travelled to the country again; during his time there he investigated allegations, made by several human rights groups, that members of the Myanma armed forces routinely raped ethnic women along the border with Thailand. He also met with Suu Kyi. In March 2003 he paid a further visit to the country.

In May 1999 the International Committee of the Red Cross (ICRC), which had withdrawn from Myanmar in 1995 but reopened its office there in October 1998, regained permission from the ruling junta to visit a limited number of prisons in the country. Despite having been initially critical of the ICRC for reaching an agreement with the SPDC, Suu Kyi was reported subsequently to have expressed her support for the Committee's work with political prisoners.

In July 2001 Minister of Foreign Affairs Win Aung travelled to Russia in order to finalize arrangements for the construction of Myanmar's first nuclear research reactor. In January 2002 the Government officially confirmed that it planned to build a reactor with Russian assistance.

Government

Following the military coup of September 1988, all state organs, including the People's Assembly, the State Council and the Council of Ministers, were abolished by the State Law and Order Restoration Council (SLORC), and the country was placed under martial law. Legislative elections took place in May 1990, but the SLORC subsequently announced that the opposition-dominated elected body was a Constituent Assembly, which was accorded no legislative power. During September 1992 a night curfew, imposed in 1988, and two martial law decrees, in force for three years, were revoked. A ban remained, however, on gatherings of more than five people. In early 1993 a National Convention, comprising members of the SLORC and representatives of the opposition parties, met to draft a new constitution; discussions continued until March 1996, when the National Convention was adjourned. The Convention remained in recess in early 2003. In November 1997 the ruling military junta

announced the dissolution of the SLORC and its replacement by the newly created State Peace and Development Council (SPDC).

Defence

Myanmar maintains a policy of neutrality and has no external defence treaties. The armed forces are largely engaged in internal security duties. In August 2002 the armed services totalled about 444,000 men, of whom a reported 325,000 were in the army, 10,000 in the navy and 9,000 in the air force. Paramilitary forces included the People's Police Force of 65,000 men and the People's Militia of 35,000 men. In 2002 the defence budget was an estimated US $555m.

Economic Affairs

In 1986, according to estimates by the World Bank, Myanmar's gross national income (GNI), measured at average 1984–86 prices, was US $7,450m., equivalent to $200 per head. In 1990–2001, it was estimated, the population increased at an annual average rate of 1.6%. According to the Asian Development Bank (ADB), Myanmar's gross domestic product (GDP) increased, in real terms, by an annual average of 7.1% between 1990/91 and 2000/01 (years ending 31 March). Real GDP growth was officially declared to be 10.9% in 1999/2000 and 13.6% in 2000/01. However, according to the IMF, GDP increased by 6.2% in the latter year.

According to the ADB, agriculture (including forestry and fishing) contributed an estimated 57.1% of GDP in 2000/01. The sector engaged an estimated 69.9% of the employed labour force in the same year. Rice is the staple crop, and has traditionally been among Myanmar's principal export commodities. Exports of rice and rice products provided 21.6% of total export earnings in 1994/95; however, the proportion had declined to 1.7% by 2000/01. In 2002 rice prices rose sharply, owing in large part to a continuing decline in rice production, exacerbated by severe flooding in that year and by an overall lack of investment in agricultural development. In 2000/01 pulses and beans accounted for 13.5% of total exports. Other crops include sugar cane, groundnuts, maize, sesame seed, tobacco and rubber. Myanmar is one of the largest sources of illicit opium in the world, and it has been speculated that the Government is involved in its export. In 2002, according to a survey conducted by the UN Office of Drug Control and Crime Prevention (see p. 37), Myanmar was the world's second biggest producer of opium, behind Afghanistan. However, ongoing government efforts to eradicate illicit poppy cultivation were achieving some success. The fishing sector is also important. Sales of teak and other hardwood provided 6.5% of total export revenue in 2000/01. (Teak is frequently felled illegally and smuggled across the border into Thailand.) Between 1990/91 and 2000/01, according to the ADB, the real GDP of the agricultural sector increased by an annual average of 5.8%. Annual agricultural GDP growth measured 11.5% in 1999/2000 and 10.9% in 2000/01.

Industry (including mining, manufacturing, construction and utilities) provided an estimated 10.4% of GDP in 2000/01, according to the ADB. The industrial sector engaged 12.2% of the employed labour force (excluding activities not adequately defined) in 1997/98. Between 1990/91 and 2000/01, according to the ADB, industrial GDP increased by an annual average of 10.7%. Industrial GDP growth measured 13.8% in 1999/2000 and 20.1% in 2000/01.

Mining and quarrying contributed an estimated 0.6% of GDP in 2000/01 and engaged 0.7% of the employed labour force in 1997/98. Production of crude petroleum decreased steadily from 1980, and from 1988 Myanmar was obliged to import petroleum. Significant onshore and offshore discoveries of natural gas and petroleum have resulted from exploration and production-sharing agreements with foreign companies, the first of which was signed in 1989. Other important minerals that are commercially exploited include tin, zinc, copper, tungsten, coal, lead, jade, gemstones, silver and gold; however, some of Myanmar's potentially lucrative mineral resources remain largely unexploited. In a five-year economic development plan issued in 1996, the ruling military junta laid emphasis on the exploitation of the country's mineral resources as a means to generate a much-needed foreign exchange. Continued efforts by the regime throughout the 1990s to attract foreign investment in the sector were largely unsuccessful, however, and in 1997 mining exports accounted for only a reported 5% of total acknowledged exports. According to the ADB, the GDP of the mining sector increased by an annual average of 18.2% between 1990/91 and 2000/01.

Growth in the GDP of the mining sector measured 36.3% in 1999/2000 and 26.7% in 2000/01.

Manufacturing contributed an estimated 7.7% of GDP in 2000/01 and engaged 9.2% of the employed labour force in 1997/98. The most important branches are food and beverage processing, the production of industrial raw materials (cement, plywood and fertilizers), petroleum refining and textiles. The sector is adversely affected by shortages of electricity and the high price of machinery and spare parts. However, the real GDP of the manufacturing sector increased, according to the ADB, at an average rate of 8.4% per year between 1990/91 and 2000/01. Manufacturing GDP rose by 14.5% in 1999/2000 and by 23.4% in 2000/01.

Energy is derived principally from natural gas, which accounted for 68.0% of electricity production in 1999; petroleum contributed 16.1% and hydroelectric power 15.9%. In January 2002 the Government announced that its third Five-Year Plan would give priority to the construction of three hydropower plants, in order to accelerate the development of the country's industrial sector. Imports of mineral fuels, lubricants, etc. accounted for 7.7% of total imports in 2000/01.

The services sector contributed 32.5% of GDP in 2000/01 and engaged 20.8% of the employed labour force in 1997/98. Tourism revenue increased substantially over the period 1992–95, and became the country's second largest source of foreign exchange in 1995/96. In 2000 tourist arrivals increased to 206,243, while revenue totalled approximately US $35m. in 1999. Following the terrorist attack on the Indonesian island of Bali in October 2002 (see the chapter on Indonesia), the number of tourists visiting Myanmar increased substantially; it was believed that the country was perceived to be a safer destination than others in the region. According to the ADB, the GDP of the services sector increased by an average of 7.3% per year between 1990/91 and 2000/01. GDP growth in the sector measured 9.2% in 1999/2000 and 13.7% in 2000/01.

In 2001 Myanmar recorded a visible trade deficit of US $268.5m., and there was a deficit of $305.5m. on the current account of the balance of payments. In the same year the principal individual source of imports (21.8%) was the People's Republic of China; other major suppliers were Singapore, Thailand, the Republic of Korea and Malaysia. The principal market for exports (26.0%) was Thailand; other significant purchasers were the USA, India, the People's Republic of China and Singapore. Illegal trade is widespread, and was estimated to be equivalent to 50% of official trade in 1995/96. The principal imports in 2000/01 were basic manufactures, machinery and transport equipment and chemicals. The principal exports in that year were pulses and beans, teak and other hardwood and base metals and ores.

In the financial year ending 31 March 2000 there was a budgetary deficit of 1,580m. kyats, equivalent to 0.07% of GDP (according to the IMF). Myanmar's external debt at the end of 2000 totalled US $6,046m., of which $5,360m. was long-term public debt; in that year the cost of servicing external debt was equivalent to 4.7% of exports of goods and services. The annual rate of inflation averaged 24.5% in 1990–2000. Having risen by 18.4% in 1999, prices declined by 0.1% in 2000. In 2001, however, the rate of inflation was 21.1%, according to the IMF. The number of registered unemployed persons in 1997/98 was equivalent to 2.5% of the labour force.

Myanmar is a member of the Asian Development Bank (see p. 143) and the Colombo Plan (see p. 339), both of which provide assistance for economic development in the region. In July 1997 Myanmar acceded to the Association of South East Asian Nations (ASEAN, see p. 146). Myanmar was granted a 10-year period from 1 January 1998 to comply with the tariff reductions (to between 0% and 5%) required under the ASEAN Free Trade Area (AFTA), which was formally established on 1 January 2002.

Following the limited liberalization of Myanmar's centrally planned economy in 1988, including the abolition of restraints on trade (although the Government retained a monopoly on exports of rice, teak, gemstones, pearls, natural gas and petroleum) and the promulgation of a liberal foreign investment law, the country attracted foreign investment and developed a small private sector. However, foreign investment was severely limited by international criticism of continued violations of human rights (culminating in the imposition of US sanctions in May 1997 and the decision of the European Union (EU) to revoke Myanmar's special trading privileges), inadequate infrastructure and widespread corruption. Consumer boycotts in the USA

and Europe of companies investing in Myanmar also led to the withdrawal from the country of several large investors from the 1990s. Although approvals of foreign direct investment increased in 2001, there was a sharp decline in the sums actually disbursed. Expansion in the economy in the 1990s largely reflected growth in the agricultural sector, which was accelerated by a system of forced labour to improve irrigation. By 1998 Myanmar was suffering extreme adverse effects from the US sanctions and, more particularly, the repercussions of the regional economic crisis that began in Thailand in mid-1997. The slow progress towards liberalization achieved since 1988 began to be reversed as most imports were banned, foreign-exchange dealers were detained, and motor spirit (petrol) was rationed. The situation was compounded by the decision of the World Bank in September 1998 to sever its ties with Myanmar, as the country had failed to service its debts. Thus, in the late 1990s Myanmar was effectively sustained by a 'parallel' economy, mostly comprising unofficial border trade with the People's Republic of China, Thailand and India. By 2001 it had become evident that Myanmar's economy had been severely weakened by the junta's policies. Although economic growth in 2000 was officially recorded as 10.9%, this was contradicted by a Deputy Minister for National Planning and Development, Brig.-Gen. Zaw Tun, who publicly claimed that the figure had been deliberately exaggerated, from about 6%. The kyat continued to depreciate sharply, declining in value from around 330 to the US dollar in early 2000 to 430 in January 2001. The depreciation continued throughout 2001. By September 2002, having appreciated by an estimated 25% following the release of Aung San Suu Kyi from house arrest in May of that year (see Recent History), the kyat had declined to a low of 1,150 to the dollar. The official exchange rate, meanwhile, remained at about six kyats to the dollar, having been fixed at the same level for nearly 40 years. In 2001 the seemingly more liberal stance shown by the SPDC began to mitigate international attitudes towards Myanmar, especially in Asia. As a direct result, in April Japan agreed to offer US $28m. in bilateral aid to Myanmar, for the purpose of the rehabilitation of a hydroelectric dam. Various ASEAN members also proclaimed interest in investment in the resource-rich country, most notably Malaysia. While most Western countries continued to await more substantial concessions from the SPDC, the EU voted to ease its sanctions in October 2001. Plans for a programme of limited humanitarian international aid met with considerable support, particularly from the EU and Japan. In March 2001 the Government implemented its third Five-Year Plan. The previous plan had, according to the SPDC, achieved an average annual growth rate of 8.4%. The plan beginning in 2001 projected average annual GDP growth rates in excess of 8% until 2005/06. The main aims of the plan were: to promote the establishment of agro-based industries; to develop the power and energy sectors; to expand the agriculture, meat and fish sectors in order to meet local demand and provide a surplus for export; to establish forest reserves; to extend the health and education sectors; and to develop the rural areas. In November 2001 a report released by the ADB stressed that the Government needed to implement a wide range of reforms if Myanmar's prospects for growth were to improve. It warned that the junta's policy of funding its annual budget deficit through an expansion of credit from the country's central bank was unsustainable in the long term and could damage the nation's economic prospects. This warning was, to some extent, borne out in 2002 as Myanmar's economic situation deteriorated, in large part due to the persistent inflation consequent upon such a policy. Prices of commodities such as rice and cooking oil increased rapidly, with fears of a rice shortage contributing to a number of outbreaks of popular unrest later in the year. In June the Government enacted an anti-money laundering law, although Myanmar remained on a list, compiled by the Financial Action Task Force on Money Laundering (FATF, see p. 343), of those countries and territories deemed to be non-co-operative in combating the practice. In early 2003 the country's private banking sector appeared to be in crisis. Although the reasons were unclear, the Government was forced to impose withdrawal limits as account holders attempted to retrieve their deposits from private banks throughout the country. While prospects for the resumption of international aid appeared to have improved following the release of Aung San Suu Kyi in May 2002, the junta's failure to resume talks with the opposition contributed to the ongoing maintenance of sanctions and to the continuing downturn in the economy.

Education

Education is provided free of charge, where available, and is compulsory at primary level. Primary education begins at five years of age and lasts for five years. Primary enrolment was equivalent to 100% of children in the relevant age-group in 1995. Secondary education, beginning at 10 years of age, lasts for a further six years, comprising a first cycle of four years and a second of two years. In 1995 enrolment at secondary schools was equivalent to 32% of children in the relevant age-group. In 1994 total enrolment at tertiary level was equivalent to 5.4% of the relevant age-group (males 4.2%; females 6.7%). Emphasis is placed on vocational and technical training.

Current expenditure on education by the central Government in 2000/01 was 31,345m. kyats, representing 14.2% of total expenditure.

Public Holidays

2003: 4 January (Independence Day), 12 February (Union Day), 2 March (Peasants' Day, anniversary of the 1962 coup), 17 March* (Full Moon of Tabaung), 27 March (Armed Forces' Day), 13–16 April* (Maha Thingyan—Water Festival), 17 April* (Myanma New Year), 1 May (Workers' Day), 15 May* (Full Moon of Kason), 13 July* (Full Moon of Waso and beginning of Buddhist Lent), 19 July (Martyrs' Day), 10 October* (Full Moon of Thadingyut and end of Buddhist Lent), 25 October* (Deepavali), 8 November* (Tazaungdaing Festival), 18 November* (National Day), December* (Kayin New Year), 25 December (Christmas Day).

2004: 4 January (Independence Day), January* (Kayin New Year), 12 February (Union Day), 2 March (Peasants' Day, anniversary of the 1962 coup), 27 March (Armed Forces' Day), March* (Full Moon of Tabaung), 13–16 April* (Maha Thingyan—Water Festival), 17 April* (Myanma New Year), 1 May (Workers' Day), May* (Full Moon of Kason), 19 July (Martyrs' Day), July* (Full Moon of Waso and beginning of Buddhist Lent), October* (Full Moon of Thadingyut and end of Buddhist Lent), November* (Tazaungdaing Festival), 12 November* (Deepavali), November/December* (National Day), 25 December (Christmas Day).

* A number of holidays depend on lunar sightings.

Weights and Measures

The imperial system is in force.

Statistical Survey

Source (unless otherwise stated): Ministry of National Planning and Economic Development, 653–691 Merchant St, Yangon; tel. (1) 272009; fax (1) 282101.

Area and Population

AREA, POPULATION AND DENSITY

Area (sq km)	676,552*
Population (census results)	
31 March 1973	28,885,867
31 March 1983†	
Males	17,507,837
Females	17,798,352
Total	35,306,189
Population (UN estimates at mid-year)‡	
1999	47,114,000
2000	47,749,000
2001	48,364,000
Density (per sq km) at mid-2001	71.5

* 261,218 sq miles.

† Figures exclude adjustment for underenumeration. Also excluded are 7,716 Myanma citizens (5,704 males; 2,012 females) abroad.

‡ Source: UN, *World Population Prospects: The 2000 Revision.*

PRINCIPAL TOWNS
(population at census of 31 March 1983)

Yangon (Rangoon)	2,513,023	Pathein (Bassein) .	144,096
Mandalay . . .	532,949	Taunggyi . . .	108,231
Mawlamyine		Sittwe	
(Moulmein) . .	219,961	(Akyab) . .	107,621
Bago (Pegu) . .	150,528	Manywa . . .	106,843

Source: UN, *Demographic Yearbook.*

Mid-2001 (UN estimate, incl. suburbs): Yangon 4,504,000 (Source: UN, *World Urbanization Prospects: The 2001 Revision*).

BIRTHS AND DEATHS
(UN estimates, annual averages)

	1985–90	1990–95	1995–2000
Birth rate (per 1,000)	31.4	29.9	26.5
Death rate (per 1,000)	13.2	12.2	11.8

Source: UN, *World Population Prospects: The 2000 Revision.*

Birth rate (1998): 27.5 per 1,000 (Source: UN, *Statistical Yearbook for Asia and the Pacific*).

Death rate (1998): 8.2 per 1,000 (Source: UN, *Statistical Yearbook for Asia and the Pacific*).

Expectation of life (WHO estimates, years at birth): 57.2 (males 54.6; females 59.9) in 2001 (Source: WHO, *World Health Report*).

EMPLOYMENT
(estimates, '000 persons aged 15 to 59 years)

	1995/96	1996/97	1997/98
Agriculture, hunting, forestry and fishing	11,848	11,960	12,093
Mining and quarrying	116	132	121
Manufacturing	1,481	1,573	1,666
Electricity, gas and water	19	21	26
Construction	354	378	400
Trade, restaurants and hotels . .	1,715	1,746	1,781
Transport, storage and communications	441	470	495
Community, social and personal services (excl. government) . .	563	577	597
Administration and other services	776	835	888
Activities not adequately defined	274	272	270
Total employed	17,587	17,964	18,359

Unemployed ('000 persons aged 18 years and over): 425.3 registered in 1998/99.

Source: mainly UN, *Statistical Yearbook for Asia and the Pacific.*

Health and Welfare

KEY INDICATORS

Total fertility rate (children per woman, 2001)	3.0
Under-5 mortality rate (per 1,000 live births, 2001) . . .	109
HIV/AIDS (% of persons aged 15–49, 1999)	1.99
Physicians (per 1,000 head, 1999)	0.30
Hospital beds (per 1,000 head, 1999)	0.30
Health expenditure (2000): US $ per head (PPP)	24
Health expenditure (2000): % of GDP	2.2
Health expenditure (2000): public (% of total)	17.1
Access to water (% of persons, 2000)	68
Access to sanitation (% of persons, 2000)	46
Human Development Index (2000): ranking	127
Human Development Index (2000): value	0.552

For sources and definitions, see explanatory note on p. vi.

Agriculture

PRINCIPAL CROPS

('000 metric tons)

	1999	2000	2001
Wheat	117	94	103*
Rice (paddy)	20,126	21,324	20,600†
Maize	349	365	524†
Millet	169	169	165*
Potatoes	245	255	319
Sweet potatoes	31	38	57
Cassava	88	77	97
Sugar cane	5,429	5,449	5,894
Other sugar crops*	240	242	242
Dry beans	1,235	1,285	1,467
Dry peas†	38	46	68
Chick-peas	68	84	119
Dry cow peas	100†	150†	150*
Pigeon peas	160	189	189*
Soybeans (Soya beans) . .	85	99	110
Groundnuts (in shell) . . .	562	634	731
Sunflower seed	189	160	268
Sesame seed	210	296	426
Cottonseed	106	118	102
Coconuts	263	240†	240*
Dry onions	476	476	593
Garlic	53	67	82
Other vegetables (incl. melons)*	2,750	2,800	2,800
Plantains	423	354	354*
Other fruits (excl. melons)* . .	910	920	920
Areca (Betel) nuts . . .	38	39	51
Tea (made)	18	19†	19†
Pimento and allspice. . .	40	40*	40*
Tobacco (leaves)	42	47	48
Jute	33	33	42
Cotton (lint)	53	59	51
Natural rubber	23	27	23

* FAO estimate(s).
† Unofficial figure(s).

Source: FAO.

LIVESTOCK

('000 head, year ending September)

	1999	2000	2001
Horses*	120	120	120
Cattle	10,740	10,964	11,218
Buffaloes	2,391	2,441	2,500
Pigs	3,715	3,914	4,139
Sheep	379	390	403
Goats	1,353	1,392	1,439
Chickens	39,529	43,522	48,269
Ducks*	5,600	5,800	6,200
Geese*	500	500	500

* FAO estimates.

Source: FAO.

LIVESTOCK PRODUCTS

('000 metric tons)

	1999	2000	2001
Beef and veal*	100.8	102.0	104.4
Buffalo meat*	20.2	20.4	20.9
Goat meat	6.8	7.0	7.3
Pig meat*	106.8	112.9	121.0
Poultry meat	176.4	198.8	220.3
Cows' milk	488.2	498.4	510.0
Buffaloes' milk	108.7	111.0	113.7
Goats' milk	7.1	7.3	7.5
Butter*	10.7	11.0	11.2
Cheese*	30.6	31.3	32.0
Hen eggs	69.9	77.5	85.9
Other poultry eggs	9.6	10.1	10.5
Cattle hides (fresh)* . . .	204.1	208.3	208.3

* FAO estimates.

Source: FAO.

Forestry

ROUNDWOOD REMOVALS

('000 cubic metres, excl. bark)

	1999	2000	2001
Sawlogs, veneer logs and logs for sleepers	2,085	2,337	2,662
Other industrial wood	1,263	1,275	1,300
Fuel wood	34,223	34,471	35,403
Total	37,571	38,083	39,365

Source: FAO.

SAWNWOOD PRODUCTION

('000 cubic metres, incl. railway sleepers)

	1999	2000	2001
Total (all broadleaved) . . .	298	545	671

Source: FAO.

Fishing

('000 metric tons, live weight, year ending 31 March)

	1997/98	1998/99	1999/2000
Capture	830.1	919.4	1,069.7
Freshwater fishes	149.3	159.7	189.7
Marine fishes	656.4	731.7	849.0
Aquaculture	82.0	91.1	98.9
Roho labeo	79.6	86.2	93.9
Total catch	912.1	1,010.5	1,168.6

Source: FAO, *Yearbook of Fishery Statistics*.

Mining

(metric tons, unless otherwise indicated)

	1999	2000	2001*
Coal and lignite	40,309	52,811	49,000
Crude petroleum ('000 barrels). .	3,394	3,538	3,300
Natural gas (million cu m)† . .	1,674	3,300*	6,800
Copper ore‡	26,736	26,711	26,300
Lead ore*‡.	1,800	1,200	1,300
Zinc ore‡	279	437	480
Tin concentrates‡	149	212	230
Chromium ore (gross weight)* . .	3,200	3,000	3,000
Tungsten concentrates‡	87	74	71
Silver ore (kilograms)‡ . . .	4,168	2,457	2,300
Gold ore (kilograms)‡‖	267	250*	200
Feldspar*‖.	12,000	12,000	10,000
Barite (Barytes)	24,651	30,370	34,000
Salt (unrefined, excl. brine)* . .	35,000	35,000	35,000
Gypsum (crude)	44,857	48,067	51,000
Rubies, sapphires and spinel ('000 metric carats)‖	8,970¶	8,351	8,630
Jade	2,342	8,318	1,700

* Estimated production.
† Marketed production.
‡ Figures refer to the metal content of ores and concentrates (including mixed concentrates).
§ Reported figure.
‖ Twelve months beginning 1 April of year stated.
¶ Excluding production of rubies from Mine-Shu.

Source: US Geological Survey.

Industry

SELECTED PRODUCTS
('000 metric tons, unless otherwise indicated)

	1997	1998	1999
Raw sugar*	52	61	53
Refined sugar†	53	53	43
Cigarettes (million)†	1,991	n.a.	n.a.
Cotton yarn†	3.7	3.9	4.8
Plywood ('000 cu m)	10	n.a.	n.a.
Printing and writing paper	11	n.a.	n.a.
Nitrogenous fertilizers‡	74	54	52
Petroleum refinery products ('000 barrels)§‖	5,414	5,815	5,605
Clay building bricks (million)	67	68	n.a.
Cement§	515,682	364,959	339,025
Tin—unwrought (metric tons)§.	228	150	150
Electric energy (million kWh, net)¶	4,261	4,377	4,813

Beer (hectolitres): 13,000 in 1994.

Woven cotton fabrics (million sq m): 16 in 1995.

* Data from FAO.

† Production by government-owned enterprises only.

‡ Production in terms of nitrogen during twelve months ending 30 June of stated year.

§ Twelve months beginning 1 April of year stated. Data from US Geological Survey.

‖ Figure includes gasoline, jet fuel, kerosene, diesel, distillate fuel oil and residual fuel oil.

¶ Data from Energy Information Administration, US Department of Energy.

Source (unless otherwise specified): UN, *Statistical Yearbook for Asia and the Pacific*.

Finance

CURRENCY AND EXCHANGE RATES

Monetary Units
100 pyas = 1 kyat

Sterling, Dollar and Euro Equivalents (31 December 2002)
£1 sterling = 10.2253 kyats
US $1 = 6.3440 kyats
€1 = 6.6530 kyats
1,000 kyats = £97.80 = $157.63 = €150.31

Average Exchange Rate (kyats per US $)
2000   6.5167
2001   6.7489
2002   6.6421

Note: Since January 1975 the value of the kyat has been linked to the IMF's special drawing right (SDR). Since May 1977 the official exchange rate has been fixed at a mid-point of SDR 1 = 8.5085 kyats. On 1 June 1996 a new customs valuation exchange rate of US $1 = 100 kyats was introduced. In September 2001 the free market exchange rate was $1 = 450 kyats.

CENTRAL GOVERNMENT BUDGET
(million kyats, year ending 31 March)

Revenue*	1998/99	1999/2000	2000/01
Tax revenue	56,653	60,294	75,727
Taxes on income, profits and capital gains	20,515	21,169	26,140
Domestic taxes on goods and services	30,748	33,750	44,101
General sales, turnover or VAT	22,720	24,576	32,961
Taxes on international trade and transactions	5,390	5,375	5,486
Other revenue	59,334	62,390	58,324
Entrepreneurial and property income	43,689	47,269	41,144
Administrative fees, nonindustrial and incidental sales	15,645	15,121	17,180
Capital revenue	79	211	257
Total	116,066	122,895	134,308

Expenditure†	1998/99	1999/2000	2000/01
Current expenditure	63,095	81,608	134,068
General public services, inc. public order	15,011	23,562	20,435
Defence	39,627	45,040	63,453
Education	9,572	12,132	31,345
Health	3,233	4,144	7,388
Social security and welfare	1,599	2,436	4,993
Recreational, cultural and religious affairs	2,114	2,013	2,668
Economic affairs and services	41,015	46,641	66,132
Agriculture, forestry, fishing and hunting	17,918	19,479	38,447
Transportation and communication	22,161	26,279	25,917
Other current expenditure	11,588	17,332	24,475
Capital expenditure	60,969	71,889	87,187
Total	124,064	153,497	221,255

* Excluding grants received from abroad (million kyats): 524 in 1998/99; 221 in 1999/2000; 242 in 2000/01.

† Excluding lending minus repayments (million kyats): −528 in 1998/99; 63 in 1999/2000; −127 in 2000/01.

Source: IMF, *Government Finance Statistics Yearbook*.

INTERNATIONAL RESERVES
(US $ million at 31 December)

	2000	2001	2002
Gold*	10.6	10.2	11.0
IMF special drawing rights	0.1	0.6	0.1
Foreign exchange	222.8	399.9	469.9
Total	233.5	410.7	481.0

* Valued at SDR 35 per troy ounce.

Source: IMF, *International Financial Statistics*.

MONEY SUPPLY
(million kyats at 31 December)

	1999	2000	2001
Currency outside banks	272,769	344,728	494,521
Demand deposits at deposit money banks	72,707	119,746	206,349
Total money (incl. others)	345,765	464,968	701,153

Source: IMF, *International Financial Statistics*.

COST OF LIVING
(Consumer Price Index for Yangon; base: 1990 = 100)

	1997	1998	1999
Food (incl. beverages)	548.2	834.6	997.0
Fuel and light	457.3	590.2	632.3
Clothing (incl. footwear)	366.0	620.3	700.4
Rent	405.1	568.9	624.1
All items (incl. others)	498.1	754.6	893.4

Source: ILO.

All items (base: 1995 = 100): 270.5 in 1999; 270.2 in 2000; 327.2 in 2001 (Source: IMF, *International Financial Statistics*).

NATIONAL ACCOUNTS
(million kyats at current prices, year ending 31 March)

National Income and Product

	1996/97	1997/98	1998/99
Domestic factor incomes. . . .	773,940	1,087,997	1,534,089
Consumption of fixed capital . .	18,040	21,557	25,907
Gross domestic product (GDP) at factor cost . .	791,980	1,109,554	1,559,996
Indirect taxes, *less* subsidies . .	—	—	—
GDP in purchasers' values . .	791,980	1,109,554	1,559,996
Net factor income from abroad . .	–116	–69	–220
Gross national product . .	791,864	1,109,485	1,559,776
Less Consumption of fixed capital	18,040	21,557	25,907
National income in market prices	773,824	1,087,928	1,533,869

Source: UN, *National Accounts Statistics*.

Expenditure on the Gross Domestic Product

	1997/98	1998/99	1999/2000
Final consumption expenditure .	987,513	1,419,709	1,906,136
Increase in stocks	–10,276	–7,604	48,325
Gross fixed capital formation . .	150,240	206,912	241,694
Total domestic expenditure. .	1,127,477	1,619,017	2,196,155
Exports of goods and services . .	6,290	7,700	9,394
Less Imports of goods and services	–14,258	–16,941	–15,248
GDP in purchasers' values . .	1,119,509	1,609,776	2,190,301
GDP at constant 1985/86 prices	75,123	79,460	88,134

Source: IMF, *International Financial Statistics*.

Gross Domestic Product by Economic Activity

	1998/99	1999/2000	2000/01
Agriculture, hunting, forestry and fishing	950,574	1,312,285	1,458,270
Mining and quarrying . . .	7,895	10,842	15,234
Manufacturing	112,774	143,244	195,876
Electricity, gas and water . .	991	2,558	3,445
Construction	37,034	40,425	50,263
Wholesale and retail trade . .	377,595	524,403	601,690
Transport, storage and communications	80,031	105,669	149,669
Finance	1,945	2,215	2,587
Government services. . . .	14,622	16,505	40,260
Other services	26,315	32,174	35,429
GDP in purchasers' values .	1,609,776	2,190,320	2,552,723

Source: Asian Development Bank, *Key Indicators of Developing Asian and Pacific Countries*.

BALANCE OF PAYMENTS
(US $ million)

	1999	2000	2001
Exports of goods f.o.b. . . .	1,281.1	1,638.4	2,294.5
Imports of goods f.o.b. . . .	–2,159.6	–2,136.9	–2,563.0
Trade balance	–878.5	–498.5	–268.5
Exports of services	507.1	471.3	419.6
Imports of services	–288.2	–323.7	–376.6
Balance on goods and services.	–659.7	–350.8	–225.5
Other income received . . .	51.1	35.0	35.6
Other income paid	–54.0	–166.2	–398.7
Balance on goods, services and income	–662.6	–482.0	–588.6
Current transfers received . . .	381.0	285.8	295.7
Current transfers paid	–0.3	–13.9	–12.6
Current balance	–281.9	–210.1	–305.5
Direct investment from abroad. .	253.1	254.8	208.3
Other investment liabilities . .	–4.3	–44.5	186.8
Net errors and omissions . . .	–12.3	–23.4	88.4
Overall balance	–45.4	–23.3	178.0

Source: IMF, *International Financial Statistics*.

External Trade

PRINCIPAL COMMODITIES*
(distribution by SITC, million kyats, year ending 31 March)

Imports c.i.f.	1998/99	1999/2000	2000/01
Food and live animals	453	620	586
Mineral fuels, lubricants, etc.	941	1,654	1,145
Animal and vegetable oils, fats and waxes	689	488	412
Chemicals and related products	1,672	1,871	1,924
Basic manufactures	4,436	4,125	4,401
Machinery and transport equipment.	6,348	4,868	3,754
Miscellaneous manufactured articles.	574	643	1,000
Total (incl. others)	16,872	16,265	14,900

Exports f.o.b.†	1998/99	1999/2000	2000/01
Food and live animals	2,543	2,237	3,206
Dried beans, peas, etc. (shelled)	1,135	1,179	1,658
Crude materials (inedible) except fuels	1,233	1,819	1,081
Teak and other hardwood . . .	789	925	803
Basic manufactures	690	602	1,559
Miscellaneous manufactured articles.	527	176	116
Total (incl. others)	6,756	8,947	12,262

* Totals include, but distribution by commodities excludes, border trade, mainly with the People's Republic of China, Thailand and Bangladesh. In 1998/99 the total value of such trade (in US $ million) was: Imports 253.1; Exports 301.6 (Source: IMF, *Myanmar: Statistical Appendix* (January 2001)).

† Excluding re-exports.

Source: Asian Development Bank, *Key Indicators of Developing Asian and Pacific Countries*.

PRINCIPAL TRADING PARTNERS
(US $ million)

Imports	1999	2000	2001
China, People's Republic . . .	447.2	546.1	611.3
Germany	61.5	44.7	25.3
Hong Kong	70.7	97.9	79.8
India	58.4	67.1	73.9
Indonesia	81.8	71.2	70.9
Japan	203.5	215.6	199.6
Korea, Republic	205.9	318.2	255.3
Malaysia	257.7	254.1	224.5
Singapore	460.2	479.7	465.6
Thailand	435.3	554.7	390.5
Total (incl. others)	2,549.7	3,027.8	2,806.2

Exports	1999	2000	2001
China, People's Republic . . .	92.3	113.5	141.1
France	56.3	71.3	71.8
Germany	54.4	77.8	99.4
Hong Kong	34.0	33.5	n.a.
India	227.3	261.3	288.5
Japan	92.2	108.4	96.5
Malaysia	52.2	63.2	74.7
Singapore	90.3	99.8	102.1
Thailand	102.6	233.0	735.4
United Kingdom	35.0	67.3	87.8
USA	222.2	442.7	456.2
Total (incl. others)	1,474.0	2,116.2	2,823.9

Source: Asian Development Bank, *Key Indicators of Developing Asian and Pacific Countries*.

Transport

RAILWAYS
(traffic, million)

	1998	1999	2000
Passenger-kilometres . . .	3,948	4,112	4,451
Freight ton-kilometres . . .	988	1,043	1,222

Source: UN, *Statistical Yearbook*.

ROAD TRAFFIC
(registered motor vehicles at 31 March)

	1994	1995	1996
Passenger cars	119,126	131,953	151,934
Trucks	39,939	36,728	42,828
Buses	19,183	14,624	15,639
Motorcycles	71,929	82,591	85,821
Others	8,377	6,251	6,611
Total	258,554	272,147	302,833

Source: Department of Road Transport Administration.

Passenger cars: 177,900 in 1997; 177,600 in 1998; 171,100 in 1999; 173,900 in 2000 (Source: UN, *Statistical Yearbook*).

Commercial vehicles: 74,800 in 1997; 75,900 in 1998; 83,400 in 1999; 90,400 in 2000 (Source: UN, *Statistical Yearbook*).

INLAND WATERWAYS
(traffic by state-owned vessels)

	1993/94	1994/95*	1995/96†
Passengers carried ('000) . . .	36,003	26,582	24,491
Passenger-miles (million) . .	617	531	544
Freight carried ('000 tons) . .	3,172	3,194	3,158
Freight ton-miles (million) . .	353	346	351

* Provisional.
† Estimates.

SHIPPING

Merchant Fleet
(registered at 31 December)

	1999	2000	2001
Number of vessels	127	123	124
Displacement (grt)	540,232	445,583	379,819

Source: Lloyd's Register-Fairplay, *World Fleet Statistics*.

International Sea-Borne Traffic
(state-owned vessels)

	1993/94	1994/95*	1995/96†
Passengers carried ('000) . . .	69	77	60
Passenger-miles (million) . . .	23	26	20
Freight carried ('000 metric tons) .	773	1,213	1,030
Freight ton-miles (million) . . .	2,655	2,765	2,807

* Provisional.
† Estimates.

CIVIL AVIATION
(traffic on scheduled services)

	1997	1998	1999
Kilometres flown (million) . . .	9	8	9
Passengers carried ('000) . . .	575	522	537
Passenger-km (million)	385	345	355
Total ton-km (million)	46	40	40

Source: UN, *Statistical Yearbook*.

Tourism

TOURIST ARRIVALS BY COUNTRY OF NATIONALITY

	1998	1999	2000
China, People's Republic . . .	n.a.	12,148	14,336
France	15,410	13,594	13,313
Germany	8,492	9,039	9,920
Japan	28,672	25,319	21,623
Malaysia	n.a.	7,583	9,938
Singapore	n.a.	11,074	11,074
Taiwan	n.a.	32,977	32,098
Thailand	18,840	19,392	19,070
United Kingdom	9,494	9,267	9,020
USA	10,700	10,270	11,554
Total (incl. others)	201,000	198,210	206,243

Source: World Tourism Organization, *Yearbook of Tourism Statistics*.

Tourism receipts (US $ million): 35 in 1998; 35 in 1999 (Source: World Bank).

Communications Media

	1999	2000	2001
Television receivers ('000 in use) .	323.3	344.3	n.a.
Telephones ('000 main lines in use)	249.1	266.2	281.2
Facsimile machines (number in use)	2,540	n.a.	n.a.
Mobile cellular telephones ('000 subscribers)	11.4	29.3	13.8
Personal computers ('000 in use) .	50	50	55
Internet users ('000)	0.5	1.0	10.0

Book production (1999): 227 titles.

Newspapers (1996): 5 dailies (average circulation 449,000).

Radio receivers (1999): 3,157,000 in use.

Sources: International Telecommunication Union; UNESCO, *Statistical Yearbook*; UN, *Statistical Yearbook*.

Education

(provisional, 1994/95)

	Institutions	Teachers	Students
Primary schools*	35,856	169,748	5,711,202
Middle schools	2,058	53,859	1,390,065
High schools	858	18,045	389,438
Vocational schools	86	1,847	21,343
Teacher training	17	615	4,031
Higher education	45	6,246	247,348
Universities	6	2,901	62,098

* Excluding 1,152 monastic primary schools with an enrolment of 45,360.

1997/98 (provisional): *Primary:* Institutions 35,877, Teachers 167,134, Students ('000) 5,145.4; *General Secondary:* Institutions 2,091, Teachers 56,955, Students ('000) 1,545.6; *Tertiary:* Institutions 923, Teachers 17,089, Students ('000) 385.3 (Source: UN, *Statistical Yearbook for Asia and the Pacific*).

Adult literacy rate (UNESCO estimates): 84.7% (males 89.0%; females 80.5%) in 2000 (Source: UN Development Programme, *Human Development Report*).

Directory

The Constitution

On 18 September 1988 a military junta, the State Law and Order Restoration Council (SLORC), assumed power and abolished all state organs created under the Constitution of 3 January 1974. The country was placed under martial law. The state organs were superseded by the SLORC at all levels with the Division, Township and Village State Law and Order Restoration Councils. The SLORC announced that a new constitution was to be drafted by the 485-member Constituent Assembly that was elected in May 1990. In early 1993 a National Convention, comprising members of the SLORC and representatives of opposition parties, met to draft a new constitution; however, the Convention was adjourned in March 1996 and remained in recess in 2003. In November 1997 the SLORC was dissolved and replaced by the newly formed State Peace and Development Council (SPDC).

The Government

HEAD OF STATE

Chairman of the State Peace and Development Council: Field Marshal THAN SHWE (took office as Head of State 23 April 1992).

STATE PEACE AND DEVELOPMENT COUNCIL
(April 2003)

Chairman: Field Marshal THAN SHWE.

Vice-Chairman: Dep. Senior Gen. MAUNG AYE.

First Secretary: Gen. KHIN NYUNT.

Second Secretary: Lt-Gen. SOE WIN.

Third Secretary: (vacant).

Other members: Rear-Adm. KYI MIN, Lt-Gen. KYAW THAN, Maj.-Gen. AUNG HTWE, Maj.-Gen. YE MYINT, Lt-Gen. KHIN MAUNG THAN, Maj.-Gen. KYAW WIN, Maj.-Gen. THEIN SEIN, Maj.-Gen. THURA SHWE MANN, Maj.-Gen. MYINT AUNG, Maj.-Gen. MAUNG BO, Maj.-Gen. THIHA THURA TIN AUNG MYINT OO, Maj.-Gen. TIN AYE.

CABINET
(April 2003)

Prime Minister and Minister of Defence: Field Marshal THAN SHWE.

Deputy Prime Ministers: (vacant).

Minister of Military Affairs: (vacant).

Minister of Agriculture and Irrigation: Maj.-Gen. NYUNT TIN.

Minister of Industry (No. 1): U AUNG THAUNG.

Minister of Industry (No. 2): (vacant).

Minister of Foreign Affairs: U WIN AUNG.

Minister of National Planning and Economic Development: U SOE THA.

Minister of Transport: Maj.-Gen. HLA MYINT SWE.

Minister of Labour: U TIN WIN.

Minister of Culture: Maj.-Gen. KYI AUNG.

Minister of Co-operatives: Lt-Gen. TIN NGWE.

Minister of Rail Transportation: Maj.-Gen. AUNG MIN.

Minister of Energy: Brig.-Gen. LUN THI.

Minister of Education: U THAN AUNG.

Minister of Health: Dr KYAW MYINT.

Minister of Commerce: Brig.-Gen. PYI SONE.

Minister of Communications, Posts and Telegraphs and Minister of Hotels and Tourism: Brig.-Gen. THEIN ZAW.

Minister of Finance and Revenue: Maj.-Gen. HLA TUN.

Minister of Religious Affairs: U AUNG KHIN.

Minister of Construction: Maj.-Gen. SAW TUN.

Minister of Science and Technology: U THAUNG.

Minister of Immigration and Population and Minister of Social Welfare, Relief and Resettlement: Maj.-Gen. SEIN HTWA.

Minister of Information: Brig.-Gen. KYAW HSAN.

Minister of Progress of Border Areas, National Races and Development Affairs: Col THEIN NYUNT.

Minister of Electric Power: Maj.-Gen. TIN HTUT.

Minister of Sports: Brig.-Gen. THURA AYE MYINT.

Minister of Forestry: U AUNG PHONE.

Minister of Home Affairs: Col TIN HLAING.

Minister of Mines: Brig.-Gen. OHN MYINT.

Minister of Livestock and Fisheries: Brig.-Gen. MAUNG MAUNG THEIN.

Ministers at the Office of the Chairman of the State Peace and Development Council: Lt.-Gen. MIN THEIN, Brig.-Gen. DAVID ABEL.

Ministers at the Office of the Prime Minister: U THAN SHWE, U PAN AUNG.

MINISTRIES

Office of the Chairman of the State Peace and Development Council: 15–16 Windermere Park, Yangon; tel. (1) 282445.

Prime Minister's Office: Ministers' Office, Theinbyu Rd, Botahtaung Township, Yangon; tel. (1) 283742.

Ministry of Agriculture and Irrigation: Thiri Mingala Lane, Kaba Aye Pagoda Rd, Yangon; tel. (1) 665587; fax (1) 664493.

Ministry of Commerce: 228–240 Strand Rd, Yangon; tel. (1) 287034; fax (1) 280679; e-mail com@mptmail.net.mm; internet www.myanmar.com/Ministry/commerce.

Ministry of Communications, Posts and Telegraphs: cnr of Merchant and Theinbyu Sts, Yangon; tel. (1) 292019; fax (1) 292977; internet www.mptp.gov.mm.

Ministry of Construction: 39 Nawaday St, Dagon Township, Yangon; tel. (1) 283938; fax (1) 289531.

Ministry of Co-operatives: 259–263 Bogyoke Aung San St, Yangon; tel. (1) 277096; fax (1) 287919.

Ministry of Culture: 131 Kaba Aye Pagoda Rd, Bahan Township, Yangon; tel. (1) 543235; fax (1) 283794; internet www.myanmar.com/Ministry/culture.

Ministry of Defence: Ahlanpya Phaya St, Yangon; tel. (1) 281611.

Ministry of Education: Theinbyu St, Botahtaung Township, Yangon; tel. (1) 285588; fax (1) 285480.

Ministry of Electric Power: Yangon.

Ministry of Energy: 23 Pyay Rd, Yangon; tel. (1) 221060; fax (1) 222964; e-mail myanmoe@mptmail.net.mm; internet www.energy.gov.mm.

Ministry of Finance and Revenue: 26(A) Setmu Rd, Yankin Township, Yangon; tel. (1) 284763; internet www.myanmar.com/Ministry/finance.

Ministry of Foreign Affairs: Pyay Rd, Dagon Township, Yangon; tel. (1) 222844; fax (1) 222950; e-mail mofa.aung@mptmail.net.mm; internet www.myanmar.com/Ministry/mofa.

Ministry of Forestry: Thirimingala Lane, Kaba Aye Pagoda Rd, Yangon; tel. (1) 289184; fax (1) 664459; internet www.myanmar .com/Ministry/Forest.

Ministry of Health: Theinbyu Rd, Botahtaung Township, Yangon; tel. (1) 277334; fax (1) 282834; internet www.myanmar.com/ Ministry/health.

Ministry of Home Affairs: cnr of Saya San St and No. 1 Industrial St, Yankin Township, Yangon; tel. (1) 549208; internet www .myanmar.com/Ministry/Moha.

Ministry of Hotels and Tourism: 77–91 Sule Pagoda Rd, Kyauktada Township, Yangon; tel. (1) 282705; fax (1) 287871; e-mail mtt .mht@mptmail.net.mm; internet www.myanmar.com/Ministry/ Hotel_Tour.

Ministry of Immigration and Population: cnr of Mahabandoola Rd and Thein Phyu Rd, Botahtaung Township, Yangon; tel. (1) 249090; internet www.myanmar.com/Ministry/imm&popu.

Ministry of Industry (No. I): 192 Kaba Aye Pagoda Rd, Yangon; tel. (1) 566066; internet www.myanmar.com/Ministry/MOI-1.

Ministry of Industry (No. II): 56 Kaba Aye Pagoda Rd, Yankin Township, Yangon; tel. (1) 666134; fax (1) 666135; e-mail dmip@ mptmail.net.mm; internet www.myanmar.com/Ministry/moi2.

Ministry of Information: 365–367 Bo Sung Kyaw St, Yangon; tel. (1) 245631; fax (1) 289274.

Ministry of Labour: Theinbyu St, Botahtaung Township, Yangon; tel. (1) 278320; fax (1) 256185.

Ministry of Livestock and Fisheries: Theinbyu St, Botahtaung Township, Yangon; tel. (1) 280398; fax (1) 289711.

Ministry of Military Affairs: Yangon.

Ministry of Mines: 90 Kanbe Rd, Yankin Township, Yangon; tel. (1) 577316; fax (1) 577455; internet www.myanmar.com/Ministry/ Mines.

Ministry of National Planning and Economic Development: Theinbyu St, Botahtaung Township, Yangon; tel. (1) 254667; fax (1) 243791.

Ministry of Progress of Border Areas, National Races and Development Affairs: Ministers' Office, Theinbyu St, Botahtaung Township, Yangon; tel. (1) 280032; fax (1) 285257.

Ministry of Rail Transportation: 88 Theinbyu St, Yangon; tel. (1) 292769.

Ministry of Religious Affairs: Kaba Aye Pagoda Precinct, Mayangone Township, Yangon; tel. (1) 665620; fax (1) 665728; internet www.myanmar.com/Ministry/religious.

Ministry of Science and Technology: 6 Kaba Aye Pagoda Rd, Yankin Township, Yangon; tel. (1) 665686.

Ministry of Social Welfare, Relief and Resettlement: Theinbyu St, Botahtaung Township, Yangon; tel. (1) 665697; fax (1) 650002; e-mail social-wel-myan@mptmail.net.mm; internet www.myanmar .com/Ministry/social-welfare.

Ministry of Sports: Ministers' Office, Botahtaung Township, Yangon; tel. (1) 553958.

Ministry of Transport: 363–421 Merchant St, Botahtaung Township, Yangon; tel. (1) 296815; fax (1) 296824; internet www .myanmar.com/Ministry/Transport.

Legislature

CONSTITUENT ASSEMBLY

Following the military coup of 18 September 1988, the 489-member Pyithu Hluttaw (People's Assembly), together with all other state organs, was abolished. A general election was held on 27 May 1990. It was subsequently announced, however, that the new body was to serve as a constituent assembly, responsible for the drafting of a new constitution, and that it was to have no legislative power. The next legislative election was provisionally scheduled for September 1997, but did not take place.

General Election, 27 May 1990

Party	% of Votes	Seats
National League for Democracy . . .	59.9	392
Shan Nationalities League for Democracy .	1.7	23
Arakan (Rakhine) League for Democracy .	1.2	11
National Unity Party	21.2	10
Mon National Democratic Front	1.0	5
National Democratic Party for Human Rights.	0.9	4
Chin National League for Democracy . .	0.4	3
Kachin State National Congress for Democracy	0.1	3
Party for National Democracy	0.5	3
Union Pa-O National Organization . . .	0.3	3
Zomi National Congress.		2
Naga Hill Regional Progressive Party . .		2
Kayah State Nationalities League for Democracy		2
Ta-ang (Palaung) National League for Democracy		2
Democratic Organization for Kayan National Unity		2
Democracy Party		1
Graduates' and Old Students' Democratic Association		1
Patriotic Old Comrades' League . . .	12.8	1
Shan State Kokang Democratic Party . .		1
Union Danu League for Democracy Party .		1
Kamans National League for Democracy .		1
Mara People's Party		1
Union Nationals Democracy Party . . .		1
Mro (or) Khami National Solidarity Organization		1
Lahu National Development Party . . .		1
United League of Democratic Parties . .		1
Karen (Kayin) State National Organization		1
Independents		6
Total	100.0	485

Political Organizations

A total of 93 parties contested the general election of May 1990. By October 1995 the ruling military junta had deregistered all except nine political parties:

Kokang Democracy and Unity Party: Yangon.

Mro (or) Khami National Solidarity Organization: f. 1988; Leader U SAN THA AUNG.

National League for Democracy (NLD): 97B West Shwegondine Rd, Bahan Township, Yangon; f. 1988; initially known as the National United Front for Democracy, and subsequently as the League for Democracy; present name adopted in Sept. 1988; central exec. cttee of 10 mems; Gen. Sec. Daw AUNG SAN SUU KYI; Chair. U AUNG SHWE; Vice-Chair. U TIN OO, U KYI MAUNG.

National Unity Party (NUP): 93C Windermere Rd, Kamayut, Yangon; tel. (1) 278180; f. 1962 as the Burma Socialist Programme Party; sole legal political party until Sept. 1988, when present name was adopted; 15-mem. Cen. Exec. Cttee and 280-mem. Cen. Cttee; Chair. U THA KYAW; Jt Gen. Secs U TUN YI, U THAN TIN.

Shan Nationalities League for Democracy: f. 1988; Leader KHUN HTUN OO.

Shan State Kokang Democratic Party: 140 40 St, Kyauktada; f. 1988; Leader U YANKYIN MAW.

Union Karen (Kayin) League: Saw Toe Lane, Yangon.

Union Pa-O National Organization: f. 1988; Leader U SAN HLA.

Wa National Development Party: Byuhar St, Yangon.

The following parties contested the general election of March 1990 but subsequently had their legal status annulled:

Anti-Fascist People's Freedom League: Bo Aung Kyaw St, Bahan Township, Yangon; f. 1988; assumed name of wartime resistance movement which became Myanmar's major political force after independence; Chair. BO KYAW NYUNT; Gen. Sec. CHO CHO KYAW NYEIN.

Democracy Party: f. 1988; comprises supporters of fmr Prime Minister U NU; Chair. U THU WAI; Vice-Chair. U KHUN YE NAUNG.

Democratic Front for National Reconstruction: Yangon; f. 1988; left-wing; Leader Thakin CHIT MAUNG.

Lahu National Development Party: f. 1988; deregistered 1994; Leader U Daniel Aung.

League for Democracy and Peace: 10 Wingaba Rd, Bahan Township, Yangon; f. 1988; Gen. Sec. U Thein Sein.

Party for National Democracy: Yangon; f. 1988; Chair. Dr Sein Win.

Union National Democracy Party (UNDP): 2–4 Shin Saw Pu Rd, Sanchaung Township, Yangon; f. 1988 by Brig.-Gen. Aung Gyi (fmr Chair. of the National League for Democracy); Chair. U Kyaw Myint Lay.

United League of Democratic Parties: 875 Compound 21, Ledauntkan St, Sa-Hsa Ward, Thingangyun Township, Yangon; f. 1989.

United Nationalities League for Democracy: Yangon; an alliance of parties representing non-Bamar nationalities; won a combined total of 65 seats at the 1990 election.

Other deregistered parties included the Arakan (Rakhine) League for Democracy, the Mon National Democratic Front, the National Democratic Party for Human Rights, the Chin National League for Democracy, the Kachin State National Congress for Democracy, the Zomi National Congress, the Naga Hill Regional Progressive Party, the Kayah State Nationalities League for Democracy, the Ta-ang (Palaung) National League for Democracy, the Democratic Organization for Kayan National Unity, the Graduates' and Old Students' Democratic Association, the Patriotic Old Comrades' League, the Union Danu League for Democracy, the Kamans National League for Democracy, the Mara People's Party and the Karen (Kayin) State National Organization.

The following groups are, or have been, in armed conflict with the Government:

Chin National Army: Chin State.

Chin National Front: f. 1988; forces trained by Kachin Independence Army 1989–91; first party congress 1993; conference in March 1996; carried out an active bombing campaign in 1996–97, mainly in the Chin State; Pres. Thomas Tang No.

Communist Party of Burma (CPB): f. 1939; reorg. 1946; operated clandestinely after 1948; participated after 1986 in jt military operations with sections of the NDF; in 1989 internal dissent resulted in the rebellion of about 80% of CPB members, mostly Wa hill tribesmen and Kokang Chinese; the CPB's military efficacy was thus completely destroyed; Chair. of Cen. Cttee Thakin Ba Thein Tin (exiled).

Democratic Alliance of Burma (DAB): Manerplaw; f. 1988; formed by members of the NDF to incorporate dissident students, monks and expatriates; Pres. Maj.-Gen. Bo Mya; Gen. Sec. U Tin Maung Win; Remaining organizations include:

  All-Burma Student Democratic Front (ABSDF): Dagwin; f. 1988; in 1990 split into two factions, under U Moe Thi Zun and U Naing Aung; the two factions reunited in 1993; Leader U Naing Aung; Sec.-Gen. Aung Thu Nyein.

  Karen (Kayin) National Union (KNU): f. 1948; Chair. Saw Ba Thin; Vice-Chair. Maj.-Gen. Bo Mya; Sec.-Gen. Mahn Sha; Military wing: **Karen (Kayin) National Liberation Army (KNLA)** ; c. 6,000 troops; Chief of Staff Gen. Tamalabaw.

  Karenni (Kayinni) National Progressive Party: agreement with the SLORC signed in March 1995 but subsequently collapsed; resumed fighting in June 1996; Chair. Gen. Aung Than Lay; Military wing: **Karenni (Kayinni) Revolutionary Army**.

God's Army: breakaway faction of the KNU; Leaders Johnny Htoo, Luther Htoo (surrendered to the Thai authorities in Jan. 2001).

National Democratic Front (NDF): f. 1975; aims to establish a federal union based on national self-determination; largely defunct.

National Socialist Council of Nagaland: Sagaing Division; comprises various factions.

Shan State Army (SSA): enlarged in Sept. 1997 through formal alliance between the following:

  Shan State National Army (SSNA): Shan State; f. 1995; breakaway group from Mong Tai Army (MTA); Shan separatists; 5,000–6,000 troops; Leaders Karn Yord, Yee.

  Shan State Peace Council (SSPC): fmrly Shan State Progressive Party; Pres. Hso Hten; Gen. Sec. Karn Yord; cease-fire agreement signed in Sept. 1989, but broken by SSA elements following establishment of above alliance in Sept. 1997; Military wing: original **Shan State Army** ; 5,000 men; Leaders Sai Nong Kai Hpa Pang Hpa.

Other MTA remnants also participated in the alliance.

Vigorous Burmese Student Warriors: f. 1999.

Most of the following groups have signed cease-fire agreements, or reached other means of accommodation, with the ruling military junta (the date given in parentheses indicates the month in which agreement with the junta was concluded):

Democratic Karen (Kayin) Buddhist Organization: Manerplaw; breakaway group from the KNU; Military wing:**Democratic Karen (Kayin) Buddhist Army**.

Kachin Democratic Army: (Jan. 1991); fmrly the 4th Brigade of the Kachin Independence Army; Leader U Zaw Maing.

Kachin Independence Organization (KIO): (Oct. 1993); Chair. Maj.-Gen. Zau Mai; Military wing: **Kachin Independence Army**.

Karen (Kayin) Solidarity Organization (KSO): f. 1997; fmrly All Karen Solidarity and Regeneration Front; breakaway group from the KNU; 21-mem. exec. cttee; advocates nation-wide cease-fire and the settlement of all national problems through negotiations; Pres. Saw W. P. Ni; Sec.-Gen. Mahn Aung Htay.

Karenni (Kayinni) National People's Liberation Front: (May 1994); Leader U Tun Kyaw.

Kayan National Guard: (Feb. 1992).

Kayan New Land Party: (July 1994); Leader U Than Soe Naing.

Myanmar National Democracy Alliance: (March 1989).

National Democracy Alliance Army: (June 1989).

New Democratic Army: Kachin; (Dec. 1989).

New Mon State Party: (June 1995); Chair. Nai Shwe Kyin; Military wing: **Mon National Liberation Army**.

Palaung State Liberation Organization: (April 1991); Military wing: **Paulung State Liberation Army** ; 7,000–8,000 men.

Pa-O National Organization: (Feb. 1991); Chair. Aung Kham Hti; Military wing: **Pa-O National Army**.

Shan State Nationalities Liberation Organization: (Oct. 1994); Chair. U Tha Kalei.

United Wa State Party: (May 1989); fmrly part of the Communist Party of Burma; Military wing: **United Wa State Army** ; 10,000–15,000 men; Leaders Chao Ngi Lai Pao Yu Chang.

Since 1991 the National Coalition Government of the Union of Burma, constituted by representatives elected in the general election of 1990, has served as a government-in-exile:

National Coalition Government of the Union of Burma (NCGUB): Washington Office, 1319 F St NW, Suite 303, Washington, DC 20004, USA; tel. (202) 639–0639; fax (202) 639–0638; e-mail ncgub@ncgub.net; internet www.ncgub.net; Prime Minister Dr Sein Win.

Diplomatic Representation

EMBASSIES IN MYANMAR

Australia: 88 Strand Rd, Yangon; tel. (1) 251810; fax (1) 246159; Ambassador Paul Grigson.

Bangladesh: 11b Thanlwin Rd, Yangon; tel. (1) 515275; fax (1) 515273; e-mail bdootygn@mptmail.mm; Ambassador Ahmed Rahim.

Brunei: 51 Golden Valley, Bahan, Yangon; tel. (1) 510422; fax (1) 512854; Ambassador Pehin Datu Pekerma Dato' Paduka Haji Hussin bin Haji Sulaiman.

Cambodia: 34 Kaba Aye Pagoda Rd, Yangon; tel. (1) 546157; fax (1) 546156; e-mail recyangon@mptmail.net.mm; Ambassador Chea Sophara.

China, People's Republic: 1 Pyidaungsu Yeiktha Rd, Yangon; tel. (1) 221281; fax (1) 227019; Ambassador Li Jinjun.

Egypt: 81 Pyidaungsu Yeiktha Rd, Yangon; tel. (1) 222886; fax (1) 222865; Ambassador Mohamed El Meneissy.

France: 102 Pyidaungsu Yeiktha Rd, POB 858, Yangon; tel. (1) 212523; fax (1) 212527; Ambassador Bernard Amaudric du Chaffaut.

Germany: 32 Nat Mauk St, POB 12, Yangon; tel. (1) 548951; fax (1) 548899; e-mail germemb@mptmail.net.mm; Ambassador Dr Klaus Wild.

India: 545–547 Merchant St, POB 751, Yangon; tel. (1) 82550; fax (1) 89562; e-mail amb.indembygn@mptmail.net.mm; Ambassador Vivek Katju.

Indonesia: 100 Pyidaungsu Yeiktha Rd, POB 1401, Yangon; tel. (1) 254465; fax (1) 254468; Ambassador Nasaruddin M. Koro.

Israel: 15 Khabaung St, Hlaing Township, Yangon; tel. (1) 515115; fax (1) 515116; e-mail yangon@israel.org; Ambassador Yaakov Avrahami Meron.

Italy: 3 Inya Myaing Rd, Golden Valley, Yangon; tel. (1) 527100; fax (1) 514565; e-mail capitani@mptmail.net.mm; Ambassador RAFFAELE MINIERO.

Japan: 100 Natmauk Rd, Yangon; tel. (1) 549644; fax (1) 549643; e-mail embassyofjapan@mptmail.net.mm; Ambassador SHIGERU TSU-MORI.

Korea, Republic: 97 University Ave, Yangon; tel. (1) 515190; fax (1) 513286; e-mail hankuk@koremby.net.mm; Ambassador LEE KYUNG-WOO.

Laos: A1 Diplomatic Quarters, Franser Rd, Yangon; tel. (1) 222482; fax (1) 227446; Ambassador LY BOUNKHAM.

Malaysia: 82 Diplomatic Quarters, Pyidaungsu Yeiktha Rd, Yangon; tel. (1) 220249; fax (1) 221840; e-mail mwyangon@mweb .com.na; Ambassador Dato' CHEAH SAM KIP.

Nepal: 16 Natmauk Yeiktha Rd, POB 84, Tamwe, Yangon; tel. (1) 545880; fax (1) 549803; e-mail rnembygn@datseco.com.mm; Ambassador DIBYA DEV BHATTA.

Pakistan: A4 Diplomatic Quarters, Pyay Rd, Dagon Township, Yangon; tel. (1) 222881; fax (1) 221147; e-mail parepygn@myanmar .com.mm; Ambassador YOUSUF SHAH.

Philippines: 50 Saya San Rd, Bahan Township, Yangon; tel. (1) 558149; fax (1) 558154; e-mail phyangon@mptmail.net.mm; Ambassador PHOEBE ABAYA GOMEZ.

Russia: 38 Sagawa Rd, Yangon; tel. (1) 241955; fax (1) 241953; e-mail rusinmyan@mptmail.net.mm; Ambassador GLEB A. IVA-SHENTSOV.

Serbia and Montenegro: 114A Inya Rd, POB 943, Yangon; tel. (1) 515282; fax (1) 504274; Chargé d'affaires a.i. VLADIMIR STAMENOVIĆ.

Singapore: 326 Pyay Rd, Yangon; tel. (1) 525688; fax (1) 525734; e-mail singemb@seygn.com.mm; internet www.mfa.gov.sg/yangon/; Ambassador SIMON TENSING DE CRUZ.

Sri Lanka: 34 Taw Win Rd, POB 1150, Yangon; tel. (1) 222812; fax (1) 221509; e-mail srilankaemb@mpt.net.mm; Ambassador UBHAYA-SEKERA MAPA.

Thailand: 437 Pyay Rd, 8 Ward, Kamayut Township, Yangon; tel. (1) 512018; fax (1) 527792; e-mail thaiygn@mfa.go.th; Ambassador OUM MAOLANON.

United Kingdom: 80 Strand Rd, POB 638, Yangon; tel. (1) 295300; fax (1) 289566; e-mail chancery@Rangoon.mail.fco.gov.uk; Ambassador VICKY BOWMAN.

USA: 581 Merchant St, POB 521, Yangon; tel. (1) 282055; fax (1) 280409; e-mail rangooninfo@state.gov; Chargé d'affaires a.i. CARMEN MARIA MARTINEZ.

Viet Nam: 36 Wingaba Rd, Bahan Township, Yangon; tel. (1) 548905; fax (1) 549302; e-mail vinaemb.myr@mptmail.net.mm; Ambassador PHAM QUANG KHON.

Judicial System

A new judicial structure was established in March 1974. Its highest organ, composed of members of the People's Assembly, was the Council of People's Justices, which functioned as the central Court of Justice. Below this Council were the state, divisional, township, ward and village tract courts formed with members of local People's Councils. These arrangements ceased to operate following the imposition of military rule in September 1988, when a Supreme Court with five members was appointed. A chief justice, an attorney-general and a deputy attorney-general were also appointed. In March 2003 a deputy chief justice, four more justices and two further deputy attorney-generals were appointed.

Office of the Supreme Court
101 Pansodan St, Kyauktada Township, Yangon; tel. (1) 280751.

Chief Justice: U AUNG TOE.

Attorney-General: U THA TUN.

Religion

Freedom of religious belief and practice is guaranteed. In 1992 an estimated 87.2% of the population were Buddhists, 5.6% Christians, 3.6% Muslims, 1.0% Hindus and 2.6% animists or adherents of other religions.

BUDDHISM

State Sangha Maha Nayaka Committee: c/o Dept of Promotion and Propagation of the Sasana, Kaba Aye Pagoda Precinct, Mayan-gone Township, Yangon; tel. (1) 660759.

CHRISTIANITY

Myanmar Naing-ngan Khrityan Athin-dawmyar Kaung-si (Myanmar Council of Churches): Myanmar Ecumenical Sharing Centre, 601 Pyay Rd, University PO, Yangon 11041; tel. (1) 533957; fax (1) 296848; f. 1974 to succeed the Burma Christian Council; 13 mem. churches; Pres. Rev. SAW MAR GAY GYI; Gen. Sec. Rt Rev. SMITH N. ZA THAWNG.

The Roman Catholic Church
Myanmar comprises three archdioceses and nine dioceses. At 31 December 2000 an estimated 1.1% of the total population were adherents.

Catholic Bishops' Conference of Myanmar
292 Pyi Rd, POB 1080, Sanchaung PO, Yangon 11111; tel. (1) 237198.
f. 1982; Pres. Rt Rev. CHARLES MAUNG BO (Bishop of Pathein).

Archbishop of Mandalay: Most Rev. ALPHONSE U THAN AUNG, Archbishop's House, 82nd and 25th St, Mandalay 05071; tel. (2) 36369.

Archbishop of Taunggyi: Most Rev. MATTHIAS U SHWE, Archbishop's Office, Bayint Naung Rd, Taunggyi 06011; tel. (81) 21689; fax (81) 22164.

Archbishop of Yangon: (vacant), Archbishop's House, 289 Theinbyu St, Botataung, Yangon; tel. (1) 246710.

The Anglican Communion
Anglicans are adherents of the Church of the Province of Myanmar, comprising six dioceses. The Province was formed in February 1970, and contained an estimated 45,000 adherents in 1985.

Archbishop of Myanmar and Bishop of Yangon: Most Rev. SAMUEL SAN SI HTAY, Bishopscourt, 140 Pyidaungsu Yeiktha Rd, Dagon PO (11191), Yangon; tel. (1) 285379; fax (1) 251405.

Protestant Churches

Lutheran Bethlehem Church: 181–183 Theinbyu St, Mingala Taung Nyunt PO 11221, POB 773, Yangon; tel. (1) 246585; Pres. Rev. JENSON RAJAN ANDREWS.

Myanmar Baptist Convention: 143 Minye Kyawswa Rd, POB 506, Yangon; tel. (1) 223231; fax (1) 221465; e-mail mbc<mbc@ mptmail.net.mm; f. 1865 as Burma Baptist Missionary Convention; present name adopted 1954; 550,104 mems (1994); Pres. Rev. U THA DIN; Gen. Sec. Rev. Dr SIMON PAU KHAN EN.

Myanmar Methodist Church: Methodist Headquarters, 22 Signal Pagoda Rd, Yangon; Bishop ZOTHAN MAWIA.

Presbyterian Church of Myanmar: Synod Office, Falam, Chin State; 22,000 mems; Rev. SUN KANGLO.

Other denominations active in Myanmar include the **Lisu Christian Church** and the **Salvation Army**.

The Press

DAILIES

Botahtaung (The Vanguard): 22–30 Strand Rd, Botahtaung PO, POB 539, Yangon; tel. (1) 274310; daily; Myanmar.

Guardian: 392–396 Merchant St, Botahtaung PO, POB 1522, Yangon; tel. (1) 270150; daily; English.

Kyehmon (The Mirror): 77 52nd St, Dazundaung PO, POB 819, Yangon; tel. (1) 282777; daily; Myanmar.

Myanmar Alin (New Light of Myanmar): 58 Komin Kochin Rd, Bahan PO, POB 21, Yangon; tel. (1) 250777; f. 1963; fmrly Loktha Pyithu Nezin (Working People's Daily); organ of the SPDC; morning; Myanmar; Chief Editor U SOE MYINT; circ. 400,000.

New Light of Myanmar: 22–30 Strand Rd, Yangon; tel. (1) 297028; internet www.myanmar.com/nlm; f. 1963; fmrly Working People's Daily; organ of the SPDC; morning; English; Chief Editor U KYAW MIN; circ. 14,000.

PERIODICALS

A Hla Thit (New Beauty): 46 90th St, Yangon; tel. (1) 287106; international news.

Dana Business Magazine: 72 8th Street, Lanmadaw Township, Yangon; tel. and fax (1) 224010; e-mail dana@mptmail.net.mm; economic; Editor-in-Chief WILLIAM CHEN.

Do Kyaung Tha: Myawaddy Press, 184 32nd St, Yangon; tel. (1) 274655; f. 1965; monthly; Myanmar and English; circ. 17,000.

Gita Padetha: Yangon; journal of Myanma Music Council; circ. 10,000.

Guardian Magazine: 392/396 Merchant St, Botahtaung PO, POB 1522, Yangon; tel. (1) 296510; f. 1953; nationalized 1964; monthly; English; literary; circ. 11,600.

Kyee Pwar Yay (Prosperity): 296 Bo Sun Pat St, Yangon; tel. (1) 278100; economic; Editor-in-Chief U Myat Khine.

Moethaukpan (Aurora): Myawaddy Press, 184 32nd St, Yangon; tel. (1) 274655; f. 1980; monthly; Myanmar and English; circ. 27,500.

Myanma Dana (Myanmar's Economy): 210A, 36th St, Kyauktada PO, Yangon; tel. (1) 284660; economic; Editor-in-Chief U Thiha Saw.

Myanmar Morning Post: Yangon; f. 1998; weekly; Chinese; news; circ. 5,000.

Myanmar Times & Business Review: Level 1, 5 Signal Pagoda Rd, Dagon Township, Yangon; tel. (1) 242711; fax (1) 242669; e-mail myanmartimes@mptmail.net.mm; internet www.myanmar.com/myanmartimes; f. 2000; Editor-in-Chief Ross Dunkley.

Myawaddy Journal: Myawaddy Press, 184 32nd St, Yangon; tel. (1) 274655; f. 1989; fortnightly; news; circ. 8,700.

Myawaddy Magazine: Myawaddy Press, 184 32nd St, Yangon; tel. (1) 274655; f. 1952; monthly; literary magazine; circ. 4,200.

Ngwetaryi Magazine: Myawaddy Press, 184 32nd St, Yangon; tel. (1) 274655; f. 1961; monthly; cultural; circ. 3,400.

Pyinnya Lawka Journal: 529 Merchant St, Yangon; tel. (1) 283611; publ. by Sarpay Beikman Management Board; quarterly; circ. 18,000.

Shwe Thwe: 529 Merchant St, Yangon; tel. (1) 283611; weekly; bilingual children's journal; publ. by Sarpay Beikman Management Board; circ. 100,000.

Taw Win Journal (Royal Journal): 149 37th St, Yangon; news; Editor-in-Chief Soe Thein.

Teza: Myawaddy Press, 184 32nd St, Yangon; tel. (1) 274655; f. 1965; monthly; English and Myanmar; pictorial publication for children; circ. 29,500.

Thwe Thauk Magazine: Myawaddy Press, 185 48th St, Yangon; f. 1946; monthly; literary.

Ya Nant Thit (New Fragrance): 186 39th St, Yangon; tel. (1) 276799; international news; Editor-in-Chief U Chit Win Mg.

NEWS AGENCIES

Myanmar News Agency (MNA): 212 Theinbyu Rd, Botahtaung, Yangon; tel. (1) 270893; f. 1963; govt-controlled; Chief Editors U Zaw Min Thein (domestic section), U Kyaw Min (external section).

Foreign Bureaux

Agence France-Presse (AFP) (France): 12L Pyithu Lane, 7th Mile, Yangon; tel. (1) 661069; Correspondent U Khin Maung Thwin.

Agenzia Nazionale Stampa Associata (ANSA) (Italy): POB 270, Yangon; tel. (1) 290039; fax (1) 290804; Rep. (vacant).

Associated Press (AP) (USA): 283 U Wisara Rd, Sanchaung PO 11111, Yangon; tel. (1) 527014; Rep. Aye Aye Win.

Xinhua (New China) News Agency (People's Republic of China): 105 Leeds Rd, Yangon; tel. (1) 221400; Correspondent Zhang Yuhfei.

Reuters (UK) and **UPI** (USA) are also represented in Myanmar.

Publishers

Hanthawaddy Press: 157 Bo Aung Gyaw St, Yangon; f. 1889; textbooks, multilingual dictionaries; Man. Editor U Zaw Win.

Knowledge Publishing House: 130 Bo Gyoke Aung San St, Yegyaw, Yangon; art, education, religion, politics and social sciences.

Kyipwaye Press: 84th St, Letsaigan, Mandalay; tel. (2) 21003; arts, travel, religion, fiction and children's.

Myawaddy Press: 184 32nd St, Yangon; tel. (1) 285996; journals and magazines; CEO U Thein Sein.

Sarpay Beikman Management Board: 529 Merchant St, Yangon; tel. (1) 283611; f. 1947; encyclopaedias, literature, fine arts and general; also magazines and translations; Chair. Aung Htay.

Shumawa Press: 146 West Wing, Bogyoke Aung San Market, Yangon; mechanical engineering.

Shwepyidan: 12A Haiaban, Yegwaw Quarter, Yangon; politics, religion, law.

Smart and Mookerdum: 221 Sule Pagoda Rd, Yangon; arts, cookery, popular science.

Thu Dhama Wadi Press: 55–56 Maung Khine St, POB 419, Yangon; f. 1903; religious; Propr U Tin Htoo; Man. U Pan Maung.

Government Publishing House

Printing and Publishing Enterprise: 228 Theinbyu St, Yangon; tel. (1) 294645; Man. Dir U Myint Thein.

PUBLISHERS' ASSOCIATION

Myanma Publishers' Union: 146 Bogyoke Market, Yangon.

Broadcasting and Communications

TELECOMMUNICATIONS

Posts and Telecommunications Department: Ministry of Communications, Posts and Telegraphs, 125 Ground Floor, Pansodan St, Yangon; tel. (1) 292019; fax (1) 292977; internet www.mptp.gov.mm; Dir-Gen. of Posts and Telecommunications Dept U Khin Soe.

Myanma Posts and Telecommunications (MPT): 43 Bo Aung Gyaw St, Kyauktada Township, Yangon; tel. (1) 285840; fax (1) 290429; internet www.mpt.net.mm; Man. Dir Col Maung Maung Tin.

BROADCASTING

Radio

Myanma TV and Radio Department (MTRD): 426 Pyay Rd, Kamayut 11041, Yangon; POB 1432, Yangon 11181; tel. (1) 531850; fax (1) 530211; radio transmissions began in 1937; broadcasts in Bamar, Arakanese (Rakhine), Shan, Karen (Kayin), Kachin, Kayah, Chin, Mon and English; Dir-Gen. U Kyi Lwin; Dir of Radio Broadcasting U Ko Ko Htway.

In 1992 the National Coalition Government of the Union of Burma (NCGUB) began broadcasting daily to Myanmar from Norway under the name Democratic Voice of Burma (DVB). In 1995 it was believed that the DVB was being operated by Myanma student activists from the Norway-Burma Council, without any formal control by the NCGUB.

Television

Myanma TV and Radio Department (MTRD): Pyay Rd, Kamayut 11041, Yangon; POB 1432, Yangon 11181; tel. (1) 531014; fax (1) 530211; colour television transmissions began in 1980; Dir-Gen. U Kyi Lwin; Dir of Television Broadcasting U Phone Myint.

TV Myawaddy: Hmawbi, Hmawbi Township, Yangon; tel. (1) 620270; f. 1995; military broadcasting station transmitting programmes via satellite.

Finance

(cap. = capital; res = reserves; dep. = deposits; m. = million; brs = branches; amounts in kyats)

BANKING

In July 1990 new banking legislation was promulgated, reorganizing the operations of the Central Bank, establishing a state-owned development institution, the Myanma Agricultural and Rural Development Bank, and providing for the formation of private-sector banks and the opening of branches of foreign banks.

Central Bank

Central Bank of Myanmar: 26A Settmu Rd, POB 184, Yankin Township, Yangon; tel. (1) 543511; fax (1) 543621; e-mail cbm.ygn@mptmail-net.mm; f. 1968; bank of issue; cap. 350m., dep. 13,545m. Gov. U Kyi Aye; 37 brs.

State Banks

Myanma Economic Bank (MEB): 1–19 Sule Pagoda Rd, Yangon; tel. (1) 289345; fax (1) 283679; provides domestic banking network throughout the country; Man. Dir U Kyaw Kyaw.

Myanma Foreign Trade Bank: 80–86 Maha Bandoola Garden St, POB 203, Yangon; tel. (1) 284911; fax (1) 289585; e-mail mftb-hoygn@mptmail.net.mm; f. 1976; cap. 110m., res 483.9m., dep. 2,425.9m. (March 1999); handles all foreign exchange and international banking transactions; Chair. U Ko Ko Gyi; Sec. U Tin Maung Aye.

Development Banks

Myanma Agricultural and Rural Development Bank (MARDB): 1–7 cnr of Latha St and Kanna Rd, Yangon; tel. (1) 226734; f. 1953 as State Agricultural Bank, reconstituted as above 1990; state-owned; cap. 60.0m., dep. 615.6m. (Sept. 1993); Man. Dir U Chit Swe.

Myanma Investment and Commercial Bank (MICB): 170/176 Bo Aung Kyaw St, Botataung Township, Yangon; tel. (1) 250509; fax (1) 281775; e-mail micb.hoygn@mpt-mail.net.mm; f. 1989; state-owned; cap. 400m., res 786m., dep. 7,035m. (March 2000); Chair. and Man. Dir U Tun Chun; 2 brs.

Private Banks

By February 1996 16 private banks were established, 14 in Yangon and one each in Mandalay and Taunggyi.

Asia Wealth Bank: 638 cnr of Maha Bandoola St and 22nd St, Latha Township, Yangon; tel. (1) 243700; fax (1) 245456; Chair. Win Maung; Vice-Chair. Aik Htun; 38 brs.

Asian Yangon International Bank Ltd: 319/321 Maha Bandoola St, Botataung Township, Yangon; tel. (1) 245825; fax (1) 245865.

Co-operative Bank Ltd: 334–336 Kanna Rd, Yangon; tel. (1) 272641; fax (1) 283063; Gen. Man. U Nyunt Hlaing.

First Private Bank Ltd (FPB): 619–621 Merchant St, Pabedan Township, Yangon; tel. (1) 289929; fax (1) 242320; e-mail fpb.hq@mptmail.net.mm; f. 1992 as the first publicly-subscribed bank; fmrly the Commercial and Development Bank Ltd; provides loans to private business and small-scale industrial sectors; cap. 654.06m. (March 2001); Chair. Dr Sein Maung; 15 brs.

Innwa Bank Ltd: cnr 35th St and Merchant St, Yangon.

Kanbawza Bank Ltd: Kanbawza Bank Headquarters Bldg, Yangon; Chair. U Aung Ko Win.

Myanma Citizens Bank Ltd (MCB): 383 Maha Bandoola St, Kyauktada Township, Yangon; tel. (1) 273512; fax (1) 245932; f. 1991; Chair. U Hla Tin.

Myanma Oriental Bank Ltd: 166–168 Pansodan St, Kyauktada Township, Yangon; tel. (1) 246594; fax (1) 253217; e-mail mobl.ygn@mptmail.net.mm; Chair. U Tin U.

Myanma Universal Bank: 81 Theinbyu Rd, Yangon; tel. (1) 297339; fax (1) 245449; f. 1995.

Myanmar Industrial Development Bank Ltd: 26–42 Pansodan St, Kyauktada Township, Yangon; tel. (1) 249536; fax (1) 249529; f. 1996; cap. US $335m.

Myanmar May Flower Bank Ltd: 1B Yadanar Housing Project, 9 Mile Pyay Rd, Mayangone Township, Yangon; tel. (1) 666112; fax (1) 666110; e-mail mmb-hq@mptmail.net.mm; Chair. U Kyaw Win.

Myawaddy Bank Ltd: 24–26 Sule Pagoda Rd, Kyauktada Township, Yangon; tel. (1) 283665; fax (1) 250093; e-mail mwdbankygn@mtpt400.stems.com; Gen. Mans U Tun Kyi, U Mya Min.

Prime Commercial Bank Ltd: 437 Pyay Rd, Kamayut Township, Yangon; tel. (1) 525990; fax (1) 522420; f. 1994; cap. 122.5m., dep. 358m. Chair. Dr Aung Khin; Man. Dir U Maung Maung Han; 2 brs.

Tun Foundation Bank Ltd: 165–167 Bo Aung Gyaw St, Yangon; tel. (1) 270710; Chair. U Thein Tun.

Yadanabon Bank Ltd: 26th St, cnr of 84th and 85th Sts, Mandalay; tel. (2) 23577.

Yangon City Bank Ltd: 12–18 Sepin St, Kyauktada Township, Yangon; tel. (1) 289256; fax (1) 289231; f. 1993; auth. cap. 500m. 100% owned by the Yangon City Development Committee; Chair. Col Myint Aung.

Yoma Bank Ltd: 1 Kungyan St, Mingala Taung Nyunt Township, Yangon; tel. (1) 242138; fax (1) 246548; Chair. Serge Pun.

Foreign Banks

By late 1996 more than 20 foreign banks had opened representative offices in Yangon. These included the Bank of Tokyo-Mitsubishi (Japan), the Development Bank of Singapore, Keppel Bank of Singapore, the Standard Chartered Bank (UK), the Thai Military Bank (Thailand), Fuji Bank (Japan), Sumitomo Bank (Japan), Tokai Bank (Japan) and Sanwa Bank (Japan).

STOCK EXCHANGE

Myanmar Securities Exchange Centre: 1st Floor, 21–25 Sule Pagoda Rd, Yangon; tel. (1) 283984; f. 1996; jt venture between Japan's Daiwa Institute of Research and Myanma Economic Bank; Man. Dir Eiji Suzuki.

INSURANCE

Myanma Insurance: 627–635 Merchant St, Yangon; tel. (1) 283376; fax (1) 289596; e-mail MYANSURE@mptmail.net.com; f. 1976; govt-controlled; Man. Dir Col Thew Lwin.

Trade and Industry

GOVERNMENT AGENCIES

Inspection and Agency Service: 383 Maha Bandoola St, Yangon; tel. (1) 276048; fax (1) 284823; works on behalf of state-owned enterprises to promote business with foreign companies; Man. Dir U Ohn Khin.

Myanmar Investment Commission: Yangon; Chair. U Thaung; Vice-Chair. Maj.-Gen. Tin Htut.

Union of Myanmar Economic Holdings: 72–74 Shwadagon Pagoda Rd, Yangon; tel. (1) 78905; f. 1990; public holding co; auth. cap. 10,000m. kyats; 40% of share capital subscribed by the Ministry of Defence and 60% by members of the armed forces.

CHAMBER OF COMMERCE

Chamber of Commerce and Industry: 504–506 Merchant St, Kyauktada Township, Yangon; tel. (1) 243151; fax (2) 248177; f. 1919; Gen. Sec. Zaw Min Win.

UTILITIES

Electricity

Myanma Electric Power Enterprise (MEPE): 197–199 Lower Kyimyindine Rd, Yangon; tel. (1) 220918; Man. Dir U Thaung Sein.

Water

Mandalay City Development Committee (Water and Sanitation Dept): cnr of 26th and 72nd Sts, Mandalay; tel. (2) 36173; f. 1992; Head of Water and Sanitation Dept U Tun Kyi.

Yangon City Development Committee (Water and Sanitation Dept): City Hall, Yangon; tel. (1) 289781; fax (1) 284910; f. 1992; Head of Water and Sanitation Dept U Zaw Win.

CO-OPERATIVES

In 1993/94 there were 22,800 co-operative societies, with a turnover of 23,603m. kyats. This was estimated to have increased to 24,760 societies, with a turnover of 20,927m. kyats, in 1994/95.

Central Co-operative Society (CCS) Council: 334/336 Strand Rd, Yangon; tel. (1) 274550; Chair. U Than Hlang; Sec. U Tin Latt.

Co-operative Department: 259–263 Bogyoke Aung San Rd, Yangon; tel. (1) 277096; Dir-Gen. U Maung Hti.

WORKERS' AND PEASANTS' COUNCILS

Conditions of work are stipulated in the Workers' Rights and Responsibilities Law, enacted in 1964. Regional workers' councils ensure that government directives are complied with, and that targets are met on a regional basis. In January 1985 there were 293 workers' councils in towns, with more than 1.8m. members. They are co-ordinated by a central workers' organization in Yangon, formed in 1968 to replace trade union organizations which had been abolished in 1964. The Myanma Federation of Trade Unions operates in exile.

Peasants' Asiayone (Organization): Yangon; tel. (1) 82819; f. 1977; peasants' representative org. Chair. Brig.-Gen. U Than Nyunt; Sec. U San Tun.

Workers' Unity Organization: Central Organizing Committee, 61 Thein Byu St, Yangon; tel. (1) 284043; f. 1968; workers' representative org. Chair. U Ohn Kyaw; Sec. U Nyunt Thein.

Transport

All railways, domestic air services, passenger and freight road transport services and inland water facilities are owned and operated by state-controlled enterprises.

RAILWAYS

The railway network comprised 3,955 km of track in 1996/97, most of which was single track.

Myanma Railways: Bogyoke Aung San St, POB 118, Yangon; tel. (1) 280508; fax (1) 284220; f. 1877; govt-operated; Man. Dir U Aung Thein; Gen. Man. U Thaung Lwin.

ROADS

In 1996 the total length of the road network in Myanmar was an estimated 28,200 km, of which an estimated 3,440 km were paved. In 2001/02 the total length of road accessible to motor vehicles was 28,598 km.

Road Transportation Department: 375 Bogyoke Aung San St, Yangon; tel. (1) 284426; fax (1) 289716; f. 1963; controls passenger and freight road transport; in 1993/94 operated 1,960 haulage trucks and 928 passenger buses; Man. Dir U OHN MYINT.

INLAND WATERWAYS

The principal artery of traffic is the River Ayeyarwady (Irrawaddy), which is navigable as far as Bhamo, about 1,450 km inland, while parts of the Thanlwin and Chindwinn rivers are also navigable.

Inland Water Transport: 50 Pansodan St, Yangon; tel. (1) 222399; fax (1) 286500; govt-owned; operates cargo and passenger services throughout Myanmar; 36m. passengers and 3.1m. tons of freight were carried in 1993/94; Man. Dir U KHIN MAUNG.

SHIPPING

Yangon is the chief port. Vessels with a displacement of up to 15,000 tons can be accommodated.

In 2001 the Myanma merchant fleet totalled 124 vessels, with a combined displacement of 379,819 grt.

Myanma Port Authority: 10 Pansodan St, POB 1, Yangon; tel. (1) 280094; fax (1) 295134; f. 1880; general port and harbour duties; Man. Dir U TIN OO; Gen. Man. U HLAING SOON.

Myanma Five Star Line: 132–136 Theinbyu Rd, POB 1221, Yangon; tel. (1) 295279; fax (1) 297669; e-mail mfsl.myr@mptmail .net.mm; f. 1959; cargo services to the Far East and Australia; Man. Dir U KHIN MAUNG KYI; Gen. Man. U KYAW ZAW; fleet of 26 coastal and ocean-going vessels.

CIVIL AVIATION

Mingaladon Airport, near Yangon, is equipped to international standards. The newly built Mandalay International Airport was inaugurated in September 2000. In December 1993 Kyauktheingan in Bago (Pegu) was selected as the location of the proposed Hantha-waddy international airport.

Department of Civil Aviation: Mingaladon Airport, Yangon; tel. (1) 662700; Dir-Gen. U TIN AYE.

Air Mandalay: 146 Dhammazedi Rd, Bahan Township, Yangon; tel. (1) 525488; fax (1) 525937; e-mail airmandalay@myanmars.net; internet www.airmandalay.com; f. 1994; Myanmar's first airline; jt venture between Air Mandalay Holding and Myanma Airways; operates domestic services and regional services to Chiang Mai and Phuket, Thailand, and Siem Reap, Cambodia; Chair. THURA U WIN MYINT; Man. Dir ERIC KANG; 242 employees.

Myanmar Airways (MA): 123 Sule Pagoda Rd, Yangon; tel. (1) 80710; fax (1) 255305; e-mail 8mpr@maiair.com.mm; internet www .maiair.com; f. 1993; govt-controlled; internal network operates services to 21 airports; Chief Operating Officer PRITHPAL SINGH.

Myanmar Airways International (MAI): 08–02 Sakura Tower, 339 Bogyoke Aung San Rd, Yangon; tel. (1) 255260; fax (1) 255305; e-mail 8mpr@maiair.com.mm; internet www.maiair.com; f. 1993; govt-owned; established by Myanmar Airways in jt venture with Highsonic Enterprises of Singapore to provide international services; operates services to Bangkok, Dhaka, Hong Kong, Kuala Lumpur and Singapore; Man. Dir GERARD DE VAZ.

Tourism

Yangon, Mandalay, Taunggyi and Pagan possess outstanding palaces, Buddhist temples and shrines. The number of foreign visitors to Myanmar declined severely following the suppression of the democracy movement in 1988. In the early 1990s, however, the Government actively promoted the revival of the tourism industry, and between 1995 and 1998 alone the number of hotel rooms almost doubled, reaching a total of nearly 14,000. In 2000 there were 206,243 foreign tourist arrivals (compared with only 5,000 in 1989). In 1999 revenue from tourism totalled an estimated US \$35m.

Myanmar Hotels and Tourism Services: 77–91 Sule Pagoda Rd, Yangon 11141; tel. (1) 282013; fax (1) 254417; e-mail mtt.mht@ mptmail.net.mm; govt-controlled; manages all hotels, tourist offices, tourist department stores and duty-free shops; Man. Dir U KYI HTUN.

Myanmar Tourism Promotion Board: 5 Signal Pagoda Rd, Yangon; tel. (1) 243639; fax (1) 245001; e-mail mtpb@mptmail.net .mm; internet www.myanmar-tourism.com.

Myanmar Travels and Tours: 77–91 Sule Pagoda Rd, POB 559, Yangon 11141; tel. (1) 287993; fax (1) 254417; e-mail mtt.mht@ mptmail.net.mm; govt tour operator and travel agent; handles all travel arrangements for groups and individuals; Gen. Man. U HTAY AUNG.

NAMIBIA

Introductory Survey

Location, Climate, Language, Religion, Flag, Capital

The Republic of Namibia (formerly known as South West Africa) lies in south-western Africa, with South Africa to the south and south-east, Botswana to the east and Angola to the north. The country has a long coastline on the Atlantic Ocean. The narrow Caprivi Strip, between Angola and Botswana in the north-east, extends Namibia to the Zambezi river, giving it a border with Zambia. The climate is generally hot, although coastal areas have relatively mild temperatures. Most of the country is subject to drought and unreliable rainfall. The average annual rainfall varies from about 50 mm (2 ins) on the coast to 550 mm (22 ins) in the north. The arid Namib Desert stretches along the west coast, while the easternmost area is part of the Kalahari Desert. The official language is English; however, most of the African ethnic groups have their own languages. At the 1991 census the most widely-spoken languages were Ovambo (used by 50.6% of the population), Nama (12.5%) and Kavango (9.7%). In addition, Afrikaans and German are widely used. About 90% of the population are Christians. The national flag (proportions 2 by 3) comprises a blue triangle in the upper hoist corner, bearing a yellow sun (a blue-bordered disc, surrounded by 12 triangular rays), separated from a green triangle in the lower fly corner by a white-bordered, broad red stripe. The capital is Windhoek.

Recent History

South West Africa became a German possession in 1884. The territory excluded the port of Walvis Bay and 12 small offshore islands, previously annexed by the United Kingdom and subsequently incorporated in South Africa. During the First World War South African forces occupied South West Africa in 1914, and in 1915 Germany surrendered the territory. In 1920 the League of Nations entrusted South Africa with a mandate to administer South West Africa. In 1925 South Africa granted a Constitution giving limited self-government to European (white) inhabitants only. No trusteeship agreement was concluded with the UN after the Second World War, and in 1946 the UN refused South Africa's request for permission to annex South West Africa. In 1949 the territory's European voters were granted representation in the South African Parliament. In 1950 the International Court of Justice (ICJ) issued a ruling that the area should remain under international mandate and that South Africa should submit it to UN control. South Africa refused to comply with this judgment. In October 1966 South Africa's security and apartheid laws were extended to South West Africa, retrospective to 1950.

Opposition within South West Africa to South African rule led to the establishment of two African nationalist organizations, the South West Africa People's Organisation (SWAPO—founded in 1957 as the Ovamboland People's Congress) and the South West African National Union (SWANU—formed in 1959). During 1966 SWAPO's military wing, the People's Liberation Army of Namibia (PLAN), launched an armed struggle for the liberation of the territory. PLAN operated from bases in Angola and Zambia, and was controlled by the external wing of SWAPO (led by Sam Nujoma—the organization's President from 1959). SWAPO also had a legal wing, which was tolerated in South West Africa.

South Africa was consistently criticized at the UN over its extension of apartheid to the territory. The UN General Assembly voted to terminate South Africa's mandate in October 1966, established a UN Council for South West Africa in May 1967, and changed the name of the territory to Namibia in June 1968. In 1971 the ICJ ruled that South Africa's presence was illegal. In 1973 the UN General Assembly recognized SWAPO as 'the authentic representative of the Namibian people', and appointed a UN Commissioner for Namibia to undertake 'executive and administrative tasks'.

In 1973 South Africa established a short-lived multiracial Advisory Council for the territory, but this was boycotted by SWAPO and most influential Africans. A multiracial constitutional conference on the territory's future, organized by the all-white South West Africa Legislative Assembly, was convened in Windhoek in September 1975, attended by representatives of the territory's 11 main ethnic groups. However, neither the UN nor the Organization of African Unity (OAU, now the African Union, see p. 130) recognized this so-called Turnhalle Conference, owing to its ethnic and non-democratic basis, and the legal wing of SWAPO refused to attend. In 1976 and 1977 proposals for procedures whereby Namibia was to achieve independence and formulate a constitution were made by the Turnhalle Conference, but rejected by SWAPO, the UN and the OAU. In September 1977 South Africa appointed an Administrator-General to govern the territory. In November the Turnhalle Conference was dissolved, and the Democratic Turnhalle Alliance (DTA), a coalition of conservative political groups representing the ethnic groups involved in the Turnhalle Conference, was formed.

In early 1978 talks were held between South Africa, SWAPO and a 'contact group' comprising Canada, France, the Federal Republic of Germany, the United Kingdom and the USA (at the time the five Western members of the UN Security Council). In March the contact group presented proposals for a Namibian settlement, including the holding of UN-supervised elections, a reduction in the numbers of South African troops in Namibia and the release of political prisoners. In September these proposals, conditionally accepted by both South Africa and SWAPO, were incorporated in UN Security Council Resolution 435. However, South Africa continued to implement its own internal solution for Namibia with an election for a Constituent Assembly in December. The election was contested by five parties, but boycotted notably by SWAPO. Of the 50 seats in the Assembly, 41 were won by the DTA. In May 1979 South Africa unilaterally established a legislative National Assembly, without executive powers, from the existing Constituent Assembly. In June, following the detention of about 40 of its activists, the legal wing of SWAPO closed its offices in Windhoek and dissolved its executive council.

All-party negotiations, held under UN auspices in Geneva, Switzerland, in January 1981, failed in their aim of arranging a cease-fire and eventual UN-supervised elections. Later in 1981 the contact group attempted to secure support for a three-phase independence plan. However, South Africa's insistence (supported by the US Government) that any withdrawal of South African forces must be linked to the withdrawal of Cuban troops from Angola was rejected by Angola and the UN. Meanwhile, the Ministerial Council, formed in 1980 and chaired by Dirk Mudge (also Chairman of the DTA), assumed much of the Administrator-General's executive power in September 1981. However, the DTA was seriously weakened in early 1982 by the resignation of its President, Peter Kalangula, the leader of the only significant movement, other than SWAPO, supported by the Ovambo (Namibia's largest ethnic group). The Ministerial Council was dissolved in January 1983, when, after several months of disagreement with the South African Government regarding the future role of the DTA in the territory, Mudge resigned as Council Chairman. South Africa disbanded the National Assembly and resumed direct rule of Namibia, with Willem van Niekerk as Administrator-General.

The Multi-Party Conference (MPC) was established in November 1983, grouping, initially, seven internal political parties. Boycotted by SWAPO, it appeared to be promoted by South Africa as a means of settling the independence issue outside the framework of Resolution 435, and of reducing SWAPO's dominance in any future post-independence government for Namibia. None the less, South Africa continued to negotiate on the independence issue with SWAPO and Angola. In February 1984 South Africa and Angola agreed to a cease-fire on the Angola–Namibia border, and set up a joint commission to monitor the withdrawal of all South African troops from Angola. Angola undertook to ensure that neither Cuban nor SWAPO forces would move into the areas vacated by the South African troops. Nujoma pledged support for the agreement, but asserted that SWAPO would not abandon the armed conflict until there was a cease-fire in Namibia itself and until South Africa had agreed to UN-supervised elections. Discussions on the independence issue in mid-1984, involving van Niekerk, SWAPO and the MPC, ended inconclusively, as did negotiations in 1984–86 between the South African Government and the US Assistant Secretary of State for African Affairs.

In April 1985 the South African Government accepted a proposal by the MPC for a 'Transitional Government of National Unity' (TGNU) in Namibia. This was formally established in Windhoek in June, although the arrangement was condemned in advance by the contact group and was declared 'null and void' by the UN Secretary-General. The TGNU consisted of an executive Cabinet, drawn from a National Assembly of 62 members who were appointed from among the parties constituting the MPC. Its establishment was accompanied by the proclamation of a 'bill of rights', drafted by the MPC, which prohibited racial discrimination. A Constitutional Council was also established to prepare a constitution for an independent Namibia. The South African Government retained responsibility for foreign affairs, defence and internal security, and all legislation was to be subject to approval by the Administrator-General. Louis Pienaar replaced van Niekerk in this post in July.

In March 1986 South Africa stipulated a deadline of 1 August for the implementation of Resolution 435, on condition that all Cuban troops be withdrawn from Angola; this was, however, abandoned in June, on the grounds that no discernible preparation had been made to comply with this provision. In January 1987 SWAPO guerrillas resumed operations in white-owned farming areas for the first time since 1983. During 1987, following the liberalization of labour laws and the legalization of trade unions for black workers in 1986, the trade union movement became increasingly active. In mid-1987 the Constitutional Council published a draft document; however, South Africa indicated that it could not accept the lack of a guarantee of minority rights in the proposal. In March 1988 the Namibian Supreme Court declared the 'AG8' law of 1980 (providing for the election of 'second-tier' legislative assemblies and for the administration of education and health facilities on an ethnic, rather than a geographical, basis) to be in conflict with the 1985 'bill of rights'. In April 1988 President P. W. Botha of South Africa expressed impatience at the slow progress towards establishing a permanent constitution, and granted the Administrator-General powers to restrict newspapers that were deemed to promote 'subversion and terrorism', and also to organize ethnically-based local elections.

Both Angola and Cuba were reported in January 1988 to have accepted, in principle, the US demand for a complete withdrawal of Cuban troops from Angola, but they reiterated that this would be conditional on the cessation of South African support for the insurgent União Nacional para a Independência Total de Angola (UNITA). In July Angola, Cuba and South Africa reached agreement on 14 'essential principles' for a peaceful settlement, and in August it was agreed that the implementation of Resolution 435 would begin on 1 November. Also in August the Governments of South Africa, Cuba and Angola announced a cease-fire, to which SWAPO agreed, and South Africa undertook to withdraw all its forces from Angola. The November deadline was not met, owing to failure to agree on an exact schedule for the evacuation of Cuban troops from Angola. In December Angola, Cuba and South Africa signed a formal treaty designating 1 April 1989 as the implementation date for Resolution 435 and establishing a joint commission to monitor the treaty's implementation. (A further agreement was signed by Angola and Cuba, requiring the evacuation of all Cuban troops from Angola by July 1991.) A Constituent Assembly was to be elected in Namibia on 1 November 1989. South African forces in Namibia were to be confined to their bases, and their numbers reduced to 1,500 by July 1989; all South African troops were to have been withdrawn from Namibia one week after the November election. SWAPO forces were to be confined to bases in Angola in April, before being disarmed and repatriated. A multinational military observer force, the UN Transition Assistance Group (UNTAG), was to monitor the South African withdrawal, and civilian administrators and an international police force were to supervise the election. At the end of February the TGNU was formally disbanded, and on 1 March the National Assembly voted to dissolve itself: until independence the territory was governed by the Administrator-General, in consultation with a Special Representative of the UN Secretary-General, Martti Ahtisaari. Pienaar and Ahtisaari were to be jointly responsible for arranging the November election.

Implementation of Resolution 435 was disrupted by large-scale movements, from April 1989, of SWAPO guerrillas into Namibia from Angola, as a result of which the South African

security forces, with the consent of the UN, suspended the cease-fire. About 280 SWAPO troops were reported to have been killed in the subsequent conflict. Following negotiations by the joint monitoring commission, conditions were arranged for an evacuation of the SWAPO forces to Angola, and in May the commission certified the cease-fire to be once more in force. In June most racially-discriminatory legislation was repealed, and an amnesty was granted to Namibian refugees and exiles: by late September nearly 42,000 people, including Nujoma, had returned to Namibia. Meanwhile, South Africa completed its troop reduction ahead of schedule.

Voting proceeded peacefully on 7–11 November 1989, with the participation of more than 95% of the electorate. The Constituent Assembly's 72 seats were contested by candidates from 10 political parties and alliances, and representatives of seven parties and fronts were elected. SWAPO received 57.3% of all votes cast and won 41 seats, while the DTA, with 28.6% of the votes, secured 21 seats. (In 1991 the South African Government admitted that it had contributed funds to the electoral campaigns of the DTA and several other political parties opposed to SWAPO.) Following the election, South Africa's remaining troops were evacuated from Namibia, while SWAPO's bases in Angola were disbanded.

In February 1990 the Constituent Assembly adopted a draft Constitution, providing for a multi-party democracy based on universal adult suffrage. Later in the month the Constituent Assembly elected Nujoma as Namibia's first President. On 21 March Namibia finally achieved independence; the Constituent Assembly was redesignated the National Assembly, and Nujoma assumed executive power. A Cabinet, headed by the Constituent Assembly Chairman, Hage Geingob (a long-serving SWAPO activist), was also sworn in. In April British military advisers arrived in Namibia to assist in training the Namibian Defence Force (NDF), comprising former members of the demobilized PLAN and the disbanded South West Africa Territory Force.

In November 1991 the DTA, formerly a coalition of ethnically-based political groupings, voted to reconstitute itself as a single party, retaining Dirk Mudge as its Chairman. In the following month, at SWAPO's first Congress, Nujoma was re-elected as the party's President. SWAPO won control of nine of the country's 13 regional councils at elections in late 1992. An advisory National Council, comprising two members from each of the regional councils, was inaugurated as the second chamber of parliament in early 1993.

Following Namibia's independence, the port of Walvis Bay, its surrounding territory of 1,124 sq km and the 12 offshore Penguin Islands remained under South African jurisdiction. In September 1991 the Namibian and South African Governments agreed to administer the disputed territories jointly, pending a final settlement on sovereignty, and in August 1992 the two countries announced the forthcoming establishment of a joint administration authority. In August 1993, however, South Africa's multi-party constitutional negotiating committee instructed the Government to prepare legislation for the transfer of sovereignty over Walvis Bay to Namibia. Accordingly, negotiations between Namibia and South Africa resulted in bilateral agreements regarding the future of South African interests in the Walvis Bay area. Namibia formally took control of Walvis Bay and its islands from 1 March 1994. In August SWAPO won eight seats, and the DTA two, in Walvis Bay's first non-racial local elections.

Namibia's first post-independence presidential and legislative elections in December 1994 resulted in overwhelming victories for Nujoma and SWAPO. Nujoma was elected for a second term as President, securing 76.3% of the votes cast; his only challenger was the President of the DTA, Mishake Muyongo. (Although he remained DTA Chairman until 1995, Mudge had effectively retired from active politics.) SWAPO secured 53 of the elective seats in the National Assembly, with 73.9% of the valid votes cast. The DTA won 15 seats (with 20.8% of the votes), and the United Democratic Front (UDF) two. The remaining two seats were won by the Democratic Coalition of Namibia (an alliance of the National Patriotic Front and the German Union) and the Monitor Action Group. Although SWAPO now had a two-thirds' majority in the National Assembly, Nujoma gave assurances that no amendments would be made to the Constitution without prior approval by national referendum. Despite opposition claims of 'gross irregularities' in electoral procedures, international observers expressed satisfaction with the conduct of voting.

At the SWAPO Congress in May 1997 Nujoma was re-elected unopposed as party President. Among the resolutions endorsed by the Congress was a proposal that Nujoma should seek re-election for a third term as national President. It was agreed that the Constitution, which stipulates that a President may serve no more than two consecutive terms, could be exceptionally amended to allow Nujoma to seek a further mandate, since the incumbent had initially been appointed by the Constituent Assembly, and had only once been elected President on a popular mandate. The proposed third term for Nujoma was denounced by SWAPO's opponents as indicative of the regime's autocratic tendencies. In August 1998 a senior SWAPO official, Ben Ulenga, resigned as Namibia's High Commissioner to the United Kingdom, in protest at the proposed arrangement to allow Nujoma to seek a renewed mandate. Ulenga also opposed Namibia's military intervention in the Democratic Republic of the Congo (DRC, see below). In October the exceptional constitutional amendment was approved by the requisite two-thirds' majority in the National Assembly, having received the support of SWAPO's members; the amendment was similarly endorsed by the National Council in November. In March 1999 it was reported that Ulenga was to establish a new political party, the Congress of Democrats (CoD), with a view to contesting the presidential and legislative elections due later in the year.

Meanwhile, SWAPO secured control of 27 of the country's 45 local councils at elections in February 1998; the DTA took nine and the UDF three. Only about 40% of the electorate were reported to have voted, compared with more than 80% at local elections in 1992. Regional elections followed in December 1998, at which SWAPO won a majority in 11 of the 13 regional councils, thereby increasing its representation in the National Council to 22 seats. Turn-out by voters was, however, only about 30%.

In August 1998 the DTA's executive announced the suspension of Muyongo as party President, and dissociated the party from Muyongo's overt support for the secession of the Caprivi Strip—a narrow area of land extending in the north-east, between Angola and Botswana, as far as the Zambezi river (Namibia's border with Zambia). In November it emerged that Muyongo, leading the so-called Caprivi Liberation Movement (CLM), was among more than 100 people who, apparently armed, had crossed into Botswana in October, and who were now seeking asylum in that country. The Namibian Government stated that it had discovered plans for a secessionist rebellion, led by Muyongo and a chief of the Mafwe tribe, Boniface Mamili, in Caprivi. Representatives of the office of the UN High Commissioner for Refugees (UNHCR) subsequently advised the Botswana authorities that the secessionists' fears of persecution, should they be returned to Namibia, were 'plausible'. In subsequent weeks many more people crossed into Botswana, claiming to be fleeing harassment and persecution by the Namibian security forces: among those who left the country were many San/Bushmen, who were not believed to be associated with the secessionist movement. (In mid-2001 it was reported that many more San/Bushmen were considering leaving Namibia, again alleging harassment by the security forces.) During a visit to Botswana in March 1999 Nujoma reached an agreement with President Festus Mogae of that country, whereby the separatist leaders (whose extradition had hitherto been sought by Namibia in order that they could be tried on terrorist charges) would be accorded refugee status, on condition that they be resettled in a third country. Muyongo and Mamili were subsequently granted asylum in Denmark. The agreement also provided for the return to Namibia, under the auspices of UNHCR and without fear of prosecution or persecution, of the estimated 2,500 refugees who had crossed into Botswana since late 1998.

A period of apparent calm in the Caprivi region ended abruptly in early August 1999 with an armed attack by members of an organization styling itself the Caprivi Liberation Army (CLA), who targeted a military base at Mpacha airport and the police headquarters and offices of the Namibian Broadcasting Corporation in the regional capital, Katima Mulilo. At least eight members of the Namibian security forces and five CLA fighters were killed during the attack and its suppression. Nujoma responded by imposing a state of emergency in the region, and as many as 500 people were reported to have been arrested on suspicion of having links with the CLA. Within Namibia support was evident for the immediate declaration of a state of emergency, although the CoD, as well as church leaders and human rights organizations, expressed concern at evidence of the ill-treatment of detainees. Several members of the Government were subsequently reported to have admitted that 'mistakes' were made in the aftermath of the attack; however, the army Chief of Staff, Maj.-Gen. Martin Shalli, maintained that the decisive response of the forces under his command had been justified. Visiting Katima Mulilo in late August, Nujoma announced an end to the state of emergency, although army and police reinforcements were to remain in Caprivi. Initially, 12 alleged rebels were remanded on charges of high treason, murder, public violence and illegal possession of firearms; the prosecution asserted that 17 known leaders of the CLA remained at large. Meanwhile, a further 47 suspects were charged with aiding and abetting the rebels, and in the following month it was reported that the trial of 30–40 alleged separatists would begin in early 2000. A total of 127 people appeared in court in November 2000, charged with offences relating to the attack on Katima Mulilo; after numerous delays, their trial was scheduled to begin in mid-June 2002, following the provision of state-funded lawyers to all the defendants. Repatriations of refugees from Botswana were halted following the attack on Katima Mulilo, although UNHCR expressed the hope that voluntary repatriations would resume as soon as the security situation in Caprivi was adequate to guarantee the safe return of refugees. In early 2000, however, following an escalation of instability in the region of the Namibian–Angolan border, a further 400 Namibian nationals were reported to have fled to Botswana. In late 2001 officials from Botswana and Namibia held talks regarding the repatriation of about 500 Namibian refugees. In September of that year, in response to a request from the Namibian Government, the Gaborone Magistrates' Court in Botswana ordered the extradition of a group of suspected Caprivi separatists who were wanted to stand trial for high treason in connection with the attack on Katima Mulilo. The Namibian Government was also seeking to extradite Muyongo from Denmark to answer similar charges; the Danish Government stated that it was awaiting advice from UNHCR before making a decision.

Meanwhile, presidential and legislative elections, which were held on 30 November and 1 December 1999, resulted in an overwhelming victory for Nujoma and SWAPO, with Ulenga and the CoD apparently winning support at the expense of the DTA. In the presidential election Nujoma was returned for a third (and final) term of office with 76.8% of the votes cast, while Ulenga took 10.5% and Katuutire Kaura (Muyongo's successor as President of the DTA) 9.6%. SWAPO won 55 of the elective seats in the National Assembly, with 76.1% of the votes cast (thus ensuring that it retained the two-thirds' majority required to amend the Constitution); the CoD and the DTA each won seven seats (taking, respectively, 9.9% and 9.5% of the total votes cast).

Geingob was reappointed Prime Minister in a reorganization of the Cabinet announced by Nujoma in March 2000. The functions of the Ministries of Foreign Affairs and of Information and Broadcasting were merged (under Theo-Ben Gurirab). A further cabinet reshuffle was effected in January 2001.

In March 2001 it emerged that the Government had banned its ministries and offices from advertising in *The Namibian*, claiming that the newspaper was too critical of government policies. Furthermore, in May Nujoma issued a directive ordering all government departments to cease purchasing *The Namibian*. In November Nujoma announced that he would not be standing for a fourth term as President on the expiry of his current mandate in 2004, which would have necessitated a constitutional amendment. In August 2002 Nujoma reorganized his Cabinet; Gurirab was appointed Prime Minister, replacing Geingob, who resigned from the Government, having declined the position of Minister of Regional and Local Government and Housing, which was accepted by Joel Kaapanda. It was reported that Nujoma considered Geingob a threat to his authority. Hidipo Hamutenya became Minister of Foreign Affairs, Information and Broadcasting.

In March 1993 UNITA alleged that members of the NDF had crossed the border into southern Angola to assist Angolan government forces in offensives against UNITA, and subsequently claimed that some 2,000 Cuban troops had landed at Namibia's southern port of Lüderitz, from where they had been transferred to Angola to assist government forces. The Namibian authorities denied any involvement in the Angolan conflict, however. In April it was disclosed that NDF troops had been dispatched to the border region to protect two hospitals that were said to be under threat of attack by UNITA, following repeated border incursions and the reported intimidation of Namibian citizens. A 550-km stretch of the Okavango river border was closed from September 1994, following the deaths of three Namibians in an attack attributed by the Namibian authorities to UNITA. In September 1995 the Namibian Government announced the formation of a border control unit to assist police and NDF troops deployed along the Okavango. In November the two countries' defence and security commission agreed new measures aimed at facilitating the work of border patrols. Namibia subsequently announced that the Government was to contribute 200 NDF troops to the UN peace-keeping mission in Angola.

Following the attack on Katima Mulilo by Caprivi separatists in August 1999, the Namibian Government alleged that UNITA was lending military and logistical support to the CLA. (Links were also reported with the separatist Barotse Patriotic Front in Zambia, and the Namibian authorities alleged that the CLA had received training on Zambian territory.) There was considerable speculation that not only was Caprivi an important supply route for UNITA, but also that the Angolan rebel movement was attempting to divert resources of the Namibian armed forces away from the conflict in the DRC (q.v.).

Tensions in the region of the Namibia–Angola border escalated from late 1999, after the two countries began joint patrols targeting UNITA, and the Namibian Government authorized the Angolan armed forces to launch attacks against UNITA from Namibian territory. In January 2000 Namibia accused UNITA of responsibility for the deaths of three French children in north-eastern Namibia; UNITA held Angolan government forces responsible for the attack on the tourists. Shortly afterwards seven members of UNITA were reportedly killed in a clash on Namibian territory. In February it was announced that Nujoma and President José Eduardo dos Santos of Angola had agreed to implement measures to restore security in the border region; by June, when a curfew was imposed on the north-eastern border with Angola, more than 50 Namibians had been killed in cross-border raids by the Angolan rebels. Continuing conflict in southern Angola resulted in a large number of refugees entering Namibia (some 6,000 arrived from Angola between November 1999 and August 2000, although increased border security subsequently reduced the flow). In October Namibian security forces announced that 82 suspected UNITA 'soldiers and collaborators', arrested several months previously, would be deported without trial. However, the deportation order on these and 15 other detainees was ruled illegal in March 2001, and 78 remained in detention in Namibia; all were released and free to return to Angola in December 2002, although their repatriation was subsequently delayed by the Angolan authorities. In March 2001 President Nujoma ordered a further reinforcement of the Namibian military presence in Caprivi. In October UNITA rebels were reported to have destroyed an electricity substation in the Kavango region, and in November a group of unidentified gunmen killed four people in western Caprivi before escaping to Angola. In February 2002 five alleged UNITA and CLA guerrillas were arrested and killed by NDF troops in western Caprivi; the NDF claimed that they were responding to an attack on a civilian vehicle in the area.

In April 2002 the Namibian Government welcomed the signing of a formal cease-fire agreement by the Angolan Government and UNITA, some six weeks after the death of Jonas Savimbi, the UNITA leader. Some stability was restored in the Kavango and Caprivi regions in mid-2002, and in August a number of Angolan refugees were repatriated; the majority of them, estimated at around 20,000, were due to return home in mid-2003, under the auspices of UNHCR.

Following independence, Namibia became a member of the UN, the Commonwealth, the OAU and the Southern African Development Co-ordination Conference—now the Southern African Development Community (SADC, see p. 311). Despite expressed concerns at South African dominance of the regional economy, the Nujoma regime has forged close links with post-apartheid South Africa, and in 1994 SWAPO contributed funds to the electoral campaigns of the African National Congress of South Africa and the Pan-Africanist Congress. President Nelson Mandela visited Namibia in August of that year, and in December South Africa announced the cancellation of Namibia's pre-independence bilateral debt; South African property in Namibia was also to be transferred to the Namibian authorities. In February 1997 legislation providing for the cancellation of the debt (now amounting to N $1,200m.) was formally approved by the South African Parliament. Nujoma made his first state visit

to South Africa in May 1996. In August 2001 the foreign ministers of Namibia and South Africa held talks regarding their 400 km border; Namibia claimed its southern border extended to the middle of the Orange river, while South Africa claimed that its territory stretched to the northern bank. (When South Africa's borders were reassessed in 1994, following its first democratic elections, the Surveyors-General of both Namibia and South Africa had agreed to place the border in the middle of the river, but the agreement was never signed.) The confusion over the location of the border has led to differences over mineral and fishing rights in the river, as well as grazing rights on its islands.

In February 1995 it was announced that Namibia and Botswana were to refer a dispute regarding the demarcation of their joint border on the Chobe river (specifically, the issue of the sovereignty of the small, uninhabited island of Kasikili-Sedudu) for adjudication by the ICJ. The dispute was formally submitted to the Court in mid-1996. The ICJ ruled in December 1999 that the island formed part of the territory of Botswana; the judgment further ruled that nationals of (and vessels flying the flags of) Botswana and Namibia should enjoy equal treatment in the two channels around the island. Meanwhile, a joint initiative was announced in March of that year to counter smuggling and illegal border crossings between the two countries. In January 1998 the two countries' Joint Commission on Defence and Security held an emergency meeting, following allegations by Namibia that troops from Botswana had taken control of a further island in disputed border territory—Setungu Island in the Caprivi Strip. The Joint Commission agreed to expedite the establishment of a Joint Technical Commission for the demarcation of the border. Relations were complicated by the issue of Caprivi secessionism (see above). Setungu is claimed as Mafwe land; furthermore, Namibia's representative in discussions regarding the island, said to be a member of the secessionist movement, was reported to have fled to Angola.

From August 1998 Namibia, which was participating in regional efforts to resolve the conflict in the DRC, supported a Zimbabwean-led initiative by members of the SADC (notably excluding South Africa) for military intervention in support of the regime of President Laurent-Désiré Kabila; as many as 2,000 Namibian troops were subsequently dispatched to the DRC, provoking vociferous criticism by opponents of Nujoma. Namibia's continuing military commitments in the DRC following the failure of the 1999 Lusaka accord (to which Namibia was a signatory), together with the need for additional army resources in north-east Namibia as a result of the Caprivi rebellion and the intensification of operations against UNITA (see above), necessitated the allocation of an additional N $173m. to defence in the supplementary budget for 1999/2000, announced in early 2000.

President Laurent-Désiré Kabila was assassinated in January 2001, and was succeeded by his son, Maj.-Gen. Joseph Kabila. Efforts to resolve the conflict in that country were accelerated, and in February proposals for the withdrawal of troops involved in the regional military intervention, including the estimated 2,000 Namibians, were approved by the participating countries, under the aegis of the UN Security Council. In March it was announced that Namibian forces would remain in the DRC until the specified date for withdrawal in May. All but an estimated 150 Namibian troops eventually withdrew from the DRC in September, although other foreign forces were still deployed in large numbers; at least 30 Namibian troops were reported to have been killed in three years of service. All Namibian troops had been withdrawn by the end of 2002. Meanwhile, the Namibian Government was criticized in February 2001, when it admitted, despite previous denials, that it owned a diamond mine in the DRC. The elder Kabila had granted the mine to a company controlled by the Namibian Government in 1999, allegedly in return for Namibian support in the conflict in the DRC.

Germany has been a major aid donor to Namibia since independence, and relations are generally close. In September 1995, none the less, during a visit by the German Chancellor, Helmut Kohl, some 300 members of the Herero ethnic group staged a demonstration outside the German embassy in Windhoek to demand compensation for suffering inflicted on the Herero under German rule. In June 1996 Nujoma made his first official visit to Germany. In March 1998 the German President, Dr Roman Herzog, made an official visit to Namibia, the first such visit by a German Head of State, and pledged his country's increased support for Namibia. In June 2001 the Herero filed a lawsuit in Washington, DC, USA, against three German companies (Deutsche Bank AG, Woermann Line and Terex Corporation), claiming US $2,000m. in reparation for the alleged exploitation and eventual extermination of some 65,000 Herero in 1904–15; a second lawsuit was filed against the German Government in September. The case against Terex Corporation was subsequently withdrawn, after the company claimed that it was under different management at the time of the atrocities, while court proceedings in the other lawsuits were expected to commence in the first half of 2003.

Government

On 21 March 1990 Namibia became independent, and the Constitution took effect. Executive authority is held by the President, who is the Head of State. According to the Constitution, the President shall be directly elected by universal adult suffrage for a term of five years, and permitted to hold office for a maximum of two terms. (In late 1998 legislation was approved whereby the Constitution was to be exceptionally amended to allow the incumbent President to seek a third term of office.) Legislative power is vested in the National Assembly, comprising 72 members directly elected by universal adult suffrage and as many as six non-voting members nominated by the President. The National Assembly has a maximum term of five years. An advisory National Council, comprising two representatives from each of the country's 13 regional councils, elected for a six-year period, operates as the second chamber of parliament. Each region has its own Governor.

Defence

In August 2002 the Namibian Defence Force numbered an estimated 9,000 men; there was also a 200-strong coastguard, operating as part of the Ministry of Fisheries and Marine Resources. In January 2002 the Government announced that it was establishing a navy, to commence operations in 2005, and constructing a naval base at Walvis Bay, with assistance from the Brazilian Government, which was also to train Namibian naval officers. Projected budgetary expenditure on defence for 2002 was N $850m.

Economic Affairs

In 2001, according to estimates by the World Bank, Namibia's gross national income (GNI), measured at average 1999–2001 prices, was US $3,520m., equivalent to US $1,960 per head (or $6,700 per head on an international purchasing-power parity basis). During 1990–2001, it was estimated, the population increased at an average annual rate of 2.4% per year, while gross domestic product (GDP) per head increased, in real terms, by an average of 1.9% per year. Overall GDP increased, in real terms, at an average annual rate of 3.9% in 1993–2001, according to the Bank of Namibia. Real GDP increased by 3.3% in 2000 and by 2.4% in 2001.

According to the Bank of Namibia, agriculture (including hunting, forestry and fishing) contributed 9.8% of GDP in 2001. About 40.5% of the labour force were employed in the sector in 2001. Namibia has potentially one of the richest fisheries in the world. Government revenue from sales of fishing concessions was projected at N $70m. in the financial year ending 31 March 1999, and exports of fish and fish products provided 28.5% of total export earnings in 1998. The principal agricultural activity is beef production; the production of karakul sheepskins is also important. In addition, sealing and ostrich farming are practised on a commercial basis. The main subsistence crops are maize, millet and root crops, although Namibia remains highly dependent on imports of basic foods, especially in drought years. Plantations of seedless grapes were being developed on the banks of the Orange river in the late 1990s, and projected growth in production was expected to make them the second largest agricultural export after beef by 2003. In 2002 the South African Government granted Namibia limited access to fish in its territorial waters. Agricultural GDP increased at an average annual rate of 2.9% in 1993–2001. Agricultural GDP increased by 8.2% in 2000, but decreased by 10.4% in 2001.

Industry (including mining, manufacturing, construction and power) contributed 30.6% of GDP in 2001, and engaged 15.0% of the employed labour force in 1991. During 1993–2001 industrial GDP increased by an average of 3.2% per year. Industrial GDP increased by 1.4% in 2000 and by 6.1% in 2001.

Mining and quarrying contributed 14.1% of GDP in 2001, and engaged 3.7% of the employed labour force in 1991. Namibia has rich deposits of many minerals, and is among the world's leading producers of gem diamonds (some 95% of diamonds mined in

Namibia are of gem quality). Diamond-mining contributed 81.8% of the sector's GDP in 2001, and diamonds are the principal mineral export, accounting for an estimated 50.6% of export earnings in 2001; in 2000 Namibia produced 5% of world diamond output by value. The mining of offshore diamond deposits is of increasing importance, with offshore recoveries of gem-quality diamonds accounting for about 56% of the country's output in 1999. Some US $500,000m. worth of diamonds were estimated to be lying on the continental shelf off the Namibian coast in 2001. A new Diamond Act, liberalizing exploration, came into force in 2000. Uranium is also an important mineral export. In addition, zinc, lead, gold, salt, fluorspar, marble and semi-precious stones are extracted, and there are also considerable deposits of hydrocarbons, lithium, manganese, tungsten, cadmium and vanadium. Namibia is also believed to have substantial reserves of coal, iron ore and platinum. Copper production, which ceased in 1998 following the liquidation of the Tsumeb Corporation, resumed at the former Tsumeb sites in September 2000. In 2000 Anglo American plc (United Kingdom) announced its intention to develop the Rosh Pinah zinc mine; production was scheduled to commence in late 2003. A mine and smelter complex for high-grade silicon metal was to be developed at Omaruru (subject to licensing agreements), in a joint venture between Namibia Metals and SMS Demag, a German company. Mining GDP increased at an average annual rate of 2.7% in 1993–2001; the sector's GDP decreased by 1.7% in 2000 and by 6.1% in 2001.

Manufacturing contributed 10.7% of GDP in 2001, and engaged 5.8% of the employed labour force in 1991. The sector has hitherto remained underdeveloped, largely owing to Namibia's economic dependence on South Africa. The principal manufacturing activities are the processing of fish (which contributed 19.4% of manufacturing GDP in 2001) and minerals for export; brewing, meat processing and the production of chemicals are also significant. Namibia's first diamond-cutting and -polishing factory was inaugurated in 1998. Manufacturing GDP increased by an average of 2.2% per year in 1993–2001. Manufacturing GDP increased by 3.6% in 2000 and by 6.0% in 2001.

In 1999 97.6% of Namibia's electricity production was derived from hydroelectric power. There is a hydroelectric station at Ruacana, on the Cunene river at the border with Angola, and a second hydroelectric power station was planned at Divundu on the Kavango river; a project to construct a power station at Epupa was stalled, following a disagreement between the Namibian and Angolan Governments over the most appropriate site. Sizeable offshore deposits of natural gas are also to be exploited commercially: a planned 750-MW power plant would supply the domestic market, and it is anticipated that a surplus will be produced for export to South Africa. Domestic electricity generation increased significantly in 2000, enabling the proportion of electrical energy imported to be reduced to 34.8% in that year. A power transmission line, linking the Namibian and South African electricity grids, was inaugurated in southern Namibia in 1999. Imports of mineral fuels and lubricants accounted for 5.9% of the value of total merchandise imports in 1997.

The services sector contributed 59.6% of GDP in 2001. Tourism is expanding rapidly, and has been the focus of a major privatization initiative. The acquisition of Walvis Bay in March 1994, and subsequent establishment there of a free-trade zone, was expected to enhance Namibia's status as an entrepôt for regional trade. The GDP of the services sector increased at an average annual rate of 4.1% in 1993–2001. Services GDP increased by 3.6% in 2000 and by 3.1% in 2001.

In 2001 Namibia recorded a visible trade deficit of N $1,572.2m., according to provisional figures, although there was a surplus of N $818.6m. on the current account of the balance of payments. South Africa is the dominant source of imports, providing 84.3% of the total in 1997. In 1993 the United Kingdom (34.4%) and South Africa (27.4%) were the principal markets for Namibian exports. The principal exports in 2001 were diamonds and other mineral products, food and live animals (notably fish and meat) and manufactured goods. The principal import groups in 1997 included food, live animals, beverages and tobacco; machinery and electrical goods; transport equipment; chemicals and chemical products; textiles, clothing and footwear; metals and metal products; and mineral fuels and lubricants.

In the financial year ending 31 March 2003 Namibia recorded an estimated overall budget deficit of N $1,221m. In 1997 South Africa officially cancelled the external public debt inherited by

Namibia at independence. At December 2000 Namibia's external debt totalled N \$909.1m. The annual rate of inflation averaged 9.9% in 1990–2001; consumer prices increased by an average of 9.2% in 2001. Some 35% of the labour force were unemployed in 2001.

Namibia is a member of the Common Market for Eastern and Southern Africa (see p. 162), of the Southern African Development Community (see p. 311), and of the Southern African Customs Union (with Botswana, Lesotho, South Africa and Swaziland).

Despite a vulnerability to drought, Namibia's potential for economic prosperity is high, given its abundant mineral reserves and rich fisheries, as well as a well-developed infrastructure, all of which were enhanced by the acquisition, in 1994, of sovereignty over Walvis Bay and of important diamond-mining rights. However, Namibia's economic progress continues to be largely influenced by its dependence on South Africa. (The Namibian dollar, introduced in 1993, is at par with the rand.) Although the average level of income per head is among the highest in the region, there remain extreme disparities in the distribution of wealth; in 1994 land-reform legislation was enacted in an effort to redress this problem, but implementation has been very slow. In April 2001 the Government announced that it had allocated N \$100m. to acquire land for redistribution on a voluntary basis over a five-year period. At this time approximately 4,000 (mainly white-owned) farms occupied 52% of the total land area, while the Government had acquired only some 6% of the land required for resettlement. In October 2002 the Government announced that it was considering the seizure of white-owned farms for redistribution to the landless black population, and criticized white farmers for taking advantage of the voluntary basis for land redistribution by charging excessively high prices for their land. In the budget presented in March 2003 the funds allocated to land reform increased from N \$20m. to N \$50m. annually. Meanwhile, a rural exodus in recent years has resulted in high rates of urban unemployment and attendant social problems such as crime. There were, furthermore, fears that the tourist industry would be adversely affected by the perceived insecurity in the north-east (see Recent History), although some stability was being restored in 2002. The Nujoma Government's first National Development Plan, covering the period 1995–2000, aimed principally to reduce poverty and encourage sustainable economic growth (averaging 5% annually during the plan period) through policies of diversification, in an attempt to prevent potential over-dependence on the mining and fishing sectors. After a disappointing performance in 1998, the economy improved in 1999 and 2000, enabling the Government to forecast the reduction of its external debt.

However, GDP growth slowed in 2001, to 2.4%, as a result of lower agricultural output, particularly in the fishing sector. The second National Development Plan, covering 2001–06, projected GDP growth of 4% per year over the period. In January 2002 it was reported that, with assistance from the Brazilian Government, Namibia planned to conduct a geological survey of the continental shelf off its shores, with the intention of extending its exclusive economic zone from 200 to 350 nautical miles. In November 2001 Namibia became eligible to export certain products to the USA free from tariffs, under the African Growth and Opportunity Act (AGOA); it was estimated that 90% of products made in Namibia would qualify for duty-free access to the US market until 2008. In December 2002 Namibia's eligibility for tariff preferences under AGOA was renewed.

Education

Under the Constitution, education is compulsory between the ages of six and 16 years, or until primary education has been completed (whichever is the sooner). Primary education consists of seven grades, and secondary education of five. In 1999/2000 enrolment at primary schools included 79.7% of children in the relevant age-group (males 76.9%; females 82.5%), while the comparable ratio for secondary enrolment in that year was 34.2% (males 28.5%; females 39.9%). Higher education is provided by the University of Namibia, the Technicon of Namibia, a vocational college and four teacher-training colleges. In 1998 12,787 students were enrolled in tertiary education. Various schemes for informal adult education are also in operation in an effort to combat illiteracy. Budget forecasts for 1998/99 allocated N \$1,700.6m. (25.2% of total government expenditure) to education. Approximately 20% of total expenditure was allocated to education under the draft budget for 2001/02.

Public Holidays

2003: 1 January (New Year's Day), 21 March (Independence Day), 18–21 April (Easter), 1 May (Workers' Day), 5 May (for Casinga Day), 26 May (for Africa Day, anniversary of the OAU's foundation), 29 May (Ascension Day), 26 August (Heroes' Day), 7 October (Day of Goodwill), 10 December (Human Rights Day), 25–26 December (Christmas).

2004: 1 January (New Year's Day), 21 March (Independence Day), 9–12 April (Easter), 1 May (Workers' Day), 4 May (Casinga Day), 20 May (Ascension Day), 25 May (Africa Day, anniversary of the OAU's foundation), 26 August (Heroes' Day), 7 October (Day of Goodwill), 10 December (Human Rights Day), 25–26 December (Christmas).

Weights and Measures

The metric system is in use.

Statistical Survey

Area and Population

AREA, POPULATION AND DENSITY*

Area (sq km)	824,292†
Population (census results)	
21 October 1991	1,409,920
28 August 2001	
Males	936,718
Females	890,136
Total	1,826,854
Density (per sq km) at September 2001	2.2

* Including data for Walvis Bay, sovereignty over which was transferred from South Africa to Namibia with effect from March 1994. Walvis Bay has an area of 1,124 sq km (434 sq miles) and had a population of 22,999 in 1991.

† 318,261 sq miles.

‡ Source: Bank of Namibia.

ETHNIC GROUPS
(population, 1988 estimate)

Ovambo . . .	623,000	Caprivian . . .		47,000
Kavango . . .	117,000	Bushmen . . .		36,000
Damara . . .	94,000	Baster		31,000
Herero . . .	94,000	Tswana		7,000
White	80,000	Others		12,000
Nama	60,000	**Total**		1,252,000
Coloured . . .	51,000			

PRINCIPAL TOWNS
(population at 1991 census)

Windhoek . . .	147,056	Oshakati . . .	21,603
Walvis Bay . . .	22,999	Rehoboth . . .	21,439

Source: Thomas Brinkoff, *City Population* (internet www.citypopulation.de).

Mid-2001 (UN estimate, including suburbs): Windhoek (capital) 216,000 (Source: UN, *World Urbanization Prospects: The 2001 Revision*).

BIRTHS AND DEATHS
(UN estimates, annual averages)

	1985–90	1990–95	1995–2000
Birth rate (per 1,000)	42.4	41.1	37.6
Death rate (per 1,000)	11.9	13.2	17.6

Source: UN, *World Population Prospects: The 2000 Revision.*

Expectation of life (WHO estimates, years at birth): 48.8 (males 48.4; females 49.0) in 2001 (Source: WHO, *World Health Report*).

ECONOMICALLY ACTIVE POPULATION
(persons aged 10 years and over, 1991 census)

	Males	Females	Total
Agriculture, hunting, forestry and fishing	99,987	89,942	189,929
Mining and quarrying	13,837	849	14,686
Manufacturing	10,773	12,111	22,884
Electricity, gas and water . . .	2,826	148	2,974
Construction	18,137	501	18,638
Trade, restaurants and hotels . .	19,678	18,142	37,820
Transport, storage and communications	8,003	1,319	9,322
Financing, insurance, real estate and business services	5,180	3,367	8,547
Community, social and personal services	3,664	2,163	5,827
Activities not adequately defined .	39,224	44,490	83,714
Total employed	221,309	173,032	394,341
Unemployed	57,263	41,976	99,239
Total labour force	278,572	215,008	493,580

Source: ILO, *Yearbook of Labour Statistics.*

Mid-2001 (FAO estimates, '000 persons): Agriculture, etc. 287; Total labour force 695 (Source: FAO).

Health and Welfare

KEY INDICATORS

Total fertility rate (children per woman, 2001)	5.0
Under-5 mortality rate (per 1,000 live births, 2001) . . .	67
HIV/AIDS (% of persons aged 15–49, 2001)	22.50
Physicians (per 1,000 head, 1997)	0.30
Health expenditure (2000): US $ per head (PPP)	366
Health expenditure (2000): % of GDP	7.1
Health expenditure (2000): public (% of total)	59.3
Access to water (% of persons, 2000)	77
Access to sanitation (% of persons, 2000)	41
Human Development Index (2000): ranking	122
Human Development Index (2000): value	0.610

For sources and definitions, see explanatory note on p. vi.

Agriculture

PRINCIPAL CROPS
('000 metric tons)

	1999	2000	2001
Wheat	4	3	6
Maize	19	32	28
Millet	48	77	65
Sorghum	4	9	8
Roots and tubers*	250	255	255
Pulses*	8	9	9
Vegetables*	10	11	11
Fruit*	10	11	11

* FAO estimates.

Source: FAO.

LIVESTOCK
('000 head, year ending September)

	1999	2000	2001
Horses	66	62	53
Mules*	7	7	7
Asses	175	168	169
Cattle	2,294	2,505	2,509
Pigs	19	23	22
Sheep	2,174	2,446	2,370
Goats	1,690	1,850	1,769
Chickens*	2,250	2,300	2,350

* FAO estimates.

Source: FAO.

LIVESTOCK PRODUCTS
(FAO estimates, '000 metric tons)

	1999	2000	2001
Beef and veal	78	64	58
Mutton and lamb	4	4	4
Goat meat	5	4	4
Pig meat	1	1	1
Poultry meat	4	4	5
Other meat	4	4	4
Cows' milk	83	89	89
Hen eggs	2	2	2
Wool (greasy)	2	2	2
Cattle hides	9	7	6
Sheepskins	0	1	1
Goatskins	1	1	1

Source: FAO.

Forestry

Separate figures are not yet available. Data for Namibia are included in those for South Africa.

Fishing*

('000 metric tons, live weight)

	1998	1999	2000
Capture	337.5	299.2	283.0
Cape hakes (Stokvisse) . . .	135.5	147.6	171.0
Orange roughy	10.7	3.2	1.5
Gobies	21.0	0.0	0.0
Devil anglerfish	16.8	13.8	14.3
Cape horse mackerel (Maasbanker)	64.9	36.0	35.0
Southern African pilchard . .	68.5	44.7	29.7
Porgies, seabreams, etc. . . .	0.0	0.0	9.9
Aquaculture†	0.0	0.0	0.1
Total catch	337.5	299.2	283.1

* Figures include quantities caught by licensed foreign vessels in Namibian waters and processed in Lüderitz and Walvis Bay. The data exclude aquatic mammals (whales, seals, etc.). The number of South African fur seals caught was: 29,475 in 1998; 25,161 in 1999; 41,753 in 2000.
† FAO estimates.

Source: FAO, *Yearbook of Fishery Statistics.*

Mining

(metric tons, unless otherwise indicated)

	1998	1999	2000
Copper ore*	7,500	—	5,070
Lead concentrates*	13,568	9,885	12,115
Zinc concentrates*	42,274	35,140	40,266
Silver ore (kilograms)*	22,670	9,670	16,669
Uranium oxide	3,257	3,171	3,201
Gold ore (kilograms)*	1,882	2,005	2,456
Fluorspar (Fluorite)†	42,139	71,011	66,129
Salt (unrefined)	507,361	503,479	542,948
Diamonds ('000 metric carats):			
gem‡	1,394	1,633	1,542
industrial‡	—	82	—

* Figures refer to the metal content of ores and concentrates.
† Figures (on a wet-weight basis) refer to acid-grade material.
‡ Estimated production.

Source: US Geological Survey.

Industry

SELECTED PRODUCTS
(metric tons)

	1998	1999	2000
Cement*	150,000	150,000	150,000
Unrefined copper (unwrought)	8,014	—	13,488
Refined lead (unwrought)	236	—	—

* Estimated production.

Source: US Geological Survey.

Finance

CURRENCY AND EXCHANGE RATES

Monetary Units
100 cents = 1 Namibian dollar (N $)

Sterling, US Dollar and Euro Equivalents (31 December 2002)
£1 sterling = N $13.9260
US $1 = N $8.6400
€1 = N $9.0608
N $1,000 = £71.81 = US $115.74 = €110.37

Average Exchange Rate (N $ per US $)
2000 6.93983
2001 8.60918
2002 10.5407

Note: The Namibian dollar was introduced in September 1993, replacing (at par) the South African rand. The rand remained legal tender in Namibia.

CENTRAL GOVERNMENT BUDGET
(N $ million, year ending 31 March)

Revenue*	2000/01	2001/02†	2002/03†
Taxation	7,550.0	7,938.0	9,116.0
Taxes on income, profits and capital gains	2,610.0	3,143.0	3,951.0
Taxes on property	63.0	60.0	70.0
Domestic taxes on goods and services	1,945.0	2,039.0	2,422.9
Taxes on international trade and transactions	2,877.0	2,641.0	2,597.1
Other taxes	55.0	55.0	75.0
Non-tax revenue	736.0	870.0	994.5
Entrepreneurial and property income	462.0	623.0	720.1
Fines and forfeitures	21.0	10.0	15.0
Administrative fees and charges	232.0	219.0	240.8
Return on capital from lending and equity	21.0	18.0	18.6
Total	8,286.0	8,808.0	10,110.5

Expenditure	2000/01	2001/02†	2002/03†
Current expenditure	7,625.0	8,697.0	9,462.8
Personnel expenditure	3,965.0	4,535.0	4,738.3
Expenditure on goods and other services	1,637.0	1,817.0	1,861.9
Interest payments	512.0	678.0	955.0
Subsidies and other current transfers	1,511.0	1,667.0	1,907.6
Capital expenditure	1,083.0	1,786.0	2,014.5
Capital investment	929.0	1,267.0	1,265.7
Capital transfers	32.0	44.0	86.8
Total lending and equity participation	122.0	475.0	662.0
Total	8,708.0	10,483.0	11,477.3

* Excluding grants received from abroad (N $ million): 57.0 in 2000/01; 204.0 in 2001/02; 145.8 in 2002/03.
† Revised estimates.

Source: Bank of Namibia.

INTERNATIONAL RESERVES
(US $ million at 31 December)

	2000	2001	2002
IMF special drawing rights	0.02	0.02	0.02
Reserve position in IMF	0.05	0.05	0.06
Foreign exchange	259.94	234.18	323.05
Total	260.01	234.25	323.13

Source: IMF, *International Financial Statistics*.

MONEY SUPPLY
(N $ million at 31 December)

	2000	2001	2002
Demand deposits at deposit money banks	5,284.8	5,805.2	6,152.4
Total money (incl. others)	5,766.0	6,312.7	6,698.2

Source: IMF, *International Financial Statistics*.

COST OF LIVING
(Consumer Price Index for Windhoek; base: December 1992 = 100)

	1999	2000	2001
Food	163.3	172.0	191.7
Beverages and tobacco	251.8	267.0	290.3
Housing, fuel and power	191.1	202.1	217.7
Clothing and footwear	179.9	183.9	196.1
All items (incl. others)	178.8	189.5	207.0

Source: Bank of Namibia, *Annual Report* (2001).

NATIONAL ACCOUNTS
(N $ million at current prices)

National Income and Product

	1999	2000	2001
Compensation of employees	8,303	9,340	10,420
Operating surplus	6,912	9,167	10,739
Domestic factor incomes	15,215	18,507	21,159
Consumption of fixed capital	2,851	3,103	3,554
Gross domestic product (GDP) at factor cost	18,066	21,610	24,713
Indirect taxes	2,771	2,995	3,189
Less Subsidies	156	610	671
GDP in purchasers' values	20,681	23,995	27,231
Factor income received from abroad	1,129	1,721	1,894
Less Factor income paid abroad	1,235	1,491	1,619
Gross national income	23,426	27,329	31,060
Less Consumption of fixed capital	2,851	3,103	3,554
National income in market prices	20,575	24,226	27,506
Other current transfers from abroad	2,906	3,272	3,297
Less Other current transfers paid abroad	363	262	312
National disposable income	23,117	27,235	30,491

Source: Bank of Namibia.

Expenditure on the Gross Domestic Product

	1999	2000	2001
Government final consumption expenditure	6,262	6,819	7,562
Private final consumption expenditure	12,240	14,192	16,500
Increase in stocks	57	171	418
Gross fixed capital formation . .	4,760	4,460	6,039
Total domestic expenditure . .	23,319	25,641	30,518
Exports of goods and services .	9,548	10,811	12,075
Less Imports of goods and services	11,773	12,119	14,785
Statistical discrepancy	−413	−338	−577
GDP in purchasers' values . .	20,681	23,995	27,231

Source: Bank of Namibia.

Gross Domestic Product by Economic Activity

	1999	2000	2001
Agriculture, hunting, forestry and fishing	2,072	2,343	2,431
Mining and quarrying . . .	1,949	2,610	3,489
Manufacturing	2,074	2,371	2,638
Electricity, gas and water . . .	541	605	662
Construction	483	476	773
Trade, restaurants and hotels . .	2,201	3,085	3,481
Transport, storage and communications	1,226	1,358	1,435
Finance, insurance, real estate and business services	2,762	3,068	3,411
Government services	4,617	5,064	5,671
Other community, social and personal services	171	201	219
Other services	392	437	486
Sub-total	18,486	21,616	24,729
Less Imputed bank service charge	259	273	328
GDP at basic prices	18,228	21,343	24,401
Taxes, less subsidies, on products	2,453	2,652	2,830
GDP in purchasers' values . .	20,681	23,995	27,231

Source: Bank of Namibia.

BALANCE OF PAYMENTS
(US $ million)

	1996	1997	1998
Exports of goods f.o.b. . . .	1,403.7	1,343.3	1,278.3
Imports of goods f.o.b. . . .	−1,530.9	−1,615.0	−1,450.9
Trade balance	−127.1	−271.7	−172.6
Exports of services	337.4	380.1	327.0
Imports of services	−580.9	−533.7	−456.9
Balance on goods and services	−370.7	−425.2	−302.4
Other income received . . .	319.2	252.0	226.7
Other income paid	−249.0	−180.6	−165.9
Balance on goods, services and income	−300.5	−353.8	−241.6
Current transfers received . .	437.3	462.2	418.2
Current transfers paid . . .	−21.0	−18.0	−14.7
Current balance	115.8	90.4	161.8
Capital account (net)	42.1	33.5	23.8
Direct investment abroad . .	21.7	−0.7	2.2
Direct investment from abroad .	128.7	91.0	96.2
Portfolio investment assets . .	−8.1	−14.6	−11.1
Portfolio investment liabilities .	31.2	26.0	−4.4
Other investment assets . .	−411.2	−289.9	−175.5
Other investment liabilities . .	63.8	116.7	−53.1
Net errors and omissions . .	39.1	15.3	15.7
Overall balance	22.9	67.8	55.8

Source: IMF, *International Financial Statistics*.

External Trade

PRINCIPAL COMMODITIES

Imports c.i.f. (US $ million)	1995	1996	1997
Food and live animals . . . .⎫			
Beverages and tobacco . . .⎭	332.2	348.7	404.0
Mineral fuels and lubricants . .	87.7	96.3	99.0
Chemicals and related products .	170.1	186.5	188.2
Wood, paper and paper products (incl. furniture)	101.2	89.3	92.2
Textiles, clothing and footwear .	117.4	125.6	126.3
Metals and metal products . .	127.4	122.3	126.3
Machinery (incl. electrical) . .	305.2	266.6	251.3
Transport equipment	275.2	274.2	246.1
Total (incl. others).	1,648.4	1,630.9	1,675.0

Source: IMF, *Namibia: Statistical Appendix* (February 1999).

Exports f.o.b. (N $ million)	1999	2000*	2001*
Food and live animals	1,202.6	1,372.8	1,399.9
Diamonds	3,022.2	4,245.4	4,506.5
Other mineral products . . .	1,123.1	1,287.9	1,672.5
Manufactured products . . .	1,867.8	794.8	1,234.9
Total (incl. others)	7,397.3	7,906.2	8,901.4

* Provisional figures.

Source: Bank of Namibia, *Annual Report* (2001).

PRINCIPAL TRADING PARTNERS

Imports c.i.f. (US $ million)	1995	1996	1997
Germany	29.7	23.7	33.3
Norway	16.2	3.4	2.9
Russia	13.4	9.5	17.3
South Africa	1,431.7	1,443.4	1,412.7
United Kingdom	25.5	15.8	7.2
USA	22.6	35.9	69.0
Zimbabwe	17.0	18.7	7.1
Total (incl. others)	1,648.6	1,630.9	1,675.0

Source: IMF, *Namibia: Statistical Appendix* (February 1999).

Exports f.o.b. (N $ million)	1993
Belgium	232
Côte d'Ivoire	70
France	87
Germany	140
Japan	411
South Africa	1,153
Spain	258
Switzerland	74
United Kingdom	1,450
USA	51
Total (incl. others)	4,213

Source: Bank of Namibia, Windhoek.

Transport

RAILWAYS

	1994/95	1995/96
Freight (million net ton-km)	1,077	1,082
Passengers carried ('000)	110	124

Source: TransNamib Ltd, Windhoek.

ROAD TRAFFIC
(motor vehicles in use at 31 December)

	1994*	1995*	1996
Passenger cars	61,269	62,500	74,875
Buses and coaches	5,098	5,200	10,175
Lorries and vans	60,041	61,300	59,352
Motorcycles and mopeds . . .	1,450	1,480	1,520

Total vehicles in use (excluding road tractors, motorcycles and mopeds): 137,650 in 1997; 137,650 in 1998*; 123,568 in 1999*.

2000: Passenger cars 68,565; Buses and coaches 1,924; Lorries and vans 73,598; Road tractors 2,912; Motorcycles and mopeds 2,849.
* Estimates.

Source: International Road Federation, *World Road Statistics*.

SHIPPING

Merchant Fleet
(at 31 December)

	1999	2000	2001
Number of vessels	105	119	121
Displacement (gross registered tons)	55,265	63,142	65,822

Source: Lloyd's Register-Fairplay, *World Fleet Statistics*.

Sea-borne Freight Traffic
('000 freight tons*, year ending 30 September)

	1997/98	1998/99
Port of Lüderitz: goods loaded	45.9	93.4
Port of Lüderitz: goods unloaded	46.1	96.6
Port of Lüderitz: goods transhipped . . .	107.9	204.2
Port of Walvis Bay: goods loaded	713.4	717.5
Port of Walvis Bay: goods unloaded . . .	1,124.5	1,023.9
Port of Walvis Bay: goods transhipped . .	45.8	44.7

* One freight ton = 40 cu ft (1.133 cu metres) of cargo capacity.

Source: Namibian Ports Authority, Walvis Bay.

CIVIL AVIATION
(traffic on scheduled services)

	1997	1998	1999
Kilometres flown (million) . . .	7	7	5
Passengers carried ('000) . . .	183	200	165
Passenger-km (million)	882	614	528
Total ton-km (million)	116	57	47

Source: UN, *Statistical Yearbook*.

Tourism

FOREIGN TOURIST ARRIVALS*

Country of origin	1996	1997	1998
Angola	144,915	158,188	177,316
Botswana	16,011	17,695	19,589
Germany	50,899	54,952	59,632
South Africa	172,544	187,687	209,318
United Kingdom	11,562	12,555	13,992
Total (incl. others)	461,310	502,012	559,674

* Excluding same-day visitors: 63,752 in 1996; 69,162 in 1997.

Source: World Tourism Organization, *Yearbook of Tourism Statistics*.

Tourism receipts (US $ million): 293 in 1996; 333 in 1997; 288 in 1998 (Source: World Bank).

Communications Media

	1999	2000	2001
Television receivers ('000 in use) .	65	67	n.a.
Telephones ('000 main lines in use)	108.2	110.2	117.4
Mobile cellular telephones ('000 subscribers)	30.0	82.0	100.0
Internet users ('000)	6.0	30.0	45.0

Source: International Telecommunication Union.

Radio receivers ('000 in use): 232 in 1997 (Source: UNESCO, *Statistical Yearbook*).

Daily newspapers (1997): 4; average circulation ('000 copies) 10 (Source: UNESCO, *Statistical Yearbook*).

Non-daily newspapers (1997): 5; average circulation ('000 copies) 9 (Source: UNESCO, *Statistical Yearbook*).

Education
(1998)

	Institutions	Teachers	Students Males	Students Females	Students Total
Primary	1,362	11,992	193,169	193,478	386,647
Secondary	n.a.	5,093	51,203	58,873	110,076
Tertiary	n.a.	619	6,537	6,250	12,787

Source: UNESCO, Institute for Statistics.

Adult literacy rate (UNESCO estimates): 82.0% (males 82.8%; females 81.2%) in 2000 (Source: UN Development Programme, *Human Development Report*).

Directory

The Constitution

The Constitution of the Republic of Namibia took effect at independence on 21 March 1990. Its principal provisions are summarized below:

THE REPUBLIC

The Republic of Namibia is a sovereign, secular, democratic and unitary State and the Constitution is the supreme law.

FUNDAMENTAL HUMAN RIGHTS AND FREEDOMS

The fundamental rights and freedoms of the individual are guaranteed regardless of sex, race, colour, ethnic origin, religion, creed or social or economic status. All citizens shall have the right to form and join political parties. The practice of racial discrimination shall be prohibited.

THE PRESIDENT

Executive power shall be vested in the President and the Cabinet. The President shall be the Head of State and of the Government and the Commander-in-Chief of the Defence Force. The President shall be directly elected by universal and equal adult suffrage, and must receive more than 50% of the votes cast. The term of office shall be five years; one person may not hold the office of President for more than two terms*.

THE CABINET

The Cabinet shall consist of the President, the Prime Minister and such other ministers as the President may appoint from members of the National Assembly. The President may also appoint a Deputy Prime Minister. The functions of the members of the Cabinet shall include directing the activities of ministries and government departments, initiating bills for submission to the National Assembly, formulating, explaining and assessing for the National Assembly the budget of the State and its economic development plans, formulating, explaining and analysing for the National Assembly Namibia's foreign policy and foreign trade policy and advising the President on the state of national defence.

THE NATIONAL ASSEMBLY

Legislative power shall be vested in the National Assembly, which shall be composed of 72 members elected by general, direct and secret ballots and not more than six non-voting members appointed by the President by virtue of their special expertise, status, skill or experience. Every National Assembly shall continue for a maximum period of five years, but it may be dissolved by the President before the expiry of its term.

THE NATIONAL COUNCIL

The National Council shall consist of two members from each region (elected by regional councils from among their members) and shall have a life of six years. The functions of the National Council shall include considering all bills passed by the National Assembly, investigating any subordinate legislation referred to it by the National Assembly for advice, and recommending legislation to the National Assembly on matters of regional concern.

OTHER PROVISIONS

Other provisions relate to the administration of justice (see under Judicial System), regional and local government, the public service commission, the security commission, the police, defence forces and prison service, finance, and the central bank and national planning commission. The repeal of, or amendments to, the Constitution require the approval of two-thirds of the members of the National Assembly and two-thirds of the members of the National Council; if the proposed repeal or amendment secures a majority of two-thirds of the members of the National Assembly, but not a majority of two-thirds of the members of the National Council, the President may make the proposals the subject of a national referendum, in which a two-thirds' majority is needed for approval of the legislation.
* In late 1998 the National Assembly and National Council approved legislation whereby the Constitution was to be exceptionally amended to allow the incumbent President to seek a third term of office.

The Government

HEAD OF STATE

President and Commander-in-Chief of the Defence Force: Dr SAMUEL DANIEL NUJOMA (took office 21 March 1990; elected by direct suffrage 7–8 December 1994; re-elected 30 November–1 December 1999).

CABINET
(May 2003)

President: Dr SAMUEL DANIEL NUJOMA.

Prime Minister: THEO-BEN GURIRAB.

Deputy Prime Minister: Rev. HENDRIK WITBOOI.

Minister of Home Affairs: JERRY EKANDJO.

Minister of Foreign Affairs: HIDIPO HAMUTENYA.

Minister of Information and Broadcasting: NANGOLO MBUMBA.

Minister of Basic Education, Sport and Culture: JOHN MUTORWA.

Minister of Higher Education, Vocational Training, Science and Technology and Sport: NAHAS ANGULA.

Minister of Mines and Energy: NICKY IYAMBO.

Minister of Justice and Attorney-General: ALBERT KAWANA.

Minister of Trade and Industry: JESAYA NYAMU.

Minister of Agriculture, Water and Rural Development: HELMUT ANGULA.

Minister of Defence: ERIKKI NGHIMTINA.

Minister of Finance: SAARAH KUUGONGELWA-AMATHILA.

Minister of Health and Social Services: Dr LIBERTINE AMATHILA.

Minister of Labour: MARCO HAUSIKU.

Minister of Regional and Local Government and Housing: JOEL KAAPANDA.

Minister of Environment and Tourism: PHILEMON MALIMA.

Minister of Works, Transport and Communications: MOSES AMWEELO.

Minister of Lands, Resettlement and Rehabilitation: HIFIKEPUNYE POHAMBA.

Minister of Fisheries and Marine Resources: ABRAHAM IYAMBO.

Minister of Prisons and Correctional Services: ANDIMBA TOIVO YA TOIVO.

Minister of Women's Development and Child Welfare: NETUMBO NANDI-NDAITWAH.

MINISTRIES

Office of the President: State House, Robert Mugabe Ave, PMB 13339, Windhoek; tel. (61) 2707111; fax (61) 221780; e-mail angolo@op.gov.na; internet www.op.gov.na.

Office of the Prime Minister: Robert Mugabe Ave, PMB 13338, Windhoek; tel. (61) 2879111; fax (61) 230648; internet www.opm.gov.na.

Ministry of Agriculture, Water and Rural Development: cnr Robert Mugabe Ave and Peter Muller St, PMB 13184, Windhoek; tel. (61) 2087111; fax (61) 229961.

Ministry of Basic Education, Sport and Culture: Troskie House, Uhland St, PMB 13186, Windhoek; tel. (61) 2933111; fax (61) 224277.

Ministry of Defence: PMB 13307, Windhoek; tel. (61) 2049111; fax (61) 232518.

Ministry of Environment and Tourism: Swabou Bldg, Post St Mall, PMB 13346, Windhoek; tel. (61) 2842111; fax (61) 221930; e-mail tourism@iwwn.com.na; internet www.tourism.com.na.

Ministry of Finance: Fiscus Bldg, John Meinert St, PMB 13295, Windhoek; tel. (61) 2099111; fax (61) 230179.

Ministry of Fisheries and Marine Resources: Brendan Simbwaye Sq., PMB 13355, Windhoek; tel. (61) 2053911; fax (61) 233286; e-mail mfmr@mfmr.gov.na; internet www.mfmr.gov.na.

Ministry of Foreign Affairs: Govt Bldgs, Robert Mugabe Ave, PMB 13347, Windhoek; tel. (61) 2829111; fax (61) 223937; e-mail headquarters@mfa.gov.na; internet www.mfa.gov.na.

Ministry of Health and Social Services: Old State Hospital, Harvey St, PMB 13198, Windhoek; tel. (61) 2039111; fax (61) 227607.

Ministry of Higher Education, Vocational Training, Science and Technology and Sport: Winco Bldg, Stuebel St, PMB 13391, Windhoek; tel. (61) 2706111; fax (61) 253672.

Ministry of Home Affairs: Cohen Bldg, Kasino St, PMB 13200, Windhoek; tel. (61) 2922111; fax (61) 2922185.

Ministry of Information and Broadcasting: Windhoek.

Ministry of Justice: Justitia Bldg, Independence Ave, PMB 13248, Windhoek; tel. (61) 2805111; fax (61) 221615.

Ministry of Labour: 32 Mercedes St, Khomasdal, PMB 19005, Windhoek; tel. (61) 2066111; fax (61) 212323.

Ministry of Lands, Resettlement and Rehabilitation: Brendan Simbwaye Bldg, Goethe St, PMB 13343, Windhoek; tel. (61) 2852111; fax (61) 254240.

Ministry of Mines and Energy: 1st Aviation Rd, PMB 13297, Windhoek; tel. (61) 2848111; fax (61) 238643; e-mail info@mme.gov.na; internet www.mme.gov.na.

Ministry of Prisons and Correctional Services: Brendan Simbwaye Bldg, Goethe St, PMB 13323; tel. (61) 2846111; fax (61) 233879.

Ministry of Regional and Local Government and Housing: PMB 13289, Windhoek; tel. (61) 2975111; fax (61) 226049.

Ministry of Trade and Industry: Govt Bldgs, PMB 13340, Windhoek; tel. (61) 2837111; fax (61) 220148; internet www.mti.gov.na.

Ministry of Women's Development and Child Promotion: Windhoek.

Ministry of Works, Transport and Communications: PMB 13341, Windhoek; tel. (61) 2088111; fax (61) 228560.

President and Legislature

PRESIDENT

Presidential Election, 30 November–1 December 1999

Candidate	% of votes
Samuel Nujoma (SWAPO)	76.8
Ben Ulenga (CoD)	10.5
Katuutire Kaura (DTA)	9.6
Justus Garoeb (UDF)	3.0
Total	100.0

NATIONAL ASSEMBLY*

Speaker: Dr MOSES TJITENDERO.

General Election, 30 November–1 December 1999

Party	% of votes	Seats
South West Africa People's Organisation of Namibia (SWAPO)	76.1	55
Congress of Democrats (CoD)	9.9	7
Democratic Turnhalle Alliance of Namibia (DTA)	9.5	7
United Democratic Front (UDF)	2.9	2
Monitor Action Group (MAG)	0.7	1
Others	0.9	—
Total	100.0	72

* In addition to the 72 directly-elected members, the President of the Republic is empowered to nominate as many as six non-voting members.

NATIONAL COUNCIL

Chairman: KANDINDIMA NEHOVA.

The second chamber of parliament is the advisory National Council, comprising two representatives from each of the country's 13 Regional Councils, elected for a period of six years.

Political Organizations

Christian Democratic Action for Social Justice (CDA): Ondwangwa; f. 1982; supported by Ovambos and mems of fmr National Democratic Party; Leader Rev. PETER KALANGULA.

Congress of Democrats (CoD): 8 Storch St, POB 40905, Windhoek; tel. (61) 256954; fax (61) 256980; internet cod.namweb.com.na; f. 1999; Leader BEN ULENGA; Sec.-Gen. IGNATIUS SHIXWAMENI.

Democratic Coalition of Namibia (DCN): Windhoek; f. 1994 as coalition of the National Patriotic Front, the South West African National Union (withdrew from coalition in Nov. 1994) and the German Union; Leader MOSES KATJIUONGUA.

Democratic Turnhalle Alliance of Namibia (DTA): POB 173, Windhoek; internet www.framework.co.za/dua/namibia/dta.html; f. 1977 as a coalition of ethnically-based political groupings; reorg. as a single party in 1991; Pres. KATUUTIRE KAURA; Chair. JOHAN DE WAAL.

Federal Convention of Namibia (FCN): Windhoek; f. 1988; Leader JOHANNES DIERGAARDT; federalist; opposes unitary form of govt for Namibia; an alliance of ethnically-based parties, including:

NUDO—Progressive Party Jo'Horongo: f. 1987; Pres. MBURUMBA KERINA.

Rehoboth Bevryde Demokratiese Party Rehoboth Free Democratic Party or **Liberation Front (RBDP):** Leader JOHANNES DIERGAARDT; coalition of the **Rehoboth Bevrydingsparty** Leader JOHANNES DIERGAARDT and the **Rehoboth Democratic Party** Leader K. G. FREIGANG.

Monitor Action Group (MAG): POB 80808, Olympia, Windhoek; tel. (61) 252008; fax (61) 229242; e-mail monitor@cyberhost.com.na; f. 1991; fmrly National Party of South West Africa; Leader KOSIE PRETORIUS.

Namibia Movement for Independent Candidate: Windhoek; f. 1997; Leader JUSTICE KAWADENGE.

Namibia National Democratic Party: Windhoek; Leader PAUL HELMUTH.

Namibia National Front: Windhoek; Leader VEKUII RUKORO.

National Democratic Party for Justice (NDPFJ): f. May 1995 as SWAPO for Justice by fmr mems of SWAPO; reorg. as a political party in Nov. 1996, when it claimed to have 3,000 mem; Pres. NGHIWETE NDJOBA.

South West Africa People's Organisation of Namibia (SWAPO): Windhoek; internet www.swapo.org.na; f. 1957 as the Ovamboland People's Congress; renamed South West Africa People's Organisation in 1960; adopted present name in 1968; Pres. Dr SAMUEL DANIEL NUJOMA; Vice-Pres. Rev. HENDRIK WITBOOI; Sec.-Gen. HIFIKEPUNYE POHAMBA.

South West African National Union (SWANU): Windhoek; f. 1959; Leader HITJEVI VEII.

United Democratic Front (UDF): POB 20037, Windhoek; tel. (61) 230683; fax (61) 237175; f. 1989 as a centrist coalition of eight parties; Nat. Chair. ERIC BIWA; Pres. JUSTUS GAROEB.

Workers' Revolutionary Party: Windhoek; f. 1989; Trotskyist; Leaders WERNER MAMUGWE, HEWAT BEUKES.

The **Caprivi Liberation Army (CLA)**, f. 1998 as the Caprivi Liberation Movement, seeks secession of the Caprivi Strip; conducts mil. operations from bases in Zambia and Angola; political wing operates from Denmark as the **Caprivi National Union**, led by MISHAKE MUYONGO and BONIFACE MAMILI.

Diplomatic Representation

EMBASSIES AND HIGH COMMISSIONS IN NAMIBIA

Algeria: 111A Gloudina St, Ludwigsdorf, POB 3079, Windhoek; tel. (61) 221507; fax (61) 236376; e-mail ambalg.wkh@iwwn.com.na; Chargé d'affaires a.i. A. I. BENGUEUEDDA.

Angola: Angola House, 3 Dr Agostinho Neto St, Ausspannplatz, PMB 12020, Windhoek; tel. (61) 227535; fax (61) 221498; Ambassador Dr GARCIA PIRES.

Botswana: 101 Nelson Mandela Ave, POB 20359, Windhoek; tel. (61) 221942; fax (61) 221948; High Commissioner TUELENYANA ROSEMARY DITLHABI-OLIPHANT.

Brazil: 52 Bismarck St, POB 24166, Windhoek; tel. (61) 237368; fax (61) 233389; e-mail orlando@iwwn.com.na; Ambassador ORLANDO GALVÊAS OLIVEIRA.

China, People's Republic: 13 Wecka St, POB 22777, Windhoek; tel. (61) 222089; fax (61) 225544; e-mail chinaemb@iafrica.com.na; Ambassador CHEN LAIYUAN.

Congo, Republic: 9 Korner St, POB 22970, Windhoek; tel. (61) 257517; fax (61) 240796; Ambassador A. KONDHO.

Cuba: 31 Omuramba Rd, Eros, POB 23866, Windhoek; tel. (61) 227072; fax (61) 231584; e-mail embacuba@iafrica.com.na; Ambassador SERGIO GONZÁLEZ GONZÁLEZ.

Egypt: 10 Berg St, POB 11853, Windhoek; tel. (61) 221501; fax (61) 228856; Ambassador HUSSEIN A. M. WAHBY.

Finland: Sanlam Centre, 5th Floor, POB 3649, Windhoek; tel. (61) 221355; fax (61) 221349; e-mail sanomat.win@formin.fi; internet www.finemb.org.na; Chargé d'affaires SINIKKA ANTILA.

France: 1 Goethe St, POB 20484, Windhoek; tel. (61) 2276700; fax (61) 276710; e-mail frambwdk@iafrica.na; internet www.ambafrance-na.org; Ambassador PHILIPPE PERRIER DE LA BATHIE.

Germany: POB 231, Windhoek; tel. (61) 273100; fax (61) 222981; e-mail info@german-embassy-windhoek.org; internet www.german-embassy-windhoek.org; Ambassador HARALD N. NESTROY.

Ghana: 5 Nelson Mandela Ave, POB 24165, Windhoek; tel. (61) 221341; fax (61) 221343; High Commissioner H. MILLS-LUTTERODT.

India: 97 Nelson Mandela Ave, POB 1209, Windhoek; tel. (61) 226037; fax (61) 237320; e-mail hicomind@mweb.com.na; High Commissioner LAL DINGLIANA.

Indonesia: 103 Nelson Mandela Ave, POB 20691, Windhoek; tel. (61) 221914; fax (61) 223811; Chargé d'affaires THEO WAYMURI.

Kenya: Kenya House, 5th Floor, 134 Robert Mugabe Ave, POB 2889, Windhoek; tel. (61) 226836; fax (61) 221409; e-mail kenyanet@mweb.com.na; High Commissioner BINSAI J. CHEPSONGOL.

Libya: 69 Burg St, Luxury Hill, POB 124, Windhoek; tel. (61) 234454; fax (61) 234471; Chargé d'affaires a.i. H. O. ALSHAOSHI.

Malawi: 56 Bismarck St, POB 13254, Windhoek; tel. (61) 221391; fax (61) 227056; High Commissioner A. MNTHAMBALA.

Malaysia: 10 Von Eckenbrecker St, POB 312, Windhoek; tel. (61) 259344; fax (61) 259343; e-mail malhicom@iwwn.com.na.

Mexico: Southern Life Tower, 3rd Floor, 39 Post St Mall, POB 13220, Windhoek; tel. (61) 229082; fax (61) 229180; e-mail embamexn@iway.na; Charge d'affaires a.i. JOSÉ LUÍS GARCÍA.

Netherlands: 2 Crohn St, PMB 564, Windhoek; tel. (61) 223733; fax (61) 223732; e-mail nlgovwin@namib.com.na.

Nigeria: 4 Omuramba Rd, Eros Park, POB 23547, Windhoek; tel. (61) 232103; fax (61) 221639; e-mail nignam@web.com.na; High Commissioner B. M. HIRSE.

Portugal: 24 Robert Mugabe Ave, POB 443, Windhoek; tel. (61) 237928; fax (61) 237929; e-mail emport@mweb.com.na; Ambassador MARIA DO CARMO ALLEGRO DE MAGALHÃES.

Russia: 4 Christian St, POB 3826, Windhoek; tel. (61) 228671; fax (61) 229061; e-mail rusembna@iafrica.com.na; Ambassador VYACHE-SLAV D. SHUMSKII.

South Africa: RSA House, cnr Jan Jonker and Nelson Mandela Aves, POB 23100, Windhoek; tel. (61) 229765; fax (61) 224140; High Commissioner B. S. S. MABIZELA.

Spain: 58 Bismarck St, POB 21811, Windhoek; tel. (61) 223066; fax (61) 223046; e-mail embespnai@mail.mae.es; Ambassador JAVIER PÉREZ-GRIFFO.

Sweden: Sanlam Centre, 9th Floor, POB 23087, Windhoek; tel. (61) 2859111; fax (61) 2859222; e-mail embassy.windhoek@sida.se; Chargé d'affaires GÖRAN HEDEBRO.

United Kingdom: 116 Robert Mugabe Ave, POB 22202, Windhoek; tel. (61) 274800; fax (61) 228895; e-mail bhc@mweb.com.na; High Commissioner ALASDAIR MACDERMOTT.

USA: 14 Lossen St, Ausspannplatz, PMB 12029, Windhoek 9000; tel. (61) 221601; fax (61) 229792; Ambassador KEVIN J. MCGUIRE.

Ukraine: Windhoek; Ambassador IHOR M. TURYANSKIY.

Venezuela: Southern Life Tower, 3rd Floor, 39 Post St Mall, PMB 13353, Windhoek; tel. (61) 227905; fax (61) 227804; e-mail embaven@com.na; Chargé d'affaires ABRAHAM QUINTERO.

Zambia: 22 Sam Nujoma Dr., cnr Mandume Ndemufayo Rd, POB 22882, Windhoek; tel. (61) 37610; fax (61) 228162; High Commissioner CHANDA SOSALA.

Zimbabwe: cnr Independence Ave and Grimm St, POB 23056, Windhoek; tel. (61) 228134; fax (61) 226859; High Commissioner MARY SIBUSISIWE MUBI.

Judicial System

Judicial power is exercised by the Supreme Court, the High Court and a number of Magistrate and Lower Courts. The Constitution provides for the appointment of an Ombudsman.

Chief Justice: SIMPSON MTAMBANENGWE (acting).

Religion

It is estimated that about 90% of the population are Christians.

CHRISTIANITY

Council of Churches in Namibia: 8 Mont Blanc St, POB 41, Windhoek; tel. (61) 217621; fax (61) 62786; e-mail ccn.windhoek@iafrica.com.na; f. 1978; eight mem. churches; Pres. Bishop HENDRIK FREDERIK; Gen. Sec. NANGULA KATHINDI.

The Anglican Communion

Namibia comprises a single diocese in the Church of the Province of Southern Africa. The Metropolitan of the Province is the Archbishop of Cape Town, South Africa.

Bishop of Namibia: Rt Rev. NEHEMIAH SHIHALA HAMUPENBE, POB 57, Windhoek; tel. (61) 238920; fax (61) 225903.

Dutch Reformed Church

Dutch Reformed Church in Namibia: 34 Feldstreet, POB 389, Windhoek; tel. (61) 225073; fax (61) 227287; e-mail ngkn@iway.na; internet www.ngkn.com.na; f. 1898; 23,724 mems in 43 congregations; Sec. Rev. CLEM MARAIS.

Evangelical Lutheran

Evangelical Lutheran Church in Namibia (ELCIN): PMB 2018, Ondangwa; tel. (56) 24241; fax (56) 240472; e-mail elcinhq@ednweb.com.na; internet www.elca.org/dgm/country_packet/packets/africa/namibia/elcin.html; Moderator Rev. HERMAN OOS-THUISEN; Presiding Bishop APOLLOS KAULINGE.

Evangelical Lutheran Church (Rhenish Mission Church): POB 5069, Windhoek; tel. (61) 224531; f. 1967; Pres. Bishop HENDRIK FREDERIK.

German Evangelical-Lutheran Church in Namibia: POB 233, Windhoek; tel. (61) 224294; fax (61) 221470; e-mail delk@namibnet.com; 5,000 mems; Pres. Bishop REINHARD KEDING.

Methodist

African Methodist Episcopal Church: Windhoek; tel. (61) 62757; Rev. B. G. KARUAERA.

Methodist Church of Southern Africa: POB 143, Windhoek; tel. (61) 228921.

The Roman Catholic Church

Namibia comprises one archdiocese, one diocese and one apostolic vicariate. At 31 December 2000 there were an estimated 218,946 adherents of the Roman Catholic Church in Namibia, comprising some 11.8% of the total population.

Bishops' Conference

Namibian Catholic Bishops' Conference, POB 11525, Windhoek; tel. (61) 224798; fax (61) 228126; e-mail ncbc@windhoek.org.na. f. 1996; Pres. Most Rev. BONIFATIUS HAUSHIKU (Archbishop of Windhoek).

Archbishop of Windhoek: (vacant), POB 272, Windhoek; tel. (61) 227595; fax (61) 229836; e-mail rcharch@iafrica.com.na.

Other Christian Churches

Among other denominations active in Namibia are the Evangelical Reformed Church in Africa, the Presbyterian Church of Southern Africa and the United Congregational Church of Southern Africa.

JUDAISM

Windhoek Hebrew Congregation: POB 563, Windhoek; tel. (61) 221990; fax (61) 226444; e-mail steinitz@nweb.com.na.

BAHÁ'Í FAITH

National Spiritual Assembly: POB 20372, Windhoek; tel. (61) 239634; e-mail don@iafrica.com.na; mems resident in 215 localities.

The Press

Abacus: POB 22791, Windhoek; tel. (61) 235596; fax (61) 236467; weekly; English; educational; circ. 31,000.

AgriForum: 114 Robert Mugabe Ave, PMB 13255, Windhoek; tel. (61) 237838; fax (61) 220193; e-mail richter@agrinamibia.com.na; monthly; Afrikaans, English; publ. by Namibia Agricultural Union; Editor RICHTER ERASMUS; circ. 5,000.

Allgemeine Zeitung: 11 Omurambaweg, POB 86695, Windhoek; tel. (61) 225822; fax (61) 220225; e-mail aznews@iway.na; internet www.az-namibia.de; f. 1916; daily; German; Editor-in-Chief EBERHARD HOFFMANN; circ. 4,800 (Mon.–Wed.), 5,900 (Thur.–Fri.).

Aloe: POB 59, Windhoek; tel. (61) 2902056; fax (61) 2902006; monthly; English; edited by the Windhoek Municipality; Editor SIMON HOABEB; circ. 45,000.

Caprivi Vision: f. 2002; regional newspaper for Caprivi region; Editor RISCO LUMAMEZI.

CCN Information: Council of Churches in Namibia, POB 41, Windhoek; f. 1980; 11 a year.

Namib Times: Seventh St., POB 706, Walvis Bay; tel. (64) 205854; fax (64) 204813; 2 a week; Afrikaans, English, German and Portuguese; Editor PAUL VINCENT; circ. 4,300.

Namibia Brief: Independence Ave, POB 2123, Windhoek; tel. and fax (61) 251044; quarterly; English; Editor CATHY BLATT; circ. 7,500.

Namibia Business Journal: POB 9355, Windhoek; tel. (61) 228809; fax (61) 228009; Editor MILTON LOUW; circ. 4,000.

Namibia Economist: 7 Schuster St, POB 49, Windhoek 9000; tel. (61) 221925; fax (61) 220615; e-mail info@economist.com.na; internet www.economist.com.na; f. 1986; weekly; English; business; Editor EDGAR BRANDT; circ. 7,000.

Namibia Focus: Windhoek; tel. (61) 227182; fax (61) 220226; monthly; English; business; Editor JOHAN ENGELBRECHT; circ. 30,000.

Namibia Review: Turnhalle Bldg, Bahnhof St, PMB 13344, Windhoek; tel. (61) 222246; fax (61) 224937; e-mail nreview@mib.gov.na; govt-owned; monthly; Editor ELIZABETH KALAMBO-MULE; circ. 5,000.

Namibia Today: POB 24669, Windhoek; tel. (61) 229150; fax (61) 229150; 2 a week; Afrikaans, English, Oshiherero, Oshiwambo; publ. by SWAPO; Editor KAOMO-VIJINDA TJOMBE; circ. 5,000.

The Namibian: John Meinert St, POB 20783, Windhoek; tel. (61) 236970; fax (61) 233980; e-mail info@namibian.com.na; internet www.namibian.com.na; daily; English; Editor GWEN LISTER; circ. 11,000.

The Namibian Worker: POB 50034, Bachbrecht, Windhoek; tel. (61) 215037; fax (61) 215589; Afrikaans, English, Oshiwambo; publ. by National Union of Namibian Workers; Editor-in-Chief C. R. HAIKALI; circ. 1,000.

New Era: PMB 13364, Windhoek; tel. (61) 234924; fax (61) 235419; govt-owned; 2 a week; English; Editor RAJAH MUNAMAVA; circ. 10,000.

Die Republikein: 49 Stuebel St, POB 3436, Windhoek; tel. (61) 2972000; fax (61) 2972025; e-mail republkn@iafrica.com.na; internet www.republikein.com.na; f. 1977; daily; Afrikaans, English and German; organ of DTA of Namibia; Editor CHRISTO RETIEF (acting); circ. 12,000 (Mon.–Wed.), 15,000 (Thur.–Fri.).

Tempo: 49 Stuebel St, POB 1794, Windhoek; tel. (61) 225822; fax (61) 223110; f. 1992; weekly; English and German; Editor DES ERASMUS; circ. 11,000.

Visitor: POB 23000, Windhoek; tel. (61) 227182; fax (61) 220226; monthly; English; tourist information; Editor JOHAN ENGELBRECHT; circ. 10,000.

The Windhoek Advertiser: 49 Stuebel St, POB 3436, Windhoek; tel. (61) 230331; fax (61) 225863; e-mail advertsr@iwwn.com.na; f. 1919; daily; English; Editor DEON SCHLECHTER; circ. 5,000 (Mon.–Wed.), 7,000 (Thur.–Fri.).

Windhoek Observer: 49 Stuebel St, POB 2255, Windhoek; tel. (61) 221737; fax (61) 226098; f. 1978; weekly; English; Editor HANNES SMITH; circ. 14,000.

NEWS AGENCIES

Namibia Press Agency (Nampa): POB 61354, Windhoek; tel. (61) 221711; fax (61) 221713; e-mail admin@nampa.org; internet www.nampa.org; Editor-in-Chief H. HAMUNIME (acting).

Foreign Bureaux

Informatsionnoye Telegrafnoye Agentstvo Rossii—Telegrafnoye Agentstvo Suverennykh Stran (ITAR—TASS) (Russia): POB 24821, Windhoek; tel. and fax (61) 232909; Correspondent PAVE MYLTSEV.

Inter Press Service (IPS) (Italy): POB 20783, Windhoek; tel. (61) 226645; Correspondent MARK VERBAAN.

South African Press Association (SAPA): POB 2032, Windhoek; tel. (61) 231565; fax (61) 220783; Representative CARMEN HONEY.

Xinhua (New China) News Agency (People's Republic of China): POB 22130, Windhoek; tel. (61) 226484; fax (61) 226484; Bureau Chief TENG WENYI.

Reuters (UK) is also represented in Namibia.

PRESS ASSOCIATIONS

Journalist Association of Namibia (JAN): Windhoek; tel. (61) 236970; fax (61) 248016; e-mail shirumbu@iafrica.com.na; f. 1992; Chair. DAVID LUSH.

Press Club Windhoek: POB 2032, Windhoek; tel. (61) 231565; fax (61) 220783; Chair. CARMEN HONEY.

Publishers

BAUM Publishers: POB 3436, Windhoek; tel. (61) 225411; fax (61) 224843; Publr NIC KRUGER.

Clarian Publishers: POB 5861, Windhoek; tel. (61) 251044; fax (61) 237251; Publr CATHY BLATT.

ELOC Printing Press: PMB 2013, Oniipa, Ondangwa; tel. and fax (6756) 40211; f. 1901; Rev. Dr KLEOPAS DUMENI.

Gamsberg McMillan Publishers (Pty) Ltd: POB 22830, Windhoek; tel. (61) 232165; fax (61) 233538; e-mail gmp@iafrica.com.na; internet www.macmillan-africa.com/contacts/namibia.htm; Man. Dir HERMAN VAN WYK.

Longman Namibia: POB 9251, Eros, Windhoek; tel. (61) 231124; fax (61) 224019; Publr LINDA BREDENKAMP.

National Archives of Namibia: Eugène Marais St, PMB 13250, Windhoek; tel. (61) 2935213; fax (61) 2935217; Man. J. KUTZNER.

New Namibia Books (Pty) Ltd: POB 21601, Windhoek; tel. (61) 221134; fax (61) 235279; Publr JANE KATJAVIVI.

Out of Africa Publishers: POB 21841, Windhoek; tel. (61) 221494; fax (61) 221720; e-mail nam00356@mweb.com.na; Man. VIDA LOCHNER.

PUBLISHERS' ASSOCIATION

Association of Namibian Publishers: POB 21601, Windhoek; tel. (61) 235796; fax (61) 235279; f. 1991; Sec. PETER REINER.

Broadcasting and Communications

TELECOMMUNICATIONS

Telecom Namibia Ltd (Telecom): POB 297, Windhoek; tel. (61) 2019211; fax (61) 248723; internet www.telecom.na; f. 1992; state-owned; Chair T. HAIMBILI; Man. Dir T. MBERIRUA.

Mobile Telecommunications Ltd (MTC): POB 23051, Windhoek; tel. (61) 249570; fax (61) 249571; f. 1994; cellular telecommunications co; Man. Dir B. GUVE.

Multicom: POB 80425, Windhoek; tel. (61) 264755; fax (61) 264756; f. 1994; Gen. Man. G. VAN WYK.

BROADCASTING

Radio

Namibian Broadcasting Corpn (NBC): POB 321, Windhoek; tel. (61) 2913111; fax (61) 216209; e-mail nbcho@iwwn.com.na; f. 1990; broadcasts on eight radio channels in 11 languages; Dir-Gen. Dr BEN MULONGENI.

Channel 7: POB 20500, Windhoek; tel. (61) 218969; fax (61) 215572; Man. NEAL VAN DEN BERGH.

Katutura Community Radio: POB 22355, Windhoek; tel. (61) 263768; fax (61) 262786; Dir FREDERICK GOWASEB.

Radio Antenna (Radio 99): POB 11849, Windhoek; tel. (61) 223634; fax (61) 230964; e-mail radio99@mweb.com.na; f. 1994; Man. Dir MARIO AITA.

Radio Energy (Radio 100): POB 11849, Windhoek; tel. (61) 224947; fax (61) 230964; Man. Dir MARIO AITA.

Television

Namibian Broadcasting Corpn (NBC): POB 321, Windhoek; tel. (61) 2913111; fax (61) 216209; e-mail nbcho@iwwn.com.na; internet www.nbc.com.na; f. 1990; operates national television channel; programmes in English; Dir-Gen. Dr BEN MULONGENI.

Multi-Choice Namibia: POB 1752, Windhoek; tel. (61) 222222; fax (61) 227605; commercial television channels; Gen. Man. HARRY AUCAMP.

Finance

(cap. = capital; res = reserves; dep. = deposits; m. = million; brs = branches; amounts in Namibian dollars)

BANKING

Central Bank

Bank of Namibia: 71 Robert Mugabe Ave, POB 2882, Windhoek; tel. (61) 2835111; fax (61) 2835067; e-mail sigrid.tjijorokisa@bon.com.na; internet www.bon.com.na; f. 1990; cap. 40.0m., res 785.0m., dep. 672.5m. (Dec. 2000); Gov. TOM ALWEENDO; Deputy Gov. L. S. IPANGELWA.

Commercial Banks

Bank Windhoek Ltd: Bank Windhoek Bldg, 262 Independence Ave, POB 15, Windhoek; tel. (61) 2991122; fax (61) 2991620; e-mail info@bankwindhoek.com.na; internet www.bankwindhoek.com.na; f. 1982; cap. 4.7m., res 283.2m., dep. 2,939.0m. (March 2002); Chair. J. C. BRANDT; Man. Dir J. J. SWANEPOEL; 22 brs.

City Savings and Investment Bank (CSIB): FGI Bldg, 2nd Floor, Post St Mall, Windhoek; tel. (61) 221262; fax (61) 221555; e-mail csib@solarium.iwwn.com.na; f. 1994; merged with South West Africa Building Society 2000.

Commercial Bank of Namibia Ltd: 12–20 Bülow St, POB 1, Windhoek; tel. (61) 2959111; fax (61) 2952046; e-mail service@c-bank.com.na; internet www.c-bank.com.na; f. 1973; controlled by SND Investment Holdings Ltd; cap. 16.0m., res 16.4m., dep. 1,648.0m. (Dec. 2001); Chair. MICHAEL J. LEEMING; Man. Dir STEPHANUS DU PLESSIS; 10 brs.

First National Bank of Namibia Ltd: 209/211 Independence Ave, POB 195, Windhoek; tel. (61) 2992109; fax (61) 2992111; e-mail info@fnbnamibia.com.na; internet www.fnbnamibia.com.na; f. 1986;

cap. 1.0m., res 427.3m., dep. 2,419.9m. (June 2000); Chair. H. D. Voigts; Man. Dir S. H. Moir; 28 brs and 22 agencies.

Namibian Banking Corpn: Carl List Haus, Independence Ave, POB 370, Windhoek; tel. (61) 225946; fax (61) 223741; Chair. J. C. Westraat; Man. Dir P. P. Niehaus; 3 brs.

Standard Bank Namibia Ltd: Mutual Platz, Post St Mall, POB 3327, Windhoek; tel. (61) 2949111; fax (61) 2942555; e-mail info@standardbank.com.na; internet www.standardbank.com.na; f. 1915; controlled by Standard Bank Investment Corpn; cap. 1.7m., res 316.0m., dep. 3,402.5m. (Dec. 2001); Chair. L. S. Hangala; Man. Dir O. M. Tidbury; 19 brs.

Agricultural Bank

Agricultural Bank of Namibia: POB 13208, Windhoek; tel. (61) 2074111; fax (61) 2074287; e-mail agribank@iafrica.com.na; f. 1922; cap. 492.7m., dep. 25.9m., total assets 659.2m. (March 1999); Chair. and Man. Dir T. Hijarunguru; Gen. Man. J. Daniels.

Merchant Bank

UAL—Namibia: Windhoek; f. 1997; subsidiary of UAL Merchant Bank Ltd (South Africa); Man. Dir Steve Galloway.

STOCK EXCHANGE

Namibian Stock Exchange (NSX): Shop 8, Kaiserkrone Centre, Post St Mall, POB 2401, Windhoek; tel. (61) 227647; fax (61) 248531; e-mail info@nsx.com.na; internet www.nsx.com.na; f. 1992; Chair. Exec. Cttee P. Hango; Gen. Man. Heiko Niedermeier.

INSURANCE

Allianz Insurance Co of Namibia Ltd: POB 3244, Windhoek; tel. (61) 226897; fax (61) 231070; e-mail mbakoh@allianz.co.na; Man. Dir H. Mbako.

W. Biederlack & Co: Metje-Behnsen Bldg, 2nd Floor, Independence Ave, POB 365, Windhoek; tel. (61) 233177; fax (61) 233178; e-mail group@w-biederlack.com; f. 1990.

Commercial Union Insurance Ltd: Bülow St, POB 1599, Windhoek; tel. (61) 37137.

FGI Namibia Ltd: POB 2516, Windhoek; tel. (61) 225450; fax (61) 229195; f. 1993; short-term insurance; Man. Dir Peter Opperman.

Incorporated General Insurance Ltd: 10 Bülow St, POB 2516, Windhoek; tel. (61) 37453; fax (61) 35647.

Insurance Co of Namibia (INSCON): POB 2877, Windhoek; tel. (61) 223425; fax (61) 233808; short-term insurance; Gen. Dir F. Otto.

Lifegro Assurance Ltd: Independence Ave, POB 23055, Windhoek; tel. (61) 33068.

Lumley Insurance Group: POB 1011, Windhoek 9000; tel. (61) 224471; fax (61) 234802; f. 1953; Chair. and Man. Dir Ingo Rix.

Metropolitan Life Ltd: Goethe St, POB 3785, Windhoek; tel. (61) 239140; fax (61) 248191; Chair. M. L. Smith; Man. Dir R. A. V. E. Fouche.

Mutual and Federal Insurance Co Ltd: Mutual and Federal Centre, 7th Floor, 227 Independence Ave, POB 151, Windhoek; tel. (61) 2077111; fax (61) 2077205; f. 1990; Gen. Man. R. I. Sanger.

Namibia National Insurance Co Ltd: Bülow St, POB 23053, Windhoek; tel. (61) 224539; fax (61) 238737; fmrly Federated Insurance Co Ltd.

Old Mutual Life Assurance Co. (Namibia) Ltd: Mutual Platz, 5th Floor, Post St Mall, POB 165, Windhoek; tel. (61) 2993999; fax (61) 223838; e-mail dkotze@oldmutual.com; internet www.oldmutual.com.na; Chair. J. S. Kirkpatrick.

Protea Assurance Co Ltd: Windhoek; tel. (61) 225891.

Sanlam Life Assurance Ltd: Bülow St, POB 317, Windhoek; tel. (61) 36680.

Santam Insurance Ltd: Independence Ave, POB 204, Windhoek; tel. (61) 238214; fax (61) 235225; Man. Dir C. J. Engelbrecht; Dep. Man. Dir H. Ochse.

Southern Life Assurance Ltd: Southern Tower, Post Street Mall, POB 637, Windhoek; tel. (61) 234056; fax (61) 231574; Man. Dir L. Lombaard.

Trade and Industry

GOVERNMENT AGENCIES

Karakul Board of Namibia—Swakara Fur Producers and Exporters: PMB 13300, Windhoek; tel. (61) 237750; fax (61) 236122; e-mail agrapels@agra.com.na.

Meat Board of Namibia: POB 38, Windhoek; tel. (61) 33180; fax (61) 228310; f. 1935; Chair. John le Roux; Gen. Man. Paul Strydom.

Meat Corpn of Namibia (MEATCO NAMIBIA): POB 3881, Windhoek; tel. (61) 216810; fax (61) 217045; e-mail hoffice@meatco.com.na; internet www.meatco.com.na.

Namibian Agronomic Board: POB 5096, Windhoek; tel. (61) 224741; fax (61) 225371; e-mail christof@nammic.com.na; Man. C. Brock.

National Petroleum Corpn of Namibia (NAMCOR): Windhoek; Man. Dir Skerf Pottas.

DEVELOPMENT ORGANIZATIONS

Namibia Development Corpn: 11 Goethe St, PMB 13252, Windhoek; tel. (61) 2069111; fax (61) 247841; e-mail info@ndc.org.na; internet www.ndc.org.na; f. 1993; promotes foreign investment and provides concessionary loans and equity to new enterprises; manages agricultural projects; undertakes feasibility studies; Chair. P. T. Damaseb; Man. Dir I. I. Namaseb.

Namibia Investment Centre: Ministry of Trade and Industry, Brendan Simbwaye Sq., Block B, Goethe St, PMB 13340, Windhoek; tel. (61) 2837335; fax (61) 220278; e-mail nic@mti.gov.na; Exec. Dir D. Nuyoma.

National Housing Enterprise: POB 20192, Windhoek; tel. (61) 2927111; fax (61) 222301; f. 1983; provides low-cost housing; Chair. V. Rukoro; CEO K. R. M. Kavekotora.

CHAMBERS OF COMMERCE

Chamber of Mines of Namibia (CMIN): POB 2895, Windhoek; tel. (61) 237925; fax (61) 222638; e-mail chammin@nweb.com.na; f. 1979; Pres. Inge Zaamwani; Gen. Man. John Rogers; 62 mems (2001).

Namibia National Chamber of Commerce and Industry (NNCCI): POB 9355, Windhoek; tel. (61) 228809; fax (61) 228009; e-mail nccihq@iwwn.com.na; internet www.ncci.org.na; f. 1990; Pres. Dr L. Hangala; CEO Sam Geiseb (acting).

Windhoek Chamber of Commerce and Industries: SWA Building Society Bldg, 3rd Floor, POB 191, Windhoek; tel. (61) 222000; fax (61) 233690; e-mail whkchamber@lianam.lia.net; f. 1920; Pres. H. Schmidt; Gen. Man. T. D. Parkhouse; 230 mems.

EMPLOYERS' ORGANIZATIONS

Construction Industries Federation of Namibia: 22 Stein St, Klein, POB 1479, Windhoek; tel. (61) 230028; fax (61) 224534; e-mail cif@namibnet.com; Pres. Ernst Keibel.

Electrical Contractors' Association: POB 3163, Windhoek; tel. (61) 37920; Pres. F. Pfaffenthaler.

Motor Industries Federation of Namibia: POB 1503, Windhoek; tel. (61) 37970; fax (61) 237251.

Namibia Agricultural Union (NAU): PMB 13255, Windhoek; tel. (61) 237838; fax (61) 220193; e-mail nau@agrinamibia.com.na; Pres. J. M. de Wet.

Namibia Chamber of Printing: POB 363, Windhoek; tel. (61) 237905; fax (61) 222927; Sec. S. G. Timm.

UTILITIES

Namibia Power Corpn Ltd (NamPower): NamPower Centre, 15 Luther St, POB 2864, Windhoek; tel. (61) 2054111; fax (61) 232805; e-mail register@nampower.com.na; internet www.nampower.com.na; Chair. M. Shikongo; Man. Dir Leake S. Hangala.

Northern Electricity: POB 891, Tsumeb; tel. (67) 222243; fax (67) 222245; private electricity supply co; Man. Dir C. G. N. Huysen.

TRADE UNIONS

There are several union federations, and a number of independent unions.

Trade Union Federations

Confederation of Labour: POB 22060, Windhoek.

National Allied Unions (NANAU): Windhoek; f. 1987; an alliance of trade unions, representing c. 7,600 mems, incl. Namibia Wholesale and Retail Workers' Union (f. 1986; Gen. Sec. T. Ngaujake;

6,000 mems), and Namibia Women Support Cttee; Pres. HENOCH HANDURA.

Namibia Trade Union (NTU): Windhoek; f. 1985; represents 6,700 domestic, farm and metal workers; Pres. ALPHA KANGUEEHI; Sec.-Gen. BEAU TJISESETA.

Namibia Trade Union Council (NTUC): Windhoek; f. 1981; affiliates include Northern Builders' Asscn.

National Union of Namibian Workers (NUNW): POB 50034, Windhoek; tel. (61) 215037; fax (61) 215589; f. 1972; Pres. PONHELE YA FRANCE; Sec.-Gen. RANGA HAIKAILI; 87,000 mems.

Affiliates include:

Mineworkers' Union of Namibia (MUN): f. 1986; Chair. ASSER KAPERE; Pres. EINO NTINDA (acting); Gen. Sec. PETER NAHOLO (acting); 12,500 mems.

Namibia Food and Allied Workers' Union: f. 1986; Chair. MATHEUS LIBEREKI; Pres. ELIFAS NANGOLO; Gen. Sec. MAGDALENA IPINGE (acting); 12,000 mems.

Namibia Metal and Allied Workers' Union: f. 1987; Chair. ANDRIES TEMBA; Gen. Sec. MOSES SHIKWA (acting); 5,500 mems.

Namibia Public Workers' Union: f. 1987; Chair. STEVEN IMMANUEL; Gen. Sec. PETER ILONGA; 11,000 mems.

Namibia Transport and Allied Workers' Union: f. 1988; Chair. TYLVES GIDEON; Gen. Sec. IMMANUEL KAVAA; 7,500 mems.

Other Unions

Association for Government Service Officials: Windhoek; f. 1981; Chair. ALLAN HATTLE; 9,000 mems.

Namibia Building Workers' Association: Windhoek; Sec. H. BOCK.

Public Service Union of Namibia: POB 21662, Windhoek; tel. (61) 213083; fax (61) 213047; f. 1981; Sec.-Gen. STEVE RUKORO.

Transport

RAILWAYS

The main line runs from Nakop, at the border with South Africa, via Keetmanshoop to Windhoek, Kranzberg, Grootfontein, Tsumeb, Swakopmund and Walvis Bay. There are three branch lines, from Windhoek to Gobabis, Otjiwarongo to Outjo and Keetmanshoop to Lüderitz. The total rail network covers 2,382 route-km. There are plans for a railway line connecting Namibia with Zambia, as part of a programme to improve transport links among the members of the Common Market for Eastern and Southern Africa; plans to extend the northern railway line by 248 km, from Tsuneb to Ondangwa, were announced in 2001.

TransNamib Holdings Ltd: TransNamib Bldg, cnr Independence Ave and Bahnhof St, PMB 13204, Windhoek; tel. (61) 2981111; fax (61) 227984; e-mail pubrelation@transnamib.com.na; internet www

.transnamib.com.na; state-owned; Chair. OTTO HERINGEL; Man. Dir Dr PEINGONDJABI T. SHIPOH.

ROADS

In 2000 the road network comprised 66,467 km of roads, of which 4,470 km were main roads. A major road link from Walvis Bay to Jwaneng, northern Botswana, the Trans-Kalahari Highway, was completed in 1998, along with the Trans-Caprivi highway, linking Namibia with northern Botswana, Zambia and Zimbabwe. The Government is also upgrading and expanding the road network in northern Namibia.

SHIPPING

The ports of Walvis Bay and Lüderitz are linked to the main overseas shipping routes and handle almost one-half of Namibia's external trade. Walvis Bay is a hub port for the region, serving land-locked countries such as Botswana, Zambia and Zimbabwe.

Namibian Ports Authority (NAMPORT): 13th Road, POB 361, Walvis Bay; tel. (64) 2082201; fax (64) 2082320; e-mail jerome@ namport.com.na; internet www.namport.com.na; f. 1994; Chair. DIRK H. CONRADIE; CEO WESSIE WESSELS.

Pan-Ocean Shipping Services Ltd: POB 2613, Walvis Bay; tel. (64) 203959; fax (64) 204199; e-mail kirovg@iafrica.com.na; f. 1995; Man. Dir JÜRGEN HEYNEMANN; Gen. Man. GEORGE KIROV.

CIVIL AVIATION

There are international airports at Windhoek and Walvis Bay, as well as a number of other airports throughout Namibia, and numerous landing strips.

Air Namibia: TransNamib Bldg, cnr Independence Ave and Bahnhof St, POB 731, Windhoek; tel. (61) 223019; fax (61) 221910; e-mail aguibeb@airnamibia.com.na; internet www.airnamibia.com .na; f. 1959 as Namib Air; state-owned; transfer to majority (70%) private ownership pending; domestic flights and services to Southern Africa and Western Europe; Chair. Dr PETRUS DAMASEB; Man. Dir PETER CHIKUMBA (acting).

Kalahari Express Airlines (KEA): POB 40179, Windhoek; tel. (61) 245665; fax (61) 245612; e-mail keaadmin@kalahariexpress .com.na; internet www.iwwn.com.na/kea/; f. 1995; domestic and regional flights; Exec. Dir PEINGONDJABI SHIPOH.

Tourism

Namibia's principal tourist attractions are its game parks and nature reserves, and the development of 'eco-tourism' is being promoted. In the late 1990s tourism was one of the fastest growing sectors of the Namibian economy. Government investment in expanding the tourism sector was expected to total N $547m. during 1993–98. Tourist arrivals in Namibia in 1998 totalled 559,674. In 1998 tourism receipts were US $288m.

Namibia Tourism: PMB 13346, Capital Bldg, Ground Floor, 272 Independence Ave, Windhoek; tel. (61) 2849111; fax (61) 284-2364; e-mail tourism@iwwn.com.na; internet www.iwwn.com.na/namtour.

NAURU

Introductory Survey

Location, Climate, Language, Religion, Flag, Capital

The Republic of Nauru is a small island in the central Pacific Ocean, lying about 40 km (25 miles) south of the Equator and about 4,000 km (2,500 miles) north-east of Sydney, Australia. Its nearest neighbour is Banaba (Ocean Island), in Kiribati, about 300 km (186 miles) to the east. The climate is tropical, with a westerly monsoon season from November to February. The average annual rainfall is about 2,060 mm (80 ins), but actual rainfall is extremely variable. Day temperatures vary between 24°C and 34°C (75°–93°F). Of the total population in 1983, 61.7% were Nauruans. Their language is Nauruan, but English is also widely understood. The majority of Nauruans are Christians, mostly adherents of the Nauruan Protestant Church. The national flag (proportions 1 by 2) is royal blue, divided by a narrow horizontal yellow stripe, with a 12-pointed white star at the lower hoist. The island state has no official capital, but the seat of the legislature and most government offices are in Yaren district.

Recent History

Nauru, inhabited by a predominantly Polynesian people, organized in 12 clans, was annexed by Germany in 1888. In 1914, shortly after the outbreak of the First World War, the island was captured by Australian forces. It continued to be administered by Australia under a League of Nations mandate (granted in 1920), which also named the United Kingdom and New Zealand as co-trustees. Between 1942 and 1945 Nauru was occupied by the Japanese, who deported 1,200 islanders to Truk (now Chuuk), Micronesia, where many died in bombing raids or from starvation. In 1947 the island was placed under UN Trusteeship, with Australia as the administering power on behalf of the Governments of Australia, New Zealand and the United Kingdom. The UN Trusteeship Council proposed in 1964 that the indigenous people of Nauru be resettled on Curtis Island, off the Queensland coast. This offer was made in anticipation of the progressive exhaustion of the island's phosphate deposits, and because of the environmental devastation resulting from the mining operations. However, the Nauruans elected to remain on the island. Between 1906 and 1968 41m. metric tons of phosphate were mined. Nauru was accorded a considerable measure of self-government in January 1966, with the establishment of Legislative and Executive Councils, and proceeded to independence on 31 January 1968 (exactly 22 years after the surviving Nauruans returned to the island from exile in Micronesia). In early 1998 Nauru announced its intention to seek UN membership and full Commonwealth membership (Nauru had hitherto been a 'special member' of the Commonwealth, not represented at meetings of Heads of Government). The decision was largely based on the islanders' desire to play a more prominent role in international policies relating to issues that affect them, most notably climate change (see below). Nauru became a full member of the Commonwealth in May 1999, and a member of the UN in September of that year.

The Head Chief of Nauru, Hammer DeRoburt, was elected President in May 1968 and re-elected in 1971 and 1973. Dissatisfaction with his increasingly personal rule led to the election of Bernard Dowiyogo (leader of the recently-established, informal Nauru Party) to the presidency in 1976. Dowiyogo was re-elected President after a general election in late 1977. However, DeRoburt's supporters adopted tactics of obstruction in Parliament, and in December 1977 Dowiyogo resigned, in response to Parliament's refusal to approve budgetary legislation; he was re-elected shortly afterwards, but was again forced to resign in April 1978, following the defeat of a legislative proposal concerning phosphate royalties. Lagumot Harris, another member of the Nauru Party, succeeded him, but resigned three weeks later when Parliament rejected a finance measure, and DeRoburt was again elected President. He was re-elected in December of that year, in December 1980 and in May and December 1983.

In September 1986 DeRoburt resigned, following the defeat of a government budget proposal; he was replaced as President by Kennan Adeang, who was elected in Parliament by nine votes to DeRoburt's eight. However, after holding office for only 14 days, Adeang was defeated in a parliamentary vote of 'no confidence', and DeRoburt subsequently resumed the presidency. Following a general election in December Adeang was again narrowly elected President. However, he was subsequently ousted by another vote of 'no confidence', and DeRoburt was reinstated as President. The atmosphere of political uncertainty generated by the absence of a clear majority in Parliament led DeRoburt to dissolve Parliament in preparation for another general election in January 1987, at which the incumbent was re-elected to the presidency by 11 votes to six. In February Adeang announced the establishment of the Democratic Party of Nauru, essentially a revival of the Nauru Party. Eight members of Parliament subsequently joined the new party, which declared that its aim was to curtail the extension of presidential powers and to promote democracy. In August 1989 a parliamentary motion of 'no confidence' in DeRoburt (proposed by Adeang) was approved by 10 votes to five, and Kenas Aroi, a former Minister for Finance, was subsequently elected President. Aroi resigned in December, owing to ill health, and after a general election in the same month Bernard Dowiyogo was re-elected President, defeating DeRoburt by 10 votes to six. The next presidential election, held shortly after a general election in November 1992, resulted in victory for Dowiyogo, by 10 votes to seven, over Buraro Detudamo.

At a general election held in November 1995, when a total of 67 candidates contested the 18 parliamentary seats, all cabinet members were re-elected. A subsequent presidential election resulted in Lagumot Harris's defeat of the incumbent Dowiyogo by nine votes to eight. The resignation of the Chairman of Air Nauru, following allegations of misconduct, prompted Parliament to vote on a motion of 'no confidence' in the Government in November 1996. The motion was narrowly approved and Harris was replaced by Dowiyogo as President. Later that month, however, Dowiyogo's new Government was itself defeated in a parliamentary vote of 'no confidence', and Kennan Adeang was elected to the presidency. A widespread perception that the new Government lacked experience was thought to be a major factor prompting a further motion of 'no confidence' in December, at which Adeang was similarly removed from office. At a subsequent presidential contest Reuben Kun, a former Minister for Finance, defeated Adeang by 12 votes to five, on the understanding that his administration would organize a general election. An election duly took place on 8 February 1997, at which four new members were elected to Parliament, following an apparent agreement between the supporters of Harris and those of Dowiyogo to end the political manoeuvring that had resulted in several months of instability in Nauru. At the election to the presidency, on 13 February, Kinza Clodumar (nominated by Dowiyogo) defeated Harris by nine votes to eight.

In early 1998 five members of Parliament (including former President Lagumot Harris) were dismissed by Adeang, the Speaker, for refusing to apologize for personal remarks about him that had been published in an opposition newsletter. At the resultant by-elections, held in late February 1998, three of the five members were re-elected. A motion expressing 'no confidence' in the President was approved in June, and Dowiyogo was consequently elected to replace Clodumar. In a further vote of 'no confidence', in late April 1999 Dowiyogo was defeated by 10 votes to seven; his replacement was Rene Harris, previously Chairman of the Nauru Phosphate Corporation. Former President Lagumot Harris died in September 1999.

Following legislative elections held on 8 April 2000, Rene Harris was re-elected President, narrowly defeating Dowiyogo by nine votes to eight. Ludwig Scotty was elected Speaker of Parliament. However, Scotty and his deputy, Ross Cairn, subsequently resigned, stating only that they were unable to continue under the 'current political circumstances'. Harris therefore tendered his resignation and was replaced by Dowiyogo, whereupon Scotty and Cairn were re-elected to their posts in the legislature. Observers attributed the manoeuvring to shifting political allegiances within the legislature.

In early 2001, in another reversal to Dowiyogo's leadership, Anthony Audoa, the Minister for Home Affairs, Culture, Health and Women's Affairs, resigned and requested that Parliament be recalled. He claimed that Dowiyogo had squandered Nauru's wealth during his various tenures as President and that in promoting the island as a tax haven he had allowed Nauru to be used by Russian criminal gangs to 'launder' their illegal funds, prompting speculation that he intended to mount a challenge for the presidency.

In late March 2001 Dowiyogo was ousted from the presidency in a parliamentary vote of 'no confidence' while he was undergoing hospital treatment in Australia. The motion, which was passed by two votes, led to Rene Harris regaining the presidency. In October, however, Harris was flown to Australia for emergency medical treatment for a diabetes-related illness, during which time Remy Namaduk performed the role of acting President. Allegations that Nauru's 'offshore' financial centre was being used extensively by Russian criminal organizations for 'laundering' the proceeds of their illegal activities had led Dowiyogo to order a full review of the industry in March 1999. The Government subsequently stated that it intended to modernize legislation governing the island's financial sector. In early 2000 President Rene Harris announced that Nauru was to suspend its 'offshore' banking services and improve the accountability of existing banks on the island, as part of the Government's efforts to bring Nauru's financial services regulations into conformity with international standards. Dowiyogo similarly reaffirmed his commitment to reform the 'offshore' sector, following his election in April 2000. However, in February 2001 11 members of Nauru's 18-member legislature signed a petition requesting that Dowiyogo attend a special session of Parliament to answer questions relating to the island's alleged role in 'laundering' significant funds from Russian criminal organizations. The allegations originated in claims by Russia's central bank that some US $70,000m. of illegal funds had been processed in 'offshore' banks in Nauru. It was estimated that 400 such banks existed on the island in early 2001. The Government subsequently drew up an Anti-Money Laundering Act in August 2001, but the Financial Action Task Force (FATF—based in Paris and operating under the auspices of the Organisation for Economic Co-operation and Development—OECD) found that the new laws contained several deficiencies, and imposed sanctions in December. The Government announced new anti-money-laundering legislation in the same month, and was considering legal action against the FATF in early 2002. Meanwhile, following Islamist attacks on New York and Washington, DC, on 11 September 2001, Nauru's tax system was subject to international scrutiny, amid suspicion that it might have been used as a conduit for the terrorists' funds.

In September 2001 Nauru agreed to accept 310 of 460 predominantly Afghan asylum-seekers who were on board a Norwegian freighter, the *MV Tampa*, unable to disembark on Christmas Island as Australia refused to grant them entry into its territory (see the chapter on Christmas Island). The Australian Government agreed to fund the processing of the asylum-seekers and to pay an undisclosed sum to Nauru, which was to house the asylum-seekers for three months while their claims for asylum were assessed. Following the interception of several other boats carrying asylum-seekers in Australian waters later the same month, Nauru received a pledge of $A20m. from the Australian Government for agreeing to host 800 asylum-seekers. In December 2001 Nauru signed an agreement with Australia's Minister for Foreign Affairs to accommodate a total of 1,200 at any one time, in return for a further $A10m. of aid, to be allocated to education, health and infrastructure programmes. During a brief visit to Australia in January 2002, the President of Nauru declared that the bilateral agreement should end as originally envisaged. However, local residents and owners of the land upon which the camps were located expressed concern over the delays in processing the asylum-seekers' claims. Processing was due to be completed by July 2002, and in May Australia offered monetary assistance to Afghan asylum-seekers as an incentive to return to their homeland. In June the President announced that he anticipated that all the asylum-seekers would have left Nauru within six months. However, in December some 700 people remained in the camps, despite the deportation of more than 100 Afghan asylum-seekers to Kabul. In the same month the President signed a new agreement with Australia's Minister for Foreign Affairs to extend the duration of the camps' operations and to accommodate up to 1,500 asylum-seekers.

On 8 January 2003 President Rene Harris was defeated in a motion of 'no confidence' by eight votes to three and was replaced by Bernard Dowiyogo. The vote followed a political crisis resulting from the defeat of the Government's budget proposals at the end of December 2002, as well as reports of increasing dissatisfaction with Harris's alleged economic mismanagement of the country. Nauru's deteriorating financial situation, in addition to the Government's decision to accept more than 1,000 asylum-seekers in return for aid from Australia, were believed to be major factors in the loss of confidence in Harris, which had led to the defection to the opposition of two cabinet ministers, two backbenchers and the Speaker in late 2002. However, Harris applied to the Supreme Court, and on 10 January 2003 an injunction was issued against Dowiyogo accepting the presidency. This decision had been based on the fact that only 11 of the 18 members of Parliament had attended the session when the vote took place, thus rendering it invalid; Harris and his Cabinet had staged a boycott of Parliament when the motion was to be proposed. Despite the injunction, Dowiyogo maintained his position and appointed a new Cabinet. Several days of confusion and political instability ensued. Finally, Harris was reinstated as President, following the intervention of Nauru's Melbourne-based Chief Justice. However, he resigned from the presidency the following day. In the resultant contest Dowiyogo defeated Kinza Clodumar by nine votes to eight to become the new President on 20 January. A lack of support for Dowiyogo within Parliament continued to create problems, however, amid appeals for an early election to resolve the impasse.

Meanwhile, a complete collapse of Nauru's telecommunications system in early January 2003 increased the problems experienced by the island. Nauru, thus, effectively became cut off from the rest of the world with external contact only possible when ships equipped with satellite telephones were calling. A speech by Dowiyogo claiming that Nauru was on the verge of bankruptcy, unable to pay its public servants or to send its sick citizens to Australia for treatment, and appealing to donor countries for emergency assistance, could not be transmitted for almost a month. Telecommunications services were restored in early March following a visit from a technician supplied by Australia's government aid agency, AusAID.

In early March 2003 Dowiyogo travelled to Washington, DC, at the request of the US Government, which had threatened to impose harsh economic sanctions on the island and to repossess Air Nauru's only aircraft, if Nauru did not discontinue its 'offshore' banking services. The administration of George W. Bush was reported to have been angered by the possibility that individuals with links to terrorist organizations might have used the island's financial services to 'launder' their funds; some 400 'offshore' banks were registered on the island in the early 2000s. Consequently, Dowiyogo agreed to sign executive orders not to renew any banking licences or to issue any further so-called 'investor passports'. Shortly after the meeting, however, Dowiyogo collapsed and, following emergency heart surgery, died on 9 March. Derog Gioura was appointed acting President and on 20 March was elected by nine parliamentary votes to seven. Legislation providing for the expiry of most 'offshore' banking licences within 30 days (and for the remainder within six months) was passed by Parliament in late March, in accordance with the agreement that Dowiyogo had signed in the USA. At the end of March acting President Derog Gioura himself suffered a heart attack and was flown to Australia for treatment.

A general election took place on 3 May 2003, at which six new members were elected to the legislature. However, the new Speaker resigned one day after his election, and with no further nominations for the position, Parliament was unable to proceed to a presidential election.

In February 1987 representatives of the British, Australian and New Zealand Governments signed documents effecting the official demise of the British Phosphate Commissioners, who from 1919 until 1970 had overseen the mining of Nauru's phosphate deposits. President DeRoburt subsequently expressed concern about the distribution of the Commissioners' accumulated assets, which were estimated to be worth $A55m. His proposal that part of this sum be spent on the rehabilitation of areas of the island that had been mined before independence was rejected by the three Governments involved. DeRoburt subsequently established a commission of inquiry to investigate proposals for rehabilitation. The commission proposed that the three Governments provide one-third ($A72m.) of the estimated rehabilitation costs. In 1989 Australia's refusal to contribute to the rehabilitation of former phosphate mining areas prompted Nauru to institute proceedings, claiming compensation from Australia for damage to its environment, at the International Court of Justice. However, in 1993, following negotiations between President Dowiyogo and the Australian Prime Minister, Paul Keating, a Compact of Settlement was signed, under which the Australian Government was to pay some $A107m. to Nauru. New Zealand and the United Kingdom subsequently agreed to contribute $A12m. each towards the settlement. An investigation into methods for the rehabilitation of the damaged areas of the island included plans to use landfill to encourage the restoration of vegetation to the mined areas, and the re-establishment of many of the species of flora and fauna that had previously been abundant on the island. In mid-1995 a report commissioned by the Government published details of a rehabilitation programme extending over the next 20–25 years and costing $A230m. The success of the rehabilitation scheme, however, was dependent on the co-operation of landowners, some of whom were expected to continue to allow areas to be mined for residual ore once phosphate reserves had been exhausted. In mid-1997 Parliament approved the Nauru Rehabilitation Corporation (NRC) Act, providing for the establishment of a corporate body to manage the rehabilitation programme. The NRC held its inaugural meeting in May 1999. The rehabilitation programme (which was to be partly financed from the Compact of Settlement with Australia) was expected to transform the mined areas into sites suitable for agriculture, new housing and industrial units.

As a result of a strike by pilots of Air Nauru, begun in 1988, the Governments of Australia and New Zealand withdrew certification of the airline, concerned that it was not complying with safety standards. Air Nauru resumed operations in 1989, and diplomatic relations with Australia (which had been suspended in the previous year) were restored. In July 1998 the airline was transferred to the Australian aviation register in order to achieve improved surveillance and safety standards. In February 2001 Nauru's transport links with the rest of the world were severed when Air Nauru suspended all its operations, following a report by the Civil Aviation Safety Authority in Australia. The organization claimed that Air Nauru had failed to maintain an effective management structure, did not have sufficiently qualified staff and that the airport in Nauru did not meet regulatory requirements owing to frequent disruptions to electricity and communications services. The suspension was lifted in the following month. It was hoped that the installation of three new electricity generators in June would resolve some of the problems outlined in the report.

Nauru was persistently critical of France's use of the South Pacific region for nuclear-weapons testing, and was one of the most vociferous opponents of the French Government's decision in mid-1995 to resume its nuclear-testing programme. Diplomatic relations, suspended between the two countries in 1995, were formally resumed in early 1998.

In early 2001 Nauru voiced strong opposition to the US Government's plans to develop a missile defence system, in which missiles are deployed to shoot down other missiles in flight. Government officials in Nauru expressed fears that testing of the system in the region could result in missile debris landing on the Pacific islands.

The President of Nauru met the Cuban Minister of Foreign Affairs in November 2001 at a UN meeting, where they agreed to establish diplomatic relations between their two countries and discussed a proposed technical and economic co-operation agreement whereby Nauru would be provided with health experts from Cuba. In 1989 a UN report on the 'greenhouse effect' (the heating of the earth's atmosphere and a resultant rise in sea-level) listed Nauru as one of the countries that might disappear beneath the sea in the 21st century, unless drastic action were taken. The Government of Nauru strongly criticized Australia's refusal, at the December 1997 Conference of the Parties to the Framework Convention on Climate Change (see UN Environment Programme, see p. 49), in Kyoto, Japan, to reduce its emission of pollutant gases known to contribute to the 'greenhouse effect'.

In August 2001 Nauru hosted the Pacific Islands Forum summit meeting, despite a problematic shortage of accommodation, caused by the presence of contingents of officials from Australia, refugee agencies, the UN and Eurest (the company subcontracted to operate Nauru's refugee camp). Fiji had been expected to perform this role, but its participation had been opposed owing to its failure to reinstate democratic rule following the coup of the previous year.

In July 2002 a political crisis emerged after President Rene Harris decided unilaterally to recognize the People's Republic of China, thus ending 22 years of diplomatic relations with Taiwan. Several cabinet ministers opposed the shift in policy, and the controversy increased after Harris immediately accepted US $60m. in aid and $77m. in debt annulment from the People's Republic of China.

Government

Legislative power is vested in the unicameral Parliament, with 18 members elected by universal adult suffrage for up to three years. Executive authority is vested in a Cabinet, which consists of the President of the Republic, elected by the Parliament, and ministers appointed by him. The Cabinet is collectively responsible to Parliament. Responsibilities for administration are divided between the Nauru Local Government Council and the Government. The Council, an elected body of nine members from the country's 14 districts, elects one of its members to be Head Chief.

Defence

Nauru has no defence forces: under an informal arrangement, Australia is responsible for the country's defence.

Economic Affairs

In 1999, according to UN estimates, Nauru's gross domestic product (GDP), measured at current prices, was US $34m., equivalent to $2,830 per head. In 1991–99, it was estimated, GDP decreased, in real terms, at an average annual rate of 5.9%. The population increased by an annual average of 2.0% per year in 1990–2000. The UN estimated that GDP declined, in real terms, by 7.3% in 1997, by 1.9% in 1998 and again by 1.9% in 1999. According to official estimates, Nauru's GDP grew by 0.8% in 2000. Real GDP growth of around 3% was predicted for 2001.

Agricultural activity comprises mainly the small-scale production of tropical fruit, vegetables and livestock, although the production of coffee and copra for export is increasingly significant. Coconuts are the principal crop. Bananas, pineapples and the screw-pine (*Pandanus*) are also cultivated as food crops, while the islanders keep pigs and chickens. However, almost all Nauru's requirements (including most of its drinking water) are imported. Increased exploitation of the island's marine resources was envisaged following the approval by Parliament of important fisheries legislation in 1997 and 1998. Funding for a new harbour for medium-sized vessels was secured from the Government of Japan in 1998, and in early 1999 the Marshall Islands Sea Patrol agreed to provide assistance in the surveillance of Nauru's exclusive economic zone. Revenue from fishing licence fees totalled $A8.5m. in 2000.

Until the early 1990s Nauru's economy was based on the mining of phosphate rock, which constituted four-fifths of the island's surface area. Phosphate extraction has been conducted largely by indentured labour, notably by I-Kiribati and Tuvaluan workers. Exports of phosphates declined to an average of 0.51m. tons annually in 1990–97 (compared with 1.58m. tons per year in the 1980s), mainly owing to the collapse of the Australian market. As a result of the Asian financial crisis, exports of phosphate declined by almost 18% in 1998 compared with the previous year. In 2001 phosphate exports were suspended in the second half of the year when a processing plant was blockaded by landowners seeking additional compensation for the use of their land by the plant. Mining production, meanwhile, decreased by 7.9% in 2000. Primary deposits of phosphate are expected to be exhausted by 2005. Feasibility studies have been conducted into the mining of secondary and residual deposits, although this activity would be less profitable. Revenue from phosphate sales has been invested in a long-term trust fund (the Nauru Phosphate Royalties Trust (NPRT), the assets of which totalled about US $900m. in 1992), in the development of shipping and aviation services, and in property purchases in Australia and elsewhere.

Energy is derived principally from imported petroleum. Output of electrical energy totalled 30m. kWh in 2000.

The country's trade balance improved significantly in 2001; imports decreased by 5.5%, while exports improved by 7.9%. This resulted in a current-account surplus in that year equivalent to nearly 12% of GDP. The principal imports are food and live animals (which comprised 83.7% of total imports in 1993/94, while beverages accounted for a further 4.1%), machinery and transport equipment (2.8%) and non-metallic mineral manu-

www.europaworldonline.com

factures (4.9%). Phosphates are the most important export, earning \$A38.1m. in 1995; exports of crude fertilizers to Australia totalled \$A8.5m. in 2001. The principal export markets in 2000 were New Zealand (45.4%), Australia (16.9%), the Republic of Korea (14.9%), the USA (5.4%) and Canada (4.3%); the principal sources of imports were Australia (48.1%), the USA (19.9%), the United Kingdom (10.8%), Indonesia (6.7%) and India (3.7%).

The national budget for 1998/99 envisaged total revenue of \$A38.7m. and expenditure of \$A37.2m. (dramatically reduced from expenditure of \$A61.8m. in the previous year). According to the Asian Development Bank (ADB, see p. 143), the budgetary deficit was projected at the equivalent of 6.1% of GDP in 1999/2000 and at 10.6% in 2000/01. A fiscal deficit of \$A40m.–\$A50m. was envisaged in 2001/02. Total public debt was equivalent to 60.8% of GDP in 2000, an improvement on figures in previous years. Development assistance from Australia amounted to \$A3.3m. in 1999/2000. Nauru's external debt was estimated at \$A280m. in 2000. In that year the cost of debt-servicing was equivalent to an estimated 13% of total revenue from the exports of goods and services. Consumer prices increased by 4.0% in 1998, by 6.7% in 1999 and by 17.9% in 2000; the annual rate of inflation averaged 4.0% in 2001. The rate of unemployment among those aged 15–19 in the late 1990s was estimated by the ADB to be 33% of males and 52% of females.

Nauru is a member of the Pacific Community (see p. 304), of the Pacific Islands Forum (see p. 306) and of the UN Economic and Social Commission for Asia and the Pacific (ESCAP, see p. 28), all of which aim to promote regional development. Nauru is also a member of the ADB.

After gaining independence in 1968, Nauru benefited from sole control of phosphate earnings and, as a result, its income per head was among the highest in the world. This, however, had serious repercussions for the country, which became excessively dependent on imported labour, imports of consumer goods and convenience foods, causing health and social problems. Another effect of phosphate mining was to render 80% of the island both uninhabitable and uncultivable, leading to chronic overcrowding. Upon the depletion of the island's phosphate resources in the early 21st century, it was hoped that Nauru would be able to derive economic security from its shipping and civil aviation services and from its position as a tax haven for international business and for 'offshore' banking. A review of Nauru's economy by the ADB in late 1998 led the organization to devise a major economic and structural adjustment programme, which aimed to ensure the island's financial security in view of the dramatic decline in revenue from phosphate and from many of its traditional investments, as well as to offset losses arising from a recent series of ill-advised investments. Moreover, the island lost a significant amount from its Phosphate Royalties Trust during the 1990s through theft and fraud by accountants and other financial advisers. In March 2000 an Australian businessman was found guilty of conspiring to defraud the fund of some \$A100m. In mid-1999 the Government stated that it had completed the first phase of the ADB-sponsored reform programme, involving some 434 redundancies in the civil service with a view to reducing personnel expenditure by 35% (although the retrenchment programme was impeded in 2000 by the appointment of some 500 additional employees to the state mining operation). Measures to reform the financial sector, in response to allegations that Nauru's 'offshore' banking services were being abused for the purposes of 'money-launder-

ing', were announced in early 2000. In September of that year the Government appointed a consultant, who, with the assistance of the ADB, was to conduct a thorough review of operations at the Bank of Nauru. However, serious allegations of 'money-laundering' re-emerged in 2001, leading the Financial Action Task Force (see above) to impose counter-measures, prescribing increased monitoring, surveillance and transparency in financial transactions. Despite these measures the US Government of George W. Bush obliged Nauru's President to sign papers effectively ending the island's 'offshore' banking industry in March 2003 or face crippling economic sanctions. Nauru received a significant financial windfall in late 2001 in exchange for co-operating with Australia in its 'Pacific Solution' to the problem of asylum-seekers (see Recent History). By the end of 2001, in addition to meeting the costs of caring for the refugees, the Australian Government had committed total aid exceeding \$A30m. The aid was allocated to various programmes, including \$A10m. towards fuel to power the island's electricity generators and \$A3m. towards the purchase of new generators. Australia also offered to cover the outstanding hospital bills incurred by Nauruans in Australia (where, owing to the shortcomings of Nauru's health service, many of the island's citizens had been obliged to seek treatment). Nauru's GDP declined throughout the 1990s, and in the early 2000s the economic outlook remained poor. It was unclear how the substantial budgetary deficit envisaged for 2001/02 would be fully financed; the Government had hitherto relied upon loans from official bilateral sources, overseas corporations or funds from the NPRT, the assets of which had been seriously depleted by 2001. The Bank of Nauru, meanwhile, another source of budgetary support and financing of phosphate royalty payments to landowners, was believed to have become practically insolvent. During 2001, furthermore, the repeated suspensions of Air Nauru's operations, owing to lack of funds, had led to serious disruptions in the provision of food, fuel and other essential supplies to the island. By early 2002 government payrolls and payments to several creditors had been severely delayed. In January 2003 President Dowiyogo broadcast an appeal for emergency aid, claiming that the island was on the verge of bankruptcy.

Education

Education is compulsory for Nauruan children between six and 16 years of age. Primary education begins at the age of six and lasts for seven years. Secondary education, beginning at 13 years of age, lasts for up to four years. In 1995 there were four pre-primary schools, six primary schools and four secondary schools with a total of 138 teachers. In 1985 there were four vocational schools with four teachers. In 1984 Nauruans studying overseas at secondary and tertiary levels numbered 88. There is a university extension centre, linked with the University of the South Pacific in Suva, Fiji. An estimated 1% of the adult population were illiterate in 1993–95.

Public Holidays

2003: 1 January (New Year's Day), 31 January (Independence Day), 18–21 April (Easter), 17 May (Constitution Day), 26 October (Angam Day), 25–26 December (Christmas).

2004: 1 January (New Year's Day), 31 January (Independence Day), 9–12 April (Easter), 17 May (Constitution Day), 26 October (Angam Day), 25–26 December (Christmas).

Statistical Survey

Source (unless otherwise stated): General Statistician, Nauru Government Offices, Yaren.

AREA AND POPULATION

Area: 21.3 sq km (8.2 sq miles).

Population: 8,042 (Nauruan 4,964; Other Pacific Islanders 2,134; Asians 682; Caucasians—mainly Australians and New Zealanders —262) at census of 13 May 1983; 9,919 (5,079 males, 4,840 females) at census of 17 April 1992; 11,845 (official estimate) at mid-2000.

Density (mid-2000): 556 per sq km.

Principal Towns (population, 1992 census): Aiwo (capital) 600; Anetan 427; Anabar 320; Anibare 165. Source: Thomas Brinkhoff, *City Population* (internet www.citypopulation.de).

Births, Marriages and Deaths (1995): Registered live births 203 (birth rate 18.8 per 1,000); Registered marriages 57 (marriage rate 5.3 per 1,000); Registered deaths 49 (death rate 4.5 per 1,000).

Expectation of Life (WHO estimates, years at birth): 61.9 (males 58.7; females 66.2) in 2001. Source: WHO, *World Health Report*.

Economically Active Population (census of 30 June 1966): 2,473 (Administration 845, Phosphate mining 1,408, Other activities 220).

HEALTH AND WELFARE

Key Indicators

Total Fertility Rate (children per woman, 2001): 4.5.

Under-5 Mortality Rate (per 1,000 live births, 2001): 30.

Physicians (per 1,000 head, 1995): 1.57.

Health Expenditure (2000): US $ per head (PPP): 525.

Health Expenditure (2000): % of GDP: 11.3.

Health Expenditure (2000): public (% of total): 98.9.
For sources and definitions, see explanatory note on p. vi.

AGRICULTURE, ETC.

Principal Crop and Livestock (FAO estimates, 2001): Coconuts 1,600 metric tons; Pigs 2,800 head; Chickens 5,000 head. Source: FAO.

Fishing (FAO estimates, metric tons, live weight of capture, 2000): Total catch 250. Source: FAO, *Yearbook of Fishery Statistics*.

MINING

Phosphate Rock ('000 metric tons): 487 in 1998; 600 (estimate) in 1999; 500 (estimate) in 2000. The phosphoric acid content (in '000 metric tons) was: 185 in 1998; 230 (estimate) in 1999; 195 (estimate) in 2000. Source: US Geological Survey.

INDUSTRY

Electric Energy (million kWh): 32 in 1996; 32 in 1997; 32 in 1998. Source: *UN, Industrial Commodity Statistics Yearbook*.

FINANCE

Currency and Exchange Rates: Australian currency: 100 cents = 1 Australian dollar ($A). *Sterling, US Dollar and Euro Equivalents* (31 December 2002): £1 sterling = $A2.8467; US $1 = $A1.7661; €1 = $A1.8522; $A100 = £35.13 = US $56.62 = €53.99. *Average Exchange Rate* (US $ per Australian dollar): 0.5823 in 2000; 0.5176 in 2001; 0.5439 in 2002.

Budget (estimates, $A '000, year ending 30 June 1999): *Revenue:* 38,700; *Expenditure:* 37,200.

EXTERNAL TRADE

Principal Commodities ($A '000, year ending 30 June 1994): *Imports:* Food and live animals 38,420; Beverages 1,890; Non-metallic mineral manufactures 2,268; Non-electrical machinery 758; Transport equipment 534; Total (incl. others) 45,906. *Exports:* Total 45,111. *1995* ($A '000): Total exports 38,081.

Trade with Australia ($A '000, year ending 30 June 2001): *Imports:* 26,000; *Exports:* 9,000. Source: Australian Bureau of Statistics, *Year Book Australia*.

Trade with New Zealand ($NZ '000, 2000): *Imports:* 166; *Exports:* 25,418. Source: Ministry of Foreign Affairs and Trade, Wellington.

TRANSPORT

Road Traffic (1989): 1,448 registered motor vehicles.

Shipping: *Merchant Fleet* (displacement, '000 grt at 31 December): 15 in 1991 (at 30 June); 5 in 1992; 1 in 1993. Source: Lloyd's Register of Shipping. *International Freight Traffic* (estimates, '000 metric tons, 1990): Goods loaded 1,650; Goods unloaded 59. Source: UN, *Monthly Bulletin of Statistics*.

Civil Aviation (traffic on scheduled services, 1998): Kilometres flown (million) 2; Passengers carried ('000) 137; Passenger-km (million) 243; Total ton-km (million) 24. Source: UN, *Statistical Yearbook*.

COMMUNICATIONS MEDIA

Radio Receivers (1997): 7,000 in use*.

Television Receivers (1997): 500 in use*.

Telephones (main lines, 2000): 1,800 in use†.

Mobile Cellular Telephones (2000): 1,200 subscribers†.
* Source: UNESCO, *Statistical Yearbook*.
† Source: International Telecommunication Union.

EDUCATION

Pre-primary (2002): 6 schools; 46 teachers; 634 pupils.

Primary (2002): 5 schools; 64 teachers; 1,566 pupils.

Secondary (2002): 4 schools; 40 teachers; 609 pupils.

Vocational (2001): 6 teachers; 38 students.
Source: Department of Education, Yaren, Nauru.
Nauruans studying at secondary and tertiary levels overseas in 2001 numbered 85.

Directory

The Constitution

The Constitution of the Republic of Nauru came into force at independence on 31 January 1968, having been adopted two days previously. It protects fundamental rights and freedoms, and vests executive authority in the Cabinet, which is responsible to a popularly elected Parliament. The President of the Republic is elected by Parliament from among its members. The Cabinet is composed of five or six members, including the President, who presides. There are 18 members of Parliament, including the Cabinet. Voting is compulsory for all Nauruans who are more than 20 years of age, except in certain specified instances.

The highest judicial organ is the Supreme Court and there is provision for the creation of subordinate courts with designated jurisdiction.

There is a Treasury Fund from which monies may be taken by Appropriation Acts.

A Public Service is provided for, with the person designated as the Chief Secretary being the Commissioner of the Public Service.

Special mention is given to the allocation of profits and royalties from the sale of phosphates.

The Government

HEAD OF STATE

President: Derog Gioura (acting—elected 20 March 2003).

CABINET
(April 2003)

President, Minister for Finance and Economic Reform, Public Service and Foreign Affairs, Minister of Civil Aviation, Minister of Foreign Affairs, Minister of Home Affairs and Culture, Minister of Industry, Minister of Investments, Minister of Public Service, and Minister of Works, Planning and Housing Development: Derog Gioura (acting).

Minister of Economic Development, Minister of Education and Vocational Training, Minister of Telecommunications, Minister of Transportation and Minister assisting the President: Remy Namaduk.

Minister of Finance and Minister of Good Governance: Aloysius Amwano.

Minister of Health and Minister of Sports: Nimrod Botelanga.

Minister of Justice and Minister of Marine Resources: Godfrey Thoma.

MINISTRIES

Office of the President: Yaren, Nauru.

Ministry of Education: Yaren, Nauru; tel. 444-3130; fax 444-3718.

Ministry of Health and Youth Affairs: Yaren, Nauru; tel. 444-3166; fax 444-3136.

Ministry of Finance: Aiwo, Nauru; tel. 444-3140; fax 555-4477.

Ministry of Justice: Yaren, Nauru; tel. 444-3160; fax 444-3108.

Ministry of Works and Community Services: Yaren, Nauru; tel. 444-3177; fax 444-3135.

Legislature

PARLIAMENT

Parliament comprises 18 members. The most recent general election took place on 3 May 2003.

Speaker: (vacant).

Political Organizations

Democratic Party of Nauru: c/o Parliament House, Yaren, Nauru; f. 1987; revival of Nauru Party (f. 1975); Leader Kennan Adeang.

Naoero Amo (Nauru First): c/o Parliament House, Yaren, Nauru; e-mail visionary@naoeroamo.com; internet www.naoeroamo.com; f. 2001; Co-Leaders David Adeang, Kieran Keke.

Diplomatic Representation

EMBASSY IN NAURU

China, People's Republic: Nauru.

Judicial System

The Chief Justice presides over the Supreme Court, which exercises original, appellate and advisory jurisdiction. The Resident Magistrate presides over the District Court, and he also acts as Coroner under the Inquests Act 1977. The Supreme Court is a court of record. The Family Court consists of three members, one being the Resident Magistrate as Chairman, and two other members drawn from a panel of Nauruans. The Chief Justice is Chairman of the Public Services Appeals Board and of the Police Appeals Board.

SUPREME COURT

tel. 444-3163; fax 444-3104.

Chief Justice: Barry Connell (non-resident).

DISTRICT COURT

Resident Magistrate: G. N. Saksena.

FAMILY COURT

Chairman: G. N. Saksena.

Religion

Nauruans are predominantly Christians, adhering either to the Nauruan Protestant Church or to the Roman Catholic Church.

Nauruan Protestant Church: Head Office, Nauru; Moderator (vacant).

Roman Catholic Church: POB 16, Nauru; tel. and fax 444-3708; Nauru forms part of the diocese of Tarawa and Nauru, comprising Kiribati and Nauru. The Bishop resides on Tarawa Atoll, Kiribati.

The Press

Central Star News: Nauru; f. 1991; fortnightly.

Nasero Bulletin: Nauru; tel. 444-3847; fax 444-3153; e-mail bulletin@cenpac.net.nr; fortnightly; English; local and overseas news; Editor Sepe Batsiua; circ. 500.

The Nauru Chronicle: Nauru; Editor Ruby Dediya.

Broadcasting and Communications

TELECOMMUNICATIONS

Nauru Telecommunications Service: Nauru; tel. 444-3324; fax 444-3111; Dir Edward W. R. H. DeYoung.

BROADCASTING

Radio

Nauru Broadcasting Service: Information and Broadcasting Services, Chief Secretary's Department, POB 77, Nauru; tel. 444-3133; fax 444-3153; e-mail ntvdirector@cenpac.net.nr; f. 1968; state-owned and non-commercial; expected to be corporatized in the late 1990s; broadcasts in the mornings in English and Nauruan; operates Radio Nauru; Station Man. Rin Tsitsi; Man. Dir Gary Turner.

Television

Nauru Television (NTV): Nauru; tel. 444-3133; fax 444-3153; e-mail ntvmanager@cenpac.net.nr; began operations in June 1991; govt-owned; broadcasts 24 hrs per day on 3 channels; most of the programmes are supplied by foreign television companies via satellite or on videotape; a weekly current affairs programme is produced locally; Man. Michael Dekarube; Dir of Media Gary Turner.

Finance

(cap. = capital; res = reserves; dep. = deposits; m. = million; amounts in Australian dollars unless otherwise stated)

BANKING

State Bank

Bank of Nauru: Civic Centre, POB 289, Nauru; tel. 444-3238; fax 444-3203; f. 1976; state-owned; cap. 12.0m., res 123.0m., dep. 141.0m. (Dec. 1994); Chair. Marcus Stephen.

Commercial Bank

Hampshire Bank and Trust Inc: Nauru Corporation Bldg, Aiwo Rd, POB 300, Aiwo, Nauru; tel. 444-3283; fax 444-3730; f. 1986; total assets 1,305m., dep. 1,139m. (Dec. 2000); Gen. Man. Roger van Zanten.

INSURANCE

Nauru Insurance Corporation: POB 82, Nauru; tel. 444-3346; fax 444-3731; f. 1974; sole licensed insurer and reinsurer in Nauru; Chair. Nimes Ekwona.

Trade and Industry

GOVERNMENT AGENCIES

Nauru Agency Corporation: POB 300, Aiwo, Nauru; tel. 555-4324; fax 444-3730; e-mail nrugrp@cenpac.net.nr; functions as a merchant bank to assist entrepreneurs in the registration of holding and trading corporations and the procurement of banking, trust and insurance licences; Chair. RENE HARRIS; Gen. Man. S. B. HULKAR.

Nauru Corporation: Civic Centre, Yaren, Nauru; f. 1925; operated by the Nauru Council; the major retailer in Nauru; Gen. Man. A. EPHRAIM.

Nauru Fisheries and Marine Resources Authority: POB 449, Nauru; tel. 444-3733; fax 444-3812; e-mail nfmra@cenpac.net.nr; f. 1997.

Nauru Phosphate Corporation: Aiwo, Nauru; tel. 444-3839; fax 444-2752; f. 1970; operates the phosphate industry and several public services of the Republic of Nauru (including provision of electricity and fresh water) on behalf of the Nauruan people; responsible for the mining and marketing of phosphate; Gen. Man. JOSEPH HIRAM.

Nauru Phosphate Royalties Trust: Nauru; e-mail nprtnau@cenpac.net.nr; statutory corpn; invests phosphate royalties to achieve govt revenue; extensive international interests, incl. hotels and real estate; Sec. NIRAL FERNANDO.

Nauru Rehabilitation Corporation (NRC): Nauru; f. 1999; manages and devises programmes for the rehabilitation of those parts of the island damaged by the over-mining of phosphate; Chair. DOGABE JEREMIAH.

UTILITIES

Nauru Phosphate Corporation: Aiwo, Nauru; tel. 555-6481; fax 555-4111; operates generators for the provision of electricity and supplies the island's water; Chair. (vacant); Gen. Man. JOSEPH HIRAM.

Transport

RAILWAYS

There are 5.2 km of 0.9-m gauge railway serving the phosphate workings.

ROADS

A sealed road, 16 km long, circles the island, and another serves Buada District. There were 1,448 registered vehicles in 1989.

SHIPPING

As Nauru has no wharves, passenger and cargo handling are operated by barge. In late 1998 finance was secured from the Japanese Government for the construction of a harbour in Anibare district. Work on the project began in 1999.

Nauru Pacific: Government Bldg, Yaren, Nauru; tel. 444-3133; f. 1969; operates cargo charter services to ports in Australia, New Zealand, Asia, the Pacific and the west coast of the USA; Man. Dir (vacant).

CIVIL AVIATION

Air Nauru: Directorate of Civil Aviation, Government of Nauru Offices, POB 40, Yaren, Nauru; tel. 444-3274; fax 444-3705; e-mail write2us@airnauru.com.au; internet www.airnauru.com.au; f. 1970; corporatized in 1996 and moved to Australian aviation register in mid-1997; operates passenger and cargo services to Kiribati, Fiji, New Caledonia, Solomon Islands, Guam, Palau, the Philippines, the Federated States of Micronesia, Hawaii (USA), Australia and New Zealand; Chair. and CEO KEN MCDONALD.

NEPAL

Introductory Survey

Location, Climate, Language, Religion, Flag, Capital

The Kingdom of Nepal is a land-locked Asian country in the Himalaya mountain range, with India to the east, south and west, and Tibet (the Xizang Autonomous Region), in the People's Republic of China, to the north. The climate varies sharply with altitude, from arctic on the higher peaks of the Himalaya mountains (where the air temperature is permanently below freezing point) to humid sub-tropical in the central valley of Kathmandu, which is warm and sunny in summer. Temperatures in Kathmandu, which is 1,337 m (4,386 ft) above sea-level, are generally between 2°C (35°F) and 30°C (86°F), with an annual average of 11°C (52°F). The rainy season is between June and October. Average annual rainfall varies from about 1,000 mm (40 ins) in western Nepal to about 2,500 mm (100 ins) in the east. The official language is Nepali, which was spoken by 48.6% of the population in 2001. Other languages include Maithir (12.3% in 2001) and Bhojpuri (7.5%). Some 80.6% of the population were Hindus in 2001, with 10.7% Buddhists and 4.2% Muslims. The national flag (proportions 4 by 3) is composed of two crimson pennants, each with a blue border. The upper section contains a white crescent moon (horns upwards and surmounted by a disc with eight rays) and the lower section a white sun in splendour. The capital is Kathmandu.

Recent History

Nepal is an hereditary monarchy, but for more than 100 years, until 1951, effective power was held by the Rana family, who created the post of hereditary Prime Minister. A popular revolution, led by the Nepali Congress Party (NCP), ousted the Ranas and restored King Tribhuvan to power. A limited constitutional monarchy was established in 1951. During most of the 1950s government was controlled by the monarchy, first under Tribhuvan and then, after his death in 1955, under his son, Mahendra. In February 1959 King Mahendra promulgated Nepal's first Constitution, providing for a bicameral parliament, including a popularly-elected lower house. Elections held later that month resulted in victory for the NCP, led by Bisweswor Prasad (B.P.) Koirala, who became Prime Minister. However, the King retained a certain degree of power, and persistent differences between the King and the Prime Minister led to a royal coup in December 1960: Nepal's first brief period of democracy was thus brought to an abrupt end. The King dismissed the Council of Ministers and dissolved Parliament. A royal decree of January 1961 banned political parties. King Mahendra accused the Koirala administration of corruption, and in December 1962 he introduced a new Constitution, reasserting absolute royal power and providing for a 'partyless' system of government, based on the Panchayat (village council), with a Prime Minister appointed by the King. This office was filled successively by Dr Tulsi Giri (1962–65), Surya Bahadur Thapa (1965–69) and Kirti Nidhi Bista (1969–70, 1971–73). King Mahendra himself was Prime Minister from April 1970 to April 1971. In January 1972 King Mahendra died and was succeeded by his son, Birendra. Nagendra Prasad Rijal became Prime Minister in July 1973, and held office until December 1975, when Dr Giri was reappointed. The new Government made major changes to the Constitution, which allowed for a widening of the franchise and more frequent elections to the Rashtriya Panchayat (National Assembly), but in no way were the King's powers eroded. In September 1977 Dr Giri resigned and was succeeded by Bista.

B. P. Koirala, the former Prime Minister and an advocate of parliamentary democracy, was acquitted of treason in February 1978. Returning from abroad a year later, he was placed under house arrest in April 1979, but then released, partly to appease students who had been demonstrating for reforms. National unrest grew and, after King Birendra announced in May that there would be a national referendum on whether to restore multi-party democracy, Bista resigned and was succeeded as Prime Minister by Thapa. In the referendum, held in May 1980, 54.8% of the voters supported the Panchayat system with reforms. As a result, the King formed a Constitutional Reforms Commission, and in December he issued a decree under which

amendments to the Constitution were made, including the proviso that the appointment of the Prime Minister by the King would henceforth be on the recommendation of the Rashtriya Panchayat. In accordance with the new provisions, direct legislative elections were held in May 1981, the first of their kind since 1959, although still on a non-party basis. Thapa was re-elected by the Rashtriya Panchayat as Prime Minister in June 1981, and the King installed a new Council of Ministers (on the recommendation of the Prime Minister). An extensive ministerial reshuffle took place in October 1982, but this failed to stem increasing official corruption and economic mismanagement. In July 1983, for the first time in the 23-year history of the Panchayat system, the incumbent Prime Minister, Surya Bahadur Thapa, was ousted, and a new Council of Ministers was formed by a former Chairman of the Rashtriya Panchayat, Lokendra Bahadur Chand, who had successfully introduced a motion expressing 'no confidence' in Thapa.

In March 1985 the NCP held a convention in Kathmandu, and in May it embarked upon a campaign of civil disobedience, aimed at restoring a multi-party political system and parliamentary rule under a constitutional monarchy. In June there was a series of bomb explosions, resulting in loss of life. The explosions were apparently co-ordinated by two newly-formed anti-monarchist and anti-Government groups, the Janawadi Morcha (Democratic Front) and the Samyukta Mukti Bahini (United Liberation Torch-bearers). These bombings united an otherwise seriously divided legislature against the terrorists, and forced the predominantly moderate opposition to abandon the campaign of civil disobedience and to disclaim any responsibility for the explosions. In August the Rashtriya Panchayat approved a stringent anti-terrorist law, and more than 1,000 people were arrested in connection with the unrest.

In January 1986 the Government announced that a general election would be held in May. In March the King accepted the resignation of the Prime Minister and the Council of Ministers, and appointed an interim Government for the pre-election period, led by a former Prime Minister, Nagendra Prasad Rijal. About 64% of the electorate voted in the election, in spite of appeals by the NCP and the pro-Beijing faction of the Communist Party of Nepal (CPN) (neither of which presented candidates) for a boycott of the polls. All the candidates in the election were nominally independents, but it was reported that among the 72 new entrants to the Rashtriya Panchayat (40 members retained their seats) were at least 16 members of the Marxist-Leninist faction of the CPN. In June the King nominated 25 additional members of the new Rashtriya Panchayat, and Marich Man Singh Shrestha (previously Chairman of the Rashtriya Panchayat) was elected unopposed by the Assembly as the new Prime Minister. A few days later, on the recommendation of the Prime Minister, the King appointed a new Council of Ministers. In late 1986, to counter the growing influence of the communist faction in the Rashtriya Panchayat, several senior figures (including Jog Meher Shrestha, a former government minister, and Chand) established a 'Democratic Panchayat Forum', which expressed full support for the non-party system.

Members of the NCP and the Marxist-Leninist faction of the CPN participated (as independents) in local elections in March–April 1987. The opposition achieved only limited success, and the NCP subsequently claimed that there had been extensive electoral fraud and intimidation of voters by supporters of the Panchayat system. NCP candidates, however, were elected to a number of important mayoral posts in Kathmandu and elsewhere.

In 1986–87 the Nepalese Government continued its policy of press censorship, in an effort to curb anti-Government criticism. In June 1987, in an apparent attempt to improve the image of the Panchayat system, the Government initiated an anti-corruption campaign, during the course of which several senior officials were arrested for drugs-trafficking and other offences. In December the Government announced plans to reorganize government ministries and departments, in an effort to make them more efficient. In early 1988 the Government continued its policy of suppressing opposition. In January the President of the

NCP was arrested, and in February more than 100 people, who were planning to demonstrate in support of the NCP mayor of Kathmandu (who had been suspended from office for his anti-Panchayat stance), were also detained. In March an extensive government reshuffle included the establishment of a new Ministry of Housing and Physical Planning. In October there was another major reorganization of the Council of Ministers.

In September 1989 the Government arrested more than 900 NCP supporters, in a seeming effort to prevent them from celebrating the anniversary of the birth of Nepal's first elected Prime Minister, B. P. Koirala (who died in 1982). During these celebrations the NCP demonstrated in protest against the failings of the country's non-party political system. In November the leaders of the NCP held a meeting in Kathmandu with members of several other left-wing and communist political groups, to discuss the proposed formation of a country-wide peaceful 'movement for the restoration of democracy'. At the meeting they stated that the aims of the movement would be the alleviation of Nepal's severe economic problems (including the trade dispute with India, see below), the restoration of full democracy, the transfer from absolute to constitutional monarchy, the immediate replacement of the Panchayat Government by an interim national government, the removal of the ban on political activities, and the introduction of a multi-party system. In January 1990 a co-ordination committee to conduct the Jana Andolan (People's Movement) was formed by the NCP and the newly-formed United Left Front (ULF, which was led by Sahana Pradhan and comprised six factions of the CPN and a labour group), despite the Government's efforts to pre-empt its inauguration by arresting hundreds of activists (including many students) and by banning, or heavily censoring, more newspapers. During the consequent violent confrontations between protesters and police that took place in February, it was officially estimated that 12 people were killed and hundreds more were arrested. Violent demonstrations, strikes and mass arrests continued throughout March. At the end of the month the Minister of Foreign Affairs, Shailendra Kumar Upadhayaya, resigned from his post, following differences with the Prime Minister regarding the Government's management of the crisis. A few days later there was an extensive government reshuffle, including the dismissal of nine ministers who allegedly opposed the Government's acts of repression against the pro-democracy movement. In an effort to end the political unrest, the King dismissed Shrestha's Government on 6 April and nominated a restricted four-member Council of Ministers, under the leadership of the more moderate Chand. King Birendra also offered to establish a body that would examine the possibility of altering the Constitution and to hold discussions with the opposition, and he promised to initiate an official inquiry into the 20 deaths that had occurred during demonstrations since February. Despite these concessions, the situation worsened later the same day. A temporary curfew was imposed on the capital, and many political agitators were arrested. The Government immediately initiated talks with the opposition, and on 8 April the King announced that the 30-year ban on political parties was to be ended, thus enabling the future holding of multi-party elections, and that a commission to study constitutional reform was to be established. At the same time, the Jana Andolan suspended its campaign of demonstrations. Many political activists continued to agitate, however, demanding the removal of the formal structure of the Panchayat system. A week later, the King accepted the resignation of Chand from his post as Prime Minister, dismissed the Council of Ministers and announced the dissolution of the Rashtriya Panchayat. King Birendra then invited the opposition alliance of the NCP and the ULF to form an interim government. On 19 April a new 11-member coalition Council of Ministers (including two ministers nominated by the King and two independents), under the premiership of the President of the NCP, Krishna Prasad (K. P.) Bhattarai, was sworn in. The new Prime Minister announced that a general election would be held, on a multi-party basis, within a year. The principal task of the interim Government was to prepare a new constitution in accordance with the spirit of multi-party democracy and constitutional monarchy. King Birendra stated that he was committed to transforming his role into that of a constitutional monarch, and, following further violent clashes in Kathmandu between anti-royalists and police, he ordered the army and the police to comply with the orders of the interim Government in order to facilitate a smooth transition to democracy.

In mid-May 1990 King Birendra announced a general amnesty for all religious and political prisoners. On 21 May he delegated the legislative powers of the dissolved Rashtriya Panchayat to the new Council of Ministers, so that the Council was empowered to enact, amend and repeal legislation in order to bring about the introduction of a multi-party democracy. At the end of the month the King formed a nine-member Constitutional Recommendation Commission, based on the suggestions of the Prime Minister, which, after consulting the various parties, was to prepare a draft constitution and present it to the King within three months. In July the death sentence was abolished and the laws restricting freedom of the press and freedom of association were repealed. In addition, the King suspended almost one-half of the articles in the Constitution to enable the interim Government to function smoothly. The draft of the new Constitution, which was published at the end of August, recommended the introduction of a constitutional monarchy; a democratic multi-party system and a bicameral legislature, composed of a 205-member House of Representatives (Pratinidhi Sabha) and a 60-member National Assembly (Rashtriya Sabha); the official guarantee of fundamental rights (including freedom of expression); an independent judiciary; and the placing of the army under the control of a three-member National Defence Council, headed by the Prime Minister. The draft Constitution recognized Hinduism as the country's dominant religion. It also, however, guaranteed freedom for religious minorities to practise their beliefs (although restrictions on proselytizing were to remain in force). Under the draft Constitution, the King would be allowed to declare a state of emergency on the advice of the Council of Ministers, but such declarations would have to be approved by the House of Representatives within three months. A crucial clause in the new Constitution required the King 'to obey and protect' the Constitution: under the old regime, the King was considered to be above the Constitution. The draft Constitution was approved by the Council of Ministers on 15 October and sent to the King for his endorsement. King Birendra, however, amended the draft in a final effort to retain sovereign authority and full emergency powers. This retrograde action provoked violent protests. The Council of Ministers rejected most of the proposed amendments in the royal counterdraft, but agreed to the King's proposal to establish a Council of State (Raj Parishad), with a standing committee headed by a royal appointee. The 15-member committee was to be composed of eight royal appointees and seven other members, including the Prime Minister, the Ministers of Defence and Foreign Affairs, the Chief Justice of the Supreme Court and the Chief of Army Staff. Bhattarai stressed, however, that the formation of this committee would not alter the democratic nature of the new Constitution, since it would not function as a parallel body to the Council of Ministers. He also emphasized that the King would only be permitted to act on judicial, executive and legislative matters on the advice of the Council of Ministers. The new Constitution was officially promulgated by the King on 9 November.

The communist movement in Nepal suffered a set-back in December 1990, when four of the seven constituent members of the ULF broke away from the front, citing their lack of representation in the interim coalition Council of Ministers. Sahana Pradhan stated, however, that the three remaining factions would continue to operate as the ULF. In January 1991 two major factions of the CPN (the Marxist and Marxist-Leninist factions) merged to form the CPN (Unified Marxist-Leninist—UML).

The process for the holding of a successful general election began with the registration of political parties and the delimitation of 205 constituencies. Of the 44 political parties registered by the election commission, however, only 20 actually participated in the general election, which was held on 12 May 1991. The NCP decided to contest the election alone and not on the basis of an electoral alignment with any of its former Jana Andolan partners. The communists interpreted the NCP's move as the result of an increased understanding between the palace and the NCP on the basis that both wanted to forestall the rise of communism in the country. Consequently, relations between the NCP and the UML became strained and competitive. The general election was not only peaceful, but was also characterized by a good turn-out (65.2% of the electorate). The NCP won a comfortable majority (110 of the 205 seats in the lower house), but it was soundly defeated by the UML in the eastern hill districts and in some parts of the Terai. In Kathmandu, supposedly an NCP stronghold, the party lost all of the seats but one. By winning 69 seats, the UML established itself as the second largest party in the House of Representatives, followed by the United People's Front (UPF), an amalgam of radical, Maoist groups, with nine seats. Two other communist organizations—the Nepal Workers' and Peasants' Party and a faction of the CPN—received two seats each, thus making a total communist tally in the House of Representatives of 82 seats. The Nepali Sadbhavana Party (NSP), which, despite the constitutional prohibition against regional-based parties, was a plains- or Terai-based party, obtained six seats, all of which were in the Terai. The National Democratic Party (Chand) and the National Democratic Party (Thapa), led by the former Prime Ministers of those names, fared badly in the election, winning only four seats —the latter one and the former three. All of the three independent candidates who won seats subsequently joined the NCP. Acting Prime Minister Bhattarai lost his seat in the capital, and was replaced in the premiership by Girija Prasad (G. P.) Koirala, the General Secretary of the NCP and brother of the late B. P. Koirala.

By the end of 1991 unity within the ruling NCP was threatened by growing internal dissent amongst its leadership, particularly between the senior leader, Ganesh Man Singh, and G. P. Koirala. In December the Prime Minister carried out a reshuffle of the Council of Ministers introducing more of his own supporters as new ministers. The Government suffered a further set-back in April 1992 when a *bandh* (general strike), organized by the communist and other opposition parties in Kathmandu in protest against price rises, water shortages and alleged government corruption, resulted in the deaths of at least seven demonstrators following violent clashes with the police. Despite the consequent imposition of curfews in the capital and in the neighbouring town of Lalitpur, the opposition staged a number of anti-Government protest marches and demonstrations during the following week. The success of a second general strike, which was held in early May, demonstrated the continuing strength of the radical left. It brought Kathmandu to a standstill and, unlike the earlier general strike, passed off without violent incidents. Despite the strikes and the rising cost of living, the NCP performed well in the local elections held throughout the country in May and June; of especial note was the party's strong showing in the Kathmandu valley where it had performed so badly in the 1991 general election. There were, however, widespread reports of corruption and malpractice.

Under the leadership of G. P. Koirala, the centrist NCP Government shifted to the right. The public image of the monarchy and leading members of the former Panchayat regime were rehabilitated with government support. No charges were brought against senior officials of the former administration for corruption or human rights violations. Replicating the patronage system of the Panchayat regime, the NCP rapidly began to dominate the public administration structure. The ruling party's persistent failure to democratize its internal bodies and the absence of open election to posts in the party leadership met with criticism both within and without the NCP.

In addition to opposition from the leadership of his own party, G. P. Koirala was faced with increasing criticism from the opposition parties themselves, which focused on an agreement drawn up by the Prime Minister in December 1991 granting India access to water from the Tanakpur barrage on the Mahakali River, the terms of which were only subsequently revealed to the Nepalese House of Representatives. Alleging that the agreement constituted a treaty affecting national sovereignty, and therefore requiring a two-thirds' majority in the House of Representatives, the opposition launched a campaign calling for the resignation of Koirala on the grounds of unconstitutional behaviour. An indeterminate Supreme Court ruling in December 1992 on Koirala's action only intensified the protest.

In January–February 1993 the national UML congress abandoned much of the party's Marxist dogma and tacitly acknowledged its commitment to working within a democratic multi-party system. However, the untimely deaths of the party's General Secretary, Madan Bhandari, and Politburo member Jiv Raj Ashrit, following a road accident in mid-May, threw the UML into disarray. The rejection by the UML of the findings of a government inquiry, which concluded that the deaths had been accidental, provoked nation-wide protests in support of demands for an independent inquiry into the so-called 'Dhasdunga Incident'. In late May Madhav Kumar Nepal was appointed as the new General Secretary of the UML.

In the mean time, the rehabilitation of officials of the former Panchayat regime continued. In January 1993 the King appointed senior figures of the old administration, including former Prime Ministers Chand and Shrestha, to the 121-member Council of State (Raj Parishad), in a move designed both to rehabilitate former Panchayat officials and to reassert his leadership role over them. In June the right-wing National Democratic Party (NDP, formed in February 1992, following a merger of the Chand and Thapa factions) held its first national conference in Kathmandu, an event that would have been inconceivable three years previously, when its leaders were forced into hiding by the democracy movement.

In August 1993 the UML signed an agreement with the NCP, providing for the permanent withdrawal of the UML from anti-Government agitation in return for the ruling party's pledge to establish an independent commission to investigate the 'Dhasdunga Incident'. The UPF and other left-wing groups, however, continued their campaign of nation-wide general strikes and demonstrations demanding, amongst other things, the Prime Minister's resignation over the Tanakpur controversy and a curb on the NCP's increasing hold on power over public life. The Government was also criticized for its apparent inability to resolve the deteriorating economic situation, for its perceived subservience to India, and for its alleged involvement in corruption. Further serious rifts became apparent within the ruling NCP when the party's President, K. P. Bhattarai, lost a legislative by-election to the UML candidate in Kathmandu in February 1994; his defeat was widely attributed to G. P. Koirala's public opposition to his candidature. At the end of the month the Prime Minister rejected demands for his resignation made by supporters of Bhattarai in the NCP's Central Executive Committee. In March the Government survived a vote of 'no confidence' (by 113 votes to 81) presented to the House of Representatives by the UML. The opposition itself suffered from internal dissension in mid-1994 when both the UPF and the CPN (Unity Centre) split into competing factions, while the UML continued to be divided between radical and conservative camps. The crisis within the NCP culminated on 10 July when followers of Ganesh Man Singh withdrew their support for Koirala, who thereby lost his parliamentary majority. Consequently the Prime Minister offered his resignation, and on the following day the King dissolved the House of Representatives. Koirala was appointed as interim Prime Minister pending the holding of a general election, which was brought forward from mid-1996 to 15 November 1994. At the general election, which attracted a turn-out of 58%, the UML unexpectedly emerged as the single largest party, winning 88 of the 205 seats in the House of Representatives, while the NCP won 85 seats. At the end of the month the UML formed a minority Government under the premiership of its moderate Chairman, Man Mohan Adhikari. In late December the communist Government won a vote of confidence in the House of Representatives (as required by the Constitution for a new administration to continue in power).

On 11 June 1995 the NCP registered a parliamentary motion of 'no confidence' against the communist Government and, in conjunction with the NDP and the NSP, submitted a memorandum to King Birendra, staking their claim to form an alternative government. On the recommendation of the Prime Minister, who wished to avert the passage of the motion, the King dissolved the legislature on 13 June and announced that fresh elections were to be held on 23 November. Adhikari and his Council of Ministers were to function as a caretaker government, pending the general election. In an apparent attempt to win popular support in the run-up to the election, Adhikari's interim administration substantially increased budgetary expenditure and implemented a number of welfare programmes. The opposition, angered by the communists' mode of electioneering, challenged the dissolution of the House of Representatives in the Supreme Court. In a controversial ruling, declared on 28 August, the Supreme Court decided that the dissolution of the lower house on the advice of a minority administration (when a majority coalition was ready to assume power) had, indeed, been unconstitutional. The House of Representatives was consequently reconvened and the election abandoned. The UML Government was defeated in a vote of 'no confidence' on 10 September, by 107 votes to 88. On 12 September a coalition Government, composed of members of the NCP, the NDP and the NSP, and headed by the NCP's parliamentary leader, Sher Bahadur Deuba, was formed.

In early March 1996 the Government introduced a number of security measures following a series of violent clashes between a group of Maoist activists and the police in western Nepal, which resulted in the deaths of at least 11 people (by the end of the year more than 100 people had been killed as a result of the insurgency). The left-wing extremists (many of whom were members of the underground Communist Party of Nepal—Maoist and the UPF) had launched a 'people's revolutionary war' in the hills of Nepal in February, demanding the abolition of the constitutional monarchy and the establishment of a republic. Later in March the Government survived a parliamentary motion of 'no confidence', tabled by the UML, by 106 votes to 90. In May G. P. Koirala was elected to replace Bhattarai as President of the NCP; for the first time since its foundation, the party elected its leader by ballot. The coalition Government was weakened by internal divisions and achieved little during 1996 (with the notable exception of the Mahakali Treaty, see below). In early December seven NDP members of the Council of Ministers resigned from their posts and the faction of the party led by Chand withdrew from the ruling coalition; the Government, however, which continued to enjoy the support of the NDP faction led by Thapa, narrowly survived a legislative vote of 'no confidence' (presented by the UML) later that month. In early January 1997 five of the former NDP ministers who had resigned from the Government in the previous month reversed their position and pledged their support for Deuba's administration; a few days later four of these politicians were reinstated in the Government as part of a ministerial reshuffle. The Government suffered a set-back at the end of the month when the UML, already the largest party in the House of Representatives, increased its strength from 87 to 90 deputies, following its success in three by-elections. Deuba's administration finally collapsed in early March when it lost a vote of confidence in the House of Representatives. Chand was appointed as the new Prime Minister (for the fourth time) at the head of a coalition Government composed of members of the NDP, the UML, the NSP and the Nepal Workers' and Peasants' Party. The new Government, however, seemed unstable from the outset, since the members of the Thapa faction of the NDP refused to support Prime Minister Chand and the ideological differences between the communists and the former pro-monarchists appeared insuperable. Although Chand held the premiership, the UML, as the largest component of the coalition, was responsible for more ministerial posts than the NDP. In May and June the communists replaced the NCP as the country's dominant force in local government, following resounding successes in local elections. These elections were marred, however, by violent clashes between supporters of the main political parties in which about 30 people were killed. In mid-June more than 10,000 NCP supporters demonstrated in Kathmandu in protest over alleged electoral irregularities on the part of the UML during the recent polls. During 1997 the UML suffered from factional infighting, with a major rift developing between Deputy Prime Minister Bam Dev Gautam and the General Secretary of the party, Madhav Kumar Nepal. This factionalism served to destabilize the coalition Government further. In August a strike organized by an alliance of left-wing groups (known as the National Democratic Front) in protest at the rise in the price of fuel and a proposed anti-terrorist law brought Kathmandu and surrounding towns to a standstill. In the following month an anti-defection bill, the aim of which was to prevent politicians from deserting their own party and thus to bring stability to Nepal's politics, was unanimously approved by the House of Representatives.

On 4 October 1997 the Government lost a parliamentary vote of 'no confidence' (by 107 votes to 94) tabled by the NCP. A few days later King Birendra appointed Thapa, the President of the NDP, to replace Chand as Prime Minister. A new coalition Government, comprising members of the NDP and the NSP, took office on the following day. On 9 October the new coalition administration won the requisite parliamentary vote of confidence (by 109 votes to two—the UML abstained). In December Prime Minister Thapa expanded the Council of Ministers in a reshuffle that introduced members of the NCP and a number of independents into the coalition. In January 1998 Nepal was once again faced with political upheaval when Thapa recommended to the King that he dissolve the House of Representatives and set a date for mid-term elections. The Prime Minister presented the petition for fresh polls following a decision by the UML and dissident members of the NDP (including Chand) to introduce a parliamentary vote of 'no confidence' against the Government. Uncertain as to how to act in this political impasse, the King referred the matter to the Supreme Court (the first time a Nepalese monarch had ever done so). In early February the Court advised King Birendra to convene a special session of the House of Representatives to discuss a 'no confidence' motion against Thapa's Government. Although the Supreme Court's advice was not binding, the King called the parliamentary session. The 'no confidence' motion, which was presented on 20 February, was, however, defeated, by 103 votes to 100. Meanwhile, in mid-January Chand and nine other rebel deputies were expelled from the NDP; they immediately re-established a breakaway faction known as the NDP (Chand). In March the UML suffered a serious reverse when about one-half of the party's parliamentary deputies formed a breakaway faction entitled the Communist Party of Nepal (Marxist-Leninist) (ML). Bam Dev Gautam was unanimously elected as the new party's leader. The creation of the new party left the UML with 49 deputies, while the ML claimed the support of 40 deputies.

Under an agreement reached in October 1997 when Thapa assumed power, the Prime Minister was to transfer the leadership of the coalition Government to the NCP within an agreed time frame. By early April 1998, however, Thapa appeared reluctant to relinquish his post, and the NCP threatened to withdraw support for the Government unless the Prime Minister resigned immediately. Thapa tendered his resignation, and the President of the NCP, G. P. Koirala, was appointed Prime Minister in mid-April, taking office with only two other ministers. After obtaining a parliamentary vote of confidence, by 144 votes to four, the Prime Minister substantially expanded his Council of Ministers. Koirala stated that amongst the top priorities of the one-party minority Government would be the tackling of the Maoist insurgency (which had escalated in recent months). In August, in a seeming attempt to strengthen his own precarious administration and to encourage the UML's communist rivals, the Prime Minister invited the ML to join in alliance with the NCP and to form a coalition government. A new coalition administration was consequently established on 26 August (with the NCP retaining the most important ministries), giving Prime Minister Koirala an adequate parliamentary majority. Meanwhile, the 'people's war' waged by the Maoist activists in the hills of west Nepal gathered momentum. In May the Government launched a large-scale police operation in an effort to curb the guerrilla violence, and in July the Minister of Home Affairs claimed that a total of 257 people had died as a result of the Maoist uprising.

In mid-October 1998 the Speaker of the House of Representatives, Ram Chandra Poudel, a member of the ruling NCP, survived a parliamentary motion introduced by opposition parties, charging him with dereliction of duty in an attempt to oust him. In December the ML withdrew from the coalition Government, alleging that its ruling partner, the NCP, had failed to implement a number of agreements drawn up between the two parties and other political groups in August. Prime Minister G. P. Koirala tendered his resignation, but was asked to head a new coalition Council of Ministers, which was to hold power in an acting capacity pending the holding of a general election. On the recommendation of the Prime Minister, the King appointed a new coalition administration, comprising members of the NCP, the UML and the NSP, and, for the first time in eight years, a nominee of the King, on 25 December. In mid-January 1999 the acting Government won a convincing vote of confidence in the House of Representatives, and on the following day the King dissolved the legislature in preparation for the forthcoming general election.

In late April 1999 the UML suffered a set-back when its veteran leader and former Prime Minister, Man Mohan Adhikari, died during the electoral campaign. In May the NCP won an outright majority in the general election (held over two rounds), securing 110 of the 205 seats in the lower house; the UML obtained 68 seats and the NDP (Thapa) took 11 seats, while the ML and the NDP (Chand) both failed to win a single seat. Voting was conducted relatively peacefully, according to government sources, despite threats by the Maoist insurgents to disrupt the electoral process. A new Council of Ministers, headed by the veteran NCP leader, K. P. Bhattarai, and composed solely of NCP members, was appointed at the end of the month. In late June the UML won all six seats in elections to the National Assembly, and in August Dr Mohammad Mohasin of the NDP was elected Chairman of the upper house.

In early October 1999 a nation-wide general strike was organized by the CPN (Maoist). In late November, in an effort to resolve the Maoist insurgency, which, according to government sources, now affected (moderately to severely) 31 of Nepal's 75 districts and had led to the deaths of more than 1,000 people, the Prime Minister offered to grant the guerrillas an amnesty and various rehabilitation measures if they surrendered their arms and entered into negotiations with the Government. In response, the insurgents (who were estimated to number 5,000–6,000 and to have the support of about 8,000 sympathizers) stated that they were not prepared to enter into peace talks until arrest warrants issued against their leaders were withdrawn, official investigations were carried out into alleged extrajudicial killings of suspected militants by the police, and imprisoned activists were released. In an attempt to facilitate the peace process, the Government established a six-member high-level negotiation commission under the convenorship of former Prime Minister Sher Bahadur Deuba, which was charged with finding a solution to the Maoist situation that met with the approval of all political parties (including the insurgents themselves).

In mid-December 1999 the ruling NCP, despite a number of by-election victories, was once again beset by internecine strife when about 80 pro-Koirala legislators initiated an attempt to oust (by means of a petition) the Prime Minister from his position as the NCP's parliamentary party leader (which would automatically lead to his removal from the premiership). Koirala had initially been supportive of Bhattarai's premiership, but had since become a vociferous critic of his rival's administration, particularly with regard to the Government's perceived mismanagement of the Maoist crisis. In February 2000, on the recommendation of Prime Minister Bhattarai, the King carried out a minor reorganization of the Council of Ministers, including the appointment of Ram Chandra Poudel, a former Speaker of the lower house, as Deputy Prime Minister; the ministerial reshuffle was prompted by the earlier resignation of the Minister of Finance, Mahesh Acharya, following a disagreement with the Prime Minister over the appointment of the new Governor of the Central Bank. A few days after the government reorganization, the Minister of Education, Yog Prasad Upadhyaya, resigned in protest at the appointment of Poudel as Deputy Prime Minister. The political unrest culminated in the registration of a vote of 'no confidence' by 58 dissident NCP legislators against Prime Minister Bhattarai; this move led to the immediate resignation of 11 government ministers. The NCP's parliamentary party was scheduled to vote on the no-confidence motion in late February; however, following the attainment of a secret agreement between the Prime Minister and the NCP President, G. P. Koirala, including Bhattarai's reported assurance that he would stand down voluntarily within a fortnight, the proposal was withdrawn. A second motion of 'no confidence' in Bhattarai, who continued to hold the premiership amid rumours that he wished to hand over the post to a younger, 'second generation' leader, was registered by 69 predominantly pro-Koirala legislators in the NCP secretariat in mid-March. Under such pressure, Prime Minister Bhattarai pre-empted the holding of a no-confidence vote and tendered his resignation to the King. It was announced that G. P. Koirala was to be the new Prime Minister (for the fourth time), following his election as parliamentary party leader of the NCP (Koirala polled 69 votes, while his rival, Deuba, secured 43 votes); this election process replaced the party's traditional method of choosing a parliamentary leader through consensus. Koirala and a new Council of Ministers were sworn in by the King on 22 March, and vowed to continue the basic programmes and policies that the previous NCP Government had adopted. In mid-April, on the recommendation of the Council of Ministers, King Birendra reduced the number of ministries from 26 to 21. In May a Human Rights Commission was formed following accusations by various bodies that both the security forces and the Maoist guerrillas had committed human rights violations, including murder and torture.

In early April 2000 Prime Minister Koirala activated the National Defence Council, which, according to the Constitution, comprised the Prime Minister, the Minister of Defence and the Commander-in-Chief of the Royal Nepal Army, to resolve the Maoist crisis. In comparison to the inadequately-trained and poorly-armed police force, which had suffered numerous casualties, the army was much better equipped to deal with the insurgency, and Koirala expressed his wish to mobilize the armed forces in the ongoing fight against militant activity. The possibility of the deployment of the armed forces met with immediate criticism from various Nepalese human rights groups, which claimed that mobilization of the army would lead to an escalation in corruption. In the same month Deuba reportedly held preliminary talks with leaders of the UPF regarding the resolution of the Maoist uprising.

In June 2000 the CPN (Maoist) accepted the Government's invitation for dialogue; however, in August the party refused to enter negotiations, owing to the Government's failure to fulfil

certain conditions. In mid-July the Government abolished bonded labour. In August the Minister for Water Resources, Khum Bahadur Khadka, was dismissed owing to his involvement in a campaign against the Prime Minister. Later that month the Government banned strikes in 'essential services', including banks and telecommunications. In the mean time, strikes took place in August and September.

Nepal experienced floods from early August 2000, causing fatalities and damage to crops and, later, food shortages. At the end of the month the Maoist crisis worsened. During two Maoist attacks in Dolpa and Lamjung, 24 police officers were killed and 44 were injured. The Royal Nepal Army was criticized for failing to intervene to protect the police from insurgents. The Minister of Home Affairs, Govinda Raj Joshi, resigned after admitting his failure to 'maintain law and order in the country'. The Prime Minister responded to the confusion over the command and control structure of the army by giving Mahesh Acharya, the Minister of Finance, the additional portfolio of defence. G. P. Koirala had hitherto always retained this portfolio personally, but it had become clear that the Government and army needed an independent defence minister, clarification of the army's ambiguous role and the development of a procedure for mobilizing the army, absent from the 1991 Constitution. It was later decided that the Government would employ a dual approach: using the army, as well as encouraging negotiations in order to resolve the Maoist crisis.

At the end of October 2000 the first direct unofficial negotiations began between the Government and the CPN (Maoist); however, they soon ended, and the violence resumed in early November. In the same month the high-level commission charged with finding a solution to the Maoist crisis (see above) produced a report advising the Government and Maoist insurgents to cease violence and participate in negotiations. The report also recommended that the Government improve and modernize its security forces. The UML leader, who had earlier held negotiations with the insurgents, ruled out any alliance with the Maoist group until it abandoned the use of force.

Strikes were organized intermittently in December 2000 and January 2001. In December 2000 56 of the ruling NCP's 113 legislators registered a no-confidence motion against Prime Minister Koirala, demanding that he be removed as leader of the party. The motion, led by the former Prime Minister, Sher Bahadur Deuba, was brought about by Koirala's perceived failure to control both the Maoist insurgency and corruption. On 4 January 2001 the no-confidence motion was defeated after 41 legislators boycotted the vote. Shortly afterwards Deuba began a nation-wide campaign to remove the Prime Minister from the NCP leadership and announced his candidacy for the party presidency, to be determined in mid-January. Nevertheless, at the party's general convention, Koirala was re-elected NCP President.

In January 2001 the Minister for Tourism and Civil Aviation, Tarani Datta Chataut, resigned following a controversial agreement to lease an Austrian aircraft to the Royal Nepal Airlines Corporation. The parliamentary Public Accounts Committee and an anti-corruption agency investigating the alleged misuse of powers by Chataut and other government members, including the Prime Minister, instructed the Government not to deliver the aircraft to Nepal until the investigation was complete; however, this directive was ignored and the transaction was performed. In early February leading opposition parties issued a memorandum to the Prime Minister, demanding his resignation over the aircraft deal and also the worsening security situation. Koirala strongly denied his involvement in the leasing of the Austrian aircraft. The King then approved a reorganization of the Council of Ministers, on the recommendation of Prime Minister Koirala. However, shortly after the new cabinet was announced, two ministers withdrew their names, criticizing Koirala for making decisions without consulting other senior leaders. Palten Gurung later reneged on his decision, but Khum Bahadur Khadka refused to join the Council of Ministers. In March the Prime Minister faced increasing opposition from within and outside his party. Further ministerial resignations followed. The opposition continued to disrupt parliamentary proceedings, and, as a result, the King prorogued the National Assembly and House of Representatives in early April. In early May the Minister of Water Resources, Baldev Sharma Majgaiya, resigned. At the end of the month the anti-corruption commission cleared the Prime Minister of involvement in the controversial aircraft agreement, but filed cases against 10 other people, including the former minister, Chataut. At the same time, Koirala was accused of accepting bribes in another aircraft deal. The opposition continued to demand his resignation and organized a nation-wide strike in protest against the Government's alleged misuse of power. Meanwhile, in the first half of 2001 several unsuccessful attempts were made by the Government and Maoist militants to embark upon a peace process.

On 1 June 2001 King Birendra, Queen Aishwarya and six other members of the royal family were shot dead; the heir to the throne, Crown Prince Dipendra, was gravely wounded. Another family member, Dhirendra Shah, died later in hospital. Initial reports suggested that Prince Dipendra had shot members of his family before shooting himself, following a dispute between himself and his mother, regarding his intentions to marry Devyani Rani (the daughter of a prominent Nepalese politician), of whom the Queen disapproved. Prince Gyanendra, the deceased King Birendra's brother, however, issued a statement claiming that the deaths were the result of an accidental discharge of an automatic weapon. Immediately after the incident Prince Dipendra was pronounced King, and Prince Gyanendra, the deceased King Birendra's brother, was appointed regent. On 4 June King Dipendra died and was succeeded by Prince Gyanendra. These events caused unrest in Kathmandu, and a curfew was imposed. In the mean time, rumours about the killings began to spread. Few believed the statement given by Gyanendra. Some suggested that Maoist insurgents were to blame; others claimed India was responsible. On 6 June three journalists of the daily newspaper, *Kantipur*, were arrested and charged with sedition for publishing an article written by a Maoist leader supporting a conspiracy theory that Gyanendra (who was not present at the incident) and his son Paras Shah, who was not harmed in the shooting, had planned the events. (The charges were withdrawn in mid-August.) Following his accession, King Gyanendra established a commission to investigate the killings. The commission, comprising the Chief Justice, K. P. Upadhyaya and Speaker of the House of Representatives, T. Ranabhat, duly concluded that Dipendra had been responsible for the shootings and that at the time had been under the influence of drugs and alcohol. It was established that prior to the incident, he had telephoned his girlfriend, Devyani Rani, three times. He then changed into his military uniform, returned to the gathering and indiscriminately shot members of his family, before shooting himself. King Gyanendra bestowed the title of Queen on his wife, Princess Komal, but did not declare his son the Crown Prince until the end of October, owing to his unpopularity among the public, caused by his profligate behaviour.

In late June 2001 elections to 16 seats in the upper house of parliament took place. The UML won eight seats, bringing its total to 23 and rendering it the largest bloc in the chamber. The NCP secured seven seats, bringing its total to 21. In June–July Maoist leaders, taking advantage of the discontent in Nepal, intensified their activities. On 13 July the Deputy Prime Minister, Ram Chandra Poudel, resigned, owing to disagreements with the Prime Minister over policy towards the insurgency. Some few days later a senior Maoist leader declared that he would enter negotiations on the condition that the Prime Minister resigned. On 19 July Prime Minister Koirala resigned, citing his failure to curb the Maoist insurgency and long-standing corruption allegations. A few days later the NCP elected former premier Sher Bahadur Deuba as its new leader; King Gyanendra appointed Deuba as Prime Minister on the same day and a new Council of Ministers were sworn in on 26 July. Prime Minister Deuba retained a number of Koirala's cabinet members in an effort to ensure stability and initially kept many of the major portfolios for himself.

Immediately after his appointment Prime Minister Deuba persuaded the Maoist leaders to reciprocate his offer of a cease-fire and agree to enter dialogue. Prior to the negotiations, both sides took a series of confidence-building measures: the Maoist activists released 31 kidnapped police officers, and the Government set free over 30 Maoist leaders and published the names of 273 guerrillas still imprisoned. At the same time parliament passed legislation to establish an Armed Police Force and to develop the co-ordination of regional development and security. The Government released a further 68 insurgents after the first two rounds of negotiations in August and September 2001. Despite the cease-fire, Maoist insurgents continued to carry out violent acts. During the peace talks tens of thousands of people held demonstrations against the fighting. The third round of negotiations, which took place in November, ended in failure, owing to the Maoists' continued demand for the dissolution of

the Constitution, the establishment of an interim government, the election of a constituent assembly and, ultimately, a republic. The Government, in contrast, was prepared to offer a much less radical set of changes. Two days later the CPN (Maoist) leader Pushpa Kamal Dahal announced the end of the cease-fire. The Maoists established a parallel central government, the 'United People's Revolutionary Government', and resumed their violent campaign. The Maoists set up parallel governments in 40 of the country's 70 districts, and established direct rule in 22 districts in western Nepal. The violence escalated; on 26 November the King declared a state of emergency and authorized, for the first time, the deployment of the army to curb the insurgency. The King termed the Maoists as 'terrorists' and promulgated the Terrorist and Disruptive Activities Ordinance 2001, which sanctioned a number of counter-terrorist measures, including the suspension of civil liberties and media restrictions. The number of people killed in the five-year 'people's war' had risen to more than 2,300 by the end of December. In mid-December Prime Minister Deuba declared that he would not resume negotiations with the Maoists until they surrendered their arms.

Meanwhile, in early September 2001 the Government implemented a radical land reform programme, which was designed to help poor, landless farmers. The programme was supported by the UML, but opposed by smaller parties. Major landowners who risked losing part of their land opposed the limit to the size of individual landholdings. In mid-August Deuba announced that discrimination against Dalits (or 'untouchables') would henceforth be illegal and pledged to pass legislation ending the caste system. A national commission for Dalit welfare and a National Women's Commission were also to be established. In mid-October the Government was reorganized and expanded.

In early January 2002 the Nepal Rastra Bank froze the bank accounts of individuals and organizations associated with Maoist militants. In mid-February Maoist insurgents launched their heaviest-ever offensive against government outposts. More than 150 people, mainly soldiers and police officers, were killed in the fighting. In response to the attacks, the army was instructed to use offensive as well as defensive measures to combat the insurgency. On 21 February the legislature voted to extend the state of emergency for three months. Although the opposition criticized the Government for its handling of the insurgency and for failing to react to warnings that major attacks were imminent, it voted for the extension after the Prime Minister agreed to establish social and economic development programmes in poor rural areas where Maoists were active, and ensured the fair use of the emergency powers. In order to mark the sixth anniversary of the Maoist insurgency and to protest against the state of emergency, the guerrillas organized a two-day nation-wide general strike.

In the mean time, in mid-February 2002 the UML and its breakaway faction, the ML, merged. The party was reunited ahead of local elections scheduled to take place in May. The merger of the more moderate communist parties was regarded largely as a move to counter the influence of the Maoist insurgents. In mid-March the Minister of Forest and Soil Conservation, Gopal Man Shrestha, resigned amid allegations of corruption. Shrestha refuted the allegations presented by his deputy, Surendra Hamal, who was also forced to resign after the UML disrupted parliamentary proceedings. Strikes occurred in March, severely affecting businesses and schools. Schools, as well as government buildings, infrastructure and army and police outposts, were attacked. Security at schools was tightened in early April during nation-wide examinations. Following appeals by students and government officials, insurgents postponed a five-day strike, originally due to take place during the examinations, to late April. The Human Rights Commission issued its first annual report in which it accused the Maoist insurgents of committing serious human rights abuses. The commission also criticized the Government for violating human rights. On 4 April the Government reduced the controversial restrictions it imposed on the media and political parties as part of the state of emergency. The violent campaign escalated in mid-April, leading to hundreds of fatalities. In May Deuba tabled a parliamentary motion proposing an extension of the six-month state of emergency (which was due to expire on 25 May), prompting strong opposition from within and outside his party. Members of the governing NCP, led by former premier G. P. Koirala, accused Deuba of not consulting them before recommending an extension and urged the Government to withdraw its parliamentary motion. The rift in the party led King Gyanendra to dissolve unexpectedly the House of Representatives on 22 May, on the recommendation of the Prime Minister. A general election was scheduled to take place on 13 November, and the incumbent Government was instructed to rule the country in the interim. Political leaders strongly condemned this decision. On 23 May Deuba was suspended from his party and three days later was expelled from the NCP for three years. In the mean time, three ministers, including the Minister of Finance, resigned in protest at the calling of early elections. In late May King Gyanendra extended by three months the state of emergency. Meanwhile, the USA agreed to provide the Nepalese army with military assistance for its campaign against the Maoist activists. India had already supplied the Nepalese Government with financial and military aid. Meanwhile, in early May the army launched a heavy attack against Maoist insurgents in Rolpa district, resulting in the deaths of, according to government sources, 548 guerrillas, three soldiers and one police officer. A series of counter-attacks and attacks ensued, leading to hundreds of fatalities; by the end of May some reports estimated that more than 4,000 people had been killed since the beginning of the insurgency. In mid-May Maoist activists set fire to Mahendra Sanskrit University, causing millions of rupees worth of damage; no-one was killed in the incident. The attack on Nepal's only Sanskrit university was motivated by the Maoists' opposition to compulsory Sanskrit education at state-managed schools on the grounds that it promoted the interests of the Brahmin caste, while disregarding other castes. On 9 May the Maoist leader made an offer of a one-month cease-fire by e-mail to newspapers in Kathmandu; Deuba promptly rejected the proposal, repeating his request for the insurgents to renounce violence. International human rights organizations voiced concern over reports of human rights violations by the army. The editor of the pro-Maoist newspaper *Janadisha* was arrested by security forces in May; it was later reported that he died while in custody, allegedly under torture.

In mid-June 2002 the NCP officially split during a 'general convention' held by the Deuba faction; at the assembly the attendees voted to expel G. P. Koirala from the party for three years and unanimously elected Deuba (who had been reinstated as a party member by the convention) as party president in his place. The Koirala faction had boycotted the convention, denouncing it as illegal, and suspended three of Deuba's leading ministerial supporters from the NCP. The Minister of Agriculture, Mahesh Acharya, resigned shortly afterwards, in response to the party crisis. Eventually, in mid-September the Election Commission recognized the faction led by G. P. Koirala as the official NCP; Deuba could either join Koirala or form a new party. Several days later Deuba's minority breakaway faction registered as a new political party, the Nepali Congress Party—Democratic (NCP—D). Meanwhile, in July interim Prime Minister Deuba was accused of acting unconstitutionally when he presented the 2002/03 budget as a royal decree, thereby undermining a 1995 Supreme Court ruling, which defined the way in which interim administrations could introduce budgets. In September the Minister of Physical Planning and Works resigned, owing to an ongoing official investigation into his property assets.

In the mean time, the state of emergency expired in late August 2002. As a result the Maoists intensified their violent campaign, leading to hundreds of fatalities in September. It was reported that by the end of September about 3,000 people had been killed since the collapse of peace negotiations in November 2001. In mid-September 2002 the Government rejected Pushpa Kamal Dahal's offer of a cease-fire, on the grounds that it lacked credibility. In response to protests by the Federation of Journalists over the alleged treatment of journalists in custody, in early September the Government issued a list of 16 journalists detained in Kathmandu under the anti-terrorism legislation.

In early October 2002 Deuba requested King Gyanendra to postpone the general election by one year, citing the deteriorating law and order situation. However, King Gyanendra dismissed the Prime Minister and the interim Council of Ministers for reportedly failing to organize the general election. The King assumed executive power and postponed indefinitely parliamentary elections scheduled for November. On 11 October King Gyanendra appointed a nine-member interim Government, headed by the former premier and monarchist Lok Bahadur Chand. Most of the members of the new cabinet were civil servants or professionals. The NCP, UML and legal experts condemned the dismissal of Deuba and his Government and the establishment of a new Council of Ministers as unconstitutional.

Furthermore, the Maoist argument appeared to be strengthened by the King's act of 'feudal absolutism'. In mid-November the King disregarded demands by political parties to create a new government composed of their members, instead reorganizing and expanding the interim Council of Ministers to include a former UML member, businessmen and independents. Interim Prime Minister Chand relinquished 14 portfolios under the government changes. At the same time, amid continuing violence and disruption, the Deputy Prime Minister stated that the interim Government was prepared to enter negotiations with the CPN (Maoists) and would consider the latter's demand for an elected constitutent assembly. In December the human rights organization Amnesty International issued a damning report on the human rights situation in Nepal since the collapse of peace talks in November 2001. The army and Armed Police Force were severely criticized for the reported 'unprecedented levels' of human rights abuses, including torture, arbitrary dentention and deaths in custody. In addition, the report accused Maoist insurgents of torturing and killing captives, taking hostages and recruiting children. The report claimed that nearly one-half of the 4,366 people who had died in the conflict since late 2001 were civilians, killed by both security forces and Maoists.

On 26 January 2003 suspected Maoist militants shot dead the chief of the Armed Police Force, Inspector-General Krishna Mohan Shrestha, in Kathmandu; his wife and bodyguard were also killed. Three days later the CPN (Maoists) and Government announced an immediate cease-fire and agreed to resume peace negotiations after the Government agreed to declassify Maoist activists as terrorists, to withdraw rewards offered for the arrest of Maoist leaders and to cancel international police warrants issued for the guerrilla leaders. In February a series of informal talks took place; at the end of the month the Maoists presented two conditions for the resumption of formal negotiations: the release of Maoist prisoners and the army to return to the barracks. A 22-point code of conduct was signed by the chief government negotiator and Minister of Physical Planning and Construction, Narayan Singh Pun, and the Maoist leader, Babu Ram Bhattarai, in mid-March. According to the code, the Government would release prisoners gradually and give Maoists equal access to the state-controlled media; there was no mention of the army moving back to the barracks, however. Both sides also agreed formally to cease hostilities. The following day a Maoist negotiator declared that, while a communist republic continued to be the CPN (Maoist)'s goal, the militant group would comply with the public's decision on the future of the monarchy. In the mean time, Chand continued unsuccessfully to involve political parties in the peace process and therefore to form a broad-based negotiating team. The political parties and the Maoists questioned the interim Government's authority to negotiate with the Maoists. At the end of March Maoist negotiators began consultations with the NCP and UML on planned peace talks. On 11 April the King dismissed three ministers in a minor government reorganization. The interim Government and Maoist representatives commenced formal negotiations at the end of the month.

In 1978 the old Trade and Transit Treaty between Nepal and India was replaced by two treaties (renewed in the mid-1980s), the one concerning bilateral trade between the two countries, the other allowing Nepal to develop trade with other countries via India. Relations with India deteriorated considerably in March 1989, however, when India decided not to renew the treaties, insisting that a common treaty covering both issues be negotiated. Nepal refused, however, stressing the importance of keeping the treaties separate, on the grounds that trade issues are negotiable, whereas the right of transit is a recognized basic right of land-locked countries. In response, India closed 13 of the 15 transit points through which most of Nepal's trade is conducted. Severe shortages of food and fuel ensued, and the prices of basic products increased significantly. It was widely believed that a major issue aggravating the dispute was Nepal's purchase of weapons (including anti-aircraft guns) from the People's Republic of China in 1988, which, according to India, violated the Treaty of Peace and Friendship concluded by India and Nepal in 1950. Diplomatic relations between Nepal and India remained strained throughout 1989, with trade at a virtual standstill. Following several rounds of senior-level talks, a joint communiqué was signed by the two countries in June 1990, restoring trade relations and reopening the transit points, and assuring mutual consultations on matters of security. A few days earlier, as an apparent gesture of goodwill to India, the

Nepalese Government had told the Chinese Government to defer indefinitely the delivery of the final consignment of weapons destined for Nepal. The visit to Kathmandu by the Indian Prime Minister in February 1991 (the first official visit to Nepal by an Indian head of government since 1977), shortly after it was announced that the first free elections there were to be held in May, helped to reaffirm the traditionally amicable ties between the two countries. Separate trade and transit treaties (valid for five and seven years respectively) were signed during a visit by Prime Minister Koirala to India in December 1991; these treaties were both subsequently renewed on expiry. A major breakthrough in Indo-Nepalese relations was achieved in February 1996, when the Prime Ministers of the two countries formally signed a treaty in New Delhi regarding the shared utilization of the waters of the Mahakali River basin (for irrigation, general consumption and the production of hydroelectric power). The costs and benefits of the project, which involved the construction of a massive hydroelectric power plant, were to be divided between Nepal and India, although not, some critics claimed, to Nepal's benefit. Despite protests by left-wing opposition parties, the Mahakali Treaty was ratified by the House of Representatives in September. During a visit to Nepal by the Indian Prime Minister in June 1997, the Mahakali Treaty was formally endorsed and India granted Nepal access to Bangladeshi ports through a new transit facility across Indian territory via the Karkavita-Phulbari road (this facility was extended and improved in 1998). Some tension in Indo-Nepalese relations, nevertheless, remained; this centred on border demarcation disputes and, in particular, on the Indian border police's use of territory that Nepal claims as its own in the far west of the country (namely the strategically-situated Kalapani junction between India, Nepal and China, which covers an area of about 35 sq km). In June 2000 the Nepalese Government announced that the border would be delineated by 2003. In early August 2000 Prime Minister Koirala paid a visit to India, around four years after the previous visit by any head of government. Koirala succeeded in improving Indo-Nepalese relations, which had been strained by the hijacking of an Indian Airlines aircraft from Kathmandu in December 1999. In June 2000 Indian Airlines' operations to Kathmandu were resumed, ending a five-month suspension. Although Nepal was keen to renegotiate the Treaty of Peace and Friendship concluded by Nepal and India in 1950, India agreed to discuss the treaty only at foreign secretary level; therefore, it was unlikely that a solution would be achieved in the immediate future. In June 2001 the Indian Government deployed paramilitary forces along the Nepalese–Indian border, owing to heightened security fears in the aftermath of the Nepalese royal family killings. In late 2001 India supplied Nepal with two helicopters and arms to assist the neighbouring country in its struggle against the Maoist insurgency. India repeated its offer of financial assistance in early 2002. In March both countries extended for five years the 1996 bilateral trade treaty. The Nepalese and Indian Governments also held talks on the civil disorder problem in Nepal; India promised to provide the necessary support. In early 2003, however, the Indian Government became increasingly concerned about King Gyanendra's perceived disregard for democracy.

The People's Republic of China has contributed a considerable amount to the Nepalese economy, and the first meeting of a joint committee on economic co-operation took place in 1984. This committee met for a second time (and thenceforth annually) in Kathmandu in 1986, when China agreed to increase its imports from Nepal in order to minimize trade imbalances. Relations between Nepal and China improved further during the late 1980s and 1990s, as indicated by reciprocal visits made by high-ranking Nepalese and Chinese officials (notably, a state visit to Nepal was conducted by the Chinese President, Jiang Zemin, in 1996). In May 2001 the leaders of Nepal and China signed a six-point co-operation agreement to improve cross-border trade, increase road and aviation links and to promote tourism.

In 1985 it was agreed that Nepal's border with Tibet (the Xizang Autonomous Region) should be opened. Following the outbreak of ethnic violence in Tibet in 1989, however, the border between Nepal and Tibet was closed indefinitely. In 1991 the interim Government of Nepal cancelled a visit by the Dalai Lama, the Tibetan leader in exile, on 'technical grounds'. The cancellation followed Chinese protests made to the Nepalese Government against the proposed visit. The Nepalese authorities have been consistent in their commitment to the 'One China' policy and in their efforts to repatriate refugees fleeing from Tibet. In 1993 G. P. Koirala paid an informal visit to Tibet

—the first visit to the region by a Nepalese Premier since the 1950s. In 1995, however, the Nepalese authorities banned a proposed peace march by Tibetans through Nepalese territory. During a visit to China by the Nepalese Minister of Foreign Affairs in August 2000, an agreement was reached to allow Nepal greater use of a new road in Tibet. Greater technological and economic co-operation was also achieved, therefore noticeably increasing bilateral trade.

Ties with Bangladesh are also significant, particularly regarding the utilization of joint water resources. Large-scale migration from Bangladesh has resulted in a notable demographic transformation in Nepal, with the Muslim population increasing from around 4% of the total in the early 1990s to about 10% by the end of the decade. In January 2001 the Nepalese Minister of Foreign Affairs visited Bangladesh, where agreements on greater economic and transport co-operation were reached. In December 1982 Nepal and Pakistan strengthened their trade links by renewing a 1962 agreement, and in 1983 they established a joint economic commission and a regular air link.

In late 1991 thousands of Bhutanese of Nepalese origin began to arrive at refugee camps in eastern Nepal, following the outbreak of political and ethnic unrest in Bhutan. By early 1996 nearly 100,000 refugees were living in eight camps in the districts of Jhapa and Morang. In the first half of 1993 talks were held between Bhutanese and Nepalese government officials regarding proposals to resolve the issues at stake. The Nepalese Government steadfastly refused to consider any solution that did not include the resettlement in Bhutan of all ethnic Nepalese refugees living in the camps. This proposal was rejected by the Bhutan Government, which claimed that the majority of the camp population were not actually Bhutanese. The deadlock was apparently broken, however, when a joint statement was signed by the Ministers of Home Affairs of Bhutan and Nepal in July, which committed each side to establishing a 'high-level joint committee' to work towards a settlement (including the categorization of the refugees). In a notable shift in strategy, in January 1996 the Nepalese Government transferred the responsibility of handling the Bhutanese refugee problem from the Ministry of Home Affairs to the Ministry of Foreign Affairs. In April 1997 more than 10,000 Bhutanese refugees gathered at a mass demonstration in the eastern Nepalese town of Damak to call for UN intervention in the crisis. They also demanded that the Nepal Government either resolve the refugee problem or, failing that, 'internationalize' it. Nepal and Bhutan finally achieved a breakthrough at the 10th round of negotiations in December 2000. Both countries agreed that nationality would be verified on the basis of the head of the refugee family for those over 25 years of age. Refugees under 25 years of age would be verified on an individual basis. By the end of January 2001 a Joint Verification Team (JVT) had concluded the inspection of refugee camps; verification of 98,897 people claiming refugee status (including 13,000 minors born in the camp) began at the end of March, commencing with the Khudanabari camp. The Nepalese press criticized the JVT for being too slow: by early July the status of 4,128 individuals had been verified. At a meeting in November the Ministers of Foreign Affairs of Nepal and Bhutan were unable to harmonize the positions of their respective governments with regard to the four categories (established in 1993) for the people in the camps. In late 2001 the verification of individuals in the Khudanabari camp was completed. However, despite two further rounds of negotiations, the process reached a standstill in early 2002, with Bhutan reluctant to accept the individuals already verified, and both Governments undecided over the most suitable way to continue the verification process. In mid-March the refugees decided to send a petition to the King of Bhutan in order to draw the attention of the international community to their difficulties.

Nepal pursues a non-aligned foreign policy, and had diplomatic relations with 113 countries in early 2000. Nepal (with six other countries) is a founder member of the South Asian Association for Regional Co-operation (SAARC, see p. 310), formally established in 1985; the Association's permanent secretariat was established in Kathmandu in 1987. Kathmandu hosted a SAARC summit meeting in January 2002, despite rising tension in the region.

Government

Under the provisions of the Constitution promulgated in November 1990, Nepal is a constitutional monarchy. The Constitution provides for a bicameral Parliament, comprising a 205-

member House of Representatives (Pratinidhi Sabha) and a 60-member National Assembly (Rashtriya Sabha), as the supreme legislative body. The House of Representatives is elected for a five-year term, and members of the National Assembly hold office for a six-year term. Executive power is vested in the King and the Council of Ministers, which is answerable to the House of Representatives. The King appoints the leader of the party that commands a majority in the House of Representatives as Prime Minister, while other ministers are appointed, from among the members of Parliament, on the recommendation of the Prime Minister.

For the purposes of local administration, Nepal is divided into five development regions, 14 zones, 75 districts, 3,995 village development committees and 36 municipalities.

Defence

In August 2002 Nepal's total armed forces numbered 51,000 men. Military service is voluntary. An Armed Police Force was formed in 2001 to counteract the Maoist insurgency and numbered 7,000 in August 2002. The defence budget for 2002/03 was projected at NRs 5,400m.

Economic Affairs

In 2001, according to estimates by the World Bank, Nepal's gross national income (GNI), measured at average 1999–2001 prices, was US $5,879m., equivalent to $250 per head (or $1,450 per head on an international purchasing-power parity basis). During 1990–2001, it was estimated, the population increased at an average annual rate of 2.4%, while gross domestic product (GDP) per head increased, in real terms, by an average of 2.6% per year. Overall GDP increased, in real terms, at an average annual rate of 5.1% in 1990–2001; growth in 2001 was 5.9%.

Agriculture (including forestry and fishing) contributed an estimated 37.9% of GDP in 2001. The sector engaged 76.1% of the employed labour force in 1999. The principal crops are rice, maize, millet, wheat, sugar cane, potatoes and vegetables and melons. During 1990–2001 agricultural GDP increased by an average of 2.6% per year. The agricultural sector grew by 4.3% in 2000/01 and an estimated 1.7% in 2001/02.

Industry (comprising mining, manufacturing, construction and utilities) employed only 9.8% of the labour force in 1999, but provided an estimated 23.1% of GDP in 2001. About 60% of Nepal's industrial output comes from traditional cottage industries, and the remainder from modern industries. During 1990–2001 industrial GDP increased at an average annual rate of 7.4%. Industrial production was estimated to have grown by 8.2% in 1999/2000, by 2.5% in 2000/01 and by an estimated 1% in 2001/02.

Mining employed only 0.08% of the labour force in 1999, and contributed an estimated 0.5% of GDP in 2001/02. Mica is mined east of Kathmandu, and there are also small deposits of lignite, copper, talc, limestone, cobalt and iron ore. Geophysical investigations have indicated that the Siwalik range and the Terai belt are potential prospective areas for petroleum.

Manufacturing contributed 10.2% of GDP in 2001, and employed about 5.8% of the labour force in 1999. Manufacturing GDP increased by an average annual rate of 10.1% in 1990–2001. Based on a census of establishments engaged in manufacturing, the principal branches of the sector, measured by value of output, in 1996/97 were textiles—including carpets and rugs (accounting for 22.6% of the total), food products (20.3%), wearing apparel (excluding footwear and fur apparel) (6.9%) and tobacco products (6.7%). Traditional cottage industries include basket-making and the production of cotton fabrics and edible oils.

Energy is derived principally from traditional sources (particularly fuelwood). Imports of mineral fuel and lubricants (mainly for the transport sector), however, comprised an estimated 9.7% of the cost of total imports in 2000/01. In addition, Nepal's rivers are exploited for hydroelectric power (HEP) production, but in July 2002 it was estimated that only about 1% of the country's huge potential generating capacity (83m. kW) was being utilized. In March 2002 the 144,000-kW Kali Gandaki A HEP project began generating electricity. The plant was expected to meet Nepal's electricity needs until 2005. Nepal was hoping to export excess electricity to India. Two other HEP projects were nearing completion in 2002. However, construction of the 750,000-kW West Seti hydroelectric dam by an Australian company was still in its early stages more than five years after production of the plant began. The US $1,000m. project in West Nepal was not only the largest, but Nepal's single biggest ever foreign investment project. Some 10% of the electricity produced

will be given free of charge to Nepal and the rest exported to India.

The services sector employed 14.0% of the labour force in 1999. The sector contributed an estimated 39.0% of GDP in 2001. The GDP of the services sector increased at an average annual rate of 6.7% in 1990–2001. By 1996 tourism had emerged as Nepal's major source of foreign exchange; in 1999/2000 revenue from tourism amounted to 12.9% of total foreign-exchange earnings. In 2000 the number of foreign visitors declined to 376,500, compared with 491,504 in the previous year, owing to the suspension of Indian Airlines flights in the first five months of the year, regular strikes and security fears. In 2001 the number of tourists declined again, to 298,066, owing to the massacre of most of the royal family in June, intermittent strikes and the escalating Maoist insurgency. The reduction in the number of foreign visitors was also due to regional tension and the attacks on the USA in September. The worsening domestic security situation caused tourist arrivals to decline by 28% in 2002.

In 2001 Nepal recorded a visible trade deficit of US $765.2m., and there was a deficit of $339.3m. on the current account of the balance of payments. In the same year the principal source of imports (supplying 36.7% of the total) was India, while the USA was the principal market for exports (30.7%). Other major trading partners were Argentina, the People's Republic of China, Singapore and Germany. The principal exports in 2001 were manufactured goods and articles, basic manufactures and food and live animals. The principal imports were basic manufactures, machinery and transport equipment, chemicals and pharmaceuticals, and mineral fuels and lubricants.

Budget proposals for the financial year ending 15 July 2003 envisaged total expenditure of NRs 86,236m. and total revenue of NRs 55,603m. Foreign aid plays a vital role in the Nepalese economy. According to the Asian Development Bank (ADB), 58% of total government development expenditure was financed by foreign aid in 2000/01. Nepal's total external debt was US $2,823m. at the end of 2000, of which $2,784m. was long-term public debt. In that year the cost of debt-servicing was equivalent to 6.5% of receipts from exports of goods and services. The annual rate of inflation averaged 8.6% in 1990–2001. The national urban consumer-price index rose by 7.5% in 1999, by 2.5% in 2000 and by 2.7% in 2001. According to the ADB, in 1999/2000 47% of Nepali workers were underemployed, while urban unemployment, a major problem, particularly among educated youths, stood at 7%.

Nepal is a member of the ADB (see p. 143), of the Colombo Plan (see p. 339) and of the South Asian Association for Regional Co-operation (SAARC, see p. 310), all of which seek to encourage regional economic development.

With an inhospitable terrain, comprising isolated valleys and very high mountains, Nepal is among the least developed countries in the world. Successive administrations since 1991 have followed a policy of economic liberalization: many state enterprises have been privatized (although there have been numerous delays in the process), and there have been attempts to reduce the fiscal deficit, to increase revenue mobilization, to restructure and improve the financial sector, and to institute and operate open trade and investment policies. In February 1993, as part of a series of economic reforms introduced in an attempt to develop industry further and to increase exports to countries other than India, the Nepalese rupee was made fully convertible for current-account transactions. Nepal's Ninth Five-Year Plan (1997–2002) was launched in July 1997, with projected expenditure of US $7,170m. The main goal of the Plan was to eliminate poverty and reduce unemployment by focusing on the vital agricultural sector. However, unemployment increased, and the rate of growth achieved during the period reached only 3.6%, compared with the targeted 6%. Exports rose by a 42% in 2000, but increased by only 3.7% in 2001, largely owing to a significant decrease in the growth rate of exports of ready-made garments and woollen carpets. The demand for these commodities continued to decline in the latter half of 2001. Imports increased by 20% in 2000, but decreased by almost 1% in 2001. Despite protests by the business sector, value-added tax (VAT) was fully implemented by the Government in August 1999. The high VAT threshold was lowered in the budget for 2000/01. For the first time in 19 years, Nepal's GDP registered a negative growth rate in 2001/02: the economy contracted by 0.6%, according to official figures, largely owing to negative growth rates in the non-agricultural sector. Tourism and foreign trade fared particularly poorly, owing to a worsening internal security situation, regional tension and the suicide attacks on the USA. Although the extension of the 1996 trade treaty with India was forecast to boost trade with India, the global economic slowdown adversely affected Nepal's export industry. However, the remittances of some 700,000 Nepalese working abroad provided a boost for the economy. Despite attempts by the Government to introduce reform programmes for poverty reduction in 2000–01, progress had been minimal, mainly as a result of the Maoist insurgency, political instability, lack of private sector development and opposition to reform. GDP growth was expected to rise to 2% in 2002/03. For the economy to improve, a revival of the tourism industry was essential. The tourism board launched Destination Nepal Campaign 2002/03 to attract foreign visitors to the country. The cease-fire and proposed peace talks encouraged the industry, but it was apparent that it would take several years to rebuild visitor confidence. In 2002 the interim Government launched the 10th five-year plan, which aimed for a 4.3%–6.2% growth rate during 2002–07. One of the objectives of the plan was to reduce the level of poverty to 30% from 42%. In order to attract foreign investment, the restoration of law and order was essential. The Government needed also to accelerate its programme of economic reforms.

Education

Primary education, beginning at six years of age and lasting for five years, is officially compulsory and is provided free of charge in government schools. Secondary education, beginning at the age of 11, lasts for a further five years, comprising a first cycle of three years (lower secondary) and a second of two years (secondary). In 1996 the total enrolment at primary and secondary schools was equivalent to 80% of the school-age population (boys 92%, girls 67%). Primary enrolment in that year was equivalent to 113% of children in the relevant age-group (boys 129%, girls 96%), while the comparable ratio for secondary enrolment was 42% (boys 51%, girls 33%). There are two state universities, the Tribhuvan University in Kathmandu and the Mahendra Sanskrit Viswavidyalaya in Beljhundi, Dang (founded in 1986), and one private university in Banepa, which, together, had a more than 120,000 students in 1999/2000. Projected expenditure on education by the central Government in the 2002/03 budget was NRs 14,286m. (16.6% of total spending). The Eighth Five-Year Plan (1992–97) included proposals to introduce free compulsory secondary education in phases over the next 10 years. By 2000 compulsory education had been implemented in only seven of Nepal's 40 districts.

Public Holidays

2003: 11 January (National Unity Day), 30 January (Martyrs' Day), 2 February (Lhosar, Tibetan New Year), 6 February (Vasant Panchami—Advent of Spring Day), 19 February (Rashtriya Prajatantra Divas—National Democracy Day), 1 March (Maha Shivaratri—in honour of Lord Shiva), 8 March (Women's Day), 18 March (Phagu Purnima—Holi Festival Day), 1 April (Ghode Jatra—Horse Festival), 10 April (Chaite Dashain), 11 April (Ram Nawami—Lord Ram's Birthday), 14 April (Navabarsha—New Year's Day), 1 May (Labour Day), 16 May (Lord Gautam Buddha's Birthday), 7 July (King Gyanendra's Birthday), 12 August (Janai Purnima—Sacred Thread Ceremony), 13 August (Gai Jatra—Cow Festival), 20 August (Janmashtami—Lord Krishna's Birthday), 21 August (Children's Day), 30 August (Haratalika Teej—Women's Festival), 9 September (Indra Jatra—Festival of Rain God), September/October (Ghatasthapana), 5 October (Dasain—Durga Puja Festival), 25 October (Diwali—Festival of Lights and, over three days, Laxmi Puja), 27 October (Bhai Tika—Brothers' Day), 9 November (Constitution Day), 29 December (King Birendra's Birthday).

2004: 11 January (National Unity Day), 26 January (Vasant Panchami—Advent of Spring Day), 29 January (Martyrs' Day), January/February (Lhosar, Tibetan New Year), 18 February (Maha Shivaratri—in honour of Lord Shiva), 19 February (Rashtriya Prajatantra Divas—National Democracy Day), 6 March (Phagu Purnima—Holi Festival Day), 8 March (Women's Day), 29 March (Chaite Dashain), 30 March (Ram Nawami—Lord Ram's Birthday), 14 April (Navabarsha—New Year's Day), 20 April (Ghode Jatra—Horse Festival), 1 May (Labour Day), 4 May (Lord Gautam Buddha's Birthday), 7 July (King Gyanendra's Birthday), 30 August (Janai Purnima—Sacred Thread Ceremony), 1 September (Gai Jatra—Cow Festival), 6 September (Janmashtami—Lord Krishna's Birthday, and Children's Day), 17 September (Haratalika Teej—Women's Festival), 27 September (Indra Jatra—Festival of Rain God), September/October (Ghatasthapana), 22 October (Dasain—Durga Puja Festival, and Bhai Tika—Brothers' Day), 9 November (Constitution Day), 12 November (Diwali—Festival of Lights and, over three days, Laxmi Puja), 29 December (King Birendra's Birthday).

Weights and Measures

The metric system has been officially adopted but traditional local and Indian systems of weights and measures are widely used.

Statistical Survey

Source (unless otherwise stated): National Planning Commission Secretariat, Singha Durbar, POB 1284, Kathmandu; tel. 4225879; fax 4226500; e-mail npcs@wlink.com.np; internet npc.gov.np:8080.

Area and Population

AREA, POPULATION AND DENSITY

Area (sq km)	147,181*
Population (census results)	
22 June 1991	18,491,097
22 June 2001†‡	11,563,921
Males	11,563,921
Females	11,587,502
Total	23,151,423
Population (official estimates at mid-year)§	
1999	22,367,048
2000	22,904,000
2001	23,593,000
Density (per sq km) at June 2001	157.3

* 56,827 sq miles.

† Population is *de jure*.

‡ Includes estimates for certain areas in 12 districts where the census could not be conducted, owing to violence and disruption.

§ Not adjusted to take account of the 2001 census results.

Capital: Kathmandu, population 1,081,845 at 2001 census.

PRINCIPAL TOWNS
(May 2001)

Kathmandu	671,846	Mahendranagar . . .	80,839
Biratnagar . .	166,674	Butwal . . .	75,384
Lalitpur . . .	162,991	Janakpur	74,192
Pokhara . . .	156,312	Bhaktapur . . .	72,543
Birgunj . . .	112,484	Hetaunda . . .	68,482
Dharan . . .	95,332	Dhangadhi . . .	67,447
Bharatpur . . .	82,323		

Source: Thomas Brinkhoff, *City Population* (internet www.citypopulation.de).

BIRTHS AND DEATHS
(UN estimates, annual averages)

	1985–90	1990–95	1995–2000
Birth rate (per 1,000)	38.6	37.9	36.3
Death rate (per 1,000)	14.5	12.9	11.2

Source: UN, *World Population Prospects: The 2000 Revision*.

2001 (estimates): Birth rate 33.1 per 1,000; Death rate 9.6 per 1,000.

Expectation of life (WHO estimates, years at birth): 58.3 (males 58.6; females 57.9) in 2001 (Source: WHO, *World Health Report*).

ECONOMICALLY ACTIVE POPULATION
(1999 labour force survey)

Agriculture, hunting, forestry and fishing	7,203,000
Mining and quarrying	8,000
Manufacturing	552,000
Electricity, gas and water	26,000
Construction	344,000
Trade, restaurants and hotels	522,000
Transport, storage and communications	135,000
Financing, insurance, real estate and business service	51,000
Community, social and personal services	614,000
Activities not adequately defined	8,000
Total employed	9,463,000

Source: Central Bureau of Statistics.

Mid-2001 (estimates in '000): Agriculture, etc. 10,352; Total labour force 11,138 (Source: FAO).

Health and Welfare

KEY INDICATORS

Total fertility rate (children per woman, 2001)	4.6
Under-5 mortality rate (per 1,000 live births, 2001)	91
HIV/AIDS (% of persons aged 15–49, 2001)	0.49
Physicians (per 1,000 head, 1995)	0.04
Hospital beds (per 1,000 head, 1997)	0.17
Health expenditure (2000): US $ per head (PPP)	66
Health expenditure (2000): % of GDP	5.4
Health expenditure (2000): public (% of total)	29.3
Access to water (% of persons, 2000)	81
Access to sanitation (% of persons, 2000)	27
Human Development Index (2000): ranking	142
Human Development Index (2000): value	0.490

For sources and definitions, see explanatory note on p. vi.

Agriculture

PRINCIPAL CROPS
('000 metric tons)

	1999	2000	2001
Wheat	1,086	1,184	1,158
Rice (paddy)	4,030	4,216	4,165
Barley	32	31	30
Maize	1,346	1,445	1,484
Millet	291	295	283
Potatoes	1,091	1,183	1,314
Other roots and tubers*	100	100	105
Sugar cane	1,972	2,103	2,212
Beans, dry	24	25	27
Lentils	132	137	143
Other pulses	55	58	56
Mustard seed	120	123	132
Vegetables and melons	1,348	1,500	1,669
Fruit (excl. melons)	561	549	590
Spices*	31	32	33
Jute and jute-like fibres	16	15	16
Tobacco (leaves)	4	4	4

* FAO estimates.

Source: FAO.

LIVESTOCK
('000 head, year ending September)

	1999	2000	2001
Cattle	7,031	7,023	6,983
Buffaloes	3,471	3,526	3,624
Pigs	825	878	913
Sheep	855	852	850
Goats	6,205	6,325	6,478
Chickens	17,797	18,620	19,790

Source: FAO.

LIVESTOCK PRODUCTS
('000 metric tons)

	1999	2000	2001
Beef and veal*	47.8	48.0	44.2
Buffalo meat	119.6	121.8	124.8
Mutton and lamb	2.9	2.9	2.9
Goat meat	36.2	36.9	37.8
Pig meat	13.9	14.6	15.2
Poultry meat	12.4	13.0	13.5
Cows' milk	328.9	337.5	342.7
Buffaloes' milk	744.0	759.6	781.4
Goats' milk*	59.0	60.5	60.5
Ghee*	19.0	19.2	19.2
Poultry eggs	24.2	23.4	25.7*
Wool: greasy	0.6	0.6	0.6
Wool: scoured*	0.4	0.5	0.5

* FAO estimate(s).

Source: FAO.

Forestry

ROUNDWOOD REMOVALS
(estimates, '000 cubic metres, excluding bark)

	1999	2000	2001
Sawlogs, veneer logs and logs for sleepers	1,260	1,260	1,260
Fuel wood*	12,678	12,763	12,744
Total	13,938	14,023	14,004

* FAO estimates.

Source: FAO.

SAWNWOOD PRODUCTION
('000 cubic metres, including railway sleepers)

	1999	2000	2001
Coniferous (softwood)*	20	20	20
Broadleaved (hardwood)	610	610	610
Total	630	630	630

* FAO estimates.

Source: FAO.

Fishing

('000 metric tons, live weight)

	1998	1999	2000
Capture	12.0	12.8	16.7
Freshwater fishes	12.0	12.8	16.7
Aquaculture	12.9	13.0	15.0
Common carp	2.6	2.6	3.0
Bighead carp	1.9	2.0	2.3
Grass carp (White amur)	0.7	0.7	0.8
Silver carp	3.9	3.9	4.5
Other cyprinids	3.8	3.8	4.4
Total catch	24.9	25.8	31.7

Source: FAO, *Yearbook of Fishery Statistics*.

Industry

SELECTED PRODUCTS
('000 metric tons, unless otherwise indicated, year ending 15 July)

	1997/98	1998/99	1999/2000
Cement	276.5	190.6	248.0
Steel rods	125.3	106.6	144.9
Jute goods	51.4	49.3	49.7
Raw sugar	67.2	75.5	77.2
Tea	2.3	2.3	3.6
Vegetable ghee	28.9	87.0	91.3
Beer and liquor (million litres)	17.0	22.1	28.9
Soft drinks (million litres)	24.0	29.1	n.a.
Paper	16.2	19.5	18.6
Cigarettes (million)	8,127	7,315	7,125
Cotton textiles (million sq metres)	3.2	3.3	26.3*
Synthetic textiles (million sq metres)	18.7	17.8	15.6*
Soap	39.1	47.7	73.7

* Million metres.

Sources: National Planning Commission Secretariat, Kathmandu, and *Far Eastern Economic Review, Asia 2001 Yearbook*.

Finance

CURRENCY AND EXCHANGE RATES

Monetary Units
100 paisa (pice) = 1 Nepalese rupee (NR)

Sterling, Dollar and Euro Equivalents (31 December 2002)
£1 sterling = NRs 126.20
US $1 = NRs 78.30
€1 = NRs 82.11
1,000 Nepalese rupees = £7.924 = $12.771 = €12.178

Average Exchange Rate (rupees per US $)
2000   71.094
2001   74.949
2002   77.877

BUDGET
(NRs million, year ending 15 July)*

Revenue†	2000/01‡	2001/02§	2002/03‖
Taxation	38,865	40,397	45,928
Taxes on income, profits and capital gains	9,114	9,248	9,863
Taxes on property	616	929	1,101
Domestic taxes on goods and services	16,583	16,580	19,205
Taxes on international trade and transactions	12,552	13,641	15,760
Other revenue	7,971	8,199	9,675
Charges, fees, fines, etc.	1,931	1,879	2,556
Sales of goods and services	1,184	1,052	1,239
Dividends	2,336	2,676	2,885
Interest receipts	1,440	860	1,066
Total	46,837	48,596	55,603

Expenditure	2000/01‡	2001/02§	2002/03‖
Regular expenditure	37,079	44,079	49,104
General administration	8,027	10,961	11,225
Defence	3,813	5,785	7,228
Social services	10,692	13,454	14,130
Education	8,226	10,413	10,968
Health	1,547	2,115	2,151
Economic services	2,533	2,965	3,260
Agriculture-related	544	575	774
Infrastructure	924	1,055	1,132
Interest payments	4,698	5,720	8,006
Other purposes	7,315	5,194	5,255
Development expenditure	35,009	30,210	37,132
Social services	12,873	11,108	16,860
Education	2,784	2,402	3,318
Health	1,972	1,702	2,748
Provision of drinking water	2,407	2,077	3,773
Economic services	22,136	19,102	20,273
Agriculture-related	6,624	5,716	5,413
Infrastructure	12,779	11,028	12,800
Total	72,087	74,289	86,236

* Figures refer to the regular and development budgets of the central Government.
† Excluding grants received (NRs million, estimates): 6,800 in 2000/01; 8,700 in 2001/02; 14,600 in 2002/03.
‡ Revised figures.
§ Estimates.
‖ Forecasts.

Source: IMF, *Nepal: Selected Issues and Statistical Appendix* (September 2002).

INTERNATIONAL RESERVES
(US $ million at mid-December)

	2000	2001	2002
Gold*	6.5	6.5	6.5
IMF special drawing rights	—	0.1	—
Reserve position in IMF	7.5	7.2	7.8
Foreign exchange	937.9	1,030.4	1,009.8
Total	951.9	1,044.2	1,024.1

* Valued at US $42.5 per troy oz.

Source: IMF, *International Financial Statistics*.

MONEY SUPPLY
(NRs million at mid-December)*

	1999	2000	2001
Currency outside banks	36,929	44,526	51,699
Private sector deposits with monetary authorities	4,346	3,160	3,570
Demand deposits at commercial banks	13,832	15,343	16,891
Total money	55,107	63,028	72,161

* Excluding Indian currency in circulation.

Source: IMF, *International Financial Statistics*.

COST OF LIVING
(National Consumer Price Index; base: 1990 = 100)

	1997	1998	1999
Food (incl. beverages)	198.9	229.5	247.1
Fuel and light	196.5	204.6	215.4
Clothing (excl. footwear)	187.7	200.3	211.5
Rent	227.2	237.8	242.0
All items (incl. others)	197.7	220.5	235.8

2000: Food 240.5; All items 241.4.

2001: Food 243.7; All items 248.0.

Source: ILO, *Yearbook of Labour Statistics*.

NATIONAL ACCOUNTS
(NRs million at current prices, year ending 15 July)

National Income and Product

	1995/96	1996/97	1997/98
Domestic factor incomes* . . .	228,991	256,891	270,641
Consumption of fixed capital . .	4,465	5,670	7,182
Gross domestic product			
(GDP) at factor cost . . .	233,456	262,561	277,823
Indirect taxes, *less* subsidies . .	15,457	17,952	18,724
GDP in purchasers' values .	248,913	280,513	296,547
Factor income from abroad . . }	3,566	4,661	6,025
Less Factor income paid abroad }			
Gross national product (GNP)	252,479	285,174	302,572
Less Consumption of fixed capital	4,465	5,670	7,182
National income in market			
prices	248,014	279,504	295,390
Other current transfers from			
abroad (net)†	900	1,009	1,157
National disposable income .	248,914	280,513	296,547

* Compensation of employees and the operating surplus of enterprises.
† Excluding official grants.

Source: UN, *National Accounts Statistics.*

Expenditure on the Gross Domestic Product

	1999/2000	2000/01	2001/02*
Government final consumption			
expenditure	34,579	40,973	45,387
Private final consumption			
expenditure	287,947	309,107	326,108
Increase in stocks	18,376	21,480	16,965
Gross fixed capital formation . .	73,314	78,017	84,165
Total domestic expenditure . .	414,216	449,577	472,625
Exports of goods and services . .	88,360	91,821	77,796
Less Imports of goods and services	123,055	131,403	123,143
GDP in purchasers' values . .	379,521	410,194†	428,033†
GDP at constant 1994/95 prices	277,751	291,139	293,595

* Provisional figures.
† Including adjustments.

Source: Central Bureau of Statistics, Kathmandu.

Gross Domestic Product by Economic Activity

	1999/2000	2000/01	2001/02*
Agriculture, forestry and fishing .	144,644	149,040	156,384
Mining and quarrying	1,815	1,981	2,091
Manufacturing	33,550	35,566	34,616
Electricity, gas and water . . .	5,942	6,989	9,339
Construction	37,373	39,571	43,984
Trade, restaurants and hotels . .	42,895	45,381	42,817
Transport, storage and			
communications	29,336	33,050	34,800
Finance and real estate	36,919	41,835	43,636
Community and social services . .	33,810	40,060	42,826
Sub-total	366,284	393,473	410,493
Less Imputed bank service charges	10,708	11,912	12,269
Indirect taxes, *less* subsidies . .	23,945	28,633	29,809
GDP in purchasers' values . .	379,521	410,194	428,033

* Provisional figures.

Source: Central Bureau of Statistics, Kathmandu.

BALANCE OF PAYMENTS
(US $ million)

	1999	2000	2001
Exports of goods f.o.b.	612.3	776.1	720.5
Imports of goods f.o.b.	−1,494.2	−1,590.1	−1,485.7
Trade balance	−881.9	−814.0	−765.2
Exports of services	655.1	505.9	413.3
Imports of services	−212.5	−199.9	−214.7
Balance on goods and services	−439.2	−508.0	−566.6
Other income received	55.8	72.2	70.3
Other income paid	−28.4	−35.2	−58.8
Balance on goods, services and			
income	−411.9	−471.0	−555.2
Current transfers received . . .	182.3	189.0	240.2
Current transfers paid	−26.9	−16.7	−24.3
Current balance	−256.5	−298.7	−339.3
Other investment assets . . .	48.2	128.6	11.2
Investment liabilities	−72.8	−52.6	−228.0
Net errors and omissions . . .	58.3	145.7	256.5
Overall balance	−222.7	−77.0	−299.6

Source: IMF, *International Financial Statistics.*

OFFICIAL DEVELOPMENT ASSISTANCE
(US $ million)

	1998	1999	2000
Bilateral donors	218.8	212.3	234.7
Multilateral donors	189.4	138.8	155.1
Total	408.2	351.1	389.8
Grants	255.1	255.0	251.6
Loans	153.1	96.1	138.2
Per caput assistance (US $) . .	18.7	15.7	17.0

Source: UN, *Statistical Yearbook for Asia and the Pacific.*

External Trade

PRINCIPAL COMMODITIES
(NRs million, year ending 15 July)

Imports c.i.f.	1998/99*	1999/2000*	2000/01
Food and live animals	7,619	10,839	5,994
Crude materials (inedible) except			
fuels	6,247	7,012	7,560
Mineral fuels and lubricants . .	8,737	9,098	11,269
Animal and vegetable oils and fats	3,329	4,446	5,589
Chemicals and pharmaceuticals .	12,476	14,474	12,942
Basic manufactures	25,638	34,420	41,188
Machinery and transport			
equipment	18,064	20,548	23,028
Miscellaneous manufactured			
articles	4,302	6,683	7,210
Total (incl. others)	87,525	108,505	115,687

Exports f.o.b.	1998/99*	1999/2000*	2000/01
Food and live animals	3,724	4,240	4,777
Animal and vegetable oils and fats	3,597	3,230	4,104
Chemicals and pharmaceuticals .	2,804	3,933	4,042
Basic manufactures	13,540	15,839	18,909
Miscellaneous manufactured			
articles	11,393	21,509	22,651
Total (incl. others)	35,676	49,823	55,654

* Revised figures.

Exports of carpets (NRs million, year ending 15 July): 9,802 in 1998/99; 9,842 in 1999/2000; 8,592 in 2000/01.

Exports of garments (NRs million, year ending 15 July): 9,702 in 1998/99; 13,942 in 1999/2000; 13,125 in 2000/01.

Source: Asian Development Bank, *Key Indicators of Developing Asian and Pacific Countries.*

PRINCIPAL TRADING PARTNERS
(US $ million)

Imports	1999	2000	2001
Argentina	196.3	225.8	248.4
China, People's Republic . . .	227.7	216.8	213.2
Hong Kong	96.1	107.5	65.3
India	464.7	534.5	587.9
Japan	29.1	34.1	24.8
Korea, Republic	29.0	21.0	16.0
Saudi Arabia	30.5	37.8	40.7
Singapore	95.5	108.4	81.6
Thailand	17.2	31.9	33.0
United Arab Emirates . . .	69.2	85.9	92.6
Total (incl. others)	1,480.3	1,626.4	1,600.1

Exports	1999	2000	2001
Argentina	37.8	43.5	48.0
Bangladesh	8.1	3.6	4.7
France	11.7	14.2	7.8
Germany	92.4	87.3	74.8
India	153.8	176.9	195.3
Italy	4.5	8.4	8.9
Japan	4.7	25.7	14.8
Switzerland	6.5	11.6	12.7
United Kingdom	16.3	16.2	12.5
USA	174.7	220.2	198.2
Total (incl. others)	565.1	679.5	645.8

Source: Asian Development Bank, *Key Indicators of Developing Asian and Pacific Countries*.

Transport

ROAD TRAFFIC
(vehicles registered at 30 June)

	2000
Cars, jeeps and vans	53,073
Buses and minibuses	12,054
Trucks and tankers.	20,011
Motorcycles	147,157
Tractors	20,469

CIVIL AVIATION

Royal Nepal Airlines Corporation
(traffic on scheduled services)

	1997	1998	1999
Kilometres flown (million) . . .	11	11	9
Passengers carried ('000) . . .	755	754	583
Passenger-km (million)	908	908	1,023
Total ton-km (million)	99	99	108

Source: UN, *Statistical Yearbook*.

Tourism

FOREIGN TOURIST ARRIVALS

Country of residence	1998	1999	2000
Australia	11,227	11,997	12,138
Bangladesh	6,677	10,003	9,365
France	21,610	23,942	24,028
Germany	23,584	25,990	25,907
India	143,627	140,672	96,995
Italy	12,571	12,656	11,384
Japan	37,069	38,566	40,841
Netherlands	14,131	16,872	15,878
Sri Lanka	10,995	12,413	16,628
United Kingdom	32,628	34,281	35,080
USA	34,968	38,681	39,377
Total (incl. others)	463,684	491,504	463,646

Tourism receipts (US $ million): 153 in 1998; 168 in 1999.

Source: World Tourism Organization, *Yearbook of Tourism Statistics*.

Visitor arrivals: 298,066 in 2001 (Source: Nepal Tourism Board, Kathmandu).

Communications Media

	1998	1999	2000
Television receivers ('000 in use) .	85	150	170
Telephones ('000 main lines in use)	208.4	253.0	266.9
Facsimile machines (number in use)*	5,000	8,000	n.a.
Mobile cellular telephones ('000 subscribers).	—	5.5	10.2
Personal computers ('000 in use)	50	60	70
Internet users ('000)	15.0	35.0	50.0
Daily newspapers (titles)* . . .	175	n.a.	189
Non-daily newspapers (titles)* . .	2,288	n.a.	2,554

1997: Radio receivers ('000 in use) 840.

2001: Telephones ('000 main lines in use) 298.1; Mobile cellular telephones ('000 subscribers) 17.3; Personal computers ('000 in use) 80; Internet users ('000) 60.0.

* Year ending 15 July.

Sources: UNESCO, *Statistical Yearbook*; International Telecommunication Union.

April 2001: Daily newspapers 193.

Education
(2000)

	Institutions	Teachers	Students
Primary	25,927	97,879	3,623,150
Lower Secondary.	7,289	25,375	957,446
Secondary.	4,350	19,498	372,914
Higher	n.a.	4,925*	129,174†

* 1991 figure (Source: UNESCO, *Statistical Yearbook*).
† Year ending 30 June.

Adult literacy rate (UNESCO estimates): 41.8% (males 59.6%; females 24.0%) in 2000 (Source: UN Development Programme, *Human Development Report*).

Directory

The Constitution

The main provisions of the Constitution, which was promulgated by the King on 9 November 1990, are summarized below:

The preamble to the Constitution envisages the guarantee of the fundamental rights of every citizen and the protection of his liberty, the consolidation of parliamentary government, the constitutional monarchy and the multi-party system, and the provision of an independent judicial system. Sovereignty resides in the Nepalese people. The Constitution is the fundamental law of the land.

Nepal is a multi-ethnic, multi-lingual, democratic, independent, indivisible, sovereign, Hindu and constitutional monarchical kingdom. Nepali is recognized as the national and official language.

FUNDAMENTAL RIGHTS

Part Three of the Constitution provides for the fundamental rights of the citizen: all citizens are equal before the law; no discrimination is to be practised on the basis of religion, race, sex, caste, tribe or ideology; no person can be deprived of his liberty except in accordance with the law; capital punishment remains abolished; freedom of expression, freedom to assemble peaceably and without arms, freedom to form trade unions and associations, and freedom of movement are also guaranteed. Similarly, pre-censorship of publications is prohibited and, thus, the right to press and publications is ensured. In the sphere of criminal justice, the following rights are specified in the Constitution: no person is to be punished unless made punishable by law; no person may be tried more than once for the same offence; no one is compelled to testify against himself; no one is to be given punishment greater than that which the law at the time of the offence has prescribed; cruelty to detainees is prohibited; no person is to be detained without having first been informed about the grounds for such an action; and the detainee must appear before the judicial authorities within 24 hours of his arrest. In addition, provision has also been made to compensate any person who is wrongfully detained. A person's right to property is ensured, and the right to protect and promote one's own language, script and culture, as well as the right to education up to primary level in the child's mother tongue, have been safeguarded. Similarly, the right to practise religion and to manage and protect religious places and trusts has been granted to the country's various religious groups. The right to secrecy and inviolability of the person, residence, property, documents, letters and other information is also guaranteed.

GOVERNMENT AND LEGISLATURE

His Majesty the King is the symbol of Nepalese nationality and of the unity of the people of Nepal. The expenditures and the privileges relating to His Majesty and the royal family are determined by law. His Majesty's income and property are exempt from tax.

The executive powers of the country are vested in His Majesty and the Council of Ministers. The direction, supervision and conduct of the general administration of the Kingdom of Nepal are the responsibility of the Council of Ministers. All official duties undertaken by His Majesty, except those which are within his exclusive domain or which are performed on the recommendation of some other institutions or officials, are discharged only on the advice of, and with the consent of, the Council of Ministers. His Majesty appoints the leader of the party that commands a majority in the House of Representatives as Prime Minister, while other Ministers are appointed, from among the members of Parliament, on the recommendation of the Prime Minister. The Council of Ministers is answerable to the House of Representatives. In the event that no single party holds an outright majority in the House, the member who commands a working majority on the basis of the support of two or more parties shall be asked to form the Government. Should this also not be the case, His Majesty may ask a member of the party with the largest number of deputies to form the Government. In the event of these exceptional circumstances, the leader forming the Government must obtain a vote of confidence in the House within 30 days. If such confidence is lacking, His Majesty is to dissolve the House and to order a fresh election to be held within six months. The Parliament is bicameral, comprising the House of Representatives and the National Assembly. His Majesty, the House of Representatives and the National Assembly together form the Parliament of the country. The House of Representatives has 205 members, and all persons who have attained the age of 18 years are eligible to vote for candidates, on the basis of adult franchise. The National Assembly has 60 members, consisting of 10 nominees of His Majesty, 35 members, including three female members, elected by the House of Representatives, and 15 members elected by the electoral college, which includes the heads of the local committees of various develop-

ment regions. The tenure of office of the members of the House of Representatives is five years, and that of the members of the National Assembly six years.

THE JUDICIARY

The judicial system has three tiers: the Supreme Court, the Appellate Courts and the District Courts. The Supreme Court is the principal Court and is also a Court of Record. The Supreme Court consists of a Chief Justice and 14 other Judges. The appointment of the Chief Justice is made on the recommendation of the Constitutional Council, while other Judges of the Supreme Court, the Appellate Courts and the District Courts are nominated on the recommendation of the Judicial Council. All Judges are appointed by His Majesty on such recommendations.

OTHER INSTITUTIONS

The Constitution also makes provisions for the establishment of a Council of State (Raj Parishad) and its standing committee, a Public Service Commission, Auditor General, Election Commission, Attorney-General, Abuse of Authority Investigation Commission, etc.

POLITICAL PARTIES

Political parties are required to register with the Election Commission, and, to be officially recognized, at least 5% of the candidates presented by a party must be female and the party should obtain at least 3% of the total votes cast at the election to the House of Representatives. It has been specifically provided that no law that bans, or imposes restrictions on, political parties may be enacted.

EMERGENCY PROVISIONS

If and when there is a grave emergency in the country, caused by threat to the sovereignty, indivisibility or security of the country (owing to war, foreign aggression, armed revolt or extreme economic depression), His Majesty may declare a state of emergency in the country. Such a declaration must obtain the approval of the House of Representatives within three months. During the period of emergency, fundamental rights, with the exception of the right of recourse to *habeas corpus*, may be suspended.

AMENDMENTS

The Constitution may be amended by a two-thirds majority in each House of Parliament. No changes, however, would be allowed to alter the spirit of the preamble.

DEFENCE

His Majesty is the Supreme Commander-in-Chief of the Royal Nepal Army. The Royal Nepal Army is administered and deployed by His Majesty on the recommendation of the National Defence Council. The Commander-in-Chief is appointed on the recommendation of the Prime Minister. The National Defence Council consists of the Prime Minister, as Chairman, the Minister of Defence and the Commander-in-Chief.

Official matters that involve, *inter alia*, the subjects of defence and strategic alliance, the boundaries of the Kingdom of Nepal, agreements on peace and friendship, and treaties concerning the utilization and distribution of natural resources, have to be approved by a two-thirds majority of the members of both Houses in a joint session of Parliament.

The Government

HEAD OF STATE

King: HM King GYANENDRA BIR BIKRAM SHAH DEV (succeeded to the throne 4 June 2001).

INTERIM COUNCIL OF MINISTERS
(April 2003)

Prime Minister and Minister of Royal Palace Affairs, of Defence, of Education and Sports, of Industry, Commerce and Supplies and of Law, Justice and Parliamentary Affairs: LOKENDRA BAHADUR CHAND.

Deputy Prime Minister and Minister of Home Affairs, of Agriculture and Co-operatives and of Local Development: BADRI PRASAD MANDAL.

Minister of Finance: Dr BADRI PRASAD SHRESTHA.

Minister of Foreign Affairs: NARENDRA BIKRAM SHAH.

Minister of Information and Communications and of General Administration: RAMESH NATH PANDEY.

Minister of Physical Planning and Construction: NARAYAN SINGH PUN.

Minister of Land Reforms and Management and of Forest and Soil Conservation: BADRI NARAYAN BASNET.

Minister of Labour and Transport Management and of Population and Environment: KAMAL PRASAD CHAULAGAIN.

Minister of Culture, Tourism and Civil Aviation: KUBER PRASAD SHARMA.

Minister of Water Resources: DEEPAK GYAWALI.

Minister of Women, Children and Social Welfare: GORE BAHADUR KHAPANGI.

Minister of Health and of Science and Technology: Dr UPENDRA DEVKOTA.

MINISTRIES

All Ministries are in Kathmandu.

Ministry of Agriculture: Singha Durbar, Kathmandu; tel. 4225108; fax 4225825; e-mail moa@fert.mos.com.np.

Ministry of Culture, Tourism and Civil Aviation: Singha Durbar, Kathmandu; tel. 4225870; fax 4227758; e-mail motca@ntc.net.np.

Ministry of Defence: Singha Durbar, Kathmandu; tel. 4228089; fax 4228204.

Ministry of Education and Sports: Keshar Mahal, Kanti Path, Kathmandu; tel. 4411599; fax 4412460.

Ministry of Finance: Foreign Aid Co-ordination Division, POB 12845, Kathmandu; tel. 4259837; internet www.facd.gov.np.

Ministry of Foreign Affairs: Shital Niwas, Maharajganj, Kathmandu; tel. 4416011; fax 4416016; e-mail mofa@mos.com.np.

Ministry of Home Affairs: Singha Durbar, Kathmandu; tel. 4226996; fax 4227186; e-mail moha@mos.com.np; internet www.south-asia.com/hmg_home.

Ministry of Industry, Commerce and Supplies: Singha Durbar, Kathmandu; tel. 4251174; fax 4220319.

Ministry of Information and Communications: Singha Durbar, Kathmandu; tel. 4220150; fax 4221729.

Ministry of Labour and Transport Management: Singha Durbar, Kathmandu; tel. 4228291; fax 4256877.

Ministry of Law, Justice and Parliamentary Affairs: Babar Mahal, Kathmandu.

Ministry of Population and the Environment: Singha Durbar, Kathmandu; tel. 4245367; fax 4242138; e-mail info@mope.gov.np; internet www.mope.gov.np.

COUNCIL OF STATE

The Council of State (Raj Parishad) has a standing committee headed by a royal appointee. The 15-member committee is composed of eight royal appointees and seven other members, including the Prime Minister, the Ministers of Defence and Foreign Affairs, the Chief Justice of the Supreme Court and the Chief of Army Staff.

Chairman of Standing Committee: Dr KESHAR JUNG RAYAMAJHI.

Legislature

NATIONAL ASSEMBLY

The National Assembly (Rashtriya Sabha) has 60 members, consisting of 10 nominees of the King, 35 members (including three women) elected by the House of Representatives, and 15 members elected by the electoral college, which includes the heads of the local committees of various development regions. The tenure of office of the members of the National Assembly is six years.

Chairman: Dr MOHAMMAD MOHASIN.

HOUSE OF REPRESENTATIVES

The 205-member House of Representatives (Pratinidhi Sabha) is elected, on the basis of adult franchise, for five years.

Speaker: TARANATH RANABHAT.

Deputy Speaker: CHITRA LEKHA YADAV.

General Election, 3 and 17 May 1999

Party	Seats
Nepali Congress Party (NCP)	111
Communist Party of Nepal (Unified Marxist-Leninist—UML)	71
National Democratic Party (NDP)	11
Rashtriya Jana Morcha	5
Nepali Sadbhavana Party	5
Nepal Workers' and Peasants' Party	1
Samyukta Janmorcha Nepal	1
Total	**205**

Notes: Polling was deferred until 8 and 23 June 1999 in four constituencies, owing to the deaths of candidates. The House of Representatives was dissolved on 22 May 2002. A general election, originally scheduled for 13 November, was postponed indefinitely on 4 October.

Political Organizations

According to the 1990 Constitution, political parties are required to register with the Election Commission, and, in order to be officially recognized, 5% of the candidates presented by a party must be female and the party should obtain at least 3% of the total votes cast in the election to the House of Representatives. The Constitution also specifies that no law may be adopted that bans, or imposes restrictions on, political parties.

Communist Party of Nepal (Maoist): underground political movement; orchestrates 'people's war' in hills of west Nepal (1996–); advocates abolition of constitutional monarchy and establishment of people's republic; Leaders PUSPA KAMAL DAHAL ('Prachandra'), Dr BABURAM BHATTARAI.

Communist Party of Nepal (Mashal): Kathmandu; Leader CHITRA BAHADUR.

Communist Party of Nepal (Unified Marxist-Leninist) (UML): Madan Nagar Balkhu, POB 5471, Kathmandu; tel. 4278081; fax 4278084; e-mail uml@mos.com.np; internet www.south-asia.com/uml/; f. 1991 when two major factions of the Communist Party of Nepal (CPN; f. 1949; banned 1960; legalized 1990)—the Marxist and Marxist-Leninist factions—merged; the Communist Party of Nepal (Marxist-Leninist—ML) seceded in 1998 and rejoined the UML in 2002; Chair. (vacant); Gen. Sec. MADHAV KUMAR NEPAL.

Communist Party of Nepal (United): Dillibazar, POB 2737, Kathmandu; tel. 4430869; fax 4411642; Leader BISHNU B. MANANDHAR.

Communist Party of Nepal (Verma): Dillibazar, Kathmandu; tel. 4414997; Leader KRISHNA RAJ VERMA.

Green Nepal Party: Kalikasthan, POB 890, Kathmandu; tel. 4411730; fax 4419497; e-mail greennp@wlink.com.np; Leader KUBER SHARMA.

Janawadi Morcha: Indrachowk, Itumbahal, Kathmandu; tel. 4211033; Leader PIRUDDHIN MIR.

National Democratic Party (NDP) (Rashtriya Prajatantra Party—RPP): Naxal, Kathmandu; tel. 4437057; fax 4434441; right-wing; Pres. SURYA BAHADUR THAPA; Vice-Pres. PRAKASH CHANDRA LOHANI; Gen. Sec. PASHUPATI SHUMSHER J. B. RANA.

National Democratic Party (NDP) (Chand) (Rashtriya Prajatantra Party—RPP): Maitighar, Kathmandu; tel. 4223044; fax 4223628; right-wing; Leader LOKENDRA BAHADUR CHAND.

National People's Council (Rashtriya Janata Parishad): Dillibazar, Kathmandu; tel. 4415150; f. 1992; royalist; aims to defend democracy, nationalism and sovereignty; Pres. MAITRIKA PRASAD KOIRALA; Vice-Pres. KIRTI NIDHI BISTA.

National People's Front (Rashtriya Jana Morcha): Mahaboudha, Kathmandu; tel. 4224226; Leader CHITRA BAHADUR.

National People's Liberation Forum: Kathmandu; left-wing; rejects 1990 Constitution as reactionary; Chair. M. S. THAPA.

Nepal Praja Parishad: Battisputali, Kathmandu; tel. 4471616; f. 1936; banned 1961; legalized 1990; Pres. RAM HARI SHRESTHA; Gen. Secs Dr MEENA ACHARYA, MAHESWOR SHARMA.

Nepal Workers' and Peasants' Party: Golmadhi Tole, 7-Bhaktapur, Kathmandu; tel. 4610974; fax 4613207; Chair. NARAYAN MAN BIJUKCHHE (ROHIT).

Nepali Congress Party (NCP): Bhansar Tole, Teku, Kathmandu; tel. 4227748; fax 4227747; e-mail ncparty@mos.com.np; internet www.nepalicongress.org.np; f. 1947; banned 1960; legalized 1990; Pres. GIRIJA PRASAD KOIRALA; Gen. Sec. SUSHIL KOIRALA; 135,000 active members, 500,000 ordinary members.

Nepali Congress Party—Democratic (NCP—D): Kathmandu; f. 2002 as a breakaway faction of the NCP; Leader SHER BAHADUR DEUBA.

Nepali Janata Dal: Samakhusi, Kathmandu; tel. 4352476; f. 1990; advocates the consolidation of the multi-party democratic system and supports the campaign against corruption; Leader KESHAR JUNG RAYAMAJHI.

Nepali National Congress: Lazimpat, Kathmandu; tel. 4411090; Pres. DILLI RAMAN REGMI.

Nepali Sadbhavana Party (NSP) (Nepal Goodwill Party): Shantinagar, New Baneshwor, Kathmandu; tel. 4488068; fax 4470797; f. 1990; promotes the rights of the Madhesiya community, who are of Indian origin and reside in the Terai; demands that the Government recognize Hindi as an official language, that constituencies in the Terai be allocated on the basis of population, and that the Government grant citizenship to those who settled in Nepal before April 1990; Pres. GAJENDRA NARAYAN SINGH; Gen. Sec. HRIDAYESH TRIPATHI.

Samyukta Janmorcha Nepal: c/o House of Representatives, Kathmandu.

United People's Front (UPF): Koteshwar, Kathmandu; tel. 4479159; fax 4470457; Maoist; involved in 'people's war' in hills of west Nepal (1996–); Chair. AMIK SHERCHAN; Leaders Dr BABURAM BHATTARAI, LILAMANI POKHAREL.

Diplomatic Representation

EMBASSIES IN NEPAL

Australia: Suraj Niwas, Bansbari, POB 879, Kathmandu; tel. 4371678; fax 4371533; Ambassador K. GARDNER.

Bangladesh: Maharajgunj Ring Rd, POB 789, Kathmandu; tel. 4372843; fax 4373265; e-mail bdootktm@wlink.com.np; Chargé d'affaires a.i. GOLAM SARWAR.

China, People's Republic: Baluwatar, POB 4234, Kathmandu; tel. 4415383; fax 4411388; Ambassador WU CONGYONG.

Denmark: Baluwatar, Lalita Niwas Rd, POB 6332, Kathmandu; tel. 4413010; fax 4411409; e-mail danemb@wlink.com.np; Chargé d'affaires GERT MEINECKE.

Egypt: Pulchowk, Lalitpur, POB 792, Kathmandu; tel. 4524844; fax 4522975; Ambassador ABD EL-HAMID MOHAMED TABAK.

Finland: Lazimpat, POB 2126, Kathmandu; tel. 4416636; fax 4416703; e-mail finembka@mos.com.np; internet www.south-asia .com/embassy-Finland; Chargé d'affaires a.i. ASKO LUUKKAINEN.

France: Lazimpat, POB 452, Kathmandu; tel. 4412332; fax 4418288; e-mail ambafr@mos.com.np; Ambassador CLAUDE ABROSINI.

Germany: Gyaneshwar, POB 226, Kathmandu; tel. 4412786; fax 4416899; e-mail gerembnp@mos.com.np; Ambassador RÜDIGER LEMP.

India: Lainchaur, POB 292, Kathmandu; tel. 4411940; fax 4413132; e-mail eipi@mos.com.np; internet www.south-asia.com/ embassy-India; Ambassador KRISHNA V. RAJAN.

Israel: Bishramalaya House, Lazimpat, POB 371, Kathmandu; tel. 4411811; fax 4413920; e-mail israelem@mos.com.np; Ambassador AVRAHIM NIR.

Japan: Panipokhari, POB 264, Kathmandu; tel. 4426680; fax 4414101; Ambassador MITSUAKI KOJIMA.

Korea, Democratic People's Republic: Jhamsikhel, Lalitpur, Kathmandu; tel. 4521084; Ambassador KIM THAE JONG.

Korea, Republic: Himshail, Red Cross Marg, Tahachal, POB 1058, Kathmandu; tel. 4270172; fax 4272041; e-mail koreasamb@mos.com .np; Ambassador HWANG BOO-HONG.

Myanmar: Chakupath, Patan Gate, Lalitpur, POB 2437, Kathmandu; tel. 4523734; fax 4523402; Ambassador U TIN LATT.

Norway: Surya Court, Pulchowk, Lalitpur, POB 20765, Kathmandu; tel. 4545307; fax 4545226; e-mail emb.kathmandu@mfa.no.

Pakistan: Panipokhari, POB 202, Kathmandu; tel. 4411421; Ambassador MUHAMMAD NASSER MIAN.

Russia: Baluwatar, POB 123, Kathmandu; tel. 4412155; fax 4416571; Ambassador VLADIMIR V. IVANOV.

Sri Lanka: Maharajgunj, POB 8802, Chundevi, Kathmandu; tel. 4413623; fax 4418128; e-mail embassy@srilanka.info.com.np; Ambassador PAMELA J. DEEN.

Thailand: Jyoti Kendra, Thapathali, POB 3333, Kathmandu; tel. 4213912; fax 4420408; Ambassador POWTHEP VANACHINDA.

United Kingdom: Lainchaur, POB 106, Kathmandu; tel. 4410583; fax 4411789; e-mail britemb@wlink.com.np; internet www.britain .gov.np; Ambassador KEITH BLOOMFIELD.

USA: Panipokhari, POB 295, Kathmandu; tel. 4411179; fax 4419963; Ambassador MICHAEL E. MALINOWSKI.

Judicial System

According to the 1990 Constitution, the judicial system is composed of three tiers: the Supreme Court (which is also a Court of Record), the Appellate Courts and the District Courts. The Supreme Court consists of a Chief Justice and up to 14 other judges. The Chief Justice, whose tenure of office is seven years, is appointed by the King on the recommendation of the Constitutional Council, while all other judges are appointed on the recommendation of the Judicial Council.

Chief Justice: KESHAV PRASAD UPADHYAYA.

Attorney-General: BADRI BAHADUR KARKI.

Religion

At the 2001 census, an estimated 80.6% of the population professed Hinduism (the religion of the Royal Family), while 10.7% were Buddhists and 4.2% Muslims. There were an estimated 101,976 Christians in Nepal in 2001.

BUDDHISM

All Nepal Bhikkhu Council: Vishwa Shanti Vihara (World Peace Temple), 465 Ekadantamarga, Minbhawan, New Baneshwar, POB 8973, Kathmandu; tel. 4482984; fax 4482250; e-mail vishwa@ntc.net .np; internet www.vishwavihara.org.

Nepal Buddhist Association: Kathmandu; tel. 45214420; Sec. Rev. BHIKKHU AMRITANANDA (Ananda Kuti, Kathmandu).

CHRISTIANITY

Protestant Church

Presbyterian Church of the Kingdom of Nepal: POB 3237, Kathmandu; tel. and fax 4524450.

The Roman Catholic Church

The Church is represented in Nepal by a single apostolic prefecture. At December 2000 there were an estimated 6,195 adherents in the country.

Apostolic Prefecture: Church of the Assumption, Everest Postal Care P. Ltd, POB 8975 EPC-343, Kathmandu; tel. 4542802; fax 4521710; e-mail anath@wlink.com.np; f. 1983 as Catholic Mission; Prefect Apostolic Fr ANTHONY FRANCIS SHARMA.

ISLAM

All Nepal Muslim Society: Durbar Marg, Kathmandu; tel. 4220534.

The Press

PRINCIPAL DAILIES

The Commoner: Naradevi, POB 203, Kathmandu; tel. 4228236; f. 1956; English; Publr and Chief Editor GOPAL DASS SHRESTHA; circ. 7,000.

Daily News: Bhimsensthan, POB 171, Kathmandu; tel. 4279147; fax 4279544; e-mail manju-sakya@hotmail.com; f. 1983; Nepali and English; Chief Editor MANJU RATNA SAKYA; Publr SUBHA LAXMI SAKYA; circ. 20,000.

Dainik Nirnaya: Bhairawa; tel. 520117; Nepali; Editor P. K. BHATTACHAN.

Gorkhapatra: Dharma Path, POB 23, Kathmandu; tel. 4221478; fax 4222921; f. 1901; Nepali; govt-owned; Editor-in-Chief KRISHNA BHAKTA SHRESTHA; circ. 75,000.

Himalaya Times: Kathmandu; Exec. Editor KUMAR PRASAD SAPKOTA.

Janadoot: Ga 2–549, Kamal Pokhari (in front of the Police Station), Kathmandu; tel. 4412501; f. 1970; Nepali; Editor GOVINDA BIYOGI; circ. 6,500.

Kantipur: Shantinagar, Naya Baneswor, POB 8559, Kathmandu; tel. 4473798; fax 4470178; internet www.kantipuronline.com; Nepali; Chief Exec. HEM RAJ GYAWALI; Editor YUBARAJ GHIMIRE.

The Kathmandu Post: Subidhnagar, Naya Baneshwor, POB 8559, Kathmandu; tel. 4480100; fax 4470178; e-mail kpost@kantipur.com.np; internet www.kantipuronline.com; f. 1993; English; Chief Editor SHYAM BAHADUR; Editor SUMAN PRADHAN; circ. 30,000.

The Motherland: POB 1184, Kathmandu; English; Editor MANINDRA RAJ SHRESTHA; circ. 5,000.

Nepal Samacharpatra: Sagarmatha Press, Ramshah Path, Kathmandu; e-mail sadhana@mail.com.np; f. 1945; Nepali; Editor NARENDRA BILAS PANDEY; circ. 1,000.

Nepali Hindi Daily: Maitidevi Phant, Shantinagar 32, Kathmandu; tel. 4436584; fax 4435931; e-mail das@ntc.net.np; f. 1954; evening; Hindi; Publr UMA KANT DAS; Chief Editor VIJOY KUMAR DAS; circ. 65,000.

Rising Nepal: Dharma Path, POB 1623, Kathmandu; tel. 4227493; fax 4224381; internet www.south-asia.com/news-ktmpost.html; f. 1965; English; Editor-in-Chief GYAN BAHADUR RAI (acting); circ. 20,000.

Samaj: National Printing Press, Dilli Bazar, Kathmandu; f. 1954; Nepali; Editor MANI RAJ UPADHYAYA; circ. 5,000.

Samaya: Kamal Press, Ramshah Path, Kathmandu; f. 1962; Nepali; Editor MANIK LAL SHRESTHA; circ. 18,000.

Swatantra Samachar: Vina Bhandranalya, Chhetrapati, Kathmandu; f. 1957; Editor MADAN DEV SHARMA; circ. 2,000.

SELECTED PERIODICALS

Agricultural Credit: Agricultural Training and Research Institute, Agricultural Development Bank, Head Office, Ramshah Path, Panchayat Plaza, Kathmandu; tel. 4220756; fax 4225329; 2 a year; publ. by the Agricultural Development Bank; Chair. Dr NARAYAN N. KHATRI; Editor RUDRA PD. DAHAL.

Arpan: Bhimsensthan, POB 285, Kathmandu; tel. 4244450; fax 4279544; e-mail manju-sakya@hotmail.com; f. 1964; weekly; Nepali; Publr and Chief Editor MANJU RATNA SAKYA; circ. 18,000.

Commerce: Bhimsensthan, POB 171, Kathmandu; tel. 4279636; fax 4279544; e-mail manju-sakya@hotmail.com; f. 1971; monthly; English; Publr and Chief Editor MANJU RATNA SAKYA; Editor SUBHA LAXMI SAKYA; circ. 12,000.

Current: Gautam Marg, Kamalpokhari, Kathmandu; tel. 4419484; fax 4413554; e-mail kiran_gautam@hotmail.com; f. 1982; weekly; Nepali; Man. Editor KIRAN GAUTAM; Publr and Editor DEVENDRA GAUTAM; circ. 10,000.

Cyber Post: Kathmandu; fortnightly; computers, electronics.

Foreign Affairs Journal: 5/287 Lagon, Kathmandu; f. 1976; 3 a year; articles on Nepalese foreign relations and diary of main news events; Publr and Editor BHOLA BIKRUM RANA; circ. 5,000.

Himal, The South Asian Magazine: POB 7251, Kathmandu; tel. 4543333; fax 4521013; e-mail info@himalmag.com; internet www.himalmag.com; f. 1987; monthly; political, business, social and environmental issues throughout South Asia; Editor-in-Chief KANAK MANI DIXIT; Marketing Man. SUMAN SHAKYA.

The Independent: Shankher Deep Bldg, Khichhapokhari, POB 3543, Kathmandu; tel. 4249256; fax 4226293; e-mail independ@mos.com.np; internet www.nepalnews.com/independent.htm; f. 1991; weekly; English; Editor SUBARNA B. CHHETRI.

Janadharana: Kathmandu; e-mail dharana@mail.com.np; internet www.nepalnews.com.np/dharana.htm; weekly; left-wing; Editor NEEMKANT PANDEY.

Janmabhumi: Janmabhumi Press, Tahachal, Kathmandu; tel. 4280979; e-mail sirishnp@hotmail.com; internet www.catmando.com; weekly; Nepali; Publr and Editor SHIRISH BALLABH PRADHAN.

Koseli: Kathmandu; weekly.

Madhuparka: Dharma Path, POB 23, Kathmandu; tel. 4222278; f. 1986; monthly; Nepali; literary; Editor-in-Chief KRISHNA BHAKTA SHRESTHA; circ. 20,000.

Mulyankan: Kathmandu; monthly, left-wing; Editor SHYAM SHRESTHA.

Matribhoomi (Nepali Weekly): Ga 2-549, Kamal Pokhari (in front of the Police Station), Kathmandu; tel. 4412501; weekly; Nepali; Editor GOVINDA BIYOGI.

Nepal Chronicle: Maruhiti; weekly; English; Publr and Editor CHANDRA LAL JHA.

Nepal Overseas Trade Statistics: Trade Promotion Centre, Pulchowk, Lalitpur, POB 825, Kathmandu; tel. 4532642; fax 4525464; e-mail tpcnep@mos.com.np; internet www.tpcnepal.org.np; annual; English.

Nepal Trade Bulletin: Trade Promotion Centre, Pulchowk, Lalitpur, POB 825, Kathmandu; tel. 4532642; fax 4525464; e-mail tpcnep@mos.com.np; internet www.tpcnepal.org.np; 3 a year; English; Editor NABIN RAJ SHARMA.

Nepali Times: Himalmedia Pvt Ltd, POB 7251, Kathmandu; tel. 4543333; fax 4521013; e-mail editors@nepalitimes.com; internet www.nepalitimes.com; f. 1955; weekly; Nepali; Publr and Editor CHANDRA LAL JHA; circ. 9,000.

People's Review: Pipalbot, Dillibazar, POB 3052, Kathmandu; tel. 4417352; fax 4438797; e-mail preview@ntc.net.np; internet www.peoplesreview.com.np; weekly; English; Editor-in-Chief PUSHPA RAJ PRADHAN; circ. 15,000.

Rastrabani: Kathmandu; weekly.

Sanibariya: Kathmandu; weekly.

Sanghu Weekly: Kathmandu; weekly; Editor GOPAL BUDHATHOKI.

Saptahik: Kathmandu; weekly.

Spotlight: POB 7256, Kathmandu; tel. 4410772; e-mail spotlight@mos.com.np; f. 1991; weekly; English; Editor MADHAV KUMAR RIMAL.

Swatantra Manch Weekly: POB 49, Kathmandu; tel. 4436374; fax 4435931; e-mail das@ntc.net.np; f. 1985; weekly; Nepali; Publr and Chief Editor V. K. DAS; circ. 30,000.

The Telegraph: Ghattekulo, Dillibazar, POB 4063, Kathmandu; tel. 4419370; e-mail tgw@ntc.net.np; weekly; English; Chief Editor NARENDRA P. UPADHYAYA.

Vashudha: Makhan, Kathmandu; monthly; English; social, political and economic affairs; Publr and Editor T. L. SHRESTHA.

Weekly Chronicle: Kathmandu.

NEWS AGENCIES

Rastriya Samachar Samiti (RSS): Prithivi Path, POB 220, Kathmandu; tel. 4227912; fax 4227698; f. 1962; state-operated; Gen. Man. MUKUNDA PARAJULI.

Foreign Bureaux

Agence France-Presse (AFP): Bhote Bahal-South, Hansa Marg, POB 402, Kathmandu; tel. 4253960; fax 4222998; e-mail afpresse@mos.com.np; Chief of Bureau KEDAR MAN SINGH.

Associated Press (AP) (USA): Thapathli Panchayan, POB 513, Kathmandu; tel. 4212767; Correspondent BINAYA GURACHARYA.

Deutsche Presse-Agentur (dpa) (Germany): KH 1-27 Tebahal Tole, POB 680, Kathmandu 44601; tel. 4224557; Correspondent K. C. SHYAM BAHADUR.

Inter Press Service (IPS) (Italy): c/o Nepal Press Institute, POB 4128, Kathmandu; tel. and fax 4228943; Correspondent DHRUBA ADHIKARY.

Kyodo News (Japan): Ga 2-502, Battisputali, POB 3772, Kathmandu; tel. 4470106; fax 4480571; e-mail macharya@kyodo.mos.com.np; Correspondent MADHAV ACHARYA.

Reuters (UK): POB 3341, Kathmandu; tel. 4372152; fax 4373814.

United Press International (UPI) (USA): POB 802, Kathmandu; tel. 4215684; Correspondent BHOLA BIKRAM RANA.

PRESS ASSOCIATIONS

Federation of Nepalese Journalists (FNJ): Kathmandu.

Nepal Journalists' Association (NJA): Maitighar, POB 285, Kathmandu; tel. 262426; fax 279544; e-mail manju-sakya@hotmail.com; 5,400 mems; Pres. MANJU RATNA SAKYA; Gen. Sec. NIRMAL KUMAR ARYAL.

Press Council: RSS Bldg, Prithvipath, POB 3077, Kathmandu; tel. 262829; fax 262894; e-mail prescoun_mdf@wlink.com.np; f. 1970; Chair. HARIHAR BIRAHI; Admin. Officer BISHNU PRASAD SHARMA.

Publishers

Educational Enterprise (Pvt) Ltd: Mahankalsthan, POB 1124, Kathmandu; tel. 4223749; e-mail ishwarbshrestha@yahoo.com; educational and technical.

International Standards Books and Periodicals (Pvt) Ltd: Bhotatity Bazaar, Chowk Bhitra, POB 3000, Kathmandu 44601; tel. 4262815; fax 4264179; e-mail u2@ccsl.com.np; f. 1991; Sr Man. Dir YOGYNDRA LALL CHHIPA; Chief Exec. and Man. Dir GANESH LALL SINGH CHHIPA.

Lakoul Press: Palpa-Tansen, Kathmandu; educational and physical sciences.

Mahabir Singh Chiniya Main: Makhan Tola, Kathmandu.

Mandass Memorials Publications: Kamabakshee Tole, Gha 3-333, Chowk Bitra, Kathmandu; tel. 4212289; fax 4223036; Man. BASANT RAJ TULADHAR.

Pilgrims Book House: Goldhunga, POB 3872, Kathmandu; tel. 4425919; fax 4424943; e-mail pilgrims@wlink.com.np; internet www.pilgrimsbooks.com; f. 1986; Asian studies, religion and travel; Propr PUSHPA TIWARI.

Pilgrims Publishing Nepal (Pvt) Ltd: Goldhunga, POB 21646, Kathmandu; tel. 4356764; e-mail johnsnepal@wlink.com.np; internet www.pilgrimsbooks.com; f. 2000; Exec. Dir JOHN SNYDER; Man. Dir BISHOW BHATTA.

Ratna Pustak Bhandar: Bhotahity Tole, POB 98, Kathmandu; tel. 4223026; fax 4248421; e-mail rpb@wlink.com.np; f. 1945; textbooks, general, non-fiction and fiction; Propr RATNA PRASAD SHRESTHA.

Royal Nepal Academy: Kamaladi, Kathmandu; tel. 4221241; fax 4221175; f. 1957; languages, literature, social sciences, art and philosophy; Dep. Admin. Chief T. D. BHANDARI.

Sajha Prakashan: Pulchowk, Lalitpur, PO Box 20259, Kathmandu; tel. 4521023; fax 4544236; e-mail amarkumal2002@hotmail.com; f. 1966; educational, literary and general; Chair. BISHNU PRASAD GHIMIRE; Gen. Man. NETRA PRASAD ADHIKARI.

Trans Asian Media Pvt Ltd: Thapathali Crossing, POB 5320, Kathmandu; tel. 4242895; fax 4223889; Man. Editor SHYAM GOENKA.

Government Publishing House

Department of Information: Ministry of Information and Communications, Singha Durbar, Kathmandu; tel. 4220150; fax 4221729.

Broadcasting and Communications

TELECOMMUNICATIONS

Nepal Telecommunications Authority: Singha Durbar, Kathmandu; tel. 4221944; fax 4260400; e-mail ntra@mos.com.np; internet www.nta.gov.np; telecommunications regulatory body; Chair. SURESH KUMAR PUDASAINI.

Nepal Telecommunications Corpn: Bhadrakali Plaza, POB 11803; Kathmandu; tel. 4246034; fax 4222424; e-mail rkt@ntc.net.np; internet www.ntc.com.np; f. 1975; monopoly provider; scheduled for transfer to private sector; Man. Dir CHET PRASAD BHATTARAI.

BROADCASTING

Radio

In 1992 radio broadcasts reached about 90% of Nepal's population.

Radio Nepal: Radio Broadcasting Service, HM Government of Nepal, Singha Durbar, POB 634, Kathmandu; tel. 4223910; fax 4221952; e-mail radio@rne.wlink.com.np; internet www.catmando.com./news/radio-nepal/radionp.htm; f. 1951; broadcasts on short and medium wave in Nepali and English for 17 hours daily (incl. two hours of regional broadcasting in the evening); short-wave station at Khumaltar and medium-wave stations at Bhaisepati, Pokhara, Surkhet, Dipayal, Bardibas and Dharan; Exec. Dir SHAILENDRA RAJ SHARMA; Dep. Exec. Dir M. P. ADHIKARI.

Television

In 1986 Nepal's first television station began broadcasting within the Kathmandu valley.

Nepalese Television Corporation: Singha Durbar, POB 3826, Kathmandu; tel. 4228447; fax 4228312; broadcasts 32 hours a week; programmes in Nepali (50%), English (25%) and Hindi/Urdu (25%); regional stations at Pokhara, Biratnagar and Hetuada; Gen. Man. TAPA NATH SHUKLA; Dep. Gen. Man. (Technical) RAVINDRA S. RANA; Dep. Gen. Man. (Productions) DURGA NATH SHARMA.

Shangri-La Channel (Pvt) Ltd: Sangharsh Chamber, Gyaneshwor, POB 5852, Kathmandu; tel. 4415299; fax 4416333; Chief Exec. NEER SHAH.

Space-Time Network: Iceberg Bldg, 3rd Floor, Putali Sadak, Kathmandu; tel. 4419133; fax 4419504; f. 1994; satellite transmission service.

Finance

(auth. = authorized; cap. = capital; p.u. = paid up; m. = million; dep. = deposits; res = reserves; brs = branches; amounts in Nepalese rupees)

BANKING

Central Bank

Nepal Rastra Bank: Central Office, Baluwatar, POB 73, Kathmandu; tel. 4419804; fax 4414553; e-mail nrb@mos.com.np; internet www.nrb.org.np; f. 1956; bank of issue; 100% state-owned; cap. 10m., res 23,623.5m., dep. 19,241.2m. (July 2000); Gov. Dr TILAK RAWAL; 9 brs.

Domestic Commercial Banks

Kumari Bank Ltd: Putalisadak, POB 21128, Kathmandu; tel. 4232112; fax 4231960; e-mail kumaribank@info.com.np; f. 2001; auth. cap 1,000m. (April 2001); Chair. NOOR PRATAP RANA.

Nepal Bank Ltd: Nepal Bank Bldg, Dharmapath, New Rd, POB 36, Kathmandu; tel. 4221185; fax 4222383; e-mail arbnbl@wlink.com.np; f. 1937; 40% state-owned, 60% owned by Nepalese public; cap. 378m., res 489.6m., dep. 21,570.5m. (July 1997); Chair. SHAMBHU SHARAN PRASAD KAYASTHA; 165 brs.

Nepal Industrial and Commercial Bank Ltd (NIC Bank): Main Rd, Koshi Zone, Morang District, POB 232, Biratnagar; tel. 521921; fax 522748; e-mail nicb@brt.wlink.com.np; internet www.nicbank.com.np; f. 1998; privately owned; cap. 499.8m., res 16.3m., dep. 3,575.8m. (July 2001); Chair. JAGDISH PRASAD AGRAWAL; CEO K. R. IYER; 6 brs.

Rastriya Banijya Bank (National Commercial Bank): Singha Durbar Plaza, Kathmandu; tel. 4252595; fax 4252931; f. 1966; 100% state-owned; cap. 1,172m., res 268m., dep. 33,329m. (July 1999); Pres. PANYA PRASAD DAHAL; 212 brs, 4 regional offices.

Joint-venture Banks

Bank of Kathmandu Ltd: Kamal Pokhari, POB 9044, Kathmandu; tel. 4418068; fax 4418990; e-mail info@bok.com.np; f. 1993; 55% owned by Nepalese public, 45% by local promoters; cap. 90m., res 10.6m., dep. 2,564.8m. (July 1999); Chair. DAMBAR BAHADUR MALLA.

Everest Bank Ltd: New Baneshwor, POB 13384, Kathmandu; tel. 44481017; fax 4482263; e-mail ebl@mos.com.np; internet www.ebl.com.np; f. 1994; 50% owned by directors, 20% by Punjab National Bank (India), 30% by the Nepalese public; cap. 235.5m., res 159.6m., dep. 4,482.1m. (Jan. 2002); Exec. Dir S. S. DABAS; 22 brs.

Himalayan Bank Ltd: Karmachari Sanchaya Kosh Bldg, Tridevi Marg, Thamel, POB 20590, Kathmandu; tel. 4227749; fax 4222800; e-mail hbl@hbl.com.np; internet www.hbl.com.np; f. 1993; 20% owned by Habib Bank Ltd (Pakistan); cap. 300m., res 200.6m., dep. 14,237.5m. (July 2000); Chair. HIMALAYA S. J. B. RANA; CEO PRITHIVI BAHADUR PANDEY; 8 brs.

Nepal Arab Bank Ltd (Nabil): Nabil House, Kamaladi, POB 3729, Kathmandu; tel. 4429546; fax 4429548; e-mail nabil@nabilbank.com.np; internet www.nabilbankltd.com; f. 1984; 50% owned by National Bank of Bangladesh, 30% by the Nepalese public and 20% by Nepalese government financial institutions; cap. 491.7m., res 623.1m., dep. 15,839.0m. (July 2001); Chair. LOK BAHADUR SHRESTHA; Vice-Chair. DAYA RAM AGRAWAL; 16 brs.

Nepal Bangladesh Bank Ltd: Bijulibazar, New Baneswor, POB 9062, Kathmandu; tel. 4490767; fax 4490824; e-mail nbblho@nbbl.com.np; f. 1994; 50% owned by International Finance Investment and Commerce Bank Ltd (Bangladesh), 20% by Nepalese promoters and 30% public issue; cap. 238.2m., res 211.2m., dep. 8,610.4m. (July 2001); Man. Dir NARENDRA BHATTARAI; Chair. JEET BAHADUR SHRESTHA; 10 brs.

Nepal Bank of Ceylon Ltd: Bagh Bazar, POB 12559, Kathmandu; tel. 4246105; fax 4244610; Man. Dir D. V. K. JAYSURYA.

Nepal Investment Bank Ltd: Durbar Marg, POB 3412, Kathmandu; tel. 4228229; fax 4226349; e-mail info@nibl.com.np; f. 1986; 50% owned by a consortium of Nepalese investors, 20% by general public, 15% by Rastriya Banijya Bank and 15% by Rastriya Beema Sansthan; cap. 170m., res 249m., dep. 4,256m. (July 2001); Chair. TIRTHA MAN SHAKYA; Chief Exec. Dir PRITHIVI B. PANDE; 6 brs.

Nepal SBI Bank Ltd: Corporate Office, Hattisar, POB 6049, Kathmandu; tel. 4435516; fax 4435612; e-mail nsblco@mos.com.np; f. 1993; 50% owned by State Bank of India, 30% by Nepalese public, 15% by Employees' Provident Fund (Nepal) and 5% by Agricultural Development Bank (Nepal); Chair. B. P. ACHARYA; Man. Dir B. B. DAS.

Nepal Sri Lanka Merchant Bank Ltd: N. B. Bldg, Bagh Bazar, POB 12248, Kathmandu; tel. 4227555; fax 4240674; Man. Dir ARJUNA HERATH.

Standard Chartered Bank Nepal Ltd: Grindlays Bhavan, Naya Baneshwor, POB 3990, Kathmandu; tel. 4246753; fax 4226762; f. 1986; 50% owned by Standard Chartered Grindlays, 33% by Nepal Bank Ltd and 17% by the Nepalese public; cap. 340m., res 673m., dep. 15,430m. (July 2001); Chair. BHOJ RAJ POKHAREL; CEO RAJEEV KULKARNI; 10 brs.

Development Finance Organizations

Agricultural Development Bank: Ramshah Path, Kathmandu; tel. 4262885; fax 4262616; e-mail info@adbn.gov.np; internet www .adbn.gov.np; f. 1968; 93.6% state-owned, 2.1% owned by the Nepal Rastra Bank, and 4.3% by co-operatives and private individuals; specialized agricultural credit institution providing credit for agricultural development to co-operatives, individuals and asscns; receives deposits from individuals, co-operatives and other asscns to generate savings in the agricultural sector; acts as Government's implementing agency for small farmers' group development project, assisted by the Asian Development Bank and financed by the UN Development Programme; operational networks include 14 zonal offices, 37 brs, 92 sub-brs, 52 depots and 160 small farmers' development projects, 3 Zonal Training Centres, 2 Appropriate Technology Units; Chair. SHYAM PRASAD MAINALI.

Nepal Development Bank: Heritage Plaza, POB 11017, Kamaladi, Kathmandu; tel. 4245753.

Nepal Housing Development Finance Co Ltd: POB 5624, Kathmandu; tel. 4223390; Chief Exec. INDRA PRASHAD KARMACHARYA.

Nepal Industrial Development Corporation (NIDC): NIDC Bldg, Durbar Marga, POB 10, Kathmandu; tel. 4228322; fax 4227428; e-mail nidc@wlink.com.np; f. 1959; state-owned; holds investments of 5,609.9m. in 1,125 industrial enterprises (2000/01); offers financial and technical assistance to private-sector industries; in 2000/01 approved a total of 9.41m. in loans and working capital, and disbursed 8.17m. Gen. Man. UTTAM NARAYAN SHRESTHA.

STOCK EXCHANGE

Nepal Stock Exchange Ltd: Singh Durbar Plaza, POB 1550, Kathmandu; tel. 4250735; fax 4262538; e-mail nepse@stock.mos .com.np; internet www.nepalstock.com; f. 1976; reorg. 1984; converted in 1993 from Securities Exchange Centre Ltd to Nepal Stock Exchange Ltd; 96 listed cos, 120 scripts; Gen. Man. MUKUNDA NATH DHUNGEL; Man. (Admin. and Market Operations) M. P. SHARMA; Man. (Information, Planning and Development) P. BHATTARAI.

INSURANCE

Alliance Insurance Co Ltd: Durbar Marg, POB 10811, Kathmandu; tel. 4222836; fax 4241411; e-mail sk@aic.wlink.com.np.

Everest Insurance Co: Kantipath, POB 8857, Kathmandu; tel. 4243631; fax 4240083.

Himalayan General Insurance Co Ltd: Durbar Marg, POB 148, Kathmandu; tel. 4231581; fax 4223906; e-mail ktm@hgi.com.np; internet www.hgi.com.np; f. 1993; CEO MAHENDRA KRISHNA SHRESTHA.

National Insurance Co Ltd: Tripureswor, POB 376, Kathmandu; tel. 4250710; fax 4261289; e-mail natinsur@ccsl.com.np; Man. A. S. KOHLI.

National Life and General Insurance Co Ltd: Lazimpat, POB 4332, Kathmandu; tel. 4412625; fax 4416427; Chief Exec. S. K. SINGH; Pres. OM SINGH.

Neco Insurance Ltd: Hattisar, POB 12271, Kathmandu; tel. 4427354; fax 4418761.

Nepal Insurance Co Ltd: Kamaladi, POB 3623, Kathmandu; tel. 4221353; fax 4225446.

The Oriental Insurance Co Ltd: Jyoti Bhavan, POB 165, Kathmandu; tel. 4221448; fax 4223419; e-mail oriental@wlink.com.np.

Premier Insurance Co (Nepal) Ltd: 1988 Ram Rukmani Sadan, Kamaladi Marg, POB 9183, Kathmandu; tel. 4417765; fax 4420554; e-mail premier@picl.com.np; internet www.premier-insurance.com .np; Man. Dir SURESH LAL SHRESTHA.

Rastriya Beema Sansthan (National Insurance Corpn): RBS Bldg, Ramshah Path, POB 527, Kathmandu; tel. 4213882; fax 4262610; e-mail beema@wlink.com.np; f. 1967; Gen. Man. BIR BIKRAM RAXAMAJHI.

Sagarmatha Insurance Co Ltd: Kathmandu Plaza, Block Y, Kamaladi, POB 12211, Kathmandu; tel. 4240896; fax 4247941;

e-mail sagarmatha@insurance.wlink.com.np; Exec. Dir K. B. BASNYAT.

United Insurance Co (Nepal) Ltd: Durbar Marg, POB 9075, Kathmandu; tel. 4246686; fax 4246687.

Trade and Industry

GOVERNMENT AGENCY

National Planning Commission (NPC): Singha Durbar, POB 1284, Kathmandu; tel. 4225879; fax 4226500; e-mail npcs@npcnepal .gov.np; internet npc.gov.np:8080; Vice-Chair. Dr NARAYAN KHADKA.

DEVELOPMENT ORGANIZATIONS

Agriculture Inputs Corporation: Teku, Kuleshwar, POB 195, Kathmandu; tel. 4279715; fax 4278790; f. 1966; govt-owned; sole supplier of inputs for agricultural development (procuring and distribution of chemical fertilizers, improved seeds, agricultural tools and plant protection material) at national level; operates seeds multiplication programme (paddy, wheat, maize and vegetable); seed processing plants at Dang, Hetauda, Itahari, Janakpur, Nepalgunj and Sidharthanagar; Chair. MOHANDEV PANT; Gen. Man. ARJUN KUMAR THAPA.

National Trading Ltd: Teku, POB 128, Kathmandu; tel. 4227683; fax 4225151; e-mail natreli@mos.com.np; f. 1962; govt-owned; imports and distributes construction materials and raw materials for industry; also machinery, vehicles and consumer goods; operates bonded warehouse, duty-free shop and related activities; brs in all major towns; Chair. SONAFI YADAV; Gen. Man. MADHAV JUNG RANA.

Nepal Foreign Trade Association: Bagmati Chamber, 1st Floor, Milanmarg, Teku, POB 541, Kathmandu; tel. 4223784; fax 4247159; e-mail nfta@mos.com.np; Pres. ASHOK KUMAR AGRAWAL; Vice-Pres. AKHIL K. CHAPAGAIN.

Nepal Productivity and Economic Development Centre: Balaju, POB 1318, Kathmandu; tel. 4350566; fax 4350530; e-mail npedc@wlink.com.np; internet www.panasia.org.sg/nepalnet/npedc/ html; functions as secretariat of National Productivity Council; provides services for industrial promotion and productivity improvement through planning research, consultancy, training, seminars and information services; Dir-Gen. VIJAY S. SHRESTHA.

Nepal Resettlement Co: Kathmandu; f. 1963; govt-owned; engaged in resettling people from the densely populated hill country to the western Terai plain.

Nepal Tea Development Corporation: Kathmandu.

Trade Promotion Centre (TPC): Pulchowk, Lalitpur, POB 825, Kathmandu; tel. 4525348; fax 4525464; e-mail tpcnep@mos.com.np; internet www.tpcnepal.org.np; f. 1971 to encourage exports; govt-owned; Exec. Dir DEB BAHADUR ROKAYA.

CHAMBERS OF COMMERCE

Federation of Nepalese Chambers of Commerce and Industry (FNCCI): Pachali Shahid Shukra FNCCI Milan Marg, Teku, POB 269, Kathmandu; tel. 4262061; fax 4261022; e-mail fncci@mos.com .np; internet www.fncci.org; f. 1965; comprises 86 District Municipality Chambers (DCCIs), 50 Commodity Associations, 424 leading industrial and commercial undertakings in both the public and private sector, and nine Bi-national Chambers; Pres. RAVI BHAKTA SHRESTHA; Sec.-Gen. BADRI PRASAD OJHA.

Birganj Chamber of Commerce and Industries: Brita, Birganj-4; tel. 522290; fax 526049; e-mail bicci@atcnet.com.np; internet www .bicci.org.np; Pres. BABU LAL CHACHAN.

Lalitpur Chamber of Commerce and Industry: Mangal Bazar, POB 26, Lalitpur; tel. 5521740; fax 5530661; e-mail lcci@mos.com .np; internet www.lcci.org.np.

Nepal Chamber of Commerce: Chamber Bhavan, Kantipath, POB 198, Kathmandu; tel. 4230947; fax 4229998; e-mail chamber@ wlink.com.np; internet www.nepalchamber.com; f. 1952; non-profit organization promoting industrial and commercial development; 8,000 regd mems and 16,000 enrolled mems; Pres. RAJESH KAZI SHRESTHA; Sec.-Gen. SURESH KUMAR BASNET.

Nepal-German Chamber of Commerce and Industry: Putalisadak, POB 201, Kathmandu; tel. 228733; fax 244417.

Nepal-India Chamber of Commerce and Industry: Shahid Shukra Brikshya, Teku, POB 13245, Kathmandu; tel. 250607; fax 250642.

INDUSTRIAL AND TRADE ASSOCIATIONS

Association of Craft Producers: Ravi Bhavan, POB 3701, Kathmandu; tel. 4275108; fax 4272676; e-mail craftacp@mos.com.np; internet acp.org.np; f. 1984; local non-profit organization providing technical, marketing and management services for craft producers, manufacturer, exporter and retailer of handicraft goods; Programme Co-ordinator REVITA SHRESTHA.

Association of Forest-based Industries and Trade: Thapathali, POB 2798, Kathmandu; tel. 4216020.

Association of Nepalese Rice and Oil Industries: Ganabahal, POB 363, Kathmandu; tel. 4250001; fax 4249723; e-mail ktm@golchha.com; Pres. PASHUPATI GIRI; Gen. Sec. HULASCHAND GOLCHHA.

Association of Pharmaceutical Producers of Nepal: 63/284, Chhetrapati, POB 4506, Kathmandu; tel. 4415330; fax 4436395; e-mail vaidya@vpharma.wlink.com.np.

Cargo Agents Association of Nepal: Thamel, POB 5355, Kathmandu; tel. 4419019.

Central Carpet Industries Association of Nepal: Bijulee Bazar, POB 2419, Kathmandu; tel. 4496108; fax 4475291; e-mail ccia@enet.com.np; internet www.nepalcarpet.org; Pres. A. G. SHERPA.

Computer Association of Nepal: 235139, Dobidhara Marg, POB 4982, Kathmandu; tel. 4432700; fax 4424043; e-mail info@can.org.np; internet www.can.org.np; f. 1992; Pres. LOCHAN LAL AMATYA.

Footwear Manufacturers' Association of Nepal: Khichapokhari, POB 648, Kathmandu; tel. 4228131; fax 4416576.

Garment Association of Nepal: Shankhamul Rd, New Baneshwor, POB 21332, Kathmandu; tel. 4482691; fax 4482173; e-mail gan@asso.wlink.com.np; internet www.ganasso.org; Pres. KIRAN P. SAAKHA.

Handicrafts Association of Nepal: Maitighar, POB 784, Kathmandu; tel. 4243015; fax 4222940; e-mail han@wlink.com.np; internet www.nepalhandicraft.com.np.

Nepal Association of Travel Agents: Gairidhara Rd, Goma Ganesh, Naxal, POB 362, Kathmandu; tel. 4418661; fax 4418684; e-mail info@nata.org.np; internet www.nata.org.np; f. 1966; 165 active mems, 14 allied mems.

Nepal Cottage and Small Industries Association: Teku, Kathmandu; tel. 4212876.

Nepal Forest Industries Association: Gyaneshwor, POB 1804, Kathmandu; tel. 4411865; fax 4413838; e-mail padmasri@ccsl.com.np.

Nepal Leather Industry and Trade Association: Baghbazar, POB 4991, Kathmandu; tel. 4410315.

Nepal Plastic Manufacturers' Association: Kupondol, Kathmandu; tel. 4211981.

Nepal Tea Planters' Association: Bhadrapur; tel. 520183.

Nepal Textile Industries Association: Kupondol, Lalitpur; tel. 5523693; Pres. MAHESH LAL PRADHAN.

Nepal Trans-Himalayan Trade Association: Kantipath, Kathmandu; tel. 4223764; Vice-Chair. NIL KANTHA CHAULAGAIN.

UTILITIES

Electricity

Butwal Power Co Ltd: POB 126, Kathmandu; tel. 4525732; fax 4527898.

Chilime Hydropower Co Ltd: Kathmandu; 51% owned by Nepal Electricity Authority; Dir DAMBER BAHADUR NEPALI.

Electricity Development Centre: Exhibition Rd, POB 2507, Kathmandu; tel. 4227262; fax 4227537; f. 1993; under Ministry of Water Resources; Dir-Gen. VIJAY SHANKER SHRESTHA.

Nepal Electricity Authority: Ratna Park, Kathmandu; tel. 4227725; fax 4227035; e-mail neamd@mos.com.np; internet www.nea.org.np; f. 1985 following merger; govt-owned; Man. Dir Dr J. L. KARMACHARYA.

Water

Nepal Water Supply Corpn: Tripureswor Marg, Kathmandu; tel. 4253656; fax 4223484; f. 1990; govt-owned; Exec. Chair. ARUN KUMAR RANJITKAR.

TRADE UNIONS

Trade unions were banned in Nepal in 1961, but were legalized again in 1990, following the success of the pro-democracy movement and the collapse of the Panchayat system.

Nepal Trade Union Centre: Tinkune Koteshower, POB 9667, Kathmandu; tel. 4480551; fax 4419148; f. 1986; Sec.-Gen. LAXMAN PRASAD PANDEY.

Democratic Confederation of Nepalese Trade Unions (DECONT): Kathmandu; Chair. KHILANATH DAHAL.

General Federation of Nepalese Trade Unions (GEFONT): Kathmandu, POB 10652; tel. 4248072; fax 4248073; e-mail info@gefont.org; internet www.gefont.org; f. 1989; Chair. MUKUNDA NEUPANE.

Transport

Ministry of Labour and Transport Management: Babar Mahal, Kathmandu; tel. 4226537; Sec. MUKTI PRASAD KAFLE.

Nepal Transport Corpn (Napal Yatayat Sansthan): Kathmandu; tel. 4222547; f. 1966; scheduled for transfer to private ownership; controls the operation of road transport facilities, railways, ropeway, trucks, trolley buses and container services; Gen. Man. A. B. SHRESTHA.

Interstate Multi-Modal Transport (Pvt) Ltd: Sabitri Sadan, Red Cross Marg, Tahachal, Kalimati, Kathmandu; tel. 4271473; fax 4271570; e-mail rauniar@mos.com.np; internet www.rauniar.com; f. 1975; provides freight forwarding, customs clearance, warehousing and shipping services, transport consultancy; Gen. Man. ANAND S. RAUNIAR.

RAILWAYS

Janakpur Railway: Khajuri, Janakpur; tel. 52082; HQ Jayanagar, India; f. 1937; 53 km open, linking Jayanagar with Janakpur and Bijalpura; narrow gauge; 11 steam engines, 25 coaches and vans, and 20 wagons; Man. J. B. THAPA.

Nepal Government Railway: Birganj; f. 1927; 48 km linking Raxaul in India to Amlekhganj, of which the 6 km between Raxaul and Birganj are used for goods traffic; 7 steam engines, 12 coaches and 82 wagons; Man. D. SINGH (acting).

ROADS

In mid-2001 there were 15,458 km of roads, of which 4,577 km were black-topped. Around Kathmandu there are short sections of roads suitable for motor vehicles, and there is a 28-km ring road round the valley. A 190-km mountain road, Tribhuwana Rajpath, links the capital with the Indian railhead at Raxaul. The Siddhartha Highway, constructed with Indian assistance, connects the Pokhara valley, in mid-west Nepal, with Sonauli, on the Indian border in Uttar Pradesh. The 114-km Arniko Highway, constructed with Chinese help, connects Kathmandu with Kodari, on the Chinese border. In the early 1990s the final section of the 1,030-km East–West Highway was under construction. A number of north–south roads were also being constructed to connect the district headquarters with the East–West Highway. In November 1999 the World Bank agreed to provide Nepal with a loan of US $54.5m. for the construction and maintenance of roads (particularly in the far west of the country).

A fleet of container trucks operates between Kolkata and Raxaul and other points in Nepal for transporting exports to, and imports from, third countries. Trolley buses provide a passenger service over the 13 km between Kathmandu and Bhaktapur.

ROPEWAY

A 42-km ropeway links Hetauda and Kathmandu and can carry 22 tons of freight per hour throughout the year. Food grains, construction goods and heavy goods on this route are transported by this ropeway.

CIVIL AVIATION

Tribhuvan international airport is situated about 6 km from Kathmandu. In 2001 Nepal had an estimated 44 airports, five of which were tarred.

Royal Nepal Airlines Corporation (RNAC): RNAC Bldg, Kanti Path, POB 401, Kathmandu 711000; tel. 4220757; fax 4225348; internet www.royalnepal.com/; f. 1958; 100% state-owned (scheduled for transfer to private ownership); scheduled services to 37 domestic airfields and international scheduled flights to Europe, the Middle East and the Far East; Chair. BAL KRISHNA MAN SINGH; Gen. Man. MOHAN PRASAD KHANAL (acting).

The monopoly of the RNAC in domestic air services came to an end in 1992. By 1999 there were about 12 private airlines in Nepal serving internal routes.

Buddha Air: Jawalakhal, Lalitpur, POB 2167, Kathmandu; tel. 4521015; fax 4537726; e-mail buddhaair@wlink.com.np; internet www.buddhaair.com; f. 1997; domestic passenger services; Man. Dir BIRENDRA BASNET.

Gorkha Airlines: New Baneshwor, POB 9451, Kathmandu; tel. 4487033; fax 4471136; e-mail gorkha@mos.com.np; internet www .yomari.com/gorkha/; f. 1996; scheduled and charter passenger and cargo flights to domestic destinations; Exec. Chair. PRAJJWAAL SHRESTHA.

Lumbini Airways (Pvt) Ltd: Kamaladi, Kathmandu; tel. 4255936; fax 4483380; e-mail lumbini@resv.wlink.com.np; f. 1996; scheduled passenger and cargo flights to domestic destinations; Man. Dir R. K. SAKYA.

Necon Air Ltd: Kalimatidole, Necon Hamlet, Airport Area, POB 10038, Kathmandu; tel. 4473860; fax 4471679; e-mail info@necon .mos.com.np; internet www.neconair.com; f. 1992; scheduled and charter flights to domestic destinations and to India; Chair./Man. Dir NARAYAN SINGH PUN.

Tourism

Tourism is being developed through the construction of new tourist centres in the Kathmandu valley, Pokhara valley and Chitwan. Regular air services link Kathmandu with Pokhara and Chitwan. Major tourist attractions include Lumbini, the birthplace of Buddha, the lake city of Pokhara, and the Himalaya mountain range, including Mt Everest, the world's highest peak. In 1989, in an effort to increase tourism, the Government abolished travel restrictions in 18 areas of north-western Nepal that had previously been inaccessible to foreigners. As expected, following the restoration of parliamentary democracy in 1990, tourist arrivals in Nepal rose considerably. Further travel restrictions in the remote areas of the kingdom were abolished in 1991, and efforts have been made to attract foreign investment in the Nepalese tourism industry. Nepal received an estimated 463,646 tourists in 2000. The number of visitor arrivals reportedly declined to 298,066 in 2001. Tourism receipts rose from US $153m. in 1998 to $168m. in 1999. Hotel bed capacity increased from 32,214 in 1999 to an estimated 34,958 in 2000. The Government granted access to a further 103 mountains, raising the total number of mountains open to climbers to 263, in an effort to promote tourism.

Nepal Tourism Board: Tourist Service Centre, Bhrikuti Mandap, Kathmandu; tel. 4256909; fax 4256910; e-mail info@ntb.wlink.com .np; internet www.welcomenepal.com.

Association of Tourism: Thamel, Kathmandu; tel. 4424740.

Hotel Association of Nepal: Kathmandu; tel. 4412705.

Tourist Guide Association of Nepal: Durbar Marg, POB 4344, Kathmandu; tel. 4225102.

Trekking Agents Association of Nepal: Naxal, POB 3612, Kathmandu; tel. 4419245.

THE NETHERLANDS

Introductory Survey

Location, Climate, Language, Religion, Flag, Capital

The Kingdom of the Netherlands is situated in western Europe, bordered to the east by Germany and to the south by Belgium. Its northern and western shores face the North Sea. The climate is temperate: the average temperature in January is 0°C (32°F), and the summer average is 21°C (70°F). The national language is Dutch. There is a Frisian-speaking minority (numbering about 400,000). About one-third of the inhabitants are Roman Catholics and about one-quarter are Protestants, while most of the remainder do not profess any religion. The national flag (proportions 2 by 3) has three equal horizontal stripes, of red, white and blue. The capital is Amsterdam, but the seat of government is The Hague ('s-Gravenhage).

Recent History

The Netherlands was occupied by Germany during the Second World War. Following its liberation in 1945, the country chose to abandon its traditional policy of neutrality, subsequently becoming a member of Western European Union (WEU, see p. 318) and the North Atlantic Treaty Organization (NATO, see p. 271). The Treaty establishing the Benelux Economic Union (see p. 339) between the Netherlands, Belgium and Luxembourg was signed in 1958 and came into force in 1960. The Netherlands was a founder member of the European Community (EC—now European Union—EU, see p. 199). Indonesia, formerly the Netherlands East Indies, was granted independence in 1949, except for West New Guinea, which was transferred to Indonesia in 1963. In 1975 Suriname became independent, leaving the Netherlands Antilles as the only remaining Dutch dependency. Aruba, formerly part of the Netherlands Antilles, was granted separate status within the Kingdom of the Netherlands in 1986.

Queen Juliana, who had reigned since 1948, abdicated in favour of her eldest daughter, Beatrix, in April 1980, following the adoption in February of a constitutional amendment that allowed for the accession of the reigning monarch's eldest child, regardless of gender.

All post-war administrations have been formed by various coalitions between the several 'confessional' Catholic and Protestant and 'progressive' Socialist and Liberal parties. At a general election held in April 1971 the left made substantial gains. In July 1972 the Government was forced to resign after losing its working majority in the Second Chamber of the States-General (see Government, below). Another general election took place in November 1972, at which the 'confessional' parties suffered a major reverse, and in May 1973 a new Government was formed by a left-of-centre coalition under the leadership of Dr Johannes (Joop) den Uyl of the Labour Party (Partij van de Arbeid—PvdA). This administration modified the fiscal structure and guaranteed minimum wage levels for all adult workers.

The coalition collapsed in March 1977, following disagreement over land-reform legislation; a general election followed in May. Attempts to form a left-of-centre coalition between the PvdA, the Christian Democratic Appeal (Christen Democratisch Appèl—CDA)—an alliance of 'confessional' groupings, which united in 1980 to form a single party—and Democraten '66 were unsuccessful, and in December 1977 Andries van Agt (of the CDA) formed a centre-right coalition Government of the CDA and the right-wing People's Party for Freedom and Democracy (Volkspartij voor Vrijheid en Democratie—VVD). The new coalition was supported by only 77 of the 150 members of the Second Chamber and was notably weakened by ministerial disagreements on NATO policy and the extent of reductions in public expenditure. Nevertheless, the Government survived its full term in office. A general election was held in May 1981, and a centre-left coalition was formed in September, led by van Agt and comprising the CDA (the party with the largest representation in the Second Chamber), the PvdA and Democraten '66. The Council of Ministers resigned after only five weeks in office, owing to its failure to agree on economic strategy. In November the three-party coalition accepted a compromise economic programme, but deep divisions within the Government continued to delay effective action on the economy. The coalition collapsed

again in May 1982: all six PvdA ministers resigned when their ambitious job-creation plan was cut, after which van Agt led a minority interim Government of the CDA and Democraten '66.

Although at a general election held in September 1982 the PvdA secured the greatest number of seats in the Second Chamber (47), the election produced a significant swing to the right. Talks on the formation of a new administration continued until November, when a centre-right CDA-VVD coalition was established under the leadership of Rudolphus (Ruud) Lubbers, a former Minister of Economic Affairs, who had recently succeeded van Agt as Chairman of the CDA. The CDA-VVD coalition was returned to power at a general election in May 1986, with (as in 1982) the two parties winning 81 of the 150 seats in the Second Chamber. A loss of nine seats by the VVD was offset by a corresponding gain by the CDA, which, with 54 seats, became the party with the largest representation in the Second Chamber. The election did, none the less, produce a shift towards the centrist parties, with the PvdA and Democraten '66 (D66—as the party was restyled) both gaining seats at the expense of smaller radical groups. Following the election, Wim Kok, a former trade unionist, replaced Joop den Uyl as parliamentary leader of the PvdA. A new CDA-VVD coalition was formed in July.

In May 1989 the VVD caused the collapse of the Government by refusing to support Lubbers' proposals for the financing of a 20-year National Environment Policy (NEP), which was to involve a reduction in government spending in sectors such as defence and housing, an increase in taxes on motor fuels, and the abolition of tax concessions for commuters using private transport. A general election was called for September, at which the CDA again secured 54 seats in the Second Chamber, while the PvdA took 49 seats (three fewer than in 1986). The VVD lost five seats to rival parties. An alliance of left-wing organizations, GroenLinks, won six seats. In October 1989 negotiations between the CDA and the PvdA culminated in the formation of a centre-left coalition, again led by Lubbers. The coalition accord envisaged increased welfare provision, to be funded by a reduction in defence expenditure, as well as a programme of job-creation and reductions in certain categories of taxation. Wim Kok was appointed Deputy Prime Minister and Minister of Finance. In August 1990 the Government introduced an amended version of the NEP, designated the National Environment Policy Plus (NEPP), which was to be financed by both the Government and the industrial sector. The NEPP was to be implemented at a faster pace than its predecessor, and placed strong emphasis on energy conservation and improvements in waste disposal and recycling. Instead of abolishing the system of tax deductions for car commuters (an unpopular proposal under the NEP), the NEPP advocated limiting the standard tax allowance for motorists and increasing excise duties on fuel. Proposals by the CDA, in mid-1991, to limit government expenditure by reforming the extensive disability benefit programme of the national welfare system were a source of friction with the PvdA. However, the PvdA eventually agreed to a compromise whereby the number of years of entitlement to full disability payments was to be restricted. The Government's decision led to widespread protest actions in September of that year.

In November 1992 the Second Chamber ratified the Treaty on European Union, which had been signed by EC Heads of Government at Maastricht in December 1991; the First Chamber similarly approved the Treaty in December 1992.

The CDA lost its leading position in the Government at the May 1994 general election, winning only 34 seats in the Second Chamber. The PvdA, which had focused its election manifesto on unemployment and reductions in social welfare, became, with 37 seats, the party with the largest representation in the Chamber. Both the VVD and D66 improved upon their performances at the previous general election, securing 31 and 24 seats respectively. The remaining 24 seats were distributed among eight smaller parties and special issue groups, including two organizations representing the interests of the elderly. As the combined seats of the CDA and PvdA amounted to less than an absolute majority, negotiations on a three-party coalition agreement commenced between the PvdA, the VVD and D66. Progress was initially retarded by deeply-entrenched disagreement between the VVD and PvdA over the latter's reluctance to sanction severe reductions in social welfare spending. Following several concessions by the PvdA (including the proposed privatization of some social benefits), a PvdA-VVD-D66 coalition, with Wim Kok as Prime Minister, was eventually agreed in August. The CDA (now led by Enneüs Heerma, Lubbers having retired from domestic politics following the May election) was thus excluded from the Council of Ministers for the first time since 1917.

In April 1996 the Government agreed that its liberal policy on the personal consumption of recreational 'soft' drugs should be subject to stricter controls, in response to protests by France and other neighbouring states that drugs-trafficking from the Netherlands would be facilitated by the withdrawal of EU border controls under the Schengen agreement.

The PvdA won increased representation at the general election to the Second Chamber held on 6 May 1998, taking 45 seats (with 29.0% of the total votes cast). The VVD also polled well, securing 38 seats (with 24.7% of the votes), while the CDA's representation was further reduced, to 29 seats (18.4%). D66 performed poorly, winning only 14 seats (with 9.0% of the poll), having lost votes to GroenLinks and the Socialist Party (Socialistische Partij). None the less, the PvdA, VVD and D66 agreed to renew their coalition (it was considered that D66 would be useful as an intermediary in conflicts of policy between the two leading partners), and a new Government, headed by Wim Kok, was inaugurated in August.

In October 1992 a cargo aircraft belonging to El Al, the Israeli national carrier, crashed into a densely-populated suburb of Amsterdam, killing at least 43 people. Following persistent speculation as to the nature of the cargo aboard the flight, and the widely-held opinion that the official response to the disaster and subsequent concerns had been inadequate, a parliamentary committee was established in October 1998 to investigate the Government's response to the crash. The inquiry was ordered after the Israeli Government had confirmed reports published in a Dutch newspaper that the cargo had included depleted uranium (used as ballast) and chemical components of sarin nerve gas, although the Israelis denied that the aircraft had been carrying 'dangerous goods'. The inquiry investigated claims that residents and workers who had been in contact with the wreckage had suffered ill health since the disaster, as well as allegations that Dutch ministers had been aware of the nature of the cargo. As hearings proceeded, it emerged that aviation officials had known of the contents of the aircraft from the time of the accident, and evidence of a lack of liaison between the transport and health ministries focused particularly on the former minister responsible for transport, Annemarie Jorritsma-Lebbink (now Deputy Prime Minister and Minister of Economic Affairs), and Els Borst-Eilers (the Deputy Prime Minister and Minister of Welfare, Public Health and Sport). The committee's report, published in April 1999, found that there was a direct link between the accident and the high incidence of ill health around the site of the crash, and was severely critical of the failure of the Prime Minister to co-ordinate government action with respect to the disaster. El Al was accused of failing to co-operate with accident investigators. The report none the less concluded that there was no evidence of attempts by the Netherlands Government to conceal details of the flight's cargo.

At provincial council elections, held on 3 March 1999, the opposition CDA took the largest share of the votes cast; the VVD outperformed the PvdA, while considerable successes for GroenLinks were largely at the expense of D66. The outcome left the Government with only a slender majority in the First Chamber, which is elected by the Provincial Councils.

In mid-May 1999 the First Chamber rejected the Government's proposal to allow the use of referendums on policy issues, a key demand of D66, after the refusal of a prominent member of the VVD to support the measure. D66 subsequently announced that it could no longer work with the VVD, and withdrew from the ruling coalition, prompting the resignation of the Council of Ministers. However, following a series of talks between the three parties, chaired by a mediator appointed by Queen Beatrix, all sides agreed to accept compromise proposals on referendums which would not require alterations to the Constitution, and in early June the Government formally withdrew its resignation. All ministers were reappointed, with the exception of the Minister of Agriculture, Nature Management and Fisheries, Haijo Apotheker, who resigned from his post,

claiming that he had not received the full support of his government colleagues for his plan to resolve legal difficulties over the proposed restructuring of the pig-farming industry. The Dutch press, however, suggested that Apotheker's resignation had in fact been provoked by public criticism of his ministry's failure to alert consumers to the risk to public health caused by the contamination of animal feed, produced in Belgium and supplied to the Netherlands, with the carcinogenic chemical dioxin (see the Recent History of Belgium). Laurens Jan Brinkhorst, a member of the outgoing European Parliament, subsequently replaced Apotheker. In January 2001 the three coalition parties reached a new agreement over the introduction of the use of referendums, subject to approval by the First Chamber. The new proposals were for a judicially non-binding referendum (i.e., the Government and the legislature would not, by law, have to act on the result of a referendum, although there would be consensus to respect the voters' will) and would not require a change to the Constitution.

In July 1999 the Government announced that it was to launch an investigation into the finances of the regional authorities after it emerged that the province of Zuid-Holland had made loans to listed companies amounting to 1,700m. guilders, more than one-and-a-half times its annual budget. The province's financial irregularities were revealed after the collapse of a Dutch company trading in Central and South America to whom the authorities had lent some 47.5m. guilders. The investigative commission, reporting its findings in October, criticized the Provincial Executive of Zuid-Holland for assuming banking functions in 1995. It stated that the decision to do so had been unauthorized and democratically inadmissible because it bypassed the Provincial Council. No adequate measures had been taken to minimize the risk involved and many rules and regulations had been transgressed.

In September 1999 anonymous allegations were made of widespread financial irregularities within Rotterdam City Council involving the Minister of Home Affairs, Dr Bram Peper, the former mayor of Rotterdam. The Council established a commission to investigate the city's financial activities, including the allegations made against Peper. In January 2000 two Dutch national newspapers reported that accountants had discovered dubious entries in the city's accounts amounting to some 100,000 guilders. Further allegations made by the press in March that Peper made use of an official car of greater value than the permitted ministerial allowance, thus transgressing the codes of ministerial conduct, and that he had withheld a report in the early 1990s criticizing his performance as mayor finally led to Peper's resignation from his government post. In its report the commission ruled that, although generally control of council expenditure was carried out lawfully and purposefully, a relatively high proportion of controls had been too lax and considerable levels of expenditure would not have met Rotterdam Council's own regulations. The commission, however, did not rule on the conduct of individual council members. In December 2000, moreover, the public prosecutor decided to drop all charges of misconduct against Peper.

In May 2000 an explosion at a fireworks depot in the middle of a residential estate in the eastern city of Enschede caused the deaths of at least 21 people and the destruction of nearly 400 homes. A commission was established to investigate public safety issues in the light of the explosion. A judicial inquiry was also held which resulted in the arrests of five police-officers and two local government officers on charges of accepting gifts of fireworks in exchange for neglecting to perform adequate safety controls of fireworks companies. The two directors of the fireworks company were also arrested on suspicion of breaching fireworks storage regulations. The commission, reporting at the end of February 2001, concluded that public authorities had not sufficiently prioritized public safety issues and that there had been inadequate supervision of the fireworks industry. The Ministries of Justice, Defence and Housing, Spatial Planning and the Environment and the Industrial Trade Supervisory Board attracted particular criticism for having failed in their duties.

In September 2000 protests by road hauliers over the high price of motor spirit (petrol), which included the blockade of the seat of government, The Hague, prompted the Council of Ministers to agree on a number of fiscal measures to help ease the pressure of high fuel prices, although the agreement did not include the reductions of taxes on fuel sought by the protesters. Also in September the First Chamber approved laws giving same-sex couples the same legal status as heterosexuals, including the right to marriage and adoption (the legislation came into effect in April 2001). Legal recognition of homosexual partnerships had been granted in 1998.

In February 2001 the Netherlands suffered an outbreak of foot and mouth disease affecting its livestock. The outbreak was concentrated primarily in the east of the country, although there were sporadic outbreaks in other regions. The Government pursued a policy of slaughter and disposal, with a cull of some 265,000 animals (although only 26 cases of the disease were actually identified), to contain the outbreak, despite the preference of a large number of farmers for vaccination. A protest by farmers in a village in the east of the country led to the arrest of some 13 people. By early May, however, the situation was considered to be under control. In July the Government announced the lifting of the remaining export restrictions that had been imposed at the outset of the epidemic.

During 1992–93 Parliament debated and approved legislation codifying a procedure for the practice of euthanasia in circumstances where it was repeatedly requested by an incurably ill patient. In April 2001 the First Chamber passed a bill legalizing euthanasia by 46 votes to 28, making the Netherlands the first country in the world to do so. (In November 2000 the Second Chamber had passed the bill by 104 votes to 40.) The practice was to be subject to strict criteria. The key conditions according to which life could lawfully be ended were that the patient was terminally ill and in unbearable pain with no prospect of improvement. Euthanasia became legal in April 2002.

In August 2001 Kok announced that he would not seek re-election for a further term in office at the general election, scheduled for May 2002. He also announced that he would step down as Party Leader of the PvdA and subsequently endorsed the appointment of Ad Melkert, the Parliamentary Leader of the party, as his successor. In September 2001 Jaap de Hoop Scheffer, the Parliamentary Leader of the CDA, resigned, claiming that he had inadequate support from senior party chiefs to lead a successful campaign in the approaching general election. He was replaced by Pieter (Peter) Balkenende the following month.

In October 2001 the Government approved a bill to allow pharmacies to handle prescriptions for cannabis. If the legislation were passed by Parliament, medicinal cannabis would thus be available free of charge on the national health service. In a further proposed liberalization of drug laws the Government requested that Parliament endorse its plan to give free heroin, in combination with methadone, to addicts deemed to be 'beyond help'. The proposal was announced in the light of research demonstrating that long-term heroin users were able to function better in society under the scheme.

In April 2002, following the publication of a report by the Netherlands Institute for War Documentation into the massacre of some 7,000 Bosnian Muslims by Bosnian Serb troops in Srebreniča (Bosnia and Herzegovina) in 1995, which blamed the Dutch Government, the Dutch military and the UN for their respective roles in failing to prevent the atrocity (the report claimed that the 100 lightly armed Dutch peace-keeping troops who had been stationed in the town at the time had been ill-trained and had no clear mandate), the entire Council of Ministers resigned. At the request of Queen Beatrix, the Government agreed to remain in office in a caretaker capacity pending the forthcoming general election, which was scheduled to be held on 15 May 2002. In addition, the Chief of Staff of the army, Gen. Ad van Baal, who had been the second-highest ranking officer in the army at the time of the massacre, also resigned.

Further investigations by a parliamentary commission, in November 2002, into the failure of the Dutch authorities to prevent the massacre at Srebreniča in 1995 revealed that the former Government had been aware of the likelihood of atrocities occurring in the UN camp. The former Minister of Development Co-operation in that administration, Jan Pronk, admitted that the possibility of such killings had in fact been discussed in a meeting of the Council of Ministers on 11 July 1995, the very day the mass murders had occurred. In January 2003 the parliamentary commission concluded that the Netherlands bore responsibility for the massacre, that the Government had failed adequately to plan the mission and that the Dutch army had suppressed details of its failures.

On 6 May 2002 the charismatic and controversial politician Pim Fortuyn was shot dead in Hilversum, in central Netherlands, just days before the holding of the general election, in which his newly established party, the populist and anti-immigration Lijst Pim Fortuyn (LPF), was expected to secure a

substantial proportion of votes. Fortuyn had formed the movement following his dismissal in January as leader of the Leefbar Nederland (LN) party for his anti-immigration rhetoric. In late November 2002 Volkert van der Graaf, an animal rights activist who had been arrested shortly after Pim Fortuyn's murder, confessed to killing the politician. At his trial, which began in late March 2003, van der Graaf claimed that he believed Fortuyn had presented a threat to vulnerable members of society. He was convicted in April and received a prison sentence of 18 years.

At the general election of 15 May 2002 the CDA won 43 of the 150 seats in the Second Chamber, with 27.9% of the valid votes cast. The LPF, aided by revulsion at Fortuyn's murder, took 26 seats (with 17.0% of the votes), the VVD won 24 seats (15.4%) and the PvdA, obtained 23 seats (15.1%). In the light of their electoral defeats, both the PvdA and the VVD changed their Parliamentary Leaders, to Jeltje van Nieuwenhoven and Gerrit Zalm, respectively.

Balkenende was inaugurated as Prime Minister on 21 July 2002, leading a coalition Government comprising the CDA, the LPF and the VVD. However, the same day, a Suriname-born LPF minister in the Ministry of Emancipation and Family Affairs, Philomena Bijhout, resigned when it was confirmed that she had been linked to a Surinamese militia group involved in political killings in the former Dutch colony in December 1982. The LPF suffered a further setback when allegations were made by a newspaper that their new leader, Mat Herben, had tried unfairly to influence the selection procedure for the LN's electoral candidates when Fortuyn was still leader and Herben a party member. Herben resigned at the end of July and was subsequently replaced by Harry Wijnschenk, a motor magazine publisher.

The new Government detailed policies to reform the health insurance and social security system and reduce the number of illegal immigrants to the Netherlands. In early October 2002 the Minister of Immigration and Integration opened a new college for the instruction of Muslim religious leaders, imams, in Dutch values and social conventions. The course was compulsory for new imams who faced deportation if they practised without passing the exam.

Meanwhile the LPF was riven by factionalism and personal acrimony. In addition to the expulsion of two party members who objected to Wijnschenk's leadership style, in early October 2002 a feud developed between the Minister of Public Health, Welfare and Sport and Deputy Prime Minister, Dr Eduard Bomhoff, and the Minister of Economic Affairs, Herman Heinsbroek. Wijnschenk approached Heinsbroek regarding his possible appointment as the party's Parliamentary Leader. Heinsbroek subsequently articulated his ambition to assume the deputy premiership resulting in a damaging dispute with the incumbent Deputy Prime Minister, Bomhoff. The party was unable to resolve the deep personal and political rivalry between the two ministers. Despite their subsequent resignation from the Council of Ministers, the LPF's coalition partners refused to co-operate further with the party and the Government resigned on 16 October after just 87 days. Balkenende presided over a minority Government, comprising the CDA and the VVD, pending a general election, which was scheduled for January 2003. In December 2002 the VVD Minister of Defence, Benk Korthals, resigned after a parliamentary inquiry accused him of misleading the legislature over corruption in the construction industry.

In the legislative elections of 22 January 2003 the CDA won 44 seats in the Second Chamber (28.6% of votes cast), while the PvdA increased its number of seats from 23 to 42 (27.3%) under its charismatic new leader, Wouter Bos. The LPF, again led by Mat Herben, following the resignation of Wijnschenk in late 2002, secured only eight seats. Although the popularity of the right-wing LPF had declined sharply, the electoral manifestos of the mainstream parties addressed the issues raised by the movement. Of these immigration became a prominent subject of debate, the VVD echoing Fortuyn's statement that the Netherlands was already 'full'. In late January negotiations began for the formation of a coalition administration led by Balkenende. Disagreements between the CDA and the PvdA over Dutch support for an impending US-led military campaign to remove the regime of Saddam Hussain in Iraq hampered progress. In mid-March, in his capacity as Prime Minister of the interim administration, Balkenende announced that while Dutch troops would not assist in the campaign, some units of the armed forces and weapons would be supplied to help defend Turkey, should the conflict escalate. The PvdA responded by proposing a motion that the Netherlands should not provide assistance for the military campaign, either in the form of personnel or of materials; the motion was defeated. Negotiations resumed in late March and as the US-led coalition entered Iraq, both parties expressed their support for the military operation. In early April, however, talks collapsed following the failure of the two sides to agree on budgetary expenditure cuts to revive a stagnant economy.

In December 2002 four men appeared in court charged with having links to the militant Islamist al-Qai'da organization, and with conspiring to attack the US embassy in Paris and a US military base in Belgium in 2001. However, the men—one Dutch national of Ethiopian origin, one French national and two Algerians—were acquitted at the end of the month when the court ruled that evidence against them had been improperly obtained by the police.

In late March 2003 the Indian Government protested angrily against the interrogation by Dutch authorities of 15 Indian employees of a subsidiary of an Indian information technology firm based in Amsterdam. Despite possessing valid visas, the workers were requested to leave the Netherlands within a week.

Government

The Netherlands is a constitutional and hereditary monarchy. Legislative power is held by the bicameral States-General. The First Chamber has 75 members and is indirectly elected for four years by members of the 12 Provincial Councils. The Second Chamber comprises 150 members and is directly elected by universal adult suffrage for four years (subject to dissolution), on the basis of proportional representation. The Head of State has mainly formal prerogatives, and executive power is exercised by the Council of Ministers, which is led by the Prime Minister and is responsible to the States-General. The monarch appoints the Prime Minister and, on the latter's recommendation, other ministers. Each of the 12 provinces is administered by a directly-elected Provincial Council, a Provincial Executive and a Sovereign Commissioner, who is appointed by Royal Decree.

Defence

The Netherlands is a member of NATO (see p. 271). Conscription to the armed forces was ended in August 1996, and a gradual reduction in the number of military personnel is ongoing. The total strength of the armed forces at 1 August 2002 was 49,580: army 23,150, navy 12,130, air force 8,850, Royal Military Constabulary 3,300 and 2,150 headquarters staff. In August 1995 a joint Dutch-German army corps, numbering 28,000 men, was inaugurated, and in January 1996 the operational units of the Royal Netherlands Navy merged with the Belgian navy under the command of the Admiral of the Benelux. Expenditure on defence in the 2002 budget totalled €6,500m. In November 2000 the Netherlands committed 5,000 troops to a proposed joint European Union rapid reaction force, which was to be ready to be deployed by 2003.

Economic Affairs

In 2001, according to estimates by the World Bank, the Netherlands' gross national income (GNI), measured at average 1999–2001 prices, was US $385,401m., equivalent to $24,040 per head (or $26,440 per head on an international purchasing-power parity basis). During 1990–2001, it was estimated, the population grew by an average annual rate of 0.6% per year, while gross domestic product (GDP) per head increased, in real terms, at an average annual rate of 2.0% in 1990–2001. Overall GDP increased, in real terms, by an average annual rate of 2.6% in 1990–2001; growth in 2001 was 1.1%.

Agriculture (including hunting, forestry and fishing) contributed 2.7% of GDP in 1999. Although only 2.9% of the employed labour force were engaged in the sector in 2001, the Netherlands is a net exporter of agricultural products: in 2001 exports of food and live animals provided 12.3% of total export earnings. The principal crops are sugar beet, potatoes, cereals, vegetables and fruit. The main agricultural activity is horticulture; market gardening is highly developed, and the production of cut flowers and bulbs has traditionally been a significant industry, although its contribution to export earnings has declined in recent years. Livestock farming is also an important activity. During 1990–99 agricultural GDP increased, in real terms, at an average annual rate of 2.5%; following a decline of 6.3% in 1997, it grew by 6.3% in 1998 and by 5.6% in 1999.

Industry (including mining, manufacturing, construction and power) contributed 25.9% of GDP in 1999. About 21.7% of the employed labour force were engaged in the sector in 2001. Industrial GDP increased, in real terms, at an average annual rate of 1.6% in 1990–99; it rose by 1.5% in 1998 and by 2.2% in 1999.

Extractive activities provided 1.9% of GDP in 1999. In 2001 about 0.1% of the employed labour force were engaged in mining and quarrying. The principal mineral resource is natural gas (of which the Netherlands was the world's seventh largest producer in 1998). Total extraction in 2001 was 74,232m. cu m. Reserves of petroleum and salts are also exploited. The GDP of the mining sector declined, in real terms, at an average annual rate of 1.2% in 1995–99; it increased by 13.4% in 1996, but subsequently decreased by 8.2% in 1997, by an estimated 2.4% in 1998 and by an estimated 6.4% in 1999.

Manufacturing contributed 16.6% of GDP in 1999. The sector accounted for 14.5% of the employed labour force in 2001. Measured by the value of output, the principal branches of manufacturing in 1999 were food products, beverages and tobacco (accounting for 22.4% of the total), electrical and optical equipment (9.8%) and basic chemicals and man-made fibres (9.8%). Several multinational companies are domiciled in the Netherlands. Manufacturing GDP increased at an average annual rate of 2.4% in 1995–99; it grew by an estimated 3.3% in 1998 and by an estimated 3.1% in 1999.

In 1999 natural gas provided 56.9% of total electricity production, coal 25.5%, petroleum 7.6%, nuclear energy 4.4% and hydroelectric power 0.1%. Imports of mineral fuels comprised 10.1% of the value of total imports in 2001; fuel exports accounted for 9.3% of total exports by value in that year. In recent years successive governments have sought to promote the utilization of 'renewable' energy resources.

The services sector contributed 71.4% of GDP in 1999, and engaged 75.4% of the employed labour force in 2001. Within the sector, financial services, tourism and transport are of considerable importance. In early 2003 the Dutch food retailing corporation, Ahold, became the subject of an inquiry by financial authorities into allegations of accounting malpractice. In mid-February the US stock market regulator, the Securities and Exchange Commission, began an investigation into reports that the group had over-reported the income of its US Foodservice subsidiary by some US $500m. The Dutch Authority for Financial Markets also began to investigate claims of insider-trading at the corporation in 2001. Two of Ahold's most senior executives resigned and the value of Ahold's shares, owned by large investors as well as thousands of the food retailer's customers, were reduced by some 75%, following news of the scandal. The Government subsequently announced plans to introduce legislation increasing the powers of the Authority for Financial Markets to supervise financial reporting by accountants and a reform of corporate governance laws. The GDP of the services sector increased, in real terms, at an average annual rate of 3.1% in 1990–99; it rose by 4.1% in 1998 and by 3.8% in 1999.

In 2002 the Netherlands recorded a visible trade surplus of €26,995m. and there was a surplus of €9,457m. on the current account of the balance of payments. In 2001 the principal source of imports was Germany (contributing 18.4% of the total); other major suppliers were the USA (9.9%), Belgium (9.2%), the United Kingdom (8.9%) and France (5.8%). Germany was also the principal market for exports (accounting for 25.6% of the total); other major purchasers in 2001 were Belgium (11.8%), the United Kingdom (11.1%), France (10.3%) and Italy (6.2%). The principal exports in 2001 were machinery and transport equipment (especially office machines), chemicals, food and live animals, and basic manufactures. The principal imports in that year were machinery and transport equipment (particularly office machines and other electrical machinery), basic manufactures and chemicals.

In 2001 the Netherlands recorded an overall budgetary deficit of €3,500, equivalent to 0.8% of GDP. In 1998 government debt was estimated to be equivalent to 7.1% of GDP. In 1990–2001 the annual rate of inflation averaged 2.6%. Consumer prices increased by 4.5% in 2001 and 3.5% in 2002. Some 2.7% of the labour force were registered as unemployed at the end of 2001.

The Netherlands is a founder member of the European Union (EU, see p. 199), of the Benelux Economic Union (see p. 339), of the Organisation for Economic Co-operation and Development (OECD, see p. 277) and of the European Bank for Reconstruction and Development (EBRD, see p. 193).

In the early 1990s the hitherto buoyant, export-led growth of the Dutch economy was undermined by a series of budget deficits, a high level of unemployment and fluctuations in international prices for natural gas. The Kok administration (1994–2002), pursuing a policy of economic consensus, which helped to limit industrial unrest, sought to reduce public expenditure, to restrain labour costs and to deregulate commercial activity, and shifted much of the burden of social-security contribution from the employer to the employee. This, together with the increasing importance of part-time work, contributed to a progressive reduction in the level of unemployment from 1992. In early 2000 it was announced that the Netherlands had recorded a budgetary surplus, equivalent to about 1% of GDP in 1999, the first such surplus for some 25 years. Between 1995 and 2000 the Netherlands recorded economic growth above the EU average. However, the weakness of the euro, the single currency adopted by the Netherlands and 10 other EU countries from January 1999, led to a rise in the real cost of imports. Together with the high level of employment, which exerted an inflationary pressure on wage demands, and the high international price for petroleum, this led to an increase in the rate of inflation. In 2001 GDP growth slowed to 1.1%, while growth for 2002 was estimated at only 0.25%. Industrial production declined throughout 2002, continuing a trend that started in September 2001. As a major trading nation the Netherlands was particularly adversely affected by the global downturn; capital gains growth slowed and the slowing of the previously booming housing market restrained consumer spending. Although the slowing of growth in the economy helped reduce the inflationary pressures of domestic consumption, the introduction of euro notes and coins in January 2002 contributed to inflation as retailers seized the opportunity to increase prices. The economic recovery of the Netherlands was likely to be slower that that of other eurozone countries owing to a decline in competitiveness, due to the effects of a tight labour market, high wage increases and lower productivity. The Dutch Central Bank urged employers and unions to moderate wages in an attempt to reduce high labour costs which were exacerbated by an overly-generous incapacity scheme, which urgently required reform. The Central Planning Board of the Netherlands forecast growth of only 0.75% in 2003, with an increase of 1.25% in unemployment, inflation to remain above 3% and real income for wage earners to decline by 2%.

Education

There are two types of school in the Netherlands: public schools, which are maintained by municipalities, and attended by about 35% of all school children; and private schools, which are, for the most part, denominational and are attended by almost 65% of the school-going population. Both types of school are fully subsidized by the State. Schools are administered by school boards, responsible to the local authorities or to the private organizations that operate them, thus providing teachers with considerable freedom. The Minister of Education, Culture and Science, advised by an education council, is responsible for educational legislation and its enforcement.

Full-time education is compulsory in the Netherlands from five to 16 years of age, and part-time education is compulsory for a further two years. Some 98% of four-year-old children also attend primary schools. Primary education lasts for eight years and is followed by various types of secondary education. Pre-university schools provide various six-year courses that prepare pupils for university education. General secondary education comprises senior and junior secondary schools, providing five- and four-year courses that prepare pupils for higher vocational institutes and senior secondary vocational education respectively. In all types there is latitude in the choice of subjects taken. In 2000/01 166,948 students were enrolled at the Netherlands' 13 universities, while some 311,000 students were enrolled at the 65 institutes of higher vocational education. In addition, 22,000 students were registered with the Open University at 1 January 2001/02. Education was allocated 10.0% of total expenditure by the central Government in the 1997 budget.

Public Holidays

2003: 1 January (New Year's Day), 18 April (Good Friday), 21 April (Easter Monday), 30 April (Queen's Day), 29 May (Ascension Day), 9 June (Whit Monday), 25–26 December (Christmas).

2004: 1 January (New Year's Day), 9 April (Good Friday), 12 April (Easter Monday), 30 April (Queen's Day), 20 May (Ascension Day), 31 May (Whit Monday), 25–26 December (Christmas).

Weights and Measures

The metric system is in force.

Statistical Survey

Source: Netherlands Central Bureau of Statistics, Prinses Beatrixlaan 428, POB 959, 2270 AZ Voorburg; tel. (70) 3373800; fax (70) 3877429; e-mail infoservice@cbs.nl; internet www.cbs.nl.

Area and Population

AREA, POPULATION AND DENSITY

Area (sq km)	
Land	33,873
Inland waters.	3,479
Coastal water.	4,175
Total	41,528*
Population (census results)†	
1 January 1991‡	15,010,445
1 January 2001‡	
Males	7,909,855
Females.	8,077,220
Total	15,987,075
Population (official estimate at 1 January)†	
2002	16,105,285
Density (per sq km of land) at 1 January 2002 . . .	475.5

* 16,034 sq miles.

† Population is *de jure*.

‡ Based on a compilation of continuous accounting and sample surveys.

PROVINCES

	Land area (sq km)*	Population (1 January 2002)†	Density (per sq km)
Groningen	2,340	570,480	244
Friesland	3,356	636,184	190
Drenthe	2,649	478,799	181
Overijssel	3,337	1,094,032	328
Flevoland	1,421	341,721	240
Gelderland	4,983	1,949,233	391
Utrecht	1,363	1,139,925	836
Noord-Holland	2,657	2,559,477	963
Zuid-Holland	2,867	3,423,780	1,194
Zeeland	1,805	377,235	209
Noord-Brabant	4,929	2,391,123	485
Limburg	2,164	1,143,296	528
Total	**33,873**	**16,105,285**	**475**

* Figures refer to area at 1 January 2000.

† Provisional.

PRINCIPAL TOWNS
(population of municipalities at 1 January 2002)*

Amsterdam (capital)†	735,526	Arnhem	140,736
Rotterdam	598,660	Zaanstad	137,669
's-Gravenhage (The		's-Hertogenbosch	131,697
Hague)†	457,726	Amersfoort	129,720
Utrecht	260,625	Maastricht	122,005
Eindhoven	204,776	Dordrecht	120,222
Tilburg	197,358	Leiden	117,170
Groningen	175,569	Haarlemmermeer	118,553
Breda	163,427	Zoetermeer	110,500
Apeldoorn	154,859	Zwolle	Zwolle
Nijmegen	154,616	Emmen	108,367
Enschede	151,346	Ede	103,708
Haarlem	147,831		
Almere	158,902		

* Provisional figures.
† Amsterdam is the capital, while The Hague is the seat of government.

BIRTHS, MARRIAGES AND DEATHS

	Live births*		Marriages		Deaths*	
	Number	Rate (per 1,000)	Number	Rate (per 1,000)	Number	Rate (per 1,000)
1994	195,611	12.7	82,982	5.4	133,471	8.7
1995	190,513	12.3	81,469	5.3	135,675	8.8
1996	189,521	12.2	85,140	5.5	137,561	8.9
1997	192,443	12.3	85,059	5.4	135,783	8.7
1998	199,408	12.7	86,956	5.5	137,482	8.8
1999	200,445	12.7	89,428	5.7	140,487	8.9
2000	206,619	13.0	88,074	5.5	140,527	8.8
2001	202,603	12.6	82,091	5.0	140,270	8.7

* Including residents outside the country if listed in a Netherlands population register.

Expectation of life (years at birth, 2001): Males 75.6; Females 80.5.

IMMIGRATION AND EMIGRATION

Immigrants from	1997*	1998*	1999
Belgium	6,100	6,400	6,022
France	3,200	3,700	3,351
Germany	9,500	9,600	8,785
Turkey	6,900	6,300	5,424
United Kingdom	5,900	6,400	6,969
Europe (unspecified)	17,800	19,400	30,571
Aruba and Netherlands Antilles	7,000	10,500	11,639
Suriname	3,500	4,600	3,139
USA	5,400	5,900	5,928
America (unspecified)	4,700	5,300	4,819
Asia	22,800	25,400	22,610
Morocco	4,800	5,400	4,692
Africa (unspecified)	10,300	11,100	10,879
Oceania	1,700	2,000	1,970
Total (incl. others)	109,900	122,400	119,151

Emigrants to	1997*	1998*	1999
Belgium	7,000	7,100	6,953
France	2,700	2,800	2,903
Germany	7,400	6,900	7,132
Spain	2,300	2,500	2,791
Turkey	1,900	1,500	1,274
United Kingdom	5,300	5,500	5,339
Europe (unspecified)	8,700	8,900	8,757
Aruba and Netherlands Antilles	4,400	3,800	3,851
Suriname	1,400	1,200	867
USA	5,200	5,400	5,343
America (unspecified)	3,100	3,100	2,890
Asia	6,700	6,200	5,445
Africa	4,300	3,800	3,433
Australia	1,400	1,300	1,552
Oceania (unspecified)	500	500	493
Total (incl. others)	62,200	60,400	59,023

* Figures are rounded to the nearest 100 persons.

2000: Total immigration 132,820; Total emigration 61,201.

2001: Total immigration 133,404; Total emigration 63,318.

ECONOMICALLY ACTIVE POPULATION*
(sample surveys, '000 persons aged 15 to 64 years)

	1999	2000	2001
Agriculture, hunting, forestry and fishing	230	248	224
Mining and quarrying	9	12	9
Manufacturing	1,111	1,121	1,115
Electricity, gas and water supply	37	35	34
Construction	471	466	508
Wholesale and retail trade†	1,238	1,291	1,254
Hotels and restaurants	281	289	291
Transport, storage and communications	465	473	486
Financial intermediation	288	276	307
Real estate, renting and business activities	891	945	944
Public administration and defence‡	517	488	541
Education	481	458	479
Health and social work	1,048	1,071	1,134
Other community, social and personal service activities	309	356	347
Private households with employed persons	17	5	3
Extra-territorial organizations and bodies	2	2	2
Activities not adequately defined	205	197	186
Total employed	7,601	7,731	7,865
Unemployed	277	262	220
Total labour force	7,879	7,993	8,086
Males	4,485	4,538	4,561
Females	3,394	3,455	3,524

* Persons working or seeking work for less than 12 hours per week are no longer included.
† Including repair of motor vehicles, motorcycles and personal and household goods.
‡ Including compulsory social security.

Source: ILO, *Yearbook of Labour Statistics*.

Health and Welfare

KEY INDICATORS

Total fertility rate (children per woman, 2001)	1.5
Under-5 mortality rate (per 1,000 live births, 2001)	5
HIV/AIDS (% of persons aged 15–49, 2001)	0.21
Physicians (per 1,000 head, 1990)	2.51
Hospital beds (per 1,000 head, 1998)	11.3
Health expenditure (2000): US $ per head (PPP)	2,255
Health expenditure (2000): % of GDP	8.1
Health expenditure (2000): public (% of total)	67.5
Access to water (% of persons, 2000)	100
Access to sanitation (% of persons, 2000)	100
Human Development Index (2000): ranking	8
Human Development Index (2000): value	0.935

For sources and definitions, see explanatory note on p. vi.

Agriculture

PRINCIPAL CROPS

('000 metric tons)

	1999	2000	2001
Wheat	851	1,143	991
Barley	365	287	387
Maize†	132	162	150
Rye	14	29	17
Triticale (wheat-rye hybrid)	11	36	21
Potatoes	8,221	8,127	7,015
Sugar beet	7,317	6,727	5,947
Cabbages	291	288	266
Lettuce	88	72	65
Spinach	39	49	35
Tomatoes	525	520	550
Cauliflower	59	54	43
Cucumbers and gherkins	455	410	425
Aubergines (Eggplants)	38	37	31
Chillies and green peppers	285	285	285
Dry onions	754	821*	765
Leeks and other alliaceous vegetables	101	95	100
Green beans	55	45*	45*
Green peas†	84	82	77
Carrots	448	385	378
Mushrooms	250	263	270
Other vegetables*	167	160	188
Apples	570	461*	160
Pears	140	203	78*
Strawberries	51	52	50*
Flax fibre and tow	28	31	25

* FAO estimate(s).

† Unofficial estimates.

Source: FAO.

LIVESTOCK

('000 head, year ending September)

	1999	2000	2001
Horses and ponies	116	118	121
Cattle	4,206	4,070	4,047
Chickens	104,767	104,015	100,334
Sheep	1,401	1,308	1,296
Goats	153	179	221
Pigs	13,567	13,118	13,037

Source: FAO.

LIVESTOCK PRODUCTS

('000 metric tons)

	1999	2000	2001
Beef and veal	508	471	371
Mutton and lamb	18	18*	20
Pig meat	1,711	1,623	1,433
Chicken meat	710	703†	700
Turkey meat	43	63*	42*
Cows' milk	11,174	11,135†	10,500†
Cheese	646	672	660*
Butter	140	126	128*
Hen eggs	647	668	658†
Cattle hides (fresh)†	50	48	48

* Unofficial figure.

† FAO estimate(s).

Source: FAO.

Forestry

ROUNDWOOD REMOVALS

('000 cubic metres, excl. bark)

	1999	2000	2001
Sawlogs, veneer logs and logs for sleepers	575	572	497
Pulpwood	215	197	148
Other industrial wood	92	110	84
Fuel wood	162	160	136
Total	1,044	1,039	865

Source: FAO.

SAWNWOOD PRODUCTION

('000 cubic metres, incl. railway sleepers)

	1999	2000	2001
Coniferous (softwood)	203	247	168
Broadleaved (hardwood)	159	143	100
Total	362	390	268

Source: FAO.

Fishing

('000 metric tons, live weight)

	1998	1999	2000
Capture	536.6	514.6	495.8
European plaice	30.6	37.5	35.1
Blue whiting	27.7	32.9	43.1
Atlantic horse mackerel	103.2	84.9	67.0
Atlantic herring	77.1	78.7	75.2
Sardinellas	110.1	115.8	112.8
Atlantic mackerel	30.2	27.8	32.4
Common edible cockle	68.1	50.9	19.6
Aquaculture	120.0	108.8	75.3
Blue mussel	113.2	100.8	66.8
Total catch	656.7	623.4	571.1

Note: Figures exclude aquatic plants and aquatic mammals. Aquatic mammals are recorded by number rather than by weight. The number of whales and porpoises caught was: 33 in 1998; 0 in 1999; 2 in 2000.

Source: FAO, *Yearbook of Fishery Statistics*.

Mining

	1999	2000	2001*
Crude petroleum ('000 barrels)	18,978	17,633	18,000
Natural gas (million cu metres)†	68,528	69,180	74,232
Salt ('000 metric tons)*	5,000	5,000	5,000

* Estimated production.

† Figures refer to gross volume of production. Marketed output (in million cu metres) was: 67,228 in 1999; 68,157 in 2000; 73,296 in 2001.

Source: US Geological Survey.

Industry

SELECTED PRODUCTS

('000 metric tons, unless otherwise indicated)*

	1995	1996	1997
Margarine.	335	297	349
Vegetable oils and fats (crude). .	521.9	479.3	n.a.
Wheat flour	1,218	1,240	n.a.
Refined sugar.	1,048	975	n.a.
Cocoa powder (metric tons). . .	161,900	175,000	180,000
Cocoa butter (metric tons) . .	156,354	164,000	178,000
Distilled alcoholic beverages ('000 hectolitres)	926	n.a.	n.a.
Beer ('000 hectolitres) . . .	22,380	22,670	23,780
Mineral waters ('000 hectolitres)	1,303	1,200	1,360
Soft drinks ('000 hectolitres) . .	16,850	16,340	16,450
Cigars (million)	1,759	1,776	1,889
Cigarettes (million)	97,727	n.a.	n.a.
Manufactured tobacco (metric tons)	41,750	n.a.	n.a.
Footwear ('000 pairs, excluding rubber footwear)	5,492	n.a.	n.a.
Veneer sheets ('000 cubic metres)†	25	19	17
Mechanical wood pulp†	148	125	138
Newsprint†	361	338	373
Other printing and writing paper†	818	840	878
Other paper and paperboard† . .	1,788	1,809	1,908
Nitrogenous fertilizers(a)†‡. . .	1,800	1,650	1,600
Phosphate fertilizers(b)†‡ . . .	335	271	402
Synthetic rubber§	185	199.3	206.7
Jet fuels	5,997	6,321	5,921
Kerosene	216	209	233
Motor spirit (petrol) and other light oils	14,857	14,882	9,569
Naphthas	11,215	10,680	11,265
Gas-diesel (distillate fuel) oil . .	20,495	21,354	21,922
Residual fuel oils	12,876	14,491	14,466
Lubricating oils	617	624	562
Petroleum bitumen (asphalt) . .	751	657	525
Liquefied petroleum gas. . . .	3,164	3,759	3,817
Coke	2,895	2,921	2,909
Coke-oven gas (terajoules) . .	26,925	27,115	26,383
Clay building bricks (million) . .	1,692	1,620	1,789
Floor and wall tiles ('000 sq metres)	14,300	14,500	n.a.
Cement‖	3,400	3,300	3,300
Pig-iron	5,530	5,544	5,805
Crude steel	6,409	6,326	6,641
Aluminium (unwrought):			
primary	216	227	231.8
secondary	191.5	150	150.4
Refined lead: secondary¶ . . .	20.2	22	19.5
Zinc (unwrought)¶	206.3	207.4	200.5
Merchant vessels launched ('000 grt)	186	189	229
Passenger motor cars ('000)[1] . .	2,254	2,334	2,458
Lorries ('000)[1].	15.8	18.8	19.7
Bicycles ('000).	766	754	880
Electricity (million kWh) . . .	80,832	85,089	86,638
Construction: new dwellings completed (number) . . .	93,836	88,934	92,315

1998 ('000 metric tons, unless otherwise indicated): Margarine 310; Cocoa powder 183; Cocoa butter 179; Beer ('000 hectolitres) 23,040; Mineral waters ('000 hectolitres) 1,330; Soft drinks ('000 hectolitres) 15,670; Cigars (million) 2,015; Veneer sheets ('000 cubic metres) 17†; Mechanical wood pulp 129†; Newsprint 349†; Other printing and writing paper 875†; Other paper and paperboard 1,956†; Nitrogenous fertilizers (a) 1,566†‡; Phosphate fertilizers (b) 405†‡; Clay building bricks (million) 1,662; Pig-iron 5,562; Crude steel 6,377; Aluminium (unwrought): primary 263.7; Aluminium (unwrought): secondary 102.0; Refined lead: secondary 17.2; Zinc (unwrought) 217.1; Merchant vessels launched ('000 grt) 194; Passenger motor cars ('000)[1]210‖; Lorries ('000) 20‖; Bicycles ('000) 1,019; Electricity (million kWh) 87,477.

1999 ('000 metric tons, unless otherwise indicated): Veneer sheets ('000 cubic metres) 19†; Mechanical wood pulp 117†; Newsprint 376†; Other printing and writing paper 892†; Other paper and paperboard 1,988†; Passenger motor cars ('000)[1]310‖; Lorries ('000)[1]17‖; Electricity (million kWh) 83,068.

2000 ('000 metric tons, unless otherwise indicated): Veneer sheets ('000 cubic metres) 19†; Mechanical wood pulp 137†; Newsprint 415†; Other printing and writing paper 930†; Other paper and paperboard 1,987†; Electricity (million KWh) 84,370.

* Official figures refer to activity by establishments employing 20 or more persons. For manufactured goods, except for petroleum, coal and basic metal products, such data relate to sales (rather than production) by the relevant establishments.
† Production figure(s) from FAO.
‡ Output during 12 months ending 30 June of the year stated. Figures are in terms of (a) nitrogen or (b) phosphoric acid.
§ Data from the International Rubber Study Group.
‖ Estimates.
¶ Data from World Metal Statistics (London).
[1] Including vehicles assembled from imported parts.

Sources: partly UN, *Industrial Commodity Statistics Yearbook* and *Monthly Bulletin of Statistics*; FAO, *Yearbook of Forest Products*; IRF, *World Road Statistics*.

Finance

CURRENCY AND EXCHANGE RATES

Monetary Units
100 cent = 1 euro (€)

Sterling and Dollar Equivalents (31 December 2002)
£1 sterling = 1.537 euros
US $1 = 0.9536 euros
100 euros = £65.06 = $104,87

Average Exchange Rate (euros per US $)
2000   1.0854
2001   1.1175
2002   1.0626

Note: The national currency was formerly the guilder. From the introduction of the euro, with the Netherlands' participation, on 1 January 1999, a fixed exchange rate of €1 = 2.20371 guilders was in operation. Euro notes and coins were introduced on 1 January 2002. The euro and local currency circulated alongside each other until 28 January, after which the euro became the sole legal tender. Some of the figures in this Survey are still in terms of guilders.

BUDGET

('000 million guilders)*

Revenue†	1995	1996	1997
Taxation	273.04	281.83	302.39
Income taxes	52.75	50.53	48.12
Corporation tax	20.85	27.55	32.34
Social security contributions . .	121.89	119.85	133.33
Taxes on property	7.40	8.63	9.66
Turnover tax	43.58	46.51	49.45
Excise duties	18.42	19.47	20.12
Entrepreneurial and property income	12.59	11.76	12.74
Administrative fees and charges, etc.	6.27	7.24	8.01
Other current revenue	0.45	0.50	0.57
Capital revenue	0.37	0.61	0.65
Total	292.72	301.94	324.36

Expenditure‡	1995	1996	1997
General public services	20.52	21.88	21.65
Defence	12.65	12.84	13.03
Public order and safety	9.21	8.75	9.63
Education	34.31	34.50	33.65
Health	47.24	45.09	49.92
Social security and welfare . . .	119.54	120.81	126.21
Housing and community amenities	9.45	4.63	5.07
Recreational, cultural and religious affairs and services	1.25	1.04	1.15
Economic affairs and services . .	18.95	17.28	20.66
Transport and communications	9.87	10.94	11.71
Other purposes	49.63	53.95	56.65
Total	322.75	320.77	337.62
Current§	307.07	308.33	325.85
Capital	15.68	12.44	11.77

* Figures refer to the consolidated accounts of the central Government. In addition to units covered by the general budget, the data include the operations of social security funds and of other government agencies with individual budgets.

† Excluding grants received ('000 million guilders): 0.12 in 1995; 0.27 in 1996; 0.17 in 1997.

‡ Excluding lending minus repayments ('000 million guilders): −30.55 in 1995; −1.71 in 1996; −1.15 in 1997.

§ Including interest payments ('000 million guilders): 30.44 in 1995; 30.34 in 1996; 30.67 in 1997.

Source: IMF, *Government Finance Statistics Yearbook*.

General Budget (million euros): *Revenue* 45,501 in 1999; 48,571 in 2000; 51,254 in 2001. *Expenditure* 178,654 in 1999; 185,463 in 2000; 202,504 in 2001.

INTERNATIONAL RESERVES
(US $ million at 31 December)*

	2000	2001	2002
Gold†	7,993	7,863	9,385
IMF special drawing rights . . .	653	759	697
Reserve position in IMF	1,988	2,352	2,849
Foreign exchange	7,004	5,930	6,017
Total	17,638	16,904	18,948

* Excluding deposits made with the European Monetary Institute (now the European Central Bank).

† Valued at market prices.

Source: IMF, *International Financial Statistics*.

MONEY SUPPLY
(million euros at 31 December)

	2000	2001	2002
Currency issued	18,730	11,394	19,357*
Demand deposits at banking institutions	131,893	150,975	152,526

* Currency put into circulation by De Nederlandsche Bank was 17,465 million euros.

Source: IMF, *International Financial Statistics*.

COST OF LIVING
(Consumer Price Index; base: 1995 = 100)

	2000	2001	2002
Food	106.3	114.3	119.0
Rent, fuel and light*	121.2	127.2	131.5
Clothing (incl. footwear) . . .	104.2	106.1	109.5
Health	107.2	110.2	112.3
Transport	113.8	116.5	117.9
Communications	98.5	96.2	96.2
Recreation and culture . . .	105.9	110.8	115.2
All items (incl. others) . . .	111.4	116.4	120.5

* Including household repairs.

NATIONAL ACCOUNTS

National Income and Product
(million euros at current prices)

	1999	2000*	2001*
Compensation of employees . .	192,347	205,533	220,470
Operating surplus	83,330	90,581	92,158
Domestic factor incomes . .	275,677	296,114	312,628
Consumption of fixed capital . .	56,549	61,317	66,158
Gross domestic product (GDP) at factor cost	332,226	357,431	378,786
Indirect taxes	49,073	52,418	57,908
Less Subsidies	7,229	7,250	7,522
GDP in purchasers' values . .	374,070	402,599	429,172
Factor income received from abroad (net)	718	4,066	−4,987
Gross national product (GNP)	374,788	406,665	424,185
Less Consumption of fixed capital .	56,549	61,317	66,158
National income in market prices	318,239	345,348	358,027
Other current transfers abroad (net)	−2,153	−3,308	−3,623
National disposable income . .	316,086	342,040	354,404

* Figures are provisional.

Expenditure on the Gross Domestic Product
(million euros at current prices)

	1999	2000*	2001*
Government final consumption expenditure	85,526	91,188	99,461
Private final consumption expenditure	187,593	201,088	212,905
Increase in stocks	524	−835	−96
Gross fixed capital formation . .	84,186	90,743	94,064
Total domestic expenditure . .	357,829	382,184	406,334
Exports of goods and services . .	225,378	271,039	280,235
Less Imports of goods and services	209,137	250,624	257,397
GDP in purchasers' values . .	374,070	402,599	429,172
GDP at constant 1995 prices . .	350,921	362,552	367,128

* Figures are provisional.

Gross Domestic Product by Economic Activity
(million guilders at current prices)

	1997	1998	1999
Agriculture, hunting, forestry and fishing	21,160	21,574	20,555
Mining and quarrying . . .	19,396	16,975	14,502
Manufacturing	115,548	121,967	125,570
Electricity, gas and water supply	11,758	12,199	13,045
Construction	36,299	38,695	43,091
Wholesale and retail trade; repair of motor vehicles, motorcycles and personal household goods	87,398	92,950	97,839
Hotels and restaurants	12,819	13,759	15,069
Transport, storage and communications	50,251	54,051	55,723
Financial and business activities	168,274	183,309	199,651
Public administration and social security	45,288	47,291	49,347
Defence	7,561	7,664	7,891
Education	26,604	27,996	29,807
Health and social work . . .	48,639	50,932	54,779
Other community, social and personal service activities . .	23,743	25,226	26,752
Private households with employed persons	2,695	2,913	3,187
Sub-total	677,433	717,501	756,808
Taxes *less* subsidies on products	76,524	82,613	91,111
Difference between imputed and paid VAT	1,354	1,472	449
Consumption of imputed bank services	−19,878	−21,106	−24,385
GDP in purchasers' values . .	735,433	780,480	823,983

BALANCE OF PAYMENTS
(million euros)

	2000	2001	2002
Exports of goods f.o.b.	221,947	228,356	223,800
Imports of goods f.o.b.	−202,828	205,088	−196,805
Trade balance	19,120	23,268	26,995
Exports of services	53,624	57,205	57,424
Imports of services	−55,839	−60,021	−58,812
Balance on goods and services	−2,214	−2,816	−1,387
Other income received . . .	47,320	45,974	37,215
Other income paid	−48,922	−49,871	−46,507
Balance on goods, services and income	15,304	16,555	16,316
Current transfers received . .	4,755	4,991	5,294
Current transfers paid . . .	−11,546	−12,528	−12,152
Current balance	8,512	9,018	9,457
Capital account (net) . . .	566	−3,571	−614
Direct investment abroad . .	−79,820	−54,215	−28,632
Direct investment from abroad	65,464	57,266	30,921
Portfolio investment assets . .	−70,047	−68,203	−70,536
Portfolio investment liabilities .	60,543	83,376	51,434
Financial derivatives assets .	89,676	97,673	75,045
Financial derivatives liabilities	−94,306	−104,209	−81,851
Other investment assets . .	−31,266	−75,761	−43,853
Other investment liabilities .	50,249	58,726	64,171
Net errors and omissions . .	737	−513	−5,688
Overall balance	−308	413	147

Source: De Nederlandsche Bank.

OFFICIAL ASSISTANCE TO DEVELOPING COUNTRIES
(million euros)

	1999	2000	2001*
Total	3,549	4,081	4,251

* Provisional figure.

External Trade

PRINCIPAL COMMODITIES
(distribution by SITC, million guilders)

Imports c.i.f.	1998	1999	2000
Food and live animals . . .	32,359.9	34,452.3	36,743.3
Crude materials (inedible) except fuels	15,629.1	15,378.1	19,047.4
Mineral fuels, lubricants, etc. .	21,372.5	26,924.2	48,519.8
Chemicals and related products	43,330.2	43,305.4	52,771.1
Organic chemicals	11,612.1	10,983.4	15,133.2
Basic manufactures . . .	53,811.5	53,117.8	59,954.8
Machinery and transport equipment . . .	146,392.8	158,512.6	185,624.1
General industrial machinery, equipment and parts	11,866.6	12,153.2	13,035.6
Office machines and automatic data-processing equipment .	49,899.2	53,864.9	59,917.5
Telecommunications and sound equipment	12,399.7	16,568.5	23,070.4
Other electrical machinery, apparatus etc. . . .	24,296.3	26,394.0	36,008.3
Road vehicles (incl. air-cushion vehicles) and parts (excl. tyres, engines, and electrical parts)	30,205.8	31,621.7	32,873.7
Miscellaneous manufactured articles	49,959.8	53,902.7	59,170.0
Clothing (excl. footwear) . .	12,780.0	12,992.5	13,701.5
Total (incl. others)*	371,204.7	393,845.7	469,780.8

2001 (million euros): Food and live animals 17,876; Crude materials (inedible) except fuels 8,549; Mineral fuels, lubricants, etc. 22,034 (Petroleum, petroleum products, etc. 17,502); Chemicals and related products 24,656 (Organic chemicals 6,646); Basic manufactures 26,756; Machinery and transport equipment 84,501 (General industrial machinery, equipment and parts 6,500; Office machines and automatic data-processing equipment 25,886; Telecommunications and sound equipment 11,509; Other electrical machinery, apparatus, etc. 16,338; Road vehicles (incl. air-cushion vehicles) and parts (excl. tyres, engines, and electrical parts) 15,181); Miscellaneous manufactured articles 28,676 (Clothing (excl. footwear) 6,457); Total (incl. others)* 217,151.
* Including victuals and stores of foreign origin supplied to Netherlands ships and aircraft.

Exports f.o.b.	1998	1999	2000
Food and live animals . . .	54,783.4	55,587.6	62,238.1
Vegetables and fruit	14,443.8	15,030.6	16,167.8
Crude materials (inedible) except fuels	20,823.1	21,939.6	27,092.8
Mineral fuels, lubricants, etc. .	22,357.7	24,528.1	43,854.6
Petroleum, petroleum products, etc.	14,653.2	17,480.4	32,441.9
Chemicals and related products	62,592.0	63,448.1	79,716.2
Organic chemicals	16,223.0	16,233.2	22,241.5
Artificial resins, plastic materials, etc.	14,147.8	14,131.3	17,722.0
Basic manufactures . . .	48,083.4	47,341.9	53,188.7
Machinery and transport equipment	131,233.7	140,963.3	168,844.1
Office machines and automatic data-processing equipment .	46,020.4	48,442.5	54,659.7
Telecommunications and sound equipment	8,725.1	11,411.9	17,029.2
Other electrical machinery, apparatus, etc. . . .	26,839.7	29,211.0	38,754.7
Road vehicles (incl. air-cushion vehicles) and parts (excl. tyres, engines, and electrical parts)	21,871.6	22,375.4	23,955.3
Miscellaneous manufactured articles	43,626.5	47,041.7	54,423.6
Total (incl. others)*	398,264.6	415,617.1	504,959.0

2001 (million euros): Food and live animals 29,531 (Vegetables and fruit 7,672); Crude materials (inedible) except fuels 12,025; Mineral fuels, lubricants, etc. 22,059 (Petroleum, petroleum products, etc. 14,291); Chemicals and related products 37,109 (Organic chemicals 9,935; Artificial resins, plastic materials, etc. 7,716); Basic manufactures 25,159; Machinery and transport equipment 82,042 (Office machines and automatic data-processing equipment 28,253; Telecommunications and sound equipment 9,773; Other electrical machinery, apparatus, etc. 17,002; Road vehicles (incl. air-cushion vehicles) and parts (excl. tyres, engines, and electrical parts) 10,950); Miscellaneous manufactured articles 26,244; Total (incl. others)* 240,833.

* Including victuals and stores supplied to foreign ships and aircraft.

PRINCIPAL TRADING PARTNERS
(million euros)

Imports c.i.f.	1999	2000	2001
Belgium	17,903.5*	19,986.0	20,177.8
Brazil	1,680.9	2,243.2	2,569.1
China, People's Republic	3,697.4	6,917.3	8,844.6
Denmark	1,932.2	2,260,405	2,148.6
France	11,565.5	12,312.0	12,617.0
Germany	34,426.2	38,485.0	40,253.0
Hong Kong	2,865.8	1,830.0	1,449.9
Ireland	3,474.4	3,926.3	3,808.9
Italy	5,651.8	6,126.0	6,173.0
Japan	7,566.1	9,272.4	8,696.3
Korea, Republic	1,590.6	2,225.2	2,146.9
Malaysia	2,493.1	3,347.3	3,696.9
Norway	3,188.0	4,831.8	4,504.1
Russia	1,510.3	2,889.8	3,463.5
Saudi Arabia	1,431.1	2,826.0	2,321.5
Singapore	2,462.8	3,401.7	3,386.0
Spain	3,772.4	4,697.6	4,741.6
Sweden	4,786.8	4,940.9	4,379.4
Switzerland	2,395.7	2,454.0	2,379.0
Taiwan	3,417.8	4,683.0	4,703.9
United Kingdom	17,371.2	20,653.4	19,458.2
USA	16,962.7	22,064.7	21,524.8
Total (incl. others)	178,719.1	216,057.2	218,329.6

Exports f.o.b.	1999	2000	2001
Austria	2,903.2	3,484.8	3,829.0
Belgium	23,029.4*	27,304.4	28,502.4
Denmark	3,038.0	3,509.4	3,430.0
France	20,306.0	24,503.0	24,944.1
Germany	49,191.5	59,654.2	61,696.9
Italy	11,236.2	13,711.3	15,076.0
Japan	1,985.3	2,323.5	2,522.3
Poland	2,002.2	2,505.9	2,587.3
Spain	6,542.3	7,575.0	8,474.1
Sweden	4,481.4	5,341.7	4,953.1
Switzerland	3,313.6	4,003.0	3,910.6
United Kingdom	20,281.3	25,066.8	26,884.3
USA	7,982.5	18,859.7	10,559.6
Total (incl. others)	188,598.7	231,854.4	241,339.0

* Includes Luxembourg.

Transport

RAILWAYS
(traffic)

	1996	1997	1998
Passenger-km (million)	14,131	14,485	14,879
Freight ton-km (million)	3,123	3,406	3,778

ROAD TRAFFIC
('000 motor vehicles in use at 1 August)

	1998	1999	2000
Passenger cars	5,931	6,120	6,343
Buses and coaches	11	11	11
Lorries and vans	648	710	779
Road tractors	49	53	57
Motorcycles	373	392	414
Mopeds	524	n.a.	n.a.

SHIPPING

Inland Waterways
(transport fleet at 1 January)

	1997	1998	1999
Number of vessels	5,067	5,003	4,577
Carrying capacity ('000 metric tons)	5,859	5,589	5,212

Inland Waterways
(freight traffic, million metric tons)

	1996	1997	1998
Internal transport: Commercial	61.2	75.7	79.3
Internal transport: Private	28.2	20.9	19.3
International transport	201.1	224.5	219.7

Merchant Fleet
(at 31 December)

	1999	2000	2001
Number of vessels	1,276	1,317	1,337
Displacement ('000 gross registered tons)	4,813.8	5,167.7	5,605.0

Source: Lloyd's Register-Fairplay, *World Fleet Statistics*.

Sea-borne Freight Traffic
('000 metric tons)

	1997	1998	1999
Goods loaded	88,667	85,137	92,000
Goods unloaded	312,864	319,684	305,000

CIVIL AVIATION*
(Netherlands scheduled air services—million)

	1994/95	1995/96	1996/97
Kilometres flown	259	283	304
Passenger-kilometres	41,767	45,531	50,350
Total ton-kilometres	7,362	8,108	8,630

* Figures refer to KLM operations only. Years from 1 April to 31 March.

Tourism

FOREIGN TOURIST ARRIVALS
('000)*

Country of origin	1998	1999	2000
Belgium	615	647	677
France	456	472	512
Germany	2,661	3,046	2,884
Italy	349	350	374
Spain	215	229	250
United Kingdom	1,595	1,726	1,838
Total (incl. others)	9,322	9,881	10,003

* Arrivals at all accommodation establishments.

Source: World Tourism Organization, *Yearbook of Tourism Statistics*.

Tourism receipts (US $ million): 6,788 in 1998; 7,092 in 1999; 6,951 (estimate) in 2000 (Source: World Tourism Organization).

Communications Media

	1999	2000	2001
Television receivers ('000 in use) .	8,500	8,600	n.a.
Telephone ('000 main lines in use)	9,610	9,879	10,000
Mobile cellular telephones ('000 subscribers).	6,746	10,710	11,900
Personal computers ('000 in use)	5,700	6,300	6,900
Internet users ('000)	3,000	3,900	5,300

1996: Daily newspapers: number 38; average circulation ('000 copies) 4,753; Non-daily newspapers: number 63; average circulation ('000 copies) 590.

1997: Radio receivers ('000 in use) 15,300; Facsimile machines ('000 in use) 600.

Book production (1993): 34,067 titles, excluding pamphlets.

Sources: UNESCO, *Statistical Yearbook*; UN, *Statistical Yearbook*; International Telecommunication Union.

Education

(2000/01—Full-time)

	Institutions	Students ('000)
Primary	7,721	1,664.0
Secondary	834	894.2
Adult and vocational	62	446.9
Higher professional.	56	306.6
University	12	164.7

* Including special secondary education.

Source: Ministry of Education, Culture and Science.

Directory

The Constitution

The Netherlands' first Constitution was adopted in 1814–15. The present Constitution, the first new one since 1848, came into force on 17 February 1983. Its main provisions are summarized below:

THE KINGDOM OF THE NETHERLANDS

The Kingdom of the Netherlands consists of territories in Europe (the Netherlands) and in the Caribbean (the Netherlands Antilles and Aruba). Under the Charter for the Kingdom of the Netherlands, signed by Queen Juliana in 1954, these territories constitute a single realm, ruled by the House of Orange-Nassau.

THE MONARCHY

The Netherlands is a constitutional monarchy with a parliamentary system of government. The Constitution regulates the royal succession and the regency in great detail. A successor to the Throne may be appointed by Act of Parliament if it appears that there will otherwise be no successor. The Bill for this purpose shall be discussed and decided upon in a joint session of the two Chambers of the States-General (Staten Generaal). The Sovereign is succeeded by his or her eldest child. The age of majority of the Sovereign is 18 years. Until the Sovereign has attained that age, the royal prerogative shall be exercised by a Regent.

ELECTORAL SYSTEM

The Parliament of the Netherlands is the Staten Generaal and is composed of two Chambers, a First and a Second Chamber. The Second Chamber, which is the more important politically, consists of 150 members, and is directly elected for four years on the basis of proportional representation. The First Chamber comprises 75 members and is elected by the (directly-elected) members of the Provincial Councils.

Nearly all Dutch nationals who have attained the age of 18 years are entitled to take part in the election for the Second Chamber. Those not entitled to vote are certain groups of non-resident nationals, mentally disordered and legally incompetent persons.

To be eligible for membership of the Staten Generaal, a person must be a Dutch national, must have attained the age of 18 years and must not have been disqualified from voting.

MINISTERIAL RESPONSIBILITY

The Ministers, led by the Prime Minister, are responsible to the Staten Generaal for all acts of government. This means, for example, that the power of the Government (Sovereign and Ministers) to dissolve one or both Chambers of the Staten Generaal is ultimately subject to the judgment of the Staten Generaal. The right to declare war and conclude treaties can, in principle, only be exercised subject to prior parliamentary approval. The Constitution contains provisions concerning the transferral of legislative, executive and judicial power to international institutions and on the legal supremacy of self-executing provisions of treaties.

The Prime Minister and the other Ministers are appointed and dismissed by Royal Decree. Ministries are established by Royal Decree.

A Council of Ministers is formed by a so-called 'formateur' (usually the future Prime Minister), who will have been assured of the support of a majority in the Second Chamber of the Staten Generaal.

A Minister may not be a member of the Staten Generaal. However, Ministers have the right to attend sittings of the Chambers and may take part in the deliberations. They must supply the Chambers, either orally or in writing, with any information requested, provided that this cannot be deemed to conflict with the interests of the State.

A statement of the policy that is to be pursued by the Government is given by the Sovereign every year on the third Tuesday in September before a joint session of the two Chambers of the Staten Generaal.

Acts of Parliament are passed jointly by the Government and the Staten Generaal. Bills, including the draft budget, must be introduced into the Second Chamber. The Second Chamber has the right to amend bills; the First Chamber can only accept or reject a bill. Revision of the Constitution requires two parliamentary readings of the bills that contain the proposed changes. In between the two readings, the Staten Generaal must be dissolved and elections held.

THE COUNCIL OF STATE

The Council of State is the Government's oldest and most important advisory body. It must be consulted on all bills and draft general administrative orders. The Council is also an important court for administrative disputes.

The Sovereign is President of the Council of State, but the day-to-day running of the Council is the responsibility of its Vice-President. Its other members—usually former politicians, scholars, judges and business executives—are appointed for life.

LOCAL GOVERNMENT

The Netherlands is divided into 12 provinces. Provinces may be dissolved and established by Act of Parliament. The provincial administrative organs are the Provincial Council, the Provincial Executive and the Sovereign's Commissioner. The Provincial Council—directly elected, as is the Second Chamber, on the basis of proportional representation—forms the provincial equivalent of the Parliament. Each Provincial Council elects, from among its members, a Provincial Executive.

The Sovereign's Commissioner is appointed and dismissed by Royal Decree. Each Commissioner presides over both the Provincial Council and the Provincial Executive. The provincial administrative organs have the constitutionally guaranteed power to regulate and administer their own internal affairs. They may also be required by, or pursuant to, Act of Parliament to provide regulation and administration. At present there are 636 municipalities in the Netherlands. The municipal administrative organs are the Municipal Council (directly elected by the local inhabitants), the Municipal Executive (chosen by the Council from among its members) and the Burgomaster (appointed and dismissed by Royal Decree). The Burgomaster (Mayor) presides over both the Municipal Council and the Municipal Executive. The Municipal Council has the power to make local regulations.

The Government

HEAD OF STATE

Queen of the Netherlands: HM Queen BEATRIX WILHELMINA ARMGARD (succeeded to the throne 30 April 1980).

COUNCIL OF MINISTERS
(April 2003)

Following the election of 22 January 2003, the country was governed by an interim administration comprising the Christen-Democratisch Appèl (CDA, Christian Democratic Appeal), the Volkspartij voor Vrijheid en Democratie (VVD, People's Party for Freedom and Democracy and the Lijst Pim Fortuyn (LPF), pending the formation of a new coalition government.

Prime Minister, Minister of General Affairs: Dr JAN PIETER (PETER) BALKENENDE (CDA).

Deputy Prime Minister, Minister of Home Affairs and Kingdom Relations: Dr JOHANNES WIJNANDUS (JOHAN) REMKES (VVD).

Deputy Prime Minister, Minister of Transport, Public Works and Water Management: ROELF HENDRIK DE BOER (LPF).

Minister of Foreign Affairs: JAKOB GIJSBERT (JAAP) DE HOOP SCHEFFER (CDA).

Minister of Finance, Minister of Economic Affairs (acting): Drs JOHANNES FRANCISCUS (HANS) HOOGERVORST (VVD).

Minister of Immigration and Integration: HILBRAND PER ANNE NAWIJN (LPF).

Minister of Justice: JAN PIETER HENDRIK DONNER (CDA).

Minister of Agriculture, Nature Management and Fisheries: Dr CORNELIS PETER (CEES) VEERMAN (CDA).

Minister of Education, Culture and Science: MARIA JOSEPHINA ARNOLDINA VAN DER HOEVEN (CDA).

Minister of Social Affairs and Employment; Minister of Public Health, Welfare and Sport (acting): AART JAN DE GEUS (CDA).

Minister of Housing, Spatial Planning and the Environment; Minister of Defence (acting): HENRICUS GREGORIUS JOZEPH (HENK) KAMP (VVD).

Minister Plenipotentiary for the Netherlands Antilles: CAREL P. DE HASETH.

Minister Plenipotentiary for Aruba: ALICIA A. TROMP-YARZAGARAY.

MINISTRIES

Office of the Prime Minister, Ministry of General Affairs: Binnenhof 20, POB 20001, 2500 EA The Hague; tel. (70) 3564100; fax (70) 3564683; internet www.minaz.nl.

Ministry of Agriculture, Nature Management and Fisheries: Bezuidenhoutseweg 73, POB 20401, 2500 EK The Hague; tel. (70) 3786868; fax (70) 3786100; internet www.minlnv.nl.

Ministry of Defence: Library, POB 20701, 2500 ES The Hague; tel. (70) 3188188; fax (70) 3187888; e-mail defensie.voorlichting@co.dnet.mindef.nl; internet www.mindef.nl.

Ministry of Economic Affairs: Bezuidenhoutseweg 30, POB 20101, 2594 EC The Hague; tel. (70) 3798911; fax (70) 3474081; e-mail info@minocw.nl; internet www.ez.nl.

Ministry of Education, Culture and Science: Europaweg 4, POB 25000, 2700 LZ Zoetermeer; tel. (79) 3232323; fax (79) 3232320; e-mail info@minocw.nl; internet www.minocw.nl.

Ministry of Finance: Korte Voorhout 7, POB 20201, 2500 EE The Hague; tel. (70) 3427540; fax (70) 3427900; internet www.minfin.nl.

Ministry of Foreign Affairs: Bezuidenhoutseweg 67, POB 20061, 2500 EB The Hague; tel. (70) 3486486; fax (70) 3484848; e-mail minbuza@buza.minbuza.nl; internet www.minbuza.nl.

Ministry of Home Affairs and Kingdom Relations: Schedelhoekshaven 200, POB 20011, 2500 EA The Hague; tel. (70) 4266426; fax (70) 3639153; e-mail info@minbzk.nl; internet www.minbzk.nl.

Ministry of Housing, Spatial Planning and the Environment: Rijnstraat 8, POB 20951, 2500 EZ, The Hague; tel. (70) 3393939; internet www.minvrom.nl.

Ministry of Immigration and Integration: operates under Ministry of Justice (see below).

Ministry of Justice: Schedelhoekshaven 100, POB 20301, 2500 EH The Hague; tel. (70) 3707911; fax (70) 3707900; e-mail voorlichting@minjus.nl; internet www.minjust.nl.

Ministry of Public Health, Welfare and Sport: Parnassusplein 5, POB 20350, 2500 EJ The Hague; tel. (70) 3407911; fax (70) 3407834; internet www.minvws.nl.

Ministry of Social Affairs and Employment: Anna van Hannoverstraat 4, POB 90801, 2509 LV The Hague; tel. (70) 3334444; fax (70) 3334033; internet www.minszw.nl.

Ministry of Transport, Public Works and Water Management: Plesmanweg 1, POB 20901, 2500 EX The Hague; tel. (70) 3516171; fax (70) 3517895; internet www.minvenw.nl.

Office of the Minister Plenipotentiary for the Netherlands Antilles: Badhuisweg 173-175, POB 90706, 2509 LS The Hague; tel. (70) 3066111; fax (70) 3066110.

Office of the Minister Plenipotentiary for Aruba: R. J. Schimmelpennincklaan 1, 2517 JN The Hague; tel. (70) 3566200; fax (70) 3451446; e-mail mail@arubahuis.nl; internet www.arubahuis.nl.

Legislature

STATEN GENERAAL
(States-General)

President of the First Chamber: GERRIT BRAKS.

President of the Second Chamber: FRANS W. WEISGLAS.

First Chamber

Election, 25 May 1999

	Seats
Christen-Democratisch Appèl	20
Volkspartij voor Vrijheid en Democratie	19
Partij van de Arbeid	15
GroenLinks	8
Democraten 66	4
Reformatorische Politieke Federatie/Gereformeerd Politiek Verbond	4
Socialistische Partij	2
Staatkundig Gereformeerde Partij	2
Independent	1
Total	75

Second Chamber

General Election, 22 January 2003

	Votes	%	Seats
Christen-Democratisch Appèl	2,763,480	28.6	44
Partij van de Arbeid	2,631,363	27.3	42
Volkspartij voor Vrijheid en Democratie	1,728,707	17.9	28
Socialistische Partij	609,723	6.3	9
Lijst Pim Fortuyn	549,975	5.7	8
GroenLinks	493,802	5.1	8
Democraten 66	393,333	4.1	6
Christen Unie	240,694	2.1	3
Staatkundig Gereformeerde Partij	150,305	1.6	2
Total (incl. others)	9,654,475	100.0	150

Advisory Councils

Raad van State (Council of State): POB 20019, 2500 EA The Hague; tel. (70) 4264426; up to 28 mems nominated by the Sovereign; advises on legislation, constitutional issues, international treaties and all matters of national importance; Vice-Pres. H. D. TJEENK WILLINK.

Sociaal-Economische Raad (Social and Economic Council): Bezuidenhoutseweg 60, 2594 AW The Hague; POB 90405, 2509 LK The Hague; tel. (70) 3499499; fax (70) 3832535; e-mail ser.info@gw.ser.nl; internet www.ser.nl; f. 1950; tripartite advisory body; to advise Govt on social and economic policy; monitors commodity and industrial boards; 33 mems, of which 11 belong to the Netherlands trade union federations, 11 belong to the employers' organizations, and 11 are independent experts in social and economic affairs appointed by the Crown; Pres. H. H. F. WIJFFELS.

Political Organizations

Centrumdemocraten (CD) (Centre Democrats): POB 84, 2501 CB The Hague; tel. (70) 3469264; internet www.xs4all.nl/centrumd/index.html; right-wing nationalist party; Chair. JOHANNES JANMAAT; Sec. W. B. SCHUURMAN; 1,500 mems.

Christen-Democratisch Appèl (CDA) (Christian Democratic Appeal): Dr Kuyperstraat 5, POB 30453, 2500 GL The Hague; tel. (70) 3424888; fax (70) 3643417; e-mail bureau@cda.nl; internet www.cda.nl; f. 1980 by merger of three 'confessional' parties; Chair. M. L. A. VAN RIJ; Parliamentary Leader JAN PIETER (PETER) BALKENENDE; 80,000 mems.

Christen Unie (Christian Union): POB 439, 3800 AK Amersfoort; tel. (33) 4226969; e-mail bureau@christenunie.nl; internet www.christenunie.nl; f. 2000 by merger of two 'evangelical' parties, the Gereformeerd Politiek Verbond (Reformed Political Asscn) and the Reformatorische Politieke Federatie (Evangelical Political Federation); interdenominational, based on biblical precepts; Chair. M. VAN DAALEN; Parliamentary Leader A. ROUVOET; c. 27,000 mems (2002).

Democraten 66 (D66): Noordwal 10, 2513 EA The Hague; tel. (70) 3566066; fax (70) 3641917; e-mail landelijk.secretariaat@D66.nl; internet www.D66.nl; f. 1966; Chair. ARNOLD PECHTOLD; Leader THOM DE GRAAF; 12,500 mems.

Fryske Nasjonale Partij (FNP) (Frisian National Party): FNP-hûs, Obrechtstrjitte 32, 8916 EN Ljouwert; tel. (58) 2131422; fax (58) 2131420; e-mail fnphus@globalxs.nl; internet www.fnp-fryslan.nl; f. 1962; promotes federalism and greater regional autonomy.

GroenLinks (The Green Left): POB 8008, 3503 RA Utrecht; tel. (30) 2399900; fax (30) 2300342; e-mail partijbureau@groenlinks.nl; internet www.groenlinks.nl; f. 1990 by merger of the Communistische Partij van Nederland, Evangelische Volkspartij, Pacifistisch Socialistische Partij and Politieke Partij Radikalen; Chair. MIRJAM DE RIJK; Parliamentary Leader FEMKE HALSEMA; 17,200 mems (August 2002).

De Groenen (Green Party): POB 1251, 3500 BG Utrecht; tel. (30) 2381700; fax (30) 2381701; e-mail info@degroenen.nl; internet www.degroenen.nl; f. 1983; Pres. JACQUES DE COO (acting).

Leefbaar Nederland (LN) (Liveable Netherlands): POB 18581, 2502 The Hague; tel. 09001419; fax (35) 6721300; e-mail info@leefbaar.nl; internet www.leefbaar-nederland.nl.

Lijst Pim Fortuyn (LPF): Albert Plesmanweg 43 M, 3088 GB Rotterdam; tel. (10) 7507050; fax (10) 7507051; e-mail info@lijst-pimfortuyn.nl; internet www.lijst-pimfortuyn.nl; f. 2002; right-wing, populist, anti-immigration; Leader MAT HERBEN.

Nieuwe Communistische Partij Nederland (NCPN) (New Communist Party of the Netherlands): Haarlemmerweg 177, 1051 LB Amsterdam; tel. (20) 6825019; fax (20) 6828276; e-mail manifest@wanadoo.nl; internet www.ncpn.nl; f. 1992.

Nieuwe Midden Partij (NMP) (New Centre Party): POB 285, 1250 AG-Laren NH; e-mail info@nmp.nl; internet www.nmp.nl; f. 1970; campaigns on economic issues; Leader MARTIN DESSING.

Partij van de Arbeid (PvdA) (Labour Party): Herengracht 54, POB 1310, 1000 BH Amsterdam; tel. (20) 5512155; fax (20) 5512250; e-mail pvda@pvda.nl; internet www.pvda.nl; f. 1946 by merger of progressive and liberal organizations; democratic socialist; Chair. RUUD KOOLE; Party Leader AD MELKERT; Parliamentary Leader WOUTER BOS; 58,527 mems (August 2002).

Socialistiese Arbeiderspartij (SAP) (Socialist Workers' Party): Sint Jacobsstraat 16, 1012 NC Amsterdam; tel. (20) 6259272; fax (20) 6203774; e-mail secretariaat@grenzloos.nl; internet www.grenzeloos.org; f. 1974; Trotskyist.

Socialistische Partij (SP) (Socialist Party): Vijverhofstraat 65, 3032 SC Rotterdam; tel. (10) 2435555; fax (10) 2435566; e-mail sp@sp.nl; internet www.sp.nl; f. 1972; Leader JAN MARIJNISSEN; 31,602 mems (August 2002).

Staatkundig Gereformeerde Partij (SGP) (Political Reformed Party): Laan van Meerdervoort 165, 2517 AZ The Hague; tel. (70) 3456226; fax (70) 3655959; e-mail partijbureau@sgp.nl; internet www.sgp.nl; f. 1918; Calvinist; female membership banned in 1993; Chair. Rev. D. J. BUDDING; Parliamentary Leader BAS J. VAN DER VLIES; Sec. A. DE BOER; 25,491 mems (2001).

Verenigde Senioren Partij (VSP) (Union Party of the Elderly): POB 26, 3100 AA Schiedam; tel. and fax (10) 4262533; internet www.vsp2001.nl; Chair. J. P. M. BOS.

Volkspartij voor Vrijheid en Democratie (VVD) (People's Party for Freedom and Democracy—Netherlands Liberal Party): POB 30836, 2500 GV The Hague; tel. (70) 3613061; fax (70) 3608276; e-mail alg.sec@vvd.nl; internet www.vvd.nl; f. 1948; advocates free enterprise, individual freedom and responsibility, but its pro-gramme also supports social security and recommends the participation of workers in profits and management; Chair. BAS EENHOORN; Parliamentary Leader GERRIT ZALM; 48,000 mems.

Diplomatic Representation

EMBASSIES IN THE NETHERLANDS

Albania: Anna Paulownastraat 109 B, 2518 BD The Hague; tel. (70) 4272101; fax (70) 4272083; e-mail albemb@euronet.nl; Ambassador QIRJAKO QIRKO.

Algeria: Van Stolklaan 1–3, 2585 JS The Hague; tel. (70) 3522954; fax (70) 3540222; Ambassador NOUREDDINE DJOUDI.

Argentina: Javastraat 20, 2585 AN The Hague; tel. (70) 3654836; fax (70) 3924900; e-mail fepbaj@mrecic.gov.ar; internet www.embassyargentina.nl; Ambassador ALBERTO LUIS DAVÉREDE.

Australia: Carnegielaan 4, 2517 KH The Hague; tel. (70) 3108200; fax (70) 3107863; internet www.australian-embassy.nl; Ambassador PETER A. HUSSIN.

Austria: van Alkemadelaan 342, 2597 AS The Hague; tel. (70) 3245470; fax (70) 3282066; e-mail austria.emb.nl@wxs.nl; Ambassador Dr JOSEPH MAGERL.

Bangladesh: Wassenaarseweg 39, 2596 CG The Hague; tel. (70) 3283722; fax (70) 3283524; e-mail bdoothague@compuserve.com; Ambassador F. A. SHAMIM AHMED.

Belarus: Anna Paulownastraat 34, 2518 BE The Hague; tel. (70) 3631566; fax (70) 3640555; Ambassador VLADIMIR GERASIMOVICH.

Belgium: Alexanderveld 97, 2585 DB The Hague; tel. (70) 3123456; fax (70) 3645579; e-mail thehague@diplobel.org; Ambassador JOHAN SWINNEN.

Bolivia: Nassaulaan 5, 2514 JS The Hague; tel. (70) 3616707; fax (70) 3620039; e-mail embolivia-lahaya@rree.gov.bo; internet www.europanas.com/Bolivia-Pbajos-en.htm; Ambassador MEDARDO NAVIA QUIROGA.

Bosnia and Herzegovina: Bezuidenhoutseweg 223, 2495 AL The Hague; tel. (70) 3588505; fax (70) 3584367; e-mail ba-emb-nl-hag@wanadoo.nl; internet www.xs4all.nl/~bih; Chargé d'affaires a.i. ZELJKO JERKIC.

Brazil: Mauritskade 19, 2514 HD The Hague; tel. (70) 3023959; fax (70) 3561273; e-mail basemb@dataweb.nl; Ambassador AFFONSO EMILIO DE ALENCASTRO MASSOT.

Bulgaria: Duinroosweg 9, 2597 KJ The Hague; tel. (70) 3503051; fax (70) 3584688; e-mail bulnedem@xs4all.nl; internet www.embassy-bulgaria.nl; Ambassador VALENTIN PORIAZOV.

Cameroon: Amaliastraat 14, 2514 JC The Hague; tel. (70) 3469715; fax (70) 3652979; internet www.cameroon-embassy.nl; Ambassador ISABELLE BASSONG.

Canada: Sophialaan 7, POB 30820, 2500 GV The Hague; tel. (70) 3111600; fax (70) 3111620; internet www.ocanada.nl; Ambassador SERGE APRIL.

Cape Verde: Burgemeester Patijnlaan 1930, 2585 CB The Hague; tel. (70) 3469623; fax (70) 3467702; e-mail embcuned@worldonline.nl; Ambassador JÚLIO VASCO DE SOUSA LOBO.

Chile: Mauritskade 51, 2514 HG The Hague; tel. (70) 3123640; fax (70) 3616227; e-mail echilenl@echile.nl; internet www.echile.nl; Ambassador CRISTIÁN DE JESÚS TOLOZA CASTILLO.

China, People's Republic: Adriaan Goekooplaan 7, 2517 JX The Hague; tel. (70) 3065061; fax (70) 3551651; Ambassador ZHU ZUSHOU.

Colombia: Groot Hertoginnelaan 14, 2517 EG The Hague; tel. (70) 3614545; fax (70) 3614636; Ambassador TELESFORO PEDRAZA ORTEGA.

Congo, Democratic Republic: Violenweg 2, 2597 KL The Hague; tel. (70) 3547904; fax (70) 3541373; Ambassador JACQUES MASANGU-A-MWANZA.

Costa Rica: Laan Copes van Cattenburg 46, 2585 GB The Hague; tel. (70) 3540780; fax (70) 3584754; e-mail embajada@embacrica.demon.nl; internet www.ambassade-costarica.nl; Ambassador GABRIELA MUÑOZ.

Croatia: Amaliastraat 16, 2514 JC The Hague; tel. (70) 3623638; fax (70) 3623195; e-mail ambassade.kroatie@worldline.nl; Ambassador JAKŠA MULJAČIĆ.

Cuba: Scheveningseweg 9, 2517 KS The Hague; tel. (70) 3606061; fax (70) 3647586; e-mail embacuba@xs4all.nl; Ambassador ELIO EDUARDO RODRÍGUEZ PERDOMO.

Cyprus: Surinamestraat 15, 2585 GG The Hague; tel. (70) 3466499; fax (70) 3924024; e-mail cyprus@xs4all.nl; Ambassador EURIPIDES L. EVRIVIADES.

Czech Republic: Paleisstraat 4, 2514 JA The Hague; tel. (70) 3469712; fax (70) 3563349; e-mail hague@embassy.mzv.cz; internet www.mfa.cz/hague; Ambassador PETR KUBERNÁT.

Denmark: Koninginnegracht 30, 2514 AB The Hague; tel. (70) 3025959; fax (70) 3025950; e-mail haaamb@um.dk; internet www.danishembassy.nl; Ambassador JOHN BERNHARD.

Ecuador: Koninginnegracht 84, 2514 AJ The Hague; tel. (70) 3463753; fax (70) 3658910; Ambassador JAIME FRANCISCO PUIG PLAZA.

Egypt: Badhuisweg 92, 2587 CL The Hague; tel. (70) 3542000; fax (70) 3543304; Ambassador MUHAMMAD NAGUIB.

Estonia: Parkstraat 15, 2514 JD The Hague; tel. (70) 3456252; fax (70) 4279243; e-mail estemb@freemail.nl; Ambassador PRIIT PALLUM.

Finland: Groot Hertoginnelaan 16, 2517 EG The Hague; tel. (70) 3469754; fax (70) 3107174; Ambassador PEKKA SÄILÄ.

France: Smidsplein 1, 2514 BT The Hague; tel. (70) 3125800; fax (70) 3725824; e-mail info@ambafrance-nl.org; internet www.ambafrance.nl; Ambassador ANNE GAZEAU-SECRET.

Germany: Groot Hertoginnelaan 18–20, 2517 EG The Hague; tel. (70) 3420600; fax (70) 3651957; e-mail ambduits@euronet.nl; internet www.duitse-ambassade.nl; Ambassador Dr EDMUND DUCKWITZ.

Ghana: Laan Copes van Cattenburch 70, 2585 GD The Hague; tel. (70) 3384384; fax (70) 3062800; e-mail info@ghanaembassy.nl; internet www.ghanaembassy.nl; Ambassador Dr GRACE AMPONSAH-ABABIO.

Greece: Amaliastraat 1, 2514 JC The Hague; tel. (70) 3638700; fax (70) 3563040; e-mail gr.emb.hague@dataweb.nl; Ambassador G. J. KAKLIKIS.

Holy See: Carnegielaan 5 (Apostolic Nunciature), 2517 KH The Hague; tel. (70) 3503363; fax (70) 3521461; Apostolic Nuncio Most Rev. FRANÇOIS BACQUÉ (Titular Archbishop of Gradisca).

Hungary: Hogeweg 14, 2585 JD The Hague; tel. (70) 3500404; fax (70) 3521749; e-mail hga@hungarianembassy.nl; internet www.hungarianembassy.nl; Ambassador TIBOR KISS.

India: Buitenrustweg 2, 2517 KD The Hague; tel. (70) 3469771; fax (70) 3617072; e-mail ambassador@indianembassy.nl; Ambassador SHYAMALA B. COWSIK.

Indonesia: Tobias Asserlaan 8, 2517 KC The Hague; tel. (70) 3108100; fax (70) 3643331; internet www.indonesia.nl; Ambassador MUHAMMAD JUSUF.

Iran: Duinweg 20–22, 2585 JX The Hague; tel. (70) 3548483; fax (70) 3503224; e-mail consulate@iranianembassy.nl; internet www.iranianembassy.nl; Ambassador HOSSEIN PANAHI AZAR.

Iraq: Johan de Wittlaan 16, 2517 JR The Hague; tel. (70) 3469683; Chargé d'affaires a. i. MAAN H. HUSSAIN.

Ireland: Dr Kuyperstraat 9, 2514 BA The Hague; tel. (70) 3630993; fax (70) 3617604; Ambassador RICHARD TOWNSEND.

Israel: Buitenhof 47, 2513 AH The Hague; tel. (70) 3760500; fax (70) 3760555; e-mail ambassade@israel.nl; internet www.israel.nl; Ambassador EITAN MARGALIT.

Italy: Alexanderstraat 12, 2514 JL The Hague; tel. (70) 3021030; fax (70) 3614932; e-mail italemb@worldonline.nl; internet www.italy.nl; Ambassador GIORGIO TESTORI.

Japan: Tobias Asserlaan 2, 2517 KC The Hague; tel. (70) 3469544; fax (70) 3106341; Ambassador HIROHARU KOIKE.

Jordan: Badhuisweg 79, 2587 CD The Hague; tel. (70) 4167200; fax (70) 4167209; e-mail jordanembassy@wanadoo.nl; internet www.jordanembassy.nl; Ambassador MAZEN M. ARMOUTI.

Kenya: Nieuwe Parklaan 21, 2597 LA The Hague; tel. (70) 3504215; fax (70) 3553594; e-mail kenre@dataweb.nl; internet www.geocities.com/ResearchTriangle/Node/9827; Ambassador LEONARD NJOGU NGAITHE.

Korea, Republic: Velengde Tolweg 8, 2517 JV The Hague; tel. (70) 3586076; fax (70) 3504712; Ambassador KIM YONG-KYOO.

Kuwait: Carnegielaan 9, 2517 KH The Hague; tel. (70) 3603813; fax (70) 3924588; internet www.kuwaitembassy.nl; Ambassador ABDULMOHSIN AL-DUAIJ.

Latvia: Balistraat 88, 2585 XX The Hague; tel. (70) 3063934; fax (70) 3062858; e-mail embassy.netherlands@mfa.gov.nl; Ambassador KARLIS EIHENBAUMS.

Lebanon: Frederikstraat 2, 2514 LK The Hague; tel. (70) 3658906; fax (70) 3620779; e-mail amb.lib@wanadoo.nl; Ambassador MICHEL EL-KHOURY.

Libya: 15 Parkweg, 2585 JH The Hague; tel. (70) 355886; fax (70) 3559075; Sec. People's Bureau HAMED AL-HOUDERI.

Luxembourg: Nassaulaan 8, 2514 JS The Hague; tel. (70) 3647589; fax (70) 3462000; Ambassador JEAN GRAFF.

Macedonia, former Yugoslav republic: Laan van Meerdervoort 50c, 2517 AM The Hague; tel. (70) 4274464; fax (70) 4274469; e-mail repmak@wanadoo.nl; Ambassador MILIJANA DANEVSCA.

Malaysia: Rustenburgweg 2, 2517 KE The Hague; tel. (70) 3506506; fax (70) 3506536; e-mail malaysia@euronet.nl; Ambassador NOOR FARIDA BINTI MOHD ARIFFIN.

Mexico: Burgermeester Patijnlaan 1930, 2585 BC The Hague; tel. (70) 3602900; fax (70) 3560543; e-mail embamex@bart.nl; internet www.embamex-nl.com; Ambassador SANTIAGO OÑATE.

Morocco: Oranjestraat 9, 2514 JB The Hague; tel. (70) 3469617; fax (70) 3614503; Ambassador NOURDINE BENOMAR ALAMI.

New Zealand: Carnegielaan 10, 2517 KH The Hague; tel. (70) 3469324; fax (70) 3632983; e-mail nzemb@bart.nl; Ambassador DAVID PAYTON.

Nicaragua: Laan Cope van Cattenburch 84, 2585 GD The Hague; tel. (70) 3225063; fax (70) 3508331; Ambassador JOSÉ FRANCISCO ARGÜELLO GÓMEZ.

Nigeria: Wagenaarweg 5, 2597 LL The Hague; tel. (70) 3501703; fax (70) 3551110; e-mail nigembassy@nigerianembassy.nl; internet www.nigerianembassy.nl; Ambassador Dr OLATOKUNBO AYOKA AWOLOWO-DOSUMU.

Norway: Lange Vijverberg 11, 2513 AC The Hague; tel. (70) 3117611; fax (70) 3659630; Ambassador JAN FLATLA.

Oman: Koninginnegracht 27, 2514 AB The Hague; tel. (70) 3615800; fax (70) 3605364; Ambassador KHADIJA HASSAN SALMAN AL-LAWATI.

Pakistan: Amaliastraat 8, 2514 JC The Hague; tel. (70) 3648948; fax (70) 3106047; e-mail parepnl@planet.nl; internet www.embassyofpakistan.com; Ambassador MUSTAFA KAMAL KAZI.

Peru: Nassauplein 4, 2585 EA The Hague; tel. (70) 3653500; fax (70) 3651929; e-mail embperu@bart.nl; internet www.europanas.com/Peru-PBajos-en.htm; Ambassador JULIO BALBUENA LÓPEZ-ALFARO.

Philippines: Laan Copes van Cattenburch 125, 2585 EZ The Hague; tel. (70) 3464820; fax (70) 3560030; e-mail ph@bart.nl; Ambassador ROMEO A. ARGUELLES.

Poland: Alexanderstraat 25, 2514 JM The Hague; tel. (70) 3602806; fax (70) 3602810; e-mail ambhaga@polamb.nl; internet www.polamb.nl; Ambassador JAN MICHALOWSKI.

Portugal: Bazarstraat 21, 2518 AG The Hague; tel. (70) 3630217; fax (70) 3615589; e-mail am.portugal@wxs.nl; Ambassador JOÃO MANUEL GUERRA SALGUEIRO.

Romania: Catsheuvel 55, 2517 KA The Hague; tel. (70) 3543796; fax (70) 3541587; e-mail sicrned@tip.nl; internet home.tiscali.nl/romanianembassy; Ambassador IULIAN BUGA.

Russia: Andries Bickerweg 2, 2517 JP The Hague; tel. (70) 3451300; fax (70) 3617960; e-mail ambrucon@ambru.nl; internet members.tripod.com/ambrunl/start_nl.htm; Ambassador ALEKSANDR G. KHODAKOV.

Saudi Arabia: Alexanderstraat 19, 2514 JM The Hague; tel. (70) 3614391; fax (70) 3630348; Ambassador ABDELMUHSEN MOHAMMED S. AL-BALLAA.

Serbia and Montenegro: Groot Hertoginnelaan 30, 2517 EG The Hague; tel. (70) 3632397; fax (70) 3602421; e-mail yuambanl@bart.nl; Ambassador MAJA MITROVIĆ.

Slovakia: Parkweg 1, 2585 JG The Hague; tel. (70) 4167777; fax (70) 4167783; e-mail embslow@bart.nl; Ambassador JÁN KUDERJAVÝ.

South Africa: Wassenaarseweg 40, 2596 CJ The Hague; tel. (70) 3924501; fax (70) 3460669; e-mail info@zuidafrika.nl; internet www.zuidafrika.nl; Ambassador PRISCILLA JANA.

Spain: Lange Voorhout 50, 2514 EG The Hague; tel. (70) 3024999; fax (70) 3617959; e-mail ambassade.spanje@worldonline.nl; internet www.users.bart.nl/~claboral; Ambassador CARLOS MANUEL DE BENAVIDES SALAS.

Sri Lanka: Jacob de Graefflaan 2, 2517 JM The Hague; tel. (70) 3655910; fax (70) 3465596; e-mail nlslmesn@wanadoo.nl; internet www.srilankanembassynl.org; Ambassador MADDUMAGE EBERT LIONEL FERNANDO.

Sudan: Laan Copes van Cattenburch 81, 2585 EW The Hague; tel. (70) 3605300; fax (70) 3617975; e-mail sudani@worldonline.nl; internet www.Sudani@Wanadoo.nl; Ambassador ABDELHALIM B. FATIH.

Suriname: Alexander Gogelweg 2, 2517 JH The Hague; tel. (70) 3650844; fax (70) 3617445; Ambassador E. S. R. AMANH.

Sweden: Burg. van Karnebeeklaan 6A, POB 85601, 2508 CH The Hague; tel. (70) 4120200; fax (70) 4120211; e-mail ambassaden

.haag@foreign.ministry.se; internet www.swedenembnl.org; Ambassador BJÖRN INGVAR SKALA.

Switzerland: Lange Voorhout 42, 2514 EE The Hague; tel. (70) 3642831; fax (70) 3561238; e-mail vertretung@hay.rep.admin.ch; internet www.eda.admin.ch/denhaag; Ambassador Dr WILHELM SCHMID.

Thailand: Laan Copes van Cattenburch 123, 2585 EZ The Hague; tel. (70) 3450632; fax (70) 3451929; Ambassador VASIN TEERAVECHYAN.

Tunisia: Gentsestraat 98, 2587 HX The Hague; tel. (70) 3512251; fax (70) 3514323; Ambassador EMNA AOULJ.

Turkey: Jan Evertstraat 15, 2514 BS The Hague; tel. (70) 3604912; fax (70) 3617969; e-mail turkije@dataweb.nl; Ambassador AYDAN KARAHAN.

Ukraine: Groot Hertoginnelaan 26, 2517 EG The Hague; fax (70) 3615565; e-mail embukr@wks.nl; Chargé d'affaires a.i. ANATOLI BURMAKOV.

United Kingdom: Lange Voorhout 10, 2514 ED The Hague; tel. (70) 4270427; fax (70) 4270345; internet www.britain.nl; Ambassador Sir COLIN BUDD.

USA: Lange Voorhout 102, 2514 EJ The Hague; tel. (70) 3109209; fax (70) 3614688; e-mail jbutterman@usemb.nl; internet www .usemb.nl; Ambassador CLIFFORD SOBEL.

Uruguay: Mauritskade 33, 2514 HD The Hague; tel. (70) 3609815; fax (70) 3562826; e-mail uruholan@wxs.nl; Ambassador OCTAVIO BRUGNINI GARCÍA LAGOS.

Venezuela: Nassaulaan 2, 2514 JS The Hague; tel. (70) 3651256; fax (70) 3656954; e-mail embvene@xs4all.nl; Ambassador NORMAN RAFAEL PINO DE LION.

Viet Nam: Prinses Mariestraat 6A, 2514 KE The Hague; tel. (70) 3648917; fax (70) 3648656; Ambassador DINH HOANG THANG.

Yemen: Surinamestraat 9, 2585 GG The Hague; tel. (70) 3653936; fax (70) 3563312; Ambassador AMAT AL-ALIM ALI AS-SOSWA.

Judicial System

Justices and judges must have graduated in law at a Dutch university, and are nominated for life by the Crown. The justices of the Supreme Court are nominated from a list of three compiled by the Second Chamber of the States-General.

SUPREME COURT

De Hoge Raad der Nederlanden
POB 20303, 2500 EH The Hague; tel. (70) 3611311; fax (70) 3658700. f. 1838; For appeals in cassation against decisions of courts of lower jurisdiction. As a court of first instance, the Supreme Court tries offences committed in their official capacity by members of the States-General and Ministers. Dealing with appeals in cassation a court is composed of five or, in more straightforward cases, of three justices (Raadsheren).

President of the Supreme Court: W. E. HAAK.

Procurator-General: TH. B. TEN KATE.

Secretary of the Court: W. J. C. M. VAN NISPEN TOT SEVENAER.

COURTS OF APPEAL

Gerechtshoven: Five courts: Amsterdam, Arnhem, 's-Hertogenbosch, Leeuwarden, The Hague. A court is composed of three judges (Raadsheren); appeal is from decisions of the District Courts of Justice. Fiscal Divisions (Belastingkamers) of the Courts of Appeal deal with appeals against decisions relating to the enforcement of the fiscal laws (administrative jurisdiction). The court of Arnhem has a Tenancy Division (Pachtkamer), composed of three judges and two assessors (a tenant and a landlord), and a Penitentiary Division (Penitentiaire Kamer), composed of three judges and two experts. The Tenancy Division hears appeals from decisions of all Canton Tenancy Divisions. The Penitentiary Division hears appeals against refusals of release on license, which is usually granted after two-thirds of a prison sentence longer than one year, unless there are special objections from the Minister of Justice. A Companies Division (Ondernemingskamer) is attached to the court at Amsterdam, consisting of three judges and two experts as assessors.

DISTRICT COURTS OF JUSTICE

Arrondissementsrechtbanken: There are 19 courts for important civil and penal cases and for appeals from decisions of the Canton Judges. A court is composed of three judges (Rechter); no jury; summary jurisdiction in civil cases by the President of the Court; simple penal cases, including economic offences, generally by a single judge (Politierechter). Offences committed by juveniles are (with certain exceptions) tried by a specialized judge (Kinderrechter), who is also competent to take certain legal steps when the upbringing of a juvenile is endangered. Economic offences, and in particular environmental offences, are also dealt with by a specialized judge sitting alone.

CANTON COURTS

Kantongerechten: There are 62 courts for civil and penal cases of minor importance. A court consists of a single judge, the Canton Judge (Kantonrechter). Each Canton Court has a Tenancy Division (Pachtkamer), presided over by the Canton Judge who is assisted by two assessors (a landlord and a tenant).

ADMINISTRATIVE COURTS

The administrative courts regulate relations between the authorities and citizens according to the provisions of the General Administrative Law Act. The majority of cases are heard by the Administrative Law Sections of the District Courts, while appeals are heard by the Administrative Law Division of the Council of State (Afdeling Bestuursrechtspraak van de Raad van State), which also acts as the court of sole and last instance in the majority of cases concerning education, the environment and spatial planning. In addition, cases relating to certain areas of administrative law are heard by the following bodies:

Central Raad van Beroep (Central Appeals Council): Utrecht; hears appeals against decisions of the District Courts in matters concerning the public service and social security.

College van Beroep voor het Bedrijfsleven (Trade and Industry Appeals Tribunal): The Hague; hears in first and last instance appeals against decisions enforcing socio-economic and agricultural legislation made by certain bodies, such as regulatory bodies and Chambers of Commerce, and by certain ministers.

Administration Law Section, Aliens Division, District Court of The Hague: court of sole and last instance in cases involving immigration; brs in Zwolle, Den Bosch, Amsterdam and Haarlem. The introduction of a limited right of further appeal is pending.

Tariefcommissie (Tariff Commission): court of sole and last instance for all customs and excise disputes.

Religion

About one-third of the population are Roman Catholics and about one-quarter are Protestants. In 1998 it was estimated that some 4.4% of the population were Muslim.

CHRISTIANITY

Raad van Kerken in Nederland (Council of Churches in the Netherlands): Kon. Wilhelminalaan 5, 3818 HN Amersfoort; tel. (33) 4633844; e-mail rvk@raadvankerken.nl; internet www .raadvankerken.nl; f. 1968; 13 mem. churches; Pres. Prof. Dr A. H. C. VAN ELJK; Gen. Sec. Drs H. J. BAKKER.

The Roman Catholic Church
The Netherlands comprises one archdiocese and six dioceses. At 31 December 2000 there were an estimated 5,203,028 adherents in the country.

Bishops' Conference
Nederlandse Bisschoppenconferentie, Biltstraat 121, POB 13049, 3507 LA Utrecht; tel. (30) 2334244; fax (30) 2332103; e-mail secrbk@ rkk.nl; internet www.omroep.nl/rkk.
f. 1986; Pres. Cardinal Dr ADRIANUS J. SIMONIS (Archbishop of Utrecht).

Archbishop of Utrecht: Cardinal Dr ADRIANUS J. SIMONIS, Aartsbisdom, Maliebaan 40, POB 14019, 3508 SB Utrecht; tel. (30) 2338030; fax (30) 2311962; e-mail secretariaat@aartsbisdom.nl; internet www.de-oase.nl.

Protestant Churches

Christelijke Gereformeerde Kerken in Nederland (Christian Reformed Churches in the Netherlands): Vijftien Morgen, POB 334, 3900 AH Veenendaal; tel. (318) 582350; e-mail lkb@cgk.nl; internet www.cgk.nl; f. 1834; Relations Dir Rev. J. G. H. VAN DER VINNE; c. 73,400 mems; 180 churches.

First Church of Christ, Scientist: c/o ACOP, Andries Bickerweg 1B, 2517 JP The Hague; tel. (70) 3208861; e-mail fccs.denhaag@ 12move.nl; churches at Amsterdam, Haarlem and The Hague.

Deutsche Evangelische Gemeinde (German Evangelical Church): Bleijenburg 3B, 2511 VC, The Hague; tel. (70) 3465727; fax (70) 3649165; Leaders Pastor D. BLAFFERT, Pastor W. BLAFFERT.

Dutch Mennonites: Algemene Doopsgezinde Sociëteit, Singel 454, 1017 AW Amsterdam; tel. (20) 6230914; fax (20) 6278919; e-mail info@ads.nl; internet www.doopsgezind.nl; f. 1811; Pres. ANNE S. DE JONG; Sec.-Gen. H. W. STENVERS; 11,000 mems; 121 parishes.

Evangelische Broedergemeente (Hernhutters): Annastr. 5C, 3062 KA Rotterdam; tel. (10) 4049224; f. 1746; Pres. Pastor J. W. TL. RAPPARLIÉ; 3,000 mems in Holland; six parishes.

Hersteld Apostolische Zendingkerk (Restored Apostolic Missionary Church): Hogerbeetsstraat 32, 2242 TR Wassenaar; tel. (70) 5113995; fax (70) 5113995; e-mail s.de.jong.hazk@hazknederland .org; internet www.hazknederland.org; f. 1863; Pres. Apostle for the Netherlands H. F. RIJNDERS; Sec. J. L. M. STRAETEMANS; 500 mems; 10 parishes.

Remonstrantse Broederschap (Remonstrant Brotherhood): Nieuwe Gracht 27A, 3512 LC Utrecht; tel. (30) 2316970; fax (30) 2311055; e-mail info@remonstranten.org; internet www .remonstranten.org; f. 1619; Pres. Dr W. VAN DER BERG; Gen. Sec. M. A. BOSMAN-HUIZINGA; 10,000 mems; 46 parishes.

Samen op Weg-Kerken (Uniting Protestant Churches): Joseph Haydnlaan 2A, POB 8504, 3503 RM Utrecht; tel. (30) 8801415; fax (30) 8801445; e-mail info@sowkerken.nl; internet www.sowkerken .nl; comprises three churches that were in the process of uniting in early 2002.

> **Evangelisch-Lutherse Kerk** (Evangelical Lutheran Church): Joseph Haydnlaan 2A, POB 8399, 3503 RJ Utrecht; tel. (30) 8801441; fax (30) 8801447; c. 15,000 mems; 55 parishes.

> **De Gereformeerde Kerken in Nederland** (The Reformed Churches in the Netherlands): Joseph Haydnlaan 2A, POB 8399, 3503 RJ Utrecht; tel. (30) 8801441; fax (30) 8801447; e-mail ldc-synodesecretariaat@sowkerken.nl; f. 1892; Calvinist; has a General Synod which is elected every two years by the 13 Particular (district) Synods; 842 churches, 1,228 officiating ministers, 676,000 mems.

> **Nederlandse Hervormde Kerk** (Netherlands Reformed Church): Joseph Haydnlaan 2A, POB 8399, 3503 RJ Utrecht; tel. (30) 8801441; fax (30) 8801447; e-mail LDC-synodesecretariaat@ sowkerken.nl; was from 16th to 18th century the State Church. Its nine church provinces are sub-divided into 75 districts, 144 fraternals and 1,400 parishes, under the jurisdiction of the General Synod; Sec.-Gen. Rev. Dr B. PLAISIER; 2.3m. mems.

Unie van Baptistengemeenten in Nederland (Union of Baptist Churches in The Netherlands): Biltseweg 10, 3735 MC Bosch en Duin; tel. (30) 2284457; fax (30) 2251798; e-mail unie-baptisten@ solcon.nl; f. 1881; Pres. J. DE BOER; Treasurer A. VAN DEN HOEF; 12,127 mems.

Other Christian Churches

Anglikaans Kerkgenootschap (Anglican Church): Riouwstraat 2, 2585 HA The Hague; tel. (70) 3555359; e-mail churchoffice@ stjohn-stphilip.org; internet www.stjohn-stphilip.org; f. 1698; British Chaplain Rev. MICHAEL SANDERS.

Katholiek Apostolische Gemeenten (Catholic Apostolic Church): 1e De Riemerstraat 3, 2513 CT The Hague; tel. (70) 3555018; f. 1867; seven parishes in the Netherlands and three in Belgium.

Oud-Katholieke Kerk van Nederland (Old Catholic Church): Kon. Wilhelminalaan 3, 3818 HN Amersfoort; tel. (33) 4620875; fax (33) 4630442; e-mail info@okkn.nl; internet www.okkn.nl; f. 1723; in the Netherlands with Jansenist influence; refuses to accept papal infallibility and other new dogmas of the Roman Catholic Church; full communion with the Anglican Churches since 1931; Leader Archbishop of Utrecht Mgr J. A. O. L. VERCAMMEN (18 parishes); Bishop of Haarlem Mgr Dr J. L. WIRIX-SPEETJENS (11 parishes); Bishop of Deventer (vacant); 10,000 mems; also churches in Europe and USA.

Vrij-Katholieke Kerk (Liberal Catholic Church): Goudvinklaan 92, 3722 VE Bilthoven; e-mail jph.draaisma@12move.nl; internet www.lcc.cc; f. 1916; Bishop Rt Rev. J. PH. DRAAISMA; 12 congregations; 35 priests; 1,400 mems.

JUDAISM

Portugees-Israëlietisch Kerkgenootschap (Portuguese-Israelite Federation): mr Visserplein 3, 1011 RD Amsterdam; tel. (20)

6245351; fax (20) 6254680; e-mail pig-amsterdam@euronet.nl; Pres. R. S. CORTISSOS.

BAHÁ'Í FAITH

National Spiritual Assembly: Riouwstraat 27, 2585 GR The Hague; tel. (70) 3554017; fax (70) 3506161; e-mail nsa@bahai.nl; internet www.bahai.nl; f. 1962; mems resident in 190 locations (1998).

The Press

Newspapers first appeared in Amsterdam in the early seventeenth century and were soon established in other cities. The Constitution guarantees the freedom of the press.

PRINCIPAL DAILIES

Alkmaar

Dagblad Kennemerland: POB 2, 1800 AA Alkmaar; tel. (70) 5196196; fax (70) 5113295; evening.

Dagblad voor West-Friesland: POB 2, 1800 AA Alkmaar; tel. (70) 5196196; fax (70) 5113295; evening.

Enkhuiser Courant: POB 2, 1800 AA Alkmaar; tel. (70) 5196196; fax (70) 5113295; evening.

Noordhollands Dagblad: POB 2, 1800 AA Alkmaar; tel. (72) 5196196; fax (72) 5126183; f. 1799; morning; Editor R. M. A. BROWN; circ. 155,000 (2001).

Alphen aan den Rijn

Rijn en Gouwe: POB 1, 2400 AA Alphen a/d Rijn; tel. (172) 487444; fax (172) 487478; f. 1871; morning; Editor L. M. HESKES; circ. 40,000 (2001).

Amersfoort

Amersfoortse Courant: POB 316, 3840 AH Harderwijk; tel. (33) 4647911; fax (33) 4647251; e-mail redacticac@un.wegener.nl; internet www.amersfoortsecourant.nl; f. 1887; evening; Editor-in-Chief J. J. LODEWIJKS; circ. 33,969 (2001).

Veluws Dagblad: POB 316, 3840 AH Harderwijk; tel. (33) 413072; fax (33) 415579; e-mail redactievd@un.wegener.nl; evening; Editor-in-Chief J. J. LODEWIJKS; circ. 11,582 (2001).

Amsterdam

Het Financieele Dagblad (Financial Daily): 85–87 Weesperstraat, POB 216, 1000 AE Amsterdam; tel. (20) 5928888; fax (20) 5928600; e-mail klantenservice@hfd.nl; internet www.fd.nl; f. 1796; morning; Editor FRED BAKKER; circ. 66,000.

Het Parool: Wibautstraat 131, POB 433, 1000 AK Amsterdam; tel. (20) 5629333; fax (20) 6681608; e-mail redactie@parool.nl; internet www.parool.nl; f. 1940; evening; Editors F. CAMPAGNE, ERIK VAN GRUIJTHUIJSEN; circ. 95,120.

De Telegraaf: POB 376, 1000 EB Amsterdam; tel. (20) 5859111; fax (20) 5858017; e-mail redactie@telegraaf.nl; internet www.telegraaf .nl; f. 1893; morning; Editors E. BOS, J. OLDE KALTER; circ. 810,000 (2001).

Trouw (Loyalty): POB 859, 1000 AW Amsterdam; tel. (20) 5629444; fax (20) 6681608; e-mail redactie@trouw.nl; f. 1943; morning; Editor F. VAN EXTER; circ. 130,000.

De Volkskrant (The People's Journal): POB 1002, 1000 BA Amsterdam; tel. (20) 5626222; fax (20) 5622448; e-mail promotie@ volkskrant.nl; internet www.volkskrant.nl; f. 1919; morning; Editor P. I. BROERTJES; circ. 372,100.

Apeldoorn

Apeldoornse Courant: POB 99, 7300 AB Apeldoorn; tel. (55) 5388388; fax (55) 5388200; internet www.apeldoornsecourant.nl; f. 1903; evening; Chief Editor D. W. H. VAN DER MOER; circ. 40,300.

Arnhemse Courant: POB 99, 7300 AB Apeldoorn; tel. (55) 5388388; fax (55) 5388200; internet www.arnhemsecourant.nl; f. 1814; evening; Editor G. DIELESSEN; circ. 31,400.

Deventer Dagblad: POB 99, 7300 AB Apeldoorn; tel. (55) 5388388; fax (55) 5388200; internet www.deventerdagblad.nl; f. 1869; Editor L. ENTHOVEN; circ. 52,400.

Het Gelders Dagblad: POB 99, 7300 AB Apeldoorn; tel. (55) 5388388; fax (55) 5388200; internet www.geldersdagblad.nl; f. 1903; evening; Editor Dr G. BIELDEREMAN.

Reformatorisch Dagblad: POB 670, 7300 AR Apeldoorn; tel. (55) 5390222; fax (55) 5412288; e-mail redactie@refdag.nl; internet www

.refdag.nl; f. 1971; evening; Editor-in-Chief C. S. L. Janse; Man. Dir J. Koetsier; circ. 58,000 (2001).

Assen

Drentse en Asser Courant: POB 36, 9400 AA Assen; tel. (592) 329500; fax (592) 329579; f. 1823; evening; Editor G. Vogelaar.

Barneveld

Barneveldse Krant: Marconistraat 33, POB 67, 3770 AB Barneveld; tel. (342) 494911; fax (342) 494240; e-mail e.v.d.brink@bdu.nl; internet www.barneveldsekrant.nl; f. 1871; evening; Editor J. van Ginkel; circ. 10,800.

Nederlands Dagblad: POB 111, 3770 AC Barneveld; tel. (342) 411711; fax (342) 411611; e-mail redactie@ud.nl; f. 1944; morning; Editors J. P. de Vries, P. A. Bergwerff; circ. 31,000.

Breda

BN/De Stem (The Voice): POB 3229, 4800 MB Breda; tel. (76) 5312311; fax (76) 5312355; e-mail l.krijneni@uitg-zwn.nl; internet www.bndestem.nl; f. 1860; morning; Man. Dir A. A. M. Verrest; circ. 145,769.

Delft

Delftsche Courant: POB 18, 2600 AA Delft; tel. (70) 3190911; internet www.delftschecourant.nl; evening; circ. 11,151 (2001).

Deventer

Gelders-Overijsselse Courant: POB 18, 7400 AA Deventer; tel. (570) 648444; fax (570) 621324; evening.

Dordrecht

De Dordtenaar: POB 54, 3300 AB Dordrecht; tel. (78) 6324711; fax (78) 6324729; e-mail redactie@dordtenaar.nl; f. 1946; morning; Editor H. Kerstiens; circ. 38,000.

Eindhoven

Eindhovens Dagblad: POB 534, 5600 AM Eindhoven; tel. (40) 2336336; fax (40) 2436954; e-mail redactie@eindhovensdagblad.nl; internet www.eindhovensdagblad.nl; circ. 130,000 (2001).

Enschede

Dagblad Tubantia: POB 28, 7500 AA Enschede; tel. (53) 4842842; fax (53) 4842230; internet www.tctubantia.nl; f. 1872; evening; Editor G. Driehuis; circ. 152,600 (incl. *De Twentsche Courant Tubantia* below).

De Twentsche Courant Tubantia: POB 28, 7500 AA Enschede; tel. (53) 4842842; fax (53) 4842230; f. 1844; circ. see Dagblad Tubantia above.

Groningen

Dagblad van het Nouden: POB 60, 9700 MC Groningen; tel. (50) 5844844; fax (50) 5844109; e-mail qijs.lensink@hazewinkel.nl; internet www.dvhn.nl; f. 1888; evening; Editors G. J. Haan, L. Bonjee; circ. 180,000.

Haarlem

Haarlems Dagblad: POB 507, 2003 PA Haarlem; tel. (23) 5150150; fax (23) 5310296; e-mail redactie.hd@damiate.hdc.nl; internet www.haarlemsdagblad.nl; f. 1656; evening; Editor J. G. C. Majoor; circ. 45,439 (2001).

IJmuider Courant: POB 507, 2003 PA Haarlem; tel. (23) 5150150; fax (23) 5317337; internet www.ijmuidercourant.nl; evening.

The Hague

Haagsche Courant: POB 16050, 2500 AA The Hague; tel. (70) 3190911; fax (70) 3906447; e-mail redactie@haagschecourant.nl; internet www.haagschecourant.nl; f. 1883; evening; Editor J. P. ter Horst; circ. 125,000.

Nederlandse Staatscourant: Chr. Plantijnstraat 2, POB 20020, 2500 EA The Hague; tel. (70) 3789422; fax (70) 3855505; e-mail staatscourant@sdu.nl; internet www.sdu.nl/staatscourant/vandaag; f. 1814; morning; Editor A. M. den Haan; circ. 14,600.

Heerlen

Limburgs Dagblad: POB 3100, 6401 DP Heerlen; tel. (45) 739911; fax (45) 5739264; internet www.limburgsdagblad.nl; f. 1918; morning; Editor R. A. M. Brown; circ. 70,748 (2001).

's-Hertogenbosch

Brabants Dagblad: POB 235, 5201 HB 's-Hertogenbosch; tel. (73) 157157; fax (73) 132229; internet www.brabantsdagblad.nl; f. 1771; morning; Editor T. van der Meulen; circ. 158,290 (2001).

Eindhovens Dagblad: POB 534, 5600 AM Eindhoven; tel. (40) 2336336; fax (40) 2436954; e-mail redactie@eindhovensdagblad.nl; internet www.eindhovensdagblad.nl; circ. 130,000 (2001).

Hilversum

De Gooi en Eemlander: POB 15, 1200 AA Hilversum; tel. (35) 6257911; fax (35) 6257246; f. 1871; evening; Editor H. van Zenderen; circ. 39,447 (2001).

Leeuwarden

Friesch Dagblad: POB 412, 8901 BE Leeuwarden; tel. (58) 2987654; fax (58) 987540; e-mail fd@frieschdagblad.nl; f. 1903; evening; Editor L. Kooistra; circ. 22,000 (2001).

Leeuwarder Courant: POB 394, 8901 BD Leeuwarden; tel. (58) 2845845; fax (58) 2845209; e-mail redactie@leeuwarder_courant.nl; internet www.leeuwarder_courant.nl; f. 1752; evening; Editors R. Mulder, P. Sypersma; circ. 112,000.

Leiden

Leidsch Dagblad: POB 54, 2300 AB Leiden; tel. (71) 5356356; fax (71) 5321429; internet www.leidschdagblad.nl; f. 1860; evening; Editor J. G. C. Majoor; circ. 41,464 (2001).

Maastricht

Dagblad De Limburger: Mercator 3, 6135 KW Sittard; tel. (6) 4116300; fax (46) 4116310; e-mail redactie@limburger.nl; internet www.limburger.nl; f. 1845; morning; Editor B. Brouwers; circ. 190,000.

Nijmegen

De Gelderlander: Voorstadslaan 2, POB 36, 6500 DA Nijmegen; tel. (24) 3650611; fax (24) 3650209; e-mail redactie@gelderlander.nl; internet www.gelderlander.nl; f. 1848; morning; Editor U. D. Jonker; circ. 164,300 (2001).

Purmurend

Nieuwe Noordhollandse Courant (NNC): POB 14, 1442 BZ Purmurend; tel. (299) 432071; fax (299) 430205.

Roosendaal

Brabants Nieuwsblad: POB 1052, 4700 BB Roosendaal; tel. (165) 578888; fax (165) 578149; f. 1862; morning; Editor G. Bielderman; circ. 55,000.

Rotterdam

Algemeen Dagblad: Marten Meesweg 35, POB 8983, 3009 TC Rotterdam; tel. (10) 4066206; fax (10) 4066958; e-mail ad@ad.nl; internet www.ad.nl; f. 1946; morning; Editor O. Garschagen; circ. 380,000 (2001).

NRC Handelsblad: PCM Landelijke Dagbladen B.V., Marten Meesweg 35, POB 8987, 3009 TH Rotterdam; tel. (10) 4066111; fax (10) 4066967; e-mail nrc@nrc.nl; internet www.nrc.nl; f. 1970; evening; Editor F. E. Jensma; circ. 271,532 (2001).

Rotterdams Dagblad: POB 1162, 3000 BD Rotterdam; tel. (10) 4004296; fax (10) 4128449; e-mail digitaal@luna.nl; internet www.rotterdamsdagblad.nl; f. 1991; evening; Editor F. Eckhardt; circ. 102,222 (2001).

Utrecht

Utrechts Nieuwsblad: POB 500, 3990 DM Houten; tel. (30) 6399911; fax (30) 6399226; e-mail info@wumn.wegener.nl; internet www.utrechtsnieuwsblad.nl; f. 1993; evening; Chief Editor R. van Zanten; circ. 86,840 (2001).

Vlissingen

Provinciale Zeeuwse Courant: POB 18, 4380 AA Vlissingen; tel. (118) 484000; fax (118) 472404; internet www.pzc.nl; f. 1758; morning; Editor A. L. Oosthoek; circ. 61,495 (2001).

Zwolle

Zwolse Courant: POB 29, 8000 AA Zwolle; tel. (38) 4275275; fax (38) 4219453; e-mail zwolsecourant@wxs.nl; internet www.zwolsecourant.nl; f. 1790; morning; Editor J. Bartelds; circ. 70,400.

SELECTED WEEKLIES

Adformatie: POB 75462, 1070 AL Amsterdam; tel. (20) 5733644; fax (20) 6793581; e-mail redactie@adformatie.nl; internet www .adformatie.nl; advertising, marketing and media; circ. 35,000.

Aktueel: POB 94210, 1090 GE Amsterdam; tel. (20) 5979600; fax (20) 5979682.

Avrobode: s'-Gravelandseweg 52, 1217 ET Hilversum; tel. (35) 6717911; fax (35) 717443; publ. by Algemene Omroepvereniging; radio and TV guide; circ. 791,986.

Boerderij: Hanzestraat 1, POB 4, 7000 BA Doetinchem; tel. (314) 349446; fax (314) 344397; e-mail boerderij@reedbusiness.nl; internet www.boerderij.nl; f. 1915; farming; Editor-in-Chief MARCEL HENST; circ. 65,000.

Donald Duck: Haaksbergsweg 75, 1101 BR Amsterdam; tel. (20) 4300300; fax (20) 4300315; f. 1952; children's interest; weekly; Publisher A. VAN DER AA; circ. 62,784.

Elsevier: POB 152, 1000 AD Amsterdam; tel. (20) 5159222; fax (20) 5159900; f. 1945; current affairs; Chief Editor H. J. SCHOO; circ. 135,000.

Fancy: POB 1610, 2130 JA Hoofddorp; tel. (23) 5565117; fax (23) 5565116; e-mail fancy@sanoma-uitgevers; internet www.fancy.nl; teenage girls interest; circ. 120,000.

HP/De Tijd (The Times): Amsterdam; tel. (20) 5734811; fax (20) 5734406; f. 1845 as daily; changed to weekly in 1974; Christian progressive; current affairs; Dir A. VISSER; circ. 37,580.

Libelle: POB 1742, 2130 JC Hoofddorp; tel. (23) 5564002; fax (23) 5564003; e-mail f.stuy@sanoma-uitgevers.nl; internet www.libelle .nl; f. 1934; women's interest; Editor-in-Chief FRANSKA STUY; circ. 670,000.

Margriet: POB 1640, 2130 JA Hoofddorp; tel. (23) 5564200; e-mail redactie@margriet.nl; internet www.margriet.nl; f. 1939; women's interest; Dir A. VISSER; circ. 499,868.

Mikro-Gids: Zeverijnstraat 6, 1216 GK Hilversum; tel. (35) 6726751; fax (35) 6726752; f. 1974; radio and TV guide; Dir C. ABBENHUIS; circ. 468,280.

NCRV-Gids: POB 25900, 1202 HW Hilversum; tel. (35) 6726801; fax (35) 6726863; f. 1966; publ. by Nederlandse Christelijke Radio Vereniging; radio and TV guide; Dir C. ABBENHUIS; circ. 419,363.

Nederlands Tijdschrift voor Geneeskunde (Dutch Journal of Medicine): POB 75971, 1070 AZ Amsterdam; tel. (20) 6620150; fax (20) 6735481; e-mail redacfie@ntvg.nl; internet ntvg.nl; f. 1856; Editors Prof. Dr J. VAN GIJN, Prof. Dr H. G. M. ROOIJMANS; Exec. Editors Dr W. HART, Prof. Dr A. J. P. M. OVERBEKE; circ. 30,000.

The Netherlander: Het Financieele Dagblad BV, Weesperstraat 85–87, 1018 VN Amsterdam; tel. (20) 5574511; fax (20) 5928600; internet www.netherlander.com; f. 1992; publ. by *Het Financieele Dagblad*; English-language financial and business news.

Nieuwe Revu: POB 1750, 2130 JD Hoofddorp; tel. (23) 5564289; fax (23) 5564290; e-mail revu@sanoma-uitgevers.nl; internet www .nieuwerevu.nl; f. 1968; general interest; Editor-in-Chief JILDOU VAN DER BIJL; circ. 110,000.

Panorama: Ceylonpoort 5-25, 2037 AA Haarlem; tel. (23) 5304304; fax (23) 5361624; internet www.panorama.nl; f. 1913; general interest; Dir R. VAN VUURE; circ. 194,466.

Privé: POB 125, 1000 AC Amsterdam; tel. (20) 5853375; fax (20) 5854111; f. 1977; women's interest; Editors W. P. J. SMITT, H. VAN DER MEYDEN; circ. 490,000.

Story: Utrecht; tel. (30) 2822511; fax (30) 2898388; f. 1974; women's interest; circ. 321,180.

TeleVizier: Zeverijnstraat 6, POB 20002, 1200 AB Hilversum; tel. (35) 6726834; fax (35) 6726712; e-mail redactie.televisier@akn.nl; publ. by Algemene Omroepvereniging; radio and TV guide; circ. 258,487.

Tina: Ceylonpoort 5-25, 2037 AA Haarlem; tel. (23) 5304304; fax (23) 5352554; f. 1967; teenage interest; circ. 112,191.

TrosKompas: POB 9430, 1090 GH Amsterdam; tel. (20) 5979580; fax (20) 5979507; f. 1966; radio and TV guide; Editor JOLANDE VOS.

TV Krant: POB 9430, 1090 GH Amsterdam; tel. (20) 5979580; fax (20) 5979507; f. 1990; radio and TV guide; Editor JOLANDE VOS.

Vara TV Magazine: POB 175, 1200 AD Hilversum; tel. (35) 6711445; fax (35) 6711429; e-mail tv.magazine@vara.nl; radio and TV guide; Editor DAAN DIJKSMAN; circ. 500,000.

Veronica: POB 22000, 1202 CA Hilversum; tel. (35) 6463333; fax (35) 6463300; e-mail michael.kroonbergs@veronica.nl; f. 1971; radio and TV guide; Editor M. KROONBERGS; circ. 1,250,000.

Viva: POB 1630, 2130 JA Hoofddorp; tel. (23) 5565165; fax (23) 5565200; e-mail redactie@viva.nl; internet www.viva.nl; women's interest; Dir HENK ROELOFS; circ. 149,461.

VNU: Ceylonpoort 5-25, 2037 AA Haarlem; POB 1, 2000 MA Haarlem; tel. (23) 5463463; fax (23) 5463912; e-mail vnupr@hq.vnu .com; circ. 174,250.

Voetbal International: POB 1050, 1000 BB Amsterdam; tel. (20) 5518711; fax (20) 6229141; f. 1965; football; Chief Editor C. VAN CUILENBORG; circ. 199,190.

VPRO-Gids: POB 11, 1200 JC Hilversum; tel. (35) 6712665; fax (35) 6712285; e-mail gids@vpro.nl; radio and TV guide; Dir B. PAANS; circ. 254,000.

Vrij Nederland: POB 1254, 1000 BG Amsterdam; tel. (20) 5518711; fax (20) 6229141; e-mail redactie.un@weenbladpers.nl; f. 1940; current affairs; Editor OSCAR GARSCHAGEN; circ. 76,668.

SELECTED PERIODICALS

Art, History and Literature

De Architect: POB 34, 2501 AG The Hague; tel. (70) 3045833; fax (70) 3045806; e-mail architect@wkths.nl; internet www.deArchitect .nl; Dir H. TILMAN; circ. 8,000.

Kunstbeeld: Bohn Stafleu van Loghum BV, POB 246, 3990 GA Houten; tel. (3403) 95711; fax (3403) 50903; monthly; art, esp. sculpture; Dir H. J. DEMOET; circ. 12,000 (2001).

Spiegel Historiael: Molukkenstraat 700, ES, 1098 TW Amsterdam; tel. (20) 6652759; fax (20) 6657831; e-mail s.h@inter.nl .net; f. 1966; monthly; history and archaeology; circ. 9,500.

Tableau Fine Arts Magazine: Capellalaan 65, 2132 JL Hoofddorp; tel. (23) 5565377; fax (23) 5565376; e-mail tableau@tijdschriften.vnu .com; every 2 months; Editor RONALD KRAAYEVELD; circ. 17,000.

Tijdschrift voor Geschiedenis (Historical Review): Instituut voor Geschiedenis RUU, Kromme Nieuwe Gracht 66, 3512 HL Utrecht; tel. (30) 2537868; e-mail tvg@let.uu.nl; f. 1886; quarterly; Editor Dr KEES RIBBENS.

Economic and Business

Computable: POB 4020, 2003 EA Haarlem; tel. (23) 5463463; fax (23) 5463931; e-mail computable@bp.vnu.com; internet www .computable.nl; Dir D. MOLMAN; circ. 96,636.

Elektronica: POB 23, 7400 GA Deventer; tel. (570) 648699; fax (570) 610918; e-mail hdevries@kluwer.nl; internet elektronica .profpages.nl; f. 1953; 11 a year; electronics design; Editor HENK DE VRIES; circ. 7,000.

Intermediair: POB 1900, 2003 BA Haarlem; tel. (23) 5463455; fax (23) 5465530; e-mail intermediair.redactie@bp.vnu.com; internet www.intermediair.nl; f. 1995; weekly; business recruitment; Editor KARIN VAN GILST; circ. 260,000.

Management Team: VNU Business Publications, POB 1907, 2003 BA Haarlem; tel. (318) 521422; fax (318) 523136; internet www.mt .nl; f. 1980; monthly; management; Editor M. TEN HOLTE; circ. 142,000 (2001).

PC Magazine (PCM): Ceylonpoort 5–25, 2037 AA Haarlem; tel. (23) 5463704; fax (23) 5465524; internet www.pcmweb.nl; f. 1982; monthly; computing; Editor-in-Chief FERDINAND SENNEMA; circ. 94,997.

Trade Channel: Holland Business Press BV, Sophiastraat 1, 2011 VT Haarlem; tel. (23) 5319022; fax (23) 5317974; e-mail pvroom@ tradechannel.com; internet www.tradechannel.com; f. 1945; monthly, 2 edns: Trade Channel Consumer Goods and Trade Channel Industrial & Technical Products; promote imports and exports; Editor HENK VAN CAPELLE; circ. 13,286 (consumer edn), 55,000 (technical edn).

Home, Fashion and General

Ariadne Women: Capellalaan 65, POB 1919, 2130 YM Hoofddorp; tel. (23) 5566770; fax (23) 5361624; f. 1946; monthly; home decoration; Editor MONIQUE WIEMEYER; circ. 169,198.

Het Beste uit Reader's Digest: POB 30, 1100 DV Amsterdam; tel. (20) 56789111; fax (20) 6976422; f. 1957; monthly; general interest; Man. Dir CAREL ROG; circ. 373,617.

Cosmopolitan: POB 1730, 2130 JC Hoofddorp; fax (23) 5565259; e-mail cosmopolitan@tijdschriften.vnu.com; internet www .uilenstein.nl/cosmo; f. 1982; monthly; women's interest; Editor M. SIFFELS; circ. 108,406.

Kijk: Ceylonpoort 5-25, 2037 AA Haarlem; tel. (20) 4300455; fax (20) 4300450; sports, science, technology and adventure; circ. 92,993.

Knipmode: POB Capellalaan 65, POB 1900, 2130 JL Hoofddorp; tel. (23) 5565006; fax (23) 5566771; internet www.knipmode.nl;

monthly; fashion and needlework; Editor-in-Chief Y. ANNEVELD-DE WIT; Publr E. ARIËUS; circ. 124,000.

Nouveau: Ceylonpoort 5-25, 2037 AA Haarlem; tel. (23) 304304; fax (23) 350621; f. 1986; women's interest; Dir K. P. M. VAN DE PAS; circ. 134,669.

Opzij: POB 1050, 1000 BB Amsterdam; tel. (20) 5518525; fax (20) 6251288; e-mail opzij@redactie.weekbladpers.nl; f. 1972; monthly; feminist themes; circ. 80,000.

Ouders van Nu: POB 1762, 2130 JP Hoofddoorp; tel. (23) 5565066; fax (23) 5565095; e-mail ouders@tijdschriften.vnu.com; internet www.oudersvannu.nl; f. 1967; monthly; childcare; Editor K. KROON-STUIVER; circ. 156,720.

Playboy: POB 1, 2000 MA Haarlem-Schalkwijk; tel. (23) 5463369; fax (23) 5463924; e-mail playboy@spaarnestad.nl; f. 1983; monthly; Publr HENK ROELOFS; circ. 103,865.

TIP Culinair: POB 1632, 2130 JA Hoofddorp; tel. (23) 5565466; fax (23) 5565488; e-mail tipculinair@tijdschriften.vnu.com; internet www.tipculinair@tijdschriften.vnu.com; f. 1977; monthly; cookery; Gen. Editor MARGOT JAMNISEK; circ. 120,000.

VT-Wonen: Ceylonpoort 5-25, 2037 AA Haarlem; tel. (30) 822511; fax (30) 898388; f. 1964; monthly; home-owning and decorating, circ. 210,374.

Leisure Interests and Sport

Autokampioen: POB 93200, 2509 BA The Hague; tel. (70) 3146688; fax (70) 3146279; e-mail autokampioen@anwb.nl; f. 1908; publ. by Royal Dutch Touring Club (ANWB); motoring; fortnightly; Editor J. VROOMANS; circ. 70,000.

Grasduinen (Browsing): Postbus 150, 3956 DG Leersum; tel. (20) 4300300; fax (20) 4300450; internet www.uilenstein.nl; monthly; leisure, healthy living, art; circ. 70,000.

Kampeer en Caravankampioen: POB 93200, 2509 BA The Hague; tel. (70) 3146691; fax (70) 3146692; f. 1941; monthly; camping and caravanning; publ. by Royal Dutch Touring Club (ANWB); Editor F. VOORBERGEN; circ. 139,601.

Kampioen: POB 93200, 2509 BA The Hague; tel. (70) 3146285; fax (70) 3146983; e-mail kampioen@anwb.nl; internet www.anwb.nl; f. 1885; monthly; recreation and tourism; publ. by Royal Dutch Touring Club (ANWB); Editor E. LODEWYKS; circ. 3,700,000.

101 Woonideeën: POB 1702, 2130 JC Hoofddorp; tel. (23) 5564590; fax (23) 5564505; e-mail 101woonideeen@sanoma-uitgevers.nl; internet www.101woonideeen.nl; f. 1957; monthly; home ideas; Editor M. WIEMEYER; circ. 95,000.

Reizen: POB 93200, 2509 BA The Hague; tel. (70) 3146670; fax (70) 3147610; e-mail reizen@anwb.nl; internet www.reizen.nl; monthly; tourism, travel; publ. by Royal Dutch Touring Club (ANWB); Editor-in-Chief HARRI THEIRLYNCK; circ. 60,000.

Sport International: POB 225, 2800 AE Gouda; tel. (182) 599366; fax (182) 516650; internet www.si.nl; f. 1981; monthly; Editor J. LINSE; circ. 47,350.

Waterkampioen: POB 93200, 2509 BA The Hague; tel. (70) 3141470; fax (70) 3242509; e-mail waterkampioen@anwb.nl; internet www.anwb.nl; f. 1927; fortnightly; water sports and yachting; publ. by Royal Dutch Touring Club (ANWB); Editor DICK WILLIAM HARINCK; circ. 54,000.

Scientific and Medical

Huisarts en Wetenschap: POB 3176, 3502 GD Utrecht; tel. (30) 2881700; fax (30) 2870668; monthly; medical; Editor Dr FRANS J. MEIJMAN; circ. 8,500.

Natuur & Techniek: Segment Special Interest Media, POB 75, 6190 AB Beek (L); tel. (46) 4389444; fax (46) 4370161; e-mail natutech@xs4all.nl; internet www.natutech.nl; f. 1932; monthly; Editor R. DOBBELAER; circ. 47,360.

Technische Revue: POB 4, 7000 BA Doetinchem; tel. (314) 349911; fax (314) 361522; internet www.ebi.nl; monthly; review of new products; Chief Editor M. L. MATSER; circ. 28,000.

Statistics

Statistisch Jaarboek van het Centraal Bureau voor de Statistiek (Statistical Year Book of the Netherlands): Prinses Beatrixlaan 428, POB 4000, 2270 JM Voorburg; tel. (70) 3373800; fax (70) 3877429; internet www.cbs.nl; f. 1899; also *Netherlands Official Statistics* (quarterly) and 300 other publs; Dir-Gen. Dr R. B. J. C. VAN NOORT.

NEWS AGENCY

Algemeen Nederlands Persbureau (ANP) (Netherlands News Agency): POB 1, 2501 AA The Hague; tel. (70) 4141414; fax (70)

4140560; e-mail redactie@anp.nl; f. 1934; official agency of the Netherlands Daily Press Asscn; Man. Dir P. F. E. TESSELAAR; Editor-in-Chief R. DE SPA.

Foreign Bureaux

Associated Press (AP) (USA): Keizersgracht 205, POB 1016, 1000 BA Amsterdam; tel. (20) 235057; Bureau Chief ABNER KATZMAN.

Deutsche Presse-Agentur (dpa) (Germany): Eisenhowerlaan 150, 2517 KP The Hague; tel. (70) 3584499; fax (70) 3521637; Correspondent EDGAR DENTER.

Dow Jones Newswires: POB 1016, 1000 BA Amsterdam; tel. (20) 6260770; fax (20) 6235616; Correspondent NEIL MOORHOUSE.

Informatsionnoye Telegrafnoye Agentstvo Rossii—Telegrafnoye Agentstvo Suverennykh Stran (ITAR—TASS) (Russia): J. van Oldenbarneveltlaan 96, 2582 NZ The Hague; tel. and fax (70) 3553876; f. 1945; Correspondent VALENTIN VOLKOV.

Reuters (UK): Drentestraat 11, 1083 HK Amsterdam; POB 74733, 1070 BS Amsterdam; tel. (20) 5045000; fax (20) 5045040; e-mail amsterdam.newsroom@reuters.com; Chief Correspondent A. LEVENE.

Rossiyskoe Informatsionnoye Agentstvo—Novosti (RIA—Novosti) (Russia): Nieuwe Parklaan 15, 2597 LA, The Hague; tel. (70) 3586958; fax (70) 3512108; Dir A. POSKAKUKHIN.

Agence France-Presse (AFP), Agenzia Nazionale Stampa Associata (ANSA) (Italy), Inter Press Service (IPS) (Italy) and UPI (USA) are also represented in the Netherlands.

PRESS ORGANIZATIONS

Buitenlandse Persvereniging in Nederland (Foreign Press Asscn in the Netherlands): Oudezijds Voorburgwal 129, 1012 EP Amsterdam; tel. (20) 4221209; fax (20) 4212411; e-mail birviss@compuserve.com; internet www.bpv-fpa.nl; f. 1925; Pres. ANNETTE BIRSCHEL; Sec. JANA SANCHEZ; 120 mems.

Centraal Bureau voor Courantenpubliciteit van de Nederlandse Dagbladpers (CEBUCO) (Central Advertising Bureau of the Netherlands Daily Press): Hoogoorddreef 5, POB 12040, 1100 AA Amsterdam; tel. (20) 4309100; fax (20) 4309129; e-mail info@cebuco.nl; internet www.cebuco.nl; f. 1935; Dir Dr M. J. KUIP.

De Nederlandse Nieuwsbladpers (NNP) (Organization of Local Newsmedia in the Netherlands): Drentsestraat 10, 3821 BP Amersfoort; tel. (33) 4481650; fax (33) 45481650; e-mail nnpnl@nnp.nl; internet www.nnp.nl; f. 1945; asscn. of publrs of non-daily local newspapers and other local newsmedia; Pres. T. ROSKAM; Dir J. M. PEKELHARING; 52 mems.

Nederlandse Vereniging van Journalisten (Netherlands Union of Journalists): Joh. Vermeerstraat 22, POB 75997, 1070 AZ Amsterdam; tel. (20) 6766771; fax (20) 6624901; e-mail vereniging@nvj.nl; internet www.villamedia.nl; f. 1884; 9,500 mems.

Vereniging De Nederlandse Dagbladpers (NDP) (Dutch Asscn of Daily Newspaper Publrs): Amsterdam; tel. (20) 6763366; fax (20) 6766777; f. 1908; Chair. W. F. DE PAGTER; Gen. Sec. J. W. D. GAST; 34 mems.

Publishers

Uitgeverij Altamira BV: Blekersvaartweg 19A, Heemstede; tel. (23) 5286882; e-mail altamira@tip.nl; f. 1985; philosophy, psychology, New Age, health and spirituality.

Uitgeverij Ankh-Hermes BV: Smyrnastraat 5, POB 125, 7400 AC Deventer; tel. (570) 678900; fax (570) 624632; e-mail info@ankh-hermes.nl; internet www.ankh-hermes.nl; health, eastern and western religions, astrology, alternative medicine, psychology, esoterics; Dir A. STEENBERGEN; Publrs E. TEN SELDAM, A. KLUWER.

Anthos: Herengracht 435–437, 1017 BR Amsterdam; tel. (20) 5245411; fax (20) 4200422; literature, cultural history, biographies, history, politics; Dir. R. AMMERLAAN.

APA (Academic Publishers Associated): POB 806, 1000 AV Amsterdam; tel. (20) 6265544; fax (20) 5285298; e-mail info@apa-publishers.com; internet www.apa-publishers.com; f. 1966; subsidiaries: Holland University Press, Fontes Pers, Oriental Press, Philo Press, van Heusden, Hissink; new and reprint edns in the arts, humanities and science; Dir G. VAN HEUSDEN.

BV Uitgeverij De Arbeiderspers: Herengracht 370–372, POB 2877, 1000 CW Amsterdam; tel. (020) 5247500; fax (20) 6224937; e-mail info@arbeiderspers.nl; participant in Weekbladpers holdings group; general, fiction and non-fiction; Dir R. C. HAANS.

A. Asher & Co BV: Zeeweg 264, POB 258, 1970 AG Ijmuiden; tel. (255) 523839; fax (255) 510352; e-mail info@asherbooks.com;

internet www.asherbooks.com; f. 1830; natural history; Dir M. J. Roos.

Bert Bakker BV: Herengracht 406, 1017 BX Amsterdam; tel. (20) 6241934; fax (20) 6225461; e-mail pbo@pbo.nl; internet www.pbo.nl; f. 1893; Dutch and international literature, sociology, history, politics, science; Dir Mai Spijkers.

John Benjamins BV: Klaprozenweg 105, POB 36224, 1020 ME Amsterdam; tel. (20) 6304747; fax (20) 6739773; e-mail customer .services@benjamins.nl; internet www.benjamins.com; f. 1964; linguistics, philology, psychology, management and organization, art history; antiquarian scholarly periodicals; Man. Dirs J. L. Benjamins, Mrs C. L. Benjamins-Schalekamp, Seline Benjamins.

Uitgeverij De Bezige Bij BV: Van Miereveldstraat 1, POB 75184, 1070 AD Amsterdam; tel. (20) 3059810; fax (20) 3059824; e-mail info@debezigebij.nl; internet www.debezigebij.nl; f. 1945; Publr Robbert Ammerlaan.

Erven J. Bijleveld: Janskerkhof 7, 3512 BK Utrecht, POB 1238, 3500 BE Utrecht; tel. (30) 2317008; fax (30) 2368675; e-mail bijleveld .publishers@wxs.nl; f. 1865; psychology, sociology, philosophy, religion and history; computer books (as Bijleveld Press); Mans J. B. Bommeljé, L. S. Bommeljé.

Boekencentrum Uitgevers: Goudstraat 50, POB 29, 2700 AA Zoetermeer; tel. (79) 3615481; fax (79) 3615489; e-mail info@ boekencentrum.nl; internet www.boekencentrum.nl; bibles, books and magazines; Dir N. A. de Waal.

Bohn Stafleu Van Hoghum BV: Het Spoor 2, POB 246, 3990 GA Houten; tel. (30) 6385838; fax (30) 6383839; e-mail klantenservice@ bsl.nl; internet www.bsl.nl; mem. of Wolters Kluwer NV holdings group; social sciences, humanities, medical, dental and nursing; Dir P. J. A. Snakkers.

Boom Uitgeverij BV: Prinsengracht 747–751, 1017 JX Amsterdam; tel. (20) 6226107; fax (20) 6253327; e-mail mail@ virgeverijboom.nl; internet www.uitgeverijboom.nl; f. 1842; fmrly Boom Pers BV, Meppel; philosophy, educational and social sciences, environment, history; Man. Dir E. A. van Ingen.

Uitgeverij Bosch & Keuning: Dorpsstraat 74, POB 24, 3730 AA De Bilt; tel. (30) 2204014; fax (30) 2202667; f. 1925; general non-fiction; Publr Chris Herschdorfer.

Bosch & Keuning Uitgeversgroep: Ericastraat 1, POB 1, 3740 AA Baarn; tel. (35) 5482411; fax (35) 5422509; f. 1925; holdings group; Dir J. Atema.

Brill Academic Publishers: Plantijnstraat 2, POB 9000, 2300 PA Leiden; tel. (71) 5353500; fax (71) 5317532; e-mail cs@brill.nl; internet www.brill.nl; f. 1683; academic books and periodicals (mainly in English); classics, medieval, renaissance and oriental studies, comparative religion, biology; Pres. R. J. Kasteleyn.

A. W. Bruna Uitgevers BV: Kobaltweg 23–25, POB 40203, 3504 AA Utrecht; tel. (30) 2470411; fax (30) 2410018; e-mail helpdesk@ awbruna.nl; internet www.awbruna.nl; f. 1868; general fiction and non-fiction; Dir J. A. A. Boezeman.

Uitgeverij G. F. Callenbach BV: Ijsseldijk 31, POB 5018, 8260 GA Kampen; tel. (38) 3392507; fax (38) 3328912; e-mail lvessen@kok.nl; f. 1854; mem. of Bosch & Keuning Uitgeversgroep; Publr J. Bijl.

Uitgeverij Cantecleer BV: Julianalaan 11, POB 309, 3740 AM Baarn; tel. (35) 5486600; fax (35) 5486645; e-mail cancleer@ worldonline.nl; f. 1948; mem. of Bosch & Keuning Uitgevers group; Man. Dir H. Schwurmans.

Elsevier NV: Van de Sande Bakhuyzenstraat 4, 1061 AG Amsterdam; POB 470, 1000 AL Amsterdam; tel. (20) 5159111; fax (20) 6832617; f. 1979 by merger; Dir-Gen. Crispin Davis; subholdings include some 60 subsidiaries in the Netherlands and abroad specializing in: reference works, handbooks, weekly magazines, newspapers, trade and technical publs, (postgraduate) scientific books and journals, audiovisual materials, further education study courses, databases; also includes.

Excerpta Medica Medical Communications: Van de Sande Bakhuyzenstraat 4, 1061 AG Amsterdam; tel. (20) 5159222; fax (20) 6854171.

Elsevier Science BV (Academic Publishing Division): Sara Burgerhartstraat 25, 1055 KV Amsterdam; POB 2400, 1000 CK Amsterdam; tel. (20) 4853911; fax (20) 4852457; incorporates the following divisions: life sciences, earth science, social sciences and economics, chemistry, engineering and technology, physics and materials sciences, computer sciences and mathematics.

Uitgeverij Van Gennep BV: Keizersgracht 524, 1017 EK Amsterdam; tel. (20) 6247033; fax (20) 6247035; e-mail vangennep@ wxs.nl; history, social theory, political science, biographies, literature; Man. Publr Chris ten Kate.

Uitgeverij J. H. Gottmer/H. J. W. Becht BV: Prof. van Vlotenweg 1A, POB 160, 2060 AD Bloemendaal; tel. (23) 5411190; fax (23) 5274404; e-mail post@gottmer.nl; internet www.gottmer.nl; f. 1937; fiction, non-fiction, children's books, religion, spirituality, travel guides; Dir C. G. A. van Wijk.

Gouda Quint BV: Willemsplein 2, POB 23, 7400 GA Arnhem; tel. (85) 454762; fax (85) 514509; f. 1735; mem. of Wolters Kluwer NV holdings group; law and taxation; Dir K. H. Mulder.

Uitgeverij Holland BV: Spaarne 110, 2011 CM Haarlem; tel. (23) 5323061; fax (23) 5342908; e-mail info@uitgeverijholland.nl; f. 1922; literature, reference, science, children's books; Dir R. van Ulzen.

Uitgeverij Hollandia BV: Eemdijk 124, POB 160, 2061 EB Bloemendaal; tel. (233) 5411190; fax (233) 5274404; e-mail tm@gottmer .nl; f. 1899; travel, yachting and nautical books; Dir Tonnis Muntinga.

Kluwer Academic Publishers BV: van Godewijckstraat 30, POB 989, 3300 AZ Dordrecht; tel. (78) 6576000; fax (78) 6576254; e-mail services@wkap.nl; internet www.wkap.nl; f. 1988; mem. of Wolters Kluwer NV holdings group; publrs of books and journals on, *inter alia*, philosophy, logic, mathematics, linguistics, sinology and oriental studies, social history, economics, econometrics, geophysics, space research, astronomy, chemistry, physics, energy, life and environmental sciences; Dir J. K. Smith.

Uitgeversmaatschappij J. H. Kok BV: Ijsseldijk 31, POB 5019, 8260 GA Kampen; tel. (38) 3392555; fax (38) 3327331; e-mail algemeen@kok.nl; f. 1894; theology, belles-lettres, science, periodicals; mem. of Bosch & Keuning holdings group; nine subsidiaries; Dir B. A. Endedijk.

Ten Have BV: Ijsseldijk 31, POB 5018, 8260 GA Kampen; tel. (38) 3392510; fax (38) 3392518; e-mail pdboer@kok.nl; f. 1831; imprint of J. H. Kok Uitgeefmaatschappij; religious; Dir B. Endedijk; Editor P. de Boer.

Kosmos-Z&K Uitgevers: St Jacobsstraat 125, POB 14095, 3508 SC Utrecht; tel. (30) 2349211; fax (30) 2349247; mem. of Veen Uitgevers Groep; Man. Dir A. de Groot.

Lemniscaat BV: Vijverlaan 48, POB 4066, 3006 AB Rotterdam; tel. (10) 2062929; fax (10) 4141560; e-mail info@lemniscaat.nl; internet www.lemniscaat.nl; f. 1963; philosophy, psychology, care of the disabled and mentally handicapped, books for juveniles and young adults, picture books; Dir J. C. Boele van Hensbroek.

Uitgeverij Leopold/Elzenga BV: Singel 262, POB 3879, 1001 AR Amsterdam; tel. (20) 5511250; fax (20) 4204699; e-mail info@leopold .nl; internet www.leopold.nl; f. 1923; mem. Weekbladpers BV; children's books; Gen. Dir R. Francissen.

Uitgeverij Luitingh-Sijthoff BV: Leidsegracht 105 A, 1017ND Amsterdam; tel. (30) 205307340; fax (30) 20626251; e-mail info@ luitingh-sijthoff.nl; Luitingh; f. 1946; Sijthoff; f. 1851; merged in 1989; mem. of Veen Bosch en Keuning Uitgevers publishing group; fiction and popular non-fiction; Man. Dir J. A. B. Leppink.

Malmberg BV: Leeghwaterlaan 16, POB 233, 5201 AE Den Bosch; tel. (73) 6288811; fax (73) 6210512; e-mail malmberg@malmberg.nl; internet www.malmberg.nl; f. 1885; educational; Dir J. M. Eijkens.

J. M. Meulenhoff BV: Herengracht 505, POB 100, 1000 AC Amsterdam; tel. (20) 5533500; fax (20) 6258511; e-mail info@ meulenhoff.nl; internet www.meulenhoff.nl; f. 1895; literature, historical, political, social/cultural, art, paperbacks and pocket books; Dir Annette Portegies.

Nienhuis Montessori International BV: Industriepark 14, POB 16, 7020 AA Zelhem; tel. (314) 627127; fax (314) 627128; f. 1800; holdings group; publrs and printers specializing in scientific books and periodicals; Dir A. J. Nienhuis.

Uitgeverij Ploegsma BV: Keizersgracht 616, POB 19857, 1000 GW Amsterdam; tel. (20) 6262907; fax (20) 6242994; subsidiary: Uitgeverij De Brink; Dir M. Brinkman.

Uitgeverij De Prom BV: Pr. Marielaan 8, POB 1, 3740 AA Baarn; tel. (35) 5422141; fax (35) 5423855; f. 1981; mem. of Bosch & Keuning holdings group; literature and art books; Dir W. Hazeu.

Em. Querido's Uitgeverij BV: Singel 262, POB 3879, 1001 AR Amsterdam; tel. (20) 5511262; fax (20) 6391968; internet www .querido.nl; f. 1915; subsidiary: Uitgeverij Nijgh & van Ditmar; participant in 'Singel 262' holdings group; general fiction, history, children's books, translations from Latin and Greek texts; Dir Ary T. Langbroek.

Uitgeverij La Rivière & Voorhoeve Kampen: Stationsplein 62, POB 133, 3740 AC Baarn; tel. (35) 5418855; fax (35) 5413174; f. 1876; mem. of Kok holdings group; general non-fiction, children's books; Dirs B. A. Endedijk, A. C. van Dam; Man. Editors K. van der Scheer, J. H. Timmerman, N. Harmsen.

Editions Rodopi BV: Tijnmuiden 7, 1046 AK Amsterdam; tel. (20) 6114821; fax (20) 4472979; e-mail orders-queries@rodopi.nl; internet www.rodopi.nl; f. 1966; Dir F. A. van der Zee.

Samsom BV: Prinses Margrietlaan 3, 2404 HA Alphen a/d Rijn; tel. (172) 466633; fax (172) 475933; e-mail heemskerk@samsom.nl; f. 1882; mem. of Wolters Kluwer NV holdings group; books and periodicals on business, social and marketing management, law, education, the environment; Dir A. M. HEEMSKERK.

SDU: Christoffel Plantijnstraat 2, POB 20025, 2500 EA The Hague; tel. (70) 3789911; fax (70) 3854321; e-mail sdu@sdu.nl; internet www.sdu.nl; Dirs S. VAN OOSTROM, B. JONGSMA.

BV Uitgeverijen 'Singel 262': Singel 262, POB 3879, 1001 AR Amsterdam; tel. (20) 5511262; fax (20) 6203509; holding group; Man. Dir P. F. M. DE JONG.

A.J.G. Strengholt Boeken, Anno 1928 BV: Hofstede Oud-Bussem, Flevolaan 41, POB 338, 1400 AH Bussum; tel. (35) 6958411; fax (35) 6946173; f. 1928; health, biography, music, current affairs, parapsychology; sports; cookery; Dir A. VAN POELGEEST.

Swets & Zeitlinger Publishers, BV: Heereweg 347B, POB 825, 2160 SZ Lisse; tel. (252) 435111; fax (252) 415888; e-mail orders@swets.nl; internet www.szp.swets.nl; f. 1901; subscription agent for periodicals worldwide; publr of books and journals; Dir P. RUSTENBURG.

Uitgeverij De Tijdstroom BV: Asschatterweg 44, 3831 JW Leusden; tel. (342) 450867; fax (342) 450365; e-mail tijdstroom@planet.nl; internet www.tijdstroom.nl; f. 1921; educational and professional publications on health and welfare, periodicals in these fields; Dir C. H. J. STAVENUITER.

Unieboek BV: Onderdoor 7, POB 97, 3990 DB Houten; tel. (30) 6377660; fax (30) 6377600; internet www.unieboek.nl; f. 1890; holdings group incorporating 10 publishing houses; general and juvenile literature, fiction, popular science, history, art, social, economics, religion, textbooks, etc. Dir W. VAN GILS.

Uitgeverij L. J. Veen BV: Herengracht 481, 1017 BT Amsterdam; tel. (20) 5249800; fax (20) 6276851; f. 1887; literature, fiction, non-fiction; Man. Dir A. DE GROOT.

Veen Bosch en Keuning Uitgevers NV: Mariaplaaks 21C POB 8049, 3503 RA Utrecht; tel. (30) 2349211; fax (30) 2300145; e-mail algemeen@veenboschenkeuning.nl; publishing group; Dir A. DE GROOT.

VNU Business Publications BV: Ceylonpoort 5-25, POB 4020, 2031 EA Haarlem; tel. (23) 5463463; fax (23) 5463931; e-mail info@bp.vnu.com; internet www.vnubp.nl; trade and fashion, careers, IT, personal computer, management, training.

West Friesland BV: Slijksteeg 4, POB 2308, 1620 EH Hoorn; tel. (229) 248820; fax (229) 218944; f. 1943; novels, biographies, children's books, paperbacks, young adults; Man. Dir B. E. ENDEDIJK; Editor-in-Chief F. H. JONKERS.

Wolters Kluwer NV: Apollolaan 153, POB 75248; 1070 AE Amsterdam; tel. (20) 6070400; fax (20) 6070490; e-mail info@wolterskluwer.com; internet www.wolters-kluwer.com; international publishing group; Chair. Dr ROBERT PIETERSE (acting).

Wolters-Noordhoff BV: Damsport 157, POB 58, 9700 MB Groningen; tel. (50) 5226922; fax (50) 5277599; e-mail info@wolters.nl; f. 1836; educational and scientific books, educational software, geographical and historical atlases and maps; Dir Dr M. J. VAN DALEN.

PUBLISHERS' ASSOCIATIONS

Koninklijke Vereniging van het Boekenvak (KVB) (Royal Association for the Book Trade): Frederiksplein 1, POB 15007, 1001 MA Amsterdam; tel. (20) 6240212; fax (20) 6208871; e-mail info@kvb.nl; internet www.kvb.nl; f. 1815; Chair. A. NUIS; Exec. Dir CONNIE VERBERNE; 928 mems.

Nederlands Uitgeversverbond (NUV) (Dutch Publrs' Asscn): Atlas Kantorenpark, Gebouw Azië, Hoogoorddreef 5, POB 12040, 1100 AA Amsterdam Zuidoost; tel. (20) 4309150; fax (20) 4309179; e-mail info@nuv.nl; internet www.nuv.nl; Chair. Prof. H. J. L. VONHOFF; Dir J. BOMMER; 140 mems.

Broadcasting and Communications

TELECOMMUNICATIONS

Regulatory Authority

Onafhankelijke Post en Telecommunicatie Autoriteit (OPTA): Babylon Bldg, Tower B, Koningin Julianaplein 30, POB 90420, 2509 LK The Hague; tel. (70) 3153500; fax (70) 3153501; e-mail mail@opta.nl; internet www.opta.nl; f. 1997; supervises compliance with legislation, settles disputes, manages the telephone number database; Chair. Prof. Dr J. C. ARNBAK.

Service Providers

A2000 Holding NV: POB 80900, 1005 DA Amsterdam; 50% owned by Telekabel; holds cable monopoly in Amsterdam.

Ben: Rijswijkseweg 60, POB 16272, 2500 BG The Hague; tel. (6) 14095000; e-mail info@ben.nl; internet www.ben.nl; majority-owned by Deutsche Telekom; mobile telephone operator.

Debitel/Cellway: POB 6700, 2130 LT Hoofddorp.

Dutchtone: POB 95313, 2509 CH The Hague; tel. (70) 8899000; fax (70) 8898000; e-mail info@dutchtone.nl; 100% owned by Orange SA.

EnerTel NV: K.P. van der Mandelelaan 130–144, POB 25226, 3001 HE Rotterdam; e-mail cst@energis.nl; internet www.enertel.nl; owned by Energis UK; Man. STEPHEN COURTE.

Koninklijke KPN NV: POB 30000, 2500 GA The Hague; tel. (70) 3434343; fax (70) 3436568; e-mail webmaster@kpn.com; internet www.kpn.com; privatized 1989; operates KPN Mobile; 31.5% state-owned; CEO ADRIANUS SCHEEPBOUWER.

KPN Broadcast: POB 850, 1200 AW Hilversum; tel. (35) 6786700; fax (35) 6246671; e-mail contact@kpnbroadcast.com; internet www.kpnbroadcast.com; provides internet services and analogue, digital and satellite broadcasting services.

Xantic: POB 30012, 2500 GA The Hague; tel. (70) 3434543; fax (70) 3434796; e-mail xantic@xantic.net; internet www.xantic.net; provides communications systems.

Libertel Netwerk: POB 1500, 6201 BM Maast; e-mail roaming@libertel.nl; internet www.libertel.nl; f. 1999; 70% owned by Vodafone/AirTouch; Chief Exec. JOHN DE WIT.

MCI WorldCom BV: Rembrandt Tower, Amstelplein 1, Amsterdam; tel. (20) 7112000; e-mail info@wcom.nl; internet www.wcom.nl; integrated voice, data and internet telecommunications products.

Talkline: POB 426, 3740 AK Baarn.

Telekabel NV: POB 8000, 6880 CA Velp.

Telfort BV: POB 23079, 1100 DN Amsterdam Zuid-Oost; tel. 0800-1771; internet www.telfort.com; owned by BT wireless, a subsidiary of British Telecom; Gen. Dir TON AAN DE STEGGE.

BROADCASTING

Under the Netherlands public broadcasting system the two co-ordinating bodies work with the seven licensed broadcasters to provide a complete range of programmes.

Co-ordinating Bodies

Nederlandse Omroep Stichting (NOS): POB 26444, 1202 JJ Hilversum; tel. (35) 6779222; fax (35) 6772649; internet www.omroep.nl; f. 1969; co-ordination of Dutch national public broadcasting and news, sports and teletext programmes on five national public radio and three TV channels; Chair. GERRIT JAN WOLFENSPERGER; Man. Dir Radio and Television RUURD BIERMAN.

Nederlandse Programma Stichting (NPS): POB 29000, 1202 MA Hilversum; tel. (35) 6779333; fax (35) 6774517; e-mail publiek@nps.nl; internet www.nps.nl; Dir W. J. M. VAN BEUSEKOM.

Broadcasting Associations

Algemene Omroepvereniging AVRO: 's-Gravelandseweg 80, POB 2, 1200 JA Hilversum; tel. (35) 6717911; fax (35) 6717439; e-mail info@avro.nl; internet www.avro.nl; f. 1923; independent; general broadcaster; 800,000 mems; Pres. M. SANDERS; Dir F. MARÉCHAL.

Evangelische Omroep (EO): Oude Amersfoortseweg 79, POB 21000, 1202 BB Hilversum; tel. (35) 6474747; fax (35) 6474727; e-mail eo@eo.nl; internet www.eo.nl; f. 1967; Protestant; Chair. A. VAN DER VEER; Man. Dirs A. P. DE BOER, A. G. KNEVEL, H. N. HAGOORT.

Katholieke Radio Omroep (KRO): 's-Gravelandseweg 80, POB 23000, 1202 EA Hilversum; tel. (35) 6713911; fax (35) 6713666; internet www.kro.nl; f. 1925; Catholic; 615,000 mems; Pres. F. C. H. SLANGEN; Dir A. C. G. VERLIND.

Nederlandse Christelijke Radio Vereniging (NCRV): Bergweg 30, POB 25000, 1202 HB Hilversum; tel. (35) 6719911; fax (35) 6719285; e-mail info@ncrv.nl; internet www.ncrv.nl; f. 1924; Protestant; more than 550,000 mems; Chair. F. BRINK; Gen. Man. H. J. HEMINK.

Omroepvereniging VARA: Sumatralaan 49, POB 175, 1200 AD Hilversum; tel. (35) 6711911; fax (35) 6711333; e-mail vara@vara.nl; internet www.vara.nl; f. 1925; social-democratic and progressive; 515,000 mems; Pres. V. M. M. KEUR.

Omroepvereniging VPRO: Media Park, Sumatralaan 49, POB 11, 1200 JC Hilversum; tel. (35) 6712911; fax (35) 6712220; e-mail info@vpro.nl; internet www.vpro.nl; f. 1926; progressive; 440,463 mems;

Pres. S. Piersma; Gen. Dir P. Schrurs; Dir of Radio A. J. Heerma van Voss; Dir of TV D. Lunenborg.

TROS: Lage Naarderweg 45i47, POB 28450, 1202 LL Hilversum; tel. (35) 6715715; fax (35) 6715236; e-mail publiekservice@tros.nl; internet www.tros.nl; f. 1964; independent; general broadcaster; 573,664 mems; Chair. K. van Doodewaerd.

Radio

There are five privately-owned national radio stations that are operated on a public-service basis, as well as 13 regional stations and about 330 local stations.

Television

Television programmes are transmitted on three public channels, each of which is allocated to a different combination of broadcasting associations and other organizations, and on the commercially-funded channels RTL4 and RTL5. Nearly all Dutch households are able to receive at least one satellite station.

SBS 6/NET5: Plantage Middenlaan 14, POB 18179, 1001 ZB Amsterdam; e-mail info@sbs6.nl; internet www.sbs6.nl; private broadcaster; Dir A. M. van Westerloo.

United Pan-Europe Communications NV: Tupolevlaan 81–89, 1119 PA Schiphol Rijk; tel. (20) 7729729; fax (20) 7729988; e-mail service@upc.nl; internet www.upc.nl; cable broadcaster; Chair Michael T. Fries.

Overseas Broadcasting

BVN TV: Witte Kruislaan 55, POB 222, 1200 JG Hilversum; tel. (35) 6724333; fax (35) 6724343; e-mail bvn@rnw.nl; internet www.bvn.nl; f. 1998 by Radio Nederland Wereldomroep, VRT and Nederlandse Omroep Stichting (NOS); daily international transmissions of news and cultural programmes from public service broadcasters in Flanders and the Netherlands; Dir of Programmes P. Landman.

Radio Nederland Wereldomroep (Radio Netherlands International): Witte Kruislaan 55, POB 222, 1200 JG Hilversum; tel. (35) 6724337; fax (35) 6724352; e-mail planning@rnw.nl; internet www.rnw.nl; f. 1947; public service broadcaster daily transmissions in Dutch, English, Indonesian, Papiamento, Portuguese and Spanish; programme and transcription services for foreign radio and TV stations; Radio Nederland Training Centre (for students from developing countries); Pres. Lodewijk W. D. Bouwens.

Finance

(cap. = capital; res = reserves; dep. = deposits; m. = million; brs = branches; all values are given in euros, unless otherwise stated)

BANKING

Central Bank

De Nederlandsche Bank NV: Westeinde 1, POB 98, 1000 AB Amsterdam; tel. (20) 5249111; fax (20) 5242500; e-mail info@dnb.nl; internet www.dnb.nl; f. 1814; nationalized 1948; cap. 500m., res 12,651m., dep. 10,305m. (Dec. 2001); Pres. D. E. Witteveen; Exec Dirs Dr H. J. Brouwer, A. Schilder, Drs J. Koning; 4 brs.

Principal Commercial Banks

ABN AMRO Bank NV: Gustav Mahlerlaan 10, POB 283, 1000 EA Amsterdam; tel. (20) 6289393; fax (20) 6287740; e-mail postbox@abnamro.com; internet www.abnamro.com; f. 1991 by merger of Algemene Bank Nederland NV and Amsterdam-Rotterdam Bank NV; cap. 1,677m., res 10,110m., dep. 492,702m. (Dec. 2001); Chair. Rijkman W. J. Groenink; 915 brs nationally.

Bank Nederlandse Gemeenten NV: Koninginnegracht 2, POB 30305, 2500 GH The Hague; tel. (70) 3750750; fax (70) 3454743; e-mail info@bng.nl; internet www.bng.nl; f. 1914; 50% state-owned; cap. 127.0m., res. 2,074.0m., dep. 55,737.0m. (Dec. 2000); Pres. P. P. van Besouw.

Banque Artesia Nederland NV: Herengracht 539-543, POB 274, 1000 AG Amsterdam; tel. (20) 5204911; fax (20) 6247502; e-mail artesia@artesia.nl; internet www.artesia.nl; f. 1863; fmrly Banque Paribas Nederland; cap. 163.9m. guilders, res 180.5m. guilders, dep. 7,856.0m. guilders (Dec. 2000); Chair. J. H. van Broeckhoven; 10 brs.

C en E Bankiers NV: Herculesplein 5, 3584 AA Utrecht; tel. (30) 2560911; fax (30) 2540919; e-mail info@CenEbankiers.nl; internet www.CenEbankiers.nl; f. 1922; present name adopted 1998; owned by ING Bank NV; cap. 5.4m., res. 200.1m., dep. 2,674.8m. (Dec. 2000); Chair. H. H. Idzerda; Gen. Mans P. A. J. Verbaas, A. A. Röell.

Commerzbank (Nederland) NV: Herengracht 571–579, POB 140, 1000 AC Amsterdam; tel. (20) 5574911; fax (20) 6272446; e-mail cbnl@commerzbank.com; f. 1973 as Europartners Bank (Nederland) NV; name changed as above 1984; cap. 40.8m., res 173.0m., dep. 3,250.7m. (Dec. 2000); Gen. Mans Dr R. W. Rutloh, G. W. Liebchen.

Dexia Bank Nederland NV: Herengracht 182, POB 11363, 1001 GJ Amsterdam; tel. (20) 5571571; fax (20) 5571414; f. 2001; formed by Oct. 2001 merger of Bank Labouchere NV (f. 1990) and Kempen and Co NV, owned by Dexia banking group; dep. 5,398.1m., total assets 7,290.1m. (Dec. 2001); Chair. J. Krant; 1 br.

Fortis Bank (Nederland) NV: Blaak 555, POB 1045, 3000 BA Rotterdam; tel. (10) 2701010; fax (10) 4148391; e-mail info@fortis.com; internet www.fortis.com; f. 1999 by merger of VSB Bank and Generale Bank Nederland; Chair Sjoerd van Keulen.

Friesland Bank NV: Zuiderstraat 1, POB 397, 8901 BD Leeuwarden; tel. (58) 2994499; fax (58) 2994591; e-mail service@frieslandbank.nl; internet www.frieslandbank.nl; f. 1913 as Coöperatieve Zuivel-Bank; dep. 10,682.0m. guilders, total assets 12,661.5m. guilders (Dec. 2000); Chair. Dr A. Offringa; Gen. Mans T. Branbergen, E. C. Lekkerkerker; 33 brs.

Indonesische Overzeese Bank NV (Indover Bank): Stadhouderskade 84, POB 526, 1000 AM Amsterdam; tel. (20) 5700700; fax (20) 6626119; e-mail info@indover.com; internet www.indoverbank.com; f. 1965; cap. 48.0m., res 98.9m., dep. 1,091.5m. (Dec. 2001); Pres. Muhamad Muchtar; Chair. Mukhlis Rasyid; Gen. Man. D. van Leeuwen.

ING Bank NV (ING Barings): POB 1800, De Amsterdamse Poort, 1000 BV Amsterdam; tel. (20) 5415411; fax (20) 5415444; e-mail fi@ingbank.com; internet www.ingbank.com; f. 1991; dep. 349,349m., total assets 406,393m. (Dec. 2000); Chair. Ewald Kist; more than 400 brs.

Kas Bank NV: Spuistraat 172, POB 24001, 1000 DB Amsterdam; tel. (20) 5575911; fax (20) 5576100; e-mail info@kasbank.com; internet www.kasbank.com; f. 1806 by merger, name change as above in Jan. 2002; cap. 15.7m., res. 161.1m., dep. 5,384.2m. (Dec. 2001); Man. Dir F. S. von Balluseck.

F. van Lanschot Bankiers NV: Hooge Steenweg 29, POB 1021, 5200 HC 's-Hertogenbosch; tel. (73) 5483548; fax (73) 5483648; e-mail vanlanschot@vanlanschot.nl; internet www.vanlanschot.nl; f. 1737; dep. 9,217.2m., total assets 10,748,821m. (Dec. 2001); Chair. (vacant); 34 brs.

Mizuho Bank Nederland NV: Apollolaan 171, POB 7075, 1007 JB Amsterdam; tel. (20) 5734343; fax (20) 5734372; e-mail dkbedp@axxel.nl; f. 2000 by merger of Dai Ichi Kangyo Bank Europe NV and Fuji Bank Nederland NV; cap. 112.7m., res 13.4m., dep. 1,686.5m. (Dec. 2000); Man. Dir T. Kondo.

NIB Capital Bank NV: Carnegieplein 4, POB 380, 2501 BH The Hague; tel. (70) 3425425; fax (70) 3651071; e-mail thehague@nibcapital.com; internet www.nibcapital.com; f. 1945 as Herstelbank; cap. 1,362.0m., res. 915.0m., dep. 14,201.0m. (Dec. 2001); Chair. M. L. Gedopt; 1 br.

Postbank NV: Haarlemmerweg 506, POB 21009, 1000 EX Amsterdam; tel. (20) 5846133; fax (20) 5846132; f. 1985; retail bank operating through post offices; owned by ING Group NV.

Rabobank Nederland (Coöperatieve Centrale Raiffeisen-Boerenleenbank BA): Croeselaan 18, POB 17100, 3500 HG Utrecht; tel. (30) 2160000; fax (30) 2161973; e-mail rabocomm@rn.rabobank.nl; internet www.rabobank.nl; f. 1898; res 15,568.0m., dep. 310,702.0m., total assets 363,619.0m. (Dec. 2000); Chair. Bert Heemskerk (acting); 1,727 brs.

SNS Bank NV: Pettelaarpark 120, POB 70053, 5201 DZ 's-Hertogenbosch; tel. (73) 6833333; fax (73) 6833600; e-mail info@snsbank.nl; internet www.sns.nl; f. 1971 as Bank der Bondsspaarbanken NV, name changed as above in 2002; cap. 340.0m., res 1,235.0m., dep. 28,309.0m. (Dec. 2000); Chair. M. W. J. Hinssen; 200 brs.

Staal Bank NV: Lange Houtsraat 8, 2511 CW The Hague; tel. (70) 3101510; fax (70) 3650819; e-mail info@staalbankiers.nl; f. 1916 as Bankierskantoor Staal & Co NV; name changed as above 1998; dep. 7,869.5m., total assets 8,980.3m. (Dec. 2000); Chair. J. S. Hesp; Man. Dirs H. W. te Best, P. F. C. Göbel.

Bankers' Association

Nederlandse Bankiersvereniging (Netherlands Bankers' Asscn): POB 3543, 1001 AH Amsterdam; tel. (20) 5502888; fax (20) 6239748; f. 1989; Pres. H. H. F. Wijffels; Gen. Man. L. M. Overmars.

STOCK EXCHANGES

A supervisory authority, the Netherlands Securities Board, commenced activities in 1989.

Euronext Amsterdam: Beursplein 5, 1012 JW Amsterdam; POB 19163, 1000 GD Amsterdam; tel. (20) 5505555; fax (20) 5504899;

e-mail info@euronext.nl; internet www.aex.nl; f. 2001 by merger of Amsterdam Exchanges, Paris Bourse and Brussels Exchanges; unitary stock and options exchange; CEO GEORGE MÖLLER.

There are also financial futures, grain, citrus fruits and insurance bourses in the Netherlands; the 'spot' market for petroleum operates from Rotterdam.

INSURANCE COMPANIES

AEGON Insurance Group: Mariahoeveplein 50, POB 202, 2501 CE The Hague; tel. (70) 3443210; fax (70) 3475238; f. 1983 by merger; life, accident, health, general and linked activities; Chair. DONALD SHEPARD.

AMEV Stad Rotterdam Verzekeringsgroep (ASR) NV: Weena 70, POB 100, 3000 AC Rotterdam; tel. (10) 4017465; fax (10) 4125490; internet www.asr.nl; f. 2000 by merger of ASR Verzekeringsgroep NV (f. 1720) and AMEV Nederland NV (f. 1883); owned by the Fortis group; Chair. C. J. DE SWART.

Delta Lloyd Verzekeringsgroep NV: Spaklerweg 4, POB 1000, 1000 BA Amsterdam; tel. (20) 5949111; fax (20) 937968; internet www.deltalloyd.nl; f. 1807; subsidiary of Commercial Union PLC (UK); Dirs A. A. ANBEEK VAN DER MEIJDEN, Baron G. W. VAN DER FELTZ, J. E. JANSEN.

De Eerste Nederlandsche: POB 325, 1170 AH Badhoevedorp; tel. (20) 6143340; fax (20) 6696556; e-mail eerstenl@pobox.com; internet www.eerste.nl; all branches.

Fiducia BV: Ruysdaelplein 42, 2282 BJ Rijswijk; tel. (70) 4140404; fax (70) 4140405; e-mail webmaster@fiducia.nl; internet www.fiducia.nl; f. 1990.

Generali Verzekeringsgroep: Diemerhof 42, 1112 XN Diemen; tel. (20) 6604444; fax (20) 3983000; e-mail info@generali.nl; internet www.generali.nl; f. 1870; life and non-life.

ING Verzekeringen NV: Strawinskylaan 2631, 1077 ZZ Amsterdam; tel. (70) 5415411; fax (70) 5415423; f. 1963; Chair. of Exec. Bd AAD G. JACOBS.

Nationale-Nederlanden Levensverzekering Maatschappij NV (Life Assurance): Weena 505, 3013 AL Rotterdam; tel. (10) 4449111; fax (10) 4449222; f. 1863; Chairs A. W. SLOOTWEG, G. M. A. M. VAN STAVEREN.

Nationale-Nederlanden Schadeverzekering Maatschappij NV (General Insurance): POB 90504, 2509 LM The Hague; tel. (70) 3418080; fax (70) 3416551; f. 1970; Chair. D. BRANDS.

RVS Levensverzekering NV: Weena 505, 3013 AL Rotterdam; tel. (10) 4012911; fax (10) 4012933; internet www.rvs.nl; f. 1838; mem. of Internationale-Nederlanden group; life; Chair. H. W. SMID.

Insurance Associations

Pensioen- en Verzekeringskamer (Chamber of Insurance and Pensions): POB 929, 7301 BD Apeldoorn; tel. (55) 3576677; fax (55) 3576565; e-mail info@pvk.nl; internet www.pvk.nl; f. 1923; Pres. D. E. WITTEVEEN.

Verbond van Verzekeraars (Asscn of Insurers): Bordewijklaan 2, POB 93450, 2509 AL The Hague; tel. (70) 3338500; fax (70) 338510; e-mail info@verzekeraars.nl; internet www.verzekeraars.nl; f. 1978; Chair. C. J. DE SWART; Gen. Man. Prof. Dr E. J. FISCHER.

Trade and Industry

GOVERNMENT AGENCIES

Nederlands Centrum voor Handelsbevordering (NCH) (Netherlands Council for Trade Promotion): Bezuidenhoutseweg 181, POB 10, 2501 CA The Hague; tel. (70) 3441544; fax (70) 3853531; internet www.handelsbervordering.nl; Man. Dir H. G. VAN BUREN.

Netherlands Foreign Investment Agency: Bezuidenhoutseweg 2, POB 20101, 2500 EC The Hague; tel. (70) 3798818; fax (70) 3796322; e-mail idcbin@minez.nl; internet www.nfia.nl; govt agency; facilitates foreign direct investment.

CHAMBERS OF COMMERCE

There are numerous Chambers of Commerce and Industry in the Netherlands. The most important are:

Kamer van Koophandel en Fabrieken voor Amsterdam (Chamber of Commerce and Industry for Amsterdam): De Ruyterkade 5, 1013 AA Amsterdam; POB 2852, 1000 CW Amsterdam; tel. (20) 5314000; fax (20) 5314799; e-mail post@amsterdam.kvk.nl; internet www.amsterdam.kvk.nl; f. 1811; Dir-Gen. Dr JACOB BEVAART.

Kamer van Koophandel Rotterdam (Chamber of Commerce for Rotterdam): Blaak 40, 3011 TA Rotterdam; POB 450, 3000 AL Rotterdam; tel. (10) 4027777; fax (10) 4145754; e-mail post@rotterdam.kvk.nl; internet www.rotterdam.kvk.nl; f. 1803; Pres. F.J LAVOOIJ.

Kamer van Koophandel voor Haaglanden (The Hague Chamber of Commerce): Koningskade 30, 2596 AA The Hague; POB 29718, 2502 LS The Hague; tel. (70) 3287100; fax (70) 3262010; e-mail info@denhaag.kvk.nl; internet www.denhaag.kvk.nl; Pres. M. J. VAREKAMP; Sec.-Gen. Dr G. ZANDSTEEG.

EMPLOYERS' ORGANIZATIONS

LTO-Nederland (Netherlands Agricultural Organization): Prinsevinkenpark 19, 2585 HK The Hague; POB 29773, 2502 LT The Hague; tel. (70) 3382700; fax (70) 3382810; f. 1995; Chair. G. J. DOORNBOS; 65,000 mems.

Netherlands Elektronica- en Radiogenootschap: POB 39, 2260 AK Leidschendam; tel. (70) 3325112; fax (70) 3326477; f. 1921; Pres. Prof. Dr W. C. VAN ETTEN; Sec. G. DE GROOT; 700 mems.

Nederlandsche Maatschappij voor Nijverheid en Handel (Netherlands Society for Industry and Trade): Herengracht 480, 1017 CB Amsterdam; tel. (20) 3831308; fax (20) 3831550; e-mail info@nmnh.nl; internet www.nmnh.nl; f. 1777; Chair. M. I. PLATSCHORRE; Dir-Gen. H. G. M. GIEZEMAN; more than 7,000 mems.

Nederlandse Tuinbouwraad (NTR) (Netherlands Horticultural Council): POB 1104, 1430 BC Aalsmeer; tel. (297) 360155; fax (297) 360156; e-mail cmoerman@vgb.nl; f. 1908; Chair. J. J. J. LANGESLAG; Sec. Ir J. M. GERRITSEN.

Vereniging VNO–NCW (Confederation of Netherlands Industry and Employers): Bezuidenhoutseweg 12, POB 93002, 2509 AA The Hague; tel. (70) 3490349; fax (70) 3490300; f. 1997 as merger of Verbond van Nederlandse Ondernemingen VNO and Nederlands Christelijk Werkgeversverbond; represents almost all sectors of the Dutch economy; Pres. JOHANNES C. BLANKERT; Dir-Gen. J. J. H. JACOBS; mems: 150 asscns representing more than 25,000 enterprises.

UTILITIES

Electricity

E.ON Benelux BV: POB 909, 2270 AX Voorburg; tel. (70) 3820028; fax (70) 3383901; e-mail info@eon-benelux.com; internet www.eon-benelux.com; f. 2000; replaced Electriciteitsbedrijf Zuid Holland (EZH) (f. 1941); supplies energy to large-volume customers and distributors.

ENECO: POB 899, 2900 AW Capelle aan den Ijssel; tel. (10) 4576979; fax (10) 4577784.

Energie Noord West NV: POB 23451, 1100 DZ Amsterdam; tel. (20) 3122500; fax (20) 3122699; internet www.enw.nl.

Essent: POB 9501, 9703 LM Groningen; internet www.essent.nl; f. 1999 by merger of Edon Group and Pnem Mega Group; electricity and gas supply.

Nuon ENW: POB 40021, 6803 HA Arnhem; e-mail nuon@nuon.com; internet www.nuon.com; f. 1999; energy and water; Dir T. SWELHEIM.

Sep: POB 575, 6800 AN Arnhem; tel. (26) 3721111; fax (26) 4430858.

Tennet BV: Utrechtseweg 310, POB 718, 6800 AS Arnhem; tel. (26) 3731111; fax (26) 3731112; e-mail servicedesu@tennet.org; internet www.tennet.org; f. 1999; independent; Dutch Transmission System Operator; manages 220/380 kV national grid and supplies electricity to direct suppliers; Chair. RUUD E. SELMAN; Dir M. KROON.

Gas

The last stage of the liberalization of the gas market in the Netherlands was scheduled to take place in January 2004 (postponed from January 2003). The functions of the wholesale and transport group, NV Nederlansdse Gasunie, were to be divided into a transport company, which would be state-owned, and a trading business, which would be shared equally by ExxonMobil and Shell.

ENECO: see above.

Essent: see above.

NV Nederlandse Gasunie: Concourslaan 17, POB 19, 9700 MA Groningen; tel. (50) 5219111; fax (50) 5211999; internet www.nunederlandsegasunie.nl.

Obragas: POB 300, 5700 AH Helmond; tel. (492) 594888; fax (492) 594990.

Water

Nuon: see above.

VEWIN: POB 1019, 2280 CA Rijswijk; tel. (70) 4144750; fax (70) 4144420; e-mail vewin@vewin.nl; internet www.vewin.nl.

TRADE UNIONS

Central Federations and affiliated unions are mainly organized on a religious, political or economic basis. The most important unions are those of the transport, metal, building and textile industries, the civil service and agriculture.

Central Federations

Christelijk Nationaal Vakverbond in Nederland (CNV) (Christian National Federation of Trade Unions): Ravellaan 1, POB 2475, 3500 GL Utrecht; tel. (30) 2913911; fax (30) 2946544; e-mail cnvinfo@cnv.nl; internet www.cnv.nl; f. 1909; Pres. D. TERPSTRA; Gen. Sec. J. WESTERBEEK-HUITINK; 359,000 mems.

Eleven affiliated unions, of which the principal unions are:

CNV Bedrijvenbond (Industry, Food and Transport): Prins Bernhardweg 69, POB 327, 3990 GC Houten; tel. (30) 6348348; fax (30) 6348200; e-mail info@cnv.net; internet www.cnv.net.

CNV Publiek Zaak (Public Sector Union): Carnegielaan 1, POB 84500, 2508 AM The Hague; tel. (70) 4160600; fax (70) 4160690; e-mail denhaag@cnvpubliekezaak.nl; internet www .cnvpubliekezaak.nl; Pres. P. J. KOESLAG; Sec. K. KRUITHOF; 84,000 mems.

Dienstenbond CNV (Service Industries, Media and Printing): Polarisave 175, POB 3135, 2130 KC Hoofddorp; tel. (23) 5651052; fax (23) 5650150; e-mail cnvdienstenbond@cnvdibo.nl; internet www .cnvdibo.nl; f. 1894; Pres. D. SWAGERMAN; Sec. R. J. ROTSHUIZEN; 35,000 mems.

Hout- en Bouwbond CNV (Wood and Building): Oude Haven 1, 3984 KT Odijk; tel. (30) 6597711; fax (30) 6571101; e-mail info@ hbbcnv.nl; internet www.hbbcnv.nl; f. 1900; Pres. D. VAN DE KAMP; Sec. A. A. VAN WIJNGAARDEN; 52,000 mems.

Onderwijsbond CNV (Education): Boerhaavelaan 5, POB 732, 2700 AS Zoetermeer; tel. (79) 3202020; fax (79) 3202195; e-mail algemeen@ocnv.nl; internet www.ocnv.nl.

Federatie Nederlandse Vakbeweging (FNV) (Netherlands Trade Union Confederation): POB 8456, 1005 AL Amsterdam; tel. (20) 5816300; fax (20) 6844541; e-mail persvoorlichting@vc.fnv.nl; internet www.fnv.nl; f. 1975 as confederation of the Netherlands Federation of Trade Unions (f. 1906) and the Netherlands Catholic Trade Union Federation (f. 1909); Pres. L. J. DE WAAL; Vice-Pres. C. E. ROOZEMOND; Gen. Sec. A. REGEER; 1,234,361 mems.

Seventeen affiliated unions, of which the principal are:

ABVAKABO FNV (Government Personnel, Civil Servants, Private Health Workers, Social Workers, Post and Telecom Workers, Public Utility Workers): Boerhaavelaan 1, POB 3010, 2700 KT Zoetermeer; tel. (79) 3536161; fax (79) 3521226; e-mail post@abvakabo.nl; internet www.abvakabo.nl; f. 1982; Pres. C. VRINS; Gen. Sec. R. CALJOUW-ROOIJACKERS; 360,000 mems.

Algemene Onderwijsbond (AOb) (Education): POB 2875, 3500 GW Utrecht; tel. (30) 2989898; fax (30) 29880; e-mail onderwijsbond@aob.nl; internet www.aob.nl; f. 1997 as merger between Algemene Bond van Onderwijspersoneel and NGL–Dordrecht; Pres. J. TICHELAAR; Gen. Sec. MARTIN KNOOP; 75,000 mems.

FNV Bondgenoten (Transport, Metal and Steel, Information Technology, Electrotechnical, Textiles, Financial Services, Retail, Wholesale, Foods, Agriculture): Goeman Borgesiuslaan 77, POB 9208, 3506 GE Utrecht; tel. (30) 2738222; fax (30) 2738225; internet www .bondgenoten.fnv.nl; f. 1998 by merger; Pres. H. VAN DER KOLK; Sec. (vacant); 500,000 mems.

FNV Bouw (Building): Houttuinlaan 3, POB 520, 3440 AM Woerden; tel. (348) 575575; fax (348) 423610; e-mail info@fnvbouw .nl; internet www.bouwenhoutbondfnv.nl; f. 1917; Pres. R. DE VRIES; Sec.-Gen. N. G. SCHOTANUS; 167,593 mems.

FNV KIEM (Printing and Allied Trades): J. Tooropstraat, POB 9354, 1006 AJ Amsterdam; tel. (20) 3553636; fax (20) 3553737; e-mail algemeen@fnv-kiem.nl; internet www.fnv.nl/kiem; Pres. R. VAN TILBORG; Gen. Sec. H. LEISINK; 51,500 mems.

Nederlandse Politiebond (Police): Boerhaavelaan 1, POB 393, 2700 AJ, Zoetermeer; tel. (79) 3536161; fax (79) 3521226; e-mail info@politieboind.nl; internet www.politiebond.nl; f. 1946; Pres. J. F. W. VAN DUIJN; Gen. Sec. FRANS VAN DER HEIDEN; 19,500 mems.

Consultative Organization

Stichting van de Arbeid (Labour Foundation): Bezuidenhoutseweg 60, 2594 AW The Hague; tel. (70) 3499577; fax (70) 3499796; internet www.stvda.nl; f. 1945; central organ of co-operation and consultation between employers and employees; 16 bd mems; Jt Pres J. H. SCHRAVEN, L. J. DE WAAL; Sec. Drs E. H. BROEKEMA.

Land Reclamation and Development

Without intensive land-protection schemes, nearly the whole of the north and west of the Netherlands (about one-half of the total area of the country) would be inundated by sea-water twice a day. A large part of the country (including a section of the former Zuiderzee, now the Ijsselmeer) has already been drained.

The Delta Plan, which was adopted in 1958 and provided for the construction of eight dams, a major canal, several locks and a system of dikes, aimed to shorten the southern coastline by 700 km and to protect the estuaries of Zeeland and Southern Holland. The final cost of the delta works project, which had originally been projected at 2,500m. guilders, totalled around 14,000m. guilders, as the result of a complex adaptation to ensure the preservation of the delta's ecological balance.

The Ministry of Transport, Public Works and Water Management is responsible for land reclamation and waterways.

Transport

RAILWAYS

About 70% of the Dutch railway network is electrified; the remaining track carries diesel electric and diesel stock. There were 2,808 km of state-operated railways in 1999, providing mainly passenger services. The infrastructure of the Dutch railway network remains wholly under public ownership. Until early 2002 the main railway operator, Nederlandse Spoorwegen (NS), was partially privatized, but, following a sharp deterioration in the quality of service, was taken back under government control. NS retains a majority of the passenger and freight rolling stock, and station premises, while there is a small number of additional, privately-owned network service providers. In 1999 the Government announced the construction of a high-speed line between Amsterdam and the Belgian border.

Lovers Rail: POB 2109, 1000 CC Amsterdam; tel. (20) 4212202; fax (20) 4210997; internet www.loversrail.nl; f. 1996; 70% owned by CGEA; operates regular services between Amsterdam and Haarlem, also seasonal trains between Amsterdam and Keukenhof.

Nederlandse Spoorwegen NV (NS): Antwoordnummer 4470, POB 2025, 3500 VE Utrecht; tel. (30) 2359111; fax (30) 2332458; internet www.ns.nl; f. 1937; partially privatized until early 2002, when the Government reassertmed management control; operates most railway lines in the Netherlands; Man. Dir (vacant).

NS Stations: POB 2534, 3500 GM, Utrecht; tel. (30) 2352500; fax (30) 2311490; station management co; Dir Z. J. J. VAN WYCK.

NS Vastgoed: POB 2319, 3500 GH, Utrecht; tel. (30) 3004310; fax (30) 3004400; property management and property development co; Dir H. E. PORTHEINE.

NoordNed Personenvervoer BV: Stationsplein 4, POB 452, 8901 BG Leeuwarden; tel. (58) 2335600; fax (58) 2335636; e-mail directie@noordned-ov.nl; internet www.noordned-ov.nl; f. 1999; operates train and bus services in North and West Friesland; operated by Arriva Nederland and NS Reizigers.

Railion Benelux NV: POB 2060, 3500 GB Utrecht; tel. (30) 2354004; fax (30) 2354334; e-mail info@railion.nl; internet www .railion.nl; international goods transport by rail.

ROADS

In 1999 there were 2,235 km of motorway, 6,650 km of main roads, 57,500 km of secondary roads and 59,400 km of other roads in the Netherlands. It was announced in 1988 that five tunnels were to be constructed under inland waterways in the 'western corridor' of the Netherlands, in an attempt to alleviate severe traffic congestion in that region. The construction of the first tunnel, under the river De Noord, was completed in 1993, and the construction of the second was under way in the mid-1990s. Cycling is a popular means of transport in the Netherlands, and in 1996 there were 19,100 km of cycle paths.

INLAND WATERWAYS

An extensive network of rivers and canals navigable for ships of 50 tons and over, totalling 5,046 km, has led to the outstanding development of Dutch inland shipping. About one-third of goods transported inside the Netherlands are carried on the canals and waterways. Dutch inland shipping has access to Germany and France along the Rhine and its branch rivers, and to France and Belgium along the the Meuse and Scheldt (including the Rhine-Scheldt link). Ocean traffic reaches Rotterdam via the New Waterway, and the 21-km long North Sea Canal connects Amsterdam to the North Sea. Following severe river flooding in early 1995, the Government announced the inauguration of a five-year programme to improve and strengthen the Netherlands' river dikes defence system.

SHIPPING

The Netherlands is one of the world's leading shipping countries. At the end of 2001 the merchant fleet comprised 1,337 vessels, with a combined displacement of 5,605,047 gross registered tons. The Rotterdam complex, incorporating the Europoort for large oil tankers and bulk carriers, is the main EU port and the busiest port in the world, handling some 3,000m. metric tons of traffic in 1998.

Principal Companies

Amasus Chartering BV: Zijlvest 26, Farmsum, POB 250, 9930 Delfzijl; tel. (596) 610744; fax (596) 616551; e-mail chartering@amasus.nl; internet www.rah-shipping.com; ship owners, managers and operators; Man. Dir S. Vonk.

Hudig & Veder's Stoomvaart Maatschappij BV: Debussystraat 2, POB 1030, 3160 AE Rhoon; tel. (10) 5066600; fax (10) 5019684; f. 1882; charter services; liner service to Ireland; Man. Dir J. G. A. Fontein.

KNSM-Kroonburgh BV: Boompjes 40, POB 958, 3000 AZ Rotterdam; tel. (10) 4007222; fax (10) 4007221; e-mail knsm.rtm@wxs.nl; liner services from Rotterdam/Antwerp/Felixstowe to southern Iberia and Morocco; Gen. Man. S. Smulders.

Koninklijke Vopak NV: Blaak 333, POB 863, 3000 AW Rotterdam; tel. (10) 4002911; fax (10) 4139829; e-mail info@vopak.com; internet www.vopak.com; f. 1839; tank storage, transportation of liquids; logistic services; Chair. C. J. van den Driest.

Royal Nedlloyd NV: POB 487, 3000 AL Rotterdam; tel. (10) 4007111; fax (10) 4006460; internet www.nedlloyd.com; Chair. Leo J. M. Berndsen.

Seatrade Groningen BV: Laan Corpus den Hoorn 200, POB 858, JS Groningen; tel. (50) 5215300; fax (50) 5215300; ship owners, managers and operators; Man. Dir J. A. N. Westerbeek.

Spliethoff's Bevrachtingskantoor BV: Radarweg 36, POB 409, 1000 AK Amsterdam; tel. (20) 4488400; fax (20) 4488500; ship owners, managers and operators; Man. P. J. M. G. Helderman.

Stena Line: Stationsweg 10, POB 2, 3150 AA Hoek van Holland; tel. (174) 389333; fax (174) 389309; e-mail info.nl@stenaline.nl; internet www.stenaline.nl; operates daily (day and night) ferry services for accompanied private cars, commercial freight vehicles and trailers between Hoek van Holland and Harwich (UK); Man. Dir W. de Lange.

Van Uden Maritime BV: POB 1123, 3000 BC, Rotterdam; tel. (10) 2973100; fax (10) 4851044; e-mail group@van-uden.nl; internet www.van-uden.nl; f. 1848; agencies in Rotterdam, Antwerp, Amsterdam; liner operators; and representatives; international chartering; Man. J. A. Dorpmans.

Vroon BV: Haven Westzijde 21, POB 28, 4510 AA Breskens; tel. (117) 384910; fax (117) 384218; ship owners, managers and operators; Chair. and Man. Dir P. W. Vroon.

Wagenborg Shipping BV: Marktstraat 10, POB 14, 9930 AA Delfzyl; tel. (596) 636911; fax (596) 636250; internet www.wagenborg.com; ship owners, managers and operators; Man. Dirs Dr E. Vuursteen, Dr G. R. Wagenborg.

Wijnne & Barends' Cargadoors- en Agentuurkantonen BV: POB 123, 9930 AC Delfzyl; tel. (596) 637777; fax (596) 637790; e-mail wyba@wijnne-barends.nl; internet www.wijnne-barends.nl;

ship owners, managers and operators; cargo services and agents; Man. Dir D. P. Makkinje.

Shipping Associations

Federatie van Werknemers in de Zeevaart (Dutch Seafarers' Federation): Heemraadssingel 323, POB 25131, 3001 HC Rotterdam; tel. (10) 4771188; fax (10) 4773846; e-mail fwz.nl@wxs.nl.

Koninklijke Nederlandse Redersvereniging (Royal Netherlands Shipowners' Asscn): Wijnhaven 65B, POB 2442, 3000 CK Rotterdam; tel. (10) 4146001; fax (10) 2330081; f. 1905; Chair. A. Korteland; Man. Dir P. A. Th. van Agtmaal; 300 mems.

Vereniging Nederlandse Scheepsbouw Industrie (Netherlands Shipbuilding Industry Association): Boerhaavelaan 40, POB 138, 2700 AC Zoetermeer; tel. (79) 3531165; fax (79) 3531155; e-mail vns@fme.nl; promotes Dutch shipbuilding on a national basis; Man. Dir R. J. Schouten; 95 mems.

CIVIL AVIATION

The main Dutch airport is at Schiphol, near Amsterdam. There are also international airports at Zestienhoven for Rotterdam, Beek for Maastricht and at Eelde for Groningen. Schiphol expanded rapidly during the late 1990s (from 25.3m. passengers in 1995 to 36.4m. in 1999), and in late 1999 plans were approved for the construction of a fifth runway, scheduled to open in 2003, while it was intended that the scheduled privatization of Schiphol would attract further investment in the airport's infrastructure.

Air Holland BV: Breguetlaan 67, POB 75116, 1117 ZR Schiphol; tel. (20) 3164444; fax (20) 3164445; e-mail info@airholland.nl; internet www.airholland.nl; f. 1991; passenger and cargo charter flights; entered administration in Nov. 1999; Man. Dir L. Sauwen.

KLM (Koninklijke Luchtvaart Maatschappij NV) (Royal Dutch Airlines): Schiphol Airport, POB 7700, 1117 ZL Schiphol; head office: Amsterdamseweg 55, 1182 GP Amstelveen; tel. (20) 6499123; fax (20) 6488069; internet www.klm.com; f. 1919; world's oldest commercial airline; regular international air services; 14% state-owned; subsidiaries: KLM Cityhopper, KLM UK; Pres.-Dir and CEO Leo van Wijk; Gen. Sec. H. E. Kuipéri.

Martinair Holland NV: POB 7507, 1118 ZG Schiphol Airport; tel. (20) 6011222; fax (20) 6011303; internet www.martinair.com; f. 1958; 50% owned by Nedlloyd; world-wide passenger and cargo services; Pres. and CEO Aart van Bochove.

Schreiner Airways: Diamantlaan 1, 2132 WV Hoofddorp; tel. (23) 5555525; fax (23) 5555520; e-mail management.saw@schreiner.nl; internet www.schreiner.nl; f. 1945; scheduled flights and leasing services; Man. Dir Tjapko van Wijk.

Transavia Airlines: POB 7777, 1118 ZM Schiphol Airport; tel. (20) 6046555; fax (20) 6484637; f. 1966; scheduled and charter services to leisure destinations; 80% owned by KLM; Pres. Peter J. Legro.

Tulip Air: POB 12059, 3004 GB Rotterdam; e-mail info@tulipair.nl; internet www.tulipair.com; f. 1988; air taxi and passenger charter services; Man. Dir J. A. van der Meer.

Tourism

The principal tourist attractions in the Netherlands are the cosmopolitan city of Amsterdam, which receives nearly one-half of all tourist visits, the old towns, the canals, the cultivated fields of spring flowers, the outlying islands, the art galleries and modern architecture. Some 10.0m. foreign tourists stayed in hotels and boarding houses in the Netherlands in 2000. Receipts from tourism totalled an estimated US $6,951m. in 2000.

Toerisme Recreatie Nederland (Netherlands Board of Tourism): Vlietweg 15, POB 458, 2260 MG Leidschendam; tel. (70) 3705705; fax (70) 3201654; e-mail info@holland.com; internet www.holland.com; f. 1968; Man. Dir F. J. van Driem.

Royal Dutch Touring Club ANWB: Wassenaarseweg 220, 2509 BA The Hague; tel. (70) 3147147; fax (70) 3146969; f. 1883; Dir-Gen. P. A. Nouwen; 50 brs in Europe; 3m. mems.

NETHERLANDS DEPENDENCIES

ARUBA

Introductory Survey

Location, Climate, Language, Religion, Flag, Capital

Aruba is one of the group of Benedenwindse Eilands or 'Leeward Islands', which it forms with part of the Netherlands Antilles (q.v.), and lies in the southern Caribbean Sea, 25 km north of Venezuela and 68 km west of the island of Curaçao (Netherlands Antilles). The climate is tropical, with an average annual temperature of 28°C (82°F), but is tempered by north-easterly winds. Rainfall is very low, averaging only about 425.5 mm (16.8 ins) annually. The official language is Dutch, but the dominant language is Papiamento (a mixture of Dutch, Spanish, English, Arawak Indian and several West African dialects). Spanish and English are also spoken. Most of the inhabitants profess Christianity and belong to the Roman Catholic Church, although a wide variety of other denominations are represented. The national flag (proportions 2 by 3) is blue, with two narrow yellow horizontal stripes in the lower section and a white-bordered four-pointed red star in the upper hoist. The capital is Oranjestad.

Recent History

The Caribbean island of Aruba was claimed for Spain in 1499, but was first colonized by the Dutch in 1636 and subsequently formed part of the Dutch possessions in the West Indies. Administered from Curaçao after 1845, in 1954 Aruba became a member of the autonomous federation of the Netherlands Antilles. The establishment in 1929 of a large petroleum refinery on the island, at San Nicolaas, led to the rapid expansion of the economy and a high standard of living for the islanders. However, many Arubans resented the administrative dominance of Curaçao, and what they regarded as the excessive demands made upon Aruban wealth and resources by the other five islands within the Netherlands Antilles. The island's principal political party, the Movimentu Electoral di Pueblo (MEP), campaigned, from its foundation in 1971 onwards, for Aruban independence and separation from the other islands. In a referendum held in Aruba in March 1977 82% of voters supported independence and withdrawal from the Antillean federation. The MEP used its position in the coalition Government of the Netherlands Antilles, formed in 1979, to press for concessions from the other islands towards early independence for Aruba. In 1981 (after the MEP had withdrawn from the Government of the Netherlands Antilles) a provisional agreement regarding Aruba's future was reached between the Dutch and Antillean Governments. Following further discussions, it was agreed in March 1983 that Aruba should receive separate status (*status aparte*), within the Kingdom of the Netherlands, from 1 January 1986, achieving full independence in 1996. The Dutch Government would remain responsible for defence and external relations until independence, while Aruba was to form a co-operative union with the Netherlands Antilles (the Antilles of the Five) in economic and monetary affairs.

At local elections in April 1983 the MEP increased its representation to 13 of the 21 seats in the Staten (parliament), and the leader of the MEP, Gilberto F. (Betico) Croes, remained as leader of the island Government. Austerity measures, introduced in an attempt to alleviate the adverse effects of the closure (announced in October 1984) of the San Nicolaas petroleum refinery, provoked a series of strikes and demonstrations by civil servants in protest at wage reductions and price rises. The MEP consequently lost popular support, and, following elections to the Staten in November 1985, the MEP was succeeded in government by a coalition of four opposition parties led by the Arubaanse Volkspartij (AVP). Aruba achieved separate status, as planned, on 1 January 1986, and Jan Hendrik Albert (Henny) Eman, leader of the AVP, became its first Prime Minister. Croes died in November 1986; he was succeeded as leader of the MEP by Nelson O. Oduber.

From 1988 Aruba began to enjoy an economic recovery, based on tourism. However, the MEP claimed that the benefits to the whole community were limited, and also criticized Eman's stated reservations about independence in 1996 and his refusal to negotiate with the Netherlands about transitional arrangements. At a general election in January 1989 the MEP came within 28 votes of securing an absolute majority in the Staten. The number of seats held by the MEP increased from eight to 10, and in February Oduber formed a Government in coalition with the Partido Patriótico Arubano (PPA) and the Accion Democratico Nacional (ADN). (Both these parties had been in the previous Government, and retained one seat each at the election.)

The MEP and the AVP each secured nine seats in the Staten at the January 1993 general election, while the three remaining seats were won by the ADN, the PPA and the Organisacion Liberal Arubano (OLA). Despite gaining fewer votes than the AVP, the MEP administration remained in office, renewing the coalition with the ADN and the PPA. In April 1994, however, Oduber announced the Government's resignation, following the withdrawal of the ADN and the PPA from the coalition. In May, following lengthy inter-party negotiations, it was agreed that a fresh general election would be held. Government functions were to be undertaken in the interim by the MEP. The general election was held on 29 July: the AVP secured 10 seats, while the MEP won nine seats and the OLA the remaining two. In late August Eman formed a Government in coalition with the OLA.

In March 1994 the Governments of Aruba, the Netherlands and the Netherlands Antilles convened in The Hague, the Netherlands, and decided to cancel plans for Aruba's transition to full independence, due to take place in 1996. The possibility of a transition to full independence at a later date was not excluded, but was not considered a priority, and would, moreover, require the approval of the Aruban people, by referendum, as well as the support of a two-thirds' majority in the Staten.

In September 1997 the Staten was dissolved after the OLA withdrew from the coalition. A general election was thus held on 12 December; this resulted in a political composition identical to that of the 1993 polls. Following protracted negotiations, the AVP and the OLA renewed their coalition in mid-1998, and a new Council of Ministers, headed by Eman, was appointed.

In October 2000 Air Aruba, the national carrier, suspended all operations after a Taiwanese lease company demanded the return of three aircraft following stalled payments amounting to US $9m. Subsequently, the US Federal Aviation Authority withdrew Air Aruba's landing rights and in November the carrier was declared bankrupt with the loss of 330 jobs.

In June 2001 the governing coalition collapsed, following the withdrawal of the OLA's support for the AVP's plan to privatize the Aruban Tourism Authority. As a result, the legislative elections that had been scheduled to be held in December were brought forward to 28 September. The MEP defeated the incumbent AVP in the elections, securing 52.4% of the votes cast and 12 seats in the Staten. The AVP legislative representation was reduced to six seats. The three remaining seats were shared between the PPA (two) and the OLA (one). The electoral turnout amongst those eligible to vote was 86.5%. Oduber was once again appointed Prime Minister and a new Government took office in November.

In August 2002 a US developer, Ralph Sanchez, won US $20.5m. in damages from the Aruban Government, to be paid over five years, at a court case in Miami, Florida (USA). Sanchez claimed that the previous Government of Henny Emman had, following environmental concerns, failed to honour a contract, signed in 2000, to build a motor-racing circuit on Aruba. In November the judge reduced the sum of damages to $19.1m. because of an accounting error by Sanchez's financial expert. None the less, the Government disputed the verdict and announced its intention to launch an appeal, which was due to be heard in early 2003. In addition, the Aruban Government announced it was commencing a criminal investigation of Sanchez and would possibly seek his extradition.

Aruba's relations with the Antilles of the Five improved after 1986. In 1987 Aruba agreed to undertake economic co-operation, and in 1988 the three Dutch 'Leeward Islands' initiated a joint project for the development of tourism. Aruba's relations with the 'metropolitan' Netherlands were dominated at this time by the latter's pressure for more control to be exercised over the large amount of aid that it gave to Aruba, and by the issue of independence, in particular the future arrangements for the island's security: Aruba's strategic position, close to the South American mainland, and the possibility of its being used as a base for drugs-trafficking, were matters of particular concern. In September 1990 Aruba announced that it was to adopt the 1988 UN Convention on measures to combat trade in illegal drugs; a joint Dutch and Aruban team was formed to conduct investigations. In December 1996, however, the USA included Aruba on its list of major drugs-producing or transit countries. New legislation to facilitate the extradition of suspected drugs-traffickers and money-launderers took effect in October 1997. US naval and air force patrols began operating from a base in Aruba in May 1999 in an effort to counter the transport of illicit drugs. In 2001 the Caribbean Financial Action Task Force commended the Government on its efforts in combating money-laundering. Following Aruba's inclusion, in June 2000, on a list of so-called 'non-co-operative tax havens' drawn up by the Organisation for Economic Co-operation and Development (OECD, based in Paris, France), in 2001 the Government of Aruba pledged to reform the territory's financial sector in order to conform to OECD's guide-lines by 2005.

After acquiring separate status, Aruba fostered relations with some of its Caribbean neighbours and with countries in Latin America. This included the development of ties with Venezuela, which had traditionally laid claim to the Dutch 'Leeward Islands', including Aruba.

Government

Aruba has separate status within the Kingdom of the Netherlands. Legislative power is held by the unicameral Staten (parliament) of 21 members, elected by universal adult suffrage for four years (subject to dissolution). Executive power in all domestic affairs is vested in the Council of Ministers (led by the Prime Minister), responsible to the Staten. The Governor, appointed by the Dutch Crown for a term of six years, represents the monarch of the Netherlands on Aruba and holds responsibility for external affairs and defence. The Governor is assisted by an advisory council.

Defence

The Netherlands is responsible for Aruba's defence and military service is compulsory. The Governor is Commander-in-Chief of the armed forces on the island. A Dutch naval contingent is stationed in Aruba, primarily to combat drugs-trafficking and organized crime. In May 1999 the USA began air force and navy patrols from a base on Aruba as part of efforts to prevent the transport of illegal drugs.

Economic Affairs

In 1997, according to the World Bank, Aruba's gross national income (GNI), measured at average 1995–97 prices, was estimated to be US $1,181m. During 1990–2000, it was estimated, the population increased at an average annual rate of 4.2% per year, while overall GDP increased, in real terms, at an average annual rate of 3.6% during 1996–2001. Gross domestic product (GDP), in current prices, according to estimates by the Central Bank, was $1,901.7m., equivalent to $18,829 per head, in 2001. In 2001 real GDP decreased by 1.2%.

Owing to the poor quality of the soil and the prohibitive cost of desalinated water, the only significant agricultural activity is the cultivation of aloes (used in the manufacture of cosmetics and pharmaceuticals); aloe-based products are exported. Some livestock is raised, and there is a small fishing industry (although in the mid-1990s fishing production contributed only some 12.5% of Aruba's annual consumption of fish and fish products). In 2000 the agricultural sector engaged 0.6% of the employed labour force.

The industrial sector, and the island's economy, was formerly based on the refining and transhipment of imported petroleum and petroleum products. In the early 1980s this sector accounted for one-quarter of GDP and provided almost all Aruba's exports. The San Nicolaas petroleum refinery ceased operations in 1985; however, in 1990 the plant partially reopened, following renovation; following further construction and revision works, production reached an estimated 202,000 b/d in 1999, an increase of 26% on the previous year's total. Following a further US $250m. renovation in 2000, production increased to 280,000 b/d. However, in April 2001 the refinery closed temporarily following an

explosion; as a result, output fell by some 42% in the final quarter of 2001, compared with the corresponding period in 2000. There is a large petroleum transhipment terminal on Aruba, and a small petrochemicals industry. An advanced-technology coker plant opened in 1995 to supply liquefied petroleum gas, largely for export to the USA. There are believed to be exploitable reserves of hydrocarbons within Aruban territory, and Aruba also has reserves of salt.

Light industry is limited to the production of beverages, building materials, paints and solvents, paper and plastic products, candles, detergents, disinfectants, soaps and aloe-based cosmetics. There is a 'free zone', and the ports of Oranjestad and Barcadera provide bunkering and repair facilities for ships. In 1996 the Ports of Aruba Masterplan was presented, proposing the relocation (over a 20-year period) of all cargo operations to Barcadera, leaving Oranjestad's port to accommodate commercial, recreation and resort activities. The construction sector, which grew steadily in the 1980s, declined in importance following a moratorium on the construction of new hotels in 1992. Industry (including mining, manufacturing, construction and power) engaged 16.4% of the employed labour force in 2000.

The service industries are Aruba's principal economic activity, employing 83.0% of the active labour force in 2000. Financial services are well established in Aruba, particularly the data-processing sector, an important service to US companies in particular. Aruba's principal source of income is tourism. The number of stop-over visitors increased by 5.3% in 2000, to 721,224. In the same year the number of cruise-ship passengers totalled 490,005, an increase of 41.0% on the previous year. However, in 2001 there was a slight decrease in the number of visitor arrivals, attributed mainly to the global economic slow-down and to the effects on tourism of the terrorist attacks on the USA in September of that year. The number of stop-over visitors decreased by 4.3%, to 691,419, while the number of cruise-ship passengers contracted by 0.6%, to 487,296. In 2002 the overall number of visitor arrivals increased, by 3.9%; however, this disguised a further 7.1% decrease in the number of stop-over visitors, to 642,627. The number of cruise-ship passengers increased by 19.5%, to 582,195. In 2002 receipts from tourism totalled US $903.3m. Tourist arrivals were reported to have increased strongly in the first two months of 2003, although the US-led military campaign against the regime of Saddam Hussain in Iraq was predicted to dampen growth for the remaining months of the year.

Aruba is obliged to import most of its requirements, particularly machinery and transport equipment, chemical products and foodstuffs. None the less, in 2001 Aruba recorded a visible trade surplus of A Fl. 138.6m., and there was a surplus on the current account of the balance of payments of A Fl. 764.3m. In 2001 the principal source of imports, excluding the petroleum sector and the 'free zone', was the USA (61.8% of the total); other major sources were the Netherlands, the Netherlands Antilles and Venezuela. The principal markets for exports in 2001 was also the USA (accounting for 26.9% of the total), followed by Venezuela, the Netherlands Antilles and the Netherlands.

In 2001 the budget deficit was A Fl. 18.0m. In 1994 the level of Dutch development assistance was approximately US $35.5m. In 1998 Aruba received $10.7m. in bilateral aid and $0.6m. in multilateral aid. At the end of 2001 total government debt was A Fl. 1,151.9m. (equivalent to 34.1% of GDP), of which 34.1% was owed to external creditors, primarily the Government of the Netherlands. The average annual rate of inflation was 3.9% in 1990–2000 and 2.9% in 1995–2002. The rate for the 12 months to December was 2.9% in 2001 and 3.3% in 2002. 6.9% of the labour force were unemployed in 2000.

As part of the Kingdom of the Netherlands, Aruba is classed as an Overseas Territory in association with the European Union (see p. 199). It forms a co-operative union with the Antilles of the Five in monetary and economic affairs. Aruba also has observer status with the Caribbean Community and Common Market (CARICOM, see p. 155).

The closure of the San Nicolaas petroleum refinery in 1985 and Aruba's separation from the rest of the Netherlands Antilles in 1986 prompted the Aruban administration to institute a policy of retrenchment and austerity, except for investment in tourism development. By the beginning of the 1990s, however, the economy was performing strongly, stimulated by rapid growth in the construction and tourism sectors, and the reopening of the refinery in 1990. In 1992, following six consecutive years of rapid economic growth, during which period there was a threefold increase in hotel capacity, a moratorium was imposed on construction in the tourism industry, partly in recognition of the adverse environmental impact on the island and also to preserve the island's reputation as an exclusive holiday destination for the wealthy. Economic growth subsequently slowed to a more sustainable level during the remainder of the decade, with real GDP growth rates at an average of between 3%–4% annually. During the 1990s Aruba maintained low levels of inflation and of unemployment, and in the early 21st century Aruba was considered to be one of the most prosperous islands in the Caribbean. Concern has, however, been expressed that Aruba's high public-sector wage bill and the generous nature of Aruba's social welfare system, combined with the island's ageing population, will threaten the future stability of public finance, which has already been hindered by a narrow taxation base and poor revenue collection. Reports in early 2002 claimed that Aruba's economic problems were worse than previously expected, with the repercussions of the terrorist attacks on the USA in September 2001 badly affecting the tourism and construction sectors, and preliminary reports showed that real GDP declined by 3.8% in that year. None the less, in early 2003 the IMF predicted growth of 4% in 2003, owing to an expectedly sharp increase in public and private investment, and a modest revival in tourism. However, following the commencement of the US-led military campaign to oust the regime of Saddam Hussain in Iraq in March 2003 and its potentially negative effect on tourism, projected growth for the year was reduced to 1%.

Education

A Compulsory Education Act was introduced in 1999, to cover the four-to-16 age-group. Kindergarten begins at four years of age. Primary education begins at six years of age and lasts for six years. Secondary education, beginning at the age of 12, lasts for up to six years. The main language of instruction is Dutch, but Papiamento (using a different spelling system from that of the Antilles of the Five) is used in kindergarten and primary education and in the lower levels of technical and vocational education. Papiamento is also being introduced onto the curriculum in all schools. In Aruba there are two institutes of higher education: the University of Aruba, comprising the School of Law and the School of Business Administration, which had 208 students in 1999/2000; and the Teachers' College, which had 180 students in 2000/01. There is also a community college. The majority of students, however, continue their studies abroad, generally in the Netherlands. The Government allocated a planned 12.6% of budget expenditure to education in 1999, equivalent to an estimated 3.4% of GDP.

Public Holidays

2003: 1 January (New Year's Day), 25 January (Gilberto F. (Betico) Croes' Birthday), 3 March (Lenten Carnival), 18 March (National Anthem and Flag Day), 18–21 April (Easter), 30 April (Queen's Day), 1 May (Labour Day), 29 May (Ascension Day), 25–26 December (Christmas).

2004: 1 January (New Year's Day), 25 January (Gilberto F. (Betico) Croes' Birthday), 23 February (Lenten Carnival), 18 March (National Anthem and Flag Day), 9–11 April (Easter), 30 April (Queen's Day), 1 May (Labour Day), 20 May (Ascension Day), 25–26 December (Christmas).

Weights and Measures

The metric system is in force.

Statistical Survey

Sources (unless otherwise stated): Department of Economic Affairs, Commerce and Industry (Direktie Economische Zaken, Handel en Industrie), Sun Plaza Bldg, L. G. Smith Blvd 160, Oranjestad; tel. (8) 21181; fax (8) 34494; e-mail deaci@setarnet .aw; internet www.arubaeconomicaffairs.com; Centrale Bank van Aruba, J. E. Irausquin Blvd 8, Oranjestad; tel. (8) 22509; fax (8) 32251; e-mail cbaua@setarnet.aw; internet www.cbaruba.org.

AREA AND POPULATION

Area: 193 sq km (74.5 sq miles).

Population: 66,687 (males 32,821, females 33,866) at census of 6 October 1991; 93,333 (males 44,664; females 48,669) at mid-2002.

Density (mid-2002): 483.6 per sq km.

Principal Towns (population estimates, 2002): Oranjestad (capital) 20,700; Sant Nicolaas 17,400. Source: Stefan Helders, *World Gazetteer* (internet www.world-gazetteer.com).

Births and Deaths (2001): Registered live births 1,266 (birth rate 13.8 per 1,000); Registered deaths 477 (death rate 5.2 per 1,000).

Expectation of Life (years at birth): Males 70.0; Females 76.0 in 2000.

Economically Active Population (persons aged 15 years and over, 2000): Agriculture, hunting and forestry 251; Manufacturing electricity, gas and water 2,940; Construction 3,892; Wholesale and retail trade, repairs 7,112; Hotels and restaurants 7,651; Transport, storage and communications 2,905; Financial intermediation 1,485; Real estate, renting and business activities 3,722; Public administration, defence and social security 3,573; Education 1,431; Health and social work 1,986; Other community, social and personal services 2,776; Private households with employed persons 1,870; Other 324; Total employed 41,918; Unemployed 3,118; Total labour force 45,036.

HEALTH AND WELFARE

Under-5 Mortality Rate (per 1,000 live births, 1996): 4.1.

Physicians (per 1,000 head, 1997): 1.28.

Hospital Beds (per 1,000 head, 1995): 37.0.

Health Expenditure (% of GDP (1994)): 6.0.

Access to Water (% of persons, 1995): 100.

Access to Sanitation (% of persons, 1995): 100 (Source: Pan American Health Organization).
For definitions, see explanatory note on p.vi.

FISHING

Total catch (metric tons, live weight, 2000): 163 (Groupers 18, Snappers and jobfishes 45, Wahoo 60, Other marine fishes 40). Source: FAO, *Yearbook of Fishery Statistics*.

INDUSTRY

Electric Energy (million kWh, 2002): 824.6.

FINANCE

Currency and Exchange Rates: 100 cents = 1 Aruban gulden (guilder) or florin (A Fl.). *Sterling, Dollar and Euro Equivalents* (31 December 2002): £1 sterling = A Fl. 2.885; US $1 = A Fl. 1.790; €1 = A Fl. 1.877; A Fl. 100 = £34.66 = $55.87 = €53.27. Note: The Aruban florin was introduced in January 1986, replacing (at par) the Netherlands Antilles guilder or florin (NA Fl.). Since its introduction, the currency has had a fixed exchange rate of US $1 = A Fl. 1.79.

Budget (A Fl. million, 2001): *Revenue:* Tax revenue 606.3 (Taxes on income and profits 302.8, Taxes on commodities 202.6, Taxes on property 27.8, Taxes on services 48.3, Foreign exchange commission 24.8); Other current revenue 125.3; Total 731.6. *Expenditure:* Wages 255.2; Employers' contributions 24.2; Wage subsidies 91.5; Goods and services 135.9; Interest payments 35.9; Investments 18.4; Other expenditure 188.4; Total 749.6.

International Reserves (US $ million at 31 December 2002): Gold 36.00; Foreign exchange 334.94; Total 370.94. Source: IMF, *International Financial Statistics*.

Money Supply (A Fl. million at 31 December 2002): Currency outside banks 127.84; Demand deposits at commercial banks 705.49; Total money (incl. others) 844.49. Source: IMF, *International Financial Statistics*.

Cost of Living (Consumer Price Index at December; base: September 2000 = 100): 115.3 in 2000; 118.6 in 2001; 122.5 in 2002.

Gross Domestic Product (US $ million at current prices): 1,745.3 in 1999; 1,860.9 in 2000; 1,901.7 in 2001.

Expenditure on the Gross Domestic Product (A. Fl. million at current prices, 2001): Government final consumption expenditure 768; Private final consumption expenditure 1,783; Increase in stocks 38; Gross fixed capital formation 675; *Total domestic expenditure* 3,264; Exports of goods and services 2,439; *Less* Imports of goods and services 2,321; *GDP in purchasers' values* 3,381.

Balance of Payments (A Fl. million, 2001): Exports of goods f.o.b. 4,366.2; Imports of goods f.o.b. -4,227.6; *Trade balance* 138.6; Exports of services 1,885.5; Imports of services -1,148.7; *Balance on goods and services* 875.4; Other income received 79.3; Other income paid -120.6; *Balance on goods, services and income* 834.1; Current transfers received 76.7; Current transfers paid -146.5; *Current account balance* 764.3; Capital account (net) -1.5; Direct investment abroad -23.1; Direct investment from abroad -580.2; Portfolio investment assets 34.7; Portfolio investment liabilities-6.1; Other investment (net) -43.8; Net errors and omissions -8.7; *Overall balance* 135.6.

EXTERNAL TRADE

Principal Commodities (US $ million, 2002): Imports c.i.f.: Live animals and animal products 50.7; Vegetable products 27.4; Food products 82.0; Chemical products 91.3; Plastic products 23.2; Pearls and other precious stones 41.6; Base metals and articles thereof 57.0; Machinery and electrical equipment 139.5; Transport equipment 66.6; Optical instruments, apparatus and equipment 32.0; Total (incl. others) 760.7. Exports f.o.b.: Live animals and animal products 9.9; Chemical products 1.9; Pearls and other precious stones 1.3; Base metals and articles thereof 3.7; Machinery and electrical equipment 6.2; Transport equipment 1.8; Optical instruments, apparatus and equipment 1.6; Art objects and collectors' items 4.7; Total (incl. others) 34.8. Note: Figures exclude transactions of the petroleum sector and those of the Free Trade Zone of Aruba.

Principal Trading Partners (A Fl. million, 2001): Imports c.i.f.: Japan 33.6; Netherlands 153.3; Netherlands Antilles 48.1; USA 811.5; Venezuela 40.3; Total (incl. others) 1,314.1. *Exports f.o.b.*: Colombia 7.0; Netherlands 7.5; Netherlands Antilles 10.3; USA 14.2; Venezuela 11.0; Total (incl. others) 52.7. Note: Figures exclude transactions of the petroleum sector and those of the Free Trade Zone of Aruba.

TRANSPORT

Road Traffic (motor vehicles in use, December 2002): Passenger cars 42,802; Lorries 804; Buses 391; Taxis 398; Rental cars 3,324; Other cars 549; Motorcycles 960; Total 49,228.

Shipping (2001): *Arrivals:* Oil tankers 390; Cruise ships 298.

Civil Aviation: *Aircraft Movements:* 36,508 in 2000; 34,566 in 2001; 33,748 in 2002. *Passenger Arrivals:* 809,087 in 2000; 821,454 in 2001; 759,085 in 2002.

TOURISM

Tourist Arrivals: 1,211,229 (721,224 stop-over visitors, 490,005 cruise-ship passengers) in 2000; 1,178,716 (691,420 stop-over visitors, 487,296 cruise-ship passengers) in 2001; 1,224,822 (642,627 stop-over visitors, 582,195 cruise-ship passengers) in 2002.

Tourism Receipts: US $903.3m. in 2002.

COMMUNICATIONS MEDIA

Radio Receivers (1997): 50,000 in use.

Television Receivers (1997): 20,000 in use.

Telephones (2001): 37,132 main lines in use.

Facsimile Machines (1996): 3,600 in use.

Mobile Cellular Telephones (2001): 53,000 subscribers.

Internet Users (2001): 7,912.

Daily Newspapers (1996): 13 titles (estimated circulation 73,000 copies per issue).

Sources: mainly UNESCO, *Statistical Yearbook*; International Telecommunication Union and UN, *Statistical Yearbook*.

EDUCATION

Pre-primary (2000/01): 23 schools; 2,737 pupils; 105 teachers.

Primary (2000/01): 33 schools; 8,849 pupils; 415 teachers.

General Secondary (2000/01): 10 schools; 4,251 pupils; 242 teachers.

Technical-Vocational (2000/01): 2 schools; 3,237 pupils; 263 teachers.

Community College (1999/2000): 1 school; 1,187 pupils; 106 teachers.

University (1999/2000): 1 university; 208 students; 24 tutors.

Teacher Training (2000/01): 1 institution; 180 students; 25 teachers.

Special Education (2000/01): 4 schools; 272 pupils; 56 teachers.

Private, Non-aided (1999/2000): 4 schools; 553 pupils; 58 teachers.

International School (2000/01): 154 pupils; 25 teachers.

Adult Literacy Rate (official estimates, 2000): Males 97.6%; Females 97.1%.

Directory

The Constitution

On 1 January 1986 Aruba acquired separate status (status aparte) within the Kingdom of the Netherlands. The form of government is similar to that for the Netherlands Antilles, which is embodied in the Charter of the Kingdom of the Netherlands (operational from 20 December 1954). The Netherlands, the Netherlands Antilles (Antilles of the Five) and Aruba each enjoy full autonomy in domestic and internal affairs, and are united on a basis of equality for the protection of their common interests and the granting of mutual assistance. In economic and monetary affairs there is a co-operative union between Aruba and the Antilles of the Five, known as the 'Union of the Netherlands Antilles and Aruba'.

The Governor, who is appointed by the Dutch Crown for a term of six years, represents the monarch of the Netherlands in Aruba. The Government of Aruba appoints a minister plenipotentiary to represent it in the Government of the Kingdom. Whenever the Netherlands Council of Ministers is dealing with matters coming under the heading of joint affairs of the realm (in practice mainly foreign affairs and defence), the Council assumes the status of Council of Ministers of the Kingdom. In that event, Aruba's Minister Plenipotentiary takes part, with full voting powers, in the deliberations.

A legislative proposal regarding affairs of the realm and applying to Aruba as well as to the 'metropolitan' Netherlands is sent, simultaneously with its submission, to the Staten Generaal (the Netherlands parliament) and to the Staten (parliament) of Aruba. The latter body can report in writing to the Staten Generaal on the draft Kingdom Statute and designate one or more special delegates to attend the debates and furnish information in the meetings of the Chambers of the Staten Generaal. Before the final vote on a draft the Minister Plenipotentiary has the right to express an opinion on it. If he disapproves of the draft, and if in the Second Chamber a three-fifths' majority of the votes cast is not obtained, the discussions on the draft are suspended and further deliberations take place in the Council of Ministers of the Kingdom. When special delegates attend the meetings of the Chambers this right devolves upon the delegates of the parliamentary body designated for this purpose.

The Governor has executive power in external affairs, which he exercises in co-operation with the Council of Ministers. He is assisted by an advisory council which consists of at least five members appointed by him.

Executive power in internal affairs is vested in a nominated Council of Ministers, responsible to the Staten. The Aruban Staten consists of 21 members, who are elected by universal adult suffrage for four years (subject to dissolution), on the basis of proportional representation. Inhabitants have the right to vote if they have Dutch nationality and have reached 18 years of age. Voting is not compulsory.

The Government

HEAD OF STATE

Queen of the Netherlands: HM Queen BEATRIX.

Governor: OLINDO KOOLMAN (took office in 1992).

COUNCIL OF MINISTERS
(April 2003)

Prime Minister and Minister of General Affairs and Utilities: NELSON ORLANDO ODUBER.

Deputy Prime Minister and Minister of Social Affairs and Infrastructure: MARISOL J. TROMP.

Minister of Education: FREDIS J. REFUNJOL.

Minister of Finance and Economic Affairs: NILO J. J. SWAEN.

Minister of Justice: HYACINTHO RUDY CROES.

Minister of Public Health and the Environment: CANDELARIO A. S. D. (BOOSHI) WEVER.

Minister of Sports, Culture and Labour: TAI FOO RAMON LEE.

Minister of Tourism and Transportation: EDISON BRIESEN.

Minister Plenipotentiary and Member of the Council of Ministers of the Realm for Aruba in the Netherlands: ALICIA A. TROMP-YARZAGARAY.

Minister Plenipotentiary of the Realm for Aruba in Washington, DC (USA): HENRY BAARH.

MINISTRIES

Office of the Governor: Plaza Henny Eman 3, Oranjestad.

Office of the Prime Minister: Government Offices, L. G. Smith Blvd 76, Oranjestad; tel. (8) 80300; fax (8) 80024.

Ministry of Education: L. G. Smith Blvd 76, Oranjestad; tel. (8) 30937; fax (8) 28328.

Ministry of Finance and Economic Affairs: L. G. Smith Blvd 76, Oranjestad; tel. (8) 80269; fax (8) 80347; e-mail minfin.ecaffairs@setarnet.aw.

Ministry of General Affairs and Utilities: L. G. Smith Blvd 76, Oranjestad; tel. (8) 39022; fax (8) 38958.

Ministry of Justice: L. G. Smith Blvd 76, Oranjestad; tel. (8) 39131; fax (8) 25388.

Ministry of Public Health and the Environment: L. G. Smith Blvd 76, Oranjestad; tel. (8) 34966; fax (8) 35082.

Ministry of Social Affairs and Infrastructure: L. G. Smith Blvd 76, Oranjestad; tel. (8) 80700; fax (8) 80032.

Ministry of Sports, Culture and Labour: L. G. Smith Blvd 76, Oranjestad; tel. (8) 39695; fax (8) 35985.

Ministry of Tourism and Transportation: L. G. Smith Blvd 76, Oranjestad; tel. (8) 39035; fax (8) 35084.

Office of the Minister Plenipotentiary for Aruba: R. J. Schimmelpennincklaan 1, 2517 JN The Hague, the Netherlands; tel. (70) 356-6200; fax (70) 345-1446.

Legislature

STATEN

President: FRANCISCO W. CROES, Staten, L. G. Smith Blvd 72, Oranjestad.

General Election, 28 September 2001

Party	% of votes	Seats
Movimentu Electoral di Pueblo	52.5	12
Arubaanse Volkspartij	26.6	6
Partido Patriótico Arubano	9.6	2
Organisacion Liberal Arubano	5.7	1
Others	5.6	—
Total	100.0	21

Political Organizations

Acción Democratico Nacional (ADN) (National Democratic Action): Oranjestad; f. 1985; Leader PEDRO CHARRO KELLY.

Aliansa Democratico Arubano (Aruban Democratic Alliance): Oranjestad; internet www.partidoaliansa.org; Leader ROBERT FREDERICK WEVER.

Arubaanse Volkspartij (AVP) (Aruba People's Party): Oranjestad; tel. (8) 33500; fax (8) 37870; f. 1942; advocates Aruba's separate status; Leader MICHIEL GODFRIED EMAN.

Conscientisacion y Liberacion Arubano (CLA) (Concentration for the Liberation of Aruba): Oranjestad; Leader MARIANO DUVERT BLUME.

Movimentu Electoral di Pueblo (MEP) (People's Electoral Movement): Santa Cruz 74D, Oranjestad; tel. (8) 54495; fax (8) 50768; e-mail mep@setarnet.aw; internet www.setarnet.aw/organisationpage/mep; f. 1971; socialist; 1,200 mems; Pres. and Leader NELSON ORLANDO ODUBER.

Organisacion Liberal Arubano (OLA) (Aruban Liberal Organization): Oranjestad; f. 1991; Leader GLENBERT FRANCOIS CROES.

Partido Patriótico Arubano (PPA) (Patriotic Party of Aruba): Oranjestad; internet www.visitaruba.com/ppa/jrpeterson; f. 1949; social democratic; opposed to complete independence for Aruba; Leader BENEDICT (BENNY) JOCELYN MONTGOMERY NISBETT.

Judicial System

Legal authority is exercised by the Court of First Instance. Appeals are heard by the Joint High Court of Justice of the Netherlands Antilles and Aruba.

Attorney-General of Aruba: THERESA D. CROES-FERNANDES PEDRA.

Courts of Justice: J. G. Emanstraat 51, Oranjestad.

Religion

Roman Catholics form the largest religious community, numbering more than 80% of the population. The Anglicans and the Methodist, Dutch Protestant and other Protestant churches have a total membership of about 6,500. There are approximately 130 Jews.

CHRISTIANITY

The Roman Catholic Church

Aruba forms part of the diocese of Willemstad, comprising the Netherlands Antilles and Aruba. The Bishop resides in Willemstad (Curaçao, Netherlands Antilles).

Roman Catholic Church: J. Yrausquin Plein 3, POB 702, Oranjestad; tel. (8) 21434; fax (8) 21409.

The Anglican Communion

Within the Church in the Province of the West Indies, Aruba forms part of the diocese of the North Eastern Caribbean and Aruba. The Bishop is resident in The Valley, Anguilla.

Anglican Church: Holy Cross, Weg Seroe Pretoe 31, Sint Nicolaas; tel. (8) 45142; fax (8) 43394.

Protestant Churches

Baptist Church: Aruba Baptist Mission, SBC, Paradera 98-C; tel. (8) 83893.

Church of Christ: Pastoor Hendrikstraat 107, Sint Nicolaas; tel. (8) 48172.

Dutch Protestant Church: Wilhelminastraat 1, Oranjestad; tel. (8) 21435.

Evangelical Church: C. Huygenstraat 17, POB 272, Oranjestad; tel. (8) 22058.

Faith Revival Center: Rooi Afo 10, Paradera; tel. (8) 31010.

Iglesia Evangelica Pentecostal: Asamblea di Dios, Reamurstraat 2, Oranjestad; tel. (8) 31940.

Jehovah's Witnesses: Guyabastraat 3, Oranjestad; tel. (8) 28963.

Methodist Church: Longfellowstraat, Oranjestad; tel. (8) 45243.

New Apostolic Church: Goletstraat SA, Oranjestad; tel. (8) 33762.

Pentacostal Apostolic Assembly: Bernhardstraat 185; tel. (8) 48710.

Seventh-day Adventist: Weststraat, Oranjestad; tel. (8) 45896.

JUDAISM

Beth Israel Synagogue: Adriaan Laclé Blvd, Oranjestad; tel. (8) 23272; fax (8) 23534.

BAHÁ'Í FAITH

Spiritual Assembly: Bucutiweg 19, Oranjestad; tel. (8) 23104.

The Press

DAILIES

Amigoe di Aruba: Patriastraat 13, POB 323, Oranjestad; tel. (8) 24333; fax (8) 22368; e-mail amigoearuba@setarnet.aw; internet amigoe.com; f. 1884; Dutch; Gen. Man. and Editor-in-Chief MICHAEL O. WILLEMSE; circ. 12,000 (in Aruba and Netherlands Antilles).

Aruba Today: Weststraat 22, Oranjestad; tel. (8) 27800; fax (8) 27093; e-mail today@bondia.com; Editor-in-Chief VANJA ODUBER.

Bon Dia Aruba: Weststraat 22, Oranjestad; tel. (8) 27800; fax (8) 27044; e-mail comment@bondia.com; internet www.bondia.com; Dir VICTOR WINKLAAR.

Diario: Engelandstraat 29, POB 577, Oranjestad; tel. (8) 826747; fax (8) 828551; e-mail diario@setanet.aw; internet www.diarioaruba.com; f. 1980; Papiamento; morning; Editor/Man. JOSSY M. MANSUR; circ. 15,000.

Extra: Dominicanessenstraat 17, Oranjestad; tel. (8) 834034; fax (8) 21639; Papiamento; Dir C. FRANKEN.

The News: Italiestraat 5, POB 300, Oranjestad; tel. (8) 24725; fax (8) 26125; f. 1951; English; Publr GERARDUS J. SCHOUTEN; Editor BEN BENNET; circ. 6,900.

Nobo: Dominicanessenstraat 17, Oranjestad; tel. (8) 34034; fax (8) 27272; Dir ADRIAAN ARENDS.

La Prensa: Bachstraat 6, POB 566 Oranjestad; tel. (8) 21199; fax (8) 28634; f. 1929; Papiamento; Editor THOMAS C. PIETERSZ.

NEWS AGENCIES

Algemeen Nederlands Persbureau (ANP) (The Netherlands): Caya G. F. (Betico) Croes 110, POB 323, Oranjestad; tel. (8) 24333; fax (8) 22368.

Aruba News Agencies: Bachstraat 6, Oranjestad; tel. (8) 21243.

Publishers

Aruba Experience Publications NV: L. G. Smith Blvd 58, Oranjestad; tel. (8) 34467.

Caribbean Publishing Co (CPC) Ltd: L. G. Smith Blvd 116, Oranjestad; tel. (8) 20485; fax (8) 20484.

De Wit Stores NV: L. G. Smith Blvd 110, POB 386, Oranjestad; tel. (8) 23500; fax (8) 21575; e-mail dewitstores@setarnet.aw; f. 1948; Man. Dir R. DE ZWART.

Gold Book Publishing: L. G. Smith Blvd 116, Oranjestad; tel. (8) 20485; fax (8) 20484.

Oranjestad Printing NV: Italiestraat 5, POB 300, Oranjestad; Man. Dir GERARDUS J. SCHOUTEN.

ProGraphics Inc: Italiestraat 5, POB 201, Oranjestad; tel. (8) 24550; fax (8) 22526; e-mail vadprinting@setarnet.aw; f. 2001; fmrly VAD Printers Inc.

Publicidad Aruba NV: Wilhelminastraat 101, Oranjestad; tel. (8) 25132.

Publicidad Exito Aruba SA: Domenicanessenstraat 17, POB 142, Oranjestad; tel. (8) 22020; fax (8) 24242; f. 1958.

Rozenstand Publishing Co: Cuquisastraat 1, Oranjestad; tel. (8) 24482.

Van Dorp Aruba NV: Caya G. F. (Betico) Croes 77, POB 596, Oranjestad; tel. (8) 23076; fax (8) 23573.

Broadcasting and Communications

TELECOMMUNICATIONS

Servicio di Telecomunicacion di Aruba (SETAR): Seroe Blanco z/n, POB 13, Oranjestad; tel. (2) 51576; fax (8) 36970; e-mail setar@setarnet.aw; internet www.setar.aw; f. 1986; Man. Dir PATRICIO NICOLAS.

BROADCASTING

Radio

Canal 90 FM Stereo: Van Leeuwenhoekstraat 26, Oranjestad; tel. (8) 24134.

Cristal Sound 1-01 7 FM: J. G. Emanstraat 124A, Oranjestad; tel. (8) 27726; fax (8) 20144.

Radio 1270: Bernardstraat 138, POB 28, Sint Nicolaas; tel. (8) 45602; fax (8) 27753; commercial station; programmes in Dutch, English, Spanish and Papiamento; Dir F. A. LEAUER; Station Man. J. A. C. ALDERS.

Radio Carina FM: Datustraat 10A, Oranjestad; tel. (8) 21450; fax (8) 31955; commercial station; programmes in Dutch, English, Spanish and Papiamento; Dir-Gen. ALBERT R. DIEFFENTHALER.

Radio Caruso Booy FM: G. M. De Bruynewijk 49, Savaneta; tel. (8) 47752; fax (8) 43351; commercial station; broadcasts for 24 hrs a day; programmes in Dutch, English, Spanish and Papiamento; Pres. HUBERT E. A. BOOY; Gen. Man. SIRA BOOY.

Radio Galactica FM: J. G. Emanstraat 120, Oranjestad; tel. (8) 20999; fax (8) 38999; f. 1990; Dir MODESTO J. ODUBER; Station Man. MAIKEL J. ODUBER.

Radio Kelkboom: Bloemond 14, POB 146, Oranjestad; tel. (8) 21899; fax (8) 34825; e-mail RadioKelkboom@setarnet.aw; f. 1954; commercial radio station; programmes in Dutch, English, Spanish and Papiamento; Owners CARLOS A. KELKBOOM; and; E. A. M. KELKBOOM; Dir EMILE A. M. KELKBOOM.

Radio Victoria: Washington 23, POB 5291, Oranjestad; tel. (8) 73444; fax (8) 73444; e-mail radiovictoria@setarnet.aw; f. 1958; religious and cultural FM radio station owned by the Radio Victoria Foundation; programmes in Dutch, English, Spanish and Papiamento; Pres. N. J. F. ARTS.

Voz di Aruba (Voice of Aruba): Van Leeuwenhoekstraat 26, POB 219, Oranjestad; tel. (8) 24134; commercial radio station; programmes in Dutch, English, Spanish and Papiamento; also operates Canal 90 on FM; Dir A. M. ARENDS, Jr.

Television

ABC Aruba Broadcasting Co NV: Royal Plaza Suite 223, POB 5040, Oranjestad; tel. (8) 38150; fax (8) 38110; e-mail 15atv@setarnet.aw.

Tele-Aruba NV: Pos Chiquito 1A, POB 392, Oranjestad; tel. (8) 57302; fax (8) 51683; e-mail telearuba@hotmail.com; internet www.telearuba.aw; f. 1963; formerly operated by Netherlands Antilles Television Co; commercial; govt-owned; Gen. Man. M. MARCHENA.

Finance

(cap. = capital; res = reserves; dep. = deposits; m. = million; brs = branches; amounts in Aruban florin)

BANKING

Central Bank

Centrale Bank van Aruba: J. E. Irausquin Blvd 8, Oranjestad; tel. (8) 22509; fax (8) 32251; e-mail cbaua@setarnet.aw; internet www.cbaruba.org; f. 1986; cap. 10.0m., res 113.1m., dep. 398.9m. (Dec. 2002); Pres. A. R. CARAM; Exec. Dirs K. A. H. POLVLIET, J. R. FIGAROA-SEMELEER.

Commercial Banks

Aruba Bank NV: Caya G. F. (Betico) Croes 41, POB 192, Oranjestad; tel. (8) 21550; fax (8) 29152; e-mail abank@setarnet.aw; internet www.arubabank.com; f. 1925; cap. and res 21m., dep. 300m. (1996); Man. Dir and CEO ILDEFONS D'ANDELO SIMON; 7 brs.

Banco di Caribe NV: Vondellaan 31, Oranjestad; tel. (8) 32168; fax (8) 32422; e-mail bdcaua@setarnet; internet www.bancodicaribe.com; f. 1987; Gen. Man. E. A. DE KORT; 1 br.

Caribbean Mercantile Bank NV: Caya G. F. (Betico) Croes 53, POB 28, Oranjestad; tel. (8) 23118; fax (8) 24373; e-mail executive_office@cmbnv.com; internet www.cmbnv.com; f. 1963; cap. 4.0m., res 43.0m., dep. 714.9m. (Dec. 2001); Pres. L. CAPRILES; Man. Dir W. G. CARSON; 5 brs.

Interbank Aruba NV: Caya G. F. (Betico) Croes 38, POB 96, Oranjestad; tel. (8) 31080; fax (8) 24058; e-mail info@interbankaruba.com; internet www.interbankaruba.com; f. 1987; owned by Fundacion Cas pa Comunidad Arubano (FCCA) since 2001; Man. Dir IRVING A. DURAND; 3 brs.

RBTT Bank Aruba NV: Italiestraat 36, Sasakiweg, Oranjestad; tel. (8) 33221; fax (8) 821756; e-mail firstet@setarnet.aw; internet www.rbtt.co.tt; f. 2001; formerly First National Bank of Aruba NV (f. 1985 and acquired by Royal Bank of Trinidad and Tobago Ltd in 1998); total assets US $125.3m. (Dec. 2000); Chair. PETER J. JULY; Pres. EDWIN L. TROMP; 6 brs.

Investment Bank

Aruban Investment Bank NV: Wilhelminastraat 32–36, POB 1011, Oranjestad; tel. (8) 27327; fax (8) 27461; e-mail aib@setarnet.aw; internet www.arubainvestmentbank.com; f. 1987; Pres. P. C. M. VAN DER VOORT VAN ZIJP.

Mortgage Banks

Fundacion Cas pa Comunidad Arubano (FCCA): Sabana Blanco 66, Oranjestad; tel. (8) 23884; fax (8) 36272.

OHRA Hypotheek & Postspaarbank NK: L. G. Smith Blvd 60, Oranjestad; tel. (8) 39666; fax (8) 39498; e-mail info@ohrabank-aua.com.

'Offshore' Banks

Inarco International Bank NV: Punta Brabo z/n, Arulex Bldg, Oranjestad; tel. (8) 22138; fax (8) 32363.

Citibank NA: Punta Brabo z/n, Arulex Bldg, Oranjestad; tel. (8) 22138; fax (8) 32363.

INSURANCE

There were nine life insurance companies active in Aruba in December 2001.

Trade and Industry

DEVELOPMENT ORGANIZATION

Department of Economic Affairs, Commerce and Industry (Direktie Economische Zaken, Handel en Industrie): Sun Plaza Bldg, L. G. Smith Blvd 160, Oranjestad; tel. (8) 21181; fax (8) 34494; e-mail deaci@setarnet.aw; internet www.arubaeconomicaffairs.com; Dir HUMPHREY O. VAN TRIKT.

CHAMBER OF COMMERCE AND INDUSTRY

Aruba Chamber of Commerce and Industry: J. E. Irausquin Blvd 10, POB 140, Oranjestad; tel. (8) 21566; fax (8) 33962; e-mail auachamber@setarnet.aw; internet www.arubachamber.com; f. 1930; Pres. ALAN H. RILEY; Exec. Dir L. C. DE SOUZA.

TRADE ASSOCIATION

Aruba Trade and Industry Association: ATIA Bldg, Pedro Gallegostraat 6, POB 562, Oranjestad; tel. (8) 27593; fax (8) 33068; e-mail atiaruba@setarnet.aw; internet www.atiaruba.org; f. 1945; Pres. G. M. PETERSON.

UTILITIES

Electricity and Water

Utilities Aruba NV: govt-owned holding co.

Electriciteit-Maatschappij Aruba (ELMAR) NV: Wilhelminastraat 110, Oranjestad; tel. (8) 23700; fax (8) 28991; e-mail elmar.aruba@setarnet.aw; internet www.elmararuba.com; independently-managed co, residing under Utilities Aruba NV; electricity distribution; Man. Dir ISMAEL W. F. WEVER.

Water en Energiebedrijf Aruba (WEB) NV: Balashi 76, POB 575, Oranjestad; tel. (8) 54600; fax (8) 57681; e-mail info@webaruba.com; internet www.webaruba.com; f. 1991; independently-managed co, residing under Utilities Aruba NV; production and distribution of industrial and potable water, and electricity generation; Gen. Dir JOSÉ LACLÉ.

Gas

Aruba Gas Supply Company Ltd (ARUGAS): Barcadera z/n, Oranjestad; tel. (8) 51198; fax (8) 52187; e-mail arubagas@setarnet.aw.

BOC Gases Aruba: Balashi 21N, POB 190, Oranjestad; tel. (8) 52624; fax (8) 52823.

TRADE UNIONS

Federashon di Trahadonan Arubano (FTA) (Aruban Workers' Federation): Bernardstraat 23, Sint Nicolaas; tel. (8) 45448; fax (8) 45504; f. 1964; independent; affiliated to World Confederation of Labour; Sec.-Gen. ANSELMO PONTILIUS.

There are also several unions for government and semi-government workers and employees.

Transport

There are no railways, but Aruba has a network of all-weather roads.

Arubus NV: Sabana Blanco 67, Oranjestad; tel. (8) 27089; fax (8) 28633; state-owned company providing public transport services.

SHIPPING

The island's principal seaport is Oranjestad, whose harbour can accommodate ocean-going vessels. There are also ports at Barcadera and Sint Nicolaas.

Aruba Ports Authority NV: L. G. Smith Blvd 23, Oranjestad; tel. (8) 26633; fax (8) 32896; e-mail aruports@setarnet.aw; f. 1981; responsible for the administration of the ports of Oranjestad and Barcadera; Dir M. H. HENRÍQUEZ.

Coastal Aruba Refining Co NV: Seroe Colorado, POB 2150, Sint Nicholas; tel. (8) 94904; fax (8) 49087; f. 1989; petroleum refinery, responsible for the administration of the port of Sint Nicolas; Man. Dir MICHAEL RENFORD.

Principal Shipping Companies

Beng Lian Shipping S. de R. L. A. V. V.: Dominicanessenstraat 22, Oranjestad.

Magna Shipping Co: Koningstraat 52, Oranjestad; tel. (8) 24349.

Rodoca Shipping and Trading SA: Parkietenbos 30, Barcadera Harbour; tel. (8) 50096; fax (8) 23371; formerly Aruba Shipping and Chartering Co NV.

Windward Island Agencies: Heyligerweg, POB 66, Oranjestad.

CIVIL AVIATION

The Queen Beatrix International Airport, about 2.5 km from Oranjestad, is served by numerous airlines, linking the island with destinations in the Caribbean, Europe, the USA and Central and South America. In November 2000 the national carrier, Air Aruba, was declared bankrupt.

Avia Air: Queen Beatrix International Airport, Oranjestad; tel. (8) 34600; fax (8) 26355; f. 1987; domestic and regional services.

Tourism

Aruba's white sandy beaches, particularly along the southern coast, are an attraction for foreign visitors, and tourism is a major industry. The number of hotel rooms increased from 2,078 in 1986 to 6,831 in 2002. In 2001 most stop-over visitors came from the USA (65.9%), Venezuela (15.8%), the Netherlands (4.7%), Colombia (3.5%) and Canada (2.7%). In 2002 642,627 stop-over visitors and 582,195 cruise-ship passengers visited Aruba. Receipts from tourism visitors totalled US $903.3m. in 2002.

Aruba Tourism Authority (ATA): L. G. Smith Blvd 172, Oranjestad; tel. (8) 23777; fax (8) 34702; e-mail ata.aruba@aruba.com; internet www.aruba.com; f. 1953; plans to make the state-controlled ATA operationally independent are pending; Man. Dir MYRNA JANSEN-FELICIANO.

Aruba Hotel and Tourism Association: L. G. Smith Blvd 174, POB 542, Oranjestad; tel. (8) 22607; fax (8) 24202; e-mail ahata@setarnet.aw; internet www.aruba.com; CEO HORACE HORD.

Cruise Tourism Authority—Aruba: POB 5254, Suite 227, Royal Plaza Mall, L. G. Smith Blvd 94, Oranjestad; tel. (8) 33648; fax (8) 35088; e-mail int1721@setarnet.aw; internet www.arubabycruise.com; Exec. Dir KATHLEEN ROJER.

THE NETHERLANDS ANTILLES

Introductory Survey

Location, Climate, Language, Religion, Flag, Capital

The Netherlands Antilles (Antilles of the Five) consists of two groups of islands in the Caribbean Sea, about 800 km (500 miles) apart. The main group, lying off the coast of Venezuela, consists of Bonaire and Curaçao which (together with Aruba, 68 km to the east of Curaçao) are known as the Benedenwindse Eilanden or 'Leeward Islands'; to the north-east lie the small volcanic islands of St (Sint) Eustatius (also known as Statia), Saba and St (Sint) Maarten (the northern half of the last island being a dependency of the French overseas department of Guadeloupe), known as the Bovenwindse Eilanden or 'Windward Islands' (although actually in the Leeward group of the Lesser Antilles). The climate is tropical, moderated by the sea, with an average annual temperature of 27.5°C (81°F) and little rainfall. The official languages are Dutch and Papiamento (a mixture of Dutch, Spanish, Portuguese, English, Arawak Indian and several West African dialects), which is the dominant language of the 'Leeward Islands'. English is the official and principal language of the 'Windward Islands'. Spanish is also widely spoken. Almost all of the inhabitants profess Christianity: the people of the 'Leeward Islands' and Saba are predominantly Roman Catholics, while those of St Eustatius and St Maarten are predominantly Protestants. The state flag (proportions 2 by 3) is white, with a red vertical stripe in the centre, crossed by a horizontal blue stripe on which there are five white five-pointed stars (one for each of the main islands) arranged in an oval. The capital is Willemstad, on the island of Curaçao.

Recent History

The 'Leeward Islands', already settled by communities of Arawak Indians, were discovered by the Spanish in 1499 and were seized by the Dutch in the 1630s. Curaçao became prosperous in the late 17th and 18th centuries as an entrepôt for trade in the Caribbean. The Dutch settled the 'Windward Islands', once settled by Carib Indians, in the mid-17th century. After frequent changes in possession, the islands (including Aruba) were finally confirmed as Dutch territory in 1816. The two groups were administered as Curaçao and Dependencies between 1845 and 1948. Slavery was abolished in 1863, and the islands suffered from an economic decline until the establishment of petroleum refineries on Curaçao and Aruba, in 1918 and 1929, respectively. During the Second World War Queen Wilhelmina of the Netherlands promised independence, and in 1954 a Charter gave the federation of six islands full autonomy in domestic affairs, and declared it to be an integral part of the Kingdom of the Netherlands.

Divisions of political allegiance within the territory have been along island, rather than policy, lines, and a series of coalition Governments has frequently paralysed decision-making. In 1969 serious rioting and looting broke out in Willemstad after a demonstration by workers in the petroleum industry. Troops had to be sent from the Netherlands to quell the disturbances and to restore order. In February 1970 the socialist Government of Ciro Kroon resigned over the nomination of a new Governor, and in 1971 the Government of E. Petronia resigned over the rejection by the Staten (parliament) of new financial measures.

Following elections to the Staten in June 1977, a coalition Government was formed, with the leader of the Democratische Partij (DP), Silvio Rozendal, as Prime Minister. After a boycott of the session by the Movimentu Electoral di Pueblo (MEP) of Aruba and the Frente Obrero i Liberashon 30 di mei (FOL), the Staten was eventually convened by a Governor's decree in October. Rozendal resigned in April 1979, and elections were held in July. A coalition administration was formed by the Movimentu Antiyas Nobo (MAN), the MEP and the Unión Patriótico Bonairiano (UPB), with Dominico (Don) Martina, the leader of the MAN, as Prime Minister. The DP joined the coalition Government in December 1980.

In Aruba resentment of the administrative dominance of Curaçao resulted, in 1971, in the establishment of the pro-independence MEP. In 1981 a series of talks regarding Aruba's future began with the Netherlands Government. However, in September the MEP representatives in the Staten withdrew their support for the Government on the question of Aruba's rights to possible discoveries of petroleum off its coast. The Government's majority was restored by the inclusion of the DP—St Maarten (DP—StM) member for the 'Windward Islands' in the coalition, but a DP resignation in January 1982 precipitated a further crisis. A general election in June failed to resolve the situation, and it was not until October that agreement was reached on the formation by Martina of a new coalition, which excluded the MEP.

In March 1983 agreement was finally reached whereby Aruba would be given separate status (*status aparte*) within the Kingdom of the Netherlands from January 1986, with the prospect of full independence in 1996 (for further details, see Aruba, q.v.). Arguments persisted regarding the division of the Antilles' financial reserves, and over rights to explore for petroleum and other minerals. In June 1984 Martina's coalition Government resigned. A five-party coalition was eventually formed in September, with Maria Liberia-Peters of the conservative Partido Nashonal di Pueblo (PNP) as Prime Minister.

At a general election in November 1985 the PNP gained the largest number of seats in the Staten for the Antilles of the Five (six out of 22), but was unable to secure enough support from other parties to form a government. Martina once again became Prime Minister and formed a coalition Government. During 1986–87 the Government was forced to introduce a series of economic austerity measures, following Aruba's separation from the Netherlands Antilles and the decline of both the petroleum-refining industry and 'offshore' financial services. The Government resigned in March 1988, after losing the support of the DP—StM and the FOL. In May Liberia-Peters formed a coalition with all the parties represented in the Staten except for the MAN and the DP—Curaçao (DP—C).

In January 1989 Martina revealed that successive Curaçao administrations had diverted revenues from the 'offshore' financial sector into a fund that had not been declared to The Hague during negotiations for budgetary support. The Netherlands had recently exerted pressure for more control to be exercised over the large amount of aid that it provided for the Netherlands Antilles. By the early 1990s it appeared that, while the 'metropolitan' Government was unwilling to allow the complete disintegration of the federation, it was prepared to consider a less centralized system or the creation of two federations in the separate island groups.

At a general election in March 1990 the PNP increased the number of its seats (all on Curaçao) to seven, again making it the largest single party in the Staten, and, after some weeks of negotiations, Liberia-Peters assumed the leadership of a broadly-based coalition. In March 1992 the FOL and its partner at the 1990 election, the Social Independiente, withdrew from the Government. Liberia-Peters formed a new coalition with the DP—StM, the UPB and the DP—C. In September 1993 the DP—StM withdrew, although the Government maintained its majority in the Staten with the support of an independent deputy and subsequently that of the Windward Islands People's Movement (WIPM).

A referendum was conducted on Curaçao in November 1993 regarding its constitutional status; 73.6% of the electorate voted for a continuance of the island's status as a member of the Antillean federation. The option of separate status, favoured by the Government, received only 17.9% of the votes cast. As a result of this defeat, the WIPM and the UPB withdrew their support, thus leaving the Government without a majority in the Staten. Liberia-Peters resigned, and Alejandro Felippe Paula, a professor at the University of the Netherlands Antilles, subsequently agreed to head an interim Government. A general election took place in February 1994, at which a new, Curaçao-based party, the Partido Antía Restrukturá (PAR), led by Miguel A. Pourier, became the largest single party (with eight seats) in the Staten. Pourier assumed the leadership of a broadly-based coalition Government, which was inaugurated in March.

Referendums on status were conducted on St Maarten, St Eustatius, Saba and Bonaire in October 1994. On St Maarten 59.8% of the electorate voted to remain within the Antillean federation, while the option of autonomy within the Kingdom of the Netherlands received 32% of the vote. On St Eustatius 86.3% of voters opted for continued membership of the Antillean federation, while the equivalent vote on Saba was 90.6%. On Bonaire (where voting took place one week later) some 88% of voters favoured continued federation.

A general election was held on 30 January 1998, at which the PAR lost four of its eight seats in the Staten. The PNP retained its three seats, while a new party, the Partido Laboral Krusada Popular (PLKP), also took three seats. The loss of support for the PAR was attributed to the unpopularity of austerity measures imposed by the outgoing Government. Pourier failed in his attempts to form a new coalition, largely owing to the opposition of the PNP, the PLKP and the FOL (which together held eight of Curaçao's 14 seats) to the PAR's economic policies. A new coalition Government, with Susanne F. C. Camelia-Römer of the PNP as Prime Minister, was finally agreed in early May, only to collapse later in the month, when it was revealed that the designated Minister of Traffic, Transport and Communication, Nelson Monte, a member of the FOL, was under criminal investigation for alleged evasion of import duties. A new Government was sworn in on 1 June. The coalition comprised six parties, with the support of 13 of the 22 members of the Staten.

In late 1998 the Government adopted a National Recovery Plan, which aimed both to reduce the government's fiscal deficit and also to generate growth in the economy through the introduction of measures intended to stimulate investment. The Government proceeded to implement several of the measures designed to increase state revenues, which had been recommended by the National Plan Committee. However, the Government's subsequent attempts to reduce state expenditure proved to be highly controversial, and proposals to reduce the public sector work-force by some 2,400—principally through cuts in the civil service of the central Government and of the island Government of Curaçao—caused great tension between Camelia-Römer's PNP and its fellow Curaçao-based coalition partners, the PLKP and the FOL, which led, in October 1999, to the collapse of both the central Government and the island Government of Curaçao.

In November 1999 former Prime Minister Pourier formed a new broadly-based coalition Government, which had the support of 18 of the 22 members of the Staten. Concerns were, however, expressed that Pourier's Government would face the same problems as the previous administration in its attempt fully to implement the National Recovery Plan, and this was, to some extent, anticipated by Pourier's appointment of Camelia-Römer as Minister for the National Recovery Plan and Economic Affairs. In September 2000 the Minister of the Interior, Labour and Social Affairs, Lucille George-Wout, resigned following a visit to the islands by International Monetary Fund (IMF) representatives, who demanded far-reaching changes in the labour market in exchange for a credit facility. These changes included a reduction in the hours and pay of employees in certain sectors, as well as the abolition of the 40-hour working week for those in the tourism industry.

A referendum on the constitutional future of St Maarten took place on 23 June 2000. Only 4% of participants in St Maarten favoured maintaining the *status quo*. Some 69% favoured obtaining *status aparte* within the Kingdom of the Netherlands, 14% favoured complete independence and 12% preferred a restructuring of the Antilles of the Five. Although the Dutch Government indicated that it would not support a request by St Maarten to receive *status aparte*, it supported the establishment of a commission to explore the possibilities of St Maarten adopting *status aparte*. In January 2001 the Dutch Minister for the Commonwealth, Klaas de Vries, suggested that he would not exclude the possibility of a *status aparte* for St Maarten, as long as certain conditions were met. However, in February 2003 Johan Remkes, the new Dutch Minister of Home Affairs, said the Netherlands would not permit St Maarten to leave the federation. Despite this setback, St Maarten had signed an agreement with the central Government in August 2002 that would permit the island's executive council to take out loans on its own initiative, without seeking permission from the central bank. Furthermore, in late 2002 the executive council proposed to the central bank that discussions should begin on a separate monetary system for St Maarten.

In December 2000 an agreement was reached with the Dutch Government on the compulsory acculturation of Antillean migrants to the Netherlands; Pourier had threatened to resign if his coalition partners opposed the accord. The high level of unemployment, particularly among the younger members of the Antillean community in the Netherlands, and the steady influx of new migrants in recent years had led the Dutch Government to propose that the Netherlands Antilles adopt legislation whereby those under 25 years of age would be granted permission to emigrate to the Netherlands only after attending acculturation classes designed to facilitate their integration into Dutch society.

The elections of 18 January 2002 were won by the FOL, led by Anthony Godett, which had campaigned against the stringent measures imposed by the IMF. The FOL won five seats in the 22-seat Staten (and 23.0% of the popular vote). Pourier's party, the PAR, won four legislative seats and 20.4% of the popular vote. The PNP won three seats (13.4% of the ballot), the PLKP, the DP—StM and the UPB each won two seats (12.1%, 5.5% and 3.6%, respectively), and the WIPM, the Democratische Partij—Statia (DP—StE), the Democratische Partij—Bonaire (DP—B) and the National Alliance (comprising the National Progressive Party and the St Maarten Patriotic Alliance) each gained one legislative seat. None the less, despite the party's victory, attempts by the FOL to form a coalition Government failed because of allegations of corruption and mismanagement of funds by party leaders. Eventually, in June 2002 a coalition Government that included representatives of the PAR, the PNP, the PLKP, the DP—StM, the UPD and the DP—StE took office, under the leadership of the new PAR leader, Etienne Ys, replacing Pourier's caretaker Government.

In January 2003 the Minister of Public and Social Development, Tilly Pikerie, resigned after an investigation was launched into allegations that she used a government car for personal, rather than work, purposes. She was replaced in the cabinet by Joan Theodora-Brewster. Earlier in the month Hendricks Abraham, a member of Curaçao's Island Council, resigned amid allegations that he had accepted bribes from a Dutch-based construction company. Two other members of the Council, Ramon Chong and David Dick, resigned in December following similar allegations, which they denied. Later in January 2003 parliament approved new anti-corruption regulations for the National Audit Chamber, which monitors government spending.

In February 2003, as part of an effort to reduce drugs-related crime, the Government implemented visa requirements for visitors from Colombia.

Government
The Governor of the Netherlands Antilles, appointed by the Dutch Crown for a term of six years, represents the monarch of the Netherlands in the territory, and has executive power over external affairs. The Governor is assisted by an advisory council.

Executive power in internal affairs is vested in the Council of Ministers. The Council is responsible to the Staten (parliament), which has 22 members elected by universal adult suffrage for four years (subject to dissolution). The administration of each island is conducted by its own Island Council, Executive Council and Lieutenant-Governor.

Defence
Although defence is the responsibility of the Netherlands, compulsory military service is laid down in an Antilles Ordinance. The Governor is the Commander-in-Chief of the armed forces in the islands, and a Dutch contingent is stationed in Willemstad, Curaçao. The Netherlands also operates a Coast Guard Force (to combat organized crime and drugs-smuggling), based at St Maarten and Aruba. In May 1999 the US air force and navy began patrols from a base on Curaçao to combat the transport of illegal drugs.

Economic Affairs
In 1994 the gross national income (GNI) of the Netherlands Antilles, measured at current prices, was an estimated US $1,550m., equivalent to some $8,800 per head. In 1990–2001 the population increased by an average of 1.2% per year, while gross domestic product (GDP) increased, in real terms, by an average of 0.4% per year during 1990–95, and stood at $1,754m. in 1995 (equivalent to $9,039 per head). GDP decreased by 4.4% in 2000.

Agriculture, together with forestry, fishing and mining, contributed only 0.6% of GDP in 1997. Agriculture, forestry and fishing employed 1.1% of the working population on Curaçao in 2000. Some 8% of the total land area is cultivated. The chief products are aloes (Bonaire is a major exporter), sorghum, divi-divi, groundnuts, beans, fresh vegetables and tropical fruit. A bitter variety of orange is used in the production of Curaçao liqueur. There is also some fishing.

Industry (comprising manufacturing, construction, power and water) contributed 16.7% of GDP in 1997. Industry (including mining, manufacturing, power and construction) employed 18.0% of the working population on Curaçao in 2000.

The mining and quarrying sector employed only 0.3% of the working population on Curaçao in 2000. Apart from some phosphates on Curaçao (exploited until the mid-1980s), and some limestone and salt on Bonaire, the islands have no other significant mineral reserves. Aggregate is quarried on St Maarten and consumed primarily by the local construction industry.

Manufacturing contributed 5.7% of GDP in 1997, and employed 9.0% of the working population on Curaçao in 2000; activities include food-processing, production of Curaçao liqueur, and the manufacture of paint, paper, soap and cigarettes. Bonaire has a textile factory, and Curaçao's 'free zone' is of considerable importance in the economy, but the 'Windward Islands' have very few manufacturing activities. Petroleum-refining (using petroleum imported from Venezuela) is the islands' principal industrial activity, with the Curaçao refinery leased to the Venezuelan state petroleum company. Production capacity at the refinery was 116.8m. barrels per year in 2001, according to the US Geological Survey; however, industrial action in Venezuela led to the closure of the refinery during December 2002–March 2003, impacting heavily upon the islands' economy. In 2000 the Government sponsored a geologic review of offshore sediments that are located 5 km south-west of Saba; results indicated the potential of a resource of 500m. barrels of petroleum. Petroleum transhipment is also important, and ship repairs at the Curaçao dry dock make a significant contribution to the economy. In 1998 fuel imports comprised 54.4% of total merchandise imports.

The services sector contributed 82.7% of GDP in 1997, and engaged 81.0% of the employed labour force on Curaçao in 2000. The Netherlands Antilles is a major 'offshore' financial centre. The financial and business services sector contributed 24.7% of GDP in 1997, and employed 14.4% of the Curaçao working population in 2000. Operational income from the offshore sector increased from NA Fl. 210.6m. in 1992 to NA Fl. 375.6m. in 1995. A major industry for all the islands (particularly St Maarten) is tourism, which is the largest employer after the public sector. In late 2001 and early 2002 the tourist industry suffered from the repercussions of the terrorist attacks on the USA in September 2001. However, the number of cruise-ship passenger arrivals rallied strongly in the second half of 2002, although the overall number of stop-over visitors declined. In addition to tourism, Curaçao, in particular, has sought to establish itself as a centre for regional trade, exploiting its excellent harbours. In 1998 a free-trade zone was established at the island's airport, with the aim of further enhancing Curaçao's entrepôt status.

In 2001 the Netherlands Antilles recorded a visible trade deficit (excluding most transactions in petroleum) of NA Fl. 1,865.7m., much of which was offset by revenue from services: there was a deficit of NA Fl. 249.4m. on the current account of the balance of payments. The petroleum industry dominates the trade figures of the Netherlands Antilles, particularly of the 'Leeward Islands'. In 1998 the principal source of imports (43.4%) was Venezuela (which provides crude petroleum), and the principal market for exports (15.3%) was the USA. The USA is an important trading partner for all the islands of the Netherlands Antilles, as are the Netherlands and other Caribbean countries. Petroleum is the principal commodity for both import and export, and accounted for 54.4% of imports and 86.0% of exports in 1998. The Netherlands Antilles also imports machinery and transport equipment, manufactured goods, and chemicals and related products, while it exports aloes, Curaçao liqueur and some light manufactures.

In 2000 the general Government (including island governments) recorded an estimated budgetary deficit equivalent to 3.3% of GDP. The deficit was expected to rise to around 5% of GDP in 2001, according to IMF projections. In 2001 the central Government recorded a deficit of NA Fl. 38.6m. on its budget. The administrations of the islands tend to operate with deficits. At the end of 1999 the combined public domestic debts of the central Government and the island Government of Curaçao were NA Fl. 2,690.3m. (64.4% of GDP). Total foreign debt stood at NA Fl. 527.3m. in 1999, owed chiefly to the Netherlands. The foreign debt in 1999 was estimated to be the equivalent of 12.6% of GDP. In 1998 the Netherlands Antilles received $125.7m. in bilateral aid and $3.4m. in multilateral aid. The average annual rate of inflation was 2.3% in 1995–2002. Consumer prices increased by an average of 15.8% in 2001 and by 0.4% in 2002. The rate of unemployment in the labour force was an estimated 16.6% for the Netherlands Antilles as a whole in 1999; 14.0% of the Curaçao work-force were unemployed in 2000. Preliminary figures from the 2001 census showed that the rate of unemployment in St Maarten stood at 12.2%, with the rate of youth unemployment at 24.1%.

The Netherlands Antilles, as part of the Kingdom of the Netherlands, has the status of an Overseas Territory in association with the European Union (see p. 199). In 1988 the Netherlands Antilles was accorded observer status by the Caribbean Community and Common Market (CARICOM, see p. 155).

The relative isolation of the individual islands has led to the development of semi-independent economies, and economic conditions vary considerably between them. Notwithstanding, the Netherlands Antilles experienced relatively strong economic growth in the 1980s and early 1990s, but the past decade witnessed a progressive weakening of the economy, leading to a prolonged recession, high unemployment and increasing rates of emigration. The direct causes of this decline were considered to be the decline in both the financial services and the petroleum-refining industries, combined with the damage to tourist infrastructure caused by Hurricanes Luis and Marilyn in September 1995. Under the terms of the structural adjustment programme (SAP), undertaken from 1996 in consultation with the IMF, which aimed to eliminate the fiscal deficit over a period of four years, the civil service was to be rationalized, public sector wages were to be frozen and pension arrangements reviewed, while new indirect taxes were to be introduced. Successive administrations, however, recorded only limited success in implementing the terms of the SAP and its successor, the National Recovery Plan, which was adopted in late 1998, in part owing to the great unpopularity of many of the measures to be undertaken. In July 2000 the Pourier Government approved legislation designed to accelerate reform of tax and finance laws. This move secured a visit from the IMF representatives in September 2000, who advised the Dutch Government to provide NA Fl. 110m. to the Netherlands Antilles in order to restore financial discipline. In May 2001 an IMF assessment of the efficacy of the structural reforms showed that the Government had made a strong start, but that it would fail in its aim to achieve medium-term fiscal sustainability unless further reforms were made to the public sector. In June 2000 the Netherlands Antilles was urged by the Organisation for Economic Co-operation and Development (OECD) to improve the accountability and transparency of its financial services and in response the Government announced that it was to review its

taxation legislation to comply more closely with OECD's standards. In April 2002 the Netherlands Antilles was removed from the list of those countries deemed to be unco-operative tax 'havens' after OECD favourably assessed the Government's legislative amendments. In the same month an agreement was signed with the USA, pledging to share information on tax matters, with the aim of combating money-laundering and associated criminal activities. In 2002 the long formation period of the new Government and the consequent lack of a government programme, coupled with the slowing world economy and weak international tourism market, damaged confidence, leading to a further estimated contraction in real GDP.

Education

Education was made compulsory in 1992. The islands' educational facilities are generally of a high standard. The education system is the same as that of the Netherlands. Dutch is used as the principal language of instruction in schools on the 'Leeward Islands', while English is used in schools on the 'Windward Islands'. Instruction in Papiamento (using a different spelling system from that adopted by Aruba) has been introduced in primary schools. Primary education begins at six years of age and lasts for six years. Secondary education lasts for a further five years. The University of the Netherlands Antilles, sited on Curaçao, had 671 students in 1996. In April 2002 the Netherlands Government made more than €12.7m. available for improvements to education provision in the Netherlands Antilles. In 1995 local government expenditure on education in the Antilles of the Five was NA Fl. 178.9m. (19.3% of total spending by the island governments).

Public Holidays

2003: 1 January (New Year's Day), 19 January (Bonaire only: Carnival Rest Day), 3 March (Curaçao and Bonaire only: Lenten Carnival), 9–12 April (Easter), 30 April (Queen's Day), 1 May (Labour Day), 8 May (St Maarten, Saba and St Eustatius only: Celebration of World War II Victory), 20 May (Ascension Day), 31 May (St Maarten, Saba and St Eustatius only: Whit Monday), 1 July (Emancipation Day), 2 July (Curaçao Day), 21 July (St Maarten, Saba and St Eustatius only: Schoelcher Day), 26 July (Carnival), 6 September (Bonaire Day), 21 October (Antillian Day), 1 November (St Maarten, Saba and St Eustatius only: All Saints' Day), 11 November (St Maarten Day), 16 November (St Eustatius Day), 6 December (Saba Day), 15 December (St Maarten, Saba and St Eustatius only: Kingdom Day), 25–26 December (Christmas).

2004: 1 January (New Year's Day), 19 January (Bonaire only: Carnival Rest Day), 11 February (Curaçao and Bonaire only: Lenten Carnival), 29 March–1 April (Easter), 30 April (Queen's Day), 1 May (Labour Day), 8 May (St Maarten, Saba and St Eustatius only: Celebration of World War II Victory), 9 May (Ascension Day), 20 May (St Maarten, Saba and St Eustatius only: Whit Monday), 1 July (Emancipation Day), 2 July (Curaçao Day), 21 July (St Maarten and St Eustatius only: Schoelcher Day), 29 July (Carnival), 6 September (Bonaire Day), 21 October (Antillian Day), 1 November (St Maarten, Saba and St Eustatius only: All Saints' Day), 11 November (St Maarten Day), 16 November (St Eustatius Day), 6 December (Saba Day), 15 December (St Maarten, Saba and St Eustatius only: Kingdom Day), 25–26 December (Christmas).

Weights and Measures

The metric system is in force.

Statistical Survey

Sources (unless otherwise stated): Centraal Bureau voor de Statistiek, Fort Amsterdam, Willemstad, Curaçao; tel. (9) 61-1329; internet www.gov.an/cbs; Bank van de Nederlandse Antillen, Breedestraat 1, Willemstad, Curaçao; tel. (9) 434-5500; fax (9) 461-5004; e-mail info@centralbank.an; internet www.centralbank .an.

AREA AND POPULATION

Area (sq km): Curaçao 444; Bonaire 288; St Maarten (Dutch sector) 34; St Eustatius 21; Saba 13; Total 800 (309 sq miles).

Population: 189,474 (males 90,707; females 98,767) at census of 27 January 1992 (excluding adjustment for underenumeration, estimated at 3.2%); 207,175 (males 99,662; females 107,513) at 31 December 1996 (official estimate); 217,000 (UN estimate) at mid-2001 (Source: UN, *Population and Vital Statistics Report*). *By island* (estimate, 31 December 1996): Curaçao 152,700; Bonaire 14,169; St Maarten (Dutch sector) 36,231; St Eustatius 2,609; Saba 1,466.

Density (per sq km, 31 December 1996): Curaçao 344; Bonaire 49; St Maarten (Dutch sector) 1,066; St Eustatius 124; Saba 113; Total 259; Total 271.3 at mid-2001.

Principal Town: Willemstad (capital), population (UN estimate, incl. suburbs): 125,000 at mid-2001. Source: UN, *World Urbanization Prospects: The 2001 Revision* .

Births, Marriages and Deaths (1999, excl. St Eustatius unless otherwise indicated): Registered live births 2,803; Birth rate 13.7 per 1,000; Registered marriages 1,418 (1996, incl. St Eustatius); Registered deaths 1,321; Death rate 6.4 per 1,000. Source: UN, *Population and Vital Statistics Report.*

Expectation of Life (UN estimates, years at birth): 75.5 (males 72.5; females 78.4) in 1995–2000. Source: UN, *World Population Prospects: The 2000 Revision.*

Economically Active Population (Curaçao only, '000 persons aged 15 years and over, 2000): Agriculture, forestry and fishing 0.56; Mining and quarrying 0.14; Manufacturing 4.68; Electricity, gas and water 0.91; Construction 3.69; Wholesale and retail trade, repairs 9.86; Hotels and restaurants 3.67; Transport, storage and communications 4.03; Financial intermediation 3.47; Real estate, renting and business activities 4.05; Public administration, defence and social security 4.99; Education 2.92; Health and social work 4.25; Other community, social and personal services 3.27; Private households with employed persons 1.70; Extra-territorial organizations and bodies 0.06; Total employed 52.24 (males 27.35, females 24.88); Unemployed 8.53 (males 3.72, females 4.81); Total labour force 60.77 (males 31.07, females 29.69). *Total employed* (Curaçao, Bonaire, St Maarten, St Eustatius, Saba): 82,980 in 1998 (Source: ILO).

HEALTH AND WELFARE

Under-5 Mortality Rate (per 1,000 live births, 1997): 18.

Physicians (per 1,000 head, 1997): 1.4.

Hospital Beds (per 1,000 head, 1996): 6.15.

Health Expenditure: % of GDP (1994): 4.8.
Source: Pan American Health Organization.
For definitions, see explanatory note on p. vi.

AGRICULTURE, ETC.

Livestock (FAO estimates, '000 head, year ending September 2001): Asses 3; Cattle 1; Pigs 2; Goats 13; Sheep 8; Poultry 135. Source: FAO.

Livestock Products (FAO estimates, metric tons, 2001): Pig meat 180; Poultry meat 300; Cows' milk 410 (FAO estimate); Hen eggs 510. Source: FAO.

Fishing (FAO estimates, metric tons, live weight, 2000): Capture 19,974 (Skipjack tuna 9,439; Yellowfin tuna 6,901; Bigeye tuna 2,627); Aquaculture 5; Total catch 19,979. Source: FAO, *Yearbook of Fishery Statistics.*

MINING

Production ('000 metric tons, 2000, estimate): Salt 500. Source: US Geological Survey.

INDUSTRY

Production ('000 metric tons, unless otherwise indicated, 1998, estimates): Jet fuel 825; Kerosene 43; Residual fuel oils 5,018; Lubricating oils 385; Petroleum bitumen (asphalt) 468; Liquefied petroleum gas 68; Motor spirit (petrol) 1,810; Aviation gasoline 12; Distillate fuel oils (gas oil) 2,225; Sulphur (recovered) 28 (1997); Electric energy (million kWh) 1,490. Source: UN, *Industrial Commodity Statistics Yearbook.*

FINANCE

Currency and Exchange Rates: 100 cents = 1 Netherlands Antilles gulden (guilder) or florin (NA Fl.). *Sterling, Dollar and Euro Equivalents* (31 December 2002): £1 sterling = NA Fl. 2.885; US $1 = NA Fl. 1.790; €1 = NA Fl. 1.877; NA Fl. 100 = £34.66 = $53.27 = €59.51. *Exchange Rate:* In December 1971 the central bank's mid-point rate was fixed at US $1 = NA Fl. 1.80. In 1989 this was adjusted to $1 = NA Fl. 1.79. The US dollar also circulates on St Maarten.

Central Government Budget (NA Fl. million, 2001): *Revenue:* Tax revenue 512.3 (Taxes on property 14.5, Taxes on goods and services 369.9, Sales tax 242.3, Licences 11.2, Taxes on international trade and transactions 122.7, Other taxes 5.2); Non-tax and capital revenue 85.0; Total 608.8 (incl. grants received 11.5). *Expenditure:* Wages and salaries 199.9; Other goods and services 82.6; Interest payments 94.8; Subsidies to public companies 4.3; Current transfers 235.0; Capital expenditure (incl. transfers and net lending) 30.8; Total 647.4. *Total General Government Budget* (incl. island governments, NA Fl. million, 2000): *Revenue:* 1,223.3; *Expenditure:* 1,367.2. (Source: IMF, *Netherlands Antilles: Recent Developments, Selected Issues and Statistical Appendix* (May 2001).

International Reserves (US $ million at 31 December 2002): Gold (national valuation) 78; Foreign exchange 406; Total 484. Source: IMF, *International Financial Statistics.*

Money Supply (NA Fl. million at 31 December 2002): Currency outside banks 235.2; Demand deposits at commercial banks 1,064.9; Total (incl. others) 1,300.1. Source: IMF, *International Financial Statistics.*

Cost of Living (Consumer Price Index; base: 1995 = 100): All items 114.9 in 2000; 117.0 in 2001; 117.5 in 2002. Source: IMF, *International Financial Statistics.*

Gross Domestic Product (million NA Fl. at current prices, 1997): Agriculture, fishing, mining, etc. 28.7; Manufacturing 271.0; Electricity, gas and water 194.4; Construction 330.6; Wholesale and retail trade 926.4; Hotels and restaurants 163.2; Transport, storage and communications 500.1; Financial intermediation 538.7; Real estate, renting and business activities 634.4; Healthcare and social services 199.5; Other community, social and personal services 196.8; Services to households 26.9; Government services 748.1; *Sub-total* 4,758.8; *Less* Imputed bank service charge 221.7; *Gross domestic product* 4,537.1. Source: IMF, *Netherlands Antilles: Recent Developments, Selected Issues and Statistical Appendix* (May 2001).

Balance of Payments (transaction basis, NA Fl. million, 2001): Exports of goods f.o.b. 984.2; Imports of goods f.o.b. –2,849.9; *Trade balance* –1,865.7; Exports of services 2,984.5; Imports of services –1,432.8; *Balance on goods and services* –314.0; Other income received 187.5; Other income paid –158.0; *Balance on goods, services and income* –284.5; Current transfers received 392.1; Current transfers paid –357.0; *Current balance* –249.4; Capital transfers (net) 66.5; Direct investment abroad –0.8; Direct investment from abroad –1.6; Portfolio investment assets –47.0; Portfolio investment liabilities –0.4; Other investment assets 292.6; Other investment liabilities 288.2; Net errors and omissions 85.1; *Overall balance* 433.0.

EXTERNAL TRADE

Principal Commodities (US $ million, 1998): *Imports c.i.f.:* Petroleum, petroleum products, etc. 1,103.4 (Crude petroleum 1,000.6); Machinery and transport equipment 178.3; Total (incl. others) 2,028.1. *Exports f.o.b.:* Petroleum, petroleum products, etc. 1,028.6; Basic manufactures 39.9; Total (incl. others) 1,195.9.

Principal Trading Partners (US $ million, 1998): *Imports c.i.f.:* Brazil 87.5; Ecuador 32.0; Germany 41.9; Iraq 127.9; Japan 24.2; Netherlands 153.1; USA 333.2; Venezuela 879.6; Total (incl. others) 2,028.1. *Exports f.o.b.:* Aruba 22.1; Bahamas 19.7; Belgium-Luxembourg 34.0; Canada 35.6; Colombia 17.3; Dominican Republic 42.8; El Salvador 20.2; France-Monaco 55.2; Germany 14.0; Guatemala 24.2; Guyana 32.8; Haiti 20.8; Honduras 40.0; Netherlands 66.5; Panama 64.4; Suriname 13.6; USA 183.4; Venezuela 163.6; Total (incl. others) 1,195.9. Source: UN, *International Trade Statistics Yearbook.*

TRANSPORT

Road Traffic (motor vehicles registered, 1996): Passenger cars 75,105, Lorries 17,031, Buses 722, Taxis 430, Other cars 2,842, Motorcycles 1,541, Total 97,671.

Shipping: *International Freight Traffic* (Curaçao, '000 metric tons, excl. petroleum, 1997): Goods loaded 215.2; Goods unloaded 516.7. *Merchant Fleet* (registered at 31 December 2001): Number of vessels 176; Total displacement 1,249,762 grt. (Source: Lloyd's Register-Fairplay, *World Fleet Statistics*).

TOURISM

Tourist Arrivals: *Stop-overs*: 722,997 in 1999; 692,376 in 2000; 672,729 in 2001. *Cruise-ship Passengers* (Bonaire, Curaçao and St Maarten only): 851,103 in 1999; 1,220,076 in 2000; 1,217,025 in 2001.

COMMUNICATIONS MEDIA

Radio Receivers (1997): 217,000 in use.

Television Receivers (1999): 71,000 in use.

Telephones (2000): 80,000 main lines in use.

Mobile Cellular Telephones (1998): 16,000 subscribers.

Internet Users (1999): 2,000.

Daily Newspapers (1996): 6 titles (estimated circulation 70,000 copies per issue).

Sources: UNESCO, *Statistical Yearbook*; UN, *Statistical Yearbook*; International Telecommunication Union.

EDUCATION

Pre-primary (1996): 77 schools; 7,720 pupils; 342 teachers.

Primary (1996): 85 schools; 24,286 pupils; 1,139 teachers.

Junior High (1996): 16 schools; 5,282 pupils; 261 teachers.

Senior High (1996): 5 schools; 3,141 pupils; 200 teachers.

Technical and Vocational (1996): 37 institutions; 8,875 pupils; 623 teachers.

Special Education (1996): 18 schools; 1,616 pupils; 204 teachers.

Teacher Training (1996): 1 institution; 217 students; 26 teachers.

University of the Netherlands Antilles (1996): 671 students; 92 teachers.

Adult Literacy Rate (UNESCO estimates): 96.5% (males 96.5%; females 96.5%) in 2000.

Directory

The Constitution

The form of government for the Netherlands Antilles is embodied in the Charter of the Kingdom of the Netherlands, which came into force on 20 December 1954. The Netherlands, the Netherlands Antilles and, since 1986, Aruba each enjoy full autonomy in domestic and internal affairs and are united on a basis of equality for the protection of their common interests and the granting of mutual assistance.

The monarch of the Netherlands is represented in the Netherlands Antilles by the Governor, who is appointed by the Dutch Crown for a term of six years. The central Government of the Netherlands Antilles appoints a Minister Plenipotentiary to represent the Antilles in the Government of the Kingdom. Whenever the Netherlands Council of Ministers is dealing with matters coming under the heading of joint affairs of the realm (in practice mainly foreign affairs and defence), the Council assumes the status of Council of Ministers of the Kingdom. In that event, the Minister Plenipotentiary appointed by the Government of the Netherlands Antilles takes part, with full voting powers, in the deliberations.

A legislative proposal regarding affairs of the realm and applying to the Netherlands Antilles as well as to the 'metropolitan' Netherlands is sent, simultaneously with its submission, to the Staten Generaal (the Netherlands parliament) and to the Staten (parliament) of the Netherlands Antilles. The latter body can report in writing to the Staten Generaal on the draft Kingdom Statute and designate one or more special delegates to attend the debates and furnish information in the meetings of the Chambers of the Staten Generaal. Before the final vote on a draft the Minister Plenipotentiary has the right to express an opinion on it. If he disapproves of the draft, and if in the Second Chamber a three-fifths' majority of the votes cast is not obtained, the discussions on the draft are suspended and further deliberations take place in the Council of Ministers of the Kingdom. When special delegates attend the meetings of the Chambers this right devolves upon the delegates of the parliamentary body designated for this purpose.

The Governor has executive power in external affairs, which he exercises in co-operation with the Council of Ministers. He is assisted by an advisory council, which consists of at least five members appointed by him.

Executive power in internal affairs is vested in the nominated Council of Ministers, responsible to the Staten. The Netherlands Antilles Staten consists of 22 members, who are elected by universal adult suffrage for four years (subject to dissolution). Each island forms an electoral district. Curaçao elects 14 members, Bonaire three members, St Maarten three members and Saba and St Eustatius one member each. In the islands where more than one member is elected, the election is by proportional representation. Inhabitants have the right to vote if they have Dutch nationality and have reached 18 years of age. Voting is not compulsory. Each island territory also elects its Island Council (Curaçao 21 members, Bonaire 9, St Maarten 7, St Eustatius and Saba 5), and its internal affairs are managed by an executive council, consisting of the Gezaghebber (Lieutenant-Governor), and a number of commissioners. The central Government of the Netherlands Antilles has the

right to annul any local island decision which is in conflict with the public interest or the Constitution. Control of the police, communications, monetary affairs, health and education remain under the jurisdiction of the central Government.

On 1 January 1986 Aruba acquired separate status (*status aparte*) within the Kingdom of the Netherlands. However, in economic and monetary affairs there is a co-operative union between Aruba and the Antilles of the Five, known as the 'Union of the Netherlands Antilles and Aruba'.

The Government

HEAD OF STATE

Queen of the Netherlands: HM Queen BEATRIX.

Governor: Dr FRITZ M. DE LOS SANTOS GOEDGEDRAG.

COUNCIL OF MINISTERS
(April 2003)

The Government comprised a six-party coalition of the Partido Antía Restrukturá (PAR), Partido Nashonal di Pueblo (PNP), Partido Laboral Krusado Popular (PLKP), the Democratische Partij—St Maarten (DP—StM), the Democratische Partij—Statia (DP—StE) and the Unión Patriótico Bonairiano (UPB).

Prime Minister, Minister of General Affairs and Foreign Relations: ETIENNE YS (PAR).

Deputy Prime Minister and Minister for the National Recovery Plan and Economic Affairs: ERROL A. COVA (PLKP).

Minister of the Interior, Labour and Social Affairs: W. RUSSELL VOGES (DP—StM).

Minister of Finance: ERSILIA T. M. DE LANNOY (PNP).

Minister of Justice: NORBERTO V. RIBEIRO (PAR).

Minister of Education, Culture, Youth and Sports: EMILY DE JONGH-ELHAGE (PAR).

Minister of Transport and Communications: HERBERT DOMACASSÉ (DP—B).

Minister of Public Health and Social Development: JOAN THEODORA BREWSTER (PNP).

Minister Plenipotentiary and Member of the Council of Ministers of the Realm of the Netherlands Antilles: CAREL DE HASETH (PAR).

Attorney-General of the Netherlands Antilles: D. A. PIAR.

GEZAGHEBBERS
(Lieutenant-Governors)

Bonaire: RICHARD N. HART, Wilhelminaplein 1, Kralendijk, Bonaire; tel. (7) 175330; fax (7) 175100; e-mail gezag@bonairelive.com.

Curaçao: LISA DINDIAL, Centraal Bestuurskantoor, Concordiastraat 24, Willemstad, Curaçao; tel. (9) 461-2900.

Saba: ANTOINE J. M. SOLAGNIER, The Bottom, Saba; tel. (416) 3215; fax (416) 3274; e-mail antoine@solagnier.com.

St Eustatius: IRWIN E. TEMMER, Oranjestad, St Eustatius; tel. (3) 2213.

St Maarten: FRANKLYN E. RICHARDS, Central Administration, Secretariat, Clem Labega Sq., POB 1121, Philipsburg, St Maarten; tel. (54) 26085; fax (54) 24172; e-mail cabgov@sintmaarten.net; internet www.sintmaarten.net/gis.

MINISTRIES

Office of the Governor: Fort Amsterdam 2, Willemstad, Curaçao; tel. (9) 461-2000; fax (9) 461-1412; e-mail kabinet@kgna.an.

Ministry of Education, Culture, Youth and Sports: Boerhavestraat 16, Otrobanda, Willemstad, Curaçao; tel. (9) 462-4777; fax (9) 462-4471.

Ministry of Finance: Pietermaai 17, Willemstad, Curaçao; tel. (9) 432-8000; fax (9) 461-3339; e-mail g.d.dirfin@curinfo.an.

Ministry of General Affairs and Development Co-operation: Plasa Horacio Hoyer 9, Willemstad, Curaçao; tel. (9) 461-1866; fax (9) 461-1268; e-mail dvmtcoop@curinfo.an.

Ministry of the Interior, Labour and Social Affairs: Schouwburgweg 24, Willemstad, Curaçao; tel. (9) 434-6503; fax (9) 461-5553; e-mail drsoza@interneeds.net.

Ministry of Justice: Willhelminaplein, Willemstad, Curaçao; tel. (9) 463-0299; fax (9) 465-8083.

Ministry for the National Recovery Plan and Economic Affairs: Scharlooweg 106, Willemstad, Curaçao; tel. (9) 465-6236; fax (9) 465-6316; e-mail info.DEZ@ibm.net.

Ministry of Public Health and Social Development: Santa Rosaweg 122, Willemstad, Curaçao; tel. (9) 736-3530; fax (9) 736-3531; e-mail vornil@cura.net.

Ministry of Transport and Communications: Fort Amsterdam 17, Willemstad, Curaçao; tel. (9) 461-3988.

Office of the Minister Plenipotentiary of the Netherlands Antilles: Antillenhuis, Badhuisweg 173–175, 2597 JP The Hague, the Netherlands; tel. (70) 306-6111; fax (70) 306-6110.

Legislature

STATEN

Speaker: D. A. S. Lucia (PNP).
General Election, 18 January 2002

Party	% of votes	Seats
Frente Obrero i Liberashon 30 di mei . .	23.0	5
Partido Antía Restrukturá	20.6	4
Partido Nashonal di Pueblo	13.4	3
Partido Laboral Krusado Popular . .	12.1	2
Unión Patriótico Bonairiano . . .	3.6	2
Democratic Party—St Maarten . . .	5.5	2
Democratische Partij—Bonaire . . .	2.6	1
National Alliance*	4.8	1
Democratic Party—Statia	0.5	1
Windward Islands People's Movement . .	0.5	1
Total (incl. others)	100.0	22

*Comprising the St Maarten Patriotic Alliance and the National Progressive Party.

Political Organizations

Democratische Partij—Bonaire (DP—B) (Democratic Party—Bonaire): Kaya America 13A, POB 294, Kralendijk, Bonaire; tel. (7) 5923; fax (7) 7341; f. 1954; also known as Partido Democratico Boneriano; liberal; Leader Jopie Abraham.

Democratische Partij—Curaçao (DP—C) (Democratic Party—Curaçao): Neptunusweg 28, Willemstad, Curaçao; tel. (9) 75432; f. 1944; Leader Raymond Bentoera.

Democratische Partij—Sint Maarten (DP—StM): Tamarind Tree Dr. 4, Union Rd, Cole Bay, St Maarten; tel. (5) 31166; fax (5) 24296; Leader Sarah Wescott-Williams.

Democratische Partij—Statia (DP—StE): Oranjestad, St Eustatius; Leader Kenneth van Putten.

Frente Obrero i Liberashon 30 di mei (FOL) (Workers' Liberation Front of 30 May): Mayaguanaweg 16, Willemstad, Curaçao; tel. (9) 461-8105; internet www.fol.an; f. 1969; socialist; Leaders Anthony Godett, Rignald Lak, Editha Wright.

Movimentu Antiyas Nobo (MAN) (Movement for a New Antilles): Landhuis Morgenster, Willemstad, Curaçao; tel. (9) 468-4781; internet www.man.an; f. 1971; socialist; Leader Dominico (Don) F. Martina.

National Progressive Party: Willemstad, Curaçao; contested the 2002 elections as the National Alliance with the St Maarten Patriotic Alliance (q.v.).

Nos Patria (Our Fatherland): Willemstad, Curaçao; Leader Chin Behilia.

Partido Antía Restrukturá (PAR) (Restructured Antilles Party): Fokkerweg 28, Willemstad, Curaçao; tel. (9) 465-2566; fax (9) 465-2622; e-mail par@partidopar.com; internet www.partidopar.com; f. 1993; social-Christian ideology; Leader Etienne Ys.

Partido Kousa Akshan Sosial (KAS): Santa Rasaweg Naast 156, Willemstad, Curaçao; tel. (9) 747-2660; Leader Bernard S. A. Demei.

Partido Laboral Krusado Popular (PLKP): Schouwburgweg 44, Willemstad, Curaçao; tel. (9) 737-0644; fax (9) 737-0831; internet www.cura.net/krusada; f. 1997; progressive; Leader Errol A. Cova.

Partido Nashonal di Pueblo (PNP) (National People's Party): Winston Churchillweg 133, Willemstad, Curaçao; tel. (9) 869-6777; fax (9) 869-6688; internet www.pnp.an; f. 1948; also known as Nationale Volkspartij; Social Christian Party; Pres. Maria Liberia-Peters; Leader Susanne F. C. Camelia-Römer.

Partido Obrero di Bonaire (Bonaire Workers' Party): Kralendijk, Bonaire.

Partido Union den Reino Ulandés (PURU): Binnenweg 11, Willemstad, Curaçao; Leader Freddy I. Antersun.

People's Democratic Party (PDP): Philipsburg, St Maarten; tel. (5) 22696; Leader Millicent de Weever.

Saba Democratic Labour Movement (SDLM): Saba; tel. (4) 63311; fax (4) 63434; Leader Steve Hassell.

Saint Eustatius Alliance (SEA): Oranjestad, St Eustatius; Leader Ingrid Whitfield.

Serious Alternative People's Party (SAPP): St Maarten; Leader Julian Rollocks.

St Maarten Patriotic Alliance (SPA): Frontstraat 69, Philipsburg, St Maarten; tel. (5) 31064; fax (5) 31065; contested the 2002 elections as the National Alliance with the National Progressive Party (q.v.); Leader Vance James, Jr.

Social Independiente (SI): Willemstad, Curaçao; f. 1986 by fmr PNP mems in Curaçao; formed electoral alliance with FOL for 1990 election; Leader George Hueck.

Unión Patriótico Bonairiano (UPB) (Patriotic Union of Bonaire): Kaya Sabana 22, Kralendijk, Bonaire; tel. (7) 8906; fax (7) 5552; 2,134 mems; christian-democratic; Leader Ramonsito T. Booi; Sec.-Gen. C. V. Winklaar.

Windward Islands People's Movement (WIPM): Windwardside, POB 525, Saba; tel. (4) 2244; Chair. and Leader Will Johnston; Sec.-Gen. Dave Levenstone.

Judicial System

Legal authority is exercised by the Court of First Instance (which sits in all the islands) and in appeal by the Joint High Court of Justice of the Netherlands Antilles and Aruba. The members of the Joint High Court of Justice sit singly as judges in the Courts of First Instance. The Chief Justice of the Joint High Court of Justice, its members (a maximum of 30) and the Attorneys-General of the Netherlands Antilles and of Aruba are appointed for life by the Dutch monarch, after consultation with the Governments of the Netherlands Antilles and Aruba.

Joint High Court of Justice

Wilhelminaplein 4, Willemstad, Curaçao; tel. (9) 463-4111; fax (9) 461-8341.

Chief Justice of the Joint High Court: Dr L. A. J. de Lannoy.
Attorney-General of the Netherlands Antilles: D. A. Piar.
Secretary-Executive of the Joint High Court: Dr N. V. Ribeiro.

Religion

CHRISTIANITY

Most of the population were Christian, the predominant denomination being Roman Catholicism. According to the 1992 census, Roman Catholics formed the largest single group on four of the five islands: 82% of the population of Bonaire, 81% on Curaçao, 65% on Saba and 41% on St Maarten. On St Eustatius the Methodists formed the largest single denomination (31%). Of the other denominations, the main ones were the Anglicans and the Dutch Reformed Church. There were also small communities of Jews, Muslims and Bahá'ís.

Curaçaose Raad van Kerken (Curaçao Council of Churches): Barenblaan 11, Willemstad, Curaçao; tel. (9) 737-3070; fax (9) 7362183; f. 1958; six member churches; Chair. Ida Visser; Exec. Sec. Paul van der Waal.

The Roman Catholic Church

The Netherlands Antilles and Aruba together form the diocese of Willemstad, suffragan to the archdiocese of Port of Spain (Trinidad and Tobago). At 31 December 2001 the diocese numbered an estimated 224,809 adherents (over 70% of the total population). The Bishop participates in the Antilles Episcopal Conference, currently based in Trinidad and Tobago.

Bishop of Willemstad: Rt Rev. Luigi Antonio Secco, Bisdom, Breedestraat 31, Otrobanda, Willemstad, Curaçao; tel. (9) 462-5857; fax (9) 462-7437; e-mail bisdomwstad@curinfo.an.

The Anglican Communion

Saba, St Eustatius and St Maarten form part of the diocese of the North Eastern Caribbean and Aruba, within the Church in the Province of the West Indies. The Bishop is resident in The Valley, Anguilla.

Other Churches

Iglesia Protestant Uni (United Protestant Church): Fortkerk, Fort Amsterdam, Willemstad, Curaçao; tel. (9) 461-1139; fax (9) 465-7481; f. 1825 by union of Dutch Reformed and Evangelical Lutheran Churches; Pres. D. J. Lopes; 3 congregations; 11,280 adherents.

Methodist Church: Oranjestad, St Eustatius.

Other denominations active in the islands include the Moravian, Apostolic Faith, Wesleyan Holiness and Norwegian Seamen's Churches, the Baptists, Calvinists, Jehovah's Witnesses, Evangelists, Seventh-day Adventists, the Church of Christ and the New Testament Church of God.

JUDAISM

Reconstructionist Shephardi Congregation Mikvé Israel-Emanuel: Hanchi di Snoa 29, POB 322, Willemstad, Curaçao; tel. (9) 461-1067; fax (9) 465-4141; e-mail board@snoa.com; internet www.snoa.com; f. 1732; on present site; about 350 mems.

Orthodox Ashkenazi Congregation Shaarei Tsedek: Leliweg 1a, Willemstad, Curaçao; tel. (9) 737-5738; 100 mems.

The Press

Algemeen Dagblad: Daphneweg 44, POB 725, Willemstad, Curaçao; tel. (9) 747-2200; fax (9) 747-2257; e-mail adcarib@cura.net; internet www.ad-caribbean.com; daily; Dutch; Editor NOUD KÖPER.

Amigoe: Kaya Fratumam di Skirpiri z/n, POB 577, Willemstad, Curaçao; tel. (9) 767-2000; fax (9) 767-4084; e-mail management@amigoe.com; internet www.amigoe.com; f. 1884; Christian; daily; evening; Dutch; Dir INGRID DE MAAIJER-HOLLANDER; Editor-in-Chief MICHAEL WILLEMSE; circ. 12,000.

Bala: Noord Zapateer nst 13, Willemstad, Curaçao; tel. (9) 467-1646; fax (9) 467-1041; daily; Papiamento.

Beurs- en Nieuwsberichten: A. M. Chumaceiro Blvd 5, POB 741, Willemstad, Curaçao; tel. (9) 465-4544; fax (9) 465-3411; f. 1935; daily; evening; Dutch; Editor L. SCHENK; circ. 8,000.

Bonaire Holiday: POB 569, Curaçao; tel. (9) 767-1403; fax (9) 767-2003; f. 1971; tourist guide; English; 3 a year; circ. 95,000.

Bonaire Reporter: Kaya Gob. Debrot 200-6, Bonaire; internet bonairereporter.com; English; weekly.

The Business Journal: Indjuweg 30A, Willemstad, Curaçao; tel. (9) 461-1367; fax (9) 461-1955; monthly; English.

Colors: Liberty Publications, Curaçao; tel. and fax (9) 869-6066; e-mail colors@curacao-online.net; internet www.curacao-online.net/colors; f. 1998; general interest magazine; 4 a year; Publr TIRZAH Z. B. LIBERT.

De Curaçaosche Courant: Frederikstraat 123, POB 15, Willemstad, Curaçao; tel. (9) 461-2766; fax (9) 462-6535; f. 1812; weekly; Dutch; Editor J. KORIDON.

Curaçao Holiday: POB 569, Curaçao; tel. (9) 767-1403; fax (9) 767-2003; f. 1960; tourist guide; English; 3 a year; circ. 300,000.

Daily Herald: Bush Rd 22, POB 828, Philipsburg, St Maarten; tel. (54) 25253; fax (54) 25913; e-mail editorial@thedailyherald.com; internet www.thedailyherald.com; daily; English.

Extra: W. I. Compagniestraat 41, Willemstad, Curaçao; tel. (9) 462-4595; fax (9) 462-7575; daily; morning; Papiamento; Man. R. YRAUSQUIN; Editor MIKE OEHLERS; circ. 20,000.

Newsletter of Curaçao Trade and Industry Association: Kaya Junior Salas 1, POB 49, Willemstad, Curaçao; tel. (9) 461-1210; fax (9) 461-5422; f. 1972; monthly; English and Dutch; economic and industrial paper.

Nobo: Scherpenheuvel w/n, POB 323, Willemstad, Curaçao; tel. (9) 467-3500; fax (9) 467-2783; daily; evening; Papiamento; Editor CARLOS DAANTJE; circ. 15,000.

Nos Isla: Refineria Isla (Curazao) SA, Emmastad, Curaçao; 2 a month; Papiamento; circ. 1,200.

La Prensa: W. I. Compagniestraat 41, Willemstad, Curaçao; tel. (9) 462-3850; fax (9) 462-5983; e-mail webmaster@laprensacur.com; internet www.laprensacur.com; f. 1929; daily; evening; Papiamento; Man. R. YRAUSQUIN; Editor SIGFRIED RIGAUD; circ. 10,750.

Saba Herald: The Level, Saba; tel. (4) 2244; f. 1968; monthly; news, local history; Editor WILL JOHNSON; circ. 500.

St Maarten Guardian: Vlaun Bldg, Pondfill, POB 1046, Philipsburg, St Maarten; tel. (5) 26022; fax (5) 26043; e-mail guardian@sintmaarten.net; f. 1989; daily; English; Man. Dir RICHARD F. GIBSON; Man. Editor JOSEPH DOMINIQUE; circ. 4,000.

St Maarten Holiday: POB 569, Curaçao; tel. (9) 767-1403; fax (9) 767-2003; f. 1968; tourist guide; English; 3 a year; circ. 175,000.

Teen Times: St Maarten; e-mail info@teentimes.com; internet www.teentimes.com; for teenagers by teenagers; sponsored by The Daily Herald; English; Editor-in-Chief MICHAEL GRANGER.

Ultimo Noticia: Frederikstraat 123, Willemstad, Curaçao; tel. (9) 462-3444; fax (9) 462-6535; daily; morning; Papiamento; Editor A. A. JONCKHEER.

La Unión: Rotaprint NV, Willemstad, Curaçao; weekly; Papiamento.

NEWS AGENCIES

Algemeen Nederlands Persbureau (ANP) (The Netherlands): Panoramaweg 5, POB 439, Willemstad, Curaçao; tel. (9) 461-2233; fax (9) 461-7431; Representative RONNIE RENS.

Associated Press (AP) (USA): Roodeweg 64, Willemstad, Curaçao; tel. (9) 462-6586; Representative ORLANDO CUALES.

Publishers

Curaçao Drukkerij en Uitgevers Maatschappij: Willemstad, Curaçao.

Ediciones Populares: W. I. Compagniestraat 41, Willemstad, Curaçao; f. 1929; Dir RONALD YRAUSQUIN.

Drukkerij Scherpenheuvel NV: Scherpenheuvel, POB 60, Willemstad, Curaçao; tel. (9) 467-1134.

Drukkerij de Stad NV: W. I. Compagniestraat 41, Willemstad, Curaçao; tel. (9) 462-3566; fax (9) 462-2175; e-mail kenrick@destad.an; f. 1929; Dir KENRICK A. YRAUSQUIN.

Holiday Publications: POB 569, Curaçao; tel. (9) 767-1403; fax (9) 767-2003.

Offsetdrukkerij Intergrafia NV: Essoweg 54, Willemstad, Curaçao; tel. (9) 464-3180.

Broadcasting and Communications

TELECOMMUNICATIONS

East Caribbean Cellular NV (ECC): 13 Richardson St, Philipsburg, St Maarten; tel. (54) 22100; fax (54) 25675; e-mail info@eastcaribbeancellular.com; internet www.eastcaribbeancellular.com; f. 1989.

Servicio de Telekomunikashon (SETEL): F. D. Rooseveltweg 337, POB 3177, Willemstad, Curaçao; tel. (9) 833-1222; fax (9) 868-2596; e-mail setel@curinfo.an; internet www.curinfo.an; f. 1979; telecommunications equipment and network provider; state-owned, but expected to be privatized; Pres. ANGEL R. KOOK; Man. Dir JULIO CONSTANSIA; 400 employees.

Smitcoms NV: Dr A. C. Wathey Cruise & Cargo Facility, St Maarten; tel. (54) 29140; fax (54) 29141; e-mail matthews@sintmaarten.net; internet smitcomsltd.com; f. 2000; international telephone network provider; Man. Dir CURTIS K. HAYNES.

St Maarten Telephone Co (TelEm): C. A. Cannegieter St 17, POB 160, Philipsburg, St Maarten; tel. (54) 22278; fax (54) 30101; e-mail lpeters@telem.an; internet www.sinmaarten.net; f. 1975; local landline and value-added services, also operates TelCell digital cellular service; 15,000 subscribers; Man. Dir CURTIS K. HAYNES.

United Telecom Services (UTS): Schouwburgweg 22, POB 103, Willemstad, Curaçao; tel. (9) 777-0101; fax (9) 777-1238; e-mail info@antele.com; f. 1908; fmrly called Antelecom NV; Chair. DAVID DICK; Man. Dir HENDRIK J. EIKELENBOOM.

BROADCASTING

Radio

Easy 97.9 FM: Arikokweg 19A, Willemstad, Curaçao; tel. (9) 462-3162; fax (9) 462-8712; e-mail radio@easyfm.com; internet www.easyfm.com; Dir KEVIN CARTHY.

Radio Caribe: Ledaweg 35, Brievengat, Willemstad, Curaçao; tel. (9) 736-9555; fax (9) 736-9569; f. 1955; commercial station; programmes in Dutch, English, Spanish and Papiamento; Dir-Gen. C. R. HEILLEGGER.

Radio Curom (Curaçaose Radio-Omroep Vereniging): Roodeweg 64, POB 2169, Willemstad, Curaçao; tel. (9) 462-6586; fax (9) 462-5796; f. 1933; broadcasts in Papiamento; Dir ORLANDO CUALES.

Radiodifusión Boneriana NV: Kaya Gobernador Debrot 2, Kralendijk, Bonaire; tel. (7) 8273; fax (7) 8220; e-mail vozdibon@bonairenet.com; Owner FELICIANO DA SILVA PILOTO.

Voz di Bonaire (PJB2) (Voice of Bonaire): broadcasts in Papiamento, Spanish and Dutch.

Ritme FM (PJB4): broadcasts in Dutch.

Radio Exito: Wolkstraat 15, Willemstad, Curaçao; tel. (9) 462-5577; fax (9) 462-5580.

Radio Hoyer NV: Plasa Horacio Hoyer 21, Willemstad, Curaçao; tel. (9) 461-1678; fax (9) 461-6528; e-mail hoyer@cura.net; internet www.radiohoyer.com; f. 1954; commercial; two stations: Radio

Hoyer I (mainly Papiamento, also Spanish) and II (mainly Dutch, also English) in Curaçao; Man. Dir HELEN HOYER.

Radio Korsou FM: Bataljonweg 7, POB 3250, Willemstad, Curaçao; tel. (9) 737-3012; fax (9) 737-2888; e-mail master@korsou.com; internet www.korsou.com; 24 hrs a day; programmes in Papiamento and Dutch; Gen. Man. ALAN H. EVERTSZ.

    Laser 101 (101.1 FM): tel. (9) 737-7139; fax (9) 737-5215; e-mail master@laser101.com; 24 hours a day; music; English and Papiamento; Gen. Man. ALAN H. EVERTSZ.

Radio Paradise: ITC Building, Piscadera Bay, POB 6103, Curaçao; tel. (9) 463-6103; fax (9) 463-6404; Man. Dir J. A. VISSER.

Radio Tropical: Willemstad, Curaçao; tel. (9) 652467; fax (9) 652470; Dir DWIGHT RUDOLPHINA.

Trans World Radio (TWR): Kaya Gouverneur N. Debrotweg 64, Kralendijk, Bonaire; tel. (717) 8800; fax (717) 8808; e-mail 800am@twr.org; internet www.twr.org; religious, educational and cultural station; programmes to South, Central and North America, Caribbean in six languages; Pres. THOMAS J. LOWELL, Jr; Station Dir RICHARD FULLER.

Voice of St Maarten (PJD2 Radio): Plaza 21, Backstreet, POB 366, Philipsburg, St Maarten; tel. (5) 22580; fax (5) 24905; also operates **PJD3** on FM (24 hrs); commercial; programmes in English; Gen. Man. DON R. HUGHES.

Voice of Saba (PJF1): The Bottom, POB 1, Saba; studio in St Maarten; tel. (5) 63213; also operates The Voice of Saba FM; Man. MAX W. NICHOLSON.

There is a relay station for Radio Nederland on Bonaire.

Television

Leeward Broadcasting Corporation—Television: Philipsburg, St Maarten; tel. (5) 23491; transmissions for approx. 10 hours daily.

Antilliaanse Televisie Mij NV (Antilles Television Co): Berg Arraret, POB 415, Willemstad, Curaçao; tel. (9) 461-1288; fax (9) 461-4138; f. 1960; operates Tele-Curaçao (formerly operated Tele-Aruba); commercial; govt-owned; also operates cable service, offering programmes from US satellite television and two Venezuelan channels; Dir JOSÉ M. CIJNTJE; Gen. Man. NORMAN K. RICHARDS.

Five television channels can be received on Curaçao, in total. Relay stations provide Bonaire with programmes from Curaçao, St Maarten with programmes from Puerto Rico, and Saba and St Eustatius with programmes from St Maarten and neighbouring islands. Curaçao has a publicly-owned cable television service, TDS.

Finance

(cap. = capital; res = reserves; dep. = deposits; m. = million; brs = branches; amounts in Netherlands Antilles guilders unless otherwise stated)

BANKING

Central Bank

Bank van de Nederlandse Antillen (Bank of the Netherlands Antilles): Breedestraat 1, Willemstad, Curaçao; tel. (9) 434-5500; fax (9) 461-5004; e-mail info@centralbank.an; internet centralbank.an; f. 1828 as Curaçaosche Bank; name changed as above 1962; cap. 30m., res 112m., dep. 439m. (Dec. 2000); Chair. M. NICOLINA; Pres. EMSLEY D. TROMP; 2 brs; on St Maarten and Bonaire.

Commercial Banks

ABN AMRO Bank NV: Kaya Flamboyan 1, POB 3144, Willemstad, Curaçao; tel. (9) 763-8000; fax (9) 737-0620; f. 1964; Gen. Man. H. V. IGNACIO; 6 brs.

Antilles Banking Corpn (Curaçao) NV: Wilhelminaplein 14–16, POB 763, Willemstad, Curaçao; tel. (9) 461-2822; fax (9) 461-2820; f. 1989 as McLaughlin Bank NV; name changed as above in 1997; Pres. SHAFFIE WIHBY; 3 brs.

Antilles Banking Corpn (St Maarten) NV: Cannegieterstreet, POB 465, Philipsburg, St Maarten; tel. (5) 25908; fax (5) 25964; f. 1988; Man. Dirs F. BOWMAN, C. A. GREIGG-DUNCAN.

Banco di Caribe NV: Schottegatweg Oost 205, POB 3786, Willemstad, Curaçao; tel. (9) 432-3000; fax (9) 461-5220; e-mail info@bancodicaribe.com; internet www.bancodicaribe.com; f. 1973; cap. 2.0m., res 30.0m., dep. 482.5m. (Dec. 1998), total assets 617.4m. (Dec.2000); Chair. P. H. DE JONGH; CEO E. DE KORT; Dir R. HENRIQUEZ; 3 brs.

Banco Mercantil CA (Banco Universal): Abraham de Veerstraat 1, POB 565, Willemstad, Curaçao; tel. (9) 461-8241; fax (9) 461-1824; f. 1988; Gen. Man. FRANK GIRIGORI.

Banco de Venezuela NV: POB 131, c/o Amicorp NV, Bronsweg 8A, Willemstad, Curaçao; tel. (9) 434-3500; fax (9) 434-3533; f. 1993; Man. Dirs H. P. F. VON AESCH, R. YANES, V.E. BORBERG.

Bank of Nova Scotia NV (Canada): Backstreet 64, POB 303, Philipsburg, St Maarten; tel. (5) 23317; fax (5) 22562; f. 1969; Man. ROBERT G. JUDD.

Barclays Bank plc (UK): 29 Front St, POB 941, Philipsburg, St Maarten; tel. (5) 23511; fax (5) 24531; f. 1959; Man. EDWARD ARMOGAN (offices in Saba and St Eustatius).

Chase Manhattan Bank NA (USA): Chase Financial Center, Vlaun Building, Cannegieter Road (Pondfill) and Mullet Bay Hotel, POB 921, Philipsburg, St Maarten; tel. (5) 23726; fax (5) 23692; f. 1971; Gen. Man. K. BUTLER.

CITCO Banking Corporation NV: Kaya Flamboyan 9, POB 707, Willemstad, Curaçao; tel. (9) 732-2322; fax (9) 732-2330; e-mail cbc@citco.com; f. 1980 as Curaçao Banking Corporation NV; Man. Dir and Gen. Man. R. F. IRAUSQUIN; Man. Dir A. A. HART.

Fortis Bank (Curaçao) NV: Berg Arrarat 1, POB 3889, Willemstad, Curaçao; tel. (9) 463-9300; fax (9) 461-3769; internet www.meespierson.com; f. 1952 as Pierson, Heldring and Pierson (Curaçao) NV, became Meespierson (Curaçao) NV in 1993, name changed as above 2000; international banking/trust company; Gen. Mans NIKO KLUIJVER, CHARLEY DE MEZA.

Giro Curaçao NV: Scharlooweg 35, Willemstad, Curaçao; tel. (9) 433-9999; fax (9) 461-7861; Gen. Dir L. C. BERGMAN; Financial Dir H. L. MARTHA.

ING Bank NV (Internationale Nederlanden Bank NV): Kaya W. F. G. (Jombi) Mensing 14, POB 3895, Willemstad, Curaçao; tel. (9) 732-7000; fax (9) 732-7502; f. 1989 as Nederlandse Middenstandsbank NV: name changed as above 1992; Gen. Man. MARK SCHNEIDERS.

Maduro & Curiel's Bank NV: Plaza Jojo Correa 2–4, POB 305, Willemstad, Curaçao; tel. (9) 466-1100; fax (9) 466-1130; e-mail info@mcb-bank.com; internet www.mcb-bank.com; f. 1916; as NV Maduro's Bank, 1931 merged with Curiel's Bank; affiliated with Bank of Nova Scotia NV, Toronto; cap. 50.0m., res 102.9m., dep. 2,609.6m. (Dec. 2001); Chair. N. D. HENRIQUEZ; Pres. LIONEL CAPRILES; Man. Dirs WILLIAM H. L. FABRO, RON GOMES CASSERES; 26 brs.

Orco Bank NV: Dr Henry Fergusonweg 10, POB 4928, Willemstad, Curaçao; tel. (9) 737-2000; fax (9) 737-6741; e-mail info@orcobank.com; internet www.orcobank.com; f. 1986; cap. 30.7m., res 27.5m., dep. 523.9m. (Dec. 1999); Chair. E. L. GARCIA; Man. Dir I. D. SIMON.

Rabobank Curaçao NV: Zeelandia Office Park, Kaya W.F.G. (Jombi), Mensing 14, POB 3876, Willemstad, Curaçao; tel. (9) 465-2011; fax (9) 465-2066; f. 1978; cap. US $53.6m., res US $52.1m., dep. US $1,126.0m. (Dec. 2000); Chair. R. MESRITZ; Gen. Man. J. S. KLEP.

SFT Bank NV: Schottegatweg Oost 44, POB 707, Willemstad, Curaçao; tel. (9) 732-2900; fax (9) 732-2902.

Windward Islands Bank Ltd: Clem Labega Square 7, POB 220, Philipsburg, St Maarten; tel. (5) 22313; fax (5) 24761; affiliated to Maduro and Curiel's Bank NV; f. 1960; cap. and res 3.6m., dep. 53.6m. (Dec. 1984); Man. Dirs VICTOR P. HENRÍQUEZ, W. G. H. STRIJBOSCH.

'Offshore' Banks
(without permission to operate locally)

ABN AMRO Bank Asset Management (Curaçao) NV: Kaya Flamboyan 1, POB 3144, Willemstad, Curaçao; tel. (9) 736-6755; fax (9) 736-9246; f. 1976; Man. D. M. VROEGINDEWEY.

Abu Dhabi International Bank NV: Kaya W. F. G. (Jombi), Mensing 36, POB 3141, Willemstad, Curaçao; tel. (9) 461-1299; fax (9) 461-5392; internet www.adibwash.com; f. 1981; cap. US $20.0m., res $30.4m., dep. $329.3m. (Dec. 2001); Pres. QAMBAR AL MULLA; Man. Dir NAGY S. KOLTA.

Banco Caracas NV: Kaya W. F. G. (Jombi) Mensing 36, POB 3141, Willemstad, Curaçao; tel. (9) 461-1299; fax (9) 461-5392; f. 1984; Pres. GEORGE L. REEVES.

Banco Consolidado NV: Handelskrade 12, POB 3141, Willemstad, Curaçao; tel. (9) 461-3423; f. 1978.

Banco Latino NV: De Ruyterkade 61, POB 785, Willemstad, Curaçao; tel. (9) 461-2987; fax (9) 461-6163; f. 1978; cap. US $25.0m., res $12.3m., dep. $450.8m. (Nov. 1992); Chair. Dr GUSTAVO GÓMEZ LÓPEZ; Pres. FOLCO FALCHI.

Banco Provincial Overseas NV: Santa Rosaweg 51–55, POB 5312, Willemstad, Curaçao; tel. (9) 737-6011; fax (9) 737-6346; Man. E. SUARES.

Banque Artesia Curaçao NV: Castorweg 22–24, POB 155, Willemstad, Curaçao; tel. (9) 461-8061; fax (9) 461-5151; f. 1976 as Banque Paribas Curaçao NV; name changed as above 1998.

Caribbean American Bank NV: POB 6087, TM1 10, WTC Bldg, Piscadera Bay, Willemstad, Curaçao; tel. (9) 463-6380; fax (9) 463-6556; Man. Dir Dr MARCO TULIO HENRÍQUEZ.

Crédit Lyonnais Bank Nederland NV: Office Park Zeelandia, Kaya W. F. G. (Jombi) Mensing 18, POB 599, Willemstad, Curaçao; tel. (9) 461-1122; fax (9) 465-6265; Gen. Man. JAN A. BROUWER.

F. Van Lanschot Bankiers (Curaçao) NV: Schottegatweg Oost 32, POB 4799, Willemstad, Curaçao; tel. (9) 737-1011; fax (9) 737-1086; f. 1962; Man. A. VAN GEEST.

First Curaçao International Bank NV: Office Park Zeelandia, Kaya W. F. G. (Jombi) Mensing 18, POB 299, Willemstad, Curaçao; tel. (9) 737-2100; fax (9) 737-2018; f. 1973; cap. and res US $55m., dep. $244m. (1988); Pres. and CEO J. CH. DEUSS; Man. M. NEUMAN-ROUIRA.

Toronto Dominion (Curaçao) NV: c/o SCRIBA NV, Polarisweg 31–33, POB 703, Willemstad, Curaçao; tel. (9) 461-3199; fax (9) 461-1099; f. 1981; Man. E. L. GOULDING.

Union Bancaire Privée (TDB): J. B. Gorsiraweg 14, POB 3889, Willemstad, Curaçao; tel. (9) 463-9300; fax (9) 461-4129.

Other offshore banks in the Netherlands Antilles include American Express Overseas Credit Corporation NV, Banco Aliado NV, Banco del Orinoco NV, Banco Mercantil Venezolano NV, Banco Principal NV, Banco Provincial International NV, Banunion NV, CFM Bank NV, Citco Banking Corporation NV, Compagnie Bancaire des Antilles NV, Deutche Bank Finance NV, Ebna Bank NV, Exprinter International Bank NV, Integra Bank NV, Lavoro Bank Overseas NV, Lombard-Atlantic Bank NV, Middenbank (Curaçao) NV, Netherlands Caribbean Bank NV, Noro Bank NV, Premier Bank International NV.

Development Banks

Ontwikkelingsbank van de Nederlandse Antillen NV: Schottegatweg Oost 3c, POB 267, Willemstad, Curaçao; tel. (9) 747-3000; fax (9) 747-3320; e-mail obna@curinfo.an; f. 1981.

Stichting Korporashon pa Desaroyo di Korsou (KORP-DEKO): Breedestraat 29c, POB 656, Willemstad, Curaçao; tel. (9) 461-6699; fax (9) 461-3013.

Other Banks

Postspaarbank van de Nederlandse Antillen: Waaigatplein 7, Willemstad, Curaçao; tel. (9) 461-1126; fax (9) 461-7561; f. 1905; post office savings' bank; Chair. H. J. J. VICTORIA; cap. 21m. 20 brs.

Spaar- en Beleenbank van Curaçao NV: MCB Salinja Bldg, Schottegatweg Oost 130, Willemstad, Curaçao; tel. (9) 466-1585; fax (9) 466-1590.

There are also several mortgage banks and credit unions.

Banking Associations

Association of International Bankers in the Netherlands Antilles: Chumaceiro Blvd 3, POB 220, Curaçao; tel. (9) 461-5367; fax (9) 461-5369; e-mail info@ibna.an; internet www.ibna.an; Pres. PETER BLESS.

Bonaire Bankers' Association: POB 288, Kralendijk, Bonaire.

Curaçao Bankers' Association (CBA): A. M. Chumaceiro Blvd 3, Willemstad, Curaçao; tel. (9) 465-2486; fax (9) 465-2476; e-mail shaffie.wihby@mcb-bank.com; Pres. SHAFFIE WIHBY; Sec. ANDY VRUTAAL.

Federashon di Kooperativanan di Spar i Kredito Antiyano (Fekoskan): Curaçaostraat 50, Willemstad, Curaçao; tel. (9) 462-3676; fax (9) 462-4995; e-mail fekoskan@attglobal.net.

International Bankers' Association in the Netherlands Antilles: Scharlooweg 55, Willemstad, Curaçao.

The Windward Islands Bankers' Association: Clem Labega Square, Philipsburg, St Maarten; tel. (5) 22313; fax (5) 24761.

INSURANCE

Amersfoortse Antillen NV: Kaya W. F. G. Mensing 19, Willemstad, Curaçao; tel. (9) 461-6399; fax 461-6709.

Aseguro di Kooperativa Antiyano (ASKA) NV: Scharlooweg 15, Willemstad, Curaçao; tel. (9) 461-7765; fax (9) 461-5991; accident and health, motor vehicle, property.

Assurantiekantoor van der Lubbe: Buncamper Rd 33, Philipsburg, St Maarten; tel. (5) 22737; fax (5) 23979; all branches except life.

Ennia Caribe Schaden NV: J. B. Gorsiraweg 6, POB 581, Willemstad, Curaçao; tel. (9) 434-3800; fax (9) 434-3873; f. 1948; general; life insurance as Ennia Caribe Leven NV; Pres. DONALD BAKHUIS; Man. Dir ALBARTUS WILLEMSEN.

ING Fatum: Cas Coraweg 2, Willemstad, Curaçao; tel. (9) 777-7777; fax (9) 461-2023; f. 1904; property insurance.

MCB Group Insurance NV: MCB Bldg Scharloo, Scharloo, Willemstad, Curaçao; tel. (9) 466-1370; fax (9) 466-1327.

Netherlands Antilles and Aruba Assurance Company (NA&A) NV: Pietermaai 135, Willemstad, Curaçao; tel. (9) 465-7146; fax (9) 461-6269; accident and health, motor vehicle, property.

Seguros Antilliano NV: S. b. N. Doormanweg/Reigerweg 5, Willemstad, Curaçao; tel. (9) 736-6877; fax 736-5794; general.

A number of foreign companies also have offices in Curaçao, mainly British, Canadian, Dutch and US firms.

Insurance Association

Insurance Association of the Netherlands Antilles (NAVV): c/o Ing Fatum, POB 3002, Cas Coraweg 2, Willemstad, Curaçao; tel. (9) 777-7777; fax (9) 736-9658; Pres. R. C. MARTINA-JOE.

Trade and Industry

DEVELOPMENT ORGANIZATIONS

Curaçao Industrial and International Trade Development Company NV (CURINDE): Emancipatie Blvd 7, Landhuis Koninsplein, Curaçao; tel. (9) 737-6000; fax (9) 737-1336; e-mail curinde@attglobal.net; internet curinde.com; f. 1980; state-owned; manages the harbor free zone, the airport free zone and the industrial zone; Man. Dir E. R. SMEULDERS.

Foreign Investment Agency Curaçao (FIAC): Scharlooweg 174, Curaçao; tel. (9) 465-7044; fax (9) 461-5788; e-mail fiac@curinfo.an.

World Trade Center Curaçao: POB 6005, Piscadera Bay, Curaçao; tel. (9) 463-6100; fax (9) 462-4408; e-mail wtccur@attglobal.net; Man. Dir HUGO DE FRANÇA.

CHAMBERS OF COMMERCE

Bonaire Chamber of Commerce and Industry: Princess Mariestraat, POB 52, Kralendijk, Bonaire; tel. (7) 5595; fax (7) 8995.

Curaçao Chamber of Commerce and Industry: Kaya Junior Salas 1, POB 10, Willemstad, Curaçao; tel. (9) 461-3918; fax (9) 461-5652; e-mail businessinfo@curacao-chamber.an; internet www.curacao-chamber.an; f. 1884; Chair. HERMAN BEHR; Exec. Dir PAUL R. J. COMENENCIA.

St Maarten Chamber of Commerce and Industry: C. A. Cannegieterstraat 11, POB 454, Philipsburg, St Maarten; tel. (54) 23590; fax (54) 23512; e-mail coci@sintmaarten.net; f. 1979; Exec. Dir J. M. ARRINDELL VAN WINDT.

INDUSTRIAL AND TRADE ASSOCIATIONS

Association of Industrialists of the Netherlands Antilles (ASINA): Kaya Junior Salas 1, Willemstad, Curaçao; tel. (9) 461-2353; fax (9) 465-8040; Pres. R. M. LUCIA.

Bonaire Trade and Industry Asscn (Vereniging Bedrijfsleven Bonaire): POB 371, Kralendijk, Bonaire.

Curaçao Exporters' Asscn: World Trade Center Curaçao, POB 6049, Piscadera Bay, Curaçao; tel. (9) 463-6151; fax (9) 463-6451; e-mail cea@curacao-inc.an; f. 1903; Business Dir MURIEL M. LARMONIE.

CIFA (Curaçao International Financial Services Asscn): Chumaceiro Blvd 3, POB 220, Curaçao; tel. (9) 461-5371; fax (9) 461-5378; e-mail info@cifa.an; internet www.cifa.an; Pres. GREGORY E. ELIAS.

Curaçao Trade and Industry Asscn (Vereniging Bedrijfsleven Curaçao—VBC): Kaya Junior Salas 1, POB 49, Willemstad, Curaçao; tel. (9) 461-1210; fax (9) 461-5652; Pres. DEANNA CHEMALY; Exec. Dir R. P. J. LIEUW.

UTILITIES

Electricity and Water

Aqualectra Production NV (KAE): Rector Zwijsenstraat 1, POB 2097, Curaçao; tel. (9) 433-2200; fax (9) 462-6685; e-mail mgmt@aqualectra.com; internet www.aqualectra.com.

GEBE NV: Pond Fill, W. J. A. Nisbeth Rd, POB 123, St Maarten; tel. (5) 22213; fax 24810; f. 1961; Man. Dir J. A. LAMBERT.

Water & Energiebedrijf Bonaire (WEB) NV: Carlos Nicolaas 3, Kralendijk; tel. (7) 8244.

TRADE UNIONS

Algemene Bond van Overheidspersoneel (ABVO) (General Union of Civil Servants): POB 3604, Willemstad, Curaçao; tel. (9) 76097; f. 1936; Pres. F. S. Britto; Sec. S. J. Heerenveen; 5,000 mems.

Algemene Federatie van Bonaireaanse Werknemers (AFBW): Kralendijk, Bonaire.

Central General di Trahado di Corsow (CGTC) (General Headquarters for Workers of Curaçao): POB 2078, Willemstad, Curaçao; tel. (9) 462-3995; fax (9) 462-7700; f. 1949; Sec.-Gen. Oscar I. Semerel.

Curaçaosche Federatie van Werknemers (Curaçao Federation of Workers): Schouwburgweg 44, Willemstad, Curaçao; tel. (9) 76300; f. 1964; Pres. Wilfred Spencer; Sec.-Gen. Ronchi Isenia; 204 affiliated unions; about 2,000 mems.

Federashon Bonaireana di Trabou (FEDEBON): Kaya Krabè 6, Nikiboko, POB 324, Bonaire; tel. and fax (7) 8845; Pres. Gerold Bernabela.

Petroleum Workers' Federation of Curaçao: Willemstad, Curaçao; tel. (9) 737-0255; fax (9) 737-5250; affiliated to Int. Petroleum and Chemical Workers' Fed. f. 1955; Pres. R. G. Gijsbertha; about 1,500 mems.

Sentral di Sindikatonan di Korsou (SSK) (Confederation of Curaçao Trade Unions): Schouwburgweg 44, POB 3036, Willemstad; tel. (9) 737-0794; 6,000 mems.

Sindikato di Trahado den Edukashon na Korsou (SITEK) (Curaçao Schoolteachers' Trade Union): Landhuis Stenen Koraal, Willemstad, Curaçao; tel. (9) 4682902; fax (9) 4690552; 1,234 mems.

Windward Islands' Federation of Labour (WIFOL): Pond Fill, Long Wall Rd, POB 1097, St Maarten; tel. (54) 22797; fax (54) 26631; e-mail wifol@sintmaarten.net; Pres. Theophilus Thompson.

Transport

RAILWAYS

There are no railways.

ROADS

All the islands have a good system of all-weather roads. There were 590 km of roads in 1992, of which 300 km were paved.

SHIPPING

Curaçao is an important centre for the refining and transhipment of Venezuelan and Middle Eastern petroleum. Willemstad is served by the Schottegat harbour, set in a wide bay with a long channel and deep water. Facilities for handling containerized traffic at Willemstad were inaugurated in 1984. A Mega Cruise Facility, with capacity for the largest cruise ships, is under construction on the Otrobanda side of St Anna Bay. Ports at Bullen Bay and Caracas Bay also serve Curaçao. St Maarten is one of the Caribbean's leading ports for visits by cruise ships and in January 2001 new pier facilities were opened which could accommodate up to four cruise ships and add more cargo space. Each of the other islands has a good harbour, except for Saba which has one inlet, equipped with a large pier. Many foreign shipping lines call at ports in the Netherlands Antilles.

Curaçao Ports Authority: Werf de Wilde, POB 3266, Willemstad, Curaçao; tel. (9) 461-4422; fax (9) 461-3907; e-mail cpamanag@cura .net; internet curports.com; Man. Dir Richard Lopez-Ramirez.

Curaçao Shipping Association: Kaya Flamboyan 11, Willemstad, Curaçao; tel. (9) 737-0600; fax (9) 737-3875; Pres. K. Ponsen.

St Maarten Ports Authorities: St Maarten; tel. (5) 22472.

Principal Shipping Companies

Caribbean Cargo Services NV: Jan Thiel w/n, POB 442, Willemstad, Curaçao; tel. (9) 467-2588.

Curaçao Dry-dock Co Inc: POB 3012, Curaçao; tel. (9) 733-0000; fax (9) 736-5580; e-mail marketing@cdmnv.com; internet www .cdmnv.com; f. 1958; Man. Dir Mario Raymond Evertsz.

Curaçao Ports Authority (CPA) NV: Werf de Wilde z/n, POB 689, Curaçao; tel. (9) 434-5999; fax (9) 461-3907; e-mail cpamanag@cura .net; internet www.curports.com; Man. Dir Richard Lopez-Ramirez.

Curaçao Ports Services Inc NV (CPS): Curaçao Container Terminal, POB 170, Curaçao; tel. (9) 461-5079; fax (9) 461-6536; e-mail cps@ibm.net; Man. Dir Karel Jan O. Aster.

Dammers & van der Heide, Shipping and Trading (Antilles) Inc: Kaya Flamboyan 11, POB 3018, Willemstad, Curaçao; tel. (9) 737-0600; fax (9) 737-3875; e-mail general@dammers-curacao.com; Man. Dir J. J. Ponsen.

Gomez Transport NV: Zeelandia, Willemstad, Curaçao; tel. (9) 461-5260; fax (9) 461-3358; e-mail gomez-shipping@ibm.net; Man. Fernando da Costa Gomez.

Hal Antillen NV: De Ruyterkade 63, POB 812, Curaçao.

Intermodal Container Services NV: Fokkerweg 30, Willemstad, POB 3747, Curaçao; tel. (9) 461-3330; fax (9) 461-3432; Mans A. R. Beaujon, N. N. Harms.

Kroonvlag Curaçao NV: Maduro Plaza, POB 231, Curaçao; tel. (9) 737-6900; fax (9) 737-1266; e-mail hekro@cura.net.

Lagendijk Maritime Services: POB 3481, Curaçao; tel. (9) 465-5766; fax (9) 465-5998; e-mail ims@ibm.net.

S. E. L. Maduro & Sons (Curaçao) Inc: Maduro Plaza, POB 3304, Willemstad, Curaçao; tel. (9) 733-1501; fax (9) 733-1506; e-mail hmeijer@madurosons.com; Man. Dir. H. Meijer; Vice Pres. R. Corsen.

St Maarten Port Services: POB 270, Philipsburg, St Maarten; tel. (5) 22304.

Anthony Veder & Co NV: Zeelandia, POB 3677, Curaçao; tel. (9) 461-4700; fax (9) 461-2576; e-mail anveder@ibm.net; Man. Dir Joop van Vliet.

CIVIL AVIATION

There are international airports at Curaçao (Dr A. Plesman, or Hato, 12 km (7.5 miles) from Willemstad), Bonaire (Flamingo Field) and St Maarten (Princess Juliana, 16 km (10 miles) from Philipsburg); and airfields for inter-island flights at St Eustatius and Saba. In 1998 a free trade zone was inaugurated at the international airport on Curaçao. A US $90m. project to expand Princess Juliana Airport was expected to commence in early 2003.

Dutch Caribbean Airlines (DCA): Hato International Airport, Curaçao; tel. (9) 733-8888; fax (9) 733-8300; e-mail anlm03@ibm.net; internet www.flydca.com; f. 1964 as Antilliaanse Luchtvaart Maatschappij (ALM—Antillean Airlines) to assume responsibilities of the Caribbean division of KLM (the Netherlands), changed name as above in 2002; majority govt-owned since 1969 and privatization pending in March 2003; internal services between Bonaire, Curaçao and St Maarten; external services to destinations in North and South America and within the Caribbean; Pres. and CEO Ir Mario R. Evertsz.

Windward Islands Airways International (WIA—Winair) NV: Princess Juliana Airport, POB 2088, Philipsburg, St Maarten; tel. (5) 452568; fax (5) 454229; e-mail info@fly-winair.com; internet www .fly-winair.com; f. 1961; govt-owned since 1974; scheduled and charter flights throughout north-eastern Caribbean; Man. Dir John Strugnell.

Tourism

Tourism is a major industry on all the islands. The principal attractions for tourists are the white, sandy beaches, marine wildlife and diving facilities. There are marine parks in the waters around Curaçao, Bonaire and Saba. The numerous historic sites are of interest to visitors. The largest number of tourists visit St Maarten, Curaçao and Bonaire. In 2001 stop-over visitors totalled 672,729 (of whom 60% were on St Maarten). In the same year 1,217,025 cruise-ship passengers visited St Maarten, Curaçao and Bonaire (of whom 71.3% were on St Maarten). The destruction caused on St Maarten by Hurricanes Luis and Marilyn in September 1995 caused a drastic decrease in tourism arrivals to the Netherlands Antilles in 1995, compared to the previous year, while there was a concomitant fall in tourism earnings of 12.1%. The sector recovered in the remainder of the decade; however, the terrorist attacks on the USA in September 2001 were expected to adversely affect the industry.

Bonaire Tourism Corporation: Kaya Grandi 2, Kralendijk, Bonaire; tel. (7) 8322; fax (7) 8408; e-mail info@tourismbonaire.com; internet www.infobonaire.com; Dir E. Beukenboom.

Curaçao Tourism Development Bureau (CTDB): Pietermaai 19, POB 3266, Willemstad, Curaçao; tel. (9) 461-6000; fax (9) 461-2305; e-mail info@ctbd.net; internet www.curacao-tourism.com; f. 1989; Dir James Hepple.

Saba Tourist Office: Windwardside, POB 527, Saba; tel. (4) 162231; fax (4) 162350; e-mail iluvsaba@unspoiledqueen.com; internet www.sabatourism.com; Dir Glenn C. Holm.

St Eustatius Tourist Office: Fort Oranje Straat z/n, Oranjestad, St Eustatius; tel. (3) 182433; fax (3) 182433; e-mail euxtour@ goldenrock.net; internet www.statiatourism.com; Dir Alida Francis.

St Maarten Tourist Bureau: Vineyard Office Park, W. G. Buncamper Rd 33, Philipsburg, St Maarten; tel. (5) 22337; fax (5) 22734; internet www.st-maarten.com; Dir Cornelius de Weever.

HOTEL ASSOCIATIONS

Bonaire Hotel and Tourism Association: Kralendijk, Bonaire; Man. Dir HUGO GERHARTS.

Curaçao Hospitality and Tourism Association (CHATA): POB 6115, Kurason Komèrsio, Curaçao; tel. (9) 465-1005; fax (9) 465-1052; e-mail information@chata.org; internet www.chata.org; Pres. ROLF SPRECHER.

St Maarten Hospitality and Trade Association: W. J. A. Nisbeth Rd 33A, POB 486, Philipsburg, St Maarten; tel. (542) 0108; fax (542) 0107; e-mail info@shta.com; internet www.shta.com.

NEW ZEALAND

Introductory Survey

Location, Climate, Language, Religion, Flag, Capital

The Dominion of New Zealand lies in the South Pacific Ocean, about 1,750 km (1,100 miles) south-east of Australia. It consists of North Island and South Island, separated by the narrow Cook Strait, and several smaller islands, including Stewart Island (or Rakiura) in the south. The climate is temperate and moist, with an average temperature of 12°C (52°F), except in the far north, where higher temperatures are reached. The official language is English, but the indigenous Maori inhabitants (an estimated 14.1% of the total population at the census of March 2001) also use their own language. At the 2001 census, 15.7% of respondents professed adherence to the Anglican Church, 13.0% being Roman Catholics and 11.5% Presbyterians. The national flag (proportions 1 by 2) is dark blue, with a representation of the United Kingdom flag as a canton in the upper hoist. In the fly are four five-pointed red stars, edged in white, in the form of the Southern Cross constellation. The capital is Wellington, on North Island.

Recent History

New Zealand is a former British colony. It became a dominion, under the British Crown, in 1907 and achieved full independence by the Statute of Westminster, adopted by the British Parliament in 1931 and accepted by New Zealand in 1947.

In 1962 Western Samoa (now Samoa, q.v.), formerly administered by New Zealand, achieved independence, and in 1965 the Cook Islands attained full internal self-government, but retained many links, including common citizenship, with New Zealand. In October 1974 Niue, one of New Zealand's island territories, obtained similar status 'in free association with New Zealand'. New Zealand retains two Dependent Territories, Ross Dependency and Tokelau (for details of New Zealand's Dependent and Associated Territories, see p. 3071).

In December 1972 the first Labour Government for more than 12 years came to power, under the leadership of Norman Kirk, after a succession of New Zealand National Party administrations. The New Zealand Labour Party took office at a time when the economy was thriving, mainly as a result of a sharp increase in international prices for agricultural commodities. However, this prosperity was accompanied by inflation. Higher domestic demand and the international energy crisis of 1973–74 led to a rapid rise in imports, a reduction in exchange reserves and a severe balance-of-payments problem. The Labour Government's foreign policy was more independent than that of its predecessors. It phased out New Zealand's military commitments under the South-East Asia Treaty Organization and established diplomatic relations with the People's Republic of China.

Norman Kirk died in August 1974, and Wallace Rowling, hitherto Minister of Finance, became Prime Minister in September. The economic recession worsened, and in November 1975 a general election resulted in victory for the National Party, which won 55 of the 87 seats in the House of Representatives, while the Labour Party took the remaining 32 seats. The new Government, under Robert (later Sir Robert) Muldoon, who had led the National Party since July 1974, introduced austere economic policies, and in 1976 reduced the annual intake of migrants from 30,000 to 5,000, while conducting a campaign against illegal immigrants.

New Zealand continued to suffer a very low rate of economic growth and increasing unemployment. Popular dissatisfaction with Muldoon's sometimes controversial leadership was reflected at the general election in November 1978. The National Party retained power, with 50 of the 92 seats in the enlarged House of Representatives, but its share of the total vote fell from 47.2% in 1975 to 39.8%. Labour won more votes (40.4% of the total) but fewer seats (41). The Social Credit Party received 17.1% of the total votes, compared with only 7.4% in 1975, but obtained only one seat. In the November 1981 election Muldoon's majority was further reduced. The National Party won 47 of the 92 seats in the House, while Labour, which again received more votes, won 43 seats and Social Credit (despite obtaining 20.6% of votes cast) only two.

In February 1984 Muldoon's Government antagonized New Zealand's trade unions by effecting legislation to ban 'closed shop' agreements with employers, thus giving employees the right to choose whether or not to join a trade union. Further legislation was used in June to compel striking construction workers to return to work. In the same month, faced with dissent within his own party, Muldoon called an early general election for July. The Labour Party obtained 43% of the total votes and secured 56 of the 95 seats in an enlarged House of Representatives, while the National Party, with 36% of the votes, took 37 seats: it was thought that the National Party had lost considerable support to the newly-formed New Zealand Party, a right-wing party which won 12.3% of the votes (but no seats) after campaigning for a minimum of government intervention in the economy. David Lange (the leader of the Labour Party since February 1983) became Prime Minister. James McLay, who had been deputy leader of the National Party since March 1984, defeated Muldoon in an election for the leadership of the party in November 1984, but he was replaced as party leader by his deputy, James (Jim) Bolger, in March 1986.

The Labour Government introduced controversial deregulatory measures to improve the country's economic situation. The initial success of these measures, together with widespread popular support for the Government's anti-nuclear policy (see below), contributed to a second victory for the Labour Party in a general election in August 1987. Of the 97 seats in the enlarged House of Representatives, the Labour Party secured 58, and the National Party 39. (The Democratic Party lost both the seats that its predecessor, the Social Credit Party, had won at the 1984 election.) Of the votes cast, the Labour Party received 47.4%, and the National Party 42.8%.

In 1987 Lange's Government initiated a controversial policy of 'privatization' of state-owned enterprises. In November 1988 policy disagreements prompted Lange to dismiss the Minister responsible for the privatization programme, Richard Prebble. Lange was accused by Cabinet colleagues of acting without consultation, and in December Roger (later Sir Roger) Douglas, the Minister of Finance, declared that he would not serve another term under Lange. Douglas was promptly dismissed from office, and later that month unsuccessfully challenged Lange for the leadership of the Labour Party. In May 1989 the formation of the NewLabour Party (led by a former president of the Labour Party, Jim Anderton) was announced: the party aimed to appeal to disillusioned Labour supporters. In early August Douglas was elected by Labour MPs to a vacant Cabinet post, thus prompting Lange to resign. Shortly afterwards, Geoffrey Palmer, hitherto the deputy leader of the Labour Party, was elected the Labour Party's parliamentary leader and Prime Minister.

In January 1990 Palmer undertook a wide-ranging government reshuffle. The return of Richard Prebble to the Cabinet, in his former post as Minister for State-Owned Enterprises, provoked considerable anger within the Labour Party. The Government also aroused hostility by its introduction of a substantial fee for tertiary-level students. The continued sale of state assets, especially that of the telecommunications company, Telecom, was also unpopular (although a portion of the proceeds from the Telecom sales was to be invested in education and health). On 4 September 1990, less than eight weeks before the next general election, Palmer resigned as Prime Minister. Public opinion polls had indicated that Labour, under his leadership, had lost support to the National Party, and members of the Cabinet had consequently urged him to resign. Michael Moore, the Minister of External Relations and Trade (who had also contested the August 1989 leadership election), replaced Palmer as Prime Minister and Labour Party leader. Moore promised to act promptly to avert the enormous budget deficit forecast for 1991/92, and, two weeks later, he secured an agreement with the country's trade union leaders regarding restricted pay settlements. In October 1990, none the less, the National Party won 47.8% of the votes at the general election, taking 67 of the 97 seats in the House of Representatives. The Labour Party, with 35.1% of the votes, won 29 seats, while the NewLabour Party retained its sole seat, obtaining 5.2% of the votes. Jim Bolger, as leader of the National Party, thus became Prime Minister at the head of a Government that promised to continue Labour's strict budgetary and monetary controls. The sale of state assets would also continue.

In November 1990 the new Government's first economic proposals were outlined. They included the repeal of legislation on equal pay for women, and envisaged reductions in public spending, particularly in the field of social welfare. In December the Government announced measures that entailed proposed reductions in unemployment benefit, family benefits, and in medical and sickness payments, and prepared for the introduction of a system whereby users of medical and educational services (hitherto provided free of charge) would be required to pay, according to a means test. These measures were received with anger by social and church groups. Protest marches took place in April 1991, and plans for a 'freeze' in the levels of old-age pensions prompted groups representing the elderly unsuccessfully to petition the British Monarch (through the Governor-General) to dismiss the Government. Two National Party members of the House of Representatives resigned from the party in August, in protest against the proposals, and the Minister of Maori Affairs, Winston Peters (who had openly criticized the Government's economic strategy), was dismissed in October. In November Sir Robert Muldoon announced that he would resign from the legislature in early 1992, in protest against the Government's economic policies. Earlier in the month criticism had prompted the Government to withdraw its stringent means-testing measures for the allocation of state pensions, but the overall level of payments remained lower than previously.

In December 1991 a coalition was formed by minor parties as a challenge to the two main parties. The grouping, known as the Alliance, consisted of the NewLabour Party, the New Zealand Democratic Party, the Green Party of Aotearoa—New Zealand and Mana Motuhake. In its first electoral test (the by-election in February 1992 that had been precipitated by Muldoon's resignation) the Alliance campaigned for the provision of education and health care free of charge and the return to the public sector of 'privatized' state assets. The National Party retained the seat in the by-election, but with a greatly reduced majority. The Alliance secured 38% of the votes, only 5% less than the National Party.

In September 1992 a preliminary referendum on proposed electoral reform was held. The electorate voted overwhelmingly in favour of the abolition of the 'first-past-the-post' system and for its replacement by a form of proportional representation; of the four alternatives offered, the mixed member proportional (MMP) system (similar to that used in Germany) received the greatest support. A second, binding referendum was to be arranged to coincide with the next general election, scheduled for late 1993. The new rules were to be implemented at the 1996 election.

In March 1993, in an attempt to improve the National Party's chances of re-election, a minor reorganization of the Government was carried out. Changes included the replacement of Simon Upton, Minister of Health responsible for the implementation of unpopular hospital reforms, by Bill Birch, a close associate of Bolger. The highly controversial charges for hospital beds were abolished by the new Minister. In the same month the outspoken Winston Peters, who had continued to embarrass the Government, resigned from his parliamentary seat in order to stand for re-election as an independent candidate. The by-election in April resulted in an overwhelming victory for Peters, the major political parties having declined to present candidates. In July Peters established New Zealand First, and announced that the party would contest all 99 seats at the forthcoming general election.

At the election, held on 6 November 1993, the National Party, which had campaigned mainly on the Government's record of economic recovery, was narrowly returned to office, receiving 35.2% of the total votes cast and securing 50 seats in the House of Representatives. The Labour Party, with 34.7% of the votes, won 45 seats, the Alliance two and New Zealand First two. At the concurrent, second referendum on electoral reform, 54% of voters favoured the adoption of the MMP system. A new Government was appointed in late November. Changes included the replacement of Ruth Richardson as Minister of Finance by Bill Birch, the latter being succeeded as Minister of Health by Jenny Shipley. Michael Moore, the parliamentary leader of the Labour Party, was replaced by Helen Clark, the former Deputy Prime Minister and Minister of Health. In August 1994 the Govern-

ment narrowly retained its majority at a by-election brought about by the unexpected resignation of Ruth Richardson from the House of Representatives.

In October 1994 a former cabinet minister, Peter Dunne, resigned from the Labour Party, following differences over the party's policy on taxation, and declared his intention to remain in the House of Representatives as an independent member. He subsequently established a new party, Future New Zealand. The traditional two-party system was further challenged in early 1995, when support for ACT New Zealand, co-founded by Sir Roger Douglas (reformist Minister of Finance in 1984–88) who had recently announced his return to politics, began to increase rapidly. In June 1995, however, the position of the ruling party was strengthened by the formation of United New Zealand by seven members of the House of Representatives (four National, two Labour and the leader of Future New Zealand, Peter Dunne). The new grouping pledged its support for the Government on issues of confidence. In February, for the first time since the early 1930s, a formal coalition Government was established when the National Party formed an official alliance with United New Zealand. In the ensuing government reorganization, Peter Dunne joined the Cabinet as Minister of Revenue and Internal Affairs. In April 1996, defections from the two major parties and realignments having continued, a National member of the House of Representatives left the ruling coalition to join New Zealand First, thus becoming the ninth member of the National Party to depart since the 1993 election. As a result, the number of parliamentary seats held by the National Party was reduced to 41. In March, meanwhile, Sir Michael Hardie Boys replaced Dame Catherine Tizard as Governor-General.

The first general election under the MMP system was held on 12 October 1996. No party achieved an outright majority. The National Party, with 34.1% of the votes, won 44 of the 120 seats in the expanded House of Representatives, the Labour Party (28.3%) secured 37 seats and New Zealand First (13.1%) garnered 17 seats, while the Alliance won 13 seats, ACT New Zealand eight and United New Zealand one. A notable development was the increase in the number of Maori MPs from six to 15, a figure almost equivalent to the proportion of Maori in the population as a whole. Although the election result initially appeared to favour the formation of a centre-left coalition under the leadership of Helen Clark, complex negotiations finally led to the establishment in December of an alliance between the National Party and New Zealand First, led by Winston Peters.

Jim Bolger thus continued as Prime Minister. Winston Peters was appointed Deputy Prime Minister and Treasurer, the latter newly-created post carrying responsibility for the drafting of the country's budget. Although Peters had previously discounted the possibility of a reconciliation and of entering into a coalition with the National Party, he had unexpectedly altered his stance in exchange for concessions on economic policy. These concessions included the deferment of proposed reductions in income tax, to enable increased expenditure in areas such as health and education. The incoming Cabinet incorporated a total of five members of New Zealand First. Don McKinnon of the National Party retained the foreign affairs portfolio, and Bill Birch continued to hold nominal responsibility for finance.

In September 1997 proposals for the introduction of a compulsory retirement savings scheme were overwhelmingly rejected by the electorate in a referendum. The holding of the referendum had been a condition of New Zealand First's participation in the ruling coalition, but the Prime Minister had also actively supported the proposed pension reforms. In the following month thousands of protesters took to the streets to demand the resignation of the Government, the latter's policies on health and education having drawn particular criticism.

In November 1997, following a leadership challenge from Jenny Shipley, a cabinet minister whose portfolios now included transport and women's affairs, the Prime Minister announced his intention to resign. Jenny Shipley was thus sworn in as New Zealand's first woman Prime Minister in December, reiterating the National Party's commitment to a continuation of the partnership with New Zealand First. In the ensuing government reorganization, most supporters of Jim Bolger retained their portfolios but were downgraded. Winston Peters continued as Deputy Prime Minister, while other members of New Zealand First also remained in the Cabinet. Wyatt Creech was appointed deputy leader of the National Party, in place of Don McKinnon, who retained the foreign affairs portfolio.

In November 1997, meanwhile, following the Alliance's rejection of a Greens' proposal to establish a coalition arrangement, the Green Party of Aotearoa decided that at the next general election it would stand as a separate political party but would remain a member of the Alliance until that time. In January 1998 the Liberal Party announced that it was to be dissolved and merge with the Alliance.

In May 1998 the outcome of a parliamentary by-election to fill the seat vacated by Jim Bolger confirmed the electorate's growing disillusionment with the coalition Government. Although the seat was retained by the National Party, its majority was decimated. The candidate of ACT New Zealand unexpectedly received more votes than his counterpart from the Labour Party. In July Tau Henare, the Minister of Maori Affairs, was removed as deputy leader of New Zealand First, upon the publication of a government report that emphasized the adverse effects on the Maori population of the various economic reforms implemented since 1987. In August 1998, following an acrimonious dispute regarding the sale of the Government's stake in Wellington airport, the Prime Minister dismissed Winston Peters from the post of Deputy Prime Minister and Treasurer. The dissolution of the coalition Government was then announced. Rejecting demands for an early general election, Jenny Shipley reallocated many cabinet portfolios. Wyatt Creech was appointed Deputy Prime Minister, while Bill Birch became Treasurer. Although Tau Henare (who in late 1998 founded a new party, Mauri Pacific) was the only former New Zealand First minister to retain his post within the Cabinet, three other erstwhile members of the National Party's former coalition partner remained as ministers outside the Cabinet. Despite the defection of Winston Peters to the opposition, the Prime Minister was able to secure the support of eight of the 16 New Zealand First representatives in the legislature, and in September she survived a vote of confidence in the House. In the same month, in an attempt to raise public concern over the social effects of government policy, in particular the plight of low-income families, the Anglican Church initiated an ecumenical 'Hikoi of Hope', in which protesters from both ends of the country marched to Wellington and converged upon the House of Representatives.

In December 1998 the minority Government's position was further weakened by the unexpected resignation of a supporting independent (and former New Zealand First) MP, following the administration's decision to proceed with its acquisition of 28 F-16 fighter aircraft from the USA. (The contract to lease the aircraft, however, was cancelled in March 2000 by the new Labour Government.) The Prime Minister was placed under further pressure in early 1999, when it was alleged that the Minister of Tourism, Murray McCully, had acted inappropriately with regard to the handling of a major contract for the advertising business of the New Zealand Tourism Board. In February, as the Prime Minister became personally implicated in the affair and as opposition MPs accused her of deliberately misleading the legislature over her association with the head of the advertising agency in question, the Government won a motion of 'no confidence' by 61 votes to 59. Claiming that the ruling party had intended to exploit its links with the agency during the next general election campaign, the Labour Party demanded an inquiry into the Government's alleged payments to departing members of the New Zealand Tourism Board and into the Board's expenditure on overseas promotions. In March the NZ$53m. marketing contract with the agency was terminated. Murray McCully relinquished the tourism portfolio in April.

During the course of 1999 the Government was also embarrassed by the award of a series of controversial severance payments to senior officers of the fire service, the work and income support services and other public bodies, in addition to the settlements reached with executives of the Tourism Board. In November, only three days before the forthcoming general election, the Prime Minister dismissed the Minister of Immigration, an independent Maori MP, following his offer of residency rights to a group of Chinese immigrants in return for substantial investment in Maori schemes.

At the election, conducted on 27 November 1999, the opposition Labour Party won the largest share of votes cast. A recount of votes in one constituency, where the Green Party candidate then unexpectedly took the seat from the incumbent National MP, combined with the incorporation of 'special votes' (which included those cast by New Zealanders overseas), led to a substantial modification of the initial results. Having secured 38.7% of the votes cast, the Labour Party was finally allocated 49 of the 120 seats in the House of Representatives, while the

National Party, which had won 30.5% of the votes, received 39 seats. The Alliance was allocated 10 seats and ACT New Zealand nine seats. Under the recently-introduced system of proportional representation, the Green Party's victory in the one constituency automatically entitled the movement to a further six seats in the legislature. New Zealand First's representation declined to five seats; the party's leader, Winston Peters, only narrowly retained his seat. United New Zealand took the one remaining seat. Having previously discounted any co-operation with the Green Party, the Labour Party was thus obliged to seek the support not only of the Alliance but also of the seven Green MPs.

The leader of the Labour Party, Helen Clark (who had served as Deputy Prime Minister in 1989–90), thus became Prime Minister. The minority Government, which incorporated several members of the Alliance, took office in December 1999. Jim Anderton, the leader of the Alliance, was appointed Deputy Prime Minister, Minister for Economic Development and Minister for Industry and Regional Development. The treasury and finance portfolios were assigned to Dr Michael Cullen, while Phil Goff became Minister of Foreign Affairs and Trade and also assumed responsibility for the justice portfolio.

In a non-binding, citizen-initiated referendum held on the same day as the general election, a majority of voters favoured a reduction in the number of members of the House of Representatives from 120 to 99; voters also favoured a reform of the criminal justice system, including the placing of greater emphasis on the needs of victims of crime.

One of the new Government's stated priorities was the 'Closing the Gaps' initiative, which aimed to address the socioeconomic disparities between the Maori and non-Maori communities, particularly in health, housing, education, income and the incidence of crime. Among its first actions were the repeal of the Employment Contracts Act, the restoration of the state monopoly in the provision of accident compensation and the cancellation of the contract to lease 28 F-16 fighter aircraft from the USA. The new Government was strongly criticized by opposition politicians and accused of racism, following its decision in mid-2000 to sell a 25% share of a lucrative radiowaves company (which auctions high frequency radio positions to telecommunications companies) to a Maori trust under its 'Closing the Gaps' policy.

In June 2000 the Prime Minister was obliged to dismiss the Minister of Maori Affairs, Dover Samuels, following allegations of sexual misconduct. Moreover, the administration suffered further controversy in February 2001 when two cabinet ministers, Marian Hobbs and Phillida Bunkle, resigned amid speculation that they had abused the system of parliamentary allowances. All three, however, were subsequently cleared of the allegations, and in late March Hobbs and Samuels were reinstated to government positions in a minor reshuffle. On 4 April 2001 Dame Silvia Cartwright (New Zealand's first female High Court Judge) took office as Governor-General. Her appointment represented a significant achievement for women in New Zealand public life, and created an unprecedented situation in which the five most important public roles in the country (those of Prime Minister, Leader of the Opposition, Attorney-General, Chief Justice and Governor-General) were all occupied by women.

The Minister of Defence, Mark Burton, rejected demands for his dismissal in August 2001, following the publication of a report critical of the tendering process that had resulted in the purchase of 105 US Lav-3 armoured vehicles costing NZ$652m., which had been described as unsuitable for the peace-keeping, rather than combat, duties for which they were intended.

In October 2001 Jenny Shipley, the leader of the opposition National Party, resigned and was replaced by Bill English, a former Minister of Health. The incoming leader renamed the party the New National Party. In December Jim Anderton was placed under considerable pressure from left-wing members of the Alliance to withdraw his support for the Government's military involvement in Afghanistan, following the Prime Minister's confirmation that New Zealand Hercules transport aircraft had landed in Afghanistan, to assist in the US-led military campaign there (see the chapter on Afghanistan). In early April 2002, after months of wrangling, the Alliance split. Anderton and six other members of the party agreed to form a breakaway party, later named the Progressive Coalition party, but continued to support the ruling coalition. The seven members of the legislature were expelled from the Alliance in late April. At the same time Laila Harré, Minister of Women's Affairs, Youth

Affairs and Statistics, succeeded Anderton as leader of the Alliance and confirmed her support for the Government until the next legislative elections. In June the Prime Minister announced that the next general election was to be held earlier than planned, in late July, largely owing to the collapse of the Alliance, and a dispute between the Labour Party and the Greens over the Government's decision not to renew a moratorium banning the commercial release of genetically modified organisms (due to expire in October 2003).

In April 2002, following extensive consultations, the Government announced the proposed replacement of the British Privy Council (based in London) as New Zealand's court of final appeal by an independent Supreme Court, consisting of five judges headed by the Chief Justice. The Government introduced the requisite legislation in December, but the new court was not expected to be functional before 2004. In mid-June 2002 the House of Representatives endorsed strict new legislation to combat the illegal trafficking of people.

Some 77% of the registered voters participated in the general election, which took place on 27 July 2002. The Labour Party won 41% of the party votes, thereby securing a second term in office. The party, failed, however, to secure an overall majority in the House of Representatives, winning 52 of the 120 seats. New Zealand First received 10% of the vote (13 seats); ACT New Zealand 7% (nine seats); the Greens 7% (nine seats) and United Future New Zealand 7% (eight seats). The Progressive Coalition won 1.7% of the party votes and secured two seats, while the Alliance failed to secure any parliamentary representation. The National Party performed badly at the election, winning only 21% of the party votes; its representation declined by 12 seats to 27. Clark, unable to reach an agreement with the Greens on the issue of genetically modified organisms, formed a minority coalition Government with the Progressive Coalition. The Labour Party leader secured the support of United Future New Zealand. In early May 2003 Mark Gosche, the Minister of Corrections, of Housing and of Pacific Island Affairs and for Racing, resigned. The Prime Minister carried out a government reorganization one week later.

During 1987, meanwhile, there were protests by the Maori (the aboriginal inhabitants of New Zealand) concerning their cultural and economic rights and, in particular, their claims to land in accordance with the Treaty of Waitangi, concluded in 1840 by the British Government and Maori leaders, whereby sovereignty had been ceded to the United Kingdom in return for the Maori people's retention of hunting and fishing grounds. In November 1987 a ruling by the Waitangi Tribunal, reconvened in 1975 to consider retrospectively the claims of Maori land rights activists, recommended the restoration of an Auckland harbour headland to the Maori people. By 1994 about 75% of the country was subject to land claims by Maori groups. In December of that year the Government offered the sum of $NZ1,000m., payable over a 10-year period from September 1992, in full and final settlement of outstanding claims for compensation. The condition that all future land claims be renounced, however, was rejected by most Maori groups. In the same month an historic agreement between the Government and the Tainui people of Waikato provided for the return of land confiscated in 1863 and for the deposit over a period of five years of $NZ65m. in a land acquisition trust.

In February 1995 the Waitangi Day celebrations were disrupted by Maori protesters, as a result of which the annual ceremony to commemorate the signing of the 1840 Treaty, attended by the Prime Minister and the Governor-General, had to be abandoned. In May the Prime Minister and the Queen of the Tainui people signed an agreement relating to a full and final settlement, valued at $NZ170m., of land grievances dating back to 1863. Increasing ethnic tension, however, was demonstrated by the destruction in September 1995 of an old school building by Maori protesters involved in a land dispute and by the burning down in October of an historic church, known as the 'Maori Cathedral', at Otaki, in an apparent retaliatory arson attack by white extremists. In November, in a significant ceremony in Wellington, Queen Elizabeth gave her personal assent to the legislation ending the Tainui grievances when she signed the Waikato Raupatu Claims Settlement Act, which implemented the $NZ170m. agreement, including the return of 15,780 ha of land, and which incorporated an apology from the Crown for the loss of lives and for the confiscation of property. A final settlement payment of $NZ13m. was made to the Tainui tribe in late 2000. In October 1996, as more modest agreements continued to be reached, the Government announced a

$NZ170m. provisional settlement with the South Island's Ngai Tahu (one of New Zealand's smallest Maori tribes) regarding the group's long-standing claim for compensation. In early 1997 Maori leaders, pursuing a claim first lodged by tribal advocates in 1991, embarked upon a lawsuit aimed at the official alteration of New Zealand's name to Aotearoa ('Land of the Long White Cloud').

In July 1997 a Maori tribe that had been driven off its land in the 1840s lodged a claim to the site of the Parliament building in Wellington. The Ngati Tama also presented claims to other areas of the capital, while declaring their willingness to negotiate. At a ceremony in Wellington in September 1997, following six years of negotiations, the Government and the Ngai Tahu reached a formal agreement, subject to approval by the tribe's members, regarding the compensation of $NZ170m. The Government's offer also included the right to name mountains and rivers, often in combination with the English equivalents, and incorporated a full apology from the Crown. In November, the tribal beneficiaries having voted overwhelmingly in favour of the arrangements, the historic deed of full and final settlement was signed by the Prime Minister and representatives of the Ngai Tahu. In March 1998 the Ngai Tahu Claims Settlement Bill was duly submitted to the House of Representatives, where it received approval six months later. In July, exercising for the first time its power of compulsory recommendation, the Waitangi Tribunal ordered the Government to return to the Ngati Turangitukua land (now valued at NZ$6.1m.) which had been confiscated from its Maori owners more than 30 years previously to permit the construction of housing for workers engaged on an electric power project in the central North Island. In early 2000 a joint land claim was lodged by five Maori tribes of the central North Island. With the forestry claim alone worth an estimated $NZ588m., the application was potentially the largest ever submitted to the Waitangi Tribunal. In March 2001 the Ngati Ruanui became the first Taranaki tribe to conclude a deed of settlement with the Government, amounting to $NZ41m. In early 2003 the Ngati Awa voted in favour of a treaty settlement with the Government, which included an apology from the Crown, the return of 64 ha of land and NZ$42m.

In response to Maori grievances over fishing rights, the Government introduced, in 1988, a Maori Fisheries Bill, under the provisions of which 2.5% of current fishing quotas were to be restored to the Maori people annually for the following 19 years. However, Maori activists alleged that the proposed legislation was racially discriminatory, since it stipulated that no other Maori fishing claim would be considered by the Waitangi Tribunal until the 19 years had elapsed. The bill was also condemned by some white New Zealanders, as, if implemented as proposed, it would guarantee the Maori people about 50% of the country's entire fishing rights by the year 2008. In August 1992, finding that the Government had failed to honour its obligations under the Treaty of 1840, the Waitangi Tribunal recommended that ownership of most of the fisheries of South Island be transferred to the Ngai Tahu. In November 1992, in the hope of reaching a permanent settlement, the Government advanced the sum of $NZ150m. to a Maori consortium to enable the latter's purchase of a 50% stake in the country's biggest inshore fishing company. In early 1996 the Treaty of Waitangi Fisheries Commission, established to resolve the issue of the allocation among Maori of resources valued at $NZ200m., had yet to deliver its recommendations. In April the Court of Appeal declared that, despite having no coastline, urban Maori constituted an *iwi* (tribe) and were therefore directly entitled to a share of these fishery assets. The case was subsequently referred to the Privy Council in London. Its decision, announced in January 1997, overruled the Court of Appeal's definition of an *iwi*. In mid-1998 the Waitangi Tribunal ruled that urban Maori without blood ties should be accorded similar negotiating rights to those of traditional *iwi*. The historic decision thus acknowledged urban Maori trusts as modern tribes. In August, however, a High Court judge ruled in favour of traditional Maori tribes, effectively declaring that urban Maori groups had no claim to fishery assets. In October 1999, furthermore, the urban Maori claim was rejected by the Court of Appeal.

In April 1997 urban Maori were outraged at a proposal by the Treaty of Waitangi Fisheries Commission to allocate up to $NZ300m. of fishery assets on a tribal basis, rather than according to *iwi* size as the populous northern tribes demanded. The Ngai Tahu and other *iwi*, meanwhile, argued that the length of coastline and traditional fishing grounds should determine the allocation of assets. In early 1998, following an incident in late 1997 when a fishing boat reportedly landed several metric tons of snapper without commercial quota rights, it was announced that new regulations were to govern the management of 'customary' fishing by *tangata whenua* (people of the land), whereby Maori are permitted to take an unlimited amount of seafood provided that it is not for pecuniary gain.

From 1984 the Lange Government's pledge to ban from New Zealand's ports all vessels believed to be carrying nuclear weapons or powered by nuclear energy caused considerable strain in the country's relations with Australia and the USA, its partners in the ANZUS military pact (see p. 348). The ban was duly imposed in February 1985. In July 1986 the US Government announced its intention to devise new, bilateral defence arrangements with Australia, and in August the USA's military obligations to New Zealand under the ANZUS Treaty were formally suspended. In February 1987 the US Government announced its decision not to renew a 1982 memorandum of understanding (due to be renegotiated in June of that year), whereby New Zealand was able to purchase military equipment from the USA at favourable prices. The Lange Government subsequently defined a new defence strategy, based on increased self-reliance for the country's military forces. In June 1987 legislation banning nuclear-armed ships was formally enacted by the House of Representatives, despite strong opposition from the National Party. In September 1989 New Zealand agreed the terms for a joint venture with Australia to build as many as 12 naval frigates to patrol the South Pacific. The decision proved to be very contentious because of the high costs and because of allegations that the Government was succumbing to political pressure from Australia to return to the ANZUS alliance and abandon its independent anti-nuclear stance. In March 1990 the opposition National Party announced its support for the anti-nuclear policy, a position that it retained after its election to office in October.

Following the US Government's decision, in September 1991, to remove nuclear weapons from surface naval vessels, Bolger announced that his administration would reconsider the law banning visits from nuclear-armed and nuclear-propelled warships. The review would focus on the nuclear propulsion ban, which was seen as the obstacle to a renegotiated alliance with Australia and the USA. In July 1992 the USA announced that its warships no longer carried tactical nuclear weapons. In December the report commissioned by the Prime Minister was released. The committee of scientists concluded that the dangers of permitting nuclear-powered vessels to enter New Zealand waters were minimal. Despite these findings, no immediate change to the anti-nuclear legislation was envisaged. In February 1994 the New Zealand Prime Minister welcomed the US decision to resume senior-level contacts with Wellington, suspended since 1985. As relations continued to improve, in December 1994 the USA announced that nuclear-armed warships would not be dispatched to New Zealand, thus acknowledging the latter's ban. In early 1995 the Prime Minister was warmly received in Washington by President Clinton. In August 1998, during a visit by the US Secretary of State, the Prime Minister of New Zealand strongly reiterated her country's longstanding ban on visits by nuclear-armed or nuclear-powered vessels. Following his attendance at the summit meeting of the Asia-Pacific Economic Co-operation forum (APEC) held in Auckland in September 1999, President Clinton announced the end of the 14-year ban on New Zealand's participation in military exercises with the USA, in preparation for the dispatch of a multinational peace-keeping force to East Timor (q.v.), of which New Zealand troops were to form part.

Meanwhile, New Zealand's trading relations with the USA were strained during 1999 by the latter's imposition of tariffs on imports of New Zealand lamb. However, in December 2000 the World Trade Organization (WTO, see p. 323) ruled in favour of New Zealand's case against the tariffs, and upheld the decision when the USA appealed against the ruling. The Prime Minister visited the USA in March 2002 for a series of meetings with the US President, Secretary of State and other senior officials, raising hopes among members of New Zealand's business community that a free-trade agreement between the two nations could be achieved, despite New Zealand's adherence to its antinuclear policy.

In July 1985 the *Rainbow Warrior*, the flagship of the antinuclear environmentalist group, Greenpeace (which was to have led a flotilla to Mururoa Atoll, in French Polynesia, to protest against France's testing of nuclear weapons in the South Pacific), was blown up and sunk in Auckland Harbour. One member of the crew was killed as a result of the explosion. Two agents of the French secret service were tried for manslaughter in November and sentenced to 10 years' imprisonment, initially in Auckland. The French Government made repeated requests for the release or repatriation of the agents, and in July 1986 the two Governments eventually reached an agreement, whereby the agents were to be transferred to detention on Hao Atoll, in French Polynesia, for three years. The French Government made a formal apology for its part in the sabotage operation, and paid the New Zealand Government $NZ7m. in compensation. By May 1988, however, both the agents had been taken back to France, ostensibly for medical reasons. When neither agent was returned to the atoll, Lange referred the matter to the UN in October: in May 1990 an arbitration panel ruled that France's repatriation of the agents constituted a substantial violation of the 1986 agreement, but it announced that the agents would not be required to return to Hao Atoll. France agreed to pay an initial US $2m. into a joint fund intended to foster close and friendly relations between the two countries. In April 1991 the French Prime Minister, Michel Rocard, visited New Zealand and again apologized for the sinking of the *Rainbow Warrior*, while reiterating that French testing of nuclear weapons in the Pacific was to continue. However, relations between the two countries deteriorated in July, following the French Government's announcement that it had conferred an honour for distinguished service on one of the two agents responsible for the sabotage of the *Rainbow Warrior*. The issue re-emerged in November, when a third French agent, also suspected of involvement in the 1985 incident, was arrested, at New Zealand's instigation, in Switzerland. In December 1991, however, the New Zealand Government decided against seeking the man's extradition, on the grounds that the case was now considered to be closed. France announced the suspension of its nuclear testing in the South Pacific in April 1992. In May 1993 the first French warship to visit New Zealand since 1985 entered Auckland Harbour. (Similarly, in June 1995 the first British warship to visit New Zealand for 12 years arrived in Wellington.)

In June 1995 President Chirac's announcement that France was to resume its nuclear-testing programme in the South Pacific aroused international condemnation. New Zealand suspended military relations with France, and the New Zealand ambassador to Paris was recalled. In August, in response to public pressure, the New Zealand Government dispatched a naval research vessel to the test area. The first in the new series of tests was carried out in early September. Later in the month the International Court of Justice ruled that it could not reopen New Zealand's case against France, brought in 1973. France's continuation of its testing programme, in defiance of world opinion, was a major issue at the Commonwealth heads of government meeting held in Auckland in November 1995. New Zealand's relations with the United Kingdom were strained by the British Prime Minister's apparent support for France's position; upon his arrival in Auckland, thousands of anti-nuclear demonstrators took to the streets to express their outrage. In March 1996 (the French tests having been concluded) France, the United Kingdom and the USA finally acceded to the South Pacific Nuclear-Free Zone Treaty (Treaty of Rarotonga—Pacific Islands Forum, see p. 306), thus opening the way to improved relations with New Zealand and other Pacific nations. In October 1997, following a two-day official visit to Paris by the New Zealand Prime Minister, the resumption of normal relations with France was declared.

In August 1996 the Prime Minister refused to comment on the disclosure that New Zealand had supplied to the United Kingdom secret intelligence information on Japan and on countries in the South Pacific region. The apparent existence of close links with the US security services, as part of an international espionage network, aroused much controversy in New Zealand. In the same month, during a visit to South Africa, the Prime Minister acknowledged that the Government's decision to permit the controversial Springbok Rugby Tour of New Zealand in 1981 (prior to the abandonment of the apartheid system) had been a mistake.

Although New Zealand's trade with the People's Republic of China is of increasing significance, relations have been strained by the issue of China's nuclear-testing programme. Relations were further strained in September 1996 when the Dalai Lama, the exiled spiritual leader of Tibet, paid a four-day visit to New Zealand, where he was welcomed by the Prime Minister. In September 1997, however, the New Zealand Deputy Prime Minister expressed support for China's bid to join the WTO. In

November 1998 New Zealand's decision to accord Taiwanese government officials similar privileges to those granted to representatives of the People's Republic provoked serious concern in China. During a visit to China in July 1999, however, the Prime Minister of New Zealand reaffirmed her country's support for the 'one China' policy. An official visit to China by the Prime Minister in April 2001 was intended to improve New Zealand's trading position with the country, prior to its accession to the WTO. A senior Chinese official, on a diplomatic tour of the Asia-Pacific region, met with New Zealand's Deputy Prime Minister in April 2002, when New Zealand reconfirmed its 'one China' policy.

New Zealand remained committed to its aim of the global elimination of all nuclear weapons, and in November 1996 was a co-sponsor of a UN resolution, overwhelmingly adopted by the General Assembly, to promote the establishment of a nuclear-weapons-free Southern Hemisphere. In December the Deputy Prime Minister of New Zealand announced that the Government was to finance a lawsuit against the United Kingdom that was being prepared by former servicemen (and veterans' widows) who had long campaigned for compensation for their exposure to the effects of British hydrogen bomb tests conducted in the South Pacific region in the late 1950s. In January 1997 New Zealand lodged a strong protest with the Japanese Government regarding the proposed route of a ship transporting nuclear waste to Japan from France. In March 1998 the New Zealand Prime Minister travelled to Japan, the first official visit by the country's head of government for 22 years. Relations with Japan, however, continued to be strained by a fishing dispute relating to Japan's perceived failure to conserve stocks of southern bluefin tuna, as agreed in a treaty of 1993, of which Australia was also a signatory. (In July 1998, following a protest to Japan's ambassador in Wellington, New Zealand closed its ports to all Japanese tuna-fishing vessels.) In August 1999 an international tribunal ruled in favour of New Zealand and Australia. In early 2000, the Labour Party's commitment to the protection of the environment having been reaffirmed, the new Government of New Zealand became embroiled in a further dispute with Japan, this time relating to the latter's controversial whaling programme. The Prime Minister, Helen Clark, announced her intention to raise the issue with Japan on an official visit to that country in April 2001, and expressed her Government's desire to pursue proposals for a southern seas whale sanctuary through the International Whaling Commission (see p. 332). In December 2000 New Zealand reiterated its opposition to nuclear waste shipments in response to the news that a shipment of high-level waste had left the United Kingdom for Japan, warning that the vessel must not enter New Zealand's exclusive economic zone. In October of that year New Zealand had ratified the Waigani Convention (signed by all South Pacific Forum members in 1995, except Marshall Islands and Tuvalu), which bans the export of hazardous and radioactive waste to the Pacific Islands.

Meanwhile, New Zealand continued to play an active role in Pacific island affairs. In 1997, in the quest for peace in Papua New Guinea, it participated in a peace-keeping force on the secessionist island of Bougainville. New Zealand hosted discussions between the Papua New Guinea Government and representatives of the secessionist movement, and in January 1998 a permanent ceasefire agreement was signed in Christchurch. The agreement was successfully implemented at the end of April. New Zealand strongly condemned the coup in Fiji in May 2000, which led to the overthrow of the Indian-led, elected Government of the country and prompted outbreaks of racially-motivated violence throughout the islands. New Zealand's Minister of Foreign Affairs and Trade, Phil Goff, led a Commonwealth delegation, together with his Australian counterpart, to negotiate with the ethnic militias involved in a coup in Solomon Islands in June 2000. The New Zealand naval frigate, *Te Kaha*, was dispatched to the islands to serve as a venue for peace talks, and the country pledged to contribute to a group of international peace-keepers following the signing of a ceasefire agreement in October.

In September 2001 relations with Australia were strained by the failure of Ansett, the Melbourne-based airline. Ansett's owner, Air New Zealand, had been unable to find a purchaser for the loss-making company, which was therefore placed in receivership. In Melbourne irate Ansett staff blockaded an aircraft upon which the New Zealand Prime Minister was due to travel, and the Australian media demanded a boycott of New Zealand products. Nevertheless, in the same month the New Zealand

Government helped Australia to resolve an international crisis, when it agreed to accept up to 150 of the refugees stranded aboard the Norwegian vessel, the MV Tampa (see the chapter on Christmas Island). Despite international pressure, neither Australia nor Indonesia (where they had embarked) were willing to accept the asylum-seekers for the duration of the processing of their claims. The Indonesian President, meanwhile, had paid an historic official visit to New Zealand in June 2001. In December, as the former Indonesian province of East Timor proceeded towards full independence, New Zealand announced that, at the request of the UN transitional administration, its 660 peace-keeping troops, would remain in the territory until November 2002.

Following lengthy negotiations, New Zealand established diplomatic relations at ambassadorial level with the Democratic People's Republic of Korea in March 2001.

As part of her golden jubilee tour of the Commonwealth, Queen Elizabeth visited New Zealand in February 2002. Having previously stated that New Zealand's eventual transition to a republic was inevitable, the Prime Minister attracted some criticism for her absence from the country on the day of the Queen's arrival. In response to the international condemnation of the conduct of Zimbabwe's presidential election of March 2002, which subsequently led to that country's suspension from the Commonwealth, New Zealand followed the EU, Canada and the USA in imposing a travel ban on senior members of the Zimbabwe Government in April. New Zealand also announced a ban on sales of armaments to Zimbabwe and that any New Zealand-based assets and investments found to belong to the Zimbabwean President or his associates would be 'frozen'.

Government

Executive power is vested in the British monarch, as Head of State, and is exercisable by an appointed representative, the Governor-General, who must be guided by the advice of the Executive Council (Cabinet), led by the Prime Minister. (In March 1994 the Prime Minister indicated that New Zealand might become a republic.) Legislative power is vested in the unicameral House of Representatives, elected for three years by universal adult suffrage. A system of mixed member proportional representation was introduced at the election of October 1996, when the legislature was expanded to 120 seats: 65 electorate members, including five seats reserved for Maoris, and 55 being chosen from party lists (adjusted to 67, six and 53, respectively, at the 1999 election). The Governor-General appoints the Prime Minister and, on the latter's recommendation, other Ministers. The Cabinet is responsible to the House.

Defence

The ANZUS Security Treaty (see p. 348) was signed by New Zealand in 1951. New Zealand also participates in the Five-Power Defence Arrangements with Australia, Malaysia, Singapore and the United Kingdom. The total strength of active forces in August 2002 was 8,710: army 4,530, navy 1,980, air force 2,200. Reserves totalled 5,870. The air combat wing of the air force was formally disbanded in December 2001. The defence budget for 2002/03 was projected at $NZ1,178m.

Economic Affairs

In 2001, according to estimates by the World Bank, New Zealand's gross national income (GNI), measured at average 1999–2001 prices, was US $47,632m., equivalent to US $12,380 per head (or $19,130 per head on an international purchasing-power parity basis). During 1990–2001, it was estimated, the population increased at an average annual rate of 1.0%, while gross domestic product (GDP) per head increased, in real terms, by an average of 1.5% per year. Overall GDP increased, in real terms, at an average annual rate of 2.6% in 1990–2001; growth was an estimated 1.8% in 2001.

Agriculture (including hunting, fishing, forestry and mining) contributed 8.8% of GDP (in constant prices) in the year ending March 2001. About 9.1% of the employed labour force were engaged in the sector (excluding mining) in 2001. The principal crops are barley, wheat and maize. Fruit (particularly kiwi fruit, apples and pears) and vegetables are also cultivated. New Zealand is a major producer of wool. In the year ending March 2002 exports of wool were worth $NZ943m. Meat and dairy products are important, contributing 13.4% and 19.5% of export earnings, respectively, in 2001. The forestry industry showed strong expansion in the early 1990s. In 2001 exports of cork and wood totalled $NZ1,679.2m. (equivalent to 5.1% of total export earnings). The fisheries sector is of increasing significance, exports in 2001 being worth $NZ1,463.6m. (equivalent to 4.5% of total export earnings). Between 1989/90 and 1999/2000 agricultural GDP (including hunting, fishing, forestry and mining) increased by an average of 4.0% per year. Compared with the previous year, agricultural GDP increased by 3.3% in 2000/01.

Industry (including mining, manufacturing, construction and utilities) engaged 22.8% of the employed labour force in 2001. The industrial sector (excluding mining) provided 22.5% of GDP (at constant prices) in the year ending March 2001. Between 1989/90 and 1999/2000 industrial GDP (excluding mining) increased at an average annual rate of 1.2%. Industrial GDP increased by 0.6% in 2000/01, compared with the previous year.

Mining contributed only 1.2% of GDP in the year ending March 2001, and employed 0.2% of the working population in 2001. New Zealand has substantial coal reserves; petroleum, natural gas, iron, gold and silica are also exploited. A considerable amount of natural gas is used to produce synthetic petrol. In April 2002 Crown Minerals announced that approximately 50,000 sq km of the offshore Canterbury Basin were to be tendered out to oil exploration companies in 2003, pending a study of the petroleum source rock potential of the basin.

Manufacturing contributed an estimated 16.6% of GDP (at constant prices) in the year ending March 2001. The sector engaged 15.9% of the employed labour force in 2001. The principal branches of manufacturing are food products, printing and publishing, wood and paper products, chemicals, metals and metal products, machinery and transport equipment. Between 1989/90 and 1999/2000 manufacturing GDP increased by an average of 1.5% per year. Manufacturing GDP expanded by 2.5% in 2000/01, compared with the previous year.

Energy is derived mainly from domestic supplies of natural gas, petroleum and coal. Hydroelectric power supplied about 61.7% of total energy output in 1999. Imports of petroleum and its products comprised 9.7% of the total value of merchandise imports in 2001.

The services sector provided 68.7% of GDP (in constant prices) in 2000/01. This sector engaged 68.1% of the employed labour force in 2001. In the year ending March 1988 tourism became the single largest source of foreign exchange. Receipts (excluding international air fares) totalled $NZ5,544m. in 2001/02. Visitor arrivals reached 1.95m. in 2001/02. Between 1989/90 and 1999/2000 the GDP of the services sector increased at an average annual rate of 2.8%. Compared with the previous year, it expanded by 3.4% in 2000/01.

In 2001 New Zealand recorded a visible trade surplus of US $1,474m., but there was a deficit of US $1,404m. on the current account of the balance of payments. In 2001 the principal sources of imports were Australia (22.2%), the USA (16.1%) and Japan (10.9%), which were also the principal markets for exports in that year (Australia 18.9%, Japan 12.5% and the USA 14.8%). The United Kingdom, other members of the European Union and Asian countries are also important trading partners. The principal exports in 2001 were meat, dairy products, vegetables and fruit, fish, cork and wood, textile fibres and machinery. The principal imports were road vehicles and other machinery and transport equipment, basic manufactures, petroleum and its products and chemicals.

In the year ending June 2002 a budgetary surplus of $NZ2,300m. was recorded, equivalent to 1.9% of GDP. In 2002/03 the surplus was expected to be around $NZ2,280m. In December 2001 New Zealand's external debt stood at $NZ122,171m., of which $NZ16,137m. was official government debt. The average rate of unemployment decreased from 7.5% of the labour force in 1998 to 5.3% in 2001. Annual inflation averaged 1.8% in 1990–2001. Consumer prices increased by 2.6% in 2001 and by 2.7% in 2002.

New Zealand is a member of the Organisation for Economic Co-operation and Development (see p. 277), APEC (see p. 139), the Pacific Community (see p. 304), the Pacific Islands Forum (see p. 306) and of the Cairns Group (see p. 389). New Zealand is also a member of the Colombo Plan (see p. 339). In 1982 New Zealand signed an agreement for a 'closer economic relationship' (CER) with Australia, aiming to eliminate trade barriers between the two countries by 1995. These were, in fact, eliminated in July 1990.

Upon taking office in late 1999, the minority Labour Government embarked upon a programme of reforms in the health, education and housing sectors. In addition, some $NZ175m. was allocated for projects aimed at the Maori population. These proposals were to be financed by an increase in income tax on those earning more than $NZ60,000 annually. The new Government also planned to curb the programme of transferring state assets to the private sector. In March 2000, in response to changing demographic trends, a controversial scheme to divert fiscal surpluses to a dedicated pension fund was announced. (The first budget surplus since 1978 had been achieved in 1994.) In August 2000 the New Zealand stock exchange initiated discussions with its Australian counterpart on the possibility of a merger and, as greater integration of the two economies continued, there was increased speculation that this might lead to the eventual establishment of a currency union. In February 2001, however, talks between the two stock exchanges collapsed, with New Zealand accusing the Australian exchange of trying to effect a take-over of its organization rather than negotiate a merger of the two companies. This development prompted fears that many New Zealand companies might move their listings 'off shore'. Having been transferred to the private sector in 1989, Air New Zealand was returned to state ownership in late 2001, following heavy financial losses. In October, in an arrangement costing $NZ885m., the Government announced that it was purchasing an 83% stake in the airline, the continued operations of which remained vital to the country's tourism industry. The bid by the Australian airline company, Qantas Airways Ltd, to buy a 22.5% stake in Air New Zealand was rejected by competition regulators in New Zealand and Australia in April 2003. Although in the short term tourist arrivals were affected by the terrorist attacks on the USA in September 2001, the consequences were less serious than originally feared, as New Zealand was regarded as a relatively safe destination. New Zealand was comparatively well placed to withstand the repercussions of the overall deceleration of the global economy in 2001, and in 2002 an increase in tourism earnings (in the year ending September 2002 tourism earnings expanded by 13.2%) and continued growth in agriculture resulted in real GDP growth of around 3.1%. The improvement in the tourism sector helped to boost employment rates. An increase in real wages and retail sales reflected a rise in business and consumer confidence. Export receipts, however, declined, owing to weakening international prices for New Zealand's export commodities, resulting in a larger trade deficit. The balance-of-payments deficit was expected to expand further in 2003 as a result of the rise in value of the New Zealand dollar against the US dollar in 2002. GDP growth was projected to decelerate to 2.4% in 2003, largely owing to the decline in exports. A budget surplus in 2002/03 was predicted, however, for the 10th successive year.

Education

State education is free and, for children between six and 16 years of age, compulsory. Primary education lasts from five to 11 years of age, after which children transfer to secondary schools until a maximum age of 18. As a proportion of children in the relevant age-groups, the enrolment ratios in 1997 were 100% in primary schools and 90% in secondary schools. In July 2001 a total of 449,491 students were enrolled in primary schools and 239,481 in secondary schools. In addition, 42,701 pupils attended composite schools, providing both primary and secondary education. There are eight universities, as well as 22 polytechnics, offering education at the post-secondary level. Changes introduced in 1991 obliged most students to pay part of their fees: parental income is tested to determine the level of allowances. Budgetary expenditure on education by the central Government in the financial year ending 30 June 2003 was projected at $NZ6,888m., representing 17.2% of total spending.

Public Holidays

2003: 1–2 January (New Year), 6 February (Waitangi Day, anniversary of 1840 treaty), 18–21 April (Easter), 25 April (ANZAC Day, anniversary of 1915 landing at Gallipoli), 2 June (Queen's Official Birthday), 27 October (Labour Day), 25 December (Christmas Day), 26 December (Boxing Day).

2004: 1–2 January (New Year), 6 February (Waitangi Day, anniversary of 1840 treaty), 9–12 April (Easter), 25 April (ANZAC Day, anniversary of 1915 landing at Gallipoli), 7 June (Queen's Official Birthday), 25 October (Labour Day), 25 December (Christmas Day), 26 December (Boxing Day).

In addition to these national holidays, each region celebrates an anniversary day.

Weights and Measures

The metric system is in force.

Statistical Survey

Source (unless otherwise stated): Statistics New Zealand, Aorangi House, 85 Molesworth St, POB 2922, Wellington 1; tel. (4) 495-4600; fax (4) 472-9135; e-mail info@stats.govt.nz; internet www.stats.govt.nz.

Area and Population

AREA, POPULATION AND DENSITY

Area (sq km)	270,534*
Population (census results)†	
5 March 1996.	3,618,303
6 March 2001	
Males	1,823,004
Females.	1,914,273
Total	3,737,277
Population (official estimates at mid-year)	
2000	3,830,800
2001	3,850,000
2002	3,940,000
Density (per sq km) at mid-2002	14.6

* 104,454 sq miles.

† Figures refer to the population usually resident. The total population (including foreign visitors) was: 3,681,546 in 1996; 3,820,749 in 2001.

PRINCIPAL CENTRES OF POPULATION
(population at census of 6 March 2001)

Auckland . . .	1,074,507	Palmerston North .	72,681
Wellington (capital) .	339,747	Hastings . . .	58,139
Christchurch . .	334,107	Napier. . . .	54,534
Hamilton . . .	166,128	Nelson. . . .	53,685
Dunedin . . .	107,088	Rotorua . . .	52,608
Tauranga . . .	95,694		

BIRTHS, MARRIAGES AND DEATHS

	Live births*		Marriages†		Deaths*	
	Number	Rate (per '000)	Number	Rate (per '000)	Number	Rate (per '000)
1993 . .	58,866	16.9	20,802	5.9	27,243	7.8
1994 . .	57,435	16.3	20,587	5.7	27,092	7.7
1995 . .	57,671	15.8	20,452	5.6	27,813	7.6
1996 . .	57,280	15.4	20,453	5.5	28,255	7.6
1997 . .	57,604	15.3	19,953	5.3	27,471	7.3
1998 . .	57,251	15.1	20,135	5.3	26,206	6.9
1999 . .	57,053	15.0	21,085	5.5	28,117	7.4
2000 . .	56,605	14.7	20,655	5.4	26,660	7.0
2001 . .	55,790	14.5	19,972	5.1	27,827	7.0

* Data for births and deaths are tabulated by year of registration rather than by year of occurrence.

† Based on the resident population concept, replacing the previous *de facto* concept.

Expectation of life (WHO estimates, years at birth): 78.5 (males 76.1; females 80.9) in 2001 (Source: WHO, *World Health Report*).

IMMIGRATION AND EMIGRATION
(year ending 31 August)*

	1998/99	1999/2000	2000/01
Long-term immigrants . . .	56,880	62,051	72,699
Long-term emigrants . . .	68,003	72,083	77,090

* Figures refer to persons intending to remain in New Zealand, or New Zealand residents intending to remain abroad, for 12 months or more.

ECONOMICALLY ACTIVE POPULATION
('000 persons aged 15 years and over, excl. armed forces)

	1999	2000	2001
Agriculture, hunting, forestry and fishing	165.6	155.5	166.1
Mining and quarrying . . .	3.6	3.9	3.7
Manufacturing	278.4	281.3	288.9
Electricity, gas and water . . .	8.9	8.5	10.1
Construction	109.5	118.4	112.2
Trade, restaurants and hotels . .	371.5	388.4	393.6
Transport, storage and communications	110.4	110.9	112.4
Finance, insurance, real estate and business services	228.6	229.5	232.0
Community, social and personal services	469.5	473.8	499.6
Activities not adequately defined	4.4	8.8	4.9
Total employed	1,750.3	1,779.0	1,823.4
Unemployed	127.8	113.4	102.3
Total labour force	1,878.1	1,892.4	1,925.7
Males	1,029.0	1,036.1	1,050.1
Females	849.1	856.3	875.6

Source: ILO, *Yearbook of Labour Statistics*.

Health and Welfare

KEY INDICATORS

Total fertility rate (children per woman, 2001)	2.0
Under-5 mortality rate (per 1,000 live births, 2001) . .	6
HIV/AIDS (% of persons aged 15–49, 2001)	0.06
Physicians (per 1,000 head, 1997)	2.18
Hospital beds (per 1,000 head, 1998)	6.2
Health expenditure (2000): US $ per head (PPP) . . .	1,623
Health expenditure (2000): % of GDP	8.0
Health expenditure (2000): public (% of total) . . .	78.0
Human Development Index (2000): ranking	19
Human Development Index (2000): value	0.917

For sources and definitions, see explanatory note on p. vi.

Agriculture

PRINCIPAL CROPS
('000 metric tons)

	1999	2000	2001
Wheat	320	326	364
Barley	304	302	296
Maize	197	181	177
Oats	42	35	36
Potatoes . . .	500	500	500
Dry peas . . .	52	64	39
Cabbages . . .	39	36	32
Lettuce. . . .	37	37	37
Tomatoes . . .	87	87	87
Cauliflower . . .	63	56	56
Pumpkins, squash and gourds . .	155	155	155*
Green onions and shallots . .	220	240	245*
Green peas . . .	57	60	60
Carrots . . .	70	77	77
Green corn . . .	95	101	101*
Other vegetables* . .	138	153	153
Grapes. . . .	80	80	71
Apples . . .	545	620	485
Pears . . .	44	42	33
Kiwi fruit . . .	217	262	271
Other fruits (excl. melons) . .	101	103	96

* FAO estimate(s).

Source: FAO.

LIVESTOCK
('000 head at 30 June)

	1999	2000	2001
Cattle	8,778	9,015	9,281
Sheep	45,956	45,385	44,002
Goats	186	183	183
Pigs	369	369	354
Horses*	80	85	85
Chickens	12,700	13,000	13,000
Ducks*	200	240	240
Geese*	65	65	65
Turkeys*	60	70	70

* FAO estimates.

Source: FAO.

LIVESTOCK PRODUCTS
('000 metric tons)

	1999	2000	2001
Beef and veal*	561.3	568.0	590.4
Mutton and lamb*	516.9	533.0	562.2
Pig meat*	47.6	46.8	46.9
Poultry meat*	99.1	106.7	115.9
Game meat	26.3*	28.0†	28.0*
Cows' milk‡	10,881.4	12,235.4	13,161.7
Butter‡	317.5	343.8	352.4
Cheese‡	238.5	296.7	289.1
Hen eggs	42.2	43.0	43.9
Other poultry eggs	2.4	2.4	2.4
Honey	9.1	9.6	9.1
Wool: greasy	252.0	257.2	236.7
Wool: scoured	220.3	202.4	198.6
Cattle hides (fresh)†	51	51	51
Sheepskins (fresh)†	100	100	100

* Twelve months ending 30 September of year stated.
† FAO estimate(s).
‡ Twelve months ending 31 May of year stated.

Source: FAO.

Forestry

ROUNDWOOD REMOVALS
('000 cubic metres, year ending 31 March)

	1999/2000	2000/01	2001/02
Sawlogs	7,043	7,273	7,268
Pulp logs	3,049	3,566	3,455
Export logs and chips	6,030	6,428	7,759
Other	2,074	2,206	2,265
Total	18,196	19,473	20,747

Source: Forestry Statistics Section, Ministry of Agriculture and Forestry, Wellington.

SAWNWOOD PRODUCTION
('000 cu m, year ending 31 March)

Species	1998/99	1999/2000	2000/2001
Radiata pine	2,996	3,583	3,625
Other introduced pines	27	28	32
Douglas fir	143	134	136
Rimu and miro	30	22	17
Total (incl. others)	3,226	3,806	3,848

Source: Forestry Statistics Section, Ministry of Agriculture and Forestry, Wellington.

Fishing

('000 metric tons, live weight)

	1998	1999	2000
Capture*	636.2	594.1	561.3
Southern blue whiting	35.1	39.0	23.0
Blue grenadier (Hoki)	267.6	236.7	234.0
Pink cusk-eel	22.2	21.4	21.6
Orange roughy	21.5	23.8	17.9
Oreo dories	21.1	22.6	22.8
Jack and horse mackerels	36.1	34.0	22.5
Snoek (Barracouta)	26.0	20.6	21.9
Wellington flying squid	42.5	27.3	20.9
Aquaculture	93.8	91.7	85.6
New Zealand mussel	75.0	71.0	76.0
Total catch	730.0	685.7	647.0

Note: Figures exclude aquatic mammals (recorded by number rather than by weight) and sponges. The number of whales and dolphins caught was: 16 in 1998; 9 in 1999; 13 in 2000. The catch of sponges (in metric tons) was: 4.1 in 1998; 14.0 in 1999; 10.0 (FAO estimate) in 2000.
* Excluding catches made by chartered vessels and landed outside New Zealand.

Source: FAO, *Yearbook of Fishery Statistics*.

Mining

('000 metric tons, unless otherwise indicated)

	1999	2000	2001
Coal (incl. lignite)	3,505.7	3,586	3,911
Gold (kg)	8,577	9,880	9,850
Crude petroleum	1,931.9	n.a.	n.a.
Gross natural gas (terajoules)	252,390	n.a.	n.a.
Liquid petroleum gas (terajoules)	12,030	11,970	n.a.
Iron sands	2,303.4	2,692	1,636
Silica sand	25.0	47.4	36.0
Limestone	2,050	4,159	4,746

Source: mainly Ministry of Commerce, Wellington.

Industry

SELECTED PRODUCTS
(metric tons, unless otherwise indicated)

	1999	2000	2001
Wine ('000 hectolitres)* . . .	602	602	533
Beer (sales, '000 hectolitres) . .	3,148	n.a.	n.a.
Wool yarn (pure and mixed) . .	23,500	n.a.	n.a.
Knitted fabrics†	3,700	n.a.	n.a.
Footwear ('000 pairs)‡ . . .	1,650	n.a.	n.a.
Chemical wood pulp§ ‖ . . .	645,032	753,885	744,991
Mechanical wood pulp§ ‖ . . .	755,707	773,680	827,286
Newsprint§ ‖	383,372	360,623	380,614
Other paper and paperboard§ ‖	430,942	469,189	490,993
Fibre board (cu m)§ ‖ . . .	600,673	744,879	801,493
Particle board (cu m)§ ‖ . . .	169,569	188,054	204,524
Veneer (cu m)§ ‖	285,825	378,282	401,590
Plywood (cu m)§ ‖	192,445	239,947	243,702
Jet fuels ('000 metric tons) . . .	839	n.a.	n.a.
Motor spirit—petrol ('000 metric tons)	1,360	n.a.	n.a.
Gas-diesel (Distillate fuel) oils ('000 barrels)	13,000	13,000¶	13,000¶
Residual fuel oils ('000 barrels)	3,500	3,500¶	3,500¶
Cement ('000 metric tons)¶ .	960	950	950
Aluminium—unwrought ('000 metric tons).			
Primary.	326.7	328.4	322.3¶
Secondary	21.4	21.5¶	21.5¶
Electric energy (million kWh)§ .	34,152	34,440	34,956

* Data from New Zealand Wines Online.
† Twelve months ending 30 September of year stated.
‡ Twelve months ending 30 June of year stated.
§ Twelve months ending 31 March of year stated.
‖ Source: Ministry of Agriculture and Forestry, Wellington.
¶ Estimate(s).

Sources (unless otherwise stated): UN, *Industrial Commodity Statistics Yearbook* and *Monthly Bulletin of Statistics*, and US Geological Survey.

2001/02 (year ending 31 March): Chemical wood pulp (metric tons) 723,054; Mechanical wood pulp (metric tons) 800,676; Newsprint (metric tons) 334,058; Other paper and paperboard (metric tons) 512,669; Fibre board (cu m) 821,994; Particle board (cu m) 198,347; Veneer (cu m) 460,619; Plywood (cu m) 263,332 (Source: Ministry of Agriculture and Forestry, Wellington).

2002 ('000 hectolitres): Wine 890 (Source: New Zealand Wines Online).

Finance

CURRENCY AND EXCHANGE RATES

Monetary Units
100 cents = 1 New Zealand dollar ($NZ).

Sterling, US Dollar and Euro Equivalents (31 December 2002)
£1 sterling = $NZ3.0613
US $1 = $NZ1.8993
€1 = $NZ1.9918
$NZ100 = £32.67 = US $52.65 = €50.21

Average Exchange Rate (US $ per New Zealand dollar)
2000 0.4574
2001 0.4206
2002 0.4642

BUDGET
($NZ million, year ending 30 June)

Revenue	1998/99	1999/2000	2000/01
Direct taxation	19,963	21,192	23,520
Individuals	14,618	15,470	16,780
Companies	3,693	4,158	4,831
Withholding taxes	1,651	1,563	1,905
Indirect taxation	11,216	11,738	12,026
Goods and services . . .	7,321	7,735	7,927
Excise duties	1,949	2,027	2,010
Other receipts	2,085	2,239	2,304
Interest, profits and dividends .	1,307	1,281	1,284
Total	33,264	35,169	37,850

Expenditure	1998/99	1999/2000	2000/01
Public administration	2,401	1,939	2,078
Defence	1,163	1,803	1,261
Law and order	1,430	1,388	1,478
Education	5,540	5,825	6,097
Health	6,085	6,247	6,761
Social welfare	12,977	13,259	13,644
Economic services	4,478	4,403	4,582
Total (incl. others)	34,202	35,020	36,024

INTERNATIONAL RESERVES
(US $ million at 31 December)

	2000	2001	2002
IMF special drawing rights . . .	13	16	22
Reserve position in IMF	320	387	459
Foreign exchange	2,997	2,605	3,258
Total	3,330	3,009	3,739

Source: IMF, *International Financial Statistics.*

MONEY SUPPLY
($NZ million at 31 December)

	2000	2001	2002
Currency outside banks	2,069	2,241	2,451
Demand deposits at banking institutions	13,460	15,463	16,157
Total money (incl. others) . . .	15,568	17,753	18,689

Source: IMF, *International Financial Statistics.*

COST OF LIVING
(Consumer Price Index; base: 1990 = 100)

	1999	2000	2001
Food (incl. beverages)	111.3	112.7	119.6
Fuel and light	149.9	151.8	152.7
Clothing (incl. footwear)	105.2	105.8	107.6
Rent	146.0	146.4	132.1
All items (incl. others)	116.0	119.1	122.2

Source: ILO, *Yearbook of Labour Statistics.*

NATIONAL ACCOUNTS
($NZ million at current prices, year ending 31 March)

National Income and Product

	1998/99	1999/2000	2000/01
Compensation of employees . .	43,183	44,462	46,756
Operating surplus	30,617	33,117	35,934
Domestic factor incomes . .	73,800	77,579	82,690
Consumption of fixed capital . .	13,928	14,262	15,205
Gross domestic product (GDP) at factor cost	87,728	91,841	97,895
Indirect taxes	13,466	14,129	14,775
Less Subsidies	298	330	353
GDP in purchasers' values . .	100,897	105,641	112,316
Net factor income from abroad . .	−4,977	−6,603	−7,736
Gross national product . . .	95,920	99,038	104,580
Less Consumption of fixed capital	13,928	14,262	15,205
National income in market prices	81,992	84,776	89,375

Expenditure on the Gross Domestic Product

	1998/99	1999/2000	2000/01
Government final consumption expenditure	18,924	20,109	20,248
Private final consumption expenditure	61,775	64,471	67,224
Increase in stocks	−114	1,480	1,143
Gross fixed capital formation	20,016	20,926	21,389
Total domestic expenditure	100,601	106,984	110,005
Exports of goods and services	30,378	33,151	41,065
Less Imports of goods and services	30,144	34,448	39,209
GDP in purchasers' values	100,835	105,687	111,861
GDP at constant 1995/96 prices	97,585	101,612	104,975

Gross Domestic Product by Economic Activity

(at constant 1995/96 prices)

	1998/99	1999/2000	2000/01
Agriculture	5,479	5,767	6,019
Hunting and fishing			
Forestry and logging	2,786	2,845	2,879
Mining and quarrying			
Manufacturing	15,643	16,329	16,731
Electricity, gas and water	2,152	2,084	2,192
Construction	3,702	4,160	3,776
Trade, restaurants and hotels	14,603	15,772	16,151
Transport, storage and communications	8,767	9,695	10,476
Finance, insurance, real estate and business services	25,133	25,356	25,881
Ownership of dwellings			
Government administration and defence	4,201	4,137	4,175
Other personal and community services	11,476	12,003	12,553
Sub-total	93,942	98,168	100,833
Goods and services tax on production			
Import duties	3,740	4,083	4,142
Other indirect taxes			
Less Imputed bank service charge			
Total	97,682	102,251	104,975

BALANCE OF PAYMENTS

(US $ million)

	1999	2000	2001
Exports of goods f.o.b.	12,657	13,530	13,920
Imports of goods f.o.b.	−13,028	−12,848	−12,446
Trade balance	−371	681	1,474
Exports of services	4,381	4,399	4,344
Imports of services	−4,573	−4,515	−4,217
Balance on goods and services	−563	565	1,601
Other income received	919	601	569
Other income paid	−4,037	−4,074	−3,714
Balance on goods, services and income	−3,681	−2,908	−1,545
Current transfers received	609	634	576
Current transfers paid	−415	−409	−435
Current balance	−3,487	−2,683	−1,404
Capital account (net)	−218	−182	439
Direct investment abroad	−803	−904	−297
Direct investment from abroad	1,412	3,330	1,731
Portfolio investment assets	−666	−2,185	−1,146
Portfolio investment liabilities	−2,285	1,926	−355
Other investment assets	−1,282	−838	−3,297
Other investment liabilities	5,597	1,945	5,291
Net errors and omissions	1,920	−552	−1,149
Overall balance	188	−143	−187

Source: IMF, *International Financial Statistics*.

External Trade

Source: Statistics New Zealand, Overseas Trade, Wellington.

PRINCIPAL COMMODITIES

($NZ million)

Imports (value for duty)	1999	2000	2001
Food and live animals	1,523.7	1,716.3	1,939.1
Mineral fuels, lubricants, etc.	1,532.6	2,976.5	2,879.0
Petroleum, petroleum products, etc.	1,528.9	2,971.1	2,872.0
Chemicals and related products	3,116.8	3,512.7	3,811.0
Medicinal and pharmaceutical products	717.5	758.7	796.7
Basic manufactures	3,553.1	3,943.1	4,013.9
Machinery and transport equipment	11,179.6	11,543.9	11,565.5
Machinery specialized for particular industries	777.2	974.3	1,127.3
General industrial machinery, equipment and parts	1,007.3	1,092.6	1,211.1
Office machines and automatic data-processing machines	1,361.1	1,587.9	1,516.1
Telecommunications and sound equipment	1,321.2	1,739.7	1,380.1
Other electrical machinery, apparatus, etc.	1,098.7	1,310.0	1,305.2
Road vehicles (incl. air-cushion vehicles) and parts*	2,980.1	3,104.8	3,449.1
Other transport equipment and parts*	2,042.4	1,183.2	1,066.4
Miscellaneous manufactured articles	3,522.3	3,962.9	4,099.2
Clothing and accessories (excl. footwear)	725.7	847.3	889.6
Total (incl. others)	25,435.7	28,851.1	29,612.7

* Excluding tyres, engines and electrical parts.

Total imports c.i.f. ($NZ million): 27,113.6 in 1999; 30,735.7 in 2000; 31,682.7 in 2001.

Exports f.o.b	1999	2000	2001
Food and live animals	10,361.4	12,298.3	14,951.4
Meat and meat preparations	3,022.7	3,745.3	4,380.3
Dairy products and birds' eggs	3,714.2	4,618.4	6,379.4
Fish (not marine mammals), crustaceans, molluscs, etc., and preparations	1,314.1	1,410.6	1,463.6
Vegetables and fruit	1,593.6	1,634.0	1,639.0
Crude materials (inedible) except fuels	3,249.9	4,180.2	4,143.8
Cork and wood	1,304.9	1,659.5	1,679.2
Textile fibres (excl. wool tops) and waste	740.6	899.3	856.0
Chemicals and related products	1,785.1	2,583.0	2,537.1
Basic manufactures	3,365.7	4,015.8	3,945.6
Non-ferrous metals	985.0	1,244.5	1,221.8
Machinery and transport equipment	2,421.3	3,074.0	3,015.4
Miscellaneous manufactured articles	1,079.6	1,204.2	1,387.6
Total (incl. others)*	23,582.9	29,257.1	32,666.5

* Including re-exports ($NZ million): 974.8 in 1999; 1,154.6 in 2000; 1,094.1 in 2001.

PRINCIPAL TRADING PARTNERS
($NZ million)

Imports (value for duty)*	1999	2000	2001
Australia	6,238.7	6,483.0	6,564.0
Belgium	196.3	222.8	296.3
Canada	342.9	443.7	429.0
China, People's Republic	1,339.9	1,803.0	2,067.2
France	633.9	552.1	573.2
Germany	1,051.2	1,226.6	1,431.4
Indonesia	245.0	267.5	387.4
Italy	511.7	566.2	677.0
Japan	3,066.3	3,186.3	3,220.8
Korea, Republic	592.1	630.8	676.2
Malaysia	572.7	756.0	912.7
Saudi Arabia	307.1	715.3	363.2
Singapore	509.0	491.1	584.6
Sweden	323.9	362.8	327.0
Taiwan	544.9	642.4	625.9
Thailand	361.0	412.7	469.6
United Arab Emirates	116.7	453.0	260.2
United Kingdom	1,039.3	1,101.2	1,144.4
USA	4,259.4	5,035.4	4,777.7
Total (incl. others)	25,435.7	28,851.1	29,612.7

* Excluding specie and gold.

Exports*	1999	2000	2001
Australia	5,133.3	5,960.4	6,180.6
Belgium	408.5	469.6	546.5
Canada	308.3	439.6	631.4
China, People's Republic	649.4	929.6	1,349.4
France	293.9	394.5	367.3
Germany	620.5	690.8	838.7
Hong Kong	610.8	790.9	786.0
Indonesia	254.7	495.4	550.5
Italy	396.3	490.1	548.5
Japan	2,979.9	3,951.8	4,083.3
Korea, Republic	995.9	1,315.1	1,440.2
Malaysia	432.9	598.3	697.7
Mexico	209.4	320.2	535.9
Philippines	276.7	403.1	564.7
Singapore	418.8	487.4	398.4
Taiwan	610.7	701.9	710.9
Thailand	250.8	336.8	412.0
United Kingdom	1,470.9	1,522.7	1,558.2
USA	3,203.7	4,241.7	4,850.6
Viet Nam	109.5	169.0	371.2
Total (incl. others)	23,582.9	29,257.1	32,666.5

* Including re-exports. Excluding specie and gold.

Transport

RAILWAYS
(traffic, year ending 30 June)

	1999/2000	2000/01	2001/02
Freight ('000 metric tons)	14,699	14,461	14,330
Passengers ('000)	12,566	12,714	12,521

Source: Tranz Rail Ltd, Wellington.

ROAD TRAFFIC
(vehicles licensed at 31 March)

	2000	2001	2002
Passenger cars	1,877,850	1,909,480	1,960,503
Goods service vehicles	368,964	364,928	366,639
Taxis	7,479	7,181	7,366
Buses and service coaches	12,264	12,667	13,339
Trailers and caravans	359,400	368,994	381,914
Motorcycles and mopeds	48,722	47,670	47,423
Tractors	20,526	21,377	22,914

Source: Ministry of Transport, Wellington.

SHIPPING
Merchant Fleet
(registered at 31 December)

	1999	2000	2001
Number of vessels	164	163	159
Displacement (grt)	264,988	180,049	174,942

Source: Lloyd's Register-Fairplay, *World Fleet Statistics*.

Vessels Handled
(international, '000 grt)

	1993	1994	1995
Entered	37,603	39,700	48,827
Cleared	35,128	37,421	42,985

Source: UN, *Statistical Yearbook*.

International Sea-borne Freight Traffic
('000 metric tons, year ending 30 June)

	1998/99	1999/2000	2000/01
Goods loaded	19,500	22,038	22,077
Goods unloaded	12,646	13,507	14,074

CIVIL AVIATION
(domestic and international traffic on scheduled services)

	1997	1998	1999
Kilometres flown (million)	173	174	172
Passengers carried ('000)	9,435	8,655	8,892
Passenger-km (million)	20,983	19,014	19,322
Total metric ton-km (million)	2,816	2,700	2,746

Source: UN, *Statistical Yearbook*.

Tourism

VISITOR ARRIVALS
(year ending 31 March)

Country of residence	1999/2000	2000/01	2001/02
Australia	537,775	592,737	633,846
China, People's Republic	26,802	39,157	59,748
Germany	48,206	53,842	49,282
Japan	145,637	157,509	149,496
Korea, Republic	53,687	70,658	93,278
United Kingdom	174,838	209,928	226,637
USA	186,842	195,551	196,121
Total (incl. others)	1,651,889	1,848,340	1,954,831

2001/02: Total tourist receipts (year ending 31 March, excl. international air fares): $NZ5,544m.

Source: New Zealand Tourism Board.

Communications Media

	1999	2000	2001
Television receivers ('000 in use) .	1,975	2,000	n.a.
Telephones ('000 main lines in use)	1,889	1,915	1,834
Mobile telephones ('000 subscribers).	1,395	2,158	2,417
Personal computers ('000 in use) .	1,250	1,380	1,500
Internet users ('000)	700	830	1,092

Radio receivers ('000 in use, 1997): 3,750.

Facsimile machines ('000 in use, year ending 31 March 1996): 65.

Daily newspapers: 26 (circulation 850,000; copies, 2002).

Non-daily newspapers: 2 (circulation 311,380; copies, 2002).

Book production (1999): 4,800 titles.

Sources: partly International Telecommunication Union; UNESCO, *Statistical Yearbook*; UN, *Statistical Yearbook*.

Education

(July 2001)

	Institutions	Teachers (full-time equivalent)	Students
Early childhood services . .	4,213	11,701[1]	171,333[2]
Primary schools[3]	2,209	25,578[4]	449,491
Composite schools[5]	126	1,496[4]	42,701
Secondary schools[6]	336	16,596[4]	239,481
Special schools	47	613[4]	2,248
Polytechnics	22	3,999	87,965
Colleges of education . . .	4	475	10,884
Universities	8	6,103	125,668
Wananga[7]	3	237	11,278
Private training establishments receiving government grants	455	3,753	51,666

[1] Excludes teaching staff of the 562 Kohanga Reo (responsible for Maori 'Language Nests' and 503 playcentres).
[2] Includes children on the regular roll of the Correspondence School, kindergartens, playcentres, Te Kohanga Reo, Early Childhood Development Unit funded playgroups, Early Childhood Development Unit funded Pacific Islands language groups, education and care centres (incl. home-based childcare).
[3] Primary schools include Full Primary Years 1–8, Contributing Years 1–6, Intermediate Years 7–8.
[4] Teachers employed in state schools at 1 March 1999.
[5] Composite schools provide both primary and secondary education (includes area schools and the Correspondence School).
[6] Secondary schools include Years 7–15, Years 9–15.
[7] Tertiary institutions providing polytechnic and university level programmes specifically for Maori students, with an emphasis on Maori language and culture.

Source: Ministry of Education, Wellington.

Directory

The Constitution

New Zealand has no written constitution. The political system is closely modelled on that of the United Kingdom (with an element of proportional representation introduced to the legislature in 1996). As in the United Kingdom, constitutional practice is an accumulation of convention, precedent and tradition. A brief description of New Zealand's principal organs of government is given below:

HEAD OF STATE

Executive power is vested in the monarch and is exercisable in New Zealand by the monarch's personal representative, the Governor-General.

In the execution of the powers and authorities vested in him or her, the Governor-General must be guided by the advice of the Executive Council.

EXECUTIVE COUNCIL

The Executive Council consists of the Governor-General and all the Ministers. Two members, exclusive of the Governor-General or the presiding member, constitute a quorum. The Governor-General appoints the Prime Minister and, on the latter's recommendation, the other Ministers.

HOUSE OF REPRESENTATIVES

Parliament comprises the Crown and the House of Representatives. At the 1996 general election, a system of mixed member proportional representation was introduced. The House of Representatives comprises 120 members: 67 electorate members (five seats being reserved for Maoris) and 53 members chosen from party lists. They are designated 'Members of Parliament' and are elected for three years, subject to the dissolution of the House before the completion of their term.

Everyone over the age of 18 years may vote in the election of members for the House of Representatives. Since August 1975 any person, regardless of nationality, ordinarily resident in New Zealand for 12 months or more and resident in an electoral district for at least one month is qualified to be registered as a voter. Compulsory registration of all electors except Maoris was introduced at the end

of 1924; it was introduced for Maoris in 1956. As from August 1975, any person of the Maori race, which includes any descendant of such a person, may enrol on the Maori roll for the particular Maori electoral district in which that person resides.

By the Electoral Amendment Act, 1937, which made provision for a secret ballot in Maori elections, Maori electors were granted the same privileges, in the exercise of their vote, as general electors.

In local government the electoral franchise is the same.

The Government

Head of State: HM Queen ELIZABETH II (acceded to the throne 6 February 1952).

Governor-General and Commander-in-Chief: Dame SILVIA CARTWRIGHT (took office 4 April 2001).

CABINET
(May 2003)

A coalition of the Labour Party and the Progressive Coalition.

Prime Minister and Minister for Arts, Culture and Heritage: HELEN CLARK.

Deputy Prime Minister, Minister of Finance, Minister of Revenue and Leader of the House: Dr MICHAEL CULLEN.

Minister for Economic Development and Minister for Industry and Regional Development: JIM ANDERTON*.

Minister for Social Development and Employment, of Housing and of Broadcasting: STEVE MAHAREY.

Minister of Foreign Affairs and Trade, of Justice and of Pacific Island Affairs: PHIL GOFF.

Minister of Health and for Food Safety: ANNETTE KING.

Minister of Agriculture, for Biosecurity, of Forestry and for Trade Negotiations: JIM SUTTON.

Minister of Education, of State Services and for Sport and Recreation: TREVOR MALLARD.

Minister of Energy, of Fisheries, of Research, Science and Technology and for Crown Research Institutes: PETE HODGSON.

Attorney-General and Minister of Labour and in Charge of Treaty of Waitangi Negotiations: MARGARET WILSON.

Minister of Maori Affairs: PAREKURA HOROMIA.

Minister of Commerce and of Immigration: LIANNE DALZIEL.

Minister of Police, of Internal Affairs, of Civil Defence and of Veteran's Affairs: GEORGE HAWKINS.

Minister of Defence, for State Owned Enterprises and of Tourism: MARK BURTON.

Minister of Transport, of Corrections, of Communications and for Information Technology: PAUL SWAIN.

Minister for the Environment and for Disarmament and Arms Control: MARIAN HOBBS.

Minister for Accident Compensation Corporation, for Senior Citizens and of Women's Affairs: RUTH DYSON.

Minister of Youth Affairs, for Land Information and of Statistics: JOHN TAMIHERE.

Minister of Conservation and of Local Government: CHRIS CARTER.

Minister for Courts and of Customs: RICK BARKER.

Minister for Racing: DAMIEN O'CONNOR.
* Denotes member of the Progressive Coalition.

In addition, there are six Ministers outside the Cabinet.

MINISTRIES AND GOVERNMENT DEPARTMENTS

Department of the Prime Minister and Cabinet: Executive Wing, Parliament Bldgs, Wellington; tel. (4) 471-9700; fax (4) 473-2508; internet www.dpmc.govt.nz.

Ministry of Agriculture and Forestry: POB 2526, Wellington; tel. (4) 474-4100; fax (4) 474-4111; internet www.maf.govt.nz.

Ministry of Civil Defence and Emergency Management: POB 5010, Wellington; tel. (4) 473-7363; fax (4) 473-7369.

Department of Conservation: POB 10-420, Wellington; tel. (4) 471-0726; fax (4) 471-1082; e-mail tsmith@doc.govt.nz; internet www.doc.govt.nz.

Ministry for Culture and Heritage: POB 5364, Wellington; tel. (4) 499-4229; fax (4) 499-4490; e-mail info@mch.govt.nz; internet www.mch.govt.nz.

Ministry of Defence: POB 5347, Wellington; tel. (4) 496-0999; fax (4) 496-0859; internet www.defence.govt.nz.

Ministry of Economic Development: POB 1473, 33 Bowen St, Wellington; tel. (4) 472-0030; fax (4) 473-4638; e-mail info@med.govt.nz; internet www.med.govt.nz.

Ministry of Education: Level 7, St Paul's Square, 45–47 Pipitea St, Thorndon, Wellington; tel. (4) 463-8000; fax (4) 463-8001; e-mail enquiries.national@minedu.govt.nz; internet www.minedu.govt.nz.

Ministry for the Environment: POB 10-362, Wellington; tel. (4) 917-7400; fax (4) 917-7523; e-mail library@mfe.govt.nz; internet www.mfe.govt.nz.

Ministry of Fisheries: POB 1020, Wellington; tel. (4) 470-2600; fax (4) 470-2601; internet www.fish.govt.nz.

Ministry of Foreign Affairs and Trade: Private Bag 18901, Wellington; tel. (4) 494-8500; fax (4) 472-9596; e-mail enquiries@mfat.govt.nz; internet www.mfat.govt.nz.

Ministry of Health: POB 5013, Wellington; tel. (4) 496-2000; fax (4) 496-2340; internet www.moh.govt.nz.

Ministry of Housing: 256 Lambton Quay, Wellington; tel. (4) 472-2753; fax (4) 499-4744; e-mail info@minhousing.govt.nz; internet www.minhousing.govt.nz.

Department of Internal Affairs: POB 805, Wellington; tel. (4) 495-7200; fax (4) 495-7222; e-mail webmaster@dia.govt.nz; internet www.dia.govt.nz.

Ministry of Justice: POB 180, Wellington; tel. (4) 494-9700; fax (4) 494-9701; e-mail reception@justice.govt.nz; internet www.justice.govt.nz.

Department of Labour: POB 3705, Wellington; tel. (4) 915-4444; fax (4) 915-0891; e-mail info@dol.govt.nz; internet www.dol.govt.nz.

Ministry of Maori Development: POB 3943, Wellington 6015; tel. (4) 922-6000; fax (4) 922-6299; e-mail tpkinfo@tpk.govt.nz; internet www.tpk.govt.nz.

Ministry of Pacific Island Affairs: POB 833, Wellington; tel. (4) 473-4493; fax (4) 473-4301; e-mail contact@minpac.govt.nz; internet www.minpac.govt.nz.

Ministry of Research, Science and Technology: POB 5336, Wellington; tel. (4) 917-2900; fax (4) 471-1284; e-mail talk2us@morst.govt.nz; internet www.morst.govt.nz.

Ministry of Social Development: Private Bag 39993, Wellington 1; tel. (4) 916-3860; fax (4) 916-3918; e-mail information@msd.govt.nz; internet www.msd.govt.nz.

Ministry of Social Policy: Private Bag 39993, Wellington 1; tel. (4) 916-3860; fax (4) 916-3910; internet www.mosp.govt.nz.

State Services Commission: POB 329, Wellington; tel. (4) 495-6600; fax (4) 495-6686; e-mail commission@ssc.govt.nz; internet www.ssc.govt.nz.

Statistics New Zealand: POB 2922, Wellington; tel. (4) 495-4600; fax (4) 495-4610; e-mail info@stats.govt.nz; internet www.stats.govt.nz.

Ministry of Tourism: POB 5640, Wellington; tel. (4) 498-7440; fax (4) 498-7445; e-mail info@tourism.govt.nz; internet www.tourism.govt.nz.

Ministry of Transport: POB 3175, Wellington; tel. (4) 472-1253; fax (4) 473-3697; e-mail reception@transport.govt.nz; internet www.transport.govt.nz.

Treasury: POB 3724, Wellington; tel. (4) 472-2733; fax (4) 473-0982; e-mail helpline@treasury.govt.nz; internet www.treasury.govt.nz.

Ministry of Women's Affairs: POB 10-049, Wellington; tel. (4) 473-4112; fax (4) 472-0961; e-mail mwa@mwa.govt.nz; internet www.mwa.govt.nz.

Ministry of Youth Affairs: POB 10–300, Wellington; tel. (4) 471-2158; fax (4) 471-2233; e-mail info@youthaffairs.govt.nz; internet www.youthaffairs.govt.nz.

Legislature

HOUSE OF REPRESENTATIVES

Speaker: JONATHAN HUNT.

General Election, 27 July 2002

Party	Number of votes	% of votes	Party seats	List seats	Total seats
NZ Labour Party . .	838,219	41.26	45	7	52
NZ National Party . .	425,310	20.93	21	6	27
New Zealand First . .	210,912	10.38	1	12	13
ACT New Zealand . .	145,078	7.14	—	9	9
Green Party . . .	142,250	7.00	—	9	9
United Future NZ. . .	135,918	6.69	1	7	8
Progressive Coalition. .	34,542	1.70	1	1	2
Total (incl. others) . .	2,031,617	100.00	69	51	120

Political Organizations

In March 2003 20 parties were registered.

ACT New Zealand: Level 1, Block B, Old Mercury Bldg, Nuffield St, POB 99-651, Newmarket, Auckland; tel. (9) 523-0470; fax (9) 523-0472; e-mail info@voteact.org.nz; internet www.act.org.nz; f. 1994; supports free enterprise, tax reform and choice in education and health; Pres. CATHERINE JUDD; Leader RICHARD PREBBLE.

The Green Party of Aotearoa—New Zealand: POB 11-652, Wellington; tel. (4) 801-5102; fax (4) 801-5104; e-mail greenparty@greens.org.nz; internet www.greens.org.nz; f. 1989; fmrly Values Party, f. 1972; Co-Leaders ROD DONALD, JEANETTE FITZSIMONS.

Mana Motuhake o Aotearoa (New Zealand Self-Government Party): Private Bag 68-905, Newton, Auckland; f. 1979; pro-Maori; promotes bicultural policies; Leader WILLIE JACKSON.

The New Zealand Democratic Party Inc: 414 Glenfield Rd, POB 40364, Glenfield, North Shore City; tel. (9) 442-2364; fax (9) 442-2438; e-mail nzdp.inc@xtra.co.nz; internet www.geocities.com/CapitolHill/Senate/2550; f. 1953 as Social Credit Political League; adopted present name 1985; liberal; Pres. PETER KANE; Leader JOHN WRIGHT.

New Zealand First: c/o House of Representatives, Wellington; fax (4) 472-8557; e-mail nzfirst@parliament.govt.nz; f. 1993 by fmr National Party mems; Leader WINSTON PETERS; Pres. DOUG WOOLERTON.

New Zealand Labour Party: POB 784, 160–162 Willis St, Wellington; tel. (4) 384-7649; fax (4) 384-8060; e-mail nzlpho@labour.org.nz; internet www.labour.org.nz; f. 1916; advocates an organized economy guaranteeing an adequate standard of living to every person able and willing to work; Pres. MIKE WILLIAMS; Parl. Leader HELEN CLARK; Gen. Sec. MIKE SMITH.

New Zealand New National Party: 14th Floor, Willbank House, 57 Willis St, POB 1155, Wellington 60015; tel. (4) 472-5211; fax (4) 478-1622; e-mail hq@national.org.nz; internet www.national.org.nz; f. 1936; centre-right; supports private enterprise and competitive business, together with maximum personal freedom; Pres. MICHELLE BOAG; Parl. Leader BILL ENGLISH.

Progressive Coalition: c/o House of Representatives, Wellington; f. 2002 to contest the general election; Leader JIM ANDERTON.

United Future New Zealand (UNZ): c/o House of Representatives, Wellington; e-mail united.nz@parliament.govt.nz; internet www.united.org.nz; f. 1995 by four mems of National Party, two mems of Labour Party and leader of Future New Zealand; joined by New Zealand Conservative Party in 1998; Leader PETER DUNNE.

Other parties that contested the 2002 election included the Alliance, the Aotearoa Legalise Cannabis Party, the Christian Heritage Party, Mana Maori Movement, One New Zealand Party and Outdoor Recreation New Zealand.

Diplomatic Representation

EMBASSIES AND HIGH COMMISSIONS IN NEW ZEALAND

Argentina: Sovereign Assurance House, 14th Floor, 142 Lambton Quay, POB 5430, Lambton Quay, Wellington; tel. (4) 472-8330; fax (4) 472-8331; e-mail enzel@arg.org.nz; internet www.arg.org.nz; Ambassador ENRIQUE J. DE LA TORRE.

Australia: 72–78 Hobson St, Thorndon, POB 4036, Wellington; tel. (4) 473-6411; fax (4) 498-7118; High Commissioner ROBERT L. COTTON.

Brazil: Wool House, 10 Brandon St, POB 5432, Wellington; tel. (4) 473-3516; fax (4) 473-3517; e-mail brasemb@ihug.co.nz; Ambassador EDGARD TELLES RIBEIRO.

Canada: 61 Molesworth St, POB 12049, Wellington 1; tel. (4) 473-9577; fax (4) 471-2082; High Commissioner VALERIE RAYMOND.

Chile: 19 Bolton St, POB 3861, Wellington; tel. (4) 471-6270; fax (4) 472-5324; e-mail embchile@ihug.co.nz; Ambassador CARLOS APPELGREN BALBONTÍN.

China, People's Republic: POB 17257, Karori, Wellington; tel. (4) 472-1382; fax (4) 499-0419; internet www.chinaembassy.org.nz; Ambassador CHEN MINGMING.

Fiji: 31 Pipitea St, Thorndon, POB 3940, Wellington; tel. (4) 473-5401; fax (4) 499-1011; e-mail viti@paradise.net.nz; internet www.fiji.org.nz; High Commissioner BAL RAM.

France: 34–42 Manners St, Open Networks Building, 12th Floor, POB 11-343, Wellington; tel. (4) 802-7787; fax (4) 384-2579; e-mail laurence.oxenberg@diplomatic.gouv.fr; internet www.ambafrance-nz.org; Ambassador JACKY MUSNIER.

Germany: 90–92 Hobson St, POB 1687, Wellington; tel. (4) 473-6063; fax (4) 473-6069; e-mail germanembassywellington@xtra.co.nz; Ambassador GUIDO HEYMER.

Greece: 10th Floor, 5–7 Willeston St, POB 24-066, Wellington; tel. (4) 473-7775; fax (4) 473-7441; e-mail info@greece.org.nz; Ambassador CHRISTOS KARAPANOS.

Holy See: Apostolic Nunciature, 112 Queen's Drive, Lyall Bay, POB 14-044, Wellington 6041; tel. (4) 387-3470; fax (4) 387-8170; e-mail nuntius@ihug.co.nz; Apostolic Nuncio Most Rev. PATRICK COVENEY (Titular Archbishop of Satriano).

India: 180 Molesworth St, POB 4045, Wellington 1; tel. (4) 473-6390; fax (4) 499-0665; e-mail hicomind@clear.net.nz; internet www.hicomind.org.nz; High Commissioner BAL ANAND.

Indonesia: 70 Glen Road, Kelburn, POB 3543, Wellington; tel. (4) 475-8699; fax (4) 475-9374; e-mail kbriwell@ihug.co.nz; internet www.indonesianembassy.org.nz; Ambassador H. E. SUTOYO.

Iran: POB 10-249, The Terrace, Wellington; tel. (4) 386-2983; fax (4) 386-3065; e-mail embassy.of.iran@xtra.co.nz; Ambassador MOHAMMAD ALI KORMI NOURI.

Israel: Equinox House, 13th Floor, 111 The Terrace, POB 2171, Wellington; tel. (4) 472-2368; fax (4) 499-0632; e-mail israel-ask@israel.org.nz; internet www.webnz.co.nz/israel; Ambassador RUTH KAHANOFF.

Italy: 34–38 Grant Rd, Thorndon, POB 463, Wellington 1; tel. (4) 473-5339; fax (4) 472-7255; e-mail ambwell@xtra.co.nz; internet www.italy-embassy.org.nz/em_well.html; Ambassador ROBERTO PALMIERI.

Japan: Levels 18–19, The Majestic Centre, 100 Willis St, POB 6340, Wellington 1; tel. (4) 473-1540; fax (4) 471-2951; Ambassador KOICHI MATSUMOTO.

Korea, Republic: ASB Bank Tower, Level 11, 2 Hunter St, POB 11-143, Wellington; tel. (4) 473-9073; fax (4) 472-3865; e-mail korembec@world-net.co.nz; Ambassador CHONG WOO-SEONG.

Malaysia: 10 Washington Ave, Brooklyn, POB 9422, Wellington; tel. (4) 385-2439; fax (4) 385-6973; e-mail mwwelton@xtra.co.nz; High Commissioner Dato' ZULKIFLY ABDUL RAHMAN.

Mexico: Perpetual Trust House, Level 8, 111–115 Customhouse Quay, POB 11-510, Manners St, Wellington; tel. (4) 472-0555; fax (4) 496-3559; e-mail mexico@xtra.co.nz; internet www.mexico.org.nz; Ambassador JORGE ALVAREZ FUENTES.

Netherlands: Investment House, 10th Floor, Cnr Featherston and Ballance Sts, POB 840, Wellington; tel. (4) 471-6390; fax (4) 471-2923; e-mail wel@minbuza.nl; internet www.netherlandsembassy.co.nz; Ambassador A. E. DE BIJLL NACHENIUS.

Papua New Guinea: 279 Willis St, POB 197, Wellington; tel. (4) 385-2474; fax (4) 385-2477; e-mail pngnz@globe.net.nz; High Commissioner LUCY BOGARI.

Peru: Cigna House, Level 8, 40 Mercer St, POB 2566, Wellington; tel. (4) 499-8087; fax (4) 499-8057; e-mail embperu@xtra.co.nz; Ambassador JAVIER LEÓN.

Philippines: 50 Hobson St, Thorndon, POB 12-042, Wellington; tel. (4) 472-9848; fax (4) 472-5170; e-mail embassy@wellington-pe.co.nz; Ambassador FRANCISCO F. SANTOS.

Poland: 17 Upland Rd, Kelburn, POB 10211, Wellington; tel. (4) 475-9453; fax (4) 475-9458; Chargé d'affaires ANDRZEJ SOŁTYSIŃSKI.

Russia: 57 Messines Rd, Karori, Wellington; tel. (4) 476-6113; fax (4) 476-3843; e-mail eor@netlink.co.nz; Ambassador GENNADII SHABANNIKOV.

Samoa: 1A Wesley Rd, Kelburn, POB 1430, Wellington; tel. (4) 472-0953; fax (4) 471-2479; e-mail samoahicom@clear.net.nz; High Commissioner FEESAGO SIAOSI FEPULEA'I.

Singapore: 17 Kabul St, Khandallah, POB 13140, Wellington; tel. (4) 470-0850; fax (4) 479-2315; e-mail shcwlg@xtra.co.nz; internet www.mfa.gov.sg/wellington; High Commissioner TAN KENG JIN.

Switzerland: Panama House, 22 Panama St, Wellington; tel. (4) 472-1593; fax (4) 499-6302; e-mail vertretung@wel.rep.admin.ch; Ambassador SYLVIE MATTEUCCI.

Thailand: 2 Cook St, Karori, POB 17-226, Wellington; tel. (4) 476-8618; fax (4) 476-3677; e-mail thaiembassynz@xtra.co.nz; Ambassador ANUCHA OSATHANOND.

Turkey: Level 8, 15–17 Murphy St, POB 12-248, Wellington; tel. (4) 472-1292; fax (4) 472-1277; e-mail turkem@xtra.co.nz; Ambassador ÜNAL MARASLI.

United Kingdom: 44 Hill St, POB 1812, Wellington; tel. (4) 924-2888; fax (4) 473-4982; e-mail bhc.wel@xtra.co.nz; internet www.britain.org.nz; High Commissioner RICHARD FELL.

USA: 29 Fitzherbert Terrace, POB 1190, Wellington; tel. (4) 462-6000; fax (4) 472-3537; internet usembassy.state.gov/wellington; Ambassador CHARLES SWINDELLS.

Judicial System

The Judicial System of New Zealand comprises a Court of Appeal, a High Court and District Courts, all of which have civil and criminal jurisdiction, and the specialist courts, the Employment Court, the Family Court, the Youth Court and the Maori Land Court. Final appeal is to the Judicial Committee of the Privy Council in the United Kingdom. In civil cases parties have an appeal to the Privy Council from the Court of Appeal as a matter of right if the case involves $NZ5,000 or more; leave to appeal is not automatically granted for criminal cases.

The Court of Appeal hears appeals from the High Court and from District Court Jury Trials, although it does have some original jurisdiction. Its decisions are final, except in cases that may be appealed to the Privy Council. Appeals regarding convictions and sentences handed down by the High Court or District Trial Courts are by leave only.

The High Court has jurisdiction to hear cases involving crimes, admiralty law and civil matters. It hears appeals from lower courts and tribunals, and reviews administrative actions.

District Courts have an extensive criminal and civil law jurisdiction. They hear civil cases up to $NZ200,000, unless the parties agree to litigate a larger sum (up to $NZ62,500 per year for rent and up to $NZ500,000 for real estate). Justices of the Peace can hear minor criminal and traffic matters if less than $NZ5,000. The Family Court, which is a division of the District Courts, has the jurisdiction to deal with dissolution of marriages, adoption, guardianship applications, domestic actions, matrimonial property, child support, care and protection applications regarding children and young persons, and similar matters.

The tribunals are as follows: the Employment Tribunal (administered by the Department of Labour), Disputes Tribunal, Complaints Review Tribunal, Residential Tenancies Tribunal, Waitangi Tribunal, Environment Court, Deportation Review Tribunal and Motor Vehicles Disputes Tribunal. The Disputes Tribunal has the jurisdiction to hear civil matters involving sums up to $NZ7,500. If the parties agree, it can hear cases involving sums up to $NZ12,000.

In criminal cases involving indictable offences (major crimes), the defendant has the right to a jury. In criminal cases involving summary offences (minor crimes), the defendant may elect to have a jury if the sentence corresponding to the charge is three months or greater.

In early 2002 the Government announced its intention to replace the system of final appeal to the Privy Council with a local Supreme Court.

Attorney-General: Margaret Wilson.

Chief Justice: Dame Sian Elias.

THE COURT OF APPEAL

President: Thomas Munro Gault.

Judges: Dame Sian Elias (ex officio), John Steele Henry, John J. McGrath, Sir Kenneth Keith, Peter Blanchard, Andrew Patrick Charles Tipping, Susan Glazebrook.

THE HIGH COURT

Permanent Judges: Dame Sian Elias (ex officio), Richard Alexander Heron, Anthony Arthur Travers Ellis, Robert Andrew McGechan, John Anthony Doogue, Noel Crossley Anderson, James Bruce Robertson, Robert Lloyd Fisher, Peter George Spenser Penlington, Robert Grant Hammond, David Stewart Morris, John W. Hansen, Hugh Williams, David Baragwanath, Lowell Goddard, Graham Panckhurst, Lester H. Chisholm, Peter M. Salmon, Barry J. Paterson, J. Warwick Gendall, Judith M. Potter, John A. Laurenson, Tony Randerson, Willie Young, Justice Nicholson, Justice Wild, E. T. Durie, Justice Chambers, Rodney Hansen.

Religion

CHRISTIANITY

Conference of Churches in Aotearoa New Zealand: POB 22-652, Christchurch; tel. and fax (3) 377-2702; e-mail ccanz@clear.net.nz; internet www.ccanz.godzone.net.nz; f. 1987 to replace the National Council of Churches in New Zealand (f. 1941); 12 mem. churches, 1 assoc. mem.; Gen. Sec. Michael Earle.

Te Runanga Whakawhanaunga i Nga Hahi o Aotearoa (Maori Council of Churches in New Zealand): Private Bag 11903, Ellerslie, Auckland, Aotearoa-New Zealand; tel. (9) 525 4179; fax (9) 525 4346; f. 1982; four mem. churches; Administrator Te Rua Gretha.

The Anglican Communion

The Anglican Church in Aotearoa, New Zealand and Polynesia comprises Te Pihopatanga o Aotearoa and eight dioceses (one of which is Polynesia). In 1996 the Church had an estimated 631,764 members in New Zealand.

Primate of the Anglican Church in Aotearoa, New Zealand and Polynesia, and Bishop of Auckland: Rt Rev. John Campbell Paterson, POB 37-242, Parnell, Auckland; tel. (9) 302-7201; fax (9) 377-6962.

General Secretary and Treasurer of the Anglican Church in Aotearoa, New Zealand and Polynesia: Robin Nairn, POB 885, Hastings; tel. (6) 878-7902; fax (6) 878-7905; e-mail gensec@hb.ang.org.nz; internet www.anglican.org.nz.

The Roman Catholic Church

For ecclesiastical purposes, New Zealand comprises one archdiocese and five dioceses. At 31 December 2000 there were an estimated 456,947 adherents.

Bishops' Conference

New Zealand Catholic Bishops' Conference, POB 1937, Wellington; tel. (4) 496-1747; fax (4) 496-1746; e-mail t.oliver@wn.catholic.org.nz.

f. 1974; Pres. Rt Rev. Peter Cullinane (Bishop of Palmerston North); Sec. Bishop John Dew (Auxiliary Bishop of Wellington); Executive Officer Terence Oliver.

Archbishop of Wellington: Cardinal Thomas Stafford Williams, POB 1937, Wellington 6015; tel. (4) 496-1795; fax (4) 496-1728; e-mail bishop.tsw@xtra.co.nz.

Other Christian Churches

Baptist Churches of New Zealand: 8 Puhinui Rd, Manukau City, POB 97543, South Auckland; tel. (9) 278-7494; fax (9) 279-7499; e-mail info@baptist.org.nz; internet www.baptist.org.nz; f. 1882; 22,456 mems; Pres. Rob Bellingham; Nat. Leader Rev. Brian Winslade.

Congregational Union of New Zealand: 10 The Close, 42 Arawa St, New Lynn, Auckland; tel. and fax (9) 827-3708; e-mail cunz@xtra.co.nz; f. 1884; 786 mems, 15 churches; Gen. Sec. Bob Franklyn; Chair. Barbara Kennett.

Methodist Church of New Zealand: Connexional Office, POB 931, Christchurch; tel. (3) 366-6049; fax (3) 366-6009; e-mail info@methodist.org.nz; 16,995 mems; Gen. Sec. Rev. Jill van de Geer.

Presbyterian Church of Aotearoa New Zealand: 100 Tory St, POB 9049, Wellington; tel. (04) 801-6000; fax (04) 801-6001; e-mail assemblyoffice@pcanz.org.nz; internet www.presbyterian.org.nz; 50,000 mems; Moderator Rt Rev. Michael Thawley; Assembly Exec. Sec. Rev. Dr Kerry M. Enright.

There are several Maori Churches in New Zealand, with a total membership of over 30,000. These include the Ratana Church of New Zealand, Ringatu Church, Church of Te Kooti Rikirangi, Absolute Maori Established Church and United Maori Mission. The Antiochian Orthodox Church, the Assemblies of God, the Greek Orthodox Church of New Zealand, the Liberal Catholic Church, and the Society of Friends (Quakers) are also active.

BAHÁ'Í FAITH

National Spiritual Assembly of the Bahá'ís of New Zealand: POB 21-551, Henderson, Auckland 1231; tel. (9) 837-4866; fax (9) 837-4898; e-mail natsec@nsa.org.nz; internet www.bahai.org.nz; CEO Suzanne Mahon.

The Press

NEWSPAPERS AND PERIODICALS

Principal Dailies

In 1999 there were 29 daily newspapers in New Zealand (eight morning, 21 evening).

Bay of Plenty Times: 108 Durham St, Private Bag TG12002, Tauranga; tel. (7) 578-3059; fax (7) 578-0047; e-mail news@boptimes.co.nz; internet www.mytown.co.nz/bayofplenty; f. 1872; evening; Gen. Man. John Wood; Editor Bruce Morris; circ. 22,920.

The Daily News: Currie St, POB 444, New Plymouth; tel. (6) 758-0559; fax (6) 758-6849; e-mail editor@dailynews.co.nz; f. 1857; morning; Gen. Man. Kevin Nielsen; Editor (vacant); circ. 27,316.

The Daily Post: 1143 Hinemoa St, POB 1442, Rotorua; tel. (7) 348 6199; fax (7) 346 0153; e-mail daily@dailypost.co.nz; f. 1885; evening; Gen. Man. Alan Sampson; Editor R. G. Mayston; circ. 13,421.

Dominion Post: Dominion Post House, 40 Boulcott St, POB 1297, Wellington; tel. (4) 474-0000; fax (4) 474-0350; e-mail editor@dompost.co.nz; internet www.wnl.co.nz; f. 2002 following merger of *Evening Post* and *The Dominion*; morning; Gen. Man. Don Churchill; Man. Editor Tim Pankhurst; circ. 101,600.

Evening Standard: POB 3, Palmerston North; tel. (6) 356-9009; fax (6) 350-9836; e-mail editor@msl.co.nz; f. 1880; evening; Gen. Man. Trevor Howes; Editor Tony Curran; circ. 21,367.

Gisborne Herald: 64 Gladstone Rd, POB 1143, Gisborne; tel. (6) 868-6655; fax (6) 867-8048; e-mail editorial@gisborneherald.co.nz; f. 1874; evening; Man. Dir M. C. Muir; Editor Iain Gillies; circ. 9,587.

Hawke's Bay Today: 113 Karamu Rd, POB 180, Hastings; tel. (6) 873-0800; fax (6) 873-0805; e-mail hb_news@hbtoday.co.nz; f. 1999; evening; conservative; Gen. Man. Ron D. Hall; Editor Louis Pierard; circ. 33,000.

Marlborough Express: 62–64 Arthur St, POB 242, Blenheim; tel. (3) 577-2950; fax (3) 577-2953; e-mail laurab@marlexpress.co.nz; internet www.malboroughexpress.co.nz; f. 1866; Gen. Man. Roger G. Rose; Editor Laura Basham; circ. 10,431.

The Nelson Mail: 15 Bridge St, POB 244, Nelson; tel. (3) 548-7079; fax (3) 546-2802; f. 1866; evening; Business Man. Mark Hughes; Editor David J. Mitchell; circ. 18,555.

New Zealand Herald: 46 Albert St, POB 32, Auckland; tel. (9) 379-5050; fax (9) 373-6421; internet www.nzherald.co.nz; f. 1863; morning; Man. Dir TIM MURPHY; Editor KEN STEINKE; circ. 215,000.

Northern Advocate: 36 Water St, POB 210, Whangarei; tel. (9) 438-2399; fax (9) 430-5669; e-mail daily@northernadvocate.co.nz; internet www.wilsonandhorton.co.nz; f. 1875; evening; Gen. Man. JOHN T. WOOD; Editor G. A. BARROW; circ. 14,602.

Otago Daily Times: Lower Stuart St, POB 517, Dunedin; tel. (3) 477-4760; fax (3) 474-7422; e-mail odt.editor@alliedpress.co.nz; internet www.odt.co.nz; f. 1861; morning; Man. Dir JULIAN C. S. SMITH; Editor ROBIN CHARTERIS; circ. 44,500.

The Press: Cathedral Sq., Private Bag 4722, Christchurch; tel. (3) 379-0940; fax (3) 364-8492; e-mail editorial@press.co.nz; internet www.press.co.nz; f. 1861; morning; Gen. Man. PETER O'HARA; Editor PAUL THOMPSON; circ. 92,000.

Southland Times: 67 Esk St, POB 805, Invercargill; tel. (3) 218-1909; fax (3) 214-9905; e-mail editor@stl.co.nz; f. 1862; morning; Gen. Man. BLAIR BURR; Editor FRED TULETT; circ. 33,300.

Timaru Herald: 52 Bank St, POB 46, Timaru; tel. (3) 684-4129; fax (3) 688-1042; e-mail editor@timaruherald.co.nz; f. 1864; morning; Gen. Man. BARRY APPLEBY; Editor DAVE WOOD; circ. 14,141.

Waikato Times: Private Bag 3086, Hamilton; tel. (7) 849-6180; fax (7) 849-9603; f. 1872; evening; independent; Gen. Man. P. G. HENSON; Editor VENETIA SHERSON; circ. 42,000.

Wanganui Chronicle: 59 Taupo Quay, POB 433, Wanganui; tel. (6) 349-0710; fax (6) 349-0722; e-mail wc_editorial@wilsonandhorton.co.nz; f. 1856; morning; Gen. Man. R. A. JARDEN; Editor J. MASLIN; circ. 14,000.

Weeklies and Other Newspapers

Best Bets: POB 1327, Auckland; fax (9) 366-4565; Sun. and Thur. horse-racing, trotting and greyhounds; Editor MIKE BROWN; circ. 10,000.

Christchurch Star: 293 Tuam St, POB 1467, Christchurch; tel. (3) 379-7100; fax (3) 366-0180; e-mail bob_cotton@christchurchstar.co.nz; f. 1868; 2 a week; Chief Reporter BOB COTTON; circ. 118,170.

MG Business: 8 Sheffield Crescent, Christchurch 8005; tel. (3) 358-3219; fax (3) 358-4490; f. 1876; fmrly *Mercantile Gazette*; fortnightly; Mon. economics, finance, management, stock market, politics; Editor BILL HORSLEY; circ. 16,300.

The National Business Review: Level 26, Bank of New Zealand Tower, 125 Queen St, POB 1734, Auckland; tel. (9) 307-1629; fax (9) 307-5129; e-mail editor@nbr.co.nz; f. 1970; weekly; Editor NEVIL GIBSON; circ. 14,328.

New Truth and TV Extra: News Media (Auckland) Ltd, 155 New North Rd, POB 1327, Auckland; tel. (9) 302-1300; fax (9) 307-0761; e-mail editor@truth.co.nz; f. 1905; Friday; local news and features; TV and entertainment; sports; Editor CLIVE NELSON; circ. 22,000.

New Zealand Gazette: Dept of Internal Affairs, POB 805, Wellington; tel. (4) 470-2930; fax (4) 470-2932; e-mail gazette@parliament.govt.nz; internet www.gazette.govt.nz; official government publication; f. 1840; weekly; Man. JANET GOOTJES; circ. 1,000.

North Shore Times Advertiser: POB 33-235, Takapuna, Auckland 9; tel. (9) 489-4189; fax (9) 486-1950; 3 a week; Editor I. DUNN; circ. 59,000.

Sunday Star-Times: POB 1409, Auckland; tel. (9) 302-1300; fax (9) 309-0258; f. 1994 by merger; Editor SUZANNE CHETWIN; circ. 207,375.

Sunday News: POB 1327, Auckland; tel. (9) 302 1300; fax (9) 358 3003; e-mail editor@sunday-news.co.nz; internet www.sundaynews.co.nz; Editor CLIVE NELSON; circ. 113,422.

Taieri Herald: POB 105, Mosgiel; tel. (3) 489-7123; fax (3) 489-7668; f. 1962; weekly; Man. Editor LEE HARRIS; circ. 10,700.

Waihi Gazette: Seddon St, Waihi; tel. (7) 863-8674; fax (7) 863-8103; weekly; Editor FRITHA TAGG; circ. 8,650.

Wairarapa News: POB 87, Masterton; tel. (6) 370-5690; fax (6) 379-6481; f. 1869; Editor ERIC TURNER; circ. 18,200.

Other Periodicals

AA Directions: AA Centre, cnr Albert and Victoria Sts, Auckland; tel. (9) 356-6444; fax (9) 357-9975; e-mail editor@nzaa.co.nz; internet www.aa.co.nz/online; quarterly; official magazine of the The New Zealand Automobile Association; Editor JOHN CRANNA; circ. 542,219.

Air New Zealand Inflight Magazine: Private Bag 47-920, Ponsonby, Auckland; tel. (9) 379-8822; fax (9) 379-8821; e-mail nzsales@pol.net.nz; monthly; in-flight magazine of Air New Zealand; circ. 61,000.

Architecture New Zealand: AGM Publishing Ltd, Private Bag 99-915, Newmarket, Auckland; tel. (9) 846-4068; fax (9) 846-8742;

e-mail johnw@agm.co.nz; f. 1987; every 2 months; Editor JOHN WALSH; circ. 10,000.

Australian Women's Weekly (NZ edition): Private Bag 92–512, Wellesley St, Auckland; tel. (9) 308-2735; fax (9) 302-0667; monthly; Editorial Dir LOUISE WRIGHT; circ. 100,550.

Computer Buyer New Zealand: 246 Queen St, Level 8, Auckland; tel. (9) 377-9902; fax (9) 377-4604; every 2 months; Man. Editor DON HILL; circ. 120,968.

Dairying Today: POB 3855, Auckland; tel. (9) 307-0399; fax (9) 307-0122; e-mail rural_news@clear.net.nz; monthly; Editor ADAM FRICKER; circ. 25,979.

Fashion Quarterly: ACP Media Centre, Private Bag 92–512, Auckland; tel. (9) 308-2735; fax (9) 302-0667; e-mail fq@acpmedia.co.nz; f. 1982; 5 a year; Editor LEONIE DALE; circ. 31,500.

Grapevine: Private Bag 92–124, Auckland; tel. (9) 624-3079; fax (9) 625-8788; monthly; family magazine; Editor JOHN COONEY; circ. 149,658.

Info-Link: AGM Publishing Ltd, Private Bag 99-915, Newmarket, Auckland; tel. (9) 846-4068; fax (9) 846-8742; e-mail pengelly@agm.co.nz; internet www.info-link.co.nz; quarterly; Editors SALLY LINDSAY, REBECCA WOOD; circ. 22,000.

Landfall: University of Otago Press, POB 56, Dunedin; tel. (3) 479-8807; fax (3) 479-8385; e-mail landfall@otago.ac.nz; f. 1947; 2 a year; literary; Editor JUSTIN PATON; circ. 1,200.

Mana Magazine: POB 1101, Rotorua; tel. (7) 349-0260; fax (7) 349-0258; e-mail editor@manaonline.co.nz; internet www.manaonline.co.nz; Maori news magazine; Editor DEREK FOX.

Management: POB 5544, Wellesley St, Auckland; tel. (9) 630-8940; fax (9) 630-1046; e-mail editor@management.co.nz; internet www.profile.co.nz; f. 1954; monthly; business; Editor REG BIRCHFIELD; circ. 12,000.

New Idea New Zealand: 48 Greys Ave, 4th Floor, Auckland; tel. (9) 979-2700; fax (9) 979-2721; weekly; women's interest; Editor ANATHEA JOHNSTON; circ. 59,039.

New Truth: 155 New North Rd, Auckland 1; tel. (9) 302-1300; fax (9) 307-0761; e-mail editor@truth.co.nz; weekly; Editor CLIVE NELSON; circ. 22,000.

New Zealand Dairy Exporter: POB 299, Wellington; tel. (4) 499-0300; fax (4) 499-0330; e-mail lance@dairymag.co.nz; f. 1925; monthly; Man. Editor L. MCELDOWNEY; circ. 22,739.

The New Zealand Farmer: Great South Rd, POB 4233, Auckland; tel. (9) 520-9451; fax (9) 520-9459; f. 1882; weekly; Editor HUGH STRINGLEMAN; circ. 18,000.

New Zealand Forest Industries: POB 5544, Auckland; tel. (9) 630-8940; fax (9) 630-1046; e-mail info@nzforest.co.nz; internet www.nzforest.co.nz; f. 1960; monthly; forestry; Publr REG BIRCHFIELD; circ. 2,500.

New Zealand Gardener: POB 6341, Wellesley St, Auckland; tel. (4) 293-4495; f. 1944; monthly; Editor P. MCGEORGE; circ. 77,077.

New Zealand Geographic: POB 37291, Parnell, Auckland; tel. (9) 303-0126; fax (9) 303-0127; e-mail editor@nzgeographic.co.nz; internet www.nzgeographic.co.nz; f. 1988; 6 a year; people, places and wildlife of New Zealand; Editor KENNEDY WARNE; circ. 24,612.

New Zealand Horse & Pony: POB 12965, Auckland; tel. (9) 634-1800; fax (9) 634-2918; e-mail editor@horse-pony.co.nz; f. 1959; monthly; Editor JOAN E. GILCHRIST; circ. 9,252.

New Zealand Medical Journal: Department of Medicine, Christchurch Hospital, POB 4345, Christchurch; tel. (3) 364-0640; fax (3) 364-0752; e-mail frank.frizell@chmeds.ac.nz; internet www.nzma.org.nz; 2 a month; Editor Prof. FRANK A. FRIZELL; circ. 5,000.

New Zealand Science Review: POB 1874, Wellington; fax (4) 389-5095; e-mail mberridge@malaghan.org.nz; internet www.rsnz.govt.nz/clan/nzmss; f. 1942; 4 a year; reviews, policy and philosophy of science; Editor M. V. BERRIDGE.

New Zealand Woman's Day: Private Bag 92–512, Wellesley St, Auckland; tel. (9) 308-2700; fax (9) 357-0978; e-mail wdaynz@acp.nz.co.nz; weekly; Editor in Chief LOUISE WRIGHT; circ. 143,420.

New Zealand Woman's Weekly: NZ Magazines Ltd, POB 90-119, Auckland Mail Centre, Auckland; tel. (9) 360-3820; fax (9) 360-3826; e-mail editor@nzww.co.nz; internet www.on-line.co.nz; f. 1932; Mon. women's issues and general interest; Editor ROWAN DIXON; circ. 130,706.

Next: Level 4, Cnr Fanshawe and Beamont Sts, Westhaven, Private Bag 92512, Auckland 1036; tel. (9) 308-2773; fax (9) 377-6725; e-mail next@acpmedia.co.nz; f. 1991; monthly; home and lifestyle; Editor LIZ PARKER; circ. 63,000.

North & South: 100 Beaumont St, Private Bag 92512, Wellesley St, Auckland; tel. (9) 308-2700; fax (9) 308-9498; e-mail northsouth@

acpmedia.co.nz; f. 1986; monthly; current affairs and lifestyle; Editor ROBYN LANGWELL; circ. 35,959.

NZ Catholic: POB 147000, Ponsonby, Auckland 1034; tel. (9) 378-4380; fax (9) 360-3065; e-mail catholic@iconz.co.nz; f. 1996; fortnightly; Roman Catholic; Editor PAT MCCARTHY; circ. 7,800.

NZ Home and Entertaining: ACP Media Centre, Cnr Fanshawe and Beaumont Sts, Private Bag 92512, Auckland; tel. (9) 308–2700; e-mail cmccall@acpmedia.co.nz; f. 1936; bi-monthly, design, architecture, lifestyle; Editor CLARE MCCALL; circ. 21,298.

NZ Listener: NZ Magazines Ltd, POB 90-119, Auckland Mail Centre, Auckland; tel. (9) 360-3820; fax (9) 360-3831; f. 1939; weekly; general features, politics, arts, TV, radio; Editor FINLAY MACDONALD; circ. 96,000.

NZ Turf Digest: News Media (Auckland) Ltd, 155 New North Rd, POB 1327, Auckland; tel. (9) 302-1310; fax (9) 366-4565; Sun./Thur. Editor MIKE BROWN; circ. 7,500.

Otago Southland Farmer: POB 805, Invercargill; tel. (3) 211-1051; fax (3) 214-3713; fortnightly; Editor REX TOMLINSON; circ. 19,000.

Pacific Wings: NZ Wings Ltd, POB 120, Otaki; tel. (6) 364-6423; fax (6) 364-7797; e-mail editor@nzwings.co.nz; internet www.nzwings.co.nz; f. 1932; monthly; Editor CALLUM MACPHERSON; circ. 20,000.

Prodesign: AGM Publishing Ltd, Private Bag 99-915, Newmarket, Auckland; tel. (9) 846-4068; fax (9) 846-8742; e-mail agm.publishing@xtra.co.nz; f. 1993; every 2 months; Man. Editor STEVE BOHLING; circ. 9,000.

PSA Journal: PSA House, 11 Aurora Terrace, POB 3817, Wellington 1; tel. (4) 917-0333; fax (4) 917-2051; e-mail enquiries@psa.org.nz; internet www.pas.org.nz; f. 1913; 8 a year; journal of the NZ Public Service Asscn; circ. 52,000.

Reader's Digest: L5/235 Broadway, Newmarket, Auckland 1015; tel. (9) 522-9777; fax (9) 522-9778; f. 1950; monthly; Editor TONY SPENCER-SMITH; circ. 105,000.

RSA Review: 181 Willis St, POB 27248, Wellington; tel. (4) 384-7994; fax (4) 385-3325; e-mail rsareview@paradise.net.nz; every 2 months; magazine of the Royal New Zealand Returned Services' Asscn; circ. 106,000.

Rural News: POB 3855, Auckland; tel. (9) 307-0399; fax (9) 307-0122; e-mail rural_news@clear.net.nz; fortnightly; Editor ADAM FRICKER; circ. 85,813.

She Magazine: Private Bag 92–512, Wellesley St, Auckland; tel. (9) 308-2735; fax (9) 302-0667; e-mail she@acpmedia.co.nz; Editor LEONIE DALE.

Spanz: POB 9049, Wellington; tel. (4) 801-6000; fax (4) 801-6001; e-mail marym@pcanz.org.nz; internet www.presbyterian.org.nz; f. 1987; bi-monthly; magazine of Presbyterian Church; Editor MARY MACPHERSON; circ. 21,500.

Straight Furrow: c/o Rural Press, POB 4233, Auckland; tel. (9) 376-9786; fax (9) 376-9780; e-mail straightfurrow@ruralpress.com; internet www.straightfurrow.co.nz; f. 1933; fortnightly; Editor SUSAN TOPLESS; circ. 85,000.

Time New Zealand: Tandem House, 18 St Martins Lane, POB 198, Auckland; fax (9) 366-4706; weekly; circ. 42,765.

TV Guide (NZ): POB 1327, Auckland; tel. (9) 302-1300; fax (9) 373-3036; e-mail editor@tv-guide.co.nz; f. 1986; weekly; Editor ANTHONY PHILLIPS; circ. 225,648.

UNANewZ: UN Asscn of NZ, POB 12324, Wellington; tel. (4) 473-0441; fax (4) 473-2339; e-mail unanz@xtra.co.nz; internet www.converge.org.nz/unanz; f. 1945; quarterly; Editor (vacant).

NEWS AGENCIES

New Zealand Press Association: Newspaper House, 93 Boulcott St, POB 1599, Wellington; tel. (4) 472-7910; fax (4) 473-7480; e-mail news@nzpa.co.nz; internet www.newsquest.co.nz; f. 1879; non-political; Chair. JULIAN SMITH.

South Pacific News Service Ltd (Sopacnews): POB 5026, Lambton Quay, Wellington; tel. and fax (3) 472-8329; f. 1948; Man. Editor NEALE MCMILLAN.

Foreign Bureaux

Agence France-Presse (AFP): POB 11-420, Manners St, Wellington; tel. (021) 688438; fax (021) 471085; e-mail afpnz@clear.net.nz; Correspondent MICHAEL FIELD.

Reuters (UK): POB 11-744, Wellington; tel. (4) 471-4277; e-mail wellington.newsroom@reuters.com; Correspondent RODNEY JOYCE.

United Press International (UPI) (USA): Press Gallery, Parliament Bldgs, Wellington; tel. (4) 471-9552; fax (4) 472-7604; Correspondent BRENDON BURNS.

Xinhua (New China) New Agency (People's Republic of China): 136 Northland Rd, Northland, Wellington; tel. (4) 475-7607; fax (4) 475-7607; e-mail xinhua@ihug.co.nz; Correspondent ZHOU CIPU.

PRESS COUNCIL

New Zealand Press Council: POB 10879, The Terrace, Wellington; tel. (4) 473-5220; fax (4) 471-1785; e-mail presscouncil@asa.co.nz; internet www.presscouncil.org.nz; f. 1972; Chair. Sir JOHN JEFFRIES; Sec. M. E. MAJOR.

PRESS ASSOCIATIONS

Commonwealth Press Union (New Zealand Section): POB 1066, Wellington; tel. (4) 472-6223; fax (4) 471-0987; Chair. G. ELLIS; Sec. L. GOULD.

Newspaper Publishers' Association of New Zealand (Inc): Newspaper House, POB 1066, 93 Boulcott St, Wellington 1; tel. (4) 472-6223; fax (4) 471-0987; e-mail npa@npa.co.nz; f. 1898; 31 mems; Pres. J. SANDERS; CEO L. GOULD; Corporate Affairs Man. H. SOUTER.

Publishers

Auckland University Press: Private Bag 92–019, University of Auckland, Auckland; tel. (9) 373-7528; fax (9) 373-7465; e-mail aup@auckland.ac.nz; internet www.auckland.ac.nz/aup; f. 1966; scholarly; Dir ELIZABETH P. CAFFIN.

Lexis-Nexis NZ Ltd: 205–207 Victoria St, POB 472, Wellington; tel. (4) 385-1479; fax (4) 385-1598; e-mail Customer.Relations@lexisnexis.co.nz; internet www.lexisnexis.co.nz; legal; Man. Dir R. W. GRAY.

Christchurch Caxton Press Ltd: 113 Victoria St, POB 25-088, Christchurch 1; tel. (3) 366-8516; fax (3) 365-7840; f. 1935; human and general interest, gardening, craft, local and NZ history, tourist publs; Man. Dir BRUCE BASCAND.

Dunmore Press Ltd: POB 5115, Palmerston North; tel. (6) 358-7169; fax (6) 357-9242; e-mail dunmore@xtra.co.nz; internet www.dunmore.co.nz; f. 1975; non-fiction, educational; Publrs MURRAY GATENBY, SHARMIAN FIRTH.

HarperCollins Publishers (New Zealand) Ltd: 31 View Rd, Glenfield, Auckland; tel. (9) 443-9400; fax (9) 443-9403; f. 1888; general and educational; Man. Dir BARRIE HITCHON.

Hodder Moa Beckett Publishers Ltd: POB 100–749, North Shore Mail Centre, Auckland 1330; tel. (9) 478-1000; fax (9) 478-1010; e-mail admin@hoddermoa.co.nz; f. 1971; Man. Dir KEVIN CHAPMAN.

Learning Media Ltd: POB 3293, Wellington; tel. (4) 472-5522; fax (4) 472-6444; e-mail info@learningmedia.co.nz; internet www.learningmedia.com; f. 1947 as School Publications; became Crown-owned company in 1993; general and educational books, audio cassettes, videos and computer software in English, Spanish, Maori, etc. International Man. TRISH STEVENSON.

Legislation Direct: Bowen State Bldg, Bowen St, POB 12-418, Wellington; tel. (4) 496-5655; fax (4) 496-5698; e-mail idenquiries@legislationdirect.co.nz; internet www.gplegislation.co.nz; general publishers and leading distributor of government publs; fmrly Govt Printing Office/GP Publications; Man. DOUGAL CABLE.

McGraw-Hill Book Co, New Zealand Ltd: 2nd Floor, Westfield Tower, Westfield Shopping Town, Manukau City, POB 97082, Wiri; tel. (9) 262-2537; fax (9) 262-2540; e-mail cservice_auckland@mcgraw-hill.com; f. 1974; educational; Man. FIRGAL ADAMS.

New Zealand Council for Educational Research: POB 3237, Wellington; tel. (4) 384-7939; fax (4) 384-7933; e-mail sales@nzcer.org.nz; internet www.nzcer.org.nz; f. 1934; scholarly, research monographs, educational, academic, periodicals; Chair. Prof. RUTH MANSELL; Dir ROBYN BAKER.

Pearson Education New Zealand Ltd: Private Bag 102908, North Shore Mail Centre, Glenfield, Auckland 10; tel. (9) 444-4968; fax (9) 444-4957; e-mail rosemary.stagg@pearsoned.co.nz; f. 1968; fmrly Addison Wesley Longman; educational; Dirs ROSEMARY STAGG, A. HARKINS, P. FIELD, E. IMPEY.

Penguin Books (NZ) Ltd: Cnr Airborne and Rosedale Rds, Albany, Private Bag 102902, North Shore Mail Centre, Auckland; tel. (9) 415-4700; fax (9) 415-4701; e-mail geoff.walker@penguin.co.nz; internet www.penguin.co.nz; f. 1973; Publ. Dir GEOFF WALKER; Man. Dir TONY HARKINS.

Wendy Pye Ltd: Private Bag 17-905, Greenlane, Auckland; tel. (9) 525-3575; fax (9) 525-4205; e-mail admin@sunshine.co.nz; children's fiction and educational; Man. Dir WENDY PYE.

Random House New Zealand Ltd: Private Bag 102950, North Shore Mail Centre, Glenfield, Auckland; tel. (9) 444-7197; fax (9)

444-7524; e-mail admin@randomhouse.co.nz; internet www .randomhouse.co.nz; f. 1977; general; Man. Dir MICHAEL MOYNAHAN.

Reed Publishing (NZ) Ltd: Private Bag 34–901, Birkenhead, Auckland 10; tel. (9) 441 2960; fax (9) 480-4999; e-mail info@reed.co .nz; internet www.reed.co.nz; children's and general non-fiction; Heinemann Education primary, secondary tertiary and library; Man. Dir ALAN L. SMITH.

University of Otago Press: POB 56, Dunedin; tel. (3) 479-8807; fax (3) 479-8385; e-mail university.press@otago.ac.nz; f. 1958; academic, trade publs; Man. Editor WENDY HARREX.

Whitcoulls Ltd: 3rd Floor, 210 Queen St, Private Bag 92–098, Auckland 1; tel. (9) 356-5410; fax (9) 356-5423; NZ, general and educational; Gen. Man. S. PRESTON.

PUBLISHERS' ASSOCIATION

Book Publishers' Association of New Zealand Inc: POB 36477, Northcote, Auckland 1309; tel. (9) 480-2711; fax (9) 480-1130; e-mail bpanz@copyright.co.nz; internet www.bpanz.org.nz; f. 1977; Pres. KEVIN CHAPMAN.

Broadcasting and Communications

TELECOMMUNICATIONS

Asia Pacific Telecom (NZ) Ltd: POB 331214, Takapuna, Auckland.

Clear Communications: Clear Centre, Cnr Northcote and Taharoto Rds, Takapuna, Private Bag 92-143, Auckland; tel. (9) 912-4200; fax (9) 912-4442; e-mail webmaster@clear.co.nz; internet www .clear.co.nz; f. 1990; business solutions, local and toll services, enhanced internet, etc. owned by British Telecommunications; CEO PETER KALIAROPOLOUS.

Compass Communications Ltd: POB 2533, Auckland.

Global One Communications Ltd: Level 15, Phillips Fox Tower, 209 Queen St, Auckland; tel. (9) 357-3700; fax (9) 357-3737.

NewCall Communications Ltd: Box 8703, Symonds St, Auckland; Man. Dir NORMAN NICHOLLS.

Singtel Optus Ltd: Level 14, ASB Centre, 135 Albert St, Auckland; tel. (9) 356–2660; fax (9) 356–2669.

Telecom Corpn of New Zealand Ltd: Telecom Networks House, 68 Jervois Quay, POB 570, Wellington; tel. (4) 801-9000; fax (4) 385-3469; internet www.telecom.co.nz; Chair. RODERICK DEANE; Chief Exec. THERESA GATTUNG.

Telecom Mobile Telecommunications: Midcity Tower, 141 Willis St, Wellington 6001; tel. (4) 801-9000; internet www.telecom .co.na; f. 1987; Gen. Man. LORRAINE WITTEN.

Telstra Saturn Ltd: Telstra Business Centre, Level 9, 191 Queen St, Auckland; tel. (9) 980-8800; fax (9) 980-8801; e-mail enquiries@ telstra.co.nz; internet www.telstra.co.nz; f. 2000 through merger of Telstra New Zealand and Saturn Communications.

Vodafone New Zealand Ltd: 21 Pitt St, Private Bag 92-161, Auckland; tel. (9) 357-5100; fax (9) 357-4836; internet www.vodafone .co.nz; fmrly Bell South; cellular network; CEO LARRY CARTER; Man. Dir GRAHAME MAHER.

WorldxChange Communications Ltd: 55 Shortland St, POB 3296, Auckland; tel. (9) 308-1300.

Regulatory Authority

Telecommunications Policy Section, Ministry of Economic Development: 33 Bowen St, POB 1473, Wellington; tel. (4) 472-0030; fax (4) 473-7010; e-mail info@med.govt.nz; internet www.med .govt.nz/pbt/telecom.html.

BROADCASTING

In December 1995 Radio New Zealand Commercial (RNZC) and New Zealand Public Radio Ltd (NZPR) became independent entities, having assumed responsibility for, respectively, the commercial and non-commercial activities of Radio New Zealand. RNZC was sold to the New Zealand Radio Network Consortium in 1996, and NZPR, which remained a Crown-owned company, assumed the name of its now-defunct parent company, to become Radio New Zealand Ltd. In late 1999 there were 190 radio stations broadcasting on a continuous basis, of which 170 were operating on a commercial basis.

Radio

Radio Broadcasters' Association (NZ) Inc: POB 3762, Auckland; tel. (9) 378-0788; fax (9) 378-8180; e-mail rba@xtra.co.nz;

represents commercial radio industry; Exec. Dir D. N. G. INNES; Sec. JANINE BLISS; 142 mems.

Radio New Zealand Ltd: RNZ House, 155 The Terrace, POB 123, Wellington; tel. (4) 474-1999; fax (4) 474-1459; e-mail rnz@radionz .co.nz; internet www.radionz.co.nz; f. 1936; Crown-owned entity, operating non-commercial national networks: National Radio and Concert FM; parliamentary broadcasts on AM Network; Radio New Zealand News and Current Affairs; the short-wave service, Radio New Zealand International; and archives; Chief Exec. SHARON CROSBIE.

The Radio Network of New Zealand Ltd: 54 Cook St, Private Bag 92–198, Auckland; tel. (9) 373-0000; e-mail enquiry@ radionetwork.co.nz; operates 87 commercial stations, reaching 1.3m. people; Chief Exec. JOHN McELHINNEY.

Television

Television New Zealand (TVNZ) Ltd: Television Centre, Cnr Hobson and Victoria Sts, POB 3819, Auckland; tel. (9) 916-7000; fax (9) 379-4907; internet www.tvnz.co.nz; f. 1960; the television service is responsible for the production of programmes for two TV networks, TV One and 2; networks are commercial all week and transmit in colour; both channels broadcast 24 hours a day, seven days a week, and reach 99.9% of the population; Chair. Dr ROSS ARMSTRONG; CEO RICK ELLIS; Gen. Man. ALAN BROOKBANKS.

Private Television

Auckland Independent Television Services Ltd: POB 1629, Auckland.

Bay Satellite TV Ltd: Hastings; tel. (6) 878-9081; fax (6) 878-5994; Man. Dir JOHN LYNAM.

Broadcast Communications Ltd: POB 2495, Auckland; tel. (9) 916-6400; fax (9) 916-6404; Man. Dir GEOFF LAWSON.

Sky Network Television Limited: 10 Panorama Rd, POB 9059, Newmarket, Auckland; tel. (9) 579-9999; fax (9) 579-0910; internet www.skytv.co.nz; f. 1990; UHF service on six channels, satellite service on 18 channels; Chief Exec. NATE SMITH.

TV3 Network Services Ltd: Private Bag 92–624, Symonds St, Auckland; tel. (9) 377-9730; fax (9) 366-5999; internet www.tv3.co .nz; f. 1989; owned by CanWest Global Corpn; Man. Dir RICK FRIESEN.

TV4 Network Ltd: Private Bag 92–624, Symonds St, Auckland; tel. (9) 377-9730; fax (9) 366-5999; e-mail di.winks@tv3.co.nz; internet www.tv4.co.nz; 'free-to-air' entertainment channel; Man. Dir RICK FRIESEN.

Finance

(cap. = capital; res = reserves; dep. = deposits; m. = million; amounts in New Zealand dollars)

BANKING

Central Bank

Reserve Bank of New Zealand: 2 The Terrace, POB 2498, Wellington; tel. (4) 472-2029; fax (4) 473-8554; e-mail rbnz-info@rbnz .govt.nz; internet www.rbnz.govt.nz; f. 1934; res 400.1m., dep. 7,123.3m. (June 2000); Gov. ALAN BOLLARD; Dep. Govs Dr M. A. SHERWIN, Dr R. M. CARR.

Registered Banks

As a result of legislation which took effect in April 1987, several foreign banks were incorporated into the domestic banking system.

ANZ Banking Group (New Zealand) Ltd: Private Bag 92-210 AMSC, Auckland; tel. (9) 374-4040; fax (9) 374-4038; internet www .nz.anz.com; f. 1979; subsidiary of Australia and New Zealand Banking Group Ltd of Melbourne, Australia; cap. 406.5m., res. 0.45m., dep. 23047.3m. (Sept 2000); Chair. R. S. DEANE; Man. Dir Dr M. J. HORN; 150 brs and sub-brs.

ASB Bank Ltd: ASB Bank Centre, Cnr Wellesley and Albert Sts, POB 35, Auckland 1; tel. (9) 377-8930; fax (9) 358-3511; e-mail helpdesk@asbbank.co.nz; internet www.asbbank.co.nz; f. 1847 as Auckland Savings Bank, name changed 1988; cap. 373.1m., res 473.8m., dep. 16,187.0m. (June 2000); Chair. G. J. JUDD; Man. Dir R. J. NORRIS; 118 brs.

Bank of New Zealand (BNZ): BNZ Centre, 1 Willis St, POB 2392, Wellington; tel. (4) 474-6999; fax (4) 474-6861; internet www.bnz.co .nz; f. 1861; owned by National Australia Bank; cap. 1,511m., dep. 29,801m. (Sept. 2000); Chair. T. K. McDONALD; Man. Dir P THODEY; 241 brs and sub-brs.

Citibank NA (USA): POB 3429, 23 Customs Street East, Auckland; tel. (9) 307-1902; fax (9) 307-1983; internet www.citibank.com; CEO ANDREW AU; 2 brs.

Deutsche Bank AG: POB 6900, Wellesley St, Auckland; tel. (9) 351-1000; fax (9) 351-1001; internet www.deutsche-bank.co.nz; f. 1986; fmrly Bankers Trust New Zealand; Chief Country Officer BRETT SHEPHERD.

Hongkong and Shanghai Banking Corporation Ltd (Hong Kong): POB 5947, Level 9, 1 Queen St, Auckland; tel. (9) 308-8888; fax (9) 308-8997; e-mail hsbcplb@clear.net.nz; internet www .asiapacific.hsbc.com; CEO S. EDWARDS; 6 brs.

Kiwibank Ltd: Private Bag 39990, Wellington; tel. (4) 4627900; fax (4) 4627996; internet www.kiwibank.co.nz; f. 2001; 100% New Zealand-owned; savings bank for small depositors; Chair. JIM BOLGER; Chief Exec. SAM KNOWLES.

National Bank of New Zealand Ltd: 1 Victoria St, POB 1791, Wellington 6000; tel. (4) 494-4000; fax (4) 494-4023; internet www .nationalbank.co.nz; f. 1873; merged with Countrywide Banking Corpn in 1999; cap. 472m., res 1,066m., dep. 28,881m. (Dec. 1999); Chair. Sir WILSON WHINERAY; Dir and CEO Sir JOHN ANDERSON; 164 brs.

Rabobank (New Zealand): POB 1069, Auckland; tel. (9) 375-3700; fax (9) 375-3710; f. 1996; full subsidiary of Rabobank Nederland.

TSB Bank Ltd: POB 240, New Plymouth; tel. (6) 757-9270; fax (6) 759-2768; f. 1850; dep. 1,400m. (March 2001); Man. Dir K. W. RIMMINGTON; 15 brs.

Westland Bank Ltd: 99 Revell St, POB 103, Hokitika; tel. (3) 755-8680; fax (3) 755-8277; full subsidiary of ASB Bank Ltd; cap. and res 6,176m., dep. 108m. (June 1992); Man. Dir K. J. BEAMS; 9 brs.

WestpacTrust: 318 Lambton Quay, POB 691, Wellington; tel. (4) 498-1000; fax (4) 498-1350; acquired Trust Bank New Zealand; New Zealand division of Westpac Banking Corpn (Australia); Chief Exec. D. T. GALLAGHER.

Other Banks

Postbank: 58–66 Willis St, Wellington 1; tel. (4) 729-809; f. 1987; owned by Australia and New Zealand Banking Corpn; 550 brs.

Association

New Zealand Bankers' Association: POB 3043, Wellington; tel. (4) 472-8838; fax (4) 473-1698; e-mail acopland@nzba.org.nz; f. 1891; CEO ERROL LIZAMORE.

STOCK EXCHANGES

Dunedin Stock Exchange: POB 298, Dunedin; tel. (3) 477-5900; Chair. E. S. EDGAR; Sec. R. P. LEWIS.

New Zealand Stock Exchange: ASB Tower, Level 9, 2 Hunter St, POB 2959, Wellington 1; tel. (4) 472-7599; fax (4) 473-1470; e-mail nzse@nzse.co.nz; internet www.nzse.co.nz; Chair. SIMON ALLEN; Man. Dir M. WELDON.

Supervisory Body

New Zealand Securities Commission: POB 1179, Wellington; tel. (4) 472-9830; fax (4) 472-8076; e-mail seccom@sec-com.govt.nz; internet www.sec-com.govt.nz; f. 1979; Chair. JANE DIPLOCK.

INSURANCE

ACE Insurance NZ Ltd: POB 734, Auckland; tel. (9) 377-1459; fax (9) 303-1909; e-mail grant.simpson@ace-ina.com; Gen. Man. GRANT SIMPSON.

AMI Insurance Ltd: 29–35 Latimer Sq., POB 2116, Christchurch; tel. (3) 371-9000; fax (3) 371-8314; e-mail amichch@es.co.nz; f. 1926; Chair. K. G. L. NOLAN; CEO JOHN B. BALMFORTH.

AMP General Insurance Ltd: 86/90 Customhouse Quay, POB 1093, Wellington; tel. (4) 498-8000; fax (4) 471-2312; f. 1958; fire, accident, marine, general; Chair. J. W. UTZ; Mans (NZ) L. ROSS, R. CUFF.

AMP General Insurance (NZ) Ltd: 86/90 Customhouse Quay, POB 1093, Wellington; tel. (4) 498-8000; fax (4) 471-2312; f. 1958; fire, accident, marine, general; Chair. GRAEME W. VALENTINE; Man. K. SHAW.

ANZ Life Assurance Co Ltd: POB 1492, Wellington; tel. (4) 496-7000; fax (4) 470-5100; Man. R. A. DEAN.

BNZ Life Insurance Ltd: POB 1299, Wellington; tel. (4) 382-2577; fax (4) 474-6883; e-mail rodger-murphy@bnz.co.nz; Gen. Man. R. J. MURPHY.

Colonial Life (NZ) Ltd: 117 Customhouse Quay, POB 191, Wellington 6000; tel. (4) 470-4700; fax (4) 470-4701; e-mail servicecentre@colonialfs.co.nz; life, accident, investment, sickness

and disability, staff superannuation; expected to adopt the name Sovereign during 2001, following its merger with Sovereign group; Man. Dir DAVID MAY.

Commercial Union General Insurance Co Ltd: 142 Featherston St, POB 2797, Wellington; tel. (4) 473-9177; fax (4) 473-7424; fire, accident, travel, engineering; Gen. Man. T. WAKEFIELD.

Farmers' Mutual Group: 68 The Square, POB 1943, Palmerston North 5330; tel. (6) 356-9456; fax (6) 356-4603; e-mail enquiries@ fimg.co.nz; internet fmg.co.nz; comprises Farmers' Mutual Insurance Asscn, Farmers' Mutual Insurance Ltd and other cos; fire, accident, motor vehicle, marine, life; CEO G. SMITH.

Gerling NCM EXGO: POB 3933, Wellington 6015; tel. (4) 472-4142; fax (4) 472-6966; e-mail info@gerlingEXGO.co.nz; internet www.gerlingEXGO.co.nz; trade credit insurance services; division of Gerling NZ Ltd since December 2001; Gen. Man. ARTHUR C. DAVIS.

Metropolitan Life Assurance Co of NZ Ltd: Sovereign Assurance House, 33–45 Hurstmere Rd, Takapuna, Auckland 1; tel. (9) 486-9500; fax (9) 486-9501; f. 1962; life; Man. Dir PETER W. FITZSIMMONS.

New Zealand Insurance: NZI House, 151 Queen St, Private Bag 92130, Auckland 1; tel. (9) 309-7000; fax (9) 309-7097; internet www .nzi.co.nz; Chief Exec. M. HANNAN.

The New Zealand Local Government Insurance Corporation Ltd (Civic Assurance): Local Government Bldg, 114–118 Lambton Quay, POB 5521, Wellington; tel. (4) 470-0037; fax (4) 471-1522; e-mail rod.mead@civicassurance.co.nz; internet www .civicassurance.co.nz; f. 1960; fire, motor, all risks, accident; Chair. K. N. SAMPSON; Gen. Man. R. D. MEAD.

QBE Insurance (International) Ltd: POB 44, Auckland; tel. (9) 366-9920; fax (9) 366-9930; e-mail gevans@qbe.co.nz; f. 1890; Gen. Man. GRAEME EVANS.

State Insurance Ltd: Microsoft House, 3–11 Hunter St, POB 5037, Wellington 1; tel. (4) 496-9600; fax (4) 476-9664; internet www.state .co.nz; f. 1905; mem. NRMA Insurance Group; Man. Dir T. C. SOLE.

Tower Insurance Ltd: 67–73 Hurstmere Rd, POB 33-144, Takapuna; tel. (9) 486-9340; fax (9) 486-9368; f. 1873; fmrly National Insurance Co of New Zealand; Chair. Sir C. J. MAIDEN; Man. Dir P. R. HUNT.

Associations

Insurance Council of New Zealand: POB 474, Wellington; tel. (4) 472-5230; fax (4) 473-3011; e-mail icnz@icnz.org.nz; internet www .icnz.org.nz; CEO CHRISTOPHER RYAN.

Investment Savings and Insurance Association of New Zealand Inc: POB 1514, Wellington; tel. (4) 473-8730; fax (4) 471-1881; e-mail isi@isi.org.nz; f. 1996; from Life Office Asscn and Investment Funds Asscn; represents cos that act as manager, trustee, issuer, insurer, etc. of managed funds, life insurance and superannuation; Chief Exec. VANCE ARKINSTALL; Exec. Officer DEBORAH KEATING.

Trade and Industry

GOVERNMENT AGENCY

New Zealand Trade and Enterprise: POB 10-341, Wellington; tel. (4) 499-2244; fax (4) 473-3193; internet www.tradenz.govt.nz; f. 2003 to combine the functions of Trade New Zealand and Industry New Zealand; CEO TIM GIBSON; Chair. PHIL LOUGH.

CHAMBERS OF COMMERCE

Auckland Regional Chamber of Commerce and Industry: POB 47, Auckland; tel. (9) 309-6100; fax (9) 309-0081; e-mail mbarnett@chamber.co.nz; internet www.chamber.co.nz; CEO MICHAEL BARNETT; Pres. DAVID TRUSCOTT.

Canterbury Employers' Chamber of Commerce: 57 Kilmore St, POB 359, Christchurch; tel. (3) 366-5096; fax (3) 379-5454; e-mail info@cecc.org.nz; internet www.cecc.org.nz; CEO PETER TOWNSEND.

Otago Chamber of Commerce and Industry Inc: Level 7, Westpac Trust Bldg, 106 George St, POB 5713, Dunedin; tel. (3) 479-0181; fax (3) 477-0341; e-mail office@otagochamber.co.nz; f. 1861; CEO J. A. CHRISTIE; Pres. BEVAN RICKERBY.

Wellington Regional Chamber of Commerce: 9th Floor, 109 Featherston St, POB 1590, Wellington; tel. (4) 914-6500; fax (4) 914-6524; e-mail info@wgtn-chamber.co.nz; internet www .wgtn-chamber.co.nz; f. 1856; Chief Exec. PHILIP LEWIN; Pres. PETER STEEL; 1,000 mems.

INDUSTRIAL AND TRADE ASSOCIATIONS

Canterbury Manufacturers' Association: POB 13-152, Armagh, Christchurch; tel. (3) 353-2540; fax (3) 353-2549; e-mail cma@cma .org.nz; internet www.cma.org.nz; f. 1879; CEO JOHN WALLEY; 500 mems.

Employers' and Manufacturers' Association (Central Inc): Federation House, 95–99 Molesworth St, POB 1087, Wellington; tel. (4) 473-7224; fax (4) 473-4501; e-mail ema@emacentral.org.nz; f. 1997 by merger of Wellington Manufacturers' Asscn and Wellington Regional Employers' Asscn; Pres. R. KERR-NEWELL; 2,200 mems.

Employers' and Manufacturers' Association (Northern Inc): 159 Khyber Pass Rd, Grafton, Private Bag 92066, Auckland; tel. (9) 367-0900; fax (9) 367-0902; e-mail ema@ema.co.nz; internet www .ema.co.nz; f. 1886; fmrly Auckland Manufacturers' Asscn; Pres. T. ARNOLD; 4,500 mems.

ENZAFRUIT: POB 279, Hastings; tel. (6) 878-1898; fax (6) 878-1850; e-mail info@enza.co.nz; fmrly New Zealand Apple and Pear Marketing Board; Man. Dir MICHAEL DOSSOR; Chair. B BIRNIE.

Federated Farmers of New Zealand (Inc): 6th Floor, Agriculture House, 12 Johnston St, Wellington 1; POB 715, Wellington; tel. (4) 473-7269; fax (4) 473-1081; e-mail wellingtonoffice@fedfarm.org.nz; internet www.fedfarm.org.nz; f. 1946; Pres. ALISTAIR POLSON; CEO TONY ST CLAIR; 16,000 mems.

Kiwifruit New Zealand: POB 4246, Mt Maunganui South; tel. (7) 574-7139; fax (7) 574-7149; Chair. PETER TRAPSKI.

National Beekeepers' Association of New Zealand (Inc): Agriculture House, 12 Johnston St, POB 715, Wellington 6015; tel. (4) 473-7269; fax (4) 473-1081; e-mail tleslie@fedfarm.org.nz; internet www.nba.org.nz; f. 1913; 1,500 mems; Pres. DON BELL; Sec. TIM LESLIE.

New Zealand Animal By-Products Exporters' Association: POB 12-222, 11 Longhurst Terrace, Christchurch; tel. (3) 332-2895; fax (3) 332-2825; 25 mems; Sec. J. L. NAYSMITH.

New Zealand Berryfruit Growers' Federation (Inc): POB 10-050, Wellington; tel. (4) 473-5387; fax (4) 473-6999; e-mail berryfed@ xtra.co.nz; 530 mems; Pres. JOHN GARELJA; Executive Officer PETER ENSOR.

New Zealand Council of Wool Exporters Inc: POB 2857, Christchurch; tel. (3) 353-1049; fax (3) 374-6925; e-mail cwe@xtra.co.nz; internet www.woolexport.net; f. 1893; Exec. Man. R. H. F. NICHOLSON; Pres. C. HALL.

The New Zealand Forest Industries Council: POB 2727, Wellington; tel. (4) 473-9220; fax (4) 473-9330; e-mail griffithsj@nzfic.org .nz; internet www.nzfic.nzforestry.co.nz; CEO JAMES GRIFFITHS.

The New Zealand Forest Owners' Association: POB 1208, Wellington; tel. (4) 473-4769; fax (4) 499-8893; e-mail robmcl@nzfoa .org.nz; internet www.nzfoa.nzforestryco.nz; CEO ROB MCCLAGAN.

New Zealand Fruitgrowers' Federation: Huddart Parker Bldg, POB 2175, Wellington, 6015; tel. (4) 472-6559; fax (4) 472-6409; e-mail hans@fruitgrowers.org.nz; internet www.fruitgrowers.org .nz; f. 1928; 5,000 mems; CEO P. R. SILCOCK.

New Zealand Fruit Wine & Cider Makers: 81 Branch Rd, New Plymouth, Taranaki; tel. and fax (6) 758-6910; e-mail admin@ fruitwines.co.nz; internet www.fruitwines.co.nz; 30 mems; Chair. BRIAN SHANKS; Exec. Officer CHRIS GARNHAM.

New Zealand Meat Board: Wool House, 10 Brandon St, POB 121, Wellington; tel. (4) 473-9150; fax (4) 474-0800; e-mail help@meatnz .co.nz; internet www.meatnz.co.nz; f. 1922; Chair. JEFF GRANT; Sec. A. DOMETAKIS; 13 mems.

New Zealand Pork Industry Board: POB 4048, Wellington; tel. (4) 385-4229; fax (4) 385-8522; e-mail info@pork.co.nz; internet www .pork.co.nz; f. 1937; Chair. C. TRENGROVE; CEO A DAVIDSON.

New Zealand Seafood Industry Council: Private Bag 24-901, Wellington; tel. (4) 385-4005; fax (4) 384-2727; e-mail info@seafood .co.nz; internet www.seafood.co.nz; CEO JOHN VALENTINE; Chair. DAVID SHARP.

New Zealand Timber Industry Federation: 2–8 Maginnity St, POB 308, Wellington; tel. (4) 473-5200; fax (4) 473-6536; e-mail enquiries@nztif.co.nz; 350 mems; Exec. Dir W. S. COFFEY.

New Zealand Vegetable and Potato Growers' Federation (Inc): POB 10232, Wellington 1; tel. (4) 472-3795; fax (4) 471-2861; e-mail information@vegfed.co.nz; internet www.vegfed.co.nz; 4,000 mems; Pres. B. GARGIULO; CEO P. R. SILCOCK.

New Zealand Wool Board: 10 Brandon St, Box 3225, Wellington; tel. (4) 472-6888; fax (4) 473-7872; e-mail info@woolboard.co.nz; internet www.woolboard.co.nz; assists research, development, production and marketing of NZ wool; Chair. B. C. MUNRO; CEO MARK O'GRADY.

NZMP: 25 The Terrace, POB 417, Wellington; tel. (4) 462-8096; fax (4) 471-8600; internet www.nzmp.com; f. 2001; through merger of New Zealand Dairy Board and Fonterra Co-operative.

Registered Master Builders' Federation (Inc): Level 6, 234 Wakefield St, POB 1796, Wellington; tel. (4) 385-8999; fax (4) 385-8995; internet www.masterbuilder.org.nz; Chief Exec. C. PRESTON.

Retail Merchants' Association of New Zealand (Inc): 8th Floor, Willbank House, 57 Willis St, Wellington; tel. (4) 472-3733; fax (4) 472-1071; e-mail bhellberg@retail.org.nz; f. 1920 as the NZ Retailers' Fed. (Inc); present name adopted in 1987, following merger with the NZ Wholesale Hardware Fed. direct membership 4,600; Pres. TERENCE DELANEY; CEO JOHN ALBERTSON.

EMPLOYERS' ORGANIZATION

Business New Zealand: Level 6, Microsoft House, 3–11 Hunter St, Wellington; tel. (4) 496-6555; fax (4) 496-6550; e-mail admin@ businessnz.org.nz; internet www.businessnz.org.nz; Chief Exec. SIMON CARLAW.

UTILITIES

Energy Efficiency and Conservation Authority (EECA): Level 1, Simpson Grierson Bldg, 44 The Terrace, Wellington; tel. (4) 470-2200; fax (4) 499-5330; e-mail eecainfo@eeca.govt.nz; internet www .eeca.govt.nz.

Electricity

Bay of Plenty Electricity Ltd: 52 Commerce St, POB 404, Whakatane; tel. (7) 307-2700; fax (7) 307-0922; f. 1995; generation of electricity, operation of distribution network; Chair. C. G. HOLMES; CEO ROB BALDEY.

Contact Energy Ltd: Level 1, Harbour City Tower, 29 Brandon St, Wellington; tel. (4) 449-4001; fax (4) 499-4003; internet www .contactenergy.co.nz; generation of electricity, wholesale and retail of energy; transferred to the private sector in 1999; Chair. PHIL PRYKE.

The Marketplace Co Ltd (M-CO): Level 2, Wool House, 10 Brandon St, POB 5422, Wellington; tel. (4) 473-5240; fax (4) 473-5247; e-mail info@m-co.co.nz; internet www.m-co.co.nz; administers wholesale electricity market; Chief Exec. CHRIS RUSSELL.

Powerco: New Plymouth; operates power networks in Wairarapa, Manawatu, Wanganui and Taranaki; Chair. BARRY UPSON.

TransAlta New Zealand Ltd: 10 Hutt Rd, Petone, Wellington; tel. (4) 576-8700; fax (4) 576-8600; e-mail transalta@transalta.co.nz; internet www.transalta.co.nz; f. 1993; retailer of electricity and gas; Chair. R. H. ARBUCKLE; Chief Exec. MURRAY NELSON.

Transpower New Zealand Ltd: Unisys House, 56 The Terrace, POB 1021, Wellington; tel. (4) 495-7000; fax (4) 495-7100; internet www.transpower.co.nz; manages national grid; Chair. Sir COLIN MAIDEN; Chief Exec. BOB THOMSON.

TrustPower Ltd: Private Bag 12–023, Tauranga, Auckland; tel. (7) 574-4800; fax (7) 574-4825; e-mail trustpower@trustpower.co.nz; internet www.trustpower.co.nz; f. 1920 as Tauranga Electric Power Board; independent generator; Chair. HAROLD TITTER.

Vector Ltd: POB 99–882, Newmarket, Auckland; tel. (9) 978-7788; fax (9) 978-7799; internet www.vector-network.co.nz; fmrly Mercury Energy Ltd; Chair. WAYNE BROWN; CEO Dr PATRICK STRANGE.

Wairarapa Electricity Ltd: 316–330 Queen St, Masterton, Auckland; tel. (6) 377-3773; fax (6) 378-2347; f. 1993; owned by South Eastern Utilities Ltd; distribution of electric power; Chair. JOHN MATHESON; CEO A. LODGE.

Gas

Natural Gas Corpn: Natural Gas Corpn House, 22 The Terrace, POB 1818, Lambton, Wellington; tel. (4) 499-0136; fax (4) 499-0993; f. 1992; purchase, processing and transport of natural gas; wholesale and retail sales; Chair. LEONARD BLEASEL; CEO RICHARD BENTLEY.

Nova Gas Ltd: POB 10-141, Wellington; tel. (4) 472-6263; fax (4) 472-6264; e-mail hansv@novagas.co.nz; internet www.novagas.co .nz.

Water

Waste Management NZ Ltd: 86 Lunn Ave, Mt Wellington, Auckland; tel. (9) 527-8044; fax (9) 570-5595; f. 1985; water and waste water services; Chair. J. A. JAMIESON; Man. Dir K. R. ELLIS.

TRADE UNIONS

In December 1998 a total of 83 unions were in operation; 306,687 workers belonged to a union.

The New Zealand Council of Trade Unions: Education House, West Block, 178–182 Willis St, POB 6645, Wellington 1; tel. (4) 385-1334; fax (4) 385-6051; e-mail ctu@nzctu.org.nz; internet www.union.org.nz; f. 1937; present name since 1987; affiliated to ICFTU; 25 affiliated unions with 250,000 mems; Pres. ROSS WILSON; Sec. PAUL GOULTER.

Principal Affiliated Unions

Association of Staff in Tertiary Education (ASTE)/Te hau Takitini O Aotearoa: POB 27141, Wellington; tel. (4) 801-5098; fax (4) 385-8826; e-mail national.office@aste.ac.nz; 3,500 mems; Nat. Sec. SHARN RIGGS.

Association of University Staff (AUS): POB 11-767, Wellington; tel. (4) 915-6690; fax (4) 915-6699; e-mail national.office@aus.ac.nz; internet www.aus.ac.nz; 6,000 mems; Gen. Sec HELEN KELLY.

Central Amalgamated Workers Union (AWUNZ): POB 27-291, 307 Willis St, Wellington; tel. (4) 384-4049; fax (4) 801-7306; e-mail centralawunz@xtra.co.nz; Sec. JACKSON SMITH.

FinSec Finance and Information Workers Union: POB 27-355, Wellington; tel. (4) 385-7723; fax (4) 385-2214; e-mail union@finsec.org.nz; internet www.finsec.org.nz/; Pres. ROBYN WOLLER; Sec. DONALD FARR.

Meat and Related Trades Workers Union of Aotearoa: POB 17056, Greenlane, Auckland; tel. (9) 520-0034; fax (9) 523-1286; e-mail meat.union@xtra.co.nz; Sec. GRAHAM COOKE.

New Zealand Dairy Workers Union, Inc: POB 9046, Hamilton; tel. (7) 839-0239; fax (7) 838-0398; e-mail nzdwu@wave.co.nz; internet www.nzdwu.org.nz; f. 1992; 5,900 mems; Sec. RAY POTROZ; Pres. J. SMITH.

New Zealand Educational Institute/Nzei Te Riu Roa: POB 466, Wellington; tel. (4) 384-9689; fax (4) 385-1772; e-mail nzei@nzei.org.nz; internet www.nzei.org.nz; f. 1883; Pres. BRUCE ADIN; Sec. LYNNE BRUCE.

New Zealand Engineering, Printing & Manufacturing Union (EPMU): POB 31-546, Lower Hutt; tel. (4) 568-0086; fax (4) 576-1173; e-mail epmunion@epmunion.org.nz; internet www.epmunion.org.nz; Sec. REX JONES.

New Zealand Meat Workers and Related Trades Union: POB 13-048, Armagh, Christchurch; tel. (3) 366-5105; fax (3) 379-7763; e-mail nzmeatworkersunion@clear.net.nz; 7,629 mems; Pres. D. WILSON; Gen. Sec. R. G. KIRK.

New Zealand Nurses' Organisation: POB 2128, Wellington; tel. (4) 385-0847; fax (4) 382-9993; e-mail nurses@nzno.org.nz; internet www.nzno.org.nz; 32,000 mems; CEO GEOFF ANNALS.

New Zealand Post Primary Teachers' Association: POB 2119, Wellington; tel. (4) 384-9964; fax (4) 382-8763; e-mail gensec@ppta.org.nz; internet www.ppta.org.nz; Pres. JEN McCUTCHEON; Gen. Sec. KEVIN BUNKER.

New Zealand Waterfront Workers Union: POB 27004, Wellington; tel. (4) 385-0792; fax (4) 384-8766; e-mail nzwwu@paradise.net.nz; 1,200 mems; Sec. TREVOR HANSON.

NZ PSA (New Zealand Public Service Association): PSA House, 11 Aurora Terrace, POB 3817, Wellington 1; tel. (4) 917-0333; fax (4) 917-2051; e-mail enquiries@psa.org.nz; internet www.psa.org.nz; 40,000 mems; Pres. IAN BAMBER.

Rail & Maritime Transport Union Inc: POB 1103, Wellington; tel. (4) 499-2066; fax (4) 471-0896; e-mail postmaster@rmtunion.org.nz; internet rmtunion.intra.net.nz; 3,497 mems; Pres. J. KELLY; Sec. W. BUTSON.

Service and Food Workers' Union: Private Bag 68–914, Newton, Auckland; tel. (9) 375-2680; fax (9) 375-2681; e-mail darien@sfwu.org.nz; 19,000 mems; Pres. SUE WETERE; Sec. DARIEN FENTON.

Other Unions

Manufacturing & Construction Workers Union: POB 11-123, Manners St, Wellington; tel. (4) 385-8264; fax (4) 384-8007; e-mail M.C.Union@TradesHall.Org.NZ; Gen. Sec. GRAEME CLARKE.

National Distribution Union (NDU): Private Bag 92-904, 120 Church St, Onehunga, Auckland; tel. (9) 622-8355; fax (9) 622-8353; e-mail ndu@nduunion.org.nz; 18,500 mems; Pres. BILL ANDERSEN; Sec. MIKE JACKSON; **Wood Sector** e-mail jjones@nduunion.org.nz; Pres. DENNIS DAWSON.

New Zealand Building Trades Union: POB 11-356, Manners St, Wellington; tel. (4) 385-1178; fax (4) 385-1177; e-mail nzbtu@tradeshall.org.nz; Pres. P. REIDY; Sec. ASHLEY RUSS.

New Zealand Seafarers' Union: POB 9288, Marion Square, Wellington; tel. (4) 385-9288; fax (4) 384-9288; e-mail admin@seafarers.org.nz; f. 1993; Pres. DAVE MORGAN.

Transport

RAILWAYS

There were 3,904 km of railways in New Zealand in 2000, of which more than 500 km were electrified.

Tranz Rail Ltd: Wellington Station, Private Bag, Wellington 1; tel. (4) 498-3000; fax (4) 498-3259; e-mail info@tranzrail.co.nz; internet www.tranzrail.co.nz; f. 1990; transferred to private ownership in 1993; fmrly New Zealand Rail; 3,904 km of railway; also provides road and ferry services; Man. Dir MICHAEL BEARD.

ROADS

In June 1999 there were a total of 92,075 km of maintained roads in New Zealand, including 10,605 km of state highways and motorways.

Transfund New Zealand: POB 2331, Customhouse Quay, Wellington; tel. (4) 916 4220; fax (4) 916 0028; e-mail reception@transfund.govt.nz; internet www.transfund.gout.nz; f. 1996; Crown agency responsible for purchasing a safe and efficient road system and efficient alternatives; Chair. DAVID STUBBS; Chief Exec. WAYNE DONNELLY.

Transit New Zealand: POB 5084, 20–26 Ballance St, Wellington; tel. (4) 499-6600; fax (4) 496-6666; e-mail deborah.willett@transit.govt.nz; internet www.transit.govt.nz; Crown agency responsible for management and development of the state highway network; Chair. ALAN BICKERS; CEO Dr ROBIN DUNLOP.

SHIPPING

There are 13 main seaports, of which the most important are Auckland, Tauranga, Wellington, Lyttleton (the port of Christchurch) and Port Chalmers (Dunedin). In December 2001 the New Zealand merchant fleet comprised 159 vessels, with a total displacement of 174,942 grt.

Principal Companies

P & O Nedlloyd Ltd: 2–10 Customhouse Quay, POB 1699, Wellington; tel. (4) 462-4000; fax (4) 462-4162; e-mail g.f.quirke@ponl.com; internet www.ponl.com; worldwide shipping services; Man. Dir GARY F. QUIRKE.

Sofrana-Unilines New Zealand Ltd: 101 Customs St, CPOB 3614, Auckland; tel. (9) 377 3279; fax (9) 377 8629; internet www.sofrana.co.nz; Chair DIDIER LEROUX; Man. Dir HANS ASSARSSON.

Other major shipping companies operating services to New Zealand include Blue Star Line (NZ) Ltd and Columbus Line, which link New Zealand with Australia, the Pacific Islands, South-East Asia and the USA.

CIVIL AVIATION

There are international airports at Auckland, Christchurch and Wellington.

Civil Aviation Authority of New Zealand: Aviation House, 1 Market Grove, POB 31441, Lower Hutt; tel. (4) 560-9400; fax (4) 569-2024; e-mail info@caa.govt.nz; internet www.caa.govt.nz; Dir of Civil Aviation JOHN JONES.

Principal Airlines

Air Nelson: Private Bag 32, Nelson 7030; tel. (3) 547-8700; fax (3) 547-8788; e-mail john.hambleton@airnewzealand.co.nz; internet www.airnewzealand.com; f. 1979; owned by Air New Zealand; changed to present name 1986; operates services throughout New Zealand; Gen. Man. JOHN HAMBLETON.

Air New Zealand: Quay Tower, 29 Customs St West, Private Bag 92007, Auckland 1; tel. (9) 366-2400; fax (9) 366-2401; internet www.airnz.co.nz; f. 1978 by merger; privatized in 1989, in process of return to state sector in late 2001; services to Australia, the Pacific Islands, Asia, Europe and North America, as well as regular daily services to 26 cities and towns in New Zealand; Chair. JOHN PALMER; Man. Dir and CEO RALPH NORRIS.

Tourism

New Zealand's principal tourist attractions are its high mountains, lakes, forests, volcanoes, hot springs and beaches. In 2001/02 New Zealand received 1,954,831 visitors. Receipts from tourism totalled almost $NZ5,544m. in 2001/02.

Tourism New Zealand: POB 95, Wellington; tel. (4) 917-5400; fax (4) 915-3817; e-mail reception@nztb.govt.nz; internet www.purenz.com; f. 1901; responsible for marketing of New Zealand as a tourism destination; offices in Auckland, Wellington and Christchurch; 13 offices overseas; Chair. WALLY STONE; Chief Exec. GEORGE HICKTON.

NEW ZEALAND'S DEPENDENT AND ASSOCIATED TERRITORIES

New Zealand's Associated Territories are the Dependent Territories of Tokelau and the Ross Dependency and the self-governing Cook Islands and Niue.

ROSS DEPENDENCY

The Ross Dependency comprises the sector of Antarctica between 160°E and 150°W (moving eastward) and the islands lying between those degrees of longitude and south of latitude 60°S. It has been administered by New Zealand since 1923 and has a total area of 750,310 sq km (289,700 sq miles), comprising a land area of 413,540 sq km and an ice shelf of 336,770 sq km. The Territory rises to a height of 3,794 m above sea-level at the peak of the volcano, Mount Erebus.

Scott Base was established in 1957 on Ross Island, and in the following year the Ross Dependency Research Committee was formed to supervise New Zealand activity on the Territory. In 1968 a new scientific station was set up at Lake Vanda, about 130 km (80 miles) west of Scott Base. In 1986 traces of petroleum were discovered in the Territory, more than 600 m below the sea-bed. The Ross Dependency Research Committee was disbanded in 1995. Legislation approved in the mid-1990s consolidated measures aimed at conserving the region's flora and fauna (which includes 18 species of penguin, six species of seal and several rare species of whale) included in the Antarctic Treaty (see p. 492), and reinforced the Convention for the Conservation of Antarctic Marine Living Resources.

TOKELAU

Introductory Survey

Location, Climate, Language, Religion, Flag, Capital

Tokelau consists of three atolls (Atafu, Nukunonu and Fakaofo), which lie about 480 km (300 miles) north of Samoa, in the Pacific Ocean. The annual average temperature is 28°C (82°F), July being the coolest month and May the warmest; rainfall is heavy but inconsistent. The principal language is Tokelauan (a Polynesian language), although English is also widely spoken. The population is almost entirely Christian, with 67% adhering to the Congregational Christian Church of Samoa (a Protestant denomination) and 30% to the Roman Catholic Church. The New Zealand flag is used in the Territory (see p. 3049). Tokelau has no capital, each atoll having its own administrative centre. However, the seat of government (the Office of the Council of Faipule) is recognized as 'the capital' and is rotated on a yearly basis among the three atolls.

Recent History

The Tokelau (formerly Union) Islands became a British protectorate in 1877. At the request of the inhabitants, the United Kingdom annexed the islands in 1916 and included them within the Gilbert and Ellice Islands Colony (now Kiribati and Tuvalu). The British Government transferred administrative control of the islands to New Zealand by legislation enacted in 1925, effective from February 1926. The group was officially designated the Tokelau Islands in 1946, and sovereignty was transferred to New Zealand by legislation of 1948, effective from January 1949. From 1962 until the end of 1971 the High Commissioner for New Zealand in Western Samoa (now Samoa) was also the Administrator of the Tokelau Islands. In November 1974 the administration of the Tokelau Islands was transferred to the Ministry of Foreign Affairs in New Zealand. In 1976 the Tokelau Islands were officially redesignated Tokelau.

New Zealand has undertaken to assist Tokelau towards increased self-government and economic self-sufficiency. The Territory was visited by the United Nations Special Committee on Decolonization in 1976 and 1981, but on both occasions the mission reported that the people of Tokelau did not wish to change the nature of the existing relationship between Tokelau and New Zealand. This opinion was reiterated by an emissary of the General Fono, the Territory's highest advisory body, in 1987, and by the Official Secretary in 1992. In June 1987, however, in a statement to the UN Special Committee, Tokelau had expressed a desire to achieve a greater degree of political autonomy, while maintaining its relationship with New Zealand. A report by the UN Special Committee in 2002 listed Tokelau as one of 16 dependent territories it was seeking to encourage towards independence. However, a UN decolonization mission which visited the islands in September of that year was told that the majority of Tokelauans wanted to remain part of New Zealand and that the Territory was far too dependent on that country to change its status.

In December 1980 New Zealand and the USA signed a treaty whereby a US claim to Tokelau, dating from 1856, was relinquished. At the same time New Zealand abandoned a claim, on behalf of Tokelau, to Swains Island, which had been administered by the USA since 1925 as part of American Samoa. The treaty was ratified in August 1983.

In 1989 Tokelau supported efforts by the South Pacific Forum to impose a regional ban on drift-net fishing (which was believed to have resulted in a serious depletion in tuna stocks). In November New Zealand prohibited drift-net fishing within Tokelau's exclusive economic zone (which extends to 200 nautical miles (370 km) from the islands' coastline). At the Pacific Islands Forum annual meeting in August 2002 New Zealand endorsed Tokelau's membership of the Forum Fisheries Agency.

In 1989 a UN report on the 'greenhouse effect' (the heating of the earth's atmosphere as a result of pollution) listed Tokelau as one of the island groups that would completely disappear beneath the sea in the 21st century, unless drastic action were taken.

A programme of constitutional change, agreed in 1992 and formalized in January 1994, provided for a more defined role for Tokelau's political institutions, as well as for their expansion. A process of relocating the Tokelau Public Service (hitherto based in Apia, Western Samoa, now Samoa) to the Territory began in 1994, and by 1995 all government departments, except Transport and Communications and part of the Administration and Finance Department, had been transferred to Tokelauan soil. The Tokelau Apia Liaison Office (formerly the Office for Tokelau Affairs) was, however, to remain in Western Samoa, owing to that country's more developed communications facilities.

The development of Tokelau's institutions at a national level has prompted renewed interest in the islands' prospects for greater internal autonomy. In June 1994 the General Fono adopted a National Strategic Plan, which gave details of Tokelau's progression (over the next five to 10 years) towards increased self-determination and, possibly, free association with New Zealand. The executive and administrative powers of the Administrator were formally transferred, in that year, to the General Fono and, when the Fono is not in session, to the Council of Faipule (cabinet). A draft Constitution was subsequently drawn up. In May 1996 the New Zealand House of Representatives approved the Tokelau Amendment Bill, granting the General Fono the power to enact legislation, to impose taxes and to declare public holidays, effective from 1 August 1996 (although New Zealand was to retain the right to legislate for Tokelau). A visit to the islands by the Prime Minister of Tuvalu in mid-1996, for the signing of a mutual co-operation agreement (covering shipping, trade and fisheries), was widely interpreted as an indication of Tokelau's increased autonomy. A further co-operation agreement was established in March 2003, following a five-day visit to the islands by the Prime Minister of Samoa. Tokelau's traditional leaders agreed a framework for annual meetings with the Samoan Government to discuss issues of concern and mutual benefit in what was regarded as a sign of the growing relationship between the two parties.

Following electoral reforms introduced in the latter half of the 1990s, delegates were, for the first time, elected to the General Fono for a three-year term in January 1999; they had previously been nominated by each Taupulega (Island Council). As part of the same reform process, the number of delegates to the General Fono was reduced from 27 to 18. At the elections two of the Territory's Faipule (political leaders) were re-elected, while the remaining Faipule and three Pulenuku (village mayor) posts were secured by new candidates. At elections in January 2002 all three incumbent Faipule and one Pulenuku were re-elected to office; two new Pulenuku were elected.

Mounting fears among islanders that, despite their wishes, New Zealand was seeking to loosen its ties with Tokelau, led the New Zealand Minister of Foreign Affairs and Trade to state in April 2000 that his country would not impose independence on the Territory and that any change in its political status would only occur with the consent of Tokelauans. In early 2001 the head of the Tokelau Public Service Commission, Aleki Silau, reiterated the islanders' reluctance to renounce New Zealand citizenship, and emphasized that both sides have until 2010 to reach a decision. Under legislation approved in 1999, management of the islands' public service was formally transferred to Tokelau in July 2001. A mission from the United Nations Special Committee on Decolonization visited the islands in September 2002 (see above).

Government

The administration of Tokelau is the responsibility of the Minister of Foreign Affairs and Trade of New Zealand, who is empowered to appoint an Administrator to the Territory. In practice, most of the Administrator's powers are delegated to the Official Secretary, who heads the Tokelau Apia Liaison Office, as well as to the General Fono and the Council of Faipule. Each atoll has its own Island Council, or Taupulega, which comprises the heads of family groups together with two elected members, the Faipule and the Pulenuku. The Faipule represents the atoll in its dealings with the administering power and the public service, and presides over the Council and the court. The Pulenuku is responsible for the administration of village affairs. The Faipule and the Pulenuku are democratically elected by universal adult suffrage every three years. The three Faipule, who hold ministerial portfolios and form the Council of Faipule, choose one of their number to hold the title Ulu-O-Tokelau (Head of Tokelau) for a term of one year. The Ulu-O-Tokelau chairs sessions of the territorial assembly, the General Fono. The General Fono is a meeting of 18 delegates, who are elected by universal adult suffrage for a three-year term (including the three Faipule and the three Pulenuku) and who represent the entire Territory. There are two or three meetings of the General Fono each year, which may take place on any of the atolls.

Economic Affairs

According to estimates by the UN Development Programme, in 1982 Tokelau's gross national product (GNP) was US $1.2m., equivalent to US $760 per head. Gross domestic product (GDP) was estimated at US $1.5m. in 1993.

Agriculture (including fishing) is, excluding copra production, of a basic subsistence nature. Coconuts (the source of copra) are the only cash crop. Pulaka, breadfruit, papayas, the screw-pine (*Pandanus*) and bananas are cultivated as food crops. Livestock

comprises pigs, ducks and other poultry. Ocean and lagoon fish and shellfish are staple constituents of the islanders' diet. The sale of fishing licences for Tokelau's exclusive economic zone to foreign fleets provides an important source of income, as do fees from shipping, radio and telegram excises and customs duties. Fisheries licensing earned $NZ1.2m. in 2000/01, although the Government projected a more modest revenue of $NZ0.9m. in 2001/02. In 2001 the sum of $NZ0.68m. of the income from fisheries licensing was used to establish the Tokelau Trust Fund.

Manufacturing chiefly comprises the production of copra and handicrafts. However, the opening on Atafu, in 1990, of a factory processing highly-priced yellowfin tuna provided another important source of income. The principal markets for the product are New Zealand and Japan.

The sale of postage stamps and souvenir coins (which are legal tender, although New Zealand currency is in general use) also makes a significant contribution to the Territory's income, as does revenue provided by remittances from Tokelauans working abroad, mainly in New Zealand. Since 1982 the General Fono has levied a tax on the salaries of public servants who are unavailable for the community service labour levy. In the mid-1990s, when the public service, which is the principal employer, engaged approximately 160 people, the tax was equivalent to 6%–12% of public servants' salaries. Public salaries and employment account for the single largest item of government expenditure (about one-third in the early 1990s).

Imports to the value of $NZ0.5m. were purchased from New Zealand in 1993/94. The principal imports are generally foodstuffs, building materials and fuel.

In 1999/2000 there was a budgetary deficit of $NZ0.9m. Tokelau's budget for 2001/02 was to include at least $NZ4.2m. from New Zealand and an estimated $NZ1.7m. to be obtained from local revenues such as fisheries licensing, duty, taxes, philatelic sales, freight charges and interest earned. Official development assistance from New Zealand totalled $NZ8.1m. in 2002/03, of which $NZ4.75m. was allocated towards budgetary support, while $NZ2.65m. was for the purposes of development projects and training, focusing on such areas as health, education, information technology, infrastructure, and financial and economic management. In addition to its links to New Zealand, Tokelau maintains a bilateral development assistance plan with Australia, centred upon human resource development. Australia provides scholarships for Tokelauan students to study in Australia or at regional academic institutions. Development assistance from Australia in 2001/02 was projected at a total of $A100,000.

Tokelau is a member of the Pacific Community (see p. 304), and, as a Dependent Territory of New Zealand, is represented by that country in the Pacific Islands Forum (see p. 306) and other international organizations.

Tokelau's agricultural development has been adversely affected by inclement weather, particularly cyclones. Moreover, the Territory's small size, remote situation, lack of land-based resources and the population's continuing migration to New Zealand severely hinder economic development. The New Zealand budget for 1989 allowed the payment of 50% of retirement income for people residing abroad, in an attempt to persuade Tokelauans to return to the islands and to contribute to the Territory's economic development. The improvement of shipping links in the late 1980s and early 1990s, although of general economic benefit, resulted in an increase in imported foods, which, according to a report published in 1992, has contributed to serious social and dietary problems in the islands. In an attempt to reduce the Territory's dependence on overseas aid, measures were taken during 1996 to augment locally-generated revenue. The measures, which included the expansion of the islands' tax base and the introduction of charges for health and education services, resulted in an increase in Tokelau's contribution to total budgetary revenue from 17% in 1995 to 25% in the following year. The proportion, however, declined to 13.8% in 1997/98. Tokelau established the Tokelau Trust Fund in 2001 (see above). In September 2002 the Ulu-O-Tokelau, Pio Tuia, announced renewed proposals for the construction of wharves and improved access for shipping to facilitate the export of fish, and of an airport to encourage tourism (fewer than 30 tourists visited the islands in 2001).

Education

Education is provided free of charge, and is compulsory between the ages of five and 14 years. The provision of an additional year for 15-year-olds is rotated among the Territory's three schools every five years. Government expenditure on education in 1998/99 totalled $NZ0.8m. (equivalent to 18% of total budgetary expenditure). The New Zealand Department of Education provides advisory services and some educational equipment. Scholarships are awarded for secondary and tertiary education and vocational training in Samoa, Fiji, Niue, Tonga and New Zealand. Australia also provides scholarships. There was a total of 474 pupils enrolled in primary and secondary education in 1991, and 97 Tokelauan students at overseas institutions in 1990. There were 30 qualified teachers, complemented by teacher aides, on the islands in 1999.

Public Holidays

2003: 1 January (New Year's Day), 6 February (Waitangi Day, anniversary of 1840 treaty), 18–21 April (Easter), 25 April (ANZAC Day, anniversary of 1915 landing at Gallipoli), 2 June (Queen's Official Birthday), 27 October (Labour Day), 25 December (Christmas Day), 26 December (Boxing Day).

2004: 1 January (New Year's Day), 6 February (Waitangi Day, anniversary of 1840 treaty), 9–12 April (Easter), 25 April (ANZAC Day, anniversary of 1915 landing at Gallipoli), 1 June (Queen's Official Birthday), 26 October (Labour Day), 25 December (Christmas Day), 26 December (Boxing Day).

Weights and Measures

The metric system is in force.

Statistical Survey

Source (unless otherwise indicated): Tokelau Apia Liaison Office, POB 805, Apia, Samoa; tel. 20822; fax 21761.

AREA AND POPULATION

Area: Atafu 3.5 sq km; Nukunonu 4.7 sq km; Fakaofo 4.0 sq km; Total 12.2 sq km (4.7 sq miles).

Population (census of March 1991): Atafu 543; Nukunonu 437; Fakaofo 597; Total 1,577. *Tokelauans resident in New Zealand:* 2,802. (Census of 1996*): Atafu 499; Fakaofo 578; Nukunonu 430; Total 1,507.
*Figures include temporary visitors. Total resident population: 1,487.

Density (resident population, 1996): 121.9 per sq km.

Births and Deaths (1996): Birth rate 33.1 per 1,000; Death rate 8.2 per 1,000.

Expectation of Life (official estimates, years at birth): Males 68; Females 70 in 1996. Source: Ministry of Foreign Affairs and Trade, Wellington.

AGRICULTURE, ETC.

Crop Production (FAO estimates, metric tons, 2001): Coconuts 3,000; Copra 45; Roots and tubers 300; Bananas 15. Source: FAO.

Livestock (FAO estimates, year ending September 2001): Pigs 1,000; Chickens 5,000. Source: FAO.

Fishing (FAO estimates, metric tons, live weight, 1999): Total catch 200. Source: FAO, *Yearbook of Fishery Statistics*.

INDUSTRY

Production (estimate, 1990): Electric energy 300,000 kWh.

FINANCE

Currency and Exchange Rates: New Zealand currency is legal tender. Tokelau souvenir coins have also been issued. New Zealand currency: 100 cents = 1 New Zealand dollar ($NZ); *Sterling, US Dollar and Euro Equivalents* (31 December 2002): £1 sterling = $NZ3.0613; US $1 = $NZ1.8993; €1 = $NZ1.9918; $NZ100 = £32.67 = US $52.65 = €50.21. *Average Exchange Rate* (US $ per $NZ): 0.4574 in 2000; 0.4206 in 2001; 0.4642 in 2002.

Budget ($NZ, year ending 30 June 1998): *Revenue:* Local 734,950; New Zealand subsidy 4,600,000; Total 5,334,950. *Expenditure:* Total 5,208,449.

Overseas Aid (projection, $NZ '000, 2001/02): Official development assistance from New Zealand 7,500 (of which Budget support 4,500, Projects and training 3,000). Source: Ministry of Foreign Affairs and Trade, Wellington.

EXTERNAL TRADE

Principal Commodities: *Imports:* Building materials WS $104,953 (1983/84) *Exports:* Copra $NZ43,542 (1982/83); Handicrafts WS $10,348 (1983/84). Note: Foodstuffs and fuel are also important import commodities. *1993/94:* Imports from New Zealand totalled $NZ500,000.

COMMUNICATIONS MEDIA

Radio Receivers (estimate, 1997): 1,000 in use.

EDUCATION

Schools (1999): 3 (one school for all levels on each atoll).

Teachers (1990): Qualified 43; Aides 8; Adult Learning Centre Co-ordinators 3. (1999): Qualified 30.

Pupils (1991): Pre-primary 133; Primary 361; General secondary 113.

Students Overseas (1990): Secondary 42; Technical and vocational 36; Teacher training 3; University 16. (1999): Secondary 22; Tertiary 20.

Directory

The Constitution

Tokelau is administered under the authority of the Tokelau Islands Act 1948 and subsequent amendments and regulations. The Act declared Tokelau (then known as the Tokelau Islands) to be within the territorial boundaries of New Zealand. The Administrator is the representative of the Crown and is responsible to the Minister of Foreign Affairs and Trade in the New Zealand Government. The office of Administrator is normally held conjointly with that of New Zealand's Secretary of Foreign Affairs and Trade, but provision is made for the offices to be held separately. Most of the powers of the Administrator are delegated to the Tokelau Apia Liaison Office, the General Fono and the Council of Faipule. The chief representative of the Administrator (and the Crown) on each atoll is the highest elected official, the Faipule, who exercises executive, political and judicial powers. The three Faipule, who hold ministerial portfolios and form the Council of Faipule, act as the representatives of the Territory in dealings with the administration and at international meetings, and choose one of their number to hold the title Ulu-O-Tokelau (Head of Tokelau) for a term of one year. The Ulu-O-Tokelau chairs sessions of the territorial assembly, the General Fono. The General Fono is a meeting of 18 delegates (including the Faipule and the Pulenuku—Village Mayor—from each atoll), representing the entire Territory. There are two or three meetings each year, which may take place on any of the atolls. The General Fono is the highest advisory body and the administration must consult it about all policy affecting the Territory. The assembly has responsibility for the territorial budget and has the power to enact legislation, to impose taxes and to declare public holidays. There are a number of specialist committees, such as the Budget Committee and the Law Committee.

Tokelau is an association of three autonomous atoll communities. Local government consists of the Faipule, the Pulenuku and the Taupulega (Island Council or Council of Elders). The Faipule, the Pulenuku and delegates to the General Fono are elected every three years on the basis of universal adult suffrage (the age of majority being 21). The Faipule represents the atoll community, liaises with the administration and the Tokelau Public Service, acts as a judicial commissioner and presides over meetings of the Taupulega. The Pulenuku is responsible for the administration of village affairs, including the maintenance of water supplies and the inspection of plantations, and, in some instances, the resolution of land disputes (practically all land is held by customary title, by the head of a family group, and may not be alienated to non-Tokelauans). The Taupulega is the principal organ of local government. The Taupulega also appoints the Failautuhi (Island Clerk), to record its meetings and transactions. The Taupulega in Atafu consists of the Faipule, the Pulenuku and the head of every family group; in Nukunonu it consists of the Faipule, the Pulenuku, the elders of the community and the nominated heads of extended families; in Fakaofo it consists of the Faipule, the Pulenuku and the elders (meetings of all the heads of family groups take place only infrequently).

The Government

(April 2003)

Administrator: LINDSAY WATT (took office March 1993).

3073

FAIPULE

At elections in January 2002, all three incumbent Faipule were re-elected to office.

Faipule of Fakaofo: KOLOUEI O'BRIEN.

Faipule of Nukunonu: PIO TUIA.

Faipule of Atafu: KURESA NASAU.

PULENUKU

At elections in January 2002, two new Pulenuku were elected to office and one was re-elected.

Pulenuku of Fakaofo: KELI NEEMIA.

Pulenuku of Nukunonu: PANAPA SAKARIA.

Pulenuku of Atafu: PAULO KITONIA.

GOVERNMENT OFFICES

Tokelau Apia Liaison Office/Ofiha o Fehokotakiga Tokelau Ma Apia: POB 865, Apia, Samoa; tel. 20822; fax 21761; responsible for transport, accounting and consular functions; Man. LOGOTASI IOSEFA.

The Tokelau Public Service has seven departments, divided among the three atolls, with a supervising administrative official located in each village. Two departments are established on each atoll, while the seventh department, the Office of the Council of Faipule, rotates on a yearly basis in conjunction with the position of Ulu-O-Tokelau. Management of the Tokelau Public Service was formally transferred to Tokelau in July 2001.

Judicial System

Tokelau's legislative and judicial systems are based on the Tokelau Islands Act 1948 and subsequent amendments and regulations. The Act provided for a variety of British regulations to continue in force and, where no other legislation applies, the law of England and Wales in 1840 (the year in which British sovereignty over New Zealand was established) was to be applicable. New Zealand statute law applies in Tokelau only if specifically extended there. In 1986 legislation formalized the transfer of High Court civil and criminal jurisdiction from Niue to New Zealand. Most cases are judged by the Commissioner established on each atoll, who has limited jurisdiction in civil and criminal matters. Commissioners are appointed by the New Zealand Governor-General, after consultation with the elders of the atoll.

Commissioner of Fakaofo: LUI KELEKOLIO.

Commissioner of Nukunonu: ATONIO EGELIKO.

Commissioner of Atafu: MAKA TOLOA.

Religion

On Atafu almost all inhabitants are members of the Tokelau Congregational Christian Church, on Nukunonu all are Roman Catholic, while both denominations are represented on Fakaofo. In the late 1990s some 70% of the total population adhered to the Congregational Christian Church, and 30% to the Roman Catholic Church.

CHRISTIANITY

Roman Catholic Church

The Church is represented in Tokelau by a Mission, established in 1992. There were an estimated 510 adherents at 31 December 2000.

Superior: Mgr PATRICK EDWARD O'CONNOR, Catholic Mission, Nukunonu, Tokelau (via Apia, Samoa); tel. 4160; fax 4236.

Broadcasting and Communications

Each atoll has a radio station to broadcast shipping and weather reports. Radio-telephone provided the main communications link with other areas until the late 1990s. A new telecommunications system established at a cost of US $2.76m. (US $1m. of which was provided by New Zealand) and operating through an earth station, linked to a communications satellite, on each atoll, became operational in 1997. A new radio station, broadcasting information and music, was to commence operations in 2002.

TELECOMMUNICATIONS

TeleTok: Fenuafala, Fakaofo.

Finance

In 1977 a savings bank was established on each atoll; commercial and other banking facilities are available in Apia, Samoa.

Trade and Industry

A village co-operative store was established on each atoll in 1977. Local industries include copra production, woodwork and plaited craft goods, and the processing of tuna. Electricity is provided by diesel generators based in the village on each atoll.

Transport

There are no roads or motor vehicles. Unscheduled inter-atoll voyages, by sea, are forbidden because the risk of missing landfall is too great. Passengers and cargo are transported by vessels that anchor off shore, as there are no harbour facilities. A scheme to provide wharves (primarily to facilitate the export of fish) was proposed in September 2002. Most shipping links are with Samoa, but a monthly service from Fiji was introduced in 1986. The vessel *Forum Tokelau*, operated by Pacific Forum Line, began a monthly service between Tokelau and Apia, Samoa, in mid-1997. A New Zealand-funded inter-atoll vessel commenced service in 1991, providing the first regular link between the atolls for 40 years. Plans to construct an airstrip on each atoll were postponed in 1987 in favour of the development of shipping links. In late 2002, however, proposals for the construction of an airport were again under consideration.

COOK ISLANDS

Introductory Survey

Location, Climate, Language, Religion, Flag, Capital

The 13 inhabited and two uninhabited islands of the Cook Islands are located in the southern Pacific Ocean and lie between American Samoa, to the west, and French Polynesia, to the east. The islands extend over about 2m. sq km (more than 750,000 sq miles) of ocean, and form two groups: the Northern Cooks, which are all atolls and include Pukapuka, Rakahanga and Manihiki, and the Southern Cooks, including Aitutaki, Mangaia and Rarotonga, which are all volcanic islands. From December to March the climate is warm and humid, with the possibility of severe storms; from April to November the climate is mild and equable. The average annual rainfall on Rarotonga is 2,012 mm (79 ins). The official languages are English and Cook Islands Maori. The principal religion is Christianity, with about 70% of the population adhering to the Cook Islands Congregational Christian Church. The islands' flag (proportions 1 by 2) displays 15 five-pointed white stars (representing the islands of the group) on a royal blue field, with the United Kingdom's Union Flag as a canton in the upper hoist. The capital is Avarua, on Rarotonga.

Recent History

The first Europeans to visit the islands were members of a British expedition, led by Capt. James Cook (after whom the islands are named), in 1773. The Cook Islands were proclaimed a British protectorate in 1888, and a part of New Zealand in 1901.

On 5 August 1965 the Cook Islands became a self-governing Territory in free association with New Zealand. The people are New Zealand citizens. Sir Albert Henry, leader of the Cook Islands Party (CIP), was elected Premier in 1965 and re-elected in 1971, 1974 and March 1978. However, in July 1978, following an inquiry into alleged electoral malpractice, the Chief Justice disallowed votes cast in the elections to the Legislative

Assembly (later renamed Parliament) by Cook Islands expatriates who had been flown from New Zealand, with their fares paid from public funds. The amended ballot gave a majority to the Demoratic Party (DP), and its leader, Dr (later Sir) Thomas Davis, was sworn in as Premier by the Chief Justice. In August 1979 Sir Albert Henry was convicted of conspiracy to defraud, and was formally stripped of his knighthood.

In May 1981 the Cook Islands' Constitution was amended to increase the membership of Parliament from 22 to 24, and to extend the parliamentary term from four to five years. In March 1983 Sir Thomas Davis lost power to the CIP, under Geoffrey (later Sir Geoffrey) Henry, cousin of the former Premier. However, with one seat already subject to re-election, Henry's majority of three was reduced by the death of one CIP member of Parliament and the transfer of allegiance to the DP by another. Henry resigned in August, and a general election in November returned the DP to power under Davis. In August 1984 Davis announced wide-ranging government changes, with three of the seven posts going to members of the CIP, to form a coalition Government, with Henry as Deputy Prime Minister. In mid-1985, however, Davis dismissed Henry, who had endorsed an unsuccessful motion expressing 'no confidence' in the Government, and Henry's supporters withdrew from the coalition. Henry's successor as Deputy Prime Minister was Dr Terepai Maoate, one of four CIP members who continued to support the Davis Government, in defiance of the CIP central committee.

Davis was forced to resign as Prime Minister in July 1987, after a parliamentary motion expressing 'no confidence' in his administration was approved. He was succeeded by Dr Pupuke Robati, a member of the Cabinet and a leading figure in the DP. Geoffrey Henry again became Prime Minister following a general election victory for the CIP in January 1989. The defection in mid-1990 of a member of Parliament, from the DP to the CIP provided the CIP with 15 seats in Parliament and thus the minimum two-thirds' majority support necessary to amend the Constitution. In August 1991 a constitutional amendment was approved to increase the number of members of Parliament to 25 and, at an election to the newly-created seat, a CIP candidate was successful. The amendment also provided for an increase in the number of cabinet members from seven to nine (including the Prime Minister).

At a general election in March 1994 the CIP increased its majority, winning 20 seats in Parliament; the DP secured three seats and the Alliance Party (established in 1992 by Norman George, the former DP parliamentary whip, who had been expelled from the party following a dispute over spending) two. Davis, who failed to win a seat, subsequently resigned as leader of the DP. A referendum held simultaneously revealed that a majority of the electorate favoured retaining the current name (69.8% of voters), national anthem (80.2%) and flag (48.5%) of the Cook Islands. (At subsequent by-elections the CIP lost two seats and the DP and Alliance Party each gained one seat.)

A financial scandal was narrowly averted following reports that during 1994 the Government had issued loan guarantees for foreign companies worth more than $NZ1,200m. (the island's total revenue for 1994/95 was estimated at $NZ50m.). An investigation into the affair by the New Zealand Reserve Bank found that the Government had not been guilty of fraud, but rather had been coerced into the activity by unscrupulous foreign business interests. However, the affair led many investors to remove their funds from the islands, provoking a financial crisis that resulted in Henry's decision in mid-1995 to withdraw the Cook Islands dollar from circulation, and to implement a programme of retrenchment measures. The crisis deepened during 1995 as new allegations emerged, and Henry's Government was severely criticized by New Zealand for failing to co-operate with an official inquiry into accusations of fraud and tax evasion involving several New Zealand companies. Henry maintained that the islands' bank secrecy laws prevented the disclosure of information relating to financial transactions. The situation deteriorated further when it was revealed that the Government had defaulted on a debt of some US $100m. to an Italian bank. In response to pressure from New Zealand, and in an attempt to restore a degree of financial stability to the islands, Henry (whose management of the crisis had been questioned both by his own party and by the opposition) announced a severe restructuring programme in April 1996. The measures included a 50% reduction in the pay of public sector workers, the closure of almost all diplomatic missions overseas, a 60% reduction in the number of government departments and ministries, and the privatization of the majority of government-owned authorities.

A marked increase in 1995/96 in the emigration rate and a decline in the number of Cook Islanders returning to the islands following a period of residency overseas was attributed to the austere economic conditions created by the financial crisis.

In August 1997 Parliament approved the Outer Islands Local Government Act, providing for a new budgetary system to allocate funds for projects in the outer islands and for increased powers for local authorities, with the aim of reducing significantly central government administration of the outer islands. As part of the plan, three new government bodies were elected in April 1998.

Henry's administration continued to attract controversy, with the announcement in December 1997 of the closure of the Ministry of Public Works, Survey, Housing, Water Supply and Environment Services for exceeding its budget. The minister responsible, Tihina Tom Marsters, resigned in protest at the closure, which resulted in the loss of more than 100 public servants' jobs, problems with the supply of utilities (particularly water) and the suspension of several development projects.

In November 1997 the northern Cook Islands were devastated by Cyclone Martin, which killed at least eight people and destroyed virtually all crops and infrastructure. The islands' important black pearl industry suffered severe losses as a result of extensive damage on Manihiki Atoll.

In April 1999 Chief Justice Sir Peter Quilliam ruled as unconstitutional an electoral amendment, submitted by the ruling CIP, to ban any electoral activity, including the formation of political parties. The amendment was contested by the DAP and NAP, which claimed that it contravened fundamental human rights and freedoms.

At legislative elections on 16 June 1999 the CIP won 11 of the 25 seats in Parliament, the Democratic Alliance Party (DAP, formerly the Democratic Party) 10 seats, and the New Alliance Party (NAP, formerly the Alliance Party) four seats. Sir Geoffrey Henry of the CIP was reappointed Prime Minister and formed a new Cabinet, following the establishment of a political coalition with the NAP; the leader of the NAP, Norman George, became Deputy Prime Minister. However, three members of the CIP subsequently left the party to form a coalition with the DAP, in protest at the alliance with the NAP, and at the end of July Henry resigned and was replaced by a 'rebel' CIP member, Dr Joe Williams. Williams was confirmed as the new Prime Minister by 13 votes to 12 in a vote of confidence by the Parliament. Williams' appointment provoked a public protest in Rarotonga, exacerbated by general discontent at the nomination of a Prime Minister whose parliamentary constituency was outside the Cook Islands. Electors also voted in a referendum on whether the parliamentary term should be reduced from five years to four. The shorter term was favoured by 63% of voters, and thus narrowly failed to receive the support of the two-thirds' majority required to amend the Constitution. The result of the contest for the Pukapuka seat, which had been won by former Prime Minister Inatio Akaruru by just one vote, was challenged by the DAP. The matter was taken to the Court of Appeal, which subsequently declared the result invalid, stripping the Government of its one-seat majority. A by-election was held in late September 1999 to decide the Pukapuka seat, however the result was again said to be invalid and a further by-election was scheduled. The Government became a minority administration in mid-October when the Prime Minister dismissed his deputy, Norman George, along with the Minister of Education, following their defection to the opposition. Despite the appointment of three new ministers, Williams failed to regain a majority in Parliament. In November Williams resigned, shortly before a vote of 'no confidence' was to be tabled against him by Dr Terepai Maoate, the leader of the opposition DAP. Maoate won the vote by 14 votes to 11 and was appointed Prime Minister, forming a new coalition Government with the NAP. He subsequently reappointed Norman George to the post of Deputy Prime Minister.

In February 2001 Maoate removed the transport portfolio from among the responsibilities of Dr Robert Woonton (whose other duties included that of Minister of Foreign Affairs). Maoate underwent medical treatment in March, prompting speculation that he might stand down as Prime Minister later in the year. In July Maoate dismissed Norman George on the grounds that he was working to undermine him; this was the second time that George had lost the position of Deputy Prime Minister. He was replaced by Dr Robert Woonton. Woonton, however, strongly criticized Maoate's leadership in the same month.

In late 2001 the rift between the Prime Minister and his Cabinet widened. Woonton announced his resignation, which Maoate refused to accept. This led to a motion of 'no confidence' in the Prime Minister, which he only narrowly survived. In February 2002 Maoate's leadership was again challenged: 15 of the 25 Members of Parliament voted against him in a second motion of 'no confidence'. He was therefore replaced by Robert Woonton. In an extensive ministerial reorganization Sir Geoffrey Henry returned to the Cabinet as Deputy Prime Minister. Woonton declared his priorities to be the encouragement of emigrant workers to return to the islands through income tax incentives and an ambitious redevelopment plan for the capital, Avarua.

The Government's decision not to name a senior civil servant in the Prime Minister's office who had been arrested and charged with fraud in August 2002 led to accusations of secrecy by the opposition. Criticism of the Government's position increased in the following month with the introduction of new media laws (which many observers believed would serve to suppress opposition to government policy), particularly when a government official stated his desire for 'Zimbabwe-style legislation to stop inaccurate reporting'.

In November 2002 Parliament approved a constitutional amendment abolishing the requirement for electoral candidates to reside in the islands for a qualifying period of three months. This action was widely interpreted as a way of retaining the overseas parliamentary seat for the CIP leader, Dr Joe Williams, who lived permanently in New Zealand. In the same month the CIP and the Democratic Party formed a coalition government (the fifth such coalition since the previous election) which left Norman George, who had been recently dismissed from his position in the Cabinet, as the sole opposition member of Parliament. The Government's action prompted a demonstration outside the parliament building by some 150 people, organized by a recently formed organization, the Group for Political Change. The protesters claimed that the virtual absence of an opposition constituted an erosion of democracy and appealed to the Prime Minister to commit to an early general election. However, in late January 2003 the CIP was ousted from the coalition. The continued political manoeuvring was widely denounced, particularly among the business community, for creating a climate of instability in the islands. Public dissatisfaction with the situation resulted in the presentation of a petition to Government in March signed by a significant percentage of the population. The petition called for a number of political reforms including a reduction in the number of members of Parliament, the introduction of a shorter parliamentary term and the abolition of the overseas seat. Moreover, businessman Teariki Heather announced the formation of a new political party, the Cook Islands National, in the same month.

The rate of emigration, meanwhile, continued to increase. In late 2000 it was announced that some 1,400 residents had left the islands during that year (compared with 641 in the previous year). This resulted in a reduction in the estimated population of the islands to 14,300 (the lowest level in more than 50 years) and prompted the Government to campaign in Australia and New Zealand to encourage former citizens to return to the Cook Islands. Private-sector businesses, many of which had experienced difficulties in recruiting workers in sufficient numbers, were also involved in the campaign. The resident population numbered only 12,900 in December 2001, and the Government feared that it could decrease to just 10,000 by 2006, the majority of the loss being from the outer islands. In August 2002 the Government announced that it would allocate US $23,350 for the campaign.

In early 2000 the islands of Penrhyn, Pukapuka, Rakahanga and Manihiki expressed their desire to become fully devolved and to take sole control over areas such as administration, public expenditure and justice. In response, the Government pledged gradually to phase out the Ministry of Outer Islands Development, as well as the post of Government Representative in the outer islands. In December of that year an additional US $2m. in funding under the Cotonou agreement was designated for projects on the outer islands.

A reported increase in the number of Russian nationals opening accounts in the Cook Islands led to allegations in early 1999 that the islands' 'offshore' financial centre was being used extensively by criminal organizations for 'laundering' the proceeds of their activities. (The facility had regularly generated some 8% of annual GDP.) The claims were vigorously denied by officials in the sector. However, in June 2000 the naming of the islands by both the Financial Action Task Force (FATF, see p. 343) and the Organisation for Economic Co-operation and Development (OECD, see p. 277) as one of a number of countries and territories that had 'failed to co-operate' in regional efforts to combat 'money-laundering' led to increased international pressure on the Government to implement stricter controls over its 'offshore' financial centre. Consequently, legislation was approved in August of that year providing for the creation of the Money Laundering Authority and the introduction of new regulations aimed at reducing criminal activity in the sector. However, in early 2003 the Cook Islands remained on the FATF list of non-co-operative countries and territories.

In August 1985 eight members of the South Pacific Forum (subsequently restyled the Pacific Islands Forum, see p. 306), including the Cook Islands, signed a treaty on Rarotonga, designating a 'nuclear-free' zone in the South Pacific. The treaty imposed a ban on the manufacture, testing, storage and use of nuclear weapons, and the dumping of nuclear waste, in the region.

In January 1986, following the rift between New Zealand and the USA in respect of the ANZUS (see p. 348) security arrangements, Sir Thomas Davis declared the Cook Islands a neutral country, because he considered that New Zealand (which has control over the islands' defence and foreign policy) was no longer in a position to defend the islands. The proclamation of neutrality meant that the Cook Islands would not enter into a military relationship with any foreign power, and, in particular, would prohibit visits by US warships. Visits by US naval vessels were allowed to resume by Henry's Government. In October 1991 the Cook Islands signed a treaty of friendship and co-operation with France, covering economic development, trade and surveillance of the islands' exclusive economic zone (EEZ). The establishment of closer relations with France was widely regarded as an expression of the Cook Islands' Government's dissatisfaction with existing arrangements with New Zealand. However, relations deteriorated considerably when the French Government resumed its programme of nuclear-weapons testing at Mururoa Atoll in September 1995. Henry was fiercely critical of the decision and dispatched a *vaka* (traditional voyaging canoe) with a crew of Cook Islands' traditional warriors to protest near the test site. The tests were concluded in January 1996. Full diplomatic relations with France were established in early 2000. Meanwhile, the islands established diplomatic relations at ambassadorial level with the People's Republic of China in July 1997. In November 1998 Henry made an official visit to China, during which the two countries signed a bilateral trade agreement and each conferred the status of 'most favoured nation' on the other. Henry stated that the move constituted a further attempt by his Government to reduce the islands' dependence on New Zealand. During her visit to the islands in June 2001, Helen Clark, the New Zealand Prime Minister, stated that if the Cook Islands desired complete independence, and membership of international organizations, the process would not be obstructed by New Zealand. Cook Islanders, however, would then be obliged to renounce their New Zealand citizenship.

Government

The Cook Islands is an internally self-governing state in free association with New Zealand, which is responsible for the Cook Islands' external affairs and defence (although the Territory has progressively assumed control over much of its foreign policy). Executive authority is vested in the British monarch, who is Head of State, and is exercised through her official representative; a representative of the New Zealand Government (redesignated High Commissioner in 1994) resides on Rarotonga. Executive government is carried out by the Cabinet, consisting of the Prime Minister and between five and seven other ministers. The Cabinet is collectively responsible to the Parliament, which is formed of 25 members who are elected by universal adult suffrage every five years (including one member elected by non-resident voters). The House of Ariki, which comprises up to 15 members who are hereditary chiefs, can advise the Government, but has no legislative powers. Each of the main islands, except Rarotonga, has an elected island council, and a government representative who is appointed by the Prime Minister.

Economic Affairs

In 2000, according to the Asian Development Bank (ADB), the Cook Islands' gross domestic product (GDP), measured at current prices, totalled an estimated $NZ171.6m. GDP increased, in real terms, at an average annual rate of 2.4% in 1990–2000.

According to official figures, GDP rose by 6.1% in 1999/2000 and by 4.3% in 2000/01.

According to estimates by the ADB, agriculture (including hunting, forestry and fishing) contributed 16.1% of GDP in 2000. The sector engaged 11.5% of employees in 1996. In 2000 only 35% of Rarotonga households were classified as being agriculturally active, compared with 74% in the southern outer islands. According to ADB estimates, the real GDP of the agricultural sector contracted by 1.0% per year in 1990–2000. Compared with the previous year, the sector's GDP decreased by 17.2% in 1998 and by 28.2% in 1999, but increased by an estimated 32.7% in 2000. In 2000 the sector provided 3.7% of export earnings (compared with 32.1% in 1995). Papaya is the Cook Islands' most important export crop, and accounted for 24.9% of total export earnings in 1996. Papaya exports were worth some $NZ250,000 in 1998. Other important cash crops are coconuts and tropical fruits such as mangoes, pineapples and bananas. Cassava, sweet potatoes and vegetables are cultivated as food crops. Pigs and poultry are kept. Plans to develop cattle-ranching, ostrich farming and the cultivation of vanilla, taro, coffee and arrowroot on Atiu, Mangaia and Mauke have been discussed. The sale of fishing licences to foreign fleets provides an important source of income. However, illegal fishing in the islands' exclusive economic zone increased during the 1990s, and in March 2003 the Government announced harsher penalties in an attempt to deal with this problem. Aquaculture, in the form of giant clam farming and pearl oyster farming, was developed during the 1980s. The pearl industry expanded considerably during the 1990s, earning an estimated $NZ16.3m. in export revenue in 2000/01 (equivalent to more than 90% of export earnings). The industry was adversely affected, however, by Cyclone Martin which devastated Manihiki Atoll in late 1997 and by a bacterial pearl shell disease in 2000. In response to the infection, the pearl industry agreed to a number of measures designed to protect the environment and reduce overfarming. In early 2001 an Australian fishing company announced plans to invest some US $60m. (including the purchase of 25 long-line fishing vessels and the construction of a fish-processing facility) in a major fishing project in the islands.

According to ADB estimates, industry (comprising mining and quarrying, manufacturing, construction and power) provided 7.5% of GDP in 2000. The sector engaged 12.1% of employees in 1993. Industrial GDP increased, in real terms, at an average rate of 2.7% per year during 1990–2000. Compared with the previous year, the industrial sector's GDP increased by some 7.0% in 1999 and by 6.8% in 2000.

Manufacturing contributed 4.1% of GDP in 1995, and engaged 4.5% of employees in 1993. The manufacturing and mining sectors together accounted for an estimated 2.2% of GDP in 2000, according to ADB estimates. The real GDP of manufacturing and mining declined at an average rate of 0.5% per year during 1990–2000. Compared with the previous year, however, the two sectors' GDP increased by 6.1% in 1999 and by 6.5% in 2000. The most important industrial activities are fruit-processing, brewing, the manufacture of garments and handicrafts. Construction contributed an estimated 2.8% of GDP in 2000 and engaged 3.4% of the employed labour force in 1993.

The islands depend on imports for their energy requirements. Mineral fuels accounted for 17.6% of total imports in 2000. In September 1997 the Government signed an agreement with a consortium of Norwegian companies to mine cobalt, nickel, manganese and copper by extracting mineral-rich nodules found in the islands' exclusive economic zone (EEZ) between Aitutaki and Penrhyn. It was estimated that the deep-sea mining project, which was expected to begin in 2003/04, could earn the islands up to US $15m. per year and US $600m. in total. Trial operations began in 1999.

Service industries contributed an estimated 76.4% to GDP in 2000 and engaged 80.8% of the employed labour force in 1993. Tourism expanded considerably in the late 1980s and early 1990s, and earned an estimated $NZ93.9m. in 2000/01. Visitor arrivals rose from 72,994 in 2000 to an estimated 74,575 in 20001 but declined to some 72,000 in 2002. The trade, restaurants and hotels sector contributed 30.2% of GDP in 2000 and engaged 20.9% of the employed labour force in 1993. 'Offshore' banking, introduced to the islands in 1982, expanded rapidly, with more than 2,000 international companies registered by 1987. In 1992 the islands were established as an alternative domicile for companies listed on the Hong Kong Stock Exchange. The financial and business services sector provided 9.9% of GDP in 2000 and engaged 3.6% of the employed labour force in 1993.

A significant proportion of the islands' revenue is provided by remittances from migrants (who outnumber the residents of the islands).

In 2001 the Cook Islands recorded a trade deficit of $NZ95.3m. The principal exports in that year were basic manufactures (which accounted for more than 90% of total exports). The principal imports were machinery and transport equipment (which cost 26.2% of total imports), food and live animals (20.6%) and basic manufactures (15.5%). The principal sources of imports in 2001 were New Zealand (74.8% of the total) and Fiji (11.2%). Japan and Australia were the principal markets for exports (37.5% and 29.1%).

According to official estimates, in the financial year ending June 2001 there was an overall budgetary surplus of an estimated $NZ10.8m., a substantial increase on the $NZ2.3m. surplus recorded in 2000. An estimated surplus of $NZ0.5m. was recorded in 2001/02 and a similar surplus forecast for 2002/03. Development assistance from New Zealand totalled $NZ6.2m. in 1999/2000, and was to remain at this level for the following three financial years (New Zealand is the guarantor of the Cook Islands' borrowing from the ADB, which had reached a total of $NZ25m. at 31 October 2001). Development assistance from Australia totalled $A10.4m. in 2002/03. It was estimated at the end of 2001 that the islands' external debt amounted to some $NZ117m. In mid-2001 net public debt amounted to $NZ128.7m., equivalent to 71.8% of GDP. The annual rate of inflation averaged 2.5% in 1990–98. Average consumer prices rose by 1.7% in 1999/2000 but the inflation rate increased substantially, according to official estimates, to 9.5% in 2000/01.

The Cook Islands is a member of the Pacific Community (see p. 304) and the Pacific Islands Forum (see p. 306) and an associate member of the UN Economic and Social Commission for Asia and the Pacific (ESCAP, see p. 28). In late 1999 the Cook Islands were granted observer status at the Lomé Conventions with the European Union (superseded by the Cotonou Agreement, see p. 234).

During the 1980s and 1990s development plans sought to expand the economy by stimulating investment in the private sector and developing the islands' infrastructure. In 1995 it was announced that the New Zealand dollar was to become the sole legal currency of the islands, following a financial crisis that led the Government to withdraw the Cook Islands dollar from circulation and to introduce a retrenchment programme. Between 1996 and 1998 the number of public-sector workers was reduced from 3,350 to 1,340, and the number of ministries from 52 to 22. In addition, a radical economic restructuring programme was announced in 1996, in response to a deepening financial crisis, which had led the Government to default on a debt of US $100m. to an Italian bank (see Recent History). Negotiations took place between the Cook Islands Government and its major creditors, the Governments of Italy and Nauru and the New Zealand Government Superannuation Fund, in late 1998, at which an agreement to reschedule the islands' external debt was concluded. The Government of France (also a major source of foreign debt) refused to participate in the arrangement. The Government subsequently adopted a policy of accumulating reserves for the purposes of debt-servicing as an annual budgetary allocation. In 2000/01 it set aside $NZ2m. and anticipated reserving at least $NZ1m. for the following financial year. In the longer term the Government aimed to invest these reserves in overseas portfolios, in order to reduce the risks arising from currency fluctuations. Plans to restructure the 'offshore' sector, announced in 1998, were expected to increase revenue. However, the islands' financial regulations were severely criticized by the Financial Action Task Force (FATF— see Recent History), which in early 2003 continued to include the Cook Islands on a list of countries and territories of which the banking systems were allegedly being used for the purposes of 'money-laundering'. Large-scale emigration remained a serious and deepening concern for the Cook Islands' economy in the late 1990s and early 2000s, and in August 2002 the Government announced that it would allocate US $23,350 to the campaign to encourage islanders resident abroad to return. Meanwhile, the success of the tourist industry and the dramatic increase in arrivals to the islands led to expressions of concern that Rarotonga, in particular, was unable to sustain the growth. Reports indicated that waste disposal and energy provision were inadequate in relation to the demands of large numbers of visitors and that pollution of the lagoon was occurring as a result. In January 2003 the Cook Islands Tourism Corporation appealed for a moratorium on all new tourism projects following an independent report into the environmental and social impact of the industry on the islands.

Education

Free secular education is compulsory for a period of ten years between six and 15 years of age. Primary education, from the age of five, lasts for six years. Secondary education, beginning at 11 years of age, comprises two cycles, each of three years. In 1998 there were 28 primary schools and 23 secondary schools. In that year 2,711 pupils were enrolled in primary and 1,779 in secondary schools and there was a total of 140 primary school teachers and 129 teachers at secondary level. Tertiary education is provided at a teacher-training college, a nursing school and through an apprenticeship scheme. Under the New Zealand Training Scheme, the New Zealand Government offers overseas scholarships in New Zealand, Fiji, Papua New Guinea, Australia and Samoa for secondary and tertiary education, career-training and short-term in-service training. There is an extension centre of the University of the South Pacific (based in Fiji) in the Cook Islands.

Public Holidays

2003: 1 January (New Year's Day), 18–21 April (Easter), 25 April (ANZAC Day, anniversary of 1915 landing at Gallipoli), 2 June (Queen's Official Birthday), 5 August (Constitution Day), 26 October (Cook Islands Gospel Day), 25 December (Christmas Day), 26 December (Boxing Day).

2004: 1 January (New Year's Day), 9–12 April (Easter), 25 April (ANZAC Day, anniversary of 1915 landing at Gallipoli), 1 June (Queen's Official Birthday), 5 August (Constitution Day), 26 October (Cook Islands Gospel Day), 25 December (Christmas Day), 26 December (Boxing Day).

Weights and Measures

The metric system is in force.

Statistical Survey

Sources (unless otherwise stated): Statistics Office, POB 125, Rarotonga; tel. 29390; Prime Minister's Department, Government of the Cook Islands, Avarua, Rarotonga; tel. 29300; fax 22856.

AREA AND POPULATION

Area: 237 sq km (91.5 sq miles).

Population: 19,103 (males 9,842; females 9,261) at census of 1 December 1996; 18,027 (males 9,303; females 8,724) at census of December 2001 (provisional); resident population 18,034 (males 9,297; females 8,737) at 1996 census; 12,900 (official estimate) at December 2001. *By island* (resident population, 1996 census): Rarotonga (including the capital, Avarua) 10,337; Aitutaki 2,272; Atiu 942; Mangaia 1,083; Manihiki 656; Mauke 643; Mitiaro 318; Nassau 99; Palmerston (Avarua) 49; Penrhyn (Tongareva) 604; Pukapuka 778; Rakahanga 249; Suwarrow 4. *Cook Island Maoris Resident in New Zealand* (census of 6 March 2001): 52,569.

Density (resident population, December 2001): 54.4 per sq km.

Principal Town (population in '000, 1986): Avarua (capital) 9.3. Source: Stefan Helders, *World Gazetteer* (internet www.world-gazetteer.com).

Births and Deaths (1999): Births: 346 (birth rate 21.1 per 1,000); Deaths: 96 (death rate 5.9 per 1,000). Source: UN, *Population and Vital Statistics Report*.

Expectation of Life (WHO estimates, years at birth): 71.9 (males 69.9; females 74.0) in 2001. Source: WHO, *World Health Report*.

Employment (September 1993): Agriculture, hunting, forestry and fishing 457; Mining and quarrying 16; Manufacturing 290; Electricity, gas and water 254; Construction 215; Trade, restaurants and hotels 1,338; Transport, storage and communications 770; Financing, insurance, real estate and business services 231; Community, social and personal services 2,835; Total employees 6,406 (males 4,069, females 2,337). Source: ILO, *Yearbook of Labour Statistics*.

1996: Agriculture hunting, forestry and fishing 600; Manufacturing, mining and quarrying 300; Activities not adequately defined 4,400; Total employed 5,200; Unemployed 800; Total labour force 6,000. Source: Asian Development Bank, *Key Indicators of Developing Asian and Pacific Countries*.

HEALTH AND WELFARE

Key Indicators

Total Fertility Rate (children per woman, 2001): 3.3.

Under-5 Mortality Rate (per 1,000 live births, 2001): 23.

Physicians (per 1,000 head, 1997): 0.90.

Health Expenditure (2000): US $ per head (PPP): 426.

Health Expenditure (2000): % of GDP: 4.7.

Health Expenditure (2000): public (% of total): 62.8.

Access to Water (% of persons, 2000): 100.

Access to Sanitation (% of persons, 2000): 100.
For sources and definitions, see explanatory note on p. vi.

AGRICULTURE, ETC.

Principal Crops (mainly FAO estimates, metric tons, 2001): Cassava 3,000; Sweet potatoes 1,400; Coconuts 5,000; Vegetables and melons 1,302; Tomatoes 500; Mangoes 2,700; Papayas 908; Pineapples 50; Bananas 230; Avocados 150. Source: FAO.

Livestock (mainly FAO estimates, head, year ending September 2001): Pigs 40,000; Goats 2,500; Poultry 80,000; Horses 300. Source: FAO.

Livestock Products (metric tons, 2001): Hen eggs 250; Goatskins 2; Pigmeat 600; Poultry meat 80. Source: FAO.

Fishing (FAO estimates, metric tons, live weight, 2000): Total catch (Groupers 60, Flyingfishes 20, Jacks and crevalles 20, Marlins and sailfishes 20, Swordfish 20, Sharks, rays and skates 20, Octopuses 100, Other marine molluscs 10). Figures exclude trochus shells: 25 metric tons (FAO estimate). Source: FAO, *Yearbook of Fishery Statistics*.

INDUSTRY

Electric Energy (million kWh): 21.8 in 1999; 24.7 in 2000; 25.8 in 2001.

FINANCE

Currency and Exchange Rates: New Zealand currency is legal tender. In mid-1995 it was announced that the Cook Islands dollar (formerly the local currency, at par with the New Zealand dollar) was to be withdrawn from circulation. New Zealand currency: 100 cents = 1 New Zealand dollar ($NZ); for details of exchange rates, see Tokelau.

Budget ($NZ '000, year ending 30 June 2001): *Revenue*: Total revenue 65,161 (Tax 54,742, Non-tax 10,419). *Expenditure*: Total expenditure 54,343.

Overseas Aid ($NZ '000): Official development assistance from New Zealand 6,200 in 1999/2000, in 2000/01 and in 2001/02. Source: Ministry of Foreign Affairs and Trade, Wellington.

Cost of Living (Consumer Price Index for Rarotonga; base: 1998 = 100): 102.7 in 2000; 112.4 in 2001.

Gross Domestic Product by Economic Activity (estimates, $NZ '000 in current prices, 2000): Agriculture, forestry and fishing 28,475; Mining, quarrying and manufacturing 4,859; Electricity, gas and water 3,524; Construction 4,940; Trade, restaurants and hotels 53,479; Transport and communications 28,883; Financial and business services 17,605; Public administration 23,156; Other services 12,194; *Sub-total* 177,115; *Less* Imputed bank service charge 5,516; *GDP in purchasers' values* 171,599. Source: Asian Development Bank, *Key Indicators of Developing Asian and Pacific Countries*.

EXTERNAL TRADE

Principal Commodities (distribution by SITC, $NZ '000, 2001): *Imports c.i.f.*: Food and live animals 22,927; Mineral fuels, lubricants, etc. 11,071; Chemicals 6,905; Basic manufactures 17,246; Machinery and transport equipment 29,171; Miscellaneous manufactured articles 16,671; Total (incl. others) 111,437. *Exports f.o.b.*: Food and live animals 861; Basic manufactures 14,612; Miscellaneous manufactured articles 498; Total (incl. others) 16,132. Source: Asian Development Bank, *Key Indicators of Developing Asian and Pacific Countries*.

Principal Trading Partners ($NZ '000, 2001): *Imports*: New Zealand 83,410; Australia 6,737; USA 1,547; Japan 1,382; Fiji 12,453; Total (incl. others) 111,437. *Exports*: Japan 6,057; New Zealand 1,411; Australia 4,698; USA 2,118; Total (incl. others) 16,132. Source: Asian Development Bank, *Key Indicators of Developing Asian and Pacific Countries*.

TRANSPORT

Road Traffic (registered vehicles, April 1983): 6,555. *New Motor Vehicles Registered* (Rarotonga, 2001): 1,698.

Shipping: *Merchant Fleet* (registered at 31 December 2001): 10 vessels, displacement 5,202 grt (Source: Lloyd's Register-Fairplay, *World Fleet Statistics*); *International Sea-borne Freight Traffic* (estimates, '000 metric tons): Goods unloaded 32.6 (2001); Goods loaded 9; Goods unloaded 32 (1990) (Source: UN, *Monthly Bulletin of Statistics*).

Civil Aviation (2001): *Aircraft Movements*: 559. *Freight Traffic* (metric tons): Goods loaded 290; Goods unloaded 659.

TOURISM

Foreign Tourist Arrivals: 55,599 in 1999; 72,994 in 2000; 74,575 in 2001.

Tourist Arrivals by Country of Residence (2000): Australia 12,128; Canada 5,992; Germany 5,232; New Zealand 22,020; United Kingdom 12,392; USA 6,734; Total (incl. others) 72,994. Source: World Tourism Organization, *Yearbook of Tourism Statistics*.

Visitor Expenditure (estimates, $NZ '000): 73,753 in 1999/2000; 93,929 in 2000/01.

COMMUNICATIONS MEDIA

Radio Receivers (1997): 14,000 in use*.

Television Receivers (1997): 4,000 in use*.

Telephones (main lines, 2000): 5,680 in use†.

Mobile Cellular Telephones (2000): 552 subscribers†.

Facsimile Machines (1990): 230 in use‡.

Daily Newspaper (1996): 1; circulation 2,000*.

Non-daily Newspaper (1996): 1; circulation 1,000*.
* Source: UNESCO, *Statistical Yearbook*.
† Source: International Telecommunication Union.
‡ Source: UN, *Statistical Yearbook*.

EDUCATION

Pre-primary (1998): 26 schools; 30 teachers; 460 pupils.

Primary (1998): 28 schools; 140 teachers; 2,711 pupils.

Secondary* (1998): 23 schools; 129 teachers; 1,779 pupils.

Higher (1980): 41 teachers; 360 pupils†.
* Includes high school education.
† Source: UNESCO, *Statistical Yearbook*.

Directory

The Constitution

On 5 August 1965 a new Constitution was proclaimed, whereby the people of the Cook Islands have complete control over their own affairs in free association with New Zealand, but they can at any time move into full independence by a unilateral act if they so wish.

Executive authority is vested in the British monarch, who is Head of State, and exercised through an official representative. The New Zealand Government also appoints a representative (from 1994 redesignated High Commissioner), resident on Rarotonga.

Executive powers are exercised by a Cabinet consisting of the Prime Minister and between five and seven other ministers including a Deputy Prime Minister. The Cabinet is collectively responsible to Parliament.

Parliament consists of 25 members who are elected by universal suffrage every five years (including one member elected by voters living overseas), and is presided over by the Speaker. The House of Ariki comprises up to 15 members who are hereditary chiefs; it can advise the Government, particularly on matters relating to land and indigenous people but has no legislative powers. The Koutu Nui is a similar organization comprised of sub-chiefs, which was established by an amendment in 1972 of the 1966 House of Ariki Act.

Each of the main islands, except Rarotonga (which is divided into three tribal districts or *vaka*), has an elected mayor and a government representative who is appointed by the Prime Minister. In January 2000 it was announced that the post of Government Representative in the outer islands was to be phased out over two years.

The Government

Queen's Representative: FRED GOODWIN.

New Zealand High Commissioner: KURT MEYER.

THE CABINET
(April 2003)

Prime Minister, Minister of Foreign Affairs and Immigration, Tourism, Marine Resources, House of Ariki, Police, Agriculture, Airport Authority, Ports Authority, Telecom and Information Services and Broadcasting and Information: Dr ROBERT WOONTON.

Deputy Prime Minister, Minister of Finance, Public Expenditure Review, Committee and Audit, Office of Offshore Financial Services, Bank of the Cook Islands, Cook Islands Investment Corporation, Cook Islands Government Property Corporation, National Research and Development Institute, National Development Council, Revenue Management, Development Investment Board, National Superannuation, Crown Law and Attorney-General: TEREPAI MAOATE.

Minister of Agriculture, Justice and Marine Resources: ROBERT WIGMORE.

Minister of Education, Culture, Public Service Commission, Natural Heritage, Ombudsman and Human Resources: JIM MARURAI.

Minister of Works, Youth, Sports and Recreation, Transport, Police, National Disaster Management and Energy: TANGATA VAVIA.

Minister of Health, Internal Affairs, Non-Government Organizations, Information Technology and Commerce Commission: PERI VAEVAE PARE.

GOVERNMENT OFFICES

Office of the Queen's Representative: POB 134, Titikaveka, Rarotonga; tel. 29311.

Office of the Prime Minister: Government of the Cook Islands, Avarua, Rarotonga; tel. 21150; fax 23792; e-mail coso@pmoffice.gov.ck.

Office of the Public Service Commissioner: POB 24, Rarotonga; tel. 29421; fax 21321; e-mail pscom@oyster.net.ck.

Department of Justice: POB 111, Rarotonga; tel. 29410; fax 29610; e-mail justice@cookislands.gov.ck.

Department of Tourism and Transport: POB 61, Rarotonga; tel. 28810; fax 28816; e-mail tourism@cookislands.gov.ck.

New Zealand High Commission: 1st Floor, Philatelic Bureau Bldg, Takuvaine Rd, POB 21, Avarua, Rarotonga; tel. 22201; fax 21241; e-mail nzhraro@oyster.net.ck.

Ministries

Ministry of Agriculture: POB 96, Rarotonga; tel. 28711; fax 21881; e-mail cimoa@oyster.net.ck.

Ministry of Cultural Development: POB 8, Rarotonga; tel. 20725; fax 23725; e-mail culture1@oyster.net.ck; internet www.cinews.co.ck/culture/index.htm.

Ministry of Education: POB 97, Rarotonga; tel. 29357; fax 28357; e-mail dieducat@oyster.net.ck.

Ministry of Energy: POB 72, Rarotonga; tel. 24484; fax 24485.

Ministry of Finance and Economic Management: POB 120, Rarotonga; tel. 22878; fax 23877; e-mail finsec@oyster.net.ck.

Ministry of Foreign Affairs and Immigration: POB 105, Rarotonga; tel. 29347; fax 21247; e-mail secfa@foraffairs.gov.ck.

Ministry of Health: POB 109, Rarotonga; tel. 22664; fax 23109; e-mail aremaki@oyster.net.ck.

Ministry of Internal Affairs: POB 98, Rarotonga; tel. 29370; fax 23608; e-mail sec1@intaff.gov.ck.

Ministry of Marine Resources: POB 85, Rarotonga; tel. 28721; fax 29721; e-mail rar@mmr.gov.ck.

Ministry of Outer Islands' Development: POB 383, Rarotonga; tel. 20321; fax 24321.

Ministry of Works and Physical Planning: POB 102, Rarotonga; tel. 20034; fax 21134; e-mail herman@mow.gov.ck.

HOUSE OF ARIKI

House of Ariki
POB 13, Rarotonga; tel. 26500; fax 21260.

President: PA TEARIKI UPOKOTINI MAIRE ARIKI.

Vice-President: TINOMANA RUTA TUORO ARIKI.

KOUTU NUI

Koutu Nui

POB 13, Rarotonga; tel. 29317; fax 21260; e-mail nvaloa@parliament.gov.ck.

President: TETIKA MATAIAPO DORICE REID.

Legislature

PARLIAMENT

Parliamentary Service

POB 13, Rarotonga; tel. 26500; fax 21260; e-mail nvaloa@parliament.gov.ck.

Speaker: PUPKE ROBATI.

Clerk of Parliament: NGA VALOA.

General Election, 16 June 1999

Party	Seats
Cook Islands Party (CIP)	11
Democratic Alliance Party (DAP)	10
New Alliance Party (NAP)	4
Total	25

Political Organizations

Cook Islands Labour Party: Rarotonga; f. 1988; anti-nuclear; Leader RENA ARIKI JONASSEN.

Cook Islands National: Rarotonga; f. 2003; Leader TEARIKI HEATHER.

Cook Islands Party (CIP): Rarotonga; f. 1965; Gen. Sec. TIHINA TOM MARSTERS; Leader Dr JOE WILLIAMS.

Democratic Alliance Party (DAP): POB 73, Rarotonga; tel. 21224; f. 1971; fmrly the Democratic Party; Leader Dr TEREPAI MAOATE; Pres. FRED GOODWIN.

Democratic Tumu Party (DTP): POB 492, Rarotonga; tel. 21224; fax 22520; split from Democratic Party in 1985; Leader VINCENT A. K. T. INGRAM.

New Alliance Party (NAP): POB 2164, Rarotonga; f. 1992; from split with Democratic Party (Coalition); fmrly the Alliance Party; Leader NORMAN GEORGE; ceased activities.

Judicial System

Ministry of Justice

POB 111, Avarua, Rarotonga; tel. 29410; fax 28610; e-mail offices@justice.gov.ck.

The judiciary comprises the Privy Council, the Court of Appeal and the High Court.

The High Court exercises jurisdiction in respect of civil, criminal and land titles cases on all the islands, except for Mangaia, Pukapuka and Mitiaro, where disputes over land titles are settled according to custom. The Court of Appeal hears appeals against decisions of the High Court. The Privy Council, sitting in the United Kingdom, is the final appellate tribunal for the country in civil, criminal and land matters; since May 1993 the Court of Appeal has been the final appellate tribunal for disputes concerning chiefly titles.

Attorney-General: NORMAN GEORGE.

Solicitor-General: JANET GRACE MAKI.

Chief Justice of the High Court: LAURENCE MURRAY GREIG.

Judges of the High Court: GLENDYN CARTER, NORMAN SMITH, DAVID WILLIAMS, HETA HINGSTON.

Religion

CHRISTIANITY

The principal denomination is the Cook Islands (Congregational) Christian Church, to which about 58% of the islands' population belong, according to figures recorded in the census conducted in 1996.

Religious Advisory Council of the Cook Islands: POB 31, Rarotonga; tel. 22851; fax 22852; f. 1968; four mem. churches; Pres. KEVIN GEELAN; Gen. Sec. TUNGANE POKURA.

The Roman Catholic Church

The Cook Islands form the diocese of Rarotonga, suffragan to the archdiocese of Suva (Fiji). At 31 December 2000 the diocese contained an estimated 3,140 adherents. The Bishop participates in the Catholic Bishops' Conference of the Pacific, based in Suva.

Bishop of Rarotonga: Rt Rev. STUART FRANCE O'CONNELL, Catholic Diocese, POB 147, Rarotonga; tel. 20817; fax 29817; e-mail sbish@oyster.net.ck.

The Anglican Communion

The Cook Islands are within the diocese of Polynesia, part of the Church of the Province of New Zealand. The Bishop of Polynesia is resident in Fiji.

Protestant Churches

Cook Islands Christian Church: Takamoa, POB 93, Rarotonga; tel. 26452; 11,193 mems (1986); Pres. Rev. TANGIMETUA TANGA; Gen. Sec. WILLIE JOHN.

Seventh-day Adventists: POB 31, Rarotonga; tel. 22851; fax 22852; e-mail umakatu@oyster.net.ck; 732 mems (1998); Pres. UMA KATU.

Other churches active in the islands include the Assembly of God, the Church of Latter-day Saints (Mormons), the Apostolic Church, the Jehovah's Witnesses and the Baptist Church.

BAHÁ'Í FAITH

National Spiritual Assembly: POB 1, Rarotonga; tel. 20658; fax 23658; e-mail nsacooks@bahai.org.ck; mems resident in eight localities; Sec. JOHNNY FRISBIE.

The Press

Cook Islands Herald: POB 126, Tutakimoa, Rarotonga; e-mail bestread@ciherald.co.ck; internet www.ciherald.co.ck; weekly.

Cook Islands News: POB 15, Avarua, Rarotonga; tel. 22999; fax 25303; e-mail editor@cinews.co.ck; internet www.cinews.co.ck; f. 1954; by Govt, transferred to private ownership 1989; daily; mainly English; Man. Dir PHIL EVANS; Editor MOANA MOEKA'A; circ. 1,800.

Cook Islands Star: POB 798, Rarotonga; tel. 29965; e-mail jason@oyster.net.ck; fortnightly; Chief Reporter JASON BROWN.

Cook Islands Sun: POB 753, Snowbird Laundry, Arorangi, Rarotonga; f. 1988; tourist newspaper; twice a year; Editor WARREN ATKINSON.

Broadcasting and Communications

TELECOMMUNICATIONS

Telecom Cook Islands Ltd: POB 106, Rarotonga; tel. 29680; fax 20990; e-mail stu@telecom.co.ck; internet www.telecom.co.ck; CEO STUART DAVIES.

BROADCASTING

Radio

Cook Islands Broadcasting Corpn (CIBC): POB 126, Avarua, Rarotonga; tel. 29460; fax 21907; f. 1989 to operate new television service, and radio service of former Broadcasting and Newspaper Corpn; state-owned; Gen. Man. EMILE KAIRUA.

Radio Cook Islands: tel. 20100; broadcasts in English and Maori 18 hours daily.

KC Radio: POB 521, Avarua, Rarotonga; tel. 23203; f. 1979 as Radio Ikurangi; commercial; operates station ZK1ZD; broadcasts 18 hours daily on FM; Man. Dir and Gen. Man. DAVID SCHMIDT.

Television

Cook Islands Broadcasting Corpn (CIBC): see Radio.

Cook Islands TV: POB 126, Rarotonga; tel. 20101; fax 21907; f. 1989; broadcasts nightly, in English and Maori, from 5 p.m. to 10.15 p.m. 10 hours of local programmes per week; remainder provided by Television New Zealand.

In early 1999 the French Société Nationale de Radio-Télévision Française d'Outre-Mer agreed to operate two or three new television channels in the islands.

Finance

Cook Islands Monetary Board: POB 594, Rarotonga; tel. 20798; fax 21798; f. 1981; exercises control of currency; controlling body for trade and industry as well as finance; registers companies, financial institutions, etc. Sec. M. BROWN.

Trustee Companies Association (TCA): Rarotonga; controlling body for the 'offshore' financial sector; Sec. LOU COLVEY.

BANKING

Development Bank

Bank of Cook Islands (BCI): POB 113, Avarua, Rarotonga; tel. 29341; fax 29343; e-mail bci@oyster.net.ck; f. July 2001; when Cook Islands Development Bank merged with Cook Island Savings Bank; finances development projects in all areas of the economy and helps islanders establish small businesses and industries by providing loans and management advisory assistance; Gen. Man. UNAKEA KAUVAI; brs on Rarotonga and Aitutaki.

Commercial Banks

Australia and New Zealand (ANZ) Banking Corpn: 1st Floor, Development Bank Bldg, POB 907, Avarua, Rarotonga; tel. 21750; fax 21760; e-mail lancaster@gatepoly.co.ck; Man. GARY RUNCIMAN.

The Wall Street Banking Corp Ltd: POB 3012, CITC House, Avarua, Rarotonga; tel. 23445; fax 23446; e-mail info@wallbank.co .ck; internet www.wallstreetbankingcorp.com; f. 1992; 100% owned by Natar Holdings Co Ltd; cap. US $15.0m., dep. US $74.9m. (Mar. 2001); Exec. Dir RIAZ PATEL.

Westpac Banking Corpn (Australia): Main Rd, POB 42, Avarua, Rarotonga; tel. 22014; fax 20802; e-mail bank@westpac.co.ck; Man. TERRY SMITH.

Legislation was adopted in 1981 to facilitate the establishment of 'offshore' banking operations.

INSURANCE

Cook Islands Insurance: POB 44, Rarotonga.

Trade and Industry

GOVERNMENT AGENCIES

Cook Islands Development Investment Board: Private Bag, Avarua, Rarotonga; tel. 24296; fax 24298; e-mail cidib@cidib.gov.ck; internet www.cookislands-invest.com; f. 1996 as replacement for Development Investment Council; promotes, monitors and regulates foreign investment, promotes international trade, advises the private sector and Government and provides training in business skills; CEO MARK SHORT.

Cook Islands Investment Corporation: Rarotonga; tel. 29391; fax 29381; e-mail ciic@oyster.net.ck; f. 1998; manages government assets and shareholding interests; Chair. TAPI TAIO; Man. JOE CAFFERTY.

Cook Islands Trading Corporation: Avarua, Rarotonga; fax 20857.

CHAMBER OF COMMERCE

Chamber of Commerce: POB 242, Rarotonga; tel. 20925; fax 20969; f. 1956; Pres. EWAN SMITH.

INDUSTRIAL AND TRADE ASSOCIATIONS

Pearl Federation of the Cook Islands, Inc: Manihiki; tel. and fax 43363; f. 1995 following the dissolution of the govt-owned Cook Islands Pearl Authority; oversees the activities and interests of pearl-producers in the northern Cook Islands.

Pearl Guild of the Cook Islands: Rarotonga; e-mail trevon@ oyster.net.ck; f. 1994; monitors standards of quality within the pearl industry and develops marketing strategies; Pres. TREVON BERGMAN.

UTILITIES

Electricity

Te Aponga Uira O Tumutevarovaro (TAUOT): POB 112, Rarotonga; tel. 20054; fax 21944.

Water

Water Supply Department: POB 102, Arorangi, Rarotonga; tel. 20034; fax 21134.

TRADE UNIONS

Airport Workers Association: Rarotonga Int. Airport, POB 90, Rarotonga; tel. 25890; fax 21890; f. 1985; Pres. NGA JESSIE; Gen. Sec. (vacant).

Cook Islands Industrial Union of Waterside Workers: Avarua, Rarotonga.

Cook Islands Workers' Association (CIWA): POB 403, Avarua, Rarotonga; tel. 24422; fax 24423; largest union in the Cook Islands; Pres. MIRIAMA PIERRE; Gen. Sec. NGAMETUA ARAKUA.

Transport

ROADS

On Rarotonga a 33-km sealed road encircles the island's coastline. A partly sealed inland road, parallel to the coastal road and known as the Ara Metua, is also suitable for vehicles. Roads on the other islands are mainly unsealed.

SHIPPING

The main ports are on Rarotonga (Avatiu), Penrhyn, Mangaia and Aitutaki. The Cook Islands National Line operates a three-weekly cargo service between the Cook Islands, Tonga, Samoa and American Samoa. In August 2002 the Government approved proposals to enlarge Avatiu Harbour. The project, work on which was due to start in September 2002, received additional funding from the Ports Authority and from New Zealand.

Apex Maritime: POB 378, Rarotonga; tel. 27651; fax 21138.

Cook Islands National Line: POB 264, Rarotonga; tel. 20374; fax 20855; 30% govt-owned; operates three fleet cargo services between the Cook Islands, Niue, Samoa, Norfolk Island, Tonga and New Zealand; Dirs CHRIS VAILE, GEORGE ELLIS.

Cook Islands Shipping Ltd: POB 2001, Arorangi, Rarotonga; tel. 24905; fax 24906.

Ports Authority: POB 84, Rarotonga and Aitutaki; tel. 21921; fax 21191.

Reef Shipping Company: Rarotonga; operates services between Rarotonga and Aitutaki.

Taio Shipping Ltd: Teremoana Taio, POB 2001, Rarotonga; tel. 24905; fax 24906.

Triad Maritime (1988) Ltd: Rarotonga; fax 20855.

CIVIL AVIATION

An international airport was opened on Rarotonga in 1974. Polynesian Airlines and Air New Zealand operate services linking Rarotonga with other airports in the region. Air Pacific (Fiji) began a twice-weekly service between Nadi and Rarotonga in June 2000, and in August of that year Air New Zealand began a direct service from Rarotonga to Los Angeles, USA.

Airport Authority: POB 90, Rarotonga.

Air Rarotonga: POB 79, Rarotonga; tel. 22888; fax 23288; e-mail bookings@airraro.co.ck; f. 1978; privately owned; operates internal passenger and cargo services and charter services to Niue and French Polynesia; Man. Dir EWAN F. SMITH.

Tourism

Tourism is the most important industry in the Cook Islands, and there were 72,944 foreign tourist arrivals in 2000, compared with 25,615 in 1984. Of total visitors in 2000, 30.2% came from New Zealand, 16.6% from Australia and 17.0% from the United Kingdom. Visitor arrivals were estimated to have increased to 74,575 in 2001. There were 1,874 beds available at hotels and similar establishments in the islands in 1999. Most of the tourist facilities are to be found on Rarotonga and Aitutaki, but the outer islands also offer attractive scenery. Revenue from tourism was estimated at some $NZ93.9m. in 2000/01.

Cook Islands Tourism Corporation: POB 14, Rarotonga; tel. 29435; fax 21435; e-mail tourism@cookislands.gov.ck; internet www .cook-islands.com; CEO CHRIS WONG.

NIUE

Introductory Survey

Location, Climate, Language, Religion, Flag, Capital

Niue is a coral island, located in the Pacific Ocean, about 480 km (300 miles) east of Tonga and 930 km (580 miles) west of the southern Cook Islands. Rainfall occurs predominantly during the hottest months, from December to March, when the average temperature is 27°C (81°F). Average annual rainfall is 7,715mm (298 ins). Niuean, a Polynesian language, and English are spoken. The population is predominantly Christian, with 66% belonging to the Ekalesia Niue, a Protestant church, in 1991. Niue's flag (proportions 1 by 2) is yellow, bearing, in the upper hoist corner, the United Kingdom's Union Flag with a yellow five-pointed star on each arm of the cross of St George and a slightly larger yellow five-pointed star on a blue disc in the centre of the cross. Some 30% of the population resides in Alofi, which is the capital and administrative centre of Niue.

Recent History

The first Europeans to discover Niue were members of a British expedition, led by Capt. James Cook, in 1774. Missionaries visited the island throughout the 19th century, and in 1900 Niue was declared a British protectorate. In 1901 Niue was formally annexed to New Zealand as part of the Cook Islands, but in 1904 it was granted a separate administration.

In October 1974 Niue attained 'self-government in free association with New Zealand'. Niueans retain New Zealand citizenship, and a sizeable resident Niuean community exists in New Zealand. The 1991 population census revealed an 11.5% decrease since 1986, and many more Niueans live in New Zealand than on Niue. Robert (from 1982, Sir Robert) Rex, who had been the island's political leader since the early 1950s, was Niue's Premier when it became self-governing, and retained the post at three-yearly general elections in 1975–90.

The migration of Niueans to New Zealand has been a cause of concern, and in October 1985 the Government of New Zealand announced its intention to review its constitutional relationship with Niue, with the express aim of preventing further depopulation of the island. In 1987 a six-member committee, comprising four New Zealanders and two Niueans, was formed to examine Niue's economic and social conditions, and to consider the possibility of the island's reversion to the status of a New Zealand-administered territory.

At the 1987 general election all except three of the 20 members of the Niue Assembly were re-elected. The newly-founded Niue People's Action Party (NPAP) secured one seat. The NPAP, Niue's only political party, criticized the Government's economic policy, and in particular its apparent inability to account for a substantial amount of the budgetary aid received from New Zealand. A declared aim of the party was to persuade Niueans residing in New Zealand to invest in projects on Niue.

In April 1989 the New Zealand Auditor-General issued a report which was highly critical of the Niuean Government's use of aid money from New Zealand, in particular Rex's preferential treatment of public servants in the allocation of grants. In June Young Vivian, leader of the unofficial NPAP opposition in the Niue Assembly, proposed a motion expressing 'no confidence' in the Government, which was defeated by 13 votes to seven. In November proposed legislation which included the replacement of New Zealand's Governor-General by a Niuean citizen was rejected by the Niue Assembly, owing to the implications for relations with New Zealand.

At the 1990 general election candidates of the NPAP and its sympathizers won 12 of the 20 seats. Earlier disagreements in the NPAP leadership, however, allowed Rex to secure the support of four members previously opposed to his Government. Rex therefore remained Premier.

The announcement in mid-1991 by the New Zealand Government that it was to reduce its aid payments to Niue by about $NZ1m. (a decrease of some 10% on the average annual allocation) caused considerable concern on the island. More than one-quarter of the paid labour force on Niue were employed by the Niue Government, and, following the reduction in aid in July, about 150 (some 25%) lost their jobs. Members of the Government subsequently travelled to New Zealand to appeal against the decision and to request the provision of redundancy payments for the dismissed employees. Their attempts failed, however, with the New Zealand Government reiterating its claim that aid had been inefficiently used in the past.

In December 1992 Sir Robert Rex died, and Young Vivian (who had been serving as acting Premier at the time of Rex's death) was unanimously elected Premier by the Government. Legislative elections took place in February 1993, and in the following month the Niue Assembly elected Frank Lui, a former cabinet minister, as Premier. Lui, who defeated Young Vivian by 11 votes to nine, announced a new Cabinet following the election; among the new Premier's stated objectives were the development of tourism and further plans to encourage Niueans resident in New Zealand to return to the island.

In March 1994 Vivian proposed an unsuccessful motion of 'no confidence' in the Government, and a further attempt by the opposition to introduce a similar motion was invalidated in the High Court in October on a procedural matter. However, during the ensuing debate, the Minister for National Planning and Economic Development, Sani Lakatani, resigned in order to join the opposition as its deputy leader, thus leaving the Government with only 10 official supporters in the Assembly. Subsequent opposition demands for the intervention of the Governor-General of New Zealand in dissolving the legislature, in preparation for a fresh general election, were rejected, and, despite Lui's assurance that an early election would take place in order to end the atmosphere of increasing political uncertainty, polls were not held until February 1996. The Premier and his three cabinet ministers were re-elected to their seats, although support among the electorate for candidates of the Niue People's Party (NPP, as the NPAP had been renamed in 1995) and independents appeared fairly equally divided; in one village the result was decided by the toss of a coin when both candidates received an equal number of votes. Frank Lui was re-elected by the Niue Assembly as Premier, defeating Robert Rex, Jr (son of Niue's first Premier) by 11 votes to nine.

The issue of Niue's declining population continued to cause concern, particularly when provisional census figures, published in late 1997, revealed that the island's population was at its lowest recorded level. The Government expressed disappointment that its policy of encouraging Niueans resident in New Zealand to return to the island had failed and announced its intention to consider introducing more lenient immigration laws in an attempt to increase the population.

At a general election on 19 March 1999 Lui lost his seat and subsequently announced his retirement from politics. The Minister for Finance, Aukuso Pavihi, also failed to be re-elected. On 29 March Sani Lakatani, leader of the NPP, was elected Premier by the new Assembly, defeating O'Love Jacobsen by 14 votes to six. Lakatani's stated priority as Premier was to increase Niue's population to at least 3,000; he claimed that the sharp decline in the number of residents constituted a threat to the island's self-governing status.

It was reported in May 1999 that New Zealand was to phase out aid to Niue by 2003; New Zealand's aid programme to the island had been reduced by $NZ250,000 annually over the previous five years. However, doubts were expressed over the legality of the New Zealand Government's action, and it was suggested that New Zealand was required by law to provide financial assistance under the 1974 act that established Niue as a self-governing state.

In December 1999 a motion of 'no confidence' in Lakatani was proposed by a number of opposition ministers, in protest at the Government's plans to fund a new national airline (Coral Air Niue). The result of the vote was inconclusive, with an equal number of votes cast for and against the motion. The proposed airline did not materialize, and the Government lost $NZ400,000 of its initial investment in the project. The New Zealand Government subsequently criticized officials in Niue for failing to secure a business plan or feasibility study for the proposed airline.

In late 1999 allegations made by a foreign news agency that Niue was being used by criminal organizations for 'laundering' the proceeds of their illegal activities were strongly denied by Lakatani. However, the naming of the island in a report by the

Financial Action Task Force (FATF, see p. 343) in June 2000 as one of a number of countries and territories that had 'failed to co-operate' in regional efforts to combat 'money-laundering' led the Government to suspend the issue of any further 'offshore' banking licences until stricter regulations governing the financial sector had been introduced. In early 2001 the USA imposed sanctions on Niue (including a ban on transactions with US banks), claiming that the island had not implemented all the recommendations of the report. Lakatani appealed directly to President George W. Bush to end the embargo, which he said was having a devastating effect on Niue's economy. The Government stressed its commitment to meeting international requirements in its financial sector but claimed that it was having difficulty doing so, given its limited legal resources. Moreover, the Premier expressed strong disapproval that a nation as powerful as the USA should choose to inflict such hardship on a small, economically-vulnerable island, and urged other Pacific islands targeted by the report to unite in protest against such impositions. In June 2001 the Government engaged a US law firm in an effort to persuade two banks, Chase Manhattan and Bank of New York, to remove their bans on the transfer of some $NZ1m. to Niue via the business registry in Panama that the Government used for its 'offshore' tax activity.

Having failed to meet an FATF deadline in August 2001, in February 2002 Niue pledged to repeal its 'offshore' banking legislation. Premier Sani Lakatani was also considering closing down international business registrations based in Niue. The FATF announced in April 2002 that, in view of the island's commitment to improving the transparency of its tax and regulatory systems, the organization was to remove Niue from its list of non-co-operative territories; the decision was duly implemented in October. The bank-licensing legislation was repealed in June.

In December 2001 the Alliance of Independents, a new political party led by Frank Lui, was formed to contest the forthcoming general election. The party's spokesperson, O'Love Jacobsen, announced that the Alliance would campaign for a direct air link to New Zealand and for increased spending on public health.

At the general election, held on 20 April 2002, all 20 incumbent members were returned to the Niue Assembly. Independent candidate Toke Talagi polled the highest number of votes (445), but overall the NPP was victorious. However, despite having polled the second-highest number of votes (428), Sani Lakatani did not command the general support of his party, and faced a leadership challenge from his deputy, Young Vivian. Following several days of lobbying within the NPP, Vivian was chosen as Premier. Vivian announced that the party had the support of 10 elected members, having formed a coalition with several independents associated with Toke Talagi. Lakatani was appointed Deputy Premier, however, later that year and following a period of ill health, the former Premier indicated that he might withdraw from politics.

One of the first tasks of the new Government was to draft a budget for 2002/03, which aimed to reduce the territory's deficit by 20%. An initial draft, in which pensions, child allowances and subsidies to village and church councils were reduced, was defeated in the Assembly. A budget that restored these elements but that still aimed to reduce the deficit was approved in late August 2002.

In March 2000 a Niue-New Zealand joint consultative committee met, for the first time, in Alofi to consider the two sides' future constitutional relationship. Later that year the committee proposed to conduct a survey of islanders' views and to consider all options, from reintegration with New Zealand to full independence. A meeting of the joint committee took place in March 2001 in Wellington at which the issues of New Zealand aid and reciprocal immigration laws were discussed, as well as options for Niue's future constitutional status. In early 2001 Hima Takelesi was appointed Niue's first High Commissioner to New Zealand. New Zealand remained committed to annual assistance of $NZ6.3m. in the years 2001–03. At New Zealand's 2001 census, a total of 20,148 Niueans were recorded as resident in New Zealand. Discussions took place in Wellington in March 2003 between the New Zealand Prime Minister, Helen Clark, and Niue's Premier, Young Vivian. Topics debated included budgetary assistance, a review of the island's development plan and the continued migration of islanders from the territory to New Zealand.

Following almost 10 years of technical and political consultations, Niue and the USA signed a maritime boundary treaty in May 1997, delineating the precise boundary between the territorial waters of Niue and American Samoa.

Government

Niue enjoys self-government in free association with New Zealand. The New Zealand Government, however, remains responsible for the island's defence and external affairs. Executive government is carried out by the Premier and three other ministers. Legislation is the responsibility of the Niue Assembly, which has 20 members (14 village representatives and six elected on a common roll), but New Zealand, if called upon to do so by the Assembly, will also legislate for the island. There is a New Zealand representative in Niue, whose status was upgraded to that of High Commissioner in 1993.

Economic Affairs

Niue's gross national product (GNP) per head was estimated at US $2,250 in 1994. The population decreased at an average annual rate of 1.8% in 1986–97. Gross domestic product (GDP) was estimated at $NZ16.7m. in 2000.

Agriculture (including fishing) employs only a small minority of the labour force as a full-time occupation, although a majority of households practise subsistence gardening. The principal crops are coconuts and root crops. Honey is also produced for export. Coconut cream was the island's major export until the closure of the coconut cream processing factory in 1989. The main subsistence crops are taro, yams, cassava and sweet potatoes. A taro export scheme was successfully introduced in the early 1990s, and production of the crop increased by more than 500% in 1993. Exports of taro and yams contributed 87% of total export earnings in 1993. Pigs, poultry, goats and beef cattle are raised, mainly for local consumption. There is no manufacturing industry on Niue.

An increase in the frequency of flights between Niue and Auckland in 1992 enhanced prospects for tourism, as did the construction of some 60 hotel rooms in the mid-1990s and a project to extend the runway at Hanan airport. A total of 2,252 people (48.8% of whom were travelling from New Zealand) visited Niue in 1999, and the industry earned US $2m. in 1997. The island's tourist industry depends upon the twice-weekly service operated by Royal Tonga, and tourism was severely affected by the cancellation of its services between Niue and New Zealand in early 2001. Niue was forced to rely upon charter flights operated by Air Fiji. Both Air Rarotonga and Royal Tongan Airlines officials were seeking subsidies for their services, based on previous passenger and freight loads. However, in November 2001 Kiribati announced plans to operate a 70-seater Airbus between Niue and Fiji. More significantly, Samoa's Polynesian Airlines signed a five-year agreement in October 2002 to provide a direct weekly air link between Niue and Auckland, New Zealand.

Niue records an annual trade deficit, with imports in 1993 exceeding exports by around 1,300%. In that year New Zealand, Niue's main trading partner, provided 86.1% of imports. The principal exports in that year were root crops (which provided 87.1% of total export earnings), coconuts (1.9%), honey and handicrafts. The principal imports were foodstuffs (which constituted 28.0% of the total cost of imports), electrical goods (11.8%), motor vehicles (10.6%) and machinery (5.4%). In 1999 imports totalled $NZ5.2m., while exports were worth only $NZ0.3m. Taro, honey and vanilla were Niue's most significant exports. Imports from New Zealand cost an estimated $NZ4.2m., while exports to that country earned an estimated $NZ0.2m. in 2002.

In 2002/03 the budgetary deficit was projected at US $0.7m. Development assistance from New Zealand totalled $NZ6.25m. in 2002/03 (compared with $NZ10.0m. in 1994/95), of which $NZ3.75m was allocated to budgetary support and $NZ2.5m. to projects and training, including such areas as human resources, the private sector, health and the development of natural resources. The annual rate of inflation averaged 2.8% in 1990–95; consumer prices increased by an average of 1.0% in 1995.

Niue is a member of the Pacific Community (see p. 304) and the Pacific Islands Forum (see p. 306), and an associate member of the UN Economic and Social Commission for Asia and the Pacific (ESCAP, see p. 28). In 2000 Niue became a signatory of the Cotonou Agreement (see p. 234) with the European Union (EU).

Niue's economic development has been adversely affected by inclement weather, inadequate transport services and the annual migration of about 10% of the population to New Zealand. Two-thirds of the land surface is uncultivable, and marine resources are variable. Measures were announced in 1993 aimed at encouraging the return to the island of Niueans resident in New Zealand. It was hoped that, by increasing the resident population, Niue's economy could be stimulated and its chances for self-sufficiency improved. However, the population continued to decline. In 1994 the Niue Assembly approved legislation allowing the island to become an 'offshore' financial centre. The Government predicted that Niue could earn up to $NZ11m. annually in fees from a financial services industry. By mid-1996 the 'offshore' centre was believed to have attracted some US $280,000. However, following the threat of financial sanctions from the Paris-based Financial Action Task Force (FATF, see Recent History), Niue declared its intention to repeal its 'offshore' banking legislation, despite fears that this would result in annual revenue losses of some US $80,000 in bank licence fees and more than US $500,000 in company registration fees. Further attempts to secure additional sources of revenue in Niue included the leasing of the island's telecommunications facilities to foreign companies for use in specialist telephone services. However, this enterprise (which earned the island an estimated $NZ1.5m. per year) caused considerable controversy when it was revealed that Niue's telephone code had been made available to companies offering personal services considered indecent by the majority of islanders. Further controversy surrounded reports in 1998 that the Government was negotiating with a Canadian company to establish a gambling website on the internet. In addition, the island earned some US $0.5m. between 1997 and 2000 from the sale of its internet domain name '.nu'. The imposition of harsh economic sanctions by the US Government in 2001, following accusations that the island was still allowing criminal organizations to 'launder' their funds through the territory's 'offshore' financial centre, led Niue's Government to investigate various alternative activities for generating revenue. In November 2001 Premier Sani Lakatani announced that the Government was negotiating a deal with a US company interested in using Nauru as the call-centre of a satellite service. It was hoped that the scheme would create hundreds of new jobs and provide significant levels of revenue (Niue was to receive 35% of total profits from the project). Other large-scale projects included a scheme by a Korean religious sect to build a US $200m. holy walled city on Niue, which was abandoned in early 2003 following strong opposition from local residents. In 1999 Premier Lakatani announced that he was seeking to gain membership of the Asian Development Bank (ADB, see p. 143) for Niue in the hope that the island might receive a low-interest loan from the ADB if the New Zealand Government proceeded with its intention to withdraw aid to the territory. In 2001, however, Niue's application was obstructed by the USA. In March 2002 Niue was in the process of concluding a 20-year development programme with the EU. Initial assistance of €2.6m., to be released in 2003, was to be used to finance renewable energy projects such as wind power generation. An island development plan for 2003 included proposals to develop Niue's fishing industry by employing a fleet of used Korean fishing vessels, to expand the agricultural sector with the introduction of vanilla cultivation, to encourage increased tourism given the availability of direct flights to New Zealand and to increase taro exports to New Zealand owing to a new regular shipping service which was expected to reduce freight costs significantly.

Education

Education is provided free of charge, and is compulsory for 10 years between five and 16 years of age. The school-leaving age was raised from 14 to 16 in 1998. Primary education, from the age of five, lasts for six years, and is followed by six years of secondary education. In 1998 a total of 54 children were enrolled in pre-primary schools and 282 pupils in primary schools. A total of 304 pupils were enrolled in secondary education in 1991. A number of school-leavers take up tertiary education, mainly in the Pacific region and, to a lesser extent, in New Zealand. There is an extension centre of the University of the South Pacific in Niue. An estimated 50 students were engaged in tertiary education in 1991. A private medical school opened in 2000. The budget for 1998 allocated $NZ1,190,386 to education.

Public Holidays

2003: 1 January (New Year's Day), 2 January (Commission Day), 6 February (Waitangi Day, anniversary of 1840 treaty), 18–21 April (Easter), 25 April (ANZAC Day, anniversary of 1915 landing at Gallipoli), 2 June (Queen's Official Birthday), 17–18 October (Constitution Day celebrations), 21 October (Peniami-

na's Day), 25 December (Christmas Day), 26 December (Boxing Day).

2004: 1 January (New Year's Day), 2 January (Commission Day), 6 February (Waitangi Day, anniversary of 1840 treaty), 9–12 April (Easter), 25 April (ANZAC Day, anniversary of 1915 landing at Gallipoli), 1 June (Queen's Official Birthday), 17–18 October (Constitution Day celebrations), 21 October (Peniamina's Day), 25 December (Christmas Day), 26 December (Boxing Day).

Weights and Measures

The metric system is in force.

Statistical Survey

Source (unless otherwise stated): Economics, Planning, Development and Statistics Unit, POB 40, Alofi; tel. and fax 4219.

AREA AND POPULATION

Area: 262.7 sq km (101.4 sq miles).

Population: 2,321 (provisional) at census of October 1994; 2,088 (provisional: males 1,053; females 1,035) at census of 17 August 1997; 1,857 (official estimate: males 944; females 913) in January 2001; 1,489 in October 2001. An estimated 20,148 Niueans lived in New Zealand in March 2001.

Density (October 2001): 5.7 per sq km.

Ethnic Groups (1997): Niueans 1,779; Europeans 115; Tongans 68; Tuvaluans 35; Fijians 22; Samoans 19; Cook Islanders 10; Others 40.

Principal Towns (population, 2001 census): Alofi (capital) 615; Hakupu 227. Source: Thomas Brinkhoff, *City Population* (internet www.citypopulation.de).

Births, Marriages and Deaths (1998): Births 28 (birth rate 18.3 per 1,000 (1991–97)); Marriages 10; Deaths 17 (death rate 6.6 per 1,000 (1991–97)).

Expectation of Life (WHO estimates, years at birth): 70.4 (males 67.6; females 73.5) in 2001. Source: WHO, *World Health Report*.

Employment (1991): Agriculture, forestry and fishing 45; Manufacturing 27; Construction 36; Trade 58; Restaurants and hotels 19; Transport 40; Finance 27; Real estate, etc. 43; Public administration 242; Education 66; Health, etc. 61; Total (incl. others) 701.

HEALTH AND WELFARE

Key Indicators

Total Fertility Rate (children per woman, 2001): 2.6.

Physicians (per 1,000 head, 1996): 1.30.

Health Expenditure (2000): US $ per head (PPP): 1,111.

Health Expenditure (2000): % of GDP: 7.6.

Health Expenditure (2000): public (% of total): 96.2.

Access to Water (% of persons, 2000): 100.

Access to Sanitation (% of persons, 2000): 100.

For sources and definitions, see explanatory note on p. vi.

AGRICULTURE, ETC.

Principal Crops (FAO estimates, metric tons, 2001): Taro 3,200; Other roots and tubers 406; Coconuts 2,500; Bananas 70. Source: FAO.

Livestock (FAO estimates, 2001): Cattle 112; Pigs 1,700; Chickens 10,000. Source: FAO.

Livestock Products (FAO estimates, year ending September 2001): Pigmeat 49; Poultry meat 14; Hens eggs 12; Honey 6. Source: FAO.

Forestry (cu m, 1985): Roundwood removals 613; Sawnwood production 201.

Fishing (FAO estimates, metric tons, 2000): Total catch 120. Source: FAO, *Yearbook of Fishery Statistics*.

INDUSTRY

Production (1998): Electric energy 3 million kWh (estimate).

FINANCE

Currency and Exchange Rates: 100 cents = 1 New Zealand dollar ($NZ). For details, see Tokelau.

Budget ($NZ '000, year ending 30 June 1990): Revenue 11,296 (New Zealand budgetary support 7,625, Niue Govt Revenue 3,671); Expenditure 11,730.6; (year ending 30 June 1993): Revenue 14,927 (New Zealand budgetary support 7,509, Niue Govt Revenue 7,418).

Overseas Aid ($NZ '000, 2001/02): Official development assistance from New Zealand 6,250 (of which Budget support 3,750, Projects and training 2,500). Source: Ministry of Foreign Affairs and Trade, Wellington.

Cost of Living (Consumer Price Index; base: 1990 = 100): 111.6 in 1993; 113.5 in 1994; 114.6 in 1995. Source: ILO, *Yearbook of Labour Statistics*.

Gross Domestic Product ($NZ '000 in current prices): 16,700 in 2000. Source: Ministry of Foreign Affairs and Trade, Wellington.

EXTERNAL TRADE

Principal Commodities ($NZ '000, 1993): *Imports c.i.f.*: Food and live animals 1,949.7; Beverages, spirits and vinegar 334.0; Mineral fuels 228.5; Wood and cork products 345.3; Iron and steel and articles thereof 278.3; Machinery and parts 374.6; Electrical goods 819.1; Motor vehicles 739.0; Total (incl. others) 6,962.1. *Exports f.o.b.*: Taro 450.5; Yams 22.6; Coconuts 10.2; Others (incl. honey and handicrafts) 50.0; Re-exports 10.0; Total 543.2. *1999* ($NZ '000): *Imports*: 5,200; *Exports*: 300 (Source: Ministry of Foreign Affairs and Trade, Wellington).

Principal Trading Partners ($NZ '000, 1993): *Imports c.i.f.*: Australia 101.7; Fiji 140.9; Japan 358.3; New Zealand 5,993.8; Samoa 47.2; USA 197.2; Total (incl. others) 6,962.1. *Exports f.o.b.*: Total 543.2. *2001/02* ($NZ '000): Trade with New Zealand: *Imports c.i.f.*: 4,182; *Exports f.o.b.*: 197 (Source: Ministry of Foreign Affairs and Trade, Wellington).

TRANSPORT

Road Traffic (registrations, 1992): Passenger cars 130; Motorcycles 301; Vans, etc. 177; Heavy lorries 36; Buses 11; Total motor vehicles 655.

International Shipping: *Ship Arrivals* (1989): Yachts 20; Merchant vessels 22; Total 42. *Freight Traffic* (official estimates, metric tons, 1989): Unloaded 3,410; Loaded 10.

Civil Aviation: *Passengers* (1992): Arrivals 3,500; Departures 3,345; Transit n.a. *Freight Traffic* (metric tons, 1992): Unloaded 41.6; Loaded 15.7.

TOURISM

Foreign Tourist Arrivals (by air): 1,736 in 1998; 2,252 in 1999; 2,010 in 2000.

Tourist Arrivals by Country of Residence (2000): Australia 172; Fiji 58; New Zealand 1,000; Tonga 58; United Kingdom 32; USA 145; Total (incl. others) 2,010.

Tourism Receipts (US $ million): 1 in 1996; 2 in 1997; 1 in 1998. Source: mainly World Tourism Organization, *Yearbook of Tourism Statistics*.

COMMUNICATIONS MEDIA

Telephones (main lines, 2000): 1,050 in use*.

Radio Receivers (1997): 1,000 in use†.

Television Receivers (1997): 340 in use.

Non-daily Newspapers (1996, estimate): 1, circulation 2,000†.
* Source: International Telecommunication Union.
† Source: UNESCO, *Statistical Yearbook*.

EDUCATION

Pre-primary (1998): 1 facility; 54 pupils.

Primary (1998): 1 school; 12 teachers; 282 pupils.

Secondary (1991): 1 school; 27 teachers; 304 pupils.

Post-secondary (March 1991): 50 students (estimate).
Source: mainly Department of Education, Niue, and UN, *Statistical Yearbook for Asia and the Pacific*.

Directory

The Constitution

In October 1974 Niue gained self-government in free association with New Zealand. The latter, however, remains responsible for Niue's defence and external affairs and will continue economic and administrative assistance. Executive authority in Niue is vested in the British monarch as sovereign of New Zealand but exercised through the government of the Premier, assisted by three ministers. Legislative power is vested in the Niue Assembly or Fono Ekepule, which comprises 20 members (14 village representatives and six elected on a common roll), but New Zealand, if requested to do so by the Assembly, will also legislate for the island. There is a New Zealand representative in Niue, the High Commissioner, who is charged with liaising between the Governments of Niue and New Zealand.

The Government

New Zealand High Commissioner: SANDRA LEE.
Secretary to Government: BRADLEY PUNU.

THE CABINET
(April 2003)

Premier and Minister for External Affairs, International Relations and Aid Co-ordination, the Niue Public Service Commission, the Crown Law Office, Community Affairs, Arts, Culture and Village Councils, Religious Affairs, Population Development and Niueans Abroad, Women's Affairs, Youth and Sport, and Private Sector Development: YOUNG VIVIAN.

Deputy Premier and Minister for Planning, Economic Development and Statistics, the Niue Development Bank, Post, Telecommunications and Information Computer Technology Development, Philatelic Bureau and Numismatics, Shipping, Investment and Trade, Civil Aviation, and Police, Immigration and Disaster Management: (vacant).

Minister for Education and Language Development, Health, Environment and Biodiversity, Justice, Finance, Customs and Revenue, and Tourism: TOKE TALAGI.

Minister for Development and Training, Public Works, Water and Utilities, Port Services, the Niue Broadcasting Corporation, and Agriculture, Forestry and Fishing: BILL VAKAAFI-MOTUFOU.

GOVERNMENT OFFICES

All ministries are in Alofi.

Office of the New Zealand High Commissioner: POB 78, Tapeu, Alofi; tel. 4022; fax 4173.

Office of the Secretary to Government: POB 40, Alofi; tel. 4200; fax 4232; e-mail secgov.premier@mail.gov.nu.

Legislature

ASSEMBLY

The Niue Assembly or Fono Ekepule has 20 members (14 village representatives and six members elected on a common roll). The most recent general election was held on 20 April 2002.

Speaker: ATAPANA SIAKIMOTU.

Political Organizations

Alliance of Independents: Alofi; f. 2001; Leader FRANK LUI; Spokesperson O'LOVE JACOBSEN.

Niue People's Party (NPP): Alofi; f. 1987 as Niue People's Action Party; name changed in 1995; Leader YOUNG VIVIAN.

Judicial System

The Chief Justice of the High Court and the Land Court Judge visit Niue quarterly. In addition, lay justices are locally appointed and exercise limited criminal and civil jurisdiction. Appeals against High Court judgments are heard in the Court of Appeal of Niue (created in 1992).

The High Court: exercises civil and criminal jurisdiction.

The Land Court: is concerned with litigation over land and titles.

Land Appellate Court
Hears appeals over decisions of the Land Court.

Chief Justice: NORMAN F. SMITH.

Religion

About 66% of the population belong to the Ekalesia Niue, a Protestant organization, which had 1,487 adherents at the time of the 1991 census. Within the Roman Catholic Church, Niue forms part of the diocese of Tonga. The Church of Jesus Christ of Latter-day Saints

(Mormon), the Seventh-day Adventists, the Jehovah's Witnesses and the Church of God of Jerusalem are also represented.

Ekalesia Niue: Head Office, POB 25, Alofi; tel. 4195; fax 4352/4010; e-mail ekalesia.niue@niue.nu; f. 1846 by London Missionary Society, became Ekalesia Niue in 1966; Pres. Rev. MATAGI VILITAMA; Gen. Sec. Rev. ARTHUR PIHIGIA.

The Press

Niue Economic review: POB 91, Alofi; tel. 4235; monthly.

Niue Star: POB 151, Alofi; tel. 4207; weekly; Niuean and English; publ. by Jackson's Photography and Video; circ. 600.

Broadcasting and Communications

TELECOMMUNICATIONS

Director of Posts and Telecommunications: Alofi; tel. 4002.

Niue Telecom: Alofi; tel. 4000; internet www.niuenet.com.

BROADCASTING

Radio

Broadcasting Corporation of Niue: POB 68, Alofi; tel. 4026; fax 4217; operates television service and radio service; govt-owned; Chair. PONI KAPAGA; CEO TREVOR TIAKIA.

Radio Sunshine: broadcasts in English and Niuean.

Television

Broadcasting Corporation of Niue: see Radio.

Television Niue: broadcasts in English and Niuean, six days a week from 5 p.m. to 11 p.m.

Trade and Industry

GOVERNMENT AGENCIES

Business Advisory Service: Alofi; tel. 4228.

Office of Economic Affairs, Planning and Development, Statistics and Trade and Investment: POB 42, Alofi; tel. 4148; e-mail business.epdsu@mail.gov.nu; responsible for planning and financing activities in the agricultural, tourism, industrial sectors, business advisory and trade and investment.

UTILITIES

Niue Power Corporation: POB 198, Alofi; tel. 4119; fax 4385; e-mail gm.npc.@mail.gov.nu.

TRADE UNION

Public Service Association: Alofi.

Finance

DEVELOPMENT BANK

Fale Tupe Atihake Ha Niue (Development Bank of Niue): POB 34, Alofi; tel. 4335; fax 4010; f. 1993; began operations July 1994; Gen. Man. TERAI MCFADZIEN.

COMMERCIAL BANK

Westpac Banking Corpn: Main St, Alofi; tel. 4221; fax 4043; e-mail westpacniue@sin.net.nu; Man. R. J. COX.

Transport

ROADS

There are 123 km of all-weather roads and 106 km of access and plantation roads. A total of 655 motor vehicles were registered in 1992.

SHIPPING

The best anchorage is an open roadstead at Alofi, the largest of Niue's 14 villages. Work to extend a small wharf at Alofi began in mid-1998 with US assistance. The New Zealand Shipping Corporation operates a monthly service between New Zealand, Nauru and Niue. Fuel supplies are delivered by a tanker (the *Pacific Explorer*) from Fiji. In December 2002 the Government signed an agreement with Reef Shipping Ltd to provide a service to New Zealand every three–four weeks.

CIVIL AVIATION

Hanan International Airport has a total sealed runway of 2,350 m, following the completion of a 700-m extension in 1995, with New Zealand assistance. Air links were seriously affected by the cessation of the Air Nauru service in 1989. In 1995 Royal Tongan Airlines began operating a weekly service between Niue and Tonga, with connections to Auckland, New Zealand, and in 1996 the airline established a twice-weekly direct service between Niue and Tonga.However, Royal Tongan Airlines discontinued its service to Niue in October 2002. Air Rarotonga (Cook Islands) operates occasional charter flights to Niue. In November 2001 Kiribati announced plans to operate a flight between Niue and Fiji. In October 2002 the Niue Government concluded negotiations with Polynesian Airlines to introduce direct weekly flights from Niue to Auckland, New Zealand, for a five-year period.

Niue Airways Ltd (NAL): Hanan International Airport; f. 1990; registered in New Zealand; Dir RAY YOUNG.

Tourism

Niue has a small but significant tourism industry (specializing in holidays based on activities such as diving, rock-climbing, caving and game fishing), which was enhanced by an increase in the frequency of flights between the island and New Zealand in the early 1990s. A new 24-room hotel opened in 1996, increasing Niue's tourist accommodation to 158 beds. However, this resort was closed in April 2001 and its 20 staff were made redundant, following numerous cancelled bookings resulting from the cessation of the Royal Tongan Airlines service to the island. A total of 2,210 people arrived by air (about 50%% of whom were from New Zealand) to visit Niue in 2000. The industry earned about US $1m. in 1998.

Niue Tourist Office: POB 42, Alofi; tel. 4224; fax 4225; e-mail niuetourism@mail.gov.nu; internet www.niueisland.com; Dir of Tourism IDA TALAGI HEKESI.

NICARAGUA

Introductory Survey

Location, Climate, Language, Religion, Flag, Capital

The Republic of Nicaragua lies in the Central American isthmus, bounded by the Pacific Ocean to the west and by the Caribbean Sea to the east. Its neighbours are Honduras, to the north, and Costa Rica, to the south. The climate is tropical, with an average annual temperature of 25.5°C (78°F). The rainy season extends from May to October. The national language is Spanish, although English is spoken by some indigenous Indians along the Caribbean coast. Almost all of the inhabitants profess Christianity, and the great majority are Roman Catholics. The national flag (proportions 3 by 5) has three equal horizontal stripes, of blue, white and blue, with the state emblem (a triangle enclosing a dark blue sea from which rise five volcanoes, in green, surmounted by a Phrygian cap from which extend white rays and, at the top, a rainbow, all encircled by the words, in gold capitals, 'República de Nicaragua' and 'América Central') in the centre of the white stripe; the same flag without the state emblem is an alternative version of the civil flag. The capital is Managua.

Recent History

Nicaragua was under Spanish rule from the 16th century until 1821. It then became part of the Central American Federation until 1838. From 1927 US troops were based in Nicaragua at the request of the Government, which was opposed by a guerrilla group, led by Augusto César Sandino. In 1933, following the establishment of the National Guard (commanded by Gen. Anastasio Somoza García), the US troops left Nicaragua. Sandino was assassinated in 1934, but some of his followers ('Sandinistas') continued actively to oppose the new regime. Somoza seized power in a coup in 1935 and took office as President in 1936. Apart from a brief interlude in the late 1940s, Somoza remained as President until September 1956, when he was assassinated. However, the Somoza family continued to dominate Nicaraguan politics until 1979.

In 1962 the left-wing Frente Sandinista de Liberación Nacional (FSLN, the Sandinista National Liberation Front) was formed with the object of overthrowing the Somozas by revolution. Gen. Anastasio Somoza Debayle, son of the former dictator, became President in May 1967, holding office until April 1972. The Congreso Nacional (National Congress) was dissolved, and a triumvirate ruled until Gen. Somoza was re-elected President in September 1974. In January 1978 the murder of Pedro Joaquín Chamorro Cardenal, the leader of the opposition coalition and the editor of La Prensa (the country's only independent newspaper), provoked violent demonstrations against the Government.

In June 1979 the FSLN announced the formation of a provisional Junta of National Reconstruction. With the FSLN in command of many towns and preparing for the final onslaught on Managua, President Somoza resigned and left the country on 17 July 1979. (He was assassinated in Paraguay in September 1980.) After the Sandinistas had gained control of the capital, the Junta and its Provisional Governing Council took power on 20 July as the Government of National Reconstruction. The 1974 Constitution was abrogated, and the bicameral Congreso Nacional dissolved. The National Guard was disbanded and replaced by the Ejército Popular Sandinista (EPS—Sandinista People's Army), officially established in August. In August the Junta issued a 'Statute on Rights and Guarantees for the Citizens of Nicaragua', providing for basic personal freedoms and restoring freedom of the press and broadcasting. Civil rights were restored in January 1980.

On taking office, the Junta had issued a Basic Statute, providing for the creation of an appointed Council of State to act as an interim legislature. In March 1981 Commdr Daniel Ortega Saavedra was appointed Co-ordinator of the Junta and of its new consultative body, the Council of Government.

By 1981 discontent at the postponement of elections and the increasing hegemony of the Sandinistas had led to the creation of counter-revolutionary forces ('Contras'), who were mostly members of the former National Guard and operated from camps in Honduras. Meanwhile, relations between the US and

Nicaraguan Governments had seriously deteriorated, culminating in the suspension of US economic aid in April 1981. In the same year the US Government donated US $10m. in support of the Contras, while covert operations by the US Central Intelligence Agency (CIA) attempted to destabilize the Sandinista regime. In March 1982 the Sandinista Government declared a state of emergency. However, the intensity of attacks by the Fuerzas Democráticas Nicaragüenses (FDN), anti-Sandinista guerrillas based in Honduras, increased. A Contra group, the Alianza Revolucionaria Democrática (ARDE), was also established in Costa Rica, led by Edén Pastora Gómez, a prominent figure in the revolution who had become disillusioned with the Sandinistas. In December the Sandinistas reaffirmed their support for the initiatives of the 'Contadora group' (Colombia, Mexico, Panama and Venezuela), which was attempting to find peaceful solutions to the disputes involving Central America, and adopted a more conciliatory approach towards the opposition.

In January 1984 the Government announced that a presidential election and elections to a constituent assembly would be held on 4 November 1984. The assembly was to draw up a constitution within two years of taking office. In August the Government restored the majority of the civil rights that had been suspended in September 1982, in order to permit parties to campaign without restrictions. At the elections in November 1984 the FSLN candidate, Daniel Ortega Saavedra, received 67% of the votes cast in the presidential election, and the party won 61 of the 96 seats in the National Constituent Assembly, which replaced the Council of State. Ortega's new Government and the National Constituent Assembly were inaugurated in January 1985.

Meanwhile, in June 1984 talks had commenced between the Nicaraguan and US Governments in order to foster the peace negotiations proposed by the Contadora group. However, although the Sandinistas agreed in September to sign a peace agreement, the USA rejected the agreement on the grounds that the forthcoming Nicaraguan elections would not be fairly conducted. In June 1985 the US Congress voted to allocate US $27m. in non-military aid to the Contras. None the less, the Nicaraguan Government reaffirmed its desire to resume negotiations with the USA. Concurrently, however, the civil conflict escalated, and clashes along Nicaragua's borders with Costa Rica and Honduras became increasingly frequent. In July thousands of Miskito Indians, who had allied themselves with the Contras in the early 1980s, began to return to their ancestral homelands in northern Nicaragua, following talks with the Government concerning autonomy for the region.

In August 1986 the US Congress approved assistance for the Contras worth US $100m. In November the US Government disclosed that funds accruing from its clandestine sales of military equipment to Iran had been used to support the Contras.

In January 1987 a new Constitution was promulgated; on the same day, however, civil liberties, guaranteed in the Constitution, were again suspended by the renewal of the five-year-old state of emergency.

In February 1987 the Governments of Costa Rica, El Salvador, Guatemala and Honduras approved a peace plan for Nicaragua, submitted by the President of Costa Rica and largely based on earlier Contadora proposals, but placing greater emphasis on democratization within Nicaragua, including the ending of the state of emergency. The proposal subsequently underwent some modification, and in August the peace plan was signed by the Presidents of the five nations, in Guatemala. In accordance with the plan's requirements, a four-member National Commission for Reconciliation was created in Nicaragua in August: it was chaired by Cardinal Miguel Obando y Bravo, the Archbishop of Managua, a leading critic of the Government. In January 1988, following a summit meeting of the five Central American Presidents, the Nicaraguan Government ended the state of emergency, and consented to participate directly in negotiations with the Contras. In March negotiations held in Nicaragua between representatives of the Government and the Contras resulted in agreement on a 60-day cease-fire (with effect from 1 April), as a prelude to detailed peace negotiations (this was later unilaterally extended by the Government until November 1989). The Government agreed to the gradual release of political prisoners and to permit the participation of the Contras in domestic political dialogue and, eventually, in elections. In August 1988 the US Senate approved the provision of US $27m. in humanitarian aid for the Contras. As the hope of further military aid diminished, the Contras retreated into Honduras.

In February 1989 the five Central American Presidents met in El Salvador to discuss the reactivation of the regional peace plan. At the meeting it was agreed that, in return for the dismantling of Contra bases in Honduras, there would be moves towards greater democracy in Nicaragua. These included a pledge to hold a general election, open to opposition parties, by February 1990. In April 1989 the Government announced that a general election would be held on 25 February 1990. A number of electoral reforms were introduced: Contra rebels were to be permitted to return to vote, on condition that they relinquished their armed struggle under a proposed demobilization plan. In June 1989 the Unión Nacional Opositora (UNO) was formed by 14 opposition parties of varying political views: the UNO was to present a joint presidential candidate and a single programme in the forthcoming elections.

In August 1989 the five Central American Presidents met in Tela, Honduras, where they signed an agreement providing for the voluntary demobilization, repatriation or relocation of the Contra forces within a 90-day period. To facilitate this process, an International Commission of Support and Verification (CIAV) was established by the UN and the Organization of American States (OAS, see p. 288). Following mediation (conducted by the former US President, Jimmy Carter), the Government concluded an agreement with the leaders of the Miskito Indians of the Caribbean coast. The rebels agreed to renounce their armed struggle and to join the political process. Meanwhile, the UNO designated Violeta Barrios de Chamorro (the owner and director of *La Prensa* since the assassination of her husband, Pedro Chamorro, in 1978), as its presidential candidate in the forthcoming elections. Daniel Ortega was nominated as the candidate of the FSLN.

In November 1989 President Ortega declared the ending of the cease-fire with the Contras, on the grounds that the rebels had made insufficient progress in implementing the Tela agreement and disbanding their forces stationed in Honduras. In response to these events, the UN Security Council established the UN Observer Group in Central America (ONUCA) to monitor compliance with the Tela agreement, to prevent cross-border incursions by rebels and to assist in supervising the forthcoming Nicaraguan elections.

The elections proceeded in February 1990, resulting in an unexpected victory for Violeta Chamorro, the UNO candidate, who obtained some 55% of votes in the presidential election, while Ortega received 41%. Foreign observers confirmed the conduct of the polls to have been free and fair. After the elections, the Sandinista Government decreed an immediate cease-fire. The President-elect pledged to 'depoliticize' the military and security forces, and urged the Contra rebels to disband and return to civilian life. However, the UNO had not secured a sufficient majority of seats in the Asamblea Nacional to make amendments to the Constitution. Consequently, the new Government would be prevented from radically reforming the armed forces, which, under the Constitution, bore the name Ejército Popular Sandinista (EPS—Sandinista People's Army) and were mandated to protect the Sandinista revolution.

During the interim period before the transfer of power, which was to take place on 25 April 1990, Ortega introduced a number of reforms. A General Amnesty and National Reconciliation Law was adopted: this was designed to pre-empt retaliatory measures against outgoing officials and to quash legal proceedings against those who had committed politically-motivated crimes against the State since 1979. In addition, legislation was introduced to protect the rights of public-sector employees.

On 19 April 1990 a cease-fire was agreed by the Contras and the Sandinista armed forces. The Contras agreed to surrender their weapons by 10 June, and to assemble in 'security zones' supervised by UN troops. A transitional agreement between the outgoing Sandinista Government and the newly-elected UNO coalition provided for a reduction in the strength of the security forces and their subordination to civilian authority. Upon taking office President Chamorro assumed the post of Minister of National Defence, but allowed the previous minister, Gen. Humberto Ortega Saavedra, temporarily to retain the post of Chief of the EPS: this provoked considerable controversy within the UNO and the Contra leadership. However, in return for a commitment from the Contras to sign the demobilization accords, the Government agreed to the establishment of a special police force, composed of former Contra rebels, in order to guarantee security within the demobilization zones. Demobilization of the Contra rebels was officially concluded on 27 June, signifying the end of 11 years of civil war in Nicaragua.

On assuming office, the UNO Government immediately attempted to reverse much Sandinista policy. The suspension of the civil service law in May 1990 provoked a public-sector strike, which paralysed the country. Chamorro was forced to concede wage increases of 100% and the establishment of a joint commission of trade union and government representatives to revise the civil service law. In July another general strike, involving 100,000 workers, was held in support of demands for wage increases and also in protest at the implementation of legislation allowing the restoration to private ownership of land that had been nationalized and redistributed under the Sandinista regime. Once again the Government made concessions, including a wage increase and the suspension of the programme to privatize land. The agreement was condemned by the Vice-President, Virgilio Godoy Reyes, who accused Chamorro of capitulating too readily to the demands of the FSLN. In October the Government announced the formation of a National Agrarian Commission to study problems of land distribution and illegal land seizures. The commission was to include members of the trade unions and former Contras. In mid-1991, however, the emergence of groups of rearmed Contra rebels (known as Re-contras) became apparent with the reported occupation of several cities in the northern province of Jinotega. The Re-contras' stated aim was to publicize the grievances of thousands of demobilized Contras in the north of the country who had not received land and aid promised them under the terms of the resettlement plan introduced by the Government prior to demobilization.

In August 1991 a National Security Commission, including a 150-strong Brigada Especial de Desarme (BED—special disarmament brigade), was established to disarm civilians. In the same month the FSLN-operated Radio Sandino acknowledged the existence of groups of rearmed Sandinistas (Re-compas), claiming that these had been formed to counter the military operations of the Re-contras. In spite of the efforts of the National Security Commission, reports of hostilities between Re-contras and Re-compas continued. The phased disarmament of the Re-contras and the Re-compas began in January 1992. However, in April groups of the former combatants began joining forces to form the 'Revueltos', demanding land and credit promised to them prior to demobilization. In May the Government allocated 800 plots of land outside the capital to the Revueltos, as a gesture of its intention to address the groups' grievances. However, rebel activity continued throughout 1992 and 1993, despite successive government ultimatums requiring the rebels to disarm or face military intervention. In July 1993 the Government deployed more than 2,000 troops to quell an uprising by a group of Re-compas in the northern town of Estelí. The ensuing hostilities resulted in the deaths of some 45 people, including several civilians, and the Government was subsequently accused of using undue force. In August the legislature approved an amnesty for all political crimes. Shortly afterwards a group of some 150 Re-contras, the Frente Norte 3-80 (FN 3-80), took hostage 38 members of the BED who had been sent to discuss the Government's amnesty proposals with the rebels. In response, a group of Re-compas, the Comando 40 por la Dignidad de la Soberanía, seized the offices of the Alianza Política Opositora (APO—as the UNO had become, see below) in the capital and took 33 hostages, including the political council of the APO. By late August all the hostages had been released in return for an amnesty for both rebel groups. The FN 3-80 received assurances that the Government would review its grievances, and a temporary truce was declared pending the group's disarmament. On 24 February 1994, following the mediation of Cardinal Obando y Bravo and the OAS, a peace agreement was signed that provided for the demobilization of the FN 3-80 by mid-April, in return for which the rebels were granted an amnesty and the right to be incorporated into the national police force. Demobilization of the FN 3-80 proceeded accordingly, but violent incidents involving further groups of armed rebels, identified as Re-contras, continued in northern and central Nicaragua. In response the Government deployed security forces to combat the rebels' activities, which, it asserted, were criminal and not related to legitimate demands for land.

In June 1991 the FSLN withdrew indefinitely its 39 deputies from the Asamblea Nacional, in protest against the introduction by conservative deputies of a draft bill revoking two laws concerning redistribution of property. The so-called *piñata* laws had been introduced by the FSLN in March 1990, immediately prior to the transfer of power to the Chamorro administration. They guaranteed the property rights of the thousands of people who had benefited from the land expropriation that had been conducted by the Sandinistas. In August 1991 the legislature approved the abrogation of the *piñata* laws, but in the following month President Chamorro vetoed parts of the bill that she deemed to be unconstitutional. In response, right-wing supporters of Vice-President Godoy accused Chamorro of yielding to pressure exerted by the Sandinistas. Disagreement over the property issue had by now led to the alienation by Chamorro of the majority of UNO deputies, and the legislature only narrowly failed to overturn the veto in December. In July, meanwhile, the first congress of the FSLN appointed Daniel Ortega to the newly-created post of General Secretary.

In January 1992 Chamorro reorganized the Cabinet; members of the UNO coalition were replaced by new ministers, in an attempt to reinforce the President's policy of national reconciliation. However, in April Lacayo (son-in-law of Violeta Chamorro and widely considered to be the principal architect of government policy) announced that the Government was seeking 'fundamental agreements' with the FSLN. This announcement served to fuel the anger of right-wing and liberal members of the UNO who, led by Godoy and the President of the Asamblea Nacional, Alfredo César Aguirre, accused both Lacayo and Chamorro of being in league with the Sandinistas. In May Humberto Ortega was summoned to appear before the Asamblea Nacional to answer charges that he was maintaining a clandestine pro-Sandinista army in the country. A possible vote of censure against Ortega was avoided when the Government secured a court injunction in June. Meanwhile in May, at the instigation of Republican US Senator Jesse Helms (a fervent anti-Sandinista), the US Congress suspended the release of US $116m. in aid to Nicaragua, on the grounds that the Nicaraguan Government had failed to compensate US citizens for land expropriated under the Sandinista regime. In August a report by the US Senate's Foreign Relations Committee claimed that the *de facto* rulers of Nicaragua were the Sandinistas who controlled the army, police and judiciary as well as much of the public administrative system. In September, in response to US and UNO criticism on the issue of the return of property expropriated under the Sandinista Government, Chamorro signed decrees establishing a property ombudsman's office and other provisions to expedite the processing of property claims. In addition, the President signed an agreement specifying that all unjustly confiscated property would be returned (or the rightful owners compensated).

A serious legislative crisis arose in September 1992, when César convened the legislature in the absence of the deputies of the FSLN and the Grupo de Centro (GC—a group of eight dissident UNO deputies who had maintained their allegiance to the Government, thus depriving the UNO of its parliamentary majority), recruiting substitute deputies in order to elect new legislative authorities. Chamorro subsequently announced that no laws approved by the legislature would be promulgated until the assembly recognized a Supreme Court decision ruling César's actions to be unconstitutional and declaring all subsequent rulings by the legislature null and void. In late December Chamorro ordered the army to occupy the assembly building and appointed a provisional administration to manage parliamentary affairs pending the election of new legislative authorities. In January 1993 a session of the legislature, boycotted by the UNO deputies, elected a GC member, Gustavo Tablada Zelaya, the Secretary-General of the Partido Socialista Nicaragüense (PSN), to be the new President of the Asamblea Nacional. On the same day, Chamorro announced cabinet changes. Excluded from the new Cabinet, the UNO declared itself an opposition party, as the Alianza Política Opositora (APO), expelling four member parties (including the PSN) for their involvement with the GC. The APO continued to boycott the Asamblea Nacional and to demand the expulsion of Sandinistas from the Government.

In May 1993, in an attempt to resolve the legislative dispute and address the country's social and economic problems, the Government held separate talks with the APO, the FSLN and representatives of the trade unions and the private sector, with a view to establishing an agenda for multilateral discussions. However, the APO withdrew from the talks, insisting that it would not participate in a national dialogue until its parliamentary majority had been restored and Lacayo and Humberto Ortega had been dismissed. Bilateral discussions between the APO and the Government resumed in September, following the announcement by Chamorro that Humberto Ortega would be replaced as Chief of the EPS in 1994. However, the APO continued to demand the dismissal of Lacayo and of the GC deputies.

In October 1993 unprecedented discussions between the APO and the FSLN resulted in a joint demand for a complete restructuring of the Government's economic policy. In addition, it was agreed that Humberto Ortega should resign as soon as a new law regulating the armed forces was enacted. Constitutional issues were also discussed, with the APO proposing the election of a constituent assembly, while the FSLN favoured the implementation of partial constitutional reform by the incumbent legislature. In late October the APO and the FSLN signed an agreement providing for the implementation of partial constitutional reforms, on condition that a consensus was reached on the substance of the reforms by the end of November (subsequently extended to mid-December). The political council of the APO stipulated that it would support the reforms (which required endorsement by 60% of deputies to be enacted) only on condition that its parliamentary majority be restored (through the dismissal of the GC deputies and their replacement by APO members) and that it gain control of the legislative authorities. In November the APO and the FSLN signed an initial agreement on issues including provisions for the creation of a council of ministers to review budget expenditure and advise on policy matters, and a planning and economic council to operate with the participation of representatives of the private sector and labour organizations. Meanwhile, divisions within the APO resulted in the Unión Demócrata Cristiana (UDC), the Movimiento Democrático Nicaragüense (MDN) and the Alianza Popular Conservadora (APC) breaking away from the alliance. The Asamblea Nacional reconvened in January 1994, and a new working alliance (with the majority necessary to approve constitutional reform), including the FSLN, the GC, the UDC, the MDN and the APC, elected new legislative authorities. The establishment of a political council, to expedite the enactment of new legislation, was also announced. The APO subsequently abandoned its boycott of the legislature, and its remaining deputies returned.

In February 1994 a widening division within the FSLN became apparent when Daniel Ortega founded the Izquierda Democrática Sandinista, an internal faction comprising what were termed 'orthodox revolutionaries' and intended to maintain the party's role as a revolutionary force; the faction declared support for 'all forms of struggle', aims not shared by the party's 'renewalist' faction, led by Sergio Ramírez Mercado. In May, in the light of increasing party disunity, the FSLN held an extraordinary congress to conduct internal elections and establish the party's political direction. The result was a victory for the orthodox faction of the party, which secured control of the party's national directorate. The orthodox faction also secured dominance in elections to the party assembly, the Asamblea Sandinista, which subsequently approved a policy of opposition to the Government. Daniel Ortega was re-elected as General Secretary of the FSLN, while Ramírez was excluded from the party's national directorate. In September Ramírez was also dismissed as leader of the FSLN bloc of deputies in the legislature. Meanwhile, the departure from the APO of the Partido Social Demócrata, in February, and of the Partido Liberal Constitucionalista, in April, reduced the alliance to just four parties.

In November 1994, despite opposition from Chamorro, the Asamblea Nacional approved amendments to some 67 of the Constitution's 202 articles. The emphasis of the reforms was to adjust the balance of authority in favour of the legislature (and thus to the disadvantage of the Government). In particular, the Government would be required to seek legislative approval for external loans, debt negotiations and international trade agreements; the legislature would also have greater powers in the allocation of the budget. A further amendment, prohibiting close relatives of a serving President from contesting the presidential election, was widely considered to be intended specifically to prevent Lacayo, Chamorro's son-in-law and Minister of the Presidency, from securing presidential office at the next election, due in 1996. Other reforms included a reduction in the presidential and legislative terms, from six to five years, and the withdrawal of the absolute ban on presidential re-election, although consecutive terms remained prohibited. The set of amendments was deemed illegal by the FSLN leadership but won the support of 32 of the 39 deputies in the FSLN bloc, reflecting the seemingly irreconcilable division within the party. Of particular concern to the FSLN leadership was the introduction of a second round of presidential elections should a single candidate fail to secure the necessary 45% of the votes to win outright in the initial round. It maintained that this was intended to allow right-wing parties to ally in order to prevent an FSLN victory. Amendments were also introduced enshrining civilian authority over the depoliticized security forces. The armed forces, which under the Constitution had previously been entitled the Ejército Popular Sandinista, were thenceforth referred to as the Ejército de Nicaragua (Nicaraguan Army).

In January 1995 the disunity within the FSLN finally resulted in members of the renewalist faction, led by Sergio Ramírez Mercado, forming a separate political party, the Movimiento Renovador Sandinista (MRS). The rupture followed the resignation of the moderate Dora María Téllez as leader of the FSLN bloc in the legislature. Téllez had complained that the FSLN-controlled press had been conducting a defamatory campaign against her. She subsequently left the party to join the MRS.

On 7 February 1995 the constitutional amendments, which had been ratified by the legislature at the beginning of the month, were signed and submitted to Chamorro for approval within 15 days. However, following Chamorro's refusal to promulgate the reforms, on 24 February the Asamblea Nacional released the amendments for publication, thereby enacting them. Chamorro condemned the decision as unconstitutional and contested the legitimacy of the amendments. Meanwhile, an application made by Lacayo to the Court of Appeal, contesting the constitutional amendment preventing him from entering the next presidential election, was rejected. In June a resolution to the dispute concerning the constitutional amendments was achieved by the signing of a political accord between the Government and the legislature. Under the terms of the agreement, many of the amendments intended to reduce presidential authority were to be moderated. Legislation defining the interpretation and implementation of the amendments was approved by the Asamblea Nacional in July, and was subsequently promulgated by Chamorro.

In May 1995 a national strike in opposition to government austerity policies received widespread support—in particular from transport workers and agricultural producers protesting, respectively, at rising fuel prices and the scarcity of available credit from state-owned banks. In June some 40 rural workers belonging to the FSLN-affiliated trade union, the Frente Nacional de Trabajadores, occupied the building of the Asamblea Nacional to support demands for the granting of titles to land allocated under the agrarian reforms of the former FSLN Government. The protest, which lasted three weeks, concluded following a government undertaking to expedite the process of issuing land titles. In November legislation was introduced legalizing the land titles of more than 200,000 families granted land under Sandinista agrarian reform.

In September 1995 Antonio Lacayo was succeeded as Minister of the Presidency by Julio Cárdenas. Lacayo, who had tendered his resignation in July, expressed his intention to pursue in the Supreme Court the right, denied him by the consanguinity clause included in the amended Constitution, to contest the forthcoming presidential election at the head of his newly-established political party, Proyecto Nacional (Pronal). In February 1996 the Supreme Court pronounced that it was not within its jurisdiction to rule on the admissibility of candidacies, and that it fell to the Consejo Supremo Electoral (CSE—Supreme Electoral Tribunal) to make such decisions in accordance with the Constitution and the law. In October 1995, meanwhile, Virgilio Godoy resigned as Vice-President in order to contest the presidency as the candidate of the Partido Liberal Independiente (under the amended Constitution, government officials must leave office at least one year in advance of contesting a presidential election); he was succeeded as Vice-President by Julia Mena Rivera. In July 1996 the CSE ruled that Antonio Lacayo was not eligible to contest the forthcoming presidential election.

Presidential and legislative elections were held, as scheduled, on 20 October 1996. According to official results eventually published in late November, Arnoldo Alemán Lacayo of the Partido Liberal Constitucionalista, who was the presidential candidate of the Alianza Liberal (an electoral alliance comprising mainly liberal parties) secured 51.03% of the votes. Ortega had won 37.75%, while a further 21 presidential candidates shared the remainder of the votes. however, although international observers declared the ballot to have been generally free and fair, the FSLN and several other parties disputed the result as fraudulent. Demands were made for a revision of the vote in many departments and for a fresh poll to be conducted in the departments of Managua and Matagalpa. Although the latter demand was dismissed by the CSE, many of the provisional results were subsequently revised. The CSE acknowledged the existence of serious anomalies, but maintained that these had been insufficient to affect the overall outcome of the poll. In the legislative election the Alianza Liberal failed to gain a majority in the Asamblea Nacional, winning 42 of 90 elective seats. The FSLN obtained 35 seats, the Camino Cristiano Nicaragüense (CCN) three, the Partido Conservador de Nicaragua (PCN) two and Proyecto Nacional two seats. Six smaller parties secured one seat each. The FSLN, the CCN and the PCN were each allocated an additional seat, on the basis of votes received by their candidates in the presidential election. The day before Alemán took office, on 10 January 1997, the FSLN boycotted the newly inaugurated Asamblea Nacional in protest at the decision of the CSE to conduct an open ballot (rather than a secret vote) to elect the legislative authorities. As a result of the boycott the Alianza Liberal secured control of the four principal posts while the PCN and the CCN obtained the remaining three.

In April 1997 the FSLN organized national protests in opposition to the Government's policy concerning the return of property expropriated under the Sandinista regime. Following four days of strike action Alemán and Ortega reached a partial accord whereby Alemán agreed to suspend, for a period of three months, the eviction of families occupying disputed land. Multiparty commissions were established to seek a solution to the property disputes, and to address other issues arising from Alemán's austerity programme, including the rationalization of the civil service. However, the commissions failed to produce agreement. In June a 'national dialogue', involving representatives of more than 50 political parties and civic organizations, was convened by the Government with a view to reaching a consensus on the resolution of issues including poverty, unemployment and property rights. The FSLN, however, declined to participate in the talks. In September the Government and the FSLN reached an agreement in principle on draft legislation concerning the property issue. The bill was subsequently submitted to the 'national dialogue' for consultation. In November the Asamblea Nacional approved the new legislation, the *Ley de la Propiedad Reformada, Urbana y Agraria*, under the terms of which occupants of small expropriated properties would be granted legal ownership of the land, while those of larger such properties would be required to return them or to compensate fully the original owners over a 15-year period.

At the second congress of the FSLN, held in May 1998, Daniel Ortega was re-elected as Secretary-General of the party, despite an earlier public declaration by his stepdaughter, Zoilamérica Narváez Murillo, accusing him of sexually abusing her when she was a child. Ortega, who maintained that Narváez's accusations were politically motivated and claimed that she was being manipulated by his political rivals within the FSLN in order to discredit him, subsequently invoked his parliamentary immunity to avoid being tried. In response, Narváez announced that she would take her case to the Inter-American Court of Human Rights. In October Ortega led demonstrations in the capital in protest at high utility charges, threatening to take up arms if the Government failed to honour its pledge to lower the cost of living for the poor. In January 1999 Ortega assumed control of the FSLN parliamentary bloc and again called for public protests against the economic policies of the Alemán administration.

In April 1999 attempts by the security services to disperse a student demonstration in the capital led to violent confrontations that resulted in the death of a student. The protest, held annually since 1996, was in support of demands for the fulfilment of the constitutional clause, introduced in 1995 but never implemented, which reserved 6% of the budget for university funding. Later in April 1999 Alemán again deployed the security services to restore order in the capital after a strike by transport workers to protest against rising fuel prices degenerated into widespread rioting. In early May the Government conceded a 9% reduction in fuel prices in order to end the strike (the strikers had sought a 40% reduction). At the same time, agreement was reached with the student demonstrators on increased university funding. Both the student and the transport workers' protests had been strongly supported by the FSLN, reflecting the progressive political polarization of the Government and the principal opposition party.

In November 1999 the Comptroller-General, Agustín Jarquín, was arrested on charges of committing fraud against the State. Jarquín, a vigorous critic of corruption in the Government, had launched numerous investigations into corrupt practices by members of the Alemán administration, the most notable of which had resulted in the publication of a report, revealing that Alemán had increased his personal wealth by 900% during his terms of office as Mayor of Managua and as President, and that he had failed to declare these assets to the Office of the Comptroller-General, as required by law. Following his detention Jarquín supporters alleged that the accusations made against him were politically motivated. The arrest had serious consequences for the international reputation of the Alemán administration and for the country's economy. Representatives of donor nations and multilateral organizations expressed concern over the case, and both Germany and Sweden suspended funding for various projects as a result of Jarquín's detention. In late December Jarquín was acquitted of the charges against him, and later that month he formally renewed the corruption charges against Alemán.

In June 1999 the Government and the FSLN reached an agreement to begin negotiations on constitutional and electoral reform. This co-operation prompted the formation of an anti-Ortega faction within the FSLN, led by the party's former parliamentary leader, Víctor Hugo Tinoco. In July these dissident Sandinistas, in alliance with former Contras and various minor right-wing and centre-right parties, protested in Managua against the pact. In January 2000 a series of constitutional reforms resulting from the negotiations came into force. The principal amendments included a reduction in the proportion of votes necessary for a President to be elected outright from 45% to 35%, thus increasing the likelihood of an FSLN victory. In return, Alemán was guaranteed a seat in the Asamblea Nacional after leaving office, thus making him virtually immune from prosecution. Other reforms included the restructuring of the judiciary, electoral authorities and the Office of the Comptroller-General—which was to be headed by a five-member board, thereby effectively removing the threat to the Alemán administration of Jarquín.

In September 2000 the Minister of Foreign Affairs, Eduardo Montealegre, resigned, allegedly following a dispute with President Alemán (he was replaced, in December, by Francisco Aguirre Sacasa). However, Montealegre's departure increased rumours that he intended to stand as a candidate in the presidential election that was scheduled to be held on 4 November 2001, as Nicaraguan law required ministers to resign from government one year before standing for an elected office. In the following month the Minister of Government, René Herrera, resigned in order to contest the presidency.

In municipal elections held on 5 November 2000 the PLC won a convincing victory, securing control of 97 of the 151 municipalities. The FSLN won control of 49 municipalities (including Managua), and the Partido Conservador Nicaragua won five. Changes to rules governing local elections made by the CSE earlier in the year meant that many smaller parties were disqualified from participating. Concern was also expressed over the high abstention rate; however, the results were upheld.

In January 2001 the FSLN elected Ortega as their presidential candidate, as expected. In the same month the Vice-President, Enrique Bolaños Geyer, resigned his position and announced his presidential candidacy, representing the PLC. In April the FSLN and the USC announced an alliance and declared that the former Comptroller-General, Agustín Jarquín Anaye, would be Ortega's running mate. The legitimacy of the vice-presidential candidates of the three main parties was questioned by the electoral authorities in mid-2001. In June Jarquín was accused of embezzling public funds, while the PLC's José Rizo and the PCN's José Antonio Alvarado, who had been born in Chile and the USA, respectively, were both challenged over their nationality. The authorities concluded that while Jarquín and Rizo could continue to stand for election, Alvarado would be prohibited from participating in the contest as he could not prove that he had relinquished his US nationality.

In his electoral manifesto, Bolaños, the PLC candidate, pledged to investigate legislative corruption and to reduce civil service salaries. The FSLN nominee Ortega sought to reassure the electorate that he had renounced the more militaristic policies of his past, pledging to demilitarize the border with Costa Rica, to return property belonging to US citizens confiscated by his Government during the 1980s and to introduce a job-creation programme. Nevertheless, Ortega proved to be a controversial choice of candidate for the FSLN. His step-daughter, Zoilamérica Narváez, continued to make allegations of abuse against him and Bolaños, his main opponent, made much of the FSLN's links with the Cuban regime of Fidel Castro Rúz and with the Libyan military leader, Col Muammar Al-Qaddafi. The US Government also made it known that it disapproved of Ortega as the FSLN's candidate. The State Governor of Florida (and brother of the US President, George W. Bush) published a full-page advertisement in one of the national newspapers expressing his support for Bolaños. When, days before the elections, the PCN candidate, Noel Vidaurre, announced his withdrawal from the contest, the US Government was accused of influencing his decision.

Presidential and legislative elections took place on 4 November 2001, amid tight security. The final results gave Bolaños 56.3% of votes cast, while Ortega secured 42.3% and Alberto Saborío of the PCN, 1.4%. The PLC also won a majority of votes (53.2%) in the elections to the Asamblea Nacional, securing 47 seats; the FSLN won 43 seats and the PCN the remaining two. In the weeks following the election the FSLN made allegations of electoral irregularities. Three FSLN magistrates on the seven-member electoral council objected to the party's allocation of seats in the Asamblea Nacional and resigned their positions in protest. However, the complaint was rejected by the Supreme Constitutional Court.

Bolaños took office on 10 January 2002. Almost immediately he encountered opposition from within his own party, when members of the PLC rejected his preferred candidate for President of Congress, Jaime Cuadra, in favour of former President Alemán. Alemán, who still enjoyed strong support from within the PLC, had already indicated that he intended to stand for re-election in 2007 and to use his position to obstruct legislation proposed by the new President. The new Cabinet, which was appointed in January, included few members of the Alemán faction of the PLC.

In late March 2002 the Attorney-General announced that former President Alemán was to face charges of fraud and embezzlement relating to the state television company, Sistema Nacional de Television Canal 6. However, in the months that followed President Bolaños made several attempts to remove Alemán's congressional immunity. However, internal divisions within the PLC (which had divided into pro-Alemán and pro-Bolaños factions) meant that the President lacked the 47 votes necessary to have the motion approved. Nevertheless, in early August, although he remained immune from prosecution through his position as congressional speaker, Alemán, along with several members of his family and former members of his Government, was formally charged with 'laundering' some US $100m. from state communications, infrastructure, insurance and petroleum enterprises during his 1997–2002 term as President. On the same day, in an emotive speech broadcast to the nation, Bolaños expressed his disappointment with his predecessor and claimed that corruption was one of the main causes of poverty in the country. The former President rejected the charges and throughout the month his supporters organized several demonstrations. As President of the Asamblea Nacional, Alemán obstructed approval of the budget and several reforms to the tax system which the Government needed to introduce in order to negotiate credit from the IMF. Furthermore, in mid-August, he announced a 20-day parliamentary recess just as President Bolaños was to propose a further vote on removing Alemán's immunity. At the end of the month thousands of protesters marched through Managua to demand an end to the former head of state's immunity. The demonstration coincided with a visit to Nicaragua of the US Assistant Secretary of State for Western Hemisphere Affairs, Otto Reich, who offered the US Administration's support in the fight against corruption.

In September 2002 the relatives and associates of Alemán accused of money-laundering in the previous month were convicted of the charges. On sentencing the guilty parties, the judge also urged the Asamblea Nacional to lift Alemán's immunity. A week later, Alemán suspended a parliamentary session at which the removal of his congressional immunity was to be discussed.

The following day, FSLN members joined the Bolaños faction of PLC to vote in favour of Alemán's dismissal and to dissolve the legislative committee, which had supported him. Jaime Cuadra was installed as President of the Asamblea and a new legislative commission, comprising supporters of Bolaños, was formed to determine whether Alemán's immunity should be revoked. Alemán denounced his removal from office as an 'act of terrorism' and declared his intention and that of his supporters further to impede the business of the Asamblea. The former President refused to attend the first session of the new legislative commission, which began in late September, claiming that its members were not impartial and therefore unfit to judge. Nevertheless, the hearing proceeded in early October. The former President's financial assets in Panama and those of his family in the USA were 'frozen' while investigations into the charges were made. The USA also suspended Alemán's right to enter its territory; several members of his family and former administration had already fled the country.

In late October 2002 Bolaños himself became the subject of allegations of fraud. In response to charges filed with the Supreme Court, that he and his Vice-President, José Rizo Castellón, had used an illegal fund controlled by Alemán to finance his 2001 electoral campaign, Bolaños promised to renounce his presidential immunity at a date named by his prosecutors. In early November Bolaños and Rizo were formally charged with embezzling US $4.1m. from public funds.

On 13 December 2002 the Asamblea Nacional approved a motion revoking Alemán's congressional immunity by a narrow majority; the former President was immediately put under house arrest. However, later in the month, the Attorney-General, Julio Centeno, warned that evidence amassed to prosecute Alemán could also be used in the case against Bolaños, who was under pressure from business leaders not to renounce his immunity from prosecution fearing that the case would cause the country's economic collapse.

Alemán's arrest further deepened divisions within the PLC. In January 2003 Bolaños' veto of parts of the budget, in order to comply with conditions stipulated by the IMF for Nicaragua to qualify for financial assistance and debt relief, was opposed by both the pro-Alemán faction of the PLC and the FSLN (the Sandinistas had supported the President in his attempts to remove Alemán). In late March the pro-Alemán faction of the PLC officially announced that they were in opposition to the Government, leaving Bolaños with the unconditional support of only nine PLC members in the Asamblea Nacional. However, six members of the Alemán faction later declared their allegiance to Bolaños.

In March 2003 the Government announced that it was to sell its remaining 49% share in the state telecommunications concern, Enitel (the company had been the subject of fraud investigations in 2001 and 2002). The company's complete privatization was recommended by the IMF and the process was expected to be concluded by September 2003.

Delays in the resolution of claims by US citizens for compensation for, or the restitution of, property expropriated under the former Sandinista Government, threatened to undermine relations with, and jeopardize inflows of aid from, the USA in 1994. In April the US Congress approved the Helms-González Amendment providing for the suspension of bilateral aid to countries where the property of US citizens had been confiscated. The amendment also obliged the US Government to veto applications by those countries to international lending agencies. However, Nicaraguan efforts to resolve US property claims prior to the July deadline stipulated in the amendment proved sufficient to avoid the suspension of aid. In May 2001 Nicaragua and the USA re-established full military relations, suspended since 1980. In early 2002 the US Government granted the Nicaraguan armed forces US $500,000 to fund anti-drugs-trafficking programmes and assist in aid programmes following natural disasters. The Ministry of National Defence announced that it was to receive an additional sum in 2003.

In June 1995, prompted by frequent disputes concerning fishing rights in the Gulf of Fonseca, Nicaragua signed an accord with Honduras providing for the visible demarcation of each country's territorial waters. Despite this agreement, in December the Honduran Government issued an official protest to Nicaragua at what it claimed to be the illegal seizure of Honduran fishing vessels by a Nicaraguan naval patrol in Honduran waters. In May 1997 a further incident, in which Nicaraguan and Honduran naval patrols exchanged fire following the seizure by the Nicaraguan navy of Honduran fishing

boats, gave renewed impetus to the demarcation issue. However, the demarcation process did not begin until May 1998. In December 1999, following further confrontations, Nicaragua initiated proceedings at the International Court of Justice (ICJ) in The Hague, Netherlands, to determine the maritime delimitation in the Gulf of Fonseca. In that month a dispute arose prompting Nicaragua to sever commercial ties with, and impose import taxes on, Honduras, in direct contravention of Central American free-trade undertakings (Nicaragua also imposed similar tariffs on Colombia, thereby violating commitments entered into with the World Trade Organization). The dispute stemmed from the Caribbean Sea Maritime Limits Treaty, which Honduras had signed with Colombia in 1986 and had finally ratified in late November 1999, thereby formally recognizing a frontier with Colombia that effectively granted Colombia territorial rights to areas of the Caribbean historically claimed by Nicaragua. Troop movements were subsequently reported on both sides of the Nicaragua–Honduras border. Following mediation by the OAS, in January 2000 Nicaragua ended its trade sanctions against Honduras, and in March both countries signed an accord committing them to observe a maritime exclusion zone in the Caribbean and to reduce troop numbers on their common border. In addition, both countries agreed to submit all issues pertaining to maritime space in the Caribbean Sea to the ruling of the ICJ, and to return to the situation prevailing immediately before the ratification by Honduras of the Caribbean Sea Maritime Limits Treaty. An agreement was also made to mount co-ordinated naval patrols in the Gulf of Fonseca. However, shortly after the new accord was signed conflict again emerged over a small islet in the disputed territory, which Nicaragua claimed had been occupied by the Honduran armed forces. Furthermore, in February 2001 the Minister of Defence, José Adán Guerra, accused Honduras of violating the March 2000 accords by carrying out military exercises in the area and, in the following month, Nicaragua submitted documentation to the ICJ contesting the Treaty. Nicaragua also refused to participate in the joint patrol of the Gulf of Fonseca. In March 2001 delegates from both Governments attended OAS-sponsored discussions in Washington, DC, USA. In June Nicaragua and Honduras concluded a confidence-building agreement, which provided for OAS observers to monitor the actions of army and navy forces on both sides of the common border. However, in August, the Nicaraguan Government claimed that Honduras was purchasing arms and anti-tank and anti-aircraft weapons and was planning to launch an attack on its border. Honduras denied the accusations. In July 2002 the situation further deteriorated when the Nicaraguan Government announced plans to sell oil-drilling rights in the disputed area. The authorities also reported that Honduras had again increased the number of armed forces in the border region; the Honduran Government maintained that the troops were deployed as part of a campaign to stop the spread of dengue fever in the area. In August Honduras threatened to impose tariffs on all Nicaraguan goods in protest. In the following month the Government announced that it had received several bids and intended to proceed with the sale of drilling rights. However, in March 2003 the Asamblea Nacional approved the suspension of import taxes on Honduran goods, imposed in 1999. The ICJ was not expected to rule on the dispute until 2004.

In 1997 relations with Costa Rica became strained when, following a change in that country's immigration policy, it began deporting Nicaraguans who were residing illegally in the country. Large numbers of Nicaraguan immigrants, who provided a source of cheap labour, had previously been tolerated, but owing to a deterioration of economic conditions in Costa Rica were now considered a burden on the country's resources. Remittances from Nicaraguans in Costa Rica represented a significant contribution to the Nicaraguan economy, averaging US $240m.–$300m. per year. During bilateral discussions held in January 1998, Costa Rica established as a condition for agreement on the immigration issue that Nicaragua grant concessions allowing Costa Rican artisan fishermen to operate in Nicaraguan territorial waters. Nicaragua, however, rejected the demand. In February 1999 Costa Rica offered one-year renewable residence permits to registering illegal Nicaraguan immigrants. The Costa Rican authorities further assured Nicaragua that, following the amnesty, the law would be firmly applied. In July 1998 further antagonism developed between the two countries when Nicaragua prohibited Costa Rican civil guards from carrying arms while navigating the San Juan river, which forms the border between the two countries. According to a long-standing treaty, the river, which is Nicaraguan territory, was only to be used by Costa Rica for commercial purposes. Following protests by Costa Rica, agreement was reached allowing for that country's civil guard to carry arms on the river while under escort by the Nicaraguan authorities. In August, however, following concerted pressure by opposition parties, the media and the Roman Catholic Church in Nicaragua, which accused the Government of surrendering part of the nation's sovereignty, Nicaragua annulled the accord. In June 2000 both Governments agreed a procedure that would allow armed Costa Rican police officers to patrol the river. In October 2001 President Alemán further announced that Costa Rican guards could patrol the river, providing they had first obtained permission from his Government, but rejected Costa Rica's submission of the dispute to the ICJ. However, in early December, President-elect Bolaños held discussions with his Costa Rican counterpart, Miguel Angel Rodríguez Echeverría, at which he pledged to seek a solution to the issue. In September 2002 the two countries appeared to have made some progress towards resolving the dispute. The Government agreed to discontinue the fees charged to Costa Ricans crossing the river in exchange for the abolition of charges levied on visas and tourist permits required by Nicaraguans to enter Costa Rica. Costa Rica also announced that it would relinquish plans to refer the matter to the ICJ. In October bilateral discussions began on the Nicaraguan Government's plans to sell oil-exploration rights in the Caribbean Sea and Pacific Ocean.

In early November 2001 a dispute with Colombia arose after a Nicaraguan fishing vessel was captured allegedly in Colombian waters. The Colombian authorities charged the crew with violating its sovereignty and misappropriating its natural resources. It was the third time in that year that a Nicaraguan vessel had been apprehended in Colombian waters. In the following month, Nicaragua presented a request to the ICJ that its claim over territorial waters in the Caribbean Sea and around the islands of San Andrés and Providencia be recognized.

Government

Executive power is vested in the President, who is elected by popular vote for a five-year term. The President is assisted by a Vice-President and an appointed Cabinet. Legislative power is held by the Asamblea Nacional (National Assembly), elected by universal adult suffrage, under a system of proportional representation, for a five-year term.

Defence

In August 2002 the armed forces were estimated to total 14,000 (army 12,000, navy 800, air-force 1,200). Compulsory military service was abolished in April 1990. In 1995 the armed forces were renamed the Ejército de Nicaragua, following a constitutional amendment removing their Sandinista affiliation. The defence budget for 2002 totalled US $322m.

Economic Affairs

In 1998, according to estimates by the World Bank, Nicaragua's gross national income (GNI), measured at average 1996–1998 prices, was US $1,783m., equivalent to $370 per head (or $1,870 per head on an international purchasing-power parity basis). During 1990–98, it was estimated, the population increased at an average annual rate of 2.9%, while gross domestic product (GDP) per head decreased, in real terms, by an average of 2.0% per year. According to the Central Bank, Nicaragua's gross domestic product (GDP) increased, in real terms, by an average of 3.4% per year in 1990–2001; GDP increased by 5.5% in 2000 and by a preliminary 3.0% in 2001.

Agriculture (including forestry and fishing) contributed an estimated 32.4% of GDP in 2001 and engaged an estimated 42.9% of the employed work-force in 2001. The principal cash crops are coffee (which accounted for an estimated 73.3% of export earnings in 2002, sugar cane, bananas and cotton. Maize, rice and beans are the principal food crops. Meat and meat preparations accounted for about 8.1% of export earnings in 2000. Production of shellfish became increasingly important, and in 2000 shrimps and lobsters accounted for some 17.4% of export earnings, although this decreased to 12.7% in 2002. Agricultural GDP increased at an average annual rate of 5.2% during 1990–2001; the sector's GDP increased by 11.4% in 2000 and by an estimated 3.1% in 2001.

Industry (including mining, manufacturing, construction and power) engaged an estimated 15.0% of the employed labour force and provided an estimated 21.7% of GDP in 2001. Industrial

GDP increased by an average of 4.0% per year during 1990–2001; it increased by 3.1% in 2000 and by an estimated 3.2% in 2001.

Mining contributed an estimated 0.7% of GDP in 2001 and engaged an estimated 0.6% of the employed labour force in 2001. Nicaragua has workable deposits of gold, silver, copper, lead, antimony, zinc and iron; its non-metallic minerals include limestone, gypsum, bentonite and marble. The GDP of the mining sector increased at an average annual rate of 11.4% in 1990–2001; the sector's GDP decreased by about 20% in 2000, but grew by an estimated 2.5% in 2001.

Manufacturing contributed some 14.2% of GDP in 2001 and engaged an estimated 7.0% of the employed labour force in 2001. Measured by the value of output, the principal branches of manufacturing in 2001 were food products, beverages and tobacco (about 67% of the total), machinery and metal products and petroleum derivatives and rubber products. The *maquila*, or offshore assembly, sector expanded rapidly in the early 1990s, although growth slowed at the end of the decade. The principal products were clothing, footwear, aluminium frames and jewellery. Manufacturing GDP increased by an average of 2.0% per year in 1990–2001; the sector's GDP grew by 2.8% in 2000 and by an estimated 2.6% in 2001.

Energy is derived principally from imported petroleum, although two hydroelectric plants in the department of Jinotega account for one-third of the electrical energy generated in the country. The construction of a geothermal generator, with a capacity of 232 MW, began in western Nicaragua in 1998. Imports of mineral fuels and lubricants comprised 8.2% of the total value of imports in 1999. In 2001 Nicaragua produced an estimated 2,613.7m. kWh of electrical energy.

The services sector contributed an estimated 45.2% of GDP in 2001 and engaged an estimated 42.5% of the employed labour force in 2001. The tourism sector expanded throughout the 1990s; in 2000 annual income reached US $116m., with arrivals reaching 485,909. The GDP of the services sector increased by an average of 1.8% per year in 1990–2001; in 2000 it grew by 3.1%, and in 2001 by an estimated 2.9%.

In 2000 Nicaragua recorded a visible trade deficit of about US $1,207.6m., and there was a deficit of $561.1m. on the current account of the balance of payments. In 2000 the principal source of imports (27.4%) was the USA; other major suppliers were Nicaragua's partners in the Central American Common Market (CACM—Costa Rica, El Salvador, Guatemala and Honduras, see p. 160), as well as Venezuela, Panama and Mexico. The USA was also the principal market for exports (32.2%) in 2002; other notable purchasers were the countries of the CACM, France, Canada and Mexico. The principal exports in 2002 were coffee, meat and lobster. The principal imports were non-durable consumer goods, intermediate goods for industry, capital goods for industry and crude and petroleum and its derivatives.

In 2001 Nicaragua recorded a budgetary deficit of an estimated 4,692.5m. gold córdobas (equivalent to 13.8% of GDP). At the end of 2000 Nicaragua's total external debt was $7,019m., of which $5,860m. was long-term public debt. The cost of servicing external debt in that year was equivalent to 23.0% of the value of goods and services. Annual inflation averaged 122.2% in 1985–95, reaching a peak of 10,205% in 1988. In 1990–2001 the average rate of increase in consumer prices was 51.9%. However, the average rate declined from 2,945% in 1991 to only 7.4% in 2001. An estimated 10.7% of the labour force were unemployed in 2001.

Nicaragua is a member of the CACM (see p. 160), which aims eventually to liberalize intra-regional trade, and of the Inter-American Development Bank (IDB, see p. 239).

On assuming power in 1990, the Chamorro administration inherited an economy devastated by the effects of a prolonged civil war and characterized by extremely low output, hyper-inflation and a large foreign debt burden. With the implementation of a comprehensive economic reform programme, supported by the IMF, inflation was brought under control, levels of foreign reserves were greatly improved, and the fiscal deficit significantly reduced. In 1998 the Alemán administration secured a three-year Enhanced Structural Adjustment Facility (ESAF) in support of its economic programme. Measures stipulated under the terms of the ESAF included a rationalization of the public sector, increases in public utility tariffs, and the continued privatization of state enterprises. In addition to facilitating further credits from multilateral sources, in December 2000 Nicaragua qualified for debt relief of some

US \$4,500m. under the 'Heavily Indebted Poor Countries' (HIPC) initiative.

In October 1998 the Nicaraguan economy was devastated by the effects of 'Hurricane Mitch'. Much of the country's infrastructure was destroyed, and as many as 1.5m. people were left homeless. The Central Bank estimated total reconstruction costs at more than US \$1,500m. Real GDP growth was reduced to 4.1% in 1998 (from the 6.0% originally forecast for that year), while inflation was estimated to have increased to 13.1%, from 9.2% in the previous year, owing partly to rising food prices resulting from uncertainty about grain supplies. Nevertheless, in 1999 the economy recovered rapidly, recording GDP growth of 7.4%, partly as a consequence of the inflow of funds for reconstruction: Nicaragua received aid commitments totalling some \$2,500m., to be disbursed in the three-year period following the hurricane. According to the Central Bank, the economy grew by 5.5% in 2000 and by a preliminary 3.0% in 2001; the decrease in the rate of growth in 2001 was partly owing to a fall in international commodity prices.

In 2001 the IMF expressed concern that Nicaragua was not fulfilling its commitments under the terms of the ESAF, crucial if an extension to the scheme was to be approved. As well as the Government's failure to adequately control public spending and the punitive 35% trade tariffs imposed on Honduran imports, of particular concern to the IMF was the lack of progress in the country's privatization programme. In 1999 the state electricity company, Empresa Nicaragüense de Electricidad (ENEL), was divided into three generating companies (one hydroelectric and two thermal plants) and two distribution companies, in preparation for its divestment. The distribution companies were sold to a Spanish company, Unión Fenosa, in November 2000; however, the Alemán Government failed to sell the generating companies. Following the change of government in January 2002, some progress was made, with the successful sale of GEOSA, one of the operating companies, to the US company Coastal Power International. In 2001 the Government succeeded in selling the telecommunications concern, Enitel, although not without some controversy. Hours before tendering for the company began, on 31 August, the mayor of Managua and FSLN member, Herty Lewites, obtained a legal injunction against its sale on the grounds that it owed the city council some US \$30m. in unpaid taxes. In spite of this, in December the sale of a 40% stake in the company to a Swedish-Honduran consortium was completed.

In December 2001 the IDB approved a debt-relief programme of US \$386m. for Nicaragua, to be implemented annually until 2019. The Government of Enrique Bolaños Geyer, which took office in January 2002, immediately began negotiations for a new accord with the IMF. The process became hindered in 2002, however, by the political feud between Bolaños and Alemán, who, as President of the Asamblea Nacional, obstructed proposed tax reform and other budgetary measures that had been stipulated by the IMF as conditions for new financing. In late October the IMF agreed to make a loan of \$100m., dependent on a number of conditions, including the reduction of the fiscal deficit to 14% of GDP over the next three years, the complete privatization of Enitel and a reduction in domestic public debt. In December the IMF approved the release of \$129m. of funds over the next three years and \$2.5m. in interim assistance through the HIPC initiative. The 'Paris Club' of creditor nations also agreed to cancel \$405m. of public external debt and to reschedule remaining payments. However, the 2003 draft budget passed by the Asamblea Nacional in the same month was deemed unacceptable by the IMF as funds formerly set aside for debt servicing were used to facilitate public-sector wage increases. Attempts by President Bolaños to veto the budget were met with strong congressional opposition and in February 2003 the IMF announced that the accord could not be fully implemented until the political situation had been resolved.

Education

Primary and secondary education have been provided free of charge since 1979. Primary education, which is officially compulsory, begins at seven years of age and lasts for six years. Secondary education, beginning at the age of 13, lasts for up to five years, comprising a first cycle of three years and a second of two years. In 1998 total enrolment at primary and secondary schools was equivalent to 82% of the school-age population (boys 79%; girls 85%). Secondary enrolment in that year was equivalent to 57% of children in the relevant age-group (boys 52%; girls 62%). There are many commercial schools and four universities. In 2000 a total of 56,558 students attended universities and other higher education institutes. Public expenditure on primary and secondary education accounted for 8.8% of total government expenditure in 1997.

Public Holidays

2003: 1 January (New Year's Day), 17 April (Maundy Thursday), 18 April (Good Friday), 1 May (Labour Day), 21 July (Liberation Day), 1 and 10 August (Managua local holidays), 15 September (for Battle of San Jacinto and Independence Day), 3 November (for Day of the Dead), 8 December (Immaculate Conception), 25 December (Christmas Day).

2004: 1 January (New Year's Day), 8 April (Maundy Thursday), 9 March (Good Friday), 1 May (Labour Day), 19 July (Liberation Day), 1 and 10 August (Managua local holidays), 14 September (for Battle of San Jacinto), 15 September (Independence Day), 2 November (for Day of the Dead), 8 December (for Immaculate Conception), 25 December (Christmas).

A considerable number of local holidays are also observed.

Weights and Measures

The metric system is officially used, although some Spanish and local units are also in general use.

Statistical Survey

Sources (unless otherwise stated): Banco Central de Nicaragua, Carretera Sur, Km 7, Apdos 2252/3, Zona 5, Managua; tel. (2) 65-0500; fax (2) 65-2272; e-mail bcn@cabcn.gob.ni; internet www.bcn.gob.ni; Instituto Nacional de Estadísticas y Censos (INEC), Las Brisas, Frente Hospital Fonseca, Managua; tel. (2) 66-2031.

Area and Population

AREA, POPULATION AND DENSITY

Area (sq km)	
Land	109,004
Inland water	11,250
Total	120,254*
Population (census results)	
20 April 1971	1,877,952
25 April 1995	
Males	2,147,105
Females	2,209,994
Total	4,357,099
Population (official estimates at mid-year)	
1999	4,935,600
2000	5,071,700
2001	5,205,000
Density (per sq km) at mid-2001	43.3

* 46,430 sq miles.

DEPARTMENTS
(population at 1995 census)

Boaco	136,949		Managua	1,093,760
Carazo	149,407		Masaya	241,354
Chinandega	350,212		Matagalpa	383,776
Chontales	144,635		Nueva Segovia	148,492
Estelí	174,894		Río San Juan	70,143
Granada	155,683		Rivas	140,432
Jinotega	257,933		Zelaya Norte	192,716
León	336,894		Zelaya Sur	272,252
Madríz	107,567		**Total**	4,357,099

PRINCIPAL TOWNS
(population at 1995 census)

Managua (capital) .	864,201	Granada	71,783
León	123,865	Estelí	71,550
Chinandega . .	97,387	Tipitaga . . .	67,925
Masaya	88,971	Matagalpa . . .	59,397

Mid-2001 (UN estimate, including suburbs): Managua 1,039,000 (Source: UN, *World Urbanization Prospects: The 2001 Revision*).

BIRTHS AND DEATHS
(UN estimates, annual averages)

	1985–90	1990–95	1995–2000
Birth rate (per 1,000)	38.9	38.0	35.3
Death rate (per 1,000)	8.3	6.4	5.6

Source: UN, *World Population Prospects: The 2000 Revision*.

Expectation of life (WHO estimates, years at birth): 69.5 (males 67.1; females 721.0) in 2001 (Source: WHO, *World Health Report*).

ECONOMICALLY ACTIVE POPULATION
('000 persons)

	1999	2000	2001*
Agriculture, forestry and fishing .	655.3	711.8	728.0
Mining and quarrying	11.7	9.4	10.8
Manufacturing	125.3	127.8	132.3
Electricity, gas and water . . .	5.8	5.9	6.1
Construction	88.1	97.3	105.2
Trade, restaurants and hotels . .	259.2	268.3	278.0
Transport and communications .	49.7	51.2	52.6
Financial services	20.1	21.8	22.5
Government services. . . .	67.5	65.0	65.0
Other services	261.5	278.8	303.3
Total employed	1,544.2	1,637.3	1,697.6
Unemployed	184.7	178.0	202.8
Total labour force	1,728.9	1,815.3	1,900.4

* Preliminary figures.

Health and Welfare

KEY INDICATORS

Total fertility rate (children per woman, 2001)	4.0
Under-5 mortality rate (per 1,000 live births, 2001) . . .	43
HIV/AIDS (% of persons aged 15–49, 2001)	0.20
Physicians (per 1,000 head, 1998)	0.86
Hospital beds (per 1,000 head, 1996)	1.48
Health expenditure (2000): US $ per head (PPP) . . .	108
Health expenditure (2000): % of GDP	4.4
Health expenditure (2000): public (% of total)	51.7
Access to water (% of persons, 2000)	79
Access to sanitation (% of persons, 2000)	84
Human Development Index (2000): ranking	118
Human Development Index (2000): value	0.635

For sources and definitions, see explanatory note on p. vi.

Agriculture

PRINCIPAL CROPS
('000 metric tons)

	1999	2000	2001
Rice (paddy)	193.0	271.2	237.4
Maize	290.8	412.2	419.9
Sorghum	75.4	81.7	88.9
Cassava (Manioc)*	51.5	52.0	51.0
Sugar cane	3,687.1	3,524.4	3,144.6
Dry beans	134.5	173.2	176.8
Groundnuts (in shell) . . .	68.2	67.0	80.6
Oil palm fruit*	53.0	53.0	53.0
Bananas	75.1	56.7	63.9
Plantains*	39.0	40.0	38.0
Oranges*	71.0	71.0	72.0
Pineapples*	46.0	47.0	47.0
Coffee (green)	91.8	82.2	66.8

* FAO estimates.

Source: FAO.

LIVESTOCK
('000 head, year ending September)

	1999	2000	2001
Cattle	1,693*	1,660†	2,280*
Pigs†	400	400	405
Goats†	6.4	6.5	6.6
Horses†	245	246	248
Asses†	8.5	8.6	8.7
Mules†	45.7	45.7	46.0
Poultry†	10,630	14,000	17,000

* Unofficial figure.
† FAO estimate(s).

Source: FAO.

LIVESTOCK PRODUCTS
('000 metric tons)

	1999	2000	2001
Beef and veal	47.9	52.6	54.1
Pig meat	5.7	5.9	6.0
Horse meat*	1.9	1.9	1.9
Poultry meat	36.8	47.3	55.4
Cows' milk	224.0	231.8	247.1
Butter*	0.9	0.7	0.5
Cheese*	16.4	22.1	22.6
Hen eggs*	30.6	30.9	31.2
Cattle hides*	7.1	7.8	8.2

* FAO estimates.

Source: FAO.

Forestry

ROUNDWOOD REMOVALS
('000 cubic metres, excl. bark)

	1999	2000	2001
Sawlogs, veneer logs and logs for sleepers	228*	228*	93
Fuel wood*	5,717	5,756	5,791
Total	5,945*	6,212*	5,884

* FAO estimate(s).

Source: FAO.

SAWNWOOD PRODUCTION
('000 cubic metres, incl. railway sleepers)

	1999*	2000*	2001
Coniferous	104	104	55
Broadleaved	44	44	10
Total	148	148	65

* FAO estimates.

Source: FAO.

Fishing

(metric tons, live weight)

	1998	1999	2000
Capture	19,892	20,569	28,008
Tilapias	—	750	680
Freshwater fishes	1,256	363	396
Snooks	—	2,000	2,150
Groupers, seabasses	—	1,040	800
Snappers	—	2,640	2,290
Yellowfin tuna	—	—	4,950
Common dolphinfish	—	710	2,540
Marine fishes	9,530	2,107	1,828
Caribbean spiny lobsters	3,729	5,141	6,327
Shrimps	4,864	5,218	4,431
Aquaculture	4,788	4,198	5,429
Whiteleg shrimp	4,544	4,000	5,140
Total catch	24,680	24,767	33,437

Source: FAO, *Yearbook of Fishery Statistics*.

Mining

	1999*	2000	2001*
Gold ('000 troy ounces)	143.0	118.1	87.6
Silver ('000 troy ounces)	57.2	51.1	58.5
Sand ('000 cubic metres)	737.3	535.6	329.2
Limestone ('000 cubic metres)	250.8	261.3	178.3
Gypsum ('000 metric tons)	26.9	28.2	27.6

* Provisional figures.

Industry

SELECTED PRODUCTS
('000 metric tons, unless otherwise indicated)

	1996	1997	1998
Raw sugar	349	351	331
Motor spirit	102	97	101
Kerosene	17	16	18
Jet fuel	19	18	18
Distillate fuel oils	174	220	224
Residual fuel oils	250	355	482
Bitumen (asphalt)*	14	14	14
Electric energy (million kWh)*	1,919	1,907	2,153
Soap (kg)	21,796	9,488	3,971
Rum ('000 litres)	12,381	11,374	8,352.1
Cigarettes (million)	1,510	1,580	n.a.

1999: Electric energy 2,069 million kWh; Soap 8,611 kg*; Rum 9,120,900 litres*.

* Provisional figure(s).

Source: mainly UN, *Industrial Commodity Statistics Yearbook*.

Finance

CURRENCY AND EXCHANGE RATES

Monetary Units
    100 centavos = 1 córdoba oro (gold córdoba).

Sterling, Dollar and Euro Equivalents (31 December 2002)
    £1 sterling = 23.65 gold córdobas
    US $1 = 14.67 gold córdobas
    €1 = 15.39 gold córdobas
    1,000 gold córdobas = £42.29 = $68.16 = €65.00.

Average Exchange Rate (gold córdobas per US dollar)
    2000   12.69
    2001   13.37
    2002   14.25

Note: In February 1988 a new córdoba, equivalent to 1,000 of the former units, was introduced, and a uniform exchange rate of US $1 = 10 new córdobas was established. Subsequently, the exchange rate was frequently adjusted. A new currency, the córdoba oro (gold córdoba), was introduced as a unit of account in May 1990 and began to be circulated in August. The value of the gold córdoba was initially fixed at par with the US dollar, but in March 1991 the exchange rate was revised to $1 = 25,000,000 new córdobas (or 5 gold córdobas). On 30 April 1991 the gold córdoba became the sole legal tender.

BUDGET
(million gold córdobas)

Revenue*	1999	2000	2001‡
Taxation	6,483.7	7,264.3	7,354.5
Direct taxes	975.8	1,169.7	1,288.4
Taxes on income and profits	985.9	1,180.4	1,302.7
Taxes on goods and services	4,585.4	5,080.3	5,136.7
General sales tax	2,617.5	2,935.0	3,079.5
Excise and selective consumption tax	1,955.5	2,134.1	2,045.3
Petroleum products	1,339.7	1,457.6	1,325.9
Stamp taxes	12.4	11.1	11.8
Taxes on international trade and transactions	585.7	650.5	590.2
Earmarked revenue	336.8	363.8	339.3
Other current revenue	246.6	273.1	291.1
Capital revenue	8.6	3.5	8.4
Total	6,738.9	7,541.0	7,654.0

Expenditure†	1999	2000	2001‡
Current expenditure	5,688.8	6,815.0	9,231.7
Personnel emoluments	1,697.5	1,885.8	2,251.1
Goods and services	1,265.0	1,420.8	1,944.9
Interest payments	1,149.1	1,331.4	2,630.8
Current transfers	1,577.2	2,177.1	2,399.9
Capital expenditure	4,491.4	5,087.9	4,920.9
Fixed capital formation	2,362.2	3,002.2	2,581.0
Capital transfers	2,129.1	2,085.6	2,339.9
Total	10,180.1	11,902.9	14,152.6

* Excluding grants received (million gold córdobas): 1,934.9 in 1999; 1,873.9 in 2000; 1,935.6 in 2001‡.

† Excluding net lending (million gold córdobas): 181.8 in 1999; 17.0 in 2000; 129.5 in 2001‡.

‡ Preliminary figures.

Source: IMF, *Nicaragua: Statistical Appendix* (December 2002).

INTERNATIONAL RESERVES*
(US $ million at 31 December)

	2000	2001	2002
IMF special drawing rights	0.06	0.03	0.03
Foreign exchange	488.40	379.60	448.10
Total	488.46	379.63	448.13

* Excluding gold reserves (US $ million at 31 December): 4.10 in 1993.

Source: IMF, *International Financial Statistics*.

MONEY SUPPLY
(million gold córdobas at 31 December)

	1999	2000	2001
Currency outside banks . . .	1,734.8	1,760.5	1,919.6
Demand deposits at commercial banks	1,406.0	1,565.5	2,348.0
Total money (incl. others)´ . .	3,151.0	3,411.7	4,529.5

Source: IMF, *International Financial Statistics*.

COST OF LIVING
(Consumer Price Index; base: 1990 = 100)

	1998	1999	2000
Food (incl. beverages)	6,541.1	6,897.5	7,243.4
Clothing (incl. footwear) . . .	4,581.0	5,118.8	5,339.4
Rent, fuel and light	19,071.9	24,283.2	29,955.7
All items (incl. others)	7,470.4	8,307.9	9,267.0

2001 (base: 1990 = 100): Food 7,869.3; All items 9,949.2.

Source: ILO.

NATIONAL ACCOUNTS
(million gold córdobas at current prices)

Expenditure on the Gross Domestic Product

	1999	2000	2001*
Government final consumption expenditure	4,927.6	5,733.7	6,874.5
Private final consumption expenditure	24,881.1	28,378.4	31,402.9
Increase in stocks	55.3	−65.3	13.1
Gross fixed capital formation . .	11,258.9	10,866.6	11,272.2
Total domestic expenditure. .	41,122.9	44,913.4	49,562.7
Exports of goods and services . .	9,021.5	11,080.0	11,093.9
Less Imports of goods and services	24,014.5	25,253.4	26,651.4
GDP in purchasers' values . .	26,129.8	30,740.0	34,005.3
GDP at constant 1980 prices †	24,018.2	25,330.2	26,102.4

* Preliminary figures.

† In million (pre-1988) córdobas.

Gross Domestic Product by Economic Activity

	1999	2000	2001*
Agriculture, hunting, forestry and fishing	8,521.3	10,091.6	11,024.4
Mining and quarrying	256.1	220.5	242.7
Manufacturing	3,878.4	4,406.7	4,833.8
Electricity, gas and water . . .	297.6	338.7	372.7
Construction	1,559.5	1,920.5	2,169.1
Wholesale and retail trade . . .	6,002.0	6,912.9	7,624.8
Transport and communications .	893.6	1,028.3	1,137.8
Finance, insurance, real estate and business services	1,347.2	1,558.3	1,735.5
Government services	2,226.2	2,615.2	3,021.3
Other services	1,417.9	1,647.4	1,843.4
Total	26,129.8	30,740.0	34,005.3

* Preliminary figures.

BALANCE OF PAYMENTS
(US $ million)

	1999	2000	2001
Exports of goods f.o.b.	552.4	652.8	601.9
Imports of goods f.o.b.	−1,698.2	−1,647.3	−1,629.5
Trade balance	−1,145.8	−994.5	−1,207.6
Exports of services	286.9	303.5	331.8
Imports of services	−334.7	−343.4	353.5
Balance on goods and services	1,193.6	−1,034.4	1,049.3
Other income received	30.7	30.7	14.7
Other income paid	−227.5	−232.5	−263.2
Balance on goods, services and income	−1,390.4	−1,236.2	−1,297.8
Current transfers received . . .	696.5	749.9	736.7
Current balance	−693.9	−486.3	−561.1
Direct investment from abroad. .	300.0	265.0	132.3
Other investment assets . . .	22.2	79.9	−60.4
Other investment liabilities . .	166.0	−284.1	−31.5
Net errors and omissions . . .	−254.6	−42.2	−13.3
Overall balance	−460.3	−467.7	−534.0

Source: IMF, *International Financial Statistics*.

External Trade

PRINCIPAL COMMODITIES
(distribution by SITC, US $ million)

Imports c.i.f.	1997	1998	1999
Food and live animals . . .	158.7	204.0	253.9
Cereals and cereal preparations .	74.0	86.1	109.3
Mineral fuels, lubricants and related materials	178.8	181.4	142.0
Petroleum, petroleum products and related materials	172.1	175.0	133.3
Crude petroleum	117.2	121.1	84.8
Petroleum products, refined . .	53.7	52.7	46.0
Animal and vegetable oils, fats and waxes.	42.2	48.0	46.2
Chemicals and related products	275.5	230.2	261.5
Medicinal and pharmaceutical products.	75.2	79.9	105.7
Medicaments (incl. veterinary)	63.8	69.1	94.7
Plastic materials	54.3	23.7	21.5
Basic manufactures	234.8	238.5	297.2
Iron and steel.	50.6	52.8	71.5
Machinery and transport equipment.	395.9	467.6	513.4
Power-generating machinery and equipment	30.4	54.1	75.6
Machinery specialized for particular industries	49.2	48.5	63.5
Road vehicles and parts. . . .	132.0	183.2	170.8
Passenger motor cars (excl. buses).	58.2	78.0	65.8
Lorries and trucks.	47.1	68.7	64.5
Miscellaneous manufactured articles.	152.2	124.6	164.4
Total (incl. others)	1,469.7	1,532.1	1,723.1

Exports f.o.b.	1997	1998	1999
Food and live animals	380.6	403.7	373.5
Meat and meat preparations	42.5	39.0	45.8
Bovine meat, fresh, chilled or frozen	40.8	37.6	41.8
Dairy products and birds' eggs	13.9	17.9	15.8
Fish, crustaceans and molluscs	81.8	84.9	78.6
Shell fish, fresh or frozen	63.8	72.5	68.9
Vegetables and fruit	36.8	33.7	35.8
Vegetables, fresh, chilled, frozen or simply preserved	16.3	7.3	17.3
Fruit and nuts, fresh or dried	20.4	26.5	18.4
Bananas (incl. plantains)	15.9	21.8	15.4
Sugar, sugar preparations and honey	56.7	44.0	31.1
Sugar and honey	56.6	43.8	30.9
Raw sugars (solid)	53.2	39.6	10.2
Refined sugars, etc.	1.2	2.6	20.3
Coffee, tea, cocoa, spices and manufactures	126.0	167.2	141.5
Green and roasted coffee, and substitutes	123.5	164.7	134.8
Beverages and tobacco	45.0	24.9	18.6
Tobacco and tobacco manufactures	42.5	23.8	17.8
Cigars and cheroots; cigarillos	31.1	14.8	9.7
Crude materials (inedible) except fuels	56.7	42.7	37.2
Oil seeds and oleaginous fruit	28.1	26.3	24.8
Seeds for 'soft' fixed oil	25.2	24.6	23.0
Groundnuts, green	14.8	19.0	19.0
Machinery and transport equipment	50.3	8.9	5.7
Office machines and automatic data-processing equipment	23.8	0.2	0.3
Office machine parts	23.7	0.0	0.1
Miscellaneous manufactured articles	90.8	11.0	13.2
Total (incl. others)	666.6	552.8	508.5

Source: UN, *International Trade Statistics Yearbook*.

2000 (US $ million): *Imports c.i.f.:* Consumer goods 536.3; Petroleum and derivatives 291.4; Intermediate goods 533,2; Capital goods 442.5; Total (incl. others) 1,805.3. *Exports f.o.b.:* Coffee 160.9; Shrimps 54.3; Lobsters 57.5; Meat 52.3; Sugar 41.3; Gold 29.3; Total (incl. others) 642.8.

2001 (US $ million): *Imports c.i.f.:* Consumer goods 554.8; Petrol and derivatives 269.8; Intermediate goods 543.3; Capital goods 406.9; Total (incl. others) 1,779.4. *Exports f.o.b.:* Coffee 103.2; Shrimps 38.4; Lobsters 38.1; Meat 65.6; Sugar 49.1; Gold 29.8; Total (incl. others) 605.0.

2002 (US $ million): *Imports c.i.f.:* Consumer goods 560.5; Petroleum and derivatives 254.2; Intermediate goods 532.8; Capital goods 443.1; Total (incl. others) 1,795.5. *Exports f.o.b.:* Coffee 73.3; Shrimps 34.5; Lobsters 41.3; Meat 73.3; Sugar 28.6; Gold 35.2; Total (incl. others) 596.3.

PRINCIPAL TRADING PARTNERS
(US $ million)

Imports c.i.f.	2000	2001	2002
Argentina	5.8	5.5	6.2
Canada	27.0	30.4	19.6
Colombia	7.4	9.2	7.2
Costa Rica	164.2	158.6	155.2
El Salvador	109.2	104.8	103.0
Germany	34.9	36.8	36.0
Guatemala	126.9	130.0	140.7
Honduras	22.8	21.5	9.5
Japan	133.5	88.3	96.3
Mexico	126.1	130.6	114.7
Netherlands	11.8	2.6	5.3
Panama	40.6	32.3	23.0
Spain	23.5	27.0	33.8
USA	449.8	493.6	492.4
Venezuela	197.3	195.2	196.1
Total (incl. others)	1,805.3	1,779.4	1,795.5

Exports f.o.b.	2000	2001	2002
Belgium	17.5	8.0	3.3
Canada	29.7	19.9	19.9
Costa Rica	37.7	37.0	49.7
El Salvador	70.8	76.6	89.4
France	8.2	6.9	15.5
Germany	53.4	31.1	13.4
Guatemala	19.7	23.4	28.6
Honduras	34.3	44.8	57.5
Mexico	23.3	27.8	25.0
Netherlands	6.7	6.3	2.7
Spain	12.3	11.0	12.3
United Kingdom	13.1	16.0	15.3
USA	246.0	190.6	192.1
Total (incl. others)	642.8	605.0	596.3

Transport

RAILWAYS
(traffic)

	1990	1991	1992
Passenger-km (million)	3	3	6

Freight ton-km (million): 4 in 1985.

Source: UN, *Statistical Yearbook*.

ROAD TRAFFIC
(motor vehicles in use at 31 December)

	1998	1999	2000
Cars	52,220	56,513	61,357
Buses and coaches	4,450	10,034	5,460
Goods vehicles	68,952	79,488	85,554
Motorcycles and mopeds	19,303	22,291	25,857

Source: IRF, *World Road Statistics*.

SHIPPING

Merchant fleet
(registered at 31 December)

	1999	2000	2001
Number of vessels	28	28	26
Total displacement ('000 grt)	4.3	4.3	3.6

Source: Lloyd's Register-Fairplay, *World Fleet Statistics*.

International Sea-Borne Freight Traffic
('000 metric tons)

	1997	1998	1999
Imports	1,272.7	1,964.7	1,180.7
Exports	329.3	204.5	183.6

CIVIL AVIATION
(traffic on scheduled services)

	1997	1998	1999
Kilometres flown (million)	1	1	1
Passengers carried ('000)	51	52	59
Passenger-km (million)	85	93	67
Total ton-km (million)	17	10	7

Tourism

TOURIST ARRIVALS BY COUNTRY OF ORIGIN

	1998	1999	2000
Canada	7,565	8,063	10,515
Costa Rica.	64,792	71,476	67,189
El Salvador	49,829	61,603	69,283
Guatemala	27,676	37,202	36,146
Honduras	119,710	133,745	122,631
Panama	9,026	12,277	11,608
Spain	8,024	8,863	8,162
USA	66,460	76,757	84,399
Total (incl. others)	405,702	468,159	485,909

Receipts from tourism (US $ million): 90 in 1998; 113 in 1999; 116 in 2000.

Sources: World Tourism Organization, *Yearbook of Tourism Statistics*; World Bank, *World Development Indicators*.

Communications Media

	1999	2000	2001
Television receivers ('000 in use)	340	350	n.a.
Telephones ('000 main lines in use)	150.3	153.7	158.6
Mobile cellular telephones ('000 subscribers).	44.2	90.3	156.0
Personal computers ('000 in use) .	40	40	50
Internet users ('000)	20	50	50

Radio receivers ('000 in use): 1,240 in 1997.

Daily newspapers: 4 in 1996 (average circulation 135,000 copies).

Sources: UNESCO, *Statistical Yearbook*; International Telecommunication Union.

Education

(2000, unless otherwise indicated)

	Institu-tions	Teachers	Students		
			Males	Females	Total
Pre-primary . .	3,968*	3,672†	83,342	83,373	166,715
Primary . . .	7,224*	21,020†	423,928	414,509	838,437
Secondary: general . .	n.a.	5,970†	147,394	167,960	315,354
Tertiary: university level‡ . .	n.a.	3,630	22,441	6,317	48,758
Tertiary: other higher‡ . .	n.a.	210	4,360	3,440	7,800

* 1998 figure.
† 1996 figure.
‡ 1997 figures.

Sources: UNESCO, *Statistical Yearbook*; Ministry of Education.

Adult literacy rate (UNESCO estimates): 66.5% (males 66.3%; females 66.8%) in 2000 (Source: UN Development Programme, *Human Development Report*).

Directory

The Constitution*

Shortly after taking office on 20 July 1979, the Government of National Reconstruction abrogated the 1974 Constitution. On 22 August 1979 the revolutionary junta issued a 'Statute on Rights and Guarantees for the Citizens of Nicaragua', providing for the basic freedoms of the individual, religious freedom and freedom of the press and abolishing the death penalty. The intention of the Statute was formally to re-establish rights which had been violated under the deposed Somoza regime. A fundamental Statute took effect from 20 July 1980 and remained in force until the Council of State drafted a political constitution and proposed an electoral law. A new Constitution was approved by the National Constituent Assembly on 19 November 1986 and promulgated on 9 January 1987. Amendments to the Constitution were approved by the Asamblea Nacional (National Assembly) in July 1995 and January 2000. The following are some of the main points of the Constitution.

Nicaragua is an independent, free, sovereign and indivisible state. All Nicaraguans who have reached 16 years of age are full citizens.

POLITICAL RIGHTS

There shall be absolute equality between men and women. It is the obligation of the State to remove obstacles that impede effective participation of Nicaraguans in the political, economic and social life of the country. Citizens have the right to vote and to be elected at elections and to offer themselves for public office. Citizens may organize or affiliate with political parties, with the objective of participating in, exercising or vying for power. The supremacy of civilian authority is enshrined in the Constitution.

SOCIAL RIGHTS

The Nicaraguan people have the right to work, to education and to culture. They have the right to decent, comfortable and safe housing, and to seek accurate information. This right comprises the freedom to seek, receive and disseminate information and ideas, both spoken and written, in graphic or any other form. The mass media are at the service of national interests. No Nicaraguan citizen may disobey the law or prevent others from exercising their rights and fulfilling their duties by invoking religious beliefs or inclinations.

LABOUR RIGHTS

All have a right to work, and to participate in the management of their enterprises. Equal pay shall be given for equal work. The State shall strive for full and productive employment under conditions that guarantee the fundamental rights of the individual. There shall be an eight-hour working day, weekly rest, vacations, remuneration for national holidays and a bonus payment equivalent to one month's salary, in conformity with the law.

EDUCATION

Education is an obligatory function of the State. Planning, direction and organization of the secular education system is the responsibility of the State. All Nicaraguans have free and equal access to education. Private education centres may function at all levels.

LEGISLATIVE POWER

The Asamblea Nacional exercises Legislative Power through representative popular mandate. The Asamblea Nacional is composed of 90 representatives elected by direct secret vote by means of a system of proportional representation, of which 70 are elected at regional level and 20 at national level. The number of representatives may be increased in accordance with the general census of the population, in conformity with the law. Representatives shall be elected for a period of five years. The functions of the Asamblea Nacional are to draft and approve laws and decrees; to decree amnesties and pardons; to consider, discuss and approve the General Budget of the Republic; to elect judges to the Supreme Court of Justice and the Supreme Electoral Council; to fill permanent vacancies for the Presidency or Vice-Presidency; and to determine the political and administrative division of the country. The Presidency of the Republic may partially or totally veto a legislative proposal within a period of 15 days following its approval by the Assembly.

EXECUTIVE POWER

The Executive Power is exercised by the President of the Republic (assisted by the Vice-President), who is the Head of State, Head of Government and Commander-in-Chief of the Defence and Security Forces of the Nation. The election of the President (and Vice-President) is by equal, direct and free universal suffrage in secret ballot. Should a single candidate in a presidential election fail to secure the necessary 35% of the vote to win outright in the first round, a second ballot shall be held. Close relatives of a serving President are prohibited from contesting a presidential election. The President shall serve for a period of five years and may not serve for two consecutive terms. All outgoing Presidents are granted a seat in the Asamblea Nacional.

JUDICIAL POWER

The Judiciary consists of the Supreme Court of Justice, Courts of Appeal and other courts of the Republic. The Supreme Court is composed of at least seven judges, elected by the Asamblea Nacional, who shall serve for a term of six years. The functions of the Supreme Court are to organize and direct the administration of justice. There are 12 Supreme Court justices, appointed for a period of seven years.

LOCAL ADMINISTRATION

The country is divided into regions, departments and municipalities for administrative purposes. The municipal governments shall be elected by universal suffrage in secret ballot and will serve a six-year term. The communities of the Atlantic Coast have the right to live and develop in accordance with a social organization which corresponds to their historical and cultural traditions. The State shall implement, by legal means, autonomous governments in the regions inhabited by the communities of the Atlantic Coast, in order that the communities may exercise their rights.

*In January 2000 a constitutional amendment established a constitutional assembly to effect further reform of the Constitution, following amendments in 1995 and 2000.

The Government

HEAD OF STATE

President: ENRIQUE BOLAÑOS GEYER (took office 10 January 2002).

Vice-President: JOSÉ RIZO CASTELLÓN.

CABINET
(April 2003)

Cabinet Chief: MARIO DE FRANCO.

Minister of Foreign Affairs: NORMAN CALDERA CARDENAL.

Minister of Government: EDUARDO URCUYO.

Minister of National Defence: JOSÉ ADÁN GUERRA PASTORA.

Minister of Finance and Public Credit: EDUARDO MONTEALEGRE RIVAS.

Minister of Development, Industry and Trade: MARIO ARANA SEVILLA.

Minister of Labour: VIRGILIO JOSÉ GURDIÁN CASTELLÓN.

Minister of the Environment and Natural Resources: ARTURO HARDING LACAYO.

Minister of Transport and Infrastructure: PEDRO SOLÓRZANO CASTILLO.

Minister of Agriculture and Forestry: JOSÉ AUGUSTO NAVARRO FLORES.

Minister of Health: JOSÉ ANTONIO ALVARADO.

Minister of Education, Culture and Sports: SILVIO DE FRANCO MONTALVÁN.

Minister of the Family: NATALIA BARILLAS CRUZ.

Secretary to the Presidency: LEANDRO MARIN ABAUNZA.

There are, in addition, five Secretaries of State.

MINISTRIES

Ministry of Agriculture and Forestry: Km 8½, Carretera a Masaya, Managua; tel. (2) 76-0235; internet www.mag.gob.ni.

Ministry of Development, Industry and Trade: Edif. Central, Km 6, Carretera a Masaya, Apdo 8, Managua; tel. (2) 78-8702; fax (2) 70-095; internet www.mific.gob.ni.

Ministry of Education, Culture and Sports: Complejo Cívico Camilo Ortega Saavedra, Managua; tel. (2) 65-1577; internet www.med.gob.ni.

Ministry of the Environment and Natural Resources: Km 12½, Carretera Norte, Apdo 5123, Managua; tel. (2) 33-1111; fax (2) 63-1274; internet www.marena.gob.ni.

Ministry of the Family: Managua.

Ministry of Finance and Public Credit: Frente a la Asamblea Nacional, Apdo 2170, Managua; tel. (2) 22-6530; fax (2) 22-6430; e-mail gobid@ibw.com.ni; internet www.hacienda.gob.ni.

Ministry of Foreign Affairs: Del Cine González al Sur sobre Avda Bolívar, Managua; tel. (2) 44-8000; fax 28-5102; e-mail gabriela.hernandez@cancilleria.gob.ni; internet www.cancilleria.gob.ni.

Ministry of Government: Apdo 68, Managua; tel. (2) 28-5005.

Ministry of Health: Complejo Cívico Camilo Ortega Saavedra, Managua; tel. (2) 89-7164.

Ministry of Labour: Estadio Nacional, 400 m al Norte, Apdo 487, Managua; tel. (2) 28-2028; fax (2) 28-2103.

Ministry of National Defence: Casa de la Presidencia, Managua; tel. (2) 66-3580; fax (2) 28-7911.

Ministry of Tourism: Managua; internet www.intur.gob.ni.

Ministry of Transport and Infrastructure: Frente al Estadio Nacional, Apdo 26, Managua; tel. (2) 28-2061; fax (2) 22-5111; e-mail webmaster@mti.gob.ni; internet www.mti.gob.ni.

President and Legislature

PRESIDENT

Election, 4 November 2001

Candidate	Votes	% of total
Enrique Bolaños Geyer (Partido Liberal Constitucionalista)	1,216,863	56.3
Daniel Ortega Saavedra (Frente Sandinista de Liberación Nacional)	915,417	42.3
Alberto Saborío (Partido Conservador de Nicaragua)	29,933	1.4
Total	**2,162,213**	**100.0**

ASAMBLEA NACIONAL
(National Assembly)

Asamblea Nacional

Avda Bolívar, Contiguo a la Presidencia de la República, Managua; e-mail webmaster@correo.asamblea.gob.ni; internet www.asamblea.gob.ni.

President: ARNOLDO ALEMÁN LACAYO.

First Vice-President: WILFREDO NAVARRO MOREIRA.

Second Vice-President: GUILLERMO OSORNO MOLINA.

Third Vice-President: RENÉ NUÑEZ TÉLLEZ.

Election, 4 November 2001

Party	Seats
Partido Liberal Constitucionalista (PLC)	47
Frente Sandinista de Liberación Nacional (FSLN)	42
Partido Conservador de Nicaragua (PCN)	1
Total	**90***

* In addition to the 90 elected members, supplementary seats in the Asamblea Nacional are awarded to the unsuccessful candidates at the presidential election who were not nominated for the legislature but who received, in the presidential poll, a number of votes at least equal to the average required for one of the 70 legislative seats decided at a regional level. On this basis, the FSLN obtained one additional seat in the Asamblea Nacional. A legislative seat is also awarded to the outgoing President. Thus, the PLC also gained an additional seat, bringing the total of seats in the Asamblea Nacional to 92.

Political Organizations

Acción Nacional Conservadora (ANC): Costado Oeste SNTV, Managua; tel. (2) 66-8755; Pres. Dr FRANK DUARTE TAPIA.

Alianza Liberal (AL): f. 1996 as electoral alliance; comprises the following parties:

Conservadores por la Democracia.

Convergencia Liberal: f. 1996 by former mems of Partido Liberal Independiente.

Partido Liberal Constitucionalista (PLC): Semáforos Country Club 100 m al Este, Apdo 4569, Managua; tel. (2) 78-8705; fax (2) 78-1800; e-mail plc@ibw.com.ni; internet www.plc .org.ni; f. 1967; Pres. Dr LEOPOLDO NAVARRO BERMÚDEZ; Exec. Dir EDMOND H. PALLAIS.

Partido Liberal Independiente de Unidad Nacional (PLIUN): Munich, 2½ c. Arriba, Managua; tel. (2) 61672; f. 1988; splinter group of PLI; Pres. EDUARDO CORONADO PÉREZ; Sec.-Gen. CARLOS ALONSO.

Partido Neo-Liberal (Pali): Cine Dorado, 2 c. al Sur, 50 m Arriba, Managua; tel. (2) 66-5166; f. 1986; Pres. Dr RICARDO VEGA GARCÍA.

Partido Unionista Centroamericano (PUCA): Cine Cabrera, 1a c. al Este, 20 m al Norte, Managua; tel. (2) 27472; f. 1904; Pres. BLANCA ROJAS ECHAVERRY.

Alianza Unidad (AU): f. 1996; an alliance of parties with social democrat tendencies.

Frente Sandinista de Liberación Nacional (FSLN) (Sandinista National Liberation Front): Costado Oeste Parque El Carmen, Managua; tel. (2) 66-0845; fax (2) 66-1560; internet www.fsln.org.ni; f. 1960; led by a 15-member directorate; embraces Izquierda Democrática Sandinista 'orthodox revolutionary' faction, led by Daniel Ortega Saavedra; 120,000 mems; Gen. Sec. DANIEL ORTEGA SAAVEDRA.

Movimiento de Acción Democrática (MAD): Managua; f. 1993; Leader EDÉN PASTORA GÓMEZ.

Movimiento Democrático Nicaragüense (MDN): f. 2000 as electoral alliance; comprises the following parties:

Camino Cristiano Nicaragüense (CCN): Managua; Pres. GUILLERMO ANTONIO OSORNO MOLINA.

Movimiento Democrático Nicaragüense (MDN): Casa L-39, Ciudad Jardín Bnd, 50 m al Sur, Managua; tel. (2) 43898; f. 1978; Leader ROBERTO URROZ CASTILLO.

Movimiento Renovador Sandinista (MRS): Tienda Katty 1 c. Abajo, Apdo 24, Managua; tel. (2) 78-0279; fax (2) 78-0268; f. 1995; former faction of Frente Sandinista de Liberación Nacional; Pres. Dr SERGIO RAMÍREZ MERCADO.

Partido Conservador de Nicaragua (PCN): Colegio Centroamérica 500 m al Sur, Managua; tel. (2) 67-0484; f. 1992 as result of merger between Partido Conservador Demócrata (PCD) and Partido Socialconservadurismo; Pres. Dr FERNANDO AGÜERO ROCHA.

Partido de Unidad Social Cristiano (PUSC).

Proyecto Nacional (PRONAL): Managua; formed an alliance with MDN, MRS and PUSC in February 2000; Leader BENJAMÍN LANZAS.

Movimiento Patria: Managua; alliance of centre parties, formed in 1998; comprising:

Alianza Popular Conservadora (APC): Iglesia El Carmen 50 m Arriba, Managua; tel. (2) 28-1247; f. 1856 as Partido Conservador de Nicaragua, name changed as above 1989; Pres. EDUARDO PALADINO CABRERA; Sec.-Gen. MYRIAM ARGÜELLO MORALES.

Movimiento Nueva Alternativa (MNA).

Partido Liberal Independiente (PLI): Ciudad Jardín, H-4, Calle Principal, Managua; tel. (2) 44-3556; fax (2) 48-0012; f. 1944; Leader VIRGILIO GODOY REYES.

Partido Resistencia Nicaragüense (PRN): Optica Nicaragüense, 100 m al Lago, Managua; tel. (2) 66-8098; f. 1991; Pres. ENRIQUE QUIÑONES.

Partido Nacional Conservador (PNC): Frente Costado Sur Galería Internacional, Managua; tel. (2) 66-9979; f. 1979; Leader Dr SILVIANO MATAMOROS LACAYO; Pres. ADOLFO CALERO PORTOCARRERO.

Partido Popular Nicaragüense (PPN): Managua; centrist; Leader ALVARO RAMÍREZ.

Partido de los Pueblos Costeños (PPC): Bluefields; f. 1997; multi-ethnic; Pres. HUGO SUJO.

Partido Social Cristiano Nicaragüense (PSCN): Ciudad Jardín, Pizza María, 1 c. al Lago, Managua; tel. (2) 22026; f. 1957; 42,000 mems; Pres. GERMÁN ALFARO OCAMPO.

Partido Social Demócrata (PSD): Frente al Teatro Aguerri, Managua; tel. (2) 28-1277; f. 1979; Pres. ADOLFO JARQUÍN ORTEL; Sec.-Gen. Dr JOSÉ PALLAIS ARANA.

Partido Socialista Nicaragüense (PSN): Hospital Militar, 100 m al Norte, 100 m al Oeste, 100 m al Sur, Managua; tel. (2) 66-2321; fax (2) 66-2936; f. 1944; social democratic party; Sec.-Gen. Dr GUSTAVO TABLADA ZELAYA.

Unión Demócrata Cristiana (UDC): De Iglesia Santa Ana, 2 c. Abajo, Barrio Santa Ana, Apdo 3089, Managua; tel. (2) 66-2576; f. 1976 as Partido Popular Social Cristiano; name officially changed as above December 1993; Pres. Dr LUIS HUMBERTO GUZMÁN; Political Sec. Dr PEDRO ARCEDA PICADO.

Unión Nacional Opositora 96 (UNO 96): f. 1996; frmly Partido Nacional Demócrata; no relation to former governing UNO; Pres. ALFREDO CÉSAR AGUIRRE.

Yatama: Atlantic Coast Miskito group.

Diplomatic Representation

EMBASSIES IN NICARAGUA

Argentina: Reparto Las Colinas, Km 8, Carretera a Masaya, de la TEXACO 1 c. Arriba, Apdo 703, Managua; tel. (2) 76-0156; fax (2) 76-0116; e-mail embargsc@tmx.com.ni; Ambassador HORACIO ALBERTO AMOROSO.

Brazil: Km 7¾, Carretera Sur, Quinta los Pinos, Apdo 264, Managua; tel. (2) 50035; e-mail ebrasil@tmx.com.ni; Chargé d'affaires PATRICIA MARIA DE OLIVEIRA LIMA SERAPIÃO.

Chile: Apdo 1289, Managua; Ambassador CARLOS DUPRÉ SILVA.

China (Taiwan): Planes de Altamira, 19-20, frente de la Cancha de Tenis, Apdo 4653, Managua 5; tel. (2) 77-1333; fax (2) 67-4025; e-mail embchina@ibw.com.ni; Ambassador ANTONIO T. S. TSAI.

Colombia: Segunda entrada a las Colinas, una cuadra arriba, media cuadra al lago, Casa 97, contiguo al Sur, Managua; tel. (2) 70247; Ambassador MELBA MARTÍNEZ LÓPEZ.

Costa Rica: De la Estatua de Montoya 2 c. al Lago y 1 c. Arriba (Callejón Zelaya), Managua; tel. (2) 66-2404; fax (2) 68-1479; e-mail embcr@ibw.com.ni; Ambassador SOLÓN CHAVARRÍA AGUILAR.

Cuba: Carretera a Masaya, 3a Entrada a las Colinas, Managua; tel. (2) 71182; fax (2) 76-0166; e-mail ecuba@ibw.com.ni; Chargé d'affaires a.i. DAMIAN ARTEAGA HERNÁNDEZ.

Denmark: De la Plaza España l c. Abajo, 2 c. al Lago, ½ c. Abajo, Apdo 4942, Managua; tel. (2) 68-0250; fax (2) 66-8095; e-mail danembassy@denmark.org.ni; internet www.denmark.org.ni; Ambassador ANDERS SERUP RASMUSSEN.

Dominican Republic: Reparto Las Colinas, Prado Ecuestre 100, con Curva de los Gallos, Apdo 614, Managua; tel. (2) 76-2029; fax (2) 76-0654; e-mail embdom@alfanumeric.com.ni; Ambassador JESÚS MARÍA TRONCOSO POU.

Ecuador: De los Pipitos 1½ c. Abajo, Apdo C-33, Managua; tel. (2) 68-1098; fax (2) 66-8081; Ambassador FRANCISCO PROAÑO ARANDI.

El Salvador: Reparto Las Colinas, Avda Las Colinas y Pasaje Los Cerros, Apdo 149, Managua; tel. (2) 76-0712; fax (2) 76-0711; Ambassador JOSÉ ROBERTO FRANCISCO IMENDIA.

Finland: Suc. Jorge Navarro, Apdo 2219, Managua; tel. (2) 66-7947; fax (2) 66-3416; e-mail finland@ibw.com.ni; Ambassador INGER HIRVELÄ LÓPEZ.

France: Km 13½, Carretera del Sur, Apdo 1227, Managua; tel. (2) 22-6210; fax (2) 28-1056; e-mail ambafrance@tmx.com.ni; internet www.ambafrance-ni.org; Ambassador MICHEL VANDEPOORTER.

Germany: Bolonia, de la Rotonda El Güegüense, 1.5 c. al Lago, Contiguo a Optica Nicaragüense, Apdo 29, Managua; tel. (2) 66-3917; fax (2) 66-7667; e-mail diploger@tmx.com.ni; internet www .embajada-managua.org; Ambassador HANS PETERSMANN.

Guatemala: Km 11½, Carretera a Masaya, Apdo E-1, Managua; tel. (2) 79609; fax (2) 79610; Ambassador RAFAEL SALAZAR GÁLVEZ.

Holy See: Apostolic Nunciature, Km 10.8, Carretera Sur, Apdo 506, Managua; tel. (2) 65-0552; fax (2) 65-7416; e-mail nunels@telesal .net; Apostolic Nuncio Most Rev. BERLOCO GIACINTO (Titular Archbishop of Fidene).

Honduras: Km 7½, Carretera Sur, Reparto Barcelona, Apdo 321, Managua; tel. (2) 78-4133; fax (2) 78-3043; e-mail embhonduras@ ideay.net.ni; Ambassador (vacant).

Italy: Rotonda El Güegüense, 1 c. al norte, Apdo 2092, ½ c. Abajo, Managua 4; tel. (2) 66-2961; fax (2) 66-3987; e-mail italdipl@tmx .com.ni; Ambassador Dr MAURIZIO FRATINI.

Japan: Del Portón del Hospital Militar, 1 c. al Lago y 1½ c. Abajo, Mano Izquierda, Bolonia, Apdo 1789, Managua; tel. (2) 62-3092; fax (2) 62-7393; Ambassador YOSHIZO KONISHI.

Korea, Democratic People's Republic: Managua; Ambassador KIM SUNG RYONG.

Libya: Mansión Teodolinda, 6 c. al Sur, ½ c. Abajo, Managua; Secretary of the People's Bureau IBRAHIM MOHAMED FARHAT.

Mexico: Frente Oficinas Telcor de Altamira, Km 4½ Carretera a Masaya, Apdo 834, Managua; tel. (2) 78-1859; fax (2) 78-2886; Ambassador FRANCISCO DEL RÍO.

Netherlands: Col. los Robles III etapa, de Plaza el Sol 1 c. al sur 1½ c. al oeste, Apdo 3688, Managua; tel. (2) 70-4505; fax (2) 70-0399; e-mail mng-az@minbuza.nl; Chargé d'affaires a.i. KEES RADE.

Panama: Reparto San Juan, Calle El Carmen 619, Managua; tel. (2) 66-2224; fax (2) 66-8633; Ambassador JOSEFA MARÍN DIEZ.

Peru: Casa 325, Barrio Bolonia, del Hospital Militar 'Alejandró Dávila', 1c. al Lago y 2 c. Abajo, Apdo 211, Managua; tel. (2) 66-8677; fax (2) 66-1408; e-mail peru1@ibw.com.ni; Chargé d'affaires a.i. PEDRO BUITRÓN BUITRÓN.

Russia: Reparto Las Colinas, Calle Vista Alegre 214, Entre Avda Central y Paseo del Club, Managua; tel. (2) 76-0374; fax (2) 76-0179; e-mail rossia@tmx.com.ni; Ambassador ANATOLII P. KUZNETSOV.

Spain: Avda Central 13, Las Colinas, Apdo 284, Managua; tel. (2) 76-0966; fax (2) 76-0937; e-mail embespni@correo.mae.es; Ambassador IGNACIO JESÚS MATELLANES MARTÍNEZ.

Sweden: Rotonda El Güegüense, 1 c. Abajo, 2 c. al Lago y ½ c. Abajo, Lado Derecho, Apdo 2307, Managua; tel. (2) 66-2762; fax (2) 66-6778; e-mail ambassaden.managua@sida.se; internet www.suecia.org.ni; Ambassador KLAS MARKENSTEN.

United Kingdom: Plaza Churchill, Reparto Los Robles, Apdo A-169, Managua; tel. (2) 78-0014; fax (2) 78-4085; e-mail britemb@ibw.com.ni; Ambassador HARRY WILES.

USA: Km 4½, Carretera Sur, Apdo 327, Managua; tel. (2) 66-6010; Ambassador BARBARA C. MOORE.

Uruguay: Managua; tel. (2) 25542; Ambassador ALFREDO LAFONE.

Venezuela: Edif. Málaga, 2°, Plaza España, Módulo A-13, Apdo 406, Managua; tel. (2) 72-0267; fax (2) 72-2265; e-mail embaveznica@cablenet.com.ni; Ambassador MIGUEL GÓMEZ.

Judicial System

The Supreme Court

Km 7½, Carretera Norte, Managua; tel. (2) 43562; fax (2) 33-0581; internet www.csj.gob.ni.

Deals with both civil and criminal cases, acts as a Court of Cassation, appoints Judges of First Instance, and generally supervises the legal administration of the country.

President: Dr IVAN ESCOBAR FORNOS.

Vice-President: Dr MARVIN AGUILAR GARCÍA.

Attorney-General: JULIO CENTENO.

Religion

All religions are tolerated. Almost all of Nicaragua's inhabitants profess Christianity, and the great majority belong to the Roman Catholic Church. The Moravian Church predominates on the Caribbean coast.

CHRISTIANITY

The Roman Catholic Church

Nicaragua comprises one archdiocese, six dioceses and the Apostolic Vicariate of Bluefields. At 31 December 2000 there were an estimated 4,689,958 adherents.

Bishops' Conference

Conferencia Episcopal de Nicaragua, Ferretería Lang 1 c. al Norte, 1 c. al Este, Zona 3, Las Piedrecitas, Apdo 2407, Managua; tel. (2) 66-6292; fax (2) 66-8069; e-mail cen@tmx.com.ni.

f. 1975; statute approved 1987; Pres. Cardinal MIGUEL OBANDO Y BRAVO (Archbishop of Managua).

Archbishop of Managua: Cardinal MIGUEL OBANDO Y BRAVO, Arzobispado, Apdo 3058, Managua; tel. (2) 77-1754; fax (2) 76-0130.

The Anglican Communion

Nicaragua comprises one of the five dioceses of the Iglesia Anglicana de la Región Central de América.

Bishop of Nicaragua: Rt Rev. STURDIE W. DOWNS, Apdo 1207, Managua; tel. (2) 25174; fax (2) 22-6701.

Protestant Churches

Baptist Convention of Nicaragua: Apdo 2593, Managua; tel. (2) 25785; fax (2) 24131; e-mail cbn@ibw.com.ni; f. 1917; 35,000 mems

(1988); Pres. Rev. ELÍAS SÁNCHEZ; Gen. Sec. Rev. ELÍAS GONZÁLEZ ARGÜELLO.

The Nicaraguan Lutheran Church of Faith and Hope: Apdo 151, Managua; tel. (2) 66-1329; fax (2) 66-4609; e-mail luterana@nicarao.org.ni; f. 1994; 4,000 mems (2000); Pres. Rev. VICTORIA CORTEZ RODRÍGUEZ.

The Press

NEWSPAPERS AND PERIODICALS

Acción: Managua; official publication of the Partido Social Demócrata.

Alternativa Liberal: Managua; f. 1984; official publication of the Partido Liberal Independiente.

Avance: Ciudad Jardín 0-30, Apdo 4231, Managua; tel. (2) 43750; f. 1972; weekly publication of the Partido Comunista de Nicaragua; circ. 10,000.

Barricada: Camino del Oriente, Apdo 576, Managua; tel. (2) 67-4885; fax (2) 67-3941; e-mail barricada@ibw.com.ni; internet www.barricada.com.ni; f. 1979; morning, daily; also publ. in English; temporary closure announced Jan. 1998; Dir TOMÁS BORGE; Editor JUAN RAMÓN HUERTA; circ. 95,000.

El Centroamericano: 4a Calle Norte, Apdo 52, León; f. 1917; evening; independent; Dir R. ABAUNZA SALINAS; circ. 3,500.

La Crónica: Managua; f. 1988; weekly; independent; Dir LUIS HUMBERTO GUZMÁN.

Diario El Pueblo: Apdo 2346, Managua; tel. (2) 23480; f. 1979; daily; owned by a co-operative; Dir CARLOS CUADRA; circ. 7,000.

La Gaceta, Diario Oficial: Avda Central Sur 604, Managua; f. 1912; morning; official.

La Información: León; weekly.

La Nación Nicaragüense: Camino de Oriente, Managua; weekly.

Novedades: Pista P. Joaquín Chamorro, Km 4, Carretera Norte, Apdo 576, Managua; daily, evening.

Nuevo Diario: Pista P. Joaquín Chamorro, Km 4, Carretera Norte, Apdo 4591, Managua; tel. (2) 49-1190; fax (2) 49-0700; e-mail ndiario@ibw.com.ni; internet www.elnuevodiario.com.ni; f. 1980; morning, daily; independent; Editor XAVIER CHAMORRO CARDENAL; circ. 45,000.

El Observador: Apdo 1482, Managua; weekly.

Paso a Paso: Managua; weekly; Dir JOAQUÍN MEJÍA.

Poder Sandinista: Managua; f. 1980; weekly.

El Popular: Managua; monthly; official publication of the Partido Socialista Nicaragüense.

La Prensa: Km 4½, Carretera Norte, Apdo 192, Managua; tel. (2) 49-8405; fax (2) 49-6926; e-mail info@laprensa.com.ni; internet www.laprensa.com.ni; f. 1926; morning, daily; independent; Pres. JAIME CHAMORRO CARDENAL; Editor PABLO ANTONIO CUADRA; circ. 30,000.

Prensa Proletaria: Managua; fortnightly; official publication of the Movimiento de Acción Popular Marxista-Leninista.

El Reportero: Managua; resumed publication Jan. 1988; Editor ARILO MEJÍA.

Revista del Pensamiento Centroamericano: Apdo 2108, Managua; quarterly; centre-left; Editor XAVIER ZAVALA CUADRA.

La Semana Cómica: Centro Comercial Bello Horizonte, Módulos 7 y 9, Apdo SV-3, Managua; tel. (2) 44909; f. 1980; weekly; Dir RÓGER SÁNCHEZ; circ. 45,000.

El Socialista: Managua; fortnightly; official publication of the Partido Revolucionario de los Trabajadores.

Tiempos del Mundo: Apdo 3525, Managua; tel. (2) 68-2945; fax (2) 68-2904; e-mail editor@com.ni; internet www.tdm.com.ni; weekly; circ. 5,000.

La Tribuna: Detrás del Banco Mercantil, Plaza España, Apdo 1469, Managua; tel. (2) 66-7583; fax (2) 66-9089; e-mail tribuna@latribuna.com.ni; internet www.latribuna.com.ni; f. 1993; morning, daily; Dir HAROLDO J. MONTEALEGRE; Gen. Man. MARIO GONZÁLEZ.

Association

Unión de Periodistas de Nicaragua (UPN): Apdo 4006, Managua; Leader LILLY SOTO VÁSQUEZ.

NEWS AGENCIES

Agencia Nicaragüense de Noticias (ANN): Managua; Dir-Gen. ROBERTO GARCÍA.

Foreign Bureaux

Agencia EFE (Spain): Ciudad Jardín S-22, Apdo 1951, Managua; tel. (2) 24928; Bureau Chief FILADELFO MARTÍNEZ FLORES.

Agenzia Nazionale Stampa Associata (ANSA) (Italy): c/o La Prensa, Km 4½, Carretera Norte, Apdo 192, Managua; tel. (2) 40139; Correspondent MARCIO VARGAS.

Deutsche Presse-Agentur (dpa) (Germany): Apdo 2095, Managua; tel. (2) 78-1862; fax (2) 78-1863; Correspondent JOSÉ ESTEBAN QUEZADA.

Informatsionnoye Telegrafnoye Agentstvo Rossii—Telegrafnoye Agentstvo Suverennykh Stran (ITAR—TASS) (Russia): Col. Los Robles, Casa 17, Managua; Correspondent ALEKSANDR TRUSHIN.

Prensa Latina (Cuba): De los Semáforos del Portón de Telcor de Villa Fontana, 25 m al Este, 2 c. al Lago, Casa 280, Managua; tel. (2) 72697; Correspondent MARIO MAINADE MARTÍNEZ.

Reuters (United Kingdom): Apdo A-150, Managua; tel. (2) 27070; Correspondent M. CAMPBELL.

Xinhua (New China) News Agency (People's Republic of China): De Policlínica Nicaragüense, 80 m al Sur, Apdo 5899, Managua; tel. (2) 62155; Bureau Chief LIU RIUCHANG.

Publishers

Academia Nicaragüense de la Lengua: Calle Central, Reparto Las Colinas, Apdo 2711, Managua; f. 1928; languages; Dir PABLO ANTONIO CUADRA; Sec. JULIO YCAZA TIGERINO.

Editora de Publicaciones, SA (EDIPSA): Detrás Edif. Corporación Industrial del Pueblo, Pista de la Resistencia Sur, Managua.

Editorial Alemana, SA: Centro Comercial, Módulo B 30, Km 18½, Carretera a Masaya, Apdo E-10, Managua.

Editorial América, SA: Ciudad Jardín K-24, Frente al Juzgado, Managua.

Editorial Artes Gráficas: Managua.

Editorial El Socorro: Cine Aguerri, 1 c. Abajo, 2½ c. al Lago, No 618, Managua.

Editorial Flórez: Centro Taller Las Palmas, 75 m al Norte, Managua; Dir JOSÉ MARÍA FLÓREZ MORALES.

Editorial Impresora Comercial: Julio C. Orozco L., 9 C.S.E. Entre 27a y 28a Avda, Apdo 10-11, Managua; tel. (2) 42258; art.

Editorial José Martí: De donde fue Bunge, 2 c. al Lago, Managua.

Editorial Nueva Nicaragua: Paseo Salvador Allende, Km 3½, Carretera Sur, Apdo 073, Managua; fax (2) 66-6520; f. 1981; Pres. Dr SERGIO RAMÍREZ MERCADO; Dir-Gen. ROBERTO DÍAZ CASTILLO.

Editorial Rodríguez: Iglesia Santa Faz, 1½ c. Abajo, B. Costa Rica, Apdo 4702, Managua.

Editorial San José: Calle Central Este 607, Managua.

Editorial Unión: Avda Central Norte, Managua; travel.

Editorial Universitaria Centroamérica: Col. Centroamérica, K-752, Managua.

Editorial Vilma Morales M.: Academia Militar David Tejada, 2 c. Abajo y ½ c. al Lago, Bello Horizonte K-1-19.

Librería y Editorial, Universidad Nacional de Nicaragua: León; tel. (311) 2612; education, history, sciences, law, literature, politics.

Broadcasting and Communications

TELECOMMUNICATIONS

Regulatory Body

Instituto Nicaragüense de Telecomunicaciones y Correos (Telcor): Edif. Telcor, Avda Bolivar diagonal a Cancillería, Apdo 2264, Managua; tel. (2) 22-7350; fax (2) 22-7554; e-mail Webmaster@telcor.gob.ni; internet www.telcor.gob.ni; Dir-Gen. MARIO GONZÁLEZ LACAYO; Deputy Dir-Gen. ANA NUBIA ALEGRÍA TREMINIO.

Major Service Providers

BellSouth: Managua; internet www.bellsouth.com.ni; US-owned mobile cellular telephone provider.

Empresa Nicaragüense de Telecomunicaciones (Enitel): Villafontana 2°, Apdo 232, Managua; tel. (2)77-3057; fax (2) 70-2128; internet www.tmx.com.ni; f. 1925; 40% stake sold to Swedish-Honduran consortium in 2001; CEO Dr CARLOS RAMOS FONES.

Servicio Inalambrico de Comunicaciones Personales de Nicaragua (PCS de Nicaragua): Managua; mobile cellular telephone operator; subsidiary of Mexican Grupo Salinas; awarded licence in 2002.

Telefonía Celular de Nicaragua (Nicacel): Managua; mobile cellular telephone operator; owned by BellSouth (USA).

BROADCASTING

Radio

Radio Cadena de Oro: Altamira 73, Managua; tel. (2) 78-1633; fax (2) 78-1220; f. 1990; Dir ALLAN DAVID TEFEL ALBA.

Radio Católica: Altamira D'Este 621, 3°, Apdo 2183, Managua; tel. (2) 78-0836; fax (2) 78-2544; e-mail catolica@ibw.com.ni; f. 1961; controlled by Conferencia Episcopal de Nicaragua; Dir Fr JOSÉ BISMARCK CARBALLO; Gen. Man. ALBERTO CARBALLO MADRIGAL.

Radio Corporación: Ciudad Jardín Q-20, Apdo 2442, Managua; tel. (2) 49-1619; fax (2) 44-3824; internet www.rc540.com.ni; Dir JOSÉ CASTILLOS OSEJO; Man. FABIO GADEA MANTILLA.

Radio Minuto: Ciudad Jardín Q-20, Apdo 2442, Managua; tel. (2) 40869; Dir CARLOS GADEA MANTILLA.

Radio Mundial: 36 Avda Oeste, Reparto Loma Verde, Apdo 3170, Managua; tel. (2) 66-6767; fax (2) 66-4630; commercial; Pres. MANUEL ARANA VALLE; Dir-Gen. ALMA ROSA ARANA HARTIG.

Radio Nicaragua: Villa Fontana, Contiguo a Enitel, Apdo 4665, Managua; tel. (2) 27-2330; fax (2) 626-71448; e-mail radio.nicaragua@netport.com.ni; internet www.radionicaragua.com.ni; f. 1960; government station; Dir-Gen. ALFONSO MONCADO CUELLAR.

Radio Noticias: Col. Robles 92, 4°, Apdo A-150, Managua; tel. (2) 49-5914; fax (2) 49-6393; e-mail fuentes@ibw.com.ni; Dir AGUSTÍN FUENTES SEQUEIRA.

Radio Ondas de Luz: Costado Sur del Hospital Bautista, Apdo 607, Managua; tel. and fax (2) 49-7058; f. 1959; religious and cultural station; Pres. GUILLERMO OSORNO MOLINA; Dir EDUARDO GUTIÉRREZ NARVÁEZ.

Radio Sandino: Paseo Tiscapa Este, Contiguo al Restaurante Mirador, Apdo 4776, Managua; tel. (2) 28-1330; fax (2) 62-4052; f. 1977; station controlled by the Frente Sandinista de Liberación Nacional; Pres. BAYARDO ARCE CASTAÑO; Dir CONRADO PINEDA AGUILAR.

Radio Tiempo: Reparto Pancasan 217, 7°, Apdo 2735, Managua; tel. (2) 78-2540; f. 1976; Pres. ERNESTO CRUZ; Gen. Man. MARIANO VALLE PETERS.

Radio Universidad: Del transfer de la UNAN 800 m al Sur, Apdo 2883, Managua; tel. (2) 78-4743; fax (2) 77-5057; f. 1984; Dir LUIS LÓPEZ RUIZ.

Radio Ya: Pista de la Resistencia, Frente a la Universidad Centroamericana, Managua; tel. (2) 78-5600; fax (2) 78-6000; f. 1990; Dir CARLOS JOSÉ GUADAMUZ P.

There are some 50 other radio stations.

Television

Nicavisión, Canal 12: Apdo 2766, Managua; tel. (2) 66-0691; fax (2) 66-1424; e-mail info@tv12-nic.com; internet www.tv12-nic.com; f. 1993; Dir MARIANO VALLE PETERS.

Nueva Imagen, Canal 4: Montoya, 1 c. Sur, 1 c. Arriba, Managua; tel. (2) 66-3420; fax (2) 66-3467; Pres. DIONISIO MARENCO; Gen. Man. ORLANDO CASTILLLO.

Sistema Nacional de Televisión Canal 6 (SNTV Canal 6): Km 3½, Carretera Sur, Contiguo a Shell, Las Palmas, Apdo 1505, Managua; tel. (2) 66-1520; fax (2) 66-2712; state-owned; Dir MARIO AMADOR RIVAS.

Televicentro de Nicaragua, S.A., Canal 2: Casa del Obrero, 6½ c. al Sur, Apdo 688, Managua; tel. (2) 68-2222; fax (2) 66-3688; e-mail canal2@canal2.com.ni; internet www.canal2.com.ni; f. 1965; Pres. OCTAVIO SACASA.

Televisora Nicaragüense, S.A., Telenica 8: De la Mansión Teodolinda, 1 c. al Sur, ½ c. Abajo, Bolonia, Apdo 3611, Managua; tel. (2) 66-5021; fax (2) 66-5024; e-mail cbriceno@nicanet.com.ni; f. 1989; Pres. CARLOS A. BRICEÑO LOVO.

Televisión Internacional, Canal 23: Planes de Altamira 7, del Sorbet-Inn 30 m Abajo, Apdo 444, Managua; tel. (2) 67-0171; fax (2) 67-0179; e-mail canal23@ibw.com.ni; f. 1993; Pres. CÉSAR RIGUERO.

Unitel, S.A., Canal 13: Calle Principal de Altamira, Managua; tel. (2) 66-5530; fax (2) 66-4862; Pres. ARNOLDO RÍOS.

Finance

(cap. = capital; res = reserves; dep. = deposits; m. = million; amounts in gold córdobas unless otherwise stated)

BANKING

All Nicaraguan banks were nationalized in July 1979. Foreign banks operating in the country are no longer permitted to secure local deposits. All foreign exchange transactions must be made through the Banco Central or its agencies. Under a decree issued in May 1985, the establishment of private exchange houses was permitted. In 1990 legislation allowing for the establishment of private banks was enacted.

Supervisory Authority

Superintendencia de Bancos y de Otras Instituciones Financieras: Edif. SBOIF, Km 7, Carretera Sur, Apdo 788, Managua; tel. (2) 65-1555; fax (2) 65-0965; e-mail correo@sibiof.gob.ni; internet www.superintendencia.gob.ni; f. 1991; Superintendent NOEL J. SACASA CRUZ.

Central Bank

Banco Central de Nicaragua: Carretera Sur, Km 7, Apdos 2252/3, Zona 5, Managua; tel. (2) 65-0500; fax (2) 65-0561; e-mail bcn@bcn.gob.ni; internet www.bcn.gob.ni; f. 1961; bank of issue and Government fiscal agent; cap. 10.6m., res 1,947.6m., dep. 20,212.5m. (Dec. 2001); Pres. Dr MARIO ALONSO ICABALCETA; Dir MARIO FLORES.

Private Banks

Banco de América Central (BAC): Pista Sub-Urbana, Frente a Lotería Popular, Managua; tel. (2) 67-0220; fax (2) 67-0224; e-mail info@BancodeAmericaCentral.com; internet www.BancodeAmericaCentral.com; f. 1991; total assets 10,516m. (1999); Pres. CARLOS PELLAS CHAMORRO; Gen. Man. CARLOS MATUS TAPIA.

Banco de Crédito Centroamericano (BANCENTRO): Edif. BANCENTRO, Km 4½, Carretera a Masaya, Managua; tel. (2) 78-0353; fax (2) 78-8030; internet www.bancentro.com; f. 1991; total assets 5,249m. (1999); Pres. ROBERTO J. ZAMORA LLANES; Gen. Man. JULIO CÁRDENAS R.

Banco de la Exportación (BANEXPO): Plaza España, Rotonda el Güegüense 20 m al Oeste, Managua; tel. (2) 78-7171; fax (2) 77-3154; e-mail info@banexpo.com.ni; internet www.banexpo.com.ni; dep. 2,553m. (Sept. 2001); Man. GILBERTO WONG.

Banco Mercantil, SA (BAMER): Plaza Banco Mercantil, Rotonda El Güegüense 1 c. al Sur, Managua; tel. (2) 66-8558; fax (2) 67-2041; e-mail bamer@tmx.com.ni; f. 1991; total assets 1,480m. (2000); Pres. HAROLDO J. MONTEALEGRE; 6 brs.

Banco Nicaragüense de Industria y Comercio (BANIC): Centro BANIC, Carretera a Masaya, Km 5½, Apdo 549, Managua; tel. (2) 67-2107; fax (2) 67-2308; e-mail rolacayo@ibw.com.ni; internet www.banconicaraguense.com; f. 1953; total assets 2,127m. (2000); Pres. RONALD LACAYO; Gen. Man. ARMANDO NÚÑEZ BRUX; 21 brs.

Foreign Bank

Citibank NA (USA): Del Sandy's ½ c. Arriba, Km 3½, Carretera a Masaya, 75 m Arriba, Apdo 3102, Managua; tel. (2) 72124; f. 1967; 1 br.

STOCK EXCHANGE

Bolsa de Valores de Nicaragua: Edif. Oscar Pérez Cassar, Centro BANIC, Km 5½, Carretera a Masaya, Managua; tel. (2) 78-3830; fax (2) 78-3836; e-mail info@bolsanic.com; internet http://bolsanic.com; f. 1993; Pres. Dr RAÚL LACAYO SOLÓRZANO; Gen. Man. CAROLINA SOLÓRZANO DE BARRIOS.

INSURANCE

State Company

Instituto Nicaragüense de Seguros y Reaseguros (INISER): Centro Comercial Camino de Oriente, Km 6, Carretera a Masaya, Apdo 1147, Managua; tel. (2) 72-2772; fax (2) 67-2121; internet www.iniser.gob.ni; f. 1979 to assume the activities of all the pre-revolution national private insurance companies; Exec. Pres. VILMA ROSA LEÓN-YORK.

Foreign Companies

American Life Insurance Company: Metrocentro Módulo 7, Apdo 601, Managua; tel. (2) 73356; Admin. Man. DOLORES LEZAMA.

British American Insurance Co.: Altamira D'Este 360, Apdo A-56, Managua; Gen. Man. CECIL E. GILL.

Citizens Standard Life Insurance Co.: Iglesia El Carmen, 2 c. al Lago, ½ c. Abajo, No 1410, Apdo 3199, Managua; Man. YAGALÍ RIVAS ALEGRÍA.

Pan American Life Insurance Co.: Edif. Kodak, Plaza de Compras, Col. Centroamérica, Managua; Man. ALEJANDRO LEIVA CABEZAS.

Trade and Industry

GOVERNMENT AGENCIES

Comisión Nacional de Promoción de Exportaciones: Km 6, Carretera a Masaya, Apdo 8, Managua; tel. and fax (2) 77-2511; e-mail promexpo@mific.gob.ni; f. 1991; promotion of exports, responsible to Ministry of Development, Industry and Trade; Tech. Sec. Dr HUMBERTO AGUELLO CH.

Empresa Nicaragüense de Alimentos Básicos (ENABAS): Salida a Carretera Norte, Apdo 1041, Managua; tel. (2) 23082; fax (2) 26185; f. 1979; controls trading in basic foodstuffs; Dir Lic. IGNACIO VÉLEZ LACAYO.

Empresa Nicaragüense del Azúcar (ENAZUCAR): Ministerio de Defensa Nacional, El Chipote, Complejo Germán Pomares, Managua; tel. (2) 27261; f. 1979; controls sugar trading; Dir NOEL CHAMORRO CUADRA.

Empresa Nicaragüense del Banano (BANANIC): Edif. Málaga, Plaza España, Apdo 3433, Managua; tel. (2) 678311; fax (2) 73633; f. 1979; controls banana trading; Dir EDUARDO HOLMANN.

Empresa Nicaragüense del Café (ENCAFE): Plaza de Compras, Contiguo al Banco de Londres (Lloyds Bank), Col. Centroamérica, Apdo 2482, Managua; tel. (2) 70337; fax (2) 67-2604; f. 1979; controls coffee trading; Dir Dr ARMANDO JARQUÍN SEQUIERA.

Empresa Nicaragüense de la Carne (ENCAR): Frente al Edif. Pérez Cassar, Apdo C-11, Managua; tel. (2) 70519; fax (2) 70621; f. 1979; controls trading and export of meat and meat products; Exec. Dir ORLANDO N. BONILLA.

Empresa Nicaragüense de Insumos Agropecuarios (ENIA): Distribuidora Vicky, 2 c. Oeste, Apdo C-11, Managua; tel. (2) 71724; f. 1979; agricultural investment goods board; f.1979; Dir EDUARDO FONSECA FÁBREGAS.

Empresa Nicaragüense de Productos del Mar (ENMAR): Frente al Cine Aguerri, Apdo 356, Managua; tel. (2) 23572; f. 1979; controls trading in all seafood products; Dir FRANKLIN MENDIETA MEDINA.

Instituto Nicaragüense de Apoyo a la Pequeña y Mediana Empresa (INPYME): De la Shell Plaza el Sol, 1 c. al Sur, 300 m Abajo, Apdo 449, Managua; tel. (2) 77-0598; fax (2) 70-1406; internet www.inpyme.gob.ni; supports small and medium-sized enterprises; Exec. Dir Dr RICARDO ALVARADO N.

Instituto Nicaragüense de Minas (INMINE): Pista de la Resistencia, Antiguo Centro Comercial El Punto, Contiguo a Migración y Extranjera, Apdo 195, Managua; tel. (2) 65-2073; fax (2) 51043; f. 1979; mines and hydrocarbons; Dir IVAN ORTEGA.

Instituto Nicaragüense de Reforma Agraria (INRA): Km 8, Entrada a Sierrita Santo Domingo, Managua; tel. (2) 73210; agrarian reform; Dir (vacant).

Instituto Nicaragüense de Seguridad Social (INSS): Frente Cementerio San Pedro, Edif. INSS, Apdo 1649, Managua; tel. (2) 22-7454; fax (2) 22-7445; f. 1955; social security and welfare; Dir EDNA BALLADARES; Deputy Dir EMILIO SELVA TAPIA.

Instituto Nicaragüense de Tecnología Agropecuaria (INTA): Managua; internet www.inta.gob.ni; f. 1993; Dir HENRY PEDROZA PACHECO.

MEDEPESCA: Km 6½, Carretera Sur, Managua; tel. (2) 67-3490; state fishing agency; Dir Ing. EMILIO OLIVARES.

DEVELOPMENT ORGANIZATIONS

Asociación Nicaragüense de Productores y Exportadores de Productos No Tradicionales (APENN): Del Hotel Intercontinental, 2 c. al Sur y 2 c. Abajo, Bolonia, Managua; tel. (2) 66-5038; fax (2) 66-5039; Pres. EMILIANO ENRÍQUEZ; Gen. Man. ROBERTO BRENES.

Cámara de Industrias de Nicaragua: Rotonda el Güegüense, 300 m al Sur, Apdo 1436, Managua; tel. (2) 66-8847; Pres. GABRIEL PACOS JACOYES.

Cámara Nacional de la Mediana y Pequeña Industria (CONAPI): Plaza 19 de Julio, Frente a la UCA, Apdo 153, Managua; tel. (2) 78-4892; fax (2) 67-0192; e-mail conapi@nicarao.org.ni; Pres. FLORA VARGAS; Gen. Man. URIEL ARGAÑEL C.

Cámara Nicaragüense de la Construcción (CNC): Bolonia de Aval Card, 2 c. Abajo, 50 vrs al Sur, Managua; tel. (2) 26-3363; fax (2) 66-3327; e-mail cncsecre@nicarao.org.ni; f. 1961; construction industry; Pres. Ing. BENJAMIN LANZAS.

Instituto Nicaragüense de Fomento Municipal (INIFOM): Edif. Central, Carretera a la Refinería, entrada principal residencial Los Arcos, Apdo 3097, Managua; tel. (2) 66-6050; fax (2) 66-6050; internet www.inifom.gob.ni; Pres. CARLOS MIGUEL DUARTE AREAS.

CHAMBERS OF COMMERCE

Cámara de Comercio de Nicaragua: Rotonda El Gueguense 300 m al Sur, 20 m al Oeste; tel. (505) 268-3505; fax (505) 268-3600; e-mail comercio@ibw.com.ni; f. 1892; 530 mems; Pres. MARCO A. MAYORGA L; Gen. Man. MARIO ALEGRÍA.

Cámara de Comercio Americana de Nicaragua: Semáforos ENEL Central, 500 m al Sur, Apdo 2720, Managua; tel. (2) 67-3099; fax (2) 67-3098; e-mail amcham@ns.tmx.com.ni; f. 1974; Pres. HUMBERTO CORRALES M.

Cámara Oficial Española de Comercio de Nicaragua: Restaurante la Marseilleisa, ½ c. Arriba, Los Robles, Apdo 4103, Managua; tel. (2) 78-9047; fax (2) 78-9088; e-mail camacoes@tmx.com.ni; Pres. JOSÉ ESCALANTE ALVARADO; Sec.-Gen. AUXILIADORA MIRANDA DE GUERRERO.

EMPLOYERS' ORGANIZATIONS

Asociación de Productores de Café Nicaragüenses: coffee producers; Pres. Dr NICOLÁS BOLAÑOS.

Consejo Superior de la Empresa Privada (COSEP): De Telcor Zacarías Guerra, 1 c. Abajo, Apdo 5430, Managua; tel. (2) 28-2030; fax (2) 28-2041; e-mail cosep@nic.gbm.net; f. 1972; private businesses; consists of Cámara de Industrias de Nicaragua (CADIN), Unión de Productores Agropecuarios de Nicaragua (UPANIC), Cámara de Comercio, Cámara de la Construcción, Confederación Nacional de Profesionales (CONAPRO), Instituto Nicaragüense de Desarrollo (INDE); mem. of Coordinadora Democrática Nicaragüense; Pres. ROBERTO TERAN; Sec. ORESTES ROMERO ROJAS.

Instituto Nicaragüense de Desarrollo (INDE): Ofs de Montoya, 1 c. al Norte, ½ c. al Oeste, Apdo 2598, Managua; tel. (2) 24047; f. 1963; organization of private businessmen; 650 mems; Pres. Ing. GILBERTO CUADRA; Exec. Sec. CARLOS ANTONIO NOGUERA P.

Unión de Productores Agropecuarios de Nicaragua (UPANIC): Reparto San Juan No 300, Detrás del Ginmasio Hércules, Managua; tel. (2) 78-3382; fax (2) 78-3291; e-mail upanic@ibw.com.ni; private agriculturalists' association; Pres. OSCAR ALEMÁN; Exec. Sec. ALEJANDRO RASKOSKY.

UTILITIES

Regulatory Bodies

Comisión Nacional de Energía: Managua; Exec. Sec. RAÚL SOLÓRZANO.

Instituto Nicaragüense de Energía (INE): Edif. Petronic, 4°, Managua; tel. (2) 28-1142; fax (2) 28-2049; internet www.ine.gob.ni; Pres. OCTAVIO SALINAS MORAZÁN.

Electricity

Unidad de Reestructuración de la Empresa Nicaragüense de Electricidad (URE): Altamira d'Este 141, de la Vicky 1 c. Abajo, 1 c. al Sur, Managua; tel. (2) 70-9989; fax (2) 78-2284; e-mail ure@ibw.com.ni; internet www.ure.gob.ni; f. 1999; to oversee the privatization of the state-owned distribution and generation companies of ENEL; Exec. Dir SALVADOR QUINTANILLA.

Empresa Nicaragüense de Electricidad (ENEL): Ofs Centrales, Pista Juan Pablo II y Avda Bolívar, Managua; tel. (2) 67-4159; fax (2) 67-2686; e-mail relapub@ibw.com.ni; internet www.enitel.gob.ni; Pres. MARIO MONTENEGRO; responsible for planning, organization, management, administration, research and development of energy resources; split into two distribution companies and three generation companies in 1999:

DISNORTE, SA: electricity distribution company; distributes some 802 gWh; sold to Union Fenosa (Spain) in 2000.

DISSUR, SA: electricity distribution company; distributes some 658 gWh; sold to Unión Fenosa (Spain) in 2000.

GECSA: electricity generation company; 79 MW capacity thermal plant; scheduled for privatization.

GEOSA: electricity generation company; 112 MW capacity thermal plant; sold to Coastal Power International (USA) in January 2002.

HIDROGESA: electricity generation company; 94 MW capacity hydro-electric plant; scheduled for privatization.

Water

Instituto Nicaragüense de Acueductos y Alcantarillados (INAA): De la Mansión Teodolinda, 3 c. al Sur, Bolonia, Apdo 1084, Managua; tel. (2) 66-7916; fax (2) 66-7917; e-mail pres.ejinaa@tmx.com.ni; internet www.inaa.gob.ni; f. 1979; water and sewerage; Pres. WILLIAM ARTILES VELÁZQUEZ.

CO-OPERATIVES

Cooperativa de Algodoneros de Managua, RL: Km 3½, Carretera Norte, Apdo 483, Managua; tel. (2) 4515; cotton-growers; Pres. Ing. GUILLERMO LACAYO; Sec. Ing. CARLOS ORTEGA M.

Cooperativa de Mercadeo de los Artesanos del Calzado: Managua; tel. (2) 4196; shoemakers and leatherworkers; Dir FÉLIX LECHADO CASTRILLO.

Empresa Cooperativa de Productores Agropecuarios: Managua; represents 13,000 members from 48 affiliated co-operatives; Chair. DANIEL NÚÑEZ.

TRADE UNIONS

Asociación de Trabajadores del Campo (ATC) (Association of Rural Workers): Apdo A-244, Managua; tel. (2) 23221; f. 1977; Gen. Sec. EDGARDO GARCÍA; 52,000 mems.

Central de Trabajadores Nicaragüenses (CTN) (Nicaraguan Workers' Congress): Iglesia Santa Ana, 1½ c. al Oeste, Managua; tel. (2) 25981; f. 1962; mem. of Coordinadora Democrática Nicaragüense; Leader CARLOS HUENDES; Sec.-Gen. ANTONIO JARQUÍN.

Confederación General de Trabajo (Independiente) (CGT(I)) (Independent General Confederation of Labour): Calle 11 de Julio, Managua; f. 1953; Sec.-Gen. CARLOS SALGADO MEMBRENO; 4,843 mems (est.) from six federations with 40 local unions, and six non-federated local unions.

Confederación de Unificación Sindical (CUS) (Confederation of United Trade Unions): Apdo 4845, Managua; tel. (2) 42039; f. 1972; affiliated to the Inter-American Regional Organization of Workers, etc. mem. of Coordinadora Democrática Nicaragüense; Leader ALVIN GUTHRIE RIVEZ; Sec. SANTOS TIJERINO.

Congreso Permanente de los Trabajadores (CPT) (Permanent Workers' Congress): 'umbrella' group for four trade unions, incl. the CTG(I) and CTN.

Consejo de Acción y Unidad Sindical (CAUS) (Council for Trade Union Action and Unity): Pauterizadora 'La Perfecta', 3 c. Abajo, Residencial Bello Horizonte, Managua; tel. (2) 44-2587; fax (2) 22-2623; f. 1973; trade-union wing of Partido Comunista de Nicaragua; Sec.-Gen. PÍO SANTOS MURILLO GONZÁLEZ.

Federación de Trabajadores de la Salud (FETSALUD) (Federation of Health Workers): Optica Nicaragüense, 2 c. Arriba ½ c. al Sur, Apdo 1402, Managua; tel. and fax (2) 66-3065; Dir GUSTAVO PORRAS CORTEZ.

Federación de Trabajadores Nicaragüenses (FTN): workers' federation; Leader ZACARÍAS HERNÁNDEZ.

Federación de Transportadores Unidos Nicaragüense (FTUN) (United Transport Workers' Federation of Nicaragua): De donde fue el Vocacional, esq. Este, 30 m al Sur, Apdo 945, Managua; f. 1952; Pres. MANUEL SABALLOS; 2,880 mems (est.) from 21 affiliated associations.

Frente Nacional de Trabajadores (FNT) (National Workers' Front): Calle Colón, Iglesia del Carmen, 1 c. Abajo, 20 m al Sur, Managua; tel. (2) 26484; e-mail fnt@nicarao.org; f. 1979; affiliated to Frente Sandinista de Liberación Nacional; Leader GUSTAVO PORRAS CORTÉS.

Frente Obrero (FO) (Workers' Front): f. 1974; radical Marxist-Leninist trade union.

Frente de Trabajadores Socialcristiano (FRETRA SC) (Social-Christian Workers' Front): f. 1980; trade-union wing of the Partido Social Cristiano Nicaragüense.

Solidaridad de Trabajadores Cristianos (STC): Christian workers; Leader DONALD CASTILLO.

Unión Nacional de Agricultores y Ganaderos (UNAG) (National Union of Agricultural and Livestock Workers): De donde fue el Cine Dorado, 1 c. Este, ½ c. Norte, frente al Restaurante Rincón Marino, Apdo 4526, Managua; tel. (2) 28-1403; fax (2) 28-1404; e-mail unag@unag.org.ni; internet www.unag.org.ni; f. 1981; Pres. DANIEL NÚÑEZ RODRÍGUEZ.

Unión Nacional de Caficultores de Nicaragua (UNCAFENIC) (National Union of Coffee Growers of Nicaragua): Reparto San Juan,

Casa 300, Apdo 3447, Managua; tel. (2) 78-2586; fax (2) 78-2587; Pres. GERARDO SALINAS C.

Unión Nacional Campesina (UNC) (National Union of Rural Workers): f. 1983; affiliated to the Unión Demócrata Cristiana.

Unión de Productores Agropecuarios de Nicaragua (Union of Agricultural Producers of Nicaragua): Reparto San Juan, Casa 300, Apdo 2351, Managua; tel. (2) 78-3382; fax (2) 78-2587; Pres. GERARDO SALINAS C.

Transport

Plans for the construction of a 377 km 'dry canal' or rail link between the Atlantic and Pacific oceans, at an estimated cost of US $1,400m., were being pursued in 2001–02. The plans included the construction of two deep-water ports, at Punta Mono (Atlantic) and Gigante (Pacific).

RAILWAYS

Ferrocarril de Nicaragua: Plantel Central Casimiro Sotelo, Del Parque San Sebastián, 5 c. al Lago, Apdo 5, Managua; tel. (2) 22-2160; fax (2) 22-2542; f. 1881; government-owned; main line from León via Managua to Granada on Lake Nicaragua (132 km), southern branch line between Masaya and Diriamba (44 km), northern branch line between León and Río Grande (86 km) and Puerto Sandino branch line between Ceiba Mocha and Puerto Sandino (25 km); total length 287 km; reported to have ceased operations in 1994; Gen. Man. N. ESTRADA.

Ferrocarril del Pacífico de Nicaragua: Plantel Central Casimiro Sotelo, Del Parque San Sebastián, 5 c. al Lago, Apdo 5, Managua; tel. (2) 22-2530; fax (2) 22-2542; Pacific railway co.

ROADS

In 2000 there were an estimated 19,032 km of roads of which 2,093 km were paved. Of the total only some 9,000–10,000 km were accessible throughout the entire year. Some 8,000 km of roads were damaged by 'Hurricane Mitch', which struck in late 1998. The Pan-American Highway runs for 384 km in Nicaragua and links Managua with the Honduran and Costa Rican frontiers and the Atlantic and Pacific Highways connecting Managua with the coastal regions.

SHIPPING

Corinto, Puerto Sandino and San Juan del Sur, on the Pacific, and Puerto Cabezas, El Bluff and El Rama on the Caribbean, are the principal ports. Corinto deals with about 60% of trade. In 2001 the US-based company Delasa was given a 25-year concession to develop and modernize Puerto Cabezas port. It was to invest some US $200m.

Empresa Portuaria Nacional (EPN): Apdo 2727-3570, Managua; tel. (2) 22-3827; fax (2) 66-3488; e-mail epn_puertos@epn.com.ni; internet www.epn.com.ni; Dir ROBERTO ZELAYA BLANCO.

Administración Portuaria de Arlen Siú: tel. (817) 0011; e-mail asiurama@ibw.com.ni.

Administración Portuaria de Bluefields-Bluff: tel. (822) 2632; e-mail Apb@ibw.com.ni.

Administración Portuaria de Corinto: De Telcor, 1 c. al Oeste, Corinto; tel. (342) 2768; e-mail corinto@epn.com.ni; f. 1956.

Administración Portuaria de San Juan del Sur: tel. (458) 2336.

Administración Portuaria de Puerto Cabezas: tel. (282) 2331.

Administración Portuaria de Sandino: tel. (312) 2212; e-mail portsand@ibw.com.ni.

CIVIL AVIATION

The principal airport is the Augusto Sandino International Airport, in Managua. There are some 185 additional airports in Nicaragua.

Aerolíneas Nicaragüenses (AERONICA): Contiguo Aeropuerto Internacional Augusto C. Sandino, Apdo 6018, Managua; tel. (2) 63-1929; fax (2) 63-1822; f. 1981; domestic services and international services to El Salvador, Costa Rica, Panama, Mexico and USA; Gen. Man. JULIO ROCHA.

Nicaragüenses de Aviación (NICA): Apdo 6018, Managua; tel. (2) 63-1929; fax (2) 63-1822; internet www.flylatinamerica.com; f. 1992; domestic services and international services to Panama, Costa Rica, Honduras, El Salvador, Guatemala and USA; Pres. ENRIQUE DREYFUS; Gen. Man. MARIO MEDRANO.

Tourism

In 1988 a campaign to attract more tourists to Nicaragua was launched, including a tourist development at Montelimar, which was supported by a US $10m. loan from Spanish investors. In 2000 tourist arrivals totalled 485,909 and receipts from tourism totalled around $116m.

Instituto Nicaragüense de Turismo (INTUR): Avda Bolívar Sur, Apdo 122, Managua; tel. (2) 22-5436; fax (2) 28-1187; internet www.intur.gob.ni; f. 1967; Pres. AUSBERTO NARVÁEZ; Vice-Pres. LEDA SÁNCHEZ DE PARRALES.

Asociación Nicaragüense de Agencias de Viajes (ANAVIT): Apdo 1045, Managua; Pres. ANTONIO ESPINO.

Cámara Nacional de Turismo: Contiguo al Ministerio de Turismo, Apdo 2105, Managua; tel. (2) 66-5071; fax (2) 66-5071; e-mail canatur@munditel.com.ni; f. 1976; Pres. MARIO MEDRANO M.

NIGER

Introductory Survey

Location, Climate, Language, Religion, Flag, Capital

The Republic of Niger is a land-locked country in western Africa, with Algeria and Libya to the north, Nigeria and Benin to the south, Mali and Burkina Faso to the west, and Chad to the east. The climate is hot and dry, with an average temperature of 29°C (84°F). The official language is French, but numerous indigenous languages, including Hausa (spoken by about one-half of the population), Tuareg, Djerma and Fulani, are also used (the 1991 sovereign National Conference identified 10 'national' languages). Some 95% of the population are Muslims, the most influential Islamic groups being the Tijaniyya, the Senoussi and the Hamallists. Most of the remainder of the population follow traditional beliefs, and there is a small Christian minority. The national flag (proportions 6 by 7) has three equal horizontal stripes, of orange, white and green, with an orange disc in the centre of the white stripe. The capital is Niamey.

Recent History

Formerly a part of French West Africa, Niger became a self-governing member of the French Community in December 1958 and was granted independence on 3 August 1960. Hamani Diori, leader of the Parti progressiste nigérien (the local section of the Ivorian-dominated Rassemblement démocratique africain) and Prime Minister since December 1958, became Head of State. Following the suppression of Djibo Bakary's left-wing nationalist Union nigérienne démocratique (or Sawaba party) in 1959, Diori was elected President in November 1960, and re-elected in 1965 and 1970. Close links were maintained with France.

The Sahelian drought of 1968–74 was particularly damaging to the Nigerien economy and was a major factor in precipitating a military coup in April 1974. Diori was arrested, and Lt-Col (later Maj.-Gen.) Seyni Kountché, the armed forces Chief of Staff, became President. The new administration, headed by a Conseil militaire suprême (CMS), suspended the Constitution; the legislature was replaced by a consultative Conseil national de développement (CND), and political activity was banned. Seeking greater national independence, Kountché obtained the withdrawal of French troops and reduced French influence over the exploitation of Niger's deposits of uranium (which France had initiated in 1968).

In August 1975 Djibo Bakary (who had lived in exile in Guinea in 1959–74, returning to Niger following the coup) was arrested, together with the Vice-Chairman of the CMS and the head of the national groundnut company, on charges of plotting to seize power. An alleged coup plot in March 1976, led by a former government minister, resulted in death sentences for nine conspirators.

Niger suffered further drought in 1977–78. From late 1977 the proportion of army officers in the Government was progressively reduced, as the unpopular and corrupt administration was gradually replaced. Senior members of Diori's administration and other political prisoners were released in March 1978, and in April 1980 both Diori and Bakary were released from prison, although Diori was kept under house arrest. In January 1983 a civilian, Oumarou Mamane, was appointed to the newly created post of Prime Minister. In October, while Kountché was overseas, ministers loyal to his regime thwarted a coup attempt by military officers. Two government ministers were among those arrested, although the suspected architects of the plot fled Niger. In November Mamane, who in August had been appointed President of the CND, was replaced as Prime Minister by Hamid Algabid. In January 1984 Kountché announced the establishment of a commission to draft a 'national charter' defined as a pre-constitutional document. The recurrence of drought in 1984–85, and the two-year closure (at Nigeria's instigation) of the land border with Nigeria from April 1984, impeded economic adjustment efforts and increased Niger's dependence on external financial assistance.

The draft 'national charter' was approved by a reported 99.6% of voters in a referendum in June 1987. On 14 November, four days after Kountché's death, while undergoing medical treatment in France, Col (later Brig.) Ali Saïbou, the army Chief of Staff, was inaugurated as Chairman of the CMS and Head of

State. Diori was released from house arrest, and an appeal was made to exiled Nigeriens to return to the country. (Diori died in Morocco in 1989.) In December 1987 an amnesty was proclaimed for all political prisoners. In July 1988 Oumarou Mamane (who had been replaced as President of the CND in September 1987) was reinstated as Prime Minister, and the CND was given the task of drafting a new constitution. In August 1988 Brig. Saïbou formed a new ruling party, the Mouvement national pour une société de développement (MNSD). In October four of those who had been implicated in the 1983 coup attempt were sentenced, in absentia, to death; 16 others received prison sentences.

In May 1989 an MNSD congress elected a Conseil supérieur d'orientation nationale (CSON) to succeed the CMS. The draft Constitution was endorsed by referendum in September, reportedly receiving the support of 99.3% of voters. At elections in December Saïbou (as President of the CSON, the sole candidate) was confirmed as President of the Republic, for a seven-year term, by 99.6% of those who voted, while 99.5% of voters endorsed a single list of CSON-approved deputies to a new, 93-member Assemblée nationale. It was subsequently announced that Niger's two remaining political prisoners were to be released, to commemorate Saïbou's inauguration as President of what was designated the Second Republic. The post of Prime Minister was abolished later in December 1989, but was restored in March 1990, and allocated to a prominent industrialist, Aliou Mahamidou, in an extensive government reorganization.

In June 1990 the labour federation, the Union des syndicats des travailleurs du Niger (USTN), organized strike action to protest against the new Government's economic austerity programme. In that month the CSON announced that the Constitution was to be amended to facilitate a transition to political pluralism. Industrial unrest persisted, and the USTN made new demands for multi-party politics and for access to the state-controlled media. Following a five-day general strike in November, Saïbou announced that a multi-party political system would be established and that less stringent austerity measures would be adopted. A national conference on political reform was to be convened in mid-1991, and multi-party national elections would take place in early 1992.

In March 1991 the armed forces Chief of Staff, in accordance with a principal demand of the opposition, announced that the armed forces were to distance themselves from the MNSD with immediate effect. In July Saïbou resigned as Chairman of the MNSD, in preparation for the National Conference. The Conference, which was convened in Niamey later that month, was attended by about 1,200 delegates, including representatives of the organs of state, 24 political organizations, the military and civic society. It declared itself sovereign, voting to suspend the Constitution and dissolve the legislature. Saïbou would remain in office as Head of State on an interim basis, but the Conference would supervise the exercise of his (now largely ceremonial) powers. The Government was deprived of its authority to make financial transactions on behalf of Niger, and links with external creditors were effectively severed when the Conference voted to suspend adherence to the IMF- and World Bank-sponsored programme of economic adjustment. The Conference also assumed control of the armed forces and the police, and in September appointed a new armed forces Chief and Deputy Chief of Staff. The Government was dissolved in September, and in October the Conference appointed Amadou Cheiffou to head a transitional Council of Ministers, which was intended to hold office until the inauguration of democratically elected institutions, now scheduled for early 1993. In October 1991 an amnesty was announced for all those who had been implicated in the 1983 coup attempt. Prior to the conclusion of the Conference, in November 1991, its President, André Salifou, was designated Chairman of a 15-member interim legislative body, the Haut conseil de la République (HCR), whose duties were to include the supervision of the drafting of a new constitution.

The process of transition to civilian rule encountered numerous difficulties. A referendum on the new Constitution, scheduled for October 1992, was delayed until 26 December, when 89.8% of those who voted approved the new document. The elections to the new Assemblée nationale, which eventually took place on 14 February 1993, were contested by 12 political parties. The MNSD won the greatest number of seats (29) in the 83-member assembly, but was prevented from resuming power by the rapid formation, following the election, of the Alliance des forces de changement (AFC), which included six parties with a total of 50 seats in the legislature. Principal members of the AFC were the Convention démocratique et sociale—Rahama (CDS), the Parti nigérien pour la démocratie et le socialisme—Tarayya (PNDS), and the Alliance nigérienne pour la démocratie et le progrès social—Zaman Lahiya (ANDPS).

At the first round of the presidential election, on 27 February 1993, which was contested by eight candidates, Col (retd) Tandja Mamadou, Saïbou's successor as leader of the MNSD, won the greatest proportion of votes cast (34.2%). He and his nearest rival, Mahamane Ousmane (the leader of the CDS, with 26.6%), proceeded to a second round on 27 March, at which Ousmane was elected President by 55.4% of voters; his inauguration took place on 16 April. Ousmane appointed a first-round candidate, Mahamadou Issoufou of the PNDS, as Prime Minister. Despite an attempt by the MNSD to block the appointment, in May another presidential candidate, Moumouni Adamou Djermakoye of the ANDP, became President of the Assemblée nationale.

The new regime's efforts to curb public expenditure, combined with the effects of the 50% devaluation of the CFA franc in January 1994, provoked considerable disquiet among workers and students. In May, following several weeks of disturbances (during which Mamadou and other opposition leaders had briefly been detained), three opposition activists were imprisoned, having been convicted of unauthorized demonstration and causing damage to public and private property.

In September 1994 the PNDS withdrew from the AFC, and Issoufou resigned the premiership, in protest at the perceived transfer of certain prime ministerial powers to the President. A new minority Government, led by Souley Abdoulaye of the CDS, failed to withstand a parliamentary motion of 'no confidence' proposed by the MNSD and the PNDS in October. Ousmane dissolved the Assemblée nationale, confirming the Abdoulaye Government in office pending new elections.

Some 774 candidates, including representatives of about 15 political parties, contested the delayed legislative elections on 12 January 1995. The MNSD, which won 29 seats, formed a 43-strong majority group with its allies in the Assemblée nationale. Although the CDS increased its representation to 24 seats, the AFC secured only 40 seats. Ousmane declined to accept the new majority's nominee to the premiership, Hama Amadou (the Secretary-General of the MNSD), instead appointing another member of that party, Amadou Aboubacar Cissé, a former official of the World Bank. The MNSD and its allies announced that they would neither participate in nor co-operate with his administration, and Cissé was expelled from the party. Meanwhile, Issoufou was elected President of the Assemblée nationale. In February the legislature approved a motion of censure against Cissé, and Ousmane accepted the nomination of Amadou as Prime Minister.

The political 'cohabitation' of Ousmane and the Amadou Government encountered serious institutional difficulties, as the President and Prime Minister disputed their respective competencies, in particular with regard to a proposed programme for the reorganization and privatization of state enterprises, which was opposed by Ousmane. Following several months of industrial and social unrest, Ousmane's rejection of the Government's draft budget, in January 1996, resulted in a new impasse in relations between the President and the Government.

On 27 January 1996 the elected organs of state were overthrown by the military. The coup leaders, who formed a Conseil de salut national (CSN), chaired by Col (later Brig.-Gen.) Ibrahim Baré Maïnassara, armed forces Chief of Staff since March 1995 and a former aide-de-camp to Kountché, asserted that their seizure of power had been necessitated by Niger's descent into political chaos. The CSN suspended the Constitution and dissolved the Assemblée nationale; political parties were suspended, and a state of emergency was imposed.

The CSN committed itself to economic restructuring, with a view to securing funding arrangements with the IMF and the World Bank, and to the restoration of peace in the north of the country (see below). A national forum was to be convened to consider the revision of the Constitution and the electoral code,

and to determine a timetable for a return to democratically elected civilian rule. None the less, Western donors withdrew all non-humanitarian assistance, and negotiations with the IMF were stalled.

The CSN appointed Boukary Adji, the Deputy Governor of the Banque centrale des états de l'Afrique de l'ouest (and Minister of Finance in 1983–87) as Prime Minister. Adji's transitional Government, named in February 1996, was composed entirely of civilians, including the former HCR President, André Salifou, although military officers were appointed to regional governorships, purportedly as a means of ensuring political neutrality in the organization of elections. In that month Ousmane, Amadou and Issoufou signed a joint text, in Maïnassara's presence, which effectively endorsed the legitimacy of the CSN and stated that the assumption of power by the military had been necessitated by the prolonged administrative difficulties that had preceded the coup. A constitutional referendum was subsequently scheduled for June, with elections to be completed by September.

Two consultative bodies were established to prepare for the restoration of civilian government, the advisory Conseil des sages (which elected Saïbou as its Chairman) and the co-ordinating committee of the national forum. The National Forum for Democratic Renewal, which was convened in April 1996, adopted revisions to the Constitution that aimed to guarantee greater institutional stability, essentially by conferring executive power solely on the republican President. In mid-April the constitutional referendum was brought forward to May, with the intention that the presidential poll could take place in July. Also in April it was announced that restrictions on the movements of Ousmane, Amadou and Issoufou, which had been enforced following the *coup d'état*, had been ended, and all three accompanied Maïnassara to northern Niger to celebrate National Concord Day, on the first anniversary of the signing of the peace agreement with the Tuareg movement (see below).

By May 1996 Maïnassara had confirmed reports of his intention, which he had initially denied, to seek election as President. The revised Constitution was approved by some 92.3% of the votes cast at the referendum on 12 May (about 35% of the electorate participated). The ban on activities by political organizations, and the state of emergency imposed in January, were lifted shortly afterwards. Ousmane, Issoufou, Mamadou and Djermakoye swiftly announced their intention to contest the presidential election. As the political consensus of recent months ended, there was much criticism among opposition groups of the appointment of a new High Court of Justice, which was to be solely responsible for trying cases of high treason and other offences committed by public figures (including past officials) in the exercise of their state duties. Moreover, tensions between the authorities and the Commission électorale nationale indépendante (CENI) became increasingly evident, as the Government disregarded the latter's recommendation that the presidential election be postponed, in response to various logistical delays.

Voting in the presidential election commenced, as scheduled, on 7 July 1996, but was quickly halted in Niamey and in several other areas where preparations were incomplete: polling took place in these areas on 8 July. Shortly before the end of voting the authorities announced the dissolution of the CENI, citing its alleged obstruction of the electoral process. A new commission was appointed to collate the election results. Meanwhile, Maïnassara's four rivals for the presidency were placed under house arrest. According to provisional results, announced by the new commission, Maïnassara won the election, with some 52.2% of the votes cast, Ousmane secured 19.8%, and Mamadou 15.7%. Security measures in Niamey were reinforced, the closure was ordered of the headquarters of the main opposition parties, and, following violent unrest, a curfew was imposed in Zinder, Ousmane's native town. The Supreme Court validated the election results on 21 July, and the release from house arrest of the defeated candidates was announced on the following day. Maïnassara was installed as President of the Fourth Republic on 7 August 1996. A new Government, with Adji as Prime Minister, also included Abdoulaye and Cissé. Members of the CDS, the MNSD and the PNDS who had accepted government posts were subsequently expelled from these parties.

In August 1996 the legislative elections, which had been scheduled for September, were postponed until 10 November. The Conseil des sages recommended a further delay, pending the resolution of difficulties—including the threatened boycott by the main opposition parties, now grouped in a Front pour la restauration et la défense de la démocratie (FRDD). At Maïnassara's instigation, the Government undertook inter-party negotiations, mediated by the Conseil des sages. The Government agreed to permit opposition access to the state media and to rescind the ban (in force since the presidential election) on public meetings and demonstrations, and in October announced the further postponement of the legislative elections, to 23 November, and the restoration of the CENI, with the same composition as that which had overseen the 1995 election. The commission's prerogatives were, however, amended, and the FRDD responded that it would not participate in the forthcoming poll unless the CENI was reinstated with its original powers and the presidential election annulled.

The legislative elections proceeded on 23 November 1996, contested by 11 parties and movements, as well as by independent candidates. According to official results, the pro-Maïnassara Union nationale des indépendants pour le renouveau démocratique (UNIRD) won 52 of the Assemblée nationale's 83 seats. International observers pronounced themselves satisfied with the organization and conduct of the election. (The Supreme Court later annulled the results in three constituencies won by the UNIRD, on the grounds of fraud.) The CSN was formally dissolved on 13 December 1996, prior to the appointment of a new Government, with Cissé as Prime Minister. The FRDD rejected an invitation to participate in the Government, and the deputy leader of the CDS, Sanoussi Jackou, was expelled from the party after accepting a ministerial post. The Assemblée nationale was inaugurated on 27 December.

In January 1997 an unauthorized opposition demonstration in Niamey degenerated into clashes with the security forces. Some 62 people were arrested, among them Ousmane, Mamadou and Issoufou, who were to be tried by the recently restored State Security Court. In response to opposition claims that neither the Constitution nor the penal code made provision for the Court (which had been in existence under the Kountché regime), the Government cited constitutional provisions that ensured the continued validity of laws in force at the time of the promulgation of the Constitution, unless specifically repealed. Nine days later, following clashes in Zinder and a further protest in Niamey, the opposition leaders were released, reportedly on Maïnassara's direct order. The FRDD rejected an invitation by the President to participate in a government of national unity, demanding the dissolution of the Assemblée nationale and the holding of free and fair elections.

A new Chief and Deputy Chief of Staff of the Armed Forces and new military regional prefects were appointed in June 1997, following unrest in military garrisons, precipitated by a failure to pay arrears in soldiers' allowances. Also in June the Assemblée nationale designated members to the High Court of Justice, including Djermakoye as the Court's President.

In November 1997 Maïnassara dismissed the entire Government, on the grounds of its failure to address Niger's political, economic and social difficulties: a resumption of hostilities in the north had been compounded by poor harvests and by further labour unrest. Maïnassara appointed Ibrahim Hassane Maiyaki, hitherto Minister of Foreign Affairs and Co-operation, as Prime Minister and named a new Council of Ministers in December.

In January 1998 it was announced that members of a commando unit had been arrested and charged with attempting to overthrow Maïnassara and other senior officials. Four of the accused made a televised confession, stating that they had been operating on the direct orders of former Prime Minister Amadou, who was himself arrested. Two other former ministers were also arrested, but were released within a week. Although all three denied involvement in any conspiracy, Maïnassara stated that Amadou had been associated with, and given financial support to, the alleged commandos. Several members of the armed forces accused of involvement in the plot were reported to have fled Niger. Amadou was released on bail shortly afterwards, charged with forming a militia, criminal conspiracy and illegal possession of weapons.

In February 1998 soldiers at three military garrisons in the Diffa region, in the south-east, mutinied, taking hostage local military commanders and civilian administrators. The rebels imposed a curfew and seized the local radio station to demand the payment of salary arrears. Despite reassurances from the Government, the mutiny spread to the north—to Agadez and Arlit—and also to Zinder. All the rebellions had been abandoned by early March, after the Government promised payment of two months' salary arrears (four months' pay was outstanding) and,

acknowledging that conditions in the north and east were particularly harsh, undertook to establish a minimum standard of living for all military personnel.

In February 1998 three parties of the presidential group (Sanoussi Jackou's Parti nigerien pour l'autogestion—al Umat, the Parti pour l'unité nationale et le développement—Salama and the ANDPS) formed the Alliance des forces démocratiques et sociales (AFDS). However, the AFDS subsequently protested against its perceived marginalization in the political process and in the state media, observing that the alliance was increasingly associated with the opposition. Meanwhile, the FRDD laid down a number of preconditions for participation at the forthcoming local elections, including the rehabilitation of the CENI and guarantees of the neutrality of regional administrators and the security forces. Clashes in Tahoua in April between the security forces and FRDD activists, who were demanding Maïnassara's resignation, were followed by violent protests by the FRDD in Maradi and in Zinder.

In July 1998 it was reported that the Government and 11 opposition parties (the eight FRDD members and the three affiliates of the AFDS) had signed an agreement, which was intended to facilitate opposition participation in the local elections scheduled for November. Revisions to electoral procedures and institutions were outlined, as well as to the manner in which senior appointments would be made to the Supreme Court. It was, moreover, agreed that all political groups should have equal access to the state media, and that freedom to demonstrate should be respected. The Government was to ensure the political neutrality of the military. The President of the CENI was to be appointed by consensus from among the country's magistrates, and was to have no voting rights. However, the opposition challenged the subsequent appointment by Maïnassara of Lawali Mahamane Danda to head the electoral body, in spite of Danda's assurances of his neutrality. The remaining members of the CENI were appointed by presidential decree in September. It was evident, however, that preparations were inadequate to allow the elections to proceed as scheduled, and in October the CENI postponed voting until February 1999.

Voting in the regional, district and municipal elections took place, accordingly, on 7 February 1999, one day after the Minister of the Interior, Souley Abdoulaye, had presented a document purportedly giving evidence of an opposition plot to obtain full control of the state. Following the discovery of overt irregularities, the CENI emphasized that it favoured by-elections in affected areas. Full results, which were not released by the Supreme Court until 7 April, gave the 11 opposition parties a slim overall majority of seats in those municipal, district and regional assemblies where the elections were deemed valid. Voting was to be rerun at some 4,000 polling stations nationwide. The FRDD and AFDS, denouncing Maïnassara as personally responsible for the disruption to voting, demanded the President's resignation.

On 9 April 1999 Maiyaki made a broadcast to the nation, announcing the death of Maïnassara in an 'unfortunate accident' at a military airbase in Niamey. The Prime Minister stated that the defence and security forces would continue to be the guarantors of republican order and national unity, and announced the dissolution of the Assemblée nationale, as well as the temporary suspension of all party political activity. Despite the official explanation for his death, it was generally perceived that members of the presidential guard had assassinated Maïnassara in a *coup d'état*. Members of the Assemblée nationale initially rejected its dissolution, stating that the 1996 Constitution remained in force and that its institutions must therefore continue to function. On 11 April 1999, however, the Constitution was suspended, and its institutions dissolved. The February local elections were annulled. A military Conseil de réconciliation nationale (CRN), under the chairmanship of Maj. Daouda Mallam Wanké (hitherto head of the presidential guard), was to exercise executive and legislative authority during a nine-month transitional period, prior to the restoration of elected civilian institutions. Wanké immediately signed an ordinance on interim political authority, which was to function as a constitutional document during the transitional period. A new Constitution was to be drafted, and it was stated that the timetable for the restoration of civilian rule, which envisaged a constitutional referendum in June, elections in November, and the installation of an elected Head of State on 31 December, would be strictly adhered to.

Maiyaki was reappointed as Prime Minister of the transitional Government on 12 April 1999; a new Council of Ministers was named shortly afterwards. New appointees notably included Danda as Minister of Justice, Keeper of the Seals. Moussa Moumouni Djermakoye, who had been succeeded as armed forces Chief of Staff by Lt-Col Soumara Zanguina, became Minister of National Defence. In July, in a minor reshuffle, the Minister of the Interior and Territorial Administration, Lt-Col Moumouni Boureima, was appointed armed forces Chief of Staff, while Zanguina became an adviser to the Head of State.

In May 1999 a consultative council of state elders was inaugurated, in order to consider proposals relating to the drafting of a constitution and the restoration of national unity. Chaired by Moumouni Adamou Djermakoye, its members included Issoufou, Abdoulaye, Amadou and Cissé. Indications that the council favoured a semi-presidential system of government were criticized by the pro-Maïnassara Rassemblement pour la démocratie et le progrès—Djamaa (RDP), and also by trade unions, as being likely to result in such institutional paralysis as had preceded the military take-over in 1996.

The draft Constitution of the Fifth Republic of Niger was submitted to referendum on 18 July 1999, when it was approved by 89.57% of those who voted (about one-third of the registered electorate). The Constitution, as promulgated by Wanké on 9 August, envisaged a balance of powers between the President, the Government and the legislature, but, none the less, vested strong powers in the Head of State, who was to be politically liable only in the case of high treason. The Government, under a Prime Minister appointed by the President, was to be responsible to the Assemblée nationale, which would be competent to remove the Prime Minister by vote of censure. A clause in the Constitution guaranteeing all those involved in the military take-overs of January 1996 and April 1999 immunity from prosecution provoked controversy and was condemned by Amnesty International, in a report in September, as undermining the rule of law. The report was regarded as particularly significant in that it published the testimony of a witness who alleged that Maïnassara had been murdered by the presidential guard under Wanké's command. The Wanké regime continued to assert that Maïnassara's death had been accidental, and that a commission of inquiry into the death had been ordered in response to a complaint lodged by the late President's family.

In mid-August 1999 the first round of the presidential election, which had been scheduled for 3 October, was postponed until 17 October, with a second round (should no candidate secure an overall majority at the first round) to be held concurrently with the legislative elections on 24 November. Voting at the presidential election, which was contested by seven candidates, proceeded as scheduled, and was considered both by the CENI and by independent observers to have been largely transparent and peaceful. Tandja Mamadou, of the MNSD, won 32.30% of the votes cast, followed by Issoufou, of the PNDS, with 22.78%, and Ousmane, of the CDS, with 22.52%. The rate of participation by voters was 43.66%. Mamadou and Issoufou thus proceeded to a second round, on 24 November. Having secured the support of Ousmane, Mamadou was elected President, with 59.89% of the votes cast. About 39% of the registered electorate voted. The MNSD was similarly successful in the concurrent elections to the Assemblée nationale, winning 38 of the 83 seats; the CDS took 17, the PNDS 16, the RDP eight and the ANDPS four.

Mamadou, who had served in the CMS under Kountché and was Minister of the Interior in the early 1990s, was inaugurated as President of the Fifth Republic on 22 December 1999. Hama Amadou, the MNSD Secretary-General, was subsequently appointed Prime Minister, and a new Council of Ministers was named in early January 2000. Mamadou urged the Government to address the problem of outstanding salaries, grants and scholarships (some 12–13 months' salaries were now outstanding in many areas of the public sector), and to adopt an emergency financial programme so as to allow the rapid resumption of international assistance. The French Government subsequently announced exceptional assistance to allow the payment of arrears.

In early January 2000 the newly inaugurated Assemblée nationale adopted draft amnesty legislation, as provided for in the Constitution. The amnesty was opposed by the RDP, and many activists of the party joined a demonstration in February to denounce the legislation and to demand an international inquiry into the death of Maïnassara. In March members of the PNDS, the RDP and the ANDPS boycotted parliament for two weeks, in protest at the ruling party's assumption of the vast majority of senior committee and bureau positions. In that month 12 opposition parties, led by the PNDS, formed a coalition, the Coordination des forces démocratiques (CFD). Similarly, 17 parties loyal to the President, most notably the MNSD and the CDS, formed the Alliance des forces démocratiques (AFD).

In May 2000 Col Bourahima Moumouni was appointed armed forces Chief of Staff. None the less, rumours persisted of dissent within the army; in June Amadou warned that, without a restoration of military discipline, the threat of further uprisings could not be ignored. Also in that month 10 soldiers were arrested, following the kidnapping and arrest of Maj. Djibrilla Hima, a spokesman for the former Wanké regime. In a speech broadcast on national radio, the Minister of Rural Development, Wassalike Boukari (in his role as acting Prime Minister), spoke of the need to create a 'republican army' as part of the re-establishment of democracy, while rejecting the suggestion that any purging of the institution was necessary. In July the army Chief of Staff refuted allegations that elements within the military had attempted or were plotting a *coup d'état*.

Opposition deputies were unsuccessful in attempts to gain majority support for two motions of 'no confidence' in the Government proposed to the Assemblée nationale in January and March 2001, the former reportedly in response to allegations of administrative corruption, the latter in response to the continued closure of the Abdou Moumouni University at Niamey, following repeated student demonstrations against a perceived decline in educational standards, a reduction in student grants and a failure to pay scholarship arrears.

In June 2001 controversy arose following the suspension of El Hadj Aboubacar Sanda from his duties as Sultan of Zinder and as President of the Association des chefs traditionnels du Niger, following his arrest on charges of involvement in criminal activity and in planning a *coup d'état*. Sanda was dismissed as Sultan by the Government in early July, prompting the CFD to accuse the authorities of acting illegally (as Sanda had yet to be charged or face trial), while supporters of Sanda threatened to instigate a campaign of civil disobedience unless he was returned to office. (In September 2002 Sanda was convicted of complicity in fraud and sentenced to two years' imprisonment.)

In September 2001 President Mamadou reshuffled the Council of Ministers, retaining Prime Minister Amadou and 10 of his ministers, although there were some 13 new appointments. In October opposition parties tabled a further censure motion against the Government in the Assemblée nationale, although the motion was withdrawn before voting could proceed, in response to concerns that it would negatively affect the Government's ongoing negotiations with the World Bank and the European Union (EU, see p. 199).

In the early 2000s demands for the introduction of Islamic *Shari'a* law became a source of tension in Niger, which, in accordance with the 1999 Constitution, retains a separation between the state and religious organizations. In November 2000 violent protests erupted in Niamey and Maradi in response to a fashion show held in the capital. Following the demonstrations, some 270 people, reportedly including prominent religious leaders, were arrested, although 240 of the protesters were released promptly without charge. Islamist leaders, who condemned the show as an incitement to debauchery, had instigated the protests. In early July 2002 two Islamist activists, who had demanded the introduction of the *Shari'a* in a letter to Mamadou, were charged with incitement to revolt.

In July 2002 the ANDP withdrew from the opposition CFD alliance and joined the AFD, thereby increasing the Government's parliamentary majority by four seats. Explaining his party's shift in allegiances, the leader of the ANDP, Moumouni Adamou Djermakoye, accused the CFD of intolerance and of failing to ease social tensions.

In late July 2002 a further mutiny broke out at a barracks in Diffa, and a number of officers were taken hostage. Several officers, in addition to the mayor of Diffa and the regional governor, were arrested by the mutinous soldiers, who also took control of a radio station to broadcast their demands for improved pay and conditions, including the payment of wage arrears. The Government declared a state of emergency in Diffa and dispatched troops to bring the rebellion, which continued for 10 days, to a halt. Six soldiers, including three officers, were arrested in connection with the rebellion, but other rebel soldiers were reported to have fled the region, while a further uprising, at a barracks in Nguigmi, to the east of Diffa, was rapidly quashed. In early August, before the rebellion in Diffa had been conclusively suppressed, a military uprising broke out in Niamey, although government forces quickly restored order in the capital. By mid-September special security measures, imposed in the Diffa region by presidential decree, had been relaxed. In mid-August the President of the national human rights league, Elhaji Bagnou Bonkoukou, was arrested on charges of disseminating false information; Bonkoukou had declared that several civilians and soldiers, in excess of the two deaths announced by the Government, had been killed during the rebellion and its suppression. In late September Bonkoukou was sentenced to 12 months' imprisonment.

In late August 2002 Amadou announced that the rebellion in Diffa had been intended to serve as a distraction, while a *coup d'état* was being prepared in Niamey. The Prime Minister also rejected demands from his party that the rebel soldiers be court-martialled, stating that a committee had been established to draft new military texts, which would be approved by the Assemblée nationale prior to the trial of the rebels. In mid-September the President and Vice-President of the Constitutional Court, Sani Koutoubi and Lawan Ari Gremah, resigned, following a ruling by the court, earlier in the month, that two decrees announced by President Mamadou in relation to the suppression of the rebellion were unconstitutional; in particular, the imposition of emergency measures by the Head of State without consulting the Prime Minister, the Assemblée nationale and the Constitutional Court was deemed a breach of constitutional requirements, while a further decree, which restricted media coverage of the uprising, was also determined to be illegal.

Meanwhile, the Minister of Sports and Culture, Issa Lamine, resigned at the end of August 2002, reportedly in protest at the failure to build proposed sporting infrastructure funded by France. Mamadou implemented a major government reshuffle in early November, as a result of which the position of allies of Prime Minister Amadou was reportedly strengthened. Among the 13 new ministerial appointments was Moumouni Adamou Djermakoye, as Minister of State, responsible for African Integration and the NEPAD (New Partnership for Africa's Development, see p. 133) Programmes, while seven ministers left the Government. Although several principal positions, including the foreign affairs and economy portfolios, remained unchanged, new appointments were made to the Ministries of National Defence and of the Interior and Decentralization. At the end of December the Assemblée nationale approved legislation providing for the creation of a special military tribunal to try those accused of involvement in the rebellion earlier in the year; elements within the opposition alleged that the legislation violated several articles of the Constitution.

Ethnic unrest followed the return to northern Niger, during the late 1980s, of large numbers of Tuareg nomads who had migrated to Libya and Algeria in the early 1980s to escape the Sahelian drought. It was widely believed that the perceived failure of the Saïbou administration to assist in the rehabilitation of returnees was a significant factor contributing to the subsequent Tuareg uprising. In May 1990 some 100 deaths were reported when the military suppressed a Tuareg attack on the prison and gendarmerie at Tchin-Tabaraden. In April 1991 44 Tuaregs were reportedly acquitted of involvement in the attack. In a renewed offensive, which began in October, numerous attacks were directed against official targets in the north, and several members of the armed forces were kidnapped. In January 1992 the transitional authorities intensified security measures in the north and, for the first time, formally acknowledged that there was a rebellion in the country. Rhissa Ag Boula, the leader of the rebel Front de libération de l'Aïr et l'Azaouad (FLAA), subsequently stated that the Tuareg rebels were seeking to achieve the establishment of a federal system of governance. Although the Government and the FLAA concluded a truce agreement in May, violence swiftly resumed.

In August 1992 the security forces launched a major offensive against the Tuareg rebellion. Military authority was reinforced in October by the appointment of senior members of the security forces to northern administrative posts. In November, none the less, a commission that had been appointed by the transitional Government recommended a far-reaching programme of decentralization, according legal status and financial authority to local communities. In December the Government announced the release from custody of 57 Tuaregs.

In January 1993 five people were killed in a Tuareg attack on a meeting of the MNSD attended by Tandja Mamadou (who was Minister of the Interior at the time of the suppression of the

Tchin-Tabaraden raid) in the northern town of Abala. Later in January 81 Tuaregs were released from detention, and a Minister of State for National Reconciliation, whose main responsibility would be to seek a solution to the Tuareg issue, was appointed to the Government. In March, following Algerian mediation, Ag Boula (who was based in Algeria) agreed that the FLAA would observe a truce for the duration of the campaign for the second round of the presidential election. Shortly afterwards Tuareg representatives in Niamey signed a similar (French-brokered) agreement. In April the outgoing transitional Government and the FLAA agreed to extend the truce indefinitely; the remaining Tuareg prisoners were subsequently released from detention, and the rebels released their hostages.

The Ousmane administration identified the resolution of the Tuareg issue as a priority. In mid-1993 a formal, three-month truce agreement between representatives of the Government and the Tuaregs, which provided for the demilitarization of the north, and envisaged negotiations on the Tuaregs' political demands, was signed in Paris, France, although the accord encountered some opposition within the Tuareg movement. A new group, the Armée révolutionnaire de libération du nord-Niger (ARLN), emerged to denounce the truce, and supporters of the truce (led by Mano Dayak, the Tuareg signatory to the agreement) broke away from the FLAA to form the Front de libération de Tamoust (FLT): Ag Boula and the remainder of the FLAA stated that they could not support any agreement that contained no specific commitment to discussion of federalism. In September the FLT and the Government agreed to extend the truce for a further three months. Although the FLAA and the ARLN refused to sign the accord, in October they joined with the FLT in a Coordination de la résistance armée (CRA), with the aim of presenting a cohesive programme in future negotiations.

Despite an escalation of violence during May 1994, as a result of which as many as 40 deaths were recorded, negotiations took place in Paris in June. Tentative agreement was reached on the creation of ethnically based autonomous regions, each of which would have its own elected assembly and governor to function in parallel with the organs of central government. Renewed unrest in August and September included a grenade attack on a meeting in Agadez of a mainly-Tuareg political organization, the Union pour la démocratie et le progrès social—Amana, as a result of which six people were killed. In late September, none the less, the CRA presented Nigerien government negotiators with a plan for the restoration of peace. Formal negotiations resumed, with mediation by the Burkinabè President, Blaise Compaoré, as well as representatives of France and Algeria, in Ouagadougou (Burkina Faso) in October. A new peace accord resulted, emphasizing that Niger was 'unitary and indivisible', while proposing the establishment of elected assemblies or councils for territorial communities, which would be responsible for the implementation of economic, social and cultural policies. The Government was to take immediate measures to ensure the rehabilitation and security of areas affected by the conflict. Provisions were also to be made to facilitate the return and resettlement of refugees. A renewable three-month truce was to take immediate effect, to be monitored by French and Burkinabè military units. By the time of the conclusion of the Ouagadougou agreement the number of deaths since the escalation of the Tuareg rebellion in late 1991 was officially put at 150. A commission was established in January 1995 to consider the administrative reorganization of the country.

Ag Boula, who had withdrawn from the CRA (having repeatedly criticized Dayak's negotiating stance), and refused to participate in the decentralization committee, in protest at alleged delays in the implementation of the provisions of the October 1994 agreement, emerged as the leader of the Tuareg delegation (now renamed the Organisation de la résistance armée—ORA) at negotiations in Ouagadougou in March 1995. In April it was announced that a lasting peace agreement had been reached. The accord provided for the establishment of a special peace committee, to be overseen by representatives of the three mediating countries. Demobilized rebels were to be integrated into the Nigerien military and public sector; particular emphasis was to be placed on the economic, social and cultural development of the north, and the Government undertook to support the decentralization process. There was to be a general amnesty for all parties involved in the Tuareg rebellion and its suppression, and a day of national reconciliation was to be instituted in memory of the victims of the conflict. The peace agreement was formally signed by Ag Boula and the Nigerien government negotiator, Mai Maigana, in Niamey on 24 April 1995, one day before the cease-fire took effect.

Meanwhile, there was increasing evidence of ethnic unrest in the Lake Chad region of south-east Niger, where several thousand (mainly Toubou) Chadian refugees had settled since the overthrow of President Hissène Habré in late 1990. The Front démocratique du renouveau (FDR) emerged in October 1994 to demand increased autonomy for the Toubou population of the south-east. In November, in compliance with a request by the UN, Niger established a committee whose stated aim was to disarm militias and to combat arms-trafficking, which was reportedly well-established in the Agadez and Lake Chad regions. The Comité spécial de la paix (CSP) was inaugurated in May 1995, under the chairmanship of Maigana, and a military observer group, comprising representatives of Burkina and France, was deployed in the north in July. The Prime Minister approved an amnesty in that month, and all Tuareg prisoners were reported to have been released shortly afterwards. The peace process was undermined, however, by evidence that Dayak and other Tuareg groups in a revived CRA were making common cause with the FDR in demanding autonomy for their respective regions. In October clashes in the north-east involving rebel Tuaregs and the armed forces were attributed to elements of the CRA. In the same month bilateral and international donors pledged some 18,700m. francs CFA in support of a two-year emergency programme for the development of the north. In December Dayak was one of three leading CRA members to be killed in an air crash. In January 1996 the new leader of the FLT (and acting leader of the CRA), Mohamed Akotai, indicated that his movement favoured inter-Tuareg reconciliation and a dialogue with the Government.

Following the *coup d'état* of January 1996, the CSN expressed its commitment to the peace process. Maïnassara had previously been involved in the work of the CSP, and the new administration, the ORA and the CRA all expressed the view that direct contacts between the military and the Tuareg movements would expedite the peace process. Although the FDR also expressed its willingness to co-operate with the new authorities, an armed assault on Dirkou in February by members of that movement, and an army counter-attack, resulted in 12 deaths. In March the Nigerien authorities, the office of the UN High Commissioner for Refugees (UNHCR) and the Governments of Algeria and Burkina signed agreements on refugee repatriation. Shortly afterwards the CRA, including the FDR, affirmed its recognition of the April 1995 agreement, and announced that it would observe a unilateral truce for one month, while negotiations continued. In April 1996 the Government and the CRA signed an agreement formalizing the latter's adherence to the peace process. The following month the ORA and the CRA agreed to establish a joint committee to co-ordinate their activities and to represent their interests in negotiations. In July the CSP and the resistance movements recommended measures aimed at curbing ongoing insecurity in northern areas. Preliminary agreement was also reached regarding the integration of demobilized fighters into the national military and civilian sectors. In September joint peace-keeping patrols of the Nigerien armed forces and former rebels were inaugurated in the north.

In late September 1996 Ag Boula announced that the ORA no longer considered itself bound by the peace treaty. The authorities asserted that this abandonment of the 1995 accord was linked primarily to the arrest of ORA members in connection with the diversion, some months previously, of a large consignment of cigarettes bound for the north. In an apparent gesture of reconciliation, the detainees were released at the end of October 1996, and the ORA surrendered the consignment to the authorities. In November it was reported that a new group had emerged from among the ORA and the CRA; led by Mohamed Anako, the Union des forces de la résistance armée (UFRA) affirmed its commitment to the peace accord. A meeting between the High Commissioner for the Restoration of Peace and 10 of the reported 12 resistance groups was followed in December by the signing of a protocol for the encampment of some 5,900 former fighters, prior to their disarmament and reintegration, from which process, however, the ORA remained excluded. Following a meeting between Maïnassara and Ag Boula in January 1997, and assurances regarding the implementation of provisions of the 1995 accord, the ORA declared its renewed support; it was announced, moreover, that the FLAA and FLT would establish a joint patrol aimed at combating insecurity and banditry. In February 1997 the UFRA joined members of the

regular armed forces, the CRA and the Comité de vigilance de Tassara in a peace-keeping patrol in Agadez. In April Maïnassara signed a decree establishing a commission, under his direct jurisdiction, to be chaired by the Minister of National Defence, charged with overseeing the reintegration of former rebels.

Insecurity persisted, none the less, particularly in the east. Violent clashes were reported in March 1997, involving several hundred soldiers and Toubou rebels: the FDR protested that the operation, which was attributed by the authorities to the need to eliminate isolated groups of armed bandits, was endangering the peace accord. In June it was announced that Toubous and Arabs of the Forces armées révolutionnaires du Sahara (FARS) had, following negotiations in Chad, agreed to join the peace process. It subsequently appeared that large numbers of armed Toubous had fled to Nigeria following the defeat of the FARS; Niger's Minister of National Defence subsequently proposed the establishment of joint patrols, to involve the armed forces of Niger, Nigeria, Chad and Cameroon, to ensure security in the Lake Chad region.

A three-day meeting took place in July 1997 to assess encampment procedures, as envisaged in the December 1996 accord, and the incorporation of demobilized groups into the regular armed and paramilitary forces and the civil service. Shortly after the meeting, however, the FDR announced its withdrawal from the peace process, stating that Nigerien and Chadian military units had attacked one of its bases; the FDR reported that 17 members of the armed forces had been killed in clashes with its fighters. The Nigerien authorities, however, denied that any engagement had taken place.

A further meeting of the parties to the peace process took place in September 1997. At this time, however, elements of Anako's UFRA, apparently frustrated at the slow progress of the implementation of the peace process, had taken up arms again. Meanwhile, the FARS was held responsible by the authorities for a number of violent incidents in the east of Niger. A total of 27 deaths resulted from an armed attack on Aderbissanat, in the Agadez region.

The conclusion of the disarmament process was officially celebrated in Tchin-Tabaraden in late October 1997. The armed forces subsequently undertook an offensive against positions held by rebel groups. In November, following two weeks of talks, a peace accord, known as the Algiers addendum protocol, providing for an immediate cease-fire, was signed in Algeria between the Nigerien Government, the UFRA and the FARS. In March 1998 the ORA and CRA surrendered their weapons stocks at Agadez. Meanwhile, Ag Boula was appointed as Minister-delegate responsible for Tourism in December 1997.

In April 1998 Maiyaki chaired a meeting in Niamey of the peace monitoring and implementation committee, now charged with overseeing the implementation of the April 1995 peace agreement and Algiers addendum protocol. In June it was reported that the last units of the UFRA had disarmed at a ceremony near Agadez. A peace agreement was signed with the FDR in August. Following the death of President Maïnassara, in April 1999, the military CRN gave assurances that the peace process would be continued. Ag Boula was promoted to the rank of minister in the transitional Government, while Anako was appointed as special adviser to Wanké. Ag Boula retained his ministerial post in the new Government of Hama Amadou, formed in January 2000. In June the final groups of fighters from the UFRA and other resistance movements participating in the peace process were disarmed near Agadez, prior to their intended integration into the national forces. Concerns remained, however, that progress still had to be made in the implementation of moves towards greater administrative decentralization, as well as regarding the delayed fulfilment of quotas for Tuaregs in military formations. In late September more than 1,200 guns, surrendered by the disarmed factions, were ceremoniously burned in Agadez, in the presence of President Tandja Mamadou, leaders of other West African nations and UN representatives. At the ceremony, Anako announced the dissolution of several of the rebel groups and militias. In September 2001 Chahayi Barkaye, the leader of the FARS, the only ethnic rebel group to have refused disarmament, was killed in heavy fighting with Nigerien soldiers near the Libyan border.

In March 1998 it was announced that voluntary repatriations from Algeria of Nigerien refugees, under the supervision of UNHCR and the Algerian Red Crescent, were to begin in that month. In November 1996, meanwhile, Niger, Mali and UNHCR had signed an agreement for the repatriation of 25,000 Malian

Tuaregs from Niger; the agreement defined the obligations and responsibilities of its signatories with regard to the voluntary return 'with dignity' of the refugees. (See also the chapter on Mali for details of the Tuareg rebellion in that country.)

In foreign affairs, there was a notable deterioration in relations with the USA in the immediate aftermath of the 1996 presidential election in Niger. In July of that year the US authorities announced the suspension of its programme of economic and military assistance. The assumption of power by the CRN in April 1999, following the death of Maïnassara, was condemned by the USA, France and Niger's other Western creditors. (The US Department of State was a principal source of reports that a coup had taken place.) Relations with the USA appeared to improve following the re-installation of an elected Government; Niger's new Minister of Foreign Affairs, Co-operation and African Integration visited Washington, DC, in February 2000, and in March the USA announced an end to the sanctions imposed after Maïnassara's death. In August President Mamadou met President Bill Clinton and other US representatives in Abuja, Nigeria, where the USA announced increased support for Niger in areas including food security, the promotion of democracy, education and healthcare.

Countries of the region with which Maïnassara had forged close relations also condemned the military take-over of April 1999: Libya notably denounced the new regime; it was reported in mid-April that Maiyaki had been made to leave a summit meeting in Libya of the Community of Sahel-Saharan States (see p. 339), although relations between the CRN and the Government of Libya had apparently normalized by the end of the year. In December the two countries signed an agreement envisaging the establishment of a joint company to distribute oil and liquefied natural gas; it was also agreed to expedite the establishment of a joint company for petroleum exploration and production. In January 2000 President Mamadou undertook an official visit to Libya and met the country's leader, Col Muammar al-Qaddafi. On a visit to Agadez in early July, Qaddafi pledged support for the Tuareg peace process. Later that month Prime Minister Amadou visited Libya and met Qaddafi. In November Libya pledged to grant financial support for the reconstruction of Agadez airport, for the construction of a road linking Agadez and Zinder and for increased agricultural development in Niger. Meanwhile, some 1,000 Nigerien citizens were repatriated from Libya in October, following instances of inter-ethnic violence between Libyan Arabs and black Africans in that country.

The EU suspended all assistance to Niger in the aftermath of the military take-over in April 1999 and made its resumption dependent on a full investigation into Maïnassara's death; the CRN subsequently stated that its report had been lodged with organizations including the EU, and EU aid recommenced in June 2000. France also suspended military and civilian co-operation with Niger in April 1999. Following a visit to France by Tandja Mamadou in January 2000, when the newly installed Nigerien President met President Jacques Chirac and Prime Minister Lionel Jospin, the resumption of French co-operation was formalized, with the announcement of exceptional assistance principally to allow payment of outstanding salaries in the public sector.

In May 2000 a long-term dispute between Niger and Benin regarding the ownership of a number of small islands along their common border at the Niger river escalated, reportedly following the sabotage of a Beninois administrative building on the island of Lété, apparently by Nigerien soldiers. A meeting between representatives of the two Governments failed to resolve the dispute, which was subsequently referred to the Organization of African Unity (now the African Union) for arbitration. Further clashes between rival groups of farmers were reported on Lété in late August. In April 2002 the two Governments officially ratified an agreement (signed in 2001) to refer the issue of ownership of the islands to the International Court of Justice in The Hague, Netherlands, for arbitration.

In June 2001 Niger and Nigeria announced that joint border patrols of their common frontier would be instigated, in order to combat increasing cross-border crime and smuggling in the region. It was reported that the introduction of *Shari'a* law in several northern Nigerian states, from 2000, had been instrumental in encouraging Nigerian criminal gangs to operate from within Niger.

Government

Following the death of President Ibrahim Baré Maïnassara, in April 1999, a military Conseil de réconciliation nationale (CRN)

was established, under the chairmanship of Maj. Daouda Mallam Wanké, to exercise executive and legislative authority during a nine-month transitional period prior to the restoration of elected organs of government. A new constitution was approved in a national referendum in July 1999. The Constitution of the Fifth Republic, promulgated on 9 August, envisages a balance of powers between the President, Government and legislative Assemblée nationale. The President, who is elected by universal adult suffrage, is Head of State, and is accorded 'broad ordinary and arbitral powers'. The Government, under a Prime Minister appointed by the President, is responsible to the Assemblée nationale, which is competent to remove the Prime Minister by vote of censure. The Assemblée nationale is similarly elected by direct adult suffrage. The new President and legislature were inaugurated in December 1999.

For the purposes of local administration, Niger comprises seven regions and the municipality of Niamey. A reorganization of Niger's administrative structures, with the aim of devolving increased autonomy to local and regional authorities, was undertaken in the second half of the 1990s.

Defence

In August 2002 Niger's armed forces totalled 5,300 men (army 5,200; air force 100). Paramilitary forces numbered 5,400 men, comprising the gendarmerie (1,400), the republican guard (2,500) and the national police force (1,500). Conscription to the armed forces is selective and lasts for two years. The 2002 budget allocated an estimated 24,000m. francs CFA to defence.

Economic Affairs

In 2001, according to estimates by the World Bank, Niger's gross national income (GNI), measured at average 1999–2001 prices, was US $1,953m., equivalent to $170 per head (or $770 on an international purchasing-power parity basis). During 1999–2001, it was estimated, the population increased at an average annual rate of 3.4%, while gross domestic product (GDP) per head declined, in real terms, by an average of 1.2% per year. Overall GDP increased, in real terms, at an average annual rate of 2.2% in 1990–2001; growth was 0.1% in 2000 and 5.1% in 2001, according to the World Bank, although the IMF reported growth of 7.6% for 2001.

Agriculture (including hunting, forestry and fishing) contributed an estimated 38.7% of GDP in 2001. About 87.5% of the labour force were employed in the sector in that year. The principal cash crops are cow-peas, onions, groundnuts and cotton. The principal subsistence crops are millet, sorghum and rice. Niger is able to achieve self-sufficiency in basic foodstuffs in non-drought years. Following a disappointing harvest in 2000, the UN's World Food Programme (WFP) appealed for donors to assist an estimated 200,000 people affected by malnutrition in the country; according to the WFP, more than 4,000 of Niger's 10,094 villages had food deficits of over 50%. However, a modest cereals surplus was achieved in 2001. Livestock-rearing is important, especially among the nomadic population: cattle accounted for an estimated 19.1% of total exports (including re-exports) by value in 2001, constituting the second most important source of export revenue, after uranium. Major anti-desertification and reafforestation programmes are in progress. According to the World Bank, agricultural GDP increased by an average of 2.9% per year in 1990–2001. Agricultural GDP declined by 4.7% in 2000, but increased by 3.9% in 2001.

Industry (including mining, manufacturing, construction and power) contributed an estimated 17.6% of GDP in 2001. Only 3.6% of the labour force were employed in industrial activities at the time of the 1988 census. According to the World Bank, industrial GDP increased by an average of 1.8% per year in 1990–2001; growth was 2.9% in 2000 and 4.1% in 2001.

Mining contributed an estimated 7.0% of GDP in 2000, but employed only 0.2% of the labour force in 1988. Niger is among the world's foremost producers of uranium (the third largest, after Canada and Australia, in 2000), although the contribution of uranium-mining to the domestic economy has declined, as production costs have exceeded world prices for the mineral. In 2001 exports of uranium accounted for an estimated 30.4% of total export earnings (including re-exports), and in 2000 the sector contributed 4% of total budgetary revenue. In addition, gypsum, coal, salt and cassiterite are also extracted, and commercial exploitation of gold (previously mined on a small scale) at the Samira Hill mine was scheduled to begin in 2002, at a rate of 10,000 metric tons of ore per day. In 2000 the Government awarded two permits for petroleum exploration in eastern Niger to two US companies. According to the IMF, the GDP of the mining sector increased at an average annual rate of 2.7% in 1995–2000; mining GDP declined by 1.2% in 1999, but increased by an estimated 0.2% in 2000.

Manufacturing contributed an estimated 6.8% of GDP in 2001, and employed 2.7% of the labour force in 1988. The processing of agricultural products (groundnuts, cereals, cotton and rice) constitutes the principal activity. Some light industries, including a textiles plant, a brewery and a cement works, supply the internal market. According to the World Bank, manufacturing GDP increased by an average of 2.3% per year in 1990–2001. Manufacturing GDP increased by 4.9% in 2000 and by 4.7% in 2001.

The domestic generation of electricity (almost entirely thermal) provides a little less than one-half of Niger's electrical energy requirements, much of the remainder being imported from Nigeria. Construction of a hydroelectric installation at Kandadji, on the Niger, is planned. Imports of mineral fuels accounted for 21.2% of the value of merchandise imports in 2000.

The services sector contributed an estimated 43.7% of GDP in 2001, and employed 15.0% of the labour force in 1988. The GDP of the sector increased by an average of 1.8% per year in 1990–2001, according to the World Bank; growth was 3.6% in 2000 and 6.7% in 2001.

In 2001 Niger recorded a visible trade deficit of an estimated 47,400m. francs CFA, while there was a deficit of 81,200m. francs CFA on the current account of the balance of payments. France is Niger's principal trading partner, supplying 20.1% of imports and purchasing 48.1% of exports in 2000. Côte d'Ivoire, Nigeria and Japan are also important trading partners. The principal exports are uranium (most of which is purchased by France), cattle, cow-peas and onions. The principal imports in 2000 were food and live animals (notably cereal and cereal preparations), refined petroleum products and machinery and transport equipment.

Niger's overall budget deficit for 2001 was estimated at 70,800m. francs CFA (equivalent to 5.1% of GDP). Niger's total external debt was US $1,638m. at the end of 2000, of which $1,481m. was long-term public debt. In that year the cost of debt-servicing was equivalent to 9.2% of the value of exports of goods and services. Consumer prices increased by an annual average of 4.1% during 1990–2001, although in 1994, following the 50% devaluation of the CFA franc, the rate of inflation averaged 36.0%. Consumer prices increased by an average of 4.0% in 2001 and by an average of 2.7% in 2002. Some 20,926 people were registered as unemployed in 1991.

Niger is a member of numerous regional organizations, including the Economic Community of West African States (see p. 187), the West African organs of the Franc Zone (see p. 238), the Conseil de l'Entente (see p. 339), the Lake Chad Basin Commission (see p. 340), the Liptako–Gourma Integrated Development Authority (see p. 341), the Niger Basin Authority (see p. 341) and the Permanent Inter-State Committee on Drought Control in the Sahel (see p. 341).

Niger's dependence on uranium mining, and its consequent narrow export base, meant that the country benefited less than most countries of the region from the 50% devaluation of the CFA franc in 1994. Agreement for a three-year Enhanced Structural Adjustment Facility (ESAF) was reached with the IMF in mid-1996, and most major creditors, having withdrawn support in the aftermath of the military coup in January, had resumed full co-operation by the end of the year. The military take-over following the sudden death of President Maïnassara in April 1999 again prompted the withdrawal of most co-operation. In September, furthermore, the World Bank suspended all credits, in view of Niger's failure to honour existing repayment deadlines. The new administration installed in late 1999 acted swiftly to re-establish contacts with the international financial

community. France resumed co-operation in early 2000, granting exceptional aid of 6,000m. francs CFA, principally to pay outstanding salaries, and in January 2001 also cancelled a proportion of Niger's debt. In December 2000 the IMF and the World Bank announced that Niger would receive US $890m. in debt-service relief under the enhanced framework of the Heavily Indebted Poor Countries initiative. Also in December the IMF announced the approval of a three-year loan, worth $76m., for Niger under the Poverty Reduction and Growth Facility (the successor to the ESAF). However, the European Commission suspended economic assistance to Niger in June 2001, after an audit revealed that some 6,500m. francs CFA granted by the Commission in 1996–2001 had been used for purposes deemed ineligible for such support. Following two years of stagnation, economic performance improved markedly in 2001, when GDP growth exceeded prior expectations by one-half, according to IMF figures, although improved agricultural output was responsible for some two-thirds of economic growth in that year. The Government undertook to eliminate corruption in public life and to expedite the previously proposed, although subsequently postponed, privatization programme. Majority shares in the state water and telecommunications companies were transferred to the private sector in 2001. Priorities for 2003 included the further restructuring of the public sector, including the divestiture of the state electricity and petroleum companies, an increase in poverty-related expenditure and the continued reduction of domestic payment arrears. GDP growth of 2.7% was projected for 2002, somewhat lower than initial forecasts, as a result of difficulties in the agricultural sector.

Education

Education is available free of charge, and is officially compulsory for eight years between the ages of seven and 15 years. Primary education begins at the age of seven and lasts for six years. Secondary education begins at the age of 13 years, and comprises a four-year cycle followed by a further, three-year cycle. Primary enrolment in 1999/2000 included only 21.2% of children in the appropriate age-group (males 20.6%; females 21.8%). Enrolment at secondary schools in that year was equivalent to only 6.5% of the relevant age-group (males 7.8%; females 5.1%), according to UNESCO estimates. The Abdou Moumouni University (formerly the University of Niamey) was inaugurated in 1973, and the Islamic University of Niger, at Say (to the south of the capital), was opened in 1987. In December 2001 the Assemblée nationale approved legislation providing for the introduction of teaching in all local languages, with the aim of improving the literacy rate—one of the lowest in the world. Expenditure on education in 2000 was 32,500m. francs CFA, representing 15.5% of total spending.

Public Holidays

2003: 1 January (New Year's Day), 12 February* (Tabaski, Feast of the Sacrifice), 5 March* (Islamic New Year), 21 April (Easter Monday), 24 April (National Concord Day), 1 May (Labour Day), 14 May* (Mouloud, Birth of the Prophet), 3 August (Independence Day), 26 November* (Aïd al-Fitr, end of Ramadan), 18 December (Republic Day).

2004: 1 January (New Year's Day), 2 February* (Tabaski, Feast of the Sacrifice), 22 March* (Islamic New Year), 12 April (Easter Monday), 24 April (National Concord Day), 1 May (Labour Day), 2 May* (Mouloud, Birth of the Prophet), 3 August (Independence Day), 14 November* (Aïd al-Fitr, end of Ramadan), 18 December (Republic Day).

*These holidays are dependent on the Islamic lunar calendar and may vary by one or two days from the dates given.

Weights and Measures

The metric system is in force.

Statistical Survey

Source (unless otherwise stated): Direction de la Statistique et de l'Informatique, Ministère des Finances et des Réformes Économiques, BP 720, Niamey; tel. 72-23-74; fax 73-33-71.

Area and Population

AREA, POPULATION AND DENSITY

Area (sq km)	1,267,000*
Population (census results)	
20 November 1977	5,098,427
20 May 1988	
Males	3,590,070
Females	3,658,030
Total	7,248,100
Population (UN estimates at mid-year)†	
1998	10,096,000
1999	10,455,000
2000	10,832,000
Density (per sq km) at mid-2000	8.5

* 489,191 sq miles.

† Source: UN, *World Population Prospects: The 2000 Revision*.

ETHNIC GROUPS (Percentage of total, 1995): Hausa 52.8; Djerma 14.7; Peul 10.4; Kanori 8.7; Songhaï 8.1; Tuareg 3.0; Toubou 0.5; Others 1.8 (Source: La Francophonie).

PROVINCES

(population at 1988 census, rounded figures)

Tillabéri*	. . .	1,725,700	Dosso	. . . .	1,018,900
Zinder	. . . .	1,411,100	Agadez	. . . .	208,800
Maradi	. . .	1,389,400	Diffa	. . . .	189,100
Tahoua	. . .	1,308,600			

* Includes Niamey, which subsequently became a separate administrative unit.

PRINCIPAL TOWNS

(population at 1988 census)

Niamey (capital)	.	398,265*	Tahoua	. . . .	51,607
Zinder	. . . .	120,892	Agadez	. . . .	50,164
Maradi	. . .	112,965	Arlit	. . . .	31,993

* Figure refers to Niamey city only. Population of the Niamey agglomeration was 550,000.

BIRTHS AND DEATHS

(UN estimates, annual averages)

	1985–90	1990–95	1995–2000
Birth rate (per 1,000)	55.8	55.3	55.4
Death rate (per 1,000)	23.6	22.0	20.7

Source: UN, *World Population Prospects: The 2000 Revision*.

Expectation of life (WHO estimates, years at birth): 42.5 (males 41.9; females 43.2) in 2001 (Source: WHO, *World Health Report*).

ECONOMICALLY ACTIVE POPULATION

(persons aged 10 years and over, 1988 census, provisional)

	Males	Females	Total
Agriculture, hunting, forestry and fishing	1,549,600	243,950	1,793,550
Mining and quarrying	4,790	960	5,750
Manufacturing	28,060	35,630	63,690
Electricity, gas and water . . .	2,330	60	2,390
Construction	14,040	390	14,430
Trade, restaurants and hotels . .	95,670	112,700	208,370
Transport, storage and communications	14,400	470	14,870
Financing, insurance, real estate and business services	1,400	450	1,850
Community, social and personal services	100,620	29,110	129,730
Activities not adequately defined .	21,250	50,270	71,520
Total employed	1,832,160	473,990	2,306,150
Unemployed	44,210	16,360	60,570
Total labour force	1,876,370	490,350	2,366,720

Source: UN, *Demographic Yearbook*.

Mid-2001 (estimates in '000): Agriculture, etc. 4,525; Total labour force 5,170 (Source: FAO).

Health and Welfare

KEY INDICATORS

Total fertility rate (children per woman, 2001)	8.0
Under-5 mortality rate (per 1,000 live births, 2001) . . .	265
HIV/AIDS (% of persons aged 15–49, 1999)	1.35
Physicians (per 1,000 head, 1997)	0.04
Hospital beds (per 1,000 head, 1998)	0.12
Health expenditure (2000): US $ per head (PPP)	22
Health expenditure (2000): % of GDP	3.9
Health expenditure (2000): public (% of total)	44.9
Access to water (% of persons, 2000)	59
Access to sanitation (% of persons, 2000)	20
Human Development Index (2000): ranking	172
Human Development Index (2000): value	0.277

For sources and definitions, see explanatory note on p. vi.

Agriculture

PRINCIPAL CROPS
('000 metric tons)

	1999	2000	2001
Wheat	12.7	10.9	6.3
Rice (paddy)	62.0	60.5	76.4
Maize	4.0*	3.9	6.4
Millet	2,296.2	1,697.2	2,414.4
Sorghum	476.1	370.7	655.7
Potatoes	4.5	7.6	4.2
Sweet potatoes . . .	33.1	46.6	29.4
Cassava (Manioc) . . .	100.8	164.5	105.5
Sugar cane	89.7	200.0	211.4
Dry cow-peas	435.8	268.7	350.0*
Other pulses*	18	19	19
Groundnuts (in shell) . .	103.7	113.2	129.3
Sesame seed	7.4	14.1	21.7
Cottonseed*	2.6	3.5	3.0
Cabbages	77.8	119.0	120.0*
Lettuce	25.6	42.0	40.0*
Tomatoes	90.1	139.9	99.2
Chillies and green peppers . .	10.7	17.2	17.0*
Dry onions	226.0	356.2	271.2
Garlic	9.8	8.2	8.0*
Carrots	9.2	18.8	18.0*
Other vegetables* . . .	39	39	39
Dates*	7.6	7.6	7.6
Other fruit*	40	40	40
Cotton (lint)	7.3	6.4	6.9
Spices*	4.8	4.9	4.9
Tobacco (leaves) . . .	4.9	4.4	0.2

* FAO estimate(s).

Source: FAO.

LIVESTOCK
('000 head, year ending September)

	1999	2000	2001*
Cattle	2,174	2,217	2,260
Sheep	4,266	4,392	4,500
Goats	6,560	6,724	6,900
Pigs*	39	39	39
Horses*	103	104	105
Asses*	570	570	580
Camels	404	410†	415*
Chickens*	23,000	23,500	24,000

* FAO estimate(s).
† Unofficial figure.

Source: FAO.

LIVESTOCK PRODUCTS
('000 metric tons)

	1999	2000	2001
Beef and veal	40.0*	41.0†	42.1†
Mutton and lamb*	14.6	14.7	14.9
Goat meat*	24.0	24.0	25.2
Camel meat*	4.8	5.0	5.0
Game meat*	15	15	15
Chicken meat*	26.6	27.2	27.8
Other meat*	3.6	3.7	3.7
Cows' milk*	176	180	184
Sheep's milk*	15.2	15.4	15.6
Goats' milk*	99.5	100.0	105.0
Camels' milk*	10.5	10.7	10.8
Cheese*	14.0	14.1	14.7
Butter*	4.8	5.0	5.1
Hen eggs*	10.0	10.2	10.4
Cattle hides*	6.2	6.3	6.4
Sheepskins*	1.8	1.8	1.9
Goatskins*	4.0	4.1	4.2

* FAO estimate(s).
† Unofficial figure.

Source: FAO.

Forestry

ROUNDWOOD REMOVALS
('000 cubic metres, excl. bark)

	1999*	2000*	2001
Industrial wood*	411	411	411
Fuel wood	7,611	7,805	2,857
Total	8,022	8,216	3,268

* FAO estimates.

Source: FAO.

SAWNWOOD PRODUCTION
(FAO estimates, '000 cubic metres, incl. railway sleepers)

	1999	2000	2001
Total (all broadleaved)	4	4	4

Source: FAO.

Fishing

(metric tons, live weight)

	1998	1999	2000
Capture (freshwater fishes) . . .	7,013	11,000	16,250
Aquaculture	12	14	15
Total catch	7,025	11,014	16,265

Source: FAO, *Yearbook of Fishery Statistics*.

Mining

('000 metric tons, unless otherwise indicated)

	1998	1999	2000
Hard coal	145*	168	158
Tin (metric tons)†	10*	32	22
Uranium (metric tons)†	3,516	2,948	2,896
Gold (metric tons)*	1	1	1
Salt*	2	2	2
Gypsum	2.0*	1.5	1.5

* Estimated production.
† Data refer to the metal content of ore.
2001: Uranium (metric tons) 2,197.

Sources: Banque centrale des états de l'Afrique de l'ouest; US Geological Survey.

Industry

SELECTED PRODUCTS
('000 metric tons, unless otherwise indicated)

	1998	1999	2000
Flour	8.5	—	—
Cement	32.8	33.5	33.1
Soap	5.6	7.9	8.1
Textile fabrics (million metres) . .	5.6	6.1	5.8
Beer ('000 bottles)	125	126	130
Electric energy (million kWh) . .	185.8	195.9	199.2

Source: IMF, *Niger: Statistical Annex* (February 2002).

Raw sugar (FAO estimates, '000 metric tons): 12.1 in 1998; 10.2 in 1999; 20.6 in 2000; 21.2 in 2001 (Source: FAO).

Finance

CURRENCY AND EXCHANGE RATES

Monetary Units
100 centimes = 1 franc de la Communauté financière africaine (CFA)

Sterling, Dollar and Euro Equivalents (31 December 2002)
£1 sterling = 1,008.17 francs CFA
US $1 = 625.50 francs CFA
€1 = 655.96 francs CFA
10,000 francs CFA = £9.919 = $15.987 = €15.245

Average Exchange Rate (francs CFA per US $)
2000   711.98
2001   733.04
2002   696.99

Note: An exchange rate of 1 French franc = 50 francs CFA, established in 1948, remained in force until January 1994, when the CFA franc was devalued by 50%, with the exchange rate adjusted to 1 French franc = 100 francs CFA. This relationship to French currency remained in effect with the introduction of the euro on 1 January 1999. From that date, accordingly, a fixed exchange rate of €1 = 655.957 francs CFA has been in operation.

BUDGET
('000 million francs CFA)

Revenue*	1998	1999	2000†
General budget	107.1	104.5	106.6
Tax revenue	96.9	100.6	102.8
Taxes on income, profits, payroll and work force	18.9	19.3	18.0
Taxes on goods and services	15.6	23.0	20.6
Taxes on international trade and transactions	56.9	51.3	58.5
Import Duties	44.7	42.2	46.2
Export duties	2.7	3.9	2.3
Other taxes	—	0.8	1.1
Non-tax revenue	10.1	3.9	3.8
Annexed budgets and special accounts	4.7	5.1	3.5
Total	111.8	109.6	110.1

* Excluding grants received ('000 million francs CFA): 65.3 in 1998; 47.8 in 1999; 52.0 in 2000.
† Estimated figures.

Expenditure*	1998	1999	2000†
General services	74.3	83.9	82.6
Defence	13.0	14.3	14.0
Security	8.0	7.1	8.0
Education	26.3	33.8	32.5
Health	18.5	25.3	24.4
Social affairs	8.5	3.4	3.7
Economic services	46.4	36.6	41.0
Agriculture	27.6	20.0	15.0
Road infrastructure	9.2	9.7	18.7
Other budgetary expenditure	83.4	95.9	81.2
Interest payments	19.2	19.7	21.6
Annexed budgets and special accounts	8.1	7.0	5.3
Sub-total	212.3	223.4	210.0
Current	142.5	154.1	143.8
Capital	69.9	69.3	66.3
Adjustment for changes in payments arrears‡	4.6	−49.1	112.0
Total (cash basis)	216.9	174.3	322.0

* Excluding net lending ('000 million francs CFA): −0.4 in 1998; −1.4 in 1999; −3.1 in 2000.
† Estimated figures.
‡ Minus sign indicates an increase in arrears.

Source: IMF, *Niger: Statistical Annex* (February 2002).

2001 ('000 million francs CFA, estimates): Total revenue 132.3 (Tax revenue 125.0, Non-tax revenue 4.1, Annexed budgets and special accounts 3.2); Total expenditure ('000 million francs CFA, estimates, cash basis) 255.8 (Current 157.5, Capital 81.3, Adjustment for changes in payments arrears 17.0). These figures exclude grants received ('000 million francs CFA, estimates): 51.9 and net lending ('000 million francs CFA, estimates): −0.8 (Source: IMF, *Niger: Third Review Under the Poverty Reduction and Growth Facility Arrangement and Requests for Modification and Waiver of Performance Criteria—Staff Report and News Brief on the Executive Board Discussion* (September 2002)).

INTERNATIONAL RESERVES
(excl. gold, US $ million at 31 December)

	2000	2001	2002
IMF special drawing rights	—	0.3	0.7
Reserve position in IMF	11.2	10.8	11.6
Foreign exchange	69.2	95.9	121.6
Total	80.4	107.0	133.9

2002 (US $ million at 31 December): IMF special drawing rights 0.7; Reserve position in IMF 11.6.

Source: IMF, *International Financial Statistics*.

MONEY SUPPLY
(million francs CFA at 31 December)

	1999	2000	2001
Currency outside banks	34,119	32,158	49,300
Demand deposits at deposit money banks*	33,892	43,289	52,413
Checking deposits at post office	255	1,205	1,943
Total money (incl. others)*	68,801	76,899	104,039

* Excluding the deposits of public enterprises of an administrative or social nature.

Source: IMF, *International Financial Statistics*.

COST OF LIVING
(Consumer Price Index for Niamey; base: 1996 = 100)

	2000	2001	2002
Food, beverages and tobacco	110.5	118.6	123.9
Clothing	104.8	104.5	106.2
Housing, water, electricity and gas	103.2	102.8	105.4
All items (incl. others)	108.8	113.1	116.1

Source: Banque centrale des états de l'Afrique de l'ouest.

NATIONAL ACCOUNTS
('000 million francs CFA at current prices)

Expenditure on the Gross Domestic Product

	1999	2000	2001
Government final consumption expenditure	199.3	153.7	161.1
Private final consumption expenditure	1,011.1	1,048.6	1,174.6
Increase in stocks	3.0	16.0	22.0
Gross fixed capital formation	124.0	152.1	171.8
Total domestic expenditure	1,337.4	1,370.4	1,529.5
Exports of goods and services	197.6	206.4	204.8
Less Imports of goods and services	292.4	296.4	335.8
GDP in purchasers' values	1,242.6	1,280.4	1,399.1*

* Including adjustment.

Source: Banque centrale des états de l'Afrique de l'ouest.

Gross Domestic Product by Economic Activity

	1998	1999	2000*
Agriculture, hunting, forestry and fishing	522.2	506.1	484.4
Mining and quarrying	83.0	83.6	87.5
Manufacturing	75.8	80.7	87.0
Electricity, gas and water	26.0	27.4	28.8
Construction	20.0	21.5	24.1
Trade, restaurants and hotels	198.9	213.2	237.1
Transport, storage and communications	54.3	56.4	60.9
Government services	102.9	105.0	109.6
Other services	118.2	122.6	131.4
GDP at factor cost	1,201.3	1,216.5	1,250.9
Import duties	23.9	26.1	29.5
GDP in purchasers' values	1,225.2	1,242.6	1,280.4

* Estimates.

Source: IMF, *Niger: Statistical Annex* (February 2002).

BALANCE OF PAYMENTS
('000 million francs CFA)

	1999	2000	2001*
Exports of goods f.o.b.	176.6	201.6	207.2
Imports of goods f.o.b.	−206.5	−230.4	−254.6
Trade balance	−29.9	−28.8	−47.4
Services and other income (net)	−76.7	−78.9	−81.3
Balance on goods, services and income	−106.6	−107.7	−128.7
Private unrequited transfers (net)	2.1	2.7	2.8
Public unrequited transfers (net)	20.0	31.0	44.7
Current balance	−84.6	−74.0	−81.2
Capital account (net)	38.2	39.6	27.7
Direct investment (net)	0.3	6.4	20.6
Portfolio investment (net)	−0.1	6.5	3.5
Other investment (net)	−1.1	14.3	9.8
Commercial banks' net foreign assets	1.1	6.8	−17.1
Net errors and omissions	−0.5	−21.3	3.0
HIPC assistance†	—	—	8.1
Overall balance	−46.6	−21.7	−25.5

* Estimated figures.

† Includes assistance from the IMF, the World Bank, the African Development Bank, and Paris Club creditors.

Sources: IMF, *Niger: Statistical Annex* (February 2002) and *Niger: Third Review Under the Poverty Reduction and Growth Facility Arrangement and Requests for Modification and Waiver of Performance Criteria—Staff Report and News Brief on the Executive Board Discussion* (September 2002).

External Trade

PRINCIPAL COMMODITIES
(Distribution by SITC, US $ million)

Imports c.i.f.	1998	1999	2000
Food and live animals	120.6	86.5	85.6
Dairy products and birds' eggs	13.9	9.5	9.4
Milk and cream	13.6	9.2	9.1
Milk and cream, preserved, concentrated or sweetened	13.1	9.0	8.8
Cereals and cereal preparations	61.4	40.9	41.2
Rice	35.3	27.7	25.4
Rice, semi-milled or wholly milled	34.9	27.6	25.3
Rice, semi-milled or milled (unbroken)	34.3	26.7	24.6
Sugar, sugar preparations and honey	23.2	17.4	16.2
Refined sugar, etc.	22.9	17.0	15.4
Beverages and tobacco	15.8	16.2	22.1
Tobacco, manufactured	13.7	14.5	20.3
Cigarettes	13.3	14.5	20.3
Crude materials (inedible) except fuel	24.4	17.5	19.8
Textile fibres (not wool tops) and their wastes (not in yarn)	12.7	9.6	11.6
Bulk textile waste, old clothing, traded in bulk or in bales	12.6	9.5	11.2
Mineral fuels, lubricants, etc (incl. electric current)	62.6	65.2	77.2
Petroleum, petroleum products, etc	57.1	57.4	69.2
Petroleum products, refined	56.4	57.2	69.0
Animal and vegetable oils, fats and waxes	25.6	28.7	19.9
Fixed vegetable oils and fats	23.7	26.9	18.4
Palm oil	21.8	25.3	15.4
Chemicals and related products	41.0	30.1	35.1
Medicinal and pharmaceutical products	12.3	7.8	11.2
Basic manufactures	52.8	49.2	41.7
Textile yarn, fabrics, made-up articles, etc	19.5	17.0	15.7
Cotton fabrics, woven (not incl. narrow or special fabrics)	15.4	14.0	12.0
Cotton fabrics, woven, bleached, dyed, etc or otherwise finished	12.0	12.1	8.4

Imports c.i.f. — *continued*	1998	1999	2000
Machinery and transport equipment	55.5	70.6	47.5
General industrial machinery, equipment and parts	13.4	9.3	6.0
Road vehicles	16.9	24.7	21.3
Passenger motor vehicles (excl. buses)	6.8	12.6	11.8
Miscellaneous manufactured articles	21.3	15.0	15.6
Total (incl. others)	420.0	379.2	364.5

Exports f.o.b.	1998*	1999	2000
Food and live animals	62.6	64.6	73.5
Live animals chiefly for food	26.2	29.8	45.5
Animals of the bovine species (incl. buffaloes), live	13.4	14.6	20.5
Animals of the bovine species (incl. buffaloes), live, other than pure bred for breeding	12.7	14.5	20.3
Sheep and goats, live	11.7	13.5	21.9
Sheep, live	5.6	7.9	12.8
Vegetables and fruit	30.0	31.3	24.3
Vegetables, fresh or simply preserved; roots and tubers	29.7	30.5	23.3
Alliaceous vegetables, fresh or chilled	22.5	20.4	6.9
Beverages and tobacco	35.2	1.0	9.2
Tobacco and tobacco manufactures	35.0	0.7	8.9
Tobacco, manufactured	35.0	0.7	8.7
Cigarettes	34.6	0.7	8.7
Crude materials (inedible) except fuels	145.4	114.3	97.4
Textile fibres (not wool tops) and their wastes (not in yarn)	10.0	5.5	6.7
Metalliferous ores and metal scrap	133.1	106.2	88.0
Ores and concentrates of uranium and thorium	133.0	106.1	88.0
Basic manufactures	31.4	9.1	9.6
Textile yarn, fabrics, made-up articles, etc.	27.2	8.5	7.3
Cotton fabrics, woven (not incl. narrow or special fabrics)	13.4	8.3	7.2
Cotton fabrics, woven, bleached, dyed, etc, or otherwise finished	13.1	8.2	7.1
Fabrics, woven, of man-made fibres (not narrow or special fabrics)	12.9	0.1	—
Fabrics, woven, less than 85% of discontinuous synthethic fibres	12.6	—	—
Fabrics, woven, less than 85% of discontinuous synthetic fibres, mixed mainly or solely with cotton	11.4	—	—
Machinery and transport equipment	44.8	2.0	10.1
Road vehicles	37.2	0.8	2.8
Passenger motor vehicles (excl. buses)	30.0	0.6	0.7
Total (incl. others)	336.8	197.0	208.5

* Including re-exports.

Source: UN, *International Trade Statistics Yearbook*.

2001 ('000 Francs CFA, estimates): Total imports 254.6 (incl. Food products 69.9, Petroleum products 69.9, Intermediate goods 19.3, Capital goods 57.0); Total exports and re-exports 207.0 (incl. Uranium 63.0, Cattle 39.6, Cowpeas 15.1, Onions 13.3; Total value of re-exports 27.0) (Source: IMF, *Niger; Third Review Under the Poverty Reduction and Growth Facility Arrangement and Requests for Modification and Waiver of Performance Criteria—Staff Report and News Brief on the Executive Board Discussion* (September 2002)).

PRINCIPAL TRADING PARTNERS
(US $ million)*

Imports c.i.f.	1998	1999	2000
Côte d'Ivoire	39	47	36
France	95	71	55
Germany	8	8	6
Italy	14	5	4
Japan	17	20	17
Nigeria	32	25	28
Total (incl. others)	362	315	273

Exports f.o.b.	1998	1999	2000
Côte d'Ivoire	10	3	3
France	97	77	90
Japan	33	31	1
Nigeria	42	47	76
Total (incl. others)	206	173	187

* Data are partly compiled on the basis of reporting by Niger's trading partners.

Source: IMF, *Niger: Statistical Annex* (February 2002).

Transport

ROAD TRAFFIC
(estimates, motor vehicles in use)

	1994	1995	1996
Passenger cars	38,610	37,620	38,220
Lorries and vans	13,160	14,100	15,200

Source: IRF, *World Road Statistics*.

CIVIL AVIATION
(traffic on scheduled services)*

	1997	1998	1999
Kilometres flown (million)	3	3	3
Passengers carried ('000)	86	91	84
Passenger-km (million)	242	258	235
Total ton-km (million)	38	38	36

* Including an apportionment of the traffic of Air Afrique.

Source: UN, *Statistical Yearbook*.

Tourism

FOREIGN TOURIST ARRIVALS BY ORIGIN*

	1997	1998	1999
Africa	19,203	20,242	20,792
America	4,311	4,544	4,668
Europe	13,325	13,633	14,427
Total (incl. others)	39,190	41,311	42,433

* Figures refer to arrivals in hotels and similar establishments.

Source: World Tourism Organization, *Yearbook of Tourism Statistics*.

Tourism receipts (US $ million): 18 in 1997; 18 in 1998; 24 in 1999 (Source: World Tourism Organization).

Communications Media

	1999	2000	2001
Television receivers ('000 in use)	285	395	n.a.
Telephones ('000 main lines in use)	20.0	20.0	21.7
Mobile cellular telephones ('000 subscribers)	n.a.	n.a.	1.8
Personal computers ('000 in use)*	4	5	6
Internet users ('000)*	3	5	12

* Estimates.

1995: Facsimile machines (number in use) 327.

1996: Daily newspapers: number 1, average circulation ('000 copies) 2; Non-daily newspapers: number 5, average circulation ('000 copies) 14.

1997: Radio receivers ('000 in use) 680.

Books published (first editions, 1991): titles 5; copies ('000) 11.

Sources: UNESCO, *Statistical Yearbook*; UN, *Statistical Yearbook*; International Telecommunication Union.

Education

(1998/99, unless otherwise indicated)

	Institutions	Teachers	Males	Females	Total
				Students	
Pre-primary	133	533	5,785	5,779	11,564
Primary	3,597	12,901	322,247	207,559	529,806
Secondary:*					
general	n.a.	4,303	60,128	38,234	98,362
technical and vocational	n.a.		3,963	2,608	6,571
teacher training*	n.a.	101	1,007	333	1,340

* 1996/97 figures.

Source: mainly UNESCO Institute for Statistics.

University level: 232 teachers; 4,569 students in 1991/92; 4,880 students in 1994/95 (Source: UNESCO, *Statistical Yearbook*).

Adult literacy rate (UNESCO estimates): 15.9% (males 23.8%; females 8.4%) in 2000 (Source: UN Development Programme, *Human Development Report*).

Directory

The Constitution

Following the death of President Ibrahim Baré Maïnassara, on 9 April 1999, a military Conseil de réconciliation nationale (CRN) was formed to exercise executive and legislative authority during a transitional period prior to the restoration of elected organs of government. A new Constitution, of what was to be designated the Fifth Republic, was approved by national referendum on 18 July 1999. The Constitution of the Fifth Republic, promulgated on 9 August, envisages a balance of powers between the President, Government and legislative Assemblée nationale. The President, who is elected by universal adult suffrage, is Head of State, and is accorded 'broad ordinary and arbitral powers'. The Government, under a Prime Minister appointed by the President, is responsible to the Assemblée nationale, which is competent to remove the Prime Minister by vote of censure. The Assemblée nationale is similarly elected by direct adult suffrage. The new President and legislature were inaugurated in December 1999.

Enshrined in the Constitution is a clause granting immunity from prosecution for all those involved in the *coups d'état* of January 1996 and April 1999. Legislation to this effect was adopted by the new Assemblée nationale in January 2000.

Among regulatory bodies provided for in the Constitution are the Conseil supérieur de la communication, responsible for the broadcasting and communications sector, and the Conseil supérieur de la défense nationale, which advises the Head of State on defence matters.

The Government

HEAD OF STATE

President: Col (retd) TANDJA MAMADOU (inaugurated 22 December 1999).

COUNCIL OF MINISTERS
(April 2003)

Prime Minister: HAMA AMADOU.

Minister of State, responsible for Sports, Culture and the Games of La Francophonie: ABDOU LABO.

Minister of State, responsible for African Integration and the NEPAD Programmes: Col (retd) MOUMOUNI ADAMOU DJERMAKOYE.

Minister of Trade and the Promotion of the Private Sector: SEYNI OUMAROU.

Minister of Tourism and Crafts: RHISSA AG BOULA.

Minister of Community Development: SABIOU DADDY GAOH.

Minister of Animal Resources: KORONEY MAOUDÉ.

Minister of Basic Education and Literacy: ARY IBRAHIM.

Minister of the Economy and Finance: ALI BADJO GAMATIÉ.

Minister of National Defence: HASSANE SOULEY BONTO.

Minister of Foreign Affairs and Co-operation: AÏCHATOU MIND-AOUDOU.

Minister of Justice, Keeper of the Seals, Minister responsible for Relations with Parliament: MATI Elhadj MOUSSA.

Minister of Water, the Environment and the Fight against Desertification: ADAMOU NAMATA.

Minister of Secondary and Higher Education, Research and Technology: HABI MAHAMADOU SALISSOU.

Minister of the Civil Service and Labour: MOUSSA SAYBOU KAS-SEYE.

Minister of Privatization and the Restructuring of State Enterprises: TRAPSIDA FATIMA.

Minister of Social Development, Population, the Promotion of Women and the Protection of Children: ABDOULWAHID HAL-IMATOU OUSSEINI.

Minister of the Interior and Decentralization: ALBADE ABOURA.

Minister of Public Health and the Fight against Epidemics: MAMADOU SOURGHIA.

Minister of Transport: SOULEYMANE KANE.

Ministry of Equipment and Territorial Administration: ZAKARIA MAMADOU.

Minister of Agricultural Development: ABARY MAÏ MOUSSA.

Minister of Mines and Energy: RABIOU HASSANE YARI.

Minister of Town Planning, the Environment and Public Property: MAMANE BACHINE YAHAYA.

Minister of Communication, Government Spokesman: Prof. SIDIKOU OUMAROU HAROUNA.

Minister of Youth and Professional Training of the Young: MOUNKAÏLA SANDA.

Secretary of State at the Ministry of Foreign Affairs and Co-operation, responsible for Co-operation: Dr SANI GONIMI.

Secretary of State at the Ministry of Public Health and the Fight against Epidemics, responsible for Hospital Reforms and the Fight against Epidemics: KARIM FATOUMA ZARA.

Secretary of State at the Ministry of Water Resources, the Environment and the Fight against Desertification, responsible for the Environment and the Fight against Desertification: CHAÏBOU MAMAN.

MINISTRIES

Office of the President: BP 550, Niamey; tel. 72-23-80; fax 72-33-96.

Office of the Prime Minister: BP 893, Niamey; tel. 72-26-99; fax 73-58-59; internet www.niger-gouv.org.

Ministry of African Integration and the NEPAD Programmes: Niamey.

Ministry of Agricultural Development: BP 12091, Niamey; tel. 73-35-41; fax 73-20-08.

Ministry of Animal Resources: BP 12091, Niamey; tel. 73-79-59; fax 73-31-86.

Ministry of Basic Education and Literacy: BP 557, Niamey; tel. 72-20-80; fax 72-21-05.

Ministry of the Civil Service and Labour: BP 11107, Niamey; tel. 73-22-31; fax 73-61-69; e-mail sani.yakouba@caramail.com.

Ministry of Communication: BP 452, Niamey; tel. 72-28-74; fax 73-36-85.

Ministry of Community Development: Niamey.

Ministry of the Economy and Finance: BP 389, Niamey; tel. 72-23-74; fax 73-59-34.

Ministry of Equipment and Territorial Administration: BP 403, Niamey; tel. 73-53-57; fax 72-21-71.

Ministry of Foreign Affairs and Co-operation: BP 396, Niamey; tel. 72-29-07; fax 73-52-31.

Ministry of the Interior and Decentralization: BP 622, Niamey; tel. 72-32-62; fax 72-21-76.

Ministry of Justice: BP 466, Niamey; tel. 72-31-31; fax 72-37-77.

Ministry of Mines and Energy: BP 11700, Niamey; tel. 72-38-51; fax 73-27-59.

Ministry of National Defence: BP 626, Niamey; tel. 72-20-76; fax 72-40-78.

Ministry of Privatization and the Restructuring of State Enterprises: Immeuble CCCP, BP 862, Niamey; tel. 73-27-50; fax 73-59-91; e-mail ccpp@intnet.ne; internet www.nigerprivatisation.com.

Ministry of Public Health and the Fight against Epidemics: BP 623, Niamey; tel. 72-28-08; fax 73-35-70.

Ministry of Secondary and Higher Education, Research and Technology: BP 628, Niamey; tel. 72-26-20; fax 72-40-40; e-mail mesnt@intnet.ne.

Ministry of Social Development, Population, the Promotion of Women and the Protection of Children: BP 11286, Niamey; tel. 72-23-30; fax 73-61-65.

Ministry of Sports, Culture and the Games of La Francophonie: BP 215, Niamey; tel. 72-32-35; fax 72-23-36.

Ministry of Tourism and Crafts: BP 480, Niamey; tel. 73-65-22; fax 72-23-87.

Ministry of Town Planning, the Environment and Public Property: Niamey.

Ministry of Trade and the Promotion of the Private Sector: BP 480, Niamey; tel. 72-34-67; fax 73-21-50; e-mail nicom@intnet.ne.

Ministry of Transport: BP 12130, Niamey; tel. 72-28-21; fax 73-36-85.

Ministry of Water, the Environment and the Fight against Desertification: BP 257, Niamey; tel. 73-47-22; fax 72-40-15.

Ministry of Youth and Professional Training of the Young: BP 12501, Niamey; tel. 73-69-88; fax 73-35-93.

President and Legislature

PRESIDENT

Presidential Election, First Round, 17 October 1999

Candidate	Votes	% of votes
Tandja Mamadou (MNSD)	617,554	32.30
Mahamadou Issoufou (PNDS)	435,693	22.78
Mahamane Ousmane (CDS)	430,571	22.52
Hamid Algabid (RDP)	207,658	10.86
Moumouni Adamou Djermakoye (ANDP)	147,979	7.74
André Salifou (UPDP)	39,797	2.08
Amadou Djibo Ali (UNIU*).	32,947	1.72
Total	1,912,199	100.00

*Union des Nigériens indépendants unis.

Second Round, 24 November 1999

Candidate	% of votes
Tandja Mamadou (MNSD)	59.89
Mahamadou Issoufou (PNDS)	40.11
Total	100.00

ASSEMBLÉE NATIONALE

Assemblée nationale: place de la Concertation, BP 12234, Niamey; tel. 72-42-29; fax 72-28-04; e-mail webmestre@niger .assemblee.ne; internet www.assemblee.ne.

President: El Hadj MAHAMANE OUSMANE.

General Election, 24 November 1999

Party	Seats
Mouvement national pour une société de développement—Nassara (MNSD)	38
Convention démocratique et social—Rahama (CDS) .	17
Parti nigérien pour la démocratie et le socialisme—Tarayya (PNDS)	16
Rassemblement pour la démocratie et le progrès—Djamaa (RDP)	8
Alliance nigérienne pour la démocratie et le progrès social—Zaman Lahiya (ANDP)	4
Total	83

Political Organizations

In mid-2003 there were some 30 political parties registered in Niger, of which the following were among the most prominent:

Alliance nigérienne pour la démocratie et le progrès social—Zaman Lahiya (ANDP): fmrly mem. of opposition Coordination des forces démocratiques (CFD); joined pro-Govt Alliance des forces démocratiques (AFD) in July 2002; Leader Col (retd) MOUMOUNI ADAMOU DJERMAKOYE.

Convention démocratique et social—Rahama (CDS): supports Govt of Hama Amadou; mem. of Alliance des forces démocratiques (AFD); Chair. MAHAMANE OUSMANE.

Front démocratique nigérien—Mountounchi (FDN): f. 1995 by fmr mems of PPN; Chair. OUMAROU YOUSSOUFOU GARBA; Sec.-Gen. MOHAMED MUDUR.

Mouvement national pour une société de développement—Nassara (MNSD): f. 1988; sole party 1988–90; Chair. Col (retd) TANDJA MAMADOU; Pres. HAMA AMADOU.

Parti nigérien pour l'autogestion—al Umat (PNA): f. 1997; Leader SANOUSSI JACKOU.

Parti nigérien pour la démocratie et le socialisme—Tarayya (PNDS): mem. of Coordination des forces démocratiques (CFD); Sec.-Gen. MAHAMADOU ISSOUFOU.

Parti progressiste nigérien—Rassemblement démocratique africain (PPN—RDA): associated with the late Pres. Diori; mem. of Coordination des forces démocratiques (CFD); Chair. ABDOULAYE DIORI.

Parti républicain pour les libertés et le progrès au Niger—Nakowa (PRLPN): Chair. ALKA ALAMOU.

Parti social-démocrate nigérien—Alheri (PSDN): Leader KAZELMA OUMAR TAYA.

Parti pour l'unité nationale et le développement—Salama (PUND): Leader AKOLI DAOUEL.

Rassemblement des verts—Ni'ima (RDV): BP 12515, Niamey; tel. and fax 74-11-25; e-mail agarba_99@yahoo.com; Pres. ADAMOU GARBA.

Rassemblement pour la démocratie et le progrès—Djamaa (RDP): party of late Pres. Maïnassara; Chair. HAMID ALGABID; Sec.-Gen. MAHAMANE SOULEY LABI.

Union pour la démocratie et le progrès—Amici (UDP): supports Govt of Hama Amadou; mem. of Alliance des forces démocratiques (AFD); Leader ABDOULAYE TONDI.

Union pour la démocratie et le progrès social—Amana (UDPS): represents interests of Tuaregs; mem. of Coordination des forces démocratiques (CFD); Chair. ISSOUF BAKO.

Union pour la démocratie et la République—Tabbat (UDR): Niamey; f. 2002; Pres. AMADOU BOUABACAR CISSÉ.

Union des forces populaires pour la démocratie et le progrès —Sawaba (UFPDP): Niamey.

Union des patriotes démocratiques et progressistes— Shamuwa (UPDP): Chair. Prof. ANDRÉ SALIFOU.

Union des socialistes nigériens—Talaka (USN): f. 2001 by mems of the UFPDP; Leader ISSOUFOU ASSOUMANE.

In March 2001 12 opposition parties, led by the PNDS, formed the **Coordination des forces démocratiques (CFD)** (Zabarkan, rue du SNEN, BP 5005, Niamey; tel. 74-05-69), while 17 parties loyal to Prime Minister Hama Amadou, headed by the MNSD, formed the **Alliance des forces démocratiques (AFD)**. In July 2002 the ANDP withdrew from the CFD and joined the AFD.

Diplomatic Representation

EMBASSIES IN NIGER

Algeria: route des Ambassades-Goudel, BP 142, Niamey; tel. 72-35-83; fax 72-35-93; Ambassador MADJID BOUGUERRA.

Benin: BP 11544, Niamey; tel. 72-28-60; Ambassador TAÏROU MAMADOU DJAOUGA.

Chad: Niamey; tel. 75-34-64; Ambassador ALI ABDOULAYE SABRE.

China, People's Republic: Niamey; tel. 72-32-83; fax 72-32-85; e-mail embchine@intnet.ne; Ambassador SUN ZHAOTONG.

Cuba: Niamey; tel. 72-46-00; Ambassador MIGUEL OTERO LÓPEZ.

Egypt: BP 254, Niamey; tel. 73-33-55; fax 73-38-91; Ambassador MOUSTAPHA OUSMAN HASSAN.

France: BP 10660, Niamey; tel. 72-24-32; fax 72-25-18; e-mail ambafrance@intnet.ne; internet www.ambafrance.ne; Ambassador DENIS VÈNE.

Germany: 71 ave du Général de Gaulle, BP 629, Niamey; tel. 72-35-10; fax 72-39-85; e-mail amballny@intnet.ne; Ambassador JOSEPH ALBERT WEISS.

Iran: ave de la Présidence, Niamey; tel. 72-21-98; Ambassador SEYED AHMAD SHOEYBI DERO.

Korea, Democratic People's Republic: Niamey; Ambassador PAK SONG IL.

Libya: Rond-point du Grand Hôtel, POB 683, Niamey; tel. 72-40-19; Ambassador HUSSEIN AL-KUNI.

Morocco: ave du Président Lubke, BP 12403, Niamey; tel. 73-40-84; fax 74-14-27; Ambassador ALI BOJJI.

Nigeria: ave du Général Ibrahim Babangida, Goudel, BP 11130, Niamey; tel. 73-24-10; fax 73-35-00; Ambassador Dr YAKUBU KWARI.

Pakistan: ave des Zermakoye, BP 10426, Niamey; tel. 75-32-57; fax 75-32-55; e-mail parepnmy@intnet.ne; internet www.brain.net.pk/ ~farata; Ambassador (vacant).

Saudi Arabia: Route de Tillabery, BP 339, Niamey; tel. 75-43-78; e-mail neemb@mofa.gov.sa; Chargé d'affaires a.i. FAHAD ALI ALDOSARY.

USA: rue des Ambassades, BP 11201, Niamey; tel. 73-31-69; fax 73-55-60; e-mail usis@intnet.ne; Ambassador GAIL DENNISE MATTHIEU.

Judicial System

The Supreme Court was dissolved following the death of President Ibrahim Baré Maïnassara in April 1999. The Conseil de réconciliation nationale established a State Court as the highest judicial authority pending the restoration of constitutional government: the State Court was composed of the four chambers of the dissolved Supreme Court. The Constitution of the Fifth Republic, promulgated in August 1999, provides for a Constitutional Court.

High Court of Justice: Niamey; internet www.assemblee.ne/ organes/hjc.htm; competent to indict the President of the Republic and all other state officials (past and present) in relation to all matters of state, including high treason; comprises seven perm. mems and three rotating mems; Pres. SÉKOU CISSÉ OUMAROU; Vice-Pres SOULEYE OUMAROU, INTAROU HASSANE DJERMAKOYE, BAKO ABOU DADAMI.

Court of State Security: Niamey; competent to try cases not within the jurisdiction of the High Court of Justice; incorporates a martial court.

Court of Appeal: Niamey; court of appeal for judgements of **Criminal** and **Assize Courts** (the latter at Niamey, Maradi, Tahoua and Zinder).

Constitutional Court: BP 10779, Niamey; tel. 72-30-81; fax 72-35-40; e-mail cconstit@intnet.ne; internet www.niger-gouv.org/courconstitutionnelle.htm; comprises a President, a Vice-President and five Councillors; Pres ABBA MOUSSA ISSOUFOU; Vice-Pres. ABDOU HASSAN.

Courts of First Instance: located at Niamey (with sub-divisions at Dosso and Tillabéri), Maradi, Tahoua (sub-divisions at Agadez, Arlit and Birni N'Konni) and Diffa (sub-division at Diffa).

Labour Courts: function at each Court of the First Instance and sub-division thereof.

Religion

It is estimated that some 95% of the population are Muslims, 0.5% are Christians and the remainder follow traditional beliefs.

ISLAM

The most influential Islamic groups in Niger are the Tijaniyya, the Senoussi and the Hamallists.

Association Islamique du Niger: Niamey; Dir CHEIKH OUMAROU ISMAEL.

CHRISTIANITY

Various Protestant missions maintain 13 centres, with a personnel of 90.

The Roman Catholic Church

Niger comprises two dioceses, directly responsible to the Holy See. The Bishops participate in the Bishops' Conference of Burkina Faso and Niger (based in Ouagadougou, Burkina Faso). At 31 December 2000 there were an estimated 20,000 adherents in Niger.

Bishop of Maradi: Rt Rev. AMBROISE OUÉDRAOGO, Evêché, BP 479, Maradi; tel. 41-03-30; fax 41-13-86; e-mail evechemi@intnet.ne.

Bishop of Niamey: Rt Rev. MICHEL CHRISTIAN CARTATÉGUY, Evêché, BP 10270, Niamey; tel. 73-32-59; fax 73-80-01; e-mail evecheny@intnet.ne; internet www.multimania.com/cathoniger.

The Press

The published press expanded considerably in Niger after 1993, when the requirement to obtain prior authoritization for each edition was lifted, although legislation continued to require that a copy of each publication be deposited at the office of the Procurator of the Republic. For the most part, however, economic difficulties have ensured that few publications have maintained a regular, sustained appearance. The following were among those newspapers and periodicals believed to be appearing regularly in mid-2003.

L'Action: quartier Yantala, Niamey; tel. 96-92-22; e-mail action_ne@yahoo.fr; internet www.tamtaminfo.com/action.pdf; f. 2003; fortnightly; popular newspaper intended for youth audience; Dir of Publication BOUSSADA BEN ALI; circ. 2,000 (2003).

L'Alternative: BP 10948, Niamey; tel. 74-24-39; fax 74-24-82; e-mail alter@intnet.ne; internet www.alternative.ne; f. 1994; weekly; Dir MOUSSA TCHANGARI; Editor-in-Chief ABDRAMANE OUSMANE.

Anfani: Immeuble DMK, rue du Damagaram, BP 2096, Niamey; tel. 74-08-80; fax 74-00-52; e-mail anfani@intnet.ne; internet www.anfani.cjb.net; f. 1992; 2 a month; Editor-in-Chief IBBO DADDY ABDOULAYE; circ. 3,000.

As-Salam: BP 451, Niamey; tel. 74-29-12; e-mail assa_lam@yahoo.fr; monthly; Dir IBBO DADDY ABDOULAYE.

Le Canard Déchaîné: BP 383, Niamey; tel. 92-66-64; satirical; weekly; Dir of Publication ABDOULAYE TIÉMOGO; Editor-in-Chief IBRAHIM MANZO.

Le Canard Libéré: BP 11631, Niamey; tel. 75-43-52; fax 75-39-89; e-mail canardlibere@caramail.com; satirical; weekly; Dir of Publication TRAORÉ DAOUDA AMADOU; Editorial Dir OUMAROU NALAN MOUSSA.

Le Démocrate: BP 11064, Niamey; tel. 73-24-25; e-mail le_democrate@caramail.com; internet www.tamtaminfo.com/democrate.pdf; weekly; independent; f. 1992; Dir of Publication ALBERT CHAÏBOU; Editor-in-Chief OUSSEINI ISSA.

Les Echos du Sahel: quartier Wadata, BP 12952, Niamey; tel. and fax 74-32-17; e-mail ecosahel@intnet.ne; f. 1999; rural development; quarterly; Dir IBBO DADDY ABDOULAYE.

L'Enquêteur: BP 172, Niamey; tel. 90-18-74; e-mail lenqueteur@yahoo.fr; fortnightly; Publr TAHIROU GOURO; Dir HAROUNDA YACOUBA.

Haské: BP 297, Niamey; tel. 74-18-44; fax 73-20-06; f. 1990; weekly; also *Haské Magazine*, quarterly; Dir CHEIKH IBRAHIM DIOP.

La Jeune Académie: BP 11989, Niamey; tel. 73-38-71; e-mail jeune.academie@caramail.com; monthly; Dir ABDOULAYE HASSOUMI GARBA.

Journal Officiel de la République du Niger: BP 116, Niamey; tel. 72-39-30; fax 72-39-43; f. 1960; fortnightly; govt bulletin; Man. Editor BONKOULA AMINATOU MAYAKI; circ. 800.

Libération: BP 10483, Niamey; tel. 73-24-25; e-mail libera.niger@usa.net; Dir BOUBACAR DIALLO.

Matinfo: BP 11631, Niamey; tel. 75-43-52; fax 75-39-89; e-mail matinfo@caramail.com; daily; independent; Dir DAOUDA AMADOU TRAORÉ.

Nigerama: BP 11158, Niamey; tel. 74-08-09; e-mail anpniger@intnet.ne; quarterly; publ. by the Agence Nigérienne de Presse.

L'Opinion: BP 11116, Niamey; tel. 74-09-84; e-mail lopinion@dounia.ne; Dir ALZOUMA ZAKARI.

Le Regard: BP 2809, Niamey; tel. 73-84-07; e-mail le_regard@usa.net; Dir MAHAMADOU TOURÉ.

Le Républicain: Nouvelle Imprimerie du Niger, Place du Petit Marché, BP 12015, Niamey; tel. 73-47-98; fax 73-41-42; e-mail nin@intnet.ne; internet www.republicain-niger.com; f. 1991; weekly; independent; Dir MAMAN ABOU; circ. 1,000.

La Roue de l'Histoire: Zabarkan, rue du SNEN, BP 5005, Niamey; tel. 74-05-69; internet www.tamtaminfo.com/roue.pdf; weekly; Propr SENOUSSI JACKOU; Dir ABARAD MOUDOUR ZAKARA.

Le Sahel Quotidien: BP 13182, ONEP, Niamey; tel. 73-34-87; fax 73-30-90; internet www.tamtaminfo.com/sahelquotidien.html; f. 1960; publ. by Office National d'Edition et de Presse; daily; Dir IBRAHIM MAMANE TANTAN; Editor-in-Chief ALASSANE ASOKOFARE; circ. 5,000; also *Sahel-Dimanche*, Sundays; internet www.tamtaminfo.com/saheldimanche.html; circ. 3,000.

Sauyi: BP 10948, Niamey; tel. 74-24-39; fax 74-24-82; e-mail sarji@alternative.ne; fortnightly; Hausa; publ. by Groupe Alternative; Hausa; rural interest; Dir SAÏDOU ARJI.

Stadium: BP 10948, Niamey; tel. 74-08-80; e-mail kiabba@yahoo.fr; sports; 2 a month; Dir ABDOU TIKIRÉ.

Le Témoin: BP 2303, Niamey; tel. 74-24-12; e-mail letemoin@usa.net; internet www.tamtaminfo.com/temoin.pdf; 2 a month; Dir of Publication IBRAHIM SOUMANA GAOH; Editors G. S. TAHIROU, OUSMANE IBRAHIM, ALASSANE ABDOU; circ. 2,000 (2003).

Ténéré Express: BP 13600, Niamey; tel. 73-35-76; fax 73-77-75; e-mail tenerefm@intnet.ne; daily; independent; current affairs; Dir ABDOULAYE MOUSSA MASSALATCHI.

La Tribune du Peuple: BP 2624, Niamey; tel. 73-34-28; e-mail tribune@intnet.ne; f. 1993; weekly; Man. Editor IBRAHIM HAMIDOU.

Le Trophée: BP 2000, Niamey; tel. 74-12-79; e-mail strophee@caramail.com; sports; 2 a month; Dir ISSA HAMIDOU MAYAKI.

NEWS AGENCIES

Agence Nigérienne de Presse (ANP): BP 11158, Niamey; tel. 74-08-09; e-mail anpniger@intnet.ne; f. 1987; state-owned; Dir ABDOURAHMANE ALILOU.

Sahel—Office National d'Edition et de Presse (ONEP): BP 13182, Niamey; tel. 73-34-86; f. 1989; Dir ALI OUSSEÏNI.

Publishers

La Nouvelle Imprimerie du Niger (NIN): Place du Petit Marché, BP 61, Niamey; tel. 73-47-98; fax 73-41-42; e-mail nin@intnet.ne; f. 1962 as Imprimerie Nationale du Niger; govt publishing house; brs in Agadez and Maradi; Dir E. WOHLRAB.

Réseau Sahélien de Recherche et de Publication: BP 11040, Niamey; tel. 73-36-90; fax 73-39-43; e-mail resadep@ilimi.uam.ne; press of the Université Abdou Moumouni; Co-ordinator BOUREIMA DIADIE.

Broadcasting and Communications

REGULATORY AUTHORITY

Conseil Supérieur de la Communication (CSC): Niamey; comprises 13 mems; one representative of the President of the Republic, one representative of the President of the Assemblée nationale, one representative apiece of the Ministers of Transport and Communication, of the Interior and Decentralization, and of Justice, three representatives of the publicly-owned communications sector, three representatives of civil society, and one representative each of private-sector employees and employers in the domain of communication; Pres. MARIAMA KEÏTA.

TELECOMMUNICATIONS

Celtel Niger: Niamey; tel. 73-85-43; fax 73-23-85; e-mail b-sghir@intnet.ne; f. 2001 to operate mobile cellular telecommunications network in Niamey and Maradi; 70% owned by MSI-Cellular Investments (United Kingdom), 30% owned by Caren Assurance; Dir-Gen. BACHAR SAGHIR.

Société Nigérienne des Télécommunications (SONITEL): BP 208, Niamey; tel. 72-20-00; fax 73-58-12; e-mail sonitel@intnet.ne; internet www.intnet.ne; f. 1998; 51% jtly-owned by ZTE Corpn (People's Republic of China) and Laaico (Libya), 46% state-owned; Dir-Gen. MOUSSA BOUBACAR.

Sahel Com: BP 208, Niamey; f. 2002; mobile cellular telecommunications in Niamey.

Telecel Niger: Niamey; f. 2001 to operate mobile cellular telecommunications network, initially in Niamey and western regions, expanding to cover Maradi and Zinder by 2003, and Tahoua and Agadez by 2004; 68% owned by Orascom Telecom (Egypt); Dir HIMA SOULEY.

BROADCASTING

Radio

Independent radio stations have been permitted to operate since 1994, although the majority are concentrated in the capital, Niamey. In 2000 the first of a network of rural stations, RURANET, which were to broadcast mainly programmes concerned with development issues, mostly in national languages, was established. Several local radio stations, funded by the Agence intergouvernementale de la francophonie, were expected to commence operations in the early 2000s.

Anfani FM: rue du Damagaram, BP 2096, Niamey; tel. 74-08-80; fax 74-00-52; e-mail anfani@intnet.ne; private radio station, broadcasting to Niamey, Zinder, Maradi and Diffa; Dir GRÉMAH BOUCAR.

Office de Radiodiffusion-Télévision du Niger (ORTN): BP 309, Niamey; tel. 72-31-63; fax 72-35-48; state broadcasting authority; Dir-Gen. ASSANE SALEY.

La Voix du Sahel: BP 361, Niamey; tel. 72-22-02; fax 72-35-48; e-mail ortny@intnet.ne; f. 1958; govt-controlled radio service; programmes in French, Hausa, Djerma, Kanuri, Fulfuldé, Tamajak, Toubou, Gourmantché, Boudouma and Arabic; Dir IBRO NA-ALLAH AMADOU.

Ténéré FM: BP 13600, Niamey; tel. 73-65-76; fax 73-46-94; e-mail tenerefm@intnet.ne; f. 1998; Dir ABIBOU GARBA; Editor-in-Chief SOULEYMANE ISSA MAÏGA.

RURANET: Niamey; internet membres.lycos.fr/nigeradio; f. 2000; network of rural radio stations, broadcasting 80% in national languages, with 80% of programmes concerned with development issues; 31 stations operative in April 2002.

La Voix de l'Hémicycle: BP 12234, Niamey; f. 2002 as the radio station of the Assemblée nationale; broadcasts parliamentary debates and analysis for 15 hours daily in French and national languages to Niamey and environs.

Sudan FM: Dosso; auth. 2000; private radio station; Dir HIMA ADAMOU.

Television

Office de Radiodiffusion-Télévision du Niger (ORTN): see Radio (see p. 3123).

Télé-Sahel: BP 309, Niamey; tel. 72-31-55; fax 72-35-48; govt-controlled television service; broadcasts daily from 13 transmission posts and six retransmission posts, covering most of Niger; Dir-Gen. ABDOU SOULEY.

Télévision Ténéré (TTV): BP 13600, Niamey; tel. 73-65-76; fax 73-77-75; e-mail tenerefm@intnet.ne; f. 2000; independent broadcaster in Niamey; Dir ABIBOU GARBA.

The independent operator, Télé Star, broadcasts several international or foreign channels in Niamey and environs, including TV5, Canal Horizon, CFI, RTL9, CNN and Euro News

Finance

(cap. = capital; res = reserves; dep. = deposits; m. = million; brs = branches; amounts in francs CFA)

BANKING

Central Bank

Banque Centrale des Etats de l'Afrique de l'Ouest (BCEAO): BP 487, Niamey; tel. 72-24-91; fax 73-47-43; HQ in Dakar, Senegal; f. 1962; bank of issue for the mem. states of the Union économique et monétaire ouest-africaine (UEMOA, comprising Benin, Burkina Faso, Côte d'Ivoire, Guinea-Bissau, Mali, Niger, Senegal and Togo); cap. and res 850,500m., total assets 5,157,700m. (Dec. 2001); Gov. CHARLES KONAN BANNY; Dir in Niger ABDOULAYE SOUMANA; brs at Maradi and Zinder.

Commercial Banks

Bank of Africa—Niger: Immeuble Sonara II, BP 10973, Niamey; tel. 73-36-20; fax 73-38-18; e-mail bofafrni@intnet.ne; f. 1994 to acquire assets of Nigeria International Bank Niamey; 42.5% owned by African Financial Holding; cap. 1,500m., total assets 20,890m. (Dec. 2000); Chair. PAUL DERREMAUX; Man. Dir KHALED SUCCARI.

Banque Commerciale du Niger (BCN): BP 11363, Niamey; tel. 73-39-15; fax 73-21-63; f. 1978; owned by private Nigerien (50%) and Libyan (50%) interests; cap. 1,440m., total assets 5,180m. (Dec. 1998); Pres. SAIDOU SIDIBE; Dir-Gen. MUFTAH ABDALLA DANDY.

Banque Internationale pour l'Afrique au Niger (BIA—Niger): ave de la Mairie, BP 10350, Niamey; tel. 73-31-01; fax 73-35-95; e-mail bia@intnet.ne; f. 1980; 35% owned by Groupe Belgolaise SA (Belgium); cap. 2,800.0m., res 1,156.8m., dep. 32,075.8m. (Dec. 2000); Pres. AMADOU HIMA SOULEY; Dir-Gen. DANIEL HASSER; 5 brs.

Banque Islamique du Niger pour le Commerce et l'Investissement (BINCI): Immeuble El Nasr, BP 12754, Niamey; tel. 73-27-30; fax 73-47-35; e-mail binci@intnet.ne; f. 1983; fmrly Banque Masraf Faisal Islami, restructured 1994–96; 33% owned by Dar al-Maal al-Islami (Switzerland), 33% by Islamic Development Bank (Saudi Arabia); cap. and res 1,416m., total assets 6,043m. (Dec. 1999); Pres. ABDERRAOUF BENESSAÏAH; Man. Dir ABDERRALMAM ZINEDDINE.

Ecobank Niger: angle blvd de la Liberté et rue des Bâtisseurs, BP 13804, Niamey; tel. 73-71-81; fax 73-72-04; e-mail ecobank@intnet.ne; internet www.ecobank.com; owned by Ecobank Transnational Inc. (Togo) and subsids (operating under the auspices of the Economic Community of West African States); cap. 1,250m., total assets 16,093m. (Dec. 1999); Man. Dir JOSEPH KODJO AGBEMEHIN.

Société Nigérienne de Banque (SONIBANK): ave de la Mairie, BP 891, Niamey; tel. 73-47-40; fax 73-46-93; e-mail sonibank@intnet.ne; f. 1990; 25% owned by Société Tunisienne de Banque; cap. 2,000m., dep. 23,592m., total assets 33,140m. (Dec. 2000); Pres. ILLA KANE; Dir-Gen. MOUSSA HAITOU.

Development Banks

Caisse de Prêts aux Collectivités Territoriales (CPCT): BP 730, Niamey; tel. 72-34-12; fax 72-30-80; f. 1970; 100% state-owned (94% by collectivités territoriales); part-privatization pending; cap. 1,395m., total assets 4,045m. (Dec. 1998); Admin. JOËLLE BOLHO (acting).

Crédit du Niger (CDN): 11 blvd de la République, BP 213, Niger; tel. 72-27-01; fax 72-23-90; f. 1958; 54% state-owned, 20% owned by Caisse Nationale de Sécurité Sociale; cap. 1,720m., total assets 2,878m. (Dec. 1999); Chair. JOËLLE BOLHO (acting).

Fonds d'Intervention en Faveur des Petites et Moyennes Entreprises Nigériennes (FIPMEN): Immeuble Sonara II, BP 252, Niamey; tel. 73-20-98; f. 1990; state-owned; cap. and res 124m. (Dec. 1991); Chair. AMADOU SALLA HASSANE; Man. Dir IBRAHIM BEIDARI.

Savings Bank

Office National de la Poste et de l'Epargne: BP 11778, Niamey; tel. 73-24-98; fax 73-35-69; fmrly Caisse Nationale d'Epargne; Chair. Mme PALFI; Man. Dir HASSOUME MATA.

STOCK EXCHANGE

Bourse Régionale des Valeurs Mobilières (BRVM): c/o Chambre de Commerce et d'Industrie du Niger, Place de la Concertation, BP 13299, Niamey; tel. 73-66-92; fax 73-69-47; e-mail imagagi@brvm.org; internet www.brvm.org; f. 1998; national branch of BRVM (regional stock exchange based in Abidjan, Côte d'Ivoire, serving the member states of UEMOA); Man. IDRISSA S. MAGAGI.

INSURANCE

Agence d'Assurance du Sahel: BP 10661, Niamey; tel. 74-05-47.

Agence Nigérienne d'Assurances (ANA): place de la Mairie, BP 423, Niamey; tel. 72-20-71; f. 1959; cap. 1.5m. owned by L'Union des Assurances de Paris; Dir JEAN LASCAUD.

Caren Assurance: BP 733, Niamey; tel. 73-34-70; fax 73-24-93; e-mail carenas@intnet.ne; insurance and reinsurance; Dir-Gen. IBRAHIM IDI ANGO.

Leyma—Société Nigérienne d'Assurances et de Réassurances (SNAR—Leyma): BP 426, Niamey; tel. 73-57-72; fax 73-40-44; f. 1973; restructured 2002; Pres. AMADOU OUSMANE; Dir-Gen. MAMADOU MALAM AOUAMI.

La Nigérienne d'Assurance et de Réassurance: BP 13300, Niamey; tel. 73-63-36; fax 73-73-37.

Union Générale des Assurances du Niger (UGAN): rue de Kalley, BP 11935, Niamey; tel. 73-54-06; fax 73-41-85; f. 1985; cap. 500m. Pres. PATHÉ DIONE; Dir-Gen. MAMADOU TALATA; 7 brs.

Trade and Industry

GOVERNMENT AGENCIES

Caisse de Stabilisation des Prix des Produits du Niger (CSPPN): BP 480, Niamey; price control agency for Nigerien goods; Dir IBRAHIM KOUSSOU.

Cellule de Coordination de la Programme de Privatisation: Immeuble Sonibanque, BP 862, Niamey; tel. 73-29-10; fax 73-29-58; responsible for co-ordination of privatization programme; Co-ordinator IDÉ ISSOUFOU.

Office des Eaux du Sous-Sol (OFEDES): BP 734, Niamey; tel. 74-01-19; fax 74-16-68; govt agency for the maintenance and development of wells and boreholes; transfer to private sector pending in 2002; Pres. DJIBO HAMANI.

Office du Lait du Niger (OLANI): BP 404, Niamey; tel. 73-23-69; fax 73-36-74; f. 1971; development and marketing of milk products; transferred to majority private ownership in 1998; Dir-Gen. M. DIENG.

Office National de l'Energie Solaire (ONERSOL): BP 621, Niamey; tel. 73-45-05; govt agency for research and development, commercial production and exploitation of solar devices; Dir ALBERT WRIGHT.

Office National des Ressources Minières du Niger (ONAREM): rond-point Kennedy, BP 12716, Niamey; tel. 73-59-28; fax 73-28-12; f. 1976; govt agency for exploration, exploitation and marketing of all minerals; Pres. MOUDY MOHAMED; Dir-Gen. A. A. ASKIA.

Office des Produits Vivriers du Niger (OPVN): BP 474, Niamey; tel. 73-44-43; fax 74-27-18; govt agency for developing agricultural and food production; Dir-Gen. M. ISSAKA.

Riz du Niger (RINI): BP 476, Niamey; tel. 71-13-29; fax 73-42-04; f. 1967; cap. 825m. francs CFA; 30% state-owned; transfer to 100% private ownership proposed; production and marketing of rice; Pres. YAYA MADOUGOU; Dir-Gen. M. HAROUNA.

Société Nigérienne de Produits Pétroliers (SONIDEP): 3 ave de l'Afrique, BP 11702, Niamey; tel. 73-33-34; fax 73-43-28; e-mail sonidep@intnet.ne; f. 1977; govt agency for the distribution and marketing of petroleum products; privatization proposed for 2003; cap. 1,000m. francs CFA (Dec. 1998); Man. Dir AMADOU DIOFFO.

DEVELOPMENT ORGANIZATIONS

Agence Française de Développement (AFD): ave Gounti-Yéna, BP 212, Niamey; tel. 72-33-93; fax 72-26-05; e-mail afdniger@intnet.ne; internet www.afd.fr; Dir in Niger OLIVIER RICHARD.

Mission Française de Coopération et d'Action Culturelle: BP 494, Niamey; tel. 72-20-66; administers bilateral aid from France; Dir JEAN BOULOGNE.

SNV (Société Néerlandais de Développement): ave des Zarma-koye, BP 10110, Niamey; tel. 75-36-33; fax 75-35-06; e-mail snvniger@snv.ne; internet www.snv.ne; present in Niger since 1978; projects concerning food security, agriculture, the environment, savings and credit, marketing, water and communications; operations in Tillabéri, Zinder and Tahoua provinces.

CHAMBERS OF COMMERCE

Chambre de Commerce d'Agriculture, d'Industrie et d'Artisanat du Niger: BP 209, Niamey; tel. 73-22-10; fax 73-46-68; e-mail cham209n@intnet.ne; f. 1954; comprises 80 full mems and 40 dep. mems; Pres. IBRAHIM IDI ANGO; Sec.-Gen. SADOU AISSATA.

Chambre de Commerce, d'Agriculture, d'Industrie et d'Artisanat du Niger, Antenne d'Agadez: BP 201, Agadez; tel. 44-01-61.

Chambre de Commerce, d'Agriculture, d'Industrie et d'Artisanat du Niger, Antenne de Diffa: BP 91, Diffa; tel. 54-03-92; f. 1988.

Chambre de Commerce, d'Agriculture, d'Industrie et d'Artisanat du Niger, Antenne de Maradi: BP 79, Maradi; tel. 41-03-66; fax 41-10-32.

Chambre de Commerce, d'Agriculture, d'Industrie et d'Artisanat du Niger, Antenne de Tahoua: BP 172, Tahoua; tel. 61-03-84; f. 1984; Sec. ILYESS HABIB.

Chambre de Commerce, d'Agriculture, d'Industrie et d'Artisanat du Niger, Antenne de Zinder: BP 83, Zinder; tel. 51-00-78.

INDUSTRIAL AND TRADE ORGANIZATIONS

Centre Nigérien du Commerce Extérieur (CNCE): place de la Concertation, BP 12480, Niamey; tel. 73-22-88; fax 73-46-68; f. 1984; promotes and co-ordinates all aspects of foreign trade; Dir AÏSSA DIALLO.

Société Nationale de Commerce et de Production du Niger (COPRO-Niger): Niamey; tel. 73-28-41; fax 73-57-71; f. 1962; monopoly importer of foodstuffs; cap. 1,000m. francs CFA; 47% state-owned; Man. Dir DJIBRILLA HIMA.

EMPLOYERS' ORGANIZATIONS

Syndicat des Commerçants Importateurs et Exportateurs du Niger (SCIMPEXNI): Chambre de Commerce, d'Agriculture, d'Industrie et d'Artisanat du Niger, Niamey; tel. 73-33-17; Pres. M. SILVA; Sec.-Gen. INOUSSA MAÏGA.

Syndicat National des Petites et Moyennes Entreprises et Industries Nigériennes (SYNAPEMEIN): Chambre de Commerce, d'Agriculture, d'Industrie et d'Artisanat du Niger, Niamey; Pres. SEYBOU SLAEY; Sec.-Gen. ADOLPHE SAGBO.

Syndicat Patronal des Entreprises et Industries du Niger (SPEIN): BP 415, Niamey; tel. 73-24-01; fax 73-47-07; f. 1994; Pres. AMADOU OUSMANE; Sec.-Gen. NOUHOU TARI.

UTILITIES

Electricity

Société Nigérienne d'Electricité (NIGELEC): 46 ave du Gen. de Gaulle, BP 11202, Niamey; tel. 72-26-92; fax 72-32-88; e-mail nigelec@intnet.ne; f. 1968; 95% state-owned; 51% transfer to private ownership proposed for 2003; production and distribution of electricity; Dir-Gen. IBRAHIM FOUKORI.

Water

Société de Patrimoine des Eaux du Niger (SPEN): Immeuble SONARA 11, BP 10738, Niamey; tel. 73-43-40; fax 73-46-40; fmrly Société Nationale des Eaux; 51% owned by Vivendi (France); production and distribution of drinking water; Pres. ABARY DAN BOUZOUA SOULEYMENE; Dir-Gen. SEYNI SALOU.

TRADE UNION FEDERATIONS

Confédération des Syndicats Libres des Travailleurs du Niger (CSLTN): BP 12271, Niamey; tel. 73-26-15; fax 72-21-71; f. 1993; 4 affiliates.

Confédération des Travailleurs du Niger (CTN): Niamey; Sec.-Gen. ISSOUFOU SEYBOU.

Union des Syndicats des Travailleurs du Niger (USTN): Bourse du Travail, BP 388, Niamey; tel. and fax 73-52-56; f. 1960; Sec.-Gen. El Hadj MAHAMANE MANSOUR; 28,000 mems in 37 affiliated unions.

Transport

ROADS

Niger is crossed by highways running from east to west and from north to south, giving access to neighbouring countries. A road is under construction to Lomé, Togo, via Burkina Faso, and the 428-km Zinder–Agadez road, scheduled to form part of the Trans-Sahara Highway, has been upgraded. Niger and Algeria appealed jointly in mid-1998 for international aid to fund construction of the Trans-Sahara Highway, development of which was suspended in the mid-

1990s because of the conflict in northern Niger. Some 2,100m. francs CFA of the budget for 2001 was allocated to road maintenance.

In 2000 there were an estimated 14,000 km of classified roads, of which 3,621 km were paved.

Société Nationale des Transports Nigériens (SNTN): BP 135, Niamey; tel. 72-24-55; fax 74-47-07; e-mail sntn@intnet.ne; f. 1963; operates passenger and freight road-transport services; 49% state-owned; Chair. MOHAMED ABDOULAHI; Man. Dir MAINA ARI ADJI KIRGAM.

RAILWAYS

There are as yet no railways in Niger.

Organisation Commune Bénin-Niger pour le Réseau Ferroviaire (OCBN): BP 38, Niamey; tel. 73-27-90; f. 1959; 50% owned by Govt of Niger, 50% by Govt of Benin; manages the Benin-Niger railway project (begun in 1978); transfer to private ownership proposed; Dir-Gen. JOSEPH KETCHIAN.

INLAND WATERWAYS

The River Niger is navigable for 300 km within the country. Access to the sea is available by a river route from Gaya, in south-western Niger, to the coast at Port Harcourt, Nigeria, between September and March. Port facilities at Lomé, Togo, are used as a commercial outlet for land-locked Niger: some 126,000 metric tons of goods imported by Niger pass through Lomé annually. An agreement providing import facilities at the port of Tema was signed with Ghana in November 1986.

Niger-Transit (NITRA): Zone Industrielle, BP 560, Niamey; tel. 73-22-53; fax 73-26-38; f. 1974; 48% owned by SNTN; customs agent, freight-handling, warehousing, etc. manages Nigerien port facilities at Lomé, Togo; Pres. OUMAROU ALI BEÏOLI; Man. Dir SADE FATIMATA.

Société Nigérienne des Transports Fluviaux et Maritimes (SNTFM): Niamey; tel. 73-39-69; river and sea transport; cap. 64.6m. francs CFA; 99% state-owned; Man. Dir BERTRAND DEJEAN.

CIVIL AVIATION

There are international airports at Niamey (Hamani Diori), Agadez (Mano Dayak) and Zinder, and major domestic airports at Diffa, Maradi and Tahoua.

Air Inter Afrique: Niamey; tel. 73-85-85; fax 73-69-73; f. 2001; operates services within West Africa; CEO CHEIKH OUSMANE DIALLO.

Air Inter Niger: Agadez; f. 1997 to operate services to Tamanrasset (Algeria).

Air Niger International: Niamey; f. 2002; principal shareholder is Conseil Nigérien des Utilisateurs des Transports Publics.

Nigeravia SA: BP 10454, Niamey; tel. 73-30-64; fax 74-18-42; e-mail nigavia@intnet.ne; f. 1991 as Trans-Niger Aviation; operates domestic and regional services; Man. Dir JEAN SYLVESTRE.

Société Nigérienne des Transports Aériens (SONITA): Niamey; f. 1991; owned by private Nigerien (81%) and Cypriot (19%) interests; operates domestic and regional services; Man. Dir ABDOULAYE MAIGA GOUDOUBABA.

Tourism

The Aïr and Ténéré Nature Reserve, covering an area of 77,000 sq km, was established in 1988. Tourism was hampered by insecurity in the north and east during the 1990s. However, the number of foreign arrivals at hotels and similar establishments increased from 39,190 in 1997 to 42,433 in 1999, when tourism receipts amounted to US $24m.

Office National du Tourisme (ONT): BP 612, ave Luebke, Niamey; tel. 73-24-47; fax 73-39-40.

NIGERIA

Introductory Survey

Location, Climate, Language, Religion, Flag, Capital

The Federal Republic of Nigeria is a West African coastal state on the shores of the Gulf of Guinea, with Benin to the west, Niger to the north, Chad to the north-east, and Cameroon to the east and south-east. The climate is tropical in the southern coastal areas, with an average annual temperature of 32°C (90°F) and high humidity. It is drier and semi-tropical in the north. Average annual rainfall is more than 2,500 mm (98 ins) in parts of the south-east, but in certain areas of the north is as low as 600mm (24 ins). In 1963 the most widely spoken languages were Hausa (20.9%), Yoruba (20.3%), Ibo (16.6%) and Fulani (8.6%). English is the country's official language. In 1963 the principal religious groups were Muslims (47.2%) and Christians (34.5%), while 18% of the total population followed animist beliefs. The national flag (proportions 1 by 2) has three equal vertical stripes, of green, white and green. The capital is Abuja, to which the Federal Government was formally transferred in December 1991; however, many non-government institutions remained in the former capital, Lagos.

Recent History

The territory of present-day Nigeria, except for the section of former German-controlled Cameroon (see below), was conquered by the United Kingdom, in several stages, during the second half of the 19th century and the first decade of the 20th century. The British dependencies of Northern and Southern Nigeria were merged into a single territory in 1914, administered largely by traditional native rulers, under the supervision of the colonial authorities. In 1947 the United Kingdom introduced a new Nigerian Constitution, establishing a federal system of government, based on three regions: Northern, Western and Eastern. The federal arrangement was an attempt to reconcile religious and regional tensions, and to accommodate Nigeria's diverse ethnic groups, notably the Ibo (in the east), the Yoruba (in the west) and the Hausa and Fulani (in the north). The Northern Region, which was predominantly Muslim, contained about one-half of Nigeria's total population.

In 1954 the federation became self-governing, and the first federal Prime Minister, Alhaji Abubakar Tafawa Balewa (a Muslim northerner), was appointed in August 1957. A constitutional conference, convened in 1958, agreed that Nigeria should become independent in 1960, and elections to an enlarged federal legislature took place in December 1959. The Northern People's Congress (NPC), which was politically dominant in the north, became the single largest party in the new legislature, although lacking an overall majority. Tafawa Balewa (a prominent member of the NPC) continued to head a coalition government of the NPC and the National Council for Nigeria and the Cameroons (NCNC), which attracted most of its support in the Eastern Region.

On 1 October 1960, as scheduled, the Federation of Nigeria achieved independence, initially as a constitutional monarchy. In June 1961 the northern part of the UN Trust Territory of British Cameroons was incorporated into Nigeria's Northern Region as the province of Sardauna, and in August 1963 a fourth region, the Mid-Western Region, was created by dividing the existing Western Region. On 1 October a revised Constitution was adopted, and the country was renamed the Federal Republic of Nigeria, although it remained a member of the Commonwealth. Dr Nnamdi Azikiwe of the NCNC took office as Nigeria's first President (then a non-executive post).

The first national election after independence, to the federal House of Representatives, took place in December 1964. Widespread electoral malpractice and violence were reported during the election campaign, prompting a boycott of the poll by the main opposition grouping, the United Progressive Grand Alliance (UPGA), a coalition of four parties, dominated by the NCNC (previously renamed the National Convention of Nigerian Citizens). The election resulted in a large majority for the Nigerian National Alliance, a seven-party coalition, which was dominated by the NPC.

On 15 January 1966 Tafawa Balewa's civilian Government was overthrown (and the Prime Minister killed) by junior army officers (mainly Ibos from the Eastern Region). Surviving federal ministers transferred power to the Commander-in-Chief of the Army, Maj.-Gen. Johnson Aguiyi-Aronsi (an Ibo), who formed a Supreme Military Council, suspended the Constitution and imposed emergency rule. On 29 July Aguiyi-Aronsi was killed in a further coup, staged by northern troops, and power was transferred to the Chief of Staff of the Army, Lt-Col (later Gen.) Yakubu Gowon, a Christian northerner. Gowon subsequently reintroduced the federal system, which had been suppressed after the January coup.

In early 1967 there was a rapid deterioration in relations between the Federal Government and the military Governor of the Eastern Region, Lt-Col Chukwuemeka Odumegwu-Ojukwu, following a dispute between the federal and regional authorities concerning the distribution of petroleum revenues. The increasing tensions in Nigeria's federal structure prompted Gowon to propose the replacement of the four existing regions by 12 states. On 30 May Ojukwu announced the secession of the Eastern Region from the Federation, and proclaimed its independence as the Republic of Biafra. Fighting between the forces of Biafra and the Federal Government began in July; federal forces eventually suppressed the rebellion in December 1969, following Ojukwu's departure into exile, and Biafran forces formally surrendered in January 1970. Meanwhile, the proposed 12-state structure replaced the four federal regions in April 1968.

In October 1974 Gowon postponed the restoration of civilian rule indefinitely. However, increasing opposition to Gowon's regime culminated in his overthrow by other senior officers in a bloodless coup on 29 July 1975. He was replaced as Head of State by Brig. (later Gen.) Murtala Ramat Muhammed, hitherto Federal Commissioner for Communications, who, in October 1975, announced a detailed timetable for a transition to civilian rule. In February 1976, however, Muhammed was assassinated during an unsuccessful coup attempt. Power was immediately assumed by Lt-Gen. (later Gen.) Olusegun Obasanjo, the Chief of Staff of the Armed Forces, who promised to fulfil his predecessor's programme for the restoration of civilian rule.

In March 1976 the number of states was increased from 12 to 19, and it was announced that a new federal capital was to be constructed near Abuja, in central Nigeria. In September 1978 a new Constitution was promulgated, and the state of emergency, in force since 1966, was ended. At the same time the 12-year ban on political activity was revoked. Elections took place in July 1979 to a new bicameral National Assembly (comprising a Senate and a House of Representatives), and for State Assemblies and State Governors. The National Party of Nigeria (NPN), which included many prominent members of the former NPC, received the most widespread support in all the elections. The NPN's presidential candidate, Alhaji Shehu Shagari (who had served as an NPC federal minister prior to 1966 and as a federal commissioner in 1970–75), was elected to the new post of executive President in August 1979. He took office on 1 October, whereupon the military regime transferred power to the newly elected civilian authorities and the new Constitution came into effect.

In August–September 1983 local government, state and federal elections took place. In the presidential election Shagari was returned for a second term of office. The NPN won 13 of the 19 state governorships, and achieved substantial majorities in the Senate and the House of Representatives. On 31 December, however, the civilian Government was deposed in a bloodless military coup, led by Maj.-Gen. Muhammadu Buhari, who had been Federal Commissioner for Petroleum in 1976–78. The Government was replaced by a Supreme Military Council (SMC), headed by Buhari; the National Assembly was dissolved, and all political parties were banned. Hundreds of politicians, including former President Shagari, were arrested on charges of corruption. Legislation that severely restricted the freedom of the press was introduced, and several journalists were subsequently detained.

On 27 August 1985 Buhari's administration was deposed in a bloodless coup, led by Maj.-Gen. (later Gen.) Ibrahim Babangida, the Chief of Staff of the Army and a member of the SMC. A new military administration, the Armed Forces Ruling Council (AFRC), was established, with Babangida as President. The decree on press censorship was revoked, and a number of journalists and other political detainees were released. (Shagari and 17 other former government officials were released in July 1986, having been acquitted of corruption charges.) In December 1985 the AFRC suppressed a coup attempt by disaffected army officers; 10 of the alleged conspirators were later executed.

In February 1986 Babangida's announcement that Nigeria had been accepted as a full member of the Organization of the Islamic Conference (OIC, see p. 295) prompted unrest in the non-Muslim sector of the population, reflecting concern at increasing 'Islamization' in Nigeria. In July 1987 Babangida announced details of a programme to transfer power to a civilian government on 1 October 1992. Local government elections, to be contested on a non-party basis, were to take place in late 1987. The ban on party politics was to be revoked in 1989, and a maximum of two political parties were to be approved to contest elections. In August 1987 the Government established a National Electoral Commission (NEC); in September the number of states was increased to 21. The local government elections were contested by some 15,000 non-party candidates in December. In May 1988 a Constituent Assembly, comprising 450 members elected by local government and 117 members nominated by the AFRC, commenced preparation of a draft constitution, which was to be based on proposals submitted by a constitutional committee. The progress of the Constituent Assembly was impeded, however, by controversy over the proposed inclusion of Islamic (*Shari'a*) courts in the new document.

In April 1989 the Constituent Assembly presented a draft Constitution to Babangida. In May Babangida announced the end of the prohibition on political parties, and the new Constitution (which was scheduled to take effect on 1 October 1992) was promulgated. Only 13 of the existing parties managed to fulfil the requirements for registration by the stipulated date in July 1989. In September the NEC submitted six political associations to the AFRC; in October, however, it was decided to dissolve all the newly formed political parties, on the grounds that they were too closely associated with discredited former parties. In their place, the AFRC created two new organizations, the Social Democratic Party (SDP) and the National Republican Convention (NRC), provoking widespread criticism. Further local elections, due to take place in December, were postponed until late 1990. In December 1989, in an extensive government reorganization, Babangida personally assumed the defence portfolio (thereby gaining greater control over the security forces), in an apparent attempt to pre-empt unrest during the transition to civilian rule.

On 22 April 1990 a coup attempt, staged by junior army officers, led by Maj. Gideon Orkar (who claimed to be acting on behalf of Nigerians in the centre and south of the country) was suppressed; some 160 members of the armed forces were subsequently arrested. In July, following their conviction by a military tribunal on charges of conspiring to commit treason, 69 prisoners, including Orkar, were executed.

Following the completion of registration for membership of the SDP and the NRC, party executives were elected for each state in July 1990, replacing government-appointed administrators. Later in August Babangida implemented extensive changes in the Government: nine ministers were dismissed, and the position of Chief of General Staff, held by Vice-Adm. (later Adm.) Augustus Aikhomu, was replaced by the office of Vice-President (to which Aikhomu was immediately appointed). Babangida subsequently announced plans to reduce substantially the size of the armed forces. In September, in an attempt to restrict military influence within the Government, three ministers were obliged to retire from the armed forces. Local government elections took place in early December; only an estimated 20% of registered voters participated.

In October 1990 the Movement for the Survival of the Ogoni People (MOSOP) was formed to co-ordinate opposition to the exploitation of petroleum reserves in territory of the Ogoni ethnic group (Ogoniland), in the south-central Rivers State, by the Shell Petroleum Development Company of Nigeria. Following a demonstration, organized by MOSOP in protest at environmental damage resulting from petroleum production, it was reported that security forces had killed some 80 Ogonis. In April 1991 some 130 people, mainly Christians, were killed in clashes between Muslims and Christians in the northern state of Bauchi.

In September 1991, in an apparent attempt to relieve ethnic tensions prior to the elections, nine new states were created, increasing the size of the federation to 30 states. On 12 December the Federal Government was formally transferred from Lagos to Abuja, the new federal capital. In the gubernatorial and state assembly elections, which took place on 14 December, the NRC secured a majority in 14 State Assemblies, while the SDP won control of 16 State Assemblies; candidates representing the NRC were elected as State Governors in 16 states. Both the SDP and the NRC disputed the election results in a number of states, on the grounds of electoral malpractice.

In January 1992 Babangida formed a new National Council of Ministers, in which several portfolios were restructured. In the same month the Government announced that elections to a bicameral National Assembly, comprising a 593-member House of Representatives and a 91-member Senate, would take place on 7 November, and would be followed by a presidential election on 5 December. The formal installation of a civilian government (and the implementation of the new Constitution) was consequently scheduled for 2 January 1993, rather than, as previously planned, on 1 October 1992.

In May 1992 some 300 people were reported to have been killed in renewed violence between the Hausa ethnic group (which was predominantly Muslim) and the Kataf (predominantly Christian) in Kaduna. Shortly afterwards the Government announced that all organizations with religious or ethnic interests were to be prohibited. Later in May further rioting occurred in Lagos, following the arrest of the Chairman of the Campaign for Democracy (CD—an informal alliance of Nigerian human rights organizations, which had been established in late 1991), Dr Beko Ransome-Kuti, who had accused the Government of deliberately provoking unrest in order to delay the transition to civilian rule. In June several human rights activists, including Ransome-Kuti, were released, pending their trial (which was later deferred) on charges of conspiring to incite the previous month's riots.

At elections to the bicameral National Assembly, which had been brought forward to 4 July 1992, the SDP secured a majority in both chambers, with 52 seats in the Senate and 314 seats in the House of Representatives, while the NRC won 37 seats in the Senate and 275 seats in the House of Representatives. The formal inauguration of the National Assembly, due to take place on 27 July, was, however, postponed until 5 December, the stipulated date for the presidential election, prompting concern at the AFRC's apparent reluctance to relinquish legislative power.

Voting in primary elections for presidential candidates took place in September 1992. In October, however, shortly before a final round of voting was due to take place, Babangida suspended the primary elections, pending the outcome of an investigation by the NEC into alleged incidents of electoral malpractice. Later that month, following a report by the NEC that confirmed malpractice, Babangida announced that the leaders of the NRC and the SDP were to be removed from office.

In November 1992 Babangida postponed the presidential election until 12 June 1993. On 2 January 1993 (hitherto the stipulated date for the completion of the transition to civilian rule) the AFRC was to be replaced by a 14-member ruling National Defence and Security Council (NDSC), and the existing Council of Ministers by a civilian Transitional Council, pending the installation of a civilian government, which was to take place on 27 August. Babangida further announced that the 23 prospective presidential candidates who had contested the discredited primary elections were to be prohibited from political activity during the transitional period: new candidates were to be nominated at a series of party congresses, to be conducted at ward, local government, state and national level.

On 5 December 1992 Babangida inaugurated the National Assembly. On 2 January 1993 the AFRC and the Council of Ministers were duly dissolved, and the Transitional Council and the NDSC (which comprised the President, Vice-President, the heads of the armed forces and senior members of the Transitional Council) were formally installed. The Chairman of the Transitional Council, Chief Ernest Adegunle Shonekan, was officially designated Head of Government (although supreme power was vested in the NDSC and the President), while Aikhomu retained the post of Vice-President. Legislation approved by the National Assembly was henceforth to be endorsed by the NDSC, and subsequently by Babangida. In accordance with the new programme for the transition to civilian rule, party congresses to select presidential candidates were conducted in February–March; the NRC elected a banker, Alhaji Bashir Othman Tofa, and the SDP a Muslim business executive, Chief Moshood Kastumawo Olawale Abiola, to contest the presidential election.

In June 1993 the Association for a Better Nigeria (ABN), a newly formed pro-Babangida pressure group, obtained an interim injunction in the Abuja High Court prohibiting the NEC from conducting the presidential election, pending an appeal by the ABN for the extension of military rule until 1997. The NEC, however, announced that the injunction was invalid, and that the election would take place as scheduled. Owing, in part, to confusion caused by the court action, only about 30% of the registered electorate voted in the presidential election, which took place on 12 June. Initial results indicated that Abiola had secured the majority of votes in 11 of 15 states. Shortly afterwards, however, the ABN obtained a further injunction suspending the promulgation of the election results. The court ruling prompted widespread demands that the results be released, and several applications were lodged in an attempt to reverse the injunction. Later in June the CD released election results (which it claimed to be official) indicating that Abiola had secured the majority of votes in 19 states, and Tofa in 11; Abiola subsequently proclaimed himself President. Amid increasing tension, the NEC announced that it was to present an application to the Court of Appeal to contest the injunction. Shortly afterwards the Abuja High Court declared the election results to be invalid, on the grounds that the NEC had failed to comply with the ruling that had cancelled the poll.

On 23 June 1993, in what it claimed was an effort to uphold the judicial system, the NDSC annulled the results of the presidential election, suspended the NEC and halted all proceedings pertaining to the election. Babangida subsequently announced that the poll had been marred by widespread irregularities (contradicting reports by international observers that voting had been conducted fairly), but insisted that he remained committed to the transition to civilian rule on 27 August. The SDP and the NRC were to select two new presidential candidates, under the supervision of a reconstituted NEC; prospective candidates would be required to comply with new electoral regulations, which effectively precluded Abiola and Tofa from contesting a further poll. (Abiola, however, continued to claim, with much popular support, that he had been legitimately elected to the presidency.) The annulment of the election attracted international criticism, particularly from the USA and the United Kingdom, which announced the imposition of military sanctions against Nigeria.

In July 1993 a general strike, organized by the CD in support of demands that Abiola be installed as President, culminated in rioting; some 20 people were subsequently killed when security forces violently suppressed the unrest. Shortly afterwards the NDSC announced that a new presidential election was to take place on 14 August, in order to fulfil the pledge to transfer power to a civilian government on 27 August. The new electoral schedule was generally viewed with scepticism, while the SDP declared its intention to boycott the poll, on the grounds that it had legitimately won the previous election. Legal proceedings initiated by Abiola in the Lagos Supreme Court, in an attempt to uphold his claim to the presidency, were abandoned after Babangida introduced legislation that prohibited any legal challenges to the annulment of the election.

At the end of July 1993 Babangida announced that an Interim National Government (ING) was to be established, on the grounds that there was insufficient time to permit the scheduled transition to civilian rule on 27 August. In August the CD continued its campaign of civil disobedience in protest at the annulment of the election, appealing for a three-day general strike (which was widely observed in the south-west of the country, where Abiola received most popular support). Later in August Babangida resigned, reportedly as a result of pressure from prominent members of the NDSC, notably the Secretary of Defence, Gen. Sani Abacha. On 27 August a 32-member interim Federal Executive Council (FEC), headed by Shonekan, was installed; the new administration, which included several members of the former Transitional Council, was to supervise the organization of local government elections later that year and a presidential election in early 1994, while the transitional period for the return to civilian rule was extended to 31 March 1994. (Shonekan was later designated Head of State and Commander-in-Chief of the Armed Forces.) Supporters of democracy criticized the inclusion in the ING of several members of the

now-dissolved NDSC, including Abacha, who was appointed to the new post of Vice-President.

At the end of August 1993 the CD staged a further three-day strike, while the Nigerian Labour Congress (NLC) and the National Union of Petroleum and Natural Gas Workers (NUPENG) also announced industrial action in support of the installation of a civilian administration, headed by Abiola. The combined strike action resulted in a severe fuel shortage and the suspension of most economic activity. Following the establishment of the ING, Shonekan pledged his commitment to the democratic process and, in an effort to restore order, initiated negotiations with the NLC and effected the release of several journalists and prominent members of the CD, including Ransome-Kuti, who had been arrested in July. In early September the NLC and NUPENG provisionally suspended strike action, after the ING agreed to consider their demands.

In September 1993 a series of military appointments, which included the nomination of Lt-Gen. Oladipo Diya to the office of Chief of Defence Staff, effectively removed supporters of Babangida from significant posts within the armed forces, thereby strengthening Abacha's position. Later in September the NRC and SDP agreed to a new timetable whereby local government elections and a presidential election would take place concurrently in February 1994. The CD subsequently announced the resumption of strike action in support of demands for the installation of Abiola as President; an ensuing demonstration by supporters of the CD in Lagos was violently dispersed by security forces, and Ransome-Kuti and other prominent members of the CD were again arrested. In October 1993 the SDP (which had previously demonstrated limited support for Abiola, as a result of dissension within the party) demanded that he be inaugurated as President, and refused to participate in the new elections.

In November 1993 the President of the Senate, a strong supporter of Abiola, was removed from office. Shortly afterwards the Lagos High Court ruled in favour of an application by Abiola, declaring the establishment of the ING to be invalid under the terms of the 1979 Constitution (whereby the President of the Senate was to act as interim Head of State). In the same month the ING dissolved the government councils, prior to local elections, and withdrew state subsidies on petroleum products. The resultant dramatic increase in the price of fuel prompted widespread anti-Government demonstrations, and the NLC announced the resumption of strike action. Meanwhile, the scheduled revision of the electoral register ended in failure, owing to a boycott by supporters of the SDP, and it became apparent that the new schedule for the transition to civilian rule was unviable.

On 17 November 1993, following a meeting with senior military officials, Shonekan resigned as Head of State and immediately transferred power to Abacha (confirming widespread speculation that the latter had effectively assumed control of the Government following Babangida's resignation). On the following day Abacha dissolved all state institutions that had been established under the transitional process, replaced the State Governors with military administrators, prohibited political activity (thereby proscribing the NRC and the SDP), and announced the formation of a Provisional Ruling Council (PRC), which was to comprise senior military officials and principal members of a new FEC. He insisted, however, that he intended to relinquish power to a civilian government, and pledged to convene a conference with a mandate to determine the constitutional future of the country. Restrictions on the media were revoked. On 21 November Abacha introduced legislation that formally restored the 1979 Constitution and provided for the establishment of the new government organs. In an apparent attempt to counter domestic and international criticism, several prominent supporters of Abiola, including Kingibe, and four former members of the ING were appointed to the PRC and FEC, which were installed on 24 November. Abacha subsequently removed 17 senior military officers who were believed to be loyal to Babangida. In the same month the NLC agreed to abandon strike action after the Government acted to limit the increase in the price of petroleum products.

In December 1993 the United Kingdom announced that member nations of the European Union (EU, see p. 199) were to impose further sanctions against Nigeria, including restrictions on the export of armaments. In April 1994 the Government announced a programme for the establishment of a National Constitutional Conference (NCC): some 273 delegates were to be elected in May, while 96 delegates were to be nominated by the

Government from a list of eligible citizens submitted by each state. The NCC was to be convened at the end of June, and was to submit recommendations, including proposals for a new draft constitution, to the PRC in October. The ban on political activity was to end in January 1995. In May 1994 a new pro-democracy organization, comprising former politicians, retired military officers and human rights activists, the National Democratic Coalition (NADECO), demanded that Abacha relinquish power by the end of that month and urged a boycott of the NCC. In the same month the leader of MOSOP, Ken Saro-Wiwa, was arrested in connection with the deaths, during political violence, of four Ogoni traditional leaders (who were reported to have a moderate attitude to the military authorities). Saro-Wiwa was alleged to have incited his supporters to commit the murders, although many critics of the Nigerian authorities believed that the charges had been fabricated by the Government in an effort to suppress the activities of MOSOP.

In June 1994 a number of prominent opposition members, including Ransome-Kuti, were also arrested after the CD urged a campaign of civil disobedience, which received the support of NADECO. Following a public gathering, at which Abiola declared himself Head of State and President of a parallel government, a warrant was issued for his arrest on charges of treason; the authorities claimed that he intended to organize an uprising to force the military administration to relinquish power. Later in June he was arrested by security forces, prompting protests from pro-democracy organizations and from the Governments of the United Kingdom and the USA. Further demonstrations in support of demands for an immediate suspension of military rule and the installation of Abiola as President ensued. At the initial session of the NCC, which was convened as scheduled, Abacha pledged to relinquish power at a date that would be determined by the conference.

In July 1994 Abiola was arraigned before a special High Court in Abuja and charged with treason. NUPENG initiated strike action in support of demands for Abiola's release and installation as President, and an improvement in government investment in the petroleum industry; the strike was subsequently joined by members of the Petroleum and Natural Gas Senior Staff Association. By mid-July several affiliated unions had joined the strike action, resulting in an effective suspension of economic activity in Lagos and other regions in the south-west of the country. At the end of the month it was reported that some 20 people had been killed when security forces violently suppressed anti-Government demonstrations. In September the union leaders announced the suspension of strike action, in view of the ensuing widespread hardship. In the same month Abacha promulgated legislation to extend the period of detention without trial to three months, prohibit legal action challenging government decisions, and officially ban three independent newspaper groups. Later in September Abacha enlarged the PRC from 11 to 25 members, all senior military officials.

Meanwhile, Abiola's trial was repeatedly adjourned following his legal action, in August 1994, challenging the jurisdiction of the special High Court in Abuja with regard to an offence that had been allegedly committed in Lagos. Despite reports that he was suffering from a medical condition necessitating immediate treatment, Abiola had refused to accept the stipulated conditions for bail, requiring him to refrain from political activity. In September Wole Soyinka, a prominent writer and critic of the Government, challenged the legitimacy of the Abacha administration at the Federal High Court in Lagos. (Soyinka was subsequently prevented from leaving the country.)

In January 1995 Abacha announced the adoption of a new programme of economic reforms, designed to secure the approval of the IMF and the World Bank. In the same month the NCC, which had been scheduled to complete the preparations for a draft constitution in October 1994, adjourned until March 1995, prompting increasing concern that its protracted deliberations served to prolong the tenure of the military administration. The trial of Saro-Wiwa and a further 14 Ogoni campaigners, on charges of complicity in the murder of the four Ogoni traditional leaders, commenced in mid-January; the defendants were to challenge the legitimacy of the government-appointed Special Military Tribunal, at Port Harcourt. In February the Federal Court of Appeal dismissed Abiola's legal action challenging the jurisdiction of the High Court in Abuja.

In February 1995 Abacha dissolved the FEC, after a number of ministers announced their intention of engaging in political activity in the forthcoming transitional period. In March some 150 military officials were arrested, apparently in response to

widespread disaffection within the armed forces. The authorities subsequently confirmed reports (which had initially been denied) of a conspiracy to overthrow the Government. (However, opponents of the Abacha administration claimed that the Government had fabricated a coup attempt, with the aim of suppressing dissent within the armed forces.) The arrest of the former Head of State Olusegun Obasanjo and his former deputy, Maj.-Gen. (retd) Shehu Musa Yar'Adua, together with other prominent critics of the Government, prompted international protests. In mid-March Abacha appointed a new, 36-member FEC, which included a number of civilians who were believed to support an extended period of military rule. In May more than 40 people, including Obasanjo, Yar'Adua and Ransome-Kuti, were arraigned before a Special Military Tribunal in Lagos, in connection with the alleged coup attempt in March.

In late June 1995 the NCC submitted a draft Constitution to Abacha, who rescinded the ban on political activity; a programme for transition to civilian rule was to be announced on 1 October. (A number of political organizations subsequently emerged, in response to the removal of the ban.) At the end of June it was reported that Yar'Adua and a further 13 military officers had been sentenced to death for conspiring to overthrow the Government, while several other defendants, including Obasanjo and Ransome-Kuti, received custodial terms. The Government subsequently confirmed that a total of 43 had been convicted in connection with the coup attempt, prompting protests and appeals for clemency from the international community. On 1 October, however, Abacha officially commuted the death sentences to terms of imprisonment and reduced the custodial sentences (although he did not withdraw the capital charges against Abiola). At the same time he announced the approval of the new Constitution (which was due to be formally adopted later that year) and the adoption of a three-year programme for transition to civilian rule, whereby a new President was to be inaugurated on 1 October 1998, following elections at local, state and national level. (The duration of the transitional period was received with disapproval by the international community.)

At the end of October 1995 Saro-Wiwa and a further eight Ogoni activists were sentenced to death by the Special Military Tribunal in Port Harcourt, having been convicted of involvement in the murder of the four Ogoni leaders in May 1994; six defendants were acquitted. Although the defendants were not implicated directly in the incident, the nine convictions were based on the premise that the MOSOP activists had effectively incited the killings. An international campaign against the convictions, and numerous appeals for clemency, ensued. However, on 10 November the nine convicted Ogonis were executed, prompting immediate condemnation by the international community. Nigeria was suspended from the Commonwealth, and threatened with expulsion if the Government failed to restore democracy within a period of two years. Later that month the EU reaffirmed its commitment to existing sanctions that had been imposed in 1993 (notably an embargo on the export of armaments and military equipment to Nigeria), and extended visa restrictions to civilian members of the administration. The Governments of the USA, South Africa and the EU member nations recalled their diplomatic representatives from Nigeria in protest at the executions. The Nigerian Government condemned the imposition of sanctions and, in turn, withdrew its diplomatic representatives from the USA, South Africa and the EU member countries. Additional security forces were dispatched to Ogoniland to deter any protests against the executions, while a further 19 Ogonis were charged with complicity in the May 1994 murders. (However, their trial was subsequently postponed, pending an appeal to the effect that the Special Military Tribunal at Port Harcourt was unconstitutional.)

In December 1995 Abacha approved the establishment of a number of committees, including the National Electoral Commission of Nigeria (NECON), to implement the transitional programme. NECON subsequently divided the country into seven regions (rather than six, as originally envisaged), prior to local government elections in early 1996. Later in December the Commonwealth Ministerial Action Group (CMAG—comprising the ministers with responsibility for foreign affairs of eight member countries), which had been established at the summit meeting in November, met to discuss further measures to be taken if the Nigerian Government failed to restore democracy, and announced that five of the ministers were to visit Nigeria to initiate negotiations with the military administration. (The diplomatic representatives who had been withdrawn following the executions in November subsequently returned to Lagos, in order to facilitate the Commonwealth mission.) In January 1996 the Government refused the Commonwealth delegation permission to visit Nigeria, and demanded that the decision to suspend Nigeria be reviewed. At the end of January the Government announced that the new Constitution would be formally adopted in 1998, upon the completion of the transitional period (rather than in late 1995).

In February 1996 the 19 Ogonis who remained in detention pending their trial appealed to the Commonwealth for assistance in securing their release. In March local government elections were contested, on a non-party basis, as part of the transitional programme; although opposition leaders had urged a boycott, NECON claimed that a high level of voter participation had been recorded. In April a UN mission visited Ogoniland to investigate the trial and execution of the nine Ogoni activists in 1995; it was reported that Ogoni and other opposition representatives were prevented from meeting the delegation. Later that month, following the Government's continued refusal to enter into negotiations with CMAG regarding human rights issues and the restoration of democracy, the Commonwealth proposed to adopt a number of sanctions against Nigeria. In May the PRC was reorganized, following the removal of a number of senior military officials.

In early June 1996 Abiola's wife, Kudirat, who had been a prominent critic of the administration, was killed by unidentified assailants. Although the authorities instigated an investigation into the incident, widespread speculation that the Government had ordered the killing increased general hostility towards the regime. Abiola's son and a number of his other immediate relatives were subsequently arrested, apparently on suspicion that they had instigated the killing as a result of feuding within the family. Later in June Nigerian officials met CMAG in an attempt to avert the threatened imposition of sanctions against Nigeria; the Nigerian delegation demanded that Nigeria be readmitted to the Commonwealth in exchange for the Government's adoption of the programme for transition to civilian rule by October 1998. The Commonwealth dismissed the programme as unsatisfactory, but remained divided regarding the adoption of consequent measures. It was finally agreed that the Commonwealth would suspend the adoption of sanctions, but that the situation would subsequently be reviewed. (Canada, however, announced its opposition to this decision and unilaterally imposed a number of sanctions.) At the end of September 1996 CMAG agreed that the Commonwealth delegation would visit Nigeria, despite conditions imposed by the military authorities, which insisted that it would not be permitted access to opposition activists or political prisoners.

In June 1996 legislation governing the formation of political parties was promulgated. Five of 15 political organizations that applied for registration were granted legal status in September. NADECO condemned the disqualification of the remaining 10 parties, which were subsequently dissolved by decree; it was widely believed that the associations that had been granted registration were largely sympathetic towards the military administration. In October Abacha announced the creation of a further six states, increasing the total size of the federation to 36 states.

In February 1997 Abacha attributed delays in the holding of local government elections to a further series of bomb attacks in Lagos, in which, it was reported, about six people had been killed; he also indicated that he intended to contest the presidential election in 1998. International observers declared that the local government elections, which took place in March 1997, had been conducted peacefully; it was reported that the United Nigerian Congress Party (UNCP) had secured the highest number of seats in the municipal councils. In the same month, after repeatedly accusing NADECO of responsibility for the bomb attacks, the Government charged Soyinka (who was now in exile) and a further 15 pro-democracy activists, including several NADECO leaders, of treason in connection with the incidents. (Soyinka and a further three of the accused were charged *in absentia*.) The Canadian Government subsequently suspended its diplomatic representation in Nigeria.

In early 1997 escalating tension between the Ijaw and Itsekiri ethnic groups in the town of Warri, in south-western Nigeria, severely disrupted operations in the region of the Niger Delta by the Shell Petroleum Development Company of Nigeria. In March a demonstration by members of the Ijaw ethnic group in Warri, in protest at the relocation of local government headquarters from Ijaw to Itsekiri territory, precipitated violent clashes. Protesters seized Shell installations and took about 100

employees hostage, in an attempt to force the Government to accede to their demands. A curfew was subsequently imposed in the region in an attempt to restore order. By mid-April it was reported that about 70 people had been killed in the disturbances, while the disruption in petroleum production had resulted in a national fuel shortage, effectively suspending the transportation system in much of the country. Further clashes and attacks on Shell installations in May were reported. Later that month the authorities established a commission of inquiry to investigate the cause of the unrest and submit recommendations for restoring order in the region.

In April 1997 Abacha issued a decree empowering himself to replace the mayors who had been elected in March and to dissolve local municipal councils if he considered that they were acting contrary to national interests. In May some 22 pro-democracy and human rights organizations, including MOSOP and the CD, formed a loose alliance, the United Action for Democracy (UAD), with the aim of campaigning for the restoration of democracy in Nigeria. In the same month four people were killed in a further series of bomb attacks in Lagos, Ibadan and Onitsha (in Anambra State). NADECO denied repeated claims by the authorities that the organization was responsible for the attacks.

In July 1997 CMAG reviewed statements from Nigerian opposition representatives, who appealed for the adoption of sanctions against Nigeria. At a subsequent summit meeting of the Commonwealth Heads of Government, which took place in Edinburgh, United Kingdom, in October, Nigeria's suspension from the organization was extended for an additional year; it was further indicated that the country would be expelled from the Commonwealth, and that a number of sanctions would be imposed, if Abacha reneged on his pledge to restore democratic rule by 1 October 1998.

In July 1997 the Government announced a new electoral timetable: elections to the State Assemblies were to take place in December, followed by elections to the National Assembly on 25 April 1998, and presidential and gubernatorial elections on 1 August of that year (although it was maintained that the new elected organs of government would be installed by 1 October 1998). Elections to the state legislatures, which were contested by the five registered parties, took place accordingly on 6 December 1997; the UNCP won 637 of the 970 contested seats, securing a majority in 29 of the 36 State Assemblies. The other four parties (the Congress for National Consensus, the Democratic Party of Nigeria, the Grassroots Democratic Movement and the National Centre Party of Nigeria) subsequently attributed the electoral success of the UNCP to malpractice on the part of the authorities, and threatened to withdraw from the remainder of the electoral process. In mid-December Abacha nominated a new FEC, in which most of the ministers who had served in the previous administration were replaced. Later that month, following reports of a bomb attack at the presidential wing of the airport at Abuja, the Government announced that an attempted coup had been thwarted. About 100 people, notably several prominent military officials (including Lt-Gen. Diya), were subsequently detained. However, there was widespread speculation that government claims of a coup attempt were a pretext for the removal of a number of army officers who were perceived to be a threat to Abacha. The incident also served to divert attention from the death in detention of Yar'Adua earlier that month. (It had also been reported that Obasanjo was receiving medical treatment for an undisclosed illness.) In February 1998, following the report of a special board of investigation, 26 people, including Diya and two ministers who had served in the previous FEC, were charged with conspiring to overthrow the Government.

In March 1998 a number of associations that supported Abacha, including the newly established Youths Earnestly Ask for Abacha, conducted rallies in favour of his re-election in August. UAD organized counter-demonstrations (which resulted in the arrest of a number of protesters by the security forces), and announced that it was to initiate a campaign of civil disobedience to oppose Abacha's candidacy in the presidential election. Later in March increasing fuel shortages prompted further unrest. In April all five registered parties voted separately to nominate Abacha as the sole presidential candidate; Abacha was therefore to contest the presidential election in August unopposed. In May about seven people were killed in clashes between members of the security forces and anti-Government protesters; a number of opposition activists, including the leader of UAD, Olisa Agbakoba, were subsequently arrested.

On 8 June 1998 Abacha died unexpectedly from heart failure. The PRC designated the Chief of Defence Staff, Maj.-Gen. Abdulsalami Abubakar, as Abacha's successor, and on 9 June he was inaugurated as Head of State (having been promoted to the rank of General). Abubakar pledged to continue the Abacha Government's scheduled transition to civilian rule. The UAD, however, urged continued protests against the military administration. In mid-June Abubakar ordered the release of about 26 political prisoners, including Obasanjo (ostensibly on grounds of ill health) and Agbakoba. In July, following discussions with UN officials, the authorities agreed to release Abiola from detention. Shortly after his release, however, Abiola collapsed and subsequently died. Violent rioting ensued, amid widespread speculation that the authorities were responsible for Abiola's death. Although an autopsy confirmed that he had died of heart failure, it was indicated that his period in detention had contributed to his poor health. Later in July Abubakar announced that the transition to civilian rule would be completed on 29 May 1999 (rather than 1 October 1998). The Government annulled the results of the elections that had previously been conducted, and dissolved the five authorized political parties, NECON and other electoral bodies. In August a new, 31-member FEC, which included a number of civilians, was appointed to remain in office pending the formal transition to civilian rule; an Independent National Electoral Commission (INEC) was also established. Later that month the INEC announced that local government elections would take place on 5 December 1998 and state legislative elections on 9 January 1999, followed by elections to a bicameral national legislature on 20 February and a presidential election on 27 February. On 7 September 1998 the Government published the draft Constitution that had been submitted by the NCC in June 1995. Abubakar announced that all charges against Nigerian exiles abroad had been abandoned, and that the 19 Ogoni activists who had been detained in connection with the killing of the four Ogoni leaders in May 1994 had been granted an unconditional release. (In October five former government opponents who had fled Nigeria in 1994 returned from exile, and Soyinka visited the country, amid acclaim from his supporters.)

Some 25 new political organizations had submitted applications for registration to the INEC by the stipulated deadline, which was extended to early October 1998. The commission provisionally approved nine political associations, notably the People's Democratic Party (PDP), which principally comprised former opponents of the Abacha administration. In the same month CMAG recommended that Commonwealth member states end sanctions against Nigeria, in preparation for the country's readmission to the Commonwealth. At the end of that month, in response to the democratization measures undertaken by the Government, the EU ended a number of sanctions against Nigeria (while maintaining the embargo on the export of arms to the country). Meanwhile, following continuing clashes between members of the Ijaw and Ilaje ethnic groups in the Niger Delta, Ijaw activists briefly seized a Shell petroleum installation in October, as part of their campaign in support of demands that the Government allocate a greater proportion of revenue from petroleum exploitation in the region to the Ijaw.

In November 1998 Obasanjo (who had joined the PDP in October) announced that he intended to seek nomination as the party's presidential candidate. At elections to Nigeria's 768 local municipal councils, which took place, as scheduled, on 5 December, the PDP secured about 60% of the votes cast. The INEC subsequently declared that the PDP, the All Nigeria People's Party (ANPP) and the Alliance for Democracy (AD) were the only political organizations to qualify for final registration, having achieved the requisite minimum of 5% of the votes cast in 24 seats. The state legislative elections, which were consequently contested only by the PDP, APP and AD, took place on 9 January 1999. The PDP, with about 50% of votes cast, secured 20 state governorships, while the ANPP obtained nine and the AP six. Elections in Bayelsa State were postponed, owing to clashes between the security forces and Ijaw activists (whose continued attacks against petroleum installations resulted in the imposition of a state of emergency at the end of December 1998).

In January 1999 several prominent members of former administrations announced that they intended to seek nomination to contest the forthcoming presidential election. In early February the ANPP and AD, which, despite the stated opposition of the INEC, had established an electoral alliance, nominated a joint candidate, Samuel Oluyemisi Falae (a former Minister of Finance in the Babangida administration). Later that month Obasanjo was elected as the presidential candidate of the PDP, defeating a former civilian Vice-President, Alex Ekwueme. At the elections to the bicameral legislature, which took place on 20 February, the PDP secured 215 seats in the 360-member House of Representatives and 66 seats in the 109-member Senate. (Voting in the Niger Delta region was postponed, owing to continued unrest, and a further by-election for the vacant seat to the National Assembly took place in March.)

On 27 February 1999 Obasanjo was elected to the presidency, with 62.8% of votes cast. Voting irregularities were reported, and Falae submitted a legal challenge to the electoral results at the Court of Appeal on the grounds of malpractice. In March the Government ordered the release of some 95 prisoners, including Diya, who had been detained in connection with the alleged coup attempt in December 1997. In April 1999 the Court of Appeal dismissed Falae's challenge to the declaration of Obasanjo as President-elect, and a further legal appeal at the Supreme Court was also rejected. The Constitution was formally promulgated on 5 May. Obasanjo was formally inaugurated as President on 29 May; on the same day Nigeria was readmitted as a full member of the Commonwealth. Obasanjo announced that measures to combat corruption would be introduced, and that all contracts awarded since the beginning of 1999 would be reviewed, following reports that the outgoing military Government had perpetrated large-scale embezzlement of state funds and assets. On 3 June the inaugural session of the National Assembly took place. Obasanjo nominated a new Cabinet, principally comprising members of the PDP, which was approved by the Senate later that month. He also undertook a reorganization of the armed forces, removing more than 150 military officers who had served under the Abacha Government.

In June 1999 about 200 people were killed in further violence between the Itsekiri, Ijaw and Urhobo ethnic communities in Warri. In July clashes between the Hausa and Yoruba ethnic groups (in which at least 100 people were killed) were reported in the town of Shagamu, near Lagos, and subsequently in Kano; government troops succeeded in restoring order at the end of the month. In August about 64 Shell petroleum workers, including several foreign nationals, were temporarily taken hostage by ethnic political activists in Warri.

In October 1999 Abacha's son, Mohammed, together with a former security officer of the Abacha administration, Maj. Hamza al-Mustapha, and two others, were charged with the killing of Kudirat Abiola in 1996. At the end of the month the Governor of the predominantly Muslim Zamfara State, in northern Nigeria, announced the introduction of Islamic *Shari'a* law in the state, in response to endemic crime. Obasanjo subsequently declared that the state imposition of *Shari'a* was in contravention of the federal Constitution. In early November Obasanjo ordered the release of 200 prisoners who had been detained without trial for more than two years. Later that month government troops were deployed to suppress unrest in the town of Odi, in Bayelsa State, following the killing of 12 members of the security forces by Ijaw activists. Obasanjo denied subsequent reports of retaliatory atrocities perpetrated by government forces against the local civilian population. Measures were subsequently introduced to grant states a higher proportion of revenue generated locally, in an effort to reduce ethnic tension in the Niger Delta. The Government had also demanded that multinational enterprises operating in the Niger Delta adopt long-term measures in response to environmental damage. Later in November about 50 people were killed in clashes between the Yoruba and Hausa in an outskirt of Lagos. Obasanjo (himself a Yoruba) accused a Yoruba nationalist organization, the O'odua People's Congress (OPC), of precipitating the violence.

In December 1999 Kano State, in the north, announced the adoption of *Shari'a* law. However, the Christian Association of Nigeria threatened to initiate a legal challenge to the introduction of *Shari'a* law by Kano and Zamfara States, on the grounds that it contravened the principle of secularity enshrined in the Constitution. In January 2000 the adoption of *Shari'a* was formally ratified by the Governor of Zamfara State. In February a demonstration by Christians in the northern town of Kaduna in protest at the proposed imposition of *Shari'a* in Kaduna State precipitated violent hostilities between Muslims and Christians, in which more than 300 people were killed; government troops eventually suppressed the unrest, and a curfew was imposed in the town. However, more than 50 people were killed in further clashes between Christians and Muslims in the south-eastern towns of Aba and Umuahia, which ensued in reprisal for the violence in the north. By the end of the month thousands of Christians had fled the north of the country, fearing possible retaliatory massacres. At an emergency meeting at the end of February, chaired by Obasanjo, the Governors of the 18 northern states agreed, in the interests of peace, to withdraw the new legislation introducing *Shari'a* law, and to revert to the provisions for *Shari'a* in the existing penal code, in accordance with the federal Constitution. However, the Governors of a number of the states subsequently announced that they would not comply with the federal government order, but would proceed with the implementation of *Shari'a* law. In March religious rioting in Niger State (where the adoption of the *Shari'a* law had been declared) was reported. In May some 150 people were killed in further clashes between Christians and Muslims in Kaduna; government troops were again deployed in the town to restore order. In early June Obasanjo reorganized the Cabinet, following media criticism of a number of ministers. In the same month the Government announced a reduction in subsidies on domestic fuel as part of planned reforms of the energy sector, precipitating riots by students in the south-west of the country and a general strike, organized by the NLC. The strike action was ended a few days later, after the authorities agreed to limit the increase in the price of fuel.

In August 2000, following persistent dissension between the executive and the legislature over the issue of government corruption, the President of the Senate was removed from office and charged with misusing public funds. In the same month *Shari'a* law was formally adopted in the northern states of Katsina, Jigawa and Yobe (to enter into effect later that year). In September the Governor of Borno State also announced the adoption of *Shari'a*. Although the Governors of most of these states had declared that Christians would be exempt from the provisions of *Shari'a,* social segregation of men and women and the application of punishments stipulated under Islamic law had been widely implemented in Zamfara and Kano States. In view of the violence in Kaduna State, the Governor announced that the form of *Shari'a* to be introduced in the state was to be modified to allow Islamic courts to exist in conjunction with special courts upholding secular laws. In early October some 100 people were killed in further severe ethnic clashes in Lagos between the Hausa and members of the Yoruba OPC; security forces, supported by troops, finally restored order in the capital. Later that month Obasanjo banned the OPC and ordered the arrest of more than 200 of the movement's prominent members, including the leader, Frederick Faseun.

At the end of January 2001 Obasanjo replaced 10 members of the Cabinet in an extensive reorganization, following widespread criticism of the Government's failure to resolve economic and social difficulties. In late March the Governors of Nigeria's 17 southern states, meeting in Benin City, urged that the Constitution be amended to provide for greater government decentralization, including the right for states to establish separate security forces. In the same month the US Supreme Court ruled that the relatives of Ken Saro-Wiwa and the other Ogoni activists executed in 1995 were entitled to continue legal proceedings against the multinational petroleum group, Royal Dutch Shell, for the alleged complicity of its Nigerian subsidiary in the alleged human rights violations perpetrated against the Ogoni ethnic group (see above). In April Obasanjo replaced the heads of the three branches of the armed forces, notably the Chief of Army Staff, who had served under Abacha. In early June a further cabinet reorganization was effected.

In mid-June 2001 religious and ethnic unrest in northern and central Nigeria intensified; some 1,000 people were killed in fighting between Christians and Muslims in Bauchi (which had become the 10th northern state to adopt *Shari'a* law). In early September hostilities between Christians and Muslims also erupted in the central town of Jos, where Christians had objected to the appointment of a Muslim to an influential post heading the state's poverty alleviation programme; it was reported that some 500 people were killed, before armed forces were deployed to restore control. In October it was reported that a further 200 civilians had been killed in Jos and the northern town of Kano, in clashes precipitated by Muslim protests at the US offensive in Afghanistan (following the terrorist attacks against the USA on 11 September). Government troops were reported to have perpetrated a massacre of about 200 Tiv villagers in the eastern state of Benue later that month, in retaliation for the abduction of 19 members of the armed forces, who had been deployed to quell unrest in the region. (In March

2002 a report by the US-based organization Human Rights Watch accused the Federal Government of supporting the military action against the civilians.)

In December 2001 the incumbent Minister of Justice, a close associate of Obasanjo, was shot and killed in the south-west town of Ibidjan (where a curfew was subsequently imposed); general speculation regarding the identity of his assailants was focused on rivalries within the Yoruba community. In early January 2002 the National Assembly rejected legislation that would have prohibited new political parties from contesting the presidential and legislative elections in 2003, instead amending the existing code, with the effect that new associations would henceforth be required to present a certain number of candidates in municipal elections. In mid-January a general strike, organized by the NLC in protest at a further government effort to increase fuel prices, caused severe disruption in principal towns. However, the Government subsequently won a legal challenge to the legitimacy of the strike (on the grounds that the NLC had not supplied the requisite period of notice to the authorities), obliging the movement to suspend action. The security forces briefly detained 10 prominent NLC officials, following a rally of supporters in Abuja. In February about 100 people were killed in further clashes between the Hausa and Yoruba in Lagos, necessitating the deployment of the armed forces to quell unrest in the town. The Hausa claimed that the OPC had destroyed large numbers of residences, in an effort to force members of that ethnic group to flee from Lagos.

In early 2002 the death sentence imposed on a woman in northern Sokoto State, who had been convicted in October 2001 under *Shari'a* law on charges of adultery, attracted increasing international attention. Following pressure from the international community, in March the Minister of Justice urged the 12 State Governors who had adopted *Shari'a* law to discontinue its strict enforcement, on the grounds that it contravened the Constitution for reasons of discrimination (applying only to Muslims). A Court of Appeal subsequently overturned the sentence against the convicted woman, ruling that there was insufficient evidence to justify the death penalty. However, the Governors of several northern states insisted that they would continue to implement *Shari'a*.

In April 2002 the Federal Government reached an agreement with Abacha's relatives and business associates, whereby Swiss banks were to return state funds appropriated by the former President, and the Nigerian authorities were to abandon legal proceedings against several members of Abacha's family (including his son, on charges of murdering Kudirat Abiola in 1996). Also in April Obasanjo announced that he intended to seek a second term in office, while the former Head of State, Muhammadu Buhari, stated that he planned to contest the forthcoming presidential election on behalf of the ANPP. In June the INEC announced that of 24 political parties that had applied for official registration only three had been recognized (increasing the total number of legal associations to six). In July several people were killed during violence in the Niger Delta, following a dispute over selecting a political candidate for forthcoming local government elections (which, however, were subsequently postponed indefinitely owing to lack of preparation). Meanwhile, in June, after a longstanding dispute between Obasanjo and the Senate over control of public finances, the President survived an impeachment attempt by the upper chamber. In August the House of Representatives adopted by an overwhelming majority a resolution demanding that Obasanjo resign from office or face impeachment, on charges of mismanagement and abuse of power. Obasanjo refused to comply with the resolution, and at the end of that month the PDP voted in favour of drafting a list of charges against the President.

In August 2002 a Court of Appeal in Katsina State upheld a sentence of death by stoning imposed in March against a woman, Amina Lawal, who had been convicted for having extramarital sexual intercourse. The case attracted international outrage, and the Minister of Justice announced that the Federal Government was opposed to the death sentence. (A further appeal against the sentence was submitted at federal level.) In the same month a *Shari'a* court in Jigawa State imposed a death sentence against a man who had been convicted for rape of a minor. In October the Federal Government announced that it would not permit executions under *Shari'a* law, after contestants threatened to boycott a 'Miss World' beauty pageant, due to be staged in Kaduna in December. Following increasing controversy over the pageant, an article in the newspaper *This Day*, referring to the Prophet Mohammed in connection with the contestants, precipitated violent protests by Muslims. Some 200 people were killed in ensuing clashes between Muslims and Christians in Kaduna, and the pageant was finally relocated to London, United Kingdom. The Deputy Governor of Zamfara State issued a *fatwa* against the female journalist responsible for the article (who had fled abroad).

In December 2002 the INEC granted registration to a further 24 political associations, after the Supreme Court upheld an appeal by five opposition parties against their exclusion, and ordered less restrictive regulations for legalization. Later that month the Commission announced that legislative elections were to be conducted on 12 April 2003, followed by a presidential election on 19 April, and elections to regional Houses of Assembly on 3 May. In January Obasanjo was formally elected as the presidential candidate of the PDP. A further 18 political leaders announced their intention to contest the presidential election, although Obasanjo and Buhari remained the two principal candidates. In March the killing of a prominent member of the ANPP in Abuja was declared by the authorities to have been politically motivated. In the same month further clashes between members of the Ijaw and Itsekiri ethnic group near Warri forced the suspension of the operations of a number of international petroleum companies; government troops were dispatched to the region to suppress the violence.

Incidences of violence and malpractice were reported during the federal legislative elections on 12 April 2003. The INEC subsequently announced that the PDP had secured an overwhelming majority in both legislative chambers. At the presidential election on 19 April (the first to be organized by civilian authorities for 19 years), Obasanjo was elected for a second term by 61.2% of the valid votes cast, while Buhari received 32.7% of votes. Opposition leaders, notably Buhari, contested the results, claiming that widespread electoral malpractice had been perpetrated, and indicated that violent protests might ensue. International monitors, although generally satisfied with the organization of the elections, declared that irregularities had taken place, particularly in the region of the Niger Delta. At gubernatorial elections, which also took place on 19 April, the PDP gained eight state governorships from the ANPP and AD, losing only one (that of Kano). Later that month Obasanjo criticized a statement by EU monitors, who claimed that they had obtained evidence of electoral malpractice perpetrated in 13 states. In late May Buhari submitted a challenge at the Court of Appeal against Obasanjo's re-election.

At the end of April 2003 four offshore petroleum rigs, operated by a US enterprise, Transocean, in the Niger Delta were seized by protesting Nigerian employees, who took hostage 97 foreign national workers. Miltary naval forces were dispatched to the region. Following negotiations between officials of NUPENG, the NLC and Transocean, all hostages were airlifted from the rigs. Obasanjo officially dissolved the Cabinet on 21 May; he was expected to form a new administration in June, following his inauguration on 29 May.

Nigeria has taken a leading role in African affairs and is a prominent member of the Economic Community of West African States (see p. 187) and other regional organizations. The Nigerian Government has contributed a significant number of troops to ECOMOG (see p. 189), which was deployed in Liberia from August 1990 in response to the conflict between government forces and rebels in that country (see the chapter on Liberia). In early 1998, following the installation of elected civilian institutions in Liberia, a number of Nigerian troops were withdrawn from ECOMOG; the remainder of the Nigerian contingent was withdrawn from Liberia in October 1999. In 1993 Nigerian troops were dispatched to Sierra Leone, in response to a formal request by the Sierra Leonean Government for military assistance to repulse attacks by rebels in that country. Following the completion of the transition to civilian rule in Nigeria in May 1999, a phased withdrawal of Nigerian troops from Sierra Leone took place. By the end of April 2000 all Nigerian troops belonging to ECOMOG had left Sierra Leone; however, Nigeria continued to contribute troops to the UN Mission in Sierra Leone (UNAMSIL), which had been deployed in that country. (In early 2002 about 8,000 Nigerian troops were stationed in Sierra Leone as part of UNAMSIL; in September UNAMSIL's mandate, which had been due to expire, was extended for a further six months.) In September an official visit to Nigeria by the US President, Bill Clinton, the first by a US Head of State since 1978, provided for a number of new trade and development initiatives.

In 1991 the Nigerian Government claimed that Cameroonian security forces had annexed several Nigerian fishing settlements in Cross River State (in south-eastern Nigeria), following a long-standing border dispute, based on a 1913 agreement between Germany and the United Kingdom that ceded the Bakassi peninsula in the Gulf of Guinea (a region of strategic significance) to Cameroon. Subsequent negotiations between Nigerian and Cameroonian officials in an effort to resolve the dispute achieved little progress. In December 1993 some 500 Nigerian troops were dispatched to the region, in response to a number of incidents in which Nigerian nationals had been killed by Cameroonian security forces. Later that month the two nations agreed to establish a joint patrol at the disputed area, and to investigate the cause of the incidents. In February 1994, however, the Nigerian Government increased the number of troops deployed in the region. Later in February the Cameroonian Government announced that it was to submit the dispute for adjudication by the UN, the Organization of African Unity (OAU, now the African Union, see p. 130) and the International Court of Justice (ICJ), and requested military assistance from France. Subsequent reports of clashes between Cameroonian and Nigerian forces in the region prompted fears of a full-scale conflict between the two nations.

In February 1996 renewed hostilities between Nigerian and Cameroonian forces in the Bakassi region resulted in several casualties. Later that month, however, Nigeria and Cameroon agreed to refrain from further military action, and delegations from the two countries resumed discussions, with mediation by President Gnassingbe Eyadéma of Togo, in an attempt to resolve the dispute. In March the ICJ ruled that Cameroon had failed to provide sufficient evidence to support its contention that Nigeria had instigated the border dispute, and ordered both nations to cease military operations in this respect, to withdraw troops to former positions, and to co-operate with a UN investigative mission that was to be dispatched to the region. In April, however, clashes continued, with each Government accusing the other of initiating the attacks. Although tension in the region remained high, diplomatic efforts to avoid further conflict increased in May; in that month a Cameroonian delegation visited Nigeria, while Abacha accepted an invitation to attend an OAU summit meeting, which was to be convened in Yaoundé in July. The UN investigative mission visited the Bakassi region in September. In December, however, the Nigerian authorities claimed that Cameroonian troops had launched further attacks in the region. In May 1997 the Cameroonian Government denied further allegations by Nigeria that it had initiated hostilities; the UN requested that the Togolese President continue mediation efforts. Further clashes between Nigerian and Cameroonian forces were reported in December 1997 and February 1998. In March the Nigerian Government contested the jurisdiction of the ICJ to rule on the Bakassi issue, on the grounds that the two countries had agreed to settle the dispute through bilateral negotiations. In June, however, the Court pronounced that it had the necessary jurisdiction.

In October 2002 the ICJ finally ruled that the disputed Bakassi region was part of Cameroon, under the terms of the 1913 agreement. However, inhabitants of the peninsula, who claimed to be more than 90% of Nigerian nationality, strongly rejected the ICJ's decision, and Obasanjo subsequently refused to recognize the ruling. It was reported that Nigeria had reinforced its military presence in the Bakassi region. Following UN mediation, a bilateral commission was established to conduct further discussions, and in December it agreed to dispatch an investigative mission to the Bakassi peninsula.

Government

Under the terms of the Constitution of the Federal Republic of Nigeria, which entered into effect on 31 May 1999, executive power is vested in the President, who is the Head of State. The President, who is elected for a term of four years, nominates a Vice-President and a Cabinet, subject to confirmation by the Senate. Legislative power is vested in the bicameral National Assembly, comprising a 360-member House of Representatives and a 109-member Senate, which is elected by universal suffrage for a four-year term. Nigeria is a federation of 36 states, comprising 774 local government areas. The executive power of a state is vested in the Governor of that state, who is elected for a four-year term, and the legislative power in the House of Assembly of that state.

Defence

In August 2002 Nigeria's total armed forces numbered 78,500 (army 62,000, navy 7,000 and air force 9,500). There was also a paramilitary force of 82,000. Military service is voluntary. Expenditure on defence by the Federal Government in 2001 was ₦63,472m. (equivalent to 8.0% of federal budget expenditure).

Economic Affairs

In 2001, according to estimates by the World Bank, Nigeria's gross national income (GNI), measured at average 1999–2001 prices, was US $37,116m., equivalent to $290 per head (or $830 per head on an international purchasing-power parity basis). During 1990–2001, it was estimated, the population increased, in real terms, at an average annual rate of 2.8%, while gross domestic product (GDP) per head remained constant. Overall GDP increased, in real terms, at an average annual rate of 2.7% in 1990–2001; growth in 2001 was 4.0%.

Agriculture (including hunting, forestry and fishing) contributed 34.6% of GDP in 2001. An estimated 32.4% of the labour force were employed in the sector in that year. The principal cash crops are cocoa (which accounted for only 0.7% of total merchandise exports in 1995), rubber and oil palm. Staple food crops include rice, maize, taro, yams, cassava, sorghum and millet. Timber production, the raising of livestock (principally goats, sheep, cattle and poultry), and artisanal fisheries are also important. According to the World Bank, agricultural GDP increased at an average annual rate of 3.6% in 1990–2000. Growth in agricultural GDP, according to IMF estimates, was 3.8% in 2001.

Industry (including mining, manufacturing, construction and power) engaged an estimated 6.9% of the employed labour force in 1990, and contributed 35.5% of GDP in 2001. According to the World Bank, industrial GDP increased at an average annual rate of 1.6% in 1990–2000. Growth in industrial GDP, according to IMF estimates, was 1.5% in 2001.

Mining contributed 30.3% of GDP in 2001, although the sector engaged less than 0.1% of the employed labour force in 1986. The principal mineral is petroleum, of which Nigeria is Africa's leading producer (providing an estimated 92.3% of total export earnings in 2001). In addition, Nigeria possesses substantial deposits of natural gas and coal. In late 1999 the Nigerian Government commenced exports of liquefied natural gas. Plans for the construction of a pipeline, which would transport natural gas from the Escravos field, in Delta State, to Benin, Togo and Ghana, were under way. Tin and iron ore are also mined, while there are plans to exploit deposits of uranium. The GDP of the mining sector was estimated by the IMF to have declined by an average of 0.1% per year in 1997–2001; mining GDP increased by 0.6% in 2001.

Manufacturing contributed 4.2% of GDP in 2001, and engaged about 4.3% of the employed labour force in 1986. The principal sectors are food-processing, brewing, petroleum-refining, iron and steel, motor vehicles (using imported components), textiles, cigarettes, footwear, pharmaceuticals, pulp and paper, and cement. According to the World Bank, manufacturing GDP increased at an average annual rate of 1.6% in 1990–2000. Growth in manufacturing GDP, according to IMF estimates, was 3.8% in 2001.

Energy is derived from natural gas, which provided some 40.8% of electricity in 1999, hydroelectric power (35.0%) and petroleum (24.2%). Petroleum-related imports comprised an estimated 14.8% of the value of merchandise imports in 2001.

The services sector contributed 29.9% of GDP in 2001, and engaged 48.5% of the employed labour force in 1986. According to World Bank estimates, the GDP of the services sector increased at an average annual rate of 2.7% in 1990–2000. Growth in the sector, according to IMF estimates, was 3.8% in 2001.

In 1999 Nigeria recorded a visible trade surplus of US $4,288m., and there was a surplus of $506m. on the current account of the balance of payments. In 2001 the principal source of imports (9.4%) was the United Kingdom; other major suppliers were the USA, the People's Republic of China, Germany and France. The USA was the principal market for exports (40.5%) in that year; other significant purchasers were Spain, Brazil, India and France. The main exports in 2000 were fuel and liquefied natural gas. The principal imports in 1997 were manufactured goods, machinery and transport equipment, chemicals, and food and live animals.

Nigeria's overall budget deficit for 2001 was ₦156,678m., equivalent to 3.3% of GDP. The country's external debt totalled US $34,134m. at the end of 2000, of which $32,735m. was long-term public debt. In that year the cost of debt-servicing was equivalent to 4.3% of the value of exports of goods and services. The annual rate of inflation averaged 28.0% in 1990–2001; consumer prices increased by 12.9% in 2002. An estimated 4.5% of the labour force were unemployed at the end of 1997.

Nigeria is a member of the African Development Bank (see p. 128), of the Economic Community of West African States (see p. 187), which aims to promote trade and co-operation in West Africa, and of the Organization of the Petroleum Exporting Countries (see p. 298).

Following high levels of economic growth in the 1970s, Nigeria's economy deteriorated as a result of the subsequent decline in international prices for petroleum. In response to democratization measures initiated by a new military Head of State in mid-1998, the European Union ended a number of sanctions against Nigeria later that year. In January 1999 the Government abolished the dual exchange rate system and ended restrictions on foreign investment. The new civilian Government, which was installed in June, benefited greatly from an increase in the international price of petroleum, and some fiscal recovery ensued. Continuing violent protests in the Niger Delta region disrupted petroleum production, however, and, together with severe religious and ethnic violence from 2000 (see Recent History), deterred potential foreign investors. Meanwhile, increasingly low levels of investment, high unemployment and declining productivity contributed to endemic crime. Progress towards the privatization of state enterprises and easing of currency controls remained slow, while repeated government efforts to reduce subsidies on domestic fuel were impeded by widespread strike action. The Government failed to adhere to a one-year IMF-endorsed economic programme, which expired in August 2001. In March 2002 the IMF ended formal relations with Nigeria, thereby ending the immediate prospect of concessionary debt relief. In July the World Bank announced that it was to halve its lending capacity to Nigeria, owing to concern over projected levels of public expenditure, prior to elections in early 2003. The Government's own economic strategy, announced in late 2002, laid emphasis on diversification, and claimed that recovery had commenced; modest growth in GDP in 2001 was generated largely by the non-petroleum sector, particularly by strong agricultural output. The IMF commended the tightening of monetary policy, which resulted in a progressive reduction in the rate of inflation by the end of 2002, and the adoption of a more market-orientated exchange rate system. However, progress in the implementation of structural reforms was considered to be limited, with reverses in efforts to privatize public utilities, and poverty continued to increase. Concern remained over the stability of the banking system and lack of fiscal control. In November Obasanjo announced a revised draft budget for 2003, following protracted disagreement between himself and the legislature over the approval of a programme. Despite widespread discontent over his perceived failure to reduce corruption, Obasanjo was returned to the presidency in April 2003.

Education

Education is partly the responsibility of the state governments, although the Federal Government has played an increasingly important role since 1970. Primary education begins at six years of age and lasts for six years. Secondary education begins at 12 years of age and lasts for a further six years, comprising two three-year cycles. Education to junior secondary level (from six to 15 years of age) is free and compulsory. In 1994 total enrolment at primary schools was equivalent to 98% of children in the relevant age-group (109% of boys; 87% of girls), while the comparable ratio for secondary enrolment was only 33% (36% of boys; 30% of girls). In 1993 383,488 students were enrolled in 133 higher education institutions. Expenditure on education by the Federal Government in 2001 was ₦59,745m., equivalent to 7.5% of total expenditure in the federal budget.

Public Holidays

2003: 1 January (New Year's Day), 12 February* (Id al-Kabir, Feast of the Sacrifice), 18–21 April (Easter), 14 May* (Mouloud, Birth of the Prophet), 1 October (National Day), 26 November* (Id al-Fitr, end of Ramadan), 25–26 December (Christmas).

2004: 1 January (New Year's Day), 2 February* (Id al-Kabir, Feast of the Sacrifice), 9–12 April (Easter), 2 May* (Mouloud, Birth of the Prophet), 1 October (National Day), 14 November* (Id al-Fitr, end of Ramadan), 25–26 December (Christmas).

*These holidays are dependent on the Islamic lunar calendar, and may vary by one or two days from the dates given.

Weights and Measures

The metric system is in force.

Statistical Survey

Source (unless otherwise stated): Federal Office of Statistics, 7 Okotie-Eboh St, SW Ikoyi, Lagos; tel. (1) 2682935.

Area and Population

AREA, POPULATION AND DENSITY

Area (sq km)	923,768*
Population (census results, 28–30 November 1991)†	
Males	44,529,608
Females	44,462,612
Total	88,992,220
Population (official estimate at mid-year)‡	
2000	115,224,000
2001	116,929,000
Density (per sq km) at mid–2001	126.6

* 356,669 sq miles.

† Revised 15 September 2001.

‡ Source: UN, *Population and Vital Statistics Report*.

STATES

(unrevised census of November 1991)*

	Population	Capital
Abia	2,297,978	Umuahia
Adamawa	2,124,049	Yola
Akwa Ibom	2,359,736	Uyo
Anambra	2,767,903	Awka
Bauchi	4,294,413	Bauchi
Benue	2,780,398	Makurdi
Borno	2,596,589	Maiduguri
Cross River	1,865,604	Calabar
Delta	2,570,181	Asaba
Edo	2,159,848	Benin City
Enugu	3,161,295	Enugu
Imo	2,485,499	Owerri
Jigawa	2,829,929	Dutse
Kaduna	3,969,252	Kaduna
Kano	5,632,040	Kano
Katsina	3,878,344	Katsina
Kebbi	2,062,226	Birnin Kebbi
Kogi	2,099,046	Lokoja
Kwara	1,566,469	Ilorin
Lagos	5,685,781	Ikeja
Niger	2,482,367	Minna
Ogun	2,338,570	Abeokuta
Ondo	3,884,485	Akure
Osun	2,203,016	Oshogbo
Oyo	3,488,789	Ibadan
Plateau	3,283,704	Jos
Rivers	3,983,857	Port Harcourt
Sokoto	4,392,391	Sokoto
Taraba	1,480,590	Jalingo
Yobe	1,411,481	Damaturu
Federal Capital Territory	378,671	Abuja
Total	88,514,501	

* In October 1996 the Government announced the creation of six new states: Bayelsa, Ebonyi, Ekiti, Gombe, Nassarawa and Zamfara (with capitals at Yenogoa, Abakaliki, Ado-Ekiti, Gombe, Lafia and Gusau respectively).

PRINCIPAL TOWNS

(unrevised census of November 1991)

Lagos (federal capital)* . . .	5,195,247	Enugu	407,756
Kano	2,166,554	Oyo	369,894
Ibadan	1,835,300	Warri	363,382
Kaduna . . .	933,642	Abeokuta . . .	352,735
Benin City . . .	762,719	Onitsha . . .	350,280
Port Harcourt . .	703,421	Sokoto	329,639
Maiduguri . . .	618,278	Okene	312,775
Zaria	612,257	Calabar . . .	310,839
Ilorin	532,089	Katsina . . .	259,315
Jos	510,300	Oshogbo . . .	250,951
Aba	500,183	Akure	239,124
Ogbomosho . . .	433,030	Bauchi	206,537

* Federal capital moved to Abuja (population 107,069) in December 1991.

Mid-2000 (UN estimates, incl. suburbs): Lagos 8,665,000; Ibadan 1,549,000.

Mid-2001 (UN estimate, incl. suburbs): Abuja (capital) 420,000.

Source: UN, *World Urbanization Prospects: The 2001 Revision*.

BIRTHS AND DEATHS

(UN estimates, annual averages)

	1985–90	1990–95	1995–2000
Birth rate (per 1,000)	44.0	44.0	41.7
Death rate (per 1,000)	16.0	15.0	14.1

Source: UN, *World Population Prospects: The 2000 Revision*.

Expectation of life (WHO estimates, years at birth): 51.6 (males 50.6; females 52.6) in 2001 (Source: WHO, *World Health Report*).

ECONOMICALLY ACTIVE POPULATION

(sample survey, '000 persons aged 14 years and over, September 1986)

	Males	Females	Total
Agriculture, hunting, forestry and fishing	9,800.6	3,458.4	13,259.0
Mining and quarrying	6.8	—	6.8
Manufacturing	806.4	457.3	1,263.7
Electricity, gas and water . . .	127.0	3.4	130.4
Construction	545.6	—	545.6
Trade, restaurants and hotels . .	2,676.6	4,740.8	7,417.4
Transport, storage and communications	1,094.7	17.2	1,111.9
Financing, insurance, real estate and business services	109.8	10.3	120.1
Community, social and personal services	3,939.5	962.6	4,902.1
Activities not adequately defined .	597.1	147.8	744.9
Total employed	19,704.1	9,797.8	29,501.9
Unemployed	809.8	453.8	1,263.6
Total labour force	20,513.9	10,251.6	30,765.5

Note: Figures are based on a total estimated population of 98,936,800, which may be an overestimate.

Source: ILO, *Yearbook of Labour Statistics*.

Mid-2001 (estimates in '000): Agriculture, etc. 15,048; Total labour force 46,450 (Source: FAO).

Health and Welfare

KEY INDICATORS

Total fertility rate (children per woman, 2001)	5.6
Under-5 mortality rate (per 1,000 live births, 2001) . .	183
HIV/AIDS (% of persons aged 15–49, 2001)	5.80
Physicians (per 1,000 head, 1992)	0.19
Hospital beds (per 1,000 head, 1990)	1.67
Health expenditure (2000): US $ per head (PPP) . . .	20
Health expenditure (2000): % of GDP	2.2
Health expenditure (2000): public (% of total) . . .	20.8
Access to water (% of persons, 2000)	57
Access to sanitation (% of persons, 2000)	63
Human Development Index (2000): ranking	148
Human Development Index (2000): value	0.462

For sources and definitions, see explanatory note on p. vi.

Agriculture

PRINCIPAL CROPS
('000 metric tons)

	1999	2000	2001
Wheat	101	73	51
Rice (paddy)	3,277	3,298	2,752
Maize	5,476	4,107	4,620
Millet	5,960	6,105	5,530
Sorghum	7,520	7,711	7,081
Potatoes	573	599	599
Sweet potatoes	2,451	2,468	2,473
Cassava	32,697	32,010	32,586
Yams	25,873	26,201	26,374
Taro (Coco yam)	3,835	3,886	3,910
Sugar cane	682	695	705
Pulses*	50	50	50
Soybeans	410	429	436
Groundnuts (in shell)	2,894	2,901	2,683
Sesame seed	69	71†	74†
Coconuts	158	160	161
Palm kernels	562	577	600*
Tomatoes	879	879*	879*
Green peppers	715	715*	715*
Carrots	231	231*	231*
Citrus fruits*	3,240	3,250	3,250
Mangoes	729	730*	730*
Pineapples	881	881*	881*
Plantains	1,902	1,999*	2,000
Papayas	748	748*	748*
Other fruit (excluding melons) . .	1,400	1,400*	1,400*
Cashew nuts	176	184	185
Cocoa beans	225	338	338*
Tobacco (leaves)*	9	9	9
Cotton (lint)*	145	147	148
Natural rubber (dry weight) . .	107	115*	115*

* FAO estimate(s).
† Unofficial figure.

Source: FAO.

LIVESTOCK
('000 head, year ending September)

	1999	2000	2001
Horses*	204	204	205
Asses*	1,000	1,000	1,000
Cattle	19,830	19,500*	19,500
Camels*	18	18	18
Pigs	4,853	5,048	5,100*
Sheep*	20,500	21,000	21,000
Goats*	26,000	26,000	26,000
Poultry*	126,000	130,000	130,000

* FAO estimate(s).
Source: FAO.

LIVESTOCK PRODUCTS
('000 metric tons)

	1998	1999	2000
Beef and veal	297	298	298*
Mutton and lamb	89	91	91*
Goat meat	151	154	154*
Pig meat	65	78	78*
Poultry meat	172	172*	172*
Other meat	100	101	101*
Cows' milk	368	386	386*
Butter and ghee	8	9	9*
Cheese	7	7	7*
Poultry eggs	419	435	435*
Cattle hides	36	37	37
Sheepskins	16	17	17
Goatskins	24	24	24

* FAO estimate.

Source: FAO.

Forestry

ROUNDWOOD REMOVALS
('000 cubic metres, excluding bark)

	1996	1997	1998
Sawlogs, veneer logs and logs for sleepers	6,200	6,800	7,100
Pulpwood	n.a.	n.a.	39
Other industrial wood*	2,279	2,279	2,279
Fuel wood*	57,673	58,661	58,418
Total	66,152	67,740	67,836

* FAO estimates.

1999–2001: Annual removals as in 1998.

Source: FAO.

SAWNWOOD PRODUCTION
('000 cubic metres, including railway sleepers)

	1995	1996	1997
Broadleaved (hardwood)	2,356	2,178	2,000

Coniferous (softwood): 6 in 1990.

1998–2000: Broadleaved (hardwood) production as in 1997.

Source: FAO.

Fishing

('000 metric tons, live weight)

	1998	1999	2000
Capture	463.0	455.6	441.4
Tilapias	16.3	19.7	13.4
Characins	19.8	11.9	12.5
Bagrid catfish	15.5	10.7	7.3
Torpedo-shaped catfishes . . .	17.2	11.0	14.0
Sea catfishes	10.9	17.0	14.9
West African croakers . . .	15.0	14.6	12.6
Sardinellas	95.5	83.6	80.9
Bonga shad	30.2	18.5	17.6
Southern pink shrimp . . .	12.4	27.3	18.8
Aquaculture	20.5	21.7	25.7
Total catch	483.5	477.4	467.1

Source: FAO, *Yearbook of Fishery Statistics*.

Mining

(estimates, metric tons, unless otherwise indicated)

	1999	2000	2001
Coal, bituminous	30,000	35,000	35,000
Crude petroleum ('000 barrels). .	770,000	783,000	823,000
Natural gas (million cu m) . . .	30,000	30,000	35,000
Tin concentrates*	130	200	130

* Metal content.

Source: US Geological Survey.

Industry

SELECTED PRODUCTS

('000 metric tons, unless otherwise indicated)

	1999	2000	2001
Palm oil*	896	899	903
Raw sugar*†	35	36	40
Plywood ('000 cubic metres)*† . .	55	55	55
Wood pulp*†	23	23	23
Paper and paperboard*† . . .	19	19	19
Jet fuels (metric tons)‡	1,000	2,000	3,000
Motor spirit—petrol ('000 barrels)‡	10,000	25,000	27,000
Kerosene ('000 barrels)‡. . .	6,000	10,000	12,000
Gas-diesel (distillate fuel) oil ('000 barrels)‡	9,000	20,000	21,000
Residual fuel oils ('000 barrels)‡	12,000	18,000	22,000
Cement‡	2,500	2,500	3,000
Tin metal—unwrought (metric tons)‡	200	300	200
Electric energy ('000 million kWh, net)‡.	9.9	n.a.	n.a.

Wheat flour: 561 in 1996.

Wine ('000 hectolitres): 68 in 1995.

Beer ('000 hectolitres): 1,461 in 1995.

Cigarettes (million): 256 in 1995.

Footwear, excl. rubber ('000 pairs): 1,255 in 1995.

Phosphatic fertilizers (phosphoric acid content): 28 in 1994.

Liquefied petroleum gas† 60 in 1996.

Crude steel‡ 2 in 1998.

* Data from FAO.
† Estimates.
‡ Estimated data from the US Geological Survey.

Source (unless otherwise indicated): UN, *Industrial Commodity Statistics Yearbook*.

Finance

CURRENCY AND EXCHANGE RATES

Monetary Units
100 kobo = 1 naira (₦)

Sterling, Dollar and Euro Equivalents (31 December 2002)
£1 sterling = 203.73 naira
US $1 = 126.40 naira
€1 = 132.56 naira
1,000 naira = £4.908 = $7.911 = €7.544

Average Exchange Rate (naira per US $)
2000   101.697
2001   111.231
2002   120.578

FEDERAL BUDGET
(₦ million)*

Revenue†	1999	2000	2001
Distribution from Federation Account	211,751	514,969	530,658
Share of value-added tax (VAT) .	7,277	8,770	13,359
Independent revenue‡	17,000	38,057	44,405
First-charge deductions from federation revenue. . . .	426,416	783,953	730,317
External debt-servicing . . .	177,610	175,034	232,192
National priority projects. .	14,000	42,459	18,124
Nigerian National Petroleum Corporation (NNPC) cash calls and priority projects . . .	206,806	284,750	480,001
Transfer from Petroleum Trust Fund (PTF) for Petroleum Special Trust Fund (PSTF) . .	21,000	0	0
Total (incl. others)	**611,449**	**1,368,233**	**1,412,949**

Expenditure§	1999	2000	2001
Recurrent expenditure	447,264	562,704	510,966
General administration . .	48,364	57,332	75,080
Defence	20,679	31,046	47,072
Internal security	28,091	26,154	38,855
Agriculture and water resources	5,239	4,806	7,065
Construction	3,895	11,480	7,202
Transport and communications .	2,632	2,427	33,935
Other economic services . .	8,686	11,102	4,809
Education	23,047	39,034	39,885
Health	8,793	11,580	24,524
Other social and community services	5,908	8,189	15,226
Interest payments due . . .	266,740	316,606	187,267
Other transfers ‖	25,190	42,948	30,046
Capital expenditure	142,979	168,337	283,074
General administration . . .	34,083	36,560	28,032
Defence	3,798	6,440	16,400
Internal security	4,856	8,397	4,814
Agriculture and water resources	6,913	8,803	57,879
Manufacturing, mining and quarrying.	9,924	10,514	7,284
Transport and communications .	3,317	7,177	19,241
Special projects	18,920	40,377	18,124
Other economic services . . .	14,103	15,098	65,524
Education	8,517	10,529	19,860
Health	7,387	8,866	10,128
Other social and community services	1,350	8,570	13,348
Transfers	24,812	0	0
Total	**585,243**	**731,041**	**794,040**

* Figures refer to the operations of the Federal Government, the 'first charges' and the Petroleum Special Trust Fund (PSTF).
† Figures for government revenue refer to federally retained revenue. This includes 48.5% of total distributed revenue of the Federation Account, more than half of which consists of proceeds from the operations of the NNPC and foreign petroleum companies. The remainder of Federation Account revenue is allocated to state governments (24%), local governments (20%) and five special funds (7.5%). The Federal Government retains 20% of federally collected VAT.
‡ Including loan repayments and proceeds from the privatization or commercialization of state enterprises.
§ Figures exclude the operations of extrabudgetary accounts. Including supplementary and extrabudgetary outlays, total expenditure (in ₦ million) was: 957,960 in 1999; 1,220,744 in 2000; 1,466,862 in 2001.
‖ Including pensions, gratuities, grants, subventions and losses from transactions in foreign exchanges.
Source: IMF, *Nigeria: Selected Issues and Statistical Appendix* (March 2003).

INTERNATIONAL RESERVES
(US $ million at 31 December)

	1999	2000	2001
IMF special drawing rights. . .	—	—	1
Foreign exchange.	5,450	9,910	10,456
Total*	**5,450**	**9,911**	**10,457**

* Excluding gold reserves (687,000 troy ounces each year). At 31 December 1998 the national valuation of these reserves (based on market-related prices) was US $1 million.

Source: IMF, *International Financial Statistics*.

MONEY SUPPLY
(₦ million at 31 December)

	2000	2001	2002
Currency outside banks	274,011	338,671	349,080
Demand deposits at commercial banks	356,954	448,021	450,377
Total money (incl. others) . . .	649,684	816,708	943,520

Source: IMF, *International Financial Statistics.*

COST OF LIVING
(Consumer Price Index for urban areas; base: September 1985 = 100)

	1999	2000	2001
Food (excl. beverages) . . .	2,922.3	3,060.8	4021.4
Clothing (incl. footwear) . . .	2,984.7	3,249.1	3,474.4
Rent, fuel and light	4,743.2	5,204.3	5,161.5
All items (incl. others) . . .	3,489.2	3,727.8	4,490.7

Source: IMF, *Nigeria: Selected Issues and Statistical Appendix* (March 2003).

NATIONAL ACCOUNTS
(₦ million at current prices)

National Income and Product
(year ending 31 March)*

	1992/93	1993/94	1994/95
Compensation of employees . .	59,100	74,546	81,048
Operating surplus	468,880	604,200	808,817
Domestic factor incomes . .	527,980	678,746	889,865
Consumption of fixed capital .	16,351	17,240	18,629
Gross domestic product (GDP) at factor cost	544,331	695,986	908,494
Indirect taxes	5,762	5,689	6,042
Less Subsidies	284	202	202
GDP in purchasers' values . .	549,809	701,473	914,334
Factor income received from abroad	2,799	1,338	1,170
Less Factor income paid abroad .	67,203	74,900	66,878
Gross national product (GNP) .	485,405	627,911	848,626
Less Consumption of fixed capital .	16,351	17,240	18,629
National income in market prices	469,053	610,671	829,997
Other current transfers from abroad	15,240	21,386	13,164
Less Other current transfers paid abroad	2,560	3,592	2,211
National disposable income .	481,733	628,465	840,950

* Figures are provisional.

Source: UN, *National Accounts Statistics.*

Expenditure on the Gross Domestic Product

	1999	2000	2001
Government final consumption expenditure	620,754	974,924	1,423,886
Private final consumption expenditure	2,119,065	1,873,700	2,157,707
Increase in stocks	728,306	757,229	952,069
Gross fixed capital formation .			
Total domestic expenditure .	3,468,126	3,605,853	4,533,662
Exports of goods and services .	1,272,198	2,279,602	2,108,131
Less Imports of goods and services	1,368,989	1,606,233	1,895,128
GDP in purchasers' values .	3,371,335	4,279,221	4,746,666
GDP at constant 1990 prices .	344,811	359,004	369,501

Source: IMF, *Nigeria: Selected Issues and Statistical Appendix* (March 2003).

Gross Domestic Product by Economic Activity

	1999	2000	2001
Agriculture, hunting, forestry and fishing	1,127,693	1,192,910	1,584,312
Mining and quarrying	959,735	1,604,218	1,388,006
Manufacturing	150,972	166,316	191,576
Electricity, gas and water . . .	2,110	2,200	2,438
Construction	27,528	30,604	40,755
Trade, restaurants and hotels . .	491,458	533,940	650,112
Transport, storage and communications	109,634	120,395	134,750
Finance, insurance, real estate and business services	174,806	211,532	229,382
Government services	159,513	226,386	288,525
Other community, social and personal services	41,246	53,963	65,470
GDP at factor cost	3,244,693	4,140,464	4,575,325
Taxes on products	128,019	140,663	174,023
Less Subsidies	1,378	1,906	2,683
GDP in purchasers' values . .	3,371,335	4,279,221	4,746,666

Source: IMF, *Nigeria: Selected Issues and Statistical Appendix* (March 2003).

BALANCE OF PAYMENTS
(US $ million)

	1997	1998	1999
Exports of goods f.o.b.	15,207	8,971	12,876
Imports of goods f.o.b.	−9,501	−9,211	−8,588
Trade balance	5,706	−240	4,288
Exports of services	786	884	980
Imports of services	−4,712	−4,166	−3,476
Balance on goods and services .	1,781	−3,552	1,792
Other income received . . .	258	333	240
Other income paid	−3,404	−2,624	−2,818
Balance on goods, services and income	−1,365	−5,813	−786
Current transfers received . . .	1,920	1,574	1,301
Current transfers paid	−4	−5	−9
Current balance	552	−4,244	506
Capital account (net)	−49	−54	−48
Direct investment from abroad . .	1,539	1,051	1,005
Portfolio investment assets . . .	9	51	50
Portfolio investment liabilities . .	−76	−59	−39
Other investment assets . . .	−2,183	−332	−3,319
Other investment liabilities . .	286	792	−1,699
Net errors and omissions . . .	−62	−77	7
Overall balance	15	−2,873	−3,538

Source: IMF, *International Financial Statistics.*

2000 (US $ million): Exports of goods (f.o.b.) 20,441.0; Imports of goods (f.o.b.) −12,372.0; *Trade balance* 8,068.0; Service and factor income (net)−7,789.0; *Balance on goods, services and income* 279.0; Current transfers (net) 1,724.0; *Current balance* 2,003.0; Capital and financial account (net) 167.0; Net errors and omissions 137.0; *Overall balance* 2,307.0 (Source: African Development Bank).

External Trade

PRINCIPAL COMMODITIES

Imports c.i.f. (₦ million)	1993	1994	1995*
Food and live animals	13,912.9	16,585.8	76,819.1
Crude materials (inedible) except fuels	4,306.4	5,636.0	27,576.1
Chemicals	28,322.6	40,578.8	172,678.8
Basic manufactures	39,751.1	35,909.0	152,324.9
Machinery and transport equipment	70,226.9	50,240.4	180,557.6
Miscellaneous manufactured articles	6,293.9	7,246.2	27,094.8
Total (incl. others)	165,629.4	161,027.0	656,572.2

Exports f.o.b. (US $ million)		1999	2000
Fuel		11,393	19,550
Liquefied natural gas		322	623
Total (incl. others)		11,927	20,441

Source: partly World Bank.

PRINCIPAL TRADING PARTNERS
(US $ million)*

Imports c.i.f.†	1999	2000	2001
Brazil	249	271	459
China, People's Repub. . . .	436	604	1,009
France	631	746	832
Germany	740	635	971
Hong Kong	195	184	198
India	211	264	263
Indonesia	226	260	252
Italy	366	458	546
Japan	271	318	487
Korea, Repub..	185	273	456
Netherlands	383	448	610
Singapore	213	257	269
Thailand	259	247	384
United Kingdom	821	881	1,082
USA	709	789	1,053
Total (incl. others)	7,609	8,842	11,484

Exports f.o.b.	1999	2000	2001
Brazil	738	738	1,372
Canada	261	311	138
Côte d'Ivoire	359	601	435
France	684	1,055	1,073
Germany	189	463	627
Ghana	439	545	588
India	1,005	1,246	1,345
Portugal	292	727	657
Spain	876	2,189	1,747
Switzerland	211	325	270
USA	4,220	9,409	8,345
Total (incl. others)	11,999	21,684	20,603

* Imports by country of production; exports by country of last consignment.
† Excluding imports related to oil and gas sectors.

Source: IMF, *Nigeria: Selected Issues and Statistical Appendix* (March 2003).

Transport

RAILWAYS
(traffic)

	1995	1996	1997
Passenger-km (million) . . .	161	170	179
Freight ton-km (million) . . .	108	114	120

Source: UN, *Statistical Yearbook*.

ROAD TRAFFIC
(estimates, motor vehicles in use)

	1995	1996
Passenger cars	820,069	885,080
Buses and coaches	1,284,251	903,449
Lorries and vans.	673,425	912,579
Motorcycles and mopeds	481,345	441,651

Source: IRF, *World Road Statistics*.

1997 ('000s of vehicles): Passenger cars: 52.3; Commercial vehicles: 13.5 (Source: *UN Statistical Yearbook*).

SHIPPING

Merchant Fleet
(registered at 31 December)

	1999	2000	2001
Number of vessels	287	296	293
Displacement ('000 grt)	432.4	438.3	404.2

Source: Lloyd's Register-Fairplay, *World Fleet Statistics*.

International Sea-borne Freight Traffic
(estimates, '000 metric tons)

	1991	1992	1993
Goods loaded	82,768	84,797	86,993
Goods unloaded	10,960	11,143	11,346

Source: UN Economic Commission for Africa, *African Statistical Yearbook*.

CIVIL AVIATION
(traffic on scheduled services)

	1997	1998	1999
Kilometres flown (million) . . .	2	2	4
Passengers carried ('000) . . .	44	49	162
Passenger-km (million)	100	122	370
Total ton-km (million) . . .	14	18	61

Source: UN, *Statistical Yearbook*.

Tourism

ARRIVALS BY NATIONALITY*

Country	1998	1999	2000
Benin	178,608	187,538	196,468
Cameroon	48,650	51,083	53,516
Chad	38,644	40,576	42,508
France	28,103	29,508	30,918
Germany	27,411	28,782	30,153
Ghana	93,680	98,364	103,048
Italy	29,794	31,284	32,770
Liberia	48,785	51,224	53,663
Niger	281,914	296,010	310,106
Sudan	28,636	30,068	31,500
Total (incl. others)	1,356,958	1,424,840	1,491,767

* Figures refer to arrival at frontiers of visitors from abroad, including same-day visitors (excursionists).

Source: World Tourism Organization, *Yearbook of Tourism Statistics*.

Tourism receipts (US $ million): 85 in 1996; 86 in 1997; 142 in 1998 (Source: World Bank).

Communications Media

	1999	2000	2001
Television receivers ('000 in use)	7,500	7,700	n.a.
Telephones ('000 main lines in use)	410	492	500
Mobile cellular telephones ('000 in use)	25	30	330
Personal computers ('000 in use)	700	750	800
Internet users ('000)	100	200	200

Radio receivers ('000 in use): 23,500 in 1997.

Book production (titles, including pamphlets): 1,314 in 1995.

Daily newspapers: 25 (estimated average circulation 2,740,000 copies) in 1996.

Sources: International Telecommunication Union; UNESCO, *Statistical Yearbook*.

Education

(1994)

	Institu-tions	Teachers	Students		
			Males	Females	Total
Primary	38,649	435,210	9,056,367	7,134,580	16,190,947
Secondary	6,162*	152,596	2,419,782	2,031,547	4,451,329
Teacher training†	135	4,531	n.a.	n.a.	108,751
Technical and vocational†	240	5,115	n.a.	n.a.	89,536
Higher education	133*	19,601‡	n.a.	n.a.	383,488*

* 1993 figure.
† 1987 figures.
‡ 1989 figure.

Sources: Federal Ministry of Education, Lagos; UNESCO, *Statistical Yearbook*.

Adult literacy rate (UNESCO estimates): 63.9% (males 72.4%; females 55.7%) in 2000 (Source: UN Development Programme, *Human Development Report*).

Directory

The Constitution

The Constitution of the Federal Republic of Nigeria was promulgated on 5 May 1999, and entered into force on 31 May. The main provisions are summarized below:

PROVISIONS

Nigeria is one indivisible sovereign state, to be known as the Federal Republic of Nigeria. Nigeria is a Federation, comprising 36 States and a Federal Capital Territory. The Constitution includes provisions for the creation of new States and for boundary adjustments of existing States. The Government of the Federation or of a State is prohibited from adopting any religion as a state religion.

LEGISLATURE

The legislative powers of the Federation are vested in the National Assembly, comprising a Senate and a House of Representatives. The 109-member Senate consists of three Senators from each State and one from the Federal Capital Territory, who are elected for a term of four years. The House of Representatives comprises 360 members, representing constituencies of nearly equal population as far as possible, who are elected for a four-year term. The Senate and House of Representatives each have a Speaker and Deputy Speaker, who are elected by the members of the House from among themselves. Legislation may originate in either the Senate or the House of Representatives, and, having been approved by the House in which it originated by a two-thirds majority, will be submitted to the other House for approval, and subsequently presented to the President for assent. Should the President withhold his assent, and the bill be returned to the National Assembly and again approved by each House by a two-thirds majority, the bill will become law. The legislative powers of a State of the Federation will be vested in the House of Assembly of the State. The House of Assembly of a State will consist of three or four times the number of seats that the State holds in the House of Representatives (comprising not less than 24 and not more than 40 members).

EXECUTIVE

The executive powers of the Federation are vested in the President, who is the Head of State, the Chief Executive of the Federation and the Commander-in-Chief of the Armed Forces of the Federation. The President is elected for a term of four years and must receive not less than one-quarter of the votes cast at the election in at least two-thirds of the States in the Federation and the Federal Capital Territory. The President nominates a candidate as his associate from the same political party to occupy the office of Vice-President. The Ministers of the Government of the Federation are nominated by the President, subject to confirmation by the Senate. Federal executive bodies include the Council of State, which advises the President in the exercise of his powers. The executive powers of a State are vested in the Governor of that State, who is elected for a four-year term and must receive not less than one-quarter of votes cast in at least two-thirds of all local government areas in the State.

JUDICIARY

The judicial powers of the Federation are vested in the courts established for the Federation, and the judicial powers of a State in the courts established for the State. The Federation has a Supreme Court, a Court of Appeal and a Federal High Court. Each State has a High Court, a *Shari'a* Court of Appeal and a Customary Court of Appeal. Chief Judges are nominated on the recommendation of a National Judicial Council.

LOCAL GOVERNMENT

The States are divided into 768 local government areas. The system of local government by democratically-elected local government councils is guaranteed, and the Government of each State will ensure their existence. Each local government council within the State will participate in the economic planning and development of the area over which it exercises authority.

Federal Government

HEAD OF STATE

President and Commander-in-Chief of the Armed Forces: Gen. (retd) OLUSEGUN OBASANJO (inaugurated 29 May 1999; re-elected 19 April 2003).

Vice-President: Alhaji ATIKU ABUBAKAR.

CABINET
(April 2003)

Minister of Finance: Alhaji ADAMU CIROMA.

Minister of Foreign Affairs: Alhaji SULE LAMIDO.

Minister of Health: Prof. ALPHONSUS NWOSU.

Minister of Industry: Chief KOLAWOLE BABALOLA JAMODU.

Minister of Information: Prof. JERRY GANA.

Minister of Internal Affairs: Chief SUNDAY M. AFOLABI.

Minister of Justice and Attorney-General: KANU AGABI.

Minister of Labour and Productivity: Alhaji MUSA GWADABE.

Minister of Police Affairs: STEVEN AKIGA.

Minister of Power and Steel: Chief SEGUN AGAGU.

Minister of Agriculture and Rural Development: ADAMU BELLO.

Minister of Commerce: MUSTAPHA BELLO.

Minister of Communications: BELLO HALIRU MOHAMMED.

Minister of Defence: Gen. THEOPHILUS (YAKUBU) DANJUMA.

Minister of Education: BABALOLA BORISHADE.

Minister of the Environment: MOHAMMED KABIR SAID.

Minister of the Federal Capital Territory: MOHAMMED ABBA-GANA.

Minister of Aviation: KEMA CHIKWE.

Minister of Culture and Tourism: BOMA BROMILLOW JACK.

Minister of Regional Integration and Co-operation: BIMBOLA OGUNKELU.

Minister of Science and Technology: TURNER ISOUN.

Minister of Solid Minerals: DUPE ADELAJA.

Minister of Transport: Chief OJO MADUEKWE.

Minister of Water Resources: Mallam MUKHTAR SHAGARI.

Minister of Sports and Social Development: STEPHEN IBN AKIGA.

Minister of Women and Youth: HAJIYA AISHAT ISMAIL.

Minister of Works and Housing: Chief TONY ANENIH.

Minister in the Presidency, with responsibility for Civil Service Matters: Alhaji BELLO USMAN.

Minister in the Presidency, with responsibility for Co-operation and Integration in Africa: Chief BIMBOLA OGUNKELU.

Minister in the Presidency, with responsibility for Economic Matters: VINCENT OGBULEAFOR.

Minister in the Presidency, with responsibility for Inter-Governmental Affairs: Alhaji IBRAHIM UMAR KIDA.

Minister in the Presidency, with responsibility for Special Projects: YOMI EDU.

There are, in addition, 18 Ministers of State.

MINISTRIES

All ministries are located in Abuja.

Office of the Head of State: New Federal Secretariat Complex, Shehu Shagari Way, Central Area District, Abuja; tel. (9) 5233536.

Ministry of Agriculture and Rural Development: Area 1, Secretariat Complex, Garki, Abuja; tel. (9) 3141185.

Ministry of Aviation: New Federal Secretariat Complex, Shehu Shagari Way, Central Area District, Abuja; tel. (9) 5232132.

Ministry of Commerce: Area 1, Secretariat Complex, Garki, Abuja; tel. (9) 2341884.

Ministry of Communications: New Federal Secretariat Complex, Shehu Shagari Way, Central Area District, Abuja; tel. (9) 5237183.

Ministry of Culture and Tourism: Area 1, Secretariat Complex, Garki, Abuja; tel. (9) 2342727; e-mail ntdc@metrong.com.

Ministry of Defence: Ship House, Central Area, Abuja; tel. (9) 2340534.

Ministry of Education: New Federal Secretariat Complex, Shehu Shagari Way, Central Area District, Abuja; tel. (9) 5232800; fax (9) 619904.

Ministry of the Federal Capital Territory: FCT Secretariat Complex, Area 11, Abuja; tel. (9) 5234014.

Ministry of Finance: Olusegun Obasanjo Way, Garki, Abuja; tel. (9) 2344686.

Ministry of Foreign Affairs: Maputo St, Zone 3, Wuse District, Abuja; tel. (9) 5230576.

Ministry of Health: New Federal Secretariat Complex, Shehu Shagari Way, Central Area District, Abuja; tel. (9) 5230576.

Ministry of Industry: Area 1, Secretariat Complex, Garki, Abuja; tel. (9) 5230576.

Ministry of Information: Radio House, Herbert Macaulay Way, Area 11, Garki, Abuja; tel. (9) 5230576.

Ministry of Internal Affairs: Area 1, Secretariat Complex, Garki, Abuja; tel. (9) 2346884.

Ministry of Justice: New Federal Secretariat Complex, Shehu Shagari Way, Central Area District, Abuja; tel. (9) 5235208.

Ministry of Labour and Productivity: New Federal Secretariat Complex, Shehu Shagari Way, Central Area District, Abuja; tel. (9) 5235980.

Ministry of Police Affairs: New Federal Secretariat Complex, Shehu Shagari Way, Central Area District, Abuja; tel. (9) 5230549.

Ministry of Power and Steel: New Federal Secretariat Complex, Shehu Shagari Way, Central Area District, Abuja; tel. (9) 5237064.

Ministry of Science and Technology: New Federal Secretariat Complex, Shehu Shagari Way, Central Area District, Abuja; tel. (9) 5233397.

Ministry of Solid Minerals: New Federal Secretariat Complex, Shehu Shagari Way, Central Area District, Abuja; tel. (9) 5235830.

Ministry of Sports and Social Development: New Federal Secretariat Complex, Shehu Shagari Way, Abuja; tel. (9) 5235905.

Ministry of Transport: National Maritime Agency Bldg, Central Area, Abuja; tel. (9) 5237053; e-mail permsec@fedtransport-gov.org.

Ministry of Water Resources: Area 1, Secretariat Complex, Garki, Abuja; tel. (9) 2342376.

Ministry of Women and Youth: New Federal Secretariat Complex, Shehu Shagari Way; tel. (9) 5237051.

Ministry of Works and Housing: Mabushi District, Garki, Abuja; tel. (9) 5211622; fax (9) 2340174.

President and Legislature

PRESIDENT

Election, 19 April 2003

Candidate	Votes	% of votes
Chief Olusegun Obasanjo (People's Democratic Party)	21,906,949	61.22
Muhammadu Buhari (All Nigeria People's Party)	11,698,593	32.69
Ojukwu Chukwuemeka Odumegwu (All Progressive Grand Alliance)	1,184,965	3.31
Others	993,957	2.78
Total*	35,784,464	100.00

*Excluding 2,135,749 invalid votes.

NATIONAL ASSEMBLY

House of Representatives

Speaker of the House of Representatives: GHALI UMAR NA'ABBA.

Election, 12 April 2003

Party	Votes	% of votes	Seats
People's Democratic Party	15,927,807	54.49	213
All Nigeria People's Party	8,021,531	27.44	95
Alliance for Democracy	2,711,972	9.28	31
United Nigeria People's Party	803,432	2.75	2
All Progressive Grand Alliance	397,147	1.36	2
National Democratic Party	561,161	1.92	1
People's Redemption Party	185,764	0.76	1
People's Salvation Party	96,550	0.33	1
Others	527,706	1.67	—
Total*	29,233,070	100.00	360

*Based on votes cast in 346 of the 360 constituencies of the House of Representatives, received on 2 May 2003. Total excludes 1,153,200 invalid votes.

Senate

Speaker of the Senate: ANYIM PIUS ANYIM.

Election, 12 April 2003

Party	Votes	% of votes	Seats
People's Democratic Party	15,585,538	53.69	73
All Nigeria People's Party	8,091,783	27.87	28
Alliance for Democracy	2,828,082	9.74	6
Others	2,524,704	8.70	—
Total*	29,030,107	100.00	109

*Based on votes cast in 107 of the 109 districts of the Senate, received on 2 May 2003. Total excludes 965,064 invalid votes.

Political Organizations

Following the death of the military Head of State in June 1998, the existing authorized political parties were dissolved. The Government established a new independent national electoral commission, which officially approved three political parties to contest elections in February 1999. Prior to legislative and presidential elections in April 2003, three political associations were granted registration in June 2002, as were a further 24 in December.

Abia Democratic Alliance (ADA): Umuahia; f. 2001; allied to the People's Democratic Party.

Alliance for Democracy (AD): Abeokuta St, Area 8, Garki, Abuja; e-mail info@alliancefordemocracy.org; internet www.afrikontakt .com/alliance; f. 1998; contested 1999 elections in alliance with the APP; breakaway faction (Leader MAMAN YUSUF) f. 2000; Chair. Senator AHMED ABDULKADIR.

All Nigeria People's Party (ANPP): internet www.appnigeria .org; f. 1998; contested 1999 elections in alliance with the AD; Leader Alhaji YUSUF GARBAH ALI.

All Progressive Grand Alliance (APGA): Abuja; regd June 2002; Leader CHEKWAS OKORIE.

Fourth Dimension: f. 2001 by fmr politicians and military officers; Chair. Adm. (retd) AUGUSTUS AIKHOMU.

IBB Vision 2003: f. 2002; supports former Pres. Ibrahim Babangida; Chair. HAMEED MAKAMA.

Ijaw Youth Congress (IYC): f. 1999; Pres. FELIX TUODOLO.

Movement for the Actualization of the Sovereign State of Biafra (MASSOB): f. 1999; Leader RALPH UWAZURIKE.

Movement for the Survival of the Ogoni People (MOSOP): f. 1990 to organize opposition to petroleum production in Ogoni territory; Leader LEDUM MITEE.

National Conscience Party (NCP): 18 Phase 1 Low Cost Housing Estate, Lake City Ave, Gwagwalada, Abuja; tel. (9) 4937279; e-mail info@nigeriancp.net; internet www.nigeriancp.net; Leader GANI FAWEHINMI.

National Democratic Party (NDP): POB 8196, Abuja; tel. (9) 6703366; regd June 2002; Chair. ALIYU HABU FARI.

National Frontier: f. 2001 by fmr Governors and military officers; Chair. Chief EDWIN UME EZEOKE.

National Solidarity Party: f. 2001 by fmr military officers; Chair. SALEH JAMBO.

O'odua People's Congress (OPC): f. 1994; banned Oct. 2000; Yoruba nationalist organization; divided into two factions, led by FREDERICK FASEUN and GANIYU ADAMS.

People's Democratic Party (PDP): f. 1998 by fmr opponents of the Govt of Gen. Sani Abacha; supports greater federalism; party of Pres. Gen. (retd) Olusegun Obasanjo; Chair. AUDU OGBEH; Sec. OKWESILIEZE NWODO.

People's Redemption Party (PRP): Abuja; regd Dec. 2002; Leader BALARABE MUSA.

People's Salvation Party (PSP): regd Dec. 2002; Chair. Alhaji WADA NAS.

Progressive Liberation Party (PLP): f. 2001; Leader EZEKIEL IZUOGU.

Reform Party of Nigeria (RPN): tel. (1) 6463826342; fax (1) 7753059912; e-mail reformnigeria@reformnigeria.com; internet www.reformnigeria.com.

United Nigeria Development Forum: f. 2001 by fmr military officers of Pres. Sani Abacha; Chair. Brig.-Gen. (retd) LAWAL JA'AFAR ISA.

United Nigeria People's Party (UNPP): Abuja; regd June 2002; Leader SALEH JAMBO.

United Progressive Grand Alliance (UPGA): Enugu; f. 2001; Chair. CHEKWAS OKORIE.

Diplomatic Representation

EMBASSIES AND HIGH COMMISSIONS IN NIGERIA

Algeria: Plot 203, Etim Inyang Crescent, POB 55238, Falomo, Lagos; tel. (1) 612092; fax (1) 2624017; Ambassador EL-MIHOUB MIHOUBI.

Angola: 5 Kasumu Ekomode St, Victoria Island, POB 50437, Falomo Ikoyi, Lagos; tel. (1) 2611135; Ambassador B. A. SOZINHO.

Argentina: 93 Awolowo Rd, SW Ikoyi, POB 51940, Lagos; tel. (1) 2690093; fax (1) 2690117; Chargé d'affaires a.i. GUSTAVO FAZZARI.

Australia: 2 Ozumba Mbadiwe Ave, Victoria Island, POB 2427, Lagos; tel. (1) 2613124; fax (1) 2618703; e-mail ahelagos@hyperia .com; High Commissioner ROBERT WHITTY.

Austria: Fabac Centre, 3B Ligali Ayorinde Ave, POB 1914, Lagos; tel. (1) 2616081; fax (1) 2617639; Ambassador Dr WILFRIED ALMO-SLECHNER.

Belgium: 1A Murtala Muhammed Dr., Ikoyi, POB 149, Lagos; tel. (1) 2691507; fax (1) 2691444; e-mail ambellagcom@infoweb.com; Ambassador CHRISTIAAN VAN DRIESSCHE.

Benin: 4 Abudu Smith St, Victoria Island, POB 5705, Lagos; tel. (1) 2614411; fax (1) 2612385; Ambassador PATRICE HOUNGAVOU.

Brazil: 257 Kofo Abayomi St, Victoria Island, POB 1931, Lagos; tel. (1) 2610135; fax (1) 2613394; e-mail nigbrem@intracom5.com; Ambassador CARLOS ALFREDO PINTO DA SILVA.

Bulgaria: 3 Walter Carrington Crescent, Victoria Island, PMB 4441, Lagos; tel. (1) 2611931; fax (1) 2619879; Ambassador (vacant).

Burkina Faso: 15 Norman Williams St, Ikoyi, Lagos; tel. (1) 617985; e-mail ebfn@nova.net.ng; Ambassador DRAMANE YAMEOGO.

Cameroon: 5 Elsie Femi Pearse St, Victoria Island, PMB 2476, Lagos; tel. (1) 2612226; fax (1) 7747510; High Commissioner ANDRÉ E. KENDECK MANDENG.

Canada: 4 Idowu Taylor St, Victoria Island, POB 54506, Ikoyi Station, Lagos; tel. (1) 2692195; fax (1) 2692919; High Commissioner IAN FERGUSON.

Chad: 2 Goriola St, Victoria Island, PMB 70662, Lagos; tel. (1) 2622590; fax (1) 2618314; Ambassador Dr ISSA HASSAN KHAYAR.

China, People's Republic: Plot 302–303, Central Area, Abuja; tel. (9) 2347081; Ambassador LIANG YINZHU.

Côte d'Ivoire: 3 Abudu Smith St, Victoria Island, POB 7786, Lagos; tel. (1) 610936; fax (1) 2613822; e-mail cotedivoire@micro.com.ng; Ambassador EMILE M'LINGUI KEFFA.

Cuba: Plot 935, Idejo St, Victoria Island, POB 328, Victoria Island, Lagos; tel. (1) 2614836; fax (1) 2617036; Ambassador GIRALDO MAZOLA.

Czech Republic: Plot 1223, Gnassingbé Eyadéma St, Asokoro District, POB 4628, Abuja; tel. (9) 3141245; fax (9) 3141248; e-mail abuja@embassy.mzv.cz; Ambassador JURAJ CHMIEL.

Denmark: 4 Walter Carrington Crescent, Victoria Island, POB 2390, Lagos; tel. (1) 2611503; fax (1) 2610841; Ambassador LARS BLINKENBERG.

Egypt: 182B Kofo Abayomi St, POB 538, Lagos; tel. (1) 2612922; fax (1) 261767; Ambassador FUAD YUSUF.

Equatorial Guinea: 7 Bank Rd, Ikoyi, POB 4162, Lagos; tel. (1) 2683717; Ambassador A. S. DOUGAN MALABO.

Ethiopia: Plot 97, Ahmadu Bello Rd, Victoria Island, PMB 2488, Lagos; tel. (1) 2613198; fax (1) 2615055; Ambassador J. K. SHINKAIYE.

Finland: Plot 13, 13 Walter Carrrington Crescent, Victoria Island, POB 4433, Lagos; tel. (1) 2610916; fax (1) 2613158; Ambassador HEIKKI LATVANEN.

France: 32 Odi St, off Aso Drive, Maitama, Abuja; tel. (9) 5235506; e-mail ambafrance.abj@micro.com.ng; internet www.ambafrance-ng .org/emb; Ambassador JEAN-MARIE SIMON.

Gabon: 8 Norman Williams St, SW Ikoyi, POB 5989, Lagos; tel. (1) 2684673; fax (1) 2690692; Ambassador E. AGUEMINYA.

Gambia: 162 Awolowo Rd, SW Ikoyi, POB 873, Lagos; tel. (1) 682192; High Commissioner OMAR SECKA.

Germany: Plot 433, Yakubu Gowon Crescent, Abuja; tel. (9) 3148005; fax (9) 3148006; e-mail asgeremb@hotmail.com; Ambassador Dr DIETMAR KREUSEL.

Ghana: 21–25 King George V Rd, POB 889, Lagos; tel. (1) 2630015; fax (1) 2630338; High Commissioner JOHN K. TETTEGAH.

Greece: Plot 1397, 9B Tiamiyu Savage St, Victoria Island, POB 1199, Lagos; tel. (1) 2614852; fax (1) 2611412; Ambassador HARIS KARABARBOUNIS.

Guinea: 8 Abudu Smith St, Victoria Island, POB 2826, Lagos; tel. (1) 2616961; Ambassador KOMO BEAVOGUI.

Holy See: Pope John Paul II Crescent, Maitama, PMB 541, Garki, Abuja; tel. (9) 4138381; e-mail nuntius@linkserve.com; Apostolic Nuncio Most Rev. OSVALDO PADILLA (Titular Archbishop of Pia).

Hungary: Plot 1685, Jose Marti Crescent, Asokoro, Abuja; tel. (1) 3141180; fax (1) 3141177; e-mail huemblgs@nova.net.ng; Ambassador GYÖRGY SZABÓ.

India: 8A Walter Carrington Crescent, POB 2322, Lagos; tel. (1) 2681297; fax (1) 2693803; High Commissioner SATINDER KUMBER UPPAL.

Indonesia: 5 Anifowoshe St, Victoria Island, POB 3473, Marina, Lagos; tel. (1) 2614601; fax (1) 2613301; e-mail indlgs@infoweb.abs .net; Ambassador SUSANTO ISMODIRDJO.

Iran: 2 Udi St, Maitama, Abuja; tel. (1) 5238048; fax (1) 5237785; e-mail irembassy_abuja@yahoo.com; Ambassador JAWAD TORKABADI.

Ireland: Plot 415, Negro Crescent, Maitama District, Abuja; tel. (9) 4131751; fax (9) 4131805; Ambassador JOE LYNCH.

Israel: Plot 636, Cowrie House, Adeyemo Alakaja St, Victoria Island, Lagos; tel. (1) 2622055; fax (1) 2622040; Ambassador GADI GOLAN.

Italy: 12 Walter Carrington Crescent, Victoria Island, POB 2161, Lagos; tel. (1) 2621046; fax (1) 2619881; e-mail ambitnig@alpha .linkserve.com; Ambassador GIOVANNI GERMANO.

Jamaica: Plot 77, Samuel Adedoyin Ave, Victoria Island, POB 75368, Lagos; tel. (1) 2611085; fax (1) 2610047; High Commissioner ROBERT MILLER (acting).

Japan: 24–25 Apese St, Victoria Island, PMB 2111, Lagos; tel. (1) 2614929; fax (1) 2614035; Ambassador TAKAHISA SASAKI.

Kenya: 53 Queen's Drive, Ikoyi, POB 6464, Lagos; tel. (1) 2682768; High Commissioner Dr I. E. MALUKI.

Korea, Democratic People's Republic: 31 Akin Adesola St, Victoria Island, Lagos; tel. (1) 2610108; Ambassador KIM PYONG GI.

Korea, Republic: Plot 934, Idejo St, Victoria Island, POB 4668, Lagos; tel. (1) 2615353; Ambassador CHAI KI-OH.

Lebanon: Plot 18, Walter Carrington Crescent, Victoria Island, POB 651, Lagos; tel. (1) 2614511; Ambassador M. SALAME.

Liberia: 3 Idejo St, Plot 162, off Adeola Odeku St, Victoria Island, POB 70841, Lagos; tel. (1) 2618899; Ambassador Prof. JAMES TAPEH.

Libya: 46 Raymond Njoku Rd, SW Ikoyi, Lagos; tel. (1) 2680880; Chargé d'affaires a.i. IBRAHIM al-BASHAR.

Malaysia: 205 Abiola Segun-Ajayi St, Victoria Island, POB 3729, Lagos; tel. (1) 3200687; fax (1) 3200787; e-mail mwlagos@hyperia .com; High Commissioner MOHAMMED ZAIN ABUBAKAR.

Morocco: Plot 1318, 27 Karimu Katun St, Victoria Island, Lagos; tel. (1) 2611682; Ambassador SAAD EDDINE TAIEB.

Namibia: Tiamiyu Savage St, Victoria Island, PMB 1395, Lagos; tel. (1) 2618606; e-mail namibiahc@alfa.linkserve.com.

Netherlands: 24 Ozumba Mbadiwe Ave, Victoria Island, POB 2426, Lagos; tel. (1) 2613005; fax (1) 617605; Ambassador B. R. KÖRNER.

Niger: 15 Adeola Odeku St, Victoria Island, PMB 2736, Lagos; tel. (1) 2612300; Ambassador Alhaji MAHAMANG DADO MANSOUR.

Norway: 3 Anifowoshe St, Victoria Island, PMB 2431, Lagos; tel. (1) 2618467; fax (1) 2618469; e-mail emb.lagos@mfa.no; Ambassador DAG NISSEN.

Pakistan: 4 Molade Okoya-Thomas St, Victoria Island, POB 2450, Lagos; tel. (1) 613909; fax (1) 614822; High Commissioner ZAFAR A. HILALY.

Philippines: Plot 152, No 302, off 3rd Ave, Victoria Island, Lagos; tel. (1) 2614048; Ambassador MUKHTAR M. MUALLAM.

Poland: 10 Idejo St, Victoria Island, POB 410, Lagos; tel. (1) 2614684; fax 2614685; e-mail poemb@linkserve.com.ng; Chargé d'affaires TOMASZ PYRCZ.

Portugal: Plot 1677, Olukunle Bakare Close, Victoria Island, Lagos; tel. (1) 2619037; fax (1) 2616071; Ambassador FILIPE ORLANDO DE ALBUQUERQUE.

Romania: Plot 498, Nelson Mandela St, Zone A4, Asokoro, POB 10376, Abuja; tel. (9) 3142304; fax (9) 3142306; e-mail romnig@ nigtel.com; Ambassador GHEORGHE DUMITRU.

Russia: 5 Walter Carrington Crescent, Victoria Island, POB 2723, Lagos; tel. (1) 2613359; fax (1) 4619994; e-mail musemlagos@vgccl .net; Ambassador GENNADY V. ILYITEHEV.

Saudi Arabia: Plot 347H, off Adetokunbo Ademola Crescent, Wuse 2, Abuja; tel. (9) 4131880; fax (9) 4134906; Ambassador ANWAR A. ABD-RABBUH.

Senegal: 14 Kofo Abayomi Rd, Victoria Island, PMB 2197, Lagos; tel. (1) 2611722; Ambassador ALIOUNE DIAGNE.

Serbia and Montenegro: 7 Maitama Sule St, SW Ikoyi, PMB 978, Lagos; tel. (1) 2680238; Chargé d'affaires a.i. DORBEJOG KAHANSKI.

Sierra Leone: 31 Waziri Ibrahim St, Victoria Island, POB 2821, Lagos; tel. (1) 2614666; High Commissioner JOSEPH BLELL.

Slovakia: POB 1290, Lagos; tel. (1) 2621585; fax (1) 2612103; e-mail obeo.sk@micro.com.ng; Ambassador VASIL HUDÁK.

Somalia: Plot 1270, off Adeola Odeka St, POB 6355, Lagos; tel. (1) 2611283; Ambassador M. S. HASSAN.

South Africa: 4 Maduike St, Ikoyi, Lagos; tel. (1) 2693842; fax (1) 2690448; High Commissioner S. G. NENE.

Spain: 21C Kofo Abayomi Rd, Victoria Island, POB 2738, Lagos; tel. (1) 2615215; fax (1) 2618225; e-mail embespng@mail.mae.es; Ambassador ALFONSO MANUEL PORTABALES VÁZQUEZ.

Sudan: 2B Kofo Abayomi St, Victoria Island, POB 2428, Lagos; tel. (1) 2615889; Ambassador AHMED ALTIGANI SALEH.

Sweden: PMB 569, Garki, Abuja; tel. (9) 3143399; fax (9) 3143398; e-mail swedemb.abuja@linkserve.com; Ambassador BIRGITTA HOLST ALANI.

Switzerland: Plot 1098, Kwami Nkrumah Crescent, Asokoro District, Abuja; tel. (9) 3142307; fax (9) 3148364; Ambassador Dr RUDOLF KNOBLAUCH.

Syria: 25 Kofo Abayomi St, Victoria Island, Lagos; tel. (1) 2615860; Chargé d'affaires a.i. MUSTAFA HAJ-ALI.

Tanzania: 8 Agoro Odiyan St, Victoria Island, POB 6417, Lagos; tel. (1) 613594; fax (1) 618908; High Commissioner CISCO MTIRO (acting).

Thailand: 1 Ruxton Rd, Old Ikoyi, POB 3095, Lagos; tel. (1) 2681337; Ambassador N. SATHAPORN.

Togo: 96 Awolowo Rd, SW Ikoyi, POB 1435, Lagos; tel. (1) 2617449; Ambassador FOLI-AGBENOZAN TETTEKPOE.

Trinidad and Tobago: 3A Tiamiyu Savage St, Victoria Island, POB 6392, Marina, Lagos; tel. (1) 2612087; fax (1) 612732; High Commissioner Dr HAROLD ROBERTSON.

Turkey: 3 Okunola Martins Close, Ikoyi, POB 56252, Lagos; tel. (1) 2691142; fax (1) 2693040; e-mail turkemb@infoweb.abs.net; Ambassador ÖMER SAHINKAYA.

United Kingdom: Shehu Shangari Way, Maitama, Abuja; tel. (9) 4132010; fax (9) 4133552; e-mail consular@abuja.mail.fco.gov.uk; High Commissioner Sir GRAHAM BURTON.

USA: 7 Mambilla St, off Aso Drive, Maitama District, Abuja; tel. (9) 5230916; fax (9) 5230353; e-mail usabuja@pd.state.gov; Ambassador HOWARD F. JETER.

Venezuela: 35B Adetokunbo Ademola St, Victoria Island, POB 3727, Lagos; tel. (1) 2611590; fax (1) 2617350; e-mail embavenez .nig@net.ng; Ambassador ALFREDO ENRIQUE VARGAS.

Zambia: 11 Keffi St, SW Ikoyi, PMB 6119, Lagos; High Commissioner B. N. NKUNIKA (acting).

Zimbabwe: 10A Tiamiyu Savage St, POB 50247, Victoria Island, Lagos; tel. (1) 2619328; High Commissioner GIFT PUNUNGUE (acting).

Judicial System

Supreme Court

Three Arms Complex, Central District, PMB 308, Abuja; tel. (9) 2346594.

Consists of a Chief Justice and up to 15 Justices, appointed by the President, on the recommendation of the National Judicial Council (subject to the approval of the Senate). It has original jurisdiction in any dispute between the Federation and a State, or between States, and hears appeals from the Federal Court of Appeal.

Chief Justice: MUHAMMADU LAWAL UWAIS.

Court of Appeal: consists of a President and at least 35 Justices, of whom three must be experts in Islamic (*Shari'a*) law and three experts in Customary law.

Federal High Court: consists of a Chief Judge and a number of other judges.

Each State has a **High Court**, consisting of a Chief Judge and a number of judges, appointed by the Governor of the State on the recommendation of the National Judicial Council (subject to the approval of the House of Assembly of the State). If required, a state may have a **Shari'a Court of Appeal** (dealing with Islamic civil law) and a **Customary Court of Appeal**. **Special Military Tribunals** have been established to try offenders accused of crimes such as corruption, drugs-trafficking and armed robbery; appeals against rulings of the Special Military Tribunals are referred to a **Special Appeals Tribunal**, which comprises retired judges.

Religion

ISLAM

According to the 1963 census, there were more than 26m. Muslims (47.2% of the total population) in Nigeria.

Spiritual Head: Alhaji MOHAMED MACCIDO (the Sultan of Sokoto).

CHRISTIANITY

The 1963 census enumerated more than 19m. Christians (34.5% of the total population).

Christian Council of Nigeria: 139 Ogunlana Drive, Surulere, POB 2838, Lagos; tel. (1) 836019; f. 1929; 12 full mems and seven assoc. mems; Pres. Rt Rev. Dr S. A. FALEYE; Gen. Sec. C. O. WILLIAMS.

The Anglican Communion

Anglicans are adherents of the Church of the Province of Nigeria, comprising 61 dioceses. Nigeria, formerly part of the Province of West Africa, became a separate Province in 1979; in 1997 it was divided into three separate provinces. The Church had an estimated 10m. members in 1990.

Archbishop of Province I and Bishop of Lagos: Most Rev. EPHRAIM A. ADEMOW, Archbishop's Palace, 29 Marina, POB 13, Lagos; tel. (1) 2635681; fax (1) 2631264.

Archbishop of Province II and Bishop of Awka: Most Rev. MAXWELL ANIKWENWA, Bishopscourt, Ifite Rd, POB 130, Awka.

Archbishop of Province III and Bishop of Abuja: Most Rev. PETER JASPER AKINOLA, Archbishop's Palace, POB 212, ADCP, Abuja; fax (9) 5230986; e-mail abuja@anglican.skannet.com.ng.

General Secretary: Ven. SAMUEL B. AKINOLA, 29 Marina, POB 78, Lagos; tel. (1) 2635681; fax (1) 2631264.

The Roman Catholic Church

Nigeria comprises nine archdioceses, 36 dioceses, two Apostolic Vicariates and one Apostolic Prefecture. At 31 December 2000 the total number of adherents represented an estimated 14% of the population.

Catholic Bishops' Conference of Nigeria

6 Force Rd, POB 951, Lagos; tel. (1) 2635849; fax (1) 2636680; e-mail cathsecl@infoweb.abs.net.

f. 1976; Pres. Most Rev. JOHN O. ONAIYEKAN (Archbishop of Abuja).

Catholic Secretariat of Nigeria: 6 Force Rd, POB 951, Lagos; tel. (1) 2635849; fax (1) 2636680; e-mail cathsecl@infoweb.abs.net.

Sec.-Gen. Rev. Fr MATTHEW HASSAN KUKAH.

Archbishop of Abuja: Most Rev. JOHN O. ONAIYEKAN, Archdiocesan Secretariat, POB 286, Garki, Abuja; tel. (9) 2340661; fax (9) 2343661; e-mail archbuja@infoweb.abs.net.

Archbishop of Benin City: Most Rev. PATRICK E. EKPU, Archdiocesan Secretariat, POB 35, Benin City, Edo; tel. (52) 253787; fax (52) 255763; e-mail cadobc@infoweb.abs.net.

Archbishop of Calabar: Most Rev. BRIAN D. USANGA, Archdiocesan Secretariat, PMB 1044, Calabar, Cross River; tel. (87) 232176; fax (87) 231407.

Archbishop of Ibadan: Most Rev. FELIX ALABA JOB, Archdiocesan Secretariat, 8 Latosa Rd, PMB 5057, Ibadan, Oyo; tel. (22) 2413544; fax (22) 2414855; e-mail archdiocese.ibadan@skannet.com.ng.

Archbishop of Jos: Most Rev. IGNATIUS AYAU KAIGAMA, Archdiocesan Secretariat, 20 Joseph Gomwalk Rd, POB 494, Jos, Plateau; tel. (73) 451548; fax (73) 451547; e-mail josarch@hisen.org.

Archbishop of Kaduna: Most Rev. PETER YARIYOK JATAU, Archbishop's House, Tafawa Balewa Way, POB 248, Kaduna; tel. (62) 236076; fax (62) 240026; e-mail catholickad@email.com.

Archbishop of Lagos: Most Rev. ANTHONY OLUBUNMI OKOGIE, Archdiocesan Secretariat, 19 Catholic Mission St, POB 8, Lagos; tel. (1) 2635729; fax (1) 2633841; e-mail arclagos@infoweb.abs.net.

Archbishop of Onitsha: Most Rev. ALBERT KANENE OBIEFUNA, Archdiocesan Secretariat, POB 411, Onitsha, Anambra; tel. (46) 210444; fax (46) 462963; e-mail obiefuna30@hotmail.com.

Archbishop of Owerri: Most Rev. ANTHONY J. V. OBINNA, Archdiocesan Secretariat, POB 85, Owerri, Imo; tel. (83) 230115; fax (83) 230760; e-mail jvobinna@primanet.

Other Christian Churches

Brethren Church of Nigeria: c/o Kulp Bible School, POB 1, Mubi, Adamawa; f. 1923; 100,000 mems; Gen. Sec. Rev. ABRAHAM WUTA TIZHE.

Church of the Lord (Aladura): Anthony Village, Ikorodu Rd, POB 308, Ikeja, Lagos; tel. (1) 4964749; f. 1930; 1.1m. mems; Primate Dr E. O. A. ADEJOBI.

Lutheran Church of Christ in Nigeria: POB 21, Numan, Adamawa; 575,000 mems; Pres. Rt Rev. Dr DAVID L. WINDIBIZIRI.

Lutheran Church of Nigeria: Obot Idim Ibesikpo, Uyo, Akwa Ibom; tel. and fax (85) 201848; f. 1936; 370,000 mems; Pres. Rev. S. J. UDOFIA.

Methodist Church Nigeria: Wesley House, 21–22 Marina, POB 2011, Lagos; tel. (1) 2631853; 483,500 mems; Patriarch Rev. SUNDAY COFFIE MBANG.

Nigerian Baptist Convention: Baptist Bldg, PMB 5113, Ibadan; tel. (2) 2412267; fax (2) 2413561; e-mail baptconv@skannet.com;

2.5m. mems; Pres. Rev. EMMANUEL O. BOLARINWA; Gen. Sec. Dr ADEMOLA ISHOLA.

Presbyterian Church of Nigeria: 26–29 Ehere Rd, Ogbor Hill, POB 2635, Aba, Imo; tel. (82) 222551; f. 1846; 130,000 mems; Moderator Rt Rev. Dr A. A. OTU; Synod Clerk Rev. UBON B. USUNG.

The Redeemed Church of Christ, the Church of the Foursquare Gospel, the Qua Iboe Church and the Salvation Army are prominent among numerous other Christian churches active in Nigeria.

AFRICAN RELIGIONS

The beliefs, rites and practices of the people of Nigeria are very diverse, varying between ethnic groups and between families in the same group. In 1963 about 10m. persons (18% of the total population) were followers of traditional beliefs.

The Press

DAILIES

Abuja Times: Daily Times of Nigeria Ltd, 2 Hasper Crescent, Wuse Zone 7, PMB 115 Gaski, Abuja; tel. (1) 4900850; f. 1992; Editor CLEMENT ILOBA.

Daily Champion: Isolo Industrial Estate, Oshodi-Apapa, Lagos; fax (1) 4526011; e-mail letters@champion-newspapers.com; internet www.champion-newspapers.com; Editor AUGSTEN ADAMU.

Daily Express: Commercial Amalgamated Printers, 30 Glover St, Lagos; f. 1938; Editor Alhaji AHMED ALAO (acting); circ. 20,000.

Daily Sketch: Sketch Publishing Ltd, Oba Adebimpe Rd, PMB 5067, Ibadan; tel. (2) 414851; f. 1964; govt-owned; Chair. RONKE OKUSANYA; Editor ADEMOLA IDOWU; circ. 64,000.

Daily Star: 9 Works Rd, PMB 1139, Enugu; tel. (42) 253561; Editor JOSEF BEL-MOLOKWU.

Daily Times: Daily Times of Nigeria Ltd, New Isheri Rd, Agidingbi, PMB 21340, Ikeja, Lagos; tel. (1) 4900850; f. 1925; 60% govt-owned; Editor OGBUAGU ANIKWE; circ. 400,000.

The Democrat: 9 Ahmed Talib Ave, POB 4457, Kaduna South; tel. (62) 231907; f. 1983; Editor ABDULHAMID BABATUNDE; circ. 100,000.

Evening Times: Daily Times of Nigeria Ltd, New Isheri Rd, Agidingbi, PMB 21340, Ikeja, Lagos; tel. (1) 4900850; Man. Dir Dr ONUKA ADINOYI-OJO; Editor CLEMENT ILOBA; circ. 20,000.

The Guardian: Rutam House, Isolo Expressway, Isolo, PMB 1217, Oshodi, Lagos; tel. (1) 524111; internet www.ngrguardiannews.com; f. 1983; independent; Publr ALEX IBRU; Editor EMEKA IZEZE; circ. 80,000.

National Concord: Concord House, 42 Concord Way, POB 4483, Ikeja, Lagos; f. 1980; Editor NSIKAK ESSIEN; circ. 200,000.

New Nigerian: Ahmadu Bello Way, POB 254, Kaduna; tel. (62) 201420; f. 1965; govt-owned; Chair. Prof. TEKENA TAMUNO; Editor (vacant); circ. 80,000.

Nigerian Chronicle: Cross River State Newspaper Corpn, 17-19 Barracks Rd, POB 1074, Calabar; tel. (87) 224976; fax (87) 224979; f. 1970; Editor UNIMKE NAWA; circ. 50,000.

Nigerian Herald: Kwara State Printing and Publishing Corpn, Offa Rd, PMB 1369, Ilorin; tel. and fax (31) 220506; f. 1973; sponsored by Kwara State Govt; Editor RAZAK EL-ALAWA; circ. 25,000.

Nigerian Observer: The Bendel Newspaper Corpn, 18 Airport Rd, POB 1143, Benin City; tel. (52) 240050; f. 1968; Editor TONY IKEAKANAM; circ. 150,000.

Nigerian Standard: 5 Joseph Gomwalk Rd, POB 2112, Jos; f. 1972; govt-owned; Editor SALE ILIYA; circ. 100,000.

Nigerian Statesman: Imo Newspapers Ltd, Owerri-Egbu Rd, POB 1095, Owerri; tel. (83) 230099; f. 1978; sponsored by Imo State Govt; Editor EDUBE WADIBIA.

Nigerian Tide: Rivers State Newspaper Corpn, 4 Ikwerre Rd, POB 5072, Port Harcourt; f. 1971; Editor AUGUSTINE NJOAGWUANI; circ. 30,000.

Nigerian Tribune: African Newspapers of Nigeria Ltd, Imalefalafi St, Oke-Ado, POB 78, Ibadan; tel. (2) 2313410; fax (2) 2317573; e-mail correspondence@nigerian-tribune.com; internet www.nigerian-tribune.com; f. 1949; Editor FOLU OLAMITI; circ. 109,000.

Post Express: 7 Warehouse Rd, PMB 1186, Apapa, Lagos; tel. (1) 5453351; fax (1) 5453436; e-mail postexpress@nova.net.ng; internet www.postexpresswired.com; Publr Chief S. ODUWU; Man. Dir Dr STANLEY MACEBUH.

The Punch: Skyway Press, Kudeti St, PMB 21204, Onipetsi, Ikeja; tel. (1) 4963580; f. 1976; Editor GBMEIGA OGUNLEYE; circ. 150,000.

This Day: 35 Creek Rd, Apapa, Lagos; tel. (1) 5871432; fax (1) 5871436; e-mail thisday@nova.net.ng; internet www.thisdayonline .com.

Vanguard: Kirikiri Canal, PMB 1007, Apapa; e-mail vanguard@ linkserve.com.ng; internet www.vanguardngr.com; f. 1984; Editor FRANK AIGBOGUN.

SUNDAY NEWSPAPERS

Sunday Chronicle: Cross River State Newspaper Corpn, PMB 1074, Calabar; f. 1977; Editor-in-Chief ETIM ANIM; circ. 163,000.

Sunday Concord: Concord House, 42 Concord Way, POB 4483, Ikeja, Lagos; f. 1980; Editor DELE ALAKE.

Sunday Herald: Kwara State Printing and Publishing Corpn, PMB 1369, Ilorin; tel. (31) 220976; f. 1981; Editor CHARLES OSAGIE (acting).

Sunday New Nigerian: Ahmadu Bello Way, POB 254, Kaduna; tel. (62) 245220; fax (62) 213778; e-mail auduson@newnigerian.com; f. 1981; weekly; Editor IBRAHIM AUDUSON; circ. 120,000.

Sunday Observer: PMB 1334, Bendel Newspapers Corpn, 18 Airport Rd, Benin City; f. 1968; Editor T. O. BORHA; circ. 60,000.

Sunday Punch: Kudeti St, PMB 21204, Ikeja; tel. (1) 4964691; fax (1) 4960715; f. 1973; Editor DAYO WRIGHT; circ. 150,000.

Sunday Sketch: Sketch Publishing Co Ltd, PMB 5067, Ibadan; tel. (2) 414851; f. 1964; govt-owned; Editor OBAFEMI OREDEIN; circ. 125,000.

Sunday Standard: Plateau Publishing Co Ltd, Owerri-Egbu Rd, PMB 1095, Owerri; tel. (83) 230099; f. 1978; sponsored by Imo State Govt; Editor EDUBE WADIBIA.

Sunday Sun: PMB 1025, Okoro House, Factory Lane, off Upper Mission Rd, New Benin.

Sunday Tide: 4 Ikwerre Rd, POB 5072, Port Harcourt; f. 1971; Editor AUGUSTINE NJOAGWUANI.

Sunday Times: Daily Times of Nigeria Ltd, New Isheri Rd, Agidingbi, PMB 21340, Ikeja, Lagos; tel. (1) 4900850; f. 1953; 60% govt-owned; Editor DUPE AJAYI; circ. 100,000.

Sunday Tribune: Imalefalafi St, POB 78, Oke-Ado, Ibadan; tel. (2) 2310886; Editor WALE OJO.

Sunday Vanguard: Kirikiri Canal, PMB 1007, Apapa; Editor DUPE AJAYI.

WEEKLIES

Albishir: Triumph Publishing Co Ltd, Gidan Sa'adu Zungur, PMB 3155, Kano; tel. (64) 260273; f. 1981; Hausa; Editor ALIYU UMAR (acting); circ. 15,000.

Business Times: Daily Times of Nigeria Ltd, New Isheri Rd, Agidingbi, PMB 21340, Ikeja, Lagos; tel. (1) 4900850; f. 1925; 60% govt-owned; Editor GODFREY BAMAWO; circ. 22,000.

Gboungboun: Sketch Publishing Co Ltd, New Court Rd, PMB 5067, Ibadan; tel. (2) 414851; govt-owned; Yoruba; Editor A. O. ADEBANJO; circ. 80,000.

The Independent: Bodija Rd, PMB 5109, Ibadan; f. 1960; English; Roman Catholic; Editor Rev. F. B. CRONIN-COLTSMAN; circ. 13,000.

Irohin Imole: 15 Bamgbose St, POB 1495, Lagos; f. 1957; Yoruba; Editor TUNJI ADEOSUN.

Irohin Yoruba: 212 Broad St, PMB 2416, Lagos; tel. (1) 410886; f. 1945; Yoruba; Editor S. A. AJIBADE; circ. 85,000.

Lagos Life: Guardian Newspapers Ltd, Rutam House, Isolo Expressway, Isolo, PMB 1217, Oshodi, Lagos; f. 1985; Editor BISI OGUNBADEJO; circ. 100,000.

Lagos Weekend: Daily Times of Nigeria Ltd, New Isheri Rd, Agidingbi, PMB 21340, Ikeja, Lagos; tel. (1) 4900850; f. 1965; 60% govt-owned; news and pictures; Editor SAM OGWA; circ. 85,000.

The News: Lagos; independent; Editor-in-Chief JENKINS ALUMONA.

Newswatch: 3 Billingsway Rd, Oregun, Lagos; tel. (1) 4935654; fax (1) 4960950; e-mail newswatchngr@aol.com; f. 1985; English; CEO RAY EKPU; Editor-in-Chief DAN AGBESE.

Nigerian Radio/TV Times: Nigerian Broadcasting Corpn, POB 12504, Ikoyi.

Sporting Records: Daily Times of Nigeria Ltd, New Isheri Rd, Agidingbi, PMB 21340, Ikeja, Lagos; tel. (1) 4900850; f. 1961; 60% govt-owned; Editor CYRIL KAPPO; circ. 10,000.

Tempo: 26 Ijaiye Rd, PMB 21531, Ogba, Ikeja, Lagos; tel. (1) 920975; fax (1) 4924998; e-mail ijc@linkserve.com.ng; news magazine.

Times International: Daily Times of Nigeria Ltd, 3–7 Kakawa St, POB 139, Lagos; f. 1974; Editor Dr HEZY IDOWU; circ. 50,000.

Truth (The Muslim Weekly): 45 Idumagbo Ave, POB 418, Lagos; tel. (1) 2668455; f. 1951; Editor S. O. LAWAL.

ENGLISH LANGUAGE PERIODICALS

Afriscope: 29 Salami Saibu St, PMB 1119, Yaba; monthly; African current affairs.

The Ambassador: PMB 2011, 1 peru-Remo, Ogun; tel. (39) 620115; quarterly; Roman Catholic; circ. 20,000.

Benin Review: Ethiope Publishing Corpn, PMB 1332, Benin City; f. 1974; African art and culture; 2 a year; circ. 50,000.

Headlines: Daily Times of Nigeria Ltd, New Isheri Rd, Agindingbi, PMB 21340, Ikeja, Lagos; f. 1973; monthly; Editor ADAMS ALIU; circ. 500,000.

Home Studies: Daily Times Publications, 3–7 Kakawa St, Lagos; f. 1964; 2 a month; Editor Dr ELIZABETH E. IKEM; circ. 40,000.

Insight: 3 Kakawa St, POB 139, Lagos; quarterly; contemporary issues; Editor SAM AMUKA; circ. 5,000.

Journal of the Nigerian Medical Association: 3–7 Kakawa St, POB 139, Apapa; quarterly; Editor Prof. A. O. ADESOLA.

Lagos Education Review: Faculty of Education, University of Lagos Akoka, Lagos; tel. (1) 820448; fax (1) 822644; f. 1978; 2 a year; African education; Editor Prof. M. N. OKENIMKPE.

The Leader: 19A Assumpta Press Ave, Industrial Layout, PMB 1017, Owerri, Imo; tel. (83) 230932; fortnightly; Roman Catholic; Editor Rev. KEVIN C. AKAGHA.

Management in Nigeria: Plot 22, Idowu Taylor St, Victoria Island, POB 2557, Lagos; tel. (1) 2615105; fax (1) 614116; e-mail nim@rcl .nig.com; quarterly; journal of Nigerian Inst. of Management; Editor Rev. DEJI OLOKESUSI; circ. 25,000.

Marketing in Nigeria: Alpha Publications, Surulere, POB 1163, Lagos; f. 1977; monthly; Editor B. O. K. NWELIH; circ. 30,000.

Modern Woman: 47–49 Salami Saibu St, Marina, POB 2583, Lagos; f. 1964; monthly; Man. Editor TOUN ONABANJO.

The New Nation: 52 Iwaya Rd, Onike, Yaba, Surulere, POB 896, Lagos; tel. (1) 5863629; monthly; news magazine.

Nigeria Magazine: Federal Dept of Culture, PMB 12524, Lagos; tel. (1) 5802060; f. 1927; quarterly; travel, cultural, historical and general; Editor B. D. LEMCHI; circ. 5,000.

Nigerian Businessman's Magazine: 39 Mabo St, Surulere, Lagos; monthly; Nigerian and overseas commerce.

Nigerian Journal of Economic and Social Studies: Nigerian Economic Society, c/o Dept of Economics, University of Ibadan; tel. (2) 8101701; fax (2) 8100079; f. 1959; 3 a year; Editor Prof. A. H. EKPO.

Nigerian Journal of Science: University of Ibadan, POB 4039, Ibadan; publ. of the Science Asscn of Nigeria; f. 1966; 2 a year; Editor Prof. L. B. KOLAWOLE; circ. 1,000.

Nigerian Worker: United Labour Congress, 97 Herbert Macaulay St, Lagos; Editor LAWRENCE BORHA.

The President: New Breed Organization Ltd, Plot 14 Western Ave, 1 Rafiu Shitty St, Alaka Estate, Surulere, POB 385, Lagos; tel. (1) 5802690; fax (1) 5831175; fortnightly; management; Chief Editor CHRIS OKOLIE.

Quality: Ultimate Publications Ltd, Oregun Rd, Lagos; f. 1987; monthly; Editor BALA DAN MUSA.

Radio-Vision Times: Western Nigerian Radio-Vision Service, Television House, POB 1460, Ibadan; monthly; Editor ALTON A. ADEDEJI.

Savanna: Ahmadu Bello University Press Ltd, PMB 1094, Zaria; tel. (69) 550054; e-mail abupl@abu.edu.ng; f. 1972; 2 a year; Prof. Alhaji I. O. ARIYO (acting); circ. 1,000.

Spear: Daily Times of Nigeria Ltd, New Isheri Rd, Agidingbi, PMB 21340, Ikeja, Lagos; tel. (1) 4900850; f. 1962; monthly; family magazine; Editor COKER ONITA; circ. 10,000.

Technical and Commercial Message: Surulere, POB 1163, Lagos; f. 1980; 6 a year; Editor B. O. K. NWELIH; circ. 12,500.

Today's Challenge: PMB 2010, Jos; tel. (73) 52230; f. 1951; 6 a year; religious and educational; Editor JACOB SHAIBY TSADO; circ. 15,000.

Woman's World: Daily Times of Nigeria Ltd, New Isheri Rd, Agidingbi, PMB 21340, Ikeja, Lagos; monthly; Editor TOYIN JOHNSON; circ. 12,000.

VERNACULAR PERIODICALS

Abokiyar Hira: Albah International Publishers, POB 6177, Bompai, Kano; f. 1987; monthly; Hausa; cultural; Editor BASHARI F. FOUKBAH; circ. 35,000.

Gaskiya ta fi Kwabo: Ahmadu Bello Way, POB 254, Kaduna; tel. (62) 201420; f. 1939; 3 a week; Hausa; Editor ABDUL-HASSAN IBRAHIM.

NEWS AGENCIES

Independent Media Centre (IMC): POB 894, Benin City; e-mail nigeriaimc@yahoo.com; internet www.nigeria.indymedia.org.

News Agency of Nigeria (NAN): Independence Avenue, Central Business Area, PMB 7006, Garki, Abuja; tel. (9) 2341189; fax (9) 2344897; e-mail nanabujaq@rd.nig.com; internet www.nannews .com; f. 1978; Man. Dir Malam WADA ABDULLAHI MAIDA; Editor-in-Chief SHEHU ABUI.

Foreign Bureaux

Agence France-Presse (AFP): 11 Awolowo Rd, SW Ikoyi, PMB 2448, Lagos; tel. (1) 2691336; fax (1) 2670925; e-mail afplagos@afp .com; Bureau Chief DAVID CLARKE.

Informatsionnoye Telegrafnoye Agentstvo Rossii– Telegrafnoye Agentstvo Suverennykh Stran (ITAR—TASS) (Russia): 401 St, POB 6465, Victoria Island, Lagos; tel. (1) 617119; Correspondent BORIS VASILIEVICH PILNIKOV.

Inter Press Service (IPS) (Italy): c/o News Agency of Nigeria, PMB 12756, Lagos; tel. (1) 5801290; Correspondent REMI OYO.

Pan-African News Agency (PANA): c/o News Agency of Nigeria, National Arts Theatre, POB 8715, Marina, Lagos; tel. (1) 5801290; f. 1979.

Xinhua (New China) News Agency (People's Republic of China): 161A Adeola Odeku St, Victoria Island, POB 70278, Lagos; tel. (1) 2612464; Bureau Chief ZHAI JINGSHENG.

Publishers

Africana-FEP Publishers Ltd: Book House Trust, 1 Africana-FEP Drive, PMB 1639, Onitsha; tel. (46) 210669; f. 1973; study guides, general science, textbooks; Man. Dir RALPH O. EKPEH.

Ahmadu Bello University Press: PMB 1094, Zaria; tel. (69) 550054; e-mail abupl@abu.edu.ng; f. 1972; history, Africana, social sciences, education, literature and arts; Man. Dir SA'IDU HASSAN ADAMU.

Albah International Publishers: 100 Kurawa, Bompai-Kano, POB 6177, Kano City; f. 1978; Africana, Islamic, educational and general, in Hausa; Chair. BASHARI F. ROUKBAH.

Alliance West African Publishers: Orindingbin Estate, New Aketan Layout, PMB 1039, Oyo; tel. (85) 230798; f. 1971; educational and general; Man. Dir Chief M. O. OGUNMOLA.

Aromolaran Publishing Co Ltd: POB 1800, Ibadan; tel. (2) 715980; f. 1968; educational and general; Man. Dir Dr ADEKUNLE AROMOLARAN.

Cross Continent Press Ltd: 25 Egbeyemi Rd, Ilupeju, POB 282, Yaba, Lagos; tel. and fax (1) 7746348; e-mail crosscontinent@yahoo .com; f. 1974; general, educational and academic; Man. Dir Dr T. C. NWOSU.

Daar Communications Ltd: Communication Village, AIT Rd, Off Lagos–Abeokuta Expressway, Ilapo Village, Alagbado, Lagos; tel. (1) 2644814; fax (1) 2644817; broadcasting and information services; Man. Dir. KENNY OGUNGBE.

Daystar Press: Daystar House, POB 1261, Ibadan; tel. (2) 8102670; f. 1962; religious and educational; Man. PHILLIP ADELAKUN LADOKUN.

ECWA Productions Ltd: PMB 2010, Jos; tel. (73) 52230; f. 1973; religious and educational; Gen. Man. Rev. J. K. BOLARIN.

Ethiope Publishing Corpn: Ring Rd, PMB 1332, Benin City; tel. (52) 243036; f. 1970; general fiction and non-fiction, textbooks, reference, science, arts and history; Man. Dir SUNDAY N. OLAYE.

Evans Brothers (Nigeria Publishers) Ltd: Jericho Rd, PMB 5164, Ibadan; tel. (2) 2414394; fax (2) 2410757; f. 1966; general and educational; Chair. Dr A. O. OJORA; Man. Dir B. O. BOLODEOKU.

Fourth Dimension Publishing Co Ltd: 16 Fifth Avenue, City Layout, PMB 01164, Enugu; tel. (42) 459969; fax (42) 456904; e-mail nwankwov@infoweb.abs.net; internet www.fdpbooks.com; f. 1977; periodicals, fiction, verse, educational and children's; Chair. ARTHUR NWANKWO; Man. Dir V. U. NWANKWO.

Gbabeks Publishers Ltd: POB 37252, Ibadan; tel. (62) 2315705; e-mail gbabeks@hotmail.com; f. 1982; educational and technical; Man. Dir TAYO OGUNBEKUN.

Heinemann Educational Books (Nigeria) Ltd: 1 Ighodaro Rd, Jericho, PMB 5205, Ibadan; tel. (2) 2412268; fax (2) 2411089; e-mail info@heinemannbooks.com; internet www.heinemannbooks.com; f.

1962; educational, law, medical and general; Chair. AIGBOJE HIGO; Man. Dir AYO OJENIYI.

Heritage Books: the Poet's Cottage, Artistes Village, Ilogbo-Eremi, Badagry Expressway, POB 610, Apapa, Lagos; tel. (1) 5871333; e-mail theendofknowledge@yahoo; internet www .theendofknowledge.com; f. 1971; general; Chair. NAIWU OSAHON.

Ibadan University Press: Publishing House, University of Ibadan, PMB 16, IU Post Office, Ibadan; tel. (2) 400550; f. 1951; scholarly, science, law, general and educational; Dir F. A. ADESANOYE.

Ilesanmi Press Ltd: Akure Rd, POB 204, Ilesha; tel. 2062; f. 1955; general and educational; Man. Dir G. E. ILESANMI.

John West Publications Ltd: Plot 2, Block A, Acme Rd, Ogba Industrial Estate, PMB 21001, Ikeja; tel. (1) 4925459; f. 1964; general; Man. Dir Alhaji L. K. JAKAUDE.

Kolasanya Publishing Enterprise: 2 Epe Rd, Oke-Owa, PMB 2099, Ijebu-Ode; general and educational; Man. Dir Chief K. OSUNSANYA.

Literamed Publications Ltd (Lantern Books): Plot 45, Alausa Bus-stop, Oregun Industrial Estate, Ikeja, PMB 21068, Lagos; tel. (1) 4962512; fax (1) 4935258; e-mail literamed@infoweb.abs.net; internet www.lantern-books.com; general; Chair. O. M. LAWAL-SOLARIN.

Longman Nigeria Ltd: 52 Oba Akran Ave, PMB 21036, Ikeja, Lagos; tel. (1) 4978925; fax (1) 4964370; e-mail longman@linkserve .com; f. 1961; general and educational; Man. Dir J. A. OLOWONIYI.

Macmillan Nigeria Publishers Ltd: Ilupeju Industrial Estate, 4 Industrial Ave, POB 264, Yaba, Lagos; tel. (1) 4962185; f. 1965; educational and general; Exec. Chair. J. O. EMMANUEL; Man. Dir Dr A. I. ADELEKAN.

Minaj Systems Ltd: Ivie House, 4–6 Ajose Adeogun St, POB 70811, Victoria Island, Lagos; tel. (1) 2621168; fax (1) 2621167; e-mail minaj@minaj.com; broadcasting, printing and publishing; Chair. Chief MIKE NNANYE I. AJEGBO.

Nelson Publishers Ltd: 8 Ilupeju By-Pass, Ikeja, PMB 21303, Lagos; tel. (1) 4961452; general and educational; Chair. Prof. C. O. TAIWO; Man. Dir R. O. OGUNBO.

Northern Nigerian Publishing Co Ltd: Gaskiya Bldg, POB 412, Zaria; tel. (69) 332087; f. 1966; general, educational and vernacular texts; Gen. Man. JA'AFAR D. MOHAMMED.

NPS Educational Publishers Ltd: Trusthouse, Ring Rd, off Akinyemi Way, POB 62, Ibadan; tel. (2) 316006; f. 1969; academic, scholarly and educational; CEO T. D. OTESANYA.

Nwamife Publishers: 10 Ibiam St, Uwani, POB 430, Enugu; tel. (42) 338254; f. 1971; general and educational; Chair. FELIX C. ADI.

Obafemi Awolowo University Press Ltd: Obafemi Awolowo University, Ile-Ife; tel. (36) 230284; f. 1968; educational, scholarly and periodicals; Man. Dir AKIN FATOKUN.

Obobo Books: the Poet's Cottage, Artistes Village, Ilogbo-Eremi, Badagry Expressway, POB 610, Apapa, Lagos; tel. and fax (1) 5871333; e-mail theendofknowledge@yahoo.com; internet www .theendofknowledge.com; f. 1981; children's books; Editorial Dir BAKIN KUNAMA.

Ogunsanya Press Publishers and Bookstores Ltd: SW9/1133 Orita Challenge, Idiroko, POB 95, Ibadan; tel. (2) 310924; f. 1970; educational; Man. Dir Chief LUCAS JUSTUS POPO-OLA OGUNSANYA.

Onibonoje Press and Book Industries (Nigeria) Ltd: Felele Layout, Challenge, POB 3109, Ibadan; tel. (2) 313956; f. 1958; educational and general; Chair. G. ONIBONOJE; Man. Dir J. O. ONIBONOJE.

Pilgrim Books Ltd: New Oluyole Industrial Estate, Ibadan/Lagos Expressway, PMB 5617, Ibadan; tel. (2) 317218; educational and general; Man. Dir JOHN E. LEIGH.

Spectrum Books Ltd: Sunshine House, 1 Emmanuel Alayande St, Oluyole Estate, PMB 5612, Ibadan; tel. (2) 2310145; fax (2) 2318502; e-mail admin1@spectrumbooksonline.com; internet www .spectrumbooksonline.com; f. 1978; educational and fiction; Man. Dir JOOP BERKHOUT.

University of Lagos Press: University of Lagos, POB 132, Akoka, Yaba, Lagos; tel. (1) 825048; e-mail library@rcl.nig.com; university textbooks, monographs, lectures and journals; Man. Dir S. BODUNDE BANKOLE.

University Press Ltd: Three Crowns Bldg, Eleyele Rd, Jericho, PMB 5095, Ibadan; tel. (2) 2411356; fax (2) 2412056; e-mail unipress@skannet.com.ng; f. 1978; associated with Oxford University Press; educational; Man. Dir WAHEED O. OLAJIDE.

University Publishing Co: 11 Central School Rd, POB 386, Onitsha; tel. (46) 210013; f. 1959; primary, secondary and university textbooks; Chair. E. O. Ugwuegbulem.

Vanguard Media Ltd: Vanguard Ave, off Mile 2/Apapa Expressway, Kirikiri Canal; tel. (1) 5871200; fax (1) 5872662; e-mail vanguard@linkserve.com.ng; Publr Sam Amuka.

Vista Books Ltd: 59 Awolowo Rd, S. W. Ikoyi, POB 282, Yaba, Lagos; tel. (1) 7746348; e-mail vista-books@yahoo.com; f. 1991; general fiction and non-fiction, arts, children's and educational; Man. Dir Dr T. C. Nwosu.

West African Book Publishers Ltd: Ilupeju Industrial Estate, 28–32 Industrial Ave, POB 3445, Lagos; tel. (1) 4970196; fax (1) 4970294; f. 1967; textbooks, children's, periodicals and general; Dir F. B. Omo-Eboh.

PUBLISHERS' ASSOCIATION

Nigerian Publishers Association: Book House, NPA Permanent Secretariat, Jericho G.R.A., POB 2541, Ibadan; tel. (2) 2413396; f. 1965; Pres. S. B. Bankole.

Broadcasting and Communications

TELECOMMUNICATIONS

Nigerian Communications Commission (NCC): Plot 19, Aguata Close, Garki 2, Abuja; tel. (9) 2344589; e-mail ncc@ncc.gov.ng; internet www.ncc.gov.ng; f. 1992 as an independent regulatory body for the supply of telecommunications services and facilities; Chair. Alhaji Ahmed Jodi.

Intercellular Nigeria Ltd: UBA House, 57, Marina, PMB 80078, Victoria Island, Lagos; tel. (1) 4703010; fax (1) 2643014; e-mail hq@intercellular-ng.com; f. 1993; internet and international telephone services; Pres. Bashir El-Rufai.

Motophone Ltd: C. & C. Towers, Plot 1684, Sanusi Fafumwa St, Victoria Island, Lagos; tel. (1) 2624168; fax (1) 2620079; e-mail motophone@hyperia.com; f. 1990; Man. Dir Eric Chamchoum.

Multi-Links Telecommunication Ltd: 231 Adeola Odeku St, Victoria Island, POB 3453, Marina, Lagos; tel. (1) 7740000; fax (1) 2622452; e-mail ccu@multilink.com; f. 1994; Man. Dir C. K. Ramani.

Nigerian Mobile Telecommunications Ltd (M-TEL): 3 M-Tel St, off Mal. Aminu Kano Crescent, Wuse 2, Abuja; tel. (9) 5237801; fax (9) 409066; f. 1996; Man. Dir Eng. Ismaila Mohammed.

Nigerian Telecommunications (NITEL): 2 Bissau St, off Herbert Macaulay Way, Wuse Zone 6, Abuja; tel. (9) 5233021; Man. Dir Dr Emmanuel Ojeba.

Telnet (Nigeria) Ltd: Plot 242, Kofo Abayomi St, Victoria Island, POB 53656, Falomi Ikoyi, Lagos; tel. (1) 2611729; fax (1) 2619945; e-mail info@iteco.com; internet www.telnetng.com; f. 1985; telecommunications engineering and consultancy services; Man. Dir Dr Nadu Denloye.

BROADCASTING

Regulatory Authority

National Broadcasting Commission: Plot 807, Ibrahim Taiwo Rd, Asokoro District, POB 5747, Garki, Abuja; tel. (9) 3147525; fax (9) 3147522; e-mail info@nbc-ng.org; internet www.nbc-ng.org; Dir-Gen. Mallam Danladi Bako.

Radio

Federal Radio Corpn of Nigeria (FRCN): Area 11, Garki, PMB 55, Abuja; tel. (9) 2345915; fax (9) 2345914; f. 1976; controlled by the Fed. Govt and divided into five zones: Lagos (English); Enugu (English, Igbo, Izon, Efik and Tiv); Ibadan (English, Yoruba, Edo, Urhobo and Igala); Kaduna (English, Hausa, Kanuri, Fulfulde and Nupe); Abuja (English, Hausa, Igbo and Yoruba); CEO Eddie Roh.

Imo Broadcasting Corpn: 14 Savage Crescent, Enugu, Imo; tel. (42) 250327; operates one radio station in Imo State.

Voice of Nigeria (VON): Radio House, Herbert Macaulay Way, Area 10, Garki, Abuja; tel. (9) 2344017; fax (9) 2346970; e-mail dgovon@nigol.net.ng; internet www.voiceofnigeria.org; f. 1990; controlled by the Fed. Govt; external services in English, French, Arabic, Ki-Swahili, Hausa and Fulfulde; Dir-Gen. Taiwo Alimi.

Menage Holding's Broadcasting System Ltd: Umuahia, Imo; commenced broadcasting Jan. 1996; commercial.

Ray Power 100 Drive: Abeokuta Express Way, Ilapo, Alagbado, Lagos; tel. (1) 2644814; fax (1) 2644817; commenced broadcasting Sept. 1994; commercial; Chair. Chief Raymond Dokpesi.

Television

Nigerian Television Authority (NTA): Television House, Ahmadu Bello Way, Victoria Island, PMB 12036, Lagos; tel. (1) 2615949; f. 1976; controlled by the Fed. Govt; comprises 32 stations (due to be increased to 67), which broadcast local programmes; Chair. Ifeanyinwa Nzeakor; Dir-Gen. Alhaji Mohammed Ibrahim.

NTA Aba/Owerri: Channel 6, PMB 7126, Aba, Abia; tel. (83) 220922; Gen. Man. Godwin Duru.

NTA Abeokuta: Channel 12, PMB 2190, Abeokuta, Ogun; tel. (39) 242971; f. 1979; broadcasts in English and local languages; Gen-Man. Victor Folivi.

NTA Abuja: PMB 55, Garki, Abuja; tel. (9) 2345915.

NTA Akure: PMB 794, Akure; tel. (34) 230351; Gen. Man. Jibola Dedenuola.

NTA Bauchi: PMB 0146, Bauchi; tel. (77) 42748; f. 1976; Man. Muhammad Al-Amin.

NTA Benin City: West Circular Rd, PMB 1117, Benin City; Gen. Man. J. O. N. Ezekoka.

NTA Calabar: 105 Marion Rd, Calabar; Man. E. Etuk.

NTA Enugu: Independence Layout, PMB 01530, Enugu, Anambra; tel. (42) 335120; f. 1960; Gen. Man. G. C. Mefo.

NTA Ibadan: POB 1460, Ibadan, Oyo; tel. (2) 713238; Gen. Man. Jibola Dedenuola.

NTA Ikeja: Tejuosho Ave, Surulere.

NTA Ilorin: PMB 1478, Ilorin; tel. and fax (31) 224196; Gen. Man. Vicky Olumudi.

NTA Jos: PMB 2134, Jos; Gen. Man. M. J. Bewell.

NTA Kaduna: POB 1347, Kaduna; tel. (62) 216375; f. 1977; Gen. Man. Alhaji Bello Abubakar.

NTA Kano: PMB 3343, Kano; tel. (64) 640072; Gen. Man. B. B. Muhammad.

NTA Lagos: Ahmadu Bello Way, Victoria Island, PMB 12005, 12036, Ikaji, Lagos; tel. (1) 2622082; fax (1) 2626239; Dir-Gen. Ben Murray-Bruce.

NTA Maiduguri: PMB 1487, Maiduguri; Gen. Man. M. M. Mailafiya.

NTA Makurdi: PMB 2044, Makurdi.

NTA Minna: TV House, PMB 79, Minna; tel. (66) 222941; fax (66) 222552; Gen. Man. Vicky Olumubi.

NTA Port Harcourt: PMB 5797, Port Harcourt; Gen. Man. Jon Ezekoka.

NTA Sokoto: PMB 2351, Sokoto; tel. (60) 232670; f. 1975; Gen. Man. M. B. Tunau.

NTA Yola: PMB 2197, Yola; Gen. Man. M. M. Saidu.

Finance

(cap. = capital; p.u. = paid up; res = reserves; dep. = deposits; m. = million; brs = branches; amounts in naira unless otherwise stated)

BANKING

In 1998 there were a total of 1,106 deposit banks (including 1,015 community banks) operating in Nigeria. There were also some 1,805 other financial institutions at that time.

Central Bank

Central Bank of Nigeria: Samuel Ladoke Akintola Way, PMB 0187, Garki, Abuja; tel. (1) 2660100; f. 1958; bank of issue; cap. and res 6,908.8m., dep. 168,187m. (1995); Gov. Chief Joseph Sanusi; 18 brs.

Commercial Banks

Afribank Nigeria Ltd: 51–55 Broad St, PMB 12021, Lagos; tel. (1) 2663608; fax (1) 2666327; e-mail anp-info@linkserve.com.ng; internet www.afribank.net; f. 1969 as International Bank for West Africa Ltd; cap. 552.1m., res 2,271.0m., dep. 58,287.3m. (March 2001); Chair. Alhaji Kola Belgore; Man. Dir Chief Raymond Ihyembe; 137 brs.

Allstates Trust Bank plc: Allstates Centre, Plot 1675, Oyin Jolayemi St, POB 73018, Victoria Island, Lagos; tel. (1) 4618445; fax (1) 2612206; e-mail enquiry@allstatesbankng.com; internet www.allstatesbankng.com; cap. 2,476.8m. (Sept. 2001); Man. Dir Duate Patmore Iyabi.

Bank of the North Ltd: Ahmadu Bello House, 2 Zaria Rd, POB 211, Kano; tel. (64) 660290; fax (64) 661361; f. 1960; cap. 600m., res 2,575.4m., dep. 42,130.1m. (Dec. 2000); Chair. MUHAMMADU LUGGA.

Chartered Bank plc: 1 Chartered Close, off Idejo St, Victoria Island, Lagos; tel. (1) 2620380; fax (1) 2615094; e-mail info@charteredbank.com; internet www.charteredbank.com; f. 1988; cap. 508.1m., res 1,267.6m., dep. 17,094.1m. (March 2001); Chair. Lt-Gen. (retd) MOHAMMED INUA WUSHISHI.

Citibank Nigeria: Commerce House, 1 Idowu Taylor St, Victoria Island, POB 6391, Lagos; tel. (1) 2622000; fax (1) 2618916; f. 1984; cap. 1,000m., res 4,433.3m., dep. 19,952.7m. (Dec. 2000); Chair. Chief CHARLES S. SANKEY; Man. Dir MICHEL ACCAD; 13 brs.

City Express Bank Ltd: Adetokunbo Ademola St, Victoria Island, PMB 12637, Marina, Lagos; tel. (1) 2622454; fax (1) 2619024; e-mail ceb@cityexpressbank.com; internet www.cityexpressbank.com; cap. 500m. (March 2000); Chair. SAMUEL ADEDOYIN; Man. Dir OLUSOLA ADEOTI.

Commercial Bank (Crédit Lyonnais Nigeria) Ltd: Elephant House, 214 Broad St, PMB 12829, Lagos; tel. (1) 2625700; fax (1) 2625699; e-mail fduntze@cbcln.com; f. 1983; cap. p.u. 570m.(1999), dep. 1,700m. (1993); Chair. ALLISON A. AYIDA; Man. Dir DOMINIQUE TISSIER; 21 brs.

Ecobank Nigeria Ltd: 2 Ajose Adeogun St, Victoria Island, POB 72688, Lagos; tel. (1) 2615242; fax (1) 2616568; e-mail ecobank@linkserve.com.ng; internet www.ecobank.com; cap. 652.7m., res 1,438.7m., dep. 15,173.4m. (Dec. 2000); Chair. OLUDAYO SONUGA; Man. Dir AMIN UDDIN.

Eko International Bank: Plot 5, Ikeja Commercial Scheme, off Obafemi, Awolowo, Alausa, Ikeja, PMB 12864, Lagos; tel. (1) 4932567; fax (1) 4932565; e-mail ekobank@ekobank.com; internet www.ekobank.com; f. 1986; cap. 573.0m., res 296.5m., dep. 5,554.1m. (Dec. 2001); Chair. Dr A. A. OGUNLEWE; Man. Dir OLATUNDE FASINA; 9 brs.

Equity Bank of Nigeria Ltd: Kingsway House, 107–113 Broad St, Lagos; tel. (1) 2665142; fax (1) 2660235; e-mail itequity@equity-bank.com.ng; internet www.equity-bank.com.ng; f. 1988 as Meridien Equity of Nigeria Ltd; name changed 1995; cap. 639.4m., res 411.3m., dep. 7,097.0m. (Dec. 2000); Chair. ALH ISYAKU UMAR; Man. Dir SAM O. OBAZE.

First Bank of Nigeria PLC: Samuel Asabia House, 35 Marina, POB 5216, Lagos; tel. (1) 2665900; fax (1) 2665934; e-mail fbn@firstbank-nig.com.ng; internet www.firstbank-nig.com.ng; f. 1894 as Bank of British West Africa; cap. 813m., res 16,280m., dep. 148,279m. (March 2001); Chair. UMAR ABDUL MUTALLAB; CEO and Man. Dir BERNARD O. LONGE; 302 brs.

FSB International Bank PLC: 23 Awolowo Rd, Ikoyi, PMB 12512, Lagos; tel. (1) 2690739; fax (1) 2690397; e-mail customerservice@fsbint.com; internet www.fsbint.com; f. 1974 as Federal Savings Bank; name changed 1989; cap. 610.2m., res 1,730.8m., dep. 16,472.8m. (March 2001); Chair. Alhaji A. O. G. OTITI; Man. Dir MOHAMMED HAYATU-DEEN.

Habib Nigeria Bank Ltd: 7–9 Bank Rd, PMB 2180, Kaduna; tel. (62) 235140; fax (62) 234584; e-mail info@habibbank.com.ng; internet www.habibbank.com.ng; f. 1983; cap. 629.8m. (Dec. 1999), res 557.8m., dep. 7,564.5m. (Dec. 1998); Chair. Mallam ADAMU BELLO; Man. Dir AKIN KEKERE-EKUN; 65 brs.

Intercontinental Bank Ltd: Danmole St, Plot 999C, Adela Odeku, Victoria Island, Lagos; tel. (1) 2622940; fax (1) 2622981; e-mail info@intercontinentalbankplc.com; internet www.intercontinentalbankplc.com; cap. 1,436m., dep. 25,510m. (Dec. 2001); Chair. RAYMOND C. OBIERI; 42 brs.

Investment Banking & Trust Co Ltd (IBTC): I.B.T.C. Place, Walter Carrington Crescent, POB 71707, Victoria Island, Lagos; tel. (1) 2626520; fax (1) 2626541; e-mail ibtc@ibtclagos.com; internet www.ibtclagos.com; f. 1989; cap. 1,000m., res 2,939m., dep. 8,910.1m. (March 2002); Chair. DAVID DANKARO; Man. Dir ATEDO A. PETERSIDE.

Lion Bank of Nigeria: 34 Ahmadu Bello Way, PMB 2126, Jos, Plateau; tel. (73) 452223; fax (73) 455602; e-mail itd@lionbankng.com; f. 1987; cap. 500m., res 370.2m., dep. 3,321.0m. (March 2000); Chair. Alhaji RAYYANU DALHATU.

Magnum Trust Bank: 67 Marina, PMB 12933, Lagos; tel. (1) 2640060; fax (1) 2640069; e-mail magnum@magnum-bank.com; internet www.magnum.addr.com; f. 1991; cap. 500m., res 90.4m., dep. 6,672.9m. (Feb. 2000); Chair. OMOTAYO ADIO SERIKI; Man. Dir WAHAB BABATUNDE DABIRI.

NBM Bank Ltd: 228A Awolowo Rd, POB 52463, Ikoyi, Lagos; tel. (1) 2690380; fax (1) 2693256; e-mail nbm@nbmbank.com; internet www.nbmbank.com; cap. 1,000m., res 389.9m., dep. 3,217.5m. (Dec. 2000); Chair. Chief N. O. IDOWU.

Omegabank (Nigeria) plc: 1 Engineering Close, PMB 80134, off Idowu Taylor, Victoria Island, Lagos; tel. (1) 2622580; fax (1) 2620761; e-mail omegabank@omegabankplc.com; internet www.omegabankplc.com; f. 1982 as Owena Bank plc; name changed 2001; 30% owned by Ondo State Govt; cap. 2,896.4m., res 208.0m., dep. 11,676.8m. (Dec. 2001); Chair. Chief ANTHONY ADENIYI; CEO Rev. Dr SEGUN AGBETUYI.

Société Générale Bank (Nigeria) Ltd: Sarah House, 13 Martins St, PMB 12471, Lagos; tel. (1) 2660315; fax (1) 2663731; e-mail infosgbn@sgbn.com.ng; internet www.sgbn.com.ng; cap. 556.5m., res 597.6m., dep. 14,470.9m. (June 2001); Chair. Dr SOLA SARAKI.

Trade Bank PLC: 2 Ilofa Rd, PMB 1496, Ilorin; tel. (31) 220062; fax (31) 223532; e-mail tradebnk@info.web.abs.net; internet www.tradebankplc.com; f. 1985; cap. 510.0m., res 189.1m., dep. 9,371.8m. (March 2001); Chair. Alhaji ALIYU ALARAPE SALMAN; Man. Dir SAMUEL EREOLA KOLAWOLE.

Union Bank of Nigeria Ltd: 36 Marina, PMB 2027, Lagos; tel. (1) 2630361; fax (1) 2669873; e-mail askubn@ng.com; internet www.unionbankng.com; f. 1969 as Barclays Bank of Nigeria Ltd; cap. 629m., res 13,157m., dep. 170,977m. (March 2001); Chair. Prof. KALU UKEH KALU; CEO G. A. T. OBOH; 255 brs.

United Bank for Africa (Nigeria) Ltd: UBA House, 57 Marina, POB 2406, Lagos; tel. (1) 2644651; fax (1) 2642243; e-mail info@ubaplc.com; internet www.ubaplc.com; f. 1961; cap. 850m., res 7,577m., dep. 133,135m. (March 2001); Chair. HAKEEM BELO-OSAGIE; Man. Dir and CEO Mallam ABBA KYARI; 213 brs.

Wema Bank Ltd: Wema Towers, PMB 12862, 54 Marina, Lagos; tel. (1) 2668105; fax (1) 2669508; e-mail info@wemabank.com; internet www.wemabank.com; f. 1945; cap. 675.0m., res 1,821.7m., dep. 29,631.3m. (March 2001); Man. Dir and CEO Alhaji I. A. DOSUNMU; 75 brs.

Merchant Banks

City Express Bank Ltd: Plot 1637, Adetokunbo Ademola St, Victoria Island, PMB 12637, Lagos; tel. (1) 2622454; fax (1) 2619024; e-mail ceb@cityexpressbank.com; internet www.cityexpressbank.com; f. 1988 as Industrial Bank Ltd; cap. 500.0m., res 135.6m., dep. 3,596m. (Dec. 2000); Chair. Dr SAMUEL ADEDOYIN.

FBN (Merchant Bankers) Ltd: 9/11 Macarthy St, Onikan, POB 12715, Lagos; tel. (1) 2600880; fax (1) 2633600; e-mail fbnmb@fbnmb.com; internet www.fbnmb.com; cap. 750m. (March 2000); Chair. BERNARD O. LONGE.

Fidelity Bank Ltd: Savannah House, 62-66 Broad St, Lagos; tel. (1) 2601960; fax (1) 2636868; e-mail fidelity@alpha.linkserve.com; f. 1988; cap. 544.0m. (June 2000), res 241.8m., dep. 2,689.1m. (June 1998); Chair. Chief EMMANUEL A. OKECHUKWU; CEO NEBOLISA O. ARAH.

First City Monument Bank Ltd: Primrose Tower, 17A Tinubu St, POB 9117, Lagos; tel. (1) 2665944; fax (1) 2665126; e-mail caf@fcmb-ltd.com; internet www.fcmb-ltd.com; internet www.fcmb-ltd.com; f. 1983; cap. 1,000m., res 1,000.8m., dep. 8,128.6m. (Dec. 2000); Chair. and CEO OTUNBA M. O. BALOGUN.

First Interstate Merchant Bank (Nigeria) Ltd: Kingsway Bldg Complex, 2/4 Davies St, off Marina, Victoria Island, POB 72295, Lagos; tel. (1) 2600500; fax (1) 2668273; e-mail merchant@fimb.metrong.com; cap. 507.6m., res 110.4m., dep. 2,055.3m. (March 2000); Chair. Prof. A. L. MABOGUNJE.

Indo-Nigerian Merchant Bank Ltd: 42 Adeola Hopewell St, Victoria Island, PMB 12656, Lagos; tel. (1) 2621323; fax (1) 2622794; e-mail mdce@indobank.com.ng; subsidiary of State Bank of India; cap. 500m. (March 2000); Chair. A. O. ABUDU; Man. Dir. P. G. R. PRASAD.

International Merchant Bank (Nigeria) Ltd: IMB Plaza, 1 Akin Adesola St, Victoria Island, PMB 12028, Lagos; tel. (1) 2612204; fax (1) 2616792; f. 1974; cap. 701.8m., res 640.1m., dep. 2,082.9m. (June 2000); Chair. Maj.-Gen. MOHAMMED SHUWA (retd); Man. Dir EDWIN CHINYE; 5 brs.

MBC International Bank Ltd: 16 Keffi St, S W Ikoyi, POB 53289, Lagos; tel. (1) 2690261; fax (1) 2690767; e-mail mbcnig@linkserve.com.ng; f. 1982 as Merchant Banking Corpn; name changed 2000; cap. 556.3m., res 526.7m., dep. 3,175.0m. (March 2000); Chair. Dr M. A. MAJEKODUNMI; Man. Dir FUNKE OSIBODU.

NAL Merchant Bank: NAL Towers, 20 Marina, PMB 12735, Lagos; tel. (1) 2600420; fax (1) 2633294; e-mail infonal@nalbank.com.ng; internet www.nalbank.com.ng; f. 1960; cap. 531.6m., res 2,015.9m., dep. 6,504.8m. (March 2000); Chair. MOUFTAH BABA-AHMED; Man. Dir BEN AKABUEZE; 6 brs.

Nigerian American Merchant Bank Ltd: Boston House, 10–12 Macarthy St, PMB 12759, Lagos; tel. (1) 2600360; fax (1) 2637568; e-mail nambl@micro.com.ng; f. 1979; affiliate of First National Bank of Boston (USA); cap. 500.0m., res 359.0m., dep. 923.7m. (Dec. 1999); Chair. Alhaji IBRAHIM DAMCIDA; Man. Dir OSARO ISOKPAN; 3 brs.

Pacific Merchant Bank Ltd: Plot 1704, Sea View House, Adetokumbo Ademola St, POB 75152, Victoria Island, Lagos; tel. (1) 2622440; fax (1) 2613302; e-mail pacific@hyperia.com; cap. 501m. (March 2000); Chair. Dr ADEDEJI T. ADELEKE; Man. Dir YINKA ADEOLA.

Stanbic Merchant Bank Nigeria Ltd: 188 Awolowo Rd, Ikoyi, POB 54746, Lagos; tel. (1) 2690402; fax (1) 2692469; internet www.stanbic.com.ng; f. 1983 as Grindlays Merchant Bank of Nigeria; cap. 500.0m., res 173.1m., dep. 1,454.8m. (Dec. 1999); Chair. Dr MATTHEW TAWO MBU; Man. Dir STEPHEN JOHN CALEY.

Development Banks

Bank of Industry (BOI) Ltd: BOI House, 63/71 Broad St, Lagos; tel. (1) 2663470; fax (1) 2667074; e-mail info@boi-ng.com; internet www.boi-ng.com; f. 1964 as the Nigerian Industrial Development Bank Ltd to provide medium and long-term finance to industry, manufacturing, non-petroleum mining and tourism; name changed as above Oct. 2001; cap. 400m. (Dec. 2001); Man. Dir Dr LAWRENCE OSS-AFIANA; 6 brs.

Nigerian Agricultural, Co-operative and Rural Development Bank Ltd (NACB): Yakubu Gowoh, PMB 2155, Kaduna; tel. (62) 243590; fax (62) 245012; e-mail nacb@infoweb.abs.net; f. 1973 for funds to farmers and co-operatives to improve production techniques; name changed as above Oct. 2000, following merger with People's Bank of Nigeria; cap. 1,000m. (2002); Chair. Alhaji ISA TATA YUSUF; Man. Dir Alhaji UMAR BABALE GIREI; 200 brs.

Bankers' Association

Chartered Institute of Bankers of Nigeria: 19 Adeola Hopewell St, POB 72273, Victoria Island, Lagos; tel. (1) 2615642; fax (1) 2611306; Chair. JOHNSON O. EKUNDAYO; CEO A. A. ADENUBI.

STOCK EXCHANGE

Securities and Exchange Commission (SEC): Mandilas House, 96–102 Broad St, PMB 12638, Lagos; f. 1979 as govt agency to regulate and develop capital market and to supervise stock exchange operations; Dir-Gen. GEORGE A. AKAMIOKHOR.

Nigerian Stock Exchange: Stock Exchange House, 2–4 Customs St, POB 2457, Lagos; tel. (1) 2660287; fax (1) 2668724; e-mail contactus@thenigerianstockexchange.com; internet www.thenigerianstockexchange.com; f. 1960; Pres. GOODY M. IBRU; Dir-Gen. Dr NDI OKEREKE-ONYIUKE; 6 brs.

INSURANCE

In December 1994 there were some 134 insurance companies operating in Nigeria. Since 1978 they have been required to reinsure 20% of the sum insured with the Nigeria Reinsurance Corpn.

Insurance Companies

African Alliance Insurance Co Ltd: 112 Broad St, POB 2276, Lagos; tel. (1) 2664398; fax (1) 2660943; e-mail alliance@infoweb.abs.net; f. 1960; life assurance and pensions; Man. Dir OPE OREDUGBA; 30 brs.

Aiico International Insurance (AIICO): AIICO Plaza, Plot PC 12, Afribank St, Victoria Island, POB 2577, Lagos; tel. (1) 2610651; fax (1) 2617433; e-mail info@aiicoplc.com; internet www.aiicoplc.com; CEO M. E. HANSEN.

Ark Insurance Group: Glass House, 11A Karimu Kotun St, Victoria Island, POB 3771, Marina, Lagos; tel. (1) 2615826; fax (1) 2615850; e-mail ark@nova.net.ng; internet www.nigeriaweb.com/ark; Chair. F. O. AWOGBORO.

Continental Reinsurance Co Ltd: Reinsurance House, 11th Floor, 46 Marina, POB 2401, Lagos; tel. (1) 2665350; fax (1) 2665370; e-mail crcl@cyberspace.net.ng; CEO ADEYEMO ADEJUMO.

Cornerstone Insurance Co Plc: POB 75370, Victoria Island, Lagos; tel. (1) 2631832; fax (1) 2633079; e-mail marketing@cornerstone.com.ng; internet www.cornerstone.com; f. 1991; Chair. CLEMENT O. BAIYE.

Equity Indemnity Insurance Co Ltd: POB 1514, Lagos; tel. (1) 2637802; fax (1) 2637479; e-mail equity@infoweb.abs.net; f. 1991; Chair. Prof. O. A. SERIKI.

Great Nigeria Insurance Co Ltd: 8 Omo-Osaghie Street, off Obafemi Awolono Road, Ikoyi S/W, Ikoyi, Lagos; tel. (1) 2695805; fax (1) 2693483; e-mail info@greatinsure-ng.com; internet www.greatinsure-ng.com; f. 1960; all classes; Man. Dir M. A. SIYANBOLA.

Guinea Insurance Co Ltd: Guinea insurance House, 21 Nnandi Azikiwe St, POB 1136, Lagos; tel. (1) 2665201; f. 1958; all classes; CEO AYO BAMMEKE.

Industrial and General Insurance Co Ltd: Plot 741, Adeola Hopewell St, POB 52592, Falomo, Lagos; tel. (1) 2625437; fax (1)

2621146; e-mail info@igi-insurers.com; internet www.igi-insurers.com; Chair. Y. GOWON.

Kapital Insurance Co Ltd: 116 Hadejia Rd, POB 2044, Kano; tel. (64) 645666; fax (64) 636962; CEO MOHAMMED GAMBO UMAR.

Law Union and Rock Insurance Co of Nigeria Ltd: 88–92 Broad St, POB 944, Lagos; tel. (1) 2663526; fax (1) 2664659; fire, accident and marine; 6 brs; CEO S. O. AKINYEMI.

Leadway Assurance Co Ltd: NN 28–29 Constitution Rd, POB 458, Kaduna; tel. (62) 200660; fax (62) 236838; f. 1970; all classes; Man. Dir OYEKANMI ABIODUN HASSAN-ODUKALE.

Lion of Africa Insurance Co Ltd: St Peter's House, 3 Ajele St, POB 2055, Lagos; tel. (1) 2600950; fax (1) 2636111; f. 1952; all classes; Man. Dir G. A. ALEGIEUNO.

National Insurance Corpn of Nigeria (NICON): 5 Customs St, POB 1100, Lagos; tel. (1) 2640230; fax (1) 2666556; f. 1969; all classes; cap. 200m. Man. Dir Alhaji MOHAMMED U. A. KARI; 28 brs.

N.E.M. Insurance Co (Nigeria) Ltd: 22A Borno Way, Ebute, POB 654, Lagos; tel. (1) 5861920; all classes; Chair. Alhaji Dr ALIYU MOHAMMED; Man. Dir J. E. UMUKORO.

Niger Insurance Co Ltd: 47 Marina, POB 2718, Lagos; tel. (1) 2664452; fax (1) 2662196; all classes; Chair. P. M. G. SOARES; 6 brs.

Nigeria Reinsurance Corpn: 46 Marina, PMB 12766, Lagos; tel. (1) 2667049; fax (1) 2668041; e-mail info@nigeriare.com; internet www.nigre.com; all classes of reinsurance; Man. Dir T. T. MIRILLA.

Nigerian General Insurance Co Ltd: 1 Nnamdi Azikiwe St, Tirubu Square, POB 2210, Lagos; tel. (1) 2662552; e-mail odua@odua.com; f. 1951; all classes; Chair. O. O. OKEYODE; Man. Dir J. A. OLANIHUN; 15 brs.

Phoenix of Nigeria Assurance Co Ltd: Mandilas House, 96–102 Broad St, POB 12798, Lagos; tel. (1) 2661160; fax (1) 2662883; e-mail phoenixassce@alpha.linkserve.com; f. 1964; all classes; cap. 10m. Chair. A. A. OJORA; Man. Dir A. A. AKINTUNDE; 5 brs.

Prestige Assurance Co (Nigeria) Ltd: 54 Marina, POB 650, Lagos; tel. (1) 2661213; fax (1) 2664110; all classes except life; Chair. Alhaji S. M. ARGUNGU; Man. Dir K. C. MATHEW.

Royal Exchange Assurance (Nigeria) Group: New Africa House, 31 Marina, POB 112, Lagos; tel. (1) 2663120; fax (1) 2664431; all classes; Chair. Alhaji MUHTAR BELLO YOLA; Man. Dir JONAH U. IKHIDERO; 6 brs.

Sun Insurance Office (Nigeria) Ltd: Unity House, 37 Marina, POB 2694, Lagos; tel. (1) 2661318; all classes except life; Man. Dir A. T. ADENIJI; 6 brs.

United Nigeria Insurance Co Ltd (UNIC): 53 Marina, POB 588, Lagos; tel. (1) 2663201; fax (1) 2664282; f. 1965; all classes except life; CEO E. O. A. ADETUNJI; 17 brs.

Unity Life and Fire Insurance Co Ltd: 25 Nnamdi Azikiwe St, POB 3681, Lagos; tel. (1) 2662517; fax (1) 2662599; all classes; Man. Dir R. A. ODINIGWE.

West African Provincial Insurance Co: WAPIC House, 119 Awolowo Rd, POB 55508, Falomo–Ikoyi, Lagos; tel. (1) 2672770; fax (1) 2693838; e-mail wapic@alpha.linkserve.com; Man. Dir D. O. AMUSAN.

Insurance Association

Nigerian Insurance Association: Nicon House, 1st Floor, 5 Customs St, POB 9551, Lagos; tel. (1) 2640825; f. 1971; Chair. J. U. IKHIDERO.

Trade and Industry

GOVERNMENT AGENCIES

Bureau of Public Enterprises: Secretariat of the National Council on Privatization, 1 Osun Crescent, off Ibib Way, Maitama District, PMB 442, Garki, Abuja; tel. (9) 4134636; tel. (9) 4134640; fax (9) 4134657; e-mail bpe@bpeng.org; internet www.bpeng.org; Dir-Gen. Mallam NASIR AHMAD EL-RUFAI.

Corporate Affairs Commission: Area 11, Garki, Abuja; tel. (9) 2342917; fax (9) 2342669; e-mail info@cac.gov.ng; internet www.cac.gov.ng; Sec. HENRIEITA O. M. TALABI.

National Council on Privatisation: Bureau of Public Enterprises, NDIC Bldg, Constitution Ave, Central Business District, PMB 442, Garki, Abuja; tel. (9) 5237405; fax (9) 5237396; e-mail bpegen@micro.com.ng; internet www.bpe.gov.ng.

Nigeria Export Processing Zones Authority: Radio House, Fourth Floor, Herbert Macaulay Way, PMB 037, Garki, Abuja; tel.

(9) 2343059; fax (9) 2343061; e-mail info@nepza.com; internet www
.nepza.com; Gen. Man. SINA A. AGBOLUAJE.

DEVELOPMENT ORGANIZATIONS

Benin–Owena River Basin Development Authority: 24 Benin-
Sapele Rd, PMB 1381, Obayantor, Benin City; tel. (52) 254415; f.
1976 to conduct irrigation; Gen. Man. Dr G. E. OTEZE.

Chad Basin Development Authority: Dikwa Rd, PMB 1130,
Maiduguri; tel. (76) 232015; f. 1973; irrigation and agriculture-allied
industries; Chair. MOHAMMED ABALI; Gen. Man. Alhaji BUNU S. MUSA.

Cross River Basin Development Authority: 32 Target Rd, PMB
1249, Calabar; tel. (87) 223163; f. 1977; Gen. Man. SIXTUS ABETIANBE.

Federal Institute of Industrial Research, Oshodi (FIIRO):
Murtala Muhammed Airport, Bilnd Centre St, Oshodi, Ikeja, PMB
21023, Lagos; tel. (1) 900121; fax (1) 4525880; f. 1956; plans and
directs industrial research and provides tech. assistance and information to industry; specializes in foods, minerals, textiles, natural
products and industrial intermediates; Dir. Prof. S. A. ODUNFA.

Industrial Training Fund: Miango Rd, PMB 2199, Jos, Plateau;
tel. and fax (73) 461887; e-mail dp@itf-nigeria.com; internet www
.itf-nigeria.com; f. 1971 to promote and encourage skilled workers in
trade and industry; Dir-Gen. Prof. OLU E. AKEREJOLA.

Kaduna Industrial and Finance Co Ltd: Investment House, 27
Ali Akilu Rd, PMB 2230, Kaduna; tel. (62) 240751; fax (62) 240754;
e-mail kifc@skannet.com; f. 1989; provides development finance;
Chair. (vacant); Man. Dir Alhaji DAHIRU MOHAMMED.

Kwara State Investment Corpn: 109–112 Fate Rd, PMB 1344,
Ilorin, Kwara; tel. (31) 220510.

Lagos State Development and Property Corpn: 1 Town Planning Way, Ilupeju, Lagos; tel. (1) 4972243; e-mail isdpc@isdpc.com;
internet www.isdpc.com; f. 1972; planning and development of
Lagos; Gen. Man. O.R. ASHAFA.

New Nigerian Development Co Ltd: 18/19 Ahmadu Bello Way,
Ahmed Talib House, PMB 2120, Kaduna; tel. (62) 249355; fax (62)
245482; e-mail nndc@skannet.com.ng; f. 1949; owned by the Govts of
19 northern States; investment finance; 8 subsidiaries, 83 assoc. cos;
Chair. Lt-Gen. (retd) GARBA DUBA.

Niger Delta Development Commission: 6 Olumeni St, Port
Harcourt; internet www.nddconline.org; f. 1976; Man. Dir GODWIN
OMENE.

Nigerian Enterprises Promotion Board: 15–19 Keffi St, S.W.
Ikoyi, Lagos; tel. (1) 2680929; f. 1972 to promote indigenization;
Chair. MINSO GADZAMA.

Northern Nigeria Investments Ltd: 4 Waff Rd, POB 138,
Kaduna; tel. (62) 239654; fax (62) 230770; f. 1959 to identify and
invest in industrial and agricultural projects in 16 northern States;
cap. p.u. 20m. Chair. Alhaji ABUBAKAR G. ADAMU; Man. Dir GIMBA H.
IBRAHIM.

Odu'a Investment Co Ltd: Cocoa House, PMB 5435, Ibadan; tel.
(2) 417710; fax (2) 413000; f. 1976; jtly owned by Ogun, Ondo and
Oyo States; Man. Dir Alhaji R. S. ARUNA.

Plateau State Water Resources Development Board: Jos;
incorporates the fmr Plateau River Basin Devt Authority and Plateau State Water Resources Devt Board.

Projects Development Institute: Emene Industrial Layout,
Proda Rd, POB 01609, Enugu; tel. (42) 451593; fax (42) 457691;
e-mail proda@rmrdc.nig.com; f. 1977; promotes the establishment of
new industries and develops industrial projects utilizing local raw
materials; Dir BASIL K. C. UGWA.

Raw Materials Research Development Council: Plot 427,
Aguiyi, Ironsi St, Maitama, Abuja; tel. (9) 5237417.

Rubber Research Institute of Nigeria: PMB 1049, Benin City;
tel. (52) 254792; f. 1961; conducts research into the production of
rubber and other latex products; Dir Dr M. M. NADOMA.

Trans Investments Co Ltd: Bale Oyewole Rd, PMB 5085, Ibadan;
tel. (2) 416000; f. 1986; initiates and finances industrial and agricultural schemes; Gen. Man. M. A. ADESIYUN.

CHAMBERS OF COMMERCE

**Nigerian Association of Chambers of Commerce, Industry,
Mines and Agriculture:** 15A Ikorodu Rd, Maryland, PMB 12816,
Lagos; tel. (1) 4964727; fax (1) 4964737; e-mail naccima@
supernet300.com; Pres. CLEMENT OBINEZE MADUAKO; Dir-Gen. L. O.
ADEKUNLE.

Aba Chamber of Commerce and Industry: UBA Bldg, Ikot
Expene Rd/Georges St, POB 1596, Aba; tel. (82) 225148; f. 1971;
Pres. KALU NNANA KALU.

Abeokuta Chamber of Commerce and Industry: 29 Kuto Rd,
Ishabo, POB 937, Abeokuta; tel. (39) 241230; Pres. Chief S. O.
AKINREMI.

Abuja Chamber of Commerce, Industry, Mines & Agriculture:
International Trade Fair Complex, KM8, Airport Road, PMB 86,
Garki, Abuja; tel. (9) 5239995; tel. (9) 6707428; fax (9) 2348808;
e-mail abuccima@hotmail.com; Pres. Sir PETER OKOLO.

Adamawa Chamber of Commerce and Industry: c/o Palace
Hotel, POB 8, Jimeta, Yola; tel. (75) 255136; Pres. Alhaji ISA HAMMA-
NYERO.

Akure Chamber of Commerce and Industry: 57 Oyemekun Rd,
POB 866, Akure; tel. (34) 242540; f. 1984; Pres. Alhaji A. A. AYEGBUSI.

Awka Chamber of Commerce and Industry: 220 Enugu Rd,
POB 780, Awka; tel. (45) 550105; Pres. Lt-Col (retd) D. ORUGBU.

Bauchi Chamber of Commerce and Industry: 96 Maiduguri Rd,
POB 911, Bauchi; tel. (77) 42620; f. 1976; Pres. Alhaji MAGAJI MU'AZU.

**Benin Chamber of Commerce, Industry, Mines and Agri-
culture:** 10 Murtala Muhammed Way, POB 2087, Benin City; tel.
(52) 255761; Pres. C. O. EWEKA.

**Benue Chamber of Commerce, Industry, Mines and Agri-
culture:** 71 Ankpa Qr Rd, PMB 102344, Makurdi; tel. (44) 32573;
Chair. Col (retd) R. V. I. ASAM.

Borno Chamber of Commerce and Industry: Grand Stand,
Ramat Sq., off Central Bank, PMB 1636, Maiduguri; tel. (76)
232832; Pres. Alhaji ZANNA BUKAR UMORU MANDARA.

Calabar Chamber of Commerce and Industry: Desan House
Bldg, 38 Ndidem Iso Rd, POB 76, Calabar, Cross River; tel. (87)
221558; 92 mems; Pres. Chief TAM OFORIOKUMA.

Enugu Chamber of Commerce, Industry and Mines: International Trade Fair Complex, Abakaliki Rd, POB 734, Enugu; tel.
(42) 250575; fax (42) 252186; e-mail eccima@infoweb.abs.net;
internet www.enuguchamber.com; f. 1963; Dir S. C. NWAEKEKE.

Franco-Nigerian Chamber of Commerce: Elf Petroleum Bldg,
35 Kofo Abayomi St, POB 70001, Victoria Island, Lagos; tel. (1)
2621423; fax (1) 2621422; e-mail fncci@nova.net.ng; internet www
.ccife.org/nigeria; f. 1985; Chair. C. VILLA; Pres. AKIN AKINBOLA.

Gongola Chamber of Commerce and Industry: Palace Hotel,
POB 8, Jimeta-Yola; tel. (75) 255136; Pres. Alhaji ALIYU IBRAHIM.

Ibadan Chamber of Commerce and Industry: Commerce
House, Ring Rd, Challenge, PMB 5168, Ibadan; tel. (2) 317223; Pres.
JIDE ABIMBOLA.

Ijebu Chamber of Commerce and Industry: 51 Ibadan Rd, POB
604, Ijebu Ode; tel. (37) 432880; Pres. DOYIN DEGUN.

Ikot Ekpene Chamber of Commerce and Industry: 47 Aba Rd,
POB 50, Ikot Ekpene; tel. (85) 400153; Pres. G. U. EKANEM.

Kaduna Chamber of Commerce, Industry and Agriculture: 24
Waff Rd, POB 728, Kaduna; tel. (62) 211216; fax (62) 214149; Pres.
Alhaji MOHAMMED SANI AMINU.

**Kano Chamber of Commerce, Industry, Mines and Agricul-
ture:** Zoo Rd, POB 10, Kano City, Kano; tel. (64) 666936; fax (64)
667138; Pres. MAL. U. J. KIRU.

Katsina Chamber of Commerce and Industry: 1 Nagogo Rd,
POB 92, Katsina; tel. (65) 31014; Pres. ABBA ALI.

**Kwara Chamber of Commerce, Industry, Mines and Agri-
culture:** 208 Ibrahim Taiwo Rd, POB 1634, Ilorin; tel. (31) 221069;
Pres. W. O. ODUDU.

Lagos Chamber of Commerce and Industry: Commerce House,
1 Idowu Taylor St, Victoria Island, POB 109, Lagos; tel. (1) 2623665;
fax (1) 610573; e-mail inform@micro.com.ng; f. 1888; 1,267 mems;
Pres. Chief J. A. ODEYEMI.

Niger Chamber of Commerce and Industry: Trade Fair Site,
POB 370, Minna; tel. (66) 223153; Pres. Alhaji U. S. NDANUSA.

Nnewi Chamber of Commerce and Industry: 31A Nnobi Rd,
POB 1471, Nnewi; tel. (46) 462258; f. 1987; Pres. AJULU UZODIKE.

Osogbo Chamber of Commerce and Industry: Obafemi Awolowo Way, Ajegunle, POB 870, Osogbo, Osun; tel. (35) 231098; Pres.
Prince VICTOR ADEMLE.

Owerri Chamber of Commerce and Industry: OCCIMA
Secretariat, 123 Okigwe Rd, POB 1640, Owerri; tel. (83) 234849;
Pres. Chief BONIFACE N. AMAECHI.

Oyo Chamber of Commerce and Industry: POB 67, Oyo; Pres.
Chief C. A. OGUNNIYI.

**Plateau State Chambers of Commerce, Industry, Mines and
Agriculture:** Shama House, 32 Rwang Pam St, POB 2092, Jos; tel.
(73) 53918; f. 1976; Pres. Chief M. E. JACDOMI.

Port Harcourt Chamber of Commerce, Industry, Mines and Agriculture: Alesa Eleme, POB 585, Port Harcourt; tel. (84) 239536; f. 1952; Pres. Chief S. I. ALETE.

Remo Chamber of Commerce and Industry: 7 Sho Manager Way, POB 1172, Shagamu; tel. (37) 640962; Pres. Chief S. O. ADEKOYA.

Sapele Chamber of Commerce and Industry: 144 New Ogorode Rd, POB 154, Sapele; tel. (54) 42323; Pres. P. O. FUFUYIN.

Sokoto Chamber of Commerce and Industry: 12 Racecourse Rd, POB 2234, Sokoto; tel. (60) 231805; Pres. Alhaji ALIYU WAZIRI BODINGA.

Umahia Chamber of Commerce: Aba Rd, Umahia; tel. (88) 220055; Pres. Dr LEVI I. NWOKEAFOR.

Uyo Chamber of Commerce and Industry: 141 Abak Rd, POB 2960, Uyo, Akwa Ibom; Pres. Chief DANIEL ITA-EKPOTT.

Warri Chamber of Commerce and Industry: Block 1, Edewor Shopping Centre, Warri/Sapele Rd, POB 302, Warri; tel. (53) 233731; Pres. MOSES F. OROGUN.

INDUSTRIAL AND TRADE ASSOCIATIONS

Nigerian Export Promotion Council: Zone 2, Block 312, Wuse, PMB 133, Abuja; tel. (9) 5230930; fax (9) 5230931; f. 1976.

Nigerian Investment Promotion Commission (NIPC): Plot 1181, Agyuiyi-Ironsi St, Maitama District, Abuja; tel. (9) 4138026; fax (9) 4138021; e-mail suraj@nipc-nigeria.org; internet www .nipc-nigeria.org; Chair. MFON AMANA; CEO Mallam YAKUBU SURAJ B.

EMPLOYERS' ORGANIZATIONS

Association of Advertising Practitioners of Nigeria: 3 William St, off Sylvia Crescent, POB 50648, Anthony Village, Lagos; tel. (1) 4970842.

Chartered Institute of Bankers: Plot PC 19, Adeola Hopewell St, POB 72273, Victoria Island, Lagos.

Institute of Chartered Accountants of Nigeria: Plot 16, Professional Layout Centre, Idowu Taylor St, Victoria Island, POB 1580, Lagos; tel. (1) 2622394; fax (1) 2610304; e-mail info.ican@ican .org.ng; f. 1965; CEO and Registrar O. OLUBUNMI SOWANDE (acting).

Nigeria Employers' Consultative Association: Commercial House, 1–11 Commercial Ave, POB 2231, Yaba, Lagos; tel. (1) 800360; fax (1) 860309; f. 1957; Pres. Chief R. F. GIWA.

Nigerian Institute of Architects: 2 Idowu Taylor St, Victoria Island, POB 178, Lagos; tel. (1) 2617940; fax (1) 2617947; f. 1960; Pres. Chief O. C. MAJOROH.

Nigerian Institute of Building: 45 Opebi Rd, Ikeja, POB 3191, Marina, Lagos; tel. (1) 4930411; f. 1970; Pres. Dr SANI HABU GUMEL.

Nigerian Institution of Estate Surveyors and Valuers: Flat 2B, Dolphin Scheme, Ikoyi, POB 2325, Lagos; tel. (1) 2673131; fax (1) 2694314; e-mail niesv@nova.net.ng; Pres. NWEKE UMEZURUIKE.

Nigerian Society of Engineers: National Engineering Centre, 1 Engineering Close, POB 72667, Victoria Island, Lagos; tel. and fax (1) 2617315; Pres. Dr O. AJAYI.

UTILITIES

Electricity

National Electric Power Authority (NEPA): Plot 1071, Area 3, Garki, Abuja; tel. (1) 5231938; f. 1972 by merger of the Electricity Corpn of Nigeria and the Niger Dams Authority; Man. Dir (vacant).

Gas

Nigerian Liquefied National Gas Co: C. and C. Towers, Plot 1684, Sanusi Fafunwa St, Victoria Island, PMB 12774, Marina, Lagos; tel. (1) 2624190; fax (1) 2617146; Man. Dir. STEVE J. OLLER-EARNSHAW.

TRADE UNIONS

Federation

Nigerian Labour Congress (NLC): 29 Olajuwon St, off Ojuelegba Rd, Yaba, POB 620, Lagos; tel. (1) 5835582; f. 1978; comprised 29 affiliated industrial unions in 1999; Pres. ADAMS OSHIOMOLE.

Principal Unions

Amalgamated Union of Public Corpns, Civil Service, and Technical and Recreational Services Employees: 9 Aje St, PMB 1064, Yaba, Lagos; tel. (1) 5863722; Sec.-Gen. SYLVESTER EJIOFOR.

National Union of Journalists: Lagos; Pres. LANRE OGUNDIPE; Sec. MOHAMMED KHALID.

National Union of Petroleum Workers and Natural Gas (NUPENG): Lagos; Sec.-Gen. FRANK KOKORI.

Nigerian Union of Civil Engineering, Construction, Furniture and Woodworkers: 51 Kano St, Ebute Metta, PMB 1064, Lagos; tel. (1) 5800263.

Nigerian Union of Mine Workers: 95 Enugu St, POB 763, Jos; tel. (73) 52401.

Petroleum and Gas Senior Staff Association of Nigeria (PENGASSAN): Lagos; Sec.-Gen. KENNETH NAREBOR.

Transport

RAILWAYS

There are about 3,505 km of mainly narrow-gauge railways. The two principal lines connect Lagos with Nguru and Port Harcourt with Maiduguri.

Nigerian Railway Corpn: Plot 739, Zone A6, Panama St, off IBB Way, Maitama, Abuja; tel. (9) 5231912; f. 1955; restructured in 1993 into three separate units: Nigerian Railway Track Authority; Nigerian Railways; and Nigerian Railway Engineering Ltd; Admin. GREG IHIKUE.

ROADS

In 1997 the Nigerian road network totalled 194,394 km, including 1,194 km of motorways, 26,500 km of main roads and 32,300 km of secondary roads; some 60,068 km were paved.

Nigerian Road Federation: Ministry of Transport, National Maritime Agency Bldg, Central Area, Abuja; tel. (9) 5237053.

INLAND WATERWAYS

Inland Waterways Department: Ministry of Transport, National Maritime Agency Bldg, Central Area, Abuja; tel. (9) 5237053; responsible for all navigable waterways.

SHIPPING

The principal ports are the Delta Port complex (including Warri, Koko, Burutu and Sapele ports), Port Harcourt and Calabar; other significant ports are situated at Apapa and Tin Can Island, near Lagos. The main petroleum ports are Bonny and Burutu.

National Maritime Authority: Michael Okpara St, Plot 1970, Wuse, Zone 5, Abuja; tel. (9) 5237016; fax (9) 5237015; f. 1987; Dir-Gen. Alhaji BUBA GALADIMA.

Nigerian Ports Authority: Olusegun Obasanjo Way, Plot 126, Central Business District, Garki, Abuja; tel. (9) 2347920; fax (9) 2347930; e-mail telnpo@infoweb.abs.net; internet www .nigeria-ports.com; f. 1955; Man. Dir Mallam IBRAHIM GWANDO.

Nigerian Green Lines Ltd: Unity House, 15th Floor, 37 Marina, POB 2288, Lagos; tel. (1) 2663303; 2 vessels totalling 30,751 grt; Chair. Alhaji W. L. FOLAWIYO.

Nigerian Unity Line: Maritime Complex, 34 Creek Rd, PMB 1175, Apapa, Lagos; tel. (1) 5804808; fax (1) 5804807; e-mail nul@hyperia .com; f. 1995 following the dissolution of the Nigerian National Shipping Line; govt-owned.

Association

Nigeria Shipping Federation: NPA Commercial Offices, Block 'A', Wharf Rd, POB 107, Apapa, Lagos; f. 1960; Chair. (vacant); Gen. Man. D. B. ADEKOYA.

CIVIL AVIATION

The principal international airports are at Lagos (Murtala Muhammed Airport), Kano, Port Harcourt, Calabar and Abuja. There are also 14 airports for domestic flights. In early 1997 a two-year programme to develop the airports at Lagos, Abuja, Port Harcourt and Kano was announced.

Federal Airport Authority of Nigeria: Murtala Muhammed Airport, PMB 21607, Ikeja, Lagos; tel. (1) 4900800; Man. Dir PETER IGBINEDION.

Principal Airlines

Kabo Air: 6775 Ashton Rd, POB 3439, Kano; tel. (64) 639591; fax (64) 645172; f. 1981; domestic services and international charters; Dir SHITU ADAMU.

Nigeria Airways: Airways House, Ikeja, PMB 136, Lagos; tel. (1) 4900470; fax (1) 2777675; f. 1958; scheduled domestic and services to

Europe, the USA, West Africa and Saudi Arabia; Man. Dir Alhaji SHEHU MALAMI.

Okada Air: 17B Sapele Rd, Benin City; tel. (19) 241054; f. 1983; domestic and international charter passenger services, domestic scheduled services; Chair. Chief GABRIEL O. IGBINEDION.

Tourism

Potential attractions for tourists include fine coastal scenery, dense forests, and the rich diversity of Nigeria's arts. A total of 1,491,767 tourists visited Nigeria in 2000. Receipts from tourism amounted to US $142m in 1998.

Nigerian Tourism Development Corpn: Old Federal Secretariat, Area 1, Garki, PMB 167, Abuja; tel. (9) 2342764; fax (9) 2342775; e-mail ntdc@metrong.com; internet www.nigeria.tourism .com; Chair. Prince ADESUYI HAASTRUP; CEO OMOTAYO OMOTOSHO.

NORWAY

Introductory Survey

Location, Climate, Language, Religion, Flag, Capital

The Kingdom of Norway forms the western part of Scandinavia, in northern Europe. It is bordered to the east by Sweden and, within the Arctic Circle, by Finland and Russia. A long, indented coast faces the Atlantic Ocean. Norway exercises sovereignty over the Svalbard archipelago, Jan Mayen island and the uninhabited dependencies of Bouvetøya and Peter I Øy. Dronning Maud Land, in Antarctica, is also a Norwegian dependency. Norway's climate is temperate on the west coast but colder inland. Average temperatures range from −2°C (28°F) to 8°C (46°F). There are two forms of the Norwegian language, which are officially recognized as equal. About 80% of children in schools use the older form, Bokmål, as their principal language, whereas only 20% use the newer form, Nynorsk (Neo-Norwegian). Lappish is also spoken by the Sámi population, in northern Norway. Almost all of the inhabitants profess Christianity: the Evangelical Lutheran Church is the established religion, with about 86% of the population professing adherence in 2000. The civil flag (proportions 8 by 11) has a dark blue cross, bordered with white, on a red background, the upright of the cross being to the left of centre; the state flag (16 by 27) displays the same cross, but forms a triple swallow-tail at the fly. The capital is Oslo.

Recent History

Norway, formerly linked to the Swedish crown, declared its independence in 1905. The union with Sweden was peacefully dissolved and the Norwegians elected their own monarch, Prince Karl of Denmark, who took the title of King Håkon VII. He reigned until his death in 1957, and was succeeded by his son, Olav V. Olav's son, Crown Prince Harald (who had acted as regent since his father suffered a stroke in May 1990), became King Harald V upon Olav's death in January 1991.

During the Second World War Norway was occupied by German forces between 1940 and 1945. Norway abandoned its traditional policy of neutrality after the war, joining the North Atlantic Treaty Organization (NATO, see p. 271) in 1949. Norway was also a founder member of the Nordic Council (see p. 266) in 1952 and of the European Free Trade Association (EFTA, see p. 195) in 1960.

Det norske Arbeiderparti (DnA—Norwegian Labour Party) governed from 1935 to 1965, except for the period of German occupation, when a pro-Nazi 'puppet' regime was administered by Vidkun Quisling, and an interlude of one month in 1963. Norway applied for membership of the European Community (EC, now European Union—EU, see p. 199) in 1962, and again in 1967. A general election to the Storting (parliament) in September 1965 resulted in a defeat for the Labour Government of Einar Gerhardsen, who had been Prime Minister almost continuously since 1955. His administration was replaced in October 1965 by a non-socialist coalition under Per Borten, leader of the Senterpartiet (Sp—Centre Party). In March 1971, however, Borten resigned, following revelations that he had deliberately disclosed confidential details of Norway's negotiations with the EC. He was succeeded by a minority DnA Government, led by Trygve Bratteli. The terms of Norway's entry into the EC were agreed in December 1971, and a preliminary Treaty of Accession was signed in January 1972. In September, however, a consultative referendum on the agreed terms produced a 53.3% majority against entering the EC. The application was withdrawn, and Bratteli resigned in October. A coalition of Venstre (Liberals), the Sp and the Kristelig Folkeparti (KrF—Christian Democrats' Party) formed a new minority Government, with Lars Korvald of the KrF as Prime Minister.

Following the general election of September 1973, Bratteli formed another minority DnA Government, dependent on the support of a socialist alliance known from 1975 as the Socialistisk Venstreparti (SV—Socialist Left Party). In January 1976 Bratteli was succeeded as Prime Minister by Odvar Nordli. Nordli resigned in February 1981, for reasons of ill health, and was succeeded by Gro Harlem Brundtland, Norway's first female Prime Minister. At the general election in September the

DnA lost support to centre-right groups. In October a minority administration, led by Kåre Willoch, became Norway's first Høyre (Conservative) Government since 1928. In June 1983 a coalition of Høyre with the Sp and the KrF was formed, with 79 of the 165 parliamentary seats. Willoch's Government was returned to power, although lacking an overall majority in the Storting, following the general election in September 1985. In May 1986, however, Willoch resigned when the Storting narrowly rejected a proposal to increase taxation on petrol. The Norwegian Constitution did not permit a general election before the expiry of the Storting's term (due in 1989). Brundtland accepted an invitation by the King to form a minority DnA administration. The new Government devalued the krone by 12%, and a revised budget was approved by the Storting in June 1986.

At the general election in September 1989 both the DnA and Høyre lost support to more radical parties. The SV gained nine seats, to achieve a total of 17 seats in the 165-seat Storting. The Fremskrittspartiet (FrP—Progress Party) increased its representation from two to 22 seats, despite attracting allegations of racism during the election campaign. Brundtland's Government resigned in October, following an agreement made by Høyre, the Sp and the KrF to form a coalition. The new Government, led by Jan Syse (Høyre leader since January 1988), controlled only 62 seats in the Storting and was dependent upon the support of the FrP. Also in September 1989 the Sámi (Lapps) of northern Norway elected 39 representatives for a new Sameting (Consultative Assembly), to be based in Karasjok. This followed an amendment to the Constitution the previous year, which recognized the Sámi as an indigenous people and an ethnic minority. There was considerable support among the Sámi for a degree of autonomy, in order to protect their traditional way of life. The Sámi had officially ceased to exist by 1900, with their culture and language being declared illegal, but by 2000 they had formed a joint council comprising Sámi populations in Norway, Sweden, Finland and Russia, and received a parliament building, opened in November by King Harald V. The issue of land rights, however, remained unresolved. This was aggravated by the discovery, in November 2001, of substantial platinum deposits in Finnmark, an area to which the Sámi laid claim.

While Høyre had supported EC membership since 1988, the Sp remained strongly opposed to it. In October 1990 the Government announced that the Norwegian krone was to be linked to the European Currency Unit. Later in that month the coalition collapsed, following disagreement between Høyre and the Sp regarding Norwegian demands in the negotiations between EFTA and the EC on the creation of a joint European Economic Area (EEA). In November the DnA formed another minority Government, led by Brundtland.

In October 1991 agreement was finally reached on the terms of the EEA treaty, including arrangements whereby EC countries were to be allowed to take extra quotas of fish from Norwegian waters, while Norwegian fish products were to have increased access to EC markets. Many Norwegians remained opposed to membership of the EC, fearing, in particular, that government subsidies that had allowed the survival of remote rural and coastal communities would no longer be permitted. In April 1992, however, Brundtland declared that she was in favour of applying for EC membership, and that Norway could not afford to remain outside the EC once most of the other Nordic countries had joined. The EEA treaty was ratified by the Storting in October. (The treaty entered into effect on 1 January 1994, following ratification by all of the countries concerned.) Brundtland's proposal to apply for EC membership was endorsed by the DnA conference in November 1992, and by the Storting later in the same month. An application was duly submitted in late November.

In November 1992 Brundtland resigned from the leadership of the DnA, and was replaced by the party's Secretary-General, Thorbjørn Jagland. At the September 1993 general election the DnA slightly increased its representation in the Storting, from 63 to 67 seats. The Sp (whose electoral campaign had been based on opposition to EC membership) increased its total from 11 to 32 seats, thereby becoming the second-largest party in the Storting, while Høyre won only 28 seats, compared with 37 at the previous election.

Negotiations on Norway's entry to the EU, as it had been restyled, were concluded in March 1994. At a national referendum held on 27–28 November, however (shortly after Sweden and Finland had voted to join the Union), 52.4% of voters rejected EU membership. The success of the campaign opposing Norway's entry to the EU was attributed to several factors: in particular, fears were expressed by farmers that the influx of cheaper agricultural goods from the EU would lead to bankruptcies and unemployment in the agricultural sector, and by workers in the fishing industry that stocks of fish would be severely depleted if EU boats were granted increased access to Norwegian waters. There was also widespread concern that national sovereignty would be compromised by the transfer to the EU of certain executive responsibilities.

In local elections held in September 1995, the DnA received 31% of the votes cast (compared with 37% at the 1993 general election), Høyre obtained 20% and the Sp 12%. The right-wing FrP, which had campaigned for more stringent policies on law and order, doubled its share of the vote to 12%, from 6% at the general election.

In October 1996 Brundtland resigned as Prime Minister. Thorbjørn Jagland, the Chairman of the DnA, succeeded her. Jagland emphasized that he would continue the previous Government's cautious fiscal policy, and declared that the priorities of his administration would be fourfold: to foster the expansion of the private sector; to develop and maintain an efficient welfare system; to invest in education, science and culture; and to encourage the development of external trade relations. By the end of the year, however, the Government's credibility had been seriously undermined, after Terje Röd-Larsen, the newly appointed Minister of National Planning, and Grete Faremo, the Minister of Petroleum and Energy, were forced to resign, following, respectively, allegations of financial irregularities and abuse of power.

A general election was conducted on 16 September 1997, at which the DnA attracted the largest level of support (35.0% of the votes cast), winning 65 seats, ahead of the FrP (with 15.3% —25 seats), Høyre (14.3%—23 seats) and the KrF (13.7%—25 seats). Prior to the election, Jagland had indicated his intention to resign as Prime Minister should the DnA fail to secure at least the 36.9% of popular support that it attracted at the 1993 poll, and in October he duly resigned. Kjell Magne Bondevik, the parliamentary leader of the KrF, had organized an alliance of the KrF, the Sp and Venstre (with representation totalling 42 seats in the Storting), and was invited to form a coalition government on that basis. A new Council of State comprising ministers from all three parties (although dominated by the KrF) was announced immediately. There was some uncertainty regarding the durability of the Government after the Prime Minister took more than three weeks' leave from his post from the end of August 1998, announcing that he was suffering from depression caused by overwork. Bondevik was reported to have been under intense pressure as a result of the recent instability of the economy, largely attributable to the sharp decline in international prices for petroleum; this had notably necessitated the postponement of the introduction of a scheme, promoted by the Prime Minister, to give financial support to parents choosing to look after their children at home. In November, furthermore, the Government was obliged to abandon proposed tax increases in order to secure the support of the FrP (and thus parliamentary approval) for the 1999 budget. A government reshuffle in mid-March 1999 included the appointment of Eldbjørg Løwer as Norway's first female Minister of Defence. Electoral support for the DnA declined further in the local elections held in September, when it received 28.2% of the votes cast; support also declined for the three parties in the coalition Government, while the most significant gains were made by the right-wing FrP, which campaigned on an anti-immigration platform and received the third largest share of the vote.

On 9 March 2000 Bondevik resigned following his defeat in a confidence motion in the Storting by 81 votes to 71. The vote was called to resolve a dispute between the majority in the Storting and the minority Government on whether to postpone the construction of gas-fired power plants pending the introduction of new technology to render them pollution-free. Bondevik favoured postponement as he opposed amending the country's strict anti-pollution laws to allow increased carbon dioxide emissions. This constituted the first time that a government had resigned over an environmental issue. Bondevik recommended that Jens Stoltenberg, who had replaced Jagland as leader of the DnA in February, be approached to form a single-party minority government. Stoltenberg, whose party controlled 65 seats in the 165-member Storting, took office as Prime Minister on 17 March. The new Council of State, which was drawn exclusively from the DnA, included the former DnA Prime Minister, Jagland, as Minister of Foreign Affairs and former Minister of Foreign Affairs Bjørn Tore Godal as Minister of Defence. The new Government pledged to reform the public sector, resume the country's privatization programme, forge stronger links with Europe and continue Norway's role as a mediator in international peace negotiations.

The Deputy Chairman of the FrP, Terje Soeviknes, resigned from his party position in February 2001, following allegations, which he denied, that he had raped a 16-year-old girl at a youth conference the previous year. Soeviknes had been viewed as the next leader of the increasingly influential right-wing FrP, which, however, suffered a decline in popularity following Soeviknes's resignation. In January the first officially recognized racially motivated murder in Norway took place. Six youths with neo-Nazi sympathies were arrested on suspicion of involvement in the murder of Benjamin Hermansen, a 15-year-old anti-racist campaigner, whose father was Ghanaian. The Government condemned the murder but counselled caution regarding demands for the banning of neo-Nazi groups. Two of the suspects were convicted of the crime in January 2002, and a third was convicted as an accessory to the crime.

In March 1999 the Storting approved compensation valued at US $57.5m. for the country's Holocaust victims and their descendants. The programme was to include compensation for plundered property, as well as funding for contemporary Jewish community projects. In October 2001 a lawsuit was brought against the Norwegian Government by surviving victims of the Nazi *Lebensborn* (Source of Life) project. The survivors, children of German soldiers and Norwegian women, were conceived during the Nazi occupation of Norway in the Second World War as part of a scheme to create a 'master race'. They alleged that, following the liberation of Norway, they and their mothers were subjected to systematic abuse and discrimination, and that the Government not only allowed this abuse to occur, but it also attempted to conceal it. The lawsuit was rejected on the grounds that the alleged offences occurred too long ago to be brought to court. However, in late 2002 the Storting's Justice Committee recommended that the Government 'make amends'.

At a general election conducted on 10 September 2001 the DnA received only 24.3% of the valid votes cast (its poorest performance in an election since 1909), thus attaining 43 of the 165 parliamentary seats. Høyre secured 21.2% of the votes cast (38 seats), the FrP 14.7% (26 seats), the SV 12.5% (23 seats) and the KrF 12.4% (22 seats). The DnA formed a minority Government, but was unable to attract enough political support to hold a majority in the Storting. Stoltenberg consequently resigned on 17 October, and the DnA was replaced in government by a minority centre-right coalition comprising Høyre, the KrF and Venstre, with Bondevik as Prime Minister. The coalition gained a majority in the Storting with the informal support of the FrP, which was expected to exert a strong influence on government policy.

In August 2002 the Government announced a minimum quota of 40% for female board members, giving state-owned companies 12 months and public companies three years to comply with this ruling. The Government stated that failure to meet these deadlines would lead to the introduction of new legislation to enforce the quota. Informal gender quotas have operated in Norway since 1981, since when some 40% of government posts have been held by women.

In February 2003 the Government announced its decision to expel Mullah Krekar, the leader of the Kurdish guerrilla organization Ansar al-Islam, who was suspected by both the USA and the United Nations of having links to terrorism, and possibly to the al-Qa'ida (Base) organization. However, Krekar, who had stated that he would not leave Norway voluntarily, was not taken into custody or otherwise compelled to leave the country. The following month the Government announced that the case, without precedent in Norway, merited further investigation, and that the launch of the US-led military action in Iraq that month posed difficulties for his repatriation, effectively granting Krekar the right to remain in the country for a further two months. A request from Jordan for him to be extradited for drugs offences was also to be investigated. Krekar was eventually detained following his appearance on Dutch television when he stated that Ansar al-Islam had suicide bombers ready to attack US citizens.

During 1993 the Norwegian Government was instrumental in conducting secret negotiations between the Israeli Government and the Palestine Liberation Organization (PLO), which led to agreement on Palestinian self-rule in certain areas occupied by Israel. Norway won international acclaim for its role in furthering peace in the Middle East through these negotiations, and continued to be involved in the advancement of the peace process in the late 1990s.

In February 2000 Norway extended its role as an international mediator, agreeing to broker negotiations between the Sri Lankan Government and Tamil separatists in an attempt to end the 17-year conflict; the negotiations were still continuing, under Norway's brokerage, in early 2003. In April 2001 Norway agreed to host peace negotiations between the Philippine Government and the Philippine dissident communist alliance, the National Democratic Front; similarly, Norway's role as mediator was continuing in these negotiations in early 2003. Norway also announced that it was donating just over US $500,000 towards the ongoing peace negotiations between Somalia and Sudan in Kenya.

Norway declared an exclusive economic zone extending to 200 nautical miles (370 km) from its coastline in 1977, and also unilaterally established a fishery protection zone around its territory of Svalbard. The declaration of an economic zone around Jan Mayen island in 1980 led to agreements with Iceland, in 1980 and 1981, over conflicting claims to fishing and mineral rights. A similar dispute with Denmark, acting for Greenland, was not resolved, and in 1988 Denmark requested arbitration by the International Court of Justice, in The Hague, Netherlands, which gave its judgment on the delimitation of the disputed zones in June 1993 (see under Jan Mayen). During 1994 incidents were reported between vessels of the Norwegian coastguard and Icelandic fishing boats, within the economic zone surrounding the Norwegian island of Spitsbergen (see under Svalbard).

Following a moratorium on commercial whaling, adopted by the International Whaling Commission (IWC, see p. 332) with effect from 1985, Norway continued to hunt small numbers of whales ostensibly for purposes of scientific research, and in 1992 the Norwegian Government declared that it would allow the resumption of commercial hunting of minke whales in 1993, claiming that (according to the findings of the IWC's scientific commission) this species was plentiful enough to allow whaling on a sustainable basis: the Government argued that many Norwegian coastal communities depended on whaling for their existence. In April 1995, amid continuing international opposition, the Norwegian Government announced that its quota for minke whales in that year was to be reduced from 301 to 232. By 1999, however, the quota had increased to 753 (this figure decreased to 655 in 2000 and to 549 in 2001). A moratorium on the hunting of seal pups, imposed in 1989, was ended by the Norwegian Government in 1995, although it was emphasized that the killing of seals would be strictly for scientific purposes. Opponents of sealing, however, expressed concern that Norway might seek to resume commercial hunting. Norway continued to campaign against the moratorium on commercial whaling, and made some progress in its attempts to exempt the minke whale from the ban on exports of whale products imposed under the Convention on International Trade in Endangered Species (CITES). In July 1999 journalists revealed that 500 metric tons of blubber had been stockpiled by the Norwegians in anticipation of a resumption of legal trading. In January 2001 the Government announced that it would resume exports of whale meat and products without waiting for the next CITES conference, scheduled for 2004. The announcement attracted criticism from environmental groups; however, many observers (including a number within the IWC) admitted that a return to controlled commercial whaling was becoming inevitable. In March 2002 Norway declared that it was to resume exports of whale meat to Japan; whale blubber, however, was not included in the trading arrangement, although it was believed that it might be added at a later date.

Relations between Norway and Sweden were strained in 1999 by disputes arising from negotiations regarding the proposed merger of Telenor and Telia, respectively the Norwegian and Swedish state-owned telecommunications companies, which collapsed acrimoniously in December amidst Swedish accusations

of Norwegian nationalism. (Four foreign takeover attempts of major Norwegian petroleum companies and banks failed in 1999.)

Government

Norway is a constitutional monarchy. Legislative power is held by the Storting (parliament), with 165 members elected for four years by universal adult suffrage, on the basis of proportional representation. For the consideration of legislative proposals, the Storting divides itself into two chambers by choosing one-quarter of its members to form the Lagting (upper house), the remainder forming the Odelsting (lower house). Executive power is nominally held by the monarch, but is, in effect, exercised by the Statsråd (Council of State), led by the Prime Minister. The Council is appointed by the monarch in accordance with the will of the Storting, to which the Council is responsible. Norway comprises 19 counties (fylker) and 435 municipalities.

Defence

Norway is a member of NATO (see p. 271), and became an associate member of the Western European Union (WEU, see p. 318) in 1992. Every male is liable for 12 months' national service at the age of 19. Periodical refresher programmes are also compulsory until the age of 44. The total strength of the armed forces in August 2002 was 26,600 (including 15,200 conscripts): army 14,700 (8,700 conscripts), navy 6,100 (3,300 conscripts), air force 5,000 (3,200 conscripts), joint services organizations 400, and Home Guard permanent staff 400. There is also a mobilization reserve of about 219,000 (army 89,000, navy 22,000, air force 25,000 and Home Guard *c.* 83,000) and a coastguard of 270. The defence budget for 2002 was projected at 27,600m. kroner. Government proposals were presented to the Storting in early 2001 to reduce the size of the armed forces to 125,000 by 2005.

Economic Affairs

In 2001, according to estimates by the World Bank, Norway's gross national income (GNI), measured at average 1999–2001 prices, was US $160,577m., equivalent to $35,530 per head (or $30,440 per head on an international purchasing-power parity basis). During 1990–2001, it was estimated, the population increased by an average of 0.6% per year, while gross domestic product (GDP) per head increased, in real terms, by an average of 2.6% per year. Norway's overall GDP increased, in real terms, at an average annual rate of 3.2% in 1990–2001. Real GDP increased by 2.3% in 2000 and by 1.4% in 2001.

The contribution of agriculture, hunting, forestry and fishing to GDP in 2001 was estimated at 1.8%. In that year these sectors (excluding hunting) engaged 3.9% of the employed labour force. Around 3.4% of the land surface is cultivated, and the most important branch of the agricultural sector is livestock-rearing. Fish-farming has been intensively developed by the Government since the early 1970s. The fishing industry provided 5.6% of total export revenue in 2001. A temporary emergency ban on cod fishing in parts of the North Sea, agreed between the European Union (EU, see p. 199) and Norway, was announced in January 2001 in an attempt to prevent the collapse of fish stocks through over-fishing. Agricultural production increased at an average annual rate of 2.1% during 1990–2000. Agricultural GDP increased by 0.6% in 1999 and by 2.1% in 2000.

Industry (including mining, manufacturing, construction, power and public utilities) contributed 38.9% of GDP in 2001, and engaged 21.6% of the employed labour force in that year. During 1990–2000 industrial GDP increased, in real terms, at an average annual rate of 3.6%. Industrial GDP declined, in real terms, by 0.8% in 1999, but increased by 2.7% in 2000.

Mining provided 22.9% of GDP in 2001, and along with the manufacturing sector engaged 14.1% of the employed labour force in that year; however, the mining sector alone engaged only 1.4% of the employed labour force in 1999. Norway possesses substantial reserves of petroleum and natural gas (exports of petroleum and petroleum products accounted for 48.5% of total export earnings in 2001). Most of the reserves are located off shore. During 1992–2000 the production of crude petroleum increased at an average annual rate of 4.3% and output of natural gas grew at an average rate of 7.1% per year. Norway's other mineral reserves include iron ore, iron pyrites, copper, lead and zinc. Substantial deposits of platinum were discovered in the northern county of Finnmark in November 2001—the area was also believed to contain deposits of gold and diamonds. During 1990–96 production in the petroleum and gas extraction sub-sector increased by an average of 10.2% per year, whereas elsewhere in the mining sector the comparable growth rate was 0.9%. Real GDP in the petroleum and gas extraction sub-sector declined by 3.4% in 1998, but increased by 1.3% in 1999; the GDP of the non-hydrocarbon mining sub-sector declined by 1.7% in 1998 and by 1.8% in 1999.

Manufacturing contributed 9.6% of GDP in 2001, and (with mining, quarry, petroleum and gas extraction) employed 14.1% of the working population in the same year; the manufacturing sector alone engaged 13.3% of the working population in 1999. In 1998 the most important branches of manufacturing, measured by gross value of output, were food products (accounting for 20.3% of the total), transport equipment (13.5%), metals and metal products (13.2%), chemicals and chemical products (7.6%), and publishing and printing (7.2%). During 1990–98 manufacturing production increased by an average of 2.3% per year. Manufacturing GDP increased, in real terms, by 1.5% in 1998, but declined by 2.3% in 1999.

In 2001, according to provisional figures, some 99.2% of Norway's installed capacity of electric energy was produced by hydroelectric power schemes; domestic energy demands are easily supplied, and Norway has exported hydroelectricity since 1993. Norway's extensive reserves of petroleum and natural gas are mainly exploited for sale to foreign markets, since the domestic market is limited.

The services sector contributed 59.2% of GDP in 2001, and engaged 74.4% of the employed labour force in that year. The GDP of the services sector increased, in real terms, by an average of 3.3% per year during 1990–2000; it grew by 2.1% in 1999 and by 2.2% in 2000.

Although shipbuilding has declined since the early 1970s, Norway remains a leading shipping nation. The establishment of the Norwegian International Ship Register in 1987 allowed an expansion of the merchant fleet by more than 300%, in terms of gross tonnage; it totalled 22.6m. grt at the end of 2001.

In 2001, according to IMF figures, Norway recorded a visible trade surplus of US $26,018m., and there was a surplus of $24,960m. on the current account of the balance of payments. In 2001 the EU provided 65.7% of imports and took 75.7% of exports: Fellow-members of the European Free Trade Association (EFTA, see p. 195) accounted for 1.6% of Norway's imports and 0.6% of exports. The principal source of imports in 2001 was Sweden (providing 15.2% of the total), followed by Germany (12.6%), the United Kingdom (7.9%) and the USA (7.1%); the principal market for exports was the United Kingdom (taking 19.6%), followed by Germany (12.2%), the Netherlands (10.4%) and France (9.4%). In 2001 the principal exports were petroleum, petroleum products and related materials (accounting for 48.5% of total exports), non-ferrous metals (5.6%), fisheries products (also 5.6%) and paper, paperboard and paper manufactures (2.1%); the principal imports were road vehicles (accounting for 8.7% of total imports), other transport equipment including ships (8.5%), electrical machinery, apparatus and appliances (5.4%) and office machines and automatic data-processing equipment (5.2%).

In the revised budget for 2001 a surplus of 220,340m. kroner was forecast (equivalent to some 14.6% of GDP in purchasers' values), compared with a surplus of 168,184m. kroner in 2000. At the end of 2000 Norway's gross public debt was estimated at an amount equivalent to 21% of GDP, and was forecast to remain at this level until 2004. During 1990–2001 the average annual rate of inflation was 2.4%; consumer prices increased by 3.0% in 2000 and by 3.0% again in 2001. The average rate of unemployment was 3.6% in 2001.

In addition to its membership of EFTA, Norway is a member of the European Economic Area (EEA), the Nordic Council (see p. 266) and the Nordic Council of Ministers (see p. 267). Although Norway is not a member of the EU, it joined the EU's Schengen Agreement along with Denmark, Finland and Sweden (all EU members) by virtue of its membership in the Nordic passport union (Iceland also joined).

The Norwegian economy, which is highly dependent on its hydrocarbons sector (Norway is the world's second largest petroleum exporter), experienced a sustained expansion during the 1990s, leading to virtually full employment, as well as rises in real incomes. Norway maintained a stable exchange rate during this period and a prudent fiscal position, and reinvested a substantial proportion of petroleum revenues abroad through the State Petroleum Fund, partly in preparation for future increased demands on pensions and also to offer limited protection to the economy against fluctuations in the petroleum

sector. During 2000 interest rates were raised to control inflation. Norway's large fiscal and current-account surpluses from continuing high international petroleum prices led to intense political pressure for an expansionary budget for 2001, increasing public expenditure on health and education. However, owing to the risk of 'overheating' the economy, the minority Government managed to agree a fiscally neutral budget with certain opposition parties. The formation of a new, centre-right coalition Government in late 2001 resulted in little immediate change in economic policy, although there was to be greater emphasis on reducing levels of taxation and on the reform of public services. Prior to the establishment of the new administration, the outgoing Government presented a budget for 2002, which included a modest increase in spending from the State Petroleum Fund, one-half of which was to contribute to tax relief. Norway's mainland GDP growth was 1.4% in 2002, driven mainly by strong growth in consumption. Investment and traditional exports slackened, however, owing to weak external demand and a strong krone. This reduced the profitability of the manufacturing sector, which further suffered from pay increases in excess of productivity gains. Unemployment remained fairly stable throughout much of the year, although by the end of the year it had risen to about 4%. Weak international demand and the low profitability of manufacturing were expected to continue to hamper investment, traditional exports and employment during 2003. (Unemployment was expected to rise, especially in the manufacturing sector.) Nevertheless, the Government forecast a budgetary surplus of 162,000m. kroner in 2003, comprised mostly of petroleum revenues. The high pay increases of 2002 and tax cuts financed by the State Petroleum Fund were expected to support disposable income and private consumption, offset only partly by rising unemployment and high electricity prices. Headline inflation was expected to increase, owing largely to the latter, although core inflation was projected to remain below government targets. On balance, mainland GDP was forecast to grow by 1.6% during 2003, and improvement in the international economy was expected to support further growth of between 2.3% and 2.5% during 2004–05. However, it remained essential that the competitiveness of vulnerable Norwegian businesses be improved in order for Norway to benefit fully. Furthermore, the effect of the US-led military action in Iraq on petroleum prices, and consequently the Norwegian economy, remained to be seen.

Education

Compulsory education begins at six years of age and lasts for 10 years. Elementary education is divided into a four-year lower stage (barnetrinnet), for children aged six to 10 years, a three-year intermediate stage (mellomtrinnet), for children aged 10 to 13 years, and a three-year upper stage (ungdomstrinnet), from the age of 13. A pupil may then transfer to an upper-secondary school for a course lasting three years. Primary enrolment in 2000 included 100% of children in the 6–13 age-group. In 1996 secondary enrolment included 97% of those in the relevant age-group (males 97%; females 98%).The comparable ratio of 16-year-olds entering upper-secondary education directly after leaving compulsory education in 2000 was 94% (males 93%; females 95%). From the second half of 2002 adults who had not completed compulsory education, or who wished to refresh their competence, were to be given a statutory right to lower-secondary education. This also applied to special education. With effect from the 2000/2001 academic year, everyone had the right to upper-secondary education. Upon completion of a three-year course in general and technical areas of study at an upper-secondary school, a pupil may seek admission to one of Norway's four universities or other colleges. From 2000 persons from the age of 25 had the right to be assessed for admittance to higher education based on non-formal learning. A broader system of higher professional education has been organized on a regional basis, including colleges of education and technology. Expenditure on education by all levels of government in 2000 was 81,091m. kroner (equivalent to 14.0% of total government expenditure).

Public Holidays

2003: 1 January (New Year's Day), 17 April (Maundy Thursday), 18 April (Good Friday), 21 April (Easter Monday), 1 May (Labour Day), 17 May (Constitution Day), 29 May (Ascension Day), 9 June (Whit Monday), 24 December (Christmas Eve)*, 25–26 December (Christmas), 31 December (New Year's Eve)*.

2004: 1 January (New Year's Day), 8 April (Maundy Thursday), 9 April (Good Friday), 12 April (Easter Monday), 1 May (Labour Day), 17 May (Constitution Day), 20 May (Ascension Day), 31 May (Whit Monday), 24 December (Christmas Eve)*, 25–26 December (Christmas), 31 December (New Year's Eve)*.

* Half day from 12 noon.

Weights and Measures

The metric system is in force.

Statistical Survey

Sources (unless otherwise stated): Statistics Norway, Kongens gt. 6, Oslo; tel. 21-09-00-00; fax 21-09-49-73; e-mail biblioteket@ssb.no; internet www.ssb .no; Nordic Statistical Secretariat (Copenhagen), *Yearbook of Nordic Statistics*.

Area and Population

AREA, POPULATION AND DENSITY

Area (sq km)	
Land	306,253
Inland water	17,506
Total	323,759*
Population (census results)	
3 November 1990	4,247,546
3 November 2001	
Males	2,240,281
Females	2,280,666
Total	4,520,947
Population (official estimates at 1 January)	
2000	4,478,497
2001	4,503,436
2002	4,524,066
Density (per sq km) at 1 January 2002†	14.8

* 125,004 sq miles.

† Excluding inland water.

COUNTIES

(1 January 2002)

	Land area (sq km)*	Population	Density (per sq km)
Østfold	3,889	252,746	65.0
Akershus	4,587	477,325	104.1
Oslo	427	512,589	1,200.4
Hedmark	26,120	187,965	7.2
Oppland	23,827	183,235	7.7
Buskerud	13,856	239,793	17.3
Vestfold	2,140	216,456	101.1
Telemark	14,186	165,710	11.7
Aust-Agder	8,485	102,945	12.1
Vest-Agder	6,817	157,851	23.2
Rogaland	8,753	381,375	43.6
Hordaland	14,780	438,253	26.7
Sogn og Fjordane	17,864	107,280	6.0
Møre og Romsdal	14,596	243,855	16.7
Sør-Trøndelag	17,839	266,323	14.9
Nord-Trøndelag	20,777	127,457	6.1
Nordland	36,434	237,503	6.5
Troms	25,015	151,673	6.1
Finnmark	45,879	73,732	1.6
Total	306,253	4,524,066	14.8

* Excluding inland waters, totalling 17,506 sq km.

PRINCIPAL TOWNS

(population at 1 January 2000)*

Oslo (capital)	773,498	Kristiansand	61,400
Bergen	205,759	Tromsø	49,372
Stavanger/Sandnest†	162,083	Tønsberg	43,346
Trondheim	140,631	Haugesund	39,112
Fredrikstad/Sarpsborg†	93,273	Sandefjord	37,229
Drammen	86,732	Ålesund/Spjelkavik†.	35,832
Porsgrunn/Skien†	83,409	Moss	33,081

* Settlement delimited independent of administrative boundaries.

† From 1 January 1999 continuous urban settlements were merged as one settlement.

BIRTHS, MARRIAGES AND DEATHS

	Registered live births		Registered marriages		Registered deaths*	
	Number	Rate (per 1,000)	Number	Rate (per 1,000)	Number	Rate (per 1,000)
1993	59,678	13.8	19,464	4.5	46,597	10.8
1994	60,092	13.9	20,605	4.8	44,071	10.2
1995	60,292	13.8	21,677	5.0	45,190	10.4
1996	60,927	13.9	23,172	5.3	43,860	10.0
1997	59,801	13.6	23,815	5.4	44,595	10.1
1998	58,352	13.2	23,354	5.3	44,112	10.0
1999	59,298	13.3	24,889	5.6	45,170	10.1
2000	59,234	13.2	26,763	6.0	44,002	9.8

* Including deaths of residents temporarily abroad.

Expectation of life (WHO estimates, years at birth): 78.8 (males 76.1; females 81.4) in 2001 ((Source: WHO, *World Health Report*).

IMMIGRATION AND EMIGRATION

	1998	1999	2000
Immigrants	36,704	41,841	36,542
Emigrants	22,881	22,842	26,854

ECONOMICALLY ACTIVE POPULATION

('000 persons aged 16 to 74 years)*

	1999	2000	2001
Agriculture, hunting and forestry	84	77 }	89
Fishing	18	16 }	
Oil and gas extraction	27	28	32
Mining and quarrying	32	34 }	290
Manufacturing	300	291 }	
Electricity, gas and water	18	20	18
Construction	146	147	152
Trade, restaurants and hotels	411	419	398
Transport and communications	170	168	169
Financing, insurance, real estate and business services	252	256	273
Public administration and defence	153	157	151
Education	179	184	190
Health and social work	397	402	417
Other services	96	94	97
Total employed	2,258	2,269	2,278
Unemployed	75	81	83
Total labour force	2,333	2,350	2,361
Males	1,250	1,258	1,260
Females	1,083	1,092	1,101

* Figures are annual averages, based on quarterly sample surveys.

Health and Welfare

KEY INDICATORS

Total fertility rate (children per woman, 2001) 1.7
Under-5 mortality rate (per 1,000 live births, 2001) . . 4
HIV/AIDS (% of persons aged 15–49, 2001) 0.08
Physicians (per 1,000 head, 1998) 4.13
Hospital beds (per 1,000 head, 1997) 14.7
Health expenditure (2000): US $ per head (PPP) . . . 2,373
Health expenditure (2000): % of GDP 7.9
Health expenditure (2000): public (% of total) 85.2
Access to water (% of persons, 2000) 100
Human Development Index (2000): ranking 1
Human Development Index (2000): value 0.942

For sources and definitions, see explanatory note on p. vi.

Agriculture

PRINCIPAL CROPS
('000 metric tons)*

	1999	2000	2001
Wheat	230	313	252
Rye	6	11	5
Barley	624	574	612
Oats	355	397	333
Potatoes	380	341	388

* Figures refer to holdings with at least 0.5 ha of agricultural area in use.
Source: FAO.

LIVESTOCK
('000 head)*

	1999	2000	2001
Horses	26	27	28
Cattle	1,047	1,019	980
Sheep	2,294	2,332	2,400
Goats	54	53	51
Pigs	439	412	391

* Figures refer to holdings with at least 0.5 ha of agricultural area in use.
Source: FAO.

LIVESTOCK PRODUCTS
('000 metric tons)

	1999	2000	2001
Beef and veal	96	91	84
Mutton and lamb	23	24	23
Pig meat	109	103	105
Horse meat	1	1	1*
Poultry meat	29	35	32
Cows' milk	1,790	1,699	1,669
Goats' milk	23	22	21
Butter	19	16	14
Cheese	84	84	82
Hen eggs	50	49	49
Honey	1	1	1
Wool: greasy	5	5	5
Wool: scoured	3	3.	3
Cattle hides (fresh)*	10	10	8
Sheepskins (fresh)*	7	7	7

* FAO estimate(s).
Source: FAO.

Forestry

ROUNDWOOD REMOVALS
('000 cubic metres, excl. bark)

	1999	2000	2001
Sawlogs, veneer logs and logs for sleepers	4,194	4,088	4,219
Pulpwood	3,483	3,366	3,444
Other industrial wood	30	24	26
Fuel wood	717	678	691
Total	**8,424**	**8,156**	**8,380**

Source: FAO.

SAWNWOOD PRODUCTION
('000 cubic metres, incl. railway sleepers)

	1999	2000	2001
Coniferous (softwood)	2,336	2,267	2,240
Broadleaved (hardwood) . . .	0	13	13
Total	**2,336**	**2,280**	**2,253**

Source: FAO.

Fishing

('000 metric tons, live weight)

	1998	1999	2000
Capture	2,861.2	2,620.1	2,703.4
Atlantic cod	321.4	256.6	220.1
Saithe (Pollock)	194.5	198.0	169.7
Blue whiting (Poutassou) . .	570.7	534.2	553.5
Sandeels (Sandlances) . . .	343.6	187.6	119.0
Capelin	88.2	92.6	374.6
Atlantic herring	831.8	821.4	799.7
Atlantic mackerel	158.3	160.8	174.2
Aquaculture	410.7	475.8	487.9
Atlantic salmon	360.8	425.2	436.7
Total catch	**3,271.9**	**3,095.9**	**3,191.3**

Note: Figures exclude aquatic plants ('000 metric tons, wet weight, capture): 179.8 in 1998; 178.5 in 1999; 192.4 in 2000. Also excluded are aquatic mammals, recorded by number rather than by weight. The number of minke whales caught was: 625 in 1998; 591 in 1999; 487 in 2000. The number of harp seals caught was: 2,689 in 1998; 1,953 in 1999; 18,678 in 2000. The number of hooded seals caught was: 6,332 in 1998; 4,446 in 1999; 1,871 in 2000.

Source: FAO, *Yearbook of Fishery Statistics*.

Mining

(estimates, '000 metric tons, unless otherwise indicated)

	1999	2000	2001
Coal (all grades)	328	330	320
Crude petroleum (million barrels) . .	1,100	1,000	1,000
Iron ore*	355	369	340
Natural gas ('000 barrels)†	42,000	41,000	41,000

* Metal content of ore.
† Marketed natural gas.

Source: US Geological Survey.

Industry

SELECTED PRODUCTS
('000 metric tons, unless otherwise indicated)

	1998	1999	2000
Margarine.	57.1	55	n.a.
Mechanical wood pulp (dry weight)	1,664	1,644	1,717
Chemical wood pulp (dry weight) .	684	655	635
Particle board ('000 cu m)	418.6	419*	433*
Paper and paperboard	2,260	2,241	2,301
Woven woollen fabrics (million sq m)	1.6	n.a.	n.a.
Motor spirit (petrol, '000 barrels)	25,000	25,000*	26,000*
Kerosene ('000 barrels) .	9,000	9,000	9,000
Gas-diesel (distillate fuel) oil ('000 barrels) .	45,000	45,000	46,000
Cement	1,676	1,700	1,720
Ferro-silicon (75% basis)	470*	460	460
Other ferro-alloys	770	740	750
Crude steel	644	611	620*
Nickel (refined): primary	70.2	74.1	58.7
Copper (refined): primary	31.7	33.3	27.0*
Aluminium (refined): primary	995.6	1,020.2	1,025.7
Zinc (refined): primary	128.0	132.6	125.8
Electricity (million kWh)	116,787	122,445	n.a.

* Estimated or unofficial figure.

Sources: mainly UN, *Industrial Commodity Statistics Yearbook*; FAO; US Geological Survey.

Finance

CURRENCY AND EXCHANGE RATES

Monetary Units
100 øre = 1 Norwegian krone (plural: kroner)

Sterling, Dollar and Euro Equivalents (31 December 2002)
£1 sterling = 11.2273 kroner
US $1 = 6.9657 kroner
€1 = 7.3049 kroner
1,000 Norwegian kroner = £89.07 = $143.56 = €136.89

Average Exchange Rate (kroner per US $)
2000   8.8018
2001   8.9917
2002   7.9838

BUDGET
(million kroner)*

Revenue	1999	2000†	2001†
Taxation‡	407,709	478,599	551,797
Taxes on income, profits and wealth‡	103,456	156,190	213,835
Social security contributions .	122,123	128,856	135,256
Value-added tax and investment levy	114,076	121,710	130,330
Property income	45,246	52,852	66,506
Interest and dividends	36,988	42,054	50,723
Compulsory fees, fines, etc..	3,147	2,350	606
Other current transfers .	40,394	109,721	88,956
From public enterprises	32,909	95,608	76,652
From Norges Bank	3,401	10,685	10,685
Capital transfers‡	1,024	1,273	1,329
Total	494,374	642,446	708,588

Expenditure§‖	1999	2000†	2001†
General public services	89,082	94,691	99,702
Defence	26,445	27,236	28,090
Public order and safety	10,522	10,908	11,798
Economic affairs	51,275	60,545	47,611
Environmental protection	1,942	2,040	2,132
Housing and community amenities	934	1,114	1,111
Health	41,125	44,699	47,987
Recreation, culture and religion	5,624	5,837	6,112
Education	27,925	29,156	31,367
Social protection	182,260	198,037	212,381
Total	437,133	474,262	488,248
Current	424,565	457,463	478,564
Capital	10,633	14,899	7,533

* Figures represent a consolidation of the operations of the central Government and local administrations (counties and municipalities), including social security funds and extrabudgetary accounts.

† Figures are provisional.

‡ Inheritance and gift taxes are excluded from tax revenue and are treated as capital transfers.

§ Excluding lending minus repayments.

‖ According to the international standard classification of the functions of government (COFOG), introduced in 2002.

INTERNATIONAL RESERVES
(US $ million at 31 December)

	2000	2001	2002
Gold*	257.1	260.3	402.8
IMF special drawing rights.	306.6	354.5	315.5
Reserve position in IMF.	583.8	725.6	992.2
Foreign exchange.	19,273.7	14,408.0	19,374.2
Total	20,421.2	15,748.3	21,084.7

* National valuation (1,184,000 troy ounces each year).

Source: IMF, *International Financial Statistics*.

MONEY SUPPLY
(million kroner at 31 December)

	2000	2001	2002
Currency outside banks .	42,524	42,038	40,280
Demand deposits at commercial and savings banks.	521,010	616,023	671,670
Total money (incl. others) .	565,223	659,562	711,950

Source: IMF, *International Financial Statistics*.

COST OF LIVING
(Consumer Price Index; base: 1998 = 100)

	1999	2000	2001
Food	103.2	105.0	103.0
Alcoholic beverages and tobacco	103.1	110.4	114.2
Housing and maintenance	102.2	107.1	115.0
Fuel and power			
Clothing and footwear.	99.2	95.0	94.2
Furnishings and household equipment	101.3	101.9	102.7
Health	104.8	108.4	111.6
Transport	102.9	108.5	111.6
Communications	93.3	90.0	87.0
Recreation and culture	102.2	103.8	104.7
Education	104.8	110.2	117.7
Restaurants and hotels	103.4	106.8	111.4
Other goods and services .	103.8	106.8	111.6
All items (incl. others)	102.3	105.5	108.7

NATIONAL ACCOUNTS
(million kroner at current prices)

National Income and Product

	1999	2000*	2001*
Compensation of employees . .	606,127	637,566	677,825
Operating surplus	274,484	444,071	429,187
Domestic factor incomes . .	880,611	1,081,637	1,107,012
Consumption of fixed capital .	188,472	207,264	219,429
Gross domestic product			
(GDP) at factor cost . . .	1,069,083	1,288,901	1,326,441
Indirect taxes . . . . . }	163,956	176,202	184,428
Less Subsidies . . . . }			
GDP in purchasers' values . .	1,223,039	1,465,103	1,510,869
Factor income received from			
abroad . . . . }	−14,821	−14,564	−8,491
Less Factor income paid abroad . }			
Gross national product (GNP)	1,218,218	1,450,539	1,502,378
Less Consumption of fixed capital	188,472	207,264	219,429
National income in market			
prices	1,029,746	1,243,275	1,282,949
Other current transfers received			
from abroad . . . . . }	−11,277	−12,300	−15,130
Less Other current transfers paid			
abroad . . . . }			
National disposable income .	1,018,469	1,230,975	1,267,819

* Figures are provisional.

Expenditure on the Gross Domestic Product

	1999	2000*	2001*
Government final consumption			
expenditure	263,730	280,116	306,064
Private final consumption			
expenditure	584,272	624,641	651,492
Increase in stocks	20,732	30,269	16,289
Gross fixed capital formation . .	271,828	283,559	280,015
Total domestic expenditure .	1,140,562	1,218,585	1,253,860
Exports of goods and services .	486,232	686,473	698,876
Less Imports of goods and services	393755	439,963	441,869
GDP in purchasers' values . .	1,233,039	1,456,095	1,510,867

* Figures are provisional.

Gross Domestic Product by Economic Activity

	1999	2000*	2001*
Agriculture and hunting . . .	11,214	10,821	10,383
Forestry and logging	4,902	4,559	4,513
Fishing and fish farming . . .	10,064	10,647	10,114
Oil and gas extraction . . .	163,370	326,102	311,274
Other mining and quarrying . .	2,500	2,772	2,769
Manufacturing	135,733	135,670	131,432
Electricity, gas and water . .	23,952	27,853	30,844
Construction	47,732	51,790	56,654
Trade, restaurants and hotels . .	125,460	137,723	141,378
Transport, storage and			
communications†	101,122	105,664	119,351
Financing, insurance, real estate			
and business services . . .	207,6172	230,587	247,619
Other private services	58,892	64,257	68,652
Government services	202,822	215,483	233,950
Sub-total	1,095,380	1,323,928	1,368,933
Value-added tax and investment			
levy	122,443	130,694	138,838
Other taxes on products (net) . .	50,740	50,808	54,880
Less Imputed bank service charge	35,524	37,824	41,872
Statistical discrepancy	—	−2,509	−9,911
GDP in purchasers' values . .	1,233,039	1,465,097	1,510,868

* Figures are provisional.

† Including transportation of petroleum and gas by pipeline.

BALANCE OF PAYMENTS
(US $ million)

	1999	2000	2001
Exports of goods f.o.b.	46,224	60,463	59,699
Imports of goods f.o.b.	−35,501	−34,520	−33,681
Trade balance	10,723	25,942	26,018
Exports of services	15,878	17,331	17,958
Imports of services	−14,882	−15,422	−15,392
Balance on goods and services	11,719	27,851	28,584
Other income received	6,100	6,641	7,590
Other income paid	−7,998	−8,295	−8,530
Balance on goods, services and			
income	9,821	26,197	27,644
Current transfers received . . .	1,681	1,321	1,473
Current transfers paid . . .	−3,124	−2,712	−3,157
Current balance	8,378	24,807	25,960
Capital account (net)	−116	−186	−93
Direct investment abroad . . .	−6,018	−8,511	1,086
Direct investment from abroad . .	8,056	5,806	1,086
Portfolio investment assets . .	−7,228	−25,144	−29,420
Portfolio investment liabilities . .	4,238	9,844	2,756
Financial derivatives assets . .	152	−329	−1,228
Financial derivatives liabilities .	92	−131	88
Other investment assets . . .	−7,663	−14,148	−2,261
Other investment liabilities . .	8,802	19,459	2,935
Net errors and omissions . . .	−2,710	−7,780	−4,104
Overall balance	5,984	3,686	−2,114

Source: IMF, *International Financial Statistics*.

OFFICIAL ASSISTANCE TO DEVELOPING COUNTRIES
(million kroner)

	1998	1999	2000
Bilateral assistance*	6,768	7,362	7,704
Technical assistance	1,469	1,054	956
Investments	n.a.	578	587
Sector-related project and			
programme aid	n.a.	2,597	2,827
Associated financing	n.a.	2,915	3,140
Multilateral assistance	2,802	2,832	2,901
Administration	450	526	563
Total official development			
assistance	10,019	10,721	11,168

* From 1999 the categories for bilateral assistance have been changed.

External Trade

(Note: Figures include all ships bought and sold but exclude trade in military supplies under defence agreements.)

PRINCIPAL COMMODITIES
(distribution by SITC, million kroner)

Imports c.i.f.*	1999	2000	2001
Food and live animals	15,173.3	15,582.8	16,553.4
Crude materials (inedible) except fuels	17,025.7	21,494.9	20,918.6
Metalliferous ores and metal scrap	9,259.7	12,478.1	12,249.2
Mineral fuels, lubricants, etc. (incl. electric current)	8,512.9	13,458.6	15,114.6
Petroleum, petroleum products, etc.	6,266.0	9,208.2	8,964.5
Chemicals and related products	24,298.2	27,362.3	28,210.8
Basic manufactures	41,209.6	43,240.1	43,698.3
Metal manufactures	9,941.3	9,027.3	9,528.5
Machinery and transport equipment	113,239.3	134,941.2	124,682.3
Machinery specialized for particular industries	10,735.3	10,222.1	10,187.5
General industrial machinery, equipment and parts	15,241.7	12,785.4	13,652.1
Office machines and automatic data-processing equipment	13,782.7	15,077.2	15,311.6
Automatic data-processing machines and units	9,072.5	9,119.1	8,938.4
Telecommunications and sound equipment	10,258.2	12,564.6	11,984.7
Telecommunications equipment and parts	8,057.6	9,715.8	8,660.2
Other electrical machinery, apparatus, etc.	13,897.2	15,299.1	16,021.2
Road vehicles and parts†	23,066.0	25,125.7	25,700.6
Passenger motor cars (excl. buses)	12,368.2	13,526.5	13,931.4
Other transport equipment†	20,556.2	38,343.6	25,043.6
Ships exceeding 100 grt	9,646.6	16,170.1	10,086.9
Miscellaneous manufactured articles	43,668.4	44,912.7	45,034.9
Clothing and accessories (excl. footwear)	10,767.7	11,341.5	11,092.5
Total (incl. others)	266,676.5	302,852.1	296,161.3

* Equipment imported directly to the Norwegian sector of the continental shelf is excluded.

† Excluding tyres, engines and electrical parts.

Exports f.o.b.	1999	2000	2001
Food and live animals	31,538.0	33,127.3	32,411.9
Fish and fish preparations*	28,454.4	30,340.5	29,576.1
Mineral fuels, lubricants, etc. (incl. electric current)	177,375.5	337,868.0	326,883.8
Petroleum, petroleum products, etc.	147,756.7	283,578.4	256,893.5
Crude petroleum	133,678.2	258,835.8	240,594.0
Gas (natural and manufactured)	28,700.5	52,052.4	68,149.1
Natural gas	25,548.5	47,789.5	61,018.2
Chemicals and related products	22,280.9	25,949.4	27,618.4
Basic manufactures	50,046.9	59,211.5	56,623.7
Non-ferrous metals	24,309.4	31,955.1	29,885.6
Aluminium	16,162.1	20,046.0	21,416.6
Machinery and transport equipment	50,950.3	49,558.7	60,188.9
Transport equipment†	19,254.4	11,103.2	19,665.0
Miscellaneous manufactured articles	12,563.7	16,048.8	18,378.2
Total (incl. others)	335,171.5	528,836.0	529,966.0

* Including crustaceans and molluscs.

† Excluding tyres, engines and electrical parts.

PRINCIPAL TRADING PARTNERS
(million kroner)

Imports c.i.f.	1999	2000	2001
Belgium	6,117.3	5,607.1	5,611.6
Canada	4,589.9	8,664.9	8,465.1
China, People's Republic	7,228.2	8,707.5	8,931.2
Denmark	18,225.5	19,298.1	20,940.5
Finland	9,222.7	10,760.1	10,218.8
France	11,338.4	12,106.0	15,292.1
Germany	34,251.8	35,964.3	37,451.4
Ireland	3,469.6	4,172.3	4,395.1
Italy	10,064.9	9,528.7	9,844.1
Japan	11,214.5	15,635.5	11,009.7
Korea, Republic	3,857.0	7,389.3	3,492.9
Netherlands	13,185.8	11,807.5	12,835.4
Poland	2,547.0	3,362.8	3,156.4
Russia	5,378.7	7,268.9	7,031.1
Spain	5,504.2	6,195.7	4,794.5
Sweden	40,197.9	44,488.3	45,147.1
Switzerland	3,070.3	3,296.5	3,770.9
Taiwan	2,237.2	3,886.6	3,373.2
United Kingdom	24,546.3	24,569.2	23,312.1
USA	21,224.4	24,714.6	20,989.3
Total (incl. others)	266,676.5	302,852.1	296,161.3

Exports f.o.b.	1999	2000	2001
Belgium	9,703.0	18,291.7	19,681.2
Canada	16,987.0	29,923.5	21,762.8
China, People's Republic	3,999.7	2,363.9	5,962.5
Denmark	18,964.0	20,231.9	19,173.7
Finland	8,326.8	11,456.6	10,035.7
France	29,533.3	53,150.3	49,985.6
Germany	35,654.4	55,425.2	64,419.3
Ireland	4,860.2	8,719.2	8,296.1
Italy	7,810.9	9,872.9	11,198.6
Japan	9,451.0	8,723.1	8,991.6
Korea, Republic	3,580.8	3,915.0	3,282.4
Netherlands	37,462.0	60,605.9	54,870.1
Portugal	4,221.0	4,010.3	4,760.6
Spain	6,528.1	8,268.2	8,351.0
Sweden	33,243.2	44,478.4	42,644.5
United Kingdom	64,507.9	109,175.20	103,942.6
USA	26,877.0	40,164.3	40,801.9
Total (incl. others)	355,171.5	529,836.0	529,966.0

Transport

STATE RAILWAYS
(traffic)

	1999	2000	2001
Passengers carried ('000)	50,019	50,773	49,396
Goods carried ('000 metric tons)	8,229	7,959	8,190
Passenger-kilometres (million)	2,668	2,635	2,536
Freight ton-kilometres (million)	2,456	2,399	2,451

ROAD TRAFFIC
(motor vehicles registered at 31 December)

	1999	2000	2001
Passenger cars (incl. station wagons and ambulances)	1,813,642	1,851,929	1,872,862
Buses	37,039	36,686	35,667
Vans	219,731	233,248	249,939
Combined vehicles	107,349	104,868	100,624
Goods vehicles, etc.	75,959	76,224	76,414
Tractors and special-purpose vehicles	227,236	229,204	231,921
Motorcycles	78,133	85,672	90,268
Snow scooters	46,648	48,305	50,468
Mopeds	114,868	115,892	121,159

SHIPPING

Merchant Fleet
(registered at 31 December)

	1999	2000	2001
Number of vessels	2,350	2,349	2,363
Total displacement ('000 grt) . .	23,446.3	22,604.1	22,590.8

Note: Figures include vessels on the Norwegian International Ship Register.

Source: Lloyd's Register-Fairplay, *World Fleet Statistics*.

International Sea-borne Freight Traffic*
('000 metric tons)

	1998	1999	2000
Goods loaded	154,116	151,116	160,080
Goods unloaded	27,264	25,788	23,400

* Figures exclude transit traffic (other than Swedish iron ore), packing and re-export.

Source: UN, *Monthly Bulletin of Statistics*.

CIVIL AVIATION
(traffic on scheduled services)*

	1997	1998	1999
Kilometres flown (million) . .	130	134	151
Passengers carried ('000) . .	13,759	14,279	15,020
Passenger-kilometres (million) . .	9,158	9,480	9,874
Total ton-kilometres (million) . .	1,061	1,082	1,154

* Including an apportionment (2/7) of the international services of Scandinavian Airlines System (SAS), operated jointly with Denmark and Sweden.

Source: UN, *Statistical Yearbook*.

Tourism

VISITOR ARRIVALS BY COUNTRY OF ORIGIN*

	1998	1999	2000
Denmark	390,834	396,339	403,830
Finland	111,285	107,604	93,279
France	243,811	260,465	245,653
Germany	1,286,973	1,202,103	1,151,073
Italy	147,342	132,364	133,293
Japan	113,882	119,233	131,493
Netherlands	344,974	351,527	345,286
Spain	135,767	138,811	139,695
Sweden	581,544	565,265	514,429
United Kingdom	316,119	309,299	295,189
USA	250,321	278,936	274,006
Total (incl. others)	4,538,221	4,481,400	4,438,039

* Non-resident staying in all types of accommodation establishments.

Tourism receipts (US $ million): 2,212 in 1998; 2,229 in 1999.

Source: mainly World Tourism Organization, *Yearbook of Tourism Statistics*.

Communications Media

	1999	2000	2001
Television receivers ('000 in use)	2,900	3,000	n.a.
Telephones ('000 main lines in use)	3,176	3,302	3,262
Mobile cellular telephones ('000 subscribers).	2,788	3,151	3,737
Personal computers ('000 in use)	2,000	2,200	2,300
Internet users ('000)	2,000	2,200	2,700

Source: International Telecommunication Union.

Radio receivers (1997): 4,030,000 in use*.

Books published (1996): 6,900 titles.*†.

Daily newspapers (2000): 64; net circulation ('000 copies) 2,252.‡.
* Source: UNESCO, *Statistical Yearbook*.
† Excluding school textbooks and government publications.
‡ Issued at least six times a week.

Education

(incl. Svalbard, 2000/2001)

	Institutions	Teachers (Full-time)	Students
Pre-primary*	5,833	52,673†	189,837
Primary and lower secondary	3,260	45,247	590,471
Upper secondary‡	696	7,791	190,229
Colleges of higher education	59	5,702	109,893
Universities and their equivalent	11	6,369	81,561

* 2000 figures.
† Of the total, 16,467 were trained as pre-school teachers.
‡ Including folk high schools and labour market courses. The figure for students excludes apprentices (30,099 in 2000/2001).

Directory

The Constitution

The Constitution was promulgated on 17 May 1814.

According to the Constitution, Norway is a 'free, independent, indivisible, inalienable Kingdom'; its form of government a 'limited and hereditary monarchy'. (In May 1990 the law of succession, which stipulated that a male heir should have precedence in succeeding to the throne, was amended to permit men and women an equal right to the throne. The previous law would still apply to those born before 1990.) The Evangelical Lutheran Church is the established religion of the State.

Executive power is vested in the King, legislative power in the Storting (parliament), and judicial power in the Judicature.

EXECUTIVE POWER

The King exercises his power through the Statsråd (Council of State). The Statsråd is composed of a Prime Minister and not fewer than seven other Councillors of State, all at least 30 years of age. The business to be dealt with in the Statsråd is prepared by the various executive Ministries, each with a Councillor of State at its head. These executive departments conduct the administrative work of the country.

The Government submits the budget estimates and introduces bills in the Storting.

Formally, the King appoints the Government, but since the introduction of the parliamentary system in 1884 it is the practice for him to act in accordance with the will of the Storting.

LEGISLATIVE POWER

The Storting is elected quadrennially by universal suffrage. All Norwegian citizens aged 18 years and over are eligible to vote and every qualified voter who has resided in Norway for at least 10 years is eligible to stand for election. The Storting has 165 members, who elect one-quarter of their own body to constitute the Lagting (upper house); the other three-quarters compose the Odelsting (lower house). All bills must first be introduced in the Odelsting, either by the Government through a Councillor of State or by a member of the Odelsting. Should the bill be passed by the Odelsting, it is sent to the Lagting, which may adopt it or return it with amendments. If a bill be passed twice by the Odelsting and rejected on both occasions by the Lagting, it is submitted to the entire Storting and decided by a two-thirds' majority. When a bill has thus been passed, it must receive the royal assent in the Statsråd.

Bills for the revision of the Constitution must be introduced in the first, second or third session after a new election. However, only the Storting, after the next election, has the power to decide whether the proposed alteration should be adopted. Bills relating to the Constitution are dealt with only by the united Storting. For the adoption of a bill of this nature, a two-thirds' majority is required, and the measure becomes law without the royal assent.

The Storting votes all state expenditure and determines state revenue, taxes, customs tariffs and other duties; the Odelsting exercises control over government administration, government appointments and so forth.

The Storting prepares its business through its committees and settles such business, with the exception of bills, in plenum. The Councillors of State may attend the Storting, having the right of speech but not of voting.

The Storting determines the duration of each session. It is opened and prorogued by the King each year. The Storting cannot be dissolved either by the King or by its own resolution until the expiry of the quadrennial period for which it has been elected.

Note: In September 1989 the Sámi (Lapps) of northern Norway elected 39 representatives to a new consultative assembly (Sameting). The Sameting is elected quadrennially and is based in the town of Karasjok, in Finnmark.

The Government

HEAD OF STATE

Monarch: King HARALD V (succeeded to the throne 17 January 1991; sworn in 21 January 1991).

COUNCIL OF STATE
(Statsråd)
(April 2003)

A minority Government, comprising Høyre (H), the Kristelig Folkeparti (KrF) and Venstre (V).

Prime Minister: KJELL MAGNE BONDEVIK (KrF).

Minister of Foreign Affairs: JAN PETERSEN (H).

Minister of Finance: PER-KRISTIAN FOSS (H).

Minister of Culture and Church Affairs: VALGERD SVARSTAD HAUGLAND (KrF).

Minister of Agriculture: LARS SPONHEIM (V).

Minister of Justice and the Police: ODD EINAR DØRUM (V).

Minister of Health: DAGFINN HØYBRÅTEN (KrF).*

Minister of International Development: HILDE FRAFJORD JOHNSON (KrF).*.

Minister of Petroleum and Energy: EINAR STEENSNÆS (KrF).

Minister of Children and Family Affairs: LAILA DÅVØY (KrF).*

Minister of Education and Research: KRISTIN CLEMET (H).

Minister of Fisheries: SVEIN LUDVIGSEN (H).

Minister of Labour and Government Administration: VICTOR DANIELSEN NORMAN (H).*

Minister of Social Affairs: INGJERD SCHOU (H).

Minister of Trade and Industry: ANSGAR GABRIELSEN (H).

Minister of Transport and Communications: TORILD SKOGSHOLM (V).*

Minister of Local Government and Regional Development: ERNA SOLBERG (H).

Minister of Defence: KRISTIN KROHN DEVOLD (H).

Minister of the Environment: BØRGE BRENDE (H).

* Not a member of the Storting.

MINISTRIES

Office of the Prime Minister: Akersgt. 42, POB 8001 Dep., 0030 Oslo; tel. 22-24-90-90; fax 22-24-95-00; e-mail postmottak@smk.dep .no; internet odin.dep.no/smk.

Ministry of Agriculture: Akersgt. 42, POB 8007 Dep., 0030 Oslo; tel. 22-24-90-90; fax 22-24-95-55; e-mail postmottak@ld.dep.no; internet odin.dep.no/ld.

Ministry of Children and Family Affairs: Akersgt. 59, POB 8036 Dep., 0030 Oslo; tel. 22-24-90-90; fax 22-24-95-15; e-mail postmottak@bfd.dep.no; internet odin.dep.no/bfd.

Ministry of Culture and Church Affairs: Akersgt. 59, POB 8030 Dep., 0030 Oslo; tel. 22-24-90-90; fax 22-24-95-50; e-mail info@kkd .dip.no; internet odin.dep.no/kkd.

Ministry of Defence: Myntgt. 1, POB 8126 Dep., 0032 Oslo; tel. 23-09-80-00; fax 23-09-23-23; e-mail postmottak@fd.dep.no; internet odin.dep.no/fd.

Ministry of Education and Research: Akersgt. 44, POB 8119 Dep., 0032 Oslo; tel. 22-24-90-90; fax 22-24-95-40; e-mail postmottak@ufd.dep.no; internet odin.dep.no/ufd.

Ministry of the Environment: Myntgt. 2, POB 8013 Dep., 0030 Oslo; tel. 22-24-90-90; fax 22-24-95-60; e-mail postmottak@md.dep .no; internet www.md.dep.no.

Ministry of Finance: Akersgt. 40, POB 8008 Dep., 0030 Oslo; tel. 22-24-90-90; fax 22-24-95-10; e-mail arkiv.postmottak@finans.dep .no; internet odin.dep.no/fin.

Ministry of Fisheries: Grubbegt. 1, POB 8118 Dep., 0032 Oslo; tel. 22-24-90-90; fax 22-24-95-85; e-mail postmottak@fid.dep.no; internet odin.dep.no/fid.

Ministry of Foreign Affairs: 7 juni pl. 1, POB 8114 Dep., 0032 Oslo; tel. 22-24-36-00; fax 22-24-95-00; e-mail post@mfa.no; internet odin.dep.no/ud; also incl. Ministry of International Development and Human Rights.

Ministry of Health and Social Affairs: Einar Gerhardsens pl. 3, POB 8011 Dep., 0030 Oslo; tel. 22-24-90-90; fax 22-24-95-75; internet odin.dep.no/hd.

Ministry of Justice and the Police: Akersgt. 42, POB 8005 Dep., 0030 Oslo; tel. 22-24-90-90; fax 22-24-95-30; e-mail postmottak@jd .dep.no; internet odin.dep.no/jd.

Minister of Labour and Government Administration: Akersgt. 59, POB 8004 Dep., 0030 Oslo; tel. 22-24-60-60; fax 22-24-95-16; e-mail postmottak@aad.dep.no; internet odin.dep.no/aad.

Ministry of Local Government and Regional Development: Akersgt. 59, POB 8112 Dep., 0032 Oslo; tel. 22-24-90-90; fax 22-24-95-45; e-mail postmottak@krd.dep.no; internet odin.dep.no/krd.

Ministry of Petroleum and Energy: Einar Gerhardsens pl. 1, POB 8148 Dep., 0033 Oslo; tel. 22-24-90-90; fax 22-24-95-65; e-mail postmottak@oed.dep.no; internet odin.dep.no/oed.

Ministry of Social Affairs: Einar Gerhardsens pl. 3, POB 8019 Dep., 0030 Oslo; tel. 22-24-90-90; fax 22-24-95-65; e-mail postmottak@sos.dep.no; internet odin.dep.no/sos.

Ministry of Trade and Industry: Einar Gerhardsens pl. 1, POB 8014 Dep., 0030 Oslo; tel. 22-24-90-90; fax 22-24-95-65; e-mail postmottak@nhd.dep.no; internet odin.dep.no/nhd.

Ministry of Transport and Communications: Akersgt. 59, POB 8010 Dep., 0030 Oslo; tel. 22-24-90-90; fax 22-24-95-71; e-mail postmottak@sd.dep.no; internet odin.dep.no/sd.

Legislature

STORTING

Stortinget
Karl Johansgt. 22, 0026 Oslo; tel. 22-31-30-50; fax 22-31-38-50; e-mail stortinget.postmottak@stortinget.no; internet www .stortinget.no.

President: KIRSTI KOLLE GRØNDAHL (DnA).

Vice-President: HANS J. RÖSJORDE (FrP).

The Storting has 165 members, one-quarter of whom sit as the upper house, the Lagting, and the rest as the lower house, the Odelsting.

President of the Lagting: ODD HOLTEN (KrF).

Vice-President: SVEIN H. LUDVIGSEN (H).

President of the Odelsting: GUNNAR SKAUG (DnA).

Vice-President: JORUNN RINGSTAD (Sp).

General Election, 10 September 2001

	Valid votes	%	Seats
Det norske Arbeiderparti (DnA) .	612,632	24.3	43
Høyre	534,852	21.2	38
Fremskrittspartiet (FrP) . .	369,236	14.6	26
Sosialistisk Venstreparti (SV) .	316,397	12.5	23
Kristelig Folkeparti (KrF) . .	312,839	12.4	22
Senterpartiet (Sp)	140,287	5.6	10
Venstre (V)	98,486	3.9	2
Kystpartiet (KP)	44,010	1.7	1
Rød Valgallianse (RV) . . .	30,015	1.2	—
Det Politiske Parti (DPP) . .	19,457	0.8	—
Pensjonistpartiet (Pp) . . .	17,940	0.7	—
Others	25,669	1.1	—
Total	**2,521,820**	**100.0**	**165**

Political Organizations

Arbeidernes Kommunistparti (Workers' Communist Party): Ostarhausgt. 27, 0183 Oslo; tel. 22-98-90-60; fax 22-98-90-55; e-mail akp@akp.no; internet www.akp.no; f. 1973; mem. of Red Electoral Alliance (see below); Leader JORUN GULBRANDSEN.

Fremskrittspartiet (FrP) (Progress Party): POB 8903 Youngstorget, 0028 Oslo; tel. 23-13-54-00; fax 23-13-54-01; internet www .frp.no; f. 1973; formerly Anders Lange's Party; anti-tax; favours privatization, the diminution of the welfare state and less immigration; Chair. CARL I. HAGEN; Sec.-Gen. GEIR MO.

FRIdemokratene (Free Democrats): POB 310 Sentrum, 0103 Oslo; tel. 22-84-45-46; e-mail fridem@online.no; internet www .fridemokratene.no.

Høyre (H) (Conservative): Stortingsgt. 20, POB 1536 Vika, 0117 Oslo; tel. 22-82-90-00; fax 22-82-90-80; e-mail hoyre@hoyre.no; internet www.hoyre.no; f. 1884; aims to promote economic growth and sound state finances, achieve a property-owning democracy, and to uphold democratic government, social security, private property, private initiative and personal liberty; 63,000 mems; Chair. JAN PETERSEN; Leader ODDVARD NILSEN; Sec.-Gen. TROND R. HOLE.

Internasjonale Sosialister (International Socialists): POB 9226 Grønland, 0134 Oslo; tel. 22-20-17-89; fax 22-20-35-70; e-mail intsos@intsos.no; internet www.intsos.no.

Kristelig Folkeparti (KrF) (Christian Democratic Party): Øvre Slottsgt. 18–20, POB 478 Sentrum, 0105 Oslo; tel. 23-10-28-00; fax 23-10-28-10; e-mail krf@krf.no; internet www.krf.no; f. 1933; aims to promote a democratic policy based on Christian outlook; Chair. VALGERD SVARSTAD HAUGLAND; Sec. INGER HELENE VENAAS.

Kystpartiet (Coastal Party): Stortingt., POB 207, 0026 Oslo; tel. 23-31-31-63; fax 23-31-38-23; internet www.kystpartiet.no; Leader STEINAR BASTESEN.

Miljøpartiet de Grønne (Green Environmental Party): POB 2169, 7001 Trondheim; tel. 73-53-09-11; fax 73-53-05-15; e-mail gronne@ gronne.no; internet www.gronne.no; f. 1988; Chief Officer TORE BERGUM.

Naturlovpartiet (Natural Law Party): 2610 Mesnali; tel. 62-36-31-30; fax 62-36-33-72; e-mail info@nlp.no; internet www.nlp.no; f. 1992; Leader ODD SVERRE LOSET.

Norges Kommunistiske Parti (Communist Party of Norway): Torborg Nedreaasgt. 20, POB 2727/Møhlenpris, 5836 Bergen; tel. 55-32-74-89; fax 55-32-93-00; e-mail nkp@nkp.no; internet www.nkp .no; f. 1923; Chair. PER LOTHAR LINDTNER.

Det norske Arbeiderparti (DnA) (Norwegian Labour Party): Youngstorget 2A, POB 8743, 0028 Oslo; tel. 24-14-40-00; fax 24-14-40-01; e-mail dna@dna.no; internet www.dna.no; f. 1887; social democratic; 66,813 mems; Leader JENS STOLTENBERG; Gen. Sec. MARTIN KOLBERG.

Pensjonistpartiet (Pensioners' Party): Nordsetavern 410, 2618 Lillehammer; tel. 61-25-17-70; fax 61-25-06-67; e-mail mona@ pensjonistpartiet.no; internet www.pensjonistpartiet.no; Leader GUNNAR BEKKEN.

Rød Valgallianse (Red Electoral Alliance): Osterhausgt. 27, 0183 Oslo; tel. 22-98-90-50; fax 22-98-90-55; e-mail rv@rv.no; internet www.rv.no; f. 1973; left-wing group; Leader ASLAK SIRA MYHRE.

Senterpartiet (Sp) (Centre Party): Kristian Augustsgt. 7B, 0130 Oslo; tel. 22-98-96-00; fax 22-20-69-15; e-mail epost@senterpartiet .no; internet www.senterpartiet.no; f. 1920 as the Bondepartiet (Agrarian Party), name changed 1959; advocates a decentralized society which will secure employment and diversified settlements in all parts of the country; opposes Norwegian membership of the EU;

encourages the development of an ecologically balanced society; Leader ODD ROGER ENOKSEN; Sec.-Gen. KJELL DAHLE.

Sosialistisk Venstreparti (SV) (Socialist Left Party): Storgt. 45, 0182 Oslo; tel. 21-93-33-00; fax 21-93-33-01; e-mail post@sv.no; internet www.sv.no; f. 1975 as a fusion of the Socialist People's Party, the Democratic Socialists and other socialist forces united previously in the Socialist Electoral League; advocates non-alignment and socialism independent of international centres, based on workers' control, decentralized powers and ecological principles; Chair. KRISTIN HALVORSEN.

Venstre (V) (Liberal): Møllergt. 16, 0179 Oslo; tel. 22-40-43-50; fax 22-40-43-51; e-mail venstre@venstre.no; internet www.venstre.no; f. 1884; in 1988 reunited with Det Liberale Folkepartiet (Liberal Democratic Party, f. 1972); advocates the promotion of national and democratic progress on the basis of the present system by gradual economic, social and cultural reforms; Leader LARS SPONHEIM; Sec.-Gen. GEIR RUNE NYHUS.

Diplomatic Representation

EMBASSIES IN NORWAY

Argentina: Drammensvn 39, 0244 Oslo; tel. 22-55-24-48; fax 22-44-16-41; e-mail enoru@online.no; Ambassador ORLANDO R. REBAGLIATI.

Austria: Thomas Heftyesgt. 19–21, 0244 Oslo; tel. 22-55-23-48; fax 22-55-43-61; e-mail oslo-ob@bmaa.gv.at; Ambassador Dr THOMAS HAJNOCZI.

Belgium: Drammensvn 103D, 0244 Oslo; tel. 23-13-32-20; fax 22-44-38-08; Ambassador CARLOS DE WEVER.

Brazil: Sigurd Syrsgt. 4, 0244 Oslo; tel. 22-55-20-29; fax 22-44-39-64; e-mail brasil@brasil.no; internet www.brasil.no; Ambassador LUIZ ANTÔNIO IARDIM GAGLIARDI.

Bulgaria: Tidemandsgt. 11, 0244 Oslo; tel. 22-55-40-40; fax 22-55-40-24; internet www.bulgaria2net.com; Chargé d'affaires MILKO MILUSHEV.

Canada: Wergelandsvn 7, 0244 Oslo; tel. 22-99-53-00; fax 22-99-53-01; e-mail oslo@dfait-maeci.gc.ca; internet www.canada.no; Ambassador SHIRLEY SERAFINI.

Chile: Meltzersgt. 5, 0244 Oslo; tel. 22-44-89-55; fax 22-44-24-21; e-mail embassy@chile.no; internet www.chile.no; Ambassador MANUEL ATRIA.

China, People's Republic: Tuengen allé 2B, Vinderen, 0244 Oslo; tel. 22-49-38-57; fax 22-92-19-78; Ambassador CHEN NAIQING.

Costa Rica: Skippergt. 33, 8th Floor, 0154 Oslo; tel. 22-42-58-23; fax 22-33-04-08; e-mail ecroslo@online.no; internet home.online.no/ ~ecroslo; Chargé d'affaires a.i. BERNAL E. MONGE.

Croatia: Drammensvn 82, 0271 Oslo; tel. 22-44-22-33; fax 22-44-39-00; e-mail embassy@online.no; Ambassador JAGODA VUKUŠIĆ.

Czech Republic: Fritznersgt. 14, 0244 Oslo; tel. 22-43-00-34; fax 22-55-33-95; e-mail oslo@embassy.mzv.cz; internet www.mfa.cz/ oslo; Ambassador PETR KYPR.

Denmark: Olav Kyrresgt. 7, 0244 Oslo; tel. 22-54-08-00; fax 22-55-46-34; e-mail oslamb@um.dk; internet www.denmark-embassy.no; Ambassador STEN LILHOLT.

Egypt: Drammensvn 90A, 0244 Oslo; tel. 22-20-00-10; fax 22-56-22-68; Ambassador NERMIN ALY MONIR MURAD.

Estonia: Parkvn 51A, 0244 Oslo; tel. 22-54-00-70; fax 22-54-00-71; e-mail saatkondoslos@estemb.no; Ambassador PEEP JAHILO.

Finland: Thomas Heftyesgt. 1, 0244 Oslo; tel. 22-12-49-00; fax 22-12-49-49; e-mail finland@online.no; internet www.finland.no; Ambassador OLE NORRBACK.

France: Drammensvn 69, 0244 Oslo; tel. 22-44-18-20; fax 22-56-32-21; Ambassador PATRICK HENAULT.

Germany: Oscarsgt. 45, 0258 Oslo; tel. 23-27-54-00; fax 22-44-76-72; e-mail post@deutschebotschaft.no; internet www .deutschebotschaft.no; Ambassador Dr HORST WINKELMANN.

Greece: Nobelsgt. 45, 0244 Oslo; tel. 22-44-27-28; fax 22-56-00-72; e-mail gremb@online.no; Ambassador YANNIS BOUCAOURIS.

Guatemala: Oscarsgt. 59, 0258 Oslo; tel. 22-55-60-04; fax 22-55-60-47; e-mail guate@online.no; Ambassador LUIS RAUL ESTEVEZ.

Hungary: Sophus Liesgt. 3, 0244 Oslo; tel. 22-55-24-18; fax 22-44-76-93; e-mail huembosl@online.no; Ambassador GÁBOR IKLÓDY.

Iceland: Stortingsgt. 30, 0244 Oslo; tel. 22-82-34-35; fax 22-83-07-04; Ambassador KRISTINN F. ÁRNASON.

India: Niels Juelsgt. 30, 0244 Oslo; tel. 22-55-22-29; fax 22-44-07-20; e-mail india@online.no; Ambassador GOPALKRISHNA GANDHI.

Indonesia: Gange-Rolvsgt. 5, 0244 Oslo; tel. 22-44-11-21; fax 22-55-34-44; e-mail kbrioslo@online.no; Ambassador AMIRUDDIN NOOR.

Iran: Drammensvn 88E, 0244 Oslo; tel. 22-55-24-08; fax 22-55-49-19; Chargé d'affaires a.i. JAVAD KAJOUYAN FINI.

Israel: POB 534 Skøyen, 0214 Oslo; tel. 21-01-95-00; fax 21-01-95-30; e-mail israel@oslo.mfa.gov.il; Ambassador LIORA HERZL.

Italy: Inkognitogt. 7, 0244 Oslo; tel. 22-55-22-33; fax 22-44-34-36; e-mail ambitalia.oslo@online.no; internet www.ambitalia.no; Ambassador ANDREA G. MOCHI ONORY DI SALUZZO.

Japan: Parkvn 33B, 0244 Oslo; tel. 22-55-10-11; fax 22-44-25-05; internet www.japan-embassy.no; Ambassador MASAO KAWAI.

Korea, Republic: Inkognitogt. 3, 0244, Oslo; tel. 22-55-20-18; fax 22-56-14-11; Ambassador PARK KYUNG-TAI.

Latvia: Bygdøy allé 76, 0268 Oslo; tel. 22-54-22-80; fax 22-54-64-26; e-mail latve@sensewave.com; Ambassador NORMUNDS POPENS.

Lithuania: Gimle Terrasse 6, 0244 Oslo; tel. 22-55-81-50; fax 22-55-67-30; e-mail litauens@online.no; internet litauens.home.online.no; Ambassador ČESLOVAS STANKEVIČIUS.

Mexico: Drammensvn 108B, 0244 Oslo; tel. 22-43-11-65; fax 22-44-43-52; Ambassador GUSTAVO IRUEGAS EVARISTO.

Morocco: Holtegt. 28, 0355 Oslo; tel. 23-19-71-50; fax 23-19-71-51; Ambassador ALI ACHOUR.

Netherlands: Oscarsgt. 29, 0244 Oslo; tel. 23-33-36-00; fax 23-33-36-01; e-mail nlgovosl@online.no; internet www .netherlands-embassy.no; Ambassador D. A. V. E. ADER.

Pakistan: Eckersbergsgt. 20, 0244 Oslo; tel. 21–33–60–80; fax 22-55-50-97; e-mail pareposlo@yahoo.com; internet www.geocities.com/pareposlo; Ambassador Mr SHAHBAZ.

Poland: Olav Kyrres pl. 1, 0244 Oslo; tel. 22-55-55-36; fax 22-44-48-39; e-mail ambpol@online.no; Ambassador ANDRZEJ JEROSZYŃSKI.

Portugal: Josefinesgt. 37, 0244 Oslo; tel. 23-33-28-50; fax 22-56-43-55; Ambassador JOAQUIM RAFAEL CAIMOTO DUARTE.

Romania: Oscarsgt. 51, 0244 Oslo; tel. 22-44-15-12; fax 22-4316-74; e-mail romemb@online.no; internet home.sol.no/romemb; Ambassador Dr VASILE GALGAU.

Russia: Drammensvn 74, 0271 Oslo; tel. 22-55-32-78; fax 22-55-00-70; Ambassador YULII A. KVITSINSKII.

Serbia and Montenegro: Drammensvn 105, 0244 Oslo; tel. 22-44-81-05; fax 22-55-29-92; Ambassador VIDA OGNJENOVIĆ.

Slovakia: Thomas Heftyes gt. 24, 0244 Oslo; tel. 22-04-94-70; fax 22-04-94-74; e-mail slovakr@online.no; Ambassador ANDREJ SOKOLIK.

South Africa: Drammensvn 88C, POB 2822 Solli, 0204 Oslo; tel. 23-27-32-20; fax 22-44-39-75; e-mail sa-emb@online.no; Ambassador HAPPY H. L. MAHLANGU.

Spain: Oscarsgt. 35, 0244 Oslo; tel. 22-92-66-80; fax 22-55-98-22; e-mail embspain@online.no; Ambassador EDUARDO GARRIGUES.

Sudan: Holtegt. 28, 0355 Oslo; tel. 22-60-33-55; fax 22-69-83-44; Ambassador CHARLES MANYANY-D'AWOL.

Sweden: Nobelsgt. 16, 0244 Oslo; tel. 24-11-42-00; fax 22-5515-96; e-mail ambassaden.oslo@foreign.ministry.se; internet www .sverigesambassad.no; Ambassador MATS RINGBORG.

Switzerland: Bygdøy allé 78, 0244 Oslo; tel. 22-43-05-90; fax 22-44-63-50; e-mail vertretung@osl.rep.admin.ch; Ambassador GIAN FEDERICO PEDOTTI.

Thailand: Eilert Sundts gt. 4, 0244 Oslo; tel. 22-12-86-60; fax 22-04-99-69; e-mail thaioslo@online.no; Ambassador THAKUR PHANIT.

Tunisia: Haakon Vllæsgt. 5B, 0161 Oslo; tel. 22-83-19-17; fax 2283-24-12; e-mail ambassade.tunisie.oslo@online.no; Ambassador HOUDA KANOUN.

Turkey: Halvdan Svartes gt. 5, 0244 Oslo; tel. 22-44-99-20; fax 22-55-62-63; e-mail postmaster@oslo-turkish-embassy.com; Ambassador BERHAN EKINCI.

United Kingdom: Thomas Heftyesgt. 8, 0244 Oslo; tel. 23-13-27-00; fax 23-13-27-41; e-mail britemb@online.no; internet www.britain .no; Ambassador MARIOT LESLIE.

USA: Drammensvn 18, 0244 Oslo; tel. 22-44-85-50; fax 22-43-07-77; e-mail oslo@usa.no; internet www.usa.no; Ambassador JOHN DOYLE ONG.

Venezuela: Drammensvn 82, POB 2820 Solli, 0204 Oslo; tel. 22-43-06-60; fax 22-43-14-70; e-mail consulado@venezuela.no; Ambassador LOURDES MOLINOS.

Judicial System

The judicial system in Norway is organized on three levels. The courts of first instance are the District (Herredsrett) and City (Byrett) Courts. The country is divided into 93 judicial areas, most of which are served by one professional judge and one or two deputies (in the major cities the number of judges ranges from three to 52). The Court of Appeal (Lagmannsrett) consists of six jurisdictions, each with between 10 and 52 judges, and two divisions (Appeals and Criminal Divisions). The Supreme Court (Høyesterett) sits in Oslo and decides cases in the last instance. The Court, which is served by 19 judges appointed by the Crown and presided over by a Chief Justice, is competent to try all factual and legal aspects of cases in civil and criminal cause. In criminal cases, however, the competence of the Court is limited to questions concerning the application of the law, the nature of the penalty, and procedural errors of the lower courts. Appeals to the Supreme Court may not be based on errors in the assessment of evidence in connection with the question of guilt.

Chief Justice of the Supreme Court: CARSTEN SMITH.

Presiding Judge of the Court of Appeal (Oslo): NILS ERIK LIE.

Presiding Judge of the Court of Appeal (Bergen): ARNE FANEBUST.

Presiding Judge of the Court of Appeal (Hamar): ODD JARL PEDERSEN.

Presiding Judge of the Court of Appeal (Skien): ARNE CHRISTIANSEN.

Presiding Judge of the Court of Appeal (Tromsø): GAUTE GREGUSSON.

Presiding Judge of the Court of Appeal (Trondheim): SVERRE DRAGSTEN.

CIVIL COURTS

In each municipality there is a Conciliation Board (Forliksråd) consisting of three lay members elected by the municipal council for four years. With a few exceptions, no case may be taken to a court of justice without a prior attempt at mediation by a Conciliation Court. In addition to mediation, the Conciliation Court has a judicial capacity and is intended to settle minor cases in a simple manner without great expense to the parties involved.

The ordinary lower courts are the District and City Courts, which decide all cases not adjudicated upon by the Conciliation Court, and they also act as courts of appeal from judgments given in the Conciliation Court. During the main hearing, the court is generally convened with only one professional judge, but each of the parties may request that the court be convened with two lay judges, in addition to the professional judge. When the court finds it advisable, it may also summon lay judges on its own initiative.

Judgments delivered in the District and City Courts may be taken, on appeal, to the Court of Appeal or to the Supreme Court. In the Court of Appeal cases are judged by three professional judges, but, if requested by one of the parties, lay judges may be summoned.

CRIMINAL COURTS

The criminal courts are: the Court of Examination and Summary Jurisdiction (Forhørsretten), the District and City Courts, the Court of Appeal and the Supreme Court. In the Court of examination and summary jurisdiction the professional judge presides alone, but in the District and City Courts two lay judges also sit. Following the implementation of a major reform in 1995, all criminal cases now begin in a District or City Court. The gravest offences were previously tried directly before a jury in the Court of Appeal and the possibilities for appeal were thus limited. Now, however, the issue of guilt can be appealed to the Court of Appeal in all cases. (Such cases are tried either by three professional judges, and four lay judges with equal votes—meddomsrett, or by three professional judges and a jury of 10 members. For a guilty verdict to be upheld in the latter case, at least seven members of the jury must support the original decision of the lower court. In other cases appeal is directly to the Supreme Court.) The maximum penalty permissible under Norwegian law is 21 years of imprisonment.

OMBUDSMAN

The office of Parliamentary Ombudsman was established in 1962. An Ombudsman is elected by the Storting after every general election for a four-year term (with the possibility of re-election). The Ombudsman is accessible to all citizens, and attempts to ensure against the public administration committing any injustice to the individual citizen. The Ombudsman does not cover private legal affairs, and does not have the right to reverse an official decision, but his pronouncements are normally complied with.

Sivilombudsmannen—Stortingets ombudsmann for forvaltningen (Parliamentary Ombudsman for Public Administration): Akersgt 8, 0158, Oslo; POB 3 Sentrum, 0101 Oslo; tel. 22-82-85-00; fax 22-82-85-11; e-mail post@sivilombudsmannen.no; ARNE FLIFLET.

Religion

CHRISTIANITY

The National Church

Church of Norway

Ministry of Culture and Church, POB 8030 Dep., 0030 Oslo; Council of Norwegian Bishoprics, POB 9307 Grønland, 0135 Oslo; tel. 22-24-90-90; fax 22-24-95-50; tel. 23-30-11-60; e-mail kirkeinfo@kirken.no; internet www.kirken.no.

The Evangelical Lutheran Church, constituted as the State Church; there are 11 dioceses, 103 archdeaconries, 620 clerical districts and 1,298 parishes. The highest representative body of the Church is the Synod, summoned for the first time in 1984. In 2000 approximately 86% of the population belonged to the State Church.

Bishop of Oslo: ANDREAS AARFLOT.

Bishop of Borg: EVEN FOUGNER.

Bishop of Hamar: ROSEMARIE KÖHN.

Bishop of Tunsberg: SIGURD OSBERG.

Bishop of Agder: HALVOR BERGAN.

Bishop of Stavanger: ERNST ODDVAR BAASLAND.

Bishop of Bjørgvin: OLE D. HAGES'THER.

Bishop of Møre: ODD BONDEVIK.

Bishop of Nidaros: FINN WAGLE.

Bishop of Sør-Hålogaland: ØYSTEIN I. LARSEN.

Bishop of Nord-Hålogaland: OLA STEINHOLT.

The Roman Catholic Church

For ecclesiastical purposes, Norway comprises the diocese of Oslo and the territorial prelatures of Tromsø and Trondheim. The diocese and the prelatures are directly responsible to the Holy See. At 31 December 2000 there were an estimated 52,276 adherents in Norway. The Bishop of Oslo participates in the Scandinavian Episcopal Conference (based in Västra Frölunda, Sweden).

Bishop of Oslo: Rt Rev. GERHARD SCHWENZER, Oslo Katolske Bispedømme, Akersvn 5, 0177 Oslo; tel. 23-21-95-00; fax 23-21-95-01; e-mail okb@katolsk.no; internet www.katolsk.no.

Other Churches

Church of England: St. Edmund's Anglican Church, Mollergt. 30, Oslo; tel. 22-69-22-14; fax 22-69-21-63; e-mail trepar@online.no; internet www.osloanglicans.net; 1,600 mems (2001); also in Stavanger, Bergen and Trondheim; Rev. Dr TREVOR PARK (Diocese of Gibraltar in Europe).

Evangelical Lutheran Free Church of Norway: POB 23, Bekkelagshøgda, 1109 Oslo; tel. 22-74-86-00; fax 22-74-86-01; e-mail delf.admin@frikirken.no; internet www.frikirken.no; f. 1877; c. 22,000 mems (1999); Chair. of Synod ARNFINN LØYNING.

Norwegian Baptist Union: Micheletsvei 62C, 1368 Stabekk; tel. 67-10-35-60; fax 67-10-35-69; f. 1860; 10,381 mems (2001); Gen. Sec. BILLY TARANGER.

Pentecostal Movement: Oslo; tel. 22-11-43-00; fax 22-11-43-43; 44,977 mems (1998).

United Methodist Church: POB 2744 St Hanshaugen, 0131 Oslo; tel. 23-33-27-00; fax 23-33-27-01; e-mail hovedkontoret@metodiskirken.no; internet www.metodistkirken.no; f. 1856; 13,178 mems (2001).

In 1998 there were 15,113 Jehovah's Witnesses in Norway and 6,188 Seventh-day Adventists. There were 7,934 members of the Missionary Alliance.

OTHER RELIGIONS

In 1998 there were 46,634 Muslims in Norway and 6,920 Buddhists. There was an Orthodox Jewish community numbering 1,048 at the beginning of 1996.

The Press

The principle of press freedom is safeguarded in the Norwegian Constitution. There is no law specifically dealing with the Press. Editors bear wide responsibility in law for the content of their papers, especially regarding such matters as libel. Although a journalist is legally entitled to conceal his source he may be required to disclose this information under penalty of imprisonment, but such instances are rare. A three-member Council of Conduct gives judgments in cases of complaint against a paper or of disputes between papers. It has no powers of enforcement but its judgments are highly respected. The Press Association has a Code of Ethics aimed at maintaining the standards and reputation of the profession.

The Eastern region dominates press activity. Oslo dailies are especially influential throughout this area, and four of these—*Aftenposten, Verdens Gang, Dagbladet* and *Arbeiderbladet*—have a national readership. Nevertheless, in Norway's other chief cities the large local dailies easily lead in their own districts. In 1999 Norway had 65 daily newspapers, with a combined circulation averaging 2,294,000 copies per issue. A few very large papers are responsible for the bulk of this circulation. In 1996 the most popular newspapers were *Verdens Gang* (Oslo), *Aftenposten* (Oslo), *Dagbladet* (Oslo), *Bergens Tidende* (Bergen) and *Adresseavisen* (Trondheim), with a combined circulation of almost 1m. At the beginning of 1994 the principal media holding company was Schibsted A/S, which owned *Aftenposten* and *Verdens Gang* and had substantial holdings in *Adresseavisen* (33.4%), *Stavanger Aftenblad* (30.5%) and several other newspapers. Orkla Media A/S had holdings of 90% or more in eight regional newspapers (and a 50% share in the major magazine publisher Hjemmet Mortensen—see below). The trade-union-owned Norsk Arbeiderpresse is the principal owner of the left-wing press.

In 1994 there were 33 weekly magazines, with a total circulation of 2.5m. The weekly magazines with the largest sales were *Se og Hør* (news, television and radio) and the 'family' magazines *Hjemmet, Allers* and *Norsk Ukeblad*. The most popular monthly and other magazines included *Illustrert Vitenskap* (science), the sports magazines *Fotball* and *Villmarksliv* the family magazine *Familien* and the home and furnishings magazine *Bonytt/Hjem og Fritid*. The principal magazine publishers in 1994 were Hjemmet Mortensen Forlag AS (with 13 titles), A/S Allers Familie-Journal (five titles) and Bonniers Spesialblader AS (eight titles).

PRINCIPAL NEWSPAPERS

Ålesund

Sunnmørsposten: POB 123, 6001 Ålesund; tel. 70-12-00-00; fax 70-12-46-42; e-mail redaksjon@smp.no; internet www.smp.no; f. 1882; Liberal; Editor HARALD H. RISE; circ. 38,478.

Arendal

Agderposten: POB 8, 4801 Arendal; tel. 37-00-37-00; fax 37-00-38-38; e-mail agderposten@agderposten.no; internet www.agderposten .no; f. 1874; independent; Editor STEIN GAUSLAA; circ. 25,660.

Bergen

Bergens Tidende: POB 875, 5001 Bergen; tel. 55-21-45-00; fax 55-21-48-48; e-mail annonse@bergens-tidende.no; internet www .bergens-tidende.no; f. 1868; Editor HANS ERIK MATRE; circ. 95,455.

Bergensavisen: Chr. Miehelsens gt. 4, POB 824 Sentrum, 5807 Bergen; tel. 55-23-50-00; fax 55-31-00-30; e-mail olav.bergo@ba.no; internet www.ba.no; f. 1927; Labour; Editor OLAV TERJE BERGO; circ. 31,000.

Dagen: POB 76/77, 5002 Bergen; tel. 55-31-17-55; fax 55-31-71-06; f. 1919; religious daily; Editor FINN JARLE SÆLE; circ. 12,351.

Bodø

Nordlands Framtid: Storgt. 9, 8002 Bodø; tel. 75-50-50-00; fax 75-50-50-10; e-mail redaksjonen@nordlands-framtid.no; internet www .nordlands-framtid.no; f. 1910; Labour; Editor THOR WOJE; circ. 20,257.

Drammen

Drammens Tidende og Buskeruds Blad A/S: POB 7033, 3007 Drammen; tel. 32-20-40-00; fax 32-20-42-10; e-mail redaksjonen@dt .no; internet www.dt.no; f. 1832 and 1883; Conservative daily; Dir FINN GRUNDT; Editor HANS ARNE ODDE; circ. 45,000.

Fremtiden: Drammen; tel. 32-82-35-80; fax 32-82-36-00; f. 1905; Labour; Editor KNUT S. EVENSEN; circ. 17,138.

Fredrikstad

Fredrikstad Blad: POB 143, 1601 Fredrikstad; tel. 69-38-80-00; fax 69-31-31-81; e-mail tips@f-b.no; internet www.f-b.no; f. 1889; Conservative; Editor ENLING OMVIK; circ. 24,185.

Gjøvik

Oppland Arbeiderblad: POB 24, 2801 Gjøvik; tel. 61-18-93-00; fax 61-17-98-56; internet www.oa-net.no; f. 1924; daily; Labour; Editor-in-Chief JENS O. JENSEN; circ. 28,500.

Hamar

Hamar Arbeiderblad: Torggt. 51, POB 333, 2301 Hamar; tel. 62-51-96-99; fax 62-51-96-18; e-mail post@ha-nett.no; internet www.ha-nett.no; f. 1925; daily; Labour; Editor ROLV AMDAL; circ. 29,000.

Harstad

Harstad Tidende: Storgt. 11, POB 85, 9481 Harstad; tel. 77-01-80-00; fax 77-01-80-05; e-mail redaksjoner@harstad-tidende.no; internet www.harstad-tidende.no; f. 1887; Conservative; Editor ODD R. OLSEN; circ. 15,556.

Haugesund

Haugesunds Avis: POB 2024, 5501 Haugesund; tel. 52-72-00-00; fax 52-72-04-44; e-mail redaksjonen@haugesunds-avis.no; internet www.haugesunds-avis.no; f. 1895; independent; Editor-in-Chief TONY NUNDAL; circ. 38,485.

Hønefoss

Ringerikes Blad: POB 68, 3502 Hønefoss; tel. 32-17-95-00; fax 32-17-95-01; e-mail redaksjonen@ringblad.no; internet www.ringblad.no; f. 1845; independent; Editor TORE ROLAND; circ. 13,152.

Kongsvinger

Glåmdalen: Gågt. 20, 2226 Kongsvinger; tel. 62-88-25-00; fax 62-88-25-01; e-mail redaksjon@glomdalen.no; internet www.glomladen.no; f. 1926; daily; Labour; Editor BJORN SAUGE; circ. 22,557.

Kristiansand

Fædrelandsvennen: POB 369, 4664 Kristiansand; tel. 38-11-30-00; fax 38-11-30-01; e-mail fep@fedrelandsvennen.no; internet www.fedrelandsvennen.no; f. 1875; daily; Liberal independent; Editor FINN HOLMER-HOVEN; circ. 46,962.

Lillehammer

Dagningen: Lillehammer; tel. 61-25-50-00; fax 61-26-34-65; f. 1924; Labour; Editor INGAR SLETTEN KOLLOEN; circ. 12,441.

Gudbrandsdølen Lillehammer Tilskuer: POB 954, 2601 Lillehammer; tel. 61-28-98-33; fax 61-26-09-60; f. 1841; and 1894; independent; Editor-in-Chief ASBJØRN RINGEN; circ. 30,018.

Lillestrøm

Akershus/Romerikes Blad: POB 235, 2001 Lillestrøm; tel. 63-80-50-50; fax 63-80-50-60; e-mail redaksjonen@rb.no; internet www.rb.no; f. 1913; Labour; Editor-in-Chief TERJE GRANERUD; circ. 42,123.

Molde

Romsdals Budstikke: POB 55, 6401 Molde; tel. 72-15-00-00; fax 71-25-00-11; f. 1843; Conservative independent; Editor ARNT SOMMERLUND; circ. 18,773.

Moss

Moss Avis: POB 248/250, 1501 Moss; tel. 69-20-50-00; fax 69-20-50-03; e-mail jan.tollefsen@moss-avis.no; internet www.moss-avis.no; f. 1876; Liberal/Conservative independent; Editor JAN TOLLEFSEN; circ. 14,561.

Oslo

Aftenposten: Akersgt. 51, POB 1178 Sentrum, 0107 Oslo; tel. 22-86-30-00; fax 22-42-63-25; e-mail aftenposten@aftenposten.no; internet www.aftenposten.no; f. 1860; Conservative independent; Editor-in-Chief EINAR HANSEID; circ. morning 262,362, evening 167,671, Sunday 229,858 (2001).

Akers Avis/Groruddalen Budstikke: POB 100 Grorud, 0905 Oslo; tel. 22-25-01-89; fax 22-16-01-05; f. 1928; 2 a week; non-political; Editor HJALMAR KIELLAND; circ. 12,536.

Arbeiderbladet: POB 1183 Sentrum, 0107 Oslo; tel. 22-72-60-00; fax 22-64-92-82; f. 1884; Labour; Editor-in-Chief ARVID JACOBSEN; circ. 51,786.

Dagbladet: POB 1184 Sentrum, 0107 Oslo; tel. 22-31-06-00; fax 22-31-05-10; e-mail annb@dagbladet.no; internet www.dagbladet.no; f. 1869; daily; Editor-in-Chief JOHN O. EGELAND; circ. 207,551.

Dagens Næringsliv: POB 1182 Sentrum, 0107 Oslo; tel. 22-00-10-00; fax 22-00-10-70; e-mail annonser@dn.nhst.no; Editor AMUND DJUVE; circ. 68,663.

Nationen: POB 9390 Grønland, 0135 Oslo; tel. 21-31-00-00; fax 21-31-00-90; e-mail nationen@nationen.no; internet www.nationen.no; f. 1918; daily; Centre; Editor-in-Chief LARS OLAV HAUG; circ. 18,500.

Verdens Gang: Akersgt. 55, POB 1185 Sentrum, 0107 Oslo; tel. 22-00-00-00; fax 22-42-58-11; e-mail annonser@vg.no; internet www.vg.no; f. 1945; independent; Editor-in-Chief BERNT OLUFSEN; circ. 370,115.

Vårt Land: POB 1180, Sentrum, 0107 Oslo; tel. 22-31-03-10; fax 22-31-03-05; e-mail annonse@vartland.no; internet www.vartland.no; f. 1945; independent, religious daily; Editor HELGE SIMONNEN; circ. 32,000.

Sandefjord

Sandefjords Blad: POB 2042, Hasle, 3202 Sandefjord; tel. 33-42-00-00; fax 33-46-29-91; e-mail redaksjonen@sandfjords-blad.no; internet www.sandefjords-blad.no; f. 1861; Conservative; Editor LEIF MAGNE FLEMMEN; circ. 15,000.

Sandvika

Asker og Baerums Budstikke: POB 133, 1376 Billingstad; tel. 66-77-00-00; fax 66-77-00-60; e-mail redaksjonen@budstikka.no; internet www.budstikka.no; f. 1898; 6 a week; Conservative; Editor ANDREAS GJØLME; circ. 31,940.

Sarpsborg

Sarpsborg Arbeiderblad: POB 87, 1701 Sarpsborg; tel. 69-11-11-11; fax 69-11-11-00; e-mail sa@ostfoldpressen.no; internet www.sarpsborg-arbeiderblad.of.no; f. 1929; independent; Editor TOM HELGESEN; circ. 19,000.

Skien

Telemarksavisa AS: POB 2833, Kjørbekk, 3702 Skien; tel. 35-58-55-00; fax 35-52-82-09; e-mail ove.mellingen@telemarksavisa.no; internet www.telemarksavisa.no; f. 1921; independent; Editor OVE MELLINGEN; circ. 22,000.

Varden: POB 2873 Kjørbekk, 3702 Skien; tel. 35-54-30-00; fax 35-52-83-23; e-mail info@varden.no; internet www.varden.no; f. 1874; Conservative; Editor MAJ-LIS STORDAL; circ. 32,986.

Stavanger

Stavanger Aftenblad: POB 229, 4001 Stavanger; tel. 51-50-00-00; fax 51-89-30-05; e-mail redaksjonen@t-a.no; internet www.t-a.no; independent; f. 1893; Editor-in-Chief JENS BARLAND; circ. 72,000.

Steinkjer

Trønder-Avisa: Hamnegt., 7738 Steinkjer; tel. 74-12-12-00; fax 74-12-13-13; e-mail redaksjonen@t-a.no; internet www.t-a.no; Centre/Liberal; Editor OLE ERIK ALMLID; circ. 25,000.

Tønsberg

Tønsbergs Blad: POB 2003, Postterminalen, 3103 Tønsberg; tel. 33-37-00-00; fax 33-37-30-10; e-mail redaksjon@tb.no; internet www.tb.no; f. 1870; Conservative; Editor-in-Chief MARIT HAUKOM; circ. 33,400.

Tromsø

Nordlys: Rådhusgt. 3, POB 2515, 9272 Tromsø; tel. 77-62-35-00; fax 77-62-35-01; e-mail nyheter@nordlys.no; internet www.nordlys.no; f. 1902; Labour; Editor JONNY HANSEN; circ. 30,924.

Trondheim

Adresseavisen: 7003 Trondheim; tel. 72-50-00-00; fax 72-50-17-54; f. 1767; Editor GUNNAR FLIKKE; circ. 88,802.

POPULAR PERIODICALS

Allers: Stenersgt. 2, 0107 Oslo; tel. 21-30-10-00; fax 21-30-12-04; e-mail allersredaktion@afj.no; family weekly; Editor-in-Chief ORY BJØRHOVDE; circ. 123,578.

Bedre Helse: Gullhaugv. 1, 0483 Oslo; POB 5001 Majorstuen, 0301 Oslo; tel. 22-58-55-30; fax 22-58-05-66; e-mail karin.schau@hm-media.no; health; circ. 33,219 (2000).

Byavisa: Munkegt. 66E, 7011 Trondheim; tel. 73-99-05-50; fax 73-99-05-60; e-mail redaksjon@byavisa.no; internet www.byavisa.no; f. 1996; weekly; circ. 82,000.

Bonytt: Gullhaugvn 1, POB 5001 Majorstuen, 0301 Oslo; tel. 22-58-58-30; fax 22-58-58-09; e-mail bonytt@hm-media.no; internet www.bonytt.com; home and furnishing; 14 a year; Editor ELISABETH HOLTE; circ. 68,000 (2001).

Facts and Fenomener: Oslo; tel. 22-37-30-50; fax 22-38-10-35; previously known as *Lexicon*; monthly; illustrated general knowledge for young people over 15 years of age; Editor ANKER TIEDEMANN; circ. 38,612.

Familien: POB 5460, Majorstua, 0305 Oslo; tel. 22-58-57-00; fax 22-58-07-64; family fortnightly; Editor-in-Chief IVAR MOE; circ. 161,195 (2001).

Foreldre & Barn: Sørkedalsvn 10, 0301 Oslo; tel. 22-96-15-00; fax 22-96-13-52; internet www.foreldre.com; 11 a year; for parents of young children; Editor EDDA ESPELAND; circ. 59,210 (2000).

Foreldremagasinet: Gullhaugvn 1, 0483 Oslo; POB 5001 Majorstuen, 0301 Oslo; tel. 22-58-55-39; e-mail vibeke.ostelie@hm-media .no; for parents; circ. 20,470 (2000).

Henne: POB 250, Økern, 0510 Oslo; tel. 22-63-60-00; fax 22-63-60-36; women's; Editor-in-Chief ELLEN ARNSTAD; circ. 45,586.

Hjemmepc: Gullhaugvn 1, 0483 Oslo; POB 5001 Majorstuen, 0301 Oslo; tel. 22-58-55-14; e-mail anita.myrvang@hm-media.no; internet www.hjemmepc.com; home computers; circ. 38,738 (2000).

Hjemmet: Gullhaugvn 1, 0483 Oslo; POB 5001 Majorstua, 0301 Oslo; tel. 22-58-50-00; fax 22-58-05-70; e-mail hjemmet@hm-media .no; internet www.hm-media.no; family weekly; Editor-in-Chief RØNNAUG GREAKER; circ. 240,008 (2001).

Hytteliv: POB 5001 Majorstua, 0301 Oslo; tel. 22-58-50-00; fax 22-58-58-59; e-mail turid.roste@hm-media.no; f. 1972; 9 a year; for second-home owners; Editor TURID RØSTE; circ. 55,000 (2000).

IdéMagasinet: Oslo; tel. 22-09-75-00; fax 22-09-75-99; women's; Editor ANNICHEN LARGE; circ. 48,257.

I form: Oslo; tel. 22-37-30-50; fax 22-38-10-35; monthly; health and fitness; Editor-in-Chief JENS HENNEBERG; circ. 46,551.

Illustrert Vitenskap: Oslo; tel. 22-37-30-50; fax 22-38-10-35; monthly; popular science; Editor-in-Chief BIRGITTE ENGEN; Editor MONA GRAVNINGEN RYGH; circ. 79,559.

Jærbladet: POB 23, 4341 Bryne; tel. 51-77-99-00; fax 51-48-37-40; 3 days a week; independent; Editor IVAR RUSDAL; circ. 12,477.

KK (Kvinner og Klær): POB 250 Økern, 0510 Oslo; tel. 22-63-60-00; fax 22-63-61-02; women's weekly; Editor-in-Chief JUNE TRØNNES HANSSEN; circ. 88,158.

Mann: Gullhaugvn 1, 0483 Oslo; POB 5001 Majorstuen, 0301 Oslo; tel. 22-58-50-00; fax 22-58-59-59; e-mail postmann.no; internet www .mann.no; men's magazine; Editor-in-Chief ROGER GROENDALEN; circ. 20,000.

Mat & Drikke: POB 250 Økern, 0510 Oslo; tel. 22-63-60-00; fax 22-63-60-36; 7 a year; food and wine; Editor-in-Chief ARNFINN HANSSEN; circ. 23,032.

Norsk Ukeblad: Gullhaugvn 1, 0483 Oslo; tel. 22-58-53-00; fax 22-58-05-69; family weekly; Editor-in-Chief ULF-ARVID MEJLÆNDER; circ. 178,119 (2000).

Det Nye: POB 5001 Majorstuen, 0301 Oslo; tel. 22-58-50-00; fax 22-58-58-09; e-mail detnye@hm-media.no; internet www.detnye.com; for young women; 14 a year; Editor-in-Chief KRISTIN MA BERG; circ. 72,000.

Programbladet: POB 1180 Sentrum, 0107 Oslo; tel. 22-31-03-10; fax 22-31-04-55; f. 1946; radio and television weekly; Editor ØYVIND RISVIK; circ. 65,000.

Romantikk: POB 148 Kalbakken, 0902 Oslo; tel. 22-25-71-90; fax 22-16-50-59; romantic weekly; Editor GUSTAV M. GALÅSEN; circ. 25,500.

Se og Hør: POB 1164 Sentrum, 0128 Oslo; tel. 22-41-51-80; fax 22-41-51-70; f. 1978; news weekly (radio and TV); Editors-in-Chief KNUT HÅVIK, ODD J. NELVIK; circ. 366,887.

Shape-Up: Sørkedalsvn 10A, 0301 Oslo; tel. 22-96-15-00; fax 22-96-13-52; 11 a year; health and beauty; Editor EVA SUNDENE LYNGAAS; circ. 30,986 (2000).

TOPP: POB 1164 Sentrum, 0107 Oslo; tel. 22-41-51-80; fax 22-41-51-70; monthly; for young people aged between 10 and 17 years; Editors ODD J. NELVIK, KNUT HÅVIK; circ. 48,011.

Vi Menn: POB 5001 Majorstuen, 0301 Oslo; tel. 22-58-50-00; fax 22-58-05-71; e-mail vimenn@hm-media.no; internet www.vimenn.com; men's weekly; Editor-in-Chief SVEIN E. HILDONEN; circ. 105,034 (2000).

SPECIALIST PERIODICALS

Alt om Fiske: Gullhaugvn 1, 0483 Olso; POB 5001 Majorstuen, 0301 Oslo; tel. 22-58-55-13; e-mail aud.haugvik@hm-media.no; angling; circ. 27,718 (2000).

Bam: Gullhaugvn 1, 0483 Oslo; POB 5001 Majorstuen, 0301 Oslo; tel. 22-58-55-15; e-mail erika-o.asker@hm-media.no; internet www .bam.no; for new parents; circ. 80,000 (2000).

Batmagasinet: POB 1169, Sentrum, 0107 Oslo; tel. 21-30-10-00; fax 21-30-12-59; e-mail hans.due@afj.no; internet www .batmagasinet.no; 10 a year; boating; Editor HANS DUE; circ. 28,555.

Bil: POB 9247 Vaterland, 0134 Oslo; tel. 23-03-66-00; fax 23-03-66-40; e-mail bil@bilforlaget.no; internet www.bilnorge.no; 10 a year; motoring; Editor KJELL-MAGNE AALBERGSJØ; circ. 51,388.

Bondebladet: POB 9367 Grønland, 0135 Oslo; tel. 21-31-44-00; fax 21-31-44-01; e-mail post@bondebladet.no; internet www .bondebladet.no; f. 1974; weekly; farming; Editor BENDIK BENDIKSEN; circ. 85,593.

Familiens Grønne Gleder: Gullhaugvn 1, 0483 Oslo; POB 5001 Majorstuen, 0301 Oslo; tel. 22-58-55-13; e-mail aud.haugvik@ hm-media.no; gardening; circ. 50,000 (2000).

Fjell og Vidde: Den Norske Turistforening, POB 7, Sentrum, 0101 Oslo; tel. 22-82-28-00; fax 22-82-28-01; e-mail redaksjonen@ turistforeningen.no; internet www.turistforeningen.no; f. 1967; 7 a year; organ of Mountain Touring Asscn; Editor HELLE ANDRESEN; circ. 135,000.

Fotball: Sørkedalsvn 10A, 0301 Oslo; tel. 22-96-15-00; fax 22-96-13-52; 8 a year; for football players and spectators; Editor ØYVIND STEEN JENSEN; circ. 98,655.

Gjør det Selv i Hjemmet: Oslo; tel. 22-37-30-50; fax 22-38-10-35; monthly; for do-it-yourself enthusiasts; Editor-in-Chief AKSEL BRINCK; circ. 27,259.

Gravid: Gullhaugvn 1, 0483 Oslo; POB 5001 Majorstuen, 0301 Oslo; tel. 22-58-55-15; e-mail erika-o.asker@hm-media.no; for pregnant women; circ. 15,301 (2000).

Hagen for alle: POB 644 Sentrum, 0106 Oslo; tel. 22-41-03-52; fax 22-42-64-71; e-mail annonsesalg@hagen-foralle.no; internet www .hagen-foralle.no; monthly; gardening; Editor KNUT LANGELAND; circ. 30,000.

Hundesport: POB 0163 Bryn, 0611 Oslo; tel. 21-60-09-00; fax 21-60-09-01; e-mail hundesport@nkk.no; internet www.nkk.no; monthly; for dog-owners; circ. 50,000.

Ingeniørnytt: POB 25 Røa, 0701 Oslo; tel. 67-16-34-99; fax 22-09-75-55; e-mail ingnytt@online.no; every 2 weeks; engineering, architecture; circ. 65,000.

Jakt & Fiske: POB 94, 1378 Nesbru; tel. 66-79-22-00; fax 66-90-15-87; e-mail viggokristiansen@njff.no; monthly; hunting and angling; Editor VIGGO KRISTIANSEN; circ. 76,710.

Jakt, Hund & Våpen: Gullhaugvn 1, 0483 Oslo; POB 5001 Majorstuen, 0301 Oslo; tel. 22-58-55-34; e-mail inger.storodegard@ hm-media.no; hunting; circ. 25,908 (2000).

Kampanje: Sandakerv. 114B, 0483 Oslo; POB Majorstuen, 0301 Oslo; tel. 22-58-50-00; fax 22-15-40-86; e-mail redaksjon@kampanje .com; internet www.kampanje.com; marketing and media; Editor-in-Chief GLENN Ø. STØLDAL; circ. 11,340 (2000).

Kapital: POB 444 Vinderen 0319 Oslo; tel. 23-29-65-50; fax 23-29-65-94; e-mail wenchew@kapital.no; internet www.hegnar.no; fortnightly; business, management; circ. 40,000.

Kommuniké: POB 9202, 0134 Oslo; tel. 21-03-36-00; fax 21-03-36-50; f. 1936; 9 a year; organ of Norwegian Confederation of Municipal Employees; Editor AUDUN HOPLAND; circ. 54,000.

Kontor & Finans: POB 14 Røa, 0701 Oslo; tel. 22-52-44-60; fax 22-52-24-80; e-mail ergjerts@sn.no; f. 1977; quarterly; business; Editor THOR O. SANDBERG; circ. 100,000.

LINUXmagasinet: POB 7183 Majorstuen, 0307 Oslo; tel. 23-36-82-00; fax 23-36-82-01; e-mail tosterud@linmag.no; internet www .linmag.no; Linux operating system, open source software; 5 a year; Editor-in-Chief SVEIN ERIK TOSTERUD; circ. 8,000.

Motor: POB 494 Sentrum, 0105 Oslo; tel. 22-34-15-55; fax 22-34-14-90; e-mail redaksjonen@motor.no; internet www.motor.no; monthly; motoring, travel and leisure; Editor SVEIN OLA HOPE; circ. 400,000.

NETTUERK: Lilleiorget 1, 0184 Oslo; tel. 23-06-33-74; fax 23-06-33-66; e-mail harald@lo-media.no; monthly; electricity and electronics; Editor HAROLD OLAU MOEN; circ. 43,500.

Norsk Hagetidend: POB 53 Manglerud, 0612 Oslo; tel. 23-03-16-00; fax 23-03-16-01; e-mail postkasse@hageselskapet.no; internet www.hageselskapet.no; f. 1885; monthly; gardening; Editor BERGLJOT GUNDERSEN; circ. 41,878.

Norsk Landbruk: POB 9303 Grønland, 0135 Oslo; tel. 23-15-89-20; fax 23-15-89-21; e-mail norsk.landbruk@landbruksforlaget.no; internet www.landbruksforlaget.no; f. 1882; 22 a year; agriculture, horticulture and forestry; Editor-in-Chief TORD LANGMOEN; circ. 16,172.

Norsk Skoleblad: Rosenkrantzgt. 15, 0160 Oslo; tel. 22-00-20-00; fax 22-00-21-90; f. 1934; weekly; teaching; Editor KNUT HOVLAND; circ. 80,018.

Okonomisk Rapport: Møllergt. 8, Inngang Skråninga, POB 1161 Sentrum, 0107 Oslo; tel. 22-40-41-00; fax 22-42-70-44; e-mail rapport@orapp.no; internet www.orapp.no; business; circ. 24,946 (2000).

PCPro: Gullhaugvn 1, 0483 Oslo; POB 5001 Majorstuen, 0301 Oslo; tel. 22-58-55-04; e-mail harvard.holmedal@hm-media.no; internet www.pcpro.no; computing; circ. 30,000 (2000).

Seilmagasinet: POB 253, 1379 Nesbru; tel. 66-77-40-60; fax 66-77-40-61; e-mail morten.jensen@seilmagasinet.no; internet www.seilmagasinet.no; f. 1975; 10 a year; sailing; Editor MORTEN JENSEN; circ. 14,000.

Skogeieren: POB 1438 Vika, 0115 Oslo; tel. 22-01-05-50; fax 22-83-40-47; f. 1914; 16 a year; forestry; Editor ANDERS HALS; circ. 48,179.

Snø og Ski: Kongevn 5, 0390 Oslo; tel. 22-92-32-00; fax 22-92-32-50; quarterly; winter and summer sports; Editor WANDA WIDERØE; circ. 45,000.

Teknisk Ukeblad (Technology Review Weekly): Oslo; tel. 22-94-76-00; fax 22-94-76-01; f. 1854; technology, industry, management, marketing and economics journal; Editor-in-Chief ERIK B. OLIMB; circ. 73,877.

Tidsskriftet Sykepleien: POB 456 Sentrum, 0104 Oslo; tel. 22-04-33-04; fax 22–04–33–756; internet www.sykepleien.no; f. 1912; 21 a year; health personnel, nursing; Editor-in-Chief MORTEN E. MATHIESEN; circ. 69,000.

Tips: Gullhaugvn 1, 0483 Oslo; POB 5001 Majorstuen, 0301 Oslo; tel. 22-58-50-00; fax 22-58-59-19; e-mail firmapost@tips.as; internet www.tips.as; football and betting; circ. 20,000 weekdays, 18,000 weekend (2000).

Utsyn: Oslo; tel. 22-42-91-30; fax 22-42-04-91; 38 a year; organ of Norsk Luthersk Misjonssamband (Norwegian Lutheran Mission); circ. 30,000.

Vi Menn Båt: Gullhaugvn 1, 0483 Oslo; POB 5001 Majorstuen, 0301 Oslo; tel. 22-58-55-34; e-mail inger.storodegard@hm-media.no; boats; circ. 25,000 (2000).

Vi Menn Bil: Gullhaugvn 1, 0483 Oslo; POB 5001 Majorstuen, 0301 Oslo; tel. 22-58-55-12; e-mail olaug.gaarder@hm-media.no; cars; circ. 113,345 (2000).

Vi Menn Fotball: Gullhaugvn 1, 0483 Oslo; POB 5001 Majorstuen, 0301 Oslo; tel. 22-58-55-15; e-mail erika-o.asker@hm-media.no; football; circ. 30,000 (2000).

Villmarksliv: POB 5928 Majorstuen, 0308 Oslo; tel. 22-58-50-00; fax 22-58-52-39; e-mail dag.kjelsaas@hm-media.no; f. 1972; monthly; angling, hunting, photography; Editor-in-Chief DAG KJELSAAS; circ. 63,645 (2000).

NEWS AGENCIES

Bulls Pressetjeneste A/S: Ebbellsgt. 3, 0158 Oslo; tel. 22-98-26-60; fax 22-20-49-78; e-mail info@bulls.no; internet www.bulls.no; Man. PAUL E. VATNE.

A/S Norsk Telegrambyrå (NTB) (Norwegian News Agency): Holbergs gt. 1, POB 6817 St Olavs pl., 0130 Oslo; tel. 22-03-44-00; fax 22-20-12-29; e-mail ntb@ntb.no; f. 1867; Editor-in-Chief THOR VIKSVEEN.

NPS Billedbyra A/S: Oslo; tel. 22-06-87-70; fax 22-06-87-71; e-mail bildc@ups.no; f. 1962; Man. Dir PER R. MORTENSEN.

Foreign Bureaux

Agence France-Presse (AFP): c/o NTB, Holbergsgt. 1, POB 6817 St Olavs pl., 0130 Oslo; tel. 22-03-44-00; fax 22-20-12-29; Correspondent OLE LUDVIG NYMOEN.

Associated Press (AP) (USA): Holbergsgt. 1, 0166 Oslo; tel. 22-20-10-30; fax 22-20-52-80; Bureau Chief DOUG MELLGREN.

Deutsche Presse-Agentur (dpa) (Germany): Holbergsgt. 1, 0166 Oslo; tel. 22-03-44-00; fax 22-20-12-29; Editor BJØRN VESETH.

Informatsionnoye Telegrafnoye Agentstvo Rossii—Telegrafnoye Agentstvo Suverennykh Stran (ITAR—TASS) (Russia): Fougstadsgt. 9, 0173 Oslo; tel. 22-60-61-91; fax 22-60-63-22; Correspondent IGOR B. PSHENICHNIKOV.

Inter Press Service (IPS) (Italy): Holbergsgt. 1, 0166 Oslo; tel. 22-11-50-80; fax 22-11-50-95; e-mail mail@ipsnor.no; Dir KRISTIN HAVGAR.

Reuters Norge A/S: Stortorvet 10, 0155 Oslo; tel. 22-93-69-00; fax 22-42-50-32; internet www.reuters.no; Country Rep. HENRIK KLAWITTER.

Rossiiskoye Informationnoye Agentstvo—Novosti (RIA—Novosti) (Russia): Oslo; tel. 22-55-55-41; fax 22-55-65-20; Editor ALEKSANDR KRASNOV.

United Press International (UPI) (USA): Holbergsgt. 1, 0166 Oslo; tel. 22-03-44-00; fax 22-20-12-29.

PRESS ASSOCIATIONS

Norsk Presseforbund (Norwegian Press Asscn): Rådhusgt. 17, POB 46 Sentrum, 0101 Oslo; tel. 22-40-50-40; fax 22-40-50-55; e-mail np@presse.no; internet www.presse.no; f. 1910; asscn of newspapermen, editors and journalists; Pres. MARIT HAUKOM; Sec.-Gen. PER EDGAR KOKKVOLD.

Norsk Journalistlag (Norwegian Union of Journalists): Torggt. 5, 5th Floor, POB 8793 Youngstorget, 0028 Oslo; tel. 22-05-39-50; fax 22-41-33-70; e-mail njpost@nj.no; internet www.nj.no; f. 1946; Sec.-Gen. TROND IDÅS; 8,550 mems.

Norske Avisers Landsforening (Norwegian Newspaper Publishers' Asscn): Tollbugt. 27, 0157 Oslo; tel. 22-86-12-00; fax 22-42-26-11; e-mail nal@nal.no; internet www.nal.no; Man. Dir KURT BORGEN.

Den Norske Fagpresses Forening (Specialized Press Asscn): Akersgt. 41, 0158 Oslo; tel. 24-14-61-00; fax 24-14-61-10.

Publishers

Andresen & Butenschøn A/S: POB 1153 Sentrum, 0107 Oslo; tel. 22-33-56-86; e-mail abforlag@online.no.

Antropos Forlag: Josefinesgt. 12, 0351 Oslo; tel. 22-46-03-74; e-mail forlag@antropos.no; internet www.antropos.no.

Ariel Lydbokforlag A/S: Solfallsv. 67, 1430 Ås; POB 1546 Vika, 0117 Oslo; tel. and fax 64-94-35-10; f. 1988; audiocassettes; Editors-in-Chief INGER SCHJOLDAGER, MARGARETE WIESE.

H. Aschehoug & Co (W. Nygaard): Sehestedsgt. 3, POB 363 Sentrum, 0102 Oslo; tel. 22-40-04-00; fax 22-20-63-95; e-mail epost@aschehoug.no; internet www.aschehoug.no; f. 1872; general non-fiction, fiction, reference, children's, educational, textbooks; Man. Dir WILLIAM NYGÅRD; Asst Man. Dir ERIK HOLST.

Atheneum Forlag A/S/Ansgarbøker: Nesset, 1433 Vinterbro; tel. 64-97-80-00; fax 64-97-80-01; e-mail atheneum@online.no; f. 1934; general, fiction, children's, religion; Publr SVENN OTTO BRECHAN.

Bladkompaniet A/S: Staælfjœra 5, POB 148 Kalbakken, 0902 Oslo; tel. 22-90-24-00; fax 22-90-24-01; e-mail bladkompaniet@bladkompaniet.no; internet www.bladkompaniet.no; f. 1915; general fiction, non-fiction, paperbacks, comics, magazines; Publr CLAUS HUITFELDT; Editorial Dir FINN ARNESEN.

Boksenteret Erik Pettersen & Co A/S: Krusesgt. 11, POB 3125 Elisenberg, 0207 Oslo; tel. 22-54-07-00; fax 22-54-07-07; e-mail bs@boksenteret.no; internet www.boksenteret.no; f. 1999; illustrated, non-fiction, craft, DIY; Man. Dir ERIK PETTERSEN.

Bokvennen Forlag: Trudvangvn 41, 0363 Oslo; tel. 22-60-80-28; fax 22-93-02-88; f. 1989; fiction, essays, biographies; Mans MORTEN CLAUSSEN, JAN M. CLAUSSEN.

F. Bruns Bokhandel og Forlag A/S: Kongensgt. 10–14, 7005 Trondheim; tel. 73-51-00-22; fax 73-50-93-20; f. 1873; local history, technology; Publr FRIDTHJOV BRUN.

Cappelen Akademisk Forlag A/S: Oslo; tel. 22-98-58-00; fax 22-95-58-41; e-mail caf@cappelen.no; internet www.cappelen.no; f. 1946; educational, textbooks, non-fiction, periodicals; Publr ESTER MOEN.

J. W. Cappelens Forlag A/S: Mariboesgt. 13, POB 350 Sentrum, 0101 Oslo; tel. 22-36-50-00; fax 22-36-50-40; e-mail web@cappelen.no; internet www.cappelen.no; f. 1829; general, educational, popular science, fiction, maps, children's, encyclopaedias; Man. Dir SINDRE GULDVOG.

N. W. Damm og Søn A/S: Fridtjof Nansensvei 14, 0055 Oslo; tel. 24-05-70-00; fax 24-05-12-99; e-mail post@damm.no; internet www.damm.no; f. 1843; children's, reference, handbooks; Man. Dir TOM HARALD JENSSEN.

Eide Forlag A/S: Sandbrugt. 11, POB 4081 Dreggen, 5835 Bergen; tel. 55-32-90-40; fax 55-31-90-18; f. 1945; general, children's, textbooks, fiction, non-fiction; Publr TRINE KOLDERUP FLATEN; Man. Dir ROALD FLATEN.

Elanders Publishing A/S: Brobekkvn 80, POB 1156 Sentrum, 0107 Oslo; tel. 22-63-64-00; fax 22-63-65-94; e-mail aina@elanders.no; internet elanderspublishing.no; f. 1844 as Elanders Forlag, present name adopted 1997; legislation, catalogues; Publr AINA THORSTENSEN.

Forlaget Fag og Kultur A/S: POB 6633 Etterstad, Biskop Jens Nilssønsgt. 5, 0607 Oslo; tel. 22-68-36-30; fax 22-68-06-25; e-mail firmapost@fagogkultur.no; internet www.fagogkultur.no; f. 1987; reference; Man. Dir MARI ETTRE OLSEN.

Fagbokforlaget: Huitfeldtsgt. 15 POB 2336 Solli, 0201 Oslo; tel. 22-55-69-06; fax 22-55-41-83; e-mail fagbokforlaget@fagbokforlaget.no; f. 1992; general and scientific; Publrs ARNO VIGMOSTAD, ARNSTEIN BJØRKE.

Falken Forlag: Osterhaugsgt. 8, 0183 Oslo; tel. 22-20-86-40; f. 1946; fiction, non-fiction; Publr KIRSTI KRISTIANSEN.

Fonna Forlag: POB 6912 St Olavs pl., 0130 Oslo; tel. 22-20-13-03; fax 22-20-12-01; f. 1940; general, fiction; Man. Dir JOHN F. SØRBØ.

Fono Forlag AS: Billingstadsletta 30, POB 169, 1376 Billingstad; tel. 66-84-64-90; fax 66-84-75-07; e-mail mail@fonoforlag.no; internet www.fonoforlag.no; f. 1991; audio books; Gen. Man. HALVOR HANEBORG.

Frifant Forlag A/S: Leinvn 10, 1453 Bjørnemyr; tel. 66-91-29-40; fax 66-91-29-41; e-mail frifor@online.no; internet www.frifant.no; f. 1997.

Genesis Forlag: Kongensgt. 22, 0153 Oslo; POB 1180 Sentrum, 0107 Oslo; tel. 22-31-03-10; fax 22-31-02-05; e-mail genesis@genesis .no; internet www.genesis.no; f. 1996; Dir MAGNE LERØ.

John Grieg Forlag A/S: Valkendosfsgt. 1A, 5012, Bergen; tel. 55-21-31-80; fax 55-12-00-05; internet www.griegforlag.no; f. 1721; children's books, art, education, aquaculture; Publr SVEIN SKOTHEIM.

Gyldendal Akademisk: Kristian IVs gt. 13, POB 6730 St Olavs pl., 0130 Oslo; tel. 22-03-43-00; fax 22-03-43-05; e-mail akademisk@ gyldendal.no; internet www.gyldendal.no/akademisk; f. 1992; university textbooks; Man. Dir FREDRIK NISSEN.

Gyldendal Norsk Forlag A/S: Sehestedsgt. 4, POB 6860 St Olavs pl., 0130 Oslo; tel. 22-03-41-00; fax 22-03-41-05; internet www .gyldendal.no; f. 1925; general, non-fiction, fiction, biography, religion, cookery, school and university textbooks, children's, manuals; Man. Dir BJØRGUN HYSING.

Gyldendal Yrkesopplaring: Sehestedsgt. 4, POB 6860 St Olavs pl., 0130 Oslo; tel. 22-99-05-10; fax 22-99-05-79; e-mail yrkesopplaring@gyldendal.no; internet www.gyldendal.no/ yrkesopplaring; f. 1979; educational, vocational and technical; Publr KÅRE KVILEKVAL.

Hjemmet Mortensen A/S: Gullhaugvn 1, POB 5001 Majorstuen, 0301 Oslo; tel. 22-58-50-00; fax 22-58-50-68; f. 1941; fiction, non-fiction, children's; Man. Dir KNUT ENGER.

Imprintforlaget A/S: POB 2336 Solli, 0201 Oslo; tel. 23-13-69-30.

Kolibri Forlag A/S: Huk aveny 2B, POB 33 Bygdøy, 0211 Oslo; tel. 22-43-87-78; fax 22-44-77-40; f. 1982; general non-fiction, cookery, children's, humour, leisure; Publr ELSE LILL BJØNNES.

Kolon Forlag: Sehestedsgt. 4, POB 6860 St Olavs pl., 0130 Oslo; tel. 22-03-42-02; fax 22-03-41-05; e-mail torleiv.grue@gyldendal.no; internet www.gyldendal.no/kolon; f. 1995; modern Norwegian poetry and fiction; Publr TORLEIV GRUE.

Kunnskapsforlaget: Kr. Augustsgt. 10, POB 6736 St Olavs pl., 0130 Oslo; tel. 22-03-66-00; fax 22-03-66-05; e-mail resepsjonen@ kunnskapsforlaget.no; internet www.kunnskapsforlaget.no; f. 1975; knowledge games; Man. Dir KRISTIN W. WIELAND; Editorial Dir ØYSTEIN EEK; Editor-in-Chief PETTER HENRIKSEN.

Landbruksforlaget: Schweigaardsgt. 34A POB 9303 Grønland, 0135 Oslo; tel. 23-15-89-20; fax 23-15-89-21; e-mail post@ landbruksforlaget.no; internet www.landbruksforlaget.no; f. 1949; outdoor, handicrafts, culture, horses, dogs, children; Editorial Man. HEIDI FANNIDU ANDERSEN.

Libretto Forlag: Eilert Sundts gt. 32, 0259 Oslo; tel. 22-44-30-11; fax 22-44-30-12; f. 1990; children's, giftbooks and handbooks; Publr TOM THORSTEINSEN.

Lunde Forlag A/S: Sinsenv. 25, 0572 Oslo; tel. 22-00-73-50; fax 22-00-73-73; e-mail akvalbein@nlm.no; internet www.lunde-forlag.no; f. 1905; religious, general, fiction, children's; Publishing Dir ASBJØRN KVALBEIN.

Luther Forlag: Grensen 15, POB 6640 St Olavs pl., 0129 Oslo; tel. 22-33-06-08; fax 22-42-10-00; e-mail postkasse@lutherforlag.no; internet www.lutherforlag.no; f. 1984; religious, fiction, general; Dir ASLE DINGSTAD.

Lydbokforlaget A/S: Søreggen 2, POB 135, 7223 Melhus; tel. 72-85-60-70; fax 72-85-60-90; e-mail herborg.hongset@lybokforlaget.no; internet www.lybokforlaget.no; f. 1987; owned by H. Aschehoug & Co (33%), Gyldendal Norsk Forlag (33%) and Stiftergruppen (34%).

Messel Forlag: St Olavsgt. 21A, 0165 Oslo; tel. 22-20-29-15; e-mail messelfo@online.no.

NKI Forlaget: Hans Burumsvn 30, POB 111, 1319 Bekkestua; tel. 67-58-88-00; fax 67-58-19-02; f. 1972; textbooks for secondary and technical schools and colleges; Publr JAN B. THOMSEN.

Norsk Bokreidingslag L/L: POB 684, 5807 Bergen; tel. 55-30-18-99; fax 55-32-03-56; e-mail post@bodonihus.no; internet www .bokreidingslaget.no; f. 1939; fiction, folklore, linguistics, cultural history; Man. FROYDIS LEHMANN.

Det Norske Samlaget: Gjerdrumsvn 12A, POB 4672 Sofienberg, 0506 Oslo; tel. 22-70-78-00; fax 22-68-75-02; e-mail det.norske@

samlaget.no; internet www.samlaget.no; f. 1868; general literature, fiction, poetry, children's, textbooks; Man. Dir AUDUN HESKESTAD.

Forlaget Oktober A/S: Kr. Augustsgt. 11, POB 6848 St Olavs pl., 0130 Oslo; tel. 23-35-46-20; fax 23-35-46-21; e-mail oktober@ aschehoug.no; internet www.aschehoug.no/oktober; f. 1970; fiction, politics, social and cultural books; Publr GEIR BERDAHL.

Orion Forlag: Søkedalsvn 10C, 0369 Oslo; tel. 23-19-60-90; internet www.boknett.no/orion.

Pantagruel Forlag A/S: POB 2370 Solli, 0201 Oslo; tel. 22-54-82-40; e-mail alle@pantagruel.no.

Pax Forlag A/S: Huitfeldtgt. 15, POB 2336 Solli, 0201 Oslo; tel. 23-13-69-00; fax 22-55-41-83; f. 1964; fiction, non-fiction, feminism, social sciences; Man. Dir BJØRN SMITH-SIMONSEN.

Sambåndet Forlag AS: Vetrlidsalm. 1 5014 Bergen; tel. 55-31-79-63; fax 55-31-09-44; e-mail vestlandskes.bokhandel@vestbok.no; f. 1945; religion, children's, poetry; Dir TARALD UELAND.

Scandinavian University Press/Universitetsforlaget: Oslo; tel. 22-57-53-00; fax 22-57-53-53; e-mail journals@scup.no; internet www.scup.no; f. 1950; publishers to the Universities of Oslo, Bergen, Trondheim and Tromsø and various learned societies; school books, university textbooks, specialized journals; Man. Dir (vacant).

Chr. Schibsteds Forlag: Akersgt. 32, POB 1178 Sentrum, 0107 Oslo; tel. 22-86-30-00; fax 22-42-54-92; f. 1839; reference, biographies, handbooks, hobbies, crafts, children's books, food and drink, sports, foreign language, guides, maps; Man. Dir THOMAS ØYBÖ.

Skolebokforlaget A/S: Stortingsgt. 30, 0161, Oslo; tel. 22-83-77-05; fax 22-83-38-32; f. 1979; educational; Man. Dir HANS B. BUTENSCHØN; Editor SVERRE MØRKHAGEN.

Snøfugl Forlag: POB 95, 7221 Melhus; tel. 72-87-24-11; fax 72-87-10-13; f. 1972; fiction, general; Man. ÅSMUND SNØFUGL.

Solum Forlag A/S: Hoffsvn 18, POB 140 Skøyen, 0212 Oslo; tel. 22-50-04-00; fax 22-50-14-53; e-mail solumfor@online.no; f. 1973; fiction, human sciences, general; Man. Dir KNUT ENDRE SOLUM.

Spartacus Forlag A/S: POB 2587 Solli, 0203 Oslo; tel. 22-44-56-70; fax 22-44-46-50; e-mail post@spartacus.no; internet www.spartacus .no; f. 1989.

Spektrum Forlag ANS: POB 363 Sentrum, 0102 Oslo; tel. 23-13-39-03; e-mail cyrus.brantenberg@spektrum-forlag.no.

Stabenfeldt A/S: Aker Base Dusavik, Bygg 19, 4029 Stavanger; tel. 51-84-54-00; fax 51-84-54-90; f. 1920; general fiction, adventure, reference; Man. Dir TOR TJELDFLÅT.

Tell Forlag A/S: Nilsemarka 5C, 1390 Vollen; tel. 66-78-09-18; fax 66-90-05-72; e-mail tell@tell.no; internet www.tell.no; f. 1987; textbooks and educational books; Man. TELL-CHR. WAGLE.

Tiden Norsk Forlag A/S: Møllergt. 39, POB 8813 Youngstorgt., 0028 Oslo; tel. 23-32-76-60; fax 23-32-76-97; e-mail tiden@tiden.no; internet www.tiden.no; f. 1933; general, political, fiction; Man. Dir LIV LYSAKER.

Universitetsforlaget AS: POB 508 Sentrum, 0105 Oslo; tel. 24-14-75-00; fax 24-14-75-01; e-mail post@universitetsforlaget.no; internet www.universitetsforlaget.no; f. 1999; professional, scientific, general non-fiction, reference; Gen. Man. LAILA STANGE.

Verbum Forlag: Underhaugsvn 15, POB 7062 Majorstuen, 0306 Oslo; tel. 22-93-27-00; fax 22-93-27-27; e-mail verbum.forlag@ bibelselskapet.no; internet www.verbumforlag.no; f. 1820; Christian literature; Man. TURID BARTH PETTERSEN.

Vett & Viten A/S: Vakåsvn. 7, POB 203, 1379 Nesbru; tel. 66-84-90-40; fax 66-84-55-90; e-mail vv@vettviten.no; internet www.vettviten .no; f. 1987; medical, technical and engineering textbooks; Publr JAN LIEN.

Wigestrand Forlag A/S: POB 621, 4001 Stavanger; tel. 51-89-49-69; e-mail forlag@wigestrand.no.

PUBLISHERS' ASSOCIATION

Den norske Forleggerforening (Norwegian Publishers' Asscn): Øvre Vollgt. 15, 0158 Oslo; tel. 22-00-75-80; fax 22-33-38-30; e-mail dnf@forleggerforeningen.no; internet www.forleggerforeningen.no; f. 1895; Chair. BJØRN SMITH-SIMONSEN; Man. Dir KRISTIN CECILIE SLØRDAHL; 52 mem. firms.

Broadcasting and Communications

TELECOMMUNICATIONS

Post- og Teletilsynet (Norwegian Post and Telecommunications Authority): Revierstredet 2, POB 447 Sentrum, 0104 Oslo; tel. 22-82-

46-00; fax 22-82-48-90; e-mail firmapost@npt.no; internet www.npt
.no; f. 1987; issues and supervises regulations, concessions and
licences; expanded to incorporate postal matters in 1997; Dir-Gen.
WILLY JENSEN.

Norkring AS: Oslo; tel. 22-77-92-86; fax 22-72-03-83; e-mail truls
.langeggen@s.norkring.telenor.no; Dir TRULS LANGEGGEN.

Telenor AS: POB 6701, St Olavs pl., 0130 Oslo; tel. 22-77-89-90; fax
22-77-87-20; state-owned; Pres. and CEO TORMOD HERMANSEN.

BROADCASTING

Radio

Norsk Rikskringkasting (NRK) (Norwegian Broadcasting
Corpn): Bj. Bjørnsons pl. 1, 0340 Oslo; tel. 23-04-70-00; fax 23-04-78-
80; e-mail info@nrk.no; internet www.nrk.no; autonomous public
corpn; operates three national services (including a youth programme), 18 regional services (including one in the language of the
Sámi—Lappish) and an international service, Radio Norway International; Chair. of Govs ANNE CARINE TANUM; Dir-Gen. JOHN G.
BERNANDER; CEO (Broadcasting) HANS-TORE BJERKAAS.

P4—Radio Hele Norge ASA: Serviceboks, 2626 Lillehammer; tel.
61-24-84-44; fax 61-24-84-45; e-mail p4@p4.no; internet www.p4.no;
f. 1993; private commercial station.

Television

Norsk Rikskringkasting (NRK) (Norwegian Broadcasting
Corpn): (see Radio, above); Dir of Television HANS-TORE BJERKAAS.

TV-2: POB 2, 5002 Bergen; tel. 55-90-80-70; fax 55-90-80-90; f. 1992;
private commercial station; Man. Dir ARNE JENSEN; Dir of Programmes FINN H. ANDREASSEN.

TV Norge: Oslo; private satellite television service.

Finance

In 1996 there were 15 commercial banks (comprising the major
banks, some large regional banks and a number of smaller regional
and local banks). In 1995 the commercial banks had total assets of
450,855m. kroner. In the same year there were 132 savings banks,
with total assets of 284,187m. kroner. There were also 10 publicly
financed government banks.

Kredittilsynet (Banking, Insurance and Securities Commission):
Østensjøvn 43, POB 100 Bryn, 0611 Oslo; tel. 22-93-98-00; fax 22-63-
02-26; e-mail post@kredittilsynet.no; internet www.kredittilsynet
.no; finance inspectorate; Dir-Gen. BJØRN SKOGSTAD AAMO.

BANKING

(cap. = capital; res = reserves; dep. = deposits; m. = millions;
brs = branches; amounts in kroner)

Central Bank

Norges Bank: Bankplassen 2, POB 1179 Sentrum, 0107 Oslo; tel.
22-31-60-00; fax 22-41-31-05; e-mail central.bank@norges-bank.no;
internet www.norges-bank.no; f. 1816; holds the exclusive right of
note issue; cap. and res 44,818m., dep. 566,730m. (Dec. 2000); Chair.
of Supervisory Bd MARY KVIDAL; Gov. SVEIN GJEDREM; 12 brs.

Principal Commercial Banks

Bank 1 Oslo A/S: POB 778, Henrik Ibsens gt. 12, Sentrum, 0106
Oslo; tel. 21-02-00-00; fax 21-02-00-01; e-mail bank1@sparebank1
.no; internet www.sparebank1.no; f. 1898; name changed as above
2000; cap. 281m., res 729m., dep. 13,536m. (Dec. 2001); CEO GUNNAR
DOLVEN; Chair. GUNN WÆRSTED; 7 brs.

Fokus Bank ASA: Vestre Rosten 77, 7466 Trondheim; tel. 72-88-
20-11; fax 72-88-20-61; e-mail fokus@fokus.no; internet www.fokus
.no; f. 1987; Den Danske Bank of Denmark took over Fokus Bank in
1999; cap. 1,130m., dep. 41,697m. (Dec. 2000); Chair. SØREN MØLLER
NIELSEN; Man. Dir and CEO THOMAS BORGEN; 65 brs.

Gjensidige Bank AS: Strandkanten 18, POB 2, 1324 Lysaker; tel.
22-96-89-00; fax 22-96-89-10; e-mail albert@gjensidige.no; internet
www.gjensidige.no; cap. 4,689m., res 7,707m., dep. 180,997m. (Dec.
2000); Man. Dir BENTHE RATHE.

Nordea Bank Norge ASA: Middelthunsgt. 17, 0368 Oslo; POB
1166 Sentrum, 0107 Oslo; tel. 22-48-50-00; fax 22-48-47-49; internet
www.nordea.com; fmrly Christiana Bank og Kreditkasse ASA, current name adopted 2001; part of Nordea Group (Finland); cap.
1,182m., res 9,069m., dep. 179,262m. (Dec. 2001).

Nordlandsbanken ASA: Molov. 16, 8002 Bodø; tel. 75-55-85-00;
fax 75-55-85-10; e-mail post@nordlandsbanken.no; internet www
.norlandsbanken.no; f. 1893; cap. 373m., res 1,208m., dep. 18,445m.

(Dec. 2001); Chair. HARALD MELLERUD; Man. Dir and CEO NILS MOE;
21 brs.

Den norske Bank ASA: Stranden 21, 0021 Oslo; tel. 22-48-10-50;
fax 22-48-18-70; e-mail dnb@dnb.no; internet www.dnb.no; f. 1990
by merger of Bergen Bank (f. 1855) and Den norske Creditbank
(f. 1857); merged with Postbanken in 1999; 47.3% state-owned; cap.
7,706m., res 18,130m., dep. 302,373m. (Dec. 2001); Chair. JANNIK
LINDBAEK; 125 brs.

Principal Savings Banks

Sparebanken Hedmark: Torggt. 12–14, POB 203, 2302 Hamar;
tel. 62-51-20-00; fax 62-53-29-75; e-mail konsern@
sparebanken-hedmark.no; internet www.sparebanken-hedmark.no;
f. 1845; cap. 2,246m., dep. 16,665m. (Dec. 2001); Chair. SYVER
AALSTAD; Man. Dir HARRY KONTERUD; 12 brs.

Sparebanken Midt-Norge: Sondregt. 4, 7005 Trondheim; tel. 73-
58-51-11; fax 73-58-64-50; e-mail smn@smn.no; internet www.smn
.no; f. 1823; cap. 605m., res 1,542m., dep. 29,175m. (Dec. 2001);
Chair. STEIN ATLE ANDERSEN; Man. Dir FINN HAUGAN; 75 brs.

Sparebanken Møre: Keiser Wilhelmsgt. 29–33, 6002 Ålesund; tel.
70-11-30-00; fax 70-12-99-12; e-mail sparebanken.more@sbm.no;
internet www.sbm.no; f. 1985; cap. 632m., res 1,023m., dep.
14,014m. (Dec. 2001); Man. Dir OLAV-ARNE FISKERSTRAND; 55 brs.

Sparebanken NOR (Union Bank of Norway): Kirkegt. 18, POB
1172 Sentrum, 0107 Oslo; tel. 22-31-90-50; fax 22-31-99-85; e-mail
marit.hebo@nor.no; internet www.nor.no; f. 1985 as Sparebanken
ABC, by merger of Sparebanken Oslo and Union Bank of Norway;
merged with four regional savings banks in 1990; Sparebanken
Telemark incorporated in 1997; cap. 4,689m., res 6,114m., dep.
180,997m. (Dec. 2000); Chair. HANS BØ; Man. Dir KJELL O. KRAN; 151
brs.

Sparebanken Nord-Norge: Storgt. 65, 9298 Tromsø; tel. 77-62-20-
00; fax 77-65-84-08; internet www.snn.no; f. 1989; cap. 660m., res
1,482m., dep. 29,508m. (Dec. 2000); Pres. HARALD OVERVAAG; Man.
Dir HANS OLAV KARDE; 106 brs.

Sparebanken Pluss: POB 200, Rådhusgt. 7–9, 4662 Kristiansand;
tel. 38-17-35-00; fax 38-02-04-70; e-mail firmapost@
sparebankenpluss.no; internet www.sparebankenpluss.no; f. 1824;
merged with four savings banks in 1987; total assets 10,032m. (Dec.
2001); Chair. JENS FREUCHEN; Man. Dir STEIN HANNEVIK.

Sparebanken Rogaland: Bjergsted Terrasse 1, 4001 Stavanger;
tel. 51-50-90-00; fax 51-53-18-64; e-mail sparebank1@sr-bank.no;
internet www.sr-bank.no; f. 1839 (as Egersund Sparebank); merged
with 22 savings banks in 1976; cap. 749m., res. 1,790m. dep.
37,329m. (Dec. 2000); Pres. TERJE VAREBERG; 57 brs.

Sparebanken Sør: POB 602, 4809 Arendal; Vestervn. 1, 4800
Arendal; tel. 37-02-50-00; fax 37-02-41-50; e-mail international@sor
.no; internet www.sor.no; f. 1825; cap. and res 1,264m., dep.
12,892m. (Dec. 2001); Chair. TOM F. EVENSEN; Man. Dir HANS A.
IVERSEN; 45 brs.

Sparebanken Vest: Kaigt. 4, 5016 Bergen; tel. 55-21-70-00; fax 55-
21-74-10; e-mail sparebank1.vest@spv.sparebank1.no; internet
www.spv.no; f. 1823 as Bergens Sparebank; merger 1982/83 of 25
savings banks; cap. 250m., res 1,924m., dep. 29,230m. (Dec. 2001);
Man. Dir KNUT RAVNÅ; 70 brs.

Bankers' Associations

Finansnaeringens Hovedorganisasjon (Norwegian Financial
Services Asscn): Hansteensgt. 2, POB 2473 Solli, 0202 Oslo; tel. 23-
28-42-00; fax 23-28-42-01; e-mail fnh@fnh.no; internet www.fnh.no;
f. 2000 by merger of Den norske Bankforening (Nowegian Bankers'
Asscn) and Norges Forsikringsforbond (Norwegian Insurance
Asscn); Chair. SVEIN AASER; Man. Dir ARNE SKAUGE; 28 brs.

Sparebankforeningen i Norge (Savings Banks Asscn): Universi-
tetsgt. 8, POB 6772, 0130 Oslo; tel. 22-11-00-75; fax 22-36-25-33; f.
1914; Pres. KJELL REMVIK (Sparebanken Møre); Man. Dir EINAR
FORSBAK; 133 mems.

STOCK EXCHANGE

Oslo Børs: Tollbugt. 2, POB 460 Sentrum, 0105 Oslo; tel. 22-34-17-
00; fax 22-41-65-90; e-mail info@ose.no; internet www.ose.no; f.
1819; Pres. SVEN ARILD ANDERSEN.

INSURANCE

Assurance Foreningen Skuld: Roald Amundsens gt. 6, 0114 Oslo;
tel. 22-00-22-00; fax 22-42-42-22; e-mail osl@skuld.com; internet
www.skuld.com; f. 1897; mutual, shipowners' protection and indemnity; Chair. H. BEUTNER; Man. Dir D. JACOBSOHN.

Gjensidige NOR Forsikring: Drammensvn 228, POB 276, 1326
Lysaker; tel. 22-96-80-00; fax 22-96-92-00; e-mail epost@

gjensidigenor.no; internet www.gjensidigenor.no; f. 1847; merged with Forenede Norge Forsikring and Forenede Skadeforsikring in 1993; Pres. HELGE KVAMME; CEO LARS AUSTIN.

Norske Liv AS: Oslo; tel. 22-44-39-50; fax 22-55-79-72; f. 1844; life insurance; Chair. PER DITLEV SIMONSEN; Man. Dir JOSTEIN SØRVOLL.

Uni Storebrand: Håkon VII's gt. 10, POB 1380 Vika, 0114 Oslo; tel. 22-31-10-20; f. 1991 by merger of Storebrand (f. 1947) and Uni Forsikring (f. 1984); group includes life, non-life and international reinsurance operations; taken over by govt administrators in 1992 and new holding co (Uni Storebrand New) formed, following suspension of payments to creditors; Chair. ERIK KEISERUD; CEO PER TERJE VOLD.

Vesta Group PLC: Folke Bernadottesvei 50, 5020 Bergen; tel. 55-17-10-00; fax 55-17-18-99; f. 1884; owned by Skandia (Sweden); includes Skadeforsikringsselskapet Vesta A/S (general insurance), Vesta Liv A/S (life insurance), Vesta Finans A/S (financial services); Chair. JAN EINAR GREVE; Man. Dir JOHAN FR. ODFJELL.

Vital Insurance: Folke Bernadottesvei 40, 5020 Bergen; tel. 55-17-80-90; fax 55-17-86-99; internet www.vital.no; f. 1990 by a merger between NKP Forsikring and Hygea; life and pension insurance; Chair. SVEIN AASEN; Pres. BJØRN ØSTBØ.

INSURANCE ASSOCIATION

Finansnaeringens Hovedorganisasjon (Norwegian Financial Services Asscn): (see Bankers' Associations above).

Trade and Industry

GOVERNMENT AGENCY

Norwegian Trade Council: Drammensvn 40, 0243 Oslo; tel. 22-92-63-00; fax 22-92-64-00; e-mail oslo@ntc.no; internet www.exportnet.ntc.no; f. 1945; promotes Norwegian exports; Dir-Gen. PER ANDREAS VOGT.

CHAMBERS OF COMMERCE

Bergen Chamber of Commerce and Industry: Olav Kyrresgt. 11, 5807 Bergen; tel. 55-55-39-00; fax 55-55-39-01; e-mail firmapost@bergen-chamber.no; f. 1915; Pres. REIDAR LIEN; Man. Dir HELGE S. DYRNES.

Oslo Chamber of Commerce: Drammensvn 30, POB 2874 Solli, 0230 Oslo; tel. 22-55-74-00; fax 22-55-89-53; e-mail chamber@online.no; internet www.chamber.no; Man. Dir TORE B. LAURITZSEN.

INDUSTRIAL AND TRADE ASSOCIATION

Norges Skogeierforbund (Norwegian Forest Owners): Stortingsgt. 30, POB 1438 Vika, 0115 Oslo; tel. 22-01-05-50; fax 22-83-40-47; e-mail nsf@skog.no; internet www.skog.no; f. 1913; aims to promote the economic and technical interests of the forest owners, a general forest policy in the interests of private ownership and co-operation between the affiliated associations; Man. Dir IVAR KORSBAKKEN; 50,000 mems.

EMPLOYERS' ASSOCIATIONS

Næringslivets Hovedorganisasjon (NHO) (Confederation of Norwegian Business and Industry): Middelthunsgt. 27, POB 5250 Majorstua, 0303 Oslo; tel. 23-08-80-00; fax 23-08-80-01; f. 1989; rep. Org. for industry, crafts and service industries; Pres. JENS ULLTVEIT-MOE; Dir-Gen. FINN BERGSEN, Jr; c. 16,500 mems who must also belong to the 23 affiliated national asscns; chief among which are the following.

> **Entreprenørforeningen—Bygg og Anlegg** (General Contractors): POB 5485 Majorstua, 0305 Oslo; tel. 23-08-75-35; fax 23-08-75-30; Admin. Dir ERIK ANSKAU; 215 mems.

> **Fiskerinæringens Landsforening** (Fishing Industry): POB 5471 Majorstua, 0305 Oslo; tel. 23-08-87-30; fax 23-08-87-31; Man. Dir TERJE E. MARTINUSSEN.

> **Flyselskapenes Landsforening** (Airlines): POB 5474 Majorstua, 0305 Oslo; tel. 23-08-85-70; fax 22-56-57-90; e-mail tor.sodeland@nho.no; Dir TOR SODELAND.

> **TBL Møbel- og Innredning** (Asscn of Norwegian Furnishing Industries): POB 7072 Majorstuen, 0306 Oslo; tel. 22-59-00-00; fax 22-59-00-01; e-mail tbl@tbl.no; internet www.tbl.no; Exec. Man. EGIL SUNDET.

> **Næringsmiddelbedriftenes Landsforening** (Food and Drink Industry): POB 5472 Majorstua, 0305 Oslo; tel. 23-08-87-00; fax 23-08-87-20; Admin. Dir GAUTE EGEBERG.

Norges Bilbransjeforbund (Norwegian Motor Car Dealers and Services): Drammensvn 97, POB 2804 Solli, 0204 Oslo; tel. 22-54-21-00; fax 22-54-21-40; e-mail firmapost@nbf.no; internet www.nbf.no; f. 1962; Admin. Dir EIRIK HØIEN.

Norges Elektroentreprenørforbund (Norwegian Electrical Contractors' Asscn): Essendropsgt. 3, POB 5467 Majorstua, 0305 Oslo; tel. 23-08-77-00; fax 23-08-77-01; e-mail iso@nelfo.no; internet www.nelfo.no; Admin. Dir JORTEIN SKREE.

Norsk Bryggeri- og Mineralvannindustris Forening (Norwegian Breweries and Soft Drink Producers): POB 7087 Majorstua, 0306 Oslo; tel. 23-08-86-90; fax 22-60-30-04; e-mail firmapost@nbmf.no; internet www.nbmf.no; Man. Dir PER UNDRUM; 21 mems.

Oljeserviceselskapenes Landsforening (Oil Industry): Lervigsxn 32, POB 547, 40003 Stavanger; tel. 51-84-65-00; fax 51-84-65-01; e-mail firmapost@olf.no; internet www.olf.no; Admin. Dir FINN ROAR AMODT.

Prosessindustriens Landsforening (Federation of Norwegian Process Industries): Essendropsgt. 3, POB 5487 Majorstua, 0305 Oslo; tel. 23-08-78-00; fax 23-08-78-99; e-mail pil@pil.no; internet www.pil.no; Man. Dir PER TERJE VOLD.

Reiselivsbedriftenes Landsforening (Hotels and Restaurants): POB 5465 Majorstua, Essendrops gt. 6, 0305 Oslo; tel. 23-08-86-20; fax 23-08-86-21; e-mail firmapost@rbl.no; f. 1997; Admin. Dir KNUT ALMQUIST.

Servicebedriftenes Landsforening (Service Industry): Essendropsgt. 6, 0368 Oslo; tel. 23-08-86-50; fax 23-08-86-59; e-mail petter.furulund@service.no; internet www.sbl.no; Admin. Dir PETTER FURULUND.

Skogbrukets Landsforening (Forestry): Essendropsgt. 3, 0368 Oslo; POB 7016 Majorstua, 0306 Oslo; tel. 23-08-79-40; fax 23-08-79-41; e-mail firmapost@skogbruk.no; internet www.skogbruk.no; f. 1927; Man. Dir KNUT BERG.

TBL Teko (Textile, Clothing, Shoe, Leather and Sporting Goods Industries): Oscarsgt. 20, POB 7086 Majorstuen, 0306 Oslo; tel. 22-59-00-00; fax 22-59-00-06; f. 1989 by merger of several asscns; Chair. JONAS HILDRE; Man. Dir ØYVIND HAUGERUD; 130 mems.

Teknologibedriftenes Landsforening (Manufacturing Industries): POB 7072 Majorstua, 0306 Oslo; tel. 22-59-00-00; fax 22-59-00-01; e-mail tbl@tbl.no; internet www.tbl.no; f. 1889; Pres. ROLF T. WAAGE; Admin. Dir KARL NYSTERUD; 1,220 mems with 72,000 employees.

Transportbedriftenes Landsforening (Norwegian Transport Companies): POB 5477, Majorstua, 0305 Oslo; tel. 23-08-86-00; fax 23-08-86-01; Admin. Dir CHRISTIAN AUBERT.

Treforedlingsindustriens Bransjeforening (TFB) (Pulp and Paper): Essendropsgt. 3, POB 5487, Majorstua, 0305 Oslo; tel. 23-08-78-00; fax 23-08-78-99; e-mail mb@pil.no; internet www.pulp-and-paper.no; Pres. PER A. SØRLIE; 27 mems.

Visuell Kommunikasjon Norge (Norwegian Federation of Visual Communications Enterprises): Tollbugt. 27, 0157 Oslo; tel. 22-47-88-70; fax 22-47-88-70; e-mail viskom@viskom.net; internet www.viskom.net; Admin. Dir CATO KJØLSTAD; 340 mems.

Handels- og Servicenæringens Hovedorganisasjon (Federation of Commercial and Service Enterprises): Drammensvn 30, POB 2900 Solli, 0230 Oslo; tel. 22-54-17-00; fax 22-56-17-00; e-mail info@hsh-org.no; internet www.hsh-org.no; f. 1990 by merger; 14,000 mem cos; Pres. EGIL THORBERG.

UTILITIES

Electricity

Bergenshalvøens Kommunale Kraftselskap A/S: POB 7050, 5020 Bergen; tel. 55-12-70-00; fax 55-12-70-01; e-mail firmapost@bkk.no; internet www.bkk.no; f. 1920.

Gjermå; Energi: POB D, 2051 Jessheim; tel. 63-94-66-00; fax 63-94-67-20; e-mail je@gjermo.telemax.no.

Haugesund Energi AS: Haugesund; tel. 52-70-80-00; fax 52-70-80-05; e-mail firmapost@haugesund-energi.no; f. 1908; joint stock co; 15,000 customers.

Nedre Eiker Energi: Evjegata 13, POB 153, 3051 Mjøndalen; tel. 32-23-28-70; fax 32-87-72-10.

Nordmøre Energiverk AS: Industrivn 1, POB 2125, 6501 Kristiansund; tel. 71-56-55-00; fax 71-58-15-21; e-mail neas@neas.mr.no.

Nord-Salten Kraftlag AL: POB 70, 8276 Ulvsvåg; tel. 75-77-10-00; fax 75-77-10-01; e-mail nskal@narvikknet.no; f. 1946.

Nord-Trøndelag Elektrisitetsverk: Steinkjer; e-mail nte@nte.nt.no; 70,343 customers.

Oslo Energi AS: Oslo; tel. 22-92-50-00; fax 22-43-50-85; 290,898 customers.

Statkraft SF: POB 494, 1322 Hovik; tel. 67-57-70-00.

Statnett SF: Husebybakken 28B, POB 5192 Maj., 0302 Oslo; tel. 22-52-70-00; fax 22-52-70-01; national power grid co; supervises and co-ordinates the operation of the entire Norwegian power system, also operates own transmission lines and submarine cables, as well as sub-stations and switching stations; state-owned co under the jurisdiction of the Ministry of Petroleum and Energy; Pres. and CEO ODD HÅKON HOELSÆTER.

Statnett Entreprenør AS: fax 22-52-71-80; subsidiary specializing in overseas sales.

Other major production and distribution companies include Akershus Energiverk, Aktieselskapet Tysselfaldene, Aust-Agder kraftverk, Bærum Energi AS, Bergen Lysverker, Elkem AS, Fredrikstad Energiverk AS, Hafslund Energi, Hamar-regionen Energiverk, Hedmark Energi AS, Helgelund Kraftlag A/L, Hydro Energi, Kraftlaget Opplandskraft, Kristiansand Energiverk, Lyse Kraft, Østfold Energiverk, I/S Øvre Otta, Sira-Kvina Kraftselskap, Skiensfjorden komm. kraftselskap, Stavanger Energi, Svelvik Everk, Trønder Energi, Trondheim Energiverk, Troms Kraftforsyning and Vest-Agder Energiverk.

TRADE UNIONS

Landsorganisasjonen i Norge (LO) (Norwegian Confederation of Trade Unions): Folkets Hus, Youngsgt. 11, 0181 Oslo; tel. 23-06-10-50; fax 23-06-17-43; e-mail lo@lo.no; f. 1899; Pres. GERD-LIV VALLA; Int. Sec. JON IVAR NÅLSUND; 800,000 mems in 25 affiliated unions (2001).

All member unions can be contacted by fax at LO, above.

The member unions are:

Arbeiderpartiets Presseforbund (Labour Press Union): Tromsø; tel. 77-68-11-70; f. 1909; Pres. SVENN A. NIELSEN; 955 mems.

EL & IT Forbundet (Electricians and Information Technology Workers): Youngsgt. 11, 0181 Oslo; tel. 23-06-34-00; fax 23-06-34-01; e-mail firmapost@elogit.no; internet www.elogit.no; f. 1999 by merger of Tele- og Dataforbundet (TD) and Norsk Elektriker- og Kraftstasjonsforbundet (NEKF); Pres. HANS OLAV FELIX; 40,000 mems.

Fellesforbundet (United Federation of Trade Unions): Lilletorget 1, 0184 Oslo; tel. 23-06-31-00; fax 23-06-31-01; e-mail fellesforbundet@fellesforbundet.no; internet www.fellesforbundet.no; f. 1988; Pres. KJELL BJØRNDALEN; 150,000 mems.

Fellesorganisasjonen for barnevernpedagoger, sosionomer og vernepleiere (Social Educators and Social Workers): POB 4693 Sofienberg, 0506 Oslo; tel. 23-06-11-70; fax 23-06-11-14; e-mail kontor@fobsv.no; internet www.fobsv.no; f. 1992; Pres. RANDI REESE; Gen. Sec. HANS CHRISTIAN LILLEHAGEN; 18,500 mems.

Forbundet for Ledelse og Teknikk (Engineers and Managers): POB 8906 Youngsgt. 11, 0028 Oslo; tel. 22-03-10-29; fax 22-03-10-17; f. 1951; Pres. MAGNUS MIDTBØ; 16,376 mems.

Handel og Kontor i Norge (Commercial and Office Employees): Youngsgt. 11, 0181 Oslo; tel. 22-03-11-80; fax 22-03-12-06; f. 1908; Pres. STURE ARNTZEN; 56,209 mems.

Hotel- og Restaurant Arbeiderforbundet (Hotel and Restaurant Workers): Storgt. 32, 0184 Oslo; tel. 23-06-21-00; fax 23-06-21-01; e-mail hraf@hraf.no; internet www.hraf.no; f. 1931; Pres. JENS HOEL; 14,827 mems.

Musikernes Fellesorganisasjon (Norwegian Musicians' Union): POB 8806 Youngstorget, 0028 Oslo; tel. 23-06-21-50; fax 23-06-21-51; e-mail mfo@musikerorg.no; internet www.musikerorg.no; f. 2001; Pres. ARNFINN BJERKESTRAND; 6,100 mems.

Norges Offiserforbund (Norwegian Military Officers): Møllergt. 10, 0179 Oslo; tel. 22-03-15-72; fax 22-03-15-77; f. 1978; Pres. PETER ANDRE MOE; 4,527 mems.

Norsk Arbeidsmandsforbund (Norwegian General Workers): POB 8704 Youngstorget, 0028 Oslo; tel. 23-06-10-50; fax 23-06-10-92; e-mail norsk@arb-mand.no; internet www.arbeidsmandsforbundet.no; f. 1895; Pres. ARNFINN NILSEN; 32,000 mems.

Norsk Fengselstjenestemannsforbund (Norwegian Prison Officers): Møllergt. 10, 0179 Oslo; tel. 22-03-15-88; fax 22-42-46-48; f. 1918; Pres. ROAR ØVREBØ; 2,438 mems.

Norsk Grafisk Forbund (Norwegian Graphic Workers): POB 8913 Youngstorget, 0028 Oslo; tel. 23-06-13-00; fax 23-06-13-25; e-mail ngf@ngf.no; internet www.ngf.no; f. 1882; Pres. ROGER ANDERSEN; 12,971 mems.

Norsk Jernbaneforbund (Norwegian Railway Workers): Møllergt. 10, 0179 Oslo; tel. 23-06-10-50; fax 23-06-13-85; f. 1892; Pres. OVE DALSHEIM; 19,920 mems.

Norsk Kjemisk Industriarbeiderforbund (Norwegian Chemical Workers): Youngsgt. 11, 0181 Oslo; tel. 22-03-13-40; fax 22-03-13-60; f. 1923; Pres. OLAV STØYLEN; 31,999 mems.

Norsk Kommuneforbund (Norwegian Municipal Employees): Kr. Augustsgt. 23, 0164 Oslo; tel. 22-36-47-10; fax 22-36-40-25; f. 1920; Pres. JAN DAVIDSEN; 226,722 mems.

Norsk Lokomotivmannsforbund (Norwegian Locomotive Workers): Svingen 2, 0196 Oslo; tel. 23-30-21-10; fax 23-30-21-11; e-mail nlf@lokmann.no; internet www.lokmann.no; f. 1893; Pres. ØYSTEIN ASLAKSEN; 2,222 mems.

Norsk Næring- og Nytelsesmiddelforbund (Norwegian Food and Allied Workers): Arbeidersamfunnets pl. 1, 0181 Oslo; tel. 22-20-66-75; fax 22-36-47-84; e-mail firmapost.nnn@loit.no; internet www.nnn.no; f. 1923; Pres. TORBJØRN DAHL; 34,813 mems.

Norsk Olje- og Petrokjemisk Fagforbund (Norwegian Oil and Petrochemical Workers): Kongensgt. 52, 4012 Stavanger; tel. 51-56-79-80; fax 51-56-79-88; f. 1977; Pres. LARS A. MYHRE; 10,654 mems.

Norsk Post- og Kommunikasjonsforbund (Norwegian Union of Postal and Communications Workers): Møllergt. 10, 0179 Oslo; tel. 23-06-22-90; fax 22-42-74-86; e-mail postkom@loit.no; f. 2000; Pres. ODD-CHRISTIAN ØVERLAND; 28,911 mems.

Norsk Sjømannsforbund (Norwegian Seamen): Grev. Wedels pl. 7, 0151 Oslo; tel. 22-82-58-00; fax 22-33-66-18; f. 1910; Pres. ERIK BRATVOLD; 12,500 mems.

Norsk Tjenestemannslag (Norwegian Civil Service Union): Møllergt. 10, 0179 Oslo; tel. 23-06-15-99; fax 23-06-15-55; internet www.ntl.no; f. 1947; Pres. TURID LILLEHEIE; 47,400 mems.

Norsk Tolkeforbund (Norwegian Interpreters): Oslo; tel. 23-06-23-80; fax 23-06-23-81; f. 1986; Pres. ONUR SAFAK JOHANSEN; 149 mems.

Norsk Transportarbeiderforbund (Norwegian Transport Workers): Youngsgt. 11, 0181 Oslo; tel. 22-20-40-55; fax 22-11-35-72; f. 1896; Pres. WALTER KOLSTAD; 16,018 mems.

Norsk Treindustriarbeiderforbund (Norwegian Wood Workers): Henrik Ibsensgt. 7, 0179 Oslo; tel. 23-06-13-90; fax 23-06-13-95; f. 1904; Pres. ANTON SOLHEIM; 5,241 mems.

Skolenes Landsforbund (School Employees): Møllergt. 20, 0179 Oslo; tel. 22-03-13-62; fax 22-03-13-83; f. 1982; Pres. GRO STANDNES; 3,466 mems.

Statstjenestemannskartellet (Government Employees): Møllergt. 10, 0179 Oslo; tel. 22-03-15-78; fax 22-42-00-75; f. 1939; Pres. TERJE MOE GUSTAVSEN; 105,867 mems.

Yrkesorganisasjonenes Sentralforbund (YS): Brugt. 19, 0134 Grønland; tel. 21-01-36-00; fax 21-01-37-20; f. 1977; Pres. RANDI BJØRGEN; 242,000 mems in 19 affiliated unions.

Transport

RAILWAYS

At 1 January 1996 there were 4,023 km of state railways (standard gauge), of which 2,422 km were electrified.

Norges Statsbaner AS (NSB) (Norwegian State Railways): Prinsensgt. 7–9, 0048 Oslo; tel. 23-15-00-00; fax 23-15-33-00; internet www.nsb.no; f. 1854 as private line; govt-owned; CEO E. ENGER.

ROADS

In 2000 there were 91,454 km of public roads in Norway, of which 143 km were motorways and 26,639 km were national main roads.

Vegdirektoratet: Grensevn 92, POB 8142 Dep., 0033 Oslo; tel. 22-07-35-00; fax 22-07-37-68; e-mail firmapost@vegvesen.no; internet www.vegvesen.no; f. 1864; Dir OLAV SØFTELAND.

SHIPPING

At 31 December 2001 the Norwegian merchant fleet numbered 2,363 vessels, with a combined displacement of 22.6m. grt. The total includes vessels on the Norwegian International Ship Register (established in 1987), with 762 vessels (19.0m. grt). The Norwegian-controlled fleet represents some 10% of the world's total fleet, making Norway one of the four largest shipping nations in the world. It has been estimated that Norwegian companies control some 23% of the world's cruise vessels, 19% of the world's gas carriers, 19% of the world's chemical tankers and 10.5% of all crude petroleum tankers.

Port Authorities

Ålesund: Ålesund Havnevesen, Skansekaia, 6002 Ålesund; tel. 70-10-12-70; fax 70-10-12-71; e-mail tortk@alesund.kommune.no; internet www.alesund.kommune.no.

Bergen: Bergen & Omland Havnevesen, Slottsgaten 1, 5003 Bergen; tel. 55-56-89-50; fax 55-56-89-86; e-mail bergen.havn@bergen-kommune.telemax.no; internet www.bergenhavn.no; Harbour Master GUNVALD ISAKSEN.

Bodø: Bodø Havnevesen, POB 138, 8001 Bodø; tel. 75-58-15-80; fax 75-58-39-90; e-mail firmapost@bodo-havnevesen.no; Harbour Master TERJE DOKSRØD.

Borg Harbour: Borg Havnevesen, Oravn 27, POB 1205 Gamle, 1631 Fredrikstad; tel. 69-35-89-00; fax 69-35-89-20; e-mail borghavnevesen@borghavn.of.no; Port Capt. SVEN-JAN JOHANSEN.

Flekkefjord: Flekkefjord Havnevesen, POB 224, 4402 Flekkefjord; tel. 38-32-80-00; fax 38-32-80-09; e-mail formannskapskontoret@flekkefjord.kommune.no; internet flekkefjord.kommune.no; Harbour Master HELGE NILSEN.

Florø: Florø Havnevesen, POB 17, 6901 Florø; tel. 57-74-14-28; fax 57-74-09-16.

Grenland: Grenland Havnevesen, POB 20, 3991 Brevik; tel. 35-93-10-00; fax 35-93-10-11; e-mail grenland-havnevesen@grenland-havn.no; internet port.of.grenland.com; Port Capt. TORJUS JOHNSEN.

Halden: Halden Havnevesen, Langbrygga 3, 1750 Halden; tel. 69-18-32-00; fax 69-18-06-80; Harbour Master ØYVIND JOHANNESSEN.

Hammerfest: Hammerfest Havnevesen, POB 123, 9615 Hammerfest; tel. 78-40-74-00; fax 78-40-74-01; e-mail post@hammerfest.havn.no; f. 1828; Harbour Master ROLL STIANSEN.

Haugesund: Karmsund Interkommunale Havnevesen, Garpaskjaerskaien, 5500 Haugesund; tel. 52-70-37-50; fax 52-70-37-69.

Horten: Borre Havnevesen, POB 167, 3192 Horten; tel. 33-03-17-17; fax 33-04-47-27; Harbour Master KJELL FJELLIN.

Kirkenes: Municipality of Sør-Varanger, Rådhusplassen, POB 406, 9915 Kirkenes; tel. 78-97-74-99; fax 78-97-75-87; e-mail post@kirkenes-havn.no.

Kopervik: Karmsund Havnevesen, POB 70, 4291 Kopervik; tel. 52-84-54-70; fax 52-84-54-71; e-mail postmattak@karmsund-havn.no; internet www.karmsund-havn.no; Harbour Master O. E. MAELAND.

Kragerø: Board of Harbour Commissioners, POB 158, 3770 Kragerø; tel. 35-98-17-50; fax 35-99-13-34; e-mail post@kragero-havnevesen.no; Harbour Master Capt. BORGAR F. THORSEN.

Kristiansand S.: Kristiansand Euro-Port Norway, Gravane 4, 4661 Kristiansand S. tel. 38-00-60-00; fax 38-02-70-99; e-mail post@kristiansand-europort.no; internet www.kristiansand-europort.no; Port Dir STEIN E. HAARTVEIT.

Kristiansünd N.: Kristiansünd Havnevesen, Kaibakken 1, 6509 Kristiansünd N. tel. 71-58-61-80; fax 71-58-61-81; e-mail jan-olav.bjerkestrand@kristiansund.kommune.no; Harbour Master JAN OLAV BJERKESTRAND.

Larvik: Larvik Havnevesen, Havnegaten 5, 3251 Larvik; tel. 33-16-57-50; fax 33-16-57-59; e-mail lvh@larvikhavn.vf.no; internet www.larvikhavn.vf.no; Port Dir JAN FREDRIK JONAS.

Malm: Malm; tel. 74-15-71-00; fax 74-15-78-76; Agent OLAV VAARDAL.

Mandal: Mandal Havnevesen, POB 57, 4501 Mandal; tel. 38-27-34-77; fax 38-26-34-76; Harbour Master ARNE O. JOHANNESSEN.

Mongstad: Statoil, Mongstad Division, 5154 Mongstad; tel. 56-34-40-00; fax 56-34-47-29; e-mail khegg@statoil.com; Port Capt. KJELL HEGGERTVEIT.

Mosjøen: Mosjøen Havnevesen, 8650 Mosjøen; tel. 75-17-52-65; fax 75-17-03-65; e-mail mosjohavn@enitel.no; Port Man. GUNNAR JOHANSEN.

Moss: Moss Havnevesen, Moss Maritime Centre, Moss; tel. 69-25-11-06; Harbour Master FINN SYVERTSEN.

Narvik: Narvik Havn KF, POB 627, 8508 Narvik; tel. 76-95-03-70; fax 76-95-03-84; e-mail havnevesenet@narvik.kommune.no; internet www.portofnarvik.no; Port Man. RUNE ARNOY.

Odda: Odda Havnevesen, 5750 Odda; tel. 53-64-84-00; fax 53-64-12-92; Harbour Master OLAV BJØERKE.

Orkanger: Orkanger Havnevesen, 7300 Orkanger; tel. 72-48-00-09; fax 72-48-10-03; e-mail tom.hamborg@orkdal.kommune.no; Port Man. TOM HAMBORG.

Oslo: Oslo Havnevesen, POB 230 Sentrum, 0103 Oslo 1; tel. 22-91-00-00; fax 22-91-00-01; e-mail firmapost@ohv.oslo.no; internet www.ohv.oslo.no; Port Capt. HARRY GRYTBAKK.

Risør: Risør Havnekontor, 4950 Risør; tel. 37-14-96-00; fax 37-14-96-01; Agent KJELL SKARHEIM.

Sandefjord: Sandefjord Havnevesen, Tollbugt. 5, 3200 Sandefjord; tel. 33-45-60-38; fax 33-46-26-13; Harbour Master LEIF ALLUM.

Sauda: Sauda Havnekontor, 4200 Sauda; tel. 52-78-25-85; fax 52-78-15-88; Harbour Master OEYSTEIN TVEIT.

Stavanger: Stavanger Havnevesen, Nedre Strandgt. 51, 4005 Stavanger; tel. 51-50-78-00; fax 51-50-78-22; e-mail info@stavanger-havn.no; internet www.stavanger-havn.no; Port Dir BJØRN HELGOY.

Tønsberg: Tønsberg Havnekontor, Nedre Langgate 36, 3110 Tønsberg; tel. 33-34-88-50; fax 33-31-19-17; Harbour Master PER SVENNAR.

Tromsø: Tromsø Havnevesen, POB 392, 9001 Tromsø; tel. 77-68-11-19; fax 77-65-85-29; Port Capt. PER JENSEN.

Trondheim: Trondheim Havn, Pirsenteret, 7462 Trondheim; tel. 73-99-17-00; fax 73-99-17-17; Port Capt. SIGURD KLEIVEN.

Vardø: Vardø Havnevesen, POB 50, 9951 Vardø; tel. 78-98-72-76; fax 78-98-78-28; Harbour Master INGOLF ERIKSEN.

Shipping Organizations

Nordisk Skibsrederforening (Northern Shipowners' Defence Club): Kristinelundvn 22, POB 3033 Elisenberg, 0207 Oslo; tel. 22-13-56-00; fax 22-43-00-35; e-mail post@nordisk.no; internet www.nordisk.org; f. 1889; Pres. MORTEN WERRING; Man. Dir GEORG SCHEEL.

Norges Rederiforbund (Norwegian Shipowners' Asscn): POB 1452 Vika, 0116 Oslo; tel. 22-40-15-00; fax 22-40-15-15; e-mail post@rederi.no; internet www.rederi.no; f. 1909; 10 regional asscns; Dir-Gen. MARIANNE LIE.

Norsk Skipsmeglerforbund (Norwegian Shipbrokers' Asscn): Fr. Nansens pl. 9, 0160 Oslo; tel. 22-20-14-85; fax 22-42-74-13; e-mail mail@shipbroker.no; internet www.shipbroker.no; f. 1919; Pres. AXEL STOVE LORENTLEN; Gen. Man. GRETE C. NOER; 150 mems.

Det Norske Veritas (DNV): Veritasvn 1, POB 300, 1322 Høvik; tel. 67-57-99-00; f. 1864; classification and certification of ships, other floating structures and fixed offshore structures, petrochemical installations, marine research and development; stations in over 100 countries throughout the world; acts on behalf of 130 national maritime authorities; CEO HELGE MIDTTUN.

Rederienes Landsforening (Federation of Norwegian Coastal Shipping): Oslo; tel. 22-42-41-20; fax 22-42-41-44; Admin. Dir HARALD THOMASSEN.

Principal Companies

Actinor Shipping ASA: Rådhusgt. 27, 0158 Oslo; tel. 22-42-78-30; fax 22-42-72-04; Pres. KRISTIAN EIDESVIK.

Bergesen d.y. ASA: Drammensvn 106, POB 2800 Solli, 0204 Oslo; tel. 22-12-05-05; fax 22-12-05-00; e-mail bergesen@bergesen.no; internet www.bergesen.no; f. 1935; merged with Havtor Management A/S in 1995; Chair. MORTEN SIG. BERGESEN; Man. Dir SVEIN ERIK AMUNDSEN.

Bergshav Management AS: POB 8, 4891 Grimstad; tel. 37-25-63-00; fax 37-25-63-01; e-mail mgmt@bergshav.com; internet www.bergshav.com; Chair. ATLE BERGSHAVEN.

Bona Shipping AS: Rådhusgt. 27, POB 470 Sentrum, 0105 Oslo; tel. 22-31-00-00; fax 22-31-00-01; internet www.bona.no; Pres. RAGNAR BELCK-OLSEN.

Grieg Shipping A/S: POB 781, 5002 Bergen; tel. 55-57-69-50; fax 55-57-69-10; Man. Dir JACOB IRGENS.

Leif Høegh & Co ASA: Wergelandsvn 7, POB 2596 Solli, 0203 Oslo; tel. 22-86-97-00; fax 22-20-14-08; e-mail ihc@hoegh.no; internet www.hoegh.no; f. 1927; vessels for the transport of liquefied gas, ores and other bulk materials, car and ro-ro ships and reefers; world-wide services; Chair. WESTYE HØEGH; Pres. THOR J. GUTTORMSEN.

Jahre-Wallem AS: Strandpromenaden 9, POB 271, 3236 Sandefjord; tel. 33-48-44-44; fax 33-48-44-43; e-mail jawa@jawa.no; Dir HENRIK LIAN.

Jebsens Management A/S: POB 4145 Dreggen, 5015 Bergen; tel. 55-31-03-20; fax 55-31-72-70; f. 1929; services in Scandinavia, and to Europe, Far East, Australia, the Americas; Owner ATLE JEBSEN.

Torvald Klaveness & Co AS: Harbitzalleen 2A, POB 183 Skøyen, 0212 Oslo; tel. 22-52-60-00; fax 22-50-67-31; Chair. T. E. KLAVENESS; Man. Dir NILS HOY-PETERSEN.

Knutsen OAS Shipping A/S: Smedasundet 40, POB 2017, 5501 Haugesund; tel. 52-70-40-00; fax 52-70-40-40; JENS ULLTVEIT MOE.

A/S J. Ludwig Mowinckels Rederi: Bradbenken 1, POB 4070 Dreggen, 5835 Bergen; tel. 55-21-63-00; fax 55-21-63-05; e-mail mailbox@jlmr.no; f. 1898; tankers and cargo services; Man. Dir BØRGE ROSENBERG.

Norbrooker Shipping & Trading A/S: POB 34, 4401 Flekkefjord; Strandgt. 36, 4400 Flekkefjord; tel. 38-32-61-00; fax 38-38-17-01; e-mail norbroke@online.no.

Odfjell ASA: Conrad Mohrsveg 29, 5073 Bergen; , POB 6101 Postterminalen, 5892 Bergen; tel. 55-27-00-00; fax 55-28-47-41; e-mail mail@odfjell.com; internet www.odfjell.com; f. 1916; transportation and storage of liquid chemicals; Chair. B. D. ODFJELL, Jr.

Rasmussen Maritime Services A/S: POB 37, 4661 Kristiansand; tel. 38-12-22-00; fax 38-07-03-58; e-mail rms@rasmussen.no; Man. Dir OIVIND STAERK.

Red Band A/S: Prinsens gt. 2B, POB 374 Sentrum, 0101 Oslo; tel. 22-34-11-00; fax 22-42-13-14; e-mail redband@redband.no; Chair. NICOLAS BRUM-LIE.

Det Stavangerske Dampskibsselskab: POB 40, 4001 Stavanger; tel. 51-84-56-11; fax 51-84-56-03; Chair. HENRIK AGER-HANSSEN.

Uglands Rederi A/S: POB 128, 4891 Grimstad; tel. 37-29-26-00; fax 37-04-47-22; e-mail jjuc@jjuc.no; internet www.jjuc.no; f. 1930; part of J. J. Ugland Cos (f. 1996; group of cos with shipping interests; tankers, bulk carriers, crane vessel, barges).

Anders Wilhelmsen & Co AS: Beddingen 8, Aker Brygge, POB 1583 Vika, 0118 Oslo; tel. 22-01-42-00; fax 22-01-43-72; e-mail thagen@awilco.no; Chair. ARNE WILHELMSEN; Man. Dir ENDRE ORDING SUND.

Wilh. Wilhelmsen ASA: Strandvn 20, POB 33, 1324 Lysaker; tel. 67-58-40-00; fax 67-58-40-80; internet www.wilh-wilhelmen.com; f. 1861; regular fast freight-reefer-mail services world-wide; Chair. LEIF T. LØDDESØL; Man. Dir WILHELM WILHELMSEN.

CIVIL AVIATION

In 1999 there were 53 scheduled airports in Norway, the principal international airport being Gardermøn Airport, 47 km north of Oslo. The airport at Gardermøn opened in October 1998, replacing the previous principal international airport, Fornebu Airport, which ceased operations in the same month.

Principal Airlines

SAS Norge ASA (Norwegian Airlines Ltd): 0800 Oslo; tel. 64-81-60-50; fax 67-58-08-20; f. 1946; partner in Scandinavian Airlines System (SAS) and SAS Commuter, with Denmark and Sweden (q.v.); Chair. HARALD NORVIK; Gen. Man. JOERGEN LINDEGAARD.

Braathens SAFE (Braathens South-American & Far East Air-transport) ASA: Oksenøyvn 3, POB 55 Lufthavn-Fornebu, 1330 Oslo Airport; tel. 67-59-70-00; fax 67-59-13-09; internet www .braathens.no; f. 1946; scheduled airline and charter company; domestic routes: all main cities in Norway and Longyearbyen, Svalbard; international routes within Europe; Pres. ERIK G. BRAATHEN; Chair. LARS A. CHRISTENSEN.

Norwegian Air Shuttle: Oksenøyvn 10, POB 115 Oslo Lufthavn, 1331 Oslo; tel. 67-58-37-77; fax 67-58-32-77; f. 1966; present name since 1993; charter and contract flights; Man. Dir STIG WILLASSEN.

Scandinavian Airlines System (SAS): Head Office: Snarøyvn 57, 0080 Oslo; tel. 64-81-60-50; internet www.sas.no; f. 1946; the national carrier of Denmark, Norway and Sweden; consortium owned two-sevenths by SAS Danmark A/S, two-sevenths by SAS Norge ASA and three-sevenths by SAS Sverige AB; parent org. is a limited co-owned 50% by Government and 50% by private shareholders; SAS group includes the consortium and the subsidiaries in which the consortium has a majority or otherwise controlling interest; the Board consists of two members from each of the parent cos and the chairmanship rotates among the three national chairmen on an annual basis; strategic alliance with Lufthansa (Germany) formed in 1995; Chair. BO BERGGREN; Pres. and CEO JAN STENBERG.

Widerøe's Flyveselskap ASA: Eyvind Lyches vei 10, POB 312, 1301 Sandvika; tel. 67-11-60-00; fax 67-11-61-95; internet www .wideroe.no; f. 1934; scheduled domestic service; Pres. PER ARNE WATLE.

Widerøe Norsk Air: POB 2047, 3202 Sandefjord; tel. 33-46-98-80; fax 33-47-03-25; f. 1961; acquired by Widerøe in 1989; regional services in Scandinavia; Technical Dir JAN RUNE NORDGARD.

Tourism

Norway is a popular resort for tourists who prefer holidays in rugged, peaceful surroundings. It is also a centre for winter sports. In 1999 receipts from tourism amounted to US $2,229m., compared with $2,212m. in the previous year. In 2000 visitor arrivals totalled 4.4m.

Norwegian Tourist Board: Drammensvn 40, POB 2893, 0230 Oslo; tel. 22-92-52-00; fax 22-56-05-05; e-mail norway@nortra.no; internet www.nortra.no.

NORWEGIAN EXTERNAL TERRITORIES

SVALBARD

Introductory Survey

Location and Climate

The Svalbard archipelago is the northernmost part of the Kingdom of Norway. It lies in the Arctic Sea, 657 km north of mainland Norway, between latitudes 74°N and 81°N and longitudes 10°E and 35°E, comprising a total area of 61,229 sq km (23,641 sq miles). The group consists of nine principal islands, Spitsbergen (formerly Vestspitsbergen), the main island, Kvitøya, Edgeøya, Barentsøya, Nordaustlandet, Prins Karls Forland, Kong Karls Land, Hopen and Bjørnøya (Bear Island), some 204 km to the south of the main island, together with numerous small islands. Mild Atlantic winds lessen the severity of the Arctic climate, but almost 60% of the land area is covered with glaciers. Average temperatures range from −22°C (−8°F) to 7°C (45°F), and precipitation in the lowlands averages some 200 mm per year.

History and Government

The existence of Svalbard has probably been known since Viking exploration in the 12th century. There were conflicting claims to sovereignty by Britain, the Netherlands and Denmark-Norway in the 17th century, when the area was an important centre for whale hunting, but interest subsequently lapsed until the early years of the 20th century, when coal deposits were discovered. On 9 February 1920 14 nations signed a treaty recognizing Norwegian sovereignty over Svalbard. International rights of access and economic exploitation were agreed, but the use of the islands for bellicose purposes and the construction of fortifications were expressly forbidden.

Svalbard has been part of the Kingdom of Norway since it was formally incorporated in 1925. The territory is administered by a Sysselmann (Governor), resident at Longyearbyen, on Spitsbergen, which is the administrative centre of the archipelago. The Sysselmann is responsible to the Polar Department of the Ministry of Justice and the Police. The Norwegian Polar Institute acts in an advisory capacity to the administration. Svalbard lies within the same judicial jurisdiction as the city of Tromsø.

In accordance with the Svalbard Treaty of 1920, the Norwegian Government prescribed a mining code in 1925, regulating all mineral prospecting and exploitation in the islands and their territorial waters extending to 4 nautical miles (7.4 km). The Mining Code is administered by a Commissioner of Mines.

In 1941 the population was evacuated by Allied forces for the duration of the war, and three years later the USSR, to which Svalbard was of considerable strategic interest, unsuccessfully sought Norway's agreement to a revision of the 1920 treaty whereby part of the archipelago would become a Soviet-Norwegian condominium. Russia currently maintains a helicopter station and a mobile radar station adjoining its coal-mining settlement at Barentsburg on Spitsbergen. Russia (and, before it, the USSR) has refused to recognize Norway's unilateral declaration of a fisheries protection zone around Svalbard from 1977.

In June 1994 vessels of the Norwegian coastguard severed the nets of Icelandic fishing boats that were alleged to be fishing within the fisheries protection zone. The Icelandic Government subsequently withdrew its boats from the zone; in August, however, Norway claimed that an Icelandic boat had opened fire on a Norwegian coastguard vessel.

Particularly since a Royal Decree of 1971, the Norwegian administration has endeavoured to protect the flora, fauna and environment of Svalbard. The protected areas total some 35,000 sq km, or 57% of the land area.

Apart from a small permanent research station established by Poland, only Norway and Russia maintain permanent settlements on Svalbard. In order to continue Norwegian occupation of Svalbard, thus ensuring its future as a Norwegian territory and protecting it from potential, rival claims for sovereignty, notably from Russia, in 2000 the Svalbard administration proposed the opening of a new coal-mine on Spitsbergen to exploit newly discovered reserves. Svalbard has also been promoted as a centre for scientific research; at the end of 2000 there were more than 20 scientific stations from foreign countries on the islands.

In November 2001 Norwegians resident on Spitsbergen conducted, for the first time, an election for a local council. The new Longyearbyen Council (Longyearbyen Lokalstyre) replaced the incumbent Svalbard Council, which had been partly appointed by the state-owned mining company, Store Norske Spitsbergen Kulkompani. The new 14-seat Council was to exercise only limited power in issues relating to health, education and the Church, which would all continue to be controlled by the State. The rate of participation in the local election was only 51.5% of the electorate; a multi-party grouping received 47.8% of the total votes cast, obtaining eight seats on the Council, while the DnA won 37.9% and secured six seats.

Social and Economic Affairs

The total population in January 2001 was 2,6167, of whom 1,704 were resident in Norwegian settlements, 903 in Russian settlements and 9 in Polish settlements. There are limited recreational, transport, financial and educational facilities on Svalbard. There is a hospital in Longyearbyen.

During 1994 a total of 212 expeditions visited Svalbard, of which the majority (169) were tourist expeditions. In 2001 27,762 guests booked in at hotels in Svalbard.

Coal is the islands' main product. In 2001 1,939,466 metric tons were shipped from mines on Svalbard (1,565,502 metric tons from Norwegian mines). The Norwegian state-owned coal company, Store Norske Spitsbergen Kulkompani (SNSK), employed 266 people at 1 January 1996. The company incurred financial losses estimated at 78m. kroner in 1993, and the principal motive for continuing to exploit the coal deposits appeared to be political rather than economic. Until 1989 SNSK operated many local services and provided most of the infrastructure, but in that year these functions were assumed by the state company Svalbard Samfunnsdrift, which employed 125 people at the beginning of 1996. By 1998 the number of people employed in the mining and quarrying sector had declined to 189. At the end of 2000 only one Norwegian coal-mining camp was operational (compared with seven at the islands' peak) and this was largely to supply the one coal-burning power station, which provides electricity for the capital, Longyearbyen. In December 2001 it was announced that Longyear Energiverk (the company which operates the power station) was considering replacing the station with three wind-powered stations. Russia still had two camps at the end of 2000, although one at Pyramiden was only being mined for scrap, while the second, at Barentsburg, was still shipping coal to Russia. A new Norwegian mine at Svea, about 60 km (38 miles) from Longyearbyen, was opened in 2001 to exploit significant newly discovered reserves of coal. The coal was of high calorific value (1,200 kilocalories per kilo more than usual) and therefore burnt more cleanly than normal coal. Svea is extremely well-placed for exporting coal to Europe, being located only 10 km from the port; the mine is linked to the port by road, and in late 2002 SNSK was in the process of constructing a conveyor belt to transport the coal directly to the ships. In October 2002 SNSK announced its intention to increase production at Svea, and that it was drilling around Svea in the hope of opening another mine there within three years. SNSK also stated that it had discovered 'overwhelmingly rich' deposits of Arctic gold near Ny-Ålesund on Spitsbergen's west coast, which it was considering exploiting.

Deep drillings for petroleum have been carried out by Norwegian and other companies, but no commercial results have been reported. Svalbard's other mineral resources include reserves of phosphate, asbestos, iron ore, anhydrite, limestone and various sulphides.

Tourism has been encouraged on Svalbard; cruise ships make stops at the islands and there is also a small industry in skiing and trekking across the wilderness.

For 2002 the Svalbard budget was 136,977m. kroner, of which 100,993m. kroner was a direct subsidy from the Norwegian state budget. Svalbard raises some revenue from the sale of fishing licences.

Statistical Survey

Source: Statistics Norway, Kongens gt. 6, Oslo; tel. 21-09-00-00; fax 21-09-49-73; e-mail biblioteket@ssb.no; internet www.ssb.no.

AREA AND POPULATION

Area: 61,229 sq km (23,641 sq miles).

Population (January 2001): 2,616 (Norwegian 1,704, Russian 903, Polish 9).

Density (2001): 0.04 per sq km.

Economically Active Population (2001): Mining and quarrying 183; Manufacturing 19; Construction 133; Wholesale and retail trade 93; Hotels and restaurants 140; Transport, storage and communication 79; Supporting and auxiliary transport activities and activities of travel agencies 52; Post and telecommunications 39; Financial intermediation, business activities etc. 104; Public administration 116; Education, health and social work 107; Other community, social and personal service activities 15; Total 1,080.

MINING

Coal Shipments ('000 metric tons): 755.5 (Norwegian mines 72.2) in 1999; 992.9 (Norwegian mines 689.9) in 2000; 1,939.5 (Norwegian mines 1,565.5) in 2001.

FINANCE

(Norwegian currency is used (100 øre = 1 Norwegian krone))

Budget (million kroner, 2002): Estimated revenue 137.0 (incl. direct grant of 101.0 from central Govt); Budgeted expenditure 137.0.

TRANSPORT AND TOURISM

Road Traffic (vehicles registered at 31 December 2000): Passenger cars 651; Buses 46; Goods vehicles 287; Mopeds and motorcycles 84.

Civil Aviation: 77,702 passengers in 2000.

Guests Arriving at Hotels: 16,896 in 1999; 23,741 in 2000; 27,762 in 2001.

EDUCATION

Pre-primary (1999/2000): Schools 3; Teachers 23; Pupils 89.

Primary and Lower Secondary (2000/01): Schools 1; Pupils 147.

Directory

The Government

(April 2003)

ADMINISTRATION

Governor (Sysselmann): Odd Olsen Ingerø.

Commissioner of Mines: Per Zakken Brekke.

OFFICES

Office of the Governor: Kontoret til Sysselmannen på Svalbard, POB 933, 9171 Longyearbyen, Svalbard; tel. 79-02-43-00; fax 79-02-11-66; e-mail firmapost@sysselmannen.svalbard.no; internet www.sysselmannen.svalbard.no.

Ministry of Justice and the Police (Polar Affairs Department): Åkersgt. 42, POB 8005 Dep., 0030 Oslo; tel. 22-24-56-01; fax 22-24-95-39; e-mail postmottak@jd.dep.no; responsible for the administration of Svalbard and Jan Mayen, and for the Norwegian 'Antarctic' dependencies.

Norsk Polarinstitutt Svalbard (Norwegian Polar Institute Svalbard): Næringsbygget, POB 505, 9071 Longyearbyen, Svalbard; tel.

79-02-26-00; fax 79-02-26-04; e-mail postmottak@npolar.no; internet www.npolar.no; f. 1928 (Norwegian Polar Institute, Oslo) as Norges Svalbard- og Ishavs-undersøkelser; adopted present name and expanded functions in 1948; mapping and research institute; responsible for advising Govt on matters concerning Svalbard, Jan Mayen and the 'Antarctic' dependencies; monitors and investigates environment of the territories; organizes regular Antarctic research expeditions; establishes and maintains aids to navigation in Svalbard waters; Dir Jan Erling Haugland.

Norsk Polarinstitutts Forskningsstasjon (Norwegian Polar Institute Research Station): Ny-Ålesund, Svalbard; tel. 79-02-71-15; fax 79-02-70-02; permanent research base in Svalbard.

Longyearbyen Lokalstyre (Longyearbyen Council): POB 350, 9171 Longyearbyen; tel. 79-02-21-50; fax 79-02-21-51; e-mail postmottak@lokalstyre.no; internet www.lokalstyre.no; f. 2002; first locally elected body in Svalbard; replaced Svalbard Council; Leader Sigmund Spjelkavik.

Svalbard, as an integral part of the Kingdom of Norway, has provision for its Norwegian inhabitants to participate in the national elections. For judicial matters Svalbard lies in the jurisdiction of Tromsø. The state Evangelical Lutheran Church provides religious services.

Press

There is only one newspaper published in the Svalbard archipelago.

Svalbardposten: POB 503, 9171 Longyearbyen; tel. 79-02-47-00; fax 79-02-47-01; e-mail post@svalbardposten.no; internet www.svalbardposten.no; f. 1948; weekly; Editor-in-Chief Nils Lorensten; circ. 3,000.

Finance

Norwegian currency is used. Most banking facilities are available.

Sparebanken Nord-Norge: POB 518, 9171 Longyearbyen, Svalbard; tel. 79-02-29-10; fax 79-02-29-11; e-mail kundeservice@snn.sparebank1.no; internet www.snn.no; savings bank.

Trade and Industry

Store Norske Spitsbergen Kulkompani A/S: 9171 Longyearbyen, Svalbard; tel. 79-02-52-00; fax 79-02-18-41; state-owned; operates coal-mines; 230 employees (2003); Admin. Dir Atle Fornes.

Store Norske Spitsbergen Grubekompani A/S (SNSG): f. 2002; manages all assets, rights, contractual obligations and liabilities in connection with the Svea Nord mine, responsible for coal production and sales in Longyearbyen and Svea, and for exploration at both its own SNSK's claims.

Store Norske Boliger A/S: f. 2002; manages the group's accommodation in Longyearbyen and some of the accommodation in Svea.

Svalbard Næringsutvikling A/S: 9170 Longyearbyen, Svalbard; tel. 79-02-21-00; fax 79-02-10-19; state-owned; encourages development of industry and trade; Admin. Dir Endre Hoflandsdal.

Svalbard Samfunnsdrift A/S: POB 475, 9171 Longyearbyen, Svalbard; tel. 79-02-23-00; fax 79-02-23-01; e-mail firmapost@ssd.no; internet www.ssd.no; state-owned; operates most local services, undertakes infrastructure development; 140 employees (1998); Admin. Dir Endre Hoflandsdal.

Transport

Shipping links operate from June to August, with weekly sailings from Honningsvåg to Longyearbyen and Ny-Ålesund and back via Tromsø. In 1975 an airport was opened near Longyearbyen. SAS and Braathens SAFE operate services to Tromsø up to five times per week. There are air strips at Ny-Ålesund and Svea, and a Russian helicopter facility at Barentsburg. Apart from helicopters, and a fixed-wing service between Longyearbyen and Ny-Ålesund, internal traffic is little developed.

AIRPORT

Svalbard Lufthavn: POB 550, 9171 Longyearbyen, Svalbard; tel. 79-02-38-00; fax 79-02-38-01; e-mail de.m.rambech@avinor.no; internet www.avinor.no.

JAN MAYEN

Location and Climate

The lofty volcanic island of Jan Mayen is located in the Arctic Ocean, some 910 km west-north-west of Bodø on the Norwegian mainland, 610 km north-north-east of Iceland and 480 km east of Greenland (Denmark). The island is 53 km in length and has a total area of 377 sq km (145 sq miles). The highest point is the summit of Mt Beerenberg (2,277 m above sea-level). The climate is severe, cold and usually misty.

History and Government

The sea north and west of Jan Mayen (which was frequented by various whalers and hunters for a brief period in the 17th century) has been an important area for sealing by Norwegians since the mid-19th century. Partly to assist their navigation, the Norwegian Meteorological Institute instigated activities on the island in the early 20th century. In 1922 Jan Mayen was declared annexed by the Institute, and on 8 May 1929 Norwegian sovereignty was proclaimed by Royal Decree. The island was made an integral part of the Kingdom of Norway by the Jan Mayen Act of 1930. Jan Mayen is not included in the Svalbard Treaty.

The island has no known exploitable mineral resources and is largely barren. Fishing in the surrounding waters is intermittently productive, and it was once considered that a base for fishing fleets could be established. This is now believed to be unlikely, particularly because of the high cost of building a harbour. In September 1970 there was a violent volcanic eruption on the island, the first since the early 19th century. In the course of the first few days of the eruption a huge glacier melted and millions of cubic metres of ice disappeared as steam. Lava poured into the sea and formed about 3.5 sq km of new land. The island's main use remains as a meteorological, navigational and radio station.

During the Second World War Jan Mayen remained the only part of Norway under Norwegian rule, following the German invasion of the mainland. Despite some conflict, the Norwegian Government and its allies maintained the strategic meteorological station and established a radio-locating station on the island during the war.

In 1946 a new base was established at Nordlaguna, both as a meteorological and a coastal radio station. As a result of a North Atlantic defence co-operation exercise in 1959–60, a long-range navigation (LORAN) network was established, with one base on Jan Mayen. At the same time, it was decided to build an airstrip near the new LORAN C base, and in 1962 the personnel of the weather and coastal radio services also moved to the same area.

After negotiations with Iceland in 1980, the Norwegian Government declared an economic zone extending for 200 nautical miles (370 km) around the coast of Jan Mayen. In 1981 a further agreement was made with Iceland, regarding mineral and fishing rights. A dispute with Denmark, acting on behalf of Greenland, concerning the delimitation of maritime economic zones between Greenland and Jan Mayen was referred by Denmark to the International Court of Justice (based in The Hague, Netherlands) in 1988. The Court delivered its judgment in June 1993, deciding that 57% of the disputed area belonged to Norway. A subsequent accord on maritime delimitation, agreed between the Governments of Norway, Greenland and Iceland in November 1997, established the boundaries of a 1,934-sq km area of Arctic sea that had been excluded from the terms of the 1993 settlement.

The commanding officer in charge of the LORAN C base is the chief administrative official of the island. The officer is responsible for the 15–25 inhabitants (who usually remain on the island for only one year at a time), and is accountable to the Chief of Police in Bodø, and the Ministry of Justice and the Police (as in Svalbard; see above). The LORAN C commander may grant permission for visits of not more than 24 hours. For longer visits, the Bodø Chief of Police or the Ministry must approve the application. Visits are normally allowed only for scientific purposes and only if private provision has been made for transport. There is no public transport or accommodation on Jan Mayen.

Officer-in-charge: MARTIN HELGE-SIMONSEN.

Chief of Police (Bodø): Kongensgt. 81, 8006, Bodø, Norway.

For the Ministry of Justice and the Police and the Norsk Polarinstitutt (Norwegian Polar Institute), see under Svalbard.

NORWEGIAN DEPENDENCIES

Norway's so-called 'Antarctic' dependencies are all uninhabited and were acquired as a result of Norwegian whaling interests in the region since the 1890s. The three territories are dependencies of the Kingdom of Norway, and are administered by the Polar Department of the Ministry of Justice and the Police, with the advice of the Norsk Polarinstitutt (Norwegian Polar Institute: for details, see under Svalbard) and the assistance of the Ministry of the Environment.

Bouvetøya

Bouvetøya (Bouvet Island) is a volcanic island in the South Atlantic Ocean, some 2,400 km south-west of the Cape of Good Hope (South Africa) and 1,600 km north of Antarctica. The island lies north of the Antarctic Circle (it is not, therefore, encompassed by the terms of the Antarctic Treaty). Bouvetøya has an area of 49 sq km, but about 93% of the surface is covered by ice. The climate is maritime antarctic, with a mean annual temperature of –1°C and a persistent heavy fog.

Regular landings on the island occurred only as part of Norwegian Antarctic expeditions in the 1920s and 1930s. Bouvetøya was claimed for Norway in 1927, placed under its sovereignty in 1928, and declared a Norwegian dependency in 1930. A Royal Decree of 1971 declared the entire island to be a nature reserve. An automatic weather station was established in 1977, and the island is regularly visited by Norwegian scientific expeditions.

Dronning Maud Land

Dronning Maud Land (Queen Maud Land) is that sector of the Antarctic continent lying between the longitudes of 20°W (adjoining the British Antarctic Territory to the west) and 45°E (neighbouring the Australian Antarctic Territory). The territory is, in area, several times the size of Norway, and 98% of its surface is covered by ice. The climate is severe, the usual temperature always being below 0°C and, in the winter months of mid-year, falling to –60°C on the coast and –88°C inland. The territory's coast is divided into five named sectors (the exact delimitations of which, and of the territory as a whole, have varied at different periods): Kronprinsesse Märtha Kyst (Crown Princess Märtha Coast), Prinsesse Astrid Kyst, Prinsesse Ragnhild Kyst, Prins Harald Kyst and Kronprins Olav Kyst.

The first Norwegian territorial claims in Antarctica were made in 1929, following many years of Norwegian involvement in the exploration and survey of the continent. Further claims were made in 1931 and 1936–37. These claims were formalized by the Norwegian authorities, and the land placed under their sovereignty, only in 1939. The extent of Dronning Maud Land then received its current limits, between the British and Australian claims. Norway now follows a policy which upholds its claim to sovereignty but supports the pattern of international co-operation, particularly that established under the terms of the Antarctic Treaty (see p. 492) (signed in 1959), to which the Kingdom of Norway is an original signatory. There are six wintering stations, staffed by personnel of various nationalities, in Dronning Maud Land.

Peter I Øy

Peter I Øy (Peter I Island) is located in the Bellingshausen Sea, some 450 km north of Antarctica and more than 1,800 km south-west of Chile, the nearest inhabited territory. It covers an area of some 156 sq km, 95% of which is covered by ice. The island lies within the Antarctic Circle and the area covered by the terms of the Antarctic Treaty. The first recorded landing on the island was not made until 1929, by a Norwegian expedition, which then claimed the island. A Royal Proclamation placed Peter I Øy under Norwegian sovereignty in 1931, and the island was declared a dependency in 1933. Few landings have been made since, but in 1987 the Norsk Polarinstitutt (Norwegian Polar Institute) conducted a relatively long survey and established an automatic weather station on the island.

OMAN

Introductory Survey

Location, Climate, Language, Religion, Flag, Capital

The Sultanate of Oman occupies the extreme east and south-east of the Arabian peninsula. It is bordered to the west by the United Arab Emirates (UAE), Saudi Arabia and Yemen. A detached portion of Oman, separated from the rest of the country by UAE territory, lies at the tip of the Musandam peninsula, on the southern shore of the Strait of Hormuz. Oman has a coastline of more than 1,600 km (1,000 miles) on the Indian Ocean, and is separated from Iran by the Gulf of Oman. In Muscat average annual rainfall is 100 mm and the average temperature varies between 21°C (70°F) and 35°C (95°F). Rainfall is heavier on the hills of the interior, and the south-western province of Dhofar is the only part of Arabia to benefit from the summer monsoon. The official language is Arabic. Islam is the official religion. The majority of the population are Ibadi Muslims, while about one-quarter are Hindus. The national flag (proportions 1 by 2) has three equal horizontal stripes, of white, red and green, with a vertical red stripe at the hoist. In the upper hoist is a representation, in white, of the state emblem, two crossed swords and a dagger (khanjar), surmounted by a belt. The capital is Muscat.

Recent History

Officially known as Muscat and Oman until 1970, the Sultanate has had a special relationship with the United Kingdom since the 19th century. Full independence was confirmed by a treaty of friendship with the United Kingdom on 20 December 1951, although the armed forces and police still have some British officers on loan service. Sultan Said bin Taimur succeeded his father in 1932 and maintained a strictly conservative and isolationist rule until July 1970, when he was overthrown by his son in a bloodless palace coup. The new Sultan, Qaboos bin Said as-Said, then began a liberalization of the regime, and spending on development was increased.

A Consultative Assembly (comprising representatives of the Government, the private sector and the regions, appointed by the Sultan) was created in 1981, in order to advise Sultan Qaboos on economic and social development. In November 1990 it was announced that the Assembly was to be replaced by a Consultative Council (Majlis ash-Shoura), comprising regional representatives, which was intended to extend participation by Omani citizens in national affairs. A selection process was duly announced whereby representatives of each of the country's 59 districts (*wilayat*) would nominate three candidates; the nominations would then be submitted to the Deputy Prime Minister for Legal Affairs, who, with the Sultan's approval, would choose one representative for each district to join the new Majlis. No government official or civil servant would be eligible for election to the new body. The President of the Consultative Council would be appointed by royal decree; other executive officers and committee members would be designated by, and from among, the 59 local delegates. Although the role of the Majlis was strictly advisory, government ministers were to be obliged to submit reports to the assembly and to answer any questions addressed to them. The Majlis was formally established by royal decree in November 1991 and was convened in January 1992, when its members were sworn in for a three-year term. In 1994 membership of the Majlis was increased from 59 to 80, to include an additional member for any district with 30,000 or more inhabitants. Women were for the first time nominated as candidates in six regions in and around the capital; two women were subsequently appointed to the enlarged Majlis.

In mid-1994 the Government was reported to be employing stringent measures to curb an apparent rise in Islamist militancy in Oman. In August the security forces arrested more than 200 members of an allegedly foreign-sponsored Islamist organization, including two junior ministers, university lecturers, students and soldiers. Most were later released, but in November several of those against whom charges had been brought were sentenced to death, having been found guilty of conspiracy to foment sedition; the Sultan subsequently commuted the death sentences to terms of imprisonment. In November 1995

139 prisoners were released, under a general amnesty granted by Sultan Qaboos.

In November 1996 Sultan Qaboos issued a decree promulgating a Basic Statute of the State, a constitutional document defining for the first time the organs and guiding principles of the State. The Statute provided for a Council of Oman, to be composed of the Majlis ash-Shoura and a new Council of State (Majlis ad-Dawlah). The latter was to be appointed from among prominent Omanis, and would liaise between the Government and the people of Oman. It was subsequently reported that 23 senior government ministers had resigned as directors of public joint-stock companies, in accordance with a stipulation in the Basic Statute that ministers should not abuse their official position for personal gain. In December a Defence Council was established by royal decree, comprising the Minister of the Royal Court, the heads of the armed and police forces, and the chief of internal security. The Basic Statute defined a process of succession to the Sultan, requiring that the ruling family determine a successor within three days of the throne's falling vacant, failing which the Defence Council would confirm the appointment of a successor predetermined by the Sultan.

Voting was organized in October 1997 to select candidates for appointment to the Majlis ash-Shoura. Of a total of 736 candidates, 164 were chosen, from whom the Sultan selected the 82 members of the new Majlis in November. The two female members of the outgoing Majlis were returned to office. (Women from all regions had been permitted to seek nomination in the October poll.) In December Sultan Qaboos issued a decree appointing the 41 members of the Majlis ad-Dawlah, which was reportedly dominated by former politicians, business leaders and academics. A further decree established the Council of Oman, which was formally inaugurated by the Sultan on 27 December.

Elections to the Majlis ash-Shoura were held on 14 September 2000. For the first time members were to be directly elected rather than appointed by the Sultan. Of a total of 541 candidates (21 of whom were women), 83 (including two women) were elected to the Majlis. The number of eligible voters had tripled, to some 150,000, since the previous election; according to official figures, an estimated 90% of the electorate participated in the poll. Publication of final election results was postponed until 20 September, following allegations that there had been incidences of vote-buying; however, the Ministry of the Interior found no evidence of electoral malpractice. A new Majlis ad-Dawlah was appointed in October, and the Council of Oman convened for its second term on 4 November. Government changes were effected in May, June and November 2001, and in February 2002.

From late 2000 the Government undertook measures aimed at reducing the number of expatriates in Oman's labour force, a process termed 'Omanization'. In April 2001 more than 100 suspected illegal immigrants were detained by the Omani authorities, who announced that all foreign nationals employed illegally in the country who had not supplied the correct documentation within a period of two months would be liable to deportation. About 130 alleged illegal immigrants were reportedly arrested in September.

In February 2003 the Government announced that the next elections to the Majlis ash-Shoura were to be held on 2 October; voting rights would be granted to all Omani citizens over 21 years of age—a total of some 820,000 people. Previously voting rights were limited to prominent business leaders, intellectuals, professionals and tribal chiefs. In March Sultan Qaboos issued a decree establishing a Public Authority for Craft Industries. The President of the Authority, Sheikha Aisha bint Khalfan bin Jumiel as-Siyabiah, was given the rank of Minister, and thus became the first female member of the Council of Ministers.

An agreement on the demarcation of Oman's border with Yemen, which had been the subject of a lengthy dispute with the former People's Democratic Republic of Yemen, was signed in October 1992 and ratified in December; demarcation was completed in June 1995. In July 1996 Oman withdrew an estimated 15,000 troops from the last of the disputed territories on the Yemeni border, in accordance with the 1992 agreement, and in

May 1997 the border demarcation maps were signed in Muscat. Several bilateral economic co-operation accords were announced in September 1998, as were plans for the establishment of a free trade zone. Oman and Yemen agreed in October 2001 to extend co-operation between their hydrocarbon industries.

In response to the invasion of Kuwait by Iraq in August 1990, Oman, together with the other members of the Co-operation Council for the Arab States of the Gulf (Gulf Co-operation Council—GCC, see p. 175), gave its support to the deployment of a US-led defensive force in Saudi Arabia. The Omani Government expressed the view that the imposition of international economic sanctions would compel Iraq to withdraw from Kuwait. In November there was evidence that Oman was attempting to mediate in the crisis, when the Iraqi Minister of Foreign Affairs, Tareq Aziz, visited Oman (the first official Iraqi visit to a GCC state, other than Kuwait, since the Gulf crisis began). By the mid-1990s Oman's stance regarding the continuation of economic sanctions against Iraq appeared ambivalent: Oman and Qatar were, notably, absent from talks held in March 1995 between the US Secretary of State, Warren Christopher, and other GCC members to discuss the issue. In November 1997 Oman stated its opposition to possible military action to force Iraq to submit to inspections of its weapons capabilities by the UN Special Commission (UNSCOM, see the Recent History of Iraq). In early 1998, as the crisis regarding UNSCOM inspections deepened, the Omani Government again urged the pursuit of a diplomatic solution, maintaining that the UN should remove the economic sanctions against Iraq once UNSCOM had been permitted to complete its task.

Although Oman was swift to condemn the September 2001 terrorist attacks in New York and Washington, DC, the Omani Government expressed concern that the US-led military campaign in Afghanistan against the al-Qa'ida (Base) network of Osama bin Laden (held by the USA to be principally responsible for the attacks) and the Taliban regime should not be extended to target any Arab state, notably Iraq. Street demonstrations were held in October by Omani students protesting against the war in Afghanistan. During an official visit to Oman by the US Secretary of Defense, Donald Rumsfeld, in that month, it was reported that the USA was to supply Oman with 12 F-16 fighter aircraft and other advanced weaponry, at a cost of some US $1,120m. From 2002 Oman opposed attempts led by the USA, as part of its 'war against terror', to garner international support for an eventual offensive against the Iraqi regime of Saddam Hussain, and advocated a diplomatic solution to the escalating crisis. In March 2003, as the US-led force began assaults on targets in Iraq, Sultan Qaboos appealed for a swift curtailment of the conflict, which he described as 'unjustified' and 'illegitimate'. During March and April there were frequent anti-war protests in various locations in Oman.

In April 1994 the Israeli Deputy Minister of Foreign Affairs, Yossi Beilin, participated in talks in Oman. This constituted the first official visit by an Israeli government member to an Arab Gulf state since Israel's declaration of independence in 1948. In September 1994, moreover, Oman and the other GCC member states announced the partial ending of their economic boycott of Israel. In December the Israeli Prime Minister, Itzhak Rabin, made an official visit to Oman to discuss the Middle East peace process, and in February 1995 it was announced that low-level diplomatic relations were to be established between Oman and Israel. An Omani trade office was opened in Tel-Aviv in August 1996, despite concerns that bilateral relations would be undermined by the uncompromising stance adopted by the new Israeli Government of Binyamin Netanyahu. In March 1997 ministers responsible for foreign affairs of the countries of the League of Arab States (the Arab League, see p. 260) recommended, in condemnation of Israeli settlement policy, the suspension of involvement in multilateral negotiations with Israel, a reassertion of the primary economic boycott and the ending, by means of closing representative offices in Tel-Aviv, of efforts to normalize bilateral relations. In April Oman prohibited Israeli participation at a Muscat trade fair. Oman attended the Middle East and North Africa economic conference in Doha, Qatar, in November, despite a boycott by most Arab League and GCC members in response to the perceived failure of Israel (which was represented at the conference) to comply with its obligations under the Middle East peace process. In October 2000, in view of the deepening crisis in Israeli–Palestinian relations, Oman closed both its trade office in Tel-Aviv and the Israeli trade office in Muscat. Oman hosted the annual summit meeting of GCC heads of state in December 2001, at the close of which a

statement was issued blaming Israel for the collapse of the peace process and expressing support for the Palestinian leadership. Two demonstrations took place in Muscat in early April 2002 to demand an end to Israeli military incursions into Palestinian territory.

Government

The Basic Statute of the State, which was promulgated by Royal Decree on 6 November 1996, defines Oman's organs of government. The Sultan, who is Head of State, is empowered to promulgate and ratify legislation. He is assisted in formulating and implementing the general policy of the State by a Council of Ministers. Members of the Council of Ministers are appointed by the Sultan, who presides, or may appoint a Prime Minister to preside, over the Council. There is no legislature. However, a Majlis ash-Shoura (Consultative Council) is now elected for three years at national polls. Voters have hitherto been nominated within the country's *wilayat*, or districts, with the franchise effectively limited to prominent business leaders, intellectuals, professionals and tribal chiefs; with effect from elections scheduled to take place in October 2003, however, voting rights were to be granted to all Omani citizens over 21 years of age. The Majlis is composed of one representative from each *wilaya* with fewer than 30,000 inhabitants, and two from each *wilaya* with 30,000 or more inhabitants. The Majlis ash-Shoura elected in September 2000 comprised 83 members. A 41-member Majlis ad-Dawlah (Council of State) is appointed by the Sultan from among prominent Omanis. The two Councils together comprise the Council of Oman.

Oman comprises three governorates, subdivided into 59 *wilayat*; each of the *wilayat* has its own governor (*wali*).

Defence

In August 2002 the Omani armed forces numbered 41,700 (excluding about 2,000 expatriate personnel): army 25,000; navy 4,200; air force 4,100; royal household 6,400. Paramilitary forces numbered 4,400: tribal home guard (*firqat*) 4,000; police coastguard 400. Military service is voluntary. Government expenditure on defence was budgeted at RO 860m. in 2002.

Economic Affairs

In 1995, according to estimates by the World Bank, Oman's gross national income (GNI), measured at average 1993–95 prices, was US $10,790m., equivalent to $5,050 per head. During 1990–2001, it was estimated, the population increased at an average annual rate of 3.8%, while real gross domestic product (GDP) per head increased, in real terms, by an average of 0.3% in 1990–1995. Overall GDP increased, in real terms, at an average annual rate of 4.6% in 1990–2000; growth in 2000 was 5.5% and in 2001 was an estimated 9.3%.

Agriculture (including fishing) engaged 9.4% of the employed population at the 1993 census, and contributed 2.0% of GDP in 2001, according to provisional figures. FAO data suggested that some 35.0% of the economically active population were engaged in agriculture in 2001, mainly at subsistence level. The major crops are dates, tomatoes, bananas, watermelons and onions. The production of frankincense, formerly an important export commodity, has been revived. Livestock and fishing are also important. The real GDP of the agricultural sector increased by an average of 4.0% annually in 1990–2000. Real agricultural GDP declined by 5.3% in 2000, but expanded by some 2.7% in 2001.

Industry (including mining and quarrying, manufacturing, construction and power) employed 27.8% of the working population in 1993, and provided 53.3% of GDP in 2001, according to provisional figures. Real industrial GDP increased by an average of 4.1% annually in 1990–2000. The sector's real GDP increased by 9.1% in 2000 and by an estimated 9.2% in 2001.

According to provisional figures, the mining sector contributed 42.0% of GDP in 2001, and engaged 2.1% of the employed labour force in 1993. The main mineral reserves are petroleum and natural gas, which together provided an estimated 41.8% of GDP in 2001. There were proven petroleum reserves of 5,500m. barrels at the end of 2001. Production in 2001 averaged 959,000 barrels per day (b/d). Petroleum reserves were estimated to be sufficient to sustain production at these levels until 2016. Under its 2001–05 Development Plan, Oman plans to increase oil output to at least 1m. b/d. Exports of Omani crude petroleum provided 80.4% of total export earnings in 2001. Natural gas is also an important mineral resource; there were proven reserves of some 830,000m. cu m at the end of 2001, sustainable for almost 62 years at 2001 production levels (output in 2001 totalled 13,400m. cu m—an increase of some 60% compared with the previous year). Official projections envisaged that gas would contribute 15% of GDP by 2002. Budget revenue from petroleum and natural gas was forecast to contribute 73.1% of the total in 2002. Chromite, gold, salt, marble, gypsum and limestone are also mined, and the exploitation of coal deposits is planned. The GDP of the mining sector increased at an average annual rate of 3.5% in 1990–2000. Mining GDP expanded by 5.6% in 2000 and by some 0.2% in 2001.

Manufacturing contributed 8.2% of GDP in 2001, according to provisional figures, and engaged 9.0% of the employed labour force in 1993. The most important branches of the sector are petroleum-refining, construction materials, cement production and copper-smelting. Assembly industries, light engineering and food-processing are being encouraged at industrial estates in Muscat, Sohar and Salalah. Completion of a US $9,000m. liquefied natural gas (LNG) plant at Sur has reduced domestic demand for petroleum and also produced a surplus for export. The GDP of the manufacturing sector increased, in real terms, at an average rate of 7.9% annually in 1990–2000. The sector's real GDP increased by 40.2% in 2000 and by an estimated 62.7% in 2001.

Energy is derived almost exclusively from domestic supplies of natural gas (which accounted for 83.3% of electricity produced in 2001) and petroleum. Imports of fuel products comprised just 1.6% of total imports in 2000.

Services provided 44.7% of GDP (according to provisional figures) in 2001, and engaged 62.0% of the employed population at the 1993 census. The GDP of the services sector increased, in real terms, at an average rate of 5.3% per year during 1990–2000. Real services GDP increased by 4.5% in 2000 and by an estimated 9.2% in 2001.

In 2001 Oman recorded a visible trade surplus of RO 5,763m., and there was a surplus of RO 2,315m. on the current account of the balance of payments. In 2001 the principal sources of imports were the United Arab Emirates and Japan (which supplied, respectively, 28.4% and 15.4% of Oman's imports). The USA and the United Kingdom are also important suppliers. By some margin, the most important market for exports in 2000 was the United Arab Emirates (taking 87.8%). Saudi Arabia, Iran and Yemen were also important markets of exports. Petroleum is, by far, the principal export; machinery and transport equipment also make a notable contribution to export earnings. The principal imports in 2001 were machinery and transport equipment, basic manufactures, food and live animals, and chemicals and related products.

Oman recorded an estimated overall budgetary deficit of RO 327.9m. in 2001 (equivalent to 4.3% of GDP in that year). At the end of 2000 Oman's total external debt was US $6,267m., of which $4,968m. was long-term public debt. The cost of debt-servicing in that year was equivalent to 7.3% of the total value of exports of goods and services. Annual inflation declined by an average of 0.2% in 1990–2001; consumer prices decreased by an annual average of 0.7% in 2002. Although Oman has traditionally relied on a high level of immigrant labour (non-Omanis accounted for 64.2% of the employed labour force in 1993), employment opportunities for young Omanis declined in the early 1990s and, according to census results, unemployment among Omanis stood at 11.9% in 1993.

Oman is a member of the Arab Fund for Economic and Social Development (see p. 136), the Islamic Development Bank (see p. 257) and the Arab Monetary Fund (see p. 138). It was a founder member of the Co-operation Council for the Arab States of the Gulf (the Gulf Co-operation Council—GCC, see p. 175), and of the Indian Ocean Rim Association for Regional Co-operation (see p. 340). Oman is not a member of the Organization of the Petroleum Exporting Countries (OPEC, see p. 298) nor of the Organization of Arab Petroleum Exporting Countries (see p. 292), but it generally respects OPEC's policies regarding levels of petroleum production and pricing. Oman was admitted to the World Trade Organization (see p. 323) in November 2000. The GCC's six members established a unified regional customs tariff in January 2003, and the organization has undertaken to establish a single market and currency no later than January 2010.

Oman's limited petroleum reserves and fluctuations in the price of petroleum have necessitated a series of five-year development plans to diversify the country's economic base, in particular through the expansion of the private sector. Under the sixth Development Plan (2001–05), emphasis was to be placed on the reduction of public expenditure, the development of the non-petroleum sector (with gas-based industry and tourism being

notable targets), and the expansion of the privatization programme (begun in mid-1994). Besides seeking to create 110,000 jobs for Omani nationals, it was also planned to increase state funding for their education and training, and to limit the employment of expatriates in certain fields. (Omanis are now reported to constitute at least 90% of employees in banking and finance.) Under the Plan, the Government aimed to achieve annual GDP growth of at least 3% and to maintain low annual rates of inflation. Oman's economy strengthened in 2000, owing to sustained high prices for petroleum and the commencement of LNG exports in April. The economy expanded further in 2001, as government efforts to maximize existing hydrocarbons reserves while strengthening the non-petroleum sector achieved some success. However, the Israeli–Palestinian crisis resulted in reduced tourism revenues for Oman, although buoyant petroleum prices continued to produce high oil revenues. Meanwhile, in late 1999 the Government approved an accelerated privatization programme in the power sector; divestment of the postal service and telecommunications and transport sectors was also planned in 2003. Ongoing industrial development included the construction of gas pipelines at Sohar and Salalah, scheduled for completion in early 2003. However, plans for the establishment of a free-trade zone at Salalah, which was expected to create new employment opportunities for Omani nationals and also encourage foreign investment, appeared to be in doubt when the major investor withdrew from the venture in late 2002, alluding to the instability of the region's politics as a reason for its withdrawal. In preparation for admittance to the WTO, the Government abolished import fees, raised the limit on foreign ownership of local industries from 49% to 70% (effective from 1 January 2001) and authorized 100% foreign ownership in banking, insurance and brokerage firms (from 1 January 2003). In January 2003 the Government approved an estimated RO 400m. deficit in its 2003 budget. The shortfall, attributed to a decrease in crude petroleum sales in 2002, was to be financed by bank loans, drawing on state reserves and adopting measures to enhance non-petroleum revenues.

Education

In 1970 there were only three schools, with a total of 909 pupils. By 2001/02 there were 1,125 schools at the primary, preparatory and secondary levels, as well as a number of private kindergartens and schools regulated by the Ministry of Education; in total, 567,997 students were in state education and 22,773 in private education in that year. According to the Basic Statute, the State endeavours to make education available to all; it provides public education and encourages the establishment of private educational institutions. However, education is still not compulsory. Primary education begins at six years of age and lasts for six years. The next level of education, divided into two equal stages (preparatory and secondary), lasts for a further six years. In 1998/99 a new system, comprising 10 years of basic education and two years of secondary education, was introduced in 17 schools; it was to be implemented gradually throughout the country. Primary enrolment in 1997/98 included 76% of children in the relevant age-group (boys 78%; girls 74%), while preparatory and secondary enrolment included 67% of children in the relevant age-group (boys 68%; girls 66%). In 2001/02 there were six teacher-training colleges and four vocational institutes, together with institutes of health sciences and banking, and five technical institutes. There were seven Islamic colleges in 1995/96. Oman's first national university, named after Sultan Qaboos, was opened in late 1986, and had 8,755 students (males 4,466; females 4,289) in 2001/02. There are three private universities: Sohar University offers degree courses in various disciplines, while the College of Administrative Sciences specializes in business studies. A tourism and hotel management institute is also being established. According to budget forecasts, of total expenditure by the central Government in 2002, RO 331m. (11.5%) was allocated to education.

Public Holidays

2003: 12 February* (Id al-Adha, Feast of the Sacrifice), 5 March* (Muharram, Islamic New Year), 14 May* (Mouloud, Birth of the Prophet), 24 September* (Leilat al-Meiraj, Ascension of the Prophet), 27 October* (Ramadan begins), 18 November (National Day), 26 November* (Id al-Fitr, end of Ramadan).

2004: 2 February* (Id al-Adha, Feast of the Sacrifice), 22 February* (Muharram, Islamic New Year), 2 May* (Mouloud, Birth of the Prophet), 12 September* (Leilat al-Meiraj, Ascension of the Prophet), 15 October* (Ramadan begins), 14

November* (Id al-Fitr, end of Ramadan), 18 November (National Day).

*These holidays are dependent on the Islamic lunar calendar and may vary by one or two days from the dates given.

Weights and Measures

The imperial, metric and local systems are all used, although the metric system was officially adopted in 1974.

Statistical Survey

Sources (unless otherwise stated): Ministry of National Economy, Information and Publication Centre, POB 881, Muscat 113; tel. 698900; fax 698467; e-mail mone@omantel.net.om; internet www.moneoman.gov.om; Central Bank of Oman, POB 1161, Ruwi 112; tel. 702222; fax 702253; e-mail cboresb@omantel.net.om; internet www.cbo-oman.org.

Area and Population

AREA, POPULATION AND DENSITY

Area (sq km)	309,500*
Population (census results)	
1 December 1993	
Males	1,178,005
Females	840,069
Total	2,018,074†
Population (official estimates at mid-year)	
1999	2,325,438
2000	2,401,256
2001	2,477,687‡
Density (per sq km) at mid-2001	8.0

* 119,500 sq miles.

† Comprising 1,483,226 Omani nationals and 534,848 non-Omanis.

‡ Comprising 1,826,124 Omani nationals and 651,563 non-Omanis.

GOVERNORATES
(mid-2001)

	Area (sq km)	Population	Density (per sq km)
Muscat	3,900	685,676	175.8
Al-Batinah	12,500	686,284	54.9
Musandam	1,800	35,045	19.5
Adh-Dhahira	44,000	221,687	5.0
Ad-Dakhliya	31,900	279,829	8.8
Ash-Sharqiya	36,400	315,584	8.7
Al-Wosta	79,700	21,019	0.3
Dhofar	99,300	232,563	2.3
Total	309,500	2,477,687	8.0

PRINCIPAL TOWNS
(population at 1993 census)

Salalah	131,802	Nizwa	58,582
Ibri	93,475	Sur	53,504
Suhar	90,814	Al-Buraymi . . .	48,287
Ar-Rustaq . . .	61,984	Muscat (capital) . .	40,856

Source: Thomas Brinkhoff, *City Population* (internet www.citypopulation.de).

2001: (UN estimates, incl. suburbs) Muscat 540,000 (Source: UN, *World Urbanization Prospects: The 2001 Revision*).

BIRTHS AND DEATHS
(official estimates, Omani nationals only)

	1999	2000	2001
Birth rate (per 1,000)	30.0	32.6	28.4
Death rate (per 1,000)	3.6	3.7	3.5

Expectation of life (years at birth): 71.6 (males 69.4; females 74.6) in 2001 (Source: WHO, *World Health Report*).

ECONOMICALLY ACTIVE POPULATION
(persons aged 15 years and over, 1993 census)

	Omanis	Non-Omanis	Total
Agriculture and fishing	21,993	40,789	62,782
Mining and quarrying	8,076	5,991	14,067
Manufacturing	4,212	55,825	60,037
Electricity, gas and water . . .	942	3,481	4,423
Construction	4,412	103,291	107,703
Trade, hotels and restaurants . .	12,201	91,041	103,242
Transport, storage and communications	11,339	12,989	24,328
Finance, insurance and real estate	5,857	11,287	17,144
Public administration and defence	134,714	25,610	160,324
Other community, social and personal services	34,178	76,205	110,383
Activities not adequately defined	2,056	3,786	5,842
Total employed	239,980	430,295	670,275
Unemployed	32,417	2,106	34,523
Total labour force	272,397	432,401	704,798
Males	248,917	387,473	636,390
Females	23,480	44,928	68,408

Health and Welfare

KEY INDICATORS

Total fertility rate (children per woman, 2001)	5.6
Under-5 mortality rate (per 1,000 live births, 2001) . . .	13
HIV/AIDS (% of persons aged 15–49, 2001)	0.11
Physicians (per 1,000 head, 1998)	1.33
Hospital beds (per 1,000 head, 1998)	2.2
Health expenditure (2000): US $ per head (PPP)	295
Health expenditure (2000): % of GDP	2.8
Health expenditure (2000): public (% of total)	82.9
Access to water (% of persons, 1999)	39
Access to sanitation (% of persons, 1999)	92
Human Development Index (2000): ranking	78
Human Development Index (2000): value	0.751

For sources and definitions, see explanatory note on p. vi.

Agriculture

PRINCIPAL CROPS
('000 metric tons)

	1999	2000	2001
Sorghum*	2.9	3.0	2.9
Potatoes	15.6	18.2	12.7
Tomatoes	42.0	39.6	46.5
Dry onions	25.0	13.9	17.4
Other vegetables*	98	98	98
Bananas	30.1	32.2	33.7
Lemons and limes	12.1	8.2	8.6
Watermelons	22.6	24.0	29.9
Mangoes	11.0	10.9	10.9
Dates	282.0	280.0	248.5
Papayas	2.0	2.7	2.4

* FAO estimates.

Source: FAO.

LIVESTOCK
('000 head, year ending September)

	1999	2000	2001
Asses*	28	29	29
Cattle	285	299	314
Camels*	97	98	98
Sheep	327	344	354
Goats	959	979	998
Poultry*	3,200	3,400	3,400

* FAO estimates.

Source: FAO.

LIVESTOCK PRODUCTS
('000 metric tons)

	1999*	2000	2001
Beef and veal*	4.7	4.9	5.1
Camel meat*	5.0	5.1	5.3
Mutton and lamb*	12.8	12.9	13.1
Goat meat*	7.0	9.8	6.5
Poultry meat*	4.2	4.3	4.4
Cows' milk*	36.8	16.8	17.6
Sheep's milk*	3.7	3.7	3.7
Goats' milk*	81.2	81.4	81.4
Hen eggs	6.8	6.8	8.8

* FAO estimates.

Source: FAO.

Fishing
('000 metric tons, live weight)

	1998	1999	2000
Capture	102.5	108.8	118.9
Groupers	5.3	4.8	5.0
Emperors (Scavengers) . .	6.6	7.0	7.7
Porgies and seabreams . .	4.0	6.1	4.4
Demersal percomorphs . .	6.9	8.8	5.7
Pelagic percomorphs . .	6.1	1.1	—
Hairtails and cutlassfishes .	4.8	1.8	4.4
Indian oil sardine	20.7	21.7	40.0
Anchovies, etc.	0.9	0.5	5.1
Longtail tuna	4.4	4.8	5.3
Yellowfin tuna	14.9	7.4	7.0
Sharks, rays, skates, etc. . .	4.8	4.0	3.7
Cuttlefish and bobtail squids	4.1	7.5	2.9
Aquaculture	0.0	0.0	4.9
Total catch	106.6	108.8	123.7

Source: FAO, *Yearbook of Fishery Statistics*.

Mining
('000 metric tons, unless otherwise indicated)

	1999	2000	2001
Crude petroleum ('000 barrels)*	328,100	340,000	352,000
Natural gas (dry, million cu m)* .	8,056	12,020	13,400
Chromite*	26.0	15.1	30.1
Silver (kg)*	3,566	4,894	3,153
Gold (kg)*	884	1,029	1,000
Marble*	188.5	147.7	156.0
Limestone	3,808.6	3,497.1	n.a.
Salt	11.2	11.7	n.a.
Gypsum*	180.1	131.9	30.0

* Estimates.

Source: partly US Geological Survey.

Industry

SELECTED PRODUCTS
('000 barrels, unless otherwise indicated)

	1998	1999	2000
Kerosene	1,127.3	1,456.6	1,643.0
Motor spirit (petrol)	5,225.0	4,710.9	4,856.5
Gas-diesel (distillate fuel) oils . .	6,029.1	6,297.0	6,362.7
Residual fuel oils	14,948.8	14,866.2	14,796.5
Electric energy (million kWh) . .	8,200	8,413	9,111

2001 (provisional figure): Electric energy 9,726 million kWh.

Finance

CURRENCY AND EXCHANGE RATES

Monetary Units
1,000 baiza = 1 rial Omani (RO)

Sterling, Dollar and Euro Equivalents (31 December 2002)
£1 sterling = 619.7 baiza
US $1 = 384.5 baiza
€1 = 403.2 baiza
100 rials Omani = £161.35 = $260.08 = €248.00

Exchange Rate: Since January 1986 the official exchange rate has been fixed at US $1 = 384.5 baiza (1 rial Omani = $2.6008).

BUDGET
(RO million)

Revenue	1998	1999	2000
Petroleum revenue (net) . . .	1,240.2	1,201.6	1,721.0
Natural gas revenue	63.3	57.6	73.4
Other current revenue . . .	522.7	519.8	455.3
Taxes and fees	177.3	187.0	156.5
Income tax on enterprises . .	40.1	36.1	41.8
Payroll tax	43.2	38.9	36.8
Customs duties	61.6	80.3	46.1
Non-tax revenue	345.4	332.8	298.8
Electricity	98.6	100.0	109.4
Surplus from public authorities	64.0	75.0	14.5
Income from government investments	46.9	37.3	34.1
Capital revenue	9.1	13.5	7.6
Capital repayments	11.0	3.6	32.6
Total	1,846.3	1,796.1	2,289.9

Expenditure	1998	1999	2000
Current expenditure	1,760.4	1,808.9	2,091.9
Defence and national security	675.8	687.2	808.6
Civil ministries	893.7	944.5	1,097.8
General public services . .	134.5	133.0	153.6
Education	262.4	276.8	208.8
Health	117.4	122.7	137.8
Social security and welfare	60.7	75.3	126.5
Housing	94.2	99.2	111.7
Fuel and energy	125.8	135.5	149.6
Interest payments	101.6	98.8	107.1
Share of PDO expenditure* . .	89.3	78.4	78.4
Investment expenditure	443.9	426.2	491.7
Civil development	206.0	201.3	225.3
Fuel and energy	48.7	85.4	76.0
Transport and communications .	59.4	35.6	50.1
Share of PDO expenditure* . .	179.3	170.1	191.2
Participation and subsidies . .	17.3	33.9	72.6
Total	2,221.6	2,269.0	2,656.2

* Referring to the Government's share of current and capital expenditure by Petroleum Development Oman.

2001 (preliminary figures, RO million): Total revenue 2,530.0 (Oil revenue 1,875.0); Total expenditure 2,857.9.

2002 (forecasts, RO million): Total revenue 2,490.0 (Oil revenue 1,819.0); Total expenditure 2,870.0.

INTERNATIONAL RESERVES
(US $ million at 31 December)

	2000	2001	2002
Gold*	68.3	80.5	0.2
IMF special drawing rights . .	4.1	6.3	8.9
Reserve position in IMF.	64.9	81.6	99.8
Foreign exchange.	2,310.9	2,277.0	3,064.8
Total	2,448.2	2,445.4	3,173.7

* Valued at RO 90.8 per troy ounce until 2000, and at market-related prices from 2001.

Source: IMF, *International Financial Statistics*.

MONEY SUPPLY
(RO million at 31 December)

	2000	2001	2002
Currency outside banks . . .	276.8	275.9	289.6
Demand deposits at commercial banks	272.5	425.7	482.0
Total money	549.3	701.6	771.6

Source: IMF, *International Financial Statistics*.

COST OF LIVING
(Consumer Price Index for Muscat; base: 1995 = 100)

	1999	2000	2001
Food, beverages and tobacco . .	102.7	101.4	100.8
Textiles, clothing and footwear	98.8	99.2	98.6
Rent, electricity, water and fuel	97.0	96.7	96.4
All items (incl. others) . . .	100.0	98.8	97.8

2002 (base: 1995 = 100): All items 97.0 in 2002 (Source: IMF, *International Financial Statistics*).

NATIONAL ACCOUNTS
(RO million in current prices)

Expenditure on the Gross Domestic Product

	1999	2000	2001
Government final consumption expenditure	1,440	1,580	1,823
Private final consumption expenditure	3,001	3,000	3,174
Increase in stocks . . . } Gross fixed capital formation . }	897	912	967
Total domestic expenditure.	5,338	5,492	5,964
Exports of goods and services .	2,937	4,515	4,392
Less Imports of goods and services	2,234	2,368	2,687
GDP in purchasers' values .	6,041	7,639	7,669
GDP at constant 1988 prices	5,356	5,650	6,175

Source: IMF, *International Financial Statistics*.

Gross Domestic Product by Economic Activity

	1999	2000	2001*
Agriculture and livestock† . . .	106.7	100.7	105.2
Fishing†	52.3	48.7	49.4
Mining and quarrying	2,381.6	3,735.9	3,282.2
Crude petroleum	2,299.2	3,616.1	3,105.5
Natural gas.	66.6	101.6	158.9
Manufacturing	262.3	414.7	640.2
Electricity and water	71.4	77.7	79.7
Construction	141.2	144.8	163.3
Trade, restaurants and hotels . .	825.4	869.9	947.3
Transport, storage and communications†	436.0	450.9	492.6
Financing, insurance, real estate and business services‡ . . .	678.2	678.3	715.0
Public administration and defence	688.2	715.9	757.7
Other community, social and personal services	496.1	543.3	567.9
Domestic services of households	16.2	16.5	16.8
Sub-total	6,155.5	7,797.1	7,817.3
Import duties†	80.3	46.1	58.6
Less Imputed bank service charge	195.2	204.0	195.2
GDP in purchasers' values . .	6,040.6	7,639.2	7,668.4

* Provisional figures.
† Excluding activities of government enterprises.
‡ Including imputed rents of owner-occupied dwellings.

BALANCE OF PAYMENTS
(US $ million)

	1999	2000	2001
Exports of goods f.o.b.	7,239	11,319	11,074
Imports of goods f.o.b.	−4,300	−4,593	−5,311
Trade balance	2,939	6,726	5,763
Exports of services	401	424	349
Imports of services	−1,511	−1,566	−1,678
Balance on goods and services .	1,829	5,584	4,434
Other income received	187	291	309
Other income paid	−869	−1,001	−897
Balance on goods, services and income	1,147	4,874	3,847
Current transfers paid	−1,438	−1,451	−1,532
Current balance	−291	3,423	2,315
Capital account (net)	−3	8	−10
Direct investment from abroad . .	21	70	42
Portfolio investment liabilities . .	26	−36	13
Other investment assets . . .	−307	−356	229
Other investment liabilities . .	325	−172	−1,170
Net errors and omissions . . .	522	−674	−384
Overall balance	215	2,262	1,034

Source: IMF, *International Financial Statistics*.

External Trade

PRINCIPAL COMMODITIES
(distribution by SITC)

Imports c.i.f. (RO million)	1999	2000	2001
Food and live animals	246.6	233.0	269.3
Dairy products and birds' eggs	59.2	54.2	67.9
Beverages and tobacco	140.2	167.5	198.2
Tobacco and tobacco manufactures	122.2	149.8	183.8
Chemicals and related products	132.5	140.4	160.0
Basic manufactures	263.0	267.9	345.8
Textile yarn, fabrics, etc.	54.8	60.0	67.2
Iron and steel	63.2	51.4	99.9
Machinery and transport equipment	744.4	838.1	881.7
Power-generating machinery and equipment	54.2	42.4	56.0
Machinery specialized for particular industries	97.1	113.6	146.4
General industrial machinery, equipment and parts	98.2	85.8	91.1
Telecommunications and sound equipment	50.2	40.4	74.1
Other electrical machinery, apparatus, etc.	61.3	61.2	76.4
Road vehicles and parts*	311.9	429.4	395.1
Miscellaneous manufactured articles	115.6	118.4	157.9
Total (incl. others)	1,797.1	1,937.6	2,229.1

Exports f.o.b. (US $ million)	1998	1999	2000
Food and live animals	180.0	188.0	215.5
Mineral fuels, lubricants, etc.	3,755.7	5,562.5	8,952.3
Petroleum, petroleum products, etc.	3,755.6	5,561.8	8,949.1
Crude petroleum oils, etc.	3,586.0	5,376.5	8,727.2
Refined petroleum products	169.6	185.3	221.9
Basic manufactures	179.8	169.3	221.3
Machinery and transport equipment	906.7	838.2	900.5
Road vehicles and parts*	588.6	521.4	611.8
Passenger motor cars (excl. buses)	377.1	282.5	365.0
Parts and accessories for cars, buses, lorries, etc.*	146.2	182.8	175.4
Miscellaneous manufactured articles	208.2	191.4	207.0
Total (incl. others)	5,518.8	7,230.9	10,852.3

* Data on parts exclude tyres, engines and electrical parts.

Source (for Exports): UN, *International Trade Statistics Yearbook*.

2001 (provisional figures, RO million): Total imports 2,229.3; Total exports 4,258.0 (Crude petroleum 2,934.8).

PRINCIPAL TRADING PARTNERS

Imports c.i.f. (RO '000)	1999	2000	2001
Australia	48,480	56,292	54,434
China, People's Republic	20,247	36,381	37,323
France	63,464	38,576	69,377
Germany	70,760	72,066	94,319
India	62,004	63,269	87,116
Iran	15,218	23,412	17,749
Italy	49,080	35,803	47,240
Japan	273,697	350,869	343,022
Korea, Republic	37,909	66,781	71,806
Malaysia	22,737	24,837	31,141
Netherlands	57,720	45,016	41,678
Pakistan	19,980	22,872	20,268
Saudi Arabia	61,167	52,942	71,149
Singapore	18,757	19,732	21,663
Switzerland	17,229	16,557	16,473
United Arab Emirates	505,314	570,891	632,726
United Kingdom	122,894	112,776	133,898
USA	115,318	103,981	151,848
Total (incl. others)	1,797,078	1,937,678	2,229,314

Exports f.o.b. (US $ million)	1998	1999	2000
China, People's Republic	482.7	689.2	1.9
Hong Kong	23.3	9.5	16.3
India	53.0	29.4	17.3
Iran	160.3	120.0	152.0
Japan	990.2	1,674.9	7.5
Korea, Republic	754.3	980.8	8.1
Philippines	208.8	166.8	1.0
Saudi Arabia	101.1	116.4	162.8
Tanzania	63.2	77.2	57.2
Thailand	977.2	1,147.0	8.2
United Arab Emirates	746.1	718.1	9,505.2
United Kingdom	53.7	79.2	73.6
USA	86.8	86.5	107.0
Yemen	136.4	91.1	151.9
Total (incl. others)	5,518.8	7,230.9	10,852.3

Source (for Exports): UN, *International Trade Statistics Yearbook*.

Transport

ROAD TRAFFIC
(registered vehicles at 31 December)

	1999	2000	2001
Private cars	254,214	280,977	309,217
Taxis	29,246	35,159	20,901
Commercial	117,615	124,582	132,920
Government	25,983	26,804	27,788
Motorcycles	4,853	5,050	5,195
Diplomatic	945	1,113	1,274
Other	14,318	22,229	23,631
Total	447,174	495,914	520,926

SHIPPING

Merchant Fleet
(registered at 31 December)

	1999	2000	2001
Number of vessels	25	26	28
Total displacement ('000 grt)	16.7	18.9	19.7

Source: Lloyd's Register-Fairplay, *World Fleet Statistics*.

International Sea-borne Freight Traffic
('000 metric tons)

	1994	1995	1996
Goods loaded	40,174	41,586	43,525
Goods unloaded	4,475	4,799	5,303

CIVIL AVIATION
(traffic on scheduled services)

	1997	1998	1999
Kilometres flown (million)	24	26	29
Passengers carried ('000)	1,507	1,590	1,768
Passenger-km (million)	3,055	3,257	3,295
Total ton-km (million)	374	404	427

Note: Figures include an apportionment (one-quarter) of the traffic of Gulf Air, a multinational airline with its headquarters in Bahrain.

Source: UN, *Statistical Yearbook*.

OMAN

Tourism

FOREIGN TOURIST ARRIVALS*

Country of nationality	1998	1999	2000
Bahrain	8,413	8,642	15,827
France	9,540	14,843	16,718
Germany	31,783	45,063	58,357
India	33,143	43,339	52,313
Netherlands	7,062	9,624	11,746
Philippines	3,506	4,752	12,704
Saudi Arabia	9,056	12,173	17,260
Switzerland	11,535	16,397	18,810
United Arab Emirates	30,373	33,862	55,984
United Kingdom	44,230	54,888	66,555
USA	13,918	18,456	26,789
Total (incl. others)	423,953	502,788	571,110

* Figures refer to international arrivals at hotels and similar establishments.

Source: World Tourism Organization, *Yearbook of Tourism Statistics*.

Tourism receipts (RO million): 43.2 in 1998; 40.4 in 1999; 45.7 in 2000 (Source: Directorate-General of Tourism).

Communications Media

	1999	2000	2001
Television receivers ('000 in use)	1,415	1,430	n.a.
Telephones ('000 main lines in use)	220.4	225.4	235.3
Mobile cellular telephones ('000 subscribers)	124.1	164.3	324.5
Personal computers ('000 in use)	65	80	85
Internet users ('000)	50	90	120
Daily newspapers (number)	5	5	5
Non-daily newspapers and other periodicals (number)	25	25	27

1996: Book production (first editions only) 7 titles.

1997 (number in use): Radio receivers 1,400,000; Facsimile machines 6,356.

Sources: mainly UNESCO, *Statistical Yearbook* and International Telecommunication Union.

Education

(2001/02)

	Institutions	Teachers	Pupils/Students Males	Females	Total
Pre-primary*	5	347	3,792	3,197	6,989
Primary	277†	8,417	122,546	114,358	236,904
Preparatory	497†	6,994	79,926	70,265	150,191
Secondary	177†	6,102	57,211	59,521	116,732
Higher*	n.a.	1,307	8,894	7,138	16,032
University	1	833‡	4,466	4,289	8,755

* Figures refer to 1997/98 (Source: UNESCO, *Statistical Yearbook*).
† Figure refers to 1998/99.
‡ Figure refers to 2000/01.

Adult literacy rate (UNESCO estimates): 71.7% (males 80.1%; females 61.6%) in 2000 (Source: UNDP, *Human Development Report*).

Directory

The Constitution

The Basic Statute of the State was promulgated by royal decree on 6 November 1996, as Oman's first document defining the organs and guiding principles of the State.

Chapter 1 defines the State and the system of government. Oman is defined as an Arab, Islamic and independent state with full sovereignty. Islamic law (*Shari'a*) is the basis for legislation. The official language is Arabic. The system of government is defined as Sultani (Royal), hereditary in the male descendants of Sayyid Turki bin Said bin Sultan. Article 6 determines the procedure whereby the Sultan is designated.

Chapter 2 defines the political, economic, social, cultural and security principles of the State. Article 11 (economic principles) includes the stipulation that 'All natural resources and revenues therefrom shall be the property of the State which will preserve and utilize them in the best manner taking into consideration the requirements of the State's security and the interests of the national economy'. The constructive and fruitful co-operation between public and private activity is stated to be the essence of the national economy. Public property is inviolable, and private ownership is safeguarded. Article 14 (security principles) provides for a Defence Council to preserve the safety and defence of the Sultanate.

Chapter 3 defines public rights and duties. Individual and collective freedoms are guaranteed within the limits of the law.

Chapter 4 concerns the Head of State, the Council of Ministers, Specialized Councils and financial affairs of the State. Article 41 defines the Sultan as Head of State and Supreme Commander of the Armed Forces. The article states that 'His person is inviolable. Respect for him is a duty and his command must be obeyed. He is the symbol of national unity and the guardian of its preservation and protection.' The Sultan presides over the Council of Ministers, or may appoint a person (Prime Minister) to preside on his behalf. Deputy Prime Ministers and other Ministers are appointed by the Sultan. The Council of Ministers and Specialized Councils assist the Sultan in implementing the general policy of the State.

Chapter 5 comprises a single Article (58). This states that the Council of Oman shall consist of the Majlis ash-Shoura (Consultative Council) and the Majlis ad-Dawlah (Council of State). The jurisdiction, terms, sessions, rules of procedure, membership and regulation of each shall be determined by the law.

Chapter 6 concerns the judiciary. Articles 59 and 60 state that the supremacy of the law shall be the basis of governance, and enshrine the dignity, integrity, impartiality and independence of the judiciary. Article 66 provides for a Supreme Council of the judiciary.

Chapter 7 defines the general provisions pertaining to the application of the Basic Statute.

The Government

HEAD OF STATE

Sultan: QABOOS BIN SAID AS-SAID (assumed power on 23 July 1970, after deposing his father).

COUNCIL OF MINISTERS
(April 2003)

Prime Minister and Minister of Foreign Affairs, Defence and Finance: Sultan QABOOS BIN SAID AS-SAID.

Deputy Prime Minister for the Council of Ministers: Sayyid FAHAD BIN MAHMOUD AS-SAID.

Personal Representative of the Sultan: Sayyid THUWAINI BIN SHIHAB AS-SAID.

Minister of National Economy, Supervisor of the Finance Ministry and Deputy Chairman of the Financial Affairs and Energy Resources Council: AHMAD BIN ABD AN-NABI MACKI.

Minister Responsible for Defence Affairs: Sayyid BADR BIN SAUD BIN HAREB.

Minister of Legal Affairs: MUHAMMAD BIN ALI BIN NASIR AL-ALAWI.

Minister of Oil and Gas: Dr MUHAMMAD BIN HAMAD BIN SAIF AR-RUMHI.

Minister of Justice: Sheikh MUHAMMAD BIN ABDULLAH BIN ZAHIR AL-HINAI.

Minister of Awqaf (Religious Endowments) and Religious Affairs: Sheikh ABDULLAH BIN MUHAMMAD BIN ABDULLAH AS-SALIMI.

Minister Responsible for Foreign Affairs: YOUSUF BIN AL-ALAWI BIN ABDULLAH.

Minister of Information: HAMAD BIN MUHAMMAD BIN MUHSIN AR-RASHIDI.

Minister of Housing, Electricity and Water: Sheikh SUHAIL BIN MUSTAHIL BIN SALEM BEIT SHAMMAS.

Minister of Education: YAHYA BIN SAUD BIN MANSOOR AS-SULAIMI.

Minister of Higher Education: YAHYA BIN MAHFOUZ AL-MANTHARI.

Minister of Social Development: Sheikh AMIR BIN SHUWAIN AL-HOSNI.

Minister of Labour: JUMA BIN ALI BIN JUMA.

Minister of Transport and Telecommunications: MALEK BIN SULAYMAN AL-MA'AMARI.

Minister of National Heritage and Culture: Sayyid HAITHAM BIN TARIQ BIN AS-SAID.

Minister of the Interior: Sayyid SAUD BIN IBRAHIM BIN SAUD AL-BUSAIDI.

Minister of Commerce and Industry: MAQBOOL BIN ALI BIN SULTAN.

Minister of Agriculture and Fisheries: Sheikh SALIM BIN HILAL AL-KHALILI.

Minister of Health: Dr ALI BIN MUHAMMAD BIN MOUSA AR-RAISI.

Minister of Regional Municipalities and the Environment: Dr KHAMIS BIN MUBARAK BIN ISA AL-ALAWI.

Minister of the Civil Service: Sheikh ABD AL-AZIZ BIN MATAR BIN SALIM AL-AZIZI.

Governor of Muscat and Minister of State: Sayyid AL-MUTASIM BIN HAMOUD AL-BUSAIDI.

Governor of Dhofar and Minister of State: Sheikh MUHAMMAD BIN ALI AL-QATABI.

Minister of the Diwan of the Royal Court: Sayyid ALI BIN HAMOUD BIN ALI AL-BUSAIDI.

Minister of the Palace Office and Head of the Office of the Supreme Commander of the Armed Forces: Maj-Gen. ALI BIN MAJID AL-MA'AMARI.

President of the Public Authority for Craft Industries with the rank of Minister: Sheikha AISHA BINT KHALFAN BIN JUMIEL AS-SIYABIAH.

MINISTRIES

Diwan of the Royal Court: POB 632, Muscat 113; tel. 738711; fax 739427; internet www.diwan.gov.om.

Ministry of Agriculture and Fisheries: POB 467, Ruwi 113; tel. 694182; fax 695909; internet www.maf.gov.om.

Ministry of Awqaf (Religious Endowments) and Religious Affairs: POB 354, Ruwi 112; tel. 697699; e-mail admin@mara.gov .om; internet www.mara.gov.om.

Ministry of the Civil Service: POB 3994, Ruwi 112; tel. 696000; fax 601365; internet www.omanmocs.gov.om.

Ministry of Commerce and Industry: POB 550, Muscat 113; tel. 774290; fax 7717238; e-mail minister@mocioman.gov.om; internet www.mocioman.gov.om.

Ministry of Defence: POB 113, Muscat 113; tel. 704096; fax 618205.

Ministry of Education: POB 3, Muscat 113; tel. 775334; fax 704465; e-mail info@edu.gov.om; internet www.edu.gov.om.

Ministry of Finance: POB 506, Muscat 113; tel. 738201; fax 737028; internet www.mof.gov.om.

Ministry of Foreign Affairs: POB 252, Muscat 113; tel. 699500; fax 699589.

Ministry of Health: POB 393, Muscat 113; tel. 602177; fax 601430; e-mail moh@moh.gov.om; internet www.moh.gov.om.

Ministry of Higher Education: POB 82, Ruwi 112; tel. 693148; internet www.mohe.gov.om.

Ministry of Housing, Electricity and Water: POB 1491, Ruwi 112; tel. 603906; fax 699180; internet www.mhew.gov.om.

Ministry of Information: POB 600, Muscat 113; tel. 603222; fax 601638; e-mail inform@omanet.com; internet www.omanet.com.

Ministry of the Interior: POB 127, Ruwi 112; tel. 602244; fax 696660.

Ministry of Justice: POB 354, Ruwi 112; tel. 697699; internet www.moj.gov.om.

Ministry of Legal Affairs: POB 578, Ruwi 112; tel. 605802.

Ministry of National Economy: POB 506, Muscat 113; tel. 698821; fax 698908; e-mail mone@omantel.net.om; internet www .moneoman.gov.om.

Ministry of National Heritage and Culture: POB 668, Muscat 113; tel. 602555; fax 602735; internet www.mnhc.gov.om.

Ministry of Oil and Gas: POB 551, Muscat 113; tel. 603333; fax 696972; internet www.mog.gov.om.

Ministry of the Palace Office: POB 2227, Ruwi 112; tel. 600841.

Ministry of Regional Municipalities and the Environment: POB 323, Muscat 113; tel. 696444; fax 602320.

Ministry of Social Affairs, Labour and Vocational Training: POB 560, Muscat 113; tel. 602444; fax 701515.

Ministry of Transport and Telecommunications: POB 338, Ruwi 112; tel. 697870; fax 696817; e-mail pttdiwan@omantel.net .om; internet www.comm.gov.om.

Ministry of Water Resources: POB 2575, Ruwi 112; tel. 703552; fax 701353; e-mail mwres@omantel.net.om.

COUNCIL OF OMAN

Majlis ash-Shoura
(Consultative Council)

President: Sheikh ABDULLAH BIN ALI AL-QATABI.

The Majlis ash-Shoura was established by royal decree in November 1991. Initially, members of the Majlis were appointed by the Sultan from among nominees selected at national polls, but in the September 2000 elections, members were directly elected. Two representatives are appointed from four candidates in each *wilaya*(region) of more than 30,000 inhabitants, and one from two candidates in each *wilaya* of fewer than 30,000 inhabitants. Members of the Majlis are appointed for a single three-year term of office. The Majlis elected in September 2000 comprised 83 members. The Majlis is an advisory body, the duties of which include the review of all social and economic draft laws prior to their enactment; public-service ministries are required to submit reports and answer questions regarding their performance, plans and achievements. The President of the Majlis ash-Shoura is appointed by royal decree.

Majlis ad-Dawlah
(Council of State)

President: Sheikh HAMOUD BIN ABDULLAH AL-HARITHI.

The Majlis ad-Dawlah was established in December 1997, in accordance with the terms of the Basic Statute of the State. It is also an advisory body, comprising 41 members appointed by the Sultan. Its function is to serve as a liaison between the government and the people of Oman. A new Majlis was appointed in October 2000.

Political Organizations

There are no political organizations in Oman.

Diplomatic Representation

EMBASSIES IN OMAN

Algeria: POB 216, Muscat 115; tel. 601698; fax 694419; e-mail algeria@omantel.net.om; Ambassador CHÉRIF DERBAL.

Austria: Moosa Complex Bldg, No. 477, 2nd Floor, Way No. 3109, POB 2070, Ruwi 112; tel. 793135; fax 793669; e-mail aeiou@omantel .net.om; Ambassador Dr CLEMENS CORETH.

Bahrain: POB 66, Madinat Qaboos, Al-Khuwair; tel. 605912; fax 605072; Chargé d'affaires AHMAD MUHAMMAD MAHMOUD.

Bangladesh: POB 3959, Ruwi 112; tel. 707462; fax 708495; Ambassador AMIN AHMED CHOWDHURY.

Brunei: POB 91, Ruwi 112; tel. 603533; fax 693014; Ambassador Pehin Dato' Haji MAHDINI.

China, People's Republic: Shati al-Qurum, Way No. 3017, House No. 1368, POB 315, Muscat 112; tel. 696698; fax 602322; Ambassador ZHAO XUECHANG.

Egypt: Diplomatic City, Al-Khuwair, POB 2252, Ruwi 112; tel. 600411; fax 603626; e-mail egyembmuscat@hotmail.com; Ambassador HANI RIAD ALI.

France: Diplomatic City, Al-Khuwair, POB 208, Madinat Qaboos 115; tel. 681800; fax 681843; e-mail diplofr1@omantel.net.om; internet www.ambafrance-om.org; Ambassador MICHEL TOURAINE.

Germany: POB 128, Ruwi 112; tel. 7732482; fax 7735690; e-mail diplofrg@omantel.net.om; Ambassador HARTMUT BLANKENSTEIN.

India: POB 1727, Ruwi 112; tel. 7714120; fax 7717503; e-mail indiamct@omantel.net.om; internet www.indemb-oman.org; Ambassador SATNAM JIT SINGH.

Iran: Madinat Qaboos East, Dal, POB 3155, Ruwi 112; tel. 696944; fax 696888; Ambassador NEMATOLLAH IAZDI.

Iraq: POB 262, Way 1737, House No. 2803, Ruwi 112; tel. 604178; fax 605112; Ambassador KHALID ABDULLAH SALEH AS-SAMIRA'I.

Italy: Qurum Area 5, Way No. 2411, House No. 842, POB 3727, Ruwi 112; tel. 564838; fax 564846; e-mail ambmasc@hotmail.net .om; Ambassador Dr MARIO QUAGLIOTTI.

Japan: Shati al-Qurum, POB 3511, Ruwi 112; tel. 601028; fax 698720; Ambassador ZENJI KAMINAGA.

Jordan: Diplomatic City, Al-Khuwair, POB 70, Al-Adhaiba 130; tel. 692760; fax 692762; e-mail embhkjom@omantel.net.om; Ambassador NABIL ALI BARTO.

Korea, Republic: POB 377, 115 Madinat Qaboos; tel. 691490; fax 691495; e-mail depkomct@omantel.net.om; Ambassador LEE YONG-HYUN.

Kuwait: Diplomatic City, Al-Khuwair, Block No. 13, POB 1798, Ruwi 112; tel. 699626; fax 600972; Ambassador ABD AL-MOHSIN SALIM AL-HAROUN.

Malaysia: Shati al-Qurum, Villa 1611, Way 3019, POB 3939, Ruwi 112; tel. 698329; fax 605031; e-mail mwmuscat@omantel.net.om; Ambassador Dato' MOHAMED ROZE BIN ABDUL RAHMAN.

Morocco: Al-Ensharah Street, Villa No. 197, POB 3125, Ruwi 112; tel. 696152; fax 601114; Ambassador ALAOUI M'HAMDI MUSTAPHA.

Netherlands: Shati al-Qurum, Way 3017, Villa 1366, POB 3302, Ruwi 112; tel. 603706; fax 603778; e-mail nethmus@omantel.net.om; internet www.nlembassyoman.org; Ambassador G. J. VAN EPEN.

Pakistan: POB 1302, Ruwi 112; tel. 603090; fax 697462; e-mail parepmct@omantel.net.om; internet www.pakemboman.ejb.net; Ambassador KARAM ELAHI.

Philippines: POB 420, Madinat Qaboos 115; tel. 605140; fax 605176; e-mail aasakkam@omantel.net.om; Ambassador AKMAD A. SAKKAM.

Qatar: Jameat ad-Duwal al-Arabiya Street, Diplomatic City, Al-Khuwair, POB 802, Muscat 113; tel. 691152; Ambassador SAAD NASSER AL-HOMIDI.

Russia: Shati al-Qurum Way 3032, Surfait Compound, POB 80, Ruwi 112; tel. 602894; fax 604189; Ambassador ALEKSANDR K. PATSEV.

Saudi Arabia: Diplomatic Area, Jamiat ad-Dowal al-Arabiya St, POB 1411, Ruwi 112; tel. 601744; fax 603540; e-mail omemb@mofa .gov.sa; Ambassador AHMAD ALI AL-KAHTANI.

Somalia: Mumtaz Street, Villa Hassan Jumaa Baker, POB 1767, Ruwi 112; tel. 564412; fax 564965; Ambassador MUHAMMAD SUBAN NUR.

Sri Lanka: POB 95, Madinat Qaboos 115; tel. 697841; fax 697336; e-mail lankaemb@omantel.net.om; Ambassador (vacant).

Sudan: Diplomatic City, Al-Khuwair, POB 3971, Ruwi 112; tel. 697875; fax 699065; Ambassador ABD AL-AZIZ MARHOUM AHMAD.

Syria: Madinat Qaboos, Al-Ensharah Street, Villa No. 201, POB 85, Muscat 115; tel. 697904; fax 603895; Chargé d'affaires ANWAR WEBBI.

Thailand: Villa No. 33–34, Madinat Qaboos East, POB 60, Ruwi 115; tel. 602684; fax 605714; Ambassador PENSAK CHARALAK.

Tunisia: Al-Ensharah Street, Way No. 1507, POB 220, Muscat 115; tel. 603486; fax 697778; Ambassador HATEM ESSAIEM.

Turkey: Bldg No. 3270, Street No. 3042, Shati al-Qurum, POB 47, Mutrah 113; tel. 697050; fax 697053; e-mail turemmus@omantel.net .om; internet www.turkishembassymuscat.org; Ambassador N. MURAT ERSAVCI.

United Arab Emirates: Diplomatic City, Al-Khuwair, POB 551, Muscat 111; tel. 600302; fax 604182; Ambassador HAMAD HELAL THABIT AL-KUWAITI.

United Kingdom: POB 300, Muscat 113; tel. 693077; fax 693087; e-mail enquiries.muscat@fco.gov.uk; internet www.uk.gov.om; Ambassador J. STUART LAING.

USA: Diplomatic City, POB 202, Muscat 115; tel. 698989; fax 699771; e-mail aemctric@omantel.net.om; internet www.usa.gov .om; Ambassador RICHARD L. BALTIMORE, III.

Yemen: Shati al-Qurum, Area 258, Way No. 2840, Bldg No. 2981, POB 105, Madinat Qaboos 115; tel. 600815; fax 605008; Ambassador AHMAD DAIFALLAH AL-AZEIB.

Judicial System

Oman's Basic Statute guarantees the independence of the judiciary. The foundation for the legal system is *Shari'a* (Islamic law), which is the basis for family law, dealing with matters such as inheritance and divorce. Separate courts have been established to deal with commercial disputes and other matters to which *Shari'a* does not apply.

Courts of the First Instance are competent to try cases of criminal misdemeanour; serious crimes are tried by the Criminal Courts; the Court of Appeal is in Muscat. There are district courts throughout the country. Special courts deal with military crimes committed by members of the armed and security forces.

The Basic Statute provides for a Supreme Council to supervise the proper functioning of the courts.

An Administrative Court, to review the decisions of government bodies, was instituted in April 2001.

The office of Public Prosecutor was established in 1999 and the first such appointment was made in June 2001.

Religion

ISLAM

The majority of the population (estimated at 53.5% in 1994) are Muslims, of whom approximately three-quarters are of the Ibadi sect and about one-quarter are Sunni Muslims.

HINDUISM

According to 1994 estimates, 28.0% of the population are Hindus.

CHRISTIANITY

It was estimated that in 1994 14.7% of the population were Christians.

Protestantism

The Protestant Church in Oman: POB 1982, Ruwi 112; tel. 702372; fax 789943; e-mail pcomct@omantel.net.om; internet www .pcomct.com; joint chaplaincy of the Anglican Church and the Reformed Church of America; four inter-denominational churches in Oman, at Ruwi and Ghala in Muscat, at Sohar and at Salalah; Senior Chaplain Rev. JOHN ALDIS.

The Roman Catholic Church

A small number of adherents, mainly expatriates, form part of the Apostolic Vicariate of Arabia. The Vicar Apostolic is resident in the United Arab Emirates.

The Press

Article 31 of Oman's Basic Statute guarantees the freedom of the press, printing and publishing, according to the terms and conditions specified by the law. Published matter 'leading to discord, harming the State's security or abusing human dignity or rights' is prohibited.

NEWSPAPERS

Oman Daily Newspaper: POB 3303, Ruwi 112; tel. 701555; e-mail editor@omandaily.com; internet www.omandaily.com; daily; Arabic; Editor-in-Chief HABIB MUHAMMAD NASIB; circ. 15,560.

Ash-Shabibah: POB 3303, 112 Ruwi; tel. 795373; fax 796711; daily; Arabic; culture, leisure and sports.

Al-Watan (The Nation): POB 643, Muscat 113; tel. 591919; fax 591280; e-mail alwatan@omantel.net.om; internet www.alwatan .com; f. 1971; daily; Arabic; Editor-in-Chief MUHAMMAD BIN SULAYMAN AT-TAI; circ. 40,000.

English Language

Khaleej Times: POB 3305, Ruwi 112; tel. 700895; fax 706512; Reg. Man. SANKAR NARAYAN.

Oman Daily Observer: POB 3303, Ruwi 112; tel. 703055; fax 790524; e-mail editor@omanobserver.com; internet www .omanobserver.com; f. 1981; daily; publ. by Oman Newspaper House; Chair. SULTAN BIN HAMAD BIN SAUD; Editor SAID BIN KHALFAN AL-HARTHI; circ. 22,000.

Times of Oman: POB 3770, Ruwi 112; tel. 701953; fax 799153; e-mail times@omantel.net.om; internet www.omantimes.com; f. 1975; daily; Founder, Propr and Editor-in-Chief MUHAMMAD AZ-ZED-JALI; Man. Dir ANIS BIN ESSA AZ-ZEDJALI; circ. 21,000.

PERIODICALS

Al-Adwaa' (Lights): POB 580, 113 Muscat; tel. 704353; fax 798187; weekly; Arabic; economic, political and social; Editor-in-Chief HABIB MUHAMMAD NASIB; circ. 15,600.

Al-'Akidah (The Faith): POB 1001, 112 Ruwi; tel. 701000; fax 709917; weekly illustrated magazine; Arabic; political; Editor SAID AS-SAMHAN AL-KATHIRI; circ. 10,000.

Business Today: Apex Press and Publishing, POB 2616, Ruwi 112; tel. 799388; fax 793316; internet www.apexstuff.com; monthly; Editor MOHANA PRABHAKAR.

The Commercial: POB 2002, Ruwi 112; tel. 704022; fax 795885; e-mail omanad@omantel.net.om; f. 1978; monthly; Arabic and English; business news; Man. AYOOB CHANKALAN; Chief Editor HAMAD BIN AMIR AL-KASBI; circ. 7,000.

Al-Ghorfa (Oman Commerce): POB 1400, Ruwi 112; tel. 707674; fax 708497; e-mail pubrel@omanchamber.org; internet www .chamberoman.com; f. 1973; bi-monthly; English and Arabic; business; publ. by Oman Chamber of Commerce and Industry; Editor RASHID AHMAD AS-SAWAFI; circ. 10,500.

Jund Oman (Soldiers of Oman): POB 113, Muscat 113; tel. 613615; fax 613369; f. 1974; monthly; Arabic; illustrated magazine of the Ministry of Defence; Supervisor Chief of Staff of the Sultan's Armed Forces.

Al-Markazi (The Central): POB 1161, Ruwi 112; tel. 702222; fax 707913; f. 1975; bi-monthly economic magazine; English and Arabic; publ. by Central Bank of Oman.

Al-Mawared at-Tabeey'iyah (Natural Resources): POB 551, Muscat; publ. by Ministries of Agriculture and Fisheries and of Oil and Gas; monthly; English and Arabic; Editor KHALID AZ-ZUBAIDI.

Al-Mazari' (Farms): POB 467, Muscat; weekly journal of the Ministry of Agriculture and Fisheries; Editor KHALID AZ-ZUBAIDI.

An-Nahda (The Renaissance): POB 979, 113 Muscat; tel. 563104; fax 563106; weekly illustrated magazine; Arabic; political and social; Editor TALEB SAID AL-MEAWALY; circ. 10,000.

Oman Today: Apex Press and Publishing, POB 2616, Ruwi 112; tel. 799388; fax 793316; internet www.apexstuff.com; f. 1981; bi-monthly; English; leisure and sports; Editor EMMA VENTURA; circ. 20,000.

Al-Omaniya (Omani Woman): POB 3303, Ruwi 112; tel. 792700; fax 707765; monthly; Arabic; circ. 10,500.

Risalat al-Masjed (The Mosque Message): POB 6066, Muscat; tel. 561178; fax 560607; issued by Diwan of Royal Court Affairs Protocol Dept (Schools and Mosques Section); Editor JOUMA BIN MUHAMMAD BIN SALEM AL-WAHAIBI.

Ash-Shurta (The Police): Directorate of Public Relations, Royal Oman Police, POB 2, Muscat 113; tel. 569216; fax 562341; quarterly magazine of Royal Oman Police; Editor Director of Public Relations.

Al-Usra (The Family): POB 440, Mutrah 114; tel. 794922; fax 795348; e-mail admeds@omantel.net.om; f. 1974; fortnightly; Arabic; socio-economic illustrated magazine; Chief Editor SADEK ABDOWANI; circ. 15,000.

NEWS AGENCY

Oman News Agency: Ministry of Information, POB 3659, Ruwi 112; tel. 696970; e-mail info@omannews.com; internet www .omannews.com; f. 1986; Dir-Gen. MUHAMMAD BIN SALIM AL-MARHOON.

Publishers

Apex Press and Publishing: POB 2616, Ruwi 112; tel. 799388; fax 793316; internet www.apexstuff.com; f. 1980; art, history, trade directories, maps, leisure and business magazines, and guidebooks; Pres. SALEH M. TALIB AL-ZAKWANI; Editors MOHANA PRABHAKAR, ANDREA DIXON.

Arabian Distribution and Publishing Enterprise: Mutrah; tel. 707079.

Dar al-Usra: POB 440, Mutrah 114; tel. 794922; fax 795348; e-mail alusra@omantel.net.om.

Muscat Press and Publishing House SAOC: POB 3112, 112 Ruwi; tel. 795373; fax 796711.

National Publishing and Advertising LLC: POB 3112, Ruwi 112; tel. 793098; fax 708445; e-mail npanet@usa.net; f. 1987; Man. ASHOK SUVARNA.

Oman Establishment for Press, Printing and Publishing: POB 463, 113 Muscat; tel. 591919; fax 591280; Chair. SULTAN BIN HAMAD BIN SAUD; Editor-in-Chief SAID BIN KHALFAN EL-HARTHY.

Oman Newspaper House: POB 3002, 112 Ruwi; tel. 701555; fax 790523; Dir ABD AL-WAHAB BIN NASSER AL-MANTHERI.

Oman Publishing House: POB 580, Muscat; tel. 704353.

Ash-Shahmi Publishers and Advertisers: POB 6112, Ruwi; tel. 703416.

Broadcasting and Communications

TELECOMMUNICATIONS

Regulatory Authority

Oman Telecommunications Regulatory Authority: Muscat; f. 2002 to oversee the privatization of OMANTEL (see below) and to set tariffs and regulate the sale of operating licences.

State-owned Company

Oman Telecommunications Company SAOC (OMANTEL): POB 789, Ruwi 112; tel. 631417; fax 697066; e-mail info@omantel .net.om; internet www.omantel.net.om; f. 1999 as successor to the General Telecommunications Organization (GTO), to facilitate transfer to private ownership; Chair. MALEK BIN SULAYMAN AL-MA'AMARI; Exec. Pres. Eng. MUHAMMAD BIN ALI AL-WAHAIBI.

BROADCASTING

Radio

Radio Sultanate of Oman: Ministry of Information, POB 600, Muscat 113; tel. 603222; fax 601393; e-mail omanfm@omanet.com; internet www.oman-radio.gov.om; f. 1970; transmits in Arabic 20 hours daily, English on FM 15 hours daily; Dir-Gen. ALI BIN ABDULLAH AL-MUJENI.

Radio Salalah: f. 1970; transmits daily programmes in Arabic and the Dhofari languages; Dir MUHAMMAD BIN AHMAD AR-ROWAS.

The British Broadcasting Corpn (BBC) has built a powerful medium-wave relay station on Masirah island. It is used to expand and improve the reception of the BBC's Arabic, Farsi, Hindi, Pashtu and Urdu services.

Television

Sultanate of Oman Television: Ministry of Information, POB 600, Muscat 113; tel. 603222; fax 605032; internet www.oman-tv.gov .om; began broadcasting in 1974; programmes broadcast via Arabsat and Nilesat satellite networks.

Finance

(cap. = capital; res = reserves; dep. = deposits; m. = million; brs = branches; amounts in rials Omani unless otherwise stated)

BANKING

In March 2002 there were 15 commercial banks (six local and nine foreign) and three specialized banks, with a total network of 363 domestic branch offices operating throughout Oman. Legislation introduced in January 2001 increased the minimum capital requirement for Omani commercial banks from RO 10m. to RO 20m., and set a minimum capital requirement of RO 3m. for foreign banks established in Oman.

Central Bank

Central Bank of Oman: POB 1161, Ruwi 112; tel. 702222; fax 702253; e-mail cboresb@omantel.net.om; internet www.cbo-oman .org; f. 1974; cap. 250.0m., res 322.7m., dep. 149.9m. (Dec. 2001); a royal decree issued in July 2002 increased the bank's capital to 300.0m. 100% state-owned; Exec. Pres. HAMOUD SANGOUR AZ-ZADJALI; 2 brs.

Commercial Banks

Bank Dhofar al-Omani al-Fransi SAOG: POB 1507, Ruwi 112; tel. 790466; fax 797246; e-mail info@bankdhofar.com; internet www.bankdhofar.com; f. 1990; cap. 33.6m., res 8.5m., dep. 283.4m. (Dec. 2001); Chair. Eng. ABD AL-HAFIDH SALIM RAJAB AL-AUJAILI; Gen. Man. AHMAD BIN ALI ASH-SHANFARI; 21 brs.

BankMuscat SAOG: POB 134, Ruwi 112; tel. 703044; fax 707806; e-mail banking@bkmuscat.com; internet www.bankmuscat.com; f. 1993 by merger as Bank Muscat Al-Ahli Al-Omani; renamed Bank Muscat International in 1998, and as above in 1999; merged with Commercial Bank of Oman Ltd SAOG in 2000 and with Industrial Bank of Oman in 2002; 89.6% owned by Omani shareholders; cap. 45.5m., res 80.8m., dep. 1,084.7m. (Dec. 2001); Chair. ABD AL-MALEK BIN ABDULLAH AL-KHALILI; CEO ABD AR-RAZAK ALI ISSA; 95 brs.

Majan International Bank SAOC: POB 2717, Ruwi 112; tel. 780388; fax 780643; e-mail majanbk@omantel.net.om; internet www.majanbank.com; f. 1998; incorporated three branches of Habib Bank AG Zurich; cap. 29.4m., res. 3.1m., dep. 101.0m. (Dec. 2001); Chair. Sheikh ADIL SAID ASH-SHANFARI; Gen. Man. SALAAM SAID ASH-SHAKSY; 6 brs.

National Bank of Oman SAOG (NBO): POB 751, Ruwi 112; tel. 708894; fax 707781; e-mail info@nbo.co.om; internet www.nbo.co.om; f. 1973; 100% Omani-owned; cap. 45.8m., res 50.2m., dep. 800.8m. (Dec. 2001); Chair. KHALFAN BIN NASSER AL-WOHAIBI; CEO JOHN P. FINIGAN; 54 brs.

Oman Arab Bank SAOC: POB 2010, Ruwi 112; tel. 706265; fax 797736; e-mail arabbank@omantel.om; internet www.omanab.com; f. 1984; purchased Omani European Bank SAOG in 1994; 51% Omani-owned, 49% by Arab Bank PLC (Jordan); cap. 22.0m., res 13.4m., dep. 271.4m. (Dec. 2001); Chair. RASHAD MUHAMMAD AZ-ZUBAIR; CEO ABD AL-QADER ASKALAN; 40 brs.

Oman International Bank SAOG: POB 1727, Muscat 111; tel. 682500; fax 682800; e-mail oibintl@omantel.net.om; internet www.oiboman.com; f. 1984; 100% Omani-owned; cap. 62.9m., res 21.9m., dep. 489.5m. (Dec. 2001); Chair. REEM OMAR ZAWAWI; CEO JOHN CARLOUGH; 82 brs.

Foreign Banks

Bank of Baroda (India): POB 231, Mutrah 114; tel. 714559; fax 714560; e-mail barbmust@omantel.net.om; internet www.bankofbaroda.com; f. 1976; Gen. Man. G. C. SHARMA; 3 brs.

Bank Melli Iran: POB 2643, Ruwi 112; tel. 7715160; fax 7715183; f. 1974; Gen. Man. ALI JAFFARI LOFTI.

Bank Saderat Iran: POB 1269, Ruwi 112; tel. 7733923; fax 7736478; e-mail bsimct@omantel.net.om; Gen. Man. MAHDI NALAEI.

Banque Banorabe (France): POB 1608, Ruwi 112; tel. 704274; fax 707782; f. 1982; fmrly Banque de l'Orient Arabe et d'Outre Mer; Man. (Oman) WALID G. HAJJAR.

Citibank NA (USA): POB 1994, Mutrah 114; tel. 795705; fax 795724; f. 1975; Vice-Pres. and Country Man. ZULFIQUAR ALI SULAYMAN.

Habib Bank Ltd (incorporated in Pakistan): POB 1326, Ruwi 112; tel. 7717139; fax 7715809; e-mail hbloman1@omantel.net.om; f. 1972; Exec. Vice-Pres. and Country Man. JAVED Z. KARIM; 13 brs.

HSBC Bank Middle East (United Kingdom): POB 234, Muscat 113; tel. 736041; fax 736043; f. 1948; CEO (vacant); 4 brs.

Standard Chartered Bank (UK): POB 2353, Ruwi 112; tel. 703999; fax 796864; internet www.standardchartered.com/om; f. 1968; Man. SAID SALIM AL-MUBARAK KUKOOR; 4 brs.

Development Banks

Alliance Housing Bank: POB 545, Mina al-Fahal 116; tel. 568845; fax 568001; e-mail info@alliance-housing.com; internet www.alliance-housing.com; f. 1997; state-owned; cap. 21.0m., res 3.2m., dep. 5.9m. (June 2002); Chair. AHMAD BIN SUWAIDAN AL-BALUSHI; Gen. Man. LAURIE COWELL; 7 brs.

Oman Development Bank SAOG: POB 309, Muscat 113; tel. 7712507; fax 7713100; e-mail odebe@omantel.net.om; f. 1977; absorbed Oman Bank for Agriculture and Fisheries in 1997; short-, medium- and long-term finance for development projects in industry, agriculture and fishing; state-owned; cap. 20.0m., res 0.4m., dep. 46.3m. (Dec. 2001); Chair. Sheikh YACOUB BIN HAMAD AL-HARTHY; Gen. Man. MURTADHA BIN MUHAMMAD FADHIL; 9 brs.

Oman Housing Bank SAOC: POB 2555, Ruwi 112; tel. 704444; fax 704071; f. 1977; long-term finance for housing development; 100% state-owned; cap. 30.0m., res 24m., dep. 31m. (1999); Chair. DARWISH ISMAIL ALI AL-BULUSHI; Gen. Man. ADNAN HAIDAR DARWISH AZ-ZA'ABI; 9 brs.

STOCK EXCHANGE

Muscat Securities Market: POB 3265, Muscat 112; tel. 7712607; fax 7716353; e-mail info@msm.gov.om; internet www.msm.gov.om; f. 1989; Dir-Gen. (acting) SULAYMAN BIN MUHAMMAD AR-RASHIDY.

Supervisory Body

Capital Markets Authority (CMA): POB 3359, Ruwi 112; tel. 7712722; fax 7716266; f. 2000 to regulate stock exchange; Exec. Pres. YAHYA BIN SAID ABDULLAH AL-JABRI.

INSURANCE

In 2000 there were 17 licensed insurance companies operating in Oman. Of these, seven were local firms and the remainder were branches of non-resident companies.

Al-Ahlia Insurance Co SAO: POB 1463, 112 Ruwi; tel. 709331; fax 797151; e-mail aicinsur@omantel.net.om; f. 1985; cap. 2.5m. Chair. ADEL ABDULLAH AR-RAISI; Gen. Man. G. V. RAO.

Dhofar Insurance Co SAOG: POB 1002, 112 Ruwi; tel. 705305; fax 793641; Gen. Man. TAHER AL-HERAKI.

Al-Ittihad al-Wattani: POB 2279, 112 Ruwi; tel. 700715; fax 705595; Area Man. GEORGE A. CHIDIAC.

Muscat Insurance Co SAOG: POB 72, 112 Ruwi; tel. 695897; fax 695847; e-mail mic@omzest.com; Gen. Man. MALCOLM A. JACK.

National Life Insurance Co SAOC: POB 798, 117 Wadi Kabir; tel. 567125; fax 567124; e-mail natlife@omantel.net.om; internet www.nlicgulf.com; Gen. Man. ANDREW BENSON.

Oman National Insurance Co SAOG (ONIC): POB 2254, Ruwi; tel. 795020; fax 702569; f. 1978; cap. 2m. Chair. SALIM BIN HASSAN MACKI; Gen. Man. MICHAEL J. ADAMS.

Oman United Insurance Co SAOG: POB 1522, Ruwi 112; tel. 703990; fax 796327; e-mail ouinsco@omantel.net.om; internet www.ouholding.com; f. 1985; cap. 2m. Chair. SAID SALIM BIN NASSIR AL-BUSAIDI; Gen. Man. KHALID MANSOUR HAMED.

Trade and Industry

GOVERNMENT AGENCY

Omani Centre for Investment Promotion and Export Development (OCIPED): POB 25, Al-Wadi Kabir 117, Muscat; tel. 7712344; fax 7710890; e-mail info@ociped.com; internet www.ociped.com; f. 1996; promotes investment in Oman and the development of non-oil Omani exports; Dir-Gen. (Investment Promotion) MALAK AHMAD ASH-SHAIBANI; Dir-Gen. (Export Development) MEHDI BIN ALI BIN JUMA.

CHAMBER OF COMMERCE

Oman Chamber of Commerce and Industry: POB 1400, Ruwi 112; tel. 707684; fax 708497; e-mail pubrel@omanchamber.org; internet www.chamberoman.com; f. 1973; Pres. Sheikh ABDULLAH BIN SALIM AR-RAWAS; 100,000 mems (2001).

STATE HYDROCARBONS COMPANIES

National Gas Co SAOG: POB 95, CPO Seeb Airport; tel. 626073; fax 626307; f. 1979; bottling of liquefied petroleum gas; Gen. Man. P. K. BAGCHI; 83 employees.

Oman Gas Co (OGC): Muscat; f. 1999; 80% government-owned, 20% Oman Oil Co; to operate gas network and build pipelines to supply power plants in Salalah and Sohar; Chair. SARHAN SARHANI; Vice-Chair. SALIM BIN MUHAMMAD BIN SHABAAN AL-OJAILY.

Oman LNG LLC: POB 560, 116 Mina al-Fahal; tel. 707807; fax 707656; internet www.oman-lng.com; f. 1992; 51% state-owned; manages 6,600 tons-per-year liquefied natural gas plant at Qalhat; manufacturing, shipping and marketing; Chair. SALIM BIN MUHAMMAD BIN SHABAAN AL-OJAILY; CEO and Gen. Man. Dr AGNUS CASSENS.

Oman Oil Co SAOC (OOC): POB 261, al-Harthy Complex, Ruwi 118; tel. 567392; fax 567386; e-mail oman-oil@oman-oil.com; internet www.oman-oil.com; f. late 1980s to invest in foreign commercial enterprises and oil trading operations; 100% state-owned; Chair. MAQBOOL BIN ALI BIN SULTAN; CEO DAVID C. DOUGLAS.

Oman Refinery Co LLC: POB 3568, Ruwi 112; tel. 561200; fax 561384; e-mail orc.oman1@omantel.net.om; production of light petroleum products; Man. Dir KAZUTOSHI SHIMMURO; 298 employees.

Petroleum Development Oman LLC (PDO): POB 81, Muscat 113; tel. 678111; fax 677106; internet www.pdo.co.om; incorporated in Sultanate of Oman since 1980 by royal decree as limited liability co; 60% owned by Oman Govt, 34% by Shell; production (2000) averaged 840,000 b/d from 100 fields, linked by a pipeline system to terminal at Mina al-Fahal, near Muscat; production averaged 834,000 b/d in 2001; Man. Dir JOHN MALCOLM.

UTILITIES

As part of its privatization programme, the Omani Government is divesting the utilities on a project-by-project basis. Private investors have already been found for several municipal waste water projects, desalination plants and regional electricity providers. Listed below are the state agencies currently responsible for each utility.

Ministry of Housing, Electricity and Water: (see The Government); plans and supervises the development of the utilities in Oman.

Electricity

Oman National Electric Co SAO: POB 1393, 112 Ruwi; tel. 796353; fax 704420; f. 1978; Chair. HAMOUD BIN SONGOR BIN HASHIM; Gen. Man. M. OSMAN BAIG.

Water

Ministry of Water Resources: (see The Government); to assess, manage, develop and conserve water resources.

Transport

ROADS

A network of adequate graded roads links all the main centres of population and only a few mountain villages are inaccessible by off-road vehicles. In 1996 there were an estimated 32,800 km of roads, of which 550 km were motorways, 2,160 km national roads and 3,720 km secondary roads. There were 8,477 km of asphalt roads in 2000. In that year contracts were awarded for the construction of around 700 km of new roads in central Oman.

Directorate-General of Roads: POB 7027, Mutrah; tel. 701577; Dir-Gen. of Roads Sheikh MUHAMMAD BIN HILAL AL-KHALILI.

Oman National Transport Co SAOG: POB 620, Muscat; tel. 590046; fax 590152; operates local, regional and long-distance bus services from Muscat; Chair. TARIQ BIN MUHAMMAD AMIN AL-MANTHERI; Man. Dir SULAYMAN BIN MUHANA AL-ADAWI.

SHIPPING

Port Sultan Qaboos (Mina Sultan Qaboos), at the entrance to the Persian (Arabian) Gulf, was built in 1974 to provide nine deep-water berths varying in length from 250 ft to 750 ft (76 m to 228 m), with draughts of up to 43 ft (13 m), and three berths for shallow-draught vessels drawing 12 ft to 16 ft (3.7 m to 4.9 m) of water. A total of 12 new berths have been opened and two of the existing berths have been upgraded to a container terminal capable of handling 60 containers per hour. The port also has a 3,000-ton-capacity cold store which belongs to the Oman Fisheries Co. In the 1990s Port Sultan Qaboos underwent a further upgrade and expansion. In 2001 1,384 ships visited the port and 2.2m. tons of cargo were handled.

The oil terminal at Mina al-Fahal can also accommodate the largest super-tankers on offshore loading buoys. Similar facilities for the import of refined petroleum products exist at Mina al-Fahal. Mina Raysut, near Salalah (now known as Salalah port), has been developed into an all-weather port, and, in addition to container facilities, has four deep-water berths and two shallow berths. In November 1998 the first phase of the Salalah port container terminal opened; phase two was completed in 1999. Salalah port is currently undergoing transformation into a free-trade zone. During 2001 591 ships called at the port. In 2002 the port handled a reported 1.2m. 20-ft equivalent units (TEU). Loading facilities for smaller craft exist at Sohar and Khasab (both of which are being expanded), Khaboura, Sur, Marbet, Ras al-Had, Al-Biaa, Masirah and Salalah.

Directorate General of Ports and Maritime Affairs: POB 684, 113 Ruwi; tel. 700986; fax 702044; e-mail dgpma@omantel.net.om; Dir-Gen. Eng. JAMAL T. AZIZ.

Port Services Corporation SAOG: POB 133, Muscat 113; tel. 714001; fax 714007; e-mail pscco@omantel.net.om; f. 1976; cap. RO 7.2m. jointly owned by the Govt of Oman and private shareholders; Exec. Pres. SAUD BIN AHMAD AN-NAHARI.

Salalah Port Services Co (SPS): POB 105, 118 Muscat; tel. 567188; fax 567166; e-mail mktg@salalahport.com; internet www .salalahport.com; port authority for Salalah port; CEO and Gen. Man. JACK HELTON.

CIVIL AVIATION

Domestic and international flights operate from Seeb International Airport. In 2001 some 2.7m. passengers passed through the airport; however, it is planned to increase annual passenger capacity to 12.5m. over a 25-year period. Seeb International Airport and Oman's second international airport, at Salalah (completed in 1978), are both earmarked for privatization. There are airports at Sur, Masirah, Khasab and Diba; most other sizeable towns have airstrips.

Directorate-General of Civil Aviation and Meteorology: POB 1, CPO Seeb Airport, 111 Muscat; tel. 519356; fax 519880; e-mail dgen@dgcam.com; internet www.dgcam.com.om; Dir-Gen. Eng. AHMAD BIN SAID BIN SALIM AR-RAWAHY.

Gulf Air: POB 138, Bahrain; tel. 531166; fax 530385; internet www .gulfairco.com; f. 1950 as Gulf Aviation Co; name changed 1974; jointly owned by the Govts of Bahrain, Oman and Abu Dhabi (UAE); international services to destinations in Europe, the USA, Africa, the Middle East, the Far East and Australasia; Chair. Sheikh HAMDAN BIN MUBARAK AN-NEHYAN; Pres. and CEO IBRAHIM ABDULLAH AL-HAMER.

Oman Aviation Services Co SAOG: POB 1058, Seeb International Airport; tel. 519223; fax 510805; internet www.oman-aviation .com; f. 1981; cap. RO 11m. 35% of shares owned by Govt, 65% by Omani nationals; air-charter, maintenance, handling and catering; operators of Oman's domestic airline (Oman Air); international services to Bangladesh, India, Kuwait, Pakistan, Qatar, Saudi Arabia, Sri Lanka and the UAE; Chair. ADEL BIN ABDULLAH AR-RAIMI; CEO ABD AR-RAHMAN AL-BUSAIDY; Gen. Man. ROBERT BURKE.

Tourism

Tourism, introduced in 1985, is strictly controlled. Oman's attractions, apart from the capital itself, include Nizwa, ancient capital of the interior, Dhofar and the forts of Nakhl, Rustaq, and Al-Hazm. The country also possesses an attractive and clean environment, including around 1,700 km of sandy beaches. The Government promotes, in a limited capacity, high-quality adventure, cultural and marine tourism. In 2000 there were 571,110 visitor arrivals in Oman, and tourism receipts for that year totalled RO 45.7m.

Directorate-General of Tourism: Ministry of Commerce and Industry, POB 550, Muscat 113; tel. 7716527; fax 7714436; e-mail dgt@mocioman.gov.om; internet www.mocioman.gov.om; Dir-Gen. MUHAMMAD ALI SAID.

PAKISTAN

Introductory Survey

Location, Climate, Language, Religion, Flag, Capital

The Islamic Republic of Pakistan lies in southern Asia, bordered by India to the east and by Afghanistan and Iran to the west. It has a short frontier with the People's Republic of China in the far north-east. The climate is dry and generally hot, with an average annual temperature of 27°C (80°F), except in the mountains, which have very cold winters. Temperatures in Karachi are generally between 13°C (55°F) and 34°C (93°F), with negligible rainfall. The principal languages are Punjabi (the language usually spoken in 48.2% of households in 1981), Pushto (Pashtu) (13.1%), Sindhi (11.8%) and Saraiki (9.8%). Urdu (7.6%) is the national language, and English is extensively used. The state religion is Islam, embracing about 97% of the population, the remainder being mainly Hindus or Christians. The national flag (proportions 2 by 3) has a vertical white stripe at the hoist, while the remainder is dark green, with a white crescent moon and a five-pointed star in the centre. The capital is Islamabad.

Recent History

Pakistan was created in August 1947 by the partition of the United Kingdom's former Indian Empire into the independent states of India and Pakistan, in response to demands by elements of the Muslim population in the subcontinent for the establishment of a specifically Islamic state. Pakistan originally comprised two distinct regions: East Pakistan and West Pakistan, separated by some 1,600 km (1,000 miles) of Indian territory, and united only by a common religion. Although the majority of the population lived in the smaller part, East Pakistan, political and military power was concentrated in the west, where the Muslim League was the dominant political movement. The leader of the Muslim League, Muhammad Ali Jinnah, popularly known as Quaid-i-Azam ('Great Leader'), became the first Governor-General of Pakistan but died in 1948. The country, formerly a dominion with the British monarch as Head of State, became a republic on 23 March 1956, when Pakistan's first Constitution was promulgated. At the same time Maj.-Gen. Iskander Mirza became Pakistan's first President.

Pakistan came under military rule in early October 1958, when President Mirza abrogated the Constitution, declared martial law, dismissed the national and provincial governments and dissolved all political parties. In late October, however, Gen. (later Field Marshal) Muhammad Ayub Khan, the Martial Law Administrator appointed by Mirza, removed Mirza from office and became President himself. Ayub Khan's autocratic but modernizing regime lasted until March 1969, when he was forced to resign following widespread unrest. Gen. Agha Muhammad Yahya Khan, the Commander-in-Chief of the Army, replaced him, and martial law was reimposed.

In December 1970 the country's first general election was held for a national assembly. Sheikh Mujibur Rahman's Awami League, which advocated autonomy for East Pakistan, won almost all the seats in the east (thus gaining an absolute majority in the National Assembly), while the Pakistan People's Party (PPP), led by Zulfikar Ali Bhutto, won a majority of seats in the west. Following the failure of negotiations to achieve a coalition government of the two parties, on 23 March 1971 East Pakistan declared its independence as the People's Republic of Bangladesh. Civil war immediately broke out, as Pakistani troops clashed with Bengali irregular forces. In December the Indian army intervened in the conflict to support the Bengalis, and the Pakistani army was forced to withdraw, thus permitting Bangladesh to establish firmly its independence. In the truncated Pakistan that remained in the west, Yahya Khan resigned, military rule was ended, and Bhutto became the new President.

A new Constitution, which came into effect in August 1973, provided for a parliamentary system of government. Bhutto became executive Prime Minister, while Fazal Elahi Chaudry, hitherto Speaker of the National Assembly, became constitutional President. The PPP won an overwhelming majority of seats in elections to the National Assembly in March 1977. However, the opposition Pakistan National Alliance (PNA) accused the PPP of widespread electoral malpractice and launched a nation-wide campaign of civil disobedience. An estimated 1,000 people died in subsequent clashes between troops and demonstrators, and some 40,000 people were arrested. Armed clashes were also reported between supporters of the PNA and the PPP. In July the armed forces intervened in the crisis: Bhutto was deposed in a bloodless military coup and a martial law regime was instituted, with Gen. Mohammad Zia ul-Haq, the Army Chief of Staff, as Chief Martial Law Administrator. President Chaudry remained in office as Head of State. Bhutto was subsequently charged with instigating the murder of a PPP dissident and a member of the dissident's family in 1974. He was sentenced to death in March 1978 and executed in April 1979, after the failure of an appeal to the Supreme Court on his behalf.

In September 1978 President Chaudry resigned and Gen. Zia became President. General elections were postponed several times by the military administration, and in October 1979 Gen. Zia announced an indefinite postponement of the polls. Opposition to the military regime was severely suppressed, particularly after new martial law orders were adopted in May 1980. In March 1981 nine political parties formed an opposition alliance, the Movement for the Restoration of Democracy (MRD), which advocated an end to military rule and a return to a parliamentary system of government. Several opposition politicians were subsequently interned or placed under house arrest. In August 1983 the MRD, led by the PPP, launched a civil disobedience campaign to press for the restoration of parliamentary democracy on the basis of the 1973 Constitution. The campaign enjoyed considerable support in Sindh province, where anti-Government protests resulted in numerous deaths. However, there was limited popular support elsewhere in the country, and the campaign ended in December 1983. Many political leaders and activists, including Benazir Bhutto (daughter of the former President and herself a leading PPP activist), were subsequently imprisoned or went into exile.

Gen. Zia's regime zealously pursued a policy of 'Islamization' of the country's institutions, including the enforcement of Islamic penal codes, and the introduction of Islamic economic principles, such as interest-free banking. In December 1984 a referendum was held, which sought affirmation of the Islamization process and, indirectly, endorsement of a further five-year term for Gen. Zia. The referendum was boycotted by the MRD, but, according to official figures, 98% of those participating supported the proposal. There were, however, widespread allegations of electoral malpractice.

In February 1985 a general election was held for a national assembly, followed shortly afterwards by elections to four provincial assemblies. The elections were held on a non-party basis, but widespread dissatisfaction with the regime was indicated by the defeat of several of Zia's cabinet ministers and close supporters. The largest two groupings in the new National Assembly were formed by a faction of the Pakistan Muslim League (PML, the successor to the Muslim League), known as the Pagara Group, and former members of the PPP. In late March Gen. Zia appointed Muhammad Khan Junejo, a member of the PML (Pagara Group), as Prime Minister, and an almost entirely civilian Cabinet was formed.

In October 1985 the National Assembly approved changes to the Constitution (the 'Eighth Amendment'), proposed by Gen. Zia, which introduced a powerful executive presidency and indemnified all actions of the military regime during the previous eight years. On 30 December Gen. Zia announced the repeal of martial law and the restoration of the Constitution (as amended in October). The military courts were dissolved, and military personnel were removed from civilian posts, with the exception of Gen. Zia, who remained as President and head of the armed forces. Junejo retained the post of Prime Minister in a new Cabinet. However, the MRD continued to demand the restoration of the unamended 1973 Constitution. In April 1986 its cause was strengthened by the return from exile of Benazir Bhutto, who travelled throughout the country holding political rallies which attracted thousands of supporters. She demanded the resignation of President Zia and the holding of a free general election, open to all political parties. In May Benazir Bhutto and her mother, Nusrat Bhutto, were elected as Co-Chairwomen of the PPP. In August the Government adopted a less tolerant approach towards the MRD by banning all rallies scheduled for Independence Day and by detaining hundreds of opposition members, including Benazir Bhutto. The arrests provoked violent anti-Government demonstrations in a number of cities.

In late 1986 violent clashes occurred in Karachi, Quetta and Hyderabad as a result of disputes between rival ethnic groups (primarily between the Pathans, originally from the North-West Frontier Province—NWFP—and Afghanistan, and the Urdu-speaking Mohajirs, who migrated from India when the subcontinent was partitioned in 1947). The violence was most severe in Karachi, where some 170 people were killed in December. The rise of ethnic communalism in Pakistan was reflected in the results of local elections held throughout the country in November 1987. The party of the Mohajirs, the Mohajir Qaumi Movement (MQM), won the majority of seats in Karachi and was also successful in other urban areas of Sindh province. Nationwide, the government-supported PML received the majority of votes, while the PPP won less than 20% of total seats.

In May 1988, in accordance with the authority vested in him through the Eighth Amendment, President Zia dismissed the Prime Minister and his Cabinet, and dissolved the National Assembly and the four provincial assemblies. Zia became head of an interim administration, which was to govern until a general election was held. In July Zia announced that the elections to the National Assembly and the provincial assemblies would be held in November. On 17 August 1988, however, President Zia was killed in an air crash in eastern Pakistan. Subsequent speculation that the cause of the crash was sabotage was not officially confirmed. The Chairman of the Senate, Ghulam Ishaq Khan, was appointed acting President, and an emergency National Council (composed of senior military officers, the four provincial governors and four federal ministers) was appointed to take charge of government.

Despite the imposition of a state of emergency after the death of Zia, the general election took place, as scheduled, in November 1988. In the elections to the National Assembly the PPP won 93 of the 207 directly-elective seats, and was the only party to secure seats in each of Pakistan's four provinces. The Islamic Democratic Alliance (IDA), a grouping of nine Islamic and right-wing parties (including the PML), gained 54 seats, with the remaining seats going to independents and candidates representing seven smaller parties. The PPP did not achieve such a high level of support, however, in the elections to the provincial assemblies, held three days later. The PPP was able to form coalition governments in Sindh and the NWFP, but the IDA took power in Punjab, the most populous province. At the federal level, a coalition Government was formed by the PPP and the MQM, which together had a working majority in the National Assembly (the MQM had 14 seats). Benazir Bhutto, the leader of the PPP, was appointed Prime Minister on 1 December, thus becoming the first female leader of a Muslim country. The state of emergency was repealed on the same day. A new Cabinet was formed, and later in December an electoral college (comprising the Senate, the National Assembly and the four provincial assemblies) elected Ghulam Ishaq Khan as President.

Benazir Bhutto's attempts, in early 1989, to repeal the Eighth Amendment to the Constitution, which severely constrained her powers as Prime Minister, were unsuccessful. Moreover, the fragile coalitions that the PPP had formed in the provincial assemblies soon came under pressure. In April the coalition Government formed by the PPP and the Awami National Party (ANP) in the NWFP collapsed. In May the coalition with the MQM in Sindh province also failed, following renewed ethnic conflict in the region. In the same month the opposition was strengthened by the formation of an informal parliamentary grouping, the Combined Opposition Party (COP), comprising the IDA, the ANP, the Jamiat-e-Ulema-e-Islam (JUI) and the Pakistan Awami Ittehad. In October the Government suffered a serious reversal when the MQM withdrew its parliamentary support for the PPP and transferred it to the opposition, claiming that the PPP had failed to honour any of the promises made in the original co-operation agreement between the two parties. In November a parliamentary motion of 'no confidence', proposed by the COP against the Government, was narrowly defeated. In January 1990 the COP organized a campaign to undermine the Government, accusing it of corruption, political bribery and mismanagement. Rallies and demonstrations in

Sindh province culminated in violence between supporters of the PPP and the MQM; in May about 100 people were killed during violent clashes between police and demonstrators in the region. Calm was temporarily restored by the deployment of army units.

By mid-1990 the initial popularity of the PPP Government appeared to have declined considerably: the maintenance of law and order had worsened; no significant new legislation had been introduced; the economic situation was deteriorating; and there were widespread allegations of corruption against high-ranking officials. On 6 August the President, in accordance with his constitutional powers, dissolved the National Assembly, dismissed the Prime Minister and her Cabinet and declared a state of emergency. He also announced that a general election would take place in late October. The President alleged that the ousted Government had violated the Constitution, accusing it of corruption, nepotism and incompetence. Ghulam Mustafa Jatoi, the leader of the COP in the National Assembly, was appointed acting Prime Minister in an interim Government. The four provincial assemblies were also dissolved, and 'caretaker' Chief Ministers appointed. Benazir Bhutto claimed that the dissolution of her administration was illegal and strongly denied the various charges made against her Government. At the end of August several of Benazir Bhutto's former ministers were arrested, and in the following month she herself was indicted on more than 10 charges of corruption and abuse of power. In early October Benazir Bhutto's husband, Asif Ali Zardari, was arrested on charges of extortion, kidnapping and financial irregularities (he was later acquitted on all counts).

At the general election, which took place, as scheduled, on 24 October 1990, the IDA doubled its representation in the National Assembly, leaving it only four seats short of an absolute majority, while the People's Democratic Alliance (PDA, an electoral alliance comprising the PPP and three smaller parties) suffered a heavy defeat. Support for the PPP also declined in the provincial elections, where it unexpectedly lost control of its traditional stronghold in Sindh and fared badly elsewhere. Regional and ethnic parties continued to expand their influence, notably the MQM in urban areas of Sindh, and the ANP in the NWFP. On 6 November Mohammad Nawaz Sharif, the leader of the IDA and the former Chief Minister of Punjab, was elected as the new Prime Minister. He officially ended the three-month-long state of emergency, and appointed a new Cabinet, which included several ministers who had served under President Zia. Nawaz Sharif promised that one of the Government's major priorities was to establish lasting peace in Sindh, where ethnic conflict and general lawlessness continued to prevail. It was alleged, however, that the Government's subsequent campaign of suppression in the province, in response to numerous local murders and kidnappings, was aimed primarily at supporters of the PPP, hundreds of whom were arrested. In January 1991 the IDA won 19 of the 25 by-elections for seats in the National Assembly and the provincial assemblies, and in March won a decisive majority in elections to 42 seats in the Senate.

In May 1991 the National Assembly adopted legislation imposing the incorporation of *Shari'a*, the Islamic legal code, in Pakistan's legal system. The Assembly also adopted legislation providing for the Islamization of the educational, economic and judicial systems. Benazir Bhutto criticized the legislation as being extreme and fundamentalist, while the right-wing JUI claimed that the new law's provisions were not stringent enough.

The fundamentalist Jamaat-e-Islami Pakistan (JIP) left the IDA in May 1992, in protest at the Government's decision to support the new moderate *mujahidin* Government in Kabul, Afghanistan. The JIP accused the Government of abandoning the extremist Afghan guerrilla leader, Gulbuddin Hekmatyar, and also of failing to effect the full Islamization of Pakistan.

In response to continuing violence in Sindh, the Government launched 'Operation Clean-up' in May 1992, whereby the army was to apprehend criminals and terrorists, and seize unauthorized weapons. A violent clash between two factions of the MQM (the majority Altaf faction and the small breakaway Haqiqi faction) in Karachi in June provided the armed forces with the opportunity to suppress the extremist elements within the MQM. More than 500 people were arrested; caches of arms were located and seized; and 'torture cells', allegedly operated by the MQM, were discovered. The leader of the MQM(A), Altaf Hussain, accused the Government of attempting to crush the MQM through the military operation. In protest, 12 of the 15 MQM members in the National Assembly and 24 of the 27 members in the Sindh assembly resigned their seats. The Government, however, repeatedly gave assurances that the operations were against criminals, and not specifically against the MQM.

In mid-November 1992 the PDA intensified its campaign of political agitation and was now supported by the majority of the components of the newly-formed opposition National Democratic Alliance (NDA), including the National People's Party (NPP—which had been expelled from the IDA in March). The large-scale demonstrations and marches organized by Benazir Bhutto were, however, ruthlessly suppressed by the Government through mass arrests, road-blocks and the imposition of a two-month ban on the holding of public meetings in Islamabad and Rawalpindi and of travel restrictions on the former Prime Minister. By mid-December tensions between the Government and opposition had eased considerably, and in January 1993, in an apparently conciliatory move on the part of Nawaz Sharif's administration, Benazir Bhutto was elected Chairperson of the National Assembly's Standing Committee on Foreign Affairs. Shortly after Benazir Bhutto had accepted the nomination, her husband was released on bail.

In March 1993 a growing rift between the Prime Minister and the President became evident when the Government initiated discussions regarding proposed modifications to the provisions of the Eighth Constitutional Amendment, which afforded the President the power to dismiss the Government and dissolve assemblies, and to appoint judicial and military chiefs. In late March three cabinet ministers resigned in protest at Nawaz Sharif's nomination as President of the PML (Junejo Group), to succeed Muhammad Khan Junejo (who had died earlier that month), and voiced their support for Ghulam Ishaq Khan in his political struggle with the Prime Minister. In a seemingly final attempt at reconciliation, the Cabinet unanimously decided, in early April, to nominate Ghulam Ishaq Khan as the PML's candidate for the forthcoming presidential election. By mid-April, however, a total of eight ministers had resigned from the Cabinet in protest at Nawaz Sharif's continued tenure of the premiership. On 18 April the President dissolved the National Assembly and dismissed the Prime Minister and his Cabinet, accusing Nawaz Sharif of 'maladministration, nepotism and corruption'. The provincial assemblies and governments, however, remained in power, despite demands by the PDA and the NDA for their dissolution. A member of the dissolved National Assembly, Mir Balakh Sher Mazari, was sworn in as acting Prime Minister. It was announced that elections to the National Assembly would be held on 14 July. In late April a broadly-based interim Cabinet, including Benazir Bhutto's husband, was sworn in. In early May the PML (Junejo Group) split into two factions: one led by Nawaz Sharif, the other by Hamid Nasir Chattha (with the support of the President).

On 26 May 1993, in an historic and unexpected judgment, the Supreme Court ordered that the National Assembly, the Prime Minister and the Cabinet (dismissed in April) should be restored to power immediately, stating that President Khan's order had been unconstitutional. The President agreed to honour the Court's ruling, and the National Assembly and Nawaz Sharif's Government were reinstated with immediate effect. On the following day Nawaz Sharif's return to power was consolidated when he won a vote of confidence in the National Assembly. A few days later, however, there was renewed political turmoil following the dissolution, through the machinations of supporters of the President, of the provincial assemblies in Punjab and the NWFP. Lacking effective authority in each of the four provinces, Nawaz Sharif resorted to the imposition of federal government's rule on Punjab through a resolution passed by the National Assembly in late June. However, the Punjab provincial government refused to obey the federal Government's orders, claiming that they subverted provincial autonomy, prompting the Government to threaten the imposition of a military administration. Meanwhile, an All Parties Conference (APC), including, amongst others, Benazir Bhutto and the Chief Ministers of Punjab and the NWFP, convened in Lahore to pass a resolution, urging the President to dissolve the legislature, dismiss Nawaz Sharif's Government and hold fresh elections. In early July the Chief of Army Staff, following an emergency meeting of senior army officers, acted as an intermediary in talks between the President and Prime Minister in an attempt to resolve the political crisis. Benazir Bhutto, supported by her APC collaborators, announced a 'long march' on 16 July, with the intention of laying siege to the federal capital and forcing Nawaz Sharif to resign. Fearing the outbreak of serious violence, the army persuaded Benazir Bhutto to postpone the

march, reportedly assuring her that both the President and the Prime Minister would resign and that a general election would be held under a neutral administration. On 18 July, in accordance with an agreement reached under the auspices of the army, both Khan and Nawaz Sharif resigned from their posts, the federal legislature and the provincial assemblies were dissolved, the holding of a general election in October was announced, and neutral administrations were established, at both federal and provincial level. As specified in the Constitution, Khan was succeeded by the Chairman of the Senate, Wasim Sajjad Jan, who was to hold the presidency for the remaining tenure of the deposed President. A small, apolitical Cabinet was sworn in, headed by Moeenuddin Ahmad Qureshi, a former Executive Vice-President of the World Bank, as interim Prime Minister.

The general election, held in early October 1993 under military supervision, was widely considered to have been fair, although the turn-out, which some officials estimated to be less than 50%, was disappointing. The polling was closely contested between the PML faction led by Nawaz Sharif—PML (Nawaz)—and the PPP (the MQM boycotted the elections to the National Assembly, claiming systematic intimidation by the army, but took part in the provincial assembly elections a few days later). However, neither of the two leading parties won an outright majority in the federal elections, and in the provincial elections an outright majority was only achieved by the PPP in Sindh. Following intensive negotiations with smaller parties and independents in the National Assembly, on 19 October Benazir Bhutto was elected to head a coalition Government. On the following day a PPP-led coalition assumed control of the provincial administration in Punjab (traditionally a PML stronghold). The provincial governments in the NWFP and in Balochistan were, however, headed by alliances led by the PML (Nawaz).

In November 1993 the PPP's candidate, the newly-appointed Minister of Foreign Affairs, Sardar Farooq Ahmad Khan Leghari, was elected President, having secured 274 votes (62% of the total) in the electoral college. The incumbent acting President, Wasim Sajjad Jan, who stood as the candidate of the PML (Nawaz), obtained 168 votes (38%). On assuming office, Leghari stated that he intended to end his political ties with the PPP and that he hoped for the early repeal or modification of the controversial Eighth Constitutional Amendment.

In January 1994 the Prime Minister announced the appointment of 11 new cabinet members. In the following month the President dismissed the Chief Minister and government in the NWFP, suspended the provincial legislature and imposed governor's rule, following the thwarted introduction of a vote of 'no confidence' against the PML (Nawaz)-led coalition by the PPP. The PPP consolidated its hold on federal power in March by winning the majority of the contested seats in elections to the Senate; however, the ruling party's candidate for the Senate's chairmanship lost to the opposition's nominee. In April a PPP member was elected as Chief Minister of the newly-revived provincial government in the NWFP; the opposition alliance boycotted the proceedings.

It was reported that at least 20 people were killed in ethnic violence, allegedly instigated by members of the MQM(A), in Karachi in May 1994. The army was deployed in an attempt to restore order; incidents were also reported in Hyderabad and Sukkur. In June 19 high-ranking members of the MQM(A), including its leader, Altaf Hussain, were each sentenced *in absentia* to 27 years' imprisonment on terrorist charges.

September 1994 witnessed an upsurge in political unrest when Nawaz Sharif organized a nation-wide general strike; in response, the Government arrested hundreds of PML supporters. Relations between the Prime Minister and the leader of the opposition deteriorated in November, when the latter's elderly father was arrested on charges of fraud and tax evasion (he was later released on health grounds). In the same month the Government was confronted with a series of uprisings staged by heavily-armed tribesmen in the mountainous regions of Malakand and Swat demanding the enforcement of *Shari'a*. The fundamentalist revolt was suppressed by paramilitary forces (but only after the deaths of several hundred people), and the *Shari'a* measures were implemented in the tribal areas. By the end of the year, however, the police and paramilitary forces appeared to be losing control of Karachi, which was riven by rapidly escalating ethnic and criminal violence; nearly 170 people were killed in the city in December alone, following the lengthy 'Operation Clean-up' and the withdrawal of the army in the previous month. Much of the violence stemmed from the bloody rivalry between the opposing factions of the MQM, whilst other killings were linked to drugs mafias and to sectarian disputes between Sunni and Shi'a Muslims. Pakistani officials primarily accused Indian intelligence agencies of fomenting the unrest and demanded the closure of the Indian consulate in Karachi.

In early 1995, despite the arrest of large numbers of suspected Islamist militants, there was an upsurge in religious violence between Sunni and Shi'a Muslims in Karachi. In March the murder of two US consular officials by unidentified gunmen in the troubled Sindh capital provoked international condemnation. There was no respite from the violence in the following months, and by June the security forces had lost control of large areas of Karachi to MQM activists. Negotiations between representatives of the MQM(A) and government officials in mid-1995 proved fruitless and, although there was a temporary abatement in urban violence in the latter half of the year, the city's problems were far from resolved. It was estimated that during 1995 almost 2,000 people (including about 250 members of the security forces) were killed as a result of the political and ethnic violence in Karachi. In September of that year the growing political instability in Pakistan was underlined by the arrest of nearly 40 army officers on suspicion of plotting to overthrow the Government and to establish an Islamist fundamentalist state. In November 18 people were killed when a car bomb exploded at the Egyptian embassy in Islamabad; within hours of the attack three militant Islamist groups in Egypt had claimed responsibility for the bombing. During the previous year the Pakistani Government had been co-operating with Egypt in attempts to apprehend and extradite members of illegal Islamist militant organizations operating in the NWFP or across the border in Afghanistan. (In 1993–95 the Pakistan authorities, concerned at the country's growing reputation as a refuge for Islamist extremists, expelled more than 2,000 Arabs, the majority of whom were reported to have been involved in the civil war in Afghanistan.) Acts of violence and terrorism in Pakistan continued throughout late 1995 and early 1996—sectarian killings continued to occur regularly in Karachi and there was an increase in bomb attacks.

A new and potentially influential political force emerged in Pakistan in early 1996, when the popular former international cricketer Imran Khan (of late a prominent benefactor of charitable causes) established a political reform movement known as the Tehrik-e-Insaf (Movement for Justice), to oppose Benazir Bhutto's administration.

In March 1996 the Supreme Court in Karachi ruled that the Government no longer had the exclusive mandate to appoint judges to the higher courts; these appointments would, in future, be required to have the consent of the Chief Justices of the High Courts and the Chief Justice of Pakistan. This ruling aroused considerable controversy since it deprived the executive of substantial authority within the national judicial system.

The Government's popularity was undermined by the necessary introduction of an austere budget, including the introduction of new taxes, in mid-June 1996, in an attempt to reduce the budget deficit. Anti-budget protests were held in Islamabad and Rawalpindi in late June, during which three JIP protesters were shot dead by the police. The volatile political situation was intensified by a bomb explosion at Lahore airport in late July, a series of debilitating public-sector strikes and by a resurgence of violence in Karachi. In addition, the appointment of the Prime Minister's unpopular husband, Asif Ali Zardari, as Minister of Investment as part of a cabinet expansion in July aroused much controversy and criticism. At the end of that month the Government's position appeared even less secure when about 16 opposition parties, including the PML (Nawaz), the MQM and the JIP, established an informal alliance with a one-point agenda to oust Prime Minister Bhutto and her Government. Pakistan was thrown into further political turmoil in mid-September following the fatal shooting of Benazir Bhutto's estranged brother, Mir Murtaza Bhutto, in a gun battle with police in Karachi. A number of opposition politicians accused the Prime Minister and her husband of complicity in the killing, while Benazir Bhutto implied in a number of public statements that she believed that the President and the army were to blame. In 1995 Mir Murtaza Bhutto had established a rival faction of the PPP, known as the PPP (Shaheed Bhutto Group), charging his sister's Government with corruption and misrule; the breakaway faction, however, attracted no substantial support and posed little threat to the Prime Minister. Meanwhile, growing discord between Benazir Bhutto and President Leghari

became more apparent, particularly over the issues of judicial appointments and alleged official corruption.

Amidst mounting public discontent, including a three-day blockade of Islamabad by thousands of JIP supporters in October 1996, President Leghari dismissed Prime Minister Benazir Bhutto and her Government and dissolved the National Assembly on 5 November (the state assemblies were dissolved over the following week), citing the deteriorating law and order situation, severe economic problems, widespread corruption, disregard for judicial authority and the violation of various constitutional provisions as justification for his action. A former Speaker of the National Assembly, Malik Meraj Khaled, who claimed no affiliation to any political party, was named as acting Prime Minister and an interim Cabinet was appointed. It was also announced that a general election would be held in February 1997. Following the dismissal of her Government, it was reported that several leading members of Benazir Bhutto's PPP, including her husband, had been arrested. In mid-November 1996 the President promulgated a decree providing for a five-year disqualification from public office of politicians (with the exception of the President and members of the judiciary and armed forces) involved in corruption and abuses of power. At the end of December the JIP, announced its intention to boycott the forthcoming general election, accusing the 'caretaker' Government of failing in its much-vaunted anti-corruption drive. Sectarian violence between Sunni and Shi'a Muslims escalated in January 1997, culminating in a bomb blast outside a district court in Lahore, which killed the leader of the Sunni extremist group Sipah-e-Sahaba Pakistan, and 25 others. Meanwhile, in early January the President instituted an official advisory role for the military, with the formation of a 10-member Council of Defence and National Security (CDNS), which was to advise the Government on a broad range of issues from national security to the economy. The President chaired the new body, which comprised the Prime Minister, four senior cabinet ministers, the Chairman of the Joint Chiefs of Staff and the three armed services chiefs, and could refer any matter to it without previously consulting the Prime Minister. In response to this unexpected development, many political parties, including the PPP—but with the notable exception of the PML (Nawaz), accused the President of an unconstitutional usurpation of authority. The Government insisted, however, that the role of the CDNS would be purely advisory.

The general election, which was held on 3 February 1997, was marred by an extremely low turn-out (an estimated 30%–40%). The PML (Nawaz) won a decisive victory, obtaining 134 of the 204 directly-elective seats in the National Assembly (voting in three seats was deferred until a later date), while the PPP was routed, both at federal and state level, winning only 18 seats. The MQM emerged as the country's third political force (obtaining 12 seats), while Imran Khan's Tehrik-e-Insaf failed to win a single seat. Nawaz Sharif was sworn in as Prime Minister on 17 February and a small Cabinet was appointed the following week. In March the PML (Nawaz) and its allies secured a two-thirds' majority in the 87-seat Senate following elections for about one-half of the seats.

Nawaz Sharif's political authority was strengthened considerably in April 1997 when both the National Assembly and the Senate unanimously voted to repeal the major components of the 1985 Eighth Constitutional Amendment, thereby divesting the President of the power to appoint and dismiss the Prime Minister and Cabinet, to dissolve the legislature, to order a national referendum on any national issue, and to appoint provincial Governors, the Chairman of the Joint Chiefs of Staff and the three armed forces chiefs (these functions and appointments were, in future, to be carried out subject to a mandatory advice from the Prime Minister). The President thus became a largely ceremonial figure whose main executive role was the appointment of judges. President Leghari was reported to have 'willingly agreed' to the constitutional changes. Nawaz Sharif employed his new powers at the end of the month when he dismissed Adm. Mansur ul-Haq as Chief of Naval Staff, following allegations of bribery.

In July 1997 Asif Ali Zardari was formally charged with ordering the killing of Mir Murtaza Bhutto; 21 other former officials were simultaneously charged with murder and conspiracy in the death. In September the Swiss police ordered four banks in Geneva to 'freeze' the accounts of Benazir Bhutto and her family after Pakistan's Accountability Commission alleged that up to US $80m. had been illegally transferred to them. Pakistani investigators later alleged that more than $3,000m. in total had been illegally siphoned out of the country by the Bhutto family. In January 1998 the British authorities, at the request of the Pakistani Government, ordered the seizure of documents relating to assets and bank accounts of Benazir Bhutto in the United Kingdom. In March the Sindh High Court issued an arrest warrant for the leader of the PPP on a charge of misuse of power during her final term in office as Prime Minister. In April the High Court in Lahore ordered that all assets belonging to Benazir Bhutto, her husband and her mother be 'frozen' as the government investigation into allegations of corruption continued.

Meanwhile, in the latter half of 1997 a serious rift developed between Nawaz Sharif and the Chief Justice of the Supreme Court, Sajjad Ali Shah, over the appointment of new judges to the Court. In early November, however, a compromise was reached between the Supreme Court and the Government, allowing the former to appoint five new judges while confirming the right of the legislature to determine the total number of judges. Yet, despite this outcome, the crisis was not over and later that month the Supreme Court charged Nawaz Sharif and five other officials with contempt for slandering the Court and defying its orders in the previous month. The Prime Minister, who, if found guilty, was liable to be disqualified from office, denied the charges. The Chief Justice was forced to adjourn Nawaz Sharif's trial in late November, however, when thousands of the Prime Minister's supporters stormed the Supreme Court in Islamabad. The constitutional crisis came to a dramatic end on 2 December when the Chief Justice was suspended from office by rebel members of the Supreme Court; on the same day President Leghari also stood down from office. The Chairman of the Senate, Wasim Sajjad Jan, assumed the position of acting President. It was widely speculated that the army, in tacitly supporting the Prime Minister, had exerted considerable influence in resolving the constitutional impasse. Nawaz Sharif strengthened his hold on power on 31 December when his nominee and fellow Punjabi, Mohammad Rafiq Tarar (a personal acquaintance of the Prime Minister and a former Supreme Court judge), won the presidential election by a record margin (winning more than 80% of the total votes cast by the electoral college).

In January 1998 sectarian violence erupted again in Lahore when at least 24 Shi'a Muslims were massacred by a clandestine Sunni group. In response, the Government approved measures to control illicit weapons in an attempt to curb terrorism. (A controversial anti-terrorist law had been passed in August 1997, giving the security forces extensive powers of arrest and enabling the Government to ban any group or association without parliamentary approval.) In late February, however, two Iranian engineers were murdered by unidentified terrorists in Karachi, and in the following month more than 20 people were killed in two bomb explosions on passenger trains in Lahore.

Despite the temporary public euphoria and heightened popularity of the Prime Minister arising from the conduct of the controversial nuclear tests in May 1998 (see below), the repercussions (particularly the international sanctions) left Pakistan in dire financial straits. A cabinet reshuffle in early August was primarily driven by Nawaz Sharif's concerns over the country's deteriorating economic situation. In late August the Prime Minister introduced the Fifteenth Constitutional Amendment Bill to the National Assembly, seeking to replace Pakistan's legal code with *Shari'a*. Nawaz Sharif attempted to allay fears of a move towards Islamist extremism by promising to uphold women's rights and to safeguard minorities.

In early October 1998 the Chief of Army Staff, General Jehangir Karamat, was forced to resign from his post after publicly criticizing the Government's economic and political policies and demanding that the armed forces be given a direct rather than advisory role in government decisions. On the following day the Fifteenth Constitutional Amendment Bill was passed in the National Assembly, by 151 votes to 16. Human rights activists in Pakistan denounced the bill as 'regressive', claiming that it would allow Islamic courts to challenge every law in the Constitution and would over-expand the mandate of the premiership.

The Government suffered a severe reverse in late October 1998 when the Muttahida Qaumi Movement—MQM(A)—(formerly known as the Mohajir Qaumi Movement) withdrew its support for the PML (Nawaz)-led provincial administration in Sindh. On 30 October the provincial legislature was suspended and the troubled province was placed under governor's rule in an effort to curb the violence. In November the Prime Minister

announced the establishment of anti-terrorist military courts in Karachi (which were designed to dispense rapid and punitive justice), and the suspension of civil rights in Sindh.

In late December 1998 a travel ban was placed on Benazir Bhutto by the Government on the grounds that there were corruption cases pending against her in several Pakistani courts; a few days later, however, a court ruling overturned the ban on her departure from the country. In April 1999 the Lahore High Court found Benazir Bhutto (now in self-imposed exile abroad) and her husband guilty of corruption; they were each sentenced to five years' imprisonment, their property was confiscated and they were jointly fined US $8.6m. The verdict automatically removed the former Prime Minister and Asif Ali Zardari (who was already in prison serving a separate sentence) from their seats in the National Assembly and Senate, respectively.

Meanwhile, in early January 1999 the Prime Minister escaped an apparent assassination attempt when a bomb exploded near his country residence in Punjab, killing four people. The following day there was an upsurge in sectarian violence in the province when unidentified gunmen murdered 17 worshippers in a Shi'a mosque near Multan. Sindh became the focus of political attention later in the month when the Supreme Court stayed all execution orders handed down by the special military courts in Karachi pending a decision on the validity of these controversial legal bodies. A day later, in response to another petition, the Supreme Court declared unlawful the central Government's decision (made in November 1998) to remove the powers of the speaker and deputy speaker of the suspended Sindh assembly. In mid-February 1999 the Supreme Court ruled that military trials could not be used for cases against civilians, thus sparing 14 people from death sentences imposed in the military tribunals in Sindh and effectively barring the establishment of military courts throughout the country (as the Government had proposed). The Supreme Court ordered the transfer of the cases to civilian anti-terrorist courts.

Opposition claims that Pakistan was being ruled in accordance with the influence and interests of Punjabis were widely disseminated during 1999 and were linked with the continuing centralization of power under the control of Nawaz Sharif. In mid-1999 various allegations of corruption (particularly involving illegal financial transactions) were aimed at the PML and the Prime Minister's family. In May supporters of Asif Ali Zardari claimed that a police allegation that Benazir Bhutto's husband had attempted suicide was a fabrication to conceal the fact that he had been tortured while in custody.

A dangerous escalation in the Kashmir crisis between Pakistan and India in mid-1999 (see below) and the former's effective defeat in the face of almost universal condemnation and diplomatic isolation appeared to represent a major turning point in the fortunes of the PML Government. Although Nawaz Sharif attempted to ensure that any blame attached to the episode would be diverted to the army, many of his opponents in Pakistan declared that his seeming haste to concede defeat and to agree to a Pakistani withdrawal in the face of US pressure constituted a national 'betrayal'. In mid-September Nawaz Sharif's position looked increasingly precarious following the formation of a Grand Democratic Alliance by 19 conservative and centrist opposition parties, including the PPP, the MQM (A) and the ANP, which demanded the Prime Minister's immediate resignation. The various Islamist parties, including the JIP, also stepped up their anti-Government protests and rallies throughout the country. The opposition was weakened to some extent, however, by the fact that Benazir Bhutto was unwilling to return to Pakistan for fear of being arrested.

Events took a dramatic turn on 12 October 1999, when, shortly after Nawaz Sharif's announcement of a decision to dismiss the Chief of Army Staff and Chairman of the Joint Chiefs of Staff Committee, Gen. Pervez Musharraf, the army chief flew back from an official tour in Sri Lanka and promptly organized a bloodless military coup in Islamabad. Nawaz Sharif and his Government were overthrown, and the deposed Prime Minister was placed under house arrest. On 15 October Gen. Musharraf assumed the position of Chief Executive, declared a nation-wide state of emergency and suspended the Constitution, the National Assembly, the Senate, the four provincial legislatures and all political officials, with the exception of the President and judiciary. He also ensured, by means of a Provisional Constitution Order, that his actions could not be challenged by any court of law, thus imposing virtual martial law. On 18 October the Commonwealth Ministerial Action Group

(CMAG) condemned the coup and demanded a time-frame for the restoration of democracy; Pakistan was suspended from participation in meetings of the Commonwealth with immediate effect. Meanwhile, on 22 October Gen. Musharraf appointed four new provincial governors, and on 26 October he installed a three-member Cabinet (which was later expanded) and named the members of a National Security Council (NSC), which was expected to be the supreme executive body of the country. The NSC initially comprised Gen. Musharraf himself, the two other chiefs of staff, and four civilian experts on law, finance and national and foreign affairs.

Following his seizure of power, Gen. Musharraf attempted to win over international opinion by portraying himself as a moderate, liberal leader. He was aided, in this respect, by the fact that the majority of the Pakistani people appeared to support the army's coup (it was a widely-held opinion that the military had no provincial bias and represented all levels of society—rather than purely the landed élite). Indeed, no large-scale popular demonstrations were organized in support of the deposed Prime Minister, Nawaz Sharif. Although expressing regret at Pakistan's effective suspension from the Commonwealth, the military regime was more concerned with the reaction of the USA and the international financial organizations (such as the IMF and the World Bank) to the coup. The US Government's initial relations with the new administration in Pakistan appeared cautious but conciliatory. Gen. Musharraf promised an eventual return to civilian rule and announced wide-ranging measures to tackle corruption, loan defaulters, tax evasion, regional instability and religious extremism. The new regime's major priority was the revival of the almost bankrupt economy.

In November 1999 Nawaz Sharif and six other senior officials (including Mohammad Shahbaz Sharif, the brother of the ousted Prime Minister and the former Chief Minister of Punjab) were arrested on charges of criminal conspiracy, hijacking (a charge that carries the maximum penalty of the death sentence), kidnapping and attempted murder in relation to the alleged refusal of landing rights to the commercial aircraft carrying Gen. Musharraf from Sri Lanka to Karachi on 12 October; the aircraft ran precariously low on fuel before troops loyal to the army chief seized control of the airport and permission to land was finally granted (although the aircraft was rerouted to Nawabshah). The military authorities also charged Nawaz Sharif and his brother in November with corruption and non-repayment of bank loans. Later that month a new law was enacted barring politicians from holding public office for 21 years if found guilty of corruption or of defaulting on loans. The bill also allowed for the establishment of special courts to conduct trials within 30 days and gave the newly-formed National Accountability Bureau far-reaching powers of investigation. In mid-November, in apparent response to the military's treatment of the deposed Prime Minister, the PML (Nawaz) filed a lawsuit in the Supreme Court demanding that the elected Government be reinstated and Nawaz Sharif be released.

In late November 1999, as part of the Chief Executive's agenda for the decentralization of power, the military authorities delegated financial and administrative powers to the Northern Areas Council, thus bringing it level (with regard to local autonomy) with other provincial administrations. In early December the military Government suffered a set-back when Dr Muhammad Yaqub, a former governor of the State Bank and a leading economic expert, resigned from the NSC.

In January 2000 Nawaz Sharif and six senior officials were formally charged with criminal conspiracy, hijacking, kidnapping and attempted murder. The neutrality and avowed fairness of the hijacking case against Nawaz Sharif, which was conducted (after much delay as a result of various legal arguments) in an anti-terrorist court in Karachi, were called into question when the presiding judge abruptly quit the proceedings in protest at the reported presence of government intelligence agents in the courtroom. In March one of Nawaz Sharif's senior defence lawyers, Iqbal Raad, was killed by unidentified gunmen in Karachi. The former Prime Minister's supporters immediately attributed responsibility for the murder to the military Government, which, in turn, denounced the killing as an act of terrorism. In early April Nawaz Sharif was sentenced to life imprisonment on charges of terrorism and hijacking, despite the prosecution having demanded the maximum penalty of the death sentence; in addition to the life sentence, all of the former Prime Minister's property in Pakistan was to be confiscated by the State. The six other defendants were acquitted. In May

Nawaz Sharif's trial on charges of corruption opened; two months later the deposed Prime Minister was convicted and sentenced to 14 years' imprisonment, and barred from holding public office for 21 years. In August the Chief Executive issued a decree disqualifying those convicted of criminal offences and of terrorist acts from holding public office. The decision was viewed by many as a ban on convicted political leaders, notably former Prime Ministers Benazir Bhutto and Nawaz Sharif. In October the Karachi high court upheld Nawaz Sharif's conviction and sentence for hijacking, but sustained the deposed Prime Minister's appeal against a conviction for terrorism

Meanwhile, in late January 2000 Gen. Musharraf was accused of undemocratic conduct and of attempting to erode the independence of the judiciary when he dismissed the country's Chief Justice, Saiduzzaman Siddiqui, together with five other judges of the Supreme Court, following their refusal to swear allegiance to the military regime under a new oath. In late March, a few days before the visit of the US President, Bill Clinton (see below), the Chief Executive announced that new-style local elections would be held nation-wide (but on a non-party basis) between December 2000 and August 2001. Gen. Musharraf claimed that, under the reformed local government system (which included the lowering of the voting age from 21 to 18), power would be transferred from the traditional ruling élite to the 'grassroots' level.

In May 2000 Gen. Musharraf's regime was strengthened by a unanimous decision by the Supreme Court to validate the October 1999 coup as having been necessary to spare the country from chaos and bankruptcy (the decision was undermined to some extent, however, by the fact that all the incumbent members of the Supreme Court had, a few months earlier, sworn allegiance to the military administration). At the same time, the Court announced that the Chief Executive should name a date not later than 90 days before the expiry of the three-year period from 12 October 1999 for the holding of elections to the National Assembly, the provincial assemblies and the Senate. Gen. Musharraf stated that he would comply with the Supreme Court ruling regarding the restoration of democracy.

In late May 2000 the sudden resignation of the Governor of Sindh, Air Marshal (retd) Mohammad Azeem Daudpota, was widely believed to be linked to his inability to control the deteriorating law and order situation in Karachi. Daudpota was replaced by a prominent banker, Mohammed Mian Soomro.

In July 2000 Gen. Musharraf issued a decree to revive the Islamic provisions of the suspended Constitution and to incorporate them in the Provisional Constitution Order, thereby supporting a ban on the passing of any law that conflicts with Islamic principles. In mid-August Gen. Musharraf confirmed that nation-wide local elections would take place from December. At the same time the NSC was reconstituted and redefined as the supreme executive body, comprising the three chiefs of staff and the four Ministers of Foreign Affairs, Interior, Finance and Commerce. The Cabinet was reorganized and expanded. At the end of August the Chief Executive announced a reshuffle of the military; the Chief of General Staff, Lt-Gen. Mohammad Aziz, was replaced by the more liberal Lt-Gen. Mohammad Yusuf.

In September 2000 an explosion in an Islamabad market killed 16 people and injured about 100. An extreme Hindu organization claimed responsibility for the attack. In early November Air Chief Marshal Mushaf Ali Mir was appointed Chief of Air Staff. At the end of the month the Cabinet was partially reorganized and expanded.

In late 2000 former leaders Nawaz Sharif and Benazir Bhutto, with 16 other smaller political parties, agreed to form the Alliance for the Restoration of Democracy (ARD), in an effort to end military rule and accelerate a return to democracy. The new alliance superseded the PPP-led Grand Democratic Alliance. On 10 December Nawaz Sharif was unexpectedly released from prison and sent into exile in Saudi Arabia, with his wife and 17 other members of his family. The Government announced that the deposed Prime Minister had been granted a 'presidential pardon' and was allowed to leave the country to seek medical treatment. In return, Nawaz Sharif relinquished his personal and business assets worth approximately Rs 500m., promised not to return to Pakistan for 10 years, and agreed to not take part in Pakistani politics for 21 years. The deal, reportedly negotiated by a member of the Saudi Arabian royal family, weakened Nawaz Sharif's prospects as a serious opponent to the Chief Executive, and adversely affected the credibility of Gen. Musharraf's campaign against political corruption.

In early April 2001 the Supreme Court ordered that Benazir Bhutto's conviction for corruption be set aside and a retrial held. Later that month the court concluded that the verdict had been politically motivated. Bhutto, in self-imposed exile, declared that she would return to Pakistan after the third phase of local elections. Meanwhile, Bhutto and her husband faced further charges of corruption. In May a warrant was issued for Benazir Bhutto's arrest on her return to Pakistan. However, owing to her continued exile in Dubai (United Arab Emirates), in June she was sentenced, *in absentia,* to three years' imprisonment for failing to appear in court to answer these latest corruption allegations; this criminal conviction effectively disqualified Bhutto from holding further public office in Pakistan.

In late December 2000 the first phase of local elections was held in 18 of 106 districts. According to the Government, the turn-out reached 43.5%. The opposition PPP, however, claimed that less than 20% of the electorate had participated, attributing the low turn-out to the ban on political parties. Of a total of 20,076 seats, 33% were reserved for female candidates, but few women were able or willing to participate in a largely male-dominated society. The next three phases of local elections took place in March, May and July 2001. Although the elections were conducted on a non-party basis, it was believed that the majority of candidates were sponsored by either the PML (Nawaz) or the PPP. Furthermore, it appeared that the election scheme had failed to challenge the dominance of Pakistani politics by local feudal families. Elections to the 40-member legislative assembly for Azad Kashmir also took place in early July. Meanwhile, Musharraf insisted that a ban on party political activity in public would be maintained until after the forthcoming parliamentary elections, and opposition attempts at organizing pro-democracy rallies in March and May were suppressed by the authorities, who detained thousands of ARD supporters prior to the planned demonstrations.

On 20 June 2001 Gen. Musharraf unexpectedly assumed the Presidency, having dismissed Mohammad Rafiq Tarar (who had reportedly refused to resign from the post). Musharraf immediately issued a formal dissolution of both houses of the federal legislature (which had been suspended since October 1999) in preparation for the elections scheduled for October 2002. In an Independence Day address to the nation in August, Musharraf confirmed that elections to the four provincial legislatures and to the bicameral federal parliament would be conducted between 1 and 11 October 2002, thereby providing for the full restoration of democratic institutes by 12 October (the deadline established by the Supreme Court). Musharraf also announced that certain 'checks and balances' would be contained in constitutional amendments to be promulgated before June 2002; these were expected to include enhanced presidential powers and an advisory executive role for the military.

In response to a continuing escalation in sectarian and ethnically motivated violence, in June 2001 the Government approved new legislation to tackle terrorist activity. Earlier in the month Musharraf had complained that Pakistan's growing reputation as a centre for militant religious intolerance and fundamentalism was having a detrimental effect on the country's international standing and on its economic prospects. The violent deaths of two prominent public sector employees from the Shi'a community in late July were attributed to an ongoing campaign of sectarian violence by the militant Sunni group, Sipah-e-Sahaba. In August it was reported that sectarian violence had claimed 108 lives between January and May 2001, compared with 37 fatalities during the same period of the previous year. In his Independence Day address to the nation later in the month, Musharraf appealed for greater tolerance and understanding and announced an immediate ban on the activities of two militant Islamist groups: the Sunni Lashkar-e-Jhangvi and the Shi'ite Sipah-e-Mohammad.

As one of only three states to have recognized the legitimacy of the Taliban administration in Afghanistan, and as the most significant trading partner and political associate of the regime, Pakistan's support was crucial to the efforts of the US-led anti-terrorism coalition in the aftermath of the 11 September 2001 terrorist attacks on the US mainland, and Musharraf was left in little doubt that his refusal to co-operate with the campaign to apprehend those members of the al-Qa'ida (Base) organization held responsible for the attacks would result in Pakistan's increased economic and political isolation. Therefore, Musharraf's political opponents in the PML and PPP appeared to accept his declaration of co-operation with US requests for shared intelligence and use of air space with resignation. (In early November, however, the PML announced that it was transferring its support to those groups opposed to co-operation with the US-led coalition—a move that prompted accusations from other moderate opponents that the party leadership was attempting to make political gains from the crisis.) However, large-scale popular opposition to the decision was inevitable, particularly in the NWFP bordering Afghanistan, which was home to large numbers of Pakhtoon (Pashtun) Pakistanis who were fiercely opposed to any assault on the Pashtun-dominated Taliban. Despite Musharraf's insistence that the US-led activities in the region did not represent an attack on Islam, protests against the action spread throughout the country, and on 21 September a grouping of more than 30 Pakistani militant Islamist organizations known as the Afghan Defence Council (ADC) organized an opposition campaign of demonstrations and industrial action nation-wide. There was further opposition to Pakistan's support for the intervention in Afghanistan from within the armed forces and the Inter-Services Intelligence (ISI) agency, both having enjoyed particularly close links with the Taliban. In early October, having extended indefinitely his term of office as Chief of Army Staff, Musharraf implemented a radical reorganization of the military high command and the intelligence service, replacing a number of senior personnel with known sympathies for the country's militant Islamist cause, including Lt-Gen. Mahmood Ahmed, head of the ISI. However, popular protests against co-operation with the US-led coalition continued, and were fuelled by reports of civilian casualties of US bombing raids in Afghanistan and by the call to *jihad* (holy war) against all non-Muslims by the ADC and by the JUI in October. None the less, Musharraf's resolve remained firm (strengthened, in part, by the promise of financial recognition of his political support from the USA and the EU—see section on Economic Affairs), and despite the uncompromising response of the security forces to sporadic rioting, an attempt to capture the Jacobad air base in Sindh province (which was providing logistical support to US forces) by some 5,000 demonstrators and an opposition rally attended by around 20,000 protesters in Karachi, there were surprisingly few casualties. In late October, however, at least 15 members of a Christian congregation celebrating mass in the town of Bahawalpur, in Sindh province, were shot dead by six gunmen. Although a Muslim policeman guarding the church door was also killed in the incident, the attack was widely believed to have been a symbolic retaliation for Muslim civilian casualties in the ongoing military action in Afghanistan. A number of militant Islamists were arrested at the end of the month in connection with the massacre. In early November the leaders of the JUI and the JIP were detained following allegations that they were continuing to promote anti-Government activities and demonstrations; a national strike organized for 9 November was only partially observed, but four protesters were shot dead during clashes with security forces in Punjab. Earlier in the month a Qatar-based Arab satellite television channel, Al-Jazeera, had broadcast details of a new communication from Osama bin Laden, the Saudi-born leader of the al-Qa'ida organization, in which he issued a renewed call to *jihad* against non-Muslims and urged Pakistanis to rise up and overthrow Musharraf's administration for its part in the US-led campaign. Bin Laden's exhortations were particularly resonant in the border regions of the NWFP and Balochistan, where reports were emerging of large numbers of armed local tribesmen crossing the border as willing recruits for the Taliban. By mid-November there were believed to be significant numbers of Pakistanis fighting in Afghanistan (and reports that supply lines were being maintained into north-western Pakistan), rekindling long-standing animosity with the forces of the United National Islamic Front for the Salvation of Afghanistan (commonly known as the United Front or Northern Alliance), whose impressive territorial gains in Afghanistan (with the support of the US-led coalition) in early November alarmed Musharraf sufficiently for him to request a suspension of all bombing in Afghanistan during the Muslim holy month of Ramadan and to seek assurances that the United Front would not be allowed to occupy Kabul (the Afghan capital) unilaterally, during an official visit to Europe and the USA in the second week of November. However, Musharraf's concerns were overtaken by events, and by mid-November the United Front had taken Kabul, leaving Musharraf to concentrate his efforts in attempting to convince the international community of the need for plural (including Pashtun, perhaps even moderate Taliban) representation in any interim administration in Afghanistan. As the rout of Taliban forces in Afghanistan continued in

December and the USA intensified its bombardment of suspected al-Qa'ida positions in the Tora Bora region of southern Afghanistan, Pakistan reinforced security personnel along its north-western border (believed to number some 125,000 by the end of 2001) in order to intercept fleeing combatants. Many ethnic Pashtuns (both Pakistani and Afghan) were believed to have evaded capture on the border and escaped into north-western Pakistan. Violent exchanges between Pakistani security forces and intercepted (mostly Arab) al-Qa'ida fighters in the border regions resulted in a number of casualties on both sides.

Meanwhile, relations with India had become openly hostile as a result of the deteriorating security situation in Kashmir and the increasingly violent activities of Pakistan's militant Islamist groups in India (see below). Following intense international pressure (particularly from the USA) to address the continuing security risk presented by these groups, in December 2001 the security forces began to detain some of their most prominent members, and financial assets were 'frozen' and offices closed down. Moreover, in January 2002, in an audacious address to the nation in which he envisaged a moderate and prosperous Pakistan of the future, Musharraf announced an indefinite ban on the activities of five predominantly separatist groups (the Tehrik-e-Nifaz-e-Shariat-e-Mohammadi, the Sipah-e-Sahaba, the Jaish-e-Mohammed, the Tehrik-e-Jafria and the Lashkar-e-Taiba) and plans to reform the country's system of *madrassa* religious schools, many of which were accused of promoting extremism and theocracy. Musharraf's counter-terrorism initiative and new moderate vision drew plaudits from the international community, but the murder of US journalist Daniel Pearl (see below) and sectarian attacks on Shi'a Muslims in a mosque in Rawalpindi in February, a grenade attack on the congregation at the Protestant International Church in Islamabad in March and a sectarian attack on Shi'a Muslims in a mosque in Punjab in late April appeared to undermine the success of Musharraf's rhetoric. Moreover, in early May a suicide bomb attack, allegedly organized by al-Qa'ida, killed 14 people, mostly French engineers, in Karachi. Nevertheless, in mid-June it was announced that the Government had approved an ordinance for the registration of *madrassas*, according to which only *madrassas* that were registered by the Madrassa Education Board within the next six months would be allowed to operate.

During early 2002 Musharraf reiterated his commitment to returning the country to democracy, beginning with the parliamentary elections scheduled for October. He also confirmed that there would be a continuing role in government for the military-dominated National Security Council beyond October. In early April the Government approved a plan to hold a national referendum seeking endorsement for Musharraf's term of office as President to be extended by five years and approval of the Government's political and economic programme. Opposition parties and the independent Human Rights Commission of Pakistan condemned the decision as unconstitutional and illegal and resolved to boycott the vote; however, on 27 April the Supreme Court ruled that the referendum was legitimate, allowing the poll to take place three days later. According to official figures, 98% of those participating supported the proposal. There were, however, widespread allegations of gross irregularities and fraud. The Government claimed that the turn-out was 70%, but opposition parties and independent monitors estimated that it was about 5%. In late June Musharraf dismissed the head of the political wing of the ISI and chief organizer of the presidential referendum, Maj.-Gen. Ehtesam Zamir, after being forced to admit that his referendum victory had been fraudulent. Musharraf had already apologized publicly after ballot boxes were found to be crammed with 'yes' votes and after it transpired that government employees had been ordered to vote. In an attempt to reduce the political influence wielded by feudal landowning families, on 24 June the President issued a Chief Executive's Order stipulating that all candidates for future elections to federal and provincial legislatures should hold a university degree. Several days later Musharraf publicly announced a set of radical proposals for constitutional reform. The reforms were strongly criticized by political parties, constitutional experts and human rights groups for attempting to remodel Pakistan's prime-ministerial system into a presidential one and to undermine the authority of any elected government. Among the changes, Musharraf proposed to reduce the parliamentary term from five years to four; to lower the voting age from 21 to 18; to restrict the number of terms premiers or provincial chief ministers could hold in office to two; and to

disqualify those members of the legislature who had criminal convictions, had defaulted on loans or had absconded. The last two amendments were widely considered to be aimed at preventing former Prime Ministers Benazir Bhutto and Nawaz Sharif from returning to office. Indeed, in early July Musharraf issued a decree barring former premiers and chief ministers from seeking a third term in office. Several days later Musharraf announced that elections to the federal and provincial legislatures would be held on 10 October. At the same time Benazir Bhutto was sentenced to three years' imprisonment for failing to appear before a court on corruption charges. Meanwhile, in early June the Minister of Foreign Affairs, Abdul Sattar, tendered his resignation on health grounds; Inamul Haque was appointed Minister of State for Foreign Affairs almost two weeks later.

Instead of presenting the constitutional amendments before the next legislature, on 21 August 2002 President Musharraf unilaterally enacted the Legal Framework Order, which introduced 29 amendments to the Constitution and validated all the military decrees approved since the coup in 1999. The amendments would take effect from 12 October. As a result, the President's powers were enlarged and the military was ensured influence in decision-making beyond the parliamentary elections in October. The above proposals were endorsed. One of the most significant amendments, the establishment of a National Security Council (NSC), which would include Musharraf in his capacity as President and Chief of Army Staff, as well as the three other armed forces chiefs, the Prime Minister, the provincial chief ministers, the leader of the parliamentary opposition and Speakers of both houses of the federal legislature, was also authorized. The NSC would provide consultation to the elected government on strategic issues. The President was also restored the right to dissolve the National Assembly, and to dismiss the Prime Minister and Cabinet; furthermore, he was given the authority to override parliamentary majorities and provincial assemblies in order to appoint a Prime Minister and Provincial Governors himself if necessary. The amendments allowed the President to appoint Supreme Court judges and to extend his term in office. The changes were heavily criticized by the PML (Sharif) and PPP. Musharraf, however, insisted that a formal role for the military in governing the country was necessary to ensure a stable transition to democracy and to forestall a potential military coup. According to the Legal Framework Order, the size of the National Assembly would be increased to 342 members, with 60 seats reserved for women and 10 seats reserved for non-Muslims. The Senate would consist of 100 members. The PML (Nawaz) and PPPP (see below) were permitted to take part in the elections.

Meanwhile, in late July 2002 Benazir Bhutto was re-elected as leader of the PPP. However, the decree barring parties from contesting an election if any of its office-holders have a criminal conviction, prompted the PPP in early August to create the Pakistan People's Party Parliamentarians (PPPP) under new leadership to contest the forthcoming general elections. At the same time Shahbaz Sharif was elected leader of the pro-Nawaz PML. Bhutto's plans to return to the political arena were thwarted in late August when election officials in Sindh province rejected her candidacy in the National Assembly elections, owing to her criminal conviction. In response, Nawaz Sharif withdrew his nomination papers (although they had been accepted by the Election Commission), reportedly in solidarity with Bhutto. In mid-September Shahbaz Sharif was disqualified from entering the general elections, for defaulting on a bank loan. Meanwhile, a pro-Musharraf faction of the PML, the Quaid-e-Azam group, was reportedly receiving covert support from the Government.

On 9 October 2002 Musharraf declared that he was resigning the title of Chief Executive. The following day elections for the National Assembly and Provincial Assemblies took place. In elections to the National Assembly the PML (Quaid-e-Azam—Q) won 77 of the directly-elective 272 seats (25.7% of the vote). The PPPP won 25.8% of the vote, but only 63 seats. A surprising outcome was the success of the Muttahida Majlis-e-Amal (MMA), an alliance of six Islamist parties, in securing 45 seats (11.3% of the vote). The PML (Nawaz) won only 14 seats (9.4% of the vote). According to the Election Commission, the turn-out at the election was 41.8%; voting to five seats was deferred to a later date. The PML (Q)'s strong performance was to be expected, since Musharraf had publicly voiced his support for the party during the election campaign. Opposition parties, independent analysts and the Human Rights Commission of Pakistan claimed that the army had provided financial and other support to the PML (Q), while hampering other parties' campaign efforts. Meanwhile, Benazir Bhutto claimed that the election had been rigged. EU election monitors reported that the poll was 'seriously flawed'. The emergence of the MMA as a third political force suggested that a significant proportion of the population objected to Musharraf's support for the US-led military action against the Taliban and al-Qa'ida in Afghanistan, and the ongoing campaign against al-Qa'ida in Pakistan. PPPP and PML (Nawaz) leaders considered the religious alliance's success to be a result of the military Government's attempts to prevent their parties from achieving power. However, many observers held the opinion that the army and ISI sponsored the MMA in an attempt to convince the West that continued military rule was necessary to contain the religious parties; to gain further concessions from the USA; and to ensure support from the new government for hostile policies towards India, particularly over the Kashmir issue. On 31 October the 60 seats reserved for women and 10 for non-Muslims were allocated by the Election Commission. The three leading parties entered intensive and protracted negotiations on forming a governing coalition: the PML (Q) and PPPP each attempted to gain the support of the MMA. However, the parties failed to reach common ground; neither the PML (Q) or PPPP was able to persuade the MMA to withdraw its candidate for prime minister. By mid-November the parties had failed to reach a compromise; nevertheless, the National Assembly convened and elected a Speaker and Deputy Speaker. Shortly beforehand, the President revived the 1973 Constitution, which had been in abeyance since he assumed power in 1999; it was believed that the Constitution incorporated the controversial Legal Framework Order. On 21 November the PML (Q) candidate Zafarullah Khan Jamali was elected Prime Minister by the National Assembly. Jamali secured a narrow majority of 172 votes after 10 members of the PPPP defected and smaller parties agreed to support him. The MMA candidate, Maulana Fazlur Rehman—known for his anti-US and pro-Taliban views—won 86 votes, and the PPPP candidate, Shah Mahmood Qureshi—a supporter of Bhutto—received 70 votes. Jamali's victory ensured a PML (Q)-led, pro-army Government with a slim majority, which was sworn in two days later. In late December Jamali won a vote of confidence in the National Assembly (according to the Constitution, the Prime Minister was required to win a vote of confidence within 60 days of assuming office). Meanwhile, Musharraf agreed to transfer power to the elected Government, but emphasized that he would continue to carry out his 'important role'. The debate about the true status of democracy was immediately under way in the lower house of the federal legislature, with almost one-half of the members refusing to accept Musharraf's constitutional amendments, and objecting to the President continuing as the Chief of Army Staff. In mid-November the Government passed an amendment to its existing anti-terrorism legislation, allowing the police force to detain suspects for up to one year without pressing charges.

The MMA won a majority in the provincial elections in the NWFP in October 2002 and formed a provincial government in late November, with Muhammad Akram Durrani elected Chief Minister. The provincial assembly immediately announced the imposition of *Shari'a* in the province. The religious alliance, opposed to the presence of US troops in Pakistan, was expected to make the already difficult search for members of the Taliban and al-Qa'ida in the Pashtun-dominated province even more challenging. The MMA and PML (Q) announced a coalition government in the province of Balochistan in late November, led by a PML (Q) Chief Minister. The PML (Q) assumed power in the Punjab province at the same time. The PPPP emerged as the single largest party in the Sindh assembly but failed to form a coalition government despite support from the MMA. Eventually, in mid-December the PML (Q), MMA and several smaller parties agreed to a power-sharing arrangement with Ali Mohammad Mahar, a PML (Q) representative, as Chief Minister. The delay in forming new federal and provincial governments meant that the Senate elections were finally held on 25–27 February 2003, rather than on 12 November 2002 as originally planned. Some 88 of the 100 seats in the Senate were elected by the four provincial assemblies. The remaining 12 seats were chosen by the National Assembly from a list of candidates provided by the Federally Administered Tribal Areas and the federal capital. The PML (Q) secured 34 seats, making it the largest single party in the Senate. The Senate convened on 12 March 2003. The PML (Q) candidate Mian Mohammad Soomro was elected unopposed as Chairman of the Senate after

the eight opposition parties boycotted the vote in protest at the Legal Framework Order endorsed by Musharraf in August 2002 and the alleged military interference in the Senate elections.

Meanwhile, in February 2003 the Chief of Air Staff, Air Chief Marshal Mushaf Ali Mir, and his wife and several senior army officers were killed in an air crash in NWFP. The cause of the crash was not immediately known, although the air force dismissed speculation of sabotage. Kaleem Saadat was promoted as Air Chief Marshal and appointed as the new Chief of Air Staff in mid-March.

Attacks against the Christian community in the latter half of 2002 continued to undermine Musharraf's counter-terrorism initiative. In August suspected Islamist militants attacked a chapel in the grounds of a Christian hospital in Taxila, killing three nurses and wounding nearly 30 others; the incident occurred four days after an attack on a Christian missionary school, in which six people were killed. In September suspected militant Islamists killed seven workers at a Christian charity in Karachi. Some four days later a bomb exploded near a village church within hours of a protest march held by about 10,000 people in Karachi demanding more protection for Christians. On Christmas Day suspected Islamist militants launched a bomb attack on a church in Punjab, killing three people and injuring 16 others. The banned Jaish-e-Mohammed was held responsible for the attack. Meanwhile, although the security forces had succeeded in curbing the number of sectarian attacks, attacks by suspected Islamist militants on Western targets continued. In late December an incident involving Pakistani and US forces along the Afghan–Pakistani border (caused by a Pakistani border guard firing on a US patrol searching for remnants of the Taliban and al-Qa'ida) provoked anti-US demonstrations across the country into early 2003. The provincial assembly in NWFP demanded the withdrawal of US forces from Pakistan.

In foreign relations Pakistan has traditionally pursued a policy of maintaining close links with Islamic states in the Middle East and Africa and with the People's Republic of China, while continuing to seek aid and assistance from the USA. Pakistan's controversial nuclear programme prompted the USA to terminate development aid in April 1979, but, as a result of the Soviet invasion of Afghanistan in December of that year, military and economic assistance was renewed in 1981. However, increased concern about Pakistan's ability to develop nuclear weapons and Pakistan's refusal to sign the Treaty on the Non-Proliferation of Nuclear Weapons led to the suspension of military and economic aid by the US Government again in 1990 (under the Pressler Amendment). In February 1992 the Pakistani Government admitted for the first time that Pakistan had nuclear-weapons capability, but added that it had 'frozen' its nuclear programme at the level of October 1989, when its capabilities were insufficient to produce a nuclear device. In September 1995 the US Senate voted in favour of the Brown Amendment, which allowed a limited resumption of defence supplies to Pakistan. The Brown Amendment (which was ratified by the US President, Bill Clinton, in January 1996) also deleted the Pressler Amendment requirements for economic sanctions, thus paving the way for the resumption of US economic aid to Pakistan. In February 1996, however, the US Government was considering delaying the delivery of military equipment worth US $368m. to Pakistan because of the latter's suspected purchase of sensitive nuclear weapons-related equipment from China in 1995. These allegations were denied by both Pakistan and China. In August 1996 the first consignment of US military equipment released by the US Government after a six-year delay arrived in Pakistan. Following US air-strikes against a suspected base of bin Laden in Afghanistan in August 1998 (which entailed the use of Pakistani airspace), the USA evacuated its non-essential embassy staff from Pakistan. In December Prime Minister Nawaz Sharif held talks with President Clinton in the US capital in an attempt to gain support for Pakistan's ailing economy and to persuade the US leader further to ease sanctions imposed on Pakistan following nuclear tests carried out by the latter in May (see below). During 1998–99 the USA lifted some of the sanctions imposed on Pakistan and India, whilst reiterating requests that the two countries sign the Comprehensive Test Ban Treaty (CTBT) and exercise restraint in their respective missile development programmes to ensure peace in South Asia. During 2000 US foreign policy appeared to favour closer co-operation with India at the expense of improved relations with Pakistan. However, Pakistan's strategic importance to US efforts to dismantle the Taliban regime in Afghanistan and thus apprehend members of the al-Qa'ida terrorist organization held responsible for the devastating attacks on New York and Washington, DC, in September 2001 resulted in attempts by the USA to promote Pakistan's political rehabilitation in the Western international community. Although in September the US Government withdrew sanctions imposed on Pakistan in May 1998, and Gen. Musharraf was warmly received on official visits to the USA in November 2001 and February 2002, a 1990 suspension order on the delivery to Pakistan of 28 US F-16 fighter aircraft was not lifted, to the evident disappointment of the Pakistani President.

Despite the international acclaim that greeted Musharraf's public declaration of his commitment to the eradication of militant religious extremism in January 2002, US concerns about the proliferation of armed fundamentalist groups in Pakistan's border regions, and the possibility of their assisting scattered al-Qa'ida units to regroup in these areas, persisted. A US journalist, Daniel Pearl, was abducted in Karachi in January by a previously unknown group called the National Movement for the Restoration of Pakistani Sovereignty, which made a number of demands for his safe return, including the release of all Pakistani nationals captured by US forces in Afghanistan and transported (together with other suspected al-Qa'ida members) to a detention centre at the US military base in Guantánamo Bay in Cuba. Despite the prompt arrest by the Pakistani authorities of a British-born militant Islamist, Ahmed Omar Saeed Sheikh, who was believed to have organized the kidnapping, it soon emerged that Pearl had been murdered by his abductors. Confounding speculation that suspects in the case would be extradited for trial in the USA, in March Saeed Sheikh and three alleged accomplices appeared in a specially instituted anti-terrorism court in Karachi on charges of kidnapping, murder and terrorism. The men were convicted of the charges in mid-July; Saeed Sheikh was sentenced to death and his co-defendants were each sentenced to life imprisonment. Following an anti-US grenade attack on the Protestant International Church in Islamabad in March, in which five people (including the wife and daughter of a US diplomat) were killed, Musharraf dismissed five senior police officers for what he considered a serious lapse in security. It was widely believed that intelligence proceeding from Pakistani investigations to discover the identities of the assailants was a crucial factor in the arrest of Abu Zubaydah, one of al-Qa'ida's most senior commanders, by officers of the US Federal Bureau of Investigation (FBI) in Faisalabad at the end of March. However, it was reported that several prominent Islamic clerics and at least 1,300 of their supporters detained in late 2001 were released in early April 2002. In early May a suicide bomber killed 14 people, mostly French engineers, in Karachi; al-Qa'ida was held principally responsible. Another attack occurred in mid-June outside the US consulate in Karachi, killing 12 people. The US consulates in Karachi, Lahore and Peshawar, and the American Embassy in Islamabad closed temporarily for security reasons as a result. The United Kingdom had already reduced the number of British diplomatic staff in Pakistan. One month later two Pakistani members of the al-Alami faction of the banned Islamist militant Harakat ul-Mujahideen claimed responsibility for the attack on the US consulate as well as other attacks on Western targets. It was reported that the car bomb used in that attack had been retrieved from a previous failed assassination attempt on Musharraf in late April. (In April 2003 four men were convicted of organizing the attack on the consulate; two were sentenced to death.) In September 2002 Pakistani security forces arrested 12 alleged members of al-Qa'ida in Karachi, including the Yemeni-born Ramzi Binalshibh, a principal suspect in the attacks on the USA on 11 September 2001. The USA took custody of Binalshibh and four other al-Qa'ida suspects. The arrests were a significant boost for Musharraf's search for closer political and economic ties with the USA; at the same time, however, they were a reminder of the dangerous presence of Islamist militants in Karachi. In December Pakistani authorities arrested Dr Ahmed Javed Khawaja, a US citizen, and his brother, for allegedly sheltering and medically treating al-Qa'ida members and their families. The two suspects were charged a month later, prompting criticisms from human rights activists. Meanwhile, Dr Amir Aziz, who was arrested in October on suspicion of aiding al-Qa'ida, was released without charge a month later. In January 2003 Pakistani security forces and the FBI arrested two suspected Islamist militants in Karachi. In an apparent breakthrough in the campaign against religious extremism, the alleged operations chief of the al-Qa'ida network, Khalid Sheikh Mohammed, suspected of planning the attacks on the USA in

September 2001, was arrested in Rawalpindi in March 2003. It was hoped that the suspect, who was promptly taken into US custody, would provide information on the identity and whereabouts of al-Qa'ida cells in Pakistan and elsewhere in the world. The ISI's involvement in the arrest of the suspected militant suggested that the intelligence agency was genuinely attempting to curb militant activity. However, the discovery of Mohammed in a house owned by an army officer's brother raised questions about links between al-Qa'ida and the Pakistani military. Furthermore, the proprietor's prominent role in the Jamaat-e-Islami generated speculation about the political party's connections with al-Qa'ida. The arrest temporarily eased US pressures to support a UN Security Council resolution authorizing the removal of the regime of Saddam Hussain in Iraq. Later that month Pakistan, influenced by widespread large-scale protest marches against military action in Iraq, decided to abstain in the UN Security Council vote.

Relations with Afghanistan were strained during the 1980s and early 1990s, as rebel Afghan tribesmen (the *mujahidin*) used areas inside Pakistan (notably the city of Peshawar) as bases for their activities. In early 1988 there were an estimated 3.2m. Afghan refugees in Pakistan, most of them in the NWFP. The presence of the refugees prompted cross-border attacks against *mujahidin* bases by Soviet and Afghan government troops. In 1988 Pakistan signed the Geneva Accords on the withdrawal of Soviet troops from Afghanistan, which included agreements on the voluntary repatriation of Afghan refugees from Pakistan. Following the withdrawal of Soviet troops from Afghanistan in 1989, Pakistan maintained its support for the guerrillas' cause, while denying accusations by the Afghan Government that it was taking an active military part in the conflict, or that it was acting as a conduit for arms supplies to the *mujahidin*. The Pakistani Government welcomed the overthrow of the Afghan regime by the guerrillas in April 1992 and supported the interim coalition Government that was formed to administer Afghanistan until the holding of free elections. Relations between Pakistan and Afghanistan deteriorated, however, in 1994. The turbulence and increasingly anti-Pakistan feeling in Afghanistan threatened not only to result in an extension of the violence into the Pakhtoon (Pashtun) areas of the NWFP, but also obstructed the trade route from the Central Asian republics of the former USSR to the Arabian Sea at Karachi. The situation worsened in September 1995 when the Pakistani embassy in Kabul was ransacked and burned down by a mob of about 5,000 Afghans protesting at Pakistan's alleged active support for the Islamist Taliban militia. In the following month the Afghan ambassador to Pakistan was expelled from the country. Following the capture of Kabul by Taliban troops in late September 1996 and their assumption of power, the Pakistani Government issued a statement in which it recognized the Taliban militia as the new Afghan Government. In December 1999 there were signs of distinct changes in Pakistan's policy towards Afghanistan. Following the imposition of UN-mandated sanctions on Afghanistan the previous month for refusing to hand over the terrorist suspect bin Laden, Pakistan appeared to be exerting pressure on the Taliban to accede to Western demands by closing down a number of Afghan banking operations in Pakistan. In May 2000 the Afghan Minister of the Interior held talks with his Pakistani counterpart in Islamabad concerning transit trade, narcotics control and the repatriation of Afghan refugees. The Afghan delegation agreed to the repatriation of 100,000 refugees annually. The Pakistani Government continued to offer financial and diplomatic support to the Taliban. Although Gen. Musharraf repeatedly and strongly denied giving military assistance to the Taliban, allegations regarding the involvement of Pakistan's special forces in the Taliban campaign grew, following the latter's successful offensive in August–September 2000. The Pakistani Government agreed to implement the UN sanctions imposed on Afghanistan in January 2001, but announced that it would attempt to mitigate the effect of the restrictions, warning of a steep increase in refugee numbers and a worsening of the civil war. Afghanistan and Pakistan continued to hold bilateral negotiations. In February the Chief Executive urged the international community to accept and integrate the Taliban, and to assist Afghanistan with its humanitarian crisis. Relations between the two countries were again strained in March following the Taliban regime's destruction of ancient statues of the Buddha in Bamian. The failure of (somewhat unconvincing) attempts by senior Pakistani military officers to persuade the Taliban administration to comply with US demands that bin Laden and members of his al-Qa'ida terrorist organization thought to be resident in Afghanistan should be handed over to the US authorities to answer charges of responsibility for the September 2001 terrorist attacks on the US mainland ultimately resulted in a US-led military campaign to remove the Taliban from power. Despite considerable opposition from ethnic Pakhtoons (Pashtuns–who comprised the majority of the Taliban administration) in north-western Pakistan and from elements of the armed forces who had spent years consolidating relations with the Taliban regime, Musharraf was forced to co-operate with the US-led coalition to avoid potentially devastating economic and political isolation. Long-standing enmity between the Pakistani Government and the tribes of the United National Islamic Front for the Salvation of Afghanistan (commonly known as the United Front or Northern Alliance) arising from Pakistani sponsorship of the Taliban regime was exacerbated by the participation of Pakistani nationals in the armed resistance to the United Front's renewed military campaign (supported by the international coalition) to recapture Afghanistan (see above). As the United Front continued to make impressive territorial gains in Afghanistan, culminating in the capture of the capital, Kabul, in mid-November, the Pakistani Government announced the closure of all Taliban consular offices in Pakistan, including the embassy in Islamabad. It was hoped that the broad-based ethnicity of the Afghan Interim Administration (which included Pashtun representatives) installed in December would help to foster improved relations between the Pakistani authorities and the tribes of the United Front. Normal relations with Afghanistan had yet to be restored by late 2002. Publicly, Musharraf supported Karzai and the new Afghan Transitional Administration. However, Afghan officials were convinced that the Pakistani ISI was giving sanctuary to senior Taliban members and other anti-Afghan Government military commanders, such as Gulbuddin Hekmatyar. In mid-February 2003 the Pakistani and Afghan military intelligence services held talks in Rome, Italy, in an attempt to resolve deep-rooted differences. The Afghan delegation repeated its claims that the ISI was harbouring Islamist militants. The ISI, in turn, expressed its discontent at the Afghan Transitional Administration for granting India, Iran and Russia, unrestricted movement around the Afghanistan. The opening of Indian consulates in Jalalabad and Qandahar, close to the Afghan–Pakistani border, particularly irritated the ISI.

Drought conditions in the region contributed to a new influx of Afghan refugees in early 2001 (there were thought to be more than 2m. in Pakistan in March), placing renewed strain on limited resources (Pakistan had also suffered severe drought) and threatening to exacerbate the country's deteriorating economy and security situation. In mid-2001 the Pakistani authorities reiterated their commitment to providing refuge for Afghans fleeing political and religious persecution but expressed regret that the country was no longer capable of providing shelter for 'economic refugees'. Military operations by the US-led anti-terrorism coalition in Afghanistan in October 2001 resulted in a new exodus of refugees. Although Pakistan had officially closed its border with Afghanistan in late September, it was estimated that as many as 80,000 refugees had crossed into Pakistan illegally before the Government agreed, at the end of October, to plans to reopen the border to allow the inflow of as many as 300,000 of the most vulnerable refugees, as part of an agreement with UNHCR that was to include the establishment of 15 new camps. (In February 2002 it was announced that thousands of refugees had been moved from the notorious Jalozai camp in northern Pakistan—which was subsequently closed—to a new UNHCR-supervised camp near Peshawar.) According to UNHCR, by April 2002 (following the decisive defeat of Taliban forces in most of Afghanistan) repatriation offices in Pakistan were processing the return of as many as 50,000 Afghan refugees each week. At the end of 2002 UNHCR announced that more than 1.5m. Afghan refugees in Pakistan had returned to their homeland, surpassing all expectations. An estimated 1.5m. refugees remained in Pakistan.

Relations with India have dominated Pakistan's foreign policy since the creation of the two states in 1947. Relations deteriorated during the late 1970s and early 1980s, owing to Pakistan's programme to develop nuclear weapons, and as a result of major US weapons deliveries to Pakistan. The other major contentious issue between the two states was the disputed region of Kashmir, where, since 1949, a cease-fire line, known as the Line of Control (LoC), has separated Indian-controlled Kashmir (the state of Jammu and Kashmir) and Pakistani Kashmir, which

comprises Azad (Free) Kashmir and the Northern Areas. While Pakistan demanded that the sovereignty of the region be decided in accordance with earlier UN resolutions (which advocated a plebiscite in both parts of the region), India argued that a solution should be reached through bilateral negotiations.

Relations between Pakistan and India reached a crisis in late 1989, when the outlawed Jammu and Kashmir Liberation Front (JKLF) and several other Muslim groups in Indian-controlled Kashmir intensified their campaigns of terrorism, strikes and civil unrest, in support of demands for an independent Kashmir or unification with Pakistan. In response, the Indian Government dispatched troops to Jammu and Kashmir. By early February 1990 it was officially estimated that about 80 people (mostly civilians) had been killed in resulting clashes between troops and protestors. The opposition parties in Pakistan organized nation-wide strikes, to express their sympathy for the Muslims in Jammu and Kashmir, and urged the Government to adopt more active measures regarding the crisis. In August and September there were reports of heavy skirmishes between Indian and Pakistani troops along the Kashmir border.

In December 1990 discussions were held between the Ministers of External Affairs of Pakistan and India, at which an agreement not to attack each other's nuclear facilities was finalized, but no solution was found to the Kashmiri problem. Further high-level talks held between the two countries during the first half of the 1990s made no progress in resolving the crisis, and skirmishes between Pakistani and Indian troops along the border in Kashmir continued throughout 1991–95 and into 1996. In December 1994 Pakistan was successful in securing the passage of a resolution condemning reported human rights abuses by Indian security forces in Kashmir at the summit meeting of the Organization of the Islamic Conference held in Casablanca, Morocco. (In the same month Pakistan's decision to close down its consulate in Mumbai (Bombay), amid claims of Indian support for acts of terrorism in Karachi, provided a further indication of the growing rift between the two countries.) In February 1995 (and again in February 1996) Benazir Bhutto's Government organized a nation-wide general strike to express solidarity with the independence movement in Jammu and Kashmir and to protest against alleged atrocities carried out by the Indian forces. In January 1996 relations between the two countries deteriorated when the Pakistani Government accused the Indian forces of having launched a rocket attack on a mosque in Azad Kashmir, which killed 20 people. In response, the Indian authorities claimed that the deaths had been caused by Pakistani rockets that had been misfired. Tensions between Pakistan and India were also exacerbated in early 1996 by allegations that each side was on the verge of conducting nuclear tests. The sharp deterioration in relations was clearly indicated by the fact that in late January the Pakistani President felt it necessary to reassure the public that there was no possibility of war between the two countries. Later that year, India's decision to hold state assembly elections in Jammu and Kashmir (described as 'farcical' by Benazir Bhutto) and its refusal to sign the CTBT did nothing to encourage an improvement in relations between Islamabad and New Delhi. In March 1997, however, talks (which had been suspended since 1994) were resumed, both at official and at ministerial level. Of most significance were the negotiations between India and Pakistan's Foreign Secretaries, which took place in Islamabad in June. These talks resulted in an agreement to establish a series of distinct working parties to consider groups of issues. One such group of issues specifically related to Jammu and Kashmir. Little progress was made, however, in improving bilateral relations during a further round of high-level talks held in New Delhi in September and tension increased at the end of the month.

In April 1998 Pakistan provoked stern condemnation from the recently-elected right-wing Government in India following its successful test-firing of a new intermediate-range missile (capable of reaching deep into Indian territory). The arms race escalated dramatically and to potentially dangerous proportions in the following month when India conducted five underground nuclear test explosions. The test programme was condemned world-wide, and the USA imposed economic sanctions against India. The US President, Bill Clinton, and the UN Security Council urged Pakistan to show restraint in not carrying out its own retaliatory test explosions. However, at the end of May Pakistan carried out six underground atomic test explosions. In early June the Pakistani Government ordered a 50% reduction in public expenditure in an attempt to mitigate the effects of the resultant economic sanctions imposed by various foreign countries, including the USA. Immediately after the nuclear tests, India and Pakistan announced self-imposed moratoriums on further testing and engaged themselves in intense diplomatic activity. In September, however, the Pakistani Minister of Foreign Affairs categorically stated that Pakistan would not sign the CTBT until all of the sanctions were lifted and other legitimate concerns addressed.

Indo-Pakistani talks at foreign secretary level regarding Kashmir and other issues were resumed in Islamabad in October 1998. In February 1999 relations appeared to improve considerably when the Indian Prime Minister, Atal Bihari Vajpayee, made an historic journey (inaugurating the first passenger bus service between India and Pakistan) over the border to Lahore. Following his welcome by the Pakistani Prime Minister, the two leaders held a summit meeting (the first to be conducted in Pakistan for 10 years), at the end of which they signed the Lahore Declaration, which, with its pledges regarding peace and nuclear security, seemed designed to allay world-wide fears of a nuclear 'flashpoint' in South Asia. The contentious subject of Jammu and Kashmir was, however, largely avoided. Concern over the escalating arms race in South Asia was again deepened in April, following a series of ballistic missile tests carried out first by India and then by Pakistan (both countries, however, appeared to have adhered to the procedures incorporated in the Lahore Declaration, by informing each other of their test plans well in advance).

In May 1999 the Kashmir conflict intensified to reach what was termed a 'near-war situation' following the reported infiltration of 600–900 well-armed Islamist militants, reinforced by regular Pakistani troops across the LoC into the area around Kargil in the Indian-held sector of Kashmir. It was widely believed that the incursion of the guerrillas had been planned months in advance by the Pakistani army and intelligence agents; the Pakistani Government, however, claimed that it had no direct involvement whatsoever with the Islamist insurgents. In response, the Indian troops launched a series of air-strikes against the militants at the end of the month, a move that represented a serious provocation to Pakistan since it constituted the first peacetime use of air power in Kashmir. Within days tensions were heightened when a militant Kashmiri group claimed responsibility for shooting down an Indian helicopter gunship and Pakistani troops destroyed two Indian fighter aircraft, which had reportedly strayed into Pakistani airspace. Artillery exchanges increased along the LoC (with both sides suffering heavy casualties) and reports of the massing of troops and evacuation of villages along the international border aroused considerable concern. In early July, however, Indian military dominance combined with US diplomatic pressure prompted Nawaz Sharif's precipitate visit to Washington in the USA for talks with President Clinton. The resultant Washington Declaration prepared the ground for an end to the Kargil crisis through the Pakistan leader's agreement to the withdrawal of all 'intruders' from Indian-controlled Kashmir. In August there was renewed tension between Pakistan and India when India shot down a Pakistani naval reconnaissance aircraft near Pakistan's border with Gujarat, killing all 16 personnel on board; Pakistan retaliated the following day by opening fire on Indian military aircraft in the same area.

In October/November 1999 there was a notable increase in terrorist incidents in Kashmir, and Indian and Pakistani forces were reported to have resumed skirmishes across the LoC. Relations between the two countries worsened in early November after the success of Vajpayee in promoting an official condemnation of the new Pakistani military regime by the Commonwealth heads of government, following the military coup in Pakistan in mid-October. In December the Indian Government stated that it would not resume dialogue with Pakistan until the latter halted 'cross-border terrorism'.

In late December 1999 the Kashmir conflict came to international attention when five Islamist fundamentalists hijacked an Indian Airlines aircraft and held its passengers captive at Qandahar airport in southern Afghanistan for one week. Among the hijackers' demands was the release of 36 Muslim militants being held in Indian prisons who supported the Kashmiri separatist movement. Under increasing domestic pressure to prioritize the safety of the hostages, the Indian Government agreed to release three of the prisoners in exchange for the safe return of the captive passengers and crew. Despite Indian accusations of complicity, the Pakistani Government denied any links with the hijackers. In late March 2000 the US President's recent visit

to the region appeared to have failed to bring Pakistan and India any closer together when Gen. Musharraf's offer of peace talks regarding Kashmir was firmly rejected by the Indian Government (which still seemed deeply suspicious of the Pakistani Chief Executive). India continued to demand that Pakistan cease 'cross-border terrorism' as a precondition for negotiations, and Pakistan repeatedly denied arming and funding militants. Gen. Musharraf emphasized that the Government's support for the Kashmiri people's self-determination was moral and diplomatic, not political. On 24 July the Kashmiri militant group, the Hizbul Mujahideen, declared a three-month cease-fire on condition that India curbed human rights violations and military operations against militants. Other militant groups denounced the cease-fire. The Pakistani army continued a policy of not firing first, at the same time emphasizing that the cease-fire was not unilateral. The Government supported the cessation of hostilities, but was allegedly under pressure from separatist groups not to become involved in peace negotiations. The Hizbul Mujahideen later demanded tripartite discussions, which included Pakistan, but India refused to involve its neighbouring state, renouncing it as 'terrorist'. The cease-fire ended in the second week of August.

In mid-August 2000 Pakistan renewed its offer to resume negotiations, despite claims of increased violence by the Indian army towards separatists. Relations, however, remained unchanged and violence in the region intensified. In November the Indian Government declared the suspension of combat operations against Kashmiri militants during the Muslim holy month of Ramadan. The unilateral cease-fire began at the end of November (and was subsequently extended, at intervals, until the end of May); Indian security forces were authorized to retaliate if fired upon. The majority of national parties and foreign governments supported the cessation of hostilities, although the Pakistani authorities described the cease-fire as 'meaningless' without simultaneous constructive dialogue. The All-Party Hurriyat Conference welcomed the development and offered to enter negotiations with Pakistani authorities in order to prepare for tripartite discussions. The Hizbul Mujahideen and other militant groups, however, rejected the offer and continued their campaign of violence, extending their activities as far as the Red Fort in Old Delhi, where three people were shot dead in December. In the same month Pakistan extended an invitation to the All-Party Hurriyat Conference to participate in joint preparations for the establishment of tripartite negotiations. At the end of December India agreed to issue passports to a delegation of All-Party Hurriyat Conference leaders to allow them to visit Pakistan; however, processing of the applications was subsequently stalled. In mid-January 2001 the Indian high commissioner to Pakistan visited Gen. Musharraf. This meeting signified the first high-level contact since the military coup in Pakistan in 1999. The two officials urged an early resumption of negotiations on the Kashmir question.

Relations with India appeared to improve following the earthquake in Gujarat in January 2001, when Pakistan offered humanitarian relief to India and the leaders of the two countries thus established contact. In May Prime Minister Vajpayee issued an unexpected invitation to Gen. Musharraf to attend bilateral negotiations in Agra in July. However, hopes for a significant breakthrough on the issue of Kashmir were frustrated by the failure of the two leaders to agree to a joint declaration at the conclusion of the dialogue; the divergent views of the two sides on the priority issue in the dispute (cross-border terrorism according to India, and Kashmiri self-determination in the opinion of Pakistan) appeared to be more firmly entrenched than ever. Tension with India was heightened considerably following a guerrilla-style attack on the state assembly building in Srinagar on 1 October. An estimated 38 people (including two of the four assailants) were killed and around 70 were wounded in the attack and in the subsequent confrontation with security forces. The Indian Government attributed responsibility for the attack to the Pakistan-based Jaish-e-Mohammed and Lashkar-e-Taiba groups. Tensions were exacerbated later in the month when Gen. Musharraf rejected official Indian requests to ban the activities of the organization in Pakistan, although he did publicly condemn the attack. Skirmishes between Indian and Pakistani security forces along the LoC threatened to erupt into open conflict later in the month.

On 13 December 2001 five armed assailants gained access to the grounds of the Indian union parliament in New Delhi and attempted to launch an apparent suicide attack on the parliament building, where some 300 MPs had congregated for a routine session. Although no parliamentary deputies were hurt in the attack, nine people were killed and some 25 were injured in the botched assault; the five assailants were also killed in the attack. The Indian authorities again attributed responsibility for the attack to the Jaish-e-Mohammed and Lashkar-e-Taiba groups, and suggested that the five assailants appeared to be of Pakistani origin. Pakistan, which had been among the many countries to express immediate condemnation of the attack (which was popularly described as an assault on democracy), now demanded to see concrete proof to support the allegations made by the Indian Government, while the US Government urged the Indian authorities to exercise restraint in their response. Tensions between India and Pakistan continued to mount when Mohammed Afzal, a member of Jaish-e-Mohammed arrested in Kashmir on suspicion of complicity in the incident, admitted his involvement and alleged publicly that Pakistani security and intelligence agencies had provided support to those directly responsible for the attack. India recalled its high commissioner from Islamabad and announced that overground transport services between the two countries would be suspended from 1 January 2002. As positions were reinforced with troops and weapons (including missiles) on both sides of the LoC, there was considerable international concern that such brinkmanship might propel the two countries (each with nuclear capabilities) into renewed armed conflict. Mindful of the potential detriment to security at Pakistan's border with Afghanistan that could result from escalated conflict in Kashmir, the USA applied increased pressure on the beleaguered Pakistani Government (already facing vociferous domestic opposition to its accommodation of US activities in Afghanistan) to adopt a more conciliatory attitude towards India's security concerns, and in late December the Pakistani authorities followed the US Government's lead in 'freezing' the assets of the two groups held responsible for the attack by India. The leaders of the two groups were later detained by the Pakistani authorities (who arrested some 80 suspected militants in the last week of December) but, despite an evident satisfaction at this development, the Indian Government continued to dismiss much of the Pakistani response as superficial and demanded that the two leaders be extradited (together with 20 other named Pakistan-based militants) to stand trial in India.

It had been hoped that tensions between the two countries might be defused by renewed dialogue between Vajpayee and Musharraf at a summit meeting of the South Asian Association for Regional Co-operation (SAARC) convened in Nepal in the first week of January 2002, but contacts between the two men were minimal, and troops on both sides of the LoC continued to exchange gunfire in the days following the conference. However, on 12 January Musharraf yielded to relentless international pressure by publicly condemning the activities of militant extremists based in Pakistan and announcing the introduction of a broad range of measures to combat terrorist activity and religious zealotry, including the proscription of five extremist organizations (among them the Jaish-e-Mohammed and the Lashkar-e-Taiba). Within two days the Pakistani authorities claimed to have closed almost 500 offices used by the five organizations and to have arrested some 1,400 suspected activists, prompting considerable international praise for the initiative. It was hoped that reports published in late January which indicated that the number of terrorist incidents in Jammu and Kashmir had halved since the introduction of Pakistan's new counter-insurgency measures earlier in the month would help foster a more substantial improvement in future relations between the two countries. However, in March 2002 India and (subsequently) Pakistan expelled a number of each other's diplomats for alleged improprieties, and in a somewhat belligerent interview with the German magazine, *Der Spiegel,* published in April, Musharraf stated that he was prepared to use nuclear weapons in the event of war. In mid-May suspected Islamist militants attacked an Indian army camp in Jammu and Kashmir, killing more than 30 people. India expelled Pakistan's high commissioner. Indo-Pakistani relations deteriorated further following the assassination of Abdul Ghani Lone, the leader of the moderate All-Party Hurriyat Conference on 21 May, by suspected Islamist militants. India accused the Pakistani Government of supporting the Islamist extremists. Despite US attempts to calm tensions, artillery fire was exchanged along the LoC. More than 1m. soldiers were mobilized on both sides of the border as the two countries appeared to be on the brink of war. Pakistan would not rule out first use of nuclear weapons, and

India declared that it would be prepared to go to war after the monsoon season ended (in September) if its neighbour refused to halt 'cross-border terrorism'. Musharraf, however, denied that Pakistan was aiding incursions into Jammu and Kashmir, and ordered several 'routine' tests of its ballistic-missile arsenal at the end of May. An attempt to broker peace at a security summit held in Kazakhstan in early June failed after the Indian Prime Minister refused to meet Musharraf. Following intense diplomatic efforts by British and US officials, the threat of war appeared to diminish. On 10 June India lifted its ban on Pakistani commercial aircraft flying over its territory and prepared to appoint a new high commissioner to Pakistan, in response to Pakistani pledges to halt cross-border infiltration. India's campaign against 'cross-border terrorism' gained impetus as a result of the US Secretary of Defense Donald Rumsfeld's declaration in mid-June that there were strong indications that al-Qa'ida was operating near the LoC. In late June Rumsfeld announced that Pakistan had significantly reduced cross-border infiltration. However, an attack on Hindus by suspected Islamist militants in Jammu and Kashmir in mid-July disrupted attempts to restore diplomatic relations between India and Pakistan, and the Indian Government decided to delay the appointment of a new high commissioner to Pakistan. Both countries conducted 'routine' ballistic-missile tests in early October. In mid-October the Indian Minister of Defence stated that India would withdraw a large number of troops from the international border with Pakistan; the number of troops along the LoC would remain unchanged, however. Pakistan reciprocated the announcement shortly afterwards. India's gradual removal of troops began in late October; Pakistan responded by withdrawing a portion of its troops in November. President Musharraf dismissed elections in Jammu and Kashmir in September–October as a 'sham' and 'farcical'. In December Pakistan announced the indefinite postponement of the next summit meeting of SAARC, scheduled for January 2003 in Islamabad, owing to India's failure to confirm its attendance.

Relations with India deteriorated in early 2003. Tensions were exacerbated by India's latest set of 'routine' ballistic-missile tests, the violence in Kashmir and India's new military agreement with Russia. In late January India ordered four officials at Pakistan's high commission in New Delhi to leave the country within 48 hours for 'indulging in activities incompatible with their official status', a euphemism for spying. Pakistan reacted by expelling four officials at the Indian high commission in Islamabad. In early February India expelled Pakistan's acting high commissioner, accusing him of funding Kashmiri separatist groups. Four other Pakistani officials were charged with spying and expelled. Pakistan retaliated by giving India's acting high commissioner and four colleagues 48 hours to leave for allegedly spying. In early May the two neighbours agreed to restore relations and civil aviation links and to resume negotiations.

Relations with Bangladesh deteriorated in September 2000 when, at the UN Millennium Summit meeting in the USA, the Bangladeshi Prime Minister condemned the Pakistani military leadership, ostensibly as part of a general request for the UN to take action against undemocratic changes of government. Gen. Musharraf subsequently cancelled forthcoming meetings with the Prime Minister of Bangladesh. Later, the Bangladeshi leader demanded that Pakistan apologize for the atrocities committed by its army during the Bangladesh war of liberation and that those involved be brought to justice. In late November Pakistan withdrew its Deputy High Commissioner to Bangladesh, following his insistence that the ruling Bangladesh Awami League, rather than the Pakistani army, was responsible for the bloodshed. The Bangladesh Government declared the diplomat *persona non grata* in mid-December and demanded his immediate departure. During his visit to Bangladesh in late July 2002, President Musharraf apologized unreservedly for the atrocities committed by Pakistani troops during Bangladesh's war of liberation.

Pakistan withdrew from the Commonwealth in January 1972, in protest at the United Kingdom's role in the East Pakistan crisis. Pakistan recognized Bangladesh in February 1974, but attempts to rejoin the Commonwealth in the late 1970s and early 1980s were thwarted by India. In January 1989, however, India announced that it would no longer oppose Pakistan's application to rejoin the organization, and in July, during an official visit to the United Kingdom by Benazir Bhutto, Pakistan was formally invited to rejoin the Commonwealth, which it did on 1 October 1989. In October 1999, however, Pakistan was suspended from participation in meetings of the Commonwealth. In November 2002 the Commonwealth Ministerial Action Group agreed to maintain Pakistan's suspension from participation in meetings, as it was not convinced that democracy had been completely restored in the country.

In early 1992 the Economic Co-operation Organization (ECO, see p. 192), comprising Pakistan, Iran and Turkey, was reactivated, and by the end of the year had been expanded to include Afghanistan and the six Central Asian, mainly Muslim, republics of the former USSR; the 'Turkish Republic of Northern Cyprus' joined ECO in 1993. Trade delegations from Turkey and the new republics visited Pakistan, and an agreement for the restoration and construction of highways in Afghanistan, to link Pakistan with these republics, was signed. In 1995 Pakistan, the People's Republic of China, Kazakhstan and Kyrgyzstan signed a transit trade agreement, restoring Pakistan's overland trade route with Central Asia, through China. During a commemorative visit to Pakistan by the Chinese Premier, organized in May 2001 to celebrate 50 years of bilateral relations, the two countries concluded a number of agreements on technical and economic co-operation. Bilateral relations were consolidated and further co-operation agreements were signed during an official visit to China made by Gen. Musharraf in December. In late November 2002 Pakistan rejected US allegations that it had provided assistance for the Democratic People's Republic of Korea's nuclear programme.

Government

The President is a constitutional Head of State, who is normally elected for five years by an electoral college, comprising the federal legislature and the four provincial assemblies. The former consists of a lower and upper house. Until August 2002 the lower house, called the National Assembly, had 207 members elected directly for a term of five years, on the basis of adult suffrage, plus 10 members representing minorities. The upper house, called the Senate, had 87 members elected directly by the provincial assemblies serving for six years, with one-third retiring every two years. The Prime Minister, who holds supreme executive authority, is elected by the National Assembly and he/she and the other ministers in the Cabinet are responsible to it.

Pakistan comprises four provinces (each with an appointed Governor and provincial government), the federal capital of Islamabad and the Federally Administered Tribal Areas.

In April 1997 many executive powers were transferred from the President to the Prime Minister as a result of the repeal of the major components of the 1985 Eighth Constitutional Amendment, which divested the President of the power to appoint and dismiss the Prime Minister and Cabinet, to dissolve the legislature, to order a national referendum, and to appoint provincial Governors, and the armed forces chiefs; these functions and appointments were, in future, to be carried out subject to a mandatory advice from the Prime Minister. The President consequently became a largely ceremonial figure whose main executive role was the appointment of judges.

Following the overthrow of the Government in a military coup on 12 October 1999, the federal legislature and the four provincial legislatures were all suspended on 15 October. On the same day a Provisional Constitution Order was promulgated, according to which executive power was transferred to a National Security Council, led by a Chief Executive. A federal Cabinet, which was to aid and advise the Chief Executive, was to be appointed by the President on the advice of the Chief Executive. The President was to act on, and in accordance with, the advice of the Chief Executive. On 22 October the military regime appointed four new provincial governors, who were to enjoy the functions and powers of a chief minister. In preparation for democratic elections, scheduled for October 2002, the Legal Framework Order was enacted in August, increasing the size of the National Assembly to 342 seats, with 272 members directly elected and 60 seats reserved for women and 10 for non-Muslims. The term of the National Assembly was reduced to four years. The size of the Senate was increased to 100 seats and its term of office reduced to five years. The term of the provincial assemblies was reduced to four years. The establishment of a National Security Council after the general election was authorized, ensuring the military a formal role in government. In all, the Legal Framework Order introduced 29 amendments to the Constitution and validated all the military decrees approved since the coup in 1999 (see The Constitution). The President was to continue his self-appointed role and remain Chief of Army Staff for a further five years.

Defence

In August 2002 the armed forces totalled 620,000 men (including 513,000 reserves): 550,000 in the army, 25,000 in the navy and 45,000 in the air force. Active paramilitary forces numbered an estimated 289,000–294,000 (including a National Guard of 185,000 men). The projected defence budget for 2002/03 was Rs 146,022m. at the federal level. Military service is voluntary.

Economic Affairs

In 2001, according to estimates by the World Bank, Pakistan's gross national income (GNI), measured at average 1999–2001 prices, was US $59,637m., equivalent to $420 per head (or $1,920 per head on an international purchasing-power parity basis). During 1990–2001, it was estimated, the population increased at an average annual rate of 2.5%, while gross domestic product (GDP) per head increased, in real terms, by an average of 1.4% per year. Overall GDP increased, in real terms, at an average annual rate of 3.9% in 1990–2001; growth in 2000/01 declined to 2.5%, before reaching 3.6% in 2001/02.

Agriculture (including forestry and fishing) contributed an estimated 24.2% of GDP in the year ending 30 June 2002. About 48.4% of the employed labour force were engaged in the sector in 2001. The principal cash crops are cotton (textile yarn and fabrics accounted for around 49.3% of export earnings in 2001/02) and rice; wheat, maize and sugar cane are also major crops. Fishing and leather production provide significant export revenues. During 1990/91–2000/01 agricultural GDP increased at an average annual rate of 3.7%; it rose by 6.1% in 1999/2000, but contracted by 2.6% in 2000/01 as a result of drought, before increasing by 1.4% in 2001/02.

Industry (including mining, manufacturing, power and construction) engaged 18.0% of the employed labour force in 2001, and provided an estimated 22.4% of GDP in 2001/02. During 1990/91–2000/01 industrial GDP increased by an average of 3.8% per year. Industrial GDP grew by 3.1% in 2000/01, and by 2.8% in 2001/02.

Mining and quarrying contributed an estimated 0.7% of GDP in 2001/02, and employed 0.1% of the labour force in 1994/95. Petroleum and petroleum products are the major mineral exports. Limestone, rock salt, gypsum, silica sand, natural gas and coal are also mined. In addition, Pakistan has reserves of graphite, copper and manganese. The GDP of the mining sector increased at an average annual rate of 1.8% during 1990/91–2000/01; mining GDP increased by 6.1% in 1999/2000, but decreased by 0.4% in 2000/01.

Manufacturing contributed an estimated 15.7% of GDP in 2001/02, and employed about 9.8% of the labour force in 1994/95. The most important sectors in 1995/96, measured by gross value of output, were textiles (accounting for 33.8% of the total), food products (17.7%) and petroleum refineries (4.9%). During 1990/91–2000/01 manufacturing GDP increased at an average annual rate of 3.9%; manufacturing GDP increased by 1.8% in 1999/2000, by 8.6% in 2000/01, and by 4.0% in 2001/02.

Energy is derived principally from petroleum (providing 35.2% of the total electrical energy supply in 1999), water (34.3%) and natural gas (29.3%). At present around 35% of Pakistan's petroleum is produced domestically. Imports of petroleum and petroleum products comprised about 27.2% of the cost of total imports in 2001/02. In 1994 Pakistan launched a wide-ranging plan to restructure and privatize its power sector.

Services engaged 35.6% of the employed labour force in 2000, and provided an estimated 53.4% of GDP in 2001/02. The combined GDP of the service sectors increased at an average rate of 4.5% per year in 1990/91–2000/01. The GDP of services expanded by 4.8% in 2000/01 and by 5.1% in 2001/02.

In 2001 Pakistan recorded a visible trade deficit of US $608m., and there was a surplus of $1,880m. on the current account of the balance of payments. Remittances from Pakistanis working abroad declined substantially during the 1990s, and by 2000/01 had levelled off to about $1,087m. In 2001/02, however, the flow of remittances increased significantly to $2,389m. The principal source of imports (11.6%) in 2001/02 was Saudi Arabia, and the principal market for exports was the USA (24.7%). Other major trading partners were Germany, Hong Kong, Japan, Kuwait, the United Arab Emirates and the United Kingdom. The principal exports in 2001/02 were textile manufactures, clothing and accessories and food and live animals. The principal imports were petroleum and petroleum products, machinery and transport equipment, chemicals and related products and food and live animals (particularly sugar).

For the financial year ending 30 June 2003 there was a projected budgetary deficit of Rs 67,065m. Pakistan's total external debt was $32,091m. at the end of 2000, of which $27,140m. was long-term public debt. The cost of debt-servicing in that year was equivalent to 26.8% of earnings from exports of goods and services. During 1990–2001 the average annual rate of inflation was 8.6%; according to official figures, consumer prices rose by 4.4% in 2000/01 and by an estimated 2.8% in 2001/02. About 7.8% of the labour force were estimated to be unemployed in 2001.

Pakistan is a member of the South Asian Association for Regional Co-operation (SAARC, see p. 310), of the Asian Development Bank (ADB, see p. 143) and of the Colombo Plan (see p. 339). Pakistan is also a founder member of the Islamic Financial Services Board.

During the 1990s economic growth was constrained by poor investment in manufacturing and inadequate agricultural production, while widespread corruption and inefficient revenue management (particularly in the collection and administration of taxes) undermined attempts to address worsening levels of poverty and deteriorating infrastructure and social services. A number of reform initiatives, undertaken with support from the international finance community, were subsequently abandoned or compromised by the Government (under pressure from a hostile public), and relations were particularly strained with the IMF as a result. The economic crisis was exacerbated by economic sanctions imposed on Pakistan by a group of countries (including the USA) in May 1998 for carrying out nuclear tests, and by further sanctions imposed in response to the military coup of October 1999. However, the new Musharraf administration demonstrated renewed commitment to radical economic reform. In September 2001 the IMF stated that it was encouraged by the economic achievements of the Government during a 12-month stand-by agreement (worth some US $596m.) concluded in November 2000. Despite the volatile political and economic climate in the aftermath of the 11 September 2001 terrorist attacks on the USA, Pakistan's support for and co-operation with the activities of the US-led anti-terrorism coalition in neighbouring Afghanistan resulted in the withdrawal of US sanctions dating from 1998, the extension of concessionary trade terms (including an increased export quota for textiles until 2004) by the EU and offers of substantial financial assistance from the ADB, the USA, Europe and (reportedly) China. In December the IMF agreed to extend a $1,320m. Poverty Reduction and Growth Facility (PRGF) to Pakistan, in support of a three-year social and economic reform programme to be implemented during October 2001–September 2004. The core of the reform programme was outlined in an Interim Poverty Reduction Strategy Paper (I-PRSP) and Memorandum of Economic and Financial Policies (MEFP), published by the Pakistani authorities in November 2001 as a draft document to be consolidated by the new government arising from parliamentary elections scheduled for October 2002. The crucial objectives identified by the I-PRSP were increased potential for economic growth, improved social provisions and reduced vulnerability to external factors. To achieve these objectives, fiscal adjustment and governance reforms were to be introduced. Poverty was also to be addressed directly through reorientation of public expenditure, increased support for rural development, job creation and social contingency programmes. Despite the economic repercussions of the suicide attacks on the USA in September 2001, the prolonged drought, and regional and domestic security problems, Pakistan made substantial progress in implementing these objectives. Real GDP grew by 3.6% in 2001/02 and inflation declined to 2.7%, one of the lowest rates in Pakistan's history. The increase in remittances (owing to the expatriate Pakistani community reinvesting capital in Pakistan after 11 September 2001 and the increased flow of capital through official channels) resulted in high GNI growth. Furthermore, an improved trade balance and a current-account surplus allowed the State Bank of Pakistan to accumulate foreign-exchange reserves at a faster rate than expected, thereby reducing its vulnerability to external factors. The fiscal deficit, including grants, remained at around 4% of GDP in 2001/02 and a shortfall in receipts prompted calls for improved revenue collection. Spending on poverty alleviation and social improvement projects increased in 2002. Devolution of social service delivery was under way in 2002, as well as tax administration reform, the implementation of greater fiscal transparency and privatization. Real GDP was projected to increase by 4.5% in 2002/03, owing to a recovery in the agricultural sector, record-low interest rates and an increase in exports (resulting from more favourable access to US and European markets). Encouraged by the IMF's extension of the PRGF, in December 2001 the 'Paris Club' of creditor governments agreed to reschedule Pakistan's entire bilateral debt stock of $12,500m. (with two-thirds rescheduled over 38 years and the remainder over 23 years). The agreement was expected to save the Pakistani Government an estimated $1,000m. per year over the next three years. However, Pakistan's high public debt continued to restrict investment in development and infrastructure in 2002/03. US-led military action in Iraq in 2003 delayed the privatization of Pakistan State Oil, scheduled for April. Analysts expressed concerns that the conflict in Iraq would put at risk other privatization plans (domestic political uncertainty during and following the elections and security problems was already deterring potential investors). In the mean time, in 2003 the new Government was required to continue fiscal adjustment, ensure greater investment in social services and implement further structural reforms in order to secure Pakistan's progress.

Education

Universal free primary education is a constitutional right, but education is not compulsory. Primary education begins at five years of age and lasts for five years. Secondary education, beginning at the age of 10, is divided into two stages, of three and four years respectively. In 1991 the total enrolment at primary and secondary schools was equivalent to 44% of all school-age children (58% of boys; 29% of girls). Primary enrolment in 1993 was equivalent to 74% of children in the relevant age-group (101% of boys; 45% of girls), while the comparable ratio for secondary enrolment in 1991 was 26% (33% of boys; 17% of girls). In 2000/01 it was estimated that there were 20,999,000 children enrolled at pre-primary and primary schools (including mosque schools), and 6,576,000 at middle and secondary schools. All institutions, except missions and an increasing number of private schools, are nationalized. From 1976 agrotechnical subjects were introduced into the school curriculum, and 25 trade schools were established in that year. There are 26 universities. Development expenditure on science and technology and education and training in 2001/02 was projected at Rs 4,343.3m. (only 3.3% of the Government's total development spending).

Public Holidays

2003: 12 February* (Id al-Adha, Feast of the Sacrifice), 5 March* (Muharram, Islamic New Year), 14 March* (Ashoura), 23 March (Pakistan Day, proclamation of republic in 1956), 18 April† (Good Friday), 21 April† (Easter Monday), 1 May (Labour Day), 14 May* (Eid-i-Milad-un-Nabi, Birth of the Prophet), 14 August (Independence Day), 6 September (Defence of Pakistan Day), 11 September (Anniversary of Death of Quaid-i-Azam), 27 October* (Ramadan begins), 9 November (Allama Iqbal Day), 26 November* (Id al-Fitr, end of Ramadan), 25 December (Birthday of Quaid-i-Azam, and Christmas), 26 December† (Boxing Day).

2004: 2 February* (Id al-Adha, Feast of the Sacrifice), 22 February* (Muharram, Islamic New Year), 2 March* (Ashoura), 23 March (Pakistan Day, proclamation of republic in 1956), 9 April† (Good Friday), 12 April† (Easter Monday), 1 May (Labour Day), 2 May* (Eid-i-Milad-un-Nabi, Birth of the Prophet), 14 August (Independence Day), 6 September (Defence of Pakistan Day), 11 September (Anniversary of Death of Quaid-i-Azam), 15 October* (Ramadan begins), 9 November (Allama Iqbal Day), 14 November* (Id al-Fitr, end of Ramadan), 25 December (Birthday of Quaid-i-Azam, and Christmas), 26 December† (Boxing Day).

* These holidays are dependent on the Islamic lunar calendar and may vary by one or two days from the dates given.

† Optional holidays for Christians only.

Weights and Measures

The metric system has been officially introduced. Also in use are imperial and local weights, including:

1 maund = 82.28 lb (37.32 kg).

1 seer = 2.057 lb (933 grams).

1 tola = 180 grains (11.66 grams).

Statistical Survey

Source (unless otherwise stated): Development Advisory Centre, Karachi; tel. (21) 2631587; e-mail arsidiqi@fascom.com.

Area and Population

AREA, POPULATION AND DENSITY*

Area (sq km)	796,095†
Population (census results)	
1 March 1981.	84,253,644
2 March 1998	
Males	67,840,137
Females.	62,739,434
Total	130,579,571
Population (official estimates at mid-year)	
1999	134,510,000
2000	137,510,000
2001	140,470,000
Density (per sq km) at mid-2001.	176.4

* Excluding data for the disputed territory of Jammu and Kashmir. The Pakistani-held parts of this region are known as Azad ('Free') Kashmir, with an area of 11,639 sq km (4,494 sq miles) and a population of 1,980,000 in 1981, and Northern Areas (including Gilgit and Baltistan), with an area of 72,520 sq km (28,000 sq miles) and a population of 562,000 in 1981. Also excluded are Junagardh and Manavadar. The population figures exclude refugees from Afghanistan (estimated to number 1.5m. in early 2003).

† 307,374 sq miles.

ADMINISTRATIVE DIVISIONS
(population at 1998 census)

	Area (sq km)	Population (provisional)	Density (per sq km)
Provinces:			
Balochistan.	347,188	6,511,358	18.8
North-West Frontier Province .	74,522	17,554,674	235.6
Punjab	205,345	72,585,430	353.5
Sindh	140,913	29,991,161	212.8
Federally Administered Tribal			
Areas	27,221	3,137,8630	115.3
Federal Capital Territory:			
Islamabad	906	799,085	882.0
Total	796,095	130,579,571	164.0

Source: Thomas Brinkhoff, *City Population* (internet www.citypopulation.de).

PRINCIPAL TOWNS
(population at 1998 census)

Karachi . . .	9,269,265	Bahawalpur . . .	403,408
Lahore. . . .	5,063,499	Sukkur	329,176
Faisalabad			
(Lyallpur) . . .	1,977,246	Jhang Maghiana	
		(Jhang Sadar) . .	292,214
Rawalpindi . . .	1,406,214	Shekhupura . . .	271,875
Multan	1,182,441	Larkana	270,366
Hyderabad . . .	1,151,274	Okara	258,324
Gujranwala . .	1,124,799	Gujrat	250,121
Peshawar . . .	988,005	Mardan	244,511
Quetta. . . .	560,307	Kasur	241,649
Islamabad (capital) .	529,180	Rahimyar Khan . .	228,479
Sargodha . . .	455,360	Sahiwal	207,388
Sialkot. . . .	417,597		

Source: Thomas Brinkhoff, *City Population* (internet www.citypopulation.de).

BIRTHS AND DEATHS
(UN estimates, annual averages)

	1985–90	1990–95	1995–2000
Birth rate (per 1,000)	41.5	39.9	37.9
Death rate (per 1,000)	13.3	12.0	10.8

Source: UN, *World Population Prospects: The 2000 Revision.*

Expectation of life (WHO estimates, years at birth): 61.3 (males 61.0; females 61.5) in 2001 (Source: WHO, *World Health Report*).

ECONOMICALLY ACTIVE POPULATION
(ISIC major divisions, '000 persons aged 10 years and over, excl. armed forces)*

	1999	2000	2001
Agriculture	17,570	17,780	18,160
Mining and manufacturing . .	3,780	4,240	4,330
Construction	2,330	2,120	2,170
Electricity and gas distribution .	260	260	260
Transport	2,040	1,850	1,890
Trade	5,160	4,960	5,060
Total employed (incl. others) .	37,190	36,720	37,500
Unemployed	2,330	3,120	3,190
Total labour force	39,520	39,840	40,690

* Excluding data for Jammu and Kashmir, Gilgit and Baltistan, Junagardh and Manavadar.

Source: *Economic Survey, 2001/02*, Government of Pakistan.

Health and Welfare

KEY INDICATORS

Total fertility rate (children per woman, 2001)	5.2
Under-5 mortality rate (per 1,000 live births, 2001)	109
HIV/AIDS (% of persons aged 15–49, 2001)	0.11
Physicians (per 1,000 head, 1997)	0.57
Hospital beds (per 1,000 head, 1993)	0.65
Health expenditure (2000): US $ per head (PPP)	76
Health expenditure (2000): % of GDP	4.1
Health expenditure (2000): public (% of total)	22.9
Access to water (% of persons, 1999)	88
Access to sanitation (% of persons, 1999)	61
Human Development Index (2000): ranking	138
Human Development Index (2000): value	0.499

For sources and definitions, see explanatory note on p. vi.

Agriculture

PRINCIPAL CROPS
('000 metric tons)

	1999	2000	2001
Wheat	17,856	21,079	19,024
Rice (paddy)	7,733	7,204	5,823
Barley	137	118	99
Maize	1,652	1,643	1,664
Millet	156	199	216
Sorghum	220	219	222
Potatoes	1,810	1,868	1,666
Other roots and tubers*	429	439	430
Sugar cane	55,191	46,333	43,606
Dry beans	119	130	143
Dry peas	93	78	61
Chick-peas	698	565	397
Other pulses	179	162	154*
Nuts*	74	57	61
Groundnuts (in shell)	99	91	101
Sunflower seed	149	150	150*
Rapeseed	279	297	231
Cottonseed	3,824	3,651	3,610
Other oil-bearing crops*	62	76	94
Cabbages	62	62	67
Spinach	80	74	76
Tomatoes	332	283	270
Cauliflower	198	197	200
Pumpkins, squash and gourds*	245	250	250
Aubergines (Eggplants)*	76	76	76
Dry onions	1,138	1,648	1,563
Garlic	83	76	64
Green peas	72	71	71
Carrots	195	186	188
Okra*	109	110	110
Other vegetables*	1,131	1,232	1,232
Watermelons*	420	400	400
Cantaloupes and other melons*	400	400	400
Bananas	125	139	151
Oranges	1,360†	1,328†	1,328*
Tangerines, mandarins, clementines and satsumas	505†	493†	493*
Lemons and limes	78†	76†	76*
Apples	377	439	438
Apricots	121	126	126
Peaches and nectarines	33	33	41
Plums	59	64	60
Grapes	40	51	51
Mangoes	938	990	1,037
Dates	580	612	632
Other fruits*	907	920	914
Pimento and allspice	115	163	163*
Other spices	45	45*	45*
Cotton (lint)	1,912	1,825	1,805
Tobacco (leaves)	109	108	85

* FAO estimate(s).
† Unofficial figure.

Source: FAO.

LIVESTOCK
('000 head, year ending September)

	1999	2000	2001
Cattle	21,592	22,004	22,424
Buffaloes	22,032	22,669	23,335
Sheep	23,900	24,100	24,200
Goats	45,800	47,400	49,100
Horses	300	300	300
Asses	3,800	3,800	3,900
Mules	150	200	200
Camels	800	800	800
Chickens*	148,000	150,000	155,000
Ducks*	3,500	3,500	3,500

* FAO estimates.

Source: FAO.

LIVESTOCK PRODUCTS
('000 metric tons)

	1999	2000	2001
Beef and veal*	407	420	428
Buffalo meat*	460	466	480
Mutton and lamb*	183	170	172
Goat meat*	312	336	348
Poultry meat	314.7	326.7	337.7
Other meat†	15.7	15.9	15.9
Cows' milk	9,863	10,049	10,240
Buffaloes' milk	20,489	21,138	21,817
Sheep's milk	30	31	31
Goats' milk	565	586	607
Ghee†	546.0	563.3	581.4
Hen eggs*	323.5	331.5	339.8
Other poultry eggs†	7.1	7.2	7.2
Wool: greasy	38.7	38.9	39.2
Wool: scoured*	23.1	23.4	23.5
Cattle hides†	51.6	52.8	53.8
Buffalo hides†	78.8	81.0	82.3
Sheepskins†	40.3	40.3	41.7
Goatskins†	96.3	99.8	103.2

* Unofficial figures.
† FAO estimates.

Source: FAO.

Forestry

ROUNDWOOD REMOVALS
('000 cubic metres, excl. bark)

	1999	2000	2001
Sawlogs, veneer logs and logs for sleepers	1,765	2,045	1,892
Other industrial wood	620	635	787
Fuel wood	30,670	30,880	30,553
Total	33,055	33,560	33,232

Source: FAO.

SAWNWOOD PRODUCTION
('000 cubic metres, incl. railway sleepers)

	1999	2000	2001
Coniferous (softwood)	410	415	435
Broadleaved (hardwood)	665	672	745
Total	1,075	1,087	1,180

Source: FAO.

Fishing

('000 metric tons, live weight)

	1998	1999	2000
Capture	597.0	654.5	614.8
Freshwater fishes	163.5	179.9	176.5
Sea catfishes	55.9	51.7	39.2
Croakers and drums	19.6	24.7	22.0
Mullets	17.6	12.3	9.6
Indian oil sardine	44.1	30.6	31.2
Requiem sharks	35.4	32.5	28.2
Penaeus shrimps	25.4	24.5	18.0
Aquaculture	17.4	23.1	12.5
Cyprinids	17.3	23.0	12.4
Total catch	614.5	674.6	627.3

Source: FAO, *Yearbook of Fishery Statistics*.

Mining

(metric tons, unless otherwise indicated, year ending 30 June)

	1999/2000*	2000/01*	2001/02†
Barytes	26,000	28,000	n.a.
Chromite	25,669	16,459	15,984
Limestone	9,589,000	10,868,000	9,805,000
Gypsum	355,000	364,000	328,000
Fireclay	139,000	164,000	n.a.
Silica sand	167,000	155,000	157,000
Rock salt	1,358,000	1,394,000	1,359,000
Coal and lignite	3,164,000	3,269,000	n.a.
Crude petroleum ('000 barrels)	20,395	21,083	23,193
Natural gas (million cu m)	23,173	24,789	26,154

* Revised figures.
† Provisional figures.

Sources: *Economic Survey, 2001/02*, Government of Pakistan; State Bank of Pakistan.

Industry

SELECTED PRODUCTS

('000 metric tons, unless otherwise indicated, year ending 30 June)

	1999/2000	2000/01	2001/02*
Cotton cloth (million sq m)	437.2	490.2	568.4
Cotton yarn	1,669.9	1,721.0	1,808.6
Jute textiles	85.5	89.4	82
Refined sugar	2,429.3	2,955.9	3,246.6
Vegetable ghee	698.1	834.8	774
Cement	9,314	9,674	9,935
Urea	3,785.0	4,005.1	4,216.2
Superphosphate	145.8	159.6	161.0
Sulphuric acid	57.7	57.1	59.4
Soda ash	245.7	217.9	215.2
Caustic soda	141.3	145.5	150.3
Chlorine gas	14.2	14.5	15.1
Cigarettes (million)	46,976	58,259	55,320
Petroleum products	11,878	7,333*	n.a.
Beverages (million bottles)	2,332.3	2,541.6	2,492
Ammonium nitrate	386.5	374.4	329.4
Nitrophosphate	261.3	282.5	305.7
Pig-iron	1,106.6	1,071.2	1,042.9
Billets	345.2	414.7	n.a.
Paperboard	228.1	246.3	256.0
Tractors ('000)	35.0	32.6	24.3
Bicycles ('000)	534.1	569.6	553.4
Motor tyres and tubes ('000)	1,346	1,404	1,463
Bicycle tyres and tubes ('000)	9,703	9,942	11,507
Sewing machines ('000)	27.6	26.9	n.a.
Electric energy (million kWh)	65,751	68,117	72,106

* Provisional figure(s).

Sources: State Bank of Pakistan; *Economic Survey, 2001/02*, Government of Pakistan; Asian Development Bank, *Key Indicators of Developing Asian and Pacific Countries*.

Finance

CURRENCY AND EXCHANGE RATES

Monetary Units

100 paisa = 1 Pakistani rupee

Sterling, Dollar and Euro Equivalents (31 December 2002)

£1 sterling = 94.35 rupees
US $1 = 58.53 rupees
€1 = 61.39 rupees
1,000 Pakistani rupees = £10.60 = $17.08 = €16.29

Average Exchange Rate (Pakistani rupees per US $)

2000   53.648
2001   61.927
2002   59.724

CENTRAL GOVERNMENT BUDGET

(million rupees, year ending 30 June)

Revenue	2000/01*	2001/02*	2002/03†
Tax revenue	406,500	414,200	460,600
Income and corporate taxes‡	125,751	142,000	143,200
Taxes on property	1,812	400	—
Other direct taxes	6,337	4,100	5,200
Excise duty	52,200	47,100	50,000
Sales tax‡	155,800	170,100	205,700
Taxes on international trade	64,600	50,500	56,500
Non-tax revenue	118,450	164,697	153,793
Surcharges‡	33,000	53,902	60,500
Total	557,950	632,799	674,893

Expenditure	2000/01*	2001/02*	2002/03†
Current expenditure	579,682	648,589	607,958
Defence‡	131,637	151,669	146,022
Debt-servicing	308,103	320,114	289,695
Current subsidies	22,706	25,580	607,958
General administration	49,743	51,186	54,928
Social services	10,390	12,289	13,869
Development expenditure	102,432	124,700	134,000
Total	682,114	773,289	741,958

* Revised estimates.
† Projected estimates.
‡ Exclusively federal.

Source: Ministry of Finance, Economic Affairs and Statistics, Islamabad.

PLANNED DEVELOPMENT EXPENDITURE

(million rupees, year ending 30 June)

	1999/2000*	2000/01†	2001/02†
Sectoral programme:			
Agriculture (incl. subsidy for fertilizers)	329.1	329.2	665.2
Water	11,298.9	10,077.9 ⎫	8,957.7
Power	2,963.0	2,682.5 ⎬	
Industry	260.1	692.3	364.0
Fuels	1,170.0	2,238.7	—
Minerals	38.0	8.1	—
Transport and communication	3,188.2	4,057.1	754.3
Physical planning and housing	13,274.7	1,748.5	221.4
Science and technology and education and training	7,129.2	4,064.6	4,343.3
Social welfare, culture, tourism, sport and manpower and employment	457.8	263.6	381.5
Health	2,566.4	2,841.4	2,547.5
Population planning	2,200.0	2,200.0	1,800.0
Rural development	117.2	2,419.8	—
Mass media	126.0	126.9	207.3
Special programmes	3,500.0	—	20,170.0
Corporation	—	—	26,678.3
Provincial Development Programme	—	—	30,000.0
Provincial Social Action Programme Tied Allocation	—	—	11,000.0
Total planned development expenditure (incl. others)	116,296.6	120,432.5	130,000.0

* Revised estimates.
† Provisional figures.

Source: Ministry of Finance, Economic Affairs and Statistics, Islamabad.

INTERNATIONAL RESERVES

(US $ million, last Thursday of the year)

	2000	2001	2002
Gold*	543	595	684
IMF special drawing rights	14	4	2
Foreign exchange	1,499	3,636	8,076
Total	2,056	4,235	8,762

* Revalued annually, in June, on the basis of London market prices.

Source: IMF, *International Financial Statistics*.

MONEY SUPPLY

(million rupees, last Thursday of the year)

	2000	2001	2002
Currency outside banks . . .	410,469	429,360	487,745
Demand deposits at scheduled banks	457,773	524,429	628,531
Total money*	876,014	964,921	1,118,403

* Including also private-sector deposits at the State Bank.

Source: IMF, *International Financial Statistics*.

COST OF LIVING

(Consumer Price Index; base: 1990/91 = 100; year ending 30 June)

	1998/99	1999/2000	2000/01
Food, beverages and tobacco . .	225.6	230.6	238.8
Clothing and footwear	200.4	211.3	217.1
Rent	208.3	217.1	223.5
Fuel and lighting.	214.2	227.0	255.9
All items (incl. others)	215.7	223.4	233.2

Source: State Bank of Pakistan, *Annual Report*.

NATIONAL ACCOUNTS

(million rupees at current prices, year ending 30 June)

National Income and Product

	1995/96	1996/97	1997/98
Domestic factor incomes* . . .	1,813,222	2,045,127	2,354,018
Consumption of fixed capital . .	138,338	156,801	179,262
Gross domestic product at factor cost.	1,951,560	2,201,928	2,533,280
Indirect taxes.	227,858	215,636	239,519
Less Subsidies	13,820	12,931	13,274
GDP in purchasers' values . .	2,165,598	2,404,633	2,759,525
Net factor income from abroad . .	−7,136	−19,127	−15,081
Gross national product (GNP) .	2,158,462	2,385,506	2,744,444
Less Consumption of fixed capital .	138,338	156,801	179,262
National income in market prices	2,020,124	2,228,705	2,565,182

* Compensation of employees and the operating surplus of enterprises. The amount is obtained as a residual.

Source: UN, *National Accounts Statistics*.

Expenditure on the Gross Domestic Product

	1999/2000	2000/01*	2001/02†
Government final consumption expenditure.	351,624	350,376	425,902
Private final consumption expenditure.	2,342,417	2,567,321	2,793,408
Increase in stocks	51,700	56,200	58,000
Gross fixed capital formation . .	452,280	488,180	459,457
Total domestic expenditure. .	3,198,021	3,462,077	3,736,767
Exports of goods and services . .	514,389	615,371	661,024
Less Imports of goods and services	565,243	661,196	671,180
GDP in purchasers' values . .	3,147,167	3,416,252	3,726,611
Net factor income from abroad . .	−44,906	−50,830	25,901
GNP in purchasers' values . .	3,102,261	3,365,422	3,752,512

* Revised figures.
† Provisional figures.

Source: *Economic Survey, 2001/02*, Government of Pakistan.

Gross Domestic Product by Economic Activity

	1999/2000	2000/01*	2001/02†
Agriculture and livestock . . .	755,348	761,979	800,563
Forestry and fishing	24,344	27,042	28,835
Mining and quarrying	17,393	20,856	22,803
Manufacturing	447,395	499,085	537,035
Electricity and gas distribution .	114,064	105,244	106,614
Construction	97,517	100,164	103,157
Commerce	443,934	488,586	511,819
Transport, storage and communications	311,630	357,644	393,799
Banking and insurance	60,255	96,467	102,814
Ownership of dwellings	135,518	146,861	162,946
Public administration and defence	249,832	263,505	321,090
Other services	264,758	294,490	336,843
GDP at factor cost.	2,921,988	3,161,923	3,428,318
Indirect taxes, *less* subsidies . .	225,179	254,329	298,293
GDP in purchasers' values . .	3,147,167	3,416,252	3,726,611

* Revised figures.
† Provisional figures.

Source: *Economic Survey, 2001/02*, Government of Pakistan.

BALANCE OF PAYMENTS

(US $ million)

	1999	2000	2001
Exports of goods f.o.b.	7,673	8,739	9,131
Imports of goods f.o.b.	−9,520	−9,896	−9,739
Trade balance	−1,847	−1,157	−608
Exports of services	1,373	1,380	1,459
Imports of services	−2,146	−2,252	−2,330
Balance on goods and services .	−2,620	−2,029	−1,479
Other income received	119	118	113
Other income paid	−1,959	−2,336	−2,192
Balance on goods, services and income	−4,460	−4,247	−3,558
Current transfers received . . .	3,582	4,200	5,499
Current transfers paid	−42	−38	−61
Current balance	−920	−85	1,880
Direct investment abroad . . .	−21	−11	−31
Direct investment from abroad .	532	308	383
Portfolio investment liabilities . .	46	−451	−192
Other investment assets . . .	−523	−437	54
Other investment liabilities . .	−2,398	−2,508	−613
Net errors and omissions . . .	768	557	716
Overall balance	−2,516	−2,627	2,197

Source: IMF, *International Financial Statistics*.

OFFICIAL DEVELOPMENT ASSISTANCE

(US $ million)

	1998	1999	2000
Bilateral donors	531.0	435.9	476.0
Multilateral donors	522.0	297.2	226.8
Total	1,053.0	733.1	702.8
Grants	294.1	296.9	206.5
Loans	758.9	436.2	496.3
Per caput assistance (US $) . .	7.9	5.3	4.9

Source: UN, *Statistical Yearbook for Asia and the Pacific*.

External Trade

Note: Data exclude trade in military goods.

PRINCIPAL COMMODITIES
(US $ million, year ending 30 June)

Imports c.i.f. (excl. re-imports)	1999/2000	2000/01	2001/02
Food and live animals	804.4	901.3	525.2
Crude materials (inedible)			
except fuels	719.0	635.9	847.8
Mineral fuels, lubricants, etc.	2,873.1	3,395.3	2,869.0
Petroleum, petroleum products, etc.	2,804.4	3,347.3	2,809.5
Animal and vegetable oils, fats and waxes	503.2	432.3	474.1
Fixed vegetable fats and oils	436.1	377.3	411.1
Chemicals and related products	1,997.2	1,903.9	1,871.0
Organic chemicals	593.9	652.8	600.5
Basic manufactures	855.7	883.5	993.1
Iron and steel	304.5	279.0	336.7
Machinery and transport equipment	1,997.7	2,073.4	2,201.9
Machinery specialized for particular industries	595.3	689.6	707.7
Road vehicles and parts (excl. tyres, engines and electrical parts)	345.5	320.6	329.2
Total (incl. others)	10,309.4	10,728.9	10,339.6

Exports f.o.b. (excl. re-exports)	1999/2000	2000/01	2001/02
Food and live animals	919.8	913.5	947.3
Rice	539.7	527.9	447.8
Crude materials (inedible) except fuels	210.9	283.7	152.1
Basic manufactures	4,628.5	4,852.4	4,832.4
Leather, leather manufactures and dressed furskins	183.8	247.5	250.5
Textile yarn, fabrics, etc.	4,383.7	4,532.2	4,502.7
Miscellaneous manufactured articles	2,550.7	2,720.5	2,770.3
Clothing and accessories (excl. footwear)	1,988.4	2,150.1	2,097.9
Total (incl. others)	8,568.6	9,201.6	9,134.6

Source: State Bank of Pakistan, *Annual Report*.

PRINCIPAL TRADING PARTNERS
(US $ million, year ending 30 June)

Imports c.i.f. (excl. re-imports)	1999/2000	2000/01	2001/02
Australia	366.7	226.2	288.6
Bahrain	114.6	80.0	59.6
Belgium	121.4	181.2	257.7
China, People's Republic	471.6	528.9	575.2
France	224.8	146.7	132.6
Germany	423.3	382.4	439.7
India	127.4	235.1	186.5
Indonesia	175.6	161.7	243.2
Iran	130.2	374.4	158.2
Italy	171.2	178.3	214.7
Japan	650.5	576.2	519.4
Korea, Republic	354.2	354.6	298.6
Kuwait	1,236.8	964.6	731.9
Malaysia	439.3	428.1	456.3
Netherlands	152.9	177.2	174.6
Saudi Arabia	923.0	1,259.2	1,200.7
Singapore	267.1	325.3	322.5
Switzerland	350.6	233.2	169.1
Thailand	159.4	209.8	178.1
Turkey	106.6	47.6	34.8
United Arab Emirates*	907.6	1,328.1	1,354.6
United Kingdom	355.7	350.2	356.8
USA	646.5	565.5	687.9
Total (incl. others)	10,309.4	10,728.9	10,339.6

* Abu Dhabi and Dubai only.

Exports f.o.b. (excl. re-exports)	1999/2000	2000/01	2001/02
Afghanistan	115.2	140.4	169.3
Australia	111.9	113.1	101.3
Bangladesh	120.4	133.4	101.1
Belgium	202.2	174.5	178.4
Canada	183.4	182.1	174.6
China, People's Republic	180.3	303.2	228.6
France	282.7	265.8	246.7
Germany	512.7	495.0	452.1
Hong Kong	524.9	504.5	442.2
Indonesia	52.9	136.4	76.8
Italy	209.3	230.3	253.0
Japan	267.5	193.6	166.5
Korea, Republic	245.4	278.4	261.9
Netherlands	229.1	233.2	257.8
Saudi Arabia	214.8	273.0	330.4
Spain	150.3	162.3	174.0
Sri Lanka	96.6	75.3	72.1
Turkey	61.0	100.5	98.3
United Arab Emirates*	493.0	626.1	727.3
United Kingdom	579.5	576.1	659.1
USA	2,123.1	2,245.6	2,257.5
Total (incl. others)	8,568.6	9,201.6	9,134.6

* Abu Dhabi and Dubai only.

Source: State Bank of Pakistan, *Annual Report*.

Transport

RAILWAYS
(year ending 30 June)

	1998/99	1999/2000	2000/01
Passenger journeys ('000)	64,990	68,000	68,800
Freight ('000 metric tons)	5,450	4,770	5,900
Net freight ton-km (million)	4,330	3,612	4,520

Source: *Economic Survey, 2001/02*, Government of Pakistan.

ROAD TRAFFIC
('000 vehicles in use)

	1999	2000	2001
Motorcycles and scooters	1,976.9	2,113.0	2,140.5
Passenger cars	700.6	748.9	758.6
Jeeps	69.5	66.8	67.6
Station wagons	79.1	84.5	85.6
Road tractors	538.7	575.8	583.2
Buses	85.9	91.9	93.0
Taxicabs	67.9	72.6	73.5
Rickshaws	87.2	93.3	94.5
Delivery vans	172.1	184.0	186.4
Trucks	148.4	158.6	160.1
Total (incl. others)	4,016.6	4,277.8	4,332.5

Source: *Economic Survey, 2001/02*, Government of Pakistan.

SHIPPING

Merchant Fleet
(displacement at 31 December)

	1999	2000	2001
Number of vessels	55	52	49
Total displacement ('000 grt)	308.0	260.3	247.4

Source: Lloyd's Register-Fairplay, *World Fleet Statistics*.

International Sea-borne Shipping
(port of Karachi, year ending 30 June)

	1998/99	1999/2000	2000/01
Goods ('000 long tons):			
loaded	5,735	5,612	5,918
unloaded	18,318	18,149	20,063

Source: State Bank of Pakistan, *Annual Report*.

CIVIL AVIATION
(PIA only, domestic and international flights, '000, year ending 30 June)

	1998/99	1999/2000	2000/01
Kilometres flown	70,697	76,155	54,830
Passengers carried	5,086	5,242	4,178
Passenger-km.	10,722,000	11,650,000	9,739,000

Source: *Economic Survey, 2000/01*, Government of Pakistan.

Tourism

FOREIGN TOURIST ARRIVALS

Country of nationality	1998	1999	2000
Afghanistan	20,275	25,586	27,913
Canada	10,931	11,429	12,956
China, People's Republic . . .	10,747	7,957	6,191
Germany	12,988	12,778	14,121
India	67,050	63,225	66,061
Japan	17,479	16,589	12,794
United Kingdom	109,772	126,532	179,758
USA	49,795	48,488	71,518
Total (incl. others)	428,781	432,217	556,805

Receipts from tourism (US $ million): 98 in 1998; 76 in 1999; 86 (estimate) in 2000.

Source: World Tourism Organization, *Yearbook of Tourism Statistics*.

Communications Media

	1998	1999	2000
Television receivers ('000 in use) .	12,500	16,000	18,500
Telephones ('000 main lines in use)	2,756.1	2,986.1	3,200.0
Mobile cellular telephones ('000 subscribers).	206.9	278.8	349.5
Facsimile machines ('000 in use)	268	n.a.	n.a.
Personal computers ('000 in use)	561	580	590
Internet users ('000)	61.9	80.0	133.9

Radio receivers ('000 in use): 13,500 in 1997 (Source: UNESCO, *Statistical Yearbook*).

Daily newspapers and periodicals: 359 in 1997 (Source: UN, *Statistical Yearbook*).

Non-daily newspapers and periodicals: 782 (with average circulation of 1,830,000 copies) in 1997 (Source: UN, *Statistical Yearbook*).

2001: Telephones ('000 main lines in use) 3,400; Mobile cellular telephones ('000 subscribers) 800; Personal computers ('000 in use) 600; Internet users ('000) 500.

Sources: *Economic Survey, 2000/01*, Government of Pakistan; International Telecommunication Union.

Education

(estimates, 2000/01)

	Institutions	Teachers	Students
Pre-primary and primary* . .	165,700	373,900	20,999,000
Middle	18,800	96,100	4,644,000
Secondary	12,800	224,000	1,932,000
Higher:			
secondary vocational institutes	580	7,062	75,000
arts and science colleges . .	853	26,942	791,000
professional†	308	8,817	162,989
universities	26	5,914	114,010

* Including mosque schools.
† Including educational colleges.

Source: *Economic Survey, 2000/01*, Government of Pakistan.

Adult literacy rate (UNESCO estimates): 43.2% (males 57.5%; females 27.9%) in 2000 (Source: UN Development Programme, *Human Development Report*).

Directory

The Constitution

The Constitution was promulgated on 10 April 1973, and amended on a number of subsequent occasions (see Amendments, below). Several provisions were suspended following the imposition of martial law in 1977. The (amended) Constitution was restored on 30 December 1985.

GENERAL PROVISIONS

The Preamble upholds the principles of democracy, freedom, equality, tolerance and social justice as enunciated by Islam. The rights of religious and other minorities are guaranteed.

The Islamic Republic of Pakistan consists of four provinces—Balochistan, North-West Frontier Province, Punjab and Sindh—and the tribal areas under federal administration. The provinces are autonomous units.

Fundamental rights are guaranteed and include equality of status (women have equal rights with men), freedom of thought, speech, worship and the press and freedom of assembly and association. No law providing for preventive detention shall be made except to deal with persons acting against the integrity, security or defence of Pakistan. No such law shall authorize the detention of a person for more than one month.

PRESIDENT

The President is Head of State and acts on the advice of the Prime Minister. He is elected by an electoral college, comprising the two chambers of the Federal Legislature and the four Provincial Assemblies, to serve for a term of five years. He must be a Muslim. The President may be impeached for violating the Constitution or gross misconduct.

FEDERAL LEGISLATURE

The Federal Legislature consists of the President, a lower and an upper house. The lower house, called the National Assembly, has 207 members elected directly for a term of five years, on the basis of universal suffrage (for adults over the age of 21 years), plus 10 members representing minorities. The upper house, called the Senate, has 87 members who serve for six years, with one-third retiring every two years. Each Provincial Assembly is to elect 19 Senators. The tribal areas are to return eight members and the remaining three are to be elected from the Federal Capital Territory by members of the Provincial Assemblies.

There shall be two sessions of the National Assembly and Senate each year, with not more than 120 days between the last sitting of a session and the first sitting of the next session.

The role of the Senate in an overwhelming majority of the subjects shall be merely advisory. Disagreeing with any legislation of the National Assembly, it shall have the right to send it back only once for reconsideration. In case of disagreement in other subjects, the Senate and National Assembly shall sit in a joint session to decide the matter by a simple majority.

GOVERNMENT

The Constitution provides that bills may originate in either house, except money bills. The latter must originate in the National

Assembly and cannot go to the Senate. A bill must be passed by both houses and then approved by the President, who may return the bill and suggest amendments. In this case, after the bill has been reconsidered and passed, with or without amendment, the President must give his assent to it.

PROVINCIAL GOVERNMENT

In the matter of relations between Federation and Provinces, the Federal Legislature shall have the power to make laws, including laws bearing on extra-territorial affairs, for the whole or any part of Pakistan, while a Provincial Assembly shall be empowered to make laws for that Province or any part of it. Matters in the Federal Legislative List shall be subject to the exclusive authority of the Federal Legislature, while the Federal Legislature and a Provincial Assembly shall have power to legislate with regard to matters referred to in the Concurrent Legislative List. Any matter not referred to in either list may be subject to laws made by a Provincial Assembly alone, and not by the Federal Legislature, although the latter shall have exclusive power to legislate with regard to matters not referred to in either list for those areas in the Federation not included in any Province.

Four provisions seek to ensure the stability of the parliamentary system. First, the Prime Minister shall be elected by the National Assembly and he and the other Ministers shall be responsible to it. Secondly, any resolution calling for the removal of a Prime Minister shall have to name his successor in the same resolution which shall be adopted by not less than two-thirds of the total number of members of the lower house. The requirement of two-thirds majority is to remain in force for 15 years or three electoral terms, whichever is more. Thirdly, the Prime Minister shall have the right to seek dissolution of the legislature at any time even during the pendency of a no-confidence motion. Fourthly, if a no-confidence motion is defeated, such a motion shall not come up before the house for the next six months.

All these provisions for stability shall apply *mutatis mutandis* to the Provincial Assemblies also.

A National Economic Council, to include the Prime Minister and a representative from each province, shall advise the Provincial and Federal Governments.

There shall be a Governor for each Province, appointed by the President, and a Council of Ministers to aid and advise him, with a Chief Minister appointed by the Governor. Each Province has a provincial legislature consisting of the Governor and Provincial Assembly.

The executive authorities of every Province shall be required to ensure that their actions are in compliance with the Federal laws which apply in that Province. The Federation shall be required to consider the interests of each Province in the exercise of its authority in that Province. The Federation shall further be required to afford every Province protection from external aggression and internal disturbance, and to ensure that every Province is governed in accordance with the provisions of the Constitution.

To further safeguard the rights of the smaller provinces, a Council of Common Interests has been created. Comprising the Chief Ministers of the four provinces and four Central Ministers to decide upon specified matters of common interest, the Council is responsible to the Federal Legislature. The constitutional formula gives the net proceeds of excise duty and royalty on gas to the province concerned. The profits on hydroelectric power generated in each province shall go to that province.

OTHER PROVISIONS

Other provisions include the procedure for elections, the setting up of an Advisory Council of Islamic Ideology and an Islamic Research Institute, and the administration of tribal areas.

AMENDMENTS

Amendments to the Constitution shall require a two-thirds majority in the National Assembly and endorsement by a simple majority in the Senate.

In 1975 the Constitution (Third Amendment) Bill abolished the provision that a State of Emergency may not be extended beyond six months without the approval of the National Assembly and empowered the Government to detain a person for three months instead of one month.

In July 1977, following the imposition of martial law, several provisions, including all fundamental rights provided for in the Constitution, were suspended.

An amendment of September 1978 provided for separate electoral registers to be drawn up for Muslims and non-Muslims.

In October 1979 a martial law order inserted a clause in the Constitution establishing the supremacy of military courts in trying all offences, criminal and otherwise.

On 26 May 1980, the President issued a Constitution Amendment Order, which amended Article 199, debarring High Courts from making any order relating to the validity of effect of any judgment or sentence passed by a military court or tribunal granting an injunction; from making an order or entering any proceedings in respect of matters under the jurisdiction or cognizance of a military court or tribunal, and from initiating proceedings against the Chief Martial Law Administrator or a Martial Law Administrator.

By another amendment of the Constitution, the Federal Shari'a Court was to replace the Shari'a Benches of the High Courts. The Shari'a Court, on the petition of a citizen or the Government, may decide whether any law or provision of law is contrary to the injunction of Islam as laid down in the Holy Koran and the Sunnah of the Holy Prophet.

In March 1981 the Government promulgated Provisional Constitution Order 1981, whereby provision is made for the appointment of one or more Vice-Presidents, to be appointed by the Chief Martial Law Administrator, and a Federal Advisory Council (*Majlis-i-Shura*) consisting of persons nominated by the President. All political parties not registered with the Election Commission on 13 September 1979 were to be dissolved and their properties made forfeit to the Federal Council. Any party working against the ideology, sovereignty or security of Pakistan may be dissolved by the President.

The proclamation of July 1977, imposing martial law, and subsequent orders amending the Constitution and further martial law regulations shall not be questioned by any court on any grounds.

All Chief Justices and Judges shall take a new oath of office. New High Court benches for the interior of the provinces shall be set up and retired judges are debarred from holding office in Pakistan for two years. The powers of the High Courts shall be limited for suspending the operation of an order for the detention of any person under any law provided for preventative detention, or release any person on bail, arrested under the same law.

The Advisory Council of Islamic Ideology, which was asked by the Government to suggest procedures for the election and further Islamization of the Constitution, recommended non-party elections, separate electorates, Islamic qualifications for candidates and a federal structure with greater devolution of power by changing the present divisions into provinces.

Under the Wafaqi Mohtasib Order 1982, the President appointed a Wafaqi Mohtasib (Federal Ombudsman) to redress injustice committed by any government agency.

In March 1985 the President, Gen. Zia ul-Haq, promulgated the Revival of the 1973 Constitution Order, which increased the power of the President by amendments such as those establishing a National Security Council, powers to dismiss the Prime Minister, the Cabinet and provincial Chief Ministers, to appoint judicial and military chiefs, and to call elections, and indemnity clauses to ensure the power of the President. The Constitution was then revived with the exception of 28 key provisions relating to treason, subversion, fundamental rights and jurisdiction of the Supreme Court. In October 1985 the Constitution (Eighth Amendment) Bill became law, incorporating most of the provisions of the Revival of the 1973 Constitution Order and indemnifying all actions of the military regime. In December the enactment of the Political Parties (Amendment) Bill allowed political parties to function under stringent conditions (these conditions were eased in 1988). In December Gen. Zia lifted martial law and restored the remainder of the Constitution.

In March 1987 the Constitution (Tenth Amendment) Bill reduced the minimum number of working days of the National Assembly from 160 days to 130 days.

In April 1997 the Constitution (Thirteenth Amendment) Bill repealed the main components of the Eighth Constitutional Amendment, thus divesting the President of the power to appoint and dismiss the Prime Minister and Cabinet, to dissolve the legislature, to order a national referendum, and to appoint provincial Governors, the Chairman of the Joint Chiefs of Staff and the three armed forces chiefs (these functions and appointments were, in future, to be carried out subject to a mandatory advice from the Prime Minister).

In October 1998 the Constitution (Fifteenth Amendment) Bill replaced the country's existing legal code with full *Shari'a*; the bill remained to be ratified by the Senate.

Note: Following the overthrow of the Government in a military coup on 12 October 1999, the Constitution was placed in abeyance on 15 October. On the same day a Provisional Constitution Order was promulgated, according to which executive power was transferred to a National Security Council, under the leadership of a Chief Executive. A federal Cabinet, which was to aid and advise the Chief Executive in the exercise of his functions, was to be appointed by the President on the advice of the Chief Executive. The President was to act on, and in accordance with, the advice of the Chief Executive. The National Assembly, Senate and the Provincial Assemblies were suspended and the Chairman and Deputy Chairman of the Senate ceased to hold office. Local elections were to be held nation-wide from December 2000. Under the reformed local government system, one-third of the seats would be reserved for women and 5% for religious minorities. The voting age would be lowered from 21 to 18. The publicly elected local councils would then select members of two higher councils in each district. The local elections were held between December 2000 and August 2001, on a non-party basis. In May 2000 the Chief Executive stated that he would comply with the Supreme Court's ruling that he should name a date, no later than 90 days before the expiry of the three-year period from 12 October 1999, for the holding of elections to the National Assembly, the Senate and provincial assemblies. In July 2000 the Chief Executive issued a decree to revive the Islamic principles of the suspended Constitution and to incorporate them in the Provisional Constitution Order. On 20 June 2001 the Proclamation of Emergency (Amendment) Order 2001 was promulgated, according to which the Chief Executive assumed the office of President of Pakistan. The National Assembly, Senate and Provincial Assemblies were dissolved with immediate effect. The Speaker and Deputy Speaker of the National Assembly and Provincial Assemblies ceased to hold office with immediate effect. The President later announced that elections to federal and provincial legislatures would be held on 10 October 2002 (see Recent History).

On 21 August 2002 the Legal Framework Order 2002 was promulgated, which sanctioned the President's 29 amendments to the Constitution, including the restoration of Article 58 (2-B), which authorized the President to dissolve the National Assembly (the article was also amended to allow the President to appoint provincial governors in consultation with the Prime Minister), the restoration of Article 243, which gave the President power to appoint the Chairman of the Joint Chiefs of Staff Committee and the three armed forces chiefs and the power to establish the National Security Council to provide consultation to the elected government on strategic matters. The President's term in office and role as Chief of Army Staff were to be extended for five years from the date of the election. Other amendments included the provision of constitutional protection to the offices of the National Accountability Bureau and the Governor of the State Bank of Pakistan, by placing them in 'Schedule Six'. Other provisions granted constitutional protection included the lowering of the voting age from 21 to 18, the Political Parties' Order and the autonomy of the Election Commission. The 1973 Constitution, incorporating the Legal Framework Order, was revived on 15 November 2002.

The Government

HEAD OF STATE

President: Gen. PERVEZ MUSHARRAF (sworn in 20 June 2001).

NATIONAL SECURITY COUNCIL
(April 2003)

Chairman: Gen. PERVEZ MUSHARRAF.

Ex-Officio Members: ZAFARULLAH KHAN JAMALI, CHAUDHRY PERVEZ ELAHI, Sardar ALI MOHAMMAD MAHER, JAM MOHAMMAD YOUSUF, MOHAMMAD AKRAM KHAN DURRANI, Gen. AZIZ AHMAD, Air Chief Marshal KALEEM SAADAT, Adm. SHAHID KARIMULLAH, Mian KHURSHID MEHMOUD KASURI, MAKHDOOM SYED FAISAL SALEH HAYAT, RIO SIKANDER.

CABINET
(April 2003)

Prime Minister: ZAFARULLAH KHAN JAMALI.

Minister of Defence: RAO SIKANDER IQBAL.

Minister of Finance, Revenue, Economic Affairs and Statistics and of Planning and Economic Development: SHAUKAT AZIZ.

Minister of Commerce: HUMAYUN AKHTAR KHAN.

Minister of Education: ZUBAIDA JALAL.

Minister of Food, Agriculture and Livestock: Sardar YAR MOHAMMAD RIND.

Minister of Foreign Affairs and of Law, Justice and Human Rights: Mian KHURSHID MEHMOUD KASURI.

Minister of Health: MOHAMMAD NASIR KHAN.

Minister of Industries and Production: LIAQAT ALI JATOI.

Minister of Information and Media Development: SHEIKH RASHID AHMAD.

Minister of Interior and of Narcotics Control: MAKHDOOM SYED FAISAL SALEH HAYAT.

Minister of Labour, Manpower and Overseas Pakistanis: ABDUL SATTAR LALEKA.

Minister of Information Technology and Telecommunications: AWAIS AHMAD KHAN LEGHARI.

Minister of Petroleum and Natural Resources: CHAUDHRY NOREZ SHAKOOR KHAN.

Minister Water and Power, of Inter-Provincial Co-ordination and of Kashmir Affairs, Northern Areas and States and Frontier Regions (SAFRON): AFTAB AHMAD KHAN SHERPAO.

Minister of Railways: GHAUS BAKHSH KHAN MAHR.

Minister of Privatization and Investment: Dr ABDUL HAFEEZ SHEIKH.

Minister of State for the Environment: Maj. (retd) TAHIR IQBAL.

Minister of State for Water and Power: KHALID AHMAD KHAN LUND.

Minister of State for Food and Agriculture: SAIKANDER HAYAT KHAN BOSAN.

Minister of State for Defence Production: Maj. (retd) HABIBULLAH WARRAICH.

Minister of State for Health: HAMID YAR HIRAJ.

Minister of State for Minorities, Culture, Sports, Tourism and Youth Affairs: RAIS MUNIR AHMED.

Minister of State for Information Technology and for Law, Justice, Human Rights and Parliamentary Affairs: MUHAMMAD RAZA HAYAT LUND.

Adviser to the Prime Minister for Foreign Affairs, Law, Justice and Human Rights: SYED SHARIFFUDIN PIRZADA.

Adviser to the Prime Minister for Women's Development, Social Welfare and Special Education: NILOFAR BAKHTYAR.

MINISTRIES

Office of the President: Aiwan-e-Sadr, Islamabad; tel. (51) 9202723; fax (51) 9211018.

Office of the Prime Minister's Secretariat: Constitution Ave, F-6/5, Cabinet Division, Cabinet Block, Islamabad; tel. (51) 9206111; internet www.pak.gov.pk.

Ministry of Commerce: Block A, Pakistan Secretariat, Islamabad; tel. (51) 9204548; fax (51) 9205241; e-mail mincom@commerce.gov.pk.

Ministry of Communications: Block D, Pakistan Secretariat, Islamabad; tel. (51) 9210344; fax (51) 9217540; internet www.moc.gov.pk/moc.

Ministry of Culture, Sports, Tourism and Youth Affairs: Block D, Pakistan Secretariat, Islamabad; tel. (51) 9204556; fax (51) 9202347; internet www.heritage.gov.pk.

Ministry of Defence: Pakistan Secretariat, No. II, Rawalpindi 46000; tel. (51) 582980; fax (51) 580464.

Ministry of Education: Block D, Pakistan Secretariat, Islamabad; tel. (51) 9212020; fax (51) 9202851; e-mail pak@yahoo.com.

Ministry of Environment, Local Government and Rural Development: 8th Floor, UBL Bldg, Jinnah Avenue, Islamabad; tel. (51) 9224291; fax (51) 9202211; e-mail envir@isb.compol.com; internet www.environment.gov.pk.

Ministry of Finance, Economic Affairs and Statistics: Block Q, Pakistan Secretariat, Islamabad; tel. (51) 9203687; fax (51) 9213780; e-mail finance@isb.paknet.com.pk; internet www.finance.gov.pk.

Ministry of Food, Agriculture, Co-operatives and Livestock: Block B, Pakistan Secretariat, Islamabad; tel. (51) 9210088; fax (51) 9221246.

Ministry of Foreign Affairs: Constitution Ave, Islamabad; tel. (51) 9211942; fax (51) 9207217; e-mail pak.fm@usa.net; internet www.forisb.org.

Ministry of Health: Block C, Pakistan Secretariat, Islamabad; tel. (51) 9208139; fax (51) 9213933.

Ministry of Housing and Works: Block B, Pakistan Secretariat, Islamabad; tel. (51) 9202952; internet www.pha.gov.pk.

Ministry of Human Rights: Pakistan Secretariat, Islamabad.

Ministry of Industries and Production: Block A, Pakistan Secretariat, Islamabad; tel. (51) 9210192; fax (51) 9206350; internet www.sec.gov.pk.

Ministry of the Interior and Narcotics Control: Block R, Pakistan Secretariat, Islamabad; tel. (51) 9212026; fax (51) 9202642.

Ministry of Kashmir Affairs and Northern Areas, States and Frontier Regions (SAFRON): Block R, Pakistan Secretariat,

Islamabad; tel. (51) 9203022; fax (51) 9202494; e-mail safron@isb
.perd.net.pk.

Ministry of Labour, Manpower and Overseas Pakistanis:
Block B, Pakistan Secretariat, Islamabad; tel. (51) 9210077; fax (51)
9203462; internet www.labour.gov.pk.

Ministry of Law, Justice and Parliamentary Affairs: Block
S&R, Pakistan Secretariat, Islamabad; tel. (51) 9212710; fax (51)
9215852; e-mail molaw1@comsats.net.pk.

Ministry of Petroleum and Natural Resources: 3rd Floor, Block
A, Pakistan Secretariat, Islamabad; tel. (51) 9208233; fax (51)
9205437; e-mail info@mpnr.gov.pk; internet www.mpnr.gov.pk.

Ministry of Planning and Development: Block P, Pakistan
Secretariat, Islamabad; tel. (51) 9202704; fax (51) 9202783.

Ministry of Railways: Block D, Pakistan Secretariat, Islamabad;
tel. (51) 9208846; fax (51) 828846.

Ministry of Religious Affairs: Plot No. 20, Markaz Ramna-6, nr
GPO, Islamabad; tel. (51) 9214856; fax (51) 821646; internet www
.mra.gov.pk.

Ministry of Science and Technology: Block D, Pakistan Secretariat, Islamabad; tel. (51) 9208026; fax (51) 9202603; e-mail
minister@most.gov.pk; internet www.most.gov.pk.

Ministry of Water and Power: Block A, 15th Floor, Shaheed-e-
Millat, Pakistan Secretariat, Islamabad; tel. (51) 9212442; fax (51)
9203187.

**Ministry of Women's Development, Social Welfare, Special
Education and Population Welfare:** State Life Building (SLIC),
Blue Area, China Chowk, Islamabad; tel. (51) 9224167; fax (51)
9203132; e-mail mowdswse@ibscomsate.net.pk.

Federal Legislature

SENATE

The Legal Framework Order, approved by the President in August
2002, increased the number of seats in the Senate to 100. Eighty-
eight of the members are elected by the four provincial legislatures;
eight are chosen by representatives of the Federally Administered
Tribal Areas; and four by the federal capital. Its term of office was
reduced to five years from six.

Chairman: Mian MOHAMMAD SOOMRO.

Deputy Chairman: KHALIL-UR-REHMAN.

Election, 25 February 2003

	Seats
Pakistan Muslim League (Quaid-e-Azam Group) . .	38
Muttahida Majlis-e-Amal*	27
Pakistan People's Party Parliamentarians	14
Muttahida Qaumi Movement	5
National Alliance†	4
Pakistan Muslim League (Nawaz Group)	3
Pakistan Muslim League (Functional Pir Pagara Group)	2
Pakistan People's Party (Sherpao Group)	2
Jamhuri Watan Party	1
Balochistan National Movement (Hai)	1
Pakhtoonkhwa Milli Awami Party	1
Awami National Party	1
Balochistan National Movement (Maingal)	1
Total	**100**

* Coalition comprising Jamaat-e-Islami Pakistan, Jamiat-e-Ulema-
e-Pakistan, Jamiat-e-Ulema-Islam (S), Jamiat-e-Ulema-Islam (F),
Islam Tehreek Pakistan and Jamiat Ahl-e-Hadith.
† Coalition comprising the National People's Party, the Millat Party,
the Sindh National Front, the Sindh Democratic Alliance and the
National Awami Party.

NATIONAL ASSEMBLY

In accordance with the Legal Framework Order, introduced by the
President in August 2002, the number of seats in the National
Assembly increased to 342, with 60 seats reserved for women and 10
for non-Muslims. Its term of office was reduced by one year to four.

Speaker: CHAUDHRY AMIR HUSSAIN.

Deputy Speaker: Sardar MOHAMMAD YAQOOB.

General Election, 10 October 2002

	Seats
Pakistan Muslim League (Quaid-e-Azam Group) . .	118
Pakistan People's Party Parliamentarians	81
Muttahida Majlis-e-Amal	60
Pakistan Muslim League (Nawaz Group)	19
Muttahida Qaumi Movement	17
National Alliance	16
Pakistan Muslim League (Functional Pir Pagara Group).	5
Pakistan Muslim League (Junejo Group)	3
Pakistan People's Party (Sherpao Group)	2
Balochistan National Party	1
Pakistan Tehrik-e-Insaf	1
Pakistan Muslim League (Ziaul Haq).	1
Jamhuri Watan Party	1
Muhajir Qaumi Movement	1
Pakistan Awami Tehreek	1
Independents	14
Vacant	1
Total	**342**

Provinces

Pakistan comprises the four provinces of Sindh, Balochistan, Punjab
and the North-West Frontier Province, plus the federal capital and
Federally Administered Tribal Areas.

GOVERNORS

Balochistan: Lt–Gen. (retd) ABDUL QADIR BALUCH.

North-West Frontier Province: Lt-Gen. (retd) SYED IFTIKHAR
HUSSAIN SHAH.

Punjab: Lt-Gen. (retd) KHALID MAQBOOL.

Sindh: ISHRATUL EBAD.

CHIEF MINISTERS

Balochistan: JAM MOHAMMAD YOUSUF.

North-West Frontier Province: MOHAMMAD AKRAM KHAN DURRANI.

Punjab: CHAUDHRY PERVEZ ELAHI.

Sindh: Sardar ALI MOHAMMAD MAHER.

Political Organizations

Some 73 parties, issued with election symbols by the Election
Commission, contested the general election on 10 October 2002.
Three alliances contested the elections: the Alliance for the Restora-
tion of Democracy (Leader NAWABZADA NASRULLAH KHAN; includes the
Pakistan Muslim League (Nawaz) and the Pakistan People's Party
Parliamentarians); the National Alliance (Chair. GHULAM MUSTAFA
JATOI; includes the National People's Party, the Millat Party, the
Sindh National Front, the Sindh Democratic Alliance and the
National Awami Party); Muttahida Majlis-e-Amal (Chair. Maulana
SHAH AHMED NOORANI; comprises Jamaat-e-Islami, Jamiat-e-Ulema-
e-Pakistan, Jamiat-e-Ulema-e-Islam (S), Jamiat-e-Ulema-e-Islam
(F), Islami Tehreek Pakistan and Jamiat Ahl-e-Hadith).

All Pakistan Jammu and Kashmir Conference: f. 1948; advocates the holding of a free plebiscite in the whole of Kashmir; Pres.
Sardar SIKANDAR HAYAT KHAN.

Awami National Party (ANP) (People's National Party): Karachi;
tel. (21) 534513; f. 1986 by the merger of the National Democratic
Party, the Awami Tehrik (People's Movement) and the Mazdoor
Kissan (Labourers' and Peasants' Party); federalist and socialist;
Leader KHAN ABDUL WALI KHAN; Pres. ASFANDAR WALI KHAN.

Awami Qiyadat Party (People's Leadership Party): Lahore; f.
1995; Chair. Gen. (retd) ASLAM BEG.

Balochistan National Party: Quetta; Central leader Dr JAHANGIR
JAMALUDDIN.

Balochistan National Movement: Quetta; Leader AYUB JATTAK.

Jamaat-e-Islami Pakistan (JIP): Mansoorah, Multan Rd, Lahore
54570; tel. (42) 5419504; fax (42) 5432194; e-mail amir@ji.org.pk;
internet www.jamaat.org; f. 1941; seeks the establishment of Islamic
order through adherence to teaching of Maulana MAUDUDI, founder
of the party; revivalist; right-wing; Chair. Amir QAZI HUSSAIN AHMAD;
Sec.-Gen. SYED MUNAWAR HASAN; c. 18,200 full mems (2003).

Jamhuri Watan Party (Bugti) Balochistan: Pres. Nawab Akbar Bugti.

Jamiat-e-Ulema-e-Islam (JUI): f. 1950; advocates adoption of a constitution in accordance with (Sunni) Islamic teachings; Leader Maulana Fazlur Rehman.

Jamiat-e-Ulema-e-Pakistan (JUP): Burns Rd, Karachi; f. 1948; advocates progressive (Sunni) Islamic principles and enforcement of Islamic laws in Pakistan; Pres. Maulana Shah Ahmed Noorani Siddiqui; Gen. Sec. Gen. (retd) K. M. Azhar Khan.

Millat Party: 21-E/3, Gulberg III, Lahore; tel. (42) 5757805; fax (42) 5756718; e-mail millat@lhr.comsats.net.pk; advocates 'true federalism'; Chair. Farooq Ahmad Khan Leghari.

Muttahida Qaumi Movement (MQM): 494/8 Azizabad, Karachi; tel. (21) 6313690; fax (21) 6329955; e-mail mqm@mqm.org; internet www.mqm.org; f. 1978 as All Pakistan Mohajir Students Organisation; name changed to Mohajir Qaumi Movement in 1984 and to Muttahida Qaumi Movement in 1997; represents the interests of Muslim, Urdu-speaking immigrants (from India) in Pakistan; seeks the designation of Mohajir as fifth nationality (after Sindhi, Punjabi, Pathan and Balochi); aims to abolish the prevailing feudal political system and to establish democracy; Pres. Aftab Sheikh.

National Awami Party: Peshawar; Pres. Ajmal Khatak; Gen. Sec. Arbab Ayub Jan.

National People's Party (NPP): 18 Kh-e-Shamsheer, Defence Housing Authority, Phase II, Karachi; tel. (21) 5854522; fax (21) 5873753; f. 1986; advocates a 10-point programme for the restoration of democracy; breakaway faction from PPP; right-wing; Chair. Ghulam Mustafa Jatoi; Chief Organizer A. B. Leghari.

Pakhtoonkhwa Milli Awami Party (Quetta): Leader Samand Achakzai.

Pakistan Awami Tehreek (PAT): 365-M Model Town, Lahore; tel. (42) 5169111; fax (42) 5169114; e-mail info@pat.com.pk; internet www.pat.com.pk; Chair. Dr Muhammad Tahrir-ul-Qadri.

Pakistan Democratic Party (PDP): f. 1969; advocates democratic and Islamic values; Pres. Nawabzada Nasrullah Khan.

Pakistan Muslim League (PML): Muslim League House, Rawalpindi (Junejo Group); Muslim League House, 33 Agha Khan Rd, Lahore (Fida Group); f. 1906; in 1979 the party split into two factions, the pro-Zia Pagara Group and the Chatta Group (later renamed the Qasim Group, see below); the Pagara Group itself split into two factions when a group of army-supported Zia loyalists, known as the Fida Group, separated from the Junejo Group in August 1988; at the November 1988 general election, however, the Junejo Group and the Fida Group did not present rival candidates; by 2002 the PML had split into two main factions, one led by Mian Mohammad Nawaz Sharif, known as the Nawaz Group (Pres. Raja Zafar-ul-Haq; Sec.-Gen. Anjaam Khan, and the other by Mian Mohammad Azhar, known as the PML Quaid-e-Azam Group (Sec.-Gen. Zafarullah Khan Jamali); other factions of the PML were led by Hamid Nasir Chatta, known as the Chatta League, and Functional PML, led by Pir Pagara.

Pakistan National Conference: Islamabad; Pres. Air Marshal (retd) Mohammad Asghar Khan; Sec.-Gen. Dr Ghulam Hussain.

Pakistan People's Party (PPP): Zardari Hse, 8, St 19, F-8/2, Islamabad; tel. (51) 255264; e-mail ppp@comsats.net.pk; internet www.ppp.org.pk; f. 1967; advocates Islamic socialism, democracy and a non-aligned foreign policy; Pres. Aftab Sherpao; Sr Vice-Pres. Makhdoom Mohammed Zaman Talib-ul-Maula; in 2002 the faction the Pakistan People's Party Parliamentarians was formed to contest the October general election; Leader Makhdoom Amin Fahim.

Pakistan People's Party (Shaheed Bhutto Group): 71 Clifton, Karachi; f. 1995 as a breakaway faction of the PPP; Chair. Ghinwa Bhutto; Sec.-Gen. Dr Mubashir Hasan.

Pakistan People's Party (Sherpao Group): Peshawar; breakaway faction of the PPP; Pres. Altab Sherpao.

Punjabi Pakhtoon Ittehad (PPI): f. 1987 to represent the interests of Punjabis and Pakhtoons in Karachi; Pres. Malik Mir Hazar Khan.

Qaumi Jamhori Party: Abbottabad; Pres. Air Marshal (retd) Asghar Khan.

Sindh National Front: Pres. Mumtaz Bhutto.

Sindh Taraqi Passand Party (STPP): Leader Dr Qadir Magsi.

Sipah-e-Sahaba Pakistan (SSP): Karachi; f. as a breakaway faction of Jamiat-e-Ulema-e-Islam; Sunni extremist; activities proscribed in January 2002; Leader Maulana Tariq Azam; Sec.-Gen. Hafiz Ahmed Bukhsh.

Tehrik-e-Insaf (Movement for Justice): Lahore; internet www.insaf.org.pk; f. 1996; Leader Imran Khan; Sec.-Gen. Miraj Mohammad Khan.

Tehrik-i-Jafria-i-Pakistan (TJP): f. 1987 as a political party; Shi'a extremist; activities proscribed in January 2002; Leader Allama Sajid Ali Naqvi.

Diplomatic Representation

EMBASSIES AND HIGH COMMISSIONS IN PAKISTAN

Afghanistan: 8, St 90, G-6/3, Islamabad; tel. (51) 2824505; fax 2824504; Ambassador Dr Nanguyalai Tarzi.

Algeria: 107, St 9, E-7, POB 1038, Islamabad; tel. (51) 2206632; fax (51) 2820912; Ambassador Seferdjeli Aissa.

Argentina: 20 Hill Rd, Shalimar, F-6/3, POB 10151, Islamabad; tel. (51) 2825561; fax (51) 2825564; e-mail epaki@worldtelmeca.com; Ambassador Horacio R. Basso.

Australia: Diplomatic Enclave 1, G-5/4, POB 1046, Islamabad; tel. (51) 2824345; fax (51) 2820189; High Commissioner Howard Brown.

Austria: 13, St 1, F-6/3, POB 1018, Islamabad 44000; tel. (51) 2279237; fax (51) 2828366; e-mail Islamabad-ob@bmaa.gv.at; Ambassador Dr Guenther Gallowitsch.

Azerbaijan: 1, Nazimuddin Rd, F-10/4, Islamabad; tel. (51) 2291141; fax (51) 2211826; Ambassador Dr Eynulla Yadalla Oglu Madatli.

Bangladesh: 1, St 5, F-6/3, Islamabad; tel. (51) 2279267; fax (51) 2279266; High Commissioner Alimul Haque.

Belgium: 14, St 17, F-7/2, POB 1016, Islamabad; tel. (51) 2827091; fax (51) 2822358; e-mail ambel-pk@isb.comsats.net.pk; Ambassador Patrick Renault.

Bosnia and Herzegovina: House No. 1, Kaghan Rd, F-8/3, Islamabad; tel. (51) 2261041; fax (51) 2261004; e-mail ambassador@bosnianembassypakistan.org; internet www.bosnianembassypakistan.org; Ambassador Avdo Abdullah Iodzić.

Brazil: 50 Atatürk Ave, G-6/3, POB 1053, Islamabad; tel. (51) 2279690; fax (51) 2823034; Ambassador Abelardo Arantes Júnior.

Brunei: 16, St 21, F-6/2, Islamabad; tel. (51) 2823038; fax (51) 2823138; High Commissioner Haji Mustappa bin Haji Sirat.

Bulgaria: Plot No. 6-11, Diplomatic Enclave, Ramna 5, POB 1483, Islamabad; tel. (51) 2279196; fax (51) 2279195; Ambassador Ivan Dantchev Petkov.

Canada: Diplomatic Enclave, Sector G-5, POB 1042, Islamabad; tel. (51) 2279100; fax (51) 2279110; e-mail ferry.de-kerchkove@dfait.maeci.gc.ca; High Commissioner Konrad Sinrad Sigurdson.

China, People's Republic: Ramna 4, Diplomatic Enclave, Islamabad; tel. (51) 2826667; fax (51) 2279602; Ambassador Zhang Chunxiang.

Czech Republic: 49, St 27, Shalimar F-6/2, POB 1335, Islamabad; tel. (51) 2274304; fax (51) 2825327; e-mail islamabd@embassy.mzv.cz; internet www.mzv.cz/islamabad; Ambassador Petr Přibík.

Denmark: 9, St 90, Ramna 6/3, POB 1118, Islamabad; tel. (51) 2824722; fax (51) 2823483; e-mail ambadane@comsats.net.pk; Chargé d'affaires a.i. Sven Bille Bjerregaard.

Egypt: 38–51, UN Blvd Diplomatic Enclave, Ramna 5/4, POB 2088, Islamabad; tel. (51) 2209072; fax (51) 2279552; Ambassador Hisham El Ziamaity.

Finland: 11, St 88, G-6/3, Islamabad; tel. (51) 2828426; fax (51) 2828427; Ambassador Tarja Laitiainen.

France: Constitution Ave, G-5, Diplomatic Enclave 1, POB 1068, Islamabad; tel. (51) 2278730; fax (51) 2822583; e-mail ambafra@isb.comsats.net.pk; Ambassador Yannick Gérard.

Germany: Ramna 5, Diplomatic Enclave, POB 1027, Islamabad 44000; tel. (51) 2279430; fax (51) 2279436; Ambassador Dr Christoph Brümmer.

Greece: 22 Margalla Rd, F-6/3, Islamabad; tel. (51) 2822558; fax (51) 2825161; e-mail greece@isb.paknet.com.pk; internet www.greekembassy.netfirms.com; Ambassador Evangelos Carokis.

Holy See: Apostolic Nunciature, St 5, Diplomatic Enclave 1, G-5, POB 1106, Islamabad 44000; tel. (51) 2278218; fax (51) 2820847; e-mail vatipak@isb.comsats.net.pk; Apostolic Nuncio Most Rev. Alessandro D'Errico (Titular Archbishop of Carini).

Hungary: House No. 12, Margalla Rd, F-6/3, POB 1103, Islamabad; tel. (51) 2823352; fax (51) 2825256; Ambassador József Kovács.

India: G-5, Diplomatic Enclave, Islamabad; tel. (51) 2206950; fax (51) 2823386; Chargé d'affaires T. C. A. Raghvan.

Indonesia: Diplomatic Enclave 1, St 5, G-5/4, POB 1019, Islamabad; tel. (51) 2278736; fax (51) 2829145; e-mail unitkom@best.net.pk; Ambassador Jack Said Gaffar.

Iran: 57, St 48, F-8/4, Islamabad; tel. (51) 2276270; fax (51) 2824839; Ambassador SYED SERAJEDDIN MOUSAVI.

Iraq: 44, St 27, F-10, Islamabad; tel. (51) 2214570; fax (51) 2214572; e-mail iraqiya@sat.net.pk; Ambassador KADHIM AL-RAWI.

Italy: 54, Margalla Rd, F-6/3, POB 1008, Islamabad; tel. (51) 2829106; fax (51) 2829026; e-mail segreter@embassy.italy.org.pk; internet www.embassy.italy.org.pk; Ambassador Dr ANGELO GABRIELE DE CEGLIE.

Japan: Plot No. 53-70, Ramna 5/4, Diplomatic Enclave 1, Islamabad 44000; tel. (51) 2279320; fax (51) 2279340; e-mail info@japanemb.org.pk; internet japanemb.org.pk; Ambassador MINORU SHIBUYA.

Jordan: 131, St 14, E-7, POB 1189, Islamabad; tel. (51) 2823459; fax (51) 2823207; e-mail jordanemb@comsats.net.pk; Ambassador Dr FAWAZ ABU TAYEH.

Kazakhstan: FT-1, Nazimuddin Rd, Islamabad; tel. (51) 2262926; fax (51) 2262806; e-mail embkaz@comsats.net.pk; Ambassador BEKZHASAR NARBAYEV.

Kenya: 10, St 9, F-7/3, Islamabad; tel. (51) 2279540; fax (51) 2279541; High Commissioner MOHAMMAD OMAAR SOBA.

Korea, Democratic People's Republic: Diplomatic Enclave, Q. A. U. Rd, Islamabad; tel. and fax (51) 2252754; Ambassador KOM WON GYU.

Korea, Republic: Block 13, St 29, G-5/4, Diplomatic Enclave 2, POB 1087, Islamabad; tel. (51) 2279380; fax (51) 2279391; e-mail koremi@isb.comsats.net.pk; Ambassador JEON BOU-GUAN.

Kuwait: Plot No.s 1, 2 and 24, University Rd, G-5, Diplomatic Enclave, POB 1030, Islamabad; tel. (51) 2279413; fax (51) 2279411; Ambassador MANSOUR ABDULLAH AL-AWADI.

Lebanon: St 27, F-62, Islamabad; tel. (51) 2278338; fax (51) 2826410; e-mail lebemb@comsats.net.pk; Ambassador AL-AMEERA LEILA CHEHAB.

Libya: 12, St 4, Faisal Chow, F-83, Islamabad; tel. (51) 2254219; fax (51) 2261459; Chargé d'affaires a.i. HADI M. AWSAJI.

Malaysia: 78, Margalla Rd, F-6/2, POB 1034, Islamabad; tel. (51) 2279570; fax (51) 2824761; e-mail mwislam@isb.comsats.net.pk; High Commissioner Gen. TAN SRI MOHAMMAD HASHIM HUSSAIN.

Mauritius: 27, St 26, F-6/2, Islamabad; tel. (51) 2824657; fax (51) 2824656; High Commissioner RAVINDRANATH DWARKA.

Morocco: 6, Gomal Rd, E-7, POB 1179, Islamabad; tel. (51) 2829656; fax (51) 2822745; e-mail sifmapk@comsats.net.pk; Ambassador AHMED EL RHAIDI.

Myanmar: 12/1, St 13, F-7/2, Islamabad; tel. (51) 822460; fax (51) 828819; Ambassador U SOE WIN.

Nepal: House No. 11, St 84, G-6/4, Islamabad; tel. (51) 2828838; fax (51) 2828839; e-mail nepemb@isb.comsats.net.pk; Ambassador PUSHKAR MAN SINGH RAJBHANDARI.

Netherlands: PIA Bldg, 2nd Floor, Blue Area, POB 1065, Islamabad; tel. (51) 2279510; fax (51) 2279512; Ambassador Prof. P. M. KURPERFHOEK.

Nigeria: Diplomatic Enclave, Bari Imam Rd, Islamabad; tel. (51) 823542; fax (51) 824104; High Commissioner ADAMU DANJUMA IDRIS WAZIRI.

Norway: 25, St 19, F-6/2, POB 1336, Islamabad; tel. (51) 2279720; fax (51) 2279726; e-mail emb.islamabad@mfa.no; internet www.norway.org.pk; Ambassador Dr JANIS BJØRN KANAVIN.

Oman: 53, St 48, F-8/4, POB 1194, Islamabad; tel. (51) 2254869; fax (51) 2255074; Ambassador SALIM MOHAMMAD SALIM AL-WAHAIBI.

Philippines: 8, St 60, F-7/4, Islamabad; tel. (51) 2824933; fax (51) 2277389; e-mail isdpe@isb.comsats.net.pk; Ambassador JORGE V. ARIZABAL.

Poland: St 24, G-5/4, Diplomatic Enclave 2, POB 1032, Islamabad; tel. (51) 2279491; fax (51) 2279498; e-mail polemb@isb.comsats.net.pk; Ambassador TOMASZ KOZLOWSKI.

Portugal: 66 Main Margalla Rd, F-7/2, POB 1067, Islamabad 44000; tel. (51) 2279531; fax (51) 2279532; e-mail portugal@isb.paknet.com.pk; Ambassador Dr ALEXANDRO LINDIM VASSALO.

Qatar: 20, Margalla Rd, Diplomatic Enclave, G-6/3, Islamabad; tel. (51) 2270768; fax (51) 2270207; Ambassador ABDULLAH FALAH ABDULLAH AD-DOSSARI.

Romania: 13, St 88, G-6/3, Islamabad; tel. (51) 2826514; fax (51) 2826515; e-mail romania@isb.comsats.net.pk; Ambassador EMIL GHITULESCU.

Russia: Khayaban-e-Suhrawardy, Diplomatic Enclave, Ramna 4, Islamabad; tel. (51) 2278670; fax (51) 2826552; e-mail russia2@comsats.net.pk; Ambassador EDWARD SHEVCHENKO.

Saudi Arabia: 14, Hill Rd, F-6/3, Islamabad; tel. (51) 2820156; fax (51) 2278816; Ambassador ALI SAYEED MOHAMMAD AL-AWAD ASSERI.

Serbia and Montenegro: 14, St 87, Ramna 6/3, Islamabad; tel. (51) 829556; fax (51) 820965; e-mail fryemy@isb.comsats.net.pk; Chargé d'affaires ZARKO MILOŠEVIĆ.

Somalia: 21, St 56, F-6/4, Islamabad; tel. (51) 2279789; fax (51) 2826117; Ambassador ABDISALAAM Haji AHMAD LIBAN.

South Africa: House No. 48, Margalla Rd, Khayban-e-Iqbal, Sector F-8/2, Islamabad; tel. (51) 262354; fax (51) 250114; e-mail xhosa@isb.comsats.net.pk; High Commissioner MOOSA MOHAMED MOOLLA.

Spain: St 6, G-5, Diplomatic Enclave 1, POB 1144, Islamabad; tel. (51) 2279480; fax (51) 2279489; Ambassador ANTONIO SEGURA MORÍS.

Sri Lanka: St 55, F-6/4, Islamabad; tel. (51) 2828723; fax (51) 2828751; e-mail srilanka@isb.comsats.net.pk; High Commissioner Gen. C. S. WEERASOORIYA.

Sudan: 7, St 1, G-6/3, Islamabad; tel. (51) 2827068; fax (51) 2827073; Ambassador AWAD MOHAMED HUSSAN SAID.

Sweden: 7, St 5, F-6/3, Islamabad; Ambassador PETER TEJLER.

Switzerland: St 6, G-5/4, Diplomatic Enclave, POB 1073, Islamabad; tel. (51) 279291; fax (51) 279286; e-mail swiemisl@isb.comsats.net.pk; Ambassador CHRISTIAN DUNANT.

Syria: Suite 33, F–81, Islamabad; tel. (51) 2279470; fax (51) 2279472; Ambassador SAIFI HAMWI.

Thailand: 10, St 33, Shalimar 8/1, Islamabad; tel. (51) 2280909; fax (51) 2256730; e-mail thailand@isb.comsats.net.pk; Ambassador SORNSILP POLTEJA.

Tunisia: 221, St 21, E-7, Islamabad; tel. (51) 827869; fax (51) 827871; Ambassador LAMINE BENZARTI.

Turkey: 58 Atatürk Ave, G-6/3, Islamabad; tel. (51) 2278748; fax (51) 2278752; e-mail turkemb@isb.comsats.net.pk; Ambassador KEMAL GUL.

Turkmenistan: H 22A, Nazim-Ud-Din Rd, Sector F-7/1, Islamabad; tel. (51) 2274913; fax (51) 2278799; e-mail turkmen@comsats.net.pk; Ambassador SAPAR BERDINIYAZOV.

Ukraine: 20, St 18, F 6/2, Islamabad; tel. (51) 2274732; fax (51) 2274643; e-mail ukremb@isb.compol.com; internet www.ukremb.org.pk; Ambassador VOLODYMYR S. PONOMARENKO.

United Arab Emirates: Plot No. 1-22, Diplomatic Enclave, Quaid-e-Azam University Rd, Islamabad; tel. (51) 2279052; fax (51) 2279063; Ambassador ALI MOHAMMED AL-SHAMSI.

United Kingdom: Diplomatic Enclave, Ramna 5, POB 1122, Islamabad; tel. (51) 2822131; fax (51) 2823439; e-mail bhcmedia@isb.comsats.net.pk; internet www.britainonline.org.pk; High Commissioner HILARY SYNNOTT.

USA: Diplomatic Enclave, Ramna 5, POB 1048, Islamabad; tel. (51) 826161; fax (51) 821193; e-mail isl@state.gov; Ambassador NANCY POWELL.

Uzbekistan: 2, St 2, F-8/3, Kohistan Rd, Islamabad; tel. (51) 2264746; fax (51) 2261739; e-mail uzbekemb@isb.comsats.net.pk; Ambassador SHUKHRAT S. KOBILOV.

Yemen: 220, St 21, E-7, POB 1523, Islamabad 44000; tel. (51) 2821146; fax (51) 2279567; Ambassador GHALEB SAEED AL-ADOOFI.

Judicial System

A constitutional amendment bill was passed in the National Assembly in October 1998 replacing the country's existing legal code with full Islamic *Shari'a*. The bill remained to be approved, however, by the Senate.

SUPREME COURT

Chief Justice: IRSHAD HUSSAN KHAN.

Attorney-General: AZIZ A. MUNSHI.

Deputy Attorney-General: KHWAJA SAEEDUZ ZAFAR.

Federal Shari'a Court

Chief Justice: FAZAL ELAHI KHAN.

Federal Ombudsman: Justice USMAN ALI SHAH.

Religion

ISLAM

Islam is the state religion. The majority of the population are Sunni Muslims, while about 5% are of the Shi'a sect and only about 0.001% are of the Ahmadi sect.

CHRISTIANITY

About 3% of the population are Christians.

National Council of Churches in Pakistan: 32-B, Shahrah-e-Fatima Jinnah, POB 357, Lahore 54000; tel. (42) 7592167; fax (42) 7569782; e-mail nccp@lhr.comsats.net.pk; f. 1949; four mem. bodies, nine associate mems; Gen. Sec. VICTOR AZARIAH.

The Roman Catholic Church

For ecclesiastical purposes, Pakistan comprises two archdioceses, four dioceses and one apostolic prefecture. At 31 December 2000 there were an estimated 1,263,934 adherents in the country.

Bishops' Conference

Pakistan Catholic Bishops' Conference, Sacred Heart Cathedral, 1 Mian Mohammad Shafi Rd, POB 909, Lahore 54000; tel. (42) 6366137; fax (42) 6368336; e-mail abishop@lhr.comsats.net.pk.

f. 1976; Pres. Most Rev. LAWRENCE J. SALDANHA (Archbishop of Lahore); Sec.-Gen. Rt Rev. ANTHONY LOBO (Bishop of Islamabad-Rawalpindi).

Archbishop of Karachi: St Patrick's Cathedral, Shahrah-e-Iraq, Karachi 74400; tel. (21) 7781533; fax (21) 7781532.

Archbishop of Lahore: Most Rev. LAWRENCE J. SALDANHA, Sacred Heart Cathedral, 1 Mian Mohammad Shafi Rd, POB 909, Lahore 54000; tel. (42) 6366137; fax (42) 6368336; e-mail abishop@lhr.comsats.net.pk; internet www.rcarchdioceselahore.org.pk.

Protestant Churches

Church of Pakistan: Moderator Rt Rev. Samuel Azariah (Bishop of Raiwind), 17 Warris Rd, POB 2319, Lahore 3; fax (42) 7577255; f. 1970 by union of the fmr Anglican Church in Pakistan, the United Methodist Church in Pakistan, the United Church in Pakistan (Scots Presbyterians) and the Pakistani Lutheran Church; eight dioceses; c. 700,000 mems (1993); Gen. Sec. (vacant).

United Presbyterian Church of Pakistan: POB 395, Rawalpindi; tel. (51) 72503; f. 1961; c. 340,000 mems (1989); Moderator Sardar FEROZE KHAN; Sec. Rev. PIYARA LALL.

Other denominations active in the country include the Associated Reformed Presbyterian Church and the Pakistan Salvation Army.

HINDUISM

Hindus comprise about 1.8% of the population.

BAHÁ'Í FAITH

National Spiritual Assembly: POB 7420, Karachi 74400; tel. (21) 7216429; fax (21) 7215467; e-mail nsapk@cyber.net.pk.

The Press

The Urdu press comprises almost 800 newspapers, with *Daily Jang, Daily Khabrain, Nawa-i-Waqt, Jasarat* and *Mashriq* among the most influential. The daily newspaper with the largest circulation is *Daily Jang*. Although the English-language press reaches only a small percentage of the population, it is influential in political, academic and professional circles. The four main press groups in Pakistan are Jang Publications (the *Daily Jang, The News* the *Daily News* and the weekly *Akhbar-e-Jehan*), the Dawn or Herald Group (the *Dawn* the *Star* the *Watan* and the monthly *Herald* and *Spider*), the Nawa-i-Waqt Group (the *Nawa-i-Waqt* and *The Nation*), and the National Press Trust (the *Mashriq*). The establishment of an independent press council was under consideration in 2003.

PRINCIPAL DAILIES

Islamabad

Al-Akhbar: Al-Akhbar House, Markaz, G-8, Islamabad; tel. (51) 852023; fax (51) 256522; Urdu; also publ. in Muzaffarabad; Editor GHULAM AKBAR.

The Nation: Nawa-i-Waqt House, Zero Point, Islamabad; tel. (51) 277631; fax (51) 278353; e-mail editor@nation.com.pk; internet www.nation.com.pk; English; Editor ARIF NIZAMI; circ. 15,000.

Pakistan Observer: Ali Akbar House, Markaz G-8, Islamabad 44870; tel. (51) 2852027; fax (51) 2262258; e-mail observer@best.net

.pk; internet www.pakobserver.com; f. 1988; English; independent; Editor-in-Chief ZAHID MALIK.

Karachi

Aghaz: 11 Japan Mansion, Preedy St, Sadar, Karachi 74400; tel. (21) 7721688; fax (21) 7722125; internet www.aghaz.com; f. 1963; evening; Urdu; Editor MOHAMMAD ANWAR FAROOQI; Man. Editor BILAL FAROOQI; circ. 62,377.

Amn: Akhbar Manzil, Elender Rd; off I. I. Chundrigar Rd, Karachi 74200; tel. (21) 2634451; fax (21) 2634454; e-mail amn@aol.net.pk; Urdu; Editor AJMAL DEHLVI.

Business Recorder: Recorder House, Business Recorder Rd, Karachi 74550; tel. (21) 7210072; fax (21) 7228644; e-mail editor@brecorder.com; internet www.brecorder.com; f. 1965; English; Editor M. A. ZUBERI.

Daily Awam: HQ Printing House, I. I. Chundrigar Rd, POB 52, Karachi; tel. (21) 2637111; fax (21) 2636066; f. 1994; evening; Urdu; Editor-in-Chief Mir SHAKIL-UR-RAHMAN.

Daily Beopar: 118 Bombay Hotel, I. I. Chundrigar Rd, Karachi; tel. (21) 214055; Urdu; Man. Editor TARIQ SAEED.

Daily Intekhab: Liaison Office, 3rd Floor, Mashhoor Mahal, Kucha Haji Usman, off I. I. Chundrigar Rd, Karachi; tel. (21) 2634518; fax (21) 2631092; Urdu; also publ. from Hub (Balochistan) and Quetta; Man. Editor SARKAR AHMAD; Publr and Editor ANWAR SAJIDI.

Daily Jang: HQ Printing House, I. I. Chundrigar Rd, POB 52, Karachi; tel. (21) 2637111; fax (21) 2634395; e-mail jang@jang-group .com.pk; internet www.jang.com.pk; f. 1940; morning; Urdu; also publ. in Quetta, Rawalpindi, Lahore and London; Editor-in-Chief Mir SHAKIL-UR-RAHMAN; combined circ. 750,000.

Daily Khabar: A-8 Sheraton Centre, F. B. Area, Karachi; tel. (21) 210059; Urdu; Exec. Editor FAROOQ PARACHA; Editor and Publr SAEED ALI HAMEED.

Daily Khabrain: Sitara Market, Markaz G-7/2, Islamabad; tel. (51) 2204751; fax (51) 2204756.

Daily Mohasaba: Imperial Hotel, M.T. Khan Rd, Karachi; tel. (21) 519448; Urdu; Editor TALIB TURABI.

Daily News: Al-Rahman Bldg, I. I. Chundrigar Rd, Karachi; tel. (21) 2637111; fax (21) 2634395; f. 1962; evening; English; Editor S. M. FAZIL; circ. 50,000.

Daily Public: Falak Printing Press, 191 Altaf Hussain Rd, New Chhali, Karachi; tel. (21) 5687522; Man. Editor INQUILAB MATRI; Editor ANWAR SANROY.

Daily Sindh Sujag: 15/4, Namco Centre, Campbell St, New Challi, Karachi; tel. (21) 2625282; fax (21) 2623918; Sindhi; political; Editor NASIR DAD BALOCH.

Daily Special: Ahbab Printers, Beauty House, nr Regal Chowk, Abdullah Haroon Rd, Sadar, Karachi; tel. (21) 7771655; fax (21) 7722776; Urdu; Editor MOHAMMAD AT-TAYYAB.

Dawn: Haroon House, Dr Ziauddin Ahmed Rd, POB 3740, Karachi 74200; tel. (21) 5670001; fax (21) 5682187; e-mail editor@dawn.com; internet www.dawn.com; f. 1947; English, Gujarati; also published from Islamabad and Lahore; Chief Exec. HAMEED HAROON; Editor AHMAD ALI KHAN; circ. 110,000 (weekdays), 125,000 (Sundays).

Deyanet: Karachi; tel. (21) 2631556; fax (21) 2631888; Urdu; also publ. in Sukkur and Islamabad; Editor NAJMUDDIN SHAIKH.

The Finance: 903–905 Uni Towers, I. I. Chundrigar Rd, Karachi; tel. (21) 2411665; fax (21) 2422560; e-mail tfinance@super.net.pk; English; Chief Editor S. H. SHAH.

Financial Post: Bldg No. 106/C, 11 Commercial St, Phase II, Extension, Defence Housing Authority, POB 300, Karachi; tel. (21) 5381628; fax (21) 5802760; e-mail fpost@webnet.com.pk; f. 1994; English; Chief Editor and CEO QUDSIA K. KHAN; Publr M. AHSAN JAWAD.

Hilal-e-Pakistan: Court View Bldg, 2nd Floor, M. A. Jinnah Rd, POB 3737, Karachi 74200; tel. (21) 2624997; fax (21) 2624996; Sindhi; Editor MOHAMMAD IQBAL DAL.

Jago: Karachi; tel. (21) 2635544; fax (21) 2628137; f. 1990; Sindhi; political; Editor AGHA SALEEM.

Jasarat: Eveready Chambers, Muhammad Bin Qasim Rd, Karachi 74200; tel. (21) 2630391; fax (21) 2632102; e-mail jasarat@cyber.net .pk; f. 1970; Urdu; Editor MAHMOOD AHMAD MADANI; circ. 50,000.

Leader: Block 5, 609, Clifton Centre, Clifton, Karachi 75600; tel. (21) 5863801; fax (21) 5872206; e-mail dailyleader@hotmail.com; f. 1958; English; independent; Editor MANZAR-UL-HASSAN; Man. Editor MUNIR M. LADHA; circ. 3,000.

Mazdur: Spencer Bldg, I. I. Chundrigar Rd, Karachi 2; f. 1984; Urdu; Editor MOHAMMAD ANWAR BIN ABBAS.

Millat: 191 Altaf Hussain Rd, Karachi 2; tel. (21) 2411514; internet www.millat.com; f. 1946; Gujarati; independent; Editor INQUILAB MATRI; circ. 22,550.

Mohasib: Karachi; fax (21) 2632763; Urdu; also publ. from Abbotabad; Chief Editor ZAFAR MAJAZI; Editor NAEEM AHMAD.

The News International: Al-Rahman Bldg, I. I. Chundrigar Rd, POB 52, Karachi; tel. (21) 2630611; fax (21) 2418343; f. 1990; English; also publ. from Lahore and Rawalpindi/Islamabad; Editor-in-Chief Mir SHAKIL-UR-RAHMAN; Sr Editor SHAHEEN SEHBAI.

Parliament: 1013 Qasimabad, Karachi; tel. (21) 422030; f. 1988; English; Chief Editor FARRUGH AHMAD SIDDIQ.

Qaum (Nation): Karachi; Urdu; Editor and Publr MUSHTAQUE SOHAIL; Man. Editor MAMNOONUR REHMAN.

Qaumi Akhbar: 14 Ramzan Mansion, Dr Bilmoria St, off I. I. Chundrigar Rd, Karachi; tel. (21) 2633381; fax (21) 2635774; f. 1988; Urdu; Editor ILYAS SHAKIR.

Roznama Special: Falak Printing Press, 191 Altaf Hussain Rd, Karachi; tel. (21) 5687522; fax (21) 5687579; Publr and Man. Editor INQUILAB MATRI; Editor ANWAR SEN ROY.

Savera: 108 Adam Arcade, Shaheed-e-Millat Rd, Karachi; tel. (21) 419616; Urdu; Editor RUKHSANA SAHAM MIRZA.

Sindh Tribune: No. 246-D/6, PECHS, Karachi; tel. (21) 4535227; fax (21) 4332680; English; political; Editor YOUSUF SHAHEEN.

Star: Haroon House, Dr Ziauddin Ahmed Rd, Karachi 74200; evening; English; Editor KAMAL MAJEEDULLAH.

The Times of Karachi: Al-Falah Chambers, 9th Floor, Abdullah Haroon Rd, Karachi; tel. (21) 7727740; e-mail iqbalmir@yahoo.com; evening; English; independent; city news; Editor Mir IQBAL AZIZ.

Lahore

Daily Pakistan: 41 Jail Rd, Lahore; tel. (42) 7576301; fax (42) 7586251; internet www.daily-pakistan.com; f. 1990; Urdu; Chief Editor MUJIBUR RAHMAN SHAMI.

Daily Times: 41-N, Industrial Area, Gulberg II, Lahore; tel. (42) 5878614; fax (42) 5878620; e-mail editorial@dailytimes.com.pk; Editor NAJAM SETHI.

Mahgribi Pakistan: Lahore; tel. (42) 53490; Urdu; also publ. in Bahawalpur and Sukkur; Editor M. SHAFAAT.

The Nation: NIPCO House, 4 Sharah-e-Fatima Jinnah, POB 1815, Lahore 54000; tel. (42) 6367580; fax (42) 6367005; e-mail editor@nation.com; internet www.nation.com.pk; f. 1986; English; Chair. MAJEED NIZAMI; Editor ARIF NIZAMI; circ. 52,000.

Nawa-i-Waqt (Voice of the Time): 4 Sharah-e-Fatima Jinnah, Lahore 54000; tel. (42) 6302050; fax (42) 6367583; internet www.nawaiwaqt.com.pk; f. 1940; English, Urdu; also publ. edns in Karachi, Islamabad and Multan; Editor MAJID NIZAMI; combined circ. 560,000.

The Sun International: 15-L, Gulberg III, Ferozepur Rd, Lahore; tel. (42) 5883540; fax (42) 5839951; Editor MAHMOOD SADIQ.

Tijarat: 14 Abbot Rd, opp. Nishat Cinema, Lahore; Urdu; Editor JAMIL ATHAR.

Wifaq: 6A Waris Rd, Lahore; tel. (42) 302862; Urdu; also publ. in Rawalpindi, Sargodha and Rahimyar Khan; Editor MOSTAFA SADIQ.

Rawalpindi

Daily Jang: Murree Rd, Rawalpindi; internet www.jang.com.pk; f. 1940; also publ. in Quetta, Karachi and Lahore; Urdu; independent; Editor Mir JAVED REHMAN; circ. (Rawalpindi) 65,000.

Daily Wifaq: 7A C/A, Satellite Town, Rawalpindi; f. 1959; also publ. in Lahore, Sargodha and Rahimyar Khan; Urdu; Editor MUSTAFA SADIQ.

The News: Murree Rd, Rawalpindi; e-mail thenews@isb.comsats.net.pk; internet www.jang-group.com; f. 1991; also publ. in Lahore and Karachi; English; independent; Chief Editor Mir SHAKIL-UR-RAHMAN.

Other Towns

Aftab: Hyderabad; Sindhi; also publ. in Multan; Editor SHEIKH ALI MOHAMMAD.

Al Falah: Al Falah Bldg, Saddar Rd, Peshawar; f. 1939; Urdu and Pashtu; Editor S. ABDULLAH SHAH.

Al-Jamiat-e-Sarhad: Kocha Gilania Chakagali, Karimpura Bazar, Peshawar; tel. (91) 2567757; e-mail sagha@brain.net.pk; f. 1941; Urdu and Pashtu; Propr and Chief Editor S. M. HASSAN GILANI.

Balochistan Times: Jinnah Rd, Quetta; Editor SYED FASIH IQBAL.

Basharat: Peshawar; Urdu; general; also publ. in Islamabad; Chief Editor ANWAR-UL-HAQ; Editor KHALID ATHER.

Daily Awaz: Peshawar; political; Man. Editor ALI RAZA MALIK.

Daily Business Report: Railway Rd, Faisalabad; tel. (41) 642131; fax (41) 621207; f. 1948; Editor ABDUL RASHID GHAZI; circ. 26,000.

Daily Hewad: 32 Stadium Rd, Peshawar; tel. (521) 270501; Pashtu; Editor-in-Chief REHMAN SHAH AFRIDI.

Daily Ibrat Hyderabad: Ibrat Building, Gadi Khata, Hyderabad; tel. (221) 28571; fax (221) 784300; e-mail ibrat@hyd.compol.com; internet www.ibratgroup.com; Sindhi; Man. Editor Qazi ASAD ABID.

Daily Khadim-e-Waten: B-2, Civil Lines, Hyderabad; Editor MUSHATAQ AHMAD.

Daily Rehbar: Jamil Market, Circular Rd, Bahawalpur; tel. (621) 884664; e-mail dailyrehber@yahoo.co.uk; f. 1954; Urdu; Chief Editor AKHTER HUSSAIN ANJUM; circ. 250,000.

Daily Sarwan: 11-EGOR Colony, Hyderabad; tel. (221) 781382; Sindhi; Chief Editor GHULAM HUSSAIN.

Daily Shabaz: Peshawar; tel. (521) 220188; fax (521) 216483; Urdu; organ of the Awami National Party; Chief Editor Begum NASEEM WALI KHAN.

Frontier Post: 32 Stadium Rd, Peshawar; tel. (521) 79174; fax (521) 76575; e-mail editor@frontierpost.com.pk; internet www.frontierpost.com.pk; f. 1985; English; left-wing; also publ. in Lahore; closed down temporarily in January 2001, reopened in June; Editor-in-Chief REHMAT SHAH AFRIDI; Editor MUZAFFAR SHAH AFRIDI.

Jihad: 15A Islamia Club Bldg, Khyber Bazar, Peshawar; tel. (521) 210522; e-mail jehad@pes.comsats.net.pk; also publ. in Karachi, Rawalpindi, Islamabad and Lahore; Editor SHARIF FAROOQ.

Kaleem: Shahi Bazar Thalla, POB 88, Sukkur; tel. (71) 22086; fax (71) 22087; e-mail kaleem1@hyd.paknet.com.pk; Urdu; Editor SHAHID MEHR SHAMSI.

Kavish: Sindh Printing and Publishing House, Civil Lines, POB 43, Hyderabad; Chief Editor MUHAMMAD AYUB QAZI; Publr/Editor ASLAM A. QAZI.

Mashriq: Quetta; Chief Editor AZIZ MAZHAR.

Nawai Asma'n: Mubarak Ali Shah Rd, Hyderabad; tel. and fax (221) 21925; Urdu, Sindhi and Pashtu; Chief Editor DOST MUHAMMAD.

The News: Qaumi Printing Press, Peshawar; English; Editor KHURSHID AHMAD.

Punjab News: Kutchery Bazar, POB 419, Faisalabad; tel. (41) 30151; f. 1968; Chief Editor PERVAIZ PASHA; Man. Editor JAVAID HIMYARITE; circ. 20,000.

Sarhad: New Gate, Peshawar.

Sindh Guardian: Tulsi Das Rd, POB 300, Hyderabad; tel. and fax (221) 21926; English; Chief Editor DOST MUHAMMAD.

Sindh News: Garikhata, Hyderabad; tel. (221) 20793; fax (221) 781867; Editor Kazi SAEED AKBER.

Sindh Observer: POB 43, Garikhata, Hyderabad; tel. (221) 27302; English; Editor ASLAM AKBER KAZI.

Sindhu: Popular Printers, Ibrat Bldg, Garhhi Khata, Hyderabad; tel. (221) 783571; fax (221) 783570; Sindhi; political.

Watan: 10 Nazar Bagh Flat, Peshawar.

Zamana: Jinnah Rd, Quetta; tel. (81) 71217; Urdu; Editor SYED FASIH IQBAL; circ. 5,000.

SELECTED WEEKLIES

Akhbar-e-Jehan: Printing House, off I. I. Chundrigar Rd, Karachi; tel. (21) 2634368; fax (21) 2635693; f. 1967; Urdu; independent; illustrated family magazine; Editor-in-Chief Mir JAVED RAHMAN; circ. 278,000.

Amal: Shah Qabool Colony, POB 185, Peshawar; tel. 275605; e-mail pakbase@brain.com.pk; f. 1958; Urdu, Pashtu and English; Chief Editor F. M. ZAFAR KAIFI; Publr MUNAZIMA MAAB KAIFI.

Asianews: 4 Amil St, off Robson Rd, Karachi 1; multilingual news for and about Asians overseas; Man. Editor AMEEN TAREEN.

Badban: Nai Zindagi Publications, Rana Chambers, Old Anarkali, Lahore; Editor MUJIBUR REHMAN SHAMI.

Chatan: Chatan Bldg, 88 McLeod Rd, Lahore; tel. (42) 6311336; fax (42) 6374690; f. 1948; Urdu; Editor MASUD SHORISH.

Family Magazine: 4 Shara-i-Fatima Jinnah, Lahore 54000; tel. (42) 6367551; fax (42) 6367583; circ. 100,000.

The Friday Times: 45 The Mall, Lahore; tel. (42) 7355079; fax (42) 7355197; e-mail tft@lhr.comsats.net.pk; internet www.thefridaytimes.com; independent; Editor/Owner NAJAM SETHI.

Hilal: Hilal Rd, Rawalpindi 46000; tel. (51) 56134605; fax (51) 565017; f. 1951; Friday; Urdu; illustrated armed forces; Editor MUMTAZ IQBAL MALIK; circ. 90,000.

Insaf: P/929, Banni, Rawalpindi; tel. and fax (51) 5550903; fax (51) 4411038; e-mail insafrwp@isb.paknet.com.pk; f. 1955; Editor Mir WAQAR AZIZ.

Lahore: Galaxy Law Chambers, 1st Floor, Room 1, Turner Rd, Lahore 5; f. 1952; Editor SAQIB ZEERVI; circ. 8,500.

Mahwar: D23, Block H, North Nazimabad, Karachi; Editor SHAHIDA NAFIS SIDDIQI.

Memaar-i-Nao: 39 KMC Bldg, Leamarket, Karachi; Urdu; labour magazine; Editor M. M. MUBASIR.

The Muslim World: 49-B, Block-8, Gulshan-e-Iqbal, Karachi 75300; POB 5030, Karachi 74000; tel. (21) 4960738; fax (21) 466878; English; current affairs.

Nairang Khayal: 8 Mohammadi Market, Rawalpindi; f. 1924; Urdu; Chief Editor SULTAN RASHK.

Nida-i-Millat: 4 Sharah-e-Fatima Jinnah, Lahore 54000.

Noor Jehan Weekly: 32A National Auto Plaza, POB 8833, Karachi 74400; tel. and fax (21) 7723946; f. 1948; Urdu; film journal; Editor KHALID CHAWLA.

Pakistan and Gulf Economist: 3A Falcon Arcade, BC-3, Block-7, Clifton, POB 4447, Karachi; tel. (21) 5869534; fax (21) 5876071; e-mail information@pak-economist.com; f. 1960; English; Editor SUHAIL ABBAS; circ. 30,000.

Pak Kashmir: Pak Kashmir Office, Soikarno Chowk, Liaquat Rd, Rawalpindi; tel. (51) 74845; f. 1951; Urdu; Editor MUHAMMED FAYYAZ ABBAZI.

Parsi Sansar and Loke Sevak: 8 Mehrabad, 5 McNeil Rd, Karachi 75530; tel. and fax (21) 5673717; e-mail ogra@cyber.net.pk; f. 1909; English and Gujarati; Editor MEHERJI P. DASTUR.

Parwaz: Madina Office, Bahawalpur; Urdu; Editor MUSTAQ AHMED.

Qallandar: Peshawar; f. 1950; Urdu; Editor M. A. K. SHERWANI.

Quetta Times: Albert Press, Jinnah Rd, Quetta; f. 1924; English; Editor S. RUSTOMJI; circ. 4,000.

Shahab-e-Saqib: Shahab Saqib Rd, Maulana St, Peshawar; f. 1950; Urdu; Editor S. M. RIZVI.

The Statesman: 260C, Central C/A, PECHS, Karachi 75400; tel. (21) 4525627; f. 1955; English; Editor MOHAMMAD OWAIS.

Takbeer: A-1, 3rd Floor, 'Namco Centre', Campbell St, Karachi 74200; tel. (21) 2626613; fax (21) 2627742; e-mail irfanfaruqi@usa .com; f. 1984; Urdu; Sr. Exec. IRFAN KALIM FAROOQ; circ. 70,000.

Tarjaman-i-Sarhad: Peshawar; Urdu and Pashtu; Editor MOHAMMAD SHAFI SABIR.

Times of Kashmir: P/929, Banni, Rawalpindi; tel. (51) 5550903; fax (51) 4411038; e-mail iqbalmir@yahoo.com; English; Editor Mir IQBAL AZIZ.

Ufaq: 44H, Block No. 2, PECHS, Karachi; tel. (21) 437992; f. 1978; Editor WAHAJUDDIN CHISHTI; circ. 2,000.

SELECTED PERIODICALS

Aadab Arz: 190 N. Ghazali Rd, Saman Abad, Lahore 54500; tel. (42) 7582449; monthly; Editor KHALID BIN HAMID.

Aalami Digest: B-1, Momin Sq., Rashid Minhas Rd, Gulshan-e-Iqbal, Karachi; monthly; Urdu; Editor ZAHEDA HINA.

Afsan Digest: B-436, Sector 11-A, North Kaveli, Karachi 36; tel. (21) 657074; Urdu; Editor SYED ASIM MAHMOOD.

Akhbar-e-Watan: 68-C, 13th Commercial St, Phase-II, Extension Defence, Karachi; tel. (21) 5886071; fax (21) 5890179; e-mail akhbarewatan@hotmail.com; f. 1977; monthly; Urdu; cricket; Man. Editor MUNIR HUSSAIN; circ. 57,000.

Albalagh: Darul Uloom, Karachi 14; monthly; Editor MOHAMMED TAQI USMANI.

Al-Ma'arif: Institute of Islamic Culture, Club Rd, Lahore 54000; tel. (42) 6363127; f. 1950; quarterly; Urdu; Dir and Editor-in-Chief Dr RASHID AHMAD JALLANDHRI.

Anchal: 24 Saeed Mansion, I. I. Chundrigar Rd, Karachi; monthly.

Architecture and Interiors: 99, Ghafoor Chambers, Abdullah Haroon Rd, Karachi; tel. (21) 7772397; fax (21) 7772417; e-mail aplusi@cyberaccess.com.pk; f. 2001; quarterly; English; Editor MUTJUBA HUSSAIN; Man. Editor MURTUZA SHIKOH.

Archi Times: Ghafoor Chambers, 7th Floor, Abdullah Haroon Rd, Karachi; tel. (21) 7772397; fax (21) 7772417; e-mail archtime@ cyberaccess.com.pk; f. 1986; monthly; English; architecture; Editor MUJTABA HUSSAIN.

Asia Travel News: 101 Muhammadi House, I. I. Chundrigar Rd, Karachi 74000; tel. (21) 2424837; fax (21) 2420797; fortnightly;

travel trade, tourism and hospitality industry; Editor JAVED MUSHTAQ.

Auto Times: 5 S. J. Kayani Shaheed Rd, off Garden Rd, Karachi; tel. (21) 713595; fortnightly; English; Editor MUHAMMAD SHAHZAD.

Bachoon Ka Risala: 108–110 Adam Arcade, Shaheed-e-Millat Rd, Karachi; tel. (21) 419616; monthly; Urdu; Editor RUKHSANA SEHAM MIRZA.

Bagh: 777/18 Federal B Area, POB 485, Karachi; tel. (21) 449662; monthly; Urdu; Editor RAHIL IQBAL.

Bayyenat: Jamia Uloom-e-Islamia, Binnori Town, Karachi 74800; tel. (21) 4927233; f. 1962; monthly; Urdu; religious and social issues; Editor Maulana MUHAMMAD YOUSUF LUDHIANVI.

Beauty: Plot No. 4-C, 14th Commercial St, Defence Housing Authority, Phase II Extension, Karachi; tel. (21) 5805391; fax (21) 5896269; e-mail mansuri@fascom.com; f. 2000; bi-monthly; English; Chief Editor RIAZ AHMED MANSURI.

Beemakar (Insurer): 85 Press Chambers, I. I. Chundrigar Rd, Karachi; monthly; Urdu; Man. Editor SHAMSHAD AHMAD; Editor A. M. HASHMI.

Chand: 190 N. Ghazali Rd, Saman Abad, Lahore 54500; tel. (42) 7582449; monthly; Editor MASOOD HAMID.

The Cricketer: Plot No. 4-C, 14th Commercial St, Defence Housing Authority, Phase II Extension, Karachi; tel. (21) 5805391; fax (21) 5896269; e-mail mansuri@fascom.com; f. 1972; monthly; English/Urdu; Chief Editor RIAZ AHMED MANSURI.

Dastarkhuan: Plot No. 4-C, 14th Commercial St, Defence Housing Authority, Phase II Extension, Karachi; tel. (21) 5805391; fax (21) 5896269; e-mail mansuri@fascom.com; f. 1998; bi-monthly; Urdu; Chief Editor RIAZ AHMED MANSURI.

Defence Journal: 16B, 7th Central St, Defence Housing Authority, POB 12234, Karachi 75500; tel. (21) 5894074; fax (21) 571710; f. 1975; monthly; English; Editor-in-Chief Brig. (retd) ABDUL RAHMAN SIDDIQI; Editor IKRAM SEHGAL; circ. 10,000.

Dentist: 70/7, Nazimabad No. 3, Karachi 18; f. 1984; monthly; English and Urdu; Editor NAEEMULLAH HUSAIN.

Dosheeza: 108–110 Adam Arcade, Shaheed-e-Millat Rd, Karachi; tel. (21) 4930470; fax (21) 4934369; monthly; Urdu; Editor RUKHSANA SEHAM MIRZA.

Duniya-e-Tibb: Eveready Chambers, 2nd Floor, Mohd Bin Qasim Rd, off I. I. Chundrigar Rd, POB 1385, Karachi 1; tel. (21) 2630985; fax (21) 2637624; e-mail mcm@digicom.net.pk; f. 1986; monthly; Urdu; modern and Asian medicine; International Co-ordinator 'Parekh'; circ. 12,000.

Economic Review: Al-Masiha, 3rd Floor, 47 Abdullah Haroon Rd, POB 7843, Karachi 74400; tel. (21) 7728963; fax (21) 7728957; f. 1969; monthly; economic, industrial and investment research; Editor AHMAD MUHAMMAD KHAN.

Engineering Horizons: 3/II Shadman Plaza, Shadman Market, Lahore 54000; tel. (42) 7581743; fax (42) 7587422; e-mail mahmood@ imtiaz-faiz.com; f. 1988; monthly; English.

Engineering Review: 305 Spotlit Chambers, Dr Billimoria St, off Chundrigar Rd, POB 807, Karachi 74200; tel. (21) 2632567; fax (21) 2639378; e-mail engineeringreview@yahoo.com; internet www .engineeringreview.com.pk; f. 1975; fortnightly; English; circ. 5,000.

Film Asia: 68-C, 13th Commercial St, Phase-II, Extension Defence, Karachi; tel. (21) 5886071; fax (21) 5890179; e-mail akhbarewatan@ hotmail.com; f. 1973; monthly; film, television, fashion, art and culture; Man. Editor MUNIR HUSSAIN; circ. 38,000.

Good Food: Plot No. 4-C, 14th Commercial St, Defence Housing Authority, Phase II Extension, Karachi; tel. (21) 5805391; fax (21) 5896269; e-mail mansuri@fascom.com; f. 1997; bi-monthly; English; Chief Editor RIAZ AHMED MANSURI.

Hamdard-i-Sehat: Institute of Health and Tibbi Research, Hamdard Foundation Pakistan, Nazimabad, Karachi 74600; tel. (21) 6616001; fax (21) 6611755; e-mail hamdard@khi.paknet.com.pk; f. 1933; monthly; Urdu; Editor-in-Chief SADIA RASHID; circ. 12,000.

Hamdard Islamicus: Hamdard Foundation Pakistan, Nazimabad, Karachi 74600; tel. (21) 6616001; fax (21) 6611755; e-mail hamdard@khi.paknet.com.pk; f. 1978; quarterly; English; Editor-in-Chief SADIA RASHID; circ. 750.

Hamdard Medicus: Hamdard Foundation Pakistan, Nazimabad, Karachi 74600; tel. (21) 6616001; fax (21) 6611755; e-mail hamdard@khi.paknet.com.pk; f. 1957; quarterly; English; Editor-in-Chief SADIA RASHID; circ. 1,000.

Hamdard Naunehal: Hamdard Foundation Pakistan, Nazimabad, Karachi 74600; tel. (21) 6616001; fax (21) 6611755; e-mail hamdard@khi.paknet.com.pk; f. 1952; monthly; Urdu; Editor MASOOD AHMAD BARAKATI; circ. 30,000.

The Herald: Haroon House, Dr Ziauddin Ahmed Road, Karachi 74200; tel. (21) 5670001; fax (21) 5687221; e-mail subscribe.Herald@Dawn.com; f. 1970; monthly; English; Editor AAMER AHMED KHAN; circ. 38,000.

Hikayat: 26 Patiala Ground, Link McLeod Rd, Lahore; monthly; Editor INAYATULLAH.

Honhar-e-Pakistan: 56 Aurangzeb Market, Karachi; monthly; Editor MAZHAR YUSAFZAI.

Hoor: Hoor St, Lahore; monthly; Editor KHULA RABIA.

Islami Jumhuria: Laj Rd, Old Anarkali, Lahore; monthly; Editor NAZIR TARIQ.

Islamic Studies: Islamic Research Institute, Faisal Masjid Campus, POB 1035, Islamabad 44000; tel. (51) 850751; fax (51) 250821; e-mail amzia555@apollo.net.pk; f. 1962; quarterly; English, Urdu (Fikro-Nazar) and Arabic (Al Dirasat al-Islamiyyah) edns; Islamic literature, religion, history, geography, language and the arts; Editor Dr ZAFAR ISHAQ ANSARI (acting); circ. 3,000.

Jamal: Institute of Islamic Culture, 2 Club Rd, Lahore 3; tel. (42) 363127; f. 1950; annual; English; Dir and Editor-in-Chief MUHAMMAD SUHEYL UMAR.

Journal of the Pakistan Historical Society: c/o Hamdard Foundation, Nazimabad, Karachi 74600; tel. (21) 6616001; fax (21) 6611755; e-mail hamdard@khi.paknet.com.pk; f. 1953; quarterly; English; Editor Dr ANSAR ZAHID KHAN; circ. 700.

Khel-Ke-Duniya: 6/13 Alyusaf Chamber, POB 340, Karachi; tel. (21) 216888.

Khwateen Digest: Urdu Bazar, M.A. Jinnah Rd, Karachi; monthly; Urdu; Editor MAHMUD RIAZ.

Kiran: 37 Urdu Bazar, M. A. Jinnah Rd, Karachi; tel. (21) 216606; Editor MAHMUD BABAR FAISAL.

Leather News: Iftikhar Chambers, opp. UNI Plaza, Altaf Hussain Rd, POB 4323, Karachi 74000; fax (21) 2631545; f. 1989; Editor ABDUL RAFAY SIDDIQI.

Medical Variety: 108–110 Adam Arcade, Shaheed-e-Millat Rd, Karachi; tel. (21) 419616; monthly; English; Editor RUKHSANA SEHAM MIRZA.

Muslim World Business: 20 Sasi Arcade, 4th Floor, Main Clifton Rd, POB 10417, Karachi 6; tel. (21) 534870; f. 1989; monthly; English; political and business; Editor-in-Chief MUZAFFAR HASSAN.

Naey-Ufaq: 24 Saeed Mansion, I. I. Chundrigar Rd, Karachi; fortnightly.

NGM Communication: Gulberg Colony, POB 3041, Lahore 54660; tel. (42) 5713849; e-mail ngm@shoa.net; internet www.ngm.web-page.net; English; lists newly-released Pakistani publications on the internet; updated weekly; Editor NIZAM NIZAMI.

Pakistan Journal of Applied Economics: Applied Economics Research Centre, University of Karachi, POB 8403, Karachi 75270; tel. (21) 9243168; fax (21) 4829730; e-mail pjae@cyber.net.pk; twice a year; Editor Prof. Dr NUZHAT AHMAD.

Pakistan Journal of Scientific and Industrial Research: Pakistan Council of Scientific and Industrial Research, Scientific Information Centre, 39 Garden Rd, Saddar, Karachi 74400; tel. (21) 9215100; fax (21) 9215107; e-mail pcsirsys@super.net.pk; f. 1958; bi-monthly; English; Exec. Editor Dr A. RASHEED KHAN; circ. 1,000.

Pakistan Management Review: Pakistan Institute of Management, Management House, Shahrah Iran, Clifton, Karachi 75600; tel. (21) 9251711; e-mail pimkhi@pim.com.pk; internet www.pim.com.pk; f. 1960; quarterly; English; Editor IQBAL A. QAZI.

Pasban: Faiz Modh Rd, Quetta; fortnightly; Urdu; Editor MOLVI MOHD ABDULLAH.

Phool: 4 Sharah-e-Fatima Jinnah, Lahore 54000; e-mail phool@nawaiwaqt.com.pk; internet www.phool.com.pk; monthly; children's; circ. 40,000.

Progress: 4th Floor, PIDC House, Dr Ziauddin Ahmed Rd, Karachi 75530; tel. 111–568–568; fax (21) 5680005; e-mail n_nusrat@ppl.com.pk; f. 1956; monthly; publ. by Pakistan Petroleum Ltd; Editor and Publr NUSRAT NASARULLAH; Chief Exec./Man. Dir S. MUNSIF RAZA.

Qaumi Digest: 50 Lower Mall, Lahore; tel. (42) 7225143; fax (42) 7233261; monthly; Editor MUJIBUR REHMAN SHAMI.

Sabrang Digest: 47–48 Press Chambers, I. I. Chundrigar Rd, Karachi 1; tel. (21) 211961; f. 1970; monthly; Urdu; Editor SHAKEEL ADIL ZADAH; circ. 150,000.

Sach-Chee Kahaniyan: 108–110 Adam Arcade, Shaheed-e-Millat Rd, Karachi; tel. (21) 4930470; fax (21) 4934369; monthly; Urdu; Editor RUKHSANA SEHAM MIRZA.

Sayyarah: Aiwan-e-Adab, Urdu Bazar, Lahore 54000; tel. (42) 7321842; f. 1962; monthly; Urdu; literary; Man. Editor HAFEEZ-UR-RAHMAN AHSAN.

Sayyarah Digest: 244, Main Market Riwaz Garden, Lahore 54000; tel. (42) 7245412; fax (42) 7325080; e-mail sayyaradigest@brain.com.pk; f. 1963; monthly; Urdu; Chief Editor AMJAD RAUF KHAN; circ. 40,000.

Science Magazine: Science Book Foundation, Haji Bldg, Hassan Ali Efendi Rd, Karachi; tel. (21) 2625647; monthly; Urdu; Editor QASIM MAHMOOD.

Seep: Alam Market, Block No. 16, Federal B Area, Karachi; quarterly; Editor NASIM DURRANI.

Show Business: 108–110 Adam Arcade, Shaheed-e-Millat Rd, POB 12540, Karachi; tel. (21) 419616; monthly; Urdu; Editor RUKHSANA SEHAM MIRZA.

Sindh Quarterly: 36D Karachi Administrative Co-operative Housing Society, off Shaheed-e-Millat Rd, Karachi 75350; tel. (21) 4531988; f. 1973; Editor SAYID GHULAM MUSTAFA SHAH.

Smash: Plot No. 4-C, 14th Commercial St, Defence Housing Authority, Phase II Extension, Karachi; tel. (21) 5805391; fax (21) 5896269; e-mail mansuri@fascom.com; f. 2000; monthly; English; Chief Editor RIAZ AHMED MANSURI.

Spider: Haroon House, Dr Ziauddin Ahmed Rd, Karachi 74200; tel. (21) 5681544; fax (21) 5685420; e-mail hr@spider.tm; internet spider.tm; f. 1998; internet monthly.

Sports International: Arshi Market, Firdaus Colony, Nazimabad, Karachi 74600; tel. (21) 6602171; fax (21) 6683768; e-mail ibp-khi@cyber.net.pk; f. 1972; fortnightly; Urdu and English; Chief Editor KANWAR ABDUL MAJEED; Editor RAHEEL MAJEED.

Taj: Jamia Tajia, St 13, Sector 14/B, Buffer Zone, Karachi 75850; monthly; Editor BABA M. ATIF SHAH ANWARI ZAHEENI TAJI.

Talimo Tarbiat: Ferozsons (Pvt) Ltd, 60 Shahrah-e-Quaid-e-Azam, Lahore 54000; tel. (42) 6301196; fax (42) 6369204; f. 1941; children's monthly; Urdu; Chief Editor A. SALAM; circ. 50,000.

Textile Times: Arshi Market, Firdaus Colony, Nazimabad, Karachi 74600; tel. (21) 6683768; e-mail ibp-khi@cyber.net.pk; f. 1993; monthly; English; Chief Editor KANWAR ABDUL MAJEED; Exec. Editor RAHEEL MAJEED KHAN.

Trade Chronicle: Iftikhar Chambers, Altaf Hussain Rd, POB 5257, Karachi 74000; tel. (21) 2631587; fax (21) 2635007; e-mail arsidiqi@fascom.com; f. 1953; monthly; English; trade, politics, finance and economics; Editor ABDUL RAB SIDDIQI; circ. 6,000.

Trade Link International: Zahoor Mansion, Tariq Rd, Karachi; monthly; English; Man. Editor M. IMRAN BAIG; Editor IKRAMULLAH QUREISHI.

TV Times: Plot No. 4-C, 14th Commercial St, Defence Housing Authority, Phase II Extension, Karachi; tel. (21) 5805391; fax (21) 5896269; e-mail mansuri@fascom.com; f. 1987; monthly; English; Chief Editor RIAZ AHMED MANSURI.

UNESCO Payami: 30 UNESCO House, Sector H-8/1, Islamabad; tel. (51) 434196; fax (51) 431815; monthly; Urdu; publ. by Pakistan National Commission for UNESCO; Editor Dr MUNIR A. ABRO.

The Universal Message: D-35, Block-5, Federal 'B' Area, Karachi 75950; tel. (21) 6349840; fax (21) 6361040; f. 1979; journal of the Islamic Research Acad. monthly; English; literature, politics, economics, religion; Editor ASADULLAH KHAN.

Urdu Digest: 21-Acre Scheme, Samanabad, Lahore 54500; tel. (42) 7589957; fax (42) 7563646; e-mail digest@lhr.paknet.com.pk; monthly; Urdu; Editor ALTAF HASAN QURESHEE.

Voice of Islam: Jamiatul Falah Bldg, Akbar Rd, Saddar, POB 7141, Karachi 74400; tel. (21) 7721394; f. 1952; monthly; Islamic Cultural Centre magazine; English; Editor Prof. ABDUL QADEER SALEEM; Man. Editor Prof. WAQAR ZUBAIRI.

Wings: 101 Muhammadi House, I. I. Chundrigar Rd, Karachi 74000; tel. (21) 2412591; fax (21) 2420797; monthly; aviation and defence; English; Editor and Publr JAVED MUSHTAQ.

Women's Own: Plot No. 4-C, 14th Commercial St, Defence Housing Authority, Phase II Extension, Karachi; tel. (21) 5805391; fax (21) 5896269; e-mail mansuri@fascom.com; f. 1987; monthly; English; Chief Editor RIAZ AHMED MANSURI.

Yaqeen International: Darut Tasnif (Pvt) Ltd, Main Hub River Rd, Mujahidabad, Karachi 75760; tel. (21) 2814432; fax (21) 2811304; f. 1952; English and Arabic; Islamic organ; Editor Dr HAFIZ MUHAMMAD ADIL.

Yaran-e-Watan: Overseas Pakistanis Foundation, Shahrah-E-Jamhuriate, G-5/2, POB 1470, Islamabad 44000; tel. (51) 9210175; fax (51) 9224518; e-mail opf@comsats.net.pk; f. 1982; monthly;

Urdu; publ. by the Overseas Pakistanis Foundation; Editor HAROON RASHID.

Youth World International: 104/C Central C/A, Tariq Rd, Karachi; tel. (21) 442211; f. 1987; monthly; English; Editor Syed ADIL EBRAHIM.

NEWS AGENCIES

Associated Press of Pakistan (APP): 18 Mauve Area, Zero Point, G-7/1, POB 1258, Islamabad; tel. (51) 2826158; fax (51) 2821292; e-mail appnews@isb.comsats.net.pk; f. 1948; Dir-Gen. ASHFAQ AHMAD GONDAL.

National News Agency (NNA): 131 Posh Arcade Plaza, Markaz G-9, POB 455, Islamabad 44000; tel. (51) 2260082; fax (51) 2255967; e-mail nna@islamabad.net; internet www.nij.8m.net; f. 1992; Chief Editor SUHAIL ILYAS.

News Network International: 410 Khyber Plaza, Blue Area, Islamabad; tel. (51) 827442; fax (51) 218549; internet nni-news.com; Editor-in-Chief HAFIZ ABDUL KHALIQ.

Pakistan International Press Agency (PIPA): 6 Ground Floor, State Life Bldg, Karachi; tel. (21) 5683618; Bureau Chief S. M. SHAKEEL.

Pakistan—International Press Agency (PPA): 6, St 39, G-6/2, Islamabad 44000; tel. (51) 2279830; fax (51) 2272405; e-mail newsatisb@yahoo.com; internet www.ppanews.com.pk; Chief Editor KHALID ATHAR.

Pakistan Press International (PPI): Press Centre, Shahrah Kamal Atatürk, POB 541, Karachi; tel. (21) 2631123; fax (21) 2637754; e-mail owais.ali@post.harvard.edu; f. 1956; Chair. OWAIS ASLAM ALI.

United Press of Pakistan (Pvt) Ltd (UPP): 1 Victoria Chambers, Haji Abdullah Haroon Rd, Karachi 74400; tel. 5683235; fax (21) 5682694; f. 1949; Man. Editor MAHMUDUL AZIZ; 6 brs.

Foreign Bureaux

Agence France-Presse (AFP): 90 Attaturk Ave, G-6/3, Islamabad; tel. (51) 111–237–475; fax (51) 2822203; e-mail islamabad@afp.com; Chief Rep. FRANÇOIS XAVIER HARISPE.

Agenzia Nazionale Stampa Associata (ANSA) (Italy): Islamabad; Bureau Chief ABSAR HUSAIN RIZVI.

Associated Press (AP) (USA): 6A, St 25, F-8/2, Islamabad; tel. (51) 260957; fax (51) 256176; Bureau Chief KATHY GANON.

Deutsche Presse-Agentur (dpa) (Germany): Islamabad; tel. (51) 821925; Correspondent ANWAR MANSURI.

Inter Press Service (IPS) (Italy): House 10, St 13, F-8/3, Islamabad; tel. (51) 853356; fax (42) 856430; Correspondent MUSHAHID HUSSAIN.

Reuters (UK): POB 1069, Islamabad; tel. (51) 2274757; e-mail simon.denyer@reuters.com; Bureau Chief SIMON DENYER.

United Press International (UPI) (USA): Islamabad; tel. (51) 821472; Bureau Chief DENHOLM BARNETSON.

Xinhua (New China) News Agency (People's Republic of China): Islamabad; tel. (51) 856614; Chief Correspondent LI JIASHENG.

PRESS ASSOCIATIONS

All Pakistan Newspaper Employees Confederation: Karachi Press Club, M. R. Kayani Rd, Karachi; f. 1976; confed. of all press industry trade unions; Pres. ABDUL HAMEED CHAPRA; Sec.-Gen. PERVAIZ SHAUKAT.

All Pakistan Newspapers Society: 32 Farid Chambers, 3rd Floor, Abdullah Haroon Rd, Karachi 3; tel. (21) 5671256; fax (21) 5671310; e-mail apns44@hotmail.com; f. 1949; Pres. HAMEED HAROON; Sec.-Gen. KAZI ASAD ABID.

Council of Pakistan Newspaper Editors: c/o United Press of Pakistan, 1 Victoria Chambers, Haji Abdullah Haroon Rd, Karachi 74400; tel. (21) 5682694; fax (21) 5682694; Gen. Sec. MUJIBUR RAHMAN SHAMI.

Publishers

Al-Hamra Publishing: Saudi Pak Tower, Jinnah Ave, Islamabad; tel. (51) 2823862; e-mail contact@alhamra.com.

Anjuman Taraqq-e-Urdu Pakistan: D-159, Block 7, Gulshan-e-Iqbal, Karachi 75300; tel. (21) 461406; f. 1903; literature, religion, textbooks, Urdu dictionaries, literary and critical texts; Pres. AFTAB AHMED KHAN; Hon. Sec. JAMIL UDDIN AALI.

Camran Publishers: Jalaluddin Hospital Bldg, Circular Rd, Lahore; f. 1964; general, technical, textbooks; Propr ABDUL HAMID.

Chronicle Publications: Iftikhar Chambers, Altaf Hussain Rd, POB 5257, Karachi 74000; tel. (21) 2631587; fax (21) 2635007; e-mail arsidiqi@fascom.com; f. 1953; reference, directories, religious books; Dir ABDUL RAUF SIDDIQI.

Economic and Industrial Publications: Al-Masiha, 3rd Floor, 47 Abdullah Haroon Rd, POB 7843, Karachi 74400; tel. (21) 7728963; fax (21) 7728434; f. 1965; industrial, economic and investment research.

Elite Publishers Ltd: D-118, SITE, Karachi 75700; tel. (21) 297035; fax (21) 295220; f. 1951; Chair. AHMED MIRZA JAMIL; Man. Dir KHALID JAMIL.

Ferozsons (Pvt) Ltd: 60 Shahrah-e-Quaid-e-Azam, Lahore; tel. (42) 626262; fax (42) 6369204; e-mail support@ferozsons.com.pk; internet www.ferozsons.com.pk; f. 1894; books, periodicals, maps, atlases, stationery products; Man. Dir A. SALAM; Dir ZAHEER SALAM.

Frontier Publishing Co: 22 Urdu Bazar, Lahore; tel. (42) 7355262; fax (42) 7247323; e-mail masim@brain.net.pk; internet www.brain.net.pk/~masim; academic and general; Execs MUHAMMAD ARIF, MUHAMMAD AMIR, MUHAMMAD ASIM.

Sh. Ghulam Ali and Sons (Pvt) Ltd: 199 Circular Rd, Lahore 54000; tel. (42) 7352908; fax (42) 6315478; e-mail niazasad@hotmail.com; internet www.ghulamali.com; f. 1887; general, religion, technical, textbooks; Dirs NIAZ AHMAD, ASAD NIAZ.

Harf Academy: G/307, Amena Plaza, Peshawar Rd, Rawalpindi.

Idara Taraqqi-i-Urdu: S-1/363 Saudabad, Karachi 27; f. 1949; general literature, technical and professional books and magazines; Propr IKRAM AHMED.

Ilmi Kitab Khana: Kabeer St, Urdu Bazar, Lahore; tel. (42) 62833; f. 1948; technical, professional, historical and law; Propr Haji SARDAR MOHAMMAD.

Indus Publications: 25 Fared Chambers, Abdullah Haroon Rd, Karachi; tel. (21) 5660242; e-mail muzaffar_indus@hotmail.com.

Islamic Book Centre: 25B Masson Rd, POB 1625, Lahore 54000; tel. (42) 6361803; fax (42) 6360955; e-mail lsaeed@paknetl.ptc.pk; religion in Arabic, Urdu and English; Islamic history, text books, dictionaries and reprints; Propr and Man. Dir SUMBLEYNA SAJID SAEED.

Islamic Publications (Pvt) Ltd: 3 Court St, Lower Mall, Lahore 54000; tel. (42) 7248676; fax (42) 7214974; e-mail islamicpak@hotmail.com; internet www.islamicpak.com.pk; f. 1959; Islamic literature in Urdu and English; Man. Dir Prof. MUHAMMAD AMIN JAVED; Gen. Man. AMANAT ALI.

Jamiatul Falah Publications: Jamiatul Falah Bldg, Akbar Rd, Saddar, POB 7141, Karachi 74400; tel. (21) 7721394; f. 1952; Islamic history and culture; Pres. MUZAFFAR AHMED HASHMI; Sec. Prof. SHAHZADUL HASAN CHISHTI.

Kazi Publications: 121 Zulqarnain Chambers, Ganpat Rd, POB 1845, Lahore; tel. (42) 7311359; fax (42) 7117606; e-mail kazip@brain.net.pk; internet www.brain.net.pk/~kazip/; f. 1978; Islamic literature, religion, law, biographies; Propr/Man. MUHAMMAD IKRAM SIDDIQI; Chief Editor MUHAMMAD IQBAL SIDDIQI.

Lark Publishers: Urdu Bazar, Karachi 1; f. 1955; general literature, magazines; Propr MAHMOOD RIAZ.

Lion Art Press (Pvt) Ltd: 112 Shahrah-e-Quaid-e-Azam, Lahore 54000; tel. (42) 6304444; e-mail alij@brain.net.pk; f. 1919; general publs in English and Urdu; Chief Exec. KHALID A. SHEIKH; Dir S. A. JAMIL.

Maktaba Darut Tasnif: Main Hub River Rd, Mujahidabad, Karachi 75760; tel. (21) 2814432; fax (21) 2811307; f. 1951; Koran, Majeed and Islamic literature; Dir ABDUL BAQI FAROOQI.

Malik Sirajuddin & Sons: Kashmiri Bazar, POB 2250, Lahore 54000; tel. (42) 7657527; fax (42) 7657490; e-mail sirajco@brain.net.pk; f. 1905; general, religion, law, textbooks; Man. MALIK ABDUL ROUF.

Malik Sons: Karkhana Bazar, Faisalabad.

Medina Publishing Co: M. A. Jinnah Rd, Karachi 1; f. 1960; general literature, textbooks; Propr HAKIM MOHAMMAD TAQI.

Mehtab Co: Ghazni St, Urdu Bazar, Lahore; tel. (42) 7120071; fax (42) 7353489; e-mail shashraf@brain.net.pk; f. 1978; Islamic literature; Propr SHAHZAD RIAZ SHEIKH.

Mohammad Hussain and Sons: 17 Urdu Bazar, Lahore 2; tel. (42) 7244114; f. 1941; religion, textbooks; Partners MOHAMMAD HUSSAIN, AZHAR ALI SHEIKH, PERVEZ ALI SHEIKH.

Sh. Muhammad Ashraf: 7 Aibak Rd, New Anarkali, Lahore 7; tel. (42) 7353171; fax (42) 7353489; e-mail shashraf@brain.net.pk; f. 1923; books in English on all aspects of Islam; Man. Dir SHAHZAD RIAZ SHEIKH.

National Book Service: 22 Urdu Bazar, Lahore; tel. (42) 7247310; fax (42) 7247323; e-mail masim@brain.net.pk; internet www.brain .net.pk/~masim; academic and primary school books; Execs MUHAMMAD ARIF, MUHAMMAD AMIR, MUHAMMAD ASIM.

Oxford University Press: Plot No. 38, Sector 15, Korangi Industrial Area, Karachi; tel. 111–693–673; fax (21) 4547640; e-mail ouppak@theoffice.net; internet www.oup.com.pk; academic, educational and general; Man. Dir AMEENA SAIYID.

Pakistan Law House: Pakistan Chowk, POB 90, Karachi 1; tel. (21) 2212455; fax (21) 2627549; e-mail plh_law_house@hotmail.com; f. 1950; importers and exporters of legal books and reference books; Man. K. NOORANI.

Pakistan Publishing House: Victoria Chambers 2, A. Haroon Rd, Karachi 75400; tel. (21) 5681457; e-mail danyalbooks@hotmail.com; f. 1959; Propr H. NOORANI; Gen. Man. AAMIR HUSSEIN.

Paramount Books: 152/0, Block 2, PECHS, Karachi 75400; tel. (21) 4310030; e-mail parabks@cyber.net.pk.

Pioneer Book House: 1 Avan Lodge, Bunder Rd, POB 37, Karachi; periodicals, gazettes, maps and reference works in English, Urdu and other regional languages.

Premier Bookhouse: Shahin Market, Room 2, Anarkali, POB 1888, Lahore; tel. (42) 7321174; Islamic and law.

Publishers International: Bandukwala Bldg, 4 I. I. Chundrigar Rd, Karachi; f. 1948; reference; Man. Dir KAMALUDDIN AHMAD.

Publishers United (Pvt) Ltd: 176 Anarkali, POB 1689, Lahore 54000; tel. (42) 7352238; textbooks, technical, reference, oriental literature in English, military and general; Man. Dir Maj. (retd) JAVED AMIN.

Punjab Religious Books Society: Anarkali, Lahore 2; tel. (42) 54416; educational, religious, law and general; Gen. Man. A. R. IRSHAD; Sec. NAEEM SHAKIR.

Reprints Ltd: 16 Bahadur Shah Market, M. A. Jinnah Rd, Karachi; f. 1983; Pakistani edns of foreign works; Chair. A. D. KHALID; Man. Dir AZIZ KHALID.

Sang-e-Meel Publications: 20 Shahrah-e-Pakistan, Lahore; tel. (42) 7220100; e-mail smp@sang-e-meel.com.

Sindhi Adabi Board (Sindhi Literary and Publishing Organization): Hyderabad; tel. (221) 771276; f. 1951; history, literature, culture of Sindh; in Sindhi, Urdu, English, Persian and Arabic; translations into Sindhi, especially of literature and history; Chair. MOHAMMAD IBRAHIM JOYO; Sec. GHULAM RABBANI A. AGRO.

Taj Co Ltd: Manghopir Rd, POB 530, Karachi; tel. (21) 294221; f. 1929; religious books; Man. Dir A. H. KHOKHAR.

The Times Press (Pvt) Ltd: C-18, Al-Hilal Society, off University Rd, Karachi 74800; tel. (21) 4932931; fax (21) 4935602; e-mail timekhi@cyber.net.pk; internet www.timespress.8m.com; f. 1948; printers, publishers and stationery manufacturers, including security printing (postal stationery and stamps); registered publishers of Koran, school textbooks, etc. Dir S. M. MINHAJUDDIN.

Tooba Publishers: 85 Sikandar Block, Allama Iqbal Town, Lahore; tel. (42) 5410185; e-mail haroonkallem@hotmail.com; f. 1983; poetry; Man. HAROON KALEEM USMANI.

Urdu Academy Sind: 16 Bahadur Shah Market, M. A. Jinnah Rd, Karachi 2; tel. (21) 2634185; f. 1947; brs in Hyderabad and Lahore; reference, general and textbooks; Editor and Man. Dir A. D. KHALID.

Vanguard Books: 45, The Mall, Lahore; tel. (42) 7243783; e-mail vbal@brain.net.pk.

West-Pak Publishing Co (Pvt) Ltd: 56N, Gulberg-II, Lahore; tel. (42) 7230555; fax (42) 7120077; f. 1932; textbooks and religious books; Chief Exec. SYED AHSAN MAHMUD.

Government Publishing House

Government Publications: Office of the Deputy Controller, Stationery and Forms, nr Old Sabzi Mandi, University Rd, Karachi 74800; tel. (21) 9231989; Dep. Controller MUHAMMAD AMIN BUTT.

PUBLISHERS' ASSOCIATION

Pakistan Publishers' and Booksellers' Association: YMCA Bldg, Shahrah-e-Quaid-e-Azam, Lahore; Chair. SYED AHSAN MAHMUD; Sec. ZUBAIR SAEED.

Broadcasting and Communications

TELECOMMUNICATIONS

Pakistan Telecommunications Authority (PTA): F-5/1, Islamabad; tel. (51) 99257246; fax (51) 456375; e-mail ddpr_pta@yahoo .com; internet www.pta.gov.pk; f. 1995; regulatory authority; Chair. Mian AKHTAR BAJWA; Dir-Gen. CH. MOHAMMAD DIN.

Carrier Telephone Industries (Pvt) Ltd: 1-9/2 Industrial Area, POB 1098, Islamabad; tel. (51) 414856; fax (51) 414859; f. 1969; Man. Dir MALIK MOHAMMAD AMIN.

Instaphone: Pakcom Ltd, World Trade Centre, 10 Khayaban-e-Roomi, Clifton, Karachi; tel. (21) 5871171; fax (21) 5869051; private mobile telephone co.

Mobilink: Pakistan Mobile Communications (Pvt) Ltd, 205-B, E. I. Lines, Dr Daud Pota Rd, Karachi; tel. (21) 5670261; fax (21) 5670268; private mobile telephone co.

Pakistan Telecommunication Co Ltd (PTCL): G-8/4 Islamabad 44000; tel. (51) 4844463; fax (51) 4843991; e-mail gmpr@ptcl.com.pk; internet www.ptcl.com.pk; f. 1990; 88% state-owned; scheduled for transfer to the public sector; Chair. AKHTAR AHMED BAJWA.

Paktel Ltd: 1st Floor, State Life Bldg No. 3, Dr Ziauddin Ahmed Rd, Karachi; tel. (21) 5689231; fax (21) 5682537; private mobile telephone co.

Other telecommunications companies operating in Pakistan include Telephone Industries of Pakistan and Alcatel Pakistan Ltd.

RADIO

Pakistan Broadcasting Corporation: National Broadcasting House, Constitution Ave, Islamabad 4400; tel. (51) 9214278; fax (51) 9223827; e-mail cnoradio@isb.comsats.net.pk; internet www.radio .gov.pk; f. 1947 as Radio Pakistan; national broadcasting network of 23 stations; home service 513 hrs daily in 17 languages and dialects; external services 10 hrs daily in 15 languages; world service 11 hrs daily in two languages; 80 news bulletins daily; Dir-Gen. TARIQ IMMAM; Chair. SYED ANWAR MAHMOOD.

Azad Kashmir Radio: Muzaffarabad; state-owned; Station Dir MASUD KASHFI; Dep. Controller (Eng.) SYED AHMED.

Capital FM: Islamabad; f. 1995; privately-owned; broadcasts music and audience participation shows 24 hrs daily.

TELEVISION

Pakistan Television Corpn Ltd: Federal TV Complex, Constitution Ave, POB 1221, Islamabad; tel. (51) 9208651; fax (51) 9202202; e-mail md@ptv.com.pk; internet www.ptv.com.pk; f. 1964; transmits 240 hrs daily; four channels; Chair. SYED ANWAR MAHMOOD; Man. Dir YOUSAF BAIG MIRZA.

Shalimar Television Network: 36, H-9, POB 1246, Islamabad; tel. (51) 9257396; fax (51) 4434830; e-mail srbc@comsats.net.pk; f. 1989 as People's Television Network; 57% state-owned, 43% privately-owned; 12 terrestrial stations throughout Pakistan; Chief Exec. ANWAR JAHANGIR.

Finance

(cap. = capital; auth. = authorized; p.u. = paid up; res = reserves; dep. = deposits; m. = million; brs = branches; amounts in rupees unless otherwise stated)

BANKING

In January 1974 all domestic banks were nationalized. In December 1990 the Government announced that it intended to transfer the five state-owned commercial banks to private ownership. By late 1991 the majority of shares in the Muslim Commercial Bank Ltd and the Allied Bank of Pakistan Ltd had been transferred to private ownership. In 1991 the Government granted 10 new private commercial bank licences, the first since banks were nationalized in 1974. In June 2002 the Supreme Court reversed its 1999 ruling that ordered the Government to abolish charging interest. Interest charges, known as 'riba', are forbidden under Islamic law. The ruling would have required all financial institutions to adopt the Islamic style of banking. In late 2002 the State Bank of Pakistan gave banks three options for the launching of Islamic banking: to establish an independent Islamic bank; to open subsidiaries of existing commercial banks; and to establish new branches to carry out Islamic banking operations.

Central Bank

State Bank of Pakistan: Central Directorate, I. I. Chundrigar Rd, POB 4456, Karachi 2; tel. (21) 9212400; fax (21) 9212433; e-mail sbp-isd@cyber.net.pk; internet www.sbp.org.pk; f. 1948; bank of issue; controls and regulates currency and foreign exchange; cap. 100m., res 9,000m., dep. 312,625m. (June 1999); Gov. Dr ISHRAT HUSSAIN; Dep. Govs MUKHTAR NABI QURESHI, RASHID AKHTAR CHUGHTAI; 18 brs.

Commercial Banks

Allied Bank of Pakistan Ltd: Allied Bank Bldg, Khayaban-e-Iqbal, Main Clifton Rd, Bath Island, Central Office, Karachi 75600; tel. (21) 5836719; fax (21) 5875189; e-mail int-div@abl.com.pk; f. 1942 as Australasia Bank Ltd; name changed as above 1974; cap. 1,063.2m., res 480.8m., dep. 93,107.3m. (Dec. 1999); 49% state-owned; Pres., Chair. and Chief Exec. KHALID A. SHERWANI; Sr Vice-Pres. IQBAL ZAIDI; 929 brs in Pakistan.

Askari Commercial Bank Ltd: AWT Plaza, The Mall, POB 1084, Rawalpindi; tel. (51) 9272150; fax (51) 9272455; e-mail askari@comsats.net.pk; internet www.askaribank.com.pk/; f. 1992; cap. US $ 17.3m., res US $25.4m., dep. US $686.7m. (Dec. 2001); Chair. Lt-Gen. JAMSHAID GULZAR; Pres. and Chief Exec. KALIM UR-RAHMAN; 46 brs.

Bank Al Habib Ltd: Mackinnon Bldg, I.I. Chundrigar Rd, Karachi; tel. 111–786–110; e-mail alhabib@cyber.net.pk; f. 1991; cap. 865.6m., res 665.5m., dep. 14,112.9m. (Sept. 2002); Chief Exec. and Man. Dir ABBAS D. HABIB; 57 brs.

Bank Alfalah Ltd: BA Bldg, I.I. Chundrigar Rd, POB 6773, Karachi; tel. (21) 2414030; fax (21) 2417006; e-mail karachi@bankalfalah.com; internet www.bankalfalah.com; f. 1992 as Habib Credit and Exchange Ltd; name changed as above 1998; cap. 600.0m., res 286.0m., dep. 15,820.5m. (Dec. 1999); 70% owned by Abu Dhabi Consortium, 30% by Habib Bank; Chief Exec. MUHAMMAD SALEEM AKHTAR; 13 brs.

The Bank of Khyber: 24 The Mall, Peshawar; tel. (521) 279977; fax (521) 278146; e-mail mdbok1@pes.comsats.net.pk; internet www.bankofkhyber.com.pk; cap. 416.0m., res 253.0m., dep. 9,630.5m. (Dec. 1998); 100% state-owned; Exec. Dir SAJID ALI ABBASI; Man. Dir SAJID ALI ABBASI; 29 brs.

The Bank of Punjab: 7 Egerton Rd, POB 2254, Lahore 54000; tel. (42) 9200421; fax (42) 9200297; e-mail bop@lhr.comsats.net.pk; internet www.punjabbank.com; f. 1989; share cap. 1,004m., res 1,251m., dep. 22,433m. (June 2002); 51.6% owned by provincial govt; Chair. TARIQ SULTAN; Man. Dir SALIM JAN; 242 brs.

Bolan Bank Ltd: 92-514/A Madresa Rd, Quetta; tel. (81) 66562; fax (81) 67595; f. 1991; auth. cap. 600m. Pres. and Chief Exec. SYED IJAZ HUSSAIN SHAH; 10 brs.

Habib Bank Ltd: 21 Habib Bank Plaza, I. I. Chundrigar Rd, Karachi 75650; tel. (21) 2418000; fax (21) 2414191; e-mail hfilsn@netvigator.com; f. 1941; cap. 12,178.5m., res 9,935.7m., dep. 258,097.1m. (Dec. 1998); 100% state-owned; scheduled for transfer to private sector; Pres. ZAKIR MAHMOOD; 1,859 brs in Pakistan.

Khushhali Bank: 94 West, 4th Floor, Jinnah Ave, Blue Area, POB 3111, Islamabad; fax (51) 9206080; Chair. and Man. Dir GHALIB NISHTAR.

Metropolitan Bank Ltd: Spencer's Bldg, I. I. Chundrigar Rd, POB 1289, Karachi; tel. (21) 2636740; fax (21) 2630404; e-mail metro@paknet3.ptc.pk; f. 1992; cap. 500.0m., res 727.0m., dep. 15,839.4m. (Dec. 1999); Chair. and Chief Exec. KASSIM PAREKH; Sr Exec. Vice-Pres. and Gen. Man. A. SUBHAN SIDDIQUI; 19 brs.

Muslim Commercial Bank Ltd: Adamjee House, I. I. Chundrigar Rd, POB 4976, Karachi 74000; tel. (21) 2414091; fax (21) 2438441; e-mail mcbintl@cyber.net.pk; internet www.mcb.com.pk; f. 1947; cap. 2,423m., res 2,147m., dep. 154,439m. (June 2001); Chair. Mian MUHAMMAD MANSHA; Pres. and CEO MUHAMMAD AFTAB MANZOOR; 1,210 brs in Pakistan, 6 brs abroad.

National Bank of Pakistan (NBP): NBP Building, I. I. Chundrigar Rd, POB 4937, Karachi 2; tel. (21) 9212208; fax (21) 9212774; e-mail info@nbp.com.pk; internet www.nbp.com.pk; f. 1949; cap. 1,463.9m., res 6,376.4m., dep. 208,283.0m. (Dec. 1995); 100% state-owned; Pres. ALI RAZA; Sr Vice-Pres. MUHAMMAD YOUSUF; 1,491 brs in Pakistan and 23 brs abroad.

PICIC Commercial Bank Ltd: I. I. Chundrigar Rd, POB 572, Karachi 74200; tel. (21) 2637161; fax (21) 2636909; e-mail gcbl-fi@cyber.net.pk; f. 1994 as Schön Bank Ltd; name changed to Gulf Commercial Bank Ltd in 1998; 60% shares and full management of bank acquired by PICIC in February 2001, name changed to above in June 2001; cap. and res 690.9m., dep. 7,552.5m. (June 2001); Chair. MOHAMMAD ALI KHOJA; Pres. and CEO MOHAMMAD BILAL SHEIKH; 20 brs.

Platinum Commercial Bank Ltd: 76B, E-1, Main Blvd (next to Hafeez Centre), Gulberg III, Lahore 54000; tel. (42) 5764288; fax (42) 5755358; e-mail pcblglh@brain.net.pk; f. 1995; cap. 500m., res 154.8m., dep. 4,821.6m. (Dec. 1999); Chair. MOHAMMED ABID; Pres. and Chief Exec. S. M. WASEEM; 16 brs.

Prime Commercial Bank Ltd: 77–Y, Phase III, Defence Housing Authority, Lahore 54792; tel. (42) 5728282; fax (42) 5728181; e-mail primebank@primebank.com.pk; internet www.primebankpk.com; f. 1991; cap. 1,008m., res 283m., dep.12,918.6m. (Sept. 2002); Pres. SAEED I. BAARMA; Chair. SAMI M. BAARMA; 33 brs.

Saudi Pak Commercial Bank Ltd: Hassan Ali St, off I. I. Chundrigar Rd, Karachi; tel. (21) 111–001–987; f. 1994 as Prudential Commercial Bank, acquired by Saudi Pak Industrial and Agricultural Investment Co (Pvt) Ltd and name changed to above in 2001; cap. 1,500m., res 74.3m., dep. 7,000m. (Dec. 2001); Chair./CEO MUHAMMAD RASHID ZAHIR; Vice-Chair. JAWED ANWAR; 24 brs.

Soneri Bank Ltd: 87 Shahrah-e-Quaid-e-Azam, POB 49, Lahore; tel. (42) 6368142; fax (42) 6368138; e-mail mainlhr@soneri.com; f. 1991; cap. 782.7m., res 760.3m., dep. 16,053.9m. (Dec. 2001); Chair. BADRUDDIN J. FEERASTA; Pres. and CEO SAFAR ALI K. LAKHANI; 24 brs.

Union Bank Ltd: New Jubilee Insurance House, I. I. Chandrigar Rd, Karachi 74200; tel. (21) 2416428; fax (21) 2400842; e-mail ubrokhi@digicom.net.pk; internet www.unionbankpk.com; f. 1991; cap. 655.0m., res 248.0m., dep. 22,900.5m. (Dec. 2000); Chair. SHAUKAT TARIN; Pres. and CEO MUNEER KAMAL; 27 brs.

United Bank Ltd: State Life Bldg, No. 1, I. I. Chandrigar Rd, POB 4306, Karachi 74000; tel. (21) 2417021; fax (21) 2413492; e-mail helpline@ubl.com.pk; internet www.ubl.com.pk; f. 1959; cap. 30,382m., res 3,961m., dep. 142,633m. (Sept. 2002); privatized in 2002; Pres.and CEO AMAR ZAFAR KHAN; 1,349 brs in Pakistan and 19 brs abroad.

Principal Foreign Banks

ABN AMRO Bank NV (Netherlands): Avari Plaza, 242–243 Fatima Jinnah Rd, POB 4096, Karachi 74000; tel. (21) 5683097; fax (21) 5683432; f. 1948; Country Man. NAVEED A. KHAN; 3 brs.

American Express Bank Ltd (USA): Shaheen Commercial Complex, Dr Ziauddin Ahmed Rd, POB 4847, Karachi; tel. (21) 2634153; fax (21) 2631803; f. 1950; Sen. Dir and Country Man. NADEEM KARAMAT; 4 brs.

ANZ Grindlays Bank Ltd (Australia): I. I. Chundrigar Rd, POB 5556, Karachi 74000; tel. (21) 2412671; fax (21) 2414914; Gen. Man. (Pakistan) AZHAR HAMID; 15 brs.

Bank of Ceylon (Sri Lanka): Ground Floor, 252A Sarwar Shaheed Rd, Saddar, Karachi; tel. (21) 5684664; fax (21) 5686817; e-mail cm@ceybank.com.pk; Country Man. M. T. PERERA.

Bank of Tokyo-Mitsubishi Ltd (Japan): Shaheen Complex, 1st Floor, M. R. Kayani Rd, POB 4232, Karachi; tel. (21) 2630171; fax (21) 2631368; e-mail btmkarwr@cyber.net.pk; f. 1953; Gen. Man. K. ENDO; 1 br.

Chase Manhattan Bank, NA (USA): 13th Floor, Commercial Tower, Sidco Ave Centre, 264 R. A. Lines, Karachi; tel. (21) 5683568; fax (21) 5681467; f. 1982; Vice-Pres. RUDOLF VON WATZDORF; 2 brs.

Citibank, NA (USA): No. 1 State Life Bldg, 1.1. Chundrigar Rd, Karachi; tel. (21) 2638222; fax (21) 2638211; internet www.citibank.com/pakistan; f. 1961; Gen. Man. ZUBYR SOOMRO; 3 brs.

Crédit Agricole Indosuez (France): Muhammadi House, I. I. Chundrigar Rd, POB 6942, Karachi 74000; tel. (21) 2413720; fax (21) 2417503; f. 1973; Gen. Man. JEAN PIERRE RAYNAUD; 2 brs.

Deutsche Bank AG (Germany): Uni Tower Bldg, I. I. Chundrigar Rd, POB 4925, Karachi; tel. (21) 2416824; fax (21) 2411130; f. 1962; Gen. Man. (Pakistan) ARIF M. ALI; 2 brs.

Doha Bank Ltd (Qatar): 36/6-2 Lalazar Drive, off M. T. Khan Rd, Karachi; tel. (21) 5611313; fax (21) 5610764; Gen. Man. (Pakistan) MASOOD H. KHAN.

Emirates Bank International PJSC (United Arab Emirates): Emirates Bank Bldg, I. I. Chundrigar Rd, POB 831, Karachi; tel. (21) 2416648; fax (21) 2416599; e-mail timgibbs@emiratesbank.com; internet www.emiratesbank.com.pk; f. 1978; Gen. Man. (Pakistan) TIMOTHY P. GIBBS; 10 brs.

Faysal Islamic Bank Ltd (Bahrain): 11/13 Trade Centre, I. I. Chundrigar Rd, POB 472, Karachi; tel. (21) 2638011; fax (21) 2637975; e-mail fblpak@cyber.net.pk; internet www.faysalbank.com.pk; f. 1995; Chief Operating Officer and Country Gen. Man. FAROOQ BENGALI; 9 brs.

Habib Bank AG Zurich (Switzerland): Hirani Centre, I. I. Chundrigar Rd, POB 1424, Karachi; tel. (21) 2630526; fax (21) 2631418; Chief Exec. (Pakistan) MUHAMMAD HAROON AHMED.

The Hongkong and Shanghai Banking Corpn Ltd (Hong Kong): Shaheen Commercial Complex, M. R. Kayani Rd, POB 121, Karachi; tel. (21) 2632143; fax (21) 2631526; f. 1982; CEO PETER WATERHOUSE; Dep. CEO NICK D. GILMOUR; 2 brs.

Mashreq Bank PSC (United Arab Emirates): Ground and 1st Floor, Bahria Complex, 24 M.T. Khan Rd, POB 930, Karachi 74000; tel. (21) 5611271; fax (21) 5610661; f. 1978; Country Man. AZMAT ASHRAF; 3 brs.

Middle East Bank PJSC (United Arab Emirates): Mac Volk Bldg, I. I. Chundrigar Rd, POB 6712, Karachi; tel. (21) 2412986; f. 1978; Gen. Man. KALIM-UR-RAHMAN; 4 brs.

Rupali Bank Ltd (Bangladesh): Unitowers, I. I. Chundrigar Rd, POB 6440, Karachi 74000; tel. (21) 2410424; fax (21) 2414322; f. 1976; Country Man. (Pakistan) MD SELIM KHAN; 1 br.

Saudi Bahrain Investment Co: Karachi; Man. Dir RASHID ZAHID.

Société Générale (France): 3rd Floor, PNSC Bldg, Maulvi Tamizuddin Khan Rd, POB 6766, Karachi 74000; tel. (21) 111331331; fax (21) 5611672; Gen. Man. PAUL HENRI RUSCH; Dep. Gen. Man. FERNAND CLOP; 2 brs.

Standard Chartered Bank (UK): I. I. Chundrigar Rd, POB 4896, Karachi 74000; tel. (21) 2419075; fax (21) 2418788; Chief Exec. (Pakistan) ZAHID RAHIM; 6 brs.

Trust Bank Ltd (Kenya): Al-Falah Court, I. I. Chundrigar Rd, Karachi; tel. (21) 2633519; fax (21) 2636534; CEO (Pakistan) HUMAYUN ZIA.

Leasing Banks (Modarabas)

The number of leasing banks (modarabas), which conform to the strictures placed upon the banking system by *Shari'a* (the Islamic legal code), rose from four in 1988 to about 45 in 2002. The following are among the most important modarabas in Pakistan.

Asian Leasing Corporation Ltd: 85-B Jail Rd, Gulberg, POB 3176, Lahore; tel. (42) 484417; fax (42) 484418.

Atlas Lease Ltd: Ground Floor, Federation House, Shahrah-e-Firdousi, Main Clifton, Karachi 75600; tel. (21) 5866817; fax (21) 5870543; e-mail all@atlasgrouppk.com; Chair. YUSUF H. SHIRAZI.

B.R.R. Capital Modaraba: Dean Arcade, Block 8, Kehkeshan, Clifton, Karachi 75600; tel. (21) 572013; fax (21) 5870324.

Dadabhoy Leasing Co Ltd: 5th Floor, Maqbool Commercial Complex, JCHS Block, Main Sharhah-e-Faisal, Karachi; tel. (21) 4548171; fax (21) 4547301; Man. (Finance) MOHAMMAD AYUB.

English Leasing Ltd: M. K. Arcade, Ground Floor, 32 Davis Rd, Lahore; tel. (42) 6303855; fax (41) 6304251; e-mail englease@hotmail.com; Chair. JAVAID MAHMOOD; CEO MANZOOR ELAHI.

First Grindlays Modaraba: Grindlays Services of Pakistan (Pvt) Ltd, ANZ Grindlays Bank Bldg, I. I. Chundrigar Rd, POB 5556, Karachi 74000; tel. (21) 223917; fax (21) 2417197.

First Habib Bank Modaraba: 18 Habib Bank Plaza, I. I. Chundrigar Rd, Karachi 75650; tel. (21) 2412294; fax (21) 2411860; f. 1991; wholly-owned subsidiary of Habib Bank Ltd; auth. cap. 500.0m., cap. p.u. 397.1m. (1996); CEO MUHAMMAD NAWAZ CHEEMA; Co Sec. NAJEEB MAHMUD.

National Development Leasing Corpn Ltd: NIC Bldg, 10th Floor, Abbasi Shaheed Rd, off Shahrah-e-Faisal, POB 67, Karachi 74400; tel. (21) 5660671; fax (21) 5680454; e-mail ndlckar@cyberaccess.com.pk; 3 brs.

Pakistan Industrial and Commercial Leasing Ltd: 504 Park Ave, 24-A, Block 6, PECHS, Shahrah-e-Faisal, Karachi 75210; tel. (21) 4551045; fax (21) 4520655; e-mail picl@super.net.pk; f. 1987; Chief Exec. MINHAJ-UL-HAQ SIDDIQI.

Co-operative Banks

In 1976 all existing co-operative banks were dissolved and given the option of becoming a branch of the appropriate Provincial Co-operative Bank, or of reverting to the status of a credit society.

Federal Bank for Co-operatives: State Bank Bldg, G-5, POB 1218, Islamabad; tel. (51) 9205667; fax (51) 9205681; f. 1976; owned jtly by the fed. Govt, the prov. govts and the State Bank of Pakistan; provides credit facilities to each of six prov. co-operative banks and regulates their operations; they in turn provide credit facilities through co-operative socs; supervises policy of prov. co-operative banks and of multi-unit co-operative socs; assists fed. and prov. govts in formulating schemes for development and revitalization of co-operative movement; carries out research on rural credit, etc. share cap. p.u. 200m., res 398m. (1998); Man. Dir M. AFZAL HUSSAIN; 4 regional offices.

Investment Banks

Al-Faysal Investment Bank Ltd: 15 West Jinnah Ave, Blue Area, Islamabad; tel. (51) 272579; fax (51) 272569; e-mail afibl@afibl.isb.sdnpk.org; f. 1991; cap. 978.7m., res 226.7m. (Dec. 1999); Pres. MOHAMMAD KHAN HOTI.

Al-Towfeek Investment Bank Ltd: 63 Shahrah-e-Quaid-e-Azam, Lahore; tel. (42) 7122395; fax (42) 2628610; e-mail atibl@lhr.comsats.pk.net; f. 1990; Chair. KHALID MAHMOOD BHAIMIA; Chief Exec. KHALID MAJID.

Asset Investment Bank Ltd: Room 1-B, 1st Floor, Ali Plaza, Khayaban-e-Quaid-e-Azam, Blue Area, Islamabad; tel. (51) 2270625; fax (51) 2272506; Chief Exec. SYED NAVEED ZAIDI.

Atlas Investment Bank Ltd: Ground Floor, Federation House, Shaheen-e-Firdoosi, Main Clifton, Karachi; tel. (21) 5832292; fax

(21) 5863984; 15% owned by The Bank of Tokyo-Mitsubishi Ltd; Chief Exec. NAEEM KHAN.

Citicorp Investment Bank (Pak) Ltd: AWT Plaza, I. I. Chundrigar Rd, Karachi; tel. (21) 111–777–777; fax (21) 2638288; f. 1992; 60% owned by Citibank Overseas Investment Corpn; Chair. SHEHZAD NAQVI; CEO MUHAMMAD AZIMUDDIN.

Franklin Investment Bank Ltd: Bandukwala Bldg, I. I. Chundrigar Rd, Karachi; tel. (21) 2429721; fax (21) 2428642; Chief Executive MUHAMMAD ANWAR SULTAN.

Development Finance Organizations

First Women Bank Ltd: A-115, 7th Floor, Mehdi Towers, Sindhi Muslim Co-operative Housing Society, Sharah-e-Faisal, POB 15549, Karachi; tel. (21) 4556093; fax (21) 4556983; e-mail fwblps@cyber.net.pk; f. 1989; cap. 200m., dep. 2,421m. (Dec. 1995); Pres. ZAREEN AZIZ; 38 brs.

House Building Finance Corpn: Finance and Trade Centre, Shahrah-e-Faisal, Karachi 74400; tel. (21) 9202314; fax (21) 9202360; provides loans for the construction and purchase of housing units; Man. Dir SOHAIL USMAN ALI.

Industrial Development Bank of Pakistan: State Life Bldg No. 2, Wallace Rd, off I. I. Chundrigar Rd, POB 5082, Karachi 74000; tel. (21) 2419160; fax (21) 2411990; e-mail idbp@idbp.com.pk; internet www.idbp.com.pk; f. 1961; provides credit facilities for small and medium-sized industrial enterprises in the private sector; cap. 157.0m., res 342.3m., dep. 20,119.9m. (June 1997); 100% state-owned; Chair. and Man. Dir JAVED SADIQ; 19 brs.

Investment Corpn of Pakistan: NBP Bldg, 5th Floor, I. I. Chundrigar Rd, POB 5410, Karachi 74400; tel. (21) 9212360; fax (21) 9212388; e-mail icp@paknet3.ptc.pk; f. 1966 by the Govt to encourage and broaden the base of investments and to develop the capital market; total assets 4,633.1m., cap. 200.0m., res 413.5m. (June 1997); Man. Dir ISTIQBAL MEHDI; Dep. Man. Dir BEHRAHM HASAN; 10 brs.

Khushhali Bank: POB 3111, Islamabad; f. 2000 by the Govt under the Asian Development Bank's micro-finance sector development programme; provides micro-loans to the poor and finances reforms in the micro-finance sector; cap. 1,705m. (Aug. 2000); Pres. GHALIB NISHTAR.

National Investment (Unit Trust) Ltd: NBP Bldg, 6th Floor, I. I. Chundrigar Rd, POB 5671, Karachi; tel. (21) 2419061; fax (21) 2430623; e-mail info@nit.com.pk; internet www.nit.com.pk; f. 1962; an open-ended Mutual Fund, mobilizes domestic savings to meet the requirements of growing economic development and enables investors to share in the industrial and economic prosperity of the country; 67,000 Unit holders (1999/2000); Man. Dir ISTIQBAL MEHDI.

Pakistan Industrial Credit and Investment Corpn Ltd (PICIC): State Life Bldg No. 1, I. I. Chundrigar Rd, POB 5080, Karachi 74000; tel. (21) 2414220; fax (21) 2417851; e-mail contact@picic.com; internet www.picic.com; f. 1957 as an industrial development bank to provide financial assistance in both local and foreign currencies, for the establishment of new industries in the private sector and balancing modernization, replacement and expansion of existing industries; merchant banking and foreign exchange activities; total assets 15,398m., cap. 736.8m., res 984.7m. (June 2001); held 91.4% and 8.7% by local and foreign investors respectively; Man. Dir MOHAMMAD ALI KHOJA; Chair. KURSHID K. MARKER; 19 brs.

Pakistan Investment Board (PIB): Rooms 108 and 109, 1st Floor, Block A, Pakistan Secretariat, Govt of Pakistan, Islamabad; tel. (51) 211870; fax (51) 215554; Vice-Chair. SAFDAR ABBAS ZAIDI.

Pakistan Kuwait Investment Co (Pvt) Ltd: Tower 'C', 4th Floor, Finance and Trade Centre, Shahrah-e-Faisal, POB 901, Karachi 74200; tel. (21) 5660750; fax (21) 5683669; jt venture between the Govt and Kuwait to promote investment in industrial and agro-based enterprises; Man. Dir ZAIGHAM H. RIZVI.

Pak-Libya Holding Co (Pvt) Ltd: Finance and Trade Centre, 5th Floor, Tower 'C', Shahrah-e-Faisal, POB 10425, Karachi 74400; tel. (21) 111–111–115; fax (21) 5682389; e-mail paklibya@paklibya.com.pk; jt venture between the Govts of Pakistan and Libya to promote industrial investment in Pakistan; Man. Dir KHALID SHARWANI.

Regional Development Finance Corpn: Ghausia Plaza, 20 Blue Area, POB 1893, Islamabad; tel. (51) 2825131; fax (51) 2201179; promotes industrial investment in the less developed areas of Pakistan; CEO MIRZA GHAGANFAR BAIG; 13 brs.

Saudi Pak Industrial and Agricultural Investment Co (Pvt) Ltd: Saudi Pak Tower, 61-A Jinnah Ave, Islamabad; tel. (51) 2273514; fax (51) 2273508; e-mail saudipak@saudipak.com; internet www.saudipak.com; f. 1981; jtly by Saudi Arabia and Pakistan to finance industrial and agro-based projects and undertake investment-related activities in Pakistan; cap. 2,000m., res. 732m., dep.

5,900m. (March 2001); CEO Muhammad Rashid Zahir; Exec. Vice-Pres. Abdul Jaleel Shaikh; 1 br.

Small Business Finance Corpn: NBP Bldg, Ground Floor, Civic Centre, Islamabad 44000; tel. (51) 9214296; fax (51) 2826007; provides loans for small businesses; Man. Dir Kaiser Haneef Naseem.

Youth Investment and Promotion Society: PIA Bldg, 3rd Floor, Blue Area, Islamabad; tel. (51) 815581; Man. Dir Ashraf M. Khan.

Zarai Taraqiati Bank Ltd (ZTBL): 1 Faisal Ave, POB 1400, Islamabad; tel. (51) 202089; fax (51) 812907; e-mail adbp@isb .paknet.com.pk; internet www.paknet.com.pk/users/adbp; f. 1961; provides credit facilities to agriculturists (particularly small-scale farmers) and cottage industrialists in the rural areas and for allied projects; auth. cap. 4,000m., res 1,739m. (June 1999); 100% state-owned; Chair. Istiqbal Mehdi; 49 regional offices and 349 brs.

Banking Associations

Investment Banks Association of Pakistan: 7th Floor, Shaheen Commercial Complex, Dr Ziauddin Ahmed Rd, POB 1345, Karachi; tel. (21) 2631396; fax (21) 2630678.

Modaraba Association of Pakistan: Chair. Waqar Ajmal Chaudhry.

Pakistan Banks' Association: National Bank of Pakistan, Head Office Bldg, 2nd Floor, I. I. Chundrigar Rd, POB 4937, Karachi 2; tel. and fax (21) 2416686; e-mail pba@cyber.net.pk; Chair. M. Younas Khan; Sec. A. Ghaffar K. Hafiz.

Banking Organizations

Pakistan Banking Council: Habib Bank Plaza, I. I. Chundrigar Rd, Karachi; tel. (21) 227121; fax (21) 222232; f. 1973; acts as a co-ordinating body between the nationalized banks and the Ministry of Finance, Economic Affairs and Statistics; Chair. Muhammad Zaki; Sec. Mir Wasif Ali.

Pakistan Development Banking Institute: 4th Floor, Sidco Ave Centre, Stratchen Rd, Karachi; tel. (21) 5688049; fax (21) 5688460.

STOCK EXCHANGES

Securities and Exchange Commission of Pakistan: NIC Bldg, 63 Jinnah Ave, Blue Area, Islamabad; tel. (51) 9205713; fax (51) 9204915; e-mail hilal-bult@seep.gov.pk; oversees and co-ordinates operations of exchanges and registration of companies; registration offices in Faisalabad (356-A, 1st Floor, Al-Jamil Plaza, People's Colony, Small D Ground, Faisalabad; tel. (41) 713841), Karachi (No. 2, 4th Floor, State Life Building, North Wing, Karachi; tel. (21) 2415855), Lahore (3rd and 4th Floors, Associated House, 7 Egerton Rd, Lahore; tel. (42) 9202044), Multan (61 Abdali Rd, Multan; tel. (61) 542609), Peshawar (Hussain Commercial Bldg, 3 Arbab Rd, Peshawar), Quetta (382/3, IDBP House, Shahrah-e-Hall, Quetta; tel. (81) 844138) and Sukkur (B-30, Sindhi Muslim Housing Society, Airport Rd, Sukkur; tel. (71) 30517); Chair. Abdul Rahman Qureshi.

Islamabad Stock Exchange: 4th Floor, Stock Exchange Bldg, 101e Faz-ul-haq Rd, Blue Area, Islamabad; tel. (51) 2829001; fax (51) 2272393; e-mail ise@ise.com.pk; internet www.ise.com.pk; f. 1991; 103 mems; Chair. Omar Iqbal Pasha; Sec. Yousuf H. Makhdoomi.

Karachi Stock Exchange (Guarantee) Ltd: Stock Exchange Bldg, Stock Exchange Rd, Karachi 74000; tel. (21) 2425502; fax (21) 2410825; e-mail gm@kse.com.pk; internet www.kse.com.pk; f. 1947; 200 mems, 762 listed cos; Chair. Saleem Chandna; Man. Dir Fudda (acting).

Lahore Stock Exchange (Guarantee) Ltd: Lahore Stock Exchange Bldg, 19 Khayaban-e-Aiwan-e-Iqbal, Lahore 54000; tel. (42) 6300070; fax (42) 6368484; e-mail lstock@paknet4.ptc.pk; internet www.lahorestock.com; f. 1970; 576 listed cos, 151 mems; Pres. Group Capt. (retd) Naseem A. Khan; Man. Dir Sameer Ahmed.

INSURANCE

In 1995 legislation came into effect allowing foreign insurance companies to operate in Pakistan.

Insurance Division: Securities and Exchange Commission, 4th Floor, NIC Bldg, Jinnah Ave, Islamabad; tel. (51), 9208887; fax (51) 9208955; internet www.secp.gov.pk; under the Ministry of Finance and Economic Affairs; Commissioner of Insurance Sharif Ejaz Ghauri; Exec. Dir Shafaat Ahmed.

Life Insurance

American Life Insurance Co (Pakistan) Ltd: Laksan Sq Bldg, Karachi 75400.

Metropolitan Life Assurance Co of Pakistan Ltd: 310-313 Qamar House, M. A. Jinnah Rd, Karachi 74000; tel. (21) 2311662;

fax (21) 2311667; e-mail myunus@cyber.net.pk; Chief Exec. Maheen Yunus.

Postal Life Insurance Organization: Tibet Centre, M. A. Jinnah Rd, Karachi; tel. (21) 723804; f. 1884; life and group insurance; Gen. Man and CEO Dr Salahuddin Ahmad.

State Life Insurance Corpn of Pakistan: State Life Bldg No. 9, Dr Ziauddin Ahmed Rd, POB 5725, Karachi 75530; tel. (21) 5683233; fax (21) 5683266; e-mail dhasp@super.net.pk; internet www .statelife.com.pk; f. 1972; life and group insurance and pension schemes; Chair. Samee ul-Hasan.

General Insurance

ACE Insurance Ltd: 6th Floor, NIC Bldg, Abbasi Shaheed Rd, off Shahrah-e-Faisal, Karachi; tel. (21) 5681320; fax (21) 5683935; Country Gen. Man. Syed Umer Ali Shah.

Adamjee Insurance Co Ltd: Adamjee House, 6th Floor, I. I. Chundrigar Rd, POB 4850, Karachi 74000; tel. (21) 2414607; fax (21) 2412627; e-mail info@adamjeeinsurance.com; internet www .adamjeeinsurance.com; f. 1960; Man. Dir and CEO Mohammed Choudhury.

Agro General Insurance Co Ltd: 612, Qamar House, M. A. Jinnah Rd, POB 5920, Karachi 74000; tel. (21) 2313182; fax (21) 2310624; f. 1987; Man. Dir M. I. Ansari.

Alpha Insurance Co Ltd: State Life Bldg No. 1B–1C, 2nd Floor, off I.I. Chungrigar Rd, POB 4359, Karachi 74000; tel. (21) 2412609; fax (21) 2419968; f. 1952; Chair. Iqbal M. Qureshi; Man. Dir V. C. Gonsalves; 9 brs.

Amicus Insurance Co Ltd: F-50, Block 7, Feroze Nana Rd, Bath Island, POB 3971, Karachi; tel. (21) 5831082; fax (21) 5870220; f. 1991; Chair. M. Irshad Uddin.

Asia Insurance Co Ltd: Asia Insurance House, 7 Egerton Rd, POB 2289, Lahore; tel. (42) 6363692; fax (42) 6368966; f. 1980; Man. Dir Zafar Iqbal Shaikh.

Askari General Insurance Co Ltd: 4th Floor, AWT Plaza, The Mall, POB 843, Rawalpindi; tel. (51) 9272425; fax (51) 9272424; f. 1995; Pres. and Chief Exec. M. Jamaluddin.

Business and Industrial Insurance Co Ltd: 65 East Pak Pavilions, 1st Floor, Fazal-e-Haq Rd, Blue Area, Islamabad; tel. (51) 2278957; fax (51) 2271914; f. 1995; Chair. and Chief Exec. Mian Mumtaz Abdullah.

Capital Insurance Co Ltd: opp. ABL Paris Rd, Sialkot; tel. (432) 587643; fax (432) 583080; e-mail cicl@skt.comsats.net.pk; f. 1998; Chief Exec. Khawaja Zakauddin; Sec. M. I. Butt.

Central Insurance Co Ltd: Dawood Centre, 5th Floor, M. T. Khan Rd, POB 3988, Karachi 75530; tel. (21) 5683194; fax (21) 5680218; f. 1960; Man. Dir M. Hussain Dawood.

Century Insurance Co Ltd: Lakson Square Bldg No. 1, 2nd Floor, Block 'D', Sarwar Sheheed Rd, Karachi 74200; tel. (21) 5653519; fax (21) 5671665; e-mail cic@cyber.net.pk; f. 1988; Chair. and Chief Exec. Iqbalali Lakhani; Dir Mir Nadir Ali.

CGU Inter Insurance PLC: 74/1-A, Lalazar, M. T. Khan Rd, POB 4895, Karachi 74000; tel. (21) 5611802; fax (21) 5611456; f. 1861; general and life insurance; Gen. Man. Abdur Rahim; 3 brs.

Commerce Insurance Co Ltd: 11 Shahrah-e-Quaid-e-Azam, POB 1132, Lahore 54000; tel. (42) 7325330; fax (42) 7230828; f. 1992; Chief Exec. Syed Moin-ud-Din.

Co-operative Insurance Society of Pakistan Ltd: Co-operative Insurance Bldg, Shahrah-e-Quaid-e-Azam, POB 147, Lahore; tel. (42) 7352306; fax (42) 7352794; f. 1949; Chief Exec. and Gen. Man. Farooq Haider Jung.

Credit Insurance Co Ltd: Asmat Chambers, 68 Mazang Rd, Lahore; tel. (42) 6316774; fax (42) 6368868; f. 1995; Chief Exec. Muhammad Ikhlaq Butt.

Crescent Star Insurance Co Ltd: Nadir House, I. I. Chundrigar Rd, POB 4616, Karachi 74000; tel. (21) 2421207; fax (21) 2415474; f. 1957; Man. Dir Munir I. Millwala.

Dadabhoy Insurance Co Ltd: 5th Floor Maqbool Commercial Complex, JCHS Block, Main Shahrah-e-Faisal, Karachi; tel. (21) 4545704; fax (21) 4548625; f. 1983; Chief Exec. Usman Dadabhoy.

Delta Insurance Co Ltd: 101 Baghpatee Bldg, Altaf Hussain Rd, New Challi, Karachi; tel. (21) 2632297; fax (21) 2422942; f. 1991; Man. Dir Syed Asif Ali.

East West Insurance Co Ltd: 410 Qamar House, M. A. Jinnah Rd, POB 6693, Karachi 74000; tel. (21) 2313304; fax (21) 2311904; f. 1983; Chief Exec. Naveed Yunus.

EFU General Insurance Ltd: EFU House, M. A. Jinnah Rd, Karachi 74000; tel. (21) 2313471; fax (21) 2310450; e-mail info@

efuinsurance.com; internet www.efuinsurance.com; f. 1932; Man. Dir and Chief Exec. SAIFUDDIN N. ZOOMKAWALA.

Excel Insurance Co Ltd: S-07, 5th Floor, KDLB Bldg, 58 West Wharf Rd, Karachi 74000; tel. (21) 7738611; fax (21) 2310314; f. 1995; Chief Exec. BASHIR H. ALIMOHAMMAD.

Gulf Insurance Co Ltd: Gulf House, 1-A Link McLeod Rd, Patiala Grounds, Lahore; tel. (42) 7312028; fax (42) 7234987; f. 1988; Chief Exec. S. ARIF SALAM.

Habib Insurance Co Ltd: Insurance House, 6 Habib Sq., M. A. Jinnah Rd, POB 5217, Karachi 74000; tel. (21) 2424038; fax (21) 2421600; f. 1942; Chair. HAMID D. HABIB; Man. Dir and Chief Exec. ALI RAZA D. HABIB.

Indus International Co Ltd: Indus House, 18-E-III, Model Town, POB 2002, Lahore 54700; tel. (42) 5865579; fax (42) 5866293; e-mail nation@paknet4.ptc.pk; f. 1993; Pres. and Man. Dir KHALID RASHID.

International General Insurance Co of Pakistan Ltd: Finlay House, 1st Floor, I. I. Chundrigar Rd, POB 4576, Karachi 74000; tel. (21) 2424976; fax (21) 2416710; e-mail igikhi@cubexs.net.pk; internet www.igi.com.pk; f. 1953; Gen. Man. BASIT HASSAN SYED.

Ittefaq General Insurance Co Ltd: H-16 Murree Rd, Rawalpindi; tel. (51) 71333; f. 1982; Man. Dir SYED ALI ASGHAR SHAH.

Jupiter Insurance Co Ltd: 4th Floor, Finlay House, I. I. Chundrigar Rd, POB 4655, Karachi 74000; tel. (21) 2427659; fax (21) 2427660; e-mail jicl20@hotmail.com; f. 1994; Chief Exec. MAHMUD HASAN.

Muslim Insurance Co Ltd: 3 Bank Sq., Shahrah-e-Quaid-e-Azam, POB 1219, Lahore; tel. (42) 7310658; fax (42) 7234742; f. 1935; Chief Exec. S. C. SUBJALLY.

National General Insurance Co Ltd: 401-B, Satellite Town, nr Commercial Market, Rawalpindi; tel. (51) 411792; fax (51) 427361; f. 1969; Gen. Man. F. A. JAFFERY.

National Insurance Corpn: NIC Bldg, Abbasi Shaheed Rd, Karachi 74400; tel. (21) 9202741; fax (21) 9202779; e-mail nicl@cyber.net .pk; internet www.niclpk.com; govt-owned; Chair. JAHAN ZEB KHAN.

New Hampshire Insurance Co: State Life Bldg No. 2, 8th Floor, Wallace Rd, POB 4693, Karachi 74000; tel. (21) 2434470; fax (21) 2419413; Country Man. for Pakistan MUJIB KHAN.

New Jubilee Insurance Co Ltd: 2nd Floor, Jubilee Insurance House, I. I. Chundrigar Rd, POB 4795, Karachi 74000; tel. (21) 2416022; fax (21) 2416728; e-mail nji@cyber.net.pk; internet www .nji.com.pk; f. 1953; Pres., Chief Exec. and Man. Dir MASOOD NOORANI.

North Star Insurance Co Ltd: 37–38 Basement, Sadiq Plaza, 69 The Mall, Lahore 54000; tel. (42) 6314308; fax (42) 6375366; e-mail northstarins@hotmail.com; f. 1995; Chief Exec./Man. Dir M. RAFIQ CHAUDHRY.

Orient Insurance Co Ltd: 2nd Floor, Dean Arcade, Block No. 8, Kahkeshan, Clifton, Karachi; tel. (21) 5865327; fax (21) 5865724; f. 1987; Man. Dir FAZAL REHMAN.

Pak Equity Insurance Co Ltd: M. K. Arcade, 32 Davis Rd, Lahore; tel. (42) 6361536; fax (42) 6365959; f. 1984; Chief Exec. CH. ATHAR ZAHOOR.

Pakistan General Insurance Co Ltd: 43 Al-Noor Bldg, Bank Square, POB 1028, Lahore; tel. (42) 7325281; fax (42) 7323051; f. 1948; Chair. CH. AZFAR MANZOOR; Pres. and Chief Exec. CH. ZAHOOR AHMAD.

Pakistan Guarantee Insurance Co Ltd: Al-Falah Court, 3rd and 5th Floors, I. I. Chundrigar Rd, POB 5436, Karachi 74000; tel. (21) 2636111; fax (21) 2638740; f. 1965; Chief Exec. SHAKIL RAZA SYED.

Premier Insurance Co of Pakistan Ltd: 2-A State Life Bldg, 5th Floor, Wallace Rd, off I. I. Chundrigar Rd, POB 4140, Karachi 74000; tel. (21) 2416331; fax (21) 2416572; f. 1952; Chair. ZAHID BASHIR; Adviser A. U. SIDDIQUI.

Prime Insurance Co Ltd: 505–507, Japan Plaza, M. A. Jinnah Rd, POB 1390, Karachi; tel. (21) 7770801; fax (21) 7725427; f. 1989; Chief Exec. ABDUL MAJEED.

Raja Insurance Co Ltd: Panorama Centre, 5th Floor, 256 Fatimah Jinnah Rd, POB 10422, Karachi 4; tel. (21) 5670619; fax (21) 5681501; f. 1981; Chair. RAJA ABDUL RAHMAN; Man. Dir SHEIKH HUMAYUN SAYEED.

Reliance Insurance Co Ltd: Reliance Insurance House, 181-A, Sindhi Muslim Co-operative Housing Society, POB 13356, Karachi 74400; tel. (21) 4539413; fax (21) 4539412; e-mail reli-ins@cyber.net .pk; Chief Exec. and Man. Dir ABDUL RAZAK AHMED.

Royal Exchange Assurance: P&O Plaza, I. I. Chundrigar Rd, POB 315, Karachi 74000; tel. (21) 2635141; fax (21) 2631369; Man. (Pakistan) Dr MUMTAZ A. HASHMI.

Seafield Insurance Co Ltd: 86-Q, Block-2, Allama Iqbal Rd, PECHS, Karachi; tel. (21) 4556895; fax (21) 4527593; f. 1989; Man. Dir ADNAN HAFEEZ.

Security General Insurance Co Ltd: Nishat House, 53A Lawrence Rd, Lahore; tel. (42) 6279192; fax (42) 6303466; f. 1996; Man. Dir SYED JAWAD GILLANI.

Shaheen Insurance Co Ltd: D-27, Block 5, Kahkashan, Clifton, POB 707, Karachi; tel. (21) 5879705; fax (21) 5879072; f. 1996; CEO NASREEN RASHID.

Silver Star Insurance Co Ltd: Silver Star House, 2nd Floor, 5 Bank Square, POB 2533, Lahore; tel. (42) 7324488; fax (42) 7229966; e-mail silvrstr@nexlinx.net.pk; f. 1984; Man. Dir ZAHIR MUHAMMAD SADIQ.

Union Insurance Co of Pakistan Ltd: Adamjee House, 9th Floor, I. I. Chundrigar Rd, Karachi; tel. (21) 2427524; fax (21) 2420174; Chair. Mian MOHAMMED HANIF; Pres. NISHAT RAFFIQ.

United Insurance Co of Pakistan Ltd: Nizam Chambers, 5th Floor, Shahrah-e-Fatima Jinnah, POB 532, Lahore; tel. (42) 6361471; fax (42) 6375036; f. 1959; Man. Dir and CEO M. A. SHAHID.

Universal Insurance Co Ltd: Universal Insurance House, 63 Shahrah-e-Quaid-e-Azam, POB 539, Lahore; tel. (42) 7322972; fax (42) 7230326; e-mail mobin@am.lcci.org.pk; f. 1958; Chief Exec. OMAR AYUB KHAN; Man. Dir SARDAR KHAN.

Insurance Associations

Insurance Association of Pakistan: Jamshed Katrak Chambers, G. Allana Rd, POB 4932, Karachi 74000; tel. (21) 2311784; fax (21) 2310798; e-mail iapho@cyber.net.pk; f. 1948; mems comprise 46 cos (Pakistani and foreign) transacting general insurance business; issues tariffs and establishes rules for insurance in the country; regional office in Lahore; Chair. M. I. ANSARI; Sec. K. A. SIDDIQI.

Pakistan Insurance Institute: Shafi Court, 2nd Floor, Mereweather Rd, Karachi 4; f. 1951 to encourage insurance education; Chair. MOHAMMAD CHOUDHRY.

Trade and Industry
GOVERNMENT AGENCIES

Agricultural Marketing and Storage Ltd: Islamabad; tel. (51) 827407; fax (51) 824607.

Board of Investment (BOI): Govt of Pakistan, Attaturk Ave, Sector G-5/1, Islamabad; tel. (51) 9206161; fax (51) 9215554; e-mail boipr@isb.comsats.net.pk; internet www.pakboi.gov.pk; Chair. WASIM HAQUEE; Sec. SHUJA SHAH.

Commission for the Islamization of the Economy: Government of Pakistan, Finance Division, 2nd Floor, SNC Centre, 12-D, Fazl-ul-Haq Rd, Blue Area, Islamabad 44000; tel. (51) 9223679; fax (51) 9223684; f. 1991; Chair. RAJA MUHAMMAD ZAFARUL HAQ; Mem./Sec. ZULFIQAR KHAN.

Corporate and Industrial Restructuring Corpn: 13-C-II, M. M. Alam Rd, Gulberg III, Lahore; tel. (42) 5871532; fax (42) 5761650; e-mail info@cir-gov.cort; internet www.circ.gov.com.

Environmental Protection Agency: Govt of Sindh, EPA Complex, ST-2/1, Sector 23, Korangi Industrial Area, Karachi; tel. (21) 5065950; fax (21) 5065940.

Export Processing Zones Authority (EPZA): Landhi Industrial Area Extension, Mehran Highway, POB 17011, Karachi 75150; tel. (21) 5082001; fax (21) 5082005; e-mail epza@super.net.pk; internet www.epza.com.pk.

Export Promotion Bureau: 5th Floor, Block A, Finance and Trade Centre, Shahrah-e-Faisal, POB 1293, Karachi; tel. (21) 9202718; fax (21) 9202713; e-mail epb@epb.kar.erum.com.pk; internet www.epb .gov.pk; Chair. TARIQ IKRAM; Vice-Chair. IQBAL PURI.

Family Planning Association of Pakistan: 24, St 30, F-6/1, Islamabad.

Geological Survey of Pakistan: Sariab Rd, POB 15, Quetta; tel. (81) 9211032; fax (81) 9211018; e-mail geophy@gsp.qta.khi.sdnpk .undp.org; Dir-Gen. S. HASAN GAUHAR; Asst Dir MOHSIN ANWAR KAZIM.

Gwadar Port Authority: 2nd Floor, PNSC Bldg, M. T. Khan Rd, Karachi; tel. (21) 9204061; fax (21) 9204196; e-mail gwadarport@ hotmail.com.

Information Technology Commission: IT and Telecom Division, Govt of Pakistan, 14, St 61, F-7/4, Islamabad; tel. (51) 9205889; fax (51) 9205992; e-mail secyitc@isb.comsats.net.pk; internet www .itcommission.gov.pk.

Investment Promotion Bureau: Kandawala Bldg, M. A. Jinnah Rd, Karachi.

Karachi Export Processing Zone (KEPZ): Landhi Industrial Area Extension, Mehran Highway, POB 17011, Karachi 75150; tel. (21) 5082011; fax (21) 5082005; e-mail epza@super.net.pk.

Karachi Metropolitan Corpn: M. A. Jinnah Rd, Karachi.

National Accountability Bureau: Government of Pakistan, Islamabad; e-mail info@nab.gov.pk; internet www.nab.gov.pk; Chair. Lt-Gen. KHALIF MAQBOOL.

National Database and Registration Authority (NADRA): Ministry of Interior, Awami Markaz, 5-A, Constitution Ave, F-5/1, Islamabad; tel. (51) 9204624; internet www.nadrapk.com.

National Economic Board: f. 1979 by the Govt as an advisory body to review and evaluate the state of the economy and to make proposals, especially to further the adoption of the socio-economic principles of Islam.

National Economic Council: supreme economic body; the governors and chief ministers of the four provinces and fed. ministers in charge of economic ministries are its mems; sr fed. and provincial officials in the economic field are also associated.

National Electric Power Regulatory Authority (NEPRA): OPF Bldg, Shahrah-e-Jamhuriat, G-5/2, Islamabad; tel. (51) 9207200; fax (51) 9210215.

National Energy Conservation Centre (ENERCON): ENERCON Bldg, G-5/2, Islamabad; tel. (51) 9206001; fax (51) 9206004; Man. Dir ARIF ALAUDDIN.

National Highway Authority: 27, Mauve Area, G-9/1, Islamabad; tel. (51) 9260563; fax (51) 9261327; e-mail nhal2@comsats.net.pk.

National Housing Authority: Prime Minister's Office, Islamabad; tel. (51) 92008539; fax (51) 92008324.

National Technical Resources Pool: 414-C, National Reconstruction Bureau, Chief Executive's Secretariat II, Islamabad; tel. (51) 9207912.

Pakistan Electronic Media Regulatory Authority: Islambad; tel. (51) 2441600; f. 2002; Chair. Mian MUHAMMAD JAVED.

Pakistan Revenue Service: national tax authority.

Pakistan Software Export Board (Guarantee) Ltd: 2nd Floor, Evacuee Trust Complex, F-5/1, Aga Khan Rd, Islamabad; tel. (51) 9204074; fax (51) 9204075; e-mail info@pseb.org.pk; internet www.pseb.org.pk.

Pakistan Telecommunication Authority: F-5/1, Islamabad; internet www.pta.gov.pk; f. to regulate telecommunications services; to arrange deregulation of telecommunications; Chair. AKHTAR BAJWA.

Privatisation Commission: Experts Advisory Cell Bldg, 5A Constitution Ave, Islamabad 44000; tel. (51) 9216514; fax (51) 9203076; e-mail info@privatisation.gov.pk; internet www.privatisation.gov.pk; supervised by Ministry of Finance, Economic Affairs and Statistics.

Sindh Katchi Abadi Authority: Karachi; tel. (21) 9211275; fax (21) 9211272; e-mail skaa@khi.compol.com; internet www.skaa.cutecity.com; govt agency established to regulate and improve slums in Pakistan's southern province; Dir-Gen. TASNEEM AHMAD SIDDIQUI.

Sindh Privatisation Commission: Sindh Secretariat, 4-A, Block 15, Court Rd, Karachi; tel. (21) 9202077; fax (21) 9202071; e-mail spcsecretary@yahoo.com; internet www.spc.gov.pk.

Sustainable Development Policy Institute: St 3, UN Boulevard Diplomatic Enclave 1; Islamabad; tel. (51) 2277146; fax (51) 2278135; e-mail yasin@sdpi.org.

DEVELOPMENT ORGANIZATIONS

Balochistan Development Authority: Civil Secretariat, Block 7, Quetta; tel. (81) 9202491; created for economic development of Balochistan; exploration and exploitation of mineral resources; development of infrastructure, water resources, etc.

Capital Development Authority: Islamabad; tel. (51) 823454; Chair. MOHAMMAD ZAFAR IQBAL.

Karachi Development Authority (KDA): Civic Centre, Gulshan-e-Iqbal, University Rd, Karachi; tel. (21) 9230653; fax (21) 9230670; responsible for planning and development of Karachi city; Dir-Gen. Brig. (retd) SYED ZAHEER KADRI.

Lahore Development Authority (LDA): LDA Plaza, Egerton Rd, Lahore.

Pakistan Industrial Technical Assistance Centre (PITAC): Maulana Jalaluddin Roomi Rd (Old Ferozepur Rd), Lahore 54600; tel. (42) 5864171; fax (42) 5862381; e-mail pitac@paknet4.ptc.pk; f. 1962 by the Govt to provide advanced training to industrial personnel in the fields of metal trades and tool engineering design and related fields; under Ministry of Industries and Production; provides

human resource development programmes; design and production of tools, moulds, jigs, dies, gauges, fixtures, etc. also operates as secretariat of National Productivity Council; Chair. SAJJAD HAIDER GILANI; Gen. Man. MOHAMMAD ABDUL JABBAR KHAN.

Pakistan Poverty Alleviation Fund: 6-A, Park Rd, F-8/2, Islamabad; tel. (51) 2253178; fax (51) 2251726; e-mail kamran@ppaf.org.pk; internet www.ppaf.org.pk; f. 1997 by the Government; funded by the World Bank; works with non-governmental organizations and private-sector institutions to alleviate poverty; Chief Exec. KAMAL HAYAT.

Peshawar Development Authority (PDA): PDA House, Phase V, Hayatabad, Peshawar; tel. (521) 9217035; fax (521) 9217030.

Sarhad Development Authority (SDA): PIA Bldg, Arbab Rd, POB 172, Peshawar; tel. (521) 73076; f. 1972; promotes industrial (particularly mining), commercial development in the North-West Frontier Province; Chair. KHALID AZIZ.

Small and Medium Enterprises Development Authority (SMEDA): 43-T, Gulberg II, Lahore 59660; fax (42) 5753545; f. 1998; 3 brs.

CHAMBERS OF COMMERCE

The Federation of Pakistan Chambers of Commerce and Industry: Federation House, Main Clifton, POB 13875, Karachi 75600; tel. (21) 5873691; fax (21) 5874332; e-mail fpcci@digicom.net.pk; internet www.fpcci.com; f. 1950; 163 mem. bodies; Sec.-Gen. Dr ANWAR-UL-HAQUE.

The Islamic Chamber of Commerce and Industry: St 2/A, Block 9, KDA Scheme No. 5, Clifton, Karachi 75600; tel. (21) 5874756; fax (21) 5870765; e-mail icci@icci-oic.org; internet www.icci-oic.org; f. 1979; Pres. SHEIKH ISMAIL ABU DAWOOD; Sec.-Gen. AQEEL AHMAD AL-JASSEM.

Overseas Investors' Chamber of Commerce and Industry: Chamber of Commerce Bldg, Talpur Rd, POB 4833, Karachi; tel. (21) 2410814; fax (21) 2427315; e-mail oicci@global.net.pk; internet www.oicci.org; f. 1860 as the Karachi Chamber of Commerce, name changed to above in 1968; 184 mem. bodies; Pres. KAMRAN MIRZA; Sec.-Gen. ZAHID ZAHEER.

Principal Affiliated Chambers

Azad Jammu and Kashmir Chamber of Commerce and Industry: 52, F/1, Kotli Rd, POB 12, Mirpur; tel. (58610) 44890; fax (58610) 39110; e-mail ajkcci@isb.paknet.com.pk; internet www.ajkcci.com; Pres. ZULFIQAR ABBASI.

Bahawalpur Chamber of Commerce and Industry: 317-C, Satellite Town, Bahawalpur; tel. and fax (621) 80283; e-mail chamber@bcci.bwp.brain.net.pk; Pres. Khawaja MOHAMMAD ILYAS.

Balochistan Chamber of Commerce and Industry: Zarghoon Rd, POB 117, Quetta; tel. (81) 821943; fax (81) 821948; e-mail qcci@hotmail.com; f. 1984; Pres. Mir WALI MUHAMMAD BADINI; Sec. MUHAMMAD AHMED.

Dadu Chamber of Commerce and Industry: Nooriabad, Dadu; tel. 4400114; fax 4547301.

Dera Ghazi Khan Chamber of Commerce and Industry: Block '34', Khakwani House, Dera Ghazi Khan, Punjab; tel. (641) 462338; fax (641) 464938; Pres. SHEIKH IFTIKHAR AHMED; Sec. MUHAMMAD MUJAHID.

Dera Ismail Khan Chamber of Commerce and Industry: Circular Rd, POB 5, D. I. Khan; tel. (961) 711334; fax (961) 811334; e-mail sjbdn@epistemics.net.

Faisalabad Chamber of Commerce and Industry: 2nd Floor, National Bank Bldg, Jail Rd, Faisalabad; tel. (41) 616045; fax (41) 615085; e-mail fcci@fsd.paknet.com.pk; Pres. Mian NAEEM-UR-REHMAN; Sec. Maj. (retd) MOHAMMAD WASIM.

Gujranwala Chamber of Commerce and Industry: Aiwan-e-Tijarat Rd, Gujranwala; tel. (431) 256701; fax (431) 254440; e-mail gcci@gjr.paknet.com.pk; internet www.gcci.org.pk; f. 1978; Pres. RANA NASIR MAHMOOD; Sec. SHAHID IMRAN RANA.

Hyderabad Chamber of Commerce and Industry: Aiwan-e-Tijarat Rd, Saddar, POB 99, Hyderabad; tel. (221) 784973; fax (221) 784972; e-mail hcci@paknet3.ptc.pk; Pres. Haji MOHAMMAD YAQOOB; Sec. A. U. MALIK.

Islamabad Chamber of Commerce and Industry: Aiwan-e-Sana't-o-Tijarat Rd, Mauve Area, Sector G-8/1, Islamabad; tel. (51) 2250526; fax (51) 2252950; e-mail icci@brain.net.pk; internet www.icci.com.pk; f. 1984; Pres. Mian AKRAM FARID; Sec. MAJID SHABBIR.

Jhelum Chamber of Commerce and Industry: Rani Nagar, GT Rd, Jhelum; tel. (541) 646532; fax (541) 646533; Pres. RAJA HABIB UR REHMAN; Sec. Capt. (retd) MUHAMMAD ZAMAN.

Karachi Chamber of Commerce and Industry: Aiwan-e-Tijarat Rd, off Shahrah-e-Liaquat, POB 4158, Karachi 74000; tel. (21) 2416091; fax (21) 2416095; e-mail ccikar@cyber.net.pk; internet www.karachichamber.com; f. 1960; 11,705 mems; Pres. A. Q. KHALIL; Sec. M. NAZIR ALI.

Khairpur Chamber of Commerce and Industry: Shop 8, Sachal Shopping Centre, Khairpur; tel. (792) 5105.

Lahore Chamber of Commerce and Industry: 11 Shahrah-e-Aiwan-e-Tijarat, POB 597, Lahore; tel. (42) 6305538; fax (42) 6368854; e-mail sect@lcci.org.pk; internet www.lcci.org.pk; f. 1923; 8,000 mems; Pres. YAWAR KHAN; Sec. M. LATIF CHAUDHRY.

Larkana Chamber of Commerce and Industry: 21–23 Kenedy Market, POB 78, Larkana, Sindh; tel. (741) 40709; fax (741) 44633; Pres. KHAIR MUHAMMAD SHEIKH.

Mirpurkhas Chamber of Commerce and Industry: Khan Chamber, New Town, POB 162, Mirpurkhas, Sindh; tel. (231) 2175; fax (231) 2195; Pres. ABDUL KHALIQUE KHAN; Sec. MOHAMMAD BASI-TULLAH BAIG.

Multan Chamber of Commerce and Industry: Sharah-e-Aiwan-e-Tijarat-o-Sanat, Multan; tel. (61) 517087; fax (61) 570463; e-mail mccimul@mul.paknet.com.pk; Pres. MUHAMMAD KHAN SADDOZAI; Sec. G. A. BHATTI.

Rawalpindi Chamber of Commerce and Industry: Chamber House, 108 Adamjee Rd, POB 323, Rawalpindi; tel. (51) 5566238; fax (51) 5586849; e-mail rcci@best.net.pk; f. 1952; Pres. SOHAIL A. SETHI; Sec. MUHAMMAD IFTIKHAR-UD-DIN.

SAARC Chamber of Commerce and Industry: H No. 5, St No. 59, F-8/4, Islamabad; tel. (51) 2281396; fax (51) 2281390; e-mail saarc@comsats.net.pk; internet www.saarc.sec.org; f. 1993; Pres. PADMA JYOTI.

Sarhad Chamber of Commerce and Industry: Sarhad Chamber House, Chacha Younis Park, G.T. Rd, Peshawar; tel. (91) 9213314; fax (91) 9213316; e-mail sccip@brain.net.pk; internet www.scci.org .pk; f. 1958; 1,861 mems; Pres. GHULAM SARWAR KHAN MOHMAND; Sec. FAQIR MUHAMMAD.

Sialkot Chamber of Commerce and Industry: Shahrah-e-Aiwan-e-Sanat-o-Tijarat, POB 1870, Sialkot 51310; tel. (432) 261881; fax (432) 268835; e-mail info@scci.com.pk; internet www .scci.com.pk; f. 1982; 4,500 mems; Pres. DAUD AHMAD CHATTHA; Sec. NAWAZ AHMED TOOR.

Sukkur Chamber of Commerce and Industry: Sukkur Chamber House, 1st Floor, Opposite Mehran View Plaza, Bunder Rd, Sukkur; tel. (71) 23938; fax (71) 23059; Pres. S. NAQEEB-UL-HUSSAIN MUSAVI; Sec. MIRZA IQBAL BEG.

Thatta Chamber of Commerce and Industry: Room D, Al-Haroon, 4th Floor, Garden Rd, Karachi; tel. (21) 7726243; fax (21) 7725628; e-mail malodhi@lodhico.khi2.erum.com.pk.

INDUSTRIAL AND TRADE ASSOCIATIONS

All Pakistan Cloth Exporters' Association: 30/7, Civil Lines, Faisalabad; tel. (41) 644750; fax (41) 617985; e-mail apcea@fsd .paknet.com.pk; Chair. CH. MOHAMMAD SIDDIQUE; Sec. AFTAB AHMAD.

All Pakistan Cloth Merchants' Association: 64, 4th Floor, Hussain Cloth Market, Dada Chambers, Mereweather Tower, M. A. Jinnah Rd, Karachi; tel. (21) 2444274; fax (21) 2419751; Chair. JAVED CHINOY.

All Pakistan Cotton Powerlooms' Association: P-79/3, Montgomery Bazaar, Faisalabad; tel. (411) 612929; fax (411) 28171; Chair. CHAUDRY JAVAID SADIQ.

All Pakistan Textile Mills' Association: APTMA House, 44A Lalazar, off Moulvi Tamizuddin Khan Rd, POB 5446, Karachi 74000; tel. (21) 5610191; fax (21) 5611305; e-mail aptma@cyber.net .pk; internet www.paktextile.com; Chair. NADEEM MAQBOOL; Sec.-Gen. Mian IFTIKHAR AFZAL.

Cigarette Manufacturers' Association of Pakistan: Mezzanine 1, Avanti Park View, 141-A, Block 2, PECHS, Allama Iqbal Rd, Karachi 75400; tel. and fax (21) 4526825; Sec. TARIQ FAROOQ.

Cotton Board: Dr Abbasi Clinic Bldg, 76 Strachan Rd, Karachi 74200; tel. (21) 215669; fax (21) 5680422; f. 1950; Chair. Mian HABIBULLAH; Dep. Sec. Dr MUHAMMAD USMAN.

Federal 'B' Area Industrial Association: F. B. Area, Karachi; Chair. (vacant).

Karachi Cotton Association: The Cotton Exchange, I. I. Chundrigar Rd, Karachi; tel. (21) 2410336; fax (21) 2413035; e-mail kca33@cyber.net.pk; internet www.kcapak.org; Chair. ZAHID BASHIR; Sec. FASIHUDDIN.

Korangi Association of Trade and Industry: ST-4/2,1st Floor, Aiwan-e-Sanat, Sector 23, Korangi Industrial Area, Karachi 74900; tel. (21) 5061211; fax (21) 5061215; e-mail korangi1@email.com; Chair. S. M. NASEEM.

Management Association of Pakistan: 36-A/4, Lalazar, opposite Beach Luxury Hotel, Karachi 74000; tel. (21) 5611683; fax (21) 5611683; e-mail info@mappk.org; Pres. SYED MASOOD ALI NAQVI; Exec. Dir FAROOQ HASSAN.

Pakistan Agricultural Machinery and Implements Manufacturers' Association: Samundari Rd, Faisalabad; tel. (41) 714517; fax (41) 722721; e-mail iqra@fsd.comsats.net.pk.

Pakistan Agricultural Pesticides Association: Karachi; Chair. ASIF MUHAMMAD KHAN.

Pakistan Art Silk Fabrics and Garments Exporters' Association: 405 Amber Estate, Shahrah-e-Faisal, Karachi; tel. (21) 4538814; fax (21) 4536164; Chair. MAHMOOD AHMED; Sec.-Gen. IFTIKHAR AHMED KHAN.

Pakistan Bedwear Exporters' Association: 245-1-V, Block 6, PECHS, Karachi; tel. (21) 4541149; fax (21) 2851429; e-mail nash2@ attglobal.net; Chair. SHABIR AHMED; Sec. S. IFTIKHAR HUSSAIN.

Pakistan Beverage Manufacturers' Association: C, 1st Floor, Kiran Centre, M-28, Model Town Extension, Lahore; tel. (42) 5167306; fax (42) 5167316.

Pakistan Canvas and Tents Manufacturers' and Exporters' Association: 15/63, Shadman Commercial Market, Afridi Mansion, Lahore 3; tel. (42) 7578836; fax (42) 7577572; e-mail pctmea@wol.net .pk; Chair. ABDUL RAZAK CHHAPRA; Sec. IJAZ HUSSAIN.

Pakistan Carpet Manufacturers' and Exporters' Association: 401-A, 4th Floor, Panorama Center, Fatima Jinnah Rd, Saddar, Karachi 75530; tel. (21) 5212189; fax (21) 5679649; e-mail pcmeaho@ gerrys.net; internet www.pakistanrug.com.pk; Chair. ABDUL LATIF MALIK; Sec. A. S. HASHMI.

Pakistan Chemicals and Dyes Merchants' Association: Chemical and Dye House, Jodia Bazar, Rambharti St, Karachi 74000; tel. (21) 2432752; fax (21) 2430117.

Pakistan Commercial Towel Exporters' Association: 207, 2nd Floor, Uni Plaza, I. I. Chundrigar Rd, Karachi; tel. (21) 2411389; fax (21) 2410135; Chair. JAMIL MAHBOOB MAGOON.

Pakistan Cotton Fashion Apparel Manufacturers' and Exporters' Association: Room 5, Amber Court, 2nd Floor, Shahrah-e-Faisal, Shaheed-e-Millat Rd, Karachi 75350; tel. (21) 4533936; fax (21) 4546711; e-mail faf@pcfa.khi.brain.net.pk; f. 1982; 650 mems; Chair. QASEEM FAZIL.

Pakistan Cotton Ginners' Association: 1119–1120, 11th Floor, Uni-Plaza, I. I. Chundrigar Rd, Karachi; tel. (21) 2411406; fax (21) 2423181; e-mail pcga@gem.net.pk; Chair. MUHAMMAD SAEED; Sec. AIJAZUDDIN GHAURI.

Pakistan Film Producers' Association: Regal Cinema Bldg, Shahrah-e-Quaid-e-Azam, Lahore; tel. (42) 7322904; fax (42) 7241264; Chair. SYED YAAR MUHAMMAD SHAH; Sec. SAMI DEHLVI.

Pakistan Footwear Manufacturers' Association: 6-F, Rehman Business Centre, 32-B-III, Gulberg III, Lahore 54600; tel. (42) 5750051; fax (42) 5750052; e-mail pfma@pfma.lcci.org.pk; internet www.pakfootwear.org; Chair. SHAHID USMAN; Sec. Col (retd) ARSHAD AYYAZ.

Pakistan Gloves Manufacturers' and Exporters' Association: 349 Khadim Ali Rd, G. H. Jones Bldg, Tajpura, POB 1330, Sialkot; tel. (432) 551847; fax (432) 550182; Chair. Khawaja ABDUL QAVI; Sec. GULZAR AHMED SHAD.

Pakistan Hardware Merchants' Association: Mandviwala Bldg, Serai Rd, Karachi 74000; tel. (21) 2420610; fax (21) 2415743; f. 1961; more than 1,500 mems; Central Chair. WAJID RAFIQ; Central Sec. SYED ZAFRUN NABI.

Pakistan Hosiery Manufacturers' Association: Karachi; tel. (21) 4522769; fax (21) 4543774; Chair. SHAHZAD AZAM KHAN; Sec. YUNUS BIN AIYOOB.

Pakistan Iron and Steel Merchants' Association: Corner House, 2nd Floor, Preedy St, Saddar, Karachi; tel. (21) 519994; fax (21) 4550699; Pres. MALIK AHMAD HUSSAIN; Gen. Sec. S. S. REHMAN.

Pakistan Jute Mills' Association: 8 Sasi Town House, Abdullah Haroon Rd, Civil Lines, Karachi 75530; tel. (21) 5676986; fax (21) 5676463; Chair. AHSAN SALEEM; Exec. Consultant M. Z. CHUGHTAI.

Pakistan Knitwear and Sweaters Exporters' Association: Rooms Nos 1014–1016, 10th Floor, Park Ave, Block 6, PECHS, Shahrah-e-Faisal, Karachi 95350; tel. (21) 4522604; fax (21) 4525747; Chair. NASIR HUSSAIN.

Pakistan Leather Garments Manufacturers' and Exporters' Association: 92-C, Khayaban-e-Ittehad, DHA Phase II (Extension), Karachi; tel. (21) 5387356; fax (21) 5388799; e-mail info@plgmea .org; internet www.plgmea.org; f. 2002; Chair. FAWAD EJAZ KHAN.

Pakistan Paint Manufacturers' Association: ST/6a, Block 14, Federal 'B' Area, Karachi 38; tel. (21) 6321103; fax (21) 2560468; f. 1953; Chair. Wassim A. Khan; Sec. Syed Azhar Ali.

Pakistan Plastic Manufacturers' Association: 410 Mashrique Shopping Centre, St 6/A, Block No. 14, Gulshan-e-Iqbal, Karachi; tel. (21) 4942336; fax (21) 4944222; e-mail pakppma@pk.netsolir .com; Sec. Fayyaz A. Chaudhry.

Pakistan Polypropylene Woven Sacks Manufacturers' Association: Karachi; Chair. Shoukat Ahmed.

Pakistan Pulp, Paper and Board Mills' Association: 402 Burhani Chambers, Abdullah Haroon Rd, Karachi 74400; tel. (21) 7726150; Chair. Kamran Khan.

Pakistan Readymade Garments Manufacturers' and Exporters' Association: Shaheen View Bldg, Mezzanine Floor, Plot No. 18A, Block IV, PECHS, Shahrah-e-Faisal, Karachi; tel. (21) 4547912; fax (21) 4539669; e-mail info@prgmea.org; Chair. Masood Naqi.

Pakistan Ship Breakers' Association: 608, S.S. Chamber, Siemens Chowrangi, S.I.T.E., Karachi; tel. (21) 293958; fax (21) 256533.

Pakistan Silk and Rayon Mills' Association: Room Nos 44–48, Textile Plaza, 5th Floor, M. A. Jinnah Rd, Karachi 2; tel. (21) 2410288; fax (21) 2415261; f. 1974; Chair. M. Ashraf Sheikh; Sec. M. H. K. Burney.

Pakistan Small Units Powerlooms' Association: 2nd Floor, Waqas Plaza, Aminpura Bazar, POB 8647, Faisalabad; tel. (411) 627992; fax (411) 633567.

Pakistan Soap Manufacturers' Association: 148 Sunny Plaza, Hasrat Mohani Rd, Karachi 74200; tel. (21) 2634648; fax (21) 2563828; e-mail pakistansma@yahoo.com; Chair. Yaqoob Karim.

Pakistan Software House Association (PASHA): Block 5, F-58, Park Lane, Clifton, Karachi 75600; tel. (21) 5870321; fax (21) 5870988; e-mail info@pasha.org.pk; internet www.pasha.org.pk; f. 1992; Pres. Syed Hamza.

Pakistan Sports Goods Manufacturers' and Exporters' Association: Paris Rd, Sialkot 51310; tel. (432) 267962; fax (432) 261774; e-mail psga@brain.net.pk; Chair. Arif Mehmood Sheikh.

Pakistan Steel Melters' Association: Lahore; Chair. Aziz Ahmed Chaudhry.

Pakistan Steel Re-rolling Mills' Association: Rashid Chambers, 6-Link McLeod Rd, Lahore 54000; tel. (42) 7227136; fax (42) 7231154; Chair. Mian Tariq Waheed; Sec. Lt-Col (retd) S. H. A. Bukhari.

Pakistan Sugar Mills' Association: Mezzanine Floor, 24D Rashid Plaza, Jinnah Ave, Islamabad; tel. (51) 270525; fax (51) 274153; Chair. Ashraf W. Tabbani; Sec.-Gen. K. Ali Qazilbash.

Pakistan Tanners' Association: Plot No. 46-C, 21st Commercial St, Phase II Extension, Defence Housing Authority, Karachi 75500; tel. (21) 5880180; fax (21) 5880093; e-mail info@pakistantanners .org; Chair. Masood Ahmed Shaikh (acting).

Pakistan Tea Association: Suite 307, Business Plaza, Mumtaz Hassan Rd, off I. I. Chundrigar Rd, Karachi; tel. (21) 2422161; fax (21) 2422209; e-mail pta@cyber.net.pk; Chair. Hanif Janoo.

Pakistan Vanaspati Manufacturers' Association: No. 5-B, College Rd, F-7/3, Islamabad; tel. (51) 2274358; fax (51) 2272529; Chair. Mian Mohammad Ibrahim.

Pakistan Wool and Hair Merchants' Association: 27 Idris Chambers, Talpur Rd, Karachi; Pres. Mian Mohammad Siddiq Khan; Sec. Khalid Lateef.

Pakistan Woollen Mills' Association: Republic Motors Bldg, 2nd Floor, Room No. 12, 87 Shahrah-e-Quaid-e-Azam, Lahore 54000; tel. (42) 6308398; fax (42) 6306879; e-mail pwma@lcci.org.pk; internet www.lcci.org.pk; Chair. Mian Muzaffar Ali; Sec. Muhammad Yasin.

Pakistan Yarn Merchants' Association: Room Nos 802–3, Business Centre, 8th Floor, Dunolly Rd, Karachi 74000; tel. (21) 2410320; fax (21) 2424896; Central Chair. Yaqoob Nagaria.

Towel Manufacturers' Association of Pakistan: 77-A, Block A, Sindhi Muslim Co-operative Housing Society, Karachi 74400; tel. (21) 4551628; fax (21) 4551628; Chair. Tahir Jahangir.

EMPLOYERS' ORGANIZATION

Employers' Federation of Pakistan: 2nd Floor, State Life Bldg No. 2, Wallace Rd, off I. I. Chundrigar Rd, Karachi 74000; tel. (21) 2411049; fax (21) 2439347; e-mail efpak@cyber.net.pk; internet www.efpak.com; f. 1950; Pres. Ashraf Wali Mohammad Tabani; Sec.-Gen. Mohammed Mustafa Sharif.

UTILITIES

Water and Power Development Authority (WAPDA): WAPDA House, Shahrah-e-Quaid-e-Azam, Lahore; tel. (42) 6366911; f. 1958 for development of irrigation, water supply and drainage, building of replacement works under the World Bank-sponsored Indo-Pakistan Indus Basin Treaty; flood-control and watershed management; reclamation of waterlogged and saline lands; inland navigation; generation, transmission and distribution of hydroelectric and thermal power; partial transfer to private ownership carried out in 1996; Chair. Lt-Gen. Zulfikar Ali Khan.

Electricity

National Electric Power Regulatory Authority (NEPRA): 2nd Floor, OPF Bldg, G-5/2, Islamabad; tel. (51) 9207200; fax (51) 9210215; e-mail info@napra.org.pk; f. 1997; fixes the power tariff.

Hub Power Co Ltd (Hubco): Islamic Chamber Bldg, Block No. 9, Clifton, POB 13841, Karachi 75600; tel. (21) 5874677; fax (21) 5870397; f. 1991; supplies electricity; Chair. Mohammad Ali Raza; Chief Exec. Vince Harris.

Karachi Electric Supply Corpn Ltd (KESC): Aimai House, Abdullah Haroon Rd, POB 7197, Karachi; tel. (21) 5685492; fax (21) 5682408; f. 1913; Chair. and Man. Dir Kamal Azfar.

Kot Addu Power Co (KAPCO): G.T.P, Kot Addu, District Muzaffargarh; tel. (697) 41336.

National Power Construction Corpn (Pvt) Ltd: 9 Shadman II, Lahore 54000; tel. (42) 7566019; fax (42) 7566022; e-mail npcc@wol .net.pk; internet www.npcc.com.pk; f. 1974; execution of power projects on turnkey basis, e.g. extra high voltage transmission lines, distribution networks, substations, power generation plants, industrial electrification, external lighting of housing complexes, etc. Man. Dir Muhammad Ajaz Malik; Gen. Man. Tauqir Ahmed Sharifi; project office in Jeddah (Saudi Arabia).

National Power International: D-15, Block-2, Khayaban-e-Ghalib, Clifton, Karachi 75600; tel. (21) 5860328; fax (21) 5860343; e-mail npower@www.fascom.com.

Pakistan Atomic Energy Commission (PAEC): POB 1114, Islamabad; tel. (51) 9209032; fax (51) 9204908; responsible for harnessing nuclear energy for development of nuclear technology as part of the nuclear power programme; operates Karachi Atomic Nuclear Power Plant—KANUPP (POB 3183, nr Paradise Point, Hawksbay Rd, Karachi 75400; tel. (21) 9202222; fax (21) 7737488; e-mail knpc@khi.comsats.net.pk) and Chasma Nuclear Power Plant (CHASNUP) at Chasma District Mianwali; building another nuclear power station at Kundian; establishing research centres, incl. Pakistan Institute of Nuclear Science and Technology (PINSTECH); promoting peaceful use of atomic energy in agriculture, medicine, industry and hydrology; searching for indigenous nuclear mineral deposits; training project personnel; Chair. Pervez Butt; Gen. Man. (KANUPP) Qamrul Hoda.

Pakistan Electric Power Co: Lahore; f. 1998; Chair. Javed Burki.

Quetta Electric Supply Co Ltd: Zarghoon Rd, Quetta Cantt, Balochistan; tel. (81) 9202211; fax (81) 836554; e-mail qesco@qta .infolink.net.pk; f. 1998; CEO Brig. Agha Gul.

Gas

Mari Gas Co Ltd (MGCL): 21 Mauve Area, 3rd Rd, Sector G–10/4, Islamabad; tel. (51) 297679; fax (51) 2297686; e-mail marigd@cyber .net.pk; 20% govt-owned; Chair. Lt-Gen. (retd) Khalid Latif Moghal.

Oil and Gas Development Corpn Ltd (OGDCL): C-6, Masood Mansion, F-8, Markaz, Islamabad; tel. (51) 9260405; fax (51) 9260467; f. 1961; plans, promotes, organizes and implements programmes for the exploration and development of petroleum and gas resources, and the production, refining and sale of petroleum and gas; transfer to private ownership pending; Man. Dir Zakauddin Malik.

Pakistan Petroleum Ltd (PPL): PIDC House, 4th Floor, Dr Ziauddin Ahmed Rd, Karachi 75530; tel. 111–568–568; fax (21) 5680005; e-mail info@ppl.com.pk; 93.7% govt-owned, 6.1% owned by International Finance Corpn; Pakistan's largest producer of natural gas; Chief Exec./Man. Dir S. Munsif Raza.

Sui Northern Gas Pipelines Ltd: Gas House, 21 Kashmir Rd, POB 56, Lahore; tel. (42) 9201277; fax (42) 9201302; f. 1964; 36% state-owned; transmission and distribution of natural gas in northern Pakistan; sales 321,957m. (June 2002); Chair. Lt-Gen. (retd) Ghulam Safdar Butt; Man. Dir Abdul Rashid Lone.

Sui Southern Gas Co Ltd: 4B Sir Shah Suleman Rd, Block 14, Gulshan-e-Iqbal, Karachi 75000; tel. (21) 9231602; fax (21) 9231604; e-mail info@ssgc.com.pk; f. 1988; 70% state-owned.

Water

Faisalabad Development Authority (Water and Sanitation Agency): POB 229, Faisalabad; tel. (411) 767606; fax (411) 782113; e-mail fwasa@fsd.paknet.com.pk; f. 1978; Man. Dir Lt-Col (retd) Syed Ghias-ud-Din.

Karachi Water and Sewerage Board: Block D, (Behind Subzazar Lawns), 9th Mile Office, Shahrae Faisal, Karachi; tel. (21) 9231882; fax (21) 9231814; e-mail water@cyber.net.pk; f. 1983; Man. Dir Brig. (retd) MUHAMMAD BAHRAM KHAN.

Lahore Development Authority (Water and Sanitation Agency): 4-A Gulberg V, Lahore; tel. (42) 5756739; fax (42) 5752960; f. 1967; Man. Dir IMRAN RAZA ZAIDI.

TRADE UNIONS

National Trade Union Federation Pakistan: Bharocha Bldg, 2-B/6, Commercial Area, Nazimabad No. 2, Karachi 74600; tel. (21) 628339; fax (21) 6622529; e-mail ntuf@super.net.pk; f. 1999; 50 affiliated unions; covers following fields: steel, agriculture, textiles, garments, leather, automobiles, pharmaceuticals, chemicals, transport, printing, food, shipbuilding, engineering and power; Pres. MUHAMMAD RAFIQUE; Gen. Sec. SALEEM RAZA.

Pakistan National Federation of Trade Unions (PNFTU): Aiwan-E-Ittehad St, 37/4, Qasba Township, Manghopir Rd, Karachi 75890; tel. (21) 6693372; fax (21) 2313077; e-mail pnftu@cyber.net .pk; f. 1962; 177 affiliated feds; 218,468 mems; Pres. MUHAMMAD SHARIF; Sec.-Gen. ABDUL GHAFOOR BALOCH.

The principal affiliated federations are:

All Pakistan Federation of Labour (Durrani Group): Durrani Labour Hall, Khyber Bazar, Peshawar; tel. (91) 216411; fax (91) 274038; f. 1951; 300 affiliated unions, with 445,000 mems; affiliated to the World Federation of Trade Unions (WFTU); Pres. AURANGZEB DURRANI; Sec.-Gen. M. ZAFER IQBAL SAIF.

All Pakistan Federation of Trade Unions (APFTU): Bakhtiar Labour Hall, 28 Nisbet Rd, Lahore; tel. (42) 7229419; fax (42) 7239529; e-mail apftu@brain.net.pk; 520,100 mems; Pres. Haji MUHAMMAD AMIN RATHORE; Gen. Sec. KHURSHID AHMED.

Muttahida Labour Federation: Labour Welfare Society, Block D, Shershah Colony, Karachi 75730; tel. (21) 291576; c. 120,000 mems; Pres. KHAMASH GUL KHATTAK; Sec.-Gen. NABI AHMED.

Pakistan Central Federation of Trade Unions: 220 Al-Noor Chambers, M. A. Jinnah Rd, Karachi; tel. (21) 728891.

Pakistan Railway Employees' Union (PREM): City Railway Station, Karachi; tel. (21) 2415721; Divisional Sec. BASHIRUDDIN SIDDIQUI.

Pakistan Trade Union Federation: Khamosh Colony, Karachi; Pres. KANIZ FATIMA; Gen. Sec. SALEEM RAZA.

Pakistan Transport Workers' Federation: 110 McLeod Rd, Lahore; 17 unions; 92,512 mems; Pres. MEHBOOB-UL-HAQ; Gen. Sec. CH. UMAR DIN.

Other affiliated federations include: Pakistan Bank Employees' Federation, Pakistan Insurance Employees' Federation, Automobile, Engineering and Metal Workers' Federation, Pakistan Teachers Organizations' Council, Sarhad WAPDA Employees' Federation, and Balochistan Ittehad Trade Union Federation.

Transport

RAILWAYS

In 1994 the Government approved a US $700m., 850-km railway project, which was to link Pakistan with Turkmenistan via Afghanistan. In 1996 work was begun on the US $590m. Karachi mass transit system (KMTS), Pakistan's first urban train network; in mid-1998, however, work on the KMTS was suspended owing to the serious economic crisis.

Pakistan Railways: 31 Sheikh Abdul Hamid Bin Badees Rd, Lahore; tel. (42) 9201771; fax (42) 9201760; e-mail gmopr@pakrail .com; internet www.pakrail.com; state-owned; 11,515 km of track and 7,791 route km; seven divisions (Karachi, Lahore, Multan, Quetta, Rawalpindi, Peshawar and Sukkur); Chair. Lt-Gen. (retd) SAEED-UZ-ZAFAR; Gen. Man. IQBAL SAMAD KHAN.

ROADS

The total length of roads was 254,410 km (motorways 339 km, main 6,587 km, secondary 211,846 km, other roads 35,638 km) in 1999. In 1978 the 800-km Karakoram highway was opened, linking Xinjiang Province in the People's Republic of China with Havelian, north of Islamabad. In November 1997 a 340-km motorway between Islamabad and Lahore was opened. The road was Pakistan's first intercity motorway and constituted the first section of a planned 2,000-km transnational motorway (the Indus Highway) from Peshawar to Karachi. In April 1997 the National Highways Authority announced a major road-building programme, the estimated cost of which was US $4,017m. Some 11 highway-building projects were under way in mid-2002.

Government assistance comes from the Road Fund, financed from a share of the excise and customs duty on sales of petrol and from development loans.

National Highways Authority: 27 Mauve Area, G–9/1, Islamabad; tel. (51) 9260717; fax (51) 9260404; e-mail info@nha.gov.pk; internet www.nha.gov.pk; f. 1991; jt venture between Govt and private sector; Chair. Maj.-Gen. (retd) FURRUKH JAVED; Dir-Gen. Maj.-Gen. (retd) HIDAYATULLAH KHAN NIAZI.

Punjab Road Transport Board: Transport House, 11A Egerton Rd, Lahore.

SHIPPING

In 1974 maritime shipping companies were placed under government control. The chief port is Karachi. A second port, Port Qasim, started partial operation in 1980. A third port, Port Gwadar, is being developed as a deep-water seaport; the first phase of construction had been completed by mid-2002. Another port, Port Pasni, which is situated on the Balochistan coast, was completed in 1988. In 1991 the Government amended the 1974 Pakistan Maritime Shipping Act to allow private companies to operate. By mid-1992 31 private companies had been granted licences.

Mercantile Marine Dept: Government of Pakistan, 70/4, Timber Pond, N. M. Reclamation, Keamari, Karachi.

Al-Hamd International Container Terminal (Pvt) Ltd: Plot K&L, K-28, Trans Lyari Quarters, Hawkesbay Rd, New Truck Stand, Karachi; tel. (21) 2352651; fax (21) 2351556; e-mail info@ aictpk.com; internet www.aicpakistan.com.

Engro Vopak Terminal Ltd: 1st Floor, Bahria Complex, 1 M. T. Khan Rd, POB 5736, Karachi 74000; tel. (21) 5610965; fax (21) 5611394; internet www.engro.com.

Karachi Port Trust (KPT): Eduljee Dinshaw Rd, Karachi 74000; tel. (21) 9214312; fax (21) 9214329; e-mail gmpd@kpt.gov.pk; internet www.kpt.gov.pk; Chair. Rear-Adm. AHMED HAYAT; Sec. FAROZUDDIN.

Karachi International Container Terminal: Administrative Bldg, Berths 28–30, Dockyard Rd, West Wharf, Karachi; tel. (21) 2316410; fax (21) 2313816; internet www.kictl.com; f. 1996; Chief Exec. KHURRAM S. ABBAS.

Karachi Shipyard and Engineering Works Ltd: West Wharf, Dockyard Rd, POB 4419, Karachi 2; tel. (21) 9214045; fax (21) 9214020; e-mail ksew@fascom.com; f. 1956; building and repairing ships; general engineering; Man. Dir Rear-Adm. ARSHAD MUNIR AHMAD; Gen. Man. (Sales and Marketing) Capt. S. A. BOKHARI.

Korangi Fisheries Harbour Authority: Ghashma Goth, Landhi, POB 15804, Karachi 75160; tel. (21) 5013315; fax (21) 5015096; e-mail kfha@sat.net.pk.

National Tanker Co (Pvt) Ltd (Pak): 15th Floor, PNSC Bldg, M. T. Khan Rd, Karachi 74000; tel. (21) 5611843; fax (21) 5610780; f. 1981 by the Pakistan National Shipping Corpn and the State Petroleum Refining and Petrochemical Corpn Ltd; aims to make Pakistan self-reliant in the transport of crude petroleum and petroleum products; Chief Exec. Vice-Adm. A. U. KHAN; Dep. Chief Exec. TURAB ALI KHAN.

Pakistan National Shipping Corpn: PNSC Bldg, M. T. Khan Rd, POB 5350, Karachi 74000; tel. (21) 9203980; fax (21) 9203974; e-mail pnsckar@paknet3.ptc.pk; f. 1979 by merger; state-owned; Chair. Vice-Adm. S. T. H. NAQVI; Sec. ARIF SAEED.

Port Qasim Authority (PQA): Bin Qasim, Karachi 75020; tel. (21) 730101; fax (21) 730108; f. 1973; Chair. NAZAR MOHAMMAD SHAIKH; Sec. SYED MUMTAZ HUSSAIN SHAH.

Terminals Association of Pakistan: Molasses Exports Wing, Keamari, Karachi; tel. (21) 2410427; fax (21) 2416791; Chair. RASHID JAN MUHAMMAD.

Qasim International Container Terminal: Berths 5–7, Marginal Wharfs, POB 6425, Port Mohammad Bin Qasim, Karachi 75020; tel. (21) 730002; fax (21) 730021; e-mail info@qict.net; internet www.qict .net; f. 1994; CEO ALI HYDER STANHOPE; Gen. Man. DARAYUS DIVECHA.

Associations

All Pakistan Shipping Association: 01-E, 1st Floor, Sattar Chambers, West Wharf Rd, Karachi; tel. (21) 2200742; fax (21) 2200743; e-mail mfqshaheen@cyber.net.pk; Chair. MUHAMMAD F. QAISER.

Pakistan Ship Agents' Association: GSA House, 19 Timber Pound, Keamari, Karachi 75620; tel. (21) 2850837; fax (21) 2851528; e-mail psaa@cyber.net.pk; internet www.shipezee.com/psaa; Chair. CYRUS R. COWASJEE.

Terminal Association of Pakistan: 8th Floor, Adamjee House, I. I. Chundrigar Rd, Karachi 74000; tel. (21) 2417131; fax (21) 2416477; Sec. AKHTAR SULTAN.

CIVIL AVIATION

Karachi, Lahore, Rawalpindi, Peshawar and Quetta have international airports.

In 1992 the Government ended the air monopoly held by the Pakistan International Airlines Corpn, and opened all domestic air routes to any Pakistan-based company.

Civil Aviation Authority: Jinnah Terminal, Karachi Airport, Karachi; tel. (21) 9248778; fax (21) 9248770; internet www.caapakistan .com; controls all the civil airports; Dep. Dir Gen. Air Vice-Marshal ALIDDIN.

Aero Asia International: 47-E/1, Block 6, PECHS, Karachi 75400; tel. (21) 4544951; fax (21) 4544940; e-mail aeroasia@cyber.net.pk; internet www.aeroasia.com; f. 1993; operates scheduled passenger and cargo services to domestic destinations and to the neighbouring Gulf states; Chair. MOHAMMED YAQUB TABANI; Man. Dir KHURSHID ANWAR.

Bhoja Air: Bhoja Air City Office, Court View Bldg, Court Road, Karachi 74200; tel. (21) 5683475; fax (21) 2625995; e-mail bhoja@ mail.digicom.net.pk; internet www.bhojaair.com.pk; f. 1993; scheduled passenger services to domestic and international destinations; Chair. M. FAROUQ BHOJA; Man. Dir Capt. AIJAZ ALI FAIZI.

Pakistan International Airlines Corpn (PIA): PIA Bldg, Quaid-e-Azam International Airport, Karachi 75200; tel. (21) 4572011; fax (21) 4570419; e-mail info@fly-pia.com; internet www.piac.com.pk; f. 1954; merged with Orient Airways in 1955; 57.7% govt-owned; operates domestic services to 35 destinations and international services to 40 destinations in 31 countries; Chair. Lt-Gen. HAMID NAWAZ KHAN; Man. Dir AHMAD SAEED.

Shaheen Air International: 157B Clifton Rd, Clifton, Karachi 75600; tel. (21) 5872191; fax (21) 5873337; f. 1993; operates scheduled domestic services and international services to the Gulf region; Man. Dir ATAUR REHMAN.

Tourism

The Himalayan hill stations of Pakistan provide magnificent scenery, a fine climate and excellent opportunities for field sports, mountaineering, trekking and winter sports. The archaeological remains and historical buildings are also impressive.

In 2000 Pakistan received 556,805 foreign visitors, and in 2000 receipts from tourism amounted to around US $86m.

Pakistan Tourism Development Corpn: House No. 170, St 36, F-10/1, Islamabad 44000; tel. (51) 294189; fax (51) 294540; e-mail tourism@isb.comsats.net.pk; internet www.tourism.gov.pk; f. 1970; Chair. MUSHAHID HUSSAIN SAYED; Man. Dir IMTIAZ A. SYED.

Related Territories

The status of Jammu and Kashmir has remained unresolved since the 1949 cease-fire agreement, whereby the area was divided into sectors administered by India and Pakistan separately. Pakistan administers Azad (Free) Kashmir and the Northern Areas as *de facto* dependencies, being responsible for foreign affairs, defence, coinage, currency and the implementation of UN resolutions concerning Kashmir.

AZAD KASHMIR

Area: 11,639 sq km (4,494 sq miles).

Population: 1,980,000 (1981 census).

Administration: Government is based on the Azad Jammu and Kashmir Interim Constitution Act of 1974. There are four administrative districts: Kotli, Mirpur, Muzaffarabad and Poonch.

Legislative Assembly: consists of 42 members: 40 directly elected and two women nominated by the other members.

Azad Jammu and Kashmir Council: consists of the President of Pakistan as Chairman, the President of Azad Kashmir as Vice-Chairman, five members nominated by the President of Pakistan, six members by the Legislative Assembly, and the Pakistan Minister of States, Northern Areas, Frontier Regions and Kashmir Affairs (ex officio).

President of Azad Kashmir: Maj.-Gen. (retd) MOHAMMAD ANWAR KHAN.

Prime Minister: Sardar SIKANDAR HAYAT.

NORTHERN AREAS

Area: 72,520 sq km (28,000 sq miles).

Population: 562,000 (1981 census).

Administration: There are three administrative districts: Baltistan, Diamir and Gilgit. The Northern Areas Council consists of 26 members (24 members are elected in a party-based election and two seats are reserved for women), headed by the federal Minister of Kashmir Affairs and Northern Areas, States and Frontier Regions (SAFRON).

PALAU

Introductory Survey

Location, Climate, Language, Religion, Flag, Capital

The Republic of Palau (also known as Belau) consists of more than 200 islands, in a chain about 650 km (400 miles) long, lying about 7,150 km (4,450 miles) south-west of Hawaii and about 1,160 km (720 miles) south of Guam. With the Federated States of Micronesia (q.v.), Palau forms the archipelago of the Caroline Islands. Palau is subject to heavy rainfall, and seasonal variations in precipitation and temperature are generally small. Palauan and English are the official languages. The principal religion is Christianity, much of the population being Roman Catholic. The flag (proportions 3 by 5) features a large golden disc (representing the moon), placed off-centre, towards the hoist, on a light blue background. The provisional capital is Koror, on Koror Island: the Constitution provides for the capital to be established on the less developed island of Babeldaob, in Melekeok state.

Recent History

The Republic of Palau's independence, under the Compact of Free Association, in October 1994 marked the end of the Trust Territory of the Pacific Islands, of which Palau was the final component (for history up to 1965, see the chapter on the Marshall Islands). From 1965 there were increasing demands for local autonomy within the Trust Territory. In that year the Congress of Micronesia was formed, and in 1967 a commission was established to examine the future political status of the islands. In 1970 the commission declared Micronesians' rights to sovereignty over their own lands, self-determination, the right to their own constitution and to revoke any form of free association with the USA. In May 1977, after eight years of negotiations, US President Jimmy Carter announced that his Administration intended to adopt measures to terminate the trusteeship agreement by 1981. In the Palau District a referendum in July 1979 approved a proposed local Constitution, which came into effect on 1 January 1981, when the district became the Republic of Palau.

The USA signed the Compact of Free Association with the Republic of Palau in August 1982, and with the Marshall Islands and the Federated States of Micronesia in October. The trusteeship of the islands was due to end after the principle and terms of the Compacts had been approved by the respective peoples and legislatures of the new countries, by the US Congress and by the UN Security Council. Under the Compacts, the four countries (including the Northern Mariana Islands) would be independent of each other and would manage both their internal and foreign affairs separately, while the USA would be responsible for defence and security. In addition, the USA was to allocate some US $3,000m. in aid to the islands.

More than 60% of Palauans voted in February 1983 to support their Compact, but fewer than the required 75% approved changing the Constitution to allow the transit and storage of nuclear materials. A revised Compact, which contained no reference to nuclear issues, was approved by 66% of votes cast in a referendum in September 1984. However, the US Government had hoped for a favourable majority of 75% of the votes cast, which would have allowed the terms of the Compact to override the provisions of the Palau Constitution in the event of a conflict between the two.

In June 1985 President Haruo Remeliik of Palau was assassinated. Relatives of a rival candidate in the 1984 presidential election, Roman Tmetuchl, were convicted of the murder, but remained at liberty pending an appeal; this was upheld, on the grounds of unreliable evidence, by Palau's Supreme Court in August 1987. Lazarus Salii was elected President in September 1985.

In January 1986 representatives of the Palau and US administrations reached a preliminary agreement on a new Compact, whereby the USA consented to provide US $421m. in economic assistance to the islands. However, the proportion of votes in favour of the new Compact at a referendum in the following month was still less than that required for the constitutional ban on nuclear material to be waived. Both Salii and US President Ronald Reagan supported the terms of the Compact, arguing that a simple majority would suffice for its approval, as the USA had guaranteed that it would observe the constitutional ban on nuclear material.

In May 1986 the UN Trusteeship Council endorsed the US Administration's request for the termination of the existing trusteeship agreement with the islands. However, a writ was subsequently submitted to the Palau High Court, in which it was claimed that approval of the Compact with the USA was unconstitutional because it had failed to obtain the requisite 75% of votes. The High Court ruled in favour of the writ, but the Palau Government appealed against the ruling and in October the Compact was approved by the US Congress. At a new plebiscite in December, however, only 66% of Palauans voted in favour of the Compact. Ratification of the Compact thus remained impossible.

A fifth plebiscite on Palau's proposed Compact with the USA, in June 1987, again failed to secure the 75% endorsement required by the Constitution. Under alleged physical intimidation by pro-nuclear supporters of the Compact, the House of Delegates (the lower house of the Palau National Congress) agreed to a further referendum in August. In this referendum an amendment to the Constitution was approved, ensuring that a simple majority would henceforth be sufficient to approve the Compact. This was duly achieved in a further referendum in the same month. When a writ was entered with the Supreme Court challenging the legality of the decision to allow approval of the Compact by a simple majority, a campaign of arson and bombing followed, and one person was murdered.

In February 1988 a team from the US General Accounting Office travelled to Palau to investigate allegations of corruption and intimidation on the part of the Palau Government. Approval of the Compact by the US Congress was to be delayed until the investigators had published their findings. However, in April a ruling by Palau's Supreme Court invalidated the procedure by which the Compact had finally been approved by a simple majority in the previous August. Three government employees, including Salii's personal assistant, were imprisoned in April, after being found guilty of firing on the home of Santos Olikong, Speaker of Palau's House of Delegates. The attack was widely considered to have been prompted by Olikong's public opposition to the Compact.

In August 1988 Salii, the principal subject of the bribery allegations, apparently committed suicide. At an election in November Ngiratkel Etpison was elected President, with just over 26% of the total votes. Although Etpison advocated the proposed Compact and was supported by the pro-Compact Ta Belau Party, his closest challenger, Tmetuchl, opposed it and was supported by the anti-nuclear Coalition for Open, Honest and Just Government, which had demanded that a special prosecutor from the USA be dispatched to Palau to investigate alleged corruption and violent attacks against opponents of the Compact.

Only 60% of voters approved the proposed Compact at a seventh referendum in February 1990. In July the US Department of the Interior declared its intention to impose stricter controls on the administration of Palau, particularly in financial matters. In the following year the leader of Palau's Council of Chiefs (a presidential advisory body), Yutaka Gibbons, initiated proceedings to sue the US Government: his claim centred on demands for compensation for the extensive damage caused to Palau's infrastructure by US forces during the Second World War and the subsequent retardation of the economy, allegedly as a result of the US administration of the islands.

During 1991 the US authorities reopened investigations into the assassination of Remeliik in 1985. In March 1992 Palau's Minister of State, John Ngiraked, his wife, Emerita Kerradel, and Sulial Heinrick (already serving a prison sentence for another killing) were charged with Remeliik's murder. In March 1993 Ngiraked and Kerradel were found guilty of aiding and abetting the assassination of the President, while Heinrick was acquitted.

Legislative and presidential elections were held in November 1992. (The electoral system had been modified earlier in the year to include primary elections for the selection of two presidential candidates.) At the presidential election the incumbent Vice-President, Kuniwo Nakamura, narrowly defeated Johnson Toribiong to become President. A concurrent referendum endorsed a proposal that, in future polls, a simple majority be sufficient to approve the adoption of the Compact of Free Association. Some 62% of voters were in favour of the proposal, which was approved in 14 of Palau's 16 states. A further referendum on the proposed Compact took place in November 1993. Some 68.3% of participating voters approved the proposed Compact, giving the Government a mandate to proceed with its adoption. Nevertheless, opposition to the changes remained fierce, and in January 1994 two legal challenges were mounted that questioned the validity of the amendments and stated that the Compact's approval had been procured by coercion. The challenges failed, however, and on 1 October Palau achieved independence under the Compact of Free Association. At independence celebrations, Nakamura appealed to opponents of the Compact to support Palau's new status. He announced that his Government's principal concern was the regeneration of the country's economy, which he aimed to initiate with an economic programme financed by funds from the Compact. Palau was admitted to the UN in December 1994, and became a member of the IMF in December 1997.

A preliminary round of voting in the presidential election took place in September 1996; Nakamura secured 52.4% of total votes, Toribiong received 33.5%, and Yutaka Gibbons 14.2%. Nakamura and Toribiong were, therefore, expected to proceed to a second election due to take place in November. However, in late September a serious crisis struck Palau when the bridge linking the islands of Koror and Babeldaob collapsed, killing two people and injuring several others. The collapse of the bridge left the capital isolated from the international airport on Babeldaob, with disastrous economic repercussions for Palau, which relies on the route for all domestic and international communications. A state of emergency was declared as the authorities sought to re-establish water and power supplies and to reconnect telephone lines. It was subsequently revealed that major repairs had recently been carried out on the bridge, at a cost of US $3.2m., and several reports implied that inappropriate changes made to its structure during the work were responsible for the disaster. Toribiong was harshly critical of Nakamura, who had commissioned the repair work, and demanded his resignation along with those of the public works officials involved. However, following the revelation that Toribiong's running-mate in the election for the vice-presidency was one of the officials involved in the work, Toribiong withdrew his candidacy from the second round of the presidential election. A new bridge linking Koror to Babeldaob opened in January 2002. Its construction was funded by the Japanese Government.

Legislative elections and the second round of the presidential poll were held on 5 November 1996. Nakamura was re-elected with 62.0% of total votes, defeating Yutaka Gibbons (who had re-entered the contest, following the withdrawal of Toribiong in October). Legislation providing for the establishment of an 'offshore' financial centre in Palau was approved by the Senate (the upper house of the Palau National Congress) in October 1998, despite strong opposition by Nakamura, who believed that the new status might attract criminal organizations seeking to 'launder' the proceeds of their illegal activities and that it might compromise the country's ability to enforce corporate law. In December 1999, following discussions with US government officials, President Nakamura signed an executive order establishing a National Banking Review Commission, with the aim of maintaining a legally-responsible banking environment in Palau: both the Bank of New York and Deutsche Bank (of Germany) had alleged that Palau's 'offshore' banks were facilitating 'money-laundering'. The new body was given wide-ranging powers to examine banking operations in the country and to evaluate current banking regulations.

At the presidential elections held on 7 November 2000, Thomas E. Remengesau, Jr, hitherto the Vice-President of Palau, was elected with 52% of the votes cast, defeating Senator Peter Sugiyama. Sandra Pierantozzi was elected as Vice-President. Remengesau was officially inaugurated on 19 January 2001, pledging to pursue Nakamura's policies of economic expansion and transparency in government. In July 2001 Remengesau introduced a formal resolution proposing the reduction of the legislature to a single chamber, to replace the existing House of Delegates and the Senate, claiming that a unicameral legislature would reduce bureaucracy. He also pro-

posed that, henceforth, the President and Vice-President base their election campaign on a joint common policy, to ensure efficient and cohesive government. However, in spite of pledges to improve transparency, there were several instances of fraudulent use of official funds in 2002–03. In December 2002 the Speaker of the House of Delegates, Mario Gulibert, was arrested on charges relating to the alleged misuse of travel expenses. In February 2003 the former Governor of Ngardmau state, Albert Ngirmekur, was fined and sentenced to six months' imprisonment, following his impeachment on allegations of theft and misuse of public funds. In March, however, the appellate division of the Supreme Court reversed an earlier ruling that had found the Governor of Ngiwal, Elmis Mesubed, along with six state legislators, liable for irregularities relating to their inauguration expenses in 2000.

In mid-1999 a delegation from Solomon Islands visited Palau to discuss the possibility of allowing Solomon Islanders to work in Palau, in an attempt to resolve the latter's severe labour shortage. In August 2001, however, the Government imposed a ban on the hiring of Indian and Sri Lankan workers, citing rising tensions and disputes with local employers which the Government claimed were largely due to religious differences. The ban was to remain in place until legislation to create official recruitment agencies in Palau had been approved. In July 2002 the Senate approved a bill that would amend the islands' immigration law in order to give greater authority over immigration affairs to the President of Palau. (Non-Palauan nationals were estimated to represent about 33% of the islands' population in 2002.) In March 2003 the Government introduced a measure to extend employment permits for foreign workers, which allowed a new maximum extension of two years. In April some 200 Chinese migrant employees of a failed clothing business were stranded on Palau and placed under house arrest. The potential cost of repatriating the migrants was estimated to be some $600,000.

Diplomatic relations were established, at ambassadorial level, with Taiwan in late 1999; the first Taiwanese Ambassador to Palau was formally appointed in April 2000. Reports in December 2000 that the Palau Government was considering establishing diplomatic relations with the People's Republic of China were denied, and President-elect Remengesau reaffirmed Palau's diplomatic ties with Taiwan. In early 2000, meanwhile, Palau and Taiwan signed an agreement pledging to develop bilateral projects in a number of areas, including agriculture, fisheries and tourism.

In October 2001 the Government sought to establish diplomatic relations with Malaysia and Indonesia in an attempt to facilitate the resolution of disputes over overlapping territorial boundaries, amid concern over increasing instances of illegal fishing in Palau waters. (Palau introduced more stringent regulations concerning illegal fishing in May 2002.)

Palau maintains strong diplomatic links with Japan, which was consistently a leading source of tourist revenue throughout the 1980s and 1990s. The Japanese Government provided US $25m. for the construction of the Koror bridge (see above) and was contributing to the construction of a new terminal building at Palau International Airport; work began in February 2002, and was expected to be completed in mid-2003. Construction of an innovative thermal energy generator and deselination plant was scheduled to begin in mid-2003. The project was to be partly funded by the Government of Japan, with technical assistance provided by a Japanese university. The President of Palau met travel and tour operators in Japan in November 2001, in an attempt to promote tourism in Palau. In June 2002 President Remengesau undertook his first state visit to the Republic of Korea, his itinerary incorporating visits to a number of infrastructural development projects.

Government

In October 1994 Palau, the last remaining component of the Trust Territory of the Pacific Islands (a United Nations Trusteeship administered by the USA), achieved independence under the Compact of Free Association. Administrative authority was transferred to the Government of Palau (with the USA retaining responsibility for the islands' defence—see below).

A locally drafted Constitution of the Republic of Palau entered into effect on 1 January 1981. Under the Constitution, executive authority is vested in the President, elected by direct suffrage for a four-year term. Legislative power is exercised by the Olbiil era Kelulau (Palau National Congress), composed of the elected House of Delegates (comprising one Delegate from each of the 16 states of Palau) and the Senate (currently comprising 14 Senators).

Local governmental units are the municipalities and villages. Elected Magistrates and Councils govern the municipalities. Village government is largely traditional.

Defence

The USA is responsible for the defence of Palau, according to the Compact of Free Association implemented in October 1994, and has exclusive military access to its waters, as well as the right to operate two military bases on the islands.

Economic Affairs

In 2001, according to estimates by the World Bank, Palau's gross national income (GNI), measured at average 1999–2001 prices, totalled US $131m., equivalent to $6,730 per head. During 1999–2001, it was estimated, the population increased at an average annual rate of 2.6%, while gross domestic product (GDP) per head decreased, in real terms, by an average of 1.6%. In 1991–2001 overall GDP increased, in real terms, at an average annual rate of 1.3%; growth in 2001 was 1.1%.

Agriculture (including fishing) is mainly on a subsistence level, the principal crops being coconuts, root crops and bananas. Pigs and chickens are kept for domestic consumption. Eggs are produced commercially, and the introduction of cattle-ranching on Babeldaob was under consideration in the late 1990s. The agricultural sector, together with mining, engaged 2.2% of the employed labour force in 2000. In 2001 FAO estimated that agricultural activities employed some 2,000 people. Agriculture and fisheries alone provided an estimated 4.0% of GDP in 2001. Fishing licences are sold to foreign fleets, including those of Taiwan, the USA, Japan and the Philippines. Palau is a signatory of the Multilateral Fisheries Treaty, concluded by the USA and member states of the South Pacific Forum (now Pacific Islands Forum) in 1987. The islands, however, are believed to lose significant amounts of potential revenue through illegal fishing activity. Revenue from the sale of fishing licences totalled US $39,000 in 1999/2000 and an estimated $76,000 in 2000/01, a considerable decline from the total of $230,000 recorded in 1994/95. Fish have traditionally been a leading export, accounting for some $13m. of exports in 1995, but earnings declined to an estimated $7m. in 2001, reportedly owing to adverse weather conditions.

The industrial sector (including mining and quarrying, manufacturing, construction and utilities) provided an estimated 13.0% of GDP in 2001. The only manufacturing activity of any significance is a factory producing garments, which in 1997 employed some 300 (mostly non-resident) workers. In 2000 the manufacturing sector engaged 3.6% of the employed labour force. In 2001 manufacturing accounted for only 1.5% of GDP. Construction is the most important industrial activity, contributing an estimated 8.0% of GDP in 2001 and engaging 11.6% of the employed labour force in 2000. Electrical energy is produced by two power plants at Aimeliik and Malakal.

Service industries dominate Palau's economy, providing an estimated 83.0% of GDP in 2001, and (with utilities) engaging 82.6% of the employed labour force in 2000. The Government is an important employer within the sector, public administration engaging some 33.3% of the total employed labour force in 2000. Tourism is an important source of foreign exchange, directly contributing an estimated 11.1% of GDP in 1998 and employing 9.4% of paid workers in 1995. In 2000/01 a total of 55,595 visitors (of whom 46,684 were tourists) arrived in the islands. Expenditure by tourists totalled an estimated US $54.3m. in 2000/01.

In the year ending September 2001 the visible trade deficit was estimated at US $80.8m. (equivalent to 66% of GDP). The deficit on the current account of the balance of payments totalled $15.7m. The principal sources of imports were the USA (which supplied 39.3% of the total), Guam (14.0%) and Japan (10.2%). The principal imports in 2000/01 were machinery and transport equipment, manufactured goods and food and live animals.

The islands record a persistent budget deficit, which was estimated at almost US $18.5m. in the year ending September 2001. Financial assistance from the USA contributes a large part of the islands' external revenue. Furthermore, upon implementation of the Compact of Free Association with the USA in 1994, Palau became eligible for an initial grant of US $142m. and for annual aid of $23m. over a period of 14 years. Assistance from the USA (including non-Compact funding) totalled $21.0m. in 1999/2000 and an estimated $20.6m. in 2000/01, a respective 28.1% and 33.5% of total budgetary revenue in those years.

Compact funding for 2001/02 was projected at $11.8m. in current grants and $2.0m. in capital grants, while non-Compact funding was budgeted at $11.2m. Palau's external debt totalled $20.0m. in 2000/01. The annual rate of inflation was thought to average between 1% and 3% in the mid-1990s. The inflation rate was about 2.5% in 2000/01, according to the IMF. In 2000 2.3% of the total labour force were unemployed.

Palau is a member of the Pacific Community (see p. 304) and of the Pacific Islands Forum (see p. 306); it is also an associate member of the UN Economic and Social Commission for Asia and the Pacific (ESCAP, see p. 28). In early 1996 Palau joined representatives of the other countries and territories of Micronesia at a meeting in Hawaii, at which a new regional organization, the Council of Micronesian Government Executives, was established. The new body aimed to facilitate discussion of economic developments in the region. In December 2002 Palau requested to join the World Trade Organization (WTO).

A period of recession in the early 1990s (caused largely by reductions in government expenditure in an attempt to offset decreases in revenue) was alleviated by substantial aid payments from the US Government, following the implementation of the Compact of Free Association in 1994, and by the dramatic expansion of tourism in the country. Subsequent policies to reduce the size of the public sector, to encourage the return of Palauans resident overseas and to attract foreign investment aimed to stimulate economic growth. Particularly strong commercial ties were forged with Taiwan during the mid-1990s, and it was hoped that the establishment of diplomatic relations at ambassadorial level between Palau and Taiwan in late 1999 would further develop bilateral economic co-operation. Trade between Palau and the Philippines was expected to increase significantly, following the signing of an agreement between the two countries in early 1998. Tourism is expected to remain essential to Palau's economic growth upon the cessation of US aid in 2009. The Government announced plans in 1998 for further expansion of the industry, which had declined in the late 1990s following the Asian financial crisis, and expressed particular interest in developing the country's potential as a destination for visitors of above-average wealth. However, an IMF report in 2002 claimed that the country's investment laws, which prohibit foreign ownership of land or businesses, contributed to a lack of transparency in financial dealings, and cautioned that the increase in tourism infrastructure projects posed a risk to the country's trade balance. A new road along the coastline of Babeldaob was none the less widely expected to increase long-term tourism revenues upon its scheduled completion in late 2003. (A new official capital was also under construction on the island.) In December 2001 the Government announced plans to develop a new regional airline to serve Palau and neighbouring Micronesian countries, which was due to begin operations in mid-2003. Meanwhile, following allegations that Palau's offshore banking system was being used for the purposes of 'money-laundering' (see Recent History), various new banking laws were approved, in an effort to restore the confidence of the international financial community. Although a number of concerns were raised by the Financial Action Task Force on Money Laundering (FATF, see p. 343), Palau was not included on the FATF's list of non-co-operative countries and territories. In June 2002 the legislature approved new measures to regulate the financial sector, which included the creation of a Financial Institutions Commission.

Education

Education is compulsory for children between the ages of six and 14 years. In 1990 there were 22 public elementary schools in Palau, with 2,125 pupils (there were also 369 pupils attending private elementary schools). After eight years of compulsory elementary education, a pupil may enrol in the government-operated high school or one of the five private (church-affiliated) high schools. In 1990 there were 610 students at the government high school, and in 1989 there were 445 at private high schools. The Micronesian Occupational College, based in Palau, provides two-year training programmes. Government spending on education in 1999/2000 totalled US $9.1m., equivalent to 10.7% of total budgetary expenditure.

Public Holidays

2003: 1 January (New Year's Day), 15 March (Youth Day), 5 May (Senior Citizens' Day), 1 June (President's Day), 9 July (Constitution Day), 1 September (Labor Day), 1 October (Independence Day), 24 October (United Nations Day), 27 November (Thanksgiving), 25 December (Christmas).

2004: 1 January (New Year's Day), 15 March (Youth Day), 5 May (Senior Citizens' Day), 1 June (President's Day), 9 July (Constitution Day), 6 September (Labor Day), 1 October (Independence Day), 24 October (United Nations Day), 25 November (Thanksgiving), 25 December (Christmas).

Weights and Measures

With certain exceptions, the imperial system is in force. One US cwt equals 100 lb; one long ton equals 2,240 lb; one short ton equals 2,000 lb. A policy of gradual voluntary conversion to the metric system is being undertaken.

Statistical Survey

AREA AND POPULATION

Area: 508 sq km (196 sq miles); Babeldaob island 409 sq km (158 sq miles).

Population: 17,225 (males 9,213, females 8,012) at census of 9 November 1995; 19,129 at census of 1 April 2000.

Density (2000): 37.7 per sq km (97.6 per sq mile).

Births and Deaths (2000, estimates): Birth rate 14.5 per 1,000; Death rate 6.5 per 1,000. Source: 2000 Census of Population and Housing, Office of Planning and Statistics, Palau.

Expectation of Life (WHO estimates, years at birth): 68.6 (males 66.9; females 70.5) in 2001. Source: WHO, *World Health Report.*

Economically Active Population (2000): Agriculture, fishing and mining 215; Construction 1,112; Manufacturing 345; Transport, communications and utilities 765; Trade, hotels and restaurants 2,619; Finance, insurance and real estate 116; Public administration 3,203; Other services 1,246; Total employed 9,621; Unemployed 224; Total labour force 9,845. Source: IMF, *Republic of Palau: Recent Economic Developments* (March 2002).

HEALTH AND WELFARE

Key Indicators

Total Fertility Rate (children per woman, 2001): 2.8.

Under-5 Mortality Rate (per 1,000 live births, 2001): 29.

Physicians (per 1,000 head, 1998): 1.10.

Health Expenditure (2000): US $ per head (PPP): 482.

Health Expenditure (2000): % of GDP: 6.4.

Health Expenditure (2000): public (% of total): 88.5.

Access to Water (% of persons, 2000): 79.

Access to Sanitation (% of persons, 2000): 100.
For sources and definitions, see explanatory note on p. vi.

AGRICULTURE, ETC.

Principal Crops, Livestock and Livestock Products: see Chapter on the Federated States of Micronesia.

Fishing (FAO estimates, metric tons, live weight, 1999): Total catch 2,000 (Marine fishes 1,330). Source: FAO, *Yearbook of Fishery Statistics.*

INDUSTRY

Production (estimate, 1997): Electric energy 208 million kWh. Source: UN, *Statistical Yearbook for Asia and the Pacific.*

FINANCE

Currency and Exchange Rates: United States currency is used: 100 cents = 1 United States dollar (US $). *Sterling and Euro Equivalents* (31 December 2002): £1 sterling = US $1.6118; €1 = US $1.05; US $100 = £62.04 = €95.36.

Budget (estimates, US $'000, year ending Sept. 2001): *Revenue:* Domestic revenue 40,186 (Tax 25,762; Other current revenues 5,907; Local trust fund 1,806; Investment income 6,711); Grants 21,307 (Compact funds 19,128); Total 61,493. *Expenditure:* Current expenditure 63,080 (Wages and salaries 29,863; Purchase of goods and services 25,360; Subsidies and other transfers 7,157); Capital expenditure 14,122; Total 77,202. Note: Figures exclude net errors and omissions (US $ '000): –2,770. Source: IMF, *Republic of Palau: Recent Economic Developments* (March 2002).

Gross Domestic Product by Economic Activity (US $'000 at current prices, 2001, estimates): Agriculture 1,399; Fishing 3,388; Mining and quarrying 245; Manufacturing 1,808; Electricity, gas and water 3,863; Construction 9,621; Trade 25,175; Hotels and restaurants 12,082; Transport and communications 11,272; Finance and insurance 4,828; Real estate and business services 5,108; Public administration 30,816; Other services 10,260; Sub-total 119,867; Import duties 3,842; *Less* Imputed bank service charges 1,250; GDP in purchasers' values 122,459. Source: IMF, *Republic of Palau: Recent Economic Developments* (March 2002).

Balance of Payments (estimates, US $'000, year ending Sept. 2001): Exports of goods f.o.b. 18,267; Imports of goods f.o.b. –99,104; *Trade balance* –80,837; Exports of services 54,307; Imports of services –21,551; *Balance on goods and services* –48,081; Other income (net) 14,028; *Balance on goods, services and income* –34,053; Private current transfers (net) –1,899; Official current transfers (net) 20,267; *Current balance* –15,685; Capital grants received 5,144; Private direct investment 1,000; Net errors and omissions –8,938; *Overall balance* –18,479. Source: IMF, *Article IV Consultation with the Republic of Palau: Staff Report* (March 2002).

EXTERNAL TRADE

Principal Commodities (US $'000, 2000/01): *Imports f.o.b.*: Food and live animals 14,534; Beverages and tobacco 7,954; Mineral fuels, lubricants etc. 9,930; Chemicals 7,134; Basic manufactures 18,203; Machinery and transport equipment 23,179; Miscellaneous manufactured articles 12,744; Total (incl. others) 95,765. *Exports (1996)*: 14,300 (including trochus, tuna, copra and handicrafts). Source: mainly IMF, *Republic of Palau: Recent Economic Developments* (March 2002).

Principal Trading Partners (US $'000, 2000/01): *Imports*: Australia 1,047; China, People's Republic 2,546; Guam 13,379; Hong Kong 3,484; Japan 9,814; Korea, Republic 6,155; Philippines 2,617; Singapore 7,343; Taiwan 5,091; USA 37,611; Total (incl. others) 95,765. *Exports*: Total 18,267. Source: IMF, *Republic of Palau: Recent Economic Developments* (March 2002).

TRANSPORT

International Shipping (1995): *Ship Arrivals*: 280. *Freight Traffic* (metric tons): Goods unloaded 64,034.

TOURISM

Tourist Arrivals: 56,466 in 1998/99; 56,502 in 1999/2000; 55,595 in 2000/01.

Tourist Arrivals by Country of Residence (2000/01): Japan 23,303, Philippines 4,164, Taiwan 14,077, USA 8,456.
Source: IMF, *Republic of Palau: Recent Economic Developments* (March 2002).

COMMUNICATIONS MEDIA

Radio Receivers (1997): 12,000 in use.

Television Receivers (1997): 11,000 in use.

EDUCATION

Elementary (1990): 22 government schools; 172 teachers (1998); 2,125 pupils at government schools; 369 pupils at private schools.

Secondary (1990): 1 government school; 5 private (church-affiliated) schools; 60 teachers (1998); 610 pupils at government schools; 445 pupils at private schools (1989).

Tertiary (1986): 305 students.

2001/02: 20 government schools (19 elementary; 1 secondary) with 3,145 pupils.

Directory

The Constitution

In October 1994 Palau, the last remaining component of the Trust Territory of the Pacific Islands (a United Nations Trusteeship administered by the USA), achieved independence under the Compact of Free Association. Full responsibility for defence lies with the USA, which undertakes to provide regular economic assistance.

From 1986 the three polities of the Commonwealth of the Northern Mariana Islands, the Republic of the Marshall Islands and the Federated States of Micronesia ceased, *de facto*, to be part of the Trust Territory. In December 1990 the United Nations Security Council agreed formally to terminate the Trusteeship Agreement for all the territories except Palau. The agreement with Palau was finally terminated in October 1994.

The islands became known as the Republic of Palau when the locally-drafted Constitution came into effect on 1 January 1981. The Constitution provides for a democratic form of government, with executive authority vested in the directly-elected President and Vice-President. Presidential elections are held every four years. Legislative power is exercised by the Olbiil era Kelulau, the Palau National Congress, which is an elected body consisting of the Senate and the House of Delegates. The Senators represent geographical districts, determined by an independent reapportionment commission every eight years, according to population. There are currently 14 Senators (four from the northern part of Palau, nine from Koror and one from the southern islands). There are 16 Delegates, one elected to represent each of the 16 states of the Republic. The states are: Kayangel, Ngerchelong, Ngaraard, Ngardmau, Ngaremlengui, Ngiwal, Melekeok, Ngchesar, Ngatpang, Aimeliik, Airai, Koror, Peleliu, Angaur, Sonsorol and Tobi. Each state elects its own Governor and legislature.

The Government

HEAD OF STATE

President: THOMAS E. REMENGESAU, Jr (took office 19 January 2001).
Vice-President: SANDRA S. PIERANTOZZI.

THE CABINET
(April 2003)

Vice-President and Minister of Health: SANDRA S. PIERANTOZZI.

Minister of Commerce and Trade: OTOICHI BESEBES.

Minister of Resources and Development: FRITZ KOSHIBA.

Minister of Education: MARIO KATOSANG.

Minister of Justice: MICHAEL ROSENTHAL.

Minister of Community and Cultural Affairs: ALEXANDER R. MEREP.

Minister of State: TEMMY L. SHMULL.

Minister of Administration: ELBUCHEL SADANG.

COUNCIL OF CHIEFS

The Constitution provides for an advisory body for the President, comprising the 16 highest traditional chiefs from the 16 states. The chiefs advise on all traditional laws and customs, and on any other public matter in which their participation is required.

Chairman: Ibedul YUTAKA GIBBONS (Koror).

GOVERNMENT OFFICES AND MINISTRIES

Office of the President: POB 100, Koror, PW 96940; tel. 488-2403; fax 488-1662; e-mail roppresoffice@palaunet.com.

Department of the Interior, Office of Insular Affairs (OIA): OIA Field Office, POB 6031, Koror, PW 96940; tel. 488-2655; fax 488-2649; Field Rep. J. VICTOR HOBSON, Jr.

Ministry of Commerce and Trade: POB 1471, Koror, PW 96940; tel. 488-4343; fax 488-3207.

Ministry of Health: POB 6027, Koror, PW 96940; tel. 488-5552; fax 488-1211; e-mail healthminister@palaunet.com.

Ministry of Resources and Development: POB 100, Koror, PW 96940; tel. 488-2701; fax 488-3380; e-mail mrd@palaunet.com.

All national government offices are based in Koror. Each state has its own administrative headquarters.

President and Legislature

PRESIDENT

At the presidential election held on 7 November 2000, Thomas E. Remengesau, Jr, who won 52% of the votes cast, narrowly defeated Sen. Peter Sugiyama.

OLBIIL ERA KELULAU
(Palau National Congress)

President of the Senate: SEIT ANDRES.

Vice-President of the Senate: HARRY R. FRITZ.

Speaker of the House of Delegates: (vacant).

Political Organizations

Palau Nationalist Party: c/o Olbiil era Kelulau, Koror, PW 96940; Leader JOHNSON TORIBIONG.

Ta Belau Party: c/o Olbiil era Kelulau, Koror, PW 96940; Leader KUNIWO NAKAMURA.

Diplomatic Representation

EMBASSIES IN PALAU

China (Taiwan): POB 9087, Koror, PW 96940; tel. 488-8150; fax 488-8151; Ambassador CLARK K. H. CHEN.

USA: POB 6028, Koror, PW 96940; tel. 488-2920; fax 488-2911; e-mail usembassykoror@palaunet.com; Chargé d'affaires RONALD A. HARMS.

Judicial System

The judicial system of the Republic of Palau consists of the Supreme Court (including Trial and Appellate Divisions), presided over by the Chief Justice, the National Court (inactive), the Court of Common Pleas and the Land Court.

Supreme Court of the Republic of Palau: POB 248, Koror, PW 96940; tel. 488-2482; fax 488-1597; e-mail a.ngiraklsong@palaunet .com; Chief Justice ARTHUR NGIRAKLSONG.

Religion

The population is predominantly Christian, mainly Roman Catholic. The Assembly of God, Baptists, Seventh-day Adventists, the Church of Jesus Christ of Latter-day Saints (Mormons), and the Bahá'í and Modignai (or Modeknai) faiths are also represented.

CHRISTIANITY

The Roman Catholic Church

Palau forms part of the diocese of the Caroline Islands, suffragan to the archdiocese of Agaña (Guam). The Bishop, who is resident in Chuuk, Eastern Caroline Islands (see Federated States of Micronesia), participates in the Catholic Bishops' Conference of the Pacific, based in Suva, Fiji.

MODIGNAI FAITH

Modignai Church: Koror, PW 96940; an indigenous, non-Christian religion; also operates a high school.

The Press

Palau Gazette: POB 100, Koror, PW 96940; tel. 488-3257; fax 488-1662; e-mail roppresoffice@palaunet.com; newsletter publ. by Govt; monthly.

Palau Horizon: POB 487, Koror, PW 96940; tel. 488-4588; fax 488-4565; weekly; Man. ABED E. YOUNIS; circ. 2,500.

Tia Belau (This is Palau): POB 569, Koror, PW 96940; tel. 488-1461; fax 488-1725; f. 1992; fortnightly; English and Palauan; Publr MOSES ULUDONG.

Broadcasting and Communications

BROADCASTING

Radio

Palau National Communications Corpn (PNCC): Bureau of Domestic Affairs, POB 279, Koror, PW 96940; tel. 587-9000; fax 587-1888; e-mail pncc@palaunet.com; internet www.palaunet.com; f. 1982; mem. of the Pacific Islands Broadcasting Asscn; operates station WSZB; broadcasts American, Japanese and Micronesian music; 18 hrs daily; Gen. Man. ED CARTER.

WSZB Broadcasting Station: POB 279, Koror, PW 96940; tel. 488-2417; fax 488-1932; Station Man. ALBERT SALUSTIANO.

KHBN: POB 66, Koror, PW 96940; tel. 488-2162; fax 488-2163; e-mail hamadmin@palaunet.com; f. 1992; broadcasts religious material; CEO JACKIE MITCHUM YOCKEY.

Television

STV-TV Koror: POB 2000, Koror, PW 96940; tel. 488-1357; fax 488-1207; broadcasts 12 hrs daily; Man. DAVID NOLAN; Technical Man. RAY OMELEN.

Island Cable Television, Inc: POB 39, Koror, PW 96940; tel. 488-1490; fax 488-1499; owned by the United Micronesian Development Asscn and Palau National Communications Corpn.

Finance

(cap. = capital; res = reserves; amounts in US dollars)

BANKING

Bank of Guam: POB 338, Koror, PW 96940; tel. 488-2697; fax 488-1384.

Bank of Hawaii (USA): POB 340, Koror, PW 96940; tel. 488-2428; fax 488-2427; Man. JOAN DEMEI.

Bank Pacific: POB 1000, Koror, PW 96940; tel. 488-5635; fax 488-4752.

Melekeok Government Bank: POB 1711, Koror, PW 96940; tel. 488-2066; fax 488-2065; e-mail mgbank@palaunet.com.

National Development Bank of Palau: POB 816, Koror, PW 96940–0816; tel. 488-2578; fax 488-2579; e-mail ndbp@palaunet .com; f. 1982; cap. and res 11.5m. (Sept. 2002); Pres. TUKANA A. BOVORO.

Pacific Savings Bank: POB 399, Koror, PW 96940; tel. 488-1859; fax 488-1858; e-mail bank@palaunet.com; internet pnccwg.palaunet .com/bank/index.htm.

In 1990 there were also 22 registered credit unions, with 1,025 members, but they were severely affected by the financial crisis in Palau.

INSURANCE

NECO Insurance Underwriters Ltd: POB 129, Koror, PW 96940; tel. 488-2325; fax 488-2880; e-mail necogroup@palaunet.com.

Poltalia National Insurance: POB 12, Koror, PW 96940; tel. 488-2254; e-mail psata@palaunet.com.

Trade and Industry

CHAMBER OF COMMERCE

Palau Chamber of Commerce: POB 1742, Koror, PW 96940; tel. 488-3400; fax 488-3401; e-mail pcoc@palaunet.com; f. 1984; Pres. (vacant).

CO-OPERATIVES

These include the Palau Fishermen's Co-operative, Palau Boat-builders' Asscn, Palau Handicraft and Woodworkers' Guild. In 1990, of the 13 registered co-operatives, eight were fishermen's co-operatives, three consumers' co-operatives (only two in normal operation) and two farmers' co-operatives (one in normal operation).

Transport

ROADS

Macadam and concrete roads are found in the more important islands. Other islands have stone and coral-surfaced roads and tracks. The Government is responsible for 36 km (22 miles) of paved roads and 25 km (15 miles) of coral- and gravel-surfaced roads. Most paved roads are located on Koror and are in a poor state of repair. A major project to construct a new 85-km (53-mile) road around Babeldaob began in 1999 and is scheduled for completion in late 2003. The project is being funded with US $150m. from the Compact of Free Association.

SHIPPING

Most shipping in Palau is government-organized. However, the Micronesia Transport Line operates a service from Sydney (Australia) to Palau. A twice-weekly inter-island service operates between Koror and Peleliu. There is one commercial port at Malakal Harbor, which is operated by the privately-owned Belau Transfer and Terminal Company.

CIVIL AVIATION

There is an international airport in the south of Babeldaob island, in Airai state, near Koror. With Japanese assistance, work began on a new terminal building in February 2002. Construction was scheduled for completion in 2003. Domestic airfields (former Japanese military airstrips) are located on Angaur and Peleliu. Continental Micronesia (Northern Mariana Islands and Guam) provides daily flights to Koror from Guam, and twice-weekly flights from Manila (Philippines). Cebu Pacific operates direct flights from Davao (Philippines) to Koror. A civil aviation agreement between Palau and Taiwan was signed in 1997, and direct charter flights between the two countries began in the following year, operated by the Far Eastern Air Transport Corpn. There is one domestic carrier.

Palau Paradise Air, Inc: POB 488, Palau Int. Airport, Airai State, Babeldaob, PW 96940; tel. and fax 488-2348; internal services between Koror, Peleliu and Angaur.

Rock Island Airlines: managed by Aloha Airlines (Hawaii).

Tourism

Tourism is becoming increasingly important in Palau, and plans for a major expansion of the industry were announced in 1998. The islands are particularly rich in their marine environment, and the Government has taken steps to conserve and protect these natural resources. The myriad Rock Islands, now known as the Floating Garden Islands, are a noted reserve in the lagoon to the west of the main group of islands. There were 1,200 hotel rooms in 1998, and a further 558 hotel rooms were expected to be opened by 2001. In 2000/01 there were 55,595 visitor arrivals, of whom 41.9% were from Japan, 25.3% from Taiwan, 15.2% from the USA and 7.5% from the Philippines. Tourist expenditure rose from US $53.2m. in 1999/2000 to $54.3m. in 2000/01.

Belau Tourism Association: POB 9032, Koror, PW 96940; tel. 488-4377; fax 488-1725; e-mail bta@palaunet.com.

Palau Visitors' Authority: POB 256, Koror, PW 96940; tel. 488-2793; fax 488-1453; e-mail pva@palaunet.com; internet www .visit-palau.com; Man. Dir MARY ANN DELEMEL.

PALESTINIAN AUTONOMOUS AREAS

Introductory Survey

Location, Climate, Language, Religion, Flag, Capital

The Palestinian Autonomous Areas are located in the West Bank and the Gaza Strip. (For a more detailed description of the location of the Palestinian territories, see Government, below.) The West Bank lies in western Asia, to the west of the Jordan river and the Dead Sea. To the north and south is the State of Israel, to the west Israel and the Gaza Strip. The Interim Agreement of September 1995 (see below) provides for the creation of a corridor, or safe passage, linking the Gaza Strip with the West Bank. A 'southern' safe passage between Hebron and Gaza was opened in October 1999 (although it has been closed since October 2000). Including East Jerusalem, the West Bank covers an area of 5,655 sq km. Precipitation ranges between 600 mm and 800 mm on the Mount Hebron massif and 200 mm in the Jordan valley. Apart from the urban centres of Beit Lahm (Bethlehem) and Al-Khalil (Hebron) to the south, the majority of the Palestinian population is concentrated in the northern localities around Ram Allah (Ramallah), Nabulus (Nablus), Janin (Jenin) and Tulkarm. The Gaza Strip, lying beside the Mediterranean Sea and Israel's border with Egypt, covers an area of 365 sq km. Annual average rainfall is 300 mm. The language of Palestinians in the West Bank and Gaza is Arabic. The majority of the Palestinian population are Muslims, with a Christian minority representing about 2% of the Palestinian population of the territories. This minority, in turn, represents about 45% of all Palestinian Christians. The national flag (proportion 1 by 2) comprises three equal horizontal stripes of black, white and green, with a red triangle with its base corresponding to the hoist. Gaza City is the main population centre and the centre of administration for the Palestinian (National) Authority (PA), appointed in May 1994. Ramallah is the PA's administrative centre in the West Bank. In November 1988 the Palestine National Council (PNC) proclaimed Jerusalem as the capital of the newly-declared independent State of Palestine. Israel (q.v.) declares Jerusalem as its capital. In 1967 East Jerusalem was formally annexed by the Israeli authorities, although the annexation has never been recognized by the UN. The permanent status of Jerusalem remains subject to negotiation on so-called 'final status' issues under the Oslo accords (detailed in the Recent History, below).

Recent History

Until the end of the 1948 Arab–Israeli War, the West Bank formed part of the British Mandate of Palestine, before becoming part of the Hashemite Kingdom of Jordan under the Armistice Agreement of 1949. It remained under Jordanian sovereignty, despite Israeli occupation in 1967, until King Hussein of Jordan formally relinquished legal and administrative control on 31 July 1988. Under Israeli military occupation the West Bank was administered by a military government, which divided the territory into seven sub-districts. The Civil Administration, as it was later termed, did not extend its jurisdiction to the many Israeli settlements that were established under the Israeli occupation; settlements remained subject to the Israeli legal and administrative system. By October 2000 approximately 17.2% of the West Bank was under exclusive Palestinian jurisdiction and security control, although Israel retained authority over access to and from the zone; about 23.8% was under Israeli military control, with responsibility for civil administration and public order transferred to the PA; the remaining 59% was under Israeli occupation.

An administrative province under the British Mandate of Palestine, Gaza was transferred to Egypt after the 1949 armistice and remained under Egyptian administration until June 1967, when it was invaded by Israel. Following Israeli occupation the Gaza Strip, like the West Bank, became an 'administered territory'. Until the provisions of the Declaration of Principles on Palestinian Self-Rule (see below) began to take effect, the management of day-to-day affairs was the responsibility of the area's Israeli military commander. Neither Israeli laws nor governmental and public bodies—including the Supreme Court —could review or alter the orders of the military command to any great extent. In 2001 an estimated 42% of the Gaza Strip was under Israeli control, including Jewish settlements, military bases, bypass roads and a 'buffer zone' along the border with Israel.

In accordance with the Declaration of Principles on Palestinian Self-Rule of 13 September 1993, and the Cairo Agreement on the Gaza Strip and Jericho of 4 May 1994, the Palestine Liberation Organization (PLO) assumed control of the Jericho area of the West Bank, and of the Gaza Strip, on 17 May 1994. In November and December 1995, under the terms of the Israeli-Palestinian Interim Agreement on the West Bank and the Gaza Strip concluded on 28 September 1995, Israeli armed forces withdrew from the West Bank towns of Nablus, Ramallah, Jenin, Tulkarm, Qalqilya and Bethlehem. (These three agreements and associated accords are referred to collectively as the Oslo accords, owing to the role played by Norwegian diplomacy in their negotiation.) In late December the PLO assumed responsibility in some 17 areas of civil administration in the town of Hebron. Under the terms of the Oslo accords, the PLO was eventually to assume full responsibility for civil affairs in the 400 surrounding villages, but Israeli armed forces were to retain freedom of movement to act against potential hostilities there. In Hebron Israel effected a partial withdrawal of its armed forces in January 1997, but retained responsibility for the security of some 400 Jewish settlers. Responsibility for security in the rest of Hebron (excluding access roads) passed to the Palestinian police force. Israel was to retain control over a large area of the West Bank (including Jewish settlements, rural areas, military installations and the majority of junctions between Palestinian roads and those used by Israeli troops and settlers) until July 1997. Following the first phase of the redeployment and the holding, on its completion, of elections to a Palestinian Legislative Council and for a Palestinian executive president, Israel was to have completed a second redeployment from rural areas by that month. The Israeli occupation was to be maintained in military installations, Jewish settlements, East Jerusalem and the settlements around Jerusalem until the conclusion of 'final status' negotiations between Israel and the Palestinians, scheduled for May 1999.

Subsequent postponements, and further negotiations within the context of the Oslo peace process, resulted in a new timetable for Israeli redeployment which envisaged two phases, subsequent to the Hebron withdrawal, to be completed by October 1997 and August 1998. Discussions on 'final status' issues—borders, Jerusalem, Jewish settlements and Palestinian refugees—were to commence within two months of the signing of the agreement on Hebron. As guarantor of the Oslo accords, the USA undertook to obtain the release from Israeli custody of Palestinian prisoners, and to ensure that Israel continued to engage in negotiations for the establishment of a Palestinian airport in the Gaza Strip and for safe passage for Palestinians between the West Bank and Gaza. The USA also undertook to ensure that the Palestinians would continue to combat terrorism, complete the revision of the Palestinian National Charter (or PLO Covenant), adopted in 1964 and amended in 1968, and consider Israeli requests to extradite Palestinians suspected of involvement in attacks in Israel.

Meanwhile, progress on redeployment entered a period of paralysis, emerging from the decision of the Israeli Government of Binyamin Netanyahu, announced in February 1997, to begin construction of a new Jewish settlement at Jabal Abu Ghunaim (Har Homa, in Hebrew), near Beit Sahur, which, if completed, would make it impossible to reach East Jerusalem from the West Bank without crossing Israeli territory, thereby prejudicing 'final status' negotiations concerning Jerusalem. In response, the PA withdrew from 'final status' talks scheduled to commence in March. The start of construction work at Jabal Abu Ghunaim provoked rioting among Palestinians and a resumption of attacks by the military wing of the Islamic Resistance Movement (Hamas) on Israeli civilian targets. Israel responded by ordering a general closure of the West Bank and Gaza. Both the Jabal Abu Ghunaim construction and Israel's unilateral decision to redeploy its armed forces from only 9% of West Bank territory (announced in March 1997) were regarded by many observers as a vitiation of both the Oslo and the subsequent post-Hebron agreements. These were further undermined by the publication, in the Israeli daily *Ha'aretz*, of the results of a US study asserting that more than 25% of Jewish settlers' homes in Gaza and the West Bank were uninhabited (the Israeli Central Bureau of Statistics stated that only 12% were unoccupied). *Ha'aretz* later reported that Israeli plans, evolved within the framework of the Oslo accords, to relinquish 90% of the West Bank had been revised to a 40% redeployment.

In June 1997 the US House of Representatives voted in favour of recognizing Jerusalem as the undivided capital of Israel and of transferring the US embassy to the city from Tel-Aviv. The vote (which was opposed by US President Bill Clinton) coincided with violent clashes between Palestinian civilians and Israeli troops in Gaza and Hebron. In July, following a series of meetings conducted by the US Department of State with representatives of the Israeli Government and the PA, it was announced that peace talks would resume in early August. At the end of July, however, on the eve of a scheduled visit by Dennis Ross, the US Special Co-ordinator to the Middle East, to reactivate the negotiations, Hamas carried out a 'suicide bomb' attack at a Jewish market in Jerusalem, in which 14 civilians were killed and more than 150 injured. Ross cancelled his visit and the Israeli Government immediately halted payment of tax revenues to the PA and closed the Gaza Strip and the West Bank. In the aftermath of the bombing the PA undertook a campaign to detain members of Hamas and another militant organization, Islamic Jihad. The closure of the Palestinian territories was briefly relaxed at the beginning of September, in anticipation of a visit to the region by the US Secretary of State, Madeleine Albright, but a further Hamas suicide bombing in Jerusalem, in which eight people died, led to the reimposition of Israeli sanctions shortly afterwards. During her visit, Albright reportedly asked Israel to halt the construction of Jewish settlements on Arab lands, cease confiscations of land and the demolition of Arab dwellings, and end its policy of confiscating Palestinian identity documents, while endorsing Israeli Prime Minister Netanyahu's demand that the PA take more effective measures to suppress militant Islamist groups. The Secretary of State was critical of Netanyahu's decision, announced in late September, to permit the construction of 300 Jewish homes in Efrat in the West Bank. None the less, it was announced at the end of the month that, as a result of US diplomacy, Israeli and Palestinian officials had agreed to resume negotiations in early October. The first round of talks was to focus on the outstanding issues of the Oslo accords, in particular the opening of an airport and seaport facilities in the Gaza Strip, the establishment of a safe corridor linking Gaza with the West Bank, and the release of Palestinian prisoners from Israeli detention. A second round of discussions, in mid-October, would address security co-operation between the PA and Israel, the long-delayed redeployment of Israeli armed forces from the West Bank, Israeli settlement expansion, and questions pertaining to 'final status' negotiations. On the day after the talks resumed, Arafat and Netanyahu held their first meeting for eight months.

Meanwhile, the attempted assassination in Amman, Jordan, in late September 1997, of Khalid Meshaal, the head of the Hamas political bureau there, provoked warnings of retaliation against Israel, even before official confirmation that agents of the Israeli security service, Mossad, had been responsible for the attack. In order to secure the release of its agents by the Jordanian authorities, Israel was obliged, at the beginning of October, to free a number of Arab political prisoners, most notably Sheikh Ahmad Yassin, the founder and spiritual leader of Hamas, who had been sentenced to life imprisonment in Israel in 1989 for complicity in attacks on Israeli soldiers. The release of Sheikh Yassin into Jordanian custody was swiftly followed by his return, on 6 October 1997, to Gaza.

In December 1997, under further US pressure, it was reported that the Israeli Cabinet had agreed in principle to withdraw troops from an unspecified area of the West Bank. In January 1998 US Special Co-ordinator Dennis Ross visited Israel in a further attempt to break the deadlock regarding redeployment. However, the Israeli Government subsequently reiterated that it would not conduct such a redeployment until the Palestinian leadership had fulfilled a series of conditions: these included the adoption of effective measures to counter terrorism, a reduction in the strength of its security forces from 40,000 to 24,000, and a revision of the Palestinian National Charter to recognize explicitly Israel's right to exist. Moreover, prior to a summit meeting that month between Clinton and Netanyahu in Wash-

ington, DC, the Israeli Cabinet issued a communiqué detailing 'vital and national interests' in the West Bank (amounting to some 60% of the entire territory) that it was not prepared to relinquish; the document asserted that Israel would, among other areas, retain control of the territory surrounding Jerusalem. At the talks the USA was reportedly seeking to persuade Israel to effect a second withdrawal of its armed forces from some 12% of the West Bank over a period of 80 days, in exchange for the PA's increased co-operation on security issues. In late January, however, direct contacts between Palestinian representatives and the Israeli Prime Minister collapsed.

In late March 1998 it emerged that the USA planned to present new proposals regarding the withdrawal of Israeli armed forces at separate meetings in Europe between the US Secretary of State and the PA President and Israeli Prime Minister. Although no details had been published, the USA was apparently proposing an Israeli withdrawal from slightly more than 13% of West Bank territory and a suspension of settlement construction, in return for further efforts by the PA to combat Palestinian organizations engaged in campaigns of violence against Israeli targets. Arafat sought an Israeli withdrawal from a further 30% of the West Bank, although there were indications that he might be prepared to accept an initial redeployment from some 13%. It was evident that, even if agreement could be reached on the extent of territory involved, the issue of whether a subsequent withdrawal should take place prior to the commencement of 'final status' talks remained far more contentious. The Israeli Cabinet rejected the new US initiative. At the end of March Madeleine Albright stated that the peace process was on the verge of collapse, and indicated that the USA was considering ending its involvement as a mediator. A month later it emerged that, during a visit to Gaza City on behalf of the European Union (EU), the British Prime Minister, Tony Blair, had persuaded Arafat to attend a conference in London, based on the most recent US initiative. Accordingly, in early May Blair hosted a summit meeting attended by Netanyahu, Arafat and Albright. At its conclusion the US Secretary of State invited Netanyahu and Arafat to attend a summit meeting with Bill Clinton in Washington, DC, to discuss the apparent US proposal that Israeli and Palestinian officials could proceed to 'final status' negotiations as soon as the scope of the next Israeli withdrawal from the West Bank had been agreed. However, the Israeli Government rejected the US initiative in advance of Clinton's direct participation. In June details of the latest US initiative were unofficially disclosed in the Israeli press: Israel would be required to agree to 'no significant expansion' of Jewish settlements and to relinquish slightly more than 13% of West Bank territory over a period of 12 weeks, in exchange for increased Palestinian co-operation. The adoption by the Israeli Cabinet later that month of a plan to extend the boundaries of Jerusalem and construct homes there for a further 1m. people prompted accusations by the PA that it amounted to a *de facto* annexation of territories that were officially subject to 'final status' discussions.

On 7 July 1998 the UN General Assembly overwhelmingly approved a resolution to upgrade the status of the PLO at the UN. The new provision, which the USA and Israel had opposed, allowed the PLO to participate in debates, to co-sponsor resolutions, and to raise points of order during discussions of Middle East affairs.

On 19–22 July 1998 Israeli and Palestinian delegations held direct negotiations for the first time since March 1997, in order to discuss the US peace initiative disclosed in June; however, the proposal was deemed unacceptable by Israel. In August 1998 Netanyahu was reported to have presented a compromise plan to his Cabinet whereby Israel would effect a full redeployment from a further 10% of the West Bank and a partial withdrawal from 3% of the Judaean desert. Arafat gave a cautious welcome to the plan. In late September Netanyahu and Arafat met for the first time since October 1997, in Washington, DC, and agreed to participate in a peace conference in the USA in the following month. The summit meeting, also attended by President Clinton, commenced at the Wye Plantation, Maryland, USA, on 15 October 1998, and culminated in the signing, on 23 October, of the Wye River Memorandum, which was intended to facilitate the implementation of the Oslo accords.

Under the terms of the Wye Memorandum, which was to be implemented within three months of its signing, Israel was to transfer a further 13.1% of West Bank territory from exclusive Israeli control to joint Israeli-Palestinian control. An additional 14% of the West Bank was to be transferred from joint Israeli-

Palestinian control to exclusive Palestinian control. The Wye Memorandum also stipulated that negotiations with regard to a third Israeli redeployment (under the terms of the Oslo accords) should proceed concurrently with 'final status' discussions; that the PA should reinforce anti-terrorism measures under the supervision of the US Central Intelligence Agency (CIA) and arrest 30 suspected terrorists; that the strength of the Palestinian police force should be reduced by 25%; that Israel should carry out the phased release of 750 Palestinian prisoners (including political detainees); that the Palestine National Council (PNC) should annul those clauses of the PLO Covenant deemed to be anti-Israeli; that Gaza International Airport was to become operational with an Israeli security presence; and that an access corridor between the West Bank and the Gaza Strip should be opened. The Memorandum was endorsed by the Israeli Cabinet on 11 November 1998 and approved by the Knesset on 17 November. Three days later Israel redeployed its armed forces from about 500 sq km of the West Bank. Of this area, some 400 sq km came under exclusive Palestinian control for both civil and security affairs. In the remaining 100 sq km the PA assumed responsibility for civil affairs, while Israel retained control over security. At the same time, Israel released some 250 Palestinian prisoners (although a majority were non-political detainees) and signed a protocol for the opening of Gaza International Airport: Israel retained the right to decide which airlines could use the airport, which was officially inaugurated by Arafat on 24 November.

However, implementation of the Wye Memorandum did not proceed smoothly. In the weeks prior to a visit by Bill Clinton to Israel and the Gaza Strip, planned for December 1998, violent clashes erupted in the West Bank between Palestinians and Israeli security forces. One cause of the unrest was a decision by the Israeli Cabinet to suspend further releases of Palestinian prisoners under the terms of the Wye Memorandum, and its insistence that no Palestinians convicted of killing Israelis, nor members of Hamas or Islamic Jihad, would be released. On 14 December, meanwhile, in the presence of President Clinton, the PNC voted to annul articles of the Palestinian National Charter that were deemed to be anti-Israeli. However, at a summit meeting the following day between Clinton, Netanyahu and Arafat at the Erez check-point between Israel and the Gaza Strip, the Israeli Prime Minister reiterated Israel's stance regarding the release of Palestinian prisoners and further demanded that the Palestinians should honour their commitments by ceasing incitement to violence and formally relinquishing plans for a unilateral declaration of Palestinian statehood on 4 May 1999 (the original deadline as established by the Oslo accords). At the conclusion of the meeting Netanyahu announced that Israel would not proceed with the second scheduled redeployment of its armed forces (under the Wye Memorandum) on 18 December 1998, and on 20 December the Israeli Cabinet voted to suspend implementation of the agreement.

Palestinians reacted to the death of King Hussein of Jordan in February 1999 with public grief—about 65% of the Kingdom's inhabitants are believed to be of Palestinian origin—especially in the West Bank, which King Hussein ruled for 15 years until June 1967. For Arafat, the death of Hussein was a major political reverse since the King had frequently supported him when the peace process with Israel appeared to be on the verge of collapse. Arafat subsequently surprised many Jordanians by proposing the establishment of a Palestinian-Jordanian confederation. The proposal (which had been put forward as part of a peace initiative in 1985, but was rejected by King Hussein) was not welcomed in Jordan, where it was considered to be premature while the West Bank was still largely under Israeli occupation.

President Arafat came under intense international pressure to postpone a unilateral declaration of Palestinian statehood, at least until after the Israeli elections scheduled for May 1999. Arafat indicated in January that he might postpone a declaration of independence if he received certain assurances from Israel and the international community regarding the issue of settlement expansion; moreover, he apparently considered that making such a declaration prior to the elections might actually improve Netanyahu's chances of re-election. The Palestinian leader undertook numerous regional and international visits during February–April, as part of a campaign of intensive diplomacy. In late April PLO chief negotiators Mahmud Abbas and Saeb Erakat (the Minister of Local Government) visited Washington, DC, in order to secure certain assurances from the USA in return for an extension of the 4 May deadline. Also in late April, following a meeting of the Palestinian Central Council (PCC), together with Hamas representatives, in Gaza, it was announced that a declaration on Palestinian statehood would be postponed until after the Israeli elections. The decision was applauded internationally, but provoked violent demonstrations among many Palestinians.

Palestinians cautiously welcomed the victory of Ehud Barak and his One Israel alliance in the Israeli elections of May 1999, and PA officials immediately urged Barak to break the deadlock in the Middle East peace process. However, the new Israeli Prime Minister asserted that he would not offer the Palestinians any fundamental concessions. After the elections there emerged a Palestinian consensus that a halt to Israel's programme of settlement expansion in the Occupied Territories (which Palestinians regarded as an attempt to predetermine the 'final status' borders) must be a precondition for any meaningful resumption of talks. Palestinians in the West Bank declared a 'day of rage' in June against continuing settlement construction; the mass protests, which were particularly violent in Hebron, followed an announcement in late May that the population of the West Bank's largest Jewish settlement, Ma'aleh Edomin, was to be expanded from 25,000 to 50,000 settlers.

One of Arafat's principal concerns following Barak's election was Israel's apparent concentration of efforts on the Lebanese and, especially, Syrian tracks of the Middle East peace process. In August 1999 a political crisis developed after the Syrian Deputy Prime Minister and Minister of Defence, Maj.-Gen. Mustafa Tlass, allegedly made hugly insulting remarks about Yasser Arafat and his stance within the peace process, leading to Palestinian demands for the Syrian minister's resignation and the issuing, by Arafat's Fatah organization, of a death warrant for Tlass. Despite Arafat's poor relations with the Syrian regime, he attended the funeral of President Hafiz al-Assad in June 2000. Relations with Syria appeared to improve under the new President, Bashar al-Assad. Arafat and al-Assad held talks during the Arab League summit in Amman in March 2001, agreeing to future bilateral co-operation, particularly with regard to the peace process.

The first direct meeting between Arafat and Prime Minister Barak was held at the Erez check-point in July 1999. Although both leaders reiterated their commitment to reviving the peace process, Arafat was reportedly alarmed by Barak's apparent opposition to full implementation of the Wye Memorandum and his seeming preoccupation with the Syrian component of the peace process (see below). Later that month, during a second meeting between the two leaders at Erez, Barak angered the Palestinians by seeking to win Arafat's approval to postpone implementation of the Wye agreement until it could be combined with 'final status' negotiations (thereby implying a 15-month delay in further Israeli troop redeployments). At the beginning of August Barak pledged to bring forward the release of 250 Palestinian prisoners if Arafat agreed to a postponement. Bilateral discussions broke down the same day, after Arafat rejected the Israeli stance; however, talks resumed in mid-August, when Israel agreed to pursue implementation of the Wye Memorandum.

Meeting at Sharm esh-Sheikh, Egypt, on 4 September 1999, during a visit to the region by US Secretary of State Albright, Barak and Arafat signed the Sharm esh-Sheikh Memorandum (or Wye Two accords), outlining a revised timetable for implementation of the outstanding provisions of the original Wye agreement. Under the terms of the Memorandum, on 9 September Israel released some 200 Palestinian 'security' prisoners, and the following day Israel transferred a further 7% of the West Bank to PA control. A ceremonial opening of 'final status' negotiations between Israel and the PA was held at the Erez check-point on 13 September; shortly afterwards details emerged of a secret meeting between Barak and Arafat to discuss an agenda for such talks. However, in early October the Palestinians' chief negotiator and Minister of Culture and Information, Yasser Abd ar-Rabbuh, warned that the PA would boycott 'final status' talks unless Israel ended its settlement expansion programme. In mid-October Barak, also under pressure from left-wing groups in Israel, responded by dismantling 12 'settlement outposts' in the West Bank which he deemed to be illegal. Meanwhile, Israel released a further 151 Palestinian prisoners under the terms of Wye Two. The first 'safe passage' between the West Bank and Gaza was inaugurated on 25 October: the opening had been delayed by almost a month owing to a dispute between Israel and the PA over security arrangements for the 44-km route, linking the Erez check-point in the

Gaza Strip to Hebron in the West Bank. Israel asserted that it would maintain almost complete control over the so-called 'southern route'.

'Final status' negotiations between Israel and the PA commenced in Ramallah on 8 November 1999, following a summit meeting held earlier in the month in Oslo, Norway, between Arafat, Barak and Clinton. Shortly before the talks opened three bombs exploded in northern Israel. (Israel claimed that Hamas was responsible, since the attack followed an alleged warning by the organization's military wing that it would intensify its activities in protest at Israel's settlement policies.) A further redeployment of Israeli armed forces from 5% of the West Bank, scheduled for 15 November, was postponed owing to disagreement over the areas to be transferred. In early December Palestinian negotiators walked out of 'final status' talks, following reports that settlement activity had intensified under Barak. Apparently in response to US pressure, the Israeli Prime Minister subsequently announced a halt to settlement construction until the close of negotiations regarding a framework agreement on 'final status'. In late December Arafat conducted talks in Ramallah with Barak, who was the first Israeli premier to hold peace discussions on Palestinian territory. At the end of the month Israel released some 26 Palestinian 'security' prisoners as a gesture of 'goodwill'. On 6–7 January 2000 Israeli armed forces withdrew from a further 5% of the West Bank; however, Israel announced in mid-January that a third redeployment from 6.1% of the territory (scheduled to take place on 20 January) would be postponed until Barak had returned from revived peace talks with Syria in the USA. During a meeting with Arafat on his return from the USA (where talks on the Israeli-Syrian track had collapsed), Barak was reported to have proposed that the deadline for reaching a framework agreement be postponed for two months. The approval by the Israeli Cabinet of a withdrawal of its troops from a sparsely-populated area of the West Bank led the PA to break off negotiations in early February. On 19–20 March Israel released 15 Palestinian 'security' prisoners, and the resumption of 'final status' talks was announced on 21 March. On the same day Israeli armed forces withdrew from a further 6.1% of the West Bank.

In mid-April 2000, following talks between Barak and Clinton in Washington, DC, Israel was said to have agreed to Palestinian demands for greater US involvement in future discussions. The Israeli premier was subsequently reported to have indicated that a Palestinian entity could be established in what was now PA-controlled territory—covering 60%–70% of the West Bank—although Barak refused to speak of a Palestinian 'state'. Later in April Arafat met with Clinton in Washington, where he reportedly sought his intervention in halting Israel's settlement expansion programme. Israel and the PA opened the third round of 'final status' talks at the Israeli port of Eilat on 30 April. Palestinian negotiators immediately denounced a recent decision by the Israeli Government to construct 174 new Jewish homes in the West Bank. At crisis talks between Arafat and Barak in Ramallah in early May, mediated by Dennis Ross, Barak reportedly proposed the transfer to full PA control of three Palestinian villages close to Jerusalem, on condition that the third West Bank redeployment (scheduled to be implemented in June) be postponed. After PA negotiators admitted that the 13 May deadline for reaching a framework agreement would not be met, 'final status' talks were suspended.

At the beginning of May 2000 up to 1,000 Palestinians held in Israeli detention began a hunger strike. Palestinians in the West Bank and Gaza initiated mass protests in support of the prisoners; the demonstrations erupted into violence on 15 May (the anniversary of the declaration of the State of Israel in 1948), which was declared to be a 'day of rage'. Three days of violent gun battles ensued between Palestinian police and civilians and Israeli troops, in which seven Palestinians (including two policemen) were killed, and several hundred injured. Meanwhile, on 15 May the PA chief negotiator, Yasser Abd ar-Rabbuh, announced his resignation (which Arafat refused to accept), in protest at 'secret' talks being conducted without his prior knowledge between Israeli and Palestinian representatives in Stockholm, Sweden. Growing anger among Palestinians over the apparent unaccountability of the PA leadership appeared to have contributed to the civil unrest. On 21 May Israel suspended the Stockholm talks, after an Israeli child was seriously wounded in continuing violence in the West Bank. The Israeli Government also reversed its decision to transfer the three Arab villages to PA control, demanding that Arafat take action to curb Palestinian unrest. Several Palestinians accused

of involvement in the recent violence were subsequently detained by the PA. The Palestinian prisoners called off their hunger strike at the end of the month.

Meanwhile, Palestinians welcomed the withdrawal of Israeli troops from southern Lebanon in late May 2000. Following a tour of Israel and the Palestinian areas by US Secretary of State Madeleine Albright in early June, on 15 June President Clinton received Arafat for discussions in Washington, DC, in an attempt to reinvigorate the Israeli-Palestinian track of the Middle East peace process. Four days later Israel released three Palestinian prisoners as a 'goodwill' gesture. On 21 June, two days prior to the scheduled date, the PA reportedly agreed to a postponement of the third redeployment of Israeli forces from the West Bank. The PCC convened on 2 July, and after two days of discussions stated that the PLO would declare a State of Palestine on or before 13 September.

On 11 July 2000 Bill Clinton inaugurated a peace summit between Arafat and Barak at the US presidential retreat at Camp David, Maryland, with the aim of achieving a framework agreement on 'final status'. Despite intensive mediation efforts the Camp David talks, which were extended beyond their original deadline, ended without agreement on 25 July. Although progress had reportedly been made regarding the borders of a future Palestinian entity and the question of Palestinian refugees, disagreements over the future status of Jerusalem had been the principal obstacle to an accord. Israel was said to have offered the Palestinians municipal authority over certain parts of East Jerusalem, as well as access to the Islamic holy sites. PA officials, however, demanded full sovereignty over the holy sites (in particular the al-Aqsa Mosque and the Dome of the Rock), with East Jerusalem as the capital of a Palestinian state. Nevertheless, Israel and the PA pledged to continue peace negotiations and to avoid 'unilateral actions'—interpreted as Arafat's threat unilaterally to declare an independent Palestinian state. In late July an attempted invasion of the al-Aqsa Mosque by Jewish extremists resulted in confrontations between Jews and Muslims in Jerusalem; a similar incident followed in early August. At the end of July the PA leadership was angered by strong indications from US officials that the USA was considering relocating its embassy from Tel-Aviv to Jerusalem. During a tour principally of Europe, the Middle East and Asia in late July and August, Arafat came under intense pressure not to announce the establishment of a Palestinian state on 13 September. Meanwhile, during August about 23 Palestinians were arrested by Israeli security forces on charges of involvement in militant Islamist 'terrorist squads'. In early September Bill Clinton held separate talks with Arafat and Barak on the sidelines of the UN Millennium Summit in New York, USA. The PCC convened in Gaza on 9–10 September and agreed to postpone the declaration of statehood for an indefinite period (although 15 November was reportedly designated as the new target date). Later in September negotiations between Israeli and PA officials resumed in the USA, and on 20 September an agreement was signed allowing for construction of the Gaza seaport to begin (the work failed to progress owing to the worsening security situation). On 26 September Barak and Arafat met at the Israeli premier's home for their first direct talks since the Camp David summit.

From late September 2000 the West Bank and Gaza Strip became engulfed in the most serious violence for many years, as Palestinians demonstrated their frustration at the lack of progress in the Oslo peace process and at their failure to achieve statehood. On 28 September Ariel Sharon, leader of Israel's right-wing Likud party, visited Temple Mount/Haram ash-Sharif in Jerusalem—the site of the al-Aqsa Mosque and the Dome of the Rock—flanked by Israeli security guards. Sharon's visit to the Islamic holy sites provoked violent protests and stone-throwing by Palestinians, to which Israeli security forces responded forcefully. The clashes spread rapidly to other Palestinian towns: by the end of October at least 140 people had died —all but eight of them Palestinians—and thousands had been wounded. On 4 October Arafat and Barak travelled to Paris, France, for negotiations led by the US Secretary of State. However, no agreement was reached on the composition of an international commission of inquiry into the causes of the violence, and while Arafat and Madeleine Albright continued talks at Sharm-esh Sheikh the following day, Barak returned to Israel. The Israeli authorities subsequently sealed off the borders of the West Bank and Gaza. On 7 October the UN Security Council issued a resolution condemning the 'provocation carried out' at Temple Mount/Haram ash-Sharif and the 'excessive use of force' employed by the Israeli security forces against Palestinians. Two days later the UN Secretary-General, Kofi Annan, arrived in the region, and international diplomatic initiatives intensified. Meanwhile, Israel accused Arafat of failing to intervene to halt the violence, as members of Arafat's own Fatah movement joined Hamas and other militant groups in what swiftly became known as the al-Aqsa *intifada* (uprising—the first *intifada* began at the end of 1987 and continued for some five years). In mid-October 2000 the Israeli army launched rocket attacks on Arafat's headquarters in the West Bank and Gaza, in retaliation for the murder of two Israeli army reservists by Palestinians in Ramallah. In an attempt to prevent the crisis from escalating into a major regional conflict, a US-sponsored summit meeting between Barak and Arafat was convened on 16–17 October at Sharm esh-Sheikh. At the close of the meeting US President Clinton announced that the Israeli and Palestinian leaders had agreed the terms of a 'truce' to halt the spiralling violence. The two sides had also reportedly agreed on the formation of a US-appointed committee to investigate the clashes. Barak, however, demanded that Arafat rearrest some 60 militant Islamists whom the PA had freed in early October. Amid further violence in the West Bank and Gaza, the League of Arab States (the Arab League, see p. 260) held an emergency summit meeting in the Egyptian capital on 21–22 October, issuing a strong condemnation of Israel's actions towards the Palestinians. Barak responded by announcing that Israel was calling a 'time-out' in the peace process.

At the end of October 2000 Islamic Jihad claimed responsibility for a suicide bombing on an Israeli army post in Gaza. The attack signalled a new campaign against Israeli forces by militant Palestinian organizations opposed to the Oslo process. Israel responded by launching air strikes on Fatah military bases, and declared a new strategy of targeting leading officials of militant Islamist groups suspected of terrorist activities. On 1 November Arafat held a crisis meeting in Gaza with the Israeli Minister for Regional Co-operation, Shimon Peres; the two sides were reported to have agreed a 'cease-fire', based on the truce brokered in Egypt in October. The following day, however, a car bomb exploded in Jerusalem, killing two Israelis. Although Islamic Jihad claimed responsibility for the attack, Barak accused the PA of being indirectly culpable by its recent release of Islamist prisoners. In early November President Clinton appointed the five-member international commission of inquiry, to be chaired by former US Senator George Mitchell. Meeting with Clinton in the USA shortly afterwards, Arafat demanded that the USA support Palestinian requests for the establishment of a UN peace-keeping force in the self-rule areas (Barak was opposed to such a force). Prior to the meeting a senior Fatah official in the West Bank was killed by Israeli troops. Israel reinforced its closure of the West Bank and Gaza in mid-November, imposing an economic blockade on the territories. Meanwhile, after completing a fact-finding mission to the region, the UN High Commissioner for Human Rights, Mary Robinson, expressed concerns regarding the deterioration of human rights in the Palestinian territories and recommended the presence there of international monitors. Israel launched air-strikes against PA offices in Gaza in late November, in reprisal for the deaths of two people in the bombing of a school bus for Jewish settlers. Despite the continuing violence, Israel and the PA resumed negotiations, partly as a result of Russian diplomacy. At the end of November the Palestinians rejected a partial peace plan, announced by Barak, whereby Israel would withdraw its armed forces from additional West Bank territory provided that the PA agreed to postpone any discussion of the remaining 'final status' issues. During late 2000 Jewish settlers increasingly became the target of Palestinian attacks. Under pressure from the US Administration, in early December Israel eased some of the sanctions imposed on the Palestinian enclaves at the outbreak of the crisis. In mid-December the US-led commission of inquiry began conducting investigations into the violence. Shortly afterwards five Palestinian policemen were killed by Israeli forces during a gun battle in the Gaza Strip.

Meanwhile, the USA was evidently keen to continue negotiations aimed at reaching a framework agreement on permanent status prior to the expiry of President Clinton's term of office in January 2001. (By this time indications were strong that George W. Bush, who had been elected to the US presidency in November 2000, intended to be less actively engaged than Clinton in the Middle East peace process.) A further round of peace talks opened in mid-December 2000, at which the US President was reported to have proposed a peace deal that included plans for a future Palestinian state covering the Gaza Strip and some 95% of the West Bank, as well as granting the Palestinians sovereignty over the Islamic holy sites in the Old City of Jerusalem. However, the US plan also required that Palestinians renounce the right of return for 3.7m. refugees, which the PA deemed unacceptable. The negotiations broke down in late December after two Israelis died in bombings by Palestinian militants in Tel-Aviv and the Gaza Strip. At the end of the month a prominent Jewish settler and a senior Fatah activist were both shot dead in the West Bank. In early January 2001 Arafat visited Washington, DC, to seek official clarification of Clinton's proposals. Meanwhile, following a car bomb explosion in northern Israel, the Israeli authorities again tightened their blockade of the West Bank and Gaza. Israel subsequently confirmed its policy of assassinating local Palestinian officials who were regarded as endangering Israeli society. Israeli-Palestinian discussions aimed at securing a breakthrough prior to the impending Israeli premiership election opened at the Egyptian resort of Taba later in January, but Israel suspended the talks two days later after two Israeli civilians were killed in a Hamas gun attack in the West Bank.

The success of Ariel Sharon in the Israeli premiership election in early February 2001 provoked violent demonstrations by Palestinians, who held Sharon responsible—as Israel's Minister of Defence at that time—for the massacre of Palestinian refugees in Lebanese camps in 1982 (see the chapters on Israel and Lebanon). Immediately after Sharon's election Palestinian militants carried out a car bombing in Jerusalem. A few days later another senior Fatah official was killed by Israeli security forces. In mid-February a Palestinian bus driver launched an attack on Israeli soldiers and civilians in Tel-Aviv, killing nine people. Israel responded by again sealing off the Palestinian territories.

Arafat delivered a 'state of the nation' address to members of the Palestinian Legislative Council (PLC), which was meeting in Gaza, in early March 2001. The Palestinian President emphasized his desire to achieve peace with Israel, but he condemned Israeli military actions in the West Bank and Gaza and urged the presence of a UN peace-keeping force to protect civilians there. This request was blocked by a US veto at the UN Security Council in mid-March. In mid-April Israeli armed forces moved tanks to the Palestinian-controlled town of Beit Hanun in the Gaza Strip, in retaliation for a mortar attack on the Israeli town of Sderot; however, Israel quickly withdrew its troops. Later in April four Fatah officials died in an explosion on the Gaza–Egypt border. The PA claimed that the men were victims of an Israeli assassination, while militants responded by launching mortar assaults on two Jewish settlements in Gaza. At the end of the month Arafat called on the Palestinian police and security forces to end all 'security breaches'; he also detained a leading Hamas activist, Abd al-Aziz ar-Rantisi, who had recently urged Palestinians to reject the Egyptian-Jordanian peace initiative then under discussion. At the beginning of June 21 Israelis were killed in a suicide bomb attack, apparently perpetrated by Hamas, at a Tel-Aviv nightclub. The PA agreed the following day to implement the recommendations listed in the final report of the international commission of inquiry under George Mitchell (the Sharm esh-Sheikh Fact-Finding Committee, or 'Mitchell Committee'), published in late May. The Mitchell Report recommended a 'freeze' on Israeli settlement expansion; a clear statement by the PA demanding an end to Palestinian violence; an 'immediate and unconditional' end to the conflict and the disengagement of forces by both sides; and the resumption of security co-operation. In mid-June the PA also agreed to an extended cease-fire brokered by the CIA Director, George Tenet. Although it appeared initially that Palestinian militant groups would maintain the truce, in early July both Hamas and Islamic Jihad formally announced that the cease-fire was ended. In late July Palestinian security forces in Gaza arrested a number of militants including members of Fatah's military wing, the *tanzim*.

In August 2001 the PA rejected a demand by Israel for the arrest of seven alleged 'terrorists', who headed a 'most wanted' list of about 100 Palestinians believed to be perpetrators of violence against Israelis. In early August, in response to a Hamas suicide bombing at a restaurant in central Jerusalem (in which at least 15 Israelis died), Israel ordered its armed forces to occupy several PA offices including Orient House, the PA's *de facto* headquarters in East Jerusalem. Israeli troops entered the West Bank town of Jenin in mid-August—the first time that Israel had reoccupied territory transferred to full PA control under the terms of the Oslo accords. Palestinian officials called the action a 'declaration of war'. Later in the month Abu Ali Moustafa, the leader of the Popular Front for the Liberation of Palestine (PFLP), was assassinated by Israeli forces in the West Bank. Moustafa was the highest-ranking Palestinian official to be killed under Israel's so-called strategy of 'targeted killings'. At the end of August Israel made a brief military incursion into Beit Jala, also in the West Bank.

The unprecedented scale of the suicide attacks launched against New York and Washington, DC, on 11 September 2001 precipitated an escalation of tensions in the Middle East. The USA held the al-Qa'ida (Base) network, led by the Saudi-born Islamist militant Osama bin Laden, principally responsible for the atrocities. As the US Administration sought to attract support for an international 'war on terror', President George W. Bush placed considerable pressure on Israel and the PA to end the violence in the Palestinian territories. In mid-September Yasser Arafat, who had condemned the attacks in the strongest terms, declared that he had ordered militant Palestinian groups to halt their actions against Israelis, while Israel agreed to withdraw from PA-controlled areas of the West Bank. However, Sharon prevented a planned meeting between Shimon Peres (Israel's Deputy Prime Minister and Minister of Foreign Affairs) and Arafat from taking place, stating that his Government required 48 hours without violence prior to any resumption of peace talks. Arafat and Peres finally met in the Gaza Strip in late September, in an attempt to consolidate the cease-fire arrangements outlined in the Mitchell Report. However, on the first anniversary of the al-Aqsa *intifada* five Palestinians were shot dead by Israeli forces in Gaza, and retaliatory attacks between the two sides resumed.

In early October 2001 President Bush disclosed for the first time that the USA would accept the creation of a Palestinian state, on condition that Israel's existence was not threatened. Meanwhile, Israel moved tanks into the Gaza Strip and shelled Palestinian police stations there, in response to the killing by Hamas gunmen of two Jewish settlers. In mid-October a prominent Hamas official was killed at Qalqilya in the West Bank; Israeli officials claimed that the man had been involved in plotting the Tel-Aviv nightclub bombing in June. Also in mid-October Yasser Arafat visited the United Kingdom for discussions with Prime Minister Tony Blair on reviving the Oslo process. Blair urged Arafat to exert his authority over Palestinian militant groups to persuade them to observe the cease-fire. However, the assassination in Jerusalem of Israel's ultra-nationalist Minister of Tourism, Rechavam Ze'evi, by three members of the PFLP—apparently in revenge for the murder of the PFLP leader in August—led Israel, in late October, to order its armed forces into six major West Bank towns. Shortly after Ze'evi's death Arafat banned all military factions of Palestinian political groups, and his security forces arrested several PFLP militants; however, the PA refused Israeli demands for their extradition. Violence flared across the Palestinian territories as Israel rejected US demands for a swift withdrawal from the recently occupied towns. At least five Palestinians reportedly died in Beit Rima, near Ramallah, in a raid by Israeli forces searching for Ze'evi's assassins. Towards the end of October Israel stated that it would carry out a phased withdrawal from the six West Bank towns; however, its 'anti-terrorist' operation continued in Jenin and Tulkarm, and Israeli tanks continued to surround Ramallah. In mid-November George W. Bush refused to hold talks with the PA President during a session of the UN General Assembly in New York, on the grounds that this would be 'inappropriate'. Meanwhile, Israeli forces entered the refugee camp of Khan Younis in the Gaza Strip after Palestinians had launched mortar attacks on a nearby Jewish settlement. At the end of November the US Assistant Secretary of State for Near Eastern Affairs, William Burns, and the newly appointed US special envoy to the Middle East, Gen. Anthony Zinni, arrived in the region in a fresh attempt to secure a cease-fire. Their arrival coincided with the assassination by Israel of another senior Hamas militant and Israeli air-strikes against Palestinian security targets in Gaza. Furthermore, at least five Israeli civilians died in two separate attacks in the West Bank and Gaza perpetrated by Islamic Jihad and another militant group, the al-Aqsa Martyrs Brigade.

Palestinian militants intensified their attacks against Israel at the beginning of December 2001. Over a 24-hour period at least 25 Israelis were killed, and more than 200 injured, as a result of a triple bombing in Jerusalem and a further suicide attack on a bus in Haifa. In the week following the attacks, for

which Hamas claimed responsibility, Palestinian security forces claimed to have arrested more than 150 (mainly Hamas and Islamic Jihad) militants, targeting in particular Jenin, the alleged base of the recent suicide bombers; it was also reported that the spiritual leader of Hamas, Sheikh Ahmad Yassin, had been placed under house arrest. Israeli forces, meanwhile, fired missiles against security targets in Jenin and targeted Arafat's official residence in Gaza, destroying two of his helicopters; the runway at Gaza International Airport was also damaged. The Palestinian leader was, at the time, in Ramallah, where Israel ordered tanks to the edge of his compound. The Israeli Prime Minister increasingly began to draw parallels between Israel's efforts to suppress the *intifada* and the USA's 'war on terror', describing the PA as a 'terror-supporting entity'. Israel demanded that Arafat arrest 33 militants held to be responsible for recent suicide attacks. In mid-December Israel responded to an assault on a settlers' bus in the West Bank (in which some 10 Israelis died) by declaring the PA leader to be 'irrelevant', owing to his failure to prevent such attacks, and announced that it was severing all contacts with Arafat. The Israeli military launched air-raids across the West Bank and Gaza, reoccupied large areas of Ramallah, and reinforced its military blockade of Arafat's headquarters; several Palestinian police and civilians were killed during the Israeli operations. Meanwhile, the USA again vetoed a proposed UN resolution calling for international observers to be deployed in the Palestinian areas. In a televised speech Arafat issued a strong condemnation of groups that carried out gun attacks and suicide bombings against Israelis, although Sharon insisted that Arafat would not be permitted to leave Ramallah until the PA arrested the perpetrators of Ze'evi's murder. Nevertheless, Israeli and Palestinian security officials resumed talks in an attempt to achieve a breakthrough.

US special envoy Anthony Zinni undertook a four-day visit to the region in early January 2002, although he failed to secure a cease-fire agreement between Israel and the Palestinians. Meanwhile, Arafat ordered an investigation into Israeli claims that the PA was complicit in a massive shipment of largely Iranian-produced weaponry—including *Katyusha* rockets, mortar shells and anti-tank missiles—which Israeli forces had intercepted in the Red Sea; the freighter, the *Karine A*, was apparently *en route* for the Gaza Strip to be used in attacks against Israeli targets. (The PA reportedly detained a number of suspects, while the USA claimed to have evidence of PA involvement: Arafat did, in February, accept responsibility on behalf of his administration for the shipment.) Israel responded to the killing by Hamas members of four of its soldiers in southern Israel by sending tanks into the Gazan town of Rafah and demolishing a number of homes there; Gaza airport was again targeted. In mid-January a senior Fatah militant died in an explosion, apparently orchestrated by Israel, in Tulkarm in the West Bank. Following a gun attack by members of the al-Aqsa Martyrs Brigade that killed six guests at a bar mitzvah ceremony in Hadera, northern Israel, Sharon ordered tanks and armoured vehicles to tighten their blockade of Arafat's Ramallah headquarters (the President had effectively been under house arrest since early December 2001), and also reoccupied Tulkarm in order to arrest known Palestinian 'terrorists'. Although the troops withdrew a day later, it was reported to be the largest military incursion since the start of the al-Aqsa *intifada*. At the end of January 2002 it appeared that for the first time in the Israeli–Palestinian conflict a female suicide bomber had acted; one Israeli was killed in the attack in West Jerusalem, for which the al-Aqsa Martyrs claimed responsibility. Meanwhile, EU officials increasingly distanced themselves from the US position towards the conflict, reaffirming their support for Arafat as a crucial partner in the peace process. The EU also issued a formal complaint to Israel, listing EU-funded projects in the West Bank and Gaza that had undergone physical damage during recent military operations.

In early February 2002 at least four members of the radical Democratic Front for the Liberation of Palestine (DFLP) were killed by an explosion in the Gaza Strip that appeared to be an Israeli 'targeted assassination'. The violence came amid renewed efforts to restart peace negotiations. Ariel Sharon met leading PA representatives, while Shimon Peres held a series of discussions with the PLC Speaker, Ahmad Quray. However, Israeli officials were angered when a large number of Palestinian militants were freed during Israeli air-strikes on the PA's security headquarters in Nablus. Requests for calm by the UN and attempts by the EU to launch a new peace initiative in the second week of February—reportedly based on the convening of new elections to the PLC—failed to prevent an escalation of violence in the territories, particularly in Gaza. As Hamas appeared to be intensifying its attacks on Israelis by firing a new type of missile, the *Qassam-2*, against Jewish settlers, four Palestinian security officers died during incursions by the Israeli army into three Gazan towns. Israel's military offensive was also accelerated in Hebron and Ramallah. In late February up to 30 Palestinians were reportedly killed in Israeli military operations across the West Bank and Gaza in retaliation for the shooting of six Israelis at an army check-point near Ramallah. The Israeli premier declared that he intended to establish 'buffer zones' between Israel and the Palestinian enclaves in an attempt to halt the rising number of militants who were infiltrating Israeli territory to launch attacks. The Israeli Cabinet subsequently agreed to withdraw its tanks from Arafat's compound in Ramallah but refused to allow the Palestinian leader freedom of movement beyond the town: Sharon stated that the travel ban would remain in place despite the arrest by Palestinian security forces of three militants believed to have been responsible for Ze'evi's murder. The Israeli position led PA security officials to suspend bilateral talks, which had recently been resumed. Gun battles raged across the West Bank at the end of February, despite efforts by Crown Prince Abdullah of Saudi Arabia to promote his proposals for peace in the Middle East prior to a summit meeting of the Arab League Council, due to be held in Beirut, Lebanon, in March. Abdullah's proposals centred on Arab recognition of the State of Israel and the normalization of diplomatic relations, in exchange for agreement by Israel to withdraw from all Arab land occupied since 1967 and on the establishment of a Palestinian state with East Jerusalem as its capital. Arafat announced that he would not attend the Beirut conference owing to threats by Sharon to prevent his return to the West Bank and Gaza should he travel abroad. Meanwhile, the number of fatalities continued to grow: in response to a suicide bombing by a Palestinian woman at an Israeli army check-point, Israel for the first time sent ground troops into two refugee camps in the West Bank which it claimed were centres of Islamist militancy: the Balata camp near Nablus and the camp at Jenin. Israeli forces were met with strong resistance from Palestinian gunmen in the two towns; at least 25 Palestinians and two Israeli soldiers reportedly died in the first few days of fighting. The PA announced subsequently that it was suspending all contacts with the Israeli Government. The USA, meanwhile, urged Israel to show restraint, while UN and EU officials demanded an immediate Israeli withdrawal from the camps.

PA officials categorically rejected an offer made by Ariel Sharon in early March 2002 that Yasser Arafat should agree to go into voluntary exile. At the same time Israel refused to allow senior UN and EU diplomats to visit Arafat. A number of Palestinians were killed as Israeli forces entered Ramallah, Bethlehem and Tulkarm in an attempt to find those responsible for two attacks apparently perpetrated by the al-Aqsa Martyrs Brigade—10 Israelis had died in a suicide attack in Jerusalem, and a further 10 had been shot dead at a West Bank check-point. Shortly afterwards Palestinian militants carried out another bus bombing and an assault on a restaurant in Tel-Aviv, leading Israel to launch missiles against targets across the West Bank and Gaza; Arafat's presidential compound in Ramallah and the police headquarters in Gaza were both hit. Three militants— believed to be from the al-Aqsa Martyrs Brigade, including an aide to the Fatah leader in the West Bank, Marwan Barghouthi —died in a helicopter raid in Ramallah. The US Secretary of State, Gen. Colin Powell, publicly criticized Sharon's declared aim of forcing the PA to return to peace talks by defeating them militarily. On 8 March five Jewish settler students were killed by Hamas gunmen in Gaza; an estimated 40 Palestinians died during the fierce fighting that ensued. The upsurge in violence followed an announcement by US President Bush that his special envoy, Anthony Zinni, was to return to the region in a renewed attempt to secure a cease-fire. As Israel re-entered Bethlehem and Tulkarm, the Israeli Prime Minister (apparently under pressure from the USA and from members of his Cabinet) suggested that he might be prepared to abandon his demand for seven days of calm prior to the resumption of peace talks. Sharon declared that Arafat had met the conditions required for his release after a fifth suspect in Ze'evi's murder was arrested by Palestinian security forces in the first week of March. However, after a suicide bombing in Jerusalem, killing 11 Israelis, and a shooting in Netanya in which two died, Israel's 'inner' Security Cabinet voted to intensify its military offensive. Tanks

entered Qalqilya and the Jabalia refugee camp in Gaza (where 18 Palestinians, including four Hamas members, were reported to have been killed), while Arafat's headquarters in Gaza were destroyed by Israeli helicopters and gunboats.

On 11 March 2002 Israel announced that it was ending its travel ban on Arafat, although the Palestinian leader would still not be permitted to travel abroad. The following day Israeli forces intensified their campaign to dismantle the 'infrastructure of terror' with a massive ground offensive (deploying some 20,000 troops) in the Palestinian territories and rounding up hundreds of Palestinian men for questioning; several civilians died during the incursions. This was reported to be the largest Israeli operation against Palestinian militants since the 1982 invasion of Lebanon. Israeli forces again took control of most of Ramallah, with tanks coming to within a short distance of Arafat's presidential compound. On 12 March 2002 the UN Security Council adopted Resolution 1397, affirming its 'vision' of both Israeli and Palestinian states 'within secure and recognized borders'; the US-drafted resolution also demanded an immediate end to 'all acts of violence' by both sides, and called upon Israel and the Palestinians to co-operate in implementation of the Mitchell Report and George Tenet's recommendations. Anthony Zinni returned to the region on the following day, and was later accompanied by US Vice-President Dick Cheney; however, Zinni's arrival coincided with more violence. Under pressure to withdraw as a 'goodwill' gesture to Zinni, the Israeli army later withdrew from Ramallah, Tulkarm and Qalqilya, although they continued to surround the towns. Following discussions between Zinni and Arafat, and US-brokered talks between Israeli and PA security officials in Jerusalem, Israel also agreed to redeploy its troops from Bethlehem and Beit Jala. The PA was angered by Cheney's refusal to meet the Palestinian leader until certain cease-fire conditions had been met. In mid-March the Israeli movement Peace Now issued a report stating that 34 new Israeli settlements had been built in the year since Sharon came to power. After the security talks ended without agreement on 21 March, the Israeli Government again ordered troops into much of the West Bank and detained several alleged militants. The security talks had been overshadowed by an Islamic Jihad bombing on a bus in northern Israel, in which seven Israelis died. A further suicide attack by the al-Aqsa Martyrs Brigade killed three Israelis in central Jerusalem; the USA responded by adding the group to its list of proscribed terrorist organizations. Three Palestinians were shot dead in Gaza shortly afterwards. Later in March two European civilian observers became the first foreign observers to be killed during the *intifada*; the PA announced that it would hold an inquiry into reports that they were the victims of Palestinian gunfire.

The Arab League summit proceeded in Beirut on 27–28 March 2002, in the notable absence of both President Hosni Mubarak of Egypt and King Abdullah of Jordan (the two leaders had apparently boycotted the meeting as a gesture of support for the PA President). Palestinian officials were angered when the Lebanese hosts refused to permit Arafat to address the session via a live satellite link from Ramallah: the Lebanese authorities had stated that they feared an Israeli disruption of such a broadcast. At the close of the conference the participating Arab states unanimously endorsed the Saudi peace initiative, which also included a clause calling for a 'just solution' to the question of Palestinian refugees. Israel rejected the plan, however, stating that its terms would lead to the destruction of the Jewish state.

The crisis deepened on 27 March 2002 when a Hamas suicide bomber blew himself up at a hotel in the Israeli town of Netanya, where Jews were celebrating the festival of Passover; 29 people died as a result of the attack and some 140 were injured. Although Arafat personally condemned the bombing, and reportedly ordered the immediate arrest of four prominent West Bank militants, Sharon blamed the PA for its failure to prevent such attacks. In response to what was swiftly called the 'Passover massacre' and a subsequent Hamas gun attack which killed at least three Jewish settlers near Nablus, Israel mobilized about 20,000 army reservists and convened an emergency cabinet meeting, at which 'extensive operational activity against Palestinian terrorism' was agreed. As the region appeared to be on the brink of a major conflagration, Israel shelled a section of Arafat's compound in Ramallah and troops took over most of the building, leaving the President in effective isolation. On 29 March Israeli armed forces began a huge campaign of incursions into West Bank towns—code-named 'Operation Defensive Shield'—with the declared aim of dismantling the Palestinian 'terrorist infrastructure' in order to prevent future suicide bombings against Israeli citizens. During the offensive Israeli forces entered and conducted house-to-house searches for militants in Ramallah, Bethlehem, Beit Jala, Qalqilya, Tulkarm, Jenin and Nablus. Meanwhile, a female suicide bomber, apparently linked to the al-Aqsa Martyrs Brigade, killed two Israelis in Jerusalem. On 30 March the UN Security Council met in emergency session and demanded, in Resolution 1402, an immediate Israeli withdrawal from all towns that had been transferred to the PA under the Oslo accords. At the end of the month a Hamas suicide bomber from Jenin killed 15 Israelis at a café in Haifa. Sharon declared that Israel was 'at war', and his 'inner' Security Cabinet gave the army permission to broaden its offensive in the West Bank. Israeli armed forces reoccupied Ramallah, declaring it to be a 'closed military area'; the invasion was reported to have resulted in many Palestinian deaths. Many leaders of the international community urged Israel to show restraint; for its part, the US Administration expressed 'grave concern' about the situation in the Palestinian areas, and President Bush again demanded that Arafat should take action to prevent attacks against Israelis. In Ramallah Israeli forces attacked the headquarters of the Palestinian Preventive Security Force, bringing about the surrender of a group of militants from the compound.

In early April 2002 Yasser Arafat again dismissed a suggestion by Sharon that the Palestinian leader should go into exile. On 2 April fighting between Israelis and Palestinians in Bethlehem escalated into a siege at the Church of the Nativity—a place of great significance to Christians since it is believed to mark the site of Christ's birth. As many as 200 people—Palestinian civilians and priests as well as some 30 armed militants wanted by Israel—sought shelter from Israeli troops inside the church. (In subsequent weeks some Palestinians left the church, among them 26 who were taken into Israeli custody for questioning at the end of April.) On 3 April Israeli tanks entered Jenin and its refugee camp. By the following day Israel had effectively reoccupied all but two major towns (Jericho and Hebron) in the West Bank and detained more than 1,000 Palestinians; Bethlehem, like Ramallah, was declared a 'closed military area'. International diplomatic efforts to calm the conflict intensified. However, Israel prevented an EU delegation from holding discussions with Arafat. George W. Bush, amid intense international pressure, demanded that Israel withdraw its forces immediately from Palestinian towns and implement the Tenet and Mitchell recommendations for a cease-fire. On 4 April Israeli troops reportedly withdrew from Nablus but entered Hebron. Israel also intensified its offensive in the Jenin refugee camp, the alleged base of several of the suicide bombers. According to PA reports, more than 80 Palestinians died during the first week of Israeli military operations in Jenin. The UN Security Council unanimously adopted a resolution (No. 1403) that demanded the implementation of Resolution 1402 (i.e. an Israeli withdrawal from Palestinian territories) 'without delay'. The following day Israel permitted a meeting to take place between Zinni and Arafat in preparation for a visit to the Middle East by the US Secretary of State, Gen. Colin Powell. On 9 April 13 Israeli army reservists were killed in ambushes in the Jenin camp, and the following day, in response to the deaths of at least eight people in a Hamas suicide bombing of a bus near Haifa, Israel ruled out the prospect of further withdrawals from the West Bank while its 'anti-terror' operation remained incomplete. Powell arrived in Israel on 11 April; he held talks with the besieged Palestinian leader in Ramallah three days later, but stated subsequently that a suggested conference on the Middle East crisis would not necessarily require the personal presence of Arafat. The Secretary of State's mission ended on 17 April without having achieved a cease-fire.

During mid-April 2002 Palestinians made increasingly vocal allegations of an Israeli 'massacre' at the Jenin refugee camp—where many buildings had been destroyed by tanks and bulldozers—and that Israeli armed forces were guilty of war crimes. There was considerable controversy regarding the number of Palestinians who had died during the Israeli incursion (at least 100 according to Palestinian sources); 23 Israelis were believed to have died. Israeli officials were angered when UN Special Coordinator Terje Roed-Larsen issued a strong criticism of Israel's failure to allow humanitarian aid agencies to enter the camp for 11 days after the Jenin battle had ended. (In early May the US-based Human Rights Watch issued a report stating that Israeli forces had been guilty of 'excessive force' and of war crimes in Jenin, but that there had been no massacre. Although a UN fact-finding mission had been scheduled to start investigations into the allegations at the end of April, in early May the UN team

was disbanded, following repeated refusals by Israel to accept both its composition and mandate. A report issued by the UN in early August stated that there was no evidence of a massacre having occurred at the Jenin camp, but criticized the methods adopted by the Israeli military during its occupation of the camp.) Although Israel's forces began to withdraw from some Palestinian-administered towns, a number of Palestinians were killed as Israeli tanks entered the town of Rafah, in the Gaza Strip, after two Israeli soldiers were injured in a suicide bombing by Islamic Jihad at a Jewish settlement. Also in mid-April Marwan Barghouthi, the Fatah leader in the West Bank (and, according to Israel, commander of the al-Aqsa Martyrs Brigade), was arrested by Israeli forces in Ramallah; his trial, on charges of leading Palestinian 'terrorist' groups in the West Bank and of orchestrating a number of suicide bombings against Israeli citizens, began in mid-August. (Barghouthi claimed that the Israeli judiciary had no jurisdiction over him, as an elected member of the PLC.) Meanwhile, Sharon announced on 21 April 2002 that the first stage of Operation Defensive Shield had been completed; however, Israeli forces were to remain in Ramallah and Bethlehem. Some reports stated that more than 4,000 Palestinians were detained during the offensive, although many were subsequently released. In late April Hebron and the Gaza Strip appeared to be the focus of Israeli military operations. According to the Palestine Red Crescent Society, by the end of April at least 1,500 Palestinians had been killed, and more than 19,000 injured, since the start of the al-Aqsa *intifada*. (At least 260 Palestinians had died since Israel's reoccupation of West Bank territory from the end of March.) According to Israeli sources, more than 470 Israelis had been killed, and many more wounded, as a result of the violence that had erupted in September 2000.

Yasser Arafat was freed by the Israeli authorities on 1 May 2002. His release came after the USA secured an arrangement whereby Israel agreed to end its siege of Ramallah, including Arafat's headquarters, on condition that the PA leader handed over six prisoners sheltering in the presidential compound who were wanted by Israel in connection with 'terrorist' activities. In late April four of the prisoners were convicted of direct involvement in the assassination of Rechavam Ze'evi by an *ad hoc* Palestinian court inside the compound and variously sentenced to between one and 18 years' imprisonment. The other two detainees were the PFLP leader, Ahmad Saadat, and a militant implicated in the *Karine A* affair. In early May the six prisoners were moved from Ramallah to a gaol in Jericho, where they were to remain in 'international custody' under US and British guard. Despite Arafat's release, US President Bush declared that he was not yet willing to meet the Palestinian leader. Meanwhile, Israeli armed forces were continuing their detention of suspected militants in a number of Palestinian towns including Hebron and Tulkarm. Following protracted negotiations, the siege at the Church of the Nativity in Bethlehem finally came to an end, after more than five weeks, on 10 May, when 13 remaining militants were transferred under international guard to Cyprus pending their dispersal to permanent exile elsewhere in Europe. The agreement ending the siege envisaged that 26 other militants who were removed to the Gaza Strip should be tried by a Palestinian court there, but it was unclear whether a trial would actually proceed; 84 Palestinian civilians and police-officers were free to leave the church; and 10 foreign pro-Palestinian activists were to be deported. It was reported in mid-June that Israel had begun construction of an electrified 'security' fence, which would eventually extend the length of its border with the West Bank, in an attempt to prevent further suicide bombings. Despite international diplomatic efforts aimed at securing a new round of peace talks between Israel and the PA, and reports of a potential US initiative involving the creation of an 'interim' Palestinian state, there was a marked increase in violence at this time: in response to a series of suicide attacks against Israeli citizens by Palestinian militants in late June (in which a number of Israelis were killed), Israel again ordered its armed forces into several towns in the West Bank and Gaza. In August an Israeli proposal to implement a gradual withdrawal of troops from the Gaza Strip and parts of the West Bank in exchange for the arrest of known militants by the Palestinian security forces (the so-called 'Gaza First' plan) failed as renewed violence swept through the territories.

As the cycle of violence between Israelis and Palestinians continued, in late September 2002 the Israeli Cabinet responded to the latest suicide bombing in Tel-Aviv by announcing that it was to 'isolate' Yasser Arafat. Israeli forces began the systematic destruction of Arafat's compound in Ramallah while the Palestinian leader reportedly remained inside one of the office buildings. Sharon declared that Arafat had failed to arrest militant Islamists known to advocate violence against Israeli citizens. At the same time Israeli armed forces launched a series of incursions into the Gaza Strip, which increasingly became the focus of Israeli military operations in late 2002 and early 2003. Meanwhile, at the end of September 2002 the Israeli siege of Arafat's headquarters was brought to an end, after the UN Security Council had issued a resolution (No. 1435), demanding the immediate cessation of Israeli military actions in and around Ramallah. However, the Israeli–Palestinian violence continued in subsequent months and the number of people killed since the start of the al-Aqsa *intifada* increased dramatically.

Legislative elections took place on 20 January 1996, with the participation of some 79% of the estimated 1m. eligible Palestinian voters, selecting 88 deputies to the 89-seat PLC. (One seat was automatically reserved for the president of the Council's executive body—the Palestinian President.) At the concurrent election for a Palestinian Executive President, Yasser Arafat defeated his only rival, Samiha Khalil, winning 88.1% of the votes cast, and took office as President on 12 February. Deputies returned to the PLC automatically became members of the PNC, the existing 483 members of which were subsequently permitted to return from exile by the Israeli authorities. The PLC held its first session in Gaza City on 7 March, electing Ahmad Quray as its Speaker.

At the 21st session of the PNC, held in Gaza City on 22–24 April 1996, the PNC voted to amend the Palestinian National Charter (or PLO Covenant) by annulling those clauses that sought the destruction of the State of Israel and those that were inconsistent with the agreement of mutual recognition concluded by Israel and the PLO in September 1993. At the close of its session the PNC elected a new Executive Committee, and in May 1996 President Arafat appointed a Palestinian Cabinet. The appointments were approved by the PLC in July.

In April 1997 Arafat's audit office disclosed evidence of the misappropriation by PA ministers of some US $326m. of public funds. The PA General Prosecutor, Khalid al-Qidram, resigned in response to the findings, and was reportedly placed under house arrest in June. The Cabinet submitted its resignation in August (in accordance with the findings of a parliamentary committee appointed by Arafat to investigate the affair); however, this was not accepted by the President until December, when it was announced that ministers would remain in office in a provisional capacity until new appointments were made in early 1998. In March the PLC threatened to hold a vote of 'no confidence' in Arafat's leadership in protest at alleged corruption within the PA, as well as at the prolonged delay in approval of budget proposals for 1998 and at the failure to hold local government elections. The Cabinet resigned in June, apparently in order to obstruct another 'no confidence' motion. The new Cabinet, appointed by Arafat in August, included several new ministers; however, only one minister from the outgoing administration was actually dismissed, and two prominent ministers immediately resigned on the grounds that the reshuffle had failed adequately to address the PA's shortcomings. The new Cabinet was also criticized by officials of the principal international organizations granting funds to the PA; however, in November donors pledged aid worth more than US $3,000m., to be disbursed over the next five years. In October 1998 the PA was again accused of financial mismanagement, after customs revenues amounting to some US $70m. allegedly failed to be deposited at the PA treasury.

In addition to persistent allegations of corruption within the PA, President Arafat himself has at times been the target of accusations of autocracy from other members of the Palestinian leadership. Furthermore, there have been frequent claims that the Palestinian security forces have resorted to intimidation and torture in their treatment of detainees. Such allegations were contained in a report published by the US-based Human Rights Watch in 1998, and in the annual report of the Palestinian Independent Commission for Citizens' Rights published in February of that year.

US officials were said to have confirmed in March 1998 that the CIA was assisting the Palestinian security forces in the spheres of espionage, information-gathering and interrogation, in an attempt to reassure the Israeli Government of the PA's ability to take effective action against groups involved in attacks on Israeli targets. Later that month the death of a senior Hamas official provoked a serious deterioration in relations between the

Islamist organization and the PA. Hamas accused the PA of colluding with the Israeli authorities in the killing of Muhi ad-Din Sharif, and its threats to wreak revenge on Israeli citizens prompted the PA to arrest many of its members. In April, however, Hamas's political leader in Jordan retracted the allegation that the PA had collaborated with Israel. In October the PA detained 11 journalists who had attempted to obtain an interview with the spiritual leader of Hamas, Sheikh Ahmad Yassin (who was subsequently placed under house arrest); Palestinian police also arrested an outspoken cleric and Islamic Jihad's chief spokesman for publicly criticizing the newly signed Wye Memorandum (see above). In subsequent weeks several radio and television stations, as well as press offices, were closed down by the PA, and numerous journalists were imprisoned. There was also a marked increase in self-censorship in the state-controlled and pro-Government media.

In January 1999 the PLC approved a motion urging an end to political detentions and the release of all those imprisoned on exclusively political charges. The motion demanded the formation of a special committee to assess the case of every political prisoner in the Palestinian territories and to recommend which prisoners should be released: the committee was duly appointed in February, under the chairmanship of the Minister of Justice. Meanwhile, the PA responded by releasing 37 political prisoners. However, in late January Hamas and Islamic Jihad activists began a hunger strike in Jericho and Nablus, in protest at their continued detention without trial. In early February some 3,000 protesters marched to the headquarters of the PA, whom they accused of 'subservience to Israel and the CIA' (under the terms of the Wye Memorandum, the CIA was to monitor the PA's compliance with the security provisions of the accord), and throughout the month thousands of Palestinians demonstrated in support of the detainees. Also in February a Gaza-based police chief, known to be an opponent of Hamas, alleged that the organization had received some US $35m. from Iran in order to carry out suicide bombings against Israeli targets. Both Iran and Hamas leaders strongly denied the allegations. Relations between the PA and Hamas were further strained following the murder of a Palestinian intelligence officer in Rafah. In March a security agent and former member of Hamas' military wing was sentenced to death for the killing, while two accomplices received lengthy prison sentences. The verdict provoked serious clashes between Palestinian police and protesters in the Gaza Strip, during which two youths were shot dead by police; Arafat was forced to curtail an official visit to Jordan to address the domestic security crisis. Security surrounding the President was intensified in June, after a group of Palestinian dissidents calling themselves 'the Free Officers and the Honest People of Palestine' released a statement accusing leading Palestinian officials of corruption and of collaboration with Israel, and containing a veiled threat to assassinate the President; nine arrests were subsequently made. In November 20 leading Palestinian intellectuals (including members of the PLC) issued a joint statement in which they criticized alleged corruption, mismanagement and abuse of power within the PA, and accused Palestinian officials of ineffectiveness in the peace talks with Israel. The authorities responded by launching a crack-down on Arafat's critics, detaining several of the document's signatories or placing them under house arrest (they were later released on bail). In December a PLC member who had signed the anti-corruption manifesto was wounded by unidentified gunmen in Nablus. The establishment, announced in January 2000, of a Higher Council for Development under Arafat's chairmanship was welcomed by foreign donors as a major step towards ending corruption and mismanagement within the Palestinian administration.

In August 1999 a Palestinian national dialogue conference was held in Cairo, Egypt, between representatives of Fatah and the PFLP. Later in August Arafat and the Secretary-General of the DFLP, Naif Hawatmeh, met, also in Cairo, for the first time since 1993. At the end of the month representatives of nine Palestinian political factions, meeting in Ramallah, agreed on an agenda for a comprehensive national dialogue; Hamas and Islamic Jihad, however, refused to participate (the PA had recently arrested several suspected activists of these two organizations). It was reported in September 1999 that the leader of the PFLP, George Habash, was to resign. In late September the organization's deputy leader, Abu Ali Moustafa, was permitted by the Israeli Government to return to the West Bank from exile in Jordan, in order to participate in reconciliation talks with Arafat. However, although in late October Israeli officials had also reportedly granted an entry permit to the DFLP leader, they subsequently cancelled Hawatmeh's right of return. Habash finally stepped down in April 2000, and Abu Ali Moustafa was elected as the new PFLP leader in July. (Following Moustafa's assassination in August 2001, Ahmad Saadat assumed the party leadership.)

In February 2000 a controversial visit to the Palestinian Autonomous Areas by the French Prime Minister, Lionel Jospin (who described Hezbollah's resistance in southern Lebanon as 'terrorism'), resulted in angry protests by university students in the West Bank, which escalated into violent clashes between Palestinian civilians and the security forces. About 120 students were arrested, and the PA declared that henceforth all marches, rallies and public gatherings would require the prior consent of the police. In March two separate incidents were reported in which senior Palestinian officials were allegedly assaulted by members of the security forces. Meanwhile, in late 1999 Human Rights Watch had urged Arafat to take action in order to increase press freedom. In May 2000 the chief news editor at the Voice of Palestine radio station, Fathi Barqawi, was arrested after publicly criticizing the PA's 'secret' talks with Israel in Sweden. During May and June the PA intensified its crackdown on political activists and journalists who criticized Arafat's administration: four television and two radio stations were reportedly shut down by the authorities. At the end of July security forces in Gaza arrested leading Hamas official Abd al-Aziz ar-Rantisi, on charges including incitement and defamation.

After Palestinians in the West Bank and Gaza began a new *intifada* against Israeli occupation in late September 2000, some analysts suggested that Arafat's influence over Palestinians might be waning, as other Fatah leaders began to pursue their own agendas and became increasingly outspoken against the President. In particular, the leader of Fatah in the West Bank, Marwan Barghouthi, was said to attract considerable support among Palestinians there. In December a court in Nablus sentenced to death a Palestinian who had been convicted of collaborating with Israeli secret services in the assassination of a Hamas commander. The harsh sentence apparently signalled a change in policy by the PA, which in January 2001 carried out the executions, by firing squad, of two alleged collaborators. In mid-January Hisham Mekki, the Chairman of Palestinian Satellite Television and a director of the state broadcasting corporation (who had been a close associate of Arafat), was assassinated by unidentified gunmen in Gaza. The al-Aqsa Martyrs Brigade claimed responsibility for the killing, and accused the President of failing to end official corruption. The PA, for its part, accused Palestinian collaborators with Israel of being behind the attack; Israel vehemently denied the claim. In August a group of Palestinians were sentenced to death, and at least 100 others arrested, on charges of having collaborated with Israeli security services in recent attacks against Hamas officials. In early October three Palestinians were killed by security forces in Gaza during violent protests in support of Osama bin Laden. Although the al-Qa'ida leader, widely considered to have planned the previous month's terrorist attacks in the USA, claimed to have acted partly in protest against Israel's occupation of Palestinian territory, the PA sought to distance itself from the atrocities.

A report published by Human Rights Watch at the end of November 2001 accused the PA of systematic abuses of human rights since the start of the *intifada*, citing incidences of arbitrary arrests and of detention without trial and torture of prisoners. When Sheikh Ahmad Yassin was placed under house arrest in early December, hundreds of Hamas supporters demanded his release, resulting in clashes between Hamas gunmen and security forces. In late December violence intensified between Palestinian militants and security forces in the Gaza Strip, resulting in the deaths of at least six people. The arrest by Palestinian security services in Ramallah of the PFLP leader, Ahmad Saadat, in mid-January 2002 provoked fierce protests by militants, as well as accusations that Arafat was bowing to pressure from Israel and the USA. Tensions within Palestinian society worsened in early February when a crowd led by members of the security services entered a military court in Jenin and killed three defendants, two of whom had just been sentenced to death for the murder of a security official; the murders appeared to have been a revenge attack related to the issue of collaboration with Israel. In mid-March a suspected collaborator was hanged in Ramallah; two others were killed in Bethlehem, on suspicion of involvement in the deaths of two militants of the al-Aqsa Martyrs Brigade the previous year. During one day in early April 2002 11 alleged collaborators were reportedly murdered by Palestinians in Tulkarm, Qalqilya and Bethlehem. There were further incidences of 'vigilante killings' in subsequent weeks.

At an emergency meeting of the PA leadership held following Arafat's release from Israeli house arrest in early May 2002, the Minister of Parliamentary Affairs, Nabil Amr, tendered his resignation, reportedly after the President had rejected his proposals for a reorganization of the Cabinet. Arafat implemented major government changes in early June: membership of the cabinet was reduced from 31 ministers to 21, with several ministries being either merged or abolished. Maj.-Gen. Abd ar-Razzaq al-Yahya was appointed Minister of the Interior—a position previously held by Arafat. Salam Fayyad was named as the new Minister of Finance. The principal task of the new Government, which was described as an 'interim' administration, was to be the preparation and supervision of far-reaching reforms, including the convening of municipal elections towards the end of 2002 and of presidential and legislative elections by early 2003. The planned reforms would also require the Palestinian security services to be streamlined. Perhaps most importantly, draft legislation was being prepared that would create a new post of Prime Minister, to be responsible for the day-to-day administration of the PA. Arafat was placed under considerable pressure by the USA and the EU to implement wide-ranging reforms of the Palestinian administration: among their demands were the preparation of a new constitution and the establishment of an independent judiciary. President Bush emphasized in late June 2002 that, if the PA undertook such reforms, the USA would give its support to the creation of a 'provisional Palestinian state'. In early July Yasser Arafat dismissed Col Jibril Rajoub as commander of the Preventive Security Force in the West Bank and replaced him with a former governor of Jenin, Brig.-Gen. Zuheir Manasra. The Palestinian chief of police, Maj.-Gen. Ghazi al-Jabali, was similarly replaced at this time by his deputy, Col Salim al-Bardini. On 11 September the entire Palestinian Cabinet resigned in order to prevent a vote of 'no confidence' being brought in the legislature; however, the Cabinet was to remain in place until the appointment of a new administration (which was finally announced in late October). On the same day the PA President set 20 January 2003 as the day on which legislative and presidential elections were to be held. However, in late December 2002 Arafat announced a postponement of the polls, claiming that it would be untenable to hold elections while Israel continued to occupy PA-controlled population centres in the West Bank and Gaza.

Palestinian representatives participated in a conference on reform of the Palestinian administration, held in London in mid-January 2003, via a video link, after the Israeli Government refused to allow the delegates to attend the talks following a double suicide bombing in Tel-Aviv (in which more than 20 Israelis died). At the conference, which was also attended by officials of the Quartet group (comprising the USA, Russia, the UN and the EU) and representatives from Jordan, Egypt and Saudi Arabia, it was agreed that a new draft Palestinian constitution would be presented within two weeks. In mid-March the PLC endorsed a bill defining the role to be played by a future Palestinian Prime Minister, after having rejected amendments to the legislation proposed by Arafat according to which the President would retain authority over the appointment of Cabinet ministers. In the proposed power-sharing arrangement, the President was reportedly to control security and foreign affairs and would also have the authority to appoint and dismiss a premier, while the Prime Minister would nominate ministers and retain responsibility for domestic affairs. Mahmud Abbas (also known as Abu Mazen), the Secretary-General of the PLO Executive Committee, formally accepted the post of Prime Minister on 19 March. There were, however, reports of strong disagreements between Abbas and Arafat regarding the composition of the new Cabinet, particularly owing to Arafat's disapproval of Abbas' proposed choice of Muhammad Dahlan as the Minister of State for Security Affairs. On 29 April Mahmud Abbas was overwhelmingly endorsed as Prime Minister by the Palestinian legislature. A newly expanded Palestinian Cabinet was announced on that day, comprising 25 ministers under the premiership of Mahmud Abbas (who also became Minister of the Interior). Muhammad Dahlan was confirmed as the Minister of State for Security Affairs, while Nabil Shaath was named as the Minister of External Affairs and Saeb Erakat as the Minister of

Negotiation Affairs. Salam Fayyad—who some had believed would become premier—retained the finance portfolio in the new administration. A suicide bombing perpetrated by Hamas in Tel-Aviv on the day after the Cabinet was formed appeared to demonstrate the opposition of the Islamist organization to the composition of the new Palestinian administration. Nevertheless, on the same day both the Israeli and Palestinian Prime Ministers were presented with copies of the Quartet-sponsored 'road map' to an Israeli-Palestinian settlement, which had originally been agreed in December 2002. In mid-May 2003, on the eve of the first meeting between Mahmud Abbas and Ariel Sharon, Saeb Erakat announced his resignation from the Cabinet (reportedly having been angered by his omission from the Palestinian delegation chosen to attend the talks).

Government

In accordance with the Declaration of Principles on Palestinian Self-Rule and the Cairo Agreement on the Gaza Strip and Jericho (see Recent History, above), the PLO assumed control of the Jericho area of the West Bank and of the Gaza Strip on 17 May 1994. In November and December 1995, under the terms of the Israeli-Palestinian Interim Agreement on the West Bank and the Gaza Strip concluded in September 1995, Israeli armed forces withdrew from the West Bank towns of Nablus, Ramallah, Jenin, Tulkarm, Qalqilya and Bethlehem. In late December the PLO assumed responsibility in some 17 areas of civil administration in the town of Hebron. The Interim Agreement divided the West Bank into three zones: Areas A, B and C. As of July 1998, the PA had sole jurisdiction and security control in Area A (2% of the West Bank), but Israel retained authority over movement into and out of the area. In Area B (26% of the West Bank) the PA had some limited authority while Israel remained in control of security. Area C, the remaining 72% of the West Bank, was under Israeli military occupation. In accordance with the Wye Memorandum of October 1998 (see Recent History), Israel effected a further redeployment of its armed forces from approximately 500 sq km of West Bank territory in November. Of this, about 400 sq km became Area A territory and the remainder Area B territory. The Sharm esh-Sheikh Memorandum of September 1999 (see Recent History) was intended to facilitate completion of outstanding commitments under agreements previously signed, as well as to enable the resumption of 'final status' negotiations with Israel. By October 2000 approximately 17.2% of the West Bank (Area A) was under sole Palestinian jurisdiction and security control, although Israel retained authority over access to and from the zone; about 23.8% (Area B) was under Israeli military control, with the PA responsible for civil administration and public order; the remaining 59% (Area C) remained under Israeli military occupation. The total area of the territory over which the PA will eventually assume control, and the extent of its jurisdiction there, remain subject to 'final status' talks.

Defence

Paramilitary forces in the Gaza Strip and in the areas of the West Bank where the PA has assumed responsibility for security totalled an estimated 29,000 in August 2002. They included a Public Security Force of 14,000 (Gaza 6,000, West Bank 8,000); a Civil Police Force of 10,000 (Gaza 4,000, West Bank 6,000); a Preventive Security Force of 3,000 (Gaza 1,200, West Bank 1,800); a General Intelligence Force of 1,000; a Military Intelligence Force of 500; and a Presidential Security Force of an estimated 500. In addition, there are small forces belonging to Coastal Police, Civil Defence, Air Force, a Customs and Excise Police Force and a University Security Service. Units of the Palestine National Liberation Army (PNLA) are garrisoned in various countries in the Middle East and North Africa. The security budget of the Palestinian Autonomous Areas was estimated at US $500m. in 1999.

Economic Affairs

In 2001, according to estimates by the World Bank, the gross national income (GNI) of the West Bank and the Gaza Strip, measured at average 1999–2001 prices, was US $4,177m., equivalent to $1,350 per head. During 1990–2001, it was estimated, the population increased at an average annual rate of 4.2%, while gross domestic product (GDP) per head decreased, in real terms, by an average of 4.6% per year. Overall GDP decreased, in real terms, at an average annual rate of 0.5% in 1994–2001; GDP declined by an estimated 11.9% in 2001.

Agriculture and fishing contributed 10.2% of the GDP of the West Bank and Gaza Strip in 2000. In 2001 agriculture (including hunting, forestry and fishing) engaged an estimated 12.2% of the employed Palestinian labour force. Although the agricultural sector is focused mainly on supplying local needs, about one-half of Palestinian exports are derived from agricultural production. Citrus fruits are the principal export crop, and horticulture also makes a significant contribution to trade. Other important crops are tomatoes, cucumbers and potatoes. The livestock sector is also significant. According to the World Bank, agricultural GDP decreased at an average annual rate of 6.7% during 1994–2000; however, it increased by 8.5% in 1999.

Industry (mining and quarrying, manufacturing, electricity and water supply and construction) contributed 23.3% of Palestinian GDP in 2000. The industrial sector (including gas utilities) engaged some 28.9% of the employed labour force of the West Bank and Gaza in 2001. Construction alone accounted for 6.5% of GDP in 2000 and employed some 14.5% of the working population in 2001. During 1994–2000 industrial GDP increased at an average rate of 0.4% annually; the sector's GDP expanded by 3.1% in 1999.

Mining and quarrying contributed 0.7% of the GDP of the Palestinian territories in 1998, and engaged an estimated 0.4% of the employed labour force in 2001. Two significant gas fields were discovered off the Gazan coast in 1999.

Manufacturing contributed 16.5% of the GDP of the West Bank and Gaza Strip in 1999, according to the World Bank. In 2001 about 13.8% of the employed labour force were engaged in the sector. Palestinian manufacturing is characterized by small-scale enterprises which typically engage in food-processing and the production of textiles and footwear. The frequent closure of the West Bank and Gaza by the Israeli authorities has prompted the development of free-trade industrial zones on the Palestinian side of the boundaries separating Israel from the territories: Israeli and Palestinian enterprises can continue to take advantage of low-cost Palestinian labour at times of closure, and the zones also benefit from tax exemptions and export incentives. Manufacturing GDP increased at an average annual rate of 3.6% during 1994–2000; the sector expanded by 1.6% in 1999.

The energy sector (comprising electricity and water supply) accounted for an estimated 2.0% of Palestinian GDP in 1998. Electricity, gas and water utilities together employed some 0.2% of the labour force of the West Bank and Gaza in 2001. In the West Bank there is no utility supplying electric power apart from the Jerusalem District Electric Company Ltd, which supplies Jerusalem, Bethlehem, Ramallah and Al-Birah. Most municipalities in the Gaza Strip purchase electricity from the Israel Electric Corporation. However, the Palestine Electric Company (established in 1999) is constructing a power plant in Gaza, while the National Electric Company (created in 2000) plans to build a second power plant in the West Bank.

In 2000 the services sector contributed 66.5% of Palestinian GDP, and engaged an estimated 58.9% of the employed labour force in 2001. Although tourism has generally contributed more than 10% of the GDP of the West Bank and Gaza, it has been all but halted by the ongoing violence in the territories. The GDP of the services sector expanded at an average rate of 2.1% per year during 1994–2000; services GDP increased by 6.4% in 1999.

In 2000, according to preliminary estimates, the West Bank and Gaza Strip recorded a visible trade deficit of US $2,303m. and a deficit of $1,029m. on the current account of the balance of payments. In 1999 the Israel's imports (c.i.f.) from the West Bank and Gaza was $280m., while the value of Israel's exports (f.o.b.) to the Palestinian areas was $1,535m. In the absence of seaport facilities and of an airport (Gaza International Airport was opened in November 1998 but has frequently been closed by the Israeli authorities), foreign trade (in terms of value) has been conducted almost exclusively with Israel since occupation. Most Palestinian exports are of agricultural or horticultural products. One notable feature of this trade is that Palestinian goods have often in the past been exported to Israel, and subsequently re-exported as originating in Israel.

In 1998, according to data published by the IMF, the PA recorded an overall budget deficit of US $144.7m., equivalent to some 3.4% of GDP. The annual rate of inflation in the West Bank and Gaza averaged 4.5% in 1996–2001; consumer prices increased by an average of 2.8% in 2000 and by 1.2% in 2001. According to official estimates, some 26% of the labour force were unemployed in 2001. However, by early 2002 the Palestinian Economic Council for Development and Reconstruction (PECDAR) estimated that unemployment had risen to 53% as a result of the Israeli economic blockade.

The prospects for an improvement in economic conditions in the Palestinian Autonomous Areas, which remain highly dependent on Israel, are inextricably linked to the full implementation of the Oslo accords (see Recent History, above) and the outcome of the (currently suspended) 'final status' negotiations between the PA and Israel. Examples of this economic dependency are the large number of Palestinian workers employed in Israel, and the reliance of the trade sector on Israel as a market for exports and source of imports. The underdevelopment of Palestinian agriculture and industry is a consequence of the Israeli occupation, when investment became orientated towards residential construction at the expense of these sectors. Agriculture remains focused mainly on meeting local demand, although the sector supplies the bulk of Palestinian exports and there is proven demand for Palestinian products beyond the Israeli market. The expansion of Palestinian agriculture is also limited by problems with irrigation: access to water supplies is subject to 'final status' discussions. Economic conditions in the West Bank and Gaza have deteriorated markedly since 1993, largely as a result of frequent border closures enforced by the Israeli authorities in reprisal for terrorist attacks by militant Islamist groups opposed to the Oslo accords. Such closures lead to an immediate rise in the rate of unemployment among Palestinians, increase transportation costs for Palestinian goods and, at times, halt trade entirely. The Oslo accords provide for the development of seaport facilities and for the opening of Gaza International Airport and of a safe passage linking the Gaza Strip with the West Bank. However, by mid-2003 the provision for a seaport at Gaza had still not been implemented, while the airport and safe passage were both closed by the Israeli authorities. From 1998 the PA has aimed to achieve current budget surpluses, and to focus public expenditure on health, education and infrastructural investment. In early 2000 the PA announced the creation of a Palestinian Investment Fund and a Higher Council for Development, the latter being charged with the preparation of a comprehensive privatization strategy. However, in the context of the renewed Palestinian *intifada*, in November 2000 Israel imposed a complete economic blockade on the West Bank and Gaza, and halted the payment of tax transfers to the PA. The closure quickly reversed any recent economic successes: in the first half of 2000 unemployment had reportedly been declining, GDP growth was strong, and private-sector investment was increasing sharply. By September 2001, however, economic losses resulting from the blockade were estimated at US $5,300m., including losses incurred as a result of the replacement of long-term investment programmes by short-term projects aimed at reducing rapidly escalating levels of unemployment and poverty. According to PECDAR, about 64% of Palestinians were living in poverty in early 2002. The economy was in a state of paralysis, with the World Bank estimating that GDP had contracted by some 12% in 2001; productive activity had virtually ceased in much of the West Bank. Amid continued border closures, military incursions by Israel into Palestinian towns, and the destruction of the PA's infrastructure, the administration was effectively bankrupt. In an attempt to ease the chronic economic situation, in October 2000 Arab states pledged aid worth US $1,000m. to the PA. The European Union authorized payments totalling $80m. in November–December. In the latter month the World Bank also announced that it was to grant $12m. for an Emergency Response Programme: the World Bank estimated that international donor funding to the PA approached $930m. in 2001. In March 2002 Arab states pledged a further $330m. in aid, and in the following month international donors agreed to grant $900m. to assist the PA in rebuilding vital infrastructure destroyed during the Israeli military offensive and a further $300m. as emergency relief. In May the UN Relief and Works Agency for Palestine Refugees in the Near East (UNRWA) assessed that, in addition to $117m. that it had previously estimated as being necessary to fund its emergency programmes for 2002, some $70m. would be required to address the immediate humanitarian needs of Palestinians in the West Bank and Gaza arising from the recent Israeli military incursions into the Palestinian areas.

Education

In the West Bank the Jordanian education system is in operation. Services are provided by the Israeli Civil Administration, the UN Relief and Works Agency for Palestine Refugees in the Near East (UNRWA) and private, voluntary organizations, which provide all university and most community college education. There are 20 community and teacher training colleges in the West Bank, and six universities (including an open university). The Egyptian system of education operates in the Gaza Strip, where there are two universities and one teaching training college. Palestinian education has been severely disrupted since 1987, and more recently as a result of the Palestinian *intifada* which began in late 2000. Since May 1994 the PA has assumed responsibility for education in Gaza and parts of the West Bank. In 2000/01 66,506 pupils attended 806 preprimary schools, while 863,730 pupils attended 1,364 primary schools. There were 83,569 students enrolled at 554 secondary institutions in that year, while 88,721 students attended universities or equivalent third-level institutions.

Since 1950 UNRWA has provided education services to all Palestinian refugees. The focus of UNRWA's education programme is basic primary and junior secondary schooling, offered free of charge to all refugee children and youth in accordance with local systems. In 2002/03 UNRWA operated 95 schools in the West Bank and 174 in the Gaza Strip, providing education to 60,003 pupils in the West Bank and to 189,317 pupils in Gaza. In addition, UNRWA operated four vocational training centres and awarded 13 university scholarships.

Public Holidays

2003: 1 January (Fatah Day), 12 February* (Id al-Adha, Feast of the Sacrifice), 15 November (Independence Day), 26 November* (Id al-Fitr, end of Ramadan).

2004: 1 January (Fatah Day), 2 February* (Id al-Adha, Feast of the Sacrifice), 14 November* (Id al-Fitr, end of Ramadan), 15 November (Independence Day).

*These holidays are dependent on the Islamic lunar calendar and may vary by one or two days from the dates given.
Christian holidays are observed by the Christian Arab community.

Statistical Survey

Source (unless otherwise indicated): Palestinian Central Bureau of Statistics (PCBS), POB 1647, Ramallah; tel. 2-2406340; fax 2-2406343; e-mail pcbshp@pcbs.pna.org; internet www.pcbs.org.

Note: Unless otherwise indicated, data include East Jerusalem, annexed by Israel in 1967.

Area and Population

AREA, POPULATION AND DENSITY

Area (sq km)	6,020*
Population (census of 9 December 1997)†	
Males	1,470,506
Females	1,425,177
Total	2,895,683
Population (official estimates at mid-year)	
2000	3,150,056
2001	3,298,951
2002	3,464,550
Density (per sq km) at mid-2002	575.5

* 2,324 sq miles. The total comprises: West Bank 5,655 sq km (2,183 sq miles); Gaza Strip 365 sq km (141 sq miles).

† Figures include an estimate of 210,209 for East Jerusalem and an adjustment of 83,805 for estimated underenumeration. The total comprises 1,873,476 (males 951,693; females 921,783) in the West Bank (including East Jerusalem) and 1,022,207 (males 518,813; females 503,394) in the Gaza Strip. The data exclude Jewish settlers. According to official Israeli estimates, the population of Israelis residing in Jewish localities in the West Bank (excluding East Jerusalem) and Gaza Strip was 208,300 at 31 December 2001.

GOVERNORATES

(official estimates, mid-2002)

	Area (sq km)	Popu-lation*	Density (per sq km)
West Bank			
Janin (Jenin)	583	236,428	405.5
Tubas	402	43,110	107.2
Tulkarm	246	156,242	635.1
Qalqilya	166	86,290	519.8
Salfit	204	57,339	281.1
Nabulus (Nablus)	605	304,347	503.1
Ram Allah (Ramallah) and Al-Birah	855	256,483	300.0
Al-Quds (Jerusalem)†	345	380,422	1,102.7
Ariha (Jericho)	593	38,968	65.7
Beit Lahm (Bethlehem)	659	161,579	245.9
Al-Khalil (Hebron)	997	481,433	482.9
Gaza Strip			
North Gaza	61	236,298	3,873.7
Gaza	74	446,416	6,032.6
Deir al-Balah	58	182,882	3,153.1
Khan Yunus (Khan Yunis) . . .	108	245,588	2,274.0
Rafah	64	150,725	2,355.1
Total	6,020	3,464,550	575.5

* Figures exclude Jewish settlers.

† Figures refer only to the eastern sector of the city.

PRINCIPAL LOCALITIES

(estimated population at mid-2002, excluding Jewish settlers)

West Bank			
Al-Quds (Jerusalem)	242,081*	Adh-Dhahiriya . .	25,348
Al-Khalil (Hebron) .	147,291	Ar-Ram and Dahiyat	
Nabulus (Nablus) .	121,344	al-Bareed	23,038
Tulkarm	41,109	Ram Allah	
		(Ramallah) . . .	22,493
Qalqilya	39,580	Halhul	19,345
Yattah (Yatta) . .	38,023	Dura	19,124
Al-Birah	34,920	Ariha (Jericho) . .	18,239
Janin (Jenin) . . .	32,300	Qabatiya	17,788
Beit Lahm			
(Bethlehem) . .	26,847		
Gaza Strip			
Ghazzah (Gaza) . .	361,651	Beit Lahya . . .	50,576
Khan Yunus (Khan		Deir al-Balah . .	43,593
Yunis)	110,677	Bani Suhaylah . .	28,761
Jabalyah (Jabalia) .	104,620	Beit Hanun . . .	27,341
Rafah	62,452	Tel as-Sultan Camp .	21,477
An-Nuseirat . . .	56,449	Al-Maghazi Camp .	21,278

* The figure refers only to the eastern sector of the city.

BIRTHS AND DEATHS

(estimates)*

	1999	2000	2001
Live births:			
West Bank	51,306	54,718	54,791
Gaza Strip	36,709	38,277	37,735
Deaths:			
West Bank	5,303	5,488	5,329
Gaza Strip	3,685	3,630	3,874

* Excluding Jewish settlers.

MARRIAGES

(number registered)

	1999	2000	2001
West Bank	16,099	14,867	14,483
Gaza Strip	8,775	9,023	10,152

ECONOMICALLY ACTIVE POPULATION*

('000 persons aged 10 years and over, labour force survey, 2001)

	Males	Females	Total
Agriculture, hunting, forestry and fishing	41	21	62
Mining and quarrying	2	—	2
Manufacturing	62	8	70
Electricity, gas and water supply .	1	—	1
Construction	73	1	74
Wholesale and retail trade . . .	83	6	89
Hotels and restaurants	10	—	10
Transport, storage and communications	28	—	28
Financial intermediation . . .	3	2	5
Real estate, renting and business activities	6	2	8
Public administration and defence	67	5	72
Education	29	24	53
Health and social work	13	6	19
Other community, social and personal service activities . .	10	2	12
Extra-territorial organizations and bodies	3	1	4
Total employed	431	78	509
Unemployed	162	13	175
Total labour force	593	91	684
West Bank	414	70	484
Gaza Strip	179	21	200

* Figures refer to Palestinians only.

2002 (Sample survey, '000 persons aged 15 years and over, April–June): *Total employed* 451 (West Bank 318; Gaza Strip 133); *Unemployed* 229 (West Bank 134; Gaza Strip 95); *Total labour force* 680 (West Bank 452; Gaza Strip 228).

Health and Welfare

KEY INDICATORS

Total fertility rate (children per woman, 1999)	5.9
Under-5 mortality rate (per 1,000 live births, 2001) . . .	24
Hospital beds (per 1,000 head, 2000)	1.4
Access to water (% of persons, 2000)	96.2
Access to sanitation (% of persons, 2000)	99.6

For sources and definitions, see explanatory note on p. vi.

Agriculture

PRINCIPAL CROPS

('000 metric tons, year ending September)

	1998/99	1999/2000	2000/01
Wheat	11.1	53.4	25.0
Barley	2.8	13.9	12.6
Maize	1.7	11.9	9.7
Potatoes	52.9	47.3	51.5
Sweet potatoes	5.0	9.5	6.7
Olives	35.3	156.5	38.5
White cabbages	11.4	13.6	16.5
Tomatoes	172.0	196.1	176.2
Cauliflower	22.2	19.2	21.3
Squash	39.1	44.8	44.4
Cucumbers	109.0	135.7	147.7
Aubergines (Eggplants) . . .	37.1	39.7	42.6
Chillies	9.9	11.0	11.2
Dry onions	14.0	25.6	19.0
Green kidney beans	4.7	6.8	6.1
Jew's mallow	10.6	10.9	10.9
Watermelons	13.3	7.6	8.3
Musk-melons	6.0	5.7	3.7
Grapes	44.5	56.9	59.4
Plums	6.7	12.7	16.0
Oranges	97.3	76.7	83.6
Mandarins and clementines . .	18.1	12.9	12.3
Lemons	23.2	20.8	23.0
Grapefruit	5.8	4.6	3.4
Bananas	26.4	9.4	5.9
Strawberries	4.6	5.5	5.6
Figs	7.3	8.2	5.4
Guava	11.9	12.7	11.9
Almonds	3.4	4.4	4.4

LIVESTOCK

('000 head, year ending September)

	1998/99	1999/2000	2000/01
Cattle	23.9	23.7	26.6
Sheep	504.1	566.4	615.8
Goats	295.0	308.8	313.6
Chickens	50,477	45,975	50,408

Fishing

Gaza Strip

(metric tons, live weight)

	1998	1999*	2000*
Bogue	162	160	160
Jack and horse mackerels . . .	115	115	115
Sardinellas	1,780	1,750	1,750
Chub mackerel	337	340	340
Shrimps and prawns	161	160	160
Cuttlefish and bobtail squids . .	144	145	145
Total catch (incl. others) . .	3,625	3,600	3,600

* FAO estimates.

Source: FAO, *Yearbook of Fishery Statistics*.

Finance

CURRENCY AND EXCHANGE RATES:
At present there is no domestic Palestinian currency in use. The Israeli shekel, the Jordanian dinar and the US dollar all circulate within the West Bank and the Gaza Strip.

BUDGET OF THE PALESTINIAN AUTHORITY
(estimates, US $ million)

Revenue	1996	1997	1998
Domestic revenue	264.6	329.4	321.1
Tax revenue	178.8	210.9	224.3
Income tax	52.4	66.0	68.4
Value-added tax	65.8	75.0	80.6
Other receipts	85.8	118.5	96.8
Revenue clearances* . . .	419.6	496.0	542.0
Value-added tax	216.7	216.5	202.1
Petroleum excise	100.4	111.3	106.8
Total	684.2	825.4	863.1

* Figures refer to an apportionment of an agreed pool of selected tax revenues arising as a result of the de facto customs union between Israel and the Palestinian territories. Israel is the collecting agent for these receipts and periodically makes transfers to the Palestinian Authority.

Expenditure†	1996	1997	1998
Current expenditure	779.3	863.2	802.6
Wages and salaries	402.5	470.9	466.8
Civil service	246.5	273.4	286.0
Police force	156.0	197.5	180.9
Other purposes	376.8	392.3	335.8
Capital expenditure	173.6	214.4	204.7
Total	952.9	1,077.6	1,007.3

† Excluding the cost of foreign-financed employment programmes (estimates, US $ million): 49.2 in 1996; 5.7 in 1997; 0.5 in 1998.
Source: IMF, *West Bank and Gaza Strip: Economic Developments in the Five Years Since Oslo* (1999).

1999 (estimates, US $ million): Total revenue 1,589; Total expenditure 1,740.

2000 (estimates, US $ million): Total revenue 1,386; Total expenditure 1,386 (Current 940; Capital 446).

COST OF LIVING
(Consumer Price Index; base: 1996 = 100)

	1999	2000	2001
Food	119.3	121.2	120.7
Beverages and tobacco	126.9	130.2	131.9
Textiles, clothing and footwear .	123.2	125.9	123.4
Housing	116.7	126.5	133.2
All items (incl. others) . . .	119.9	123.3	124.8

NATIONAL ACCOUNTS
(US $ million at current prices)

Expenditure on the Gross Domestic Product

	1998	1999	2000
Government final consumption expenditure	979.5	893.1	1,114.1
Private final consumption expenditure	4,286.9	4,235.2	4,131.4
Increase in stocks	107.5	179.3	63.1
Gross fixed capital formation . .	1,448.5	1,523.6	1,327.6
Statistical discrepancy*	15.4	10.2	7.3
Total domestic expenditure .	5,266.3	5,128.3	5,245.5
Exports of goods and services . .	887.0	798.3	842.1
Less Imports of goods and services	3,482.4	3,216.2	3,053.6
GDP in purchasers' values . .	4,242.3	4,413.5	4,432.0

* Referring to the difference between the sum of the expenditure components and official estimates of GDP, compiled from the production approach.

Gross Domestic Product by Economic Activity

	1998	1999	2000
Agriculture and fishing	481.1	482.8	420.6
Mining, manufacturing, electricity and water	839.6	664.2	689.9
Construction	534.9	386.6	268.0
Wholesale and retail trade . . .	406.7	545.8	520.9
Transport	209.1	231.1	227.6
Financial intermediation . . .	123.6	150.0	180.9
Public administration and defence	403.9	455.7	571.1
Domestic services of households .	7.8	7.4	7.9
Public-owned enterprises . . .	114.5	163.5	184.1
Other services	935.4	1,024.2	1,045.0
Sub-total	3,762.4	4,093.4	4,116.0
Financial intermediation services indirectly measured	−99.0	−116.2	−144.1
Taxes on imports (net)	578.9	436.3	460.3
GDP in purchasers' values . .	4,242.3	4,413.5	4,432.0

BALANCE OF PAYMENTS
(preliminary estimates, US $ million, excluding East Jerusalem)

	1998	1999	2000
Exports of goods f.o.b.	610.6	602.8	697.4
Imports of goods f.o.b.	−3,021.7	−3,220.7	−3,000.0
Trade balance	−2,411.1	−2,617.8	−2,302.7
Exports of services	394.5	471.3	393.1
Imports of services	−507.5	−522.1	−524.7
Balance on goods and services	−2,524.1	−2,668.7	−2,434.3
Other income received	931.5	960.6	867.4
Other income paid	−29.9	−23.2	−42.4
Balance on goods, services and income	−1,622.4	−1,731.3	−1,609.3
Current transfers received . . .	540.2	545.9	702.0
Current transfers paid	−134.7	−173.8	−121.5
Current balance	−1,216.9	−1,359.2	−1,028.8
Capital account (net)	261.1	237.3	198.1
Direct investment abroad . . .	−160.1	−169.4	−439.5
Direct investment from abroad .	218.2	188.6	62.0
Portfolio investment (net) . . .	−80.3	−106.0	−101.0
Other investment (net)	656.9	918.6	1,315.8
Net errors and omissions . . .	286.3	255.0	77.4
Overall balance	52.9	35.1	84.1

External Trade

PRINCIPAL COMMODITIES
(US $ '000)

Imports c.i.f.	1998	1999	2000
Food and live animals	447,195	524,314	431,837
Beverages and tobacco	97,494	104,929	101,711
Crude materials (inedible) except fuels	67,185	73,321	62,136
Mineral fuels, lubricants, etc. . .	409,881	391,547	455,507
Animal and vegetable oils and fats	19,558	23,528	17,942
Chemicals and related products .	189,739	225,559	230,765
Basic manufactures	565,422	715,674	522,204
Machinery and transport equipment	386,625	619,903	352,360
Miscellaneous manufactured articles	175,642	321,232	199,200
Other commmodities and transactions	14,363	10,221	9,145
Total	2,375,102	3,007,227	2,382,807

Exports f.o.b.	1998	1999	2000
Food and live animals	61,793	60,878	84,552
Beverages and tobacco	25,432	26,348	13,573
Crude materials (inedible) except fuels	17,566	13,406	15,760
Mineral fuels, lubricants, etc. . .	7,006	4,952	3,671
Animal and vegetable oils and fats	5,343	4,133	5,713
Chemicals and related products .	24,631	30,250	29,687
Basic manufactures	165,862	151,240	153,239
Machinery and transport equipment	20,736	20,758	23,958
Miscellaneous manufactured articles	64,397	71,545	70,596
Other commodities and transactions	1,080	419	198
Total	394,846	372,148	400,857

Transport

ROAD TRAFFIC
(registered motor vehicles holding Palestinian licence, December 2000)

	West Bank	Gaza Strip	Total
Private cars	53,026	37,098	90,124
Taxis	6,090	1,173	7,263
Buses and minibuses . . .	865	177	1,042
Trucks and commercial cars . .	13,310	8,500	21,810
Motorcycles and scooters . . .	38	253	291
Tractors	1,207	1,291	2,498
Special service and other vehicles .	112	169	281
Total	74,854	49,014	123,868

Tourism

ARRIVALS OF VISITORS AT HOTELS*

	1999	2000	2001
Total	316,949	335,711	60,208

* Including Palestinians (16,598 in 1999; 25,520 in 2000; 17,432 in 2001).

Communications Media

	1999	2000	2001
Telephones ('000 main lines in use)	222.2	270.0	256.9
Mobile cellular telephones ('000 subscribers)	117	285	300
Internet users ('000)	n.a.	35	60

Source: International Telecommunication Union.

Book production (1996): 114 titles; 571,000 copies (Source: UNESCO, *Statistical Yearbook*).

Education

(2000/01)

	Institutions	Teachers	Students
Pre-primary	806	2,550	66,506
Primary . .	1,364*		863,730
Secondary:		33,532	
general	545†		79,663
vocational	9		3,906
Higher:			
universities, etc.	15	1,848	53,563
distance learning	1	219	29,845
other	21	438	5,313

* Schools for primary education only.
† Including schools for primary and secondary education, and including 30 schools providing both general and vocational education.

Adult literacy rate (official estimates): 90.2% (males 95.3%; females 85.0%) in 2001.

Directory

Administration

PALESTINIAN NATIONAL AUTHORITY

Appointed in May 1994, the Palestinian National Authority (PNA), generally known internationally as the Palestinian Authority (PA), has assumed some of the civil responsibilities formerly exercised by the Israeli Civil Administration in the Gaza Strip and parts of the West Bank.

Executive President: YASSER ARAFAT (assumed office 12 February 1996).

CABINET
(May 2003)

Prime Minister and Minister of the Interior: MAHMUD ABBAS (Fatah).

Minister of Cabinet Affairs: YASSER ABD AR-RABBUH (Independent).

Minister of External Affairs: Dr NABIL SHAATH (Fatah).

Minister of Finance: Dr SALAM FAYYAD (Independent).

Minister of Planning: NABIL QASSIS (Independent).

Minister of Economy and Trade: MAHER AL-MASRI (Fatah).

Minister of Negotiation Affairs: (vacant).

Minister of Education and Higher Education: Dr NA'IM ABU AL-HUMMUS (Fatah).

Minister of Health: KAMAL ASH-SHIRAFI (Independent).

Minister of Local Government: JAMAL SHOBAKI (Fatah).

Minister of Justice: ABD AL-KARIM ABU SALAH (Independent).

Minister of Public Works and Housing: HAMDAN ASHOUR (Fatah).

Minister of Social Affairs: INTISAR AL-WASIR (Fatah).

Minister of Agriculture: RAFIK AN-NATSHEH (Fatah).

Minister of Culture: ZIAD ABU AMR (Independent).

Minister of Information: NABIL AMR (Fatah).

Minister of Energys: Dr AZZAM ASH-SHAWWA (Fatah).

Minister of Labour: GHASSAN AL-KHATIB (Hezb ash-Sha'ab).

Minister of Tourism: MITRI ABU AYTAH (Fatah).

Minister of Telecommunications and Information Technology: AZZAM AL-AHMAD (Fatah).

Minister of Transport: SA'ADI AL-KRUNZ (Fatah).

Minister of Prisoners' Affairs: HISHAM ABD AR-RAZZAQ (Fatah).

Minister of State for Security Affairs: MUHAMMAD DAHLAN (Fatah).

Minister of State without Portfolio: ABD AL-FATTAH HAMAYEL (Fatah).

Minister of Awqaf (Religious Endowments): (vacant).

MINISTRIES

Ministry of Agriculture: POB 197, Ramallah; tel. (2) 2961080; fax (2) 2961212; e-mail moa@planet.edu.

Ministry of Awqaf (Religious Endowments): POB 54825, Jerusalem; tel. (2) 6282085; fax (2) 2986401.

Ministry of Civil Affairs: Ramallah; tel. (2) 2987336; fax (2) 2987335.

Ministry of Culture: POB 147, Ramallah; tel. (2) 2986205; fax (2) 2986204; e-mail moc@gov.ps; internet www.moc.gov.ps.

Ministry of Economy and Trade: POB 1629, Ramallah; POB 402, Gaza; tel. (2) 2981214; fax (2) 2981207; tel. (8) 2826139; fax (8) 2866700; e-mail info@met.gov.ps.

Ministry of Education: POB 576, Ramallah; tel. (2) 2983254; fax (2) 2983261; e-mail moe@planet.com; internet www.moe.gov.ps.

Ministry of Finance: Sateh Marhaba, Al-Birah/Ramallah; POB 4007, Gaza; tel. (2) 2400372; fax (2) 2405880; e-mail mofdep@hally .edu; tel. (8) 2829243; fax (8) 2820696.

Ministry of Health: POB 14, al-Mukhtar St, Nablus; POB 1035, Abu Khadra Center, Gaza; tel. (9) 2384772; fax (9) 2384777; e-mail moh@gov.ps; internet www.moh.gov.ps; tel. (8) 2829173; fax (8) 2826295; e-mail mohgaza@palnet.com.

Ministry of Higher Education: POB 17360, Ramallah; tel. (2) 2982600; fax (2) 2954518; e-mail minhed@planet.edu; internet www .mohe.gov.ps.

Ministry of Housing: POB 4034, Gaza; tel. (8) 2822233; fax (8) 2822235.

Ministry of Industry: POB 2073, Ramallah; POB 4053, Gaza; tel. (2) 2987641; fax (2) 2987640; tel. (8) 2826463; fax (8) 2824884; e-mail industry_wb@gov.ps; internet www.industry.gov.ps.

Ministry of Information: POB 224, Al-Birah/Ramallah; Gaza; tel. (2) 2986465; fax (2) 2954043; tel. (8) 2866888; fax (8) 2821672; e-mail minfo@gov.ps; internet www.minfo.gov.ps.

Ministry of the Interior: Gaza; tel. (8) 2829185; fax (8) 2862500.

Ministry of Jerusalem Affairs: POB 20479, Jerusalem; tel. (2) 6273330; fax (2) 6286820.

Ministry of Justice: Gaza; tel. (8) 2822231; fax (8) 2867109.

Ministry of Labour: POB 350, Ramallah Industrial Zone, Ramallah; POB 4021, Gaza; tel. (2) 2900375; fax (2) 2900607; e-mail narman@gov.ps; internet www.mol.gov.ps; tel. (8) 2829146; fax (8) 2822400.

Ministry of Local Government: Jericho; tel. (2) 2321260; fax (2) 2321240; internet www.p-ol.com/~molg.

Ministry of Planning and International Co-operation: Ramallah; POB 4017, Gaza; tel. (2) 5747045; fax (2) 5747046; tel. (8) 2829260; fax (8) 2824090; e-mail info@nmopic.pna.net; internet www.mopic.gov.ps.

Ministry of Public Works: Gaza; tel. (8) 2829232; fax (8) 2823653; e-mail mopgaza@palnet.com.

Ministry of Social Affairs: POB 3525, Ramallah; tel. (2) 2986181; fax (2) 2985239.

Ministry of Supply: Gaza; tel. (8) 2824324; fax (8) 2826430.

Ministry of Telecommunications and Information Technology: Ramallah; Gaza; tel. (2) 9986555; fax (2) 9986556; tel. (8) 2829171; fax (8) 2824555.

Ministry of Tourism and Antiquities: POB 534, Manger St, Bethlehem; tel. (2) 2741581; fax (2) 2743753; e-mail mota@ visit-palestine.com; internet www.visit-palestine.com.

Ministry of Transport: POB 399, Ramallah; tel. (2) 2986945; fax (2) 2986943.

Ministry of Youth and Sports: POB 52, Ramallah; tel. (2) 2985981; fax (2) 2985991.

President

The first election for a Palestinian Executive President was contested on 20 January 1996 by two candidates: Yasser Arafat and Samiha Khalil. Arafat received 88.1% of the votes cast and Khalil 9.3%; the remaining 2.6% of the votes were spoilt.

Legislature

PALESTINIAN LEGISLATIVE COUNCIL

Speaker: AHMAD QURAY.

General Election, 20 January 1996

Party	Seats
Fatah	54
Independent Fatah	12
Independent Islamists	4
Popular Front for the Liberation of Palestine (PFLP)	1
Palestinian Democratic Union (FIDA)	1
Independents	16
Total	**88***

* The total number of seats in the Palestinian Legislative Council—including one which is automatically reserved for the Palestinian President—is 89.

The first Palestinian legislative elections took place in 16 multi-member constituencies (including East Jerusalem) on 20 January 1996. An estimated 79% of eligible voters participated in the elections. Prior to the polls European Union observers criticized the election commission appointed by Yasser Arafat for late alterations to electoral procedure, which, it was felt, might prejudice the prospects of some candidates. Although irregularities were reported during voting, these were not regarded as sufficiently serious to compromise the final outcome. The elections were officially boycotted by all sections of the so-called Palestinian 'rejectionist' opposition, including the Islamic Resistance Movement (Hamas) and Islamic Jihad, although Hamas did endorse a list of 'approved' candidates for those voters who chose to participate. All deputies elected to the Palestinian Legislative Council (PLC) automatically became members of the Palestine National Council (PNC), the existing 483 members of which were subsequently permitted to return from exile by the Israeli authorities, in order, among other things, to consider amendments to the Palestinian National Charter (or PLO Covenant), which has largely been superseded by the agreements concluded between Israel and the PLO since September 1993. Under Palestinian legislation, the tenure of the PLC was scheduled to expire after the Israeli Government has implemented all of its outstanding obligations under the terms of the Interim Agreement of 1995 (see Recent History). Elections to the PLC were, however, scheduled to take place concurrently with presidential elections on 20 January 2003, although in late December 2002 Arafat announced a postponement of the polls, owing to the continued Israeli occupation of PA-controlled areas in the West Bank and Gaza.

Political Organizations

Palestine Liberation Organization (PLO): Gaza City; after the conclusion of the Cairo Agreement on the Gaza Strip and Jericho, signed by the PLO and Israel on 4 May 1994, the PLO gradually transferred its headquarters from Tunis, Tunisia, to the Gaza Strip; f. 1964; the supreme organ of the PLO is the Palestine National Council (PNC; Speaker SALIM AZ-ZA'NUN), while the PLO Executive Committee (Chair. YASSER ARAFAT; Sec.-Gen. MAHMUD ABBAS) deals with day-to-day business. Fatah (the Palestine National Liberation Movement) joined the PNC in 1968, and all the guerrilla organizations joined the Council in 1969. In 1973 the Palestinian Central Council (PCC Chair. SALIM AZ-ZA'NUN) was established to act as an intermediary between the PNC and the Executive Committee. This 95-member Council meets when the PNC is not in session and approves major policy decisions on its behalf. Chair. YASSER ARAFAT.

The most important guerrilla organizations are:

Fatah (The Palestine National Liberation Movement): e-mail fateh@fateh.org; internet www.fateh.net; f. 1957; the largest single Palestinian movement, embraces a coalition of varying views from conservative to radical Leader YASSER ARAFAT; Sec.-Gen. FAROUK KADDOUMI; Central Cttee (elected by Fatah's 530-member Congress, 31 May 1980): YASSER ARAFAT, SALAH KHALAF, FAROUK KADDOUMI, MAHMUD ABBAS, KHALID AL-HASSAN, HAYIL ABD AL-HAMID, MUHAMMAD GHUNAIM, SALIM AZ-ZA'NUN, RAFIK AN-NATSHEH, HANI AL-HASSAN.

Popular Front for the Liberation of Palestine (PFLP): POB 12144, Damascus, Syria; e-mail pflp@p-ol.com; internet www .pflp-pal.org; f. 1967; Marxist-Leninist; publ. *Democratic Palestine* (monthly, in English); Sec.-Gen. AHMAD SAADAT; in 1994 the PFLP announced the formation of the Democratic National Action Front (DNAF), which it described as an open political, popular forum, an extension of the PFLP.

Democratic Front for the Liberation of Palestine (DFLP): Damascus, Syria; Marxist; split from the PFLP in 1969; Sec.-Gen. NAIF HAWATMEH.

Arab Liberation Front (ALF): f. 1968; Iraqi-backed; Leader (Gaza) IBRAHIM ZAANEN.

Palestinian Popular Struggle Front (PPSF): f. 1967; Sec.-Gen. Dr SAMIR GHOSHEH.

Hezb ash-Sha'ab (Palestine People's Party): POB 54224, Jerusalem; tel. (2) 2960104; fax (2) 2960640; e-mail shaab@palpeople.org; internet www.palpeople.org; formerly Palestine Communist Party, admitted to the PNC at its 18th session in 1987; Sec.-Gen. (vacant).

Palestine Liberation Front (PLF): split from PFLP—GC in April 1977; the PLF split into two factions at the end of 1983, both of which retained the name PLF; one faction (Leader MUHAMMAD 'ABU' ABBAS) based in Tunis, Tunisia, and Baghdad, Iraq, and remaining nominally loyal to Yasser Arafat; the other faction belonging to the anti-Arafat National Salvation Front and having offices in Damascus, Syria, and Libya. A third group derived from the PLF was reportedly formed by its Central Cttee Secretary, Abd al-Fattah Ghanim, in June 1986. At the 18th session of the PNC, a programme for the unification of the PLF was announced, with Talaat Yaqoub (died November 1988) named as Secretary-General and 'Abu Abbas' appointed to the PLO Executive Committee, while unification talks were held. The merging of the two factions was announced in June 1987, with 'Abu Abbas' becoming Deputy Secretary-General.

Palestinian Democratic Union (FIDA): split from the DFLP in March 1990; Leader YASSER ABD AR-RABBUH; Sec.-Gen. SALEH RA'FAT.

The anti-Arafat National Salvation Front includes the following organizations:

Popular Front for the Liberation of Palestine—General Command (PFLP—GC): Damascus, Syria; split from the PFLP in 1968; pro-Syrian; Leader AHMAD JIBRIL.

Popular Front for the Liberation of Palestine—National General Command: Amman, Jordan; split from the PFLP—GC in 1999; aims to co-operate with the PNA; Leader ATIF YUNUS.

As-Saiqa (Vanguard of the Popular Liberation War): f. 1968; Syrian-backed; Leader ISSAM AL-QADI.

Palestine Revolutionary Communist Party: Damascus, Syria; Sec.-Gen. ARBI AWAD.

Alliance of Palestinian Forces: f. 1994; 10 members representing the PFLP, the DFLP, the PLF, the PPSF, the Palestine Revolutionary Communist Party and the PFLP—GC; opposes the Declaration of Principles on Palestinian Self-Rule signed by Israel and the PLO in September 1993, and subsequent agreements concluded within its framework (the 'Oslo accords'). The **Fatah Revolutionary Council**, headed by Sabri Khalil al-Banna, alias 'Abu Nidal', split from Fatah in 1973. Its headquarters were formerly in Baghdad, Iraq, but the office was closed down and its staff expelled from the country by the Iraqi authorities in November 1983; a new base was established in Damascus, Syria, in December. Al-Banna was readmitted to Iraq in 1984, having fled Syria. With 'Abu Musa' (whose rebel Fatah group is called **Al-Intifada**, or 'Uprising'), 'Abu Nidal' formed a joint rebel Fatah command in February 1985, and both had offices in Damascus until June 1987, when those of 'Abu Nidal' were closed by the Syrian Government. Forces loyal to 'Abu Nidal' surrendered to Fatah forces at the Rashidiyeh Palestinian refugee camp near Tyre, northern Lebanon, in 1990. 'Abu Nidal' was reported to have been found dead in Baghdad in August 2002.

The militant Islamist organizations, **Islamic Jihad** (Gen. Sec. RAMADAN ABDULLAH SHALLAH) and the **Islamic Resistance Movement** (Hamas; Spiritual Leader Sheikh AHMAD YASSIN), are also active in the West Bank and Gaza. Like the organizations represented in the Alliance of Palestinian Forces, they are strongly opposed to the Oslo accords. The formation of the **Right Movement for Championing the Palestinian People's Sons** by former members of Hamas was announced in April 1995. The movement, based in Gaza City, was reported to support the PA.

Diplomatic Representation

Countries with which the PLO maintains diplomatic relations include:

Afghanistan, Albania, Algeria, Angola, Austria, Bahrain, Bangladesh, Benin, Bhutan, Botswana, Brunei, Bulgaria, Burkina Faso, Burundi, Cambodia, Cameroon, Cape Verde, Central African Republic, Chad, China (People's Rep.), Comoros, Congo (Dem. Rep.), Congo (Rep.), Cuba, Cyprus, Czech Republic, Djibouti, Egypt, Equatorial Guinea, Ethiopia, Gabon, Gambia, Ghana, Guinea, Guinea-Bissau, Hungary, India, Indonesia, Iran, Iraq, Jordan, Korea (Dem. People's Rep.), Kuwait, Laos, Lebanon, Libya, Madagascar, Malaysia, Maldives, Mali, Malta, Mauritania, Mauritius, Mongolia, Morocco, Mozambique, Nepal, Nicaragua, Niger, Nigeria, Norway, Oman, Pakistan, Philippines, Poland, Qatar, Romania, Russia, Rwanda, São Tomé and Príncipe, Saudi Arabia, Senegal, Serbia and Montenegro, Seychelles, Sierra Leone, Somalia, Sri Lanka, Sudan, Swaziland, Sweden, Tanzania, Togo, Tunisia, Turkey, Uganda,

United Arab Emirates, Vanuatu, the Vatican City, Viet Nam, Yemen, Zambia and Zimbabwe.

The following states, while they do not recognize the State of Palestine, allow the PLO to maintain a regional office: Belgium, Brazil, France, Germany, Greece, Italy, Japan, the Netherlands, Portugal, Spain, Switzerland and the United Kingdom.

A Palestinian passport has been available for residents of the Gaza Strip and the Jericho area only since April 1995. In September of that year the passport was recognized by 29 states, including: Algeria, Bahrain, Bulgaria, China (People's Rep.), Cyprus, Egypt, France, Germany, Greece, India, Israel, Jordan, Malta, Morocco, the Netherlands, Pakistan, Qatar, Romania, Saudi Arabia, South Africa, Spain, Sweden, Switzerland, Tunisia, Turkey, the United Arab Emirates, the United Kingdom and the USA.

Judicial System

In the Gaza Strip, the West Bank towns of Jericho, Nablus, Ramallah, Jenin, Tulkarm, Qalqilya, Bethlehem and Hebron, and in other, smaller population centres in the West Bank, the PA has assumed limited jurisdiction with regard to civil affairs. However, the situation is confused owing to the various and sometimes conflicting legal systems which have operated in the territories occupied by Israel in 1967: Israeli military and civilian law; Jordanian law; and acts, orders-in-council and ordinances that remain from the period of the British Mandate in Palestine. Religious and military courts have been established under the auspices of the PA. In February 1995 the PA established a Higher State Security Court in Gaza to decide on security crimes both inside and outside the PA's area of jurisdiction; and to implement all valid Palestinian laws, regulations, rules and orders in accordance with Article 69 of the Constitutional Law of the Gaza Strip of 5 March 1962. As of September 2000 the PLC had passed a total of 30 laws; others were being drafted, reviewed or awaited approval by the President.

General Prosecutor of the PA: KHALID AL-QIDRA.

The Press

NEWSPAPERS

Akhbar an-Naqab: Gaza City; internet www.akhbarna.com; Arabic.

Al-Ayyam: e-mail info@al-ayyam.com; internet www.al-ayyam .com; Arabic; weekly.

Al-Ayyam al-Arabi: Ramallah; f. 1999; Arabic; daily newspaper published by PA; Editor-in-Chief SALIM SALAMAH.

Filastin ath-Thawra (Palestine Revolution): normally published in Beirut, but resumed publication from Cyprus in November 1982; Arabic; weekly newspaper of the PLO.

Al-Hadaf: organ of the PFLP; Arabic; weekly.

Al-Haria (Liberation): organ of the DFLP; Arabic.

Al-Hayat al-Jadidah: West Bank; e-mail alhayat@p-ol.com; internet www.alhayat-j.com; f. 1994; Arabic; weekly; Editor NADIL AMR.

Al-Istiqlal: Gaza City; e-mail alesteqlal@p-i-s.com; internet www .alesteqlal.com; organ of Islamic Jihad; Arabic; weekly.

Al-Quds (Jerusalem): Jerusalem; internet www.alquds.com; Arabic; daily.

Ar-Risala (Letter): Gaza City; organ of the Islamist Construction and Democracy Party; Arabic; weekly; Editor-in-Chief GHAZI HAMAD.

Al-Watan: Gaza City; supports Hamas; Arabic; weekly.

PERIODICALS

Filastin (Palestine): Gaza City; f. 1994; Arabic; weekly.

Palestine Report: Jerusalem Media and Communications Centre, POB 25047, Nablus Rd, Jerusalem; tel. (2) 5819777; fax (2) 5829534; e-mail palreport@jmcc.org; internet www.jmcc.org/media/reportonline; f. 1990; English; weekly; current affairs.

Shu'un Filastiniya (Palestine Affairs): POB 5614, 92 Gr. Afxentiou St, Nicosia, Cyprus; tel. 461140; Arabic; monthly.

NEWS AGENCY

Wikalat Anbaa' Filastiniya (WAFA, Palestine News Agency): Gaza City; tel. (8) 2824056; fax (8) 2824046; e-mail wafa15@palnet .com; internet www.wafa.pna.net; formerly based in Beirut, but resumed activities in Cyprus and Tunis, November 1982; official PLO news agency; Editor ZIAD ABD AL-FATTAH.

Broadcasting and Communications

TELECOMMUNICATIONS

Palestine Telecommunications Co PLC (PalTel): POB 1570, Nablus; tel. (9) 2376225; fax (9) 2376227; e-mail paltel@palnet.net; internet www.paltel.net; f. 1995; privately-owned monopoly; launched cellular telephone service (Palcel) in 1999; Chair. HATEM AL-HALAWANI; Dir-Gen. WALID IRSHAID.

Palestine Cellular Co (Jawal): Rafeedia St, Nablus; tel. (9) 2337370; fax (9) 2337366; internet www.myjawwal.com; f. 1999; 65% owned by PalTel, 35% state-owned; CEO HAKAM KANAFANI.

BROADCASTING

Palestinian Broadcasting Corpn (PBC): POB 984, Al-Birah/Ramallah; tel. (2) 2959894; fax (2) 2959893; e-mail pbc@planet.edu; Chair. RADWAN ABU AYYASH.

Sawt Filastin (Voice of Palestine): c/o Police HQ, Jericho; tel. (2) 921220; internet www.bailasan.com/pinc; f. 1994; official radio station of the PA; broadcasts in Arabic from Jericho and Ramallah; Dir RADWAN ABU AYYASH.

Palestine Television: f. 1994; broadcasts from Ramallah and Gaza City; Dir RADWAN ABU AYYASH.

Finance

(cap. = capital; dep. = deposits; brs = branches; m. = million)

BANKING

Palestine Monetary Authority

It is intended to develop the Palestine Monetary Authority (PMA), which was established in December 1994, into the Central Bank of Palestine. In July 1995 the PMA began to license, inspect and supervise the Palestinian and foreign commercial banks operating in the Gaza Strip and the Jericho enclave in the West Bank at that time. In December of that year the PMA assumed responsibility for 13 banks in the Palestinian Autonomous Areas over which the Central Bank of Israel had hitherto exercised control. Three currencies circulate in the Palestinian economy—the Jordanian dinar, the Israeli shekel and the US dollar. The PMA, which is seeking a reserve base of US $10m. from donors, currently has no right of issue. According to the PMA, there were 22 banks with a total of 126 branches operating in the West Bank and Gaza in December 2001. In January 2002 the banks' deposit base amounted to $3,275m. Gov. FOUAD HAMDI BESEISO; Nablus Rd, Ramallah; tel. (2) 2964786; fax (2) 2959922; e-mail info@pma-ram.pna.net; POB 4026, An-Nassera St, Gaza; tel. (8) 2825713; fax (8) 2824487; e-mail pmgaza@ palnet.com; internet www.pma-palestine.org.

National Banks

Bank of Palestine Ltd: POB 50, Omar al-Mukhtar St, Gaza City; tel. (8) 2843059; fax (8) 2846025; e-mail info@bankofpalestine.com; internet www.bankofpalestine.com; f. 1960; cap. US $15.2m., res US $4.9m., dep. US $213.6m., total assets US $239.2m. (Dec. 2000); Pres., Chair. and Gen. Man. HASHEM ATA SHAWA; 19 brs in West Bank and Gaza.

Commercial Bank of Palestine PLC: POB 1799, Michael Tanous Bldg, Alawda St, Ramallah; tel. (2) 2954141; fax (2) 2953888; e-mail cbp@cbpal.palnet.com; f. 1992; total assets US $87m. Gen. Man. KHALID MUHAMMAD GHABEISH; 4 brs.

Palestine International Bank: Al-Birah/Ramallah; tel. (2) 2983300; fax (2) 2983344; e-mail pib@pib.palnet.com; f. 1996; cap. US $20m; Chair. ABD AS-SALAM ABU ISSA.

Investment Banks

Arab Palestinian Investment Bank: POB 1260, Al-Harji Bldg, Ramallah; tel. (2) 2987126; fax (2) 2987125; e-mail apibank@palnet .com; f. 1996; Arab Bank of Jordan has a 51% share; cap. US $15m.

Palestine Investment Bank PLC: POB 3675, Al-Helal St, Al-Birah/Ramallah; tel. (2) 2407880; fax (2) 2407887; e-mail pibc@alami.net; f. 1995 by the PA; some shareholders based in Jordan and the Gulf states; cap. US $20m. provides full commercial and investment banking services throughout the West Bank and Gaza; Man. YOUSUF AL-QADI; 6 brs.

Al-Quds Bank for Development and Investment: POB 2384, Ramallah; tel. (2) 2961750; fax (2) 2961753; e-mail qudsbkhq@palnet.com; f. 1996; merchant bank; Dirs EID GHAYADAH, MUHAMMAD SALMAN; 3 brs.

Islamic Banks

Arab Islamic Bank: POB 631, Nablus St, Al-Birah/Ramallah; tel. (2) 2407060; fax (2) 2407065; e-mail aib@aibnk.com; internet www .aibnk.com; Gen. Man. ATIYEH A. SHANANIER; 6 brs.

Palestine Islamic Bank: POB 1244, Omar al-Mukhtar St, Gaza City; tel. (8) 2825259; fax (8) 2825269.

Foreign Banks

Arab Bank PLC (Jordan): Regional Management: POB 1476, Ramallah; tel. (2) 2982400; fax (2) 2982444; e-mail arabbank@palnet .com; internet www.arabbank.com; f. 1930; dep. of some US $1,800m. (Jan. 2001); Senior Exec. Vice-Pres. SHUKRY BISHARA; 18 brs in the West Bank and Gaza.

Bank of Jordan PLC: POB 1328, Bahour Bldg, Al-Quds St, Ramallah; tel. (2) 2952702; fax (2) 2952705; e-mail bojreg@palnet.com; internet www.boj.com.jo; Chair. TAWFIK FAKHOURY; Gen. Man. AZIZ SHAKER; 4 brs.

Cairo Amman Bank (Jordan): POB 1870, Ramallah; tel. (2) 2983500; fax (2) 2952764; e-mail cabl@attmail.com; internet www .ca-bank.com; Regional Man. MAZEN ABU HAMDEN; 11 brs.

Jordan National Bank PLC: POB 550, Az-Zahra St, Ramallah; tel. (2) 2986310; fax (2) 2986311; e-mail jnb-ram@alqudsnet.com; internet www.ahli.com; f. 1995; Chair. ABD AL-QADER M. TASH; Regional Man. HANNA GHATTAS; 6 brs.

Other foreign banks include Egyptian Arab Land Bank, Housing Bank for Trade and Finance (Jordan), HSBC Bank Middle East (United Kingdom), Jordan Gulf Bank, Jordan Kuwait Bank, Principal Bank for Development and Agricultural Credit (Egypt), Standard Chartered Grindlays Bank Ltd (United Kingdom) and Union Bank for Savings and Investment (Jordan).

STOCK EXCHANGE

Palestine Securities Exchange (PSE): POB 128, Nablus; tel. (9) 2375946; fax (9) 2375945; e-mail psexchng@palnet.com; internet www.p-s-e.com; f. 1997; Chair. SABEIH MASRI; Gen. Man. NAIM KHUSHASHI.

INSURANCE

A very small insurance industry exists in the West Bank and Gaza.

Arab Insurance Establishment Co Ltd (AIE): POB 166, Nablus; tel. (9) 2384040; fax (9) 2384032; f. 1975; Man. Dir IBRAHIM ABD AL-HADI; Gen. Man. SHAKER HATER.

Gaza Ahliea Insurance Co Ltd: POB 1214, Al-Jalaa Tower, Remal, Gaza; tel. (8) 2824035; fax (8) 2824015; e-mail gaicnet@palnet.com; f. 1994; Chair. and Gen. Man. Dr MUHAMMAD SABAWI; 6 brs.

National Insurance Co: POB 1819, 34 Municipality St, Al-Birah/Ramallah; tel. (2) 2983800; fax (2) 2407460; e-mail nic@palnet .com; f. 1992; Chair. MUHAMMAD MAHMOUD MASROUJI; Gen. Man. AZIZ MAHMOUD ABD AL-JAWAD; 8 brs.

DEVELOPMENT FINANCE ORGANIZATIONS

Arab Palestinian Investment Co. Ltd: POB 2396, Kharaz Center, Yafa St, Industrial Zone, Ramallah; tel. (2) 2984242; fax (2) 2984243; e-mail apic@palnet.com; internet www.apic-pal.com.

Jerusalem Real Estate Investment Co: POB 1876, Ramallah; tel. (2) 2965215; fax (2) 2965217; e-mail jrei@palnet.com; f. 1996; Man. Dir WALID AL-AHMAD.

Palestine Development & Investment Co (PADICO): POB 316, Nablus; tel. (9) 2384354; fax (9) 2384355; e-mail padico@padico.com; internet www.padico.com; f. 1993; Chair. MUNIB R. AL-MASRI; Vice-Chair. NABIL GHATTAS SARRAF.

Palestinian Economic Council for Development and Reconstruction (PECDAR): POB 54910, Dahiyat Al-Barid, Jerusalem; tel. (2) 2362300; fax (2) 2347041; e-mail info@pecdar.pna.net; internet www.pecdar.org; privately-owned; Dir-Gen. Dr MUHAMMAD SHTAYYEH.

Palestine Real Estate Investment Co (Aqaria): POB 4049, Gaza; tel. (8) 2824815; fax (8) 2824845; e-mail aqaria@rannet.com; internet www.aqaria.com; f. 1994; Chair. NABIL SARRAF; Man. MUHAMMAD ISMAEL.

Trade and Industry

CHAMBERS OF COMMERCE

Bethlehem Chamber of Commerce and Industry: POB 59, Bethlehem; tel. (2) 2742742; fax (2) 2764402; e-mail bcham@palnet .com; internet www.pal-chambers.com; f. 1952; 2,500 mems.

Federation of Chambers of Commerce, Industry and Agriculture: tel. (2) 6280727; fax (2) 6280644; e-mail fpccia@palnet.com; internet www.pal-chambers.com.

Hebron Chamber of Commerce and Industry: POB 272, Hebron; tel. (2) 2228218; fax (2) 2227490; e-mail hebcham@hebronet .com; internet www.pal-chambers.com; f. 1954; 5,500 mems.

Jenin Chamber of Commerce, Industry and Agriculture: Jenin; tel. (4) 2501107; fax (4) 2503388; e-mail jencham@hally.net; internet www.pal-chambers.com; f. 1953; 3,800 mems.

Jericho Chamber of Commerce, Industry and Agriculture: POB 91, Jericho; tel. (2) 2323313; fax (2) 2322394; e-mail jercom@ hally.net; internet www.pal-chambers.com; f. 1953; 400 mems.

Jerusalem Chamber of Commerce and Industry: Jerusalem; tel. (2) 6282351; fax (2) 6272615; e-mail chamber@alqudsnet.com; internet www.pal-chambers.com; 2,050 mems.

Nablus Chamber of Commerce and Industry: POB 35, Nablus; tel. (9) 2380335; fax (9) 2377605; e-mail nablus@palnet.com; internet www.pal-chambers.com; f. 1941; 4,800 mems.

Palestine Chamber of Commerce in the Gaza Strip: POB 33, Sabra Quarter, Gaza; tel. (8) 2864588; fax (8) 2821172; e-mail gazacham@palnet.com; internet www.pal-chambers.com; f. 1954; Chair. Muhammad al-Qudwah; 14,000 mems.

Palestinian-European Chamber of Commerce: tel. (2) 894883.

Qalqilya Chamber of Commerce, Industry and Agriculture: POB 13, Qalqilya; tel. (9) 2941473; fax (9) 2940164; e-mail chamberq@hally.net; internet www.pal-chambers.com; f. 1972; 1,068 mems.

Ramallah Chamber of Commerce and Industry: POB 256, Al-Birah/Ramallah; tel. (2) 2955052; fax (2) 2984691; e-mail info@ ramallahcci.org; internet www.ramallahcci.org; f. 1950; Chair. Muhammad Ahmad Amin; Vice-Chair. Yousuf ash-Sharif; 3,700 mems.

Salfit Chamber of Commerce, Industry and Agriculture: Salfit; tel. (2) 2395970; fax (2) 2574762; e-mail salfeet-chamb@hally .net; internet www.pal-chambers.com.

Tulkarm Chamber of Commerce, Industry and Agriculture: POB 51, Tulkarm; tel. (9) 2671010; fax (9) 2675623; e-mail tulkarm@ zaytona.com; internet www.pal-chambers.com; f. 1945; 625 mems.

TRADE AND INDUSTRIAL ORGANIZATIONS

Union of Industrialists: POB 1296, Gaza; tel. (8) 2866222; fax (8) 2862013; Chair. Muhammad Yazıji.

UTILITIES

Electricity

Palestinian Energy Authority (PEA): POB 3591, Nablus St, Al-Birah/Ramallah; POB 3041, Gaza; tel. (2) 2986190; fax (2) 2986191; tel. (8) 2808484; fax (8) 2808488; e-mail pea@palnet.com; internet www.pea.gov.ps; f. 1994; Chair. Dr Abd ar-Rahman T. Hamad.

Jerusalem District Electricity Co Ltd (JDECO): internet www .jdeco.net.

National Electric Co (NEC): West Bank; f. 2000.

Palestine Electric Co (PEC): Gaza; f. 1999; Chair. Said Khoury; Man. Dir Samir Shawwa.

Water

Palestinian Water Authority (PWA): POB 2174, Ramallah; internet www.pwa.pna.org; Dir Eng. Nabil ash-Sharif.

Transport

CIVIL AVIATION

Palestinian Civil Aviation Authority (PCAA): Gaza International Airport, Gaza; tel. (8) 2822800; fax (8)2823109; e-mail fzaidan@palairlines.com; internet www.palairlines.com; f. 1994; Gaza International Airport was formally inaugurated in November 1998 to operate services by Palestinian Airlines (its subsidiary), Egypt Air and Royal Jordanian Airline; Royal Air Maroc began to operate services to Amman, Abu Dhabi, Cairo, Doha, Dubai, Jeddah, İstanbul and Larnaca, and intend to expand their network to Europe; the airport was closed by the Israeli authorities in February 2001 and the runway seriously damaged by Israeli air-strikes in late 2001 and early 2002; Chair. and Dir-Gen. Fayez A. Zaidan.

Palestinian Airlines: POB 4043, Gaza; tel. (8) 2822800; fax (8) 2821309; e-mail fzaidan@palairlines.com; internet www.palairlines .com; f. 1994; state-owned; Chair. and Dir-Gen. Fayez A. Zaidan; Commercial Dir Yousuf Shaath.

Tourism

Although the tourist industry in the West Bank was virtually destroyed as a result of the 1967 Arab–Israeli war, by the late 1990s the sector was expanding significantly, with a number of hotels being opened or under construction. Much of the tourism in the West Bank centres around the historical and biblical sites of Jerusalem and Bethlehem. However, the renewed outbreak of Israeli–Palestinian conflict in the West Bank and Gaza Strip from late 2000 has prevented the recovery of the tourist industry.

Ministry of Tourism and Antiquities: POB 534, Manger St, Bethlehem; tel. (2) 2741581; fax (2) 2743753; e-mail mota@ visit-palestine.com; internet www.visit-palestine.com.

Near East Tourist Agency: POB 19015, 18 Azzahra St, Jerusalem; tel. (2) 6282515; fax (2) 6282415; e-mail operations@netours.com.

PANAMA

Introductory Survey

Location, Climate, Language, Religion, Flag, Capital

The Republic of Panama is a narrow country situated at the southern end of the isthmus separating North and South America. It is bounded to the west by Costa Rica and to the east by Colombia in South America. The Caribbean Sea is to the north, and the Pacific Ocean to the south. Panama has a tropical maritime climate (warm, humid days and cool nights). There is little seasonal variation in temperatures, which average 23°C–27°C (73°F–81°F) in coastal areas. The rainy season is from April until December. Spanish is the official language. Almost all of the inhabitants profess Christianity, and some 85% are Roman Catholics. The national flag (proportions 2 by 3) is composed of four equal rectangles: on the top row the quarter at the hoist is white, with a five-pointed blue star in the centre, while the quarter in the fly is red; on the bottom row the quarter at the hoist is blue, and the quarter in the fly is white, with a five-pointed red star in the centre. The capital is Panamá (Panama City).

Recent History

Panama was subject to Spanish rule from the 16th century until 1821, when it became independent as part of Gran Colombia. Panama remained part of Colombia until 1903, when it declared its separate independence with the support of the USA. In that year the USA purchased the concession for construction of the Panama Canal, which was opened in 1914. The 82-km Canal links the Atlantic and Pacific Oceans, and is a major international sea route. Under the terms of the 1903 treaty between Panama and the USA concerning the construction and administration of the Canal, the USA was granted ('in perpetuity') control of a strip of Panamanian territory, known as the Canal Zone, extending for 8 km on either side of the Canal route. The treaty also established Panama as a protectorate of the USA. In exchange for transferring the Canal Zone, Panama was to receive an annuity from the USA. The terms of this treaty and its successors have dominated relations between Panama and the USA since 1903.

In 1939 a revised treaty with the USA ended Panama's protectorate status. A new Constitution for Panama was adopted in 1946. Following a period of rapidly changing governments, the 1952 presidential election was won by Col José Antonio Remón, formerly Chief of Police. During his term of office, President Remón negotiated a more favourable treaty with the USA, whereby the annuity payable to Panama was increased. In January 1955, however, before the treaty came into force, Remón was assassinated. He was succeeded by José Ramón Guizado, hitherto the First Vice-President, but, less than two weeks after assuming power, the new President was implicated in the plot to assassinate Remón. Guizado was removed from office and later imprisoned. Remón's Second Vice-President, Ricardo Arias Espinosa, then completed the presidential term, which expired in 1956, when Ernesto de la Guardia was elected President. The next presidential election was won by Roberto Chiari, who held office in 1960–64, and his successor was Marco Aurelio Robles (1964–68). During this period there were frequent public demands for the transfer to Panama of sovereignty over the Canal Zone.

Presidential and legislative elections took place in May 1968. The presidential contest was won by Dr Arnulfo Arias Madrid, the candidate supported by the coalition Unión Nacional (which included his own Partido Panameñista). Dr Arias had been President in 1940–41 and 1949–51, but both terms had ended in his forcible removal from power. He took office for a third term in October 1968 but, after only 11 days, he was deposed by the National Guard (Panama's only military body), led by Col (later Brig.-Gen.) Omar Torrijos Herrera, who accused him of planning to establish a dictatorship. The Asamblea Nacional (National Assembly) was dissolved, and political activity suspended. Political parties were banned in February 1969.

In August 1972 elections were held to a new legislative body, the 505-member Asamblea Nacional de Corregidores (National Assembly of Community Representatives). In October the Asamblea conferred extraordinary powers on Gen. Torrijos as Chief of Government for six years.

In February 1974 representatives of Panama and the USA concluded an agreement on principles for a new treaty whereby the USA would surrender its jurisdiction over the Canal Zone. Discontent arising from the Government's handling of subsequent protracted negotiations, combined with deteriorating living standards, culminated in student riots in 1976. Intensified talks in 1977 resulted in two new Canal treaties, which were approved by 66% of voters at a referendum in October. The treaties became effective from October 1979. Panama assumed control of the former Canal Zone, which was abolished. Administration of the Canal was placed under the control of a joint Panama Canal Commission until the end of 1999. US military forces in Panama were to remain until 2000, and the USA was to be entitled to defend the Canal's neutrality thereafter.

In August 1978 elections were held to the Asamblea Nacional de Corregidores; in October the new representatives elected Dr Arístides Royo Sánchez, hitherto Minister of Education, to be President for a six-year term. Gen. Torrijos resigned as Chief of Government but continued in the post of Commander of the National Guard, and effectively retained power until his death in an air crash in July 1981. President Royo failed to gain the support of the National Guard, and in July 1982 he was forced to resign by Col Rubén Darío Paredes, who had ousted Col Florencio Flores as Commander-in-Chief in March. The Vice-President, Ricardo de la Espriella, was installed as President, and, under the direction of Col Paredes, promoted business interests and pursued a foreign policy more favourable to the USA.

In April 1983 a series of amendments to the Constitution were approved by referendum. However, in spite of new constitutional measures to limit the power of the National Guard, de facto power remained with the armed forces, whose position was strengthened by a decision in September to unite all security forces within one organization (subsequently known as the National Defence Forces). In June Paredes was succeeded as Commander-in-Chief by Brig. (later Gen.) Manuel Antonio Noriega Morena. In February 1984 Dr Jorge Illueca, hitherto the Vice-President, became Head of State after the sudden resignation of President de la Espriella, who was believed to have been ousted from power by the National Defence Forces.

Elections to the presidency and the legislature (the new 67-member Asamblea Legislativa—Legislative Assembly) took place in May 1984. Despite allegations of extensive electoral fraud, Dr Nicolás Ardito Barletta, the candidate of the Partido Revolucionario Democrático (PRD) who received the electoral support of the armed forces, was eventually declared President-elect, narrowly defeating Arias Madrid, standing as candidate of the Partido Panameñista Auténtico (PPA). However, as a result of protracted opposition to his economic policies, President Ardito was unable to secure a political base to support his administration, and in September 1985 he resigned. Ardito claimed that his resignation had been prompted by the deterioration in his relations with the legislature and with the National Defence Forces, although there was considerable speculation that he had been forced to resign by Gen. Noriega, to prevent a public scandal over the alleged involvement of the National Defence Forces in the murder of Dr Hugo Spadafora, a former deputy minister under Torrijos and a leading critic of Noriega. Ardito was succeeded as President in September by Eric Arturo Delvalle, formerly First Vice-President.

In June 1986 US sources alleged that Noriega was involved in the trafficking of illegal drugs and weapons and in the transfer of proceeds from these activities through Panamanian banks. In addition, Noriega was implicated in the sale of US national security information and restricted technology to Cuba. There were also renewed allegations of his involvement in the murder of Dr Spadafora and in electoral fraud during the 1984 presidential election. Strikes and demonstrations in support of demands for Noriega's dismissal resulted in violent clashes with the National Defence Forces. Following this outbreak of violence, the US Senate approved a resolution urging the establishment of democracy in Panama, the suspension of Noriega and the holding of an independent investigation into the allegations against him. The Panamanian Government responded by accusing the USA of interfering in Panamanian affairs, and a wave of anti-US sentiment was unleashed, including an attack on the US embassy building by protesters in July 1987. The USA subsequently suspended economic and military aid to Panama and downgraded its official links with the country. Protests against Noriega continued, in an atmosphere of mounting political and economic insecurity.

In February 1988 Noriega was indicted by two US Grand Juries on charges of drugs-smuggling and racketeering. On 25 February President Delvalle dismissed Noriega from his post, following his refusal to resign voluntarily. However, leading members of the ruling coalition and the National Defence Forces united in support of their Commander-in-Chief, and on the following day the Asamblea Legislativa voted to remove President Delvalle from office because of his 'failure to abide by the Constitution'. The Minister of Education, Manuel Solís Palma, was appointed acting President. Delvalle refused to accept his dismissal, and the US Administration affirmed its support for the ousted President by declining to recognize the new leadership. Delvalle, who went into hiding, became the figurehead of the USA's attempts to oust Noriega, and in late February, following Delvalle's demand that the US Government impose an economic boycott on Panama, US courts authorized a 'freeze' on some US $50m. of Panamanian assets held in US banks. This move, coupled with a general strike organized by the Cruzada Civilista Nacional (a broadly-based opposition grouping led by the business sector) after Delvalle's dismissal, brought economic chaos to Panama, prompting the closure of all banks for more than two months.

In March 1988 a coup attempt by the chief of police, Col Leónidas Macías, was thwarted by members of the National Defence Forces loyal to Noriega. The attempted coup represented the first indication of opposition to Noriega from within the security forces. The Government announced a state of emergency (which was revoked in April) and the suspension of civil rights. Negotiations between Noriega and a representative of the US Administration, during which the USA was reported to have proposed the withdrawal of charges against Noriega in exchange for his retirement and departure into exile before the elections scheduled for 1989, ended acrimoniously in late March. The US Administration subsequently reinforced economic sanctions against Panamanian interests.

Presidential, legislative and municipal elections were scheduled for 7 May 1989. The presidential candidate of the pro-Government electoral alliance, the Coalición de Liberación Nacional (COLINA), was Carlos Duque Jaén, the leader of the PRD and a close associate of Noriega. The opposition alliance, the Alianza Democrática de Oposición Civilista (ADOC), selected Guillermo Endara Galimany of the PPA as its presidential candidate. The election campaign was dominated by accusations of electoral malpractice, and, following the elections, both ADOC and COLINA claimed victory, despite indications from exit polls and unofficial sources that ADOC had received between 50% and 75% of votes cast. A group of international observers declared that the election had been conducted fraudulently. A delay in announcing the results of the election was interpreted by the opposition as an attempt by the Government to falsify the outcome. Endara declared himself President-elect; in subsequent demonstrations crowds clashed with the National Defence Forces, and many members of the opposition, including Endara and other leaders, were severely beaten. On 10 May the election results were annulled by the Electoral Tribunal, which cited US interference.

On 31 August 1989, following intervention by the Organization of American States (OAS, see p. 288), Panama's General State Council announced the appointment of a provisional Government and a 41-member Legislative Commission to preserve 'institutional order'. The holding of elections was to be considered within six months, but this was to be largely dependent upon the cessation of US 'hostilities' and the withdrawal of US economic sanctions. On 1 September Francisco Rodríguez, a known associate of Noriega, was inaugurated as President, and Carlos Ozores Typaldos as Vice-President. The USA immediately severed diplomatic relations with Panama and expressed its intention to impose more stringent economic sanctions upon the new Government, including a ban on the use of US ports by Panamanian-registered ships. In October an attempted coup, led by middle-ranking officers seeking to replace Noriega at the

head of the *de facto* military dictatorship, was suppressed by forces loyal to Noriega.

In November 1989 the Asamblea Nacional de Corregidores was provisionally restored. This body, now numbering 510 members, was intended to fulfil a consultative and (limited) legislative function. Noriega was elected as its 'national co-ordinator'. In mid-December the Asamblea adopted a resolution declaring Noriega to be Head of State and 'leader of the struggle for national liberation', and announced that a state of war existed with the USA. On 20 December a US military offensive ('Operation Just Cause'), involving some 24,000 troops, was launched against Noriega and the headquarters of the National Defence Forces from US bases within Panama. The objects of the assault were swiftly brought under US control, although sporadic attacks on US bases by loyalist forces continued for several days, and Noriega eluded capture long enough to take refuge in the residence of the Papal Nuncio in Panama. On 21 December Endara, who had been installed as Head of State in a ceremony attended by a Panamanian judge at the Fort Clayton US military base only hours before the invasion, was officially inaugurated as President. President Endara declared that the Panamanian judicial system was inadequate to try Noriega. Following his surrender to US forces on 3 January 1990, Noriega was immediately transported to the USA and arraigned on several charges of involvement in drugs-trafficking and money-laundering operations. (Noriega, who claimed the status of a prisoner of war, refused to recognize the right of jurisdiction of a US court.) The trial, delayed by legal and procedural complications, finally began in September 1991, and in April 1992 Noriega was found guilty on eight charges of conspiracy to manufacture and distribute cocaine; in July he was sentenced to 40 years' imprisonment.

International criticism of the USA's military operation was widespread, although the administration cited the right to self-defence, under Article 51 of the UN Charter, as a legal justification for armed intervention, and US President George Bush asserted that military action was necessary for the protection of US citizens, the protection of the Panama Canal, support for Panama's 'democratically elected' officials and the pursuit of an indicted criminal. According to the US Government, 'Operation Just Cause' resulted in about 500 Panamanian casualties, but a total of at least 1,000 Panamanian deaths was estimated by the Roman Catholic Church and other unofficial sources; 26 US troops were killed, and more than 300 wounded, during the invasion.

Following the appointment of a new Cabinet (comprising members of the ADOC alliance) in late December 1989, the Endara administration declared itself to be a 'democratic Government of reconstruction and national reconciliation'. Shortly afterwards the Electoral Tribunal revoked its annulment of the May elections and announced that ADOC had obtained 62% of the votes cast in the presidential election, according to copies of incomplete results (covering 64% of total votes) that had been held in safe keeping by the Bishops' Conference of the Roman Catholic Church. In February 1990 the composition of the Asamblea Legislativa was announced, based on the same documentation, with 51 seats awarded to ADOC and six to COLINA; fresh elections were to be held for nine seats that could not be reliably allocated. The National Defence Forces were officially disbanded, and a new, 'non-political' Public Force was created.

Although the overthrow of Noriega immediately released US $375m. in assets that had previously been withheld by the US Government, the new administration inherited serious economic difficulties. The cost of 'Operation Just Cause', in terms of damage and lost revenues alone, was estimated to be at least $2,000m. Although the Administration of US President George Bush agreed to provide aid amounting to more than $1,000m., the US Congress was slow to approve the appropriation of funds. In April 1990 the USA revoked the economic restrictions that had been imposed two years previously, and in May Congress approved financial assistance to Panama totalling $420m. Disbursement of a substantial tranche was to be dependent upon the successful negotiation of a Mutual Legal Assistance Treaty (MLAT) between the two countries, whereby the US authorities sought to gain greater access to information amassed by Panama City's 'offshore' international finance centre, in order to combat the illegal laundering of money obtained through drugs-related activities. In August the Endara Government announced its 'Strategy of Development and Economic Modernization', which included provisions for the transfer to private ownership of several state-controlled enterprises. The new economic measures encountered vociferous political opposition from the Partido Demócrata Cristiano (PDC—one of the parties in the ruling coalition), and prompted widespread disaffection among public-sector workers whose jobs were threatened by the short-term divestment programme.

Accusations from public and political opponents that the security forces had not been adequately purged following the ousting of Noriega were seemingly justified by a succession of coup attempts during the early 1990s. Meanwhile, growing public concern at the Government's failure to restore civil and economic order was reflected in the results of elections held in January 1991 for the nine seats in the Asamblea Legislativa that had not been awarded by the Electoral Tribunal following the elections of May 1989 (see above), together with elections for 170 local officials. Member parties of the former electoral alliance COLINA, which had supported the previous regime, secured five of the contested seats: three were won by the PRD and one each by the Partido Laborista (PALA) and the Partido Liberal (PL). Parties represented in the governing alliance secured only four seats—two for the Movimiento Liberal Republicano Nacionalista (MOLIRENA) and two for the PDC. President Endara's recently formed Partido Arnulfista (PA, formerly a faction of the PPA) failed to secure a single seat. Serious concern had been expressed at the increasing level of influence exerted by the US Government over the President, particularly when it became known that in July 1990 the Government had accepted US funds to establish, by decree, a 100-strong Council for Public Security, which would maintain close links with the US Central Intelligence Agency.

Long-standing political differences within the Government reached a crisis in March 1991, when the PDC initiated proceedings to impeach Endara for involving the US armed forces in suppressing an uprising in December 1990 (a technical violation of the 1977 Panama Canal Treaty). Although the proposal was dismissed by the Asamblea Legislativa (since his action had been widely considered to be justifiable at the time of the uprising), Endara and his supporters strongly criticized leaders of the PDC, accusing them of participating in illegal activities to gather intelligence information and of obtaining armaments in preparation for a coup attempt. The PDC, which had repeatedly expressed reservations concerning aspects of government policy (particularly regarding the economy and judicial procedure), threatened to withdraw from the governing alliance, but was pre-empted by Endara's decision, in April 1991, to dismiss the five PDC members of his Cabinet, including the First Vice-President, Ricardo Arias Calderón, who had occupied the Government and Justice portfolio. Arias Calderón retained the vice-presidency, however, since he had been elected to the position in May 1989. Endara significantly increased the representation of the PA in the Cabinet.

In July 1991 the Asamblea Legislativa approved the terms of the MLAT, following indications in US intelligence documents that drugs-related activities in Panama (and money-laundering in particular) had returned to the levels that had prevailed prior to the removal of Gen. Noriega. The Panamanian Government's urgent need of direct financial aid (the disbursement of which the USA had made dependent on the MLAT) prompted it to sign the treaty with only minor modifications to the terms of the agreement.

In October 1991 and February 1992 two further alleged coup attempts were immediately suppressed, and resulted in the detention of several more members of the former National Defence Forces, and the creation, in March 1992, of a presidential police force to be directly responsible to the Head of State. In November, however, the President suffered a serious political reverse, when proposals for more than 50 reforms (including the constitutional abolition of the armed forces and the creation of the post of ombudsman to protect the rights of Panamanian citizens) were rejected by 64% of voters in a referendum organized by the Government in an attempt to consolidate popular support. Opposition groups reiterated demands for the creation of a constituent assembly to draft a new constitution, and stressed popular concerns regarding the future security of the Panama Canal in the absence of an effective Panamanian military force. Following the defeat, at the referendum, of the reform proposals for which he had campaigned, First Vice-President Arias Calderón resigned in December.

The acquittal, in September 1993, of seven former soldiers tried for involvement in the 1985 assassination of Dr Spadafora provoked widespread public outrage. Noriega was tried in connection with the affair *in absentia* and, in October 1993, was found guilty and sentenced to 20 years' imprisonment for ordering his murder. In March 1994 Noriega was also convicted *in absentia* for the 1989 murder of an army major who had led an unsuccessful military coup against him; he was sentenced to a further 20 years' imprisonment for this offence. Furthermore, in August 2001 he was sentenced to a further eight years' imprisonment after being convicted *in absentia* of corruption charges.

In January 1994 MOLIRENA announced its withdrawal from the ruling alliance in order to support the presidential candidature of Rubén Darío Carles, as part of the Cambio 94 alliance—also comprising the Partido Renovación Civilista (PRC) and the Movimiento de Renovación Nacional (Morena). The Alianza Democrática was subsequently formed by the PA—in alliance with the PL, the Partido Liberal Auténtico (PLA), the Unión Democrática Independiente and the Partido Nacionalista Popular (PNP)—with Mireya Moscoso de Gruber, the widow of former President Arias Madrid, as candidate for the presidency. A third electoral alliance, the Pueblo Unido (comprising the PRD, the Partido Liberal Republicano and the PALA), selected Ernesto Pérez Balladares as its presidential candidate.

The presidential poll, conducted on 8 May 1994, resulted in a narrow victory for Pérez Balladares, with 33.2% of the votes cast, ahead of Moscoso de Gruber, with 29.5%. The failure of the Pueblo Unido alliance to secure a majority in the legislature (the PRD and its supporters won 34 of the seats in the expanded, 72-seat Asamblea Legislativa) was reflected in the broad political base of Pérez Balladares' proposed Cabinet, announced in May. Post-electoral political manoeuvring resulted in the creation of the Alianza Pueblo Unido y Solidaridad, Pérez Balladares' electoral alliance having secured the additional support of the Partido Solidaridad in the Asamblea. The Alianza secured another seat in the Asamblea (increasing its representation to exactly one-half of the 72 seats) following a repeat election in a district where the original results had been annulled. Pérez Balladares assumed the presidency on 1 September 1994. A new Cabinet, installed on the same day, included former members of the PA and the PDC who had been obliged to resign their party membership in order to take up their cabinet posts. (An earlier invitation to participate in a coalition government had been rejected by the PA.) The outgoing legislature had in August approved a constitutional amendment that again sought to abolish the armed forces. However, this required the formal endorsement of the new Asamblea, and the PRD continued to express concern that a credible alternative for national defence must first be established.

Industrial unrest in 1995 was prompted by the Government's unpopular five-year economic modernization programme. Plans for tax reform encountered considerable opposition from the financial sector and from traders in the Colón Free Zone. In August trade union opposition to planned reforms to the labour code, under discussion in the Asamblea, resulted in an extended general strike during which demonstrators clashed with security forces, leaving more than 40 injured and at least four dead. Nevertheless, the reforms were approved by the Asamblea. In September it was reported that the Partido Solidaridad had withdrawn from the Alianza Pueblo Unido y Solidaridad (subsequently known as the Alianza de Consenso Nacional) following its criticism of the Government's reform of the labour code and the party's subsequent exclusion from a new legislative executive committee.

In May 1996 the credibility of the Government was damaged by the discovery that a private Panamanian bank (Banaico, which had collapsed earlier in the year), in whose activities senior PRD members were implicated, had been a centre for money-laundering. In June, moreover, the position of President Pérez Balladares was undermined by reports that an alleged drugs-trafficker had contributed some US $51,000 to his 1994 presidential campaign. Pérez Balladares was forced to admit that his campaign fund had 'unwittingly' received the payment; the Procurator-General subsequently announced a thorough investigation into the origin of the 1994 campaign funds.

In July 1997, in the light of the increasing number of incursions by Colombian guerrillas and paramilitary groups into Panamanian territory, the Government deployed more than 1,200 members of the security forces to Darién Province to secure the border with Colombia. In previous months Colombian paramilitary members were reported to have forcibly occupied several settlements in the area while in pursuit of guerrillas who had taken refuge over the border. The death of a member of the Panamanian security forces during an attack by Colombian guerrillas on a settlement in the border area in November prompted discussions between Pérez Balladares and his Colombian counterpart, Andrés Pastrana Arango; these resulted in agreement on improved co-operation concerning border security.

In late 1997 the Asamblea Legislativa approved legislation providing for a constitutional amendment that would allow the election of the President to a second consecutive term in office. However, the proposed amendment was rejected at a national referendum held in August 1998. The outcome was widely considered to reflect public discontent with the neo-liberal economic policies of the Pérez Balladares administration, and prompted the resignations of the Ministers of Housing and Labour and Social Welfare.

At a presidential election conducted on 2 May 1999, Mireya Moscoso de Gruber, the candidate of the Unión por Panamá alliance (comprising the PA, MOLIRENA, Morena and Cambio Democrático), was elected with 44.8% of the votes, ahead of Martín Torrijos Espino, the candidate of the Nueva Nación alliance (comprising the PRD, the Partido Solidaridad, the Partido Liberal Nacional—PLN—and the Movimiento Papa Egoró—MPE), who secured 37.8%, and Alberto Vallarino, the candidate of the Acción Opositora alliance (comprising the PDC, the PRC, the PNP and the PL). However, the Unión por Panamá failed to secure a majority in the concurrent legislative election, obtaining 24 of the 71 contested seats in the Asamblea Legislativa, while Nueva Nación secured 41 seats and Acción Opositora won six seats. Moscoso assumed the presidency on 1 September. A new Cabinet, installed on the same day, included members of the Partido Solidaridad, the PLN, the PDC and the PRC, each of which had abandoned their respective electoral alliances in order to form a 'Government of national unity' with Unión por Panamá, thereby giving Moscoso a narrow majority in the legislature.

In June 1999, following further incursions by Colombian guerrillas into Darién Province, Panama and Colombia reached agreement on the strengthening of military patrols on both sides of the countries' joint border. However, in October 2000 one person was killed and 12 people were injured when Colombian paramilitaries attacked the town of Nazaret. In late October President Moscoso met her Colombian counterpart to discuss a further reinforcement of the border. Nevertheless, incursions by Colombian guerrillas continued; in early 2002 an escalation in the conflict in Colombia led to fears of an influx of refugees into Darién and prompted the Panamanian Government to reinforce its border.

In July 1999 the Commander-in-Chief of the US Southern Command, Gen. Charles Wilhelm, caused considerable unease in Panama when he indicated that the USA had contingency plans for defending the Panama Canal, following US withdrawal at the end of 1999, should violence spread from Colombia into Panama: according to the 1977 Canal treaties, the USA was entitled unilaterally to intervene if it had reason to suppose that the security of the Canal was threatened. Further concern that the USA might attempt to invoke this provision in order to re-establish a military presence in Panama followed claims by senior members of the US Senate that the concession, awarded in 1997 to Hutchison Whampoa of Hong Kong, to operate the ports at each end of the Canal would give the People's Republic of China 'undue influence' over Canal operations after US withdrawal. In November the USA completed its withdrawal from Howard air base, and at the end of the month the last of the US military bases, Fort Clayton, was ceded to Panama. In December, following discussions with military representatives of the USA and other countries, the Panamanian Government announced that a national security plan was under negotiation to ensure the security of the Canal and to combat border incursions, drugs-trafficking and international crime. While the plan included the provision of training and equipment from other countries, including the USA, the Government denied that a foreign military presence was being negotiated. On 31 December 1999 the USA officially relinquished ownership of the Canal to Panama. In early 2000 a five-year canal-modernization project was initiated. In February the Government negotiated a counter-narcotics agreement with the USA, which it hoped, would facilitate the provision of US financing and training for the Panamanian security forces. Accusations by the opposition PRD that the accord undermined national sovereignty were denied.

In August 2000 the governing coalition lost its narrow legislative majority after the PRD and the PDC formed an alliance. The PDC leader, former First Vice-President Ricardo Arias Calderón, claimed that a strong parliamentary opposition was necessary for a functioning democracy. In October 2001 the Minister of the Interior and Justice, Dr Winston Spadafora, resigned to take up a post as a Supreme Court judge; he was replaced by Aníbal Raúl Salas Céspedes. In February 2002 the effective impasse in the legislature was ended following the defection of three opposition deputies.

In November 2000 four people were arrested in Panama City following the discovery of a plot to assassinate the Cuban head of state, Fidel Castro Ruz, who was attending the 10th Ibero-American Summit. Among those detained was Luis Posada Carriles, an alleged member of the Cuban-American National Foundation. In April 2001 the Panamanian Government rejected a Cuban request for the extradition of the detainees.

Following the discovery of human remains in a former military barracks in Tocumen, in December 2000 President Moscoso announced the establishment of a Truth Commission, headed by Alberto Santiago Almanza Henriquez, to investigate 'disappearances' during the military dictatorships of 1968–89. In October 2001 the Commission reported that, following excavations in 12 separate areas, it was able to confirm that 72 of the 189 people believed to have 'disappeared' had been killed or tortured by state forces. The Commission was scheduled to continue its investigations in other areas of the country.

The Government was beset with accusations of corruption in early 2002. In January three PRD members were accused of having received payment in exchange for voting for two Supreme Court candidates not approved by their party. The situation was exacerbated after PRD member Carlos Afú confessed that he had accepted a bribe to vote in favour of a Caribbean port-development project. Public protests ensued, led by the Movimiento Nacional por la Defensa de la Soberanía. In late February an anti-corruption commission made several recommendations for changes to the civil service system and the Attorney-General, José Antonio Sossa, urged legislators to renounce their congressional immunity in order to allow for a more thorough investigation.

President Moscoso's administration encountered further problems following the signature of an agreement with the USA in February 2002, which provided for US authorities to join the Panamanian National Maritime Service in patrolling its territorial waters. The measure, which was designed to control the illegal trade in narcotics, was strongly criticized by opposition members. A lawsuit was filed against the Minister of the Interior and Justice, Aníbal Salas, alleging that he had damaged Panama's international legal status. An additional accord, which provided the USA with increased powers to inspect Panama's financial and tax records as part of its campaign against money-laundering, similarly provoked protests from opposition parties. The Government had already introduced legislation in 2000 and 2001 aimed at eliminating the abuse of the financial system, which had facilitated the removal of Panama from the USA's blacklist of so-called tax 'havens'. However, the Ministry of Foreign Affairs expressed its concern that failure to comply with subsequent US demands for a further accord would have resulted in possible economic and political sanctions. In April 2002 Panama was also removed from the Organisation for Economic Co-operation and Development's (OECD) list of 'unco-operative tax havens', after the Government committed to making its financial sector more transparent.

In June 2002 a contract, due to be awarded to the Panamá Ports Company to fund the development of Balboa port, was criticized by the PRD after it was revealed that the Government proposed to waive a US $22.2m. leasing fee. An amended agreement was subsequently concluded in August.

In July 2002 members of a national dialogue forum, established by President Moscoso, reached a preliminary agreement on the need to reform taxation and the country's social security system. However, the delegates, comprising representatives of the political parties as well as business and trade union leaders, disagreed on the nature of the changes. The Government wished to raise income and corporate tax, as well as to impose sales tax on a number of previously exempt goods and services, in order to improve the country's prospects at impending loan negotiations with the IMF. These proposals were rejected by the opposition parties and business leaders, who warned that they would lead to an increase in labour costs. In September the PRD withdrew from the forum, in protest at the Government's support of a PRD dissident, Carlos Alvarado Acosta, in elections to the presidency of the Asamblea Legislativa. In addition, a number of defections from the opposition to the governing coalition gave Moscoso a working majority in the Asamblea for the first time since taking office. At the end of the month the Government was able to make further amendments to the controversial bilateral maritime agreement with the USA, which gave both countries' security forces the right to search vessels and pursue criminals in each other's territorial waters.

Following a further decline in profits in 2002, at the end of that year the US Chiquita Brands company announced the closure of its Pafco fruit plantations in Colón. However, in March 2003 it was announced that Chiquita had agreed to sell the operation to a plantation workers' co-operative.

At the end of January 2003 the national dialogue forum reached agreement on a number of reforms to the tax system. These included the extension of sales tax to luxury goods and services; nevertheless, the level of taxation on income and business corporations remained unchanged. In the same month the Cabinet was reorganized, following the resignation of several ministers who wished to present their candidacy for legislative elections scheduled for May 2004. Also in January four Panamanians were killed in a cross-border incursion by Colombian paramilitaries. President Moscoso announced that police presence in the Colombian border area would be reinforced. In March former President Endara announced his intention to stand in the 2004 presidential elections, as a candidate for the Partido Solidaridad.

In October 1993 President Endara signed a protocol to establish Panama's membership of the Central American Parliament (Parlacen), a regional political forum with its headquarters in Guatemala. Later in the month Endara, together with the five Presidents of the member nations of the Central American Common Market (CACM, see p. 160), signed a protocol to the 1960 General Treaty on Central American Integration, committing Panama to fuller economic integration in the region. However, at a meeting of Central American Presidents, convened in Costa Rica in August 1994, Pérez Balladares (attending as an observer) stated that his administration considered further regional economic integration to be disadvantageous to Panama, owing to the differences between Panama's services-based economy and the reliance on the agricultural sector of the other Central American states. In March 2000, however, Panama began negotiations with other Central American countries on a free-trade accord. Negotiations continued throughout 2001 and led to the conclusion of a free-trade agreement with El Salvador in March 2002. Discussions with Nicaragua were reported to be nearing agreement in the same month and it was hoped that similar agreements with other Central American countries would follow. Discussions regarding a free-trade agreement with the USA opened in December 2001. Progress was made at a further meeting in March 2002, and negotiations between the two Governments were scheduled to resume in July. Panama has observer status within the Andean Community of Nations (see p. 133, formerly Andean Group).

Government

Legislative power is vested in the unicameral Asamblea Legislativa (Legislative Assembly), which replaced the Asamblea Nacional de Corregidores (National Assembly of Community Representatives) in 1984 (except for its brief reintroduction in late 1989), with a total of 71 members elected for five years by universal adult suffrage. Executive power is held by the President, also directly elected for a term of five years, assisted by two elected Vice-Presidents and an appointed Cabinet. Panama is divided into nine provinces and three autonomous Indian Reservations. Each province has a governor, appointed by the President.

Defence

In 1990, following the overthrow of Gen. Manuel Noriega, the National Defence Forces were disbanded and a new Public Force was created. This numbered 11,800 men in August 2002, comprising the National Police (11,000 men), the National Air Service (400 men) and the National Maritime Service (an estimated 400 men). Defence expenditure for 2001 was US $372m.

Economic Affairs

In 2001, according to estimates by the World Bank, Panama's gross national income (GNI), measured at average 1999–2001 prices, was US $9,532m., equivalent to $3,290 per head (or $5,720 on an international purchasing-power parity basis). During 1990–2001, it was estimated, the population increased at an average annual rate of 1.7%, while gross domestic product (GDP) per head increased, in real terms, by an average of 2.5%

per year. Overall GDP increased, in real terms, at an average annual rate of 4.1% in 1990–2001; growth in 2001 was 0.3%.

Agriculture (including hunting, forestry and fishing) contributed an estimated 6.7% of GDP in 2000 and engaged some 21.7% of the employed labour force in 2001. Rice, maize and beans are cultivated as subsistence crops, while the principal cash crops are bananas (which accounted for an estimated 15.1% of total export earnings in 2001), sugar cane and coffee. Cattle-raising, tropical timber and fisheries (particularly shrimps for export) are also important. In 2000 the banana sector employed some 15,000 people, directly and indirectly. The following year, however, the banana-producing industry was adversely affected by industrial action and poor weather conditions. Owing to low world commodity prices, the coffee sector also experienced a reversal in 2001/02. In the 1990s, in an attempt to diversify the agricultural sector, new crops such as oil palm, cocoa, coconuts, various winter vegetables and tropical fruits were introduced. Fish exports increased steadily throughout that decade, and in 1999 Panama claimed to be the world's third largest exporter of shrimps. However, the shrimp industry was severely affected in 2000 by an outbreak of the white-spot virus. According to the World Bank, agricultural GDP increased by an average of 1.9% annually during 1990–2000; according to official figures, agricultural GDP increased by 2.1% in 1999 and by an estimated 1.6% in 2000.

Industry (including mining, manufacturing, construction and power) contributed an estimated 16.2% of GDP in 2000 and engaged 16.8% of the employed labour force in 2001. According to World Bank figures, industrial GDP increased at an average annual rate of 6.1% during 1990–2000; the sector's GDP increased by 3.9% in 1999 and by an estimated 1.1% in 2000.

Mining contributed an estimated 0.4% of GDP in 2000 and engaged 0.2% of the employed labour force in 2001. Panama has significant deposits of copper and coal. In 1995 the Government, encouraged by the discovery of significant new deposits of copper and molybdenum, announced plans to develop the sector with a view to increasing mining exports to some US $350m. by 2005. However, a decline in world metal prices in the late 1990s served to delay the implementation of these plans. The GDP of the mining sector increased by an estimated average of 25.7% per year in 1996–2000; the sector decreased by 6.0% in 2002.

Manufacturing contributed an estimated 7.0% of GDP in 2000 and engaged an estimated 9.0% of the employed labour force in 2001. In 1999 the most important sectors, measured by output in producers' prices, were refined petroleum products, food-processing, beverages, and cement, lime and plaster. Labour-intensive light assembly operations are conducted in the Colón Free Zone (CFZ), which accommodated more than 1,500 companies in 1998. According to World Bank estimates, manufacturing GDP increased by an average of 3.4% annually during 1990–2000; however, it decreased by 7.5% in 1999, and by an estimated 5.3% in 2000.

The country's topography and climate make it ideal for hydroelectric power, and in 2001 approximately 52.5% of Panama's total output of electricity was water-generated. Construction of a 120-MW hydroelectric plant was scheduled to begin in 2001. In the same year imports of mineral products accounted for an estimated 14.4% of the value of merchandise imports.

Panama's economy is dependent upon the services sector, which contributed an estimated 77.1% of GDP in 2000, and engaged 61.4% of the employed labour force in 2001. The Panama Canal Commission contributed an estimated 6.4% of the country's GDP in 1998/99. Panama is an important 'offshore' financial centre, and in 2000 financial and business services contributed an estimated 26.1% of GDP. Important contributions to the economy are also made by trade in the CFZ (in which some 1,944 companies were situated in 2000, and which was scheduled to double in size in the early 2000s), and by the registration of merchant ships under a 'flag of convenience' in Panama. The tourism sector also increased steadily, contributing 7.5% of GDP in 1999, a 9.0% increase on the previous year. In 2000 income from tourism increased by an estimated 21.3% and, during the first half of 2001, the Instituto Panameño de Turismo announced that the number of visitors arriving by cruise ship had almost doubled from the previous year. According to the World Bank, the GDP of the services sector increased by an average of 4.3% per year in 1990–2000; it grew by 2.8% in 1999 and by an estimated 2.9% in 2000.

In 2001 Panama recorded a visible trade deficit of US $825.7m., and there was a deficit of $499.5m. on the current account of the balance of payments. In 2000 the principal source of imports (32.8%) was the USA, which was also the principal market for exports (46.1% in 2002). Other major trading partners are Costa Rica, Japan, Ecuador, Germany, and Mexico. The principal exports in 2001 were bananas, shrimps and petroleum products. The principal imports in 2001 were consumer and intermediate goods, capital goods and crude petroleum.

In 2000 there was an overall budgetary surplus of 30.2m. balboas (equivalent to 0.3% of GDP). Panama's external debt at the end of 2000 was US $7,056m. In that year the cost of debt-servicing was equivalent to 10.1% of the value of exports of goods and services. Annual inflation averaged 1.1% in 1992–2001, and stood at 0.3% in 2001. Some 13.7% of the economically active population were unemployed in 2001.

Panama is a member of the Inter-American Development Bank (IDB, see p. 239). In September 1997 Panama joined the World Trade Organization (WTO, see p. 323). In March 2002 Panama concluded a free-trade agreement with El Salvador. In 2003 discussions were under way with four other Central American countries (Costa Rica, Guatemala, Honduras and Nicaragua) and the USA on the proposed establishment of a Central American Free Trade Agreement.

The political problems that developed between Panama and the USA in the late 1980s, and the resultant US economic sanctions, adversely affected most sectors of the Panamanian economy during that period. The Pérez Balladares administration, which took office in September 1994, undertook a five-year programme of economic modernization based on a reform of the labour code, the dismantling of trade barriers and attracting greater foreign investment through renewed commitment to the privatization of major state-owned concerns. In 1996 the Panama Canal Commission announced increases in the Canal's general toll rate to finance an acceleration in an extensive maintenance and capital improvements programme. Meanwhile, from January 1997 legislation was introduced that would exempt businesses in the CFZ from paying taxes on their profits. It was estimated that the measure would cost the Government US $40m. annually in lost revenue; however, it was expected to strengthen the competitiveness of the CFZ, and result in higher levels of investment in Panama. In December 1997 the IMF approved a credit of $162m., under an Extended Fund Facility, to support the Government's economic programme for 1998–2000. The programme sought to broaden existing structural reforms while maintaining strict budgetary control and containing inflation. The economic plan of the Moscoso administration, which took office in September 1999, envisaged export-led growth, while aiming to reduce poverty (which affected 37% of the population) and unemployment. The plan committed the Government to the continued privatization of state assets, the proceeds of which, it proposed, would be used to repurchase outstanding external debt bonds, thereby producing substantial savings on interest payments. Increased tax collection (by some $120m. in 2000) was also envisaged, in an attempt to increase revenue and thus reduce dependence on foreign borrowing. In September 2001 the IDB approved a $35m. loan to Panama to help fund improvements in the health care system. In order to allay concerns in the business community regarding its populist tendencies, the Government's budget for 2000 included only a modest rise in expenditure of 4.3%, compared with the previous year. However, election pledges to increase social expenditure were honoured, with 49.7% of the budget allocated to this area. In 2000 economic growth declined for the third successive year, with GDP expanding by 2.5%. This was owing principally to the continuing recession in the CFZ (the result of a deceleration in economic activity elsewhere in Latin America and the financial crisis in Asia), as well as a decline in investment and a reduction in domestic demand. GDP growth in 2001 was 0.3%, falling far short of the earlier predictions of 3.9%–4.3%. The main causes of the slowdown in economic

growth in 2001 were thought to be an increase in petroleum prices and a reduction in demand from Panama's main trading partner, the USA. Following the cession to Panamanian control of the Panama Canal at the end of 1999, the waterway was operated as a profit-making venture, providing the Government with a considerable source of funds. (In 1998 toll revenues from the Canal totalled $546m.) In June 2001 the 'Plan Puebla-Panamá', intended to promote regional development extending from the Mexican state of Puebla, to Panama, was inaugurated. In December the Plan received support from the Spanish power group Endesa, which announced plans for the construction of an electricity network connecting Costa Rica, El Salvador, Guatemala, Honduras and Panama. In 2002 revenue from the CFZ fell by 10.7% and there was also a sharp decline in the principal export sectors of bananas, sugar and coffee. This decline was, to some extent, offset by a growth of 20% in tourism; overall economic growth in 2002 was estimated at 0.8%. In November the Government sold some $430m. in bonds on the international markets to help finance the budget and reduce the country's debt. In January 2003 the Asamblea Legislativa approved a number of tax reforms, including the extension of sales tax to luxury items and some professional services to increase revenue. Additional efforts to reduce the fiscal deficit in preparation for negotiations for a loan from the IMF in 2003 were evident in the 2003 budget, which sought to reduce public expenditure by 17%.

Education

The education system is divided into elementary, secondary and university schooling, each of six years' duration. Education is free up to university level, and is officially compulsory for six years between six and 15 years of age. Primary education begins at the age of six, and secondary education, which comprises two three-year cycles, at the age of 12. The enrolment at primary schools of children in the relevant age-group was 89.9% (males 89.6%; females 90.2%) in 1997, and secondary enrolment was 71.3% (males 70.9%; females 71.7%) in the same year. There are three universities, with regional centres in the provinces. Budgetary expenditure on education by the central Government in 2000 totalled 465.4m. balboas (equivalent to 16.6% of total expenditure).

Public Holidays

2003: 1 January (New Year's Day), 9 January (National Martyrs' Day), 3–4 March (Carnival), 5 March (Ash Wednesday), 17 April (Maundy Thursday), 18 April (Good Friday), 1 May (Labour Day), 15 August (Foundation of Panama City, Panama City only)*, 13 October (Revolution Day), 1 November (National Anthem Day)*, 2 November (Day of the Dead), 3 November (Independence from Colombia), 4 November (Flag Day)*, 5 November (Independence Day, Colón only), 10 November (First Call for Independence), 28 November (Independence from Spain), 8 December (Immaculate Conception, Mothers' Day), 25 December (Christmas).

2004: 1 January (New Year's Day), 9 January (National Martyrs' Day), 23–24 February (Carnival), 25 February (Ash Wednesday), 8 April (Maundy Thursday), 9 April (Good Friday), 1 May (Labour Day), 16 August (Foundation of Panama City, Panama City only)*, 11 October (Revolution Day), 1 November (National Anthem Day)*, 2 November (Day of the Dead), 3 November (Independence from Colombia), 4 November (Flag Day)*, 5 November (Independence Day, Colón only), 10 November (First Call for Independence), 29 November (Independence from Spain), 8 December (Immaculate Conception, Mothers' Day), 25 December (Christmas).

* Official holiday: banks and government offices closed.

Weights and Measures

Both the metric and the imperial systems of weights and measures are in use.

Statistical Survey

Sources (unless otherwise stated): Dirección de Estadística y Censo, Contraloría General de la República, Avda Balboa y Federico Boyd, Apdo 5213, Panamá 5; tel. 210-4777; internet www.contraloria.gob.pa; Banco Nacional de Panamá, Casa Matriz, Vía España, Apdo 5220, Panamá; tel. 263-5151; e-mail bnpvalores@cwp.net.pa; internet www.banconal.com.pa; Viceministerio del Comercio Exterior, Plaza Edison, 3°, Avda El Paical, Apdo 55-2359, Panamá; e-mail secomex@mici.gob.pa; internet www.vicomex.gob.pa.

Note: The former Canal Zone was incorporated into Panama on 1 October 1979.

Area and Population

AREA, POPULATION AND DENSITY

Area (sq km)	75,517*
Population (census results)	
13 May 1990	2,329,329
14 May 2000	
Males	1,432,566
Females	1,406,611
Total	2,839,177
Population (official estimates at mid-year)	
2001	2,897,000
Density (per sq km) at mid-2001	38.4

* 29,157 sq miles.

ADMINISTRATIVE DIVISIONS
(population at census of May 2000)

Province	Population	Capital (and population)*
Bocas del Toro	89,269	Bocas del Toro (9,916)
Chiriquí	368,790	David (124,280)
Coclé	202,461	Penonomé (72,448)
Colón	204,208	Colón (42,133)
Comarca Emberá . . .	8,246	—
Comarca Kuna Yala . .	32,446	—
Comarca Ngöbe Buglé .	110,080	—
Darién	40,284	Chepigana (27,461)
Herrera	102,465	Chitré (42,467)
Los Santos	83,495	Las Tablas (24,298)
Panamá	1,388,357	Panamá (708,438)
Veraguas	209,076	Santiago (74,679)
Total	**2,839,177**	—

* Population of district in which capital is located.
Note: Population figures include the former Canal Zone.

PRINCIPAL TOWNS
(population at 2000 census)

Panamá (Panama City, capital) . .	463,093	Pacora	57,232
San Miguelito . .	291,769	Santiago . . .	55,146
Tocumen . . .	81,250	La Chorrera . .	54,823
David . . .	76,481	Colón . . .	52,286
Nuevo Arraiján . .	63,753	Changuinola . .	45,063
Puerto Armuelles . .	60,102	Pedregal . . .	45,033

BIRTHS, MARRIAGES AND DEATHS

	Registered live births		Registered marriages*		Registered deaths	
	Number	Rate (per 1,000)	Number	Rate (per 1,000)	Number	Rate (per 1,000)
1992 . .	59,905	24.1	12,547	5.4	10,143	4.1
1993 . .	59,191	23.3	13,744	5.8	10,669	4.2
1994 . .	59,947	23.2	13,523	5.2	10,983	4.3
1995 . .	61,939	23.5	8,841	3.4	11,032	5.1
1996 . .	63,401	23.7	10,206	3.8	11,161	4.2
1997 . .	68,009	25.0	10,357	3.8	12,179	4.5†
1998 . .	62,351	22.6	n.a.	n.a.	11,824	4.3†
1999 . .	64,248	22.9	n.a.	n.a.	11,938	4.2†

* Excludes tribal Indian population.
† Estimate.

1999 (estimates): Registered live births 64,248 (birth rate 22.9 per 1,000) (Source: UN, *Demographic Yearbook*).

Expectation of life (WHO estimates, years at birth): 74.9 (males 72.1; females 78.1) in 2001 (Source: WHO, *World Health Report*).

EMPLOYMENT
('000 persons aged 15 years and over, August of each year)

	1999	2000*	2001
Agriculture, hunting and forestry	157.2	191.4	208.9
Fishing	10.4	11.6	11.8
Mining and quarrying	0.9	1.8	2.2
Manufacturing	94.0	93.6	91.3
Electricity, gas and water supply .	7.0	8.3	9.9
Construction	73.0	77.6	67.8
Wholesale and retail trade; repair of motor vehicles, motorcycles and personal and household goods	182.7	179.5	181.3
Hotels and restaurants . . .	39.5	43.1	38.7
Transport, storage and communications	73.0	72.4	77.7
Financial intermediation . . .	23.9	24.5	21.9
Real estate, renting and business activities	39.4	41.3	33.6
Public administration and defence; compulsory social service . . .	68.1	65.6	66.6
Education	50.2	54.1	56.3
Health and social work . . .	30.8	34.8	36.7
Other community, social and personal service activities	57.5	42.5	57.1
Private households with employed persons	51.2	58.0	54.0
Extra-territorial organizations and bodies	2.4	1.1	0.4
Total employed	**961.4**	**1,010.8**	**1,016.6**
Unemployed	128.4	150.8	161.4
Total labour force	**1,089.4**	**1,161.6**	**1,177.9**

* Figures refer to persons aged 10 years and over at the May 2000 census.

Source: partly ILO, *Yearbook of Labour Statistics*.

Health and Welfare

KEY INDICATORS

Total fertility rate (children per woman, 2001)	2.5
Under-5 mortality rate (per 1,000 live births, 2001) . . .	25
HIV/AIDS (% of persons aged 15–49, 2001)	1.50
Physicians (per 1,000 head, 1998)	1.69
Hospital beds (per 1,000 head, 1996)	2.21
Health expenditure (2000): US $ per head (PPP)	464
Health expenditure (2000): % of GDP	7.6
Health expenditure (2000): public (% of total)	69.2
Access to water (% of persons, 1999)	87
Access to sanitation (% of persons, 1999)	99
Human Development Index (2000): ranking	57
Human Development Index (2000): value	0.787

For sources and definitions, see explanatory note on p. vi.

Agriculture

PRINCIPAL CROPS
('000 metric tons)

	1999	2000	2001
Rice (paddy)	224.3	207.4	279.3
Maize	88.6	94.0	37.2
Sugar cane	1,773.9	1,788.5	1,789.0
Bananas	800.0†	660.4	489.4
Plantains	112.0†	104.2	100.0†
Coffee (green)	11.4	9.4	12.4
Tobacco (leaves)	1.8*	1.8†	2.1†

* Unofficial figure.
† FAO estimate.

Source: FAO.

LIVESTOCK
('000 head, year ending September)

	1999	2000	2001
Horses*	166.0	166.0	166.0
Mules*	4.0	4.0	4.0
Cattle	1,359.8	1,342.8	1,342.4
Pigs	278.3	279.5	277.9
Goats	5.3*	5.2	5.2
Chickens	11,793	14,451	14,451
Ducks*	200	200	200
Turkeys*	25	25	25

* FAO estimate(s).

Source: FAO.

LIVESTOCK PRODUCTS
('000 metric tons)

	1999	2000	2001
Beef and veal	60.3	69.6	56.7
Pig meat	20.5*	21.6	19.0
Poultry meat	67.0*	100.4	76.8
Cows' milk	150.0*	165.6	170.6
Cheese	9.5*	8.1	7.9
Hen eggs	12.0*	12.4	12.7

* FAO estimate.

Source: FAO.

Forestry

ROUNDWOOD REMOVALS
('000 cubic metres, excluding bark)

	1999	2000	2001
Sawlogs, veneer logs and logs for sleepers	48	32	42
Fuel wood*	1,290	1,280	1,264
Total*	1,338	1,342	1,306

* FAO estimates.

Source: FAO.

SAWNWOOD PRODUCTION
('000 cubic metres, incl. railway sleepers)

	1999	2000	2001
Coniferous (softwood)	2	2	2*
Broadleaved (hardwood) . . .	44	46	40
Total	46	48	42*

* FAO estimate.

Source: FAO.

Fishing

('000 metric tons, live weight)

	1998	1999	2000
Capture	202.7	120.6	223.5
Snappers and jobfishes . . .	5.4	10.4	8.5
Pacific thread herring . . .	49.5	38.7	63.5
Pacific anchoveta	107.7	27.4	86.7
Skipjack tuna	1.5	6.3	15.8
Yellowfin tuna	5.6	7.5	7.9
Marine fishes	15.4	15.6	18.3
Aquaculture	10.2	3.2	2.4
Whiteleg shrimp	9.1	2.6	1.2
Total catch	212.8	123.7	225.9

Source: FAO, *Yearbook of Fishery Statistics*.

Industry

SELECTED PRODUCTS
('000 metric tons, unless otherwise indicated)

	1997	1998	1999
Salt*	22.0	22.5†	23.0
Raw sugar‡	142	166	177
Condensed milk	32.1	34.7	29.2
Powdered milk	4.6	4.6	4.6
Electricity (million kWh, net)§ .	4,680	4,880	4,890

Tomato derivatives ('000 metric tons): 10,081 in 2001.

Fishmeal ('000 metric tons): 23.1 in 1996.

Fish oil ('000 metric tons): 3.2 in 1996.

Cigarettes (million): 1,253.2 in 1996.

Alcoholic beverages ('000 litres): 12,150 in 2001.

Electricity ('000 kWh): 4,858,133 in 2001.

* Data from US Geological Survey.
† Estimate.
‡ Data from FAO.
§ Data from Energy Information Administration, US Department of Energy.

Source (unless otherwise specified): mainly UN, *Industrial Commodity Statistics Yearbook*.

Finance

CURRENCY AND EXCHANGE RATES

Monetary Units
100 centésimos = 1 balboa (B)

Sterling, Dollar and Euro Equivalents (31 December 2002)
£1 sterling = 1.6118 balboas;
US $1 = 1.0000 balboas;
€1 = 1.0487 centésimos;
100 balboas = £62.04 = $100.00 = €95.36

Exchange Rate: The balboa's value is fixed at par with that of the US dollar.

BUDGET
(million balboas)*

Revenue†	1998	1999	2000
Tax revenue	1,608.2	1,737.6	1,683.6
Taxes on income, profits, etc. .	399.5	508.4	494.2
Corporate.	115.0	186.8	155.2
Social security contributions . .	431.4	472.1	497.8
Taxes on property	35.1	41.5	33.9
Other tax revenue	68.6	69.6	77.8
Other current revenue . . .	721.6	923.7	1,003.6
Entrepreneurial and property income	402.3	492.6	567.1
Administration fees, charges and non-industrial sales. . . .	181.3	156.7	118.0
Capital revenue	1.4	3.2	1.2
Total revenue	2,331.2	2,664.5	2,688.4

Expenditure‡	1998	1999	2000
General public services	213.1	211.2	209.7
Public order and safety	195.2	211.2	199.4
Education	459.7	450.1	465.4
Health	485.3	470.2	482.1
Social security and welfare . . .	528.7	496.0	586.4
Housing and community amenities	103.1	95.0	80.6
Recreational, cultural and religious affairs	22.8	28.0	27.9
Economic affairs and services . .	195.7	208.2	196.1
Transportation and communications	100.8	106.9	92.4
Other expenditures	403.2	481.0	556.3
Total	2,606.8	2,650.9	2,803.9
Current§	2,331.7	2,429.6	2,551.7
Capital.	275.1	221.3	252.2

* Figures refer to the consolidated accounts of the central Government.
† Excluding grants received (million balboas): 72.3 in 1998; 6.8 in 1999; 17.8 in 2000.
‡ Excluding lending minus repayments (million balboas): −139.1 in 1998; −14.0 in 1999; −127.9 in 2000.
§ Including interest payments (million balboas): 401.6 in 1998; 481.0 in 1999; 556.3 in 2000.

INTERNATIONAL RESERVES
(US $ million at 31 December*)

	2000	2001	2002
IMF special drawing rights .	0.3	1.4	1.1
Reserve position in IMF . .	15.5	14.9	16.1
Foreign exchange	706.8	1,075.5	1,165.7
Total	722.6	1,091.8	1,182.8

* Excludes gold, valued at US $476,000 in 1991–93.

Source: IMF, *International Financial Statistics*.
Note: US treasury notes and coins form the bulk of the currency in circulation in Panama.

COST OF LIVING
(Consumer Price Index, Panamá (Panama City); base: 1990 = 100)

	1999	2000	2001
Food (incl. beverages)	110.3	111.1	110.6
Fuel and light	103.1	110.5	108.2
Clothing (incl. footwear). . .	105.7	106.0	110.5
Rent	121.1	123.0	128.2
All items (incl. others)	110.6	112.3	112.6

Source: ILO.

NATIONAL ACCOUNTS
(million balboas at current prices)

National Income and Product

	1998	1999	2000*
Compensation of employees. . .	4,724.2	4,856.7	4,984.8
Operating surplus	3,103.9	3,170.4	3,430.8
Domestic factor incomes. . .	7,828.1	8,027.1	8,415.6
Consumption of fixed capital . .	667.8	723.2	747.2
Gross domestic product (GDP) at factor cost	8,495.9	8,750.3	9,162.8
Indirect taxes	891.2	935.2	893.3
Less Subsidies	42.4	48.9	37.1
GDP in purchasers' values . .	9,344.7	9,636.6	10,019.0
Factor income received from abroad	1,547.9	1,380.7	1,469.0
Less Factor income paid abroad .	2,156.7	2,171.4	2,169.5
Gross national product . . .	8,735.9	8,845.9	9,318.5
Less Consumption of fixed capital .	667.8	723.2	747.2
National income in market prices	8,068.1	8,122.7	8,571.3
Other current transfers from abroad (net)	159.0	171.1	175.5
National disposable income. .	8,227.1	8,293.8	8,746.8

* Preliminary figures.

Expenditure on the Gross Domestic Product

	1998	1999	2000*
Government final consumption expenditure.	1,507.6	1,500.0	1,605.3
Private final consumption expenditure.	5,283.4	5,331.8	5,672.8
Increase in stocks	372.3	278.0	239.4
Gross fixed capital formation . .	2,624.9	2,908.1	2,634.1
Total domestic expenditure. .	9,788.2	10,017.9	10,151.6
Exports of goods and services . .	8,396.4	7,390.4	7,941.1
Less Imports of goods and services	8,839.9	7,771.7	8,073.7
GDP in purchasers' values . .	9,344.7	9,636.6	10,019.0
GDP at constant 1982 prices .	6,947.2	7,169.9	7,345.7

* Preliminary.

Gross Domestic Product by Economic Activity

	1998	1999	2000
Agriculture, hunting, forestry and fishing	659.1	669.4	682.7
Mining and quarrying . . .	37.2	47.2	42.8
Manufacturing	753.7	728.9	712.9
Electricity, gas and water . . .	320.4	349.6	399.0
Construction	427.9	480.5	492.8
Wholesale and retail trade, restaurants and hotels . . .	1,826.0	1,725.2	1,758.8
Transport, storage and communications	1,389.7	1,536.5	1,727.5
Finance, insurance, real estate and business services	2,332.6	2,507.6	2,659.6
Government, community, social and personal services	1,644.4	1,686.4	1,716.2
Sub-total	9,391.0	9,731.1	10,192.3
Import duties and other taxes . .	307.8	304.7	276.0
Less Imputed bank service charge	354.1	399.4	449.3
GDP in purchasers' values . .	9,344.7	9,636.6	10,019.0

BALANCE OF PAYMENTS
(US $ million)*

	1999	2000	2001
Exports of goods f.o.b.	5,303.3	5,836.8	5,883.7
Imports of goods f.o.b.	−6,689.4	−7,026.6	−6,709.5
Trade balance	−1,386.1	−1,189.8	−825.7
Exports of services	1,793.2	1,829.6	1,816.9
Imports of services	1,143.1	1,137.8	−1,144.0
Balance on goods and services	−736.0	−498.0	−152.9
Other income received	1,503.3	1,580.4	1,398.7
Other income paid	−2,258.6	2,192.4	−1,944.0
Balance on goods, services and income	−1,491.3	−1,110.0	−698.2
Current transfers received	202.7	208.6	226.8
Current transfers paid	−31.6	−31.7	−28.1
Current balance	−1,320.2	−933.1	−499.5
Capital account (net)	3.0	1.7	1.6
Direct investment from abroad.	652.4	603.4	512.6
Portfolio investment assets	−550.2	−109.3	−778.3
Portfolio investment liabilities	−99.2	−86.8	−66.2
Other investment assets	1,983.0	358.5	856.3
Other investment liabilities	−587.8	763.7	62.7
Net errors and omissions	−228.7	602.4	−387.7
Overall balance	−147.7	−327.0	−298.5

* Including the transactions of enterprises operating in the Colón Free Zone.

Source: IMF, *International Financial Statistics*.

External Trade

PRINCIPAL COMMODITIES
('000 balboas)

Imports c.i.f.	1996	1997	1998*
Vegetable products	104,135	90,448	121,936
Food products, beverages and tobacco	155,315	171,838	211,703
Mineral products	455,636	440,978	349,300
Chemicals and chemical products	318,330	324,638	327,051
Plastics and synthetic resins	130,202	149,742	161,573
Paper and paper products	129,487	126,911	134,181
Textiles and textile manufactures	153,293	168,556	188,398
Basic metals and metal manufactures	174,567	205,382	210,073
Electrical and electronic equipment	498,163	580,378	779,238
Transport equipment	354,184	402,686	514,808
Total (incl. others)	2,781,071	2,992,404	3,398,342

* Preliminary figures.

1999 ('000 balboas): Capital goods 839,428; Crude petroleum 301,973; Foodstuffs 342,787; Other consumer and intermediate goods 2,031,577; Total imports c.i.f. 3,515,765.

2000 ('000 balboas, preliminary figures): Capital goods 688,032; Crude petroleum 447,007; Foodstuffs 347,981; Other consumer and intermediate goods 1,895,634; Total imports c.i.f. 3,378,654.

2001 (US $ '000): Capital goods 514,702; Crude petroleum 425,984; Foodstuffs 317,949; Other consumer and intermediate goods 1,704,949; Total imports c.i.f. 2,963,584 (Source: Ministry of Finance and Treasury, *Informe Económico Anual 2002*).

Exports f.o.b.	1998	1999	2000*
Raw sugar	25,549	14,455	19,887
Bananas	138,748	182,312	148,329
Coffee	23,931	19,999	16,045
Shrimps	136,730	70,233	62,710
Yellowfin tuna	2,505	12,617	29,844
Other fish (fresh, dried and frozen)	62,620	85,750	124,018
Clothing	25,635	21,879	19,472
Petroleum products	24,827	63,902	52,066
Cigarettes	1,588	7,089	37,677
Total (incl. others)	705,458	707,131	771,514

* Preliminary figures.

2001 (US $ '000): Bananas 122,158; Coffee 11,112; Shrimps 79,374; Clothing 14,281; Petroleum products 57,176; Total exports f.o.b. (incl. others) 809,537 (Source: Ministry of Finance and Treasury, *Informe Económico Anual 2002*).

PRINCIPAL TRADING PARTNERS
(US $ '000)

Imports c.i.f.	1998	1999	2000*
Brazil	27,702	34,312	37,943
Canada	27,804	30,110	40,312
Colombia†	65,044	91,097	115,568
Costa Rica	101,861	114,423	118,548
Ecuador	108,754	185,236	243,094
Finland	1,741	52,813	31,517
Germany	45,110	47,542	52,749
Guatemala	55,590	63,414	61,789
Hong Kong	33,971	27,971	25,501
Japan	304,256	254,119	185,954
Korea, Republic	89,162	123,760	79,524
Mexico	163,932	172,293	132,880
Netherlands Antilles‡	20,477	11,604	61,410
Spain	44,634	53,961	60,723
Trinidad and Tobago	8,375	43,619	5,076
United Kingdom	39,830	34,651	31,949
USA	1,349,990	1,241,865	1,109,183
Venezuela	106,900	100,403	222,039
Total (incl. others)	3,365,510	3,515,766	3,378,655

Exports f.o.b.	2000	2001	2002
Belgium-Luxembourg	39,165	36,515	32,778
Colombia†	8,620	6,199	5,749
Costa Rica	40,536	38,959	36,167
Dominican Republic	12,071	7,799	15,774
Ecuador	3,999	4,814	3,903
El Salvador	9,455	6,033	7,675
Germany	9,858	25,832	6,443
Guatemala	21,243	17,171	15,916
Honduras	22,313	20,075	33,560
Hong Kong	8,068	6,360	5,220
Italy	24,907	22,137	7,563
Japan	11,824	12,067	10,111
Mexico	24,095	15,397	14,821
Nicaragua	18,020	41,098	20,900
Portugal	7,994	13,827	28,627
Puerto Rico	15,613	13,434	12,506
Spain	13,112	18,123	21,867
Sweden	62,320	30,306	44,239
Taiwan	14,898	11,699	4,495
USA	338,162	388,607	348,266
Venezuela	4,127	18,192	8,582
Total (incl. others)	771,514	809,537	755,747

* Preliminary figures.
† Excl. San Andrés island.
‡ Curaçao only.

Transport

RAILWAYS
(traffic)

	1995	1996	1997
Passenger-km (million)*	39,240	11,740	5,684
Freight ton-km (million)†	34,119	27,971	24,115

* Panama Railway and National Railway of Chiriquí.
† Panama Railway only.

Source: UN, *Statistical Yearbook*.

ROAD TRAFFIC
(motor vehicles registered)

	1996	1997*	1998*
Cars	203,760	214,899	228,722
Buses	15,492	16,181	16,072
Lorries	59,145	62,057	67,948
Others	7,243	7,532	n.a.

* Estimates.

Source: IRF, *World Road Statistics*.

SHIPPING

Merchant Fleet

(registered at 31 December)

	1999	2000	2001
Number of vessels	6,143	6,184	6,245
Total displacement ('000 grt) . .	105,248.1	114,382.3	122,352.1

Source: Lloyd's Register-Fairplay, *World Fleet Statistics*.

International Sea-borne Freight Traffic

('000 metric tons)

	1995*	1996	1997*
Goods loaded	1,645.0	362.2	2,916.5
Goods unloaded	2,167.8	3,255.4	4,440.3

* Preliminary figures.

Panama Canal Traffic

	2000	2001	2002
Transits	13,653	13,492	13,185
Cargo (million long tons) . . .	193.7	193.2	187.8

Source: Panama Canal Authority.

CIVIL AVIATION

(traffic on scheduled services)

	1997	1998	1999
Kilometres flown (million) . .	18	21	24
Passengers carried ('000) . .	772	856	933
Passengers-km (million). . .	1,094	1,373	1,697
Total ton-km (million)	152	174	215

Source: UN, *Statistical Yearbook*.

Tourism

VISITOR ARRIVALS BY COUNTRY OF ORIGIN

	1999	2000	2001
Argentina	5,889	7,394	8,946
Canada	5,797	5,872	13,854
Chile	4,413	5,335	5,823
Colombia	64,261	70,823	77,047
Costa Rica	61,327	21,962	19,870
Dominican Republic	8,712	9,229	8,693
Ecuador	11,966	14,298	19,006
El Salvador	8,298	5,628	5,188
Germany	4,612	3,378	3,635
Guatemala	11,419	10,289	10,542
Haiti	6,613	5,330	3,823
Honduras	9,419	4,785	4,004
Jamaica	8,450	8,314	8,446
Mexico	17,805	20,019	19,852
Nicaragua	12,513	5,666	5,061
Peru	5,412	7,124	8,141
Puerto Rico	6,669	5,330	3,823
Spain	7,662	8,188	7,585
USA	119,169	111,858	108,273
Venezuela	16,225	16,956	17,413
Total (incl. others)	445,957	395,551	410,605

Receipts from tourism (US $ million): 379 in 1998; 387 in 1999; 576 in 2000.

Sources: World Tourism Organization, *Yearbook of Tourism Statistics*; IMF, *Panama: Recent Economic Developments* (February 2001).

Communications Media

	1999	2000	2001
Television receivers ('000 in use) .	540	550	n.a.
Telephones ('000 main lines in use)	463	429	430
Mobile cellular telephones ('000 subscribers).	232.9	410.0	600.0
Personal computers ('000 in use) .	90	n.a.	110
Internet users ('000)	45	90	90

Radio receivers ('000 in use): 815 in 1997.

Daily newspapers: 7 in 1997.

Sources: UNESCO, *Statistical Yearbook*; International Telecommunication Union.

Education

(1997)

	Institutions	Teachers	Pupils
Pre-primary.	1,084	2,063	45,340
Primary	2,866	15,058	377,898
Secondary	417	12,327	223,155
University	5	5,454	84,452
Special*	24	483	6,205
Supplementary*	27	206	4,819

* 1996 figures.

Sources: Ministry of Education; UNESCO, *Statistical Yearbook*.

Adult literacy rate (UNESCO estimates): 91.9% (males 92.5%; females 91.3%) in 2000 (Source: UN Development Programme, *Human Development Report*).

Directory

The Constitution

Under the terms of the amendments to the Constitution, implemented by the adoption of Reform Acts No 1 and No 2 in October 1978, and by the approval by referendum of the Constitutional Act in April 1983, the 67 (later 71) members of the unicameral Asamblea Legislativa (Legislative Assembly) are elected by popular vote every five years. Executive power is exercised by the President of the Republic, who is also elected by popular vote for a term of five years. Two Vice-Presidents are elected by popular vote to assist the President. The President appoints the Cabinet. The armed forces are barred from participating in elections.

The Government

HEAD OF STATE

President: MIREYA ELISA MOSCOSO DE GRUBER (took office 1 September 1999).

First Vice-President: ARTURO ULISES VALLARINO.

Second Vice-President: DOMINADOR KAISER BALDOMERO BAZÁN.

THE CABINET
(April 2003)

Minister of the Interior and Justice: ARNULFO ESCALONA AVILA.

Minister of Foreign Affairs: HARMODIO ARIAS CERJACK.

Minister of Public Works: EDUARDO ANTONIO QURIÓS.

Minister of Finance and the Treasury: NORBERTO DELGADO DURÁN.

Minister of Agricultural Development: LYNETTE MARIA STANZIOLA APOLAYO.

Minister of Commerce and Industry: JOAQUÍN E. JÁCOME DÍEZ.

Minister of Public Health: FERNANDO J. GRACIA GARCÍA.

Minister of Labour and Social Welfare: JAIME A. MORENO DIAZ.

Minister of Education: Dr DORIS ROSAS DE MATA.

Minister of Housing: MIGUEL ANGEL CÁRDENAS.

Minister of the Presidency: IVONNE YOUNG VALDÉS.

Minister of Youth, Women, Family and Childhood: ROSABEL VERGARA B.

Minister of Canal Affairs: JERRY SALAZAR.

MINISTRIES

Office of the President: Palacio Presidencial, Valija 50, Panamá 1; tel. 227-4062; fax 227-0076; internet www.presidencia.gob.pa.

Ministry of Agricultural Development: Edif. 576, Calle Manuel E. Melo, Altos de Curundú, Apdo 5390, Panamá 5; tel. 232-6254; fax 232-5044; e-mail infomida@mida.gob.pa; internet www.mida.gob.pa.

Ministry of Commerce and Industry: El Paical 2° y 3°, Plaza Edison, Apdo 9658, Panamá 4; tel. 360-0600; fax 360-0280; e-mail uti@mici.gob.pa; internet www.mici.gob.pa.

Ministry of Education: Edif. Poli y Los Rios, Avda Justo Arosemena, Calles 26 y 27, Apdo 2440, Panamá 3; tel. 262-2645; fax 262-9087; e-mail me@sinfo.net; internet www.meduc.gob.pa.

Ministry of Finance and the Treasury: Central Postal Balboa, Ancón, Apdo 5245, Panamá 5; tel. 225-3431; fax 227-2357; e-mail mhyt@mhyt.gob.pa; internet www.mef.gob.pa.

Ministry of Foreign Affairs: Altos de Ancón, Complejo Narciso Garay, Panamá 4; tel. 227-0013; fax 227-4725; e-mail prensa@mire.gob.pa; internet www.mire.gob.pa.

Ministry of Housing: Avda Ricardo J. Alfaro, Edif. Plaza Edison, 4°, Apdo 5228, Panamá 5; tel. 279-9200; fax 321-0028; internet www.mivi.gob.pa.

Ministry of the Interior and Justice: Avda Central, entre calle 2da y 3era, San Felipe, Apdo 1628, Panamá 1; tel. 212-2000; fax 212-2126; e-mail informa@gobiernoyjusticia.gob.pa; internet www.gobiernoyjusticia.gob.pa.

Ministry of Labour and Social Welfare: Avda Ricardo J. Alfaro, Plaza Edison, 5°, Apdo 2441, Panamá 3; tel. 260-9087; fax 260-4466; e-mail mitrabs2@sinfo.net; internet www.mitradel.gob.pa.

Ministry of the Presidency: Valija 50, Apdo 2189, Panamá 1; tel. 227-9600; fax 227-6944; e-mail ofasin@presidencia.gob.pa; internet www.presidencia.gob.pa.

Ministry of Public Health: Apdo 2048, Panamá 1; tel. 225-6080; fax 227-5276; e-mail daimimsa@yahoo.com; internet www.minsa.gob.pa.

Ministry of Public Works: Edif. 1619, Curundú, Zona 1, Apdo 1632, Panamá 1; tel. 232-5333; fax 232-8776; internet www.mop.gob.pa.

Ministry of Youth, Women, Family and Childhood: Avda Ricardo J. Alfaro, 4°, Edison Plaza, Apdo 680-50, El Dorado, Panamá; tel. 279-0702; fax 279-0714; e-mail minjufa@sinfo.net; internet www.dinamu.gob.pa.

Office of the Minister of Canal Affairs: Edif. Bancomer, 5°, Calle 50, Apdo 832-0003, Panamá; tel. 263-4545; fax 263-0267; e-mail valerio@psinet.pa.

President and Legislature

PRESIDENT

Election, 2 May 1999

Candidate	Votes	% of votes
Mireya Moscoso de Gruber (Unión por Panamá)	572,717	44.8
Martín Torrijos Espino (Nueva Nación)	483,501	37.8
Alberto Vallarino (Acción Opositora)	222,250	17.4
Total	**1,278,468**	**100.0**

ASAMBLEA LEGISLATIVA
(Legislative Assembly)

President: CARLOS R. ALVARADO ACOSTA.

General Election, 2 May 1999

Affiliation/Party	% of votes	Seats
Nueva Nación		
Partido Revolucionario Democrático (PRD)*	47.9	34
Partido Solidaridad	5.6	4
Partido Liberal Nacional (PLN)	4.2	3
Unión por Panamá		
Partido Arnulfista (PA)	25.3	18
Movimiento Liberal Republicano Nacionalista (MOLIRENA)	4.2	3
Cambio Democrático	2.8	2
Movimiento de Renovación Nacional (Morena)	1.4	1
Acción Opositora		
Partido Demócrata Cristiano (PDC)	7.0	5
Partido Renovación Civilista (PRC)	1.4	1
Total (incl. others)	**100.0**	**71**

*In September 2002 two members of the PRD were officially excluded from the party; CARLOS ALVARADO ACOSTA joined the governing coalition as an independent and the other became a member of the Partido Solidaridad. A further three dissident PRD members also regularly voted with the Government.

Political Organizations

Movimiento Laborista Agrario (MOLA): Panamá; tel. 263-7055; fax 264-5981; formally registered 1993.

Movimiento Liberal Republicano Nacionalista (MOLIRENA): Calle Venezuela, Casa No 5, entre Vía España y Calle 50, Panamá; tel. 213-5928; fax 265-6004; internet www.sinfo.net/molirena; formally registered 1982; conservative; Pres. JESUS L. ROSAS.

Movimiento Nacional por la Defensa de la Soberanía (Monadeso): Panamá; Leader CONRADO SANJUR.

Movimiento de Renovación Nacional (Morena): Panamá; tel. 236-4930; formally registered 1993; Pres. PEDRO VALLARINO COX; Sec.-Gen. DEMETRIO DECEREGA.

Partido Arnulfista (PA): Avda Perú y Calle 38E, No 37–41, (al lado de Casa la Esperanza), Apdo 9610, Panamá 4; tel. 227-1267; f. 1990; formed by Arnulfista faction of the Partido Panameñista Auténtico; Pres. MIREYA MOSCOSO DE GRUBER; Sec.-Gen. CARLOS RAÚL PIAD H.

Partido Cambio Democrático (CD): Parque Lefevre, Plaza Carolina, arriba de la Juguetería del Super 99, Panamá; formally registered 1998; Pres. RICARDO A. MARTINELLI BERROCAL; Sec.-Gen. ROBERTO ORTÍZ.

Partido Demócrata Cristiano (PDC): Avda Perú (frente al Parque Porras), Apdo 6322, Panamá 5; tel. 227-3204; fax 227-3944; f. 1960; Pres. RUBÉN AROSEMENA.

Partido Liberal Auténtico (PLA): Panamá; tel. 227-1041; fax 227-4119; formally registered 1988; Pres. ARNULFO ESCALONA RIOS; Sec.-Gen. JULIO C. HARRIS.

Partido Liberal Nacional (PLN): Vía Fernandez de Córdoba, Vista Hermosa, Plaza Córdoba, antigua Ersa, Local 6–7, Panamá; tel. 229-7523; fax 229-7524; e-mail pln@sinfo.net; internet www.sinfo.net/liberal-nacional; f. 1979; mem. of Liberal International, and founding mem. of Federación Liberal de Centroamérica y el Caribe (FELICA); 40,645 mems; Pres. VIOLA ICAZA DE GARCÍA; Sec.-Exec. RICARDO ANGUIZOLA.

Partido Liberal Republicano (Libre): Panamá; tel. 261-4659; formally registered 1993; Pres. GONZALO TAPIA COLLANTE; Sec.-Gen. CARLOS ORILLAC.

Partido Revolucionario Democrático (PRD): Calle 42 Bella Vista, entre Avda Perú y Avda Cuba, bajando por el teatro Bella Vista, Panamá 9; tel. 225-1050; e-mail secreprd@sinfo.net; f. 1979; supports policies of late Gen. Omar Torrijos Herrera; combination of Marxists, Christian Democrats and some business interests; Pres. HUGO H. GUIRAUD; Sec.-Gen. MARTÍN TORRIJOS ESPINO.

Partido Solidaridad: Panamá; tel. 263-4097; internet www.sinfo.net/solidaridad; formally registered 1993; Pres. MAROIA ESTHER VILLALAZ DE ARIAS; Sec.-Gen. ENRIQUE LAU CORTÉZ.

The following political alliances were formed to contest presidential and legislative elections conducted on 2 May 1999:

Acción Opositora (AO): comprising the PDC, the Partido Renovación Civilista (PRC), the Partido Liberal (PL) and the Partido Nacionalista Popular (PNP); Presidential Candidate ALBERTO VALLARINO (PDC).

Nueva Nación (NN): comprising the PRD, Partido Solidaridad, the PLN and the Movimiento Papa Egoró (MPE); Presidential Candidate MARTÍN TORRIJOS (PRD).

Unión por Panamá (UPP): comprising the PA, MOLIRENA, Morena and CD; Presidential Candidate MIREYA MOSCOSO DE GRUBER (PA).

Diplomatic Representation

EMBASSIES IN PANAMA

Argentina: Edif. del Banco de Iberoamérica, 7°, Avda 50 y Calle 53, Apdo 1271, Panamá 1; tel. 264-6561; fax 269-5331; e-mail embargen@c-com.net.pa; Ambassador ERNESTO MARIO PFIRTER.

Bolivia: Calle Eric Arturo del Valle, Bella Vista 1, Panamá; tel. 269-0274; fax 264-3868; e-mail embolivia-panama@rree.gov.bo; Ambassador GUILLERMO GUITÉRREZ DE LAS HERAS.

Brazil: Edif. El Dorado, 1°, Calle Elvira Méndez y Avda Ricardo Arango, Urb. Campo Alegre, Apdo 4287, Panamá 5; tel. 263-5322; fax 269-6316; e-mail brasemb@sifo; Ambassador PEDRO PAULO PINTO ASSUMPÇAO.

Canada: Edif. World Trade Center, Galería Comercial, 1°, Urb. Marbella, Apdo 0832-2446, Panamá; tel. 264-7115; fax 263-8083; Ambassador DAVID ADAM.

Chile: Edif. Banco de Boston, 11°, Calle Elvira Méndez y Vía España, Apdo 7341, Panamá 5; tel. 223-9748; fax 263-5530; e-mail echilepa@cw.panama.net; Ambassador JAIME ROCHA MANRIQUE.

China (Taiwan): Calle 8, Ave Roosevelt, Casa 10-084, Colón; tel. 441-3403; fax 441-3784; e-mail embchina@hotmail.com; Ambassador GUANG-PU SHYU.

Colombia: Edif. World Trade Center, Of. 1802, Calle 53, Urb. Marbella, Panamá; tel. 264-9644; fax 223-1134; e-mail emcolpan@sinfo.net; Ambassador GINA BENEDETTI DE VELEZ.

Costa Rica: Edif. Plaza Omega, 3°, Calle Samuel Lewis, Apdo 8963, Panamá; tel. 264-2980; fax 264-4057; e-mail embarica@pan.gbm.net; Ambassador ALVARO DE LA CRUZ MARTÍNEZ.

Cuba: Avda Cuba y Ecuador 33, Apdo 6-2291, El Dorado, Panamá; tel. 227-5277; fax 225-6681; e-mail embacuba@cableonda.net; Ambassador CARLOS RAFAEL ZAMORA RODRÍGUEZ.

Dominican Republic: Casa 40A, Calle 75, Apdo 6250, Panamá 5; tel. 270-3884; fax 270-3886; e-mail embajdom@sinfo.net; Ambassador RODOLFO LEYBA POLANCO.

Ecuador: Edif. Torre 2000, 6°, Calle 50, Marbella, Bellavista, Panamá; e-mail panamaecuador@hotmail.com; tel. 264-2654; fax 223-0159; Ambassador HUMBERTO PLAZA LAVEZZARI.

Egypt: Calle 55, No 15, El Cangrejo, Panamá; tel. 263-5020; Ambassador MOUSTAFA MOHAMED AHMED EL HATEER.

El Salvador: Edif. Metropolis, 4°, Avda Manuel Espinosa Batista, Panamá; tel. 223-3020; fax 264-1433; e-mail patriasa@sinfo.net; Ambassador AÍDA ELENA MINERO.

France: Plaza de Francia 1, Las Bovedas, San Felipe, Apdo 869, Panamá 1; tel. 228-8290; fax 228-7852; internet www.ambafrance-pa.org; Ambassador PATRICK BOURSIN.

Germany: Edif. World Trade Center, 20°, Calle 53E, Marbella, Apdo 0832-0536, Panamá 5; tel. 263-7733; fax 223-6664; e-mail germpanama@cwp.net; internet www.embajada-alemana-panama.org; Ambassador GEORG HEINRICH VON NEUBRONNER.

Guatemala: Edif. Altamira, Of. 925, Vía Argentina, El Cangrejo, Corregimiento de Bella Vista, Panamá 9; tel. 269-3475; fax 223-1922; Ambassador GUISELA ATALIDA GODÍNEZ DE GUTIÉRREZ.

Haiti: Edif. Dora Luz, 2°, Calle 1, El Cangrejo, Apdo 442, Panamá 9; tel. 269-3443; fax 223-1767; Ambassador JOSEPH ETIENNE.

Holy See: Punta Paitilla, Avda Balboa y Vía Italia, Apdo 4251, Panamá 5 (Apostolic Nunciature); tel. 269-2102; fax 264-2116; e-mail nuncio@sinfo.net; Apostolic Nuncio Most Rev. GIACOMO GUIDO OTTONELLO (Titular Archbishop of Sasabe).

Honduras: Edif. BayMall, 1°, 112 Avda Balboa, Apdo 8704, Panamá 5; tel. 264-5513; fax 224-5513; e-mail ehpan@cableonda.net; Ambassador RAÚL CARDONA LÓPEZ.

India: Avda Federico Boy y Calle 51, Alado de Torre Universal, Panamá; tel. 264-3043; fax 264-2855; e-mail indempn@panama.c-com.net; Ambassador TARA SINGH.

Italy: Torre Banco Exterior, 25°, Avda Balboa, Apdo 2369, Panamá 9; tel. 225-8950; fax 227-4906; e-mail panitamb@cwp.net.pa; Ambassador MARCO ROCCA.

Japan: Calle 50 y 60 E, Obarrio, Apdo 1411, Panamá 1; tel. 263-6155; fax 263-6019; e-mail taiship2@sinfo.net; internet www.embjapon.net; Ambassador MITSUI MATSUZU.

Korea, Republic: Edif. Plaza, planta baja, Calle Ricardo Arias y Calle 51E, Campo Alegre, Apdo 8096, Panamá 7; tel. 264-8203; fax 264-8825; e-mail korm@cwp.net.pa; Ambassador KEUN SEOP OHM.

Libya: Avda Balboa y Calle 32 (frente al Edif. Atalaya), Apdo 6-894 El Dorado, Panamá; tel. 227-3342; fax 227-3886; Chargé d'affaires ABDULMAJID MILUD SHAHIN.

Mexico: Edif. Torre ADR, 10°, Avda Samuel Lewis y Calle 58, Urb. Obarrio, Corregimiento de Bella Vista, Panamá; tel. 263-4900; fax 263-5446; e-mail embamexpan@cwpanama.net; Ambassador JOSÉ IGNACIO PIÑA ROJAS.

Nicaragua: Quarry Heights, 16°, Ancon, Apdo 772, Zona 1, Panamá; tel. 211-2113; fax 211-2116; e-mail embapana@sinfo.net; Ambassador EDGARD ESCOBAR FORNOS.

Peru: Edif. World Trade Center, 12°, Panamá; tel. 223-1112; fax 269-6809; e-mail embaperu@pananet.com; Ambassador JOSÉ ANTONIO BELLINA ACEVEDO.

Russia: Torre IBC, 10°, Avda Manuel Espinosa Batista, Apdo 6-4697, El Dorado, Panamá; tel. 264-1408; fax 264-1588; e-mail emruspan@sinfo.net; Ambassador NIKOLAI MIKHAILOVICH VLADIMIR.

Saudi Arabia: Calle Manuel M. Icaza y Avda Samuel Lewis, Panamá; tel. 263-2599; fax 264-2116; Ambassador SOULIMAN TAYEB AHMED SALEM.

Spain: Calle 53 y Avda Perú (frente a la Plaza Porras), Apdo 1857, Panamá 1; tel. 227-5122; fax 227-6284; e-mail embespa@cwp.net.pa; Ambassador CARLOS DE LOJENDIO Y PARDO MANUEL DE VILLENA.

United Kingdom: Torre Swiss Bank, 4°, Urb. Marbella, Calle 53, Apdo 889, Panamá 1; tel. 269-0866; fax 223-0730; e-mail britemb@cwp.net.pa; Ambassador JAMES MALCOLM.

USA: Avda Balboa y Calle 38, Apdo 6959, Panamá 5; tel. 207-7000; fax 227-1964; e-mail usembisc@cwp.net.pa; Ambassador LINDA ELLEN WATT.

Uruguay: Edif. Vallarino, 5°, Of. 4, Calle 32 y Avda Justo Arosemena, Apdo 8898, Panamá 5; tel. 225-0049; fax 225-9087; e-mail urupanan@sinfo.net; Ambassador TABARÉ BOCALANDRO.

Venezuela: Torre Banco Unión, 5°, Avda Samuel Lewis, Apdo 661, Panamá 1; tel. 269-1014; fax 269-1916; e-mail embvenp@panama.ce .net; Ambassador FLAVIO GRANADOS POMENTA.

Judicial System

The judiciary in Panama comprises the following courts and judges: Corte Suprema de Justicia (Supreme Court of Justice), with nine judges appointed for a 10-year term; 10 Tribunales Superiores de Distrito Judicial (High Courts) with 36 magistrates; 54 Jueces de Circuito (Circuit Judges) and 89 Jueces Municipales (Municipal Judges).

Panama is divided into four judicial districts and has seven High Courts of Appeal. The first judicial district covers the provinces of Panamá, Colón, Darién and the region of Kuna Yala and contains two High Courts of Appeal, one dealing with criminal cases, the other dealing with civil cases. The second judicial district covers the provinces of Coclé and Veraguas and contains the third High Court of Appeal, located in Penonomé. The third judicial district covers the provinces of Chiriquí and Bocas del Toro and contains the fourth High Court of Appeal, located in David. The fourth judicial district covers the provinces of Herrera and Los Santos and contains the fifth High Court of Appeal, located in Las Tablas. Each of these courts deals with civil and criminal cases in their respective provinces. There are two additional special High Courts of Appeal. The first hears maritime, labour, family and infancy cases; the second deals with antitrust cases and consumer affairs.

Corte Suprema de Justicia
Edif. 236, Ancón, Calle Culebra, Apdo 1770, Panamá 1; tel. 212-0587; e-mail pcsjrp@cw.net.pa; internet www.organojudicial.gob.pa.

President of the Supreme Court of Justice: ADNÁN ARNULFO ARJONA.

Attorney-General: JOSÉ ANTONIO SOSSA.

Religion

The Constitution recognizes freedom of worship and the Roman Catholic Church as the religion of the majority of the population.

CHRISTIANITY

The Roman Catholic Church
For ecclesiastical purposes, Panama comprises one archdiocese, five dioceses, the territorial prelature of Bocas del Toro and the Apostolic Vicariate of Darién. There were an estimated 2,404,446 adherents at 31 December 2000.

Bishops' Conference
Conferencia Episcopal de Panamá, Secretariado General, Apdo 870933, Panamá 7; tel. 223-0075; fax 223-0042.

f. 1958; statutes approved 1986; Pres. Rt Rev. JOSÉ LUIS LACUNZA MAESTROJUÁN (Bishop of David).

Archbishop of Panamá: Most Rev. JOSÉ DIMAS CEDEÑO DELGADO, Arzobispado Metropolitano, Calle 1a Sur Carrasquilla, Apdo 6386, Panamá 5; tel. 261-0002; fax 261-0820.

The Baptist Church

The Baptist Convention of Panama (Convención Bautista de Panamá): Apdo 6212, Panamá 5; tel. 264-5585; fax 264-4945; f. 1959; Pres. Rev. DIMAS JIMÉNEZ; Exec. Sec. Rev. EDUARDO HENNINGHAM.

The Anglican Communion
Panama comprises one of the five dioceses of the Iglesia Anglicana de la Región Central de América.

Bishop of Panama: Rt Rev. CLARENCE W. HAYES-DEWAR, Box R, Balboa; fax 262-2097; e-mail furriola@sinfo.net.

BAHÁ'Í FAITH

National Spiritual Assembly of the Bahá'ís: Apdo 815-0143, Panamá 15; tel. 231-1191; fax 231-6909; e-mail panbahai@sinfo.net; mems resident in 550 localities; National Sec. EMELINA RODRÍGUEZ.

The Press

DAILIES

Crítica Libre: Vía Fernández de Córdoba, Apdo B-4, Panamá 9A; tel. 261-0575; fax 230-0132; e-mail esotop@epasa.com; internet www .epasa.com; f. 1925; morning; independent; Pres. ROSARIO ARIAS DE GALINDO; Editor ANTONIO AMAT; circ. 40,000.

La Estrella de Panamá: Calle Demetrio H Brid 7-38, Panamá; tel. 222-0900; fax 227-1026; f. 1853; morning; independent; Pres. ALEJANDRO A. DUQUE; Editor JAMES APARICIO; circ. 20,000.

El Matutino: Vía Fernández de Córdoba, Apdo B-4, Panamá 9A; tel. 261-2300; morning; pro-Govt; circ. 7,000.

El Panamá América: Vía Ricardo J. Alfaro, al lado de la USMA, Apdo B-4, Panamá 9A; tel. 230-1666; fax 230-1035; e-mail director@ epasa.com; internet www.epasa.com; f. 1958; morning; independent; Pres. ROSARIO ARIAS DE GALINDO; Editor OCTAVIO AMAT; circ. 25,000.

La Prensa: Avda 11 de Octubre y Calle C. Hato Pintado, Apdo 6-4586, El Dorado, Panamá; tel. 221-7515; fax 221-7328; e-mail editor@prensa.com; internet www.prensa.com; f. 1980; morning; independent; closed by Govt 1988–90; Pres. RICARDO ALBERTO ARIAS; Editor GILBERTO SUCRE; circ. 38,000.

La República: Vía Fernández de Córdoba, Apdo B-4, Panamá 9A; tel. 261-0813; evening; circ. 5,000.

El Siglo: Avda Juan XXIII 3, Punta Paitilla, Apdo W, Panamá 4; tel. 263-5735; fax 269-6954; e-mail siglonet@pananet.com; f. 1985; morning; independent; Editor JAIME PADILLA BÉLIZ; circ. 42,000.

El Universal: Avda Justo Arosemena, entre Calles 29 y 30, Panamá; tel. 225-7010; fax 225-6994; e-mail eluniver@sinfo.net; f. 1995; Pres. TOMÁS GERARDO DUQUE ZERR; Editor MILTON HENRÍQUEZ; circ. 16,000.

PERIODICALS

Análisis: Edif. Señorial, Calle 50, Apdo 8038, Panamá 7; tel. 226-0073; fax 226-3758; monthly; economics and politics; Dir MARIO A. ROGNONI.

El Camaleón: Calle 58E, No 12, Apdo W, Panamá 4; tel. 269-3311; fax 269-6954; weekly; satire; Editor JAIME PADILLA BÉLIZ; circ. 80,000.

Diálogo Social: Apdo 9A-192, Panamá; tel. 229-1542; fax 261-0215; f. 1967; published by the Centro de Capacitación Social; monthly; religion, economics and current affairs; Pres. CELIA SANJUR; circ. 3,000.

Estadística Panameña: Apdo 5213, Panamá 5; tel. 210-4800; fax 210-4801; e-mail cgrdec@contraloría.gob.pa; internet www .contraloria.gob.pa; f. 1941; published by the Contraloría General de la República; statistical survey in series according to subjects; Controller-General ALVIN WEEDEN GAMBOA; Dir of Statistics and Census LUIS ENRIQUE QUESADA.

FOB Colón Free Zone: Apdo 6-3287, El Dorado, Panamá; tel. 225-6638; fax 225-0466; e-mail focusint@sinfo.net; internet www .colonfreezone.com; annual; bilingual trade directory; circ. 35,000.

Focus on Panama: Apdo 6-3287, Panamá; tel. 225-6638; fax 225-0466; e-mail focusint@sinfo.net; internet www.focuspublicationsint .com; f. 1970; 2 a year; visitors' guide; separate English and Spanish editions; Dir KENNETH JONES; circ. 70,000.

Informativo Industrial: Apdo 6-4798, El Dorado, Panamá 1; tel. 230-0482; fax 230-0805; monthly; organ of the Sindicato de Industriales de Panamá; Pres. ALBERTO PONS Z.

Maga: Panamá 4; monthly; literature, art and sociology; Dir ENRIQUE JARAMILLO LEVY.

Sucesos: Calle 58E, No 12, Apdo W, Panamá 4; tel. 269-3311; fax 269-6854; 3 a week; Editor JAIME PADILLA BÉLIZ; circ. 50,000.

PRESS ASSOCIATION

Sindicato de Periodistas de Panamá: Avda Ecuador y Calle 33, Apdo 2096, Panamá 1; tel. 225-0234; fax 225-0857; f. 1949; Sec.-Gen. EUCLIDES FUENTES ARROYO.

FOREIGN NEWS BUREAUX

Agencia EFE (Spain): Edif. Comosa, 22°, Avda Samuel Lewis y Calle Manuel María Icaza, Apdo 479, Panamá 9; tel. 223-9020; fax 264-8442; Bureau Chief HUGO FABIÁN ORTIZ DURÁN.

Agenzia Nazionale Stampa Associata (ANSA) (Italy): Edif. Banco de Boston, 17°, Vía España 601, Panamá; tel. 260-6166; Dir LUIS LAMBOGLIA.

Central News Agency (Taiwan): Apdo 6-693, El Dorado, Panamá; tel. 223-8837; Correspondent HUANG KWANG CHUN.

Deutsche Press-Agentur (dpa) (Germany): Panamá; tel. 233-0396; fax 233-5393.

Inter Press Service (IPS) (Italy): Panamá; tel. 225-1673; fax 264-7033; Correspondent SILVIO HERNÁNDEZ.

Prensa Latina (Cuba): Edif. Doña Luz, Apto 3, Avda Quinta Norte 35, Apdo 6-2799, Panamá; tel. 264-3647; Correspondent RAIMUNDO LÓPEZ MEDINA.

Xinhua (New China) News Agency (People's Republic of China): Vía Cincuentenario 48, Viña del Mar, Panamá 1; tel. 226-4501; Dir HU TAIRAN.

Publishers

Editora 'La Estrella de Panamá': Avda 9a Sur 7-38, Apdo 159, Panamá 1; tel. 222-0900; f. 1853.

Editora Renovación, SA: Vía Fernández de Córdoba, Apdo B-4, Panamá 9A; tel. 261-2300; newspapers; govt-owned; Exec. Man. ESCOLÁSTICO CALVO.

Editora Sibauste, SA: Panamá; tel. 269-0983; Dir ENRIQUE SIBAUSTE BARRÍA.

Editorial Litográfica, SA (Edilito): Panamá 10; tel. 224-3087; Pres. EDUARDO AVILES C.

Editorial Universitaria: Vía José de Fábrega, Panamá; tel. 264-2087; f. 1969; history, geography, law, sciences, literature; Dir CARLOS MANUEL GASTEAZORO.

Focus Publications: Apdo 6-3287, El Dorado, Panamá; tel. 225-6638; fax 225-0466; e-mail focusint@sinfo.net; internet www .focuspublicationsint.com; f. 1970; guides, trade directories and yearbooks.

Fondo Educativo Interamericano: Edif. Eastern, 6°, Avda Federico Boyd 10 y Calle 51, Apdo 6-3099, El Dorado, Panamá; tel. 269-1511; educational and reference; Dir ALICIA CHAVARRÍA.

Industrial Gráfica, SA: Vía España entre Calles 95 y 96 (al lado de Orange Crush), Apdo 810014, Panamá 10; tel. 224-3994; Pres. EDUARDO AVILES C.

Publicaciones Panameñas, SA: Edif. YASA, 2°, Of. 1, Urb. Obarrio, Calle 59, Apdo 9-103, Panamá 9; tel. 263-5190; Dir EMPERATRIZ S. DE CÁRDENAS.

Publicar Centroamericana, SA: Edif. Banco de Boston, 7°, Vía España 200 y Calle Elvira Méndez, Apdo 4919, Panamá 5; tel. 223-9655; fax 269-1964.

Government Publishing House

Editorial Mariano Arosemena: Instituto Nacional de Cultura, Apdo 662, Panamá 1; tel. 222-3233; f. 1974; literature, anthropology, social sciences, archaeology; Dir ESTHER URIETA DE REAL.

Broadcasting and Communications

TELECOMMUNICATIONS

The telecommunications sector was to be liberalized from 2002.

Dirección Nacional de Medios de Comunicación Social: Avda 7a Central y Calle 3a, Apdo 1628, Panamá 1; tel. 262-3197; fax 262-9495; Dir EDWIN CABRERA.

Instituto Nacional de Telecomunicaciones (INTEL): Gerencia Executiva Internacional, Apdo 659, Panamá 9A; tel. 269-0656; fax 264-5743; f. 1973; 49% share acquired by Cable & Wireless (United Kingdom) in 1997; Gen. Man. JUAN RAMÓN PORRAS; 3,600 employees.

Cable & Wireless Panama: Apdo 659, Panamá 9A; internet www .cwpanama.com.pa; major telecommunications provider.

BROADCASTING

Radio

In March 1990 the Government approved the creation of the National State Radio Broadcasting Directorate, which was to be a department of the Ministry of the Presidency.

Asociación Panameña de Radiodifusión: Apdo 7387, Estafeta de Paitilla, Panamá; tel. 263-5252; fax 226-4396; Pres. FERNANDO ELETA CASSANOVA.

In 1995 there were 88 AM (Medium Wave) and 118 FM stations in Panama. Most stations are commercial.

Television

Fundación para la Educación en la Televisión—FETV (Canal 5): Edif. Proconsa, 8°, Calle 51 y Calle Manuel María Icaza, Apdo 6-7295, El Dorado, Panamá; tel. 264-6555; fax 223-5966; e-mail fetvadm@sinfo.net; f. 1992; Pres. JOSÉ DIMAS CEDEÑO DELGADO; Dir MANUEL SANTIAGO BLANQUER I PLANELLS; Gen. Man. MARÍA EUGENIA FONSECA M.

Medcom: Calle 50, No. 6, Apdo 116, Panamá 8; tel. 210-6700; fax 210-6797; e-mail murrutia@medcom.com.pa; f. 1998 by merger of RPC Televisión (Canal 4) and Telemetro (Canal 13); commercial; also owns Cable Onda 90; Pres. FERNANDO ELETA; CEO NICOLÁS GONZÁLEZ-REVILLA.

Panavisión del Istmo, SA: Panamá; tel. 269-6816; f. 1983; Dir ALFONSO DE LA ESPRIELLA.

Sistema de Televisión Educativa (Canal 11): Universidad de Panamá, Estafeta Universitaria, Calle José de Fábrega, Panamá; tel. 269-3755; fax 223-2921; f. 1978; educational and cultural; Pres. GERARDO MALLONEY; Dir-Gen. I. VELÁSQUEZ DE CORTES.

Tele-Carrier Inc: Panamá; f. 2000; commercial; Pres. JOSÉ GUANTI.

Telemetro: Apdo 8-116, Zona 8, Panamá; tel. 269-2122; fax 269-2720.

Televisora Nacional—TVN (Canal 2): Vía Bolívar, Apdo 6-3092, El Dorado, Panamá; tel. 236-2222; fax 236-2987; e-mail tvn@tvn-2 .com; f. 1962; Dir JAIME ALBERTO ARIAS.

In 1995 there were 32 television channels broadcasting in Panama.

Finance

(cap. = capital; res = reserves; dep. = deposits; m. = million; amounts in balboas, unless otherwise stated)

BANKING

In February 1998 new banking legislation was approved, providing for greater supervision of banking activity in the country, including the creation of a Superintendency of Banks. In 2002 a total of 84 banks operated in Panama: two official banks, 47 with general licence, 29 with international licence, and six representative offices.

Superintendencia de Bancos (Banking Superintendency): Torre HSBC, 18°, Apdo 2397, Panamá 1; tel. 206-7800; fax 264-9422; internet www.superbancos.gob.pa; f. 1970 as Comisión Bancaria Nacional (National Banking Commission) to license and control banking activities within and from Panamanian territory; Comisión Bancaria Nacional superseded by Superintendencia de Bancos June 1998 with enhanced powers to supervise banking activity; Superintendent DELIA CÁRDENAS.

National Bank

Banco Nacional de Panamá: Torre BNP, Vía España, Apdo 5220, Panamá 5; tel. 263-5151; fax 269-0091; e-mail bnpvalores@cwp.net .pa; internet www.banconal.com.pa; f. 1904; govt-owned; cap. 500.0m., dep. 2,855m. (Dec. 1999); Pres ROOSEVELT THAYER G, JORGE BATINOVICH C; Man. BOLIVAR PARIENTE C; 51 brs.

Development Banks

Banco de Desarrollo Agropecuario (BDA): Avda de los Mártires, Apdo 5282, Panamá 5; tel. 262-0140; fax 262-1713; internet www .mida.gob.pa/bda; f. 1973; govt-sponsored agricultural and livestock credit org. Pres. (vacant) (Minister of Agricultural Development); Gen. Man. ABELARDO AMO ZAKAY.

Banco Hipotecario Nacional: Edif. Peña Prieta, Avda Balboa y Calle 40 Bella Vista, Apdo 222, Panamá 1; tel. 227-0055; fax 225-6956; e-mail bhn@sinfo.net; f. 1973; govt-sponsored; finances national housing projects and regulates national savings system; Pres. MINISTER OF HOUSING; Gen. Man. WALDO ARROCHA.

Savings Banks

Banco General, SA: Calle Aquilino de la Guardia, Apdo 4592, Panamá 5; tel. 227-3200; fax 265-0210; e-mail info@bgeneral.com; internet www.bgeneral.com; f. 1955; cap. 300.0m., res 13.2m., dep. 1,866.0m., total assets 2,317m. (2001); purchased Banco Comercial de Panamá (BANCOMER) in 2000; Chair. and CEO FEDERICO HUMBERT, Jr; Exec. Vice-Pres. and Gen. Man. RAÚL ALEMÁN Z; 35 brs.

Banco Panameño de la Vivienda (BANVIVIENDA): Casa Matriz-Bella Vista, Avda Chile y Calle 41, Apdo 8639, Panamá 5; tel. 227-4020; fax 227-5433; e-mail bpvger@pty.com; internet www .banvivienda.com; f. 1981; Pres. ORLANDO SANCHEZ AVILES; Gen. Man. MARIO L. FÁBREGA AROSEMENA; 3 brs.

Caja de Ahorros: Vía España y Calle Thays de Pons, Apdo 1740, Panamá 1; tel. 263-6233; fax 269-3674; f. 1934; govt-owned; cap. and res 10.1m., dep. 310.7m., total assets 359.6m. (1987); Chair. RAMÓN MORALES; Man. CARLOS RAÚL PIAD; 37 brs.

Domestic Private Banks

Banco Atlántico (Panamá), SA: Edif. Banco Iberóamerica, Calle 50 y Calle 53, Apdo 6553, Panamá 5; tel. 263-5656; fax 269-1616; e-mail ibergeren@pan.gbm.net; internet www.iberban.org; f. 1975 as Banco de Iberoamerica, SA, current name adopted in 2000; Pres. JOSÉ M. CHIMENO CHILLÓN; Gen. Man. RUBÉN FABREGAT BRACCO; 4 brs.

Banco Continental de Panamá, SA: Calle 50 y Avda Aquilino de la Guardia, Apdo 135, Panamá 9A; tel. 215-7000; fax 215-7134; e-mail bcp@bcocontinental.com; internet www.bcocontinental.com; f. 1972; merged with Banco Internacional de Panamá in Jan. 2002; cap. 90.4m., dep. 626.1m., total assets 728.3m. (June 2000); Pres. ROBERTO MOTTA; Gen. Man. OSVALDO MOUYNÉS; 7 brs.

Banco Internacional de Panamá (BIPAN): Complejo Plaza Marbella, Avda Aquilino de la Guardia y Calles 47 y 48, Apdo 11181, Panamá 6; tel. 263-9000; fax 263-9514; e-mail bipan@bipan.com; internet www.bipan.com; f. 1973; merged with Banco Continental de Panamá in Jan. 2002; total assets 456.2m. (June 2001); Gen. Man. RENÉ A. DÍAZ; 10 brs.

Banco Mercantil del Istmo, SA: Edif. Interocéanio, Calle 50 y Calle Margarita A de Vallarino, Apdo 484, Panamá 9A; tel. 263-6262; fax 263-6664; e-mail mguerra@banistmo.com; internet www .banistmo.com; f. 1967 as Banco de Santander y Panamá; current name adopted in 1992; cap. 19.5m., res 0.3m., dep. 306.9m., total assets 354.9m. (Dec. 1999); Pres. SAMUEL LEWIS GALINDO; Gen. Man. MANUEL JOSÉ BARREDO MARTÍNEZ.

Banco Panamericano, SA (PANABANK): Edif. Panabank, Casa Matriz, Calle 50, Apdo 1828, Panamá 1; tel. 263-9266; fax 269-1537; e-mail panabank@sinfo.net; internet www.panabank.com; f. 1983; Exec. Vice-Pres. GUIDO J. MARTINELLI, Jr.

Global Bank Corporation: Torre Global Bank, Calle 50, Apdo 55-1843, Paitilla, Panamá; tel. 206-2000; fax 263-3518; e-mail global@ pan.gbm.net; internet www.globalbank.com.pa; f. 1994; total assets 458.6m. (June 2001); Pres. JORGE VALLARINO S.

Multi Credit Bank Inc: Edif. Prosperidad, planta baja, Vía España 127, Apdo 8210, Panamá 7; tel. 269-0188; fax 264-4014; e-mail banco@grupomulticredit.com; internet www.grupomulticredit.com; f. 1990; total assets 343.9m. (Dec. 2000); Gen. Man. MOISÉS D. COHEN M.

Primer Banco del Istmo, SA: Edif. Banco del Istmo, Calle 77 y Calle 50, San Francisco, Panamá; tel. 270-0015; fax 270-1667; internet www.banistmo.com; f. 1984 as Banco del Istmo; current name adopted in 2000 following merger of Primer Grupo Nacional and Banco del Istmo; cap. US $222.3m., dep. US $2,678.3m. (Dec. 2000); Chair. SAMUEL LEWIS GALINDO; Gen. Man. L. J. MONTAGUE BELANGER.

Towerbank International Inc: Edif. Tower Plaza, Calle 50 y Beatriz M de Cabal, Apdo 6-6039, Panamá; tel. 269-6900; fax 269-6800; e-mail towerbank@towerbank.com; internet www.towerbank .com; f. 1971; cap. US $401.1m. (Dec. 2000); Pres. SAM KARDONSKI; Gen. Man. GYSBERTUS ANTONIUS DE WOLF; 1 br.

Foreign Banks

Principal Foreign Banks with General Licence

BAC International Bank (Panamá), Inc (USA): Avda de la Guardia, planta baja, Apdo 6-3654, Panamá; tel. 213-0822; fax 269-3879; e-mail rcucalon@bacbank.com; internet www.bacbank.com; Dir and Sec.-Gen. BARNEY VAUGHAN.

BANCAFE (Panamá), SA (Colombia): Avda Manuel María Icaza y Calle 52E, No 18, Apdo 384, Panamá 9A; tel. 264-6066; fax 263-6115; e-mail bancafe@bancafe-panama.com; internet www.bancafe-pa .com; f. 1966 as Banco Cafetero; current name adopted in 1995; cap. 27.6m., dep. 299.5m. (Dec. 1994); Pres. PEDRO NEL OSPINA S; Gen. Man. ALVARO NARANJO SALAZAR; 2 brs.

Banco Atlántico, SA: Apdo 6553, Panamá 5; tel. 263-5366; fax 264-2341; e-mail ibegeren@pan.gbm.net.com; internet www.iberban .com; f. 1975; Gen. Man. RUBEN FABREGAT BRACCO.

Banco Bilbao Vizcaya Argentaria (Panamá), SA (Spain): Torre BBVA, Avda Balboa, Apdo 8673, Panamá 5; tel. 227-0973; fax 227-3663; e-mail fperezp@bbvapanama.com; internet www.bbvapanama .com; f. 1982; cap. 10.0m., res 34.1m., dep. 355.4m. (Dec. 1997); Chair. MANUEL ZUBIRÍA PASTOR; Gen. Man. FRANCISCO JAVIER LEJARRAJA.

Banco de Bogotá, SA (Colombia): Centro Comercial Plaza Paitilla, Avda Balboa y Vía Italia, Apdo 8653, Panamá 5; tel. 264-6000; fax 263-8037; e-mail banbogo@sinfo.net; internet www .bancobogota-panama.com; f. 1967; cap. 17.7m., dep. 351.3m., total assets 394.8m. (Dec. 1999); merged with Banco del Comercio, SA (Colombia) in 1994; Gen. Man. FABIO RIAÑO.

Banco do Brasil, SA: Edif. Interseco, planta baja, Calle Elvira Méndez 10, Apdo 87-1123, Panamá 7; tel. 263-6566; fax 269-9867; e-mail bdbrasil@bbpanama.com; internet www.bancodobrasil.com .br; f. 1973; cap. and res 52.3m., dep. 1,248.1m., total assets 1,320.2m. (Dec. 1993); Gen. Man. LUIZ EDUARDO JACOBINA; 1 br.

Banco Internacional de Costa Rica, SA: Apdo 600, Panamá 1; tel. 263-6822; fax 263-6393; e-mail bicsapty@pananet.com; internet www.bicsa.com; f. 1976; total assets 15,382m. (1999); Gen. Man. JOSÉ FRANCISCO ULATE.

Banco de Latinoamerica, SA (BANCOLAT): Calle 50 y Calle 56 este, Apdo 4401, Panamá 5; tel. 210-7100; fax 263-7368; e-mail bancolat@bancolat.com; internet www.bancolat.com; f. 1982; total assets 11,060m. (1999); Pres. JUAN JOSÉ GARCÍA; Gen. Man. RAMÓN GILBERTO PÉREZ.

Banco Latinoamericano de Exportaciones (BLADEX) (Multinational): Casa Matriz, Calles 50 y Aquilino de la Guardia, Apdo 6-1497, El Dorado, Panamá; tel. 210-8500; fax 269-6333; e-mail infobla@blx.com; internet www.blx.com; f. 1979; groups together 254 Latin American commercial and central banks, 22 international banks and some 3,000 New York Stock Exchange shareholders; cap. US $148.7m., dep. $4,836.2m., total assets $5,660.7m. (Dec. 2000); Exec. Pres. JOSÉ CASTAÑEDA VELEZ; Chief Operating Officer JAIME RIVERA.

Banco Unión, SACA (Venezuela): Torre Hongkong Bank, 1°, Avda Samuel Lewis, Apdo 'A', Panamá 5; tel. 264-9133; fax 263-9985; e-mail bcounion@orbi.net; internet www.bancunion.com; f. 1974; cap. and res 15.6m., dep. 177.1m. (Dec. 1993); Gen. Man. MARÍA M. DE MÉNDEZ; 1 br.

Bancolombia (Panama), SA: Calle Manuel María Icaza 11, Apdo 8593, Panamá 5; tel. 263-6955; fax 269-1138; e-mail mdebetan .bicpma@mail.bic.com.co; internet www.bancolombia.com; f. 1973; current name adopted in 1999; cap. US $14.0m., res $1.4m., dep. $713.5m. (Dec. 2000); Gen. Man. MARÍA ISABEL URIBE.

Bank of China: Apdo 87-1056, Panamá 7; tel. 263-5522; fax 223-9960; e-mail heqr@bank-of-china.com; f. 1994; Gen. Man. QUINGBO WANG.

Bank of Nova Scotia (Canada): Edif. P. H. Scotia Plaza, Avda Federico Boyd y Calle 51, Apdo 7327, Panamá 5; tel. 263-6255; fax 263-8636; e-mail scotiabk@sinfo.net; Gen. Man. TERENCE S. McCOY.

Bank of Tokyo-Mitsubishi Ltd (Japan): Vía España y Calle Aquilino de la Guardia, Apdo 1313, Panamá 1; tel. 263-6777; fax 263-5269; f. 1973; cap. and res 8.3m., dep. 1,574.0m., total assets 1,615.8m. (March 1998); Gen. Man. SHIGEYUKI ONISHI.

Bank Leumi Le-Israel, BM (Israel): Edif. Grobman, planta baja, Calle Manuel María Icaza, Apdo 6-4518, El Dorado, Panamá; tel. 263-9377; fax 269-2674; Gen. Man. URI ROM.

Banque Sudameris, SA (Multinational): Avda Balboa y Calle 41, Apdo 1847, Panamá 9A; tel. 227-2777; fax 227-5828; e-mail banque .sudameris@sudameris.com.pa; internet www.sudameris.com.pa; Gen. Man. JULIO A. CORTÉS; 2 brs.

BNP Paribas (Panama), SA: Edif. Omanco, Vía España 200, Apdo 1774, Panamá 1; tel. 263-6600; fax 263-6970; e-mail bnpparibas .panama@americas.bnpparibas.com; internet www.bnpparibas.com; f. 1948; name changed as above in 2000; cap. 10.0m., res 6.7m., dep 194.9m., total assets 224.0m. (Dec. 1999); Gen. Man. CHRISTIAN GIRAUDON.

Citibank NA (USA): Vía España 124, Apdo 555, Panamá 9A; tel. 210-5900; fax 210-5901; internet www.citibank.com.pa; f. 1904; Gen. Man. FRANCISCO CONTO; 10 brs.

Credicorp Bank, SA: Apdo 833-0125, Panamá; tel. 210-1111; fax 210-0069; e-mail sistemas@plazapan.com; internet www .credicorpbank.com; f. 1993; Gen. Man. CARLOS GUEVARA.

Dai Ichi Kangyo Bank, SA (Japan): Edif. Plaza Internacional, Vía España, Apdo 2637, Panamá 9A; tel. 269-6111; fax 269-6815; f. 1979; cap. and res 2.0m., dep. 216.1m., total assets 218.4m. (Sept. 1991); Gen. Man. GAKUO FUKUTOMI.

Dresdner Bank Lateinamerika AG (Germany): Torre Banco Germánico, Calles 50 y 55E, Apdo 5400, Panamá 5; tel. 206-8100; fax 206-8109; e-mail panama@dbla.com; internet www.dbla.com; f. 1971; affiliated to Dresdner Bank AG; Gen. Mans KLAUS MÜLLER, BERND KLEINWORTH.

HSBC Bank USA: Apdo 9A-76, Panamá 9A; tel. 263-5855; fax 263-6009; e-mail hsbcpnm@info.net; internet www.hsbcpnm.com; dep. 477m. (1999); in 2000 it acquired the 11 branch operations of the Chase Manhattan Bank, with assets of US $752m. Gen. Man. JOSEPH L. SALTERIO; 3 brs.

International Commerical Bank of China (Taiwan): Calles 50 y 56E, Apdo 4453, Panamá 5; tel. 263-8565; fax 263-8392; Gen. Man. SHOW-LOONG HWANG.

Korea Exchange Bank (Republic of Korea): Torre Global Bank, Calle 50, Apdo 8358, Panamá 7; tel. 269-9966; fax 264-4224; Gen. Man. KWANG-SUCK KOH.

Lloyds TSB Bank Plc (United Kingdom): Calles Aquilino de la Guardia y 48, Apdo 8522, Panamá 5; tel. 263-6277; fax 264-7931; e-mail lloydspa@sinfo.net; Gen. Man. J. E. FRANKE; 3 brs.

Principal Foreign Banks with International Licence

Atlantic Security Bank: Apdo 6-8934, El Dorado, Panamá; tel. 269-5944; fax 215-7302; internet www.credicorpnet.com; f. 1984; Gen. Man. JORGE PONCE MENDOZA.

Banco Alemán Platina, SA: Panamá; tel. 269-2666; fax 269-0910; e-mail baplatina@balppa.com; internet www.bancoalemanplatina .com; f. 1965 as Banco Alemán-Panameño; current name adopted in 1993; cap. US $42.0m., res $10.3m., dep. $244.6m. (Aug. 2001); Pres. DANIEL PFISTER; Gen. Man. RALF FISCHER.

Banco de Crédito (Panama), SA: Apdo 0832-1700, Panamá; tel. 214-9613; fax 214-9715; internet www.bancredito.com; f. 1998; Gen. Man. CARLOS HUMBERTO ROJAS MARTÍNEZ.

Banco de la Nación Argentina: Avda Federico Boyd y Calle 51, Apdo 6-3298, El Dorado, Panamá; tel. 269-4666; fax 269-6719; e-mail bna@panama.phoenix.net; internet www.bna.com.ar; f. 1977; Man. OLGA SOLÍS.

Banco de Occidente (Panama), SA: Calle 50 y Aquilino de la Guardia, Apdo 6-7430, El Dorado, Panamá; tel. 263-8144; fax 269-3261; e-mail boccipan@pty.com; f. 1982; cap. US $6.3m., res $1.5m., dep. $188.2m. (Dec. 2000); Pres. EFRAÍN OTERO ALVAREZ.

Banco del Pacífico (Panama), SA: Apdo 6-3100, El Dorado, Panamá; tel. 263-5833; fax 269-2640; e-mail bpacificopanama@ pacifico.fin.ec; f. 1980; Chair. MARCEL J. LANIADO.

Banco de la Provincia de Buenos Aires (Argentina): Torre Banco Continental, 26°, Calle 50, Apdo 6-4592, El Dorado, Panamá; tel. 215-7703; fax 215-7718; e-mail bpbapma@psianet.pa; internet www .bapro.com; f. 1982; total assets 15,000m. (Dec. 2000); Gen. Man. JUAN CARLOS STURLESI.

BNP Paribas: Edif. Omanco, Vía España 200, 6°, Apdo 201, Panamá; tel. 264-8555; fax 263-6970; e-mail bnpsuc@sinfo.net; f. 1972; Gen. Man. CHRISTIAN GIRUADON.

Discount Bank and Trust Co: Edif. Discount Bank and Trust Co, Calles 50 y 57, Zona 7, Panamá; tel. 269-4011; fax 269-6266; Man. L. A. QUINTERO SAURI (acting).

Popular Bank and Trust Ltd: Apdo 0816-00265, Panamá; tel. 269-4166; fax 269-1309; e-mail gversari@bpt.com.pa; f. 1983 as Banco Popular Dominicano (Panama) SA; current name adopted in 2000; cap. 16.4m., res 8.2m., dep. 309.0m. Pres. RAFAEL A. RODRÍGUEZ; Gen. Man. GIANNI VERSARI.

Societé Générale: Panamá; tel. 264-9611; fax 264-0295; e-mail panama.branch@pa.socgen.com; f. 1981; Gen. Man. CELESTIN CUQ.

UBS (Panama), SA: Apdo 61, Panamá 9A; tel. 206-7100; fax 206-7100; internet www.ubs.com/panama; f. 1968; Chair. MARTIN WIRZ.

Banking Association

Asociación Bancaria de Panamá (ABP): Torre Hong Kong Bank, 15°, Avda Samuel Lewis, Apdo 4554, Panamá 5; tel. 263-7044; fax 223-5800; e-mail abp@orbi.net; internet www.asociacionbancaria .com; f. 1962; 79 mems; Pres. LUIS A. NAVARRO L; Exec. Vice-Pres. MARIO DE DIEGO, Jr.

STOCK EXCHANGE

Bolsa de Valores de Panamá: Edif. Vallarino, planta baja, Calles Elvira Méndez y 52, Apdo 87-0878, Panamá; tel. 269-1966; fax 269-2457; e-mail bvp@pty.com; f. 1960; Gen. Man. ROBERTO BRANES P.

INSURANCE

Aseguradora Mundial, SA: Edif. Aseguradora Mundial, Avda Balboa y Calle 41, Apdo 8911, Panamá 5; tel. 207-8700; fax 207-8787; e-mail ymarti@mundial.com; internet www.amundial.com; general; f. 1937; Vice-Pres. and Dir-Gen. JUAN LUIS CHEVALIER.

ASSA Cía de Seguros, SA: Edif. ASSA, Avda Nicanor de Obarrio (Calle 50), Apdo 5371, Panamá 5; tel. 269-0443; fax 263-9623; f. 1973; Pres. LORENZO ROMAGOSA; Gen. Man. CARLOS A. RABAT MALLOL.

Cía Internacional de Seguros, SA: Avda Cuba y Calles 35 y 36, Apdo 1036, Panamá 1; tel. 227-4000; f. 1910; Pres. RICHARD A. FORD; Gen. Man. MANUEL A. ESKILDSEN.

Cía Nacional de Seguros, SA: Edif. No 62, Calle 50, Apdo 5303, Panamá 5; tel. 205-0300; fax 223-1146; f. 1957; Pres. RAÚL DELVALLE; CEO RAÚL NOVEY.

La Seguridad de Panamá, Cía de Seguros SA: Edif. American International, Calle 50 esq. Aquilino de la Guardia, Apdo 5306, Panamá 5; tel. 263-6700; Man. COURTNEY STEMPEL.

LARSA Latin American Reinsurance Co Inc: Apdo 810, Panamá 1; tel. 263-5866; fax 263-5713; Pres. LAURENCIO JAÉN O.

Trade and Industry

Colón Free Zone (CFZ): Avda Roosevelt, Apdo 1118, Colón; tel. 445-1033; fax 445-2165; e-mail zonalibre@zolicol.org; internet www .colonfreezone.com; f. 1948 to manufacture, import, handle and re-export all types of merchandise; some 1,800 companies were established by 2002. Well-known international banks operate in the CFZ, where there are also customs, postal and telegraph services. In the first six months of 2001 the value of imports was an estimated 2,267.8m. balboas. Re-exports amounted to an estimated 2,536.6m. balboas in the same period. The main exporters to the CFZ are Japan, the USA, Hong Kong, Taiwan, the Republic of Korea, Colombia, France, Italy and the United Kingdom. The main importers from the CFZ are Brazil, Venezuela, Mexico, Ecuador, the Netherlands Dependencies, Bolivia, the USA, Chile, Argentina and Colombia. The total area of the CFZ was 485.3 ha. Gen. Man. RICARDO ALEMÁN.

GOVERNMENT AGENCIES

Consejo Nacional de Inversiones (CNI): Edif. Banco Nacional de Panamá, Apdo 2350, Panamá; tel. 264-7211; f. 1982; national investment council; promotes private local and foreign investments; Exec. Dir Lic. JULIO E. SOSA.

Corporación Financiera Nacional (COFINA): Apdo 6-2191, Estafeta El Dorado, Panamá; f. 1976 to develop state and private undertakings in productive sectors; Dir-Gen. WINSTON WELCH.

Instituto Panameño de Comercio Exterior (IPCE): Edif. Banco Exterior, Torre Chica, 3° y 4°, Apdo 55-2359, Paitilla, Panamá; tel. 225-7244; fax 225-2193; f. 1984; foreign trade and investment promotion organization; Dir KENIA JAÉN RIVERA.

CHAMBER OF COMMERCE

Cámara de Comercio, Industrias y Agricultura de Panamá: Avda Cuba y Ecuador 33A, Apdo 74, Panamá 1; tel. 227-1233; fax 227-4186; e-mail infocciap@panacamara.com; f. 1915; Pres. IVÁN COHEN S; First Vice-Pres. JOSÉ JAVIER RIVERA; 1,300 mems.

INDUSTRIAL AND TRADE ASSOCIATIONS

Cámara Oficial Española de Comercio: Calle 33E, Apdo 1857, Panamá 1; tel. 225-1487; Pres. EDELMIRO GARCÍA VILLA VERDE; Sec.-Gen. ATILIANO ALFONSO MARTÍNEZ.

Cámara Panameña de la Construcción: Calle Aquilino de la Guardia No 19, Apdo 6793, Panamá 5; tel. 265-2500; fax 265-2571; e-mail ryburilo@pty.com; represents interests of construction sector; Pres. Ing. JOSÉ A. SOSA.

Codemín: Panamá; tel. 263-7475; state mining organization; Dir JAIME ROQUEBERT.

Corporación Azucarera La Victoria: Transístmica, San Miguelito; tel. 229-4794; state sugar corpn; scheduled for transfer to private ownership; Dir Prof. ALEJANDRO VERNAZA.

Corporación para el Desarrollo Integral del Bayano: Avda Balboa, al lado de la estación del tren, Estafeta El Dorado, Panamá 2; tel. 232-6160; f. 1978; state agriculture, forestry and cattle-breeding corpn; Dir Ing. JOSÉ MARÍA CHAVERRI.

Dirección General de Industrias: Edif. Plaza Edison, 3°, Apdo 9658, Panamá 4; tel. 360-0720; govt body which undertakes feasibility studies, analyses and promotion; Dir-Gen. LUCÍA FUENTES DE FERGUSON; Nat. Dir of Business Development FRANCISCO DE LA BARRERA.

Sindicato de Industriales de Panamá: Vía Ricardo J. Alfaro, Entrada Urb. Sara Sotillo, Apdo 6-4798, Estafeta El Dorado, Panamá; tel. 230-0169; fax 230-0805; e-mail sip@sinfo.net; f. 1945; represents and promotes activities of industrial sector; Pres. ANTONIO MIRO E.

EMPLOYERS' ORGANIZATIONS

Asociación Panameña de Ejecutivos de Empresas (APEDE): Edif. APEDE, Calle 42, Bella Vista y Avda Balboa, Apdo 1331, Panamá 1; tel. 227-3511; fax 227-1872; e-mail apede@sinfo.net; Pres. IRVING H. BENNETT N.

Consejo Nacional de la Empresa Privada (CONEP): Calle 41, Bella Vista, Apdo 1276, Panamá 1; tel. 225-5306; fax 225-2663; Pres. DARÍO SELLES.

Consejo Nacional para el Desarrollo de la Pequeña Empresa: Ministry of Commerce and Industry, Apdo 9658, Panamá 4; tel. 227-3559; fax 225-1201; f. 1983; advisory and consultative board to the Ministry of Commerce and Industry.

UTILITIES

Electricity

Instituto de Recursos Hidráulicos y Electrificación (IRHE): Edif. Poli, Avda Justo Arosemena y 26E, Apdo 5285, Panamá 5; tel. 262-6272; state organization responsible for the national public electricity supply; partial divestment of generation and distribution operations completed Dec. 1998; transmission operations remain under complete state control; Dir-Gen. Dr FERNANDO ARAMBURÚ PORRAS.

Water

Instituto de Acueductos y Alcantarillados Nacionales (IDAAN) (National Waterworks and Sewage Systems Institute): Panamá; Dir-Gen. ELIDA DÍ.

TRADE UNIONS

In 1981 the Labour Code which had been promulgated in 1977 was amended, establishing the right to strike and increasing compensation for dismissal. Collective bargaining is permitted and employers must pay workers' salaries during the whole period of a legal strike.

Central Istmeña de Trabajadores (CIT) (Isthmian Labour Confederation): Vía España 16, Of. 1, Apdo 6308, Panamá 5; tel. 264-0509; f. 1971; Sec.-Gen. JULIO CÉSAR PINZÓN.

Confederación de Trabajadores de la República de Panamá (CTRP) (Confederation of Workers of the Republic of Panama): Calle 31, entre Avdas México y Justo Arosemena 3-50, Apdo 8929, Panamá 5; tel. 225-0293; fax 225-0259; f. 1956; admitted to ICFTU/ORIT; Sec.-Gen. ANIANO PINZÓN REAL; 62,000 mems from 13 affiliated groups.

Consejo Nacional de Trabajadores Organizados (CONATO) (National Council of Organized Labour): Ancón 777, 2°, Panamá; tel. 228-0224; e-mail conato@sinfo.net; 150,000 mems.

Federación Nacional de Asociaciones de Empleados Públicos (FENASEP) (National Federation of Associations of Public Employees): Panamá; Pres. HÉCTOR ALEMÁN.

A number of unions exist without affiliation to a national centre.

Transport

RAILWAYS

In 1998 there were an estimated 485 km of track in Panama. In 2000 a US \$75m. project to modernize the line between the ports at either end of the Panama Canal began. In July 2001 the 83-km transisthmian railway, originally founded in 1855, reopened. The Ministry of Public Works also announced that construction on a light railway network for Panama City would begin in late 2002.

Chiriquí Land Co: Panamá; tel. 770-7243; fax 770-8064; operates two lines: the Northern Line (Almirante–Guabito in Bocas del Toro Province) and the Southern Line (Puerto Armuelles–David in Chiriquí Province); purchased by the Govt in 1978; Gen. Man. FRED JOHNSON.

Ferrocarril Nacional de Chiriquí: Apdo 12B, David City, Chiriquí; tel. 775-4241; fax 775-4105; 126 km linking Puerto Armuelles and David; Gen. Man. M. ALVARENGA.

Ferrocarril de Panamá: Apdo 2023, Estafeta de Balboa, Panamá; tel. 232-6000; fax 232-5343; govt-owned; 83 km linking Panama City and Colón, running parallel to Panama Canal; operation on concession by Kansas City Southern (USA); modernization programme completed in 2001; operates daily passenger and cargo service; Dir-Gen. VÍCTOR MANUEL DANELO.

ROADS

In 1999 there were an estimated 11,400 km of roads, of which some 3,944 km were paved. The two most important highways are the Pan-American Highway and the Boyd-Roosevelt or Trans-Isthmian, linking Panama City and Colón. The Pan-American Highway to Mexico City runs for 545 km in Panama and was being extended towards Colombia. There is a highway to San José, Costa Rica. A plan to build a 183-km road from Panama City to Darién Province was expected to be completed by 2004.

SHIPPING

The Panama Canal opened in 1914. In 1984 more than 4% of all the world's seaborne trade passed through the waterway. It is 82 km long, and ships take an average of eight hours to complete a transit. In 2000 some 12,303 transits were recorded. The Canal can accommodate ships with a maximum draught of 12 m and beams of up to approximately 32.3 m (106 ft) and lengths of up to about 290 m (950 ft), roughly equivalent to ships with a maximum capacity of 65,000–70,000 dwt. In 2000 a five-year modernization project was begun. The project included: a general improvement of facilities; the implementation of a satellite traffic-management system; the construction of a bridge; and the widening of the narrowest section of the Canal, the Culebra Cut (which was completed in 2001). Plans were also announced to construct a 203 ha international cargo-handing platform at the Atlantic end of the Canal, including terminals, a railway and an international airport. Terminal ports are Balboa, on the Pacific Ocean, and Cristóbal, on the Caribbean Sea.

Autoridad del Canal de Panamá (ACP): Balboa Heights, Panamá; tel. 272-3202; fax 272-2122; e-mail info@pancanal.com; internet www.pancanal.com; in Oct. 1979 the Panama Canal Commission, a US govt agency, was established to perform the mission, previously accomplished by the Panama Canal Co, of managing, operating and maintaining the Panama Canal. The Autoridad del Canal de Panamá (ACP) was founded in 1997 and succeeded the Panama Canal Commission on 31 December 1999, when the waterway was ceded to the Govt of Panama. The ACP is the autonomous agency of the Govt of Panama; there is a Board of 11 mems; Chair. RICARDO MARTINELLI; Administrator ALBERTO ALEMÁN ZUBIETA; Dep. Administrator RICAURTE VÁSQUEZ.

Autoridad Marítima de Panamá: Edif. 5534, Antigua escuela de Diablo, Ancón, Apdo 8062, Panama 7; tel. 232-5528; fax 232-5527; e-mail autoport@sinfo.net; f. 1998 to unite and optimize the function of all state institutions with involvement in maritime sector; Admin. JERRY SALAZAR.

Autoridad de la Región Interoceánica (ARI): Panamá; tel. 228-5668; fax 228-7488; e-mail ari@sinfo.net; f. 1993; govt body created to administer the land and property of the former Canal Zone following their transfer from US to Panamanian control, after 1999; legislation approved in early 1995 transferred control of the ARI to the Pres. of the Republic; Pres. ALFREDO ARIAS.

Panama City Port Authority and Foreign Trade Zone 65: Apdo 15095, Panamá; FL 32406, USA; Dir RUDY ETHEREDGE.

There are deep-water ports at Balboa and Cristóbal (including general cargo ships, containers, shipyards, industrial facilities); Coco Solo (general cargo and containers); Bahía Las Minas (general bulk and containers); Vacamonte (main port for fishing industry); Puerto Armuelles and Almirante (bananas); Aguadulce and Pedregal (export of crude sugar and molasses, transport of fertilizers and chemical products); and Charco Azul and Chiriquí Grande (crude oil).

The Panamanian merchant fleet was the largest in the world in December 2001, numbering 6,245 vessels with an aggregate displacement of 122.4m. gross registered tons. In November 2000 construction was completed on the largest container terminal in Latin America, in Balboa.

CIVIL AVIATION

Tocumen (formerly Omar Torrijos) International Airport situated 19 km (12 miles) outside Panamá (Panama City), is the country's principal airport and is served by many international airlines. The France Airport in Colón and the Rio Hato Airport in Coclé province have both been declared international airports. There are also 11 smaller airports in the country.

Aerolíneas Pacífico Atlántico, SA (Aeroperlas): Apdo 6-3596, El Dorado, Panamá; tel. 315-7500; fax 315-0331; e-mail info@aeroperlas.com; internet www.aeroperlas.com; f. 1970; fmrly state-owned, transferred to private ownership in 1987; operates scheduled regional and domestic flights; in 2000 initiated international flights; Pres. GEORGE F. NOVEY; Gen. Man. EDUARDO STAGG.

Compañía Panameña de Aviación, SA (COPA): Avda Justo Arosemena 230 y Calle 39, Apdo 1572, Panamá 1; tel. 227-2522; fax 227-1952; e-mail proquebert@mail.copa.com.pa; internet www.copaair.com; f. 1947; scheduled passenger and cargo services from Panamá (Panama City) to Central America, South America, the Caribbean and the USA; Chair. ALBERTO MOTTA; Exec. Pres. PEDRO O. HEILBRON.

Tourism

Panama's attractions include Panamá (Panama City), the ruins of Portobelo and 800 sandy tropical islands, including the resort of Contadora, one of the Pearl Islands in the Gulf of Panama, and the San Blas Islands, lying off the Atlantic coast. The number of foreign visitors to Panama declined from 370,369 in 1982 to 200,436 in 1989, partly as a result of internal and regional instability. By 2001 the number of visitors had increased to 410,605. Income from tourism was some US $576m. in 2000. In 2000 there were some 5,700 hotel rooms in Panama. In that year hotel and recreation projects to the value of $600m. were under way in Panama; these included plans for a cruise-ship terminal at either end of the Canal.

Instituto Panameño de Turismo (IPAT): Centro de Convenciones ATLAPA, Vía Israel, Apdo 4421, Panamá 5; tel. 226-7000; fax 226-3483; internet www.ipat.gob.pa; f. 1960; Dir-Gen. César Tribaldos.

Asociación Panameña de Agencias de Viajes y Turismo (APAVIT): Apdo 55-1000 Paitilla, Panamá 3; tel. 269-9584; fax 264-0309; Pres. Michelle de Guizado.

PAPUA NEW GUINEA

Introductory Survey

Location, Climate, Language, Religion, Flag, Capital

The Independent State of Papua New Guinea lies east of Indonesia and north of the north-eastern extremity of Australia. It comprises the eastern section of the island of New Guinea (the western section being Papua (West Papua), formerly Irian Jaya, which forms part of Indonesia) and about 600 smaller islands, including the Bismarck Archipelago (mainly New Britain, New Ireland and Manus) and the northern part of the Solomon Islands (mainly Bougainville and Buka). The climate is hot and humid throughout the year, with an average maximum temperature of 33°C (91°F) and an average minimum of 22°C (72°F). Rainfall is heavy on the coast but lower inland: the annual average varies from about 1,000 mm (40 ins) to 6,350 mm (250 ins). There are an estimated 742 native languages, but Pidgin and, to a lesser extent, standard English are also spoken, and, together with Motu, are the official languages in Parliament. More than 90% of the population profess Christianity. The national flag (proportions 3 by 4) is divided diagonally from the upper hoist to the lower fly: the upper portion displays a golden bird of paradise in silhouette on a red ground, while the lower portion has five white five-pointed stars, in the form of the Southern Cross constellation, on a black ground. The capital is Port Moresby.

Recent History

Papua New Guinea was formed by the merger of the Territory of Papua, under Australian rule from 1906, with the Trust Territory of New Guinea, a former German possession which Australia administered from 1914, first under a military Government, then under a League of Nations mandate, established in 1921, and later under a trusteeship agreement with the UN. During the Second World War, parts of both territories were occupied by Japanese forces from 1942 to 1945.

A joint administration for the two territories was established by Australia in July 1949. The union was named the Territory of Papua and New Guinea. A Legislative Council was established in November 1951 and was replaced by a House of Assembly, with an elected indigenous majority, in June 1964. The territory was renamed Papua New Guinea in July 1971. It achieved internal self-government in December 1973 and full independence on 16 September 1975, when the House of Assembly became the National Parliament.

Michael Somare, who from 1972 served as Chief Minister in an interim coalition Government, became Prime Minister on independence. He remained in office until 1980, despite widespread allegations of inefficiency in government ministries and of discrimination against the Highland provinces. The first elections since independence were held in June and July 1977, and Somare's Pangu (Papua New Guinea Unity) Pati formed a governing coalition, first with the People's Progress Party (PPP) and later with the United Party (UP).

In March 1980 the Government lost a vote of confidence, the fourth in 15 months, and Sir Julius Chan, the leader of the PPP and a former Deputy Prime Minister, succeeded to the premiership. Somare became Prime Minister again following a general election in June 1982. In 1983 the Somare Government effected a constitutional change to provide the central authorities with greater control of the provincial governments as a means of preventing abuse of their powers. As a result, between 1983 and 1991 a total of nine provincial governments were suspended by the central Government for alleged maladministration.

In March 1985 a motion expressing 'no confidence' in Somare's Government was introduced in Parliament by Chan, who nominated Paias Wingti (hitherto Deputy Prime Minister and a member of the Pangu Pati) as alternative Prime Minister. Somare quickly formed a coalition, comprising the ruling Pangu Pati, the National Party (NP) and the Melanesian Alliance (MA), and the 'no confidence' motion was defeated. Fourteen members of Parliament who had supported the motion were expelled from the Pangu Pati, and subsequently formed a new political party, the People's Democratic Movement (PDM), under the leadership of Wingti.

In August 1985 the NP withdrew from Somare's coalition Government, and in November Chan presented another motion of 'no confidence', criticizing Somare's handling of the economy. Somare was defeated and Wingti took office as Prime Minister of a new five-party coalition Government (comprising the PDM, the PPP, the NP, the UP and the MA), with Chan as Deputy Prime Minister.

At the mid-1987 general election to the National Parliament Somare's Pangu Pati won 26 of the 109 elective seats, while Wingti's PDM obtained 18. However, by forming a coalition with minor parties, Wingti succeeded in securing a parliamentary majority and was re-elected Prime Minister. In July 1988 Wingti was defeated in a 'no confidence' motion, proposed by Rabbie Namaliu, who had replaced Somare as leader of the Pangu Pati. As a result, Namaliu took office as Prime Minister and announced a new coalition Government, comprising members of the Pangu Pati and five minor parties: the People's Action Party (PAP), the MA, the NP, the League for National Advancement (LNA) and the Papua Party. In August Ted Diro, the leader of the PAP, was acquitted on a charge of perjury by the Supreme Court (having been accused of illegally appropriating funds for his party). An amendment to the Constitution, whereby a motion expressing 'no confidence' in the Prime Minister could not be proposed until he or she had completed 18 months in office, was approved by Parliament in August 1990 and incorporated into the Constitution in July 1991.

Apart from the continued unrest on Bougainville (see below), the principal cause for concern in Papua New Guinea's domestic affairs during the 1980s and 1990s was the increase in serious crime. In 1991 the National Parliament approved a programme of severe measures to combat crime, including the introduction of the death penalty and the tattooing of the foreheads of convicted criminals.

In September 1991 a leadership tribunal found Ted Diro, the leader of the PAP, guilty of 81 charges of misconduct in government office. However, the Governor-General, Sir Serei Eri, refused to ratify the tribunal's decision and reinstated Diro as Deputy Prime Minister, despite recommendations that he be dismissed. A constitutional crisis subsequently arose, during which a government envoy was sent to the United Kingdom to request that the monarch dismiss Eri. However, on 1 October the resignation of the Governor-General was announced; this was followed shortly afterwards by that of Diro.

In 1992 the Government continued to be troubled by allegations of corruption and misconduct (notably bribery and misuse of public funds). Campaigning for the 1992 general election began amid serious fighting among the various political factions, which led to rioting, in April, by some 10,000 supporters of rival candidates. At the election in June a total of 59 members of the legislature (including 15 ministers) lost their seats. The final result gave the Pangu Pati 22 of the 109 elective seats, while the PDM secured 15. Independent candidates won a total of 31 seats. Paias Wingti of the PDM was subsequently elected Prime Minister by the National Parliament, defeating Rabbie Namaliu of the Pangu Pati by a single vote. Wingti formed a coalition Government, comprising PDM, PPP and LNA members, as well as several independents. As part of the new administration's anti-corruption policy, Wingti suspended six provincial governments for financial mismanagement in October, and threatened to abolish the entire local government system.

In early 1993 a resurgence of tribal violence, mainly in the Enga Province, resulted in the deaths of more than 100 people. This development, together with a continued increase in violent crime throughout the country (despite the severe measures introduced in 1991), prompted the National Parliament to approve a new internal security act in May 1993. The measures —which included an amendment of the legal system that required defendants accused of serious crimes to prove their innocence, rather than be proven guilty—were criticized by the opposition as oppressive. In May 1994 the Supreme Court nullified six of the 26 sections of the act (most of which concerned the extension of police powers), denouncing them as unconstitutional.

In September 1993 Prime Minister Wingti announced his resignation to Parliament. The Speaker immediately requested nominations for the premiership, and Wingti was re-elected unopposed with 59 of the 109 votes. According to the Constitution (as amended in 1991), a motion of 'no confidence' in the Prime Minister could not be presented for at least 18 months, and Wingti claimed that his action had been necessary in order to secure a period of political stability for the country. Opposition members, however, described the events as an abuse of the democratic process, and several thousand demonstrators gathered in the capital to demand Wingti's resignation. In December the National Court rejected a constitutional challenge from the opposition to Wingti's re-election. However, in August 1994 the Supreme Court declared Wingti's re-election in September 1993 invalid. Wingti did not contest the ensuing parliamentary vote for a new Prime Minister, in which Sir Julius Chan of the PPP defeated the Speaker, Bill Skate, by 66 votes to 32; Chris Haiveta, the leader of the Pangu Pati, was appointed Deputy Prime Minister.

The abolition of the directly-elected provincial government system, as proposed by Wingti, was rejected by Chan's Government. However, there was still considerable support among the opposition for the planned changes, and, as a result, it was decided that Parliament would vote on a series of motions to amend the Constitution accordingly; the first of these was approved in March 1995. However, in June the Pangu Pati withdrew its support for the reforms, and considerable opposition to the proposals was expressed by the provincial governments. Nevertheless, the controversial legislation was approved later that month on condition that Chan lent his support to several opposition amendments to be considered later in the year. Chan subsequently dismissed six ministers for failing to vote for the legislation and effected a major reorganization of portfolios. The new regional authorities, comprising national politicians and selected local councillors and led by appointed governors, were appointed in that month. Wingti resigned as parliamentary leader of the opposition in order to assume the post of Governor in the Western Highlands Province, and was replaced by another PDM member, Roy Yaki.

Meanwhile, the country continued to experience serious problems relating to crime and tribal violence throughout 1995–96, and in November 1996 the Government imposed a nation-wide curfew to combat the increasing lawlessness.

The mercenary affair on Bougainville in early 1997 (see below) led to a period of extreme instability throughout the country, culminating in Chan's temporary resignation and the appointment of John Giheno as acting Prime Minister for about two months. The atmosphere of political uncertainty was exacerbated by serious outbreaks of violence in the weeks preceding the general election (which had been set for mid-June). The Government imposed a dusk-to-dawn curfew and a nation-wide ban on the sale of alcohol, and dispatched security personnel across the country in an attempt to quell the politically-motivated disturbances. Many senior politicians failed to be re-elected in the general election, including Giheno and Wingti. Outbreaks of violence were reported in several Highlands constituencies as the results were declared. A period of intense political manoeuvring followed the election, as various members sought to form coalitions and groupings in an attempt to achieve a majority in Parliament. On 22 July Bill Skate of the People's National Congress (PNC), who was the former Speaker and Governor of the National Capital District, was elected Prime Minister, defeating Sir Michael Somare (who had established a new party—the National Alliance—in 1996) by 71 votes to 35. Skate was supported by a coalition of the PNC, PDM, PPP, Pangu Pati and independent members. A new Government was appointed in late July, and extensive changes in the functional responsibilities of ministries were announced.

In September 1997 the Government declared a national disaster following a prolonged period of drought believed to have been caused by El Niño (a periodic warming of the tropical Pacific Ocean). By December more than 1,000 people had died, and as many as 1.2m. were threatened by starvation, as a result of the drought, which was the most severe in the country's recorded history. Several countries and organizations that had provided relief funds during the disaster were highly critical of the Government's management of the aid it received. The Minister for Finance, Roy Yaki, was dismissed, in part for his role in the affair, and responsibility for the administration of relief funds was subsequently transferred from the Department of Finance to the Department of Provincial Affairs. In March 1998

(when the drought was deemed to have ended following heavy rainfall) it was revealed that less than one-half of the relief aid received had been deployed to help the victims of the disaster.

On 14 November 1997 Silas (later Sir Silas) Atopare was appointed Governor-General, defeating Sir Getake Gam, head of the Evangelical Lutheran Church, by 54 votes to 44 in the legislature.

A serious political scandal erupted in late November 1997, following allegations of corruption against Skate. The accusations centred on a videotape broadcast on Australian television, which appeared to show Skate arranging bribes and boasting of his strong connections with criminal elements in Port Moresby. The Prime Minister dismissed his recorded comments (and the resultant allegations) saying that he had been drunk at the time of filming. Several senior politicians, including Somare, demanded his resignation over the affair. Meanwhile, Skate dismissed the leaders of the Pangu Pati and the PPP (Chris Haiveta and Andrew Baing, respectively), his coalition partners, accusing them of conspiring against him. The situation intensified with the resignation of seven Pangu Pati members from the Government in early December, and the announcement that the Pangu Pati and the PPP would join the opposition. However, the PPP rejoined the Government shortly afterwards, having voted to replace Baing as leader of the party with Michael Nali. Similarly, four Pangu Pati ministers rejoined the Government, thereby restoring Skate's majority in the National Parliament. A major ministerial reorganization was subsequently announced, in which Nali was appointed Deputy Prime Minister.

In April 1998 Skate announced the formation of a new political grouping, the Papua New Guinea First Party (which absorbed the PNC, the Christian Country Party and several other minor parties), and effected a ministerial reorganization. The Government's majority was subsequently undermined, however, following a series of decisions by the Court of Disputed Returns during mid-1998, which declared the election of seven government MPs (at the 1997 general election) null and void. Furthermore, in June the Pangu Pati officially joined the opposition, thereby reducing the Government's representation to 61 members in the National Parliament.

Rumours of a motion expressing 'no confidence' in the Prime Minister prompted the formation of a new pro-Skate coalition in the National Parliament in late July 1998. In the same month Skate announced a number of major reforms in the structure of the Government, including the merging of several ministerial portfolios, the establishment of new departments for Private Enterprise and Rural Development, a series of new appointments to various public bodies and an extensive ministerial reorganization.

In July 1998 a state of national disaster was declared, following a series of tsunamis (huge tidal waves caused by undersea earthquakes) which obliterated several villages on the north-west coast of the country and killed an estimated 3,000 people. An estimated K10m. was subsequently received for disaster relief operations, although widespread concern at the apparently inefficient distribution of the funds was expressed in the following months.

In October 1998 the PPP left the governing coalition and, in a subsequent ministerial reorganization, the party's leader, Nali, was replaced as Deputy Prime Minister by Iairo Lasaro.

In late 1998 there was a series of scandals relating to the various serious misdemeanours of a number of provincial governors. Moreover, outbreaks of tribal fighting continued to cause problems (particularly in the Highlands) in 1998–99. A serious conflict in the Eastern Highlands in early 1999 involved villagers using rocket launchers and grenades, and resulted in numerous deaths. In mid-1999 a state of emergency was declared in the Southern Highlands, following serious disturbances provoked by the death of a former provincial Governor, Dick Mune, in a road accident.

The establishment of a new political party, the PNG Liberal Party (PNGLP), in May 1999 by the Speaker, John Pundari (relaunched in June as the Advance PNG Party—APP), encouraged rumours of a forthcoming vote of 'no confidence' against the Prime Minister. In early June, as part of a government reorganization, Skate dismissed the PDM leader, Sir Mekere Morauta, and three other PDM ministers, replacing them with four Pangu Pati members, including Haiveta. Later that month both the PDM and the United Resource Party (URP) announced their decision to withdraw completely from the coalition Government, following the resignation of nine government ministers. Both parties were expected to support the APP, in an attempt to subject Skate to a vote of 'no confidence'. On 7 July, however, Skate unexpectedly resigned, but declared that he would remain in power, in an acting capacity, until the appointment of a new Prime Minister. The opposition alliance announced Morauta as their candidate for the premiership. On the day before the National Parliament was due to reconvene. Skate claimed that the APP had pledged support for the Government, thereby ensuring that it would have a sufficient majority to defeat any motion of 'no confidence'. At the opening session of the National Parliament in mid-July, Lasaro, the incumbent Prime Minister's nominee, defeated the opposition candidate, Bernard Narokobi of the PDM by 57 votes to 45, to become Speaker. However, on the next day Morauta was elected as new Prime Minister with an overwhelming majority, following his nomination by Pundari, who had transferred his allegiance from Skate, having refused to accept the latter's nomination of himself as candidate for the premiership. Lasaro immediately resigned as Speaker, and Narokobi was elected unopposed to the position. Morauta subsequently appointed a new coalition Government, with Pundari as Deputy Prime Minister.

In early August 1999 Morauta, a former Governor of the central bank, presented a 'mini-budget', in an attempt to combat various economic problems which, he claimed, were a consequence of the previous Government's mismanagement. As part of a series of measures aimed at stabilizing the political situation in the country, legislation was drafted in October 1999 to prevent ministers transferring political allegiances. In early December Prime Minister Morauta expelled the APP from the coalition Government and dismissed Pundari from his post as Deputy Prime Minister, claiming that this constituted a further move towards the restoration of political stability. (Pundari was rumoured to have conspired with the opposition leader, Skate, to oust the Prime Minister.) Pundari was replaced by the former Minister of Works and deputy leader of the PDM, Mao Zeming. Following Pundari's sudden dismissal, four small political parties within the governing coalition—the National Alliance, the People's National Party, the Melanesian Alliance and the Movement for Greater Autonomy—joined to form the People's National Alliance. Also in that month, Skate (who was faced with a charge of attempted fraud during his term in office as Governor of the National Capital District Commission), announced that his party, the People's National Congress (PNC, which had 10 MPs), was to join the coalition Government; in May he assumed leadership of the party. Later in December, the resignation of the Minister of Agriculture and Livestock, Ted Diro, prompted Morauta to carry out a government reshuffle, including the appointment of three new ministers. In February 2000 it was announced that about 25,000 inhabitants of the Duke of York Islands, which are situated in East New Britain Province, were expected to be resettled by the Government, following the publication of a UN report indicating that the islands were becoming uninhabitable owing to rising sea levels resulting from the 'greenhouse effect' (the heating of the earth's atmosphere as a consequence of pollution).

Morauta dismissed three ministers in March 2000, on the grounds that they had allegedly conspired to introduce a parliamentary motion of 'no confidence' in the Prime Minister. The parliamentary strength of the ruling coalition was increased to 76 MPs in April, following the readmission of the APP to government, including the appointment of Pundari, to the post of Minister of Lands and Physical Planning. In an attempt to increase government stability, Morauta proposed legislation in August that would restrict the ability of MPs to change their party allegiance within a parliamentary session. Moreover, Morauta also announced the adjournment of Parliament between January and July 2001, the only period during which votes of 'no confidence' could be tabled. (The Constitution forbids such votes in the 18 months following the election of a Prime Minister, and in the 12 months prior to a general election.) In November, however, a revolt by 25 government MPs (including six cabinet ministers) prevented a vote on the so-called Political Parties Integrity Bill. The rebellion prompted a major cabinet reshuffle, in which all of the ministers involved in the revolt, including the Deputy Prime Minister, Mao Zeming, were dismissed. Further changes to the composition of the cabinet were made in December, notably the dismissal of Michael Somare, the Minister for Foreign Affairs and Trade, following which Morauta secured the parliamentary approval of the bill. The Prime Minister claimed that the introduction of the new legislation represented the most important constitutional change in Papua

New Guinea since independence and would greatly enhance the political stability of the country, as it required members of Parliament who wished to change party allegiance to stand down and contest a by-election.

Allegations of corruption and mismanagement resulted in the suspension of four provincial governments (Western Province, Southern Highlands, Enga and NCD) in late 2000 and early 2001. The central Government claimed that a failure to deliver services had resulted from the misuse of public funds. Moreover, in January 2001 the Minister for Provincial and Local Government, Iairo Lasaro, was arrested for the alleged misappropriation of public funds, and in mid-March Bill Skate was charged with the same crime, having been acquitted earlier in the month of conspiring to defraud an insurance company (the trial was to be abandoned in December 2001 owing to lack of evidence).

A Commonwealth report into the Papua New Guinea Defence Force published in January 2001 recommended reducing the number of army personnel by one-third. Subsequent plans by the Government to make more than 2,000 soldiers redundant (equivalent to some 50% of the entire Defence Force) resulted in a revolt at the Port Moresby barracks in March. It was believed that senior officers had helped to distribute arms to the rebels, who demanded the resignation of the Prime Minister and the transfer of power to a caretaker administration. The rebellion ended some two weeks later with an amnesty for the soldiers involved, during which hundreds of looted weapons were surrendered. In March 2002 another rebellion by soldiers protesting against the proposed reductions in defence personnel took place at the Moem barracks on the northern coast. The leader of the rebellion, Nebare Dege, was sentenced to 15 years' imprisonment in December 2002.

In April 2001 the Advance PNG Party, led by John Pundari, was dissolved and merged with the PDM, led by the Prime Minister. In May, following a minor ministerial reorganization in March, Morauta expelled the National Alliance from the ruling coalition and dismissed the party's ministers (including Bart Philemon, Minister for Foreign Affairs) from the National Executive Council, accusing Somare, its leader, of attempting to destabilize the Government.

In late June, following several days of protests against the Government's economic reforms, police used tear gas to disperse hundreds of demonstrators outside the Prime Minister's office in Port Moresby. In a separate incident, four students were killed and several injured when riot police allegedly entered the premises of the University of Papua New Guinea and opened fire. A temporary curfew was imposed, and a Commission of Inquiry was established; in December relatives of one of the dead students began legal action against the police force.

In October 2001 the Prime Minister effected another reallocation of ministerial portfolios. At the end of the month, furthermore, the Minister for Foreign Affairs, John Pundari, was dismissed. His removal from office followed his criticism of the Government's participation in Australia's 'Pacific Solution', whereby 216 refugees, who had attempted to enter Australia illegally, were being housed on Manus Island. In December negotiations with Australia were under way to accommodate a further 1,000 asylum-seekers, and Australia had requested the Government to hold the refugees for an additional six months, although no formal agreement was made. In January 2002 the Government decided to accept 784 additional asylum-seekers. It was understood that they were to remain only until their asylum claims were processed. The agreement with Australia to accommodate the asylum-seekers on Manus Island was extended for a further 12 months in October 2002 and was to provide for the housing of an additional 1,000 people.

A general election was held in the latter part of June 2002. Voting commenced on 15 June and was to extend over a two-week period. Many polling stations, however, failed to open as scheduled, amid reports of the theft of ballot papers and subsequent strike action by electoral staff. Some 25 people were killed and dozens injured in election-related violence, much of which occurred in the Highlands provinces as a result of disputes between clan-based candidates. A Commonwealth inquiry was subsequently planned to investigate the events surrounding the election, which was described as the worst in the country's history. In the final results announced in August six seats in the Highlands provinces remained vacant where voting had been unable to proceed. Of the 103 seats determined, Somare's National Alliance won 19 and Morauta's PDM secured 12. Independent candidates won 17 seats, with the remainder divided among a large number of minor parties, many of which had been formed specifically to contest the election.

On 5 August 2002 Sir Michael Somare was elected Prime Minister, with 88 parliamentary votes. No candidates stood against him, and Morauta and his supporters abstained from the vote. Bill Skate, who had played an important part in Somare's campaign, was elected Speaker. After appointing a 28-member Cabinet (which was dominated by 19 newly elected MPs), Somare began his third term as Prime Minister, pledging to restore stability, halt the privatization programme and reduce expenditure. Instability within the parliamentary opposition in late 2002 resulted in the dismissal of Morauta as Leader of the Opposition in December; he was replaced in that role by John Muinepe. Morauta was replaced as PDM leader by Paias Wingti, who had been expelled from the party in the previous August. However, in February 2003 a court ruled that this action had been unlawful and Morauta was subsequently reinstated as party leader.

In early 2003 it was announced that elections for the six Highlands constituencies, where elections had failed to take place in the previous year, would be held in April/May 2003.

Tribal conflicts, principally between the Ujimap and Wagia tribes, broke out near Mendi, the capital of Southern Highlands province, in December 2001. It was alleged that national and local politicians, along with tribal leaders, had made little effort to end the fighting, which had originated in a dispute over the governorship of the province in 1997; furthermore, many were dissatisfied at the election of Tom Tomiape as Governor, in late November, and at the widespread political corruption and deteriorating public services in the province. Tomiape's election was ruled invalid by the Supreme Court in December, and Wambi Nondi was appointed acting Governor. A brief cease-fire was brokered in early January and an independent peace commission was formed in February, headed by Francis Awesa, a local businessman. By early 2002 more than 120 people had been killed since the onset of the fighting.

The status of the province of Bougainville was increasingly questioned in the late 1980s, a problem that developed into civil unrest and a long-term national crisis. In April 1988 landowners on the island of Bougainville submitted compensation claims amounting to K10,000m., for land mined by the Australian-owned Bougainville Copper Ltd since 1972. When no payment was forthcoming, acts of sabotage were perpetrated in late 1988 by the Bougainville Revolutionary Army (BRA), led by Francis Ona, a former mine surveyor and landowner, and the mine was obliged to suspend operations for an initial period of six days. However, when repairs had been completed, the mine's owners refused to resume operations for fear of further attack, and the President, Rabbie Namaliu, was forced to deploy members of the security forces in the area. Production at the mine recommenced in December, but, after further violence in January 1989, a curfew was imposed. In early 1989 it was announced that, in an attempt to appease landowners, their share of mining royalties was to be increased from 5% to 20%.

The BRA's demands increasingly favoured secession from Papua New Guinea for Bougainville (and for North Solomons Province as a whole), together with the closure of the mine until their demands for compensation and secession had been met. In May 1989, as the violent campaign on the island intensified, the mine was forced once more to suspend production, and in June the Papua New Guinea Government declared a state of emergency on Bougainville, sending 2,000 security personnel to the island. In September a minister in the Bougainville provincial government, who had been negotiating an agreement with Bougainville landowners to provide them with financial compensation, was shot dead. The signing of the accord, due to take place the following day, was postponed indefinitely. Diro, who had been reinstated in the Government in May, as Minister of State with responsibility for overseeing the Bougainville crisis, responded by offering a reward for the capture or killing of Ona and seven of his deputies, including the BRA's military commander, Sam Kauona. In January 1990 the owners of the Bougainville mine made redundant 2,000 of the remaining 2,300 staff.

The escalation of violence on Bougainville led the Australian Government to announce plans to send in military forces to evacuate its nationals trapped on the island, and to withdraw the remaining 300 personnel of Bougainville Copper Ltd. Criticism of the Government's failure to resolve the dispute, the rising death toll among the security forces, rebels and civilians and a worsening economic crisis, which was aggravated by the

conflict, led the Government to negotiate a cease-fire with the BRA, with effect from the beginning of March 1990. The Government undertook to withdraw its security forces and to release 80 detainees. Bougainville came under the control of the BRA in mid-March, after the sudden departure of the security forces. The premature withdrawal of the troops was seen as an attempt by Paul Tohian, the police commissioner who had been in charge of the state of emergency on Bougainville, to disrupt the peace process, and was followed by an apparent abortive coup, allegedly led by Tohian, who was summarily dismissed from his post.

In late March 1990 the Government imposed an economic blockade on Bougainville; this was intensified in May, when banking, telecommunications and public services on the island were suspended. On 17 May the BRA, apparently in response to the Government's implementation of economic sanctions, proclaimed Bougainville's independence, renaming the island the Republic of Bougainville. The unilateral declaration of independence, made by Ona, who also proclaimed himself interim President, was immediately dismissed by Namaliu as unconstitutional and invalid. In July negotiations between the BRA and the Government finally began on board a New Zealand naval vessel, *Endeavour*. In the resulting 'Endeavour Accord', the BRA representatives agreed to defer implementation of the May declaration of independence and to hold further discussions on the political status of the island. The Government agreed to end the blockade, and to restore essential services to the island. However, despite assurances from Namaliu that troops would not be sent to the island, the first two ships that left for Bougainville with supplies were found to be carrying 100 security personnel, intending to disembark on the island of Buka, north of Bougainville. The BRA accused the Government of violating the accord, and a week later the security forces and the two ships, together with the supplies, withdrew. In mid-September the Government sent armed troops to take control of Buka, stating that this was in response to a petition for help from Buka islanders. Violent clashes ensued between the BRA and the armed forces on Buka, in which many people were reported to have been killed.

In January 1991 further negotiations took place between representatives of the Papua New Guinea Government and of Bougainville in Honiara, the capital of Solomon Islands, which resulted in the 'Honiara Accord'. The agreement stated that the Papua New Guinea Government would not station its security forces on Bougainville if the islanders agreed to disband the BRA and to surrender all prisoners and weapons to a multinational peace-keeping force. The Bougainville secessionists were guaranteed immunity from prosecution. The agreement, however, made no provision for any change in the political status of Bougainville, and by early March it appeared to have failed. Government troops launched a further attack on Bougainville in April 1991. In June Col Leo Nuia was dismissed from his post as Commander of the Papua New Guinea Defence Force, after admitting that his troops had committed atrocities during fighting on Bougainville in early 1990. Further allegations of human rights abuses and summary executions of BRA members and sympathizers by government troops prompted Namaliu to announce plans for an independent inquiry into the claims.

Fighting continued throughout 1991 and the situation deteriorated further in early 1992 when, in an attempt to force the Government to end its economic blockade of the island, the BRA intercepted and set fire to a supply ship, and held its crew hostage. As a result, all shipping and air services to Bougainville were suspended.

In October 1992 government troops began a major offensive against rebel-held areas of Bougainville and, later in the month, announced that they had taken control of the main town, Arawa. The BRA, however, denied the claim and began a campaign of arson against government offices and public buildings in Arawa. Violence on the island intensified in early 1993, and allegations of atrocities and violations of human rights by both sides were widely reported.

Talks between government representatives and secessionists in Honiara during 1994 led to the signing of a cease-fire agreement in September. Under the terms of the agreement, a regional peace-keeping force, composed of troops from Fiji, Vanuatu and Tonga, was deployed in October (with the Governments of Australia and New Zealand in a supervisory role) and the economic blockade of Bougainville was lifted. In the following month Chan and a group of non-BRA Bougainville leaders signed the Charter of Mirigini, which provided for the establishment of a transitional Bougainville government. The

BRA declared its opposition to the proposed authority, reiterating its goal of outright secession.

In April 1995, following the suspension of the Bougainville provincial government, 27 members of the 32-member transitional administration were sworn in at a ceremony on Buka Island, attended by the Prime Minister and several foreign dignitaries. Theodore Miriong, a former legal adviser to Ona, was elected Premier of the authority. However, the three seats reserved for the BRA leaders, Ona, Kauona and Joseph Kabui (a former Premier of North Solomons Province), remained vacant, as the rebels urged their supporters to reject the new administration and to continue the violent campaign for independence. An amnesty, declared in May by the transitional administration and the Government, for all who had committed crimes during the conflict, was rejected by the BRA. Violence escalated during July and August, and a campaign of arson against public buildings was conducted by BRA rebels. Meanwhile, the Government denied any involvement in a series of attacks on BRA leaders, including an assassination attempt on Kabui. The murder of several more members of the security forces in March 1996 led the Government to abandon all talks with the secessionists and to reimpose a military blockade on Bougainville. An escalation of violence in mid-1996 culminated in a major military offensive against rebel-held areas in June. Civilians on the island were encouraged to seek refuge in government 'care centres', and by August it was estimated that some 67,000 Bougainvilleans were being accommodated in 59 such centres. In the same month defence forces arrested Miriong, accusing him of incitement regarding the killing of 13 government soldiers at an army camp. The incident, in which Miriong was removed from Bougainville and kept under surveillance on Buka, caused the Government considerable embarrassment, particularly as it followed a number of similar cases in which the security forces had chosen to act independently of government policy. On 12 October Miriong was assassinated at his home in south-west Bougainville by unidentified gunmen. The following month an official inquiry concluded that a group of government soldiers was responsible for the killing, assisted by pro-Government civilians (known as 'resistance fighters'). Meanwhile, Gerard Sinato was elected as the new Premier of the Bougainville Transitional Government.

An apparent deterioration in the situation on Bougainville in late 1996 was characterized by an increase in BRA attacks against civilian targets and a similar escalation in violence by government troops and 'resistance fighters'. The Red Cross temporarily suspended its operations on the island following an attack on one of its vehicles, and human rights organizations repeated demands that observers be allowed to monitor incidents on the island, following a series of attacks on civilians (for which both sides denied responsibility). A report commissioned by the Government and published in late 1996 recommended a thorough reorganization of the country's armed forces. The report identified a number of problems which had contributed to a lack of cohesion and discipline and a marked decline in morale among troops, which had resulted in many soldiers refusing to serve in Bougainville.

In February 1997 unofficial reports suggested that the Government was planning to engage the services of a group of mercenaries on Bougainville. Chan reacted angrily to the reports, which he claimed were inaccurate; however, he confirmed that a company based in the United Kingdom, Sandline International (a subsidiary of Executive Outcomes, a notorious supplier of private armed forces in Africa), had been commissioned to provide military advice and training for soldiers on Bougainville. Subsequent reports of mercenary activity on the island and of the large-scale purchase of military equipment and weapons provoked expressions of condemnation from numerous interests in the region, including the British High Commission in Port Moresby, and, in particular, from the Government of Australia. The situation developed into a major crisis when on 16 March the Commander of the Defence Force, Brig.-Gen. (later Maj.-Gen.) Jerry Singirok, announced on national radio and television that the country's armed forces were refusing to co-operate with the mercenary programme and demanded the immediate resignation of Chan. He explained that the mercenaries (most of whom were from South Africa) had been captured by the armed forces and were being detained while arrangements were made for their deportation. Singirok denied that his actions constituted a coup attempt. The following day Chan dismissed Singirok, replacing him with Col Alfred Aikung. However, the armed forces rejected the new leadership,

remaining loyal to Singirok. Popular support for the army's stance became increasingly vocal, as several thousand demonstrators rampaged through the streets of the capital, looting and clashing with security forces. Armed forces in Australia were reported to be prepared for deployment to Papua New Guinea in the event of any worsening of the situation. In view of the escalation in civil unrest, Chan announced the suspension of the contract with Sandline International on 20 March, pending an inquiry into the affair. The following day the remaining mercenaries left the country and Aikung was replaced as Commander of the Defence Force by Col Jack Tuat. Despite these attempts at conciliation, however, demands for Chan's resignation intensified, with military, political and religious leaders, as well as the Governor-General, urging him to leave office. Moreover, four government ministers resigned their posts in an attempt to increase the pressure on Chan to do likewise. On 25 March the National Parliament voted on a motion of 'no confidence' in the Prime Minister. When the vote was defeated protesters laid siege to the parliament building, effectively imprisoning more than 100 members inside the building until the next day, while an estimated 15,000 demonstrators marched on Parliament from across the capital. The following day Chan announced his resignation, along with that of the Deputy Prime Minister and the Minister for Defence. John Giheno, the erstwhile Minister for Mining and Petroleum, was subsequently elected acting Prime Minister.

In April 1997 an inquiry was initiated into the mercenary affair. The chief executive of Sandline International, Col (retd) Tim Spicer, was questioned over his alleged acceptance of bribes and in connection with various firearms offences. During the inquiry it was revealed that the company had requested part-ownership of the Panguna copper mine as payment for its military services. Criminal charges against Spicer were withdrawn within several days. The inquiry concluded in early June that Chan had not been guilty of misconduct in relation to the mercenary affair, and, as a result (despite Giheno's stated intention to continue as acting Prime Minister until a general election had taken place), Chan announced his immediate resumption of his former position. Shortly after resuming office, Chan again provoked controversy by appointing Col Leo Nuia to the position of Commander of the Defence Force. (Nuia had been dismissed from the post in 1991, following an admission that his troops had committed atrocities during fighting on Bougainville.)

Following the election of a new Government, it was announced in August 1997 that a second inquiry into the mercenary affair, based on broader criteria, would be conducted. Meanwhile, government soldiers reacted angrily to the prosecution of military leaders involved in the operation to oust Sandline mercenaries from Bougainville in March. Nuia was imprisoned in his barracks by members of the Defence Force, while Maj. Walter Enuma, who was being held while awaiting trial on charges of 'raising an illegal force', was freed by rebel soldiers. The second inquiry concluded in September 1998 that Chris Haiveta (the former Deputy Prime Minister) had been the beneficiary of corrupt payments from Sandline and upheld the first inquiry's finding that Chan had not been guilty of any wrongdoing in the affair. In the same month an international tribunal ruled that the Government owed $A28m. to Sandline in outstanding payments under the mercenary contract. In May 1999 the Government agreed to pay this debt and the two parties undertook to end all legal action against each other. The Papua New Guinea Defence Force was to be allowed to retain Sandline military equipment stored on Bougainville.

In July 1997 talks were held in New Zealand (at the Burnham army base) between secessionists and representatives of the Bougainville Transitional Government. As a result of the negotiations, Sinato and Kabui signed the 'Burnham Declaration', which recommended the withdrawal of government troops from Bougainville and the deployment of a neutral peace-keeping force. Persistent reports of internal divisions within the BRA were refuted by the leadership, despite Ona's declared opposition to the 'Burnham Declaration'. However, hopes for a significant improvement in the political climate on Bougainville were encouraged by an official visit by the new Prime Minister, Bill Skate, in August (the first such visit since 1994) and by the resumption of talks in New Zealand in the following month. Negotiations concluded on 10 October 1997 with the signing of the 'Burnham Truce', in which representatives from both sides agreed to a series of interim measures, which included refraining from acts of armed confrontation pending a formal meeting of government and secessionist leaders in early 1998. Ona (who appeared to be becoming increasingly marginalized within the BRA) refused to be a party to the truce, however, claiming that similar agreements had not been honoured by government troops and 'resistance fighters' in the past, and indirectly threatened the members of an unarmed group of regional representatives, established to monitor the truce. The Prime Ministers of both Papua New Guinea and Solomon Islands made an extended visit to Bougainville in December 1997 to demonstrate their united support for the truce. Further talks held at Lincoln University in Christchurch, New Zealand, in January 1998 resulted in the 'Lincoln Agreement', providing for an extension to the truce, the initiation of a disarmament process and the phased withdrawal of government troops from the island. Skate also issued a public apology for mistakes made by successive administrations during the conflict, which was estimated to have resulted in the deaths of some 20,000 people and to have cost a total of K200m.

In accordance with the provisions of the 'Burnham Truce', a permanent cease-fire agreement was signed in Arawa on 30 April 1998. The occasion was attended by senior government members from Australia, New Zealand, Solomon Islands and Vanuatu, as well as Papua New Guinea government representatives and secessionist leaders. Ona declined to take part in the ceremony, reiterating his opposition to the peace agreement. In the following month he attracted statements of condemnation from Kabui and Kauona for issuing a 'shoot-to-kill' order against the peace-keeping troops on Bougainville to the small band of rebels who remained loyal to him. In June government troops were withdrawn from Arawa under the terms of the agreement and reconstruction projects on Bougainville, financed by funds from various sources, including an aid package of $NZ1m. from the New Zealand Government, were initiated. An increase in crime and arson attacks, however, was reported in the demilitarized zones in the following months.

In August 1998 more than 2,000 representatives from different groups in Bougainville met in Buin (in the south of the island) to discuss their response to the 'Burnham Truce'. The resultant 'Buin Declaration' stated that the islanders were united in their aspiration for independence through peaceful negotiation. In October the National Parliament voted to amend the Constitution to allow the Bougainville Reconciliation Government to replace the Bougainville Transitional Government. The new authority came into existence on 1 January 1999, following the renewed suspension of the Bougainville provincial government, and at its first sitting elected Sinato and Kabui as its co-leaders. In April an agreement signed by Bougainville and Papua New Guinea government representatives (although not acknowledged by the BRA), known as the Matakana and Okataina Understanding, reaffirmed both sides' commitment to the cease-fire, while undertaking to discuss options for the political future of the island. Elections to the Bougainville People's Congress (BPC, formerly the Bougainville Reconciliation Government) were held in early May 1999, and were reported to have proceeded smoothly. At the first sitting of the BPC, Kabui was elected President by an overwhelming majority, securing 77 of the 87 votes, thus defeating his former co-leader, Sinato, who received only 10 votes. Kabui subsequently appointed 29 members to the Congressional Executive Council, and Linus Konukong was elected Speaker. Ona refused Kabui's offer to join the BPC, stating that he did not wish to co-operate with the Government. At a subsequent session of the Council, Kabui announced his intention to campaign for independence for Bougainville. In response, Prime Minister Bill Skate stated that, although there was no possibility of independence (as this was not provided for in the Constitution), Parliament would consider terms for greater autonomy for the island. Plans for the disposal of weapons on Bougainville were expected to be drafted by the UN under terms agreed upon at a meeting with the Peace Process Consultative Committee in June. In August the suspension of the Bougainville provincial government was extended for a further six months in an attempt to find a peaceful resolution to the issue of autonomy for Bougainville; the decision was confirmed at a parliamentary session the following month. Following a visit to Bougainville, the Minister for Bougainville Affairs and for Foreign Affairs, Sir Michael Somare (as he had become), stated that the Government was willing to grant the island a greater degree of autonomy. Somare proposed that Bougainville be self-governing in all matters except foreign affairs, defence and policing, all of which would remain the responsibility of the central Government. The proposal was

welcomed as an important development by members of the BPC, although they also announced their intention not to surrender their weapons until the Government had agreed to the holding of a referendum on independence. Following further talks between Somare and Kabui, the former reiterated Skate's earlier comments that there was no provision for a referendum on independence in the Constitution.

In October 1999 a Supreme Court ruling declared the suspension of the Bougainville provincial government illegal on technical grounds. On 9 December the provincial government was formally recognized, in theory, despite protests by members of the BPC and concerns that this development would hinder the peace process. In effect, however, the provincial government comprised only four members—the Bougainville Regional Member of Parliament, John Momis, who thus became Governor-elect (although he agreed not to exercise his powers for the mean time) and the three other Bougainville parliamentarians. Following talks in mid-December between Somare and members of the BPC, the BRA and elders of the island, Somare declared, in the consequent agreement, to considering the possibility of a referendum on independence for Bougainville. The agreement, known as the Hutjena Record, stated that the highest possible degree of autonomy should be accorded to the island. Further talks regarding the future status of Bougainville commenced in early March 2000. However, following the rejection of an initial proposal on the island's autonomy by secessionist leaders, the talks were suspended. Negotiations resumed in mid-March, and on 23 March an agreement, known as the Loloata Understanding, allowing for the eventual holding of a referendum on independence, once full autonomy had been implemented, and the formal establishment of the Bougainville Interim Provincial Government (BIPG), composed of an Executive Council and a 25-member Provincial Assembly (including the four original members), was signed by Somare and Kabui.

On 30 March 2000 the Provincial Assembly and the Executive Council were sworn in by the Governor-General. Another six seats were left vacant in the Provincial Assembly for other Bougainville officials such as Kabui and Ona; Kabui, however, stated that, rather than joining the BIPG, he would wait until the establishment of a fully autonomous government (which he hoped would be set up by early 2001). In May 2000 the Office of Bougainville Affairs was renamed the Office of Peace and Reconstruction. In July Somare approved an allocation of K200,000, as part of a scheme co-ordinated by the United Nations Development Programme (UNDP), to facilitate the collection and disposal of weapons held by dissident groups. Although an initial deadline of 15 September to determine the form and date of a referendum was not met, a further round of negotiations that month was presented as a significant advance in the peace process. Uncertainties regarding the proposed date of a referendum continued to delay the progress of negotiations; Somare's statement in May that the referendum would be held 15 years hence contradicted a previously-stated deadline of December 2000. Concerns about renewed Australian funding of the Papua New Guinea Defence Force troops stationed on Bougainville and the failure of the BRA to begin disarmament before the implementation of political autonomy, further impeded progress. In October the BRA's commander, Ishmael Toroama, threatened to abandon the organization's cease-fire. Following a further round of peace talks in November, Kabui confirmed that he had secured an agreement from Somare that a future referendum would include a legally-binding option of independence, although disagreement over how soon the vote should be held persisted. In the following month Somare was abruptly dismissed from his ministerial position and replaced by Bart Philemon; Morauta believed Somare was impeding the progress of the Political Parties Integrity Bill.

In February 2001 agreement on the terms of the referendum was finally reached following the intervention of the Australian Minister for Foreign Affairs. The agreement stated that the referendum would be held in 10–15 years' time and would contain the option of independence. In the interim the provincial government was to be granted increased autonomy and the BRA would be expected to disarm. Despite a temporary breakdown in negotiations, in early May commanders of the BRA and the Bougainville Resistance Force (a militia that was allied to the Government during the civil conflict on Bougainville) signed an agreement to surrender their weapons. In the same month, in Port Moresby, the Government and the BPA held negotiations on autonomy for Bougainville. In late June Moi Avei, who had replaced Philemon as Minister for Bougainville Affairs in May, announced that further talks had resulted in a comprehensive agreement on autonomy for the island, with the Government ceding to the BPA's demands that Bougainville be accorded its own system of criminal law and an autonomous police force. It was also agreed that the Papua New Guinea Defence Force's jurisdiction on the island would be strictly limited. On 30 August the Government and island leaders signed the Bougainville peace agreement in Arawa. Although he signed the accord, which was still to be approved by the National Parliament, Toroama stated that the BRA would campaign for the referendum to be held in three–five years' time and would continue to seek full independence. Francis Ona did not attend the signing ceremony.

The weapons disposal process was threatened in late November 2001 when Henry Kiumo, a former commander of the pro-Government Bougainville Resistance Force (BRF) militia, was murdered. However, weapons disposal by the BRA and BRF began in early December, and the UN Observer Mission on Bougainville (UNOMB) formally acknowledged the Bougainville Peace Agreement later in that month. In January 2002 the National Parliament unanimously endorsed the Organic Law enacting the Bougainville peace agreement, along with a bill containing the requisite constitutional amendment. A second vote, held in late March, ratified the legislation, and the Papua New Guinea Defence Force began its withdrawal from Bougainville. The withdrawal of troops was completed in late December. In the same month, however, the peace process was jeopardized by the theft of 360 weapons from containers being used in the weapons disposal process.

In January 2003 it was announced that the BIPG and the BPC would be merged to form the Bougainville Constituent Assembly. The new body, which was expected to be composed of some 90 members, would debate and approve a proposed constitution for the island and complete the weapons disposal process. It was not expected to be established until further changes had been made to Papua New Guinea's Constitution, although a subsequent announcement indicated that elections to the authority might take place in July 2003.

In September 2000 a group of landowners from Bougainville initiated legal action in a US court against Rio Tinto, the operator of the Panguna copper mine between 1972 and 1988. The group was reported to be suing the company for the environmental and social damage caused by its activities, including health problems experienced by workers and islanders living near the mine. Moreover, their case alleged that the company had effectively transformed the Papua New Guinea Defence Force into its own private army and was therefore responsible for the deaths of some 15,000 civilians in military action and a further 10,000 as a result of the economic blockade on the island.

In 1984 more than 9,000 refugees crossed into Papua New Guinea from the Indonesian province of Irian Jaya (officially known as Papua from January 2002), as a consequence of operations by the Indonesian army against Melanesian rebels of the pro-independence Organisasi Papua Merdeka (Free Papua Movement—OPM). For many years relations between Papua New Guinea and Indonesia had been strained by the conflict in Irian Jaya, not least because the independence movement drew sympathy from many among the largely Melanesian population of Papua New Guinea. A new border treaty was signed in October 1984, and attempts were made to repatriate the refugees, based on assurances by the Indonesian Government that there would be no reprisals against those who returned. In October 1985 representatives of the Papua New Guinea and Indonesian Governments signed a treaty providing for the settlement of disputes by consultation, arbitration and 'other peaceful means'. The treaty, however, provoked strong criticism among opposition politicians in Papua New Guinea, who claimed that it effectively precluded the censure of any violation of human rights in Irian Jaya. In 1988 the Government condemned the incursions by Indonesian soldiers into Papua New Guinea, in search of OPM members, and the resultant violence and killings as a breach of bilateral accords, and affirmed that Papua New Guinea would not support Indonesia in its attempt to suppress the OPM. In late 1995 the Indonesian consulate in the border town of Vanimo was attacked by OPM rebels and a subsequent increase in Indonesian troops along the border was reported. Violent confrontations resulted in the killing of several rebels and security personnel and the kidnapping by OPM activists of some 200 villagers. Australia urged the Papua New Guinea Government to accept several thousand refugees living in camps along the border, and in May 1996 the Government announced that 3,500 Irian Jayans would be allowed to remain in Papua New Guinea on condition that they were not involved in OPM activities. In mid-1998, on an official visit to Indonesia, the Prime Minister, Bill Skate, signed a memorandum of understanding on bilateral relations, which was expected to provide the basis for closer co-operation in political, economic and defence matters. Under the terms of the agreement, troop numbers along the border were increased in March 1999. In May of that year 11 Javanese people were taken hostage and three people were reported to have been killed by OPM rebels in the West Sepik Province of Papua New Guinea. The hostages were later released as a result of the intervention of Papua New Guinea security forces. The OPM subsequently demanded an inquiry into the operation leading to the release of the hostages, after its communications director was allegedly shot dead at a border post. During 2000 hundreds of refugees were voluntarily repatriated to Indonesia (including more than 600 in a major operation in early September), although approximately 7,000 were believed to remain in Papua New Guinea in September. In late 2000 it was reported that Indonesian security forces had made some 400 incursions into Papua New Guinea in the previous two months while pursuing separatists. In December the border with Irian Jaya was officially closed, while Morauta reaffirmed his recognition of Indonesia's sovereignty over the region.

In January 2003 the Papua New Guinea Government denied a number of security breaches, which were reported to have occurred along its border with Indonesia. Concerns grew following a dramatic increase in the numbers of Indonesian troops along the border, from some 150 in late 2002 to a reported 1,500 in early 2003. In late January the Government of Papua New Guinea ordered its security forces to arrest OPM rebels believed to be staying in refugee camps along the border, following complaints from the Indonesian authorities that rebels based there were carrying out operations in the province of Papua. The Government also confirmed in April that it had been unable to persuade more than 400 Papuans living in a camp near the border town of Vanimo to return to Indonesia, despite assurances that their safety would not be at risk.

Since 1990 relations with Solomon Islands have been overshadowed by the conflict on Bougainville. Solomon Islands (whose inhabitants are culturally and ethnically very similar to Bougainville islanders) has protested against repeated incursions by Papua New Guinea defence forces into Solomon Islands' territorial waters, while the Papua New Guinea Government has consistently accused Solomon Islands of harbouring members of the BRA and providing them with supplies. Despite several attempts during the 1990s to improve the situation between the two countries (including an agreement by Solomon Islands in 1993 to close the BRA office in the capital, Honiara), relations remained tense. In April 1997 the Solomon Islands Government announced that it was considering the initiation of proceedings against the Papua New Guinea Government concerning the latter's attempted use of mercenaries on Bougainville. In June of that year Papua New Guinea and Solomon Islands concluded a maritime border agreement, following several years of negotiations. The purpose of the agreement (which came into effect in January 1998) was not only to delineate the sea boundary between the two countries but also to provide a framework for co-operation in matters of security, natural disaster, customs, quarantine, immigration and conservation. In March 2000 relations between Papua New Guinea and Solomon Islands were further strengthened following the opening of a Solomon Islands High Commission in Port Moresby.

In March 1988 Papua New Guinea signed an agreement with Vanuatu and Solomon Islands to form the 'Melanesian Spearhead Group', dedicated to the preservation of Melanesian cultural traditions and to achieving independence for the French Overseas Territory of New Caledonia. In 1989 Papua New Guinea increased its links with South-East Asia, signing a Treaty of Amity and Co-operation with the Association of South East Asian Nations (ASEAN, see p. 146).

The growing exploitation of Papua New Guinea's natural resources in the 1990s led to considerable concern over the impact of the activities of numerous foreign business interests on the country's environment. Activity in the forestry sector increased dramatically in the early 1990s, and an official report published in 1994 indicated that the current rate of logging was three times the sustainable yield of the country's forests. Attempts to introduce new regulations to govern the industry, however, were strongly opposed by several Malaysian logging companies with operations in the country. In early 2000, however, environmentalists welcomed a commitment by the Papua New Guinea Government to impose a moratorium on all new forestry licences and to review all existing licences. The exploitation of Papua New Guinea's extensive mineral resources has resulted in considerable environmental damage. In 1989 the Government gave the operators of the Ok Tedi gold and copper mine permission to discharge 150,000 metric tons of toxic waste per day into the Fly River. In 1994 6,000 people living in the region began a compensation claim against the Australian company operating the mine for damage caused by the resultant pollution. A settlement worth some $A110m. was reached in an Australian court in 1995 (and a further settlement worth $A400m. for the establishment of a containment system was concluded in mid-1996), despite opposition from the Papua New Guinea Government, which feared that such action might adversely affect the country's prospects of attracting foreign investment in the future. Similar claims were initiated by people living near the Australian-controlled Porgera gold-mine in early 1996 for pollution of the Strickland River system, as well as by landowners near the Kutubu oilfield. The results of an independent study into the effects of mining activities by the Ok Tedi mine, published in mid-1999, showed that damage to the environment might be greater than originally believed, casting doubts over the future of the mine. The Government, however, announced that it would await the findings of an independent review, carried out by the World Bank. The results of this report, which were published in March 2000, found that closure of the mine was necessary on environmental grounds. However, it also emphasized the potentially damaging impact of the mine's early closure on both the local economy and world copper markets. In May BHP, the Australian operator, endorsed the World Bank report and reaffirmed its intention to close the mine. In October 2001 BHP Billiton announced its withdrawal from the Ok Tedi mine and in early 2002 transferred its 52% stake to a development fund called the PNG Sustainable Development Programme Ltd.

Government

Executive power is vested in the British monarch (the Head of State), represented locally by the Governor-General, who is appointed on the proposal of the National Executive Council (the Cabinet) in accordance with the decision of the National Parliament by simple majority vote. The Governor-General acts on the advice of the National Executive Council, which is led by the Prime Minister. The Prime Minister is appointed and dismissed by the Head of State on the proposal of the National Parliament. Legislative power is vested in the unicameral National Parliament, with 109 members elected by universal adult suffrage for a term of five years. The National Executive Council is responsible to the National Parliament. The local government system underwent extensive reform in 1995, when the 19 directly-elected provincial governments were replaced by new regional authorities, composed of members of the National Parliament and local councillors, and led by an appointed Governor. The National Capital District has its own governing body.

Defence

In August 2002 Papua New Guinea's national Defence Force numbered an estimated 3,100, comprising an army of 2,500, a navy of 400 and an air force of 200. In addition, 55 foreign troops (including 35 from Australia) were stationed in the country as part of the Bougainville Truce Monitoring Group. Military service is voluntary. Budget estimates for 2002 allocated K54m. to defence.

Economic Affairs

In 2001, according to estimates by the World Bank, Papua New Guinea's gross national income (GNI), measured at average 1999–2001 prices, was US $3,026m., equivalent to $580 per head (or $2,150 per head on an international purchasing-power parity basis). During 1990–2001, it was estimated, the population increased at an average annual rate of 2.6%, while gross domestic product (GDP) per head increased, in real terms, by an average of 1.4% per year. Overall GDP increased, in real terms, at an average annual rate of 4.0% in 1990–2001. Real GDP declined by 3.5% in 2001.

Agriculture (including hunting, forestry and fishing) contributed 26.0% of GDP in 2001, and engaged an estimated 73.6% of the labour force in that year. The principal cash crops are coffee (which accounted for 3.1% of export earnings in 2001), cocoa (1.8%), coconuts (for the production of copra and coconut oil), palm oil (which accounted for 4.7% of export earnings in 2001), rubber and tea. Roots and tubers, vegetables, bananas and melons are also grown as food crops. The sale of fishing licences to foreign fleets provides a substantial source of revenue, estimated at US $15m. in 1998. In the late 1990s Papua New Guinea was one of the world's largest exporters of unprocessed tropical timber. In 1999, however, low prices for tropical hardwoods on the international market, together with the Asian financial crisis, led to a contraction in the industry. Exports of logs accounted for 5.1% of total export revenue in 2001. An estimated 1.5m. cu m of logs were exported in that year, the lowest volume (and at the lowest prices) for 10 years. However, exports of processed timber products rose by 15% in that year and earned some US $30m. of revenue. There is serious concern about the environmental damage caused by extensive logging activity in the country, much of which is illegal. Concern regarding the unsustainability of the industry increased in 1999, when tax incentives for logging operators resulted in a dramatic increase in production. In late 1999 the Government reinstated higher taxes on logging and introduced a moratorium on all new forestry licences, in an attempt to control logging activity. During 1990–2001 agricultural GDP increased by an average annual rate of 3.1%. The GDP of the agricultural sector contracted by 5.7% in 2001.

Industry (including mining, manufacturing, construction and power) contributed an estimated 42.0% of GDP in 2001. During 1990–2001 industrial GDP increased by an average of 6.6% per year. Industrial GDP decreased by 3.6% in 2001.

Mining and quarrying provided an estimated 27.2% of GDP in 2001 and 77.3% of total export earnings in 2000. Petroleum (which accounted for 30.9% of export revenue in 2001), gold (34.7% in that year) and copper (14.1%) are the major mineral exports. Papua New Guinea also has substantial reserves of natural gas, and deposits of silver, chromite, cobalt, nickel and quartz. Production of petroleum began at the Kutubu oilfield, at a rate of about 150,000 barrels per day, in 1992 (although by early 2000 output had decreased to some 36,000 barrels per day). Production from two new major oilfields (Moran and Gobe), which began in early 1998, was expected to double the volume of exported petroleum. However, production declined by 20.2% in 2000. The Napa Napa facility, the country's largest petroleum refinery, was expected to begin production in late 2003 and to process some 33,000 barrels per day by 2004. In early 2002 plans were concluded for the construction of a gas pipeline to Queensland, Australia, expected to be completed by 2007, in which the Government held a 15% stake. Large gold deposits were discovered at several sites during the 1980s (including the largest known deposit outside South Africa at Lihir, which began operations in mid-1997), and annual gold production subsequently rose at a steady rate, reaching an estimated 74.0 metric tons in 2000 (compared with some 55 tons in 1996). A new medium-sized gold-mining project at Kainantu in the Eastern Highlands was announced in December 2002. Moreover, the important Ramu cobalt-nickel project was launched in February 2003. In 1997 an agreement was signed to allow for the deep-sea mining of gold, silver and zinc deposits. According to Asian Development Bank (ADB) figures, the GDP of the mining sector increased at an average annual rate of 9.0% during 1990–2001. However, the sector's GDP declined by 4.0% in 2000 and by an estimated 9.0% in 2001.

Manufacturing contributed an estimated 8.7% of GDP in 2001, and employed 1.9% of the working population in 1980. Measured by the value of output, the principal branches of manufacturing are food products, beverages, tobacco, wood products, metal products, machinery and transport equipment. Several fish canneries were established in the 1990s and exports of canned tuna were expected to increase significantly, following the signing of a new quota agreement with the European Union (EU) in March 2003. During 1990–2001 manufacturing GDP increased by an average of 3.7% per year. In 2001, however, the sector's GDP contracted for the second consecutive year, declining by almost 8.9%.

Energy is derived principally from hydroelectric power, which is estimated to account for more than 30% of electricity supplies. A diesel power station to be constructed by South Korean interests in Port Moresby in 1999 was expected to supply 30% of the capital's electricity needs.

The services sector contributed an estimated 32.0% of GDP in 2001. Tourism is an expanding sector, although political instability and reports of widespread crime have had a detrimental effect on the industry. During the late 1980s and early 1990s annual foreign tourist arrivals barely exceeded 40,000, but the total increased significantly to 66,143 in 1997 and to 67,465 in 1998, before declining slightly to 67,357 in 1999 and further to 58,448 in 2000. The World Bank estimated that tourism receipts were worth US $104m. in 1999. The GDP of the services sector expanded at an average annual rate of 2.7% in 1990–2001. However, the sector's GDP declined by 6.0% in 2000 and by almost 1.5% in 2001.

In 2001 Papua New Guinea recorded a visible trade surplus of US $880.5m., and a surplus of $282.0m. on the current account of the balance of payments. In that year the principal source of imports (51.3%) was Australia; other major suppliers were Singapore (18.3%) and Japan (4.5%). In 2001 Australia was also the principal market for exports (25.6%), followed by Japan (10.4%), the People's Republic of China (7.3%) and Germany (4.3%). The principal exports in the early 2000s were gold, copper ore and concentrates, petroleum, coffee, cocoa, palm oil and logs. The principal imports were machinery and transport equipment, basic manufactures, food and live animals, miscellaneous manufactured articles, chemicals and mineral fuels.

The budgetary deficit decreased from K249.1m. in 2001 to an estimated K214.5m. in 2002. A deficit of some K200m., equivalent to 2% of GDP, was projected for 2003. Papua New Guinea receives grants for budgetary aid from Australia, and Australian aid was projected at $A351.4m. in 2002/03. Papua New Guinea's external debt totalled US $2,604m. at the end of 2000, of which $1,502m. was long-term public debt. In that year the cost of debt-servicing was equivalent to 13.5% of the value of exports of goods and services. At the end of 2001 the external debt stood at an estimated K4,982.1m., of which K4,822.0m. was owed to various international agencies. The rate of unemployment in 2001 was estimated to be as high as 50% in Port Moresby, while in the rural areas underemployment remained a serious problem. According to the ADB, the annual rate of inflation averaged 9.5% in 1990–2001. Consumer prices increased by 9.3% in 2001.

Papua New Guinea is a member of Asia-Pacific Economic Co-operation (APEC, see p. 139), the ADB (see p. 143), the Colombo Plan (see p. 339), the Pacific Community (see p. 304), the Pacific Islands Forum (see p. 306), the International Cocoa Organization (see p. 336) and the International Coffee Organization (see p. 336).

In recent years Papua New Guinea has remained dependent on aid from Australia and other international donors for its economic development, and in the early 2000s it was estimated that at least 70% of the population were within the subsistence sector of the economy. The country's difficult terrain, vulnerability to extreme climatic conditions (such as droughts and tidal waves) and lack of infrastructure, the limited domestic market and a shortage of skilled workers all impeded industrial development, and an increase in migration from rural areas to urban centres led to a rise in unemployment. Civil unrest on Bougainville also adversely affected the economy. Strong economic growth in the early 1990s was attributed largely to the success of the new Porgera gold-mine and an increase in petroleum production at the Kutubu oilfield. However, the country's petroleum resources were expected to be exhausted by 2010, and the Porgera operation planned to cease mining activity by 2007. Financial problems in the late 1990s, caused partly by a dramatic decrease in the value of the kina, prompted the Government to reduce public expenditure and to announce plans for the reduction of the public-service sector by some 7,000 employees. Growing ethnic and environmental problems, widespread crime and concern over foreign exploitation also continued to threaten Papua New Guinea's prospects for long-term economic success. A 'recovery' budget for 2000 included the privatization of government assets, the proceeds of which were to be used to repay a proportion of the national debt. A joint funding programme, valued at US $500m., was agreed upon by the IMF and the World Bank to assist the Government in the implementation of the economic reforms. Australia pledged a total of US $1,000m. in programme aid over a period of three years. Almost 1,500 public servants were made redundant in late 2000, as part of ongoing government retrenchment measures. The IMF commended the Government for its structural reform policies; however, the organization expressed concern in early 2001 over the continued high incidence of official corruption in the country, and in February the World Bank resident representative (who had been monitoring the implementation of structural economic reforms) was deported for allegedly interfering in domestic politics. Papua New Guinea received exceptional financing of US $91m. in December 2001 from the World Bank, the ADB and the Japan Bank for International Cooperation. In late 2001 the controversial sale of the Papua New Guinea Banking Corporation to the locally-owned Bank of South Pacific was concluded, thus generating revenue of some K155m. It was envisaged that the 2002 budget deficit would be largely financed by revenue from the partial privatization of state assets, including Air Niugini, Telikom, Elcom and the Harbours Board, to offset disappointing tax revenues and increasing external financing. The value of the kina, meanwhile, continued to decline during 2001, losing almost 20% against the US dollar between January and December. In April 2002 the Prime Minister announced that, as part of the public-sector reform programme, more than 3,000 civil servants were to be made redundant by the end of the year. However, the Government suffered a conclusive defeat at a general election in June, and the newly elected Prime Minister, Sir Michael Somare, announced that one of his Government's most urgent priorities was the immediate cessation of the World Bank-endorsed privatization programme. A marked increase in the country's debt, as well as a continued decline in the value of the kina (which fell by some 10% between October and November) resulted in serious financial difficulties for the new Government, particularly when a request to the Australian Government to help restructure US $180m. of debt was refused. Expenditure in the 2003 budget was significantly reduced in an attempt to control the growing deficit, although a large proportion of this was allocated to major infrastructure projects, such as the Highlands Highway (which, it was hoped, would stimulate the economy, particularly the agricultural sector). Despite the success of Papua New Guinea's agricultural exports (notably coffee, cocoa and palm oil) in 2002, owing to high commodity prices and the low value of the kina, it seemed likely that additional revenue would need to be raised in 2003 through a resumption of the asset sales programme.

Education

Education is not compulsory. Primary education, available at community schools, begins at seven years of age and lasts for six years. Secondary education, beginning at the age of 13, lasts for up to six years (comprising two cycles, the first of four years, the second two). Originally, schooling was free; fees and charges for equipment were introduced, although the 2002 budget provided for the reinstatement of free education. In 1995 the total enrolment at primary schools was equivalent to 80% of children in the relevant age-group (87% of boys; 74% of girls). In the same year total secondary enrolment was equivalent to 14% of children in the relevant age-group (boys 17%; girls 11%). Tertiary education is provided by the University of Papua New Guinea and the University of Technology. There are also teacher-training colleges and higher institutions, which cater for specific professional training. Budget estimates for 2002 allocated K150.0m. to education.

Public Holidays

2003: 1 January (New Year's Day), 18–21 April (Easter), 9 June (Queen's Official Birthday), 18 July (Provincial Government Day), 23 July (Remembrance Day), 16 September (Independence Day and Constitution Day), 25 December (Christmas Day), 26 December (Boxing Day).

2004: 1 January (New Year's Day), 9–12 April (Easter), 8 June (Queen's Official Birthday), 18 July (Provincial Government Day), 23 July (Remembrance Day), 16 September (Independence Day and Constitution Day), 25 December (Christmas Day), 26 December (Boxing Day).

Weights and Measures

The metric system is in force.

Statistical Survey

Source (unless otherwise stated): Papua New Guinea National Statistical Office, Post Office, Wards Strip, Waigani, NCD; tel. 3011229; fax 3251869; e-mail nsuvulo@nso.gov.pg; internet nso.gov.pg.

Area and Population

AREA, POPULATION AND DENSITY

Area (sq km)	462,840*
Population (census results)	
11 July 1990†	3,607,954
9 July 2000	
Males	2,661,091
Females.	2,469,274
Total	5,130,365
Density (per sq km) at July 2000	11.1

* 178,704 sq miles.

† Excluding North Solomons Province (estimated population 154,000).

PRINCIPAL TOWNS
(census of 9 July 2000)

Port Moresby			
(capital). . . .	254,158	Mount Hagen. . .	27,782
Lae.	78,038	Madang	27,394
Arawa	36,443	Kokopo/Vunamami .	20,262

Source: Thomas Brinkhoff, *City Population* (internet www.citypopulation.de).

BIRTHS AND DEATHS (1996 estimates): Birth rate 32.6 per 1,000; Death rate 10.1 per 1,000

Expectation of life (WHO estimates, years at birth): 59.8 (males 58.4; females 61.3) in 2001 (Source: WHO, *World Health Report*).

ECONOMICALLY ACTIVE POPULATION*
(estimates based on 1980 census results)

Agriculture, hunting, forestry and fishing†	564,500
Mining and quarrying	4,300
Manufacturing	14,000
Electricity, gas and water	2,800
Construction	21,600
Trade, restaurants and hotels	25,100
Transport, storage and communications	17,400
Financing, insurance, real estate and business services .	4,500
Community, social and personal services	77,100
Others (incl. activities not stated or not adequately	
described)	1,500
Total labour force †	732,800

* Figures refer to citizens of Papua New Guinea only.

† Excluding persons solely engaged in subsistence agriculture, hunting, forestry and fishing.

1990 census (citizens aged 10 years and over, excl. North Solomons Province): Total employed 1,582,518 (Agriculture, hunting, forestry and fishing 1,269,744); Unemployed 132,812; Total labour force 1,715,330 (males 1,002,891, females 712,439).

Mid-2001 (estimates in '000): Agriculture, etc. 1,745; Total 2,372 (Source: FAO).

Health and Welfare

KEY INDICATORS

Total fertility rate (children per woman, 2001). . . .	4.4
Under-5 mortality rate (per 1,000 live births, 2001) . . .	94
HIV/AIDS (% of persons aged 15–49, 2001).	0.65
Physicians (per 1,000 head, 1998)	0.07
Hospital beds (per 1,000 head, 1990)	4.02
Health expenditure (2000): US $ per head (PPP)	147
Health expenditure (2000): % of GDP	4.1
Health expenditure (2000): public (% of total)	88.6
Access to water (% of persons, 1999).	42
Access to sanitation (% of persons, 1999)	82
Human Development Index (2000): ranking	133
Human Development Index (2000): value	0.535

For sources and definitions, see explanatory note on p. vi.

Agriculture

PRINCIPAL CROPS
('000 metric tons)

	1999	2000	2001
Maize*	7	7	7
Sorghum	3†	3†	4*
Sweet potatoes	480†	480†	485*
Cassava (Manioc)*	120	120	120
Yams*	220	230	230
Taro (Coco yam)*.	170	172	172
Other roots and tubers* . . .	270	277	277
Sugar cane*	430	350	367
Pulses*	3	3	3
Coconuts	1,020†	1,032†	1,032*
Oil palm fruit*	1,000	1,030	1,050
Vegetables and melons*. . .	461	474	474
Pineapples*	12	12	12
Bananas*	700	710	710
Other fruit (excl. melons)* . .	502	512	512
Coffee (green).	83	83†	63†
Cocoa beans†	36	47	43
Tea (made)*	10	10	10
Natural rubber (dry weight) . .	7†	7†	7*

* FAO estimate(s).

† Unofficial figure(s).

Source: FAO.

LIVESTOCK
(FAO estimates, '000 head, year ending September)

	1999	2000	2001
Horses	1.8	1.8	2
Cattle	87	87	88
Pigs	1,550	1,550	1,650
Sheep	6.2	6.3	6.5
Goats	2.2	2.3	2.4
Chickens	3,600	3,700	3,700

Source: FAO.

LIVESTOCK PRODUCTS
(FAO estimates, '000 metric tons)

	1999	2000	2001
Beef and veal	3	3	3
Pig meat	44	44	47
Poultry meat	5	5	5
Other meat	19	19	19
Poultry eggs	4	5	5

Source: FAO.

Forestry

ROUNDWOOD REMOVALS
('000 cubic metres, excluding bark)

	1998	1999	2001
Sawlogs, veneer logs and logs for sleepers	3,064	3,064	3,064
Fuel wood	5,533	5,533	5,533
Total	8,597	8,597	8,597

Source: FAO.

SAWNWOOD PRODUCTION
(estimates, '000 cubic metres, including railway sleepers)

	1999	2000	2001
Coniferous (softwood)	43	43	43
Broadleaved (hardwood)	175	175	175
Total	218	218	218

Source: FAO.

Fishing

('000 metric tons, live weight)

	1998	1999	2000
Capture*	71.3	59.7	50.5
Mozambique tilapia*	2.3	2.3	2.3
Other freshwater fishes*	6.7	6.7	6.7
Sea catfishes*	1.9	1.9	1.9
Skipjack tuna	31.9	24.0	15.9
Yellowfin tuna	9.7	7.4	5.4
Aquaculture*	0.0	0.0	0.0
Total catch *	71.3	59.7	50.6

* FAO estimates.

Source: FAO, *Yearbook of Fishery Statistics*.

Mining

	1998	1999	2000†
Petroleum, crude('000 barrels)	29,479	32,020	33,000
Copper ('000 metric tons)*	152.2	187.9	200.9
Silver (metric tons)*	59.2	66.5	73.2
Gold (metric tons)*	61.6	65.7	74.3

* Figures refer to metal content of ore.
† Preliminary figures.

Source: US Geological Survey.

Industry

SELECTED PRODUCTS

	1999	2000	2001
Palm oil ('000 metric tons)*	326	365	355
Raw sugar ('000 metric tons)*	52	42	44

* Unofficial figures.

Beer ('000 litres): 39,029 in 1997; 34,826 in 1998.

Electric energy (estimates, million kWh): 1,795 in 1997.

Sources: FAO, *Production Yearbook*; UN, *Industrial Commodity Statistics Yearbook*; and Papua New Guinea National Statistical Office.

Finance

CURRENCY AND EXCHANGE RATES

Monetary Units
100 toea = 1 kina (K)

Sterling, Dollar and Euro Equivalents (31 December 2002)
£1 sterling = 6.478 kina
US $1 = 4.019 kina
€1 = 4.215 kina
100 kina = £15.44 = $24.88 = €23.72

Average Exchange Rate (US $ per kina)
2000   0.3617
2001   0.2964
2002   0.2573

Note: The foregoing information refers to the mid-point exchange rate of the central bank. In October 1994 it was announced that the kina would be allowed to 'float' on foreign exchange markets.

BUDGET
(million kina)*

Revenue†	1999	2000‡	2001‡
Taxation	1,662	1,917	2,476
Taxes on income, profits,etc.	818	910	1,342
Individual	524	565	650
Corporate	293	345	692
Excises	171	169	185
Taxes on international trade and transactions	551	666	771
Import duties	472	542	636
Export duties	79	124	135
Non-tax revenue	1,148	600	383
Entrepreneurial and property income	1,066	483	111
Total	2,810	2,517	2,859

Expenditure§	1997	1998	1999
Recurrent expenditure	1,768	1,895	2,020
National and statutory	941	994	1,091
National	820	858	970
Salaries and wages	367	384	393
Goods and services	453	475	428
Statutory authorities	120	136	121
Provincial departments	530	566	537
Salaries and wages	288	307	384
Goods and services	73	125	89
Conditional grants	169	135	65
Interest payments	298	335	393
Domestic	206	228	261
External	91	107	132
Development expenditure	428	596	786
National and statutory	318	495	698
Provinces	110	101	88
Total	2,196	2,491	2,806

* Figures refer to the operations of the General Budget and of superannuation and retirement funds. The transactions of other central government units with individual budgets are excluded.
† Excluding grants received from abroad (million kina): 477 in 1999; 555 (estimate) in 2000; 551 (estimate) in 2001.
‡ Estimate(s).
§ Excluding net lending (million kina): –3 in 1997; –5 in 1998; –5 in 1999.

Source: partly IMF, *Papua New Guinea: Recent Economic Developments* (October 2000).

2000 (million kina): *Expenditure:* Recurrent expenditure 2,218.6 (Salaries and wages 836.3; Goods and services 760.4; Interest payments 428.6); Development expenditure 904.7; Total 3,123.3 (Source: IMF, *Papua New Guinea: Recent Economic Developments* (October 2001)).

INTERNATIONAL RESERVES
(US $ million at 31 December)

	2000	2001	2002
Gold (national valuation)	9.08	7.42	19.69
IMF special drawing rights	12.17	8.71	6.06
Reserve position in IMF	0.23	0.38	0.49
Foreign exchange	274.45	413.56	323.30
Total	295.95	430.06	349.54

Source: IMF, *International Financial Statistics*.

MONEY SUPPLY
(million kina at 31 December)

	2000	2001	2002
Currency outside banks . . .	306.93	308.98	379.94
Demand deposits at deposit money banks	1,061.86	1,104.17	1,256.39
Total money (incl. others) . . .	1,372.69	1,416.95	1,644.9

Source: IMF, *International Financial Statistics.*

COST OF LIVING
(Consumer Price Index; base: 1977 = 100)

	1998	1999	2000
Food	390.2	456.5	518.5
Clothing	286.1	324.8	375.9
Rent, fuel and power . . .	216.5	225.6	242.2
All items (incl. others) . . .	411.0	472.4	546.1

Source: National Statistical Office, *Statistical Digest 2000.*

2001 (base: 2000 = 100): All items 109.3 (Source: IMF, *International Financial Statistics*).

NATIONAL ACCOUNTS
(million kina at current prices)

National Income and Product

	1997	1998	1999
Compensation of employees . .	1,778.3	1,751.6	1,852.4
Operating surplus	3,963.2	4,804.6	5,519.4
Domestic factor incomes . .	5,741.5	6,556.2	7,371.8
Consumption of fixed capital .	535.2	539.6	526.5
Gross domestic product (GDP) at factor cost . . .	6,276.7	7,095.8	7,898.3
Indirect taxes . . . . . . } *Less* Subsidies . . . . . . }	787.0	692.6	882.4
GDP in purchasers' values . .	7,063.7	7,788.5	8,780.8
Net factor income from abroad .	−310.4	−343.3	−360.1
Gross national product . .	6,753.3	7,445.2	8,420.7
Less Consumption of fixed capital*	535.2	539.6	526.5
National income in market prices	6,218.1	6,905.6	7,894.2

Expenditure on the Gross Domestic Product

	1997	1998	1999
Government final consumption expenditure	1,361.3	1,406.6	1,488.3
Private final consumption expenditure	4,118.8	4,619.5	6,122.8
Increase in stocks	408.9	306.7	376.6
Gross fixed capital formation . .	1,079.4	1,088.6	1,062.7
Total domestic expenditure . .	6,968.3	7,421.4	9,050.4
Exports of goods and services . .	3,312.0	3,942.3	4,153.2
Less Imports of goods and services	3,216.5	3,575.1	4,422.8
GDP in purchasers' values . .	7,063.7	7,788.5	8,780.8
GDP at constant 1983 prices .	3,674.6	3,536.1	3,803.5

Sources: National Statistical Office and Bank of Papua New Guinea.

Gross Domestic Product by Economic Activity

	1999	2000*	2001*
Agriculture, hunting, forestry and fishing	2,520.6	2,638.0	2,847.7
Mining and quarrying . . .	2,086.6	2,662.7	2,745.1
Manufacturing	797.6	793.6	857.9
Electricity, gas and water . . .	100.2	113.1	131.8
Construction	364.1	356.5	349.3
Wholesale and retail trade . . .	834.4	833.6	866.1
Transport, storage and communications	429.6	430.9	430.9
Finance, insurance, real estate and business services . . .	89.7†	321.6	358.1
Community, social and personal services (incl. defence) . . .	1,096.1	1,179.9	1,253.4
Sub-total	8,318.9	9,329.9	9,840.3
Import duties	461.9	320.6‡	237.5‡
GDP in purchasers' values . .	8,780.8	9,650.5	10,077.8

* Estimates.
† After deducting imputed bank service charge.
‡ After deducting imputed bank service charge and subsidies.

Source: Asian Development Bank, *Key Indicators of Developing Asian and Pacific Countries.*

BALANCE OF PAYMENTS
(US $ million)

	1999	2000	2001
Exports of goods f.o.b.	1,927.4	2094.1	1812.9
Imports of goods f.o.b.	−1,071.4	-998.8	-932.4
Trade balance	856.0	1095.3	880.5
Exports of services	247.5	242.7	285.1
Imports of services	−727.9	-772.3	-662.0
Balance on goods and services	375.6	565.7	503.7
Other income received	18.6	32.0	20.0
Other income paid	−291.1	-242.1	-250.2
Balance on goods, services and income	103.1	355.6	273.4
Current transfers received . .	60.3	62.4	75.9
Current transfers paid	−68.7	-72.7	-67.3
Current balance	94.7	345.3	282.0
Direct investment from abroad .	296.5	95.9	62.5
Portfolio investment assets . .	89.0	-123.8	-72.7
Other investment assets . . .	10.7	-41.0	-66.9
Other investment liabilities . .	−380.2	-185.2	-74.7
Net errors and omissions . .	14.3	13.1	-1.6
Overall balance	125.0	104.5	128.6

Source: IMF, *International Financial Statistics.*

External Trade

PRINCIPAL COMMODITIES

Imports f.o.b. (US $ million)*	1998	1999	2000
Food and live animals	220.2	128.7	168.6
Meat and meat preparations	44.0	25.4	41.6
Fresh, chilled or frozen meat	40.9	24.2	38.0
Cereals and cereal preparations	105.3	61.1	73.5
Rice	75.0	42.1	46.3
Milled or semi-milled rice	49.1	25.5	39.1
Chemicals and related products	130.5	86.1	71.0
Basic manufactures	275.7	198.0	159.5
Iron and steel	44.1	38.7	31.3
Iron or steel structures and parts	53.1	3.4	3.6
Machinery and transport equipment	529.1	481.9	305.3
Power-generating machinery and equipment	47.8	33.3	18.0
Machinery specialized for particular industries	71.7	82.6	43.0
General industrial machinery and equipment	105.2	58.9	53.9
Electrical machinery, apparatus and appliances, etc.	49.9	39.1	26.6
Road vehicles and parts†	145.1	172.7	119.6
Motor vehicles for goods transport	66.8	79.8	51.5
Other transport equipment and parts†	56.3	38.3	24.4
Miscellaneous manufactured articles	111.9	87.6	64.2
Total (incl. others)	1,360.1	1,086.4	1,035.1

* Figures include migrants' and travellers' dutiable effects, but exclude military equipment and some parcel post.
† Data on parts exclude tyres, engines and electrical parts.

Source: UN, *International Trade Statistics Yearbook*.

Exports f.o.b. (million kina)	1999	2000	2001
Coffee	417	295	189
Logs	266	309	310
Copper	574	595	859
Petroleum	1,382	1,922	1,884
Palm oil	338	307	289
Gold	1,546	1,951	2,115
Cocoa	85	85	110
Total (incl. others)	5,006	5,813	6,093

Source: Asian Development Bank, *Key Indicators of Developing Asian and Pacific Countries*.

PRINCIPAL TRADING PARTNERS
(US $ million)

Imports f.o.b. (excl. gold)	1999	2000	2001
Australia	607.7	553.2	543.1
China, People's Republic	29.2	24.9	24.6
Hong Kong	15.7	13.8	9.6
Indonesia	33.4	33.5	33.4
Japan	63.6	45.0	48.0
Malaysia	41.0	38.0	30.7
New Zealand	47.1	42.8	40.9
Singapore	146.4	221.9	193.5
Thailand	20.0	19.3	–
USA	41.0	24.0	22.3
Total (incl. others)	1,143.5	1,113.4	1,058.0

Exports f.o.b. (excl. gold)	1999	2000	2001
Australia	733.8	843.3	711.0
China, People's Repub.	77.7	182.5	203.9
Germany	185.4	116.7	120.2
Indonesia	69.8	76.7	–
Japan	324.9	317.3	287.5
Korea, Repub.	132.0	106.8	78.4
Philippines	52.7	17.2	29.2
United Kingdom	96.6	77.6	51.7
USA	127.5	35.5	39.5
Total (incl. others)	2,792.0	2,820.3	2,777.1

Source: Asian Development Bank, *Key Indicators of Developing Asian and Pacific Countries*.

Transport

ROAD TRAFFIC
(licensed vehicles)

	1986	1987	1988
Cars and station wagons	16,574	17,121	17,532
Commercial vehicles	26,989	26,061	29,021
Motorcycles	1,246	1,232	1,204
Tractors	1,287	1,313	1,414

1996 (estimates): Passenger cars 31,000; Lorries and vans 85,000.
Source: IRF, *World Road Statistics*.

SHIPPING

Merchant Fleet
(registered at 31 December)

	1999	2000	2001
Number of vessels	105	112	114
Total displacement ('000 grt)	64.8	72.5	77.0

Source: Lloyd's Register-Fairplay, *World Fleet Statistics*.

International Sea-borne Freight Traffic

	1997	1998	1999
Cargo unloaded ('000 metric tons)	2,208.6	2,209.0	2,062.8
Cargo loaded ('000 metric tons)	735.9	823.3	788.1

Source: Papua New Guinea Harbours Board, *Monthly Shipping Register Form*.

CIVIL AVIATION
(traffic on scheduled services)

	1997	1998	1999
Kilometres flown (million)	15	15	12
Passengers carried ('000)	1,114	1,110	1,102
Passenger-km (million)	735	736	641
Total ton-km (million)	86	87	80

Source: UN, *Statistical Yearbook*.

Tourism

FOREIGN TOURIST ARRIVALS

Country of origin	1998	1999	2000
Australia	35,403	33,818	29,285
Canada	912	923	1,762
Japan	1,834	2,427	3,244
New Zealand	3,661	3,712	2,648
United Kingdom	3,087	3,067	2,279
USA	6,101	5,619	5,429
Total (incl. others)	67,465	67,357	58,448

Source: World Tourism Organization, *Yearbook of Tourism Statistics*.

Receipts from tourism (US $ million): 75 in 1998; 76 in 1999 (Source: World Tourism Organization).

Communications Media

	1998	1999	2000
Television receivers ('000 in use)	20	60	80
Telephones ('000 main lines in use)	56.9	59.8	64.8
Mobile cellular telephones ('000 subscribers).	5.6	7.1	8.6
Internet users ('000).	n.a.	2.0	135.0

Daily newspapers (1996): 2 (combined circulation 65,000 copies).

Radio receivers (1997): 410,000 in use.

Facsimile machines (1994): 795 in use.

Personal computers (estimate, 2001): 300,000 in use.

Sources: UNESCO, *Statistical Yearbook*; International Telecommunication Union.

Education

(1999, unless otherwise indicated)

	Institutions*	Teachers	Students
Pre-primary	29	3,816	119,147
Primary	2,790	16,297	594,444
Secondary	n.a.	3,046	74,042
Tertiary	n.a.	815	13,761

* 1995 figures.

Sources: National Department of Education, *The state of education in PNG* (March 2001); UNESCO, *Statistical Yearbook*.

Adult literacy rate (UNESCO estimates): 63.9% (males 70.6%; females 56.8%) in 2000 (Source: UN Development Programme, *Human Development Report*).

Directory

The Constitution

The present Constitution came into effect on 16 September 1975, when Papua New Guinea became independent. The main provisions of the Constitution are summarized below:

PREAMBLE

The national goals of the Independent State of Papua New Guinea are: integral human development, equality and participation in the development of the country, national sovereignty and self-reliance, conservation of natural resources and the environment and development primarily through the use of Papua New Guinean forms of social, political and economic organization.

BASIC HUMAN RIGHTS

All people are entitled to the fundamental rights and freedoms of the individual whatever their race, tribe, place of origin, political opinion, colour, creed or sex. The individual's rights include the right to freedom, life and the protection of the law, freedom from inhuman treatment, forced labour, arbitrary search and entry, freedom of conscience, thought, religion, expression, assembly, association and employment, and the right to privacy. Papua New Guinea citizens also have the following special rights: the right to vote and stand for public office, the right to freedom of information and of movement, protection from unjust deprivation of property and equality before the law.

THE NATION

Papua New Guinea is a sovereign, independent state. There is a National Capital District which shall be the seat of government.

The Constitution provides for various classes of citizenship. The age of majority is 19 years.

HEAD OF STATE

Her Majesty the Queen of the United Kingdom of Great Britain and Northern Ireland is Queen and Head of State of Papua New Guinea. The Head of State appoints and dismisses the Prime Minister on the proposal of the National Parliament and other ministers on the proposal of the Prime Minister. The Governor-General and Chief Justice are appointed and dismissed on the proposal of the National Executive Council. All the privileges, powers, functions, duties and responsibilities of the Head of State may be exercised or performed through the Governor-General.

Governor-General

The Governor-General must be a citizen who is qualified to be a member of Parliament or who is a mature person of good standing who enjoys the respect of the community. No one is eligible for appointment more than once unless Parliament approves by a two-thirds majority. No one is eligible for a third term. The Governor-General is appointed by the Head of State on the proposal of the National Executive Council in accordance with the decision of Parliament by simple majority vote. He may be dismissed by the Head of State on the proposal of the National Executive Council in accordance with a decision of the Council or of an absolute majority of Parliament. The normal term of office is six years. In the case of temporary or permanent absence, dismissal or suspension he may be replaced temporarily by the Speaker of the National Parliament until such time as a new Governor-General is appointed.

THE GOVERNMENT

The Government comprises the National Parliament, the National Executive and the National Judicial System.

National Parliament

The National Parliament, or the House of Assembly, is a single-chamber legislature of members elected from single-member open or provincial electorates. The National Parliament has 109 members elected by universal adult suffrage. The normal term of office is five years. There is a Speaker and a Deputy Speaker, who must be members of Parliament and must be elected to these posts by Parliament. They cannot serve as government ministers concurrently.

National Executive

The National Executive comprises the Head of State and the National Executive Council. The Prime Minister, who presides over the National Executive Council, is appointed and dismissed by the Head of State on the proposal of Parliament. The other ministers, of whom there shall be not fewer than six nor more than a quarter of the number of members of the Parliament, are appointed and dismissed by the Head of State on the proposal of the Prime Minister. The National Executive Council consists of all the ministers, including the Prime Minister, and is responsible for the executive government of Papua New Guinea.

National Judicial System

The National Judicial System comprises the Supreme Court, the National Court, Local Courts and Village Courts. The judiciary is independent.

The Supreme Court consists of the Chief Justice, the Deputy Chief Justice and the other judges of the National Court. It is the final court of appeal. The Chief Justice is appointed and dismissed by the Head of State on the proposal of the National Executive Council after consultation with the minister responsible for justice. The Deputy Chief Justice and the other judges are appointed by the Judicial and Legal Services Commission. The National Court consists of the Chief Justice, the Deputy Chief Justice and no fewer than four nor more than six other judges.

The Constitution also makes provision for the establishment of the Magisterial Service and the establishment of the posts of Public Prosecutor and the Public Solicitor.

THE STATE SERVICES

The Constitution establishes the following State Services which, with the exception of the Defence Force, are subject to ultimate civilian control.

National Public Service

The Public Service is managed by the Department of Personnel Management which is headed by a Secretary, who is appointed by the National Executive Council on a four-year contract.

Police Force

The Police Force is subject to the control of the National Executive Council through a minister and its function is to preserve peace and good order and to maintain and enforce the law.

Papua New Guinea Defence Force

The Defence Force is subject to the superintendence and control of the National Executive Council through the Minister of Defence. The functions of the Defence Force are to defend Papua New Guinea, to provide assistance to civilian authorities in a civil disaster, in the restoration of public order or during a period of declared national emergency.

The fourth State Service is the Parliamentary Service.

The Constitution also includes sections on Public Finance, the office of the Auditor-General, the Public Accounts Commission and the declaration of a State of National Emergency.

The Government

Head of State: HM Queen ELIZABETH II.

Governor-General: Sir SILAS ATOPARE (appointed 14 November 1997).

NATIONAL EXECUTIVE COUNCIL
(April 2003)

Prime Minister: Sir MICHAEL SOMARE.

Deputy Prime Minister and Minister for Trade and Industry: Dr ALLAN MARAT.

Minister for Agriculture and Livestock: MOSES MALADINA.

Minister for Communications and Information: BEN SEMRI.

Minister for Correctional and Institutional Services: PETER ORESI.

Minister for Culture and Tourism: (vacant).

Minister for Defence: YARKA KAPPA.

Minister for Education, Science and Technology: MICHAEL LAIMO.

Minister for Environment and Conservation: SASA ZIBE.

Minister for Finance and Treasury: BART PHILEMON.

Minister for Fisheries: ANDREW BAING.

Minister for Foreign Affairs and Immigration: Sir RABBIE NAMALIU.

Minister for Forestry: PATRICK PRUAITCH.

Minister for Health: MELCHIOR PEP.

Minister for Housing and Urban Resettlement: YUNTUVI BAO.

Minister for Inter-Government Relations: Sir PETER BARTER.

Minister for Internal Security: YAWA SILUPA.

Minister for Justice: MARK MAIPAKAI.

Minister for Labour and Industrial Relations: PETER O'NEILL.

Minister for Lands and Physical Planning: ROBERT KOPAOL.

Minister for Mining: SAM AKOITAI.

Minister for National Planning and Monitoring: SINAI BROWN.

Minister for Petroleum and Energy: Sir MOI AVEI.

Minister for Privatization: VINCENT AUALI.

Minister for Public Services: Dr PUKA TEMU.

Minister for Science and Technology: ALPHONESE MOROI.

Minister for Transport and Civil Aviation: DON POLYE.

Minister for Welfare and Social Development: Lady CAROL KIDU.

Minister for Works: GABRIEL KAPRIS.

GOVERNMENT DEPARTMENTS AND OFFICES

Office of the Prime Minister: POB 639, Waigani, NCD; tel. 3276544; fax 3277380; e-mail primeminister@pm.gov.pg; internet www.pm.gov.pg/pmsoffice/PMsoffice.nsf.

Department of Agriculture and Livestock: Spring Garden Rd, POB 417, Konedobu 125, NCD; tel. 3231848; fax 3230563; internet www.agriculture.gov.pg.

Department of the Attorney-General: POB 591, Waigani, NCD; tel. 3230138; fax 3230241.

Department of Commerce and Industry: Central Government Offices, Kumul Ave, Post Office, Wards Strip, Waigani, NCD; tel. 3271115; fax 3271750.

Department of Corrective Institution Services: POB 6889, Boroko, NCD; tel. 3214917; fax 3217686.

Department of Defence: Murray Barracks, Free Mail Bag, Boroko 111, NCD; tel. 3242480; fax 3256117; internet www.defence.gov.pg.

Department of Education: POB 446, Waigani, NCD 131, Fin Corp Haus; tel. 3013555; fax 3254648; internet www.education.gov.pg.

Department of Environment and Conservation: POB 6601, Boroko 111, Kamul Ave, Waigani, NCD; tel. 3011607; fax 3011691.

Department of Family and Church Affairs: Ori Lavi Haus, Nita St, POB 7354, Boroko, NCD; tel. 3254566; fax 3251230; internet ww3.datec.com.pg/government/famchurch/default.htm.

Department of Finance and Treasury: POB 710, Waigani, Vulupindi Haus, NCD; internet www.treasury.gov.pg.

Department of Fisheries and Marine Resources: POB 2016, Port Moresby; tel. 3271799; fax 3202074; internet www.fisheries.gov.pg.

Department of Foreign Affairs: Central Government Offices, Kumul Ave, Post Office, Wards Strip, Waigani, NCD; tel. 3271311; fax 3254467.

Department of Health: POB 3991, Boroko, Aopi Centre, Waigani Drive, Waigani; tel. 3254648; fax 3013555; internet www.health.gov.pg.

Department of Housing and Urban Resettlement: POB 1550, Boroko, NCD; tel. 3247200; fax 3259918.

Department of Inter-Government Relations: Somare Haus, Independence Drive, Waigani, POB 1287, Boroko, NCD; tel. 3011002; fax 3250553; e-mail paffairs@dalton.com.pg; internet www.dplga.gov.pg.

Department of Justice: Port Moresby; internet www.justice.gov.pg.

Department of Labour and Employment: POB 5644, Boroko, NCD; tel. 3272262; fax 3257092.

Department of Lands and Physical Planning: POB 233, Boroko, NCD; tel. 3013175; fax 3013299; e-mail lubena@lands.gov.pg; internet www.datec.com.pg/government/lands.

Department of Mineral Resources: PMB PO, Konedobu, Port Moresby 121; tel. 3227600; fax 3213701; internet www.mineral.gov.pg.

Department of Mining: Private Mailbag, Port Moresby Post Office; tel. 3227670; fax 3213958.

Department of Personnel Management: POB 519, Wards Strip, Waigani, NCD; tel. 3276422; fax 3250520; e-mail perrtsiamalili@dpm.gov.pg.

Department of Petroleum and Energy: POB 1993, Port Moresby, NCD; tel. 3224200; fax 3224222; e-mail joseph_gabut@petroleum.gov.pg; internet www.petroleum.gov.pg.

Department of Planning and Implementation: POB 710, Waigani 131, Vulupindi Haus, Port Moresby, NCD; tel. 3288302; fax 3288375.

Department of Police: Police Headquarters, POB 85, Konedobu, NCD; tel. 3226100; fax 3226113; internet www.police.gov.pg.

Department of Private Enterprise: Central Government Offices, Kumul Ave, Post Office, Wards Strip, Waigani, NCD.

Department of Social Welfare and Development, Youth and Women: Maori Kiki Bldg, 2nd Floor, POB 7354, Boroko, NCD; tel. 3254967; fax 3213821.

Department of State: Haus To Makala, 5th Floor, Post Office, Wards Strip, Waigani, NCD; tel. 3276758; fax 3214861.

Department of Trade and Industry: Heduru Haus, Waigani Drive, POB 375, Waigani 131, NCD; tel. 3255311; fax 3254482; internet www.trade.gov.pg.

Department of Transport and Civil Aviation: POB 1489, Port Moresby; tel. 3222580; fax 3200236; e-mail dotdirectro@datec.com.pg.

National Forest Authority: POB 5055, Boroko, Frangipani St, Hohola, Port Moresby; tel. 3277800; fax 3254433; internet ww3.datec.com.pg/government/forest/default.htm.

Office of Peace and Reconstruction (fmrly Office of Bougainville Affairs): Morauta Haus, POB 343, Waigani 131, NCD; tel. 3276760; fax 3258038; internet www.oba.gov.pg.

Office of Civil Aviation: POB 684, Boroko 111, NCD; tel. 3257077; fax 3251919; e-mail dgoca@datec.net.pg; internet www.oca.gov.pg.

Office of Information and Communication: Port Moresby; internet www.communication.gov.pg.

Office of Works: POB 1489, Port Moresby 121, cnr Champion Parade and Musgrave St; tel. 3222500; fax 3200236; internet www.works.gov.pg.

Legislature

NATIONAL PARLIAMENT

The unicameral legislature has 109 elective seats: 89 representing open constituencies and 20 representing provincial constituencies. There is constitutional provision for up to three nominated members.

Speaker: BILL SKATE.

General Election, 15 June–29 July 2002

Party	Seats
National Alliance	19
People's Democratic Movement	12
People's Progress Party	8
Pangu Pati	6
People's Action Party	5
People's Labour Party	4
Christian Democratic Party	3
Melanesian Alliance	3
National Party	3
United Party	3
National Transformation Party	2
Pan-Melanesian Congress Party	2
People's National Congress	2
People's Solidarity Party	2
Pipol First Party	2
Rural Pipol's Pati	2
Others and undeclared	14
Independents	17
Total	**109**

Note: In many cases party affiliations were subject to review in the immediate aftermath of the election.

Autonomous Region

BOUGAINVILLE INTERIM PROVINCIAL GOVERNMENT—BIPG

The BIPG was formally established following the signing of the 'Loloata Understanding' on 23 March 2000, and is responsible for the island's budget, judicial system and local administration. It is composed of an Executive Council and a 25-member Provincial Assembly, which was appointed by the National Executive Council on the recommendation of the four Bougainville Members of Parliament (who themselves joined the Assembly).

BOUGAINVILLE PEOPLE'S CONGRESS

Prior to the establishment of the BIPG, the Bougainville People's Congress (BPC) officially represented the island of Bougainville. Elections to the Congress were held over several days starting on 3 May 1999. Joseph Kabui was elected President, winning 77 of the 87 votes. A Congressional Executive Council, comprising 29 members, was subsequently appointed by Kabui. Although the BPC unanimously endorsed the 'Loloata Understanding', it did not actively participate in the newly-established BIPG.

President: JOSEPH KABUI.

Vice-President: JAMES TANIS.

Speaker: LINUS KONUKONG.

Political Organizations

Bougainville Revolutionary Army (BRA): demands full independence for island of Bougainville; Leaders FRANCIS ONA, ISMAEL TOROAMA.

League for National Advancement (LNA): POB 6101, Boroko, NCD; f. 1986; Leader JOHN NILKARE.

Melanesian Labour Party: Port Moresby; Leader PAUL MONDIA.

Melanesian United Front: Boroko, NCD; f. 1988; fmrly Morobe Independent Group; Leader UTULA SAMANA.

National Alliance Party: c/o National Parliament, Port Moresby; f. 1996 to combat corruption in public life; Leader Sir MICHAEL SOMARE.

National Party (NP): Private Bag, Boroko, NCD; f. 1979; fmrly People's United Front; Leader MICHAEL MEL.

Pangu (Papua New Guinea Unity) Pati: POB 289, Waigani, NCD; tel. 3277628; fax 3277611; f. 1968; urban and rural-based; Leader CHRIS HAIVETA.

People's Action Party (PAP): Boroko, NCD; tel. 3251343; f. 1985; Leader TED DIRO.

People's Democratic Movement (PDM): POB 972, Boroko, NCD; f. 1985; merged with Advance PNG Party in 2001; Leader Sir MEKERE MORAUTA.

People's National Alliance (PNA): c/o National Parliament, Port Moresby; f. 1999 by merger of following:

   Melanesian Alliance (MA): Port Moresby; tel. 3277635; f. 1978; socialist; Chair. Fr JOHN MOMIS; Gen. Sec. FABIAN WAU KAWA.

   Movement for Greater Autonomy: Manus Province; Leader STEPHEN POKAWIN.

   People's National Party: Port Moresby.

People's National Congress (PNC): c/o National Parliament, Port Moresby; Leader BILL SKATE.

People's Progress Party (PPP): POB 6030, Boroko, NCD; f. 1970; Leader MICHAEL NALI; Nat. Chair. GLEN KUNDIN.

People's Unity Party: c/o National Parliament, Port Moresby; Leader ALFRED KAIABE.

United Resource Party (URP): Port Moresby; f. 1997; aims to secure greater representation in Government for resource owners; Leader MASKET IANGALIO; Chair. PITA IPATAS.

Diplomatic Representation

EMBASSIES AND HIGH COMMISSIONS IN PAPUA NEW GUINEA

Australia: POB 129, Waigani, NCD; tel. 3259333; fax 3259183; High Commissioner NICK WARNER.

China, People's Republic: POB 1351, Boroko, NCD; tel. 3259836; fax 3258247; e-mail chnempng@daltron.com.pg; Ambassador ZHAO ZHENYU.

Fiji: Defence House, 4th Floor, Champion Parade, Port Moresby, NCD; tel. 3211914; fax 3217220; e-mail ert_rakai@yahoo.co,uk; High Commissioner RATU INOKE KUBUABOLA.

France: Pacific Place, 12th Floor, Musgrave St, POB 1155, Port Moresby; tel. 3215550; fax 3215549; e-mail ambfrpom@global.net.pg; Ambassador THIERRY BERNADAC.

Holy See: POB 98, Port Moresby; tel. 3256021; fax 3252844; e-mail nunciaturepng@datec.net.pg; Apostolic Nuncio Archbishop ADOLFO TITO YLLANA.

India: Port Moresby; tel. 3254757; fax 3253138; e-mail hcipom@datec.net.pg; High Commissioner BASANT K. GUPTA.

Indonesia: 1-2/410 Kiroki St, Sir John Guise Dr., Waigani, NCD; tel. 3253116; fax 3253544; e-mail kbripom@daltron.com.pg; Ambassador (vacant).

Japan: Cuthbertson House, Cuthbertson St, POB 1040, Port Moresby; tel. 3211800; fax 3217906; Ambassador (vacant).

Korea, Republic: Pacific View Apts, Lot 1, sec. 84, Pruth St, Korobosea, Port Moresby; tel. 3254755; fax 3259996; Ambassador Dr SEO HYUN-SEOP.

Malaysia: POB 1400, Pacific View Apts, Units 1 and 3, 2nd floor, Pruth St, Kovobosea, Port Moresby; tel. 3252076; fax 3252784; e-mail mwpom@datec.com.pg; High Commissioner MOHAMAD FADZIL AYOB.

New Zealand: Embassy Drive, POB 1051, Waigani, NCD; tel. 3259444; fax 3250565; e-mail nzhcpom@dg.com.pg; High Commissioner LAURIE MARKES.

Philippines: POB 5916, Boroko, NCD; tel. 3256577; fax 3231803; e-mail pomphpem@datec.com.pg; Ambassador BIENVENIDO TEJANO.

Solomon Islands: Port Moresby; High Commissioner PHILIP KAPINI.

United Kingdom: Kiroki St, POB 212, Waigani 131, NCD; tel. 3251677; fax 3253467; e-mail bhcpng@datec.com.pg; High Commissioner SIMON SCADDAN.

USA: Douglas St, POB 1492, Port Moresby; tel. 3211455; fax 3213423; internet www.altnews.com.au/usembassy; Ambassador-designate ROBERT FITTS.

Judicial System

The Supreme Court is the highest judicial authority in the country, and deals with all matters involving the interpretation of the Constitution, and with appeals from the National Court. The National Court has unlimited jurisdiction in both civil and criminal matters. All National Court Judges (except acting Judges) are Judges of the

Supreme Court. District Courts are responsible for civil cases involving compensation, for some indictable offences and for the more serious summary offences, while Local Courts deal with minor offences and with such matters as custody of children under the provision of Custom. There are also Children's Courts, which judge cases involving minors. Appeal from the District, Local and Children's Courts lies to the National Court. District and Local Land Courts deal with disputes relating to Customary land, and Warden's Courts with civil cases relating to mining. In addition, there are other courts with responsibility for determining ownership of government land and for assessing the right of Customary landowners to compensation. Village Courts, which are presided over by Magistrates with no formal legal qualification, are responsible for all Customary matters not dealt with by other courts.

Supreme Court of Papua New Guinea
POB 7018, Boroko, NCD; tel. 3245700; fax 3234492.

Chief Justice Sir MARI KAPI.

Attorney-General: MICHAEL GENE.

Religion

The belief in magic or sorcery is widespread, even among the significant proportion of the population that has adopted Christianity (nominally 97% in 1990). Pantheism also survives. There are many missionary societies.

CHRISTIANITY

Papua New Guinea Council of Churches: POB 1015, Boroko, NCD; tel. 3259961; fax 3251206; f. 1965; seven mem. churches; Chair. EDEA KIDU; Gen. Sec. SOPHIA W. R. GEGEYO.

The Anglican Communion
Formerly part of the Province of Queensland within the Church of England in Australia (now the Anglican Church of Australia), Papua New Guinea became an independent Province in 1977. The Anglican Church of Papua New Guinea comprises five dioceses and had 246,000 members in 2000.

Archbishop of Papua New Guinea and Bishop of Aipo Rongo: Most Rev. JAMES AYONG, POB 893, Mount Hagen, Western Highlands Province; tel. 5421131; fax 5421181; e-mail acpnghgn@global.net.pg.

General Secretary: MARTIN GARDHAM, POB 673, Lae, Morobe Province; tel. 4724111; fax 4721852; e-mail acpng@global.net.pg.

The Roman Catholic Church
For ecclesiastical purposes, Papua New Guinea comprises four archdioceses and 14 dioceses. At 31 December 2000 there were 1,630,289 adherents.

Catholic Bishops' Conference of Papua New Guinea and Solomon Islands
POB 398, Waigani, NCD; tel. 3259577; fax 3232551; e-mail cbc@dg.com.pg.
f. 1959; Pres. Most Rev. STEPHEN REICHERT (Bishop of Mendi); Gen. Sec. LAWRENCE STEPHENS.

Archbishop of Madang: Most Rev. WILLIAM KURTZ, Archbishop's Residence, POB 750, Madang; tel. 8522946; fax 8522596; e-mail Kurtz_caom@global.net.pg.

Archbishop of Mount Hagen: Most Rev. MICHAEL MEIER, Archbishop's Office, POB 54, Mount Hagen, Western Highlands Province; tel. 5421285; fax 5422128; e-mail archdios@online.net.pg.

Archbishop of Port Moresby: Most Rev. BRIAN BARNES, Archbishop's House, POB 1032, Boroko, NCD; tel. 3251192; fax 3256731; e-mail archpom@daltron.com.pg.

Archbishop of Rabaul: Most Rev. KARL HESSE, Archbishop's House, POB 357, Kokopo, East New Britain Province; tel. 9828369; fax 9828404; e-mail abkhesse@online.net.pg.

Other Christian Churches
Baptist Union of Papua New Guinea Inc: POB 705, Mount Hagen, Western Highlands Province; tel. 5522364; fax 5522402; f. 1976; Administrator JOSEPH SILIPIN; 36,000 mems.

Evangelical Lutheran Church of Papua New Guinea: Bishop Rt Rev. WESLEYKIGASUNG POB 80, Lae, Morobe Province; tel. 4723711; fax 4721056; e-mail bishop@elcpng.org.pg; f. 1956; Sec. REUBEN KURE; 815,000 mems.

Gutnius Lutheran Church of Papua New Guinea: Bishop Rev. DAVIDP.PISO POB 111, 291 Wabag, Enga Province; tel. 5471002; f. 1948; Gen. Sec. RICHARD R. MOSES; 95,000 mems.

Papua New Guinea Union Mission of the Seventh-day Adventist Church: POB 86, Lae, Morobe Province 411; tel. 4721488; fax 4721873; Pres. Pastor WILSON STEPHEN; Sec. Pastor BRADLEY RICHARD KEMP; 200,000 adherents.

The United Church in Papua New Guinea: POB 1401, Port Moresby; tel. 3211744; fax 3214930; f. 1968 by union of the Methodist Church in Melanesia, the Papua Ekalesia and United Church, Port Moresby; Moderator Rev. SAMSON LOWA; 600,000 mems; Gen. Sec. DEMAS TONGOGO APELIS.

BAHÁ'Í FAITH

National Spiritual Assembly: Private Mail Bag, Boroko, NCD; tel. 3250286; fax 3236474; e-mail nsapng@datec.net.pg.

ISLAM

In 2000 the Muslim community in Papua New Guinea numbered about 1,500, of whom approximately two-thirds were believed to be expatriates. The religion was introduced to the island in the 1970s. The first mosque there was opened in late 2000 at Poreporena Highway, Hohola, Port Moresby; Imam KHALID ARAI (acting).

The Press

There are numerous newspapers and magazines published by government departments, statutory organizations, missions, sporting organizations, local government councils and regional authorities. They are variously in English, Tok Pisin (Pidgin), Motu and vernacular languages.

Ailans Nius: POB 1239, Rabaul, East New Britain Province; weekly.

Foreign Affairs Review: Dept of Foreign Affairs, Central Government Offices, Kumul Ave, Post Office, Wards Strip, Waigani, NCD; tel. 3271401; fax 3254886.

Hailans Nius: Mount Hagen, Western Highlands Province; weekly.

The Independent: POB 1982, Boroko, NCD; tel. 3252500; fax 3252579; e-mail word@global.net.pg; internet www.niugini.com/independent; f. 1995 to replace the Times of Papua New Guinea; weekly; English; published by Word Publishing Co Pty Ltd; Publr ANNA SOLOMON; Editor DOMINIC KAKAS; circ. 9,000.

Lae Nius: POB 759, Lae, Morobe Province; 2 a week.

The National: POB 6817, Boroko, NCD; tel. 3246731; fax 3246868; e-mail national@thenational.com.pg; internet www.thenational.com.pg; f. 1993; daily; Editor FRANK SENGE KOLMA; circ. 21,036.

Niugini Nius: POB 3019, Boroko, NCD; tel. 3252177; e-mail niusedita@pactok.net; internet pactok.net.au/docs/nius/; daily.

Papua and New Guinea Education Gazette: Dept of Education, PSA Haus, POB 446, Waigani, NCD; tel. 3272413; fax 3254648; monthly; Editor J. OBERLENTER; circ. 8,000.

Papua New Guinea Post-Courier: POB 85, Port Moresby; tel. 3091000; fax 3212721; e-mail postcourier@ssp.com.pg; internet www.postcourier.com.pg; f. 1969; daily; English; published by News Corpn; Gen. Man. TONY YIANNI; Editor OSEAH PHILEMON; circ. 25,044.

PNG Business: POB 1982, Boroko, NCD; tel. 3252500; fax 3252579; e-mail word@global.net.pg; monthly; English; Editor ABBY YADI; circ. 12,000.

Wantok (Friend) Niuspepa: POB 1982, Boroko, NCD; tel. 3252500; fax 3252579; e-mail word@global.net.pg; f. 1970; weekly in New Guinea Pidgin; mainly rural readership; Publr ANNA SOLOMON; Editor LEO WAFIWA; circ. 15,300.

Publishers

Gordon and Gotch (PNG) Pty Ltd: POB 107, Boroko, NCD; tel. 3254855; fax 3250950; e-mail ggpng@online.net.pg; f. 1970; books, magazines and stationery; Gen. Man. PETER G. PORTER.

Scripture Union of Papua New Guinea: POB 280, University, Boroko, NCD; tel. and fax 3253987; f. 1966; religious; Chair. RAVA TAVIRI.

Word Publishing Co Pty Ltd: POB 1982, Boroko, NCD; tel. 3252500; fax 3252579; e-mail word@global.net.pg; f. 1979; 60% owned by the Roman Catholic Church, 20% by Evangelical Lutheran, 10% by Anglican and 10% by United Churches; Gen. Man. (acting) and Publr ANNA SOLOMON.

Broadcasting and Communications

TELECOMMUNICATIONS

Office of Information and Communication: POB 639, Waigani; tel. 3256853; fax 3250412; internet www.communication.gov.pg.

Papua New Guinea Telecommunication Authority (Pangtel): POB 8444, Boroko, NCD; tel. 3258633; fax 3256868; internet www.pangtel.gov.pg; f. 1997; CEO PHILIP AEAVA.

Telikom PNG Pty Ltd: POB 1349, Boroko, NCD; tel. 3004010; fax 3250665; CEO SUNIL ANDRADI; Chair. PILA NININGI.

BROADCASTING

Radio

National Broadcasting Corporation of Papua New Guinea: POB 1359, Boroko, NCD; tel. 3255233; fax 3230404; e-mail md.nbc@global.net.pg; f. 1973; commercial and free govt radio programmes services; broadcasting in English, Melanesian, Pidgin, Motu and 30 vernacular languages; Chair. CHRIS RANGATIN; Man. Dir Dr KRISTOFFA NINKAMA.

Kalang Service (FM): POB 1359, Boroko, NCD; tel. 3255233; commercial radio co established by National Broadcasting Commission; Chair. CAROLUS KETSIMUR.

Nau FM/Yumi FM: POB 774, Port Moresby; tel. 3201996; fax 3201995; internet www.naufm.com.pg; f. 1994; Gen. Mans MARK ROGERS, JUSTIN KILI.

Television

EM TV: POB 443, Boroko, NCD; tel. 3257322; fax 3254450; e-mail emtv@emtv.com.pg; internet www.emtv.com.pg; f. 1988; operated by Media Niugini Pty Ltd; CEO STEPHEN SMITH.

Media Niugini Pty Ltd: POB 443, Boroko, NCD; tel. 3257322; fax 3254450; e-mail emtv@emtv.com.pg; internet www.emtv.com.pg; f. 1987; owned by Nine Network Australia; CEO STEPHEN SMITH.

Finance

(cap. = capital; res = reserves; dep. = deposits; m. = million; brs = branches; amounts in kina unless otherwise stated)

BANKING

Central Bank

Bank of Papua New Guinea: Douglas St, POB 121, Port Moresby; tel. 3227200; fax 3211617; e-mail bpng@datec.com.pg; internet www.datec.com.pg/bpng/bpng.nsf; f. 1973; bank of issue since 1975; sold to Bank of South Pacific in 2002; cap. 62.0m., res 271.5m., dep. 375.8m. (Dec. 1999); Gov. WILSON KAMIT.

Commercial Banks

Australia and New Zealand Banking Group (PNG) Limited: Defens Haus, 3rd Floor, cnr of Champion Parade and Hunter St, POB 1152, Port Moresby; tel. 3223333; fax 3223306; f. 1976; cap. 4.7m., res 1.1m., dep. 494.1m. (Sept. 1998); Chair. R. G. LYON; Man. Dir A. MARLIN; 8 brs.

Bank of Hawaii (PNG) Ltd: Burns House, Champion Parade, POB 1390, Port Moresby; tel. 3213533; fax 3213115; e-mail bohpng@datec.com.pg; f. 1983 as Indosuez Niugini Bank Ltd, name changed in 1997; the bank was expected to cease operations in 2001/02; cap. 3.0m., res 0.8m., dep. 121.1m. (Dec. 1997); Chair. M. BAVER; Man. Dir JOHN SHEATHER; 2 brs.

Bank of South Pacific Ltd: Douglas St, POB 173, Port Moresby; tel. 3212444; fax 3200053; e-mail service@bsp.com.pg; internet www.bsp.com.pg; f. 1974; acquired from National Australia Bank Ltd by Papua New Guinea consortium (National Investment Holdings, now BSP Holdings Ltd) in 1993; cap. 17.9m., res 13.8m., dep. 519.8m. (Dec. 2000); Chair. NOREO BEANGKE; Man. Dir NOEL R. SMITH; 8 brs and 2 sub-brs.

Maybank (PNG) Ltd: Waigani, NCD; f. 1995.

MBf Finance (PNG) Ltd: Elsa Beach Towers, Ground Floor, cnr of Musgrave St, POB 329, Port Moresby; tel. 3213555; fax 3213480; f. 1989.

Papua New Guinea Banking Corporation: cnr of Douglas and Musgrave Sts, POB 78, Port Moresby; tel. 3229700; fax 3211683; f. 1974; corporatized in 2001; cap. 11.3m., res 72.9m., dep. 978.8m. (Dec. 1997); Chair. ROGER PALME; Man. Dir HENRY FABILA; 34 brs.

Westpac Bank—PNG—Ltd: Mogoru Motu Bldg, 5th Floor, Champion Parade, POB 706, Port Moresby; tel. 3220800; fax 3213367; e-mail westpacpng@westpac.com.au; f. 1910 as Bank of New South Wales, present name since 1982; 90% owned by Westpac Banking Corpn, Australia; cap. 5.8m., res 6.1m., dep. 554.7m. (Sept. 1999); Chair. ALAN WALTER; Man. Dir SIMON MILLETT; 15 brs.

Development Bank

Rural Development Bank of Papua New Guinea: Somare Crescent, POB 686, Waigani, NCD; tel. 3247500; fax 3259817; f. 1967; cap. 32.6m., res U17.1m. (Dec. 1992); statutory govt agency; Chair. ROGER PALME; Man. Dir SHEM M. PAKE; 10 brs.

Savings and Loan Societies

Registry of Savings and Loan Societies: Financial System Supervision Dept, POB 121, Port Moresby; tel. 3227200; fax 3214548; 101 savings and loan societies; 125,306 mems (2001); total funds 163.5m., loans outstanding 90.0m., investments 21.4m. (June 2001); CEO ELIZABETH GIMA.

STOCK EXCHANGE

Port Moresby Stock Exchange (POMSoX) Ltd: Level 4, Defens Haus, POB 1531, Port Moresby; tel. 3201980; fax 3201981; e-mail pomsox@datec.com.pg; internet www.pomsox.com.pg; f. 1999; Chair. Sir ANTHONY SIAGURU; Gen. Man. EMILY GEORGE TAULE.

INSURANCE

Niugini Insurance Corporation Ltd: POB 331, Port Moresby; tel. 3214077; fax 3217898; f. 1978; govt-owned; Chair. JACOB POPUNA; Man. Dir DARRYL G. NATHAN.

Pan Asia Pacific Assurance (PNG) Pty Ltd (PAPA): Port Moresby; f. 1993; Chair. BENIAS SABUMEI.

There are branches of several Australian and United Kingdom insurance companies in Port Moresby, Rabaul, Lae and Kieta.

Trade and Industry

GOVERNMENT AGENCIES

Investment Corporation of Papua New Guinea: Hunter St, POB 155, Port Moresby; tel. 3212855; fax 3211240; f. 1971 as govt body to support local enterprise and to purchase shares in foreign businesses operating in Papua New Guinea; partially transferred to private ownership in 1993.

Investment Promotion Authority (IPA): POB 5053, Boroko, NCD 111; tel. 3217311; fax 3212819; e-mail iepd@ipa.gov.pg; internet www.ipa.gov.pg; f. 1992 following reorganization of National Investment and Development Authority; a statutory body responsible for the promotion of foreign investment; the first contact point for foreign investors for advice on project proposals and approvals of applications for registration to conduct business in the country; contributes to planning for investment and recommends priority areas for investment to the Govt; also co-ordinates investment proposals; Man. Dir SIMON PETER (acting).

Privatization Commission: Port Moresby; f. 1999 to oversee transfer of state-owned enterprises to private ownership; Exec. Chair. BEN MICAH.

DEVELOPMENT ORGANIZATIONS

CDC Capital Partners Ltd: CDC Haus, 2nd Floor, POB 907, Port Moresby; tel. 3212944; fax 3212867; e-mail png@cdc.com.pg; internet www.cdcgroup.com; fmrly Commonwealth Development Corpn; Man. Dir ASHLEY EMBERSON-BAIN.

Industrial Centres Development Corporation: POB 1571, Boroko, NCD; tel. 3232913; fax 3231109; promotes foreign investment in non-mining sectors through establishment of manufacturing facilities.

CHAMBERS OF COMMERCE

Papua New Guinea Chamber of Commerce and Industry: POB 1621, Port Moresby; tel. 3213057; fax 3210566; e-mail pngcci@global.net.pg; Pres. MICHAEL MAYBERRY; Vice-Pres. PHILIP FRANKLIN.

Papua New Guinea Chamber of Mines and Petroleum: POB 1032, Port Moresby; tel. 3212988; fax 3217107; e-mail ga@pngchamberminpet.com.pg; internet www.pngchamberminpet.com.pg; Exec. Dir GREG ANDERSON; Pres. PETER BOTTEN.

Port Moresby Chamber of Commerce and Industry: POB 1764, Port Moresby; tel. 3213077; fax 3214203; Pres. CES IEWAGO.

Lae Chamber of Commerce and Industry: POB 265, Lae, Morobe Province.

INDUSTRIAL AND TRADE ASSOCIATIONS

Cocoa Board of Papua New Guinea: POB 1165, Madaney; tel. 8823253; fax 8822198; f. 1974; Chair. JIMMY SIMITAB.

Coffee Industry Corpn Ltd: POB 137, Goroka, Eastern Highlands Province; tel. 721266; fax 721431; e-mail webmaster@gka.coffeecorp .org.pg; internet www.coffeecorp.org.pg; CEO BADIRA VARI.

Fishing Industry Association (PNG) Inc: POB 2340, Boroko, NCD; e-mail netshop1@daltron.com.pg; Chair. MAURICE BROWNJOHN.

Forest Industries Association: POB 5055, Boroko, NCD; Pres. GARY HONEY; CEO ROBERT TATE.

Higaturu Oil Palms Pty Ltd: POB 28, Popondetta, Oro Province; tel. 3297177; fax 3297137; f. 1976; jtly owned by the Commonwealth Development Corpn (UK) and the Papua New Guinea Govt; major producer of palm oil and cocoa; Gen. Man. RICHARD CASKIE.

Kopra Indasrti Korporesen (KIK): Port Moresby; markets all copra in Papua New Guinea; consists of a chair. and mems representing producers; formerly known as the Copra Marketing Board of Papua New Guinea; Chair. ROBINSON NAMALIU; Gen. Man. TED SITAPAI.

Manufacturers' Council of Papua New Guinea: POB 598, Port Moresby; tel. 3259512; fax 3230199; e-mail pngmadecouncil@datec .com.pg; internet www.pngmade.org.pg; Chair. WAYNE GOLDING; CEO MARYANNE MCDONALD.

National Contractors' Association: Port Moresby; formed by construction cos for the promotion of education, training and professional conduct in the construction industry; Pres. ROY THORPE.

National Fisheries Authority: POB 2016, Port Moresby; tel. 3212643; fax 3202074; Man. Dir TONY LEWIS; Dep. Man. Dir MICHAEL BATTY.

National Housing Corpn (NHC): POB 1550, Boroko NCD; tel. 3247000; fax 3254363; Man. Dir GABRIEL TOVO.

New Britain Palm Oil Ltd: POB 389, Kimbe, West New Britain; tel. 9852177; fax 9852003; e-mail nbpol@nbpol.com.pg; f. 1967; 80% owned by Kulim (Malaysia), 20% owned by Govt, employees and local producers; major producer of palm oil, coffee trader and exporter, supplier of high quality oil palm seed; Man. Dir NICK THOMPSON; Sec. ALLAN MORROW.

Niugini Produce Marketing Pty Ltd: Lae, Morobe Province; f. 1982; govt-owned; handles distribution of fruit and vegetables throughout the country.

Palm Oil Producers Association: Port Moresby; Exec. Sec. ALLAN MAINO.

Papua New Guinea Forest Authority: POB 5055, Boroko, NCD; tel. 3277800; fax 3254433; Man. Dir THOMAS NEN.

Papua New Guinea Growers Association: Port Moresby; Pres. VALENTINE KAMBORI.

Papua New Guinea Holdings Corpn: POB 131, Port Moresby; fax 3217545; f. 1992; responsible for managing govt privatization programme; Chair. MICHAEL MEL; Man. Dir PETER STEELE.

Papua New Guinea Log Carriers Association: f. 1993.

Pita Lus National Silk Institute: Kagamuga, Mount Hagen, Western Highlands Province; f. 1978; govt silk-producing project.

Rural Industries Council: Chair. PETER COLTON.

UTILITIES

Electricity

PNG Electricity Commission (Elcom): POB 1105, Boroko, NCD; tel. 3243200; fax 3214051; plans to privatize the organization were announced in 1999; Chair. PAUL AISA; Chief Exec. SEV MASO.

Water

Eda Ranu (Our Water): POB 1084, Waigani, NCD; tel. 3122100; fax 3122190; e-mail enquiries@edaranu.com.pg; internet www .edaranu.com.pg; fmrly Port Moresby Water Supply Company; Gen. Man. BILLY IMAR.

PNG Waterboard: POB 2779, Boroko, NCD; tel. 3235700; fax 3236317; e-mail pamini@pngwater.com.pg; f. 1986; govt-owned; operates 12 water supply systems throughout the country; Man. Dir PATRICK AMINI.

TRADE UNIONS

The Industrial Organizations Ordinance requires all industrial organizations that consist of no fewer than 20 employees or four employers to register. In 1977 there were 56 registered industrial organizations, including a general employee group registered as a workers' association in each province and also unions covering a specific industry or profession.

Papua New Guinea Trade Unions Congress (PNGTUC): POB 254, Boroko, NCD; tel. 3212132; fax 3212498; e-mail tucl@daltron .com.pg; Pres. GASPER LAPAN; Gen. Sec. JOHN PASKA; 52 affiliates, 76,000 mems.

The following are among the major trade unions:

Bougainville Mining Workers' Union: POB 777, Panguna, North Solomons Province; tel. 9958272; Pres. MATHEW TUKAN; Gen. Sec. ALFRED ELISHA TAGORNOM.

Central Province Building and Construction Industry Workers' Union: POB 265, Port Moresby.

Central Province Transport Drivers' and Workers' Union: POB 265, Port Moresby.

Employers' Federation of Papua New Guinea: POB 490, Port Moresby; tel. 3214772; fax 3214070; f. 1963; Pres. G. J. DUNLOP; Exec. Dir TAU NANA; 170 mems.

National Federation of Timber Workers: Madang; f. 1993; Gen. Sec. MATHIAS KENUANGI (acting).

Papua New Guinea Communication Workers' Union: Pres. GASPER LAPAN; Gen. Sec. EMMANUEL KAIRU.

Papua New Guinea National Doctors' Association: Pres. Dr BOB DANAYA; 225 mems.

Papua New Guinea Teachers' Association: POB 1027, Waigani, NCD; tel. 3262588; f. 1971; Pres. TAINA DAI; Gen. Sec. LEONARD JONLI; 13,345 mems.

Papua New Guinea Waterside Workers' and Seamen's Union: Port Moresby; f. 1979; an amalgamation of four unions; Sec. AUGUSTINE WAVIKI.

Police Association of Papua New Guinea: POB 903, Port Moresby; tel. 3214172; f. 1964; Pres. A. AVIAISA; Gen. Sec. (vacant); 4,596 mems.

Port Moresby Council of Trade Unions: POB 265, Boroko, NCD; Gen. Sec. JOHN KOSI.

Port Moresby Miscellaneous Workers' Union: POB 265, Boroko, NCD.

Printing and Kindred Industries Union: Port Moresby.

Public Employees' Association: POB 965, Boroko, NCD; tel. 3252955; fax 3252186; f. 1974; Pres. NAPOLEON LIOSI; Gen. Sec. JACK N. KUTAL; 28,000 mems.

Transport

There are no railways in Papua New Guinea. The capital city, Port Moresby, is not connected by road to other major population centres. Therefore, air and sea travel are of particular importance.

ROADS

In 1999 there were an estimated 19,600 km of roads in Papua New Guinea, of which 3.5% were paved. In 1995 the Australian Government announced that it was to donate $A155m. over five years for major road-building projects in Papua New Guinea. In 1998 the European Union (EU) committed €24m. over two years to upgrade the Lae–Madang Highway. Japan offered a grant-in-aid in 1998 of 940m. yen for the reconstruction of a bridge on the Highlands Highway. In October 2000 it was announced that this highway was also to be upgraded over six years at a cost of 26.3m. kina financed through a loan negotiated with the Asian Development Bank (ADB).

SHIPPING

Papua New Guinea has 16 major ports and a coastal fleet of about 300 vessels. In early 1999 a feasibility study was commissioned to investigate the possible relocation of port facilities in Port Moresby.

Papua New Guinea Harbours Board: POB 671, Port Moresby; tel. 3211400; fax 3211546; Chair. TIMOTHY BONGA.

Port Authority of Kieta: POB 149, Kieta, North Solomons Province; tel. 9956066; fax 9956255; Port Man. SAKEUS GEM.

Port Authority of Lae: POB 563, Lae, Morobe Province; tel. 4422477; fax 4422543; Port Man. JOSHUA TARUNA.

Port Authority of Madang: POB 273, Madang; tel. 8523381; fax 8523097; Port Man. WILLIE WANANGA.

Port Authority of Port Moresby: POB 671, Port Moresby; tel. 211400; fax 3211546; Gen. Man. T. AMAO.

Port Authority of Rabaul: POB 592, Rabaul, East New Britain Province; tel. 9821533; fax 9821535.

Shipping Companies

Coastal Shipping Pty Co Ltd: Sulphur Creek Rd, POB 423, Rabaul, East New Britain Province; tel. 9828518; fax 9828519.

Lutheran Shipping: POB 1459, Lae, Morobe Province; tel. 4722066; fax 4725806.

Morehead Shipping Pty Ltd: POB 1908, Lae, Morobe Province; tel. 4423602.

New Guinea Australia Line Pty Ltd: POB 145, Port Moresby; tel. 3212377; fax 3214879; e-mail ngal@daltron.com.pg; f. 1970; operates regular container services between Australia, Papua New Guinea, Singapore, Indonesia, Vanuatu, Tuvalu and Solomon Islands; Chair. (vacant); Gen. Man. GEOFFREY CUNDLE.

P & O PNG Ltd (trading as Century Shipping Agencies): MMI House, 3rd Floor, Champion Parade, POB 1403, Port Moresby; tel. 3229200; fax 3229251; e-mail cgcpom@popng.com.pg; owned by P & O (Australia); Gen. Man. ANDREW CRIDLAND.

Papua New Guinea Shipping Corporation Pty Ltd: POB 634, Port Moresby; tel. 3220290; fax 3212815; e-mail shipping@steamships.com.pg; f. 1977; owned by Steamships Trading Co Ltd; provides a container/break-bulk service to Australia and the Pacific islands; Chair. CHRISTOPHER PRATT; Man. Dir JOHN DUNLOP.

South Sea Lines Proprietary Ltd: POB 5, Lae, Morobe Province; tel. 4423455; fax 4424884; Man. Dir R. CUNNINGHAM.

Western Tug & Barge Co P/L: POB 175, Port Moresby; tel. 3212099; fax 3217950; shipowning arm of P & O PNG; operates 24 vessels.

CIVIL AVIATION

There is an international airport at Port Moresby, Jackson's Airport, and there are more than 400 other airports and airstrips throughout the country. International services from Lae and Mount Hagen airports began in March 1999. A programme to upgrade eight regional airports over three years, with finance of $A30m. from the Australian Government, was initiated in mid-1997. New domestic and international terminal buildings were opened at Jackson's Airport in 1998, following a 13-year project financed with K120m. from the Japanese Government. A project to redevelop Tari airport was announced in late 1999. It was expected that, following redevelopment, the airport would receive international flights.

Air Niugini: POB 7186, Boroko, NCD; tel. 3259000; fax 3273482; e-mail airniugini@airniugini.com.pg; internet www.airniugini.com.pg; f. 1973; govt-owned national airline (plans to privatize the airline were announced in 1999); operates scheduled domestic cargo and passenger services within Papua New Guinea and international services to Australia, Solomon Islands, Philippines and Singapore; a new service to Tokyo, Japan, was expected to commence in 2002; Chair. JOSEPH PHILLIP KAPAL; CEO PETER ROBERTS; Man. Dir MICHAEL BULEAU (acting).

MBA Pty Ltd: POB 170, Boroko, NCD; tel. 3252011; fax 3252219; e-mail mba@mbapng.com; internet www.mbapng.com; f. 1984; operates domestic scheduled and charter services; Chair. and CEO JOHN R. WILD; Gen. Man. SIMON D. WILD.

Tourism

Despite Papua New Guinea's spectacular scenery and abundant wildlife, tourism makes only a small contribution to the economy. In 1998 there were 4,280 hotel beds. In 2000 visitor arrivals totalled some 58,448. The industry earned an estimated US $76m. in 1999.

PNG Tourism Promotion Authority: POB 1291, Port Moresby; tel. 3200211; fax 3200223; e-mail tourismpng@dg.com.pg; internet www.paradiselive.org.pg; CEO JOHN KAMBOWA.

PARAGUAY

Introductory Survey

Location, Climate, Language, Religion, Flag, Capital

The Republic of Paraguay is a land-locked country in central South America. It is bordered by Bolivia to the north, by Brazil to the east, and by Argentina to the south and west. The climate is sub-tropical. Temperatures range from an average maximum of 34.3°C (93.7°F) in January to an average minimum of 14°C (51°F) in June. The official language is Spanish, but the majority of the population speak Guaraní, an indigenous Indian language. Almost all of the inhabitants profess Christianity, and some 85% adhere to the Roman Catholic Church, the country's established religion. There is a small Protestant minority. The national flag (proportions 3 by 5) has three equal horizontal stripes, of red, white and blue. It is the only national flag with a different design on each side, having a varying emblem in the centre of the white stripe: the obverse side bears the state emblem (a white disc with a red ring bearing the words 'República del Paraguay', in yellow capitals, framing a blue disc with the five-pointed 'May Star', in yellow, surrounded by a wreath, in green), while the reverse side carries the seal of the Treasury (a white disc with a red ribbon bearing the words 'Paz y Justicia' in yellow capitals above a lion supporting a staff, surmounted by the red 'Cap of Liberty'). The capital is Asunción.

Recent History

Paraguay, ruled by Spain from the 16th century, achieved independence in 1811. In 1865 Paraguay was involved in a disastrous war against Brazil, Argentina and Uruguay (the Triple Alliance), resulting in the loss of more than one-half of its population. Paraguay also suffered heavy losses in the Chaco Wars of 1928–30 and 1932–35 against Bolivia, but won a large part of the disputed territory when the boundary was fixed in 1938. Gen. Higinio Morínigo established an authoritarian regime in 1940, but the return of a number of political exiles in 1947 precipitated a civil war in which supporters of the right-wing Asociación Nacional Republicana (Partido Colorado) defeated the Liberals and the Partido Revolucionario Febrerista, leading to the overthrow of Gen. Morínigo in June 1948. A period of great instability ensued. In May 1954 Gen. Alfredo Stroessner Mattiauda, the Army Commander-in-Chief, assumed power in a military coup. He nominated himself for the presidency, as the Colorado candidate, and was elected unopposed in July to complete the term of office of his predecessor, Federico Chávez. In 1955 Stroessner assumed extensive powers, and established a state of siege. Regular purges of the Partido Colorado membership, together with the mutual co-operation of the ruling party, the armed forces and the business community, enabled Stroessner to become the longest-serving dictator in Latin America: he was re-elected President, by large majorities, at five-yearly elections in 1958–88.

In February 1978 President Stroessner revoked the state of siege in all areas except Asunción. The assassination of the former Nicaraguan dictator, Gen. Anastasio Somoza Debayle, in Asunción in September 1980, however, caused President Stroessner to doubt the security of his own position, and the state of siege was reimposed throughout the country; harassment of leaders of the political opposition and of peasant and labour groups continued. The leader of the Partido Demócrata Cristiano, Luis Alfonso Resck, was expelled from the country in June 1981, and Domingo Laíno, leader of the Partido Liberal Radical Auténtico (PLRA), was deported in December 1982. After Ronald Reagan took office as President of the USA in 1981, Paraguay encountered less pressure from the US Administration to curb abuses of human rights, and the use of torture against detainees reportedly became widespread once more. It was estimated at this time that more than 60% of all Paraguayans resided outside the country.

The majority of opposition parties boycotted the presidential and legislative elections of February 1983, enabling Stroessner to obtain more than 90% of the votes cast in the presidential poll, and in August he formally took office for a further five-year term. In May 1983 the Government instigated a campaign of repression against students and trade unionists. There was, however, some indication of a moderation in government policy when, in January 1984, Stroessner, alarmed by a recent decline in his popularity, granted an amnesty to politicians in exile, with the notable exceptions of Luis Alfonso Resck and Domingo Laíno. In February 1984 opposition parties organized demonstrations in Asunción for the first time in 30 years.

Divisions over Stroessner's continuance in office led to factionalism within the Partido Colorado in the mid-1980s. In April 1987 Stroessner announced that the state of siege was to be ended, since extraordinary security powers were no longer necessary to maintain peace. (Later in the month Laíno was finally allowed to return to Paraguay.) However, the suppression of civil liberties and of political activity continued under the new penal code that replaced the state of siege. The level of participation in the 1988 presidential election (which took place simultaneously with legislative elections) was reported to be 92.6% of eligible voters, and it was announced that Stroessner had received 88.6% of the votes cast. However, opposition leaders (who had urged voters to boycott the elections) complained of electoral malpractice, and denounced Stroessner's re-election as fraudulent.

On 3 February 1989 Gen. Stroessner was overthrown in a coup, led by Gen. Andrés Rodríguez, the second-in-command of the armed forces. Stroessner was allowed to leave for exile in Brazil, as Gen. Rodríguez assumed the presidency (in a provisional capacity) and appointed a new Council of Ministers. The interim President pledged to respect human rights, to strengthen links with neighbouring countries and to improve relations with the Roman Catholic Church. Presidential and legislative elections, open to all political parties except the Partido Comunista Paraguayo (PCP), were scheduled for the 1 May, and Gen. Rodríguez confirmed that he would be the presidential candidate of the Partido Colorado. He also gave assurances that, if elected, he would relinquish power to a civilian successor in 1993, and promised constitutional reforms. At the election Rodríguez was confirmed as President, receiving 74.2% of the votes cast; his closest rival, Laíno, secured 19.6% of the votes. The Partido Colorado, having won 72.8% of the votes in the congressional election, automatically took two-thirds of the seats in both the Cámara de Diputados (Chamber of Deputies) and the Senado (Senate—48 and 24, respectively). The most successful opposition party was the PLRA, which obtained 19 seats in the Cámara and 10 in the Senado. Despite widespread allegations of electoral fraud, all parties agreed to respect the results.

In July 1989 the Cámara ratified the San José Pact on Human Rights, adopted by the Organization of American States (OAS, see p. 288) in 1978. In August 1989 the Congreso Nacional (National Congress—comprising the Cámara de Diputados and the Senado) initiated judicial proceedings against former government officials for violations of human rights. In December the Secretary-General of the PCP, Ananías Maidana (who had been expelled from Paraguay in 1978), returned to the country: the repeal, in August 1989, of laws that had provided a basis for political repression under the Stroessner regime had allowed the formal legalization of the PCP. In November 1990, however, Rodríguez vetoed congressional proposals for the establishment of a legislative commission to investigate alleged violations of human rights.

Divisions within the Partido Colorado became evident at its annual convention in December 1989, when the 'Tradicionalistas' attempted to elect new party officials drawn exclusively from their own membership. The newly-emerged Coloradismo Democrático faction, led by Blás Riquelme (a vice-president of the party at that time), succeeded in obtaining a judicial annulment of all decisions of the convention. The political crisis led to the resignation of the entire Council of Ministers. However, Rodríguez subsequently reappointed all but one of the out-going ministers to their former posts. In February 1990 a new electoral code was adopted; this banned party affiliation for serving members of the armed forces and the police, and reformed procedures for the election of party officials. In March the 'Tradicionalista' President of the Partido Colorado, Juan Ramón Chaves, resigned. In July Dr Luis María Argaña, the acting

President of the party, was dismissed from his post as Minister of Foreign Affairs, after having publicly vowed that the Partido Colorado would never relinquish power and would retain control by whatever means possible.

Paraguay's first direct municipal elections took place in May 1991. Although the Partido Colorado secured control of a majority of municipalities, the important post of mayor of Asunción was won by a relatively unknown candidate, Carlos Filizzola, the representative of a new centre-left coalition, Asunción Para Todos (APT). Defeat in the capital precipitated mutual recriminations within the increasingly fragmented Partido Colorado, and, shortly after Filizzola's election, the ruling party's youth wing, Juventud Colorada, organized a demonstration to demand the resignation of Argaña from the party presidency.

In August 1991 the Congreso Nacional approved proposals for a complete revision of the 1967 Constitution. In anticipation of the elections to a National Constituent Assembly, President Rodríguez and military leaders made concerted efforts to forge unity within the Partido Colorado, with the result that the party's three main factions, the 'Renovadores', the 'Democráticos' and the 'Autónomos' were persuaded to present a single list of candidates, under the title 'Tradicionalistas', to represent the ruling party. In the elections, held on 1 December 1991, the Partido Colorado won 55.1% of the votes cast, thus securing an overwhelming majority of the Assembly's 198 seats. The PLRA won 27.0% of the votes, while Constitución Para Todos, formed as a result of APT's success in the municipal elections, won 11.0% of the votes. The new body was convened in January 1992.

In November 1991 new legislation, drafted by President Rodríguez in co-operation with military leaders, was approved by the Congreso Nacional. The law appeared to guarantee the autonomy of the armed forces, and the definition of the role of the military was expanded to include responsibility, at the request of the Head of State, for civil defence and internal order. Apparently in contradiction of the 1990 electoral code, no restrictions were placed on political activities by serving members of the armed forces. Provision was made for the President to delegate the functions of Commander-in-Chief of the Armed Forces to a senior military officer (with the Head of State retaining only ceremonial powers as the military commander). Opposition parties protested that, should the new legislation be entrenched in the new Constitution, the armed forces would remain a 'parallel' political force, following the transition to civilian rule.

On 20 June 1992 the new Constitution was promulgated before the Constituent Assembly. Under the new Constitution, the President and the Vice-President (a new post) were to be elected by a simple majority of votes. The Constituent Assembly had ostensibly disregarded the November 1991 military legislation by confirming the President as Commander-in-Chief of the Armed Forces and excluding officers on active duty from participating directly in politics. Other significant changes in the Constitution included the abolition of the death penalty and the granting of the right to unionize and to strike to public-sector employees (excluding the armed forces and police).

In August 1992, following the party's first direct internal elections, Blás Riquelme was appointed President of the Partido Colorado. However, serious divisions within the party persisted. An internal election, conducted in December, to select the party's presidential candidate was declared to have been won by Argaña (who had resigned the position in 1992), the candidate of the far-right. However, the candidate believed to be favoured by Rodríguez, Juan Carlos Wasmosy, refused to recognize the result, claiming that the vote had been fraudulent. An electoral tribunal failed to resolve the issue, and, following intense pressure and alleged death threats by both factions, several members of the tribunal resigned. Party leaders organized an extraordinary national convention in February 1993, at which a new electoral tribunal was to be chosen. Wasmosy was eventually confirmed as the presidential candidate of the Partido Colorado. The decision was denounced by Argaña, whose supporters threatened to resign *en masse* from the party.

At the general election of 9 May 1993, Wasmosy was elected President with 39.91% of the votes cast, ahead of Laíno (32.13%) and Guillermo Caballero Vargas of Encuentro Nacional (EN) (23.24%). However, the Partido Colorado failed to gain a majority in either the Cámara or the Senado. Moreover, the faction of the Partido Colorado led by Argaña, the Movimiento de Reconciliación Colorada (MCR), negotiated with the PLRA and the EN to exclude supporters of the President-elect from appointment to important posts in the Congreso Nacional (with the

support of the MCR, the overall opposition strength stood at 35 of a total of 45 seats in the Senado and 64 of the 80 seats in the Cámara, sufficient to approve legislation affecting the Constitution).

Wasmosy was inaugurated as President on 15 August 1993. The opposition expressed some concern over the composition of Wasmosy's first Council of Ministers, many of whom had served in the administrations of Rodríguez and Stroessner. Despite Wasmosy's apparent desire to restrict the influence of the military (he notably appointed a civilian to the post of Minister of National Defence), the designation of Gen. Lino César Oviedo Silva as Commander of the Army provoked further criticism, since, prior to the elections, Oviedo had publicly stated that the army would not accept an opposition victory.

A preliminary agreement on a 'governability pact' between the Government and the opposition, initiated in an attempt to facilitate the implementation of a coherent economic and legislative programme, was signed in October 1993, and this, in turn, facilitated an agreement between the Government and the legislature towards resolving the controversial question of judicial reform. Under the latter agreement, the two were to appoint members of the Supreme Court and the Supreme Electoral Tribunal by consensus. (The new members of the Supreme Court, enlarged from five to nine justices in accordance with the 1992 Constitution, were eventually elected in April 1995). In January 1994 Blás Riquelme resigned as President of the Partido Colorado, following disagreements with Wasmosy, specifically with regard to the Government's implementation of a programme of price increases for public utilities, to which Riquelme was opposed. By early 1995 speculation concerning unrest in the armed forces, prompted by Wasmosy's recent uncompromising manipulation of the ranks of the military high command, and by a reported clash of interests between the President and Gen. Oviedo, had reached such a level that Wasmosy was forced to issue a public statement discounting the possibility of a military coup. In February Wasmosy announced a further reorganization of the military high command, thus consolidating his position of authority.

In May 1995 an investigation into corruption at the Banco Central del Paraguay (the country's Central Bank) revealed the existence of an illegal 'parallel' financial system involving a network of institutions, including the Central Bank. The investigation precipitated the collapse of the system and a severe liquidity crisis. In June the President of the Central Bank resigned. In December the Government issued an emergency decree extending the powers of intervention of the Central Bank, with the aim of resolving the financial crisis and restoring confidence in the banking sector. By late December the Central Bank had disbursed almost $400m. of reserves in order to contain the liquidity crisis—which had resulted in the closure of four banks, four finance companies, one savings and loan institution and one insurance company.

In early March 1996 some 30,000 farm workers conducted a demonstration outside the building of the Congreso Nacional, in support of demands for agrarian reform and improved working conditions, and in protest at government economic policy—in particular the privatization of state assets and Paraguay's membership of Mercosur (see below), which, its opponents maintained, led to excessive competition from agricultural imports. The demonstration prompted the resignation of the Minister of Agriculture and Livestock. In late March labour confederations organized a 24-hour general strike in support of demands for a 31% increase in all salaries, measures to alleviate rural poverty, a referendum on the privatization of state assets and a renegotiation of Paraguay's involvement in Mercosur. The strike was notable for the support it received from the Confederación Paraguaya de Trabajadores, a labour confederation dominated by supporters of the Partido Colorado. The Government's failure to respond to the protesters' demands prompted a further, 48-hour general strike in early May, when additional demands were made for the reversal of government plans to privatize the social security system and for the dismissal of the Minister of Justice and Labour. Violent confrontations between demonstrators and the security forces resulted in numerous injuries and the arrest of several leading labour representatives.

In April 1996 a serious confrontation arose between President Wasmosy and Gen. Oviedo, with the result that a military coup was only narrowly averted. Following an attempt by Oviedo to postpone the internal elections of the Partido Colorado (widely interpreted as an effort to manipulate the proceedings to suit his own political ambitions), Wasmosy accused Oviedo of contravening the ban on political activity by serving members of the military, and, on 22 April, demanded his resignation as Commander of the Army. When Oviedo refused to resign, Wasmosy promptly announced his dismissal, naming Gen. Oscar Rodrigo Díaz Delmas as his successor. Oviedo rejected the decision, and installed himself at the army headquarters in Asunción, from where he issued demands for Wasmosy's resignation and (it was later revealed) threatened, with the support of the army, violently to overthrow the Government. Wasmosy took refuge in the US embassy building. The following day, in a demonstration of popular support for Wasmosy, thousands rallied outside the presidential palace. Declarations of support were also issued by the Commanders of the Navy and the Air Force, and by the Congreso Nacional. External pressure for Wasmosy to resist the overthrow of democratic rule came from the USA, which immediately suspended military aid, and from neighbouring South American countries, and was sufficient to prompt Wasmosy to seek a compromise: in return for his retirement from military service, Oviedo was offered, and accepted, the position of Minister of Defence. However, the measure was condemned by the legislature, which threatened to initiate impeachment proceedings against Wasmosy should Oviedo be appointed. Public opinion was also strongly opposed to the appointment, and on 25 April, following Oviedo's retirement from military service and his replacement by Gen. Díaz, Wasmosy withdrew the offer of the defence portfolio. Despite fears of an outright coup, Oviedo accepted the final outcome of the dispute and announced that, as a private citizen, he would now dedicate himself to the political campaign of the Partido Colorado.

In late April 1996 the internal elections of the Partido Colorado resulted in victory for Dr Luis María Argaña, the leader of the Movimiento de Reconciliación Colorada faction, who was appointed President of the party. In May Gen. (retd) Oviedo announced the creation of a new faction of the Partido Colorado, the Unión Nacional de Colorados Eticos (Unace). In that month, in an effort to purge the armed forces of officers sympathetic to Oviedo, Wasmosy announced the retirement of some 20 high-ranking officers, including the Commander of the First Army Corps and the Chief of Staff of the Army. In June Oviedo was placed under house arrest on charges of insurrection and insubordination with respect to the events of April. In July Oviedo's assets were seized and the order for his detention was revised from house arrest to preventative imprisonment. This development provoked protest by Oviedo's supporters, who rallied outside the Congreso Nacional to demand his release. Wasmosy continued to reorganize the military hierarchy, replacing several senior officers. In August an appeal court acquitted Oviedo of the charge of insurrection, ruling that there was insufficient evidence to suggest that he had made military preparations to overturn the constitutional order. Shortly after his release Oviedo expressed publicly his intention to contest the forthcoming presidential election due in 1998. In December 1996 Oviedo was acquitted of the lesser charge of insubordination.

At municipal elections conducted in November 1996 the Partido Colorado secured control of a majority of municipalities, although the opposition parties gained considerable support. Moreover, the influential post of mayor of Asunción was again won by an opposition candidate, Martín Burt, the candidate of the PLRA in alliance with the EN. In early January 1997, therefore, Wasmosy indicated his willingness to effect a *rapprochement* with Argaña's faction of the Partido Colorado, with a view to uniting in support of a single nominee—the Minister of Education and Culture, Dr César Nicanor Duarte Frutos—as the party's presidential candidate. However, in February Wasmosy withdrew from negotiations with Argaña's faction and announced his intention to support his own nominee—the Minister of Finance, Carlos Facetti Masulli. The decision provoked Duarte's resignation from the Government. The Ministers of the Interior and of Integration, both staunch supporters of efforts to reunify the Partido Colorado, similarly resigned in protest at Wasmosy's actions.

In June 1997 further evidence of illegal 'parallel' operations in the nation's banking sector emerged when the Central Bank was forced to intervene in the operations of three financial institutions (Banco de Ahorros Paraguayos, Banco Unión, SAECA and Banco de Inversiones del Paraguay, SA) that were experiencing serious liquidity problems. In view of the crisis, the Minister of Industry and Commerce, who was a shareholder in Banco Unión and brother of the bank's president, resigned from the Council of Ministers in late June.

In August 1997 Juan Carlos Galaverna, a Partido Colorado senator and prominent supporter of Dr Argaña, presented a motion to the Senado seeking the impeachment of President Wasmosy on the grounds that he had contravened the Constitution by attempting to influence the outcome of the forthcoming Partido Colorado primary election. Wasmosy had conducted a meeting with senior party officials and military commanders in July, but denied allegations that the internal elections had been discussed. Although the impeachment motion was unsuccessful, it illustrated the extent of division between rival factions of the Partido Colorado in advance of the forthcoming general election, scheduled for 10 May 1998. Also in August 1997 the PLRA and the EN formally established an electoral alliance, the Alianza Democrática (AD), to contest the general election. In September Gen. Oviedo succeeded in securing the Partido Colorado's presidential nomination, defeating Wasmosy's preferred candidate, Facetti, and Argaña himself, in the party's primary. However, Argaña's faction, which effectively controlled the party's executive board, refused to accept the outcome of the ballot, claiming that it had been fraudulent, and presented a legal challenge to the result.

In early October 1997 Wasmosy issued an executive order for the 'disciplinary arrest', for a period of 30 days, of Gen. Oviedo; the grounds for the detention was contempt of the President and Commander-in-Chief of the Armed Forces, after Oviedo had publicly accused Wasmosy of corruption. An appeal court subsequently issued an injunction suspending the arrest order, prompting Wasmosy to file a petition requesting that the Supreme Court uphold his order. Oviedo, meanwhile, had gone into hiding. In December, following a ruling by the Supreme Court endorsing the arrest order issued by Wasmosy in October, Oviedo surrendered to the military authorities in order to serve the 30-day period of confinement. Later that month the Supreme Electoral Tribunal rejected the petition by Argaña's faction of the Partido Colorado to have the results of the party's primary election annulled, and in early January 1998 it registered Oviedo as the official presidential candidate of the Partido Colorado, without the endorsement of the party's executive board. Oviedo completed his period of confinement on 11 January; however, a special military tribunal, established by Wasmosy to investigate the events of the coup attempt led by Oviedo in April 1996, ordered that he be detained indefinitely pending the results of the investigation. In March the special military tribunal found Oviedo guilty of crimes committed against the order and security of the armed forces, and also of sedition, and sentenced him to 10 years' imprisonment. In the following month the Supreme Court ratified the military tribunal's decision and the Supreme Electoral Tribunal consequently annulled Oviedo's presidential candidacy. In accordance with the law, the candidacy of the Partido Colorado was assumed by Raúl Cubas Grau, hitherto the vice-presidential nominee; Argaña was to be the new candidate for the vice-presidency.

The presidential election of 10 May 1998 resulted in victory for candidate Raúl Cubas Grau, who secured some 55.4% of the votes cast, ahead of the candidate of the AD, Domingo Laíno, who received 43.9% of the votes. Partido Colorado candidates were also most successful at legislative elections conducted concurrently with the presidential poll (securing 51.7% of the votes and 24 seats in the Senado and 53.8% of the votes and 45 seats in the Cámara—the AD won 20 seats in the Senado and 35 in the Cámara) and at elections for provincial administrators organized at the same time. The elections were generally considered to have been free and fair, and turn-out was estimated at an impressive 85%. Cubas Grau's election campaign had emphasized his support for his long-time political ally, Oviedo, and his intention to grant Oviedo a presidential pardon on his inauguration (scheduled for 15 August). In June, therefore, the out-going Congreso Nacional (in which the Partido Colorado had no majority) endorsed new legislation which restricted the terms of application of presidential pardons; henceforth, recipients would first be required to complete one-half of the original sentence, and would still be subject to any attendant long-term restrictions on their constitutional rights (such as a ban on holding public office). The new legislation was promulgated by Wasmosy later in the month. Also prior to the inauguration of the new administration, in July Vice-President-elect Argaña (a staunch opponent of Oviedo) concluded an informal political pact involving his faction of the Partido Colorado and the opposition PLRA and EN, effectively depriving Cubas Grau of a congressional majority, while in early August President Wasmosy implemented a comprehensive reorganization of the military high command, which promoted the interests of many of Oviedo's military opponents.

Cubas Grau duly took office on 15 August 1998, and a new Council of Ministers, largely composed of supporters of Gen. Oviedo, was sworn in on the same day. (Out-going President Wasmosy assumed a seat in the Senado on 20 August.) On 18 August, deliberately circumventing the new law restricting presidential pardons, Cubas Grau issued a decree commuting Oviedo's prison sentence to time already served. On the following day the Congreso Nacional voted to condemn the decree and to initiate proceedings to impeach the President for unconstitutional procedure. (A successful impeachment would result in the promotion of Oviedo's severest critic, Vice-President Argaña, to the presidency.) The new President's confrontational stance (and the release of Oviedo) also provoked dissent among his own supporters and associates; Cubas Grau's brother, Carlos, resigned the industry and commerce portfolio in the new Council of Ministers later that month. The increasingly symbolic struggle for authority to decide the fate of Gen. Oviedo between President Cubas Grau (with the support of Oviedo's military allies—Cubas Grau reorganized the military high command and reinstated some 200 officers dismissed by Wasmosy) and the legislature (with the support of the judiciary) intensified in late 1998, both sides indulging in increasingly threatening rhetoric. Meanwhile, on 5 December, the Argaña faction-controlled central apparatus of the Partido Colorado expelled Oviedo from the party. While the Congreso Nacional was unable to muster the two-thirds' majority support necessary to impeach President Cubas Grau, the country remained in effective political deadlock, prompting serious concerns in the business community that the country's mounting economic difficulties would not be addressed.

In March 1999, however, the political impasse ended dramatically. On 23 March Vice-President Argaña was assassinated by an unknown assailant, prompting nation-wide speculation that Oviedo was behind the attack, and galvanizing the Congreso Nacional sufficiently to secure the support of the two-thirds' majority needed to initiate Cubas Grau's impeachment. Mounting tensions were exacerbated, on 26 March, by the murders of six protesters who were demonstrating in Asunción, in support of demands for the resignation of the President, in the light of Argaña's assassination. On 28 March Cubas Grau resigned the presidency and sought refuge in Brazil, while Oviedo crossed the border to Argentina. (In February 2002 Cubas Grau surrendered to the Paraguayan authorities to face trial for the killings of the protesters and was placed under house arrest.) In early April the judicial authorities ordered the arrest of Oviedo for involvement in the death of Argaña, after three of his close collaborators were identified as the assassins. (In October 2000 Maj.-Gen. Reinaldo Servin, Constantino Rodas and Pablo Vera Esteche were sentenced to long prison terms for their roles in the assassination.) However, the Argentine Government rejected Paraguay's request for extradition, resulting in a rapid deterioration in the relationship between the two countries. When the extradition request was rejected for the second time in early September, the Paraguayan Government recalled its ambassador to Argentina (and the ambassador to Uruguay, which at the same time rejected a request to extradite the former Minister of National Defence, José Segovia Boltes). The Argentine authorities did, however, banish Oviedo to Tierra del Fuego in the extreme south after he repeatedly violated the terms of his asylum by making political statements. However, Oviedo left Argentina in early December in order to avoid being extradited by the new Argentine Government of Fernando de la Rúa.

Meanwhile, in accordance with the terms of the Constitution, in the absence of the elected President and Vice-President, the President of the Congreso Nacional, the pro-Argaña Partido Colorado senator, Luis González Macchi, was swiftly installed as Head of State and he announced the composition of a multiparty Government of National Unity at the end of March 1999. In late April, following careful scrutiny of the articles of the Constitution, the Supreme Court ruled that González Macchi should serve the remainder of Cubas Grau's presidential term (scheduled to expire in 2003). The Court also ruled that elections to select a new Vice-President should be conducted in late 1999. (The date eventually set was 13 August 2000.) Hoping to consolidate the Government of National Unity, González Macchi announced that his own party (the Partido Colorado) would not present a vice-presidential candidate. However, prominent figures within the party decided to contest the election none the

less, precipitating tension with the PLRA (the main opposition and largest coalition partner), which had effectively been promised the post. Meanwhile, factionalism within the PLRA placed increasing strains on the Government of National Unity. Luis Alberto Wagner of the PLRA was dismissed as Minister of Agriculture and Livestock by González Macchi in late August 1999, apparently in response to pressure by the party's leadership to replace him because he was from the opposing 'Laíno' faction. The PLRA leadership was angered when Miguel Abdón Saguier was replaced as Minister of Foreign Affairs in early September by José Fernández Estigarribia, a 'Laíno' faction member of the PLRA. Events culminated in February 2000 when PLRA members voted to withdraw from the ruling coalition. Accordingly, Fernández Estigarribia resigned and was replaced by Juan Esteban Aguirre Martínez of the Partido Colorado. Meanwhile, Oscar Denis resigned as Minister of Agriculture and Livestock at the end of December 1999, after his faction had decided to support the move to withdraw from the administration; he was replaced by Enrique Zúñiga. The withdrawal of the PLRA deprived the Government of a legislative majority. The Partido Colorado's remaining coalition partner, the EN, was, furthermore, divided over the issue of its continuing participation in the Government.

In late May 1999 González Macchi forcibly retired more than 100 army officers, including several high-ranking supporters of Gen. Oviedo. By mid-November another 45 senior commanders, who were thought to be supporters of Oviedo, had been replaced. However, the reorganization did not prevent a coup attempt, in mid-May 2000, by rebellious soldiers thought to be sympathetic to Oviedo. It was swiftly defeated by the Government (most army brigades and the air force remained loyal to the President), which declared a 30-day nation-wide state of emergency, assuming extraordinary powers that resulted in the arrest of more than 70 people, mostly members of the security forces. Oviedo denied any involvement with the coup, but in mid-June he was arrested by Brazilian police in Foz do Iguaçú, near the Brazilian border with Paraguay. He was transferred to Brasília to await a Supreme Court decision on an extradition request from Paraguay. In March 2001 the Brazilian Chief Prosecutor ruled that Oviedo could be extradited; however, in December the Supreme Court rejected the ruling, stating that Oviedo was a victim of political persecution, and released him from imprisonment.

The initial popularity of the Government of National Unity collapsed as thousands of peasants, assembled by rural organizations, mobilized on several occasions during 1999 to protest against the Government's lack of action on rural issues. In response to the protests, in November the Government offered a US $168m. rescue package for the agricultural and livestock sector, mostly for debt-refinancing schemes. In March 2000 the Government announced a scheme valued at $30m., with assistance from the UN Development Programme, to assist 250,000 small farmers. However, by the end of the month there were an estimated 10,000 smallholders camped outside the Congreso building. (The protest continued until March 2001, when government concessions were eventually secured.) Also during March 2000 thousands of power and telecommunications workers undertook strike action to protest against the Government's privatization plans. In June public-sector workers held a 48-hour general strike to protest against the privatization programme. However, it did not receive the same level of support as previous demonstrations and the Government insisted it would continue with its 'state restructuring' programme. In mid-November the Congreso Nacional approved legislation allowing for the sale of the state railway, water and telecommunications companies. At the end of January 2001 the announcement of utility price increases led to an upsurge of protests by farmers and opposition groups. The Government responded by reducing the increase in the price of petrol from 36% to 25% for the rest of the year and by lowering the cost of diesel for a provisional period.

In April 2000 the Partido Colorado nominated Félix Argaña, son of the late Vice-President, to be its candidate in the forthcoming vice-presidential ballot. However, at the election, which was finally held on 13 August, the 53-year Colorado monopoly on power was ended when Argaña was narrowly defeated (by less than 1% of the votes cast) by the PLRA candidate, Julio César Franco. The election of Franco, whose candidacy was endorsed by Oviedo, increased the divisions within the Partido Colorado and resulted in the resignation of the Minister of National Defence, Nelson Argaña, another son of the late Vice-President.

A cabinet reshuffle subsequently took place, in which Francisco Oviedo Brítez replaced Federico Zayas as Minister of Finance, while Wálter Bower Montalto, hitherto interior minister and often criticized for his authoritarian style, was moved to the public works and communications ministry.

In January 2001 the new Minister of National Defence, José Ocampos Alfaro, resigned in protest at a presidential decree that eliminated civilian posts at the armed forces' main training institute. He was replaced in the following month by Adm. Miguel Angel Candia Fleitas, hitherto Commander of the Armed Forces. In February the Minister of Education and Culture, Nicanor Duarte Frutos, resigned in order to campaign for the presidency of the Partido Colorado, which he secured, with almost 50% of the vote, in elections in early May. At the same time, the Government was further undermined by tensions between the President and the Vice-President; Franco, as the most senior elected government official, demanded the resignation of President González Macchi in the name of democratic legitimacy. In mid-March the Government's problems intensified when the three EN representatives in the Council of Ministers threatened to resign in response to allegations that the President's car was a stolen vehicle, illegally smuggled into the country. In an attempt to restore confidence, González Macchi swiftly carried out a cabinet reshuffle that included the appointment of José Antonio Moreno Rufinelli to the post of Minister of Foreign Affairs, replacing Juan Esteban Aguirre. On the same day, some 10,000 farmers marched through Asunción to protest against the Government's economic policy and to demand greater action on rural issues.

Another corruption scandal emerged in early May 2001, which forced the President of the Central Bank, Washington Ashwell, to resign over his alleged involvement in the fraudulent transfer of US $16m. to a US bank account. Later that month, in response to allegations that the President had been a beneficiary of the misappropriated funds, opposition parties attempted to impeach him; however, the bid was defeated by the Cámara de Diputados in August. In September several thousand protesters marched in Asunción to demand the resignation of González Macchi. Nevertheless, in spite of the unpopularity of the National Government, and a united opposition, in municipal elections in November the Partido Colorado candidate, Enrique Riera, was elected to the politically significant post of Mayor of Asunción. In April 2002 González Macchi was formally charged with involvement in the corruption scandal.

In late January 2002 the credibility of the Government was further undermined after two leaders of the left-wing party Movimiento Patria Libre (MPL) alleged that they had been illegally detained for 13 days and tortured by the police, with the knowledge of government ministers, as part of an investigation into a kidnapping case. In response to the allegations, in early February the head of the national police force and his deputy, as well as the head of the judicial investigations department, were dismissed. Following sustained public and political pressure the Minister of the Interior, Julio César Fanego, and the Minister of Justice and Labour, Silvio Ferreira Fernández, resigned soon afterwards, although both protested their innocence. They were replaced by Francisco Oviedo Brítez (who was succeeded by James Spalding at the finance ministry) and Diego Abente Brun, respectively. In addition, the national intelligence agency, the Secretaría Nacional de Informaciones, was disbanded. The Cámara de Diputados issued a statement assigning some responsibility for the detention of the MPL leaders to the President and the Attorney-General, and describing the event as 'state terrorism'. Later that month 2,000 police officers were deployed to prevent a demonstration by peasants protesting against such 'state terrorism' from reaching government buildings.

Throughout 2002 an alliance of farmers, trade unions and left-wing organizations staged mass protests throughout the country to call for an end to the Government's free-market policies and to protest at widely-perceived government corruption. In response to the mounting opposition, in June the Government suspended its planned privatization of the state telecommunications company, Corporación Paraguaya de Comunicaciones (COPACO). Nevertheless, the protests continued as the economic situation worsened, prompting González Macchi to declare a state of emergency in July, which was lifted two days later after clashes between anti-Government protesters and security forces resulted in two fatalities. A further mass demonstration in Asunción in early September, organized by opposition parties, including Gen. Oviedo's Unace grouping, led to further clashes with security forces. The protest had been prompted by the publication of a report by the non-governmental organization Transparency International, which claimed that Paraguay was the most corrupt country in Latin America.

In August 2002 the IMF approved, subject to conditions, a US $200m. stand-by loan to Paraguay. However, in November the Congreso failed to approve the financial reforms necessary to fulfil the Fund's conditions. As a result of the congressional impasse, the Minister of Finance, James Spalding, resigned. He was replaced by Alcides Jiménez, the Minister of Public Works, who, in turn, was succeeded by Adam Nill. Earlier in November the President of the Central Bank, Raúl Vera Bogado, had stepped down, also in protest at the Congreso Nacional's failure to approve the reform package. In early December the lower house of the Congreso voted in favour of the impeachment of President González Macchi on five charges of corruption. In an attempt to avoid the charges, González Macchi offered to step down early from office, immediately following the presidential elections that were scheduled to be held on 27 April 2003 (his term of office officially ended in August 2003). However, in February 2003 the Senate voted narrowly against impeachment. It was thought that the absence of a Vice-President to take over from González Macchi had influenced the senators' decision. (In October 2002 Julio César Franco had resigned as Vice-President in order to stand as the PLRA presidential candidate.)

Presidential and legislative elections were held on 27 April 2003. According to preliminary results, the Colorado presidential candidate, Nicanor Duarte Frutos, was victorious in the presidential ballot, attracting 37% of the votes cast. His main opponent, the PLRA candidate, former Vice-President Franco, won 24% of the ballot, followed by Pedro Fadul, representing the newly created Patria Querida party, with 22%. The Unace grouping performed unexpectedly well, with its nominee, Guillermo Sánchez, winning some 13% of the votes (the Unace leader, Gen. Oviedo, remained exiled in Brazil). However, the Colorados performed less well in the concurrently held legislative elections, losing their majority in the Congreso Nacional. The party's lower-house representation fell from 45 to 37, according to preliminary results, and it won only 16 senate seats, compared with 24 in the previous Congreso. In May agreement had not been reached on the formation of a governing coalition; none the less, President-elect Duarte Frutos began to seek a solution to the country's pressing economic concerns (see Economic Affairs) prior to his official inauguration, scheduled for August.

In March 1991 the Presidents and Ministers of Foreign Affairs of Argentina, Brazil, Uruguay and Paraguay signed a formal agreement in Asunción creating a common market of the 'Southern Cone' countries, the Mercado Común del Sur (Mercosur, see p. 316). The agreement allowed for the dismantling of trade barriers between the four countries, and entered into full operation in 1995.

Government

Under the 1992 Constitution, legislative power is held by the bicameral Congreso Nacional (National Congress), whose members serve for five years. The Senado (Senate) has 45 members, and the Cámara de Diputados (Chamber of Deputies) 80 members. Elections to the legislature are by universal adult suffrage. Executive power is held by the President, directly elected for a single term of five years at the same time as the legislature. The President of the Republic governs with the assistance of a Vice-President and an appointed Council of Ministers. Paraguay is divided into 17 departments, each administered by an elected governor.

Defence

The armed forces totalled 18,600 men (including 11,200 conscripts) in August 2002. There was an army of 14,900 men and an air force of 1,700. The navy, which is largely river-based, had 2,000 men, including 900 marines. There is also a 14,800-strong paramilitary police force. Military service, which is compulsory, lasts for 12 months in the army and for two years in the navy. The defence budget for 2001 totalled an estimated 262,000m. guaraníes.

Economic Affairs

In 2001, according to estimates by the World Bank, Paraguay's gross national income (GNI), measured at average 1999–2001 prices, was US $7,345m., equivalent to $1,300 per head (or

$4,400 per head on an international purchasing-power parity basis). During 1990–2001, it was estimated, the population increased at an average annual rate of 2.7%, while gross domestic product (GDP) per head decreased, in real terms, by an average of 0.9% per year. Overall GDP increased, in real terms, at an average annual rate of 1.7% in 1990–2001; growth in 2001 was 2.7%.

Agriculture (including forestry and fishing) contributed an estimated 25.1% of GDP in 2000. In that year an estimated 35.2% of the economically active population were employed in the sector. The principal cash crops are soya bean seeds, which accounted for an estimated 32.8% of total export revenue in 2000, and cotton (an estimated 9.0%). Other significant crops are sugar cane, cassava, wheat and maize. Timber and wood manufactures provided an estimated 5.8% of export revenues in 2000. The raising of livestock (particularly cattle and pigs) is also important. Meat accounted for an estimated 8.3% of export earnings in 2000. According to the World Bank, agricultural GDP increased at an average annual rate of 1.7% in 1990–2000; real agricultural GDP increased by 3.2% in 1999, but decreased by 4.7% in 2000. An outbreak of foot and mouth disease in September 2002 was expected to adversely affect growth in the sector in 2003.

Industry (including mining, manufacturing, construction and power) contributed an estimated 26.1% of GDP in 2000 and employed 16.0% of the working population. According to the World Bank, industrial GDP increased by an average of 3.1% per year in 1990–2000; the sector increased by 3.9% in 1999 and by 2.8% in 2000.

Paraguay has almost no commercially exploited mineral resources, and the mining sector employed only 0.1% of the labour force in 2000 and contributed 0.4% of GDP in the same year. Production is confined to gypsum, kaolin and limestone. However, foreign companies have been involved in exploration for gold and petroleum deposits, and deposits of natural gas were discovered in 1994. In March 2002 Bolivia and Paraguay signed an agreement, pending congressional approval, to build a 3,300-mile gas pipeline through Bolivia, Paraguay, Argentina and Brazil. Construction was expected to begin in 2003 and to be completed in 2005.

Manufacturing contributed an estimated 13.7% of GDP in 2000 and employed 11.2% of the working population in the same year. In 1999 the production of food and beverages (measured in terms of value added) comprised 49.5% of total manufacturing output. The other principal sectors were wood and wood products, handicrafts, paper, printing and publishing, hides and furs, and non-metallic mineral products. According to the World Bank, manufacturing GDP increased at an average annual rate of 0.8% in 1990–2000. Manufacturing GDP increased by just 0.1% in 1999 and by 1.0% in 2000.

Energy is derived almost completely from hydroelectric power. Imports of fuels and lubricants comprised an estimated 13.6% of the value of total merchandise imports in 2000. Ethyl alcohol (ethanol), derived from sugar cane, is widely used as a component of vehicle fuel.

The services sector contributed an estimated 48.7% of GDP in 2000, and engaged 48.8% of the working population in the same year. Paraguay traditionally serves as an entrepôt for regional trade. According to the World Bank, the GDP of the services sector increased by an average of 1.5% per year in 1990–2000; the sector declined by 2.9% in 1999, but grew by 0.6% in 2000.

In 2001 Paraguay recorded a visible trade deficit of US $545.7m., and there was a deficit of $207.0m. on the current account of the balance of payments. In 2000 the principal source of registered imports (31.6%) was Argentina; other major suppliers in this year were Brazil, the People's Republic of China and the USA. Brazil was the principal market for registered exports (38.7%) in 2000; other notable purchasers were Uruguay, Argentina and the Netherlands. The principal exports in 2000 were soya bean seeds, raw cotton and wood and wood manufactures. The principal imports were machinery and transport equipment, fuels and lubricants, beverages and tobacco, and foodstuffs.

In 2001 there was an estimated overall general budget deficit of 229,670m. guaraníes (equivalent to 0.8% of GDP). Paraguay's total external debt was US $3,091m. at the end of 2000, of which $2,061m. was long-term public debt. In that year the cost of debt-servicing was equivalent to 10.4% of the total value of exports of goods and services. Annual inflation averaged 12.9% in 1990–2001; consumer prices increased by an average of 9.0% in 2000 and by 7.3% in 2001. An estimated 14% of the labour force were unemployed in 2000.

Paraguay is a member of the Inter-American Development Bank (IDB, see p. 239), of the Latin American Integration Association (ALADI, see p. 259), of the Latin American Economic System (SELA, see p. 340) and of the Mercado Común del Sur (Mercosur, see p. 316).

The discovery of widespread corruption in the financial sector provoked a serious liquidity crisis in 1995, resulting in the closure of several significant financial institutions (see above). By 1998 only five state enterprises identified for privatization had been divested (at a net loss to the Government). The Government was paralysed by a lack of resources until the end of August 1999, when Taiwan agreed to underwrite a $400m. bond issue. In the previous month the Government had agreed on a long-term structural reform strategy with the IMF and World Bank, which involved acceleration of the privatization of the remaining state assets. However, in May 2002 the Government was again forced to postpone the sale of the state telecommunications company, Corporación Paraguaya de Comunicaciones (COPACO), following mass protests. In July 2000 the IDB announced the approval of three loans totalling $56m. to support modernization of the state and to finance education and agricultural programmes. Faced by growing levels of debt owed by the private sector to state-owned banks, in February 2001 the Government launched a rescue programme to cover $200m. worth of bad debts and it was hoped that a 'shadow' agreement, reached in April with the IMF, would reduce the fiscal deficit. Although the fiscal deficit was contained during 2001, this was achieved by implementing only one-half of the budgeted investments for that year in public works. In real terms, tax revenues continued to decline and by January 2002 the Government was only able to pay public-sector workers in arrears. A request was made to the IMF for a stand-by credit of $50m.–$70m. to strengthen Paraguay's international monetary reserves as a number of debt repayments were delayed in late 2001 and early 2002. Economic growth was 2.7% in 2001. In 2002 the economic situation worsened, partly as a result of the continuing financial crisis in neighbouring Argentina. Political instability meant that the Government was forced to postpone the planned sales of state assets, revenues from which had been intended to reduce the fiscal deficit. This, in turn, jeopardized the granting of a US $200m. stand-by loan from the IMF. Although, the loan was approved in August, it was conditional on the Government implementing a fiscal reform programme. These controversial reforms, known as the 'economic transition law' or 'el impuestazo' (the 'big tax'), involved raising value-added tax (VAT) to 12%, as well as imposing tax increases on various goods, including cigarettes. However, the proposed legislation, which exceeded the limit on tax rises set by the Congreso, was rejected by the legislature in November, thus jeopardizing the IMF loan. The economy was estimated to have contracted by 4.0% in 2002 and the value of the guaraní fell by 30% in that year. In March 2003 the Government narrowly avoided defaulting on its debt obligations by borrowing from the Central Bank. The solution, however, was short-term, and the new Government that was due to take office in mid-2003 would inherit severe economic problems; as well as convincing foreign investors that it would not be plagued by the corruption scandals of its predecessors, the incoming administration would have to undertake the economic austerity measures laid down by the IMF as a condition of funding.

Education

Education is, where possible, compulsory for six years, to be undertaken between six and 12 years of age, but there are insufficient schools, particularly in the remote parts of the country. Primary education begins at the age of six and lasts for six years. Secondary education, beginning at 12 years of age, lasts for a further six years, comprising two cycles of three years each. In 1996 91% of children in the relevant age-group were enrolled at primary schools (males 91%; females 91%), while secondary enrolment included 38% of children in the relevant age-group (males 37%; females 39%). There is one state and one Roman Catholic university in Asunción. Expenditure by the Ministry of Education in 1996 amounted to 777,652m. guaraníes, equivalent to some 18.6% of total government spending.

Public Holidays

2003: 1 January (New Year's Day), 3 February (San Blás, Patron Saint of Paraguay), 1 March (Heroes' Day), 17 April (Maundy Thursday), 18 April (Good Friday), 1 May (Labour

Day), 14–15 May (Independence Day celebrations), 29 May (Ascension Day), 12 June (Peace of Chaco), 19 June (Corpus Christi), 15 August (Founding of Asunción), 25 August (Constitution Day), 29 September (Battle of Boquerón), 12 October (Day of the Race, anniversary of the discovery of America), 1 November (All Saints' Day), 8 December (Immaculate Conception), 25 December (Christmas Day).

2004: 1 January (New Year's Day), 3 February (San Blás, Patron Saint of Paraguay), 1 March (Heroes' Day), 8 April (Maundy Thursday), 9 April (Good Friday), 1 May (Labour Day),

14–15 May (Independence Day celebrations), 20 May (Ascension Day), 10 June (Corpus Christi), 12 June (Peace of Chaco), 15 August (Founding of Asunción), 25 August (Constitution Day), 29 September (Battle of Boquerón), 12 October (Day of the Race, anniversary of the discovery of America), 1 November (All Saints' Day), 8 December (Immaculate Conception), 25 December (Christmas Day).

Weights and Measures

The metric system is in force.

Statistical Survey

Sources (unless otherwise stated): Dirección General de Estadística, Encuestas y Censos, Humaitá 473, Asunción; tel. (21) 47900; internet www.dgeec.gov .py/index.htm; Banco Central del Paraguay, Avda Pablo VI y Avda Sargento Marecos, Casilla 861, Asunción; tel. (21) 60-8019; fax (21) 60-8150; internet www.bcp.gov.py; Secretaría Técnica de Planificación, Presidencia de la República, Iturbe y Eligio Ayala, Asunción.

Area and Population

AREA, POPULATION AND DENSITY

Area (sq km)	406,752*
Population (census results)†	
11 July 1982	3,029,830
26 August 1992	
Males	2,085,905
Females.	2,066,683
Total	4,152,588
Population (official estimates at mid-year)‡	
1999	5,355,843
2000	5,496,450
2001	5,830,583§
Density (per sq km) at mid-2001	14.3

* 157,048 sq miles.
† Excluding adjustments for underenumeration.
‡ Not revised to take account of the 1992 census results.
§ Not comparable with figures for earlier years.

DEPARTMENTS
(1 July 2000)

	Area (sq km)	Population (estimates)	Density (per sq km)	Capital
Alto Paraguay (incl. Chaco)	82,349	14,669	0.2	Fuerte Olimpo
Alto Paraná . . .	14,895	705,137	47.3	Ciudad del Este
Amambay	12,933	136,910	10.6	Pedro Juan Caballero
Asunción	117	561,386	4,798.2	—
Boquerón (incl. Nueva Asunción) . . .	91,669	38,451	0.4	Doctor Pedro P. Peña
Caaguazú	11,474	461,937	40.3	Coronel Oviedo
Caazapá	9,496	143,889	15.2	Caazapá
Canindeyú . . .	14,667	145,841	9.9	Salto del Guairá
Central.	2,465	1,333,889	541.1	Asunción
Concepción. . . .	18,051	191,911	10.6	Concepción
Cordillera	4,948	215,516	43.6	Caacupé
Guairá	3,846	175,121	45.5	Villarrica
Itapúa	16,525	490,969	29.7	Encarnación
Misiones	9,556	100,385	10.5	San Juan Bautista
Ñeembucú	12,147	88,285	7.3	Pilar
Paraguarí	8,705	247,175	28.4	Paraguarí
Presidente Hayes .	72,907	83,193	1.1	Pozo Colorado
San Pedro	20,002	361,786	18.1	San Pedro
Total	406,752	5,496,450	13.5	—

PRINCIPAL TOWNS
(population at 1992 census)

Asunción (capital) .	500,938	Luque	84,877
Ciudad del Este*.	133,881	Capiatá . . .	83,773
San Lorenzo . .	133,395	Encarnación . .	56,261
Lambaré	99,572	Pedro Juan	
Fernando de la Mora	95,072	Caballero . . .	53,566

* Formerly Puerto Presidente Stroessner.

2001: Asunción 627,239.

BIRTHS AND DEATHS
(UN estimates, annual averages)

	1985–90	1990–95	1995–2000
Birth rate (per 1,000)	36.6	34.1	31.3
Death rate (per 1,000)	6.7	6.0	5.4

Source: UN, *World Population Prospects: The 2000 Revision.*

Expectation of life (WHO estimates, years at birth): 70.6 (males 68.3; females 72.9) in 2001 (Source: WHO, *World Health Report*).

ECONOMICALLY ACTIVE POPULATION
(household survey, August–December 2000)

	Males	Females	Total
Agriculture, hunting, forestry and fishing	689,825	212,497	902,322
Mining and quarrying	2,500	—	2,500
Manufacturing	186,322	99,864	286,186
Electricity, gas and water . . .	10,432	3,300	13,732
Construction	107,340	—	107,340
Trade, restaurants and hotels . .	281,928	306,039	587,967
Transport, storage and communications	62,788	11,461	74,249
Financing, insurance, real estate and business services	55,836	28,950	84,786
Community, social and personal services	174,747	326,571	501,318
Activities not adequately described	208	—	208
Total employed	1,571,926	988,682	2,560,608

Health and Welfare

KEY INDICATORS

Total fertility rate (children per woman, 2001).	3.9
Under-5 mortality rate (per 1,000 live births, 2001)	30
HIV/AIDS (% of persons aged 15–49, 1999).	0.11
Physicians (per 1,000 head, 1997)	1.10
Hospital beds (per 1,000 head, 1996)	1.34
Health expenditure (2000): US $ per head (PPP)	323
Health expenditure (2000): % of GDP	7.9
Health expenditure (2000): public (% of total)	38.3
Access to water (% of persons, 1999)	79
Access to sanitation (% of persons, 1999)	95
Human Development Index (2000): ranking	90
Human Development Index (2000): value	0.740

For sources and definitions, see explanatory note on p. vi.

Agriculture

PRINCIPAL CROPS
('000 metric tons)

	1999	2000	2001
Wheat	188	220	359
Rice (paddy)	128	101	106
Maize	817	647	947
Sorghum	23	34	43
Sweet potatoes	79	69	131
Cassava (Manioc)	3,694	2,719	3,568
Sugar cane	2,872	2,244	2,396
Dry beans	43	37	53
Soybeans (Soya beans)	3,053	2,980	3,511
Oil palm fruit*	125	125	125
Sunflower seed	73	82	40
Tung nuts	41	39	45
Cottonseed†	202	247	294
Tomatoes	66	61	55
Dry onions*	34	34	34
Bananas	70	57	64
Oranges	231	202	209
Tangerines, mandarins clementines and satsumas	30	22	24
Grapefruit and pomelo	60	48	48
Watermelons*	110	110	115
Cantaloupes and other melons*	30	30	28
Mangoes*	30	30	29
Pineapples	41	39	41
Cotton (lint)†	67	82	97
Maté	67	59	69

* FAO estimates.
† Unofficial figures.

Source: FAO.

LIVESTOCK
('000 head, year ending September)

	1999	2000	2001
Cattle	9,647	9,737	9,889
Horses	400*	400*	358
Pigs*	2,500	2,700	2,700
Sheep	398	402	406
Goats	122	123	124
Chickens	15,047	15,198	15,350
Ducks*	710	710	715
Geese*	75	80	80
Turkeys*	90	90	95

* FAO estimate(s).

Source: FAO.

LIVESTOCK PRODUCTS
('000 metric tons)

	1999	2000	2001
Beef and veal	246*	239	250†
Pig meat†	120	148	151
Poultry meat†	38	58	59
Cows' milk†	445	330	331
Hen eggs	45†	68	70†
Cattle hides†	38	39	39

* Unofficial figure.
† FAO estimate(s).

Source: FAO.

Forestry

ROUNDWOOD REMOVALS
('000 cubic metres, excluding bark)

	1999	2000*	2001*
Sawlogs, veneer logs and logs for sleepers	3,515	3,515	3,515
Other industrial wood	529	529	529
Fuel wood*	5,508	5,551	5,646
Total	9,552	9,595	9,680

* FAO estimates.

Source: FAO.

SAWNWOOD PRODUCTION
('000 cubic metres, including railway sleepers)

	1995	1996	1997
Total (all broadleaved)	400	500	550

1998–2001: Annual production as in 1997 (FAO estimates).
Source: FAO.

Fishing

(FAO estimates, '000 metric tons, live weight)

	1996	1997	1998
Capture	22.0	28.0	25.0
Characins	8.0	10.0	9.0
Freshwater siluroids	10.0	13.0	12.0
Other freshwater fishes	4.0	5.0	4.0
Aquaculture	0.4	0.4	0.1
Total catch	22.4	28.4	25.1

Note: Figures exclude crocodiles, recorded by number rather than by weight. The number of spectacled caimans caught was: 725 in 1996; 503 in 1997; 4,445 in 1998; 0 in 1999; 9,750 in 2000.

1999–2000: Total catch as in 1998 (FAO estimates).
Source: FAO, *Yearbook of Fishery Statistics*.

Industry

SELECTED PRODUCTS
('000 metric tons, unless otherwise indicated)

	1999	2000	2001
Soya bean oil*	126.2	138.4	174.0
Sugar (raw)†	151	135	130
Hydraulic cement‡	680	700*	750

* Unofficial figure(s).
† FAO estimates.
‡ Data from US Geological Survey.

Source (unless otherwise indicated): FAO.

Finance

CURRENCY AND EXCHANGE RATES

Monetary Units
100 céntimos = 1 guaraní (G)

Sterling, Dollar and Euro Equivalents (31 December 2002)
£1 sterling = 11,449.6 guaraníes
US $1 = 7,103.6 guaraníes
€1 = 7,449.5 guaraníes
10,000 guaraníes = £0.873 = $1.407 = €1.342

Average Exchange Rate (guaraníes per US dollar)
2000   3,486.4
2001   4,105.9
2002   5,716.3

BUDGET
('000 million guaraníes)

Revenue*	1999	2000	2001
Taxation	2,397.7	2,676.8	2,851.5
Taxes on income, profits, etc. .	551.3	478.5	458.8
Domestic taxes on goods and			
services	1,357.9	1,591.1	1,781.9
General sales, turnover or			
value-added tax . . .	1,048.4	1,150.3	1,204.3
Excises	308.2	440.1	476.8
Taxes on international trade and			
transactions	398.8	487.6	498.5
Import duties	398.8	487.6	498.5
Other taxes	88.8	119.0	106.9
Other current revenue . . .	1,603.0	1,523.9	1,984.7
Entrepreneurial and property			
income	1,116.5	992.9	1,342.1
Administrative fees, charges and			
non-industrial sales . .	195.8	225.8	264.7
Contributions to government			
employee pension and welfare			
fund	288.0	300.5	313.4
Capital revenue	3.4	1.0	2.5
Total	4,004.0	4,201.7	4,838.7

Expenditure†	1999	2000	2001
Current expenditure . . .	3,530.1	4,169.6	4,370.4
Expenditure on goods and			
services	2,316.4	2,666.5	2,718.1
Wages and salaries . . .	2,021.4	2,338.7	2,400.1
Interest payments	174.4	303.9	364.3
Subsidies and other transfers .	1,039.3	1,199.2	1,288.1
Transfers to other levels of			
national government . . .	283.8	336.1	338.8
Transfers to non-profit			
institutions and households .	732.0	852.4	940.7
Capital expenditure	1,157.2	1,046.7	831.0
Acquisition of fixed capital assets	700.7	895.9	668.0
Transfers	445.8	149.1	159.7
Total	4,687.3	5,216.3	5,201.4

* Excluding grants received ('000 million guaraníes): 49.7 in 1999; 46.1 in 2000; 135.9 in 2001.
† Excluding lending minus repayments ('000 million guaraníes): 172.6 in 1999; 112.0 in 2000; 2.8 in 2001.

Source: IMF, *Government Finance Statistics Yearbook*.

INTERNATIONAL RESERVES
(US $ million at 31 December)

	2000	2001	2002
Gold*	9.60	9.70	12.10
IMF special drawing rights . .	102.26	102.21	113.18
Reserve position in IMF . .	27.98	26.99	29.20
Foreign exchange	630.40	584.30	486.80
Total	770.24	723.20	641.28

* National valuation of gold reserves (35,000 troy ounces in each year), based on market-related prices.

Source: IMF, *International Financial Statistics*.

MONEY SUPPLY
('000 million guaraníes at 31 December)

	2000	2001	2002
Currency outside banks . .	1,327.19	1,377.21	1,451.20
Demand deposits at commercial			
banks	1,192.53	1,326.51	1,273.39
Total money (incl. others) . .	2,562.25	2,743.15	2,759.53

Source: IMF, *International Financial Statistics*.

COST OF LIVING
(Consumer Price Index for Asunción; base: 1990 = 100)

	1999	2000	2001
Food (incl. beverages) . . .	283.6	307.2	319.0
Housing (incl. fuel and light) . .	347.6	370.2	413.1
Clothing (incl. footwear) . . .	234.2	241.9	249.5
All items (incl. others)	323.5	352.5	378.2

Source: ILO.

NATIONAL ACCOUNTS
('000 million guaraníes at current prices)

National Income and Product

	1997	1998	1999
Compensation of employees . .	6,610.5	7,360.3	7,764.3
Operating surplus*	10,912.5	12,331.2	12,736.9
Domestic factor incomes . .	17,523.0	19,691.5	20,501.2
Consumption of fixed capital . .	1,639.2	1,835.0	1,889.6
Gross domestic product (GDP)			
at factor cost	19,162.2	21,526.5	22,390.8
Indirect taxes, *less* subsidies . .	1,772.2	1,910.4	1,753.6
GDP in purchasers' values . .	20,934.4	23,437.0	24,144.3
Factor income received from			
abroad, *less* factor income paid			
abroad	221.7	304.5	132.2
Gross national product . .	21,156.1	23,741.5	24,276.5
Less Consumption of fixed capital	1,639.2	1,835.0	1,889.6
National income in market			
prices	19,516.9	21,906.5	22,386.9

* Obtained as a residual.

Expenditure on the Gross Domestic Product

	1999	2000	2001
Government final consumption			
expenditure	2,135.4	2,601.6	2,639.9
Private final consumption			
expenditure	19,762.5	22,406.8	25,912.0
Increase in stocks	221.7	242.5	265.5
Gross fixed capital formation . .	5,342.1	5,638.6	5,294.6
Total domestic expenditure . .	27,461.7	30,889.6	34,112.0
Exports of goods and services . .	5,548.6	5,260.1	6,170.1
Less Imports of goods and services	8,866.1	9,228.7	10,696.0
GDP in purchasers' values . .	24,144.3	26,921.0	29,586.1
GDP at constant 1982 prices .	1,130.7	1,126.4	1,157.0

Source: IMF, *International Financial Statistics*.

Gross Domestic Product by Economic Activity

	1998	1999	2000
Agriculture, hunting, forestry and			
fishing	5,716.4	6,067.7	6,764.1
Mining and quarrying . . .	79.5	89.0	97.2
Manufacturing	3,631.5	3,272.1	3,689.2
Construction	1,433.1	1,502.9	1,615.1
Electricity, gas and water . . .	1,148.9	1,394.9	1,635.7
Trade, finance and insurance . .	6,309.9	5,887.1	6,250.4
Transport, storage and			
communications	913.9	1,063.4	1,303.2
Government services	1,181.8	1,360.3	1,537.8
Real estate and housing . . .	515.8	561.5	610.1
Other services	2,506.2	2,945.3	3,418.3
GDP in purchasers' values . .	23,437.0	24,144.3	26,921.0

Source: UN Economic Commission for Latin America and the Caribbean.

BALANCE OF PAYMENTS
(US $ million)

	1999	2000	2001
Exports of goods f.o.b.	2,312.4	2,225.8	2,408.5
Imports of goods f.o.b.	−2,904.0	−2,905.0	−2,954.2
Trade balance	−440.5	−678.2	−545.7
Exports of services	575.4	618.5	580.1
Imports of services	−493.0	−436.1	−409.7
Balance on goods and services	−358.1	−495.8	−375.3
Other income received	212.5	247.9	218.2
Other income paid	−195.0	−219.4	−216.3
Balance on goods, services and income	−340.6	−467.3	−373.4
Current transfers received	176.7	178.3	168.0
Current transfers paid	−1.5	−1.5	−1.6
Current balance	−165.4	−290.5	−207.0
Capital account (net)	19.6	3.0	15.2
Direct investment abroad	−5.6	−5.7	−5.8
Direct investment from abroad	94.5	118.6	79.2
Portfolio investment assets	−9.0	2.0	0.4
Portfolio investment liabilities	—	0.5	−0.1
Other investment assets	−117.7	−209.1	190.4
Other investment liabilities	127.0	121.1	13.9
Net errors and omissions	−244.3	−79.3	−136.4
Overall balance	−300.9	−339.4	−50.2

Source: IMF, *International Financial Statistics*.

External Trade

(excl. border trade)

PRINCIPAL COMMODITIES
(distribution by SITC, US $ million)

Registered imports c.i.f.	1998	1999	2000
Food and live animals	158.3	86.9	148.2
Beverages and tobacco	452.4	230.7	218.6
Beverages	105.7	65.0	78.7
Alcoholic beverages	95.5	95.5	68.0
Tobacco and manufactures	346.7	165.7	139.9
Tobacco, manufactured	323.6	144.5	111.5
Cigarettes	318.8	135.3	95.6
Mineral fuels, lubricants and related materials	208.9	220.8	297.4
Petroleum, petroleum products and related materials	190.2	208.8	274.6
Petroleum products, refined	163.9	190.4	260.8
Gasoline, other light oils	137.6	177.6	230.7
Motor spirit (incl. aviation spirit)	117.8	154.1	198.6
Chemicals and related products	316.5	227.0	306.6
Basic manufactures	339.5	225.4	273.0
Machinery and transport equipment	1,101.7	686.3	637.2
Machinery specialized for particular industries	84.9	53.8	50.4
General industrial machinery equipment and parts	109.4	75.9	100.2
Office machines and automatic data-processing equipment	95.3	89.1	114.0
Telecommunications and sound equipment	155.9	119.0	106.8
Road vehicles and parts	495.0	189.7	161.3
Passenger motor cars (excl. buses)	153.9	88.0	84.7
Goods vehicles	80.3	55.8	35.4
Miscellaneous manufactured articles	287.8	209.8	281.2
Total (incl. others)	2,896.7	1,905.9	2,193.0

Registered exports f.o.b.*	1998	1999	2000
Food and live animals	211.3	132.1	210.7
Meat and preparations	69.4	35.4	72.7
Bovine meat, fresh, chilled or frozen	65.9	33.4	70.3
Bovine meat, boneless	37.4	21.3	54.3
Cereals and preparations	34.0	15.3	32.0
Feeding stuff for animals	69.6	58.0	81.8
Oil-cake and residues of soya beans	64.2	52.3	75.2
Crude materials (inedible) except fuels	582.7	424.6	429.7
Oil seeds and oleaginous fruit	448.9	317.4	291.8
Soya beans	440.3	307.1	285.9
Cork and wood	48.7	38.7	50.3
Wood, shaped, non-coniferous	45.2	35.1	46.7
Wood, sawn, non-coniferous	25.9	13.6	15.9
Textile fibres and waste	77.5	62.8	80.7
Raw cotton (excl. linters)	75.4	61.5	78.6
Animal and vegetable oils, fats and waxes	72.3	49.5	42.4
Fixed vegetable oils and fats	70.2	49.1	41.7
Fixed vegetable oils, 'soft'	65.4	45.8	38.9
Soya bean oil	60.9	36.0	31.0
Basic manufactures	87.8	69.4	110.5
Leather and manufactures, dressed furskins	37.2	35.1	55.9
Leather	35.2	33.3	52.6
Total (incl. others)	1,014.1	740.8	870.9

* Excluding re-exports.

Source: UN, *International Trade Statistics Yearbook*.

PRINCIPAL TRADING PARTNERS
(US $ million)

Imports f.o.b.	1998	1999	2000
Argentina	481.1	312.2	521.4
Brazil	822.4	509.6	502.1
Chile	20.6	4.8	32.5
France (incl. Monaco)	29.8	22.8	21.9
Germany	69.2	57.8	57.9
Hong Kong	33.3	16.1	14.8
Italy	37.2	25.1	44.5
Japan	135.1	102.7	92.5
Korea, Republic	53.1	31.4	24.6
Spain	36.9	54.4	30.0
Sweden	25.3	21.2	24.3
Switzerland	11.6	10.4	34.7
Taiwan	195.0	121.7	40.5
United Kingdom	61.4	39.6	29.0
USA	260.8	235.9	147.0
Uruguay	79.9	68.2	78.3
Total (incl. others)	2,470.8	1,725.1	2,050.4

Exports f.o.b.	1998	1999	2000
Argentina	152.7	53.3	92.0
Brazil	349.3	235.0	336.6
Chile	40.0	23.1	49.9
France (incl. Monaco)	8.1	7.5	5.4
Germany	4.5	11.4	6.7
Italy	20.5	20.1	30.3
Netherlands	241.2	137.1	61.7
Taiwan	11.9	19.7	15.4
United Kingdom	3.5	95.4	3.6
USA	81.7	57.9	33.6
Uruguay	28.7	19.2	123.0
Total (incl. others)	1,014.1	740.8	869.4

Transport

RAILWAYS
(traffic)

	1988	1989	1990
Passengers carried	178,159	196,019	125,685
Freight (metric tons)	200,213	164,980	289,099

1991–93: Passenger-km 1m.; Net ton-km 3m.

Source: UN, *Statistical Yearbook*.

ROAD TRAFFIC
(vehicles in use)

	1999	2000
Cars	267,587	274,186
Buses	8,991	9,467
Lorries	41,329	42,992
Vans and Jeeps	134,144	138,656
Motorcycles	6,872	8,825

Source: Organización Paraguaya de Cooperación Intermunicipal.

SHIPPING

Merchant Fleet
(registered at 31 December)

	1999	2000	2001
Number of vessels	40	44	44
Total displacement ('000 grt)	39.4	45.0	47.1

Source: Lloyd's Register-Fairplay, *World Fleet Statistics*.

CIVIL AVIATION
(traffic on scheduled services)

	1997	1998	1999
Kilometres flown (million)	4	5	4
Passengers carried ('000)	196	222	217
Passenger-km (million)	215	247	239
Total ton-km (million)	19	22	21

Source: UN, *Statistical Yearbook*.

Tourism

ARRIVALS BY NATIONALITY

	1998	1999	2000
Argentina	111,006	98,381	153,800
Bolivia	7,926	6,044	10,855
Brazil	77,304	62,695	50,782
Chile	45,997	16,146	13,277
Germany	7,093	6,110	6,880
Peru	4,534	5,148	9,723
Spain	5,806	7,357	5,977
USA	15,066	10,174	12,372
Uruguay	11,022	9,424	8,238
Total (incl. others)	349,592	269,021	323,041

Source: World Tourism Organization, *Yearbook of Tourism Statistics*.

Tourism receipts (US $ million): 111 in 1998; 81 in 1999; 66 in 2000 (Source: World Tourism Organization).

Communications Media

	1999	2000	2001
Television receivers ('000 in use)	1,100	1,200	n.a.
Telephones ('000 main lines in use)	268.1	n.a.	288.8
Mobile cellular telephones ('000 subscribers)	435.6	820.8	1,150.0
Personal computers ('000 in use)	60	70	80
Internet users ('000)	20	40	60

Radio receivers ('000 in use): 925 in 1997.

Facsimile machines (number in use): 1,691 in 1992.

Daily newspapers: 5* in 1996 (average circulation 213,000* copies).

Non-daily newspapers: 2 in 1988 (average circulation 16,000* copies).

Book production: 152 titles (incl. 23 pamphlets) in 1993.
* Estimates.

Sources: UNESCO, *Statistical Yearbook*; UN, *Statistical Yearbook*; International Telecommunication Union.

Education

(1999, unless otherwise indicated)

	Institutions	Teachers*†	Students
Pre-primary schools	4,071	4,188	123,597
Primary	7,456	24,526	1,036,770
Secondary: general	1,844	21,052	260,500
Secondary: vocational	305		31,136
Tertiary: university level‡	2	n.a.	37,009
Tertiary: other higher‡	109	1,135	20,283

* 1998 figures.
† Full-time teachers only.
‡ Excluding private universities.

Source: partly UNESCO Institute for Statistics.

Adult literacy rate: 91.6% (males 93.1%; females 90.2%) in 2001.

Directory

The Constitution

A new Constitution for the Republic of Paraguay came into force on 22 June 1992, replacing the Constitution of 25 August 1967.

FUNDAMENTAL RIGHTS, DUTIES AND FREEDOMS

Paraguay is an independent republic whose form of government is representative democracy. The powers accorded to the legislature, executive and judiciary are exercised in a system of independence, equilibrium, co-ordination and reciprocal control. Sovereignty resides in the people, who exercise it through universal, free, direct, equal and secret vote. All citizens over 18 years of age and resident in the national territory are entitled to vote.

All citizens are equal before the law and have freedom of conscience, travel, residence, expression, and the right to privacy. The freedom of the press is guaranteed. The freedom of religion and ideology is guaranteed. Relations between the State and the Catholic Church are based on independence, co-operation and autonomy. All citizens have the right to assemble and demonstrate peacefully. All public- and private-sector workers, with the exception of the Armed Forces and the police, have the right to form a trade union and to strike. All citizens have the right to associate freely in political parties or movements.

The rights of the indigenous peoples to preserve and develop their ethnic identity in their respective habitat are guaranteed.

LEGISLATURE

The legislature (Congreso Nacional—National Congress) comprises the Senado (Senate) and the Cámara de Diputados (Chamber of Deputies). The Senado is composed of 45 members, the Cámara of 80 members, elected directly by the people. Legislation concerning national defence and international agreements may be initiated in the Senado. Departmental and municipal legislation may be initiated in the Cámara. Both chambers of the Congreso are elected for a period of five years.

GOVERNMENT

Executive power is exercised by the President of the Republic. The President and the Vice-President are elected jointly and directly by the people, by a simple majority of votes, for a period of five years. They may not be elected for a second term. The President and the Vice-President govern with the assistance of an appointed Council of Ministers. The President participates in the formulation of legislation and enacts it. The President is empowered to veto legislation sanctioned by the Congreso, to nominate or remove ministers, to direct the foreign relations of the Republic, and to convene extraordinary sessions of the Congreso. The President is Commander-in-Chief of the Armed Forces.

JUDICIARY

Judicial power is exercised by the Supreme Court of Justice and by the tribunals. The Supreme Court is composed of nine members who are appointed on the proposal of the Consejo de la Magistratura, and has the power to declare legislation unconstitutional.

The Government

HEAD OF STATE

President: Luis González Macchi (took office 28 March 1999).

President-elect: Nicanor Duarte Frutos (scheduled to take office 1 August 2003).

Vice-President-elect: Luis Alberto Castiglioni Soria.

COUNCIL OF MINISTERS
(April 2003)

Following the election of Nicanor Duarte Frutos to the presidency in April 2003, a new Council of Ministers was due to be announced in May.

Minister of the Interior: Francisco Oviedo Brítez.

Minister of Foreign Affairs: José Antonio Moreno Rufinelli.

Minister of Finance: Alcides Luciano Jiménez.

Minister of Industry and Commerce: Eúclides Acevedo.

Minister of Public Works and Communications: Adam Nill.

Minister of National Defence: Adm. Miguel Angel Candia Fleitas.

Minister of Public Health and Social Welfare: Martín Antonio Chiola.

Minister of Justice and Labour: Diego Abente Brun.

Minister of Agriculture and Livestock: Dario Baumgarten.

Minister of Education and Culture: Dario Zárate Arellano.

MINISTRIES

Ministry of Agriculture and Livestock: Presidente Franco 472, Asunción; tel. (21) 44-9614; fax (21) 49-7965.

Ministry of Education and Culture: Chile, Humaitá y Piribebuy, Asunción; tel. (21) 44-3078; fax (21) 44-3919; internet www2 .paraguaygobierno.gov.py/mec.

Ministry of Finance: Chile 128 esq. Palmas, Asunción; tel. (21) 44-0010; fax (21) 44-8283; e-mail info@hacienda.gov.py; internet www .hacienda.gov.py.

Ministry of Foreign Affairs: Juan E. O'Leary y Presidente Franco, Asunción; tel. (21) 49-4593; fax (21) 49-3910; internet www .mre.gov.py.

Ministry of Industry and Commerce: Avda España 323, Asunción; tel. (21) 20-4638; fax (21) 21-3529; internet www.mic.gov.py.

Ministry of the Interior: Estrella y Montevideo, Asunción; tel. (21) 49-3661; fax (21) 44-8446.

Ministry of Justice and Labour: G. R. de Francia y Estados Unidos, Asunción; tel. (21) 49-3515; fax (21) 20-8469; e-mail mjt@ conexion.com.py.

Ministry of National Defence: Avda Mariscal López y Vice-Presidente Sánchez, Asunción; tel. (21) 20-4771; fax (21) 21-1583.

Ministry of Public Health and Social Welfare: Avda Pettirossi y Brasil, Asunción; tel. (21) 20-7328; fax (21) 20-6700; internet www .mspbs.gov.py.

Ministry of Public Works and Communications: Oliva y Alberdi, Asunción; tel. (21) 44-4411; fax (21) 44-4421; internet www .mopc.gov.py.

President and Legislature

PRESIDENT

Election, 27 April 2003*

Candidate	% of votes
Nicanor Duarte Frutos (Partido Colorado) . . .	37.1
Julio César Ramón Franco Gómez (PLRA)	24.0
Pedro Nicolás Fadul Niella (Patria Querida) . . .	21.3
Guillermo Sánchez Guffanti (Unace)	13.5
Total (incl. others)	100.0

* Preliminary results.

CONGRESO NACIONAL
(National Congress)

President: Juan Carlos Galaverna.

General Election, 27 April 2003*

	Seats	
Party	Cámara de Diputados	Senado
Partido Colorado	37	16
Partido Liberal Radical Auténtico . .	21	12
Patria Querida	10	8
Unión Nacional de Ciudadanos Eticos . .	10	7
Partido País Solidario	2	2
Total	80	45

* Preliminary results.

Political Organizations

Asociación Nacional Republicana—Partido Colorado (National Republican Party): Asunción; 19th century, ruling party since 1940; principal factions include: Movimiento de Reconciliación Colorada; Coloradismo Unido, led by Dr Angel Roberto Seifart; Coloradismo Democrático, led by Blás Riquelme; Acción Democrática Republicana, led by Carlos Facetti Masulli; Frente Republicano de Unidad Nacional, led by Wálter Bower Montalto; 947,430 mems (1991); Pres. Nicanor Duarte Frutos.

Asunción Para Todos (APT): Asunción; f. 1991 to contest municipal elections; also campaigned nationally; Leader Dr Carlos Filizzola.

Encuentro Nacional (EN): Asunción; coalition comprising factions of PRF, PDC, APT and a dissident faction of the Partido Colorado formed to contest presidential and legislative elections of May 1993; Leader Eúclides Acevedo.

Movimiento Patria Libre (MPL): Asunción; left-wing; Sec.-Gen. Anuncio Marti.

Partido Comunista Paraguayo (PCP): Asunción; f. 1928; banned 1928–46, 1947–89; Sec.-Gen. Ananías Maidana.

Partido Demócrata Cristiano (PDC): Colón 871, Casilla 1318, Asunción; f. 1960; 20,500 mems; Pres. Prof. Dr Jerónimo Irala Burgos; Vice-Pres Dr José M. Bonín, Juan C. Descalzo Buongermini; Gen. Sec. Dr Luis M. Andrada Nogués.

Partido Liberal Radical Auténtico (PLRA): Asunción; f. 1978; centre party; Leader Julio César ('Yoyito') Franco.

Partido País Solidario: Asunción.

Partido Revolucionario Febrerista (PRF): Casa del Pueblo, Manduvira 552, Asunción; tel. (21) 494041; e-mail partyce@mixmail .com; f. 1951; social democratic party; affiliated to the Socialist International; President Carlos María Ljubetic.

Partido de los Trabajadores (PT): Asunción; f. 1989; Socialist.

Patria Querida: Asunción; f. 2002; Leader PEDRO NICOLÁS FADUL NIELLA.

Unión Nacional de Ciudadanos Eticos (Unace): Asunción; breakaway faction of the Partido Colorado; Leader Gen. (retd) LINO CÉSAR OVIEDO SILVA (exiled in Brazil).

Diplomatic Representation

EMBASSIES IN PARAGUAY

Argentina: Avda España esq. Avda Perú, Asunción; tel. (21) 21-2320; fax (21) 21-1029; e-mail embarpy@personal.net.py; internet www.embajada-argentina.org.py; Ambassador FÉLIX CÓRDOVA MOYANO.

Bolivia: América 200 y Mariscal Lopez, Asunción; tel. (21) 22-7213; fax (21) 21-0440; e-mail embolivia-asuncion@rree.gov.bo; Chargé d'affaires a.i. RAÚL ZELADA BOBARRUBIAS.

Brazil: Col Irrazábal esq. Eligio Ayala, Asunción; tel. (21) 21-4534; fax (21) 21-2693; Ambassador LUIZ CASTRO NEVES.

Chile: Guido Spano 1687, Calle Juan B. Motta, Asunción; tel. (21) 66-0344; Ambassador EMILIO RUIZ TAGLE.

China (Taiwan): Avda Mariscal López 1043, Casilla 503, Asunción; tel. (21) 21-3362; fax (21) 21-3681; e-mail giopy@telesurf.com.py; internet www.roc-taiwan.org.py; Ambassador BING-FAN YEN.

Colombia: Avda Mariscal López 2240, Asunción; tel. (21) 66-2131; Ambassador CARLOS ALBERTO BERNAL ROMÁN.

Costa Rica: San José 447, Casilla 1936, Asunción; tel. and fax (21) 21-3535; Ambassador FERNANDO JOSÉ GUARDIA ALVARADO.

Cuba: San Rafael 698 esq. Nuestra Señora del Carmen, Asunción; tel. (21) 60-2747; fax (21) 61-2228; Ambassador ANTONIO MIGUEL PARDO SÁNCHEZ.

Ecuador: Edif. Inter-Express, 9°, Of. 901, Herrera 195 esq. Yegros, Asunción; tel. (21) 44-6150; Ambassador ROBERTO PONCE ALVARADO.

France: Avda España 893, Calle Pucheu, Casilla 97, Asunción; tel. (21) 21-2449; fax (21) 21-1690; e-mail chancellerie@ambafran.gov.py; Ambassador JEAN-PIERRE DANIEL LAFOSSE.

Germany: Avda Venezuela 241, Casilla 471, Asunción; tel. (21) 21-4009; fax (21) 21-2863; e-mail aaasun@pla.net.py; Ambassador PETER KIEWITT.

Holy See: Calle Ciudad del Vaticano 350, casi con 25 de Mayo, Casilla 83, Asunción (Apostolic Nunciature); tel. (21) 21-5139; fax (21) 21-2590; e-mail nunapos@conexion.com; Apostolic Nuncio Most Rev. ANTONIO LUCIBELLO (Titular Archbishop of Thurio).

Italy: Calle Luis Morales 680, esq. Luis de León, Apdo 521, Asunción; tel. (21) 20-7429; fax (21) 21-2630; e-mail ambasu@uninet.com.py; Ambassador GIULIO CESARE PICCIRILLI.

Japan: Avda Mariscal López 2364, Casilla 1957, Asunción; tel. (21) 60-4616; fax (21) 60-6901; Ambassador SHOSUKE ITO.

Korea, Republic: Avda Rep. Argentina 678, Asunción; tel. (21) 60-5606; fax (21) 60-1376; Ambassador CHOU UCK KIM.

Mexico: Calle Denis Roa 1559, Barrio Ykua Sati, Asunción; tel. (21) 60-8645; fax (21) 66-3161; e-mail embamex@embamex.com.py; Ambassador ANTONIO VILLEGAS VILLALOBOS.

Panama: Edif. Betón I, 11ᴮ°, Calle Eduardo Víctor Haedo 179, Asunción; tel. (21) 44-5545; fax (21) 44-6192; Ambassador REYMUNDO HURTADO LAI.

Peru: Agustín Barrios 852, Barrio Manorá, Asunción; tel. (21) 60-7431; fax (21) 60-7327; Ambassador NORAH NALVARTE CHÁVEZ.

Spain: Yegros 437, Asunción; tel. (21) 49-0686; Ambassador IGNACIO GARCÍA-VALDECASAS.

Switzerland: Edif. Parapití, 4°, Juan E. O'Leary 409 y Estrella, Asunción; tel. (21) 44-8022; e-mail swiemasu@pla.net.py; Ambassador URS STEMMLER.

United Kingdom: Avda Boggiani 5848, C/R 16 Boquerón, Asunción; tel. (21) 61-2611; fax (21) 60-5007; e-mail brembasu@rieder.net.py; Ambassador ANTHONY CANTOR.

USA: Avda Mariscal López 1776, Casilla 402, Asunción; tel. (21) 21-3715; fax (21) 21-3728; internet www.usembparaguay.gov.py; Ambassador JOHN F. KEANE.

Uruguay: 25 de Mayo 1894 esq. General Aquino, Asunción; tel. (21) 22-3970; fax (21) 22-5022; Ambassador RODOLFO OLAVARRIA.

Venezuela: Edif. Delime II, 1°, Juan E. O'Leary esq. Eduardo Víctor Haedo, Apdo 94, Asunción; tel. (21) 44-4242; e-mail bolivar@conexion.com.py; internet www.embvenezuela.org.py; Ambassador NELSON PINEDA.

Judicial System

The Corte Suprema de Justicia (Supreme Court of Justice) is composed of judges (usually nine) appointed on the recommendation of the Consejo de la Magistratura (Council of the Magistracy).

Corte Suprema de Justicia: Palacio de Justicia, Asunción; CARLOS FERNÁNDEZ GADEA (President), ENRIQUE SOSA ELIZECHE, FELIPE SANTIAGO PAREDES, RAÚL SAPENA BRUGADA, WILDO RIENZI GALEANO, BONIFACIO RÍOS ÁVALOS, JERÓNIMO IRALA BURGOS, LUIS LEZCANO CLAUDE, ANTONIO FRETES.

Consejo de la Magistratura
Palacio de Justicia, Asunción.

FEDERICO CALLIZO NICORA (President), CÉSAR MANUEL DIESEL (Vice-President), CARLOS FERNÁNDEZ GADEA, EVELIO FERNÁNDEZ AREVALOS, MARCELO DUARTE, FLORENTÍN LÓPEZ C, SIXTO VOLPE RÍOS, RAÚL SILVA ALONSO.

Attorney-General: OSCAR LATORRE.

Under the Supreme Court are the Courts of Appeal, the Tribunal of Jurors and Judges of First Instance, the Judges of Arbitration, the Magistrates (Jueces de Instrucción), and the Justices of the Peace.

Religion

The Roman Catholic Church is the established religion, although all sects are tolerated.

CHRISTIANITY

The Roman Catholic Church
For ecclesiastical purposes, Paraguay comprises one archdiocese, 11 dioceses and two Apostolic Vicariates. At 31 December 2000 there were an estimated 4,707,737 adherents in the country, representing about 79% of the total population.

Bishops' Conference
Conferencia Episcopal Paraguaya, Calle Alberdi 782, Casilla 1436, Asunción; tel. (21) 49-0920; fax (21) 49-5115; e-mail cep@infonet.com.py.

f. 1977; statutes approved 2000; Pres. Rt Rev. JORGE ADOLFO CARLOS LIVIERES BANKS (Bishop of Encarnación).

Archbishop of Asunción: Most Rev. FELIPE SANTIAGO BENÍTEZ AVALOS, Arzobispado, Avda Mariscal López 130 esq. Independencia Nacional, Casilla 654, Asunción; tel. (21) 44-4150; fax (21) 44-7510.

The Anglican Communion
Paraguay constitutes a single diocese of the Iglesia Anglicana del Cono Sur de América (Anglican Church of the Southern Cone of America). The Presiding Bishop of the Church is the Bishop of Northern Argentina.

Bishop of Paraguay: Rt Rev. JOHN ELLISON, Iglesia Anglicana, Casilla 1124, Asunción; tel. (21) 20-0933; fax (21) 21-4328; e-mail jellison@pla.net.py; internet www.paraguay.anglican.org.

The Baptist Church
Baptist Evangelical Convention of Paraguay: Casilla 1194, Asunción; tel. (21) 22-7110; Exec. Sec. Lic. RAFAEL ALTAMIRANO.

BAHÁ'Í FAITH

National Spiritual Assembly of the Bahá'ís of Paraguay: Eligio Ayala 1456, Apdo 742, Asunción; tel. (21) 22-0250; fax (21) 22-5747; e-mail bahai@uninet.com.py; Sec. MIRNA LLAMOSAS DE RIQUELME.

The Press

DAILIES

ABC Color: Yegros 745, Asunción; tel. (21) 49-1160; fax (21) 49-3059; e-mail azeta@abc.una.py; internet www.ubc.com.py; f. 1967; independent; Propr ALDO ZUCCOLILLO; circ. 75,000.

El Día: Avda Mariscal López 2948, Asunción; tel. (21) 60-3401; fax (21) 66-0385; e-mail eldia@infonet.com.py; Dir HUGO OSCAR ARANDA; circ. 12,000.

La Nacion: Avda Zavala Cue y Cerro Col, Fernando de la Mora, Asunción; tel. (21) 51-2520; fax (21) 44-4827; e-mail lanacion@infonet.com.py; internet www.lanacion.com.py; f. 1995; Dir-Gen. OSVALDO DOMÍNGUEZ DIBB; circ. 10,000.

Noticias: Avda Artigas y Avda Brasilia, Casilla 3017, Asunción; tel. (21) 29-2721; fax (21) 29-2841; e-mail director@diarionoticias.com .py; internet www.diarionoticias.com.py; f. 1984; independent; Dir NÉSTOR LÓPEZ MOREIRA; circ. 55,000.

Patria: Tacuari 443, Asunción; tel. (21) 92011; f. 1946; Colorado Party; Dir JUAN RAMÓN CHÁVEZ; circ. 8,000.

Popular: Avda Mariscal López 2948, Asunción; tel. (21) 60-3401; fax (21) 60-3400; Dir HUGO OSCAR ARANDA; circ. 125,000.

Ultima Hora: Benjamín Constant 658, Asunción; tel. (21) 49-6261; fax (21) 44-7071; e-mail ultimahora@uhora.com.py; internet www .ultimahora.com; f. 1973; independent; Dir DEMETRIO ROJAS; circ. 45,000.

PERIODICALS

Acción: Casilla 1072, Asunción; tel. (21) 37-0753; e-mail oliva@uninet.com.py; internet www.uninet.com.py/accion; monthly; Dir MARIANO GARCÍA.

La Opinión: Boggiani esq. Luis Alberto de Herrera, Asuncíon; tel. (21) 50-7501; fax (21) 50-2297; weekly; Dir FRANCISCO LAWS; Editor BERNARDO NERI.

Tiempo 14: Mariscal Estigarribia 4187, Asunción; tel. (21) 60-4308; fax (21) 60-9394; weekly; Dir HUMBERTO RUBÍN; Editor ALBERTO PERALTA.

NEWS AGENCIES

Agencia Paraguaya de Noticias (APN): Asunción; e-mail apn@supernet.com.py; internet www.supernet.com.py/usuarios/apn.

Foreign Bureaux

Agence France-Presse (AFP): Edif. Segesa, Of. 602, Oliva y Alberdi, Asunción; tel. (21) 44-3725; fax (21) 44-4312; Correspondent HUGO RUIZ OLAZAR.

Agencia EFE (Spain): Yegros 437, Asunción; tel. (21) 49-2730; fax (21) 49-1268; Bureau Chief LUCIO GÓMEZ-OLMEDO.

Agenzia Nazionale Stampa Associata (ANSA) (Italy): Edif. Interexpress, 4°, Of. 403, Luis Alberto de Herrera 195, Asunción; tel. (21) 44-9286; fax (21) 44-2986; Agent VÍCTOR E. CARUGATI.

Associated Press (AP) (USA): Calle Caballero 742, Casilla 264, Asunción; tel. (21) 60-6334.

Deutsche Presse-Agentur (dpa) (Germany): Edif. Segesa, Of. 705, Oliva 309, Asunción; tel. (21) 45-0329; fax (21) 44-8116; Correspondent EDUARDO ARCE.

Inter Press Service (IPS) (Italy): Edif. Segesa, 3°, Of. 5, Oliva 393 y Alberdi, Asunción; tel. and fax (21) 44-6350; Legal Rep. CLARA ROSA GAGLIARDONE.

TELAM (Argentina) is also represented in Paraguay.

Publishers

La Colmena, SA: Asunción; tel. (21) 20-0428; Dir DAUMAS LADOUCE.

Ediciones Diálogo: Calle Brasil 1391, Asunción; tel. (21) 20-0428; f. 1957; fine arts, literature, poetry, criticism; Man. MIGUEL ANGEL FERNÁNDEZ.

Ediciones Nizza: Eligio Ayala 1073, Casilla 2596, Asunción; tel. (21) 44-7160; medicine; Pres. Dr JOSÉ FERREIRA MARTÍNEZ.

Editorial Comuneros: Cerro Corá 289, Casilla 930, Asunción; tel. (21) 44-6176; fax (21) 44-4667; e-mail rolon@conexion.com.py; f. 1963; social history, poetry, literature, law; Man. OSCAR R. ROLÓN.

Librería Intercontinental: Caballero 270, Asunción; tel. (21) 49-6991; fax (21) 44-8721; e-mail agatti@pla.net.py; internet www .libreriaintercontinental.com.py; political science, law, literature, poetry; Dir ALEJANDRO GATTI VAN HUMBEECK.

R. P. Ediciones: Eduardo Víctor Haedo 427, Ascunción; tel. (21) 49-8040; Man. RAFAEL PERONI.

ASSOCIATION

Cámara Paraguaya del Libro: Nuestra Señora de la Asunción 697 esq. Eduardo Víctor Haedo, Asunción; tel. (21) 44-4104; fax (21) 44-7053; Pres. PABLO LEÓN BURIAN; Sec. EMA DE VIEDMA.

Broadcasting and Communications

TELECOMMUNICATIONS

Corporación Paraguaya de Comunicaciones (COPACO): Edif. Morotí, 1°–2°, esq. Gen. Bruguéz y Teodoro S. Mongelos, Casilla 2042, Asunción; tel. (21) 20-3800; fax (21) 20-3888; formerly Administración Nacional De Telecomunicaciones (ANTELCO); changed name to the above in December 2001 as part of the privatization process; privatization suspended in June 2002; Pres. OSCAR STARK ROBLEDO.

Comisión Nacional de Telecomunicaciones (CONATEL): Edif. San Rafael, 2° Yegros 437 y 25 de Mayo, Asunción; tel. (21) 44-0020; fax (21) 49-8982; Pres. VICTOR ALCIDES BOGADO.

BROADCASTING

Radio

Radio Arapysandu: Avda Mariscal López y Capitán del Puerto San Ignacio, Misiones; tel. (82) 2374; fax (82) 2206; f. 1982; Gen. Man. HECTOR BOTTINO FRANCO.

Radio Asunción: Avda Artígas y Capitán Lombardo 174, Asunción; tel. (21) 29-5375; fax (21) 29-2718; Dir MIGUEL G. FERNÁNDEZ.

Radio Cáritas: Kubitschek y 25 de Mayo, Asunción; tel. (21) 21-3570; fax (21) 20-4161; f. 1936; station of the Franciscan order; medium-wave; Pres. Most Rev. FELIPE SANTIAGO BENÍTEZ AVALOS (Archbishop of Asunción); Dir MARIO VELÁZQUEZ.

Radio Cardinal: Río Paraguay 1334 y Guariníes Lambaré, Casilla 2532, Asunción; tel. (21) 31-0555; fax (21) 31-0557; f. 1991; Pres. NÉSTOR LÓPEZ MOREIRA.

Radio City: Edif. Líder III, Antequera 652, 9°, Asunción; tel. (21) 44-3324; fax (21) 44-4367; f. 1980; Dir. GREGORIO RAMÓN MORALES.

Radio Concepción: Coronel Panchito López 241, entre Schreiber y Profesor Guillermo A. Cabral, Casilla 78, Concepción; tel. (31) 42318; fax (31) 42254; f. 1963; medium-wave; Dir SERGIO E. DACAK; Gen. Man. JULIÁN MARTÍ IBÁÑEZ.

Radio Emisoras Paraguay: Avda General Santos 2525 y 18 de Julio, Asunción; tel. (21) 31-0644; FM; Gen. Man. GUILLERMO HEISECKE.

Radio Encarnación: General Artigas 798 y Caballero, Encarnación; tel. (71) 3345; fax (71) 4099; medium- and short-wave; Dir BIENVENIDA KRISTOVICH.

Radio Guairá: Presidente Franco 788 y Alejo García, Villarica; tel. (541) 42130; fax (541) 42385; f. 1950; medium-, long- and short-wave; Dir LÍDICE RODRÍGUEZ DE TRAVERSI.

Radio Itapirú S.R.L.: Avda San Blás esq. Coronel Julián Sánchez, Ciudad del Este, Alto Paraná; tel. (61) 57-2206; fax (61) 57-2210; f. 1969; Gen. Man. ANTONIO ARANDA ENCINA.

Radio La Voz de Amambay: 14 de Mayo y Cerro León, Pedro Juan Caballero, Amambay; tel. (36) 72537; f. 1959; Gen. Man. LUÍS ROLÓN PEÑA.

Radio Nacional del Paraguay: Blas Garay 241 y Iturbe, Asunción; tel. (21) 39-0374; fax (21) 39-0376; medium- and short-wave and FM; Dir GILBERTO ORTÍZ BAREIRO.

Radio Ñandutí: Choferes del Chaco y Carmen Soler, Asunción; tel. (21) 60-4308; fax (21) 60-6074; internet www.infonet.com.py/holding/nanduam/; f. 1962; Dirs HUMBERTO RUBÍN, GLORIA RUBÍN.

Radio Nuevo Mundo: Coronel Romero y Flórida, San Lorenzo, Asunción; tel. (21) 58-6258; fax (21) 58-2424; f. 1972; Dir JULIO CÉSAR PEREIRA BOBADILLA.

Radio Oriental: Avda Mariscal López 450 y San Lorenzo, Caaguazú; tel. (522) 42790; Dir HECTOR OMAR YINDE.

Radio Primero de Marzo: Avda General Perón y Concepción, Casilla 1456, Asunción; tel. (21) 31-1564; fax (21) 33-3427; Dir-Gen. ANGEL GUERREROS A.

Radio Santa Mónica FM: Avda Boggiani y Herrera, 3°, Asunción; tel. (21) 50-7501; fax (21) 50-9494; f. 1973; Exec. Dir. GUSTAVO CANATTA.

Radio Uno: Avda Mariscal López 2948, Asunción; tel. (21) 61-2151; f. 1968 as Radio Chaco Boreal; Dir. BENJAMÍN LIVIERES.

Radio Venus: República Argentina y Souza, Asunción; tel. (21) 61-0151; e-mail venus@infonet.com.py; internet www.venus.com.py; f. 1987; Dir ANGEL AGUILERA.

Radio Ysapy: Independencia Nacional 1260, 1°, Asunción; tel. (21) 44-4037; Dir JOSÉ CABRIZA SALVIONI.

Television

Teledifusora Paraguaya—Canal 13: Chile 993, Asunción; tel. (21) 33-2823; fax (21) 33-1695; f. 1980; Gen. Man. NESTOR LÓPEZ MOREIGA.

Televisión Cerro Corá—Canal 9: Avda Carlos A. López 572, Asunción; tel. (21) 42-4222; fax (21) 48-0230; f. 1965; commercial; Dir Gen. ISMAEL HADID.

Televisora del Este: San Pedro, Calle Pilar, Area 5, Ciudad del Este; tel. (61) 8859; commercial; Dir Lic. JALIL SAFUAN; Gen. Man. A. VILLALBA V.

Televisión Itapúa—Canal 7: Encarnación; tel. (71) 20-4450; commercial; Dir Lic. JALIL SAFUAN; Station Man. JORGE MATEO GRANADA.

Finance

(cap. = capital; res = reserves; dep. = deposits; m. = million; amounts in guaraníes, unless otherwise indicated)

BANKING

Superintendencia de Bancos: Edif. Banco Central del Paraguay, Avda Federacíon Rusa y Avda Sargento Marecos, Barrio Santo Domingo, Asunción; tel. (21) 60-8011; fax (21) 60-8149; e-mail supban@bcp.gov.py; internet www.bcp.gov.py/supban/principal .htm; Superintendent ANGEL GABRIEL GÓNZALEZ.

Central Bank

Banco Central del Paraguay: Avda Federación Rusa y Sargento Marecos, Casilla 861, Barrio Santo Domingo, Asunción; tel. (21) 60-8011; fax (21) 60-8149; e-mail ccs@bcp.gov.py; internet www.bcp .com.py; f. 1952; cap. and res 19,300m. (June 1985); Pres. (vacant); Gen. Man. GILBERTO RODRÍGUEZ GARCETE.

Development Banks

Banco Nacional de Fomento: Independencia Nacional y Cerro Corá, Casilla 134, Asunción; tel. (21) 44-3762; fax (21) 44-4502; e-mail consubnf@connexion.com.py; internet www.bnf.gov.py; f. 1961 to take over the deposit and private banking activities of the Banco del Paraguay; cap. 59,168m., res 49,120m., dep. 807,587m. (Dec. 1997); Pres. JUAN JOSÉ GALEANO; 52 brs.

Crédito Agrícola de Habilitación: Caríos 362 y Willam Richardson, Asunción; tel. (21) 56-9010; fax (21) 55-4956; e-mail cah@quanta.com.py; f. 1943; Pres. Ing. Agr. WALBERTO FERREIRA.

Fondo Ganadero: Avda Artigas 1921, Asunción; tel. (21) 29-4361; fax (21) 44-6922; Pres. GUILLERMO SERRATTI G.

Commercial Banks

Banco Amambay, SA: Avda Aviadores del Chaco, casi San Martín, Asunción; tel. (21) 60-8831; fax (21) 60-8813; e-mail bcoama@ bcoamabancoamambay.com.com.py; internet www.bancoamambay .com.py; f. 1992; Pres. GUIOMAR DE GÁSPERI; Gen. Man. HUGO PORTILLO SOSA.

Banco Continental, SAECA: Estrella 621, Casilla 2260, Asunción; tel. (21) 44-2002; fax (21) 44-2001; e-mail contil@connexion.com.py; f. 1980; cap. US $4.2m.,res $2.5m., dep. $44.6m. (Dec. 2001). Chair. GUILLERMO GROSS BROWN; First Vice-Pres. JAVIER GONZÁLEZ PÉREZ.

Banco Finamérica SA: Chile y Oliva, Casilla 1321, Asunción; tel. (21) 49-1021; fax (21) 44-5199; f. 1988; Pres. Dr GUILLERMO HEISECKE VELÁZQUEZ; Gen. Man. ENRIQUE FERNÁNDEZ ROMAY.

Interbanco, SA: Oliva y Chile 349, Casilla 392, Asunción; tel. (21) 49-4992; fax (21) 44-8587; e-mail interban@infonet.com.py; internet www.interbanco.com.py; f. 1978; cap. 19,000.0m., res 6,443.4m., dep. 373,940.8m. (Dec. 2000); Pres. SERGIO ZAPPA; Gen. Man. CARLOS EDUARDO CASTRO; 5 brs.

Multibanco, SA: Ayolas 482 esq. Oliva, Asunción; tel. (21) 44-7066; fax (21) 48-8496; e-mail iresck@mulitbanco.com.py; Pres. PEDRO DANIEL MIRAGLIO; Gen. Man. JUAN LUÍS HERRERO.

Foreign Banks

ABN AMRO Bank NV (Netherlands): Alberdi y Estrella, Casilla 1180, Asunción; tel. (21) 49-0001; fax (21) 49-1734; internet www .abnamronet.com; f. 1965; Gen. Man. PETER BALTUSSEN.

Banco de Asunción, SA: Palma esq. 14 de Mayo, Asunción; tel. (21) 49-3191; fax (21) 49-3190; f. 1964; major shareholder Banco Central Hispano (Spain); cap. 10,000.0m., res 62,588.1m., dep. 434,799.0m. (Dec. 1999); Pres. LIZARDO PELÁEZ ACERO; Gen. Man. RODRIGO CORREA GONZÁLEZ; 2 brs.

Banco Bilbao Vizcaya Argentaria Paraguaya, SA (Spain): Yegros 437 y 25 de Mayo, Casilla 824, Asunción; tel. (21) 49-2072; fax (21) 44-7874; e-mail bbva.paraguay@bbva.com.py; f. 1961 as Banco Exterior de España, SA; renamed Argentaria Banco Exterior in 1999, name changed to above in 2000; cap. 1,126m., res 1,931m., dep. 30,455m. (Dec. 1987); Pres. JESUS PERÉZ ESTEBAN; Gen. Man. ANGEL SORIA TABUENCA; 5 brs.

Banco do Brasil, SA: Oliva y Nuestra Señora de la Asunción, Casilla 667, Asunción; tel. (21) 49-0121; fax (21) 44-8761; e-mail bbasu@connexion.com.py; f. 1941; Gen. Man. MARÍA AZEVEDO BRETAS.

Banco Central Hispano (Spain): Palma esq. 14 de Mayo, Asunción; tel. (21) 49-3191; fax (21) 49-3190.

Banco do Estado de São Paulo SA (BANESPA) (Brazil): Independencia Nacional esq. Fulgencio R. Moreno, Casilla 2211, Asunción; tel. (21) 49-4981; fax (21) 49-4985; e-mail banesspa@infonet .com.py; Gen. Man. AROLDO SALOMÃO.

Banco de la Nación Argentina: Chile y Palma, Asunción; tel. (21) 44-8566; fax (21) 44-4365; e-mail bnaasn@bna.com.py; f. 1942; Man. ALDO DARIO PAVIOTTI; 3 brs.

Banco del Paraná, SA: Chile esq Eduardo V. Haedo 2298, Asunción; tel. (21) 44-6691; fax (21) 44-8909; e-mail banco.parana@ bancodelparana.com.py; internet www.bancodelparana.com.py; f. 1980; cap. US $12.6m., dep. US $32.3m. (Dec. 2001); Pres. ANTONIO CARLOS GENOVEZE; Dir MIRAMAR BOTTINI FILHO; 5 brs.

Banco Sudameris Paraguay, SA: Independencia Nacional y Cerro Corá, Casilla 1433, Asunción; tel. (21) 49-4542; fax (21) 44-8670; e-mail sudameri@conexion.com.py; f. 1961; savings and commercial bank; subsidiary of Banque Sudameris; cap. 33,613m., res 22,571m., dep. 726,078m. (Dec. 2000); Pres. Dr JOSÉ ANTONIO MORENO RUFFINELLI; Man. GIUSEPPE DI FRANCESCO; 6 brs.

Citibank NA (USA): Avda Mariscal López 3794 y Cruz del Chaco, Asunción; tel. (21) 620-2000; fax (21) 620-2540; e-mail citservi .paraguay@citicorp.com; internet www.citibank.com/paraguay; f. 1958; dep. 55,942.2m. total assets 1,316,258.1m. (Dec. 1997); Gen. Man. HENRY COMBER.

Lloyds Bank PLC (United Kingdom): Palma esq. Juan E. O'Leary, Apdo 696, Asunción; tel. (21) 49-7000; fax (21) 44-7361; e-mail lbpyitec@connexion.com.py; f. 1920; Man. STUART DUNCAN.

Banking Associations

Asociación de Bancos del Paraguay: Jorge Berges 229 esq. EEUU, Asunción; tel. (21) 21-4951; fax (21) 20-5050; e-mail abp .par@pla.net.py; mems: Paraguayan banks and foreign banks with brs in Asunción; Pres. CELIO TUNHOLI.

Cámara de Bancos Paraguayos: 25 de Mayo esq. 22 de Setiembre, Asunción; tel. (21) 22-2373; Pres. MIGUEL ANGEL LARREINEGABE.

STOCK EXCHANGE

Bolsa de Valores y Productos de Asunción SA: Estrella 540, Asunción; tel. (21) 44-2445; fax (21) 44-2446; e-mail bupasa@pla.net .py; f. 1977; Pres. GALO EGUEZ.

INSURANCE

La Agrícola SA de Seguros Generales: Mariscal Estigarribia 1173, Casilla 1349, Asunción; tel. (21) 21-3746; fax (21) 21-3685; f. 1982; general; Pres. Dr VICENTE OSVALDO BERGUES; Gen. Man. CARLOS ALBERTO LEVI SOSA.

ALFA SA de Seguros y Reaseguros: Yegros 944, Asunción; tel. (21) 44-9992; fax (21) 44-9991; e-mail alfa.seg@conexion.com.py; Pres. ARNALDO RAMÍREZ GONZÁLEZ.

América SA de Seguros y Reaseguros: Alberdi esq. Manduvirá, 1°, Asunción; tel. (21) 49-1713; fax (21) 44-8036; Pres. EDUARDO NICOLÁS BO.

Aseguradora Paraguaya, SA: Israel 309 esq. Rio de Janeiro, Casilla 277, Asunción; tel. (21) 21-5086; fax (21) 22-2217; e-mail asepasa@asepasa.com.py; f. 1976; life and risk; Pres. GERARDO TORCIDA CONEJERO.

Atalaya SA de Seguros Generales: Independencia Nacional 565, 1°, esq. Azara y Cerro Corá, Asunción; tel. (21) 49-2811; fax (21) 49-6966; e-mail ataseg@telesurf.com.py; f. 1964; general; Pres. KARIN M. DOLL.

Cenit de Seguros, SA: Ayolas 1082 esq. Ibáñez del Campo, Asunción; tel. (21) 44-9972; fax (21) 44-9502; e-mail cenitsa@rieder.net .py; Pres. Dr FELIPE OSCAR ARMELE BONZI.

Central SA de Seguros: Edif. Betón I, 1° y 2°, Eduardo Víctor Haedo 179, Independencia Nacional, Casilla 1802, Asunción; tel. (21) 49-4654; fax (21) 49-4655; e-mail censeg@conexion.com.py; f. 1977; general; Pres. MIGUEL JACOBO VILLASANTI; Gen. Man. Dr FÉLIX AVEIRO.

El Comercio Paraguayo SA Cía de Seguros Generales: Alberdi 453 y Oliva, Asunción; tel. (21) 49-2324; fax (21) 49-3562; e-mail elcomericopy@mmail.com.py; f. 1947; life and risk; Dir Dr BRAULIO OSCAR ELIZECHE.

La Consolidada SA de Seguros y Reaseguros: Chile 719 y Eduardo Víctor Haedo, Casilla 1182, Asunción; tel. (21) 44-5788; fax (21) 44-5795; e-mail info@laconsolidada.com.py; f. 1961; life and risk; Pres. Dr JUAN DE JESÚS BIBOLINI; Gen. Man. Lic. JORGE PATRICIO FERREIRA FERREIRA.

Fénix SA de Seguros y Reaseguros: Iturbe 823 y Fulgencio R. Moreno, Asunción; tel. (21) 49-5549; fax (21) 44-5643; e-mail fenix@quanta.com.py; Pres. VICTOR MARTÍNEZ YARYES.

Grupo General de Seguros y Reaseguros, SA: Edif. Grupo General, Jejuí 324 y Chile, 3°, Asunción; tel. (21) 49-7897; fax (21) 44-9259; e-mail general_de_seguros@ggeneral.com.py; Pres. JORGE OBELAR LAMAS.

La Independencia de Seguros y Reaseguros, SA: Edif. Parapatí, 1°, Juan E. O'Leary 409 esq. Estrella, Casilla 980, Asunción; tel. (21) 44-7021; fax (21) 44-8996; e-mail la_independencia@par.net.py; f. 1965; general; Pres. REGINO MOSCARDA; Gen. Man. JUAN FRANCISCO FRANCO LÓPEZ.

Intercontinental SA de Seguros y Reaseguros: Iturbe 1047, Teniente Fariña, Altos, Asunción; tel. (21) 49-2348; fax (21) 49-1227; e-mail intercontinentalseguros@usa.net.py; f. 1978; Pres. Dr JUAN MODICA.

Mapfre Paraguay, SA: Avda Mariscal López 910 y General Aquino, Asunción; tel. (21) 44-1983; fax (21) 49-7441; e-mail mafpy@conexión.com.py; Pres. LUIS MARÍA ZUBIZARRETA.

La Meridional Paraguaya SA de Seguros: Iturbe 1046, Teniente Fariña, Asunción; tel. (21) 49-8827; fax (21) 49-8826; Pres. JUAN PASCUAL BURRÓ MUJICA.

Mundo SA de Seguros: Estrella 917 y Montevideo, Asunción; tel. (21) 49-2787; fax (21) 44-5486; f. 1970; risk; Pres. JUAN MARTÍN VILLALBA DE LOS RÍOS; Gen.-Man. BLÁS MARCIAL CABRAL BARRIOS.

La Paraguaya SA de Seguros: Estrella 675, 7°, Asunción; tel. (21) 49-1367; fax (21) 44-8235; e-mail lps@rieder.net.py; f. 1905; life and risk; Pres. JUAN BOSCH.

Patria SA de Seguros y Reaseguros: General Santos 715, Asunción; tel. (21) 22-5250; fax (21) 21-4001; e-mail patria@conexion.com.py; f. 1968; general; Pres. Dr MARCOS PERERA R.

Porvenir SA de Seguros y Reaseguros: Rca Argentina 222, Asunción; tel. (21) 61-3132; e-mail porvenir@telemail.com.py; Pres. Dr JOSÉ DE JESÚS TORRES AGUILERA.

La Previsora SA de Seguros Generales: Estrella 1003, 5°, Asunción; tel. (21) 49-2442; fax (21) 49-4791; e-mail laprevisora@laprevisora.com.py; f. 1964; general; Pres. RUBÉN ODILIO DOMECQ M; Man. JORGE ENRIQUE DOMECQ F.

El Productor SA de Seguros y Reaseguros: Ind. Nacional 811, 8°, Asunción; tel. (21) 49-1576; fax (21) 49-1599; e-mail elproductor@uninet.com.py; Pres. REINALDO PAVÍA.

Real Paraguaya de Seguros, SA: Edif. Banco Real, 1°, Estrella esq. Alberdi, Casilla 1442, Asunción; tel. (21) 49-3171; fax (21) 49-8129; e-mail realscc@pla.net.py; f. 1974; general; Pres. PETER M. BALTUSSEN.

Rumbos SA de Seguros: Estrella 851, Ayolas, Casilla 1017, Asunción; tel. (21) 44-9488; fax (21) 44-9492; e-mail rumbos@conexion.com.py; f. 1960; general; Pres. Dr ANTONIO SOLJANCIC; Man. Dir ROBERTO GÓMEZ VERLANGIERI.

La Rural del Paraguay SA Paraguaya de Seguros: Avda Mariscal López 1082 esq. Mayor Bullo, Casilla 21, Asunción; tel. (21) 49-1917; fax (21) 44-1592; e-mail larural@mmail.com.py; f. 1920; general; Pres. YUSAKU MATSUMIYA; Gen. Man. EDUARDO BARRIOS PERINI.

Seguros Chaco SA de Seguros y Reaseguros: Mariscal Estigarribia 982, Casilla 3248, Asunción; tel. (21) 44-7118; fax (21) 44-9551; e-mail segucha@conexion.com.py; f. 1977; general; Pres. EMILIO VELILLA LACONICH; Exec. Dir ALBERTO R. ZARZA TABOADA.

Seguros Generales, SA (SEGESA): Edif. SEGESA, 1°, Oliva 393 esq. Alberdi, Casilla 802, Asunción; tel. (21) 49-1362; fax (21) 49-1360; e-mail segesa@conexion.com.py; f. 1956; life and risk; Pres. CÉSAR AVALOS.

El Sol del Paraguay, Cía de Seguros y Reaseguros, SA: Cerro Corá 1031, Asunción; tel. (21) 49-1110; fax (21) 21-0604; e-mail elsolpar@pla.net.py; f. 1978; Pres. Dr ANGEL ANDRÉS MATTO; Vice-Pres. JALIL SAFUÁN.

Universo de Seguros y Reaseguros, SA: Edif. de la Encarnación, 9°, 14 de Mayo esq. General Díaz, Casilla 788, Asunción; tel. (21) 44-8530; fax (21) 44-7278; f. 1979; Pres. BRAULIO GONZÁLEZ RAMOS.

Yacyretá SA de Seguros y Reaseguros: Oliva 685 esq. Juan E. O'Leary y 15 de Agosto, Asunción; tel. (21) 45-2374; f. 1980; Pres. OSCAR A. HARRISON JACQUECT.

Insurance Association

Asociación Paraguaya de Cías de Seguros: 15 de Agosto esq. Lugano, Casilla 1435, Asunción; tel. (21) 44-6474; fax (21) 44-4343; e-mail apcs@uninet.com.py; f. 1963; Pres. EMILIO VELILIA LACONICH; Sec. D. GERARDO TORCIDA CONEJERO.

Trade and Industry

GOVERNMENT AGENCIES

Consejo Nacional para las Exportaciones: Asunción; f. 1986; founded to eradicate irregular trading practices; Dir Minister of Industry and Commerce.

Consejo de Privatización: Edif. Ybaga, 10°, Presidente Franco 173, Asunción; fax (21) 44-9157; responsible for the privatization of state-owned enterprises; Exec. Dir RUBÉN MORALES PAOLI.

Instituto Nacional de Tecnología y Normalización (INTN) (National Institute of Technology and Standardization): Avda General Artigas 3973 y General Roa, Casilla 967, Asunción; tel. (21) 29-3748; fax (21) 29-0873; national standards institute; Dir. Gen. JOSÉ MARTINO.

Instituto de Previsión Social: Constitución y Luis Alberto de Herrera, Casilla 437, Asunción; tel. (21) 22-5719; fax (21) 22-3654; f. 1943; responsible for employees' welfare and health insurance scheme; Pres. Lic. BONIFACIO IRALA AMARILLA.

DEVELOPMENT ORGANIZATIONS

Secretaría Técnica de Planificación de la Presidencia de la República: Edif. AYFRA, 3°, Presidente Franco y Ayolas, Asunción; tel. (21) 44-8074; fax (21) 49-6510; govt body responsible for overall economic and social planning; Exec. Sec. Dr GUILLERMO SOSA; Sec.-Gen. Dr MARÍA VICTORIA DIESEL DE COSCIA.

Consejo Nacional de Coordinación Económica: Presidencia de la República, Paraguayo Independiente y Juan E. O'Leary, Asunción; responsible for overall economic policy; Sec. FULVIO MONGES OCAMPOS.

Consejo Nacional de Desarrollo Industrial (National Council for Industrial Development): Asunción; national planning institution.

Instituto de Bienestar Rural (IBR): Tacuary 276, Asunción; tel. (21) 44-0578; fax (21) 44-6534; responsible for rural welfare and colonization; Pres. ANTONIO IBAÑEZ.

Instituto Nacional del Indígena (INDI): Don Bosco 745, Asunción; tel. (21) 49-7137; fax (21) 447-154; f. 1981; responsible for welfare of Indian population; Pres. ELENA PANE PÉREZ.

ProParaguay: Edif. Ayfra, 12°, Pdte Franco y Ayolas, Asunción; tel. (21) 49-3625; fax (21) 49-3862; e-mail ppy@proparaguay.gov.py; internet www.proparaguay.gov.py; f. 1991; responsible for promoting investment in Paraguay and the export of national products; Exec. Dir Ing. FRANCISCO GUTIÉRREZ CAMPOS.

CHAMBER OF COMMERCE

Cámara y Bolsa de Comercio: Estrella 540, Asunción; tel. (21) 49-3321; fax (21) 44-0817; f. 1898; Pres. NICOLÁS GONZÁLEZ ODDONE; Gen. Man. Dr RICARDO FRANCO L.

EMPLOYERS' ORGANIZATIONS

Federación de la Producción, Industria y Comercio (FEPRINCO): Palma 751 y 15 de Agosto, Asunción; tel. (21) 46638; organization of private sector business executives; Pres. GUILLERMO STANLEY.

Unión Industrial Paraguaya (UIP): Cerro Corá 1038, Casilla 782, Asunción; tel. (21) 21-2556; fax 21-3360; f. 1936; organization of business entrepreneurs; Pres. NÉSTOR MÉNDEZ NÚÑEZ.

UTILITIES

Electricity

Administración Nacional de Electricidad (ANDE): Avda España 1268, Asunción; tel. (21) 21-1001; fax (21) 21-2371; e-mail ande@ande.gov.py; internet www.ande.gov.py; f. 1949; national electricity board, scheduled for privatization in 2002; Pres. MARIO CÉSAR ORUE DELGADO.

Water

Empresa de Servicios Sanitarios del Paraguay (ESSAP): José Berges 516, entre Brasil y San José, Asunción; tel. (21) 21-0319; fax 21-5061; internet www.corposana.com; formerly called Corporación de Obras Sanitarias (CORPOSANA); responsible for public water supply, sewage disposal and drainage; scheduled for privatization in Sept. 2002; Pres. Carlos Antonio López Rodríguez.

TRADE UNIONS

Central Nacional de Trabajadores (CNT): Piribebuy 1078, Asunción; tel. (21) 44-4084; fax (21) 49-2154; e-mail cnt@uninet.com.py; Sec.-Gen. Eduardo Ojeda.

Central de Sindicatos de Trabajadores del Estado Paraguayo (Cesitep): Asunción; Pres. Reinaldo Barreto Medina.

Central Unitaria de Trabajadores (CUT): San Carlos 836, Asunción; tel. (21) 44-3936; fax (21) 44-8482; f. 1989; Pres. Alan Flores; Sec.-Gen. Jorge Alvarenga.

Confederación Paraguaya de Trabajadores (CPT) (Confederation of Paraguayan Workers): Yegros 1309–33 y Simón Bolívar, Asunción; tel. (21) 44-3184; f. 1951; Pres. Gerónimo López; Sec.-Gen. Julio Etcheverry Espinola; 43,500 mems from 189 affiliated groups.

Federación Nacional Campesina de Paraguay (FNC): Nangariry 1196 esq. Cacique Cará Cará, Asunción; tel. (21) 51-2384; national peasants' federation; Pres. Odilón Espínola; Sec.-Gen. Alberto Areco.

Transport

RAILWAYS

Ferrocarril Presidente Carlos Antonio López: México 145, Casilla 453, Asunción; tel. (21) 44-3273; fax (21) 44-7848; f. 1854; state-owned since 1961; 370 km of track, of which 8 km, from Encarnación to Argentine border, in service in 1997; scheduled for privatization; Pres. Jorge Jara Serván.

ROADS

In 1999 there were an estimated 29,500 km of roads, of which 3,067 km were paved. The Pan-American Highway runs for over 700 km in Paraguay and the Trans-Chaco Highway extends from Asunción to Bolivia.

SHIPPING

Administración Nacional de Navegación y Puertos (ANNP) (National Shipping and Ports Administration): Cólon y El Paraguayo Independiente, Asunción; tel. (21) 49-5086; fax (21) 49-7485; e-mail annp@mail.pla.net.py; internet www.annp.gov.py; f. 1965; responsible for ports services and maintaining navigable channels in rivers and for improving navigation on the Rivers Paraguay and Paraná; Pres. Milciades Rabery Ocampos.

Inland Waterways

Flota Mercante Paraguaya SA (FLOMEPASA): Estrella 672-686, Casilla 454, Asunción; tel. (21) 44-7409; fax (21) 44-6010; boats and barges up to 1,000 tons displacement on Paraguay and Paraná rivers; cold storage ships for use Asunción–Buenos Aires-Montevideo; Pres. Capt. Aníbal Gino Pertile R; Commercial Dir Dr Emigdio Duarte Sostoa.

Ocean Shipping

Compañía Paraguaya de Navegación de Ultramar, SA: Presidente Franco 625, 2°, Casilla 77, Asunción; tel. (21) 49-2137; fax (21) 44-5013; f. 1963 to operate between Asunción, USA and European ports; 10 vessel; Exec. Pres. Juan Bosch B.

Navemar S.R.L.: B. Constant 536, 1°, Casilla 273, Asunción; tel. (21) 49-3122; 5 vessels.

Transporte Fluvial Paraguayo S.A.C.I.: Edif. de la Encarnación, 13°, 14 de Mayo 563, Asunción; tel. (21) 49-3411; fax (21) 49-8218; e-mail tfpsaci@tm.com.py; Admin. Man. Daniella Charbonnier; 1 vessel.

CIVIL AVIATION

The major international airport, Aeropuerto Internacional Silvio Pettirossi is situated 15 km from Asunción. A second airport, Aeropuerto Internacional Guaraní, 30 km from Ciudad del Este, was inaugurated in January 1996.

National Airlines

Aerolíneas Paraguayas (ARPA): Terminal ARPA, Aeropuerto Internacional Silvio Pettirossi, Asunción; tel. (21) 21-5072; fax (21) 21-5111; f. 1994; domestic service; wholly-owned by Transportes Aéreos del Mercosur (TAM Mercosur).

Transportes Aéreos del Mercosur (TAM Mercosur): Aeropuerto Internacional Silvio Pettirossi, Hangar TAM/ARPA, Luque, Asunción; tel. (21) 49-1039; fax (21) 64-5146; e-mail tammercosur@uninet.com.py; internet www.tam.com.py; f. 1963 as Líneas Aéreas Paraguayas (LAP), name changed as above in 1997; services to destinations within South America; 80% owned by TAM Linhas Aereas (Brazil); Pres. Rolím Adolfo Amaro.

Tourism

Tourism is undeveloped, but, with recent improvements in infrastructure, efforts were being made to promote the sector. Tourist arrivals in Paraguay in 2000 totalled 323,041. In that year tourist receipts were US $66m.

Secretaría Nacional de Turismo: Palma 468, Asunción; tel. (21) 44-1530; fax (21) 49-1230; e-mail senatur1@pla.net.py; internet www.senatur.gov.py; f. 1998; Exec. Sec. Hugo Galli Romañach.

PERU

Introductory Survey

Location, Climate, Language, Religion, Flag, Capital

The Republic of Peru lies in western South America, bordered by Ecuador and Colombia to the north, by Brazil and Bolivia to the east, and by Chile to the south. Peru has a coastline of more than 2,300 km (1,400 miles) on the Pacific Ocean. The climate varies with altitude, average temperatures being about 11°C (20°F) lower in the Andes mountains than in the coastal plain. The rainy season is between October and April, with heavy rainfall in the tropical forests. Temperatures in Lima are usually between 13°C (55°F) and 28°C (82°F). The three official languages are Spanish, Quechua and Aymará. Almost all of the inhabitants profess Christianity, and the great majority are adherents of the Roman Catholic Church. The civil flag (proportions 2 by 3) has three equal vertical stripes, of red, white and red. The state flag additionally has the national coat of arms (a shield divided into three unequal segments: red, with a golden cornucopia spilling coins of yellow and white at the base, blue, with a yellow vicuña in the dexter chief, and white, with a green tree in the sinister chief; all surmounted by a green wreath, and framed by branches of palm and laurel, tied at the bottom with a red and white ribbon) in the centre of the white stripe. The capital is Lima.

Recent History

Since independence from Spain, declared in 1821 and finally achieved in 1824, Peruvian politics have been characterized by alternating periods of civilian administration and military dictatorship. In the early 1920s opposition to the dictatorial regime of President Augusto Bernardino Leguía resulted in the creation of the Alianza Popular Revolucionaria Americana (APRA—also known as the Partido Aprista Peruano), Peru's oldest political party to command mass support. The party, founded as a nationalist revolutionary movement, was formally established in Peru in 1930, when Leguía was deposed and the party's founder (and its leader for more than 50 years), Dr Víctor Raúl Haya de la Torre, returned from enforced exile in Mexico. A longstanding tradition of hostility developed between APRA and the armed forces, and the party was banned in 1931–45, and again in 1948–56.

During 1945–63 political power shifted regularly between the armed forces and elected government. In 1948 Dr José Luis Bustamente y Rivera was deposed by Gen. Manuel Odría, following a right-wing military rebellion. Odría established a military junta which governed until 1950, when the General was elected unopposed to the presidency, and subsequently appointed a cabinet composed of military officers and civilians. In 1956 Odría was succeeded by Dr Manuel Prado y Ugartache (who had been President in 1939–45). An inconclusive presidential election in 1962 precipitated military intervention, and power was assumed by Gen. Ricardo Pérez Godoy, at the head of a military junta. In March 1963, however, Pérez was supplanted by his second-in-command, Gen. Nicolás Lindley López.

Fernando Belaúnde Terry, the joint candidate of his own Acción Popular (AP) party and the Partido Demócrata Cristiano, emerged as the successful contestant at presidential elections conducted (together with a congressional poll) in June 1963, and was inaugurated as President in the following month. An increase in internal disturbances in predominantly Indian areas was attributed to communist subversion, and resulted in the temporary suspension of constitutional guarantees in 1965–66 and an intensive military campaign of counter-insurgency. Although the Belaúnde administration successfully promoted agrarian reform, lack of congressional support for the Government contributed to a succession of ministerial crises which, together with continuing internal unrest, prompted renewed military intervention in October 1968, when Gen. Juan Velasco Alvarado assumed the presidency, dissolved Congress and appointed a military cabinet.

Despite the re-emergence of internal disturbances and dissension within the armed forces, provoked by the introduction of radical reforms and austerity measures, Velasco retained power until August 1975, when he was overthrown and replaced by Gen. Francisco Morales Bermúdez. In July 1977 President

Morales announced plans for the restoration of civilian rule. Accordingly, a national election was conducted in June 1978 to select the members of a constituent assembly, which was to draft a new constitution in preparation for presidential and congressional elections. In the election, APRA emerged as the largest party, and in July the assembly elected the 83-year-old Dr Haya de la Torre to be its President. The new Constitution, adopted in July 1979, provided for elections by universal adult suffrage, and extended the franchise to the sizeable illiterate population.

The presidential contest of May 1980 was won decisively by Belaúnde. At the same time, the AP won an outright majority in the Cámara de Diputados (Chamber of Deputies) and also secured the greatest representation in the Senado (Senate). The new organs of state were inaugurated in July, when the new Constitution became fully effective. While Belaúnde sought to liberalize the economy and to reverse many of the agrarian and industrial reforms implemented under Velasco, much of his term of office was dominated by the increasing threat to internal stability posed by the emergence, in the early 1980s, of the Maoist terrorist group, the Sendero Luminoso (SL—Shining Path). The situation deteriorated following the uncompromising response of the armed forces to terrorist activity in a designated emergency zone, which extended to 13 provinces (primarily in the departments of Ayacucho, Huancavelica and Apurímac) by mid-1984, and a dramatic increase in violent deaths and violations of human rights was reported.

At elections in April 1985 Alan García Pérez (the candidate for APRA) received 45.7% of the total votes in the presidential poll, while APRA secured a majority in both houses (the Cámara and the Senado) of the Congreso (legislature). García's victory was ensured in May, prior to a second round of voting, when his closest opponent, Dr Alfonso Barrantes Lingán (of the left-wing Izquierda Unida coalition), withdrew his candidature. At his inauguration in July, García announced that his Government's priorities would be to arrest Peru's severe economic decline and to eradicate internal terrorism. However, efforts to establish a Peace Commission to investigate acts of terrorism and to uphold human rights failed, apparently owing to lack of political conviction on the part of the Government.

Despite APRA successes at municipal elections in 1986, widespread opposition to the Government's economic programme was manifested in a succession of well-supported general strikes in 1987 and 1988. Plans for the nationalization of Peru's banks and private financial and insurance institutions, announced by García in July 1987, encountered considerable opposition from the banking community, and prompted the creation of Libertad, a 'freedom movement' expressing opposition to the plans (which were subsequently modified), which was established under the leadership of a well-known writer, Mario Vargas Llosa. The authority of the García administration was further undermined by persistent rumours of military unrest, allegations of links between members of the Government and the right-wing paramilitary 'death squad', the Comando Rodrigo Franco, and by the continuing terrorist activities of SL and a resurgence of activity by the Movimiento Revolucionario Tupac Amarú (MRTA) guerrilla group, in north-east Peru. In addition, the Government was criticized by international human rights organizations for its methods of combating political violence.

Despite the capture of leading members of both groups in 1988 and 1989, violent attacks by SL and, to a lesser extent, by the MRTA against political and industrial targets and rural self-defence groups (or 'rondas campesinas') had reached an unprecedented level in 1989 during the campaign for local government elections, and persisted into 1990. General elections took place on 8 April 1990, despite the attempts of SL to disrupt the elections with another 'armed strike' and a campaign of bombing and looting. In the presidential poll Vargas Llosa, the candidate of the centre-right FREDEMO alliance (established in 1988 by the AP, Libertad and the Partido Popular Cristiano), obtained the largest percentage of the total votes cast, but failed to attain the required absolute majority by only narrowly defeating a hitherto little-known agronomist, Alberto Fujimori, the candidate of the Cambio 90 group of independents. In a second round of voting, conducted on 10 June, Fujimori, whose campaign had advocated 'hard work, honesty and technology', emerged as the successful candidate with some 57% of the votes cast, having attracted late support from left-wing parties and from APRA. Following his inauguration in July, Fujimori announced the composition of a new centre-left Council of Ministers, with Juan Carlos Hurtado Miller, a member of the AP, as Prime Minister and Minister of Economy and Finance.

Proposals for economic readjustment announced in August 1990 abolished subsidies for consumers, thereby increasing prices by more than 3,000% for petrol and by as much as 600% for basic foods. In February 1991 Hurtado announced his resignation from the Council of Ministers, following several weeks of internal dispute regarding the efficacy of anti-inflationary economic measures. The former Minister of Labour, Carlos Torres y Torres Lara, was appointed Prime Minister and Minister of Foreign Affairs, while the finance and economy portfolio was assumed by a right-wing economist, Carlos Boloña Behr.

Despite the success of the Government's economic reforms in securing Peru's rehabilitation within the international financial community, the adverse consequences of adjustment provoked widespread domestic opposition and industrial unrest. In November 1991, despite public and congressional dissent, Fujimori took advantage of a 150-day period of emergency legislative powers (granted to him in June in order that the country's potentially destabilizing economic and security problems might be addressed) to issue a series of economic decrees that represented a continuation of policies which had been initiated with the deregulation of the docks and of maritime, air and public transport, and concerned the elimination of state monopolies of telecommunications, postal networks and railways, the opening to private investment of the power sector, the privatization of schools and a reform of the health and social security services. Torres resigned at the end of October, in response to criticism of his handling of renewed border tension with Ecuador (see below); he was succeeded as Prime Minister by the Minister of Labour, Alfonso de los Heros Pérez Albela.

The increasing divergence of interests of President Fujimori and the Congreso (which had expressed considerable disaffection with the President's reliance upon emergency legislative powers and his attempts to govern by decree) was exacerbated in January 1992 by congressional approval of that year's draft budget, which Fujimori had opposed on the grounds that it contained provisions for excessive expenditure. On 5 April Fujimori announced the immediate suspension of the 1979 Constitution and the dissolution of the Congreso, pending a comprehensive restructuring of the legislature. The President maintained that the reform of the Congreso was essential in order to eradicate 'corruption and inefficiency', to enable him to implement a programme of 'pacification' of the nation by combating terrorism and drugs-trafficking, and also fully to implement free-market economic policies. In the interim an Emergency and National Reconstruction Government would govern the country, in accordance with a draft 'basic law' whereby legislative power would be exercised by the President, with the approval of the Council of Ministers. Fujimori also announced a reform of the judiciary. The constitutional coup (or 'autogolpe') was implemented, without recorded casualties, with the full co-operation and support of the armed forces. On the following day the Prime Minister resigned in protest, and was replaced by Oscar de la Puente; most government ministers, however, elected to remain in office. Members of the dissolved parliament declared Fujimori to be incapable of continuing in office, although an attempt to establish Máximo San Román, the First Vice-President, as the head of an alternative 'constitutional government' was undermined by a lack of domestic and international support. Moreover, while Fujimori's actions prompted outrage from politicians, the judiciary and the media, popular reaction to the 'autogolpe' was less hostile. Bolstered by demonstrations of public support for his actions, Fujimori proceeded to dismiss 13 of Peru's 28 Supreme Court judges, whom he accused of corruption, and attempted to undermine support for political opponents with the detention of prominent opposition party figures.

Indications that a return to constitutional government would be undertaken within a 12–18-month period did little to alleviate mounting international pressure upon the Government to take immediate steps to return to full democracy. The Organization of American States (OAS, see p. 288), deplored Fujimori's actions, and dispatched a mission to attempt to effect a reconciliation between the legislature and the executive. Later in April Fujimori defined a more comprehensive timetable for the

restoration of democracy, with congressional elections to be conducted in February 1993. The Minister of Foreign Affairs, Augusto Blacker Miller, and the Minister of Industry, Commerce, Tourism and Integration resigned. The President of the Central Bank was also removed from office, as were 134 judges; 12 provisional members of the Supreme Court were later appointed.

The threat posed to Fujimori's programme of radical reform by economic constraints resulting from the suspension of international financial aid to Peru prompted the revision of the timetable for a return to democracy, and in June 1992 Fujimori confirmed that national elections would be conducted in October to a unicameral constituent congress, which would then draft a new constitution (to be submitted for approval in a national referendum at a later date). The President also announced that, pending approval of a new document, the 1979 Constitution would be reinstated without certain articles that might 'impede the progress of the Government'. (In April 2003 the Congreso voted to restore a bicameral legislature; the new Congreso would comprise a 150-member lower house and a 50-member upper chamber.)

A 'National Dialogue for Peace and Development', comprising a series of discussions with representatives of the political opposition and with the public, sought to identify important issues for future consideration by the new Congreso Constituyente Democrático (CCD). Elections to the CCD, conducted on 22 November 1992 and attended by OAS observers, were a qualified success for pro-Government parties. An electoral coalition of Cambio 90 and the Nueva Mayoría (a new independent party supported by many former cabinet ministers), headed by Fujimori's former Minister of Energy and Mines, Jaime Yoshiyama Tanaka (who was subsequently elected President of the CCD), secured 44 of the 80 congressional seats. The only significant opposition party not to boycott the elections, the Partido Popular Cristiano, took eight seats. In December, at the inaugural meeting of the CCD, Yoshiyama identified its immediate aims as the restoration of the autonomy of the judiciary, the eradication of terrorism, the generation of employment and of favourable conditions for foreign investment, and the projection of an enhanced national image abroad. In January 1993, having formally reinstated the 1979 Constitution, the CCD confirmed Fujimori as constitutional Head of State. In the same month Carlos Boloña Behr resigned the economy and finance portfolio, following a disagreement with Fujimori arising from the latter's efforts to attract increased popular support through the temporary relaxation of economic restrictions. Following the resignation of de la Puente's Government in July, Alfonso Bustamente y Bustamante (hitherto Minister of Industry, Commerce, Tourism and Integration) was appointed Prime Minister in August.

The final text of the draft Constitution, which enhanced presidential powers and provided for the establishment of a unicameral legislature, was approved by the CCD in September 1993. A national referendum to ascertain the level of popular support for the new Constitution was scheduled for 31 October—the first occasion on which such popular consultation had been sought in Peru. Among the text's most controversial articles were the introduction of the death penalty for convicted terrorists and a provision permitting a President of the Republic to be re-elected for a successive five-year term of office. At the referendum the Constitution was narrowly approved, by an overall 52.2% of the votes cast. The Constitution was promulgated on 29 December, at a ceremony boycotted by opposition members of the CCD.

In April 1993 members of the army staged a demonstration in Lima, in support of the Commander-General of the Army and President of the Joint Command of the Armed Forces, Gen. Nicolás Hermoza Ríos, following accusations by opposition members of the CCD of the involvement of paramilitary forces in the 'disappearance' of 10 alleged SL supporters from the Enrique Guzmán y Valle University at La Cantuta, east of Lima, in July 1992. The bodies of the La Cantuta 'activists' were later discovered, and in December civil proceedings were initiated against 11 army officers who were accused of involvement in their kidnap and murder. In February 1994, however, controversial new legislation was promulgated allowing the Supreme Court to rule that the case be tried by a military court. This judicial manoeuvring provoked outrage among opposition parties and independent legal and humanitarian groups. The US Government issued a formal protest at what it regarded as a breach of the autonomy of the judiciary. Bustamente, dissociating himself from the process, resigned as Prime Minister: he was replaced by the Minister of Foreign Affairs, Efraín Goldenberg Schreiber. Later in February, after a brief trial at the Supreme Council of Military Justice, nine officers received prison sentences of between one and 20 years for their part in the La Cantuta murders. The conduct and outcome of the proceedings were denounced both within Peru and internationally.

Presidential and legislative elections were scheduled for April 1995. However, there was little political campaigning, as Peru's border conflict with Ecuador (see below) resulted in cross-party consensus on the need to maintain national unity. In the presidential election, conducted on 9 April, Fujimori secured an unexpected outright victory over his closest opponent, Javier Pérez de Cuéllar (the former UN Secretary-General and the candidate of the Unión por el Perú—UPP), obtaining 64.4% of the total votes. In the concurrent legislative elections, Fujimori's coalition movement, Cambio 90-Nueva Mayoría (C90-NM), also secured a majority in the unicameral Congreso, winning 67 of the 120 seats. The composition of the new Government, installed following Fujimori's inauguration in July, was largely unaltered. Goldenberg was replaced as Prime Minister by Dante Córdova Blanco, and as Minister of Foreign Affairs by Francisco Tudela van Breugal-Douglas.

In mid-June 1995 new legislation was approved by the Congreso granting an amnesty to all members of the military, police and intelligence forces who had been convicted of human rights violations committed since 1980 in the internal conflict against separatist violence. The legislation was promulgated by Fujimori and entered into immediate effect, with the declared objective of promoting national reconciliation—although it was also widely thought to have been introduced by the President in order to consolidate his relationship with the military leadership. The legislation attracted broad criticism from opposition parties, and internationally. In August an international warrant was issued for the arrest of former President Alan García, who had been accused of receiving bribes and other corrupt practices during his term of office. In September Peru requested García's extradition from Colombia, where he was believed to be living in exile.

In April 1996 the sudden resignation of the Prime Minister demonstrated the extent of disunity within the Government: Córdova's departure followed intense economic debate within the Council of Ministers, and reflected the Prime Minister's fundamental opposition to the policies (fully supported by Fujimori) of the Minister of Economy and Finance, Jorge Camet Dickman. While the entire Council of Ministers was subsequently obliged to resign, the only ministers who were not invited to resume their responsibilities were those who shared Córdova's concerns at the adverse social impact of the economic reform programme. Alberto Pandolfi Arbulu was appointed Prime Minister, and the Government's privatization programme was intensified. Meanwhile, Fujimori was attempting to formulate legislation that would allow him to stand for election for a third presidential term. A congressional committee approved a new 'interpretation' of the Constitution in August (on the grounds that Fujimori was first elected under the 1979 Constitution), and the legislation was approved by the Congreso later in that month (with a boycott of the vote by the majority of opposition politicians). In January 1997 the Constitutional Court ruled the new interpretation of the Constitution to be invalid.

On 17 December 1996 MRTA activists launched an assault on the residence of the Japanese ambassador in Lima, and detained by force more than 500 people attending an evening reception. After several hours of negotiations, led by a local representative of the International Committee of the Red Cross (ICRC, see p. 251), the release of all women and elderly persons was secured. Among those remaining inside the residence were the Peruvian Ministers of Foreign Affairs and of Agriculture, at least nine foreign ambassadors and other diplomatic personnel, leading police and security officials and representatives of the business community. After an initial threat by the activists to commence systematic assassinations of the captives in order to secure their demands (which included the release of all 458 MRTA prisoners in detention in Peru, safe passage to an area in Peru's central highlands, greater economic assistance to the country's poorest people and payment of a 'war tax'), the deadline passed without incident and the immediate tension was defused. Large numbers of hostages were gradually released, while those remaining inside the residence received adequate supplies of food, clothes

and medicines. On 27 December Fujimori declared a state of emergency in Lima, effectively suspending all constitutional rights regarding arrest and the search of property. On 22 April 1997 Peruvian troops launched an unexpected assault on the ambassador's residence, ending the MRTA siege. Two soldiers and all 14 of the MRTA activists were killed in the operation, and one of the 72 remaining hostages, a member of the Supreme Court, died of heart failure. President Fujimori presented the assault as a measure of his Government's uncompromising stance against terrorism; however, as details emerged of the military action, Fujimori was confronted by criticism that some of the MRTA members might have been killed after having surrendered to army officers.

The Fujimori administration came under renewed attack for its authoritarian style of government in May 1997, following the dismissal, by the Government-dominated Congreso, of three members of the Tribunal Constitucional (Constitutional Tribunal) who had opposed the Congreso's endorsement of Fujimori's bid to seek a third term of office. The plummeting popularity of the administration prompted a number of ministerial resignations in July. Meanwhile, the opposition took advantage of the disarray of the Government to announce the creation of a number of attractive new political alliances to contest forthcoming elections, including a revived and reorganized Coordinación Democrática (Code), to be led by the former Minister of the Economy, Carlos Boloña, with support from Renovación and prominent APRA dissidents.

Fujimori's immediate hopes for election to a third presidential term were encouraged in February 1998 by the Supreme Court's announcement that it could foresee no significant obstacle to Fujimori's candidature in 2000. However, a final decision on his eligibility was to be decided by the Jurado Nacional Electoral (JNE—National Electoral Board). The Government was accused of further supporting the subversion of normal judicial processes in March, when the Congreso approved a new law whereby the regulatory powers of the National Council of the Judiciary were severely reduced. The legislation prompted the resignation of all seven members of the Council, and the cancellation, by the World Bank, of a substantial loan to the Peruvian Government, intended for judicial reform projects.

Further concerns were expressed at Fujimori's manipulation of the judiciary in April 1998, when People's Rights ombudsman Jorge Santiestevan de Noriega warned that the rule of law was being systematically undermined and a senior public prosecutor Miguel Aljovín complained that his powers were being eroded by the newly instituted Comisión Ejecutiva del Ministerio Público. There was considerable media speculation that political opponents of the Government were being harassed by government agencies with fabricated charges of technical violations of the law. There was further evidence of the President's circumvention of the traditional role of the judiciary in May when Fujimori introduced draconian anti-crime legislation by decree (subsequently approved by the Congreso) which sought to extend the extreme powers and penalties employed in the recent successful anti-terrorism initiatives (see below) to other areas of criminal activity. Among the provisions of the new law were plans to increase the powers of military tribunals to try civilians. A report by the Geneva-based UN monitoring committee of the 1984 Convention against Torture and Other Cruel, Inhuman or Degrading Treatment or Punishment, published in the same month, contained reports of continuing abuses of human rights in Peru, and made an urgent recommendation that some form of independent judicial authority should be inaugurated in the country as soon as possible. However, in December the Congreso voted to extend the period of judicial reorganization initiated by Fujimori's administration for a further two-year period, frustrating opposition hopes that political interference in legal processes might soon be curtailed.

Fujimori's popularity continued to wane during 1998 (the ruling party chose not to field candidates for local elections conducted in October, as a consequence), and the President's attempts to consolidate his position and reassert his authority resulted in repeated changes to the Council of Ministers. In early June, in a move widely perceived as an attempt to demonstrate an increased commitment to political tolerance and economic recovery, Fujimori replaced the Prime Minister and the Minister of Economy and Finance. An outspoken lawyer and former opposition senator, Javier Valle Riestra, took over from Alberto Pandolfi as Prime Minister, while Jorge Camet was replaced at the economy portfolio by Jorge Baca Campodónico.

The appointment of Valle Riestra, a staunch defender of human rights who had been highly critical of many aspects of Fujimori's authoritative style of leadership, was considered a courageous one by many political observers. By August 1998, however, Valle Riestra's overt opposition to Fujimori's plans for re-election and a recurring conflict of interests between the Prime Minister and the more uncompromising supporters of the President in the various branches of government and the armed forces had forced his resignation. In early August Fujimori reappointed Alberto Pandolfi to the premiership. Other cabinet changes followed later that year.

A major cabinet reshuffle was implemented in January 1999, with the President of the Congreso, Víctor Joy Way Rojas, replacing Pandolfi as Prime Minister. However, the entire Council of Ministers resigned in mid-April, amid a rift over corruption allegations brought by the Minister of Labour and Social Promotion against officials at the state customs authority. Another mass cabinet resignation followed in early October, in accordance with the law requiring those public officials intending to stand for election to resign their posts six months before the April 2000 polls. A new cabinet was sworn in mid-October, with Alberto Bustamante Belaúnde as Prime Minister and Minister of Justice.

Meanwhile, Fujimori's continuing efforts to secure support for a third presidential term were encouraged by the defeat in the Congreso, in September 1998, of an opposition proposal to decide the question of Fujimori's eligibility by a national referendum. (In July a 7,000-strong opposition delegation had presented a petition containing 1.4m. signatures in support of this proposal to the JNE.) Opposition to Fujimori's election bid was vociferously expressed when a broad range of labour unions and political parties participated in late April 1999 in a one-day general strike, the biggest ever protest against the Fujimori regime. However, this, together with a demonstration involving some 20,000 people in mid-October, failed to prevent the announcement in late December of Fujimori's candidature on behalf of the Perú 2000 alliance (a new movement formed to support the incumbent's re-election campaign) for the presidency. On 1 January 2000 the JNE, which was dominated by Fujimori's supporters, ratified his registration as a candidate in response to a legal challenge issued by the political opposition. The election board's rationale was that although the Constitution did not permit a President to serve three terms, Fujimori had only served one term under the current Constitution, as amended in 1993, and therefore was eligible for re-election. The ruling precipitated further street protests. In early November 1999 the US Senate Foreign Relations Committee adopted a resolution expressing concern at the 'erosion of the independence' of the judiciary and the electoral authorities, and at the harassment of journalists in Peru. Allegations of electoral fraud and campaign misconduct were widespread. Complaints by opposition leaders included government manipulation of the media to deny them equal access, the use of state resources (including the military and the intelligence services) to promote Fujimori's campaign, and alleged falsification of more than 1m. signatures by members of Perú 2000 to register Fujimori's candidacy. (The Frente Nacional Independiente, a member of Perú 2000, subsequently withdrew its candidates for the elections in response to the allegations.) In December 14 leaders of political parties and political movements signed a 'governability agreement', which contained proposals to guarantee democracy, justice and respect for human rights. However, opposition plans to reach a consensus on a single candidate to challenge Fujimori did not materialize, and in January 2000 seven opposition candidates registered to stand for election to the presidency. Initially, Fujimori's closest opponents were Alberto Andrade Carmona, Mayor of Lima, and Luis Castañeda Lossio, former head of the Social Security Institute, but both their campaigns were severely undermined by the solidly pro-Fujimori media.

The general election proceeded on 9 April 2000. During the vote count opposition candidates and international observers, including representatives of the OAS and the US-based Carter Center, alleged that the vote was marred by fraud. There were reports of unexplained delays in counting the votes, discrepancies in early official tallies and ballot tampering. US officials issued increasingly strong statements stressing the need for a second round of voting as the only credible proof of legitimacy. At the final count Fujimori officially received 49.9% of the vote and Alejandro Toledo (the first presidential candidate of Indian descent) 40.2%. A second round was scheduled for 28 May. In the congressional elections Perú 2000 won 52 of the 120 seats while

Perú Posible (PP), which supported Toledo, won 29 seats. Disputes persisted regarding the legitimacy of the electoral process, with the political opposition and international election monitors accusing the Government of failing to ensure that irregularities of the first round were corrected before the second poll. The JNE resisted both domestic and external pressure for a postponement, and in response Toledo withdrew his candidature one week before the election and urged his supporters to spoil their votes in protest. Violent incidents, including the fire-bombing of the presidential palace, followed the JNE decision. The OAS and Carter Center suspended monitoring of the election, citing difficulties with the computer system for tabulating votes. Amid further mass demonstrations, Fujimori contested the election effectively unopposed (although the JNE ruled that Toledo remained a candidate and refused to remove his name from the ballot papers), taking 51.2% of the total votes; Toledo received 17.7%. Excluding spoilt (29.9%) and blank (1.2%) papers, the incumbent was thus returned to office with 74.3% of the valid votes cast. The result was denounced as invalid by the political opposition and by the US Government (though it later moderated its position, describing the outcome as imperfect). The OAS dispatched a mission to Peru to explore options for strengthening democracy. Fujimori's inauguration on 28 July was accompanied by violent protests in Lima.

In September 2000 a major political scandal erupted after the disclosure of a video that allegedly showed Vladimiro Montesinos, the head of the national intelligence service and a close ally of the President, bribing an opposition member of the Congreso. In response, on 16 September Fujimori declared that new elections would be held, in which he would not participate. He also announced that the national intelligence service would be disbanded. At the same time, 10 Perú 2000 deputies defected to the opposition, thus depriving Fujimori of his majority in the legislature. Demonstrations, led by Toledo, demanded the immediate resignation of Fujimori and the arrest of Montesinos, who fled to Panama. On 5 October the Congreso approved OAS-mediated proposals paving the way for power to be transferred from Fujimori to his successor in mid-2001, as well as the disbandment of the Congreso to make way for a newly-elected legislature. Later in the month Fujimori announced the replacement of the most senior commanders of the armed forces.

In late October 2000 the political crisis deepened, when Montesinos returned from Panama, after failing to obtain political asylum there. His apparent impunity supported the widely-held view that the armed forces were protecting him. At the same time, the first Vice-President, Francisco Tudela, resigned in protest at government attempts to make new elections conditional upon an amnesty for those in the armed forces accused of human rights violations. Further OAS-sponsored negotiations between opposition and Government led to the announcement, at the end of the month, that new elections would be held on 8 April 2001, without any conditions attached. An investigation into Montesinos' activities was launched, with charges ranging from corruption to torture and murder. In mid-November the Congreso voted to replace its pro-Fujimori President, Martha Hildebrandt Pérez Treviño, with Valentín Paniagua, effectively giving the opposition control of the legislature. The following day, amid rumours that he was planning to seek political asylum, Fujimori travelled to Japan, from where, on 20 November, he resigned the presidency. The Congreso, however, refused to accept the resignation, and instead voted to dismiss Fujimori. The second Vice-President, Ricardo Márquez, resigned several hours later.

On 22 November 2000 Paniagua was appointed interim President. A new cabinet was sworn in three days later, which included Javier Pérez de Cuellar, the former UN Secretary-General, as Prime Minister and Minister of Foreign Affairs. The aims of the interim Government, the mandate of which would last until 28 July 2001, included the achievement of a balanced budget and the strengthening of democracy. Several days later the new Minister of Defence, Walter Ledesma Rebaza, announced the decision to retire 13 generals, who were known to be associates of Montesinos (including Gen. Chacón Malaga, the former armed forces commander). A congressional commission, established in the same month to investigate the activities of Montesinos, uncovered hundreds of secret videotapes which compromised the integrity of judges, politicians, military officers, businessmen and even bishops. In early December it was announced that the commission's investigations were to extend to Fujimori. In mid-December it was announced that Fujimori had taken up Japanese citizenship and was thus, in effect, protected from the threat of extradition from Japan. Nevertheless, in February 2001 corruption charges were formally filed against him. Furthermore, in August the Congreso voted unanimously to lift Fujimori's constitutional immunity and issued an international warrant for his arrest on the charge of dereliction of duty. Further charges of embezzlement and illicit enrichment were subsequently filed against the former President. However, the Japanese Government proved unresponsive to diplomatic pressure and stated that it had no intention of allowing Fujimori's extradition. A new warrant for Fujimori's arrest, issued by the International Criminal Police Organization, INTERPOL, in March 2003, was found to be unenforceable, owing to the lack of any formal extradition treaty between Peru and Japan.

In June 2001 Venezuelan military intelligence officers, assisted by the US Federal Bureau of Investigation and the Peruvian police force, arrested Montesinos in the Venezuelan capital, Caracas. (The President of Venezuela, Hugo Chávez Frías, denied allegations that his security forces had obstructed the arrest and had only co-operated following widespread diplomatic intervention.) Montesinos was sent back to Peru and, in July 2002, sentenced to nine years' imprisonment on charges relating to 'usurpation of power'. However, investigating judges subsequently brought a further 57 indictments against him, including murder, bribery and the illegal sale of weapons and narcotics. Following his first public trial in February 2003, Montesinos was convicted on corruption charges and sentenced to a further five years' imprisonment, with proceedings in further trials (on charges carrying harsher penalties) yet to take place. In April arrest warrants were issued for six former finance ministers and three defence ministers, who were sought in connection with the alleged theft and illegal transfer of US $100m. to the national intelligence service during the Fujimori presidency.

In January 2001, only a few days after corruption charges against him were ruled to have expired under the statute of limitations, the former President, Alan García Pérez, returned to Peru to launch his campaign for the presidential elections, scheduled to be held in April. The other leading candidate for the presidential contest was the conservative Lourdes Flores Nano of the Unidad Nacional alliance. The first round of the presidential election was held on 8 April, following a bitter campaign. Toledo won 36.5% of the votes cast, while García attracted 25.8% of the ballot and Flores 24.3%. García's strong performance surprised most commentators and, as no candidate won a majority of the votes, was enough to earn him a place in a second ballot. In concurrently-held elections to the 120-seat Congreso, no party secured a majority: PP gained 45 seats, APRA 27 and the Unidad Nacional 17, while the right-wing Frente Independiente Moralizador won 12 seats. Election monitors declared the election process to have been open and fair. In the second round of the presidential election, held on 3 June, Toledo won with 53.1% of the vote against García's 46.9%. Toledo was inaugurated on 28 July. A broad-based 15-member cabinet was appointed, headed by lawyer Roberto Dañino and with Pedro Pablo Kuczynski as Minister of the Economy and Finance. The new Government promised to create more jobs, to reduce poverty and to put an end to the corruption of the Fujimori regime. In the previous month a congressional commission implicated 180 people in corruption scandals that took place during Fujimori's presidencies, including Gen. Walter Chacón Malaga, the recently appointed head of the armed forces.

However, the popularity of the Toledo Government declined sharply after only a few months in power, as high expectations were not matched by an increase in economic prospects. In late September and October 2001 popular protests erupted throughout Peru as workers demanded more jobs and improvements to transport infrastructure and health care. In January 2002 Toledo implemented a partial cabinet reshuffle, in which Aurelio Loret de Mola replaced David Waisman as the Minister of Defence and Fernando Carbone and Cecilia Blondet replaced the Ministers of Health (Luis Solari) and Women's Affairs (Doris Sánchez), respectively. The reshuffle caused a rift within the PP as all three dismissed ministers were from Toledo's own party. Hundreds of former public workers protested in central Lima in January 2002 to demand reinstatement and in February cotton producers and fishery workers both staged demonstrations to demand more government aid. The protests proliferated, and in late June, following a week of violent demonstrations in protest at government plans to privatize two regional electricity companies in Arequipa, the Minister of the Interior, Fernando Rospigliosi, resigned and the privatization process was suspended

indefinitely (see Economic Affairs). An extensive cabinet reshuffle was carried out in July, in which the Secretary-General of the PP, Luis Solari, replaced Dañino as prime minister and Kuczynski was succeeded as Minister of Economy and Finance by Javier Silva Ruete. Although the composition of the new cabinet was widely considered to be a shift to the left, the Council of Ministers' stated objectives were to promote economic growth through private-sector investment and to continue the reform of the political process. Nevertheless, popular dissatisfaction with the reform process continued, and in late January 2003 difficulties in the reform of the police service led to the resignation of the Minister of the Interior, Gino Costa Santolaya. He was succeeded by Alberto Sanabria Ortiz. Revelations concerning the personal lives of President Toledo and his wife, which were reported from mid-2002 onwards, also attracted strong public disapproval. In January 2003 the ruling party's congressional majority was reduced after five PP deputies resigned from the party in order to form a new movement, to be known as Perú Ahora.

In November 2002 the results of the elections to the newly-created regional authorities represented a further example of the dramatic decline in popular support for President Toledo. The PP secured just one of the 25 new regional presidencies, compared with the 12 secured by APRA (with the majority of the remaining presidencies largely won by independent candidates). The poor result for the PP was widely attributed to the Government's inability to translate strong economic growth and an improving fiscal balance into a tangible increase in employment. Moreover, despite the approval, in March, of a basic legal frameworkfor the new decentralized authorities, an 'organic law' to define the extent of their powers, did not receive congressional approval until December.

The regional presidencies were inaugurated in January 2003. Almost immediately, the new regional Presidents posed problems for the Government. Several threatened to organize popular protests if their demands were not met. The APRA leader of Arequipa, David Vera Ballén, announced that any further plans to privatize two state-owned regional electricity companies would be met with more protests. His threat had been prompted by the news that the sole bidder for the power companies, the Belgian company Tractebel, had withdrawn its offer in light of the continuing impasse between central and regional government. In mid-January President Toledo attempted to create a consensus on the legal status of the new regional authorities, under the auspices of a national decentralization council (Consejo Nacional de Descentralización). However, APRA boycotted the talks, although further negotiations were held in April.

In early January 2003 a constitutional tribunal ruled that anti-terrorism legislation passed by the Fujimori administration had violated the Constitution. In order to alleviate the potential pressure on the judiciary, and to prevent the release of large numbers of alleged terrorists, in the same month the Congreso granted President Toledo exceptional temporary powers to legislate by decree on security issues. In February the Government announced that all military sentences passed during Fujimori's presidency were to be annulled. The courts would have 60 days to decide whether to release convicted individuals or commit them for retrial. In March anti-terrorism legislation received congressional approval.

In February 2003 coca growers staged demonstrations to demand the suspension of the Government's coca-eradication policy. Roads were blocked throughout the department of Huánuco and some 70 people were injured as security forces attempted to disperse the protesters. The demonstrations escalated after a coca growers' federation leader, Nelson Palomino La Serna, was arrested on terrorism charges. At the end of the month the Government announced that some US $3,000m. was to be invested in a coca-eradication plan by 2020. It was hoped that the plan, which envisaged the eradication of coca plantations and the promotion of alternative development schemes, would convince the US Administration to grant more aid to anti-drugs programmes. Following 11 days of protests, in early March a temporary truce was declared between the coca growers and the Government, although the Government refused to release Palomino La Serna and pledged to continue with its eradication strategy. Following 20 days of negotiations, the Government agreed to give $11m. in direct aid to farmers affected by the eradication efforts, although the success of economic incentives remained threatened by the high market price of coca in relation to other crops. In April thousands of coca growers began a protest march towards Lima to demand subsidies for alternative crops and an increase in the amount of coca that could legally be grown.

Assassination attempts and bomb attacks against government and military targets, strategic power installations, commercial enterprises and rural defence groups by the SL intensified in the early 1990s. Following Fujimori's 'autogolpe' of April 1992 (effected partly in response to continuing congressional opposition to his efforts to expand the role of the armed forces), considerable concern was expressed by human rights organizations that the security forces would be permitted an increasing degree of autonomy, with unprecedented rights of civil intervention. In September 1992 government forces succeeded in capturing SL's founder and leader, Abimael Guzmán Reynoso, together with 20 prominent SL members. Guzmán was tried by a military court, where he was found guilty of treason and sentenced to life imprisonment. (In March 2003 it was announced that Guzmán was to be retried, following a ruling that military sentencing under Fujimori was unconstitutional—see above.) SL, however, remained highly active, and in early 1993 was held responsible for the assassination of 20 candidates campaigning in local elections, and for attacks on rural communities that had formed self-defence militia units. In October Guzmán made several appeals to the Government to commence a dialogue for peace, and urged his organization to co-operate. The Government actively pursued its offensive against terrorist organizations in the mid-1990s, and publicized the detention of leading members of SL, the MRTA and the dissident SL 'Sendero Rojo' faction (which advocated a continuation of the armed struggle). In 1999 Oscar Ramírez Durand (alias 'Comrade Feliciano'), the leader of Sendero Rojo, was captured and sentenced to life imprisonment.

However, the SL emerged again in 2001, with at least 31 deaths attributed to the terrorist organization in that year. In late August President Toledo ordered more than 100 army and police posts to be reopened in remote parts of the jungle where the SL was thought to be active. The resurgence of the drugs trade, partly displaced from Colombia, was believed to be financing the SL's activities. In March 2002, three days before the US President, George W. Bush, was due to visit Peru, the first such visit by a serving US head of state, a car bomb killed nine people and injured at least 40 more near the US embassy in Lima. The attack was attributed to a radical wing of the SL. Nevertheless, President Bush's visit proceeded as planned and the attack was not thought to herald a return to a sustained campaign of terrorism. In April 2003 the Government increased the defence budget by US $203.5m., which included substantial funds to support alternative development strategies, in order to help combat the illegal drugs trade.

The Peruvian Government attracted criticism from human rights organizations for its methods in achieving the apparent subjugation of the terrorist movements in the 1990s. In May 1996 Amnesty International reported that some 600 people had been wrongly imprisoned under the anti-terrorism legislation (local groups estimated the number to be as high as 1,400). In July 1999 Peru withdrew from the jurisdiction of the Inter-American Court of Human Rights (IACHR), a branch of the OAS, after the court ruled the previous month that new trials should be held for four Chilean MRTA activists who were serving life sentences. Human rights activists condemned the military trials that had sentenced them, but Fujimori dismissed the possibility of a new civil trial on the grounds of national security. However, in January 2000, the Government ended its boycott of the IACHR, apparently as part of its effort to improve the country's international image, and in January 2001 the Congreso approved Peru's return to the jurisdiction of the IACHR. In the same month, a Truth Commission was established, composed of church leaders and civil and military representatives, to investigate the fate of an estimated 4,000 people who had disappeared during the campaign against the guerrilla groups in the 1980s and 1990s. In March, one week after the IACHR ruled that a military amnesty law approved in 1995 was incompatible with the American Convention on Human Rights, two former intelligence generals, Julio Salazar Monroe and Juan Rivera Lazo, were arrested on charges of involvement in the early 1990s with a right-wing death squad, known as the Colina group. Later that month the Supreme Court ruled that a new investigation should take place into the killing of 15 people, apparently mistaken for SL members, in 1991 by the Colina group. In September 2001 the Attorney-General charged Fujimori with responsibility for two mass killings by the Colina group that took place in the early 1990s.

In February 1990, in Cartagena, Colombia, the Presidents of Peru, Colombia, Bolivia and the USA signed the Cartagena Declaration, pledging the intensification of efforts to combat the consumption, production and trafficking of illegal drugs. However, financial commitments to fund subsequent anti-drugs schemes in Peru were suspended by the US Administration as a result of international criticism of the Peruvian Government's record on human rights and its flouting of accepted democratic processes. In January 1996 responsibility for combating the drugs trade was transferred from the military to the national police force, following a series of allegations that army officers had themselves been involved in illegal trafficking. A new bilateral agreement to combat the drugs trade was signed with the USA in July, and US aid to counter the problem, amounting to US $14m., was extended in October. Following the approval of the Andean Trade Promotion and Drug Eradication Act by the US Congress in August 2002, it was announced that Peru qualified for expanded US benefits and trade preferences under the new legislation. Some $19m. was restored to the US Administration's anti-drugs funding for Peru, following an apparent improvement in government efforts to eradicate coca production, which increased the total direct assistance budget for 2003 to some $135m. In March 2003 a new $3,000m. development strategy for the regions of Peru affected by coca cultivation was announced; the plans envisaged the reforestation of 1m. hectares of arable land judged to be capable of producing coca, and the replanting of some 500,000 ha with alternative crops. The Government also envisaged that the new initiatives would lead to the creation of some 2.5m. jobs by 2020, with the complete elimination of coca in the area under illegal cultivation (which totalled approximately 24,600 ha). However, in the same month a team of officials travelled to the USA in order to voice concerns over the viability of the eradication strategy, which remained the cornerstone of US anti-drugs policy in Peru. In response to the apparently increasing sophistication of Peruvian drugs cartels, it was argued that the emphasis should be changed from eradication of coca crops towards broader attempts to disrupt the entire supply chain of the illegal narcotics industry. Moreover, prompted in part by increasing fears of a potential 'overspill' of drugs-traffickers displaced from Colombia, the Peruvian Government's representatives urged the resumption of air patrols, which had been suspended in April 2001 following the accidental destruction of an aircraft carrying two US missionaries.

Meeting in Caracas, Venezuela, in May 1991, the Presidents of the five South American nations comprising the Andean Group (now the Andean Community of Nations, see p. 133) formalized their commitment to the full implementation of an Andean free-trade area by the end of 1995, to be achieved by a gradual reduction in tariffs and other trade barriers. In April 1994 Peru, which had suspended its membership of the organization in 1992, was readmitted as a full member of the Group, although it was to participate solely as an observer in the negotiations to establish a common external tariff (CET). An agreement to restructure the Group into the Andean Community, thus strengthening regional integration, was signed, in March 1996, in Trujillo. In June 1997 the Peruvian Government announced plans to abolish tariffs on some 2,500 goods entering Peru from within the Community (with immediate effect), and its intention to remove tariffs on a further 3,500 goods (including more than 600 deemed 'sensitive') by 2005. In April 1998 the Community agreed to co-operate with Mercosur (see p. 316) in establishing an enlarged free-trade area, encompassing both organizations, by 1 January 2000 (although this was subsequently postponed until mid-2002). Following a visit to the country by US President Bush in March 2002, hopes were raised that the favourable trade terms granted to Peru under the US Andean Trade Preferences Act (ATPA), which had expired in December 2001, would be extended. Such expectations were realized with the Andean Trade Promotion and Drug Eradication Act (ATPDEA) of August 2002, which awarded Peru significant new tariff reductions on exports to the USA, including clothing and manufactures. New trade discussions between the Andean Community and Canada were also expected to take place in May 2003.

A long-standing border dispute with Ecuador over the Cordillera del Cóndor descended into armed conflict in January 1981. A cease-fire was declared a few days later, under the auspices of the guarantors (Argentina, Brazil, Chile and the USA) of the Rio de Janeiro Protocol of 1942, which had awarded the area, affording access to the Amazon river basin, to Peru. However, the Protocol has never been recognized by Ecuador, and, despite mutual efforts to achieve a constructive dialogue, the matter continued to be a source of tension and recurrent skirmishes between the two countries. In January 1995 serious fighting broke out. In February representatives of both countries, meeting in Brazil under the auspices of the Rio de Janeiro Protocol guarantors, approved a provisional cease-fire. Following further negotiations, and the announcement of a unilateral cease-fire by Peru, on 17 February both countries signed the Itamaraty Peace Declaration. Foreign affairs ministers from both countries, meeting in Uruguay at the end of the month, signed the Montevideo Declaration, which ratified the Itamaraty agreement. An observer mission, representing the Rio de Janeiro guarantors, was subsequently dispatched to the border to oversee the separation of forces and the demilitarization of the border area. The withdrawal of forces from the disputed border area was achieved by mid-May. None the less, reports of further armed clashes prompted requests from both countries for an extension of the observer mission. Agreement on the delimitation of a demilitarized zone in the disputed Cenepa river region came into effect on 1 August. In September Fujimori agreed to reopen the border with Ecuador for commercial purposes, and in November both countries agreed to pursue further confidence-building measures. In October 1996 the Ministers of Foreign Affairs of both countries, meeting in Chile under the auspices of the guarantor countries, signed the Santiago Agreement, which was to provide a framework for a settlement of the border issue.

Following further negotiations in early 1998 a number of commissions were established to examine specific aspects of a potential agreement between Peru and Ecuador, including a trade and navigation treaty and the fixing of frontier markers on the ground in the Cordillera del Cóndor. Talks culminated in the signing of an accord in Brasília on 26 October by the Ministers of Foreign Affairs of Peru and Ecuador in the presence of the two countries' Presidents and of six other regional leaders. The accord confirmed Peru's claim regarding the delineation of the border, but granted Ecuador navigation and trading rights on the Amazon and its tributaries and the opportunity to establish two trading centres in Peru (although this was not to constitute sovereign access). Moreover, Ecuador was given 1 sq km of territory, as private property, at Tiwintza in Peru where many Ecuadorean soldiers, killed during the conflict in 1995, were buried. Both countries were committed to establish ecological parks along the border where military personnel would not be allowed access. Although considerable opposition to the accord was expressed in Peru, notably in the town of Iquitos, international reaction was very favourable and resulted in several offers of finance from multilateral agencies for cross-border development projects. The border integration treaties received congressional approval in both countries during November. The physical demarcation of the frontier was completed by May 1999. The Presidents of Peru and Ecuador met in May at the Peru–Ecuador frontier to mark the placing of the last boundary stone on the border. In February 2003 a new river bridge between the two countries was opened. In April 2003 relations improved still further with the creation of a bilateral 'integration forum' to increase co-operation in agriculture, mining and tourism. A number of large infrastructure projects were also discussed, including the proposed merger of the two countries' oil export pipelines.

In January 1992 the Presidents of Peru and Bolivia concluded an agreement whereby Bolivia would be granted access to the Pacific Ocean via the Peruvian port of Ilo (which would be jointly developed as a free zone). In return, Bolivia agreed to help facilitate Peruvian access to the Atlantic Ocean (through Brazil) by way of the Bolivian town of Puerto Suárez.

Government

A new Constitution, drafted by the Congreso Constituyente Democrático, was approved by a national referendum on 31 October 1993, and was promulgated on 29 December. Under the terms of the Constitution, executive power is vested in the President, who is elected for a five-year term by universal adult suffrage and is eligible for re-election for a successive term of office. Two Vice-Presidents are also elected. The President governs with the assistance of an appointed Council of Ministers. Legislative power is vested in a single chamber Congreso, elected for five years by a single national list system. However, in April 2003, the Congreso voted to restore a bicameral legislature. A new lower chamber would comprise 150 members, elected for a five-year term, and would include at least one representative from each electoral district. A 50-member Senate would also be created. For administrative purposes, Peru comprises 25 regional presidencies, 278 regional authorities and 12,138 municipal authorities, following amendments to the Constitution approved in December 2002.

Defence

Military service is selective and lasts for two years. At 1 August 2002 the armed forces numbered 110,000 men (including an estimated 64,000 conscripts): an army of 70,000, a navy of 25,000 and an air force of 15,000. There are paramilitary police forces numbering 77,000 men. The 2002 budget allocated 2,700m. new soles for defence and domestic security.

Economic Affairs

In 2001, according to estimates by the World Bank, Peru's gross national income (GNI), measured at average 1998–2001 prices, was US $52,147m., equivalent to $2,000 per head (or $4,680 per head on an international purchasing-power parity basis). During 1990–2001, it was estimated, the population increased by an average of 1.7% per year, while gross domestic product (GDP) per head increased, in real terms, at an average annual rate of 1.9%. Overall GDP increased, in real terms, at an average annual rate of 3.6% in 1990–2001; growth was 0.2% in 2001.

Agriculture (including forestry and fishing) contributed 8.5% of GDP, measured at current prices, in 2001 and the sector (including forestry and fishing) engaged 8.8% of the total working population in that year. Rice, maize and potatoes are the principal food crops. The principal cash crop is coffee. Peru is the world's leading producer of coca, and the cultivation of this shrub, for the production of the illicit drug cocaine, reportedly generated revenue of US $1,500m.–$2,500m. per year. Undeclared revenue from the export of coca is believed to exceed revenue from legal exports. Fishing, particularly for the South American pilchard and the anchoveta, provides another important source of revenue, and the fishing sector contributed an estimated 0.8% of GDP, measured at current prices, in 2001. Fishing accounted for 13.0% of the total value of exports in 2001. During 1990–2001 agricultural GDP (including fishing) increased at an average annual rate of 4.7%; the sector's GDP increased by 6.4% in 2000, but declined by 0.6% in 2001.

Industry (including mining, manufacturing, construction and power) provided an estimated 29.8% of GDP in 2001, measured at current prices, and the sector employed 17.9% of the working population in the same year. During 1990–2001 industrial GDP increased by an average of 4.3% per year; in 2000 industrial GDP increased by 3.4%, but in 2001 the sector grew by only 0.7%.

Mining (including petroleum) contributed 5.8% of GDP in 2001, measured at current prices, and employed 0.6% of the working population in the same year. Copper (which accounted for 10.6% of total export earnings in 2001), zinc, gold, petroleum and its derivatives, lead and silver are the major mineral exports. During 1994–2000 the GDP of the mining and petroleum sector increased at an average annual rate of 6.2%; real GDP growth in the sector was 12.9% in 1999 and 2.4% in 2000.

Manufacturing contributed 15.9% of GDP in 2001, measured at current prices, and employed 12.6% of the working population in the same year. In 1996 the principal branches of manufacturing, measured by gross value of output, were food products (19.2%), petroleum refineries, non-ferrous metals, beverages and textiles and clothing. During 1990–2001 manufacturing GDP increased by an average of 3.2% per year. The sector's GDP increased by 6.7% in 2000, before declining by 1.1% in 2001.

Energy is derived principally from domestic supplies of hydroelectric power (76% of total electricity production in 1999) and petroleum (18%). Imports of fuel comprised 12.6% of the value of merchandise imports in 2001. In early 2003 a new $4,500m. project to construct a pipeline exporting liquid natural gas to the USA was announced.

The services sector contributed an estimated 61.7% of GDP in 2001, measured at current prices, and employed 73.3% of the working population in the same year. Tourism is gradually emerging as an important source of foreign revenue (US $1,001m. in 2000). In 1990–2001 the GDP of the services sector increased by an average annual rate of 3.0%. The sector's GDP grew by 4.0% in 2000 and by 3.2% in 2001.

In 2001 Peru recorded a visible trade surplus of US $92m. and there was a deficit of $1,098m. on the current account of the balance of payments. In 2000 the principal source of imports (23.4%) was the USA, which was also the principal market for exports (28.0%). Other major trading partners were Japan,

Colombia and Venezuela for imports, and the United Kingdom, Switzerland and Japan for exports. The principal exports in 2001 were metals (particularly gold and copper) and fish. The principal imports in the same year were raw materials and capital goods for industry.

In 2001 there was an estimated budgetary deficit of 5,339m. new soles. Peru's external debt at the end of 2000 was US $28,560m., of which $24,045m. was long-term public debt. In that year the cost of debt-servicing was equivalent to 42.8% of the value of exports of goods and services. The annual rate of inflation averaged 34.3% in 1990–2001. Consumer prices increased by an average of 2.0% in 2001. An estimated 7.9% of the urban labour force were unemployed in 2001. Some 52.5% were underemployed in the December 2001–February 2002.

Peru is a member of the Andean Community of Nations (see p. 133), the Inter-American Development Bank (see p. 239) and the Latin American Integration Association (see p. 259), all of which encourage regional economic development, and of the Rio Group (formerly the Group of Eight, see p. 351), which attempts to reduce regional indebtedness. Peru became a member of the Asia-Pacific Economic Co-operation group (APEC, see p. 139) in 1998.

During the early 1990s the Fujimori administration undertook a major reform of the economy, achieving considerable success in restoring international reserves and in reducing the rate of inflation. Tax reforms increased central government revenue and contributed to a reduction of the public sector deficit, while the implementation of economic liberalization measures and the repayment of arrears improved relations with the international financial community. However, the contraction in domestic demand in the late 1990s led to a widening of the fiscal deficit. The political crisis in 2000 (see above) led to a sharp decrease in investment as well as consumer demand and revenue from privatization remained below target. The interim Government of Valentín Paniagua announced a policy of fiscal austerity as well an investigation into the whereabouts of unallocated profits from the privatization programme of the Fujimori Government. In March 2001 the IMF approved a one-year stand-by credit equivalent to SDR 128m. to ensure macroeconomic stability during the transition to a new administration. The new Government of Alejandro Toledo, which took office in July, hoped to alleviate poverty and lower unemployment. As political instability abated and investor confidence gradually increased, a main priority was also the resumption of the privatization process (concentrating on the energy and infrastructure sectors) to reduce the fiscal deficit. However, violent protests led to the indefinite suspension of the privatization programme in mid-2002 and by mid-2003 it was widely feared that the Government would fail to meet its IMF-approved privatization revenue target of US $700m. for the year. In January 2003 the Belgian electricity company Tractebel cancelled plans to buy two state-owned generating firms, Egasa and Egesa. None the less, in February the Government attempted to revive the privatization process, announcing the auction of 10 regional electricity distribution companies, despite reduced investor confidence in the strategy. In February 2002 the IMF approved a new two-year stand-by credit for Peru, worth about $340m., to support the Government's economic programme for 2002–03, and disbursed a further $38m. in April. In 2003 the Toledo Government earned the praise of the IMF for its competent management of the economy, which resulted in one of the highest rates of GDP growth in the region. A surplus in the balance of trade in 2002 of some $260m. was attributed to the Government's aggressive exports strategy. Notably, economic growth in 2002 was led by sectors unrelated to the exploitation of mineral resources, thus indicating a substantial real improvement in the overall economy. Moreover, the Government met the IMF's fiscal deficit target in 2002, and enhanced collection measures allowed tax receipts to increase by an annualized rate of 40% in March 2003. However, the level of government indebtedness remained high in 2002. Growth in 2002 was 5.2%, compared with 0.6% in 2001.

Education

Reforms that were introduced after the 1968 revolution have instituted a three-level educational system. The first is for children up to six years of age in either nurseries or kindergartens. Basic (primary) education is free and compulsory, and is received between six and 11 years of age. Secondary education, beginning at the age of 12, is divided into two stages, of two and three years, respectively. In 1997 some 91% of children in the relevant age-group were enrolled at primary schools, while secondary enrolment included 55% of the appropriate age-group. Higher education includes the pre-university and university levels. There are 25 national and 10 private universities. There is also provision for adult literacy programmes and bilingual education. Under the new Constitution, adopted in 1993, the principle of free university education was abolished. Total central government expenditure on education was estimated at 2.9% of GDP in 2000.

Public Holidays

2003: 1 January (New Year's Day), 17 April (Maundy Thursday), 18 April (Good Friday), 1 May (Labour Day), 24 June (Day of the Peasant, half-day only), 29 June (St Peter and St Paul), 28–29 July (Independence), 30 August (St Rose of Lima), 8 October (Battle of Angamos), 1 November (All Saints' Day), 8 December (Immaculate Conception), 25 December (Christmas Day).

2004: 1 January (New Year's Day), 8 April (Maundy Thursday), 9 April (Good Friday), 1 May (Labour Day), 24 June (Day of the Peasant, half-day only), 29 June (St Peter and St Paul), 28–29 July (Independence), 30 August (St Rose of Lima), 8 October (Battle of Angamos), 1 November (All Saints' Day), 8 December (Immaculate Conception), 25 December (Christmas Day).

Weights and Measures

The metric system is in force.

Statistical Survey

Sources (unless otherwise stated): Banco Central de Reserva del Perú, Jirón Miró Quesada 441, Lima 1; tel. (1) 4276250; fax (1) 4275880; internet www .bcrp.gob.pe; Instituto Nacional de Estadística e Informática, Avda General Garzón 658; tel. (1) 4334223; fax (1) 4333159; internet www.inei.gob.pe.

Area and Population

AREA, POPULATION AND DENSITY
(excluding Indian jungle population)

Area (sq km)	
Land	1,280,086
Inland water	5,130
Total	1,285,216*
Population (census results)†	
12 July 1981	17,005,210
11 July 1993	
Males	10,956,375
Females	11,091,981
Total	22,048,356
Population (official estimates at mid-year)	
2000	25,939,329
2001	26,346,840
2002	26,749,947
Density (per sq km) at mid-2002	20.8

* 496,225 sq miles.

† Excluding adjustment for underenumeration, estimated at 4.1% in 1981 and 2.35% in 1993.

DEPARTMENTS
(30 June 2002)

	Area (sq km)	Population (estimated)	Density (per sq km)	Capital
Amazonas . .	39,249	428,095	10.9	Chachapoyas
Ancash . . .	35,877	1,107,828	30.9	Huaráz
Apurimac . .	20,896	463,131	22.2	Abancay
Arequipa . .	63,345	1,101,005	17.4	Arequipa
Ayacucho . .	43,814	550,751	12.6	Ayacuchu
Cajamarca . .	33,318	1,498,567	45.0	Cajamarca
Callao* . . .	147	787,154	5,354.8	Callao
Cusco . . .	72,104	1,208,689	16.8	Cusco (Cuzco)
Huancavelica .	22,131	443,213	20.0	Huancavelica
Huánuco . .	36,887	811,865	22.0	Huánuco
Ica	21,328	687,334	32.2	Ica
Junín . . .	44,197	1,246,663	28.2	Huancayo
La Libertad . .	25,500	1,506,122	59.1	Trujillo
Lambayeque . .	14,231	1,121,358	78.8	Chiclayo
Lima	34,802	7,748,528	222.6	Lima
Loreto . . .	368,852	907,341	2.5	Iquitos
Madre de Dios .	85,183	99,452	1.2	Puerto Maldonado
Moquegua . .	15,734	156,750	10.0	Moquegua
Pasco . . .	25,320	264,702	10.5	Cerro de Pasco
Piura . . .	35,892	1,636,047	45.6	Piura
Puno . . .	71,999	1,263,995	17.6	Puno
San Martín . .	51,253	757,740	14.8	Moyabamba
Tacna . . .	16,076	294,214	18.3	Tacna
Tumbes . . .	4,669	202,088	43.3	Tumbes
Ucayali . . .	102,411	456,340	4.5	Pucallpa
Total . . .	1,285,216	26,748,972	20.8	

* Province.

PRINCIPAL TOWNS
(estimated population of towns and urban environs at 1 July 1998)

Lima (capital) .	7,060,600*	Piura	308,155
Arequipa . . .	710,103	Huancayo . . .	305,039
Trujillo . . .	603,657	Chimbote . . .	298,800
Callao	515,200†	Cusco (Cuzco) . .	278,590
Chiclayo . . .	469,200	Pucallpa . . .	220,866
Iquitos	334,013	Tacna	215,683

* Metropolitan area (Gran Lima) only.

† Estimated population of town, excluding urban environs, at mid-1985.

2001 (UN projection, incl. suburbs): Lima 7,594,000 (Source: UN, *World Urbanization Prospects: The 2001 Revision*).

BIRTHS AND DEATHS
(excluding Indian jungle population)*

	Registered live births		Registered deaths	
	Number	Rate (per 1,000)	Number	Rate (per 1,000)
1994	663,239	28.7	171,476	7.4
1995	617,300	26.2	156,000	6.6
1996	615,300	25.7	156,800	6.5
1997† . . .	613,500	25.2	157,500	6.5
1998† . . .	611,600	24.7	158,500	6.4
1999	609,800	24.2	159,900	6.3
2000	607,800	23.7	161,000	6.3
2001	630,947	23.9	164,296	6.2

* Data are tabulated by year of registration rather than by year of occurrence. Registration is incomplete but the figures include an upward adjustment for under-registration.

† Provisional.

Sources: partly UN, *Demographic Yearbook* and *Population and Vital Statistics Report*.

Expectation of life (WHO estimates, years at birth): 68.5 (males 66.3; females 70.9) in 2001 (Source: WHO,*World Health Report*).

ECONOMICALLY ACTIVE POPULATION
('000 persons aged 14 and over, urban areas)

	1999	2000	2001
Agriculture, hunting and forestry .	355.0	456.4	620.7
Fishing	65.3	25.8	47.1
Mining and quarrying	31.3	52.5	45.9
Manufacturing	897.6	963.5	956.4
Electricity, gas and water . . .	41.3	28.1	20.4
Construction	378.2	299.5	341.3
Wholesale and retail trade; repair of motor vehicles, motorcycles and personal and household goods	2,077.0	2,060.5	2,124.5
Hotels and restaurants	470.6	431.9	593.8
Transport, storage and communications	618.2	639.0	641.0
Financial intermediation . . .	76.3	66.6	47.9
Real estate, renting and business activities	407.5	413.4	342.6
Public administration and defence; compulsory social security . .	349.0	346.7	298.1
Education	551.5	479.7	552.1
Health and social work	165.1	169.7	213.5
Other services	372.9	368.2	406.2
Private households	353.8	326.8	366.3
Not classifiable	—	—	1.9
Total employed	7,211.2	7,128.4	7,619.9
Unemployed	624.9	566.5	651.5
Total economically active population	7,836.1	7,694.9	8,271.4

Source: ILO.

Health and Welfare

KEY INDICATORS

Total fertility rate (children per woman, 2001)	2.7
Under-5 mortality rate (per 1,000 live births, 2001) . . .	39
HIV/AIDS (% of persons aged 15–49, 2001)	0.35
Physicians (per 1,000 head, 1997)	0.93
Hospital beds (per 1,000 head, 1996)	1.47
Health expenditure (2000): US $ per head (PPP)	238
Health expenditure (2000): % of GDP	4.8
Health expenditure (2000): public (% of total)	59.2
Access to water (% of persons, 1999).	77
Access to sanitation (% of persons, 1999)	76
Human Development Index (2000): ranking	82
Human Development Index (2000): value	0.747

For sources and definitions, see explanatory note on p. vi.

Agriculture

PRINCIPAL CROPS
('000 metric tons)

	1999	2000	2001
Wheat	169.9	189.0	181.8
Rice (paddy)	1,955.0	1,892.1	2,040.9
Barley	169.8	186.2	177.3
Maize	1,058.7	1,240.8	1,319.7
Potatoes	3,066.2	3,273.8	2,670.5
Sweet potatoes	244.2	245.1	253.4
Cassava (Manioc)	868.1	882.0	858.8
Sugar cane*	6,900.0	7,750.0	7,950.0
Dry beans	70.4	69.8	61.6
Oil palm fruit	198.9	180.0†	190.0*
Cottonseed	134.9	153.8	133.5
Cabbages	51.6	52.8	47.8
Asparagus	174.9	168.4	183.9
Tomatoes	165.5	250.4	188.7
Dry onions	366.1	379.8	415.5
Green peas	76.0	73.9	83.5
Green broad beans	64.8	67.3	65.8
Carrots	134.6	145.8	145.0
Green corn	340.9	340.0	341.0*
Plantains	1,385.0	1,414.9	1,450.0*
Oranges	257.4	270.7	287.0
Tangerines, mandarins clementines and satsumas	116.8	131.8	128.2
Lemons and limes	234.4	238.2	212.8
Apples	150.0	157.8	137.8
Grapes	98.3	107.2	127.4
Watermelons	71.5	61.2	64.3
Mangoes	191.5	128.4	140.1
Avocados	79.1	84.5	93.3
Pineapples	144.7	147.3	150.7
Papayas	171.0	171.4	163.4
Cotton (lint)	51.9	58.3*	48.0*
Coffee (green)	144.9	158.3	161.5

* FAO estimate(s).
† Unofficial figure.

Source: FAO.

LIVESTOCK
('000 head, year ending September)

	1999	2000	2001
Horses*	675	690	700
Mules*	235	250	260
Asses*	535	550	570
Cattle	4,903	4,927	4,978
Pigs	2,788	2,819	2,780
Sheep	14,297	14,686	14,259
Goats	2,068	2,023	2,004
Poultry	81,304	92,610	90,000

* FAO estimates.

Source: FAO.

LIVESTOCK PRODUCTS
('000 metric tons)

	1999	2000	2001
Beef and veal	133.5	136.2	137.8
Mutton and lamb	29.8	31.0	31.8
Pig meat	92.9	94.7	95.0
Poultry meat	553.6	609.8	622.1
Cows' milk	1,013.3	1,067.0	1,115.0
Hen eggs	161.3	162.3	162.8
Wool (greasy)	12.0	12.7	12.9

Source: FAO.

Forestry

ROUNDWOOD REMOVALS
('000 cubic metres, excluding bark)

	1999	2000	2001
Sawlogs, veneer logs and logs for sleepers	1,424	1,325	1,070
Other industrial wood	146	176	1
Fuel wood	7,625	7,777	7,299
Total	9,195	8,704	8,370

Source: FAO.

SAWNWOOD PRODUCTION
('000 cubic metres, including railway sleepers)

	1999	2000	2001
Coniferous (softwood)	44	3	3*
Broadleaved (hardwood) . . .	791	643	491
Total	835	646	494

* FAO estimate.

Source: FAO.

Fishing

('000 metric tons, live weight)

	1998	1999	2000
Capture	4,338.4	8,428.6	10,658.6
Chilean jack mackerel . . .	386.9	184.7	296.6
South American pilchard .	908.3	187.8	226.3
Anchoveta (Peruvian anchovy) .	1,206.3	6,740.2	9,575.7
Other anchovies	706.2	11.2	3.9
Chub mackerel	401.9	527.7	73.3
Aquaculture	7.7	8.3	6.8
Total catch	4,346.1	8,436.9	10,668.4

Note: Figures exclude aquatic plants ('000 metric tons): 1.8 (capture 1.7, aquaculture 0.1) in 1998; 1.8 (capture 1.7, aquaculture 0.1) in 1999; 1.3 (capture 1.3, aquaculture 0.0) in 2000. Also excluded are aquatic mammals, recorded by number rather than by weight. The number of toothed whales caught was: 48 in 1998; 0 in 1999; 0 in 2000.

Source: FAO, *Yearbook of Fishery Statistics*.

Mining

('000 metric tons, unless otherwise indicated)*

	2000	2001	2002
Crude petroleum ('000 barrels)† .	36,313.5	35,440.5	n.a.
Copper	404.7	557.8	647.5
Lead	239.1	255.9	263.7
Zinc	792.4	919.8	1,063.3
Iron ore	2,812.8	3,081.0	3,105.0
Gold (metric tons)	131.2	137.3	155.6
Silver (kg)	2,230.0	2,445.4	2,521.1

* Figures for metallic minerals refer to metal content only.
† Data from IMF, *Peru—Statistical Appendix* (March 2003).

Industry

SELECTED PRODUCTS
('000 metric tons, unless otherwise indicated)

	1998	1999	2000
Canned fish	54.5	n.a.	n.a.
Wheat flour	841	n.a.	n.a.
Raw sugar	462	613	710
Beer ('000 hectolitres)	6,556	n.a.	n.a.
Cigarettes (million)	3,061	n.a.	n.a.
Rubber tyres ('000)*	1,033	n.a.	n.a.
Motor spirit (petrol, '000 barrels)	10,134	9,449	9,291
Kerosene ('000 barrels)	5,103	4,910	5,235
Distillate fuel oils ('000 barrels)	15,040	13,622	12,355
Residual fuel oils ('000 barrels)	20,640	17,437	18,348
Cement	4,340	3,799	3,906
Crude steel†	510	510	510
Copper (refined)	309.6	318.9	324.4
Lead (refined)	109.5	121.1	116.4
Zinc (refined)	174.7	197.0	199.8
Electric energy (million kWh)‡	18,582.5	19,049.6	19,922.5

* Tyres for road motor vehicles.
† Estimated production.
‡ Data from the Ministry of Energy and Mines.

Sources (unless otherwise indicated): FAO; UN, *Industrial Commodity Statistics Yearbook*; US Geological Survey.

Finance

CURRENCY AND EXCHANGE RATES

Monetary Units
100 céntimos = 1 nuevo sol (new sol)

Sterling, Dollar and Euro Equivalents (31 December 2002)
£1 sterling = 5.664 new soles
US $1 = 3.514 new soles
€1 = 3.685 new soles
100 new soles = £17.66 = $28.46 = €27.14

Average Exchange Rate (new soles per US $)
2000   3.490
2001   3.507
2002   3.517

Note: On 1 February 1985 Peru replaced its former currency, the sol, by the inti, valued at 1,000 soles. A new currency, the nuevo sol (equivalent to 1m. intis), was introduced in July 1991.

GENERAL BUDGET
(million new soles)

Revenue	1999	2000	2001
Taxation	21,483	22,376	22,626
Taxes on income, profits, etc.	5,072	5,130	5,630
Taxes on payroll and work force.	1,000	1,038	847
Domestic taxes on goods and services	14,475	15,418	15,341
Value-added tax.	11,029	11,996	11,808
Excises	3,446	3,421	3,533
Import duties	2,848	2,913	2,740
Other taxes	229	648	902
Adjustment to tax revenue	−2,142	−2,769	−2,834
Other current revenue	3,810	5,038	4,121
Resources of ministries and other non-tax revenues	3,548	4,893	4,088
Interest on privatization funds	262	145	33
Capital revenue	624	530	291
Total (incl. grants)	25,916	27,944	27,039

Expenditure	1999	2000	2001
Current non-interest expenditure	21,797	23,757	23,853
Labour services	11,778	12,394	12,566
Wages and salaries	7,774	8,180	8,385
Pensions	3,281	3,418	3,432
Social security contributions	724	796	750
Goods and non-labour services	6,210	7,068	7,067
Transfers	3,808	4,294	4,219
Private sector	1,095	1,140	821
Non-financial public sector	2,714	3,154	3,397
Interest payments	3,680	4,076	4,059
Capital expenditure	5,900	5,232	4,467
Gross capital formation	5,652	4,749	3,898
Total	31,378	33,065	32,378

Source: IMF, *Peru—Statistical Appendix* (March 2003).

INTERNATIONAL RESERVES
(US $ million at 31 December)

	2000	2001	2002
Gold*	254.1	261.6	386.7
IMF special drawing rights	1.5	1.7	0.7
Foreign exchange	8,372.5	8,670.1	9,338.3
Total	8,628.1	8,933.4	9,725.7

* National valuation.

Source: IMF, *International Financial Statistics*.

MONEY SUPPLY
(million new soles at 31 December)

	2000	2001	2002
Currency outside banks	4,537	4,945	5,612
Demand deposits at commercial and development banks	9,110	8,977	8,398
Total money (incl. others)	21,072	21,445	22,084

Source: IMF, *International Financial Statistics*.

COST OF LIVING
(Consumer Price Index, Lima metropolitan area; base: 1990 = 100)

	1999	2000	2001
Food (incl. beverages)	1,918.1	1,932.6	1,942.0
Housing (incl. fuel and light)	6,303.9	6,969.0	7,371.3
Clothing (incl. footwear)	1,686.1	1,867.2	1,913.0
All items (incl. others)	2,427.4	2,517.9	2,568.3

Source: ILO, *Yearbook of Labour Statistics*.

NATIONAL ACCOUNTS
(million new soles at current prices)

National Income and Product

	1998	1999	2000
Compensation of employees	41,424	43,972	46,486
Operating surplus	96,921	101,629	109,873
Domestic factor incomes	138,345	145,601	156,359
Consumption of fixed capital	11,183	12,305	12,998
Gross domestic product (GDP) at factor cost	149,527	157,906	169,358
Indirect taxes	16,987	16,813	17,399
GDP in purchasers' values	166,514	174,719	186,756
Factor income received from abroad. *Less* Factor income paid abroad	−4,297	−5,128	—
Gross national product	162,217	169,591	186,756
Less Consumption of fixed capital	11,183	12,305	12,998
National income in market prices	151,035	157,286	173,758
Other current transfers from abroad. *Less* Other current transfers paid abroad.	2,666	3,189	—
National disposable income	153,701	160,475	173,758

Source: UN Economic Commission for Latin America and the Caribbean.

PERU

Expenditure on the Gross Domestic Product

	1999	2000	2001
Government final consumption expenditure	19,038	20,866	21,173
Private final consumption expenditure	122,196	131,831	136,264
Increase in stocks	−303	−27	137
Gross fixed capital formation	37,841	37,582	34,742
Total domestic expenditure	178,772	190,252	192,316
Exports of goods and services	25,855	29,851	29,975
Less Imports of goods and services	29,907	33,346	32,758
GDP in purchasers' values*	174,719	186,756	189,532
GDP at constant 1994 prices	117,590	121,267	121,513

* Including adjustment.

Source: IMF, *International Financial Statistics*.

Gross Domestic Product by Economic Activity

	1999	2000	2001
Agriculture, hunting and forestry	12,842.9	13,116.2	13,218.1
Fishing	1,478.3	1,642.3	1,318.2
Mining and quarrying	8,544.6	9,788.0	10,021.5
Manufacturing	24,393.3	27,067.4	27,230.2
Electricity and water	3,883.5	4,208.2	4,447.7
Construction	10,179.4	9,822.9	9,389.6
Wholesale and retail trade	23,753.4	25,268.0	25,442.7
Restaurants and hotels	7,313.1	7,630.3	7,779.7
Transport and communications	13,700.6	15,116.6	15,386.0
Government services	12,489.4	13,573.2	13,908.1
Finance, insurance, real estate, business and other services	39,947.8	41,716.0	43,208.1
Sub-total	158,526.3	168,949.0	171,349.7
Import duties	2,874.9	3,012.4	2,755.0
Other taxes on products	12,819.4	13,181.9	13,146.3
GDP in purchasers' values	174,220.6	185,143.3	187,251.0

BALANCE OF PAYMENTS
(US $ million)

	1999	2000	2001
Exports of goods f.o.b.	6,116	7,033	7,106
Imports of goods f.o.b.	−6,748	−7,350	−7,198
Trade balance	−632	−317	−92
Exports of services	1,589	1,578	1,491
Imports of services	−2,258	−2,374	−2,291
Balance on goods and services	−1,301	−1,113	−892
Other income received	650	739	634
Other income paid	−1,798	−2,190	−1,837
Balance on goods, services and income	−2,449	−2,564	−2,095
Current transfers received	993	1,004	1,006
Current transfers paid	−27	−8	−9
Current balance	−1,483	−1,568	−1,098
Capital account (net)	−54	−68	−67
Direct investment abroad	−128	—	—
Direct investment from abroad	1,939	662	1,064
Portfolio investment assets	−228	−539	−298
Portfolio investment liabilities	−125	75	−6
Other investment assets	130	198	66
Other investment liabilities	−1,056	483	205
Net errors and omissions	138	628	533
Overall balance	−867	−129	399

Source: IMF, *International Financial Statistics*.

External Trade

PRINCIPAL COMMODITIES
(distribution by SITC, US $ million)

Imports c.i.f.	1998	1999	2000
Food and live animals	1,111.7	865.7	742.8
Cereals and cereal preparations	535.5	404.5	335.7
Mineral fuels, lubricants, etc.	651.3	662.6	1,159.6
Petroleum, petroleum products etc.	590.0	596.6	1,058.7
Crude petroleum oils, etc.	403.4	381.3	614.4
Refined petroleum products	176.7	207.3	436.5
Chemicals and related products	1,047.5	1,001.4	1,109.6
Medicinal and pharmaceutical products	194.6	207.4	200.1
Basic manufactures	1,256.2	1,052.6	1,133.9
Iron and steel	338.1	203.1	239.8
Machinery and transport equipment	3,071.8	2,380.8	2,410.7
Power-generating machinery and equipment	176.8	144.4	142.3
Machinery specialized for particular industries	541.6	373.8	386.3
General industrial machinery equipment and parts	500.2	394.8	377.3
Office machines and automatic data-processing equipment	290.4	252.2	278.0
Telecommunications and sound equipment	412.9	342.6	367.1
Parts and accessories for telecommunications and sound equipment	300.3	253.8	249.7
Other electrical machinery apparatus, etc.	318.8	285.3	313.1
Road vehicles and parts (excl. tyres, engines and electrical parts)	767.7	549.7	513.2
Passenger motor cars (excl. buses)	333.8	188.8	196.2
Lorries and special purposes motor vehicles	250.2	207.3	164.0
Miscellaneous manufactured articles	667.5	570.5	591.1
Total (incl. others)	8,220.3	6,822.9	7,415.0

Statistical Survey

Exports f.o.b.	1998	1999	2000
Food and live animals . . .	1,201.8	1,354.5	1,634.2
Fish and fish preparations . . .	224.2	189.2	185.8
Vegetables and fruit	199.6	264.7	249.5
Coffee, tea, cocoa and spices . .	313.2	298.1	248.0
Coffee (not roasted); husks and skins	281.6	265.1	223.7
Feeding stuff for animals (excl. unmilled cereals)	413.3	564.9	902.0
Flours and meals of meat, fish, etc. (unfit for human consumption)	396.8	531.0	873.8
Crude materials (inedible) except fuels	846.1	839.5	963.9
Metalliferous ores and metal scrap	717.9	684.8	775.6
Ores and concentrates of base metals	605.0	612.4	669.0
Zinc ores and concentrates. .	315.3	326.7	347.8
Mineral fuels, lubricants, etc. .	252.2	250.2	403.7
Petroleum, petroleum products etc.	252.2	250.1	403.6
Basic manufactures	1,536.6	1,462.6	1,746.8
Non-ferrous metals	1,255.7	1,205.6	1,457.0
Silver, platinum, etc. . . .	197.3	177.1	180.1
Unwrought silver . . .	159.6	171.1	179.9
Copper and copper alloys . .	751.6	725.8	866.2
Unwrought copper and alloys .	699.4	672.5	788.6
Refined copper (excl. master alloys)	625.0	623.3	724.4
Zinc and zinc alloys . . .	195.0	210.9	223.3
Unwrought zinc and alloys .	162.8	182.2	189.3
Miscellaneous manufactured articles	593.4	528.4	634.8
Non-monetary gold (excl. gold ores and concentrates) . .	954.5	1,192.1	1,144.2
Total (incl. others)	5,671.8	5,932.1	6,866.0

Source: UN, *International Trade Statistics Yearbook.*

2001 (US $ million): *Imports f.o.b.*: Consumer goods 1,566.7 (Non-durable 938.8, Durable 627.8); Raw materials and intermediate goods 3,611.1 (Fuels 908.5, Raw materials for agriculture 231.8, Raw materials for industry 2,470.8); Capital goods 1,912.8 (Construction materials 169.0, Capital goods for industry 1,352.2, Transportation equipment 371.4); Other goods 110.3; Total 7,200.9. *Exports f.o.b.*: Traditional products 4,742.8 (Minerals 3,187.9, Petroleum and derivatives 421.4, Agricultural products 207.4, Fishing 926.2); Non-traditional products 2,186.3 (Agriculture and livestock 436.9, Textiles 663.5, Fishing products 207.2, Chemicals 246.1, Steel and metallurgical products 189.1, Other 231.6); Other 171.1; Total 7,100.2.

PRINCIPAL TRADING PARTNERS
(US $ million)

Imports c.i.f.	1998	1999	2000
Argentina	372.3	236.9	333.5
Bolivia	128.8	60.0	45.5
Brazil	381.5	301.8	377.6
Canada	217.5	146.5	218.0
Chile	285.6	300.7	395.2
China, People's Republic . .	213.3	227.7	288.9
Colombia	440.8	422.6	399.7
Ecuador	206.4	197.3	329.9
France (incl. Monaco) . . .	188.0	157.3	129.6
Germany	319.1	240.3	217.0
Italy	187.1	131.9	123.2
Japan	536.4	476.2	485.9
Korea, Republic	309.0	225.7	220.5
Mexico	298.9	238.6	237.6
Spain	220.0	191.7	176.9
Sweden	100.1	80.4	68.4
United Kingdom	99.9	82.9	93.5
USA	2,233.3	1,879.6	1,736.9
Venezuela	406.1	351.8	621.7
Total (incl. others)	8,220.3	6,822.9	7,415.0

Exports f.o.b.	1998	1999	2000
Belgium-Luxembourg	138.7	—	—
Bolivia	115.5	99.9	95.4
Brazil	180.3	172.8	221.3
Canada	126.0	118.8	123.2
Chile	138.5	173.3	262.7
China, People's Republic . .	233.2	215.5	442.7
Colombia	143.4	103.9	144.4
Ecuador	106.4	50.2	97.3
France (incl. Monaco) . . .	88.2	78.6	65.8
Germany	230.2	245.7	215.5
Italy	189.8	137.0	121.6
Japan	216.4	257.7	325.4
Korea, Republic	42.0	61.0	137.6
Mexico	137.3	171.1	150.5
Netherlands	135.7	114.1	132.7
Spain	150.7	177.5	187.4
Switzerland-Liechtenstein . .	484.0	559.5	549.6
United Kingdom	272.2	554.8	578.9
USA	1,835.2	1,725.7	1,919.9
Venezuela	108.0	92.3	110.9
Total (incl. others)	5,671.8	5,932.1	6,866.0

Source: UN, *International Trade Statistics Yearbook.*

Transport

RAILWAYS
(traffic)*

	1997	1998	1999
Passenger-km (million)	210	180	144
Freight ton-km (million)	833	892	891

* Including service traffic.

Source: UN, *Statistical Yearbook.*

ROAD TRAFFIC
(motor vehicles in use)

	1997	1998	1999
Passenger cars	595,825	645,934	684,533
Buses and coaches	43,506	43,366	44,192
Lorries and vans	325,121	343,195	359,460

Source: IRF, *World Road Statistics.*

SHIPPING

Merchant Fleet
(registered at 31 December)

	1999	2000	2001
Number of vessels	724	721	717
Total displacement ('000 grt) . .	284.9	256.5	239.6

Source: Lloyd's Register-Fairplay, *World Fleet Statistics.*

International Sea-borne Freight Traffic
('000 metric tons)

	1999	2000	2001
Goods loaded	475	542	551
Goods unloaded	579	575	596

Source: UN, *Monthly Bulletin of Statistics.*

CIVIL AVIATION
(traffic on scheduled services)

	1997	1998	1999
Kilometres flown (million) . . .	40	41	27
Passengers carried ('000) . . .	2,725	2,774	1,900
Passenger-km (million)	2,964	3,014	1,590
Total ton-km (million)	276	286	149

Source: UN, *Statistical Yearbook.*

Tourism

ARRIVALS BY NATIONALITY

	1996	1997	1998
Argentina	28,705	32,595	36,039
Bolivia	24,671	27,082	25,553
Brazil	19,557	21,936	23,894
Canada	14,393	16,601	18,232
Chile	88,698	117,052	136,763
Colombia	17,595	20,266	19,339
Ecuador	15,998	17,526	15,860
France	23,841	23,144	29,976
Germany	27,768	28,084	28,865
Italy	20,046	18,995	21,528
Japan	21,012	14,560	13,970
Mexico	10,985	13,174	15,641
Spain	25,362	25,210	28,732
United Kingdom	19,720	22,888	29,603
USA	125,603	141,577	162,039
Venezuela	11,472	12,568	12,995
Total (incl. others)	584,388	649,287	723,668

Source: World Tourism Organization, *Yearbook of Tourism Statistics*.

Tourism receipts (US $ million): 845 in 1998; 890 in 1999; 1,001 in 2000 (Source: World Tourism Organization).

Total tourist arrivals: 943,917 in 1999; 1,026,867 in 2000; 1,009,512 in 2001 (Source: Dirección General de Migraciones y Naturalización del Perú).

Communications Media

	1999	2000	2001
Television receivers ('000 in use) .	3,700	3,800	n.a.
Telephones ('000 main lines in use)	1,628.3	1,635.9	2,022.3
Mobile cellular telephones ('000 subscribers)	820.7	1,222.6	1,545.0
Personal computers ('000 in use) .	900	1,050	1,250
Internet users ('000)	1,500	2,500	3,000

1995: Facsimile machines ('000 in use): 15 (estimate).

1996: Book production: 612 titles; 74 daily newspapers.

1997: 6,650,000 radio receivers in use; 3,060,000 television receivers in use.

Sources: UNESCO, *Statistical Yearbook*; International Telecommunication Union.

Education

(2000)

	Institutions	Teachers	Pupils
Nursery	15,727	37,925	767,125
Primary	33,709	173,877	4,254,384
Secondary	8,879	137,431	2,257,400
Higher: universities	78	33,177	435,637
Higher: other third-level . .	2,083	24,697	1,060,320

Source: Ministerio de Educación del Perú.

Adult literacy rate (UNESCO estimates): 89.9% (males 94.7%; females 85.3%) in 2000 (Source: UN Development Programme, *Human Development Report*).

Directory

The Constitution

In 1993 the Congreso Constituyente Democrático (CCD) began drafting a new constitution to replace the 1979 Constitution. The CCD approved the final document in September 1993, and the Constitution was endorsed by a popular national referendum that was conducted on 31 October. The Constitution was promulgated on 29 December 1993.

EXECUTIVE POWER

Executive power is vested in the President, who is elected for a five-year term of office by universal adult suffrage; this mandate is renewable once. The successful presidential candidate must obtain at least 50% of the votes cast, and a second round of voting is held if necessary. Two Vice-Presidents are elected in simultaneous rounds of voting. The President is prohibited from serving two consecutive terms. The President is competent to initiate and submit draft bills, to review laws drafted by the legislature (Congreso) and, if delegated by the Congreso, to enact laws. The President is empowered to appoint ambassadors and senior military officials without congressional ratification, and retains the right to dissolve parliament if two or more ministers have been censured or have received a vote of 'no confidence' from the Congreso. In certain circumstances the President may, in accordance with the Council of Ministers, declare a state of emergency for a period of 60 days, during which individual constitutional rights are suspended and the armed forces may assume control of civil order. The President appoints the Council of Ministers.

LEGISLATIVE POWER

Legislative power is vested in a single-chamber Congreso (removing the distinction in the 1979 Constitution of an upper and lower house) consisting of 120 members.* The members of the Congreso are elected for a five-year term by universal adult suffrage. The Congreso is responsible for approving the budget, for endorsing loans and international treaties and for drafting and approving bills. It may conduct investigations into matters of public concern, and question and censure the Council of Ministers and its individual members. Members of the Congreso elect a Standing Committee, to consist of not more than 25% of the total number of members (representation being proportional to the different political group-

ings in the legislature), which is empowered to make certain official appointments, approve credit loans and transfers relating to the budget during a parliamentary recess, and conduct other business as delegated by parliament.

ELECTORAL SYSTEM

All citizens aged 18 years and above, including illiterate persons, are eligible to vote. Voting in elections is compulsory for all citizens aged 18–70, and is optional thereafter.

JUDICIAL POWER

Judicial power is vested in the Supreme Court of Justice and other tribunals. The Constitution provides for the establishment of a National Council of the Judiciary, consisting of nine independently elected members, which is empowered to appoint judges to the Supreme Court. An independent Constitutional Court, comprising seven members elected by the Congreso for a five-year term, may interpret the Constitution and declare legislation and acts of government to be unconstitutional.

The death penalty may be applied by the Judiciary in cases of terrorism or of treason (the latter in times of war).

Under the Constitution, a People's Counsel is elected by the Congreso with a five-year mandate which authorizes the Counsel to defend the constitutional and fundamental rights of the individual. The Counsel may draft laws and present evidence to the legislature.

According to the Constitution, the State promotes economic and social development, particularly in the areas of employment, health, education, security, public services and infrastructure. The State recognizes a plurality of economic ownership and activity, supports free competition, and promotes the growth of small businesses. Private initiative is permitted within the framework of a social market economy. The State also guarantees the free exchange of foreign currency.

* In April 2003 the Congreso voted to restore a bicameral legislature. A new lower chamber would comprise 150 members, elected for a five-year term, and would include at least one representative from each electoral district. A 50-member Senate would also be created.

The Government

HEAD OF STATE

President: ALEJANDRO TOLEDO (took office 28 July 2001).

Vice-President and Minister of International Trade and Tourism: RAÚL DÍEZ CANESCO TERRY.

COUNCIL OF MINISTERS
(April 2003)

President of the Council of Ministers: LUIS SOLARI.

Minister of Foreign Affairs: ALLAN WAGNER TIZÓN.

Minister of Defence: AURELIO LORET DE MOLA.

Minister of the Interior: ALBERTO SANABRÍA ORTIZ.

Minister of Justice: FAUSTO HUMBERTO ALVARADO DODERO.

Minister of Economy and Finance: JAVIER SILVA RUETE.

Minister of Labour and Social Promotion: FERNANDO VILLARÁN.

Minister of Transport and Communications: JAVIER REÁTEGUI ROSELLO.

Minister of Housing, Construction and Sanitation: CARLOS RICARDO BRUCE MONTES DE OCA.

Minister of Health: FERNANDO IGNACIO CARBONE.

Minister of Agriculture: ALVARO QUIJANDRÍA.

Minister of Energy and Mines: JAIME QUIJANDRÍA.

Minister of the Presidency: CARLOS BRUCE.

Minister of Production: EDUARDO IRIARTE JIMENEZ.

Minister of Education: GERARDO AYZANOA DEL CARPIO.

Minister for the Advancement of Women and Social Development: ANA MARÍA ROMERO-LOZADA LAUEZZARI.

MINISTRIES

Prime Minister's Office: Ucayali 363, Lima; tel. (1) 4471322; fax (1) 4475728; internet www.pcm.gob.pe.

Ministry for the Advancement of Women and Social Development: Avda Emancipación 235, esq. Jirón Camaná 616, Lima 1; tel. (1) 4286185; fax (1) 4287478; e-mail postmaster@lima.promudeh.gob.pe; internet www.minmimdes.gob.pe.

Ministry of Agriculture: Avda Salaverry s/n, Jesús María, Lima 11; tel. (1) 4310424; fax (1) 4310109; e-mail postmaster@mimdes.gob.pe; internet www.minag.gob.pe.

Ministry of Defence: Avda Arequipa 291, Lima 14; tel. (1) 4338344; fax (1) 4333636; e-mail oip@mindef.gob.pe; internet www.mindef.gob.pe.

Ministry of Economy and Finance: Jirón Junín 339, 4°, Lima; tel. (1) 4264275; fax (1) 4282101; e-mail postmaster@mef.gob.pe; internet www.mef.gob.pe.

Ministry of Education: Avda Van Develde 160, (cuadra 33 Javier Prado Este), San Borja, Lima 41; tel. (1) 4371613; fax (1) 4370471; e-mail postmaster@minedu.gob.pe; internet www.minedu.gob.pe.

Ministry of Energy and Mines: Avda Las Artes s/n, San Borja, Apdo 2600, Lima 41; tel. (1) 4750206; fax (1) 4750689; internet www.mem.gob.pe.

Ministry of Foreign Affairs: Palacio de Torre Tagle, Jirón Ucayali 363, Lima 1; tel. (1) 3112402; fax (1) 3112406; internet www.rree.gob.pe.

Ministry of Health: Avda Salaverry Cuadra 8, Jesús María, Lima 11; tel. (1) 4310408; fax (1) 4310093; e-mail etitos@minsa.gob.pe; internet www.minsa.gob.pe.

Ministry of Housing, Construction and Sanitation: Avda Paseo de la República 3361, San Isidro, Lima; tel. (1) 2117930; e-mail webmaster@vivienda.gob.pe; internet www.vivienda.gob.pe.

Ministry of the Interior: Plaza 30 de Agosto 150, San Isidro, Lima 27; tel. (1) 2242406; fax (1) 2242405; e-mail ofitel@mininter.gob.pe; internet www.mininter.gob.pe.

Ministry of International Trade and Tourism: Calle 1 Oeste, Urb. Corpac, San Isidro, Lima 27; tel. (1) 2243347; fax (1) 2243264; e-mail webmaster@mincetur.gob.pe; internet www.mincetur.gob.pe.

Ministry of Justice: Scipion Llona 350, Miraflores, Lima 18; tel. (1) 4222654; fax (1) 4223577; internet www.minjus.gob.pe.

Ministry of Labour and of Social Promotion: Avda Salaverry cuadra 8, Jesús María, Lima 11; tel. (1) 4337012; fax (1) 4338126; e-mail webmaster@mintra.gob.pe; internet www.mintra.gob.pe.

Ministry of the Presidency: Avda Paseo de la República 4297, Lima 1; tel. (1) 4465886; fax (1) 4470379; internet www.perugobierno.gob.pe.

Ministry of Production: Calle 1 Oeste 60, Urb. Corpac, San Isidro, Lima 27; tel. (1) 2243336; fax (1) 2243233; internet www.produce.gob.pe.

Ministry of Transport and Communications: Avda 28 de Julio 800, Lima 1; tel. (1) 4330010; fax (1) 4339378; internet www.mtc.gob.pe.

Regional Presidents
(April 2003)

Amazonas: MIGUEL REYES CONTRERAS (APRA).

Ancash: FREDDY GHILARDI ALVAREZ (APRA).

Apurímac: LUIS BELTRÁN PACHECO (APRA).

Arequipa: DANIEL ERNESTO VERA BALLÓN (APRA).

Ayacucho: WERNER QUEZADA MARTÍNEZ (APRA).

Cajamarca: LUIS FELIPE PITA GASTELUMENDI (APRA).

Callao: ROGELIO CANCHES (PP).

Cusco: CARLOS CUARESMA SÁNCHEZ (FIM).

Huancavelica: SALVADOR ESPINOZA HUAROC (Ind.).

Huánuco: LUZMILA TEMPLO CONDESO (Ind.).

Ica: MANUEL TELLO CÉSPEDES (APRA).

Junín: MANUEL DUARTE VELARDE (Ind.).

La Libertad: HOMERO BURGOS LIVEROS (APRA).

Lambayeque: YEHUDE SIMON MUNARO (UPP).

Lima: MIGUEL ANGEL MUFARECH (APRA).

Loreto: ROBINSON RIVADENEYRA (Ind.).

Madre de Díos: RAFAEL EDWIN RÍOS LÓPEZ (Ind.).

Moquegua: MARÍA CONSTANTINIDES (SP).

Pasco: VÍCTOR RAÚL ESPINOZA SOTO (Ind.).

Piura: CÉSAR TRELLES LARA (APRA).

Puno: DANIEL ANÍBAL JIMÉNEZ SARDÓN (Ind.).

San Martín: MAX HENRY RAMÍREZ GARCÍA (APRA).

Tacna: JULIO ANTONIO ALVA CENTURIÓN (APRA).

Tumbes: IRIS MEDINA FEIJOÓ (APRA).

Ucayali: EDWIN VÁSQUEZ LÓPEZ (Ind.).

President and Legislature

PRESIDENT

Elections, 8 April and 3 June 2001

Candidate	First round % of votes	Second round % of votes
Alejandro Toledo (PP)	36.51	53.08
Alan García (APRA)	25.78	46.92
Lourdes Flores (UN)	24.30	—
Fernando Olivera Vega (FIM)	9.85	—
Carlos Boloña (Solución Popular)	1.69	—
Ciro A. Gálvez (Renacimiento Andino)	0.81	—
Marco A. Arrunategui (Proyecto País)	0.75	—
Ricardo Noriega (Todos por la Victoria)	0.31	—
Total	100.00	100.00

CONGRESO

President: CARLOS FERRERO COSTA.

General Election, 8 April 2001

Parties	Seats
Perú Posible (PP)	45
Alianza Popular Revolucionaria Americana (APRA)	27
Unidad Nacional (UN)	17
Frente Independiente Moralizador (FIM)	12
Unión por el Perú	6
Somos Perú	4
Acción Popular (AP)	3
Cambio 90-Nueva Mayoría (C90-NM)	3
Renacimiento Andino	1
Solución Popular	1
Todos por la Victoria	1
Total	**120**

Political Organizations

Acción Popular (AP): Paseo Colón 218, Lima 1; tel. (1) 3321965; fax (1) 3321965; e-mail ap_sgn@telefonica.net.pe; internet accionpopular.tripod.com.pe; f. 1956; 1.2m. mems; pro-USA; liberal; Leader FERNANDO BELAÚNDE TERRY; Sec.-Gen. LUIS ENRIQUE GÁLVEZ DE LA PUENTE.

Alianza Popular Revolucionaria Americana (APRA): Avda Alfonso Ugarte 1012, Lima 5; tel. (1) 4281736; f. in Mexico 1924; in Peru 1930 as Partido Aprista Peruano (PAP); legalized 1945; democratic left-wing party; Leader ALAN GABRIEL GARCÍA PÉREZ; 700,000 mems.

Cambio 90 (C90): Jr Santa Isabel 590, Urb. Colmenares, Pueblo Libre, Lima; tel. (1) 9441739; group of independents formed to contest the 1990 elections, entered into coalition with Nueva Mayoría(see below) in 1992 to contest elections to the CCD, local elections in 1993, the presidential and congressional elections in 1995 and 2000 and the 2001 congressional elections; Leader PABLO CORREA.

Coordinación Democrática (CODE): Lima; f. 1992 by dissident APRA members; Leader JOSÉ BARBA CABALLERO.

Frente Independiente Moralizador (FIM): Pancho Fierro 133, San Isidro, Lima; tel. (1) 4220583; e-mail fim@fr.fm; internet www .fim.fr.fm; f. 1990; right-wing; Leader FERNANDO OLIVERA VEGA.

Frente Nacional de Trabajadores y Campesinos (FNTC/FRENATRACA): Lima; tel. (1) 4272868; f. 1968; left-wing party; Pres. Dr RÓGER CÁCERES VELÁSQUEZ; Sec.-Gen. Dr EDMUNDO HUANQUI MEDINA.

Frente Popular Agrícola del Perú (Frepap): Avda Morro Solar 1234; Santiago de Surco, Lima; tel. (1) 2753847; f. 1989; Leader EZEQUIEL ATAUCUSI GAMONAL.

Nueva Mayoría: Lima; f. 1992; group of independents, including former cabinet ministers, formed coalition with Cambio 90 in 1992 in order to contest elections to the CCD, and local elections in 1993; Leader JAIME YOSHIYAMA TANAKA.

Partido Comunista Peruano (PCP): Jirón Lampa 774, Lima 1; f. 1928; Pres. JORGE DEL PRADO.

Partido Demócrata Cristiano (PDC): Avda España 321, Lima 1; tel. (1) 4238042; f. 1956; 95,000 mems; Chair. CARLOS BLANCAS BUSTAMANTE.

Partido Popular Cristiano (PPC): Avda Alfonso Ugarte 1484, Lima; tel. (1) 4238723; fax (1) 4238721; e-mail estudio@flores-araoz .com; f. 1967; splinter group of Partido Demócrata Cristiano; 250,000 mems; Pres. Dr ANTERO FLORES-ARAOZ; Vice-Pres RAÚL CASTRO STAGNARO, EMMA VARGAS DE BENAVIDES.

Perú Ahora: Lima; f. 1998; relaunched in 2003 by fmr mems of Perú Posible; Leaders JORGE CHÁVEZ SIBINA, LUIS GUERRERO, RONNIE JURADO, MANUEL OLAECHEA, EDGAR VILLANUEVA.

Perú Posible (PP): Avda Faustino Sánchez Carrión, Lima; tel. (1) 4620303; f. 1994 to support Toledo's candidacy for the 1995 presidential election in alliance with CODE, contested the 2000 and 2001 presidential and congressional elections unaligned; Leader ALEJANDRO TOLEDO; Sec.-Gen. LUIS SOLARI.

Proyecto País: Avda General Garzón 820, Lima; tel. (1) 4233996; internet www.proyectopais.org.pe; f. 1998; Leader MARCO A. ARRUNATEGUI.

Renacimiento Andino: Jr Bambas 451, Lima; tel. (1) 4286516; f. 2001; Leader CIRO ALFREDO GÁLVEZ HERRERA.

Renovación: c/o Edif. Complejo 510, Avda Abancay 251, Lima; tel. (1) 4264260; fax (1) 4263023; f. 1992; Leader RAFAEL REY REY.

Solidaridad Nacional (SN): Armando Blondet 106, San Isidro, Lima; tel. (1) 2218948; e-mail psnpt@hotmail.com; internet www .psn.org.pe; f. 1999; centre-left; Leader LUIS CASTAÑEDA LOSSIO.

Solución Popular: Avda Guzmán Blanco 240, Of. 1001, Lima; tel. (1) 4263017; internet www.solucionpopular.com; Leader CARLOS BOLOÑA.

Somos Perú (SP): Avda Arequipa 3990, Miraflores, Lima; tel. (1) 4219363; e-mail andrade@somosperu.org.pe; internet www .somosperu.org.pe; f. 1998; Leader ALBERTO ANDRADE.

Todos por la Victoria: Avda Grau 122, La Victoria, Lima; tel. (1) 4242446; f. 2001; Leader RICARDO MANUEL NORIEGA SALAVERRY.

Unión de Izquierda Revolucionaria (UNIR) (Union of the Revolutionary Left): Jirón Puno 258, Apdo 1165, Lima 1; tel. (1) 4274072; f. 1980; Chair. Senator ROLANDO BREÑA PANTOJA; Gen. Sec. JORGE HURTADO POZO.

Unidad Nacional (UN): Calle Ricardo Palma 1111, Miraflores, Lima; tel. (1) 2242773; f. 2000; centrist alliance; Leader LOURDES FLORES.

Unión por el Perú (UPP): Pablo de Olavide 270, San Isidro, Lima; tel. (1) 4403227; independent movement; f. 1994 to contest presidential and legislative elections; Leader MÁXIMO SAN ROMÁN CÁCERES.

Vamos Vecino: Lima; f. 1998; Leader ABSALON VÁSQUEZ.

Other parties include Frente Obrero Campesino Estudiantil y Popular (FOCEP), Partido Unificado Mariateguista (PUM), Partido Comunista del Perú—Patria Roja and Movimiento Amplio País Unido.

Guerrilla groups

Sendero Luminoso (Shining Path): f. 1970; began armed struggle 1980; splinter group of PCP; based in Ayacucho; advocates the policies of the late Mao Zedong and his radical followers, including the 'Gang of Four' in the People's Republic of China; founder Dr ABIMAEL GUZMÁN REYNOSO (alias Commdr Gonzalo—arrested September 1992); Current leaders MARGIE CLAVO PERALTA (arrested March 1995), PEDRO DOMINGO QUINTEROS AYLLÓN (alias Comrade Luis —arrested April 1998).

Sendero Rojo (Red Path): dissident faction of Sendero Luminoso opposed to leadership of Abimael Guzmán; Leader FILOMENO CERRÓN CARDOSO (alias Comrade Artemio).

Movimiento Revolucionario Tupac Amarú (MRTA): f. 1984; began negotiations with the Government to end its armed struggle in September 1990; Leader VÍCTOR POLAY CAMPOS (alias Comandante Rolando—arrested Feb. 1989; escaped in 1990; rearrested 1992).

Diplomatic Representation

EMBASSIES IN PERU

Argentina: Avda 28 de Julio 828, Lima; tel. (1) 4339966; fax (1) 4330769; Ambassador JORGE ALBERTO VÁZQUEZ.

Austria: Avda Central 643, 5°, San Isidro, Lima 27; tel. (1) 4420503; fax (1) 4428851; e-mail austria@terra.com.pe; Ambassador GERHARD DOUJAK.

Belgium: Avda Angamos 380, Lima 18; tel. (1) 2417566; fax (1) 4474478; e-mail lima@diplobel.org; Ambassador WILLY TILEMANS.

Bolivia: Los Castaños 235, San Isidro, Lima 27; tel. (1) 4423836; fax (1) 4402298; e-mail jemis@emboli.attla.com.pe; Ambassador ELOY AVILA ALBERDI.

Brazil: Avda José Pardo 850, Miraflores, Lima; tel. (1) 4216763; fax (1) 4452421; e-mail embajada@embajadabrasil.org.pe; internet www .embajadabrasil.org.pe; Ambassador ANDRÉ MATTOSO MAIA AMADO.

Bulgaria: Jirón Paul Harris 289, San Isidro, Lima; tel. and fax (1) 4221145; Ambassador DIMITAR STANOEV.

Canada: Calle Libertad 130, Miraflores, Lima 18; tel. (1) 4444015; fax (1) 4444347; e-mail lima-gr@dfait-maeci.gc.ca; Ambassador HUGUES ROUSSEAU.

Chile: Avda Javier Prado Oeste 790, San Isidro, Lima; tel. (1) 2212080; fax (1) 2211258; e-mail emchile@terra.com.pe; internet www.civila.com/chile/chileper; Ambassador JUAN PABLO LIRA BIANCHI.

China, People's Republic: Jirón José Granda 150, San Isidro, Lima 27; tel. (1) 4429458; fax (1) 4429467; e-mail chiemba@terra .com.pe; Ambassador GUOYAN MAI.

Colombia: Avda J. Basadre 1580, San Isidro, Lima 27; tel. (1) 4410954; fax (1) 4419806; e-mail emperu@terra.com.pe; Ambassador MARÍA CRISTINA ZULETA DE PATIÑO.

Costa Rica: Avda Emilio Cavanecia 175, Miraflores, Lima; tel. (1) 4409982; fax (1) 4406392; e-mail corobici@amauta.rcp.net.pe; Ambassador JULIO SUÑOL LEAL.

Cuba: Coronel Portillo 110, San Isidro, Lima; tel. (1) 2642053; fax (1) 2644525; e-mail embacuba@chavin.rcp.net.pe; Ambassador BENIGNO PÉREZ FERNÁNDEZ.

Czech Republic: Baltazar La Torre 398, San Isidro, Lima 27; tel. (1) 2643381; fax (1) 2641708; e-mail lima@embassy.mzv.cz; internet www.mfa.cz/lima; Ambassador JAN KOPECKÝ.

Dominican Republic: Calle Tudela y Varela 360, San Isidro, Lima; tel. (1) 4219765; fax (1) 2220639; e-mail embdomperu@terra.com.pe; Ambassador IVÁN TOMÁS BAÉZ BRUGAL.

Ecuador: Las Palmeras 356 y Javier Prado Oeste, San Isidro, Lima; tel. (1) 4409991; fax (1) 4411144; e-mail embjecua@amauta.rcp.net .pe; Ambassador HORACIO SEVILLA.

Egypt: Avda Jorge Basadre 1470, San Isidro, Lima 27; tel. (1) 4402642; fax (1) 4402547; e-mail emb-egypt@amauta.rcp.net.pe; Ambassador SHADIA SHOUKRI.

El Salvador: Calle Rubens 205, San Borja Norte, Lima; tel. (1) 4758673; fax (1) 4759050; e-mail embasalv@nexoperu.com.pe; internet www.embajadaelsalvador.org.pe; Ambassador RAÚL SOTO RAMIREZ.

Finland: Avda Víctor Andrés Belaúnde 147, Edif. Real Tres, 502°, San Isidro, Lima; tel. (1) 2224466; fax (1) 2224463; e-mail embajada@finlandiaperu.org.pe; internet www.finlandiaperu.org .pe; Ambassador KIMMO PULKKINEN.

France: Avda Arequipa 3415, Lima; tel. (1) 2158400; fax (1) 2158410; e-mail france.embajada@ambafrance-pe.org; internet www.ambafrance-pe.org; Ambassador JEAN-PAUL ANGELIER.

Germany: Avda Arequipa 4210, Miraflores, Lima 18; tel. (1) 2125016; fax (1) 4226475; e-mail kanzlei@embajada-alemana.org .pe; Ambassador HERBERT BEYER.

Greece: Avda Principal 190, 6°, Urb. Santa Catalina, Lima 13; tel. (1) 4761548; fax (1) 4761329; e-mail emgrecia@terra.com.pe; Ambassador JEAN NEONAKIS.

Guatemala: Inca Ripac 309, Lima 27; tel. (1) 4602078; fax (1) 4635885; e-mail embperu@minex.gob.gt; Chargé d'affaires a.i. GUSTAVO FERNANDO ABADÍA CASTELLANOS.

Haiti: Avda Orrantia 910, San Isidro, Lima; tel. (1) 4223362; Ambassador ANTOINE BERNARD.

Holy See: Avda Salaverry 6a cuadra, Apdo 397, Lima 100 (Apostolic Nunciature); tel. (1) 4319436; fax (1) 4315704; e-mail nuntius@ amauta.rop.net.pe; Apostolic Nuncio Most Rev. RINO PASSIGATO (Titular Archbishop of Nova Caesaris).

Honduras: Avda Larco 930, Miraflores, Lima 18; tel. (1) 4442345; fax (1) 4466577; e-mail embhonpe@qnet.com.pe; Ambassador Dr EDGAR PAZ BÁRNICA.

Hungary: Avda Jorge Basadre 1580, San Isidro, Lima; tel. (1) 4410954; fax (1) 4419806; Ambassador JÁNOS TÓTH.

India: Avda Salaverry 3006, San Isidro, Lima 27; tel. (1) 4602289; fax (1) 4610374; e-mail hoc@indembassy.org.pe; internet www .indembassy.org.pe; Ambassador BUTSHIKAN SINGH.

Israel: Edif. El Pacifico, 6°, Plaza Washington, Natalio Sánchez 125, Santa Beatriz, Lima; tel. (1) 4334431; fax (1) 4338925; e-mail emisrael@electrodata.com.pe; Ambassador YUVAL METSER.

Italy: Avda Gregorio Escobedo 298, Apdo 0490, Lima 11; tel. (1) 4632727; fax (1) 4635317; e-mail italemb@chavin.rcp.net.pe; internet www.italembperu.org.pe; Ambassador SERGIO BUSETTO.

Japan: Avda San Felipe 312, Apdo 3708, Jesús María, Lima; tel. (1) 4630000; fax (1) 4630302; Ambassador YUBEN NARITA.

Korea, Democratic People's Republic: Los Nogales 227, San Isidro, Lima; tel. (1) 4411120; fax (1) 4409877; Ambassador RI IN CHUN.

Korea, Republic: Avda Principal 190, 7°, Lima 13; tel. (1) 4760815; fax (1) 4760950; e-mail korembj-pu@tmofat.go.kr; Ambassador JIN-HO CHUNG.

Malaysia: Calle 41 894, 3°, Urb. Corpac, San Isidro, Lima 27; tel. (1) 2256699; fax (1) 2227573; e-mail mwlima@terra.com.pe; Ambassador YUSOF AHMAD.

Mexico: Avda Jorge Basadre 710, San Isidro, Lima; tel. (1) 2211173; fax (1) 4404740; e-mail info@mexico.org.pe; Ambassador RICARDO VILLANUEVA HALLAL.

Morocco: Manuel Ugarte y Moscoso 790, Lima 27; tel. (1) 2643323; fax (1) 2640006; e-mail sifamlim@chavin.rcp.net.pe; Ambassador MAHMOUD RMIKI.

Netherlands: Avda Principal 190, 4°, Urb. Santa Catalina, La Victoria, Lima; tel. (1) 4761069; fax (1) 4756536; e-mail nlgovlim@

terra.com.pe; internet www.terra.com.pe/nl; Ambassador S. E. RAMONDT.

Nicaragua: Pasaje Los Piños 156, Miraflores, Lima 18; tel. (1) 4461555; fax (1) 4459274; Chargé d'affaires a.i. MARITZA ROSALES GRANERA.

Panama: Coronel Portillo 521, San Isidro, Lima; tel. (1) 4404874; fax (1) 4406592; e-mail linclark@mauta.rcp.net.pe; Ambassador DIANA VARELA DE ROBISON.

Paraguay: Alcanfores 1286, Miraflores, Lima; tel. (1) 4474762; fax (1) 4441391; Ambassador Dra JULIA VELILLA LACONICH.

Poland: Avda Salaverry 1978, Jesús María, Lima; tel. (1) 4713920; fax (1) 4713925; e-mail wojciech@amauta.rcp.net.pe; Ambassador WOJCIECH TOMASZEWSKI.

Portugal: Avda Central 643, 4°, Lima 27; tel. (1) 4409905; fax (1) 4429655; Ambassador Dr ALEXANDRE DE ALMEIDA FERNANDES.

Romania: Avda Jorge Basadre 690, San Isidro, Lima; tel. (1) 4224587; fax (1) 4210609; e-mail ambrom@terra.com.pe; Ambassador GHEORGHE LICIU.

Russia: Avda Salaverry 3424, San Isidro, Lima 27; tel. (1) 2640038; fax (1) 2640130; e-mail embrusa@amauta.rcp.net.pe; Ambassador VIKTOR A. TKACHENKO.

Serbia and Montenegro: Carlos Porras Osores 360, San Isidro, Lima 27; Apdo 0392, Lima 18; tel. (1) 4212423; fax (1) 4212427; Chargé d'affaires a.i. MILIVOJ SUCEVIĆ.

Slovakia: Avda Angamos 1626, San Isidro, Lima 27; tel. (1) 4418272; fax (1) 4222249; e-mail embajador@ddm.com.pe; Chargé d'affaires a.i. Dr PAVOL SÍPKA.

South Africa: Edif. Real Tres, Of. 801, Vía Principal 155, San Isidro, Lima 27; tel. (1) 4409996; fax 4223881; e-mail saemb@ amauta.rcp.net.pe; Chargé d'affaires a.i. ABBEY MATOTO PINDELO.

Spain: Jorge Basadre 498, San Isidro, Lima 27; tel. (1) 2125155; fax (1) 4410084; e-mail embesppe@correo.mae.es; Ambassador GONZALO DE BENITO.

Switzerland: Avda Salaverry 3240, San Isidro, Lima 27; tel. (1) 2640305; fax (1) 2641319; e-mail vertretung@lim.rep.admin.ch; internet www.eda.admin.ch/lima_emb/s/home.html; Ambassador ERIC MARTIN.

United Kingdom: Edif. El Pacífico, 12°, Plaza Washington, Natalio Sánchez 125, Lima; tel. (1) 4334738; fax (1) 4334735; e-mail britemb@terra.com.pe; Ambassador ROGER DUDLEY HART.

USA: Avda La Encalada 17, Surco, Lima 33; tel. (1) 4343000; fax (1) 4343037; internet ekeko.rcp.net.pe/usa; internet usembassy.state .gov/lima; Ambassador JOHN R. DAWSON.

Uruguay: Calle José D. Anchorena 84, San Isidro, Lima; tel. (1) 2640099; fax (1) 2640112; e-mail embajada_uruguay@terra.com.pe; Ambassador TABARE BOCALANDRO.

Venezuela: Avda Arequipa 298, Lima; tel. (1) 4334511; fax (1) 4331191; e-mail embavenez@amauta.rcp.net.pe; Ambassador GONZALO JESÚS GÓMEZ JAÉN.

Judicial System

The Supreme Court consists of a President and 17 members. There are also Higher Courts and Courts of First Instance in provincial capitals. A comprehensive restructuring of the judiciary was implemented during the late 1990s.

SUPREME COURT

Corte Suprema

Palacio de Justicia, 2°, Avda Paseo de la República, Lima 1; tel. (1) 4284457; fax (1) 4269437.

President: OSCAR ALFARO ALVAREZ.

Attorney-General: NELLY CALDERÓN NAVARRO.

Religion

CHRISTIANITY

The Roman Catholic Church

For ecclesiastical purposes, Peru comprises seven archdioceses, 18 dioceses, 11 territorial prelatures and eight Apostolic Vicariates. At 31 December 2000 89% of the country's population (an estimated 26.8m.) were adherents of the Roman Catholic Church.

Bishops' Conference

Conferencia Episcopal Peruana, Jr. Estados Unidos 838, Apdo 310, Lima 100; tel. (1) 4631010; fax (1) 4636125; e-mail ezamora@iglesiacatolica.org.pe; internet www.rcp.net.pe/IAL/cep. f. 1981; statutes approved 1987, revised 1992 and 2000; Pres. Mgr LUIS BAMBARÉN GASTELUMENDI (Bishop of Chimbote).

Archbishop of Arequipa: LUIS SÁNCHEZ-MORENO LIRA, Arzobispado, Moral San Francisco 118, Apdo 149, Arequipa; tel. (54) 234094; fax (54) 242721; e-mail arzaqp@planet.com.pe.

Archbishop of Ayacucho or Huamanga: LUIS ABILIO SEBASTIANI AGUIRRE, Arzobispado, Jirón 28 de Julio 148, Apdo 30, Ayacucho; tel. and fax (64) 812367; e-mail arzaya@mail.udep.edu.pe.

Archbishop of Cuzco: ALCIDES MENDOZA CASTRO, Arzobispado, Herrajes, Apdo 148, Cuzco; tel. (84) 225211; fax (84) 222781; e-mail arzobisp@telser.com.pe.

Archbishop of Huancayo: JOSÉ PAULINO RÍOS REYNOSO, Arzobispado, Jirón Puno 430, Apdo 245, Huancayo; tel. (64) 234952; fax (64) 239189; e-mail arzohyo@lima.business.com.pe.

Archbishop of Lima: Cardinal JUAN LUIS CIPRIANI THORNE, Arzobispado, Plaza Mayor, Apdo 1512, Lima 100; tel. (1) 4275980; fax (1) 4271967; e-mail arzolim@terra.com.pe; internet www.arzobispadodelima.org.

Archbishop of Piura: OSCAR ROLANDO CANTUARIAS PASTOR, Arzobispado, Libertad 1105, Apdo 197, Piura; tel. and fax (74) 327561; e-mail ocordova@upiura.edu.pe.

Archbishop of Trujillo: MIGUEL CABREJOS VIDARTE, Arzobispado, Jirón Mariscal de Orbegoso 451, Apdo 42, Trujillo; tel. (44) 231474; fax (44) 231473; e-mail arzobispado-tr@terra.com.pe.

The Anglican Communion

The Iglesia Anglicana del Cono Sur de América (Anglican Church of the Southern Cone of America), formally inaugurated in April 1983, comprises seven dioceses, including Peru. The Presiding Bishop of the Church is the Bishop of Northern Argentina.

Bishop of Peru: Rt. Rev. HAROLD WILLIAM GODFREY, Apdo 18-1032, Miraflores, Lima 18; tel. and fax (1) 4229160; e-mail wgodfrey@amauta.rcp.net.pe.

The Methodist Church

There are an estimated 4,200 adherents of the Iglesia Metodista del Perú.

President: Rev. JORGE FIGUEROA, Baylones 186, Lima 5; Apdo 1386, Lima 100; tel. (1) 4245970; fax (1) 4318995; e-mail iglesiamp@computextos.com.pe.

Other Protestant Churches

Among the most popular are the Asamblea de Dios, the Iglesia Evangélica del Perú, the Iglesia del Nazareno, the Alianza Cristiana y Misionera, and the Iglesia de Dios del Perú.

BAHÁ'Í FAITH

National Spiritual Assembly of the Bahá'ís of Peru: Horacio Urteaga 827, Jesús María, Apdo 11-0209, Lima 11; tel. (1) 4316077; fax (1) 4333005; e-mail bahai@terra.com.pe; mems resident in 220 localities; Nat. Sec. MARÍA LORETO JARA DE ROEDER.

The Press

DAILIES

Lima

El Bocón: Jirón Jorge Salazar Araoz 171, Urb. Santa Catalina, Apdo 152, Lima 1; tel. (1) 4756355; fax (1) 4758780; f. 1994; Editorial Dir JORGE ESTÉVES ALFARO; circ. 90,000.

El Comercio: Empresa Editora 'El Comercio', SA, Jirón Antonio Miró Quesada 300, Lima; tel. (1) 4264676; fax (1) 4260810; e-mail sugerencias@comercio.com.pe; internet www.elcomercioperu.com.pe/Online/; f. 1839; morning; Editorial Dir AURELIO MIRÓ QUESADA; Gen. Man. CÉSAR PARDO-FIGUEROA; circ. 150,000 weekdays, 220,000 Sundays.

Expreso: Jirón Libertad 117, Miraflores, Lima; tel. (1) 4447088; fax (1) 4447117; e-mail direccion@expreso.com.pe; f. 1961; morning; conservative; Editor-in-Chief MANUEL D'ORNELLAS; circ. 100,000.

Extra: Jirón Libertad 117, Miraflores, Lima; tel. (1) 4447088; fax (1) 4447117; e-mail extra@expreso.com.pe; f. 1964; evening edition of *Expreso*; Dir CARLOS SÁNCHEZ; circ. 80,000.

Gestión: Avda Salaverry 156, Miraflores, Lima 18; tel. (1) 4776919; fax (1) 4476569; e-mail gestion@gestion.com.pe; internet www.gestion.com.pe; f. 1990; News Editor JULIO LIRA; Gen. Man. OSCAR ROMERO CARO; circ. 131,200.

Ojo: Jirón Jorge Salazar Araoz 171, Urb. Santa Catalina, Apdo 152, Lima; tel. (1) 4709696; fax (1) 4761605; f. 1968; morning; Editorial Dir AGUSTÍN FIGUEROA BENZA; circ. 100,000.

El Peruano (Diario Oficial): Avda Alfonso Ugarte, cuadra 7, Lima 7; tel. (1) 4283460; fax (1) 4249507; f. 1825; morning; official State Gazette; Editorial Dir ENRIQUE SÁNCHEZ HERNANI; circ. 27,000.

La República: Jirón Camaná 320, Lima 1; tel. (1) 4276455; fax (1) 4265678; e-mail otxoa@larepublica.com.pe; internet www.larepublica.com.pe; f. 1982; left-wing; Dir GUSTAVO MOHME SEMINARIO; circ. 50,000.

Arequipa

Arequipa al Día: Avda Jorge Chávez 201, IV, Centenario, Arequipa; tel. (54) 215515; fax (54) 217810; f. 1991; Editorial Dir CARLOS MENESES CORNEJO.

Correo de Arequipa: Calle Bolívar 204, Arequipa; tel. (54) 235150; e-mail correoperu@mail.interplace.com.pe; Editorial Dir MARTHA VALENCIA; circ. 70,000.

El Pueblo: Sucre 213, Apdo 35, Arequipa; tel. (54) 211500; fax (54) 213361; f. 1905; morning; independent; Editorial Dir EDUARDO LAIME VALDIVIA; circ. 70,000.

Chiclayo

La Industria: Tacna 610, Chiclayo; tel. (74) 238592; fax (74) 235493; f. 1952; Dir JOSÉ RAMIREZ RUIZ; circ. 20,000.

Cuzco

El Diario del Cuzco: Centro Comercial Ollanta, Avda El Sol 346, Cuzco; tel. (84) 240792; e-mail correo@diariodelcusco.com; internet www.diariodelcusco.com; morning; independent; Dir-Gen. JOSÉ FERNANDEZ NUÑEZ.

Huacho

El Imparcial: Avda Grau 203, Huacho; tel. (34) 2392187; fax (34) 2321352; e-mail el.imparcial@USA.net; f. 1891; evening; Dir ADAN MANRIQUE ROMERO; circ. 5,000.

Huancayo

Correo de Huancayo: Jirón Cuzco 337, Huancayo; tel. (64) 235792; fax (64) 233811; evening; Editorial Dir RODOLFO OROSCO.

La Opinión Popular: Huancayo; tel. (64) 231149; f. 1922; Dir MIGUEL BERNABÉ SUÁREZ OSORIO.

Ica

La Opinión: Avda Los Maestros 801, Apdo 186, Ica; tel. (34) 235571; f. 1922; evening; independent; Dir GONZALO TUEROS RAMÍREZ.

La Voz de Ica: Castrovirreyna 193, Ica; tel. and fax (34) 232112; e-mail lavozdeica@terra.com.pe; f. 1918; Dir ATILIO NIERI BOGGIANO; Man. MARIELLA NIERI DE MACEDO; circ. 4,500.

Pacasmayo

Ultimas Noticias: 2 de Mayo 33, Pacasmayo; tel. and fax (44) 646969; e-mail unabs@terramail.com.pe; internet www.pacasmayo.net/ultimasnoticias; f. 1973; evening; independent; Dir LUIS ALBERTO BALLENA SÁNCHEZ; circ. 3,000.

Piura

Correo: Zona Industrial Mzna 246, Lote 6, Piura; tel. (74) 321681; fax (74) 324881; Editorial Dir ROLANDO RODRICH ARANGO; circ. 12,000.

El Tiempo: Ayacucho 751, Piura; tel. (74) 325141; fax (74) 327478; e-mail direccion@eltiempo.com.pe; internet www.eltiempo.com.pe; f. 1916; morning; independent; Dir LUZ MARÍA HELGUERO; circ. 18,000.

Tacna

Correo: Jirón Hipólito Unanue 636, Tacna; tel. (54) 711671; fax (54) 713955; Editorial Dir RUBÉN COLLAZOS ROMERO; circ. 8,000.

Trujillo

La Industria: Gamarra 443, Trujillo; tel. (44) 234720; fax (44) 427761; e-mail industri@united.net.pe; internet www.unitru.edu.pe/eelitsa; f. 1895; morning; independent; Gen. Man. ISABEL CERRO DE BURGA; circ. 8,000.

PERIODICALS AND REVIEWS

Lima

Alerta Agrario: Avda Salaverry 818, Lima 11; tel. (1) 4336610; fax (1) 4331744; f. 1987 by Centro Peruano de Estudios Sociales; monthly review of rural problems; Dir BERTHA CONSIGLIERI; circ. 100,000.

The Andean Report: Pasaje Los Pinos 156, Of. B6, Miraflores, Apdo 531, Lima; tel. (1) 4472552; fax (1) 4467888; e-mail perutimes@amauta.rcp.net.pe; internet www.perutimes.com; f. 1975; weekly newsletter; economics, trade and commerce; English; Publisher ELEANOR GRIFFIS DE ZÚÑIGA; circ. 1,000.

Caretas: Jirón Huallaya 122, Portal de Botoneros, Plaza de Armas, Lima 1; Apdo 737, Lima 100; tel. (1) 4289490; fax (1) 4262524; e-mail info@caretas.com.pe; internet www.caretas.com.pe; weekly; current affairs; Editor ENRIQUE ZILERI GIBSON; circ. 90,000.

Debate: Apdo 671, Lima 100; tel. (1) 4467070; fax (1) 4455946; f. 1980; every 2 months; Editor AUGUSTO ALVAREZ-RODRICH.

Debate Agrario: Avda Salaverry 818, Lima 11; tel. (1) 4336610; fax (1) 4331744; e-mail cepes@cepes.org.pe; f. 1987 by Centro Peruano de Estudios Sociales; every 4 months; rural issues; Dir FERNANDO EGUREN L.

Gente: Eduardo de Habich 170, Miraflores, Lima 18; tel. (1) 4465046; fax (1) 4461173; e-mail correo@genteperu.com; internet www.genteperu.com; f. 1958; weekly; circ. 25,000.

Hora del Hombre: Lima; tel. (1) 4220208; f. 1943; monthly; cultural and political journal; illustrated; Dir JORGE FALCÓN.

Industria Peruana: Los Laureles 365, San Isidro, Apdo 632, Lima 27; f. 1896; monthly publication of the Sociedad de Industrias; Editor ROLANDO CELI BURNEO.

Lima Times: Pasaje Los Pinos 156, Of. B 6, Miraflores, Apdo 531, Lima 100; tel. (1) 4469120; fax (1) 4467888; e-mail perutimes@amauta.rcp.net.pe; internet www.perutimes.com; f. 1975; monthly; travel, cultural events, general news on Peru; English; Editor ELEANOR GRIFFIS DE ZÚÑIGA; circ. 10,000.

Mercado Internacional: Lima; tel. (1) 4445395; business.

Monos y Monadas: Lima; tel. (1) 4773483; f. 1981; fortnightly; satirical; Editor NICOLÁS YEROVI; circ. 17,000.

Oiga: Pedro Venturo 353, Urb. Aurora, Miraflores, Lima; tel. (1) 4475851; weekly; right-wing; Dir FRANCISCO IGARTUA; circ. 60,000.

Onda: Jorge Vanderghen 299, Miraflores, Lima; tel. (1) 4227008; f. 1959; monthly cultural review; Dir JOSÉ ALEJANDRO VALENCIA-ARENAS; circ. 5,000.

Orbita: Parque Rochdale 129, Lima; tel. (1) 4610676; weekly; f. 1970; Dir LUZ CHÁVEZ MENDOZA; circ. 10,000.

Perú Económico: Apdo 671, Lima 100; tel. (1) 4467070; fax (1) 4455946; f. 1978; monthly; Editor AUGUSTO ALVAREZ-RODRICH.

Quehacer: León de la Fuente 110, Lima 17; tel. (1) 2641316; fax (1) 2640128; e-mail postmaster@desco.org.pe; f. 1979; 6 a year; supported by Desco research and development agency; circ. 5,000.

Runa: Lima; f. 1977; monthly; review of the Instituto Nacional de Cultura; Dir MARIO RAZZETO; circ. 10,000.

Semana Económica: Apdo 671, Lima 100; tel. (1) 4455237; fax (1) 4455946; f. 1985; weekly; Editor AUGUSTO ALVAREZ-RODRICH.

Unidad: Jirón Lampa 271, Of. 703, Lima; tel. (1) 4270355; weekly; Communist; Dir GUSTAVO ESTEVES OSTOLAZA; circ. 20,000.

Vecino: Avda Petit Thouars 1944, Of. 15, Lima 14; tel. (1) 4706787; f. 1981; fortnightly; supported by Yunta research and urban publishing institute; Dirs PATRICIA CÓRDOVA, MARIO ZOLEZZI; circ. 5,000.

NEWS AGENCIES

Government News Agency

Agencia de Noticias Andina: Jirón de la Unión 264, Lima; tel. (1) 4273602.

Foreign Bureaux

Agence France-Presse (AFP): F. Masías 544, San Isidro, Lima; tel. (1) 4214012; fax (1) 4424390; e-mail yllorca@amautarcp.net.pe; Bureau Chief YVES-CLAUDE LLORCA.

Agencia EFE (Spain): Manuel González Olaechea 207, San Isidro, Lima; tel. (1) 4412094; fax (1) 4412422; Bureau Chief FRANCISCO RUBIO FIGUEROA.

Agenzia Nazionale Stampa Associata (ANSA) (Italy): Avda Gen. Córdoba 2594, Lince, Lima 14; tel. (1) 4225130; fax (1) 4229087; Correspondent ALBERTO KU-KING MATURANA.

Deutsche Presse-agentur (dpa) (Germany): Schell 343, Of. 707, Miraflores, Apdo 1362, Lima 18; tel. (1) 4441437; fax (1) 4443775; Bureau Chief GONZALO RUIZ TOVAR.

Inter Press Service (IPS) (Italy): Daniel Olaechea y Olaechea 285, Lima 11; tel. and fax (1) 4631021; Correspondent ABRAHAM LAMA.

Prensa Latina (Cuba): Edif. Astoria, Of. 303, Avda Tacna 482, Apdo 5567, Lima; tel. (1) 4233908; Correspondent LUIS MANUEL ARCE ISAAC.

Reuters (United Kingdom): Avda Paseo de la República 3505, 4°, San Isidro, Lima 27; tel. (1) 2212111; fax (1) 4418992; Man. EDUARDO HILGERT.

Xinhua (New China) News Agency (People's Republic of China): Parque Javier Prado 181, San Isidro, Lima; tel. (1) 4403463; Bureau Chief WANG SHUBO.

PRESS ASSOCIATIONS

Asociación Nacional de Periodistas del Perú: Jirón Huancavélica 320, Apdo 2079, Lima 1; tel. (1) 4270687; fax (1) 4278493; e-mail anpofip@attmail.com; f. 1928; 7,400 mems; Pres. and Sec.-Gen. ROBERTO MEJÍA ALARCÓN.

Federación de Periodistas del Perú (FPP): Avda Abancay 173, Lima; tel. (1) 4284373; f. 1950; Pres. ALBERTO DELGADO ORÉ; Sec.-Gen. JORGE PAREDES CABADA.

Publishers

Asociación Editorial Bruño: Avda Arica 751, Breña, Lima 5; tel. (1) 4244134; fax (1) 4251248; f. 1950; educational; Man. FEDERICO DÍAZ PINEDO.

Biblioteca Nacional del Perú: Avda Abancay 4a cuadra, Apdo 2335, Lima 1; tel. (1) 4287690; fax (1) 4277331; e-mail jefatura@binape.gob.pe; internet www.binape.gob.pe; f. 1821; general non-fiction, directories; Dir SINESIO LÓPEZ JIMÉNEZ.

Colección Artes y Tesoros del Perú: Calle Centenario 156, Urb. Las Laderas de Melgarejo, La Molina, Lima 12; tel. (1) 3493128; fax (1) 3490579; e-mail acarulla@bcp.com.pe; f. 1971; Dir ALVARO CARULLA.

Editorial Colegio Militar Leoncio Prado: Avda Costanera 1541, La Perla, Callao; f. 1946; textbooks and official publications; Man. OSCAR MORALES QUINA.

Editorial D.E.S.A.: General Varela 1577, Breña, Lima; f. 1955; textbooks and official publications; Man. ENRIQUE MIRANDA.

Editorial Desarrollo, SA: Ica 242, 1°, Apdo 3824, Lima; tel. and fax (1) 4286628; f. 1965; business administration, accounting, auditing, industrial engineering, English textbooks, dictionaries, and technical reference; Dir LUIS SOSA NÚÑEZ.

Editorial Horizonte: Avda Nicolás de Piérola 995, Lima 1; tel. (1) 4279364; fax (1) 4274341; e-mail damonte@terra.com.pe; f. 1968; social sciences, literature, politics; Man. HUMBERTO DAMONTE.

Editorial Labrusa, SA: Los Frutales Avda 670-Ate, Lima; tel. (1) 4358443; fax (1) 4372925; f. 1988; literature, educational, cultural; Gen. Man. ADRIÁN REUILLA CALVO; Man. FEDERICO DÍAZ TINEO.

Ediciones Médicas Peruanas, SA: Lima; f. 1965; medical; Man. ALBERTO LOZANO REYES.

Editorial Milla Batres, SA: Lima; f. 1963; history, literature, art, archaeology, linguistics and encyclopaedias on Peru; Dir-Gen. CARLOS MILLA BATRES.

Editorial Navarrete SRL-Industria del Offset: Manuel Tellería 1842, Apdo 4173, Lima; tel. (1) 4319040; fax (1) 4230991; Man. LUIS NAVARRETE LECHUGA.

Editorial Salesiana: Avda Brasil 218, Apdo 0071, Lima 5; tel. (1) 4235225; f. 1918; religious and general textbooks; Man. Dir Dr FRANCESCO VACARELLO.

Editorial Universo, SA: Lima; f. 1967; literature, technical, educational; Pres. CLEMENTE AQUINO; Gen. Man. Ing. JOSÉ A. AQUINO BENAVIDES.

Fundación del Banco Continental para el Fomento de la Educación y la Cultura (EDUBANCO): Avda República de Panamá 3055, San Isidro, Apdo 4687, Lima 27; tel. (1) 2111000; fax (1) 2112479; f. 1973; Pres. PEDRO BRESCIA CAFFERATA; Man. FERNANDO PORTOCARRERO.

Industrial Gráfica, SA: Jirón Chavín 45, Breña, Lima 5; fax (1) 4324413; f. 1981; Pres. JAIME CAMPODONICO V.

INIDE: Van de Velde 160, Urb. San Borja, Lima; f. 1981; owned by National Research and Development Institute; educational books; Editor-in-Chief ANA AYALA.

Librerías ABC, SA: Avda Paseo de la República 3440, Local B-32, Lima 27; tel. (1) 4422900; fax (1) 4422901; f. 1956; history, Peruvian art and archaeology; Man. Dir. HERBERT H. MOLL.

Librería San Pablo: Jirón Callao 198, Lima 1; tel. (1) 4269493; fax (1) 4269496; e-mail paulinaslperu@hys.com.pe; f. 1981; religious and scholastic texts; Man. Sister MARÍA GRACIA CAPALBO.

Librería Studium, SA: Lima; tel. (1) 4326278; fax (1) 4325354; f. 1936; textbooks and general culture; Man. Dir EDUARDO RIZO PATRÓN RECAVARREN.

Pablo Villanueva Ediciones: Lima; f. 1938; literature, history, law etc. Man. AUGUSTO VILLANUEVA PACHECO.

Pontificia Universidad Católica: Fondo Editorial, Plaza Francia 1164, Lima; tel. 3307410; fax (1) 3307405; e-mail feditor@pucp.edu .pe; internet www.pucp.edu.pe; Dir DANTE ANTONIOLI DELUCCHI.

Sociedad Bíblica Peruana, AC: Avda Petit Thouars 991, Apdo 14-0295, Lima 100; tel. (1) 4335815; fax (1) 4336389; internet www .members.tripod.com/sbpac; f. 1821; Christian literature and bibles; Gen. Sec. PEDRO ARANA-QUIROZ.

Universidad Nacional Mayor de San Marcos: Oficina General de Editorial, Avda República de Chile 295, 5°, Of. 508, Lima; tel. (1) 4319689; f. 1850; textbooks, education; Man. Dir JORGE CAMPOS REY DE CASTRO.

Association

Cámara Peruana del Libro: Avda Cuba 427, Apdo 10253, Lima 11; tel. (1) 2650737; fax (1) 2650735; e-mail postmaster@cbclim.inv .pe; internet www.cbc.org.pe/camara/index1.htm; f. 1946; 120 mems; Pres. CARLOS A. BENVIDES AGUIJE; Exec. Dir LOYDA MORÁN BUSTAMANTE.

Broadcasting and Communications

TELECOMMUNICATIONS

Regulatory Authorities

Dirección de Administración de Frecuencias: Ministerio de Transportes y Comunicaciones, Avda 28 de Julio 800, Lima 1; tel. (1) 4331990; e-mail dgcdir@mtc.gob.pe; manages and allocates radio frequencies; Dir JOSÉ VILLA GAMBOA.

Dirección General de Telecomunicaciones: Ministerio de Transportes y Comunicaciones, Avda 28 de Julio 800, Lima 1; tel. (1) 4330752; fax (1) 4331450; e-mail dgtdir@mtc.gob.pe; Dir-Gen. MIGUEL OSAKI SUEMITSU.

Instituto Nacional de Investigación y Capacitación de Telecomunicaciones (INICTEL): Avda San Luis 17, esq. Bailetti, San Borja, Lima 41; tel. (1) 3360993; fax (1) 3369281; e-mail postmaster@inictel.gob.pe; Pres. MANUEL ADRIANZEN.

Organismo Supervisor de Inversión Privada en Telecomunicaciones (OSIPTEL): Calle de la Prosz 136, San Borja, Lima 41; tel. (1) 2251313; fax (1) 4760563; e-mail jkunigami@ospitel.gob.pe; internet www.ospitel.gob.pe; body established by the Peruvian Telecommunications Act to oversee competition and tariffs, to monitor the quality of services and to settle disputes in the sector; Pres. JORGE KUNIGAMI K.

Major Service Provider

Telefónica del Perú, SA: Avda Arequipa 1155, Santa Beatriz, Lima 1; tel. (1) 2101013; fax (1) 4705950; e-mail mgarcia@tp.com.pe; Exec. Pres. MANUEL GARCÍA G.

BROADCASTING

In 1999 there were 1,425 radio stations and 105 television stations in Peru.

Regulatory Authorities

Asociación de Radio y Televisión del Perú (AR&TV): Avda Roma 140, San Isidro, Lima 27; tel. (1) 4703734; Pres. HUMBERTO MALDONADO BALBÍN; Dir DANIEL LINARES BAZÁN.

Coordinadora Nacional de Radio: Santa Sabina 441, Urb. Santa Emma, Apdo 2179, Lima 100; tel. (1) 5640760; fax (1) 5640059; e-mail postmaster@cnr.org.pe; internet www.cnr.org.pe; f. 1978; Pres. RODOLFO AQUINO RUIZ.

Instituto Nacional de Comunicación Social: Jirón de la Unión 264, Lima; Dir HERNÁN VALDIZÁN.

Unión de Radioemisoras de Provincias del Perú (UNRAP): Mariano Carranza 754, Santa Beatriz, Lima 1.

Radio

Radio Agricultura del Perú, SA—La Peruanísima: Casilla 625, Lima 11; tel. (1) 4246677; e-mail radioagriculturadelperu@yahoo .com; f. 1963; Gen. Man. LUZ ISABEL DEXTRE NÚÑEZ.

Radio América: Montero Rosas 1099, Santa Beatriz, Lima 1; tel. (1) 2653841; fax (1) 2653844; e-mail kcrous@americatv.com.pe; f. 1943; Dir-Gen. KAREN CROUSILLAT.

Radio Cadena Nacional: Los Angeles 129, Miraflores, Lima; tel. (1) 4220905; fax (1) 4221067; Pres. MIGUEL DÍEZ CANSECO; Gen. Man. CÉSAR LECCA ARRIETA.

Cadena Peruana de Noticias: Gral Salaverry 156, Miraflores, Lima; tel. (1) 4461554; fax (1) 4457770; e-mail webmastercpn@gestion.com.pe; internet www.cpnradio.com.pe; f. 1996; Pres. MANUEL ROMERO CARO; Gen. Man. OSCAR ROMERO CARO.

Radio Cutivalú, La Voz del Desierto: Jirón Ignacio de Loyola 300, Urb. Miraflores, Castilla, Piura; tel. (74) 342802; fax (74) 342965; e-mail postmaster@cipcaperu-pe; f. 1986; Pres. MARÍA ISABEL REMY SIMATOVIC; Dir RODOLFO AQUINO RUIZ.

Emisoras 'Cruz del Perú': Victorino Laynes 1402, Urb. Elio, Lima 1; tel. (1) 4521028; Pres. FERNANDO CRUZ MENDOZA; Gen. Man. MARCO CRUZ MENDOZA M.

Emisoras Nacionales: León Velarde 1140, Lince, Lima 1; tel. (1) 4714948; fax (1) 4728182; Gen. Man. CÉSAR COLOMA R.

Radio Inca del Perú: Pastor Dávila 197, Lima; tel. (1) 2512596; fax (1) 2513324; e-mail corporacion@corporacionradial.com.pe; f. 1951; Gen. Man. ABRAHAM ZAVALA CHOCANO.

Radio Nacional del Perú: Avda Petit Thouars 447, Santa Beatriz, Lima; tel. (1) 4331712; fax (1) 4338952; Pres. LUIS ALBERTO MARAVÍ SÁENZ; Gen. Man. CARLOS PIZANO PANIAGUA.

Radio Panamericana: Paseo Parodi 340, San Isidro, Lima 27; tel. (1) 4226787; fax (1) 4221182; e-mail mad@radiopanamericana.com; internet www.radiopanamericana.com; f. 1953; Dir RAQUEL DELGADO DE ALCÁNTARA.

Radio Programas del Perú: Alejandro Tirado 217, 7°, Santa Beatriz, Lima; tel. (1) 4338720; Pres. MANUEL DELGADO PARKER; Gen. Man. ROLANDO ESTREMADOYRO.

Radio Santa Rosa: Jirón Camaná 170, Apdo 206, Lima; tel. (1) 4277488; fax (1) 4269219; e-mail santarosa@viaexpresa.com.pe; f. 1958; Dir P. JUAN SOKOLICH ALVARADO.

Sonograbaciones Maldonado: Mariano Carranza 754, Santa Beatriz, Lima; tel. (1) 4715163; fax (1) 4727491; Pres. HUMBERTO MALDONADO B; Gen. Man. LUIS HUMBERTO MALDONADO.

Television

América Televisión, Canal 4: Jirón Montero Rosas 1099, Santa Beatriz, Lima; tel. (1) 265-7361; fax (1) 2656979; e-mail infoamerica@americatv; internet www.americatv.com; Gen. Man. MARISOL CROUSILLAT.

ATV, Canal 9: Avda Arequipa 3570, San Isidro, Lima; tel. (1) 4426666; fax (1) 4217263; e-mail andinatelevision@atv.com.pe; f. 1983; Gen. Man. MARCELLO CÚNEO LOBIANO.

Frecuencia Latina, Canal 2: Avda San Felipe 968, Jesús María, Lima; tel. (1) 4707272; fax (1) 4714187; Pres. BARUCH IVCHER.

Global Televisión, Canal 13: Gen. Orbegoso 140, Breña, Lima; tel. (1) 3303040; fax (1) 4238202; f. 1989; Pres. GENARO DELGADO PARKER; Gen. Man. RAFAEL LEGUÍA.

Nor Peruana de Radiodifusión, SA: Avda Arequipa 3520, San Isidro, Lima 27; tel. (1) 403365; fax (1) 419844; f. 1991; Dir FRANCO PALERMO IBARGUENGOITIA; Gen. Man. FELIPE BERNINZÓN VALLARINO.

Panamericana Televisión SA, Canal 5: Avda Arequipa 1110, Lima 1; tel. (1) 4113201; fax (1) 2659541; e-mail panamericanatv@pantel.com.pe; internet www.pantel.com.pe; Pres. RAFAEL RAVETTINO FLORES; Gen. Man. FREDERICO ANCHORENA VÁSQUEZ.

Cía Peruana de Radiodifusión, Canal 4 TV: Mariano Carranza y Montero Rosas 1099, Santa Beatriz, Lima; tel. (1) 4728985; fax (1) 4710099; f. 1958; Dir JOSÉ FRANCISCO CROUSILLAT CARREÑO.

RBC Televisión, Canal 11: Avda Manco Cápac 333, La Victoria, Lima; tel. (1) 4310169; fax (1) 4331237; Pres. FERNANDO GONZÁLEZ DEL CAMPO; Gen. Man. JUAN SÁENZ MARÓN.

Radio Televisión Peruana, Canal 7: Avda José Galvez 1040, Santa Beatriz, Lima 1; tel. (1) 4718000; fax (1) 4726799; f. 1957; Pres. LUIS ALBERTO MARAVÍ SÁENZ; Gen. Man. CARLOS ALBERTO PIZZANO P.

Cía de Radiodifusión Arequipa SA, Canal 9: Centro Comercial Cayma, R2, Arequipa; tel. (54) 252525; fax (54) 254959; e-mail crasa@ibm.net; f. 1986; Dir ENRIQUE MENDOZA NÚÑEZ; Gen. Man. ENRIQUE MENDOZA DEL SOLAR.

Uranio, Canal 15: Avda Arequipa 3570, 6°, San Isidro, Lima; e-mail agamarra@atv.com.pe; Gen. Man. ADELA GAMARRA VASQUEZ.

Finance

In April 1991 a new banking law was introduced, which relaxed state control of the financial sector and reopened the sector to foreign banks (which had been excluded from the sector by a nationalization law promulgated in 1987).

BANKING

(cap. = capital; res = reserves; dep. = deposits; m. = million; amounts in new soles, unless otherwise stated)

Superintendencia de Banca y Seguros: Jirón Huancavelica 240, Lima 1; tel. (1) 4288210; fax (1) 4287259; e-mail mostos@sbs.gob.pe; internet www.sbs.gob.pe; f. 1931; Superintendent SOCORRO HEYSEN ZEGARRA; Sec.-Gen. NORMA SOLARI PRECIADO.

Central Bank

Banco Central de Reserva del Perú: Jirón Antonio Miró Quesada 441, Lima 1; tel. (1) 4276250; fax (1) 4275880; internet www.bcrp.gob.pe; f. 1922; refounded 1931; cap. 50.0m. res 300.9m., dep. 31,803.1m. (Dec. 1998); Pres. RICHARD WEBB DUARTE; Gen. Man. JAVIER DE LA ROCHA MARIE; 7 brs.

Other Government Banks

Banco Central Hipotecario del Perú: Carabaya 421, Apdo 1005, Lima; tel. (1) 4273845; fax (1) 4319729; f. 1929; Pres. AUSEJO RONCAGLIOLO CARLOS; 63 brs.

Banco de la Nación: Avda Canaval y Moreyra 150, San Isidro, Lima 1; tel. (1) 4405858; fax (1) 2218814; e-mail gergeneral@bn.com.pe; internet www.bn.com.pe; f. 1966; cap. 538.2m., res 203.6m., dep. 2,919.9m. (Dec. 2000); conducts all commercial banking operations of official government agencies; Pres. KURT BURNEO FARFÁN; Gen. Man. PEDRO ERNESTO MENÉNDEZ RICHTER; 350 brs.

Corporación Financiera de Desarrollo (COFIDE): Augusto Tamayo 160, San Isidro, Lima 27; tel. (1) 4422550; fax (1) 4423374; e-mail postmaster@cofide.com.pe; f. 1971; Pres. AURELIO LORET DE MOLA BÖHME; Gen. Man. MARCO CASTILLO TORRES; 11 brs.

Commercial Banks

Banco de Comercio: Avda Paseo de la República 3705, San Isidro, Lima; tel. (1) 4229800; fax (1) 4405458; e-mail postmaster@bancomercio.com.pe; internet www.bancomercio.com.pe; f. 1967; formerly Banco Peruano de Comercio y Construcción; cap. 41.0m., res 5.9m., dep. 411.4m. (Dec. 1998); Chair. PERCY TABORY; Gen. Man. HÉCTOR QUEZADA M. ILLA; 24 brs.

Banco Continental: Avda República de Panamá 3050–3065, San Isidro, Lima 27; tel. (1) 2111000; fax (1) 2111788; e-mail telematica@grupobbv.com.pe; internet www.continental.grupobbv.com; f. 1951; cap. 726.6m., res 112.4m., dep. 8,315.3m. (Dec. 1999); Pres. PEDRO BESCIA CAFFERATA; Dir-Gen. JOSÉ ANTONIO COLOMER GUIU; 190 brs.

Banco de Crédito del Perú: Calle Centenario 156, Urb. Las Laderas de Melgarejo, Apdo 12–067, Lima 12; tel. (1) 3490606; fax (1) 3490548; internet www.viabcp.com; f. 1889; cap. US $295.8m., res $190.3m., dep. $5,278.5m., total assets $6,300.2m. (Sept. 2001); Pres. DIONISIO ROMERO SEMINARIO; Gen. Man. RAIMUNDO MORALES DASSO; 217 brs.

Banco Exterior de los Andes y de España (EXTEBANDES): Avda Enrique Canaval y Moreyra 454, Lima 27; tel. (1) 4422121; f. 1982; cap. and res US $53.0m., dep. $371.9m. (Dec. 1987); Pres. ROSARIO ORELLANA YÉPEZ; Regional Gen. Man. HENRY BARCLAY REY DE CASTRO; 3 brs.

Banco Latino (BCOLATIN): Avda Paseo de la República 3505–3515, Lima 27; tel. (1) 4221290; fax (1) 4426200; e-mail clientelatino@bcolatino.com.pe; internet www.bcolatino.com.pe; f. 1982; cap. 229.9m., res 7.0m., dep. 815.5m. (Nov. 1999); Pres. RICHARD WEBB DUARTE; Gen. Man. HENRY BARCLAY REY DE CASTRO; 10 brs.

Banco Santander Central Hispano Perú: Avda Riviera Navarrete 698, San Isidro, Lima; tel. (1) 2158000; fax (1) 4415406; e-mail banco@bsch.com.pe; internet www.bsch.com.pe; f. 1995 as Banco Santander Perú following acquisition by Banco Santander of Banco Mercantil del Perú and Banco Interandino; name changed to above in 2000 following merger with Bancosur; cap. 410.1m., res 36.4m., dep. 3,027.2m. (Dec. 2000); Gen. Man. LEOPOLDO QUINTANO; 25 brs.

Banco Sudamericano: Avda Camino Real 815, San Isidro, Lima 27; tel. (1) 2211111; fax (1) 4423892; e-mail servicios@bansud.com

.pe; internet www.bansud.com.pe; f. 1981; cap. 101.2m., res 28.4m., dep. 1,431.1m. (Dec. 1998); Pres. ROBERTO CALDA CAVANNA; Gen. Man. RICARDO WENZEL FERRADAS; 9 brs.

Banco del Trabajo: Avda Paseo de la República 3587, San Isidro, Lima; tel. (1) 4219000; fax (1) 2214096; e-mail bravo@bantra.com.pe; Chair. CARLOS CARRILLO QUIÑONES; Gen. Man. JORGE SABAG SABAG; 46 brs.

Banco Wiese Sudameris: Jirón Cuzco 245, Apdo 1235, Lima 100; tel. (1) 4286000; fax (1) 4263977; internet www.wiese.com.pe; f. 1943; cap. 251.9m., dep. 6,647.2m., total assets 10,656.7m. (Dec. 1998); taken over by Govt in Oct. 1987; returned to private ownership in Oct. 1988 as Banco Wiese Ltdo; merged with Banco de Lima-Sudameris in Sept. 1999; Pres. and Chair. AUGUSTO FELIPE WIESE DE OSMA; Dir and Gen. Man. EUGENIO BERTINI VINCI.

INTERBANK (Banco Internacional del Perú): Carlos Villaran 140, Urb. Santa Catalina, Lima 13; tel. (1) 2192000; fax (1) 2192336; e-mail krubin@intercorp.com.pe; internet www.interbank.com.pe; f. 1897; commercial bank; cap. 299.8m., res 91.4m., dep. 4,687.8m. (Dec. 1999); Chair. CARLOS RODRÍGUEZ PASTOR; Gen. Man. ISMAEL BENAVIDES FERREYROS; 94 brs.

Provincial Banks

Banco Regional del Norte: Esq. Libertad e Ica 723, Apdo 131, Piura; tel. (74) 325992; fax (74) 332742; f. 1960; cap. and res US $9.6m., dep. $67.6m. (Dec. 1992); Pres. JUAN ARTURO ATKINS MORALES; CEO FRANCISCO GONZÁLEZ GARCÍA; 10 brs.

Foreign Banks

Banco do Brasil, SA: Avda Camino Real 348, San Isidro, Lima; tel. (1) 2212280; fax (1) 4424208.

Banco Arabe Latinoamericano (ARLABANK): Calle Juan de Arona 830, San Isidro, Apdo 10070, Lima 100; tel. (1) 4413150; fax (1) 4414277; f. 1977; Chair. CÉSAR RODRÍGUEZ BATILE; Gen. Man. FERNANDO ACCAME FEIJOO.

Citibank NA (USA): Torre Real, 5°, Avda Camino Real 456, Lima 27; tel. (1) 4214000; fax (1) 4409044; internet www.citibank.com/peru/homepage/index-e-htm; f. 1920; cap. US $47,520m., res $1,936m., dep. $139,627m. (Nov. 1997); Vice-Pres. GUSTAVO MARÍN; 1 br.

Banking Association

Asociación de Bancos del Perú: Calle 41, No 975, Urb. Corpac, San Isidro, Lima 27; tel. (1) 2241718; fax (1) 2241707; e-mail earroyo@asbanc.com.pe; f. 1929; refounded 1967; Pres. JOSÉ NICOLINI LORENZONI; Gen. Man. JUAN KLINGENBERGER LOMELLINI.

STOCK EXCHANGE

Bolsa de Valores de Lima: Pasaje Acuña 106, Lima 100; tel. (1) 4260714; fax (1) 4267650; e-mail tfreire@bvl.com.pe; f. 1860; Exec. Pres. CARLOS SEMINARIO PIZZORNI; CEO MIGUEL RIVERA AGUIRRE.

INSURANCE

Lima

Cía de Seguros La Fénix Peruana: Avda Cte Espinar 689, Miraflores, Lima 18; Apdo 1356, Lima 100; tel. (1) 2412430; fax (1) 4455840; e-mail fenix@lafenix.com.pe; internet www.lafenix.com; f. 1927; Pres. RAÚL BARRIOS ORBEGOSO; Gen. Man. RAFAEL PADIAL.

Generali Perú, Cía de Seguros y Reaseguros: Jirón Antonio Miró Quesada 191, Apdo 1751, Lima 100; tel. (1) 3111000; fax (1) 3111004; e-mail boac@generali-peru-com.pe; internet www.generali-peru.com.pe; f. 1942; Pres. PIERO SACCHI CHECCUCI; Gen. Man. BRUNO ORLANDINI ALVAREZ CALDERÓN.

El Pacífico-Peruano Suiza, Cía de Seguros y Reaseguros: Avda Arequipa 660, Apdo 595, Lima 100; tel. (1) 4333626; fax (1) 4333388; f. 1993 by merger; Pres. CALIXTO ROMERO SEMINARIO; Gen. Man. ARTURO RODRIGO SANTISTEVAN.

Panamericana Cía de Seguros y Reaseguros: Jirón Augusto Tamayo 180, San Isidro, Lima; tel. (1) 4715070; fax (1) 4703769; f. 1958; Pres. JUAN BANCHERO ROSSI; Gen. Man. RODOLFO GORDILLO TORDOYA.

La Positiva Cía de Seguros y Reaseguros SA: Esq. Javier Prado Este y Francisco Masías, Apdo 1456, Lima 27; tel. (1) 4426250; fax (1) 4401124; internet www.lapositiva.com.p; f. 1937; Pres. Ing. JUAN MANUEL PEÑA ROCA; Gen. Man. JAIME PÉREZ RODRÍGUEZ.

La Real, Cía de Seguros Generales, SA: Avda San Luis 2002, San Borja, Lima; tel. (1) 4758650; fax (1) 4769941; e-mail segureal@cbd.com.pe; f. 1980; Pres. CÉSAR VILCHEZ VIVANCO CAHUAS BONINO; Gen. Man. JOSÉ ANTONIO LEÓN ROCA.

Reaseguradora Peruana, SA: Chinchón 890, San Isidro, Apdo 3672, Lima 100; tel. (1) 4425065; fax (1) 4417959; f. 1965; state-controlled; Pres. RAFAEL VILLEGAS CERRO; Gen. Man. ERNESTO BECERRA MEJÍA.

Rimac Internacional, Cía de Seguros: Las Begonias 475, 3°, San Isidro, Lima 27; Apdo 245, Lima 100; tel. (1) 4222780; fax (1) 4210570; internet www.rimac.com; f. 1896; Pres. Ing. PEDRO BRESCIA CAFFERATA; Gen. Man. ALEX FORT BRESCIA.

SECREX, Cía de Seguro de Crédito y Garantías: Avda Angamos Oeste 1234, Miraflores, Apdo 0511, Lima 18; tel. (1) 4424033; fax (1) 4423890; e-mail ciaseg@secrex.com.pe; f. 1980; Pres. Dr RAÚL FERRERO COSTA; Gen. Man. JUAN A. GIANNONI.

El Sol, Nacional Cía de Seguros y Reaseguros: Avda 28 de Julio 873, Miraflores, Apdo 323, Lima 100; tel. (1) 4444515; fax (1) 4468456; f. 1950; Pres. Ing. ROBERTO CALDA CAVANNA; Gen. Man. RENZO CALDA GIURATO.

Sul América Cía de Seguros, SA—Sul América Seguros: Jirón Sinchi Roca 2728, Apdo 5569, Lince, Lima 14; tel. (1) 4210515; fax (1) 4418730; e-mail postmaster@sulamerica.com.pe; internet www .sulamerica.com; f. 1954; Pres. OSWALDO MARIO PEGO DE AMORIM AZEVEDO; Gen. Man. LUIS SALCEDO MARSANO.

Wiese Aetna, Cia de Seguros: Calle Tudela y Varela 102, San Isidro, Lima; tel. (1) 2222222; fax (1) 4427550; e-mail seguros@ wieseaetna.com; internet www.wieseaetna.com; f. 1980 as Cía de Seguros Condor; changed name to above in 1996; Pres. GONZALO DE LA PUENTE Y LAVALLE; Gen. Man. JOSÉ ANTONIO CACHO-SOUSA DE CÁRDENAS.

Insurance Association

Asociación Peruana de Empresas de Seguros (APESEG): Arias Araguez 146, Miraflores, Apdo 1684, Lima 100; tel. (1) 4442294; fax (1) 4468538; f. 1904; Pres. GUILLERMO CARRILLO FLECHA; Gen. Man. MANUEL PORTUGAL MARIÁTEGUI.

Trade and Industry

GOVERNMENT AGENCIES

Agencia de Promoción de la Inversión (ProInversión): Avda Paseo de la República 3361, 9°, San Isidro, Lima 27; tel. (1) 6121200; fax (1) 2212942; e-mail nrovegno@proinversion.com; internet www .proinversion.com; f. 2002 to promote economic investment; Dir LUIS GUIULFO.

Consejo Nacional de Conciliación Agraria (CNCA): Lima; f. 1988; acts as mediator between the Government and producers in agricultural sector; Pres. Minister of Agriculture.

Comisión Nacional de Inversiones y Tecnologias Extranjeras (CONITE): Jr. Antonio Miró Quesada 320, Lima; tel. (1) 4289358; fax (1) 4277696; e-mail CONITE@mef.gob.pe; internet www.mef.gob .pe/peruinv; f. 1991; responsible for supervision and promotion of foreign investment.

Empresa Nacional de Comercialización de Insumos (Enci): Galerías San Felipe 111, Cuadra 7, Avda Gregorio Escobedo, Apdo 1834, Lima 11; tel. (1) 4632122; fax (1) 4626242; f. 1974; controls the import, export and national distribution of agricultural and basic food products; Gen. Man. JUAN MASAO OKUMA ISA.

Fondo Nacional De Compensación Y Desarrollo Social (FONCODES): Avda Paseo de la República 3101, Lima; e-mail consultas@foncodes.gob.pe; internet www.foncodes.gob.pe; f. 1991; responsible for social development and eradicating poverty; Exec. Dir ALEJANDRO NARVÁEZ LICERAS.

Perupetro: Luis Aldana 320, San Borja; tel. (1) 4759590; fax (1) 4759644; internet www.perupetro.com.pe; f. 1993; responsible for promoting the investment of hydrocarbon exploration and exploitation activities; Chair ANTONIO CUETO.

DEVELOPMENT ORGANIZATIONS

Asociación de Dirigentes de Ventas y Mercadotecnia del Perú (ADV—PERU): Lima; tel. (1) 4419988; fax (1) 4410303; f. 1958; Pres. FRANCO CARABELLI PACE; Gen. Man. STEFAN ARIE SINGER; 1,500 mems.

Asociación de Exportadores (ADEX): Javier Prado Este 2875, Lima 41; Apdo 1806, Lima 1; tel. (1) 3462530; fax (1) 3461879; e-mail postmaster@adexperu.org.pe; internet www.adexperu.org.pe; f. 1973; Pres. CARLOS BRUCE MONTES DE OCA; Gen. Man. JAIME RODRÍGUEZ FAVARATO; 600 mems.

Comisión de Promoción de la Inversión Privada (COPRI): Avda Las Artes Sur 260, San Borja, Lima; tel. (1) 2217008; fax (1) 2212942; internet www.copri.org; Dir Minister of Labour and Social Promotion.

Consejo Nacional de Desarrollo (CONADE): Avda Agusto Tamayo 160, Lima 27; national development council; Chair. JOSÉ PALOMINO.

Sociedad Nacional de Industrias (SNI) (National Industrial Association): Los Laureles 365, San Isidro, Apdo 632, Lima 27; tel. (1) 4218830; fax (1) 4422573; internet www.sni.org.pe; f. 1896; comprises permanent commissions covering various aspects of industry including labour, integration, fairs and exhibitions, industrial promotion; its Small Industry Committee groups over 2,000 small enterprises; Pres. Ing. EMILIO NAVARRO CASTAÑEDA; Gen. Man. PABLO CARRIQUIRY BLONDET; 90 dirs (reps of firms); 2,500 mems; 60 sectorial committees.

Centro de Desarrollo Industrial (CDI): c/o SNI; tel. (1) 4419101; fax (1) 4407702; e-mail cdi@sni.org.pe; internet www.sni .org.pe/comites/cdi/PortalCDI.html; f. 1986; supports industrial development and programmes to develop industrial companies; Exec. Dir LUIS TENORIO PUENTES.

CHAMBER OF COMMERCE

Cámara de Comercio de Lima (Lima Chamber of Commerce): Avda Gregorio Escobedo 398, Lima 11; tel. (1) 4633434; fax (1) 4632820; internet www.camaralima.org.pe; f. 1888; Pres. SAMUEL GLEISER KATZ; Gen. Man. JOSÉ ROSAS BERNEDO; 3,500 mems.

There are also Chambers of Commerce in Arequipa, Cuzco, Callao and many other cities.

EMPLOYERS' ORGANIZATIONS

Asociación Automotriz del Perú: Dos de Mayo 299, Apdo 1248, Lima 27; tel. (1) 4404119; fax (1) 4428865; e-mail aap@terra.com.pe; f. 1926; association of importers of motor cars and accessories; 360 mems; Pres. CARLOS BAMBARÉN GARCÍA-MALDONADO; Gen. Man. CÉSAR MARTÍN BARREDA.

Asociación de Ganaderos del Perú (Association of Stock Farmers of Peru): Pumacahua 877, 3°, Jesús María, Lima; f. 1915; Gen. Man. Ing. MIGUEL J. FORT.

Comité de Minería de la Cámara de Comercio e Industria de Arequipa: Apdo 508, Arequipa; mining association; Pres. F. C. WILLFORT.

Confederación Nacional de Instituciones Empresariales Privadas (CONFIEP): Pasaje Acuña 106, Lima; e-mail postmaster@ confiep.org.pe; internet www.cosapi.org.pe; f. 1984; association of private companies; Pres. JULIO FAVRE CARRANZA.

Instituto Peruano del Café: Lima; f. 1965; representatives of Government and industrial coffee growers.

Sociedad Nacional de Minería y Petróleo: Francisco Graña 671, Lima 17; tel. (1) 4601560; fax (1) 4601616; e-mail infsnmp@mail .cosapidata.com.pe; internet www.snmpe.org.pe/; f. 1940; Pres. HANS FLURY; Vice-Pres. KURT SCHULTZE-RHONHOF; Gen. Man. CARLOS DIEZ CANSECO; association of companies involved in mining, petroleum and energy; 205 mems.

Sociedad Nacional de Pesquería (SNP): Lima; f. 1952; private sector fishing interests; Pres. JOSÉ SARMIENTO MADUEÑO.

UTILITIES

Regulatory Authority

Comisión de Tarifas Eléctricas (CTE): Avda Canadá 1470, San Borja, Lima 41; tel. (1) 2240487; fax (1) 2240491.

Electricity

Electrolima, SA: Jirón Zorritos 1301, Lima 5; tel. (1) 4324153; fax (1) 4323042; f. 1906; produces and supplies electricity for Lima and the surrounding districts; Pres. LUIS CARLOS RODRÍGUEZ MARTÍNEZ.

ElectroPerú: Avda Pedro Miotta, Ant. Carretera Panamericana Sur, km 14.5, Lima 29; tel. (1) 4661849; fax (1) 4661899; state-owned; Pres. JESÚS BEOUTIS LEDESMA; Gen. Man. LUIS NICHO DÍAZ.

Empresa Regional de Servicio Público de Electricidad Norte (Electronorte, SA): Vicente de la Vega 318, Chiclayo; tel. (74) 231580; fax (74) 243260; Gen. Man. HERACLIO PRADA MARTÍNEZ.

Sociedad Eléctrica del Sur-Oeste, SA: Consuelo 310, Arequipa; tel. (54) 212946; fax (54) 213296; e-mail seal@sealperu.com; internet www.sealperu.com; f. 1905; Man. ADOLFO VÉLEZ DE CÓRDOVA.

TRADE UNIONS

The right to strike was restored in the Constitution of July 1979. In 1982 the Government recognized the right of public employees to form trade unions.

Central Unica de Trabajadores Peruanos (CUTP): Lima; f. 1992; Pres. JULIO CÉSAR BAZÁN; comprises:

Central de Trabajadores de la Revolución Peruana (CTRP): Lima.

Confederación General de Trabajadores del Perú (CGTP): Ayacucho 173, Lima; tel. (1) 4282253; f. 1968; Pres. MARIO HUAMÁN; Sec.-Gen. JUAN JOSÉ GORRITI.

Confederación Nacional de Trabajadores (CNT): Avda Iquitos 1198, Lima; tel. (1) 4711385; affiliated to the PPC; 12,000 mems (est.); Sec.-Gen. ANTONIO GALLARDO EGOAVIL.

Confederación de Trabajadores Peruanos (CTP): Lima; affiliated to APRA; Gen. Sec. JULIO CRUZADO EZCURRA.

Confederación Intersectorial de Trabajadores Estatales (CITE) (Union of Public Sector Workers): Lima; tel. (1) 4245525; f. 1978; Leader CÉSAR PASSALACQUA PEREYRA; Sec.-Gen. RAÚL CABALLERO VARGAS; 600,000 mems.

Federación de Empleados Bancarios (FEB) (Union of Bank Employees): Leader ANTONIO ZÚÑIGA; Sec.-Gen. AUGUSTO GARCÍA DUQUE.

Federación Nacional de Trabajadores Mineros, Metalúrgicos y Siderúrgicos (FNTMMS) (Federation of Peruvian Mineworkers): Lima; Pres. VÍCTOR TAIPE; Vice-Pres. LEONARDO RAMÍREZ; 70,000 mems.

Movimiento de Trabajadores y Obreros de Clase (MTOC): Lima.

Sindicato Unico de Trabajadores de Educación del Perú (SUTEP) (Union of Peruvian Teachers): Lima; fax (1) 4762792; Sec.-Gen. JOSÉ RAMOS.

Independent unions, representing an estimated 37% of trade unionists, include: Comité para la Coordinación Clasista y la Unificación Sindical, Confederación de Campesinos Peruanos (CCP—Sec.-Gen. Andrés Luna Vargas), Confederación Nacional Agraria (Pres. Felipe Humán Yayahuanca).

Confederación Nacional de Comunidades Industriales (CONACI): Lima; co-ordinates worker participation in industrial management and profit-sharing.

The following agricultural organizations exist:

Consejo Unitario Nacional Agrario (CUNA): f. 1983; represents 36 farmers' and peasants' organizations, including:

Confederación Campesina del Perú (CCP): radical left-wing; Pres. ANDRÉS LUNA VARGAS; Sec. HUGO BLANCO (arrested Feb. 1989).

Organización Nacional Agraria (ONA): organization of dairy farmers and cattle-breeders.

Transport

RAILWAYS

In 2000 there were some 2,123 km of track. A programme to develop a national railway network (Sistema Nacional Ferroviario) was begun in the early 1980s, aimed at increasing the length of track to about 5,000 km initially. The Government also plans to electrify the railway system and extend the Central and Southern Railways.

Ministerio de Transportes y Comunicaciones: see section on The Government (Ministries).

Consorcio de Ferrocarriles del Peru: following the privatization of the state railway company Enafer, the above consortium won a 30-year concession in July 1999 to operate the following lines:

Empresa Minera del Centro del Perú SA—División Ferro-carriles (Centromín-Perú SA) (fmrly Cerro de Pasco Railway): Edif. Solgas, Avda Javier Prado Este 2175, San Borja, Apdo 2412, Lima 41; tel. (1) 4761010; fax (1) 4769757; 212.2 km; acquired by Enafer-Perú in 1997; Pres. HERNÁN BARRETO; Gen. Man. GUILLERMO GUANILO.

Ferrocarril del Centro del Perú (Central Railway of Peru): Ancash 201, Apdo 1379, Lima; tel. (1) 4276620; fax (1) 4281075; 591 km open; Man. DAVID SAN ROMÁN B.

Ferrocarril del Sur del Perú ENAFER, SA (Southern Railway): Avda Tacna y Arica 200, Apdo 194, Arequipa; tel. (54) 215350; fax (54) 231603; 915 km open; also operates steamship service on Lake Titicaca; Man. C. NORIEGA.

Tacna–Arica Ferrocarril (Tacna–Arica Railway): Avda Aldarracín 484, Tacna; 62 km open.

Ferrocarril Pimentel (Pimentel Railway): Pimentel, Chiclayo, Apdo 310; 56 km open; owned by Empresa Nacional de Puertos; cargo services only; Pres. R. MONTENEGRO; Man. LUIS DE LA PIEDRA ALVIZURI.

Private Railways

Ferrocarril Ilo–Toquepala–Cuajone: Apdo 2640, Lima; 219 km open, incl. five tunnels totalling 27 km; owned by the Southern Peru Copper Corporation for transporting copper supplies and concentrates only; Pres. OSCAR GONZÁLEZ ROCHA; Gen. Man. WILLIAM TORRES.

Ferrocarril Supe–Barranca–Alpas: Barranca; 40 km open; Dirs CARLOS GARCÍA GASTAÑETA, LUIS G. MIRANDA.

ROADS

In 1999 there were an estimated 78,128 km of roads in Peru, of which approximately 13% were paved. The most important highways are: the Pan-American Highway (3,008 km), which runs southward from the Ecuadorean border along the coast to Lima; Camino del Inca Highway (3,193 km) from Piura to Puno; Marginal de la Selva (1,688 km) from Cajamarca to Madre de Dios; and the Trans-Andean Highway (834 km), which runs from Lima to Pucallpa on the River Ucayali via Oroya, Cerro de Pasco and Tingo María.

SHIPPING

Most trade is through the port of Callao but there are 13 deep-water ports, mainly in northern Peru (including Salaverry, Pacasmayo and Paita) and in the south (including the iron ore port of San Juan). There are river ports at Iquitos, Pucallpa and Yurimaguas, aimed at improving communications between Lima and Iquitos, and a further port is under construction at Puerto Maldonado.

Empresa Nacional de Puertos, SA (Enapu): Avda Contralmirante Raygada 110, Callao; tel. (1) 4299210; fax (1) 4691011; e-mail enapu@inconet.net.pe; internet www.enapu.gob.pe; f. 1970; government agency administering all coastal and river ports; Pres. LUIS E. VARGAS CABALLERO; Gen. Man. OTTO BOTTGER R.

Asociación Marítima del Perú: Avda Javier Prado Este 897, Of. 33, San Isidro, Apdo 3520, Lima 27; tel. and fax (1) 4221904; f. 1957; association of 20 international and Peruvian shipping companies; Pres. LUIS FELIPE VILLENA GUTIÉRREZ.

Consorcio Naviero Peruano, SA: Avda Central 643, San Isidro, Apdo 18-0736, Lima 1; tel. (1) 4116500; fax (1) 4116599; e-mail cnp@cnpsa.com; f. 1959.

Naviera Humboldt, SA: Edif. Pacífico–Washington, 9°, Natalio Sánchez 125, Apdo 3639, Lima 1; tel. (1) 4334005; fax (1) 4337151; e-mail postmast@sorcomar.com.pe; internet www.humbolt.com.pe; f. 1970; cargo services; Pres. AUGUSTO BEDOYA CAMERE; Man. Dir LUIS FREIRE R.

Agencia Naviera Maynas, SA: Avda San Borja Norte 761, San Borja, Lima 41; tel. (1) 4752033; fax (1) 4759680; e-mail lima@navieramaynas.com.pe; f. 1996; Pres. R. USSEGLIO D; Gen. Man. ROBERTO MELGAR B.

Naviera Universal, SA: Calle 41 No 894, Urb. Corpac, San Isidro, Apdo 10307, Lima 100; tel. (1) 4757020; fax (1) 4755233; Chair. HERBERT C. BUERGER.

Petrolera Transoceánica, SA (PETRANSO): Víctor Maúrtua 135, Lima 27; tel. (1) 4422007; fax (1) 4403922; internet www.petranso.com.pe; Gen. Man. JUAN VILLARÁN.

A number of foreign lines call at Peruvian ports.

CIVIL AVIATION

Of Peru's 294 airports, the major international airport is Jorge Chávez Airport near Lima. Other important international airports are Coronel Francisco Secada Vignetta Airport, near Iquitos, Velasco Astete Airport, near Cuzco, and Rodríguez Ballón Airport, near Arequipa.

Corporación Peruana de Aeropuertos y Aviación Comercial: Aeropuerto Internacional Jorge Chávez, Callao; tel. (1) 5750912; fax (1) 5745578; internet www.corpac.gob.pe; f. 1943; Pres. LEOPOLDO PFLUCKER LLONA; Gen. Man. ROBERT McDONALD ZAPFF.

Domestic Airlines

Aero Condor: Juan de Arona 781, San Isidro, Lima; tel. (1) 4425215; fax (1) 2215783; internet www.aerocondor.com.pe; domestic services; Pres. CARLOS PALACÍN FERNÁNDEZ.

Aero Continente: Avda José Pardo 605, Lima 18; tel. (1) 2414816; fax (1) 2413074; internet www.aerocontinente.com.pe; f. 1992; domestic services; Pres. LUPE L. Z. GONZALES.

Tourism

Tourism is centred on Lima, with its Spanish colonial architecture, and Cuzco, with its pre-Inca and Inca civilization, notably the 'lost city' of Machu Picchu. Lake Titicaca, lying at an altitude of 3,850 m. above sea-level, and the Amazon jungle region to the north-east also form popular resorts. In the mid-1990s there was evidence of a marked recovery in the tourist sector, which had been adversely affected by health and security concerns. In 2001 Peru received 1,009,512 visitors, compared with 584,388 in 1996. Receipts from tourism generated US $1,001m. in 2000.

Comisión de Promoción del Perú (PromPerú): Edif. Mitinci, Calle Uno Oeste 13°, Urb. Corpac, San Isidro, Lima 27; tel. (1) 2243279; fax (1) 2247134; e-mail postmaster@promperu.gob.pe; internet www.peru.org.pe; f. 1993; Head of Tourism IBETH ACUÑA.

THE PHILIPPINES

Introductory Survey

Location, Climate, Language, Religion, Flag, Capital

The Republic of the Philippines lies in the western Pacific Ocean, east of mainland South-East Asia. The island of Borneo is to the south-west, and New Guinea to the south-east. The principal islands of the Philippine archipelago are Luzon, in the north, and Mindanao, in the south. Between these two (which together account for 66% of the country's area) lie the 7,000 islands of the Visayas. The climate is maritime and tropical. It is generally hot and humid, except in the mountains. There is abundant rainfall, and the islands are frequently in the path of typhoons. At the 1995 census there were 102 languages; the most frequently used were Tagalog (by 29.3% of the population), Cebuano (21.2%), Ilocano (9.3%), Hiligaynon (Ilongo—9.1%) and Bicol (5.7%). Filipino, based on Tagalog, is the native national language. English is widely spoken, and Spanish is used in some communities. In 1991 94.2% of the population were Christians (84.1% Roman Catholics, 6.2% belonged to the Philippine Independent Church (Aglipayan) and 3.9% were Protestants). In 1990 an estimated 4.6% of the population were Muslims. The national flag (proportions 1 by 2) has two equal horizontal stripes, of blue and red, with a white triangle, enclosing a yellow 'Sun of Liberty' (with eight large and 16 small rays) and three five-pointed yellow stars (one in each corner), at the hoist. The capital is Manila, on the island of Luzon.

Recent History

The Philippines became a Spanish colony in the 16th century. During the Spanish–American War, the independence of the Philippines was declared on 12 June 1898 by Gen. Emilio Aguinaldo, leader of the revolutionary movement, with the support of the USA. Under the Treaty of Paris, signed in December 1898, Spain ceded the islands to the USA. A new Constitution, ratified by plebiscite in May 1935, gave the Philippines internal self-government and provided for independence after 10 years. During the Second World War the islands were occupied by Japanese forces from 1942, but, after Japan's surrender in 1945, US rule was restored. The Philippines became an independent republic on 4 July 1946, with Manuel Roxas as its first President. A succession of Presidents, effectively constrained by US economic interests and the Filipino land-owning class, did little to help the peasant majority or to curb disorder and political violence.

At elections in November 1965 the incumbent President, Diosdado Macapagal of the Liberal Party, was defeated by Ferdinand Marcos of the Nacionalista Party (NP). Rapid development of the economy and infrastructure followed. President Marcos was re-elected in 1969. His second term was characterized by civil unrest and economic difficulties. During the early 1970s there was also an increase in guerrilla activity, by the New People's Army (NPA), the armed wing of the outlawed (Maoist) Communist Party of the Philippines (CPP), in the north of the country, and by the Moro National Liberation Front (MNLF), a Muslim separatist movement, in the south.

In September 1972, before completing the (then) maximum of two four-year terms of office, Marcos declared martial law in order to deal with subversive activity and to introduce drastic reforms. The bicameral Congress was suspended, opposition leaders were arrested, the private armies of the landed oligarchs were disbanded, stringent press censorship was introduced, and Marcos began to rule by decree. In November a new Constitution was approved by a constitutional convention, and in January 1973 it was ratified by Marcos. It provided for a unicameral National Assembly and a Constitutional President, with executive power held by a Prime Minister, to be elected by the legislature. Transitional provisions gave the incumbent President the combined authority of the presidency (under the 1935 Constitution) and the premiership, without any fixed term of office. Under martial law, the definitive provisions of the new Constitution remained in abeyance.

A referendum in July 1973 approved Marcos's continuation in office beyond his elected term. Referendums in February 1975 and October 1976 approved the continuation of martial law and the adoption of constitutional amendments, including a provi-

sion for the formation of an interim assembly. In December 1977 a fourth referendum approved the extension of Marcos's presidential term.

Criticism of Marcos became more widespread after November 1977, when a sentence of death was imposed by a military tribunal on the principal opposition leader, Benigno Aquino, Jr (a former senator and Secretary-General of the Liberal Party, who had been detained since 1972), for alleged murder, subversion and the possession of firearms. Marcos allowed a stay of execution, and conceded some relaxation of martial law in 1977. Elections to the interim National Assembly took place in April 1978. Opposition parties were allowed to participate, but the pro-Government Kilusang Bagong Lipunan (KBL—New Society Movement), founded in 1978 by Marcos and former members of the NP, won 151 of the Assembly's 165 elective seats. The Assembly was inaugurated in June, when Marcos was also confirmed as Prime Minister. Martial law remained in force, and Marcos retained the power to legislate by decree. Local elections, the first to be held in eight years, took place in January 1980, resulting in decisive victories for the KBL. In May Aquino was released from prison to undergo medical treatment in the USA, where he renewed his opposition to Marcos's regime.

In January 1981 martial law was ended, although Marcos retained most of his former powers. A referendum in April approved constitutional amendments that permitted Marcos to renew his mandate by direct popular vote and to nominate a separate Prime Minister. In June, amid allegations of electoral malpractice, Marcos was re-elected President for a six-year term. In April 1982 the United Nationalist Democratic Organization (UNIDO), an alliance of opposition groups, formed an official coalition: it included Lakas ng Bayan (the People's Power Movement, founded by Aquino in 1978) and the Pilipino Democratic Party (PDP), which merged to form PDP-Laban in 1983.

In August 1983 Aquino, returning from exile in the USA, was shot dead on arrival at Manila airport. Rolando Galman, the alleged communist assassin, was killed immediately by military guards. A commission of inquiry, nominated by the Government, concluded that Aquino's murder had been a military conspiracy. The Supreme Court announced in December 1985, however, that the evidence submitted to the commission was inadmissible, acquitted the 26 military personnel who had been accused of conspiring to murder Aquino and upheld the Government's assertion that the assassin was Galman.

Aquino's death proved to be a turning-point in Philippine politics, uniting the opposition in its criticism of Marcos. At elections to the National Assembly in May 1984, public participation was high, and, after numerous accusations by the opposition of electoral fraud and corruption by Marcos, the opposition won 59 of the 183 elective seats, compared with 14 in 1978.

In November 1985, in response to US pressure (and after continued appeals for domestic reform), Marcos announced that a presidential election would be held in February 1986, 18 months earlier than scheduled. Corazon Aquino, the widow of Benigno Aquino, was chosen as the UNIDO presidential candidate, in spite of her lack of political experience. More than 100 people were killed in violence during the election campaign. Vote-counting was conducted by the government-controlled National Commission on Elections (Comelec) and by the independent National Citizens' Movement for Free Elections (Namfrel). Allegations of large-scale electoral fraud and irregularities, apparently perpetrated by supporters of Marcos, were substantiated by numerous international observers. On 16 February 1986 the National Assembly declared Marcos the winner of the presidential election, with 10.8m. votes, compared with 9.3m. for Aquino, according to figures from Comelec. According to Namfrel figures (based on 69% of the total votes), Aquino was in the lead. Marcos immediately announced the resignation of the Cabinet, and declared his intention to establish a council of presidential advisers. Aquino rejected an offer to participate in the council, and launched a campaign of non-violent pressure on the Government, including a boycott of many organizations connected with the Marcos family.

On 22 February 1986 Lt-Gen. (later Gen.) Fidel Ramos, the acting Chief of Staff of the Armed Forces, and Juan Enrile, the Minister of National Defense, along with about 300 troops, established a rebel headquarters in the Ministry of National Defense in Manila (later moving to the police headquarters), stating that they no longer accepted Marcos's authority and asserting that Aquino was the rightful President. Attempts by forces loyal to Marcos to attack the rebels were foiled by large unarmed crowds which gathered to protect them at the instigation of the Catholic Archbishop of Manila, Cardinal Jaime Sin. Troops supporting Ramos subsequently secured control of the government broadcasting station, with little bloodshed. On 25 February rival ceremonies were held, at which both Marcos and Aquino were sworn in as President. Later the same day, however, under pressure from the USA, Marcos finally agreed to withdraw, and left the Philippines for Hawaii.

President Aquino received worldwide recognition, including that of the US Government, upon her inauguration. She appointed her Vice-President, Salvador Laurel (the President of UNIDO), to be Prime Minister and Minister of Foreign Affairs, while Enrile retained the post of Minister of National Defense. Ramos was appointed Chief of Staff of the Armed Forces. At the end of February 1986 Aquino ordered the controversial release of all political prisoners, including communist leaders. In March the Government announced the restoration of habeas corpus, the abolition of press censorship and the suspension of local government elections (scheduled for May). The Government also secured the resignation of all Justices of the Supreme Court, as well as the resignation of Comelec members. On 25 March Aquino announced that the 1973 Constitution was to be replaced by an interim document, providing for the immediate abolition of the National Assembly and for the inauguration of a provisional government, with the President being granted emergency powers. The post of Prime Minister was temporarily abolished, and in May a commission was appointed to draft a new constitution.

During 1986 and 1987 the Aquino Government struggled to maintain control over the army (which was divided into reformist and pro-Marcos factions) while, at the same time, appeasing left-wing labour movements and endeavouring to bring to an end the 17-year insurgency by the NPA and the 14-year war of secession in Mindanao by Muslim separatists. These problems were compounded by dissension within the Government regarding major policies and by the near-bankruptcy of the country's economy.

In March 1986 military leaders pledged their loyalty to Aquino as President and Commander-in-Chief of the Armed Forces. The Government then began to implement a programme of military reform, in accordance with the demands of officers of the Rebolusyonaryong Alyansang Makabayan (RAM—Nationalist Revolutionary Alliance—also known as the Reform the Armed Forces Movement), who had supported the February revolution. In September the Supreme Court ordered the retrial of the members of the military who had earlier been acquitted of the murder of Benigno Aquino. In September 1990, following a trial lasting more than three years, a special court convicted 16 members of the armed forces of the murder of both Aquino and Galman; a further 20 defendants were acquitted.

In July 1986 an abortive coup took place in Manila, led by Arturo Tolentino, a former Minister of Foreign Affairs and Marcos's vice-presidential candidate, and a group of 300 pro-Marcos troops. One of the principal reasons for military dissatisfaction was the new Government's conciliatory attitude towards communist insurgents. In June the Government had attempted to bring guerrilla activity by the NPA (estimated to number 25,000–30,000 members at that time) to an end, announcing that formal negotiations for a cease-fire agreement would begin with representatives of the National Democratic Front (NDF—a left-wing group that included the CPP and the NPA). In October, however, increasing pressure from Enrile and the RAM prompted Aquino to threaten the insurgents with open warfare if a solution were not reached by the end of November. In late November a group of army officers attempted to gain control of several military camps and to replace Aquino with Nicanor Yniguez, a former Speaker of the National Assembly. The rebellion was quelled by Ramos and troops loyal to Aquino; Enrile was dismissed from the Cabinet, and replaced by his deputy, Gen. Rafael Ileto. In January 1987 there was a further coup attempt by 500 disaffected troops; an attempt by Marcos to return to the Philippines was thwarted by US officials, and the two-day rebellion was suppressed by forces loyal to Aquino.

In February 1987 a new Constitution was approved by 76% of voters in a national plebiscite. The new Constitution gave Aquino a mandate to rule until 30 June 1992, and established an executive presidency (see Government, below). All members of the armed forces swore an oath of allegiance to the new Constitution. An order followed disbanding all 'fraternal organizations' (such as the RAM) within the armed forces, because they 'encouraged divisiveness'. Elections to the bicameral Congress of the Philippines took place on 11 May 1987 (as provided for in the new Constitution), at which more than 83% of the electorate participated. Aquino's Lakas ng Bayan coalition secured 180 of the 200 elective seats in the House of Representatives and 22 of the 24 seats in the Senate.

In August 1987 Ramos and troops loyal to Aquino averted a serious coup attempt, when rebel officers (led by Col Gregorio Honasan, an officer closely associated with Enrile) occupied the army headquarters, and captured a radio and television station. In the intense fighting that ensued in Manila and Cebu, 53 people were killed. Honasan and his supporters fled the following day, successfully evading capture by government forces until December. (Honasan, however, escaped from detention in April 1988.) In December 1990 a military court sentenced 81 members of the armed forces to prison terms of up to 32 years for their part in the rebellion.

In October 1988 Marcos and his wife, Imelda, were indicted in the USA and charged with the illegal transfer into the country of some US $100m. that had allegedly been obtained by embezzlement and racketeering. Marcos was said to be too ill to attend the proceedings. In November thousands of civilian supporters of Marcos entered Manila and distributed leaflets demanding a military rebellion to overthrow Aquino, before being dispersed by the armed forces. In February 1989 Laurel (who had formally dissociated himself from Aquino in August) visited Marcos in hospital in Hawaii, and began to campaign for Marcos to be permitted to return to the Philippines. In May Marcos's NP was revived, with Laurel as President and Enrile as Secretary-General.

In September 1989 the Philippine Government began the first of 35 planned civil suits against Marcos *in absentia*, following charges of corruption filed in Manila in July 1987. After Marcos's death in Hawaii at the end of September 1989, the opposition, particularly Laurel, aligned themselves with Marcos loyalists to exert pressure on Aquino to allow Marcos a funeral in the Philippines. In October the Supreme Court upheld (by a narrow majority) its previous ruling prohibiting the return of Marcos's body, in response to a petition, submitted by the former President's supporters, asking the court to overrule the ban. The trial of Imelda Marcos, on charges of fraud and of the illegal transfer of stolen funds into the USA, began in New York in April 1990; she was acquitted of all charges in July.

In December 1989 an abortive coup was staged by members of two elite military units, in collusion with the now illicit RAM and officers loyal to Marcos. Aquino subsequently addressed a rally of 100,000 supporters, during which she accused Laurel and Enrile (who were both included in an eight-member provisional junta named by the rebels) of involvement in the coup attempt. At the end of August 1990 Aquino expressed willingness to hold discussions with both dissident troops (who had perpetrated a series of bombings of allegedly corrupt businesses owned by US interests or associated with the Aquino Government) and communist rebels (who had unilaterally declared a cease-fire in Manila and in northern areas affected by an earthquake in July), in an effort to achieve a general reconciliation. Opposition leaders, including Enrile (who had been charged with rebellion), were also invited to attend. In early September Aquino belatedly suspended offensives against the NPA in the affected areas. Later that month, however, the NPA ended the truce and threatened to intensify the insurgency. The dissident members of the armed forces also continued their campaign to destabilize the Government: between mid-August and the beginning of October about 40 incendiary devices were planted (allegedly by members of the armed forces) in and around Manila.

In July 1991 Ramos resigned as Secretary of National Defense in order to contest the presidential election (scheduled for 1992). Having failed to secure the nomination for the presidential election of the ruling party, Laban ng Demokratikong Pilipino (LDP, formed in 1988 by members of pro-Government parties), Ramos, with Aquino's endorsement, resigned from the LDP and registered a new party, EDSA-LDP, with the support of 25 former LDP members of Congress. (EDSA was the popular

acronym for the Epifanio de los Santos Avenue, the main site of
the February 1986 uprising.) The party, which subsequently
altered its title to Lakas ng EDSA, formed an alliance with the
National Union of Christian Democrats to become Lakas-
NUCD. The Roman Catholic Church extended its support to the
LDP's candidate, Ramon Mitra, and criticized Ramos, a Protestant, for his involvement in the Marcos regime.

In February 1992 a prominent human rights organization,
Amnesty International, published a report accusing the Aquino
administration of acquiescence in violations of human rights by
the armed forces. The report, which followed previous documents critical of the Aquino Government, alleged that 550 extra-
judicial killings had taken place during 1988–91. The armed
forces denied the report's findings, and accused Amnesty International of ignoring rebel atrocities. The NPA had killed 563
members of the armed forces between January and April 1991.

On 11 May 1992 elections took place to select the President,
Vice-President, 12 senators, 200 members of the House of Representatives and 17,014 local officials. More than 100 people
were killed in outbreaks of violence during the pre-election
period. Ramos was subsequently elected to the presidency, with
23.6% of the votes cast; his closest rivals were Miriam Defensor
Santiago, a former Secretary of Agrarian Reform (with 19.7%)
and Eduardo Cojuangco (Aquino's estranged cousin, whose wing
of the NP had been renamed the Nationalist People's Coalition
—NPC) (18.2%). The election was relatively free and fair, and
Santiago's allegations of electoral fraud were largely unsubstantiated. (In February 1996 Santiago's electoral protest was
finally quashed by the Supreme Court on a technicality.) The
success of Ramos and the high level of support for Santiago
(whose electoral campaign had emphasized the need to eradicate corruption) was widely regarded as a rejection of traditional patronage party politics, since neither candidate was
supported by a large-scale party organization. In the legislative
elections, however, the LDP (the only party that had local bases
in every province) won 16 of the 24 seats in the Senate and 89 of
the 200 elective seats in the House of Representatives.

Following his inauguration on 30 June 1992, Ramos formed a
new administration that included six members of the outgoing
Government, among them Gen. Renato de Villa, who remained
Secretary of National Defense, and many senior business executives. Despite his party's poor representation in Congress,
Ramos managed to gain the support of Cojuangco's NPC, the
Liberal Party and 55 defectors (now known as Laban) from the
LDP, to form a 'rainbow coalition', comprising 145 of the 200
elected members of the House of Representatives. The Senate
remained nominally under the control of the LDP, but Ramos
ensured that he maintained good relations with individual
senators.

In July 1992 Ramos formed the Presidential Anti-Crime Commission (PACC), to combat organized crime in the Philippines.
Joseph Estrada, who was elected Vice-President with a large
majority, following the withdrawal of his presidential candidacy
to support that of Cojuangco, was appointed to head the Commission. A principal concern of the PACC was the alarming
increase in abduction, mainly of wealthy ethnic Chinese Filipinos, for ransom, owing to its detrimental effect on investment.
It emerged that members of the Philippine National Police
(PNP) were largely responsible for the abductions, and in
August the Chief of Police resigned. In April 1993, following a
complete review of the PNP, Ramos ordered the discharge of
hundreds of personnel, including 63 of the 194 senior officers.
There was also a serious decline in public respect for the
judiciary, following allegations that seven Supreme Court
judges were accepting bribes from drugs-dealers and other
criminal syndicates. In February Congress adopted legislation
(which was signed into law in December) to reinstate the death
penalty, which had been banned under the 1987 Constitution
with a provision for its reintroduction under extreme circumstances.

On assuming power, Ramos undertook to give priority to the
restoration of order by persuading mutinous right-wing soldiers,
communist insurgents and Muslim separatists to abandon their
armed struggle. In July 1992 two communist leaders were
conditionally released, and Ramos submitted to Congress an
amnesty proclamation for about 4,500 members of the NPA, the
MNLF and renegade former members of the armed forces who
had already applied for amnesty. In August the National Unification Commission (NUC) was formed to consult rebel groups
and formulate a viable amnesty programme. Later that month
Ramos ordered the temporary release from prison of more

communist leaders, including the Commander of the NPA,
Romulo Kintanar, and the NDF Spokesman, Saturnino Ocampo,
and also of 16 rebel soldiers. In the same month the Government
began discussions with exiled representatives of the NDF in the
Netherlands.

In September 1992 Ramos repealed anti-subversion legislation, in place since 1957, that proscribed the CPP. However,
the exiled leadership of the NDF issued a statement to the effect
that the CPP would continue its armed struggle, although there
was a widening division within the CPP over the issue of co-
operation with the NUC. Jose Maria Sison, a founder member of
the CPP who had been based in the Netherlands since his
release from prison in 1986, resumed the party chairmanship in
April 1992. The party's command structure was thrown into
disarray, however, as his election to the leadership was not
recognized by all party members. In December Sison, who
adopted an intransigent stance towards the Government's peace
moves and who initiated a (largely ignored) purge in the CPP of
those members who had deviated from Maoist orthodoxy,
accused his opponents, including Kintanar, of collusion with the
Ramos administration.

In July 1993 the CPP's influential Manila-Rizal regional
committee publicly broke away from the CPP Central Committee led by Sison. This followed the attempted dissolution by
Sison of the region's leading committee and its armed unit, the
Alex Boncayao Brigade (ABB), accused of factionalism and
military excesses. The Manila-Rizal organization, which comprised about 40% of CPP members, was subsequently joined by
the CPP regional committee of the Visayas. In October four
communist leaders, including Kintanar and Arturo Tabara, the
Secretary-General of the Central Philippine Command of the
NPA, were expelled from the CPP and the NPA for refusing to
recognize the authority of Sison.

Negotiations between the Government and the NDF in 1994–
96 were marred by the failure of the two sides to agree terms for
the granting of immunity for NDF members and the arrest and
subsequent release of a number of leading members of the
organization. In March 1997, however, peace negotiations,
which had resumed between the Government and the NDF in
the Netherlands, were reported to have achieved some success.
In March 1998, despite the intensification during 1997 of both
attacks by communist rebels and security operations by the
Government, the Government and the NDF signed a Comprehensive Agreement on Respect for Human Rights and International Law, the first of four agreements that would complete
the peace process.

In September 1992 seven military renegades, including Honasan, were granted passes of safe conduct to enable peace talks
to proceed. In December the seven fugitives emerged from
hiding to sign a preliminary agreement to take part in talks with
the Government. Discussions between the NUC and representatives of the RAM and the Young Officers' Union (YOU—a
progressive offshoot of the RAM, which was alleged to have
played an important role in the December 1989 coup attempt)
began in January 1993, were suspended (owing to disagreement), resumed in February and were subsequently suspended
again. In February 1994 it was announced that peace negotiations with the RAM and the YOU would remain suspended,
pending the release of six military detainees. The following
month Ramos proclaimed a general amnesty for all rebels and
for members of the security forces charged with offences committed during counter-insurgency operations, as recommended
by the NUC in a report submitted to Ramos in July 1993; the
amnesty did not, however, include persons convicted of torture,
arson, massacre, rape and robbery. The RAM rejected the
amnesty on the grounds that it failed to address the causes of
the rebellion, while Ocampo dismissed the proclamation as
being biased against the communist rebels. Following agreement between the RAM and the Government during 1994 on
certain government programmes and the issue of electoral
reform, in 1995 formal negotiations resumed. In October the
RAM and the YOU signed a peace agreement with the Government, which provided for the return of the rebels' military
weapons within 90 days and the reintegration of members of the
two organizations into the armed forces.

In August 1992 Ramos gave permission (which had been
denied by Aquino) for the remains of Ferdinand Marcos to be
brought from Hawaii to the Philippines for a private burial in
his native province of Ilocos Norte. In September 1993 Marcos's
remains were returned to the Philippines, and a funeral service
was conducted in Ilocos Norte, attended by only a few thousand

supporters. Later that month Imelda Marcos (who had returned to the Philippines in 1991, with Aquino's permission, to stand trial on charges of fraud and tax evasion) was convicted of corruption and sentenced to 18 years' imprisonment; she remained at liberty pending an appeal against the conviction. In February 1994 a district court in Honolulu, Hawaii, awarded US $2,000m. in punitive damages to 10,000 Filipinos tortured under President Marcos's administration, following a court ruling in October 1992 that victims of abuses of human rights under the Marcos regime could sue his estate for compensation. Imelda Marcos announced that she would appeal against the decision. Further charges of embezzlement were filed against her in April and June 1994 and in September 1995.

In March 1995 Imelda Marcos announced that she would seek election to the House of Representatives. Comelec disqualified her candidacy, ruling that she failed to fulfil residency criteria; however, she appealed to the Supreme Court to overturn the disqualification, and was allowed to contest the election pending the outcome of her appeal. Although her candidacy was successful, she was not permitted to take her seat in Congress until November, following a ruling in her favour by the Supreme Court. Marcos's son, Ferdinand 'Bong-Bong' Marcos II, contested (unsuccessfully) a seat in the Senate, and in July was sentenced to nine years' imprisonment following a conviction for tax evasion. He was released in August.

On 8 May 1995 elections were held to contest 12 of the 24 seats in the Senate, the 204 elective seats in the House of Representatives, 76 provincial governorships and more than 17,000 local government positions. Prior to the elections, in which an estimated 80% of all eligible voters participated, more than 80 people were killed in campaign violence. During the campaign Ramos declared that the elections should be regarded as a referendum on his three years in office and emphasized his administration's progress towards economic liberalization. Lakas-NUCD formed an electoral alliance with a small Mindanao-based moderate Islamic party for the election to the House of Representatives, in order to attract broad national support.

In the event the ruling coalition won the vast majority (about 70%) of seats in the House of Representatives and an electoral alliance between Lakas-NUCD and the LDP (Lakas-Laban) won nine of the 12 seats in the Senate. One of the three opposition seats was secured by Honasan, despite a campaign by Aquino against his candidacy. In his opening address to Congress in July Ramos urged the adoption of radical legislation to reduce public bureaucracy and eliminate corruption in the police force and in the justice system.

During 1995–97 Ramos's supporters campaigned to amend the constitutional stipulation that restricted the President to a single term of office; the Senate, however, opposed any such amendment. In September a rally organized by Cardinal Sin (to coincide with the 25th anniversary of the declaration of martial law by Marcos), to protest against any constitutional changes aimed at enabling Ramos to contest the forthcoming presidential election, was attended by more than 500,000 demonstrators. The rally was supported by Corazon Aquino as well as opposition politicians and influential business executives, who attributed the rapid decline of the peso, in part, to the insecurity created by speculation regarding Ramos's ambitions for a second term of office. Prior to the rally, in an attempt to defuse negative sentiment, Ramos finally stated categorically that he would not contest the presidential election.

The formation of an opposition grouping, the Laban ng Makabayang Masang Pilipino (LaMMP—Struggle of Nationalist Filipino Masses), to contest the elections scheduled for May 1998 was announced in June 1997. The LaMMP was composed of the Partido ng Masang Pilipino, led by Estrada, the LDP, led by Edgardo Angara (which had withdrawn from its alliance with Lakas-NUCD in February 1996), and the NCP, led by Ernesto Maceda. In December Estrada and Angara were formally endorsed as the LaMMP's presidential and vice-presidential candidates respectively. By the end of the registration period in February 83 candidates had registered to contest the presidential election, of whom 72 were subsequently disqualified by Comelec. Following the withdrawal of Imelda Marcos in April, a total of 10 candidates contested the election. The campaign was characterized by an emphasis on personalities and scandals and failed to address substantive policy issues. Estrada's immense popularity was apparently unaffected by personal attacks, including an unsubstantiated allegation that he had attempted to assassinate Ramos, and by the opposition of the Catholic Church to his candidacy, owing to his reputedly dissolute lifestyle.

Elections to the presidency, vice-presidency, the Senate, the House of Representatives, provincial governorships and local government positions took place on 11 May 1998; an estimated 80% of the electorate participated in the polls. Although an estimated 51 people were killed in pre-election violence (mostly in the southern province of Mindanao), the elections were considered relatively orderly and free. Estrada was subsequently elected to the presidency with 39.9% of the votes cast. His closest rival was the Lakas-NUCD candidate, Jose de Venezia (who was responsible for progress in negotiations with both the Islamist separatists and the NDF), who secured 15.9% of the votes. The vice-presidency was won by Gloria Macapagal Arroyo (the daughter of former President Diosdado Macapagal), who had been second in the opinion polls as a presidential candidate before agreeing to support de Venezia's candidacy. She won 47% of the votes cast, while her closest rival, Angara, secured 21%. According to Comelec, seven of the victorious senators were members of the LaMMP, while the other five were Lakas-NUCD candidates. However, Lakas-NUCD dominated the House of Representatives, gaining 106 seats compared with only 66 for the LaMMP. In a development indicative of the weakness of the party system, many congressional members subsequently defected to Estrada's party, which was renamed Laban ng Masang Pilipino (Fight of the Filipino Masses).

Estrada's election altered the political climate considerably for the family and former associates of Marcos. In June 1998 the Solicitor-General, Romeo de la Cruz, recommended that the Supreme Court acquit Imelda Marcos of charges of corruption. A ruling by the Supreme Court in January had upheld her appeal against one charge of corruption but dismissed an appeal against her conviction in 1993 on a second corruption charge, which carried a sentence of between nine and 12 years' imprisonment. She remained at liberty pending the reconsideration of the verdict by the court. Ramos, however, dismissed de la Cruz and his appointed successor, Silvestre Bello, and withdrew the Government's petition for acquittal. Marcos was, nevertheless, acquitted in October 1998, although numerous civil suits remained pending against her. In December Marcos announced plans to initiate a legal appeal to recover 500,000m. pesos in assets allegedly belonging to her husband, including shares in the Philippine Long Distance Telephone Co, the San Miguel Corporation and Philippine Airlines (PAL). Marcos claimed her husband had entrusted the money to his close associates who had refused to return it. The election of the Marcoses' daughter, Imee, to Congress and of their son, Ferdinand Jr, to the governorship of Ilocos Norte was indicative of the general rehabilitation of the Marcos family. Estrada favoured a negotiated settlement with the Marcos family to resolve the dispute over funds misappropriated by the former President and also gave his support to the burial of Marcos in the cemetery of National Heroes. However, popular outrage and public protests supported by Aquino and Ramos towards the end of June prompted Imelda Marcos to postpone the burial indefinitely in the national interest.

Following a ruling in January 1998 by the Swiss Supreme Court that the total sum of US $560m. of Marcos's wealth in Swiss bank accounts be released (to be disbursed by the Philippine courts), the transfer of $280m. was halted, owing to an appeal by Marcos's lawyers. The final appeal was rejected by the Swiss Supreme Court in June. In February 1999 the Marcos family agreed to pay a total of $150m. in damages to 9,539 victims of human rights abuses. However, the court subsequently ruled against the release of funds from those sequestered by the Government from Swiss bank accounts. In March 1999 the Supreme Court upheld a 1990 decision by the Bureau of Internal Revenue assessing the unpaid inheritance tax owed by the heirs of Ferdinand Marcos at 23,500m. pesos.

Estrada was inaugurated as President on 30 June 1998. In his inaugural address he reiterated campaign pledges to eradicate poverty and corruption, but also assured the business sector that he would continue Ramos's programme of economic reform. His new Cabinet, which elicited widespread approval, comprised members from a wide political and social spectrum, including wealthy ethnic Chinese business executives, former associates of Marcos, and allies from Estrada's career as mayor and senator, as well as former activists from the communist movement and left-wing non-governmental organizations. Five members of Lakas-NUCD were allocated portfolios and Ramos accepted a post as Senior Adviser. Estrada was, however, criticized for appointing friends and relatives to lucrative and influential positions. Additional concerns about a reversion to the Marcos era of 'cronyism' were raised by the return to prominence of former Marcos associates, some of whom had made substantial financial contributions to Estrada's presidential campaign fund. Estrada also dismissed political adversaries, such as the Chairman of the Subic Bay Metropolitan Authority, Richard Gordon, whose appointment had previously been extended by Ramos for a further six years.

Estrada's administration was criticized for factionalism, although supporters maintained that the competing aims of several influential groups minimized the risk of corruption and ensured balanced advice. In spite of widespread apprehension regarding his leadership abilities, Estrada was credited with several successes during his first year in office. His creation in July 1998 of the Presidential Anti-Organized Crime Task Force resulted in a dramatic reduction in kidnappings for ransom. The elimination of several large organized syndicates was achieved by granting autonomy from the PNP (which had been implicated in many incidents) to the head of the Task Force, Brig.-Gen. Panfilo Lacson. (Lacson's appointment, however, attracted criticism from human rights organizations, owing to his conviction with other military officers in 1993 for the illegal detention and torture of anti-Government dissidents in the 1970s.) Estrada effectively abolished 'pork barrel' funds (state funds from which congressmen finance projects in their constituencies), which had led to corruption and the reinforcement of patronage politics. He was also praised for his handling of a crisis involving the national airline, which was threatened with collapse and did cease operations briefly in September/October 1998. Estrada unexpectedly eschewed the populist solution of allocating funds to the ailing airline in favour of a private-sector arrangement to prevent its closure. Subsequently, however, Estrada became the target of renewed criticism in the media, some of it apparently justified, which he attributed to a conspiracy to discredit his administration. In February 1999 *The Manila Times* described Estrada as an 'unwitting godfather' to an allegedly improper government contract. Estrada sued the newspaper for 101m. pesos and only abandoned his legal complaint after he received an apology in April. Concerns about the administration's attitude towards the freedom of the press were exacerbated by an effective advertising boycott of the *Philippine Daily Inquirer*, following claims by Estrada in July that the newspaper was biased against him.

The hitherto strained relationship between Estrada and Ramos deteriorated in March 1999 when the Senate Blue Ribbon Committee, which had been established to investigate anomalies in government and was led by a member of Estrada's party, Aquilino Pimentel, recommended the prosecution of Ramos and five members of his Cabinet for the misapplication of public funds to celebrate the centennial anniversary of Philippine independence in June 1998. Ramos was issued with a summons to this effect in April 1999 and was obliged to justify his actions before a newly-formed Independent Citizens' Committee. Ramos claimed that the accusations were politically motivated and designed to distract attention from investigations into misconduct by Estrada's friends and relatives. The Committee's final report recommended the indictment for graft of the former Vice-President, Salvador Laurel, who had led the centennial celebration committee, and fines for Ramos and his Secretary of Finance, Salvador Enrique, for failing to prevent Laurel's abuses.

In late 1999 Estrada's hitherto excellent popularity ratings began to decline amid increasing concern that 'cronyism' and corruption in his administration were undermining the gains secured by the overthrow of Marcos in 1986. In August 1999 Aquino and Cardinal Sin mobilized 100,000 demonstrators in a Rally for Democracy held in protest against such perceived erosions, in particular government plans to amend the 1987 Constitution. Estrada's stated aim in amending the Constitution was to extend economic deregulation by altering the provisions limiting to 40% foreign ownership of land and public utilities. While in any case opposed to these proposals, critics feared the potential removal from the Constitution of the stipulation limiting the President to a single term of office. Later in August 1999 Estrada relaunched the ruling coalition, restyling it the Lapian ng Masang Pilipino (LAMP—Party of the Filipino Masses) in order to support his campaign for constitutional change, which was termed Constitutional Correction for Development (Concord).

Estrada's popularity was also adversely affected by his failure to fulfil his pledges to alleviate poverty. Little progress had been made with regard to land redistribution or 'food security' apart from the rehousing of 25,000 poor in Manila in the year to September 1999. The perceived lack of focus in economic policy and Estrada's failure to enact reformist economic legislation attracted further censure.

Following a report by the World Bank in November 1999 alleging that 20% of the Philippine budget was lost to corruption, Estrada pledged to intensify investigations of officials suspected of dishonesty. (The former chief of police, Roberto Lastimoso, and the former Secretary of the Interior and Local Government, Ronaldo Puno, were indicted on charges of graft in February 2000.) In the same month, in a further attempt to dispel criticism, Estrada established the EDSA People Power Commission to promote the ideals of the 1986 uprising; its 15 members included Aquino, Ramos and Estrada. In order to dispel allegations of media censorship, the advertising boycott against the *Philippine Daily Inquirer* was lifted. Also in November Lacson was appointed to head the PNP; having achieved significant reductions in kidnappings for ransom in his previous post, his promotion received popular support but prompted concern from human rights activists, who condemned his methods. All of these measures, however, proved inadequate to reverse a trend that was compounded by the unexpected resignation of the respected Secretary of Finance, Edgardo Espiritu, in January 2000 and his subsequent accusations concerning the undue influence exerted by unelected associates of Estrada. In January 2000 Estrada responded to growing public dissatisfaction by announcing the reform of his administration. He dismissed his informal advisers, replacing them with a six-member Economic Co-ordinating Council to promote coherence in economic affairs, and recruited five eminent business leaders to act as an economic advisory council. The proposed constitutional reforms were suspended and replaced by plans to achieve economic liberalization through legislation. Estrada's attempts to improve his popularity were, however, swiftly undermined by the testimony in January of the Chairman of the Securities and Exchange Commission (SEC), Perfecto Yasay, to a Senate Committee investigating possible illegal share trading. Yasay alleged that Estrada had pressed him to exonerate his close associate, Dante Tan, who was suspected of illegally manipulating the share price of BW Resources Corporation. Estrada denied the intervention, although he admitted telephoning Yasay four times in relation to the investigation. Despite frequent rumours of an impending coup attempt and a request for Estrada's resignation from Teofisto Guingona, the President of Lakas-NUCD, an attempt to mobilize anti-Estrada sentiment in a mass protest in early April received very little support.

In October 2000 the Philippines was engulfed by a political crisis that arose as a result of allegations, made to an investigative committee of the Senate by the Governor of Ilocos Sur, Luis Singson, that President Estrada had accepted large sums of money as bribes from illegal gambling businesses. Despite the President's denial of these allegations in a televised statement to the nation, in late October opposition parties announced their intention to begin the process of impeaching him. Earlier in the month Vice-President Gloria Macapagal Arroyo had announced her resignation from the Cabinet, in which she served as Secretary of Social Welfare and Development. The fact that she did not relinquish the vice-presidency at the same time led to speculation that she was preparing to succeed Estrada in the event of his being forced out of office. Following her resignation from the Cabinet, Macapagal Arroyo established an alliance of opposition parties.

In early November 2000 anti-Government protests throughout the Philippines intensified. Vice-President Macapagal Arroyo announced that a transitional government was prepared to assume power should the President resign. On 13 November the House of Representatives endorsed the impeachment of the President after more than one-third of its members signed a petition favouring this action. Supporters of Estrada condemned the impeachment proceedings as unconstitutional since they had not been submitted to a formal vote in the House of Representatives. (The Speaker of the House had ruled that such a vote was unnecessary because more than one-third of its members had signed the petition.) Estrada himself welcomed an impeachment trial in the Senate as an opportunity to prove his innocence and declared that he would not resign. On 20 November the Senate formally summoned the President.

The legal action pursued by Estrada in order to force the Senate to dismiss the charges against him was unsuccessful, and at the beginning of December 2000 he pleaded not guilty to charges of bribery, corruption, betrayal of public trust and violation of the Constitution. Having begun in early December, Estrada's impeachment trial in the Senate was adjourned indefinitely in mid-January 2001, after prosecutors failed to obtain the disclosure of bank records as evidence against him. This effective acquittal of the President provoked mass demonstrations against him, although it was notable that the majority of the participants were members of the middle class. Estrada had lost the support of many members of his Cabinet, the police and the armed forces, and, in response to a request by Vice-President Gloria Macapagal Arroyo, the Supreme Court declared the presidency to be vacant. Macapagal Arroyo was sworn in as the new President on 20 January. Estrada had earlier offered to hold a presidential election in May at which he would not be a candidate. He did not formally resign, however, in response to the Supreme Court's declaration.

By late January 2001 most of the positions in President Macapagal Arroyo's new Cabinet had been filled. The new administration moved quickly to prevent Estrada, members of his family and his associates from leaving the Philippines and insisted that the former President would be prosecuted for his alleged crimes. The manner in which Macapagal Arroyo had assumed the presidency, however, exacerbated the continued political crisis and raised fears of an impending military *coup d'état*. Estrada continued to assert that he remained the legitimate Head of State and, in an address to his supporters, pledged to take legal action to regain the presidency. In March, however, the Supreme Court affirmed the legitimacy of Macapagal Arroyo's office. In April Estrada was formally indicted for a number of alleged offences, including one of economic plunder, which was punishable by the death penalty. Estrada was arrested for the first time on 16 April and charged with graft and perjury. At the beginning of May there was violent unrest in Manila when supporters of Estrada attempted to storm the presidential palace. Three members of the Senate were arrested for having allegedly conspired to bring down the Government, and President Macapagal Arroyo declared a state of rebellion, which permitted her to deploy the armed forces to quell the unrest. Estrada, who had been rearrested on 25 April, was removed to a detention centre outside Manila, having had his application for bail denied.

Legislative and local elections were held on 14 May 2001. Lakas-NUCD secured 87 seats in the House of Representatives, followed by the NPC with 62. The People Power Coalition (PPC) —a coalition of Lakas-NUCD, the Liberal Party (LP) and several smaller parties which had been formed by President Macapagal Arroyo to contest the election—won eight seats in the Senate, while allies of the Laban ng Demokratikong Pilipino-Puwersa ng Masa (LDP-PnM)—the opposition coalition formed to support Estrada—secured four. The remaining seat went to an independent candidate. President Macapagal Arroyo thus succeeded in securing a majority in both chambers. As a result of the violence which had been endemic throughout the election period, 83 people died. The elections were further marred by reports of widespread corruption.

In early October 2001 Estrada's trial on charges of perjury and plunder finally commenced; he had refused to enter a plea to any of the charges against him at the pre-trial hearings. Later in the month Estrada won an initial victory when the prosecution case for perjury was effectively dismissed; the judge had refused to permit the presentation of crucial evidence owing to a legal technicality. In November, having recommenced, the trial was overshadowed by a feud between two of the judges involved, presiding judge Justice Anacleto Badoy and his senior colleague, Justice Francis Garchitorena. The trial was interrupted further when the chief prosecutor, Aniano Desierto, was accused of corruption. Shortly afterwards the Supreme Court rejected a legal challenge brought by Estrada against his ongoing trial and affirmed the constitutionality of the anti-plunder law under which he was being tried. At the end of November the Supreme Court suspended Justice Garchitorena following complaints that cases under his remit, including that of Estrada, were proceeding too slowly. In December Justice Badoy was also suspended indefinitely, following defence allegations that he lacked impartiality. The trial was subsequently adjourned and resumed in January 2002 in a special anti-graft court. In February Estrada instructed his entire legal team to resign in protest at what he alleged to be a prejudiced court. The Govern-

ment stated that the trial would proceed once it had appointed new legal representation for the defendant, despite Estrada's insistence that he would deny government lawyers access to the evidence amassed by his defence team. Estrada's trial continued to proceed, slowly, in early 2003.

In October 2001 Jose Miguel Arroyo, husband of President Macapagal Arroyo, was investigated by the Senate over allegations that he had diverted funds from a state lottery in order to finance electoral campaigns for prospective senators. In the same month Imelda Marcos was rearrested on four charges of corruption, connected to the suspected plunder of the economy under the regime of her late husband, before being released on bail. In November the widow of President Marcos appeared in court and denied all the charges. She was reported to be seeking huge damages from the Government over the claims that had been made against her. In December the court ruled that Imelda Marcos could leave the country for one month to seek medical treatment in the People's Republic of China.

In June 2002 the Government's control over the legislature was threatened when Senator John Osmeña defected to the opposition, depriving the PPC of its narrow majority in the Senate. Owing to the simultaneous absence abroad of another senator, proceedings in the Senate were suspended for almost two months. The Government was weakened further in July when Vice-President Teofisto Guingona announced his resignation from his concurrent position as Secretary of Foreign Affairs, owing largely to his disagreement with the Government's decision to allow the deployment of US troops in the country. Blas Ople was appointed to the post later in that month. In August the Secretary of Education, Culture and Sport, Raul Roco, resigned in protest at the President's endorsement of a corruption investigation being carried out into his use of public money; he was later succeeded by Edilberto de Jesus.

In October 2002 the Senate gave its assent to the Absentee Voting Bill, which rendered Filipino citizens living and working abroad eligible to vote in future legislative and presidential elections. The bill was enacted in February 2003. In November President Macapagal Arroyo announced her intention to adopt a strict policy aimed at ending the corruption apparently endemic within the Government. Shortly afterwards the Secretary of Agriculture, Leonardo Montemayor, and the Secretary of the Environment and Natural Resources, Heherson Alvarez, were dismissed from the Cabinet; they were replaced, respectively, by Luis Lorenzo, Jr, and Elisea Gozun. In the following month the Director-General of the National Economic and Development Authority, Dante Canlas, resigned from his post at the request of the President; he was replaced by Romulo Neri. Later in December the President announced that she did not intend to contest the presidential elections scheduled to take place in 2004, claiming that her decision was motivated by a desire to spare the country further political division. She subsequently stated her intention to revive the Council of State, an advisory body originally established by her father, Diosdado Macapagal, during his time in power, whilst holding exploratory talks with leading members of the opposition with the possible aim of forming a 'government of national unity'. Meanwhile, Secretary of Justice Hernando Perez resigned and denied corruption allegations that had been made against him. The justice portfolio was assumed by the former Secretary of Public Works and Highways, Simeon Datumanong, who was succeeded by Bayani Fernando. At the same time the Secretary of Agrarian Reform, Hernani Braganza, became Press Secretary; he was replaced by Roberto Pagdanganan.

Meanwhile, despite Estrada's inclusion of former communist activists in the Government, including the former head of the proscribed NDF, Horacio Morales, Jr, as Secretary of Agrarian Reform, the leadership of the NDF-CPP-NPA condemned his administration. In July 1998 Estrada approved the human rights agreement that had been reached by the NDF and the Ramos administration, and invited the exiled leadership of the NDF to the Philippines to resume peace negotiations. In February 1999, however, Estrada suspended peace talks with the communists following the NPA's abduction of three hostages, including one of the Philippines' most senior military commanders, Brig.-Gen. Victor Obillo. The Government also suspended the Joint Agreement on Safety and Immunity Guarantees, exposing NDF-CPP-NPA members to the risk of arrest. Estrada subsequently agreed to suspend military operations at the end of March to allow for the release of the hostages. A total of five hostages, including Obillo, were released by the NPA in

April, although the communists continued to reject other conditions for negotiations.

At the end of May 1999 the NDF withdrew from peace negotiations in response to the Senate's ratification of a defence treaty with the USA (see below). Estrada, who had already expressed dissatisfaction with the progress of negotiations, subsequently adopted a position of outright hostility towards the movement. The intensification of NPA attacks, including a series of attacks on police stations in southern provinces, however, adversely affected his popularity. The NDF-CPP-NPA were recruiting increasing numbers of members, who were disillusioned with the Estrada administration and the continued social inequalities in the Philippines. In an attempt to divide the communist movement, Estrada entered into negotiations with several breakaway factions, but failed to make substantial progress. In January 2000 the Government suspended military operations against the communists to facilitate the release of two NPA hostages, whom the NDF offered to release within six weeks in an attempt to foster an improved atmosphere for negotiations. In December Estrada announced that a peace agreement had been concluded with the Revolutionary Proletarian Army (RPA)-ABB. The agreement, which applied only to the central Philippines, was accompanied by a presidential amnesty for some political prisoners whose death sentences had been upheld by the Supreme Court, and by the release of an additional 235 political detainees. In the same month the NPA rejected an offer by the Government of a truce and subsequently attacked a police station in Sorsogan province, killing one policeman.

In April 2001, after obtaining the agreement of NDF leaders in February, the Government of President Macapagal Arroyo held its first round of peace talks with the NDF in Oslo, Norway. The talks were reported to have made some progress, with both sides agreeing to undertake confidence-building measures, including the release of political prisoners. Further discussions were held at the end of May 2001. However, the negotiations were suspended in June when the NDF was implicated in the assassination of Congressman Rodolfo Aguinaldo during a campaign rally near Manila. The Government insisted that the NDF was to carry out no further political killings during the peace process. However, the rebels refused, claiming that such actions were integral to their political agenda. In November a total of 28 people were killed on the island of Mindanao when fighting broke out between the NPA and government soldiers. Despite the renewal of violence, however, exiled NDF members announced shortly afterwards that they had agreed to resume peace talks with the Government in Oslo in December 2001. In the same month President Macapagal Arroyo announced a temporary cease-fire with the NDF, following its offer to suspend hostilities for one month if the Government made a reciprocal gesture. However, the arrival of US troops in the Philippines in 2002 (see below) threatened further peace negotiations, as the NDF continued to oppose any US involvement in the country. In May President Macapagal Arroyo called off further peace negotiations after a number of political assassinations occurred.

In August 2002 the USA added the CPP and the NPA to its list of international terrorist organizations and requested that the Government of the Netherlands cease benefit payments to all group members resident there. In the same month government representatives met with members of the NDF in Quezon City, with the intention of resuming peace talks. However, the chairman of the CPP, Jose Maria Sison, continued to oppose any negotiations while President Macapagal Arroyo remained in power. In October the Government formally designated the NDF a terrorist organization, while emphasizing that it remained willing to continue peace negotiations. In December the NPA rejected the Government's offer of a unilateral cease-fire over the Christmas period. In January 2003 police officials announced that they intended to charge Sison with involvement in several murders, including those of Congressman Rodolfo Aguinaldo and former NPA army leader Romulo Kintanar (who was killed by unidentified gunmen in that month), and to seek his extradition to face trial in the Philippines.

During 1986 the Aquino Government conducted negotiations to seek a solution to the conflict with Muslim separatists in the south. A cease-fire was established with the MNLF in September, following an announcement by the Government that it would grant legal and judicial autonomy to four predominantly Muslim provinces in Mindanao. Further talks ensued, under the auspices of the Organization of the Islamic Conference (OIC, see p. 295), and on 5 January 1987 the MNLF signed an agreement to relinquish demands for complete independence in Mindanao, and to accept autonomy. In February 1988, however, the MNLF resumed its offensive against the Government, which had attempted to prevent the MNLF from gaining membership of the OIC (which would imply that the MNLF was regarded as representing an independent state). The 1987 Constitution granted eventual autonomy to Muslim provinces in Mindanao, which had been promised by President Marcos in 1976. In November 1989 a referendum was held, in the country's 13 southern provinces and nine cities in Mindanao, on proposed legislation that envisaged the autonomy of these provinces and cities, with direct elections to a unicameral legislature in each province; this contrasted with the MNLF's demand for autonomy in 23 provinces, to be granted without a referendum. Four provinces (Lanao del Sur, Maguindanao, Tawi-Tawi and Sulu) voted in favour of the government proposal, and formed the autonomous region of Muslim Mindanao.

In February 1990 the candidate favoured by Aquino, Zacaria Candao (formerly the legal representative of the MNLF), was elected to the governorship of Muslim Mindanao. In October the autonomous regional government was granted limited executive powers. The MNLF boycotted the election, on the grounds that the provisions for autonomy were more limited than those reached with Marcos in 1976. Under Ramos's programme of reconciliation, the MNLF participated in discussions with the NUC. In October 1992 the leader of the MNLF, Nur Misuari, agreed to return to the Philippines from exile in Libya to facilitate negotiations. In January 1993 talks were suspended, and violence in Mindanao escalated prior to the impending elections for the region's Governor and Assembly. At the elections, which took place on 25 March, a former ambassador, Lininding Pangandaman, won 72% of the votes cast in the gubernatorial contest, with the unofficial support of Ramos; 81% of the electorate voted.

In April 1993 exploratory discussions in Jakarta, Indonesia, between Nur Misuari and representatives of the Philippine Government led to an agreement on the resumption of formal peace talks under the auspices of the OIC. Further exploratory talks took place in Saudi Arabia in June, prior to the first formal negotiations in October in Jakarta, where the MNLF demanded the creation of an autonomous Islamic state in the south, as agreed in 1976. In November 1993 the two sides signed a memorandum of understanding and an interim cease-fire was agreed.

The second round of formal peace negotiations between the Government and the MNLF took place in Jakarta in April. Agreement was subsequently reached on government administration in the proposed autonomous region, Islamic law, education and revenue-sharing between Manila and the autonomous zones. In August 1995 Misuari agreed for the first time to a referendum (which was required under the Constitution) prior to the establishment of an autonomous zone, but demanded the immediate establishment of a provisional MNLF government to ensure that the referendum was conducted fairly.

In June 1996 it was announced that the MNLF and the Government had finally reached agreement on a proposal by Ramos for the establishment of a transitional administrative council, to be known as the Southern Philippines Council for Peace and Development (SPCPD), which was to derive powers from the Office of the President. The five-member SPCPD, which was to be headed by Misuari, was to co-ordinate peacekeeping and development efforts in 14 provinces and 10 cities in Mindanao, with the assistance of an 81-member Consultative Assembly and a religious advisory council. After a period of three years a referendum was to be conducted in each province and city to determine whether it would join the existing Autonomous Region of Muslim Mindanao (ARMM—the MNLF had abandoned its demands for autonomy in 23 provinces in Mindanao). In July 1996 government officials announced that, under the peace agreement, Muslims were to be allocated one cabinet post, and were to be granted representation in state-owned companies and constitutional commissions. In addition, Ramos offered to support the candidacy of Misuari in the forthcoming gubernatorial election in the ARMM. In early September the Government and the MNLF signed a final draft of the peace agreement in Jakarta. In the same month elections took place peacefully in the ARMM for the region's Governor and Assembly; Misuari, who, as agreed, contested the gubernatorial election with the support of Lakas-NUCD, was elected unopposed. In October it was announced that Misuari had been officially appointed Chairman of the SPCPD. In March 1997 more than 1,000 former members of the MNLF were integrated into the armed forces under the terms of the peace accord.

In August 2001, after some delay, the referendum was finally held. As a result, the city of Marawi and the province of Basilan elected to join the ARMM. However, 10 provinces and 13 cities rejected the offer of membership and the electoral turn-out was low. In November around 600 supporters of Governor Misuari (who had been dismissed from the leadership of the MNLF in April owing to his widespread unpopularity) led an armed uprising against military and police outposts on the island of Jolo, resulting in the deaths of more than 100 people. The violence was reportedly intended to prevent an election to the governorship of the ARMM, scheduled for late November, from taking place. By instigating the rebellion Misuari had violated the terms of his five-year peace accord with the Government, although he claimed that by holding an election the Government was itself breaking the terms of the agreement. Shortly afterwards President Macapagal Arroyo suspended Misuari from his post. A spokesman for Misuari claimed that the attacks were in retaliation for an alleged army raid on his supporters in the previous month. Later in November Misuari and six of his supporters were arrested by the Malaysian authorities for attempting to gain illegal entry into the country. On 26 November polls to elect a new governor, vice-governor and 44 regional legislators for the province were conducted. The turn-out was low, a fact partly attributed to the escalating military presence in the region. The next day government forces launched air strikes on MNLF insurgents who remained in the city of Zamboanga, killing 25 rebels and one civilian. As they attempted to flee, the rebels took several local residents hostage. The next day the hostages were released in return for the rebels' safe passage out of the city, thus bringing an end to the confrontation. In early December the President's favoured candidate, former MNLF member Farouk Hussein, was declared Governor. He immediately urged the establishment of peace in the troubled region and stated that he would seek to open a dialogue with the remaining followers of Misuari and other radical groups in the area, including Abu Sayyaf (see below). Meanwhile, President Macapagal Arroyo indicated that she would prefer the Malaysian authorities to keep Misuari in custody as the Government feared that he would become a focal point for disaffected Muslims upon his return. In January 2002 Misuari was finally deported from Malaysia to face trial in Manila on charges of inciting a rebellion. Misuari remained in custody, awaiting trial, in early 2003, having refused to enter a plea to the charges against him. Meanwhile, in January the four factions comprising the MNLF signed a declaration of unity in advance of the election of a new leadership; significantly, Misuari's name was excluded from the statement, preventing him from regaining the chairmanship of the group.

The Moro Islamic Liberation Front (MILF), an Islamist fundamentalist grouping demanding secession for Mindanao, which was formed as a breakaway movement from the MNLF in 1978, was covered by the government cease-fire agreed in January 1994 but was not a party to the peace talks. The grouping was widely suspected of having taken advantage of negotiations between the MNLF and the Government to strengthen its position, both by an accumulation of arms and the recruitment of young militants disaffected with the compliance of the MNLF. During early 1996 the MILF initiated further attacks on villages and churches in Mindanao and was engaged in clashes with government troops. In April the Government and the MILF agreed to a cease-fire in North Cotabato.

In August 1996, for the first time, MILF and government officials met in Davao City for preliminary peace discussions. The MILF had rejected the peace agreement with the MNLF and continued to demand separatism for 23 provinces in Mindanao. In September a newly-emerged faction, the Mindanao Christian Unified Command (which claimed to comprise forces of 15,000), pledged to take military action to defend Christian territory in Mindanao.

Alternating hostilities and short-term cease-fires, together with a high incidence of abductions by the rebels, characterized relations between the Government and the MILF between late 1996 and late 1997. In November 1997 a further cease-fire agreement was signed in which so-called terrorist acts (including abduction and arson) were banned as well as public executions based on Islamic (*Shari'a*) law. However, when the leader of the MILF, Hashim Salamat, returned to the Philippines (after living in Libya for 20 years) in December, he announced that public executions would continue in defiance of the government ban. Despite further clashes between the MILF and the Government in January 1998, with mutual accusations of violations of the cease-fire agreement, peace negotiations continued in February when the MILF demanded recognition of 13 MILF camps in Mindanao as 'legitimate territories'. In March the two sides agreed to create a 'quick response team' to resolve conflicts and confrontations before they escalated into serious clashes. In October the MILF and the Government agreed to disclose the location of their forces to prevent accidental encounters. However, in January 1999, following a statement by the MILF advocating independence for Mindanao, Estrada conducted successive offensives against the MILF, causing the collapse of the 1997 cease-fire agreement. Up to 60 people were estimated to have died in the ensuing fighting and 90,000 residents were displaced. A new cease-fire was implemented at the end of January 1999 and at the beginning of February the Presidential Adviser, Robert Aventajado, was sent to Mindanao to meet Salamat inside an MILF camp. They agreed to the resumption of peace negotiations and to a meeting between Salamat and Estrada to re-establish goodwill between the two sides. However, Estrada cancelled the meeting, as a result of a dispute over its location and security considerations. In March 1999 Salamat and Nur Misuari met for the first time in 20 years in an attempt to promote the peace process.

Estrada continued to vacillate between supporting the economic development of Mindanao to eradicate insurrection and threatening to eliminate the rebels through military action. Negotiations between the Government and the MILF took place in October 1999, despite MILF protests at continued government attacks on MILF camps in Mindanao. Clashes between the Government and the MILF continued despite reports of a renewed cease-fire agreement in November. Formal peace negotiations, originally scheduled for December, finally commenced in January 2000 but failed to achieve substantial progress. In that month Estrada announced a new anti-insurgency programme, the National Peace and Development Plan, which aimed to remove the causes of insurgency in Mindanao, including poverty, injustice and disease. Peace talks resumed in March after negotiations scheduled for February were suspended owing to escalating violence, during which the Government claimed to have captured an important MILF base, Camp Omar. Several incendiary devices planted on buses in Mindanao in February, which resulted in nearly 50 civilian deaths, were attributed by government sources to the MILF. The MILF, however, claimed that the bombings were perpetrated by government agents in an attempt to justify the intensification of the military campaign against the MILF. At a second round of talks in March a protocol was signed with improved cease-fire provisions, whereby the Government agreed to recognize 39 MILF camps as 'safe areas' while the MILF representatives agreed to carry a government identity card during talks (which they had formerly claimed would represent a surrender of sovereignty). However, intense fighting took place between the MILF and government forces in March and April in Lanao del Norte and Maguindanao Provinces. The MILF, which captured a small town in Lanao del Norte, claimed the attacks were designed to pressure government forces into the immediate cessation of its offensive against the MILF in central Mindanao. The escalation of violence in Mindanao prompted Estrada to convene a meeting of the National Security Council in March.

In May 2000 the MILF was reported to have withdrawn from a section of the Narciso Ramos highway, a strategically significant route which it had controlled for more than five years. The withdrawal appeared to augur well for the resumption of peace negotiations, although the Government held Islamist separatist movements responsible for bomb attacks in Manila and Mindanao in the same month. Peace negotiations between the Government and the MILF resumed later in May, and in June the MILF was reported to be assessing an improved offer of autonomy by the Government. However, the MILF subsequently rejected the extension of the deadline for its acceptance of this offer from 1 July to 15 December, owing to a stipulation that it should meanwhile abandon its pursuit of independence. In late June, following a major offensive, government forces captured the MILF's military headquarters at Abubakar. In July the MILF rejected an offer by the Government to resume peace talks, insisting that such negotiations should be held outside the Philippines in an Islamic country. The MILF also withdrew from a subsequent commitment to resume peace talks in August. In December the MILF appeared to have resumed its armed struggle after an attack on government forces on Jolo island was attributed to the movement. Bomb explosions in Manila at the end of the month, in which more than 20 people died, were blamed on the group.

The new Cabinet appointed by President Macapagal Arroyo in January 2001 included two members who originated from Mindanao. The incoming President stated that she would seek to resume the peace negotiations with the MILF, and in February the Government's military campaign against the MILF ceased. The MILF welcomed the Government's offer to resume talks, although sporadic clashes between its forces and those of the Government continued throughout February. In late March the Government announced that it had reached an agreement with the MILF to resume peace negotiations, and appeared prepared to accept the MILF's condition that renewed talks should be held in an OIC member state. In April the MILF announced a unilateral cease-fire, declaring its intention to observe this until the conclusion of a peace agreement. In June government representatives initiated talks with the MILF in Libya, leading to the conclusion of a preliminary cease-fire agreement in July, which would pave the way for further negotiations aimed at bringing an end to the conflict. Later in the same month a new round of peace talks commenced and in August a further cease-fire agreement was signed. In the same month the MILF also reached an accord with the MNLF. In September sporadic fighting between the MILF and army troops on Mindanao, which led to the deaths of 15 rebels, threatened to undermine the peace process. However, in October the MILF signed a pact with the Government to safeguard the recent cease-fire agreement. In November 2001 the Pentagon Gang—formed in 2000 and mainly comprised of renegade members of the MILF—kidnapped an Italian priest, Father Giuseppe Pierantoni, in northern Manila. The leader of the faction, Akiddin Abdusalem, was shot dead as he attempted to escape from custody after being captured by government troops. In January 2002 39 separatist MILF guerrillas surrendered to government forces, following a series of negotiations, and relinquished a large cache of weapons. While the cease-fire remained in place the army had accused the MILF of encroaching on some villages in southern Mindanao. In February 2002 the MILF announced that it was to hold a new series of discussions with the Government as the situation had been complicated by the arrival of US troops on the island of Basilan (see below). In April government troops finally secured the release of Father Pierantoni after conducting intensive operations against the Pentagon Gang.

In May 2002 the Government signed several new peace agreements with the MILF in Putrajaya, Malaysia. In December the MILF denied responsibility for an ambush on Mindanao that resulted in the deaths of 12 employees of a Canadian mining company, as well as for a bomb attack that killed 17 people in the same week; the group claimed that it continued to observe the cease-fire agreed upon in 2001. Meanwhile, President Macapagal Arroyo succeeded in deterring the US Government from classifying the MILF as an international terrorist organization, citing concerns that the ongoing negotiation process might be undermined by such an action. In February 2003 peace negotiations broke down when government troops assumed control of the important MILF base of Pikit, on Mindanao, in violation of the cease-fire arrangement. The Government claimed that it had ordered the military action in an attempt to capture members of the Pentagon Gang, whom it believed were being sheltered by the MILF. Although President Macapagal Arroyo called for a halt to the operation several days later and proposed a peace agreement, many rebels were believed to have been killed in the fighting that had resulted. Insurgency in the area continued to intensify, as the MILF refused to negotiate unless government troops withdrew from Pikit. A number of attacks occurred, the most serious of which took place in March when a bomb exploded near Davao Airport, resulting in the deaths of 21 people. Although the MILF denied responsibility for the attack, the police subsequently filed charges against 150 of its members; four of the group's leaders were charged with murder and warrants issued for their arrest. In late March the MILF sent representatives for preliminary discussions with government officials in Malaysia, following which a statement was issued declaring that peace negotiations would restart. However, shortly afterwards the MILF was responsible for several further outbreaks of violence in the area and, in May, the Government abandoned peace talks and renewed its military offensive against the organization.

In early June 1994 the Government undertook a major offensive against Abu Sayyaf, a Muslim secessionist group held responsible for numerous attacks, principally on the islands of Jolo and Basilan, to the south of Mindanao. In retaliation for the capture by the armed forces of its base on Jolo, the group took a number of Christians hostage on Basilan, killing 15 of them. All but one of the remaining 21 hostages were released in mid-June, following the apparent payment of a ransom and the intercession of the MNLF. Later in June government troops captured the group's main headquarters in Basilan. In early August the group's remaining hostage was released, and the authorities announced that Abu Sayyaf had been 'eliminated'. In April 1995, however, the group was believed to be responsible for an attack on the town of Ipil, in Mindanao, in which as many as 100 people were killed. Some of the assailants were also believed to belong to a splinter group of the MNLF, the Islamic Command Council. Some 14 hostages were reportedly killed as the army pursued the rebels in their retreat from Ipil. Despite intense counter-insurgency measures by government troops, Abu Sayyaf perpetrated a further assault on the Tungawan, in which six civilians were killed. In April 1996 two bomb explosions in Zamboanga City were widely attributed to Abu Sayyaf or to other groups opposed to the peace negotiations between the Government and the MNLF. Abu Sayyaf subsequently denounced the MNLF's peace agreement with the Government. Clashes between government forces and Abu Sayyaf were reported on the island of Basilan in March 1998. In December the leader of Abu Sayyaf, Abdurajat Abubakar Janjalani, was killed in an exchange of fire with government security forces. Terrorist attacks by Abu Sayyaf increased in January 1999 to avenge Janjalani's death.

In April 2000 armed Abu Sayyaf troops abducted 21 people, including 10 foreign tourists, from the island resort of Sipadan in Malaysia, and held them hostage on Jolo. One month earlier members of a separate Abu Sayyaf group had seized a number of Filipino hostages on the island of Basilan where, demanding the release of convicted Islamist terrorists held in US prisons, they had at the end of April managed to evade capture by government forces by which they had been besieged. The Government's military response to the hostage crisis remained largely ineffective, and a stalemate lasting several months ensued, punctuated by both formal and informal negotiations and a partially successful intervention, involving the payment of ransoms, by Libyan mediators. While sporadic releases were secured, however, some hostages were also killed by their captors. In early April 2001 President Macapagal Arroyo declared 'all-out war' against Abu Sayyaf.

In May 2001 Abu Sayyaf rebels abducted 20 people, including three US tourists, from a holiday resort off the western island of Palawan. President Macapagal Arroyo immediately ordered a military response, although the group threatened to kill the hostages if it was attacked. In early June the rebels succeeded in fleeing from under military siege; nine Filipino captives escaped as a result. Later in the same month the Government was forced to bring in a Malaysian mediator in order to avert the threatened execution of the three US hostages still being held. It was reported that one, Guillermo Sobero, had already been beheaded, although his body had not been found. In early July two Filipino hostages were released, but Abu Sayyaf stated that it intended to continue attacking US and European citizens until government forces had been withdrawn from the southern Philippines. Shortly afterwards Nadzmie Sabtulah, the rebel leader alleged to have planned the May abductions, was arrested, together with three other members of the group. However, the arrests failed to bring an end to Abu Sayyaf activities, and in August a group of Abu Sayyaf guerrillas raided the town of Lamitan on the island of Basilan, taking at least 36 hostages and beheading 10. The next day 11 hostages were released and soon afterwards 13 more were freed, following an armed raid by government troops. However, the military failed to capture any members of the Abu Sayyaf leadership and 21 hostages remained in captivity, leading to allegations of collusion between Abu Sayyaf and the Philippine military. Soon afterwards three Chinese nationals were abducted as they tried to negotiate the release of a Chinese engineer who had been held by the group since June 2001. Two of the Chinese hostages were later killed following a clash between the kidnappers and government forces in Sultan Kudurat province. The Chinese embassy in Manila expressed its concern at the incident.

In October 2001 the Abu Sayyaf group was responsible for two explosions in the city of Zamboanga. Meanwhile, government soldiers were reported to have cornered the kidnappers and their hostages following two days of fighting which had resulted in the deaths of 21 guerrillas. Shortly afterwards the group threatened to behead its two US hostages—Martin and Gracia Burnham—prior to President Macapagal Arroyo's scheduled November visit to the USA unless the military halted its offensive. In late October an explosion in Zamboanga, which killed six people, was attributed to the group. In the following month a Canadian man was abducted by men claiming to be Abu Sayyaf separatists. Shortly afterwards the group released one hostage, followed one week later by a further seven. In December government troops succeeded in rescuing the Canadian man. Three hostages remained—the Burnhams and Ediborah Yap, a Filipino nurse. The military offensive against the guerrilla group was intensified by the arrival of US troops on Basilan in 2002. In March a series of bombs exploded in the southern city of General Santos, killing 15 people and prompting President Macapagal Arroyo to declare a state of emergency in the area. The police later arrested five men in connection with the attacks. While the suspects were initially thought to be connected to the MILF, Abu Sayyaf claimed responsibility for the bombings. Shortly afterwards four men reported to be members of Abu Sayyaf were killed during a gun battle with police in the area. In June 2002 Gracia Burnham was rescued in a military operation. Her husband and Ediborah Yap, however, were killed. Later in the same month it was reported that Abu Sabaya, a senior member of the organization, had died during a gunfight at sea.

In July 2002 the joint US-Philippine military exercises that had been conducted on Basilan were formally concluded; President Macapagal Arroyo subsequently ordered the redeployment of government forces to combat insurgency elsewhere in the country. Although it was thought that the exercises had achieved some success in defeating Abu Sayyaf, in August the group was responsible for the kidnapping of eight members of a Christian sect on Jolo; although two of the hostages were released, a further two were beheaded. Following the group's threat to perpetrate attacks in retaliation for the military offensive being conducted against it, in early October a bomb exploded in the city of Zamboanga, resulting in the deaths of three people, including a US soldier. Responsibility for the attack was attributed to Abu Sayyaf. Later in the same month two further explosions in Zamboanga, which led to the deaths of seven people, were also suspected to have been carried out by members of Abu Sayyaf, although there was speculation that the regional terrorist organization Jemaah Islamiah could have been involved. The bombings followed the terrorist attack on the island of Bali, Indonesia, several days previously (see the chapter on Indonesia). Meanwhile, a bomb exploded on a bus in the capital Manila, killing at least three people.

In January 2003 three government soldiers were killed during a battle with Abu Sayyaf rebels on the island of Jolo. In the following month further fighting broke out in advance of the resumption of counter-terrorism exercises between US and Philippine troops in the area. Abu Sayyaf continued to hold four Filipino Christian women and three Indonesian seamen hostage. In late February 2003 President Macapagal Arroyo imposed a 90-day deadline upon military commanders for the elimination of the threat posed by Abu Sayyaf. In March one of the Indonesian hostages succeeded in escaping from captivity.

Meanwhile, at the end of November 1991 the US military formally transferred management of the Clark Air Base to the Philippines, in accordance with the Constitution's stipulation that foreign military bases should not be allowed in the country after 1991. In late December negotiations for an extended withdrawal period of US forces from Subic Bay naval base collapsed, owing principally to the USA's policy of refusing to confirm or deny the presence of nuclear weapons (prohibited from the Philippines under the 1987 Constitution) on board naval vessels. US personnel withdrew from Subic Naval Bay at the end of September 1992, and from the Cubi Point Naval Air Station towards the end of November.

In November 1994 the Philippine Government rejected draft proposals (presented by President Bill Clinton of the USA during a visit to the Philippines earlier in the month) intended to facilitate access for US naval vessels to ports in the Philippines. Relations between the USA and the Philippines improved, however, following the Chinese occupation of a reef in the Spratly Islands claimed by the Philippines (see below). A joint naval exercise between US and Philippine forces took place in July 1995 about 100 km from the Spratly Islands. In January 1998 the Philippine and US Governments signed a Visiting Forces Agreement (VFA), which provided legal status for US

military visits to Philippine territory and for the holding of joint military exercises, pending ratification by the Senate. However, the powerful Catholic Church opposed the agreement and the communist guerrillas announced that they would terminate peace talks if the VFA were ratified; in September popular protests against the VFA took place. Owing to the intensification of the dispute with the People's Republic of China concerning the Spratly Islands, the Philippines signed an agreement with the USA in October to allow for the formal resumption of joint military exercises. The Senate ratified the VFA on 27 May. The first phase of joint military exercises between the USA and the Philippines, which took place in January 2000, provoked popular protests outside the US embassy against the return to the Philippines of US troops. In July Estrada visited the USA where he requested financial assistance to combat rebel movements in the Philippines.

Following the terrorist attacks on the USA in September 2001 (see chapter on the USA) President Macapagal Arroyo offered President George W. Bush her unqualified support for the US campaign against terrorism. President Macapagal Arroyo committed medical personnel and supplies of food and medicine to international troops conducting military strikes upon any countries suspected of harbouring terrorists; she also signed into law a bill to combat money laundering in an attempt to financially incapacitate the Abu Sayyaf group and other suspected Philippine terrorist organizations. In October the President stated that she had volunteered logistical and intelligence assistance, the use of Philippine airspace, and the former US military bases at Clark and Subic Bay to the US Government. An offer of combat troops had also been made, pending congressional approval. In November President Macapagal Arroyo left for the USA to address the UN General Assembly and to hold talks with President Bush. In return for the ongoing support of the Philippines in the US anti-terrorist campaign, the US President promised the country US $100m. in military assistance and further development aid for Mindanao. The funds included $39m. to aid the Government in its continuing war against Abu Sayyaf, which had proven links to the al-Qa'ida terrorist network thought to be responsible for the attacks on the USA. President Macapagal Arroyo declined an offer of direct US military involvement, limiting its role to the provision of technical and financial assistance for the offensive.

In January 2002 it was reported that the US Government had sent 660 soldiers to the southern Philippines. While they would engage in joint training exercises with Philippine troops, they would not participate in any direct combat as this would contravene the Constitution. The deployment marked the first significant extension of the US war on terrorism beyond Afghanistan. Despite some popular opposition to the deployment, President Macapagal Arroyo's stance was considerably strengthened when she succeeded in winning support for the US military presence from the National Security Council, which accepted that it was authorized under the terms of the VFA. In February more than 20 people died following clashes in the city of Jolo between police and soldiers; a later bomb blast in the city killed a further five people. A second explosion in Zamboanga—serving as a temporary base for US servicemen—occurred on the same day. The incidents were attributed to opponents of the ongoing military exercises. President Macapagal Arroyo also faced fierce criticism from many members of Congress over her decision to allow the deployment, with several claiming that the exercises were intended to conceal a US offensive against Abu Sayyaf. Her most outspoken critic was the Vice-President and Secretary of Foreign Affairs, Teofisto Guingona, whose stance was a decisive factor in his resignation from the foreign affairs portfolio in July of that year. In April 2002 President Macapagal Arroyo sanctioned the deployment of hundreds more US troops to the region and extended the deadline for their departure, owing to the apparent success of the exercises in containing terrorist activities in the Philippines. The exercises were formally concluded at the end of July.

In late 2002 the US Government signed a five-year military agreement with the Philippines, pledging to extend co-operation between the armed forces of the two countries and to facilitate the movement of heavy equipment and logistical supplies. In January 2003 an advance deployment of US Special Forces troops arrived in Zamboanga to commence anti-terrorism training exercises. In February the USA announced that it intended to send a new deployment of soldiers to the island of Jolo, a stronghold of Abu Sayyaf; it specified, controversially, that the troops would assume a combat role for the first time.

However, the Philippine Government criticized the announcement as premature, fearing that it would exacerbate popular resentment at the presence of US troops in the country. President Macapagal Arroyo stressed later that US forces would play an entirely non-combative role in any military operation against terrorism. In March the President stated that, owing to local opposition, military exercises would not be conducted on Jolo; negotiations as to the exact nature of the deployment continued.

Following his inauguration in mid-1992, President Ramos visited Brunei, Thailand, Malaysia, Singapore and Japan, demonstrating an increasing interest in regional relations. The Philippines' commitment to the Association of South East Asian Nations (ASEAN, see p. 146) also deepened. Relations with Malaysia were somewhat strained, owing to the Philippines' claim to the Malaysian state of Sabah, dating from 1962, before Sabah joined the Federation of Malaysia. Sabah was ruled by the Sultan of Sulu, in the southern Philippines, until 1878, when it was leased to what was to become the British North Borneo Company. The Malaysian Government continues to pay a nominal rent to the Sultan. Attempts by both Presidents Marcos and Aquino to abandon the claim were thwarted by the Senate. In August 1993 the Philippine and Malaysian ministers responsible for foreign affairs signed a memorandum creating a commission to address bilateral issues, including the Philippines' claim to Sabah. Following his inauguration in June 1998, Estrada pledged to continue Ramos's commitment to regional relations. At the ASEAN ministerial meeting in Manila in July, Domingo Siazon, Jr, whom Estrada had retained as Secretary of Foreign Affairs, joined his Thai counterpart in expressing support for 'constructive intervention' in member countries' internal affairs, in marked contrast to ASEAN's policy of non-interference hitherto. Later that year relations with Malaysia were strained by Estrada's public condemnation of the arrest and beating of the former Malaysian Deputy Prime Minister, Dato' Seri Anwar Ibrahim. Despite Malaysian opposition, Estrada held a private meeting with Anwar's wife, Wan Azizah Wan Ismail, during her visit to the Philippines in May 1999. In August 2001 President Macapagal Arroyo visited Malaysia on her first overseas trip since assuming the presidency. In November, however, relations were jeopardized again when the Malaysian authorities detained rebel leader Nur Misuari for attempting to enter the country illegally. After some vacillation, Misuari was finally deported in January 2002 and relations remained cordial. However, in August 2002 the bilateral relationship deteriorated following the implementation of stringent new laws in Malaysia under which all illegal immigrants remaining in the country faced harsh penalties and deportation. Many of those affected were Filipino workers. The Philippine Government filed a formal complaint against Malaysia over its treatment of the immigrants and sent an official delegation to investigate allegations of maltreatment. Malaysia subsequently suspended implementation of the legislation.

In late November 1999 an informal summit meeting took place of the leaders of ASEAN and of the People's Republic of China, Japan and the Republic of Korea, the third such meeting in three years. It was formally agreed to hold annual East Asian summit meetings of all 13 nations and to strengthen present economic co-operation with the distant aim of forming an East Asian bloc, with a common market and monetary union. In August 2001 Indonesian President Megawati Sukarnoputri visited the Philippines on her first overseas trip since assuming power. During her brief stay she met with President Macapagal Arroyo, and the two leaders promised to assist each other in overcoming the separatist violence endemic in both their countries. In March 2002 bilateral relations threatened to become strained when the Philippine police filed charges against three Indonesian men who had been arrested at Manila Airport for illegal possession of explosives. One of those arrested was believed to be a member of the Majlis Mujahidin Indonesia (MMI—Indonesian Mujahidin Council), an extremist Islamist organization, and to have links to Jemaah Islamiah. The Indonesian Government was reported to have been angered by the arrests and stated that the detentions should not be used as a pretext to portray Indonesia as a haven for Islamist extremists. However, in early 2003 it was reported that Philippine rebels were engaged in smuggling arms to militant groups in Indonesia, despite increased anti-terrorism co-operation between the two countries.

The Philippines contributed 1,000 troops to a UN multinational force to restore peace and security in East Timor (which became Timor-Leste upon its accession to independence in May 2002), following the violence that erupted after the East Timorese voted in a referendum for independence from Indonesia; the International Force for East Timor (Interfet) was deployed in the territory in September 1999. The transfer of military command from Interfet to the newly-established United Nations Transitional Administration in East Timor (UNTAET) took place in February 2000; the military component of UNTAET was commanded by a Filipino, Gen. Jaime de los Santos. The two East Timorese independence leaders, José Alexandre (Xanana) Gusmão and José Ramos Horta, visited the Philippines in that month and held a meeting with President Estrada.

Diplomatic relations were established with the People's Republic of China in 1975, at which time the Philippine Government recognized Taiwan as an 'inalienable' part of the People's Republic. Conflicting claims to the Spratly Islands, in the South China Sea, were, however, a source of tension between the Philippines and the People's Republic of China. (Viet Nam, Brunei, Malaysia and Taiwan also claimed sovereignty over some or all of the islands.) In February 1989 Chinese and Philippine warships exchanged gunfire in the vicinity of the Spratly Islands, although it was later declared that the incident occurred as a result of 'confusion over rules of engagement'. Indonesia hosted six rounds of negotiations over the sovereignty of the Spratly Islands between January 1990 and October 1995; all parties agreed to reach a settlement by peaceful means and to develop jointly the area's natural resources. In December 1993 the Philippines and Malaysia agreed to co-operate on fishing rights for the disputed Spratly Islands in the area not claimed by the other four countries. Following a visit to Viet Nam (the first official visit by a Philippine Head of State to that country) in March 1994, Ramos appealed for the six countries with claims to the Spratly Islands to remove all armed forces from the area.

In May 1994 the People's Republic of China made an official protest after the Philippine Government granted a permit to a US company to explore for petroleum off Palawan, in an area including part of the disputed territory of the Spratly Islands. In February 1995 the Philippine Government formally protested when it was revealed that Chinese armed forces had occupied a reef, Mischief Reef, which lay within the Philippines' 200-mile exclusive economic zone established by a UN Convention on the Law of the Sea. Tensions in the disputed region were exacerbated during March by the arrest, by the Philippine naval forces, of more than 60 Chinese fishermen, as well as the seizure of vessels and the destruction of territorial markers allegedly deployed by the People's Republic of China. (Most of the fishermen were released in October and the remainder in January 1996.) Following two days of consultations in August 1995, however, the Chinese Government agreed for the first time to settle disputes in the South China Sea according to international law, rather than insisting that historical claims should take precedence. The Chinese and Philippine Governments issued a joint statement agreeing on a code of conduct to reduce the possibility of a military confrontation in the area. A similar agreement was signed with Viet Nam in November 1995. In March 1996 the Philippines and China agreed to co-operate in combating piracy, which was also a source of tension between the two countries as pirate vessels in the area often sailed under Chinese flags. Despite these agreements, sporadic tension continued during 1996–98.

In August 1998 the Philippines rejected an offer from China for the joint use of the Chinese structures on Mischief Reef. In the same month Philippine and US warships staged military exercises in the South China Seas. The Philippines lodged a diplomatic protest against the People's Republic of China in November, claiming that China was extending its structures on Mischief Reef, in contravention of the mutually agreed code of conduct. China insisted that it was only reinforcing existing structures. Estrada ordered increased naval and air patrols around the Spratly Islands to block entry and exit to the reef. A further 20 Chinese fishermen were arrested by the Philippine navy in November for violating Philippine waters. In January 1999 the National Security Council was convened for the first time in three years to discuss the Spratly Islands and Muslim unrest in Mindanao. The Philippines favoured a multilateral solution to the problems, whereas China opposed any external intervention. China rebuffed the Philippines' attempts to involve the UN through a meeting with the Secretary-General, Kofi Annan, in the USA and threatened to leave the Asia-Europe meeting in Berlin, Germany, if the Spratly issue were discussed. A meeting in Manila achieved little progress, with the Chinese dismissing a Philippine proposal for joint use of the facility, owing to the allegedly aggressive behaviour of the Philippine armed forces. ASEAN, which had failed to condemn China strongly at its summit meeting in December 1998, supported the proposal by the Philippines to draft a regional code of conduct in the South China Sea to prevent the escalation of conflict in the area. In April 1999 the Philippines and Viet Nam agreed to joint operations and leisure activities to reduce the risk of military confrontation. In October, however, the Philippines lodged a protest at the Vietnamese embassy, following an incident in which Vietnamese forces had fired on a Philippine aircraft patrolling in the area of the Spratly Islands.

In early November 1999 a Philippine navy ship ran aground on the disputed Scarborough Shoal in the Spratlys. China warned that the stranded vessel could jeopardize relations, and the Philippines pledged to remove it. Later in November ASEAN officials agreed on a regional code of conduct drafted by the Philippines to prevent conflicts in the Spratlys. In the same month the Chinese Premier, Zhu Rongji, visited the Philippines, and he and Estrada agreed to strengthen co-operation between the two countries. However, China rejected the proposed regional code of conduct although it agreed to participate in further discussions on the draft. In early 2000 China proposed a new draft code omitting previous references to a ban on construction on islands or atolls and excluded the Paracel Islands, which China had seized from Viet Nam in 1974. However, China did meet with all the ASEAN representatives to discuss the draft, a departure from its previously exclusively bilateral approach. In May 2000 Estrada made a visit to China where he met President Jiang Zemin and signed a joint statement on the framework for co-operation between China and the Philippines.

In mid-2002 relations with China were jeopardized when the Secretary of Justice, Hernando Perez, demanded that the Chinese ambassador be expelled from the country. His request marked the culmination of a dispute regarding the fate of more than 100 Chinese fishermen, who had been arrested over the preceding months and accused of fishing illegally in Philippine waters. Perez accused the ambassador of reneging on an agreement whereby the fishermen would be freed on condition that they entered guilty pleas and paid fines; he claimed that the ambassador had attempted to coerce the Philippine Government into releasing the fishermen without penalty. Perez subsequently withdrew his expulsion demand and, shortly afterwards, the Chinese Minister of Defence, Chi Haotian, paid a goodwill visit to the country. In November 2002 the improvement in bilateral relations was demonstrated when a high-level delegation from the Chinese Communist Party arrived in the Philippines.

Relations between the Philippines and Taiwan deteriorated in October 1999, following Estrada's termination of all flights between Taipei and Manila after a failure to settle a dispute over passenger quotas. The Philippine authorities demanded that two Taiwanese airlines reduce passengers from the previously agreed 9,600 per week to 3,000 per week, in order to protect PAL's share of the market. Following negotiations it was agreed in January 2000 that flights would resume in February. However, a disagreement over the interpretation of the new agreement (the Taiwanese authorities claimed the new quota of 4,800 passengers per week applied only to the Manila–Taipei flights whereas the Philippines sought to include the Manila–Kaohsiung route) led the Philippines to sever air links again after only six weeks, despite Taiwanese threats of an investment boycott and curbs on Filipino workers in Taiwan. The dispute was finally resolved in September 2000 when the Philippines and Taiwan agreed to reinstate a bilateral accord concluded in 1996. The Philippines had reportedly accepted that Taiwanese airlines should be allowed to fly passengers on to other destinations after arrival in the Philippines.

Government

The Constitution, which was approved by a national referendum on 2 February 1987, provides for a bicameral Congress, comprising a Senate, with 24 members directly elected by universal suffrage (for a six-year term, with one-half of the membership being elected every three years), and a House of Representatives (with a three-year mandate), with a maximum of 250 members, one to be directly elected from each legislative district: in addition, one-fifth of the total number of representatives can be elected under a party list system from lists of nominees proposed by minority groups. Elections are supervised by a Commission on Elections, which registers political parties.

The President is Head of State, Chief Executive of the Republic and Commander-in-Chief of the Armed Forces. The President is elected by the people for a six-year term, and is not eligible for re-election. The President cannot prevent the enactment of legislative proposals if they are approved by a two-thirds' majority vote in Congress. The President may declare martial law in times of national emergency, but Congress is empowered to revoke such actions at any time by a majority vote of its members. The President appoints a Cabinet and other officials, with the approval of the Commission on Appointments (drawn from members of both chambers of Congress).

Local government is by Barangays (citizens' assemblies), and autonomy is granted to any region where its introduction is endorsed in a referendum.

Defence

The total strength of the active armed forces in August 2002 was an estimated 106,000, comprising an army of 66,000, a navy of approximately 24,000 and an air force of 16,000. There were also reserve forces of 131,000. Paramilitary forces included the Citizens Armed Forces Geographical Units, which comprised about 40,000 men. The 2002 budget allocated an estimated 69,600m. pesos to defence.

Economic Affairs

In 2001, according to estimates by the World Bank, the Philippines' gross national income (GNI), measured at average 1999–2001 prices, was US $80,845m., equivalent to $1,050 per head (or $4,360 per head on an international purchasing-power parity basis). During 1990–2001, it was estimated, the population increased at an average annual rate of 2.1%, while gross domestic product (GDP) per head increased, in real terms, by an average of 0.8% per year. According to the Asian Development Bank (ADB), overall GDP increased, in real terms, at an average annual rate of 2.9% in 1990–2001. Real GDP increased by 3.2% in 2001 and by 4.6% in 2002.

Agriculture (including hunting, forestry and fishing) contributed 15.1% of GDP in 2001, and engaged 37.0% of the employed labour force in 2003. Rice, maize and cassava are the main subsistence crops. The principal crops cultivated for export are coconuts, sugar cane, bananas and pineapples. The sector is generally constrained by inadequate irrigation infrastructure and distribution facilities and insufficient fertilizers. Livestock (chiefly pigs, buffaloes, goats and poultry) and fisheries are important. Exports of logs, an important source of foreign exchange, were suspended in 1986, owing to the effects of deforestation. In 1989 exports of sawnwood were banned in an attempt to increase the value of forestry-related exports by encouraging the manufacture of wood products. Deforestation continues at a high rate, however, owing to illegal logging and to 'slash-and-burn' farming techniques. According to the ADB, agricultural GDP increased at an average annual rate of 1.9% during 1990–2001. Agricultural GDP increased by 3.7% in 2001 and by 3.5% in 2002.

Industry (including mining, manufacturing, construction and power) contributed 31.6% of GDP in 2001, and engaged 15.1% of the employed labour force in 2003. According to the ADB, industrial GDP increased at an average annual rate of 2.5% in 1990–2001. According to the National Economic Development Authority (NEDA), industrial GDP increased by 1.3% in 2001 and by 4.1% in 2002.

Mining contributed 0.6% of GDP in 2001, and engaged 0.3% of the employed labour force in 2003. Copper is the Philippines' leading mineral product (although only two producers were still operating in 1999); gold, silver, chromium, nickel and coal are also extracted and there are plans to resuscitate the iron ore industry. Commercial production of crude petroleum began in 1979. A substantial natural gas field and petroleum reservoir, off the island of Palawan, has proven recoverable reserves of 100m. barrels of crude petroleum and an estimated 54,000m.–100,000m. cu m of gas. Production from the deposits began in October 2001. Legislation introduced in March 1995 to liberalize the mining sector failed to stimulate the industry, although 46 exploration permits had been granted by the end of 1998. Legislation, which was implemented in November, giving tribal groups the right to negotiate terms for the exploration and exploitation of minerals on ancestral lands proved a further impediment to investment. A legal challenge to the legislation was initiated in 1999. According to the ADB, mining GDP declined by an annual average of 0.9% in 1990–2001. The GDP of the mining sector declined by 6.6% in 2001, but increased by 49.2% in 2002.

Manufacturing contributed 22.8% of GDP in 2001, and engaged 9.2% of the employed labour force in 2003. In the late 1990s the most important branches of manufacturing were food products and beverages, electronic products and components (mainly telecommunications equipment), petroleum refineries and chemicals. According to the ADB, the GDP of the manufacturing sector increased by an annual average of 2.6% in 1990–2001; manufacturing GDP increased by 2.9% in 2001 and by 3.3% in 2002.

Energy had been derived principally from oil-fired thermal plants, relying chiefly on imported petroleum. In 1999 petroleum accounted for 28.3% of the total amount of electrical energy produced, coal for 27.1% and hydroelectric power for 19.0%. However, by 2003 the energy sector's reliance on petroleum had decreased significantly as new sources of power were exploited. In October 2001 the Malampaya gasfield project, approved in 1998, was completed. A 504-km pipeline had been constructed under the sea, at a cost of US $4,500m., to transport gas to three generating plants (with a combined capacity of 2,700 MW) on Luzon Island. The gasfield was expected to supply 16% of the electrical capacity of the Philippines and would limit its reliance on imported petroleum as a source of energy. It became fully operational in mid-2002. In June 2001 an Electric Power Industry Reform Act was finally enacted; this provided the legislative framework urgently needed to enable the deregulation of the power industry and the privatization and restructuring of the National Power Corporation. In 2000 imports of mineral fuels accounted for 12.1% of the value of total merchandise imports.

The services sector contributed 53.3% of GDP in 2001, and engaged 47.9% of the employed labour force in 2003. Remittances from Filipino workers abroad, which totalled an estimated US $6,500m. in 1998, constitute the Government's principal source of foreign exchange. Tourism, although periodically affected by political unrest, remains a significant sector of the economy. In 2000 almost 2.0m. tourists visited the Philippines. However, the number of arrivals declined to fewer than 1.8m. in 2001, owing partly to the effects of the September terrorist attacks on the USA. It was feared that the terrorist attack on the Indonesian island of Bali in October 2002 (see the chapter on Indonesia), combined with escalating terrorist activity in the Philippines itself (see Recent History), would cause a decline in tourist arrivals. However, according to the Department of Tourism, approximately 1.9m. tourists visited the country in 2002, an increase of 7.6% compared to the previous year. Revenue from tourism was estimated at $2,534m. in 1999. The Philippine banking sector was less affected by the financial crisis in 1997 than its regional counterparts, although the ratio of non-performing loans to total loans was estimated at 15.1% in December 2000. The imposition of higher capital requirements forced a process of consolidation among smaller banks. According to the ADB, the GDP of the services sector increased at an average annual rate of 3.7% in 1990–2001. The GDP of the services sector increased by 4.4% in 2001 and by 5.4% in 2002.

In 2001 the Philippines recorded a visible trade surplus of US $2,763m. and there was a surplus of $4,150m. on the current account of the balance of payments. In early 2003, however, the Government announced that, owing to an understatement of the cost of imports of electronic parts used in manufacturing, it had significantly overestimated the size of the current-account surplus since 2000; the figures were subsequently revised. In 2001 the principal source of imports (accounting for 20.3% of the total) was Japan; other significant suppliers were the USA (18.5%), Singapore, the Republic of Korea and Hong Kong. The USA was the principal market for exports (28.4%); other major purchasers were Japan (16.6%), Singapore and the Netherlands. The principal imports were machinery and transport equipment, mineral fuels, basic manufactures, chemical products and food and live animals. The principal exports were machinery and transport equipment, which accounted for 38.5% of total exports in that year. Electronic products destined for the computer and related industries have become a major export sector in recent years, although a decline in the global demand for exports had a particularly damaging effect on the sector in 2001.

In 2002 there was an overall budgetary deficit of 212,683m. pesos, equivalent to approximately 5.3% of GDP. The Philippines' external debt totalled US $50,063m. at the end of 2000, of which $33,429m. was long-term public debt. In that year the cost of servicing the debt was equivalent to 13.6% of the value of exports of goods and services. The annual rate of inflation averaged 8.3% in 1990–2001; consumer prices increased by an average of 6.1% in 2001 and 3.1% in 2002. In January 2003 10.6% of the labour force was unemployed.

The Philippines is a member of the Asian Development Bank (see p. 143), the Association of South East Asian Nations (ASEAN, see p. 146), the Asia-Pacific Economic Co-operation forum (APEC, see p. 139) and the Colombo Plan (see p. 339). In January 1993 the establishment of an ASEAN Free Trade Area (AFTA) commenced; a reduction in tariffs to a maximum of 5% was originally to be implemented over 15 years but this was later advanced to 2003 before being formally initiated on 1 January 2002. In November 1999 the target date for zero tariffs in ASEAN was brought forward from 2015 to 2010.

In the final quarter of 2000, as the value of the peso fell to a record low against the US dollar, interest rates were raised and investor confidence declined, it was feared that political turmoil would plunge the Philippine economy into recession. Following the inauguration of President Gloria Macapagal Arroyo in January 2001, however, the Government seemed to have regained control of economic affairs. The peso had stabilized, the rate of inflation had declined and interest rates had been returned to the levels prevailing before the political crisis. The return of a significant number of pro-Arroyo delegates to Congress in the May 2001 legislative elections allowed the new Government to pursue its programme of economic liberalization in a climate of relative political stability. It was generally acknowledged that efforts to boost revenue collection (estimated at only 80%–85% of the total due) and, perhaps, the deployment of the proceeds of privatization were unlikely to bring about any significant improvement in the fiscal position for at least two years. In June 2001 the Financial Action Task Force (FATF, see p. 339), urged the Philippine Government to impose effective measures to combat money laundering and thus eradicate the perception of the Philippines as synonymous with corruption. An Anti-Money Laundering Act was subsequently enacted, although it contained important deficiencies. In February 2003 further anti-money laundering legislation was approved in an effort to avert the imposition of sanctions by FATF member states before the March deadline. While the legislation was initially deemed to be deficient by the FATF, shortly before the deadline amendments were passed which were considered adequate to prevent the threatened sanctions. However, the Philippines remained on the FATF's list of non-co-operative countries pending the implementation of the new laws and a subsequent assessment of their efficacy. Despite the adverse effects of a global economic slowdown, recession was averted in 2001 (when GDP expanded by 3.2%), owing to the continuing strength of domestic demand and to expansion in the agricultural sector stimulated by favourable climatic conditions. In 2002 GDP expanded by 4.6%, exceeding forecasts, owing largely to growth in the agricultural sector later in the year. It was hoped that President Macapagal Arroyo's decision not to seek re-election in 2004, but instead to concentrate upon implementing economic reforms for the remainder of her time in office, would prove beneficial. However, at the end of 2002 the record budget deficit (which had reached almost 212.7m. pesos) remained the most significant obstacle to the pursuit of a more ambitious programme of economic liberalization. In March 2003 the outbreak of the US-led war against Iraq threatened to disrupt the Philippines' primary source of foreign exchange, remittances from the many Filipinos working in the Middle East, as well as contributing to a sharp rise in world petroleum prices. Continued political insurgency in the southern Philippines was also expected to discourage foreign investment in the country. The ADB forecast growth of 3.9% in 2003.

Education

Elementary education, beginning at seven years of age and lasting for six years, is officially compulsory, and is provided free of charge at public (government-administered) schools. In 1995 100% of all children in the relevant age-group were enrolled at primary schools. Secondary education begins at the age of 13 and lasts for up to four years: there is a common general curriculum for all students in the first two years, and more varied curricula in the third and fourth years, leading to either college or technical vocational courses. In 1999 enrolment at secondary level was equivalent to 28.9% of the total number of students enrolled. Instruction is in both English and Filipino. In the same year total enrolment at tertiary level was equivalent to 13.9% of total students enrolled. In the Government's budget proposals for 2002 105,300m. pesos (13.5% of total expenditure) was allocated to education.

Public Holidays

2003: 1 January (New Year's Day), 9 April (Bataan Day), 17 April (Maundy Thursday), 18 April (Good Friday), 1 May (Labour Day), 6 May (Araw ng Kagitingan), 12 June (Independence Day, anniversary of 1898 declaration), 24 June (Araw ng Maynila)*, 19 August (Quezon Day)†, 29 August (National Heroes' Day), 1 November (All Saints' Day), 30 November (Bonifacio Day), 25 December (Christmas Day), 30 December (Rizal Day), 31 December (Last Day of the Year).

2004: 1 January (New Year's Day), 8 April (Maundy Thursday), 9 April (Good Friday and Bataan Day), 1 May (Labour Day), 6 May (Araw ng Kagitingan), 12 June (Independence Day, anniversary of 1898 declaration), 24 June (Araw ng Maynila)*, 19 August (Quezon Day)†, 29 August (National Heroes' Day), 1 November (All Saints' Day), 30 November (Bonifacio Day), 25 December (Christmas Day), 30 December (Rizal Day), 31 December (Last Day of the Year).

* Observed only in Metro Manila.

† Observed only in Quezon City.

Weights and Measures

The metric system is in force.

Statistical Survey

Source (unless otherwise stated): National Statistics Office, Solicarel 1, Magsaysay Blvd, cnr Ampil St, POB 779, Metro Manila; tel. (2) 7160807; fax (2) 610794; internet www.census.gov.ph.

Area and Population

AREA, POPULATION AND DENSITY

Area (sq km)	300,000*
Population (census results)	
1 September 1995	68,616,536
1 May 2000	
Males	38,524,267
Females	37,979,810
Total	76,504,077
Population (official estimates at mid-year)†	
2001	77,925,894
Density (per sq km) at mid-2001	259.8

* 115,831 sq miles.

† Figures not adjusted to take account of the May 2000 census results.

REGIONS
(population at 2000 census)

	Area (sq km)	Population	Density (per sq km)
National Capital Region	636.0	9,932,560	15,617
Ilocos	12,840.2	4,200,478	327
Cagayan Valley	26,837.7	2,813,159	105
Central Luzon	18,230.8	8,030,945	441
Southern Tagalog	46,924.0	11,793,655	251
Bicol	17,632.5	4,686,669	266
Western Visayas	20,223.2	6,211,038	307
Central Visayas	14,951.5	5,706,953	382
Eastern Visayas	21,431.7	3,610,355	173
Western Mindanao . . .	15,997.3	3,091,208	193
Northern Mindanao . . .	14,033.0	2,747,585	196
Southern Mindanao . . .	27,140.7	5,189,335	263
Central Mindanao	14,372.7	2,598,210	179
Cordillera Administrative Region .	18,293.7	1,365,412	75
Autonomous Region of Muslim Mindanao	11,608.3	2,412,159	211
Caraga	18,847.0	2,095,367	111
Total*	300,000.3	76,504,077†	255

* Total includes a statistical adjustment.

† Including Filipinos in Philippine embassies, consulates and missions abroad (2,851 persons).

PRINCIPAL TOWNS
(population at 2000 census)

Manila (capital)* .	1,581,082		Gen. Santos City .	411,822
Quezon City* . .	2,173,831		Marikina City . .	391,170
Caloocan City* . .	1,177,604		Muntinlupa City* .	379,310
Davao City . .	1,147,116		Iloilo City . . .	365,820
Cebu City . . .	718,821		Pasay City* . .	354,908
Zamboanga City .	601,794		Iligan City . .	285,061
Pasig City* . . .	505,058		Mandaluyong City* .	278,474
Valenzuela City . .	485,433		Butuan City . .	267,279
Las Piñas City . .	472,780		Angeles City . .	263,971
Cagayan de Oro City .	461,877		Mandaue City . .	259,728
Parañaque City . .	449,811		Baguio City . .	252,386
Makati City* . .	444,867		Olongapo City . .	194,260
Bacolod City . .	429,076		Cotabato City . . .	163,849

* Part of Metropolitan Manila.

BIRTHS, MARRIAGES AND DEATHS*

	Registered live births		Registered marriages		Registered deaths	
	Number	Rate (per 1,000)	Number	Rate (per 1,000)	Number	Rate (per 1,000)
1991 . .	1,643,296	25.8	445,526	7.0	298,063	4.7
1992 . .	1,684,395	25.8	454,155	7.0	319,579	4.9
1993 . .	1,680,896	25.1	474,407	7.1	318,546	4.8
1994 . .	1,645,011	24.0	490,164	7.2	321,440	4.7
1995 . .	n.a.	n.a.	n.a.	7.4	324,737	4.7
1996 . .	1,608,468	22.9	525,555	7.5	344,363	4.9
1997 . .	1,653,236	23.1	562,808	7.9	339,400	4.7
1998 . .	1,632,859	22.3	549,265	7.5	352,992	4.8

2000 (estimates, adjusted for under-registration): Birth rate 25.7; Death rate 5.77.

2001 (estimates, adjusted for under-registration): Birth rate 26.2; Death rate 5.83.

* Registration is incomplete. According to UN estimates, the average annual rates were: births 31.6 per 1,000 in 1990–95, 28.4 in 1995–2000; deaths 6.3 per 1,000 in 1990–95, 5.5 in 1995–2000 (Source: UN, *World Population Prospects: The 2000 Revision*).

Expectation of life (WHO estimates, years at birth): 67.7(males 64.2; females 71.5) in 2001 (Source: WHO, *World Health Report*).

ECONOMICALLY ACTIVE POPULATION*
('000 persons aged 15 years and over, January)

	2001	2002	2003†
Agriculture, hunting, forestry and fishing	10,252	11,006	11,146
Mining and quarrying	118	115	98
Manufacturing	2,885	2,830	2,767
Electricity, gas and water . . .	116	120	117
Construction	1,563	1,531	1,578
Wholesale and retail trade, restaurants and hotels . . .	5,632	6,194	6,332
Transport, storage and communications	2,081	2,167	2,252
Financing, insurance, real estate and business services	775	836	845
Public administration and defence.	1,380	1,424	1,463
Community, social and personal services	2,132	2,167	2,204
Other services	1,161	1,316	1,318
Total employed	28,096	29,705	30,119
Unemployed	3,597	3,393	3,559
Total labour force	31,693	33,098	33,678

* Figures refer to civilians only and are based on annual household surveys (excluding institutional households).

† Preliminary figures.

Health and Welfare

KEY INDICATORS

Total fertility rate (children per woman, 2001).	3.4
Under-5 mortality rate (per 1,000 live births, 2001) . . .	38
HIV/AIDS (% of persons aged 15–49, 2001)	0.10
Physicians (per 1,000 head, 1996)	1.23
Hospital beds (per 1,000 head, 1993)	1.07
Health expenditure (2000): US $ per head (PPP)	167
Health expenditure (2000): % of GDP	3.4
Health expenditure (2000): public (% of total)	45.7
Access to water (% of persons, 1999).	87
Access to sanitation (% of persons, 1999)	83
Human Development Index (2000): ranking	77
Human Development Index (2000): value	0.754

For sources and definitions, see explanatory note on p. vi.

Agriculture

PRINCIPAL CROPS
('000 metric tons)

	1999	2000	2001
Rice (paddy)	11,787	12,389	12,955
Maize	4,585	4,511	4,525
Potatoes	64	64	66
Sweet potatoes	557	554	545
Cassava (Manioc)	1,890	1,766	1,652
Yams	25	26	24
Taro	97	96	97
Sugar cane	23,780	24,491	24,962
Dry beans	29	26	26*
Other pulses*	29	29	29
Groundnuts (in shell) . . .	26	27	26
Coconuts	12,142	12,995	13,208
Oil palm fruit*	199	212	200
Cabbages	87	88	90
Tomatoes	145	148	146
Pumpkins, squash and gourds . .	61	62*	63*
Aubergines (Eggplants) . . .	160	166	165*
Dry onions	85	84	83
Green peas	28	28	29*
Other vegetables (incl. melons)*	4,077	4,158	4,262
Watermelons	63	59	58
Mangoes	866	848	884
Avocados	39	38	37
Pineapples	1,530	1,560	1,620
Papayas	72	76	77
Bananas	4,571	4,930	5,061
Oranges	26†	25†	29*
Tangerines, mandarins, clementines and satsumas . .	51†	49†	53*
Lemons and limes	46†	45†	52*
Grapefruit and pomelos . . .	22†	46	43
Other fruits*	3,080	3,040	3,265
Garlic	9	14	15
Coffee (green).	117	126	132
Cocoa beans	8	7	7
Tobacco (leaves)	52	49	48
Natural rubber†	71	71	73

* FAO estimate(s).

† Unofficial figure(s).

Source: FAO.

LIVESTOCK
('000 head, year ending 30 June)

	1999	2000	2001
Cattle	2,426	2,479	2,496
Pigs	10,397	10,713	11,063
Buffaloes	3,006	3,024	3,066
Horses*	230	230	230
Goats*	6,800	6,930	6,950
Sheep*	30	30	30
Chickens	114,000	115,187	115,606
Ducks*	11,000	12,000	12,500

* FAO estimates.

Source: FAO.

LIVESTOCK PRODUCTS
('000 metric tons)

	1999	2000	2001
Beef and veal	190	190	183
Buffalo meat	69	72	72
Pig meat	973	1,008	1,064
Poultry meat	517	555	610
Cows' milk	10	10	11
Hen eggs*	440	445	445
Other poultry eggs*	68	69	69
Cattle and buffalo hides* . . .	23	26	24

* FAO estimates.

Source: FAO.

Forestry

ROUNDWOOD REMOVALS
('000 cubic metres, excl. bark)

	1999	2000	2001
Sawlogs, veneer logs and logs for sleepers	568	384	260
Pulpwood	160	400	130
Other industrial wood	2,242	2,295	2,295
Fuel wood	40,011*	40,950	41,699
Total	42,981	44,029	44,384

* FAO estimate.

Source: FAO.

SAWNWOOD PRODUCTION
('000 cubic metres, incl. railway sleepers)

	1999	2000	2001
Total	288	151	199

Source: FAO.

Fishing

('000 metric tons, live weight)

	1998	1999	2000
Capture	1,833.5	1,870.5	1,892.8
Scads (Decapterus) . . .	250.8	254.2	261.0
Sardinellas	302.6	279.9	298.5
'Stolephorus' anchovies . .	77.0	78.1	79.6
Frigate and bullet tunas . .	106.4	111.3	112.2
Skipjack tuna	116.7	108.8	113.0
Yellowfin tuna	80.0	91.3	90.8
Freshwater molluscs . . .	90.2	87.3	85.6
Aquaculture	312.1	328.4	387.7
Nile tilapia	60.7	62.9	77.4
Milkfish	162.4	170.7	204.2
Total catch	2,145.6	2,198.8	2,280.5

Note: Figures exclude aquatic plants ('000 metric tons): 643.0 (capture 0.4, aquaculture 642.6) in 1998; 621.1 (capture 0.4, aquaculture 620.6) in 1999; 657.0 (capture 0.4, aquaculture 656.6) in 2000.

Source: FAO, *Yearbook of Fishery Statistics*.

Mining

('000 metric tons, unless otherwise indicated)

	1999	2000	2001†
Coal	1,300	1,300	1,500
Crude petroleum ('000 barrels) . .	400	400†	400
Chromium ore (gross weight) . .	19.6	20.9	2.6‡
Copper ore*	34.6	129.8	20.3‡
Salt (unrefined)	704.3	589.5	600.0
Nickel ore*	20.7	17.4	27.4‡
Gold (metric tons)*	31.1	36.5	33.8‡
Silver (metric tons)*	18.2	23.5	33.6
Limestone	16,738	22,244	23,000

* Figures refer to the metal content of ores and concentrates.
† Estimate(s).
‡ Reported figure.

Source: US Geological Survey.

Industry

SELECTED PRODUCTS
('000 metric tons, unless otherwise indicated)

	1999	2000	2001
Raw sugar*†	1,682	1,676	1,868
Plywood ('000 cubic metres)* . .	268	326	348
Mechanical wood pulp*‡ . .	28	28	28
Chemical wood pulp*	145†	147†	147‡
Paper and paperboard* . . .	1,010	1,107	1,056
Nitrogenous fertilizers (a)§ . . .	184	n.a.	n.a.
Phosphate fertilizers (b)§ . .	193	n.a.	n.a.
Jet fuels ('000 barrels)‖	6,500	6,500	7,000‡
Motor spirit—petrol	1,460	n.a.	n.a.
Kerosene ('000 barrels)‖	4,500	4,500	5,000‡
Distillate fuel oils ('000 barrels)‖	40,000	40,000	40,000‡
Residual fuel oils ('000 barrels)‖	47,000	47,000	47,000‡
Liquefied petroleum gas‖ . . .	5,500	5,500	6,000‡
Cement‖	12,566	11,959	8,653‡
Smelter (unrefined) copper‖ . .	162	n.a.	n.a.
Electric energy (million kWh)‡ . .	41,337	n.a.	n.a.

* Source: FAO.
† Unofficial figure(s).
‡ Estimate(s).
§ Production of fertilizers is in terms of (a) nitrogen or (b) phosphoric acid.
‖ Source: US Geological Survey.

Sources: mainly UN, *Industrial Commodity Statistics Yearbook*; UN, *Statistical Yearbook for Asia and the Pacific*.

Finance

CURRENCY AND EXCHANGE RATES

Monetary Units
    100 centavos = 1 Philippine peso

Sterling, Dollar and Euro Equivalents (31 December 2002)
    £1 sterling = 85.58 pesos
    US $1 = 53.10 pesos
    €1 = 55.68 pesos
    1,000 Philippine pesos = £11.68 = $18.83 = €17.96

Average Exchange Rate (pesos per US $)
    2000   44.192
    2001   50.993
    2002   51.604

GENERAL BUDGET
(million pesos)

Revenue	2000	2001	2002
Tax revenue	460,034	489,869	492,424
Taxes on net income and profits	202,635	223,417	n.a.
Excise tax	61,678	58,698	n.a.
Sales taxes and licences . .	78,405	87,044	n.a.
Import duties and taxes . . .	95,006	96,232	96,250
Non-tax revenue	53,352	71,882	72,880
Bureau of the Treasury income .	30,764	46,413	47,194
Fees and other charges . . .	17,936	24,296	24,172
Total	514,762	563,732	566,034

Expenditure	2000	2001	2002
Current expenditure	585,396	648,893	n.a.
Personnel services	182,723	190,893	n.a.
Maintenance and operating subsidy	149,313	155,622	n.a.
Allotment to local government units	99,816	118,179	140,540
Interest payments	140,894	174,834	185,799
Capital outlay	60,408	57,434	n.a.
Infrastructure	17,295	15,895	n.a.
Equity investment	536	484	1,486
Net lending	2,634	3,944	3,918
Total	648,974	710,755	778,717

Source: Bureau of the Treasury.

INTERNATIONAL RESERVES
(US $ million at 31 December)

	2000	2001	2002
Gold*	1,973	2,216	3,043
IMF special drawing rights . . .	2	14	10
Reserve position in IMF	113	110	119
Foreign exchange	12,936	13,319	13,007
Total	15,024	15,659	16,179

* Valued at market-related prices.

Source: IMF, *International Financial Statistics*.

MONEY SUPPLY
(million pesos at 31 December)

	1999	2000	2001
Currency outside banks	218,474	192,300	208,909
Demand deposits at commercial banks	172,874	192,982	191,940
Total money (incl. others) . .	395,557	390,548	406,483

Source: IMF, *International Financial Statistics*.

COST OF LIVING
(Consumer Price Index; base: 1994 = 100)

	1999	2000	2001
Food (incl. beverages and tobacco)	142.6	145.5	151.4
Fuel, light and water	132.8	146.6	164.4
Clothing (incl. footwear)	136.7	140.2	145.4
Rent	165.5	174.3	186.1
Services	163.7	182.8	203.8
Miscellaneous	121.3	122.9	129.3
All items	145.9	152.3	161.6

NATIONAL ACCOUNTS

National Income and Product
(million pesos at current prices)

	1998	1999	2000
Compensation of employees . .	184,967	222,793	281,672
Operating surplus	2,241,651	2,499,941	2,746,549
Domestic factor incomes . .	2,426,618	2,722,734	3,028,221
Consumption of fixed capital . .	238,442	254,170	274,368
Gross domestic product (GDP) at factor cost	2,665,060	2,976,904	3,302,589
Factor income from abroad . .	246,701	272,989	359,872
Less Factor income paid abroad .	109,629	113,725	171,327
Gross national product (GNP) .	2,802,132	3,136,168	3,491,134
Less Consumption of fixed capital .	238,442	254,170	274,368
National income in market prices	2,563,690	2,881,998	3,216,766
Other current transfers from abroad	146,932	66,027	7,736
Less Other current transfers paid abroad	13,169	6,457	5,129
National disposable income . .	2,697,453	2,941,568	3,219,373

Expenditure on the Gross Domestic Product
('000 million pesos at current prices)

	2000	2001	2002
Government final consumption expenditure	438.9	464.5	507.6
Private final consumption expenditure	2,335.5	2,565.0	2,747.0
Increase in stocks	-6.6	10.7	-1.7
Gross fixed capital formation . .	614.3	629.3	663.9
Statistical discrepancy	-276.3	-82.4	17.2
Total domestic expenditure . .	3,105.8	3,587.1	3,934.0
Exports of goods and services . .	1,859.4	1,764.5	1,946.2
Less Imports of goods and services	1,656.9	1,711.6	1,902.8
GDP in purchasers' values . .	3,308.3	3,640.0	3,977.4
GDP at constant 1985 prices .	955.0	987.4	n.a.

Source: IMF, *International Financial Statistics*.

Gross Domestic Product by Economic Activity
('000 million pesos at current prices)

	1999	2000	2001
Agriculture, hunting, forestry and fishing	510.5	525.9	549.4
Mining and quarrying	18.0	21.2	21.2
Manufacturing	644.0	745.9	831.6
Electricity, gas and water . . .	86.1	97.5	116.3
Construction	162.9	174.4	182.4
Wholesale and retail trade, restaurants and hotels . .	419.3	473.0	517.5
Transport, storage and communications	159.3	199.0	247.6
Finance, insurance, real estate and business services . . .	141.6	149.1	160.1
Public administration and defence	290.8	319.8	343.6
Other services	544.3	602.6	670.3
GDP in purchasers' values . .	2,976.9	3,308.3	3,640.0

Source: Asian Development Bank, *Key Indicators of Developing Asian and Pacific Countries*.

BALANCE OF PAYMENTS
(US $ million)

	1999	2000	2001
Exports of goods f.o.b.	34,210	37,295	31,243
Imports of goods f.o.b.	-29,252	-30,377	-28,480
Trade balance	4,958	6,918	2,763
Exports of services	4,802	3,972	3,148
Imports of services	-7,515	-6,084	-5,104
Balance on goods and services	2,245	4,806	807
Other income received . . .	8,081	7,804	7,152
Other income paid	-2,910	-4,588	-4,256
Balance on goods, services and income	7,416	8,022	3,703
Current transfers received . . .	610	552	517
Current transfers paid	-116	-115	-70
Current balance	7,910	8,459	4,150
Capital account (net)	-9	38	-12
Direct investment abroad . . .	59	107	161
Direct investment from abroad . .	573	1,241	1,792
Portfolio investment assets . . .	-278	-806	234
Portfolio investment liabilities . .	5,094	693	178
Other investment assets . . .	-5,669	-15,311	-13,897
Other investment liabilities . .	-714	7,579	7,211
Net errors and omissions . . .	-3,307	-2,481	-610
Overall balance	3,659	-481	-680

Source: IMF, *International Financial Statistics*.

External Trade

PRINCIPAL COMMODITIES
(distribution by SITC, US $ million)

Imports c.i.f.	1998	1999	2000
Food and live animals . .	2,473.6	2,253.5	2,252.6
Cereals and cereal preparations .	1,148.1	822.7	734.7
Crude materials (inedible)			
except fuels	973.1	1,221.4	1,088.7
Mineral fuels, lubricants, etc. .	2,237.1	2,581.9	4,102.9
Petroleum, petroleum products,			
etc.	1,924.7	2,267.9	3,683.7
Crude petroleum oils, etc. . .	1,524.5	2,066.8	3,170.8
Chemicals and related			
products	2,429.8	2,703.7	2,857.6
Basic manufactures	3,537.2	3,931.4	3,992.8
Textile yarn, fabrics, etc. . .	1,195.0	1,238.5	1,250.6
Iron and steel	849.7	1,061.1	991.6
Machinery and transport			
equipment	18,118.7	17,994.2	17,723.2
Machinery specialized for			
particular industries . . .	1,183.0	1,030.0	1,164.8
General industrial machinery,			
equipment and parts . .	944.9	868.7	833.1
Office machines and automatic			
data-processing equipment . .	2,950.1	2,457.1	2,428.4
Parts and accessories for office			
machines, etc. . .	2,751.9	2,220.3	2,202.5
Telecommunications and sound			
equipment	1,269.5	1,207.6	1,949.1
Other electrical machinery,			
apparatus, etc.	10,051.3	10,679.1	9,347.4
Switchgear, resistors, printed			
circuits, switchboards, etc. .	1,031.2	712.3	702.7
Thermionic valves, tubes, etc. .	7,912.4	8,926.6	7,604.7
Electronic microcircuits .	1,841.5	2,058.8	1,603.7
Road vehicles and parts (excl. tyres,			
engines and electrical parts) .	630.6	883.9	1,086.7
Miscellaneous manufactured			
articles	1,462.9	1,520.5	1,470.8
Total (incl. others)	31,529.9	32,568.2	33,807.4

Source: UN, *International Trade Statistics Yearbook*.

2001 (US $ million): Food and live animals 2,105; Crude materials (inedible) except fuels 853; Mineral fuels, lubricants, etc. 3,372; Chemicals and related products 2,515; Basic manufactures 3,072; Machinery and transport equipment 11,517; Miscellaneous manufactured articles 924; Total (incl. others) 31,358.

Source: Asian Development Bank, *Key Indicators of Developing Asian and Pacific Countries*.

Exports f.o.b.	1998	1999	2000
Food and live animals . . .	1,262.6	1,175.3	1,285.0
Basic manufactures	1,102.7	1,234.1	1,415.9
Machinery and transport			
equipment	21,266.1	27,218.5	28,989.5
Office machines and automatic			
data-processing equipment . .	4,533.9	5,985.9	7,208.1
Automatic data-processing			
machines and units . .	2,411.1	3,610.0	4,643.8
Peripheral units	2,396.7	3,114.9	3,966.6
Parts and accessories for office			
machines, etc.	2,082.3	2,344.8	2,517.1
Telecommunications and sound			
equipment	1,165.4	985.6	1,266.9
Other electrical machinery,			
apparatus, etc.	14,707.8	19,169.7	19,251.0
Switchgear, resistors, printed			
circuits, switchboards, etc. .	1,105.2	1,321.6	1,622.4
Thermionic valves, tubes, etc. .	12,925.3	17,068.1	16,662.8
Diodes, transistors, etc. . .	880.9	982.6	1,070.2
Electronic microcircuits . .	11,750.3	15,544.4	14,937.6
Miscellaneous manufactured			
articles	3,972.1	3,814.2	4,365.6
Clothing and accessories (excl.			
footwear)	2,351.1	2,275.5	2,575.9
Total (incl. others)	29,496.4	35,036.9	38,078.3

Source: UN, *International Trade Statistics Yearbook*.

2001 (US $ million): Food and live animals 1,297; Animal and vegetable oils, fats and waxes 432; Basic manufactures 1,055; Machinery and transport equipment 12,378; Miscellaneous manufactured articles 2,431; Total (incl. others) 32,150.

Source: Asian Development Bank, *Key Indicators of Developing Asian and Pacific Countries*.

PRINCIPAL TRADING PARTNERS
(US $ million)

Imports f.o.b.	1998	1999	2000
Australia	682.9	756.8	815.6
China, People's Republic . . .	1,198.9	1,039.8	767.9
France (incl. Monaco)	492.1	305.8	347.7
Germany	822.0	800.6	734.2
Hong Kong	1,299.7	1,226.2	1,217.0
Indonesia	592.0	704.9	692.7
Iran	526.0	666.2	795.6
Japan	6,030.0	6,136.0	6,027.4
Korea, Republic	2,188.8	2,723.4	2,350.8
Malaysia	924.1	978.7	1,141.7
Netherlands	219.2	245.5	323.9
Saudi Arabia	606.7	810.5	1,048.1
Singapore	1,740.4	1,742.0	2,115.0
Taiwan	1,415.2	1,614.4	1,948.0
Thailand	793.8	821.7	846.0
United Kingdom	327.3	340.2	355.3
USA	6,560.2	6,365.1	5,323.3
Viet Nam	375.8	209.3	156.8
Total (incl. others)	29,659.9	30,742.5	31,387.4

Source: National Statistical Coordination Board.

2001 (US $ million): China, People's Republic 918; Germany 860; Hong Kong 1,642; Japan 7,258; Korea, Republic 2,250; Malaysia 1,166; Saudi Arabia 1,197; Singapore 2,365; Thailand 1,092; USA 6,602; Total (incl. others) 35,772.

Source: Asian Development Bank, *Key Indicators of Developing Asian and Pacific Countries*.

Exports f.o.b.	1998	1999	2000
China, People's Republic . . .	343.7	574.8	663.3
Germany	1,035.1	1,229.0	1,328.6
Hong Kong	1,325.9	1,947.1	1,907.3
Japan	4,233.9	4,664.2	5,608.7
Korea, Republic	508.8	1,031.5	1,172.5
Malaysia	1,141.6	1,479.3	1,372.4
Netherlands	2,319.2	2,864.6	2,982.5
Singapore	1,832.3	2,466.7	3,124.2
Taiwan	1,757.1	2,993.4	2,861.3
Thailand	634.4	841.7	1,206.5
United Kingdom	1,756.9	1,766.4	1,506.3
USA	10,097.9	10,445.5	11,365.3
Total (incl. others)	29,496.4	35,036.9	38,078.3

Source: National Statistical Coordination Board.

2001 (US $ million): Germany 1,444; Hong Kong 1,732; Japan 5,725; Korea, Republic 1,223; Malaysia 1,331; Netherlands 2,146; Singapore 2,305; Thailand 1,327; United Kingdom 1,211; USA 9,762; Total (incl. others) 34,425.

Source: Asian Development Bank, *Key Indicators of Developing Asian and Pacific Countries*.

Transport

RAILWAYS
(traffic)

	1994	1995	1996
Passengers ('000)	427	598	291
Passenger-km (million)	106	164	70
Freight ('000 metric tons) . . .	13	14	6
Freight ton-km ('000)	3,080	4,000	1,476

Source: Philippine National Railways.

Passenger-km (million): 172 in 1997; 181 in 1998; 171 in 1999; 123 in 2000 (Source: UN, *Statistical Yearbook*).

ROAD TRAFFIC
(registered motor vehicles)

	1998	1999	2000
Passenger cars	749,204	773,835	767,948
Utility vehicles	1,244,019	1,310,865	1,422,033
Buses	31,806	33,193	
Lorries and vans	231,342	243,443	248,369
Motorcycles and mopeds* . . .	1,032,594	1,144,666	1,236,241
Trailers	27,852	27,730	26,612

* Includes tricycles.

Sources: Land Transportation Office, Manila, and International Road Federation, *World Road Statistics*.

SHIPPING

Merchant Fleet
(registered at 31 December)

	1999	2000	2001
Number of vessels	1,897	1,865	1,697
Total displacement (grt) . . .	7,650,058	7,002,097	6,029,876

Source: Lloyd's Register-Fairplay, *World Fleet Statistics*.

International Sea-borne Shipping
(freight traffic)

	1994	1995	1996
Vessels ('000 net registered tons):			
entered	53,453	61,298	n.a.
cleared	53,841	61,313	n.a.
Goods ('000 metric tons):			
loaded	14,581	16,658	15,687
unloaded	38,222	42,418	51,830

CIVIL AVIATION
(traffic on scheduled services)

	1997	1998	1999
Kilometres flown (million) . . .	96	40	53
Passengers carried ('000) . . .	7,475	3,944	5,004
Passenger-km (million)	16,392	7,503	10,292
Total ton-km (million)	2,086	925	1,303

Source: UN, *Statistical Yearbook*.

Tourism

FOREIGN TOURIST ARRIVALS

Country of residence	1999	2000	2001
Australia	77,732	75,706	68,541
Canada	64,986	61,004	54,942
Germany	62,044	51,131	40,605
Hong Kong	160,152	146,858	134,408
Japan	387,513	390,517	343,840
Korea, Republic	133,068	174,966	207,957
Malaysia	49,667	42,067	30,498
Singapore	51,244	50,276	44,155
Taiwan	143,810	75,722	85,231
United Kingdom	88,920	74,507	60,147
USA	463,600	445,043	392,099
Total (incl. others)*	2,170,514	1,992,169	1,796,893

* Including Philippine nationals resident abroad (199,290 in 1999; 150,386 in 2000), not distributed by country.

Tourism receipts (US $ million): 2,831.2 in 1997; 2,412.9 in 1998; 2,534 in 1999.

Source: mainly Department of Tourism, Manila.

Communications Media

	1999	2000	2001
Television receivers ('000 in use) .	8,200	11,000	n.a.
Telephones ('000 main lines in use)	2,892.4	3,061.4	3,100.0
Mobile cellular telephones ('000 subscribers).	2,850.0	6,454.4	10,568.0
Personal computers ('000 in use) .	1,260	1,480	1,700
Internet users ('000)	1,320	2,000	2,000

Source: International Telecommunication Union.

Radio receivers ('000 in use): 11,500 in 1997.

Facsimile machines (estimated number in use): 50,000 in 1995.

Book production (titles, excluding pamphlets): 1,380 in 1999.

Daily newspapers: 47 (with average circulation of 5,700,000 copies) in 1996.

Non-daily newspapers: 243 (with average circulation of 153,000 copies) in 1995.

Sources: UN, *Statistical Yearbook*; UNESCO, *Statistical Yearbook*.

Periodicals (1990): 1,570 (estimated circulation 9,468,000).

Education

(1998/99)

	Institutions	Teachers	Pupils
Pre-primary.	8,647	9,644*	n.a.
Primary schools	39,011	328,517	12,474,886
Secondary schools	7,021	108,981	5,066,190
University level	1,316	66,876†	2,481,809
Other tertiary level institutions .	1,033	n.a.	4,134‡

* 1990/91 figure.
† 1993/94 figure.
‡ 1995/96 figure.

Sources: Department of Education, Culture and Sports; UNESCO, *Statistical Yearbook*.

Adult literacy rate (UNESCO estimates): 95.3% (males 95.1%; females 95.5%) in 2000 (Source: UN Development Programme, *Human Development Report*).

Directory

The Constitution

A new Constitution for the Republic of the Philippines was ratified by national referendum on 2 February 1987. Its principal provisions are summarized below:

BASIC PRINCIPLES

Sovereignty resides in the people, and all government authority emanates from them; war is renounced as an instrument of national policy; civilian authority is supreme over military authority.

The State undertakes to pursue an independent foreign policy, governed by considerations of the national interest; the Republic of the Philippines adopts and pursues a policy of freedom from nuclear weapons in its territory.

Other provisions guarantee social justice and full respect for human rights; honesty and integrity in the public service; the autonomy of local governments; and the protection of the family unit. Education, the arts, sport, private enterprise, and agrarian and urban reforms are also promoted. The rights of workers, women, youth, the urban poor and minority indigenous communities are emphasized.

BILL OF RIGHTS

The individual is guaranteed the right to life, liberty and property, under the law; freedom of abode and travel, freedom of worship, freedom of speech, of the press and of petition to the Government are guaranteed, as well as the right of access to official information on matters of public concern, the right to form trade unions, the right to assemble in public gatherings, and free access to the courts.

The Constitution upholds the right of habeas corpus and prohibits the intimidation, detention, torture or secret confinement of apprehended persons.

SUFFRAGE

Suffrage is granted to all citizens over 18 years of age, who have resided for at least one year previously in the Republic of the Philippines, and for at least six months in their voting district. Voting is by secret ballot.

LEGISLATURE

Legislative power is vested in the bicameral Congress of the Philippines, consisting of the Senate and the House of Representatives, with a maximum of 274 members. All members shall make a disclosure of their financial and business interests upon assumption of office, and no member may hold any other office. Provision is made for voters to propose laws, or reject any act or law passed by Congress, through referenda.

The Senate shall be composed of 24 members; Senators are directly elected for six years by national vote, and must be natural-born citizens, at least 35 years of age, literate and registered voters in their district. They must be resident in the Philippines for at least two years prior to election, and no Senator shall serve for more than two consecutive terms. One-half of the membership of the Senate

shall be elected every three years. No treaty or international agreement may be considered valid without the approval, by voting, of at least two-thirds of members.

A maximum of 250 Representatives may sit in the House of Representatives. Its members may serve no more than three consecutive three-year terms. Representatives must be natural-born citizens, literate, and at least 25 years of age. Each legislative district may elect one representative; the number of legislative districts shall be determined according to population and shall be reapportioned following each census. Representatives must be registered voters in their district, and resident there for at least one year prior to election. In addition, one-fifth of the total number of representatives shall be elected under a party list system from lists of nominees proposed by indigenous, but non-religious, minority groups (such as the urban poor, peasantry, women and youth).

The Senate and the House of Representatives shall each have an Electoral Tribunal which shall be the sole judge of contests relating to the election of members of Congress. Each Tribunal shall have nine members, three of whom must be Justices of the Supreme Court, appointed by the Chief Justice. The remaining six members shall be members of the Senate or of the House of Representatives, as appropriate, and shall be selected from the political parties represented therein, on a proportional basis.

THE COMMISSION ON APPOINTMENTS

The President must submit nominations of heads of executive departments, ambassadors and senior officers in the armed forces to the Commission on Appointments, which shall decide on the appointment by majority vote of its members. The President of the Senate shall act as ex-officio Chairman; the Commission shall consist of 12 Senators and 12 members of the House of Representatives, elected from the political parties represented therein, on the basis of proportional representation.

THE EXECUTIVE

Executive power is vested in the President of the Philippines. Presidents are limited to one six-year term of office, and Vice-Presidents to two successive six-year terms. Candidates for both posts are elected by direct universal suffrage. They must be natural-born citizens, literate, at least 40 years of age, registered voters and resident in the Philippines for at least 10 years prior to election.

The President is Head of State and Chief Executive of the Republic. Bills (legislative proposals) that have been approved by Congress shall be signed by the President; if the President vetoes the bill, it may become law when two-thirds of members in Congress approve it.

The President shall nominate and, with the consent of the Commission on Appointments, appoint ambassadors, officers of the armed forces and heads of executive departments.

The President is Commander-in-Chief of the armed forces and may suspend the writ of habeas corpus or place the Republic under martial law for a period not exceeding 60 days when, in the President's opinion, public safety demands it. Congress may revoke either action by a majority vote.

The Vice-President may be a member of the Cabinet; in the event of the death or resignation of the President, the Vice-President shall become President and serve the unexpired term of the previous President.

THE JUDICIARY

The Supreme Court is composed of a Chief Justice and 14 Associate Justices, and may sit *en banc* or in divisions comprising three, five or seven members. Justices of the Supreme Court are appointed by the President, with the consent of the Commission on Appointments, for a term of four years. They must be citizens of the Republic, at least 40 years of age, of proven integrity, and must have been judges of the lower courts, or engaged in the practice of law in the Philippines, for at least 15 years.

The Supreme Court, sitting *en banc*, is the sole judge of disputes relating to presidential and vice-presidential elections.

THE CONSTITUTIONAL COMMISSIONS

These are the Civil Service Commission and the Commission on Audit, each of which has a Chairman and two other Commissioners, appointed by the President (with the approval of the Commission on Appointments) to a seven-year term; and the Commission on Elections, which enforces and administers all laws pertaining to elections and political parties. The Commission on Elections has seven members, appointed by the President (and approved by the Commission on Appointments) for a seven-year term. The Commission on Elections may sit *en banc* or in two divisions.

LOCAL GOVERNMENT

The Republic of the Philippines shall be divided into provinces, cities, municipalities and barangays. The Congress of the Philippines shall enact a local government code providing for decentralization. A region may become autonomous, subject to approval by a majority vote of the electorate of that region, in a referendum. Defence and security in such areas will remain the responsibility of the national Government.

ACCOUNTABILITY OF PUBLIC OFFICERS

All public officers, including the President, Vice-President and members of Congress and the Constitutional Commissions, may be removed from office if impeached for, or convicted of, violation of the Constitution, corruption, treason, bribery or betrayal of public trust.

Cases of impeachment must be initiated solely by the House of Representatives, and tried solely by the Senate. A person shall be convicted by a vote of at least two-thirds of the Senate, and will then be dismissed from office and dealt with according to the law.

SOCIAL JUSTICE AND HUMAN RIGHTS

The Congress of the Philippines shall give priority to considerations of human dignity, the equality of the people and an equitable distribution of wealth. The Commission on Human Rights shall investigate allegations of violations of human rights, shall protect human rights through legal measures, and shall monitor the Government's compliance with international treaty obligations. It may advise Congress on measures to promote human rights.

AMENDMENTS OR REVISIONS

Proposals for amendment or revision of the Constitution may be made by:
  i) Congress (upon a vote of three-quarters of members);
  ii) A Constitutional Convention (convened by a vote of two-thirds of members of Congress);
  iii) The people, through petitions (signed by at least 12% of the total number of registered voters).

The proposed amendments or revisions shall then be submitted to a national plebiscite, and shall be valid when ratified by a majority of the votes cast.

MILITARY BASES

Foreign military bases, troops or facilities shall not be allowed in the Republic of the Philippines following the expiry, in 1991, of the Agreement between the Republic and the USA; except under the provisions of a treaty approved by the Senate, and, when required by Congress, ratified by the voters in a national referendum.

The Government

HEAD OF STATE

President: GLORIA MACAPAGAL ARROYO (inaugurated 20 January 2001).

Vice-President: TEOFISTO T. GUINGONA, Jr.

THE CABINET
(April 2003)

Executive Secretary: ALBERTO G. ROMULO.

Secretary of Agrarian Reform: ROBERTO PAGDANGANAN.

Secretary of Agriculture: LUIS LORENZO, Jr.

Secretary of the Budget and Management: EMILIA T. BONCODIN.

Secretary of Education, Culture and Sports: EDILBERTO C. DE JESUS.

Secretary of Energy: VICENTE S. PEREZ, Jr.

Secretary of Finance: JOSE ISIDRO N. CAMACHO.

Secretary of Foreign Affairs: BLAS F. OPLE.

Secretary of Health: MANUEL M. DAYRIT.

Secretary of the Interior and Local Government: JOSE D. LINA, Jr.

Secretary of Justice: SIMEON A. DATUMANONG.

Secretary of Labor and Employment: PATRICIA A. SANTO THOMAS.

Secretary of National Defense: Gen. (retd) ANGELO T. REYES.

Secretary of Public Works and Highways: BAYANI F. FERNANDO.

Secretary of Science and Technology: ESTRELLA F. ALABASTRO.

Secretary of Social Welfare and Development: CORAZON JULIANO N. SOLIMAN.

Secretary of Tourism: RICHARD J. GORDON.

Secretary of Trade and Industry: MANUEL A. ROXAS II.

Secretary of Transportation and Communications: LEANDRO MENDOZA.

Secretary of the Environment and Natural Resources: ELISEA GOZUN.

Director-General of the National Economic and Development Authority: ROMULO NERI.

Press Secretary: HERNANI A. BRAGANZA.

MINISTRIES

Office of the President: New Executive Bldg, Malacañang Palace Compound, J. P. Laurel St, San Miguel, Metro Manila; tel. (2) 7356047; fax (2) 7358006; e-mail opnet@ops.gov.ph; internet www.opnet.ops.gov.ph.

Office of the Vice-President: PICC, 2nd Floor, CCP Complex, Roxas Blvd, Pasay City, Metro Manila; tel. (2) 8312658; fax (2) 8312614; e-mail gma@easy.net.ph.

Department of Agrarian Reform: DAR Bldg, Elliptical Rd, Diliman, Quezon City, Metro Manila; tel. (2) 9287031; fax (2) 9292527; e-mail nani@dar.gov.ph; internet www.dar.gov.ph.

Department of Agriculture: DA Bldg, 4th Floor, Elliptical Rd, Diliman, Quezon City, Metro Manila; tel. (2) 9288741; fax (2) 9285140; e-mail dnotes@da.gov.ph; internet www.da.gov.ph.

Department of the Budget and Management: DBM Bldg, Gen. Solano St, San Miguel, Metro Manila; tel. (2) 7354807; fax (2) 7354927; e-mail dbmbiss@dbm.gov.ph; internet www.dbm.gov.ph.

Department of Education, Culture and Sports: Ultra Complex, Meralco Ave, Pasig City, 1600 Metro Manila; tel. (2) 6321361; fax (2) 6320805; internet www.deped.gov.ph.

Department of Energy: Energy Center, Merritt Rd, Fort Bonifacio, Taguig, Metro Manila; tel. (2) 8441021; fax (2) 8442495; e-mail v_perez@doe.gov.ph; internet www.doe.gov.ph.

Department of the Environment and Natural Resources: DENR Bldg, Visayas Ave, Diliman, Quezon City, 1100 Metro Manila; tel. (2) 9296626; fax (2) 9204352; e-mail sechta@denr.gov.ph; internet www.denr.gov.ph.

Department of Finance: DOF Bldg, Roxas Blvd, cnr Pablo Ocampo St, Metro Manila; tel. (2) 5234955; fax (2) 5212950; e-mail camacho@dof.gov.ph; internet www.dof.gov.ph.

Department of Foreign Affairs: DFA Bldg, 2330 Roxas Blvd, Pasay City, Metro Manila; tel. (2) 8344000; fax (2) 8321597; e-mail webmaster@dfa.gov.ph; internet www.dfa.gov.ph.

Department of Health: San Lazaro Compound, Rizal Ave, Santa Cruz, 1003 Metro Manila; tel. (2) 7438301; fax (2) 7431829; e-mail mmdayrit@doh.gov.ph; internet www.doh.gov.ph.

Department of the Interior and Local Government: A. Francisco Gold Condominium II, Epifanio de los Santos Ave, cnr Mapagmahal St, Diliman, Quezon City, 1100 Metro Manila; tel. (2) 9250349; fax (2) 9250386; e-mail dilgmail@dilg.gov.ph; internet www.dilg.gov.ph.

Department of Justice: Padre Faura St, Ermita, Metro Manila; tel. (2) 5213721; fax (2) 5211614; e-mail sechbp@info.com.ph; internet www.asti.dost.gov.ph/doj.

Department of Labor and Employment: DOLE Executive Bldg, 7th Floor, Muralla Wing, Muralla St, Intramuros, 1002 Metro Manila; tel. (2) 5272131; fax (2) 5273494; e-mail osec@dole.gov.ph; internet www.dole.gov.ph.

Department of National Defense: DND Bldg, 3rd Floor, Camp Aguinaldo, Quezon City, Metro Manila; tel. (2) 9113300; fax (2) 9116213; e-mail osnd@philonline.com; internet www.dnd.gov.ph.

Department of Public Works and Highways: DPWH Bldg, Bonifacio Drive, Port Area, Metro Manila; tel. (2) 5274111; fax (2) 5275635; e-mail pilorin.beth.p@dpwh.gov.ph; internet www.dpwh.gov.ph.

Department of Science and Technology: DOST Compound, Gen. Santos Ave, Bicutan, Taguig, Metro Manila; tel. (2) 8372071; fax (2) 8372937; e-mail wgp@sunl.dost.gov.ph; internet www.dost.gov.ph.

Department of Social Welfare and Development: Batasang Pambansa, Constitution Hills, Quezon City, Metro Manila; tel. (2) 9317916; fax (2) 9318191; e-mail dinky@mis.dswd.gov.ph; internet www.dswd.gov.ph.

Department of Tourism: DOT Bldg, Teodoro F. Valencia Circle, Rizal Park, Metro Manila; tel. (2) 5251805; fax (2) 5256538; e-mail dotmprd@info.com.ph; internet www.tourism.gov.ph.

Department of Trade and Industry: Industry and Investments Bldg, 385 Sen. Gil J. Puyat Ave, Buendia, Makati City, 3117 Metro Manila; tel. (2) 8953611; fax (2) 8956487; e-mail mis@dti.dti.gov.ph; internet www.dti.gov.ph.

Department of Transportation and Communications: Columbia Tower, Ortigas Ave, Pasig City, 1555 Metro Manila; tel. (2) 7267106; fax (2) 7267104; e-mail dotc@i-next.net; internet www.dotcmain.gov.ph.

National Economic and Development Authority (NEDA—Department of Socio-Economic Planning): NEDA-sa-Pasig Bldg, 12 Blessed Josemaria Escriva St, Pasig City, 1605 Metro Manila; tel. (2) 6313747; fax (2) 6313282; e-mail info@neda.gov.ph; internet www.neda.gov.ph.

Philippine Information Agency (Office of the Press Secretary): PIA Bldg, Visayas Ave, Diliman, Quezon City, Metro Manila; tel. (2) 9247703; fax (2) 9204347; e-mail pia@ops.gov.ph; internet www.pia.ops.gov.ph.

President and Legislature

PRESIDENT

Election, 11 May 1998*

Candidate	Votes	% of votes
Joseph Ejercito Estrada (LaMMP)	10,722,295	39.86
Jose C. de Venecia, Jr (Lakas-NUCD)	4,268,483	15.87
Paul S. Roco (Aksyon Demokratiko)	3,720,212	13.83
Emilio R. Osmeña (PROMDI)	3,347,631	12.44
Alfredo S. Lim (LP)	2,344,362	8.71
Renato S. de Villa (Reporma)	1,308,352	4.86
Miriam Defensor Santiago (PRP)	797,206	2.96
Juan Ponce Enrile (Independent)	343,139	1.28
Santiago F. Dumlao, Jr (Bago)	32,212	0.12
Manuel L. Morato (PBM)	18,644	0.07
Total	**26,902,536**	**100.00**

* In January 2001, after the impeachment trial of President Estrada had been adjourned indefinitely, the Supreme Court declared the presidency vacant. Vice-President Gloria Macapagal Arroyo was sworn in as Estrada's successor.

THE CONGRESS OF THE PHILIPPINES

Senate

President of the Senate: FRANKLIN M. DRILON.

Elections for 12 of the 24 seats in the Senate took place on 11 May 1998. The Laban ng Makabayang Masang Pilipino (LaMMP) won seven seats, while Lakas ng EDSA-National Union of Christian Democrats (Lakas-NUCD) won five seats. Elections for 13 of the 24 seats were held on 14 May 2001. The People Power Coalition (PPC) won eight seats and the Laban ng Demokratikong Pilipino-Puwersa ng Masa (LDP-PnM) won four. The remaining seat was taken by an independent candidate. The result thus gave President Macapagal

Arroyo a narrow majority in the upper house, with 13 of the 24 seats being occupied by her supporters.

House of Representatives

Speaker of the House: JOSE DE VENECIA.

General Election, 14 May 2001

	Seats
Lakas ng EDSA-National Union of Christian Democrats (Lakas-NUCD)	87
Nationalist People's Coalition (NPC)	62
Liberal Party (LP)	20
Laban ng Demokratikong Pilipino (LDP)	18
Independents	8
Partido ng Masang Pilipino (PMP)	4
Bayan Muna	3
Partido para sa Demokratikong Reporma-Lapiang Manggagawa Coalition (Reporma)	2
Aksyon Demokratiko	2
Alayon	2
Others	6
Total*	**214**

*Total includes five members of minority and cause-orientated groups allocated seats in the House of Representatives under the party list elections, which also took place on 14 May 2001.
Note: Results were provisional.

Autonomous Region

MUSLIM MINDANAO

The Autonomous Region of Muslim Mindanao (ARMM) originally comprised the provinces of Lanao del Sur, Maguindanao, Tawi-Tawi and Sulu. The Region was granted autonomy in November 1989. Elections took place in February 1990, and the formal transfer of limited executive powers took place in October. In August 2001 a plebiscite was conducted in 11 provinces and 14 cities in Mindanao to determine whether or not they would become members of the ARMM. The city of Marawi and the province of Basilan subsequently joined the Region. The regional Assembly, for which elections were held in November 2001, comprises 21 legislative seats.

Governor: FAROUK HUSSEIN (elected 26 November 2001).

Vice-Governor: MAHID MUTILAN.

In October 1996 a transitional administrative council was established, which derived powers from the office of the President, to co-ordinate peace-keeping and development activities.

Southern Philippines Council for Peace and Development Chairman: MUSLIMIN SEMA.

Vice-Chairman: EDWARD S. HAGEDORN.

Political Organizations

Akbayan (Citizens' Action Party): 14 Mapagkumbaba St, Sikatuna Village, Quezon City, Metro Manila; tel. (2) 4336933; fax (2) 9252936; e-mail secretariat@surfshop.net; internet www.akbayan.org; f. 1998; left-wing; Pres. JOEL ROCAMORA; Sec.-Gen. MARIE VICTA LABAJO.

Aksyon Demokratiko (Democratic Action Party): 16th Floor, Strata 2000 Bldg, Emerald Ave, Ortigas Centre, Pasig City, 1600 Metro Manila; tel. (2) 6385381; fax (2) 6343073; e-mail kabataan@raulroco.com; f. 1997 to support presidential candidacy of RAUL ROCO; Chair. JAIME GALVEZ TAN; Pres. RAUL ROCO.

Alayon: c/o House of Representatives, Metro Manila.

Bayan Muna: c/o House of Representatives, Metro Manila; e-mail bayanmuna@bayanmuna.net; internet www.bayanmuna.net; f. 1999; Pres. SATUR OCAMPO; Chair. Dr REYNALDO LESACA, Jr.

Gabay ng Bayan (Nation's Guide): Metro Manila; fmrly Grand Alliance for Democracy; Leader FRANCISCO TADAD.

Kabalikat ng Malayang Pilipino (KAMPI): c/o House of Representatives, Metro Manila; f. 1997.

Kilusang Bagong Lipunan (KBL) (New Society Movement): Metro Manila; f. 1978 by Pres. Marcos and fmr mems of the Nacionalista Party; Sec.-Gen. VICENTE MELLORA.

Kilusan para sa Pambansang Pagpapanibago (BAGO): Metro Manila; f. 1997 to support presidential candidacy of SANTIAGO F. DUMLAO, Jr.

Laban ng Demokratikong Pilipino (LDP) (Fight of Democratic Filipinos): Metro Manila; f. 1987; reorg. 1988 as an alliance of Lakas ng Bansa and a conservative faction of the PDP-Laban Party; mem. of Lapian ng Masang Pilipino (LAMP) until Jan. 2001; formed alliance with Puwersa ng Masa (PnM) to contest the 2001 elections to the Senate; Pres. EDGARDO ANGARA; Sec.-Gen. JOSE COJUANGCO.

Lakas ng EDSA (Power of EDSA)-National Union of Christian Democrats (Lakas-NUCD): Metro Manila; e-mail mail@LAKAS-NUCD.com; internet www.lakas-nucd.com; f. 1992 as alliance to support the presidential candidacy of Gen. FIDEL V. RAMOS; formed alliance with UMDP to contest 1998 and 2001 elections, joined People Power Coalition (PPC) in Feb. 2001; Pres. TEOFISTO T. GUINGONA, Jr; Sec.-Gen. GLORIA MACAPAGAL ARROYO.

Lapian ng Masang Pilipino (LAMP) (Party of the Filipino Masses): Metro Manila; f. 1997 as Laban ng Makabayang Masang Pilipino (LaMMP, Struggle of Nationalist Filipino Masses), renamed Laban ng Masang Pilipino (LMP, Struggle of Filipino Masses) in 1998, present name adopted in 1999; originally coalition of Laban ng Demokratikong Pilipino (LDP), Nationalist People's Coalition (NPC) and Partido ng Masang Pilipino (PMP) until split in Jan. 2001.

Liberal Party (LP): Metro Manila; f. 1946; represents centre-liberal opinion of the fmr Nacionalista Party, which split in 1946; endorsed ALFREDO LIM as presidential candidate in 1998 election; joined People Power Coalition (PPC) in Feb. 2001; Leader FLORENCIO ABAD.

Nacionalista Party (NP): Metro Manila; tel. (2) 854418; fax (2) 865602; Pres. ARTURO TOLENTINO; Sec.-Gen. RENE ESPINA.

Nationalist People's Coalition (NPC): Metro Manila; f. 1991; breakaway faction of the Nacionalista Party led by EDUARDO COJUANGCO; mem. of Lapian ng Masang Pilipino (LAMP) from 1997 until Jan. 2001.

New National Alliance: Metro Manila; f. 1998; left-wing; Dep. Sec.-Gen. TEDDY CASINO.

Partido Bansang Marangal (PBM): Metro Manila; f. 1997 to support the presidential candidacy of MANUEL L. MORATO.

Partido Demokratiko Sosyalista ng Pilipinas (PDSP) (Philippine Democratic Socialist Party): Metro Manila; f. 1981 by mems of the Batasang Pambansa allied to the Nacionalista (Roy faction), Pusyon Visaya and Mindanao Alliance parties; joined People Power Coalition (PPC) in Feb. 2001; Leader NORBERTO GONZALES.

Partido Komunista ng Pilipinas (PKP) (Communist Party of the Philippines): f. 1930; Pres. FELICISIMO MACAPAGAL.

Partido Nacionalista ng Pilipinas (PNP) (Philippine Nationalist Party): Metro Manila; f. 1986 by fmr mems of KBL; Leader BLAS F. OPLE.

Partido ng Bayan (New People's Alliance): f. May 1986 by JOSE MARIA SISON (imprisoned in 1977–86), the head of the Communist Party of the Philippines (CPP); militant left-wing nationalist group.

Partido ng Manggagawang Pilipino (PMP) (Filipino Workers' Party): f. 2002 by fmr supporters of the CPP (see below).

Partido ng Masang Pilipino (PMP): Metro Manila; mem. of Lapian ng Masan Pilipino (LAMP) from 1997 until Jan. 2001; Leader JOSEPH EJERCITO ESTRADA.

Partido para sa Demokratikong Reporma-Lapiang Manggagawa Coalition (Reporma): c/o House of Representatives, Metro Manila; joined People Power Coalition (PPC) in Feb. 2001; Leader RENATO DE VILLA.

PDP-Laban Party: c/o House of Representatives, Metro Manila; f. February 1983 following merger of Pilipino Democratic Party (f. 1982 by fmr mems of the Mindanao Alliance) and Laban (Lakas ng Bayan—People's Power Movement, f. 1978 and led by BENIGNO S. AQUINO, Jr until his assassination in August 1983); centrist; formally dissolved in Sept. 1988, following the formation of the LDP, but a faction continued to function as a political movement; Pres. JUANITO FERRER; Sec.-Gen. AUGUSTO SANCHEZ.

People Power Coalition (PPC): c/o House of Representatives, Metro Manila; internet www.ppc.ph; formed to contest 2001 elections to the Senate; coalition of Aksyon Demokratiko, Lakas-NUCD, Liberal Party, PDSP, PROMDI and Reporma.

People's Reform Party (PRP): f. 1991 by MIRIAM DEFENSOR SANTIAGO to support her candidacy in the 1992 presidential election.

Probinsya Muna Development Initiatives (PROMDI): 7 Pasteur St, Lahug, Cebu City; tel. (32) 2326692; fax (32) 2313609; e-mail emro@cebu.pw.net.ph; internet www.col.net.ph/emro; f. 1997; joined People Power Coalition (PPC) to contest 2001 elections; Leader EMILIO ('LITO') OSMEÑA.

Puwersa ng Masa (PnM): c/o House of Representatives, Metro Manila; f. 2001 by ex-President JOSEPH EJERCITO ESTRADA; formed an alliance with Laban ng Demokratikong Pilipino (LDP) to contest the 2001 elections to the Senate.

United Muslim Democratic Party (UMDP): Mindanao; moderate Islamic party; formed an electoral alliance with Lakas-NUCD for the election to the House of Representatives in May 2001.

United Negros Alliance (UNA): Negros Occidental.

The following organizations are, or have been, in conflict with the Government:

Abu Sayyaf (Bearer of the Sword): Mindanao; radical Islamic group seeking the establishment of an Islamic state in Mindanao; breakaway grouping of the MILF; est. strength 1,500 (2000); Leader KHADAFI JANJALANI.

Alex Boncayao Brigade (ABB): communist urban guerrilla group, fmrly linked to CPP, formed alliance with Revolutionary Proletarian Party in 1997; est. strength 500 (April 2001); Leader NILO DE LA CRUZ.

Islamic Command Council (ICC): Mindanao; splinter group of MNLF; Leader MELHAM ALAM.

Maranao Islamic Statehood Movement: Mindanao; f. 1998; armed grouping seeking the establishment of an Islamic state in Mindanao.

Mindanao Independence Movement (MIM): Mindanao; claims a membership of 1m. Leader REUBEN CANOY.

Moro Islamic Liberation Front (MILF): Camp Abubakar, Lanao del Sur, Mindanao; aims to establish an Islamic state in Mindanao; comprises a faction that broke away from the MNLF in 1978; its armed wing, the Bangsa Moro Islamic Armed Forces, est. 10,000 armed regulars; Chair. HASHIM SALAMAT; Vice-Chair. and Chief of Armed Forces Haji MURAD.

Moro Islamic Reform Group: Mindanao; breakaway faction from MNLF; est. strength of 200 in 2000.

Moro National Liberation Front (MNLF): internet www.mnlf .org; seeks autonomy for Muslim communities in Mindanao; signed a peace agreement with the Govt in Sept. 1996; its armed wing, the Bangsa Moro Army, comprised an est. 10,000 mems in 2000; Chair. and Pres. of Cen. Cttee (vacant); Sec.-Gen. USTADZ MURSHI D. IBRAHIM.

Moro National Liberation Front—Islamic Command Council (MNLF—ICC): Basak, Lanao del Sur; f. 2000; Islamist separatist movement committed to urban guerrilla warfare; breakaway faction from MNLF; Cmmdr DATU FIJRODIN, Cmmdr MUDS BAIRODIN, Cmmdr CALEB BEN MUHAMAD, Cmmdr ZAIDA BULLH, Cmmdr OMEN.

National Democratic Front (NDF): a left-wing alliance of 14 mem. groups; Chair. MARIANA OROSA; Spokesman GREGORIO ROSAL.

The NDF includes:

Communist Party of the Philippines (CPP): f. 1968; a breakaway faction of the PKP; legalized Sept. 1992; in July 1993 the Metro Manila-Rizal and Visayas regional committees, controlling 40% of total CPP membership (est. 15,000 in 1994), split from the Central Committee; Chair. JOSE MARIA SISON; Gen. Sec. BENITO TIAMZON.

New People's Army (NPA): f. 1969 as the military wing of the CPP; based in central Luzon, but operates throughout the Philippines; est. strength 9,500; Leader JOVENCIO BALWEG; Spokesman GREGORIO ROSAL.

Revolutionary Proletarian Party: Metro Manila; f. 1996; comprises mems of the Metro Manila-Rizal and Visayas regional committees, which broke away from the CPP in 1993; has a front organization called the Bukluran ng Manggagawang Pilipino (Association of Filipino Workers); Leader ARTURO TABARA.

Diplomatic Representation

EMBASSIES IN THE PHILIPPINES

Argentina: 8th Floor, Liberty Center, 104 H. V. de la Costa St, Salcedo Village, Makati City, 1262 Metro Manila; tel. (2) 8453218; fax (2) 8453220; e-mail embarfil@eastern.com.ph; Ambassador ISMAEL MARIO SCHUFF.

Australia: Doña Salustiana Dee Ty Bldg, 1st–5th Floors, 104 Paseo de Roxas, cnr Perea St, Makati City, 1200 Metro Manila; tel. (2) 7502850; fax (2) 7546268; e-mail public_affairs@mydestiny.net; internet www.australia.com.ph; Ambassador RUTH PEARCE.

Austria: Prince Bldg, 4th Floor, 117 Rada St, Legaspi Village, Makati City, 1200 Metro Manila; tel. (2) 8179191; fax (2) 8134238; Ambassador Dr CHRISTIAN KREPELA.

Bangladesh: Universal-Re Bldg, 2nd Floor, 106 Paseo de Roxas, Legaspi Village, Makati City, Metro Manila; tel. (2) 8175001; fax (2)

8164941; e-mail bdoot.manila@pacific.net.ph; Ambassador Munir uz Zaman.

Belgium: Multibancorporation Centre, 9th Floor, 6805 Ayala Ave, Makati City, Metro Manila; tel. (2) 8451869; fax (2) 8452076; e-mail manila@diplobel.org; Ambassador Christiaan Tanghe.

Brazil: 16th Floor, Liberty Center, 104 H. V. de la Costa St, Salcedo Village, Makati City, 1229 Metro Manila; tel. (2) 8453651; fax (2) 8453676; e-mail brascom@info.com.ph; Ambassador Claudio Maria Henrique do Couto Lyra.

Brunei: Bank of the Philippine Islands Bldg, 11th Floor, Ayala Ave, cnr Paseo de Roxas, Makati City, 1226 Metro Manila; tel. (2) 8162836; fax (2) 8916646; Ambassador Maimunah Dato' Paduka Haji Elias.

Cambodia: Unit 7a, 7th Floor, Country Space One Bldg, Sen. Gil J. Puyat Ave, Makati City, Metro Manila; tel. (2) 8189981; fax (2) 8189983; e-mail cam.emb.ma@netasia.net; Ambassador Ek Sereywath.

Canada: Allied Bank Center, 9th and 11th Floors, 6754 Ayala Ave, Makati City, 1200 Metro Manila; tel. (2) 8670001; fax (2) 8403547; e-mail manil@dfait-maeci.gc.ca; internet www.dfait-maeci.gc.ca/manila; Ambassador Robert Collette.

Chile: 17th Floor, Liberty Center, 104 H. V. de la Costa St, cnr Leviste St, Salcedo Village, Makati City, 1261 Metro Manila; tel. (2) 8433461; fax (2) 8431976; e-mail echileph@mnl.sequel.net; Ambassador Carmen Lynam.

China, People's Republic: 4896 Pasay Rd, Dasmariñas Village, Makati City, Metro Manila; tel. (2) 8443148; fax (2) 8452465; e-mail emb-chn@pacific.net.ph; Ambassador Wang Chungui.

Colombia: Aurora Tower, 18th Floor, Araneta Center, Quezon City, Metro Manila; tel. (2) 9113101; fax (2) 9112846; Ambassador Miguel Duran Ordoñez.

Cuba: 101 Aguirre St, cnr Trasierra St, Cacho-Gonzales Bldg Penthouse, Legaspi Village, Makati City, Metro Manila; tel. (2) 8171192; fax (2) 8164094; Ambassador Ramón Domingo Alonso Medina.

Czech Republic: 30th Floor, Rufino Pacific Tower, Ayala Ave, cnr Herrera St, Makati City, Metro Manila; tel. (2) 8111155; fax (2) 8111020; e-mail manila@embassy.msv.cz; internet www.mzv.cz/manila; Ambassador Stanislav Slavicky.

Egypt: 2229 Paraiso cnr Banyan St, Dasmariñas Village, Makati City, Metro Manila; tel. (2) 8439232; fax (2) 8439239; Ambassador Saber Abdel Kader Mansour.

Finland: 21st Floor, Far East Bank and Trust Center, Sen. Gil J. Puyat Ave, Makati City, Metro Manila; tel. (2) 8915011; fax (2) 8914107; e-mail sanomat.mni@formin.fi; Ambassador Raimo Anttola.

France: Pacific Star Bldg, 16th Floor, Makati Ave, cnr Sen. Gil J. Puyat Ave, Makati City, Metro Manila; tel. (2) 8101981; fax (2) 8175047; e-mail consulat@france.com.ph; internet www.france.com.ph; Ambassador Renée Veyret.

Germany: Globalbank Centre, 6th Floor, 777 Paseo de Roxas, Makati City, 1226 Metro Manila; tel. (2) 8924906; fax (2) 8104703; e-mail germanembassymanila@surfshop.net.ph; internet www.germanembassy-philippines.com; Ambassador Herbert D. Jess.

Holy See: 2140 Taft Ave, POB 3364, 1099 Metro Manila (Apostolic Nunciature); tel. (2) 5210306; fax (2) 5211235; e-mail nuntiusp@info.com.ph; Apostolic Nuncio Most Rev. Antonio Franco.

India: 2190 Paraiso St, Dasmariñas Village, POB 2123, Makati City, Metro Manila; tel. (2) 8430101; fax (2) 8158151; e-mail amb@embindia.org.ph; internet www.embindia.org.ph; Ambassador Navrekha Sharma.

Indonesia: 185 Salcedo St, Legaspi Village, Makati City, Metro Manila; tel. (2) 8925061; fax (2) 8925878; e-mail kbri@impactnet.com; Ambassador Soeratmin.

Iran: 2224 Paraiso St, cnr Pasay Rd, Dasmariñas Village, Makati City, Metro Manila; tel. (2) 8884757; fax (2) 8884777; e-mail sefarati@info.com.ph; Ambassador Gholamreza Yousefi.

Iraq: 2261 Avocado St, Dasmariñas Village, Makati City, Metro Manila; tel. (2) 8439838; fax (2) 8439839; Ambassador Faisal Hussein.

Israel: Trafalgar Plaza, 23rd Floor, H. V. de la Costa St, Salcedo Village, Makati City, 1200 Metro Manila; POB 1697, Makati Central Post Office, 1256 Metro Manila; tel. (2) 8940441; fax (2) 8941027; e-mail israinfor@pacific.net.ph; Ambassador Irit Ben-Abba.

Italy: Zeta Bldg, 6th Floor, 191 Salcedo Village, Legaspi Village, Makati City, Metro Manila; tel. (2) 8924531; fax (2) 8171436; e-mail ambitaly@iname.com; Ambassador Umberto Colesanti.

Japan: 2627 Roxas Blvd, Pasay City, 1300 Metro Manila; tel. (2) 5515710; fax (2) 5515780; e-mail info@embjapan.ph; internet www.embjapan.ph; Ambassador Kojiro Takano.

Korea, Republic: Pacific Star Bldg, 10th Floor, Sen. Gil J. Puyat Ave, cnr Makati Ave, Makati City, 1226 Metro Manila; tel. (2) 8116139; fax (2) 8116148; Ambassador Son Sang-Ha.

Kuwait: 1230 Acacia Rd, Dasmariñas Village, Makati City, Metro Manila; tel. (2) 8876880; fax (2) 8876666; Ambassador Ibrahim Muhanna Al-Muhanna.

Laos: 34 Lapu-Lapu St, Magallanes Village, Makati City, Metro Manila; tel. and fax (2) 8525759; Ambassador Phiane Philakone.

Libya: 1644 Dasmarinas St, cnr Mabolo St, Dasmariñas Village, Makati City, Metro Manila; tel. (2) 8177331; fax (2) 8177337; e-mail lpbmanila@skynet.net; Ambassador Salem M. Adam.

Malaysia: 107 Tordesillas St, Salcedo Village, Makati City, 1200 Metro Manila; POB 1967, Makati City, 1299 Metro Manila; tel. (2) 8174581; fax (2) 8163158; e-mail mwmanila@asiagate.net; Ambassador Mohamed Taufik bin Mohamed Noor.

Malta: 6th Floor, Cattleya Condominium, 235 Salcedo St, Legaspi Village, Makati City, Metro Manila; tel. (2) 8171095; fax (2) 8171089; e-mail syquia@intlaw.com.ph; Ambassador Enrique P. Syquia.

Mexico: 2157 Paraiso St, Dasmarinas Village, Makati City, Metro Manila; tel. (2) 8122211; fax (2) 8929824; e-mail ebmexfil@info.com.ph; Ambassador Enrique Hubbard.

Myanmar: Zanland Center, 8th Floor, 152 Amorsolo St, Legaspi Village, Makati City, Metro Manila; tel. (2) 8172373; fax (2) 8175895; Ambassador U Tin Tun.

Netherlands: King's Court Bldg, 9th Floor, 2129 Chino Roces Ave, POB 2448, Makati City, 1264 Metro Manila; tel. (2) 8125981; fax (2) 8154579; e-mail man@minbuza.nl; internet www.dutchembassy.ph; Ambassador Theo Arnold.

New Zealand: BPI Buendia Centre, 23rd Floor, Sen. Gil J. Puyat Ave, POB 3228, MCPO, Makati City, Metro Manila; tel. (2) 8915358; fax (2) 8915353; e-mail newzealand@embassy.com.ph; Ambassador Terry Baker.

Nigeria: 2211 Paraiso St, Dasmariñas Village, Makati City, 1221 Metro Manila; POB 3174, MCPO, Makati City, 1271 Metro Manila; tel. (2) 8439866; fax (2) 8439867; e-mail embnigmanila@pacific.net.ph; Ambassador Chief Ray O. Inije.

Norway: Petron Mega Plaza Bldg, 21st Floor, 358 Sen. Gil J. Puyat Ave, Makati City, 1209 Metro Manila; tel. (2) 8863245; fax (2) 8863244; e-mail emb.manila@mfa.no; internet www.norway.ph; Ambassador Pål Moe.

Pakistan: Alexander House, 6th Floor, 132 Amorsolo St, Legaspi Village, Makati City, Metro Manila; tel. (2) 8172772; fax (2) 8400229; e-mail parepmnl@info.co.ph; Ambassador Iftikhar Hussain Kazmi.

Panama: 10th Floor, MARC 2000 Tower, 1973 Taft Ave and San Andres St, cnr Quirino Ave, Malate, 1004 Metro Manila; tel. (2) 5212790; fax (2) 5215755; e-mail panaembassy@i-manila.com.ph; Ambassador Juan Carlos Escalona Avila.

Papua New Guinea: 3rd Floor, Corinthian Plaza Condominium Bldg, cnr Paseo de Roxas and Gamboa St, Makati City, Metro Manila; tel. (2) 8113465; fax (2) 8113466; e-mail kundumnl@pngembmnl.com.ph; Ambassador Graham Ainui.

Peru: Unit 1604, 16th Floor, Antel Corporate Centre, 139 Valero St, Salcedo Village, Makati City, Metro Manila; tel. (2) 8138731; fax (2) 8929831; e-mail leprumanila@embassyperu.com.ph; internet www.embassyperu.com.ph; Ambassador Jorge Chavez Soto.

Portugal: 14th Floor, Unit D, Trafalgar Plaza, 105 H. V. de la Costa St, Salcedo Village, Makati City, Metro Manila; tel. (2) 8483789; fax (2) 8483791; Ambassador João Caetano da Silva.

Qatar: 1601 Cypress St, Dasmariñas Village, Makati City, Metro Manila; tel. (2) 8874944; fax (2) 8876406; Ambassador Saleh Ibrahim Al-Kuwari.

Romania: 1216 Acacia Rd, Dasmariñas Village, Makati City, Metro Manila; tel. (2) 8439014; fax (2) 8439063; Ambassador Radu Homescu.

Russia: 1245 Acacia Rd, Dasmariñas Village, Makati City, Metro Manila; tel. (2) 8930190; fax (2) 8109614; e-mail RusEmb@i-manila.com.ph; Ambassador Anatoly Nebogatov.

Saudi Arabia: Saudi Embassy Bldg, 389 Sen. Gil J. Puyat Ave Ext., Makati City, Metro Manila; tel. (2) 8909735; fax (2) 8953493; e-mail phemb@mofa.gov.sa; Ambassador (vacant).

Singapore: The Enterprise Centre, Tower I, 35th Floor, 6766 Ayala Ave, cnr Paseo de Roxas, Makati City, Metro Manila; tel. (2) 7512345; Ambassador Jacky Foo.

Spain: ACT Tower, 5th Floor, 135 Sen. Gil J. Puyat Ave, Makati City, 1200 Metro Manila; tel. (2) 8183561; fax (2) 8102885; e-mail embesphh@mail.mae.es; Ambassador Ignacio Sagaz.

Sri Lanka: 2260 Avocado Ave, Dasmariñas Village, Makati City, Metro Manila; tel. (2) 8439813; Ambassador Pitiduwa Gamage Karunasiri.

Sweden: Equitable PCI Bank Tower II, 16th Floor, Makati Ave, Makati City, Metro Manila; POB 2322, MCPO 1263, Makati City, Metro Manila; tel. (2) 8191951; fax (2) 8153002; e-mail ambassaden.manila@foreign.ministry.se; internet www.swedemb-manila.com; Ambassador Ulf Håkansson.

Switzerland: Equitable Bank Tower, 24th Floor, 8751 Paseo de Roxas, Makati City, 1226 Metro Manila; tel. (2) 7579000; fax (2) 7573718; e-mail vertretung@man.rep.admin.ch; Ambassador Lise Favre.

Thailand: 107 Rada St, Legaspi Village, Makati City, 1229 Metro Manila; tel. (2) 8154220; fax (2) 8154221; e-mail thaimnl@pacific.net.ph; Ambassador Busba Bunnag.

Turkey: 2268 Paraiso St, Dasmariñas Village, Makati City, Metro Manila; tel. (2) 8439705; fax (2) 8439702; Ambassador Tanju Sumer.

United Arab Emirates: Renaissance Bldg, 2nd Floor, 215 Sakedo St, Legaspi Village, Makati City, Metro Manila; tel. (2) 8173906; fax (2) 8183577; Ambassador Mohammed Ebrahim Abdullah al-Jowaid.

United Kingdom: Locsin Bldg, 15th–17th Floors, 6752 Ayala Ave, cnr Makati Ave, Makati City, 1226 Metro Manila; tel. (2) 8167116; fax (2) 8197206; e-mail uk@info.com.ph; internet www.britishembassy.org.ph; Ambassador Paul Dimond.

USA: 1201 Roxas Blvd, Metro Manila; tel. (2) 5231001; fax (2) 5224361; e-mail manila1@pd.state.gov; internet manila.usembassy.gov; Ambassador Francis Ricciardone.

Venezuela: Unit 17A, Multinational Bancorporation Center, 6805 Ayala Ave, Makati City, Metro Manila 1200; tel. (2) 8452841; fax (2) 8452841; e-mail embavefi@compass.com.ph; Ambassador Milena Santana-Ramírez.

Viet Nam: 554 Pablo Ocampo St, Malate, Metro Manila; tel. (2) 5252837; fax (2) 5260472; e-mail sqvnplp@qinet.net; Ambassador Dinh Tich.

Judicial System

The February 1987 Constitution provides for the establishment of a Supreme Court comprising a Chief Justice and 14 Associate Justices; the Court may sit *en banc* or in divisions of three, five or seven members. Justices of the Supreme Court are appointed by the President from a list of a minimum of three nominees prepared by a Judicial and Bar Council. Other courts comprise the Court of Appeals, Regional Trial Courts, Metropolitan Trial Courts, Municipal Courts in Cities, Municipal Courts and Municipal Circuit Trial Courts. There is also a special court for trying cases of corruption (the Sandiganbayan). The Office of the Ombudsman (Tanodbayan) investigates complaints concerning the actions of public officials.

Supreme Court
Taft Ave, cnr Padre Faura St, Ermita, 1000 Metro Manila; tel. (2) 5268123; e-mail infos@supremecourt.gov.ph; internet www.supremecourt.gov.ph.

Chief Justice: Hilario G. Davide, Jr.

Court of Appeals
Consists of a Presiding Justice and 50 Associate Justices.

Presiding Justice: Jesus M. Elbinias.

Islamic Shari'a courts were established in the southern Philippines in July 1985 under a presidential decree of February 1977. They are presided over by three district magistrates and six circuit judges.

Religion

In 1991 94.2% of the population were Christians: 84.1% were Roman Catholics, 6.2% belonged to the Philippine Independent Church (Aglipayan) and 3.9% were Protestants. There is an Islamic community, and an estimated 43,000 Buddhists. Animists and persons professing no religion number approximately 400,000.

CHRISTIANITY

Sangguniang Pambansa ng mga Simbahan sa Pilipinas (National Council of Churches in the Philippines): 879 Epifanio de los Santos Ave, Diliman, Quezon City, Metro Manila; tel. (2) 9288636; fax (2) 9267076; e-mail nccp-ga@philonline.com; f. 1963; 11

mem. churches, 10 assoc. mems; publishes NCCP news magazine quarterly and TUGON periodically; Gen. Sec. Sharon Rose Joy Ruiz-Duremdes.

The Roman Catholic Church
For ecclesiastical purposes, the Philippines comprises 16 archdioceses, 50 dioceses, six territorial prelatures and seven apostolic vicariates. In December 2000 there were an estimated 66,548,331 adherents in the country, representing 82.1% of the total population.

Catholic Bishops' Conference of the Philippines (CBCP) 470 General Luna St, Intramuros, 1002 Metro Manila; POB 3601, 1076 Metro Manila; tel. (2) 5274138; fax (2) 5274063; e-mail cbcp@cbcpnet.net; internet www.cbcp.com.

f. 1945; statutes approved 1952; Pres. Most Rev. Orlando B. Quevedo (Archbishop of Cotabato).

Archbishop of Caceres: Most Rev. Leonardo Z. Legaspi, Archbishop's House, Elias Angeles St, POB 6085, 4400 Naga City; tel. (54) 4738483; fax (54) 4732800.

Archbishop of Cagayan de Oro: Most Rev. Jesus B. Tuquib, Archbishop's Residence, POB 113, 9000 Misamis Oriental, Cagayan de Oro City; tel. (88) 8571357; fax (88) 726304; e-mail orochan@cdo.weblinq.com.

Archbishop of Capiz: Most Rev. Onesimo C. Gordoncillo, Chancery Office, POB 44, 5800 Roxas City; tel. (36) 6215595; fax (36) 6211053.

Archbishop of Cebu: Cardinal Ricardo J. Vidal, Archbishop's Residence, cnr P. Gomez St and P. Burgos St, POB 52, 6000 Cebu City; tel. (32) 2530123; fax (32) 2530616; e-mail adelito@skynet.net.

Archbishop of Cotabato: Most Rev. Orlando B. Quevedo, Archbishop's Residence, Sinsuat Ave, POB 186, 9600 Cotabato City; tel. (64) 4212918; fax (64) 4211446.

Archbishop of Davao: Most Rev. Fernando R. Capalla, Archbishop's Residence, 247 Florentino Torres St, POB 80418, 8000 Davao City; tel. (82) 2271163; fax (82) 2279771; e-mail bishop-davao@skynet.net.

Archbishop of Jaro: Most Rev. Angel N. Lagdameo, Archbishop's Residence, Jaro, 5000 Iloilo City; tel. (33) 3294442; fax (33) 3293197; e-mail abpjaro@skynet.net.

Archbishop of Lingayen-Dagupan: Most Rev. Oscar V. Cruz, Archbishop's House, 2400 Dagupan City; tel. (75) 52353576; fax (75) 5221878; e-mail oscar@rezcom.com.

Archbishop of Lipa: Most Rev. Gaudencio B. Rosales, Archbishop's House, St Lorenzo Ruiz St, Lipa City, 4217 Batangas; tel. (43) 7562573; fax (43) 7562964; e-mail rcalipa@batangas.net.ph.

Archbishop of Manila: Cardinal Jaime L. Sin, Arzobispado, 121 Arzobispo St, Intramuros, POB 132, 1099 Metro Manila; tel. (2) 5277631; fax (2) 5273955; e-mail aord@mailstation.net; internet www.geocities.com/aocmanila.

Archbishop of Nueva Segovia: Most. Rev. Edmundo M. Abaya, Archbishop's House, Vigan, 2700 Ilocos Sur; tel. (77) 7222018; fax (77) 7221591.

Archbishop of Ozamis: Most Rev. Jesus A. Dosado, Archbishop's House, POB 2760, 7200 Ozamis City; tel. (65) 5212820; fax (65) 5211574.

Archbishop of Palo: Most Rev. Pedro R. Dean, Archdiocesan Chancery, Bukid Tabor, Palo, 6501 Leyte; POB 173, Tacloban City, 6500 Leyte; tel. (53) 3232213; fax (53) 3235607; e-mail rcap@mozcom.com.

Archbishop of San Fernando (Pampanga): Most Rev. Paciano B. Aniceto, Chancery House, San José, San Fernando, 2000 Pampanga; tel. (45) 9612819; fax (45) 9616772; e-mail rca@pamp.pworld.net.ph.

Archbishop of Tuguegarao: Most Rev. Diosdado A. Talamayan, Archbishop's House, Tuguegarao, 3500 Cagayan; tel. (78) 8441663; fax (78) 8462822; e-mail rcat@cag.pworld.net.ph.

Archbishop of Zamboanga: Most Rev. Carmelo Dominador F. Morelos, Sacred Heart Center, POB 1, Justice R. T. Lim Blvd, 7000 Zamboanga City; tel. (62) 9911329; fax (62) 9932608; e-mail aofzam@jetlink.com.ph.

Other Christian Churches

Convention of Philippine Baptist Churches: POB 263, 5000 Iloilo City; tel. (33) 3290621; fax (33) 3290618; e-mail gensec@iloilo.net; f. 1935; Gen. Sec. Rev. Dr Nathaniel M. Fabula; Pres. Donato Enabe.

Episcopal Church in the Philippines: 275 E. Rodriguez Sr Ave, Quezon City, 1102 Metro Manila; POB 10321, Broadway Centrum, Quezon City, 1112 Metro Manila; tel. (2) 7228478; fax (2) 7211923; e-mail ecpi@info.com.ph; internet www.episcopalphilippines.net; f. 1901; six dioceses; Prime Bishop Most Rev. IGNACIO C. SOLIBA.

Iglesia Evangélica Metodista en las Islas Filipinas (Evangelical Methodist Church in the Philippines): Beulah Land, Iemelif Center, Greenfields 1, Subdivision, Marytown Circle, Novaliches, Quezon City, Metro Manila; tel. (2) 9356519; fax (2) 4185017; e-mail iemelifph@yahoo.com; internet www.iemelif.com.ph; f. 1909; 40,000 mems (2000); Gen. Supt Bishop NATHANAEL P. LAZARO.

Iglesia Filipina Independiente (Philippine Independent Church): 1500 Taft Ave, Ermita, 1000 Metro Manila; tel. (2) 5237242; fax (2) 5213932; e-mail ifiphil@hotmail.com; internet www.ifi.dpinoyweb.com; f. 1902; 39 dioceses; 6.0m. mems; Obispo Maximo (Supreme Bishop) Most Rev. TOMAS MILLAMENA.

Iglesia ni Cristo: 1 Central Ave, New Era, Quezon City, 1107 Metro Manila; tel. (2) 9814311; fax (2) 9811111; f. 1914; 2m. mems; Exec. Minister Brother ERAÑO G. MANALO.

Lutheran Church in the Philippines: 4461 Old Santa Mesa, 1008 Metro Manila; POB 507, 1099 Metro Manila; tel. (2) 7157084; fax (2) 7142395; f. 1946; Pres. Rev. EDUARDO LADLAD.

Union Church of Manila: cnr Legaspi St and Rada St, Legaspi Village, Makati City, Metro Manila; tel. (2) 8126062; fax (2) 8172386; e-mail ucm@amdg.com.ph; internet www.unionchurch.ph; Interim Pastor Dr DOUGLAS BEYER.

United Church of Christ in the Philippines: 877 Epifanio de los Santos Ave, West Triangle, Quezon City, Metro Manila; POB 718, MCPO, Ermita, 1099 Metro Manila; tel. (2) 9240215; fax (2) 9240207; e-mail uccpnaof@manila-online.net; f. 1948; 900,000 mems (1996); Gen. Sec. Rev. ELMER M. BOLOCON (Bishop).

Among other denominations active in the Philippines are the Iglesia Evangélica Unida de Cristo and the United Methodist Church.

ISLAM

Some 14 different ethnic groups profess the Islamic faith in the Philippines, and Muslims comprised 4.6% of the total population at the census of 1990. Mindanao and the Sulu and Tawi-Tawi archipelago, in the southern Philippines, are predominantly Muslim provinces, but there are 10 other such provinces, each with its own Imam, or Muslim religious leader. More than 500,000 Muslims live in the north of the country (mostly in, or near to, Manila).

Confederation of Muslim Organizations of the Philippines (CMOP): Metro Manila; Nat. Chair. JAMIL DIANALAN.

BAHÁ'Í FAITH

National Spiritual Assembly: 1070 A. Roxas St, cnr Bautista St, Singalong Subdiv., Malate, 1004 Metro Manila; POB 4323, 1099 Metro Manila; tel. (2) 5240404; fax (2) 5245918; e-mail nsaphil@skyinet.net; mems resident in 129,949 localities; Chair. GIL MARVEL TABUCANON; Sec.-Gen. VIRGINIA S. TOLEDO.

The Press

The Office of the President implements government policies on information and the media. Freedom of the press and freedom of speech are guaranteed under the 1987 Constitution.

METRO MANILA

Dailies

Abante: Monica Publishing Corpn, Rooms 301–305, BF Condominium Bldg, 3rd Floor, Solana St, cnr. A. Soriano St, Intramuros, Metro Manila; tel. (2) 5273385; fax (2) 5274470; e-mail abante@abante-tonite.com; internet www.abante.com.ph; morning; Filipino and English; Editor NICOLAS QUIJANO, Jr; circ. 417,000.

Abante Tonite: Monica Publishing Corpn, Rooms 301–305, BF Condominium Bldg, 3rd Floor, Solana St, cnr. A. Soriano St, Intramuros, Metro Manila; tel. (2) 5273385; fax (2) 5274470; e-mail tonite@abante-tonite.com; internet www.abante-tonite.com; afternoon; Filipino and English; Man. Editor NICOLAS QUIJANO, Jr; circ. 277,000.

Ang Pilipino Ngayon: 202 Railroad St, cnr 13th St, Port Area, Metro Manila; tel. (2) 401871; fax (2) 5224998; Filipino; Publr and Editor JOSE M. BUHAIN; circ. 286,452.

Balita: Liwayway Publishing Inc, 2249 China Roces Ave, Makati City, Metro Manila; tel. (2) 8193101; fax (2) 8175167; internet www.balita.org; f. 1972; morning; Filipino; Editor MARCELO S. LAGMAY; circ. 151,000.

Daily Tribune: Penthouse Suites, Plywood Industries Bldg, T. M. Kalaw St, cnr A. Mabini St, Ermita, Metro Manila; tel. (2) 5215511; fax (2) 5215522; e-mail nco@tribune.net.ph; internet www.tribune.net.ph; f. 2000; English; Publr and Editor-in-Chief NINEZ CACHO-OLIVARES.

Malaya: People's Independent Media Inc, 575 Atlanta St, Port Area, Metro Manila; tel. (2) 5277651; fax (2) 5271839; e-mail opinion@malaya.com.ph; internet www.malaya.com.ph; f. 1983; English; Editor JOEY C. DE LOS REYES; circ. 175,000.

Manila Bulletin: Bulletin Publishing Corpn, cnr Muralla and Recoletos Sts, Intramuros, POB 769, Metro Manila; tel. (2) 5271519; fax (2) 5277534; e-mail bulletin@mb.com.ph; internet www.mb.com.ph; f. 1900; English; Publr EMILIO YAP; Editor BEN RODRIGUEZ; circ. 265,000.

Manila Standard: Leyland Bldg, 21st St, cnr Railroad St, Port Area, Metro Manila; tel. (2) 5278351; e-mail infoms@philonline.com; internet www.manilastandard.net; morning; English; Editor-in-Chief JULLIE YAP DAZA; circ. 96,000.

Manila Times: Liberty Bldg, 13th St, Port Area, Metro Manila; tel. (2) 5245664; fax (2) 5216887; e-mail newsboy1@manilatimes.net; internet www.manilatimes.net; f. 1945; morning; English; Publr, Chair. and Pres. DANTE. A. ANG; Editor-in-Chief CIPRIANO S. ROXAS.

People Tonight: Philippine Journalist Inc, Railroad St, cnr 19th and 20th Sts, Port Area, Metro Manila; tel. (2) 5278421; fax (2) 5274627; f. 1978; English and Filipino; Editor FERDIE RAMOS; circ. 500,000.

People's Bagong Taliba: Philippine Journalist Inc, Railroad St, cnr 19th and 20th Sts, Port Area, Metro Manila; tel. (2) 5278121; fax (2) 5274627; Filipino; Editor MATEO VICENCIO; circ. 229,000.

People's Journal: Philippine Journalist Inc, Railroad St, cnr 19th and 20th Sts, Port Area, Metro Manila; tel. (2) 5278421; fax (2) 5274627; English and Filipino; Editor ROSAURO ACOSTA; circ. 219,000.

Philippine Daily Globe: Nova Communications Inc, 2nd Floor, Rudgen Bldg, 17 Shaw Blvd, Metro Manila; tel. (2) 6730496; Editor-in-Chief YEN MAKABENTA; circ. 40,000.

Philippine Daily Inquirer: Philippine Daily Inquirer Bldg, cnr Mascardo St and Yague St, Pasong Tamo, Makati City, 1220 Metro Manila; tel. (2) 8978808; fax (2) 8914793; e-mail feedback@inquirer.com.ph; internet www.inquirer.net; f. 1985; English; Chair. MARIXI R. PRIETO; Editor-in-Chief RIGOBERTO TIGLAO; circ. 250,000.

Philippine Herald-Tribune: V. Esguerra II Bldg, 140 Amorsolo St, Legaspi Village, Makati City, Metro Manila; tel. (2) 853711; f. 1987; Christian-orientated; Pres. AMADA VALINO.

Philippine Star: 13th and Railroad Sts, Port Area, Metro Manila; tel. (2) 5277901; fax (2) 5276851; e-mail philippinestar@hotmail.com; internet www.philstar.com; f. 1986; Editor BOBBY DE LA CRUZ; circ. 275,000.

Tempo: Bulletin Publishing Corpn, Recoletos St, cnr Muralla St, Intramuros, Metro Manila; tel. (2) 5278121; fax (2) 5277534; internet www.tempo.com.ph; f. 1982; English and Filipino; Editor BEN RODRIGUEZ; circ. 230,000.

Today: Independent Daily News, JAKA Macrima Bldg, 1666 Epifanio de los Santos Ave, cnr Escuela St, Makati City, Metro Manila; tel. (2) 8186133; fax (2) 8193982; f. 1993; Editor-in-Chief TEODORO L. LOCSIN, Jr; Man. Editor LOURDES MOLINA-FERNANDEZ; circ. 106,000.

United Daily News: 812 and 818 Benavides St, Binondo, Metro Manila; tel. (2) 2447171; f. 1973; Chinese; Editor-in-Chief CHUA KEE; circ. 85,000.

Selected Periodicals

Weeklies

Banawag: Liwayway Bldg, 2249 Pasong Tamo, Makati City, Metro Manila; tel. (2) 8193101; fax (2) 8175167; f. 1934; Ilocano; Editor DIONISIO S. BULONG; circ. 42,900.

Bisaya: Liwayway Bldg, 2249 Pasong Tamo, Makati City, Metro Manila; tel. (2) 8193101; fax (2) 8175167; f. 1934; Cebu-Visayan; Editor SANTIAGO PEPITO; circ. 90,000.

Liwayway: Liwayway Bldg, 2249 Pasong Tamo, Makati City, Metro Manila; tel. (2) 8193101; fax (2) 8175167; f. 1922; Filipino; Editor RODOLFO SALANDANAN; circ. 102,400.

Panorama: Manila Bulletin Publishing Corpn, POB 769, cnr Muralla and Recoletos Sts, Intramuros, Metro Manila; tel. and fax (2) 5277509; f. 1968; English; Editor RANDY V. URLANDA; circ. 239,600.

Philippine Starweek: 13th St, cnr Railroad St, Port Area, Metro Manila; tel. (2) 5277901; fax (2) 5275819; e-mail starweek@pacific.net.ph; internet www.philstar.com; English; Publr MAXIMO V. SOLIVEN; circ. 268,000.

SELECTED REGIONAL PUBLICATIONS

The Aklan Reporter: 1227 Rizal St, Kalibo, Panay, Aklan; tel. (33) 3181; f. 1971; weekly; English and Aklanon; Editor ROMAN A. DE LA CRUZ; circ. 3,500.

Baguio Midland Courier: 16 Kisad Rd, POB 50, Baguio City; English and Ilocano; Editor SINAI C. HAMADA; circ. 6,000.

Bayanihan Weekly News: Bayanihan Publishing Co, P. Guevarra Ave, Santa Cruz, Laguna; tel. (645) 1001; f. 1966; Mon. Filipino and English; Editor ARTHUR A. VALENOVA; circ. 1,000.

Bohol Chronicle: 56 B. Inting St, Tagbilaran City, Bohol; tel. (32) 3100; internet www.boholchronicle.com; f. 1954; 2 a week; English and Cebuano; Editor and Publr ZOILO DEJARESCO; circ. 5,500.

The Bohol Times: 100 Gallares St, Tagbilaran City, Bohol; tel. (38) 4112961; fax (38) 4112656; e-mail times@bit.fapenet.org; internet www.calamay.bit.fapenet.org/btimes; Pblr Dr LILIA A. BALITE; Editor-in-Chief ATTY SALVADOR D. DIPUTADO.

The Kapawa News: 10 Jose Abad Santos St, POB 365, 6100 Bacolod City; tel. and fax (34) 4441941; e-mail ethel-lyn2001@yahoo.com; f. 1966; weekly; Sat. Hiligaynon and English; Editor ETHELYN MOLES; circ. 15,000.

Mindanao Star: 44 Kolambagohan-Capistrano St, Cagayan de Oro City; internet www.mindanaostar.com; weekly; Editor ROMULFO SABAMAL; circ. 3,500.

Mindanao Times: UMBN Bldg, Ponciano Reyes St, Davao City, Mindanao; tel. 2273252; e-mail timesmen@mozcom.com; internet www.mindanaotimes.com.ph; daily; Pblr JOSEFINA SAN PEDRO (acting); Editor-in-Chief VIC SUMALINOG; circ. 5,000.

Pagadian Times: Pagadian City, 7824 Zamboanga del Sur; tel. 586; e-mail pagtimes@mozcom.com; internet www.pagadian.mozcom.com/pagtimes; f. 1969; weekly; English; Publr PEDE G. LU; Editor JACINTO LUMBAY; circ. 5,000.

Palihan: Diversion Rd, cnr Sanciangco St, Cabanatuan City, Luzon; f. 1966; weekly; Filipino; Editor and Publr NONOY M. JARLEGO; circ. 5,000.

Sorsogon Today: 2886 Burgos St, POB 20, East District, 4700 Sorsogon; tel. and fax (56) 2111340; e-mail sorsogontoday@mailcity.com; f. 1977; weekly; Publr and CEO MARCOS E. PARAS, Jr; circ. 2,400.

The Tribune: Maharlika Highway, 2301 Cabanatuan City, Luzon; f. 1960; weekly; English and Filipino; Editor and Publr ORLANDO M. JARLEGO; circ. 8,000.

The Valley Times: Daang Maharlika, San Felipe, Ilagan, Isabela; f. 1962; weekly; English; Editor AUREA A. DE LA CRUZ; circ. 4,500.

The Visayan Tribune: 826 Iznart St, Iloilo City; tel. (33) 75760; f. 1959; weekly; Tue. English; Editor HERBERT L. VEGO; circ. 5,000.

The Voice of Islam: Davao City; tel. (82) 81368; f. 1973; monthly; English and Arabic; official Islamic news journal; Editor and Publr NASHIR MUHAMMAD AL'RASHID AL HAJJ.

The Weekly Negros Gazette: Broce St, San Carlos City, 6033 Negros Occidental; f. 1956; weekly; Editor NESTORIO L. LAYUMAS, Sr; circ. 5,000.

NEWS AGENCIES

Philippines News Agency: PIA Bldg, 2nd Floor, Visayas Ave, Diliman, Quezon City, Metro Manila; tel. (2) 9206551; fax (2) 9206566; e-mail philna@ops.gov.ph; internet www.pna.ops.gov.ph; f. 1973; Gen. Man. GEORGE REYES; Exec. Editor SEVERINO SAMONTE.

Foreign Bureaux

Agence France-Presse (AFP): Kings Court Bldg 2, 5th Floor, Pasong Tamo, cnr de la Rosa St, Makati City, Metro Manila; tel. (2) 8112028; fax (2) 8112664; Bureau Chief MONICA EGOY.

Agencia EFE (Spain): 5th Floor, Singapore Airlines Bldg, 138 H. V. de la Costa St, Salcedo Village, Makati City, 1227 Metro Manila; tel. (2) 8173663; fax (2) 8153395; e-mail efe@i-next.net; Bureau Chief MARÍA LUISA RUBIO.

Associated Press (AP) (USA): S&L Bldg, 3rd Floor, 1500 Roxas Blvd, Ermita, 1000 Metro Manila; tel. (2) 5259217; fax (2) 5212430; Bureau Chief DAVID THURBER.

Deutsche Presse Agentur (dpa) (Germany): Physicians Tower Bldg, 533 United Nations Ave, Ermita 1000, Metro Manila; tel. (2) 5221919; fax (2) 5221447; Representative GIRLIE LINAO.

Inter Press Service (IPS) (Italy): Amberland Plaza, Room 510, J. Vargas Ave, Ortigas Complex, Pasig City, 1600 Metro Manila; tel. (2) 6353421; fax (2) 6353660; Correspondent JOHANNA SON.

Jiji Tsushin (Jiji Press) (Japan): Legaspi Tower, Suite 21, 3rd Floor, 2600 Roxas Blvd, Metro Manila; tel. (2) 5211472; fax (2) 5211474; Correspondent IPPEI MIYASAKA.

Kyodo News Service (Japan): Pacific Star Bldg, 4th Floor, Makati Ave, cnr Sen. Gil J. Puyat Ave, Makati City, Metro Manila; tel. (2) 8133072; fax (2) 8133914; Correspondent KIMIO OKI.

Reuters (UK): L.V. Locsin Bldg, 10th Floor, Ayala Ave, cnr Makati Ave, Makati City, 1226 Metro Manila; tel. (2) 8418900; fax (2) 8176267; Country Man. RAJU GOPALAKRISHNAN.

United Press International (UPI) (USA): Manila Pavilion Hotel, Room 526C, United Nations Ave, Ermita, 1000 Metro Manila; tel. (2) 5212051; fax (2) 5212074; Bureau Chief MICHAEL DI CICCO.

Xinhua (New China) News Agency (People's Republic of China): 705B Gotesco Twin Towers, 1129 Concepcion St, Ermita, Metro Manila; tel. (2) 5271404; fax (2) 5271410; Chief Correspondent CHEN HEGAO.

PRESS ASSOCIATION

National Press Club of the Philippines: National Press Club Bldg, Magallanes Drive, 1002 Intramuros, Metro Manila; tel. (2) 494242; f. 1952; Pres. MARCELO LAGMAY; Vice-Pres. RECAH TRINIDAD; 942 mems.

Publishers

Abiva Publishing House Inc: Abiva Bldg, 851 Gregorio Araneta Ave, Quezon City, 1113 Metro Manila; tel. (2) 7120245; fax (2) 7320308; e-mail mmrabiva@i-manila.com.ph; internet www.abiva.com.ph; f. 1937; reference and textbooks; Pres. LUIS Q. ABIVA, Jr.

Ateneo de Manila University Press: Bellarmine Bldg, Ateneo de Manila University, Katipunan Rd, Loyola Heights, Quezon City, Metro Manila; tel. (2) 4265984; fax (2) 4265909; e-mail unipress@admu.edu.ph; internet www.ateneouniversitypress.com; f. 1972; literary, textbooks, humanities, social sciences, reference books on the Philippines; Dir CORAZON E. BAYTION.

Bookman, Inc: 373 Quezon Ave, Quezon City, 1114 Metro Manila; tel. (2) 7124813; fax (2) 7124843; e-mail bookman@info.com.ph; f. 1945; textbooks, reference, educational; Pres. MARIETTA PICACHE MARTINEZ; Vice-Pres. LINA PICACHE ENRIQUEZ.

Capitol Publishing House, Inc: 13 Team Pacific Bldg, Jose C. Cruz St, cnr F. Legaspi St, Barrio Ugong, Pasig City, Metro Manila; tel. (2) 6712662; fax (2) 6712664; e-mail cacho@mozcom.com; f. 1947; Gen. Man. MANUEL L. ATIENZA.

Heritage Publishing House: 33 4th Ave, cnr Main Ave, Cubao, Quezon City, POB 3667, Metro Manila; tel. (2) 7248114; fax (2) 6471393; e-mail heritage@iconn.com.ph; internet www.iconn.com.ph/heritage; art, anthropology, history, political science; Pres. MARIO R. ALCANTARA; Man. Dir RICARDO S. SANCHEZ.

The Lawyers' Co-operative Publishing Co. Inc: 1071 Del Pan St, Makati City, 1206 Metro Manila; tel. (2) 5634073; fax (2) 5642021; e-mail lawbooks@info.com.ph; f. 1908; law, educational; Pres. ELSA K. ELMA.

Liwayway Publishing Inc: 2249 Chino Roces Ave, Makati City, Metro Manila; tel. (2) 8193101; fax (2) 8175167; magazines and newspapers; Pres. RENE G. ESPINA; Chair. DIONISIO S. BULONG.

Mutual Books Inc: 429 Shaw Blvd, Mandaluyong City, Metro Manila; tel. (2) 7257538; fax (2) 7213056; f. 1959; textbooks on accounting, management and economics, computers and mathematics; Pres. ALFREDO S. NICDAO, Jr.

Phoenix—SIBS Publishing House Inc: 927 Quezon Ave, Quezon City, 1104 Metro Manila; tel. (2) 3724733; fax (2) 3724732; e-mail sibsbook@info.com.ph; internet www.sibs.com.ph; f. 1958; sciences, languages, religion, literature, history; Pres. JESUS ERNESTO SIBAL; Gen. Man. JUAN CARLOS SIBAL.

Reyes Publishing Inc: Mariwasa Bldg, 4th Floor, 717 Aurora Blvd, Quezon City, 1112 Metro Manila; tel. (2) 7221827; fax (2) 7218782; e-mail reyespub@skyinet.net; f. 1964; art, history and culture; Pres. LOUIE REYES.

Sinag-Tala Publishers Inc: GMA Lou-Bel Plaza, 6th Floor, Chino Roces Ave, cnr Bagtikan St, San Antonio Village, Makati City, 0712 Metro Manila; tel. (2) 8971162; fax (2) 8969626; e-mail info@sinagtala.com; internet www.sinagtala.com; f. 1972; educational textbooks; business, professional and religious books; Man. Dir LUIS A. USON.

University of the Philippines Press: Epifanio de los Santos Ave, U. P. Campus, Diliman, Quezon City, 1101 Metro Manila; tel. (2) 9252930; fax (2) 9282558; e-mail press@up.edu.ph; internet www.upd.edu.ph/~uppress; f. 1965; literature, history, political science, sociology, cultural studies, economics, anthropology, mathematics; Officer in Charge RUTH JORDANA L. PISON.

Vibal Publishing House Inc: G. Araneta Ave, cnr Maria Clara St, Talayan, Quezon City, Metro Manila; tel. (2) 7122722; fax (2) 7118852; internet www.vibalpublishing.com; f. 1955; linguistics, social sciences, mathematics, religion; CEO ESTHER A. VIBAL.

PUBLISHERS' ASSOCIATIONS

Philippine Educational Publishers' Asscn: 84 P. Florentino St, Quezon City, 1104 Metro Manila; tel. (2) 7402698; fax (2) 7115702; e-mail dbuhain@cnl.net; Pres. DOMINADOR D. BUHAIN.

Publishers' Association of the Philippines Inc: Gammon Center, Alfaro St, Salcedo Village, Makati City, Metro Manila; f. 1974; mems comprise all newspaper, magazine and book publrs in the Philippines; Pres. KERIMA P. TUVERA; Exec. Dir ROBERTO M. MENDOZA.

Broadcasting and Communications

National Telecommunications Commission (NTC): NTC Bldg, BIR Rd, East Triangle, Diliman, Quezon City, Metro Manila; tel. (2) 9244042; fax (2) 9217128; e-mail ntc@ntc.gov.ph; internet www.ntc.gov.ph; f. 1979; supervises and controls all private and public telecommunications services; Commr ARMI JANE R. BORJE.

TELECOMMUNICATIONS

BayanTel: Benpres Bldg, 5th Floor, Meralco Ave, cnr Exchange Rd, Pasig City, Metro Manila; tel. (2) 4493000; fax (2) 4492511; e-mail bayanserve@bayantel.com.ph; internet www.bayantel.com.ph; 359,000 fixed lines (1999); Pres. RODOLFO SALAZAR.

Bell Telecommunications Philippines (BellTel): Pacific Star Bldg, 3rd and 4th Floors, Sen. Gil J. Puyat Ave, cnr Makati Ave, Makati City, Metro Manila; tel. (2) 8400808; fax (2) 8915618; e-mail info@belltel.ph; internet www.belltel.ph; f. 1997; Pres. EDRAGDO REYES.

Capitol Wireless Inc: Dolmar Gold Tower, 6th Floor, 107 Carlos Palanca, Jr, St, Legaspi Village, Makati City, Metro Manila; tel. (2) 8159961; fax (2) 8941141; Pres. EPITACIO R. MARQUEZ.

Digital Telecommunications Philippines Inc: 110 Eulogio Rodriguez, Jr, Ave, Bagumbayan, Quezon City, 1110 Metro Manila; tel. (2) 6330000; fax (2) 6339387; provision of fixed line telecommunications services; 564,304 fixed lines (1998); cap. and res 10,928m. pesos, sales 3,060m. pesos (1998); Chief Exec. RICARDO J. ROMULO; Pres. JOHN GOKONGWEI.

Domestic Satellite Philippines Inc (DOMSAT): Solid House Bldg, 4th Floor, 2285 Pasong Tamo Ext., Makati City, 1231 Metro Manila; tel. (2) 8105917; fax (2) 8671677; Pres. SIEGFRED MISON.

Globe Telecom (GMCR) Inc: Globe Telecom Plaza, 57th Floor, Pioneer St, cnr Madison St, 1552 Mandaluyong City, Metro Manila; tel. (2) 7302701; fax (2) 7302586; e-mail custhelp@globetel.com.ph; internet www.globe.com.ph; 700,000 fixed and mobile telephone subscribers (1999); Pres. and CEO GERARDO C. ABLAZA, Jr.

Philippine Communications Satellite Corpn (PhilcomSat): 12th Floor, Telecoms Plaza, 316 Sen. Gil J. Puyat Ave, Makati City, Metro Manila; tel. (2) 8158406; fax (2) 8159287; Pres. MANUEL H. NIETO.

Philippine Global Communications, Inc (PhilCom): 8755 Paseo de Roxas, Makati City, Metro Manila; tel. (2) 8162851; fax (2) 8162872; e-mail aong@philcom.com; internet www.philcom.com; Pres. EVELYN SINGSON.

Philippine Long Distance Telephone Co: Ramon Cojuangco Bldg, Makati Ave, POB 2148, Makati City, Metro Manila; tel. (2) 8168883; fax (2) 8186800; e-mail media@pldt.com.ph; internet www.pldt.com.ph; f. 1928; monopoly on overseas telephone service until 1989; retains 94% of Philippine telephone traffic; 2,516,748 fixed lines (1998); Chair. ANTONIO COJUANGCO; Pres. and CEO MANUEL PANGILINAN.

Pilipino Telephone Corpn (Piltel): Bankers Center, 9th Floor, 6764 Ayala Ave, Makati City, Metro Manila; tel. (2) 8913888; fax (2) 8171121; major cellular telephone provider; 400,000 subscribers (1999); Chair. ROBERTO V. ONGPIN; Pres. and CEO NAPOLEON L. NAZARENO.

Smart Communications, Inc (SCI): Rufino Pacific Tower, 12th Floor, Ayala Ave, cnr Herrera St, Makati City, Metro Manila; tel. (2) 8110213; fax (2) 5113400; 900,000 mobile telephone subscribers (1999); Pres. ORLANDO B. VEA.

BROADCASTING

Radio

Banahaw Broadcasting Corpn: Broadcast City, Capitol Hills, Diliman, Quezon City, 3005 Metro Manila; tel. (2) 9329949; fax (2) 9318751; 14 stations; Station Man. BETTY LIVIOCO.

Cebu Broadcasting Co: FJE Bldg, 105 Esteban St, Legaspi Village, Makati City, Metro Manila; tel. (2) 8159131; fax (2) 8125592; Chair. HADRIAN ARROYO.

Far East Broadcasting Co Inc: POB 1, Valenzuela, 0560 Metro Manila; 62 Karuhatan Rd, Karuhatan, Valenzuela City, 1441 Metro Manila; tel. (2) 2921152; fax (2) 2925790; e-mail febcomphil@febc.org.ph; internet www.febc.org.ph; f. 1948; 18 stations; operates a classical music station, eight domestic stations and an overseas service in 64 languages throughout Asia; Pres. CARLOS L. PEÑA.

Filipinas Broadcasting Network: Legaspi Towers 200, Room 306, Paseo de Roxas, Makati City, Metro Manila; tel. (2) 8176133; fax (2) 8177135; Gen. Man. DIANA C. GOZUM.

GMA Network Inc: GMA Network Center, EDSA cnr Timog Ave, Diliman, Quezon City, 1103 Metro Manila; tel. (2) 9287021; fax (2) 4263925; e-mail yourgmafamily@gmanetwork.com; internet www.igma.tv; f. 1950; fmrly Republic Broadcasting System Inc; transmits nationwide through 44 television stations; Chair., Pres. and CEO FELIPE L. GOZON; Exec. Vice-Pres. GILBERTO R. DUAVIT, Jr.

Manila Broadcasting Co: FJE Bldg, 4th Floor, 105 Esteban St, Legaspi Village, Makati City, Metro Manila; tel. (2) 8177043; fax (2) 8400763; f. 1946; 10 stations; Pres. RUPERTO NICDAO, Jr; Gen. Man. EDUARDO L. MONTILLA.

Nation Broadcasting Corpn: NBC Broadcast Center, Jacinta II Bldg, Epifanio de los Santos Ave, Guadelupe, Makati City, 1200 Metro Manila; tel. (2) 8821622; fax (2) 8821360; e-mail joey@nbc.ph; internet www.nbc.com.ph; f. 1963; 31 stations; Pres. FRANCIS LUMEN.

Newsounds Broadcasting Network Inc: Florete Bldg, Ground Floor, 2406 Nobel, cnr Edison St, Makati City, 3117 Metro Manila; tel. (2) 8430116; fax (2) 8173631; 10 stations; Gen. Man. E. BILLONES; Office Man. HERMAN BASBANO.

Pacific Broadcasting System: c/o Manila Broadcasting Co, FJE Bldg, 105 Esteban St, Legaspi Village, Makati City, Metro Manila; tel. (2) 8921660; fax (2) 8400763; Pres. RUPERTO NICDAO, Jr; Vice-Pres. RODOLFO ARCE.

PBN Broadcasting Network: Ersan Bldg, 3rd Floor, 32 Quezon Ave, Queen City, Metro Manila; tel. (2) 7325424; fax (2) 7438162; e-mail pbn@philonline.com.ph; Pres. JORGE BAYONA.

Philippines Broadcasting Service (PBS): Bureau of Broadcast Services, Office of the Press Sec., Philippine Information Agency Bldg, 4th Floor, Visayas Ave, Quezon City, Metro Manila; tel. (2) 9242607; fax (2) 9242745; Philippine overseas service (Radyo Pilipinas), Bureau of Broadcasts, Office of Media Affairs; Dir FERNANDO G. GAGELONIA.

Philippine Broadcasting System: FJE Bldg, 105 Esteban St, Legaspi Village, Makati City, Metro Manila; tel. (2) 8177043; fax (2) 8400763; Pres. RUPERTO NICDAO, Jr.

Philippine Federation of Catholic Broadcasters: 2307 Pedro Gil, Santa Ana, POB 3169, Metro Manila; tel. (2) 5637319; fax (2) 5637316; 48 radio stations and four TV channels; Pres. Fr FRANCIS LUCAS.

Radio Philippines Network, Inc: Broadcast City, Capitol Hills, Diliman, Quezon City, Metro Manila; tel. (2) 9318627; fax (2) 984322; f. 1969; seven TV stations, 14 radio stations; Pres. EDGAR SAN LUIS; Gen. Man. FELIPE G. MEDINA.

Radio Veritas Asia: Buick St, Fairview Park, POB 2642, Quezon City, Metro Manila; tel. (2) 9394692; fax (2) 9381940; e-mail rveritas-asia@rveritas-asia.org; internet www.rveritas-asia.org; f. 1969; Catholic short-wave station, broadcasts in 17 languages; Pres. and Chair. Cardinal JAIME L. SIN; Gen. Man. Fr CARLOS S. LARIOSA (SVD).

UM Broadcasting Network: Xanland Corporate Center, Room 7B, 152 Amorsolo St, Legaspi Village, Makati City, Metro Manila; tel. (2) 8158754; fax (2) 8173505; e-mail umbmmkt@mozcom.com; Exec. Vice-Pres. WILLY TORRES.

Vanguard Radio Network: J & T Bldg, Room 208, Santa Mesa, Metro Manila; tel. (2) 7161233; fax (2) 7160899; Pres. MANUEL GALVEZ.

Television

In July 1991 there were seven originating television stations and 105 replay and relay stations. The seven originating stations were ABS-CBN (Channel 2), PTV4 (Channel 4), ABC (Channel 5), GMA (Channel 7), RPN (Channel 9), IBC (Channel 13) and SBN (Channel 21). The following are the principal operating television networks:

ABC Development Corpn: APMC Bldg, 136 Amorsolo St, cnr Gamboa St, Legaspi Village, Makati City, Metro Manila; tel. (2) 8923801; fax (2) 8128840; CEO EDWARD U. TAN.

ABS-CBN Broadcasting Corpn: ABS-CBN Broadcasting Center, Sgt E. Esguerra Ave, cnr Mother Ignacia Ave, Quezon City, 1103 Metro Manila; tel. (2) 9244101; fax (2) 9215888; Chair. EUGENIO LOPEZ III; Gen. Man. FEDERICO M. GARCIA.

AMCARA Broadcasting Network: Mother Ignacia St, cnr Sgt Esguerra Ave, Quezon City, Metro Manila; tel. (2) 4152272; fax (2) 4119646; Man. Dir MANUEL QUIOGUE.

Banahaw Broadcasting Corpn: Broadcast City, Capitol Hills, Quezon City, 3005 Metro Manila; tel. (2) 9329949; fax (2) 9318751; Station Man. BETTY LIVIOCO.

Channel V Philippines: Sagittarius Bldg, 6th Floor, H. V. de la Costa St, Salcedo Village, Makati City, Metro Manila; tel. (2) 8173747; fax (2) 8184192; e-mail channelv@i-next.net; Pres. JOEL JIMENEZ; Gen. Man. MON ALCARAZ.

GMA Network, Inc: RBS Bldg, Epifanio de los Santos Ave, Diliman, Quezon City, 1103 Metro Manila; tel. (2) 9287021; fax (2) 9243055; internet www.gmanetwork.com; f. 1950; transmits nationwide through 44 TV stations and in South-East Asia through Aguila 2 satellite; Chair. FELIPE L. GOZON; Pres. and CEO MENARDO R. JIMENEZ.

Intercontinental Broadcasting Corpn: Broadcast City Complex, Capitol Hills, Diliman, Quezon City, Metro Manila; tel. (2) 9318781; fax (2) 9318743; 19 stations; Pres. and Chair. BOOTS ANSON-ROA.

Maharlika Broadcasting System: Metro Manila; tel. (2) 9220880; jtly operated by the Bureau of Broadcasts and the National Media Production Center; Dir ANTONIO BARRIERO.

People's Television Network Inc (PTV4): Broadcast Complex, Visayas Ave, Quezon City, Metro Manila; tel. (2) 9206514; fax (2) 9204342; f. 1992; public television network; Chair. LOURDES I. ILLUSTRE.

Radio Mindanao Network: State Condominium, 4th Floor, Salcedo St, Legaspi Village, Makati City, Metro Manila; tel. (2) 8191073; fax (2) 8163680; Chair. HENRY CANOY; Pres. ERIC S. CANOY.

Radio Philippines Network, Inc: Broadcast City, Capitol Hills, Diliman, Quezon City, Metro Manila; tel. (2) 9315080; fax (2) 9318627; 7 primary TV stations, 14 relay stations; Pres. EDGAR SAN LUIS; Gen. Man. FELIPE G. MEDINA.

RJ TV 29: Save a Lot Bldg, Pasong Tamo Ext., Makati City, Metro Manila; tel. (2) 8942320; fax (2) 8942360; Gen. Man. BEA J. COLAMONICI.

Southern Broadcasting Network, Inc: Strata 200 Bldg, 22nd Floor, Ortigas Center, Emerald Ave, Pasig City, Metro Manila; tel. (2) 6365496; fax (2) 6365495; Pres. LUIS B. PACQUING.

United Broadcasting Network: FEMS Tower 1, 11th Floor, 1289 Zobel Roxas, cnr South Superhighway, Malate; tel. (2) 5216138; fax (2) 5221226; Gen. Man. JOSEPH HODREAL.

Association

Kapisanan ng mga Brodkaster sa Pilipinas (KBP) (Association of Broadcasters in the Philippines): LTA Bldg, 6th Floor, 118 Perea St, Legaspi Village, Makati City, Metro Manila; tel. (2) 8151990; fax (2) 8151989; e-mail kbp@pacific.net.ph; Chair. CERGE REMONDE; Pres. RUPERTO S. NIODAO, Jr.

Finance

(cap. = capital; res = reserves; dep. = deposits; m. = million; brs = branches; amounts in pesos, unless otherwise stated)

BANKING

Legislation enacted in June 1993 provided for the establishment of a new monetary authority, the Bangko Sentral ng Pilipinas, to replace the Central Bank of the Philippines. The Government was thus able to restructure the Central Bank's debt (308,000m. pesos).

In May 1994 legislation was promulgated providing for the establishment in the Philippines of up to 10 new foreign bank branches over the following five years (although at least 70% of the banking system's total resources were to be owned by Philippine entities). Prior to this legislation only four foreign banks (which had been in operation when the law restricting the industry to locally-owned banks was enacted in 1948) were permitted to operate. Two other foreign banks were subsequently licensed to organize locally-incorporated banks with minority Filipino partners. By the end of 2001 the number of foreign banks had increased to 17; at that time some 45 principal commercial banks were operating in the Philippines.

Central Bank

Bangko Sentral ng Pilipinas (Central Bank of the Philippines): A. Mabini St, cnr Vito Cruz St, Malate, 1004 Metro Manila; tel. (2) 5234832; fax (2) 5231252; e-mail bspmail@bsp.gov.ph; internet www.bsp.gov.ph; f. 1993; cap. 10,000m., res 97,851m., dep. 396,093m. (1998); Gov. RAFAEL B. BUENAVENTURA; 20 brs.

Principal Commercial Banks

Allied Banking Corpn: Allied Bank Centre, 6754 Ayala Ave, cnr Legaspi St, Makati City, 1200 Metro Manila; tel. (2) 8187961; fax (2) 8160921; internet www.alliedbank.com.ph; f. 1977; cap. 495m., res 12,950m., dep. 83,587m. (Dec. 2001); Chair. PANFILO O. DOMINGO; Pres. REYNALDO A. MACLANG; 285 brs.

AsianBank Corporation: AsianBank Center, 328 Sen. Gil J. Puyat Ave, Salcedo Village, Makati City, 1200 Metro Manila; tel. (2) 8190611; fax (2) 8103867; e-mail francisv@mnl.sequel.net; f. 1978; cap. 3,877m., res 32,613m., dep. 22,424m. (Dec. 1998); merged with the Philippine Bank of Communications in early 1999 and into Globalbank in 2000; Chair. RAMON R. DEL ROSARIO; Pres. EDWARD S. GO; 98 brs.

Banco de Oro Universal Bank: 12 ADB Ave, Mandaluyong City, 1550 Metro Manila; tel. (2) 6366060; fax (2) 6317810; e-mail bancoro@bdo.com.ph; f. 1996; cap. 10,690m., res 77,880m., dep. 56,617m. (Dec. 2001); Chair. TERESITA T. SY; Pres. NESTOR V. TAN; 125 brs.

Bank of Commerce: Bankers' Center, 6764 Ayala Ave, Makati City, 1226 Metro Manila; tel. (2) 8174906; fax (2) 8172426; e-mail bk_commerce@mp.bkcomp.bridge.com; internet www.bankcom.com.ph; f. 1983; fmrly Boston Bank of the Philippines; cap. 2,812m., dep. 8,621m. (Jan. 1999); Chair. ANTONIO COJUANGCO; Pres. RAUL B. DE MESA; 38 brs.

Bank of the Philippine Islands: BPI Bldg, Ayala Ave, cnr Paseo de Roxas, POB 1827, MCC, Makati City, 0720 Metro Manila; tel. (2) 8185541; fax (2) 8910170; f. 1851; merged with Far East Bank and Trust Co in Apr. 2000; cap. 15,323m., res 30,707m., dep. 296,254m. (Dec. 2000); Pres. XAVIER P. LOINAZ; Chair. JAIME ZOBEL DE AYALA; 340 brs.

China Banking Corpn: CBC Bldg, 8745 Paseo de Roxas, cnr Villar St, Makati City, 1226 Metro Manila; tel. (2) 8855555; fax (2) 8920220; e-mail postmaster@chinabank.com.ph; internet www.chinabank.com.ph; f. 1920; cap. 2,979m., res 2,082m., dep. 47,021m. (Dec. 2000); Chair. GILBERT U. DEE; Pres. and CEO PETER S. DEE; 138 brs.

DBS Bank Philippines, Inc: The Enterprise Center, 6766 Ayala Ave, cnr Paseo de Roxas, Makati City, Metro Manila; tel. (2) 8865888; internet www.dbs.com.ph; cap. 2,220m., dep. 6,099m. (Dec. 2000); Chair. CHONG KIE CHEONG; Pres. PASCUAL M. GARCIA III; 20 brs.

Development Bank of the Philippines: DBP Bldg, Makati Ave, cnr Sen. Gil J. Puyat Ave, Makati City, 1200 Metro Manila; POB 1996, Makati Central PO, Makati City, 1200 Metro Manila; tel. (2) 8189511; fax (2) 8128089; e-mail info@devbankphil.com.ph; internet www.devbankphil.com.ph; f. 1947 as the Rehabilitation Finance Corpn; govt-owned; provides medium- and long-term loans for agricultural and industrial developments; cap. 18,558m., dep. 36,740m. (June 2002); Chair. VITALIANO N. NAÑAGAS II; Pres. and CEO SIMON R. PATERNO; 77 brs; 16 area management offices.

East West Banking Corpn: 349 Sen. Gil J. Puyat Ave, Makati City, 1200 Metro Manila; tel. (2) 8905371; fax (2) 8928682; f. 1994; cap. 1,341m., dep. 2,857m. (March 1997); Chair. ANDREW L. GOTIANUM; Pres. ELREY T. RAMOS; 20 brs.

Equitable PCI Bank: Equitable PCI Bank Towers, 262 Makati Ave, cnr H. V. de la Costa St, Makati City, 1200 Metro Manila; tel. (2) 8407000; fax (2) 8941893; internet www.equitablepcib.com; f. 1950; formed by a merger between Equitable Banking Corpn and Philippine Commercial International (PCI) Bank in 1999; cap. 7,270m., res 37,396m., dep. 141,078m. (Dec. 2001); Chair. ANTONIO L. GO; Pres. RENE J. BUENAVENTURA; 420 brs.

Export and Industry Bank: 30 Paseo de Roxas, Makati City, 1226 Metro Manila; tel. (2) 8963311; fax (2) 8963310; cap. 1,638m., dep. 2,767m. (Dec. 1997); Chair. SERGIO R. ORTIZ-LUIS, Jr; Pres. BENJAMIN P. CASTILLO.

Global Business Bank (Globalbank): 777 Paseo de Roxas, cnr Sedeño St, Makati City, Metro Manila; tel. (2) 8948888; jt venture between Metrobank and Tokai Bank Ltd (Japan); merged with Philbank and Asianbank in 2000; Pres. ROBIN KING; 143 brs.

Land Bank of the Philippines: LBP Bldg, 319 Sen. Gil J. Puyat Ave, Makati City, 1200 Metro Manila; tel. (2) 8189411; fax (2) 8172536; e-mail corplan@mail.landbank.com; internet www.landbank.com; f. 1963; specialized govt bank with universal banking licence; cap. 14,220m., dep. 142,400m. (Dec. 1999); Chair. JOSE T. PARDO; Pres. FLORIDO P. CASUELA; 343 brs.

Maybank Philippines Inc: Legaspi Towers 300, Vito Cruz St, cnr Roxas Blvd, Malate, 1004 Metro Manila; POB 124, 1099 Metro Manila; tel. (2) 5216169; fax (2) 5218513; f. 1961; cap. 1,671m., dep. 2,701m. (Dec. 1997); Pres. and CEO YONG YUR WONG; 60 brs.

Metropolitan Bank and Trust Co (Metrobank): Metrobank Plaza, Sen. Gil J. Puyat Ave, Makati City, 1200 Metro Manila; tel. (2) 8988000; fax (2) 8176248; e-mail metrobank@metrobank.com.ph; internet www.metrobank.com.ph; f. 1962; cap. 32,673m., res 8,123m., dep. 350,486m. (Dec. 2000); Chair. GEORGE S. K. TY; Pres. ANTONIO S. ABACAN, Jr; 344 local brs, 6 overseas brs.

Philippine Bank of Communications: PBCOM Tower, 6795 Ayala Ave, cnr Herrera St, 1226 Makati City; tel. (2) 8307000; fax (2) 8182598; e-mail info@pbcom.com.ph; internet www.pbcom.com.ph; f. 1939; cap. 4,174m., dep. 23,904m. (Dec. 1998); merged with AsianBank Corporation in early 1999; Chair. LUY KIM GUAN; Pres. ISIDRO C. ALCANTARA, Jr; 45 brs.

Philippine Banking Corpn (Philbank): Philbank Bldg, 6797 Ayala Ave, Makati City, 1226 Metro Manila; tel. (2) 8170872; fax (2) 8170892; internet www.philbank.com.ph; f. 1935 as Square Deal Inc; present name adopted 1957; cap. 1,435m., dep. 12,104m. (Dec. 1999); Chair. SIY YAP CHUA; Pres. and CEO NORBERTO C. NAZARENO; 63 brs.

Philippine National Bank (PNB): PNB Financial Center, Roxas Blvd, Pasay City, POB 1844, 1300 Metro Manila; tel. (2) 5263131; fax (2) 8331245; e-mail mainbranch@pnb.com.ph; internet www.pnb .com.ph; f. 1916; partially transferred to the private sector in 1996 and 2000, 17% govt-owned; cap. and res 20,471m., dep. 119,812m. (Dec. 2000); Chair. ROBERTO C. NAZARENO; Pres. and CEO FELICIANO L. MIRANDA, Jr; 324 local brs, 5 overseas brs.

Philippine Veterans Bank: 101 Herrera St, cnr de la Rosa St, Legaspi Village, Makati City, Metro Manila; tel. (2) 8943919; fax (2) 8940625; cap. 3.600m., dep. 10,400m. (June 1998); Chair. EMMANUEL DE OCAMPO; Pres. SUNDAY LAVIN; 38 brs.

Philtrust Bank (Philippine Trust Co): Philtrust Bank Bldg, United Nations Ave, cnr San Marcelino St, Ermita, 1045 Metro Manila; tel. (2) 5249061; fax (2) 5217309; e-mail ptc@bancnet.net; f. 1916; cap. 1,500m., dep. 20,540m. (Dec. 1999); Pres. ANTONIO H. OZAETA; Chair. EMILIO T. YAP; 32 brs.

Prudential Bank: Prudential Bank Bldg, 6787 Ayala Ave, Makati City, 1200 Metro Manila; tel. (2) 8178981; fax (2) 8175146; e-mail feedback@prudentialbank.com; f. 1952; merged with Pilipinas Bank in May 2000; cap. 829m., res 6,890m., dep. 39,456m. (Dec. 2000); Chair. and Pres. JOSE L. SANTOS; 117 brs.

Rizal Commercial Banking Corpn: Yuchengco Tower, RCBC Plaza, 6819 Alaya Ave, Makati City, POB 2202, 1200 Metro Manila; tel. (2) 8949000; fax (2) 8949958; f. 1960; cap. 8,281m., dep. 53,287m. (March 1997); Chair. ALFONSO T. YUCHENGCO; Pres. VALENTIN A. ARANETA; 166 brs.

Security Bank Corpn: 6776 Ayala Ave, Makati City, 1200 Metro Manila; tel. (2) 8676788; fax (2) 8132069; e-mail inquiry@ securitybank.com.ph; internet www.securitybank.com; f. 1951; fmrly Security Bank and Trust Co; cap. 9,500m. (Sept. 2002), res 4,951m. (Dec. 2000), dep. 39,200m. (Sept. 2002); Pres. RAFAEL F. SIMPAO, Jr; Chair. FREDERICK Y. DY; 117 brs.

TA Bank of the Philippines: Octagon Bldg, 4th Floor, San Miguel Ave, Ortigas Complex, Pasig City, Metro Manila; tel. (2) 6376162; fax (2) 6376279; cap. 1,378m., dep. 579m. (June 1998); Chair. Datuk TIAH THEE KIAN; Pres. EXEQUIEL VILLACORTA, Jr.

Traders Royal Bank: TRB Tower, Roxas Blvd, Pasay City, 1300 Metro Manila; tel. (2) 8312821; fax (2) 8312494; e-mail trbm@mnl .sequel.net; internet www.sequel.net; f. 1963; cap. 1,323.2m., dep. 6,553m. (Dec. 1999); Chair. JULITA C. BENEDICTO; Pres. RENATO H. PERONILLA; 55 brs.

Union Bank of the Philippines: SSS Makati Bldg, Ayala Ave, cnr Herrera St, Makati City, 1200 Metro Manila; tel. (2) 8920011; fax (2) 8186058; e-mail online@unionbankph.com; internet www .unionbankph.com; f. 1954; cap. 6,970m., dep. 19,694m. (Dec. 1998); Chair. JUSTO A. ORTIZ; Pres. and CEO ARMAND F. BRAUN, Jr; 120 brs.

United Coconut Planters' Bank: UCPB Bldg, Makati Ave, Makati City, 0728 Metro Manila; tel. (2) 8119000; fax (2) 8119706; e-mail crc@ucpb.com.ph; internet www.ucpb.com; f. 1963; cap. 10,727m., dep. 87,425m. (Dec. 2000); Chair. JERONIMO U. KILAYKO; Pres. LORENZO V. TAN; 178 brs.

United Overseas Bank Philippines: 17th Floor, Pacific Star Bldg, Sen. Gil J. Puyat Ave, cnr Makati Ave, Makati City, Metro Manila; tel. (2) 8788686; fax (2) 8115917; e-mail crd@uob.com.ph; internet www.uob.com.ph; f. 1999; cap. 2,731m., dep. 15,021m. (Dec. 1999); Chair. WEE CHO YAW; Pres. CHUA TENG HUI; 97 brs.

Urban Bank, Inc: Urban Bank Plaza, Urban Ave, Makati City, 1200 Metro Manila; tel. (2) 8164666; fax (2) 8879900; f. 1995; cap. 7,706m., dep. 4,103m. (March 1997); Chair. ARESENIO M. BARTOLOME; Pres. TEODORO C. BORLONGAN; 36 brs.

Rural Banks

Small private banks have been established with the encouragement and assistance (both financial and technical) of the Government in order to promote and expand the rural economy. Conceived mainly to stimulate the productive capacities of small farmers, merchants and industrialists in rural areas, and to combat usury, their principal objectives are to place within easy reach and access of the people credit facilities on reasonable terms and, in co-operation with other agencies of the Government, to provide advice on business and farm management and the proper use of credit for production and marketing purposes. The rural banks numbered 1,942 in 1998; their registered resources totalled 59,970m. pesos at 31 December 1998.

Thrift Banks

Thrift banks mobilize small savings and provide loans to lower income groups. The thrift banking system comprises savings and mortgage banks, stock savings and loan associations and private development banks. In 1998 there were 1,474 thrift banks; their registered resources totalled 216,440m. pesos.

Development Bank

1st e-Bank: 1st e-Bank Tower, 8737 Paseo de Roxas, Makati City, 1226 Metro Manila; tel. (2) 8158536; fax (2) 8195376; e-mail 1stecare@1stebank.com.ph; internet www.1stebank.com.ph; f. 1963 with World Bank assistance, as Private Development Corporation of the Philippines; 1992 converted into a development bank; name changed as above in May 2000; banking and lending services; financial advisory, trust and investment services; training and consultancy; insurance brokerage; cap. and res 2,079.7m., dep. 7,244.6m. (1996); Pres. and CEO CARLOS A. PEDROSA; 60 brs.

Foreign Banks

ANZ Banking Group Ltd (Australia and New Zealand): Ayala Triangle, Tower One, 3rd Floor, Ayala Ave, cnr Paseo de Roxas, Makati City, 1226 Metro Manila; tel. (2) 8485091; fax (2) 8485086; e-mail labrooyM2@anz.com; f. 1995; cap. 250m., dep. 2,000m. (Dec. 1999); Pres. MICHAEL LA BROOY.

Banco Santander Philippines, Inc: Tower One, 27th Floor, Ayala Triangle, Ayala Ave, cnr Paseo de Roxas, Makati City, 1200 Metro Manila; tel. (2) 7594144; fax (2) 7594190; cap. 1,351m., dep. 3,943m. (March 1997); Chair. ANA PATRICIA BOTIN; Dir and Pres. VICENTE B. CASTILLO.

Bangkok Bank Public Company Ltd (Thailand): Far East Bank Bldg, 25th Floor, Sen. Gil J. Puyat Ave, Makati City, 1200 Metro Manila; tel. (2) 8914011; fax (2) 8914037; f. 1995; cap. 266m. (Dec. 1996), dep. 647m. (March 1997); Pres. PREYAMIT HETRAKUL.

Bank of America NA (USA): BA–Lepanto Bldg, 2nd Floor, 8747 Paseo de Roxas, POB 1767, Makati City, 1257 Metro Manila; tel. (2) 8155000; fax (2) 8155895; f. 1947; cap. 210m. (Dec. 1996), dep. 5,015m. (June 1999); Sr Vice-Pres. and Country Man. JOSE L. QUERUBIN.

Bank of Tokyo-Mitsubishi Ltd (Japan): 6750 Ayala Ave, 5th Floor, Makati City, Metro Manila; tel. (2) 8921976; fax (2) 8160413; f. 1977; cap. 200m. (Dec. 1996), dep. 2,940m. (March 1997); Gen. Man. HISAO SAKASHITA.

Citibank NA (USA): Citibank Plaza, 8741 Paseo de Roxas, Makati City, 1226 Metro Manila; tel. (2) 8947700; fax (2) 8157703; f. 1948; cap. 2,536m., dep. 30,167m. (March 1997); CEO SURESH MAHARAJ; 3 brs.

Dao Heng Bank Inc: Pearl Bank Bldg, 11th Floor, 146 Salero St, Salcedo Village, Makati City, 1227 Metro Manila; tel. (2) 8403003; fax (2) 8178794; cap. 1,416m., dep. 2,797m. (March 1997); Chair. Tan Sri QUEK LENG CHAN; Pres. RENATO H. PERONILLA; 5 brs.

Deutsche Bank AG (Germany): Ayala Triangle, Tower One, 26th Floor, Ayala Ave, cnr Paseo de Roxas, Makati City, 1226 Metro Manila; tel. (2) 8946900; fax (2) 8946901; f. 1995; cap. 625m. (Dec. 1996), dep. 2,595m. (March 1997); Chief Country Officer PETER VERHOEVEN.

Development Bank of Singapore: Citibank Tower, 32nd Floor, Valero St, cnr Villar St, Legaspi Village, Makati City, 1229 Metro Manila; tel. (2) 8480461; fax (2) 8480478; f. 1995; cap. 202m. (Dec. 1996), dep. 13m. (March 1997); Gen. Man. SADASIVAN VIJAYAKUMAR.

Fuji Bank Ltd (Japan): Citibank Tower, 26th Floor, Valero St, cnr Villar St, Legaspi Village, Makati City, 1229 Metro Manila; tel. (2) 8480001; fax (2) 8153770; f. 1995; cap. 202m. (Dec. 1996), dep. 858m. (March 1997); Gen. Man. TAKUJI IWASAKI.

Hongkong and Shanghai Banking Corpn (Hong Kong): Enterprise Center, Tower I, 6766 Ayala Ave, cnr Paseo de Roxas, Makati City 1200; tel. (2) 8305300; fax (2) 8865343; internet www .asiapacific.hsbc.com; cap. HK $113,520m., res HK $42,280m., dep. HK $1,419,076m. (June 2002); CEO PAUL LAWRENCE; 5 brs.

ING Bank NV (The Netherlands): Ayala Triangle, Tower One, 21st Floor, Ayala Ave, cnr Paseo de Roxas, Makati City, 1200 Metro Manila; tel. (2) 8408888; fax (2) 8151116; f. 1995; cap. 643m., dep. 2,594m. (March 1997); Country Man. MANUEL SALAK.

International Commercial Bank of China (Taiwan): Pacific Star Bldg, Ground and 3rd Floors, Sen. Gil J. Puyat Ave, cnr Makati Ave, Makati City, 1200 Metro Manila; tel. (2) 8115807; fax (2) 8115774; cap. 188m., dep. 458m. (March 1997); Gen. Man. HERMAN C. CHEN.

Korea Exchange Bank: Citibank Tower, 33rd Floor, 8741 Paseo de Roxas, Makati City, 1229 Metro Manila; tel. (2) 8481988; fax (2) 8195377; cap. 257m., dep. 271m. (March 1997); Gen. Man. TAE-HONG JIN.

Standard Chartered Bank (Hong Kong): 6788 Ayala Ave, Makati City, 1226 Metro Manila; tel. (2) 8867888; fax (2) 8866866; f. 1873; cap. 1,500m. (Dec. 1996), dep. 3,770m. (March 1997); CEO EIRVIN B. KNOX.

Islamic Bank

Al-Amanah Islamic Investment Bank of the Philippines: 2nd Floor, Classica Tower I, H. V. de la Costa St, Salcedo Village, Makati City, Metro Manila; tel. (2) 8164258; fax (2) 8195249; internet www.islambnk@amanet.net/; f. 1989; Chair. and CEO FAROUK A. CARPIZO; Pres. ABDUL GAFFOOR ASHROOF.

Major 'Offshore' Banks

ABN AMRO Bank, NV (Netherlands): LKG Tower, 18th Floor, 6801 Ayala Ave, Makati City, 1200 Metro Manila; tel. (2) 8842000; fax (2) 8843954; Gen. Man. CARMELO MARIA L. BAUTISTA.

American Express Bank Ltd (USA): Ayala Bldg, 11th Floor, 6750 Ayala Ave, Makati City, Metro Manila; tel. (2) 8186731; fax (2) 8172589; f. 1977; Senior Dir and Country Man. VICENTE L. CHUA.

BankBoston NA (USA): 6750 Ayala Ave, 23rd Floor, Makati City, Metro Manila; tel. (2) 8170456; fax (2) 8191251; Country Man. BENJAMIN C. SEVILLA.

Bank Dagang Nasional Indonesia: Ayala Tower and Exchange Plaza, 19th Floor, Unit B, Ayala Ave, Makati City, Metro Manila; tel. (2) 8486189; fax (2) 8486176; Man. CONSUELO N. PADILLA.

Bank of Nova Scotia (Canada): Solidbank Bldg, 9th Floor, 777 Paseo de Roxas, Makati City, 1200 Metro Manila; tel. (2) 8179751; fax (2) 8178796; f. 1977; Man. M. S. (CORITO) SEVILLA.

Bankers Trust Co (USA): Pacific Star Bldg, 12th Floor, Makati Ave, Makati City, Metro Manila; tel. (2) 8190231; fax (2) 8187349; Man. Dir JOSE ISIDRO N. CAMACHO.

BNP Paribas (France): PCIB Tower Two, Makati Ave, cnr H. V. de la Costa St, Makati City, 1227 Metro Manila; tel. (2) 8158821; fax (2) 8179237; f. 1977; Country Man. PIERRE IMHOF.

Chase Manhattan International Finance Ltd: Corinthian Plaza, 4th Floor, 121 Paseo de Roxas, Makati City, Metro Manila; tel. (2) 8113348; fax (2) 8781290; Man. HELEN S. CIFRA.

Crédit Agricole Indosuez (France): Citibank Tower, 17th Floor, 8741 Paseo de Roxas, Makati City, 1200 Metro Manila; tel. (2) 8481344; fax (2) 8481380; f. 1977; Gen. Man. MARC MEULEAU.

Crédit Lyonnais (France): Pacific Star Bldg, 14th Floor, Makati Ave, cnr Sen. Gil J. Puyat Ave, Makati City, Metro Manila; POB 1859 MCC, 3117 Makati City, Metro Manila; tel. (2) 8171616; fax (2) 8177145; f. 1981; Gen. Man. PIERRE EYMERY.

KBC Bank, NV (Belgium): Far East Bank Center, 22nd Floor, Sen. Gil J. Puyat Ave, Makati City, 1200 Metro Manila; tel. (2) 8915331; fax (2) 8915352; Gen. Man. EDWIN YAPTANGCO.

PT Lippo Bank (Indonesia): Rufino Pacific Tower, 31st Floor, 6784 Ayala Ave, Makati City, Metro Manila; tel. (2) 8110515; fax (2) 8110516; Vice-Pres. and Gen. Man. EDNA D. REYES.

Overseas Union Bank Ltd: Corinthian Plaza, 7th Floor, Paseo de Roxas, Makati City, Metro Manila; tel. (2) 8179951; fax (2) 8113168; f. 1977; Man. TAN LYE OON.

Société Générale (France): Antel Corporate Center, 21st Floor, 139 Valero St, Salcedo Village, Makati City, Metro Manila; tel. (2) 8492000; fax (2) 8492940; f. 1980; CEO CLAUDE I. TOUITOU.

Standard Chartered Bank Ltd: 9th Floor, 6788 Ayala Ave, Makati City, Metro Manila; tel. (2) 8867888; fax (2) 8866866; Vice-Pres. and Gen. Man. IMELDA B. CAPISTRANO.

Union Bank of California (USA): ACE Bldg, 8th Floor, cnr Rada and de la Rosa Sts, Legaspi Village, Makati City, Metro Manila; tel. (2) 8923056; fax (2) 8170102; f. 1977; Branch Man. TERESITA MALABANAN.

Banking Associations

Bankers Association of the Philippines: Sagittarius Cond. Bldg, 11th Floor, H. V. de la Costa St, Salcedo Village, Makati City, Metro Manila; tel. (2) 8103858; fax (2) 8103860; Pres. Dr PLACIDO L. MAPA, Jr; Exec. Dir LEONILO CORONEL.

Chamber of Thrift Banks: Cityland 10 Condominium Tower 1, Unit 614, H. V. de la Costa St, Salcedo Village, Makati City, Metro Manila; tel. (2) 8126974; fax (2) 8127203; Pres. DIONISIO C. ONG.

Offshore Bankers' Association of the Philippines, Inc: MCPO 3088, Makati City, 1229 Metro Manila; tel. (2) 8103554; Chair. ANTONIO DELOS ANGELES.

Rural Bankers' Association of the Philippines: RBAP Bldg, A. Soriano Ave, cnr Arzobispo St, Intramuros, Manila; tel. (2) 5272968; fax (2) 5272980; Pres. CARLITO B. FUENTES.

STOCK EXCHANGES

Securities and Exchange Commission: SEC Bldg, Epifanio de los Santos Ave, Greenhills, Mandaluyong City, Metro Manila; tel. (2) 7274543; fax (2) 7254399; e-mail mis@sec.gov.ph; internet www.sec.gov.ph; f. 1936; Chair. LILIA R. BAUTISTA.

Philippine Stock Exchange: Philippine Stock Exchange Center, Exchange Rd, Ortigas Centre, Pasig City, 1605 Metro Manila; tel. (2) 6360122; fax (2) 6345113; e-mail piac@pse.org.ph; internet www.pse.com.ph; f. 1994 following the merger of the Manila and Makati Stock Exchanges; Chair. VIVIAN YUCHENGCO; Pres. ERNEST C. LEUNG.

INSURANCE

At the end of 2000 a total of 156 insurance companies were authorized by the Insurance Commission to transact in the Philippines. Foreign companies were permitted to operate in the country.

Principal Domestic Companies

BPI/MS Insurance Corpn: BPI Bldg, 16th–18th Floors, Ayala Ave, Makati City, 1226 Metro Manila; tel. (2) 8409000; fax (2) 8910147; e-mail fguinsce@globe.com.ph; internet www.fguonline.com; f. 2002 as result of merger of FGU Insurance Corpn and FEB Mitsui Marine Insurance Corpn; jt venture of Bank of the Philippine Islands and Sumitomo Insurance Co (Japan); cap. 150m. (1997); Chair. JAIME AUGUSTO ZOBEL DE AYALA; Pres. ALFONSO L. SALCEDO, Jr.

Central Surety & Insurance Co: UniversalRe Bldg, 2nd Floor, 106 Paseo de Roxas, Legaspi Village, Makati City, 1200 Metro Manila; tel. (2) 8174931; fax (2) 8170006; f. 1945; bonds, fire, marine, casualty, motor car; Pres. CONSTANCIO T. CASTAÑEDA, Jr.

Commonwealth Insurance Co: Manila Bank Bldg, 4th Floor, Ayala Ave, Makati City, Metro Manila; tel. (2) 8187626; fax (2) 8138575; f. 1935; Chair. MARIO NOCHE.

Co-operative Insurance System of the Philippines: 80 Malakas St, Diliman, Quezon City, Metro Manila; tel. (2) 9240333; fax (2) 9240471; Chair. BIENVENIDO P. FAUSTINO; Gen. Man. ARTURO J. JIMENEZ.

Domestic Insurance Co of the Philippines: 5th Floor, Champ Bldg, Anda Circle, Bonifacio Drive, Port Area, Manila; tel. (2) 5278181; fax (2) 5273052; e-mail gdicp@skyinet.net; f. 1946; cap. 10m. Pres. and Chair. MAR S. LOPEZ.

Dominion Insurance Corpn: Zeta II Annex Bldg, 6th Floor, 191 Salcedo St, Legaspi Village, Makati City, Metro Manila; tel. (2) 8925787; fax (2) 8183630; f. 1960; fire, marine, motor car, accident, engineering, bonds; Pres. JUAN DOMINO.

Empire Insurance Co: Prudential Life Bldg, 2nd Floor, 843 Arnaiz Ave, Legaspi Village, Makati City, 1229 Metro Manila; tel. (2) 8159561; fax (2) 8152599; f. 1949; fire, bonds, marine, accident, motor car, extraneous perils; Chair. SERGIO CORPUS; Pres. and CEO JOSE MA G. SANTOS.

Equitable Insurance Corpn: Equitable Bank Bldg, 4th Floor, 262 Juan Luna St, Binondo, POB 1103, Metro Manila; tel. (2) 2430291; fax (2) 2415768; e-mail info@equitableinsurance.com.ph; internet www.equitableinsurance.com.ph; f. 1950; fire, marine, casualty, motor car, bonds; Exec. Vice-Pres. ANTONIO C. OCAMPO; Vice-Pres. ERLINDA D. SANTIAGO.

Insular Life Assurance Co Ltd: Insular Life Corporate Center, Insular Life Drive, Filinvest Corporate City, Alabang, 1781 Muntinlupa City; POB 8097, Parañaque Central Post Office, 1700 Parañaque City; tel. (2) 7711818; fax (2) 7711717; e-mail headofc@insular.com.ph; internet www.insularlife.com.ph; f. 1910; members' equity 8,300m. (Dec. 2000); Chair., Pres. and CEO VICENTE R. AYLLÓN.

Makati Insurance Co Inc: Far East Bank Center, 19th Floor, Sen. Gil J. Puyat Ave, Makati City, 1200 Metro Manila; tel. (2) 8459576; fax (2) 8915229; f. 1965; non-life; Pres. and Gen. Man. JAIME L. DARANTINAO; Chair. OCTAVIO V. ESPIRITU.

Malayan Insurance Co Inc: Yuchengco Tower, 4th Floor, 500 Quintin Paredes St, POB 3389, 1099 Metro Manila; tel. (2) 2428888; fax (2) 2412449; e-mail malayan@malayan.com; internet www

.malayan.com; f. 1949; cap. 100m. (1998); insurance and bonds; Pres. YVONNE S. YUCHENGCO.

Manila Surety & Fidelity Co Inc: 66 P. Florentino, Quezon City, Metro Manila; tel. (2) 7122251; fax (2) 7124129; f. 1945; Pres. MA LOURDES V. PEÑA; Vice-Pres. EDITHA LIM.

Metropolitan Insurance Co: Ateneum Bldg, 3rd Floor, Leviste St, Salcedo Village, Makati City, Metro Manila; tel. (2) 8108151; fax (2) 8162294; f. 1933; non-life; Pres. JOSÉ M. PERIQUET, Jr; Exec. Vice-Pres. ROBERTO ABAD.

National Life Insurance Co of the Philippines: National Life Insurance Bldg, 6762 Ayala Ave, Makati City, Metro Manila; tel. (2) 8100251; fax (2) 8178718; f. 1933; Pres. BENJAMIN L. DE LEON; Sr Vice-Pres. JOSE L. BURGOS.

National Reinsurance Corpn of the Philippines: PS Bank Tower, 18th Floor, Sen. Gil J. Puyat Ave, cnr Tindalo St, Makati City, Metro Manila; tel. (2) 7595801; fax (2) 7595886; e-mail nrcp@nrcp.com.ph; internet www.nrcp.com.ph; f. 1978; Chair. WINSTON F. GARCIA; Pres. and CEO WILFRIDO C. BANTAYAN.

Paramount General Insurance Corpn: Sage House, 15th Floor, 110 Herrera St, Makati City, Metro Manila; tel. (2) 8127956; fax (2) 8133043; e-mail insure@paramount.com.ph; internet www.paramount.com.ph; f. 1950; fire, marine, casualty, motor car; Chair. PATRICK L. GO; Pres. GEORGE T. TIU.

Philippine American Life and General Insurance Co (Philamlife): Philamlife Bldg, United Nations Ave, Metro Manila; POB 2167, 0990 Metro Manila; tel. (2) 5216300; fax (2) 5217057; internet www.philamlife.com.ph; Pres. JOSE CUISIA.

Pioneer Insurance and Surety Corpn: Pioneer House-Makati, 108 Paseo de Roxas, Makati City, Metro Manila; tel. (2) 8179071; fax (2) 8171461; e-mail info@pioneer.com.ph; f. 1954; cap. 172.5m. (1997); Pres. and CEO DAVID C. COYUKIAT.

Rizal Surety and Insurance Co: Prudential Life Bldg, 3rd Floor, 843 Arnaiz Ave, Legaspi Village, Makati City, Metro Manila; tel. (2) 8403610; fax (2) 8173550; e-mail rizalsic@mkt.weblinq.com; f. 1939; fire, bond, marine, motor car, accident, extraneous perils; Chair. TOMAS I. ALCANTARA; Pres. REYNALDO DE DIOS.

Standard Insurance Co Inc: Standard Insurance Tower, 999 Pedro Gil St, cnr F. Agoncillo St, Metro Manila; tel. (2) 5223230; fax (2) 5261479; f. 1958; Chair. LOURDES T. ECHAUZ; Pres. ERNESTO ECHAUZ.

Tico Insurance Co Inc: Trafalgar Plaza, 7th Floor, 105 H. V. de la Costa St, Salcedo Village, Makati City, 1227 Metro Manila; tel. (2) 8140143; fax (2) 8140150; f. 1937; fmrly Tabacalera Insurance Co Inc; Chair. and Pres. CARLOS CATHOLICO.

UCPB General Insurance Co Inc: 24th and 25th Floors, LKG Tower, 6801 Ayala Ave, Makati City, Metro Manila; tel. (2) 8841234; fax (2) 8841264; e-mail ucpbgen@ucpbgen.com; internet www.ucpbgen.com; f. 1989; non-life; Pres. ISABELO P. AFRICA; Chair. JERONIMO U. KILAYKO.

Universal Reinsurance Corpn: Ayala Life Bldg, 9th Floor, 6786 Ayala Ave, Makati City, Metro Manila; tel. (2) 7514977; fax (2) 8173745; f. 1949; life and non-life; Chair. JAIME AUGUSTO ZOBEL DE AYALA II; Pres. HERMINIA S. JACINTO.

Regulatory Body

Insurance Commission: 1071 United Nations Ave, Metro Manila; tel. (2) 5252015; fax (2) 5221434; e-mail oic@i-manila.com.ph; internet www.ic.gov.ph; regulates the private insurance industry by, among other things, issuing certificates of authority to insurance companies and intermediaries and monitoring their financial solvency; Commr EDUARDO T. MALINIS.

Trade and Industry

GOVERNMENT AGENCIES

Asset Privatization Trust: North Davao Mining Bldg, 104 Gamboa St, Legaspi Village, Makati City, 1229 Metro Manila; tel. (2) 8932383; fax (2) 8933453; f. 1986 to handle the privatization of govt assets; Chief Exec. RENATO V. VALDECANTOS.

Board of Investments: 385 Sen. Gil J. Puyat Ave, Makati City, Metro Manila; tel. (2) 8976682; fax (2) 8953521; e-mail OSAC@_boi .gov.ph; internet www.boi.gov.ph; Chair. MANUEL A. ROXAS II; Gov. JOSE ANTONIO C. LEVISTE.

Cagayan Economic Zone Authority: Westar Bldg, 7th Floor, 611 Shaw Blvd, Pasig City, 1603 Metro Manila; tel. (2) 6365781; fax (2) 6313997; e-mail cagayanecozone@pacific.net.ph; Administrator RODOLFO REYES.

Clark Development Corpn: Bldg 2127, C. P. Garcia St, cnr E. Quirino St, Clark Field, Pampanga; JMT Corporate Condominium, 15th Floor, ADB Ave, Ortigas Center, Pasig City, Metro Manila; tel. (2) 6338671; fax (2) 6338672; Pres. and CEO RUFO B. COLAYCO.

Industrial Technology Development Institute: DOST Complex, Gen. Santos Ave, Bicutan, Taguig, Metro Manila; tel. (2) 8372071; fax (2) 8373167; Man. Dr ROGELIO PANLASIGUI.

Maritime Industry Authority (MARINA): PPL Bldg, 1000 United Nations Ave, cnr San Marcelino St, Ermita, Metro Manila; tel. (2) 5238651; fax (2) 5242746; e-mail feedback@marina.gov.ph; internet www.marina.gov.ph; f. 1974; development of inter-island shipping, overseas shipping, shipbuilding and repair, and maritime power; Administrator OSCAR M. SEVILLA.

National Tobacco Administration: NTA Bldg, Scout Reyes St, cnr Panay Ave, Quezon City, Metro Manila; tel. (2) 3743987; fax (2) 3742505; e-mail nta_miscsd@pacific.net.ph; f. 1987; Administrator CARLITOS S. ENCARNACION.

Philippine Coconut Authority (PCA): Elliptical Rd, Diliman, Quezon City, 1104 Metro Manila; POB 3386, Metro Manila; tel. (2) 9278116; fax (2) 9216173; f. 1972; Administrator DANILO M. CORONACION.

Philippine Council for Advanced Science and Technology Research and Development (PCASTRD): DOST Main Bldg, Gen. Santos Ave, Bicutan, Taguig, 1631 Metro Manila; tel. (2) 8377522; fax (2) 8373168; e-mail aal@dost.gov.ph; internet www.dostweb.dost.gov.ph/pcastrd; f. 1987; Exec. Dir Dr IDA F. DALMACIO.

Philippine Economic Zone Authority: Roxas Blvd, cnr San Luis St, Pasay City, Metro Manila; tel. (2) 5513454; fax (2) 8916380; e-mail info@peza.gov.ph; internet www.peza.gov.ph; Dir-Gen. LILIA B. DE LIMA.

Subic Bay Metropolitan Authority: SBMA Center, Bldg 229, Waterfront Rd, Subic Bay Freeport Zone, 2222 Zambales; tel. (47) 2524895; fax (47) 2523014; e-mail fcpayumo@sbma.com; internet www.sbma.com; Chair. FELICITO PAYUMO.

DEVELOPMENT ORGANIZATIONS

Bases Conversion Development Authority: Metro Manila; internet www.bcda.gov.ph; f. 1992 to facilitate the conversion, privatization and development of fmr military bases; Chair. ROGELIO SINGSON.

Bureau of Land Development: DAR Bldg, Elliptical Rd, Diliman, Quezon City, Metro Manila; tel. (2) 9287031; fax (2) 9260971; Dir EUGENIO B. BERNARDO.

Capital Market Development Council: Metro Manila; Chair. ROMAN AZANZA.

Co-operatives Development Authority: Benlor Bldg, 1184 Quezon Ave, Quezon City, Metro Manila; tel. (2) 3723801; fax (2) 3712077; Chair. JOSE C. MEDINA, Jr; Exec. Dir CANDELARIO L. VERZONA, Jr.

National Development Co (NDC): NDC Bldg, 8th Floor, 116 Tordesillas St, Salcedo Village, Makati City, Metro Manila; tel. (2) 8404898; fax (2) 8404862; e-mail corplan@info.com; internet www.dti.gov.ph/ndc; f. 1919; govt-owned corpn engaged in the organization, financing and management of subsidiaries and corpns incl. commercial, industrial, mining, agricultural and other enterprises assisting national economic development, incl. jt industrial ventures with other ASEAN countries; Chair. MANUEL A. ROXAS; Gen. Man. OFELIA V. BULAONG.

Philippine National Oil Co: Energy Complex, Bldg 6, 6th Floor, Merritt Rd, Fort Bonifacio, Makati City, Metro Manila; tel. (2) 5550254; fax (2) 8442983; internet www.pnoc.com.ph; f. 1973; state-owned energy development agency mandated to ensure stable and sufficient supply of oil products and to develop domestic energy resources; sales 3,482m. pesos (1995); Chair. VINCENT S. PEREZ, Jr; Pres. and CEO THELMO Y. CUNANAN.

Southern Philippines Development Authority: Basic Petroleum Bldg, 104 Carlos Palanca, Jr, St, Legaspi Village, Makati City, Metro Manila; tel. (2) 8183893; fax (2) 8188907; Chair. ROBERTO AVENTAJADO; Manila Rep. GERUDIO 'KHALIQ' MADUENO.

CHAMBERS OF COMMERCE AND INDUSTRY

American Chamber of Commerce of the Philippines: Corinthian Plaza, 2nd Floor, Paseo de Roxas, Makati City, 1229 Metro Manila; tel. (2) 8187911; fax (2) 8113081; e-mail info@amchamphilippines.com; internet www.amchamphilippines.com; Pres. TERRY J. EMRICK.

Cebu Chamber of Commerce and Industry: CCCI Center, cnr 11th and 13th Ave, North Reclamation Area, Cebu City 6000; tel. (32) 2321421; fax (32) 2321422; e-mail ccci@esprint.com; internet www.esprint.com/~ccci; f. 1921; Pres. SABINO R. DAPAT.

European Chamber of Commerce of the Philippines: PS Bank Tower, 19th Floor, Sen. Gil J. Puyat Ave, cnr Tindalo St, Makati City, 1200 Metro Manila; tel. (2) 8451324; fax (2) 8451395; e-mail info@eccp.com; internet www.eccp.com; f. 2000; 900 mems; Pres. WILLIAM BAILEY; Exec. Vice-Pres. HENRY J. SCHUMACHER.

Federation of Filipino-Chinese Chambers of Commerce and Industry Inc: Federation Center, 6th Floor, Muelle de Binondo St, POB 23, Metro Manila; tel. (2) 2419201; fax (2) 2422361; e-mail ffccci@bell.com.ph; internet www.ffcccii.com.ph; Pres. JOHN K. C. NG; Sec.-Gen. JOAQUIN SY.

Japanese Chamber of Commerce of the Philippines: Jaycem Bldg, 6th Floor, 104 Rada St, Legaspi Village, Makati City, Metro Manila; tel. (2) 8923233; fax (2) 8150317; e-mail jccipi@jccipi.com.ph; internet www.jccipi.com.ph; Pres. MASAHARU TAMAKI.

Philippine Chamber of Coal Mines (Philcoal): Rm 1007, Princeville Condominium, S. Laurel St, cnr Shaw Blvd, 1552 Mandaluyong City; tel. (2) 5330518; fax (2) 5315513; f. 1980; Exec. Dir BERTRAND GONZALES.

Philippine Chamber of Commerce and Industry: 14th Floor, Multinational Bancorporation Centre, 6805 Ayala Ave, Makati City, Metro Manila; tel. (2) 8445713; fax (2) 8434102; e-mail pcciintr@mozcom.com; internet www.philcham.com; f. 1977; Pres. SERGIO R. ORTIZ-LUIS, Jr.

Philippine Chamber of Mines: Rm 204, Ortigas Bldg, Ortigas Ave, Pasig City, Metro Manila; tel. (2) 6354123; fax (2) 6354160; e-mail comp@vasia.com; f. 1975; Chair. GERARD H. BRIMO; Pres. ARTEMIO DISINI.

FOREIGN TRADE ORGANIZATIONS

Bureau of Export Trade Promotion: New Solid Bldg, 5th–8th Floors, 357 Sen. Gil J. Puyat Ave, Makati City, 1200 Metro Manila; tel. (2) 8990133; fax (2) 8904707; e-mail betpod@dti.gov.ph; internet www.dti.gov.ph/betp; Dir SERAFIN N. JULIANO.

Bureau of Import Services: Oppen Bldg, 3rd Floor, 349 Sen. Gil J. Puyat Ave, Makati City, Metro Manila; tel. (2) 8905418; fax (2) 8957466; e-mail bis@dti.gov.ph; internet www.dti.gov.ph/bis; Exec. Dir ALEXANDER B. ARCILLA.

Philippine International Trading Corpn (PITC): Philippines International Center, 46 Sen. Gil J. Puyat Ave, 1200 Makati City; POB 2253 MCPO; tel. (2) 8454376; fax (2) 8454476; e-mail pitc@info.com.ph; internet www.dti.gov.ph/pitc/; f. 1973; state trading company to conduct international marketing of general merchandise, industrial and construction goods, raw materials, semi-finished and finished goods, and bulk trade of agri-based products; also provides financing, bonded warehousing, shipping, cargo and customs services; Pres. ARTHUR C. YAP.

INDUSTRIAL AND TRADE ASSOCIATIONS

Chamber of Automobile Manufacturers of the Philippines: Metro Manila; Sec.-Gen. MARIO DE GRANO.

Cotton Development Administration: Rudgen Bldg 1, 2nd Floor, 17 Shaw Blvd, Pasig City, Metro Manila; tel. (2) 6312104; fax (2) 6312113; e-mail cotton@pworld.net.ph; Administrator Dr EUGENIO D. ORPIA, Jr.

Fiber Industry Development Authority: 1424 Asia Trust Annex Bldg, Quezon Ave, Quezon City, Metro Manila; tel. (2) 3739236; fax (2) 3739238; e-mail jjmt@i-manila.com.ph; Administrator JOAQUIN M. TEOTICO.

Philippine Fisheries Development Authority: Union Square 1 Bldg, 7th Floor, 145 15th Ave, Cubao, Quezon City, Metro Manila; tel. (2) 9113829; fax (2) 9113018; f. 1976; Gen. Man. PABLO B. CASIMINA.

Semiconductor and Electronic Industries in the Philippines (SEIPI): Unit 1102, Alabang Business Tower 1, Acacia Ave, Madrigal Business Park, Ayala Alabang, Muntinlupa City, 1780 Metro Manila; tel. (2) 8078458; fax (2) 8078459; e-mail philelectronics@seipi.org; internet www.seipi.org; Exec. Dir ERNIE SANTIAGO.

EMPLOYERS' ORGANIZATIONS

Employers' Confederation of the Philippines (ECOP): ECC Bldg, 4th Floor, 355 Sen. Gil J. Puyat Ave, Makati City, Metro Manila; tel. (2) 8904845; fax (2) 8958576; e-mail ecop@webquest.com; internet www.ecop.org.ph; f. 1975; Pres. MIGUEL B. VARELA; Dir-Gen. VICENTE LEOGARDO, Jr.

Filipino Shipowners' Association: Victoria Bldg, Room 503, United Nations Ave, Ermita, 1000 Metro Manila; tel. (2) 5227318; fax (2) 5243164; e-mail filiship@info.com.ph; f. 1950; 34 mems; Chair. and Pres. CARLOS C. SALINAS; Exec. Dir AUGUSTO Y. ARREZA, Jr.

Philippine Cigar and Cigarette Manufacturers' Association: Unit 508, 1851 Dr Antonio Vasquez St, Malate, Metro Manila; tel. (2) 5249285; fax (2) 5249514; Pres. ANTONIO B. YAO.

Philippine Coconut Producers' Federation, Inc: Wardley Bldg, 2nd Floor, 1991 Taft Ave, cnr San Juan St, Pasay City, 1300 Metro Manila; tel. (2) 5230918; fax (2) 5211333; e-mail cocofed@pworld.net.ph; Pres. MARIA CLARA L. LOBREGAT.

Philippine Sugar Millers' Association Inc: 1402 Security Bank Centre, 6776 Ayala Ave, Makati City, 1226 Metro Manila; tel. (2) 8911138; fax (2) 8911144; e-mail psma@netasia-mnl.net; internet www.psma.com.ph; f. 1922; Pres. V. FRANCISCO VARUA; Exec. Dir JOSE MA T. ZABALETA.

Philippine Retailers' Association: Unit 2610, Jollibee Plaza, Emerald Ave, Ortigas Centre, Pasig City; tel. (2) 6874180; fax (2) 6360825; e-mail pra@nwave.net; internet www.philretailers.com; Pres. BIENVENIDO V. TANTOCO III.

Textile Mills Association of the Philippines, Inc (TMAP): Ground Floor, Alexander House, 132 Amorsolo St, Legaspi Village, Makati City, 1229 Metro Manila; tel. (2) 8186601; fax (2) 8183107; e-mail tmap@pacific.net.ph; f. 1956; 11 mems; Pres. HERMENEGILDO C. ZAYCO; Chair. JAMES L. GO.

Textile Producers' Association of the Philippines, Inc: Downtown Center Bldg, Room 513, 516 Quintin Paredes St, Binondo, Metro Manila; tel. (2) 2411144; fax (2) 2411162; Pres. GO CUN UY; Exec. Sec. ROBERT L. TAN.

UTILITIES

Energy Regulatory Commission: Pacific Center Bldg, San Miguel Ave, Ortigas Center, Pasig City, 1600 Metro Manila; tel. (2) 6334556; fax (2) 6315871; e-mail info@erc.gov.ph; internet www.erc.gov.ph; Chair. LETICIA V. IBAY (acting); Exec. Dir ARNIDO O. INUMERABLE.

Electricity

Davao Light and Power Co: 163 C. Bangoy Sr St, Davao City 8000; tel. (82) 2212191; fax (82) 2212105; e-mail davaolight@davao-online.com; internet www.davaolight.com; the country's third largest electric utility with a peak demand of 175 MW in 2000.

Manila Electric Co (Meralco): Lopez Bldg, Meralco Center, Ortigas Ave, Pasig City, 0300 Metro Manila; tel. (2) 6312222; fax (2) 6328501; e-mail wmtirona@meralco.com.ph; internet www.meralco.com.ph; f. 1903; supplies electric power to Manila and seven provinces in Luzon; largest electricity distributor, supplying 54% of total consumption in 2000; privatized in 1991, 34% govt-owned; cap. and res 54,382m., sales 85,946m. (1998); Chair. and CEO MANUEL M. LOPEZ; Pres. JESUS P. FRANCISCO.

National Power Corpn (NAPOCOR): Quezon Ave, cnr BIR Rd, Quezon City, Metro Manila; tel. (2) 9213541; fax (2) 9212468; e-mail pad@napocor.com.ph; internet www.napocor.com.ph; f. 1936; state-owned corpn supplying electric and hydroelectric power throughout the country; scheduled for privatization; installed capacity in 1998, 11,810 MW; sales 86,611m. pesos (Dec. 1998); 12,043 employees; Pres. JESUS ALCORDO; Chair. MARIO V. TIAOQUI.

Gas

First Gas Holdings Corpn: Benpres Bldg, 4th Floor, Exchange Rd, cnr Meralco Ave, Pasig City, Metro Manila; tel. (2) 6343428; fax (2) 6352737; internet www.firstgas.com.ph; major interests in power generation and distribution; Pres. PETER GARRUCHO.

Water

Regulatory Authority

Metropolitan Waterworks and Sewerage System: Katipunan Rd, Balaran, Quezon City, 1105 Metro Manila; tel. (2) 9223757; fax (2) 9212887; e-mail mwssoch@epic.net; govt regulator for water supply, treatment and distribution within Metro Manila; Administrator ORLANDO C. HONDRADE.

Distribution Companies

Davao City Water District: Km 5, J. P. Laurel Ave, Bajada, Davao City; tel. (82) 2219400; fax (82) 2264885; e-mail dcwd@interasia.com.ph; f. 1973; public utility responsible for the water supply of Davao City; Gen. Man. WILFRED G. YAMSON.

Manila Water: MWSS Compound, 2nd Floor, 489 Katipunan Rd, Balaran, Quezon City, Metro Manila; tel. (2) 9267999; fax (2) 9281223; e-mail info@manilawateronline.com; internet www.manilawateronline.com; f. 1998 following the privatization of Metro Manila's water services; responsible for water supply to Manila East until 2023; Pres. ANTONINO T. AQUINO.

Maynilad Water: MWSS Compound, Katipunan Rd, Balaran, Quezon City, Metro Manila; tel. (2) 4353583; fax (2) 9223759; e-mail dal@maniladwater.com.ph; f. 1998 following the privatization of Metro Manila's water services; responsible for water supply, sewage and sanitation services for Manila West until 2021; Pres. RAFAEL M. ALUNAN III.

Metropolitan Cebu Water District: M. C. Briones St, cnr P. Burgos St, Cebu City 6000; tel. (32) 2560413; fax (32) 2545391; e-mail mcwd@cvis.net.ph; f. 1974; public utility responsible for water supply and sewerage of Cebu City and surrounding towns and cities; Chair. RUBEN D. ALMENDRAS; Gen. Man. DULCE M. ABANILLA.

TRADE UNION FEDERATIONS

In 1986 the Government established the Labor Advisory Consultation Committee (LACC) to facilitate communication between the Government and the powerful labour movement in the Philippines. The LACC granted unions direct recognition and access to the Government, which, under the Marcos regime, had been available only to the Trade Union Congress of the Philippines (KMP-TUCP). The KMP-TUCP refused to join the Committee.

In May 1994 a new trade union alliance, the Caucus for Labor Unity, was established; its members included the KMP-TUCP and three groups that had dissociated themselves from the former Kilusang Mayo Uno.

Katipunang Manggagawang Pilipino (KMP-TUCP) (Trade Union Congress of the Philippines): TUCP Training Center Bldg, TUCP-PGEA Compound, Masaya St, cnr Maharlika St, Diliman, Quezon City, 1101 Metro Manila; tel. (2) 9222185; fax (2) 9219758; e-mail tucp@easy.net.ph; internet www.tucp.org.ph; f. 1975; 1.5m. mems; Pres. DEMOCRITO T. MENDOZA; Gen. Sec. ERNESTO F. HERRERA; 39 affiliates:

Associated Labor Unions—Visayas Mindanao Confederation of Trade Unions (ALU—VIMCONTU): ALU Bldg, Quezon Blvd, Port Area, Elliptical Rd, cnr Maharlika St, Diliman, Quezon City, 1101 Metro Manila; tel. (2) 9222185; fax (2) 9223199; f. 1954; 350,000 mems; Pres. DEMOCRITO T. MENDOZA.

Associated Labor Union for Metalworkers (ALU—METAL): TUCP-PGEA Compound, Diliman, Quezon City, 1101 Metro Manila; tel. (2) 9222575; fax (2) 9223199; 29,700 mems; Pres. CECILIO T. SENO.

Associated Labor Union for Textile Workers (ALU—TEXTILE): TUCP-PGEA Compound, Elliptical Rd, Diliman, Quezon City, 1101 Metro Manila; tel. (2) 9222575; fax (2) 9223199; 41,400 mems; Pres. RICARDO I. PATALINJUG.

Associated Labor Unions (ALU—TRANSPORT): 1763 Tomas Claudio St, Baclaran, Paranaque, Metro Manila; tel. (2) 8320634; fax (2) 8322392; 49,500 mems; Pres. ALEXANDER O. BARRIENTOS.

Associated Professional, Supervisory, Office and Technical Employees Union (APSOTEU): TUCP-PGEA Compound, Elliptical Rd, Diliman, Quezon City, 1101 Metro Manila; tel. (2) 9222575; fax (2) 9223199; Pres. CECILIO T. SENO.

Association of Independent Unions of the Philippines: Vila Bldg, Mezzanine Floor, Epifanio de los Santos Ave, Cubao, Quezon City, Metro Manila; tel. (2) 9224652; Pres. EMMANUEL S. DURANTE.

Association of Trade Unions (ATU): Antwel Bldg, Room 1, 2nd Floor, Santa Ana, Port Area, Davao City; tel. (82) 2272394; 2,997 mems; Pres. JORGE ALEGARBES.

Confederation of Labor and Allied Social Services (CLASS): Doña Santiago Bldg, TUCP Suite 404, 1344 Taft Ave, Ermita, Metro Manila; tel. (2) 5240415; fax (2) 5266011; f. 1979; 4,579 mems; Pres. LEONARDO F. AGTING.

Federation of Agrarian and Industrial Toiling Hands (FAITH): Kalayaan Ave, cnr Masigla St, Diliman, Quezon City, Metro Manila; tel. (2) 9225244; 220,000 mems; Pres. RAYMUNDO YUMUL.

Federation of Consumers' Co-operatives in Negros Oriental (FEDCON): Bandera Bldg, Cervantes St, Dumaguete City; tel. (32) 2048; Chair. MEDARDO VILLALON.

Federation of Filipino Civilian Employees Association (FFCEA): 14 Murphy St, Pagasa, Olongapo City; tel. (2) 8114267; fax (2) 8114266; 21,560 mems; Pres. ROBERTO A. FLORES.

Federation of Unions of Rizal (FUR): Perpetual Savings Bank Bldg, 3rd Floor, Quirino Ave, Parañaque, Metro Manila; tel. and fax (2) 8320110; 10,853 mems; Officer-in-Charge EDUARDO ASUNCION.

Lakas sa Industriya ng Kapatirang Haligi ng Alyansa (LIKHA): 32 Kabayanihan Rd Phase IIA, Karangalan Village, Pasig City, Metro Manila; tel. (2) 6463234; fax (2) 6463234; e-mail jbvlikha@yahoo.com; Pres. JESUS B. VILLAMOR.

National Association of Free Trade Unions (NAFTU): CVC Bldg, Room 3, AD Curato St, Butuan City; tel. (8822) 3620941; 7,385 mems; Pres. JAIME RINCAL.

National Congress of Unions in the Sugar Industry of the Philippines (NACUSIP): 7431-A Yakal St, Barangay San Antonio, Makati City, Metro Manila; tel. (2) 8437284; fax (2) 8437284; e-mail nacusip@compass.com.ph; 32 affiliated unions and 57,424 mems; Nat. Pres. ZOILO V. DELA CRUZ, Jr.

National Mines and Allied Workers' Union (NAMAWU): Unit 201, A. Dunville Condominium, 1 Castilla St, cnr Valencio St, Quezon City, Metro Manila; tel. (2) 7265070; fax (2) 4155582; 13,233 mems; Pres. ROBERTO A. PADILLA.

Pambansang Kilusan ng Paggawa (KILUSAN): TUCP-PGEA Compound, Elliptical Rd, Diliman, Quezon City, 1101 Metro Manila; tel. (2) 9284651; 13,093 mems; Pres. AVELINO V. VALERIO; Sec.-Gen. IGMIDIO T. GANAGANA.

Philippine Agricultural, Commercial and Industrial Workers' Union (PACIWU): 5 7th St, Lacson, Bacolod City; fax (2) 7097967; Pres. ZOILO V. DELA CRUZ, Jr.

Philippine Federation of Labor (PFL): FEMII Bldg, Suite 528, Aduana St, Intramuros, Metro Manila; tel. (2) 5271686; fax (2) 5272838; 8,869 mems; Pres. ALEJANDRO C. VILLAVIZA.

Philippine Federation of Teachers' Organizations (PFTO): BSP Bldg, Room 112, Concepcion St, Ermita, Metro Manila; tel. (2) 5275106; Pres. FEDERICO D. RICAFORT.

Philippine Government Employees' Association (PGEA): TUCP-PGEA Compound, Elliptical Rd, Diliman, Quezon City, Metro Manila; tel. (2) 6383541; fax (2) 6375764; e-mail eso_pgea@hotmail.com; f. 1945; 65,000 mems; Pres. ESPERANZA S. OCAMPO.

Philippine Integrated Industries Labor Union (PIILU): Mendoza Bldg, Room 319, 3rd Floor, Pilar St, Zamboanga City; tel. (992) 2299; f. 1973; Pres. JOSE J. SUAN.

Philippine Labor Federation (PLF): ALU Bldg, Quezon Blvd, Port Area, Cebu City; tel. (32) 71219; fax (32) 97544; 15,462 mems; Pres. CRISPIN B. GASTARDO.

Philippine Seafarers' Union (PSU): TUCP-PGEA Compound, Elliptical Rd, Diliman, Quezon City, 1101 Metro Manila; tel. (2) 9222575; fax (2) 9247553; e-mail psumla@info.com.ph; 10,000 mems; Pres. DEMOCRITO T. MENDOZA; Gen. Sec. ERNESTO F. HERRERA.

Philippine Transport and General Workers' Organization (PTGWO—D): Cecilleville Bldg, 3rd Floor, Quezon Ave, Quezon City, Metro Manila; tel. (2) 4115811; fax (2) 4115812; f. 1953; 33,400 mems; Pres. VICTORINO F. BALAIS.

Port and General Workers' Federation (PGWF): Capilitan Engineering Corpn Bldg, 206 Zaragoza St, Tondo, Manila; tel. 208959; Pres. FRANKLIN D. BUTCON.

Public Sector Labor Integrative Center (PSLINK): 9723 C. Kamagong St, San Antonio Village, Makati City, Metro Manila; tel. (2) 8961573; fax (2) 9243525; 35,108 mems; Pres. ERNESTO F. HERRERA; Gen. Sec. ANNIE GERON.

United Sugar Farmers' Organization (USFO): SPCMA Annex Bldg, 3rd Floor, 1 Luzuriaga St, Bacolod City; Pres. BERNARDO M. REMO.

Workers' Alliance Trade Unions (WATU): Delta Bldg, Room 300, Quezon Ave, cnr West Ave, Quezon City, Metro Manila; tel. (2) 9225093; fax (2) 975918; f. 1978; 25,000 mems; Pres. TEMISTOCLES S. DEJON, Sr.

INDEPENDENT LABOUR FEDERATIONS

The following organizations are not affiliated to the KMP-TUCP:

Associated Marine Officers and Seamen's Union of the Philippines (AMOSUP): Seaman's Centre, cnr Cabildo and Sta Potenciana Sts, Intramuros, Metro Manila; tel. (2) 495415; internet www.amosup.org/; f. 1960; 23 affiliated unions with 55,000 mems; Pres. GREGORIO S. OCA.

Federation of Free Workers (FFW): FFW Bldg, 1943 Taft Ave, Malate, Metro Manila; tel. (2) 5219435; fax (2) 4006656; f. 1950; affiliated to the Brotherhood of Asian Trade Unionists and the World Confed. of Labour; 300 affiliated local unions and 400,000 mems; Pres. RAMON J. JABAR.

Lakas ng Manggagawa Labor Center: Rm 401, Femii Bldg Annex, A. Soriano St, Intramuros, Metro Manila; tel. and fax (2) 5280482; a grouping of 'independent' local unions; Chair. OSCAR M. ACERSON.

Manggagawa ng Komunikasyon sa Pilipinas (MKP): 22 Libertad St, Mandaluyong City, Metro Manila; tel. (2) 5313701; fax (2) 5312109; f. 1951; Pres. PETE PINLAC.

National Confederation of Labor: Suite 402, Carmen Bldg, Ronquillo St, cnr Evangelista St, Quiapo, Metro Manila; tel. and fax (2) 7334474; f. 1994 by fmr mems of Kilusang Mayo Uno; Pres. ANTONIO DIAZ.

Philippine Social Security Labor Union (PSSLU): Carmen Bldg, Suite 309, Ronquillo St, Quiapo, Metro Manila; f. 1954; Nat. Pres. Antonio B. Diaz; Nat. Sec. Ofelia C. Alavera.

Samahang Manggagawang Pilipino (SMP) (National Alliance of Teachers and Office Workers): Fersal Condominium II, Room 33, 130 Kalayaan Ave, Quezon City, 1104 Metro Manila; tel. and fax (2) 9242299; Pres. Adelisa Raymundo.

Solidarity Trade Conference for Progress: Rizal Ave, Dipolog City; tel. and fax (65) 2124303; Pres. Nicolas E. Sabandal.

Trade Unions of the Philippines and Allied Services (TUPAS): Med-dis Bldg, Suites 203–204, Solana St, cnr Real St, Intramuros, Metro Manila; tel. (2) 493449; affiliated to the World Fed. of Trade Unions; 280 affiliated unions and 75,000 mems; Nat. Pres. Dioscoro O. Nuñez; Sec.-Gen. Vladimir R. Tupaz.

Transport

RAILWAYS

The railway network is confined mainly to the island of Luzon.

Light Rail Transit Authority (Metrorail): Adm. Bldg, LRTA Compound, Aurora Blvd, Pasay City, Metro Manila; tel. (2) 8320423; fax (2) 8316449; e-mail lrt.authority@lrta.gov.ph; internet www.lrta .gov.ph; managed and operated by Light Rail Transit Authority (LRTA); electrically-driven mass transit system; Line 1 (15 km, Baclaran to Monumento) began commercial operations in Dec. 1984; Line 1 South Extension (12 km, Baclaran to Bacoot) expected to start construction in 2004 and Line 2 (13.8 km, Santolan to Recto) scheduled to become operational in April 2003; Administrator Teodoro B. Cruz, Jr.

Philippine National Railways: PNR Management Center, Torres Bugallon St, Kalookan City, Metro Manila; tel. (2) 3654716; fax (2) 3620824; internet www.pnr.gov.ph; f. 1887; govt-owned; northern line services run from Manila to Caloocan, 6 km (although the track extends to San Fernando, La Union) and southern line services run from Manila to Legaspi, Albay, 479 km; Chair. and Gen. Man. Jose M. Sarasola II.

ROADS

In 2000 there were 201,994 km of roads in the Philippines, of which 30,013 km were highways and 49,992 km were secondary roads; an estimated 42,419 km of the network were paved. Bus services provided the most widely-used form of inland transport.

Department of Public Works and Highways: Bonifacio Drive, Port Area, Metro Manila; tel. (2) 5274111; fax (2) 5275635; e-mail pilorin.beth.p@dpwh.gov.ph; internet www.dpwh.gov.ph; responsible for the construction and maintenance of roads and bridges; Sec. Gregorio R. Vigilar.

Land Transportation Franchising and Regulatory Board: East Ave, Quezon City, Metro Manila; tel. (2) 4262505; fax (2) 4262515; internet www.ltfrb.gov.ph; f. 1987; Chair. Dante Lantin.

Land Transportation Office (LTO): East Ave, Quezon City, Metro Manila; tel. (2) 9219072; fax (2) 9219071; internet www.lto .gov.ph; f. 1987; plans, formulates and implements land transport rules and regulations, safety measures; registration of motor vehicles; issues licences; Assistant Sec. Roberto Lastimoso.

SHIPPING

In 2000 there were 102 national and municipal ports, 20 baseports, 58 terminal ports and 270 private ports. The eight major ports are Manila, Cebu, Iloilo, Cagayan de Oro, Zamboanga, General Santos, Polloc and Davao.

Pangasiwaan ng Daungan ng Pilipinas (Philippine Ports Authority): Marsman Bldg, 22 Muelle de San Francisco St, South Harbour, Port Area, 1018 Metro Manila; tel. (2) 5274856; fax (2) 5274853; e-mail alcusi@ppa.com.ph; internet www.ppa.com.ph; f. 1977; supervises all ports within the Philippine Ports Authority port system; Gen. Man. Alfonso G. Cusi.

Domestic Lines

Albar Shipping and Trading Corpn: 2649 Molave St, United Parañaque 1, Parañaque, Metro Manila; tel. (2) 8232391; fax (2) 8233046; e-mail admin@albargroup.com.ph; internet www .albargroup.com.ph; f. 1974; manning agency (maritime), trading, ship husbanding; Chair. Akira S. Kato; Pres. Jose Albar G. Kato.

Candano Shipping Lines, Inc: Victoria Bldg, 6th Floor, 429 United Nations Ave, Ermita, 2802 Metro Manila; tel. (2) 5238051; fax (2) 5211309; f. 1953; inter-island chartering and Far East, cargo shipping; Pres. and Gen. Man. Jose Candano.

Carlos A. Gothong Lines, Inc: Quezon Blvd, Reclamation Area, POB 152, Cebu City; tel. (32) 211181; fax (32) 212265; Exec. Vice-Pres. Bob D. Gothong.

Delsan Transport Lines Inc: Magsaysay Center Bldg, 520 T. M. Kalaw St, Ermita, Metro Manila; tel. (2) 5219172; fax (2) 2889331; Pres. Vicente A. Sandoval; Gen. Man. Carlos A. Buenafe.

Eastern Shipping Lines, Inc: ESL Bldg, 54 Anda Circle, Port Area, POB 4253, 2803 Metro Manila; tel. (2) 5277841; fax (2) 5273006; e-mail eastship@skyinet.net; f. 1957; services to Japan; Pres. Erwin L. Chiongbian; Exec. Vice-Pres. Roy L. Chiongbian.

Loadstar Shipping Co Inc: Loadstar Bldg, 1294 Romualdez St, Paco, 1007 Metro Manila; tel. (2) 5238381; fax (2) 5218061; Pres. and Gen. Man. Teodoro G. Bernardino.

Lorenzo Shipping Corpn: Birch Tree Plaza Bldg, 6th Floor, 825 Muelle dela Industria St, Binondo, Metro Manila; tel. (2) 2457481; fax (2) 2446849; Pres. Capt. Romeo L. Malig.

Luzteveco (Luzon Stevedoring Corpn): Magsaysay Bldg, 520 T.M. Kalaw St, Ermita, Metro Manila; f. 1909; two brs; freight-forwarding, air cargo, world-wide shipping, broking, stevedoring, salvage, chartering and oil drilling support services; Pres. Jovino G. Lorenzo; Vice-Pres. Rodolfo B. Santiago.

National Shipping Corpn of the Philippines: Knights of Rizal Bldg, Bonifacio Drive, Port Area, Metro Manila; tel. (2) 473631; fax (2) 5300169; services to Hong Kong, Taiwan, Korea, USA; Pres. Tony Chow.

Negros Navigation Co Inc: Rufino Pacific Tower, 33rd Floor, 6784 Ayala Ave, cnr Herrera St, Makati City, Metro Manila; tel. (2) 8110115; fax (2) 8183707; Chair. Daniel L. Lacson; Man. Dir Manuel Garcia.

Philippine Pacific Ocean Lines Inc: Delgado Bldg, Bonifacio Drive, Port Area, POB 184, Metro Manila; tel. (2) 478541; Vice-Pres. C. P. Carandang.

Philippine President Lines, Inc: PPL Bldg, 1000–1046 United Nations Ave, POB 4248, Metro Manila; tel. (2) 5249011; fax (2) 5251308; trading world-wide; Chair. Emilio T. Yap, Jr; Pres. Enrique C. Yap.

Sulpicio Lines, Inc: 1st St, Reclamation Area, POB 137, Cebu City; tel. (32) 73839; Chair. Enrique S. Go; Man. Dir Carlos S. Go.

Sweet Lines Inc: Pier 6, North Harbour, Metro Manila; tel. (2) 201791; fax (2) 205534; f. 1937; Pres. Eduardo R. Lopingco; Exec. Vice-Pres. Sonny R. Lopingco.

Transocean Transport Corpn: Magsaysay Bldg, 8th Floor, 520 T. M. Kalaw St, Ermita, POB 21, Metro Manila; tel. (2) 506611; Pres. and Gen. Man. Miguel A. Magsaysay; Vice-Pres. Eduardo U. Manese.

United Philippine Lines, Inc: UPL Bldg, Santa Clara St, Intramuros, POB 127, Metro Manila; tel. (2) 5277491; fax (2) 5271603; e-mail uplines@skyinet.net; services world-wide; Pres. Fernando V. Lising.

WG & A Philippines, Inc: South Harbour Center 2, cnr Railroad St, South Harbour, Metro Manila; tel. (2) 5274605; fax (2) 5360945; internet www.wgasuperferry.com; f. 1996 following the merger of William Lines, Aboitiz Shipping and Carlos A. Gothong Lines; passenger and cargo inter-island services; Pres. Endica Aboitiz; Chair. W. L. Chiongbian.

CIVIL AVIATION

In March 1999 there were 92 national and 103 private airports in the Philippines. In addition to the international airports in Metro Manila (the Ninoy Aquino International Airport), Cebu (the Mactan International Airport), Angeles City (the Clark International Airport), and Olongapo City (the Subic Bay International Airport), there are five alternative international airports: Laoag City, Ilocos Norte; Davao City; Zamboanga City; Gen. Santos (Tambler) City; and Puerto Princesa City, Palawan. A further international airport was being developed in Laguindingan, Mindanao. The upgrading of the airport at the former US military installation, Clark Air Base (which was to be the country's principal airport), commenced in mid-1996, when a new international terminal (with an initial capacity of 300 passengers on charter flights) was opened.

Air Transportation Office: MIA Rd, Pasay City, Metro Manila; tel. (2) 8323308; fax (2) 8340143; internet www.ato.gov.ph; implements govt policies for the development and operation of a safe and efficient aviation network; Dir Gen. Capt. Jacinto F. Ortega, Jr; Gen. Man. Gen. (retd) Adelberto F. Yap.

Civil Aeronautics Board: Airport Rd, Pasay City, Metro Manila; tel. (2) 8317266; fax (2) 8336911; internet www.cab.gov.ph; exercises general supervision and regulation of, and jurisdiction and control over, air carriers, their equipment facilities and franchise; Dir Manuel C. San Jose.

Air Philippines: Multinational Bancorporation Center, 15th Floor, Ayala Ave, Makati City, 6805 Metro Manila; tel. (2) 8437001; fax (2) 8451983; internet www.airphilippines.com; f. 1994; operates flights between Manila, Cebu City and Davao City; was expected to commence regional services in 1996; Chair. and Pres. WILLIAM GATCHALIAN.

Asian Spirit: G & A Bldg, 3rd Floor, 2303 Don Chino Roces Ave, Makati City, Metro Manila; tel. (2) 8403811; fax (2) 8130183; e-mail info@asianspirit.com; internet www.asianspirit.com; Man. ANTONIO BUENDIA.

Cebu Pacific Air: 30 Pioneer St, cnr Epifanio de los Santos Ave, Mandaluyong City, Metro Manila; tel. (2) 6371810; fax (2) 6379170; e-mail feedback@cebupacificair.com; internet www.cebupacificair.com; f. 1995; domestic and international services; Pres. LANCE GOKONGWEI; Vice-Pres. (Corporate Planning and External Affairs) PEGGY P. VERA.

Grand Air: Philippines Village Airport Hotel, 8th Floor, Pasay City, Metro Manila; tel. (2) 8312911; fax (2) 8917682; f. 1994; Pres. REBECCA PANLILI.

Manila International Airport Authority (MIAA): NAIA Complex, Pasay City, Metro Manila; tel. (2) 8322938; fax (2) 8331180; e-mail gm@miaa.gov.ph; internet www.miaa.gov.ph; Gen. Man. EDGARDO C. MANDA.

Philippine Airlines Inc (PAL): PAL Corporate Communications Dept, PAL Center, Ground Floor, Legaspi St, Legaspi Village, Makati City, Metro Manila; tel. (2) 8316541; fax (2) 8136715; e-mail rgeccd@pal.com.ph; internet www.philippineairlines.com; f. 1941; in Jan. 1992 67% of PAL was transferred to the private sector; operates domestic, regional and international services to destinations in the Far East, Australasia, the Middle East, the USA and Canada; Chair. LUCIO TAN; Pres. AVELINO ZAPANTA.

Tourism

Tourism, although adversely affected from time to time by political unrest, remains an important sector of the economy. In 2001 arrivals totalled 1,796,893, compared with 1,992,169 in the previous year. An estimated 1.9m. people visited the country in 2002. Visitor expenditure totalled US $2,534m. in 1999 (compared with $2,412.9m. in 1998).

Philippine Convention and Visitors' Corpn: Legaspi Towers, 4th Floor, 300 Roxas Blvd, Metro Manila; tel. (2) 5259318; fax (2) 5216165; e-mail pcvcnet@info.com.ph; internet www.dotpcvc.gov.ph; Chair. RICHARD J. GORDON; Exec. Dir DANIEL G. CORPUZ.

Philippine Tourism Authority: Department of Tourism Bldg, T. M. Kalaw St, Ermita, 1000 Metro Manila; tel. (2) 5241032; fax (2) 5232865; e-mail info@philtourism.com; internet www.philtourism.com; Gen. Man. NIXON T. KUA.

POLAND

Introductory Survey

Location, Climate, Language, Religion, Flag, Capital

The Republic of Poland is situated in Eastern Europe, bounded to the north by the Baltic Sea and an exclave of the Russian Federation, to the north-east by Lithuania, to the east by Belarus, to the south-east by Ukraine, to the west by Germany and to the south by the Czech Republic and Slovakia. The climate is temperate in the west but continental in the east. Poland has short summers and cold, snowy winters. Temperatures in Warsaw are generally between –6°C (21°F) and 24°C (75°F). Most of the inhabitants profess Christianity: more than 95% are adherents of the Roman Catholic Church, but there are numerous other denominations, the largest being the Polish Autocephalous Orthodox Church. The official language is Polish, spoken by almost all of the population, and there is a small German-speaking community. The national flag (proportions 5 by 8) has two equal horizontal stripes, of white and red. The capital is Warsaw (Warszawa).

Recent History

Poland, partitioned since the 18th century, was declared an independent republic on 11 November 1918, at the end of the First World War. The country was ruled by a military regime from 1926 until 1939, when Poland was invaded by both Germany and the USSR and partitioned between the two powers. After Germany declared war on the USSR, in June 1941, its forces occupied the whole of Poland until they were expelled by Soviet troops in March 1945.

At the end of the Second World War a pro-communist 'Polish Committee of National Liberation', established under Soviet auspices in July 1944, was transformed into a Provisional Government. Under the Potsdam Agreement, signed by the major Allied powers in 1945, the former German territories lying east of the rivers Oder and Neisse (which now comprise one-third of Poland's total area) came under Polish sovereignty, while Poland's frontier with the USSR was shifted westward. These border changes were accompanied by a major resettlement of the population in the affected areas.

Non-communist political groups suffered severe intimidation during national elections in January 1947, and the communist-led 'democratic bloc' claimed an overwhelming victory. A People's Republic was established in February, with the Polish Workers' Party (PWP), led by Władysław Gomułka, as the dominant group. Gomułka's reluctance to implement certain aspects of Soviet economic policies, notably the collectivization of agriculture, led to his dismissal as First Secretary of the PWP in 1948. In December of that year the PWP merged with the Polish Socialist Party to form the Polish United Workers' Party (Polska Zjednoczona Partia Robotnicza—PZPR). Two other parties, the United Peasants' Party (Zjednoczone Stronnictwo Ludowe—ZSL) and the Democratic Party (Stronnictwo Demokratyczne—SD), were permitted to remain in existence, but were closely controlled by the PZPR, and Poland effectively became a one-party state.

The PZPR's strict control over public life eased slightly following the death of Stalin, the Soviet leader, in 1953. In 1956 mass demonstrations by industrial workers, provoked by food shortages, were suppressed by security forces. In the ensuing political crisis Gomułka was returned to office, despite the opposition of the Soviet leadership. A period of stability and some liberalization followed, and in 1964–70 limited economic reforms were implemented, although the standard of living remained low. In December 1970 a sharp rise in food prices led to strikes and demonstrations in the Baltic port of Gdańsk and in other cities. Many demonstrators were killed or injured in clashes with the police and army, and Gomułka was forced to resign as First Secretary of the PZPR; he was succeeded by Edward Gierek.

In July 1980 an increase in meat prices prompted widespread labour unrest, and shipyard employees in the Baltic ports, notably at Gdańsk, demanded the right to form free trade unions. Following negotiations with the Government, permission was finally granted to establish several self-governing trade unions, under the guidance of Solidarity (Solidarność), the

organization involved in the Gdańsk strike, which was led by a local worker, Lech Wałęsa. In September, as mass labour unrest continued, Gierek was replaced as First Secretary of the PZPR by Stanisław Kania, a member of the party's Politburo. Under the growing influence of Solidarity (which claimed an estimated 10m. members in 1981), strikes continued throughout the country, and in February Józef Pińkowski resigned as Chairman of the Council of Ministers. He was succeeded by Gen. Wojciech Jaruzelski, Minister of Defence (a post he retained) since 1968. Despite further concessions to Solidarity, the crisis persisted, forcing Kania's resignation in October; he was succeeded by Jaruzelski, who thus held the leading posts in both the PZPR and the Government.

On 13 December 1981 martial law was imposed throughout Poland. A governing Military Council of National Salvation, led by Jaruzelski, was established; all trade-union activity was suspended, and Wałęsa and other Solidarity leaders were detained. Violent clashes between workers and security forces ensued, and thousands of protesters were arrested. Sporadic disturbances continued in 1982, particularly in response to legislation (imposed in October) abolishing all trade unions. Wałęsa was released in November, and in December martial law was suspended and some other prisoners were freed. (During 1982 about 10,000 prisoners had been detained, and at least 15 demonstrators killed.) In July 1983 martial law was formally ended; the Military Council of National Salvation was dissolved, and an amnesty was declared for most political prisoners and underground activists. In October Wałęsa was awarded the Nobel Peace Prize.

In July 1984, to mark the 40th anniversary of the Polish communist regime, a wide-ranging amnesty was announced, under which some 35,000 detainees were released. In August US sanctions (imposed following the declaration of martial law) were relaxed. However, the murder, in October, of Fr Jerzy Popiełuszko, a well-known pro-Solidarity Roman Catholic priest, provoked renewed unrest. In February 1985 four officers from the Ministry of Internal Affairs were found guilty of the murder, and received lengthy prison sentences. (The case was subsequently reopened; two generals, accused of directing the murder, were acquitted in August 1994, but the verdict was overturned in March 1996, and it was announced that the case was to be re-examined.)

Legislative elections (postponed from March 1984) took place in October 1985. New regulations gave voters a choice of two candidates for 410 of the Sejm's 460 seats, the remaining 50 deputies being elected unopposed on a national list. Solidarity appealed to voters to boycott the poll, and subsequently disputed the Government's claim that 79% of the electorate had participated. In November Jaruzelski resigned as Chairman of the Council of Ministers, in order to become President of the Council of State (Head of State). His former post was taken by Prof. Zbigniew Messner (hitherto a Deputy Chairman of the Council of Ministers).

A Party Congress of the PZPR, in June 1986, re-elected Jaruzelski as First Secretary. In December, in an effort to increase popular support for the regime, Jaruzelski established a 56-member Consultative Council, which was attached to the Council of State and comprised mainly non-PZPR members—among them independent Roman Catholic activists and former members of Solidarity. Nevertheless, public discontent intensified in 1987. Solidarity activists attempted to disrupt the official May Day celebrations in several cities, and in June there were violent clashes between police and protesters during a visit by Pope John Paul II to his native country. Significant price rises were imposed in early 1988, and in April and May widespread protests were organized to demand compensatory wage increases, and the May Day celebrations were again disrupted by Solidarity supporters. In August a strike by pro-Solidarity coalworkers rapidly spread to other sectors, leading to the most serious industrial unrest since 1981.

The Messner Government resigned in September 1988. Dr Mieczysław Rakowski, Deputy Chairman in 1981–85, was appointed Chairman of a new Council of Ministers, which included several non-PZPR members and younger, reformist politicians. However, the new administration failed to commence talks that had been scheduled for October among representatives of the Government, Solidarity and other groups. Moreover, the Government's announcement that the Lenin Shipyard in Gdańsk was to be closed, ostensibly for economic reasons, provoked further strike action, despite Wałęsa's appeals to trade-union activists to remain at work. By April 1989 agreement had been reached on the restoration of legal status to Solidarity, as well as on the holding of elections to a new, bicameral legislature, the Zgromadzenie Narodowe (National Assembly). Solidarity and other non-communist groups were to be permitted to contest all the seats in a new upper chamber, the Senat, which would have a limited right of veto over the lower chamber, the Sejm. Just 35% of the seats in the Sejm were to be subject to free elections, with the remainder open only to candidates of the PZPR and its associate organizations. A new post of executive President was also to be introduced. The necessary amendments to the Constitution were duly approved by the Sejm, and Solidarity was formally legalized. In May the Roman Catholic Church was accorded legal status.

Elections to the new legislature took place on 4 and 8 July 1989, with 62% of eligible voters participating in the first round, but only 25% in the second. The Solidarity Citizens' Committee, the electoral wing of the trade-union movement, achieved a decisive victory in the elections to the Senat, securing all but one of the 100 seats. In the elections to the 460-member Sejm, Solidarity secured all the 161 seats that it was permitted to contest, while the other 299 seats were divided between the PZPR (173 seats), its allied parties—the ZSL (76) and the SD (27)—and members of Roman Catholic organizations (23).

The new legislature narrowly elected Jaruzelski, unopposed, to the post of executive President (with a six-year mandate). He was replaced as First Secretary of the PZPR by Rakowski. President Jaruzelski accepted Wałęsa's proposal of a coalition of Solidarity, the SD and the ZSL, and the appointment of Tadeusz Mazowiecki, a newspaper editor and moderate member of Solidarity, as Chairman of the Council of Ministers, was approved by the Sejm on 24 August 1989, thus ending almost 45 years of exclusive communist rule in Poland. A Solidarity-dominated administration was formed in September.

The new Government's programme of radical political and economic reforms emphasized the creation of democratic institutions and the introduction of a market economy. In December 1989 the legislature voted to rename the country the Republic of Poland, and the national symbols of pre-communist Poland were reintroduced. Economic reforms announced in January 1990 aimed to free prices by removing subsidies, while restraining wages to limit inflation; exports were to be encouraged by introducing limited convertibility of the national currency, the złoty. In the same month the PZPR was dissolved to allow the establishment of a new left-wing party, Social Democracy of the Republic of Poland (Socjaldemokracji Rzeczypospolitej Polskiej —SdRP). Local elections held in May were the first entirely free elections in Poland for more than 50 years. Candidates of the Solidarity Citizens' Committee won more than 41% of the seats, while nominally independent candidates secured 38%. However, a low rate of participation (only 42% of the electorate) apparently reflected general disenchantment with the Government's austere economic policies. By mid-1990 tension had developed between Wałęsa, who advocated an acceleration of economic reform and privatization, and the more cautious Mazowiecki. In July pro-Mazowiecki activists within Solidarity formed the Citizens' Movement-Democratic Action (Ruch Obywatelski-Akcja Demokratyczna—ROAD), presenting a direct challenge to the Centre Alliance (Porozumienie Centrum—PC), which had been formed in May by supporters of Wałęsa.

In September 1990 Jaruzelski agreed to resign, to permit direct presidential elections to take place. In the first round, held on 25 November, Mazowiecki unexpectedly received fewer votes than either Wałęsa or a little-known *émigré* business executive, Stanisław Tymiński. Wałęsa and Tymiński proceeded to a second round of voting on 9 December, at which Wałęsa won 74.3% of the votes cast. Wałęsa resigned the chairmanship of Solidarity (he was replaced in February 1991 by Marian Krzaklewski), and in late December 1990 was inaugurated as the country's President for a five-year term. Jan Krzysztof Bielecki, a radical economist, became Prime Minister. Bielecki's Council of Ministers retained only two ministers from the outgoing administration. The new regime quickly encountered public and political challenges to its reform programme. At the end of May

1991 Solidarity organized a nation-wide day of strikes and demonstrations, in protest at the Government's stringent economic policies. Moreover, the Sejm increasingly opposed, and thus delayed, economic legislation.

Legislative elections took place on 27 October 1991, with the participation of only 43.2% of the electorate. A total of 29 parties won representation in the Sejm, but none acquired a decisive mandate. The party with the largest number of deputies (62) was Mazowiecki's Democratic Union (Unia Demokratyczne— UD), formed in May by the merger of ROAD and two other organizations. The Democratic Left Alliance (Sojusz Lewicy Demokratycznej—SLD), an electoral coalition of the SdRP and the All Poland Trade Unions Alliance (Ogólnopolskie Porozumienie Związków Zawodowych), won 60 seats. In the Senat the UD was also the largest single party, with 21 seats, while Solidarity returned 11 senators. After Bronisław Geremek of the UD failed to form a government, Wałęsa nominated Jan Olszewski of the PC as Prime Minister. Criticism of his economic programme by the President and the withdrawal of two parties from the coalition negotiations caused Olszewski to submit his resignation. This was, however, rejected by the Sejm, which proceeded, in late December, to approve a new centre-right Council of Ministers, incorporating members of the PC, the pro-Solidarity Peasant Alliance and the Christian National Union (Zjednoczenie Chrześcijańsko-Narodowe—ZChN).

In June 1992, following controversy regarding government attempts to expose alleged communist conspirators, the Sejm approved a motion of 'no confidence' in the Olszewski Government. Waldemar Pawlak, the leader of the Polish People's Party (Polskie Stronnictwo Ludowe—PSL), failed to form a government, whereupon Hanna Suchocka of the UD was proposed as Prime Minister. Her appointment was approved by the Sejm later in July, and she proceeded to form a seven-party coalition, dominated by the UD and the ZChN. The new Government was, however, immediately challenged by a month-long strike by 40,000 workers at a copper plant in Legnica, supported by several transport and power workers' unions.

In December 1992 an interim 'Small Constitution' entered into effect; this was to remain in force while a comprehensive revision of the 1952 Constitution was in progress. A motion of 'no confidence' in the Suchocka administration, proposed by the Solidarity group after the failure of negotiations between the Government and striking teachers and health workers, was narrowly approved by the Sejm in late May 1993. Wałęsa refused to accept Suchocka's resignation; instead, he dissolved the Sejm, scheduling new elections to both houses of parliament for September. Subsequent amendments to the electoral code achieved greater political stability by reducing the number of political parties represented in parliament. The principal reform was a new stipulation that a party (with the exception of organizations representing national minorities) must secure at least 5% of the total votes cast (8% in the case of an electoral alliance) in order to gain parliamentary representation.

The general election resulted in an overwhelming victory for parties of the left, as voters demonstrated their dissatisfaction with the adverse consequences of recent economic reforms. The SLD and the PSL, both dominated by former communists and their allies, won, respectively, 171 and 132 seats in the Sejm, and 37 and 36 seats in the Senat. The two parties, which together won 35.8% of the total votes in the elections to the Sejm, benefited from the new law to secure more than 65% of the seats in the lower chamber. The UD took 74 seats in the Sejm (with 10.6% of the votes cast) and four in the Senat, while Solidarity won 10 Senat seats (although none in the Sejm). Wałęsa's Non-Party Bloc for Reform (Bezpartyjny Blok Wspierania Reform), established in June in an attempt to consolidate support for the President in parliament, won 16 seats in the Sejm (with 5.4% of the votes cast) and two seats in the Senat. The PC and the ZChN notably failed to win representation in either chamber. Almost 35% of the votes cast in elections to the Sejm were for parties that received fewer than 5% of the total votes, and therefore secured no representation; the rate of participation by voters was 52.1%.

In October 1993 Pawlak formed a coalition Government, dominated by members of his PSL and the SLD. The new Prime Minister expressed his commitment to a continuation of market-orientated reforms, but pledged new measures to alleviate their adverse social effects. In early 1994 the Deputy Prime Minister and Minister of Finance, Marek Borowski (of the SLD) resigned. Wałęsa subsequently threatened to dissolve parliament in response to a proposal, made by PSL-SLD deputies, for an amendment to the Small Constitution, whereby the Sejm, and not the Head of State, would be ultimately responsible for ratifying government appointments. In February, meanwhile, at least 20,000 people took part in a Solidarity-led demonstration in Warsaw, to demand increased government investment in the public sector and improved measures to combat unemployment. Solidarity began a nation-wide programme of strike action in March.

In January 1995 Wałęsa refused to endorse legislation to increase rates of personal income tax, and urged the population not to pay the new rates; his actions were subsequently ruled unconstitutional by the Constitutional Tribunal, and he was obliged to approve the legislation. Relations between the Government and the President deteriorated sharply in February, when Wałęsa threatened to dissolve parliament if the Prime Minister did not resign; the Sejm voted to begin impeachment proceedings against the President should he attempt to dissolve the legislature. Further conflict was averted by Pawlak's departure, and in March Józef Oleksy, a member of the SLD and hitherto Marshal (Speaker) of the Sejm, took office as Prime Minister; his Government comprised members of the SLD, the PSL and independents.

The first round of the 1995 presidential election took place on 5 November, contested by 13 candidates. The two leading candidates, Aleksander Kwaśniewski, the Chairman of the SdRP (and formerly a leading member of the PZPR), and Wałęsa proceeded to a second round, on 19 November, when Kwaśniewski achieved a narrow victory, with 51.7% of the votes cast. An appeal by Wałęsa's supporters for the election to be declared invalid—on the grounds that Kwaśniewski had falsely claimed to have received a postgraduate degree, and had failed to reveal details of his wife's financial assets—was disallowed by the Supreme Court, and the new President formally took office on 23 December. Kwaśniewski asserted his commitment to the further integration of Poland into Western institutions, and to the continuation of policies of economic liberalization.

Following Kwaśniewski's election, the ministers responsible for foreign affairs, the interior and national defence (all effectively presidential appointees) submitted their resignations. The outgoing Minister of Internal Affairs, Andrzej Milczanowski, claimed that Oleksy had acted on behalf of Soviet (and subsequently Russian) espionage agents since the 1980s; although Oleksy vehemently denied the charges, he resigned as Prime Minister in January 1996 (he was fully exonerated in an official report published in October). He was subsequently elected Chairman of the SdRP, replacing Kwaśniewski, who had resigned the post and his party membership following his election as President. Negotiations between the SLD and the PSL resulted in the appointment of Włodzimierz Cimoszewicz (the SLD's deputy leader and hitherto Deputy Marshal of the Sejm) as Prime Minister in February.

Legislation regulating the commercialization and privatization of state-owned enterprises was adopted in June 1996. In that month the Government's decision to file for bankruptcy for the loss-making Gdańsk shipyard prompted Solidarity-led demonstrations. Also in June some 25 centre-right political parties, including Solidarity, the PC and the ZChN, established Solidarity Electoral Action (Akcja Wyborcza Solidarność—AWS) to contest the 1997 parliamentary elections. Tensions became evident within the governing coalition in September 1996, when the Prime Minister dismissed the PSL's Jacek Buchacz as Minister of Foreign Economic Relations, in response to evidence that he had violated official policy on granting export and credit guarantees; the decision to dismiss the minister, apparently made without consulting his party, prompted the withdrawal of the PSL from government negotiations on proposed administrative reforms. Talks resumed, none the less, at the end of September, after Cimoszewicz conceded that he had reneged on the coalition accord. Agreement was subsequently reached on the distribution of ministerial portfolios, whereby the PSL was accorded responsibility for the new Ministry of the Treasury, while the SLD secured the Ministry of Internal Affairs and Administration and the new Ministry of the Economy.

In February 1997 a six-day strike by workers at the Belchatow lignite mine led to severe shortages at the Belchatow power plant, and the announcement that 3,000 workers at the Gdańsk shipyard were to lose their jobs prompted nation-wide demonstrations in March. On 2 April, after four years of parliamentary negotiations, the National Assembly adopted a new Constitution, which was approved by 52.7% of votes cast by some 42.9% of the electorate in a national referendum on 25 May. Right-wing parties, notably AWS and the Movement for the Reconstruction of Poland (ROP), had opposed the parliamentary draft, having demanded a more positive affirmation of Christian beliefs, and that their own 'citizens draft' be included in the referendum. The Constitution slightly reduced presidential powers, and committed Poland to a social market economy based on the freedom of economic activity and private ownership. In July the Supreme Court ruled the referendum result to be valid. The new Constitution was subsequently signed by the President, and came into force on 17 October.

In the general election of 21 September 1997, the right-wing dominated AWS secured 201 seats in the Sejm (with 33.8% of the valid votes cast) and 51 in the Senat, while the SLD won 164 seats in the Sejm (with 27.1% of the votes) and 28 in the Senat. The PSL retained only 27 seats in the Sejm (with 7.3% of the votes) and three in the Senat. The rate of voter participation was 48%. Marian Krzaklewski, the leader of AWS, subsequently initiated coalition talks with the Freedom Union (Unia Wolności —UW) and the ROP, which had won, respectively, 60 and six seats in the Sejm, and eight and five in the Senat. Jerzy Buzek (a member of Solidarity since its formation in 1980) was nominated as Prime Minister in mid-October 1997. (Solidarity's leader, Krzaklewski, had already announced that he had no wish to assume the premiership.) Following lengthy negotiations regarding the distribution of ministerial portfolios, AWS and the UW signed a coalition agreement later that month, despite some opposition from the ZChN and the PC (both members of AWS), which objected to several of the UW's ministerial nominations. A new Council of Ministers was subsequently appointed, which included Leszek Balcerowicz, leader of the UW, as Deputy Prime Minister, Minister of Finance and Chairman of the Economic Committee. Former Prime Minister Hanna Suchocka became Minister of Justice, a portfolio allocated to the UW. In early November the Sejm approved the new Government's programme, which prioritized rapid integration with NATO and the European Union (EU, see p. 199) and accelerated privatization and government reform. Shortly afterwards the Social Movement of Solidarity Electoral Action (Ruch Społeczny Akcja Wyborcza Solidarność), which was to replace Solidarity within AWS, applied for registration as a new political party. In December Lech Wałęsa officially formed the Christian Democratic Party of the Third Republic. In January 1998 the Concordat, an agreement reached with the Vatican in 1993 governing relations between the State and the Church, approval of which had been repeatedly delayed by the SLD-led coalition, was finally ratified by the National Assembly.

In late July 1998, following substantial debate, new legislation, which divided Poland into 16 provinces (voivodships) and 308 newly created districts (powiats), was enacted; it entered into effect on 1 January 1999. Local elections were held in the 16 provinces on 11 October 1998. In nine provinces the opposition SLD was returned as the largest party, although the governing AWS-UW coalition won the largest number of seats overall, and secured control of the seven remaining provinces. Meanwhile, the Government's programme of industrial restructuring continued to provoke public unrest, as well as discord among the governing parties. In April Solidarity organized a 10-day strike at Poland's largest copper mine at Rudna, in protest at planned redundancies. Government proposals to restructure the coalmining industry were presented to the Sejm in that month: these included job losses for about one-half of the country's 237,000 miners and the closure of 24 of its 65 mines. The proposed restructuring contradicted pre-election pledges made by the AWS that the coal sector would receive state protection from mass redundancies. In May trade unions succeeded in securing certain concessions from the Government, which agreed to reduce the number of job losses in the sector. Railway workers took industrial action in June, and in July around 10,000 farmers took part in a demonstration in Warsaw, to demand increased government protection for the agricultural sector. During August farmers organized nation-wide road blockades and, in December, after two months of inconclusive talks with government officials, there was further unrest. The farmers ended their blockades in late January 1999, when the Government agreed to a 50% increase in the state subsidy for pork. However, the leader of the Self-Defence Trade Union (Samoobrona, which had organized the protests), Andrzej Lepper, rejected government concessions, and farmers' protests continued in February, when it was announced that Lepper was to stand trial for having organized illegal road blocks.

There was further opposition to the Government's economic programme following its approval, in July 1998, of the sale of the Gdańsk shipyard (which was completed in September). Six AWS deputies withdrew their support from the Government in protest at the decision. (In preceding weeks nine other deputies had also left the ruling coalition.) In mid-December a strike by coal miners over imminent changes to the pensions system spread to more than 50 mines, and resulted in government concessions; industrial unrest also affected the steel, armaments and railway sectors. In early January 1999 Poland's hospitals entered a period of crisis, following industrial action by anaesthetists. In late January a preliminary agreement to increase anaesthetists' wages was reached.

In June 1998 the Sejm adopted a resolution condemning the communist regime imposed on post-war Poland by the USSR; the resolution, which was opposed by PZPR's successor SLD, held the PZPR responsible for offences committed during the communist period. A new penal code entered effect in early September, in conformity with EU criteria, which abolished the death penalty. In late September the Sejm approved legislation granting access for Polish citizens to files compiled on them by the security services during the communist era.

During March 1999 the Prime Minister undertook a major government reorganization, with the aim of creating a smaller chancellery, in preparation for a more significant reform of state administration, which took effect in April. The new legislation granted additional powers to the Prime Minister to review the performance of ministries and to adjust ministers' powers, subject to the approval of other leaders of the ruling coalition. The Secretary-General of the UW resigned in protest at the appointment of two ministers. Meanwhile, in late May the Sejm approved amendments to the vetting legislation, including a stipulation that any person found to have lied in a vetting declaration was to be disqualified from contesting the presidency for 10 years. In July the PC—a member of the governing AWS—and the Party of Christian Democrats (Partia Chrzescijanskich Demokratów—PChD) announced the formation of a new organization, the Alliance of Polish Christian Democrats (Porozumienie Polskich Chrzescijanskich Demokratów—PPChD); the alliance was officially founded in September.

During May 1999 farmers resumed their campaign of blockading roads in protest against agricultural policy. In mid-June workers from the Lucznik weapons factory in Radom took part in a demonstration in Warsaw, demanding government action in support of the plant; the protest resulted in violent clashes between the police and demonstrators. Nurses and midwives also held protests in the capital during late June and early July, demanding wage increases and an end to redundancies in the health service; about 25,000 others began hunger strikes. The nurses agreed to a temporary suspension of their protests in mid-July, after pay negotiations with the Government were resumed. In mid-August farmers, led by Andrzej Lepper's Self-Defence Trade Union, joined demonstrations against the low price of grain; an estimated 80 people were injured when violence erupted between police and farmers in northern Poland. Lepper subsequently announced his intention of forming a new anti-Government coalition with other farmers' organizations and trade unions: the Self Defence Party of the Republic of Poland was formally established in January 2000. Protests against the economic slowdown and the implementation of government reforms in education, health and pension provision culminated, in late September 1999, in a march through Warsaw by some 35,000 agricultural and industrial workers (as well as leaders from the opposition SLD and PSL parties).

Meanwhile, during September 1999 Buzek came under growing criticism from leading members of his governing coalition, who accused him of weak leadership. At the beginning of the month the Deputy Prime Minister and Minister of Internal Affairs and Administration, Janusz Tomaszewski, announced his resignation. A minor government reorganization took place in early October 1999. At the same time the AWS and the UW renewed their coalition agreement for a further two years. In late October the Government reached a compromise with miners' representatives from Solidarity regarding the restructuring of the industry, following miners' protests in the capital during that month. It was announced in early December that Solidarity was to withdraw from political activities and become an 'organization of employees'; the movement's voting rights within the AWS were transferred to the Social Movement of Solidarity Electoral Action (Ruch Społeczny Akcja Wyborcza Solidarność—RS AWS).

In mid-May 2000 the ruling coalition entered its most serious crisis, when the Prime Minister suspended the Government of Warsaw's central commune (a coalition of the UW and the SLD) and replaced it with an AWS-affiliated commissioner, prompting threats by the UW to withdraw from the Government. At the end of May the UW announced its withdrawal from the ruling coalition, in protest at the blocking of Balcerowicz's proposals for economic reform by AWS deputies. Negotiations aimed at maintaining the coalition collapsed in early June, and Buzek subsequently formed a minority AWS Government. Jarosław Bauc was appointed to succeed Balcerowicz as Minister of Finance, and Władysław Bartoszewski was appointed Minister of Foreign Affairs. In August the treasury minister, Emil Wąsacz, who had survived two motions of 'no confidence' in the Sejm, and faced a third, was dismissed, following long-standing controversy surrounding his privatization policies.

In August 2000 a Vetting Court cleared President Kwaśniewski and the former President, Lech Wałęsa, of charges of collaborating with communist-era security services, thereby allowing both to contest the presidential election scheduled to take place in October. In the same month the radical farmers' leader, Andrzej Lepper, who also intended to stand as a candidate in the election, was detained, after having failed to appear in court to answer charges associated with the farmers' blockades of 1998–99. (He was sentenced to 16 months in jail in May 2001.) In September 2000 one of the President's most senior aides resigned, following the release of footage from 1997, in which he appeared to parody Pope John Paul II, in the presence of Kwaśniewski. In the presidential election, held as scheduled on 8 October 2000, Kwaśniewski was re-elected, with 53.9% of the valid votes cast. The second-placed candidate, an independent and a former foreign minister, Andrzej Olechowski, secured 17.3% of the valid votes; Marian Krzaklewski obtained 15.6% of the votes, Andrzej Lepper 3.1% and Lech Wałęsa just 1.0%. The rate of voter participation was 61.1%. Following his electoral defeat, Wałęsa announced that he was to retire from politics, although he was to remain Honorary Chairman of the ChDTRP. Similarly, Marian Krzaklewski resigned as leader of the AWS in January 2001, and was succeeded by Prime Minister Jerzy Buzek. (Krzaklewski remained Chairman of Solidarity until September 2002.) Meanwhile, Leszek Balcerowicz resigned the leadership of the UW, and became President of the central bank in December 2000.

In January 2001 Andrzej Olechowski, together with the Marshal of the Sejm, Maciej Plazyński of the AWS, and a Vice-Marshal of the Senat, Donald Tusk of the UW, founded a new political movement, known as the Citizens' Platform (PO). In March the Conservative Peasant Party, a constituent party of the AWS, announced its intention to form an electoral alliance with the PO, although it was to remain in government until the election. Kwaśniewski signed a new electoral law at the end of April, which introduced a new method for the calculation of voting under the system of proportional representation, favouring small and medium-sized parties. Following the enactment of the law, legislative elections were scheduled for 23 September. Thereafter, significant political realignment took place, and in May the AWS was restructured as Solidarity Electoral Action of the Right (AWSP), in alliance with the ROP. At the end of May the Christian, nationalist League of Polish Families (LPR), which opposed membership of the EU, was registered as a party. In August the legislature rejected an austerity plan proposed by the Minister of Finance, Jarosław Bauc, in an attempt to address the predicted deficit in the budget for 2002. In late August Buzek announced Bauc's dismissal, on the grounds that he had failed to give the Government sufficient warning of the impending crisis; Halina Wasilewska-Trenkner was appointed as his replacement.

The legislative election took place as scheduled, on 23 September 2001, with a rate of voter participation of 46.3%. Neither the AWSP nor its former coalition party, the UW, received the requisite 8% of the votes to obtain seats in the Sejm, although both parties contested the election to the Senat as part of the Blok Senat 2001 (also comprising the PO, the Law and Justice Party—PiS and the UW), which obtained 15 of the 100 seats. The low proportion of votes obtained by the AWSP in the election to the Sejm (5.6%) was thought to reflect popular disillusionment with rising levels of unemployment and the party's internal divisions. Right-wing support was, instead, divided between the new PiS, which obtained 44 seats in the Sejm (with 9.5% of the votes), and the LPR, which obtained 38 seats in the Sejm (with 7.9% of the votes) and two seats in the Senat.

Another party elected to the Sejm for the first time was the agrarian Self Defence Party of Andrzej Lepper, which took 53 seats in the Sejm (with 10.2% of the votes) and two seats in the Senat, and which also opposed accession to the EU. A leftist electoral coalition of the SLD and the UP won 216 seats in the Sejm (with 41.0% of the votes) and 75 seats in the Senat, but failed to achieve an overall majority. The PO, which received 65 seats in the Sejm (with 12.7% of the votes), rejected an initial proposal to form a coalition with the SLD-UP. Instead, on 9 October the SLD and the UP signed a coalition agreement with the PSL, which had obtained 42 seats in the election to the Sejm (with 9.0% of the votes) and 4 seats in the Senat. The leader of the SLD, Leszek Miller, was sworn in as Prime Minister and Chairman of the European Integration Committee on 19 October; the PSL's leader, Jarosław Kalinowski, and the leader of the UP, Marek Pol, were appointed as Deputy Prime Ministers. Pol was also awarded responsibility for the new Ministry of Infrastructure, which was introduced to replace the transport ministry, and which was also to control communications and regional policy. Miller declared that the salaries of senior government officials, including members of the Council of Ministers, would be 'frozen' for at least one year, and pledged to revive economic progress and accelerate negotiations towards admission to the EU. Miller also announced that a referendum on entry to the EU would be held in mid-2003, and gave assurances that his Government would resign should the referendum fail to register support for Poland's admission to the Union.

In late November 2001 Andrzej Lepper was dismissed as Vice-Marshal of the Sejm, accused of having insulted the Minister of Foreign Affairs over concessions made to the EU on the issue of land sales. In January 2002 the Conservative Peasant Party and the PChD merged to form the Conservative Peasant Party-New Poland Movement, with Artur Balazs as its Chairman, in an attempt to unite the country's fractured right wing. Meanwhile, in the same month the Sejm voted to remove Lepper's parliamentary immunity from prosecution. He was subsequently fined for having insulted the President; in the following month he was also charged with seven counts of slander, and in March received a suspended one-year prison sentence for his role in the organization of illegal farmers' blockades in 1999. In early July 2002 Marek Belka resigned as Minister of Finance, prompting concern among the financial community; Grzegorz Kołodko subsequently assumed the post (which he had previously held in 1994–97). Also in early July the Minister of Culture, Andrzej Celinski, resigned, and was replaced by Waldemar Dąbrowski; the Minister of Justice, Barbara Piwniek, was dismissed, and succeeded by Grzegorz Kurczuk.

On 27 October 2002 direct local elections were held; the ruling coalition of the SLD and the UP won 33.7% of the votes cast, the Self Defence Party won 18.0% of the votes and the LPR secured 16.4%. A second round of voting took place on 10 November. In mid-December Kołodko survived a vote of 'no confidence' in the Sejm, after a controversial tax-amnesty bill, which was supported by the Minister of Finance, was rejected by a Consitutional Tribunal. In January 2003 the Prime Minister reshuffled the cabinet, and dismissed Minister of the Economy Jacek Piechota, creating a new Ministry of the Economy, Labour and Social Policy under the former Minister of Labour and Social Policy Jerzy Hausner. In the same month a large-scale political corruption scandal, which first emerged at the end of 2002, continued to attract widespread media attention. A national newspaper, *Gazeta Wyborcza*, alleged that a government intermediary had attempted to a solicit a bribe from the publication, in return for the approval of amendments to controversial legislation on media ownership, which would have enabled the newspaper's parent company to purchase a private television station. Although the Government denied the allegations, the passage of the legislation was suspended pending the results of an inquiry.

On 1 March 2003 Miller expelled the junior coalition partner, the PSL, from the Government, after it voted with opposition deputies against new legislation, supported by the SLD and UP, in the Sejm. Adam Tański consequently replaced Jarosław Kalinowski as Minister of Agriculture and Rural Development, and Czesław Sleziak succeeded Stanisław Żelichowski as Minister of the Environment. On 13 March the Sejm rejected a motion, proposed by the LPR, to dissolve parliament. The following day the SLD-UD governing coalition formed a parliamentary alliance with the Peasant Democratic Party (PLD), although it remained 13 seats short of a majority. At the beginning of April the Minister of Health, Marek Balicki,

resigned; Leszek Sikorski was appointed as his replacement. The recently appointed Minister of the Treasury, Slawomir Cytrycki, also resigned in early April, and was succeeded by Piotr Czyżewski. Although the Prime Minister pledged that no further cabinet changes were planned, the Council of Ministers was widely regarded as fragile. Miller proposed holding new legislative elections in June 2004, one year earlier than required, at the same time as the election of the first deputies to the European Parliament; commentators considered this to be a judicious decision, in light of the difficult financial situation predicted in 2005, following Poland's anticipated entry to the EU in 2004. Meanwhile, public dissatisfaction at the state of the economy and the high rate of unemployment was expressed in often-violent protest demonstrations led by the Solidarity trade union; in late April 2003 some 20,000 people attended one such gathering. Meanwhile, in February the Government had finally reached agreement with the EU on the level of direct farm subsidies following Poland's accession, and a national referendum on membership was scheduled to take place on 8 June, although a low rate of voter participation was predicted.

In foreign affairs, Poland's formal links with other Eastern European states, through its membership of the Warsaw Pact (the defence grouping of the former Soviet bloc) and the Council for Mutual Economic Assistance, were ended in 1991 upon the dissolution of these two organizations. Close relations were retained with the Czech Republic, Hungary and Slovakia through the structures of the Visegrad Group and Central European Free Trade Agreement, and also with other countries of the Baltic region. In 1991–92 Poland established diplomatic relations with the former republics of the USSR, developing particularly strong links with Ukraine. In May 1997 the Polish and Ukrainian Presidents signed a declaration of reconciliation, which included the condemnation of the killing of tens of thousands of Poles by Ukrainian nationalists in 1942–43, and of the 'Wisła Operation' of 1947, in which more than 100,000 Ukrainians were forcibly deported from their homes in south-east Poland. During 1998 and early 1999 Poland sought to reassure Ukraine (as well as Russia) that good relations and mutual co-operation between their two countries would continue following Poland's entry into NATO in March 1999 and its eventual membership of the EU. Relations with neighbouring Lithuania were initially strained by concerns regarding the status of the Polish minority in that country. Relations improved in 1993–94, and in April 1994 Poland and Lithuania signed a treaty of friendship and co-operation, in which both countries renounced any claims on each other's territory. All former Soviet combat troops had been withdrawn from Poland by November 1992, and the last remaining (non-combat) Russian military presence was withdrawn in September 1994.

Relations between Poland and Russia deteriorated as a result of Poland's decision to join NATO in March 1999, and remained tense in late January 2000, when nine Russian diplomats were expelled from Poland for their alleged involvement in espionage activities; the Russian authorities responded by expelling nine Polish diplomats from the Russian capital, Moscow. Tensions eased in July, when President Kwaśniewski became the first Polish head of state to pay an official visit to Moscow since the collapse of communist rule. Relations with Russia improved further in January 2002, when Putin paid an official visit to Poland, in what was his first visit to a former Eastern bloc country. However, the Polish Government continued to oppose Russia's plans to construct a natural gas pipeline to Slovakia via Poland, bypassing Ukraine, as it feared that the project threatened to affect adversely Polish-Ukrainian relations.

In May 1996 relations with Belarus became strained, following the arrest and deportation of four Solidarity leaders, who had been invited to Minsk by the Free Trade Union of Belarus. In September 1998 a visit by a high-level Polish delegation to a non-parliamentary national minorities committee in Belarus angered the Belarusian Government, which had not been informed of the visit. In late 1998 Belarus and Russia signed several agreements with the aim of pursuing further political and economic integration, and in December the Polish Government announced that it would continue to monitor closely the development of the Union of Russia and Belarus. Tension between Poland and Belarus increased further in January 1999 when the Sejm sent a 'message to the Belarusian nation', which included the demand that Belarusian deputies who were serving prison sentences for their opposition to the regime should be released; the Belarusian authorities described the message as 'openly hostile'. The Polish Government was to introduce visa requirements for Belarusian, Russian and Ukrainian citizens from 1 July 2003, in accordance with EU policy.

In November 1990 Poland and Germany signed a border treaty confirming their post-1945 borders, and in June 1991 the two countries signed a treaty of 'good neighbourliness and friendly co-operation'. Poland welcomed the announcement made by the German Government in February 1999 of the establishment of a compensation fund for over 2m. Poles who were employed as forced labour in German companies during the Second World War. Following a vociferous campaign by Polish veteran groups, in May Polish and German representatives began complex negotiations regarding the payment of compensation by several leading German firms. The payment was expected to begin in September; however, disagreements arose concerning the exact amount of compensation to be paid and the number of victims deemed to be eligible. Nevertheless, in mid-December a compensation agreement was signed, whereby DM 10,000m. would be paid by German companies into the compensation fund. However, payments were subject to delays.

Poland joined the Council of Europe (see p. 181) in November 1991. In December Poland signed an association agreement with the European Community (now EU), as part of its continuing efforts for closer integration with western European institutions. The agreement became fully effective from February 1994, and in April Poland made a formal application for membership of the EU. In January 1997 Poland's European Integration Committee adopted a National Integration Strategy outlining the economic, security and legal reforms deemed necessary to ensure full EU membership; formal accession negotiations began in March 1998. Despite numerous obstacles to negotiations in 2002, in December Poland, and nine other countries, were formally invited to join the EU in May 2004. In February 2003 the Government finally reached agreement with the EU on farm subsidies, and a national referendum on membership was scheduled to be held in June 2003.

Following the disintegration of the communist bloc, Poland, in common with the other Eastern European countries, regarded membership of NATO as a major priority in guaranteeing regional security. In January 1994 Poland announced that it was to join that organization's newly formulated 'Partnership for Peace' programme, and a defence co-operation agreement was duly signed by Poland and NATO in March. In May Poland was granted associate partnership status in Western European Union (see p. 318). Despite Russian opposition, in July 1997 Poland, together with the Czech Republic and Hungary, was officially invited to join NATO. Formal negotiations began in September; a protocol providing for the accession of the three states to NATO was signed in December, and was subsequently ratified by the legislatures of member states in February 1999. Poland, the Czech Republic and Hungary secured full membership of NATO on 12 March. Poland was among the most forthright supporters of the USA in the US-led military campaign to remove from power the regime of the Iraqi President, Saddam Hussein, in early 2003, despite the disapproval of some NATO and EU member countries, notably France.

Government

Under the Constitution, which came into force in October 1997, legislative power is vested in the bicameral National Assembly (Zgromadzenie Narodowe), which is elected for a four-year term and comprises the 100-member Senat (upper chamber) and the 460-member Sejm (lower chamber). The Senat reviews the laws adopted by the Sejm and may propose their rejection. Senators and deputies are elected by universal, direct suffrage. In the Sejm deputies are elected under a system of proportional representation. Executive power is vested in the President of the Republic, who is directly elected (a second ballot being held if necessary), for a five-year term, and may be re-elected only once, and in the appointed Council of Ministers, led by the Prime Minister. The Council of Ministers is responsible for its activities to the Sejm.

Prior to 1998, Poland was divided into 49 provinces (voivodships), each administered by an appointed governor. However, in July of that year, as part of a major programme of local government reform, the Government passed legislation to reduce the number of provinces to 16.

Defence

At 1 August 2002 the strength of Poland's active armed forces was estimated to be 163,000 (including 81,000 conscripts and 8,200 centrally controlled staff): army 104,050, air force 36,450 and navy 14,300. Paramilitary forces of some 21,400 comprised border guards (14,100) and police prevention units (7,300). In 1988 legislation was enacted permitting conscientious objectors to perform an alternative community service, and from January 1999 compulsory military service was reduced from 18 months to one year. In September 1997 the Government adopted a 15-year programme for the modernization of the armed forces; a further reform plan, providing for an eventual reduction in strength to 150,000, was approved in January 2001. State budget expenditure on defence in 2001 was projected at 14,800m. new złotys. In 1994 Poland joined NATO's 'Partnership for Peace' programme of military co-operation, and it became a full member of NATO in March 1999.

Economic Affairs

In 2001, according to the World Bank, Poland's gross national income (GNI), measured at average 1999–2001 prices, was US $163,907m., equivalent to $4,240 per head (or $9,280 per head on an international purchasing-power parity basis). During 1990–2001, it was estimated, the population increased at an average annual rate of 0.1%, while gross domestic product (GDP) per head grew, in real terms, at an average annual rate of 3.3%. Overall GDP increased, in real terms, at an average annual rate of 3.4% in 1990–2001; growth was 4.0% in 2000 and 1.2% in 2001.

Agriculture (including hunting, forestry and fishing) contributed 3.0% of GDP in 2001, and engaged 29.3% of the employed labour force. The principal crops are potatoes, sugar beet, wheat, rye and barley. Livestock production is important to the domestic food supply. During 1990–2001 the average annual GDP of the agricultural sector declined, in real terms, by 0.5%. Real agricultural GDP declined by 6.0% in 2000, before increasing by 1.5% in 2001.

Industry (including mining, manufacturing, power and construction) accounted for 31.6% of GDP in 2001, and engaged 25.2% of the employed labour force. During 1990–2001 industrial GDP increased, in real terms, by an average of 2.3% per year; real industrial GDP increased by 6.5% in 2000, and by 2.0% in 2001.

Mining and quarrying contributed 2.6% of GDP in 1999, and it engaged 1.5% of the employed labour force in 2001. Poland is a significant producer of copper, silver and sulphur, and there are also considerable reserves of natural gas. The mining sector experienced a marked decline in the 1990s; however, from 1998 the sector underwent significant restructuring. During 1992–96 mining GDP declined at an average annual rate of 1.5%; the sector's GDP declined by 4.3% in 1997, and by an estimated 4.6% in 1998.

The manufacturing sector contributed 16.6% of GDP in 2001, and it engaged 17.1% of the employed labour force in 2001. Measured by the value of sold production, the principal branches of manufacturing in 1998 were food products and beverages (accounting for 24.7% of the total), road motor vehicles, chemicals and chemical products, basic metals and non-electric machinery. During 1990–97 manufacturing output increased at an average annual rate of 7.6%. Manufacturing GDP increased by 8.8% in 1996, by 14.4% in 1997, and by an estimated 9.8% in 1998.

Energy is derived principally from coal, which satisfied 96.3% of the country's total energy requirements in 1999. In 1998 the Government announced plans to reduce Poland's dependence on coal: it was projected that by 2010 15% of power generation would be fuelled by imported natural gas. Mineral fuels and lubricants accounted for 10.1% of the value of merchandise imports in 2001; some 6.5% of electricity generated was exported in 2000.

In 2001 the services sector contributed 65.4% of GDP, and engaged 45.5% of the employed labour force. Services expanded rapidly from the early 1990s, with considerable growth in financial services, retailing, tourism and leisure. The GDP of the services sector increased, in real terms, by an average of 3.9% per year in 1990–2000. Real services GDP increased by 7.3% in 1999, and by 3.1% in 2000.

In 2001 Poland recorded a visible trade deficit of US $7,660m., and there was a deficit of $5,357m. on the current account of the balance of payments. The principal source of imports in 2000 was Germany (23.9%); other major suppliers were Russia, Italy and France. Germany was also the principal market for exports (34.9%) in that year; other significant purchasers included Italy, France and the Netherlands. The principal exports in 2001 were machinery and transport equipment, basic manufactures, miscellaneous manufactured articles, and food and live animals.

The principal imports in that year were machinery and transport equipment, basic manufactures, chemicals and related products, and mineral fuels and lubricants. According to government figures, imports increased by 8.2% in 2002, and exports increased by 11.4%.

Poland's overall budget deficit for 2000 was 15,391m. new złotys (equivalent to 2.2% of GDP). Poland's external debt totalled US $63,561m. at the end of 1999, of which $30,785m. was long-term public debt. In that year the cost of debt-servicing was equivalent to 20.9% of the value of exports of goods and services. In 1990–2000 the annual rate of inflation averaged 27.0%. The average rate of increase in consumer prices was 5.5% in 2001 and 1.9% in 2002. At the end of January 2003 18.7% of the labour force were registered as unemployed, the highest level since the communist era.

Poland is a member, as a 'Country of Operations', of the European Bank for Reconstruction and Development (EBRD, see p. 193), and of the Central European Free Trade Association. A free-trade agreement with the European Free Trade Association (see p. 195) came into force in November 1993. An association agreement with the EU became fully effective from February 1994; in December 2002 Poland was invited to become a full member from May 2004. Poland joined the World Trade Organization (WTO, see p. 323) in July 1995, and of the Organisation for Economic Co-operation and Development (OECD, see p. 277) in November 1996.

In the 1990s Poland undertook an ambitious, market-orientated programme of economic reform with assistance from the international financial community. Measures to maintain the value of the złoty at a realistic level achieved some success; a devalued 'new złoty' was introduced in January 1995, and was allowed to 'float' on international currency markets from May of that year. Poland's foreign debt—identified as a serious impediment to growth at the beginning of the 1990s—was significantly alleviated by concessions from the 'Paris Club' of official creditors, agreed in 1994. Following the agreement, foreign investment in Poland increased significantly; none the less, the high rate of unemployment continued to cause concern. Poland's economic performance worsened following the Russian financial crisis in August 1998, which reduced the level of demand in Poland and in other Eastern European markets and resulted in the re-orientation of export markets towards the West. In late 1999 the economy began to recover, and in April 2000 all foreign-exchange controls on the złoty were lifted. However, a decline in international petroleum prices in 2000 prompted a second economic reverse, and a sharp increase in unemployment. Following the election of a new, leftist Government in September 2001, the Government immediately reduced planned spending, in an attempt to control the expanding budgetary deficit; tax increases were approved in November. In late January 2002 the Government approved a four-year economic plan to combat unemployment, revive economic growth and increase spending on infrastructure, in particular housing and roads. However, there was concern that the Government was reluctant to implement scheduled privatizations, and the IMF warned that there was an urgent need to restructure loss-making state enterprises in the coal, steel and rail sectors. In 2002 slow economic recovery was evident. Political instability was regarded as being the greatest threat to the Polish economy in 2003; the need to curb public spending and implement labour-market reforms were also pressing concerns. The budget for 2003, passed in November 2002, envisaged GDP growth of 3.5% and inflation of 2.2%; the projected budgetary deficit for 2003 was equivalent to 4.8% of GDP.

Education

Education is free and compulsory for eight years between the ages of seven and 14 years. Before the age of seven, children may attend crèches (złobki) and kindergartens (przedszkola). In 1998/99 49.6% of children between the ages of three and six years attended kindergarten, and in 2000/01 95.4% of six-year olds attended pre-school educational establishments. A reform of primary and secondary education was undertaken from 1999, and was to be fully implemented by the 2004/05 academic year. Basic schooling begins at seven years of age with primary school (szkoła podstawowa), for which there is a common curriculum throughout the country. Primary education lasts for six years, divided into two equal cycles. Lower secondary education (at the gimnazjum) is compulsory for three years. In 2000/01 enrolment at primary and lower secondary schools was equivalent to 100% of children in the relevant age-group. Three years of education at general secondary schools (liceum ogólnokształcące) commence at the age of 16 years, for pupils who successfully complete the entrance examination; in 2000/01 enrolment at secondary schools was equivalent to 90.1% of children in the appropriate age-group. At this level, there are general secondary schools (accounting for 34%), vocational technical schools (technika zawodowe—56%) and basic vocational schools (zasadnicze szkoły—20%). The last provide courses providing three days' theoretical and three days' practical training per week, and in addition some general education is given. New post-secondary schools (szkoła policealna) were introduced in the 1999 reforms to prepare students from technical and vocational schools for skilled jobs. Curricula are standardized throughout Poland. In 1993/94 there were 985 private schools, administered under state supervision. In 1989 the Roman Catholic Church was granted the right to operate its own schools. In 2000/01 there were 310 higher education establishments in Poland and there were 15 universities in 1999/2000. State budgetary expenditure on basic education and the care of children in 2000 was 1,959.9m. new złotys (1.3% of total expenditure), while 5,326.7m. złotys (3.5%) were allocated to higher education. Of total budgetary expenditure by local governments in 1998, 17,195.0m. złotys (36.2%) was for education.

Public Holidays

2003: 1 January (New Year's Day), 21 April (Easter Monday), 1 May (Labour Day), 3 May (Polish National Day, Proclamation of 1791 Constitution), 19 June (Corpus Christi), 15 August (Assumption), 1 November (All Saints' Day), 11 November (Independence Day), 25–26 December (Christmas).

2004: 1 January (New Year's Day), 12 April (Easter Monday), 1 May (Labour Day), 3 May (Polish National Day, Proclamation of 1791 Constitution), 10 June (Corpus Christi), 15 August (Assumption), 1 November (All Saints' Day), 11 November (Independence Day), 25–26 December (Christmas).

Weights and Measures

The metric system is in force.

Statistical Survey

Source (unless otherwise indicated): Główny Urząd Statystyczny (Central Statistical Office), 00-925 Warsaw, Al. Niepodległości 208; tel. (22) 6252215; fax (22) 6251525; internet www.stat.gov.pl.

Area and Population

AREA, POPULATION AND DENSITY

Area (sq km)	
Land	304,465
Inland water	8,220
Total	312,685*
Population (census results)†	
7 December 1988.	37,878,641
17 May 1995 (provisional)	
Males	18,771,000
Females.	19,849,000
Total	38,620,000
Population (official rounded estimates at 31 December)†	
2000	38,644,200
2001	38,632,500
2002	38,610,000‡
Density (per sq km) at 31 December 2002	123.5

* 120,728 sq miles.

† Figures exclude civilian aliens within the country and include civilian nationals temporarily outside the country.

‡ Rounded figure.

VOIVODSHIPS
(estimated population at 31 December 2001)

	Area (sq km)	Total ('000)	Density (per sq km)
Dolnośląskie	19,948	2,970.1	148.9
Kujawsko-Pomorskie . . .	17,970	2,101.7	117.0
Lubelskie	25,114	2,227.6	88.7
Lubuskie	13,984	1,024.5	73.3
Łódzkie	18,219	2,632.9	144.5
Malopolskie	15,144	3,240.9	214.0
Mazowieckie	35,597	5,079.0	142.7
Opolskie	9,412	1,080.5	114.8
Podkarpackie	17,926	2,131.4	118.9
Podlaskie	20,180	1,219.9	60.5
Pomorskie	18,293	2,204.4	120.5
Śląskie	12,294	4,830.4	392.9
Świętokrzyskie	11,672	1,319.6	113.1
Warmińsko-Mazurskie . . .	24,203	1,469.3	60.7
Wielkopolskie	29,826	3,366.0	112.9
Zachodniopomorskie . . .	22,902	1,734.3	75.7
Total	312,685	38,632.5	123.6

PRINCIPAL TOWNS
(estimated population at 31 December 1998)

Warszawa (Warsaw)	1,618,468	Olsztyn	170,904
Łódź	806,728	Rzeszów	162,049
Kraków (Cracow) .	740,666	Ruda Śląska . . .	159,665
Wrocław . . .	637,877	Rybnik	144,582
Poznań	578,235	Wałbrzych . . .	136,923
Gdańsk	458,988	Tychy	133,178
Szczecin . . .	416,988	Dąbrowa Górnicza .	131,037
Bydgoszcz. . . .	386,855	Płock	131,011
Lublin	356,251	Elbląg	129,782
Katowice . . .	345,934	Opole	129,553
Białystok . . .	283,937	Gorzów Wielkopolski	126,019
Częstochowa . . .	257,812	Włocławek . . .	123,373
Gdynia	253,521	Chorzów	121,708
Sosnowiec. . . .	244,102	Tarnów	121,494
Radom.	232,262	Zielona Góra . .	118,182
Kielce	212,383	Koszalin . . .	112,375
Gliwice	212,164	Legnica	109,335
Toruń	206,158	Kalisz	106,641
Bytom	205,560	Grudziądz. . . .	102,434
Zabrze.	200,177	Słupsk	102,370
Bielsko-Biała . .	180,307	Jastrzębie-Zdrój .	102,294

BIRTHS, MARRIAGES AND DEATHS

	Registered live births		Registered marriages		Registered deaths	
	Number	Rate (per 1,000)	Number	Rate (per 1,000)	Number	Rate (per 1,000)
1994 . .	481,285	12.5	207,689	5.4	386,398	10.0
1995 . .	433,109	11.2	207,081	5.4	386,084	10.0
1996 . .	428,203	11.1	203,641	5.3	385,496	10.0
1997 . .	412,635	10.7	204,850	5.3	380,201	9.8
1998 . .	395,619	10.2	209,430	5.4	375,354	9.7
1999 . .	382,002	9.9	219,398	5.7	381,415	9.9
2000 . .	378,348	9.8	211,150	5.5	368,000*	9.5
2001 . .	368,205	9.5	195,122	5.0	363,200*	9.4

* Number rounded to the nearest 100.

Expectation of life (WHO estimates, years at birth): 74.0 (males 69.9; females 78.1) in 2001 (Source: WHO, *World Health Report*).

IMMIGRATION AND EMIGRATION*

	1999	2000	2001
Immigrants	7,525	7,331	6,625
Emigrants.	21,536	26,999	23,368

* Figures refer to immigrants arriving for permanent residence in Poland and emigrants leaving for permanent residence abroad.

ECONOMICALLY ACTIVE POPULATION*
('000 persons aged 15 years and over)

	1999†	2000‡	2001‡
Agriculture, hunting and forestry	4,322.4	4,304.6	4,289.7
Fishing	11.6	10.3	7.1
Mining and quarrying. . . .	256.7	223.2	216.5
Manufacturing	2,923.0	2,674.7	2,501.5
Electricity, gas and water supply	246.9	236.5	245.6
Construction	915.0	814.6	737.1
Wholesale and retail trade; repair of motor vehicles, motorcycles and personal and household goods	2,093.9	2,074.6	1,969.2
Hotels and restaurants . .	216.3	225.7	217.2
Transport, storage and communications	838.2	779.3	714.4
Financial intermediation . . .	388.7	298.6	286.5
Real estate, renting and business activities	775.8	822.6	842.2
Public administration and defence; compulsory social security	439.5	492.6	525.7
Education	908.3	902.8	907.9
Health and social work . . .	967.0	908.2	869.0
Other community, social and personal service activities . .	388.4	390.9	341.0
Total employed	15,691.7	15,159.2	14,670.6
Unemployed	2,177.8	2,702.6	3,115.1
Total labour force	17,869.5	17,861.8	17,785.7
Males	9,165.1	n.a.	n.a.
Females	8,704.4	n.a.	n.a.

* Excluding persons employed in budgetary entities conducting activity within the scope of national defence and public safety ('000 at 30 September): 317.2 (males 257.6, females 59.6) in 1999; ('000 at 31 December) n.a. in 2000; n.a. in 2001.

† At 30 September.

‡ At 31 December.

Health and Welfare

KEY INDICATORS

Total fertility rate (children per woman, 2001)	1.3
Under-5 mortality rate (per 1,000 live births, 2000) . . .	10
HIV/AIDS (% of persons aged 15–49, 1999)	0.10
Physicians (per 1,000 head, 1997)	2.36
Hospital beds (per 1,000 head, 1998)	5.3
Health expenditure (2000): US $ per head (PPP) . . .	578
Health expenditure (2000): % of GDP	6.0
Health expenditure (2000): public (% of total) . . .	69.7
Human Development Index (2000): ranking	37
Human Development Index (2000): value	0.833

For sources and definitions, see explanatory note on p. vi.

Agriculture

PRINCIPAL CROPS
('000 metric tons)

	1999	2000	2001
Wheat	9,051.3	8,502.9	9,283.0
Barley	3,401.1	2,783.4	3,330.5
Maize	599.4	923.3	1,361.9
Rye	5,180.7	4,003.0	4,863.6
Oats	1,446.3	1,070.2	1,305.2
Buckwheat and millet	60.3	73.4	58.7
Triticale (wheat-rye hybrid) . . .	2,096.9	1,901.0	2,697.9
Mixed grain	3,914.3	3,083.4	4,059.5
Potatoes	19,926.7	24,232.4	19,378.9
Sugar beet	12,563.6	13,134.4	11,363.9
Dry beans	44.3	47.2	40.9
Dry peas	55.1	45.6	39.8
Other pulses	217.5*	221.3†	233.9
Rapeseed	1,131.9	958.1	1,063.6
Cabbages	1,709.2	1,899.0	1,709.6
Tomatoes	333.1	311.5	273.7
Cauliflowers	225.4	248.2	250.4
Cucumbers and gherkins . . .	385.0	356.0	350.0†
Dry onions	688.3	720.3	625.9
Carrots	906.5	946.7	921.9
Mushrooms†	100	100	100
Other vegetables*	1,277.5	1,309.6	1,206.5
Apples	1,604.2	1,450.4	2,433.9
Pears	66.5	81.6	77.4
Cherries (incl. sour)	179.6	178.1	224.4
Plums	90.7	106.9	131.9
Strawberries	178.2	171.3	242.1
Raspberries	43.2	39.7	44.8
Currants	153.4	146.8	175.3
Other fruit*	69.0	69.1	70.2
Tobacco (leaves)	43.7	29.5	23.9

* Unofficial figure(s).
† FAO estimate(s).

Source: FAO.

LIVESTOCK
('000 head year ending September)

	1999	2000	2001
Horses	551	550	550*
Cattle	6,455	6,093	5,734
Pigs	18,538	17,122	17,106
Sheep	392	362	343
Chickens	50,017	49,526	48,274
Geese	608	764	614
Turkeys	672	713	802
Ducks	2,953	3,551	3,571

* FAO estimate.

Source: FAO.

LIVESTOCK PRODUCTS
('000 metric tons)

	1999	2000	2001
Beef and veal	384.6	348.5	316.3
Pig meat	2,043.0	1,923.0	1,849.1
Horse meat	9.1	9.1*	9.1*
Game meat*	12.1	11.0	11.0
Chicken meat	573.1	585.2	691.5
Duck meat*	11.0	13.0	15.0
Turkey meat*	18.0	19.0	20.0
Goose meat*	7.4	9.2	7.5
Cows' milk	12,284.4	11,889.3	11,884.0
Cheese	481.1	475.3	460.1
Butter	166.0	161.6	178.9
Hen eggs	414.9	423.7	449.3
Honey	8.9	8.6	9.5
Cattle hides (fresh)* . . .	43	39	34

* FAO estimate(s).

Source: FAO.

Forestry

ROUNDWOOD REMOVALS
('000 cubic metres, excl. bark)

	1999	2000	2001
Sawlogs, veneer logs and logs for sleepers	10,946	11,609	10,641
Pulpwood	9,901	10,988	11,171
Other industrial wood . . .	1,995	1,892	1,765
Fuel wood	1,426	1,536	1,691
Total	24,268	26,025	25,268

Source: FAO.

SAWNWOOD PRODUCTION
('000 cubic metres, incl. railway sleepers)

	1999	2000	2001
Coniferous (softwood)	3,349	3,532	2,850
Broadleaved (hardwood) . . .	788	730	700
Total	4,137	4,262	3,550

Source: FAO.

Fishing

('000 metric tons, live weight)

	1998	1999	2000
Capture	247.0	235.1	218.4
Atlantic cod	27.7	28.1	23.3
Alaska pollock	81.9	65.5	33.2
Atlantic herring . . .	21.9	19.2	24.5
European sprat . . .	59.1	71.7	84.3
Antarctic krill . . .	15.6	18.6	20.7
Aquaculture	29.8	33.7	35.8
Common carp . . .	19.4	21.4	22.6
Rainbow trout . . .	9.0	11.1	11.4
Total catch	276.8	268.8	254.1

Source: FAO, *Yearbook of Fishery Statistics*.

Mining

('000 metric tons, unless otherwise indicated)

	1998	1999	2000
Hard coal	115,726	111,894	103,331
Brown coal (incl. lignite)	62,820	60,839	59,484
Crude petroleum	360	425	653
Salt (unrefined)	3,284	3,411	4,307
Native sulphur (per 100%)	1,348	1,175	1,369
Copper ore (metric tons)*	436,200	523,120	525,000†
Lead ore (metric tons)*	73,814	81,849	65,000†
Magnesite ore—crude	38,300	54,800	50,000†
Silver (metric tons)*	1,108	1,100	1,144
Zinc ore (metric tons)*	157,874	160,082	155,000†
Natural gas (million cu metres)	4,852	4,757	4,956

* Figures refer to the metal content of ores.
† Estimate.

Source: US Geological Survey.

Industry

SELECTED PRODUCTS
(metric tons, unless otherwise indicated)

	1998	1999	2000
Sausages and smoked meat	888,000	873,000	n.a.
Refined sugar ('000 metric tons)	2,102	1,821	2,014
Margarine	363,000	367,000	n.a.
Wine and mead ('000 hectolitres)	4,500	4,490	n.a.
Beer ('000 hectolitres)	21,000	23,400	24,900
Cigarettes (million)	96,700	95,100	83,500
Cotton yarn[1]	82,200	67,300	n.a.
Woven cotton fabrics ('000 metres)[2]	207,000	179,000	n.a.
Wool yarn[1]	27,100	18,200	n.a.
Woven woollen fabrics ('000 metres)[2]	29,500	22,400	n.a.
Cellulosic staple and tow	3,700	2,400	n.a.
Leather footwear ('000 pairs)	24,400	22,600	16,800
Mechanical wood pulp	113,000	126,000	130,000
Chemical wood pulp	722,000	698,000	746,000
Newsprint ('000 metric tons)	92.2	149.0	211.0
Other paper ('000 metric tons)	1,434	1,484	n.a.
Paperboard	192,000	206,000	n.a.
Synthetic rubber	95,000	97,500	n.a.
Rubber tyres ('000)[3]	14,410	14,660	23,329
Sulphuric acid—100% ('000 metric tons)	1,707	1,482	n.a.
Nitric acid—100% ('000 metric tons)	1,671	1,635	n.a.
Caustic soda—96% ('000 metric tons)	807	737	394
Soda ash—98% ('000 metric tons)	983	910	1,018
Nitrogenous fertilizers (a) ('000 metric tons)[4]	1,406	1,272	1,610
Phosphate fertilizers (b) ('000 metric tons)[4]	593	535	530
Plastics and synthetic resins ('000 metric tons)	940	1,114	1,340
Motor spirit—Petrol ('000 metric tons)[5]	n.a.	n.a.	4,435
Distillate fuel oils ('000 metric tons)	6,031	6,041	n.a.
Residual fuel oils ('000 metric tons)	4,129	4,758	n.a.
Coke-oven coke ('000 metric tons)	9,944	8,575	9,000*
Cement ('000 metric tons)	14,970	15,600	14,800
Pig-iron ('000 metric tons)[6]	6,129	5,233	6,492
Crude steel ('000 metric tons)	9,915	8,853	10,504
Rolled steel products ('000 metric tons)	7,987	6,991	7,530
Aluminium—unwrought[7]	54,168	50,974	46,941
Refined copper—unwrought	446,837	470,494	486,002
Refined lead—unwrought	64,300	63,895	45,412
Zinc—unwrought[7]	178,016	177,804	161,000
Radio receivers ('000)	154	138	109
Television receivers ('000)	4,436	5,121	6,287

— continued	1998	1999	2000
Merchant ships launched (gross reg. tons)	598,000	n.a.	n.a.
Passenger motor cars (number)	592,355	647,232	532,427
Lorries and tractors (number)	56,100	62,714	58,112
Domestic washing machines (number)	416,000	448,000	457,000
Domestic refrigerators (number)	714,000	726,000	693,000
Construction: dwellings completed (number)	80,594	81,979	n.a.
Electric energy (million kWh)	142,789	142,128	145,148
Manufactured gas from cokeries (million cu metres)	4,145	3,876	n.a.

* Estimate.
[1] Pure and mixed yarns. Cotton includes tyre cord yarn.
[2] Pure and mixed fabrics, after undergoing finishing processes. Cotton and wool include substitutes.
[3] Tyres for passenger motor cars and commercial vehicles, including inner tubes and tyres for animal-drawn road vehicles, and tyres for non-agricultural machines and equipment.
[4] Fertilizer production is measured in terms of (a) nitrogen or (b) phosphoric acid. Phosphate fertilizers include ground rock phosphate.
[5] Including synthetic products.
[6] Including blast-furnace ferro-alloys.
[7] Figures refer to both primary and secondary metal. Zinc production includes zinc dust and remelted zinc.

Sources: partly UN, *Industrial Commodity Statistics Yearbook* and *Monthly Bulletin of Statistics*; IRF, *World Road Statistics*.

Finance

CURRENCY AND EXCHANGE RATES

Monetary Units
100 groszy (singular: grosz) = 1 new złoty

Sterling, Dollar and Euro Equivalents (31 December 2002)
£1 sterling = 6.187 new złotys
US $1 = 3.839 new złotys
€1 = 4.026 new złotys
100 new złotys = £16.16 = $26.05 = €24.84

Average Exchange Rate (new złotys per US dollar)
2000 4.3461
2001 4.0939
2002 4.0800

Note: On 1 January 1995 Poland introduced a new złoty, equivalent to 10,000 of the former units.

STATE BUDGET
(million new złotys)

Revenue	1998	1999	2000
Domestic revenue	126,552.3	125,856.8	135,530.1
Taxation	113,949.5	112,776.9	119,643.9
Value-added tax	42,868.6	48,803.6	51,749.8
Excises	21,068.5	25,208.1	27,312.0
Taxes on earnings	49,473.0	38,175.6	39,956.3
Other current revenue	12,602.8	13,079.9	15,886.2
Customs duties	6,076.5	5,566.0	5,080.3
External revenue	7.6	65.4	133.8
Total	126,559.9	125,922.2	135,663.9

Expenditure	1998	1999	2000
Education	6,987.5	2,920.2	1,959.9
Higher education.	4,272.3	5,070.5	5,326.7
Health care	20,919.5	6,312.6	4,300.0
Social welfare.	9,287.6	10,142.8	11,978.1
State administration. . . .	5,851.5	5,972.5	6,655.9
Public safety	5,575.7	6,473.2	7,040.1
Finance	21,316.5	20,975.2	20,578.3
Social security	25,218.7	29,436.4	36,698.6
National defence	8,358.7	9,448.4	9,943.7
Subsidies	2,129.2	2,573.0	n.a.
Total (incl. others) . . .	139,751.5	138,401.2	151,054.9
Current	130,315.4	131,012.5	143,627.2
Capital.	9,436.1	7,388.7	7,427.7

2001 ('000 million new złotys): *Revenue:* Tax revenue 123.2 (Taxes on earnings 36.6; Value-added tax 52.9; Excises 28.9); Non-tax revenue 16.2; Total revenue (incl. others) 140.5. *Expenditure:* Current 166.3; Capital 6.6; Total expenditure 172.9 (Source: IMF, *Republic of Poland: Selected Issues and Statistical Appendix*, June 2002).

INTERNATIONAL RESERVES
(US $ million at 31 December)

	2000	2001	2002
Gold*	901.5	914.7	1,134.0
IMF special drawing rights . .	17.7	25.8	39.5
Reserve positition in IMF . .	224.4	461.0	651.0
Foreign exchange.	26,319.9	25,161.6	27,959.2
Total	27,463.5	26,563.1	29,783.7

* National valuation (US $400 per troy ounce).

Source: IMF, *International Financial Statistics*.

MONEY SUPPLY
(million new złotys at 31 December)

	2000	2001	2002
Currency outside banks . . .	34,112.7	38,212.6	42,192.7
Demand deposits at commercial banks	48,419.6	51,940.9	70,683.1
Total money (incl. others) . .	82,574.2	94,157.8	112,889.0

Source: IMF, *International Financial Statistics*.

COST OF LIVING
(Consumer Price Index; base: 1998 = 100)

	1999	2000	2001
Food (incl. beverages) . . .	102.0	111.6	116.8
Fuel and light	106.1	115.4	n.a.
Clothing (incl. footwear). . .	107.7	113.6	n.a.
Rent	120.2	114.4	n.a.
All items (incl. others) . . .	107.3	118.1	124.6

Source: ILO, *Yearbook of Labour Statistics*; UN, *Monthly Bulletin of Statistics*.

NATIONAL ACCOUNTS
(million new złotys at current prices)

Composition of the Gross National Product

	1998	1999	2000
Compensation of employees . .	250,314.0	276,363.0	297,820.6
Operating surplus . . . . . }	227,649.6	250,783.0	293,518.2
Consumption of fixed capital . . }			
Gross domestic product (GDP) at factor cost . .	477,963.6	527,146.0	591,338.8
Indirect taxes	82,681.1	94,680.5	100,153.3
Less Subsidies	6,763.1	6,711.2	6,566.0
GDP in purchasers' values .	553,881.6	615,115.3	684,926.1
Factor income received from abroad. . . . . . . }	−4,115.6	−4,007.2	−6,350.1
Less Factor income paid abroad }			
Gross national product . .	549,766.0	611,108.1	678,576.0

Expenditure on the Gross Domestic Product

	1998	1999	2000
Government final consumption expenditure.	85,497.3	95,586	106,314
Private final consumption expenditure.	352,062.7	396,361	447,397
Increase in stocks	5,800.6	5,595	8,132
Gross fixed capital formation . .	139,204.5	156,690	170,430
Total domestic expenditure. .	582,565.1	654,232	732,272
Exports of goods and services .	155,873.8	160,787	201,001
Less Imports of goods and services	184,878.8	199,904	248,347
GDP in purchasers' values . .	553,560.1	615,115	684,926

Gross Domestic Product by Economic Activity

	1999	2000	2001
Agriculture, hunting and forestry .	21,083.5	22,083.3	24,533.2
Fishing	229.0	201.4	198.7
Mining and quarrying . . .	14,117.8	16,067.9	15,283.4
Manufacturing	112,938.6	124,416.7	118,590.1
Electricity, gas and water . . .	18,155.0	19,607.1	24,213.6
Construction	47,142.7	51,292.1	44,194.5
Trade and repairs	110,605.5	126,799.7	134,351.1
Hotels and restaurants . . .	6,724.9	7,990.4	8,293.9
Transport, storage and communications	36,259.1	42,981.8	48,191.9
Financial intermediation . . .	11,580.0	14,302.9	13,830.5
Real estate, renting and business activities* . .	63,282.8	77,509.7	86,856.7
Public administration and defence .	26,892.3	39,663.0	45,155.9
Education	23,770.7	28,724.0	33,679.8
Health care and social work . .	21,210.8	25,591.0	26,575.3
Other community, social and personal services	21,831.8	25,604.2	28,140.6
Private households with employed persons	4.5	5.1	5.5
GDP at basic prices	535,829.0	622,840.3	656,094.7
Taxes, *less* subsidies, on products .	87,969.3	100,506.1	105,261.5
GDP in purchasers' values . .	623,798.3	723,346.4	761,356.2

* Including imputed rents of owner-occupied dwellings.

BALANCE OF PAYMENTS
(US $ million)

	1999	2000	2001
Exports of goods f.o.b.	30,060	35,902	41,664
Imports of goods f.o.b.	−45,132	−48,210	−49,324
Trade balance	−15,072	−12,308	−7,660
Exports of services	8,363	10,387	9,755
Imports of services	−6,982	−8,994	−8,951
Balance on goods and services.	−13,691	−10,915	−6,856
Other income received	1,837	2,250	2,625
Other income paid	−2,847	−3,713	−4,015
Balance on goods, services and income	−14,701	−12,378	−8,246
Current transfers received . . .	2,898	3,008	3,737
Current transfers paid	−684	−628	−848
Current balance	−12,487	−9,998	−5,357
Capital account (net)	55	32	75
Direct investment abroad . . .	−31	−17	89
Direct investment from abroad. .	7,270	9,341	5,713
Portfolio investment assets . .	−548	−89	46
Portfolio investment liabilities . .	691	3,422	1,067
Financial derivatives assets . .	579	269	n.a.
Financial derivatives liabilities . .	−10	—	−336
Other investment assets . . .	−3,339	−3,870	−4,071
Other investment liabilities . .	5,850	1,148	664
Net errors and omissions . . .	2,126	387	1,682
Overall balance	156	625	−428

Source: IMF, *International Financial Statistics*.

External Trade

PRINCIPAL COMMODITIES
(US $ million)

Imports c.i.f.	1999	2000	2001
Food and live animals	2,537	2,558	2,724
Crude materials (inedible) except			
fuels	1,419	1,643	1,578
Mineral fuels, lubricants, etc. . .	3,281	5,297	5,081
Chemicals and related products .	6,584	6,881	7,337
Basic manufactures	9,526	9,789	10,333
Machinery and transport			
equipment	17,544	18,114	18,324
Miscellaneous manufactured			
articles	4,380	4,218	4,416
Total (incl. others)	45,911	48,940	50,275

Exports f.o.b.	1999	2000	2001
Food and live animals	2,328	2,366	2,669
Crude materials (inedible) except			
fuels	839	894	915
Mineral fuels, lubricants, etc. . .	1,377	1,610	2,043
Chemicals and related products .	1,695	2,151	2,278
Basic manufactures	6,986	7,856	8,614
Machinery and transport			
equipment	8,278	10,820	13,055
Miscellaneous manufactured			
articles	5,750	5,804	6,355
Total (incl. others)	27,407	31,651	36,092

Source: IMF, *Republic of Poland: Selected Issues and Statistical Appendix* (June 2002).

PRINCIPAL TRADING PARTNERS
(million new złotys)*

Imports c.i.f.	1998	1999	2000
Austria	3,154.5	3,512.0	4,141.8
Belgium	4,625.6	5,149.4	5,543.4
China, People's Republic . . .	4,092.7	4,850.1	6,015.8
Czech Republic	5,110.5	5,854.9	6,810.6
Denmark	3,207.9	3,274.6	3,414.4
Finland	2,766.0	3,334.1	3,854.9
France	10,599.0	12,444.0	13,701.9
Germany	42,036.7	45,968.5	50,938.6
Hungary	2,072.8	2,486.5	3,353.5
Italy	15,371.1	17,061.4	17,726.9
Japan	3,161.1	3,682.0	4,587.1
Korea, Republic	4,488.3	4,705.4	3,225.9
Netherlands	6,257.2	6,825.3	7,570.6
Russia	8,278.7	10,680.1	20,116.2
Slovakia	2,060.4	2,253.2	3,144.5
Spain	4,191.1	4,508.3	5,191.6
Sweden	4,748.3	5,757.2	6,121.4
Switzerland	2,255.8	2,698.2	2,830.7
Taiwan	1,719.8	1,918.3	2,001.6
United Kingdom	8,057.2	8,362.7	9,476.1
USA	6,167.0	6,523.6	9,423.4
Total (incl. others)	162,963.0	182,400.0	213,071.8

Exports f.o.b.	1998	1999	2000
Austria	1,929.4	2,200.0	2,783.9
Belgium	2,422.1	3,016.6	4,067.4
Czech Republic	3,574.5	4,130.2	5,228.1
Denmark	2,712.6	3,332.5	3,724.5
France	4,637.9	5,269.9	7,156.4
Germany	35,767.8	39,240.9	48,078.1
Hungary	1,641.8	2,141.1	2,837.9
Italy	5,790.7	7,110.5	8,702.4
Netherlands	4,732.7	5,725.1	6,960.5
Norway	810.4	1,354.6	1,472.3
Russia	5,566.3	2,829.6	3,770.5
Slovakia	1,179.0	1,418.1	1,913.4
Spain	1,365.1	1,649.8	2,201.8
Sweden	2,359.9	2,690.9	3,753.6
Ukraine	3,790.0	2,800.1	3,488.0
United Kingdom	3,845.0	4,366.5	6,178.8
USA	2,643.1	2,996.3	4,342.2
Total (incl. others)	98,647.9	108,757.9	137,908.7

* Imports by country of purchase; exports by country of sale.

Transport

POLISH STATE RAILWAYS
(traffic)

	1998	1999	2000
Paying passengers ('000 journeys)	401,509	395,850	360,687
Freight ('000 metric tons) . .	206,391	186,846	187,247
Passenger-kilometres (million) . .	25,664	26,198	24,092
Freight ton-kilometres (million) .	61,760	55,471	54,448

ROAD TRAFFIC
(motor vehicles registered at 31 December)

	1998	1999	2000
Passenger cars	8,890,763	9,282,816	9,991,260
Lorries and vans	1,578,818	1,682,887	1,783,008
Buses and coaches	80,827	78,717	82,356
Motorcycles and scooters . .	1,563,513	1,441,691	802,618
Road tractors	79,212	85,013	97,348

Source: IRF, *World Road Statistics*.

INLAND WATERWAYS
(traffic)

	1998	1999	2000
Passengers carried ('000) . .	955	1,121	1,265
Freight ('000 metric tons) . . .	9,376	8,382	10,433
Passenger-kilometres (million) . .	18	18	26
Freight ton-kilometres (million) .	1,100	1,028	1,173

SHIPPING

Merchant Fleet
(registered at 31 December)

	1999	2000	2001
Number of vessels	439	429	393
Displacement ('000 gross registered			
tons)	1,319.1	1,119.2	618.3

Source: Lloyd's Register-Fairplay, *World Fleet Statistics*.

Sea Transport
(Polish merchant ships only)

	1998	1999	2000
Passengers carried ('000) . .	609	622	625
Freight ('000 metric tons) . . .	25,362	22,747	22,774
Passenger-kilometres (million) . .	172	131	129
Freight ton-kilometres (million) .	166,095	164,236	133,654

International Sea-borne Shipping at Polish Ports

	1998	1999	2000
Vessels entered ('000 net reg. tons)	41,164	40,565	n.a.
Passengers ('000): arrivals . . .	1,175	1,572	2,260
Passengers ('000): departures . .	1,134	1,545	2,205
Cargo ('000 metric tons): loaded* .	32,314	33,361	31,524
Cargo ('000 metric tons): unloaded*	18,294	15,866	15,810

* Including ships' bunkers and transhipments.

Source: Ministry of Transport and Maritime Economy.

CIVIL AVIATION

Polish Airlines—'LOT'
(scheduled and non-scheduled flights)

	1998*	1999	2000
Passengers carried ('000) . . .	2,589	2,621	2,880
Passenger-kilometres (million) . .	5,382	5,629	6,034
Cargo (metric tons)	28,053	29,000	29,000
Cargo ton-kilometres ('000) . . .	104,089	94,000	88,000

* Including EuroLOT SA.

Source: partly Ministry of Transport and Maritime Economy.

Tourism

FOREIGN TOURIST ARRIVALS
('000, including visitors in transit)

Country of residence	1999	2000	2001
Belarus	4,640	5,920	5,197
Czech Republic	13,491	11,985	9,276
Germany	53,788	48,903	31,010
Lithuania	1,450	1,414	1,393
Russia	2,114	2,275	1,969
Slovakia	4,234	3,914	2,642
Ukraine	5,303	6,184	6,418
Total (incl. others)	89,118	84,515	61,431

Receipts from tourism (US $ million): 6,104.4 in 1999.

Source: Institute of Tourism.

Communications Media

	1998	1999	2000
Radio licences ('000)*	9,577	9,461	n.a.
Television receivers ('000 in use)‡	14,500	15,000	15,500
Telephones ('000 main lines in use)*	8,808	10,076	10,740
Mobile cellular telephones ('000 subscribers).	1,944	3,956	6,748
Personal computers ('000 in use)‡	1,900	2,400	2,670
Internet users ('000)‡	1,581	2,100	2,800
Book production: titles†	16,462	19,192	21,647
Book production: copies ('000)† . .	84,999	78,078	102,800
Daily newspapers: number . . .	52	46	42
Daily newspapers: average circulation ('000 copies) . . .	4,167	3,870	3,928
Non-daily newspapers: number .	29	28	n.a.§
Non-daily newspapers: average circulation ('000 copies) . . .	871	722	n.a.§
Other periodicals: number . . .	5,297	5,518	5,314
Other periodicals: average circulation ('000 copies) . . .	72,336	65,997	68,368

* At 31 December.
† Including pamphlets (1,753 titles and 7,461,000 copies in 1998; 1,644 titles and 5,554,000 copies in 1999).
‡ Source: International Telecommunication Union.
§ In 2000 there were 71 daily and non-daily newspapers, with a combined average circulation of 4,566,000 copies.

Facsimile machines (estimate, 1995): 55,000 in use (Source: UN, *Statistical Yearbook*).

2001: Telephones ('000 main lines in use) 11,400; Mobile cellular telephones ('000 subscribers) 10,050; Personal computers ('000 in use) 3,300; Internet users ('000) 3,800 (Source: International Telecommunication Union).

Education

(2000/01)

	Institutions	Teachers ('000)	Students ('000)
Pre-primary*	20,429	74.8	956.8
Primary	16,766	226.4	3,220.6
Lower secondary	6,295	70.1	1,189.9
Secondary	10,573	135.3	2,452.1
General	2,292	45.6	924.2
Technical and vocational	8,281	89.7	1,527.9
Post-secondary	2,567	n.a.	200.1
Tertiary	310	79.9	1,584.8

* 1998/99 figures.

Adult literacy rate (UNESCO estimates): 99.7% (males 99.7%; females 99.7%) in 2000 (Source: UN Development Programme, *Human Development Report*).

Directory

The Constitution

The Constitution of the Republic of Poland was adopted by the National Assembly on 2 April 1997 and endorsed by popular referendum on 25 May of that year. The following is a summary of the main provisions of the Constitution, which came into force on 17 October 1997:

THE REPUBLIC

The Republic of Poland shall be a unitary, democratic state, ruled by law, and implementing the principles of social justice. The Republic of Poland shall safeguard the independence and integrity of its territory, ensure the freedom and rights of persons and citizens, and safeguard the national heritage. The Constitution shall be the supreme law of the Republic of Poland, which shall respect international law binding upon it. Legislative power shall be vested in the Sejm and the Senat, executive power shall be vested in the President and the Council of Ministers, and judicial power shall be vested in courts and tribunals.

The Republic of Poland shall ensure freedom for the creation and functioning of political parties, trade unions and other voluntary associations. The financing of political parties shall be open to public inspection. Political parties and other organizations whose programmes are based upon totalitarian methods and the modes of activity of nazism, fascism and communism, as well as those whose programmes or activities sanction racial or national hatred, or the application of violence for the purpose of obtaining power or to influence the State's policy, or provide for the secrecy of their own structure or membership, shall be forbidden. The Republic of Poland shall ensure freedom of the press and other means of social communication.

A social market economy, based on the freedom of economic activity, private ownership, and solidarity, dialogue and co-operation between social partners, shall be the basis of the economic system of Poland.

Churches and other religious organizations shall have equal rights. Public authorities shall be impartial in matters of personal conviction, whether religious or philosophical, or in relation to outlooks on life, and shall ensure their freedom of expression within public life. The Armed Forces shall observe neutrality regarding political matters and shall be subject to civil and democratic control.

Polish shall be the official language in the Republic of Poland. The image of a crowned eagle upon a red field shall be the coat-of-arms, and white and red shall be the colours of the Republic of Poland. The national anthem shall be the *Mazurka Dąbrowskiego*. The capital of the Republic of Poland shall be Warsaw.

THE FREEDOMS, RIGHTS AND OBLIGATIONS OF PERSONS AND CITIZENS

All persons shall be equal before the law. Men and women shall have equal rights. The Republic of Poland shall ensure Polish citizens belonging to national or ethnic minorities the freedom to maintain and develop their own language, to maintain customs and traditions, and to develop their own culture.

The Republic of Poland shall ensure the legal protection of the life of every human being; the inviolability of the person and of the home; freedom of movement; freedom of faith and religion; and the freedom to express opinions. The freedom of peaceful assembly and association shall be guaranteed. At the age of 18 every citizen shall have the right to participate in a referendum, and to vote in presidential, legislative and local elections. Everyone shall have the right to own property; the freedom to choose and pursue his occupation; the right to health protection; and the right to education. Everyone shall have the right to compensation for any harm done to him by any action of an organ of public authority contrary to law.

SOURCES OF LAW

The sources of universally binding law of the Republic of Poland shall be the Constitution, statutes, ratified international agreements, and regulations.

THE SEJM AND THE SENAT

The Sejm shall be composed of 460 Deputies. Elections to the Sejm shall be universal, equal, direct and proportional and conducted by secret ballot. The Senat shall be composed of 100 Senators. Elections to the Senat shall be universal, direct and conducted by secret ballot. The Sejm and the Senat shall be elected for a four-year term of office. At the ages of 21 and 30, respectively, every citizen having the right to vote shall be eligible for election to the Sejm and the Senat.

The Sejm shall elect from amongst its members a Marshal and Vice-Marshals. The Sejm adopts laws; may adopt a resolution on a state of war; may order a nationwide referendum; and may appoint investigative committees to examine particular matters.

The Senat reviews laws adopted by the Sejm; it may adopt amendments or resolve upon complete rejection. The Senat can be overriden by the Sejm by an absolute majority vote in the presence of at least one-half of the statutory number of Deputies.

In instances specified in the Constitution, the Sejm and the Senat, sitting in joint session, shall act as the National Assembly (Zgromadzenie Narodowe). The right to introduce legislation shall belong to Deputies, to the Senat, to the President of the Republic, to the Council of Ministers, and to a group of at least 100,000 citizens having the right to vote in elections to the Sejm.

THE PRESIDENT OF THE REPUBLIC OF POLAND

The President of the Republic of Poland shall be the supreme representative of the Polish State and the guarantor of the continuity of state authority. The President shall ensure observance of the Constitution, safeguard the sovereignty and security of the State, as well as the inviolability and integrity of its territory. The President shall be elected in universal, equal and direct elections by secret ballot. The President shall be elected for a five-year term, and may be re-elected only once. Only a Polish citizen aged over 35 years, with full electoral rights in elections to the Sejm, may be elected President. Any such candidature shall be supported by the signatures of at least 100,000 citizens having the right to vote in elections to the Sejm. If the President of the Republic is unable to discharge the duties of his office, the Marshal of the Sejm shall temporarily assume presidential duties.

The President's duties include the calling of elections to the Sejm and the Senat; heading the Armed Forces; nominating and appointing the Prime Minister; appointing senior public officials; and representing the State in foreign affairs.

Bringing an indictment against the President shall be done by resolution of the National Assembly, passed by a majority of at least two-thirds of the statutory number of members, on the motion of at least 140 members.

THE COUNCIL OF MINISTERS AND GOVERNMENT ADMINISTRATION

The Council of Ministers shall conduct the internal affairs and foreign policy of the Republic of Poland, and shall manage the government administration. The President shall nominate a Prime Minister who shall propose the composition of a Council of Ministers. The Prime Minister shall, within 14 days following his appointment, submit a programme of activity of the Council of Ministers to the Sejm, together with a motion requiring a vote of confidence.

The members of the Council of Ministers shall be responsible to the Sejm, both collectively and individually. The Sejm shall pass a vote of no confidence in the Council of Ministers by a majority of votes of the statutory number of Deputies, on a motion of at least 46 Deputies, specifying the name of a candidate for Prime Minister.

LOCAL SELF-GOVERNMENT

The commune (*gmina*) shall be the basic unit of local self-government. Other units of regional and/or local self-government shall be specified by statute. Public duties aimed at satisfying the needs of a self-governing community shall be the direct responsibility of such units. Units of local self-government shall perform their duties through constitutive and executive organs. Units of local self-government shall be assured public funds for the performance of the duties assigned to them.

COURTS AND TRIBUNALS

The courts and tribunals shall constitute a separate and independent power. The administration of justice in the Republic of Poland shall be implemented by the Supreme Court, the common courts, administrative courts and military courts. Judges, within the exercise of their office, shall be independent and subject only to the Constitution and statutes. A judge shall not belong to a political party or trade union, or perform public activities incompatible with the principles of independence of the courts and judges. The Supreme Court shall exercise supervision over common and military courts.

The Constitutional Tribunal

The Constitutional Tribunal shall adjudicate on the conformity of statutes and other normative acts issued by central state organs to the Constitution. Its judgments shall be universally binding and final. Judges of the Tribunal shall be independent and subject only to the Constitution.

The Tribunal of State

Persons holding high state positions (as specified in the Constitution) shall be accountable to the Tribunal of State for violations of the Constitution or statutes. The First President of the Supreme Court shall be chairperson of the Tribunal. Its members shall be independent and subject only to the Constitution and statutes.

ORGANS OF STATE CONTROL AND FOR THE DEFENCE OF RIGHTS

The Supreme Chamber of Control shall be the chief organ of state order, and shall be subordinate to the Sejm. It shall audit the activity of the organs of government administration, the National Bank of Poland, state legal persons and other state organizational units. The Commissioner for Citizens' Rights shall safeguard the freedoms and rights of persons and citizens as specified in the Constitution and other normative acts. The National Council of Radio and Television Broadcasting shall safeguard freedom of speech and the right to information, as well as the public interest regarding radio and television broadcasting.

PUBLIC FINANCES

The National Bank of Poland, as the central bank of the State, shall have an exclusive right to issue money as well as to formulate and implement monetary policy. It shall be responsible for the value of the Polish currency.

The Council for Monetary Policy, presided over by the President of the National Bank, shall annually formulate the aims of monetary policy and present them to the Sejm at the same time as the submission of the Council of Ministers' draft Budget.

EXTRAORDINARY MEASURES

In situations of particular danger, if ordinary constitutional measures are inadequate, any of the following appropriate extraordinary measures may be introduced in a part or upon the whole territory of the State: martial law, a state of emergency or a state of natural disaster.

The Government

HEAD OF STATE

President: ALEKSANDER KWAŚNIEWSKI (elected 19 November 1995; re-elected 8 October 2000).

COUNCIL OF MINISTERS
(April 2003)

Prime Minister and Chairman of the European Integration Committee: LESZEK MILLER (SLD).

Deputy Prime Minister and Minister of Finance: GRZEGORZ KOŁODKO (SLD).

Deputy Prime Minister and Minister of Infrastructure: MAREK POL (UP).

Minister of Foreign Affairs: WŁODZIMIERZ CIMOSZEWICZ (SLD).

Minister of National Defence: JERZY SZMAJDZIŃSKI (SLD).

Minister of the Economy, Labour and Social Policy: JERZY HAUSNER (SLD).

Minister of the Treasury: PIOTR CZYŻEWSKI (SLD).

Minister of Justice: GRZEGORZ KURCZUK (SLD).

Minister of Internal Affairs and Administration: KRZYSZTOF JANIK (SLD).

Minister of Education: KRYSTYNA ŁYBACKA (SLD).

Minister of Culture: WALDEMAR DĄBROWSKI (Ind.).

Minister of Health: LESZEK SIKORSKI (SLD).

Minister of the Environment: CZESŁAW ŚLEZIAK (SLD).

Minister of Science: MICHAŁ KLEIBER (SLD).

Minister of Agriculture and Rural Development: ADAM TAŃSKI (SLD).

Minister without Portfolio: LECH NIKOLSKI (SLD).

MINISTRIES

Chancellery of the Prime Minister: 00-583 Warsaw, Al. Ujazdowskie 1/3; tel. (22) 6946000; fax (22) 6252637; e-mail cirinfo@kprm .gov.pl; internet www.kprm.gov.pl.

Ministry of Agriculture and Rural Development: 00-930 Warsaw, ul. Wspólna 30; tel. (22) 6231000; fax (22) 6232750; e-mail kanceleria@minrol.gov.pl; internet www.minrol.gov.pl.

Ministry of Culture: 00-71 Warsaw, ul. Krakowskie Przedmieście 15/17; tel. (22) 8267331; fax (22) 8261922; e-mail rzecznik@mk.gov .pl; internet www.mk.gov.pl.

Ministry of the Economy, Labour and Social Policy: 00-513 Warsaw, ul. Nowogrodzka 1/3/5; tel. (22) 6610100; e-mail bpi@mpips .gov.pl; internet www.mpips.gov.pl.

Ministry of Education and Sport: 00-918 Warsaw, Al. Szucha 25; tel. (22) 6280461; fax (22) 6288561; e-mail minister@menis.waw.pl; internet www.men.waw.pl.

Ministry of the Environment: 02-922 Warsaw, ul. Wawelska 52/54; tel. (22) 5792377; fax (22) 5792511; e-mail info@mos.gov.pl; internet www.mos.gov.pl.

Ministry of Finance: 00-916 Warsaw, ul. Świętokrzyska 12; tel. (22) 6945555; fax (22) 8260180; internet www.mf.gov.pl.

Ministry of Foreign Affairs: 00-580 Warsaw, Al. Szucha 23; tel. (22) 5239000; fax (22) 6290287; e-mail dsi@msz.gov.pl; internet www .msz.gov.pl.

Ministry of Health: 00-952 Warsaw, ul. Miodowa 15; tel. (22) 6349600; fax (22) 6358783; e-mail kancelaria@mz.gov.pl; internet www.mz.gov.pl.

Ministry of Infrastructure: 00-928 Warsaw, ul. Chałubińskiego 4/6; tel. (22) 6301000; fax (22) 6301116; e-mail info@mtigm.gov.pl; internet www.mi.gov.pl.

Ministry of Internal Affairs and Administration: 02-514 Warsaw, ul. Batorego 5; tel. (22) 6014427; fax (22) 8497494; e-mail wp@mswia.gov.pl; internet www.mswia.gov.pl.

Ministry of Justice: 00-950 Warsaw, Al. Ujazdowskie 11; tel. (22) 5212888; fax (22) 6215540; e-mail nagorska@ms.gov.pl; internet www.ms.gov.pl.

Ministry of National Defence: 00-909 Warsaw, ul. Klonowa 1; tel. (22) 6280031; fax (22) 8455378; e-mail bpimon@wp.mil.pl; internet www.wp.mil.pl.

Ministry of Science: 00529 Warsaw, ul. Wspólna 1/3; tel. (22) 5292718; internet www.mnii.gov.pl.

Ministry of the Treasury: 00-522 Warsaw, ul. Krucza 36; tel. (22) 6958000; fax (22) 6280872; e-mail minister@mst.gov.pl; internet www.msp.gov.pl.

Other Government Departments

European Integration Committee: 00-918 Warsaw, Al. Ujazdowskie 9; tel. (22) 4555500; fax (22) 6294888; e-mail info@mail.ukie .gov.pl; internet www.ukie.gov.pl.

Government Centre for Strategic Studies: 00-926 Warsaw, ul. Wspólna 4; tel. (22) 6618600; e-mail info@mail.rcss.gov.pl; internet www.rcss.gov.pl.

President and Legislature

PRESIDENT

Presidential election, 8 October 2000

	Votes	%
Aleksander Kwaśniewski	9,485,224	53.90
Andrzej Olechowski	3,044,141	17.30
Marian Krzaklewski	2,739,621	15.57
Jarosław Kalinowski	1,047,949	5.95
Andrzej Lepper	537,570	3.05
Janusz Korwin-Mikke	252,499	1.43
Lech Wałęsa	178,590	1.01
Jan Lopuszanski	139,682	0.79
Dariusz Grabowski	89,002	0.51
Piotr Ikonowicz	38,672	0.22
Tadeusz Wilecki	28,805	0.16
Bogdan Pawlowski	17,164	0.10
Total*	17,789,231	100.00

* Including 190,312 invalid votes.

ZGROMADZENIE NARODOWE
(National Assembly)

Senat

Senat: 00-072 Warsaw, ul. Wiejska 4/6; tel. (22) 6942500; fax (22) 2290968; internet www.senat.gov.pl.

Marshal: Longin Hieronim Pastusiak (SLD-UP).

Vice-Marshals: Jolanta Danielak (SLD-UP), Ryszard Jarzembowski (SLD-UP), Kazimierz Kutz (Blok Senat 2001).

Election, 23 September 2001

Parties and alliances	Seats
Democratic Left Alliance (SLD)/Union of Labour (UP)	75
Blok Senat 2001*	15
Polish People's Party (PSL)	4
Self Defence Party of the Republic of Poland	2
League of Polish Families (LPR)	2
Independents	2
Total	**100**

* An electoral alliance comprising Solidarity Electoral Action of the Right, the Citizens' Platform, the Law and Justice Party, the Freedom Union and the Movement for the Reconstruction of Poland.

Sejm

Sejm: 00-902 Warsaw, ul. Wiejska 4/6; tel. (22) 285927; internet www.sejm.gov.pl.

Marshal: Marek Borowski (SLD-UP).

Vice-Marshals: Tomasz Nałęcz (SLD-UP), Donald Tusk (PO), Janusz Wojciechowski (PSL).

Election, 23 September 2001

Parties and alliances	% of votes	Seats
Democratic Left Alliance (SLD)/Union of Labour (UP)	41.0	216
Civic Platform (PO)	12.7	65
Self Defence Party of the Republic of Poland	10.2	53
Law and Justice Party (PiS)	9.5	44
Polish People's Party (PSL)	9.0	42
League of Polish Families (LPR)	7.9	38
Solidarity Electoral Action of the Right (AWSP)	5.6	—
Freedom Union (UW)	3.1	—
German Minority (MN)	0.4	2
Others	0.6	—
Total	**100.0**	**460**

Political Organizations

Under the 1990 law, political parties are not obliged to file for registration. By January 1998 the number of registered parties operating in Poland had declined from some 360 to 60, as a result of new regulations, which obliged existing parties to apply for re-registration by the end of 1997, presenting a list of a minimum of 1,000 supporting signatures, instead of the previous 15.

Alliance of Polish Christian Democrats (Porozumienie Polskich Chrzescijanskich Demokratów—PPChD): e-mail biuro@chadecja .org.pl; internet www.ppchd.org.pl; f. 1999 by the merger of the Centre Alliance, the Movement for the Republic of Poland and the Party of Christian Democrats; Chair. Antoni Tokarczuk; Head of Political Council Paweł Laczkowski.

All-Polish Alliance of the Unemployed (OSB): f. 2001; leader Beata Chorazy-Ryszko.

Christian Democratic Party of the Third Republic (ChDTRP): Warsaw, Al. Jerozolimskie 11/19; tel. (22) 6291329; fax (22) 6291081; e-mail chdrp@chdrp.org.pl; internet www.chdrp.org .pl; f. 1997; Chair. Marek Gumowski.

Christian National Union (Zjednoczenie Chrześcijańsko Narodowe—ZChN): Warsaw, ul. Mokotowska 555/50; tel. (22) 6227120; e-mail biuro@zchn.waw.pl; internet www.zchn.waw.pl; f. 1989; about 10,000 mems; Chair. Stanisław Zajac.

Civic Platform (PO): 00-548 Warsaw, al. Ujazdowskie 18; tel. (22) 6227548; fax (22) 6225386; internet www.platforma.org.pl; f. 2001 by a popular independent presidential candidate and factions of the UW and the AWS; also known as the Citizens' Platform; contested the elections to the Senat in 2001 as part of the Blok Senat; formed co-operation agreement with the Law and Justice Party for the 2002 local elections; Leader Donald Tusk.

Confederation for an Independent Poland (Konfederacja Polski Niepodległej—KPN): 00-920 Warsaw, ul. Nowy Świat 18/20; tel. (22) 8261043; fax (22) 8261400; e-mail kpnwa@poczta.onet.pl; internet www.lion.transprojekt.krakow.pl/sk; f. 1979; centre-right; about 35,000 mems; Chair. Leszek Moczulski.

Confederation for an Independent Poland (Patriotic Camp—KPN OP): e-mail skus@kpn.org.pl; Leader Adam Slomka.

Conservative Peasant Party-New Poland Movement (SKL-RNP): Warsaw; e-mail webmaster@skl.org.pl; f. 2002 by the merger of the Conservative Peasant Party and the Alliance of Polish Christian Democrats right-wing; Chair. Artur Balazs.

Democratic Left Alliance (Sojusz Lewicy Demokratycznej—SLD): Warsaw; internet www.sld.org.pl; f. 1991; electoral coalition of Social Democracy of the Republic of Poland (Socjaldemokracja Rzeczypospolitej Polskiej—SdRP) and the All Poland Trade Unions Alliance; reorganized as a party in 1999, when the SdRP was disbanded; formed electoral and government alliance with the Union of Labour in 2001; led by Leszek Miller.

All Poland Trade Unions Alliance (Ogólnopolskie Porozumienie Związków Zawodowych—OPZZ): see section on Trade and Industry (Trade Unions).

Democratic Party (Stronnictwo Demokratyczne—SD): 00-021 Warsaw, ul. Chmielna 9; tel. (22) 269571; fax (22) 274051; f. 1937; 12,000 mems (1999); Chair. Andrzej Arendarski.

Freedom Union (Unia Wolności—UW): 00-683 Warsaw, ul. Marszałkowska 77/79; tel. (22) 8275047; fax (22) 8277851; e-mail uw@uw.org.pl; internet www.uw.org.pl; f. 1994 by merger of Democratic Union (Unia Demokratyczna—UD) and the Liberal Democratic Congress (Kongres Liberalno-Demokratyczny—KLD); contested the election to the Senat in 2001 as part of the Blok Senat; 12,500 mems; Leader Władysław Frasyniuk; Dep. Leader Tadeusz Syryjczyk.

German Minority (Mniejszość Niemiecka—MN): Leader Henryk Król.

Labour Party (Stronnictwo Pracy—SP): Warsaw; tel. (22) 291611; fax (22) 6252095; f. 1937; reactivated 1989; merged with Christian Democracy group in 1994; merged with Peasant-Independence Coalition in 2000; formerly known as the Christian Democratic Labour Party; 2,750 mems; Chair. Tomasz Jackowski; Gen. Sec. Zbigniew Jeczmyk.

Law and Justice Party (Prawo i Sprawieliwość—PiS): 00-564 Warsaw, ul. Koszykowa 10; tel. (22) 6216767; fax (22) 6215035; e-mail biuro@pis.org.pl; internet www.pis.org.pl; f. 2001; conservative; contested the election to the Senat in 2001 as part of the Blok Senat; formed co-operation agreement with the Civic Platform for the 2002 local elections; Leader Lech Kaczynski.

League of Polish Families (Liga Polskich Rodzin—LPR): f. 2001 as alliance comprising the National Party, All-Poland Youth, the Polish Accord Party, the Catholic National movement and the Peasant National Bloc; Christian, nationalist, anti-EU; Leader Roman Giertych; Chief of Staff Zygmunt Wrzodak.

Movement for the Reconstruction of Poland (Ruch Odbudowy Polski—ROP): Warsaw; f. 1995; conservative; contested the election to the Senat in 2001 as part of the Blok Senat; 12,000 mems; Leader Jan Olszewski.

National Pensioners' Party (Krajowa Partia Emerytówi Rencistów—KPEiR): Chair. Zenon Zumiński.

Non-Party Bloc in Support of Reforms (Bezpartyjny Blok Wspierania Reform—BBWR): Warsaw; f. 1993 by Lech Wałęsa; Leader Leszek Zieliński; Chair. Prof. Zbigniew Religa.

Party of Real Politics (Stronnictwo Polityki Realnej): Warsaw; f. 1996 following a split in the Polish Union of Real Politics; right-wing; Chair. Mariusz Dzierzawsky.

Party X: Warsaw; tel. (22) 427160; f. 1991; advocates free-market economy, expansion of industry and agriculture, gradual elimination of unemployment and universal access to education, culture and health; 9,000 mems; Leader Józef Kossecki.

Peasant Democratic Party (Partia Ludowo Demokratyczna—PLD): f. 1998; Leader Roman Jagieliński.

Polish People's Party (Polskie Stronnictwo Ludowe—PSL): 00-131 Warsaw, ul. Grzybowska 4; tel. (22) 6206020; fax (22) 6543583; e-mail biuronkw@nkw.psl.org.pl; internet www.psl.org.pl; f. 1990 to replace United Peasant Party (Zjednoczone Stronnictwo Ludowe; 1949) and Polish Peasant Party—Rebirth (Polskie Stronnictwo Ludowe—Odrodzenie; f. 1989); centrist, stresses development of agriculture and social-market economy; 200,000 mems; Chair. Jarosław Kalinowski.

Polish Socialist Party (Polska Partia Socjalistyczna—PPS): 00-325 Warsaw, ul. Krakowskie Przedmieście 6; tel. (22) 8262054; fax (22) 8266908; e-mail info@polskapartiasocjalisticzyna.org; internet www.pps.org.pl; f. 1892; re-established 1987; 5,000 mems; Leader Piotr Ikonowicz.

Self Defence Party of the Republic of Poland (Partia Samoobrona Rzeczypospolitej Polskiej): 00-024 Warsaw, Al. Jerozolimskie 30; tel. (22) 6250472; fax (22) 6250477; e-mail samoobrona@ samoobrona.org.pl; internet www.samoobrona.org.pl; f. 2000 by trade union leaders opposed to the Government's social and economic policies to contest the parliamentary elections in 2001; agrarian, conservative, anti-EU; Leader ANDRZEJ LEPPER.

Social Movement (Ruch Społeczny—RS): 00-683 Warsaw, ul. Marszałkowska 77/79; tel. (22) 6223146; fax (22) 6218224; e-mail biuro@rsaws.pl; internet www.rsaws.pl; f. 1997 as the political wing of the Solidarity trade union; name shortened from Social Movement of Solidarity Electoral Action—RS AWS in 2002; Chair. KRZYSZTOF PIESIEWICZ.

Socio-Cultural Association of Germans of Upper Silesia (Towarzystwo Społeczno-Kulturalne Niemców Województwa Katowickiego): Katowice.

Solidarity Electoral Action of the Right (AWSP): Warsaw; f. 1996 as Solidarity Electoral Action, an electoral alliance of over 30 centre-right parties; formed a renewed alliance of four principal parties, Social Movement of Solidarity Electoral Action, the Christian National Union, the Alliance of Polish Christian Democrats and the Conservative Peasant Party, in Dec. 2000; name changed as above in 2001, upon the withdrawal of the latter party; formed an alliance with the Movement for the Reconstruction of Poland in 2001, and contested the election to the Senat as part of the Blok Senat; Leader JERZY BUZEK; Gen. Sec. MAREK KOTLARSKI.

Union of Labour (Unia Pracy—UP): 00-513 Warsaw, ul. Nowogrodzka 4; tel. and fax (22) 6256776; e-mail biuro@uniapracy.org.pl; internet www.uniapracy.org.pl; f. 1993; formed electoral and government coalition with the Democratic Left Alliance in 2001; Leader MAREK POL.

Union of Real Politics (Unia Polityki Realnej—UPR): 00-042 Warsaw, ul. Nowy Świat 41; tel. and fax (22) 8267477; internet www.upr.org.pl; f. 1996; Leader STANISŁAW MICHALKIEWICZ.

Diplomatic Representation

EMBASSIES IN POLAND

Afghanistan: 03-930 Warsaw, ul. Nobla 3; tel. (22) 6173173; fax (22) 6163777; Chargé d'affaires a.i. ABDUL H. HAIDER.

Albania: 00-789 Warsaw, ul. Słoneczna 15; tel. (22) 8498427; fax (22) 8484004; e-mail albos@warman.com.pl; Ambassador SOKOL GJOKA.

Algeria: 03-932 Warsaw, ul. Dąbrowiecka 21; tel. (22) 6175855; fax (22) 6160081; e-mail ambalgva@zigzag.pl; Ambassador TEDJINI SALAOUANDJI.

Angola: 02-635 Warsaw, ul. Balonowa 20; tel. (22) 6463529; e-mail embaixada@emb-angola.pl; Ambassador LISETH NAWANGA SATUMBO PENA.

Argentina: 03-973 Warsaw, ul. Brukselska 9; tel. (22) 6176028; fax (22) 6177162; e-mail secons@ikp.atm.com.pl; Ambassador CARLOS ALBERTO PASSALACQUA.

Armenia: 02-908 Warsaw, ul. Waszkowskiego 11; tel. (22) 8408130; fax (22) 6420643; e-mail main@embarmenia.it.pl; Ambassador ASHOT HOVAKIMIAN.

Australia: 00-513 Warsaw, ul. Nowogrodzka 11, Nautilus Bldg, 3rd Floor; tel. (22) 5213444; fax (22) 6273500; e-mail ambasada@ australia.pl; internet www.australia.pl; Ambassador PATRICK LAWLESS.

Austria: 00-748 Warsaw, ul. Gagarina 34; tel. (22) 8410081; fax (22) 8410085; e-mail austria@it.com.pl; Ambassador GEORG WEISS.

Bangladesh: Warsaw; tel. (22) 8483200; fax (22) 8484974; e-mail bangla@it.com.pl; Ambassador ASHFAQUR RAHMAN.

Belarus: 03-978 Warsaw, ul. Ateńska 67; tel. (22) 6172391; fax (22) 6178441; Ambassador PAVEL LATUSHKA.

Belgium: 00-095 Warsaw, ul. Senatorska 34; tel. (22) 8270233; fax (22) 8285711; e-mail ambabel.warsaw@pol.pl; e-mail warsaw@ diplobel.org; Ambassador BRUNO NÈVE DE MÉVERGNIES.

Brazil: 03-931 Warsaw, ul. Poselska 11, Saska Kepa; tel. (22) 6174800; fax (22) 6178689; e-mail polbrem@polbrem.it.pl; Ambassador CARLOS ALBERTO DE AZEVEDO PIMENTEL.

Bulgaria: 00-540 Warsaw, Al. Ujazdowskie 33/35; tel. (22) 6294071; fax (22) 6282271; e-mail office@bgemb.com.pl; Ambassador LATCHEZAR Y. PETKOV.

Canada: 00-481 Warsaw, ul. Matejki 1/5; tel. (22) 5843100; fax (22) 5843190; e-mail wsaw@dfait-maeci.gc.ca; Ambassador RALPH J. LYSYSHYN.

Chile: 02-925 Warsaw, ul. Okrężna 62; tel. (22) 8582330; fax (22) 8582329; e-mail embajada@embachile.pl; Ambassador LEOPOLDO DURÁN VALDÉS.

China, People's Republic: 00-203 Warsaw, ul. Bonifraterska 1; tel. (22) 8313836; fax (22) 6354211; e-mail ambchina@pol.pl; Ambassador ZHOU XIAOPEI.

Colombia: 03-936 Warsaw, ul. Zwycięzców 29; tel. (22) 6177157; fax (22) 6176684; e-mail embcol@medianet.com.pl; Ambassador DORY SÁNCHEZ DE WETZEL.

Costa Rica: 02-954 Warsaw, ul. Kubickiego 9, m. 5; tel. (22) 8589112; fax (22) 6427832; e-mail embajada.cr@supermedia.pl; Chargé d'affaires JOHNNY SÁUREZ SANDÍ.

Croatia: 02-628 Warsaw, ul. Ignacego Krasickiego 10; tel. (22) 8441225; fax (22) 8440567; e-mail croemb@pol.pl.

Cuba: 02-516 Warsaw, ul. Rejtana 15, m. 8; tel. (22) 8481715; fax (22) 8482231; e-mail embacuba@medianet.pl; Ambassador JORGE FERNANDO LEFEBRE NICOLÁS.

Czech Republic: 00-555 Warsaw, ul. Koszykowa 18; tel. (22) 6287221; fax (22) 6298045; e-mail warsaw@embassy.mzv.cz; internet www.mfa.cz/warsaw; Ambassador BEDŘICH KOPECKÝ.

Denmark: 02-517 Warsaw, ul. Rakowiecka 19; tel. (22) 8482600; fax (22) 8487580; e-mail wawamb@wawamb.um.dk; internet www.danskeambassade.pl; Ambassador LAURIDS MIKAELSEN.

Ecuador: 02-516 Warsaw, ul. Rejtana 15, m. 15; tel. (22) 8487230; fax (22) 8488196; e-mail mecuapol@it.com.pl; Ambassador GALO FERNANDO LARREA DONOSO.

Egypt: 03-972 Warsaw, ul. Alzacka 18; tel. (22) 6176973; fax (22) 6179058; e-mail embassyofegypt@zigzag.pl; Ambassador HAMDI SANAD LOZA.

Estonia: 02-639 Warsaw, ul. Karwińska 1; tel. (22) 6464480; fax (22) 6464481; e-mail saatkond@varssavi.vm.ee; internet www.estemb.pl; Ambassador AIVO ORAV.

Finland: 00-559 Warsaw, ul. Chopina 4/8; tel. (22) 6294091; fax (22) 6213442; e-mail sanomat.var@formin.fi; Ambassador HANNU HÄMÄLÄINEN.

France: 02-515 Warsaw, ul. Pulawska 17; tel. (22) 5293000; fax (22) 5293001; e-mail presse@ambafrance.org.pl; internet www.france.org.pl; Ambassador PATRICK GAUTRAT.

Germany: 03-932 Warsaw, ul. Dąbrowiecka 30; tel. (22) 6173011; fax (22) 6173582; internet www.ambasadaniemiec.pl; e-mail info@ ambasadaniemiec.pl; Ambassador REINHARD SCHWEPPE.

Greece: 00-432 Warsaw, ul. Górnośląska 35; tel. (22) 6229460; fax (22) 6229464; e-mail embassy@greece.pl; internet www.greece.pl; Ambassador NIKOLAOS VAMVOUNAKIS.

Holy See: 00-582 Warsaw, Al. J. Ch. Szucha 12, POB 163 (Apostolic Nunciature); tel. (22) 6288488; fax (22) 6284556; e-mail nuncjatura@ episkopat.pl; Apostolic Nuncio Most Rev. JÓZEF KOWALCZYK (Titular Archbishop of Eraclea).

Hungary: 00-559 Warsaw, ul. Chopina 2; tel. (22) 6284451; fax (22) 6218561; e-mail magyar@optimus.waw.pl; Ambassador MIHÁLY GYŐR.

India: 02-516 Warsaw, ul. Rejtana 15, m. 2–7; tel. (22) 8495800; fax (22) 8496705; e-mail ss-com@it.com.pl; Ambassador RAJAMANI LAKSHMI NARAYAN.

Indonesia: 03-903 Warsaw, ul. Estońska 3–5, POB 33; tel. (22) 6175179; fax (22) 6121885; e-mail comwar@polbox.pl; internet www.indonezja.plocman.pl; Ambassador IBNU SANYOTO.

Iran: 03-928 Warsaw, ul. Królowej Aldony 22; tel. (22) 6174293; fax (22) 6178452; e-mail iranemb@warman.com.pl; internet www.iranemb.warsaw.pl; Ambassador SEYED MOUSA KAZEMI.

Ireland: 00-789 Warsaw, ul. Humańska 10; tel. (22) 8496633; fax (22) 8498431; e-mail ambasada@irlandia.pl; internet www.irlandia.pl; Ambassador THELMA DORAN.

Israel: 02-078 Warsaw, ul. Krzywickiego 24; tel. (22) 8250923; fax (22) 8251607; e-mail itonut@israel.pl; internet www.israel.pl; Ambassador Prof. SHEWACH WEISS.

Italy: 00-055 Warsaw, Pl. Dąbrowskiego 6; tel. (22) 8263471; fax (22) 8278507; e-mail ambvars@polbox.com.pl; Ambassador GIANCARLO LEO.

Japan: 00-464 Warsaw, ul. Szwoleżerów 8; tel. (22) 6965000; fax (22) 6965001; e-mail info-cul@emb-japan.pl; internet www.emb-japan.pl; Ambassador HIDEAKI UEDA.

Kazakhstan: 02-954 Warsaw, ul. Królowej Marysieńki 14; tel. (22) 6425388; fax (22) 6423427; e-mail kazdipmis@hot.pl; Ambassador KONSTANTIN ZHIGALOV.

Korea, Democratic People's Republic: 00-728 Warsaw, ul. Bobrowiecka 1A; tel. (22) 8405813; fax (22) 8405710; Ambassador KIM PYONG IL.

Korea, Republic: 00-867 Warsaw, ul. Chłodna 51, Warsaw Trade Tower, 24th Floor; tel. (22) 8483337; fax (22) 52825000; e-mail jnchung89@mofat.go.kr; Ambassador SONG MIN-SOON.

Laos: 02-516 Warsaw, ul. Rejtana 15, m. 26; tel. (22) 8484786; Chargé d'affaires a.i. SENGPHET HOUNGBOUNGNUANG.

Latvia: 02-516 Warsaw, ul. Rejtana 15, m. 28; tel. (22) 8481947; fax (22) 8480201; e-mail amlotewl@warman.com.pl; Ambassador ULDIS VĪTOLIŅŠ.

Lebanon: 02-516 Warsaw, ul. Starościńska 1B,m. 10–11; tel. (22) 8445065; fax (22) 6460030; e-mail embleban@pol.pl; Ambassador AHMED IBRAHIM.

Libya: 03-934 Warsaw, ul. Kryniczna 2; tel. (22) 6174822; fax (22) 6175091; e-mail alfath2@ikp.atm.com.pl; Ambassador GIUMA IBRAHIM FERJANI.

Lithuania: 00-580 Warsaw, Al. J. Ch. Szucha 5; tel. (22) 6253368; fax (22) 6253440; e-mail litwa_amb@waw.pdi.net; Ambassador DARIUS DEGUTIS.

Macedonia, former Yugoslav republic: 02-954 Warsaw, ul. Królowej Marysieńki 40; tel. (22) 6517291; fax (22) 6517292; e-mail ambrmwar@zigzag.pl; Ambassador KOSTE STOIMENOVSKI.

Malaysia: 03-902 Warsaw, ul. Gruzińska 3; tel. (22) 6174413; fax (22) 6177920; e-mail emwwarsaw@it.com.pl; Ambassador Dato NG BAK HAI.

Mexico: 02-516 Warsaw, ul. Starościńska 1B, m. 4/5; tel. (22) 6468800; fax (22) 6464222; e-mail embamex@ikp.pl; Ambassador FRANCISCO JOSÉ CRUZ GONZÁLEZ.

Moldova: 02-634 Warsaw, ul. Miłobędzka 12; tel. (22) 8447278; fax (22) 6462099; e-mail ammd_pol@yahoo.com; Ambassador EUGEN CARPOV.

Mongolia: 02-516 Warsaw, ul. Rejtana 15, m. 16; tel. (22) 8482063; fax (22) 8499391; e-mail mongamb@ikp.atm.com.pl; internet www .ambmong.net7.pl; Ambassador TUGALKHUU BAASANSUREN.

Morocco: 02-516 Warsaw, ul. Starościńska 1, m. 11/12; tel. (22) 8496341; fax (22) 8481840; e-mail sifamava@pol.pl; Ambassador HASSAN ABADI.

Netherlands: 00-791 Warsaw, ul. Chocimska 6; tel. (22) 8492351; fax (22) 8488345; e-mail nlgovwar@ikp.pl; Ambassador JAN EDWARD CRAANEN.

Nigeria: 00-791 Warsaw, ul. Chocimska 18; tel. (22) 8486944; fax (22) 8485379; e-mail nigemb@ant.pl; Ambassador ZUBAIRU DADA.

Norway: 00-559 Warsaw, ul. Chopina 2A ; tel. (22) 6964030; fax (22) 6280938; e-mail emb.warsaw@mfa.no; Ambassador STEN LUNDBO.

Pakistan: 02-516 Warsaw, ul. Starościńska 1, m. 1/2; tel. (22) 8494808; fax (22) 8491160; e-mail parepwarsaw@mailer.cst.tpsa.pl; Ambassador FAUZIA NAZREEN.

Peru: 02-516 Warsaw, ul. Starościńska 1, m. 3–4; tel. (22) 6468806; fax (22) 6468617; e-mail embperpl@atomnet.pl; internet www .perupol.pl; Ambassador MARTÍN YRIGOYEN YRIGOYEN.

Portugal: 03-941 Warsaw, ul. Zwycięzców 12; tel. (22) 6176021; fax (22) 6174498; Ambassador MARIA MARGARIDA DE ARAÚJO DE FIGUEIREDO.

Romania: 00-559 Warsaw, ul. Chopina 10; tel. (22) 6283156; fax (22) 6285264; e-mail embassy@roembassy.com.pl; Ambassador IRENI COMAROSCHI.

Russia: 00-761 Warsaw, ul. Belwederska 49; tel. (22) 6213453; fax (22) 6253016; e-mail ambrus@poczta.fm; Ambassador NIKOLAI AFANASIEVSKII.

Saudi Arabia: 00-739 Warsaw, ul. Stępińska 55; tel. (22) 8400000; fax (22) 8406003; Ambassador OSAMAH A. AL-SANOSI.

Serbia and Montenegro: 00-540 Warsaw, Al. Ujazdowskie 23/25; tel. (22) 6285161; fax (22) 6297173; e-mail yuabapl@zigzag.pl; Ambassador ZORAN NOVAKOVIĆ.

Slovakia: 00-581 Warsaw, ul. Litewska 6; tel. (22) 5258110; fax (22) 5258122; e-mail slovakia@waw.pdi.net; internet www .ambasada-slovacji.pdi.pl; Ambassador MAGDALÉNA VÁŠÁRYOVÁ.

Slovenia: 02-516 Warsaw, ul. Starościńska 1, m. 23–24; tel. (22) 8498282; fax (22) 8484090; e-mail sloemb@it.com.pl; Ambassador ZVONE DRAGAN.

South Africa: 00-675 Warsaw, 6th floor, IPC Business Centre, ul. Koszykowa 54; tel. (22) 6256228; fax (22) 6256270; e-mail saembassy@supermedia.pl; Ambassador SIKOSI MIJI.

Spain: 00-459 Warsaw, ul. Myśliwiecka 4; tel. (22) 6224250; fax (22) 6225408; e-mail embesp@medianet.pl; Ambassador MIGUEL ÁNGEL NAVARRO PORTERA.

Sri Lanka: 02-520 Warsaw, ul. Wiśniowa 40, m.12–13; tel. (22) 6464394; fax (22) 6464435; e-mail lankaemb@medianet.pl; Ambassador RATNAYAKE MUDIYANSELANGE RANJITH CHULA BANDARA.

Sweden: 00-585 Warsaw, ul. Bagatela 3; tel. (22) 6408900; fax (22) 6408983; e-mail ambassaden.warszawa@foreign.ministry.se; internet www.swedishembassy.pl; Ambassador MATS STAFFANSSON.

Switzerland: 00-540 Warsaw, Al. Ujazdowskie 27; tel. (22) 6280481; fax (22) 6210548; e-mail swiemvar@mailer.cst.tpsa.pl; Ambassador ANDRÉ VON GRAFFENREID.

Syria: 02-536 Warsaw, ul. Narbutta 19A ; tel. (22) 8491456; fax (22) 8491847; Chargé d'affaires a.i. FARES CHAHINE.

Thailand: 00-790 Warsaw, ul. Willowa 7; tel. (22) 8492655; fax (22) 8492630; e-mail thaiemb@ids.pl; Ambassador VONGTIVA SURAPOLBHICHET.

Tunisia: 00-459 Warsaw, ul. Myśliwiecka 14; tel. (22) 6286330; fax (22) 6216298; e-mail at.varsovie@it.com.pl; Ambassador ALI BOUSNINA.

Turkey: 02-622 Warsaw, ul. Malczewskiego 32; tel. (22) 6464323; fax (22) 6463757; e-mail turkemb@it.com.pl; Ambassador CANDAN AZER.

Ukraine: 00-580 Warsaw, Al. J. Ch. Szucha 7; tel. (22) 6250127; fax (22) 6298103; e-mail emb_pl@mfa.gov.ua; Ambassador OLEKSANDR NYKONENKO.

United Kingdom: 00-556 Warsaw, Al. Róż 1; tel. (22) 6281001; fax (22) 6217161; e-mail info@britishembassy.pl; internet www .britishembassy.pl; Ambassador MICHAEL PAKENHAM.

USA: 00-540 Warsaw, Al. Ujazdowskie 29/31; tel. (22) 6283041; fax (22) 6288298; internet www.usaemb.pl; Ambassador CHRISTOPHER HILL.

Uruguay: 02-516 Warsaw, ul. Rejtana 15, m. 12; tel. (22) 8495040; fax (22) 6466887; e-mail uropol@ikp.atm.com.pl; Ambassador CARLOS AMORIN.

Venezuela: 02-516 Warsaw, ul. Rejtana 15, m. 10/11; tel. (22) 6461846; fax (22) 6468761; e-mail embavenez.pl@qdnet.pl; Ambassador DANIELA SZOKOLOCZI.

Viet Nam: 02-589 Warsaw, ul. Kazimierzowska 14; tel. (22) 8446021; fax (22) 8446723; e-mail vso@warman.com.pl; Ambassador DINH XUAN LUU.

Yemen: 03-941 Warsaw, ul. Zwycięzców 18; tel. (22) 6176025; fax (22) 6176022; Ambassador ABDULAZIZ AHMED ALI BAEISA.

Judicial System

SUPREME COURT

Supreme Court

00-951 Warsaw, pl. Krasińskich 2/4/6; tel. (22) 5308213; fax (22) 5309065; e-mail press@sn.pl; internet www.sn.pl.

The highest judicial organ; exercises supervision over the decision-making of all other courts; its functions include: the examination of cassations of final decisions made by courts of appeal; the adoption of resolutions aimed at providing interpretation of legal provisions that give rise to doubts. Justices of the Supreme Court are appointed by the President of the Republic on motions of the National Council of Judiciary and serve until the age of retirement. The First President of the Supreme Court is appointed (and dismissed) from among the Supreme Court Justices by the Sejm on the motion of the President of the Republic, and serves a six-year term. The other presidents of the Supreme Court are appointed by the President of the Republic from among the Supreme Court Justices.

First President: Prof. Dr hab. LECH GARDOCKI.

OTHER COURTS

The Supreme Administrative Court examines, in one procedure, complaints concerning the legality of administrative decisions; it is vested exclusively with the powers of court of cassation.

President: Prof. Dr hab. WALERIAN SANETRA.

Religion

CHRISTIANITY

The Roman Catholic Church

The Roman Catholic Church was granted full legal status in May 1989, when three laws regulating aspects of relations between the Church and the State were approved by the Sejm. The legislation guaranteed freedom of worship, and permitted the Church to administer its own affairs. The Church was also granted access to the media, and allowed to operate its own schools, hospitals and other charitable organizations. A Concordat, agreed by the Polish Government and the Holy See in 1993, was ratified in January 1998.

For ecclesiastical purposes, Poland comprises 14 archdioceses (including one for the Catholics of the Byzantine-Ukrainian rite) and 26 dioceses (including one for the Catholics of the Byzantine-Ukrainian Rite and one Military Ordinariate). In 2000 95.7% of the population were adherents of the Roman Catholic Church.

Bishops' Conference: Konferencja Episkopatu Polski, 01-015 Warsaw, Skwer Kardynała Stefana Wyszyńskiego 6; tel. (22) 8389251; fax (22) 8380967; f. 1969; statutes approved 1995; Pres. Cardinal JÓZEF GLEMP (Archbishop of Warsaw).

Latin Rite

Archbishop of Warsaw and Primate of Poland: Cardinal JÓZEF GLEMP, Sekretariat Prymasa Polski, 00-246 Warsaw, ul. Miodowa 17/19; tel. (22) 5317200; fax (22) 6354324; e-mail prymas@perytnet.pl.

Archbishop of Białystok: Most Rev. WOJCIECH ZIEMBA, 15-087 Białystok, Pl. Jana Pawła II 1, Kuria Metropolitalna; tel. and fax (85) 7416473; e-mail kuria@bialystok.opoka.org.pl.

Archbishop of Częstochowa: Most Rev. STANISŁAW NOWAK, 42-200 Częstochowa, Al. Najśw. Maryi Panny 54, Kuria Metropolitalna; tel. (34) 3241044; fax (34) 3651182; e-mail kuria@czestochowaopoka.org.pl.

Archbishop of Gdańsk: Most Rev. TADEUSZ GOCŁOWSKI, 80-330 Gdańsk (Oliwa), ul. Cystersów 15, Kuria Metropolitalna; tel. (58) 5520051; fax (58) 5522775; e-mail kuria@gsd.gda.pl.

Archbishop of Gniezno: Most Rev. HENRYK MUSZYŃSKI, 62-200 Gniezno, ul. Kanclerza Jana Łaskiego 7; tel. (61) 4262102; fax (61) 4262105; e-mail kuriagni@gniezno.opoka.org.pl.

Archbishop of Katowice: Most Rev. DAMIAN ZIMOŃ, 40-043 Katowice, ul. Jordana 39, Kuria Metropolitalna; tel. (32) 2512160; fax (32) 2514830; e-mail kuria@katowice.opoka.org.pl.

Archbishop of Kraków: Cardinal FRANCISZEK MACHARSKI, 31-004 Kraków, ul. Franciszkańska 3, Kuria Metropolitalna; tel. (12) 6288100; fax (12) 4294617; e-mail kuria@diecezja.krakow.pl.

Archbishop of Łódź: Most Rev. WŁADYSŁAW ZIÓŁEK, 90-458 Łódź, ul. Ks Ignacego Skorupki 1, Kuria Arcybiskupia; tel. (42) 6375844; fax (42) 6361696; e-mail kuria@archidiecezja.lodz.pl.

Archbishop of Lublin: Most Rev. JÓZEF MIROSŁAW ŻYCIŃSKI, 20-105 Lublin, ul. Ks Prymasa Stefana Wyszyńskiego 2, Skr. p. 198, Kuria Metropolitalna; tel. (81) 5321058; fax (81) 5346141; e-mail j.zycinski@kuria.lublin.pl.

Archbishop of Olsztyn(Warmia): Most Rev. EDMUND PISZCZ, 10-006 Olsztyn, ul. Pieniężnego 22; tel. and fax (89) 5272280.

Archbishop of Poznań: Most Rev. STANISŁAW GĄDECKI, 61-109 Poznań ul. Ostrów Tumski 2, Kuria Arcybiskupia; tel. (61) 8524282; fax (61) 8519748; e-mail kuria@archpoznan.org.pl.

Archbishop of Przemyśl: Most Rev. JÓZEF MICHALIK, 37-700 Przemyśl, Pl. Katedralny 4A, Kuria Metropolitalna; tel. (16) 6786694; fax (16) 6782674; e-mail kuria@przemysl.opoka.org.pl.

Archbishop of Szczecin-Kamień: Most Rev. ZYGMUNT KAMIŃSKI, 71-459 Szczecin, ul. Papieża Pawła VI 4, Kuria Metropolitalna; tel. (91) 4542292; fax (91) 4536908; e-mail kuria@szczecin.opoka.org.pl.

Archbishop of Wrocław: Cardinal HENRYK ROMAN GULBINOWICZ, 50-328 Wrocław, ul. Katedralna 13, Kuria Metropolitalna; tel. (71) 3271111; fax (71) 3228269; e-mail kuri@archidiecezja.wroc.pl.

Byzantine-Ukrainian Rite

Archbishop of Przemyśl-Warsaw: Most Rev. IVAN MARTYNIAK, 37-700 Przemyśl, ul. Basztowa 13; tel. and fax (16) 6787868.

Old Catholic Churches

Mariavite Catholic Church in Poland (Kościół Katolicki Mariawitów w RP): Felicjanów, 09-470 Bodzanów, k. Płocka; tel. (24) 2607010; f. 1893; 2,470 mems (2002); Archbishop JÓZEF M. RAFAEL WOJCIECHOWSKI.

Old Catholic Mariavite Church (Kościół Starokatolicki Mariawitów): 09-400 Płock, ul. Wielkiego 27; tel. and fax (24) 2623086; f. 1906; 25,250 mems (1992); Chief Bishop ZDZISŁAW WŁODZIMIERZ JAWORSKI.

Polish Catholic Church in Poland (Kościół Polskokatolicki w RP): 02-635 Warsaw, ul. Balonowa 7; tel. (22) 8484617; f. 1920; 52,400 mems (1995); Prime Bishop Most Rev. WIKTOR WYSOCZAŃSKI.

The Orthodox Church

Polish Autocephalous Orthodox Church (Polski Autokefaliczny Kościół Prawosławny): 03-402 Warsaw, Al. Solidarności 52; tel. (22) 6190886; 870,600 mems (1989); Archbishop of Warsaw and Metropolitan of All Poland SAWA (MICHAŁ HRYCUNIAK); Archbishop of Łódź and Poznań SZYMON (SZYMON ROMAŃCZUK); Archbishop of Przemyśl and Nowy Sącz ADAM (ALEKSANDER DUBEC); Archbishop of Wrocław and Szczecin JEREMIASZ (JAN ANCHIMIUK); Archbishop of Lublin and Chełm ABEL (ANDRZEJ POPŁAWSKI); Bishop of Białystok and Gdańsk JAKUB (JAKUB KOSTIUCZUK); Bishop of Hajnówka MIRON (MIROSŁAW CHODAKOWSKI); Bishop of Bielsk Podlaski GRZEGORZ (JERZY CHARKIEWICZ).

Protestant Churches

In 1999 there were an estimated 148,738 Protestants in Poland.

Baptist Union of Poland (Kościół Chrześcijan Baptystów w RP): 00-865 Warsaw, ul. Waliców 25; tel. and fax (22) 6242783; e-mail baptist@hsn.com.pl; f. 1844; 4,000 baptized mems; Pres. Rev. Dr GRZEGORZ BEDNARCZYK; Gen. Sec. RYSZARD GUTKOWSKI.

Evangelical Augsburg(Lutheran) Church in Poland (Kościół Ewangelicko-Augsburski w RP): 00-246 Warsaw, ul. Miodowa 21; tel. (22) 8870200; fax (22) 8870218; e-mail biskup@luteranie.pl; internet www.luteranie.pl; 87,000 mems, 132 parishes (2002); Bishop and Pres. of Consistory JANUSZ JAGUCKI.

Evangelical-Reformed Church (Kościół Ewangelicko-Reformowany): 00-145 Warsaw, Al. Solidarności 76A ; tel. (22) 8314522; fax (22) 8310827; e-mail reformanda@wp.pl; f. 16th century; 4,500 mems (1996); Bishop MAREK IZDEBSKI; Pres. of the Consistory WITOLD BRODZINSKI.

Pentecostal Church (Kościół Zielonoświątkowy): 00-825 Warsaw, ul. Sienna 68/70; tel. (22) 6248575; fax (22) 6204073; e-mail nrk@kz.pl; f. 1910; 20,000 mems (2000); Pres. Bishop MIECZYSŁAW CZAJKO.

Seventh-day Adventist Church in Poland (Kościół Adwentystów Dnia Siódmego): 00-366 Warsaw, ul. Foksal 8; tel. (22) 8277611; fax (22) 8278619; f. 1921; 10,024 mems, 81 preachers (1997); Pres. WŁADYSŁAW POLOK; Sec. ANDRZEJ SICINSKI.

United Methodist Church (Kościół Ewangelicko-Metodystyczny w RP): 00-561 Warsaw, ul. Mokotowska 12; tel. and fax (22) 6285328; e-mail tep@elc.com.pl; internet www.kem.com.pl; f. 1921; 5,000 mems; Gen. Supt/Bishop Rev. Dr EDWARD PUŚLECKI.

There are also several other small Protestant churches, including the Church of Christ, the Church of Evangelical Christians, the Evangelical Christian Church and the Jehovah's Witnesses.

ISLAM

In 1999 there were about 5,125 Muslims of Tartar origin in Białystok Province (eastern Poland), and smaller communities in Warsaw, Gdańsk and elsewhere.

Religious Union of Muslims in Poland (Muzułmański Związek Religijny): 15-426 Białystok, Rynek Kosciuszki 26, m. 2; tel. (85) 414970; Chair. STEFAN MUCHARSKI.

JUDAISM

Union of Jewish Communities in Poland (Związek Gmin Wyznaniowych Żydowskich w Rzeczypospolitej Polskiej): 00-950 Warsaw, ul. Twarda 6; tel. (22) 6204324; fax (22) 6201037; 14 synagogues and about 2,500 registered mems; Pres. PAWEŁ WILDSTEIN.

The Press

Legislation to permit the formal abolition of censorship and to guarantee freedom of expression was approved in April 1990. In 1999 there were 46 daily newspapers in Poland, with a total circulation of 3,870,000. A total of 71 daily and non-daily newspapers were published in 2000, with a total circulation of 4,566,000. In that year there were 5,314 periodicals, with a combined circulation of 68.4m. copies.

PRINCIPAL DAILIES

Białystok

Gazeta Współczesna (Contemporary Daily): 15-950 Białystok, POB 193, ul. Suraska 1; tel. (85) 420935; f. 1951; Editor JERZY KOSTRZEWSKI; circ. 35,000.

Bydgoszcz

Gazeta Pomorska: Bydgoszcz; tel. (52) 221928; fax (52) 221542; f. 1948; local independent newspaper for the provinces of Bydgoszcz,

Toruń and Włocławek; Editor MACIEJ KAMIŃSKI; circ. 100,000 (weekdays), 300,000 (weekends).

Gdańsk

Dziennik Bałtycki (Baltic Newspaper): 80-886 Gdańsk, Targ Drzewny 3/7; tel. (58) 3012651; fax (58) 3013560; f. 1945; non-party; Editor KRZYSZTOF KRUPA; circ. 180,000.

Głos Wybrzeża: Gdańsk; tel. (58) 3011572; f. 1991; Editor-in-Chief MAREK FORMOLA; circ. 50,000.

Katowice

Dziennik Zachodni: 40-950 Katowice, ul. Młyńska 1; tel. (32) 1539084; fax (32) 1538196; e-mail dziennik@dz.com.pl; internet www.dz.com.pl; f. 1945; non-party; Chief Editor MAREK CHYLIŃSKI; circ. 510,000.

Trybuna Śląska (Silesian Tribune): 40-098 Katowice, ul. Młyńska 1; tel. (32) 2537822; fax (32) 2537997; e-mail tsl@trybuna-slaska.com .pl; internet www.trybuna-slaska.com.pl; f. 1945; fmrly Trybuna Robotnicza; independent; Editor ROMUALD ORZET; circ. 180,000 (weekdays), 800,000 (weekends).

Kielce

Słowo Ludu (Word of the People): 25-363 Kielce, ul. Wesoła 47/49; tel. (41) 3442480; fax (41) 3446979; e-mail redakcja@slowoludu.com .pl; internet www.slowoludu.com.pl; f. 1949; independent; Editor GRZEGORZ ŚCIWIARSKI; circ. 50,000 (weekdays), 130,000 (weekends).

Koszalin

Głos Pomorza (Voice of Pomerania): 75-604 Koszalin, ul. Zwycięstwa 137/139; tel. (94) 422693; fax (94) 423309; f. 1952; Editor-in-Chief WIESŁAW WIŚNIEWSKI; circ. 60,000 (weekdays), 130,000 (weekends).

Kraków

Czas Krakowski (Cracow Time): Kraków; tel. (12) 4225355; fax (12) 4217502; f. 1848; reactivated 1990; independent; Editor JAN POLKOWSKI; circ. 150,000 (weekdays), 260,000 (weekends).

Dziennik Polski: 31-072 Kraków, ul. Wielopole 1; tel. (12) 6199200; fax (12) 6199276; e-mail redakcja@dziennik.krakow.pl; internet www.dziennik.krakow.pl; Editor PIOTR ALEKSANDROWICZ.

Echo Krakowa: Kraków; tel. (12) 4224678; f. 1946; independent; evening; Editor WITOLD GRZYBOWSKI; circ. 60,000 (weekdays), 90,000 (weekends).

Gazeta Krakowska: Kraków; tel. (12) 4220985; fax (12) 4221563; f. 1949; Editor-in-Chief JERZY SADECKI; circ. 60,000 (weekdays), 150,000 (weekends).

Łódź

Dziennik Łódzki: 90-532 Łódź, ul. ks. Skorupki 17/19; tel. (42) 6303565; fax (42) 6377364; e-mail dziennik@dziennik.lodz.pl; internet www.dziennik.lodz.pl; f. 1945; non-party; Editor JULIAN BECK; circ. 50,000 (weekdays), 110,000 (weekends).

Lublin

Dziennik Lubelski: 20-601 Lublin, ul. Zana 38c ; tel. (81) 558000; f. 1990; fmrly Sztandar Ludu; Editor ALOJZY LESZEK GZELLA; circ. 45,000 (weekdays), 210,000 (weekends).

Dziennik Wschodni: 20-081 Lublin, ul. Staszica 20; tel. (81) 5340600; fax (81) 5340601; e-mail redakcja@dw.lublin.pl; internet www.dw.lublin.pl; Editor STANISŁAW SOWA.

Kurier Lubelski: 20-950 Lublin, POB 176; tel. (81) 5326634; fax (81) 5326835; e-mail redakcja@kurierlubelski.pl; internet www .kurier.lublin.pl; f. 1830; independent; evening; Editor PAWEŁ CHROMCEWICZ; circ. 40,000 (weekdays), 100,000 (weekends).

Olsztyn

Gazeta Olsztyńska (Olsztyn Gazette): 10-417 Olsztyn, ul. Towarowa 2; tel. (889) 330277; fax (889) 332691; f. 1886; renamed 1970; independent; Editor-in-Chief TOMASZ SRUTKOWSKI; circ. 45,000 (weekdays), 90,000 (weekends).

Opole

Nowa Trybuna Opolska: 45-086 Opole, ul. Powstańców Śląskich 9; tel. (77) 4567041; fax (77) 4543737; e-mail nto@nto.com.pl; internet www.nto.com.pl; f. 1952; independent; Editor WOJCIECH POTOCKI; circ. 80,000.

Poznań

Gazeta Poznańska: 60-782 Poznań, ul. Grunwaldzka 19; tel. (61) 8665568; e-mail gp@gp.pl; internet www.gp.pl; f. 1991; part of the Polskapresse group; Editor JAROSŁAW GOJTOWSKI; circ. 80,000 (weekdays), 320,000 (weekends).

Głos Wielkopolski (Voice of Wielkopolska): 60-959 Poznań, ul. Grunwaldzka 19; tel. (61) 8694100; fax (61) 8659672; e-mail glosmar@sylaba.poznan.pl; internet www.glos.com; f. 1945; independent; Editor-in-Chief MAREK PRZYBYLSKI; circ. 110,000 (weekdays), 160,000 (weekends).

Rzeszów

Gazeta Codzienna 'Nowiny': 35-959 Rzeszów, ul. Unii Lubelskiej 3; tel. (17) 628471; fax (17) 628836; f. 1949; evening; Editor JAN MUSIAŁ; circ. 100,000.

Szczecin

Głos Szczeciński (Voice of Szczecin): 70-550 Szczecin, Pl. Hołdu Pruskiego 8; tel. (91) 4341306; fax (91) 4345472; e-mail glos@dragon .com.pl; internet www.glosszczecinski.com.pl; f. 1947; Editor-in-Chief ROBERT CIEŚLAK; circ. 30,000 (weekdays), 100,000 (weekends).

Kurier Szczeciński: 70-550 Szczecin, Pl. Hołdu Pruskiego 8; tel. and fax (91) 4345741; e-mail redakcja@kurier.szczecin.pl; internet www.kurier.szczecin.pl; Editor ANDRZEJ ŁAPCIEWICZ.

Warsaw

Express Wieczorny (Evening Express): 02-017 Warsaw, Al. Jerozolimskie 125/127; tel. (22) 6285231; fax (22) 6284929; f. 1946; non-party; Editor ANDRZEJ URBAŃSKI; circ. 140,000 (weekdays), 400,000 (weekends).

Gazeta Wyborcza: 00-732 Warsaw, ul. Czerska 8/10; tel. (22) 415513; fax (22) 416920; e-mail listy@gazeta.pl; internet wyborcza .gazeta.pl; f. 1989; non-party; national edn and 20 local edns; weekend edn: Gazeta Świateczna; special supplements; Editor-in-Chief ADAM MICHNIK; circ. 516,000 (daily); 686,000 (weekends).

Kurier Polski: 00-018 Warsaw, ul. Zgoda 11; tel. (22) 8278081; fax (22) 8270552; e-mail kpkurier@kurier.pl; f. 1729; Editor BOŻENA SKUPIŃSKA; circ. 150,000 (weekdays), 190,000 (weekends).

Nasz Dziennik (Our Newspaper): 04-476 Warsaw, ul. Żeligowskiego 16/20; tel. (22) 6734819; fax (22) 6734817; e-mail redakcja@ naszdziennik.pl; internet www.naszdziennik.pl; national; Editor EWA SOŁOWIEJ; circ. 250,000.

Nowa Europa: Warsaw; tel. (22) 6200966; fax (22) 6209145; Editorial Dir ANDRZEJ WROBLEWSKI.

Polska Zbrojna: 00-950 Warsaw, ul. Grzybowska 77; tel. (22) 6204293; fax (22) 6242273; f. 1943; fmrly Żolnierz Wolności, name changed 1990; Editor JERZY ŚLĄSKI; circ. 50,000.

Przegląd Sportowy (Sports Review): 02-017 Warsaw, Al. Jerozolimskie 125/127, POB 181; tel. (22) 6289116; fax (22) 218697; f. 1921; Editor MACIEJ POLKOWSKI; circ. 110,000.

Rzeczpospolita (The Republic): 02-015 Warsaw, Pl. Starynkiewicza 7; tel. (22) 6283401; fax (22) 6280588; e-mail p .aleksandrowicz@rzeczpospolita.pl; internet www.rzeczpospolita.pl; f. 1982; 51% owned by Orkla (Norway); Editor-in-Chief MACIEJ LUKASIEWICZ; circ. 275,000.

Super Express: 00-939 Warsaw, ul. Jubilerska 10; tel. (22) 5159000; fax (22) 5159010; e-mail listy@superexpress.com.pl; internet www.se.com.pl; f. 1991; Pres. and Chief Exec. IZABELLA JABLONSKA; Editor-in-Chief EWA JAROSŁAWSKA; circ. 371,106.

Trybuna: 00-835 Warsaw, ul. Miedziana 11; tel. (22) 6253015; fax (22) 6204100; e-mail redakcja@trybuna.com.pl; f. 1990; fmrly Trybuna Ludu; organ of Social Democracy of the Republic of Poland; Editor-in-Chief ANDRZEJ URBAŃCZYK; circ. 110,000 (weekdays), 150,000 (weekends).

Wprost: 02-017 Warsaw, Al. Jerozolimskie 123, Reform Plaza; tel. (22) 5291100; fax (22) 8529016; e-mail redakcja@wprost.pl; internet www.wprost.pl; Editor MAREK KRÓL.

Życie Warszawy (Warsaw Life): Warsaw; tel. (22) 6256990; fax (22) 6226031; e-mail zycie@zw.com.pl; internet www.zw.com.pl; f. 1944; independent; Editor-in-Chief ANDRZEJ BOBER; circ. 250,000 (weekdays), 460,000 (weekends).

Wrocław

Gazeta Robotnicza: 50-010 Wrocław, ul. Podwale 62; tel. (71) 335756; fax (71) 335756; f. 1948; Editor ANDRZEJ BUŁAT; circ. 30,000 (weekdays), 315,000 (weekends).

Gazeta Wrocławska: Wrocław; e-mail redakcja@gazeta.wroc.pl; internet www.gazeta.wroc.pl; part of the Polskapresse group; circ. 48,600.

Zielona Góra

Gazeta Lubuska: 65-042 Zielona Góra, POB 120, Al. Niepodległości 25; tel. (68) 3254661; fax (68) 3253555; e-mail redakcja@gazetalubuska.pl; internet www.gazetalubuska.pl; f. 1952; independent; Editor MIROSŁAW RATAJ; circ. 60,000 (weekdays), 150,000 (weekends).

PERIODICALS

Computerworld Poland: 04-228 Warsaw, ul. Tytoniowa 10; tel. (22) 121390; fax (22) 154495; internet www.comnet.com.pl/cw; weekly; information technology; circ. 14,400.

Le Courrier de Varsovie: Warsaw; internet www .courrierdevarsovie.pl; daily, monthly; in French; Dir JAN KRAUZE.

Dom i Wnętrze (House and Interior): Warsaw; tel. (22) 6211038; fax (22) 6211030; e-mail ipaco@domiwnetrze.com.pl; f. 1991; illustrated monthly; Editor WIESŁAW KEDZIERSKI.

Dziecko (Child): 02-651 Warsaw, ul. Garażowa 7; tel. (22) 6077700; fax (22) 6077704; e-mail dziecko@proszynski.com.pl; f. 1995; monthly; women's magazine concerning children's affairs; Editor JUSTYNA DĄBROWSKI; circ. 95,000.

Dziewczyna (Girl): Warsaw; tel. (22) 6363681; fax (22) 6365281; e-mail mpc@saxon.pip.com.pl; f. 1990; monthly; lifestyle magazine for young women; Editor AGNIESZKA LESIAK; circ. 420,000.

Elle: 02-119 Warsaw, ul. Pruszkowska 17; tel. (22) 6689083; fax (22) 6689183; e-mail elle@elle.com.pl; f. 1994; monthly; women's fashion; Editor-in-Chief MARZENA WILKANOWICZ DEVOUD; circ. 190,000 (1998).

Filipinka: Warsaw; tel. (22) 312221; f. 1957; fortnightly; illustrated for teenage girls; Editor HANNA JAWOROWSKA-BŁOŃSKA; circ. 125,600.

Film: Warsaw; tel. (22) 455325; fax (22) 454651; f. 1946; monthly; illustrated magazine; Editor-in-Chief LECH KURPIEWSKI; circ. 105,000.

Forum: 00-656 Warsaw, ul. Śniadeckich 10; tel. (22) 6289503; fax (22) 6256150; f. 1965; weekly; political, social, cultural and economic; Editor-in-Chief BOGDAN HERBICH; circ. 33,000.

Gazeta Bankowa: Warsaw; tel. (22) 6287272; fax (22) 6212653; e-mail bankowa@ikp.atm.com.pl; internet www.bankowa.com.pl; f. 1988; weekly; business and finance; Editor-in-Chief ADA KOSTRZ-KOSTECKA; circ. 35,000.

Gazeta Targowa: 61-707 Poznań, ul. Libelta; tel. (61) 8528582; fax (61) 8526108; e-mail gazetarg@soho.online.com; finance; Editor-in-Chief SAWOMIR ERKIERT.

Głos Nauczycielski (Teachers' Voice): 00-389 Warsaw, ul. Smulikowskiego 6/8; tel. (22) 276630; fax (22) 276630; f. 1917; weekly; organ of the Polish Teachers' Union; Editor WOJCIECH SIERAKOWSKI; circ. 40,000.

Gromada-Rolnik Polski: Warsaw; tel. (22) 278815; fax (22) 278815; f. 1951; 3 a week; agricultural; Editor ZBIGNIEW LUBAK; circ. 281,800.

Kobieta i Życie (Woman and Life): Warsaw; tel. and fax (22) 6283030; f. 1946; weekly; women's; Editor ZOFIA KAMIŃSKA; circ. 400,000.

Lubie Gotować (I Love Cooking): 02-651 Warsaw, ul. Garażowa 7; tel. (22) 6077620; fax (22) 6461270; e-mail kuchnia@proszynski.com.pl; internet www.proszynski.com.pl; f. 1988; monthly; cookery; Editor HANNA GRYKALOWSKA; circ. 202,727.

Nie (No): 00-789 Warsaw, ul. Słoneczna 25; tel. (22) 8484420; fax (22) 8497258; e-mail nie@redakija.nie.com.pl; internet www.nie.com.pl; f. 1990; satirical weekly; Editor JERZY URBAN; circ. 500,000.

Nie z tej Ziemi (Out of this World): Warsaw; tel. (22) 241485; fax (22) 241481; f. 1990; monthly; para-science, ghost stories, etc. Editor TADEUSZ LACHOWICZ; circ. 150,000.

Nowa Fantastyka: 00-640 Warsaw, ul. Mokotowska 5/6; tel. (22) 8253475; fax (22) 8252089; f. 1982; monthly; science fiction and fantasy; Editor MACIEJ PAROWSKI; circ. 57,000.

Nowa Wieś: Warsaw; tel. and fax (22) 6284583; f. 1948; weekly; illustrated peasant magazine; Editor KAZIMIERZ DŁUGOSZ; circ. 60,000.

Panorama: 40-082 Katowice, ul. Sobieskiego 11; tel. (3) 1538595; fax (3) 1538374; f. 1960; weekly; socio-cultural magazine; Editor ADAM JAZWIECKI; circ. 150,000.

Państwo i Prawo (State and Law): 00-330 Warsaw, ul. Nowy Świat 72; tel. (22) 6288296; f. 1946; monthly organ of the Polish Academy of Sciences; Editor Dr LESZEK KUBICKI; circ. 3,000.

Polityka (Politics): 00-835 Warsaw, ul. Miedziana 11, POB 86; tel. (22) 6353491; fax (22) 6351797; e-mail polityka@polityka.com.pl; internet polityka.onet.pl; f. 1957; weekly; political, economic, cultural; Editor JERZY BACZYŃSKI; circ. 340,000.

Poradnik Gospodarski (Farmers' Guide): 60-837 Poznań, ul. A. Mickiewicza 33; tel. and fax (61) 8476001; f. 1889; monthly; agriculture; Editor-in-Chief WAWRZYNIEC TRAWIŃSKI; circ. 10,000.

Prawo i Gospodarka: Warsaw; tel. (22) 6727961; fax (22) 6727976; e-mail z.maciag@pg.com.pl; internet www.seonet.pl; Editor ZBIGNIEW MACIĄG.

Przegląd Tygodniowy (Weekly Review): Warsaw; tel. (22) 6207290; fax (22) 6544711; e-mail przegtyg@medianet.pl; internet www.przeglad-tygodniowy.pl; f. 1981; weekly; political, economic, social, historical, cultural, scientific and artistic; Editor-in-Chief JERZY DOMAŃSKI; circ. 150,000.

Przekrój (Review): 00-490 Warsaw, ul. Wiejska 16; tel. (22) 6272306; fax (22) 6272305; e-mail nowy.przekroj@edipresse.pl; f. 1945; weekly; illustrated; cultural; Editor-in-Chief JACEK RAKOWIECKI; circ. 77,500.

Przyjaciółka (Friend): 00-490 Warsaw, ul. Wiejska 16; tel. (22) 6280583; fax (22) 6285866; f. 1948; weekly; women's magazine; Editor EWA NIEZBECKA; circ. 720,000.

Res Publica Nowa: 00-950 Warsaw 1, POB 856, ul. Smolna 12; tel. (22) 263047; fax (22) 262329; f. 1987; monthly; political and cultural; Editor MARCIN KRÓL; circ. 5,000.

Sport: 40-082 Katowice, ul. Sobieskiego 11, POB 339; tel. (3) 1539995; fax (3) 1537138; f. 1945; 5 a week; Editor ADAM BARTECZKO; circ. 135,000.

Spotkania (Meetings): Warsaw; tel. (22) 399022; fax (22) 241423; f. 1990; weekly; illustrated; political, social, economic, cultural and scientific magazine; Editor MACIEJ IŁOWIECKI; circ. 80,000.

Sprawy Międzynarodowe (International Affairs): 00-950 Warsaw, ul. Warecka 1A ; tel. (22) 5239086; fax (22) 5239027; e-mail warecka@qdnet.pl; internet www.qdnet.pl/warecka; f. 1948; quarterly; published by the Polish Foundation of International Affairs; also English edition, *The Polish Quarterly of International Affairs* (f. 1992); Editor HENRYK SZLAJFER; circ. 900.

Swiat Nauki (World of Science and Technology): 02-651 Warsaw, ul. Garażowa 7; tel. (22) 6077640; fax (22) 6077645; e-mail swiatnauki@proszynski.com.pl; internet www.proszynski.com.pl/swiatnauki; f. 1991; monthly; Editor-in-Chief JOANNA ŻIMAKOWSKA.

Szpilki: Warsaw; tel. (22) 6280429; f. 1935; weekly; illustrated satirical; Editor JACEK JANCZARSKI; circ. 100,000.

Teatr: 03-902 Warsaw, ul. Jakubowska 14; tel. (22) 6175594; fax (22) 6174298; f. 1945; monthly; illustrated; theatrical life; Editor JANUSZ MAJCHEREK; circ. 4,000.

Tygodnik Gospodarczy (Economic Weekly): 00-511 Warsaw, ul. Nowogrodzka 31; tel. (22) 6280593; fax (22) 6299614; e-mail redakcja@tygodnikgospodarczy.pl; internet www.waw.pdi.net/sigma/; f. 1991; weekly; international business and economics; Publr TADEUSZ JACEWICZ; circ. 52,000.

Tygodnik Solidarność: Warsaw; tel. (22) 6352037; fax (22) 317858; f. 1981; reactivated 1989; weekly; Editor ANDRZEJ GELBREG; circ. 60,000.

The Warsaw Voice: 00-950 Warsaw, POB 28; tel. (22) 8375138; fax (22) 8371995; e-mail voice@warsawvoice.com.pl; internet www .warsawvoice.com.pl; f. 1988; weekly; economic, political, social, cultural and economic; in English; Editor ANDRZEJ JONAS; Gen. Dir JULIUSZ KŁOSOWSKI; circ. 15,000.

Wiedza i Życie (Knowledge and Life): 02-651 Warsaw, ul. Garażowa 7; tel. (22) 6077630; fax (22) 6077645; e-mail wiedza@proszynski.com.pl; internet www.proszynski.com.pl/wiedzaizycie; f. 1926; monthly; popular science; Editor ANDRZEJ GORZYM; circ. 112,000.

Żołnierz Polski (Polish Soldier): 00-800 Warsaw, ul. Grzybowska 77; tel. (22) 204286; fax (22) 202127; f. 1945; monthly; illustrated magazine primarily about the armed forces; Editor IRENEUSZ CZYŻEWSKI; circ. 40,000.

Życie Gospodarcze (Economic Life): Warsaw; tel. (22) 6289493; fax (22) 6210034; f. 1945; weekly; economic; Editor STANISŁAW CHETSTOWSKI; circ. 35,700.

NEWS AGENCIES

Polska Agencja Informacyjna (PAI) (Polish Information Agency): 04-028 Warsaw, Al. Stanów Zjednoczonych 53; tel. (22) 134605; fax (22) 134924; f. 1967; bulletins and news services on Polish culture, foreign policy and economics; Editor-in-Chief JAN FOROWICZ.

Polska Agencja Prasowa (PAP) (Polish Press Agency): 00-950 Warsaw, Al. Jerozolimskie 7; tel. (22) 6280001; fax (22) 6286407; e-mail webmaster@pap.com.pl; internet www.pap.com.pl; f. 1944; brs in 28 Polish towns and 22 foreign capitals; 274 journalist and photojournalist mems; information is transmitted abroad in English only; Pres. ROBERT BOGDAŃSKI; Vice-Pres. PIOTR CIOMPA.

Foreign Bureaux

Agence France-Presse (AFP): 00-582 Warsaw, Al. Szucha 16, m. 34; tel. (22) 6272409; fax (22) 6223499; e-mail afpwaw@pol.pl; Correspondent PIERRE-ANTOINE DONNET.

Agencia EFE (Spain): 00-656 Warsaw, ul. Śniadeckich 18, Lokal 16; tel. (22) 6282567; fax (22) 6215989; Bureau Chief JORGE RUIZ LARDIZÁBAL.

Agenzia Nazionale Stampa Associata (ANSA) (Italy): 00-672 Warsaw, ul. Piękna 68, p. 301; tel. (22) 298413; fax (22) 299843; Bureau Chief MAURIZIO SALVI.

Associated Press (AP) (USA): 00-433 Warsaw, ul. Profesorska 4; tel. (22) 6287231; fax (22) 6295240; internet www.ap.org; Correspondent ANDRZEJ STYLIŃSKI.

Bulgarska Telegrafna Agentsia (BTA) (Bulgaria): Warsaw; tel. (22) 278059; Correspondent WESELIN JANKOW.

Česká tisková kancelář (ČTK) (Czech News Agency): 03-946 Warsaw, ul. Brazylioska 14A/9; tel. and fax (22) 6728780; e-mail ctk@ctk.if.pl; Correspondent JAN MELICHAR.

Deutsche-Presse Agentur (dpa) (Germany): 03-968 Warsaw, ul. Saska 7A; tel. (22) 6171058; fax (22) 6178481; Correspondent DANIEL BRÖSSLER.

Informatsionnoye Telegrafnoye Agentstvo Rossii—Telegrafnoye Agentstvo Suverennykh Stran (ITAR—TASS) (Russia): Warsaw; tel. (22) 292192; fax (22) 296131; Correspondent ALEKSANDR L. POTEMKIN.

Kyodo News Service (Japan): 05-220 Warsaw, Zielonka Prosta 14; tel. and fax (22) 7810246; Chief JUN IWAWAKI.

Magyar Távirati Iroda Rt. (MTI) (Hungary): 02-954 Warsaw, ul. Jakuba Kubickiego 19, m. 11; tel. (22) 6517675; e-mail pkovacs@ipgate.pl; Correspondent PÉTER KOVÁCS.

Reuters (United Kingdom): 00-854 Warsaw, Al. Jana Pawła II 23; tel. (22) 6539700; fax (22) 6539780; internet www.reuters.com.pl; Correspondent ANTHONY BARKER.

Rossiiskoye Informatsionnoye Agentstvo—Novosti (RIA—Novosti) (Russia): Warsaw; tel. (22) 6283092; 6 correspondents.

Tlačová agentúra Slovenskej republiky (TASR) (Slovakia): Warsaw; tel. and fax (22) 6780399; Correspondent IGOR RABATIN.

Xinhua (New China) News Agency (People's Republic of China): 00-203 Warsaw, ul. Bonifraterska 1; tel. (22) 313876; Correspondents TANG DEQIAO, DONG FUSHENG, SCHAO JIN.

PRESS ASSOCIATION

Stowarzyszenie Dziennikarzy Polskich (SDP) (Polish Journalists' Association): 00-366 Warsaw, ul. Foksal 3/5; tel. and fax (22) 8278720; f. 1951; dissolved 1982, legal status restored 1989; 2,320 mems; Pres. KRYSTYNA MOKROSIŃSKA; Vice-Pres. ANDRZEJ KRAJEWSKI; Gen. Sec. J. MARCIN MAKOWIECKI.

Publishers

Bertelsmann Media Sp. z o.o.: 02-786 Warsaw, ul. Rosoła 10; tel. (22) 6458200; fax (22) 6484732; e-mail poczta@swiatksiazki.com.pl; internet www.swiatksiazki.com.pl; f. 1994 as Bertelsmann Publishing Świat Książki Sp. z o.o. belles-lettres, science-fiction, popular science, albums, books for children and teenagers; Pres. ANDRZEJ KOSTARCZYK; Editor-in-Chief BOGUSŁAW DĄBROWSKI.

Dom Wydawniczy ABC Sp. z o.o.: 01-231 Warsaw, ul. Płocka 5A; tel. (22) 5358000; fax (22) 5358001; e-mail info@abc.com.pl; internet www.abc.com.pl; f. 1989; legal, business and financial books; part of Polskie Wydawnictwa Profesjonalne Sp. z o.o. owned by Wolters Kluwer (Netherlands); Owners WŁODZIMIERZ ALBIN, KRZYSZTOF BRZESKI.

Dom Wydawniczy Bellona: 00-844 Warsaw, ul. Grzybowska 77; tel. (22) 6204291; fax (22) 6522695; e-mail bellona@bellona.pl; f. 1947; fiction, history and military; Dir ZBIGNIEW CZERWIŃSKI; Pres. Col JÓZEF SKRZYPIEC.

Dom Wydawniczy Rebis Sp. z o.o.: 60-171 Poznań, ul. Żmigrodzka 41/49; tel. (61) 8678140; fax (61) 8673774; e-mail rebis@rebis.com.pl; internet www.rebis.com.pl; f. 1990; psychology, self-help books and parental guides; Pres. and Man. Dir TOMASZ SZPONDER.

Drukarnia i Księgarnia św. Wojciecha (St Adalbert Printing and Publishing Co): 60-967 Poznań, Pl. Wolności 1; tel. (61) 8529186; fax (61) 8523746; e-mail wydawnictwo.ksw@archpoznan.org.pl; f. 1895;

textbooks and Catholic publications; Dir Rev. BOGDAN REFORMAT; Editor-in-Chief BOŻYSŁAW WALCZAK.

Egmont Sp. z o.o.: 00-810 Warsaw, ul. Srebrna 16; tel. (22) 6255005; fax (22) 6252949; f. 1990; books and comics for children and teenagers; Dir JACEK BEŁDOWSKI; Editor-in-Chief HANNA BALTYN.

Instytut Wydawniczy Pax (Pax Publishing Institute): 00-390 Warsaw, Wybrzeże Kościuszkowskie 21A; tel. (22) 6253398; fax (22) 6251378; e-mail iwpax@it.com.pl; internet www.iwpax.com.pl; f. 1949; theology, philosophy, religion, history, literature; Man. Dir JACEK KRZEKOTOWSKI; Editor-in-Chief KAROL KLAUZA.

Ludowa Spółdzielnia Wydawnicza (People's Publishing Co-operative): 00-131 Warsaw, ul. Grzybowska 4/8; tel. (22) 6205718; fax (22) 6207277; f. 1949; fiction, poetry and popular science; Chair. and Editor-in-Chief JAN RODZIM.

Muza SA: 00-590 Warsaw, ul. Marszałkowska 8; tel. (22) 6211776; fax (22) 6292349; e-mail muza@muza.com.pl; f. 1991; albums, encyclopedias, lexicons, handbooks, dictionaries, belles-lettres, books for children and youth; Man. Dir MARCIN GARLINSKI.

Niezależna Oficyna Wydawnicza NOWA (Independent Publishing House NOWA): 00-251 Warsaw, ul. Miodowa 10; tel. and fax (22) 6359994; f. 1972; belles-lettres, memoirs, essays, recent history, politics; Pres. GRZEGORZ BOGUTA; Editor-in-Chief MIROSŁAW KOWALSKI.

Oficyna Literacka: Kraków; tel. (12) 4117365; f. 1982; clandestinely, 1990 officially; belles-lettres, poetry, including débuts, essays; Editor-in-Chief HENRYK KARKOSZA.

Oficyna Wydawnicza Volumen: Warsaw; tel. and fax (22) 6357557; f. 1984 (working clandestinely as WERS), 1989 officially; science, popular history, anthropology and socio-political sciences; Dir ADAM BOROWSKI.

Pallottinum—Wydawnictwo Stowarzyszenia Apostolstwa Katolickiego: 60-959 Poznań, Al. Przybyszewskiego 30, POB 23; tel. (61) 8675233; fax (61) 8675238; e-mail pallottinum@pallottinum.pl; internet www.pallottinum.pl; f. 1947; religious and philosophical books; Dir Mgr STEFAN DUSZA.

Państwowe Wydawnictwo Rolnicze i Leśne (State Agricultural and Forestry Publishers): 00-950 Warsaw, Al. Jerozolimskie 28; tel. and fax (22) 8276338; f. 1947; professional publications on agriculture, forestry, health and veterinary science; Dir and Editor-in-Chief JOLANTA KUCZYŃSKA.

Państwowy Instytut Wydawniczy (State Publishing Institute): 00-372 Warsaw, ul. Foksal 17; tel. (22) 8260201; fax (22) 8261536; e-mail piw@piw.pl; internet www.piw.pl; f. 1946; Polish and foreign classical and contemporary literature, fiction, literary criticism, biographies, performing arts, culture, history, popular science and fine arts; Dir and Editor-in-Chief TADEUSZ NOWAKOWSKI.

Polskie Przedsiębiorstwo Wydawnictw Kartograficznych im. E. Romera SA (Romer Polish Cartographical Publishing House Co): 00-410 Warsaw, ul. Solec 18; tel. (22) 5851800; fax (22) 5851801; e-mail ppwk@ppwk.com.pl; internet www.ppwk.com.pl; f. 1951; maps, atlases, travel guides, books on geodesy and cartography; Man. Dir JACEK BŁASZCZYŃSKI.

Polskie Wydawnictwa Profesjonalne: 01-231 Warsaw, ul. Płocka 5A; tel. (22) 5358000; fax (22) 5358001; e-mail info@abc.com.pl; internet www.abc.com.pl; country's largest legal publisher, produces CD-rom databases and periodicals; online; Pres. ALBIN WŁODZIMIERZ.

Polskie Wydawnictwo Ekonomiczne SA (Polish Publishing House for Economic Literature): 00-099 Warsaw, ul. Canaletta 4; tel. (22) 8264182; fax (22) 8275567; e-mail pwe@pwe.com.pl; internet www.pwe.com.pl; f. 1949; economics books and magazines; Man. Dir ALICJA RUTKOWSKA; Editor MARIOLA ROMUS.

Polskie Wydawnictwo Muzyczne (Polish Publishing House for Music): 31-111 Kraków, Al. Krasińskiego 11A; tel. (12) 4227044; fax (12) 4220174; e-mail pwm@pwm.com.pl; internet www.pwm.com.pl; f. 1945; music and books on music; Man. Dir and Editor LESZEK POLONY.

Prószyński i S-ka: 02-651 Warsaw, ul. Garazowa 7; tel. (22) 6077700; fax (22) 8497317; e-mail ksiazki@proszynski.pl; internet www.proszynski.pl; f. 1990; poetry, fiction, non-fiction, educational text and reference books, popular science etc.;; 400 employees.

Spółdzielnia Wydawnicza Czytelnik (Reader Co-operative Publishing House): 00-490 Warsaw, ul. Wiejska 12A; tel. (22) 6289508; fax (22) 6283178; e-mail sekretariat@czytelnik.pl; internet www.czytelnik.pl; f. 1944; general, especially fiction and contemporary Polish literature; Pres. MAREK ŻAKOWSKI; Editor-in-Chief HENRYK CHŁYSTOWSKI.

Spółdzielnia Wydawniczo-Handlowa 'Książka i Wiedza' (Trade Co-operative Publishing House): 00-375 Warsaw, ul. Smolna 13; tel. (22) 8275401; fax (22) 8279423; e-mail publisher@kiw.com.pl;

internet www.kiw.com.pl; f. 1948; philosophy, religion, linguistics, literature and history; Dir STANISŁAW SOŁTYS; Editor MARIA ZWOLAK.

Wydawnictwa Artystyczne i Filmowe (Art and Film Publications): 02-595 Warsaw, ul. Puławska 61; tel. (22) 8455301; fax (22) 8455584; f. 1959; theatre, cinema, photography and art publications and reprints; Pres. and Dir JANUSZ FOGLER.

Wydawnictwa Komunikacji i Łączności (Transport and Communications Publishing House): 02-546 Warsaw, ul. Kazimierzowska 52; tel. (22) 8492314; fax (22) 8492322; e-mail wkl@wkl.com .pl; internet www.wkl.com.pl; f. 1949; technical books on motorization, electronics, radio engineering, television and telecommunications, road, rail and air transport; Dir JERZY KOZŁOWSKI; Editor-in-Chief BOGUMIŁ ZIELIŃSKI.

Wydawnictwa Naukowo-Techniczne (Scientific-Technical Publishers): 00-048 Warsaw, ul. Mazowiecka 2/4, POB 359; tel. (22) 8267271; fax (22) 8268293; e-mail wnt@pol.pl; internet www.wnt .com.pl; f. 1949; scientific and technical books on mathematics, physics, chemistry, foodstuffs industry, electrical and electronic engineering, computer science, automation, mechanical engineering, light industry; technological encyclopedias and dictionaries; Man. Dir and Editor Dr ANIELA TOPULOS.

Wydawnictwa Normalizacyjne ALFA-WERO (Standardization Publishing House): 01-067 Warsaw, ul. Piaskowa 6/8/10; tel. and fax (22) 6366925; f. 1956; standards, catalogues and reference books on standardization, periodicals, political and historical literature, science fiction, general; Man. Dir ANDRZEJ ŚWIĘCICKI; Editor MAREK NOWOWIEJSKI.

Wydawnictwa Polskiej Agencji Ekologicznej SA (Polish Ecological Publishing House): Warsaw; tel. (22) 8494927; fax (22) 8495081; e-mail ekologia@pae.com.pl; f. 1953; geology; Dir JERZY CHODKOWSKI.

Wydawnictwa Szkolne i Pedagogiczne (WSiP) (Polish Educational Publishers): 00-950 Warsaw, POB 480, Pl. Dąbrowskiego 8; tel. (22) 8265451; fax (22) 8279280; e-mail wsip@wsip.com.pl; internet www.wsip.com.pl; f. 1945; privatized in 1998; joint-stock co; school textbooks and popular science books, scientific literature for teachers, visual teaching aids, periodicals for teachers and youth; Chair. RAFAŁ GRUPIŃSKI.

Wydawnictwo Amber Sp. z o.o.: 00-108 Warsaw, ul. Zielna 39; tel. (22) 6204013; fax (22) 6201393; e-mail right@amber.supermedia.pl; reference books, fiction, biography and autobiography; Dir ZBIGNIEW FONIOK; Editor MAŁGORZATA CEBO-FONIOK.

Wydawnictwo Arkady: 00-959 Warsaw, ul. Dobra 28, POB 137; tel. (22) 8269316; fax (22) 8274194; e-mail arkady@arkady.com.pl; internet www.arkady.com.pl; f. 1957; publications on building, town planning, architecture and art; Dir and Pres. JANINA KRYSIAK.

Wydawnictwo Buffi: 43-300 Bielsko-Biała, ul. Poniatowskiego 6; tel. (33) 8146927; fax (33) 8149535; f. 1992; albums, calendars, postcards; Dir MAREK BUFFI.

Wydawnictwo C. H. Beck.: 01-518 Warsaw, ul. Gen. Zajączka 9; tel. (22) 3377600; fax (22) 3377601; e-mail redakcja@beck.pl; internet www.beck.pl; f. 1993; law and economics; Man. Dir PAWEŁ ESSE.

Wydawnictwo Czasopism i Książek Technicznych SIGMA NOT, Sp. z o.o. (Sigma Publishers of Technical Periodicals and Books, Ltd): 00-950 Warsaw, ul. Ratuszowa 11, POB 1004; tel. (22) 8180918; fax (22) 6192187; e-mail infor.sigma@pol.pl; internet www .pol.pl/sigma_not; f. 1949; popular and specialized periodicals and books on general technical subjects; Dir and Editor-in-Chief Dr ANDRZEJ KUSYK.

Wydawnictwo Dolnośląskie Sp. z o.o.: 50-206 Wrocław, ul. Strażnicza 1/3; tel. (71) 3288914; fax (71) 3288954; e-mail sekretariat@wd.wroc.pl; internet www.wd.wroc.pl; f. 1986; belles-lettres, essays, memoirs, translations, general non-fiction; Pres. of Bd ANDRZEJ ADAMUS.

Wydawnictwo Europa: 50-011 Wrocław, ul. Kościuszki 35; tel. (71) 3463010; fax (71) 3463015; e-mail europa@wydawnictwo-europa .pl; internet www.wydawnictwo-europa.pl; f. 1990; belles-lettres, non-fiction, educational publications, dictionaries, encyclopedias and atlases; Man. Dir and Editor WOJCIECH GŁUCH.

Wydawnictwo Gebethner: Warsaw; tel. (22) 8310113; fax (22) 8311417; f. 1990; publishes and distributes foreign language teaching material, imports scientific books; Pres. ZYGMUNT GEBETHNER.

Wydawnictwo Infor Sp. z o.o.: 01-938 Warsaw, ul. Wóycickiego 1/3; tel. (22) 7514400; fax (22) 7514411; f. 1987; law, economics, marketing, management; Pres. DARIUSZ PIEKARSKI.

Wydawnictwo Interpress Polskiej Agencji Informacyjnej SA (Polish Information Agency's Interpress Publishers): 00-585 Warsaw, ul. Bagatela 12; tel. (22) 6282818; fax (22) 6289331; f. 1968;

Poland past and present, handbooks, monographs, guide-books; publishing co-operation; Editor-in-Chief ANDRZEJ TUŁOWIECKI.

Wydawnictwo 'Iskry' Sp. z o.o. (Iskry Publishing House Ltd): 00-375 Warsaw, ul. Smolna 11; tel. and fax (22) 8279415; e-mail iskry@ polbox.pl; f. 1952; travel, Polish and foreign fiction, science fiction, essays, popular science, history, memoirs; Dir Dr WIESŁAW UCHAŃSKI; Editor KRZYSZTOF OBŁUCKI.

Wydawnictwo Kurpisz: 01-341 Poznań, ul. Przemysłwa 46; tel. (61) 8331517; f. 1991; belles-lettres, reprints, dictionaries, encyclopedias, periodicals; Dir KAZIMIERZ GRZESIAK.

Wydawnictwo Lekarskie PZWL Sp. z o.o. (Medical Publishers Ltd): 00-238 Warsaw, ul. Długa 38/40; tel. (22) 8312161; fax (22) 8310054; e-mail promocja@pzwl.pl; internet www.pzwl.pl; f. 1945; medical literature and manuals, lexicons, encyclopedias; Pres. ZOFIA ŻAKOWSKA.

Wydawnictwo Literackie (Literary Publishing House): 31-147 Kraków, ul. Długa 1; tel. (12) 4232254; fax (12) 4225423; e-mail redakcja@wl.net.pl; internet www.wl.net.pl; f. 1953; works of literature and belles-lettres; Dir BARBARA DRWOTA; Editor-in-Chief MAŁGORZTA NYCZ.

Wydawnictwo Nasza Księgarnia Sp. z o.o. (Nasza Księgarnia Publishing House Ltd): 02-868 Warsaw, ul. Sarabandy 24c; tel. (22) 6439389; fax (22) 6437028; e-mail naszaksiegarnia@nk.com.pl; f. 1921; books and periodicals for children and young readers; educational publications; Pres. AGNIESZKA TOKARCZYK; Editor JOLANTA SZTUCZYŃSKA.

Wydawnictwo Naukowe PWN SA (Polish Scientific Publishers PWN): 00-251 Warsaw, ul. Miodowa 10; tel. (22) 6954001; fax (22) 6954288; e-mail international@pwn.com.pl; internet www.pwn.com .pl; f. 1951; publications and journals on sciences and humanities, university textbooks, encyclopedias, dictionaries, multimedia; Pres. PETER WHISKERD-WĘGORZEWSKI; Man. Dir MICHAŁ SZEWIELOW; Editor-in-Chief RYSZARD BUREK.

Wydawnictwo Ossolineum (Ossolineum Publishing House): 50-062 Wrocław, Pl. Solny 14A ; tel. (71) 3436961; fax (71) 3448103; e-mail osso-bn@pwr.wroc.pl; internet www.ossolineum.wroc.pl; f. 1817; privatized; publishing house of the Polish Academy of Sciences; academic publications in humanities and sciences; Man. Dir Dr WOJCIECH KARWACKI.

Wydawnictwo Podsiedlik-Raniowski Sp. z o.o.: 60-171 Poznań, ul. Żmigrodzka 41/49; tel. (61) 8679546; fax (61) 8676850; e-mail office@priska.com.pl; f. 1990; popular and children's literature, poetry, prose, classical works, educational books; Pres. KRZYSZTOF RANIOWSKI; Dir MICHAŁ STECKI.

Wydawnictwo Prawnicze Sp. z o.o. (Legal Publishing House Ltd): 02-520 Warsaw, ul. Wiśniowa 50; tel. (22) 494151; fax (22) 499410; e-mail wp@wp.com.pl; f. 1952; Dir and Editor-in-Chief Dr JERZY KOWALSKI.

Wydawnictwo Prószyński Ska SA: 02-651 Warsaw, ul. Garażowa 7; tel. (22) 6077000; fax (22) 8497317; e-mail wydawnictwo@ proszynski.com.pl; internet www.proszynski.com.pl; f. 1990; handbooks, belles-lettres, educational books; Pres. MIECZYSŁAW PRÓSZYŃSKI; Editor DOROTA MALINOWSKA.

Wydawnictwo RTW: 01-780 Warsaw, ul. Broniewskiego 9A ; tel. (22) 6337010; fax (22) 6637474; e-mail rtw@wydawrtw.media.pl; internet www.wydawrtw.media.pl; f. 1992; education, geography, geology, history, science, atlases, dictionaries, encyclopedias and audio books.

Wydawnictwo Śląsk Sp. z o.o. (Silesia Publishing House Ltd): 40-161 Katowice, Al. W. Korfantego 51; tel. (32) 580756; fax (32) 583229; e-mail biuro@slaskwn.com.pl; f. 1952; social, popular science, technical and regional literature; Pres. TADEUSZ SIERNY.

Wydawnictwo Wam: 31-501 Kraków, ul. Kopernika 26; tel. (12) 4291888; fax (12) 4295003; e-mail wam@wydawnictwowam.pl; internet www.wydawnictwowam.pl; f. 1872; textbooks, encyclopedias, non-fiction, fiction and children's books; Dir HENRYK PIETRAS.

Wydawnictwo Wiedza Powszechna (General Knowledge): 00-054 Warsaw, ul. Jasna 26; tel. and fax (22) 8269592; e-mail wiedza@ medianet.pl; internet www.wiedza.pl; f. 1952; popular science books, Polish and foreign language dictionaries, foreign language textbooks, encyclopedias and lexicons; Dir TERESA KORSAK.

Wydawnictwo Wilga Sp. z o.o.: 00-389 Warsaw, ul. Smulikowskiego 1/3; tel. (22) 8260882; fax (22) 8260643; e-mail wilga@ternet .pl; f. 1993; education and fiction; Pres. JAN WOJNITKO; Editor-in-Chief OLGA WOJNITKO.

Wydawnictwo Zysk SA: 64-774 Poznań, ul. Wielka 10; tel. (61) 8532767; fax (61) 8532751; f. 1994; belles-lettres, popular, scientific and religious literature; Pres. TADEUSZ ZYSK.

Zakład Wydawnictw Statystycznych (Statistical Publishing Establishment): 00-925 Warsaw, Al. Niepodległości 208; tel. (22)

6083210; fax (22) 6083867; f. 1971; statistics and theory of statistics, economics, social sciences, periodicals; Dir ANDRZEJ STASIUN.

Znak Społeczny Instytut Wydawniczy (Znak Social Publishing Institute): 30-105 Kraków, ul. Kościuszki 37; tel. (12) 4219776; fax (12) 4219814; e-mail redakcja@znak.com.pl; internet www.znak.com .pl; f. 1959; religion, philosophy, belles-lettres, essays, history; Chief Exec. HENRYK WOŹNIAKOWSKI; Editor-in-Chief JERZY ILLG.

PUBLISHERS' ASSOCIATION

Polskie Towarzystwo Wydawców Książek (Polish Society of Book Editors): 00-048 Warsaw, ul. Mazowiecka 2/4; tel. and fax (22) 8260735; f. 1921; Pres. JANUSZ FOGLER; 500 mems.

Broadcasting and Communications

TELECOMMUNICATIONS

Telecommunications Regulatory Office (URT): 00-582 Warsaw, ul. Kasprzaka 18/20; tel. (22) 6088270; e-mail prasowy@urt .gov.pl; internet www.urt.gov.pl; f. 2001; Chair. MAREK ZDROJEWSKI.

Polkomtel SA: 02-001 Warsaw, Al. Jerozolimskie 81; tel. (22) 6071905; fax (22) 6071902; f. 1996; operates the Plus GSM mobile cellular telephone network; Chair. JAROSŁAW PACHOWSKI; Pres. WŁADYSŁAW BARTOSZEWICZ.

Polska Telefonia Cyfrowa (PTC) Sp zoo: Warsaw; tel. (22) 6996000; fax (22) 6996109; f. 1996; operates the Era GSM mobile cellular telephone network; largest mobile phone operator; Chair. and Gen. Dir BOGUSŁAW KUŁAKOWSKI; 1,000 employees.

Telekomunikacja Polska (TPSA): 00-945 Warsaw, ul. Swiętokrzyska 3; tel. (22) 8268742; fax (22) 8268528; internet www.tpsa.pl; f. 1992; partial privatization in 1998, a further 35% sold in 2000; Chief Exec. PAWEŁ RZEPKA; 72,000 employees.

BROADCASTING

Regulatory Authority

Polish National Radio and Television Broadcasting Council (KRRiTV): 00-015 Warsaw, Skwer Kardinala Wyszyńskiego, Prymasa Polski 9; tel. (22) 6359925; fax (22) 8383501; internet www .krrit.gov.pl; f. 1993; f. 1992.

Radio

There are 180 radio broadcasting institutions, of which 17 are public, and seven national channels, of which four are public.

Polskie Radio SA (Polish Radio): 00-977 Warsaw, Al. Niepodległości 77/85; tel. (22) 6459259; fax (22) 6455924; e-mail polskie.radio@radio.com.pl; internet www.radio.com.pl; Pres. KRZYSZTOF MICHALSKI; Dir of International Relations HANNA DĄBROWSKA.

    Home Service: there are four national channels broadcasting 90 hours per day; one long-wave transmitter (600 kW) broadcasting on 225 kHz; 11 medium-wave transmitters and 18 relay stations; 137 VHF transmitters covering all four programmes and 17 local programmes.

    Foreign Service: Five transmitters broadcast on 10 frequencies on short-wave, one transmitter broadcasting on medium-wave. Programmes in Polish, English, Esperanto, German, Russian, Belarusian, Ukrainian, Lithuanian, Slovak and Czech.

Radio Maryja: 87-100 Torun, ul. Zwirki i Wigury 80; tel. (56) 552361; fax (56) 552362; internet www.radiomaryja.pl; Catholic station; Dir TADEUSZ RYDZYK.

Radio Musyka Fakty (RMF FM): 30-204 Kraków, Al. Waszyngtona 1, Kopiec Kosciuszki; tel. (12) 4219696; fax (12) 4217895; e-mail redakcja@rmf.pl; internet www.rmf.pl; Pres. STANISŁAW TYCZYNSKI; Dir JOLANTA WIŚNIEWSKA.

Radio Zet: 00-503 Warsaw, ul. Żurawia 8; tel. (22) 5833382; fax (22) 5833356; e-mail radiozet@radio.com.pl; internet www.radiozet .com.pl; f. 1990; independent; 24 hours; has broadcast nationally since 1994; wholly owned by the Eurozet media group; Pres. and Editor-in-Chief ROBERT KOZYRA.

Television

There are 26 television broadcasting institutions, of which 12 are public. Of the national public channels, one broadcasts for 22 hours, the other for 16 hours per day via 84 transmitters and 134 relay stations. A third national public channel was launched in early 2002. In addition, there is one national private channel, broadcasting for 18 hours per day, and one satellite channel of Polish Television, TV Polonia, broadcasting for 16 hours per day. As well as the various

local programmes for Gdańsk, Katowice, Szczecin, Wrocław (seven hours per day) and Lublin (four hours per day), there are regional programmes for Bydgoszcz, Kraków, Łódź, Poznań, Rzeszów and Warsaw (three hours per day). Poland's first private (commercial) TV station began operating in Wrocław in early 1990. Broadcasting is regulated by the Broadcasting Bill, enacted in 1993. Poland's first digital television service was launched in April 1998.

Telewizja Polska SA (Polish Television): 00-999 Warsaw, ul. J. P. Woronicza 17, POB 211; tel. (22) 5476550; fax (22) 5477719; e-mail pr@tvp.pl; internet www.tvp.pl; f. 1952; Chair. ROBERT KWIATKOWSKI; Vice-Chair. ANNA POPOWICZ; 6,730 employees.

PolSat: 04-028 Warsaw, Al. Stanów Zjednoczonyck 53; tel. (22) 104001; fax (22) 134295; internet www.polsat.com.pl; f. 1992; Polish satellite company, awarded Poland's first national, private television licence in 1994; Propr. ZYGMUNT SOLORZ.

TVN Sp. z o.o.: 02-981 Warsaw, ul. Augustówka 3; tel. (22) 8566060; fax (22) 8566666; e-mail widzowie@tvn.pl; internet www.tvn.pl; f. 1997; broadcasts in northern Poland, Łódź and Warsaw; Pres. PIOTR WALTER.

Finance

(cap. = capital; res = reserves; dep. = deposits; m. = million; amounts in new złotys unless otherwise indicated; brs = branches)

BANKING

In accordance with Poland's association agreement with the EU, foreign banks were permitted to operate freely in the country from 1997. In September 1996 Poland's first banking group was created, the Grupa Pekao SA. In 2000 there were 75 commercial banks and 757 co-operative banks operating in Poland.

On 1 January 1995 a new złoty, equivalent to 10,000 old złotys, was introduced. All figures given below are in terms of new złotys.

National Bank

Narodowy Bank Polski—NBP (National Bank of Poland): 00-919 Warsaw, ul. Świętokrzyska 11/21, POB 1011; tel. (22) 6531000; fax (22) 6208518; e-mail nbp@nbp.pl; internet www.nbp.pl; f. 1945; state central bank; cap. 400.0m., res 22,283.3m., dep. 61,688.2m. (Dec. 2001); Pres. LESZEK BALCEROWICZ; First Deputy Pres. JERZY STOPYRA; 16 brs.

Other Banks

ABN Amro Bank (Polska) SA: 02-134 Warsaw, ul. l-go Sierpnia 8A, Wisniowy Business Park, POB 417; tel. (22) 5730500; fax (22) 5730501; internet www.abnamro.com; f. 1994 through takeover of Interbank SA; 100% owned by ABN AMRO Bank, NV (Netherlands); cap. 146.2m., res 48.3m., dep. 3,003.4m (Dec. 2001); Man. H. KESSELER.

Bank Amerykański w Polsce SA—AmerBank (American Bank in Poland Inc.): 00-102 Warsaw, ul. Marszałkowska 115; tel. (22) 6248505; fax (22) 6249981; e-mail amerbank@amerbank.pl; internet www.amerbank.pl; f. 1991; 95.2% owned by DZ Bank AG Deutsche Zentral-Genossenschaftsbank (Germany); commercial bank; cap. 23.1m., res 91.9m., dep. 1,450.3m. (Dec. 2001); Chair of Bd. PETER DIECKMAN; Pres. SŁAWOMIR SIKORA.

Bank Gospodarki Żywnościowej SA—BGZ (Bank of Food Economy): 01-211 Warsaw, ul. Kasprzaka 10/16; tel. (22) 8604000; fax (22) 8605000; e-mail info@bgz.pl; internet www.bgz.pl; f. 1919; present name adopted 1994; universal commercial bank; finances agriculture, forestry and food processing; cap. 23.1m., res 874.6m., dep. 15,596.6m. (Dec. 2001); Exec. Pres. MICHAŁ MACHLEID; Man. Dir JERZY BUSZ; 353 brs and sub-brs.

Bank Gospodarstwa Krajowego—BGK (National Economy Bank): 00-955 Warsaw, Al. Jerozolimskie 7, POB 41; tel. (22) 5229127; fax (22) 6270378; e-mail bgk@bgk.com.pl; internet www .bgk.com.pl; f. 1924; state-owned; cap. 178.9 m., res 1,942.0m., dep. 1,669.7m. (Dec. 2001); Pres.of Bd RYSZARD PAZURA; 7 brs.

Bank Handlowy w Warszawie SA (Trade Bank of Warsaw): 00-923 Warsaw, ul. Senatorska 16; tel. (22) 6903000; fax (22) 8300113; e-mail listybh@citicorp.com; internet www.citihandlowy.pl; f. 1870; merged with Citibank (Poland) SA in 2001; trade and finance bank; specializes in corporate and investment banking; 92.1% owned by Citibank Overseas Investment Corpn (USA); cap. 430.3m., res 5,311.7m., dep. 22,317.9m. (Dec. 2001); Pres. CEZARY STYPULKOWSKI; Chair. STANISŁAW SOLTYSINSKI; 61 brs.

Bank Millennium: 00-924 Warsaw, ul. Kopernika 36/40; tel. (22) 6575720; fax (22) 8267180; e-mail wojciech.kaczorowski@ bankmillennium.pl; internet www.bankmillennium.pl; f. 1989 as Bank Inicjatyw Gospodarczych BIG SA; renamed BIG Bank Gdański SA in 1997, present name adopted 2001; 50.0% owned by

Banco Comercial Portugues (Portugal); cap. 849.2m., res 520.3m., dep. 15,867.2m. (Dec. 2001), total assets 18,612.5m. (Dec. 2002); Chair. BOGUSŁAW KOTT; 172 brs.

Bank Ochrony Środowiska SA—BOS (Environmental Protection Bank): 00-950 Warsaw 1, Al. Jana Pawła II 12, POB 150; tel. (22) 8508735; fax (22) 8508891; e-mail bos@bosbank.pl; internet www.bosbank.pl; f. 1991; 47.0% owned by Skandinaviska Enskilda Banken AB (Sweden), 44.36% by Polish National Fund for the Protection of the Environment and Water; cap. 132.0m., res 435.8m., dep. 4,394.2m. (Dec. 2001); Pres.of Exec. Bd JOSEF KOZIOL; 48 brs.

Bank Polska Kasa Opieki—Bank Pekao SA: 00-950 Warsaw, ul. Grzybowska 53/57; tel. (22) 6560000; fax (22) 6560004; e-mail info@pekao.com.pl; internet www.pekao.com.pl; f. 1929; universal bank; absorbed Bank Depozytowo-Kredytowy, Pomorski Bank Kredytowy and Powszechny Bank Gospodarczy in 1999; 53.2% owned by Uno-Credito Italiano SpA (Italy); cap. 165.8m., res 5,431.8m., dep. 60,628.1m. (Dec. 2001); Chair. ALESSANDRO PROFUMO; 720 brs and sub-brs.

Bank Przemysłowo-Handlowy PBK SA—Bank BPH-BPK (Industrial and Commercial Bank): 31-548 Kraków, Al. Pokoju 1; tel. (12) 6186888; fax (12) 6186863; e-mail bank@bphpbk.pl; internet www.bphpbk.pl; f. 1988; merged with Hypovereinsbank Polska (1999), Powszechny Bank Kredytowy (2000) and Bank Przemy-slowo-Handlowy (2001); present name adopted 2002; cap. 143.6m., res 5,159.4m., dep. 38,252.1m. (Dec. 2001); Chair. of Sup. Bd ALICJA KORNASIEWICZ; Pres. JÓZEF WANCER; 75 brs and 172 sub-brs.

Bank Współpracy Europejskiej—BWE SA (European Co-operative Bank): 00-082 Warsaw, ul. Senatorska 14, POB 85; tel. (22) 8299800; fax (22) 8260261; e-mail promocja@bwe.pl; internet www.bwe.pl; f. 1990; commercial bank for tourism industry; present name adopted 1997; cap. 117.3m., res 40.1m., dep. 946.8m. (Dec. 2001); Exec. Pres. PIOTR PUCZYNSKI (acting); 9 brs.

Bank Zachodni WBK SA (Western Bank): 50-950 Wrocław, Rynek 9/11; tel. (71) 3701000; fax (71) 3702771; e-mail dorota.bernatowicz@bzwbk.pl; internet www.bzwbk.pl; f. 1989; present name adopted 2001; absorbed Wielkopolski Bank Kredytowy SA in 2001; 70.5% owned by AIB European Investments Ltd (Ireland); cap. 729.6m., res 1,276.3m., dep. 20,884.1m. (Dec. 2001); Pres. JACEK KSEŃ; 433 brs.

BNP Paribas Bank Polska SA: 00-108 Warsaw, ul. Zielna 41/43; tel. (22) 6972308; fax (22) 6972309; e-mail warsaw.office@bnpparibas.com; internet www.bnpparibas.com; f. 1994; 100% owned by BNP Paribas (France); present name adopted 2001; cap. 193.4m., res 104.1m., dep. 1,207.5m. (Dec. 2001); Man. Dir YVES DRIEUX.

BRE Bank SA: 00-950 Warsaw, ul. Senatorska 18, POB 728; tel. (22) 8290000; fax (22) 8290033; e-mail info@brebank.com.pl; internet www.brebank.com.pl; f. 1987 as Bank Rozwoju Eksportu; 50% owned by Commerzbank AG (Germany); present name adopted 1999; specializes in corporate banking; cap. 91.9m., res 2,004.6m., dep. 16,637.8m. (Dec. 2001); Chair. of Bd KRZYSZTOF SWARC; Pres., Chief Exec. and Gen. Man. WOJCIECH KOSTRZEWA; 12 brs.

Crédit Lyonnais Bank Polska SA: 00-697 Warsaw, al. Jerozolimskie 65/97, LIM Centre, POB 50; tel. (22) 6306888; fax (22) 6354500; f. 1991 as Międzynarodowy Bank w Polsce SA; present name adopted 1997; 100% owned by Crédit Lyonnais Global Banking (France); cap. 22.8m., res 145.6m., dep. 1,088.5m. (Dec. 2001); Chair. of Bd BERNARD MIGNUCCI; Pres. BERNARD SZLACHETKA.

Deutsche Bank 24 SA: 31-047 Kraków, ul. Józefa Sarego 2/4, POB 234; tel. (12) 6182116; fax (12) 4295686; e-mail info@db-24.pl; internet www.db-24.pl; f. 1991; present name adopted 2001; 92.6% owned by Deutsche Bank 24 Aktiengesellschaft (Germany); cap. 336.3m., res −166.5m., dep. 1,704.8m. (Dec. 2001); Chair. of Sup. Bd and Chief Exec. Dr HERBERT WALTER; Pres. MAREK KULCZYCKI.

Deutsche Bank Polska SA: 00-609 Warsaw, al. Armii Ludowej 26; tel. (22) 5799000; fax (22) 5799001; e-mail public.relations@db.com; internet www.deutsche-bank.pl; f. 1995; 100% owned by Deutsche Bank AG (Germany); cap. 230.0m., res 273.4m., dep. 2,802.2m. (Dec. 2001); Chief Exec. STAN SZCZUREK; Dir-Gen. WOLFGANG NIEDENHOFF.

Fortis Bank Polska SA: 02-676 Warsaw, ul. Postępu 15; tel. (22) 5669000; fax (22) 5669010; e-mail info@fortisbank.com.pl; internet www.fortisbank.com.pl; f. 1990; fmrly Pierwszy Polsko-Amerykański Bank Kraków SA; present name adopted 2000; 99.1% owned by Fortis Bank (Belgium); cap. 30.2m., res 448.8m., dep. 3,417.3m. (Dec. 2001); Pres. JEAN-MARIE DE BAERDEMAEKER; Chair. LUC DELVAUX.

Górnośląski Bank Gospodarczy—GBG Bank SA: 40-006 Katowice, ul. Warszawska 6, POB 1138; tel. (32) 2008500; fax (32) 2008685; e-mail gbg@gbg.com.pl; internet www.gbg.com.pl; f. 1990; 68.8% owned by Bank Przemysłowy-Handlowy PBK SA; cap. 62.2m., res 77.5m., dep. 2,760.9m. (Dec. 2001); Pres. TADEUSZ WNUK (acting); Chair. ANDRZEJ PODSIADLO; 44 brs.

ING Bank Śląski SA: 40-086 Katowice, ul. Sokolska 34; tel. (32) 3577000; fax (32) 588308; e-mail info@ing.pl; internet www.ing.pl; f. 1989; present name adopted 2001; acquired Wielkopolski Bank Rolniczy SA in 2001; 87.8% owned by ING Bank NV (Netherlands); cap. 130.1m., res 2,380.5m., dep. 22,112.6m. (Dec. 2001); Chair. ANDRZEJ WROBLEWSKI; Pres. MARIAN CZAKANSKI; 332 brs and sub-brs.

Kredyt Bank SA: 01-211 Warsaw, ul. Kasprzaka 2/8, POB 93; tel. (22) 6345400; fax (22) 6345335; e-mail bew@kredytbank.com.pl; internet www.kredytbank.com.pl; f. 1997 by merger; present name adopted 1999; 58.2% owned by KBC Bank NV (Belgium), 18.4% by Deutsche Bank Trust Co Americas (USA); cap. 739.5m., res 1,598.0m., dep. 18,204.6m. (Dec. 2001); Chair. ANDRZEJ WITKOWSKI; Pres. STANISŁAW PACUK; 75 brs.

LG Petro Bank SA: 93-172 Lódź, ul. Rzgowska 34/36; tel. (42) 819060; fax (42) 6846192; internet www.lgpetro.com.pl; f. 1990; present name adopted 1996; cap. 111.3m., res 131.5m., dep. 1,372.9m. (Dec. 1999); Pres. DONG CHANG PARK.

Powszechna Kasa Oszczędności Bank Państwowy—PKO Bank Polski SA (PKO BP SA) (State Savings Bank): 00-975 Warsaw, ul. Pulawska 15, POB 183; tel. (22) 5218067; fax (22) 5218068; internet www.pkobp.pl; f. 1919; state-owned joint-stock co; cap. 1,340.3m., res 1,457.4 m., dep. 71,039.1m. (Dec. 2001); Pres. of Man. Bd. ANDRZEJ PODSIADLO; Chair. of Sup. Bd. KRZYSZTOF PIETRASZKIEWICZ; 1,153 brs and sub-brs.

Powszechny Bank Kredytowy SA w Warszawie (Warsaw Credit Bank): 00-958 Warsaw, ul. Towarowa 25A, POB 3; tel. (22) 5318000; fax (22) 5318786; e-mail info@pkb.pl; internet www.pbk.pl; f. 1989; privatized, and absorbed Bank Morski in 1997; in 1999 acquired Pierwszy Komercyjny Bank SA; in 2000 merged with Bank Austria Creditanstalt Poland SA; cap. 146.7m., res 1,939.0m., dep. 19,130.4m. (Dec. 2000); Chair. CHRISTINE BOGDANOWICZ-BINDERT; Pres. of Bd ANDRZEJ PODSIADLO; 338 brs.

Raiffeisen Bank Polska SA: 00-549 Warsaw, ul. Piekna 20, POB 53; tel. (22) 5852000; fax (22) 5852585; internet www.raiffeisen.pl; f. 1991; present name adopted 2000; 100% owned by Raiffeisen Zentralbank Österreich AG (Austria); cap. 332.0m., res 126.8m. dep. 5,011.0m. (Dec. 2001); Chair. HERBERT STEPIC; 21 brs.

STOCK EXCHANGE

The Warsaw Stock Exchange was re-established in April 1991. In March 1999 it had 37 member companies and listed shares in 205 firms, in addition to 43 issues of Treasury bonds. In January 1998 a derivatives market was launched, listing index and USD futures.

Warsaw Stock Exchange: 00-498 Warsaw, ul. Książęca 4; tel. (22) 6283232; fax (22) 6281754; e-mail gielda@wse.com.pl; internet www.wse.com.pl; opened for trading in 1991; Pres. and Chief Exec. Dr WIESŁAW ROZUCKI.

INSURANCE

In early 2000 there were 56 insurance companies operating in Poland. The largest companies were Polish National Insurance (Państwowy Zakład Ubezpieczeń—PZU), which dominated the property insurance market, and Warta Insurance and Reinsurance, which specialized in vehicle insurance, and foreign business. PZU's subsidiary, PZU Life, was the largest life insurance company.

Grupa Powszechny Zakład Ubezpieczeń (PZU) (Polish National Insurance Group): 00-133 Warsaw, Al. Jana Pawła II 24; tel. (22)5823400; fax (22) 5823401; e-mail poczta@pzu.pl; internet ww.pzu.pl; f. 1803; insurance group comprising two principal companies dealing in various areas of insurance, and six support companies; 55% state-owned; Pres. ZDISŁAW MONTKIEWICZ; 400 brs; 14,000 employees.

> **PZU SA:** internet www.pzu.pl/pzusa; property insurance products; claimed 55.5% of the market in 1999; owner of the PZU Capital Group.

> **PZU Życie SA:** e-mail kontact@pzuzycie.pl; internet www.pzuzycie.com.pl; life insurance products; claimed 56.4% of the market in 1999; 99.9% of shares held by PZU SA; founder of Powsechne Towarzystwo Emerytalne PŻU SA—PZU SA Pension Society; President BOGUSŁAW KASPRZYK.

Towarzystwo Ubezpieczeń i Reasekuracji Warta SA (Warta Insurance and Reinsurance Co Ltd): 00-805 Warsaw, ul. Chmielna 85/87; tel. (22) 5810100; fax (22) 5811374; e-mail info@warta.pl; internet www.warta.pl; f. 1920; marine, air, motor, fire, luggage and credit; deals with all foreign business; Pres. AGENOR JAN GAWRZYAL; 25 brs; representatives in London (United Kingdom) and New York (USA).

Trade and Industry

GOVERNMENT AGENCIES

Mass Privatization Programme: c/o Department of National Investment Funds, Ministry of the Treasury, 00-522 Warsaw, ul. Krucza 36; tel. (22) 6958453; fax (22) 6958701; responsible for the divestment of various state-owned enterprises.

Polish Agency for Foreign Investment (PAIZ): 00-599 Warsaw, Al. Róż 2; tel. (22) 6210706; fax (22) 6226169; e-mail post@paiz.gov .pl; internet www.paiz.gov.pl; Pres. ADAM PAWŁOWICZ.

DEVELOPMENT ORGANIZATION

State Office for Housing and Urban Development: 00-926 Warsaw, ul. Wspólna 2; tel. (22) 6618111; fax (22) 6284030; e-mail umieszk@umirm.gov.pl; internet www.umirm.gov.pl; f. 1997; development of government housing policy; Pres. SŁAWOMIR NAJNIGIER.

CHAMBERS OF COMMERCE

Krajowa Izba Gospodarcza (Polish Chamber of Commerce): Head Office, 00-074 Warsaw, ul. Trębacka 4, POB 361; tel. (22) 6309600; fax (22) 8274673; internet www.kig.pl; f. 1990; Pres. ANDRZEJ ARENDARSKI; Chair. KAZIMIERZ PAZGAN; 150 mems.

Izba Przemysłowo-Handlowa Inwestorów Zagranicznych (Chamber of Industry and Trade for Foreign Investors): 00-071 Warsaw, ul. Krakowskie Przedmieście 47/51; tel. (22) 8261822; fax (22) 8268593.

UTILITIES

Electricity

Polish Power Grid Company (Polskie Sieci Elektroenergetyczne SA—PSE): 00-496 Warsaw, ul. Mysia 2; tel. (22) 6931580; fax (22) 6285964; f. 1990; Pres. Prof. Dr hab. STANISŁAW DOBRZAŃSKI.

State Atomic Energy Agency (Państwowa Agencja Atomistyki): 00-921 Warsaw, ul. Krucza 36; tel. (22) 6282722; fax (22) 6290164; e-mail niewodniczanski@paa.gov.pl; internet www.paa.gov.pl; f. 1982; responsible for the development and safe application of nuclear technologies, as well as for nuclear research and radiation protection; Pres. Prof. JERZY NIEWODNICZAŃSKI.

STOEN Stołeczny Zakład Energetyczny SA (STOEN Capital Power Distribution Company Ltd): 00-347 Warsaw, Wybrzeże Kopciuszkowskie 41; tel. (22) 8213387; fax (22) 8213122; f. 1993; distributes electric energy; Pres. KRZYSZTOF ZIĘBA; Chair. KAZIMIERZ PAWE BISEK.

Gas

EuRoPol GAZ SA: 04-028 Warsaw, Al. Stanów Zjednoczonych 61; tel. (22) 5174000; fax (22) 5174040; e-mail konto@europolgaz.com.pl; f. 1993; joint venture between PGNiG and the Russian gas company, Gazprom; Pres. KAZIMIERZ ADAMCZYK.

Polish Oil and Gas Company (PGNiG): 00-537 Warsaw, 6 ul. Krucza 14; tel. (22) 6235601; fax (22) 6235856; e-mail nowak@pgnig .com.pl; internet www.pgnig.com.pl; f. 1982; state-owned natural-gas producer and supplier; Pres. ALEKSANDER FINDZIŃSKI; 47,300 employees.

TRADE UNIONS

All Poland Trade Unions Alliance (Ogólnopolskie Porozumienie Związków Zawodowych—OPZZ): 00-924 Warsaw, ul. Kopernika 36/40; tel. (22) 8267106; fax (22) 8265102; e-mail opzz@opzz.org.pl; internet www.opzz.org.pl; f. 1984; 2.3m. mems (2000); Chair. MACIEJ MANICKI.

Independent Self-governing Trade Union—Solidarity (NSZZ Solidarność): 80-855 Gdańsk, Wały Piastowskie 24; tel. (58) 3016737; fax (58) 3010143; e-mail zagr@solidarnosc.org.pl; internet www.solidarnosc.org.pl; f. 1980; outlawed 1981–89; 1.2m. mems; Chair. JANUSZ SNIADEK.

Rural (Private Farmers') Solidarity: Leader ROMAN WIERZBICKI.

Transport

RAILWAYS

At the end of 2000 there were 22,560 km of railway lines making up the state network, of which 11,826 km were electrified and 985 km were narrow gauge. Substantial modernization, with assistance from the World Bank and other sources, was planned.

General Railway Inspectorate (Główny Inspektorat Kolejnictwa): 00-928 Warsaw, ul. Chałubinskiego 4/6; e-mail gik@gik.gov .pl; internet www.gik.gov.pl; Gen. Inspector BOLESŁAW MUSIAŁ; Dir-Gen. LIDIA OSTROWSKA.

Polish State Railways Plc (Polskie Koleje Państwowe Spółka Akcyjna—PKP SA): 00-973 Warsaw, ul. Szczęśliwicka 62; tel. (22) 5249000; fax (22) 5249020; e-mail infopkp@pkp.com.pl; internet www.pkp.com.pl; f. 1926; freight and passenger transport; scheduled for privatization after 2001; Pres. KRZYSZTOF CELIŃSKI; 152,586 employees.

ROADS

In December 2000 there were 364,656 km of roads, of which 358 km were motorways. Poland launched a road construction scheme in mid-2002, partly funded by the European Union, which aimed to enhance the country's position as a major transit route between Western Europe and the countries of the former USSR. The project, which was to concentrate on road construction, also aimed to modernize some 1,500 km of existing roads.

General Directorate of Public Roads and Motorways (Generalna Dyrekcja Dróg Krajowych i Autostrad): 00-921 Warsaw, ul. Wspólna 3; tel. (22) 6217072; fax (22) 6219557; internet www.gddp .gov.pl; Dir TADEUSZ SUVARA.

Państwowa Komunikacja Samochodowa (PKS) (Polish Motor Communications): Warsaw; tel. (22) 363594; fax (22) 366733; f. 1945; state enterprise organizing inland road transport for passengers and goods. Bus routes cover a total of 121,000 km; passengers carried 1,039,409 (1995).

Pekaes SA: 01-204 Warsaw, ul. Siedmiogrodzka 1/3; tel. (22) 6322251; fax (22) 6321092; e-mail info@pekaes.com.pl; f. 1958; road transport of goods to all European and Middle Eastern countries; Pres. ALBERT BOROWSKI.

INLAND WATERWAYS

Poland has 6,850 km of waterways, of which 3,813 km were navigable in 2000. The main rivers are the Wisła (Vistula, 1,047 km), Odra (Oder, 742 km in Poland), Bug (587 km in Poland), Warta (808 km), San, Narew, Noteć, Pilica, Wieprz and Dunajec. There are some 5,000 lakes, the largest being the Śniardwy, Mamry, Łebsko, Dąbie and Miedwie. In addition, there is a network of canals (approximately 348 km).

About 1,265,000 passengers and 10.4m. metric tons of freight were carried on inland water transport in 2000.

SHIPPING

Poland has three large harbours on the Baltic Sea: Gdynia, Gdańsk and Szczecin. At 31 December 2001 the Polish merchant fleet had 56 cargo-carrying ships, with a total displacement of 457,890 grt.

Authority of Szczecin and Świnoujście Authority SA: 70-603 Szczecin, ul. Bytomska 7; tel. (91) 4308240; fax (91) 4624842; e-mail info@port.szczecin.pl; internet www.port.szczecin.pl; f. 1950; Pres. and Man. Dir ANDRZEJ MONTWIŁŁ.

Port of Gdańsk Authority SA: 80-955 Gdańsk, ul. Zamknieta 18; tel. (58) 3439300; fax (58) 3439485; e-mail info@portgdansk.pl; internet www.portgdansk.pl; Pres. and Gen. Dir MARIAN SWITEK.

Port of Gdynia Authority SA: 81-337 Gdynia, ul. Rotterdamska Str. 9; tel. (58) 6274002; fax (58) 6203191; e-mail marketing@port .gdynia.pl; internet www.port.gdynia.pl; f. 1922; Pres. JANUSZ JAROSINSKI.

Principal shipping companies:

Polskie Linie Oceaniczne (PLO) (Polish Ocean Lines): 81-364 Gdynia, ul. 10 Lutego 24, POB 265; tel. (58) 6278222; fax (58) 6278480; e-mail pol@pol.com.pl; internet www.pol.com.pl; f. 1951; holding co for six shipping cos operating within PLO group; Dir-Gen. KRZYSZTOF KREMKY.

Polska Żegluga Bałtycka SA— Polferries (Polish Baltic Shipping Co—POLFERRIES): 78-100 Kołobrzeg, ul. Portowa 41; tel. (94) 3552102 (from June 2003); fax (94) 3526612; e-mail info@polferries .pl; internet www.polferries.pl.

Polska Żegluga Morska (PZM) (Polish Steamship Co): 70-419 Szczecin, Pl. Rodła 8; tel. (91) 3595595; fax (91) 4340574; e-mail pzmmanagement@polsteam.com.pl; internet www.polsteam.com.pl; f. 1951; world-wide tramping; fleet of 103 vessels for bulk cargoes totalling nearly 3m. dwt; Gen. Dir PAWE BRZEZICKI.

CIVIL AVIATION

Okęcie international airport is situated near Warsaw. There are also international airports at Kraków, Gdańsk and Katowice. Domestic flights serve Gdańsk, Gołeniow, Katowice, Kraków, Poznań, Rzeszów, Szczecin, Warsaw and Wrocław.

General Inspectorate of Civil Aviation (Główny Inspektorat Lotnictwa Cywilnego): 00-928 Warsaw, ul. Chałubinskiego 4/6; tel. and fax (22) 6298689; e-mail gilc@polbox.pl; internet www.gilc.gov .pl; Gen. Inspector ZBIGNIEW MĄCKA.

Air Silesia: Katowice; f. 2002; low-cost regional passenger and cargo carrier; Chair. EUGENIUSZ PIECHOCZEK.

Polskie Linie Lotnicze (LOT SA) (Polish Airlines—LOT): 00-906 Warsaw, ul. 17 Stycznia 39; tel. (22) 6066111; fax (22) 8460909; e-mail lot@lot.com; internet www.lot.com; f. 1929; 90 air routes, domestic services and international services to the Middle East, Africa, Asia, Canada, USA, and throughout Europe; due to be privatized in 2003; Pres. JAN LITWIŃSKI; Vice-Pres. ZBIGNIEW KISZCZAK.

Tourism

The Polish Tourist and Country-Lovers' Association is responsible for tourism and maintains about 420 branches across the country.

The Association runs about 250 hotels, hostels and campsites. Poland is rich in historic cities, such as Gdańsk, Wrocław, Kraków, Poznań and Warsaw. There are 30 health and climatic resorts, while the mountains, forests and rivers provide splendid scenery and excellent facilities for touring and sporting holidays. In 2001 Poland was visited by some 61.4m. foreign tourists, 50.5% of whom were from Germany.

National Administration of Tourism and Physical Culture (Urząd Kultury Fizycznej i Turystyki): 00-916 Warsaw, ul. Świętokrzyska 12; tel. (22) 6945555; fax (22) 8262172.

Polish Tourist and Country-Lovers' Society (Polskie Towarzystwo Turystyczno-Krajoznawcze): 00-075 Warsaw, ul. Senatorska 11; tel. (22) 265735; fax (22) 262505; f. 1950; Chair. ADAM CHYŻEWSKI; the Society has about 250 tourist accommodation establishments; 89,919 mems (1998).

PORTUGAL

Introductory Survey

Location, Climate, Language, Religion, Flag, Capital

The mainland portion of the Portuguese Republic lies in western Europe, on the Atlantic side of the Iberian peninsula, bordered by Spain to the north and east. The country also includes two archipelagos in the Atlantic Ocean, the Azores and the Madeira Islands. The climate is mild and temperate, with an annual average temperature of 16°C (61°F). In the interior the weather is drier and hotter. Almost all of the inhabitants speak Portuguese and are Christians of the Roman Catholic Church. The national flag (proportions 2 by 3) has two vertical stripes, of green and red, the green occupying two-fifths of the total area; superimposed on the stripes (half on the green, half on the red) is the state coat of arms: a white shield, containing five small blue shields (each bearing five white roundels) in the form of an upright cross, with a red border containing seven yellow castles, all superimposed on a yellow armillary sphere. The capital is Lisbon (Lisboa).

Recent History

The monarchy that had ruled Portugal from the 11th century was overthrown in 1910, when the King was deposed in a bloodless revolution, and a republic was proclaimed. A period of great instability ensued until a military coup installed the regime of the Estado Novo (New State) in 1926. Dr António de Oliveira Salazar became Minister of Finance in 1928 and Prime Minister in 1932, establishing a right-wing dictatorial regime, influenced by Italian Fascism. A new Constitution, establishing a corporate state, was adopted in 1933. Only one political party was authorized, and suffrage was limited. Portugal remained neutral during the Second World War. The Government strove to achieve international acceptance, but Portugal was not admitted to the UN until 1955. Unlike the other European colonial powers, Portugal insisted on maintaining its overseas possessions, regarding them as 'inalienable'. In 1961 Portuguese enclaves in India were successfully invaded by Indian forces, and in the same year a rebellion against Portuguese rule began in Angola. Similar rebellions followed, in Portuguese Guinea (1963) and Mozambique (1964), and protracted guerrilla warfare ensued in the three African provinces. Salazar remained in power until illness forced his retirement in September 1968. He was succeeded by Dr Marcello Caetano, who had been Deputy Prime Minister in 1955–58. Caetano pursued slightly more liberal policies. Opposition parties were legalized for elections to the National Assembléia in October 1969, but the União Nacional, the government party, won all 130 seats. Immediately after the elections, the opposition groups were outlawed again. The government party, renamed Acção Nacional Popular in February 1970, also won every seat at the next elections to the Assembly, in October 1973, following the withdrawal of all opposition candidates.

The drain on Portugal's economy by the long wars against nationalist forces in the overseas provinces contributed to the overthrow of Caetano in a bloodless coup on 25 April 1974, initiated by the Movimento das Forças Armadas (MFA), a group of young army officers. Gen. António Ribeiro de Spínola, head of the Junta da Salvação Nacional (Junta of National Salvation) which had then assumed power, became President in May and promised liberal reforms. In July Brig.-Gen. Vasco dos Santos Gonçalves replaced Prof. Adelino da Palma Carlos as Prime Minister. The new Government recognized the right of Portugal's overseas territories to self-determination. The independence of Guinea-Bissau (formerly Portuguese Guinea), proclaimed in September 1973, was recognized by Portugal in September 1974. The remaining African territories were all granted independence in 1975. Portugal also withdrew from Portuguese (East) Timor in 1975.

Following a split between the Junta's right and left wings, President Spínola resigned in September 1974 and was replaced by Gen. Francisco da Costa Gomes. An abortive counter-coup by senior officers in March 1975 resulted in a move to the left. All existing organs of the MFA were dissolved, a Supreme Revolutionary Council (SRC) was created, and six of the country's political parties agreed that the SRC would stay in power for five years. On 25 April, the first anniversary of the overthrow of the Caetano regime, a general election was held for a Constituent Assembly. Of the 12 parties contesting the election, the Partido Socialista (PS) obtained the largest share of the votes cast and won 116 of the Assembly's 250 seats. Disputes between Socialists and Communists, however, provoked withdrawals from the new coalition Government, and Gen. Vasco Gonçalves was dismissed from the premiership. Admiral José Pinheiro de Azevedo became Prime Minister in August. In September the provisional Government resigned and a new Government of 'united action' was formed, including members of the armed forces, the PS, the Partido Popular Democrático (PPD) and the Partido Comunista Português (PCP). In November the Government suspended its activities, owing to a lack of support from the armed forces. An abortive leftist military coup resulted from the political turmoil. Changes took place within the SRC, and in December the armed forces announced a plan to reduce its political power.

A new Constitution, committing Portugal to make a transition to socialism, took effect on 25 April 1976. The SRC was renamed the Council of the Revolution, becoming a consultative body, headed by the President, with powers to delay legislation and the right of veto in military matters. At the general election for the new Assembléia da República (Assembly of the Republic), the PS won 107 of the Assembléia's 263 seats. In June the Army Chief of Staff, Gen. António Ramalho Eanes, a non-party candidate supported by the PS, the PPD and the Centro Democrático Social (CDS), was elected President. He took office in July, when a minority Socialist Government was formed under Dr Mário Lopes Soares, who had been Minister of Foreign Affairs in 1974–75. The Government resigned in December 1977, but the President again invited Dr Soares to take office as Prime Minister. A new PS-CDS coalition was established in January 1978, but it collapsed after only six months. A new Government was formed in November under Prof. Carlos Mota Pinto, but he resigned in July 1979.

President Eanes appointed Dr Maria de Lourdes Pintasilgo to head a provisional Government. In September 1979 the President dissolved the Assembléia da República and announced that an early general election would be held in December. The centre-right alliance, Aliança Democrática (AD), which included the Partido Social Democrata (PSD, formerly the PPD) and the CDS, won 128 of the 250 seats in the Assembléia. Dr Francisco Sá Carneiro, the leader of the PSD, was appointed Prime Minister. At the general election held in October 1980, the AD increased its majority of seats in the Assembléia from six to 18. In December Dr Sá Carneiro and his Minister of Defence were killed in an apparent air accident. (New evidence revealed in 1995, however, indicated that a bomb had exploded on board the aircraft—see below.) The presidential election took place as planned, however, and President Eanes won a clear victory over five rival candidates, receiving 56.4% of the valid votes cast. Dr Francisco Pinto Balsemão, co-founder of the PSD, was appointed Prime Minister. In March 1981 the offices of the President of the Republic and the Chief of Staff of the Armed Forces were formally separated.

In August 1982 the Assembléia da República approved the final draft of the new Constitution, which abolished the Council of the Revolution and reduced the powers of the President, thus completing the transition to full civilian government. Following divisions within the PSD, and losses at local elections in December 1982, Dr Balsemão resigned as Prime Minister. In addition, the Deputy Prime Minister and leader of the CDS, Prof. Diogo Freitas do Amaral, announced his resignation from all party and political posts. President Eanes dissolved the Assembléia, and announced that a premature general election would be held. In February 1983 Dr Balsemão was replaced as leader of the PSD by Prof. Carlos Mota Pinto. At the general election, held in April, the PS, led by the former Prime Minister, Dr Mário Soares, won 101 of the Assembléia's 250 seats. Dr Soares succeeded in forming a coalition Government with the PSD (the AD having been dissolved), which took office in June.

Following an increase in urban terrorism, for which the radical left-wing group Forças Populares de 25 Abril (FP-25) claimed responsibility, controversial legislation proposing the establishment of a security intelligence agency, was introduced in the Assembléia da República in June 1984. The arrest of more than 40 terrorist suspects, including Lt-Col Otelo Saraiva de Carvalho, the former revolutionary commander, coincided with the introduction of the legislation. Further guerrilla suspects were subsequently arrested (see below).

In February 1985 Prof. Carlos Mota Pinto resigned as leader of the PSD, and subsequently as Deputy Prime Minister and Minister of Defence, following his failure to secure adequate support from within his party, and was replaced by Rui Machete, the Minister of Justice. In May Machete was replaced as leader of the PSD by Prof. Aníbal Cavaco Silva, a former Minister of Finance. In June 1985, on the day after Portugal signed its treaty of accession to the European Community (EC—now European Union—EU, see p. 199), the PS-PSD coalition disintegrated, following disagreements over labour and agricultural reforms. Dr Mário Soares resigned as Prime Minister, and President Eanes called a general election for October, at which the PSD won 88 of the 250 seats in the Assembléia da República, while the PS won 57 seats and the Partido Renovador Democrático (PRD, a new party founded in early 1985 by supporters of President Eanes) won 45 seats. Prof. Aníbal Cavaco Silva was able to form a minority Government acceptable to President Eanes.

In January 1986 four candidates contested the presidential election. As no candidate achieved the requisite 50% majority, a second round of voting was held in February: having secured the support of all the leftist parties, Dr Mário Soares, the former Prime Minister, narrowly defeated Prof. Diogo Freitas do Amaral, former leader of the CDS, to become Portugal's first civilian President for 60 years, taking office in March.

The Government of Cavaco Silva hoped to embark on a reformist programme, but, owing to its lack of a majority, encountered difficulties in securing the adoption of legislation. In June 1986, following the legislature's rejection of his proposals to amend the labour laws in order to permit the dismissal of surplus workers, Cavaco Silva survived a vote of 'no confidence'. President Soares made use of his right of veto for the first time in September, when he rejected legislation to revise the autonomy statute of the Azores.

In April 1987 Cavaco Silva resigned, following his defeat in a motion of censure. President Soares dissolved the Assembléia da República, prior to the holding of an early general election in July. The election resulted in a decisive victory for the PSD, which secured 148 of the 250 seats in the Assembléia and thus became the first party since 1974 to win an absolute majority. The PS won 60 seats, and the Coligação Democrático Unitária (CDU, a new left-wing coalition comprising mainly the PCP) won 31 seats. The PRD suffered a serious reverse, winning only seven seats, compared with 45 at the 1985 election. Gen. Eanes announced his resignation from the presidency of the party. Cavaco Silva was reappointed as Prime Minister.

Upon his return to the office of Prime Minister, Cavaco Silva appointed Eurico de Melo to the post of Deputy Prime Minister, and made several other changes to the Council of Ministers. Cavaco Silva announced a programme of radical economic reform. The gradual partial privatization of state industries was to continue, and fundamental changes in the sectors of agriculture, education and the media were proposed. The most controversial aspect of the programme, however, was the Government's renewed attempt to reform the restrictive labour laws. In March 1988 an estimated 1.5m. workers, fearing for the security of their jobs, took part in a 24-hour general strike to protest against the Government's proposed legislation. Nevertheless, in April the labour laws were approved by the Assembléia da República; the following month, however, the Constitutional Court ruled that the new legislation violated the Constitution. Opposition to the new labour legislation was renewed in January 1989, when 10,000 demonstrators took part in a protest in Lisbon. The legislation was approved by President Soares in February, although labour unrest persisted.

In October 1988 the PSD and the opposition PS reached agreement on proposed constitutional revisions. Marxist elements were to be removed from the Constitution, subject to approval by the requisite two-thirds' majority of the Assembléia da República. Having gained this approval, and also the agreement of President Soares, the constitutional amendments entered into force in August 1989.

In October 1989 the Government survived a motion of censure, presented by the PS, which was highly critical of the

Government's 'lack of ethics'. The opposition party's accusations related to two scandals earlier in the year involving the Minister of Finance, who was alleged to have evaded property-transfer tax, and the Minister of Health, who was suspected of irregularities regarding hospital contracts. At municipal elections, held in December, the PS, supported by the PCP and the Greens, took control of Lisbon; Jorge Sampaio, the new Secretary-General of the PS, became Mayor of the capital. The PSD also lost other major cities. In January 1990 the Deputy Prime Minister and Minister of Defence, Eurico de Melo, was reported to have resigned shortly before Cavaco Silva's announcement of a government reshuffle. A new Deputy Prime Minister was not appointed. Other changes included the replacement of the Ministers of Finance and of Health, both accused of misconduct during 1989. In February 1990 a financial scandal relating to the Government of the Portuguese overseas territory of Macao threatened to jeopardize relations between the Prime Minister and the socialist President. It was alleged that Carlos Melancia, the socialist Governor of Macao, had accepted 50m. escudos from a German company which hoped to secure a consultancy contract for the construction of an airport in Macao. The integrity of President Soares was therefore called into question. Although he denied any involvement in the affair, the Governor of Macao resigned. Melancia was acquitted of bribery charges in August 1993, but in February 1994 it was announced that he was to be retried; Melancia was definitively absolved of all charges by the Supreme Court in October 2002.

In October 1990 President Soares confirmed his intention to seek a renewal of his mandate at the forthcoming presidential election. The campaign was dominated by the Macao scandal. Nevertheless, at the election, held in January 1991 and contested by four candidates, Soares secured an outright victory. Supported by both the PS and the PSD, the incumbent President received more than 70% of the votes cast. Basílio Horta of the CDS won 14%, Carlos Carvalhas of the PCP received 13% and Carlos Marques of the extreme left won less than 3%.

At legislative elections held in early October 1991 the PSD renewed its absolute majority, winning 135 of the 230 seats in the Assembléia da República. The PS secured 72 seats, the CDU 17 and the CDS five. A new Government was appointed in late October. Following the electorate's clear endorsement of the PSD's policies, Prof. Diogo Freitas do Amaral resigned from the leadership of the CDS (a post to which he had returned in 1988), not being succeeded until March 1992, upon the appointment of Manuel Monteiro. In February of that year the Secretary-General of the PS, Jorge Sampaio, was replaced by António Guterres.

During 1992 tension between President Soares and Cavaco Silva became more evident, owing to the President's increasingly frequent use of his power of veto in order to obstruct the passage of legislation. At a PSD congress in November the Prime Minister was highly critical of the President's use of the veto and of his repeated recourse to the Constitutional Court. Relations between the Head of State and the Prime Minister were strained once again in August 1993 when, upon the President's exercise of his right of veto, an extraordinary session of the Assembléia da República was convened to discuss controversial legislation entailing severe restrictions on the statutory right of refugees to asylum in Portugal. The law was adopted in modified form. In December 1993 Cavaco Silva effected a ministerial reorganization. Changes included the replacement of the Ministers of Finance and of Health, following much public dissatisfaction with the shortcomings of the country's health service. Local elections were held in the same month. The opposition PS secured 36% of the votes, while the PSD received 34%. The PS retained control of Lisbon and Porto. The PCP, with 13% of the votes, maintained its position, particularly in southern Portugal.

In June 1994 Miguel Beleza, the governor of the central bank, was obliged to resign, following differences with the Government over monetary policy. The independence of the central bank was called into question upon Beleza's replacement by António de Sousa Franco, hitherto the Secretary of State for Finance and a close associate of the Prime Minister. In October the Government survived a vote of 'no confidence' in the legislature.

In January 1995 Cavaco Silva announced his intention to resign as leader of the PSD. At the party congress in the following month the Minister of Defence, Joaquim Fernando Nogueira, narrowly defeated his principal rival, the Minister of Foreign Affairs, José Manuel Durão Barroso, in the contest for the leadership. In March Fernando Nogueira resigned as Minister of Defence, following the President's veto of the former's proposed appointment as Deputy Prime Minister.

In July 1995, following a five-year investigation, the PS was embarrassed by the announcement that 23 senior officials of the socialist trade union, União Geral dos Trabalhadores de Portugal (UGTP), including the Secretary-General and his predecessor, were to stand trial on charges of fraud relating to the alleged misappropriation of subsidies from the European Social Fund. Nevertheless, at a general election held in October the PS took 112 of the 230 seats in the Assembléia da República. The PSD won 88 seats, the Partido Popular (PP, formerly the CDS) 15 and the CDU also 15. António Guterres was appointed Prime Minister, heading a minority administration which incorporated several non-party ministers. The incoming Government included Jaime Gama as Minister of Foreign Affairs, a portfolio he had held in 1983–85.

In November 1995 Jorge Sampaio, former Secretary-General of the PS, announced his resignation as Mayor of Lisbon, and declared his candidacy for the forthcoming presidential election. At the election, held in January 1996, Jorge Sampaio secured 53.9% of the votes cast, while the other remaining candidate, Cavaco Silva, received 46.1%. Upon his defeat, the former Prime Minister announced his retirement from politics. President Sampaio took office in March. Following the presidential election, Fernando Nogueira resigned from the leadership of the PSD, and was replaced by Marcelo Rebelo de Sousa.

In August 1996 the Prime Minister announced proposals for radical reforms of the country's political system. A reduction in the number of deputies to the legislature, the opening of electoral lists to independent citizens (thus ending the monopoly of the major parties) and provision for the holding of referendums were among the changes envisaged. In early 1997 the ruling PS and the opposition PSD reached a broad consensus on these proposals for constitutional reform. The two parties also agreed upon the gradual establishment of a professional army and a reduction in compulsory military service. In September the Assembléia da República gave its approval to the various constitutional reforms, thus permitting the future holding of referendums on issues of national interest.

In February 1997, in a free vote, the Assembléia da República narrowly rejected proposals to liberalize the country's restrictive abortion law. The issue aroused bitter controversy, and created a deep division within the ruling PS. The Prime Minister, a practising Catholic, expressed his strong opposition, while certain PS veterans supported the proposed change in the legislation. In February 1998 the legislature voted by a narrow margin to relax the law on abortion. A referendum on the issue was held in June. Although 51% of those casting a vote favoured the liberalization of the law, only 31% (compared with the requisite minimum of 50%) of the electorate participated in the country's first referendum, thereby rendering the result null and void.

In November 1997 the Deputy Prime Minister and Minister of Defence, António Vitorino, resigned as a result of allegations that he had failed to pay municipal taxes on the purchase of a farmhouse in 1989. In the ensuing government reorganization Vitorino was replaced as Minister of Defence by José Veiga Simão. The Minister of Economy was among other members of the Council of Ministers to be replaced. At local elections in December 1997 the PS consolidated its position, receiving more than 38% of the votes cast and retaining control of Lisbon and Porto. The PSD obtained 33% of the votes, while the PCP lost considerable support.

In October 1998 the Prime Minister announced the establishment of an anti-corruption unit and various other measures, in response to repeated accusations that political parties and public officials had been in receipt of illicit payments in return for the awarding of public-works contracts; the most recent scandal involved road-building projects. In the same month President Sampaio urged all political parties to establish a 'pact of courage and understanding', with regard to party financing and in particular to expenditure on election campaigning. Meanwhile, as an atmosphere of impunity continued to prevail (many serious corruption and other criminal cases taking up to 15 years to reach the courts), both the Government and the opposition reiterated their concerns over the extraordinarily tardy procedures of the country's judicial system.

The Prime Minister suffered a reverse in November 1998 when a referendum on the question of regional devolution resulted in an overwhelming rejection (by 63.6% of voters) of the Government's proposals to divide mainland Portugal into eight administrative regions (each with a proposed elected local assembly and regional president). However, owing to the high abstention rate (over 50%), the referendum result was declared invalid.

In March 1999 Marcelo Rebelo de Sousa announced his resignation as leader of the opposition PSD and the termination of the party's recently established electoral alliance with the PP, citing disloyalty on the part of the President of the PP, Paulo Portas. The accusation apparently arose from the latter's disclosure in a television broadcast of details of a private conversation between the two politicians.

In May 1999 the Minister of Defence, José Veiga Simão, was obliged to resign, following the revelation by a weekly newspaper that he had disclosed confidential details of the identity, and information on the operations, of members of the country's intelligence service. This disclosure to a parliamentary committee was not only regarded as a serious breach of state security, but also brought into question the relationship between the Government and the legislature.

The general election conducted on 10 October 1999 was partially overshadowed by the crisis in the former Portuguese colony of East Timor (see below). Nevertheless, the PS won 44.0% of the votes cast, thus securing 115 of the 230 seats in the Assembléia da República. The PSD, with 32.3% of the votes, was allocated 81 seats. The left-wing CDU won 17 seats (including two seats allocated to the 'green' Partido Ecologista Os Verdes—PEV), while the recently established Bloco Esquerda, a militant left-wing grouping, unexpectedly obtained two seats. Thus, one seat short of an absolute majority, António Guterres was returned to office and a new Council of Ministers was subsequently appointed. In November the incoming Government announced a programme of reforms aimed at narrowing the disparity between Portugal and the more developed member countries of the EU. Concerned by the high level of abstention at the recent election, the Prime Minister proposed a radical reform of the Portuguese political system, envisaging in particular drastic reductions in electoral campaigning expenses and greater controls over party financing. Other plans included reforms of the health service, judicial procedures and taxation system.

During the mid-1980s terrorist attacks by FP-25 and other groups had continued, targets including both Portuguese and foreign business interests, NATO installations and the US embassy in Lisbon. In July 1985 the trial of more than 70 alleged members of FP-25 (including Lt-Col Otelo Saraiva de Carvalho) opened, but was adjourned, owing to the fatal shooting of a key prosecution witness. However, the trial later resumed and upon its conclusion in May 1987, Saraiva de Carvalho was found guilty of subversion and sentenced to 15 years' imprisonment (subsequently increased to 18 years). In May 1989, however, the Supreme Court ruled that irregularities had occurred at his trial and Saraiva de Carvalho was released (along with 28 others convicted on similar charges), pending a decision on a new hearing. Despite his renunciation of the armed struggle and his request for an amnesty in February 1990, Saraiva de Carvalho's conviction was confirmed by the Supreme Court in December and he was again imprisoned. In March 1996, following a personal initiative by President Soares, the Assembléia da República approved a pardon for Saraiva de Carvalho and other members of FP-25. However, in December 1999 Saraiva de Carvalho was placed on trial on renewed charges of terrorism relating to his alleged leadership of FP-25. More than 60 other defendants also faced charges. The opening of this retrial, however, coincided with a decision not to proceed with an investigation into the circumstances surrounding the death in 1980 of the then Prime Minister, Dr Sá Carneiro. The Ministry of Justice's denial of the existence of new evidence relating to the air crash provoked a public outcry.

In early May 2000 civil service and transport unions went on strike, in protest at the 2.5% salary increase for that year announced by the Government after the collapse of negotiations in March, severely disrupting services throughout the country. Guterres claimed that the policy of moderate wage increases was necessary to ensure that inflation levels comply with those required by the EU.

A reorganization of the Council of Ministers in September 2000 included the separation of the finance and economy portfolios. The Government came under increasing pressure in late 2000, although a motion of 'no confidence', presented by the opposition PSD in September, was defeated by 117 votes to 96, following the PCP's decision to abstain from voting. In the same month the head of Portugal's privatization programme resigned, citing personal reasons, although it was widely believed that his resignation had also been precipitated by disagreements over the Government's economic policy. In October the Government failed to gain the support of at least one opposition deputy in the Assembléia da República, required to obtain a majority, to ensure the approval of the budget for 2001. Guterres subsequently announced that, rather than accept the amendments to the budgetary proposals demanded by the opposition, he would resign. In the event, however, an independent deputy abstained from the vote, thereby assuring that the budget was passed. In mid-December the Minister of Youth and Sports, Armando Vara, and the Secretary of State for the Interior, Luís Patrão, resigned following the revelation that they had been involved in a number of financial irregularities surrounding the funding of a state-financed foundation.

At a presidential election held on 14 January 2001 Sampaio was re-elected for a second term, obtaining 55.8% of the votes cast. Sampaio defeated four candidates, including the PSD candidate, Joaquim Ferreira do Amaral, who secured 34.5% of the votes.

The collapse of a bridge over the river Douro, in northern Portugal, in March 2001, killed 70 people and led to the resignation of the Minister of the Presidency and of Infrastructure, Jorge Paulo Sacadura Coelho. It subsequently emerged that concerns over the bridge's safety had been repeatedly expressed by local officials. A full investigation into the incident was announced by the Government, which also accepted responsibility for the deaths and pledged to compensate the families of the victims.

A major government reshuffle was effected in June 2001, in an apparent attempt to appease opposition members who were demanding the holding of an early general election. Significantly, the Minister of Finance, Joaquim Augusto Nunes de Pina Moura, was replaced, following criticism of his economic policies. He was succeeded by Guilherme Waldemar Pereira D'Oliveira Martins, who was also responsible for the presidency portfolio.

In October 2001 the Assembléia da República ratified the Treaty of Nice, which aimed to reform the institutions of the EU in anticipation of its forthcoming enlargement. The PS, the PSD and the PP voted in favour of the ratification, while the left-wing Bloco de Esquerda (BE) and the PCP rejected the Treaty. Earlier that month the Government had excluded the PCP's suggestion of altering the Constitution to ensure that all future treaties on the EU be subject to approval by referendum. A number of constitutional amendments were approved by the Assembly; these included the incorporation of reciprocal political rights for citizens of lusophone countries, a ban on strike action by police trade unions, and official recognition of the UN International Criminal Court.

The PS was overwhelmingly defeated at municipal elections held in December 2001, at which the party lost control of Lisbon and Porto to the PSD. In response, Guterres resigned as Prime Minister and relinquished the leadership of the PS. The poor electoral results were widely attributed to a decline in the economy as well to discontent with public services, which had been adversely affected by reductions in government expenditure. President Sampaio announced that legislative elections would be held in early 2002. Guterres, who remained Prime Minister in an interim capacity pending the elections, was replaced as Secretary-General of the PS in January 2002 by Eduardo Ferro Rodrigues. At the elections, held on 17 March, the PSD, whose campaign had featured reductions in corporate taxation and public expenditure and the privatization of state services, emerged victorious, winning 40.2% of the votes cast and securing 105 seats in the Assembléia da República, although the party did not obtain an overall majority. The PS secured 37.8% of the votes and 96 seats, the PP 8.8% and 14 seats, the PCP-PEV coalition 7.0% and 12 seats, and the BE 2.8% and three seats. The leader of the PSD, José Manuel Durão Barroso, was appointed Prime Minister and formed a centre-right coalition Government with the PP; the new administration, which included three PP ministers, took office on 6 April. Paulo Portas of the PP was given the position of Minister for State and National Defence, while Manuela Ferreira Leite, a former PSD Minister for Education, was placed in charge of a finance portfolio enlarged to include the defunct Ministries of State Reform and Planning.

Durão Barroso's Government swiftly expressed its intention to introduce austerity measures to counter the large public deficit created by the previous left-wing administration in contravention of the country's obligations under the regulations for the EU single currency (see Economic Affairs). One such measure was a complete suspension of civil service recruitment from May 2002. Meanwhile, in July a new Labour Code was proposed that would clarify in a single document 80 previously independent laws. The code was designed to combat low productivity by increasing the ease of recruitment and dismissal of staff and limiting power to the unions; it aroused protests over the possibility of employers being able to prosecute unions responsible for a strike. In November and December 2002 two public-sector one-day general strikes involving up to 500,000 workers were organized to protest against the introduction of the labour legislation and other recent austerity measures.

In October 2002 Gen. Alvarenga Sousa Santos, the Chief of Staff of the Armed Forces, was dismissed for criticising a 2% increase in military expenditure for 2003 as inadequate. The PCP demanded the resignation of the Minister of State and National Defence, Paulo Portas, for allegedly disseminating information concerning Sousa Santos's dismissal before its official announcement. Sousa Santos was temporarily replaced by the Chief of Staff of the Navy, Adm. Mendes Cabecadas. In early November 2002 Prime Minister, Durão Barroso, confirmed his support for Portas and announced that he would be seeking a second four-year term in office.

In April 2003 the publication of an article in *O Independente* alleging tax evasion by the Minister of Towns, Territorial Planning and the Environment, Isaltino Morais, led to his immediate resignation, though he denied the accusations. Luís Valente de Oliveira, the Minister of Public Works, Transport and Housing, also resigned, citing health reasons, as did seven state secretaries, precipitating the first cabinet reshuffle of the administration.

Portugal's leaders were deeply divided over the issue of the proposed US-led military campaign to remove the regime of Saddam Hussein in Iraq in early 2003. Despite domestic popular opposition to a proposed US-led military response and general support for a diplomatic solution to the Iraqi problem, Durão Barroso was a vocal supporter of the US stance on Iraq and Portugal was one of eight European countries to sign a letter, sponsored by the United Kingdom, published in support of the US administration's policy on Iraq in January 2003. In the same month Barroso announced that his Government had authorized the USA to use an airbase in the Portuguese mid-Atlantic archipelago of the Azores in the event of war. The left-wing President Sampaio was, however, resolutely opposed to any military action in Iraq without a UN mandate and clashed publicly with the Prime Minister over the issue (although under the Constitution foreign policy is the responsibility of the Government, the President is empowered to veto decisions by the Council of Ministers). In early March Durão Barroso affirmed Portuguese support for US-led military action without UN endorsement and subsequently hosted an emergency summit on Iraq between leaders of the USA, the United Kingdom and Spain, at which it was announced that they would launch a military strike with or without UN support. However, following the failure of the coalition to gain support for a second UN Security Council resolution endorsing military action, President Sampaio announced a compromise agreed between himself and Durão Barroso: Portuguese armed forces would not participate in the conflict, although Portugal would render transit facilities to their allies. At the end of March all four left-wing opposition parties, reflecting public discontent with the Government's handling of the crisis, submitted censure motions against the Government for hosting the Azores summit, claiming that Durão Barroso had linked Portugal to a war and had contributed to the weakening of international institutions; the Government defeated the motions owing to its majority in the Assembléia da República. Durão Barroso announced in April that Portugal was prepared to deploy military forces in Iraq for humanitarian and peace-keeping purposes. The opposition subsequently affirmed its support for the deployment only if it took place under the auspices of the UN.

Relations with Spain improved in the late 1980s, and in May 1989 King Juan Carlos became the first Spanish monarch to address the Portuguese Assembléia da República. Both Portugal and Spain were admitted to Western European Union (see p. 318) in November 1988. By the mid-1990s the principal bilateral issue had become that of the division of water resources. (However, in November 1998 Portugal and Spain signed an historic accord relating to the sharing of river resources.) In 1997 bilateral relations were severely strained by the Portuguese authorities' decision to release a Basque terrorist suspect, despite the Spanish Government's request for the prisoner's extradition. In June 2002 Spanish border police refused entry to two representatives of the Portuguese legislature attending an anti-globalization conference in Seville. Although the Spanish Government apologized for the incident, in which the representatives claimed they were assaulted by the police, relations between the Governments deteriorated (they had already been strained by the Portuguese refusal to extradite a suspected Basque terrorist and the exclusion of Spanish companies from a motorway-construction project). In the aftermath of the sinking of the oil-tanker *Prestige* in November, off the coast of Galicia, Spain, the Governments disputed responsibility for the disaster after both countries refused to allow the boat to dock. The Spanish administration was additionally accused of irresponsibility in dealing with the wreck and of concealing the possibility of further spills from the sunken tanker; Portuguese authorities claimed their own studies showed leakage, which was subsequently confirmed. This was followed in January 2003 by Lisbon's initiation of legal proceedings against Spanish fishermen accused of operating in Portuguese territorial waters.

Negotiations with the People's Republic of China on the question of the Portuguese overseas territory of Macao commenced in June 1986, and in April 1987 Portugal and China signed an agreement whereby Portugal would transfer the administration of Macao to China in December 1999. At midnight on 19 December 1999 the sovereignty of Macao was duly transferred.

The former Portuguese territory of East Timor was unilaterally annexed by Indonesia in 1976. UN-sponsored negotiations between Portugal and Indonesia began in 1983 but proved inconclusive. Under UN auspices, talks between Portugal and Indonesia on the East Timor issue were resumed in December 1992, but again ended without agreement. In January 1995 Portugal and Indonesia agreed to the holding of discussions, under UN auspices, between the factions of East Timor. In early 1996, the UN-sponsored discussions having continued, Portugal offered to re-establish a diplomatic presence in Jakarta in return for the release of the East Timorese resistance leader, Xanana Gusmão, who had been sentenced to life imprisonment in 1993. In August 1998, following President Suharto's replacement in May and the subsequent implementation of a series of Indonesian troop withdrawals from the disputed region, the UN Secretary-General announced that Portugal and Indonesia had agreed to hold discussions on the possibility of autonomy for East Timor. In March 1999 it was announced that Portugal and Indonesia had reached an accord providing for the holding of a referendum in the territory on the question of either autonomy or independence. In late August, following two postponements and despite continuing intimidation and violence, the referendum on the future of East Timor finally proceeded, and resulted in an overwhelming endorsement of proposals for full independence for the territory. The announcement of the result, however, precipitated a rapid decline in the security situation, leading to the declaration of martial law in the territory. In mid-September a multinational peace-keeping force, led by Australia, was deployed in the territory. Following the restoration of order in East Timor and the Indonesian Government's acceptance of the result of the referendum, in December 1999 Portugal and Indonesia resumed full diplomatic relations, which had remained severed since 1975, and in January 2001 a new Indonesian ambassador to Portugal was appointed. Meanwhile, Portugal committed an initial 700 troops to the UN peace-keeping force that was to replace the Australian-led multinational force in early 2000. The Portuguese Government also pledged an annual sum of US $75m. towards the reconstruction of East Timor. Official diplomatic relations with East Timor, now officially known as Timor Leste, were established with the creation of an embassy in Lisbon during 2002.

In early 1988 Portugal announced that it was to review the terms of the 1983–91 agreement permitting the continued use by the USA of the Portuguese air base at Lajes in the Azores, in return for US economic and military aid. On a visit to the USA in February 1988, the Portuguese Prime Minister, Cavaco Silva, expressed his disappointment at the decline in the level of US aid since 1983, but nevertheless stated that he did not intend to reduce the facilities at Lajes. In February 1989 the USA agreed to increase its level of compensation for its use of the base. In January 1990, on a visit to Washington, Cavaco Silva reiterated his desire to negotiate a new treaty with the USA. Discussions

on the renewal of the treaty began in January 1991. In June 1995 the two countries signed a five-year accord whereby the USA undertook to supply to Portugal weapons and military equipment worth US $173m. In January 2003 Portugal agreed to US use of the Azores base in the event of war in Iraq, but only if action was ratified by the UN. This was later modified and use was granted without a UN resolution

Portugal played a significant role in the peace process in Angola, a former Portuguese overseas possession. Several meetings between representatives of the Angolan Government and the rebel group UNITA were held in Lisbon, culminating in the signing of a peace accord in 1991. In January 1993, following the resumption of hostilities, President Soares issued an appeal for peace. In June UNITA rejected Portugal's status as an observer in the peace process; however, in May 1994 a UNITA spokesman welcomed the possibility of further Portuguese mediation. A new peace agreement was signed in November of that year. In early 1995, however, the neutrality of the Portuguese Government was undermined by allegations that it had given technical assistance to the Angolan Government. In July 1998, following renewed hostilities in Angola, Portugal requested the intervention of the UN Secretary-General. In August UNITA severed its links with Portugal and the other observers in the peace process, accusing them of bias towards the Angolan Government. In March 2000 tensions between Angola and Portugal increased, following comments by the Angolan Minister of Social Communication, accusing the former Portuguese President, Mario Soares, and his son, João Soares, of benefiting from UNITA's illegal trade in diamonds. The allegations were strongly denied by UNITA. However, in May it was announced that military co-operation between Portugal and the government forces was to be increased. Following the cessation of hostilities in Angola in April 2002, Portugal was one of three states with representatives observing the peace process according to the Lusaka Protocol. Portugal was to continue with military support, including overseeing the integration of UNITA soldiers into a new armed forces and the establishment of a military academy.

Portugal was also active in the quest for peace in Mozambique. Relations with Mozambique, however, deteriorated in March 1989, when a Mozambican diplomat was expelled from Portugal, following his implication in the assassination, in Lisbon in April 1988, of a Mozambican resistance leader. Nevertheless, in January 1992 Portugal received a formal invitation to attend the peace talks as an observer, and in October a peace treaty was signed in Italy.

In July 1996 Portugal hosted the inaugural meeting of the Comunidade dos Países de Língua Portuguesa (CPLP, see p. 349), a new grouping of lusophone countries (including Angola, Mozambique and Guinea-Bissau), which aimed to promote closer political and economic co-operation. In late 1998, as part of a CPLP initiative, Portugal played a major role in the implementation of a peace agreement in Guinea-Bissau, ending several months of conflict between government and rebel forces in the former colony (q.v.). Following a coup in May 1999, the deposed President of Guinea-Bissau, João Vieira, was granted asylum in Portugal. During 2002/03 the possibility of establishing a CPLP legislative parliamentary assembly was broached.

Government

A new Constitution, envisaging the construction of a socialist society in Portugal, was promulgated in 1976 and revised in 1982. Subsequent revisions included the provision in 1997 for the holding of referendums on issues of national interest. The organs of sovereignty are the President, the Assembléia da República and the Government. The President, elected by popular vote for a five-year term, appoints the Prime Minister and, on the latter's proposal, other members of the Government, principally the Council of Ministers. The Council of State (Conselho de Estado) is a consultative body. Following the election of October 1995, the unicameral Assembléia had 230 members, including four representing Portuguese abroad, elected by universal adult suffrage for four years (subject to dissolution). The mainland comprises 18 administrative districts. Proposals to divide the mainland into eight administrative regions, with elected assemblies, were rejected in a referendum in November 1998. The Azores and Madeira (integral parts of the Portuguese Republic) were granted autonomy in 1976. The overseas territory of Macao was governed by special statute until December 1999, when it reverted to Chinese sovereignty.

Defence

Compulsory military service lasts from four to eight months in the army and from four to 12 months in the navy and air force, but was to be abolished in 2004. Conscientious objectors are allowed to perform an alternative community service. Portugal is a member of NATO (see p. 271) and of Western European Union (see p. 318). In August 2002 the total strength of the armed forces was 43,600 (including 8,130 conscripts), comprising: army 25,400, navy 10,800 (including 1,580 marines) and air force 7,400. There were reserves of 210,930. The paramilitary National Republican Guard and the Public Security Police totalled 25,600 and 20,800 respectively. In mid-2002 a total of 770 US troops were stationed in Portugal, mainly at the air force base at Lajes in the Azores. Defence expenditure for 2002 was budgeted at €1,300m.

Economic Affairs

In 2001, according to estimates by the World Bank, Portugal's overall gross national income (GNI), measured at average 1999–2001 prices, was US $109,156m., equivalent to $10,670 per head (or $17,270 on an international purchasing-power parity basis). During 1990–2001, it was estimated, the population increased at an average rate of 0.3% per year, while gross domestic product (GDP) per head increased, in real terms, by an average of 2.2% per year. Overall GDP expanded, in real terms, at an average annual rate of 2.6% in 1990–2001; growth in 2001 was 1.9%.

Agriculture (including forestry and fishing) contributed an estimated 4.1% of GDP in 2002 and the sector engaged 12.6% of the employed labour force in 2001. The principal crops are wheat, maize, potatoes, olives, tomatoes, oranges, grapes and sugar beets. The production of wine, particularly port, is significant. The European Union (EU, see p. 199) imposed a ban on Portuguese beef exports in late 1998 as a result of the detection of bovine spongiform encephalopathy (BSE) in Portuguese cattle. By January 2001 500 cases of BSE had been diagnosed in Portugal, although the number of new cases was declining. The fishing industry is important, the sardine catch, at 66,319 metric tons in 2000, being by far the largest. According to the World Bank, agricultural GDP declined, in real terms, by an average of 0.1% per year during 1990–2000; agricultural GDP increased by 10.5% in 1999, but fell by 2.5% in 2000.

Industry (comprising mining, manufacturing, construction and power) contributed an estimated 29.0% of GDP in 2002. In 2001 the sector engaged 34.3% of the employed labour force. According to the World Bank, the GDP of the industrial sector increased, in real terms, by an average of 2.0% per year during 1990–2000; industrial GDP grew by 2.2% in 1999 and by 2.6% in 2000. The mining and quarrying industry makes a minimal contribution to GDP, employing 0.3% of the working population in 2001. Limestone, granite, marble, copper pyrites, gold and uranium are the most significant products.

Manufacturing provided 19.1% of GDP in 2002 and engaged 21.6% of the employed labour force in 2001. According to the World Bank, manufacturing GDP grew by an annual average of 5.0% in 1995–99. The textile and clothing industry is the most important branch of manufacturing; clothing alone accounted for 11.6% of total export earnings in 2000. Other significant manufactured products include footwear, cork items, chemicals, electrical appliances, ceramics and paper pulp. Manufacturing GDP increased, in real terms, by 3.2% in 1998 and by 1.4% in 1999.

In 1999 35.2% of electricity production was derived from coal, 16.9% from hydroelectric power, 25.6% from petroleum and 18.8% from natural gas. Total electricity production was 42,930.0m. kWh. In 2000 imports of fuel accounted for an estimated 10.4% of total import costs. Portugal's heavy dependence on petroleum was reduced in 1997 when a pipeline carrying natural gas from Algeria (via Morocco and Spain) was inaugurated.

Services provided 66.9% of GDP in 2002, and engaged 53.1% of the employed labour force in 2001. The tourism industry remained a significant source of foreign exchange earnings in 2000, when receipts totalled an estimated US $5,206m. In 2001 there were 12.2m. tourist arrivals in Portugal. Emigrants' remittances are also important to the Portuguese economy, reaching an estimated $3,100m. in 2000. According to the World Bank, the GDP of the services sector increased, in real terms, by an average of 2.5% per year during 1990–2000; services GDP rose by 3.2% in 1999 and by 4.1% in 2000.

In 2001 Portugal recorded a visible trade deficit of US $12,979m., and a deficit of $9,959m. on the current account

of the balance of payments. Most of Portugal's trade is with other members of the EU. In 2000 Spain, Germany and France (including Monaco) supplied an estimated 25.3%, 13.7% and 10.6%, respectively, of total imports. The principal export market was Spain (which purchased 19.2% of the total); other major purchasers were Germany (17.6%) and France (including Monaco) (12.5%). The main exports in 2000 were road vehicles and parts (13.5%), clothing (11.6%), textiles (6.9%), footwear (5.7%), and wood and cork manufactures (3.9%). The principal imports were foodstuffs, textile yarn, chemicals, petroleum and petroleum products, and transport equipment.

In 2002 the budget deficit was equivalent to 2.6% of GDP (according to preliminary government figures), compared with 4.1% in 2001. In 1998 Portugal's external debt totalled 2,537,600m. escudos, equivalent to 13.2% of GDP. In 1990–2001 the annual rate of inflation averaged 4.8%. The average rate of inflation declined from 4.4% in 2001 to 3.6% in 2002. The level of unemployment declined from 4.4% of the labour force in 1999 to 4.0% in 2000, but grew to 4.1% in 2001.

Portugal became a member of the EC (now EU) in January 1986. The Maastricht Treaty on European Union was ratified by the Portuguese legislature in December 1992. In April 1992 Portugal joined the exchange rate mechanism of the European Monetary System (see p. 225). Portugal is also a member of the Organisation for Economic Co-operation and Development (OECD, see p. 277) and of the Comunidade dos Países de Língua Portuguesa (CPLP, see p. 349), which was established in Lisbon in 1996.

From 1997 the developments in Portugal's economy were strongly influenced by Portugal's participation in the single European currency. the euro, under economic and monetary union (EMU, see p. 225). Portugal adopted the euro at its inception in January 1999 as a single currency unit for transactions throughout the euro zone and as an internationally traded currency, and as legal tender in cash from 1 January 2002. Preparations for entry included a reduction in interest rates in order to achieve European integration, which had a strong positive effect on the growth of domestic demand. Consumption and investment also increased as a result of economic confidence stemming from participation in the euro area. Since its entry into the EU in 1986, Portugal has been a net recipient of large-scale financial transfers from the EU, through the Community Support Framework. However, EU funds to Portugal were expected to decrease from around 3% of GDP in 2002 to 1.7% by 2006. Furthermore, a period of strong growth, full employment, low inflation and inexpensive credit ended in 2000, as a result of rising interest rates and an increase in inflation owing to high international petroleum prices. A further cause for concern was the unsustainable expansion in credit, which was partly responsible for the increase in the current-account deficit from 4.7% of GDP in 1998 to 12% in 1999. Economic growth slowed considerably in the early 2000s and, as a consequence, government revenue from taxes declined substantially, necessitating amendments to the 2001 budget, including a €750m. reduction in public expenditure. Moreover, concerns were expressed that Portugal's more traditional industries (notably clothing, textiles and footwear) would be adversely affected by increased competition from less developed countries. In early April 2002 the new Government announced that overspending by the previous administration had led to a budget deficit of 4.1% in 2001, exceeding the 3% stipulated in the EU's stability and growth pact and thus contravening the regulations for the single currency, exposing Portugal to potential punitive measures from the European Commission including the imposition of a fine of up to 0.5% of GDP. Durão Barroso's administration responded with the announcement in May of severe austerity measures. In a revised budget for 2002 value-added tax (VAT) was increased from 17% to 19%, recruitment to the civil service was suspended, while local governments were prohibited from incurring further debt and 70 public companies were scheduled for closure or merger. The deficit for 2002 was reduced to 2.6% in 2002, but Portugal became the first euro-zone country to enter into recession, with a 1.3% decline in GDP in the last quarter of 2002 relative to the same period in 2001. In October 2002, parliamentary approval was granted for a 2003 budget that provided for the privatization of the Portuguese state airline, TAP, the energy corporation, Galp Energia, and the water utility company, Aguas de Portugal. Overall GDP growth in 2002 was only 0.5%, below the Government's estimate of 0.7%, which cast some doubt on a prediction of 1.25% growth in 2003, although Durão Barroso maintained his intention to progress with further austerity measures and institutional reforms and a commitment to the European stability and growth pact.

Education

Formal education at all levels is provided at both public and private institutions. Pre-school education, for three- to six-year olds, is not compulsory, and is available free of charge. Basic education is compulsory for nine years, between the ages of six and 15, and is provided free of charge in public schools. It is divided into three cycles: the first lasts for four years, the second for two years and the third for three years. Secondary education, which is not compulsory, lasts for three years, and comprises a single three-year cycle, with two types: general and vocational. In 1994 the total enrolment in primary education was equivalent to 100% of the school-age population. Enrolment in secondary education in that year included 78% of children in the relevant age-group.

Higher education comprises two systems—education provided in universities, which award the following academic degrees: the licenciatura, after four to six years of study, the mestrado, after one or two years of study and research work, and the doutoramento (doctorate); the second system is provided in regional polytechnic institutes, grouping technical, management, educational and fine arts schools, which offer three-year courses leading to the bacharel, and specialized studies leading to a diploma after one to two years. Expenditure on education in 2002 was €5,548.2m.

Public Holidays

2003: 1 January (New Year's Day), 4 March (Carnival Day), 17 April (Maundy Thursday*), 18 April (Good Friday), 25 April (Liberty Day), 1 May (Labour Day), 10 June (Portugal Day), 13 June (St Anthony—Lisbon only), 19 June (Corpus Christi), 24 June (St John the Baptist—Porto only), 15 August (Assumption), 5 October (Proclamation of the Republic), 1 November (All Saints' Day), 1 December (Restoration of Independence), 8 December (Immaculate Conception), 24 December (Christmas Eve), 25 December (Christmas Day).

2004: 1 January (New Year's Day), 24 February (Carnival Day), 8 April (Maundy Thursday*), 9 April (Good Friday), 26 April (for Liberty Day), 1 May (Labour Day), 10 June (Corpus Christi, and Portugal Day), 13 June (St Anthony—Lisbon only), 24 June (St John the Baptist—Porto only), 15 August (Assumption), 5 October (Proclamation of the Republic), 1 November (All Saints' Day), 1 December (Restoration of Independence), 8 December (Immaculate Conception), 24 December (Christmas Eve), 25 December (Christmas Day).

*Afternoon only.

Weights and Measures

The metric system is in force.

Statistical Survey

Source (unless otherwise stated): Instituto Nacional de Estatística (INE), Av. de António José de Almeida 5, 1078 Lisbon; tel. (21) 8470050; fax (21) 7951507; internet www.ine.pt.

Area and Population

AREA, POPULATION AND DENSITY

Area (sq km)	
Land	91,906
Inland water	439
Total	92,345*
Population (census results)	
15 April 1991	9,862,540
1 March 2001 (provisional)	
Males	5,000,141
Females	5,355,976
Total	10,356,117
Population (official estimates 31 December)	
1997	9,957,300
1998	9,979,500
1999	9,997,600
Density (per sq km) at 1 March 2001	112.1

* 35,655 sq miles.

REGIONS

(2001 census)

	Area (sq km)*	Population	Density (per sq km)
Continental Portugal	88,796	9,869,343	111.1
Norte	21,278	3,687,293	173.3
Centro	23,668	2,348,397	99.2
Lisboa e Vale do Tejo	11,931	2,661,850	223.1
Alentejo	26,931	776,585	28.8
Algarve	4,988	395,218	79.2
Autonomous Region: Açores (Azores)	2,330	241,763	103.8
Autonomous Region: Madeira	779	245,011	314.5
Total	91,905	10,356,117	112.7

* Excluding river estuaries (439 sq km).

PRINCIPAL TOWNS

(provisional population at 2001 census)

Lisboa (Lisbon, the capital)	556,797	Carnaxide	82,489
Porto (Oporto)	262,928	Aqualva-Cacém	81,366
Amadora	174,788	Vila Nova de Gaia	69,167
Braga	105,000*	Alguierão-Mem Martins	63,373
Coimbra	103,000*	Odivelas	53,641
Funchal	102,521	Guimarães	53,000*
Setúbal	91,108	Amora	50,571
Queluz	89,245		

* Estimate.

Source: Thomas Brinkhoff, *City Population* (internet www.citypopulation.de).

BIRTHS, MARRIAGES AND DEATHS

	Registered live births		Registered marriages		Registered deaths	
	Number	Rate (per 1,000)	Number	Rate (per 1,000)	Number	Rate (per 1,000)
1993	114,030	11.5	68,176	6.9	106,384	10.7
1994	109,287	11.0	66,003	6.7	99,621	10.0
1995	107,184	10.8	65,776	6.6	103,939	10.4
1996	110,363	11.1	63,672	6.4	107,259	10.8
1997	113,047	11.4	65,770	6.6	105,157	10.5
1998	116,038	11.6	68,710	6.9	108,268	10.8
1999	116,002	11.6	68,710	6.9	108,268	10.8
2000	120,008	12.0	63,752	6.4	105,813	10.6

2001: Registered live births 112,774; Registered marriages 58,390; Registered deaths 105,092.

Expectation of life (WHO estimates, years at birth): 76.5 (males 72.7; females 80.1) in 2001 (Source: WHO, *World Health Report*).

ECONOMICALLY ACTIVE POPULATION
(ISIC Major Divisions, '000 persons aged 15 years and over)

	1999	2000	2001
Agriculture, hunting and forestry	593.9	597.1	609.2
Fishing	19.2	19.2	19.5
Mining and quarrying	13.1	16.0	16.2
Manufacturing	1,106.5	1,081.2	1,081.9
Electricity, gas and water supply	33.9	28.9	36.2
Construction	540.9	593.5	581.2
Wholesale and retail trade; repair of motor vehicles, motorcycles and personal and household goods	693.5	723.1	752.2
Hotels and restaurants	248.9	253.6	255.0
Transport, storage and communications	167.8	180.4	194.2
Financial intermediation	84.4	88.1	86.7
Real estate, renting and business activities	203.2	205.4	224.5
Public administration and defence; compulsory social security	307.1	319.3	321.5
Education	277.8	271.2	280.6
Health and social work	231.9	243.1	252.0
Other community, social and personal service activities*	165.7	151.8	145.7
Private households with employed persons	144.6	146.9	140.9
Extra-territorial organizations and bodies	3.5	2.3	1.8
Total employed *	4,836.9	4,921.1	4,999.8
Unemployed	221.6	204.6	211.5
Total labour force	5,058.5	5,125.7	5,211.3
Males	2,769.0	2,795.2	2,835.7
Females	2,289.5	2,330.5	2,375.5

* Including regular members of the armed forces, but excluding persons on compulsory military service.

Source: ILO, *Yearbook of Labour Statistics*.

Health and Welfare

KEY INDICATORS

Total fertility rate (children per woman, 2001)	1.5
Under-5 mortality rate (per 1,000 live births, 2001)	6
HIV/AIDS (% of persons aged 15–49, 2001)	0.52
Physicians (per 1,000 head, 1998)	4.0
Hospital beds (per 1,000 head, 1998)	3.12
Health expenditure (2000): US $ per head (PPP)	1,469
Health expenditure (2000): % of GDP	8.2
Health expenditure (2000): public (% of total)	71.2
Human Development Index (2000): ranking	28
Human Development Index (2000): value	0.880

For sources and definitions, see explanatory note on p. vi.

Agriculture

PRINCIPAL CROPS
('000 metric tons)

	1999	2000	2001
Wheat	373	353	159
Rice (paddy)	157	149	143†
Barley	31	33	13
Maize	965	905	975
Rye	56	47	28
Oats	100	113	45
Triticale (wheat-rye hybrid)	33	40	16
Potatoes	1,367	1,250*	1,200*
Sweet potatoes*	22	22	22
Sugar beets	507	475†	460*
Olives	334	260†	271†
Sunflower seeds	31	30	33†
Other oilseeds*	160	160	20
Cabbages*	140	140	140
Lettuce	94	95*	95*
Tomatoes	1,152	1,000†	1,072†
Cauliflower	34	35*	35*
Onions (dry)	121	120*	110*
Broad beens (green)*	30	30	30
Beans (green)	21	20*	20*
Carrots	174	150*	150*
Carobs*	20	20	20
Chesnuts	31	33	27
Other fresh vegetables*	580	580	580
Bananas*	30	30	30
Oranges	215	254	230*
Tangerines, mandarins, clementines and satsumas	40	61	45*
Apples	262	254	316†
Pears	118	110	126†
Peaches and nectarines	89	66	75*
Grapes	1,041	900*	980*
Cantaloupes and other melons*	20	20	20

* FAO estimate(s).
† Unofficial figure.

Source: FAO.

LIVESTOCK
('000 head, year ending September)

	1999	2000	2001
Horses*	19	17	17
Mules*	50	45	45
Asses*	135	135	130
Cattle	1,267†	1,421	1,414
Pigs	2,350	2,350	2,338
Sheep	5,850*	3,584	3,578
Goats	750	630	623
Chickens*	34,000	35,000	35,000
Turkeys*	7,500	7,000	7,000

* FAO estimate(s).
† Unofficial figure.

Source: FAO.

LIVESTOCK PRODUCTS
('000 metric tons)

	1999	2000	2001
Beef and veal	97	100	94
Mutton and lamb	22	24	22*
Pig meat	346	327	315
Poultry meat	268	266†	266†
Cows' milk	1,978	1,995	1,860*
Sheep's milk	98	104	98*
Goats' milk	34	34	35*
Cheese	73	76	76
Butter	25	25	24*
Hen eggs	110	117	108*
Cattle hides	11	11†	10†

* Unofficial figure.
† FAO estimate.

Source: FAO.

Forestry

ROUNDWOOD REMOVALS

('000 cubic metres, excluding bark)

	1998	1999	2000
Sawlogs, veneer logs and logs for sleepers	3,372	3,230	2,734
Pulpwood	4,396	4,968	5,936
Other industrial wood	180	180	180*
Fuel wood	600	600	600*
Total	8,548	8,978	9,450

* FAO estimate.

Source: FAO.

SAWNWOOD PRODUCTION

('000 cubic metres, including railway sleepers)

	1998	1999	2000
Coniferous (softwood)	1,120	1,080	1,020
Broadleaved (hardwood)	370	350	407
Total	1,490	1,430	1,427

Source: FAO.

Fishing

('000 metric tons, live weight)

	1998	1999	2000
Capture	224.2	208.4	187.2
Greenland halibut	3.3	4.0	4.7
Atlantic cod	6.0	4.2	3.8
Atlantic horse mackerel	21.4	15.5	15.5
European pilchard (sardine)	83.0	72.0	66.3
Silver scabbardfish	5.5	3.3	0.1
Black scabbardfish	7.6	7.2	7.1
Atlantic redfishes	6.6	10.5	9.7
Chub mackerel	7.8	15.0	11.6
Octopuses	6.5	9.5	9.8
Aquaculture	7.5	7.5	7.5
Total catch	231.5	215.2	194.7

Note: Figures exclude aquatic plants ('000 metric tons): 1.0 in 1998; 1.9 in 1999; 1.2 in 2000.

Source: FAO, *Yearbook of Fishery Statistics*.

Mining

('000 metric tons, unless otherwise indicated)

	1999	2000	2001*
Iron ore: gross weight	16.0	15.0	14.5
Iron ore: metal content	11.7	11.8*	11.0
Copper ore†	99.5	76.2	83.0‡
Tin ore (metric tons)†	2,163.0	1,227.0	1,200.0
Tungsten ore (metric tons)†	434.0	743.0	700.0
Silver ore (metric tons)†	26.5	20.4	23.1‡
Uranium ore (metric tons)†	12.0	16.0	5.0‡
Marble	1,215.0*‡	933.0*‡	1,000.0
Granite (crushed and ornamental)	22,858.0*‡	20,631.0*‡	20,500.0
Kaolin	221.3	162.7	146.4
Salt (rock)	558.8‡	584.5	625.8‡
Gypsum and anhydrite	550.0*	698.7*	700.0
Talc (metric tons)	9,554	7,407	7,500

* Estimated production.

† Figures refer to the metal content of ores.

‡ Reported figures.

Source: US Geological Survey.

Industry

SELECTED PRODUCTS

('000 metric tons, unless otherwise indicated)

	1997	1998	1999
Frozen fish	32.6	35.1	35.7
Tinned fish	37.7	48.2	45.6
Margarine and other prepared fats	58.9	57.5	n.a.
Flour	630	701	645
Refined sugar	339	381	359
Prepared animal feeds	3,742	3,812	3,674
Distilled alcoholic beverages ('000 hectolitres)	214	241	270
Wine ('000 hectolitres)	4,409	3,463	4,479
Beer ('000 hectolitres)	6,766	7,072	6,947
Cigarettes (million units)	13,234	15,781	17,742
Wool yarn (pure and mixed)	7.5	5.8	5.7
Cotton yarn (pure and mixed)	122.8	120.6	112.9
Woven cotton fabrics (million sq. metres)	410	444	405
Woven woollen fabrics (million sq. metres)	6.5	7.7	9.0
Knitted fabrics	94.3	99.7	87.6
Footwear, excl. rubber ('000 pairs)	71,949	68,179	75,054
Wood pulp (sulphate and soda)	1,628	1,624	1,670
Caustic soda (Sodium hydroxide)	77*	71*	n.a.
Soda ash (Sodium carbonate)	205*	187*	n.a.
Nitrogenous fertilizers	113	135	n.a.
Jet fuels	1,023	1,048†	n.a.
Motor spirit (petrol)	2,835	2,792†	n.a.
Naphthas	900	904†	n.a.
Distillate fuel oils	3,970	4,368†	n.a.
Residual fuel oils	3,023	3,185†	n.a.
Liquefied petroleum gas	454	410†	n.a.
Coke	340	352†	n.a.
Gas from cokeries (terajoules)	3,047	n.a.	n.a.
Household ware of porcelain or china (metric tons)	26,265	26,723	22,747
Household ware of other ceramic materials (metric tons)	90,412	102,168	107,848
Clay building bricks	3	4	5
Cement	9,395	9,784	10,079
Pig-iron	431†	365†	389
Crude steel (ingots)	879†	907†	1,013
Refrigerators for household use ('000)	211	257	300
Radio receivers ('000)	4,552	5,076	5,939
Electric energy (million kWh)	34,187	n.a.	n.a.
Gas from gasworks (terajoules)	3,163	3,419†	n.a.

* Data from the UN Economic Commission for Europe, Geneva.

† Estimated or provisional output. Figure from the US Geological Survey.

Source: UN, *Industrial Commodity Statistics Yearbook*.

Finance

CURRENCY AND EXCHANGE RATES

Monetary Units

100 cent = 1 euro (€)

Sterling and Dollar Equivalents (31 December 2002)

£1 sterling = 1.5370 euros

US $1 = 0.9536 euros

100 euros = £65.06 = $104.87

Average Exchange Rate (euros per US dollar)

2000	1.0854
2001	1.1175
2002	1.0626

Note: The national currency was formerly the Portuguese escudo. From the introduction of the euro, with Portuguese participation, on 1 January 1999, a fixed exchange rate of €1 = 200.482 escudos was in operation. Euro notes and coins were introduced on 1 January 2002. The euro and local currency circulated alongside each other until 28 February, after which the euro became the sole legal tender. Some of the figures in this Survey are still in terms of escudos.

BUDGET
('000 million escudos)*

Revenue	1999	2000	2001†
Taxation	4,851.9	5,217.0	5,380.7
Taxes on incomes, profits and capital gains	2,011.2	2,268.7	2,290.3
Domestic taxes on goods and services	2,779.6	2,881.6	3,013.7
General sales, turnover or value-added taxes	1,585.0	1,738.7	1,834.7
Duties, fines and other penalties	61.1	66.7	76.7
Other current revenue	197.7	184.5	259.2
Entrepreneurial and property income	96.0	85.6	74.8
Capital revenue	151.0	161.4	70.2
Other	102.5	136.7	83.3
Total	5,303.0	5,699.6	5,793.4

Expenditure	1999	2000	2001†
Current expenditure	5,057.5	5,576.3	5,904.8
Expenditure on goods and services	2,065.3	2,243.8	2,382.0
Wages and salaries	1,838.2	2,000.6	2,157.2
Other purchases of goods and services	227.1	243.2	224.8
Interest payments	591.2	706.8	754.9
Subsidies and other current transfers	2,354.8	2,575.4	2,720.8
Subsidies	129.8	123.7	123.5
Transfers to public administrative bodies	1,866.6	2,084.4	2,230.8
Other transfers	358.4	367.3	366.5
Capital expenditure	663.3	628.1	712.0
Acquisitions of fixed capital assets	140.0	106.5	125.4
Capital transfers	517.8	517.0	582.0
Total	5,720.8	6,204.3	6,616.8

* Figures refer to the consolidated accounts of the central Government, excluding assets and liabilities.
† Estimates.
Source: Direcção-Geral do Orçamento, Ministério das Finanças.

INTERNATIONAL RESERVES
(US $ million at 31 December)*

	2000	2001	2002
Gold†	5,353	5,394	6,522
IMF special drawing rights	54	62	76
Reserve position in IMF	316	376	447
Foreign exchange	8,539	9,228	10,656
Total	14,261	15,060	17,968

* Reserves are defined in accordance with the Eurosystem's statistical definition.
† Valued at $274.4 per ounce in 2000, at $276.5 per ounce in 2001 and at $342.7 per ounce in 2002.
Source: IMF, *International Financial Statistics*.

MONEY SUPPLY
(million euros at 31 December)

	2000	2001	2002
Currency in circulation	6,532	5,918	8,460*
Demand deposits at banking institutions	42,500	46,947	45,920

* Currency put into circulation by the Banco de Portugal was 5,968 million euros.
Source: IMF, *International Financial Statistics*.

COST OF LIVING
(Consumer Price Index; base: 1997 = 100)

	1998	1999
Food and non-alcoholic beverages	103.5	105.7
Alcoholic beverages and tobacco	104.9	112.5
Clothing and footwear	99.0	99.4
Housing, utilities, etc.	102.7	103.6
Furnishings, household equipment and routine maintenance	102.1	104.4
Health	104.6	108.9
Transport	102.5	105.4
Communications	96.1	92.6
Recreation and culture	99.7	100.4
Education	118.7	124.5
Hotels, cafés and restaurants	103.4	106.3
Other goods and services	103.5	107.4
All items	102.8	105.2

All items (base: 1995 = 100): 112.6 in 2000; 117.6 in 2001; 121.9 in 2002 (Source: IMF, *International Financial Statistics*).

NATIONAL ACCOUNTS
(at current prices)

Composition of the Gross National Product
(provisional, million euros)

	2000	2001	2002
Gross domestic product at market prices	115,546.2	123,052.8	129,339.8
Primary incomes received from abroad	5,657.5	6,579.9	6,313.8
Less Primary incomes paid abroad	8,440.6	9,891.3	9,654.4
Gross national income (GNI)	112,763.1	119,741.4	125,999.2
Less Consumption of fixed capital	20,002.3	21,411.6	22,231.8
Net national income	92,760.8	98,329.8	103,767.4
Current transfers from abroad	4,818.1	4,989.9	5,395.6
Less Current transfers paid abroad	1,539.2	1,941.5	2,477.4
Net national disposable income	96,039.7	101,378.2	106,685.6

Expenditure on the Gross Domestic Product
(million euros)

	2000	2001	2002
Final consumption expenditure	94,812.1	100,541.3	105,734.3
Households	69,302.9	73,016.9	76,101.3
Non-profit institutions serving households	1,812.5	1,955.8	2,105.4
General government	23,696.8	25,568.6	27,527.6
Gross capital formation	33,702.9	34,550.9	33,353.0
Gross fixed capital formation	32,656.0	33,470.1	32,226.2
Changes in inventories	871.1	926.9	974.3
Acquisitions, less disposals, of valuables	175.8	153.9	152.5
Total domestic expenditure	128,514.9	135,092.2	139,087.3
Exports of goods and services	36,563.3	38,096.8	38,096.8
Less Imports of goods and services	49,505.2	50,136.2	48,704.4
GDP in market prices	115,546.2	123,052.8	129,339.8
GDP at constant 1995 prices	97,932.7	99,538.9	100,008.5

Gross Domestic Product by Economic Activity
(provisional, million euros)

	2000	2001	2002
Agriculture, hunting, forestry and fishing	3,532.9	4,019.0	4,083.8
Electricity, gas and water	2,877.0	3,022.6	3,151.4
Manufacturing	19,378.5	20,354.6	20,958.2
Construction	7,999.6	8,451.5	8,450.8
Trade, restaurants and hotels	17,599.5	18,886.5	19,816.9
Transport, storage and communications	6,574.0	6,928.8	7,171.9
Finance, insurance and real estate	13,092.6	13,598.3	13,920.6
Other services	33,590.3	36,425.9	38,982.0
Sub-total	94,706.0	101,102.4	106,144.6
Less Financial intermediation services indirectly measured	4,969.2	5,292.4	5,195.5
Gross value added in basic prices	99,675.2	106,394.8	111,340.1
Taxes on products (net)	15,956.3	16,547.8	17,750.3
Statistical discrepancy	−85.3	110.2	249.4
GDP in market prices	115,546.2	123,052.8	129,339.8

BALANCE OF PAYMENTS
(US $ million)

	1999	2000	2001
Exports of goods f.o.b.	25,468	25,219	25,795
Imports of goods f.o.b.	−39,227	−39,155	−38,774
Trade balance	−13,758	−13,936	−12,979
Exports of services	8,659	8,472	8,787
Imports of services	−6,801	−6,593	−6,193
Balance on goods and services	−11,900	−12,057	−10,385
Other income received	4,261	4,793	5,128
Other income paid	−6,048	−7,101	−8,182
Balance on goods, services and income	−13,669	−14,365	−13,439
Current transfers received	6,048	5,386	5,626
Current transfers paid	−2,143	−1,983	−2,145
Current balance	−9,764	−10,962	−9,959
Capital account (net)	2,459	1,512	1,067
Direct investment abroad	−3,019	−7,749	−7,874
Direct investment from abroad	1,235	6,518	5,945
Portfolio investment assets	−6,737	−4,583	−6,430
Portfolio investment liabilities	9,945	2,792	68,405
Financial derivatives assets	2,682	3,673	3,086
Financial derivatives liabilities	−2,485	−3,351	−2,830
Other investment assets	421	−10,262	−4,743
Other investment liabilities	7,055	24,146	14,827
Net errors and omissions	−1,577	−1,363	−642
Overall balance	216	371	852

Source: IMF, *International Financial Statistics*.

External Trade

PRINCIPAL COMMODITIES
(distribution by SITC, US $ million)

Imports c.i.f.	1998	1999	2000
Food and live animals	3,840.8	4,083.1	3,742.1
Crude materials (inedible) except fuels	1,519.5	1,331.5	1,337.6
Mineral fuels, lubricants, etc.	2,072.3	2,716.3	4,122.6
Petroleum, petroleum products, etc.	1,659.7	2,173.3	3,307.7
Crude petroleum oils, etc.	1,218.4	1,640.7	2,436.5
Chemicals and related products	3,518.2	3,691.7	3,626.3
Basic manufactures	7,437.0	7,412.2	7,365.5
Textile yarn, fabrics, etc.	2,165.2	1,993.9	1,892.5
Iron and steel	1,282.4	1,224.2	1,255.0
Machinery and transport equipment	14,066.3	15,569.1	14,902.9
Machinery specialized for particular industries	1,323.0	1,402.8	1,367.5
General industrial machinery, equipment and parts	1,332.0	1,435.7	1,432.1
Office machines and automatic data-processing equipment	977.9	1,112.8	981.4

Imports c.i.f. — *continued*	1998	1999	2000
Telecommunications and sound equipment	1,280.9	1,433.2	1,444.7
Other electrical machinery, apparatus, etc.	2,354.4	2,506.5	2,500.2
Road vehicles and parts*	5,365.1	6,044.3	5,617.8
Passenger motor cars (excl. buses)	2,824.0	3,366.1	2,922.4
Parts and accessories for cars, buses, lorries, etc.*	1,341.7	1,380.2	1,301.1
Miscellaneous manufactured articles	3,924.7	4,304.3	4,105.5
Total (incl. others)	37,048.5	39,828.6	39,946.6

* Data on parts exclude tyres, engines and electrical parts.

Exports f.o.b.	1998	1999	2000
Food and live animals	962.9	941.3	956.6
Crude materials (inedible) except fuels	986.0	1,006.3	1,073.0
Chemicals and related products	1,137.8	1,170.6	1,332.7
Basic manufactures	5,775.1	5,804.3	5,898.6
Cork and wood manufactures (excl. furniture)	932.1	929.7	947.2
Cork manufactures	735.7	746.4	766.7
Textile yarn, fabrics, etc.	1,777.9	1,769.7	1,688.4
Made-up articles, chiefly of textile materials	823.8	823.6	790.5
Non-metallic mineral manufactures	873.9	874.1	814.6
Machinery and transport equipment	7,991.1	8,352.3	8,379.1
General industrial machinery, equipment and parts	603.6	788.0	783.4
Telecommunications and sound equipment	805.6	976.9	1,015.2
Other electrical machinery, apparatus, etc.	2,153.9	2,312.2	2,458.4
Equipment for distributing electricity	927.3	923.1	998.7
Insulated electric wire, cable, etc.	915.9	906.1	950.2
Road vehicles and parts (excl. tyres, engines and electrical parts)	3,703.9	3,599.8	3,290.6
Passenger motor cars (excl. buses)	2,595.3	2,515.7	2,224.4
Miscellaneous manufactured articles	6,179.2	5,974.3	5,326.8
Clothing and accessories (excl. footwear)	3,462.4	3,265.8	2,826.4
Outerwear, knitted or crocheted	1,129.5	1,055.0	860.4
Undergarments, knitted or crocheted	791.9	785.0	759.0
Footwear	1,605.2	1,581.0	1,395.1
Leather footwear	1,524.8	1,532.6	1,345.8
Total (incl. others)	24,217.9	24,493.6	24,364.8

Source: UN, *International Trade Statistics Yearbook*.

PRINCIPAL TRADING PARTNERS
(US $ million)

Imports c.i.f.	1998	1999	2000
Belgium	1,261.8*	1,246.9	1,218.3
Brazil	521.0	390.9	442.8
France-Monaco	4,132.1	4,547.8	4,240.9
Germany	5,513.6	5,863.4	5,483.4
Italy-San Marino-Vatican City	2,941.6	3,086.3	2,851.1
Japan	1,055.1	1,075.2	976.6
Korea, Republic	311.6	408.7	421.2
Netherlands	1,805.5	1,903.0	1,833.2
Nigeria	275.6	325.0	814.2
Norway	399.3	562.7	702.0
Spain	8,910.2	10,058.9	10,347.7
Sweden	550.7	538.8	498.2
Switzerland-Liechtenstein	411.0	392.1	326.0
United Kingdom	2,459.5	2,711.4	2,392.7
USA	1,055.6	1,124.6	1,181.4
Total (incl. others)	37,048.5	39,828.6	39,946.6

* Including Luxembourg.

Exports f.o.b.	1998	1999	2000
Angola	410.7	294.3	342.7
Austria	239.2	251.0	201.2
Belgium	1,170.6*	1,155.7	1,446.2
Denmark	372.7	354.7	295.7
France-Monaco	3,485.1	3,415.2	3,087.0
Germany	4,788.1	4,837.8	4,397.4
Italy-San Marino-Vatican City	982.2	1,022.0	968.0
Netherlands	1,171.9	1,079.9	1,031.2
Spain	3,755.9	4,430.8	4,701.7
Sweden	475.7	443.5	403.8
Switzerland-Liechtenstein	302.1	272.3	248.8
United Kingdom	2,926.3	2,949.8	2,649.2
USA	1,191.2	1,212.9	1,408.6
Total (incl. others)	24,217.9	24,493.6	24,364.8

* Including Luxembourg.

Source: UN, *International Trade Statistics Yearbook*.

Transport

RAILWAYS
(traffic)

	1996	1997	1998
Passenger journeys ('000)	177,094	178,130	177,965
Passenger-kilometres (million)	4,503	4,563	4,602
Freight ('000 metric tons)	9,064	10,457	10,101
Freight ton-kilometres (million)	2,178	2,632	2,340

ROAD TRAFFIC
(motor vehicles registered at 31 December)

	1996	1997	1998
Light and heavy vehicles	5,308,542	5,668,326	5,862,511
Motorcycles	243,877	274,715	265,166
Tractors	242,672	253,822	301,045
Trailers and semi-trailers	291,354	303,904	316,956

SHIPPING

Merchant Fleet
(registered at 31 December)

	1999	2000	2001
Number of vessels	462	471	456
Total displacement (grt)	1,164,767	1,191,492	1,199,244

Source: Lloyd's Register-Fairplay, *World Fleet Statistics*.

International Sea-borne Freight Traffic

	1996	1997	1998*
Vessels entered ('000 gross registered tons)	96,453	n.a.	n.a.
Goods loaded ('000 metric tons)	15,301	14,788	14,342
Goods unloaded ('000 metric tons)	40,571	42,498	42,490

* Figures exclude Madeira and the Azores.

CIVIL AVIATION
(TAP and SATA only, '000)

	1996	1997	1998
Kilometres flown	88,017	84,225	n.a.
Passenger-kilometres (million)	8,034	8,833	10,104
Freight ton-kilometres	209,956	235,101	232,000
Mail ton-kilometres	16,520	16,657	15,000

Tourism

FOREIGN TOURIST ARRIVALS BY COUNTRY OF RESIDENCE

Country of Origin	1999	2000	2001
Belgium	232,500	242,500	252,400
France	727,200	763,300	802,300
Germany	931,300	931,300	883,300
The Netherlands	500,400	500,400	495,400
Italy	269,600	290,900	312,400
Spain	5,736,900	5,864,900	5,927,000
United Kingdom	1,847,700	1,877,800	1,966,600
USA	227,900	258,900	238,000
Total (incl. others)	11,632,000	12,096,700	12,167,200

Source: Direcção-Geral do Turismo.

Receipts from tourism (US $ million): 5,302 in 1998; 5,131 in 1999; 5,206 in 2000 (provisional) (Source: World Tourism Organization).

Communications Media

	1999	2000	2001
Telephones ('000 main lines in use)	4,229.8	4,313.6	4,369.7
Mobile cellular telephones ('000 subscribers)	4,671.5	6,665.0	7,977.5
Personal computers ('000 in use)	930	1,050	1,210
Internet users ('000)	1,000	2,500	3,600
Television receivers ('000 in use)	5,600	6,319	n.a.

Source: International Telecommunication Union.

Facsimile machines ('000 in use): 70 in 1997.

Radio receivers ('000 in use): 3,020 in 1997.

Books published (titles): 7,868 in 1996.

Daily newspapers (number of titles, 1998): 38 (total distribution 258 million copies in 1996).

Sources: mainly UN, *Statistical Yearbook*; UNESCO, *Statistical Yearbook*.

Education

(2001/02)

	Institutions	Teachers	Students
Pre-school	5,378*	13,011	238,222
Basic: 1st cycle	9,215*	30,941	471,322
Basic: 2nd cycle			249,675
Basic: 3rd cycle	3,420	111,756	377,306
Secondary			373,607
Professional	215*	6,895†	31,159
Higher	282‡	16,192‡	346,034*

* 1998//99 figure.

† 1995/96 figure.

‡ 1996/97 figure.

Source: partly Ministério da Educação.

2001/02 (Institutions): Public 14,100; Private 2,650 (Source: Ministério da Educação).

Adult literacy rate (UNESCO estimates): 92.2% (males 94.7%; females 89.9%) in 2000 (Source: UN Development Programme, *Human Development Report*).

Directory

The Constitution

The Constitution of the Portuguese Republic was promulgated on 2 April 1976, and came into force on 25 April. It was revised in 1982, when ideological elements were diminished and the Council of the Revolution was abolished; in 1989, to permit economic reforms and a greater role for the private sector; in 1992, prior to the ratification of the Treaty on European Union (also known as the Maastricht Treaty); in 1997 when changes included provision for the holding of referendums on questions of national interest; and in 2001 to incorporate reciprocal political rights for citizens of lusophone countries, to instate a ban on strike action by police trade unions and officially to recognize the UN International Criminal Court. The following is a summary of the Constitution's main provisions:

FUNDAMENTAL PRINCIPLES

Portugal is a sovereign Republic based on the dignity of the individual and the will of the people, which strives to create a just, caring and free society and to realize economic, social and cultural democracy. It comprises the territory defined by history on the European continent and the archipelagos of the Azores and Madeira. The Azores and Madeira shall constitute autonomous regions.

The fundamental duties of the State include the following: to safeguard national independence; to guarantee fundamental rights and freedoms; to defend political democracy and to encourage citizens' participation in the solving of national problems; and to promote the welfare, quality of life and equality of the people.

FUNDAMENTAL RIGHTS AND DUTIES

All citizens are equal before the law. Rights, freedoms and safeguards are upheld by the State and include the following: the right to life; of *habeas corpus*; to the inviolability of the home and of correspondence; to freedom of expression and of conscience; to freedom of movement, emigration and of assembly. Freedom of the press is guaranteed.

Rights and duties of citizens include the following: the right and the duty to work; the right to vote (at 18 years of age); the right to form and participate in political associations and parties; the freedom to form trade unions and the right to strike; the right to set up co-operatives; the right to private property; the right to social security and medical services; the duty of the State and of society to protect the family and the disabled; the right to education, culture and sport; consumer rights.

ECONOMIC ORGANIZATION

The economic and social organization of Portugal shall be based on the subordination of economic power to political power, the co-existence of the public, private, co-operative and social sectors of ownership, and the public ownership of the means of production and land, in accordance with the public interest, as well as natural resources; and on the democratic planning of the economy, and democratic intervention by the workers. Enterprises nationalized after 25 April 1974 may be reprivatized. The aims of economic and social development plans include the promotion of economic growth, the harmonious development of sectors and regions, the fair individual and regional distribution of the national product and the defence of the environment and of the quality of life of the Portuguese people. The consultative Economic and Social Council participates in the formulation of development plans. It comprises representatives of the Government, workers' organizations, economic enterprises and representatives of autonomous regions and local organizations.

The aims of agrarian policy are to improve the situation of farm workers and to increase agricultural production and productivity. *Latifúndios* (large estates) will be adjusted in size, and property which has been expropriated, with compensation, shall be handed over to small farmers or co-operatives for exploitation. *Minifúndios* (small estates) will be adjusted in size, through the granting of incentives to integrate or divide. The aims of commercial policy include the development and diversification of foreign economic relations. The aims of industrial policy include an increase in production in the context of modernization and adjustment, greater competition, the support of small and medium enterprises and the support of industrial and technological innovation. The financial and fiscal system aims at encouraging savings and achieving the equal distribution of wealth and incomes. The State Budget shall be supervised by the Accounts Court and the Assembly of the Republic (Assembléia da República). Economic policy includes the stimulation of competition, the protection of consumers and the combating of speculative activities and restrictive trade practices.

POLITICAL ORGANIZATION

Political power shall lie with the people. The organs of sovereignty shall be: the President of the Republic, the Assembly of the Republic, the Government and the Courts. Direct, secret and regular elections shall be held. No-one shall hold political office for life.

PRESIDENT OF THE REPUBLIC

The President of the Republic shall represent the Republic. The President guarantees national independence, the unity of the State, and the proper working of democratic institutions. The President shall be elected by direct and secret universal adult suffrage. The candidate who obtains more than one-half of the valid votes will be elected President. The President shall hold office for five years. The President may not be re-elected for a third consecutive term of office.

The duties of the President include the following: to preside over the Council of State; to set dates for elections; to convene extraordinary sessions of the Assembly of the Republic; to dissolve the Assembly; to appoint and dismiss the Prime Minister; to appoint and dismiss the members of the Government at the proposal of the Prime Minister; to promulgate laws; to veto laws; to apply to the Constitutional Court; to nominate ambassadors, upon the proposal of the Government; to accredit diplomatic representatives; to ratify international treaties, after they have been duly approved; to dismiss the Government if and when the normal functioning of institutions is at stake.

COUNCIL OF STATE

The Council of State (Conselho de Estado) is the political consultative organ of the President of the Republic. It is presided over by the President of the Republic and comprises the President of the Assembly of the Republic, the Prime Minister, the President of the Constitutional Court, the Superintendent of Justice, the Presidents of the Regional Governments, certain former Presidents of the Republic, five citizens nominated by the President of the Republic and five citizens elected by the Assembly.

ASSEMBLY OF THE REPUBLIC

The Assembly of the Republic (Assembléia da República) represents all Portuguese citizens, and shall have a minimum of 180 and a maximum of 230 members, elected under a system of proportional representation by the electoral constituencies. The duties of the Assembly include the following: to present and approve amendments to the Constitution and to approve the political and administrative statutes of the Autonomous Regions; to enact legislation; to confer legislative authority on the Government; to approve plans and the Budget; to approve international conventions and treaties; to propose to the President of the Republic that questions of national interest be submitted to referendum; to supervise the fulfilment of the Constitution and laws. The Assembly supports the participation of Portugal in the process of building the European Union. Each legislative period shall last four years. The legislative session shall run from 15 September to 15 June each year.

GOVERNMENT

The Government formulates the general policy of the country and is the highest organ of public administration. It shall comprise the Prime Minister, Ministers, Secretaries and Under-Secretaries of State and may include one or more Deputy Prime Ministers. The Prime Minister is appointed and dismissed by the President. Other members of the Government are appointed by the President at the proposal of the Prime Minister. The Government shall be responsible to the President and the Assembly. The Government's programme shall be presented to the Assembly of the Republic for scrutiny within 10 days of the appointment of the Prime Minister.

JUDICIARY

The courts are independent organs of sovereignty with competence to administer justice. There shall be Courts of First Instance (District Courts), Courts of Second Instance (Courts of Appeal), the Supreme Administrative Court and the Supreme Court of Justice, in addition to the Constitutional Court. There shall also be military courts (when the State is at war) and an Accounts Court. There may be maritime courts and courts of arbitration.

The jury shall comprise the judges of the plenary court and the jurors. People's judges may be created. It is the duty of the Ministério Público to represent the State. Its highest organ is the Procuradoria-Geral which is presided over by the Procurador-Geral, who is appointed and dismissed by the President of the Republic.

AUTONOMOUS REGIONS

The special political and administrative arrangements for the archipelagos of the Azores and Madeira shall be based on their geographical, economic and social conditions and on the historic aspirations of the people to autonomy. The State is represented in each of the Autonomous Regions by a Minister of the Republic.

The organs of government in the Autonomous Regions (which are subject to dissolution by the President of the Republic if a major breach of the Constitution occurs) are: the Regional Legislative Assembly, elected by direct and secret universal adult suffrage, and the Regional Government which shall be politically responsible to the Regional Legislative Assembly. Its Chairman is appointed by the Minister of the Republic. The Minister shall appoint or dismiss members of the Regional Government on the proposal of its Chairman.

LOCAL GOVERNMENT

The local authorities shall be territorial bodies corporate with representative organs serving the particular interests of the local population. The local authorities on the mainland shall be the parishes, municipal authorities and administrative regions. The Autonomous Regions of the Azores and Madeira shall comprise parishes and municipal authorities.

PUBLIC ADMINISTRATIVE AUTHORITIES

The public administrative authorities shall seek to promote the public interest whilst respecting the legal interests and rights of all citizens. Citizens shall have the right to be informed of, and to have redress against, the public administrative authorities when the matter directly concerns them.

ARMED FORCES

The President of the Republic is Supreme Commander-in-Chief of the Armed Forces, and appoints and dismisses the Chiefs of Staff. The defence forces shall safeguard national independence and territorial integrity. Military service shall be compulsory. The right to conscientious objection is recognized.

SAFEGUARDS AND REVISION OF THE CONSTITUTION

Changes in the Constitution shall be approved by a majority of two-thirds of the members of the Assembly of the Republic present, provided that the number of such members exceeds an absolute majority of the members entitled to vote. Constitutional revisions must comply with the independence, unity and secularism of the State; the rights, freedoms and safeguards of citizens; universal, direct and secret suffrage and the system of proportional representation, etc.

The Government

HEAD OF STATE

President: Dr JORGE FERNANDO BRANCO DE SAMPAIO (took office 9 March 1996; re-elected 14 January 2001).

COUNCIL OF MINISTERS
(April 2003)

The Government is a coalition, comprising the Partido Social Democrata (PSD) and the Partido Popular (PP).

Prime Minister: JOSÉ MANUEL DURÃO BARROSO (PSD).

Minister of State and of Finance: MANUELA FERREIRA LEITE (PSD).

Minister of State and of National Defence: PAULO PORTAS (PP).

Minister of Foreign Affairs and Portuguese Communities Abroad: ANTÓNIO MARTINS DA CRUZ (PSD).

Minister of Internal Affairs: ANTÓNIO FIGUEIREDO LOPES (PSD).

Minister of Justice: MARIA CELESTE CARDONA (PP).

Minister of the Presidency: NUNO MORAIS SARMENTO (PSD).

Minister of Parliamentary Affairs: LUÍS MARQUES MENDES (PSD).

Minister in assistance to the Prime Minister: JOSÉ LUÍS ARNAUT (PSD).

Minister of the Economy: CARLOS TAVARES (PSD).

Minister of Agriculture, Rural Development and Fisheries: ARMANDO SEVINATE PINTO (PSD).

Minister of Education: DAVID JUSTINO (PSD).

Minister of Science and Higher Education: PEDRO LYNCE (PSD).

Minister of Culture: PEDRO ROSETA (PSD).

Minister of Health: LUÍS FILIPE PEREIRA (PSD).

Minister of Social Security and Labour: ANTÓNIO JOSÉ BAGÃO FÉLIX (PP).

Minister of Public Works, Transport and Housing: ANTÓNIO CARMONA RODRIGUES (PSD).

Minister of Towns, Territorial Planning and the Environment: AMÍLCAS THEIAS (PSD).

MINISTRIES

Office of the President: Presidência da República, Palácio de Belém, 1300-004 Lisbon; tel. (21) 3614600; fax (21) 3610570; e-mail belem@presidenciarepublica.pt; internet www.presidenciarepublica.pt.

Office of the Prime Minister: Presidência do Conselho de Ministros, Rua da Imprensa à Estrela 4, 1200-888 Lisbon; tel. (21) 3974091; fax (21) 3951616; e-mail pm@pm.gov.pt; internet www.primeiro-ministro.gov.pt.

Ministry of Agriculture, Rural Development and Fisheries: Praça do Comércio, 1149-010 Lisbon; tel. (21) 3234652; fax (21) 3234604; e-mail gabinete.ministro@min-agricultura.pt; internet www.min-agricultura.pt.

Ministry of Culture: Rua D. Francisco Manuel de Melo, 15, 1070–085, Lisbon; tel. (21) 3848400; fax (21) 3848439; e-mail sgmc@mail.min-cultura.pt; internet www.min-cultura.pt.

Ministry of the Economy: Rua da Horta Seca 15, 1200-221 Lisbon; tel. (21) 3228600; fax (21) 3228713; e-mail secretaria.geral@sg.min-economia.pt; internet www.min-economia.pt.

Ministry of Education: Av. 5 de Outubro 107, 1069-018 Lisbon; tel. (21) 7931603; fax (21) 7164119; e-mail secsg@min-edu.pt; internet www.min-edu.pt.

Ministry of Finance: Rua da Alfândega, 5 1100–006, Lisbon; tel. (21) 8816800; fax (21) 8816862; e-mail relacoes.publicas@sgmf.pt; internet www.min-financas.pt.

Ministry of Foreign Affairs and Portuguese Communities Abroad: Palácio das Necessidades, Largo do Rilvas, 1399-030 Lisbon; tel. (21) 3946472; fax (21) 3946053; e-mail ministro@mne.gov.pt; internet www.min-nestrangeiros.pt.

Ministry of Health: Av. João Crisóstomo 9, 1049-062 Lisbon; tel. (21) 3305166; fax (21) 3305175; e-mail gms@ms.gov.pt; internet www.min-saude.pt.

Ministry of Internal Affairs: Praça do Comércio, 1149-015 Lisbon; tel. (21) 3233000; fax (21) 3427372; e-mail ministro@mai.gov.pt; internet www.mai.gov.pt.

Ministry of Justice: Rua de Ouro, 6 1149–019, Lisbon; tel. (21) 3222300; fax (21) 3423198; e-mail correio@sg.mj.gov.pt; internet www.mj.gov.pt.

Ministry of National Defence: Av. Ilha de Madeira, 1400-204 Lisbon; tel. (21) 3034500; fax (21) 3034525; e-mail ministro@mdn.gov.pt; internet www.mdn.gov.pt.

Ministry of the Presidency: Rua da Imprensa à Estrela 4, 1200-888 Lisbon; tel. (21) 3923570; fax (21) 3964468; e-mail mp@mp.gov.pt; internet www.mp.gov.pt.

Ministry of Public Works, Transport and Housing: Palácio Penafiel, Rua de S. Mamede (ao Caldas) 21, 1149-050 Lisbon; tel. (21) 8815204; fax (21) 8863827; e-mail ministro@mes.gov.pt; internet www.mes.gov.pt.

Ministry of Science and Higher Education: Palácio de Laranjeiras, Estrada de Laranjeiras, 197–05 1649–018, Lisbon; tel. (21) 7231000; fax (21) 7231160; e-mail mces@mces.gov.pt; internet www.mces.pt.

Ministry of Social Security and Labour: Praça de Londres 2, 1049-056 Lisbon; tel. (21) 8424106; fax (21) 8424108; e-mail mts@mts.gov.pt; internet www.mts.gov.pt.

Ministry of Towns, Territorial Planning and the Environment: Rua de O Século 51, 1200-433 Lisbon; tel. (21) 3232500; fax (21) 3232531; e-mail ministro@maot.gov.pt; internet www.ambiente.gov.pt.

Presidency of the Council of Ministers: Rua Professor Gomes Teixeira 1399–022, Lisbon; tel. (21) 3927600; fax (21) 3927615; e-mail relacoes.publicas@pcm.gov.pt; internet www.portugal.gov.pt.

COUNCIL OF STATE

The Council of State (Conselho de Estado) is a consultative body, presided over by the President of the Republic (see The Constitution).

President and Legislature

PRESIDENT

Election, 14 January 2001

Candidate	Votes	% of votes
Jorge Sampaio (PS)	2,411,453	55.8
Joaquim Ferreira do Amaral (PSD)	1,493,858	34.5
António Abreu (PCP)	221,971	5.1
Fernando Rosas (Bloco de Esquerda)	145,019	3.0
Garcia Pereira (PCTP/MRPP) . . .	68,577	1.6

ASSEMBLÉIA DA REPÚBLICA

Assembléia da República: Palácio de S. Bento 1249-068, Lisbon; tel. (21) 3919000; fax (21) 3197440; e-mail correo@centro.parlamento.pt; internet www.parlamento.pt.

President: JOÃO BOSCO SOARES MOTA AMARAL.

General Election, 17 March 2002

Party	Seats
Partido Social Democrata (PSD)	105
Partido Socialista (PS)	96
Partido Popular (PP)	14
Partido Comunista Português (PCP)-Partido Ecologista Os Verdes (PEV)	12
Bloco de Esquerda	3
Total	**230**

Autonomous Regions

THE AZORES

President of the Regional Government: CARLOS MANUEL DO VALE CÉSAR.

Assembléia Legislativa Regional: 9900 Horta; tel. (292) 207600; e-mail presidencia@alra.pt; internet www.alra.pt; Pres. FERNANDO MANUEL MACHADO MENEZES.

MADEIRA

President of the Regional Government: Dr ALBERTO JOÃO JARDIM.

Assembléia Legislativa Regional: Av. do Mar e das Comunidades Madeirenses, 9004-506 Funchal; tel. (291) 210500; fax (291) 232977; e-mail presidencia@alrm.pt; internet www.alrm.pt; Pres. JOSÉ MIGUEL JARDIM D'OLIVAL MENDONÇA.

Political Organizations

Bloco de Esquerda: Av Almirante Reis 131–2°, 1150-015 Lisbon; tel. (21) 3510510; fax (21) 3510519; e-mail bloco.esquerda@bloco.org; internet www.bloco.org; Leader MIGUEL PORTAS.

Movimento O Partido de Terra (MPT) (The Earth Party Movement): Avda Eng. Arantes Oliveira 11, 1°A, 1900-221, Lisbon; tel. (21) 8438021; fax (21) 8438029; e-mail terra@mpt.pt; internet www.mpt.pt.

Partido Comunista Português (PCP) (Portuguese Communist Party): Rua Soeiro Pereira Gomes 3, 1600-196 Lisbon; tel. (21) 7813800; fax (21) 7969126; e-mail pcp@pcp.pt; internet www.pcp.pt; f. 1921; legalized 1974; theoretical foundation is Marxism-Leninism; aims are the defence and consolidation of the democratic regime and the revolutionary achievements, and ultimately the building of a socialist society in Portugal; 140,000 mems (1996); Sec.-Gen. CARLOS CARVALHAS.

Partido Comunista dos Trabalhadores Portugueses/Movimento Revolucionário Português do Proletariado (PCTP/MRPP) (Communist Workers' Party/Proletarian Portuguese Revolutionary Movement): Rua Palma 159, 2°D, 1000-391 Lisbon; f. 1970 as Movimento Reorganizativo do Partido do Proletariado; name changed in 1976; Leader GARCIA PEREIRA.

Partido da Solidariedade Nacional (Party of National Solidarity): Rua João Deus 1, 9050-027 Funchal; tel. (291) 223131.

Partido Democrático do Atlântico (PDA) (Democratic Party of the Atlantic): Largo 2 Março 65, 2500-152 Ponta Delgada; tel. (296) 284033.

Partido Ecologista Os Verdes (PEV) (The Greens): Calçada Salvador Correia de Sá 4-1°-D, 1200-399 Lisbon; tel. (21) 3432762; fax (21) 3432764; e-mail osverdes@mail.telepac.pt; internet www.osverdes.pt; f. 1982; ecological party.

Partido Nacional Renovador (PNR): Apto 14271 1064-004, Lisbon; tel. (96) 8747607; e-mail info@partidonacional.org; internet www.partidonacional.org; right-wing.

Partido Operário de Unidade Socialista (POUS) (Workers' Party of Socialist Unity): Rua do Salitre, 139G, 1250-198 Lisbon; tel. (21) 3159284; fax (21) 3524162; internet pous.pt.vu.

Partido Popular (PP) (Popular Party): Largo Adelino Amaro da Costa 5, 1149-063 Lisbon; tel. (21) 8869735; fax (21) 8860454; e-mail cds-pp@esoterica.pt; internet www.partido-popular.pt; f. 1974; fmrly Centro Democrático Social; centre-right; mem. of International Democratic Union; supports social market economy and reduction of public-sector intervention in the economy; defended revision of 1976 Constitution; Pres. PAULO PORTAS.

Partido Social Democrata (PSD) (Social Democratic Party): Rua de São Caetano 9, 1249-087 Lisbon; tel. (21) 3952140; fax (21) 3976967; e-mail psd@psd.pt; internet www.psd.pt; f. 1974; fmrly Partido Popular Democrático—PPD; aims to promote market economy, taking into account the welfare of the community; encourages European integration; 60,000 mems; Leader JOSÉ MANUEL DURÃO BARROSO; Sec.-Gen. JOSÉ LUÍS ARNAUT.

Partido Socialista (PS) (Socialist Party): Largo do Rato 2, 1269-143 Lisbon; tel. (21) 3822000; fax (21) 3822016; e-mail info@ps.pt; internet www.ps.pt; f. 1973; from former Acção Socialista Portuguesa (Portuguese Socialist Action); affiliate of the Socialist International and Party of European Socialists; advocates a society of greater social justice and co-operation between public, private and co-operative sectors, while respecting public liberties and the will of the majority attained through free elections; 100,000 mems; Sec.-Gen. EDUARDO FERRO RODRIGUES; Pres. ANTÓNIO ALMEIDA SANTOS.

Partido Socialista Revolucionário (PSR) (Revolutionary Socialist Party): Rua da Palma 268, 1100-394 Lisbon; tel. (21) 8864643; fax (21) 8882736; f. 1978; through merger of two Trotskyist groups.

Política XXI (PXXI): Rua Comandante Almoster 100, 1°D, 1500-197 Lisbon; tel. (21) 7740647.

União Democrática Popular (UDP) (People's Democratic Union): Rua de S. Bento 698-1°, 1250-223 Lisbon; tel. (21) 3885034; fax (21) 3885035; e-mail udpnacional@hotmail.com; internet www.udp.pt; f. 1974; Marxist-Leninist; comprises various political groups of the revolutionary left; Leader LUÍS FAZENDA.

Diplomatic Representation

EMBASSIES IN PORTUGAL

Algeria: Rua Duarte Pacheco Pereira 58, 1400-140 Lisbon; tel. (21) 3016356; fax (21) 3010393; e-mail embaixada-argelia@clix.pt; internet www.emb-argelia.pt; Ambassador EL-HAOUES RIACHE.

Angola: Av. da República 68, 1069-213 Lisbon; tel. (21) 7961830; fax (21) 7971238; e-mail emb.angola@mail.telepac.pt; internet www.embaixadadeangola.org; Ambassador OSVALDO SERRA VAN DUNEN.

Argentina: Av. João Crisóstomo 8 r/c, Esq., 1000-178 Lisbon; tel. (21) 7977311; fax (21) 7959255; e-mail embarpor@mailtelepac.pt; Ambassador JORGE MARCELO FAURIE.

Australia: Av. da Liberdade 200, 2nd Floor, 1250-147 Lisbon; tel. (21) 3101500; fax (21) 3101555; e-mail austemb@dfat.gov.au; internet www.portugal.embassy.gov.au; Ambassador Dr JANET GARDINER.

Austria: Av. Infante Santo 43-4°, 1399-046 Lisbon; tel. (21) 3958220; fax (21) 3958224; e-mail lissabon.ob@bmaa.gv.at; Ambassador Dr WOLFGANG KRIECHBAUM.

Belgium: Praça Marquês de Pombal 14-6°, 1269-024 Lisbon; tel. (21) 3170510; fax (21) 3561556; e-mail lisbon@diplobel.org; internet www.diplobel.org/portugal; Ambassador MICHEL CZETWERTYNSKI.

Brazil: Quinta de Milflores, Estrada das Laranjeiras 144, 1949-021 Lisbon; tel. (21) 7248510; fax (21) 7267623; e-mail geral@emb-brasil.pt; internet www.emb-brasil.pt; Ambassador JOSÉ GREGORI.

Bulgaria: Rua do Sacramento à Lapa 31, 1200-792 Lisbon; tel. (21) 3976364; fax (21) 3979272; e-mail ebul@mail.telepac.pt; Ambassador ALIOSHA NEDELCHEV.

Canada: Avda da Liberdade 196/200, 3°, 1269-121 Lisbon; tel. (21) 3164600; fax (21) 3164991; e-mail lisbon@dfait-maeci.gc.ca; internet www.dfait-maeci.gc.ca/lisbon; Chargé d'affaires a.i. JACQUES BÉLEC.

Cape Verde: Av. do Restelo 33, 1449-025 Lisbon; tel. (21) 3015271; fax (21) 3015308; e-mail emb.caboverde@mail.telepac.pt; Ambassador JOÃO HIGINO SILVA.

Chile: Av. Miguel Bombarda 5-1°, 1000-207 Lisbon; tel. (21) 3148054; fax (21) 3150909; e-mail echile.pt@mail.telepac.pt; internet www.emb.chile.pt; Ambassador BELISARIO VELASCO BARAONA.

China, People's Republic: Rua de São Caetano 2, 1249-024 Lisbon; tel. (21) 3928440; fax (21) 3975632; internet www .embaixadachina.pt; Ambassador LU BOYUAN.

Colombia: Av. Conde Valbom 30-9°, 1050-068 Lisbon; tel. (21) 3557096; fax (21) 3528665; e-mail embconslp@mail.telepac.pt; Ambassador JORGE GABRIEL PERDOMO MARTÍNEZ.

Congo, Democratic Republic: Av. Fontes Pereira de Melo 31-7°, 1050-117 Lisbon; tel. (21) 3522895; fax (21) 3544862; Chargé d'affaires SHAKEMBO KAMANGO.

Croatia: Rua D. Lourenço de Almeida 24, 1400-126 Lisbon; tel. (21) 3021033; fax (21) 3021251; e-mail croemblis@sapo.pt; Chargé d'affaires a.i. TEA KARAMAN.

Cuba: Rua Pero da Covilhã 14 (Restelo), 1400-297 Lisbon; tel. (21) 3015317; fax (21) 3011895; e-mail embaixada.cuba@mail.telepac.pt; Ambassador MERCEDES AGUIAR PENA.

Cyprus: Av. da Liberdade 229, 1°, 1250-142 Lisbon; tel. (21) 3194180; fax (21) 3194189; e-mail chipre@clix.pt.

Czech Republic: Rua Pero de Alenquer 14, 1400-294 Lisbon; tel. (21) 3010487; fax (21) 3010629; e-mail lisbon@embassy.mzv.cz; internet www.mfa.cz/lisbon; Ambassador JAROMÍR KVAPIL.

Denmark: Rua Castilho 14-C-3°, 1269-077 Lisbon; tel. (21) 3512960; fax (21) 3554615; e-mail lisamb@um.dk; Ambassador THEIS TRUELSEN.

Egypt: Av. D. Vasco da Gama 8, 1400-128 Lisbon; tel. (21) 3018301; fax (21) 3017909; e-mail egyptembassy@ip.pt; Ambassador DAWLAT HASSAN.

Estonia: Rua Camilo Castelo Branco 34-4°, 1050-045 Lisbon; tel. (21) 3194150; fax (21) 3194155; e-mail embassy@embest.pt; Chargé d'affaires a.i. PAUL LETTENS.

Finland: Rua Miguel Lupi 12-5°, 1249-080 Lisbon; tel. (21) 3933040; fax (21) 3904758; e-mail sanomat.lis@formin.fi; internet www.emb-finlandia.pt; Ambassador ESKO KIURU.

France: Rua de Santos-o-Velho 5, 1249-079 Lisbon; tel. (21) 3939100; fax (21) 3939151; e-mail ambafrance@hotmail.com; internet www.ambafrance-pt.org; Ambassador DANIEL LEQUERTIER.

Germany: Campo dos Mártires da Pátria 38, 1169-043 Lisbon; tel. (21) 8810210; fax (21) 8853846; e-mail embaixada.alemanha@clix .pt; internet www.embaixada-alemanha.pt; Ambassador Dr HANS-BODO BERTRAM.

Greece: Rua do Alto do Duque 13, 1449-026 Lisbon; tel. (21) 3031260; fax (21) 3011205; e-mail ambagrelis@mail.telepac.pt; Ambassador JEAN C. VAVVAS.

Guinea-Bissau: Rua de Alcolena 17, 1400-004 Lisbon; tel. (21) 3030440; fax (21) 3030450; Ambassador JOÃOZINHO VIEIRA CÓ.

Holy See: Av. Luís Bivar 18, 1069-147 Lisbon; tel. (21) 3171130; fax (21) 3171149; Apostolic Nuncio Most Rev. ALFIO RAPISARDA (Titular Archbishop of Canne).

Hungary: Calçada de Santo Amaro 85, 1349-042 Lisbon; tel. (21) 3645928; fax (21) 3632314; Ambassador JÁNOS BALLA.

India: Rua Pêro da Covilhã 16, 1400-297 Lisbon; tel. (21) 3041090; fax (21) 3016576; e-mail indiaembcom@mail.telepac.pt; Ambassador MADHU BITADURI.

Indonesia: Rua Miguel Lupi 12, 1°, 1249-080 Lisbon; tel. (21) 3932070; fax (21) 3932079; Ambassador HARRY HARYONO.

Iran: Rua do Alto do Duque 49, 1400-009 Lisbon; tel. (21) 3010871; fax (21) 3010777; Ambassador RASOUL MOHAVEDIAN.

Iraq: Rua de Arriaga à Lapa 9, 1200 Lisbon; tel. (21) 3960944; fax (21) 3960962; e-mail iraqem-lisboa@netcabo.pt; Chargé d'affaires a.i. SABBAR A. REJAB.

Ireland: Rua da Imprensa à Estrela 1-4°, 1200-684 Lisbon; tel. (21) 3929440; fax (21) 3977363; Ambassador PATRICK O'CONNOR.

Israel: Rua António Enes 16-4°, 1050-025 Lisbon; tel. (21) 3553640; fax (21) 3553658; e-mail press@lisboa.mfa.gov.il; internet www .israel.org.br/lisboa; Ambassador SHMUEL TEVET.

Italy: Largo Conde de Pombeiro 6, 1150-100 Lisbon; tel. (21) 3515320; fax (21) 3551420; e-mail amblisb@embital.pt; internet www.embital.pt; Ambassador MICHELE COSENTINO.

Japan: Av. da Liberdade 245–6, 1269-033 Lisbon; tel. (21) 3110560; fax (21) 3534802; e-mail bunka@ip.pt; internet www.pt.emb-japan .go.jp; Ambassador TAKERU SASAGUCHI.

Korea, Republic: Edif. Presidente, Av. Miguel Bombarda 36-7°, 1051-802 Lisbon; tel. (21) 7937200; fax (21) 7977176; e-mail rokempo@ip.pt; Ambassador SEUNG KOOK BYUN.

Latvia: Av. Miguel Bombarda 36-5C, 1050-165 Lisbon; tel. (21) 7815120; fax (21) 7963242; e-mail emb.letonia@mail.eunet.pt; Ambassador INTS UPMACIS.

Libya: Av. das Descobertas 24, 1400-092 Lisbon; tel. (21) 3016301; fax (21) 3012378; Head of People's Bureau OMAR HAMAD JADALLAH ALOKLY.

Lithuania: Av. 5 de Outubro 81-1° Esq., 1050-050 Lisbon; tel. (21) 7990110; fax (21) 7996363; e-mail emb.lituania@mail.telepac.pt; Ambassador DALIUS CEKUOLIS.

Luxembourg: Rua das Janelas Verdes 43, 1200-690 Lisbon; tel. (21) 3931940; fax (21) 3901410; e-mail embaixada.luxemburgo@clix .pt; Ambassador PAUL DUHR.

Mexico: Estrada de Monsanto 78, 1500-462 Lisbon; tel. (21) 7621290; fax (21) 7620045; e-mail embamex.port@mail.telepac.pt; internet www.sre.gob.mx/portugal; Ambassador JOSÉ MARÍA PÉREZ GAY.

Morocco: Rua Alto do Duque 21, 1400-099 Lisbon; tel. (21) 3020842; fax (21) 3020935; e-mail sifmar@emb-maroccos.pt; internet www .emb-maroccos.pt; Ambassador ABDELLAH SALAH-EDDINE TAZI.

Mozambique: Av. de Berna 7, 1050-036 Lisbon; tel. (21) 7961672; fax (21) 7932720; Ambassador PEDRO COMISSÁRIO AFONSO.

Netherlands: Av. Infante Santo 43-5°, 1399-011 Lisbon; tel. (21) 3914900; fax (21) 3966436; e-mail nlgovlis@mail.telepac.pt; internet www.emb-paisesbaixos.pt; Ambassador H.R.R.V. FROGER.

Nigeria: Av. D. Vasco da Gama 3, 1400-127 Lisbon; tel. (21) 3016189; fax (21) 3018152; e-mail nigerlis@mail.telepac.pt; Ambassador BAPPA L. TORO.

Norway: Av. D. Vasco da Gama 1, 1400-127 Lisbon; tel. (21) 3015344; fax (21) 3016158; e-mail emb.lisbon@mfa.no; internet ud50 .mogul.no; Ambassador ARNT MAGNES RINDAL.

Pakistan: Av. da República 20-1°, 1050-192 Lisbon; tel. (21) 3538446; fax (21) 3158805; e-mail parep.lisbon.1@mail.telepac.pt; Ambassador SHIREEN SAFDAR.

Panama: Av. Helen Keller, 15 Lote C, 4° Esq., 1400-197 Lisbon; tel. (21) 3642899; fax (21) 3644589; e-mail panemblisboa@netc.pt; Ambassador Dra LOURDES C. VALLARINO.

Paraguay: Rua Camilo Castelo Branco 34, 1°, 1050 Lisbon; tel. (21) 3571709; fax (21) 3153296; e-mail embaparlisboa@kpnet.pt; Chargé d'affaires a.i. ANTONIO RIVAS PALACIOS.

Peru: Rua Castilho 50-4° Dto, 1250-071 Lisbon; tel. (21) 3827470; fax (21) 3827479; e-mail embperuport@mail.telepac.pt; Ambassador MANUEL VERAMENDI I SERRA.

Poland: Av. das Descobertas 2, 1400-092 Lisbon; tel. (21) 3012350; fax (21) 3010202; e-mail embpol@telepac.pt; internet www .emb-polonia.pt; Ambassador Dr ADAM HALAMSKI.

Romania: Rua de São Caetano a Lapa 5, 1200-828 Lisbon; tel. (21) 3960866; fax (21) 3960984; e-mail ambrom@mail.telepac.pt; Ambassador TEODOR BACONSKY.

Russia: Rua Visconde de Santarém 59, 1000-286 Lisbon; tel. (21) 8462424; fax (21) 8479327; e-mail np71fn@telepac.pt; internet www .portugal.mid.ru; Ambassador GENNADII TARASSOV.

São Tomé and Príncipe: Av. Gago Coutinho 26-6°, Edif. EPAC, Areeiro, 1000-017 Lisbon; tel. (21) 8461917; fax (21) 8461895; e-mail embstp@mail.telepac.pt; Ambassador ARLINDO PEREIRA BRAGANÇA GOMES.

Saudi Arabia: Av. do Restelo 42, 1400-315 Lisbon; tel. (21) 3010317; fax (21) 3014209; Ambassador MOHAMED AL-RASHID.

Serbia and Montenegro: Av. das Descobertas 12, 1400-092 Lisbon; tel. (21) 3015311; fax (21) 3015313; e-mail yuemba@netcabo .pt; Ambassador DANILO VUCETIĆ.

Slovakia: Av. Fontes Pereira de Melo 19-7° Dto, 1050-116 Lisbon; tel. (21) 3583300; fax (21) 3583309; e-mail emslovak@mail.telepac .pt; Ambassador PETER RUSIŇÁK.

Slovenia: Av. da Liberdade 49-6°, Esq., 1250-139 Lisbon; tel. (21) 3423301; fax (21) 34223305; e-mail vli@mzz-dkp.gov.si; Ambassador BOGDAN BENKO.

South Africa: Av. Luís Bivar 10, 1069-024 Lisbon; tel. (21) 3192200; fax (21) 3535713; e-mail safrican@mail.eunet.pt; Ambassador E. J. DRY.

Spain: Rua do Salitre 1, 1296-052 Lisbon; tel. (21) 3472381; fax (21) 3472384; e-mail embesppt@correo.mae.es; Ambassador CARLOS CARDERERA SOLER.

Sweden: Rua Miguel Lupi 12-2°, 1249-077 Lisbon; tel. (21) 3942260; fax (21) 3942261; e-mail emb.suecia.lis@mail.telepac.pt; internet www.embsuecia.pt; Ambassador GUNILLA OLOFSSON.

Switzerland: Travessa do Jardim 17, 1350-185 Lisbon; tel. (21) 3944090; fax (21) 3955945; e-mail vertretung@lis.rep.admin.ch; Ambassador BERNARD DE RIEDMATTEN.

Thailand: Rua de Alcolena 12–12A, 1400-005 Lisbon; tel. (21) 3014848; fax (21) 3018181; e-mail thai.lis@mail.telepac.pt; Ambassador BUNTHAN BAIRAJ-VINICHAI.

Timor Leste: Avda Infante Santo 17, 6°, 1350-175 Lisbon; tel. (21) 3933730; e-mail capctl@mail.telepac.pt; Ambassador PASCOELA BARRETO.

Tunisia: Rua de Alcolena 35, 1400-004 Lisbon; tel. (21) 3010330; fax (21) 3016817; Ambassador LAZHAR BOUOUNY.

Turkey: Av. das Descobertas 22, 1400-092 Lisbon; tel. (21) 3014275; fax (21) 3017934; e-mail turkish.embassy@netcabo.pt; internet turquia.planetaclix.pt; Ambassador DENIZ BÖLÜKBASI.

Ukraine: Rua Rodrigues Sampaio 19-4°A, 1150-278 Lisbon; tel. (21) 3530046; fax (21) 3530048; e-mail emb_pt@mfa.gov.ua; Ambassador KONSTYANTYN TYMOSHENKO.

United Kingdom: Rua de São Bernardo 33, 1249-082 Lisbon; tel. (21) 3924000; fax (21) 3924185; e-mail ppa@fco.gov.uk; internet www.uk-embassy.pt; Ambassador Dame GLYNNE EVANS.

USA: Av. das Forças Armadas (Sete Rios), 1600-081 Lisbon; tel. (21) 7273300; fax (21) 7269109; e-mail ref@american-embassy.pt; internet www.american-embassy.pt; Ambassador JOHN PALMER.

Uruguay: Rua Sampaio e Pina 16-2°, 1070-249 Lisbon; tel. (21) 3889265; fax (21) 3889245; e-mail urulusi1@mail.telepac.pt; Ambassador ERNESTO MARTÍNEZ GARIAZO.

Venezuela: Av. Duque de Loulé 47-4°, 1050-086 Lisbon; tel. (21) 3573803; fax (21) 3527421; e-mail embavenez@mail.telepac.pt; Ambassador MANUEL QUIJADA.

Judicial System

The judicial system of the Portuguese Republic comprises several categories of courts which, according to the Constitution, are sovereign bodies. The country is divided into four judicial districts, which are, in turn, divided into 37 judicial circuits. The principle of *habeas corpus* is recognized. Citizens who have been unjustly convicted are entitled to a review of their sentence and to compensation. The death penalty is prohibited by the Constitution. The jury system, reintroduced for certain types of crime in 1976, operates only at the request of the Public Prosecutor or defendant.

Judges are appointed for life and are irremovable. Practising judges may not hold any other office, whether public or private, except a non-remunerated position in teaching or research in the legal field. The Conselho Superior da Magistratura controls their appointment, transfer and promotion and the exercise of disciplinary action.

PUBLIC PROSECUTION

The State is represented in the courts by the Public Prosecution, whose highest organ is the Procuradoria-Geral da República (Attorney-General's Office).

Procuradoria-Geral da República: Rua da Escola Politécnica 140, 1269-269 Lisbon; tel. (21) 3921900; fax (21) 3975255; e-mail mailpgr@pgr.pt; internet www.pgr.pt; Attorney-General Dr JOSÉ ADRIANO MACHADO SOUTA DE MOURA.

Gabinete de Documentação e Direito Comparado: Rua Vale de Pereiro 2, 1269-113 Lisbon; tel. (21) 3820300; fax (21) 3820301; e-mail mail@gddc.pt; internet www.gddc.pt.

SUPREME COURT

Supremo Tribunal de Justiça
Praça do Comércio, 1149-012 Lisbon; tel. (21) 3218900; fax (21) 3474919; internet www.stj.pt.

the highest organ of the judicial system; has jurisdiction over Metropolitan Portugal, The Azores and Madeira; it consists of 64 judges, incl. the President.

President: JORGE ALBERTO ARAGÃO SEIA.

COURTS OF SECOND INSTANCE
There are four Courts of Second Instance (or Courts of Appeal):

Tribunal da Relação de Coímbra: Palácio da Justiça, 3049 Coimbra; tel. (239) 852950; fax (239) 824310; e-mail trc@netcabo.pt; internet www.trc.pt; 46 judges, incl. the President; Pres. Dr CARLOS MANUEL GASPAR LEITÃO.

Tribunal da Relação de Evora: tel. (266) 758800; fax (266) 701529; internet www.tre.pt; 39 judges, incl. the President; Pres. Dr ARMINDO RIBEIRO LUIS.

Tribunal da Relação de Lisboa: Rua Arsenal, 1100-038 Lisbon; tel. (21) 3222900; fax (21) 3222934; internet www.trl.pt; 108 judges, incl. the President; Pres. Dr EDUARDO NUNES DA SILVA BAPTISTA.

Tribunal da Relação de Porto: Campo Mártires de Pátria, 4099-012 Porto; tel. (22) 2008531; fax (22) 2000715; e-mail info@trp.pt; internet www.trp.pt; 91 judges, incl. the President; Pres. Dr JOSÉ FERREIRA CORREIA DE PAIVA.

COURTS OF FIRST INSTANCE
There are 258 courts of first instance within Portuguese territory: 195 comarca hear cases of a general nature, while 46 labour courts hear specific matters. There are five family courts and two courts for the enforcement of sentences. Circuit Courts total 33.

CONSTITUTIONAL COURT

Tribunal Constitucional
Palácio Ratton, Rua de O Século 111, 1249-117 Lisbon; tel. (21) 3233600; fax (21) 3233664; e-mail tribunal@tribconstitucional.pt; internet www.tribunalconstitucional.pt.

rules on matters of constitutionality according to the terms of the Constitution of the Portuguese Republic; exercises jurisdiction over all Portuguese territory; consists of 13 judges.

President: Prof. JOSÉ MANUEL MOREIRA CARDOSO DA COSTA.

SUPREME ADMINISTRATIVE COURT

Supremo Tribunal Administrativo
Rua de S. Pedro de Alcântara 75, 1269-137 Lisbon; tel. (21) 3216200; fax (21) 3466129; e-mail suptriadm@mail.telepac.pt; internet www.sta.mj.pt.

highest organ of the administrative system; has jurisdiction over metropolitan Portugal, the Azores and Madeira; consists of 44 judges, incl. the President.

President: MANUEL FERNANDO DOS SANTOS SERRA.

Religion

There is freedom of religion in Portugal. The dominant Christian denomination is Roman Catholicism, but a number of Protestant Churches have been established.

CHRISTIANITY

Conselho Português de Igrejas Cristãs (COPIC) (Portuguese Council of Christian Churches): Rua da Lapa 9-2°, Sala 1, 3080-045 Figueira da Foz; tel. (233) 428279; fax (233) 422603; f. 1971; three mem. churches, two observers; Gen. Sec. (vacant).

The Roman Catholic Church
For ecclesiastical purposes, Portugal comprises 17 dioceses, grouped into three metropolitan sees (the patriarchate of Lisbon and the archdioceses of Braga and Évora). At 31 December 2000 more than 9.4m. Portuguese were adherents of the Roman Catholic Church, representing 93.1% of the population.

Bishops' Conference
Conferência Episcopal Portuguesa, Campo dos Mártires da Pátria 43-1 Esq., 1150-225 Lisbon; tel. (21) 8852123; fax (21) 8850559.

f. 1932; Pres. Cardinal JOSÉ DA CRUZ POLICARPO (Patriarch of Lisbon).

Patriarch of Lisbon: Cardinal JOSÉ DA CRUZ POLICARPO, Mosteiro de S. Vicente de Fora, Campo de Santa Clara, 1149-085 Lisbon; tel. (21) 8810500; fax (21) 8810530; e-mail gabinete.patriarca@patriarcado-lisboa.pt; internet www.patriarcado-lisboa.pt.

Dir P. AGOSTINHO JARDIN GONÇALVES.

Archbishop of Braga: Most Rev. JORGE FERREIRA DA COSTA ORTIGA, Cúria Arquiepiscopal, Rua de Santa Margarida 181, 4710-306 Braga; tel. (253) 203180; fax (253) 203190; e-mail jorge.ortiga@diocese-braga.pt.

Archbishop of Évora: Most Rev. MAURÍLIO JORGE QUINTAL DE GOUVEIA, Cúria Arquiepiscopal, Largo Marquês de Marialva 6, 7000-809 Évora; tel. (266) 705375; fax (266) 744819; e-mail curia-evora@clix.pt.

The Anglican Communion

Church of England: Rua João de Deus 5, Alcoitão, 2645-128 Alcabideche; tel. and fax (21) 4692303; e-mail gl-chaplaincy@clix.pt; Chaplain Canon MICHAEL BULLOCK.

Igreja Lusitana Católica Apostólica Evangélica (Lusitanian Catholic Apostolic Evangelical Church): Apdo 392, 4431-905 Vila Nova de Gaia; tel. (22) 3754018; fax (22) 3752016; e-mail centrodiocesano@igreja-lusitana.org; f. 1880; Bishop Rt Rev. FERNANDO LUZ SOARES.

Other Christian Churches

Assembleia de Deus (Assembly of God): Rua Neves Ferreira 13-3°, 1170 Lisbon; tel. (21) 8142040; Pastor JOSÉ NEVES, Pastor DINIS RODRIGUES.

Associação de Igrejas Baptistas Portuguesas (Asscn of Portuguese Baptist Churches): Rua da Escola, 18 Maceira, 2715 Pero Pinheiro; tel. (21) 9271150; f. 1955; Pres. Rev. JOÃO S. REGUEIRAS.

Convenção Baptista Portuguesa (Portuguese Baptist Convention): Queluz; tel. (21) 4343370; fax (21) 4343379; e-mail convbaptport@mail.telepac.pt; f. 1920; Pres. Dr JOSÉ P. DE SOUSA; Sec. MARIA HERCÍLIA MELO.

Igreja Evangélica Alemã de Lisboa (German Evangelical Church in Lisbon): Av. Columbano Bordalo Pinheiro 48, 1070-064 Lisbon; tel. (21) 7260976; fax (21) 7274839; e-mail dekl@deutsche-kirche-portugal.org/dekl; internet www.deutsche-kirche-portugal.org/dekl; Pastor Rev. DIRK VOOS.

Igreja Evangélica Metodista Portuguesa (Portuguese Evangelical Methodist Church): Praça Coronel Pacheco 23, 4050-453 Porto; tel. (22) 2007410; fax (22) 2086961; e-mail sede-geral@igreja-metodista.pt; internet www.igreja-metodista.pt; Bishop SIFREDO TEIXEIRA.

Igreja Evangélica Presbiteriana de Portugal (Presbyterian Church of Portugal): Rua Tomás da Anunciação, 56-1° Dto, 1350-328 Lisbon; tel. (21) 3974959; fax (21) 3956326; e-mail office@iepp.org; internet www.iepp.org; f. 1952; Pres. EUNICE LEITE; Gen. Sec. ANDREAS M. DING.

ISLAM

Muslims number an estimated 15,000.

Comunidade Islamica de Lisboa: Mesquita Central de Lisboa, Avda José Malhoa, Lisbon 1070; tel. (21) 3874142; fax (21) 3872230.

JUDAISM

There are Jewish communities in Lisbon and Porto, estimated to total 2,000.

Comunidade Israelita de Lisboa: Rua Alexandre Herculano, 59, Lisbon; tel. (1) 3858604; fax (1) 3884304; Pres. Dr JOSHUA B. RUAH.

The Press

Under the 1976 Constitution, the freedom of the press is guaranteed. In 1997 28 morning and three evening daily newspapers were published.

PRINCIPAL DAILIES

Aveiro

Diário de Aveiro: Av. Dr Lourenço Peixinho 15-1°-G, 3800 Aveiro; tel. (234) 422608; fax (234) 428965; f. 1985; morning; Dir ADRIANO CALLÉ LUCAS; circ. 4,500.

Braga

Correio do Minho: Praçeta Escola do Magisterio 34, Maximinos 4700-236 Braga; tel. (253) 309500; fax (253) 309525; morning; Dir A. COSTA GUIMARÃES; circ. 1,573.

Diário do Minho: Rua de Santa Margarida 4, 4710-306 Braga; tel. (253) 609460; fax (253) 609465; e-mail diariominho@mail.telepac.pt; f. 1919; morning; Dir JOÃO AGUIAR CAMPOS; circ. 4,000.

Coímbra

Diário as Beiras: Rua 25 de Abril, Apdo 44, 3040-935 Taveiro, Coímbra; tel. (239) 980280; fax (239) 983574; Dir JOAQUIM ROSA DE CARVALHO.

Diário de Coímbra: Rua Adriano Lucas, Apdo 542, 3020-264 Coímbra; tel. (239) 492133; fax (239) 492128; f. 1930; morning; *Domingo* publ. on Sun. (f. 1974; circ. 8,000); Dir Eng. ADRIANO MÁRIO DA CUNHA LUCAS; circ. 9,000.

Évora

Diário do Sul: Travessa de Santo André 8, 7021 Évora, Apdo 2037; tel. (266) 703144; fax (266) 741252; f. 1969; morning; Dir MANUEL MADEIRA PIÇARRA; circ. 8,500.

Notícias d' Évora: Rua do Raimundo 41–43, 7002 Évora; tel. (266) 22348; f. 1900; morning; Dir ROSA SOUTO ARMAS; circ. 3,000.

Leiria

Diário de Leiria: Edif. Maringa, Rua S. Franciso 7-4°, Esq., 2400-232 Leiria; tel. (244) 833881; fax (244) 812498; f. 1987; morning; Dir ADRIANO CALLÉ LUCAS; circ. 3,500.

Lisbon

A Bola: Travessa da Queimada 23-2°D R/C Esq., 1294 Lisbon; tel. (21) 3463981; fax (21) 3432275; f. 1945; sport; Dir VICTOR SERPA; circ. 180,000.

A Capital: Av. Infante D. Henrique 334, 1800-224 Lisbon; tel. (21) 8542000; fax (21) 8531427; e-mail acapital@acapital.pt; f. 1968; evening; Dir ANTÓNIO MATOS; circ. 40,000.

Correio da Manhã: Av. João Crisóstomo 72, 1069-043 Lisbon; tel. (21) 3185200; fax (21) 3156146; e-mail luisbcm@mail.telepac.pt; internet www.correio.manha.pt; f. 1979; morning; independent; Dir AGOSTINHO DE AZEVEDO; circ. 85,000.

Diário de Notícias: Av. da Liberdade 266, 1250-149 Lisbon; tel. (21) 3187500; fax (21) 3187515; e-mail dnot@mail.telepac.pt; internet www.dn.pt; f. 1864; morning; Editor-in-Chief MÁRIO BETTENCOURT RESENDES; circ. 75,561.

Jornal de O Dia: Lisbon; tel. (21) 8583421; fax (21) 8584421; f. 1975 as *O Dia*; morning; right-wing; Dir ADELINO ALVES.

Público: Rua Agostinho Neto 16-C, Quinta do Lambert, 1769-010 Lisbon; tel. (21) 7501075; fax (21) 7587638; e-mail publico@publico.pt; internet www.publico.pt; f. 1990; morning; Dir JOSÉ MANUEL FERNANDES; circ. 75,000.

Record: Av. Conde Valbom 30, 4-5°, 1050-068 Lisbon; tel. (21) 0124900; fax (21) 3476279; e-mail record@record.pt; internet www.record.pt; f. 1949; sport; Dir JOÃO MARCELINO; Editor-in-Chief JOÃO MANHA; circ. 132,000.

24 Horas: Av. 5 de Outubro 17, 2b, 1050-047 Lisbon; tel. (21) 3186500; fax (21) 3155787; e-mail 24horas@mail.prodiario.pt; Dir JORGE ALBERTO MONTEIRO MORAIS.

Porto

O Comércio do Porto: Rua Fernandes Tomás 352-7°, 4000 Porto; tel. (22) 563571; fax (22) 575095; f. 1854; morning; Dir LUÍS DE CARVALHO; circ. 30,295.

O Jogo: Rua de Gil Vicente 129-1°, 4000-814 Porto; tel. (22) 5071900; fax (22) 5504550; e-mail ojogo@mail.telepac.pt; internet www.ojogo.pt; sporting news; Dir MANUEL TAVARES.

Jornal de Notícias: Rua Gonçalo Cristóvão 195–219, 4049-011 Porto; tel. (22) 2096111; fax (22) 2006330; e-mail noticias@jn.pt; internet www.jn.pt; f. 1888; morning; Dir FREDERICO MARTINS MENDES; circ. 105,000.

O Primeiro de Janeiro: Rua Coelho Neto 65, 4000 Porto; tel. (22) 5103282; fax (22) 5103291; e-mail pjaneiro@mail.telepac.pt; f. 1868; independent; morning; Dir CARLOS MOURA; circ. 20,200.

Viseu

Diário Regional Viseu: Rua Alexandre Herculano 198-1°. Esq., 3510-033; tel. (232) 425795; fax (232) 424514; Dir ADRIANO CALLÉ LUCAS.

Noticias de Viseu: Av. do Convento 1, Apt. 3115, 3511-689 Viseu; tel. (232) 410410; fax (232) 410418; e-mail noticiasviseu@portugalmail.pt; internet www.noticiasdeviseu.com; f. 1974.

Madeira
(Funchal)

Diário de Notícias: Rua Dr Fernão de Ornelas 56-3°, 9054-514 Funchal; tel. (291) 202300; fax (291) 202306; e-mail dnmad@mail.telepac.pt; internet www.dnoticias.pt; f. 1876; morning; independent; Dir JOSÉ BETTENCOURT DA CÂMARA; circ. 19,000.

Jornal da Madeira: Rua Dr Fernão de Ornelas 35 R/C, 9000 Funchal; tel. (291) 220014; fax (291) 231400; e-mail jornaldamadeira@mail.telepac.pt; f. 1927; morning; Catholic; Dir Canon MANUEL TOMÉ TEIXEIRA VELOSA; circ. 8,000.

The Azores

Açoriano Oriental: Rua Dr Bruno Tavares Carreiro 36, 9500-055 Ponta Delgada; tel. (296) 202800; fax (296) 202826; e-mail pub.ao@acorianooriental.pt; internet www.acorianooriental.pt; f. 1835; morning; Dir JOÃO MANUEL ALVES; circ. 6,000.

O Correio da Horta: Rua Ernesto Rebelo 5, 9900 Horta; tel. (292) 292821; fax (292) 392234; e-mail correiodahorta@ciberacores.net;

internet www.ciberacores.net/correiodahorta; f. 1930; evening; Dir RÚBEN RODRIGUES; circ. 1,410.

Correio dos Açores: Rua Dr João Francisco de Sousa 14, 9500 Ponta Delgada; tel. (296) 201060; fax (296) 286119; e-mail redaccao@correiodosazores.com; internet www.correiodosazores.com; f. 1920; morning; Dir AMÉRICO NATALINO VIVEIROS; circ. 4,460.

Diário dos Açores: Rua do "Diário dos Açores" 5, 9500-178 Ponta Delgada; tel. (296) 286902; fax (296) 284840; e-mail diario@virtualazores.net; internet www.virtualazores.net/diario; f. 1870; morning; Dir PAULO HUGO VIVEIROS; circ. 2,380.

Diário Insular: Av. Infante D. Henrique 1, 9700-098 Angra do Heroísmo, Terceira; tel. (295) 401050; fax (295) 214246; e-mail diarioins@mail.telepac.pt; internet www.diarioinsular.com; f. 1946; morning; Dir JOSÉ LOURENÇO; circ. 3,400.

O Telégrafo: Rua Conselheiro Medeiros 30, 9902 Horta; tel. (292) 22245; fax (292) 22245; f. 1893; morning; Dir RUBEN RODRIGUES; circ. 3,200.

A União: Rua da Palha 11–17, 9700-144 Angra do Heroísmo; tel. (295) 214275; fax (295) 214062; e-mail a.uniao@mail.telepac.pt; internet www.viaoceanica.com/auniao; f. 1893; morning; Dir ÁLVARO MONJARDINO; circ. 1,500.

PRINCIPAL PERIODICALS

In 1994 an estimated total of 984 periodicals were published in Portugal. Among the more widely known are:

Activa: Rua Calvet de Magalhães 242, Laveiras, 2770-022 Paço de Arcos; tel. (21) 4143078; fax (21) 4107050; e-mail acj@acj.pt; internet www.acj.pt; f. 1991; monthly; for women; Editor-in-Chief CLARA MARQUES; circ. 90,000.

Africa Hoje: Rua Joaquim António de Aguiar 45-5° Esq., 1070 Lisbon; tel. (21) 557175; fax (21) 3557667; e-mail geral@lucidus.pt; internet africa.sapo.pt; f. 1985; monthly; African affairs; circ. 30,000; Dir ALBÉRICO CARDOSO.

Anglo-Portuguese News: Apt. 113, 2766-902 Estoril, Lisbon; tel. (21) 4661471; fax (21) 4660358; e-mail apn@mail.telepac.pt; f. 1937; every Thursday; English language newspaper; Publr and Editor NIGEL BATLEY; circ. 30,000.

Autosport: Rua Rúben A. Leitão 2-1°, 1200-392 Lisbon; tel. (21) 3220780; fax (21) 3473891; e-mail autosport@mail.telepac.pt; internet www.autosport.pt; weekly; motoring; Dir RUI FREIRE; circ. 23,500.

Avante: Av. Gago Coutinho, 121 - 1700-024Lisbon; tel. (21) 769725; e-mail avante.pcp@mail.telepac.pt; internet www.pcp.pt/avante; weekly; organ of the Communist Party; Dir JOSÉ CASANOVA.

Brotéria—Revista de Cultura: Rua Maestro António Taborda 14, 1293 Lisbon; tel. (21) 3961660; fax (21) 3956629; internet www.companhia-jesus.pt/publica/broteria/pubbro.htm; f. 1926; monthly; review of culture; Dir LUÍS ARCHER.

Casa e Decoração: Av. Duque d'Avila 26-3°, 1049-042 Lisbon; tel. (21) 3168500; fax (21) 3168578; e-mail casadeco@meriberica.pt; internet www.meriberica.pt; f. 1981; 12 a year; home and interior decoration; Dir URSULA BASTOS; circ. 20,000.

Casa & Jardim: Rua da Misericórdia 137–5/loja, 1249-037 Lisbon; tel. (21) 3472127; fax (21) 3421490; e-mail direcção@casajardim.jazznet.pt; internet www.casajardim.net; f. 1978; monthly; home, interior and exterior design, fine arts, exhibitions and antique fairs; Dir EDUARDO FORTUNATO DE ALMEIDA; circ. 20,000.

Colecções Moda & Beleza: Av. Duque d'Avila 26, 1049-132 Lisbon; tel. (21) 3168500; fax (21) 3268578; e-mail geral@meriberica.pt; internet www.meriberica.pt; 5 a year; fashion and beauty; Editor CRISTINA COSTA; circ. 240,000.

Colóquio/Letras: Av. de Berna 45a, 1067-001 Lisbon; tel. (21) 7823000; fax (21) 7823021; e-mail info@gulbenkian.pt; internet www.gulbenkian.pt/educacao/revista.asp; f. 1971; 4 a year; literary; Dir Dra JOANA VARELA; circ. 3,600.

Correio da Madeira: Rua do Carmo 19-3° Dto, 9000 Funchal; tel. (291) 20738; f. 1987; weekly newspaper; Dir JOSÉ CAMPOS; circ. 5,000.

Cosmopolitan: Rua Calvet de Magalhães 242, Laveiras, 2770-022 Paço de Arcos; tel. (21) 4698861; e-mail cosmopolitan@acj.pt; internet www.acj.pt; f. 1992; monthly; women's magazine; Editor ISABEL CANHA.

O Diabo (The Devil): Rua Alexandre Herculano 7-5° Esq., 1100 Lisbon; tel. (21) 572367; fax (21) 570263; e-mail diabo@esoterica.pt; f. 1976; weekly newspaper; Dir VERA LAGOA; circ. 46,000.

Eles e Elas: Rua das Flores 105-1° Esq., 1200-194 Lisbon; tel. (21) 3224660; fax (21) 3224679; e-mail gabinete1@gabinete1.pt; internet www.gabinete1.pt; f. 1983; monthly; fashion, culture, social events; Dir MARIA DA LUZ DE BRAGANÇA.

Elle: Rua Filipe Folque 40-4°, 1050 Lisbon; tel. (21) 3156907; fax (21) 3164205; e-mail elle@hachette.pt; f. 1988; monthly; women's magazine; Dir FÁTIMA COTTA; circ. 48,916.

Expresso: Rua Duque de Palmela 37-3° Dto, 1296 Lisbon; tel. (21) 3114000; fax (21) 3543858; e-mail info@mail.expresso.pt; internet www.expresso.pt; weekly newspaper; Dir JOSÉ ANTÓNIO PAULA SARAIVA; Vice-Dir NICOLAU SANTOS; circ. 160,000.

Gente e Viagens: Rua Joaquim António de Aguiar 45, 1099-058 Lisbon; tel. (21) 3839810; fax (21) 862746; e-mail lucidus@mail.telepac.pt; internet genteviagens.sapo.pt; f. 1980; monthly; tourism; Dir ALBÉRICO CARDOSO; circ. 30,000.

Guia—Revista Prática: Av. Almirante Gago Coutinho 113, 1749-087 Lisbon; tel. (21) 8474410; fax (21) 8474396; e-mail mpcorreia@tvguia.pt; weekly women's magazine; fashion and housekeeping; Dir MARGARIDA PINTO CORREIA; Editor-in-Chief PALMIRA SIMÕES; circ. 40,000.

O Independente: Rua Actor Taborda 27-1°, 1000 Lisbon; tel. (21) 3526306; fax (21) 3531766; f. 1988; weekly; Propr SOCI; Dir PAULO PORTAS; circ. 103,500.

JL (Jornal de Letras, Artes e Ideias): Rua Calvet de Magalhães 242, Laveiras, 2770-022 Paço de Arcos; tel. (21) 574520; e-mail jl@acj.pt; internet www.acj.pt; weekly; Dir JOSÉ CARLOS DE VASCONCELOS; Editor MANUEL BECA MURIAS; circ. 80,000.

Manchete: Rua das Flores 105-1° Esq., 1200-194 Lisbon; tel. (21) 3224660; fax (21) 3224679; e-mail gabinete1@gabinete1.pt; internet www.gabinete1.pt; f. 1992; monthly; national and international events; Dir MARIA DA LUZ DE BRAGANÇA.

Maria: Av. Miguel Bombarda 33, 2745 Queluz; tel. 4364401; fax 4365001; internet www.impala.pt/maria; f. 1977; weekly; women's magazine; Dir JACQUES RODRIGUES; Editor-in-Chief PAULA RODRIGUES; 392,000.

Máxima: Av. Joáe Crisóstemo 72-3°, 1069-043 Lisbon; tel. (21) 3309400; fax (21) 3540410; e-mail maximaonline@edimoda.pt; internet www.maxima.pt; f. 1989; women's magazine; Dir LAUZA LUZES TORRES; circ. 45,000.

Moda & Moda: Rua Braamcamp 12, R/C Esq., 1250-050 Lisbon; tel. (21) 3886068; fax (21) 3862426; e-mail modaemoda@netcabo.pt; f. 1984; 5 a year; fashion, beauty and art; Dir MARIONELA GUSMÃO; circ. 20,000.

Mulher Moderna: Av. Miguel Bombarda 33, 2745 Queluz; tel. 4364401; fax 4365001; f. 1988; weekly; women's magazine; Dir JACQUES RODRIGUES; Editor-in-Chief PAULA RODRIGUES; circ. 60,000.

Nova Gente: Av. Miguel Bombarda 33, 2745 Queluz; tel. 4364388; fax 4365001; f. 1979; weekly; popular; Dir JACQUES RODRIGUES; Editor-in-Chief ANTÓNIO SIMÕES; circ. 200,000.

Portugal Socialista: Largo do Rato 2, 1250 Lisbon; tel. (21) 3464375; f. 1967; quarterly; organ of the Socialist Party; Dir JOSÉ LEITÃO; circ. 5,000.

Povo Livre: Rua S. Caetano 9, 1249-087 Lisbon; tel. (21) 3952140; fax (21) 3976967; weekly; organ of the Social Democratic Party; Dir LUÍS ÁLVARO CAMPOS FERREIRA.

Revista ACP: Rua Rosa Araújo 24, 1250-195 Lisbon; tel. (21) 3180100; fax (21) 3180170; internet www.acp.pt; f. 1908; monthly; motoring and tourism; Propr Automóvel Club de Portugal; Editor ANTÓNIO RAPOSO DE MAGALHÃES; circ. 190,000.

Revista Exame: Rua Calvet de Magalhães 242, Laveiras, 2770-022 Paço de Arcos; e-mail exame@acj.pt; tel. (21) 4143078; fax (21) 4107050; monthly; finance; circ. 21,000.

Revista Negócios: Rua do Norte 14-2°, 1200 Lisbon; tel. (21) 3471259; monthly; business and finance; circ. 10,000.

Segredos de Cozinha: Edif. do Grupo Impala, Ranholas, 2710-460 Sintra; tel. (21) 92398033; fax (21) 9238044; e-mail gracamorais@impala.pt; f. 1985; weekly; cookery; Dir GRAÇA MORAIS; Editor-in-Chief PAULA RODRIGUES; circ. 40,000.

Selecções do Reader's Digest: Rua D. Francisco Manuel de Melo 21, 1070 Lisbon; tel. (21) 3810000; fax (21) 3859203; internet www.looksmart.com; monthly magazine; Dir ISABEL BIVAR; circ. 200,000.

Semanário: Rua S. Cabral 26–30, 1495 Lisbon; tel. (21) 4198065; fax (21) 4243328; weekly newspaper; Dir Dr ALVARO MENDONÇA; circ. 55,000.

Semanário Económico: Av. Almirante Reis 113-8°, Sala 803, 1150 Lisbon; tel. (21) 3528525; fax (21) 3148847; e-mail seconomico@ip.pt; weekly; economic newspaper; Dir HORÁCIO PIRIQUITO; circ. 20,000.

Tal & Qual: Av. 5 de Outubro 17, 1200 Lisbon; tel. (21) 3115200; fax (21) 3155793; weekly; popular newspaper; Editor JOÃO FERREIRA; circ. 61,000.

TV Guia: Av. Almirante Gago Coutinho 113, 1749-087 Lisbon; tel. (21) 8474410; fax (21) 8474395; e-mail jgobern@tvguia.pt; weekly;

TV programmes and general features; Dir João Gobern; circ. 108,500.

TV 7 Dias: Av. Miguel Bombarda 33, 2745 Queluz; tel. 4364401; fax 4365001; f. 1985; weekly; television magazine; Dir Ventura Martins; Editor-in-Chief Frederico Valarinho; circ. 100,000.

Vida Económica: Rua Gonçalo Cristovão 111-5°, 6°, 7°, 4049-037 Porto; tel. (22) 3399400; fax (22) 2058098; e-mail redaccao@ vidaeconomica.pt; internet www.vidaeconomica.pt; weekly; financial; Dir João Peixoto de Sousa; Editor-in-Chief João Luís de Sousa.

Visão: Lisbon; tel. (21) 3116100; fax (21) 3540575; weekly magazine; Dir Cáceres Monteiro; circ. 58,172.

NEWS AGENCIES

Agência Europeia de Imprensa, Lda (AEI): Largo da Rosa 6, 1149-054 Lisbon; tel. (21) 0307860; fax (21) 8875725; e-mail aei@ mail.aei.pt; internet www.aei.pt; Man. Dir Dr Alexandre Cordeiro.

Agência Lusa de Informação: Rua Dr João Couto, Lote C, 1500 Lisbon; tel. (21) 7144099; fax (21) 7145443; e-mail dinformacao@lusa .pt; internet www.lusa.pt; f. 1987; Chair. Maria Rosa Simões.

Agência de Representações Dias da Silva, Lda (ADS): Av. Almirante Reis 82-6° Dto, 1169-163 Lisbon; tel. (21) 8110270; fax (21) 8154542; e-mail adspress@mail.telepac.pt; f. 1964; pictorial news, features, photographic reports, news, comic strips, literary material, etc.; Dir Júlio Calderon Dias da Silva.

Foreign Bureaux

Agence France-Presse (AFP) (France): Rua Rosa Araújo 34-3°, 1250-195 Lisbon; tel. (21) 3527193; fax (21) 3520866; e-mail lisboa@ afp.com; Dir Isabelle Hourcade.

Agencia EFE (Spain): Rua Castilho 13 D-5°A Lisbon; tel. (21) 8875712; fax (21) 8875713; internet agencia.efe@mail.telepac.pt; Dir Nemesio Rodríguez López.

Angola Press (ANGOP) (Angola): Rua Luciano Cordeiro 89, 4°, 1150-213 Lisbon; tel. (21) 3139706; e-mail angop@mail.telepac.pt.

Associated Press (AP) (USA): P. Duque de Saldanha 1-10°-B, 1050-094 Lisbon; tel. (21) 3191860; fax (21) 3191885; Admin. Dir Emma E. A. Gilbert.

Deutsche Presse-Agentur (dpa) (Germany): Praça da Alegria 58-5°-B, 1200 Lisbon; tel. (21) 3469837; Bureau Chief Artur Margalho.

Maghreb Arabe Presse (Morocco): Rua Chagas 20, 2°D, 1200–107 Lisbon; tel. (21) 3257982.

Reuters Portugal—Agência Noticiosa Lda (UK): Rua Laura Alves 12-5°, 1050-138 Lisbon; tel. (21) 7910400; fax (21) 7957432; e-mail portugal@reuters.com; Chief Correspondent Richard Waddington.

Rossiyskoye Informatsionnoye Agentstvo—Novosti (RIA-Novosti) (Russia): Praça Andrade Caminha 3, 1700-039 Lisbon; tel. (21) 7934700; fax (21) 7934717; e-mail rialisboa@mail.telepac.pt; Dir Vitali Mirnyi.

Xinhua (New China) News Agency (People's Republic of China): Rua Gonçalo Velho Cabral 11A, Restelo, Lisbon 3; tel. (21) 615783; Chief Correspondent Xiao Ziaoquan.

ČTK (Czech Republic) is also represented in Portugal

PRESS ASSOCIATIONS

Associação da Imprensa Diária (Association of the Daily Press): Rua de Artilharia Um 69-2°, 1297 Lisbon; tel. (21) 3857584; fax (21) 3873541; f. 1976; 27 mems; Pres. António Freitas Cruz; Sec. Jorge Moura.

Associação da Imprensa (AIND) (Portuguese Press Association): Rua Gomes Freire 183-4° Esq., 1169-041 Lisbon; tel. (21) 3555092; fax (21) 3142191; e-mail geral@aind.pt; internet www.aind.pt; f. 1960; represents 500 publications, both local and national; Pres. João Palmeiro; Sec.-Gen. Joana Ramada Curto.

Publishers

Assírio & Alvim: Rua de Arroios 154 B, 1150-056 Lisbon; tel. (21) 3583030; fax (21) 3583039; f. 1972; poetry, fiction, essays, gastronomy, photography, art, children's literature, history, social science; Man. Graça Ferreira.

Bertrand Editora, SA: Rua Anchieta 31-1°, 1200 Lisbon; tel. (21) 3420081; fax (21) 3479728; literature, arts, humanities, educational; Man. Mario Correia.

Brasília Editora: Rua José Falcão 173, 4050-317 Porto; tel. and fax (22) 2055854; internet www.geocities.com/brasilia_pt; f. 1960; liter-

ature, history, general; Dirs Dr J. Carvalho Branco, Dra Zulmira Carvalho Branco, Dra Isabel Carvalho Branco.

Coímbra Editora, Lda: Rua do Arnado, Apdo 101, 3002 Coímbra; tel. (239) 25459; fax (239) 37531; f. 1920; law, education, linguistics; Man. Dr João Carlos A. Oliveira Salgado.

Contexto Editora, Lda: Rua da Rosa 105-2° Dto, 1200 Lisbon; tel. (21) 3479769; fax (21) 3479770; fiction, poetry, children's literature; Dir Manuel de Brito.

Difusão Cultural—Sociedade Editorial e Livreira, Lda: Rua Pinheiro Chagas 27, R/C, 1050-175 Lisbon; tel. (21) 3173620; fax (21) 3528215; f. 1986; art, biographies, cinema, photography, literature, history, economics, philosophy, children's books, educational; Man. Nuno de Carvalho.

Distri Editora—Grupo Electroliber: Rua Vasco da Gama 4, 2685 Sacavém; tel. (21) 9425089; fax (21) 9425214; f. 1977; fiction, poetry, essays, educational; Man. Dir Pedro Ricardo Anschel de Vasconcelos.

Edições Afrontamento, Lda: Rua de Costa Cabral 859, 4200-225 Porto; tel. (22) 5074220; fax (22) 5074229; e-mail afrontamento@ mail.telepac.pt; f. 1963; fiction, poetry, cinema, children's books, history, sociology, philosophy, economics, politics, etc. Dirs J. Sousa Ribeiro, A. Sousa Luís.

Edições Asa: Avda de Boavista 3625, S/4.1, Edif. Oceanus, 4100-138 Porto; tel. (22) 6166030; fax (22) 6155346; e-mail edicoes@asa.pt; internet www.asa.pt; f. 1951; literature, arts, schoolbooks, children's books, educational equipment; Gen. Man. Américo A. Areal.

Edições Cosmos: Av. Júlio Dinis 6c-4° Dto, 1050-131 Lisbon; tel. (21) 7999950; fax (21) 7999979; internet www.liv-arcoiris.pt/; f. 1938; paperback classics; new collections of history, human sciences, sociology and law; Dir M. Mário Reis.

Edições Rolim, Lda: Rua Fialho de Almeida 38-2D, 1000 Lisbon; tel. (21) 553375; f. 1976; fiction, history, politics, law; Man. Dir Maria Rolim Ramos.

Edições João Sá da Costa, Lda: Av. do Brasil 120-1°, Esq., 1700-074 Lisbon; tel. (21) 8400428; fax (21) 8401056; e-mail edijsc@mail .telepac.pt; f. 1984; linguistics, poetry, dictionaries, geography, history, reference books; Man. Dirs Idalina Sá da Costa, João Sá da Costa.

Edições 70, Lda: Rua Luciano Cordeiro 123-2° Esq., 1069-157 Lisbon; tel. (21) 3190240; fax (21) 3190249; e-mail edi.70@mail .telepac.pt; f. 1970; history, linguistics, anthropology, philosophy, psychology, education, art, architecture, science, reference books; Dir Joaquim José Soares da Costa.

Editora A Educação Nacional, Lda: Rua do Almada 125, 4000 Porto; tel. (22) 2005351; fax (22) 7123377; school textbooks and review, *Educação Nacional*.

Editora Pergaminho, Lda: Rua de Alegria 486, 2645-167 Alcabideche; tel. (21) 4646110; fax (21) 4674008; e-mail pergaminho@mail .telepac.pt; internet www.editorapergaminho.pt; f. 1990; cinema, music, humour, fiction; Dir Mário Mendes de Moura.

Editora Portugalmundo, Lda: Rua Gonçalves Crespo 47, r/c, 1150-184 Lisbon; tel. (21) 3304685; fax (21) 3304687; children's books, poetry, biographies, law, music, fiction, theatre; Dir Maria Helena Matos.

Editora Replicação, Lda: Rua Pedro de Sintra 26A, Alto do Restrelo, 1400-277 Lisbon; tel. (21) 3021583; fax (21) 3021584; e-mail replic@mail.telepac.pt; f. 1982; textbooks, children's books, dictionaries, language materials; Dir José Carlos Anaia Cristo.

Editorial Avante!, SA: Av. Almirante Gago Coutinho 121, 1700-029 Lisbon; tel. (21) 8429836; fax (21) 8429849; affiliated with the Partido Comunista Português; fiction, politics, history, philosophy, economics; Dir Francisco Melo.

Editorial Confluência: Calçada do Combro 99, 1200-112 Lisbon; tel. (21) 3471709; fax (21) 3159259; e-mail livroshorizonte@mail .telepac.pt; f. 1945; dictionaries; Man. Rogério Mendes de Moura.

Editorial Estampa, Lda: Rua da Escola do Exército 9, R/C Dto, 1169-090 Lisbon; tel. (21) 3555663; fax (21) 3141911; e-mail estampa@mail.telepac.pt; internet www.editorialestampa.pt; sociology, economics, occult, fiction, sport, history, art, alternative medicine, children's; Dir António Carlos Manso Pinheiro.

Editorial Futura: Rua João Frederico Ludovica, 16A 1500-310, Lisbon; tel. and fax (21) 4945995; e-mail editorialfutura@netcabo.pt; literature, comics.

Editorial Inquérito, Lda: Estrada Lisboa–Sintra, Km 14, Edif. CETOP, Apdo 33, 2726-901 Mem Martins; tel. (21) 9170096; fax (21) 9170130; e-mail inquerito@iol.pt; f. 1938; sciences, politics, literature, history, classics, philosophy; Man. Francisco Lyon de Castro.

Editorial Minerva: Rua Luz Soriano 31–33-1°, 1200 Lisbon; tel. (21) 322535; fax (21) 3464720; f. 1927; literature, politics, children's; Man. JOÃO DOMINGUES.

Editorial Notícias: Rua Padre Luís Aparício 10-1°, 1150-248 Lisbon; tel. (21) 3552130; fax (21) 3552168; e-mail editnoticias@mail .telepac.pt; internet www.editorialnoticias.pt; fiction, politics, religion, history, economics, biographies, linguistics, law, management, education, dictionaries, ethnology, children's books, CD-ROMs.

Editorial Nova Ática, SA: Calçado Nova de S. Francisco, 10, 1°esq., 1200-300 Lisbon; tel. (21) 3420557; fax (21) 3420305; f. 1935; poetry, literature, essays, theatre, history, philosophy; Chief Execs VASCO SILVA, JOSÉ RODRIGUES.

Editorial Presença, Lda: Rua Augusto Gil 35A, 1049-043 Lisbon; tel. (21) 7992200; fax (21) 7977560; e-mail info@editpresenca.pt; internet www.editpresenca.pt; f. 1960; social sciences, fiction, textbooks, computer books, business, leisure, health, children's books, etc.; Dir FRANCISCO ESPADINHA.

Editorial Verbo SA: Av. António Augusto de Aguiar 148, 2b, 1069-019 Lisbon; tel. (21) 3801100; fax (21) 3865397; e-mail verbo@ editorialverbo.pt; internet www.editorialverbo.pt; f. 1959; encyclopaedias, dictionaries, reference, history, general science, textbooks, education and children's books; Dir FERNANDO GUEDES.

Europress—Editores e Distribuidores de Publicações, Lda: Praceta da República, Loja A, 2675-183 Póvoa de Santo Adrião; tel. (21) 9381450; fax (21) 9381452; e-mail europress@mail.telepac.pt; internet www.europress.pt; f. 1982; academic, children's, law, poetry, health, novels, history, social sciences, medicine, etc. Man. ANTÓNIO BENTO VINTÉM.

FCA (Editora de Informática): Rua D. Estefânia 183-1° Esq., 1000-154 Lisbon; tel. (21) 3532735; fax (21) 3577827; e-mail fca@fca.pt; internet www.fca.pt; f. 1991; computer science.

Gradiva—Publicações, Lda: Rua Almeida e Sousa 21-R/C Esq., 1399-041 Lisbon; tel. (21) 3974067; fax (21) 3953471; e-mail gradiva@ip.pt; internet www.gradiva.pt; f. 1981; philosophy, education, history, fiction, science, social science, children's books; Man. Dir GUILHERME VALENTE.

Guimarães Editores Lda: Rua da Misericórdia 68–70, 1200-273 Lisbon; tel. (21) 3243120; fax (21) 3243129; e-mail geral@ guimaraes-ed.pt; internet www.guimaraes-ed.pt; literature, philosophy, history, etc.

Ibis Editores: Av. D. Vasco da Gama 30, 1300 Lisbon; tel. (21) 3018387; history, literature, anthology, ethnography, poetry, photography, etc.; Dirs MARINA TAVARES DIAS, JOÃO PAULO CAXARIA.

Impala, Sociedade Editorial, Lda: Estrada Sintrelos ed Impala Ranholas, 2710-460 Sintra; tel. (21) 9238000; fax (21) 9238041; e-mail geral@impala.pt; internet www.impala.pt; f. 1983; magazines and children's books; Dir JACQUES RODRIGUES.

Imprensa Nacional—Casa da Moeda, SA (INCM): Avda António de José de Almeida, Edif. Casa da Moeda, 1000-042 Lisbon; tel. (21) 7810700; e-mail dco@incm.pt; internet www.incm.pt; f. 1972 as Imprensa Nacional—Casa da Moeda, EP; changed status as above in 1999; Portuguese literature, arts, philosophy, history, geography, sociology, economics, encyclopedias, dictionaries, and the *Diário da República*; Pres. Dr ANTÓNIO MANUEL DA ASSUNÇÃO BRAZ TEIXEIRA.

Lello & Irmão: Rua Cândida dos Reis 46, 3°–10, 4050-151 Porto; tel. (22) 3326084; fax (22) 3326086; fiction, poetry, history, reference, biography, religion; Man. JOSÉ MANUEL BERNARDES PEREIRA LELLO.

Lidel—Edições Técnicas, Lda: Rua D. Estefânia 183 R/C Dto, 1049-057 Lisbon; tel. (21) 3511442; fax (21) 3577827; e-mail lidel@ lidel.pt; internet www.lidel.pt.lidel/on-line; f. 1963; Portuguese as a foreign language, management, technology, computer science; Man. Dir Eng. FREDERICO CARLOS DA SILVA ANNES.

Lisboa Editora, Lda: Avda Estados Unidos da América, 1B, 1700-163 Lisbon; tel. (21) 8430910; fax (21) 8430911; e-mail geral@ lisboaeditora.pt; internet www.lisboaeditora.pt; textbooks.

Livraria Civilização Editora: Avda Almirante Reis 102 r/c-D1150-022 Lisbon, ; tel. (21) 8161460; f. 1920; social sciences, politics, economics, history, art, medicine, fiction, children's; Man. Dir MOURA BESSA.

Livraria Clássica Editora: Rua do Vale Formoso 37, 1900 Lisbon; tel. (21) 8681183; fax (21) 8685012; fiction, social sciences, linguistics, economics, etc.; Dir FRANCISCO PAULO.

Livraria Editora Figueirinhas, Lda: Rua do Almada 47, 4050-036 Porto; tel. (22) 3325300; fax (22) 3325907; f. 1898; literature, school textbooks; Dir FRANCISCO GOMES PIMENTA.

Livraria Multinova: Av. Santa Joana Princesa 12E, 1700 Lisbon; tel. (21) 8421820; fax (21) 8483436; f. 1970; schoolbooks, general, religion, Brazilian works; Dir CARLOS SANTOS.

Livraria Romano Torres: Rua Marcos Portugal 20A, 1200 Lisbon; tel. (21) 3901244; f. 1885; fiction; Dir FRANCISCO NORONHA E ANDRADE.

Livraria Sá da Costa Editora: Rua Garrett 100–102, 1200 Lisbon; tel. (21) 3460721; fax (21) 3460722; literature, history, philosophy sociology, politics, etc.; Dir MANUEL SÁ DA COSTA.

Livros do Brasil, SA: Rua dos Caetanos 22, 1200-079 Lisbon; tel. (21) 3462621; fax (21) 3428487; e-mail livbrasil@livbrasil.com; internet www.livbrasil.com; f. 1944; literature, history, politics, science, management, health, children's books; Dir ANTÓNIO DE SOUZA-PINTO.

Livros Horizonte, Lda: Rua das Chagas 17-1° Dto, 1200-106 Lisbon; tel. (21) 3466917; fax (21) 3159259; e-mail livroshorizonte@ mail.telepac.pt; f. 1953; art, pedagogy, history; Chair. ROGÉRIO MENDES DE MOURA.

Joaquim Machado, Lda—Livraria Almedína: Arco de Almedína 15, 3004-509 Coímbra; tel. (239) 851907; fax (239) 851901; e-mail geral@almedina.net; internet www.almedina.net; law, education; Dir JOAQUIM MACHADO.

McGraw-Hill de Portugal: Rua Barata Salgueiro, 51A, 1250–043 Lisbon; tel. (21) 3553180; fax (21) 3553189; e-mail servico_clientes@ macgraw-hill.com; internet www.mcgraw-hill.pt; scientific, technical and medical; Gen. Man. ANTÓNIO DE MARCO.

Mosaico Editores Lda: Rua de Campolide 31-5° Esq., 1070-026 Lisbon; tel. (21) 3881902; fax (21) 3871081; e-mail mosaico@mail .telepac.pt; f. 1986; Dir JOÃO PAULO ARAGÃO.

PAULUS Editora: Rua Dom Pedro de Cristo 10, 1700-136 Lisbon; tel. (21) 8437620; fax (21) 8437629; e-mail editora@paulus.pt; internet www.paulus.pt; religion, theology, psychology, etc.; Dir AGOSTINHO DE FRANÇA CORREIA.

Plátano Editora, SARL: Av. de Berna 31-2°, Esq., 1069 Lisbon; tel. (21) 7979278; fax (21) 7954019; e-mail platanoeditora@mail.telepac .pt; f. 1972; literature, educational, science, technical, dictionaries, etc.; Dir FRANCISCO PRATA GINJA.

Porto Editora, Lda: Rua da Restauração 365, 4099 Porto; tel. (22) 6088300; fax (22) 6088301; e-mail pe@portoeditora.pt; internet www .portoeditora.pt; f. 1944; general literature, school books, dictionaries, children's books, multimedia; Dirs VASCO TEIXEIRA, JOSÉ ANTÓNIO TEIXEIRA, ROSÁLIA TEIXEIRA.

Publicações Alfa, SA: Estrada Lisboa/Sintra Km 14, Edif. CETOP, 2725-377 Mem Martins; tel. (21) 9172807; fax (21) 9170130; art, natural sciences, cinema, reference, history, medicine, encyclopaedias, literary history, thematic dictionaries; Man. Dir FRANCISCO LYON DE CASTRO.

Publicações Europa-América, Lda: Estrada Nacional 249, Km 14, Apdo 8, 2726–901 Mem Martins; tel. (21) 9267700; fax (21) 9267777; e-mail secretariado@europa-america.pt; internet www .europa-america.pt; f. 1945; fiction, current affairs, economics, reference, history, technical, children's; Dir TITO LYON DE CASTRO.

Publicações Dom Quixote: Av. Cintura do Porto de Lisboa, Urb. da Matinha, Lote A-2°-C, 1900 Lisbon; tel. (21) 8610430; fax (21) 8610435; e-mail ndematas@dquixote.pt; f. 1965; general fiction, poetry, history, philosophy, psychology, politics, didactics and sociology; university text books; children's books; Dir NELSON DE MATOS.

Quimera Editores Lda: Rua Actor Isidoro 17, r/c Esq., 1900-015 Lisbon; tel. (21) 8455950; fax (21) 8455951; e-mail quimera@ quimera-editores.pt; internet www.quimera-editores.pt; f. 1987; literature, art, history, photography, etc.; Dirs JOSÉ ALFARO, LUÍS VEIGA.

Rés—Editora, Lda: Praça Marquês de Pombal 78, 4000-390 Porto; tel. (22) 5024174; fax (22) 5026098; e-mail res-editora@res-editora .pt; internet www.res-editora.pt; economics, philosophy, law, sociology; Dir REINALDO DE CARVALHO.

Texto Editora, Lda: Estrada de Paço de Arcos 66 e 66A, 2735-336 Cacém; tel. (21) 4272200; fax (21) 4272201; e-mail info@textoeditora .pt; internet www.textoeditora.pt; f. 1977; school textbooks, management, pedagogy, health, beauty, cooking, children's books, multimedia; Man. Dir MANUEL JOSÉ DO ESPÍRITO SANTO FERRÃO.

Ulisseia Editora, Lda: Avda António Augusto de Aguiar, 148, 2°, 1069–019 Lisbon; tel. (21) 3801100; fax (21) 3865396; internet www .editorialverbo.pt; owned by Grupo Verbo; classical and contemporary literature and translations, history, politics, economics; Contact Dr JOSÉ LUÍS FONSECA.

Vulgus Editora, Lda: Qta Galiza 8 R/C Esq., 2765 Estoril; tel. (21) 4689072; fax (21) 4571306; f. 1982; school textbooks, linguistics, psychology, law, education; Man. Dir FERNANDO MONTEIRO.

PUBLISHERS' ASSOCIATION

Associação Portuguesa de Editores e Livreiros: Av. dos Estados Unidos da América 97-6° Esq., 1700-167 Lisbon; tel. (21) 8435180; fax (21) 8489377; e-mail cdb@apel.pt; internet www.apel .pt; f. 1939; Pres. GRAÇA DIDIER; Sec.-Gen. CRISTINA RODRIGUES.

Broadcasting and Communications

TELECOMMUNICATIONS

Portugal Telecom, SA: Av. Fontes Pereira de Melo 40-6°, 1089 Lisbon; tel. (21) 5002000; fax (21) 3562624; e-mail antonio.g .azevedo@telecom.pt; internet www.telecom.pt; f. 1994 by merger of three regional telecommunications operators; state holding reduced to 25% in 1997; relinquished monopoly on fixed-line operations in Jan. 2000; Chair. FRANCISCO MURTEIRA NABO; CEO MIGUEL HORTA E COSTA.

Optimus Telecomunicações, SA: Edif. Green Park, Av. do Combatentes 43-13° e 14°-A, 1600 Lisbon; tel. (21) 7233600; fax (21) 7546275; internet www.optimus.pt; f. 1998; provides mobile telephone services.

Telecel—Comunicações Pessoais, SA: Rua Tomás da Fonseca, Centro Empresarial Torres de Lisboa, Torre A, 1649-032 Lisbon; tel. (21) 7225000; fax (21) 7225200; internet www.telecel.pt; f. 1992; provides mobile telephone services; 51% owned by Vodafone-AirTouch PLC (United Kingdom/USA); Exec. Officer A. RUI DE LACERDA CARRAPATOSO.

TMN (Telecomunicações Móveis Nacionais), SA: Av. Álvaro Pais 2, 1649-041 Lisbon; tel. (21) 7914400; fax (21) 7914500; e-mail 1696@tmn.pt; internet www.tmn.pt; commenced mobile telephone services in 1989; part of Portugal Telecom.

Following the abolition of Portugal Telecom's monopoly in January 2000, several new operators, including Novis (controlled by the Sonae Group), Oni (owned by Electricidade de Portugal) and Jazztel (a Spanish company) commenced activities.

Regulatory Authority

Instituto das Comunicações de Portugal (ICP): Av. José Malhoa 12, 1070 Lisbon; tel. (21) 7211000; fax (21) 7211001; e-mail info@icp.pt; internet www.icp.pt; Pres. Dr LUÍS FILIPE NAZARÉ.

BROADCASTING

In 1997 a total of 560 radio broadcasters and 386 television broadcasters were licensed.

Radio

RDP
(Radiodifusão Portuguesa, SA)

Av. Eng. Duarte Pacheco 6, 1070 Lisbon; tel. (21) 3820117; fax (21) 3871402; e-mail ruimartins@rdp.pt; internet www.rdp.pt.

f. 1975; after the nationalization of nine radio stations and their merger with the existing national broadcasting company; Chair. ALMERINDO MARQUES.

Domestic Services:

Antena 1
tel. (21) 3820000; fax (21) 3873977.

Dir JOÃO COELHO; broadcasts 24 hours daily on medium-wave and FM; news, sport, music, etc.

Antena 2
tel. (21) 3820000; fax (21) 3873986.

Dir JOÃO PEREIRA BASTOS; broadcasts classical music 24 hours daily on FM.

Antena 3
tel. (21) 3820000; fax (21) 3873977.

Dir JORGE ALEXANDRE LOPES; broadcasts 24 hours daily on FM; music and entertainment for young people.

Regional Centres:

RDP/Norte (Northern Zone)
Rua Cândido dos Reis 74-1°, 4050-151 Porto; tel. (22) 3399900; fax (22) 3399902; e-mail rdpnorte@rdp.pt.

Dir JOSÉ AUGUSTO MACEDO.

RDP/Centro (Central Zone)
Rua Dr José Alberto dos Reis, 3049 Coímbra; tel. (239) 404010; fax (239) 724253.

Dir DOMINGOS GRILO.

RDP/Sul (Southern Zone)
Campo da Sra da Saúde, 8000 Faro; tel. (89) 805931; fax (89) 802192.

Dir JORGE AMORIM.

RDP/Açores
Rua Dr Aristides Moreira da Mota 33, 9500 Ponta Delgada, São Miguel, Azores; tel. (296) 22045; fax (296) 629379.

Dir CARLOS MELO TAVARES.

RDP/Madeira
Rua Tenente Coronel Sarmento 15, 9000 Funchal, Madeira; tel. (291) 229155; fax (291) 230753.

One medium-wave transmitter on 1,332 kHz and one FM transmitter on 94.1 mHz; Dir LEONEL DE FREITAS.

Overseas Services:

RDP/International—Radio Portugal
Av. Eng. Duarte Pacheco 26, 1070-110 Lisbon; tel. (21) 3820000; fax (21) 3820165; e-mail rdpinternacional@rdp.pt; internet www .rdp.pt.

Daily programmes on short wave in Portuguese to Europe, North America, South America, Africa and Middle East/India; Dir JAIME MARQUES DE ALMEIDA.

RDP/Africa
Av. Eng. Duarte Pacheco 6-5°, 1000 Lisbon; tel. (21) 3820000; fax (21) 3820081.

Broadcasts 20 hours daily on FM to Lisbon area and on short wave to lusophone countries of Africa; African news, sport, music, etc. Dir DAVID BORGES.

Private Stations

National Stations

RR
(Rádio Renascença)

Rua Capelo 5, 1294-108 Lisbon; tel. (21) 3239200; fax (21) 3239220; e-mail info@rr.pt.

f. 1937; Roman Catholic station; broadcasts 24 hours a day on Rádio Renascença (FM, medium-wave and satellite; internet www.rr.pt; Dir António Sala), on RFM (FM and satellite; internet www.rfm.pt; Dir Pedro Tojal) and on MEGA FM (FM and satellite; internet www.mega.fm.pt; Dir Nelson Ribeiro); Chair. FERNANDO MAGALHÃES CRESPO.

Regional Centres:

RR/Centro-Sul
Rua Ivens 14, 1294-108 Lisbon; tel. (21) 3239327; fax (21) 3239326.

Dir FERNANDO DE ALMEIDA.

RR/Porto
Rua Sá da Bandeira 766-1°, 4000 Porto; tel. (22) 2005678; fax (22) 325924.

Co-ordinator CARMO DA FONSECA.

There are nine RR regional stations.

Rádio Comercial, SA: Rua Sampaio Pina 24/26, 1000 Lisbon; tel. (21) 3821500; fax (21) 3821559; e-mail geral@radiocomercial.pt; internet www.radiocomercial.pt; f. 1979; as RDP-3, transferred to private ownership in 1993; broadcasts music, news and sport 24 hours daily on **Rádio Comercial** (FM); and since March 1998 on **Rádio Nacinal** on MW to central and southern Portugal, also music, news and sport; Head LUÍS MONTEZ; Dir of Programmes MIGUEL CRUZ.

Regional Stations

Rádio Nostalgia: Rua Sampaio e Pina 26, 1099-044 Lisbon; tel. (21) 3821500; fax (21) 3821559; e-mail internet@radiocomercial.pt; f. 1992; fmrly Radio Commercial; broadcasts music 24 hours daily on FM; Head LUÍS MONTEZ; Dir of Programmes MIGUEL CRUZ.

TSF-Press: Rua das Mercês 58/62, 4200 Porto; tel. (22) 5573500; fax (22) 557352; f. 1990; fmrly Radiopress; broadcasts news, sport, music, etc. 24 hours daily on FM; Dir CARLOS ANDRADE.

Local Stations

At March 1998 a total of 322 licensed local radio stations were operating in Portugal (including the Azores and Madeira).

TSF—Rádio Jornal: Av. de Ceuta, Edif. Urbiceuta 1-5°, 1300 Lisbon; tel. (21) 3622977; fax (21) 3622429; internet www.tsf.pt; broadcasts news and sport 24 hours daily on FM; Dir CARLOS ANDRADE.

Other Stations

The first 'thematic' radio stations were classified in November 1997 13 as musical programming and three as news programming.

Music Channels

Memória FM: Rua João de Barros 265, 4000 Porto; tel. (22) 6101390; fax (22) 6101421; internet www.memoria.esoterica.pt; one FM transmitter; broadcasts 24 hours a day.

Orbital FM: Av. S. José 20-4° Esq., 2686 Sacavém; tel. (21) 9414311; fax (21) 9414302; one FM transmitter; broadcasts 24 hours a day.

Rádio Activa: Rua das Mercês 58–62, 4200 Porto; tel. (22) 5573500; fax (22) 5505567; one FM transmitter; broadcasts 24 hours a day.

Rádio Arremesso: Lisbon; tel. (21) 8401147; fax (21) 8401150; one FM transmitter; broadcasts 24 hours a day.

Rádio Capital: Rua Torcato José Clavine 17D, Piso 02, Pragal, 2804-526 Almada; tel. (21) 2721380; fax (21) 2740781; one FM transmitter; broadcasts 24 hours a day.

Rádio Cidade: Praceta Notícias da Amadora, Loja 2, 2700 Amadora; tel. (21) 4922972; fax (21) 490789; internet www.rcidade.pt; one FM transmitter; broadcasts 24 hours a day.

Rádio Cidade de Vila Nova de Gaia—Rádio Satélite: Rua Álvares Cabral 54-1°, Sala 18, 4400 Vila Nova de Gaia; tel. (22) 3701031; one FM transmitter; broadcasts 24 hours a day.

Rádio Clube de Gondomar: Rua Cosme Ferreira de Castro 527, 4420 Gondomar; tel. (22) 4837134; fax (22) 4837134; one FM transmitter; broadcasts 24 hours a day.

Rádio Juventude: Av. 1 de Maio, 23 C/V Dta, 6000 Castelo Branco; tel. (72) 26536; fax (72) 27660; one FM transmitter; broadcasts seven hours a day.

Rádio Paris Lisboa: Rua Latino Coelho, 50-1°, 1050-137 Lisbon; tel. (21) 3510580; fax (21) 3510598; e-mail geral@rpl.frm; internet www.rpl.frm; one FM transmitter; broadcasts 24 hours a day.

Rádio 7 FM: Av. Visconde Barreiros 89-5°, 4470 Maia; tel. (22) 9439380; fax (22) 9439381; one FM transmitter; broadcasts 18 hours a day.

News Channels

Rádio Santa Maria: Rua Sotto Mayor 7-3° Dto, 8000 Faro; tel. (289) 21115; one FM transmitter; broadcasts 17 hours a day.

Rádio Viriato: Complexo Conventurispress, Orgens, Apdo 3115, 3511-689 Viseu; tel. (232) 410416; fax (232) 410418; e-mail inforadio@viriato.fm.com; internet www.viriatofm.com; f. 1987; one FM transmitter; broadcasts 24 hours a day; Dir ANABELA ABREU.

TSF—Rádio Jornal: see local stations above.

Radio Associations

Associação Portuguesa de Radiodifusão (APR) (Portuguese Radio Association): Av. das Descobertas, 17, 1400-091 Lisbon; tel. (21) 3016999; fax (21) 3016536; e-mail apr@apradiodifusao.pt; internet www.apradiodifusao.pt; fmrly Instituto das Rádios Locais; f. 1987; Pres. JOSÉ FAUSTINO.

Associação das Rádios de Inspiração Cristã (ARIC) (Christian Radio Association): Rua da Prata 224-2° Esq., 1100 Lisbon; tel. (21) 8873723; fax (21) 8873903.

Television

RTP (Radiotelevisão Portuguesa, SA): Av. 5 de Outubro 197, Apdo 2934, 1050-054 Lisbon; tel. (21) 7947000; fax (21) 7947570; e-mail rtp@rtp.pt; internet www.rtp.pt; f. 1956; nationalized in 1975; became joint-stock co (with 100% public capital) in August 1992; 12 studios incl. Lisbon, Porto, Ponta Delgada and Funchal; Chair. MANUEL ROQUE; Dir of Programmes MARIA ELISA DOMINGUES.

Regional Centres:

RTP/Porto: Rua Conceição Fernandes, Apdo 174, 4402 Vila Nova de Gaia; tel. (22) 7156000; fax (22) 7110963; Dir DJALME NEVES.

RTP/Açores: Rua Ernesto Canto 40, 9500 Ponta Delgada, São Miguel; tel. (296) 202700; fax (296) 202771; Dir MARIA DO CARMO FIGUEIREDO.

RTP/Madeira: Sítio da Madalena, Caminho Santo António 145, 9000 Funchal; tel. (291) 709100; fax (291) 741859; Dir CARLOS ALBERTO FERNANDES.

In addition to the three regional centres, there are seven RTP regional studios.

RTP/Internacional (RTPi): e-mail rtpi@rtp.pt; internet rtpi.rtp .pt; commenced satellite transmissions in June 1992; broadcasts in Portuguese 24 hours a day; Dir FERNANDO BALSINHA.

RTP/Africa: commenced transmissions to lusophone countries of Africa in 1997; broadcasts 24 hours a day; Dir AFONSO RATO.

The Radiotelevisão Portuguesa network serves 99% of the population of Portugal on RTP-1 (VHF) and 91% on TV-2, its second channel (UHF). Both channels also broadcast on cable. From Jan-uary 1997 commercial advertising was reduced on RTP-1 and banned on RTP-2.

Private Stations

SIC (Sociedade Independente de Comunicação, SA): Estrada da Outurela, Carnaxide, 2795 Linda-a-Velha; tel. 4179400; fax 4173118; e-mail administrator@sic.pt; internet www.sic.pt; commenced transmissions in 1992; news and entertainment; Head FRANCISCO PINTO BALSEMÃO; Dir of Programmes EMÍDIO RANGEL.

TVI (Televisão Independente, SA): Rua Mário Castelhano 40, 2740-502 Barcarena; tel. (21) 4347500; fax (21) 434756; internet www.tvi.pt; commenced transmissions in 1993; Pres. MIGUEL PAIS DO AMARAL; Gen. Man. JOSÉ EDUARDO MONIZ.

Cable Television

By 1997 cable television subscribers totalled 383,000.

Regional Companies

Cabo TV Açoreana: Av. Antero de Quental 9-C-1°, 9500-160 Ponta Delgada; tel. (296) 302400; fax (296) 302405.

Cabo TV Madeirense: Av. Estados Unidos da América, Nazaré, 9050 Funchal; tel. (291) 700800; fax (291) 766132.

TV Cabo Douro: Av. da Liberdade 424-8°, 4700 Braga; tel. (253) 215870; fax (253) 215851.

TV Cabo Guadiana: Rua do Sol 24-2°, 8000 Faro; tel. (89) 807070; fax (89) 807077.

TV Cabo Lisboa: Rua Soeiro Pereira Gomes 7, Edif. América—Escritório 10, 1600 Lisbon; tel. (21) 7956768; fax (21) 7956769.

TV Cabo Mondego: Rua do Carmo 82, 3000 Coímbra; tel. (239) 851050; fax (239) 832932.

TV Cabo Porto: Av. da Boavista 253/267-9°, Edif. Mundial Confiança, Centro Comercial Brasília, 4000 Porto; tel. (22) 6006050; fax (22) 6006075.

TV Cabo Sado: Rua Galileu Saúde Correia 13, 2800 Almada; tel. (21) 2725555; fax (21) 2730238.

TV Cabo Tejo: Taguspark, Edif. Inovação II, Sala 414, 2780 Oeiras; tel. (21) 4227700; fax (21) 4211828; e-mail mafalda.soares@tvcabo .pt; internet www.tvcabo.pt; f. 1994; CEO JOSÉ GRAÇA BAU.

Other licensed cable television enterprises are:

Bragatel—Companhia de TV por Cabo de Braga, SA: Av. 31 de Janeiro177, Apdo 17, 4710-452 Braga; tel. (253) 616600; fax (253) 616998; authorized to operate in Braga area.

Cabovisão—Sociedade de Televisão por Cabo, SA: Lugar de Poços, Vale de Touros, 2950-425 Palmela; tel. (21) 0801080; fax (21) 0801000; e-mail info@cabovisao.pt; internet www.cabovisao.pt; authorized to operate in 156 municipalities (4.5m. homes).

Pluricanal Aveiro: Rua Dr Nascimento Leitão 28, 3810 Aveiro; tel. (34) 384555; fax (34) 384556.

Pluricanal Gondomar: Rua S. João de Deus 145, 4420 Gondomar; tel. (22) 4636600; fax (22) 4636601.

Pluricanal Leiria: Av. General Humberto Delgado 2, 2400 Leiria; tel. (244) 824925; fax (244) 824943.

Pluricanal Santarém: Estrada Nacional 3, Edif. Ribatel, S. Pedro, 2000 Santarém; tel. (244) 824925; fax (244) 824943.

PT Multimédia—Serviços de Telecomunicações e Multimédia, SGPS, SA: Avda 5 de Outubro, 208 1069–203, Lisbon; tel. (21) 782–4725; fax (21) 782–4735; e-mail ir@pt-multimedia.pt; internet www.pt-multimedia.pt; 54% owned by Portugal Telecom; CFO LUÍS PACHECO DE MELO; 1.7m customers.

Finance

(cap. = capital; res = reserves; dep. = deposits; m. = million; brs = branches; amounts in escudos, unless otherwise stated)

BANKING

Central Bank

Banco de Portugal: Rua do Ouro 27, 1100-150 Lisbon; tel. (21) 3213200; fax (21) 3464843; e-mail info@bportugal.pt; internet www .bportugal.pt; f. 1846; reorganized 1931 with the sole right to issue notes; nationalized Sept. 1974; cap. €1.0m., res. €2,468.8m., dep. €11,622.0m. (Dec. 2001); chief br. Porto, with 10 others including Madeira and Azores; Gov. VÍTOR CONSTÂNCIO.

Locally-Incorporated Banks

Banco Bilbao Vizcaya Argentaria (Portugal), SA: Av. da Liberdade 222, 1250-148 Lisbon; tel. (21) 3117200; fax (21) 3117500; e-mail bbv.imagem@meganet.pt; internet www.bbva.pt; f. 1991 as Banco Bilbao Vizcaya; name changed 2000; cap. €125.0m., res €42.1m., dep. €2,560.1m. (Dec. 2001); Pres. JOSÉ VERA JARDIN; Gen Man. JOSÉ LUÍS JOLÓ MARÍN; 69 brs.

Banco BPI, SA: Rua Sá da Bandeira 20, 4000-427 Porto; tel. (22) 2075000; fax (22) 2063980; internet www.bancobpi.pt; f. 1998; upon absorption of Banco Fonsecas e Burnay and Banco Borges e Irmão by Banco de Fomento e Exterior; 51.4% owned by Banco Português de Investimento, SA; cap. €450.0m., res €374.9m., dep. €20,973.4m. (Dec 2001); Chair. ARTUR SANTOS SILVA.

Banco Comercial dos Açores: Edif. BCA, Rua Dr José Bruno Tavares Carreiro, 9500-119 Ponta Delgada, São Miguel, Azores; tel. (296) 629070; fax (296) 629657; e-mail bca@mail.telepac.pt; internet www.bca.pt; f. 1912; fmrly Banco Micaelense; 73.98% owned by Banif Comercial SGPS, SA, 15.00% owned by the Azores Autonomous Region; cap. €51,892,365, res €9,143,964, dep. €760,979,055 (Dec. 2002); Chair. HORÁCIO DA SILVA ROQUE; Pres. and CEO Dr JOAQUIM MARQUES DOS SANTOS; 42 brs.

Banco Comercial Português (BCP): Praça D João I 28, POB 4744, P-4050 Porto; tel. (22) 2064000; fax (22) 2064193; internet www.bcp.pt; f. 1985; merged with Banco Pinto e Sotto Mayor in 2000; cap. €2,101.6m., res €281.1m., dep. €53,854.9m. (Dec. 2000); Chair and Chief Exec. Eng. JORGE JARDIM GONÇALVES; 751 brs.

Banco Efisa SA: Av. Antonio Augusto de Aguiar 134-4°, 1050-020 Lisbon; tel. (21) 3117800; fax (21) 3117908; e-mail dcb@bancoefisa.pt; internet www.bancoefisa.it; f. 1994 by merger; cap. 3,650m., res 853.2m., dep. 14,491.7m. (Dec. 2000); Pres. and Chair. ADBOOL VAKIL.

Banco Espírito Santo, SA: Av. da Liberdade 195, 1250-142 Lisbon; tel. (21) 3501000; fax (21) 3501033; e-mail info@bes.pt; internet www.bes.pt; f. 1937 by merger; nationalized in 1975; transfer to private sector completed in Feb. 1992; fmrly Banco Espírito Santo e Comercial de Lisboa; cap. €1,000m., res €206.0m., dep. €33,736.0m. (Dec. 2001); Pres. RICARDO ESPÍRITO SANTO SILVA SALGADO; Chair. ANTÓNIO LUIS ROQUETTE RICCIARDI; 490 brs.

Banco Expresso Atlantico, SA: Rua de S. Nicolau 120, 1110 Porto; tel. (22) 6005579; fax (22) 6005597; f. 1974 as Banco Comercial de Macau; cap. 8,019.3m., res 3,762.9m., dep. 10,672.5m. (Dec. 2000); Chair. Dr M. C. CARVALHO FERNANDES; 32 brs.

Banco Finantia: Rua General Firmino Miguel 5-1°, 1600 Lisbon; tel. (21) 7202000; fax (21) 7202030; e-mail finantia@finantia.com; internet www.finantia.com; f. 1987; investment bank; cap. €50m., res €47.9m., dep. €1,158.3m. (Dec. 2001); Pres. ANTÓNIO MANUEL AFONSO GUERREIRO.

Banco Internacional de Crédito (BIC), SA: Av. Fontes Pereira de Melo 27, 1050-117 Lisbon; tel. (21) 3115555; fax (21) 3146165; e-mail mkt@bic.pt; internet www.bic.pt; f. 1986; wholly-owned by Banco Espírito Santo, SA; cap. €150.0m., res €55.3m., dep. €7,411.6m. (Dec. 2001); Pres. Dr JOSÉ MANUEL FERREIRA NETO; 122 brs.

Banco Itaú Europa, SA: Centro Comercial Amoreiras, Rua Tierno Galvan, Torre 3-11°, 1099-048 Lisbon; tel. (21) 3811000; fax (21) 3887219; e-mail bie.global@itaueuropa.pt; internet www.itaueuropa .pt/itaueuropa; f. 1994; cap. €144.5m., res €18.5m., dep. €1,367.8m. (Dec. 2001); Pres. and Chair. ROBERTO EGYDIO SETUBAL; Chief Exec. ALMIR VIGNOTO.

Banco Português de Investimento—BPI, SA: Largo Jean Monnet 1-9, 1269-067 Lisbon; tel. (21) 3101000; fax (21) 3535650; e-mail investor_relations@bpi.pt; internet www.bpi.pt; f. 1984; from Sociedade Portuguesa de Investimentos, SARL; restructured 1995; cap. €175.2m., res €131.9m., dep. €5,562.7m. (Dec. 2001); Pres. Dr ARTUR SANTOS SILVA; Vice-Pres. FERNANDO ULRICH.

Banco Privado Português, SA: Rua Mouzinho da Silveira 12, 1250-167 Lisbon; tel. (21) 3137000; fax (21) 3137092; internet www .bpp.pt; f. 1996; cap. €100m., res €27.5m., dep. €353.6m. (Dec. 2001); Chair. Dr JOÃO OLIVEIRA RENDEIRO.

Banco Santander Portugal, SA: Praça Marquês de Pombal 2, 1250-161 Lisbon; tel. (21) 3107000; fax (21) 3107243; e-mail superlinha@santander.pt; internet www.santander.pt; f. 1985 as Banco de Comércio e Indústria, name changed 1998; cap. 31,191m., res 10,524.4m., dep. 671,916.6m. (Dec. 2000); Chair. ANTÓNIO HORTA OSÓRIO; 121 brs.

Banco Totta e Açores, SA: Rua do Ouro 88, 1100-063 Lisbon; tel. (21) 3211549; fax (21) 3211694; e-mail bta@bta.pt; internet www.bta .pt; f. 1970 by merger; privatized in 1989–90; 99.32% owned by Santander Central Hispano Group (Spain); cap. €525.0m., res €318.2m., dep. €23,606.4m. (Dec. 2001); Chair. EURICO DE MELO; CEO ANTÓNIO HORTA OSÓRIO; 301 brs.

BANIF (Banco Internacional do Funchal): Rua de João Tavira 30, 9000 Funchal, Madeira; tel. (291) 207700; fax (291) 224822; e-mail infoa@banif.pt; internet www.banif.pt; f. 1988; cap. €150.0m., res €88.7m., dep. €5,116.08m. (Dec. 2001); Chair. HORÁCIO DA SILVA ROQUE; 134 brs.

BNC (Banco Nacional de Crédito Imobiliário): Rua do Comércio 85, 1100-149 Lisbon; tel. (21) 3238500; fax (21) 3238695; e-mail bncdfi@comnexo.pt; internet www.bnc.pt; f. 1991; mortgage institution; cap. €175.0m., res €37.4m., dep. €2,966.6m. (Dec. 2001); Pres. Dr ALBERTO ALVES DE OLIVEIRA PINTO; 104 brs.

BPN (Banco Português de Negócios, SA): Av. França 680/694, 4250-213 Porto; internet www.bpn.pt; tel. (22) 8341400; fax (22) 8341480; f. 1993; cap. €250m., res €10.7m., dep. €2,152.3m. (Dec. 2001); Chair. Dr JOSÉ DE OLIVEIRA COSTA; Gen. Man. JOSÉ CASTELO BRANCO.

Caixa Central de Crédito Agrícola Mútuo CRL: Rua Castilho 233–233A, 1099-004 Lisbon; tel. (21) 386006; fax (21) 3860166; e-mail int.cccam@creditoagricola.pt; internet www.creditoagricola .pt; f. 1984; co-operative bank; cap. €481.3m., res −€59.1m., dep. €6,611.6m. (Dec. 2001); Chair DIAMANTINO DIOGO; Chief Exec. JOSÉ MANUEL MARQUES DA SILVA LEMOS.

Caixa Económica Montepio Geral: POB 2882, Rua do Ouro 219/241, 1100-062 Lisbon; tel. (21) 3476361; fax (21) 3426766; internet www.montepiogeral.pt; f. 1844; cap. 49,118.1m., res 28,278.7m., dep. 1,819,885.7m. (Dec. 2001); Pres. Dr ANTÓNIO DE SEIXAS DA COSTA LEAL; 55 brs.

Caixa Geral de Depósitos (CGD): POB 1795, Av. João XXI 63, 1000-300 Lisbon; tel. (21) 7953000; fax (21) 7905050; e-mail cgd@cgd .pt; internet www.cgd.pt; f. 1876; wholly state-owned; grants credit for agriculture, industry, building, housing, energy, trade and tourism; cap. €2,450.0m., res €363.2m., dep. €58,845.5m. (Dec. 2001); Chair. ANTÓNIO DE SOUSA; 522 brs.

Crédibanco—Banco de Crédito Pessoal, SA: Rua Prof. Mira Fernandes Lt 17, 1900 Lisbon; tel. (21) 8427200; fax (21) 8427372; f. 1992 as Banco Central Hispano; owned by Banco Comercial Português Empresas; Pres. JORGE JARDIM GONÇALVES.

Crédito Predial Português: Rua Augusta 237, 1000-051 Lisbon; tel. (21) 3214000; fax (21) 3211694; internet www.cpp.pt; f. 1864 to further building development for industrial, commercial and residential purposes; owned by Banco Totta & Açores, SA; cap. 33,000m., res 14,164.1m., dep. 1,336,916.1m. (Dec. 1999); Chair. EURICO DE MELO; 166 brs.

Deutsche Bank (Portugal) SA: Rua Castilho 20, 1250-069 Lisbon; tel. (21) 3111200; fax (21) 3535241; f. 1990 as Deutsche Bank de Investimento; name changed 1999; cap. 8,450m., res 2,756.2m., dep. 689,907.5m. (Dec 2000); Pres. Dr HONERO JOSÉ DE PINHO COUTINHO.

Finibanco SA: Rua Júlio Dinis 157, 4050-323 Porto; tel. (22) 6084500; fax (22) 6084501; e-mail finibanco.online@finibanco.pt; internet www.finibanco.pt; f. 1993; cap. €80m., res €16.0m., dep. €1,233.8m. (Dec. 2001); Pres. ALVARO COSTA LEITE; 80 brs.

Foreign Banks

ABN-AMRO Bank NV (Netherlands): POB 10070, Av. da Liberdade 131-5°, 1269-036 Lisbon; tel. (21) 3211800; fax (21) 3211900; Country Man. Dr JAN C. PANMAN.

Banco do Brasil: Praça Marquês de Pombal 16, 1269-134 Lisbon; tel. (21) 3585000; fax (21) 3585022; Gen. Man. Dr LUIZ CARLOS DE BRITO LOURENÇO.

Bank of Tokyo-Mitsubishi Ltd (Japan): Avda da Liberdade, 180 E-6Esq., 1250–146 Lisbon; tel. (21) 3514550; Man. Dir MIKIHIKO OHIRA.

Barclays Bank PLC (UK): Av. da República 50-2°, 1050-196 Lisbon; tel. (21) 7911100; fax (21) 7911123; e-mail marketing@ barclays.pt; f. 1987; Gen. Man. Dr JOÃO FREIXA.

BNP Paribas, SA (France): Edificio BNP, Av. 5 de Outubro 206, 1050 Lisbon; tel. (21) 7910200; fax (21) 7955616; f. 1985; Dir-Gen. FRANÇOIS FALQUE PIERROTIN.

Fortis Bank NV (Belgium): Rua Alexandre Herculano 50-6°, P-1250 Lisbon; tel. (21) 3139300; fax (21) 3139350; f. 1986; Dir-Gen. YVES DE CLERCK.

Banking Association

Associação Portuguesa de Bancos (APB): Av. da República 35-5°, 1050-186 Lisbon; tel. (21) 3510070; fax (21) 3579533; Pres. Dr JOÃO SALGUEIRO; Sec.-Gen. Dr JOÃO MENDES RODRIGUES.

STOCK EXCHANGE

Bolsa de Valores de Lisboa e Porto: Edif. da Bolsa, Rua Soeiro Pereira Gomes, 1600 Lisbon; tel. (21) 7900000; fax (21) 7952021;

e-mail bvlp@bvlp.pt; internet www.bvlp.pt; f. 1769; Chair. RICARDO ESPÍRITO SANTO SALGADO; Chief Exec MANUEL ALVES MONTEIRO.

Regulatory Authority

Comissão do Mercado de Valores Mobiliários (CMVM): Av. Fontes Pereira de Melo 21, 1056-801 Lisbon; tel. (21) 3177000; fax (21) 3537077; e-mail cmvm@cmvm.pt; f. 1991; independent securities exchange commission; Pres. FERNANDO TEIXEIRA DOS SANTOS.

INSURANCE

The Portuguese insurance market is developing in accordance with EU regulations and practices. Total premiums amounted to 1,352,074m. escudos at the end of 1999, life assurance premiums having increased by 28.1% and non-life by 8.3%, compared with the previous year.

Supervisory Authority

Instituto de Seguros de Portugal (ISP): Av. de Berna 19, 1050-037 Lisbon; tel. (21) 7938542; fax (21) 7938568; e-mail isp@isp.pt; internet www.isp.pt; f. 1982; office in Porto; Pres. Dr RUI LEÃO MARTINHO.

Representative Bodies

Associação das Empresas Gestoras de Fundos de Pensões (AEGFP): Rua da Misericórdia 76, 1200-273 Lisbon; tel. (21) 3210147; fax (21) 3210264; e-mail aegfp.pensoes@mail.telepac.pt; f. 1990; pension funds; Pres. Dr RUI PEDRAS; Sec.-Gen. Dr FRANCISCO J. DE MEDEIROS CORDEIRO.

Associação Nacional dos Agentes e Corretores de Seguros (ANACS): Rua da Xabregas, Lote A, Sala 138, 1900-440 Lisbon; tel. (21) 8688013; fax (21) 8688014; e-mail anacsegur@netc.pt; Pres. MANUEL GASPAR DA CUNHA.

Associação Portuguesa de Seguradores (APS): Rua Rodrigo da Fonseca 41, 1250-190 Lisbon; tel. (21) 3848100; fax (21) 3831422; e-mail aps@apseguradores.pt; internet www.apseguradores.pt; f. 1982; Pres. ANTÓNIO PAIVA DE ANDRADA REIS.

Associação Portuguesa dos Produtores Profissionais de Seguros (APROSE): Praça da República 93-S/301, 4050-497 Porto; tel. (22) 2003000; fax (22) 3322519; e-mail aprose@aprose.pt; internet www.aprose.pt; f. 1976; Pres. ANTÓNIO VILELA; Exec. Dir PAULO CORVACEIRA GOMES.

Principal Companies

Axa-Portugal—Companhia de Seguros, SA: Rua Gonçalo Sampaio 39, 4169-001 Porto; tel. (22) 6081100; fax (22) 6081136; non-life; cap. 6,908m. (Dec. 1999); Pres. Dr CARLOS PEDRO BRANDÃO DE MELO DE SOUSA E BRITO.

Axa-Portugal—Companhia de Seguros de Vida, SA: Praça Marquês de Pombal 14-7°, 1250-162 Lisbon; tel. (21) 3506100; fax (21) 3506145; life and pension funds; cap. €10m. (Dec. 1999); Pres. Dr CARLOS PEDRO BRANDÃO DE MELO DE SOUSA E BRITO.

BPN Vida Seguros, SA: Av. França 316, Edif. Capitólio, 4050-276 Porto; tel. (22) 8330100; fax (22) 8301670; e-mail info@realseguros.pt; internet www.realseguros.pt; f. 1989; life and pension funds; cap. 1,500m. (Dec. 1997); Pres. Eng. FERNANDO FERREIRA.

Bonança Vida, Companhia de Seguros de Vida, SA: Av. José Malhoa 9, 1070-157 Lisbon; tel. (21) 7216000; fax (21) 7216112; f. 1808; life and pension funds; cap. 1,500m. (Dec. 1999); Pres. Eng. JOÃO LUÍS RAMALHO DE CARVALHO TALONE.

BPA, Seguros de Vida, SA: Rua Azevedo Coutinho 39-2°, 4100-100 Porto; tel. (22) 6072610; fax (22) 6072619; f. 1991; life; cap. 1,804m. (Dec. 1999); Chair. Dr CASTRO HENRIQUES.

BPI Vida—Companhia de Seguros de Vida, SA: Rua Braamcamp 11-5°, 1250-049 Lisbon; tel. (21) 3111020; fax (21) 3524494; life and pension funds; cap. €18.0m. (Dec. 2000); Pres. Dr FERNANDO MARIA COSTA DUARTE ULRICH.

Companhia de Seguros Açoreana, SA: Largo da Matriz 45/52, 9500-094 Ponta Delgada, S. Miguel, Azores; tel. (296) 653521; fax (296) 653516; f. 1892; life and non-life; cap. 4,000m. (Dec. 1999); Pres. Dr HORÁCIO DA SILVA ROQUE.

Companhia de Seguros Allianz Portugal, SA: Rua Andrade Corvo 19, 1069-014 Lisbon; tel. (21) 3522911; fax (21) 3522943; f. 1907; fmrly Allianz Portugal; life, non-life and pension funds; cap. 7,909m. (Dec. 1999); Pres. Dr FRANCISCO JOSÉ PEREIRA PINTO BALSEMÃO.

Companhia de Seguros Eagle Star Vida, SA: Rua Castilho 44-1°, 1250-071 Lisbon; tel. (21) 3862004; fax (21) 3862721; life; cap. 1,570m. (Dec. 1999); Pres. Dr NUNO SOARES DA FONSECA.

Companhia de Seguros Fidelidade, SA: Largo do Calhariz 30, 1249-001 Lisbon; tel. (21) 3238000; fax (21) 3237001; f. 1980; from merger of four companies; life, non-life and pension funds; cap. 30,000m. (Dec. 1999); Pres. Dr ALVARO JOÃO DUARTE PINTO CORREIA.

Companhia de Seguros Mundial—Confiança, SA: Largo do Chiado 8, 1249-125 Lisbon; tel. (21) 3401500; fax (21) 3401790; f. 1980; life, non-life and pension funds; cap. 48,600m. (Dec. 1999); Pres. Dr VITOR MANUEL LOPES FERNANDES.

Companhia de Seguros Tranquilidade, SA: Av. da Liberdade 242, 1250-149 Lisbon; tel. (21) 3503500; fax (21) 3156062; e-mail infogeral@tranquilidade.pt; internet www.tranquilidade.pt; f. 1871; non-life; cap. €135m. (Dec. 2002); 100% privatized in 1990; Pres. PETER DE BRITO E CUNHA.

Companhia de Seguros Tranquilidade Vida, SA: Av. da Liberdade 230, 1250-148 Lisbon; tel. (21) 3167500; fax (21) 3163194; e-mail correio@tranquilidade-vida.pt; life and pension funds; cap. €250m. (Dec. 2001); Pres. Dr LUÍS FREDERICO REDONDO LOPES.

Companhia Europeia de Seguros, SA (Winterthur Seguros): Av. Fontes Pereira de Melo 6, 1069-001 Lisbon; tel. (21) 3183500; fax (21) 3183800; internet www.winterthur.pt; f. 1922; life and non-life; cap. 3,948m. (Dec. 1999); Pres. Dr ANTÓNIO CARVALHO NUNES DA MOTA; Gen. Man. WOLFGANG GEMUND.

Cosec (Companhia de Seguro de Créditos, SA): Av. da República 58, 1069-057 Lisbon; tel. (21) 7913700; fax (21) 7913720; e-mail cosec@cosec.pt; internet www.cosec.pt; f. 1969; domestic and export credit insurance; bond insurance; cap. €7,500m.; Chair. Eng. JOSÉ MIGUEL GOMES DA COSTA.

Espírito Santo—Companhia de Seguros, SA: Ave. da Liberdade 230, 1250-149 Lisbon; tel. (21) 3167100; fax (21) 3167101; non-life; cap. 3,000m. (Dec. 1999); Pres. Dr PEDRO GUILHERME BEAUVILLAIN DE BRITO E CUNHA.

Europ Assistance—Companhia de Seguros de Assistência, SA: Av. Alvares Cabral 41-3°, 1250-015 Lisbon; tel. (21) 3860003; fax (21) 3860308; non-life; cap. 500,000m. (Dec. 1999); Pres. Dr PEDRO GUILHERME BEAUVILLIAN DE BRITO E CUNHA.

Global—Companhia de Seguros, SA: Av. Duque de Avila 171, 1069-031 Lisbon; tel. (21) 3137500; fax (21) 3559060; non-life; cap. 3,250m. (Dec. 1999); Pres. Dr DIAMANTINO PEREIRA MARQUES.

Imperio Arag—Seguros de Protecção Jurídica, SA: Av. Alvares Cabral 27-3°, 1269-151 Lisbon; tel. (21) 3827100; fax (21) 3827122; non-life; cap. 500,000m. (Dec. 1999); Pres. Dr DOMINGOS MARTINS RODRIGUES.

Império Bonança—Companhia de Seguros, SA: Av. José Malhoa 9, 1070-157 Lisbon; tel. (21) 7216000; fax (21) 7216112; by merger of Companhia de seguros Bonança, SA and Companhia de Seguros Império, SA; Chair. Dr CARLOS SANTOS FERREIRA.

Lusitânia—Companhia de Seguros, SA: Rua São Domingos à Lapa 35–41, 1200-833 Lisbon; tel. (21) 3926970; fax (21) 3973099; non-life; cap. 3,850m. (Dec. 1999); Pres. Dr ANTÓNIO DE SEIXAS DA COSTA LEAL.

Mapfre Seguros Gerais, SA: Rua Castilho 52-1°, 1250-071 Lisbon; tel. (21) 3819700; fax (21) 3819799; e-mail reibarata@mapfre.pt; internet www.mapfre.pt; non-life; cap. 7,274m. (Dec. 2000); Pres. Dr RAFAEL GALARRAGA SOLORES.

Ocidental—Companhia Portuguesa de Seguros, SA/Ocidental—Companhia Portuguesa de Seguros de Vida, SA/Seguros y Pensões: Av. da República 26, 1069-058 Lisbon; tel. (21) 3121300; fax (21) 3121313; non-life; cap. 2,500m., life cap. 2,550m. (Dec. 1999); Pres. Eng. JOÃO LUÍS RAMALHO DE CARVALHO TALONE.

Real Seguros, SA: Av. de França 316, Edif. Capitólio, 4050-276 Porto; tel. (22) 8330100; fax (22) 8301670; e-mail info@realseguros.pt; internet www.realseguros.pt; f. 1988; cap. 3,000m. (Dec. 1999); non-life; Pres. Dr JOSÉ DE OLIVEIRA COSTA.

Rural Seguros—Companhia de Seguros de Ramos Reais, SA: Rua Castilho 223-233, 1070-051 Lisbon; tel. (21) 3815632; fax (21) 3815643; non-life; cap. 3,000m. (Dec. 1999); Pres. Dr JERÓNIMO CAMPOS DE ESPÍRITO SANTO.

O Trabalho—Companhia de Seguros, SA: Rua Engenheiro Vieira da Silva 12, 1069-009 Lisbon; tel. (21) 3537174; fax (21) 3545377; e-mail webmaster@o-trabalho.pt; internet www.o-trabalho.pt; f. 1921; non-life; cap. 2,500m. (Dec. 1999); Pres. Dr FERNANDO LUÍS RODRIGUES BAPTISTA.

Via Directa—Companhia de Seguros, SA: Av. Visconde de Valmor 66-2°, 1050-542 Lisbon; tel. (21) 7991920; fax (21) 7991922; non-life; cap. 4,200m. (Dec. 1999); Pres. Dr JOSÉ LUÍS CARVALHO CARDOSO.

Victoria—Seguros de Vida, SA/Victoria—Seguros, SA: Edif. Victoria, Av. da Liberdade 200, 1250-147 Lisbon; tel. (21) 3134110; fax (21) 3134710; f. 1930/1981; transferred to private sector in 1993; life and pensions; cap. 1,500m. non-life; cap. 5,000m. (1998); Chair. GERHARD JOACHIM DASSOW.

Zurich—Companhia de Seguros, SA: Rua Barata Salgueiro 41, Edif. Zurich, 1269-058 Lisbon; tel. (21) 3133100; fax (21) 3561024; f. 1918; fmrly Companhia de Seguros Metrópole; non-life; cap. 2,000m. (Dec. 1999); Pres. Dr NUNO MARIA SERRA SOARES DA FONSECA; Chief Exec JOSÉ M. COELHO.

Mutual Companies

Mútua dos Armadores da Pesca do Arrasto: Av. António Augusto de Aguiar 7-1°, 1069-145 Lisbon; tel. (21) 3561051; fax (21) 3561058; f. 1942; marine and workers' compensation, personal accident, sickness, fire, etc. cap. 750m. (Dec. 1996); Pres. Dr ANTÓNIO ALBERTO CARVALHO DA CUNHA.

Mútua dos Pescadores (Sociedade Mútua de Seguros): Av. Brasília ES2, Pedruços, 1449-030 Lisbon; tel. (21) 3017375; fax (21) 3016489; e-mail mutuap@telepac.mail.pt; f. 1936; privately owned; personal accident, marine, fire, workers' compensation, etc.; cap. 1,500m. (Dec. 1997).

Foreign Companies

In 1999 43 foreign companies were in operation in Portugal. These branches took 6.1% of all Portuguese premiums in that year.

Trade and Industry

DEVELOPMENT ORGANIZATIONS

Centro para o Desenvolvimento e Inovação Tecnológicos (CEDINTEC): Rua de São Domingos à Lapa 117-2° Dto, 1200 Lisbon; tel. (21) 3955302; fax (21) 3961203; f. 1982; supports the creation of technological infrastructures; Pres. Eng. JOÃO PEDRO DE SALDANHA VERSCHNEIDER GONÇALVES.

Gabinete de Estudos e Prospectiva Económica (GEPE): Rua José Estevão 83A-4° Dto., 1169-153 Lisbon; tel. (21) 3110770; fax (21) 3110773; e-mail gep@mail.telepac.pt; internet www.gepe.pt; economic studies and analyses (Ministry of the Economy); Dir JOÃO ABEL DE FREITAS.

ICEP Portugal—Investimentos, Comércio e Turismo: Av. 5 de Outubro 101, 1050-051 Lisbon; tel. (21) 7909500; fax (21) 7935028; e-mail icep@mail2.icep.pt; internet www.icep.pt; f. 1982; promotes Portuguese exports of goods and services, foreign direct investment in Portugal, Portuguese investment abroad and tourism; Pres. Dr LUÍS NETO.

Instituto de Apoio às Pequenas e Médias Empresas e ao Investimento (IAPMEI): Rua Rodrigo da Fonseca 73, 1099-063 Lisbon; tel. (21) 3836000; fax (21) 3836283; internet www.iapmei.pt; financial and technical support to small and medium-sized enterprises; Pres. Prof. HENRIQUE MACHADO JORGE.

Instituto para a Cooperação Económica (ICE): Av. da Liberdade 192-2°, 1200 Lisbon; tel. (21) 549311; fax (21) 527897; an official body for economic co-operation; Pres. FERNANDO D'OLIVEIRA NEVES.

Instituto de Financiamento e Apoio ao Desenvolvimento da Agricultura e Pescas (IFADAP): Rua Castilho 45–51, 1250-068 Lisbon; tel. (21) 3116200; fax (21) 3525925; e-mail ifadap@ifadap.min-agricultura.pt; internet www.ifadap.min-agricultura.pt; f. 1977; provides loans for agriculture and fisheries, acts as intermediary with the European Agricultural Guidance and Guarantee Fund (EAGGF) and the Financing Instrument for Fisheries Guidance (FIFG); Chair. CARLOS FIGUEIREDO.

Instituto Nacional de Engenharia e Tecnologia Industrial (INETI): Estrada do Paço do Lumiar, 1649-038 Lisbon; tel. (21) 7165181; fax (21) 7160901; internet www.ineti.pt; f. 1977; industrial and technological research; Pres. Dr CARLOS MORAIS.

Instituto Português da Qualidade (IPQ): Rua António Gião 2, 2829-513 Caparica; tel. (21) 2948100; fax (21) 2948101; manages and develops the Portuguese Quality System (SPQ); Pres. ANTÓNIO RAMOS PIRES.

Instituto do Vinho do Porto: Rua Ferreira Borges, 4050 Porto; tel. (22) 2071600; fax (22) 2080465; e-mail ivp@ivp.pt; internet www.ivp.pt; an official body dealing with quality control and the promotion of port wine; also gives technical advice to exporters; Pres. Eng. JORGE MONTEIRO.

Sociedade de Desenvolvimento da Madeira (SDM): Rua da Mouraria 9-1°, 9000-047 Funchal, Madeira; tel. (291) 201333; fax (291) 201399; e-mail sdm@sdm.pt; internet www.sdm.pt; concessionaire of Madeira's International Business Centre; Chair. Dr FRANCISCO COSTA.

Sociedade Nacional de Empreendimentos e Desenvolvimento Económico: Av. Fontes Pereira de Melo 35–19A, 1050-118 Lisbon; tel. (21) 3549043; fax (21) 3143099; e-mail snede@mail.telepac.pt; internet www.snede.pt; private consultancy co in economy and management; Pres. Dr ALFREDO GONZALEZ ESTEVES BELO.

CHAMBERS OF COMMERCE AND TRADE ASSOCIATIONS

Associação Comercial e Industrial do Funchal (ACIF)/Câmara de Comércio e Indústria da Madeira (CCIM): Av. Arriaga 41, 9000 Funchal; tel. (291) 230137; fax (291) 222005; f. 1836; Pres. ANTHONY MILES.

Associação Comercial de Lisboa/Câmara de Comérico e Indústria Portuguesa: Palácio do Comércio, Rua das Portas de Santo Antão 89, 1194 Lisbon; tel. (21) 3427179; fax (21) 3424304; f. 1834; Pres. Eng. VASCO PINTO BASTO; Gen. Sec. ANTÓNIO MONICA; 2,100 mems.

Associação Comercial do Porto/Câmara de Comércio e Indústria do Porto: Palácio da Bolsa, Rua Ferreira Borges, 4050-253 Porto; tel. (22) 3399000; fax (22) 3399090; e-mail cciporto@mail.telepac.pt; internet www.cciporto.com; f. 1834; Pres. Dr RUI MOREIRA; 800 mems.

Câmara de Comércio e Indústria dos Açores (CCIA): Rua Ernesto do Canto 13/15, 9504-531 Ponta Delgada, Azores; tel. (296) 305000; fax (296) 305050; e-mail ccipd@ccipd.pt; internet www.ccipd.pt; f. 1979; Dir CARLOS ALBERTO DA COSTA MARTINS.

OTHER INDUSTRIAL AND TRADE ASSOCIATIONS

Associação dos Comerciantes e Industriais de Bebidas Espirituosas e Vinhos (ACIBEV): Largo do Carmo 15-1°, 1200 Lisbon; tel. (21) 3462318; fax (21) 3427517; spirit and wine traders and manufacturers; Pres. LUÍS GONZAGA MORAIS CARDOSO.

Associação Empresarial de Portugal: 4450-617 Leça da Palmeira; tel. (22) 9981500; fax (22) 9964213; e-mail aep@aeportugal.com; internet www.aeportugal.pt; f. 1849; represents industry in northern Portugal in all sectors; organizes trade fairs, exhibitions, congress, etc. Pres. Eng. ANGELO LUDGERO MARQUES; 2,500 mems.

Associação dos Industriais e Exportadores de Cortiça: Av. Duque d'Avila 169-2° Esq., 1000 Lisbon; tel. (21) 3521173; fax (21) 570878; national asscn of cork manufacturers and exporters; Pres. EDMUNDO PEREIRA.

Associação Industrial Portuguesa (AIP): Praça das Indústrias, Apdo 3200, 1304 Lisbon; tel. (21) 3601000; fax (21) 3635808; f. 1837; Pres. Dr JORGE ROCHA DE MATOS; 3,500 mems.

Associação Nacional de Comerciantes e Industriais de Produtos Alimentares (ANCIPA): Largo de S. Sebastião da Pedreira 31, 1050-205 Lisbon; tel. (21) 3528803; fax (21) 3154665; e-mail ancipa@netcabo.pt; internet www.ancipa.pt; f. 1975; national asscn of food products manufacturers and traders; Pres. MANUEL FULGÉNCIO TARRE FERNANDES; Gen. Sec. DOMITÍLIA LOPES DE ALMEIDA.

Associação Nacional das Indústrias de Vestuário e Confecção (ANIVEC): Av. da Boavista 3.523-7°, 4100 Porto; tel. (22) 6100050; fax (22) 6100049; e-mail anivec@mail.telepac.pt; clothing manufacturers' asscn; Pres. Dr AURÉLIO SILVA; Vice-Pres. JORGE DE LEMOS DA COSTA.

Associação Portuguesa de Cerâmica: Rua Artilharia Um 104-2° Andar, CP 1070, 1000 Lisbon; tel. (21) 3875262; fax (21) 3852986; ceramics asscn; Pres. JOSÉ FILIPE NOBRE GUEDES; Gen. Sec. (vacant).

Associação Portuguesa de Cortiça (APCOR) (Portuguese Cork Association): Av. Comendador Henrique Amorim 580, 4536-904 Sta Maria de Lamas; tel. (22) 7474040; fax (22) 7474049; e-mail info@apcor.pt; internet www.corkmasters.com; www.apcor.pt; asscn of cork manufacturers and exporters; Pres. ANTÓNIO RIOS DE AMORIM.

Associação Portuguesa dos Exportadores de Têxteis: Porto; tel. (22) 6002106; fax (22) 6065870; textile exporters' asscn; Pres. MADATH ALY JAMAL.

Associação Portuguesa das Indústrias de Malha a de Confecção (APIM): Rua Guillhermina Suggia, 224, 1°, sala 8, 4200–318 Porto; tel. (22) 5074250; fax (22) 5029210; e-mail apim@apim.pt; internet www.apim.pt; knitwear and ready-to-wear clothing industries; Pres. Dr CARLOS BRAVO.

Associação Portuguesa dos Industriais de Calçado, Componentes, e Artigos de Pele e seus Sucedâneos (APICCAPS): Rua Alves Redol 372, Apdo 4643, 4011-001 Porto; tel. (22) 5074150; fax (22) 5074179; e-mail apiccaps@mail.telepac.pt; internet www.apiccaps.pt; footwear and leather goods manufacturers' asscn; Pres. FORTUNATO FREDERICO.

Associação Portuguesa de Têxteis e Vestuário: Rua Gonçalo Cristovão 96-1°, 4000 Porto; tel. (22) 2057961; fax (22) 2050343; e-mail aptv@mail.telepac.pt; textile and clothing manufacturers' asscn; Pres. HENRY TILLO.

Confederação dos Agricultores de Portugal (CAP): Av. do Colégio Militar, Lote 1786, 1500 Lisbon; tel. (21) 7100000; fax (21)

7166122; e-mail cap@cap.pt; internet www.cap.pt; farmers' confederation; Pres. João Pedro Gorjão Cyryllo Machado.

Confederação do Comércio Português (CCP): Lisbon; tel. (21) 3477430; fax (21) 3478638; f. 1977; Pres. Vasco Sousa da Gama; Gen. Sec. José António Cortez; mems 143 trade asscns.

Confederação da Indústria Portuguesa (CIP): Av. 5 de Outubro 35-1°, 1000 Lisbon; tel. (21) 547454; fax (21) 545094; f. 1974; represents employers; Pres. Dr Pedro Ferraz da Costa; over 35,000 mems.

Gabinete Portex: Porto; tel. (22) 6068758; fax (22) 600058; textile manufacturers; Pres. Alexandre Pinheiro; Gen. Sec. Dr José Luís Soares Barbosa.

UTILITIES

Electricity

Rede Electrica Nacional—REN, SA: Av. Estados Unidos da América 55-12°, 1749-061 Lisbon; tel. (21) 0013500; fax (21) 0013950; concessionaire of the Portuguese Transmission Grid and Transmission System Operator in mainland Portugal; since Jan. 2002, it is also a Public Telecommunications Network Operator through its subsidiary company RENTELECOM—Comunicações SA.

Electricidade de Portugal—EDP, SA: Av. José Malhoa, Lote A/13, 1070 Lisbon; tel. (21) 7263013; fax (21) 7265029; internet www.edp.pt; production, purchase, transport, distribution and sale of electrical energy; Pres. Francisco de la Fuente Sánchez.

EDP Produção—Gestão de Produção de Energia, SA: Av. Barbosa du Bocage 45, Apt. 14125, 1064-002 Lisbon; tel. (21) 3525353; fax (21) 7992420; internet www.edp.pt; production and sale of electrical energy; Pres. Eng. António Pita de Abreu; Vice Pres. Eng. Jorge Ribeirinho Machado.

Regional Distribution Companies

Electricidade do Centro—CENEL, SA: Rua do Brasil 1, 3030 Coímbra; tel. (239) 400800; fax (239) 29028; internet www.edp.pt/edp.empresas/cenel.

Hidrocenel—Energia do Centro, SA: Quintela, 6270 Seia; tel. (238) 320000; fax (238) 320027; e-mail isidora.dinis@cenel.edp.pt; internet www.edp.pt/edp/empresa/hidrocenel; Pres. António Eduardo da Silva Oliva.

Electricidade de Lisboa e Vale do Tejo—LTE, SA: Rua Camilo Castelo Branco 43, 1050 Lisbon; tel. (21) 3538833; fax (21) 3534094; internet www.edp.pt/edp/empresas/lte.

EDP Energia, SA: Praça Marquês de Pombal 13, 1250-162 Lisbon; tel. (21) 0021400; fax (21) 0021610; internet www.edp.pt; Pres. Eng. Francisco de la Fuente Sánchez.

Electricidade do Norte—EN, SA: Rua Duque de Loulé 148, 4000 Porto; tel. (22) 321514; fax (22) 2078375; internet www.edp.pt/edp/empresas/en.

Energia do Norte—HDN, SA: Rua do Caires 292-2°, 4700 Braga; tel. (253) 6003050; fax (253) 618836; internet www.edp.pt/edp/empresas/hdn; Pres. Eng. António Eduardo da Silva Oliva.

Electricidade do Sul—SLE, SA: Rua D. Francisco Manuel de Melo 23A, 1070 Lisbon; tel. (21) 3500000; fax (21) 3888037; internet www.edp.pt/edp/empresas/sle.

Regulatory Authority

Entidade Reguladora dos Serviços Energéticos (ERSE): Rua Dom Cristovão da Gama 1, 1400-113 Lisbon; tel. (21) 3033200; fax (21) 3033201; e-mail erse@erse.pt; internet www.erse.pt; regulator of electricity and natural gas in Portugal; Chair. Jorge Vasconcelos.

Gas

Sociedade Portuguesa de Gás Natural—Transgás, SA: Av. da República 35-7°, 1050 Lisbon; tel. (21) 8478280; fax (21) 8474486; natural gas utility; also operates public telecommunications network.

Galp Energia, SGPS, SA: Edif. Galp Energia, Rua Tomás de Fonseca, 1600-209 Lisbon; tel. (21) 7242500; fax (21) 7242965; e-mail dci@galpenergia.com; internet www.galpenergia.com; Pres. António Mexia.

LABOUR ORGANIZATIONS

Confederação Geral dos Trabalhadores Portugueses-Intersindical Nacional (CGTP-IN): Rua Victor Cordon 1-2°, 1249-102 Lisbon; tel. (21) 3236500; fax (21) 3236695; e-mail cgtp@mail.telepac.pt; f. 1970; reorganized 1974; 107 affiliated unions; 704,048 mems; Gen. Sec. Manuel Carvalho da Silva.

União Geral dos Trabalhadores de Portugal (UGTP): Rua de Buenos Aires 11, 1200 Lisbon; tel. (21) 3976503; fax (21) 3974612;

e-mail ugt@mail.telepac.pt; internet www.ugt.pt; f. 1978; pro-socialist; 942,325 mems; Pres. Manuel Araujo dos Santos; Sec.-Gen. João Proença.

Transport

RAILWAYS

In 1999 the total length of the railtrack totalled 3,038 km, of which 863 km was electrified.

Rede Ferroviária Nacional—REFER, E.P.: Estação de Santa Apolónia, Largo dos Caminhos de Ferro, 1100-105 Lisbon; tel. (21) 8816000; fax (21) 8815439; internet www.refer.pt; f. 1997; assumed responsibility for rail infrastructure in 1999; Pres. Francisco José Cardoso dos Reis.

Caminhos de Ferro Portugueses, EP (CP): Calçada do Duque 20, 1294-109 Lisbon; tel. (21) 3215700; fax (21) 3215879; e-mail webmaster@mail.cp.pt; internet www.cp.pt; f. 1856; nationalized in 1975; incorporated Sociedade Estoril Caminhos de Ferro from Cais do Sodré to Cascais in 1977; Pres. António Crisóstomo Teixeira.

Metropolitano de Lisboa, EP (ML): Av. Fontes Pereira de Melo 28, 1069-095 Lisbon; tel. (21) 3558457; fax (21) 3574908; e-mail metro.relpub@mail.telepac.pt; internet www.metrolisboa.pt; opened 1959; operates the 30-km underground system; Pres. Dr Manuel Frasquilho.

ROADS

The country is divided into 18 road districts and 4 regions: North, Centre, Lisbon and South. At the end of 1999 there were an estimated 68,732 km of roads in continental Portugal, of which 797 km were motorway. In September 1999 the final section of a motorway linking Lisbon with Madrid (Spain) was inaugurated.

Brisa—Auto-Estradas de Portugal, SA: Edif. Brisa, Quinta da Torre da Aguilha, 2785-599 São Domingos de Rana; tel. (21) 4448500; fax (21) 4448773; e-mail contacto@brisa.pt; internet www.brisa.pt; f. 1972; responsible for construction, maintenance and operation of motorways; Pres. Eng. Manuel van Hoof Ribeiro.

Instituto para a Conservação e Exploração da Rede Rodoviária (ICERR): Avenida Cónego Urbano Duarte, 3000 Coimbra; tel. (239) 794500; fax (239) 853270; internet www.i.iestradas.pt; f. 1999; public authority; maintenance of roads and bridges; Pres. Eng. Pedro Eduardo da Cunha Serra.

Instituto para a Construção Rodoviária (ICOR): Praça da Portagem, 2800-225 Almada; tel. (21) 2947215; fax (21) 2947228; e-mail info@icor-construcao.pt; internet www.iestradas.pt; f. 1999; construction of roads, bridges and tunnels and the reconstruction of the existing network; Pres. Eng. Pedro Cunha Serra.

Instituto das Estradas de Portugal (IEP): Praça da Portagem, 2804-534 Almada; tel. (21) 2947100; fax (21) 2951997; internet www.iestradas.pt; f. 1999; road infrastructure policy; Pres. Eng. José Ribeiro dos Santos.

SHIPPING

The principal Portuguese ports are Lisbon, Leixões (Porto), Setúbal and Funchal (Madeira), and the Viana do Castelo port is being developed. The ports of Portimão (Algarve) and the Azores regularly receive international cruise liners.

Principal Shipping Companies

Portline—Transportes Marítimos Internacionais, SA: Av. Infante D. Henrique 332-3°, 1800-224 Lisbon; tel. (21) 8391800; fax (21) 8376680; e-mail pinto-magalhaes@portline.pt; f. 1984; marine transport; Gen. Man. Manuel Pinto de Magalhães.

Sacor Maritima, SA: Lisbon; tel. (21) 3921200; fax (21) 3922907; tanker transport; Chair. Luís Martins Carneiro.

Soponata (Sociedade Portuguesa de Navios Tanques, SA): Largo Rafael Bordalo Pinheiro 20-5°, 1249-050 Lisbon; tel. (21) 3224440; fax (21) 3476772; e-mail soponata@soponata-sa.pt; internet www.soponata.pt; f. 1947; oil tankers; CEO Eng. Pedro de Mello.

CIVIL AVIATION

There are international airports at Lisbon, Porto, Faro (Algarve), Funchal (Madeira), Santa Maria (Azores) and São Miguel (Azores).

TAP (Air Portugal, SA): Aeroporto de Lisboa, Apdo 50194, 1704-801 Lisbon; tel. (21) 8415000; fax (21) 8415881; e-mail gcrp.com@tap-airportugal.pt; internet www.tap-airportugal.pt; f. 1945; national airline serving destinations in Europe, Africa, North, Central and South America; scheduled, international, domestic, passenger and cargo services; Pres. NORBERTO PILAR; CEO FERNANDO PINTO.

PGA (Portugália Airlines (Companhia Portuguesa de Transportes Aéreos) SA: Aeroporto de Lisboa, Rua C, Edif. 70, 1749-078 Lisbon; tel. (21) 8425500; fax (21) 8425623; e-mail pga@mail.telepac .pt; internet www.pga.pt; f. 1988; regional airline operating scheduled and charter, international and domestic flights from Lisbon; Chair. JOÃO RIBEIRO DA FONSECA.

SATA (Air Açores—Serviço Açoreano de Transportes Aéreos —EP): Av. Infante D. Henrique 55, 9505-528 Ponta Delgada, São Miguel, 9500 Azores; tel. (296) 209727; fax (296) 209722; e-mail pdlsd@sata.pt; internet www.sata.pt; f. 1941; owned by the regional government of the Azores; inter-island services in the Azores archipelago; Pres. and Chief Exec. ANTÓNIO CANSADO.

TRANSPORT ASSOCIATION

Federação Portuguesa dos Transportes: Rua Viriato 5-1°, 1000 Lisbon; tel. (21) 577562; fax (21) 574104; Pres. Eng. JOSÉ CARLOS GONÇALVES VIANA.

Tourism

Portugal is popular with visitors because of its mild and clement weather. Apart from Lisbon and the Algarve on the mainland, Madeira and the Azores are much favoured as winter resorts. Earnings from tourism were an estimated US $5,206m. in 2000; in 2001 the number of tourist arrivals totalled 12.2m., compared with 7.0m. in 1980. In 2000 there were 222,958 hotel beds.

Secretaria de Estado do Turismo: Av. da República 79-7°, 1050 Lisbon; tel. (21) 7936199; fax (21) 7954127; Sec. of State Dr VÍTOR JOSÉ CABRITA NETO.

Direcção-Geral do Turismo: Av. António Augusto de Aguiar 86, Apdo 1929, 1069-021 Lisbon; tel. (21) 3586400; fax (21) 3586666; e-mail dgturismo@dgturismo.pt; internet www.dgturismo.pt; Dir-Gen. Dr JOSÉ SANCHO SILVA.

ICEP Portugal—Comércio, Investimento e Turismo: Tourism Promotion Dept: Av. Duque d'Avila 185-4°, 1050-082 Lisbon; tel. (21) 7909500; fax (21) 3556896; e-mail turismo@icep.pt; internet www .portugalinsite.pt; Exec. Vice-Pres. responsible for Tourism Dr CARLOS COSTA.

Fundo de Turismo: Rua Ivone Silva, Lote 6, 1050 Lisbon; tel. (21) 7937490; fax (21) 524221; Pres. Eng. RUI MIL HOMENS.

Instituto Nacional de Formação Turística: Escola de Hotelaria e Turismo de Lisboa, Rua Américo Durão, 12A, 1900–060 Lisbon; tel. (21) 8426900; fax (21) 84993130; e-mail ehtlisboa@inftur .min-economia.pt; internet www.inftur.pt; Dir Dra CLARA FREITAS.

QATAR

Introductory Survey

Location, Climate, Language, Religion, Flag, Capital

The State of Qatar occupies a peninsula, projecting northwards from the Arabian mainland, on the west coast of the Persian (Arabian) Gulf. It is bordered, to the south, by Saudi Arabia and the United Arab Emirates. The archipelago of Bahrain lies to the north-west. On the opposite side of the Gulf lies Iran. The climate is exceptionally hot in the summer, when temperatures may reach 49°C (120°F), with high humidity on the coast; conditions are relatively mild in the winter. Rainfall is negligible. The official language is Arabic. Almost all of the inhabitants are adherents of Islam. Native Qataris, who comprise less than one-third of the total population, belong mainly to the strictly orthodox Wahhabi sect of Sunni Muslims. The national flag (proportions 11 by 28) is maroon, with a broad vertical white stripe at the hoist, the two colours being separated by a serrated line. The capital is Doha.

Recent History

Qatar was formerly dominated by the Khalifa family of Bahrain. The peninsula became part of Turkey's Ottoman Empire in 1872, but Turkish forces evacuated Qatar at the beginning of the First World War (1914–18). The United Kingdom recognized Sheikh Abdullah ath-Thani as Ruler of Qatar, and in 1916 made a treaty with him, providing British protection against aggression in return for supervision of Qatar's external affairs. A 1934 treaty extended fuller British protection to Qatar.

In October 1960 Sheikh Ali ath-Thani, Ruler of Qatar since 1949, abdicated in favour of his son, Sheikh Ahmad. In 1968 the British Government announced its intention to withdraw British forces from the Persian (Arabian) Gulf area by 1971. Qatar thus attempted to associate itself with Bahrain and Trucial Oman (now the United Arab Emirates—UAE) in a proposed federation. In April 1970 Sheikh Ahmad announced a provisional Constitution, providing for a partially-elected Consultative Assembly, although he retained effective power. In May the Deputy Ruler, Sheikh Khalifa ath-Thani (a cousin of Sheikh Ahmad), was appointed Prime Minister. After the failure of attempts to agree terms for union with neighbouring Gulf countries, Qatar became fully independent on 1 September 1971, whereupon the Ruler took the title of Amir. The 1916 treaty was replaced by a new treaty of friendship with the United Kingdom.

In February 1972 the Amir was deposed in a bloodless coup. Claiming support from the royal family and the armed forces, Sheikh Khalifa proclaimed himself Amir. Sheikh Khalifa, who retained the premiership, adopted a policy of wide-ranging social and economic reform, and the previous extravagance and privileges of the royal family were curbed. In accordance with the 1970 Constitution, the Amir appointed an Advisory Council in April 1972 to complement the ministerial Government. The Council was expanded from 20 to 30 members in 1975 and to 35 members in 1988. Its term was extended for four years in 1978, and for further terms of four years in 1982, 1986, 1990, 1994 and 1998.

On 27 June 1995 the Deputy Amir, Heir Apparent, Minister of Defence and Commander-in-Chief of the Armed Forces, Maj.-Gen. Sheikh Hamad bin Khalifa ath-Thani, deposed his father in a bloodless coup. Sheikh Hamad proclaimed himself Amir, claiming the support of the royal family and the Qatari people. Sheikh Khalifa, who was in Switzerland at the time of the coup, immediately denounced his son's actions, and vowed to return to Qatar. Although Sheikh Khalifa had effectively granted Sheikh Hamad control of the emirate's affairs (with the exception of the treasury) in 1992, a power struggle was reported to have emerged between the two in the months prior to the coup: Sheikh Khalifa was particularly opposed to his son's independent foreign policy (notably the strengthening of relations with both Iran and Iraq, and with Israel), and had attempted to regain influence in policy-making. Sheikh Hamad, however, reputedly enjoyed widespread support both nationally and internationally, and his domestic reforms were perceived as having contributed to Qatar's stability at a time when social unrest and Islamic extremism were emerging in the region. The

United Kingdom, the USA and Saudi Arabia swiftly recognized the new Amir. In July 1995 Sheikh Hamad reorganized the Council of Ministers and appointed himself Prime Minister, while retaining the posts of Minister of Defence and Commander-in-Chief of the Armed Forces.

Meanwhile, the deposed Amir took residence in the UAE, and visited several other countries of the region in an apparent attempt to assert his legitimacy as ruler of Qatar. In January 1996 it was confirmed that Sheikh Khalifa had gained control of a substantial part of Qatar's financial reserves. In the following month security forces in Qatar were reported to have foiled an attempted coup. As many as 100 people were arrested, and a warrant was issued for the arrest of Sheikh Hamad bin Jasim bin Hamad ath-Thani, a former government minister and a cousin of the Amir. Sheikh Khalifa denied any involvement, although he was quick to imply that the alleged plot indicated popular support for his return. In July legal proceedings were initiated in Qatar, Europe and the USA in an attempt to recover some US $3,000m.–$8,000m. in overseas assets that were asserted by the new Amir to have been amassed by his father from state oil and investment revenues. In October, however, it was reported that Sheikh Hamad and Sheikh Khalifa had been reconciled and had reached an out-of-court settlement regarding the return of state funds. By early 1997 all lawsuits issued against the former Amir had been withdrawn. In November 1997, meanwhile, the trial began of 110 people (40 of whom were charged *in absentia*) accused of involvement in the attempted coup of February 1996. Hearings were immediately adjourned. A number of those being tried *in absentia* were apprehended during 1998, including Qatar's former deputy head of intelligence, who was extradited from Yemen.

In October 1996 Sheikh Hamad named the third of his four sons, Sheikh Jasim bin Hamad bin Khalifa ath-Thani, as Heir Apparent. The Amir subsequently appointed his younger brother, Sheikh Abdullah bin Khalifa ath-Thani (the Minister of the Interior), as Prime Minister. Further to the ending of media censorship earlier in the year, the post of Minister of Information and Culture was abolished. (The relevant ministry was dissolved in March 1998.) In November 1996 Sheikh Hamad announced the creation of a new Defence Council, over which he would preside. The Council, to be comprised of senior ministers and armed forces and security personnel, was expected to function in an advisory and consultative capacity. In the same month it was reported that the Amir had appointed the Gulf region's first female member of government (as Under-secretary of State for Education and Culture).

Elections to Qatar's new central Municipal Council, held by universal suffrage on 8 March 1999, were the first in the country's history. Announced by Sheikh Hamad in November 1997 and provided for by law in July 1998, the Municipal Council was to have a consultative role in the operations of the Ministry of Municipal Affairs and Agriculture. Six of the 227 candidates were women, although none was elected. The rate of participation by voters reportedly exceeded 90% in Doha, and was estimated at 60%–70% of the registered electorate in rural areas. However, the number of registered voters was low: only some 22,000 of an eligible 40,000 actually participated in the elections.

In July 1999 a 32-member constitutional committee was established to draft a permanent constitution; this was to include provision for the direct election of a new National Assembly. The committee produced a draft constitution in July 2002, which provided for a separation of the executive, the judiciary and the legislature, but which would retain executive power in the hands of the Amir and the Council of Ministers. The draft constitution also guaranteed freedom of expression, religion and association, and provided for the establishment of an independent judiciary and of a new 45-member Consultative Council, comprising 30 elected and 15 appointed members. Under the proposed constitution the Amir would be obliged to provide reasons for rejecting draft laws adopted by the Council. The Amir would be required to approve such legislation sent to him a second time by the Council with two-thirds' majority support, although he would have a discretionary right to halt implementation of laws in question on a temporary basis if he deemed this to be in the greater interests of the country. The parliament was to have a four-year mandate, and suffrage was to be extended to all citizens, including women, aged 18 years and above. On 29 April 2003 a referendum open to all citizens of 18 years of age or above was held to determine whether or not the Amir should approve the new document. An overwhelming majority (96.6%) of the 71,406 voters approved the new Constitution, and it was expected that the affirmative vote would lead to the holding of legislative elections before the end of 2005.

Sheikh Hamad bin Jasim bin Hamad ath-Thani was arrested in July 1999 for his alleged role in the coup plot of 1996. The trial of those accused of involvement in the coup ended in February 2000, with the former minister and 32 co-defendants sentenced to life imprisonment; 85 others were acquitted. Appeal proceedings were subsequently lodged by all 33 who had been convicted. Meanwhile, in June a new suspect was reportedly arrested in connection with the coup attempt. In May 2001 the Court of Appeal overruled the previous sentences of life imprisonment, sentencing to death 19 of the defendants (including Sheikh Hamad bin Jasim bin Hamad); the court was also reported to have sentenced 26 defendants to terms of life imprisonment, and acquitted two others.

In early January 2001 the Minister of State for the Interior, Sheikh Abdullah bin Khalid ath-Thani, was promoted to the office of Minister of the Interior, a post previously held by the Prime Minister. The Ministry of Finance, Economy and Trade was reorganized in accordance with an Amiri decree issued in late January 2002: the former minister, Yousuf bin Hussein Kamal, was redesignated Minister of Finance, while Sheikh Hamad bin Faisal bin Thani ath-Thani, previously Assistant Under-secretary at the ministry, was appointed to the new post of Minister of Economy and Trade.

In early January 2002 it was reported that a group styling itself the General Congress of the Qatari Opposition had emerged to demand that the Amir stand down in favour of his son, Crown Prince Jasim. The group, which claimed to include former members of the armed forces, tribal chiefs, businessmen, students and officials who had served under the previous regime, accused the Amir of pursuing 'reckless' policies, of corruption and of alienating Qatar's Gulf neighbours. This last charge was interpreted as possibly referring not only to Qatar's pursuit of an increasingly independent foreign policy but also to the activities of Al-Jazeera, a satellite television station linked to the ath-Thani with a wide audience throughout the region. Al-Jazeera's reporting style and scope of coverage had on occasions caused several governments to threaten to restrict its freedom to operate in their country: notably, in May 2002 authorities in Bahrain announced that the station was to be banned from reporting there, apparently in response to its recent unauthorized coverage of anti-US demonstrations in Bahrain, and in June the Jordanian Government ordered the closure of Al-Jazeera's Amman office after the station broadcast programmes considered unfavourable to Jordan.

In early July 2002 the former Minister of State for Council of Ministers' Affairs, Ali bin Saad al-Kawari, was appointed Minister of Municipal Affairs and Agriculture, replacing Ali bin Muhammad al-Khatir. Muhammad bin Isa Hamad al-Mehannadi was named as the new Minister of State for Council of Ministers' Affairs.

The second elections to the Municipal Council were held on 7 April 2003. A turn-out of about 50% was estimated for the country as a whole, but the rate of participation was reportedly as low as 25%–35% of the registered electorate at several polling stations, including in the largest constituency, al-Kharitaat. A female candidate was elected unopposed after the competing candidates stood aside, and thus became the first woman in the Gulf region to hold elected office, but none of the other five women who contested the elections was successful. Three further candidates were also elected unopposed, and the remaining 25 seats were contested by 85 candidates, including 18 incumbents. In early May the Amir appointed Sheikha bint Ahmad al-Mahmoud as Minister of Education; she replaced Dr Ahmad bin Khalifa Busherbak al-Mansouri and became the first woman to join the Council of Ministers.

In July 1991 Qatar instituted proceedings at the International Court of Justice (ICJ) regarding sovereignty of the Hawar islands (in 1939 a British judgment had awarded sovereignty of the islands to Bahrain), the shoals of Fasht ad-Dibal and Qit'at Jaradah (over which the British had recognized Bahrain's 'sov-

ereign rights' in 1947), together with the delimitation of the maritime border between Qatar and Bahrain. Bahrain's insistence that the two countries seek joint recourse to the ICJ was rejected by Qatar. The matter was further confused in April 1992, when the Government of Qatar issued a decree redefining its maritime borders to include territorial waters claimed by Bahrain. It was also reported that Bahrain had attempted to widen the issue to include its long-standing claim to the area around Zubarah, in mainland Qatar. In February 1994 a hearing of the ICJ opened in The Hague, Netherlands, in order to determine whether the court was competent to rule on the dispute. In July the ICJ requested that Qatar and Bahrain resubmit their dispute by 30 November, either jointly or separately. The two countries failed to reach agreement on joint presentation to the court, and at the end of November Qatar submitted a unilateral request to pursue its case through the ICJ. In February 1995, while the ICJ declared that it would have authority to adjudicate in the dispute (despite Bahrain's refusal to accept the principle of an ICJ ruling), Saudi Arabia also proposed to act as mediator between the two countries. Qatar subsequently indicated its willingness to withdraw the case from the ICJ if Saudi arbitration proved successful.

Relations with Bahrain subsequently deteriorated, and in December 1996 Bahrain boycotted the annual summit meeting of the Co-operation Council for the Arab States of the Gulf (Gulf Co-operation Council—GCC, see p. 175), which took place in Doha. The meeting none the less decided to establish a quadripartite committee, comprising those GCC countries not involved in the dispute, to mediate between Qatar and Bahrain. The committee's efforts achieved a degree of success, and meetings between senior Qatari and Bahraini representatives in London, United Kingdom, and Manama, Bahrain, in early 1997 resulted in the announcement that diplomatic relations at ambassadorial level were to be established. In September, however, Bahrain challenged the authenticity of documents presented to the ICJ by Qatar in support of its territorial claim; the ICJ subsequently directed Qatar to produce a report on the authenticity of the documents by September 1998. Following the submission of the report, in which four experts differed in their opinion of the documents, Qatar announced its decision to disregard them, to enable the case to proceed 'without further procedural complications'. Relations between the two countries improved during 1999: in December Qatar's Amir made his first official visit to Manama. During his visit it was agreed that a joint committee, headed by the Crown Princes of Bahrain and Qatar, would be established to encourage bilateral co-operation. Qatar also agreed to withdraw its petition from the ICJ in the event of the joint committee's reaching a solution to the territorial disputes. A second senior-level meeting was held in January 2000, when the new Amir of Bahrain made his first visit to Qatar. The two countries agreed to expedite the opening of embassies in Manama and Doha. In February, following the first meeting of the Bahrain-Qatar Supreme Joint Committee, it was announced that the possibility of constructing a causeway to link the two states was to be investigated. In May Bahrain announced its decision to suspend the activities of the Supreme Joint Committee pending the ICJ ruling on the dispute. Hearings at the ICJ, which began later that month, ended in June. The final verdict, issued in mid-March 2001, was virtually identical to the British judgment of 1939. Bahrain was found to have sovereignty over the Hawar islands and Qit'at Jaradah, while Qatar held sovereignty over Zubarah, Janan island and the low-tide elevation of Fasht ad-Dibal; the Court drew a single maritime boundary between the two states. Both Qatar and Bahrain accepted the ICJ ruling, and declared that their territorial dispute was ended. Later in March 2001, following a high-profile visit by the Bahraini Amir to Doha, it was announced that meetings of the Supreme Joint Committee would resume. In September a Danish consortium was appointed to carry out a feasibility study for the construction of the planned causeway linking Qatar to Bahrain (the Friendship Bridge), with an anticipated completion date of 2006.

Following the multinational military operation to liberate Kuwait from Iraq in early 1991, Qatar resumed tentative contact with Iraq in 1993. In March 1995, during the first official visit to the country by a senior Iraqi official since the Gulf War, Iraq's Minister of Foreign Affairs met with his Qatari counterpart to discuss the furtherance of bilateral relations; the Qatari Minister subsequently indicated Qatar's determination to pursue a foreign policy independent from that of its GCC neighbours when he announced his country's support for the ending of

UN sanctions against Iraq. In early 1998, as the crisis deepened regarding UN weapons inspections in Iraq (see the Recent History of Iraq), Qatar urged a diplomatic solution, and appealed to Iraq to comply with all pertinent UN Security Council resolutions. In February the Qatari Minister of Foreign Affairs, Sheikh Hamad bin Jasim bin Jaber ath-Thani, became the most senior official from the Gulf states to visit Iraq since 1990. In late 2000 Iraq's Minister of Foreign Affairs visited Qatar, as part of a regional tour, and Qatari officials visited Iraq. In subsequent months Qatar continued to advocate an end to sanctions against Iraq, and in December 2001 a meeting took place in Doha between the new Iraqi Minister of Foreign Affairs, Naji Sabri, and Qatari and Omani officials.

In September 1992 tension arose with Saudi Arabia (with which Qatar has generally enjoyed close ties) when Qatar accused Saudi forces of attacking a Qatari border post, killing two border guards and capturing a third in the process. In protest, in October Qatar suspended a 1965 border agreement with Saudi Arabia (which had never been fully ratified) and temporarily withdrew its 200-strong contingent from the Saudi-based GCC 'Peninsula Shield' force (at the time stationed in Kuwait). The Saudi Government denied the involvement of its armed forces, claiming that the incident had been caused by fighting between rival Bedouin tribes within Saudi territory. Relations between the two countries reportedly improved as a result of Kuwaiti mediation, and the Qatari hostage was released later in October 1992; Qatar nevertheless registered its disaffection by not attending meetings of GCC ministers which took place in Abu Dhabi and Kuwait in November. In December, after mediation by Egypt, Sheikh Khalifa and King Fahd of Saudi Arabia signed an agreement whereby a committee was to be established formally to demarcate the border between the two states. In November 1994, however, Qatar boycotted a GCC ministerial meeting in Saudi Arabia, in protest at what it alleged to have been armed incidents on the border with Saudi Arabia in March and October. Bilateral relations appeared to improve in August 1995, when the new Amir held talks with King Fahd in Saudi Arabia. In December, nevertheless, Qatar boycotted the closing session of the annual GCC summit, following the appointment of a Saudi national as the next GCC Secretary-General (in preference to a Qatari candidate). In March 1996 the dispute was reported to have been settled, after mediation by Oman, and in April Qatar and Saudi Arabia agreed to establish a joint committee to complete the demarcation of their mutual border. Officials from both countries met in Saudi Arabia in June 1999 to sign the border demarcation maps. In late March 2001, at a ceremony held in Doha, Saudi and Qatari officials signed a final agreement concerning the land and maritime demarcation of their joint border; the accord included provision for a joint Saudi-Qatari committee, whose task was to ensure that all provisions of the 1965 accord were implemented. In October 2002 relations between Saudi Arabia and Qatar worsened, however, when the Saudi ambassador to Qatar was recalled following the airing of a television programme via the Al-Jazeera network that was deemed to be critical of the Saudi regime. Relations had already been strained by the expansion of US military facilities in Qatar and by the relocation, in late April, of the main US air operations in the Gulf region from Saudi Arabia to Doha (see the chapter on Saudi Arabia).

In January 1994 Qatar was reported to have commenced discussions with Israel regarding the supply of natural gas to that country, in apparent disregard for the Arab economic boycott of Israel. Following pressure from its GCC allies, Qatar subsequently announced that the proposed sale would depend on Israel's withdrawal from all Arab territories occupied in 1967. In September 1994, however, Qatar, along with the other GCC states, revoked aspects of the economic boycott of Israel. In October 1995 Qatar's Minister of Foreign Affairs expressed his country's support for the cancellation of the direct economic boycott of Israel prior to the achievement of a comprehensive peace settlement in the Middle East. In the following month Israel signed a memorandum of intent to purchase Qatari liquefied natural gas (LNG). Relations between the two countries were consolidated further in April 1996, when Shimon Peres made the first official visit to Qatar by an Israeli Prime Minister. However, in late 1996 Israel declared that the memorandum of intent had expired, although negotiations would continue, and in November Qatar stated that any deal would be dependent on progress in the peace process. In late 1997 Israel indicated that Qatar and Israel were considering reviving the LNG purchase scheme. The fourth Middle East and North

Africa economic summit was scheduled to take place in Doha in November 1997. However, in protest at the intended presence of representatives of Israel, which was regarded by the Arab states as failing to comply with its obligations with regard to the Middle East peace process, most of Qatar's fellow members of the League of Arab States (the Arab League, see p. 260) and the GCC refused to attend. As a result of the boycott, the summit was downgraded to a conference, and was attended by representatives of only seven Arab states; a 'low-level' Israeli delegation attended, as did the US Secretary of State, Madeleine Albright.

In March 1998, however, the Qatari Government stated that it was reviewing its relations with Israel, given the severe difficulties in the Middle East peace process; it was also suggested that Israel's trade office in Doha might be closed. Qatar was criticized by other Arab states in September 2000 following a meeting in New York at the UN Millennium Summit between the Amir and the Israeli Prime Minister, Ehud Barak. However, in October, as the crisis in Israeli–Palestinian relations deepened, it was reported that Qatar was again considering the closure of its Israeli trade office. Prior to the ninth conference of the Organization of the Islamic Conference (OIC, see p. 295), held in Doha in November, several Arab states (notably Saudi Arabia and Iran) threatened to boycott the summit unless Qatar agreed to sever its low-level diplomatic relations with Israel. The Qatari leadership apparently bowed to regional pressure when, in early November, it announced that the Israeli trade office in Doha was to be closed, although there were subsequent reports that the office was still functioning. An emergency session of the OIC was convened in Doha in December 2001 to demonstrate solidarity with the Palestinians as the crisis deepened still further; Sheikh Hamad proposed the establishment of a panel comprising prominent representatives of the Islamic community to lobby Western governments to support an independent Palestinian state. In March 2002 Qatar's Minister of Foreign Affairs travelled to the Palestinian territories for talks with the leader of the Palestinian (National) Authority, Yasser Arafat, who at that time remained under Israeli siege in Ramallah. In late 2002 it was reported that the Israeli trade office in Doha was still functioning; Qatar's continuing refusal to close the establishment exacerbated tensions with Saudi Arabia in particular.

An emergency summit meeting of the OIC was convened in Doha in October 2001, in response to the previous month's suicide attacks against New York and Washington, DC, and the subsequent commencement of US-led military action against targets in Afghanistan linked to the Taliban regime and to the al-Qa'ida (Base) organization of Osama bin Laden, the Saudi-born fundamentalist Islamist held principally responsible for the attacks in the USA.

Despite Qatar's active support for an end to UN sanctions against Iraq, and its pursuit of contacts with the incumbent regime of Saddam Hussain (see above), by the time US Vice-President Dick Cheney visited Qatar in mid-March 2002—as part of a tour of the Gulf aimed at garnering support for a potential extension of the US-led 'war against terror' to target the incumbent Iraqi regime, Qatar was apparently alone among the Gulf states in indicating that it would allow the use of its territory as a base for action against Saddam Hussain. During the decade after the Gulf War the Government had signed a number of defence agreements with the USA and there was reported to have been a significant increase in the amount of US military personnel and equipment positioned in Qatar since September 2001; some 5,000 US troops had arrived at a military base south of Doha in late 2001 for what a Qatari official had described as 'routine' exercises. Furthermore, the construction of a major air facility at the Al-Udaid military base enhanced its strategic importance within the US military network in the region; in December 2002 the US Department of Defense dispatched more than 600 personnel from the US military command centre to the base, which, headed by Gen. Tommy Franks, was to act as the main US command post in the Gulf. Also in December Qatar signed an agreement with the USA for the further upgrade of its military bases, which a US-led force could use in the event of action against Iraq. None the less, Qatar, concerned about the popular reaction to a US-led war in Iraq and the regional implications such a conflict might have, continued to advocate a diplomatic solution to the crisis. In March 2003, as war became increasingly likely, Qatar supported an initiative put forward by the UAE that urged Saddam Hussain to step down as ruler of Iraq and go into permanent exile. By the time of the commencement of hostilities in that month the USA had stationed some 3,000 air force personnel and 36 tactical jets at Al-Udaid. In addition, a further 26 jets from the United Kingdom and Australia were awaiting deployment at the base. In April, in the immediate aftermath of the war, Qatar's Minister of Foreign Affairs, Sheikh Hamad bin Jasim bin Jaber ath-Thani, urged the USA to reject the possibility of pursuing its 'war against terror' to target the Syrian regime of President Bashar al-Assad.

Government

Qatar is an absolute monarchy, with full powers vested in the Amir as Head of State. A provisional Constitution took effect in 1970. Executive power is exercised by the Council of Ministers, which is appointed by the Head of State. An Advisory Council was formed in April 1972, with 20 nominated members, and was expanded to 30 members in 1975 and to 35 members in 1988. The Advisory Council's constitutional entitlements include the power to debate legislation drafted by the Council of Ministers before ratification and promulgation. It also has the power to request ministerial statements on matters of general and specific policy, including the draft budget. In March 1999 elections took place, by universal adult suffrage, for a 29-member Municipal Council which was to have a consultative role in the operations of the Ministry of Municipal Affairs and Agriculture; further elections were held in April 2003. Meanwhile, in 2002 a 32-member constitutional committee, established in 1999, produced a new draft constitution, recommending, among other proposals, the establishment of a partially elected legislature. The draft constitution was approved at a referendum held on 29 April 2003. It was expected that legislative elections would take place before the end of 2005.

Defence

In August 2002 the armed forces comprised an estimated 12,400 men: army 8,500; navy an estimated 1,800 (including Marine Police); air force 2,100. Government expenditure on defence was budgeted at an estimated QR 6,000m. in 2002.

Economic Affairs

In 1995, according to estimates by the World Bank, Qatar's gross national income (GNI), measured at average 1993–95 prices, was US $7,448m., equivalent to $11,600 per head. During 1990–2001, it was estimated, the population increased at an average annual rate of 1.9%. Non-Qataris accounted for some 80% of the total population by the beginning of the 21st century. Qatar's gross domestic product (GDP) was estimated to have increased, in real terms, at an average rate of 7.6% per year in 1993–2001; growth was estimated at 10.0% in 2000 and at 6.2% in 2001, with growth in 2002 put at 6.0%.

Agriculture (including fishing) contributed an estimated 0.5% of GDP in 2001, and employed an estimated 1.3% of the economically active population in that year. All agricultural land is owned by the Government, and most farm managers are immigrants employing a largely expatriate work-force. The main crops are cereals (principally barley), vegetables and dates. Qatar is self-sufficient in winter vegetables and nearly self-sufficient in summer vegetables. Some vegetables are exported to other Gulf countries. The Government has prioritized education in agricultural techniques and experimentation with unconventional methods of cultivation (including the use of sea water and solar energy to produce sand-based crops). Livestock-rearing and fishing are also practised. The GDP of the agricultural sector was estimated to have declined at an average annual rate of 5.8% during 1993–2001. Real agricultural GDP increased by an estimated 1.9% in 2000, although it declined by an estimated 0.7% in 2001.

Industry (including mining, manufacturing, construction and power) contributed an estimated 66.9% of GDP in 2001, and employed 32.2% of the economically active population at March 1986. Industrial GDP was estimated to have increased by an average of 10.1% per year during 1993–2001. Growth in the sector's real GDP was estimated at 13.8% in 2000 and at 7.3% in 2001.

The extraction and processing of petroleum and natural gas provided an estimated 56.4% of GDP in 2001, and mining and quarrying employed 2.4% of the economically active population at March 1986. Petroleum is currently the major mineral export. Proven recoverable petroleum reserves at the end of 2001 were 15,200m. barrels, sufficient to maintain production for 55.5 years at 2001 levels—averaging some 783,000 barrels per day (b/d). With effect from February 2003, Qatar's production quota

within the Organization of the Petroleum Exporting Countries (OPEC, see p. 298) was 635,000 b/d. Proven gas reserves were 14,400,000m. cu m at the end of 2001 (representing 9.3% of known world reserves at that date), primarily located in the North Field, the world's largest gas reserve not associated with petroleum. The real GDP of the mining and quarrying sector was estimated to have increased at an average annual rate of 12.1% in 1993–2001. Growth was estimated at 17.9% in 2000 and at 8.5% in 2001.

Manufacturing contributed an estimated 5.9% of GDP in 2001 (excluding activities related to petroleum and natural gas), and the sector employed 6.9% of the economically active population at March 1986. The principal manufacturing activities are linked to the country's oil and gas resources—petroleum refining and the production of liquefied natural gas (LNG—developed as part of the North Field project), together with industrial chemicals (particularly fertilizers) and steel production. Bids for development of the region's first gas-to-liquids complex were invited in early 2002. Manufacturing GDP (excluding hydrocarbons) was estimated to have increased by an average of 4.2% per year in 1993–2001. The sector's real GDP was estimated to have increased by 13.7% in 2000 and by 5.7% in 2001.

Electrical energy is derived almost exclusively from Qatar's natural gas resources (91.6% in 2001). Solar energy is being developed in conjunction with desalination.

The services sector contributed an estimated 32.6% of GDP in 2001, and engaged 64.4% of the employed labour force at March 1986. The establishment of a formal stock exchange (which commenced trading in 1997) was expected to stimulate further activity in the sector. The GDP of the services sector was estimated to have increased by an average of 6.4% per year in 1993–2001. Services GDP increased by an estimated 4.9% in 2000 and by 6.9% in 2001.

Preliminary figures indicate that in 2001 Qatar recorded a trade surplus of QR 27,244m., while there was a surplus of QR 15,950m. on the current account of the balance of payments. In 2000 the principal source of imports (11.0%) was Japan; other important suppliers in that year were the USA, Germany, the United Kingdom, the United Arab Emirates (UAE), Italy, Saudi Arabia and France. In 1989 Japan took 19% of Qatar's exports, and this percentage is thought to have increased significantly in the 1990s. The principal exports are petroleum and gas and their derivatives (mineral fuels and lubricants provided 81.2% of domestic export revenues in 1999). By 2000 LNG exports alone accounted for almost 35% of export revenues. The principal imports in 2000 were machinery and transport equipment, basic manufactures, food and live animals, miscellaneous manufactured articles and chemicals.

In the financial year ending 31 March 2001, according to preliminary figures, Qatar recorded a budget surplus of QR 4,396m. The annual rate of inflation averaged 1.6% in 1990–2001; consumer prices increased by an average of 1.7% in 2000 and by 1.4% in 2001. The Qatari economy is dependent on immigrant workers, owing to a shortage of indigenous labour.

Other than its membership of OPEC (see p. 298), Qatar is a member of the Organization of Arab Petroleum Exporting Countries (OAPEC, see p. 292), the Co-operation Council for the Arab States of the Gulf (GCC, see p. 175), the Arab Fund for Economic and Social Development (AFESD, see p. 136), the Arab Monetary Fund (see p. 138) and the Islamic Development Bank (see p. 257). GCC member states created a unified regional customs tariff in January 2003, and have undertaken to establish a single market and currency no later than January 2010.

A priority following the assumption of power by Sheikh Hamad in 1995 was the maximizing of Qatar's energy-derived wealth so as to replenish state reserves, much of which were under the control of the deposed Amir. The development of the North Field gas project has been of prime importance, with the aim that Qatar should become a major regional and international supplier of gas and associated products. One of the most notable recent generators of income has been LNG, exports of which began in 1997 and by 2000 were valued at some US $3,000m.: LNG was expected to outstrip petroleum as Qatar's principal export commodity by 2005. In the petroleum sector, meanwhile, efforts have been made to expand production capacity (which was expected to reach 1m. b/d in the early years of the 21st century—considerably in excess of Qatar's recent OPEC production quotas). The investment of some $30,000m. in oil and gas projects since 1995 has entailed the accumulation of an external debt equivalent to almost 90% of GDP by 2000.

However, there was confidence both within Qatar and in the international financial community that revenues from the gas industry (particularly sales of LNG under long-term sales contracts with companies in the Far East and Europe) would be sufficient to ensure the prompt dispatch of debt. Meanwhile, partnership agreements have been sought with overseas interests for a number of schemes in the hydrocarbons sector—notably the Dolphin project, under which it is intended to supply gas to the UAE, Oman and, eventually, Pakistan. Petroleum revenues increased considerably in excess of budgeted levels, in conjunction with the maintenance of strict controls on public spending, resulted in 2000/01 in Qatar's first budget surplus for more than a decade; preliminary indications were that there was a further surplus in 2001/02, despite the decline in oil prices from the latter part of 2001, and increased gas exports in 2003 were expected to result in a continued budgetary surplus in 2002/03, despite higher spending. Meanwhile, the sale of a 45% holding in the state telecommunications company in 1998 was to be followed by the partial privatization of the power and water utilities in 2003. Shares in the state petrochemical, fertilizer, vinyl and chemical companies were also expected to be sold in 2003. However, despite the enactment in 2002 of legislation allowing 100% foreign ownership of companies involved in areas of agriculture, manufacturing, education, health and tourism, and the inauguration in early 2002 of Qatar's first semi-private company in the energy sector (engaged in the sale of liquefied petroleum gas), the State retained responsibility for some 75% of GDP. Having restored financial reserves, a priority for the early part of the 21st century was to be the resumption of much-needed investment in infrastructure: the budget for 2003/04 provided for a 16% rise in overall expenditure, with spending on public projects, including health, social services, low-cost housing and education and youth projects, all set to increase. Furthermore, Doha's status as the venue for the 2006 Asian Games tournament was expected to entail infrastructural expenditure of some $1,800m. over three years.

Education

A state education system was introduced in 1956. Education is free at all levels, although not compulsory. In the academic year 1999/2000 there was a combined total of some 75,000 students at all levels of regular education in Qatar; there were about 44,000 students in private schools. Primary education begins at six years of age and lasts for six years. The next level of education, beginning at the age of 12, is divided into two cycles of three years (preparatory and secondary). In 1995 the equivalent of 86% of children in the relevant age-group (boys 87%; girls 86%) were enrolled at primary schools, while the comparable ratio for secondary enrolment was equivalent to 80% (boys 80%; girls 79%). There are specialized religious, industrial, commercial and technical secondary schools for boys; the technical school admitted its first students in 1999/2000, as did two scientific secondary schools (one for girls). In 1996/97 there were 8,475 students and a teaching staff of 643 at the University of Qatar. The Qatar Foundation for Education, Science and Community Development, established in 1995, is involved in programmes including the development of a faculty of medicine, in association with a US university, and a technology college, in association with a Canadian educational body and an international university, as part of its Education City complex. The 2002/03 budget allocated QR 418m. to expenditure on education and youth welfare.

Public Holidays

2003: 12 February* (Id al-Adha, Feast of the Sacrifice), 5 March* (Islamic New Year), 27 June (Anniversary of the Amir's Accession), 3 September (National Day), 24 September* (Leilat al-Meiraj, Ascension of the Prophet), 27 October* (Ramadan begins), 26 November* (Id al-Fitr, end of Ramadan).

2004: 2 February* (Id al-Adha, Feast of the Sacrifice), 22 February* (Islamic New Year), 27 June (Anniversary of the Amir's Accession), 3 September (National Day), 12 September* (Leilat al-Meiraj, Ascension of the Prophet), 15 October* (Ramadan begins), 14 November* (Id al-Fitr, end of Ramadan).

*These holidays are dependent on the Islamic lunar calendar and may differ by one or two days from the dates given.

Weights and Measures

The metric system has been adopted legally, but imperial measures are still used.

Statistical Survey

Sources (unless otherwise stated): Press and Publications Dept, Ministry of Education, POB 80, Doha; Dept of Economic Policies, Qatar Central Bank, POB 1234, Doha; tel. 4456456; fax 4413650; e-mail elzainys@qcb.gov.qa; internet www.qcb.gov.qa.

AREA AND POPULATION

Area: 11,437 sq km (4,416 sq miles).

Population: 369,079 at census of 16 March 1986; 522,023 (males 342,459, females 179,564) at census of 1 March 1997; 597,000 (provisional) at mid-2001.

Density (mid-2001): 52.2 per sq km.

Principal Towns (population of municipalities, 1997 census): Ad-Dawhah (Doha, the capital) 264,009; Ar-Rayyan 169,774; Al-Wakrah 31,702; Umm Salal 18,392; Al-Khawr (Al-Khor) 17,793.

Births and Deaths (2000): Registered live births 11,250 (birth rate 19.4 per 1,000); Registered deaths 1,173 (death rate 2.0 per 1,000). Source: mainly UN, *Population and Vital Statistics Report*.

Expectation of Life (years at birth): 71.7 (males 70.7; females 74.3) in 2001. Source: WHO, *World Health Report*.

Economically Active Population (persons aged 15 years and over, March 1986): Agriculture and fishing 6,283; Mining and quarrying 4,807; Manufacturing 13,914; Electricity, gas and water 5,266; Building and construction 40,523; Trade, restaurants and hotels 21,964; Transport and communications 7,357; Finance, insurance and real estate 3,157; Community, social and personal services 96,466; Activities not adequately defined 501; Total employed 200,238 (Qatari nationals 20,807, non-Qataris 179,431). Figures include 1,025 unemployed persons with previous work experience, but exclude 944 persons seeking work for the first time. *Mid-2001* (estimates in '000): Agriculture, etc. 4; Total labour force 317 (Source: FAO).

HEALTH AND WELFARE

Key Indicators

Total Fertility Rate (children per woman, 2001): 3.4.

Under-5 Mortality Rate (per 1,000 live births, 2001): 16.

Physicians (per 1,000 head, 1998): 0.09.

Hospital Beds (per 1,000 head, 1997): 1.65.

Health Expenditure (2000): US $ per head (PPP): 940.

Health Expenditure (2000): % of GDP: 3.2.

Health Expenditure (2000): public (% of total): 77.5.

Human Development Index (2000): ranking: 51.

Human Development Index (2000): value: 0.803.

For sources and definitions, see explanatory note on p. vi.

AGRICULTURE, ETC.

Principal Crops ('000 metric tons, 2001): Barley 4.7; Maize 1.0; Cabbages 2.3; Tomatoes 11.0; Cauliflowers 1.7; Pumpkins, squash and gourds 8.5*; Cucumbers and gherkins 4.8*; Aubergines (Eggplants) 5.0*; Chillies and green peppers 1.2; Dry onions 4.0; Other vegetables 11.4*; Watermelons 1.4; Cantaloupes and other melons 4.3*; Dates 16.1; Other fruits 1.5*.
* FAO estimate. Source: FAO.

Livestock (FAO estimates, '000 head, year ending September 2001): Horses 3.8; Cattle 15.0; Camels 50.0; Sheep 214.5; Goats 179.0; Poultry 3,835. Source: FAO.

Livestock Products (FAO estimates, '000 metric tons, 2001): Mutton and lamb 8.2; Camel meat 1.2; Poultry meat 4.2; Other meat 1.2; Cows' milk 11.2; Camel's milk 13.3; Sheep's milk 5.5; Goats' milk 6.2; Hen eggs 3.6. Source: FAO.

Fishing (metric tons, live weight, 2000): Groupers 1,215; Grunts and sweetlips 789; Emperors (Scavengers) 1,442; Porgies and sea-breams 248; Spinefeet (Rabbitfishes) 387; Narrow-barred Spanish mackerel 768; Jacks and crevalles 409; Carangids 420; Total catch (incl. others) 7,142. Source: FAO, *Yearbook of Fishery Statistics*.

MINING

Production (estimates, 2001): Crude petroleum ('000 barrels) 237,000; Natural gas (million cu m) 37,132. Source: US Geological Survey.

INDUSTRY

Production (estimates, 2001, unless otherwise indicated): Wheat flour (including bran, '000 metric tons) 40 (1999); Ammonia (nitrogen content, '000 metric tons) 1,097 (reported figure, 2000); Urea (nitrogen content, '000 metric tons) 748 (2000); Motor spirit (petrol, '000 barrels) 4,948; Kerosene ('000 barrels) 3,911; Gas-diesel (Distillate-fuel) oils ('000 barrels) 3,824; Residual fuel oils ('000 barrels) 4,492; Other refinery products ('000 barrels) 514; Liquefied natural gas ('000 barrels) 26,726; Cement ('000 metric tons) 1,050; Crude steel ('000 metric tons) 907.6 (reported figure); Electric energy (million kWh) 8,170 (1998). Source: mainly US Geological Survey.

FINANCE

Currency and Exchange Rates: 100 dirhams = 1 Qatar riyal (QR). *Sterling, Dollar and Euro Equivalents* (31 December 2002): £1 sterling = 5.867 riyals; US $1 = 3.640 riyals; €1 = 3.817 riyals; 100 Qatar riyals = £17.04 = $27.47 = €26.20. *Exchange Rate* : Since June 1980 the official mid-point rate has been fixed at US $1 = QR 3.64.

Budget (QR million, year ending 31 March): 2000/01 (provisional): *Revenue*: 23,291; *Expenditure*: 18,895 (Salaries and wages 4,999, Other current expenditure 10,849, Major works and projects 1,879, Other capital expenditure 1,168).

International Reserves (US $ million at 31 December 2002): Gold 6.7; IMF special drawing rights 27.2; Reserve position in IMF 135.4; Foreign exchange 1,404.2; Total 1,573.5. Source: IMF, *International Financial Statistics*.

Money Supply (QR million at 31 December 2002): Currency outside banks 1,921; Demand deposits at commercial banks 4,368; Total money 6,289. Source: IMF, *International Financial Statistics*.

Cost of Living (Consumer Price Index for Doha; base: 1988 = 100): 137.0 in 1999; 139.3 in 2000; 141.3 in 2001.

Expenditure on the Gross Domestic Product (provisional, QR million at current prices, 1999): Government final consumption expenditure 11,810; Private final consumption expenditure 9,515; Increase in stocks 405; Gross fixed capital formation 9,107; *Total domestic expenditure* 30,837; Exports of goods and services 26,550; *Less* Imports of goods and services 12,990; *GDP in purchasers' values* 44,397. Source: UN Economic and Social Commission for Western Asia, *National Accounts Studies of the ESCWA Region* (2000).

Gross Domestic Product by Economic Activity (provisional, QR million at current prices, 2001): Agriculture and fishing 266; Petroleum and natural gas 33,180; Manufacturing 3,460; Electricity and water 675; Construction 2,030; Trade, restaurants and hotels 3,387; Transport and communications 2,180; Finance, insurance, real estate and business services 4,821; Other services 8,795; Total 58,794.

Balance of Payments (estimates, QR million, 2001): Exports f.o.b. 39,567; Imports f.o.b. –12,323; *Trade balance* 27,244; Services, private and official transfers (net) –11,294; *Current balance* 15,950; Capital (net) –5,050; *Overall balance* 10,900.

EXTERNAL TRADE

Imports c.i.f. (QR million): 12,219 in 1998; 9,098 in 1999; 11,838 in 2000.

Exports f.o.b. (QR million): 18,311 in 1998; 26,258 in 1999; 42,202 in 2000.

Principal Commodities (distribution by SITC, QR million): *Imports c.i.f.* (2000): Food and live animals 1,212.8; Crude materials (inedible) except fuels 303.3; Chemicals and related products 754.6; Basic manufactures 2,461.5; Machinery and transport equipment 5,308.6; Miscellaneous manufactured articles 1,573.8; Total (incl. others) 11,838.0. *Exports f.o.b.* (1994): Mineral fuels and lubricants 9,297.4 (Petroleum, petroleum products, etc. 8,148.9, Gas (natural and manufactured) 1,148.5); Chemicals and related products 1,187.9 (Manufactured fertilizers 420.2, Plastics in primary forms 372.3); Basic manufactures 676.0 (Iron and steel 673.6); Total (incl. others) 11,452.8 (excl. re-exports 242.3).

Principal Trading Partners (QR million): *Imports c.i.f.* (2000): Australia 224; Bahrain 145; Brazil 113; People's Republic of China 354; France 648; Germany 967; India 335; Indonesia 113; Italy 796; Japan 1,304; Republic of Korea 634; Malaysia 150; Netherlands 285; Pakistan 120; Saudi Arabia 667; Spain 152; Sweden 135; Switzerland 215; Taiwan 117; Thailand 127; United Arab Emirates 820; United Kingdom 919; USA 1,220; Total (incl. others) 11,838. *Exports f.o.b.* (incl. re-exports, 1994): States of the Co-operation Council for the Arab States of the Gulf (Gulf Co-operation Council—GCC) 1,170.0; USA 233.5; Asia (except Arab countries) 9,448.0; Australia and New Zealand 475.3; Total (incl. others) 11,695.1.

TRANSPORT

Road Traffic ('000 motor vehicles in use, 2000): Passenger cars 199.6; Commercial vehicles 92.9. Source: UN, *Statistical Yearbook*.

Shipping (international sea-borne freight traffic, '000 metric tons, 1994): *Goods loaded*: 5,853; *Goods unloaded*: 2,500. *Merchant Fleet* (registered at 31 December 2001): 68 vessels; 690,812 gross registered tons (Source: Lloyd's Register-Fairplay, *World Fleet Statistics*).

Civil Aviation (scheduled services, 1999): Kilometres flown (million) 21; Passengers carried ('000) 1,307; Passenger-km (million) 2,836; Total ton-km (million) 387. Figures include an apportionment (one-quarter) of the traffic of Gulf Air, a multinational airline with its headquarters in Bahrain. Source: UN, *Statistical Yearbook*.

TOURISM

Tourist Arrivals ('000 foreign visitors, hotel occupants only): 327 in 1996; 435 in 1997; 451 in 1998. Source: World Tourism Organization, *Yearbook of Tourism Statistics*.

COMMUNICATIONS MEDIA

Radio Receivers ('000 in use, 1997): 256*.

Television Receivers ('000 in use, 2000): 520†.

Telephones ('000 main lines in use, 2001): 167.4†.

Facsimile Machines ('000 in use, 1996): 10.4‡.

Mobile Cellular Telephones ('000 subscribers, 2001): 178.8†.

Personal Computers ('000 in use, 2001): 100†.

Internet Users ('000, 2001): 40†.

Daily Newspapers (1996): 5 (circulation 90,000 copies)*.

Non-daily Newspapers (estimates, 1995): 1 (circulation 7,000 copies)*.

Book Production (titles, 1996): 209*.

*Source: UNESCO, *Statistical Yearbook*.
†Source: International Telecommunication Union.
‡Source: UN, *Statistical Yearbook*.

EDUCATION

Pre-primary (1995/96): 64 schools; 321 teachers; 7,018 pupils.

Primary (1995/96): 174 schools; 5,864 teachers; 53,631 pupils.

Secondary (1994/95): 126 schools (general 123, vocational 3—1993/94); 3,858 teachers (general 3,738, vocational 120); (1995/96) 38,594 pupils (general 37,924, vocational 670).

University (1996/97): 1 institution; 643 teaching staff; 8,475 students.
Source: partly UNESCO, *Statistical Yearbook*.

Adult Literacy Rate (UNESCO estimates): 81.2% (males 80.4%; females 83.1%) in 2000 (Source: UNDP, *Human Development Report*).

Directory

The Constitution

A provisional Constitution was adopted on 2 April 1970. Executive power is vested in the Amir, as Head of State, and exercised by the Council of Ministers, appointed by the Head of State. The Amir is assisted by the appointed Advisory Council of 20 members (increased to 30 in 1975 and to 35 in 1988), whose term was extended for six years in 1975, for a further four years in 1978, and for further terms of four years in 1982, 1986, 1990, 1994 and 1998. All fundamental democratic rights are guaranteed. In 1975 the Advisory Council was granted power to summon individual ministers to answer questions on legislation before promulgation. Previously the Advisory Council was restricted to debating draft bills and regulations before framing recommendations to the Council of Ministers. In March 1999 elections took place, by universal adult suffrage, for a 29-member Municipal Council, which was to have a consultative role in the operations of the Ministry of Municipal Affairs and Agriculture. In July a 32-member constitutional committee was established to draft a permanent constitution by 2002. According to the draft document, presented in July 2002, the Amir was to remain head of the executive, while a 45-member unicameral parliament, of which two-thirds were to be directly elected (the remainder being appointed by the Amir), was to have powers to legislate, review the state budget, monitor government policy and hold ministers accountable for their actions. The parliament was to have a four-year mandate. Suffrage was to be extended to all citizens, including women, aged 18 years and above. The document also guaranteed freedom of association, expression and religious affiliation and provided for the establishment of an independent judiciary. The Amir formally adopted the draft Constitution following a referendum on 29 April 2003. Elections to the new parliament were expected to be conducted before the end of 2005.

The Government

HEAD OF STATE

Amir: Maj.-Gen. Sheikh HAMAD BIN KHALIFA ATH-THANI (assumed power 27 June 1995).

Crown Prince: Sheikh JASIM BIN HAMAD BIN KHALIFA ATH-THANI.

COUNCIL OF MINISTERS
(April 2003)

Amir, Minister of Defence and Commander-in-Chief of the Armed Forces: Maj.-Gen. Sheikh HAMAD BIN KHALIFA ATH-THANI.

Prime Minister: Sheikh ABDULLAH BIN KHALIFA ATH-THANI.

Deputy Prime Minister: Sheikh MUHAMMAD BIN KHALIFA ATH-THANI.

Minister of the Interior: Sheikh ABDULLAH BIN KHALID ATH-THANI.

Minister of Foreign Affairs: Sheikh HAMAD BIN JASIM BIN JABER ATH-THANI.

Minister of Finance: YOUSUF BIN HUSSEIN KAMAL.

Minister of Economy and Trade: Sheikh HAMAD BIN FAISAL BIN THANI ATH-THANI.

Minister of Awqaf (Religious Endowments) and Islamic Affairs: AHMAD BIN ABDULLAH SALEM AL-MARRI.

Minister of Municipal Affairs and Agriculture: ALI BIN SAAD AL-KAWARI.

Minister of Justice: HASSAN BIN ABDULLAH AL-GHANIM.

Minister of Communication and Transport: Sheikh AHMAD BIN NASSER ATH-THANI.

Minister of Education: Sheikha BINT AHMAD AL-MAHMOUD.

Minister of Energy, Industry, Electricity and Water: ABDULLAH BIN HAMAD AL-ATTIYA.

Minister of Public Health: Dr HAJAR BIN AHMAD HAJAR.

Minister of Civil Service Affairs and Housing: Sheikh FALAH BIN JASIM ATH-THANI.

Minister of State for Foreign Affairs: AHMAD BIN ABDULLAH AL-MAHMOUD.

Minister of State for Council of Ministers' Affairs: MUHAMMAD BIN ISA HAMAD AL-MEHANNADI.

Minister of State for the Interior: Sheikh HAMAD BIN NASSER BIN JASIM ATH-THANI.

Ministers of State without Portfolio: Sheikh AHMAD BIN SAIF ATH-THANI, Sheikh HASSAN BIN ABDULLAH BIN MUHAMMAD ATH-THANI, Sheikh HAMAD BIN SAHIM ATH-THANI, Sheikh HAMAD BIN ABDULLAH ATH-THANI, Sheikh MUHAMMAD BIN KHALID ATH-THANI, Sheikh MUHAMMAD BIN ID ATH-THANI.

MINISTRIES

Ministry of Amiri Diwan Affairs: POB 923, Doha; tel. 43882553; fax 4361212; e-mail adf@diwan.gov.qa; internet www.diwan.gov.qa.

Ministry of Awqaf (Religious Endowments) and Islamic Affairs: POB 422, Doha; tel. 4470777; fax 4327383; e-mail minister@islam.gov.qa.

Ministry of Civil Service Affairs and Housing: POB 36, Doha; tel. 4335335; fax 4446298; internet www.mcsah.gov.qa.

Ministry of Communication and Transport: POB 22228, Doha; tel. 4835522; fax 4835101.

Ministry of Defence: Qatar Armed Forces, POB 37, Doha; tel. 4404111.

Ministry of Economy and Trade: Doha.

Ministry of Education: POB 80, Doha; tel. 4333444; fax 4413886; internet www.moe.edu.qa.

Ministry of Energy, Industry, Electricity and Water: POB 2599, Doha; tel. 4832121; fax 4832024; internet www.kahramaa.com.

Ministry of Finance: POB 3322, Doha; tel. 4461444; fax 4431177.

Ministry of Foreign Affairs: POB 250, Doha; tel. 4334334; fax 4442777; e-mail webmaster@mofa.gov.qa; internet www.mofa.gov.qa.

Ministry of the Interior: POB 115, Doha; tel. 4330000; fax 4429565; internet www.moi.gov.qa.

Ministry of Justice: POB 917 (Dept of Legal Affairs), Doha; tel. 4835200; fax 4832868.

Ministry of Municipal Affairs and Agriculture: POB 820, Doha; tel. 4336336; fax 4430239; e-mail mmaa@mmaa.gov.qa; internet www.mmaa.gov.qa.

Ministry of Public Health: POB 42, Doha; tel. 4441555; fax 4446294; internet www.hmc.gov.qa.

ADVISORY COUNCIL

The Advisory Council was established in 1972, with 20 nominated members. It was expanded to 30 members in 1975, and to 35 members in 1988.

Speaker: MUHAMMAD BIN MUBARAK AL-KHOLAIFI.

Diplomatic Representation

EMBASSIES IN QATAR

Algeria: POB 2494, Doha; tel. 4662900; fax 4663658; Ambassador MOHAMED BOUROWABA.

Bahrain: POB 24888, Doha; tel. 4839360; fax 4839360; Ambassador ABD AR-RAHMAN MUHAMMAD AL-FATHEL.

Bangladesh: POB 2080, Doha; tel. 4671927; fax 4671190; Ambassador ABU TAHER NAJRUL ISLAM.

Bosnia and Herzegovina: POB 876, Doha; tel. 4670194; fax 4670595; e-mail info@bosnianembassyqatar.org; internet www.bosnianembassyqatar.org; Ambassador HUSEIN OMERSPAHIC.

China, People's Republic: POB 17200, Doha; tel. 4824200; fax 4873959; Ambassador ZHAO HUIMIN.

Cuba: POB 12017, Doha; tel. 4672072; fax 4672074; Ambassador JORGE LEÓN CRUZ.

Egypt: POB 2899, Doha; tel. 4832555; fax 4832196; Ambassador MUHAMMAD ABD AL-FATTAH ABDULLAH.

France: POB 2669, Doha; tel. 4832281; fax 4832254; e-mail ambadoha@qatar.net.qa; internet www.qatar.net.qa/ambadoha/ambaf; Ambassador ALAN AZOUAOU.

Germany: POB 3064, Doha; tel. 4876959; fax 4876949; e-mail germany@qatar.net.qa; Ambassador ROLF MEYER-OLDEN.

India: POB 2788, Doha; tel. 4672021; fax 4670448; e-mail indembdh@qatar.net.qa; internet www.indianembassy.gov.qa; Ambassador RANJAN MATHAI.

Iran: POB 1633, Doha; tel. 4835300; fax 4831665; Ambassador DHABEEH ALLAH NOUVERSTI.

Iraq: POB 1526, Doha; tel. 4672237; fax 4673347; Ambassador FAKHRI HAMMUDI AD-DULAYMI.

Italy: POB 4188, Doha; tel. 4436842; fax 4446466; e-mail itembqat@ qatar.net.qa; internet www.qatar.net.qa/itembqat; Ambassador PIO LUIGI TEODORANI FABBRI POZZI.

Japan: POB 2208, Doha; tel. 4831224; fax 4832178; Ambassador KATZUYA IKEDA.

Jordan: POB 2366, Doha; tel. 4832202; fax 4832173; Ambassador OMAR AL-AHMAD.

Korea, Republic: POB 3727, Doha; tel. 4832238; fax 4833264; Ambassador JAE-GOUK KIM.

Kuwait: POB 1177, Doha; tel. 4832111; fax 4832042; Ambassador FAISAL SULAYMAN AL-MUKHAZEEM.

Lebanon: POB 2411, Doha; tel. 4477778; fax 4478817; Ambassador AFIF AYYUB.

Libya: POB 574, Doha; tel. 4429546; fax 4429548; Chargé d'affaires RAFAE ABD AL-QADIR AMANENA.

Mauritania: POB 3132, Doha; tel. 4836003; fax 4836015; Ambassador MUHAMMAD AL-AMIN AS-SALEM WALD DADA.

Morocco: POB 3242, Doha; tel. 4831885; fax 4833416; e-mail moroccoe@qatar.net.qa; Ambassador EL-HOUSSINE AZIZ.

Nepal: POB 23002, Doha; tel. 4675681; fax 4675680; e-mail rnedoha@qatar.net.qa; Ambassador SHYAMANANDA SUMAN.

Oman: POB 1525, Doha; tel. 4670744; fax 4670747; Ambassador NASSER BIN KHALFAN AL-KHAROOSI.

Pakistan: POB 334, Doha; tel. 4832525; fax 4832227; Ambassador KAMAL ARIF.

Philippines: POB 24900, Doha; tel. 4831585; fax 4831595; e-mail dohape@qatar.net.qa; Ambassador AMADO S. TOLENTINO.

Romania: POB 22511, Doha; tel. 4426740; fax 4444346; e-mail romamb@qatar.net.qa; Ambassador MIHAI STUPARU.

Russia: POB 15404, Doha; tel. 4329117; fax 4329118; Ambassador VIKTOR KUDRYAVTSEV.

Saudi Arabia: POB 1255, Doha; tel. 4832030; fax 4832720; Ambassador HAMAD BIN SALEH AT-TUAIMI (recalled Sept. 2002).

Somalia: POB 1948, Doha; tel. 4832200; fax 4832182; Ambassador SHARIF MUHAMMAD OMAR.

Sudan: POB 2999, Doha; tel. 4423007; fax 4351366; Ambassador MUHAMMAD AHMAD MUSTAFA AD-DABY.

Syria: POB 1257, Doha; tel. 4831844; fax 4832139; Chargé d'affaires HAJEM ABD AL-HAMED IBRAHIM.

Tunisia: POB 2707, Doha; tel. 4832645; fax 4832649; Ambassador MOUSTAFA TLILI.

Turkey: POB 1977, Doha; tel. 4835553; fax 4835206; Ambassador OYA INKAYA.

United Arab Emirates: POB 3099, Doha; tel. 4838880; fax 4836186; e-mail emarat@qatar.net.qa; Ambassador ABDUL REDHA ABDULLAH KHORI.

United Kingdom: POB 3, Doha; tel. 4421991; fax 4438692; e-mail bembcomm@qatar.net.qa; Ambassador DAVID MACLENNAN.

USA: POB 2399, Doha; tel. 4884101; fax 4884298; e-mail usisdoha@ qatar.net.qa; internet www.usembassy.org.qa; Ambassador MAUREEN E. QUINN.

Yemen: POB 3318, Doha; tel. 4432555; fax 4429400; Ambassador ABD AS-SALAM HUSSEIN AL-ANSI.

Judicial System

Independence of the judiciary is guaranteed by the provisional Constitution. All aspects pertaining to the civil judiciary are supervised by the Ministry of Justice, which organizes courts of law through its affiliated departments. The *Shari'a* judiciary hears all cases of personal status relating to Muslims, other claim cases, doctrinal provision and crimes under its jurisdiction. Legislation adopted in 1999 unified all civil and *Shari'a* courts in one judicial body, and determined the jurisdictions of each type of court. The law also provided for the establishment of a court of cassation; this was to be competent to decide on appeals relating to issues of contra-

vention, misapplication and misinterpretation of the law, and on disputes between courts regarding areas of jurisdiction. The law also provided for the establishment of a supreme judiciary council, to be presided over by the head of the court of cassation and comprising, *inter alia*, the heads of the *Shari'a* and civil courts of appeal. The establishment of a judicial inspection system was also envisaged. An amiri decree published in June 2002 sought to establish an independent public prosecution system. Further elaboration of provisions for the creation of an independent judiciary were contained in the draft Constitution formally adopted by the Amir in April 2003.

Chief Justice: MUBARAK BIN KHALIFA AS-ASARI.

Public Prosecutor: Col ABDULLAH AL-MAL.

Presidency of Shari'a Courts: POB 232, Doha; tel. 4452222; Pres. Sheikh ABD AR-RAHMAN BIN ABDULLAH AL-MAHMOUD.

Religion

The indigenous population are Muslims of the Sunni sect, most being of the strict Wahhabi persuasion.

CHRISTIANITY

The Anglican Communion

Within the Episcopal Church in Jerusalem and the Middle East, Qatar forms part of the diocese of Cyprus and the Gulf. The Anglican congregation in Qatar is entirely expatriate. The Bishop in Cyprus and the Gulf is resident in Cyprus, while the Archdeacon in the Gulf is resident in Qatar.

Archdeacon in the Gulf: POB 3, Doha; Archdeacon Ven. IAN YOUNG.

The Roman Catholic Church

An estimated 60,000 adherents in Qatar, mainly expatriates, form part of the Apostolic Vicariate of Arabia. The Vicar Apostolic is resident in the United Arab Emirates.

The Press

Al-'Arab (The Arabs): POB 6334, Doha; tel. 4325874; fax 4440016; f. 1972; daily; Arabic; publ. by Dar al-Ouroba Printing and Publishing; Editor-in-Chief KHALID NAAMA; circ. 25,000.

Ad-Dawri (The Tournament): POB 310, Doha; tel. 4328782; fax 4447039; f. 1978; weekly; Arabic; sport; publ. by Abdullah Hamad al-Atiyah and Ptnrs; Editor-in-Chief Sheikh RASHID BIN OWAIDA ATH-THANI; circ. 6,000.

Gulf Times: POB 2888, Doha; tel. 4350478; fax 4350474; e-mail editor@gulf-times.com; internet www.gulf-times.com; f. 1978; daily and weekly editions; English; political; publ. by Gulf Publishing and Printing Co; Editor-in-Chief ABD AR-RAHMAN SAIF AL-MADHADI; circ. 15,000 (daily).

Al-Jawhara (The Jewel): POB 2531, Doha; tel. 4414575; fax 4671388; f. 1977; monthly; Arabic; women's magazine; publ. by al-Ahd Est. for Journalism, Printing and Publications Ltd; Editor-in-Chief ABDULLAH YOUSUF AL-HUSSAINI; circ. 8,000.

Nada (A Gathering): POB 4896, Doha; tel. 4445564; fax 4433778; f. 1991; weekly; social and entertainment; published by Akhbar al-Usbou'; Editor-in-Chief ADEL ALI BIN ALI.

Al-Ouroba (Arabism): POB 663, Doha; tel. 4325874; fax 4429424; f. 1970; weekly; Arabic; political; publ. by Dar al-Ouroba Printing and Publishing; Editor-in-Chief YOUSUF NAAMA; circ. 12,000.

The Peninsula: POB 3488, Doha; tel. 4663945; fax 4663965; e-mail penqatar@qatar.net.qa; f. 1996; daily; English; political; publ. by Dar ash-Sharq Printing, Publishing and Distribution; Editor-in-Chief ABD AL-AZIZ AL-MAHMOUD; Man. Editor GEORGE ABRAHAM; circ. 8,000.

Qatar Lil Inshaa (Qatar Construction): POB 2203, Doha; tel. 4424988; fax 4432961; f. 1989; publ. by Almaha Trade and Construction Co; Gen. Man. MUHAMMAD H. AL-MIJBER; circ. 10,000.

Ar-Rayah (The Banner): POB 3464, Doha; tel. 4466555; fax 4350476; e-mail www.edit@raya.com; internet www.raya.com; f. 1979; daily and weekly editions; Arabic; political; publ. by Gulf Publishing and Printing Co; Editor NASSER AL-OTHMAN; circ. 25,000.

Saidat ash-Sharq: POB 3488, Doha; tel. 4662445; fax 4662450; f. 1993; monthly; Arabic; women's magazine; publ. by Dar ash-Sharq Printing, Publishing and Distribution; Editor NASSER AL-OTHMAN; circ. 15,000.

Ash-Sharq (The Orient): POB 3488, Doha; tel. 4662444; fax 4662450; e-mail webmaster@al-sharq.com; internet www.al-sharq

.com; f. 1985; daily; Arabic; political; publ. by Dar ash-Sharq Printing, Publishing and Distribution House; Gen. Supervisor NASSER AL-OTHMAN; circ. 45,018.

At-Tarbiya (Education): POB 9865, Doha; tel. 4861412; fax 4880911; f. 1971; quarterly; publ. by Qatar National Commission for Education, Culture and Science; Editor-in-Chief YOUSEF BIN ALI AL-KHATER; circ. 2,000.

This is Qatar and What's On: POB 4015, Doha; tel. 4413813; fax 4413814; f. 1978; quarterly; English; tourist information; publ. by Oryx Publishing and Advertising Co; Editor-in-Chief YOUSUF J. AD-DARWISH; circ. 10,000.

Al-Ummah: POB 893, Doha; tel. 4447300; fax 4447022; e-mail m_dirasat@islam.gov.qa; internet www.islam.gov.qa; f. 1982; bi-monthly; Islamic thought and affairs, current cultural issues, book serializations.

Al-Watan: POB 22345, Doha; tel. 4652244; fax 4660440; e-mail feedback@al-watan.com; internet www.al-watan.com; f. 1995; daily; Arabic; political; publ. by Dar al-Watan Printing, Publishing and Distribution; Editor-in-Chief AHMAD ALI AL-ABDULLAH; circ. 25,000.

NEWS AGENCIES

Qatar News Agency (QNA): POB 3299, Doha; tel. 4450319; fax 4438316; e-mail qna@qatar.net.qa; internet www.qatarnewsagency .com; f. 1975; affiliated to Ministry of Foreign Affairs; Dir and Editor-in-Chief AHMAD JASSIM AL-HUMAR.

Publishers

Qatar National Printing Press: POB 355, Doha; tel. 4448453; fax 4449550; Man. ABD AL-KARIM DEEB.

Ali bin Ali Media and Publishing: POB 75, Doha; tel. 4313245; fax 4411251; e-mail publishing@alibinali.com; internet www .alibinali.com; publishers of *Qatar Telephone Directory and Yellow Pages*.

Dar al-Ouroba Printing and Publishing: POB 52, Doha; tel. 4423179.

Dar ash-Sharq Printing, Publishing and Distribution: POB 3488, Doha; tel. 4662444; fax 4662450; e-mail webmaster@al-sharq .com; Editor-in-Chief ABD AL-AZIZ AL-MAHMOUD; circ. 22,000.

Gulf Publishing and Printing Co: POB 533, Doha; tel. 4466555; fax 4424171; e-mail gm@gulftimes.com; internet www.gulf-times .com; Gen. Man. MUHAMMAD ALLAM ALI.

Oryx Publishing and Advertising Co: POB 3272, Doha; tel. 413813; fax 4413814.

Broadcasting and Communications

TELECOMMUNICATIONS

Qatar Telecommunications Corpn (Q-Tel): POB 217, Doha; tel. 4400400; fax 4413904; e-mail webmaster@qtel.com.qa; internet www.qtel.com.qa; f. 1987; majority state-owned; provides telecommunications services within Qatar; Chair. Sheikh ABDULLAH BIN MUHAMMAD ATH-THANI; Gen. Man. HAMAD AL-ATTIYA.

BROADCASTING

Regulatory Authority

Qatar Radio and Television Corpn (QRTC): Doha; f. 1997; autonomous authority reporting directly to the Council of Ministers.

Radio

Qatar Broadcasting Service (QBS): POB 3939, Doha; tel. 4894444; fax 4882888; f. 1968; govt service transmitting in Arabic, English, French and Urdu; programmes include Holy Quran Radio and Doha Music Radio; Dir MUHAMMAD A. AL-KUWARI.

Television

Al-Jazeera Satellite Channel: POB 23123, Doha; tel. 4890890; fax 4885333; internet www.aljazeera.net; f. 1996; 24-hr broadcasting; Arabic; English-language service planned; Pres. HAMAD BIN THAMER ATH-THANI; Editor-in-Chief IBRAHIM HELAL; Man. Dir MUHAMMAD J. AL-ALI.

Qatar Television Service: POB 1944, Doha; tel. 4894444; fax 4874170; f. 1970; operates two channels; Dir MUHAMMAD JASIM AL-ALI (acting); Asst Dir ABD AL-WAHAB MUHAMMAD AL-MUTAWA'A.

Finance

(cap. = capital; res = reserves; dep. = deposits; m. = million; brs = branches; amounts in Qatar riyals unless otherwise stated)

BANKING

Central Bank

Qatar Central Bank: POB 1234, Doha; tel. 4456456; fax 4413650; e-mail webmaster@qcb.gov.qa; internet www.qcb.gov.qa; f. 1966 as Qatar and Dubai Currency Board; became Qatar Monetary Agency in 1973; renamed Qatar Central Bank in 1993; cap. and res 1,318.1m., dep. 1,368.0m., currency in circulation 2,048.1m. (Dec. 2001); Gov. ABDULLAH BIN KHALID AL-ATTIYA; Dep. Gov. Sheikh ABDULLAH BIN SAID ABD AL-AZIZ ATH-THANI.

Commercial Banks

Al-Ahli Bank of Qatar QSC: POB 2309, Doha; tel. 4326611; fax 4444652; e-mail ahlibk@qatar.net.qa; f. 1984; cap. 182.8m., res 23.5m., dep. 1,866.7m. (Dec. 2001); Chair. SALEH BIN MUBARAK AL-KHULAIFI; Gen. Man. QASIM M. QASIM; 8 brs.

Commercial Bank of Qatar QSC: Grand Hamad Ave, POB 3232, Doha; tel. 4900000; fax 4438182; e-mail info@cbq.com.qa; internet www.cbq.com.qa; f. 1975; owned 30% by board of directors and 70% by Qatari citizens and organizations; cap. 197.8m., res 357.3m., dep 4,449.2m. (Dec. 2001); Chair. ABDULLAH BIN KHALIFA AL-ATTIYA; Gen. Man. ANDREW C. STEVENS; 12 brs.

Doha Bank: Grand Hamad Ave, POB 3818, Doha; tel. 4456600; fax 4416631; e-mail dohabank@qatar.net.qa; internet www.dohabank .com.qa; f. 1979; cap. 184.6m., res 494.5m., dep. 5,689.3m. (Dec. 2001); Chair. Sheikh FAHAD BIN MUHAMMAD BIN JABER ATH-THANI; Gen. Man. SALAH MUHAMMAD JAIDAH; 13 brs in Qatar and 1 overseas.

Grindlays Qatar Bank QSC: POB 2001, Suhaim bin Hamad St, Doha; tel. 4473700; fax 4473710; e-mail qatarenq@qa .standardchartered.com; f. 2000; previously a branch of ANZ Grind-lays Bank, f. 1956; cap 75.0m. total assets 1,043.4m. (Dec. 2001); Gen. Man. J. F. MURRAY.

Qatar Industrial Development Bank: POB 22789, Doha; tel. 4421600; fax 4350433; e-mail qidb@qatar.net.qa; internet www.qidb .com.qa; f. 1996; inaugurated Oct. 1997; state-owned; provides long-term low-interest industrial loans; cap. 200m. Chair. Sheikh ABDULLAH BIN SAUD ATH-THANI.

Qatar International Islamic Bank QSC: POB 664, Doha; tel. 4332600; fax 4444101; e-mail qiibit@qatar.net.qa; f. 1990; cap. 100.0m., res 91.0m., dep. 2,258.1m. (Dec. 2001); Chair. THANI BIN ABDULLAH AL-THANI; Gen. Man. ABD AL-BASIT ASH-SHAIBEI; 3 brs.

Qatar Islamic Bank SAQ: POB 559, Doha; tel. 4409409; fax 4412700; e-mail qibt@qatar.net.qa; f. 1983; cap. 250.0m., res 119.4m., dep. 3,659.6m. (Dec. 2001); Chair., Man. Dir and Pres. KHALID BIN AHMAD AS-SUWAIDI; Gen. Man. MAHER MAHMOUD DUWEIK; 7 brs.

Qatar National Bank SAQ: POB 1000, Doha; tel. 4407407; fax 4413753; e-mail webmaster@qatarbank.com; internet www .qatarbank.com; f. 1965; owned 50% by Govt of Qatar and 50% by Qatari nationals; cap. 1,038.2m., res 3,439.3m., dep. 23,358.6m. (Dec. 2001); Chair. Minister of Finance; Chief Exec. SAID BIN ABDULLAH AL-MISNAD; 30 brs in Qatar and 3 abroad.

Foreign Banks

Arab Bank PLC (Jordan): POB 172, Doha; tel. 4437979; fax 4410774; e-mail arabbank@qatar.net.qa; f. 1957; total assets 1,100m. (Dec. 1996); Regional Man. GHASSAN BUNDAKJI; Dep. Man. SAAD AD-DIN ELAYAN; 2 brs.

Bank Saderat Iran: POB 2256, Doha; tel. 4414646; fax 4430121; e-mail bsiiran@qatar.net.qa; f. 1970; Man. MUHAMMAD ZAMANI.

BNP Paribas (France): POB 2636, Doha; tel. 4433844; fax 4410861; e-mail qatar.paribas@paribas.com; internet qatar.bnpparibas.com; f. 1973; Gen. Man. CHRISTIAN DE LA TOUCHE.

HSBC Bank Middle East (United Kingdom): POB 57, Doha; tel. 4382222; fax 4416353; e-mail hsbcqa@qatar.net.qa; internet www .britishbank.com; f. 1954; total assets US $550m. (1999); CEO CHRIS MEARES; Gen. Man. J. P. PASCOE; 2 brs.

Mashreq Bank PSC (UAE): POB 173, Doha; tel. 4413213; fax 4413880; f. 1971; Gen. Man. KHALED GAMAL ELDIN.

Standard Chartered PLC (UK): POB 29, Doha; tel. 4414252; fax 4413739; f. 1950; total assets 725m. Gen. Man. ARIF MANSOOR.

United Bank Ltd (Pakistan): POB 242, Doha; tel. 4424400; fax 4424600; e-mail ubldoha@qatar.net.qa; f. 1970; Gen. Man. and Vice-Pres. RAI MANSOOR AHMAD KHAN.

STOCK EXCHANGE

Doha Securities Market (DSM): Al-Khaleej Insurance Co Bldg, Doha; f. 1997; 23 cos listed; Dir GHANIM AL-HAMMADI.

INSURANCE

Doha Insurance Co: POB 7171, Doha; tel. 4335000; fax 4657777; e-mail dohainsco@qatar.net.qa; f. 1999 as public shareholding co; cap. 127m. (1999); Chair. Sheikh NAWAF BIN NASSER BIN KHALID ATH-THANI; Gen. Man. BASSAM HUSSAIN.

Al-Khaleej Insurance Co (SAQ): POB 4555, Doha; tel. 4414151; fax 4430530; e-mail alkhalej@qatarnet.qa; internet www.alkhalej .com; f. 1978; cap. 24m. all classes except life; Chair. ABDULLAH BIN MUHAMMAD JABER ATH-THANI; Gen. Man. MUHAMMAD AMER TAHA.

Qatar General Insurance and Reinsurance Co SAQ: POB 4500, Doha; tel. 4417800; fax 4437302; e-mail management@qgirc.com; internet www.qgirc.com; f. 1979; cap. 30m. (1997); all classes; Chair. and Man. Dir Sheikh ALI BIN SAUD ATH-THANI; Gen. Man. GHAZI ABU NAHL.

Qatar Insurance Co SAQ: POB 666, Doha; tel. 4490490; fax 4831569; e-mail qatarins@qatar.net.qa; f. 1964; cap. 36m. (1995); all classes; the Govt has a majority share; Chair. Sheikh KHALID BIN MUHAMMAD ALI ATH-THANI; Gen. Man. KHALIFA A. AS-SUBAY'I; br. in Dubai.

Qatar Islamic Insurance Co: POB 12402, Doha; tel. 4413413; fax 4447277; f. 1993; cap. 20m. (1995).

Trade and Industry

DEVELOPMENT ORGANIZATION

Department of Industrial Development: POB 2599, Doha; tel. 4832121; fax 4832024; govt-owned; conducts research, development and supervision of new industrial projects; Dir-Gen. MAJID ABDULLAH AL-MALKI.

CHAMBER OF COMMERCE

Qatar Chamber of Commerce and Industry: POB 402, Doha; tel. 4621131; fax 4622538; e-mail qcci@qatar.net.qa; internet www .qatar.net.qa/qcci; f. 1963; 17 elected mems; Pres. MUHAMMAD BIN KHALID AL-MANA; Dir-Gen. Dr MAJID ABDULLAH AL-MALKI.

STATE HYDROCARBONS COMPANIES

Qatar Petroleum (QP): POB 3212, Doha; tel. 4491491; fax 4831125; e-mail webmaster@qp.com.qa; internet www.qp.com.qa; f. 1974 as the Qatar General Petroleum Corpn (QGPC), name changed 2001; cap. QR 20,000m. the State of Qatar's interest in companies active in petroleum and related industries has passed to the Corpn; has responsibility for all phases of oil and gas industry both onshore and offshore, including exploration, drilling, production, refining, transport and storage, distribution, sale and export of oil, natural gas and other hydrocarbons; Chair. Minister of Energy, Industry, Electricity and Water; Vice-Chair. HUSSAIN KAMAL.

Qatar Petroleum wholly or partly owns: Qatar Fertilizer Co (QAFCO), Ras Laffan LNG Co Ltd (Rasgas), Gulf Helicopters Co (GHC), Qatar Vinyl Co (QVC), Qatar Chemical Co (Q-Chem), Qatar Fuel Additives Co Ltd (QAFAC), Qatar Clean Energy Co (QACENCO), Qatar Electricity and Water Co (QEWC), Qatar Shipping Co (Q-Ship), Arab Maritime Petroleum Transport Co (AMPTC), Arab Petroleum Pipelines Co (SUMED), Arab Shipbuilding and Repair Yard Co (ASRY), Arab Petroleum Services Co (APSC) and Arab Petroleum Investments Corpn (APICORP); and also the following:

Qatar Liquefied Gas Co (QATARGAS): POB 22666, Doha; tel. 4736000; fax 4736666; internet www.qatargas.com; f. 1984 to develop the North Field of unassociated gas; cap. QR 500m. QP has a 65% share; ExxonMobil and TotalFinaElf hold 10% each; the Marubeni Corpn and Mitsui and Co of Japan hold 7.5% each; Chair. Minister of Energy, Industry, Electricity and Water; Vice-Chair. and Man. Dir FAISAL MUHAMMAD AS-SUWAIDI.

Qatar Petrochemical Co (QAPCO) SAQ: POB 756, Doha; tel. 4777111; fax 4771346; e-mail information@qapco.com.qa; internet www.qapco.com; f. 1974; QP has an 80% share; 20% is held by ATOFINA (France); total assets QR 2,439m. (2001); operation of petrochemical plant at Umm Said; produced 535,215 metric tons of ethylene, 382,029 tons of low-density polyethylene, and 40,873 tons of solid sulphur in 2001; Gen. Man. HAMAD RASHID AL-MOHANNADI.

UTILITIES

Qatar General Electricity and Water Corpn (Kahramaa): POB 41, Doha; tel. 4845484; fax 4845496; internet www.kahramaa.com; f. 2000; state authority for planning, implementation, operation and maintenance of electricity and water sectors; Chair. Minister of Energy, Industry, Electricity and Water.

Qatar Electricity and Water Co (QEWC): POB 22046, Doha; tel. 4858585; fax 4831116; e-mail qewc@qatar.net.qa; f. 1990; 57% privately-owned; has responsibility for adding new generating capacity in Qatar; Gen. Man. FAHAD HAMAD AL-MOHANNADI.

Transport

ROADS

In 1991 there were some 1,191 km of surfaced road linking Doha and the petroleum centres of Dukhan and Umm Said with the northern end of the peninsula. The total road network in 1999 was estimated to be 1,230 km. A 105-km road from Doha to Salwa was completed in 1970, and joins one leading from Al-Hufuf in Saudi Arabia, giving Qatar land access to the Mediterranean. A 418-km highway, built in conjunction with Abu Dhabi, links both states with the Gulf network. A major upgrading of the national road network was planned for the first years of the 21st century. In September 2001 a Danish consortium was appointed to carry out a feasibility study for the construction of a planned causeway (the Friendship Bridge) linking Qatar with Bahrain, with an anticipated completion date of 2006.

SHIPPING

Doha Port has nine general cargo berths of 7.5 m–9.0 m depth. Total length of berths is 1,699 m. In addition, there is a flour mill berth, and a container terminal (with a depth of 12.0 m and a length of 600 m) with a roll-on roll-off berth at the north end, is currently under construction. Cold storage facilities exist for cargo of up to 500 tons. At Umm Said Harbour the Northern Deep Water Wharves consist of a deep-water quay 730 m long with a dredged depth alongside of 15.5 m, and a quay 570 m long with a dredged depth alongside of 13.0 m. The General Cargo Wharves consist of a quay 400 m long with a dredged depth alongside of 10.0 m. The Southern Deep Water Wharves consist of a deep water quay 508 m long with a dredged depth alongside of 13.0 m. The North Field gas project has increased the demand for shipping facilities. A major new industrial port was completed at Ras Laffan in 1995, providing facilities for LNG and condensate carriers and roll-on-roll-off vessels.

Customs and Ports General Authority: POB 81, Doha; tel. 4457457; fax 4413563; Dir of Ports G. A. GENKEER.

Qatar National Navigation and Transport Co Ltd (QNNTC): West Bay, Al-Tameen St, POB 153, Doha; tel. 4468666; fax 4468777; e-mail navigation@qnntc.com; internet www.qatar.net.qa/qnntc; f. 1957; 100%-owned by Qatari nationals; shipping agents, stevedoring, chandlers, forwarding, shipowning, repair, construction, etc. Chair. SALEH MUBARAK AL-KHOLEILI; Vice-Chair. and Chair. of Exec. Cttee Sheikh ABDULLAH MUHAMMAD JABER ATH-THANI.

Qatar Shipping Co QSC (Q-Ship): POB 22180, Doha; tel. 4315500; fax 4315565; e-mail qshipops@qship.com; internet www .qship.com; f. 1992; oil and bulk cargo shipping; Chair. SALEM B. AN-NAIMI; Gen. Man. NASSER AR-ROMAIHI.

CIVIL AVIATION

Doha International Airport is equipped to receive all types of aircraft. In 1998 some 2.4m. passengers used the airport. Upgrading of the airport, at an estimated cost of US $600m., was expected to increase passenger-handling capacity to 8m. by 2006. Qatar withdrew from Gulf Air, which it had owned jointly with Bahrain, Oman and Abu Dhabi, in May 2002.

Civil Aviation Authority: POB 3000, Doha; tel. 4428177; fax 4429070; Chair. and Man. Dir ABD AL-AZIZ MUHAMMAD AN-NOAIMI.

Doha International Airport: POB 73, Doha; tel. 4622222; fax 4622044; Dir ABDULLAH BIN AHMAD ATH-THANI.

Gulf Helicopters: POB 811, Doha; tel. 4333888; fax 4352287; e-mail mohd@gulfhelicopters.com; internet www.gulfhelicopters .com; f. 1974; owned by QP; Chair. ABDULLAH BIN HAMAD AL-ATTIYA.

Qatar Airways: POB 22550, Doha; tel. 4621717; fax 4621533; e-mail infodesk@qatarairways.com; internet www.qatarairways .com; f. 1993; services to more than 20 international destinations; CEO AKBAR AL-BAKER.

Tourism

Qatar's tourist industry is small, owing to its limited infrastructure. Some 451,000 tourists visited the country in 1998. By 2000, however, tourism was being actively promoted, and Qatar's reputation as a venue for international conferences and sporting events was growing.

General Tourism Authority (GTA): Doha; f. 2002; affiliated with Council of Ministers; Chair. Sheikh ABDULLAH BIN AHMAD ATH-THANI; Gen. Man. DAVID TEWELDE.

ROMANIA

Introductory Survey

Location, Climate, Language, Religion, Flag, Capital

Romania (formerly the Socialist Republic of Romania) lies in south-eastern Europe, bounded to the north and east by Ukraine, to the north-east by Moldova, to the north-west by Hungary, to the south-west by Serbia and to the south by Bulgaria. The south-east coast is washed by the Black Sea. Romania has hot summers and cold winters, with a moderate rainfall. The average summer temperature is 23°C (73°F) and the winter average is –3°C (27°F). The official language is Romanian, although minority groups speak Hungarian (Magyar), German and other languages. Most of the inhabitants profess Christianity, and about 83% of believers are adherents of the Romanian Orthodox Church. The national flag (proportions 3 by 5) consists of three equal vertical stripes, of blue, yellow and red. The capital is Bucharest (Bucureşti).

Recent History

Formerly part of Turkey's Ottoman Empire, Romania became an independent kingdom in 1881. During the dictatorship of the Fascist 'Iron Guard' movement, Romania entered the Second World War as an ally of Nazi Germany. Soviet forces entered Romania in 1944, however, when the pro-German regime was overthrown. Under Soviet pressure, King Michael accepted the appointment of a communist-led coalition Government in March 1945. At elections in November 1946 a communist-dominated bloc claimed 89% of the votes cast, but the results were widely believed to have been fraudulent. In 1947 the small Romanian Communist Party (RCP) merged with the Social Democratic Party to become the Romanian Workers' Party (RWP). King Michael was forced to abdicate on 30 December 1947, when the Romanian People's Republic was proclaimed. The republic's first Constitution was adopted in 1948, and in the same year the nationalization of the main industrial and financial institutions was begun. In 1949 private landholdings were expropriated and amalgamated into state and collective farms. The implementation of Soviet-style economic policies was accompanied by numerous arrests of non-communists and the establishment of full political control by the RWP.

In 1952, following a purge of the RWP membership, a new Constitution, closer to the Soviet model, was adopted. Gheorghe Gheorghiu-Dej, the First Secretary of the RWP, became Romania's unchallenged leader and proceeded to implement large-scale plans for industrialization, despite the Soviet leadership's preference for Romania to remain as a supplier of agricultural goods. Gheorghiu-Dej died in 1965; he was succeeded as First Secretary of the RWP by Nicolae Ceauşescu, a Secretary of the RWP Central Committee since 1954. In June 1965 the RWP again became the RCP, and Ceauşescu's post of First Secretary was restyled General Secretary. A new Constitution, adopted in August, changed the country's name to the Socialist Republic of Romania.

Ceauşescu continued his predecessor's relatively independent foreign policy, criticizing the invasion of Czechoslovakia by troops of the Warsaw Pact (the former defence grouping of the Soviet bloc) in 1968, and establishing links with Western states and institutions. However, the use of foreign loans for investment led to severe economic problems by the early 1980s. In order to strengthen his position, Ceauşescu (who had become President of the Republic in 1974) implemented frequent changes in the RCP leadership and the Government. In March 1980 his wife, Elena, became a First Deputy Chairman of the Council of Ministers, and numerous other family members held government and party posts.

At an RCP Congress in November 1984 Ceauşescu was re-elected General Secretary for a further five-year term. Legislative elections were held in March 1985, when only 2.27% of the total number of voters (99.99% of the electorate were claimed to have participated) were reported to have voted against the candidates approved by the RCP. The Grand National Assembly subsequently re-elected Ceauşescu as President of Romania. In October an energy crisis resulted in a declaration of a state of emergency in the electric-power industry and the dismissal of ministers and senior officials. Shortages of fuel and power led to strict energy rationing in early 1987, and strikes, to protest against food shortages and delays in the payment of wages, were organized in provincial factories. In November thousands of people marched through the city of Braşov and stormed the local RCP headquarters, protesting against the decline in living standards and in working conditions. Hundreds of arrests were made, and similar protests followed in other cities. Ceauşescu announced improvements in food supplies and increases in wages, but continued to oppose any reform of the system. In March he announced details of a rural urbanization programme, to entail the demolition of some 8,000 villages, located mainly in Transylvania, and the resettlement of their residents (mostly ethnic Hungarians) in multi-storey housing complexes, which were to form part of new 'agro-industrial centres'. The plan attracted much domestic and international criticism, but Ceauşescu maintained that the programme would raise living standards and ensure social equality.

During 1988 and 1989 Romania became increasingly isolated from the international community, largely owing to the rural urbanization programme and continuing abuses of human rights. On a visit to the capital, Bucharest, in May 1987, the Soviet leader, Mikhail Gorbachev, had emphasized the desirability of economic and political reforms, a view reiterated during a visit by Ceauşescu to the USSR in October 1988. Romania continued to obstruct progress at the Vienna Conference on Security and Co-operation in Europe (begun in November 1986); on adoption of the final document by the Conference in January 1989, Romania declared that it did not consider itself bound by certain provisions relating to human rights, considering them to constitute the right of interference in a country's internal affairs. In early 1989 France and the Federal Republic of Germany recalled their ambassadors from Bucharest.

There were also signs of increasing criticism of the regime within Romania. In March 1989, in an open letter to the President, six retired RCP officials accused Ceauşescu of disregard for the Constitution and economic mismanagement, and were particularly critical of the rural urbanization programme. It was subsequently reported that the signatories had been detained. In November Ceauşescu, who continued to denounce reforms under way elsewhere in Eastern Europe, was re-elected at an RCP Congress as the party's General Secretary for a further five-year term.

In December 1989 there was unrest in Timişoara as supporters of a Protestant clergyman (an ethnic Hungarian who had repeatedly criticized the Government's policies) demonstrated their opposition to his eviction from his church. A further protest, at which considerable criticism of the regime was expressed, was attended by thousands of local residents. Security forces opened fire on the crowd, reportedly killing several hundred people. There were reports of protests in other towns, and the country's borders were closed.

On 21 December 1989 President Ceauşescu attended a mass rally in Bucharest, intended to demonstrate popular support. Instead, his address was interrupted by hostile chanting, and anti-Government demonstrations followed later in the day, leading to clashes between protesters and members of the Securitate (the secret police force), during which many civilians were killed. The disturbances quickly spread to other parts of the country, and on the following day Ceauşescu declared a state of emergency; however, soldiers of the regular army declared their support for the protesters. Nicolae and Elena Ceauşescu escaped by helicopter from the roof of the RCP Central Committee headquarters as demonstrators stormed the building. They were captured near Târgovişte and, on 25 December, after a summary trial, were executed by firing squad. Fighting continued for several days, mainly between Securitate forces and regular soldiers.

Meanwhile, a revolutionary, 145-member National Salvation Front (NSF) was formed, and a provisional Government, comprising liberal communists, intellectuals and members of the armed forces, was established. Ion Iliescu, a former Secretary of the RCP Central Committee, became interim President, and

Petre Roman, an academic, was appointed Prime Minister. The new Government immediately decreed an end to the RCP's constitutional monopoly of power, and cancelled the rural urbanization programme. The RCP was banned, it was announced that free elections would be held in 1990, and the designation of Socialist Republic was abandoned. By early January 1990 the army had restored order, and the Securitate was abolished. According to official figures, 689 people were killed during the revolution.

Special military tribunals were established to try Ceaușescu's former associates. In February 1990 four senior RCP officials were found guilty of responsibility for the shootings in Timișoara and Bucharest and were sentenced to life imprisonment. Numerous other former government and RCP members were similarly charged. In September Ceaușescu's son, Nicu, who was found to have ordered security forces to open fire on demonstrators in Sibiu in December 1989, received a 20-year prison sentence. (He was released in November 1992 on the grounds of ill health, and died in September 1996.) Gen. Iulian Vlad, the former head of the Securitate, was sentenced to 12 years' imprisonment, following his conviction in 1991 on several charges; in January 1994, however, he was released as part of a general amnesty. In December 1991 eight associates of the former President were sentenced to prison terms of up to 25 years for their part in the shootings in Timișoara.

Despite the widespread jubilation that followed the downfall of Ceaușescu, the NSF did not enjoy total public support. Many citizens believed that the Front's leadership was too closely linked with the Ceaușescu regime, and were particularly critical of the NSF's control of the media. Furthermore, the NSF's announcement, in January 1990, that it was to contest the forthcoming elections, and its reversal of a decision to abolish the RCP, increased fears that members of the disgraced regime were attempting to regain power. The NSF was weakened by the resignation of Doina Cornea, a veteran dissident, and Dumitru Mazilu, the interim First Deputy President, later in the month. There were, moreover, clashes between supporters and opponents of the NSF. In January the offices of two opposition parties, the National Liberal Party (NLP) and the National Peasants' Party, were attacked by NSF supporters. In February, after negotiations among representatives of 29 political parties, the NSF agreed to share power, pending the elections, with the opposition, in a 180-member Provisional National Unity Council (PNUC). Each of the political parties represented in the talks was allocated three seats on the Council, and the PNUC was subsequently expanded to 253 members to permit representation by other political parties; nevertheless, NSF members and supporters occupied 111 seats in the Council. The PNUC elected an Executive Bureau, with Ion Iliescu as its President. Opposition to the NSF persisted, particularly in the armed forces. The Minister of National Defence was replaced in compliance with demands from within the military, but shortly afterwards thousands of anti-Government demonstrators demanded the resignation of Iliescu, and some 250 protesters forcibly entered the NSF headquarters.

As the elections approached there were mass anti-communist demonstrations daily in central Bucharest, with protesters in University Square demanding the resignation of Iliescu and his Government. The election campaign was acrimonious, and there were widespread accusations of systematic intimidation and harassment of the NSF's opponents. At the presidential and legislative elections, held on 20 May 1990, the NSF achieved an overwhelming victory. Allegations of irregularities were, however, confirmed by international observers. According to official figures, Iliescu won 85.1% of the valid votes cast in the presidential poll. In the elections to the bicameral legislature, the NSF won 65% of the votes cast, securing 263 of the 387 seats in the Chamber of Deputies and 91 of the 119 seats in the Senate.

Unrest continued, and in mid-June 1990, after seven weeks of occupation, the protest in University Square was forcibly broken up by the police. The brutal treatment of the demonstrators provoked renewed clashes, in which the armed forces opened fire on rioters. Following an appeal for support by Iliescu, some 7,000 miners and other workers from the Jiu Valley were transported to the capital, where they swiftly seized control of the streets, attacking suspected opponents of the Government. The disturbances resulted in several deaths and hundreds of injuries, and more than 1,000 people were detained. Following President Iliescu's inauguration, in late June, Roman was reappointed Prime Minister, and a new Council of Ministers was

formed, in which nearly all the members of the interim administration were replaced.

In August 1990 there were further anti-Government demonstrations in Bucharest and Brașov. In the following months, as popular discontent at the deteriorating economic situation intensified, there was widespread strike action. In October Roman announced extensive economic reforms, including privatizations and the removal of price controls. In the following month, however, price increases led to demonstrations in Bucharest, including a protest march by some 100,000 people, organized by a new (non-parliamentary) opposition grouping, the Civic Alliance. In December workers in Timișoara, demanding the resignation of the President and the Government, began a general strike. Nevertheless, the Government proceeded with its (slightly modified) reform programme, resulting in further large price rises in April. At the end of that month Roman allocated three government portfolios to opposition politicians.

In September 1991 miners in the Jiu Valley, by this time opposed to President Iliescu, began a strike in support of demands for pay increases, a 'freeze' on prices and the resignation of the Government. Thousands of miners travelled to Bucharest, where they attacked government offices and ransacked the parliament building. Four people were killed and hundreds injured during violent clashes with the security forces, as a result of which Roman and the Council of Ministers were obliged to resign. The outgoing Prime Minister was replaced by Teodor Stolojan, a former Minister of Finance. In October Stolojan formed a coalition Government, comprising members of the NSF, the NLP, the Agrarian Democratic Party of Romania (ADPR) and the Romanian Ecological Movement.

A new Constitution, enshrining a multi-party system, a free-market economy and guarantees of the respect of human rights, was approved by the legislature in November 1991 and was endorsed by some 77.3% of voters in a referendum in December. The results of local elections, which took place between February and April 1992, confirmed the decline in support for the NSF. Many seats were won by the centre-right Democratic Convention of Romania (DCR), an alliance of 18 parties and organizations opposed to the NSF, including the Christian Democratic National Peasants' Party (CDNPP) and the Party of the Civic Alliance. Meanwhile, disputes within the NSF led to a formal rift in March 1992, following the confirmation of Roman as the party's President. The NSF divided into two factions, and in April the faction loyal to Iliescu was registered as the Democratic National Salvation Front (DNSF), a moderate left-wing party that favoured only limited reforms.

Against a background of renewed labour unrest, legislative and presidential elections took place on 27 September 1992. The DNSF won 117 of the 328 elective seats in the Chamber of Deputies and 49 of the 143 seats in the Senate, making it the largest party in the new Parliament. Its closest rival was the DCR, with 82 seats in the Chamber of Deputies and 34 in the Senate. The NSF secured only 43 and 18 seats, respectively. The DCR appealed unsuccessfully for a recount, after it was revealed that some 15% of the votes cast had been declared invalid. In the presidential election, the two leading candidates, Iliescu and Emil Constantinescu, representing the DCR, proceeded to a second round of voting on 11 October, at which Iliescu won 61.4% of the votes cast. In November, following protracted negotiations, Nicolae Văcăroiu, an economist with no professed political party affiliation, formed a Government comprising equal numbers of DNSF members and independents.

In February 1993 thousands of people protested in Bucharest against rising prices, low wages and unemployment. The abolition of price subsidies for many basic commodities and services, from the beginning of May, precipitated renewed labour unrest. A threat of strike action by public-sector employees obliged the Government to increase the minimum wage in the sector by some 75%; later in the month workers in the steel industry withdrew their labour, demanding wage increases commensurate with the level of price rises, and strikes and demonstrations spread across the country. None the less, in mid-1993 the implementation of further measures aimed at liberalizing the monetary system led to the largest price increases in Romania since 1989. The Government's position was further undermined by successive confidence motions, and two political scandals uncovered in mid-1993. In June the Government was accused of involvement in an allegedly corrupt shipping deal, and in the following month three senior government officials, including the Deputy Prime Minister and Minister of Finance, Florin Georgescu, were implicated in another corruption scandal. Meanwhile, the DNSF had changed its name to the Party of Social Democracy of Romania (PSDR) in July and absorbed three other left-wing parties. In May, in an apparently similar attempt to distance itself from the events of 1989–90, Roman's NSF had renamed itself the Democratic Party—National Salvation Front (DP—NSF).

By late 1993 Văcăroiu's administration appeared increasingly unstable. In November a protest march in Bucharest, demanding rapid economic reforms, was the largest public demonstration in the country since the overthrow of the Ceauşescu regime. The Government defeated a vote of 'no confidence' in January 1994, and in February renewed industrial unrest led to a general strike. A government reshuffle in March continued the pattern of single-party (PSDR) rule supplemented by independent 'technocrats' (although later in the year two members of the Romanian National Unity Party—RNUP—were appointed to the Council of Ministers).

In April 1995 a mass demonstration was held in Bucharest to protest against legislation linking public-sector wage rises to improvements in productivity and other indices of economic efficiency. In June a three-day strike by workers in the energy sector caused considerable disruption, which was exacerbated as mineworkers and railway employees organized support strikes. Moreover, from mid-1995 the Government was further weakened by the erosion of parliamentary support and damaging political scandals. In August the distribution of vouchers for the mass privatization scheme was instigated: all Romanian citizens aged over 18 years received vouchers, which could be exchanged for shares in approximately 4,000 state-owned enterprises. In November Iliescu approved legislation providing for the restitution of property confiscated by the communist regime in the late 1940s and 1950s.

In May 1996 the PSDR terminated its parliamentary co-operation with the RNUP, having accused the latter of conducting an aggressive campaign for the forthcoming local elections. Also in May thousands of trade unionists demonstrated in Bucharest in protest against the Government's social policies. Although the PSDR secured the largest number of mayoral and council seats at the local elections in June, the results indicated a decline in support for the party, and the DCR and the Social Democratic Union (SDU), formed by the DP—NSF and the Romanian Social Democratic Party in January, won control of many major cities, including Bucharest, where the DCR's Victor Ciorbea (a former trade unionist) achieved election. In September the RNUP ministers were dismissed from the Government: the breakdown in relations with the PSDR had been exacerbated by the RNUP's opposition to the signing of a treaty with Hungary (see below).

Legislative and presidential elections took place on 3 November 1996. The DCR won the largest number of parliamentary seats, with 122 of the 328 elective seats in the Chamber of Deputies and 53 of the 143 seats in the Senate. The PSDR took 91 and 41 seats in the respective chambers, and the SDU 53 and 23. The DCR and the SDU subsequently reached agreement on political co-operation. In the first round of the presidential election, which was contested by 16 candidates, Iliescu won 32.3% of the valid votes cast, and Constantinescu 28.2%. With the support of nearly all the opposition parties, Constantinescu was duly elected in a second round on 17 November, with 54.4% of the votes cast. Constantinescu had pledged to combat corruption and accelerate economic reform, and had asserted his commitment to the integration of Romania into Western political, economic and defence institutions. At the end of November Ciorbea was nominated as Prime Minister, and in mid-December a new coalition Government, comprising the DCR, the SDU and the Democratic Alliance of Hungarians in Romania (DAHR), was officially sworn in.

In January 1997 Romania's Alternative Party (RAP—a member of the DCR alliance), apparently dissatisfied with the positions that it had been allocated in the Government and local administration, withdrew its unconditional support for government policy. Despite protests from opposition parties, the Government restored citizenship to former King Michael, who visited Romania in February. Meanwhile, in January a National Council for Action against Corruption and Organized Crime, headed by Constantinescu, was established; a number of leading bankers were subsequently arrested, principally on charges of fraud, and several senior members of the security forces were dismissed. The arrest of Miron Cozma, the leader of the miners' demonstrations in Bucharest in June 1990 and September 1991,

prompted angry protests from miners and their trade-union leaders; Cozma was subsequently charged with undermining state authority.

In June 1997 the Government survived two votes of 'no confidence' tabled by opposition parties. Meanwhile, trade unions organized marches throughout the country to protest against rising prices and the Government's socio-economic policies. A strike in the Jiu Valley by miners demanding pay rises prompted fears that they would march on Bucharest; industrial action was discontinued at the end of the month, however, when the Government agreed to increase its pay offer. Meanwhile, in August the announcement of plans to close 17 unprofitable state-owned enterprises, which would have resulted in the loss of more than 29,000 jobs, prompted nation-wide unrest; some 20,000 workers were reported to have attended demonstrations, blocking roads and railway lines. (It was subsequently decided that a number of the enterprises proposed for closure would remain in operation.) Public discontent intensified in October. It was reported that 10,000 trade-union members participated in a march in Bucharest, to protest against increasing poverty, and later that month an anti-Government demonstration was attended by some 5,000 people. An estimated 40,000 people attended a further rally in Bucharest in November, to protest against declining living standards.

Meanwhile, several prominent members of the PSDR resigned from the party in June 1997, and formed a new centre-left party, the Alliance for Romania (AFR), which claimed, by August, to hold 13 seats in the Chamber of Deputies, and two in the Senate. A government reshuffle in December, which included the appointment of a number of technocrats to key portfolios, failed to ease mounting tensions within the coalition, and the DAHR temporarily suspended its participation in the Government in protest at the rejection of amendments to legislation on education, in favour of ethnic minorities, by DCR senators.

Adrian Severin, Minister of State and Minister of Foreign Affairs, and a member of the DP (formerly DP—NSF), resigned in December 1997, after a judicial investigation failed to confirm his allegations that certain political leaders and newspaper editors were working with foreign intelligence services. In January 1998 the resignation of the Minister of Transport, Trăian Băsescu of the DP, owing to his criticism of Ciorbea's Government, led the DP to demand his reinstatement. The CDNPP's rejection of demands by the DP for Ciorbea's resignation eventually resulted in the withdrawal of DP ministers from the Government. However, the DP agreed to remain in the coalition, and to give parliamentary support to a minority DCR-DAHR Government, provided that the economic reform programme was accelerated. A new coalition agreement was signed in February, and a Council of Ministers was subsequently formed. Social unrest continued to mount, however, and widely supported anti-Government rallies took place in Bucharest and Braşov.

At the end of March 1998, in response to increasing pressure within the coalition, Ciorbea and his Government resigned. Radu Vasile, the Secretary-General of the CDNPP and a Vice-President of the Senate, was designated Prime Minister in April, with the approval of all the coalition parties, including the DP. A new Council of Ministers was appointed, which, together with its programme for accelerated market reform, was endorsed by the Chamber of Deputies and the Senate in mid-April. A new coalition protocol was designed to strengthen the authority of the Prime Minister and improve co-operation between government members. In June the Senate's approval of legislation that debarred former secret police agents from holding public office led to the resignation of the Minister of Health, Francis Baranyi.

As Romania's economic situation worsened and reforms appeared to have stalled, the Minister of Finance, Daniel Dăianu, was dismissed from the Government in September; he was replaced by Decebal Trăian Remes. Dăianu's departure was followed, in October, by the resignation of Sorin Dimitriu as Minister of Privatization and head of the State Ownership Fund. Shortly afterwards the RAP withdrew from the governing coalition and from the DCR, apparently in protest at the slow pace of reform. Meanwhile, in early September the DAHR threatened to leave the ruling coalition unless Parliament adopted controversial legislation providing for the establishment of a minority-language university. At the end of the month the Government duly agreed to create an independent university in Cluj for Hungarian and German minorities, despite considerable opposition. In December proposals for government restructuring were approved, and the number of ministries was reduced to 17.

Protests against austerity measures, which had begun the previous month, intensified in December 1998, following inconclusive talks between the Prime Minister and trade-union leaders. In January 1999 a strike by miners in the Jiu Valley, in support of demands that included increased pay and the reversal of a government decision to close two mines, escalated when Vasile refused to go to the Jiu Valley, or to negotiate with the miners' leader, Miron Cozma, who had been released from prison in July 1998, after serving an 18-month sentence for the possession of firearms and ammunition. In defiance of the Government's declaration that the strike was illegal and encouraged by nationalist politicians (notably from the Greater Romania Party—GRP), 10,000–20,000 miners marched towards Bucharest. On the fourth day of the march, in Costeşti, some 190 km north-west of Bucharest, violent clashes broke out between the security forces and the miners, who reportedly received support from local residents. Following emergency talks between the Prime Minister and miners' leaders, the march ended on the following day, and a temporary agreement was reached. The Minister of the Interior, Gavril Dejeu, was obliged to resign amid severe criticism of the security forces' failure to halt the march; he was replaced by Constantin Dudu Ionescu. In February the Supreme Court of Justice sentenced Cozma, *in absentia*, to 18 years' imprisonment for undermining state authority, and a warrant was issued for his arrest. In response, some 2,000–4,000 miners, led by Cozma, again decided to travel to Bucharest, accusing the Government of failing to honour the agreement made in January and protesting against Cozma's sentence. The miners were stopped by the security forces at Stoneşti, some 160 km west of Bucharest, where more than 100 people were injured and one miner died during the violence that ensued; Cozma and several hundred miners were arrested.

Public discontent with declining standards of living was evident in March 1999, when the rate of unemployment was reported to have reached its highest level since 1990. Some 6,000 people participated in a protest rally organized in Braşov, while four major trade unions planned a series of strikes and demonstrations against the Government's economic policies. Labour unrest intensified in June, and in Braşov some 11,000 engineering workers demonstrated in protest at unpaid wages and the threat of factory closures; the protests were suspended after a visit to the town by a delegation of government ministers who promised to provide loans for the restructuring of two plants.

In May 1999 Pope John Paul II spent three days in Romania, marking the first visit by the head of the Roman Catholic Church to a principally Orthodox country. In early June the Chamber of Deputies approved amendments to the electoral law, increasing the threshold for parliamentary representation from 3% to 5%, with alliances required to secure a further 3% for each member party. Later that month the Chamber voted in favour of providing public access to the files of the Securitate (although many documents were already believed to have been destroyed); the President promulgated the legislation in December. Also in June amendments to the law on education, in favour of ethnic minorities, were finally approved by the legislature, providing for the possibility of minority-language education at every level of the education system.

In July 1999 Gen. Victor Stănculescu and Gen. Mihai Chiţac were sentenced to 15 years' imprisonment by the Supreme Court, which found them guilty of the murders of 72 people, through having ordered the security forces to open fire on protesters during the Timişoara uprising in December 1989. The ruling was severely criticized by a number of senior politicians from both ruling and opposition parties, including Victor Babiuc, the Minister of National Defence, whose ministry, together with Stănculescu and Chiţac, was ordered to pay damages to those wounded in the shootings and the relatives of the dead.

In late 1999 public discontent increased, as the average monthly salary continued to decline, while consumer prices rose. Romania's economic difficulties and tensions within the ruling coalition appeared to have led to increased support for the PSDR. In November students undertook strike action and some 10,000 trade union members participated in protest rallies in Bucharest and Iaşi to demand the resignation of the Government. In mid-December, as labour unrest continued, Constantinescu dismissed Vasile and appointed Alexandru Athanasiu, the Minister of Labour and Social Protection, as interim Prime Minister, after all seven CDNPP government ministers, fol-

lowed by the three NLP ministers, resigned from the Government and withdrew their support for Vasile. Vasile initially refused to accept his dismissal, but finally resigned four days later; Constantinescu nominated Mugur Isărescu, hitherto Governor of the National Bank of Romania (and without affiliation to any political party), as Prime Minister. The legislature subsequently approved the appointment of Isărescu and his Council of Ministers, which remained largely unchanged, although Petre Roman joined the new Government as Minister of State and Minister of Foreign Affairs, and Mircea Ciumara was named Minister of State and President of a new Economic-Financial Co-ordination Council. Vasile was expelled from the CDNPP later that month, and in February formed a new far-right party, the Romanian People's Party, with 11 defectors from the CDNPP.

In February 2000 the parliamentary constituent parties of the DCR (the CDNPP, the NLP, the Romanian Ecological Party and the Romanian Ecological Federation—REF), signed a protocol on co-operation in legislative elections due later that year. However, the NLP and the REF were to contest local elections (which were to be held in June) separately from the DCR. Meanwhile, the PSDR formed an electoral alliance with the Humanist Party of Romania. Tension between the ruling parties, particularly the DP and the NLP, prompted fears that the former might withdraw from the coalition in mid-March. However, the DP finally signed a coalition accord, already agreed by the other ruling parties, in which it promised to honour the Government's programme and agreed priorities for the current parliamentary session. Sorin Frunzaverde of the DP was appointed to replace Victor Babiuc, who had resigned from both the party and the Government, as Minister of National Defence.

In the local elections, held on 4 June 2000, the PSDR won the majority of votes cast (36.7%), followed by the DP, with 12.7%. Anca Boangiiu replaced Trăian Băsescu as Minister of Transport in June, following Băsescu's election as Mayor of Bucharest. In July President Constantinescu unexpectedly announced that he would not stand for re-election. In August the Minister of Finance, Decebal Trăian Remes of the NLP, submitted his resignation, in protest at the party's apparent intention to form a left-wing alliance to contest the forthcoming legislative elections; his resignation was, however, rejected by Isărescu. In August Remes, who supported Isărescu's presidential candidacy, resigned from the NLP, when the party nominated former Prime Minister Teodor Stolojan as its presidential candidate. Isărescu, who was to stand as an independent candidate, in order to preserve his non-partisan status in governing the ruling coalition until the elections took place, prompted disaffection from NLP members of the governing coalition by retaining Remes as Minister of Finance, despite his expulsion from the party. Meanwhile, a number of alliances were formed in the weeks preceding the elections. In early August the RNUP and the PNR merged to form the National Alliance and, later that month, after prolonged negotiations, five parties, including the CDNPP and the Union of Right-Wing Forces, established an alliance known as the Democratic Convention of Romania 2000 (DCR). In early September the RSDP withdrew from the governing coalition, announcing that it was to merge with the main opposition party, the PSDR, in order to form a new Social Democratic Party (SDP—the two parties were to contest the general election on common lists, and merge subsequently).

Legislative and presidential elections took place, as scheduled, on 26 November 2000. The PSDR secured 155 seats in the Chamber of Deputies and 65 in the Senate, while the GRP obtained 84 and 37 seats, respectively. The rate of voter participation was the lowest recorded since the collapse of communism, at 57.5%. Representatives of the PSDR and the GRP were also the principal candidates in the presidential election, in which the former President, Ion Iliescu, obtained 36.4% of the votes cast and Corneliu Vadim Tudor of the GRM achieved 28.3%. As neither candidate secured an overall majority, a 'run-off' election was held on 10 December, in which Iliescu won 66.8% of the votes cast. Iliescu immediately rejected the possibility of forming a coalition government with the GRP. The election results represented a rejection of the incumbent socialist Government, which was perceived as having been fraught with political infighting; the increased support for the right wing was thought to reflect popular disillusionment with escalating economic hardship and unemployment levels.

Emil Constantinescu formally handed over the presidency on 21 December 2000. On 27 December the Prime Minister-designate, Adrian Năstase of the PSDR, signed a joint statement on priorities for the development of Romania, with the leaders of the DAHR, the NLP and the DP. Although Năstase insisted that the declaration did not represent a coalition agreement, the support of those parties enabled the PSDR to form a minority government, and ensured the isolation of the GRP. The new, expanded cabinet was sworn in the following day. Despite their shared objective of implementing reform with a view to attaining membership of the European Union (EU, see p. 199), the new President and Prime Minister came from different ideological backgrounds, and Iliescu pledged to reverse any 'improper' privatizations.

In mid-January 2001 the Chamber of Deputies approved a law, which aimed to return some 300,000 properties nationalized during the communist era to their original owners, with the exception of public buildings, including hospitals and schools. President Iliescu endorsed the law in early February, after the Constitutional Court rejected a challenge by 78 members of the Chamber of Deputies; the law was to supersede the law on the restitution of property that had been approved in 1995. (In August 2001 former King Michael began legal measures to recover property confiscated by the communist authorities.)

In late February 2001 the Supreme Court convicted two military officers of manslaughter for their roles in the deaths of dozens of people at Bucharest airport during the revolution of December 1989. In early March 2001 the Chamber of Deputies passed a new secrecy law, in preparation for eventual NATO membership, which made individual citizens responsible for the security of state secrets. However, critics of the law, including human rights organizations, stated that the legislation granted excessive powers to the country's intelligence agencies. In June a five-month labour strike in western Romania ended with a mass protest against the planned privatization of the Reşiţa steel factory. Some 1,500 protestors took part in anti-Government demonstrations, and the deal was cancelled later that month.

Meanwhile, the outcome of the general election led to political restructuring and the appointment of new leaders to several parties, including the CDNPP, the senior party in the 1996–2000 coalition, which had failed to win any seats in Parliament. Victor Ciorbea became Chairman of the CDNPP in early July 2001, following the resignation of Andrei Marga (who had assumed the position in January). In May Petre Roman was replaced as leader of the DP by Trăian Băsescu, the Mayor of Bucharest. In mid-June the PSDR and the RSDP merged, as planned, to form the SDP, under the leadership of Prime Minister Năstase. In late September the Socialist Party of National Revival, which had been formed as a breakaway faction of the GRP, held its inaugural conference, and elected Ioan Radu, the Deputy Mayor of Bucharest, as its Chairman. In late October an anti-Ciorbea faction of the CDNPP formed a new party, the Popular Christian Party, under the leadership of Andrei Marga, Vasile Lupu, and Calin Catalin Chirita. In November the NLP and the AFR agreed to merge under the name of the former party, a process that was finalized in late January 2002.

Continuing popular dissatisfaction with the Government's programme of reform resulted in a 15,000-strong demonstration against poverty and government austerity in Bucharest in late November 2001. In early December some 10,000 workers from major factories in Braşov participated in a further protest, against declining living standards and job insecurity. In late December the Chamber of Deputies rejected a motion of 'no confidence' in the Government proposed by three opposition parties.

Attempts to tackle corruption led the Government to announce, in March 2002, the establishment of a new National Anti-corruption Prosecution office, which was to act as an autonomous body within the Ministry of Justice from the beginning of September. Also in March the Government sought to moderate the power of labour organizations through the signature of a 'social pact' with three of the five largest trade unions, which provided for an increased minimum wage, and the creation of 10,000 jobs. In a separate development, the Supreme Court sentenced Tudor Postelnicu, a former chief of the Securitate, and Gheorghe Homostean, a former Minister of the Interior, to 14 years' imprisonment for their role in the deaths of a group of escaped prisoners in 1981; the case formed part of an ongoing investigation of crimes committed during the communist era.

In August 2002 former Prime Minister Theodor Stolojan was elected as the new Chairman of the NLP. In the following month the Senate approved a new law on political parties, which required all parties to re-register by 31 December, and to be composed of a minimum of 10,000 members from at least 21 of Romania's 41 administrative regions. On 10 November local elections took place in 21 regions, in which the SDP was the most successful party. In early 2003 a number of prominent CDNPP members were expelled from the party after participating in the foundation of the new Popular Action civic movement, led by former President Constantinescu; in February it was confirmed that the movement was to become a political party. Meanwhile, in the same month the SDP and the DAHR renewed a co-operation agreement, originally signed in January 2002, according to which the latter party agreed not to give its support to confidence motions brought against the Government, and the SDP pledged to implement measures to improve the rights of ethnic Hungarians. In late March 2003 the Government survived a vote of 'no confidence' brought by opposition parties, which regarded its anti-corruption proposals as insufficiently effective. In April the NLP absorbed the extra-parliamentary Union of Right-Wing Forces.

Romania experienced frequent occurrences of ethnic unrest after the fall of Ceauşescu. In 1991 there were organized attacks on Roma (Gypsy) communities throughout Romania, resulting in the emigration of many Roma to Germany. In September 1992 Germany repatriated 43,000 Romanian refugees, more than one-half of whom were Roma, having agreed to provide financial assistance for their resettlement in Romania. Repatriations continued in 1993–94, during which time the incidence of physical attacks against Roma in Romania was reported to have increased. The migration of Roma to the member countries of the EU strained relations with Romania throughout the remainder of the 1990s. In May 2001 the GRP unexpectedly proposed new legislation to improve the rights and integration of the Roma population. However, in October the Mayor of the northern town of Piatra Neamt, Ion Rotaru, caused public outrage by suggesting that the local Roma population be moved to a special compound under the surveillance of the security forces, a proposal that was denounced by the Government. In January 2002 the Council of Europe (see p. 181) published a report condemning police brutality and widespread discrimination against Roma communities in Romania.

Following the overthrow of Ceauşescu, ethnic Hungarians (a sizeable minority, numbering more than 7% of the total population at the 1992 census) attempted to increase their cultural and linguistic autonomy in Transylvania. In March 1990 demonstrations by ethnic Hungarians demanding such rights were attacked by Romanian nationalists in Târgu Mureş. Tanks and troops were deployed to quell the unrest, in which several people were killed, and a state of emergency was declared in the town. In mid-1992 there was renewed tension when the Mayor of Cluj-Napoca, Gheorghe Funar (later head of the right-wing RNUP), ordered the removal of Hungarian-language street signs in the city, and ethnic Hungarian prefects in Covasna and Harghita were replaced by ethnic Romanians. The Government attempted to calm the situation by appointing 'parallel' prefects of ethnic Hungarian background, but further controversy was caused by the removal, in September, of the only ethnic Hungarian State Secretary in the Government. In June 1993 talks between government representatives and leaders of the ethnic Hungarian community led to an agreement, signed in July, on Hungarian minority rights, which included guarantees of the training of Hungarian-speaking schoolteachers and bilingual street signs in areas with Hungarian populations of at least 30%. In June 1994 the Hungarian Prime Minister-designate, Gyula Horn, appealed for an 'historic reconciliation' with Romania. In August Béla Markó, the President of the DAHR, insisted that any Hungarian-Romanian state treaty should enshrine a 'special status' for ethnic Hungarians in Romania. Markó's proposals included the equal status of the Hungarian and Romanian languages in predominantly Hungarian-populated areas and greater control for the minority over educational and cultural affairs. The DAHR became increasingly isolated from the other opposition parties, and in June the DCR rejected the DAHR's application to join its ranks. In May Romania ratified the Framework Convention of the Council of Europe on the general protection of national minorities. During July–September, none the less, there were sustained protests by ethnic Hungarians in Romania against the promulgation of an education bill that specified Romanian as the sole language of tuition and examination in all universities and colleges (with the exception of a small number of subjects), thus effectively denying the right of ethnic minorities to pursue higher education in their native language. In late September the Romanian

Government presented three draft documents to its Hungarian counterpart concerning Romanian-Hungarian reconciliation, a bilateral co-operation agreement and a code of behaviour with regard to ethnic minorities. In September 1996, despite right-wing opposition, the two countries signed a treaty of friendship, whereby Romania agreed to safeguard the rights of ethnic Hungarians and Hungary relinquished any claim to territory in Transylvania. In December two DAHR leaders were appointed to the new Government. Relations between Romania and Hungary improved further in February 1997 with an agreement on the establishment of a joint peace-keeping battalion, and on the protection of classified military information. The agreement on the peace-keeping battalion was fully ratified by Hungary in September 1998, and by Romania in March 1999, and the battalion conducted its first exercise in November in Arad, western Romania. However, proposals to amend legislation on education, in favour of ethnic minorities, provoked controversy in Romania in 1997 and 1998; the amendments were finally approved in June 1999. Meanwhile, in February 2000 Romania and Hungary established a joint commission of experts to examine issues surrounding a major spill of cyanide from a gold smelter in Baia Mare, north-western Romania, which had killed thousands of fish and other wildlife in Hungarian rivers and in the Danube; the smelter, which was partly owned by the Romanian government, subsequently accepted responsibility for the incident, and compensation was to be awarded.

In January 2001 the Chamber of Deputies approved a new public administration law, which made compulsory bilingual place names and signs, and the use of a given minority's language in local administration, in towns where that minority formed at least 20% of the population; the law was denounced by the GRP. In June the Government condemned Hungary's intention to introduce a new 'Status Law', which was to grant education, employment and medical rights to ethnic Hungarians living in neighbouring countries (including Romania) from January 2002. The Romanian Government feared that Hungary was seeking to increase its influence in Romania and other countries with large Hungarian communities, thereby bypassing the Treaty of Trianon of 1920, which had awarded large parts of Hungary to its neighbours. In late December 2001 the Prime Ministers of the two countries signed a memorandum of understanding, which extended the short-term employment rights offered to ethnic Hungarians under the terms of the Law to all Romanian citizens. However, some Hungarian politicians feared that the agreement would encourage Romanian Roma to claim Hungarian origin. In October 2002 Hungarian President Ferenc Mádl visited Romania, in the first official visit from a Hungarian head of state.

Diplomatic relations with the former Soviet republic of Moldova (where a majority of the population are ethnic Romanians and much of which formed part of Romania until 1940) were established in August 1991, and some political groups began advocating the unification of the two states. The Romanian leadership opposed unification, but encouraged the development of closer cultural and economic ties with Moldova. The support of the Russian military in Moldova for the secessionist movement in the self-proclaimed 'Transdnestrian Moldovan Soviet Socialist Republic' damaged relations between Romania and Russia. In March 1994 a plebiscite was held in Moldova on the question of reunification with Romania; more than 95% of those who took part in the referendum voted for an independent state, effectively signalling the demise of the pro-unification movement. In 2000, as formal negotiations on Romania's accession to the EU commenced, hundreds of Moldovans applied for Romanian citizenship, in anticipation of the eventual tightening of border regulations. Relations with Moldova deteriorated in late 2001 and early 2002. In October 2001 Năstase cancelled a planned visit to Moldova, after President Voronin of Moldova accused Romania of 'expansionism'. The communist-dominated Government elected in Moldova in that year also accused Romania of interfering in Moldova's internal affairs by supporting protests against the perceived 'russification' of that country in early 2002; in February the Russian State Duma also adopted a resolution condemning Romanian involvement in Moldova's domestic concerns. Romania, for its part, denied the accusations, and warned that Moldova was threatening the stability of the region. A Romanian diplomat was expelled from Moldova in March, and Romania responded by expelling a Moldovan attaché. Relations had improved by 2003, following a meeting between the respective Presidents at a conference in Beirut, Lebanon, in September 2002, and inter-ministerial co-

operation was restored in April 2003, when the updating of the Basic Political Treaty between the two countries and the initiation of negotiations regarding a border agreement were discussed. In March Romania followed the EU and the USA in implementing a travel ban on senior officials in the separatist Transnistria region of Moldova, who were regarded as obstructing negotiations towards a peaceful resolution to the dispute.

A basic treaty between Romania and Ukraine, signed in early June 1997, guaranteed the inviolability of their joint border, and provided for separate treaties to be established regarding the administration of the frontier and the disputed ownership of the Black Sea continental shelf. In January 2002 Anatoliy Kinakh became the first Ukrainian Prime Minister officially to visit Romania, where talks on economic co-operation and border delimitation took place.

President Ceaușescu's resistance to reform left Romania internationally isolated and, even after his overthrow in 1989, Romania's relations with other countries only slowly improved. President François Mitterrand of France visited Romania in April 1991, and in April 1992 Romania and Germany signed a treaty of friendship and co-operation. Relations with other Western European countries took longer to develop, but an association agreement with the European Community (now EU) was signed in February 1993; in June 1995 Romania formally applied for full membership of the EU. Romania applied for membership of the Council of Europe in May 1993, but was initially rejected, owing to its poor record on civil liberties. In October, however, Romania was admitted to the Council of Europe; Hungary abstained from voting. In July 1997 the European Commission recommended that negotiations on Romania's accession to the EU should be deferred. Despite Romania's efforts to have the Commission's proposal overruled, it was endorsed in December of that year at a meeting of EU ministers of foreign affairs in Luxembourg, where it was agreed that further economic reform was necessary. In December 1999 Romania was one of six countries invited to begin negotiations on possible entry to the EU. Formal accession talks commenced in February 2000. In December the EU decided to impose conditions on Romania before granting its citizens the right to visa-free travel in Europe, partly in response to Romania's failure to combat illegal immigration. In May 2001 an EU parliamentary commission warned that it would recommend the suspension of Romania's negotiations with the EU if the former did not resolve its long-standing problem of child abandonment. In November France proposed that Romania be included in the next phase of EU expansion in 2004; however, although Romania hoped to join the EU in 2007, many observers did not expect it to accede until 2010. In December 2001 the EU announced that Romania was to receive some €286.7m. in 2002, in support of its entry preparations. On 1 January 2002 the EU abolished visa requirements for Romanians.

Attempts by the Romanian authorities to enforce the UN embargo on Yugoslavia (Serbia and Montenegro), by preventing the passage of vessels to or from that country via the Danube, encountered fierce opposition from the Yugoslav authorities, including threats of petroleum spillages if tankers were not permitted to pass. In January 1993 Yugoslavia impounded 22 Romanian ships in retaliation for the detention of 40 Yugoslav vessels by Romania, and in February 12 Yugoslav tugboats blockaded the Danube. Romania reiterated its commitment to upholding the UN embargo in February 1993, but proceeded to sign a treaty with Yugoslavia on bilateral political relations in April 1994. A further treaty of friendship was signed in May 1996. In 1998 the Romanian Government expressed its support for international efforts to find a diplomatic solution to hostilities between the Serbian authorities and ethnic Albanian separatists in the Yugoslav province of Kosovo, and in October the legislature approved Romania's participation in the Kosovo Verification Mission of the Organization for Security and Co-operation in Europe (OSCE, see p. 283). In March 1999, however, following the failure of peace negotiations, NATO launched a campaign of airstrikes against Serb military and strategic targets; in April Romania approved a NATO request for unrestricted access to its airspace, but was not to become militarily involved in the conflict. Meanwhile, economic losses resulting from the conflict were heavy, amounting to some US $900m. by the end of 1999, according to government officials. In early September 1999 Romanian shippers blockaded the river Danube for three days in protest at the losses they had suffered because of blockages resulting from the destruction of bridges during the NATO airstrikes (which had been suspended in June) and an ongoing EU oil embargo against Yugoslavia. With the support of the Minister of Transport, Trăian Băsescu, ship-owners demanded that Yugoslavia allow Romanian ships to use an alternative channel, bypassing the blockages, to which Bulgaria, Russia and Ukraine had already apparently been granted access. Băsescu subsequently announced that Yugoslav vessels were to be forbidden to navigate on Romania's Danube–Black Sea Canal. In October, however, the Romanian authorities permitted 12 Yugoslav barges that had been held for one month in the port of Constanța to enter the canal, and several days later Romanian cargo ships were allowed to enter Yugoslav territorial waters for the first time since the Kosovo conflict. In February 2000 the President of Romania hosted a summit meeting of the South-East European Co-operation Process, which was also attended by the heads of state or government of Albania, Bulgaria, Greece, the former Yugoslav republic of Macedonia and Turkey. The participants signed a charter on good neighbourly relations, stability, security and co-operation in South-Eastern Europe. In June 2000 Bulgaria and Romania reached agreement on the construction of a new bridge across the Danube, which was to be one of the first projects to receive funding from an EU-led Stability Pact for reconstruction in the region that had been created in June 1999; relations with Bulgaria were further strengthened in August 2001 by an agreement by the two countries to campaign jointly for member-ship of both the EU and NATO. In late November 2001 the Danube Commission declared the river safe for navigation for the first time since the NATO airstrikes. Meanwhile, a Romanian consortium was strongly urging the construction of a US $1,500m. petroleum pipeline from Constanța to Trieste, Italy, via Hungary and Slovenia, which would enable Romania to become a transit point for the delivery of Caspian Sea oil to the countries of the EU.

In June 1992 Romania, together with 10 other countries (including six of the former Soviet republics), established the Organization of the Black Sea Economic Co-operation (see p. 293), which aimed to encourage regional trade and co-oper- ation in developing transport and infrastructure. In December Romania signed a free trade accord with the European Free Trade Association (see p. 195). In May 1994 Romania was granted associate partnership status of Western European Union (see p. 318).

In early 1997 Romania appealed directly to NATO member countries to support its candidacy for admittance to that Organization; in July, however, Romania was not among those countries invited to commence accession negotiations and in April 1999, at a summit meeting held in Washington, DC, the USA, NATO failed to specify a date for the country's anticipated accession. Following the large-scale suicide attacks against the USA on 11 September 2001, attributed by the USA to the Saudi-born Islamist fundamentalist, Osama bin Laden (see US chapter), Romania immediately pledged full co-operation with US efforts to assemble a coalition of allied countries to combat global terrorism, and opened its airspace to US military flights to and from Afghanistan, the Taliban regime of which was harbouring militants of bin Laden's al-Qa'ida (Base) organization. As the strategic importance of the Black Sea increased, Romania also made available basing facilities in the port city of Constanța, and offered the USA the use of its airbases. None the less, concerns remained about the presence in the Romanian intelligence services of former members of the communist-era Securitate, and there were doubts about Romania's economic preparedness for NATO membership. However, the intelligence services were restructured in January 2002, and Romania secured an invitation to join NATO at a summit meeting held in Prague, the Czech Republic, in November, after which US President George W. Bush paid a visit to the country; protocols of accession were signed in early 2003. Romania was forthright in its support for US-led military action in Iraq in early 2003 (despite some criticism from within the EU, notably France), opening its airspace and offering other resources to the coalition, particularly following Turkey's refusal to allow US troops the use of its territory.

Government

Under the 1991 Constitution (drafted to replace that of 1965), legislative power is vested in the bicameral, 486-seat Parliament, comprising the Chamber of Deputies (lower house) and the Senate (upper house). Parliament is elected by universal adult suffrage on the basis of proportional representation for a term of four years. Executive power is vested in the President of the Republic, who may serve a maximum of two four-year terms and who is directly elected by universal adult suffrage. The President appoints the Prime Minister, who in turn appoints the Council of Ministers.

For administrative purposes, Romania comprises 40 administrative divisions (counties) and the municipality of Bucharest.

Defence

In January 1994 Romania became the first former Warsaw Pact state to join NATO's 'Partnership for Peace' programme (see p. 273). In August 1995 Romanian peace-keeping troops were dispatched to Angola as the first Romanian forces to participate in an international UN military operation.

Military service is compulsory; in 2003 the term of service was reduced from 12 to eight months. At 1 August 2002 active forces totalled 99,200 (including an estimated 35,000 conscripts and 10,000 in centrally controlled units), of whom: army 66,000 (including 21,000 conscripts), navy 6,200 and air force 17,000. There were also 22,900 border guards and a gendarmerie of 57,000 (which are under the control of the Ministry of the Interior). The Government increased expenditure on defence in 2001, in anticipation of achieving membership of NATO; the state budget allocated some 28,400,000m. lei to defence in that year.

Economic Affairs

In 2001, according to the World Bank, Romania's gross national income (GNI), measured at average 1999–2001 prices, totalled US $38,388m., equivalent to $1,710 per head (or $6,980 on an international purchasing-power parity basis). During 1990–2001, it was estimated, the population decreased at an average annual rate of 0.3%, while gross domestic product (GDP) per head declined, in real terms, at an average annual rate of 0.7%. Overall GDP, decreased, in real terms, by an average of 1.1% annually during 1990–2001. However, real GDP increased by 1.8% in 2000 and by 5.3% in 2001.

In 2001 agriculture (including hunting, fishing and forestry) contributed 12.4% of GDP, and employed 42.3% of the employed labour force. The principal crops are maize, wheat, potatoes, sugar beet, barley, apples and grapes. Wine production plays a significant role in Romanian agriculture. Forestry, the cropping of reeds (used as a raw material in the paper and cellulose industry) and the breeding of fish are also significant activities. Under the Government's decollectivization programme, 46% of agricultural land had been returned to its original owners and their heirs by early 1994. By 1999, according to the IMF, some 97.2% of agricultural land was privately owned. During 1990–2001, according to the World Bank, agricultural GDP declined, in real terms, by an average of 2.2% per year. Real agricultural GDP declined by 15.9% in 2000, but increased by 3.0% in 2001.

In 2001 industry (including mining, manufacturing, construction, power and water) accounted for 37.1% of GDP, and employed 26.2% of the working population. According to the World Bank, industrial GDP declined, in real terms, by an average of 1.1% annually in 1990–2001. Real industrial GDP increased by 6.2% in 2000 and by 7.0% in 2001.

The mining sector employed 1.4% of the employed labour force in 2001. As part of a major restructuring of the sector, some 83,000 miners were made redundant in 1999, and in 1997–98 operations were halted in 180 mines and quarries. In 1999 the World Bank granted a loan worth US $44.5m. to assist the Government in meeting the costs involved in the closure of a further 29 mines. Brown coal, hard coal, salt, iron ore, bauxite, copper, lead and zinc are mined. Onshore production of crude petroleum began to increase in the early 1990s and in 2002 Romania had proven reserves of 955m. barrels of petroleum, remaining the largest producer in Central and Eastern Europe, despite a dramatic decline in production. At the beginning of the 1990s seven offshore platforms were operating in the Romanian sector of the Black Sea, accounting for more than 10% of annual hydrocarbon production. Methane gas is also extracted. In April 1996 Romania launched an international invitation to tender for exploration and production rights on 15 new blocks in the Black Sea. Mining output decreased by 9.6% in 1999, but increased by 7.3% in 2000.

Manufacturing employed 18.9% of the employed labour force in 2001 and accounted for some 27.8% of GDP. The sector is based mainly on the metallurgical, mechanical engineering, chemical and timber-processing industries. However, many industries (particularly iron and steel) have been hampered by shortages of electricity and raw materials. According to the World Bank, manufacturing GDP increased, in real terms, by an average of 0.1% annually in 1994–2001. Real sectoral GDP increased by some 6.2% in 2000, and by 8.0% in 2001.

Energy is derived mainly from petroleum, natural gas and coal. A number of hydroelectric power stations are also in operation. In 2000 hydroelectric power accounted for 28.6% of domestic electricity production. According to the World Bank, in 1999 29.4% of gross electricity production was derived from coal, and 16.6% was derived from natural gas. The initial unit of Romania's first nuclear power station, at Cernavoda, became operational in December 1996. By 2000 it was estimated that Cernavoda's output represented some 10% of Romania's total energy production; the second unit was scheduled for completion in 2005. According to provisional data, 32.5% of energy resources were imported in 2000. In 2000 fuel imports represented 12.1% of total imports.

In 2001 the services sector contributed 50.6% of GDP, and engaged 31.5% of the working labour force. According to the World Bank, the GDP of the services sector declined, in real terms, by an average of 1.5% per year in 1990–2001; the real GDP of the sector increased by 6.7% in 2000, but declined by 5.7% in 2001.

In 2001 Romania recorded a visible trade deficit of US $2,969m., while there was a deficit of $2,317m. on the current account of the balance of payments. In 2000 the principal source of imports was Italy, which provided 18.7% of the total. Germany was also a major supplier, as were Russia and France. The main market for exports in that year was Italy (accounting for 22.4%); other important purchasers were Germany, France and Turkey. In 1999 the principal imports were machinery and transport equipment, basic manufactures (particularly textile yarn and fabrics), mineral fuels and chemical products. Textiles (notably clothing and accessories), base metals, machinery and transport equipment, and mineral products were among the country's major exports.

Romania's overall budget deficit for 2001 was estimated at 35,818m. lei. Romania's total external debt at the end of 2000 was US $10,224m., of which $6,430m. was long-term public debt. In that year the cost of debt-servicing was equivalent to 18.1% of revenue from exports of goods and services. The annual rate of inflation averaged 78.0% in 1992–2001; the rate of inflation was 34.5% in 2001 and 22.5% in 2002. In December 2001 8.6% of the civilian labour force were registered as unemployed.

Romania is a member (as a 'Country of Operations') of the European Bank for Reconstruction and Development (EBRD, see p. 193). In February 1993 Romania signed an association agreement with the European Union (EU, see p. 199), and a free-trade agreement with the European Free Trade Association (EFTA, see p. 195) came into effect in May 1993. In June 1995 Romania formally applied for full membership of the EU; accession negotiations commenced in February 2000. In July 1997 Romania joined the Central European Free Trade Association.

During the 1990s Romania's progress towards the development of a market economic system was considerably slower than that of many other post-communist states of Central and Eastern Europe. The economy contracted for a third consecutive year in 1999, and the Yugoslav conflict adversely affected the financial situation, severely disrupting regional trade and transport infrastructure. Further difficulties arose in 2000, in the form of increased petroleum prices and the worst drought for 50 years, which severely affected agricultural production. In an attempt to stimulate the private business sector, the new Government restored tax concessions and tariff exemptions to small and medium-sized businesses at the beginning of 2001. An extensive programme, also announced in 2001, for the privatization of 63 large state-owned enterprises, encountered strong opposition, although in October the Government succeeded in divesting the Sidex steel works at Galaţi, in what was Romania's most significant privatization to date. Overall, by 2001 Romania's economic prospects were regarded as more positive, and in late October 2001 the IMF, which had been withholding further assistance pending substantive progress on reform, approved a stand-by credit of some US $383m. None the less, many observers considered membership of the EU by 2007 to be a challenging objective. In March 2003 the National Bank replaced the US dollar with the euro as its reference currency for the exchange rate of the leu. In April the IMF assessed Romania's macroeconomic performance, despite further suspensions of lending in 2002, to have been favourable, with strong growth, declining inflation and an improved external current-account balance. In 2003 Romania aimed to focus its efforts on achieving the status of a functioning market economy in the assessment of the EU and the IMF; it was granted such status by the USA in March. Other efforts were to be focused on increased privatization and the introduction of further structural reforms. Some concern was expressed over the financial implications of the large increase in the minimum-wage level, introduced in early 2003, although this measure was expected to lead to increased domestic consumption, which would be a primary factor in stimulating economic growth, owing to the general downturn in the world economy. Economic growth for 2003 was forecast at 4.9% and it was predicted that inflation would rise by up to 16% in that year.

Education

Children under the age of six years may attend crèches (creşe), and kindergartens (grădiniţe de copii). In 1999/2000 65.2% of pre-school age children were attending kindergarten. Between the ages of six and 16 years children are obliged to attend the general education school (şcoală de cultură generală de zece ani). The general secondary school (liceul), for which there is an entrance examination, provides a specialized education suitable for entering college or university. There are also specialized secondary schools, where the emphasis is on industrial, agricultural and teacher training, and art schools, which correspond to secondary schools, but cover several years of general education. Vocational secondary schools (şcoli profesionale de ucenici) train pupils for a particular career. Tuition in minority languages, particularly Hungarian and German, is available. In 1998 primary enrolment included 95.7% of children in the relevant age-group, while the comparable ratio for secondary education in 1996 was 73% (males 72%; females 74%). In 2000/2001 the total enrolment in secondary education was 687,919. There are 49 public higher education establishments in Romania, 38 of which are universities; enrolment in tertiary education was equivalent to 28.0% in 1999/2000. Expenditure on education by the state budget in 2000 amounted to 20,173.4m. lei (representing 19.0% of total expenditure).

Public Holidays

2003: 1–2 January (New Year), 6 January (Epiphany), 27–28 April (Orthodox Easter), 1 May (Labour Day), 1 December (National Day), 25–26 December (Christmas).

2004: 1–2 January (New Year), 6 January (Epiphany), 11–12 April (Orthodox Easter), 1 May (Labour Day), 1 December (National Day), 25–26 December (Christmas).

Weights and Measures

The metric system is in force.

Statistical Survey

Source (unless otherwise indicated): Institutul National de Statistică (National Institute of Statistics), Bucharest, Bd. Libertatii 16; tel. (1) 3124875; fax (1) 3124873; e-mail romstat@insse.ro; internet www.insse.ro/index.html.

Area and Population

AREA, POPULATION AND DENSITY

Area (sq km)	238,391*
Population (census results)	
7 January 1992	22,810,035
18–27 March 2002 (preliminary)	
Males	10,581,350
Females.	11,116,831
Total	21,698,181
Population (official estimates at 1 January)	
1999	22,489,000
2000	22,456,000
2001	22,430,000
Density (per sq km) at 2002 census†	91.0

* 92,043 sq miles.
† Based on preliminary results.

POPULATION BY ETHNIC GROUP
(2002 census*)

	Number	% of total
Romanian.	19,409,400	89.5
Hungarian	1,434,377	6.6
Gypsy	535,520	2.5
Ukrainian	61,091	0.3
German	60,088	0.3
Carpathio-Rusyns . . .	36,397	0.2
Turks	32,596	0.2
Others and unknown . .	128,712	0.6
Total	21,698,181	100.0

* Based on preliminary results.

ADMINISTRATIVE DIVISIONS
(at 1 July 2000)

	Area (sq km)	Estimated population	Density (per sq km)	Administrative capital (with population)
Alba	6,242	395,941	63.4	Alba Iulia (71,638)
Arad	7,754	476,272	61.4	Arad (182,846)
Argeş	6,826	671,514	98.4	Piteşti (186,163)
Bacău	6,621	752,761	113.7	Bacău (207,573)
Bihor	7,544	620,517	82.3	Oradea (220,626)
Bistriţa-Năsăud .	5,355	326,278	60.9	Bistriţa (86,556)
Botoşani . . .	4,986	463,808	93.0	Botoşani (126,621)
Brăila	4,766	385,749	80.9	Brăila (230,962)
Braşov	5,363	628,643	117.2	Braşov (309,671)
Buzău	6,103	504,540	82.7	Buzău (145,610)
Călăraşi . . .	5,088	331,843	65.2	Călăraşi (76,636)
Caraş-Severin . .	8,520	353,209	41.5	Reşiţa (92,776)
Cluj	6,674	719,864	107.9	Cluj-Napoca (329,310)
Constanţa . . .	7,071	746,041	105.5	Constanţa (337,216)
Covasna . . .	3,710	230,537	62.1	Sfântu Gheorghe (66,341)
Dâmboviţa. . .	4,054	551,414	136.0	Târgovişte (98,028)
Dolj.	7,414	744,243	100.4	Craiova (312,358)
Galaţi	4,466	644,077	144.2	Galaţi (326,956)
Giurgiu . . .	3,526	294,000	83.4	Giurgiu (71,893)
Gorj.	5,602	394,809	70.5	Târgu Jiu (97,259)
Harghita . . .	6,639	341,570	51.4	Miercurea-Ciuc (46,021)
Hunedoara . .	7,063	523,073	74.1	Deva (75,515)
Ialomiţa . . .	4,453	304,327	68.3	Slobozia (55,308)
Iaşi	5,476	836,751	152.8	Iaşi (345,795)
Ilfov*	1,593	275,482	172.9	Bucharest (2,009,200)
Maramureş . .	6,304	530,955	84.2	Baia Mare (149,780)
Mehedinţi. . .	4,933	321,853	65.2	Drobeta-Turnu-Severin (115,979)
Mureş	6,714	601,558	89.6	Târgu Mureş (163,184)
Neamţ	5,896	586,229	99.4	Piatra-Neamţ (124,189)
Olt	5,498	508,213	92.4	Slatina (86,351)
Prahova . . .	4,716	855,539	181.4	Ploieşti (249,054)
Sălaj	3,864	256,307	66.3	Zalău (70,015)
Satu Mare . . .	4,418	390,121	88.3	Satu Mare (129,153)
Sibiu	5,432	443,993	81.7	Sibiu (167,737)
Suceava . . .	8,553	717,224	83.9	Suceava (117,615)
Teleorman. . .	5,790	456,831	78.9	Alexandria (57,377)
Timiş	8,697	688,575	79.2	Timişoara (329,554)
Tulcea	8,499	262,692	30.9	Tulcea (94,706)
Vâlcea	5,765	430,713	74.7	Râmnicu Vâlcea (119,249)
Vaslui	5,318	466,719	87.8	Vaslui (77,900)
Vrancea . . .	4,857	391,220	80.5	Focşani (96,300)
Bucharest Municipality* .	228	2,009,200	8,812.3	Bucharest (2,009,200)
Total	238,391	22,435,205	94.1	

* The Bucharest Municipality is a separate administrative division, but the city is also the capital of the adjacent Ilfov region. The area and population of Bucharest are included only in figures for the municipality.

PRINCIPAL TOWNS
(estimated population at 1 July 2000)

Bucureşti (Bucharest, the capital) . . .	2,009,200	Bacău	207,573
Iaşi.	345,795	Piteşti	186,163
Constanţa. . .	337,216	Arad	182,846
Timişoara. . .	329,554	Sibiu	167,737
Cluj-Napoca . .	329,310	Târgu Mureş . . .	163,184
Galaţi	326,956	Baia Mare . . .	149,780
Craiova . . .	312,358	Buzău	145,610
Braşov. . . .	309,671	Satu Mare . . .	129,153
Ploieşti . . .	249,054	Botoşani . . .	126,621
Brăila	230,962	Piatra-Neamţ. . .	124,189
Oradea	220,626	Râmnicu-Vâlcea . .	119,249
		Suceava	117,615
		Drobeta-Turnu-Severin	115,979

BIRTHS, MARRIAGES AND DEATHS

	Registered live births Number	Rate (per 1,000)	Registered marriages Number	Rate (per 1,000)	Registered deaths Number	Rate (per 1,000)
1993 . .	249,994	11.0	161,595	7.1	263,323	11.6
1994 . .	246,736	10.9	154,221	6.8	266,101	11.7
1995 . .	236,640	10.4	153,943	6.8	271,672	12.0
1996 . .	231,348	10.2	150,388	6.7	286,158	12.7
1997 . .	236,891	10.5	147,105	6.5	279,316	12.4
1998 . .	237,297	10.5	145,000	6.5	269,166	12.0
1999 . .	235,000	10.5	140,000	6.2	265,000	11.8
2000 . .	233,000	10.4	136,000	6.1	255,100	11.4

Sources: partly UN, *Demographic Yearbook* and *Population and Vital Statistics Report*.

Expectation of life (WHO estimates, years at birth): 71.1 (males 67.8; females 74.5) in 2001 (Source: WHO, *World Health Report*).

ECONOMICALLY ACTIVE POPULATION
(labour force surveys, '000 persons aged 15 years and over)

	1999	2000	2001
Agriculture, hunting and forestry	4,491.6	4,598.7	4,523.1
Fishing	7.6	7.9	3.7
Mining and quarrying	186.3	163.2	150.0
Manufacturing	2,164.8	2,053.8	2,024.8
Electricity, gas and water . . .	223.5	195.8	198.9
Construction	397.0	403.4	430.0
Wholesale and retail trade; repair of motor vehicles, motorcycles and personal and household goods	926.3	928.4	951.9
Hotels and restaurants	123.9	122.8	130.9
Transport, storage and communications	499.8	511.3	519.4
Financial intermediation . . .	87.0	92.6	75.9
Real estate, renting and business services	141.1	132.3	124.1
Public administration	532.7	563.1	581.4
Education	423.2	415.0	409.3
Health and social assistance . .	340.5	345.8	350.6
Other services	230.3	229.6	222.9
Total employed.	10,775.7	10,763.8	10,696.9
Unemployed	789.9	821.2	750.0
Total labour force	11,565.6	11,585.0	11,446.9
Males	6,261.6	6,253.8	6,155.4
Females	5,304.0	5,331.2	5,291.5

Registered unemployed ('000 persons): 1,130.3 in 1999; 1,007.1 in 2000; 826.9 in 2001.

Source: ILO.

Health and Welfare

KEY INDICATORS

Total fertility rate (children per woman, 2001)	1.3
Under-5 mortality rate (per 1,000 live births, 2001) . . .	21
HIV/AIDS (% of persons aged 15–49, 2001)	<0.10
Physicians (per 1,000 head, 1994)	1.84
Hospital beds (per 1,000 head, 1998)	7.56
Health expenditure (1998): US $ per head (PPP)	190
Health expenditure (1998): % of GDP	2.9
Health expenditure (1998): public (% of total)	63.8
Access to water (% of persons, 1999).	58
Access to sanitation (% of persons, 1999)	53
Human Development Index (2000): ranking	63
Human Development Index (2000): value	0.775

For sources and definitions, see explanatory note on p. vi.

Agriculture

PRINCIPAL CROPS
('000 metric tons)

	1999	2000	2001
Wheat	4,661.4	4,434.4	7,735.1
Barley	1,018.6	867.0	1,580.0
Maize	10,934.8	4,898.0	9,119.2
Rye.	21.1	21.8	28.6
Oats	389.6	244.0	382.4
Potatoes	3,957.1	3,469.8	3,997.1
Sugar beet.	1,414.9	666.9	875.5
Dry beans	47.7	21.8	36.5
Dry peas	27.0	14.2	21.7
Walnuts	33.1	31.5	33.9
Soybeans (Soya beans) . . .	183.4	69.5	72.7
Sunflower seed	1,300.9	721.0	823.5
Rapeseed	108.2	76.1	101.8
Cabbages	885.4	731.9	819.2
Lettuce.	24.0	20.0†	26.2†
Tomatoes	708.6	628.7	651.7
Pumpkins, squash and gourds .	154.0†	120.0†	152.0*
Cucumbers and gherkins . .	145.0†	110.0†	138.0*
Chillies and green peppers . .	212.3	174.8	184.8
Dry onions	401.1	296.3	396.5
Garlic	84.5	68.3	82.9
Green beans	52.4	40.1	50.8
Green peas	22.2	17.7	22.6
Other vegetables†	333.2	296.8	335.3
Apples	315.0	490.3	507.4
Pears	63.5	70.6	71.6
Cherries	71.6	73.7	91.2
Apricots	31.5	28.4	28.3
Peaches	16.1	18.3	16.7
Plums	361.3	549.6	557.2
Strawberries	14.6	11.7	18.4
Grapes	1,117.4	1,295.3	1,121.7
Cantaloupes and other melons .	853.2	900.0*	945.0*
Other fruits†	102.5	97.0	41.4
Pimento*	28	30	30
Tobacco (leaves)	14.8	10.9	10.1

* FAO estimate(s).

† Unofficial figure(s).

Source: FAO.

LIVESTOCK
('000 head, year ending September)

	1999	2000	2001
Horses	839	858	860*
Cattle	3,143	3,051	2,870
Pigs	7,194	5,848	4,797
Sheep	8,409	8,121	7,657
Goats	585	558	538
Chickens	69,480	69,143	70,076

* FAO estimate.

Source: FAO.

LIVESTOCK PRODUCTS

('000 metric tons)

	1999	2000	2001
Beef and veal .	153	162	145
Mutton and lamb.	54	49	49
Goat meat .	4.3	4.0	3.8
Pig meat .	595.1	502.3	460.1
Horse meat†	8.6	9.0	9.0
Poultry meat .	268.5	259.4	283.9
Other meat†	7.8	7.8	8.0
Cows' milk †	4,360.3	4,301.3	4,457.4
Sheep's milk .	342.4	321.5	323.7
Cheese .	42.4	40.6	38.7
Butter .	9.2	6.0	6.5
Hen eggs .	266.2	262.8	276.2
Other poultry eggs .	28.3	22.7	23.8
Honey .	11.2	11.7	12.6
Wool: greasy .	19.0	18.0	16.9
Wool: scoured .	11.4	10.8	12.0*
Cattle hides (fresh)* .	32.5	30.7	31.2
Sheepskins (fresh)* .	14.1	13.4	11.8

* Unofficial figure(s).
† FAO estimates.

Source: FAO.

Forestry

ROUNDWOOD REMOVALS

('000 cubic metres, excluding bark)

	1999	2000	2001
Sawlogs, veneer logs and logs for sleepers .	5,287	6,146	5,638
Pulpwood .	1,425	1,652	2,150
Other industrial wood .	2,772	2,318	2,018
Fuel wood .	3,220	3,032	2,618
Total .	12,703	13,148	12,424

Source: FAO.

SAWNWOOD PRODUCTION

('000 cubic metres, including railway sleepers)

	1999	2000	2001
Coniferous (softwood) .	1,845	2,077	1,805
Broadleaved (hardwood).	973	1,319	1,254
Total .	2,818	3,396	3,059

Source: FAO.

Fishing

('000 metric tons, live weight)

	1998	1999	2000
Capture .	9.0	7.8	7.4
Goldfish .	1.1	1.2	1.2
Silver carp .	0.4	1.3	0.6
Whiting .	0.6	0.3	0.3
European sprat .	3.3	1.9	1.8
Aquaculture .	9.6	9.0	9.7
Common carp .	1.9	1.9	2.3
Goldfish .	1.8	1.5	1.3
Bighead carp .	1.4	1.0	2.1
Silver carp .	3.6	3.1	3.2
Total catch .	18.6	16.8	17.1

Source: FAO, *Yearbook of Fishery Statistics.*

Mining

('000 metric tons, unless otherwise indicated)

	1998	1999	2000
Brown coal (incl. lignite) .	26,037	22,881	29,279
Crude petroleum .	6,309	6,154	6,038
Iron ore* .	459	365	290
Bauxite .	161.9	136	135
Copper concentrates† .	19.1	16.5	16.1
Lead concentrates† .	15.1	17.5	18.7
Zinc concentrates† .	25.7	26.5	27.5
Salt (unrefined) .	2,220	2,133	2,215
Natural gas (million cu metres) .	14,441	14,577	14,577

* Figures refer to gross weight.
† Figures refer to the metal content of concentrates.

Source: US Geological Survey.

Industry

SELECTED PRODUCTS

('000 metric tons, unless otherwise indicated)

	1997	1998	1999
Refined sugar .	243	321	246
Margarine .	25.8	36.1	36.1
Wine ('000 hectolitres) .	7,314	5,071	5,661
Beer ('000 hectolitres) .	7,651	9,989	11,133
Tobacco products .	26	29	31
Cotton yarn—pure and mixed .	43	36	28
Cotton fabrics—pure and mixed (million sq metres) .	173	170	143
Woollen yarn—pure and mixed .	28	20	17
Woollen fabrics—pure and mixed (million sq metres) .	34	22	18
Silk fabrics—pure and mixed (million sq metres)* .	52	40	32
Flax and hemp yarn—pure and mixed .	5	5	4
Linen, hemp and jute fabrics—pure and mixed (million sq metres) .	17	8	7
Chemical filaments and fibres .	75	48	28
Footwear (million pairs).	36	31	31
Chemical wood pulp .	197	162	178
Paper and paperboard .	330	306	302
Synthetic rubber .	29	23	16
Rubber tyres ('000) .	3,110	3,002	2,834
Sulphuric acid .	329	229	234
Caustic soda (sodium hydroxide) .	323	310	297
Soda ash (sodium carbonate) .	547	462	415
Nitrogenous fertilizers (a)† .	669	318	612
Phosphatic fertilizers (b)† .	136	99	101
Pesticides .	8	5	4
Plastics and resins .	338.6	319.9	298.4
Motor spirit (petrol) .	3,642	3,627	3,017
Kerosene and white spirit .	168	181	205
Distillate fuel oils .	3,952	4,035	3,137
Residual fuel oils .	2,083	1,941	1,825
Petroleum bitumen (asphalt) .	305	241	204
Liquefied petroleum gas .	242	304	261
Coke .	3,317	3,312	1,716
Cement .	6,553	7,300	6,252
Pig-iron .	4,556	4,541	2,969
Crude steel .	6,675	6,336	4,392
Aluminium—unwrought .	164	175	174
Refined copper—unwrought .	23	21	21
Radio receivers ('000) .	28	10	n.a.
Television receivers ('000) .	89	134	56
Merchant ships launched ('000 deadweight tons) .	43	58	231
Passenger motor cars ('000).	109	104	89
Motor tractors, lorries and dump trucks (number) .	1,956	1,263	900
Tractors ('000) .	10.5	9.6	4.5
Sewing machines ('000) .	3	1	1
Domestic refrigerators ('000) .	429	366	323
Domestic washing machines ('000)	82	36	28
Domestic cookers ('000) .	339	310	285
Electric energy (million kWh) .	57,148	53,496	50,713

* Including fabrics of artificial silk.
† Production in terms of (a) nitrogen or (b) phosphoric acid.

Finance

CURRENCY AND EXCHANGE RATES

Monetary Units

100 bani (singular: ban) = 1 Romanian leu (plural: lei)

Sterling, Dollar and Euro Equivalents (31 December 2002)

£1 sterling = 53,995.3 lei

US $1 = 33,500.0 lei

€1 = 35,131.5 lei

100,000 Romanian lei = £1.852 = $2.985 = €2.846

Average Exchange Rate (lei per US $)

2000   21,708.7
2001   29,060.8
2002   33,055.4

STATE BUDGET

('000 million lei)

Revenue*	1998	1999	2000
Current revenue	62,681.0	88,649.7	119,763.5
Tax revenue	60,677.9	85,019.0	114,394.5
Direct taxes	22,714.2	26,560.8	31,472.5
On profits	10,845.6	16,646.0	19,927.3
Indirect taxes	37,963.6	58,458.2	82,922.0
Value-added tax . . .	22,493.2	32,471.2	50,438.7
Customs duties . . .	5,741.4	7,846.7	8,702.4
Excises	8,431.3	16,167.9	20,636.3
Other indirect taxes . . .	1,297.8	1,972.3	3,144.7
Non-tax revenue	2,003.1	3,630.7	5,369.0
Capital revenue	3,228.1	4,201.2	121.0
Total	65,909.1	92,850.9	119,884.5

Expenditure†	1998	1999	2000
General public services	2,866.9	4,108.5	7,683.1
Defence	6,707.6	8,347.2	14,060.0
Public order and safety . . .	5,205.1	7,535.6	13,947.7
Education	10,801.6	13,996.2	20,173.4
Health	3,183.9	3,517.5	3,710.4
Social security and welfare . . .	6,815.7	9,069.9	11,242.1
Housing and community amenities	946.8	1,827.8	2,762.0
Recreational, cultural and religious affairs	1,466.4	1,746.6	3,077.3
Economic affairs	10,682.6	15,817.7	24,388.3
Agriculture	4,539.8	4,974.6	9,091.8
Transport and communications	3,357.5	7,211.3	9,769.7
Other	10,196.1	6,994.4	4,879.4
Total	58,872.7	72,931.4	105,923.1

* Excluding grants received ('000 million lei): 1,306.5 in 1998; 388.9 in 1999; 211.3 in 2000.

† Excluding lending minus repayments ('000 million lei): 18,743.9 in 1998; 33,955.3 in 1999; 43,244.1 in 2000.

2001 ('000 million lei): Revenue 148,203.1; Expenditure 184,021.2.

INTERNATIONAL RESERVES

(US $ million at 31 December)

	2000	2001	2002
IMF special drawing rights . . .	1	7	2
Foreign exchange . . .	3,921	5,435	7,209
Total (excl. gold)	3,922	5,442	7,211

Source: IMF, *International Financial Statistics*.

MONEY SUPPLY

('000 million lei at 31 December)

	2000	2001	2002
Currency outside banks . . .	25,742	35,635	45,577
Demand deposits at deposit money banks	18,579	25,968	38,329
Total money	44,320	61,603	83,907

Source: IMF, *International Financial Statistics*.

COST OF LIVING

(Consumer Price Index; base: Oct. 1990 = 100)

	1998	1999	2000
Food and beverages	53,830.6	68,822.0	98,906.8
Other goods	50,346.8	76,686.9	110,426.6
Services	64,032.5	117,842.6	181,315.3
All items	53,437.7	77,914.2	113,494.9

NATIONAL ACCOUNTS

('000 million lei at current prices)

Expenditure on the Gross Domestic Product

	1998	1999	2000
Government final consumption expenditure	51,649.8	81,179.5	99,634.6
Private final consumption expenditure	255,886.2	388,984.5	588,303.6
Increase in stocks	−1,350.9	−4,546.0	7,680.6
Gross fixed capital formation . .	61,209.8	97,169.8	147,209.6
Total domestic expenditure .	367,394.9	539,356.9	842,828.4
Exports of goods and services . ⎫			
Less Imports of goods and services ⎬	−28,724.9	−23,430.9	−46,294.7
GDP in purchaser' values . ⎭	338,670.0	539,356.9	796,533.7

Gross Domestic Product by Economic Activity

	1998	1999	2000
Agriculture, hunting, fishing and forestry	54,077.1	72,096.0	90,929.3
Mining and quarrying . . . . ⎫			
Manufacturing . . . . . ⎬	107,305.6	146,054.2	219,861.1
Electricity, gas and water . . . ⎭			
Construction	17,496.6	26,260.2	38,127.3
Services	128,050.1	243,648.6	370,916.4
Sub-total	306,929.4	488,059.0	719,834.1
Less Imputed bank service charge	1,567.4	7,970.8	9,600.8
GDP at basic prices	305,362.0	480,088.2	710,233.3
Taxes (less subsidies) on products	33,308.0	59,268.7	86,300.4
GDP in purchasers values .	338,670.0	539,356.9	796,533.7

BALANCE OF PAYMENTS

(US $ million)

	1999	2000	2001
Exports of goods f.o.b.	8,503	10,366	11,385
Imports of goods f.o.b.	−9,595	−12,050	−14,354
Trade balance	−1,092	−1,684	−2,969
Exports of services	1,365	1,767	1,994
Imports of services	−1,785	−2,021	−2,203
Balance on goods and services	−1,512	−1,938	−3,178
Other income received	152	325	455
Other income paid	−563	−606	−737
Balance on goods, services and income	−1,923	−2,219	−3,460
Current transfers received . .	804	1,079	1,417
Current transfers paid	−178	−219	−274
Current balance	−1,297	−1,359	−2,317
Capital account (net)	45	36	95
Direct investment abroad . . .	−16	11	17
Direct investment from abroad . .	1,041	1,025	1,157
Portfolio investment assets . . .	9	28	−8
Portfolio investment liabilities . .	−724	74	583
Other investment assets . . .	246	−407	−44
Other investment liabilities . .	141	1,212	1,233
Net errors and omissions . . .	794	286	819
Overall balance	239	906	1,535

Source: IMF, *International Financial Statistics*.

External Trade

PRINCIPAL COMMODITIES
(US $ million)

Imports c.i.f.	1997	1998	1999
Prepared foodstuffs beverages and tobacco	426	524	416
Mineral products	2,408	1,687	1,252
Mineral fuels and oils; bituminous substances; mineral waxes	2,131	1,431	1,051
Chemical products	940	1,028	974
Plastics, rubber and articles thereof	444	512	477
Plastics and articles thereof	325	392	385
Textiles and textile articles	1,565	1,825	1,937
Synthetic or man-made filaments	236	295	316
Synthetic or man-made staple fibres	320	369	392
Base metals and articles of base metal	670	790	687
Machinery and mechanical appliances; electrical equipment; sound and image recorders and players	2,593	2,723	2,435
Boilers, turbines, engines mechanical apparatus and devices, parts thereof	1,685	1,516	1,344
Electric machinery, appliances and equipment; TV sound and image recorders and players	908	1,207	1,091
Vehicles and associated transport equipment	384	485	314
Vehicles, tractors and other ground vehicles	292	423	236
Total (incl. others)	11,280	11,838	10,395

Exports f.o.b.	1997	1998	1999
Mineral products	638	507	502
Mineral fuels and oils; bituminous substances; mineral waxes	518	393	414
Chemical products	560	336	327
Wood and articles of wood, excl. furniture	338	385	495
Wood, wood charcoal and articles of wood	330	378	489
Textiles and textile articles	1,942	2,162	2,197
Knitted or crocheted clothing and accessories	310	409	454
Non-knitted clothing and accessories	1,415	1,544	1,571
Footwear, headgear, umbrellas and similar articles	545	609	683
Footwear and parts thereof	540	603	678
Base metals and articles of base metal	1,557	1,583	1,310
Pig-iron, iron and steel	917	865	665
Products of pig-iron, iron and steel	315	374	288
Aluminium and articles thereof	253	247	255
Machinery and electrical appliances; electrical equipment; sound and image recorders and players	737	790	968
Boilers, turbines, engines mechanical apparatus and devices, parts thereof	485	432	555
Electrical machinery appliances and equipment; TV sound and image recorders and players	252	358	413
Vehicles and associated transport equipment	448	427	466
Miscellaneous manufactured articles	526	519	502
Furniture; lighting fittings and other similar articles; prefabricated buildings	475	473	457
Total (incl. others)	8,431	8,302	8,503

PRINCIPAL TRADING PARTNERS
(US $ million)*

Imports c.i.f.	1998	1999†	2000†
Austria	347.4	311	332
Belgium-Luxembourg	226.6	194	203
Brazil	143.4	128	181
China, People's Republic	177.5	145	174
Czech Republic	194.9	173	196
France (incl. Monaco)	815.4	704	799
Germany	2,064.5	1,841	1,923
Greece	204.6	198	372
Hungary	546.9	414	513
Israel	110.8	98	84
Italy	2,060.7	2,062	2,443
Japan	84.8	118	170
Korea, Republic	254.6	277	212
Netherlands	277.8	243	284
Poland	145.5	160	193
Russia	1,062.3	704	1,120
Spain	121.3	109	130
Sweden	147.7	145	177
Switzerland-Liechtenstein	138.1	128	154
Turkey	271.5	237	271
Ukraine	167.5	109	196
United Kingdom	396.8	444	536
USA	499.0	370	391
Total (incl. others)	11,835.4	10,557	13,055

Exports f.o.b.	1998	1999	2000†
Austria	249.2	242.5	251
Belgium-Luxembourg	155.1	151.0	178
Bulgaria	77.9	136.7	290
Egypt	184.0	153.2	171
France (incl. Monaco)	491.5	530.4	722
Germany	1,628.6	1,510.0	1,627
Greece	201.4	216.7	324
Hungary	219.2	270.8	355
Israel	95.0	65.7	77
Italy	1,839.9	1,990.4	2,319
Moldova	128.6	101.0	142
Netherlands	313.1	327.0	329
Poland	82.2	120.0	102
Spain	84.2	106.9	114
Turkey	323.0	469.4	627
United Kingdom	303.2	412.9	546
USA	320.0	316.9	380
Yugoslavia	118.6	85.9	138
Total (incl. others)	8,300.9	8,487.0	10,367

* Imports by country of production; exports by country of last consignment.
† Figures are rounded.

Source: partly UN, *International Trade Statistics Yearbook*.

Transport

RAILWAYS
(traffic)

	1998	1999	2000
Passenger journeys (million)	146.8	129.3	117.5
Passenger-km (million)	13,422	12,304	11,632
Freight transported (million metric tons)	76.5	62.9	71.5
Freight ton-km (million)	19,708	15,927	17,982

ROAD TRAFFIC
(motor vehicles in use at 31 December)

	1998	1999	2000
Passenger cars	2,822,254	2,980,014	3,128,782
Buses and coaches	45,546	47,305	48,142
Lorries and vans	380,312	410,159	413,493
Motorcycles and mopeds	325,675	325,150	315,685

Source: IRF, *World Road Statistics*.

INLAND WATERWAYS
(traffic)

	1998	1999	2000
Passenger journeys ('000) . . .	1,923	1,654	133
Passenger-km (million)	13.1	11.0	15.0
Freight transported ('000 metric tons)	14,856	13,976	13,102
Freight ton-km (million) . . .	4,203	2,802	2,634

SHIPPING

Merchant Fleet
(registered at 31 December)

	1999	2000	2001
Number of vessels	325	264	240
Total displacement ('000 grt) . .	1,220.6	766.9	637.7

Source: Lloyd's Register-Fairplay, *World Fleet Statistics*.

International Sea-borne Freight Traffic
('000 metric tons)

	1998	1999	2000
Goods loaded	10,860	14,376	12,648
Goods unloaded	17,344	11,100	12,828

Sources: Ministry of Transport, Bucharest, and UN, *Monthly Bulletin of Statistics*.

CIVIL AVIATION
(traffic)

	1998	1999	2000
Passenger journeys ('000) . . .	1,008	1,048	1,282
Passenger-km (million)	1,827	1,887	2,212
Freight transported ('000 metric tons)	10.0	8.0	8.0
Freight ton-km (million) . . .	22.0	20.0	19.0

Tourism

FOREIGN VISITOR ARRIVALS
('000)*

Country of origin	1998	1999	2000
Bulgaria	464	489	363
Germany	259	249	255
Hungary	829	1,031	1,203
Italy	151	158	189
Moldova	1,192	1,455	1,436
Poland	105	103	102
Russia	124	78	83
Slovakia	107	92	80
Turkey	263	281	253
Ukraine	424	319	330
Yugoslavia	112	152	143
Total (incl. others)	4,830	5,224	5,264

* Figures refer to arrivals at frontiers of visitors from abroad. Excluding same-day visitors (excursionists), the total number of tourist arrivals (in '000) was: 2,966 in 1998; 3,209 in 1999; 3,274 in 2000 .
Source: World Tourism Organization, *Yearbook of Tourism Statistics*).

Receipts from Tourism (US $ million): 260 in 1998; 254 in 1999; 364 in 2000 (Source: World Bank, *World Bank Atlas*).

Communications Media

	1999	2000	2001
Television receivers ('000 in use)	7,000	8,500	n.a.
Telephones ('000 main lines in use)	3,740.0	3,899.2	4,094.0
Mobile cellular telephones ('000 subscribers)	1,355.5	2,499.0	3,860.0
Personal computers ('000 in use) .	600	713	800
Internet users ('000)	600	800	1,000

1996: Book production (incl. pamphlets) 7,199 titles (38,374,000 copies); Daily newspapers 106; Other periodicals 1,207.

1997: Radio receivers ('000 in use) 7,200.

Sources: mostly UNESCO, *Statistical Yearbook*; UN, *Statistical Yearbook*; International Telecommunication Union.

Education

(2000/01)

	Institutions	Pupils	Teachers
Kindergartens	10,080	611,036	34,023
Primary and gymnasium schools	12,709	2,411,505	162,606
Secondary schools	1,367	687,919	64,018
Vocational schools	93	239,550	4,894
Specialized technical schools	108	91,105	1,493
Higher education	126	533,152	27,959

Adult literacy rate (UNESCO estimates): 98.1% (males 99.0%; females 97.3%) in 2000 (Source: UN Development Programme, *Human Development Report*).

Directory

The Constitution

Following its assumption of power in December 1989, the National Salvation Front decreed radical changes to the Constitution of 1965. The name of the country was changed from the Socialist Republic of Romania to Romania. The leading role of a single political party was abolished, a democratic and pluralist system of government being established.

The combined chambers of the legislature elected in May 1990, working as a constituent assembly, drafted a new Constitution (based on the Constitution of France's Fifth Republic), which was approved in a national referendum on 8 December 1991.

Under the 1991 Constitution, political power in Romania belongs to the people and is exercised according to the principles of democracy, freedom and human dignity, of inviolability and inalienability of basic human rights. Romania is governed on the basis of a multi-party democratic system and of the separation of the legal, executive and judicial powers. Romania's 486-seat legislature, consisting of the Chamber of Deputies (the lower house) and the Senate (the upper house), and Romania's President are elected by universal, free, direct and secret vote, the President serving a maximum of two terms. The term of office of the legislature and of the President is four years. Citizens have the right to vote at the age of 18, and may be elected at the age of 21 to the Chamber of Deputies and at the age of 30 to the Senate, with no upper age limit. Those ineligible for election include former members of the Securitate (the secret police of President Ceauşescu) and other former officials guilty of repression and abuses. Independent candidates are eligible for election to the Chamber of Deputies and to the Senate if supported by at least 251 electors and to the Presidency if supported by 100,000 electors. Once elected, the President may not remain a member of any political party. The President appoints the Prime Minister, who in turn appoints the Council of Ministers.

The Government

HEAD OF STATE

President: Ion Iliescu (elected 10 December 2000).

COUNCIL OF MINISTERS
(April 2003)

Prime Minister: Adrian Năstase.

Minister of Foreign Affairs: Mircea Geoană.

Minister of European Integration: Hildegard Carola Puwak.

Minister of Public Finance: Mihai Nicolae Tănăsescu.

Minister of Justice: Rodica Mihaela Stănoiu.

Minister of National Defence: Ioan Mircea Paşcu.

Minister of the Interior: Ioan Rus.

Minister of Development and Prognosis: Gheorghe Romeo Leonard Cazan.

Minister of Labour and Social Solidarity: Marian Sârbu.

Minister of Industry and Resources: Dan Ioan Popescu.

Minister of Agriculture, Food and Forestry: Ilie Sârbu.

Minister of Water and Environmental Protection: Petru Lificiu.

Minister of Public Works, Transport and Housing: Miron Tudor Mitrea.

Minister of Tourism: Dan Matei-Agathon.

Minister of Small and Medium-sized Enterprises: Silvia Ciornei.

Minister of Education and Research: Ecaterina Andronescu.

Minister of Culture and Religious Affairs: Răzvan Theodorescu.

Minister of Health and Family: Daniela Bartoş.

Minister of Youth and Sports: Giorgiu Gingăraş.

Minister of Communications and Information Technology: Dan Nica.

Minister of Public Administration: Octav Cosmâncă.

Minister of Public Information: Vasile Dâncu.

Minister Co-ordinating the General Secretariat of Government: Petru Şerban Mihăilescu.

Minister for Relations with Parliament: Acsinte Gaspar.

Minister of the Privatization Authority: Ovidiu Tiberiu Muşetescu.

Minister-delegate, attached to the Prime Minister, for European Integration: Vasile Puşcaş.

Minister-delegate, attached to the Prime Minister, for Education and Research: Şerban Constantin Valeca.

MINISTRIES

Office of the Prime Minister: 71201 Bucharest, Piaţa Victoriei 1; tel. (1) 3131450; fax (1) 3122436; e-mail prim.ministru@guv.ro; internet www.guv.ro.

Ministry of Agriculture, Food and Forestry: 70312 Bucharest, Bd. Carol I 24; tel. (1) 6144020; fax (1) 3124410; internet www.maap.ro.

Ministry of Communications and Information Technology: Bucharest, Bd. Libertatii 14; internet www.mcti.ro.

Ministry of Culture and Religious Affairs: 71341 Bucharest, Piaţa Presei Libere 1; tel. (1) 2228479; fax (1) 2245440; e-mail tudor.maruntelu@cultura.ro.

Ministry of Development and Prognosis: Bucharest, Str. Ministerului 2–4; tel. (1) 2226137; fax (1) 3140809; internet www.mdp.ro.

Ministry of Education and Research: 70738 Bucharest, Str. Gen. Berthelot 28–30, Sector 1; tel. (1) 6133315; fax (1) 3124719; internet www.edu.ro.

Ministry of European Integration: Bucharest, Str. Apolodor 17, Sector 5; tel. (1) 3011502; fax (1) 3368509; internet www.mie.ro.

Ministry of Foreign Affairs: 71274 Bucharest, Al. Alexandru 33; tel. (1) 2302071; fax (1) 2314090; e-mail maero@mae.kappa.ro; internet www.mae.ro.

Ministry of Health and Family: 70109 Bucharest, Str. Ministerului 1–3; tel. (1) 2223850; fax (1) 3124916; internet www.ms.ro.

Ministry of Industry and Resources: Bucharest, Calea Victoriei 152; tel. (1) 2310262; fax (1) 3120513; internet www.minind.ro.

Ministry of the Interior: 70622 Bucharest, Sector 6, Str. Mihai Vodă 6; tel. (1) 3158616; fax (1) 3149718; e-mail drp@mi.ro; internet www.mi.ro.

Ministry of Justice: 70663 Bucharest, Str. Apolodor 17; tel. (1) 3112266; fax (1) 3155389; internet www.just.ro.

Ministry of Labour and Social Solidarity: 70119 Bucharest, Str. Demetru Dobrescu 2в, Sector 1; tel. (1) 3156563; fax (1) 3122768; internet www.mmss.ro.

Ministry of National Defence: 77303 Bucharest, Str. Izvor 13–15, Sector 5; tel. (1) 4106876; fax (1) 3120863; e-mail drp@mapn.ro; internet www.mapn.ro.

Ministry of Public Administration: 71201 Bucharest, Piaţa Victoriei 1; tel. (1) 3123687; fax (1) 3113641; internet www.mapgov.ro.

Ministry of Public Finance: 70663 Bucharest, Str. Apolodor 17; tel. (1) 4103400; fax (1) 3122077; e-mail presa@mail.mfinante.ro; internet www.mfinante.ro.

Ministry of Public Information: Bucharest, Piaţa Victoriei 1; tel. (1) 3134947; fax (1) 2223694; internet www.publicinfo.ro.

Ministry of Public Works, Transport and Housing: Bucharest, Bd. Dinicu Golescu 38; tel. (1) 4101933; fax (1) 4111138; internet www.mt.ro.

Ministry for Relations with Parliament: 07000 Bucharest, Piaţa Victoriei 1; tel. (1) 2223677; fax (1) 2223652; e-mail mrp-ministru@gov.ro.

Ministry of Small and Medium-sized Enterprises: Bucharest, Str. Poterasi 11; tel. (1) 3352630; fax (1) 3353413; e-mail publicinfo@mimmc.ro; internet www.mimmc.ro.

Ministry of Tourism: Bucharest, Str. Apolodor 17, Sector 5; tel. (1) 3123731; fax (1) 4112346; internet www.ministerulturismului.ro.

Ministry of Water and Environmental Protection: 76106 Bucharest, Bd. Libertăţii 12; tel. (1) 4100482; fax (1) 3124227; internet www.mappm.ro.

Ministry of Youth and Sports: 70139 Bucharest, Str. Vasile Conta 16; tel. (1) 2115550; fax (1) 2111710; internet www.mts.ro.

President

Presidential Election, 26 November and 10 December 2000

Candidates	First ballot votes cast %	Second ballot votes cast Number	%
Ion Iliescu (PSDR)	36.35	6,696,623	66.8
Corneliu Vadim Tudor (GRP)	28.34	3,324,247	33.2
Teodor Dumitru Stolojan (NLP)	11.78	—	—
Constantin Mugurel Isărescu (Ind.)	9.54	—	—
Gheorghe Frunda (DAHR)	6.22	—	—
Petre Roman (DP)	2.99	—	—
Teodor Melescanu (Ind.)	1.91	—	—
Others	2.87	—	—
Total	100.00	10,020,870	100.0

In addition, a total of 160,264 invalid votes were cast in the second ballot.

Legislature

PARLIAMENT

Chairman of the Chamber of Deputies: Valeriu Dorneanu.

Chairman of the Senate: Nicolae Văcăroiu.

General Election, 26 November 2000

Parties	Seats	
	Chamber of Deputies	Senate
Party of Social Democracy of Romania (PSDR)	155	65
Greater Romania Party (GRP)	84	37
Democratic Party (DP)	31	13
National Liberal Party (NLP)	30	13
Democratic Alliance of Hungarians in Romania (DAHR)	27	12
Minority parties*	19	0
Total	346	140

* These included the 'Bratstvo' Community of Bulgarians in Romania; the Community of Lipovenian Russians in Romania; the Croatian Union of Romania; the Cultural Union of Albanians in Romania; the Cultural Union of Ruthenians in Romania; the Democratic Union of Czechs and Slovaks in Romania; the Democratic Union of Serbs and Carasovenians in Romania; the Democratic Union of the Turco-Muslim Tatars in Romania; the Federation of Jewish Communities in Romania; the German Democratic Forum of Romania; the General Union of Ethnic Associations of Romania; the Hellenic Union of Romania; the Italian Community of Romania; the Roma Party; the Slav Macedonian Association of Romania; the Turkish Democratic Union of Romania; the Union of Armenians in Romania; the Union of Poles in Romania; the Union of Ukrainians in Romania.

Political Organizations

Following the downfall of President Ceauşescu in December 1989, numerous political parties were formed or re-established in preparation for the holding of free elections. By 1996 there were some 90 registered political parties. A law approved in September 2002 required all political parties to re-register by 31 December.

Christian Democratic National Peasants' Party of Romania (CDNPP) (Partidul Naţional Ţărănesc Creştin-Democrat din România—PNȚCD): 73231 Bucharest, Bd. Carol I 34; tel. (1) 6154533; fax (1) 6143277; internet www.pntcd.ro; f. 1989; by merger of centre-right Christian Democratic Party and traditional National Peasant Party; f. 1869; banned 1947, revived Dec. 1989 original party re-established in Aug. 1990 by separate group; supports pluralist democracy and the restoration of peasant property; 615,000 mems; Chair. VICTOR CIORBEA; Sec.-Gen. CONSTANTIN DUDU IONESCU.

Civic Alliance (Alianța Civică): Bucharest, Piața Amzei 13, etaj 2, Sector 1; tel. and fax (1) 6595903; f. 1990 as alliance of opposition groupings outside legislature; Chair. ANA BLANDIANA.

Democratic Alliance of Hungarians in Romania (DAHR) (Uniunea Democrată Maghiară din România—UDMR): Bucharest, Str. Avram Iancu 8; tel. (1) 3146849; fax (1) 3144583; e-mail elhivbuk@dial.kappa.ro; internet www.rmdsz.ro; f. 1990; supports the rights of Hungarians in Romania; Pres. BÉLA MARKÓ; Exec. Pres. CSABA TAKÁCS.

Democratic Alliance Party: Sibiu; f. 1995; supports the rights of Gypsies in Romania; Leader FLORIN CIOABĂ.

Democratic Convention of Romania 2000 (DCR): 70401 Bucharest, Splaiul Independenței 7, Bl. 101, Sector 5; tel. and fax (1) 3124014; alliance of 5 centre-right parties and other organizations formed to contest the legislative election of November 2000; Pres. ION DIACONESCU.

Democratic Party (DP) (Partidul Democrat—PD): 71274 Bucharest, Al. Modrogan 1; tel. and fax (1) 2301332; e-mail office@pd.ro; internet www.pd.ro; f. 1993; fmrly Democratic Party—National Salvation Front; was to absorb the National Alliance in mid-2001; centre-left; advocates a modern and social-democratic Romania, with a free-market economy, and respect for the rights and freedoms of national minorities; Pres. TRĂIAN BĂSESCU; Sec.-Gen. VASILE BLAGA.

Greater Romania Party (GRP) (Partidul România Mare—PRM): 70101 Bucharest, Str. G. Clemenceau 8–10; tel. (1) 6130967; fax (1) 3126182; internet www.romare.ro; f. 1991; nationalist; Chair. CORNELIU VADIM TUDOR; Sec.-Gen. GHEORGHE FUNAR.

Humanist Party of Romania (Partidul Umanist din România): Bucharest, Calea Victoriei 118, etaj 5, Sector 1; tel. (1) 2125302; fax (1) 2125301; e-mail pur@itcnet.ro; internet www.pur.ro; f. 1991; Pres. DAN VOICULESCU.

Liberal Monarchist Party of Romania (Partidul Liberal Monarhist din România): Bucharest, Bd. George Coşbuc 1; tel. (1) 6134940; f. 1990; advocates the restoration of the monarchy; Pres. DAN CERNOVODEANU.

National Liberal Alliance: Bucharest; f. 1996; alliance of the Party of the Civic Alliance and the Liberal Party 1993; Leader NICOLAE MANOLESCU.

National Liberal Party (NLP) (Partidul Naţional Liberal—PNL): 70112 Bucharest, Bd. Aviatorilor 86; tel. (1) 2310795; fax (1) 2317511; e-mail dre@pnl.ro; internet www.pnl.ro; f. 1869; banned 1947; merged with Liberal Party in 1993, and with Party of the Civic Alliance and Liberal Party of Romania in 1998, absorbed Alliance for Romania AFR in 2002 and the Union of Right-Wing Forces in 2003; supports EU and NATO integration, advocates freedom of expression and religion, observance of the equal rights of all minorities, the privatization of enterprises, decentralization of state powers and a free and competitive market; Chair. THEODOR STOLOJAN.

National Union of the Centre: f. 1996; alliance of the Agrarian Democratic Party of Romania and the Romanian Humanistic Party; supports agrarian, ecological and humanitarian policies.

Patriotic Party of Reconciliation (PPR): Bucharest; f. 1998; centre-right; Leader Prince PAUL of Romania.

Popular Action (Actiunea Populara): f. 2003 by members of the Christian Democratic National Peasant's Party of Romania; Leader EMIL CONSTANTINESCU.

Popular Christian Party (PPC): Bucharest; f. 2001 by former members of the CDNPP; Leaders ANDREI MARGA, VASILE LUPU, CALIN CATALIN CHIRITA.

Romanian Communist Party: fmrly Romanian Workers' Party renamed as above in 1997; Leader CRISTIAN ION NICULAE.

Romanian Ecological Federation (REF) (Federaţia Ecologistă din România): 73226 Bucharest, Str. Matei Voievod 102; tel. (1) 6352743; alliance incl. the Romanian Ecological Movement; Leader GUGUI EDWARD.

Romanian Ecological Movement (Mişcarea Ecologistă din România): 70259 Bucharest, Str. Alexandru Phillippide 11; tel. (1) 2116943; fax (1) 2116858; f. 1990; advocates protection of the environment and the pursuit of democratic, pacifist and humanist values; Chair. TOMA GHEORGHE MAIORESCU.

Romanian Ecological Party (Partidul Ecologist Român): 70476 Bucharest, Str. Stelea Spătarul 10A; tel. (1) 6158285; merged with the Green Alternative Party of Ecologists and the Ecologist Convention in 2003; Chair. CORNELIU PROTOPOPESCU.

Romanian People's Party: f. 2000; far-right; Pres. RADU VASILE; Exec. Pres. SORIN LEPSA.

Social Democratic Party (SDP) (Partidul Social Democrat—PSD): 71271 Bucharest 2, Str. Kiseleff 10; tel. (1) 2222958; fax (1) 2223272; internet www.psd.ro; f. 2001; by the merger of the Romanian Social Democratic Party and the Party of Social Democracy of Romania; absorbed the Party of Moldovans in 2002; Chair. ADRIAN NĂSTASE; Pres. of National Council ALEXANDRU ATHANASIU; Sec.-Gen. COSMIN GUSA.

Socialist Labour Party (SLP) (Partidul Socialist al Muncii—PSM): 70481 Bucharest, Str. Negustori 3; tel. and fax (1) 3112211; f. 1990 by Romanian Socialist Party members and left-wing Democratic Labour Party; Chair. ION SASU.

Socialist Party of National Revival (PRSN): Bucharest; f. 2001 as a breakaway faction of the GRP; Leader IOAN RADU.

Traditional National Liberal Party (PNL-T): Bucharest; f. 2000; previously known as PNL-Bratianus; part of Romanian Democratic Convention 2000; Leader DECEBAL TRĂIAN REMES.

Traditional Social Democratic Party of Romania (Partidul Social Democrat Tradiţional din România): 70208 Bucharest 2, Str. Aaron Florian 1; tel. (1) 2110479; fax (1) 2101707; f. 1991; by merger of Traditional Social Democratic Party and National Democratic Party; supports the Party of Social Democracy of Romania; centre-left; Pres. LUCIAN CERNESCU.

Diplomatic Representation

EMBASSIES IN ROMANIA

Albania: 71274 Bucharest, Str. Duiliu Zamfirescu 7, Sector 1; tel. (1) 2119829; fax (1) 2108039; e-mail albemb@dataline.ro; Ambassador LEONIDHA MERTIRI.

Algeria: 71111 Bucharest, Bd. Lascar Catargiu 29; tel. (1) 2115150; fax (1) 2115695; Ambassador MOHAMED LAICHOUBI.

Argentina: 70258 Bucharest, Str. Drobeta 11; tel. (1) 2117290; fax (1) 2101412; Ambassador DIANA BERRUHET.

Armenia: Bucharest 3, Str. Calotesti 1, ap. 2; tel. (1) 3215930; fax (1) 3125679; e-mail armembro@starnets.ro; Ambassador YEGISHE SARKISSIAN.

Austria: 70254 Bucharest, Str. Dumbrava Roşie 7; tel. (1) 2104354; fax (1) 2100885; e-mail bukarest-ka@bmaa.gv.at; Ambassador Dr CHRISTIAN ZEILEISSEN.

Azerbaijan: Bucharest, Str. Ion Caragea Voda 23; tel. (1) 2113044; fax (1) 2110513.

Belarus: Bucharest, Şos. Pavel Kiseleff 55, Vila 6; tel. (1) 2233510; fax (1) 2231763; e-mail ambasada.belarus@vipnet.ro; Ambassador ANATOLY I. BUTEVICH.

Belgium: 70256 Bucharest, Bd. Dacia 58; tel. (1) 2102969; fax (1) 2102803; e-mail ambabuc@ines.ro; Ambassador XAVIER VAN MIGEM.

Bolivia: Bucharest, Str. Mihai Eminescu 44–48, ap. 14; tel. (1) 2102600; fax (1) 2101338; e-mail embolivia@mail.roknet.ro; Ambassador HERNANDO GARCÍA SUÁREZ.

Brazil: 71248 Bucharest, Str. Praga 11; tel. (1) 2301130; fax (1) 2301599; e-mail braembuc@starnets.ro; Ambassador JERONIMO MOSCARDO DE SOUZA.

Bulgaria: 71272 Bucharest, Str. Rabat 5; tel. (1) 2122150; fax (1) 2307654; Ambassador NIKOLAI MILKOV.

Canada: 71118 Bucharest, Str. Nicolae Iorga 36; tel. (1) 3075000; fax (1) 3075015; e-mail bucst@dfait-maeci.gc.ca; internet www.dfait-maeci.gc.ca/Bucharest; Ambassador RAPHAEL A. GIRARD.

Chile: 71113 Bucharest, Str. Sevastopol 13–17; tel. (1) 3127239; fax (1) 3127246; e-mail embachile@consuladochile.ro; Ambassador MANUEL ENRIQUE HINOJOSA MUÑOZ.

China, People's Republic: 71512 Bucharest, Şos. Nordului 2; tel. (1) 2328858; fax (1) 2330684; Ambassador CHEN DELAI.

Colombia: 70188 Bucharest, Str. Poloná 35, ap. 3; tel. (1) 2115106; fax (1) 2100155; e-mail embcolro@bx.logicnet.ro; Ambassador ENRIQUE ARIAS JIMÉNEZ.

Congo, Democratic Republic: Bucharest, Str. Mihai Eminescu 50–54, ap. 15, Sector 2; tel. (1) 2108265; Ambassador GOMEZ DUMBA KIMBAYA.

Congo, Republic: Bucharest, Bd. Pachge Protopopescu 14; tel. and fax (1) 3153371; Chargé d'affaires GEORGES AMBARA.

Croatia: Bucharest, Str. Dr Burghelea 1, Sector 2; tel. (1) 3130457; fax (1) 3130384; e-mail crobuc@canad.ro; Ambassador ŽELJKO KUPRESAK.

Cuba: 71148 Bucharest, Str. Mihai Eminescu 44–48; tel. and fax (1) 2118916; Ambassador LÁZARO MÉNDEZ CABRERA.

Czech Republic: 70418 Bucharest, Str. Ion Ghica 11; tel. (1) 3159142; fax (1) 3122539; e-mail bukurest@ines.ro; Ambassador RADEK PECH.

Denmark: 73102 Bucharest, Str. Dr Burghelea 3; tel. (1) 3120352; fax (1) 3120358; e-mail buhamb@um.dk; Ambassador ERIK BOM.

Ecuador: Bucharest; tel. (1) 2103791; fax (1) 2103790; Chargé d'affaires a.i LEÓN PABLO AVILES SALGADO.

Egypt: 70185 Bucharest, Bd. Dacia 21; tel. (1) 2110938; fax (1) 2100337; e-mail egyptemb@canad.ro; Ambassador WAFAA ASHRAF MOUHARAM BASSIMN.

Finland: 71217 Bucharest, Str. Atena 2 bis; tel. (1) 2307504; fax (1) 2307505; e-mail finland@dnt.ro; internet www.finlandia.ro; Ambassador PEKKA HARTTILA.

France: 70172 Bucharest, Str. Biserica Amzei 13–15; tel. (1) 3120217; fax (1) 3120200; internet www.ambafrance-ro.org; Ambassador PHILIPPE ETIENNE.

Germany: 71272 Bucharest, Str. Aviator Gh. Demetriade 68; tel. (1) 2029830; fax (1) 2305846; e-mail botshaft@deutschebotshaft-bukarest.ro; Ambassador ARMIN HILLER.

Greece: 71108 Bucharest, Str. Orlando 6; tel. (1) 2125688; fax (1) 2125690; e-mail hellas@com.pcnet.ro; internet www.grembassy.ro; Ambassador THEODORA GROSSOMANIDOU.

Holy See: 70749 Bucharest, Str. Pictor C. Stahi 5–7 (Apostolic Nunciature); tel. (1) 3139490; fax (1) 3120316; e-mail nuntius@fx.ro; Apostolic Nuncio Most Rev. JEAN-CLAUDE PÉRISSET (Titular Archbishop of Iustiniana prima).

Hungary: 70203 Bucharest, Str. Jean-Louis Calderon 63; tel. (1) 6146621; fax (1) 3120467; e-mail hunembro@ines.ro; internet hungaryemb.ines.ro; Ambassador ISTVÁN IJGYÁRTÓ.

India: 712663 Bucharest, Str. Uruguay 11; tel. (1) 2225451; fax (1) 2232681; e-mail indem@dnt.ro; Ambassador JAWAHAR LAL.

Indonesia: 71108 Bucharest, Str. Orlando 10; tel. (1) 3120742; fax (1) 3120214; e-mail indo.bucharest@itcner.ro; Ambassador TOTO SOEGIHARTO.

Iran: 71112 Bucharest 1, Bd. Lascar Catargiu 39; tel. (1) 3120493; fax (1) 3120496; Ambassador Dr AHMAD FARD HOSSEINI.

Israel: 751211 Bucharest, Bd. Dimitrie Cantemir 1; tel. (1) 3304149; fax (1) 3300750; e-mail israel.embassy@algoritma.ro; Ambassador SANDU MAZOR.

Italy: 711192 Bucharest, Str. Henri Coandă 7–9; tel. (1) 3113465; fax (1) 3124269; e-mail primosegretario@ambitalia.ro; internet www.ambitalia.ro; Ambassador ANNA BLEFARI MELAZZI.

Japan: 70189 Bucharest 1, Str. Polonă 4; tel. (1) 2100790; fax (1) 2100272; e-mail embjpn@mb.roknet.ro; Ambassador HIDEKATA MITSUHASHI.

Jordan: 702542 Bucharest, Str. Dumbrava Roşie 1; tel. (1) 2104705; fax (1) 2100320; e-mail jordan.embassy@pcnet.ro; Ambassador AZMI A. MIRZA.

Korea, Democratic People's Republic: 715145 Bucharest, Şos. Nordului 6; tel. and fax (1) 2329665; Ambassador KIM CHUN GIL.

Korea, Republic: 71293 Bucharest, Bd. Mircea Eliade 14; tel. (1) 2307198; fax (1) 2307629; e-mail koreaemb@kappa.ro; internet www.uriel.net/~romemb; Ambassador KIM EUN-KI.

Lebanon: 71271 Bucharest, Str. Atena 28, ap.1; tel. (1) 2309205; fax (1) 2307534; e-mail embassy.Lebanon@allnet.ro; Ambassador ABDEL MAJID EL KASSIR.

Liberia: 72111 Bucharest, Str. Mihai Eminescu 82–88, etaj 1, ap. 19–20; tel. (1) 6193029; Chargé d'affaires G. MARCUS KELLEY.

Libya: 71111 Bucharest, Bd. Lascar Catargiu 15; tel. (1) 6507105; fax (1) 3120232; Chargé d'affaires SALEH KHALIFA GWEIDA.

Macedonia, former Yugoslav Republic: Bucharest, Str. Gral Eremia Grigorescu 16; tel. (1) 2100880; fax (1) 2117295; e-mail ammakbuk@mb.roknet.ro; Ambassador BLAGOJ ZASOV.

Malaysia: Bucharest, Str. Mihai Eminescu 124A, etaj 3, ap. 8; tel. (1) 2113801; fax (1) 2100270; e-mail mwbucrst@itcnet.ro; Chargé d'affaires AZIZAN ISMAIL.

Mexico: 702281 Bucharest, Str. Armeneasca 35, Sector 2; tel. (1) 2104417; fax (1) 2104713; Ambassador ENRIQUE FERNÁNDEZ ZAPATA.

Moldova: 71273 Bucharest 1, Al. Alexandru 40; tel. (1) 2300474; fax (1) 2307790; e-mail moldova@customers.digiro.net; Ambassador EMIL CIOBU.

Morocco: 70256 Bucharest, Bd. Dacia 75; tel. (1) 2102945; fax (1) 2102767; e-mail ambmarbuc@xnet.ro; Ambassador TAHAR NEJJAR.

Netherlands: 72271 Bucharest, Str. Atena 18; tel. (1) 2086030; fax (1) 2307620; e-mail bkr@minbuza.nl; internet www.olanda.ro; Ambassador P. J. WOLTHERS.

Nigeria: 71108 Bucharest, Str. Orlando 9; tel. (1) 3128685; fax (1) 3120622; e-mail nigeremb@canad.ro; Ambassador M. G. S. SAMAKI.

Norway: 70254 Bucharest, Str. Dumbrava Roşie 4; tel. (1) 2100274; fax (1) 2100275; e-mail emb.bucharest@mfa.ro; Ambassador ARNT MAGNE RINDAL.

Pakistan: 71304 Bucharest 1, Str. Barbu Delavrancea 22; tel. (1) 2225736; fax (1) 2225737; e-mail parepbuc@k.ro; Ambassador NAZAR ABBAS.

Peru: Bucharest, Şos. Kiseleff 18; tel. (1) 2231253; fax (1) 2231088; e-mail embaperu@bx.logicnet.ro; Ambassador JOSÉ AUGUSTO TENORIO BENAVIDES.

Philippines: 71039 Bucharest, Str. Carol Davila 107; tel. (1) 2248058; fax (1) 2233500; e-mail daciafil@dnt.ro; Ambassador MARIA ROSARIO JANOLO.

Poland: 71273 Bucharest, Al. Alexandru 23; tel. (1) 2302330; fax (1) 2307832; e-mail ampolemb@mail.flamingo.ro; internet ampolbuk.kappa.ro/ambassada.html; Ambassador MICHAL KLINGER.

Portugal: 71249 Bucharest 1, Str. Paris 55; tel. (1) 2304136; fax (1) 2304117; e-mail embporrom@fx.ro; Ambassador ZOZIMO JUSTO DA SILVA.

Qatar: Bucharest, Str. Venezuela 10A; tel. (1) 2304741; fax (1) 2305446; Ambassador ALI SULTAN AL-ZAMAN.

Russia: 71269 Bucharest, Şos. Kiseleff 6; tel. (1) 2223170; fax (1) 2229450; e-mail rab@mb.roknet.ro; internet www.romania.mid.ro; Ambassador ALEKSANDR TOLKACH.

Serbia and Montenegro: 71132 Bucharest, Calea Dorobanţilor 34; tel. (1) 2119871; fax (1) 2100175; Ambassador DUŠAN FRANCUSKI.

Slovakia: 70206 Bucharest 2, Str. Oţetari 3; tel. (1) 3126822; fax (1) 3122435; e-mail zusrbuh@fx.ro; Ambassador JAN SOTH.

Spain: 71274 Bucharest, Str. Tirana 1; tel. (1) 2121730; fax (1) 2307626; Ambassador JESÚS ATIENZA SERNA.

Sudan: 70256 Bucharest, Bd. Dacia 71; tel. (1) 2114967; fax (1) 2111217; e-mail sudanbuc@mb.roknet.ro; internet www.sudanbuc.net; Ambassador BASHIR MOHAMED EL-HASSAN.

Sweden: 71276 Bucharest, Str. Sofia 5; tel. (1) 2302184; fax (1) 2306256; e-mail ambassaden.bukarest@foreign.ministry.se; Ambassador SVANTE KILANDER.

Switzerland: 70152 Bucharest 1, Str. Pitar Moş 12; tel. (1) 2100299; fax (1) 2100324; e-mail vertretung@buc.rep.admin.ch; Ambassador FRANÇOIS CHAPPUIS.

Syria: 71114 Bucharest, Bd. Lascar Catargiu 50; tel. (1) 2124186; fax (1) 3129554; e-mail embsyrom@yahoo.com; Ambassador Dr BECHARA KHAROUF.

Thailand: Bucharest, Str. Vasile Conta 12; tel. (1) 3110031; fax (1) 3110044; Ambassador SURIYA ROSHANABUDDI.

Turkey: 71142 Bucharest, Calea Dorobanţilor 72; tel. (1) 2100279; fax 2100407; e-mail bozkir@easynet.ro; Ambassador OMER ZEYTI-NOĞLU.

Ukraine: 71132 Bucharest, Calea Dorobanţilor 16; tel. (1) 2116986; fax (1) 2116949; e-mail emb_ro@mfa.gov.ua; Ambassador ANTON BUTEIKO.

United Kingdom: 70154 Bucharest, Str. Jules Michelet 24; tel. (1) 2017200; fax (1) 2017299; e-mail press.bucharest@fco.gov.uk; internet www.britain.ro; Ambassador QUINTON QUAYLE.

USA: Bucharest, Str. Tudor Arghezi 7–9; tel. (1) 2104042; fax (1) 2100395; internet www.usembassy.ro; Ambassador MICHAEL GUEST.

Uruguay: 70188 Bucharest, Str. Polonă 35, Scara A, ap. 5; tel. (1) 2118212; fax (1) 2100348; e-mail urubucar@bx.logicnet.ro; Ambassador JUAN DELMIRO PODESTÁ PIÑON.

Venezuela: 71312 Bucharest 1, Str. Pictor G.D. Mirea 18; tel. (1) 2225874; fax (1) 2226183; e-mail embavero@kappa.ro; Ambassador (vacant).

Viet Nam: 73112 Bucharest, Str. C. A. Rosetti 35; tel. (1) 3111604; fax (1) 3121626; e-mail ambviet@ebony.ro; Ambassador LE VAN TOAN.

Yemen: 71279 Bucharest, Bd. Aviatorilor 50; tel. (1) 2313272; fax (1) 2307679; Chargé d'affaires ABDELELAH M. AL-ERYANY.

Judicial System

SUPREME COURT

The Supreme Court of Justice, which was reorganized under Law 56 of 9 July 1993, exercises control over the judicial activity of all courts. It ensures the correct and uniform application of the law. The members of the Supreme Court are appointed by the President of Romania at the proposal of the Superior Council of Magistrates.

President: Prof. Dr GHEORGHE UGLEAN, 70503 Bucharest, Calea Rahovei 2–4; tel. (1) 3353750; fax (1) 3125890; internet www.sjc.ro.

CONSTITUTIONAL COURT

According to the Constitution approved by referendum on 8 December 1991, a Constitutional Court was to be established within six months. The first Constitutional Court of Romania was duly established in June 1992, under Law 47 of 18 May.

President: NICOLAE POPA, Bucharest, Parliament Palace, Calea 13 Septembrie 2, Sector 5; tel. (1) 3132531; fax (1) 3125480; e-mail ccr@ccr.ro; internet www.ccr.ro.

COUNTY COURTS AND LOCAL COURTS

The judicial organization of courts at the county and local levels was established by Law 92 of 4 August 1992. In each of the 40 counties of Romania there is a county court and between three and six local courts. The county courts also form 15 circuits of appeal courts, where appeals against sentences passed by local courts are heard, which are generally considered courts of first instance. There is also a right of appeal from the appeal courts to the Supreme Court. In both county courts and local courts the judges are professional magistrates.

MILITARY COURTS

Military courts were reorganized through Law 54 of 9 July 1993. Generally they judge contraventions of the law by service personnel at one of the two military courts in the country. These are the Territorial Military Court, with a right of appeal to the Appeal Military Court. There is also a military department within the Supreme Court which judges appeals in some special cases. The judges are professional lawyers and career officers.

GENERAL PROSECUTING MAGISTRACY

The General Prosecuting Magistracy functions under Law 92 of 4 August 1992. There are prosecuting magistracies operating through each court, under the authority of the Minister of Justice.

Prosecutor-General: TANASE JOITE, 76105 Bucharest 5, Bd. Liber-tăţi i 14; tel. (1) 4102727; fax (1) 3113939; e-mail pg@kappa.ro; internet www.mp.pcnet.ro.

Religion

In Romania there are 15 religious denominations and more than 400 religious associations recognized by the state. According to census figures, about 87% of the population belonged to the Romanian Orthodox Church in January 1992.

State Secretariat for Religious Affairs: 70136 Bucharest, Str. Nicolae Filipescu 40; tel. (1) 2118116; fax (1) 2109471; e-mail ssc@mediasat.ro; f. 1990; Minister Sec. of State LAURENŢIU TÁNASE.

CHRISTIANITY

The Romanian Orthodox Church

The Romanian Orthodox Church is the major religious organization in Romania (with more than 19m. believers) and is organized as an autocephalous patriarchate, being led by the Holy Synod, headed by a patriarch. The Patriarchate consists of five metropolitanates, nine archbishoprics and 12 bishoprics.

Holy Synod: 70666 Bucharest, Str. Antim 29; tel. (1) 3570803; fax (1) 3370822; Sec. Bishop TEOFAN SINAITUL.

Romanian Patriarchate
(Patriarhia Română)

70526 Bucharest, Al. Dealul Mitropoliei 25; tel. (1) 3374035; fax (1) 3370097; e-mail patriarhia@dnt.ro; internet www.patriarhia.ro.

Patriarch, Metropolitan of Muntênia and Dobrogea and Archbishop of Bucharest: TEOCTIST ARĂPAŞU, 70526 Bucharest, Str. Patriarhiei 21; tel. (1) 3372776.

Metropolitan of Banat and Archbishop of Timişoara and Caransebeş: Dr NICOLAE CORNEANU, 1900 Timişoara, Bd. Constantin Diaconovici Loga 7; tel. (56) 190960.

Metropolitan of Moldova and Bucovina and Archbishop of Iaşi: Dr DANIEL CIOBOTEA, 6600 Iaşi, Bd. Ştefan cel Mare şi Sfânt 16; tel. (32) 214771; fax (32) 212656; e-mail iecum@mail.dntis.ro.

Metropolitan of Oltenia and Archbishop of Craiova: TEOFAN, 1100 Craiova, Str. Mitropolit Firmilian 3; tel. (51) 415054; fax (51) 418369; e-mail mitrop_teofan@m-ol.ro; internet www.m-ol.ro.

Metropolitan of Transylvania, Crişana and Maramureş and Archbishop of Sibiu: Dr ANTONIE PLĂMĂDEALĂ, 2400 Sibiu, Str. Mitropoliei 24; tel. (69) 412867.

Archbishop of Suceava and Rădăuti: PIMEN ZAINEA, 5800 Suceava, Str. Ioan Vodă Viteazul 2; tel. (30) 215796.

Archbishop of Târgovişte: Dr NIFON MIHAITA, 0200 Târgovişte, Str. Mihai Bravu 5-8; tel. (45) 211588; e-mail ips-nifon@k.ro.

Archbishop of Tomis: LUCIAN FLOREA, 8700 Constanţa, Str. Muzeelov 23; tel. (41) 614257.

Archbishop of Vad, Feleac and Cluj: BARTOLOMEU ANANIA, 3400 Cluj-Napoca, Piaţa Avram Iancu 18; tel. (64) 559010; e-mail rev-renasterea@personal.ro.

The Roman Catholic Church

Catholics in Romania include adherents of the Armenian, Latin and Romanian (Byzantine) Rites.

Latin Rite

There are two archdioceses and four dioceses. At 31 December 2000 there were 1,258,804 adherents of the Latin Rite (about 5.6% of the total population).

Archbishop of Alba Iulia: Most Rev. GYÖRGY-MIKLÓS JAKUBÍNYI, 2500 Alba Iulia, Str. Mihai Viteazul 21; tel. (58) 811689; fax (58) 811454; e-mail albapress@apulum.ro.

Archbishop of Bucharest: Most Rev. IOAN ROBU, 70749 Bucharest, Str. Gen. Berthelot 19; tel. (1) 3154955; fax (1) 3121208.

Romanian Rite

There is one metropolitan and four dioceses. At 31 December 2000 there were 783,716 adherents of the Romanian Rite.

Metropolitan of the Romanian Uniate Church and Archbishop of Făgăraş and Alba Iulia: Most Rev. LUCIAN MUREŞAN, 3175 Blaj, Str. Petru Pavel Aron 2; tel. (58) 712057; fax (58) 710608.

Protestant Churches

Baptist Union of Romania: 78152 Bucharest 1, Str. Dîmbovitei 9–11, Sector 6; tel. (1) 2205053; fax (1) 4302942; 1,450 churches; Pres. Pastor VASILE ALEXANDRU TALOŞ.

Evangelical Church of the Augsburg Confession in Romania: 2400 Sibiu, Str. General Magheru 4; tel. and fax (69) 217864; e-mail ev.landeskon@logon.ro; founded in the 16th century; comprises some 15,813 mems; mainly of German nationality; Bishop of Sibiu Dr CHRISTOPH KLEIN (tel. (69) 230202; fax (69) 217864); Gen. Sec. FRIEDRICH GUNESCH.

Reformed (Calvinist) Church

700,000 mems; two bishoprics.

Bishop of the Transylvanian Reformed Church District: Rev. GÉZA PAP, 3400 Cluj-Napoca, Str. I. C. Brătianu 51; tel. (64) 197472; fax (64) 195104; e-mail office@reformatus.ro.

Bishop of Oradea: LÁSZLÓ TÖKÉS, 3700 Oradea, Str. J. Calvin 1; tel. (59) 432837; e-mail partium@rdsor.ro; internet www .kiralyhagomellek.ro.

Romanian Evangelical Church: 76207 Bucharest, Str. Carol Davila 48; tel. (1) 6381004.

Evangelical-Lutheran Church of the Augsburg Confession in Romania: 3400 Cluj-Napoca, Bul. 22 Decembrie 1; tel. (64) 196614; fax (64) 193897; e-mail luthphkolozsvar@zortec.ro; comprises about 26,500 Hungarians, 4,000 Slovaks and 200 Romanians; Superintendent ÁRPÁD MÓZES.

Unitarian Church: 3400 Cluj-Napoca, Str. 21 Decembrie 9; tel. (64) 193236; fax (64) 195927; e-mail unitarian@mail.dntcj.ro; f. 1568; comprises about 75,000 mems of Hungarian nationality; 125 churches and 30 fellowships; Bishop ÁRPÁD SZABÓ.

Other Christian Churches

Armenian-Gregorian Church: 70228 Bucharest, Str. Armenească 9; tel. (1) 6139070; fax (1) 3121083; 5,000 mems; Archbishop TIRAIR MARTICHIAN.

Bulgarian Church: 70014 Bucharest, Str. Doamnei 18, Sector 4; tel. (1) 6135881.

Jehovah's Witnesses: 73217 Bucharest, Str. Teleajen 84, Sector 2; tel. (1) 3027500; fax (1) 3027501; e-mail ormi@zappmobile.ro.

Old-Rite Christian Church: 6100 Brăila, Str. Zidari 5; tel. (39) 647023; 50,000 mems of Russian nationality; Metropolitan TIMON GAVRILA.

Open Brethren Church: Head MELITON LAZAROVICI.

Pentecostal Church: 76252 Bucharest, Str. Carol Davila 81; tel. (1) 2126419; fax (1) 2204303; e-mail cuvadev@fx.ro; f. 1922; 2,455 churches, 525 pastors (Dec. 2001); 450,000 mems; Pres. Rev. RIVIS TIPEI PAVEL; Gen. Sec. Rev. IOAN GURĂU.

Serbian Orthodox Church: 1900 Timişoara, Piaţa Unirii 4; tel. and fax (56) 130426; Administrator Bishop LUKIJAN.

Seventh-day Adventist Church: 72900 Voluntari, Ilfov, Str. Erou Iancu Nicolae 38; tel. (1) 4908590; fax (1) 4908570; e-mail communicatii@adventist.ro; internet www.adventist.ro; f. 1920; 67,000 mems; Pres. of the Union Rev. ADRIAN BOCANEANU; Sec.-Gen. TEODOR HUTANU.

Ukrainian Orthodox Church: 4925 Sighetu Marmaţiei, Str. Bogdan Vodă 12; tel. (62) 511879.

Union of Brethren Assemblies: 72461 Bucharest, Andronache 60A; tel. and fax (1) 2407865; f. 1925; Pres. MIRCEA CIOATĂ.

BAHA'I FAITH

Baha'i Community: 70122 Bucharest, Bd. Nicolae Bălcescu 38, etaj 7, ap. 28; tel. (1) 6506120.

ISLAM

The Muslim Community comprises some 55,000 members of Turkish-Tatar origin.

Grand Mufti: OSMAN NEGEAT, 8700 Constanţa, Bd. Tomis 41; tel. (41) 611390.

JUDAISM

In 1999 there were about 14,000 Jews, organized in some 70 communities, in Romania.

Federation of Jewish Communities: 70478 Bucharest, Str. Sf. Vineri 9–11; tel. (1) 3132538; fax (1) 3120869; e-mail asivan@pcnet .ro; Great Rabbi MENACHEM HACOHEN; Pres. Prof. Dr NICOLAE CAJAL.

The Press

The Romanian press is highly regionalized, with newspapers and periodicals appearing in all of the administrative districts. In 1996 there were a total of 1,313 newspapers and periodicals in circulation in Romania, including 106 daily newspapers. Some 106 newspapers and periodicals are published in the languages of co-inhabiting nationalities in Romania, including Hungarian, German, Serbian, Ukrainian, Armenian and Yiddish. The Ministry of Culture relinquished control of the press in June 1990.

The publications listed below are in Romanian, unless otherwise indicated.

PRINCIPAL DAILY NEWSPAPERS

Adevărul (Truth): 71341 Bucharest, Piaţa Presei Libere 1; tel. (1) 2240067; fax (1) 2243612; e-mail redactia@adevarul.kappa.ro; internet adevarul.kappa.ro; f. 1888; daily except Sun.; independent; Dir CHRISTIAN TUDOR POPESCU; circ. 200,000.

Azi (Today): 70101 Bucharest, Calea Victoriei 39A; tel. (1) 3144215; fax (1) 3120128; e-mail office@cicero.kappa.ro; f. 1990; independent; Editor-in-Chief OCTAVIAN ŞTIREANU.

Cotidianul (The Daily): 77107 Bucharest, Calea Plevnei 114; tel. (1) 3102052; fax (1) 3123764; e-mail rhpress@cotidianul.ro; internet www.cotidianul.ro; f. 1991; daily except Sun.; Dir of Marketing IOANA SAMAREANU; circ. 120,000.

Cronica Română: 75121 Bucharest, Calea Şerban Vodă 22–24; tel. (1) 3126363; fax (1) 3126813; f. 1992; daily; Dir HORIA ALEXANDRESCU; circ. 29,000.

Curierul Naţional (National Messenger): 70109 Bucharest, Str. Ministerului 2–4; tel. (1) 3159512; fax (1) 3121300; e-mail curiernr@bx.logicnet.ro; f. 1991; Dir-Gen. VALENTIN PAUNESCU; Editor-in-Chief MARIUS PETREAN; circ. 55,000.

Dimineata (Morning): Bucharest, Str. Roma 48; tel. (1) 2120337; fax (1) 2120496; f. 1990; Dir SORIN STEFAN STANCIU.

Evenimentul Zilei (Event of the Day): 71341 Bucharest, Piaţa Presei Libere 1; tel. (1) 2226381; fax (1) 2226382; f. 1991; tabloid; Editor-in-Chief GHEORGHE VOICU; circ. 200,000.

Gazeta Sporturilor (Sports Gazette): 70139 Bucharest, Str. Vasile Conta 16; tel. (1) 2111135; fax (1) 2100153; f. 1924; daily except Sun. independent; Editor-in-Chief AURELIAN BREBEANU; circ. 50,000.

Jurnalul National (National Journal): Bucharest, Şos. Ficusului 44A; tel. (1) 2322467; fax (1) 2307944; f. 1993; Editor-in-Chief MARIUS TUCĂ; circ. 70,000.

Libertatea (Freedom): 70711 Bucharest, Şos. Fabrica de Glucoza Nr. 5, Sector 2; tel. (1) 2035646; fax (1) 2030830; internet www .libertatea.ro; f. 1989; daily except Sun.; morning paper; Editor-in-Chief ADRIAN HALPERT; circ. 140,000.

România Liber (Free Romania): 71341 Bucharest, Piaţa Presei Libere 1; tel. (1) 2224770; fax (1) 2232071; f. 1877; daily except Sun.; independent; Exec. Dir PETRE MIHAI BACANU; circ. 100,000.

Tineretul Liber (Free Youth): 71341 Bucharest, Piaţa Presei Libere 1; tel. (1) 2225040; fax (1) 2223313; f. 1989; daily except Sun. and Mon.; Editor-in-Chief ARISTOTEL BUNESCU.

Vocea Romaniei (Romanian Voice): Bucharest; tel. (1) 2227205; fax (1) 2226347; f. 1993; govt newspaper; Dir D.D. RUJAN.

Zina (The Day): Bucharest, Str. Ion Cimpineanu 4; tel. and fax (1) 3113155; f. 1930; Dir SORIN ROSCA STANESCU.

DISTRICT NEWSPAPERS

Alba

Ardealul: Alba Iulia; tel. (58) 13026; f. 1990; daily; Editor-in-Chief IOAN MAIER.

Unirea (The Union): 2500 Alba Iulia, Str. Decebal 27; tel. (58) 811420; f. 1990; independent; daily except Sun.; Gen. Man. GHEORGHE CIUL; Editor-in-Chief GHEORGHE YURCA; circ. 32,000.

Arad

Adevărul (The Truth): 2900 Arad, Bd. Revoluţiei 81; tel. (57) 213302; fax (57) 280655; f. 1989; independent; daily; Dir DOREL ZAVOIANU; circ. 53,000.

Argeş

Argeşul Liber (Free Argeş): Piteşti; tel. (76) 30490; f. 1990; independent; daily; Editor-in-Chief MARIN MANOLACHE.

Bacău

Deşteptărea (The Awakening): 5500 Bacău, Str. Vasile Alecsandri 63; tel. (34) 111272; fax (34) 124794; f. 1989; Man. CORNEL GALBEN; Editor-in-Chief IOAN ENACHE; circ. 50,000.

Bihor

Erdélyi Napló: 3700 Oradea, Sirul Canonicilor 25; tel. (59) 417158; fax (59) 417126; e-mail erdelyinaplo@rdslink.ro; internet www.hhrf .org/erdelyinaplo/; f. 19901; in Hungarian; weekly; Editor-in-Chief LÁSZLÓ DÉNES.

Bistriţa-Năsăud

Răsunetul (Sound): 4400 Bistriţa, Str. Bistricioarei 6; tel. (90) 11684; f. 1990; journal of the National Salvation Front, Bistriţa-Năsăud County; Editor-in-Chief VASILE TABĂRĂ.

Botoşani

Gazeta de Botoşani: 6800 Botoşani, Bd. Mihai Eminescu 91; tel. (40) 851106; f. 1990; fmrly Clopotul; daily; Editor-in-Chief GHEORGHE ZANEA.

Brăila

Libertatea (Freedom): 6100 Brăila, Piaţa Independenţei 1; tel. (94) 635946; f. 1989; independent; daily; Editor-in-Chief RODICA CANĂ.

Braşov

Bună Zina Braşov (Good Afternoon Braşov): Braşov; tel. (68) 411073; fax (68) 411072; f. 1995; Dir DORU ŞUPEALĂ; circ. 30,000.

Gazeta de Transilvania (Transylvanian Gazette): 2200 Braşov, Str. M. Sadoveanu 3; tel. (68) 8142029; fax (68) 8152927; f. 1838; ceased publication 1946, re-established 1989; daily except Mon.; independent; Editor-in-Chief EDUARD HUIDAN.

Buzău

Opinia (Opinion): Buzău; tel. (38) 412764; fax (38) 711063; f. 1990; independent; daily; Editor-in-Chief CALIN BOSTAN.

Călăraşi

Pământul (Free Earth): 8500 Călăraşi, Str. Bucureşti 187; tel. (911) 15840; fax (911) 313630; f. 1990; socio-political; weekly; Editor-in-Chief GHEORGHE FRANGULEA.

Caraş-Severin

Timpul (The Times): 1700 Reşiţa, Piaţa Republicii 7; tel. (40) 412739; fax (40) 416709; f. 1990; independent daily; Editor-in-Chief GHEORGHE JURMA.

Cluj

Adevărul de Cluj (Truth of Cluj): 3400 Cluj-Napoca, Str. Napoca 16; tel. (64) 111032; fax (64) 192828; f. 1989; daily; independent; Editor-in-Chief ILIE CĂLIAN; circ. 200,000.

Szabadság (Freedom): 3400 Cluj-Napoca, Str. Napoca 16, POB 340; tel. (64) 198985; fax (64) 197206; e-mail szabadsag@mail.dntcj.ro; internet www.hhrf.org/szabadsag/szamok.htm; f. 1989; daily except Sun.; in Hungarian; Editor-in-Chief ÁRON BALLÓ; circ. 12,000.

Constanţa

Cuget Liber (Free Thinking): 8700 Constanţa, Bd. I. C. Brătianu 5; tel. (41) 665110; fax (41) 665606; f. 1989; independent; daily; Dir ARCADI STRAHILEVICI.

Covasna

Cuvântul nou (New Word): 4000 Sfântu Gheorghe, Str. Pieţei 8; tel. (40) 2311388; f. 1968; new series 1990; daily except Mon.; Editor-in-Chief DUMITRU MĂNOLĂCHESCU.

Háromszék (Three Chairs): 4000 Sfântu Gheorghe, Str. Presei 8A; tel. (40) 67351504; fax (40) 67351253; e-mail hpress@3szek.ro; internet www.3szek.ro; f. 1989; socio-political; daily; in Hungarian; Editor-in-Chief FARKAS ÁRPÁD.

Dâmboviţa

Dâmboviţa: 0200 Târgovişte, Str. Unirii 32; f. 1990; independent; daily; Editor-in-Chief ALEXANDRU ILIE.

Dolj

Cuvântul Libertăţii (Word of Liberty): 1100 Craiova, Str. Lyon 8; tel. (51) 2457; fax (51) 4141; f. 1989; daily except Sun.; Editor-in-Chief DAN LUPESCU; circ. 40,000.

Galaţi

Viaţa Libera (Free Life): 6200 Galaţi, Str. Domnească 68; tel. (3) 6456800; fax (3) 6457528; f. 1990; independent; daily; Dir RADU MACOVEI.

Giurgiu

Cuvântul Liber (Free Word): 8375 Giurgiu, Str. 1 Decembrie 1918 60A; tel. (912) 21227; f. 1990; weekly; Editor-in-Chief ION GAGHII; circ. 10,000.

Gorj

Gorjanul: 1400 Târgu Jiu, Str. Constantin Brăncuşi 15; tel. (929) 17464; f. 1990; socio-political; daily; Editor-in-Chief NICOLAE BRÎNZAN.

Harghita

Adevărul Harghitei (Truth of Harghita): 4100 Miercurea-Ciuc, Str. Leticeni 45; tel. (58) 13019; f. 1990; independent; daily; Editor-in-Chief MIHAI GROZA.

Új Sport (New Sport): 4100 Miercurea-Ciuc; tel. (958) 15940; fax (58) 152514; independent sports; daily; in Hungarian; Editor-in-Chief PÉTER LÁSZLÓ.

Hunedoara

Cuvântul Liber (Free Word): 2700 Deva, Str. 1 Decembrie 35; tel. (56) 11275; fax (56) 18061; f. 1949; daily except Mon.; Editor-in-Chief NICOLAE TÎRCOB; circ. 25,000.

Ialomiţa

Tribuna Ialomiţei (Ialomiţa Tribune): 8400 Slobozia, Str. Dobrogeanu-Gherea 2; f. 1969; weekly; Editor-in-Chief TITUS NIŢU.

Iaşi

Evenimentul: 6600 Iaşi, Str. Ştefan cel Mare 4; tel. (32) 112023; fax (32) 112025; e-mail evenimentul@mail.dntis.ro; f. 1991; daily; Editor-in-Chief CONSTANTIN PALADUTA.

Monitorul: 6600 Iaşi, Str. Smârdan 5; tel. (32) 271271; fax (32) 270415; daily; Editor-in-Chief DAN RADU; circ. 40,000.

Opinia (Opinion): 6600 Iaşi, Str. Vasile Alecsandri 8; tel. (32) 452105; f. 1990; social, political and cultural; daily; Editor-in-Chief VASILE FILIP.

Maramureş

Graiul Maramureşului (Voice of Maramureş): 4800 Baia Mare, Bd. Bucureşti 25; tel. (62) 221017; fax (62) 224871; e-mail graiul@ sintec.ro; f. 1989; independent; daily; Editor-in-Chief AUGUSTIN COZMUŢA.

Bányavidéki Új Szó (Miner's New Word): 4800 Baia Mare, Bd. Bucureşti 25; tel. (62) 274465; fax (62) 432585; e-mail genius@sintec .ro; f. 1989; weekly; in Hungarian; Editor-in-Chief MARIA SZILVESZTER.

Mehedinţi

Datina (Tradition): 1500 Drobeta-Turnu-Severin, Str. Traâan 89; tel. (978) 119950; f. 1990; independent; daily; Editor-in-Chief GHEORGHE BUREŢEA.

Mureş

Cuvântul Liber (Free Word): 4300 Târgu Mureş, Str. Gh. Doja 9; tel. (65) 36636; f. 1990; independent; daily; Editor-in-Chief LAZĂR LADARIU.

Népújság (People's Journal): 4300 Târgu Mureş, Str. Gh. Doja 9; tel. (65) 166780; fax (65) 166270; e-mail impress@netsoft.ro; f. 1990; daily; in Hungarian; Editor-in-Chief JÁNOS MAKKAI.

Neamţ

Ceahlăul: 5600 Piatra-Neamţ, Al. Tiparului 14; tel. and fax (33) 625282; f. 1989; daily; Editor-in-Chief VIOREL TUDOSE; circ. 20,000.

Olt

Glasul Adevărului (Voice of the Truth): 0500 Slatina, Str. Filimon Sârbu 5; tel. (44) 22131; f. 1990.

Prahova

Prahova: 2000 Ploieşti, Bd. Republicii 2; tel. (44) 141245; fax (44) 111206; f. 1870; Editor-in-Chief DUMITRU CÂRSTEA; circ. 17,000.

Sălaj

Graiul Sălajului (Voice of Sălaj): 4700 Zalău, Piaţa Unirii 7; tel. (99) 614120; f. 1990; daily; Editor-in-Chief IOAN LUPA.

Szilágyaság (Word from Sălaj): 4700 Zalău, Piaţa Libertăţii 9, POB 68; tel. (99) 633736; f. 1990; organ of Hungarian Democratic Union of Romania; weekly; Editor-in-Chief János Kui.

Satu Mare

Ardealul: 3900 Satu Mare; tel. (61) 730661; f. 1990; organ of Christian Democratic National Peasants' Party; weekly; Dir Nae Antonescu.

Szatmári Friss Újság: 3900 Satu Mare, Str. M. Viteazu 32; tel. (61) 712024; fax (61) 714654; e-mail szfu@multiarea.ro; internet www .hhrf.org/frissujsag; f. 1990; daily except Sun.; in Hungarian; Editor-in-Chief Veres István.

Sibiu

Tribuna: Sibiu, Str. Dr Ratiu 7; tel. (92) 413833; fax (92) 412026; f. 1884; daily; independent; Editor-in-Chief Octavian Rusu; circ. 40,000.

Suceava

Crai nou: 5800 Suceava, Str. Mihai Viteazul 32; tel. (30)214723; fax (30) 530285; e-mail redactie@crainou.ro; f. 1990; daily; Editor-in-Chief Teodorescu Dumitru.

Teleorman

Teleormanul Liber (Free Teleorman): 0700 Alexandria, Str. Ion Creangă 63, jud. Teleorman; tel. (47) 311950; fax (47) 323871; e-mail etl@starnets.ro; f. 1990; daily; Editor-in-Chief Gheorghe Filip.

Timiş

Renasterea Banateana: Timisoara, Bd. Revolutiei 8; tel. (56) 197176; fax (56) 190370; f. 1990; Editor-in-Chief Adrian Pop; circ. 50,000.

Timişoara: 1900 Timişoara, Str. Brediceanu 37A; tel. (56) 123401; fax (56) 146170; f. 1990; daily; Dirs George Serban, Lucian Vasile Szabo.

Tulcea

Delta (The Delta): 8800 Tulcea, Str. Spitalului 4; tel. (405) 12406; fax (405) 16616; f. 1885; new series 1990; daily except Mon.; Editor-in-Chief Neculai Amihulesei.

Vaslui

Adevărul (Truth): 6500 Vaslui, Str. Ştefan cel Mare 79; tel. (983) 12203; socio-cultural publication; twice weekly; f. 1990; Editor-in-Chief Teodor Praxiu.

Vâlcea

Curierul de Vâlcea (Courier of Vâlcea): 1000 Râmnicu Vâlcea, Calea lui Traian 127; tel. (50) 718394; fax (50) 732423; f. 1990; independent; daily except Mon.; commerce; Dir Ioan Barbu.

Vrancea

Milcovul Liber (Free Milcov): 5300 Focşani, Bd. Unirii 18; tel. (37) 614579; fax (37) 613588; f. 1989; weekly; Dir Ovidiu Butuc.

PRINCIPAL PERIODICALS

Bucharest

22: 70179 Bucharest, Calea Victoriei 120; tel. (1) 3141776; fax (1) 3112208; e-mail r22@r22.sfos.ro; f. 1990; weekly; published by the Group for Social Dialogue; Editor-in-Chief Gabriela Adameşteanu; circ. 13,000.

Academia Catavencu (Dubious Academy): Bucharest; tel. (1) 4209459; fax (1) 6362760; f. 1991; weekly; satirical; Dir Mircea Dinescu; circ. 85,000.

Astrologia (Astrology): Bucharest, Piaţa Presei Libere 1; f. 1996; monthly; Editor-in-Chief Aurora Indan.

Auto Pro: Bucharest; tel. (1) 4113225; fax (1) 4111043; f. 1994; monthly; motor-vehicles; Editor-in-Chief Dan Vardie; circ. 50,000.

Bursa: Bucharest, Str. Balcesti 7, Sector 3; tel. (1) 3228691; fax (1) 3124556; e-mail marketing@bursa.ro; f. 1990; finance; Editor-in-Chief Florian Goldstein; circ. 35,000.

Capital: Bucharest, Şos. Fabrica de Glucoza 5, Sector 2; tel. (1) 2030802; fax (1) 2425359; e-mail office@capital.ro; internet www .capital.ro; f. 1990; weekly; Editor-in-Chief Ionut Popescu; circ. 60,000.

Doina: 71341 Bucharest, Piaţa Presei Libere 1; tel. (1) 2223346; fax (1) 2244801; f. 1991; monthly; Dir Vasile Tincu.

Economistul (The Economist): Bucharest, Calea Grivitei 21; tel. (1) 6507820; fax (1) 3129717; f. 1990; daily; Editor-in-Chief Ioan Erhan.

Contemporanul—Ideea Europeană: 71341 Bucharest, Piaţa Presei Libere 1; tel. (1) 177316; f. 1881; weekly; cultural, political and scientific review, published by the Ministry of Culture; Dir Nicolae Breban.

Expres Magazin: 71341 Bucharest 1, Piaţa Presei Libere 1; tel. (1) 2225119; fax (1) 3128381; independent; weekly; Dir Cornel Nistorescu; circ. 98,000.

Familia Moderna (Modern Family): 71341 Bucharest, Piaţa Presei Libere 1; tel. (1) 2223209; fax (1) 2227810; f. 1995; Dir Vasile Tincu.

Femeia Moderna (Modern Woman): 71341 Bucharest, Piaţa Presei Libere 1; tel. (1) 2223346; fax (1) 2224801; f. 1868; monthly; Dir Vasile Tincu.

Flacăra (The Flame): 71341 Bucharest 1, Piaţa Presei Libere 1; tel. (1) 2243688; fax (1) 2273713; e-mail redactia@flacara21.ro; internet www.flacara21.ro; f. 1911; monthly; Editor-in-Chief Alexandru Arion; circ. 30,000.

Fotbal (Football): 79778 Bucharest, Vasile Conta 16; tel. (1) 2111288; fax (1) 2100153; f. 1966; weekly; independent; Editor-in-Chief Laurentiu Dumitrescu; circ. 55,000.

Jurnalul Afacerilor (Business Journal): Bucharest, Piaţa Presei Libere 1; tel. (1) 2223760; fax (1) 2230691; f. 1990; Dir Marcel Barbu; circ. 25,000.

Luceafărul (The Morning Star): 71102 Bucharest, Calea Victoriei 133; tel. (1) 596760; f. 1958; weekly; published by the Writers' Union; Dir Laurentiu Ulici.

Magazin (The Magazine): Bucharest, Piaţa Presei Libere 1; tel. (1) 2225111; fax (1) 2230866; f. 1958; Dir Filip Dumitru.

Magazin istoric (Historical Magazine): 70711 Bucharest, Piaţa Valter Mărăcinea; tel. (1) 3126877; fax (1) 3150991; e-mail mistoric@ itcnet.ro; internet www.itcnet.ro/history/magazin.htm; f. 1967; monthly; review of historical culture; Chief Editor Dorin Matei; circ. 35,000.

Meridian: Bucharest; tel. (1) 6155332; fax (1) 3121706; f. 1993; Editor-in-Chief Constantin Zlibut.

Panoramic Radio-TV: 79757 Bucharest, Str. Molière 2–4; tel. (1) 2307501; fax (1) 156992; e-mail micara.dumutrescu@tvr.ro; f. 1990; weekly; Dir Stefan Dimitriu; Editor-in-Chief Adrian Ionescu; circ. 50,000.

PC World Romania: 71316 Bucharest, Bd. Mareşal Averescu 8–10, Sector 1; tel. and fax (1) 2241132; e-mail pcworld@idg.ro; internet www.pcworld.ro; f. 1993; monthly; computing and internet magazine; Editor-in-Chief Bogdan Learschi; circ. 15,000.

Revista Română de Statistică (Romanian Review of Statistics): 70542 Bucharest, Bd. Libertăţii 16; tel. (1) 4106744; fax (1) 3124873; e-mail munteanu@cns.kappa.ro; f. 1952; monthly; organ of the National Statistics Commission; Editor-in-Chief Nicolae Gârceag.

România Literară (Literary Romania): 71102 Bucharest, Calea Victoriei 133; tel. (1) 6506286; fax (1) 6503369; e-mail romlit@romlit .ro; internet www.romlit.ro; f. 1968 as successor to Gazeta Literară; weekly; literary, artistic and political magazine; published by the Fundation Rômânia Literară (Writers' Union); Dir Nicolae Manolescu; Editor-in-Chief Alex Ştefănescu.

România Mare (Greater Romania): 70101 Bucharest, Calea Victoriei 39A; tel. (1) 6156093; fax (1) 3125396; f. 1990; weekly; independent nationalist; Editor-in-Chief Corneliu Vadim Tudor; circ. 90,000.

Romanian Panorama: 71341 Bucharest, Piaţa Presei Libere 1, Corp B, POB 33–38; tel. (1) 2242162; fax (1) 2243608; e-mail rps@ dial.kappa.ro; internet www.wsp.ro; f. 1955; monthly; in English, French, German, Russian and Spanish; economy, politics, social questions, science, history, culture, sport, etc. published by the Foreign Languages Press Group; Dir Nicolae Şarambei; circ. 166,000.

Super Magazin: Bucharest, Piaţa Presei Libere 1; tel. (1) 2223323; fax (1) 2226382; f. 1993; Editor-in-Chief Gheorghe Voicu; circ. 200,000.

Tehnium: 79784 Bucharest, Piaţa Presei Libere 1; tel. (1) 2223374; f. 1970; monthly; hobbies; Editor-in-Chief Ing. Ilie Mihăescu; circ. 100,000.

Telecom Romania: Bucharest; tel. (1) 2120340; f. 1994; bimonthly; networking and telecommunications; Editor-in-Chief Andrei Savu.

Tribuna economică (Economic Tribune): 70159 Bucharest, Bd. Magheru 28–30; tel. (1) 6592270; fax (1) 6595158; e-mail tribunae@ dnt.ro; f. 1886; weekly; Editor-in-Chief Bogdan Padure; circ. 25,000.

Vânătorul şi Pescarul Român (The Romanian Hunter and Angler): 70344 Bucharest, Calea Moşilor 128; tel. (1) 3133363; fax (1) 3136804; f. 1948; monthly review; published by the General Association of Hunters and Anglers; Editor-in-Chief GABRIEL CHEROIU.

Cluj-Napoca

Korunk (Our Time): 3400 Cluj-Napoca, Str. Iasilor 14; tel. and fax (64) 432154; e-mail korunk@mail.dntcj.ro; internet www.hhrf.org/korunk; f. 1926; monthly; social review; in Hungarian; Editor-in-Chief LAJOS KÁNTOR; circ. 1,500.

Napsugár (Sun Ray): 3400 Cluj-Napoca, Str. L. Rebreanu 58/28, POB 137; tel. and fax (64) 141323; e-mail napsugar@mail.dntcj.ro; internet www.dntcj.ro/ngos/napsugar; f. 1956; monthly illustrated literary magazine for children aged 7–10 years; in Hungarian; Editor-in-Chief EMESE ZSIGMOND; circ. 18,000.

Szivárvány (Rainbow): 3400 Cluj-Napoca, Str. L. Rebreanu 58/28, POB 137; tel. and fax (64) 141323; e-mail napsugar@mail.dntcj.ro; f. 1980; monthly illustrated literary magazine for children aged 3–6 years; in Hungarian; Editor-in-Chief EMESE ZSIGMOND; circ. 21,500.

Tribuna: 3400 Cluj-Napoca, Str. Universităţii 1; tel. (64) 117548; f. 1884; weekly; cultural review; Editor-in-Chief AUGUSTIN BUZURA.

Iaşi

Cronica: 6600 Iaşi, Str. Vasile Alecsandri 6; tel. (32) 146433; fax (32) 211086; e-mail valerist@mail.dntis.ro; f. 1966; monthly; cultural review; Editor-in-Chief VALERIU STANCU; circ. 5,000.

Timişoara

Orizont (Horizon): 1900 Timişoara, Piaţa Sf. Gheorghe 3; tel. and fax (56) 133376; f. 1949; weekly; review of the Writers' Union (Timişoara branch); Editor-in-Chief MIRCEA MIHAIES.

Târgu Mureş

Erdélyi Figyelö (Transylvanian Observer): 4300 Târgu-Mureş, Str. Primăriei 1; tel. (65) 166910; fax (65) 168688; f. 1958; fmrly Új Élet; trimestrial; illustrated magazine; in Hungarian; Editor-in-Chief JÁNOS LÁZOK.

Látó (Visionary): 4300 Târgu Mureş, Str. Tuşnad 5; tel. and fax (65) 167087; f. 1953; fmrly Igaz Szó; monthly; in Hungarian; literature; Editor-in-Chief BÉLA MARKÓ; circ. 1,000.

NEWS AGENCIES

ROMPRES (Romanian National News Agency): 71341 Bucharest, Piaţa Presei Libere 1; tel. (1) 2228340; fax (1) 2220089; e-mail webmaster@rompres.ro; internet www.rompres.ro; f. 1949; fmrly Agerpres; provides news and photo services to more than 110 subscribers in Romanian media and 40 overseas news agencies; daily news released in English and French; publs news and feature bulletins in English and French; Chamber of Deputies reassumed control in Feb. 2002; Gen. Man. CONSTANTIN BADEA.

Nord-Est Press: 6600 Iaşi, Str. Smirdan 5; tel. and fax (32) 144776; independent regional news agency for north-east Romania; Editor MONA DIRTU.

Foreign Bureaux

Agence France-Presse (AFP): 70151 Bucharest, Str. Pitar Moş 25, ap. 26; tel. (1) 2100261; Correspondent FRANÇOISE MICHEL.

Agenzia Nazionale Stampa Associata (ANSA) (Italy): 70401 Bucharest, Bd. Unirii 8, Bl. 7A; tel. and fax (1) 6335325; f. 1970; Chief Correspondent GIAN MARCO VENIER.

Allgemeiner Deutscher Nachrichtendienst (ADN) (Germany): Bucharest; tel. (1) 111214; Correspondent MICHAEL HUBE.

Associated Press (AP) (USA): 70122 Bucharest, Bd. Nicolae Bălcescu 30, ap. 14; tel. (1) 3120288.

Bulgarska Telegrafna Agentsia (BTA) (Bulgaria): Bucharest, Str. Mihai Eminescu 124, Inter B, etaj 5, ap. 12; tel. (1) 191880; Correspondent PETYO PETKOV.

Deutsche Presse-Agentur (dpa) (Germany): Bucharest; tel. (1) 121481; fax (1) 123079; Correspondent JOACHIM SONNENBERG.

Informatsionnoye Telegrafnoye Agentstvo Rossii– Telegrafnoye Agentstvo Suverennykh Stran (ITAR—TASS) (Russia): Bucharest, Str. Armeneasca 41; tel. (1) 2106050; fax 2107490; e-mail itartass@mb.roknet.ro; Correspondent NIKOLAI N. MOROZOV.

Magyar Távirati Iroda (MTI) (Hungary): 72238 Bucharest, Al. Alexandru 10, ap. 1; tel. and fax (1) 2307741; e-mail mtibuc@pcnet.ro; internet www.mti.hu; Correspondent ISTVÁN GOZON.

Polska Agencja Prasowa (PAP) (Poland): Bucharest; tel. (1) 206870; Correspondent STANISŁAW WOJNAROWICZ.

Reuters (UK): Bucharest; tel. (1) 3158772; fax (1) 6158448.

Rossiiskoye Informatsionnoye Agentstvo—Novosti (RIA—Novosti) (Russia): 76100 Bucharest, Pandur Hw. 15, Block P18, ap. 6, Sector 5; tel. (1) 4108855; fax (1) 4115812; Correspondent VYACHESLAV SAMOSHIN.

Xinhua (New China) News Agency (People's Republic of China): 71512 Bucharest, Şos. Nordului 2; tel. (1) 2329675; fax (1) 2320258; e-mail xinhua@dial.kappa.ro; Correspondent CHEN JIN.

PRESS ASSOCIATIONS

Society of Romanian Journalists—Federation of All Press Unions (Societatea Ziariştilor din România—Federaţia Sindicatelor din Întreaga Presă): Bucharest, Piaţa Presei Libere 1; tel. (1) 2228351; fax (1) 2224266; f. 1990; affiliated to International Organization of Journalists and to International Federation of Journalists; Pres. RADU SORESCU; 5,000 mems.

The Union of Professional Journalists (Pres. ŞTEFAN MITROI) was established in 1990, as was the Democratic Journalists' Union (Pres. P. M. BACANU). There is also an Association of Hungarian Journalists of Romania (Pres. LAJOS KANTOR).

Publishers

Editura Academiei Române (Publishing House of the Romanian Academy): 76117 Bucharest, Calea 13 Septembrie 13; tel. (1) 4119008; fax (1) 4103983; e-mail edacad@ns.ear.ro; internet www.ear.ro; f. 1948; important books and periodicals on original scientific work, 96 periodicals in Romanian and foreign languages; Dir GHEORGHE MIHĂILĂ.

Editura Albatros: 71341 Bucharest, Piaţa Presei Libere 1, Of. 33; tel. (1) 2228493; f. 1971; Editor-in-Chief GEORGETA DIMISIANO.

Editura Artemis (Artemis Publishing House): 71341 Bucharest, Piaţa Presei Libere 1; tel. (1) 2226661; f. 1991; fine arts, fiction, children's literature, history; Dir MIRELLA ACSENTE.

Editura Cartea Românească (Publishing House of the Romanian Book): Bucharest; tel. (1) 3123733; fax (1) 3110025; f. 1969; Romanian contemporary literature; Dir DAN CRISTEA.

Editura Ceres: 71341 Bucharest, Piaţa Presei Libere 1; tel. (1) 2224836; f. 1953; books on agriculture and forestry; Dir MARIA DAMIAN.

Editura Dacia SA (Dacia Publishing House): 3400 Cluj-Napoca, Str. Paul Chinezul 2; tel. and fax (64) 194912; f. 1969; classical and contemporary literature, science fiction, academic, technical, philosophical and scientific books in Romanian and Hungarian; Gen. Man. IOAN VĂDAN.

Editura Didactică şi Pedagogică (Educational Publishing House): 70738 Bucharest, Str. Spiru Haret 12; tel. and fax (1) 3122885; e-mail edp@totalnet.ro; internet www.edituradp.ro; f. 1951; school, university, technical and vocational textbooks; pedagogic literature and methodology; teaching materials; Gen. Man. Prof. MIHAELA ZĂRNESCU-ENCEANU.

Editura Eminescu (Eminescu Publishing House): 701141 Bucharest, bd. Nicolae Bălcescu 33, Bloc UMIC, sc. B, Ap. 7; tel. and fax (1) 3137410; e-mail edituraeminescu@yahoo.com; internet www.edituraeminescu.com; f. 1969; contemporary original literary works and translations of world literature; Dir SILVIA CINCA.

Editura Enciclopedică (Encyclopaedic Publishing House): 71341 Bucharest, Piaţa Presei Libere 1; tel. and fax (1) 2243667; f. 1968; merged with Scientific Publishing House, as Editura Ştiinţifică şi Enciclopedică, 1974–90; encyclopaedias, dictionaries, bibliographies, chronologies, monographs, reference books and children's books; popular and informational literature; provides photographs and encyclopaedic and statistical data about Romania for publishing houses abroad; Dir MARCEL POPA.

Editura Humanitas (Humanitas Publishing House): 79734 Bucharest, Piaţa Presei Libere 1; tel. (1) 2228546; fax (1) 2243632; e-mail editors@agora.humanitas.ro; internet www.humanitas.ro; f. 1990; philosophy, religion, political and social sciences, economics, history, fiction, textbooks, art, literature, practical books; Dir GABRIEL LIICEANU.

Editura Ion Creangă SA (Ion Creangă Publishing House): 71341 Bucharest, Piaţa Presei Libere 1; tel. (1) 2223254; fax (1) 2231112; f. 1969; children's books; Dir DANIELA CRĂSNARU.

Editura Junimea (Junimea Publishing House): 6600 Iaşi, Str. Cuza Vodă 29, POB 28; tel. (32) 117290; f. 1969; Romanian literature, art books, translations, scientific and technical books; Dir CONSTANTIN DRAM.

Editura Kriterion (Kriterion Publishing House): 70002 Bucharest, str. Franceža 6/1; tel. and fax and fax (1) 3146246; e-mail krit@dnt.ro; internet www.kriterion.ro; f. 1969; classical and contemporary literature, reference books in science and art in Hungarian, German, Romanian, Russian, Serbian, Slovak, Tatar, Turkish, Ukrainian and Yiddish; translations in Romanian, Hungarian and German; Dir GYULA H. SZABÓ.

Editura Litera (The Letter Publishing House): Bucharest; tel. and fax (1) 2224829; f. 1969; original literature; Dir VIORICA OANCEA.

Editura Medicală SA (Medical Publishing House): 70406 Bucharest, Str. Smârdan 5; tel. (1) 6143252; fax (1) 3124879; f. 1954; medical literature; Dir Prof. AL. C. OPROIU.

Editura Meridiane (Meridiane Publishing House): 71341 Bucharest, Piaţa Presei Libere 1; tel. (1) 2243623; fax (1) 2223037; f. 1952; arts, history, biographies, religion, social sciences, cultural studies, media, anthropology, essays, medicine, travel, archaeology, linguistics; Dir ELENA-VICTORIA JIQUIDI; Senior Editors LIVIA SZASZ CÂMPEANU, ANDREI NICULESCU.

Editura Militară (Military Publishing House): 70764 Bucharest, Str. Gen. Constantin Cristescu 3–5; tel. and fax (1) 3112191; f. 1950; military history, theory, science, technics, medicine and fiction; Dir LUCIAN JUMÂTATE.

Editura Minerva (Minerva Publishing House): 71341 Bucharest, Piaţa Presei Libere 1; tel. and fax (1) 2224823; f. 1969; Romanian classical literature, world literature, original literary works, literary criticism and history; Dir ONDINE DASCĂLIŢA.

Editura Muzicală (Musical Publishing House): 71102 Bucharest, Calea Victoriei 141; tel. and fax (1) 3129867; e-mail editura_muzicala@hotmail.com; f. 1957; books on music, musicology and musical scores; Dir MARIUS VASILEANU.

Editura pentru Turism (Tourism Publishing House): 70161 Bucharest 1, Bd. Gh. Magheru 7; tel. (1) 6145160; f. 1990; tourism; Dir VICTOR CRĂCIUN.

Editura Porto-Franco (Porto-France Publishing House): 6200 Galati, Bd. George Coşbuc 223A; tel. (36) 464602; fax (36) 461204; f. 1990; literary and scientific books, translations; Dir ADRIANA ALDEA.

Editura Presa Libera (Free Press Publishing House): 71341 Bucharest, Piaţa Presei Libere 1; f. 1954; newspapers, magazines.

Editura Scrisul Românesc (Romanian Writing Publishing House): 1100 Craiova, Str. Mihai Viteazul 4; tel. (41) 413763; fax (1) 419506; e-mail scrisulromanesc@topedge.ro; internet www.topedge.ro; f. 1922; socio-political, technical, scientific and literary works; Dir MARIUS GHICA.

Editura Sport-Turism (Sport-Tourism Publishing House): 79736 Bucharest, Str. Vasile Conta 16; tel. (1) 107480; f. 1968; sport, tourism, monographs, translations, postcards, children's books; Dir MIHAI CAZIMIR.

Editura Ştiinţifică (Scientific Publishing House): 71341 Bucharest, Piaţa Presei Libere 1; tel. and fax (1) 2223330; f. 1990; fmrly Editura Ştiinţifică şi Enciclopedică; language dictionaries, bibliographies, monographs, chronologies, reference books, popular and informational literature; Dir DINU GRAMA.

Editura Tehnică (Technical Publishing House): 71341 Bucharest, Piaţa Presei Libere 1; tel. (1) 2228348; fax (1) 2242164; e-mail tehnica@mail.tehnica.ro; internet www.tehnica.ro; f. 1950; technical and scientific books, technical dictionaries; Dir ROMAN CHIRILĂ.

Editura Univers: 79379 Bucharest, Piaţa Presei Libere 1; tel. (1) 2226629; fax (1) 2243765; e-mail univers@rnc.ro; f. 1961; translations from world literature, criticism, essays, literary history, philosophy of culture, educational; Dir Prof. Dr MIRCEA MARTIN.

Editura de Vest (West Publishing House): 1900 Timişoara, Piaţa Sfântul Gheorghe 2; tel. (61) 18218; fax (1) 14212; f. 1972 as Editura Facla; socio-political, technical, scientific and literary works in Romanian, Hungarian, German and Serbian; Dir VASILE POPOVICI.

Rao International Publishing: 78217 Bucharest, Bd. 1 Mai 125; tel. (1) 2104588; fax (1) 2228059; educational books.

Tribuna Press and Publishing House: 2400 Sibiu, Str. George Coşbuc 38; tel. (24) 12810; fax (24) 12026; f. 1991; Dir EMIL DAVID.

PUBLISHERS' ASSOCIATIONS

Cultura Naţională: 79715 Bucharest, Piaţa Presei Libere 1; tel. (1) 6181255; state organization attached to Ministry of Culture; administration, production and distribution of literary magazines and books of national interest; organization of imports and exports.

Romanian Association of Publishers (Societatii Patronilor de Edituri din România): Braşov, Bd. 15 Noeimbrei 3; tel. (68) 114876; fax (68) 150394; f. 1993; 50 mems; Pres. DANIEL DRAGAN.

WRITERS' UNION

Romanian Writers' Union (Uniunea Scriitorilor din România): 71102 Bucharest, Calea Victoriei 115; tel. (1) 6507245; fax (1) 3129634; f. 1949; Pres. LAURENTIU ULICI.

Broadcasting and Communications

TELECOMMUNICATIONS

Mobi Fon: f. 1996; operates mobile cellular telephone network in 10 cities; Pres. AL TOLSTOY.

Mobil Rom: f. 1996; operates mobile cellular telephone network; Exec. Dir PIERRE MATTEI.

Romtelecom SA: 70060 Bucharest 5, Bd. Libertăţii 14–16; tel. (1) 4001212; fax (1) 4105581; e-mail contact@romtelecom.ro; internet www.romtelecom.ro; f. 1933; joint-stock co; former state monopoly; 54% owned by Hellenic Telecommunications Organization (Greece); Dir-Gen. FLORIN ANGHEL.

Telemobil SA: Bucharest; f. 1999; operates mobile cellular telephone network; Man. Dir and Chief Exec. DIWAKER SINGH.

BROADCASTING

Radio

Radiodifuziunea Română: 70747 Bucharest, Str. Gral Berthelot 60–64, POB 63-1200; tel. (1) 3031432; fax (1) 3121057; e-mail adimitriu@radio.ror.ro; f. 1928; 39 transmitters on medium-wave, 69 transmitters on VHF; 114 relays; News, Cultural, Youth and Music Programmes, plus two local and six regional programmes; foreign broadcasts on one medium-wave and eight short-wave transmitters in Arabic, Bulgarian, Chinese, English, German, Greek, Hungarian, Italian, Portuguese, Romanian, Russian, Serbian, Spanish, Turkish and Ukrainian; Chair. DRAGOS SEULEANU.

Radioteleviziunea Română (Romanian Radio and Television): 71281 Bucharest 1, Calea Dorobanţilor 191, POB 63-1200; tel. (1) 2307032; fax (1) 2300381; e-mail tcr@tvr.ro; internet www.tvr.ro; f. 1955; Pres. CRISTIAN HADJI-CULEA; Exec. Dir ALEXANDRU LAZESCU.

Radio 'Nord-Est': 6600 Iaşi, Str. Gării 22; tel. (32) 211570; fax (32) 146363; e-mail rneiasi@mail.dntis.ro; f. 1992; independent; Station Man. ANCA CIOBANU.

Societatea Natională de Radiocommunicaţii, SA (National Radiocommunications Co.): 70060 Bucharest, Bd. Libertaţii 14; tel. (1) 4001101; fax (1) 4001228; e-mail rarmanag@com.pcnet.ro; state-owned.

Television

Romania's first regional television station (at Timişoara) was registered in 1989. The first satellite television channel, Tele 7 ABC, was launched in 1994.

Televiziunea Română—Telecentrul Bucureşti (Romanian Television—Bucharest TV Centre): 71281 Bucharest, Calea Dorobanţilor 191, POB 63-1200; tel. (1) 6334710; fax (1) 2121427; state-owned; 39 transmitters; daily transmissions; Pres. and Dir-Gen. CRISTIAN-VALERIU HADJI-CULEA.

Antena Independenta: 71561 Bucharest, Şos. Bucureşti-Ploieşti 25–27; tel. (1) 2121844; first independent television station.

Channel 2 TV Română: Bucharest; f. 1992 as a jt venture; 80% owned by Atlantic Television Ltd (UK-Canada), 20% by Radioteleviziunea Română; independent commercial channel; to broadcast six hours of programmes daily; Man. Dir ROBIN EDWARDS.

Pro TV: Bucharest, Bd. Carol I 109, etaj 2; tel. (1) 3124218; fax (1) 3124228.

Radioteleviziunea Română (Romanian Radio and Television): see Radio.

Finance

(cap. = capital; res = reserves; dep. = deposits; m. = million; amounts in lei (unless otherwise indicated); brs = brs)

BANKING

In April 1997 legislation providing for the privatization of state-owned banks was approved; Banca Română Pentru Dezvoltare SA was the first to be sold, in December 1998.

Central Bank

National Bank of Romania (Banca Naţională a României): 70421 Bucharest 3, Str. Lipscani 25; tel. (1) 3130410; fax (1) 3123831; internet www.bnro.ro; f. 1880; central bank and bank of issue; manages monetary policy; supervises commercial banks and credit business; cap. and res 25,578,300m., dep. 152,782,700m. (Dec. 2001); Gov. MUGUR CONSTANTIN ISARESCU; 22 brs.

Other Banks

Alpha Bank Romania SA: 712811 Bucharest 1, Calea Dorobantilor 237B; tel. (1) 2092100; fax (1) 2316570; e-mail bbr@alphabank.ro; internet www.alphabank.ro; f. 1994 as Banca Bucureşti, present name since 2000; cap. US $22,995.0m.(Dec. 2002), res 641,281m., dep. 7,955,599m. (Dec. 2000); Pres. ELEFTHERIOS IOANNOU.

Banc Post SA: 761062 Bucharest 5, Bd. Libertăţii, Bl. 104; tel. (1) 3361124; fax (1) 3360772; e-mail bpt@bancpost.ro; internet www.bancpost.ro; f. 1991; 19.3% owned by EFG Eurobank Ergasias SA (Greece), 17.0% by Banco Portugues de Investimento SA (Portugal); cap. 2,086,946m., res 844,282m., dep. 11,038,684m. (Dec. 2001); Pres. Chair. and Chief Exec. ELENA PETCULESCU.

Banca Comercială Carpatica SA: 2400 Sibiu, Bd. Mihai Viteazu 42; tel. (69) 233815; fax (69) 233371; e-mail extern@carpatica.ro; internet www.carpatica.ro; f. 1999; cap. 278,978m., dep. 365,824m., total assets 654,771m. (Dec. 2001); Pres. and Chair. NICOLAE HOANTA.

Banca Comercială 'Ion Tiriac'—Banca Tiriac: 74228 Bucharest, Str. Nerva Traian 3, Complex M101; tel. (1) 3032600; fax (1) 3025700; e-mail bancatriac@cbit.ro; internet www.bancatiriac.ro; f. 1991; cap. 5,621,450m., res 61,815m., dep. 9,705,328m. (Dec. 2001); Chair. and Chief Exec. ANTHONY VAN DER HEIJDEN; 44 brs and sub-brs.

Banca Comercială Robank—Robank SA: 741382 Bucharest 3, Bd. Unirii 59; tel. (1) 3225700; fax (1) 3226885; e-mail office@robank.ro; internet www.robank.ro; f. 1995; cap. 165,468m., res 232,589m., dep. 2,335,259m. (Dec. 2001); Pres. and Chair. MUSTAFA AYAN; 5 brs.

Banca Comercială Română SA—BCR (Romanian Commercial Bank): 70348 Bucharest 3, Bd. Regina Elisabeta 5; tel. (1) 3126185; fax (1) 3122096; e-mail marketing@bcr.ro; internet www.bcr.ro; f. 1990; absorbed operations of Banca Română de Comert Exterior (BANCOREX) in Oct. 1999; commercial banking services for domestic and foreign customers; 70% state-owned, pending privatization in 2002; cap. 7,924,688mm., res 14,464,916m., dep. 92,235,741m. (Dec. 2001); Pres. and Chair. NICOLAE DĂNILĂ; 285 brs and agencies.

Banca Comercială West Bank: 2900 Arad, Bd. Revolutiei 88; tel. (57) 284888; fax (57) 285998; e-mail westbank@rdslink.ro; f. 1996; 72.4% owned by Sanpaolo IMI SpA (Italy); cap. 270,428m., res 180,963m., dep. 1,150,106m. (Dec. 2001); Pres. CORNEL PIRTEA.

Banca Daewoo (Romania) SA: Bucharest, 1/F, International Business Centre, Bd. Carol I 34–36; tel. (1) 2505711; fax (1) 2505831; e-mail daewoo@fx.ro; f. 1996; 99.99% owned by Daewoo Securities Co Ltd (Rep. of Korea); cap. US $22.7m., dep. US $39.9m., total assets US $67.6m. (Dec. 2000); Pres. BUM-SHIK BAE.

Banca de Credit şi Dezvoltare (ROMEXTERRA) SA (Bank of Credit and Development): 4300 Târgu Mureş, Mureş, bd. 1 Decembrie 1918 93; tel. (65) 166640; fax (65) 166047; e-mail info@romexterra.ro; internet www.romexterra.ro; f. 1993; cap. 444,000m., res 1,458,5330m., dep. 2,228,120m. (Dec. 2002); Pres. VASILE IFRIM; 22 brs.

Banca de Export-Import a României—Eximbank SA: 761042 Bucharest 5, Str. Splaiul Independentei 15; tel. (1) 3361134; fax (1) 3366176; e-mail relatii@eximbank.ro; f. 1992; 87.4% owned by State Privatization Agency; cap. 316,986m., res 6,367,845m., dep. 1,304,820m. (Dec. 2001); Chair. and Chief Exec. Dr MARIANA DIACONESCU.

Banca Pentru Mică- Industrie şi Liberă-Iniţiativă SA—MINDBANK) (Bank for Small Industry and Free Enterprise—MINDBANK): 78104 Bucharest 1, Calea Grivitei 24; tel. (1) 3030700; fax (1) 3030732; e-mail mindbank@bx.logicnet.ro; f. 1990; cap. 200,000m., res 240,733m., dep. 720,106m. (Dec. 2001); privately-owned; Chair. IOAN PRUNDUS; Dep. Chair. EMIL RADU, SERGIU IOAN MANEA; 12 brs.

Banca Română Pentru Dezvoltare SA-Groupe Société Générale (Romanian Bank for Development): 70016 Bucharest 3, Str. Doamnei 4; tel. (1) 3130571; fax (1) 3159600; e-mail communication@brd.ro; internet www.brd.ro; f. 1990 to replace Investment Bank (f. 1923); financial and banking services and operations to individual and private and small cos, etc.; 51.9% owned by Société Générale (France); cap. 1,742,253m., res 13,938,420m., dep. 44,662,823m. (Dec. 2001); Chair. BOGDAN BALTAZAR; Chief Exec. PATRICK GELIN; 191 brs.

Banca Română Pentru Relansare Economica—Libra Bank SA (Romanian Bank for Economic Revival–Libra Bank): 712791 Bucharest 1, Bd. Aviatorilor 46; tel. (1) 2303333; fax (1) 2306565; e-mail informatii@librabank.ro; internet www.librabank.ro; f. 1996; cap. 182,248m. (Dec. 2001), dep. 187,258m., total assets 405,774m. (Dec. 2000); Pres. DAN CONSTANTINESCU.

Banca Românească SA (Romanian Bank): 70401 Bucharest, Bd. Unirii 35, Bloc A3; tel. (1) 3211601; fax (1) 3213624; e-mail office@brom.ro; internet www.brom.ro; f. 1993; 71.9% owned by Romanian-

American Enterprise Fund (USA); cap. 692,064m., res 71,432m., dep. 1,696,253m. (Dec. 2001); Chief Exec. and Chair. of Bd PETRU RARES.

Banca Transilvania SA (Transylvanian Bank): 3400 Cluj-Napoca, Bd. Eroilor 36; tel. (64) 198833; fax (64) 198832; e-mail bancatransilvania@bancatransilvania.ro; internet www.bancatransilvania.ro; f. 1994; cap. 396,160m., res 666,102m., dep. 3,953,515m. (Dec. 2001); Pres. IOSIF POP; 32 brs.

Casa de Economii şi Consemnaţiuni—CEC SA (Savings and Consignation Bank): 79104 Bucharest 3, Calea Victoriei 13; tel. (1) 3122895; fax (1) 3143970; e-mail office@rsb.ro; internet www.rsb.ro; f. 1864; state-owned; handles private savings, loans for the inter-banking market and mortgages; cap. 642,000m., res 1,409,830m., dep. 19,522,479m. (Dec. 2000); Chair. CONSTANTIN TECULESCU; 42 brs.

Citibank Romania SA: 712042 Bucharest 1, Bd. Lancu de Hunedoara 8, POB 63-5; tel. (1) 2101850; fax (1) 2101854; internet www.citibank.ro; f. 1996; 99.6% owned by Citigroup Overseas Investment Corpn (USA); cap. US $22.0m., dep. US $317.9m., total assets US $370.4m (Dec. 2001); Pres. and Chair. ZDENEK TUREK.

Commercial Bank of Greece (Romania) SA: 70759 Bucharest 1, Str. Berzei 19, Sector 1; tel. (1) 3159783; fax (1) 3103964; e-mail bank@cbg.ro; internet www.cbg.ro; f. 1996; cap. 338,915.7m., dep. 640,163.4m., total assets 999,889,4m. (Dec. 2001); Pres. SPYRIDON KOSKINAS.

Egnatia Bank (Romania) SA: 70744 Bucharest, Str. Gral. C. Budisteanu 28C, BP 22-155; tel. (1) 3032100; fax (1) 3032181; f. 1998 as BNP-Dresdner Bank (Romania) SA; present name adopted 2001; 99.9% owned by Egnatia Bank SA (Greece); Pres. MARINIS STRATOPOULOS.

Eurom Bank SA: 71000 Bucharest, Bd Aviatorilor 45; tel. (1) 2067077; fax (1) 2067050; e-mail office@eurombank.ro; internet dacia-felix.ro; f. 1991 as Banca Dacia Felix SA; present name adopted 2001; 94.0% owned by Kolal BV (Netherlands); cap. 58,609m., res 1,540,064m., dep. 1,319,203m. (Dec. 1999); Chair. BENESH AVITAL.

Finansbank (Romania) SA: 751012 Bucharest 4, Str. Splaiul Unirii 12, Bl. B6; tel. (1) 3017100; fax (1) 3310970; e-mail hoffice@finansbank.ro; internet www.finansbank.ro; f. 1993; adopted present name 2000; 63.6% owned by Finansbank AS (Turkey); cap. 671,661m., dep. 1,956,994m., total assets 2,370,614m. (Dec. 2001); Pres. BEKIR DILDAR.

HVB Bank Romania SA: 71278 Bucharest 1, Str. Dr Grigore Mora 37; tel. (1) 2032222; fax (1) 2308485; e-mail contact@ro.hwb-cee.com; internet www.hvb.ro; f. 1997 as Creditanstalt SA; present name adopted 2001; 99.7% owned by Bank Austria Creditanstalt AG; cap. 100,001m., res 104,337m., dep. 4,067,163m. (Dec. 2000); Pres. and Chair. DAN PASCARIU.

Nova Bank SA: 71411 Bucharest 2, Bd. D. Cantemir 2, Bl. P3, T II; tel. (1) 3360856; fax (1) 3362414; e-mail office@nova-bank.ro; internet www.nova-bank.ro; f. 1997 as Banca Comerciala Unirea; Gen. Man. ZOE GHINESCU.

Piraeus Bank Romania SA: Bucharest 2, Bd. Carol I 34–36, International Business Centre; tel. (1) 2506798; fax (1) 2501799; internet www.piraeusbank.ro; f. 1995; present name adopted 2000; 99.99% owned by Piraeus Bank (Greece); cap. 521,090.6m., dep. 610,067.0m., total assets 1,078,355.8m. (Dec. 2000); Pres., Chief Exec. and Chair. EMANUEL ODOBESCU; Dir-Gen. SOFRONIS STRINOPOULOS; 3 brs.

Raiffeisen Bank SA: 742141 Bucharest 3, Bd. Mircea Voda 44; tel. (1) 3230031; fax (1) 3236027; e-mail centrala@raiffesien.ro; f. 2002 by merger of Banca Agricola-Raiffeisen SA and Raiffeisenbank (Romania) SA; 94.2% owned by Raiffeisen Zentralbank Osterreich AG (Austria); Pres. STEVEN VAN GRONIGEN.

Romanian International Bank: 70401 Bucharest 3, Bd. Unirii 68, Bloc K2; tel. (1) 3227005; fax (1) 3237272; e-mail office@roib.ro; f. 1998; privately owned; Chair. of Bd ION GHICA.

Unicredit Romania SA: 70401 Bucharest 4, Bd. Splaiul Unirii 16; tel. (1) 3302900; fax (1) 3303992; e-mail office@unicredit.ro; internet www.unicredit.ro; f. 1997 as DEMiRBANK Romania SA; name changed as above in 2001; 99.84% owned by Unicredito Italiano (UCI); cap. 404,066m., res 110,010m., dep. 1,134,548m. (Dec. 2001); Pres. of Man. Bd FAUSTO PETTENI; Chief Exec. SELÇUK SALDIRAK; 15 brs.

BANKING ASSOCIATION

Romanian Banking Association (Asociaţia Română a Băncilor): 76100 Bucharest, Str. Mihai Eminescu 88; tel. (1) 2112007; fax (1) 2112100; e-mail arb@arexim.ro; Chair. RADU GILŢEA; Sec.-Gen. RADU NEGREA.

STOCK EXCHANGE

Bucharest Stock Exchange (Bursa de Valori Bucureşti): 70421 Bucharest, Str. Doamnei 8; tel. (1) 3158209; fax (1) 3158149; e-mail bvbrel@ccir.ro; internet bse.ccir.ro; f. 1882; reopened 1995 (ceased operations 1948); 128 listed cos; Pres. SERGIU OPRESCU; Gen. Man. STERE FARMACHE.

INSURANCE

Allianz-Tiriac Asigurări: 71139 Bucharest, Cáderea Bastiliei 80–84; tel. (1) 2082222; fax (1) 2082211; e-mail office@allianztiriac.ro; internet www.allianztiriac.ro.

Arad: 71421 Bucharest, Şos. Ştefan cel Mare 7–9; tel. (1) 6113162; fax (1) 6113279.

Asigurareo Românescŏ SA (ASIROM) (Romanian Insurance): 70332 Bucharest 2, Bd. Carol I 31–33; tel. (1) 2504271; fax (1) 2504145; f. 1991; all types of insurance, including life insurance; Gen. Man. ANGELA TONCESCU; 41 brs.

Astra SA: 71291 Bucharest, Str. Puşkin 10; tel. (1) 2305288; fax (1) 2305248.

Carom SA: 70406 Bucharest, Str. Smârdan 5; tel. (1) 6150519; fax (1) 3124710.

Cascom SA: 77102 Bucharest, Calea Plevnei 46–48; tel. (1) 6151810.

Metropol SA: 75121 Bucharest, Bd. Dimitrie Cantemir 1; tel. (1) 3304706; fax (1) 3304725; f. 1991; all types of insurance and reinsurance; Chair. and Man. Dir Dr JOSEPH NOUPADJA.

Romanian-Canadian Insurance Co (AROCA) SA: 70414 Bucharest, Str. Doamnei 17–19; tel. and fax (1) 3135605; e-mail aroca@fx.ro.

Insurance Association

Uniunea Naţională a Societăţilor de Asigurare şi Reasigurare din România: 70406 Bucharest, Str. Smârdan 5; tel. (1) 6130358.

Trade and Industry

GOVERNMENT AGENCIES

Agency for Foreign Investments: Bucharest; f. 2002 to promote investment in Romania.

Romanian Development Agency (Agenţia Română de Dezvoltare): 70161 Bucharest, Bd. Magheru 7; tel. (1) 3122886; fax (1) 3120371; f. 1991; promotes foreign investment in Romanian industry; Pres. SORIN FODOREANU.

State Privatization Agency (APAPS): 70205 Bucharest, Str. C.A. Rosetti 21; tel. (1) 2118018; fax (1) 2104459; successor org. to the State Ownership Fund; Gen. Dir GABRIEL MIHUT.

CHAMBER OF COMMERCE

Chamber of Commerce and Industry of Romania and the Municipality of Bucharest: Bucharest 3, Bd. Octavian Goga 2; tel. (1) 3229536; fax (1) 3229542; e-mail ccir@ccir.ro; internet www.ccir.ro; f. 1868; non-governmental organization; Pres. GHEORGE COJOCARU.

EMPLOYERS' ASSOCIATIONS

National Confederation of Romanian Employers (Confederaţia Naţională a Patronatului Român): 70169 Bucharest, Str. Mendeleev 36–38; tel. (1) 3124715; fax (1) 3124745.

Romanian Private Farmers' Federation (Federaţia agricultorilor privatizaţi din România): 70111 Bucharest 1, Bd. Nicolae Bălcescu 17–19; tel. (1) 6131869; fax (1) 6133043; f. 1991; represents 4,000 farming co-operatives and 41 district unions; Pres. GHEORGHE PREDILA.

UTILITIES

Electricity

Regia Autonomă a Distribuţiei şi Exploatării Filmelor România Film (Film): 70231 Bucharest, Str. Thomas Masaryk 25; tel. (1) 2107930; fax (1) 2117674.

National Electricity Company (CONEL SA): 70164 Bucharest, Bd. Magheru 33; tel. (1) 6596000; fax (1) 3120291; e-mail public.relations@renel.ro; internet www.renel.ro; f. 1990; state electricity authority; pending restructuring and privatization; Chair. THEODOR BUFTEA; Dir-Gen. TUDOR SERBAN; 72,000 employees.

Gas

Transgaz SA: 3125 Mediaş, Str. Unirii 4; tel. (69) 842262; fax (69) 839031; e-mail cabinet@romgaz.ro; state-owned; exploration, transmission and distribution of natural gas; Pres. and Gen. Dir GABRIEL COCONEA.

TRADE UNIONS

The regulations governing trade unions were liberalized in early 1990. The Uniunea Generală a Sindicatelor din România (UGSR) was dissolved. Several new trade union organizations have since been established.

Alpha Cartel (Cartelul Alfa): f. 1990; 1.1m. mems; Leader BOGDAN HOSSU.

Confederation of Democratic Trade Unions of Romania: Bucharest; f. 1994; 34 branch federations; 640,000 mems; Leader IACOB BACIU.

Confederation of Romanian Miners' Trade Unions: Pres. ILIE DORSAN.

COSIN Confederation (Confederaţia COSIN): f. 1990; 10,000 mems.

Fides Confederation (Confederaţia Fides): 180,000 mems; Leader CĂTĂLIN CROITORU.

Hercules Confederation (Confederaţia Hercules): Bucharest; f. 1990; transport workers.

Inter-union Confederative Alliance of 15 November (Alianţa Confederativă Intersindicală 15 Noiembrie): 2200 Braşov, Str. Michael Weiss 13; tel. and fax (68) 151936; f. 1991; 120,000 mems; Pres. ADRIAN LAHARIA.

National Trade Union Bloc (Blocul Naţional Sindical): 77208 Bucharest, Splaiul Independenţei 202A; tel. (1) 4115184; fax (1) 4115185; e-mail bns@bns.ro; internet www.bns.ro; f. 1991; merged with National Free Trade Union Confederation of Romania–Brotherhood; c. 3.4m. mems; Pres. DUMITRU COSTIN; Gen. Sec. MATEI BRĂTIANU.

Other organizations include Infratirea, the Justice and Brotherhood Union and the Convention of Non-Aligned Union Confederations (Pres. ION MACHEDON).

Transport

RAILWAYS

In 1998 there were 11,010 km of track, of which 3,929 km were electrified lines. In January 1996 the World Bank approved a loan of US $120m. to help finance the restructuring of Romania's railways. In September 1998 the Societatea Nationale a Căilor Ferate Române (SNCFR—National Romanian Railway Company) was divided into five companies.

Company for Railways Assets Management (SAAF): 77113 Bucharest, Bd. Dinicu Golescu 38; tel. (1) 6373252; fax (1) 2227877; Gen. Man. MIRCEA DINU.

National Railways Company for Freight Traffic (CFR Marfa SA): 77113 Bucharest, Bd. Dinicu Golescu 38; tel. (1) 2249336; fax (1) 3124700; e-mail vtulbure@marfa.cfr.ro; f. 1988; after the reorganization of the SNCFR; main railway freight transport operator in Romania; Gen. Man. VASIK TULBURE.

National Passenger Railway Transport Co (CFR Calatori): 77113 Bucharest, Bd. Dinicu Golescu 38; tel. (1) 2222518; fax (1) 4112054; e-mail irina.vlad@cfr.ro; internet www.cfr.ro; divided into eight regional administrations since 1999; reorganized in Feb. 2001 and merged with eight regional companies; operates all local, regional, long-distance and international rail services; Gen. Man. VALENTIN BOTA.

National Railways Company (CFR SA): 77113 Bucharest, Bd. Dinicu Golescu 38; tel. (1) 2223637; fax (1) 3123200; e-mail virgil.daschievici@cfr.ro; internet www.cfr.ro; management railway infrastructure; Gen. Dir MIHAI MECOLAICIUC; 41,486 employees.

Rail Management Services Company (SMF): 77113 Bucharest, Bd. Dinicu Golescu 38; tel. (1) 2233560; fax (1) 6384530; e-mail spopeanga@central.cfr.ro; provides financial, judicial and accounting services; Gen. Man. SILVIA POPEANGA.

Societatea de Constructii Cai de Comunicatii SA: Bucharest 1, Bd. Dinicu Golescu 38; tel. (1) 2223615; fax (1) 3125903; f. 1876; production of materials for railway construction and vehicles; Pres. NICOLAE CONSTANTINESCU; 13,300 employees.

Metropolitan Transport

The Bucharest underground railway network totals 63.5 km in length. There are currently plans to modernize the underground system.

Societatea Comerciala de Transport cu Metroul Bucureşti–METROREX SA: 79917 Bucharest 1, Bd. Dinicu Golescu 38; tel. (1) 2248975; fax (1) 3125149; e-mail contact@metrorex.ro; internet www.metrorex.ro; f. 1977; Gen. Man. MARIUS IONEL LAPADAT.

ROADS

At the end of 2000 there were 198,603 km of roads, of which 113 km were motorways, 14,711 km national roads and 63,791 km secondary roads. Under the 1991–2005 road development programme, more than 3,000 km of motorways were to be built and 4,000 km of existing roads were to be modernized.

CCCF Bucharest SA: 77113 Bucharest 1, Bd. Dinicu Golescu 38; tel. (1) 6387375; fax (1) 6385335; f. 1879; construction of roads, railways, bridges and tunnels; Gen. Man. NICOLAE CONSTANTINESCU; 8,000 employees.

National Administration of Roads (Regia Autonomă Administraţia Naţională a Drumurilor——AND): Ministerul Transporturilor, 77113 Bucharest 1, Bd. Dinicu Golescu 38, Rm 55; tel. (1) 2232606; fax (1) 3120984; Dir-Gen. Dr Ing. DANILA BUCSA.

Road and Bridge Corporation (Regia Autonomă de Drumuri şi Poduri): Bucharest, Şos. Bucureşti-Ploieşti, km 18; tel. (1) 6130123.

INLAND AND OCEAN SHIPPING

Navigation on the River Danube is open to shipping of all nations. The Danube–Black Sea Canal was officially opened to traffic in 1984, and has an annual handling capacity of 80m. metric tons. Work on the 85-km Danube–Bucharest Canal was abandoned in early 1990. The first joint Romanian-Yugoslav Iron Gates (Porţile de Fier) power and navigation system on the Danube was completed in 1972, and Iron Gates-2 opened to navigation in 1984. Romania's principal seaports are Constanţa (on the Black Sea), Tulcea, Galaţi, Brăila and Giurgiu (on the Danube). In August 1995 Romania launched its first ferry service to Turkey, operating between Constanţa and Samsun. In 2001 Romania's merchant fleet had 240 vessels, with a total displacement of 637,700 grt.

Galaţi Corporation for the Administration of the Lower Danube (Regia Autonomă Administraţia Fluvială a Dunării de Jos Galaţi): 6200 Galaţi, Str. Portului 28–30; tel. (36) 460812; fax (36) 460847; Gen. Man. MIHAI OCHIALBESCU.

National Company for the Administration of the Maritime Port of Constanţa SA: 8700 Constanţa, Portului Incinta, Gara Maritima; tel. (41) 611540; fax (41) 619512; e-mail apmc@constantza-port.ro; internet www.constantza-port.ro; f. 1991; also administrates Midia, Mangalia and Tomis ports; Gen. Man. GHEORGHE MOLDOVEANU.

National Company for the Administration of Maritime Ports on the Danube: 6200 Galaţi, Str. Portului 34; tel. (36) 460660; fax (36) 460140; Gen. Man. ALEXANDROS GALIATATOS.

National Company for the Administration of Navigable Canals SH: 8700 Constanţa, Str. Ecluzei Agigea 1, POB 93; tel. (41) 738505; fax (41) 639402; e-mail compania@acn.ro; internet www.acn.ro; fmrly Constanţa Corpn for Navigable Channels; Gen. Man. SEVASTIAN STEFAN.

National Company for the Administration of River Ports on the Danube: 8375 Giurgiu, Şos. Portului 1; tel. (46) 213003; fax (46) 3110521; e-mail apdf@infogrup.pcnet.ro; internet www.intelsev.ro/apdf; f. 1998; Gen. Man. CRISTIAN NEMTESCU.

NAVROM—Romanian Shipping Co: 8700 Constanţa, Portului Incinta; tel. (41) 615166; fax (41) 618413; organizes sea transport; operates routes to most parts of the world; Gen. Man. MANEA GHIOCEL.

Petromin Shipping Co: Constanţa, Portului Incinta, Poarta 2; tel. (41) 617802; fax (41) 619690; e-mail office@petromin.cunet.ro; merchant fleet of 30 ships and tankers totalling 1.778m. gross registered tons; Chair. ANDREI CARAIANI.

Romline: 8700 Constanţa, Poarta 2 Hostel; tel. (41) 617285; fax (41) 615647; f. 1990; merchant shipping company.

CIVIL AVIATION

There are international airports at Bucharest-Baneasa, Bucharest-Otopeni, M. Kogălniceanu-Constanţa, Timişoara, Arad, Sibiu, Oradea and Târgu Mureş.

Romanian Civil Aeronautic Authority (Regia Autonomă Autoritatea Aeronautică Civilă Romană): 71557 Bucharest, Şos. Bucureşti–Ploieşti, km 16.5; tel. (1) 3121938; fax (1) 2302942; Gen. Man. GAVRIL GHEORGHE.

Angel Airlines: 712961 Bucharest, Str. 18 Amiral Constantin Basescu; tel. (1) 2315944; fax (1) 2315947; internet www.angelairlines.ro; f. 2001; scheduled domestic flights; Chair. and Chief Exec. KHOSRO AZAD.

Carpatair: Bucharest, 1 Dr Iacob Felix 55; tel. (1) 3130308; fax (1) 3130500; internet www.carpatair.com; f. 1998 as Veg Air, assumed present name in 1999; scheduled domestic and regional flights to Hungary, Italy and Moldova; Pres. NICOLAE PETROV.

Compania Nationala de Transporturi Aeriene Române SA—TAROM (Romanian Air Transport): 79154 Bucharest, Şos. Bucureşti–Ploieşti, km 16.5, Otopeni Airport; tel. (1) 2322494; fax (1) 3125686; e-mail secrgen@tarom.logicnet.ro; internet www.tarom.digiro.net; f. 1954; joint-stock company; scheduled to be privatized in 2002; services to 43 cities throughout Europe, the Middle East, Asia and the USA and extensive internal flights; Pres. GHEORGHE RACARU.

Jaro International: Bucharest; tel. (1) 2322273; fax (1) 2307781; f. 1990; private charter airline; Pres. and Dir-Gen. MIRICA DIMITRESCU.

Liniile Aeriene Române (LAR) (Romanian Airlines): 70733 Bucharest, Şos. Ştirbei Vodă 2–4; tel. (1) 3153206; fax (1) 3120148; e-mail dorin@baneasa.biz; f. 1975 by TAROM to operate passenger charter services; re-established as independent airline in 1990; Man. Dir DORIN IVASCU.

Romavia Romanian Aviation Co: 75121 Bucharest, Bd. Dimitrie Cantemir 1; tel. (1) 3301160; fax (1) 3301049; f. 1991; owned by Ministry of National Defence; state VIP and chartered and scheduled passenger and cargo flights; Man. Dir IULIU-ADRIAN GOLEANU.

Tourism

The Carpathian Mountains, the Danube delta and the Black Sea resorts (Mamaia, Eforie, Mangalia and others) are the principal attractions. In 2000 there were almost 5.3m. tourist arrivals (including same-day visitors).

Ministry of Tourism Promotion Office: 70663 Bucharest, Str. Apolodor 17; tel. (1) 4100491; fax (1) 4100579; e-mail turism@kappa.ro; govt org. Gen. Dir CRISTIAN CUTAS.

National Association of Travel Agencies (Asociaţia Natională a Agenţiilor de Turism——ANAT): 74288 Bucharest 3, Str. Foişorului 8, Bloc 3C, Sc. 2, ap. 41; tel. (1) 3230855; fax (1) 3211908; e-mail anatr@starnets.ro; Pres. CORNEL GAINA.

THE RUSSIAN FEDERATION

Introductory Survey

Location, Climate, Language, Religion, Flag, Capital

The Russian Federation, or Russia, constituted the major part of the USSR, providing some 76% of its area and approximately 51% of its population in 1990. It is bounded by Norway, Finland, Estonia and Latvia to the north-west and by Belarus and Ukraine to the west. The southern borders of European Russia are with the Black Sea, Georgia, Azerbaijan, the Caspian Sea and Kazakhstan. The Siberian and Far Eastern regions have southern frontiers with the People's Republic of China, Mongolia and the Democratic People's Republic of Korea. The eastern coastline is on the Sea of Japan, the Sea of Okhotsk, the Pacific Ocean and the Barents Sea, and the northern coastline is on the Arctic Ocean. The region around Kaliningrad (formerly Königsberg in East Prussia), on the Baltic Sea, became part of the Russian Federation in 1945. Separated from the rest of Russia by Lithuania and Belarus, it borders Poland to the south, Lithuania to the north and east and has a coastline on the Baltic Sea. The climate of Russia is extremely varied, ranging from extreme Arctic conditions in northern areas and much of Siberia to generally temperate weather in the south. The average temperature in Moscow in July is 19°C (66°F); the average for January is –9°C (15°F). Average annual rainfall in Moscow is 575 mm (23 ins). The official language is Russian, but many other languages are also used. Christianity is the major religion, mostly adhered to by ethnic Russians and other Slavs, with the Russian Orthodox Church the largest denomination. The main concentrations of adherents of Islam are among the Tatar, Bashkir and Chuvash peoples of the Middle Volta, and the peoples of the northern Caucasus, including the Chechen, Ingush, Kabardins and the peoples of Dagestan. Buddhism is the main religion of the Buryats, the Tyvans and the Kalmyks. The large pre-1917 Jewish population has been depleted by war and emigration, but there remained some 400,000 Jews in the Russian Federation in 1998. The national flag (proportions 2 by 3) consists of three equal horizontal stripes of (from top to bottom) white, blue and red. The capital is Moscow (Moskva).

Recent History

By the late 19th century the Russian Empire extended throughout vast territories in Eastern Europe, and included much of northern and central Asia, a result of the territorial expansionism of the Romanov dynasty, which had ruled Russia as an autocracy since 1613. Growing dissatisfaction with economic conditions in urban areas, combined with the adverse effect of defeats in the Russo–Japanese War (1904–05) led Tsar Nicholas (Nikolai) II (1894–1917) to issue a manifesto in October 1905, which promised respect for civil liberties and the introduction of some constitutional order, although the ensuing attempt at reforms failed to placate the increasingly restive workers and peasants. In 1917 there were strikes and demonstrations in the capital, Petrograd (as St Petersburg had been renamed in 1914). In March 1917 the Tsar was forced to abdicate and a liberal Provisional Government, composed mainly of landowners, took power. However, most real authority lay with the soviets (councils), composed largely of workers and soldiers, which were attracted to socialist ideas.

The inability of the Provisional Government, led first by Prince Georgii Lvov and then by the moderate socialist Aleksandr Kerenskii, to implement land reforms, or to effect a withdrawal from the First World War, allowed more extreme groups, such as the Bolshevik faction of the Russian Social Democratic Labour Party (RSDLP), led by a prominent interpreter of Marxist theory, Vladimir Ulyanov (Lenin), to foster support among disaffected soldiers and workers. On 7 November 1917 (25 October in the Old Style calendar, which remained in use until February 1918) the Bolsheviks, who had come to dominate the Petrograd Soviet, seized power in the capital, with minimal use of force, and proclaimed the Russian Soviet Federative Socialist Republic (RSFSR or Russian Federation). The Bolsheviks subsequently adopted the name All-Russian Communist Party (Bolsheviks).

The Russian Federation was presented as the territorial successor to the Russian Empire, but the Bolsheviks asserted that they would respect the self-determination of the Empire's many nations. Poland, Finland and the Baltic States (Estonia, Latvia and Lithuania) achieved independence, but other independent states established in 1917–18 were forced, militarily, to declare themselves Soviet Republics. These were proclaimed as 'independent' socialist republics, in alliance with the Russian Federation, but the laws, Constitution and Government of the Russian Federation were supreme in all of them. This recentralization of power was recognized as politically damaging by the Bolsheviks. Thus, in 1922 the Russian Federation joined the Belarusian, Ukrainian and Transcaucasian republics as constitutionally equal partners in a Union of Soviet Socialist Republics (USSR, or Soviet Union), and institutions of the RSFSR were re-formed as institutions of the new Union. The USSR eventually numbered 15 constituent Soviet Socialist Republics (SSR). Moscow, the Russian Federation's seat of government since 1918, became the capital of the USSR.

The Russian Federation, in common with the other republics, experienced hardship as a result of the collectivization campaign of the early 1930s and the widespread repression under Iosif Dzhugashvili (Stalin), who established a brutal dictatorship after the death of Lenin in 1924. The Five-Year Plans, introduced in the late 1920s to effect rapid industrialization, directed considerable investment towards the previously neglected eastern regions, a process that was reinforced by the removal of strategic industries from the west of the republic to the Ural regions during the Second World War (or 'Great Patriotic War'), which the USSR entered in 1941. Under the Nazi-Soviet Treaty of Non-Aggression (the 'Molotov-Ribbentrop Pact') of August 1939, the USSR annexed the Baltic states as well as other territories. Victory over Germany and Japan in 1945 led to further territorial gains for the Russian Federation. In the west it gained part of East Prussia around Königsberg (now Kaliningrad) from Germany, a small amount of territory from Estonia and those parts of Finland annexed during the Soviet–Finnish War (1939–40). In the east it acquired the Kurile Islands from Japan. The nominally independent People's Republic of Tuva, situated between the USSR and Mongolia, was annexed in 1944 and subsequently became the Republic of Tyva within the Russian Federation. The present territorial extent of the Russian Federation was achieved in 1954, when Crimea was ceded to the Ukrainian SSR.

Shortly after the death of Stalin in March 1953, Nikita Khrushchev took over the post of First Secretary of the Communist Party of the Soviet Union (CPSU—as the Communist Party had been renamed in 1952), and gradually assumed predominance over his main rivals, Georgii Malenkov and Vyacheslav Molotov. The most brutal aspects of the Stalinist regime were ended under Khrushchev, and in 1956 Khrushchev admitted for the first time the existence of large-scale repression under Stalin. Khrushchev was dismissed in 1964, largely as a result of his erratic attempts to reform the Soviet bureaucracy and economy, as well as his conduct of international relations. He was replaced as First Secretary (later General Secretary) of the CPSU by Leonid Brezhnev, who remained in power until his death in 1982. During the 1970s relations with the West, which had, since the late 1940s, been generally characterized by the intense mutual hostility of the 'Cold War', experienced a considerable *détente*; however, this was ended by the Soviet invasion of Afghanistan in 1979. Brezhnev's successor as CPSU General Secretary, Yurii Andropov, undertook an anti-corruption campaign and attempted very cautious economic reforms. He was succeeded upon his death, in February 1984, by Konstantin Chernenko, who, however, died in March 1985.

Chernenko's successor as General Secretary was Mikhail Gorbachev, the youngest member of the Politburo, the executive committee of the CPSU. During 1986–87 Gorbachev replaced many leading state and CPSU officials, and appointed several reformists to the Politburo. A policy of *glasnost* (openness) provided a greater degree of freedom for the mass media and for discussion. In November 1987, however, supporters of *perestroika* (restructuring), as Gorbachev's programme of gradual political and economic reform came to be known, seemed to suffer a reverse, with the dismissal from the Politburo of Boris Yeltsin (a former party Secretary in Sverdlovsk—Yekaterinburg), after he severely criticized senior members of the leadership for their apparent opposition to reform. In June 1988 Gorbachev announced plans for comprehensive changes in the political system, with the introduction of a two-tier legislature, elected largely by competitive elections. In elections to the new USSR Congress of People's Deputies, held in March 1989, many reformist politicians were successful in achieving election (Yeltsin notably won an overwhelming victory in the Moscow City constituency). In May the Congress elected Gorbachev to the new post of executive President of the USSR.

Within the USSR the Russian Federation was clearly pre-eminent, both economically and politically, and ethnic Russians dominated the Soviet élite. However, this prominence meant that Russia developed few autonomous institutions. The initial stage in the process of instituting Russian sovereignty was the election of the RSFSR Congress of People's Deputies in March 1990 by largely free and competitive elections. In May the Congress elected Yeltsin to the highest state post in the RSFSR, the Chairman of the Supreme Soviet (the permanent working body of the Congress). Ruslan Khasbulatov, a Chechen economist, was elected First Deputy Chairman. On 12 June the Congress adopted a declaration asserting that the RSFSR was a sovereign republic and that the laws of the RSFSR had primacy over all-Union legislation. Thereafter, the political, cultural and scientific institutions that Russia had lacked began to be established.

In March 1991, when a referendum was held in nine republics to determine whether a restructured USSR should be retained, voters in the RSFSR also approved an additional question on the introduction of a Russian presidency. Direct presidential elections, held in June, were won by Yeltsin and his Vice-President, Aleksandr Rutskoi, with 57.3% of the votes cast. Direct election as President gave Yeltsin a popular mandate to challenge the jurisdiction of Gorbachev and the all-Union authorities. Yeltsin's reform programme included the expedited creation of the basis for a market economy. He remained committed, none the less, to a restructured Soviet federation, with extensive autonomy for the union republics.

On 19 August 1991, one day before the new union treaty was due to be signed, a self-proclaimed State Committee for the State of Emergency (SCSE), led by the Soviet Vice-President, Gennadii Yanayev, and comprising a number of conservative communists, seized power in Moscow, taking advantage of Gorbachev's absence from the capital. The *coup d'état* collapsed within three days, and Yeltsin asserted control over all-Union bodies, appointing Russian Federation ministers to head central institutions.

In October 1991 Yeltsin announced a programme of radical economic reforms. In November a new Government was announced, with Yeltsin as Chairman (Prime Minister). The CPSU and the Russian Communist Party (RCP—created in mid-1990 by opponents of Yeltsin), which had been suspended after the attempted coup, were banned. In November the Congress granted Yeltsin special powers for one year, including the right to issue decrees with legislative force and to appoint government ministers without parliamentary approval, and elected Khasbulatov to succeed Yeltsin as Chairman of the Supreme Soviet.

Yeltsin agreed to the creation of an economic community, which was founded by eight republics in October 1991, and appeared to favour Gorbachev's proposal for a Union of Sovereign States to replace the USSR. Following the reorganization of the Government in November, however, opposition to the creation of a new federation increased. On 8 December the leaders of Belarus, Ukraine and Russia announced the annulment of the 1922 Union Treaty and declared, thereby, that the USSR had ceased to exist; the Commonwealth of Independent States (CIS, see p. 172), defined as a co-ordinating organization rather than a new state, was created in its place. The Alma-Ata (Almaty) Declaration of 21 December 1991 formally established a commonwealth of 11 states. Of the Soviet republics, only Georgia, Estonia, Latvia and Lithuania remained outside the new body, although Georgia was eventually admitted to the CIS in December 1993. On 25 December 1991 Gorbachev resigned as the final President of the USSR, and the Russian Supreme Soviet formally changed the name of the RSFSR to the Russian Federation.

Political life in the Russian Federation in the early 1990s was characterized by heightened tensions between the legislature and the executive, as the two institutions sought to determine their respective powers. Following criticism of its economic policies at the Congress of People's Deputies in April 1992, the Government tendered its resignation, but the offer was rejected by Yeltsin, and an attempt by the Congress to deprive Yeltsin of some of the additional powers granted him in November 1991 was unsuccessful. In June 1992 Yeltsin appointed Yegor Gaidar, an advocate of radical economic reform, as acting Chairman; in the same month the Supreme Soviet adopted legislation permitting large-scale privatization.

In October 1992 Yeltsin banned, *inter alia*, the National Salvation Front (NSF), which united a number of extreme nationalist and neo-communist groups. The Constitutional Court subsequently decreed that the banning of the NSF and local Communist Party branches was illegal. Communist groups immediately announced that they would attempt to establish a new party and in early 1993 the Communist Party of the Russian Federation (CPRF) was founded.

In December 1992 the Congress of People's Deputies refused to endorse Gaidar as acting Chairman, and Yeltsin was forced to appoint a new premier, Viktor Chernomyrdin, who was regarded as less sympathetic to economic reform. Following the annulment, in March 1993, of a compromise agreement on constitutional reform by the Congress, Yeltsin announced that he would rule by decree prior to the holding of a referendum on a draft constitution, and that decisions of the Supreme Soviet and the Congress would have no legal force in the interim. An extraordinary session of the Congress of People's Deputies imposed four questions for consideration at the referendum, which was held on 25 April 1993. The first question (on confidence in Yeltsin as President) received a positive response from 57.4% of voters, while 53.7% responded positively to the second, which sought approval of Yeltsin's socio-economic policies. Support for early presidential elections (the subject of the third question) was only 49.1%, but 70.6% of voters favoured early elections to the Congress of People's Deputies.

By mid-1993 Rutskoi, while nominally remaining Vice-President, had been divested of his official responsibilities by Yeltsin. Meanwhile, there was renewed disagreement between Yeltsin and the Congress of People's Deputies over the balance of powers to be provided for by the new Constitution. In July the Constitutional Conference approved a draft that provided for a presidential system with a bicameral parliament—the Federal Assembly—comprising a lower chamber (State Duma) and an upper chamber (Federation Council), with the Government subordinate to both the President and the legislature; however, the Congress of People's Deputies rejected this draft.

The long-standing impasse between the presidential administration and the legislature eventually resulted in violent confrontation. On 21 September 1993 Yeltsin suspended the Congress of People's Deputies and the Supreme Soviet, and announced that elections to the new bicameral Federal Assembly would be held in December. The Supreme Soviet consequently dismissed Yeltsin as President, announcing the appointment of Rutskoi in his place; an emergency session of the Congress of People's Deputies confirmed this appointment, and voted to impeach Yeltsin. On 27 September government troops surrounded the parliament building: some 180 deputies, including Rutskoi and Khasbulatov, remained inside, with armed supporters. Conflict erupted in early October, as supporters of the rebel deputies attempted to seize control of strategic buildings in Moscow, and Yeltsin declared a state of emergency in the capital. On 4 October army tanks bombarded the parliament building, forcing the surrender of the rebels. The leaders of the rebellion were imprisoned, and subsequently charged with inciting 'mass disorder'. According to official figures, some 160 people were killed in the fighting.

In the immediate aftermath of the rebellion, Yeltsin temporarily strengthened government control of the media and briefly suspended several parties that had either supported or participated in the conflict, including the CPRF. Yeltsin announced that the presidential election, provisionally scheduled for mid-1994, would not take place, and that he would remain in office for the duration of his mandate, until June 1996.

The new draft constitution, which guaranteed broad powers for the President and a much-diminished role for the legislature, and divested Russia's constituent republics of their right to secede from the Federation, was submitted to a national referendum on 12 December 1993, held simultaneously with elections to the two houses of the Federal Assembly. Of the 54.8% of the registered electorate that participated in the plebiscite,

58.4% endorsed the draft. In the legislative elections, Vladimir Zhirinovskii's nationalist Liberal Democratic Party of Russia (LDPR) secured a total of 64 seats, the largest number obtained by any single party or alliance. (Of the 450 members of the State Duma, 225 were elected by proportional representation on the basis of party lists, and 225 within single-member constituencies.) Russia's Choice (a new alliance of pro-reform groups, led by Gaidar, regarded as sympathetic to Yeltsin) secured 58 seats. Pro-communist parties also performed strongly: the CPRF took 48 seats, while the Agrarian Party of Russia (APR) won 33 seats. With the ensuing alignment of parties and the 130 independents into parliamentary factions, Russia's Choice emerged as the largest group in the Duma (controlling 76 seats in early 1994), although it failed to ensure an overall pro-Government majority in the legislature. The Federation Council was to comprise two representatives from each of Russia's 89 federal subjects (as the constituent republics, oblasts—regions, okrugs—districts and krais—territories of the Federation were known), although in December 1993 representatives were not elected in the separatist republics of Tatarstan and Chechnya, owing to a voter boycott, nor in Chelyabinsk Oblast, and in two other districts only one representative was elected. The majority of the Council's members were republican or regional leaders, few of whom held party affiliation; however, it was reported that supporters of Yeltsin outnumbered the communist and nationalist opposition. A new, smaller Government was appointed in January 1994. In February the combined strength of opposition groupings in the State Duma was demonstrated by a vote in favour of granting amnesties to Rutskoi, Khasbulatov and other leaders of the 1993 rebellion, as well as to the SCSE and to the organizers of violent demonstrations in May 1993 by neo-communist and nationalist groups in Moscow.

In October 1994 a sudden decline in the value of the rouble prompted the resignation or dismissal of government members, including the Chairman of the Central Bank, Viktor Gerashchenko. In November the reformist Anatolii Chubais, who had hitherto been responsible for the privatization programme, was promoted to the post of First Deputy Chairman, although other government appointments appeared to advance those opposed to further economic liberalization.

In late 1994 Russia commenced military intervention in the separatist Republic of Chechnya (see p. 3474); an apparent lack of progress there, together with the continued deterioration of the economy, were instrumental in the approval by the State Duma, in June 1995, of a motion expressing 'no confidence' in the Government. Yeltsin subsequently dismissed a number of ministers; however, Gen. Pavel Grachev, whose resignation had been demanded by the Duma, notably retained his post as Minister of Defence. In early July a second vote of 'no confidence' (as required by the Constitution) failed to secure the necessary majority.

Elections to the State Duma took place on 17 December 1995. In accordance with a new electoral law, which introduced a minimum requirement of 5% of the votes cast for seats allocated on the basis of party lists, only four parties (the CPRF, the LDPR, Chernomyrdin's Our Home is Russia—OHR and the liberal Yabloko) secured representation, while an additional 10 parties and 77 independent candidates obtained seats through voting in single-member constituencies. Overall, the CPRF emerged as the largest single party in the State Duma, with 157 of the 450 deputies, although its ability to achieve a majority in the legislature depended on the support of the APR (which had 20 deputies) and of smaller parties and independent deputies. OHR won 55 seats, the LDPR 51 and Yabloko 45.

In January 1996 Yeltsin enacted a ministerial reshuffle, in which Yevgenii Primakov (hitherto Director of the Foreign Intelligence Service) was appointed as Minister of Foreign Affairs, and Chubais was dismissed from the post of First Deputy Chairman. In the same month the Duma elected Gennadii Seleznev, a CPRF deputy, as its Chairman. Yegor Stroyev, Governor of Orel Oblast in central Russia, was elected Chairman of the Federation Council, by this time comprising the heads of the legislatures and executives of the 89 federal subjects.

Of the 10 candidates to contest the first round of the presidential election, on 16 June 1996, Yeltsin won the greatest number of votes (35.8%), narrowly defeating Gennadii Zyuganov (of the CPRF), with 32.5%. Gen. Aleksandr Lebed, who had until recently commanded Russian forces in the separatist Transnistria region of Moldova, and whose Congress of Russian Communities held five seats in the Duma, achieved an unexpectedly

high level of support, with 14.7%. Since neither had received the 50% of the votes required for outright victory, Yeltsin and Zyuganov proceeded to a second round of voting. Yeltsin consequently formed a political alliance with Lebed, appointing him Secretary of the Security Council and National Security Adviser, and granted him particular responsibility for resolving the crisis in Chechnya. Yeltsin also dismissed Grachev, whose support for the military action in Chechnya had become progressively more unpopular. Despite increasingly infrequent public appearances, apparently a result of poor health, Yeltsin was re-elected as President in the second ballot, on 3 July, with some 54% of the total votes cast. Chernomyrdin was subsequently re-appointed as premier, and Chubais was promoted to head the Presidential Administration. The powers of the Security Council were significantly widened, and Gen. Igor Rodionov, an ally of Lebed, was appointed Minister of Defence.

Despite the successful negotiation of a cease-fire agreement in Chechnya in August 1996 (see p. 3474), Yeltsin was openly critical of Lebed for failing to resolve the conflict sooner. The announcement, in September, that Yeltsin was to undergo heart surgery, raised fears that an internal struggle for power would ensue between rival factions loyal to Chernomyrdin and Lebed. In October Yeltsin dismissed Lebed, following allegations that he had been preparing to attempt a *coup d'état*. Yeltsin established a new committee, comprising Chubais, Chernomyrdin, Stroyev and Seleznev, in an attempt to introduce a more cohesive administration, but the President's appointment of Boris Berezovskii, a prominent business executive, as Deputy Secretary of the Security Council, led to a boycott by Seleznev of the committee's inaugural session. In November Yeltsin underwent heart surgery, temporarily transferring his presidential authority to Chernomyrdin, amid nation-wide unrest over wage arrears and demands for the resignation of the Government. Yeltsin assumed full presidential duties in late December, but was again hospitalized shortly afterwards, and there was growing pressure from the Duma for his resignation.

Although Yeltsin delivered a vehement criticism of the Government in his annual address to the Federal Assembly in March 1997, in a subsequent government reorganization Chernomyrdin retained his post, thereby avoiding the need to seek parliamentary approval of the new, largely reformist, cabinet. Chubais was appointed First Deputy Chairman and Minister of Finance, and Boris Nemtsov, hitherto Governor of Nizhnii Novgorod Oblast, was brought into the Government, also as First Deputy Chairman, with responsibility for dismantling the large state monopolies. He was subsequently allocated the fuel and energy portfolio. A restructuring of the gas, electricity and transport monopolies, including the sale of government holdings in six petroleum companies, was announced, in an attempt to increase tax revenue in order to settle wages' and pensions' arrears. (In March some 2m. people nation-wide had participated in demonstrations protesting at the non-payment of wages and pensions.) In May Rodionov was replaced as Minister of Defence by Gen. Igor Sergeyev, hitherto commander of the Strategic Rocket Forces, and a new Chief of the General Staff was appointed. In the following month the State Duma rejected government proposals to reduce budgetary expenditure. In August the Deputy Chairman and head of the State Committee for the Management of State Property, Alfred Kokh, resigned following criticism of his management of the privatization programme; it was subsequently alleged that he had accepted bribes in exchange for the placing of contracts.

In November 1997 Berezovskii, who had recently been implicated in improprieties relating to the privatization programme, was dismissed from his post as Deputy Secretary of the Security Council; Berezovskii attributed his dismissal to his purportedly having supported rival banking interests to Chubais in the recent round of privatizations. Chubais was dismissed as Minister of Finance in the same month, but he retained the deputy premiership until March 1998, despite requests by the Duma for his dismissal. In addition, Nemtsov lost the fuel and energy portfolio. (In late April Berezovskii was appointed as the Executive Secretary of the CIS.)

Meanwhile, a cabinet reshuffle in January 1998 significantly consolidated Chernomyrdin's authority. In the same month a new rouble, equivalent to 1,000 of the former units, was introduced. Yeltsin, whose erratic behaviour during several overseas tours had again given rise to concerns about his health, had been absent from public life in late 1997. In late March 1998 Yeltsin removed Chernomyrdin from office, thereby effectively dismissing the entire Government, citing the need to revitalize the

process of economic reform. Parliamentary deputies were reluctant to endorse Yeltsin's nominee for the premiership, the
hitherto Minister of Fuel and Energy and a close ally of Nemtsov, Sergei Kiriyenko, principally owing to the summary nature
of the dismissal of the Government. Kiriyenko's appointment as
Chairman was finally confirmed at the Duma's third vote in
mid-April, following threats by Yeltsin to dissolve the legislature. Several ministers, including Nemtsov, retained their
portfolios in the new Government formed during April–May.
Chubais, meanwhile, was appointed Chairman of the electricity
monopoly, Unified Energy System of Russia. Tensions between
the legislature and executive intensified in mid-1998, but an
attempt by the CPRF to initiate impeachment charges against
Yeltsin was ruled unconstitutional by a parliamentary commission in late July. In mid-August, however, the State Duma
succeeded in approving a resolution demanding the voluntary
resignation of Yeltsin.

In August 1998 mounting political instability was exacerbated by severe economic difficulties. The value of the rouble
declined rapidly. Yeltsin dismissed Kiriyenko and his Government, reappointing Chernomyrdin as Chairman. However,
Chernomyrdin's plans to restore financial stability failed to win
legislative approval, despite his attempts to broker an agreement to accord deputies in the State Duma increased influence
over the composition of the Government, and Chernomyrdin's
candidacy to the premiership was twice rejected by the Duma. In
mid-September Yeltsin (aware that should his candidate be
rejected for a third time he would be constitutionally obliged to
dissolve the Duma) nominated Primakov as Chairman, a candidacy that was endorsed by a large majority, despite Primakov's
lack of economic experience and an impending default on Russia's foreign debt. Gerashchenko was also re-appointed as
Chairman of the Central Bank, a position he retained until early
2002.

An audit of the Central Bank, conducted in February 1999
following allegations that funds issued by the IMF had been
misused, revealed that some US $50,000m. in reserves had been
diverted into an 'offshore' company, over a period of five years,
for the personal gain of bank staff. An investigation into irregularities involving business executives resulted, in early April,
in the arrest of Berezovskii, who had been dismissed by Yeltsin
as CIS Executive Secretary in early March, and a former official
of Aeroflot, the national airline; both were charged with illegal
entrepreneurship and 'money-laundering' (the processing of illegally obtained funds into legitimate accounts). However, the
charges, which Berezovskii insisted were politically motivated,
were withdrawn in November.

Meanwhile, in May 1999 Yeltsin dismissed Primakov and his
Government. Sergei Stepashin, hitherto First Deputy Chairman
and Minister of Internal Affairs, was appointed as Chairman,
and a new Government was formed later in the month. Meanwhile, a further attempt in the State Duma to impeach Yeltsin
failed in mid-May, as the five charges brought against the
President (the destruction of the USSR in 1991; the violent
disbandment of the elected legislature in 1993; the dispatch of
troops to war in Chechnya; undermining the armed forces and,
thus, national defences; and bringing 'genocide' on the people of
Russia through economic reforms that had resulted in a lower
birth-rate and reduced average life expectancy) failed to secure
the necessary majority of two-thirds of the chamber's membership. New appointments to the Security Council, decreed by
Yeltsin in mid-June 1999, included the replacement of Primakov
by Stepashin. Yeltsin dismissed Stepashin as Chairman of the
Government in early August. (In April 2000 Stepashin was
appointed as Chairman of the Audit Chamber of the State
Duma.) Despite the expression of significant opposition to Stepashin's removal within the Duma, his replacement by Vladimir
Putin, a former colonel in the Soviet Committee for State
Security (KGB), First Deputy Chairman of St Petersburg City
Government in 1994–96, and hitherto head of the Federal
Security Service (FSB) and Secretary of the Security Council, in
mid-August, was, none the less, endorsed by a majority vote in
the chamber; Yeltsin also named Putin as his preferred successor as President. Putin was replaced as head of the FSB by
his deputy, Nikolai Patrushev. In mid-November Yeltsin
appointed Sergei Ivanov, deputy head of the FSB, to succeed
Putin as Secretary of the Security Council.

The issue of media control assumed growing importance from
1999. In July 1999 Berezovskii purchased a 15% share of the
Kommersant (*Businessman*) newspaper, which had published a
number of unfavourable articles about him; it was suspected

that the purchase of the remaining 85% in the same month was
also effected on Berezovskii's behalf. The editor of *Kommersant*
was dismissed in August and in the same month the publication
of the newspaper was suspended, ostensibly for its failure to
comply with the demands of safety inspectors. Also in July, a
new Ministry for the Press, Broadcasting and Mass Media was
established by presidential decree.

In the months leading up to State Duma elections on 19
December 1999 several new political alliances were formed; in
August the centrist party of the Mayor of Moscow, Yurii
Luzhkov, Fatherland, merged with a grouping of regional gov-
ernors, All Russia, to form Fatherland-All Russia (FAR). Later
that month Primakov accepted the first place on the new bloc's
electoral list, ahead of Luzhkov; the Mayor of St Petersburg,
Vladimir Yakovlev, was subsequently appointed as leader of the
All Russia faction within the alliance. The APR, formerly a close
ally of the CPRF, joined FAR, although it seceded from the bloc
after the Duma elections and resumed co-operation with the
CPRF. Apparently in response to the formation of FAR, a pro-
Government bloc, Unity (also known as the Bear) was formed in
September by 31 leaders of Russia's regions and republics,
under the leadership of Sergei Shoigu, the Minister for Civil
Defence, Emergencies and Clean-up Operations. Meanwhile,
Kiriyenko and Nemtsov were among the leaders of a new liberal,
reformist bloc, the Union of Rightist Forces (URF), which also
incorporated Gaidar's Russia's Democratic Choice party.

Meanwhile, tensions relating to the unresolved status of
Chechnya and the apparent emergence there of militant
Islamist groups were heightened, following a number of incursions by Chechen militants into the neighbouring Republic of
Dagestan in early August 1999 (see p. 3475). Moreover, in late
August and September more than 300 people were killed in a
series of bomb explosions in Moscow, in Dagestan and in Volgodonsk, in Rostov Oblast, southern Russia, which Putin attributed to Chechen militant groups. Citing the threat posed by
militants in the separatist republic, Putin announced that military operations in Chechnya (which the Government described
as an 'anti-terrorist operation') were to re-commence and, prior
to the large-scale deployment of ground troops, the aerial bombardment of Chechnya commenced on 23 September.

A total of 29 parties and blocs contested the elections to the
State Duma on 19 December 1999, in which some 62% of the
electorate participated. Six parties obtained the 5% of the votes
required for representation in the Duma on the basis of the
party-list system, while an additional eight parties and blocs,
and 106 independent candidates, secured representation from
single-member constituency ballots. As in the previous Duma,
the CPRF, with 24.3% of the votes, obtained the largest number
of seats, although its quota of 113 deputies (67 of whom were
elected on the basis of party lists) was significantly smaller than
that achieved in the 1995 elections. Unity, which received 23.3%
of the votes cast, was the second largest party in the Duma, with
72 seats (64 of them elected from party lists). FAR won 67 seats
(37 from party lists), the URF 29 (24 from party lists), the
Zhirinovskii bloc (a court ruling, relating to an irregularity in
the party's registration, had led to the LDPR being forbidden to
contest the elections under that designation; the bloc comprised
the LDPR and two small 'national-patriotic' groups) won 17
seats (all of which were party-list seats), and Yabloko 21 (16
from party lists). Eight other groups, including OHR, won
constituency seats, and Berezovskii was elected as a deputy for
Unity. In eight constituencies, where the option to vote 'against
all candidates' had secured greater support than any candidate,
repeat by-elections were held in March 2000; owing to difficulties in organizing elections there, no candidate was elected in
Chechnya. (A by-election held in Chechnya in August 2000 was
won by a senior official in the Russian Ministry of the Interior.)

On 31 December 1999 Boris Yeltsin unexpectedly resigned as
President. Putin assumed the presidency in an acting capacity
prior to a presidential election, scheduled for 26 March 2000.
Putin granted Yeltsin immunity from prosecution on criminal
and administrative charges, and removed from office key members of Yeltsin's administration.

When the new State Duma convened in mid-January 2000,
the ideologically dissimilar CPRF and Unity factions formed an
alliance, meaning that, for the first time since the dissolution of
the USSR, pro-Government forces held a majority in the legislature. To protest against what they regarded as an attempt by
the CPRF and Unity to divide decisive posts in the Duma
between themselves, the FAR, Yabloko and URF factions,
together with the newly formed Regions of Russia group of

(primarily independent) deputies, withdrew from the chamber. The boycott ended later in the month following intervention by Putin and the reallocation of committee chairmanships, and the appointment of an additional Deputy Chairman of the Duma from the Regions of Russia group.

Putin effected a reorganization of the Government in January 2000. Putin's position in the forthcoming presidential election appeared to be strengthened, following an announcement, in early February, that the FAR bloc was to support Putin's candidacy; consequently, Primakov and Luzhkov, who had been expected to present a serious challenge to Putin at the elections, declined to be nominated.

Putin achieved a clear victory in the presidential election, held, as scheduled, on 26 March 2000, and contested by 11 candidates, in which he received 52.9% of the votes cast. His closest rival was Zyuganov, of the CPRF, with 29.2%. Putin was inaugurated as President on 7 May. In mid-May Mikhail Kasyanov, hitherto First Deputy Chairman and Minister of Finance, was approved as Chairman of the Council of Ministers and a new Government was appointed shortly afterwards.

Concerns regarding the freedom of the media in Russia were heightened following the approval by Putin, in September 2000, of a new information doctrine, which had been presented by the Security Council, and media coverage of the conflict in Chechnya remained subject to strict control. Meanwhile, Vladimir Gusinskii, the owner of the Mediya-Most holding company (comprising a number of concerns, including Russia's only wholly independent national television broadcaster, NTV, which had, notably, presented critical coverage of the Government's campaign in Chechnya), was arrested in June and charged with fraud. All charges were withdrawn in late July, ostensibly owing to a lack of evidence. In September, however, Gusinskii, who had fled to Spain, stated that he had been forced to agree to the sale of Mediya-Most to Gazprom-Mediya, a subsidiary of the state-controlled gas monopoly, Gazprom, to which Mediya-Most was heavily indebted, in return for the withdrawal of the charges against him. In the same month Gazprom brought charges of criminal embezzlement against Mediya-Most's management. Gusinskii lost control of the company in November, and the deal reached with the head of Gazprom-Mediya, the former deputy premier, Kokh, gave the State a controlling stake in all Mediya-Most enterprises, with the exception of NTV. In December the Moscow fiscal authorities demanded that Mediya-Most be closed, on grounds of insolvency, and Gusinskii, for the arrest of whom an international warrant had been issued, was detained in Spain in the same month.

Meanwhile, other prominent businessmen were subjected to examinations of their business affairs, in what was seen as an attempt by the Government to reduce the powers of the 'oligarchs', as a number of wealthy businessmen, who in many cases had acquired control of formerly nationalized industries in the 1990s, were widely known. In July 2000 Berezovskii, one of the wealthiest and most politically active 'oligarchs', had relinquished his seat in the State Duma and, therefore, his immunity from prosecution, accusing Putin of having adopted an increasingly authoritarian style of governance. (Berezovskii also subsequently resigned from Unity, which was becoming regarded as increasingly sympathetic to presidential policies and initiatives.) In September Berezovskii announced his intention to relinquish his 49% of shares in the state-controlled television station, ORT, claiming that he had received an ultimatum that he should surrender his holding to the state or risk imprisonment; the sale finally took place in February 2001, following which members of the company's board of directors were replaced by representatives of the state. None the less, a warrant for Berezovskii's arrest was issued in November 2000, after he failed to return to Russia from France to answer questions relating to the Aeroflot case (see above), which had recently been reopened.

Putin introduced significant changes to regional governance during 2000. In May, as part of measures intended to promote structures of 'vertical power', seven Federal Okrugs (Districts) were created, each of which was headed by a presidential appointee, and to whom regional governors were to be answerable. Additionally, a new consultative body, the State Council, comprising the heads of the 89 federal subjects, was created by presidential decree in September; participation in the Council was, however, to be voluntary.

A severe energy crisis in the Russian Far East, resulting from the non-payment of bills, prompted the resignation of the Minister of Energy, Aleksandr Gavrin, in February 2001, although

the State Duma defeated a proposal by the CPRF for the dismissal of Chubais from the chairmanship of the electricity monopoly. In mid-March a motion of 'no confidence' in the Government, proposed by Zyuganov, was rejected by the Duma; notably, Seleznev was among those communist deputies who refused to give assent to the bill. In late March Putin implemented a minor ministerial reshuffle, appointing Boris Gryzlov, hitherto the head of the Unity faction in the Duma, as Minister of Internal Affairs, in place of Vladimir Rushailo, and Sergei Ivanov as Minister of Defence; Rushailo replaced the latter as Secretary of the Security Council. In April it was announced that the Unity faction in the State Duma was, henceforth, to form an alliance with FAR, in preference to the CPRF, a measure that ensured Unity would retain a majority of seats in the lower legislative chamber with the support of an ideologically similar party; in the same month Luzhkov announced that FAR and Unity were to merge later in the year.

Following the refusal of the Spanish authorities to extradite Gusinskii to Russia, and the annulment of all travel restrictions pertaining to him, in late April 2001 he took up residence in Israel, where he held dual citizenship, purportedly in an attempt to complicate extradition procedures. None the less, Russia issued a fresh warrant for Gusinskii's arrest, on charges of 'money-laundering'. Meanwhile, in early April, upon the majority acquisition of NTV by Gazprom-Mediya, journalists occupied the company's studios to protest against the perceived loss of editorial freedom. Following the dismissal of NTV's management by its new board of directors, many journalists, led by the company's former Director-General and Editor-in-Chief, Yevgenii Kiselyev, moved to TNT, a less widely broadcast network, which remained under Gusinskii's ownership; subsequently, Kiselyev was appointed General Manager of a small television channel owned by Berezovskii, TV6, to which the majority of the former NTV journalists transferred. Meanwhile, the staff at the two newspapers published by Mediya-Most, *Segodnya* (*Today*) and *Itogi* (*Results*) were dismissed and the publications closed. In May Berezovskii, who remained outside Russia, announced his intention to form a new party to promote politically and economically liberal policies; the party, Liberal Russia, was launched later in the year. In July the legislature approved a new law, which banned foreign citizens, as well as those Russians holding dual citizenship (thus including Gusinskii), from acquiring a majority stake in Russian television channels.

During 2001 a number of further legal reforms were approved. In mid-July Putin signed a law imposing new conditions on political parties; henceforth, parties would be required to have a minimum of 10,000 members, including no fewer than 100 members from at least 50 of the 89 federal subjects, in order to be registered with the Ministry of Justice, which measure would permit them to participate in elections. Moreover, from 2003 any party that received more than 3% of the votes cast in a legislative election would be eligible for state funding. In late October Putin signed a new Land Code, which permitted the sale of commercial and residential plots; however, the law applied to less than one-10th of land, and the sale or purchase of agricultural plots remained prohibited, pending the introduction of additional legislation, approved by the Duma in late June 2002. In December 2001 Putin signed three judicial reform bills, with the stated intention of, *inter alia*, increasing the use of juries comprising members of the public (at that time jury trials were conducted, in limited conditions, in just nine of the 89 federal subjects). At the beginning of February 2002 a new Labour Code, which included provisions tightening conditions for the recognition of trade unions, was introduced.

In mid-October 2001 the Ministry of Federal Affairs, Nationality and Migration Policy was abolished, and its responsibilities absorbed into those of the Ministry of Internal Affairs. At the beginning of December the first congress of Unity and Fatherland–United Russia (UF-UR), the successor to FAR and Unity, marked the formal establishment of the party, which held a majority of seats in both parliamentary houses. Although not a member of the party or of any other, Putin attended the founding congress. Also in early December Vladimir Zorin was appointed as Minister without Portfolio, responsible for Nationalities Policy. In early January the Minister of Railways, Nikolai Aksenenko, was dismissed, after having been charged with abuse of office; he was replaced by Gennadii Fadayev, who had held the position in 1992–96.

In January 2002 TV6 ceased transmissions, following a court case brought by LUKoil Garant, a minority shareholder, a subsidiary of the state-controlled petroleum company LUKoil, which had demanded the television company's liquidation on the grounds of unprofitability. Suggestions that the ruling may have been at least partly motivated by political considerations, since Berezovskii had become one of the most vocal opponents of Putin from his self-imposed exile, were heightened at the beginning of January by the repeal of the law under which the case had been brought, particularly in view of the increasing profitability of TV6.

In mid-January 2002 a new session of the Federation Council opened, with a reformed composition. In place of regional leaders and chairmen of regional legislative assemblies, the Council comprised their full-time appointees, who were obliged to surrender their commercial interests during their term of office; several high-profile 'oligarchs' were appointed to the new Council, and the formation of political factions and groups in the Council was to be prohibited. Sergei Mironov, an ally of Putin, had replaced Stroyev as Chairman of the Council in early December 2001.

In mid-February 2002 Ilya Klebanov was demoted from the position of Deputy Chairman of the Government, although he retained his position as Minister of Industry, Science and Technology. In late March it was announced that a new non-profit organization, Mediya-Sotsium, headed by Primakov and the Chairman of the Russian Union of Industrialists and Entrepreneurs, Arkadii Volskii, had been awarded the contract to broadcast on the channel vacated by TV6; many former journalists from that station, including Kiselyev, were expected to transfer to the new channel, which commenced operations under the name TVS–The Sixth TV Channel. Meanwhile, Berezovskii presented a video-recording in London, the United Kingdom, which purported to demonstrate the FSB's involvement, and Putin's acquiescence, in the apartment block bombings of mid-1999; although 100 copies of the recording were confiscated by Russian customs authorities in mid-March, the programme was broadcast at meetings held by Liberal Russia in several cities.

Meanwhile, tensions heightened between the factions of UF-UR and the CPRF in the State Duma. In mid-March 2002 the Duma voted to remove the deciding vote in the governing body of the chamber, the Duma Council, from the Chairman, CPRF deputy Seleznev. In early April the Duma voted to revoke seven of the nine committee chairmanships held by the CPRF, as that party, in alliance with the APR, announced that it was to assume a more aggressively oppositional role. Attempts in April by the centrist majority to remove Seleznev from the position of speaker were unsuccessful, and Putin requested that Seleznev remain as Chairman of the Duma. Seleznev was subsequently expelled from the CPRF, and founded his own, socialist, political movement, Rossiya, which was registered, in October, as the Party of the Rebirth of Russia.

In late June 2002 the State Duma approved legislation, proposed by Putin, permitting the authorities to disband any organization or movement deemed to be 'extremist'; the legislation resulted from concern at the apparent growth of neo-Nazi and anti-Semitic groups, and came after several apparently racially-motivated attacks in Moscow. However, concern was also expressed that the new legislation, which was formally approved by the Federation Council in mid-July, and came into force at the end of the month, lacked specificity in defining the activities that were to be prohibited.

A criminal case against Berezovskii was opened by the Office of the Procurator-General in Moscow in August 2002. In late October Berezovskii was charged, *in absentia*, with defrauding the state, in his capacity as the Director-General of the automobile manufacturing company, LogoVAZ, which he had founded in 1991. In early November 2002 the Russian authorities requested Berezovskii's extradition from the United Kingdom, where he was resident; earlier in the month Berezovskii had announced that he would support the Chechen rebel leader Akhmed Zakayev in his attempts to avoid extradition to Russia from Denmark, and subsequently from the United Kingdom (see below). Meanwhile, in mid-October, following the publication of an interview in the nationalist journal, *Zavtra* (*Tomorrow*), in which Berezovskii appeared to support the formation of a united opposition front by liberal and left-wing forces, he was suspended from Liberal Russia; one week later the Ministry of Justice agreed to register the party, which had hitherto been denied registration on several occasions, reportedly because of irregularities with its documentation. In early December supporters of Berezovskii within Liberal Russia held an extraordinary congress in St Petersburg, in which a vote to re-admit

Berezovskii to the party and to expel the Co-chairmen of the party was agreed; however, neither decision was approved by the party at large nor recognized by the Ministry of Justice. Berezovskii was arrested by the British authorities in late March 2003. In mid-April one of the co-chairmen of Liberal Russia, Sergei Yushenkov, was assassinated in Moscow. (Another deputy of the party, Vladimir Golovlev, had been assassinated in August 2002.)

Meanwhile, in late October 2002, following the deaths of at least 129 people as the result of an armed siege at a Moscow theatre by heavily-armed militants, linked to Chechen extremists (see below), the Government implemented a number of personnel changes in Chechnya, in what was described as an attempt to bring about a military and political resolution to the conflict. In particular, the appointment, in mid-November, of Stanislov Ilyasov, hitherto the Prime Minister of Chechnya, to the federal Government as Minister without Portfolio, responsible for the Social and Economic Development of Chechnya, was regarded as indicating a redoublement of efforts by the Government to bring peace to the republic, as it represented the first occasion on which a minister whose responsibilities were specifically related to Chechnya had been appointed to the federal Government. In December Putin announced that a referendum on a draft republican constitution was to be held in Chechnya in March 2003 (see below); it was intended that this referendum would be followed by elections to the presidency and legislature of Chechnya.

On 11 March 2003 Putin removed Valentina Matviyenko from her post as Deputy Chairman of the Government, responsible for Social Affairs, appointing her as Presidential Representative in the North-Western Federal Okrug; on the same date several presidential decrees provided for a re-organization of the federal security agencies, as a result of which additional powers were transferred to the FSB. On 24 April two additional Deputy Chairmen were appointed to the Government: Boris Aleshin, latterly Chairman of the State Committee for Standards and Metrology, assumed responsibility for Industrial Policy, and Galina Karelova, hitherto First Deputy Minister of Labour and Social Development, assumed the position vacated by Matviyenko in the previous month.

Although a number of reforms that purported to strengthen constitutional order were introduced in the early 2000s, Putin's stated intention of ensuring a 'dictatorship of law' raised concerns with regard to the apparently incipient authoritarian tendencies within his administration. Notably, several measures reminiscent of the Soviet period were reintroduced during the first three years of Putin's presidency: from 2001 a 'cult of personality' (a device used by the majority of Soviet leaders, but which had been shunned by Gorbachev and Yeltsin) appeared to be developing around the President, promoted by, among others, a large national youth organization, Moving Together, which was established in 2001 (although it was not officially endorsed by the President). The Soviet national anthem was reintroduced in 2001, with new lyrics by the original composer; a number of Soviet holidays were restored; and by early 2002 the industrial Siberian city of Norilsk had successfully campaigned for its former 'closed' status, with restrictions on residency and access for foreign citizens, to be reintroduced, and other cities were seeking similar status.

In the early 1990s the Russian Federation encountered difficulties in attempting to satisfy the aspirations of its many nationalities for self-determination. In March 1992 18 of Russia's 20 nominally autonomous republics signed a federation treaty. The two dissenters, both predominately Islamic and petroleum-producing regions, were Tatarstan, which had voted for self-rule earlier in the month and Checheno-Ingushetiya, which had declared independence from Russia in November 1991 (as the Republic of Chechnya). The new treaty granted the regions greater authority, including control of natural resources and formal borders, and allowed them to conduct their own foreign trade. An agreement signed with the Russian Government in February 1994 accorded Tatarstan a considerable measure of sovereignty. Other power-sharing agreements, granting varying degrees of sovereignty, were eventually signed by some 42 of the 89 federal subjects during Yeltsin's presidency, although from 2000 Putin implemented a number of measures intended to curtail the power of regional governors, which led to the rescission of the vast majority of the power-sharing treaties by mid-2002. As a result of reforms implemented in stages between 2000 and 2002, regional governors lost their seats in the Federation Council, being replaced by unelected appointees of regional legislatures and executives. Other bills approved by the State Duma in May 2000 served to strengthen 'vertical' power relationships within the Federation, according the President the right to dismiss regional governors, a prerogative that was extended to governors with regard to those elected officials subordinate to them.

In March 1992, in response to the unilateral declaration of independence by Chechnya, the Ingush inhabitants of the former Checheno-Ingush Republic demanded the establishment of a separate Ingush republic. The formation of the new republic was approved by the federal Supreme Council in June. Additionally, Ingush activists claimed territories in neighbouring North Osetiya—Alaniya, which had formed part of the Ingush autonomous republic prior to the Second World War, when the Ingush (and Chechens, in common with several other nationalities of the USSR) were deported *en masse* to Central Asia. In October 1992 violent conflict broke out in the Prigorodnyi district in North Osetiya. By November more than 300 people had died in the conflict and some 50,000 Ingush had fled the region. In September 1997, following mediation by Yeltsin, a treaty on normalizing relations was signed by the republican Governments of North Osetiya and Ingushetiya.

In late 1993 armed hostilities commenced in Chechnya between forces loyal to the republican and separatist leader, Gen. Dzhokhar Dudayev (who had been elected President of the Republic in October 1991, following a *coup d'état* against the republic's communist Government, led by Doku Zavgayev), and his opponents. Chechnya boycotted the Russian general election and referendum of December 1993; in August 1994 an unsuccessful attempt to overthrow the Dudayev regime was reputedly aided by the federal security services. Following the defeat of a further offensive in November, federal troops entered Chechnya in December, with the stated aim of reintroducing constitutional rule in the republic. The troops rapidly gained control of the lowland area of northern Chechnya, where support for Dudayev was weakest. Dudayev's forces, estimated to number some 15,000 irregular troops, were concentrated in the Chechen capital, Groznyi, a city upon which federal troops launched an assault in late December, following heavy bombardment from the air. Despite sustaining significant casualties, federal troops gradually took control of the city and seized the presidential palace (the headquarters of Dudayev's forces) in January 1995. Groznyi suffered great devastation during the assault, and there were reported to be thousands of civilian casualties.

By May 1995 federal troops claimed to control some two-thirds of the republic's territory, including all the major towns, although rebel resistance continued from bases in the southern, mountainous regions. In June Chechen gunmen engaged local security forces in Budennovsk, in Stavropol Krai, some 200 km from the border with Chechnya, and took hostage more than 1,000 people in the city hospital. The rebels demanded that the Russian Government initiate talks with Dudayev on the immediate withdrawal of troops from Chechnya. Following the failure of attempts by federal army units to free the hostages, telephone negotiations were conducted between the rebel leader, Shamil Basayev, and federal premier Chernomyrdin, by which time some 100 people had reportedly been killed. Subsequently, as a cease-fire took effect in Chechnya, the rebels (who were permitted to re-enter Chechnya) began gradually to release hostages. Peace talks between a delegation from the federal Government and the Chechen leadership commenced in Groznyi in late June, and a cease-fire agreement was formalized in July.

Chechen fighters began to surrender weapons to government authorities during August 1995, although skirmishes continued. In October, following an assassination attempt on the Commander of the federal Forces in Chechnya, Lt-Gen. Anatolii Romanov, the federal Government announced a temporary suspension of the July agreement. In response, the Chechen leadership announced its complete rejection of the accord. Meanwhile, the Russian Government sought to establish a viable pro-Moscow administration in Chechnya. In November the Chechen Supreme Council elected Zavgayev Head of State of the Chechen Republic. In that month fears of a terrorist campaign in Russia were heightened by the discovery, in a park in central Moscow, of radioactive materials, which had been buried, apparently as a threat, by Chechen militants allegedly associated with Basayev. In December elections took place in Chechnya, both to the Russian State Duma and to the Chechen presidency. According to official figures, some 74.8% of eligible voters participated in the poll, although both separatist Chechens, who declined to propose a candidate, and independent observers disputed this

figure. Zavgayev was elected President of the Republic of Chechnya, reportedly receiving some 93% of the votes cast. Dudayev rejected the elections as invalid, and rebel forces attempted to disrupt voting by increasing attacks on federal troops.

In January 1996 Chechen militants seized about 2,000 civilians in the town of Kizlyar, in neighbouring Dagestan, and held them hostage in a hospital. Following negotiations, most were released, and the rebels departed, accompanied by some 150 hostages, for Chechnya. Federal troops halted the rebels in the border village of Pervomaiskoye and demanded the release of the remaining hostages. After further negotiations failed, federal forces attacked and captured the village. Although the rebels' leader, Salman Raduyev, escaped to Chechnya with some of his forces and around 40 hostages, some 150 rebels, and a number of their captives, were reportedly killed in the assault.

In March 1996 Dudayev's forces launched a major offensive against Groznyi, reportedly causing federal troops considerable losses, but after three days of fighting the rebel forces withdrew. In late March Yeltsin announced a peace plan for Chechnya, although fighting continued, and at the end of April Dudayev was killed, reportedly after his use of a satellite telephone enabled federal forces to discover his location. He was succeeded as leader of the separatists by Zemlikhan Yandarbiyev, who subsequently developed an association with the Islamist Taliban regime in Afghanistan, which, in return, announced its recognition of Chechnya's independence. Sporadic fighting persisted, but, following negotiations in Moscow between Yandarbiyev and the federal Government, a new cease-fire agreement was reached in May. A formal military agreement, concluded in June, envisaged a withdrawal of the federal troops by the end of August and the disarmament of the separatist fighters. The accord contained no provisions for the future political status of the republic, and Chechen legislative elections, scheduled for mid-June, were to be postponed until the federal troop withdrawal had been completed. Voting in the Russian presidential election in June–July was, however, conducted in Chechnya: according to results released by the Zavgayev administration, Yeltsin received a higher proportion of the votes cast in Chechnya than in Moscow City. Widespread violations of electoral procedures were reported, and international monitors declared that the election in Chechnya had been neither free nor fair.

The cease-fire was interrupted in July 1996 when federal troops attacked Chechen forces in several rebel-controlled villages, after issuing an ultimatum for the release of Russian prisoners. Fighting continued, but towards the end of the month federal and Chechen negotiators met to discuss the exchange of prisoners. In August separatist forces, led by Basayev, launched a sustained offensive against Groznyi, routing many of the federal troops stationed in the city and trapping thousands of civilians. Yeltsin granted Gen. Lebed, the recently appointed Secretary of the Security Council, extensive powers to co-ordinate federal operations in the republic and to conduct a negotiated settlement. Following discussions involving Yandarbiyev and the Chechen military leader, Gen. Khalid ('Aslan') Maskhadov, a fresh cease-fire was brokered in mid-August. Following further negotiations, the withdrawal of troops commenced, and on 31 August Lebed and Maskhadov signed a conclusive peace agreement (known as the Khasavyurt Accords) in Dagestan, according to which any decision regarding Chechnya's future political status was to be deferred until December 2001. Meanwhile, arrangements were made for the withdrawal of all federal troops, and a joint commission was to be established to supervise the implementation of the Accords and to monitor relations between Moscow and Chechnya in the interim.

The withdrawal of federal troops and the exchange of prisoners of war began, and it was reported that the cease-fire was largely respected. In September 1996, following a congress of political parties and public movements in Groznyi, a Chechen Government was created, with Maskhadov as Prime Minister, and Yandarbiyev as Chairman of the cabinet. Nevertheless, despite the official cessation of hostilities in Chechnya, sporadic violence continued: by early 1997 it was estimated that the conflict had caused some 80,000 deaths, and resulted in the displacement of 415,000 civilians.

All federal troops were withdrawn before the regional presidential and legislative elections, held on 27 January 1997. Maskhadov was elected President, with some 59.3% of the total votes cast. Of the 12 remaining candidates, Basayev won 23.5% of the votes, and Yandarbiyev 10.1%. The rate of voter participation was reported to be 79.4%, and international observers reported no serious discrepancies in the electoral process. Maskhadov declined his seat in the Russian Federation Council, and affirmed his support for Chechen independence. Elections to the Chechen legislature were inconclusive and, after a second round of voting, only 45 of the 63 seats had been filled; further rounds of voting were held in May and June. On 12 May Yeltsin and Maskhadov signed a formal peace treaty, defining the principles of future relations between Chechnya and the Russian Federation, and renouncing the use of violence as a means of resolving differences. The treaty, however, did not address the issue of Chechnya's constitutional status and, moreover, was refused ratification by the State Duma.

Attacks and, in particular, hostage-taking, continued to be perpetrated by rebels opposed to the peace agreement (Russia claimed that some 800 hostages had been captured during 1997). Meanwhile, Chechnya's introduction of elements of *Shari'a* (Islamic religious) law in 1997, in particular the holding of public executions, was strongly opposed by the federal authorities and was, moreover, in breach of the Russian Constitution. In January 1998 Maskhadov dismissed his cabinet and entrusted Basayev (who had been indicted by the federal authorities on charges of terrorism), hitherto Chechen First Deputy Prime Minister, but now appointed acting Prime Minister, with the formation of a new government. In late March the republican parliament unilaterally renamed the capital Dzhokhar Gala, in honour of Dudayev, and announced that the territory was henceforth to be known as the 'Chechen Republic of Ichkeriya'. Increasing lawlessness and militancy was reported in the republic: an attack on an army base in Dagestan in December 1997 was widely believed to have been perpetrated by Chechen rebels opposed to the peace process, and in April 1998 at least four deaths were reported following an ambush of a federal military convoy. In May Chechen rebels kidnapped Yeltsin's special representative to Chechnya, Vladimir Vlasov; he was freed in November by interior ministry troops. In September two British aid workers who had been held captive for 14 months were released. Four employees of a British telecommunications company were kidnapped in Chechnya in October; their decapitated bodies were found several weeks later. Meanwhile, in July Maskhadov was the target of an assassination attempt, which occurred following his declaration of a state of emergency and curfew in the republic. As disorder increased, Maskhadov dismissed the entire Chechen administration in October, and declared a further state of emergency in December. Meanwhile, it became apparent that militant Islamist groups, including factions linked to the Saudi-born dissident, Osama bin Laden, and led in Chechnya by Omar ibn al-Khattab, a militant believed to be of Saudi or Jordanian origin, were increasingly implicated in the violence in Chechnya, as Maskhadov's authority apparently became more restricted.

In mid-June 1999 50 of the 60 check-points along the border of Chechnya were closed, following serious clashes in the region. None the less, Islamist miltants, led by Basayev and al-Khattab, invaded Dagestan from Chechnya in early August, with the apparent intention of promoting a *jihad* (holy war) across the Russian North Caucasus. Federal troops were dispatched to the area, and after two weeks of fighting and aerial bombardment the rebels withdrew. However, there were renewed incursions and fighting in September. Meanwhile, in mid-August Maskhadov declared a one-month state of emergency in Chechnya, following threats by the federal authorities to bomb alleged terrorist bases in the republic. In late August and September an unprecedented series of bombings occurred across Russia. Responsibility for explosions that destroyed entire apartment blocks on 9 and 13 September in Moscow, and in which more than 200 people were killed, was claimed by the previously unfamiliar Dagestan Liberation Army, but no claims of responsibility were issued for an attack against a Russian military base at Buynaksk, Dagestan, or for a bomb attack on a vehicle in Volgodonsk, in Rostov Oblast. None the less, the authorities officially attributed the attacks to Chechen militants, although allegations (subsequently reiterated by the exiled 'oligarch' Boris Berezovskii—see above) persisted that sources associated with the FSB had ordered the attacks, in order to justify a renewed military campaign in Chechnya and to increase the Government's popularity prior to the forthcoming legislative and presidential elections; notably, the discovery of an apparent attempt to initiate a further bombing in an apartment block in Ryazan, some 200 km south-east of Moscow, heightened con-

cerns of FSB involvement, although the authorities insisted that the incident was simply an exercise designed to ensure a heightened state of public vigilance. Public fear and outrage over the bombings gave impetus to a renewed large-scale deployment of federal forces in Chechnya, ordered by the recently appointed Chairman of the Government, Vladimir Putin, in late September.

Following air and ground offensives, federal troops had advanced to within 10 km of Groznyi by late October 1999, and both sides claimed to have inflicted heavy losses on the other. Meanwhile, repeated requests by Maskhadov for negotiations to end the conflict were rejected by the Russian Government, which announced that it would deal only with the Moscow-based State Council of the Chechen Republic, formed in early October by exiled members of the former pro-Government legislature. In mid-November federal forces claimed to have gained control of Chechnya's second city, Gudermes, although Groznyi remained under the control of rebel forces. In December the federal Government issued an ultimatum, urging citizens to leave Groznyi immediately, or face death; many republican and federal administrative bodies were relocated to Gudermes. In February 2000 federal forces obtained control of Groznyi and proceeded to destroy much of the city.

In May 2000 President Putin decreed that, henceforth, Chechnya would be governed federally. Mufti Akhmad Kadyrov was inaugurated as administrative leader (Governor) of the republic in June. Kadyrov, a former ally of Maskhadov, was directly responsible to Putin and to the presidential representative to the recently created Southern Federal Okrug, Col-Gen. Viktor Kazantsev. In September the elected chairman of the Chechen legislature, Ruslan Alikhadzhiyev, who had been imprisoned in Moscow for three months, died; Chechen rebels imputed the death to torture. In January 2001 Putin signed a decree transferring control of operations in Chechnya from the Ministry of Defence to the FSB, and announced the intention of withdrawing the majority of the 80,000-strong federal forces from the region, in order to leave a 15,000-strong infantry division and 7,000 interior ministry troops. The FSB was, meanwhile, to strengthen its presence in Chechnya, in order to combat insurgency. The local administration in Chechnya was restructured to allow it greater autonomy, and Stanislav Ilyasov, a former Governor of Stavropol Krai, was appointed as the Chechen premier.

Despite announcements from March 2000 that the initial, military phase of the 'anti-terrorist operation' in Chechnya had ended, the proposed withdrawal of federal troops from the republic was postponed repeatedly throughout 2001 as rebel forces continued to wage guerrilla warfare. Concern escalated in the first half of 2001 among international human rights organizations about the allegedly widespread use of torture and detention by federal troops, particularly in the course of so-called 'cleansing' operations, in which entire towns or areas were searched for rebels; in particular, the purported discovery of a mass grave in an abandoned village, which contained several severely mutilated corpses, reported in January, prompted outrage. The Council of Europe and the UN Commissioner for Human Rights also recorded numerous instances of human rights abuses in Chechnya in early 2001.

In early 2001 a number of violent incidents outside Chechnya were staged by rebels, with the intention of drawing attention to the ongoing conflict. In mid-March three armed Chechen rebels hijacked a passenger aeroplane en route from Istanbul, Turkey, to Moscow, causing it to be flown, instead, to Medina, Saudi Arabia. The rebels demanded that federal forces withdraw from Chechnya and reportedly demanded to be taken to Qandahar, Afghanistan. However, following the intervention of Saudi security forces, three hijackers were detained; three people, including one of the hijackers, were killed in the struggle. Later in the month 23 people were killed, and more than 140 were injured in three simultaneous bomb attacks in southern Russia, which were allegedly perpetrated by associates of al-Khattab.

In early May 2001 the continuing disorder in Chechnya was demonstrated by the announcement, by Minister of Defence Sergei Ivanov, that the withdrawal of troops from the province had been terminated; by this time only 5,000 federal troops had left Chechnya. Meanwhile, tensions increased between federal forces and the Governor of Chechnya. In July Kadyrov accused the federal army of engaging in 'criminal conduct' during the course of raids on three villages at the beginning of the month, stating that the troops had targeted civilians; although six soldiers were later arrested in connection with these allegations,

Kadyrov demanded that senior military commanders also face charges. In late August, writing in the parliamentary journal, *Parlamentskaya Gazeta*, Kadyrov called for an expedited end to the Government's campaign.

In early September 2001 a bomb was detonated in the offices of the regional Government, which had, by this time, relocated to Groznyi; both Kadyrov and Ilyasov escaped unharmed. There was an upsurge of rebel activity in Chechnya in mid-September, incorporating co-ordinated attacks in Gudermes and Argun, on the outskirts of Groznyi, in the middle of the month. However, at the end of September Putin announced his willingness to participate in negotiations, for the first time since the beginning of the renewed conflict in 1999. He urged the rebels to 'halt all contacts with international terrorists' and to establish contact with the federal authorities, citing a 72-hour period during which arms could be surrendered without charge; however, only a negligible quantity of weapons was surrendered during the amnesty. (The authorities persistently issued reports purporting that Chechen militants were associated with bin Laden's al-Qa'ida—Base—organization, which had organized devastating attacks in the USA earlier that month, although evidence to confirm these allegations appeared inconclusive.) In mid-September Kadyrov visited the leaders of a number of Arab countries, notably conveying a message from Putin to the Iraqi President, Saddam Hussain, who expressed support for the federal campaign in Chechnya. Also in mid-September, in response to growing concerns regarding abuses by federal troops in Chechnya, a list of 15 servicemen (identified by their initials and ranks) who had been convicted of crimes against civilians in the republic was published; further such lists were released later in 2001 and in early 2002.

In mid-October 2001 Kadyrov reformed the Chechen administration; although Ilyasov (who remained resident in Stavropol) was maintained as republican Prime Minister, a new, more senior position, the Chief of Staff of the Chechen Administration, was assigned to Lt-Gen. Yan Sergunin, hitherto responsible for the judicial system in Chechnya. In mid-November the trial of Raduyev, the only prominent Chechen rebel leader to have been captured by federal forces, began in Makhachkala, Dagestan, on 10 charges, including murder, terrorism and hostage-taking; in late December Raduyev was sentenced to life imprisonment, and three of his associates also received custodial sentences. (Raduyev died in prison in December 2002; the federal authorities denied allegations, by supporters of Maskhadov, that he had been beaten.) Meanwhile, on 18 November 2001 the first direct negotiations between the warring factions since the renewal of hostilities in 1999, held in Moscow between Kazantsev and Maskhadov's deputy, Akhmed Zakayev, reached no substantive agreement, and no further high-level meetings were planned, although contacts with federal representatives continued into early 2002. A new rebel offensive was launched in mid-December 2001, and a special operation by federal forces at the end of the month led to fierce fighting in Argun and surrounding areas in early January 2002.

In late December 2001 Maskhadov, whose five-year mandate as President of Chechnya was to expire in late January 2002, announced the extension of his presidency for an additional year. (None the less, Maskhadov, who was believed to be in hiding in the mountainous regions of southern Chechnya, remained unable to exercise any presidential prerogatives.) In early March Kadyrov criticized the conduct of renewed large-scale 'cleansing' operations that were under way near Groznyi. Meanwhile, the federal authorities rejected renewed demands by human rights organizations for international involvement in the conflict in Chechnya, and meetings between Zakayev and representatives of the US, British and French Governments earlier in 2002 were condemned by the Russian federal authorities. Later in March further progress towards a negotiated settlement of the conflict was reported. A newly established 'Chechen Consultative Council', comprising both Chechens supportive of, and opposed to, the independence of the republic, held its first meeting in the building of the Federal Assembly in Moscow; among its members was Ruslan Kutayev, who had served as a deputy premier under Maskhadov. However, the federal Government criticized informal negotiations held that month in Paris and Strasbourg, France, under the auspices of the Parliamentary Assembly of the Council of Europe, by Chechens opposed to the continuation of the conflict, owing to the participation of three members of Maskhadov's former Government. At the end of March the federal authorities announced new measures intended to ensure greater respect for human rights in the conduct of military actions in Chechnya. Human rights activists largely dismissed the efficacy of these measures, and it was suggested that an attack on Kadyrov's convoy by federal troops, in early April, was a deliberate attempt to discredit the republican administration in the light of the new regulations. Although Putin again announced that the military stage of the conflict in Chechnya had ended, rebel activity appeared to increase markedly during April. In late April it was reported, and subsequently confirmed by Zakayev, that al-Khattab had been killed by federal forces. On 9 May, during celebrations in Kaspiisk, Dagestan, to mark 'Victory Day', some 45 people were killed and more than 130 injured in an explosion, which the federal authorities attributed to Chechen rebels. In late July the UN announced, for the second time in one year, the suspension of its humanitarian operations in Chechnya, following the kidnapping of an aid worker in the republic. In mid-August federal forces experienced their single largest loss of life since the recommencement of operations in 1999, when a military helicopter was shot down by rebels in Groznyi, killing some 118 troops; at the end of the month a second federal helicopter was attacked, killing its two crew members, and two further helicopters had been shot down by early November. Meanwhile, an explosion outside a police station in Groznyi in mid-October resulted in the deaths of at least 24 people.

On 23–26 October 2002 over 40 heavily armed rebels, led by Movsar Barayev, the cousin of a Chechen rebel leader who had been killed by federal troops in 2001, held captive more than 800 people in a Moscow theatre, and demanded the withdrawal of federal troops from the republic. The rebels described themselves as members of a 'suicide battalion' and, notably, included several women, reported to be carrying explosive devices. The siege ended when élite federal forces stormed the theatre, having initially filled the building with an (initially unidentified) incapacitating gas. The rebels were killed, and it subsequently emerged that some 129 hostages had also died, in almost all cases owing to the toxic effects of the gas. Putin stated that the siege had been planned outside Russia, by international terrorist groups, citing evidence that the hostage-takers had communicated with their purported sponsors in Qatar, Saudi Arabia and the United Arab Emirates during the course of the siege. Maskhadov issued a statement condemning the rebels' use of terrorist methods, but, despite denials by the Chechen authorities of their involvement in the incident, Zakayev was arrested at the end of October, reportedly on the orders of the federal Government, while attending a World Chechen Congress in Copenhagen, Denmark. (In early November Basayev announced that groups linked to him had perpetrated the hostage-taking in Moscow, and stated that Maskhadov had not known of the incident.) In early December the Danish authorities refused to extradite Zakayev to Russia, citing a lack of credible evidence of his involvement in terrorist activities. Zakayev's presence in Denmark resulted in the relocation to Brussels, Belgium, of the EU-Russia summit that had been scheduled to take place in Copenhagen in November. Zakayev subsequently fled to the United Kingdom, where extradition proceedings commenced in late January 2003. Meanwhile, in the aftermath of the theatre siege the federal Minister of Defence, Sergei Ivanov, announced that the Government was to intensify its military offensive in Chechnya, and that the previously planned withdrawal of troops had been cancelled. Representative offices of the Maskhadov-led 'Chechen Republic of Ichkeriya' were closed in several countries, including Azerbaijan, Georgia and Turkey, in November, as the result of pressure from the Russian Government.

In mid-November 2002 Ilyasov was removed from his position as Prime Minister of Chechnya and, in what was widely perceived as a promotion, and which followed persistent reports of conflict between Ilyasov and Kadyrov, appointed as Minister without Portfolio in the federal Government, responsible for the Social and Economic Development of Chechnya; Ilyasov was succeeded as the premier of Chechnya by Capt (retd) Mikhail Babich, who had previously held senior positions in the regional administrations of Ivanovo and Moscow Oblasts. In late November Ilyasov announced that a referendum on a new draft Chechen constitution, which would, *inter alia*, determine the status of the republic within the Russian Federation, was to be held in March 2003; this measure was confirmed by Putin, in his annual speech to mark Constitution Day on 12 December 2002. Later that month Putin dismissed the Commander of the federal troops in Chechnya, Col-Gen. Gennadii Troshev, replacing him with Col-Gen. Vladimir Boldyrev. At the end of December at least 83 people died, and more than 150 others were injured, when suicide bombers detonated bombs in two vehicles stationed outside the headquarters of the republican Government in Groznyi; no senior officials were killed. In early January 2003 Babich was appointed to head a committee that was to organize the planned referendum on the future administration of Chechnya. However, on 23 January Babich was dismissed as premier, reportedly following a disagreement with Kadyrov regarding the appointment of a republican finance minister. On 10 February Anatolii Popov was appointed as the new Prime Minister of Chechnya; Popov had been appointed as deputy chairman of the state commission for the reconstruction of Chechnya in August 2002, having served as General Director of the state company responsible for reconstruction since mid-2001.

The referendum on the draft constitution for Chechnya, describing the republic as an integral part of the Russian Federation and providing for strengthened powers for the republican President (Governor), proceeded, as scheduled, on 23 March 2003, despite concerns that the instability of the republic would prevent the poll from being free and fair. The draft constitution also provided for the holding of fresh elections to the republican presidency and legislature. According to the official results, some 88.4% of the electorate participated in the plebiscite, of whom 96.0% supported the draft constitution. Two further questions, on the method of electing the President and the Parliament of the Republic of Chechnya, were supported by 95.4% and 96.1% of participants, respectively. However, independent observers challenged the results, reporting that the rate of participation by the electorate had been much lower than officially reported. In early May at least 59 people were killed when suicide bombers attacked government offices in Znamenskoye, in the north of Chechnya. Two days later another suicide bombing at a religious festival attended by Kadyrov in Ilishkan Yurt, near Gudermes, resulted in at least 14 deaths, although Kadyrov escaped unhurt; Basayev claimed responsibility for the organization of both attacks. None the less, in mid-May Putin presented draft legislation to parliament, providing for an amnesty for rebels in the republic who surrendered their weapons; the proposed amnesty was also to apply to federal soldiers accused of abuses committed in Chechnya.

Following the dissolution of the USSR in December 1991, Russia's most immediate foreign policy concerns were with the other former Soviet republics, generally referred to in Russia as the 'near abroad'. Relations with Ukraine were, initially, dominated by a dispute over the division of the former Soviet Black Sea Fleet, based mainly in Sevastopol, Crimea (Ukraine). Russia and Ukraine signed an agreement on the division of the Fleet in June 1995, but Russia subsequently refused to implement the accord, owing to continued disagreement concerning the status of Sevastopol. In May 1997 an agreement was concluded with Ukraine, whereby Russia was to lease part of the city's naval base for a period of 20 years, and was to provide financial compensation for ships and equipment received from Ukraine. A Treaty on Friendship, Co-operation and Partnership was signed by the two countries in that month. In 1999 Ukraine's inability to pay for Russian energy supplies, and accusations that Ukraine had diverted gas from Russia's export pipelines, temporarily caused difficulties between the two countries. In March 2000, despite Ukraine having 'frozen' the accounts of the Black Sea Fleet and having detained officials of the company, as part of an investigation into alleged fiscal malpractice, the two countries signed seven agreements relating to payment for the operation and services of jointly used facilities. An agreement was reached in December permitting the payment of Ukraine's energy debts to Russia over a period of 10 years. In February 2001 Putin visited Ukraine to mark the signature of a number of accords, including an agreement to reconnect the Russian and Ukrainian power grids. In May 2001 former premier Viktor Chernomyrdin was appointed as ambassador to Ukraine, in what was interpreted as an indication of strengthening ties between the two countries.

In April 1996 Russia and Belarus signed an agreement creating a 'Community of Russia and Belarus', according to which the two countries would pursue economic integration and close co-ordination of foreign and defence policies. In May 1997 a 'Charter of the Union of Belarus and Russia' was concluded, which, while promoting greater co-operation between the two countries, moved away from advocating full union, although in June the first official session of the Union's joint Parliamentary Assembly was convened. During 1998 the Union was strength-

ened by the decision to grant joint citizenship to residents, and the establishment of a joint legislative and representative body to deal with union issues. The bicameral assembly was to comprise an upper chamber, the Council of the Union, to which deputies would be delegated by the Russian Federal Assembly and the Belarusian National Assembly, and a lower chamber, the Council of Representatives, elected on the basis of universal suffrage, with 25 deputies from Belarus and 75 from Russia. A treaty on unification, which came into force on 26 January 2000, when the President of Belarus, Alyaksandr Lukashenka, was appointed Chairman of the High State Council of the Union, did not satisfy the Belarusian President's wishes for the formation of a single state. Although a union budget was passed at a session of the Parliamentary Assembly (established under the 1996 Treaty, and comprising 36 members from the legislature of each country) in May, President Putin remained more reticent than Lukashenka, in particular with regard to the formation of joint armed forces. In November an agreement on the introduction of a single currency was signed. The Russian rouble was to be used initially, from 2005, with a new currency to be introduced in 2008. Although agreement was reached, in March 2002, on the harmonization of the two countries' customs and tax laws, and on the removal of trade barriers, Putin was increasingly dismissive of Lukashenka's proposals for a closer union of the two states. In August Putin presented Lukashenka with a new unification plan, which effectively provided for the absorption of Belarus' seven Oblasts (regions) into the Russian Federation and, following referendums on unification in May 2003, for parliamentary and presidential elections to the new state to be held in late 2003 and early 2004, respectively, at the same time as the elections to the Russian State Duma and presidency; the plan also provided for the introduction of the Russian rouble as the currency of Belarus from January 2004. The proposals were, however, conclusively rejected by Lukashenka, who stated that the introduction of such measures would undermine Belarusian sovereignty.

Concern at the treatment and status of ethnic Russians in the three Baltic states remained a particular source of tension, and the demarcation of mutual frontiers also created difficulties. In the early 2000s Russia expressed particular concern for its citizens in the Russian exclave of Kaliningrad, which is separated from the remainder of the Russian Federation by Belarus and Lithuania. Russian premier Kasyanov attempted to ensure that residents of the exclave would be exempted from visa requirements that were to be imposed by Lithuania and Poland prior to the two countries' anticipated accession to the EU in 2004. In November 2002, at an EU-Russia summit meeting, held in Brussels, Russia finally agreed to an EU proposal for simplified visa arrangements. According to the compromise accord, multiple-transit travel documentation would be made available to residents of the exclave travelling by motor vehicle. The EU also agreed to undertake a feasibility study on the possibility of allowing high-speed, sealed trains to operate between the exclave and the remainder of the Federation, thus negating the need for transit documents.

Following the dissolution of the USSR, the Russian Federation maintained significant political and military influence in many former Soviet republics, especially in those areas involved in civil or ethnic conflicts. Russian troops were deployed in Tajikistan to support the Tajik Government against rebel forces during the civil war of 1992–97, and remained thereafter to ensure the security of the Tajik–Afghan border (see chapter on Tajikistan).

Allegations persisted throughout the 1990s and early 2000s that the Russian Government provided military support for separatist factions in Moldova and Georgia. In 1999 it was announced that all Russian troops in the separatist Transnistria region of Moldova were to be withdrawn by the end of 2002, although the proposed withdrawal was subsequently postponed until December 2003. Meanwhile, in December 1998 Russia and Georgia signed an agreement that provided for the incremented transfer of the control of their mutual frontiers, from Russian to Georgian guards. (Control of the frontier was, however, complicated by the existence of separatist and rebel-controlled regions on both sides of the border—Chechnya within Russia— see p. 3474, and Abkhazia and South Ossetia within Georgia—see chapter on Georgia.) The lifting of restrictions, in September 1999, on the border between Russia and Abkhazia heightened tensions with Georgia, which subsequently increased further as the result of allegations, denied by Georgia, that the state was harbouring Chechen rebels and selling arms to the rebel elements within Chechnya. Although Georgia refused Russian federal forces permission to use its territory to launch attacks against the rebels, occasional Russian incursions into Georgian airspace were reported. Meanwhile, it was agreed in November 1999 that two of the four Russian bases on Georgian territory would be withdrawn by mid-2001. Russian troops left the two bases in Georgia by November 2001; the Russian authorities stated that the two remaining bases would be vacated by 2015, instead of the deadline of 2005 requested by Georgia. In October 2001, as the conflict in Abkhazia intensified, Chechen rebels made incursions into the Kodori Gorge, on the Abkhazia–Georgia border, and into the Pankisi Gorge, south of Chechnya. Following the aerial bombardment of villages in the Kodori Gorge by unmarked aircraft at the end of the month, Russia and Georgia each accused the other of having commanded the bombings. In September 2002 the Russian authorities accused Georgia of permitting Chechen rebels to operate from bases within its territory, and declared that Russia reserved the right to instigate 'pre-emptive' military action, in self-defence, should the situation persist. However, in early October tensions abated somewhat, when Russia and Georgia agreed to commence joint patrols of their common border.

After December 1991 the Russian Federation was recognized as the successor to the USSR. It was granted the USSR's permanent seat on the UN Security Council and, additionally, was to be responsible for the receipt and destruction of all nuclear weapons of the former USSR located in other newly independent republics (Belarus, Kazakhstan and Ukraine), a process that was successfully completed by the mid-1990s. In January 1993 Russia and the USA signed the second Strategic Arms' Reduction Treaty (START II), which envisaged a reduction in the strategic nuclear weapons of both powers. The Russian legislature ratified START II in April 2000. Despite initial impressions of a deterioration in relations between the USA and Russia in the months following the assumption of office by US President George W. Bush, in January 2001, the expulsion of 51 Russian diplomats from the USA, in March, was not reciprocated fully by Russia; initial reports that the same number of US diplomats would be asked to leave Russia were subsequently denied, and only four representatives were obliged to leave immediately. Indeed, following the first meeting of the two Presidents, in Ljubljana, Slovenia, in June, relations appeared to improve markedly. Putin assumed a notably measured approach towards the proposed abrogation by the USA of the Anti-Ballistic Missiles (ABM) treaty (signed with the USSR in 1972), which formed a principal part of the Bush administration's foreign defence policy.

Russia offered assistance and gave vocal support to the USA in its attempts to form a global coalition against terrorism, after the suicide air attacks of 11 September 2001, attributed to militant Islamists of al-Qa'ida, which destroyed the World Trade Center, New York, and damaged the Pentagon, near Washington, DC, killing some 3,000 (see chapter on the USA). Although Russia refused to commit troops to participate in the aerial bombardment against targets of the Taliban regime in Afghanistan, which commenced on 7 October, and the subsequent ground offensive, it provided military intelligence, and allowed the coalition access to its airspace. Russia also increased logistical and military support to the anti-Taliban forces of the United Islamic Front for the Salvation of Afghanistan. Putin sought to present Russia's campaign in Chechnya as targeted against associates of al-Qa'ida and also gave tacit approval to the deployment of US and allied troops at former Soviet bases in Central Asia during the US-led campaign, and to the deployment, from April 2002, of US military instructors in Georgia, despite widespread opposition expressed, in particular, by members of the Russian military.

In mid-November 2001, at a meeting in Crawford, Texas, Bush and Putin announced that significant reductions would be made to their countries' nuclear arsenals over the following decade; Putin did not specify how many weapons would be destroyed, and emphasized his desire to formalize the agreement by means of a treaty, together with clear verification procedures, in contrast to the more informal measures envisaged by Bush. In mid-December, following the USA's announcement that it was to withdraw unilaterally from the ABM treaty, with effect from June 2002, Putin reiterated earlier claims that, while he did not support the abrogation of the treaty, and would have been prepared to engage in attempts to renegotiate it, its abandonment did not pose a security threat to Russia; he further emphasized that Russia would continue to seek to develop

increasingly co-operative relations with the USA. In mid-May 2002 Russia and the USA announced that agreement had been reached on the reduction of their nuclear arsenals by approximately two-thirds, and a nuclear accord and a declaration on strategic partnership were duly signed by Presidents Putin and Bush on 24 May. The USA withdrew from the ABM treaty on 13 June, and the following day Russia withdrew from START II, which had been superseded by the treaty signed with the USA in the previous month.

The Russian Government consistently condemned intermittent US missile attacks on Iraq during the 1990s and early 2000s; additionally, in 1996, in contravention of a UN embargo, Russia concluded an agreement with Iraq on the development of petroleum fields in that country. In late 1997, following Iraq's refusal to permit weapons inspectors of the UN Special Commission (UNSCOM) access to contentious sites, the Russian Government intervened in an attempt to avert a renewal of hostilities, and the conclusion of an agreement between the UN and Iraq in late February 1998 was regarded by Russia as a significant diplomatic success. In response to US and British air attacks on Iraq in mid-December, Russia temporarily recalled its ambassadors from the USA and the United Kingdom. Russia resumed scheduled flights to Iraq in late 2000, in contravention of UN sanctions. In mid-2001 Russia, which supported Iraq in its demands that the sanctions regime in force since 1990 should be revoked, effectively obstructed a British-drafted proposal before the Security Council for the introduction of a new, US-advocated, programme of 'smart' sanctions. As the US Administration of George W. Bush, from the second half of 2002, utilized increasingly bellicose rhetoric against Iraq, Russia urged the USA to avoid the use of unilateral force, and encouraged Iraq's compliance with UN demands regarding weapons inspections, so as to facilitate the lifting of sanctions. Although Russia voted to support UN Security Council Resolution 1441, approved in November 2002, which provided for the expedited return of weapons inspectors to Iraq under the auspices of the UN Monitoring, Verification and Inspection Commission (UNMOVIC), it was a leading opponent, with France and Germany, of attempts, led by the USA and the United Kingdom in February–March 2003, to approve a further Security Council resolution to approve military action in Iraq. None the less, President Putin, in particular, emphasized the importance of maintaining co-operative relations with the USA.

In June 1994 Russia joined NATO's 'Partnership for Peace' (see p. 273) programme of military co-operation with former Eastern bloc states. In 1996 NATO's proposals for a strategic security partnership with Russia, to be formalized in a politically- but not legally-binding charter (which would have required parliamentary ratification), were initially opposed by Russia, which warned of a potential destabilization of Russia's domestic situation and a deterioration in relations with the West should NATO extend its military infrastructure to Russia's western border. NATO confirmed, however, that it did not intend to transfer nuclear warheads to the former Eastern bloc countries, but that an upgrading of existing military systems and a deployment of conventional forces would be undertaken. The 'Founding Act on Mutual Relations, Co-operation and Security between NATO and the Russian Federation' was signed in May 1997. The Act provided for enhanced Russian participation in all NATO decision-making activities, equal status in peace-keeping operations and representation at the Alliance headquarters at ambassadorial level. A NATO-Russian Permanent Joint Council was established, which met for the first time in July; the Council provided each side the opportunity for consultation and participation in the other's security decisions, but without a right of veto.

Russia's relations with NATO became increasingly strained in 1999, in particular after the failure of Russian attempts to achieve a diplomatic solution to the situation in the predominantly ethnic Albanian province of Kosovo and Metohija (Kosovo), in the republic of Serbia, Yugoslavia (now Serbia and Montenegro) precipitated the aerial bombardment of Yugoslav targets to be initiated by NATO forces later in March (see chapter on Serbia and Montenegro). Russia condemned the air offensive, and suspended its relations with the Alliance. Following the capitulation of federal Yugoslav forces in mid-June, and their withdrawal from Kosovo, Russian troops were the first to enter the province, before NATO forces. Contacts were resumed between Russia and NATO in February 2000, during a visit to Moscow by the NATO Secretary-General, Lord Robertson of Port Ellen, and parliamentary contacts resumed in

March 2001. In July Putin called for a pan-European security pact to be established in place of NATO, to incorporate Russia, and emphasized that he regarded NATO as neither an 'enemy', nor a 'tragedy', nor necessary. In the latter part of 2001, particularly after Russia expressed support for the military action undertaken by the USA and its NATO allies in Afghanistan (see p. 3478), proposals were advanced for the establishment of a closer relationship between Russia and NATO than that permitted by the Permanent Joint Council. On 28 May 2002 Putin and the heads of state and of government of the 19 NATO member states, meeting in Italy, signed the Rome Declaration, inaugurating a new NATO-Russia Council to replace the Permanent Joint Council. Although Russia was not to be granted the right of veto over any decisions of the Alliance, the new Council would enable Russia to enter into negotiations with the Organization's members on a range of issues, including terrorism, non-proliferation, defence and peace-keeping.

In January 1996 Russia was admitted as a member of the Council of Europe (see p. 181). As a condition of membership, Russia was to abolish the death penalty by the end of February 1999. By mid-2003, however, the Duma had yet to approve its abolition, although capital punishment had been subject to a moratorium since Russia's admission to the organization. Russia's voting rights were suspended in April 2000, as a result of allegations of human rights abuses committed during Russia's renewed military campaign in Chechnya. Russia's voting rights were suspended in April, but were restored in January 2001. In late January 2003 the chief rapporteur for Chechnya of the Parliamentary Assembly of the Council of Europe (PACE), Lord Judd of Portsea, resigned in protest at preparations for a proposed referendum in the republic (see p. 3477), stating that the necessary conditions for the holding of such a plebiscite had not been achieved. In early April PACE voted, by a large majority, in favour of the establishment of an international tribunal to try those suspected of war crimes in the republic.

Russia's relations with Iran in the late 1990s and early 2000s were a cause of concern for the USA. In mid-1997 Iran and Russia held discussions on nuclear co-operation, primarily focusing on the development of a nuclear power plant in Bushehr, Iran. In December 2000 Igor Sergeyev, the Russian Minister of Defence, paid the first official visit to Iran by a Russian official since 1979, with a view to increasing military and technical co-operation. In March 2001, during a visit to Moscow by the Iranian President, Muhammad Khatami, Russia agreed to resume the sale of conventional weapons to Iran and to assist with the construction of the Bushehr power plant; an agreement for arms sales worth some US $300m., the first such agreement between the two countries since 1995, was signed in October. Moreover, in December 2002 it was announced that Russia was to increase its nuclear co-operation with Iran, although the Russian Minister of Foreign Affairs, Igor Ivanov, reiterated that this co-operation was of a civilian nature.

Relations with Japan were complicated by a continuing dispute over the status of the Kurile Islands (in Sakhalin Oblast, and known in Japan as the Northern Territories), which became part of the USSR at the end of the Second World War; Japan maintained its long-standing demand that four of the islands be returned to Japanese sovereignty. In November 1997 an agreement was concluded between Yeltsin and the Japanese Prime Minister, Ryutaro Hashimoto, which aimed, by 2000, to resolve the territorial dispute and conclude a formal peace treaty to end the Second World War. Despite further high-level negotiations, little progress was made. Although Putin repudiated Japan's claim to the islands during his first official visit to the Japanese capital, Tokyo, in September 2000, Russia subsequently offered to abide by a 1956 declaration that it would hand over two of the islands following the signature of a peace treaty; Japan initially rejected this partial solution, and by mid-2003 the signature of any peace treaty remained in abeyance.

Relations with the People's Republic of China improved significantly during the 1990s, and in April 1996 several bilateral agreements were concluded during a visit by Yeltsin to China. Following a visit to Russia by the Chinese President, Jiang Zemin, in April 1997, a joint declaration that envisaged a heightened strategic partnership between the two countries was issued. In 1999 several agreements on bilateral economic and trade co-operation, and a final accord on the demarcation of a common border between the two countries, were signed. Meanwhile, negotiations in the mid-1990s that initially focused on defining the mutual borders of China, Kazakhstan, Kyrgyzstan, Russia and Tajikistan appeared to be instrumental in bringing about closer co-operation between these countries, which in 1996 formed the so-called Shanghai Five group. The group subsequently broadened its areas of activity to include trade, cultural, military and security co-operation; in June 2001 Uzbekistan joined the grouping, which was renamed the Shanghai Co-operation Organization (see p. 351). Kasyanov visited the Chinese capital, Beijing, in August 2002, to discuss strategic issues, and Putin visited China in December, when he met President Jiang and his appointed successor, Hu Jintao. The two countries issued a joint declaration on a number of global strategic issues, particularly urging a peaceful resolution to the USA's diplomatic crisis with Iraq, and for the USA and the Democratic People's Republic of Korea (the DPRK—North Korea) to normalize relations, and for the latter to abandon its nuclear weapons programme.

In February 2000 the Minister of Foreign Affairs, Igor Ivanov, visited the DPRK, and signed a Treaty of Friendship, Neighbourliness and Co-operation. In July Vladimir Putin became the first Russian or Soviet leader to visit North Korea. During Putin's visit the DPRK leader, Kim Jong-Il, declared himself willing to halt missile development, in exchange for access to space-rocket technology funded by other countries, and Putin expressed a desire to assist reconciliation on the Korean Peninsula. In July 2001 Kim Jong-Il, visiting Moscow, signed a joint declaration with Putin, stating that the missile programme of the DPRK represented no threat to any country that respected North Korean sovereignty. In August 2002 Kim travelled to Vladivostok, in the Russian Far East, where he met Putin, to discuss a proposed inter-Korean railway, which would also connect with Russia. In January 2003, as part of measures intended to defuse the crisis in relations between the USA and North Korea that resulted from the admission, in October 2002, that the DPRK was pursuing a nuclear programme, the Russian Deputy Minister of Foreign Affairs, Aleksandr Losyukov, visited the DPRK's capital, Pyongyang, and met Kim, with the aim of promoting the acceptance of a three-stage process that would, *inter alia*, result in a nuclear-free Korean peninsula, together with guarantees for the security of the North Korean regime; however, the DPRK continued to insist that direct negotiations with the USA take place.

Government

Under the Constitution of December 1993, the Russian Federation is a democratic, federative, multi-ethnic republic, in which state power is divided between the legislature, executive and judiciary, which are independent of one another. The President of the Russian Federation is Head of State and Commander-in-Chief of the Armed Forces, but also holds broad executive powers. The President, who is elected for a term of four years, renewable once, by universal direct suffrage, appoints the Chairman (Prime Minister) of the Government. Supreme legislative power is vested in the bicameral Federal Assembly. The Assembly's upper chamber is the 178-member Federation Council, which comprises two representatives from each of the country's federal territorial units (appointed by the legislature and the executive in each region); its lower chamber is the 450-member State Duma, which is elected by direct universal suffrage for a period of four years.

The Russian Federation comprises 21 nominally autonomous republics, one autonomous oblast (region), 49 administrative oblasts and six krais (provinces). There are also 10 autonomous okrugs (districts), of which nine are under the jurisdiction of the oblast or krai within which they are situated. The republics and the autonomous oblast and okrugs are nominally representative of ethnic groups, and the administrative oblasts and krais of geographic regions. The cities of Moscow and St Petersburg have special administrative status. In May 2000 these 89 administrative entities ('federal subjects') were grouped into seven federal okrugs, each of which is headed by a presidential appointee, by presidential decree. It was announced in 2000 that, henceforth, the separatist Republic of Chechnya was to be governed federally.

Defence

In May 1992 the Russian Federation established its own armed forces, on the basis of former Soviet forces on the territory of the Russian Federation, and former Soviet forces outside its territory not subordinate to other former republics of the USSR. In August 2002 the total Russian armed forces numbered an estimated 988,100 (including an estimated 330,000 conscripts). These comprised 200,000 staff of the Ministry of Defence, an estimated 149,000 permanent members of the Strategic Deterrent Forces, an estimated 321,000 in the army (including some 190,000 conscripts), 171,500 in the navy (16,000 conscripts), and an estimated 184,600 in the air force, following its merger with the air defence troops. There were a further estimated 409,100 paramilitary troops. Conscription is compulsory for males over the age of 18 years, and lasts for 18–24 months. However, the rate of conscription evasion is reported to be extremely high. In November 2000 it was announced that the armed forces were to be reduced in number by some 600,000 by 2005. In late 2001 proposals to phase out conscription in 2004–10 were announced, subject to parliamentary approval. Budgetary expenditure on defence for 2002 was 262,900m. roubles.

Economic Affairs

In 2001, according to estimates by the World Bank, Russia's gross national income (GNI), measured at average 1999–2001 prices, was US $253,413m., equivalent to $1,750 per head (or $8,660 per head on an international purchasing-power parity basis). Between 1990 and 2001, it was estimated, the population declined by an annual average of 0.2%, while gross domestic product (GDP) per head, decreased, in real terms, at an average annual rate of 3.1%. According to the World Bank, overall GDP decreased, in real terms, at an average annual rate of 3.3% in 1990–2001. However, real GDP increased by 9.0% in 2000 and by 5.0% in 2001.

Agriculture and forestry (excluding fishing) contributed an estimated 5.8% of GDP in 2002. In 2000 13.9% of the employed labour force were engaged in the agricultural sector. The principal agricultural products are grain, potatoes and livestock. In 1990 the Russian Government began a programme to encourage the development of private farming, to replace the state and collective farms. Legislation to permit the sale and purchase of agricultural land from 2003 was approved by the State Duma in June 2002. According to World Bank estimates, real agricultural GDP declined at an average annual rate of 3.3% in 1992–2001; however, the GDP of the sector increased by 5.0% in 2000 and by 10.8% in 2001.

Industry (including mining, manufacturing, construction, power and fishing) contributed an estimated 34.6% of GDP in 2002. In 2000 the industrial sector (excluding fishing) accounted for 29.7% of employment. According to estimates by the World Bank, industrial GDP declined, in real terms, by an annual average of 5.5% in 1990–2001. Industrial GDP increased by 11.8% in 2000 and by 6.0% in 2001.

Mining and quarrying employed 1.7% of the total labour force in 2000. Russia has considerable reserves of energy-bearing minerals, including one-third of the world's natural gas reserves and substantial deposits of petroleum, coal and peat. It also has large supplies of palladium, platinum and rhodium. Other minerals exploited include bauxite, cobalt, copper, diamonds, gold, iron ore, mica, nickel and tin.

In 2000 the manufacturing sector provided 18.5% of employment. In 1999 the principal branches of manufacturing, measured by gross value of output, were food products (accounting for 18.9% of the total), transport equipment (12.0%), iron and steel (11.4%), machinery (9.2%), and chemicals and chemical products (9.6%). Production in the sector decreased, in real terms, by 14.5% in 1996, but increased by 1.6% in 1997.

Electric energy is derived from petroleum-, gas- and coal-fired power stations, nuclear power stations and hydroelectric installations. In 1999 Russia's 29 nuclear reactors supplied some 14.4% of total electricity generation, while coal accounted for some 19.1% of Russia's generating capacity, hydroelectric power accounted for 19.0% of electricity production, and 42.4% of the country's generating capacity originated from natural gas. Russia is a major exporter of natural gas and crude petroleum, and Russia's largest company, Gazprom, is also the world's largest producer of natural gas. Countries of the CIS remain highly dependent on Russia for imports of these fuels. However, owing to high levels of non-payment from certain countries for these deliveries, from the late 1990s Russia sought, with some success, to increase its exports of mineral fuels to other countries, particularly to the countries of central and western Europe. The construction of the 'Blue Stream' pipeline, which was to carry natural gas from Novorossiisk, Krasnodar Krai, in southern Russia, to Ankara, Turkey, was completed in October 2002, and was expected to facilitate further growth in Russia's energy exports. Discussions with the People's Republic of China concerning the proposed construction of a pipeline to carry petroleum from Siberia to that country commenced in mid-2001. Imports of fuel comprised just 3.3% of the value of Russia's total merchandise imports in 2000.

The services sector contributed an estimated 59.7% of GDP in 2002, and provided 56.4% of employment in 2000. According to estimates by the World Bank, the GDP of the services sector declined, in real terms, at an annual average rate of 0.2% in 1992–2001. However, the GDP of the sector increased by 6.7% in 2000, and by 4.3% in 2001.

In 2001 Russia recorded a visible trade surplus of US $47,853m., and there was a surplus of $34,854m. on the current account of the balance of payments. In 2000 the most significant source of imports was Germany (accounting for 8.6% of the total), followed by Belarus (8.3%), Ukraine (8.0%) and the USA (5.9%). The largest market for Russian exports in 2000 was Germany (purchasing 9.0% of the total), followed by Italy (7.0%). Other leading customers were the Belarus (5.4%) and the People's Republic of China (5.1%). The principal exports in 2000 were mineral fuels and lubricants (comprising 51.3% of Russia's total exports), followed by basic manufactures (17.8%), and machinery and transport equipment (5.9%). The principal imports in 2000 were machinery and transport equipment (accounting for 16.9% of total imports), followed by food and live animals (11.6%), basic manufactures (10.5%), and chemicals and related products (8.2%).

In 2001 Russia recorded a surplus on the federal budget of 272,075.4m. roubles. At the end of 2000 the country's total external debt was US $160,300m., of which $111,419m. was long-term public debt. In that year the cost of debt-servicing was equivalent to 10.1% of the value of exports of goods and services. In 1991–2001 the average annual rate of inflation was 154.4%. Following the collapse of the rouble in 1998, the rate of inflation was 85.6% in 1999, but it declined to 20.8% in 2000 and to 21.5% in 2001. In December 2000 about 1.0m. people were registered as unemployed, although, according to the methodology of the International Labour Organization, the actual number of unemployed was some 5.1m. in October 2002, compared with 7.1m. in 2000

Russia became a member of the World Bank and the IMF in 1992. Russia is also a member (as a 'Country of Operations') of the European Bank for Reconstruction and Development (EBRD, see p. 193). In June 1994 Russia signed an agreement of partnership and co-operation with the European Union (EU, see p. 199). In 1996 Russia expressed an interest in joining the Organisation for Economic Co-operation and Development (OECD, see p. 277). It is also pursuing membership of the World Trade Organization (WTO, see p. 323). Russia joined the Asia-Pacific Economic Co-operation forum (APEC, see p. 139) in November 1998.

Following the dissolution of the USSR, a programme of economic reforms was initiated to effect the transition from a centrally planned economy to a market-orientated system. Following a severe financial crisis, in August 1998 Russia defaulted on its rouble-denominated bonds, and announced unilateral terms for debt conversion. The trade surplus increased appreciably in 1999, although the recovery was largely attributable to the high international prices for petroleum, natural gas and metals, Russia's principal exports, rather than the result of structural reforms. Although severe fuel shortages in the Russian Far East were reported in late 2000, precipitating the dismissal of the Minister of Energy, confidence in the Russian economy increased markedly. However, in November an IMF mission failed to agree terms for further lending, after the Government proved unwilling to accept its recommendations for banking reform, although the World Bank approved loans worth US $537m. in July 2001, following the introduction of a number of legal reforms. In early 2001 the Government introduced several measures that were intended to regularize and simplify the country's fiscal code, including the introduction of a uniform rate of income tax, of 13%, in order to discourage the high levels of tax evasion that had occurred throughout the 1990s; the introduction of a new labour code later that year was also regarded as a positive measure. None the less, the transfer to private ownership of the petroleum company, Slavneft (Slavonic Oil Co), in late 2002, which raised some $1,700m., raised concerns regarding the degree of transparency in the privatization process: the proceeds of the sale were substantially below the Audit Chamber of the State Duma's estimate of the company's value, $3,000m., and six bidders were disqualified or forced to withdraw from the auction in conditions that remained largely opaque. The privatization programme for 2003 envisaged the transfer to private ownership of the State's holding in more than 600 companies, including over 100 companies that formed part of the military-industrial complex, 25 lending institutions, 23 machine-building companies, 44 companies of the wood industry and 22 companies related to the inland waterway network. In the short term economic growth, which remained positive, appeared largely dependent on continued high international petroleum and natural gas prices, and further reforms, in the national resources and energy sectors, as well as in public administration and the social sector, seemed necessary to permit sustained expansion.

Education

Education is compulsory for nine years, to be undertaken between the ages of six and 15 years. State education is generally provided free of charge, although in 1992 some higher education establishments began charging tuition fees. Students of selected courses in higher education receive a small stipend from the state. Primary education usually begins at seven years of age and lasts for three years. Secondary education, beginning at 10 years of age, lasts for seven years, comprising a first cycle of five years and a second of two years. In 1997 the total enrolment at primary schools was equivalent to 99.9% of the school-age population. Secondary enrolment in that year was equivalent to 87.6% of children in the appropriate age-group.

The level of education in the Russian Federation is relatively high, and 4.7m. students were enrolled at institutes of higher education in 2000/01. Although Russian is the principal language used in educational establishments, a number of local languages are also in use. Budgetary expenditure on education (excluding scientific research and technology) in 2001 was an estimated 54,498,800m. roubles (representing 4.1% of total federal government expenditure).

All educational institutions were state-owned under Soviet rule, but a wide range of independent schools and colleges commenced operations in the early 1990s. In 2000/01 there were some 635 independent schools and 358 independent higher education institutions. In the early 1990s there were extensive changes to the curriculum in all branches of the education system, including an end to the study of politically-inspired subjects, a new approach to the study of Soviet and Russian history, and the introduction of study of previously prohibited literary works.

Public Holidays

2003: 1–2 January (New Year), 7 January (Orthodox Christmas), 23 February (Defenders of the Fatherland Day), 8 March (International Women's Day), 28 April (Orthodox Easter Monday), 1–2 May (Spring Holiday and Labour Day), 9 May (Victory Day), 12–13 June (Day of Sovereignty of the Russian Federation), 7 November (Day of Concord and Reconciliation), 12 December (Constitution Day), 31 December (New Year's Eve).

2004: 1–2 January (New Year), 7 January (Orthodox Christmas), 23 February (Defenders of the Fatherland Day), 8 March (International Women's Day), 12 April (Orthodox Easter Monday), 1–2 May (Spring Holiday and Labour Day), 9 May (Victory Day), 12 June (Day of Sovereignty of the Russian Federation), 7 November (Day of Concord and Reconciliation), 12 December (Constitution Day), 31 December (New Year's Eve).

Weights and Measures

The metric system is in force.

Statistical Survey

Sources (unless otherwise indicated): State Committee of Statistics of the USSR; State Committee of Statistics of the Russian Federation, 103450 Moscow, ul. Myasnitskaya 39; tel. (095) 207-49-41; fax (095) 207-42-80; internet www.gks.ru.

Area and Population

AREA, POPULATION AND DENSITY

Area (sq km)	17,075,400*
Population (census results)†	
17 January 1979	137,409,921
12 January 1989	
Males	68,713,869
Females.	78,308,000
Total	147,021,869
Population (official estimates at 1 January)	
2000	145,559,200
2001	144,819,100
2002	143,954,400
Density (per sq km) at 1 January 2002	8.4

* 6,592,850 sq miles.

† Figures refer to *de jure* population. The *de facto* total at the 1989 census was 147,400,537.

POPULATION BY ETHNIC GROUP*
(census of 12 January 1989)

	'000	%
Russian	119,865.9	81.5
Tatar†	5,522.1	3.8
Ukrainian	4,362.9	3.0
Chuvash	1,773.6	1.2
Bashkir	1,345.3	0.9
Belarusian	1,206.2	0.8
Mordovian	1,072.9	0.7
Chechen	899.0	0.6
German	842.3	0.6
Udmurt	714.5	0.5
Mari	643.7	0.4
Kazakh	635.9	0.4
Avar	544.0	0.4
Jewish‡	536.8	0.4
Armenian	532.4	0.4
Others	6,524.4	4.4
Total	**147,021.9**	**100.0**

* According to official declaration of nationality.

† Excluding Crimean Tatars, numbering 21,275.

‡ Excluding Mountain Jews, numbering 11,282.

REPUBLICS WITHIN THE FEDERATION

(estimates, 1 January 2002, except where otherwise indicated)

Republic	Area (sq km)	Population ('000)	Capital (with population, '000)*
Adygeya	7,600	444.9	Maikop (167.0)
Altai	92,600	204.9	Gorno-Altaisk (52.7)
Bashkortostan	143,600	4,090.6	Ufa (1,086.8)
Buryatiya	351,300	1,019.4	Ulan-Ude (368.9)
Chechnya†	n.a.	624.6	Groznyi (182.7‡)
Chuvashiya	18,300	1,346.3	Cheboksary (461.2)
Dagestan	50,300	2,179.5	Makhachkala (327.6)
Ingushetiya†	n.a.	466.3	Magas (0.1)§
Kabardino-Balkariya	12,500	782.0	Nalchik (228.4)
Kalmykiya	76,100	305.6	Elista (107.8)
Karachayevo-Cherkessiya	14,100	428.6	Cherkessk (120.7)
Kareliya	172,400	756.4	Petrozavodsk (282.9)
Khakasiya	61,900	575.4	Abakan (167.9)
Komi	415,900	1,117.2	Syktyvkar (227.7)
Marii-El	23,200	750.3	Ioshkar-Ola (248.5)
Mordoviya	26,200	910.0	Saransk (313.2)
North Osetiya (Alaniya)	8,000	678.2	Vladikavkaz (310.6)
Sakha (Yakutiya)	3,103,200	982.9	Yakutsk (197.8)
Tatarstan	68,000	3,768.2	Kazan (1,090.2)
Tyva	170,500	310.3	Kyzyl (101.5)
Udmurtiya	42,100	1,616.2	Izhevsk (650.3)

* Estimated population at 1 January 2001.

† Until 1992 the territories of the Republic of Chechnya and the Republic of Ingushetiya were combined in the Checheno-Ingush autonomous republic (area 19,300 sq km).

‡ Estimated population at 1 January 1995.

§ In October 1998 Magas replaced Nazran (estimated population 113,400 at 1 January 2001) as the capital.

PRINCIPAL TOWNS

(estimated population at 1 January 2001)

Town	Population	Town	Population
Moskva (Moscow, the capital)	8,304,600	Tyumen	500,200
Sankt Peterburg (St Petersburg)*	4,627,800	Tula	495,500
		Kemerovo	487,200
Novosibirsk	1,393,200	Tomsk	483,100
Nizhnii Novgorod*	1,343,300	Astrakhan	479,700
Yekaterinburg*	1,256,900	Vyatka*	466,300
Samara*	1,146,400	Cheboksary	461,200
Omsk	1,138,400	Ivanovo	452,100
Kazan	1,090,200	Bryansk	450,600
Ufa	1,088,800	Tver*	447,100
Chelyabinsk	1,081,100	Kursk	437,400
Perm	1,004,800	Magnitogorsk	427,100
Rostov-na-Donu (Rostov-on-Don)	997,800	Kaliningrad	421,000
Volgograd	982,900	Nizhnii Tagil	386,900
Voronezh	901,800	Murmansk	370,700
Saratov	864,400	Ulan-Ude	368,900
Krasnoyarsk	758,700	Kurgan	359,700
Tolyatti	724,300	Arkhangelsk (Archangel)	358,500
Ulyanovsk	662,100	Smolensk	347,600
Izhevsk*	650,300	Belgorod	342,000
Krasnodar	634,700	Stavropol	339,500
Yaroslavl	608,800	Orel	338,800
Khabarovsk	603,500	Kaluga	335,300
Vladivostok	596,600	Sochi	332,900
Irkutsk	587,200	Vladimir	331,700
Barnaul	573,300	Makhachkala	327,600
Novokuznetsk	564,500	Cherepovets	323,300
Penza	524,900	Saransk	313,200
Ryazan	523,400	Vladikavkaz*	310,600
Lipetsk	519,200	Tambov	308,000
Naberezhnye Chelny*	518,300	Chita	303,300
Orenburg	516,600		

* Some towns that were renamed during the Soviet period have reverted to their former names: St Petersburg (Leningrad); Nizhnii Novgorod (Gorkii); Yekaterinburg (Sverdlovsk); Samara (Kuibyshev); Izhevsk (Ustinov); Naberezhnye Chelny (Brezhnev); Vyatka (Kirov); Tver (Kalinin); Vladikavkaz (Ordzhonikidze).

BIRTHS, MARRIAGES AND DEATHS

	Registered live births		Registered marriages		Registered deaths	
	Number	Rate (per 1,000)	Number	Rate (per 1,000)	Number	Rate (per 1,000)
1994	1,408,159	9.5	1,080,600	7.3	2,301,366	15.6
1995	1,363,806	9.2	1,075,219	7.3	2,203,811	14.9
1996	1,304,638	8.8	866,651	5.9	2,082,249	14.1
1997	1,259,943	8.6	928,411	6.3	2,015,779	13.7
1998	1,283,292	8.8	848,691	5.8	1,988,744	13.6
1999	1,214,689	8.3	911,162	6.2	2,143,174	14.7
2000	1,266,789	8.7	789,999	5.4	2,225,332	15.3
2001	1,308,596	9.1	1,001,100*	6.9*	2,251,814	15.6

* Provisional figure.

Sources: mainly Council of Europe, *Demographic Year Book*; UN, *Population and Vital Statistics Report*.

Expectation of life (WHO estimates, years at birth): 65.2 (males 58.9; females 72.3) in 2001 (Source: WHO, *World Health Report*).

EMPLOYMENT

(sample surveys, '000 persons aged 15 to 72 years, at October)

	1998	1999*	2000
Agriculture, hunting and forestry	8,978.7	9,076.7	8,911.7
Mining and quarrying	1,409.6	1,071.8	1,086.0
Manufacturing	11,524.6	11,714.3	11,911.2
Electricity, gas and water supply	1,370.1	1,400.9	1,505.4
Construction	4,643.9	4,649.0	4,590.7
Wholesale and retail trade, restaurants and hotels	9,634.0	9,621.5	9,761.6
Transport, storage and communications	4,848.1	4,928.1	5,035.2
Financial intermediation, real estate, renting and business activities	5,297.1	5,128.0	5,074.6
Public administration and defence; compulsory social security	2,894.2	3,001.6	3,061.3
Education	5,772.3	5,816.4	5,742.1
Health and social work	4,295.3	4,341.4	4,355.8
Other community, social and personal service activities	3,055.0	3,178.9	3,271.6
Total employed (including others)	63,812.0	63,963.4	64,327.0
Unemployed	8,876.0	9,094.0	6,999.0
Total labour force	72,688	73,057.4	71,326.0

* Sample survey conducted in November.

Source: UN, *Statistical Yearbook for Asia and the Pacific*.

2001 (sample survey, '000 persons, November): Total employed 64,664; Unemployed 6,303; Total labour force 70,968 (males 36,846, females 34,122).

Health and Welfare

KEY INDICATORS

Total fertility rate (children per woman, 2001)	1.2
Under-5 mortality rate (per 1,000 live births, 2001)	21
HIV/AIDS (% of persons aged 15–49, 2001)	0.90
Physicians (per 1,000 head, 1998)	4.21
Hospital beds (per 1,000 head, 1997)	12.1
Health expenditure (2000): US $ per head (PPP)	405
Health expenditure (2000): % of GDP	5.3
Health expenditure (2000): public (% of total)	72.5
Access to water (% of persons, 1999)	99
Human Development Index (2000): ranking	60
Human Development Index (2000): value	0.781

For sources and definitions, see explanatory note on p. vi.

Agriculture

PRINCIPAL CROPS

('000 metric tons)

	1999	2000	2001
Wheat	30,995.2	34,500.0	46,871.0
Rice (paddy)	444.0	586.0	497.0
Barley	10,602.6	14,100.0	19,500.0
Maize	1,069.2	1,500.0	831.0
Rye	4,782.0	5,400.0	6,600.0
Oats	4,396.9	6,000.0	7,700.0
Millet	924.8	1,122.0	600.0
Sorghum	31.8	116.0	12.5*
Buckwheat	578.8	998.0	574.0
Potatoes	31,343.9	34,000.0	35,000.0
Sugar beet.	15,227.2	14,040.8	14,539.0
Dry peas	598.1	800.0	1,300.0
Soybeans (Soya beans) . . .	334.5	342.0	350.0
Sunflower seed	4,149.6	3,900.0	2,700.0
Rapeseed	135.1	197.8	115.7
Cabbages	3,940.1	4,000.0*	4,300.0*
Tomatoes	1,696.4	1,750.0*	1,850.0*
Cucumbers and gherkins* . . .	555.0	593.0	625.0
Dry onions	1,129.8	1,150.0*	1,200.0*
Garlic	180.7	198.0*	202.0*
Carrots	1,372.2	1,405.0*	1,480.0*
Other vegetables*	3,427.9	3,408.0	3,647.0
Apples	1,060	1,832*	1,643*
Cherries (incl. sour cherries)* . .	174	255	253
Plums*.	100	135	125
Strawberries	115*	128*	125†
Raspberries*	100	102	90
Currants	206	220*	203*
Watermelons†‡	540	475	435
Grapes	248.4	279.0	280.0†
Other fruits*	351	450	362

* Unofficial figure(s).
† FAO estimate(s).
‡ Including melons, pumpkins and squash.

Source: FAO.

LIVESTOCK

('000 head at 1 January, unless otherwise indicated)

	1999	2000	2001
Horses	1,800	1,750*	1,750*
Cattle	28,480	28,000	27,294
Pigs	17,248	18,271	15,708
Sheep†	13,413	12,715†	12,734†
Goats	2,144	2,036†	2,309†
Chickens	350,168	341,400†	332,500†
Turkeys*	2,500	2,400	2,500
Geese*	3,200	3,000	3,000

* FAO estimate(s).
† Unofficial figure.

Source: FAO.

LIVESTOCK PRODUCTS

('000 metric tons)

	1999	2000	2001
Beef and veal	1,868.0	1,895.0	1,837.0
Mutton and lamb.	123.6	123.0*	120.0*
Pig meat	1,485.4	1,569.0	1,547.0
Poultry meat	748.0	766.0	871.0
Other meat*	99.3	51.0	99.0
Cows' milk	32,000.6	31,977.0*	32,571.0*
Goats' milk	299.0	322.5*	328.5*
Cheese	364.6	390.7	433.0
Butter	261.7	267.0	269.0
Hen eggs	1,846.4	1,894.6	1,950.0*
Honey	51.0	53.9	54.0†
Wool: greasy	40.2	40.0	40.0†
Wool: scoured	24.2	20.0	20.0†
Cattle hides	229.3	232.6†	228.0†

* Unofficial figure(s).
† FAO estimate.

Source: FAO.

Forestry

ROUNDWOOD REMOVALS

('000 cubic metres, excl. bark)

	1999	2000	2001
Sawlogs, veneer logs and logs for sleepers	46,500	49,700	63,360
Pulpwood	39,200	46,400	42,300
Other industrial wood	8,900	9,700	12,300
Fuel wood	49,000	52,300	44,340
Total	143,600	158,100	162,300

Source: FAO.

SAWNWOOD PRODUCTION

('000 cubic metres, incl. railway sleepers)

	1999	2000	2001
Coniferous (softwood)	16,635	17,460	17,500
Broadleaved (hardwood). . . .	2,465	2,540	2,500
Total	19,100	20,000	20,000

Source: FAO.

Fishing*

('000 metric tons, live weight)

	1998	1999	2000
Capture	4,454.8	4,141.2	3,973.5
Pink (humpback) salmon . . .	191.4	187.1	157.1
Azov sea sprat	116.4	152.9	122.8
Atlantic cod.	248.7	215.6	171.0
Alaska (Walleye) pollock . . .	1,930.7	1,500.5	1,215.1
Blue whiting (Poutassou) . . .	130.0	182.6	241.9
Atlantic herring	139.6	170.6	174.2
Pacific herring	395.6	359.2	361.2
Aquaculture	63.2	68.6	74.1
Total catch	4,518.0	4,209.8	4,047.7

Source: FAO, *Yearbook of Fishery Statistics*.

* Figures exclude seaweeds and other aquatic plants ('000 metric tons): 30.3 in 1998; 25.7 in 1999; 53.7 in 2000. Also excluded are aquatic mammals (whales, seals, etc.).

Mining

('000 metric tons, unless otherwise indicated)

	1998	1999	2000
Hard coal	153,100	165,700	173,110
Lignite	78,800	83,400	83,740
Crude petroleum	303,300	305,000*	325,000*
Natural gas (million cu metres)	591,400	591,641	538,878
Iron ore: gross weight	72,343	81,311	86,630
Iron ore: metal content	41,700	46,900	50,000
Copper ore†	500	530*	570*
Nickel ore*†	250	260	270
Bauxite*	3,450	3,750	4,200
Lead ore†	13	13*	13*
Zinc ore†	115*	132*	136
Tin (metric tons)*†	4,500	4,500	5,000
Manganese ore*†	21	22	23
Chromium ore*	130	100	100
Tungsten concentrates (metric tons)*†	3,000	3,500	3,500
Molybdenum (metric tons)*.	2,000	2,400	2,400
Antimony ore (metric tons)*†	4,000	4,000	4,500
Cobalt ore (metric tons)*†	3,200	3,300	3,600
Mercury (metric tons)*	50	50	50
Silver (metric tons)*†	350	375	370
Uranium concentrate (metric tons)*†	2,000	2,000	2,500
Gold (metric tons)†	114.9	125.9	143.0
Platinum (metric tons)*.	30	32	35
Palladium (metric tons)*	70	75	84
Kaolin (concentrate)	50	41	45*
Magnesite	852	900*	1,000*
Phosphate rock (Apatite)‡	3,735	4,161	4,150
Potash*§	3,500	4,200	3,700
Native sulphur*	50	50	50
Fluorspar (concentrate)*	120.2	153.8	187.6*
Barite (Barytes)*.	60	60	60
Salt (unrefined)	2,200	3,200	3,200*
Diamonds: gems ('000 metric carats):			
gem*	11,600	11,500	11,600
industrial*	11,600	11,500	11,600
Gypsum (crude)	609	650	700*
Graphite*	6	6	6
Asbestos	600*	675	752
Mica*	100	100	100
Talc	79	90*	100*
Feldspar*	40	45	45
Peat (fuel use)	1,700	2,000	2,000*

* Estimated production.

† Figures refer to the metal content of ores.

‡ Figures refer to the phosphoric acid content. The data exclude sedimentary rock (estimates, '000 metric tons): 300 per year in 1998–2000.

§ Figures refer to the potassium oxide content.

Source: mainly US Geological Survey.

Industry

SELECTED PRODUCTS

('000 metric tons, unless otherwise indicated)

	1997	1998	1999
Margarine	222.3	238.7	379.4
Wheat flour	10,400	10,112	10,789
Raw sugar	3,777.7	4,744.6	6,807.6
Vodka and other spirits (million hectolitres)	8.3	8.7	13.4
Wine ('000 hectolitres)	1,230	1,260	1,830
Beer ('000 hectolitres)	26,100	33,600	44,500
Cigarettes (million)	140,077	198,506	266,031
Wool yarn (pure and mixed)	27.7	23.5	29.2
Cotton yarn (pure and mixed)	175.1	149.1	191.4
Flax, ramie and hemp yarn	31.6	17.1	20.1
Cotton fabrics (million sq metres)	1,374	1,241	1,455
Woollen fabrics (million sq metres)	62.6	51.8	61.1
Linen fabrics (million sq metres)	106.4	61.2	74.9
Leather footwear ('000 pairs)	34,541	24,998	30,821
Plywood ('000 cubic metres)	943.0	1,101.8	1,324.0

— continued	1997	1998	1999
Particle board ('000 cubic metres)	1,490	1,568	1,969
Mechanical wood pulp	899	981	1,160
Chemical and semi-chemical wood pulp	2,851	3,010	3,922
Newsprint	1,195	1,395	1,620
Other printing and writing paper	441	474	569
Other paper and paperboard	1,983	2,222	3,184
Sulphuric acid	6,247	5,840	7,148
Caustic soda (sodium hydroxide)	946	847	1,036
Soda ash (sodium carbonate)	1,652	1,538	1,918
Nitrogenous fertilizers (a)*	4,272	4,082	5,159
Phosphate fertilizers (b)*	1,787	1,703	2,044
Potassic fertilizers (c)*	3,487	3,596	4,294
Synthetic rubber	703.9	621.7	736.3
Aviation gasoline	39	31†	n.a.
Jet fuels	9,189	9,189†	n.a.
Motor spirit (petrol)	27,178	25,923†	26,300
Kerosene	107	51†	n.a.
Gas-diesel (distillate fuel) oils	47,226	45,102†	46,800
Residual fuel oils	63,887	56,701†	50,100
Lubricating oils	2,145	1,885†	n.a.
Petroleum wax (paraffin)	70	157†	n.a.
Petroleum coke	794	997†	n.a.
Petroleum bitumen (asphalt)	3,139	4,294†	n.a.
Liquefied petroleum gas	5,041	4,808†	n.a.
Coke	21,879	19,772†	n.a.
Rubber tyres ('000)‡	22,954	22,008	26,155
Rubber footwear ('000 pairs)	20,447	20,687	20,085
Cement	26,688	26,018	28,529
Pig-iron: foundry	890	1,061	1,032
Pig-iron: steel-making	36,387	33,521	39,663
Crude steel: for castings	2,758	2,459	3,125
Crude steel: ingots	45,744	41,214	48,392
Copper (refined, unwrought)†	600	620	750
Aluminium (unwrought): primary	2,906	3,005	3,146
Tractors (number)§	12,438	9,771	15,417
Domestic refrigerators ('000)	1,186.2	1,042.7	1,172.7
Domestic washing machines ('000)	799.7	862.4	998.5
Television receivers ('000)	327.2	329.0	280.7
Radio receivers ('000)	342	235	332
Passenger motor cars ('000)	986.2	840.1	954.5
Buses and motor coaches ('000)	46.0	45.7	50.0
Lorries ('000)	145.9	141.5	174.6
Cameras: photographic ('000)	143	60	81
Watches ('000)	4,983	3,763	6,304
Electric energy (million kWh)	834,100	827,200	846,200

* Production in terms of (a) nitrogen; (b) phosphoric acid; or (c) potassium oxide.

† Provisional or estimated figure(s).

‡ Tyres for road motor vehicles, excluding bicycles and motorcycles.

§ Tractors of 10 horse-power and over, excluding industrial tractors and tractors for tractor-trailer combinations.

Source: mainly UN, *Industrial Commodity Statistics Yearbook*.

Raw sugar ('000 metric tons): 6,076.6 in 2000.

Vodka and other spirits (million hectolitres): 12.3 in 2000.

Wine ('000 hectolitres): 2,410 in 2000.

Beer ('000 hectolitres): 51,600 in 2000.

Plywood ('000 cubic metres): 1,484.4 in 2000.

Motor spirit (petrol) ('000 metric tons): 27,200 in 2000; 27,500 in 2001.

Gas-diesel (distillate fuel) oils ('000 metric tons): 49,200 in 2000; 50,200 in 2001.

Residual fuel oils ('000 metric tons): 48,200 in 2000; 50,200 in 2001.

Rubber tyres ('000): 27,819 in 2000; 31,100 in 2001.

Cement ('000 metric tons): 32,389 in 2000; 35,100 in 2001.

Crude steel ('000 metric tons): 59,150 in 2000.

Tractors (number): 19,200 in 2000; 15,200 in 2001.

Domestic refrigerators ('000): 1,326.8 in 2000; 1,714.0 in 2001.

Domestic washing machines ('000): 953.9 in 2000.

Television receivers ('000): 1,115.5 in 2000; 1,004.0 in 2001.

Passenger motor cars ('000): 969.2 in 2000; 1,022.0 in 2001.

Electric energy (million kWh): 877,800 in 2000; 888,000 in 2001.

Source: mainly Ministry of Economic Development and Trade, Moscow.

Finance

CURRENCY AND EXCHANGE RATES

Monetary Units

100 kopeks = 1 Russian rubl (ruble or rouble)

Sterling, Dollar and Euro Equivalents (31 December 2002)

£1 sterling = 51.23 roubles
US $1 = 31.78 roubles
€1 = 33.33 roubles
1,000 roubles = £19.52 = $31.46 = €30.00

Average Exchange Rate (roubles per US dollar)

2000	28.1292
2001	29.1685
2002	31.3485

Note: On 1 January 1998 a new rouble, equivalent to 1,000 of the former units, was introduced. Figures in this Survey are expressed in terms of new roubles, unless otherwise indicated.

FEDERAL BUDGET
(million roubles)

Revenue	1999	2000	2001
Tax revenue	509,507.2	964,782.2	1,460,398.0
Taxes on corporate profit and			
capital gains	101,129.2	205,650.2	217,366.0
Taxes on goods and services . .	307,383.5	504,931.6	845,546.5
Taxes on the use of natural			
resources	10,496.0	18,569.0	49,692.9
Taxes on international trade and			
transactions	86,261.8	229,224.2	331,340.4
Other current revenue	43,105.3	74,104.4	119,068.5
Income from state property and			
activities	6,773.0	31,274.4	56,990.6
Income from external economic			
activity	31,047.1	37,406.3	51,506.4
Special budgetary funds. . . .	55,183.4	92,115.3	14,511.5
Total (incl. others)	611,709.6	1,131,801.8	1,593,978.1

Expenditure	1999	2000	2001
State administration.	14,832.4	25,003.6	41,971.4
International organizations, etc.	58,080.3	10,342.8	23,765.9
National defence	116,127.5	191,727.6	247,703.0
Public order and safety	55,445.5	105,393.1	148,909.4
Scientific and technical research	11,196.8	17,396.4	23,687.7
Industry, energy and construction	16,921.3	35,099.1	44,153.2
Agriculture and fisheries . . .	9,068.0	13,392.5	23,712.1
Transport, communications and			
information technology . . .	941.6	1,852.2	37,122.4
Education	20,945.4	38,127.6	54,498.8
Health and sport	10,141.0	16,879.3	23,085.1
Social security and welfare . . .	49,096.0	67,991.8	112,285.4
Servicing of government debt . .	162,582.7	248,656.4	231,104.1
Federal transfers.	62,145.0	101,208.2	230,007.0
Special budgetary funds. . . .	55,275.3	97,679.8	14,526.7
Total (incl. others)	664,673.8	1,019,116.8	1,321,902.7

Source: Ministry of Finance, Moscow.

INTERNATIONAL RESERVES
(US $ million at 31 December)

	2000	2001	2002
Gold*	3,707.8	4,079.8	3,739.3
IMF special drawing rights . . .	0.5	2.9	1.2
Reserve position in IMF. . . .	1.2	1.4	1.6
Foreign exchange.	24,262.6	32,538.1	44,050.8
Total	27,972.1	36,622.2	79,792.9

* Valued at US $300 per troy ounce.

Source: IMF, *International Financial Statistics.*

MONEY SUPPLY
(million roubles at 31 December)

	2000	2001	2002
Currency outside banks	419,261	584,328	764,406
Demand deposits at banks . . .	443,021	585,469	706,240
Total money (incl. others) . . .	879,309	1,192,627	1,499,165

Source: IMF, *International Financial Statistics.*

COST OF LIVING
(Consumer Price Index; base: 1991 = 100)

	1998	1999	2000
Food	412,043.8	810,254.3	952,103.8
All items	416,814.0	773,814.0	934,450.5

Source: ILO.

2001 (rounded figures): Food 1,148,070; All items 1,135,160 (Source: UN, *Monthly Bulletin of Statistics*).

NATIONAL ACCOUNTS
('000 million roubles at current prices)

Expenditure on the Gross Domestic Product

	2000	2001	2002
Final consumption expenditure .	4,476.8	5,896.8	7,402.0
Households	3,295.2	4,321.1	5,421.9
Non-profit institutions serving			
households	79.1	99.9	143.2
General government . . .	1,102.5	1,475.8	1,836.9
Gross capital formation . . .	1,365.8	1,993.8	2,287.3
Gross fixed capital formation .	1,232.0	1,685.8	1,947.7
Changes in inventories . . ⎫			
Aquisitions, less disposals, of ⎬	133.8	308.0	339.6
valuables . . . . . . ⎭			
Total domestic expenditure .	5,842.6	7,890.6	9,689.3
Exports of goods and services			
(net)	1,463.1	1,150.0	1,148.5
Sub-total	7,305.7	9,040.7	10,837.8
Statistical discrepancy* . . .	—	—	25.6
GDP in market prices . . .	7,305.7	9,040.7	10,863.4

* Referring to the difference between the sum of the expenditure components and official estimates of GDP, compiled from the production approach.

Source: IMF, *International Financial Statistics.*

Gross Domestic Product by Economic Activity

	2000	2001	2002*
Agriculture and forestry . . .	420.3	526.9	565.5
Industry†	2,049.2	2,271.7	2,605.1
Construction	428.8	604.4	713.5
Other production sectors . . .	41.4	61.8	79.0
Market services	3,041.3	3,872.5	4,912.0
Transport and communications .	586.4	749.1	977.7
Trade and catering	1,545.5	1,811.8	2,238.5
Non-market services	549.5	738.4	957.2
GDP at factor cost	6,530.5	8,075.7	9,832.3
Indirect taxes, *less* subsidies . .	775.2	965.0	1,031.1
GDP at market prices . . .	7,305.7	9,040.7	10,863.4

* Provisional figures.
† Comprising manufacturing (except printing and publishing), mining and quarrying, electricity, gas, water, logging and fishing.

BALANCE OF PAYMENTS
(US $ million)

	1999	2000	2001
Exports of goods f.o.b.	75,549	105,034	101,618
Imports of goods f.o.b.	−39,537	−44,862	−53,765
Trade balance	36,012	60,172	47,853
Exports of services	9,071	9,565	10,719
Imports of services	−13,352	−16,229	−18,999
Balance on goods and services	31,731	53,508	39,573
Other income received	3,878	4,752	6,800
Other income paid	−11,599	−11,491	−10,761
Balance on goods, services and income	24,010	46,769	35,612
Current transfers received . .	1,183	808	381
Current transfers paid	−582	−737	−1,139
Current balance	24,611	46,840	34,854
Capital account (net)	−326	10,675	−9,376
Direct investment abroad . . .	−2,206	−3,177	−2,533
Direct investment from abroad .	3,309	2,713	2,468
Portfolio investment assets . .	254	−411	76
Portfolio investment liabilities . .	−1,881	−12,809	−732
Other investment assets . . .	−13,218	−17,662	81
Other investment liabilities . .	−3,692	−3,089	−3,441
Net errors and omissions . . .	−8,555	−9,158	−10,132
Overall balance	−1,704	13,922	11,265

Source: IMF, *International Financial Statistics*.

External Trade

PRINCIPAL COMMODITIES
(distribution by SITC, US $ million)*

Imports c.i.f.	1998	1999	2000
Food and live animals . . .	7,681.8	5,846.5	5,287.1
Meat and meat preparations . .	2,061.9	1,244.0	1,050.4
Fresh, chilled or frozen meat and edible offal	1,758.8	1,168.6	985.0
Sugar, sugar preparations and honey	1,335.4	1,260.1	895.3
Beverages and tobacco . . .	1,967.5	1,108.5	1,129.4
Crude materials (inedible) except fuels	1,975.5	1,911.5	2,451.8
Metalliferous ores and metal scrap	1,298.8	1,133.7	1,554.0
Mineral fuels, lubricants, etc. .	1,495.4	796.0	1,508.1
Chemicals and related products	4,065.3	2,920.0	3,715.8
Basic manufactures	5,292.0	3,956.5	4,778.3
Iron and steel	1,438.4	1,087.4	1,424.4
Machinery and transport equipment	12,429.6	7,566.4	7,698.3
Machinery specialized for particular industries . . .	2,115.6	1,602.8	1,677.0
General industrial machinery, equipment and parts . . .	2,622.7	1,755.3	1,762.9
Miscellaneous manufactured articles	3,338.3	1,973.2	2,452.1
Total (incl. others)†	58,996.4	40,429.0	45,452.8

Exports f.o.b.	1998	1999	2000
Crude materials (inedible) except fuels	5,541.0	4,437.3	4,670.9
Metalliferous ores and metal scrap	2,304.1	1,393.6	984.0
Mineral fuels, lubricants, etc. .	28,190.9	31,192.0	52,846.0
Petroleum, petroleum products, etc.	13,682.5	18,905.7	34,500.4
Crude petroleum oils, etc. . .	9,456.4	13,466.8	23,644.3
Refined petroleum products .	4,174.4	5,364.5	10,717.5
Natural and manufactured gas .	13,406.7	11,531.8	16,990.7
Petroleum gases, etc., in the gaseous state	13,242.9	11,446.4	16,823.7
Chemicals and related products	3,940.5	3,894.0	4,966.1
Basic manufactures	18,546.2	14,853.6	18,367.0
Iron and steel	5,532.8	4,759.1	6,166.5
Ingots and other primary forms	2,643.5	2,409.5	3,099.0

Exports f.o.b. — *continued*	1998	1999	2000
Non-ferrous metals	8,901.1	6,826.1	8,140.8
Aluminium	4,206.9	4,156.8	4,777.4
Aluminium and aluminium alloys, unwrought . . .	3,780.0	3,612.9	4,141.8
Machinery and transport equipment	5,628.7	5,096.8	6,033.3
Total (incl. others)†	74,160.0	74,663.0	103,008.2

* Figures are provisional. Including adjustments (e.g. for barter trade), the revised totals (in US $ million) are: Imports c.i.f. 63,817 in 1998, 43,588 in 1999, 49,125 in 2000; Exports f.o.b. 74,884 in 1998, 75,665 in 1999, 105,565 in 2000 (Source: IMF, *International Financial Statistics*).

† Including commodities not classified according to kind (US $ million): Imports 20,309.3 in 1998, 13,822.9 in 1999, 15,975.4 in 2000; Exports 9,389.8 in 1998, 12,348.7 in 1999, 12,574.2 in 2000.

Source: UN, *International Trade Statistics Yearbook*.

PRINCIPAL TRADING PARTNERS
(US $ million)*

Imports	1998	1999	2000
Belarus	4,555.2	3,236.0	3,764.2
Belgium-Luxembourg . . .	689.5	n.a.	n.a.
Brazil	654.4	717.4	387.6
China, People's Republic . .	1,160.0	893.5	948.7
Finland	1,446.9	947.5	958.0
France (incl. Monaco) . . .	1,597.8	1,233.3	1,187.8
Germany	5,508.6	4,201.6	3,895.9
Hungary	607.8	313.3	403.5
India	668.3	677.2	556.2
Italy	1,820.8	1,160.1	1,211.3
Japan	819.3	455.7	571.8
Kazakhstan	1,885.0	1,397.5	2,199.7
Korea, Republic . . .	1,009.7	316.7	358.6
Netherlands	917.0	688.6	739.2
Poland	1,047.9	602.7	716.2
Sweden	704.1	477.2	465.4
Switzerland	426	315	279
Ukraine	3,282.2	2,528.4	3,650.2
United Kingdom	1,229.1	676.2	860.7
USA	4,123.4	2,389.5	2,703.2
Uzbekistan	537.4	467.6	662.6
Total (incl. others) . . .	58,996.4	40,429.0	45,452.8

Exports	1998	1999	2000
Belarus	4,622.6	3,759.3	5,535.2
British Virgin Islands . . .	1,131.7	1,751.8	3,324.1
China, People's Republic . .	3,199.7	3,526.8	5,234.7
Czech Republic	1,396.7	1,325.0	1,744.5
Estonia	516.3	691.7	1,234.8
Finland	2,076.3	2,414.0	3,104.5
France (incl. Monaco) . . .	1,456.0	1,218.1	1,913.7
Germany	5,720.7	6,202.3	9,230.9
Hungary	1,485.9	1,549.0	2,405.5
India	585.1	1,177.3	1,081.7
Italy	3,221.7	3,755.0	7,255.4
Japan	2,193.7	2,124.7	2,763.3
Kazakhstan	1,967.3	1,225.6	2,247.1
Korea, Republic . . .	508.1	826.2	972.1
Latvia	681.9	981.4	1,625.7
Lithuania	1,053.6	1,163.0	2,065.4
Netherlands	3,994.0	3,673.4	4,341.0
Poland	2,780.2	2,607.8	4,451.9
Slovakia	1,373.3	1,428.3	2,121.2
Sweden	853.2	1,190.4	1,729.4
Switzerland-Liechtenstein . .	3,256.0	3,479.1	3,976.3
Turkey	1,936.8	1,630.8	3,098.2
Ukraine	5,563.4	4,792.4	5,024.5
United Kingdom	3,024.8	2,885.7	4,668.9
USA	5,138.0	4,714.0	4,647.8
Total (incl. others) . . .	74,160.0	74,663.0	103,008.2

* The figures are compiled on the basis of reporting by Russia's trading partners. Adjusted totals (in US $ million) are: Imports c.i.f. 63,817 in 1998, 43,588 in 1999, 49,125 in 2000; Exports f.o.b. 74,884 in 1998, 75,665 in 1999, 105,565 in 2000 (Source: IMF, *International Financial Statistics*).

Source: UN, *International Trade Statistics Yearbook* (April 2002).

2001 (US $ million): Total imports c.i.f. 58,992; Total exports f.o.b. 103,139 (Source: IMF, *International Financial Statistics*).

Transport

RAILWAYS
(traffic)

	1998	1999	2000
Paying passengers ('000 journeys) .	1,471,306	1,337,509	1,418,780
Freight carried ('000 metric tons) .	834,800	947,400	1,046,800
Passenger-km (million)	152,900	141,000	167,100
Freight ton-km (million) . . .	1,019,500	1,204,500	1,373,000

ROAD TRAFFIC
(motor vehicles in use)

	1998	1999	2000
Passenger cars	18,819,600	19,717,800	20,353,000
Buses and coaches . . .	627,500	633,200	640,100
Lorries and vans	4,260,000	4,387,800	4,400,600
Motorcycles and mopeds . . .	7,165,900	6,328,600	n.a.

Source: IRF, *World Road Statistics.*

SHIPPING

Merchant Fleet
(registered at 31 December)

	1999	2000	2001
Number of vessels	4,694	4,755	4,727
Total displacement ('000 grt) . .	10,649.0	10,485.1	10,247.8

Source: Lloyd's Register-Fairplay, *World Fleet Statistics.*

International Sea-borne Freight Traffic
('000 metric tons)

	1999	2000	2001
Goods loaded	7,092	8,280	8,976
Goods unloaded	744	840	660

Source: UN, *Monthly Bulletin of Statistics.*

CIVIL AVIATION
(traffic on scheduled services)

	1997	1998	1999
Kilometres flown (million) . .	609	581	550
Passengers carried ('000) . . .	20,419	18,685	18,600
Passenger-km (million) . . .	49,278	46,158	45,863
Total ton-km (million) . . .	5,269	4,931	5,036

Source: UN, *Statistical Yearbook.*

Passenger-km (million): 42,948 in 2000; 73,812 in 2001 (Source: UN, *Monthly Bulletin of Statistics*).

Tourism

FOREIGN VISITOR ARRIVALS
('000, incl. excursionists)

Country of nationality	1998	1999	2000
Armenia	259.6	185.8	234.9
Azerbaijan.	601.5	930.5	1,074.1
Belarus	218.7	190.0	243.7
China, People's Republic . .	464.2	445.9	493.8
Estonia	271.1	463.9	418.4
Finland	1,260.3	1,406.7	1,453.5
Georgia	924.7	1,044.4	948.0
Germany	316.5	361.4	363.2
Kazakhstan	203.3	358.8	2,189.4
Latvia	209.4	259.8	329.9
Lithuania	752.1	980.4	1,048.8
Moldova	663.1	493.7	599.9
Poland	803.6	958.7	947.9
Tajikistan	101.9	156.1	314.1
Ukraine	6,412.8	7,757.1	7,391.7
USA	212.9	184.0	198.8
Uzbekistan	155.9	223.9	489.3
Total (incl. others) . . .	15,805.2	18,493.0	21,169.1

Tourism receipts (US $ million): 6,508 in 1998; 7,510 in 1999.

Source: World Tourism Organization, *Yearbook of Tourism Statistics.*

Communications Media

	1999	2000	2001
Television receivers ('000 in use)	74,000	79,000	n.a.
Telephones ('000 main lines in use)	30,949	32,070	35,700
Mobile cellular telephones ('000 subscribers).	1,370.6	3,263.2	5,560.0
Personal computers ('000 in use) .	5,500	6,300	7,300
Internet users ('000)	1,500	3,100	4,300

Source: International Telecommunication Union.

Radio receivers ('000 in use): 61,500 in 1997.

Facsimile machines (number in use): 52,900 in 1998.

Book production (including pamphlets): 36,237 titles in 1996 (421,387,000 copies).

Daily newspapers: 285 in 1996 (average circulation 15,517,000 copies).

Non-daily newspapers: 4,596 in 1996 (average circulation 98,558,000 copies).

Other periodicals: 2,751 in 1996 (average circulation 387,832,000 copies).

Sources: UNESCO, *Statistical Yearbook*; and UN, *Statistical Yearbook.*

Education

(2000/2001)

	Institutions	Teachers	Students
Pre-primary	51,329	608,700	4,263,000
Primary		330,200	5,911,800
Secondary:	} 67,063		
general		} 1,350,200	{ 15,837,600
vocational	3,893		1,679,300
Higher	965	n.a	4,741,400*

* Excluding foreign students registered at Russian institutions.

Source: partly UN, *Statistical Yearbook for Asia and the Pacific.*

Adult literacy rate (UNESCO estimates): 99.6% (males 99.7%; females 99.4%) in 2000 (Source: UN Development Programme, *Human Development Report*).

Directory

The Constitution

The current Constitution of the Russian Federation came into force on 12 December 1993, following its approval by a majority of participants in a nation-wide plebiscite. It replaced the Constitution originally adopted on 12 April 1978, but amended many times after 1990.

THE PRINCIPLES OF THE CONSTITUTIONAL SYSTEM

Chapter One of Section One declares that the Russian Federation (Russia) is a democratic, federative, law-based state with a republican form of government. Its multi-ethnic people bear its sovereignty and are the sole source of authority. State power in the Russian Federation is divided between the legislative, executive and judicial branches, which are independent of one another. Ideological pluralism and a multi-party political system are recognized. The Russian Federation is a secular state and all religious associations are equal before the law. All laws are made public and in accordance with universally acknowledged principles and with international law.

HUMAN AND CIVIL RIGHTS AND FREEDOMS

Chapter Two states that the basic human rights and freedoms of the Russian citizen are guaranteed regardless of sex, race, nationality or religion. It declares the right to life and to freedom and personal inviolability. The principles of freedom of movement, freedom of expression and freedom of conscience are upheld. Censorship is prohibited. Citizens are guaranteed the right to vote and stand in state and local elections and to participate in referendums. Individuals are to have equal access to state employment, and the establishment of trade unions and public associations is permitted. The Constitution commits the State to protection of motherhood and childhood and to granting social security, state pensions and social benefits. Each person has the right to housing. Health care and education are free of charge. Basic general education is compulsory. Citizens are guaranteed the right to receive qualified legal assistance. Payment of statutory taxes and levies is obligatory, as is military service.

THE ORGANIZATION OF THE FEDERATION

Chapter Three names the 89 members (federal territorial units) of the Russian Federation. Russian is declared the state language, but all peoples of the Russian Federation are guaranteed the right to preserve their native tongue. The state flag, emblem and anthem of the Russian Federation are to be established by a federal constitutional law. The Constitution defines the separate roles of the authority of the Russian Federation, as distinct from that of the joint authority of the Russian Federation and the members of the Russian Federation. It also establishes the relationship between federal laws, federal constitutional laws and the laws and other normative legal acts of the subjects of the Russian Federation. The powers of the federal executive bodies and the executive bodies of the members of the Russian Federation are defined.

THE PRESIDENT OF THE RUSSIAN FEDERATION

Chapter Four describes the powers and responsibilities of the Head of State, the President of the Russian Federation. The President is elected to office for a term of four years by universal, direct suffrage. The same individual may be elected to the office of President for no more than two consecutive terms. The President may appoint the Chairman of the Government (Prime Minister) of the Russian Federation, with the approval of the State Duma, and may dismiss the Deputy Chairmen and the federal ministers from office. The President is entitled to chair sessions of the Government. The President's responsibilities include scheduling referendums and elections to the State Duma, dissolving the State Duma, submitting legislative proposals to the State Duma and promulgating federal laws. The President is responsible for the foreign policy of the Russian Federation. The President is Commander-in-Chief of the Armed Forces and may introduce martial law or a state of emergency under certain conditions.

If the President is unable to carry out the presidential duties, these will be assumed by the Chairman of the Government. The acting President, however, will not possess the full powers of the President, such as the right to dissolve the State Duma or to order a referendum. The President may only be removed from office by the Federation Council on the grounds of a serious accusation by the State Duma.

THE FEDERAL ASSEMBLY

Chapter Five concerns the Federal Assembly, which is the highest representative and legislative body in the Russian Federation. It consists of two chambers: the Federation Council (upper chamber) and the State Duma (lower chamber). The Federation Council comprises two representatives from each member of the Russian Federation, one appointed by its legislative and one by its executive body (178 senators in total). The State Duma, which is composed of 450 deputies, is elected for a term of four years. The procedures for forming the Federation Council and for electing the State Duma are to be determined by federal legislation. The deputies of the Russian Federation must be over 21 years of age and may not hold government office or any other paid job. The Federal Assembly is a permanent working body.

Both chambers of the Federal Assembly may elect their Chairman and Deputy Chairmen, who preside over parliamentary sessions and supervise the observance of their regulations. Each chamber adopts its code of procedure. The powers of the Federation Council include the approval of the President's decrees on martial law and a state of emergency, the scheduling of presidential elections and the impeachment of the President. The State Duma has the power to approve the President's nominee to the office of Chairman of the Government. Both chambers of the Federal Assembly adopt resolutions by a majority vote of the total number of members. All federal and federal constitutional laws are adopted by the State Duma and submitted for approval first to the Federation Council and then to the President. If the Federation Council or the President reject proposed legislation it is submitted for repeat consideration to one or both chambers of the Federal Assembly.

The State Duma may be dissolved by the President if it rejects all three candidates to the office of Chairman of the Government or adopts a second vote of 'no confidence' in the Government. However, it may not be dissolved during a period of martial law or a state of emergency or in the case of charges being lodged against the President. A newly elected State Duma should be convened no later than four months after dissolution of the previous parliament.

THE GOVERNMENT OF THE RUSSIAN FEDERATION

The executive authority of the Russian Federation is vested in the Government, which is comprised of the Chairman, the Deputy Chairmen and federal ministers. The Chairman is appointed by the President and his nomination approved by the State Duma. If the State Duma rejects three candidates to the office of Chairman, the President will appoint the Chairman, dissolve the State Duma and order new elections. The Government's responsibilities are to submit the federal budget to the State Duma and to supervise its execution, to guarantee the implementation of a uniform state policy, to carry out foreign policy and to ensure the country's defence and state security. Its duties also include the maintenance of law and order.

Regulations for the activity of the Government are to be determined by a federal constitutional law. The Government can adopt resolutions and directives, which may be vetoed by the President. The Government must submit its resignation to a newly elected President of the Russian Federation, which the President may accept or reject. A vote of 'no confidence' in the Government may be adopted by the State Duma. The President can reject this decision or demand the Government's resignation. If the State Duma adopts a second vote of 'no confidence' within three months, the President will announce the Government's resignation or dissolve the State Duma.

JUDICIAL POWER

Justice is administered by means of constitutional, civil, administrative and criminal judicial proceedings. Judges in the Russian Federation must be aged 25 or over, have a higher legal education and have a record of work in the legal profession of no less than five years. Judges are independent, irremovable and inviolable. Proceedings in judicial courts are open. No criminal case shall be considered in the absence of a defendant. Judicial proceedings may be conducted with the participation of a jury.

The Constitutional Court comprises 19 judges. The Court decides cases regarding the compliance of federal laws and enactments, the constitutions, statutes, laws and other enactments of the members of the Russian Federation, state treaties and international treaties that have not yet come into force. The Constitutional Court settles disputes about competence among state bodies. Enactments or their individual provisions that have been judged unconstitutional by the Court are invalid. At the request of the Federation Council, the Court will pronounce its judgment on bringing an accusation against the President of the Russian Federation.

The Supreme Court is the highest judicial authority on civil, criminal, administrative and other cases within the jurisdiction of the common plea courts. The Supreme Arbitration Court is the highest authority in settling economic and other disputes within the jurisdiction of the courts of arbitration.

The judges of the three higher courts are appointed by the Federation Council on the recommendation of the President. Judges of other federal courts are appointed by the President.

The Prosecutor's Office is a single centralized system. The Prosecutor-General is appointed and dismissed by the Federation Council on the recommendation of the President. All other prosecutors are appointed by the Prosecutor-General.

LOCAL SELF-GOVERNMENT

Chapter Eight provides for the exercise of local self-government through referendums, elections and through elected and other bodies. The responsibilities of local self-government bodies include: independently managing municipal property; forming, approving and executing the local budget; establishing local taxes and levies; and maintaining law and order.

CONSTITUTIONAL AMENDMENTS AND REVISION OF THE CONSTITUTION

Chapter Nine states that no provision contained in Chapters One, Two and Nine of the Constitution is to be reviewed by the Federal Assembly, while amendments to the remaining Chapters may be passed in accordance with the procedure for a federal constitutional law. If a proposal for a review of the provisions of Chapters One, Two and Nine wins a three-fifths majority in both chambers, a Constitutional Assembly will be convened.

CONCLUDING AND TRANSITIONAL PROVISIONS

Section Two states that the Constitution came into force on the day of the nation-wide vote, 12 December 1993. Should the provisions of a federal treaty contravene those of the Constitution, the constitutional provisions will apply. All laws and other legal acts enforced before the Constitution came into effect will remain valid unless they fail to comply with the Constitution. The President of the Russian Federation will carry out the presidential duties established by the Constitution until the expiry of his term of office. The Council of Ministers will acquire the rights, duties and responsibility of the Government of the Russian Federation established by the Constitution and henceforth be named the Government of the Russian Federation. The courts will administer justice in accordance with their powers established by the Constitution and retain their powers until the expiry of their term.

The Government

HEAD OF STATE

President of the Russian Federation: VLADIMIR V. PUTIN (elected 26 March 2000; inaugurated 7 May).

THE GOVERNMENT
(April 2003)

Chairman (Prime Minister): MIKHAIL M. KASYANOV.

Deputy Chairman and Minister of Agriculture and Foodstuffs: ALEKSEI V. GORDEYEV.

Deputy Chairman and Minister of Finance: ALEKSEI L. KUDRIN.

Deputy Chairman, responsible for Industrial Policy: BORIS S. ALESHIN.

Deputy Chairman, responsible for Social Affairs: GALINA N. KARELOVA.

Deputy Chairman: VIKTOR B. KHRISTENKO.

Minister for Antimonopoly Policy and Support for Entrepreneurship: ILYA A. YUZHANOV.

Minister of Atomic Energy: ALEKSANDR YU. RUMYANTSEV.

Minister of Civil Defence, Emergencies and Clean-up Operations: Lt-Gen. SERGEI K. SHOIGU.

Minister of Communications and Information Technology: LEONID D. REIMAN.

Minister of Culture: MIKHAIL YE. SHVYDKOI.

Minister of Defence: SERGEI B. IVANOV.

Minister of Economic Development and Trade: GERMAN O. GREF.

Minister of Education and Vocational Training: VLADIMIR M. FILIPPOV.

Minister of Energy: IGOR KH. YUSUFOV.

Minister of Foreign Affairs: IGOR S. IVANOV.

Minister of Health: YURII L. SHEVCHENKO.

Minister of Industry, Science and Technology: ILYA I. KLEBANOV.

Minister of Internal Affairs: BORIS V. GRYZLOV.

Minister of Justice: YURII YA. CHAIKA.

Minister of Labour and Social Development: ALEKSANDR P. POCHINOK.

Minister of Natural Resources: VITALII G. ARTYUKHOV.

Minister of the Press, Broadcasting and Mass Media: MIKHAIL YU. LESIN.

Minister of Railways: GENNADII M. FADEYEV.

Minister of State Property: FARIT R. GAZIZULLIN.

Minister of Transport: SERGEI O. FRANK.

Minister of Taxes and Levies: GENNADII I. BUKAYEV.

Head of the Presidential Administration and Minister Without Portfolio: IGOR I. SHUVALOV.

Minister without Portfolio, responsible for the Social and Economic Development of Chechnya: STANISLAV ILYASOV.

Minister without Portfolio, responsible for Nationalities Policy: VLADIMIR YU. ZORIN.

Minister without Portfolio: VLADIMIR V. YELAGIN.

MINISTRIES

Office of the President: 103073 Moscow, Kremlin; tel. (095) 925-35-81; fax (095) 206-51-73; e-mail president@gov.ru; internet president.kremlin.ru.

Office of the Government: 103274 Moscow, Krasnopresnenskaya nab. 2; tel. (095) 205-57-35; fax (095) 205-42-19; internet www.government.ru.

Ministry of Agriculture and Foodstuffs: 107139 Moscow, Orlikov per. 1/11; tel. (095) 207-83-86; fax (095) 207-95-80; e-mail info@aris.ru; internet www.aris.ru.

Ministry for Antimonopoly Policy and Support for Entrepreneurship: 123231 Moscow, ul. Sadovaya-Kudrinskaya 11; tel. (095) 254-74-45; fax (095) 254-75-21; e-mail gak1@infpres.ru; internet www.maprf.ru.

Ministry of Atomic Energy: 109017 Moscow, ul. B. Ordynka 24/26; tel. (095) 239-45-45; fax (095) 230-24-20; e-mail info@minatom.ru; internet www.minatom.ru.

Ministry of Civil Defence, Emergencies and Clean-up Operations: 103012 Moscow, Teatralnyi proyezd 3; tel. (095) 926-39-01; fax (095) 924-19-46; e-mail pressa@emercom.gov.ru; internet www.emercom.gov.ru.

Ministry of Communications and Information Technology: 103375 Moscow, ul. Tverskaya 7; tel. (095) 292-71-44; fax (095) 292-74-55; internet www.minsvyaz.ru.

Ministry of Culture: 103074 Moscow, Kitaigorodskii proyezd 7; tel. (095) 925-11-95; fax (095) 928-17-91; e-mail root@mincult.isf.ru; internet www.mincultrf.ru.

Ministry of Defence: 105175 Moscow, ul. Myasnitskaya 37; tel. (095) 293-38-54; fax (095) 296-84-36; internet www.mil.ru.

Ministry of Economic Development and Trade: 125818 Moscow, ul. Tverskaya-Yamskaya 1/3; tel. (095) 200-03-53; e-mail presscenter@economy.gov.ru; internet www.economy.gov.ru.

Ministry of Education and Vocational Training: 113833 Moscow, ul. Lyusinovskaya 51; tel. (095) 237-61-55; fax (095) 237-83-81; e-mail mail@ministry.ru; internet www.ed.gov.ru.

Ministry of Energy: 103074 Moscow, Kitaigorodskii proyezd 7/191; tel. (095) 220-51-33; fax (095) 220-56-56; e-mail abs@cdu.oilnet.ru; internet www.mte.gov.ru.

Ministry of Finance: 103097 Moscow, ul. Ilinka 9; tel. (095) 298-91-01; fax (095) 925-08-89; internet www.minfin.ru.

Ministry of Foreign Affairs: 121200 Moscow, Smolenskaya–Sennaya pl. 32/34; tel. (095) 244-16-06; fax (095) 230-21-30; e-mail ministry@mid.ru; internet www.mid.ru.

Ministry of Health: 101431 Moscow, ul. Neglinnaya 25; tel. (095) 927-28-48; fax (095) 928-58-15; e-mail press-center@minzdrav-rf.ru; internet www.minzdrav-rf.ru.

Ministry of Industry, Science and Technology: 125889 Moscow, pl. Miusskaya 3; tel. (095) 972-70-51; fax (095) 229-55-49; e-mail info@mpnt.gov.ru; internet www.mptn.gov.ru.

Ministry of Internal Affairs: 117049 Moscow, ul. Zhitnaya 16; tel. (095) 237-754-85; fax (095) 293-59-98; e-mail uimvd@mvdinform.ru; internet www.mvdinform.ru.

Ministry of Justice: 109830 Moscow, ul. Vorontsovo Pole 4A; tel. (095) 206-05-54; fax (095) 916-29-03; internet www.minjust.ru.

Ministry of Labour and Social Development: 101999 Moscow, Birzhevaya pl. 1; tel. (095) 298-88-88; fax (095) 230-24-07; e-mail press_mt@zanas.ru; internet www.mintrud.ru.

Ministry of Natural Resources: 123812 Moscow, ul. B. Gruzinskaya 4/6; tel. (095) 254-48-00; fax (095) 254-43-10; e-mail admin@mnr.gov.ru; internet www.mnr.gov.ru.

Ministry of the Press, Broadcasting and Mass Media: 127994 Moscow, Strastnoi bulv. 5; tel. (095) 229-66-93; fax (095) 200-22-81; internet www.mptr.ru.

Ministry of Railways: 107174 Moscow, ul. Novobasmannaya 2; tel. (095) 262-10-02; e-mail info@mps.ru; internet www.mps.ru.

Ministry of State Property: 103685 Moscow, Nikolskii per. 9; tel. (095) 298-75-62; fax (095) 206-11-19; e-mail mgi1@ftcenter.ru; internet www.mgi.ru.

Ministry of Taxes and Levies: 103381 Moscow, ul. Neglinnaya 23; tel. (095) 200-38-48; fax (095) 200-11-78; e-mail mns@nalog.ru; internet www.nalog.ru.

Ministry of Transport: 109012 Moscow, ul. Rozhdestvenka 1/1; tel. (095) 926-10-00; fax (095) 200-33-56; e-mail mcc@morflot.ru; internet www.mintrans.ru.

President and Legislature

PRESIDENT

Presidential Election, 26 March 2000

Candidates	Votes	%
Vladimir V. Putin	39,740,434	52.9
Gennadii A. Zyuganov	21,928,471	29.2
Grigorii A. Yavlinskii	4,351,452	5.8
Aman M. Tuleyev	2,217,361	3.0
Vladimir V. Zhirinovskii	2,026,513	2.7
Konstantin A. Titov	1,107,269	1.5
Ella A. Pamfilova	758,966	1.0
Others	824,659	1.1
Against all candidates	1,414,648	1.9
Invalid votes	701,003	0.9
Total	**75,070,776**	**100.0**

FEDERAL ASSEMBLY

The Federal Assembly is a bicameral legislative body, comprising the Federation Council and the State Duma.

Federation Council

The Federation Council is the upper chamber of the Federal Assembly. It comprises 178 deputies, two appointed from each of the constituent members (federal territorial units) of the Russian Federation, representing the legislative and executive branches of power in each republic and region.

Federation Council: 103426 Moscow, ul. B. Dmitrovka 26; tel. (095) 203-90-74; fax (095) 203-46-17; e-mail post_sf@gov.ru; internet www.council.gov.ru.

Chairman: SERGEI M. MIRONOV.

First Deputy Chairman: VALERII P. GOREGLYAD.

Deputy Chairmen: ANDREI A. VIKHARYEV, MIKHAIL YE. NIKOLAYEV, ALEKSANDR P. TORSHIN.

State Duma

The State Duma is the 450-seat lower chamber of the Federal Assembly, members of which are elected for a term of four years. Elections to the State Duma were held on 19 December 1999.

State Duma

103265 Moscow, Okhotnyi ryad 1; tel. (095) 292-83-10; fax (095) 292-94-64; e-mail www@duma.ru; internet www.duma.ru.

Chairman: GENNADII N. SELEZNEV.

First Deputy Chairman: LYUBOV K. SLISKA.

Deputy Chairmen: VLADIMIR A. AVERCHENKO, GEORGII V. BOOS, VLADIMIR V. ZHIRINOVSKII, VLADIMIR P. LUKIN, PETR V. ROMANOV, GENNADII YU. SEMIGIN, IRINA M. KHAKAMADA, ARTUR N. CHILINGAROV.

General Election, 19 December 1999

Parties and blocs	Federal party lists		
	% of votes	Seats	Total seats*
Communist Party of the Russian Federation	24.29	67	113
Unity	23.32	64	72
Fatherland—All Russia	13.33	37	67
Union of Rightist Forces	8.52	24	29
Zhirinovskii bloc	5.98	17	17
Yabloko	5.93	16	21
Our Home is Russia	1.19	—	7
Pensioners' Party	1.95	—	1
Communists and Workers of Russia—for the Soviet Union	2.22	—	—
Women of Russia	2.04	—	—
Others	5.99	—	8
Independents	—	—	106
Against all lists	3.30	—	—
Total	**100.00‡**	**225**	**441§**

* Including seats filled by voting in single-member constituencies, totalling 225.
† There were 16 other groups, of which six obtained representation in the Duma.
‡ Including spoilt ballot papers (1.95% of the total).
§ Repeat elections were held in March 2000 in eight constituencies where the electorate had voted against all candidates. The remaining constituency, Chechnya, was to remain vacant, owing to the impossibility of holding elections while the conflict in the republic continued.

THE STATE COUNCIL

The State Council is a consultative body, established in September 2000, and intended to improve co-ordination between federal and regional government, and to strengthen federal control in the regions. The membership of the Council comprises the leaders of the 89 federal subjects and the President of the Russian Federation, who chairs the Council. The President appoints a presidium, comprising seven-members of the Council, who serve for a period of six months.

Political Organizations

In 1999 numerous political parties and movements were formed, in anticipation of the election to the State Duma in December of that year, for which the Central Electoral Commission approved a list of 29 electoral associations and blocs. Each electoral association was based on one registered political party or movement, and each electoral bloc represented an alliance of two or more parties or movements. All 29 presented federal lists of candidates. In accordance with a law signed by President Putin in July 2001, a political party must have at least 10,000 members, including no fewer than 100 members in at least 50 of the 89 subjects of the Russian Federation, in order to register and to function legally.

By December 2002 some 46 parties had registered with the Ministry of Justice, in accordance with the conditions imposed by the legislation signed in July 2001, of which the following were among the most significant.

Agrarian Party of Russia (APR) (Agrarnaya partiya Rossii): 107045 Moscow, per. B. Golovin 20/1; tel. (095) 207-99-51; fax (095) 921-31-76; e-mail chuprina@duma.gov.ru; internet www.apr.h1.ru; f. 1993; left-wing, supports the agricultural sector; member of the Fatherland-All Russia alliance in 1999–2002; Leader MIKHAIL I. LAPSHIN; 41,477 mems (2002).

Communist Party of the Russian Federation (CPRF) (Kommunisticheskaya partiya Rossiiskoi Federatsii—KPRF): 103051 Moscow, per. M. Sukharevskii 3/1; tel. (095) 928-71-29; fax (095) 292-90-50; e-mail cprf2000@mail.ru; internet www.kprf.ru; f. 1993; claims succession to the Russian Communist Party, which was banned in 1991; Chair. of Central Committee GENNADII A. ZYUGANOV; 19,013 mems (2002).

Democratic Party of Russia (Demokraticheskaya Partiya Rossiya): 103287 Moscow, ul. Poltavskaya 18; tel. (095) 214-39-91; fax (095) 213-11-08; e-mail demparty@fromru.com; internet www.demparty.ru; f. 1990; liberal-conservative; Chair. MIKHAIL M. PRUSAK; 12,086 mems (2001).

Eurasia Political Party of Russia (Politicheskaya Partiya 'Yevraziya'): 117418 Moscow, ul. Novocheremushkinskaya 69; tel. (095) 310-51-72; promotes the re-integration of the Russian Federation with the countries of the CIS; Leader ALEKSANDR G. DUGIN; 10,794 mems (2002).

Liberal Democratic Party of Russia (LDPR) (Liberalno-demokraticheskaya partiya Rossii): 103045 Moscow, Lukov per. 9; tel. (095) 925-07-15; fax (095) 924-08-69; e-mail pressldpr@duma.gov.ru; internet www.ldpr.ru; nationalist; contested 1999 general election as Zhirinovskii bloc; Chair. VLADIMIR V. ZHIRINOVSKII; 19,098 mems (2002).

Liberal Russia (Liberalnaya Rossiya): 103064 Moscow, ul. Zemlyanoi val 4; tel. and fax and fax (095) 722-53-08; e-mail info@librussia.ru; internet librussia.ru; f. 2001; co-founded by fmr Deputy Secretary of the Security Council, and Executive Secretary of the Commonwealth of Independent States, Boris Berezovskii; registered in Oct. 2002, following expulsion of Berezovskii (in exile); a faction of the party voted to re-admit Berezovskii as its leader in Dec. 2002, and to expel the party's co-chairmen, although this vote was not officially recognized by the party or by the Ministry of Justice; Co-Chair. VIKTOR POKHMELKIN, BORIS ZOLOTUKHIN; 11,889 mems (2002).

Party of the Rebirth of Russia (Partiya vozrozhdeniya Rossii): c/o 103625 Moscow, Okhotnyi ryad 1, State Duma; internet seleznev.on.ru/party; f. 2002 on the basis of the Russia (Rossiya) movement; socialist, aims to re-establish Russia as a great power; Leader GENNADII N. SELEZNEV.

People's Party of the Russian Federation (Narodnaya Partiya Rossiiskoi Federatsii): 109017 Moscow, Klimentovskii per. 9/1; f. 2001 on the basis of the People's Deputy movement; Chair. GENNADII N. RAIKOV; 39,293 mems (2002).

Rebirth (Vozrozhdeniye): 117049 Moscow, POB 621; tel. and fax 234-16-18; internet www.vozrod.ru; f. 1991; liberal, nationalist; Chair. YEVGENII P. ISHCHENKO; 20,282 mems (2002).

Russian Communist Workers' Party-Revolutionary Party of Communists (RCWP-RPC) (Rossiiskaya Kommunisticheskaya Rabochaya Partiya-Revolyutsionnaya Partiya Kommunistov—RKRP-RPK): 125167 Moscow, ul. Planetnaya 26/3/70; tel. and fax (095) 155-90-63; e-mail rkrprpk@mail.ru; internet www.rkrp-rpk.ru; f. 2001 by merger; advocates the restoration of a planned socialist economy; the RCWP contested the 1999 legislative election as Communists and Workers of Russia—For the Soviet Union; First Sec. VIKTOR TYULKIN; Chair. of Political Bureau A. V. KRYUCHKOV; 14,056 mems (2002).

Russian Democratic Party—Yabloko (Rossiiskaya Demokraticheskaya Partiya—Yabloko): 119034 Moscow, per. M. Levshinskii 7/3; tel. (095) 201-43-79; fax (095) 292-34-50; e-mail admin@yabloko.ru; internet www.yabloko.ru; f. 1993 on the basis of the Yavlinskii-Boldyrev-Lukin electoral bloc; democratic-centrist; Chair. GRIGORII A. YAVLINSKII; 12,183 mems (2002).

Russian Ecological Party—Greens (Rossiiskaya Ekologicheskaya Partiya—Zelenye): 103045 Moscow, per. Poslednyi 26; Chair. ANATOLII A. PANFILOV; 13,195 mems (2002).

Russian Pensioners' Party (Rossiiskaya Partiya Pensionerov): 101000 Moscow, Sretenskii bulv. 6/1/57; tel. (095) 923-09-42; f. 1998; aims to achieve prosperity, health protection and respect for pensioners; Leader SERGEI P. ATROSHENKO; 18,415 mems (2002).

Social-Democratic Party of Russia (Sotsial-Demokraticheskaya Partiya Rossii): 107066 Moscow, per. Tokmakov 23/1; tel. (095) 921-91-04; fax (095) 923-65-56; Leader MIKHAIL S. GORBACHEV; 12,671 mems (2002).

Union of Rightist Forces (URF) (Soyuz Pravikh Sil—SPS): 109544 Moscow, ul. M. Andronyevskaya 15; tel. (095) 232-04-06; fax (095) 201-26-15; e-mail edit@sps.ru; internet www.sps.ru; f. 1998 as alliance of nine movements, which merged to form one party in 2001; supports moderate pro-market reform; Chair. of the Federal Political Council BORIS YE. NEMTSOV; 14,647 mems (2002).

Unity and Fatherland-United Russia (UF-UR) (Yedinstvo i Otechestvo-Yedinaya Rossiya—YeO-YeR): 129110 Moscow, Bannyi per. 3A; tel. (095) 786-86-78; fax (095) 975-30-78; internet www.edinros.ru; f. 2001 on the basis of Unity (Yedinstvo—f. 1999, incorporating Our Home is Russia—Nash Dom-Rossiya), Fatherland (Otechestvo—f. 1999, and led by Mayor of Moscow Yurii Luzhkov) and the All Russia (Vsya Rossiya) grouping of regional governors; centrist, reformist; supports Govt of Pres. Putin; Chair. of Supreme Council YURII VOLKOV; Chair. of Gen. Council VALERII BOGOMOLOV; 19,579 mems (2001).

Diplomatic Representation

EMBASSIES IN RUSSIA

Afghanistan: 101000 Moscow, Sverchkov per. 3/2; tel. (095) 928-72-78; fax (095) 924-04-78; e-mail afghanem@online.ru; Ambassador AHMAD ZIA MASUD.

Albania: 117049 Moscow, ul. Mytnaya 3/23; tel. (095) 230-77-32; fax (095) 230-76-35; e-mail embassy@cnt.ru; Chargé d'affaires a.i. ALBERT JERASI.

Algeria: 103051 Moscow, Krapivinskii per. 1A; tel. (095) 200-66-42; fax (095) 200-22-22; Ambassador AMAR ABBA.

Angola: 119590 Moscow, ul. U. Palme 6; tel. (095) 923-02-98; fax (095) 956-18-80; e-mail angomosc@garnet.ru; Ambassador ROBERTO LEAL RAMOS MONTEIRO.

Argentina: 119017 Moscow, ul. B. Ordynka 72; tel. (095) 502-10-20; fax (095) 502-10-21; e-mail efrus@co.ru; Ambassador JUAN CARLOS SÁNCHEZ ARNAU.

Armenia: 101000 Moscow, Armyanskii per. 2; tel. (095) 924-12-69; fax (095) 924-45-35; e-mail armembru@df.ru; internet www.armenianembassy.ru; Ambassador ARMEN SMBATIAN.

Australia: 119034 Moscow, Kropotkinskii per. 13; tel. (095) 956-60-70; fax (095) 956-61-70; e-mail austem@comail.ru; internet www.australianembassy.ru; Ambassador LESLIE A. ROWE.

Austria: 119034 Moscow, Starokonyushennyi per. 1; tel. (095) 201-73-79; fax (095) 937-42-69; e-mail moscau-ob@bmaa.qv.at; Ambassador Dr FRANZ CEDE.

Azerbaijan: 103009 Moscow, Leontyevskii per. 16; tel. (095) 229-16-49; fax (095) 202-50-72; e-mail incoming@azembassy.msk.ru; internet azembassy.msk.ru; Ambassador RAMIZ G. RIZAYEV.

Bahrain: 109017 Moscow, ul. B. Ordynka 18/1; tel. (095) 203-00-13; fax (095) 230-24-01; Ambassador TAWFEEQ AHMED KHALIL ALMANSOOR.

Bangladesh: 119121 Moscow, Zemledelcheskii per. 6; tel. (095) 246-79-00; fax (095) 248-31-85; e-mail moscow.bangla@com2com.ru; Ambassador S. K. SHARJIL HASSAN.

Belarus: 101000 Moscow, ul. Maroseika 17/6; tel. (095) 777-66-44; fax (095) 777-66-33; e-mail mail@embassybel.ru; internet www.embassybel.ru; Ambassador VLADIMIR V. GRIGORYEV.

Belgium: 121069 Moscow, ul. M. Molchanovka 7; tel. (095) 937-80-40; fax (095) 937-80-38; e-mail ambabelmos@co.ru; Ambassador ANDRÉ MERNIER.

Benin: 103006 Moscow, Uspenskii per. 7; tel. (095) 299-23-60; fax (095) 200-02-26; e-mail ambabeninmoscou@hotmail.com; Ambassador HUBERT SYLVESTRE DÉGUÉNON.

Bolivia: 119034 Moscow, Lopukhinskii per. 5; tel. (095) 201-25-13; fax (095) 201-25-08; e-mail embolivia-moscu@rree.gov.bo; Chargé d'affaires a.i. RUBÉN VIDAURRE ANDRADE.

Bosnia and Herzegovina: 119590 Moscow, ul. Mosfilmovskaya 50/1/484; tel. (095) 147-64-88; fax (095) 147-64-89; e-mail embassybih@mail.cnt.ru; Ambassador GORDAN MILINIĆ.

Brazil: 121069 Moscow, ul. B. Nikitskaya 54; tel. (095) 363-03-66; fax (095) 363-03-67; e-mail brasrus@brasemb.ru; internet www.brasemb.ru; Ambassador JOSÉ VIEGAS FILHO.

Brunei: 121059 Moscow, Berezhkovskaya nab. 2, Radisson-Slavyanskaya Hotel, kom. 440–441; tel. (095) 941-82-16; fax (095) 941-82-14; e-mail brumos@mosbusiness.ru; Ambassador Dato PADUKA MAHADI bin Haji WASLI.

Bulgaria: 119590 Moscow, ul. Mosfilmovskaya 66; tel. (095) 143-90-22; fax (095) 232-33-02; e-mail bulemrus@bolgaria.ru; internet www.bolgaria.ru; Ambassador ILIYAN VASILEV.

Burundi: 117049 Moscow, Kaluzhskaya pl. 1/226–227; tel. (095) 230-25-64; fax (095) 230-20-09; e-mail bdiam@mail.cnt.ru; Ambassador GERMAIN NKESHIMANA.

Cambodia: 121002 Moscow, Starokonyushennyi per. 16; tel. (095) 201-24-03; fax (095) 956-65-73; e-mail cambodia@mail.cnt.ru; Ambassador ROS KONG.

Cameroon: 121069 Moscow, ul. Povarskaya 40, BP 136; tel. (095) 290-65-49; fax (095) 290-61-16; Ambassador ANDRÉ NGONGANG OUANDJI.

Canada: 121002 Moscow, Starokonyushennyi per. 23; tel. (095) 105-60-00; fax (095) 105-60-25; e-mail mosco@dfait-maeci.gc.ca; Ambassador RODNEY IRWIN.

Cape Verde: 121615 Moscow, Rublevskoye shosse 26/180–181; tel. (095) 415-45-04; fax (095) 415-45-05; e-mail pts287@ipc.ru; Chargé d'affaires HÉRCULES DO NASCIMENTO CRUZ.

Central African Republic: 117571 Moscow, ul. 26-i Bakinskikh Kommissarov 9/124–125; tel. (095) 434-45-20; Ambassador CLAUDE BERNARD BELOUM.

Chad: 121615 Moscow, Rublevskoye shosse 26/1/20–21; tel. (095) 415-41-39; fax (095) 415-29-41; Ambassador DJIBRINE ABDOUL.

Chile: 121002 Moscow, Denezhnii per. 7/1; tel. (095) 241-01-45; fax (095) 241-68-67; e-mail echileru@aha.ru; Ambassador PABLO CABRERA GAETE.

China, People's Republic: 117330 Moscow, ul. Druzhby 6; tel. (095) 938-20-06; fax (095) 938-21-32; e-mail chinaembassy_ru@ fmprc.gov.cn; internet www.chinaembassy.ru; Ambassador ZHANG DEGUANG.

Colombia: 119121 Moscow, ul. Burdenko 20/2; tel. (095) 248-30-42; fax (095) 248-30-25; e-mail emoscu@minrelaxt.gov.co; Ambassador MIGUEL SANTAMARIA DAVILA.

Congo, Democratic Republic: 113556 Moscow, Simferopolskii bulv. 7A/ 49–50; tel. and fax (095) 113-83-48; Chargé d'affaires a.i. SOPHIE MUIKA BAKENGE.

Congo, Republic: 117049 Moscow, ul. Donskaya 18/7; tel. (095) 236-33-68; fax (095) 236-41-16; Ambassador JEAN-PIERRE LOUYEBO.

Costa Rica: 121615 Moscow, Rublevskoye shosse 26/1/23; tel. (095) 415-40-42; fax (095) 415-40-14; e-mail embaric2@rol.ru; Ambassador PLUTARCO HERNÁNDEZ SANCHO.

Côte d'Ivoire: 119034 Moscow, Korobeinikov per. 14/9; tel. (095) 201-24-00; fax (095) 230-20-45; e-mail ambacimow@hotmail.com; Ambassador JEAN-CLAUDE KALOU-DJÈ.

Croatia: 119034 Moscow, per. Korobeinikov 16/10; tel. (095) 201-38-68; fax (095) 201-46-24; e-mail admin@croemba.msk.ru; Chargé d'affaires a.i. MIRKO VLASTELICA.

Cuba: 103009 Moscow, Leontiyevskii per. 9; tel. (095) 290-28-82; fax (095) 202-53-92; e-mail embacuba@online.ru; Ambassador CARLOS PALMAROLA CORDERO.

Cyprus: 121069 Moscow, ul. B. Nikitskaya 51; tel. (095) 290-21-54; fax (095) 200-12-54; e-mail piocypmos@col.ru; Ambassador CHAR-ALOMBOS G. IOANNIDES.

Czech Republic: 123056 Moscow, ul. Yu. Fuchika 12/14; tel. (095) 251-05-40; fax (095) 250-15-23; e-mail moscow@embassy.mzv.cz; internet www.mfa.cz/moscow; Ambassador JAROSLAV BAŠTA.

Denmark: 119034 Moscow, Prechistenskii per. 9; tel. (095) 201-78-68; fax (095) 201-53-57; e-mail mowamb@mowamb.um.dk; internet www.danishembassy.ru; Ambassador LARS VISSING.

Ecuador: 103064 Moscow, Gorokhovskii per. 12; tel. (095) 261-55-44; fax (095) 267-70-79; e-mail mosecua@online.ru; Ambassador XIMENA MARTÍNEZ DE PÉREZ.

Egypt: 121069 Moscow, Kropotkinskii per. 12; tel. (095) 246-30-96; fax (095) 246-10-64; Ambassador RAOUF SAAD.

Equatorial Guinea: 109017 Moscow, Pogorelskii per. 7/1; tel. (095) 953-27-66; fax (095) 953-20-84; Ambassador LUIS OBIANG MENGUE.

Eritrea: 129090 Moscow, ul. Meshchanskaya 17; tel. (095) 971-06-20; fax (095) 971-37-67; Ambassador NAIZGHI KEFLU BAHTA.

Estonia: 103009 Moscow, M. Kislovskii per. 5; tel. (095) 737-36-40; fax (095) 737-36-46; e-mail embassy@estemb.ru; internet www .estemb.ru; Ambassador KARIN YAANI.

Ethiopia: 129041 Moscow, Orlovo-Davydovskii per. 6; tel. (095) 280-16-16; fax (095) 280-66-08; e-mail eth-emb@col.ru; Ambassador ASAMINEW BEDANIE AREGGIE.

Finland: 119034 Moscow, Kropotkinskii per. 15/17; tel. (095) 787-41-74; fax (095) 247-33-80; e-mail sanomat.mos@formin.fi; internet www.finemb-moscow.fi; Ambassador RENÉ NYBERG.

France: 117049 Moscow, ul. B. Yakimanka 45; tel. (095) 937-15-00; fax (095) 937-14-30; e-mail amba@ambafrance.ru; internet www .ambafrance.ru; Ambassador CLAUDE BLANCHEMAISON.

Gabon: 121002 Moscow, Denezhnyi per. 16; tel. (095) 241-00-80; fax (095) 244-06-94; Ambassador BENJAMIN LÉGNONGO-NDUMBA.

Georgia: 121069 Moscow, M. Rzhevskii per. 6; tel. (095) 290-46-57; fax (095) 291-21-36; e-mail ineza@got.mmtel.ru; Ambassador ZURAB I. ABASHIDZE.

Germany: 119285 Moscow, ul. Mosfilmovskaya 56; tel. (095) 937-95-00; fax (095) 938-23-54; e-mail germanmo@aha.ru; internet www .deutschebotschaft-moskau.ru; Ambassador Dr HANS-FRIEDRICH VON PLOETZ.

Ghana: 121069 Moscow, Skatertnyi per. 14; tel. (095) 202-18-71; fax (095) 202-29-41; e-mail embghmos@astelit.ru; Ambassador Maj.-Gen. FRANCIS YAHAYA MAHAMA.

Greece: 103009 Moscow, Leontiyevskii per. 4; tel. (095) 290-14-46; fax (095) 771-65-10; e-mail gremb.mow@mfa.gr; internet www .hellas.ru; Ambassador DIMITRIOS PARASKEVOPOULOS.

Guatemala: 117049 Moscow, ul. Korovyi val 7/92; tel. (095) 238-59-14; fax (095) 238-22-14; e-mail embguarus@online.ru; Ambassador ALFONSO MATTA FAHSEN.

Guinea: 119034 Moscow, Pomerantsev per. 6; tel. (095) 201-36-01; fax (502) 220-21-38; Ambassador Lt-Col AMARA BANGOURA.

Guinea-Bissau: 113556 Moscow, Simferopolskii bulv. 7A /183; tel. and fax (095) 317-95-82; Ambassador ROGERIO ARAUGO ADOLPHO HER-BERT.

Holy See: 127055 Moscow, Vadkovskii per. 7/37 (Apostolic Nuncia-ture); tel. (095) 726-59-30; fax (095) 726-59-32; e-mail nuntius@ cityline.ru; Apostolic Nuncio Most Rev. ANTONIO MENNINI (Titular Archbishop of Ferrento).

Hungary: 119590 Moscow, ul. Mosfilmovskaya 62; tel. (095) 796-93-70; fax (095) 796-93-80; e-mail email@huembmow.macomnet.ru; internet www.huembmow.macomnet.ru; Ambassador Dr FERENC KONTRA.

Iceland: 101000 Moscow, Khlebnyi per. 28; tel. (095) 956-76-05; fax (095) 956-76-12; e-mail icemb.moscow@utn.stjr.is; Ambassador BEN-EDIKT JÓNSSON.

India: 101000 Moscow, ul. Vorontsovo Polye 6/8; tel. (095) 917-40-44; fax (095) 917-42-09; e-mail indianembas@pol.ru; internet www .indianembassy.ru; Ambassador KRISHNAN RAGHUNATH.

Indonesia: 109017 Moscow, ul. Novokuznetskaya 12/14; tel. (095) 951-95-50; fax (095) 230-64-31; e-mail kbrimos@online.ru; Ambas-sador Prof. JOHN ARIO KATILI.

Iran: 117292 Moscow, Pokrovskii bulv. 7; tel. (095) 917-72-82; fax (095) 230-28-97; Ambassador GHOLMREZA SHAFEHEE.

Iraq: 110121 Moscow, ul. Pogodinskaya 12; tel. (095) 246-55-08; fax (095) 230-33-93; e-mail iraqimoscow@yahoo.com; Ambassador ABBAS KHALAF KUNFUD.

Ireland: 129010 Moscow, Grokholskii per. 5; tel. (095) 937-59-11; fax (095) 975-20-66; e-mail ireland@col.ru; Ambassador JAMES A. SHARKEY.

Israel: 113095 Moscow, ul. B. Ordynka 56; tel. (095) 230-67-00; fax (095) 238-13-46; e-mail moscow@israel.org; Ambassador ARKADII MELMAN (designate).

Italy: 121002 Moscow, Denezhnyi per. 5; tel. (095) 796-96-91; fax (095) 253-92-89; e-mail embitaly@ambmosca.ru; internet www .ambmosca.ru; Ambassador GIANFRANCO FACCO BONETTI.

Japan: 103009 Moscow, Kalashnyi per. 12; tel. (095) 291-85-00; fax (095) 200-12-40; e-mail embjapan@mail.cnt.ru; internet www .embjapan.ru; Ambassador ISSEI NOMURA.

Jordan: 103001 Moscow, Mamonovskii per. 3; tel. (095) 299-43-44; fax (095) 299-43-54; Ambassador AHMAD ALI AL-MUBAYDEEN.

Kazakhstan: 101000 Moscow, Chistoprudnyi bulv. 3A; tel. (095) 927-17-15; fax (095) 208-26-50; e-mail kazembassy@kazembassy.ru; internet www.kazembassy.ru; Ambassador ALTYNBEK SARSENBAIULY.

Kenya: 101000 Moscow, ul. B. Ordynka 70; tel. (095) 237-47-02; fax (095) 230-23-40; e-mail kenya@cityline.ru; Ambassador Dr MESHAK G. NYAMBATI.

Korea, Democratic People's Republic: 107140 Moscow, ul. Mos-filmovskaya 72; tel. (095) 143-62-49; fax (095) 143-63-12; Ambas-sador PAK HUI CHUN.

Korea, Republic: 131000 Moscow, ul. Spiridonovka 14; tel. (095) 956-14-74; fax (095) 956-24-34; e-mail info@koreamb.ru; Ambas-sador CHONG TAE-IK.

Kuwait: 119285 Moscow, ul. Mosfilmovskaya 44; tel. (095) 147-00-40; fax (095) 956-60-32; Ambassador MOHAMMED SAAD UDAHA AL-SALLAL.

Kyrgyzstan: 109017 Moscow, ul. B. Ordynka 64; tel. (095) 237-48-82; fax (095) 237-44-52; Ambassador KEMELBEK NANAYEV.

Laos: 131940 Moscow, ul. M. Nikitskaya 18; tel. (095) 290-25-60; fax (095) 290-49-24; Chargé d'affaires a.i. SODOM PHETRASY.

Latvia: 103062 Moscow, ul. Chaplygina 3; tel. (095) 925-27-07; fax (095) 923-92-95; e-mail embassy.russia@mfa.gov.lv; Ambassador NORMANS PENKE.

Lebanon: 103051 Moscow, ul. Sadovaya-Samotechnaya 14; tel. (095) 200-00-22; fax (095) 200-32-22; Ambassador BOUTROS ASSAKER.

Libya: 131940 Moscow, ul. Mosfilmovskaya 38; tel. (095) 143-03-54; fax (095) 938-21-62; Secretary of Peoples' Bureau (Ambassador) SALLEH ABDALLAH SALLEH.

Lithuania: 121069 Moscow, Borisoglebskii per. 10; tel. (095) 785-86-05; fax (095) 785-86-00; e-mail ltemb@ltembassy.ru; internet amb .urm.lt/rusija; Ambassador RIMANTAS ŠIDLAUSKAS.

Luxembourg: 119034 Moscow, Khrushchevskii per. 3; tel. (095) 202-53-81; fax (095) 200-52-43; e-mail amb.amluxru@lbg.ru; Ambas-sador CAMILLE WEIS.

Macedonia, former Yugoslav republic: 117292 Moscow, ul. D. Ulyanova 16/2/509–510; tel. (095) 124-33-57; fax (095) 124-33-59; e-mail mkambmos@mail.tascom.ru; Ambassador DIMITAR DIMITROV.

Madagascar: 119034 Moscow, Kursovoi per. 5; tel. (095) 290-02-14; fax (095) 202-34-53; Ambassador ELOI MAXIME DOVO.

Malaysia: 117192 Moscow, ul. Mosfilmovskaya 50; tel. (095) 147-15-14; fax (095) 937-96-02; e-mail mwmoscow@co.ru; Ambassador Dato KAMARUDDIN MUSTAFA.

Mali: 113184 Moscow, ul. Novokuznetskaya 11; tel. (095) 951-06-55; fax (095) 230-28-89; e-mail amalirus@orc.ru; Ambassador (vacant).

Malta: 117049 Moscow, ul. Korovyi val 7/219; tel. (095) 237-19-39; fax (095) 237-21-58; e-mail maltamsk@online.ru; Ambassador Dr JOSEPH CASSAR.

Mauritania: 109017 Moscow, ul. B. Ordynka 66; tel. (095) 237-37-92; fax (095) 237-28-61; e-mail embarim@hotmail.com; Ambassador MOHAMMAD MAHMOUD OULD MOHAMMAD VALL.

Mexico: 119034 Moscow, B. Levshinskii per. 4; tel. (095) 201-48-48; fax (095) 230-20-42; e-mail embmxru@online.ru; Ambassador LUCIANO EDUARDO JOUBLANC MONTAÑO.

Moldova: 103031 Moscow, ul. Kuznetskii most 18; tel. (095) 924-53-53; fax (095) 924-95-90; e-mail moldemb@online.ru; internet www .moldova.ru; Ambassador VLADIMIR TSURCAN.

Mongolia: 121069 Moscow, Borisoglebskii per. 11; tel. (095) 290-67-92; fax (095) 291-46-36; e-mail mongolia@online.ru; Ambassador SANJAA BAYAR.

Morocco: 119034 Moscow, Prechistenskii per. 8; tel. (095) 201-73-51; fax (095) 230-20-67; e-mail sifmamos@df.ru; Ambassador ABDEL-MALEK EL-JEDDAOUI.

Mozambique: 129090 Moscow, ul. Gilyarovskogo 20; tel. (095) 284-40-07; fax (095) 200-42-35; e-mail embamocru@netscape.ru; Ambassador GREGÓRIO ELTON PAULO LINGANDE.

Myanmar: 121069 Moscow, ul. B. Nikitskaya 41; tel. (095) 291-05-34; fax (095) 956-31-86; e-mail mofa.aung@mptmail.net.mm; Ambassador U TIN SOE.

Namibia: 113096 Moscow, 2-i Kazachii per. 7; tel. (095) 230-01-13; fax (095) 230-22-74; e-mail namibembrf@glasnet.ru; Ambassador MARTEN N. KAPEWASHA.

Nepal: 119121 Moscow, 2-i Neopalimovskii per. 14/7; tel. (095) 244-02-15; fax (095) 244-00-00; e-mail nepal@orc.ru; Ambassador LILA PRASAD SHARMA.

Netherlands: 103009 Moscow, Kalashnyi per. 6; tel. (095) 797-29-00; fax (095) 797-29-04; e-mail nederl@sovintel.ru; internet www .netherlands.ru; Ambassador TIDDO P. HOFSTEE.

New Zealand: 121069 Moscow, ul. Povarskaya 44; tel. (095) 956-35-79; fax (095) 956-35-83; e-mail nzembmos@online.ru; internet www .nzembassy.msk.ru; Ambassador GEOFF K. WARD.

Nicaragua: 117192 Moscow, ul. Mosfilmovskaya 50/1; tel. (095) 938-20-82; fax (095) 938-27-01; e-mail embanic_moscu@mail.ru; Ambassador CARLOS IVÁN OTERO CASTAÑEDA.

Nigeria: 121069 Moscow, ul. M. Nikitskaya 13; tel. (095) 290-37-83; fax (095) 956-28-25; e-mail nigeriamosco@glasnet.ru; internet www .nigerianembassy-moscow.ru/; Ambassador Maj.-Gen. (retd) ABDUL-LAHI SARKI MUKHTAR.

Norway: 131940 Moscow, ul. Povarskaya 7; tel. (095) 933-14-10; fax (095) 933-14-11; e-mail emb.moscow@mfa.no; internet www .norvegia.ru; Ambassador ØYVIND NORDSLETTEN.

Oman: 109180 Moscow, Staromonetnii per. 14/1; tel. (095) 230-15-87; fax (095) 230-15-44; e-mail amoman@ipc.ru; Ambassador MUHAMMAD BIN SAID BIN MUHAMMAD AL-LAWATI.

Pakistan: 103001 Moscow, ul. Sadovaya-Kudrinskaya 17; tel. (095) 254-97-91; fax (095) 956-90-97; e-mail chancery@interanet.ru; Ambassador S. IFTIKHAR MURSHED.

Panama: 119590 Moscow, ul. Mosfilmovskaya 50/1; tel. (095) 956-07-29; fax (095) 956-07-30; e-mail empanrus@aha.ru; Ambassador HARRY ALBERTO DÍAZ STRUNZ.

Peru: 121002 Moscow, Smolenskii bulv. 22/14/15; tel. (095) 248-77-38; fax (095) 230-20-00; e-mail leprumoscu@mtu-net.ru; Ambassador Dr PABLO HUGO PORTUGAL RODRIGUEZ.

Philippines: 121099 Moscow, Karmanitskii per. 6; tel. (095) 241-05-63; fax (095) 241-26-30; e-mail moscowpe@co.ru; internet phil_embassy_moscow.tripod.com; Ambassador Dr JAIME S. BAUTISTA.

Poland: 123557 Moscow, ul. Klimashkina 4; tel. (095) 231-15-00; fax (095) 231-15-15; e-mail pol.amb@g23.relcom.ru; Ambassador STEFAN MELLER.

Portugal: 129010 Moscow, Botanicheskii per. 1; tel. (095) 280-62-68; fax (095) 280-92-03; e-mail embptrus@deltacom.ru; Ambassador JOÃO DIOGO NUNES BARATA.

Qatar: 117049 Moscow, ul. Korovyi val 7/196–198; tel. (095) 230-15-77; fax (095) 230-22-40; e-mail moscow@mofa.gov.qa; Ambassador SHAMLAN MARZOUQ AL-SHAMLAM.

Romania: 101000 Moscow, ul. Mosfilmovskaya 64; tel. (095) 143-04-24; fax (095) 143-04-49; e-mail bucur@dol.ru; Ambassador AUREL CONSTANTIN ILIE.

Saudi Arabia: 119121 Moscow, 3-i Neopalimovskii per. 3; tel. (095) 245-39-70; fax (095) 246-94-71; Ambassador MOHAMED H. ABDULWALI.

Serbia and Montenegro: 119285 Moscow, ul. Mosfilmovskaya 46; tel. (095) 147-41-06; fax (095) 147-41-04; e-mail ambasada@co.ru; Ambassador DANILO VUKSANOVIĆ.

Sierra Leone: 121615 Moscow, Rublevskoye shosse 26/1/58–59; tel. (095) 415-41-66; fax (095) 415-29-85; Ambassador MELROSE BEYON KAI-BANYA.

Singapore: 121099 Moscow, per. Kamennoi Slobody 5; tel. (095) 241-37-02; fax (095) 241-78-95; e-mail sinemb@online.ru; Chargé d'affaires a.i. CHRISTOPHER CHEANG.

Slovakia: 123056 Moscow, ul. Yu. Fuchika 17/19; tel. (095) 250-10-70; fax (095) 973-20-81; e-mail skem@col.ru; Ambassador IGOR FURDIK.

Slovenia: 103006 Moscow, ul. M. Dmitrovka 14/1; tel. (095) 209-02-03; fax (095) 200-15-68; e-mail vmo@mzz-dkp.sigov.si; internet www .gov.si/mzz/vmo; Ambassador Dr FRANCI DEMŠAR.

Somalia: 121248 Moscow, Simferopolskii bulv. 7A /145; tel. and fax (095) 317-06-22; Chargé d'affaires a.i. MAYE MAO DERE.

South Africa: 113054 Moscow, B. Strochenovskii per. 22/25; tel. (095) 230-68-69; fax (095) 230-68-65; e-mail info@saembassy.ru; internet saembassy.ru; Ambassador Dr MOCHUBELA JACOB SEEKOE.

Spain: 121069 Moscow, ul. B. Nikitskaya 50/8; tel. (095) 202-21-61; fax (095) 291-91-71; e-mail ispan@aha.ru; internet www.ispania.aha .ru; Ambassador JOSÉ MARIA ROBLES FRAGA.

Sri Lanka: 129090 Moscow, ul. Shchepkina 24; tel. (095) 288-16-20; fax (095) 288-17-57; e-mail lankaemb@com2com.ru; Ambassador N. SIKKANDER.

Sudan: 103006 Moscow, Uspenskii per. 9; tel. (095) 290-33-13; fax (095) 290-39-85; e-mail sudy@com2com.ru; Ambassador Dr IBRAHIM AL-BASHIR OSMAN AL-KABASHI.

Sweden: 119590 Moscow, ul. Mosfilmovskaya 60; tel. (095) 937-92-00; fax (095) 937-92-02; e-mail sweden@aha.ru; internet www .sweden.ru; Ambassador SVEN HIRDMAN.

Switzerland: 100100 Moscow, per. Ogorodnoi Slobody 2/5; tel. (095) 258-38-30; fax (095) 200-17-28; e-mail swiss.embassy@g23.relcom .ru; internet www.eda.admin.ch/moscow_emb/e/home.html; Ambassador WALTER FETSCHERIN.

Syria: 119034 Moscow, Mansurovskii per. 4; tel. (095) 203-15-21; fax (095) 956-31-91; Ambassador WAHIB AL-FADEL.

Tajikistan: 103001 Moscow, Granatnyi per. 13; tel. (095) 290-38-46; fax (095) 291-89-98; e-mail tajikistan@tajikistan.ru; internet www .tajikistan.ru; Ambassador SAFAR G. SAFAROV.

Tanzania: 109017 Moscow, ul. Pyatnitskaya 33; tel. (095) 953-82-21; fax (095) 956-61-30; e-mail tzmos@wm.west.call.com; Ambassador EVA LILIAN NZARO.

Thailand: 129090 Moscow, ul. B. Spasskaya 9; tel. (095) 208-08-17; fax (095) 207-53-43; e-mail thaiemb@nnt.ru; Ambassador SORAYOUTH PROMPOJ.

Tunisia: 113105 Moscow, ul. M. Nikitskaya 28/1; tel. (095) 291-28-58; fax (095) 291-75-88; Ambassador KHALIFA EL HAFDHI.

Turkey: 119121 Moscow, 7-i Rostovskii per. 12; tel. (095) 246-00-09; fax (095) 245-63-48; e-mail turemb@dol.ru; internet www .turkishline.ru/embassy; Ambassador KURTULUS TASKENT.

Turkmenistan: 121019 Moscow, Filippovskii per. 22; tel. (095) 291-66-36; fax (095) 291-09-35; Ambassador KHALNAZAR A. AGAKHANOV.

Ukraine: 103009 Moscow, Leontiyevskii per. 18; tel. (095) 229-10-79; fax (095) 924-84-69; e-mail ukremb@online.ru; Ambassador MYKOLA P. BILOBLOTSKIY.

United Arab Emirates: 101000 Moscow, ul. U. Palme 4; tel. (095) 147-00-66; fax (095) 234-40-70; e-mail uae@mail.cnt.ru; Ambassador TARIQ AHMED AL-HAIDAN.

United Kingdom: 121099 Moscow, Smolenskaya nab. 10; tel. (095) 956-72-00; fax (095) 956-72-01; e-mail moscow@britishembassy.ru; internet www.britemb.msk.ru; Ambassador Sir RODERIC LYNE.

USA: 121099 Moscow, B. Devyatinskii per. 8; tel. (095) 728-50-00; fax (095) 728-50-90; e-mail pamoscow@pd.state.gov; internet www .usembassy.ru; Ambassador ALEXANDER R. VERSHBOW.

Uruguay: 117330 Moscow, Lomonosovskii pr. 38; tel. (095) 143-04-01; fax (095) 938-20-45; e-mail ururus.embajada@mtu-net.ru; Ambassador ALBERTO LEOPOLDO FAJARDO KLAPPENBACH.

Uzbekistan: 109017 Moscow, Pogorelskii per. 12; tel. (095) 230-75-52; fax (095) 238-89-18; Ambassador SHAKASYM I. SHAISLAMOV.

Venezuela: 103051 Moscow, B. Karetnyi per. 13/15; tel. (095) 299-40-42; fax (095) 956-61-08; e-mail karakas@mail.cnt.ru; Ambassador PAULINO PAREDES.

Viet Nam: 119021 Moscow, ul. B. Pirogovskaya 13; tel. (095) 247-02-12; fax (095) 245-10-92; e-mail dsqvn@com2com.ru; Ambassador NYUGEN VAN NGANG.

Yemen: 119121 Moscow, 2-i Neopalimovskii per. 6; tel. (095) 246-15-40; fax (095) 230-23-05; Ambassador ABDO ALI ABDULRAHMAN.

Zambia: 129041 Moscow, pr. Mira 52A; tel. (095) 288-50-01; fax (095) 975-20-56; Ambassador Prof. LYSON POTIPHER TEMBO.

Zimbabwe: 119121 Moscow, per. Serpov 6; tel. (095) 248-43-67; fax (095) 230-24-97; e-mail zimbabwe@rinet.ru; Ambassador Brig. (retd) AGRIPPAH MUTAMBARA.

Judicial System

In January 1995 the first section of a new code of civil law came into effect. It included new rules on commercial and financial operations, and on ownership issues. The second part of the code was published in January 1996. The Constitutional Court rules on the conformity of government policies, federal laws, international treaties and presidential enactments with the Constitution. Following its suspension in October 1993, the Court was reinstated, with a new membership of 19 judges, in April 1995. The Supreme Arbitration Court rules on disputes between commercial bodies. The Supreme Court oversees all criminal and civil law, and is the final court of appeal from lower courts. A system of Justices of the Peace, to deal with certain civil cases, and with criminal cases punishable by a maximum of two years' imprisonment, was established in 1998. In December 2001 President Putin approved several reforms to the judicial system, including the introduction of trials by jury across the Russian Federation, and procedures to guarantee the independence of judges, which were to be implemented from 2003.

Constitutional Court of the Russian Federation: 103132 Moscow, ul. Ilinka 21; tel. (095) 206-16-72; fax (095) 206-19-78; e-mail ksrf@ksmail.rfnet.ru; internet ks.rfnet.ru; f. 1991; Chair. VALERII D. ZORKIN; Dep. Chair. VLADIMIR G. STREKOZOV; Sec.-Gen. YURII V. KUDZYAVTSEV.

Office of the Prosecutor-General: 103793 Moscow, ul. B. Dmitrovka 15A; tel. (095) 292-88-69; fax (095) 292-88-48; Prosecutor-General VLADIMIR V. USTINOV; Dep. Prosecutor-General VLADIMIR KOLESNIKOV.

Supreme Arbitration Court of the Russian Federation: 101000 Moscow, M. Kharitonevskii per. 12; tel. (095) 208-11-19; fax (095) 208-11-62; internet www.arbitr.ru; f. 1993; Chair. VENYAMIN F. YAKOVLEV.

Supreme Court of the Russian Federation: 103289 Moscow, ul. Ilinka 7/3; tel. (095) 924-23-47; fax (095) 202-71-18; e-mail gastello@ilinka.supcourt.ru; internet www.supcourt.ru; Chair. VYACHESLAV M. LEBEDEV.

Religion

The majority of the population of the Russian Federation are adherents of Christianity, but there are significant Islamic, Buddhist and Jewish minorities.

In September 1997 legislation concerning the regulation of religious organizations was approved, whereby only those religious groups able to prove that they had been established in Russia for a minimum of 15 years were to be permitted to operate. Russian Orthodoxy, Islam, Buddhism and Judaism, together with some other Christian denominations, were deemed to comply with the legislation. Religious organizations failing to satisfy this requirement were, henceforth, obliged to register annually for 15 years, before being permitted to publish literature, hold public services or invite foreign preachers into Russia. Moreover, foreign religious groups were additionally obliged to affiliate themselves to Russian organizations in order to be able to carry out their activities in Russia. An extension of this law, announced in August 1998, decreed that foreign religious workers were permitted to remain in Russia for a maximum of three months per visit. In March 2000 President Putin signed a decree that required all non-registered religious groups to be dissolved by the end of the year; however neither this decree nor the legislation passed in 1997 was applied consistently across the Russian Federation, and some constituent regions introduced legislation that was more restrictive than the 1997 law.

CHRISTIANITY

The Russian Orthodox Church (Moscow Patriatchate)

The Russian Orthodox Church (Moscow Patriarchate) is the dominant religious organization in the Russian Federation, with an estimated 75m. adherents. In 2001 there were 128 dioceses, some 19,000 communities and 480 monasteries. There were also five theological academies and 26 seminaries in Russia. In 1988–2001 more than 12,000 churches were established or returned to religious use. The Patriarchate's jurisdiction is challenged by the Russian Orthodox Church Abroad (operating in Russia as the Free Russian Orthodox Church), the jurisdiction of which was established in 1921 in Yugoslavia and which primarily operated in the USA, rejecting the canonical legitimacy of the Moscow Patriarchate. It re-established operations in Russia after 1988.

The Russian Orthodox Church (Moscow Patriarchate) is governed by the Holy Synod, consisting of six bishops (permanent members), the Patriarch, and several temporary member bishops. The supreme ruling organ of the Church is the Local Synod, which comprises representatives of bishops, clergy, monks and laity and convenes once every five years.

Moscow Patriarchate: 115191 Moscow, Danilov Monastery, ul. Danilovskii val 22; tel. (095) 230-24-39; fax (095) 230-26-19; e-mail commserv@mospat.dol.ru; internet www.russian-orthodox-church.org.ru; Patriarch of Moscow and all Rus ALEKSEI II (Ridiger).

The Roman Catholic Church

At 31 December 1999 there were an estimated 300,000 Roman Catholics in European Russia and 1,050,200 in Siberia. In 1991 administrative structures of the Roman Catholic Church in Russia were restored, with the establishment of two apostolic administratures for European Russia and Siberia, respectively. In 1999 each administrature was sub-divided, establishing two additional administratures. In February 2002 the administratures were replaced by four dioceses, the Diocese of the Mother of God at Moscow, of St Clement at Saratov, of the Transfiguration at Novosibirsk, and of St Joseph at Irkutsk.

Bishops' Conference

107078 Moscow, POB 116, ul. Novaya Basmannaya 16/31; tel. and fax (095) 261-67-14; e-mail peterpaul@starnet.ru.

Pres. Most. Rev. TADEUSZ KONDRUSIEWICZ (Archbishop of the Diocese of the Mother of God at Moscow).

Archbishop of the Diocese of the Mother of God at Moscow: Most Rev. TADEUSZ KONDRUSIEWICZ, 107078 Moscow, POB 116, ul. Novaya Basmannaya 16/31; tel. and fax (095) 261-67-14; e-mail cathmos@dol.ru; internet www.catholic.ru.

Protestant Churches

Euro-Asiatic Federation of the Union of Evangelical Christians-Baptists: 109028 Moscow, Trekhsvyatitelnyi per. 3; tel. (095) 227-39-90; fax (095) 975-23-67; e-mail moderator@baptist.org.ru; internet baptist.org.ru; 231 communities, 16,530 adherents in the Russian Federation and other former republics of the USSR (2000); Pres. GRIGORII I. KOMENDANT.

Russian Union of Evangelical Christians-Baptists: 109028 Moscow, ul. M. Trekhsvyatitelskii 3; tel. (095) 985-13-36; fax (095) 954-92-31; e-mail ecb@hotbox.ru; internet ecb.hotbox.ru; 1,380 communities and 85,000 adherents (2001); Pres. PETR B. KONOVALCHIK.

Russian Union of Christians of the Evangelical Faith—Pentecostalists ('Pyatidesyatnikov'): 123363 Moscow, ul. Fabritsiusa 31A; tel. and fax (095) 493-15-41; e-mail pentecostalunion@mtu-net.ru; internet www.pentecostalunion.ru; f. 1907, re-established 1990; 1,350 parishes and more than 300,000 adherents in 2001; Chair. Dr PAVEL N. OKARA.

Other Christian Churches

Armenian Apostolic Church: 123022 Moscow, ul. S. Makeyeva 10; tel. (095) 255-50-19.

Russian Autonomous Orthodox Church: 125212 Moscow, Church of the New Martyrs and Confessors of Russia, Golovinskoye shosse 13A; tel. (095) 152-50-76; formally established in 1990 by separation from the Moscow Patriarchate; 100 parishes in 2001; First Hierarch Metropolitan of Suzdal and Vladimir VALENTIN (Rusantsov).

Old Believers (The Old Ritualists): 109052 Moscow, ul. Rogozhskii pos. 29; tel. (095) 361-51-92; e-mail tarasburnos@mail.ru; internet www.staroobryad.narod.ru; f. 1652 by separation from the Moscow Patriarchate; divided into two main branches: the *popovtsi* (which have priests) and the *bespopovtsi* (which reject the notion of ordained priests and the use of all sacraments, other than that of baptism). Both branches are further divided into various groupings. The largest group of *popovtsi* are those of the Belokrinitskii Concord, under the Metropolitan of Moscow and All-Rus ALIMPYI, (ALEKSANDR K. GUSEV); c. 120 parishes, four bishops in Russia, Ukraine and Moldova; a further significant group of *popovtsi* Old Believers are those of the Beglopopovtsyi Concord, under the Archbishop of Novozybkov, Moscow and All Rus (AFANASII KALININ).

ISLAM

Most Muslims in the Russian Federation are adherents of the Sunni sect. Islam is the predominant religion among many peoples of the North Caucasus, such as the Chechens, the Ingush and many smaller groups, and also in the Central Volga region, among them the Tatars, Chuvash and Bashkirs. In 2000 there were some 7,000 mosques in Russia, and there were estimated to be between 19m. and 20m. Muslims in Russia in 2001.

Central Muslim Spiritual Board for Russia and European Countries of the CIS: 450057 Bashkortostan, Ufa, ul. Tukaya 50; tel. (3472) 50-80-86; e-mail rdumpo@permonline.ru; internet muslim-board.narod.ru; f. 1789; 27 regional branches in the Russian Federation, and one branch in Ukraine; Chair. Mufti Sheikh-ul Islam Talgat-Khozrat Tadzhuddin.

Council of Muftis of Russia: 129090 Moscow, per. Vypolzov 7; tel. and fax (095) 281-49-04; Chair. Mufti Sheikh Ravil Khazrat Gainutdin.

JUDAISM

At the beginning of the 20th century approximately one-half of the world's Jews lived in the Russian Empire (primarily in those regions that form part of present-day Ukraine, Belarus, Moldova and Lithuania). Although many Jews emigrated from the USSR in the 1970s and 1980s, there is still a significant Jewish population (400,000 at the end of 1998) in the Russian Federation, particularly in the larger cities. There are a small number of Jews (accounting for less than 4% of the population) in the Jewish Autonomous Oblast, in the Far East of the Russian Federation, which was established in the 1920s. There is an Orthodox Jewish Seminary (yeshiva) in Moscow. In the Jewish Autonomous Oblast Yiddish has the status of an official language; however, the first permanent appointment of a Rabbi in the oblast took place only in mid-2001.

Congress of Jewish Religious Communities and Organizations of Russia: 101000 Moscow, B. Spaso Glinishevskii per. 8, Moscow Choral Synagogue; tel. (095) 924-24-24; fax (095) 956-75-40; e-mail synrus@corbina.ru; f. 1996; co-ordinates activities of 120 Jewish communities throughout Russia; Chief Rabbi Adolf Shayevich; Dir Zinovy Kogan.

Federation of the Jewish Communities of the CIS: 103055 Moscow, ul. 2-i Vysheslaytzev per. 5a; tel. (095) 281-45-23; fax (095) 281-26-72; e-mail office@fjc.ru; internet www.jewish.ru/fjcnews.asp; f. 1999; Exec. Dir Avraham Berkovitz; Chair. Lev Leviyev.

Federation of the Jewish Communities of Russia: 103055 Moscow, ul. 2-i Vysheslaytzev per. 5a; tel. (095) 281-45-23; fax (095) 281-26-72; e-mail russia@fjc.ru; internet www.fjc.ru/russiafr.htm; unites 130 communities in Russia; Chief Rabbi of Russia, Chair. of Rabbinical Alliance of Russia and the CIS Berel Lazar.

Russian Jewish Congress: 121265 Moscow, ul. Novyi Arbat 36; tel. (095) 290-81-02; fax (095) 290-80-47; e-mail rjc@rjc.ru; internet www.rjc.ru; Pres. Yevgenii Satanovskii.

BUDDHISM

Buddhism (established as an official religion in Russia in 1741) is most widespread in the Republic of Buryatiya, where the Central Spiritual Department of Buddhists of Russia has its seat, the Republics of Kalmykiya and Tyva and in the Irkutsk and Chita Oblasts. There are also newly established communities in Moscow and St Petersburg. Before 1917 there were more than 40 datsans (monasteries) in Buryatiya, but in 1990 only two of these remained in use. By December 1999 19 datsans had been built or restored. There were believed to be 1m. Buddhists in Russia in 1997.

Central Spiritual Department of Buddhists: 670000 Buryatiya, Ulan-Ude, Ivolginskii datsan; Chair. Lama Nimazhap Ilyukhinov.

Representative of the Central Spiritual Department of Buddhists: 119034 Moscow, ul. Ostozhenka 49; tel. (095) 245-09-39.

BAHÁ'Í FAITH

National Office of the Bahá'ís of Russia: 129515 Moscow, POB 55; tel. (095) 956-24-96; e-mail secretariat@bahai.ru; internet www.bahai.ru; over 3,500 adherents in more than 400 locations.

The Press

In 1999 there were 15,836 officially registered newspaper titles published in the Russian Federation. There were also 7,577 periodicals. Almost all newspapers and periodicals suffered a sharp decrease in circulation in the early 1990s. Despite having lost over 25m. subscribers, *Argumenty i Fakty* remained the best-selling Russian weekly newspaper in 1998, while in 2001 *Moskovskii Komsomolets* and *Komsomolskaya Pravda* were the most popular dailies.

Russian Federation Press Committee: 101409 Moscow, Strastnoi bulv. 5; tel. (095) 229-33-53; fax (095) 200-22-81; e-mail komitet@presscom.ru; f. 1993 to replace the Ministry of Press and Information and the Federal Information Centre of Russia; central organ of federal executive power; Chair. Ivan D. Laptev.

PRINCIPAL NEWSPAPERS

Moscow

Argumenty i Fakty (Arguments and Facts): 101000 Moscow, ul. Myasnitskaya 42; tel. (095) 923-35-41; fax (095) 925-61-82; e-mail n-boris@aif.ru; internet www.aif.ru; f. 1978; weekly; Editor Vladislav A. Starkov; circ. 2,880,000 (2000).

Izvestiya (News): 101999 Moscow, ul. Tverskaya 18/1. POB 9; tel. (095) 209-05-81; fax (095) 209-36-20; e-mail info@izvestia.ru; internet www.izvestia.ru; f. 1917; owned by Prof-Mediya; Editor-in-Chief Mikhail Kozhokin; circ. 263,250 (2001).

Kommersant (Businessman): 125080 Moscow, ul. Vrubelya 4/1; tel. (095) 943-97-71; fax (095) 195-96-36; e-mail kommersant@kommersant.ru; internet www.kommersant.ru; f. 1989; daily; Editor Andrei Vasiliyev; circ. 117,340 (2002).

Komsomolskaya Pravda (Young Communist League Truth): 125866 Moscow, ul. Pravdy 24, POB A-137; tel. (095) 257-51-39; fax (095) 200-22-93; e-mail kp@kp.ru; internet www.kp.ru; f. 1925; fmrly organ of the Lenin Young Communist League (Komsomol); independent; weekly supplements *KP-Tolstushka* (KP-Fat volume), *KP-Ponedelnik* (KP-Monday); managed by Prof-Mediya; Editor Vladimir Sungorkin; circ.785,000 (2000).

Konservator (The Conservative): 109240 Moscow, ul. Goncharnaya 1; tel. (095) 915-28-07; fax (095) 915-70-40; e-mail egk@egk.ru; internet www.egk.ru; f. 2002 to replace *Obshchaya Gazeta*; weekly; Pres.and Editor-in-Chief Vyacheslav Leibman.

Krasnaya Zvezda (Red Star): 123007 Moscow, Khoroshevskoye shosse 38; tel. (095) 941-21-58; fax (095) 941-40-66; e-mail redstar@mail.cnt.ru; internet www.redstar.ru; f. 1924; organ of the Ministry of Defence; Editor N. N. Yefimov; circ. 80,000 (2000).

Krestyanskaya Rossiya (Peasant Russia): 123022 Moscow, ul. 1905 Goda 7; tel. and fax (095) 259-41-49; weekly; f. 1906; Editor-in-Chief Konstantin Lysenko; circ. 94,000 (2000).

Megapolis-Ekspress (Megalopolis-Express): 113184 Moscow, ul. B. Tatarskaya 29; tel. (095) 953-50-40; fax (095) 959-08-61; e-mail megapol@megapolis.garnet.ru; f. 1990; weekly; popular; Editor Lev Kulakov; circ. 500,000.

Moskovskaya Pravda (The Moscow Truth): 123846 Moscow, ul. 1905 Goda 7, POB D-22; tel. (095) 259-82-33; fax (095) 259-63-60; e-mail newspaper@mospravda.ru; internet www.mospravda.ru; f. 1918; fmrly organ of the Moscow city committee of the CPSU and the Moscow City Council; 5 a week; independent; Editor Shod S. Muladzhanov; circ. 325,000 (2000).

Moskovskii Komsomolets (The Moscow Young Communist): 123995 Moscow, ul. 1905 Goda 7; tel. (095) 259-50-36; fax (095) 259-46-39; e-mail letters@mk.ru; internet www.mk.ru; f. 1919; 6 a week; independent; Editor-in-Chief Pavel Gusev; circ. 800,000 (2001), the largest circulation of any daily newspaper in Russia; also *MK-Voskresenye* (Sundays); Editor-in-Chief Pavel Gusev.

Moskovskiye Novosti (The Moscow News): 103829 Moscow, ul. Tverskaya 16/2; tel. (095) 200-07-67; fax (095) 209-17-28; e-mail info@mn.ru; internet www.mn.ru; f. 1930; weekly; in English and in Russian; independent; Editor-in-Chief Viktor Loshak; circ. 118,000 in Russian, 40,000 in English (2000).

Moscow Times: 125212 Moscow, ul. Vyborgskaya 16/4; tel. (095) 937-33-99; fax (095) 937-33-93; e-mail webeditor@imedia.ru; internet www.themoscowtimes.com; f. 1992; daily; in English; independent; Publr Stephan Grootenboer; Editor Lynn Berry.

Nezavisimaya Gazeta (NG) (The Independent): 101000 Moscow, ul. Myasnitskaya 13; tel. (095) 928-48-50; fax (095) 975-23-46; e-mail info@ng.ru; internet www.ng.ru; f. 1990; 5 a week; regular supplements include *NG-Nauka* (NG-Science), *NG-Regiony* (NG-Regions), *NG-Politekonomiya* (NG-Political Economy), *NG-Dipkuryer* (NG-Diplomatic Courier); Gen. Man. Rustam Narzikulov; Editor-in-Chief Tatiana Koshkareva; circ. 50,000 (2001).

Novaya Gazeta (New Newspaper): 101000 Moscow, Potapovskii per. 3; tel. (095) 921-57-39; fax (095) 923-68-88; e-mail gazeta@novayagazeta.ru; internet www.novayagazeta.ru; f. 1993; weekly; Editor Dmitrii A. Muratov; circ. 670,000 (2001).

Parlamentskaya Gazeta (Parliamentary Newspaper): 125190 Moscow, ul. Pravdy 24; tel. (095) 257-50-90; fax (095) 257-50-82; e-mail pg@pnp.ru; internet www.pnp.ru; f. 1998; 5 a week; organ of the Federal Assembly of the Russian Federation; Editor-in-Chief Leonid P. Kravchenko; circ. 55,000 (2001).

Pravda (Truth): 125867 Moscow, ul. Pravdy 24; tel. (095) 257-31-00; fax (095) 251-26-97; e-mail pravda@cnt.ru; internet www.gazeta-pravda.ru; f. 1912; fmrly organ of the Cen. Cttee of the CPSU; independent; communist; Editor-in-Chief ALEKSANDR ILYIN; circ. 70,200 (2001).

Pravda.ru: Moscow; e-mail post@pravda.ru; internet pravda.ru; f. 1999; online only, in Russian, English and Portuguese; has no asscn with the newspaper *Pravda*; Editor-in-Chief VADIM V. GORSHENIN.

Rossiiskaya Gazeta (Russian Newspaper): 125881 Moscow, ul. Pravdy 24; tel. (095) 257-52-52; fax (095) 973-22-56; e-mail www@rg.ru; internet www.rg.ru; f. 1990; organ of the Russian Govt; 5 a week; Gen. Man. ALEKSANDR N. GORBENKO; Editor-in-Chief VLADISLAV A. FRONIN; circ. 482,700 (2002).

Rossiiskiye Vesti (Russian News): 127006 Moscow, ul. M. Dmitrovka 3/10; tel. and fax (095) 937-64-36; fax (095) 937-64-25; e-mail mail@rosvesty.ru; internet www.rosvesty.ru; f. 1991; weekly; Editor-in-Chief ALEKSEI TITKOV; circ. 50,000 (2000).

Rossiya (Russia): 103811 Moscow, Kostyanskii per. 13; e-mail agalakov@rgz.ru; internet www.rgz.ru; f. 2000; controlled by Sistema Mass-Mediya; weekly supplement *Gubernskaya Rossiya—Regions of Russia* (Mondays), of news from the territories of the Russian Federation; circ. 50,000 (2001).

Selskaya Zhizn (Country Life): 125869 Moscow, ul. Pravdy 24, POB 137; tel. (095) 257-51-51; fax (095) 257-58-39; e-mail sg@sgazeta.ru; internet www.sgazeta.ru; f. 1918 as *Bednota* (Poverty), present name adopted in 1960; 2 a week; fmrly organ of the Cen. Cttee of the CPSU; independent; Editor-in-Chief and Gen. Man. SHAMUN M. KAGERMANOV; circ. 102,000 (2002).

Sovetskaya Rossiya (Soviet Russia): 125868 Moscow, ul. Pravdy 24; tel. (095) 257-53-00; fax (095) 200-22-90; e-mail sovross@aha.ru; internet www.rednews.ru; f. 1956; fmrly organ of the Cen. Cttee of the CPSU and the Russian Federation Supreme Soviet and Council of Ministers; 3 a week; reflects views of left-wing of Communist Party; Editor VIKTOR CHIKIN; circ. 300,000 (2002).

Tribuna (Tribune): 125993 Moscow, ul. Pravdy 24, POB A-40; tel. (095) 257-59-13; fax (095) 973-20-02; e-mail tribuna@adi.ru; internet www.tribuna.ru; f. 1969; national industrial daily; Editor-in-Chief VIKTOR ANDRIYANOV; circ. 201,943 (2000).

Trud (Labour): 103792 Moscow, Nastasinskii per. 4; tel. (095) 299-39-06; fax (095) 299-47-40; e-mail letter@trud.ru; internet www.trud.ru; f. 1921; 5 a week; independent trade union newspaper; Editor ALEKSANDR S. POTAPOV; circ. 1,700,000 (2001).

Vechernyaya Moskva (Evening Moscow): 123849 Moscow, ul. 1905 Goda 7; tel. (095) 256-20-11; fax (095) 259-05-26; e-mail post@vm.ru; internet www.vm.ru; f. 1923; independent; Editor-in-Chief VALERII YEVSEYEV; circ. 300,000 (2001).

Vedomosti (Gazette): 125212 Moscow, ul. Vyborgskaya 16; tel. (095) 232-32-00; fax (095) 956-07-16; e-mail vedomosti@media.ru; internet www.vedomosti.ru; f. 1999; independent business newspaper, publ. jointly with the *Financial Times* (United Kingdom) and the *Wall Street Journal* (USA); Editor LEONID BERSHIDSKII; circ. 42,000 (2001).

Vremya-MN (Time-Moscow News): 103829 Moscow, ul. Tverskaya 16/2; tel. (095) 209-05-20; fax (095) 209-17-28; e-mail vremya@mn.ru; internet www.vremyamn.ru; f. 1995; Pres. ALEKSANDR VAINSHTEIN; Editor VLADIMIR V. UMNOV; circ. 54,000 (2001).

Vremya Novosti (Time News): 113326 Moscow, ul. Pyatniyskaya 25; tel. (095) 231-18-17; fax (095) 959-33-40; e-mail info@vremya.ru; internet www.vremya.ru; f. 2000; 5 a week; Editor-in-Chief VLADIMIR GUREVICH; circ. 51,000.

Zhizn (Life): 101970 Moscow, ul. Maroseika 13/3; tel. (095) 206-88-56; fax (095) 206-85-48; e-mail info@zhizn.ru; weekly; Editor-in-Chief VLADIMIR TOPORKOV; circ. 1,068,000 (2002).

St Petersburg

Peterburgskii Chas Pik (Petersburg Rush Hour): 191040 St Petersburg, Nevskii pr. 81; tel. (812) 279-25-65; fax (812) 279-19-12; e-mail nabor2@chaspik.spb.ru; internet www.chaspik.spb.ru; f. 1990; weekly; Editor-in-Chief NATALIYA CHAPLINA; circ. 33,000 (2002).

Novosti Peterburga (Petersburg News): St Petersburg; tel. and fax (812) 312-35-66; e-mail press@neva.spb.ru; f. 1997; Editor-in-Chief ALEKSANDR V. MARKOV; circ. 25,000 (2001).

Sankt-Peterburgskiye Vedomosti (St Petersburg Gazette): 191023 St Petersburg, ul. Fontanka 59; tel. (812) 327-22-00; fax (812) 310-51-41; e-mail post@spbvedomosti.ru; internet www.spbvedomosti.ru; f. 1728; re-established 1991; Editor OLEG KUZIN; circ. 90,000 (2002).

Smena (The Rising Generation): 191119 St Petersburg, ul. Marata 69; tel. (812) 315-04-76; fax (812) 315-03-53; e-mail info@smena.ru;

internet www.smena.ru; f. 1919; 6 a week, controlled by Sistema Mass-Mediya; Editor-in-Chief LEONID DAVYDOV; circ. 80,000 (2002).

The St Petersburg Times: 190000 St Petersburg, Isaakevskaya pl. 4; tel. and fax (812) 325-60-80; e-mail letters@sptimesrussia.com; internet www.sptimes.ru; f. 1993; 2 a week; in English; independent; Publr TATYANA SHALYGINA; Man. Dir SERGEI PODOINTITSIN; Editor THOMAS RYMER.

Vechernii Peterburg (Evening Petersburg): 191023 St Petersburg, ul. Fontanka 59; tel. (812) 311-88-75; fax (812) 314-31-05; e-mail gazeta@vspb.spb.ru; f. 1992; Editor VLADIMIR GRONSKII; circ. 20,000 (2001).

PRINCIPAL PERIODICALS

Agriculture, Forestry, etc.

Agrarnyi Zhurnal (Agrarian Journal): Moscow; tel. (095) 204-49-80; fax (095) 207-44-78; e-mail mobilecenter@mtu-net.ru; f. 2000; monthly; Editor-in-Chief ALEKSANDR MORGACHEV.

Agrokhimiya (Agricultural Chemistry): 119991 Moscow, Maronovskii per. 26; tel. (095) 238-24-00; e-mail ovpes@mail.ru; f. 1964; monthly; journal of the Russian Academy of Sciences; results of theoretical and experimental research work; Editor V. N. KUDEYAROV; circ. 400 (2002).

Doklady Rossiiskoi Akademii Selskokhozyaistvennykh Nauk (Reports of the Russian Academy of Agricultural Sciences): 117218 Moscow, ul. Krzhizhanovskii 15, POB B-2; tel. and fax (095) 207-76-60; f. 1936; 6 a year; developments in agriculture; Editor-in-Chief N. S. MARKOVA; circ. 1,000.

Ekologiya i Promlyshlennost Rossii (The Ecology and Industry of Russia): 119911 Moscow, Leninskii pr. 4; tel. (095) 247-23-08; fax (095) 955-00-58; e-mail ecip@online.ru; internet ecip.newmail.ru; f. 1996; monthly; environmental protection, forestry, wood and paper products, nature conservation; Editor-in-Chief V. D. KALNER.

Ekonomika Selskokhozyaistvennykh i Pererabatyvayushchikh Predpriyatii (Economics of Agricultural and Processing Enterprises): 107996 Moscow, ul. Sadovaya-Spasskaya 18/423; tel. (095) 207-15-80; fax (095) 207-18-56; internet www.reason.ru/economy; f. 1926; monthly; publ. by Ministry of Agriculture and Foodstuffs; Editor S. K. DEVIN; circ. 4,500 (1998).

Lesnaya Promyshlennost (Forest Industry): 101934 Moscow, Arkhangelskii per. 1/234; tel. (095) 207-91-53; f. 1926; 3 a week; publ. by the state forest industrial company, Roslesprom; Editor V. G. ZAYEDINOV; circ. 250,000.

Mezhdunarodnyi Selskokhozyaistvennyi Zhurnal (International Agricultural Journal): 107996 Moscow, ul. Sadovaya-Spasskaya 18; tel. and fax (095) 207-23-11; f. 1957; 6 a year; Editor-in-Chief VIKTOR P. KOROVKIN; circ. 4,000.

Molochnoye i Myasnoye Skotovodstvo (Dairy and Meat Cattle Breeding): 107996 Moscow, ul. Sadovaya-Spasskaya 18; tel. (095) 207-19-46; f. 1956; 6 a year; Editor V. V. KORGENEVSKII; circ. 791 (1996).

Selskokhozyaistvennaya Biologiya (Agricultural Biology): 117218 Moscow, ul. Krzhizhanovskogo 15; tel. (095) 921-93-88; f. 1966; 6 a year; publ. by the Russian Academy of Agricultural Sciences; Editor E. M. BORISOVA; circ. 1,000.

Tekhnika v Selskom Khozyaistve (Agricultural Technology): 117218 Moscow, ul. Krzhizhanovskogo 15/2; tel. (095) 207-37-62; fax (095) 207-28-70; e-mail jurali@mail.ru; internet www.tehnvsh.by.ru; f. 1941; 6 a year; journal of the Ministry of Agriculture and Foodstuffs and the Russian Academy of Agricultural Sciences; Editor-in-Chief PETR S. POPOV; circ. 2,000 (1998).

Veterinariya (Veterinary Science): 107996 Moscow, ul. Sadovaya-Spasskaya 18; tel. (095) 207-10-60; fax (095) 207-28-12; f. 1924; monthly; Editor V. A. GARKAVTSEV; circ. 4,860 (2000).

Zashchita i Karantin Rastenii (The Protection and Quarantine of Plants): 107996 Moscow, ul. Sadovaya-Spasskaya 18, POB 6; tel. (095) 207-21-30; fax (095) 207-21-40; e-mail fitopress@ropnet.ru; f. 1932; monthly; Editor V. E. SAVZDARG; circ. 5,200 (2000).

Zemledeliye (Farming): 107996 Moscow, ul. Sadovaya-Spasskaya 18; tel. (095) 207-24-66; fax (095) 207-28-70; f. 1939; 6 a year; publ. by Ministry of Agriculture and Foodstuffs, Russian Academy of Agricultural Sciences, Russian Scientific Research Institute of Farming; Editor V. IVANOV; circ. 4,000 (1998).

For Children

Koster (Campfire): 193024 St Petersburg, ul. Mytninskaya 1/20; tel. (812) 274-15-72; fax (812) 274-46-26; e-mail root@kostyor.spb.org; internet www.kostyor.ru; f. 1936; monthly; journal of the International Union of Children's Organizations (UPO-FCO); fiction, poetry, sport, reports and popular science; for ages 10–14 years; Editor-in-Chief N. B. KHARLAMPIYEV; circ. 7,500 (2000).

Murzilka: 125015 Moscow, ul. Novodmitrovskaya 5A; tel. and fax (095) 285-18-81; e-mail documents@mtu-net.ru; internet www .murzilka.km.ru; f. 1924; monthly; illustrated; for first grades of school; Editor TATYANA ANDROSENKO; circ. 115,000 (2000).

Pioner (Pioneer): 101459 Moscow, Bumazhnyi proyezd 14; tel. (095) 257-34-27; f. 1924; monthly; fmrly journal of the Cen. Cttee of the Lenin Young Communist League (Komsomol); fiction; illustrated; for children of fourth–eighth grades; Editor A. S. MOROZ; circ. 7,000 (2000).

Pionerskaya Pravda (Pioneers' Truth): 127994 Moscow, ul. Sus-hchevskaya 21; tel. (095) 972-22-38; fax (095) 972-10-28; e-mail pionerka@hotmail.ru; f. 1925; 3 a week; fmrly organ of the Union of Pioneer Organizations (Federation of Children's Organizations) of the USSR; Editor O. I. GREKOVA; circ. 60,000 (2000).

Veselye Kartinki (Merry Pictures): 107076 Moscow, Stromynskii per. 4; tel. (095) 269-52-96; fax (095) 268-49-68; e-mail merrypictures@mtu-net.ru; internet vkids.km.ru/subjects .asp?id_sect=5&id_subj=4; f. 1956; monthly; publ. by the Molodaya Gvardiya (Young Guard) Publishing House; humorous; for pre-school and first grades; Editor R. A. VARSHAMOV; circ. 140,000 (1999).

Yunyi Naturalist (Young Naturalist): 125015 Moscow, ul. Novo-dmitrovskaya 5A; tel. (095) 285-89-67; f. 1928; monthly; fmrly journal of the Union of Pioneer Organizations (Federation of Child-ren's Organizations) of the USSR; popular science for children of fourth–10th grades, who are interested in biology; Editor B. A. CHASHCHARIN; circ. 16,350 (2000).

Yunyi Tekhnik (Young Technician): 125015 Moscow, ul. Novo-dmitrovskaya 5A; tel. (095) 285-44-80; e-mail yt@got.mmtel.ru; f. 1956; monthly; publ. by the Molodaya Gvardiya (Young Guard) Publishing House; popular science for children and youth; Editor BORIS CHEREMISINOV; circ. 13,050 (2000).

Culture and Arts

7 Dnei (7 Days): 125871 Moscow, Leningradskoye shosse 5A; tel. (095) 195-92-76; fax (095) 753-41-32; e-mail 7days@7days.ru; internet www.7days.ru; f. 1967; celebrity news and television list-ings magazine; Editor V. V. ORLOVA; circ. 937,000 (2000).

Dekorativnoye Iskusstvo (Decorative Art): 103009 Moscow, ul. Tverskaya 9; tel. (095) 229-19-10; fax (095) 229-68-75; f. 1957; 4 a year; all aspects of visual art; illustrated; Editor A. KURCHI; circ. 1,500 (1999).

Iskusstvo Kino (The Art of the Cinema): 125319 Moscow, ul. Usievicha 9; tel. (095) 151-56-51; fax (095) 151-02-72; e-mail kino@ kinoart.ru; internet www.kinoart.ru/main.html; f. 1931; monthly; journal of the Russian Film-makers' Union; Editor DANIIL DONDUREI; circ. 5,000 (1998).

Knizhnoye Obozreniye (Book Review): 129272 Moscow, ul. Sus-hchevskii val 64; tel. and fax (095) 281-62-66; f. 1966; weekly; sum-maries of newly published books; Editor S. V. YATSENKO; circ. 15,280 (1999).

Kultura (Culture): 127055 Moscow, ul. Novoslobodskaya 73; tel. (095) 285-06-40; fax (095) 200-32-25; e-mail kultura@dol.ru; internet www.kulturagz.ru; f. 1929; controlled by Sistema Mass-Mediya; weekly; Editor YURII I. BELYAVSKII; circ. 29,200 (2002).

Literaturnaya Gazeta (Literary Newspaper): 103811 Moscow, Kostyanskii per. 13; tel. (095) 208-96-60; fax (095) 206-62-25; e-mail litera@nettaxi.com; internet www.lgz.ru; f. 1831; publ. restored 1929; weekly; literature, politics, society; controlled by Sistema Mass-Mediya; Editor-in-Chief LEV GUSHIN; circ. 57,000 (2002).

Literaturnaya Rossiya (Literary Russia): 103051 Moscow, Tsvetnoi bulv. 30; tel. (095) 200-50-10; fax (095) 921-40-00; f. 1958; weekly; essays, verse, literary criticism, political reviews; Editor VLADIMIR V. YEREMENKO; circ. 24,000 (2000).

Muzykalnaya Akademiya (Musical Academy): 103006 Moscow, ul. Sadovaya-Triumfalnaya 14/12; tel. (095) 209-23-84; f. 1933; quar-terly; publ. by the Kompozitor (Composer) Publishing House; journal of the Union of Composers of the Russian Federation and the Ministry of Culture; Editor YU. S. KOREV; circ. 1,000 (1998).

Muzykalnaya Zhizn (Musical Life): 103006 Moscow, ul. Sadovaya-Triumfalnaya 14/12; tel. (095) 209-75-24; f. 1957; fortnightly; publ. by the Kompozitor (Composer) Publishing House; journal of the Union of Composers of the Russian Federation and the Ministry of Culture; development of music; Editor J. PLATEK; circ. 10,000 (2000).

Neva (The River Neva): 191186 St Petersburg, Nevskii pr. 3; tel. and fax (812) 312-65-37; fax (812) 312-65-37; e-mail office@nevajournal .spb.ru; internet www.nevajournal.spb.ru; f. 1955; monthly; journal of the St Petersburg Writers' Organization; fiction, poetry, literary criticism; Editor B. N. NIKOLSKII; circ. 4,000 (2000).

Oktyabr (October): 125040 Moscow, ul. Pravdy 11/13; tel. (095) 214-62-05; fax (095) 214-50-29; internet magazines.russ.ru/october; f. 1924; monthly; independent literary journal; new fiction and essays by Russian and foreign writers; Editor-in-Chief IRINA N. BARMETOVA; circ. 4,500 (2002).

Teatr (Theatre): 121835 Moscow, ul. Arbat 35; tel. and fax (095) 248-07-45; monthly; publ. by the Izvestiya (News) Publishing House; journal of the Theatrical Workers' Union and the Russian Feder-ation Union of Writers; new plays by Russian and foreign play-wrights; Editor V. SEMENOVSKII; circ. 5,000 (2000).

Znamya (Banner): 103001 Moscow, ul. B. Sadovaya 2/46; tel. (095) 299-52-38; e-mail znamlit@dialup.ptt.ru; internet magazines.russ .ru/znamia; f. 1931; monthly; independent; novels, poetry, essays; Editor-in-Chief SERGEI CHUPRININ; circ. 10,000 (2000).

Economics, Finance

Dengi (Money): 123308 Moscow, Khoroshevskoye shosse 41; tel. (095) 943-91-17; fax (095) 956-18-13; e-mail dengi@kommersant.ru; internet www.kommersant.ru/k-money; weekly; publ. by the Kom-mersant Publishing House; Editor SERGEI YAKOVLEV; circ. 85,500 (2002).

Dengi i Kredit (Money and Credit): 103016 Moscow, ul. Neglinnaya 12; tel. (095) 771-99-87; fax (095) 771-99-85; e-mail ggv@cbr.ru; f. 1927; monthly; publ. by the Central Bank; all aspects of banking and money circulation; Editor Y. G. DMITRIYEV; circ. 5,430 (2002).

Ekonomika i Matematicheskiye Metody (Economics and Mathematical Methods): 117418 Moscow, Nakhimovskii pr. 47; tel. (095) 332-46-39; internet www.cemi.rssi.ru/emm; f. 1965; 4 a year; publ. by the Nauka (Science) Publishing House; theoretical and methodological problems of economics, econometrics; Editor V. L. MAKAROV; circ. 796 (2000).

Ekonomika i Zhizn (Economics and Life): 101462 Moscow, Bu-mazhnyi proyezd 14; tel. (095) 257-30-62; fax (095) 250-55-58; e-mail gazeta@ekonomika.ru; f. 1918; weekly; fmrly *Ekonomicheskaya gazeta*; news and information about the economy and business; Editor YURII YAKUTIN; circ. 460,000 (1999).

Ekspert (Expert): 125866 Moscow, ul. Pravdy 24, Novyi Gazetnyi kor. tel. (095) 257-47-27; fax (095) 250-52-09; e-mail ask@expert.ru; internet www.expert.ru; weekly; business and economics; financial and share markets; policy and culture; owned by Prof-Mediya; Editor-in-Chief VALERII FADEYEV; circ. 60,000 (2002).

Finansy (Finances): 103009 Moscow, ul. Tverskaya 22B; tel. and fax (095) 299-96-16; e-mail finance@df.ru; internet www.df.ru/~finance; f. 1926; monthly; publ. by the Finansy (Finances) Publishing House; fmrly journal of the Ministry of Finance; theory and information on finances; compilation and execution of the state budget, insurance, lending, taxation etc. Editor YU. M. ARTEMOV; circ. 10,000 (2002).

Finansovaya Rossiya (Financial Russia): 103051 Moscow, B. Sukharevskii per. 19/1; tel. (095) 207-57-55; e-mail fr@fr.ru; internet www.fr.ru; f. 1996; weekly; economics, business, finance, society; Editor-in-Chief ANDREI A. MIROSHNICHENKO; circ. 103,000 (2001).

Kompaniya (The Firm): 125047 Moscow, ul. Usachyeva 11; tel. (095) 755-87-88; fax (095) 755-87-21; e-mail info@ko.ru; internet www.ko.ru; f. 1998; weekly; politics, economics, finance; Editor-in-Chief ANDREI GRIGORYEV; circ. 40,000 (2002).

Mirovaya Ekonomika i Mezhdunarodniye Otnosheniya (World Economy and International Relations): 117859 Moscow, ul. Profsoyuznaya 23; tel. (095) 128-08-83; fax (095) 310-70-27; e-mail memojour@imemo.ru; f. 1957; monthly; publ. by the Nauka (Science) Publishing House; journal of the Institute of the World Economy and International Relations of the Russian Academy of Sciences; prob-lems of theory and practice of world socio-economic development, international policies, international economic co-operation, the eco-nomic and political situation in Russia and different countries of the world, etc. Editor A. V. RYABOV; circ. 4,000 (2002).

Profil (Profile): 109544 Moscow, ul. B. Andronyevskaya 17; tel. (095) 745-94-01; fax (095) 278-72-05; e-mail profil@orc.ru; internet www.profil.orc.ru; f. 1997; weekly; Editor-in-Chief ALEKSANDR PEROV; circ. 103,000 (2001).

Rossiiskii Ekonomicheskii Zhurnal (Russian Economic Journal): 109542 Moscow, Ryazanskii pr. 99; tel. and fax (095) 377-25-56; e-mail rem@mail.magelan.ru; f. 1958; monthly; fmrly *Ekono-micheskiye Nauki* (Economic Sciences); theory and practice of eco-nomics and economic reform; Editor A. YU. MELENTEV; circ. 6,074 (2000).

Vek (The Age): 125124 Moscow, ul. Pravdy 24, POB 35; tel. (095) 257-30-38; fax (095) 251-72-00; e-mail wek@wek.ru; internet www .wek.ru; f. 1992; Editor-in-Chief ALEKSANDR KOLODNYI.

Voprosy Ekonomiki (Questions of Economics): 117218 Moscow, Nakhimovskii pr. 32; tel. and fax (095) 124-52-28; e-mail mail@

vopreco.ru; internet www.vopreco.ru; f. 1929; monthly; journal of the Institute of Economics of the Russian Academy of Sciences; theoretical problems of economic development, market relations, social aspects of transition to a market economy, international economics, etc. Editor L. ABALKIN; circ. 7,000 (2002).

Education

Pedagogicheskii Vestnik (Pedagogical Herald): 117393 Moscow, ul. Profsoyuznaya 62; tel. (095) 125-95-01; weekly; Editor-in-Chief LEONID RUVINSKII; circ. 120,000 (2002).

Pedagogika (Pedagogy): 119905 Moscow, ul. Pogodinskaya 8; tel. (095) 248-51-49; f. 1937; monthly; publ. by Academy of Education; Chief Editor V. P. BORISENKOV; circ. 4,550 (2000).

Semya (Family): 107996 Moscow, Orlikov per. 5; tel. (095) 975-05-29; fax (095) 975-00-76; e-mail mail@semya.ru; internet www.semya.ru; f. 1988; weekly; fmrly publ. by Soviet Children's Fund; Editor-in-Chief SERGEI A. ABRAMOV; circ. 100,000 (1999).

Semya i Shkola (Family and School): 129278 Moscow, ul. P. Korchagina 7; tel. (095) 283-82-21; fax (095) 283-86-14; e-mail semia_i_shkola@mtu-net.ru; f. 1871; monthly; for parents and children; Gen. Man. V. F. SMIRNOV; Editor-in-Chief P. I. GELAZONIYA; circ. 5,000 (2002).

Shkola i Proizvodstvo (School and Production): 127254 Moscow, ul. Sh. Rustaveli 10/3; tel. (095) 219-08-40; e-mail marketing@shkolapress.ru; f. 1957; 8 a year; publ. by the Shkola-Press (School-Press) Publishing House; Editor YU. YE. RIVES-KOROBKOV; circ. 14,700 (2000).

Uchitelskaya Gazeta (Teachers' Gazette): 109012 Moscow, Vetoshnyi per. 13/15; tel. (095) 928-82-53; fax (095) 924-29-27; e-mail ug@ug.ru; internet www.ug.ru; f. 1924; weekly; independent pedagogical newspaper; distributed throughout the CIS; Editor PETR POLOZHEVETS; circ. 98,500 (2002).

Vospitaniye Shkolnikov (The Upbringing of Schoolchildren): 129278 Moscow, ul. P. Korchagina 7; tel. (095) 283-86-96; f. 1966; 6 a year; publ. by Pedagogika (Pedagogics) Publishing House; Editor L. V. KUZNETSOVA; circ. 41,000 (2000).

International Affairs

Ekho Planety (Echo of the Planet): 103860 Moscow, Tverskoi bulv. 10/12; tel. (095) 202-67-48; fax (095) 290-59-11; e-mail echotex@itar-tass.com; internet www.explan.ru; f. 1988; weekly; publ. by ITAR—TASS; international affairs, economic, social and cultural; Editor-in-Chief VALENTIN VASILETS; circ. 29,000 (2002).

Mezhdunarodnaya Zhizn (International Life): 103064 Moscow, Gorokhovskii per. 14; tel. (095) 265-37-81; fax (095) 265-37-71; e-mail inter_affairs@mid.ru; f. 1954; monthly; Russian and English; publ. by the Pressa Publishing House; problems of foreign policy and diplomacy of Russia and other countries; Editor B. D. PYADYSHEV; circ. 70,530 (2002).

Novoye Vremya (New Times): 127994 Moscow, M. Putinkovskii per. 1/2, POB 4; tel. (095) 229-88-72; fax (095) 200-41-92; e-mail contact@newtimes.ru; internet www.newtimes.ru; f. 1943; weekly; Russian, English; publ. by the Moskovskaya Pravda Publishing House; foreign and Russian affairs; Editor-in-Chief ALEKSANDR PUMPYANSKII; circ. 25,000 (2002).

Language, Literature

Ex Libris-NG: 113935 Moscow, ul. Myasnitskaya 13; tel. (095) 928-48-50; fax (095) 975-23-46; e-mail info@ng.ru; internet exlibris.ng.ru; weekly; literature; Editor-in-Chief IGOR ZOTOV.

Filologicheskiye Nauki (Philological Sciences): Moscow; tel. (095) 203-36-23; f. 1958; 6 a year; publ. by the Vysshaya Shkola (Higher School) Publishing House; reports of institutions of higher learning on questions of literary studies and linguistics; Editor P. A. NIKOLAYEV; circ. 900 (1999).

Russkaya Literatura (Russian Literature): 199034 St Petersburg, nab. Makarova 4; tel. (812) 328-16-01; fax (812) 328-11-40; f. 1958; quarterly; journal of the Institute of Russian Literature of the Russian Academy of Sciences; development of Russian literature from its appearance up to the present day; Editor N. N. SKATOV; circ. 1,467 (1999).

Russkaya Rech (Russian Speech): 121019 Moscow, ul. Volkhonka 18/2; tel. (095) 290-23-78; f. 1967; 6 a year; publ. by the Nauka (Science) Publishing House; journal of the Institute of Russian Language of the Academy of Sciences; popular; history of the development of the literary Russian language; Editor V. G. KOSTOMAROV; circ. 1,092 (2000).

Voprosy Literatury (Questions of Literature): 125009 Moscow, B. Gnezdnikovskii per. 10; tel. (095) 229-49-77; fax (095) 229-64-71; internet magazines.russ.ru/voplit; f. 1957; 6 a year; joint edition of the Institute of World Literature of the Academy of Sciences and the

Literary Thought Foundation; theory and history of modern literature and aesthetics; Editor L. I. LAZAREV; circ. 2,400 (2002).

Voprosy Yazykoznaniya (Questions of Linguistics): 121019 Moscow, ul. Volkhonka 18/2; tel. (095) 201-25-16; f. 1952; 6 a year; publ. by the Nauka (Science) Publishing House; journal of the Department of Literature and Language of the Russian Academy of Sciences; Editor T. M. NIKOLAYEVA; circ. 1,448 (2000).

Leisure and Sport

Afisha (Poster): 103009 Moscow, per. B. Gnezdnikovskii 7/28/1; tel. (095) 785-17-00; fax (095) 785-17-01; e-mail inf@afisha.net; internet www.afisha.ru; f. 1999; every 2 weeks; listings and reviews of events in Moscow; Editor-in-Chief ILYA OSKOLKOV-TSENTSIPER; circ. 80,000 (2002).

Avtopilot (Autopilot): 123308 Moscow, Khoroshevskoye shosse 41; tel. (095) 493-91-44; fax (095) 493-91-64; e-mail autopilot@kommersant.ru; internet www.autopilot.ru; cars; publ. by the Kommersant Publishing House; Editor-in-Chief ALEKSANDR FYODOROV; circ. 96,500 (2002).

Dosug v Moskve (Leisure in Moscow): 101000 Moscow, Potapovskii per. 3; tel. and fax (095) 924-09-27; internet dosug-v-moskve.chat.ru; weekly; Thursday; listings and reviews of events in Moscow; circ 70,000.

Filateliya (Philately): 121069 Moscow, Khlebnyi per. 6; tel. (095) 291-14-32; fax (095) 254-85-84; f. 1966; monthly; journal of the Publishing and Trading Centre 'Marka'; Editor-in-Chief Y. G. BEKHTEREV; circ. 2,900 (2000).

Fizkultura i Sport (Exercise and Sport): 125130 Moscow, per. 6-i Novopodmoskovnii 3, POB 198; tel. (095) 786-60-62; fax (095) 786-61-39; e-mail fisemail@mtu-net.ru; f. 1922; monthly; activities and development of Russian sports, health; Editor I. SOSNOVSKII; circ. 37,600 (2001).

Rossiiskaya Okhotnichya Gazeta (Russian Hunters' Magazine): 123848 Moscow, ul. 1905 Goda 7; tel. (095) 256-94-74; e-mail rog@mk.ru; internet www.mk.ru/rog.asp; weekly; hunting, shooting, fishing; Editor-in-Chief OLEG MALOV.

Sovetskii Sport (Soviet Sport): 101913 Moscow, B. Spasoglinishchevskii per. 8; tel. and fax (095) 925-36-26; e-mail org@sovsport.ru; internet www.sovsport.ru; f. 1924; weekly; owned by Prof-Mediya; Editor-in-Chief ALEKSANDR KOZLOV; circ. 450,215 (2002).

Teoriya i Praktika Fizicheskoi Kultury (Theory and Practice of Exercise): 105122 Moscow, Sirenevyi bulv. 4; tel. and fax (095) 166-37-74; e-mail tpfk@infosport.ru; internet www.infosport.ru/press/tpfk; f. 1925; monthly; fmrly journal of the USSR State Committee for Exercise and Sport; Editor L. I. LUBYSHEVA; circ. 1,500 (1999).

Turist (Tourist): 107078 Moscow, B. Kharitonevskii per. 14; tel. (095) 923-64-23; fax (095) 959-23-36; f. 1929; every two months; publ. by the Intour Central Council for Tourism; articles, photo-essays, information, recommendations about routes and hotels for tourists, natural, cultural and historical places of interest; Editor BORIS V. MOSKVIN; circ. 3,000 (2000).

Za Rulem (Behind The Wheel): 103045 Moscow, per. Selivyerstov 10; tel. (095) 207-23-82; e-mail stas@zr.ru; internet www.zr.ru; f. 1928; monthly; cars and motorsport; Gen. Man. VIKTOR PANYARSKII; Editor-in-Chief PETR S. MENSHIKH; circ. 580,000 (2001).

Politics and Military Affairs

Gazeta: 123242 Moscow, ul. Zoologicheskaya 4; tel. (095) 787-39-99; fax (095) 787-39-98; e-mail info@gzt.ru; internet www.gzt.ru; f. 2001; Editor-in-Chief RAF SHAKIROV; circ. 35,000 (2002).

Litsa (People): 121099 Moscow, Smolenskaya pl. 13/21, POB 99; tel. (095) 241-37-92; e-mail litsa@aha.ru; f. 1996; monthly; Editor-in-Chief ARTEM BOROVIK; circ. 100,000 (2002).

Na Dne (The Lower Depths): 191025 St Petersburg, POB 110; tel. (812) 310-54-12; fax (812) 310-52-09; e-mail office@nadne.ru; internet www.nadne.ru; f. 1994; current affairs; social issues; 2 a month.

Nezavisimoye Voyennoye Obozreniye (Independent Military Review): 101000 Moscow, ul. Myasnitskaya 13; tel. (095) 928-48-50; fax (095) 975-23-46; internet nvo.ng.ru; Editor VADIM SOLOVYEV; circ. 26,998 (2002).

Rossiiskaya Federatsiya Segodnya (The Russian Federation Today): 103800 Moscow, ul. M. Dmitrovka 3/10; tel. (095) 299-40-55; fax (095) 200-30-80; e-mail rfs@rfnet.ru; f. 1994; journal of the State Duma; Editor YURII A. KHRENOV; circ. 50,000 (1999).

The Russia Journal: 113054 Moscow, nab. Ozerkovskaya 50/451; e-mail info@russiajournal.com; internet www.russiajournal.com; f. 1998; published by Norasco Publishing Ltd; Editor JON WRIGHT.

Shchit i Mech (Shield and Sword): 127434 Moscow, ul. Ivanovskaya 24; tel. (095) 976-66-44; fax (095) 977-21-72; e-mail ormvd@ itar-tass.com; f. 1989; weekly; military, security, geopolitical concerns; publ. by the Ministry of Internal Affairs; Editor-in-Chief VALERII KULIK; circ. 45,000 (2002).

Sovershenno Sekretno (Top Secret): 121099 Moscow, Smolenskaya pl. 13/21, POB 255; tel. (095) 241-68-73; fax (095) 241-75-55; e-mail topsec@dol.ru; internet www.topsecret.ru; f. 1989; monthly; Editor ARTEM BOROVIK; circ. 2,300,000 (2002).

Svobodnaya Mysl (Free Thought): 107140 Moscow, ul. Mosfilmovskaya 40; tel. (095) 788-65-00; f. 1924; fmrly *Kommunist* (Communist); monthly; politics, philosophy, economics; Editor-in-Chief N. B. BIKKENNIN; circ. 4,600 (2002).

Vlast (Power): 123308 Moscow, Khoroshevskoye shosse 41; tel. (095) 195-96-36; fax (095) 234-16-60; e-mail vlast@kommersant.ru; internet www.kommersant.ru/k-vlast; f. 1997; weekly; publ. by the Kommersant Publishing House; Editor MAKSIM KOVALSKII; circ. 73,500 (2002).

Yezhenedelnii Zhurnal (Weekly Magazine): 129110 Moscow, Pereyaslavskii per. 4; tel. (095) 785-82-50; fax (095) 785-82-51; e-mail info@ej.ru; internet www.ej.ru; f. 2001; Editor-in-Chief SERGEI PARKHOMENKO.

Zakon (Law): 127994 Moscow, ul. Tverskaya 18/1; tel. (095) 209-46-24; fax (095) 209-75-60; e-mail zakon@izvestia.ru; f. 1992; monthly; publ. by the editorial board of Izvestiya JSC; publishes thematic legislation and commentaries relating to business and commerce; legal issues for businessmen; Editor-in-Chief NIKOLAI KAPINUS; circ. 8,000 (2002).

Zavtra (Tomorrow): 119146 Moscow, Komsomolskii pr. 13; tel. (095) 247-13-37; fax (095) 245-37-10; e-mail zavtra@zavtra.ru; internet zavtra.ru; extreme left, nationalist; Editor-in-Chief ALEKSANDR A. PROGANOV; circ. 100,000 (2002).

Popular, Fiction and General

Akh! (Ah!): 129090 Moscow, ul. Novyi Arbat 21, POB 36; e-mail info@ahmagazine.ru; internet www.ahmagazine.ru; f. 1998; monthly; general; Editor LARISA BORUZDNIA.

Alfavit (Alphabet): 129090 Moscow, ul. Novyi Arbat 21, POB 36; e-mail alphabet@alphabet.ru; internet www.alphabet.ru; f. 1998; weekly; general; Editor-in-Chief MIKHAIL POLYACHEK; circ. 25,000 (2002).

Druzhba Narodov (The Friendship of Peoples): 121827 Moscow, ul. Povarskaya 52; tel. (095) 291-62-27; fax (095) 291-63-54; e-mail dn@mail.sitek.ru; internet magazines.russ.ru/druzhba; f. 1939; monthly; independent; prose, poetry and literary criticism; Editor A. EBANOIDZE; circ. 7,000 (2002).

Geo: 123056 Moscow, per. Krasina 16; tel. (095) 937-60-90; fax (095) 937-60-91; e-mail geo@gjrussia.com; f. 1998; monthly; travel magazine; Editor YEKATERINA SEMINA; circ. 175,000 (2000).

Inostrannaya Literatura (Foreign Literature): 109017 Moscow, ul. Pyatnitskaya 41; tel. (095) 953-51-47; fax (095) 953-50-61; e-mail inolit@rinet.ru; internet magazines.russ.ru/inostran; f. 1891; monthly; independent; Russian translations of modern foreign authors and literary criticism; Editor-in-Chief ALEKSEI SLOVESNII; circ. 10,000 (2002).

Krokodil (Crocodile): 101455 Moscow, Bumazhnyi proyezd 14; tel. (095) 257-31-14; f. 1922; monthly; publ. by the Pressa Publishing House; satirical; Editor A. S. PYANOV; circ. 40,900 (2000).

Molotok (Little Hammer): 125080 Moscow, vul. Vrubelya 4; tel. (095) 209-11-32; fax (095) 200-40-55; e-mail molotok@unity .kommersant.ru; internet www.zabey.ru; f. 2000; weekly; popular culture.

Moskva (Moscow): 119002 Moscow, ul. Arbat 20; tel. (095) 291-71-10; fax (095) 291-07-32; e-mail jurmos@cityline.ru; f. 1957; monthly; fiction; Editor LEONID I. BORODIN; circ. 7,100 (2002).

Nash Sovremennik (Our Contemporary): 103051 Moscow, Tsvetnoi bulv. 30; tel. (095) 200-24-24; fax (095) 200-23-05; e-mail nashsovr@chat.ru; internet www.friends-partners.org/partners/ rpiac/nashsovr/; f. 1956; monthly; publ. by the Union of Writers of Russia; contemporary prose and 'patriotic polemics'; Editor STANISLAV KUNAYEV; circ. 13,000 (1999).

Novaya Rossiya (New Russia): 103772 Moscow, Petrovskii per. 8; tel. (095) 229-14-19; fax (095) 232-37-99; f. 1930; monthly; in Russian and English; illustrated; Editor A. N. MISHARIN; circ. 15,000 (1999).

Novyi Mir (New World): 103806 Moscow, M. Putinkovskii per. 1/2; tel. and fax (095) 200-08-29; e-mail nmir@aha.ru; internet magazines.russ.ru/novyi_mi; f. 1925; monthly; publ. by the Izvestiya (News) Publishing House; new fiction and essays; Editor ANDREI V. VASILEVSKII; circ. 14,700 (2000).

Ogonek (Beacon): 191456 Moscow, Bumazhnyi proyezd 14; tel. (095) 250-22-30; fax (095) 943-00-70; e-mail ogonyok@ropnet.ru; internet www.ropnet.ru/ogonyok; f. 1899; weekly; independent; politics, popular science, economics, literature; Editor VLADIMIR B. CHERNOV; circ. 50,000 (2002).

Rodina (The Motherland): 103025 Moscow, ul. Novyi Arbat 19; tel. (095) 203-75-98; fax (095) 203-47-45; e-mail rodina@istrodina.com; f. 1989; monthly; popular historical; supplement *Istochnik* (Source), every two months, documents state archives; Editor V. DOLMATOV; circ. 20,000 (2000).

Roman Gazeta (Novels): 107078 Moscow, ul. Novobasmannaya 19; tel. 261-95-87; fax (095) 261-11-63; f. 1927; fortnightly; contemporary fiction including translations into Russian; Editor VICTOR MENSHIKOV; circ. 15,000 (2000).

Rossiiskii Kto Yest Kto (Russian Who's Who): 117335 Moscow, POB 81; tel. (095) 234-46-92; e-mail zhurnal@whoiswho.ru; internet www.whoiswho.ru; 2 a year; biographical and directory material; Editor-in-Chief SVYATOSLAV RYBAS; circ. 10,000.

Sobesednik (Interlocutor): 101484 Moscow, ul. Novoslobodskaya 73, POB 4; tel. (095) 285-56-65; fax (095) 973-20-54; e-mail info@ sobesednik.ru; internet www.sobesednik.ru; f. 1984; weekly; Editor-in-Chief YURII PILIPENKO; circ. 227,500 (2002).

SPID-Info: 125284 Moscow, POB 42; tel. (095) 255-02-99; fax (095) 252-09-20; e-mail mail@si.ru; internet www.s-info.ru; f. 1991; monthly; satirical; Editor-in-Chief ANDREI MANN; circ. 2,910,000.

Vokrug Sveta (Around the World): 125015 Moscow, ul. Argunovskaya 12/1/6A; tel. and fax (095) 215-01-65; e-mail vokrugsveta_g@onlin.ptt.ru; f. 1861; monthly; geographical, travel and adventure; illustrated; Editor A. DMITRII ZAKHAROV; circ. 145,000 (2002).

Zvezda (Star): 191028 St Petersburg, ul. Mokhovaya 20; tel. (812) 272-89-48; fax (812) 273-52-56; e-mail arjev@zvezda.spb.su; internet magazines.russ.ru/zvezda; f. 1923; monthly; publ. by the Zvezda Publishing House; novels, short stories, poetry and literary criticism; Editors A. YU. ARYEV, YA. A. GORDIN; circ. 10,000 (2003).

Popular Scientific

Meditsinskaya Gazeta (Medical Gazette): 129090 Moscow, B. Sukharevskaya pl. 1/2; tel. (095) 208-86-95; fax (095) 208-69-80; e-mail mggazeta@online.ru; internet www.medgazeta.rusmedserv .com; f. 1938; 2 a week; professional international periodical; Editor ANDREI POLTORAK; circ. 52,000 (2002).

Modelist-Konstruktor (Modelmaker-Designer): 125015 Moscow, ul. Novodmitrovskaya 5A; tel. (095) 285-80-46; fax (095) 285-27-57; f. 1962; monthly; information about amateur cars, planes, cross-country vehicles; designs of cars, planes, ships, tanks, garden furniture etc. Editor A. RAGUZIN; circ. 22,000 (1999).

Nauka i Zhizn (Science and Life): 101990 Moscow, ul. Myasnitskaya 24; tel. (095) 924-18-35; fax (095) 200-22-59; e-mail mail@ nauka.relis.ru; internet nauka.relis.ru; f. 1890, resumed 1934; monthly; recent developments in all branches of science and technology; Chief Editor I. K. LAGOVSKII; circ. 49,800 (2002).

PC Week: 109047 Moscow, ul. Marksistskaya 34/10; tel. (095) 974-22-60; fax (095) 974-22-63; e-mail editorial@pcweek.ru; internet www.pcweek.ru; f. 1995; 48 a year; Editor-in-Chief EDUARD PROYDAKOV; circ. 35,000 (2000).

Priroda (Nature): 117810 Moscow, Maronovskii per. 26; tel. (095) 238-24-56; fax (095) 238-26-33; f. 1912; monthly; publ. by the Nauka (Science) Publishing House; journal of the Presidium of the Academy of Sciences; natural sciences; Editor A. F. ANDREYEV; circ. 2,500 (1999).

Radio: 103045 Moscow, per. Seliverstov 10; tel. (095) 207-31-18; fax (095) 208-77-13; f. 1924; monthly; audio, video, communications, practical electronics, computers; Editor Y. I. KRYLOV; circ. 70,000 (2000).

Tekhnika-Molodezhi (Engineering—For Youth): 125015 Moscow, ul. Novodmitrovskaya 5A; tel. (095) 285-16-87; fax (095) 234-16-78; f. 1933; monthly; engineering and science; Editor A. N. PEREVOZCHIKOV; circ. 50,000 (1999).

Vrach (Physician): 119881 Moscow, ul. B. Pirogovskaya 2/6; tel. (095) 248-57-27; fax (095) 248-02-14; f. 1990; monthly; medical, scientific and socio-political; illustrated; Editor-in-Chief MIKHAIL A. PALTSEV; circ. 6,000 (1999).

Zdorovye (Health): 127994 Moscow, Bumazhnyi proyezd 14; tel. (095) 250-58-28; fax 257-32-51; e-mail zdorovie@zdr.ru; internet zdorovie.ad.ru; f. 1955; monthly; medicine and hygiene; Editor T. YEFIMOVA; circ. 195,000 (2002).

Zemlya i Vselennaya (The Earth and The Universe): 117810 Moscow, Maronovskii per. 26; tel. (095) 238-42-32; f. 1965; 6 a year; publ. by the Nauka (Science) Publishing House; jt edition of the

Academy of Sciences and the Society of Astronomy and Geodesy; current hypotheses of the origin and development of the earth and the universe; astronomy, geophysics and space research; Chief Editor V. K. ABALAKIN; circ. 1,000 (2000).

The Press, Printing and Bibliography

Bibliografiya (Bibliography): 119019 Moscow, Kremlevskaya nab. 1/9; tel. and fax (095) 298-25-82; e-mail bookch@postman.ru; f. 1929; 6 a year; publ. by the Book Chamber International Publishing House; theoretical, practical and historical aspects of bibliography; Editor G. A. ALEKSEYEVA; circ. 2,200 (2002).

Poligrafist i Izdatel (Printer and Publisher): 129272 Moscow, ul. Suchevskii val 64/105; tel. (095) 288-93-17; fax (095) 288-94-44; e-mail pub@online.ru; f. 1994; monthly; Editor A. I. OVSYANNIKOV; circ. 5,000 (2000).

Poligrafiya (Printing): 129272 Moscow, ul. Sushchevskii val 64; tel. (095) 281-74-81; fax (095) 288-97-66; e-mail polimag@aha.ru; internet www.aha.ru/~polimag; f. 1924; 6 a year; equipment and technology of the printing industry; Dir N. N. KONDRATIYEVA; circ. 5,000 (1999).

Slovo (Word): 121069 Moscow, ul. Povarskaya 11/2; tel. and fax (095) 202-50-51; f. 1936; monthly; fmrly *V Mire Knig* (In the World of Books); reviews of new books, theoretical problems of literature, historical and religious; Editor A. V. LARIONOV; circ. 4,000 (1999).

Vitrina Chitayushchei Rossii (Through the Window of Reading Russia): 127550 Moscow, Listvennichnaya alleya 2A; tel. (095) 921-11-56; fax (095) 977-12-11; e-mail vitrina@souzpechat.ru; internet www.souzpechat.ru/vitrina; f. 1994; monthly; Editor MARINA DMITRIEVA.

Zhurnalist (Journalist): 101453 Moscow, Bumazhnyi proyezd 14; tel. (095) 257-30-58; fax (095) 257-31-27; f. 1920; monthly; publ. by Ekonomicheskaya Gazeta Publishing House; Editor G. P. MALTSEV; circ. 6,200 (2002).

Religion

Bratskii Vestnik (Herald of the Brethren): 109028 Moscow, M. Vuzovskii per. 3; tel. (095) 917-96-26; f. 1945; 6 a year; organ of the Russian Union of Evangelical Christians-Baptists; Chief Editor YU. AGAPOV; circ. 10,000 (1998).

Istina I Zhizn (Truth and Life): 105215 Moscow, POB 38; tel. (095) 965-00-07; e-mail istina@aha.ru; inter-confessional Christian magazine; Editor Fr ALEKSANDR KHMELNITSKII.

Mezhdunarodnaya Yevreyskaya Gazeta (International Jewish Newspaper): 107005 Moscow, Pleteshkovskii per. 3A; tel. and fax (095) 265-08-69; e-mail tankred@aha.ru; internet www.jig.nm.ru; f. 1989; weekly; Editor-in-Chief NIKOLAI PROPIRNYI; circ. 15,000 (2002).

NG-Religii (The Independent-Religions): 101000 Moscow, ul. Myasnitskaya 13; tel. (095) 923-42-40; fax (095) 921-58-47; e-mail ngr@ng.ru; internet religion.ng.ru; f. 1997; analysis of religious affairs and their social and political implications both within Russia and worldwide; 2 a month; Editor-in-Chief MAKSIM SHEVCHENKO; circ. 50,000 (2002).

Russkii Yevrey (Russian Jew): 107005 Moscow, Pleteshkovskii per. 3A; tel. and fax (095) 265-08-69; f. 1879; re-established 1996; quarterly.

Zhurnal Moskovskoi Patriarkhii (Journal of the Moscow Patriarchate): 119435 Moscow, ul. Pogodinskaya 20/2; tel. (095) 246-98-48; fax (095) 246-21-41; e-mail pressmp@jmp.ru; internet www.jmp.ru; f. 1934; monthly; Editor Archpriest VLADIMIR (SILOVYEV); circ. 6,000 (1999).

Trade, Trade Unions, Labour and Social Security

Chelovek i Trud (Man and Labour): 103064 Moscow, Yakovoapostolskii per. 6/3; tel. and fax (095) 916-10-00; monthly; employment issues and problems of unemployment; Editor-in-Chief G. L. PODVOISKII; circ. 20,000 (1999).

Profsoyuzy (Trade Unions): 101000 Moscow, ul. Myasnitskaya 13/18/231; tel. (095) 924-57-40; fax (095) 975-23-29; e-mail iidprof@cityline.ru; f. 1917; monthly; fmrly publ. by the General Confederation of Trade Unions of the USSR; Editor Y. I. KOROBKO; circ. 3,200 (1999).

Vneshnyaya Torgovlya (External Trade): 121108 Moscow, ul. Minskaya 11; tel. (095) 145-68-94; fax (095) 145-51-92; e-mail vneshtorg@mtu-net.ru; internet www.trade-point.ru/vt; f. 1921; monthly; Russian and English; organ of the Ministry of Economic Development and Trade; Editor-in-Chief YURII DEOMIDOV; circ. 7,000 (1999).

Transport and Communication

Grazhdanskaya Aviyatsiya (Civil Aviation): 125836 Moscow, Leningradskii pr. 37; tel. and fax (095) 155-59-23; f. 1931; monthly; journal of the Union of Civil Aviation Workers; development of air transport; utilization of aviation in construction, agriculture and forestry; Editor A. M. TROSHIN; circ. 10,000 (2000).

Radiotekhnika (Radio Engineering): 103031 Moscow, Kuznetskii most 20/6/31; tel. (095) 921-48-37; fax (095) 925-92-41; e-mail iprzhr@online.ru; internet www.webcenter.ru/~iprzhr/; f. 1937; monthly; publ. by the Svyaz (Communication) Publishing House; journal of the A. S. Popov Scientific and Technical Society of Radio Engineering, Electronics and Electrical Communication; theoretical and technical problems of radio engineering; other publications include *Advances in Radio Science*, *Radio Systems* and *Antennae*; Editor YU. V. GULYAYEV; circ. 1,500 (1999).

Radiotekhnika i Elektronika (Radio Engineering and Electronics): 103907 Moscow, ul. Mokhovaya 11; tel. (095) 203-47-89; f. 1956; monthly; journal of the Russian Academy of Sciences; theory of radio engineering; Editor Y. V. GULYAYEV; circ. 468 (2000).

Vestnik Svyazi (Herald of Communication): 101000 Moscow, Krivokolennyi per. 14/1; tel. (095) 925-42-57; fax (095) 921-27-97; e-mail irais@vestnik-sviazy.ru; internet www.vestnik-sviazy.ru; f. 1917; monthly; publ. by the IRIAS Agency; mechanization and automation of production; Editor E. B. KONSTANTINOV; circ. 10,000 (2002).

For Women

Domovoi (House-Sprite): 113035 Moscow, ul. B. Ordynka 16; tel. (095) 956-77-02; fax (095) 956-22-09; e-mail info@domovoy.ru; internet www.domovoy.ru; monthly; Editor-in-Chief KSENIYA MAKHNENKO; circ. 105,000 (2000).

Elle: 101959 Moscow, ul. Myasnitskaya 35; tel. (095) 204-17-77; fax (095) 795-08-15; e-mail elle@hfm.ru; f. 1996; monthly; fashion; Editor-in-Chief YELENA SOTNIKOVA; circ. 180,000 (1998).

Krestyanka (Peasant Woman): 101460 Moscow, Bumazhnyi proyezd 14; tel. (095) 257-39-39; fax (095) 257-39-63; e-mail mail@krestyanka.ru; internet www.krestyanka.ru; f. 1922; monthly; publ. by the Krestyanka Publishing House; popular; supplements *Khozyayushka* (Dear Hostess), *On i ona* (He and She), *Moda v dome* (Fashion at Home), *Obyvatel* (The Ordinary Person), *Samochuvstvie* (Health), *Nasha Usadba* (Our Garden), *Pyatnashki* (Game of Tag); Pres and Editor-in-Chief ANASTASIYA V. KUPRIYANOVA; circ.120,000 (2002).

Mir Zhenshchiny (Woman's World): 101999 Moscow, Glinitchevskii per. 6; tel. and fax (095) 209-95-33; f. 1945; monthly; fmrly *Zhenshchina* (Woman); in Russian, Chinese, English, French, German and Spanish; fmrly publ. by the Soviet Women's Committee and the General Confederation of Trade Unions; popular; illustrated; Editor-in-Chief V. I. FEDOTOVA; circ. 50,000 (2000).

Modeli Sezona (Models of the Season): 103031 Moscow, Kuznetskii most 7/9; tel. (095) 921-73-93; fax (095) 928-77-93; f. 1957; 4 a year; Editor-in-Chief N. A. KASATKINA; circ. 45,000 (1999).

Rabotnitsa (Working Woman): 101458 Moscow, Bumazhnyi proyezd 14; tel. (095) 257-36-49; fax (095) 956-90-94; e-mail webmaster@rabotnitsa.ru; internet www.rabotnitsa.ru; f. 1914; monthly; publ. by the Pressa Publishing House; popular; Editor ZOYA P KRYLOVA; circ. 223,000 (2000).

Zhurnal Mod (Fashion Journal): 103031 Moscow, Kuznetskii most 7/9; tel. (095) 921-73-93; f. 1945; 4 a year; illustrated; Editor-in-Chief N. A. KASATKINA; circ. 45,000 (1999).

Youth

Molodaya Gvardiya (Young Guard): 125015 Moscow, ul. Novodmitrovskaya 5A; tel. (095) 285-88-29; fax (095) 285-56-90; f. 1922; monthly; fiction, poetry, criticism, popular science; Editor Y. YUSHIN; circ. 6,000 (2000).

Rovesnik (Contemporary): 125015 Moscow, ul. Novodmitrovskaya 5A; tel. (095) 285-89-20; fax (095) 285-06-27; e-mail rovesnik@rovesnik.ru; f. 1962; publ. by the Molodaya Gvardiya (Young Guard) Publishing House; fmrly journal of the Cen. Cttee of the Leninist Young Communist League; popular illustrated monthly of fiction, music, cinema, sport and other aspects of youth culture; Editor I. A. CHERNYSHKOV; circ. 100,000 (2000).

Selskaya Molodezh (Rural Youth): 125015 Moscow, ul. Novodmitrovskaya 5A; tel. (095) 285-80-04; fax (095) 285-08-30; f. 1925; monthly; publ. by the Molodaya Gvardiya (Young Guard) Publishing House; supplements *Podvigi* (Heroic Deeds) and *Detektivy selskoy molodezhi* (Rural Youth Detective Stories); popular illustrated, fiction, verses, problems of rural youth; Editor-in-Chief MICHAEL MASSUR; circ. 10,000 (1999).

Smena (The Rising Generation): 101457 Moscow, Bumazhnyi proyezd 14; tel. (095) 212-15-07; fax (095) 250-59-28; e-mail smena@garnet.ru; internet www.smena-id.ru; f. 1924; monthly; publ. by the Pressa Publishing House; popular illustrated, short stories, essays and problems of youth; Editor-in-Chief M. G. Kizilov; circ. 50,000 (2001).

Yunost (Youth): 101524 Moscow, ul. Tverskaya-Yamskaya 8/1; tel. (095) 251-31-22; fax (095) 251-74-60; f. 1955; monthly; novels, short stories, essays and poems by beginners; Editor V. Lipatov; circ. 15,000 (2000).

NEWS AGENCIES

ANI (News and Information Agency): 103009 Moscow, Kalashnyi per. 10, bldg 2; tel. (095) 202-37-06; fax (095) 202-54-03; e-mail ani@ani.ru; internet www.ani.ru; f. 1991; Editor-in-Chief Marianna Medovaya.

Federal News Service (FNS): 119992 Moscow, per. Obolenskyi 10; tel. (095) 245-58-00; fax 245-58-23; e-mail commerce@fednews.ru; internet www.fednews.ru; f. 1992; Bureau Chief Vyacheslav Nemodruk.

Interfax: 103006 Moscow, ul. 1-aya Tverskaya-Yamskaya 2; tel. (095) 250-92-03; fax (095) 250-89-94; e-mail webmaster@interfax.ru; internet www.interfax.ru; f. 1989; independent news agency; Gen. Dir M. Komissar.

ITAR—TASS (Information Telegraphic Agency of Russia—Telegraphic Agency of the Sovereign Countries): 103009 Moscow, Tverskoi bulv. 10/12; tel. (095) 292-36-14; fax (095) 291-83-72; e-mail dms@itar-tass.com; internet www.itar-tass.com; f. 1904; state information agency; 74 bureaux in Russia and the states of the former USSR, 65 foreign bureaux outside the former USSR; Dir-Gen. Vitalii N. Ignatenko.

Prima Human Rights News Agency: 111399 Moscow, POB 5; tel. and fax (095) 455-30-11; e-mail prima@prima-news.ru; internet www.prima-news.ru; f. 2000; Editor-in-Chief Aleksandr Podrabinek.

RIA—Novosti (Russian Information Agency—News): 103786 Moscow, Zubovskii bulv. 4; tel. (095) 201-82-09; fax (095) 201-45-45; e-mail marketing@rian.ru; internet www.rian.ru; f. 1961; collaborates by arrangement with foreign press and publishing organizations in 110 countries; provider of Russian news features and photographs; Chair. Svetlana Mironyuk.

RosBalt Information Agency: 190000 St Petersburg, Konnogvardeiskii bulv. 7; tel. (812) 320-50-30; fax (812) 320-50-31; e-mail rosbalt@rosbalt.ru; internet www.rosbalt.ru; news coverage of European Russia and other countries in northern Europe; bureau in Moscow; Chair. Nataliya Cherkesova; Gen. Man. Aleksandr Kadyrov.

Rossiiskoye Informatsionnoye Agentstvo 'Oreanda' (RIA 'Oreanda'): 117342 Moscow, POB 21; tel. (095) 330-98-50; fax (095) 23-04-39; e-mail info@oreanda.ru; internet www.oreanda.ru; f. 1994.

Strana-Ru (Country-Russia): 119021 Moscow, Zubovskii bulv. 4, podyezd 8; tel. (095) 201-81-34; fax (095) 201-41-17; e-mail mail@strana.ru; internet www.strana.ru; f. 2000; news agency; central bureau in Moscow, regional bureaux in each of the 7 Federal Okrugs, and in Groznyi, Chechnya; controlled by the All-Russian State Television and Radio Broadcasting Company (VGTRK) from 2002; Gen Man. Marina A. Litvinovich.

Foreign Bureaux

Agence France-Presse (AFP): 103006 Moscow, ul. Dolgorukovskaya 18/3; tel. (095) 926-59-69; fax (095) 931-95-85; e-mail desk.moscou@afp.com; internet www.afp.com; Dir Bernard Estrade.

Agencia EFE (Spain): 103051 Moscow, ul. Sadovaya-Samotechnaya 12/24/23; tel. (095) 200-15-32; fax (095) 956-37-38; e-mail efemos@co.ru; internet www.efe.es; Bureau Chief Manuel Velasco.

Agenzia Nazionale Stampa Associata (ANSA) (Italy): 121248 Moscow, Kutuzovskii pr. 9/1/12–14; tel. (095) 243-73-93; fax (095) 243-06-37; e-mail ansamos@online.ru; internet www.ansa.it; Bureau Chief Giulio Gelibter.

Anatolian News Agency (Turkey): 121552 Moscow, Rublevskoye shosse 26/1/279; tel. (095) 415-44-19; e-mail roonni@hotmail.com; Correspondent Remzi Oner Ozkan.

Associated Press (AP) (USA): 121248 Moscow, Kutuzovskii pr. 7/4, kor. 5, kv. 33; tel. (095) 234-43-53; fax (095) 974-18-45; e-mail mosed@ap.org; internet www.ap.org; Bureau Chief Deborah Seward.

Athens News Agency (Greece): 121148 Moscow, Kutuzovskii pr. 13/91; tel. and fax (095) 243-73-73; internet www.ana.gr; Correspondent Dimitrios Konstanta kopoulos.

Baltic News Service (News Agency of Estonia, Latvia and Lithuania): 121069 Moscow, ul. Povarskaya 24/15; tel. and fax (095) 202-38-05; e-mail juri@bns.ee; internet www.bns.ee; f. 1990; Bureau Chief Jüri Maloverjan; also maintains bureau in Kaliningrad.

Česká tisková kancelář (ČTK) (Czech Republic): 125047 Moscow, ul. 3-aya Tverskaya-Yamskaya 31-35/5/106; tel. and fax (095) 251-

71-63; e-mail bwanamar@glas.apc.org; internet www.ctk.cz; Correspondent Alexandra Malachovska.

Deutsche Presse-Agentur (dpa) (Germany): 121248 Moscow, Kutuzovskii pr. 7/4/210; tel. (095) 243-97-90; fax (095) 243-14-46; internet www.dpa.de; Bureau Chief Günther Chalupa.

Iraqi News Agency: 119121 Moscow, ul. Pogodinskaya 12; tel. (095) 316-99-75; fax (095) 246-77-76; Correspondent Muhammad Abdel Muttalib.

Islamic Republic News Agency (IRNA) (Iran): 121609 Moscow, Rublevskoye shosse 36/2/264; tel. (095) 415-43-62; fax (095) 415-42-88; e-mail irna@garnet.ru; Bureau Chief Mahmoud Hidaji.

Jiji Tsushin (Jiji Press) (Japan): 117049 Moscow, ul. Korovyi val 7/35; tel. (095) 564-81-02; fax (095) 564-81-13; Bureau Chief Kitagata Kazuya.

Korea Central News Agency (KCNA) (Democratic People's Republic of Korea): 119590 Moscow, ul. Mosfilmovskaya 72; tel. (095) 143-62-31; fax (095) 143-63-12; Bureau Chief Kan Chu Min.

Kuwait News Agency (KUNA): 117049 Moscow, ul. Korovyi val 7/52; tel. (095) 230-25-10; fax (095) 956-99-06; Correspondent Adib al-Sayyed.

Kyodo News (Japan): 121059 Moscow, B. Dorogomilovskaya 12; tel. (095) 956-60-22; fax (095) 956-60-26; Bureau Chief Yoshida Shigeyuki.

Magyar Távirati Iroda (MTI) (Hungary): 129010 Moscow, ul. B. Spasskaya 12/46; tel. (095) 280-04-25; fax (095) 280-04-21; Bureau Chief Sándor Tamassy.

Middle East News Agency (MENA) (Egypt): 107113 Moscow, ul. Sokolnicheskii val 24/2/176; tel. (095) 264-82-76; fax (095) 269-60-93; Correspondent Dr Mamdouh Mustafa.

Mongol Tsahilgaan Medeeniy Agentlag (Montsame) (Mongolia): 117333 Moscow, ul. Vavilova 79/52; tel. (095) 950-55-16; fax (095) 229-98-83; Bureau Chief Shagdar.

News Agencies of Sweden, Norway, Denmark and Finland: 121248 Moscow, Kutuzovskii pr. 7/4/5/30; tel. (095) 956-60-50; fax (095) 974-81-52; Correspondent Thomas Hamberg.

Notimex News Agency (Mexico): 123182 Moscow, ul. Akademika Bochvara 5/2/30–1; tel. and fax (095) 196-47-75; Correspondent Fernando Orozco Lloreda.

Novinska Agencija Tanjug (Serbia and Montenegro): 129085 Moscow, pr. Mira 74/124; tel. (095) 971-01-77; Bureau Chief Dragan Glumičić.

Polska Agencja Prasowa (PAP) (Poland): 117334 Moscow, Leninskii pr. 45/411; tel. and fax (095) 135-11-06; e-mail papmos@online.ru; Chief Correspondent Andrzej Lomanowski.

Prensa Latina (Cuba): 123182 Moscow, ul. Akademika Bochvara 5/2/30–1; tel. and fax (095) 196-47-75; Chief Correspondent Antonio Rondón.

Press Trust of India: 129041 Moscow, ul. B. Pereyaslavskaya 7/133–134; tel. and fax (095) 437-43-60; Correspondent Vinay Kumar Shukla.

Reuters (United Kingdom): 121059 Moscow, Radisson-Slavyanskaya Hotel, Berezhkovskaya nab. 2; tel. (095) 941-85-20; fax (095) 941-88-01; Man. Michal Broniatowski.

Rompres (Romania): Moscow, 121248 Kutuzovskii pr. 14/21; tel. (095) 243-67-96; Bureau Chief Nicolae Cretu.

Schweizerische Depeschenagentur (Switzerland): 121059 Moscow, B. Dorogomilovskaya 8/19; tel. and fax (095) 240-90-78; Bureau Chief Christoph Güdel.

Syrian Arab News Agency (SANA): 121248 Moscow, Kutuzovskii pr. 7/4/184–185; tel. (095) 243-13-00; fax (095) 243-75-12; Dir Fahed Kamnakesh.

Tlačová agentúra Slovenskej republiky (TASR) (Slovakia): 123056 Moscow, ul. Yu. Fuchika 17–19/43; tel. and fax (095) 250-24-89; Correspondent Blazej Pánik.

United Press International (UPI) (USA): 117334 Moscow, Leninskii pr. 45/426; tel. (095) 135-32-55; fax (095) 564-86-61; internet www.upi.com; Bureau Chief Anthony Louis.

Viet Nam News Agency (VNA): 117334 Moscow, Leninskii pr. 45/326–327; tel. (095) 135-11-08; fax (095) 137-38-67; e-mail pxmoscow@online.ru; Bureau Chief Ngo Gia Son.

Xinhua (New China) News Agency (People's Republic of China): 109029 Moscow, ul. M. Kalitnikovskaya 9A; tel. (095) 270-47-41; fax (095) 270-44-85; Dir Wei Zhengqiang.

Yonhap (United) News Agency (Republic of Korea): 103009 Moscow, Tverskoi bulv. 10/425; tel. and fax (095) 290-65-75; Correspondent Chi Il-Woo.

PRESS ASSOCIATIONS

Russian Guild of Publishers of Periodical Press: 125047 Moscow, ul. Sesnaya 20/6-211; tel. and fax (095) 978-41-89.

Union of Journalists of Russia: 119021 Moscow, Zubovskii bulv. 4; tel. (095) 201-51-01; fax (095) 201-35-47; f. 1991; Sec.-Gen. IGOR YAKOVENKO.

Publishers

Ad Marginem-Ad Patres: 119034 Moscow, Kropotkinskii per. 23; tel. and fax (095) 201-52-62; e-mail robot@rosd.org.ru; internet ad-marginem.pp.ru; f. 1994; fiction, philosophy, artistic and literary criticism; Dir SERGEI DATSYUK.

AST: 129085 Moscow, Zvezdnyi bulv. 21; tel. (095) 215-01-01; fax (095) 215-51-10; e-mail astpub@aha.ru; internet www.ast.ru; original and translated fiction and non-fiction, children's and school-books.

Avrora (Aurora): 191186 St Petersburg, Nevskii pr. 7/9; tel. (812) 312-37-53; fax (812) 312-54-60; f. 1969; fine arts; published in foreign languages; Dir ZENOBIUS SPETCHINSKII.

Bolshaya Rossiiskaya Entsiklopediya (The Great Russian Encyclopedia): 109028 Moscow, Pokrovskii bulv. 8; tel. (095) 917-94-86; fax (095) 917-71-39; e-mail gnibre2000@mail.ru; f. 1925; universal and specific encyclopedias; Dir A. P. GORKIN.

Detskaya Entsiklopediya (Children's Encyclopedia): 107042 Moscow, ul. Bakuninskaya 55; tel. (095) 269-52-76; f. 1933; science fiction, literature, poetry, biographical and historical novels.

Detskaya Literatura (Children's Literature): 103720 Moscow, M. Cherkasskii per. 1; tel. (095) 928-08-03; e-mail detlit@detlit.ru; f. 1933; State Publishing House of Children's Literature (other than school books); Dir E. A. NORTSOVA.

Drofa: 127018 Moscow, ul. Sushchevskii val. 49; tel. (095) 795-05-50; fax (095) 795-05-44; e-mail info@drofa.ru; internet www.drofa .ru; f. 1991; school textbooks, children's fiction; Dir-Gen. KONSTANTIN M. DRAGAN.

Ekonomika (Economy): 121864 Moscow, Berezhkovskaya nab. 6; tel. (095) 240-48-77; fax (095) 240-58-28; f. 1963; various aspects of economics, management and marketing; Dir G. I. MAZIN.

Eksmo: 125190 Moscow, Leningradskii pr. 80/16/3; tel. and fax (095) 956-24-11; e-mail osipova.eg@eksmo.ru; internet www.eksmo .ru; f. 1991; popular fiction; Gen. Dir OLEG YE. NOVIKOV.

Energoatomizdat (Atomic Energy Press): 113114 Moscow, Shluzovaya nab. 10; tel. (095) 925-99-93; f. 1981; different kinds of energy, nuclear science and technology; Dir A. P. ALESHKIN.

Finansy i Statistika (Finance and Statistics): 101000 Moscow, ul. Pokrovka 7; tel. (095) 925-47-08; fax (095) 925-09-57; e-mail mail@ finstat.ru; internet www.finstat.ru; f. 1924; education, economics, science, finance, statistics, banking, insurance, accounting, computer science; Dir Dr A. N. ZVONOVA.

Fizkultura i Sport (Exercise and Sport): 101421 Moscow, ul. Dolgorukovskaya 27; tel. (095) 978-26-90; fax (095) 200-12-17; f. 1923; books and periodicals relating to all forms of sport, chess and draughts, etc. Gen. Dir T. BALYAN.

Forum: 101831 Moscow, Kolpachnyi per. 9A; tel. and fax (095) 925-01-97; e-mail forum-books@mail.ru; internet www.infra-m.ru/forum .htm; f. 2001; general and professional educational textbooks; Gen. Man. IRINA S. MONAKHOVA.

GALART: 125319 Moscow, ul. Chernyakhovskogo 4; tel. (095) 151-25-02; fax (095) 151-37-61; f. 1969; fmrly *Sovetskii Khudozhnik* (Soviet Artist); art reproduction, art history and criticism; Gen. Dir V. V. GORYAINOV.

Gorodets: 117419 Moscow, 2-i Roshchinskii pr. 8/7/1201; tel. (095) 955-71-28; fax (095) 234-39-67; e-mail info@gorodets.com; internet www.gorodets.com; law, politics, international relations, economics.

INFRA-M: 127214 Moscow, Dmitrovskoye shosse 107; tel. (095) 485-7077; fax (095) 485-5317; e-mail office@infra-m.ru; internet www.infra-m.ru; f. 1992; economics, law, computing, history, reference works, encyclopaedias; Gen. Man. YELENA V. MELCHUK.

Iskusstvo (Art): 103009 Moscow, M. Kislovskii per. 3; tel. (095) 203-58-72; f. 1936; fine arts, architecture, cinema, photography, television and radio, theatre; Dir O. A. MAKAROV.

Izobrazitelnoye Iskusstvo (Fine Art): 129272 Moscow, ul. Sushchevskii val 64; tel. (095) 281-65-48; fax (095) 281-41-11; reproductions of pictures, pictorial art, books on art, albums, calendars, postcards; Dir V. S. KUZYAKOV.

Khimiya (Chemistry): 107976 Moscow, ul. Strominka 21/2; tel. (095) 268-29-76; f. 1963; chemistry and the chemical industry; Dir BORIS S. KRASNOPEVTSEV.

Khudozhestvennaya Literatura (Fiction): 107078 Moscow, ul. Novobasmannaya 19; tel. (095) 261-88-65; fax (095) 261-83-00; fiction and works of literary criticism, history of literature, etc. Dir A. N. PETROV; Editor-in-Chief V. S. MODESTOV.

Kniga and Business Ltd (Books and Business): 125047 Moscow, ul. 1-aya TverskayaYamskaya 22; tel. (095) 251-60-03; fax (095) 250-04-89; fiction, biographies, history, commerce, general; Dir VIKTOR N. ADAMOV.

Kolos (Ear of Corn): 107807 Moscow, ul. Sadovaya-Spasskaya 18; tel. (095) 207-29-92; fax (095) 207-28-70; f. 1918; all aspects of agricultural production; Dir ANATOLII M. ULYANOV.

Kompozitor (Composer): 103006 Moscow, ul. Sadovaya-Triumfalnaya 12–14; tel. (095) 209-41-05; fax (095) 209-54-98; e-mail music@ spica-eng.ru; f. 1957; established by the Union of Composers of the USSR; music and music criticism; Dir GRIGORII A. VORONOV.

Malysh (Dear Little One): 121352 Moscow, ul. Davydkovskaya 5; tel. (095) 443-06-54; fax (095) 443-06-55; f. 1958; books, booklets and posters for children aged three to 10 years; Dir V. A. RYBIN.

Meditsina (Medicine): 101838 Moscow, Petroverigskii per. 6/8; tel. (095) 924-87-85; fax (095) 928-60-03; e-mail meditsina@iname.com; internet www.medlit.ru; f. 1918; state-owned; imprint of Association for Medical Literature; books and journals on medicine and health; Dir A. M. STOCHIK; Editor-in-Chief Prof. NIKOLAI R. PALEYEV.

Metallurgiya (Metallurgy): 119034 Moscow, 2-i Obydenskii per. 14; tel. (095) 202-55-32; f. 1939; metallurgical literature; Dir A. G. BELIKOV.

Mezhdunarodnye Otnosheniya (International Relations): 107078 Moscow, ul. Sadovaya-Spasskaya 20; tel. (095) 207-67-93; fax (095) 200-22-04; f. 1957; international relations, economics and politics of foreign countries, foreign trade, international law, foreign language textbooks and dictionaries, translations and publications for the UN and other international organizations; Dir B. P. LIKHACHEV.

Mir (The World): 107996 Moscow, l-i Rizhskii per. 2; tel. (095) 286-17-83; fax (095) 288-95-22; e-mail akhp@mir-publishers.net; internet www.mir-publishers.net; f. 1946; Russian translations of foreign scientific, technical and science fiction books; translations of Russian books on science and technology into foreign languages; Dir KHABIB P. ABDULLAYEV.

Molodaya Gvardiya (The Young Guard): 103030 Moscow, ul. Sushchevskaya 21; tel. (095) 972-05-46; fax (095) 972-05-82; f. 1922; fmrly publishing and printing combine of the Lenin Young Communist League (Komsomol); joint-stock co; books and magazines, newspaper for children and for adolescents; Gen. Dir V. F. YURKIN.

Moscow University Press: 119899 Moscow, ul. Khokhlova 11; tel. and fax (095) 939-33-23; e-mail kd_mgu@df.ru; f. 1756; more than 200 titles of scientific, educational and reference literature annually, 19 scientific journals; Dir N. S. TIMOFEYEV.

Moskovskii Rabochii (Moscow Worker): 101854 Moscow, Chistoprudnyi bulv. 8; tel. (095) 921-07-35; f. 1922; publishing house of the Moscow city and regional soviets; all types of work, including fiction; Dir D. V. YEVDOKIMOV.

Muzyka (Music): 103031 Moscow, ul. Neglinnaya 14; tel. (095) 921-51-70; fax (095) 928-33-04; f. 1861; sheet music, music scores and related literature; Dir IGOR P. SAVINTSEV.

Mysl (Thought): 119071 Moscow, Leninskii pr. 15; tel. (095) 952-42-48; fax (095) 955-04-58; f. 1963; science, popular science, economics, philosophy, demography, history, political science, geography; Editor-in-Chief I. V. USHAKOV.

Nauka (Science): 117997 Moscow, ul. Profsoyuznaya 90; tel. (095) 336-02-66; fax (095) 420-22-20; e-mail secret@naukaran.ru; f. 1964; publishing house of the Academy of Sciences; general and social science, mathematics, physics, chemistry, biology, earth sciences, oriental studies, books in foreign languages, university textbooks, scientific journals, translation, export, distribution, typesetting and printing services; Dir-Gen. V. VASILIYEV.

Nauka i Tekhnologiya (Science and Technology): 107076 Moscow, Stromynskii per. 4; tel. (095) 269-51-96; fax (095) 269-49-96; e-mail admin@nauka-technology.ru; f. 2000; journals on chemistry, electronics and telecommunications; Gen. Dir MAKSIM A. KOVALEVSKII.

Nedra Biznestsentr (Natural Resources Business Centre): 125047 Moscow, Tverskaya zastava 3; tel. (095) 251-31-77; fax (095) 250-27-72; e-mail business@nedrainform.ru; internet www.nedrainform.ru; f. 1964; geology, natural resources, mining and coal industry, petroleum and gas industry; Dir V. D. MENSHIKOV.

Norma (The Norm): 101831 Moscow, Kolpachnyi per. 9A; tel. and fax (095) 925-45-05; e-mail norma@norma-verlag.com; internet www

.infra-m.ru/norma.htm; f. 1995; law and jurisprudence, philosophy, psychology, sociology, economics; Gen. Man. EDUARD I. MACHULSKII.

Novosti (News): 105082 Moscow, ul. B. Pochtovaya 7; tel. (095) 265-63-35; fax (095) 975-20-65; f. 1964; politics, economics, fiction, translated literature; Dir ALEKSANDR YEIDINOV.

Olma Press: 129075 Moscow, Zvezdnyi bulv. 23/12; tel. (095) 784-67-74; fax (095) 215-80-53; e-mail info@olmapress.ru; internet www.olmapress.ru; f. 1991; fiction, history, reference; children's books, popular science; general; Pres. VLADIMIR I. UZUN; Gen. Man. OLEG P. TKACH.

Pedagogika Press (Pedagogy Press): 119034 Moscow, Smolenskii bulv. 4; tel. and fax (095) 246-59-69; f. 1969; scientific and popular books on pedagogics, didactics, psychology, developmental physiology; young people's encyclopaedia, dictionaries; Dir I. KOLESNIKOVA.

Planeta (Planet): 103779 Moscow, ul. Petrovka 8/11; tel. (095) 923-04-70; fax (095) 200-52-46; f. 1969; postcards, calendars, guidebooks, brochures, illustrated books; co-editions with foreign partners; Dir V. G. SEREDIN.

Pressa (The Press): 125865 Moscow, ul. Pravdy 24; tel. (095) 257-46-21; fax (095) 250-52-05; f. 1934 as Pravda (Truth) Publishing House; publishes booklets, books and many newspapers and periodicals; Dir V. P. LEONTEV.

Profizdat (Professional Publishers): 101000 Moscow, ul. Myasnitskaya 13/18; tel. (095) 924-57-40; fax (095) 975-23-29; e-mail profizdat@profizdat.ru; f. 1930; books and magazines; Gen. Dir VLADIMIR SOLOVIEV.

Progress (Progress): 119992 Moscow, Zubovskii bulv. 17; tel. (095) 246-90-32; fax (095) 230-24-03; e-mail progress@mcn.ru; f. 1931; translations of Russian language books into foreign languages and of foreign language books into Russian; political and scientific, fiction, literature for children and youth; encyclopedias; Dir-Gen. SARKIS V. OGANIAN.

Prosveshcheniye (Enlightenment): 127521 Moscow, 3-i proyezd M. Roshchi 41; tel. (095) 789-30-40; fax (095) 789-30-41; e-mail prosv@prosv.ru; internet www.prosv.ru; f. 1930; school textbooks, fiction; Dir A. P. SUDAKOV.

Radio i Svyaz (Radio and Communication): 103473 Moscow, 2-i Shchemilovskii per.4/5; tel. (095) 978-54-10; fax (095) 978-53-51; f. 1981; radio engineering, electronics, communications, computer science; Dir YE. N. SALNIKOV; Editor-in-Chief I. K. KALUGIN.

Raduga (Rainbow): 121839 Moscow, per. Sivtsev Vrazhek 43; tel. (095) 241-68-15; fax (095) 241-63-53; e-mail raduga@pol.ru; f. 1982; translations of Russian fiction into foreign languages and of foreign authors into Russian; Dir TANYANA ZIMINA.

Respublika (Republic): 125811 Moscow, Miusskaya pl. 7; tel. (095) 251-42-44; fax (095) 200-22-54; e-mail respublik@dataforce.net; f. 1918; fmrly *Politizdat* (Political Publishing House); dictionaries, books on politics, human rights, philosophy, history, economics, religion, fiction, arts, reference; Dir ALEKSANDR P. POLYAKOV.

Russkaya Kniga (Russian Book): 123557 Moscow, Tishinskii per. 38; tel. (095) 205-33-77; fax (095) 205-34-27; f. 1957 as Sovetskaya Rossiya; fiction, politics, history, social sciences, health, do-it-yourself, children's; Dir M. F. NENASHEV.

Russkii Yazyk (Russian Language): 117303 Moscow, ul. M. Yushunski 1; tel. (095) 319-83-14; fax (095) 319-83-12; e-mail russlang@mtu-net.ru; f. 1974; textbooks, reference, dictionaries; Dir IRINA KAINARSKAYA.

Sovremennyi Pisatel (The Contemporary Writer): 121069 Moscow, ul. Povarskaya 11; tel. (095) 202-50-51; f. 1934; fiction and literary criticism, history, biography; publ. house of the International Confederation of Writers' Unions and the Union of Russian Writers; Dir A. N. ZHUKOV.

Stroyizdat (Construction Publishing House): 101442 Moscow, ul. Kalyayevskaya 23A; tel. (095) 251-69-67; f. 1932; building, architecture, environmental protection, fire protection and building materials; Dir V. A. KASATKIN.

Sudostroyeniye (Shipbuilding): 191186 St Petersburg, ul. M. Morskaya 8; tel. (812) 312-44-79; fax (812) 312-08-21; f. 1940; shipbuilding, ship design, navigation, marine research, underwater exploration, international marine exhibitions; Dir and Editor-in-Chief A. A. ANDREYEV.

Transport (Transport): 103064 Moscow, Basmannyi tupik 6A; tel. (095) 262-67-73; fax (095) 261-13-22; f. 1923; publishes works on all forms of transport; Dir V. G. PESHKOV.

Vagrius: 129090 Moscow, ul. Troitskaya 7/1; tel. (095) 785-09-62; fax (095) 785-09-69; e-mail vagrius@vagrius.com; internet www.vagrius.com; f. 1992; fiction, politics, history; Pres. and Dir-Gen. GLEB USPENSKII.

Ves Mir (The Whole World): 101831 Moscow, Kolpachnyi per. 9A; tel. (095) 923-68-39; fax (095) 925-42-69; e-mail info@vesmirbooks.ru; internet www.vesmirbooks.ru; f. 1994; university textbooks, scholarly works, history, encyclopaedias, in Russian and European languages; Dir Dr OLEG ZIMARIN; Editor-in-Chief TATYANA KOMAROVA.

Vneshtorgizdat (External Trade Printing and Publishing Association): 125047 Moscow, ul. Fadeyev 1; tel. (095) 250-51-62; fax (095) 253-97-94; f. 1925; publishes foreign technical material translated into Russian, and information on export goods, import and export firms, joint ventures; in several foreign languages; Dir-Gen. V. I. PROKOPOV.

Voyenizdat (Military Publishing House): 103160 Moscow, ul. Zorgye 1; tel. (095) 195-25-95; fax (095) 195-24-54; military theory and history, general fiction; Dir YURII I. STADNYUK.

Vysshaya Shkola (Higher School): 101439 Moscow, ul. Neglinnaya 29/14; tel. (095) 200-04-56; fax (095) 973-21-80; f. 1939; textbooks for higher-education institutions; Dir MIKHAIL I. KISELEV.

Yuridicheskaya Literatura (Legal Literature): 121069 Moscow, ul. M. Nikitskaya 14; tel. (095) 203-83-84; fax (095) 291-98-83; f. 1917; law subjects; official publishers of enactments of the Russian President and Govt; Dir I. A. BUNIN.

Znaniye (Knowledge): 101835 Moscow, proyezd Serova 4; tel. (095) 928-15-31; f. 1951; popular books and brochures on politics and science; Dir V. K. BELYAKOV.

Broadcasting and Communications

TELECOMMUNICATIONS

Delta Telecom: 191014 St Petersburg, per. Manezhnyi 14; tel. (812) 314-61-26; fax (812) 275-01-30; e-mail delta@deltatel.ru; internet www.deltatelecom.net; f. 1991; provides mobile cellular telecommunications services in St Petersburg, Kareliya, and Leningrad, Novgorod and Pskov Oblasts; Man. Dir SERGEI SOLDATENKOV.

Petersburg Telephone Network (PTS): 119186 St Petersburg, ul. B. Morskaya 24; tel. (812) 314-15-50; fax (812) 110-68-34; e-mail office@ptn.ru; internet www.ptn.ru; f. 1993; subsidiary of Severo-Zapadnyi Telekom (North-Western Telecom); Dir IGOR N. SAMYLIN.

Rostelekom: 125047 Moscow, ul.1-aya Tverskaya-Yamskaya 14; tel. (095) 787-28-49; fax (095) 787-28-50; e-mail info@rostelecom.ru; internet www.rt.ru; 50.7% owned by Svyazinvest; dominant long-distance and international telecommunications service provider; seven regional subsidiary cos based in St Petersburg, Samara, Novosibirsk, Yekaterinburg, Khabarovsk, Moscow and Rostov-on-Don; Dir ALEKSEI YE. SHEVCHENKO.

Sistema Telecom: 125047 Moscow, ul. 1–aya Tverskaya-Yamskaya 5; tel. (095) 105-74-21; fax (095) 105-74-58; e-mail info@sistel.ru; internet www.sistel.ru; subsidiary of Sistema; Pres. ALEKSANDR GONCHARUK.

Mobile TeleSystems (MTS): 109147 Moscow, ul. Marksistskaya 4; tel. (095) 766-01-77; e-mail info@mts.ru; internet www.mts.ru; f. 1993; 776,000 subscribers (Dec. 2000); provides mobile cellular telecommunications services in 25 regions of Russia; majority-owned by Sistema Telecom; Pres. M. A. SMIRNOV.

Moscow City Telephone Network (MGTS): 127994 Moscow, Petrovskii bulv. 12/3; tel. (095) 950-00-00; fax (095) 950-06-18; e-mail mgts@mgts.ru; internet www.mgts.ru; f. 1882; provides telecommunications services to over 4.2m. subscribers (2001) in Moscow City; 56% owned by Sistema Telecom; Gen. Man. VLADIMIR S. LAGUTIN.

Svyazinvest: 119121 Moscow, ul. Plyushchikha 55/2; tel. (095) 248-24-71; fax 248-24-53; e-mail dms@svyazinvest.ru; internet www.sinvest.ru; f. 1995; 51%-state-owned telecommunications co; holds controlling stakes in 75 regional telecommunications operators, 2 inter-city and international telephone exchanges, and non-controlling stakes in 5 regional and city telecommunications cos; Gen. Dir VALERII N. YASHIN.

Teleross: 111250 Moscow, ul. Krasnokazarmennaya 12; tel. (095) 787-10-00; fax (095) 787-10-10; e-mail info@goldentelecom.ru; internet www.teleross.ru; f. 1994; operates mobile cellular telecommunications network in 16 cities in the Russian Federation, and in Almaty (Kazakhstan) and Kiev (Ukraine); subsidiary of the Golden TeleSystems Group (USA); Dir-Gen. STAN ABBELOOS.

Vympelcom-Beeline: 125083 Moscow, ul. 8 Marta 10/14; tel. and fax (095) 725-07-00; e-mail info@beeline.ru; internet www.beeline.ru; operates mobile cellular telecommunications networks in Moscow City and Moscow Oblast, and in Yaroslavl, Nizhnii Novgorod, Novosibirsk, Omsk, Ufa, Rostov-on-Don and Volgograd; 25% owned by Telenor (Norway), 25% owned by Alfa-Bank; 1,800,000 subscribers (Nov. 2001); Chief Exec. Jo Lunder; Pres. Dmitrii B. Zimin.

BROADCASTING

In December 1993 the Federal Television and Radio Broadcasting Service was established to replace the Ministry of Press and Information and the Federal Information Service of Russia. Its function was to co-ordinate the activity of national and regional state television and broadcasting organizations. In 1995 there was extensive reorganization of Russian broadcasting, and a new organization, Public Russian Television (ORT), was formed to take over the broadcasting responsibilities of the Ostankino Russian State Television and Radio Broadcasting Company. Pervyi Kanal (First Channel), as ORT's Channel 1 was renamed in 2002, is received throughout Russia and many parts of the CIS. All-Russian State Television broadcasts Telekanal—Rossiya, which reaches some 92% of the Russian population.. In 1997 it began broadcasting Telekanal —Kultura channel, founded for the purpose of broadcasting Russian-made programmes. In addition to the nation-wide television channels, there are local channels, and the Independent Television (NTV) channel is broadcast in most of central Russia. In the regions, part of Rossiya's programming is devoted to local affairs, with broadcasts in minority languages. In late 2001 there were some 550 television stations in the Russian Federation, of which approximately 150 were state-owned.

Association of Regional State Television and Radio Broadcasters: 113326 Moscow, ul. Pyatnitskaya 25/226; tel. and fax (095) 950-60-28; e-mail fstratyv@rzn.rosmail.com; Chair. of Bd Aleksandr N. Levchenko.

Regulatory Authority

Russian Television and Radio Broadcasting Network: 113326 Moscow, ul. Pyatnitskaya 25; tel. (095) 233-66-03; fax (095) 233-28-93; f. 2001; Gen. Man. Gennadii I. Sklyar.

Radio

All-Russian State Television and Radio Broadcasting Company (VGTRK): 125124 Moscow, ul. 5-aya Yamskogo Polya 19/21; tel. (095) 214-42-58; fax (095) 975-26-11; e-mail info@vesti-rtr.com; internet www.tvradio.ru; f. 1991; broadcasts 'Rossiya' and 'Kultura' television channels, 89 regional television and radio cos, and national radio stations 'Radio Rossiya', 'Radio Mayak', 'Radio Orfei' and 'Radio Nostalzhi'; Chair. Olga Dobrodeyeva.

Radio Mayak (Radio Beacon): 113326 Moscow, ul. Pyatnitskaya 25; tel. (095) 950-67-67; fax (095) 959-42-04; e-mail inform@ radiomayak.ru; internet www.radiomayak.ru; f. 1964; state-owned; Chair. Irina A. Gerasimova.

Radio Nostalzhi (Radio Nostalgia): 113162 Moscow, ul. Shabolovka 37; tel. (095) 955-84-00; e-mail nostalgie@vimain.vitpc.com; f. 1993; Gen. Man. Irina A. Gerasimova.

Radio Orfei (Radio Orpheus): 121069 Moscow, ul. M. Nikitskaya 24; tel. and fax (095) 290-19-16; e-mail orphei@dol.ru; internet www.mmv.ru/orphei; f. 1991; broadcasts classical music; Gen. Dir Olga A. Gromova.

Radio Rossiya (Radio Russia): 125040 Moscow, ul. 5-aya Yamskogo Polya 19/21; tel. (095) 214-07-30; fax (095) 214-53-66; e-mail mail@radiorus.ru; internet www.radiorus.ru; f. 1990; broadcasts information, social, political, musical, literary and investigate progamming; Gen. Man. Aleksei V. Abakumov.

Ekho Moskvy (Moscow Echo): 119992 Moscow, ul. Novyi Arbat 11; tel. (095) 202-92-29; e-mail info@echo.msk.ru; internet www.echo.msk.ru; f. 1990; stations in Moscow, St Petersburg, Rostov-on-Don and Vologda; also broadcasts from Moscow to Chelyabinsk, Krasnoyarsk, Novosibirsk, Omsk, Perm, Saratov and Yekaterinburg; majority-owned by Gazprom-Mediya; Gen. Man. Yurii Fedutinkov.

Golos Rossii (The Voice of Russia): 113326 Moscow, ul. Pyatnitskaya 25; tel. (095) 950-64-40; fax (095) 230-28-28; e-mail letters@ vor.ru; internet www.vor.ru; fmrly Radio Moscow International; international broadcasts in 31 languages; Man. Dir Armen G. Oganesian.

Radio Arsenal: 119992 Moscow, ul. Novyi Arbat 11; tel. (095) 202-92-29; e-mail info@radioarsenal.ru; internet www.echo.msk.ru/headings/arsenal.html; f. 2002 by the former staff of Ekho Moskvy (Moscow Echo—q.v.); broadcasts news, interviews and conversation; Dir Aleksei Venediktov.

Yevropa Plyus (Europa Plus): 127427 Moscow, ul. Akademika Koroleva 19; tel. (095) 217-82-57; fax (095) 956-35-08; e-mail main@ europaplus.ru; internet www.europaplus.ru; FM station, broadcasting music, entertainment and information programmes to 500 cities; Pres. Zhorzh Polinski; Gen. Man. Aleksandr Polesitskii.

Television

All-Russian State Television and Radio Broadcasting Company (VGTRK): see Radio.

Telekanal—Kultura (Television Channel—Culture): 123995 Moscow, ul. M. Nikitskaya 24; e-mail kultura@tvkultura.ru; internet www.tvkultura.ru; f. 1997; Gen. Dir Aleksandr S. Ponomarev.

Telekanal—Rossiya (Television Channel—Russia): 115162 Moscow, ul. Shabolovka 37; tel. (095) 924-63-74; fax (095) 234-87-71; e-mail info@rutv.ru; internet www.rutv.ru; fmrly RTR-TV; name changed as above in 2002; Dir-Gen. Aleksandr S. Ponamarev.

NTV—Independent Television: 127000 Moscow, ul. Akademika Koroleva 12; tel. (095) 217-51-03; fax (095) 217-92-74; e-mail info@ ntv-tv.ru; internet www.ntv-tv.ru; f. 1993; 65% owned by Gazprom-Mediya; also NTV International, broadcasting to Russian communities in Israel, Western Europe and the USA; Chief Exec. Aleksandr Dybal; Dir-Gen. Nikolai Yu. Senkevich.

Pervyi Kanal—First Channel: 127000 Moscow, ul. Akademika Koroleva 12; tel. (095) 215-82-47; fax (095) 215-82-47; e-mail ort_int@ortv.ru; internet www.1tv.ru; f. 1995; fmrly ORT—Public Russian Television; name changed as above in 2002; 51% state-owned; 49% owned by private shareholders; broadcasts Russia's main television channel; Chair. Vitalii Ignatenko; Dir-Gen. Konstantin Ernst.

Ren-TV Network: 119843 Moscow, Zubovskii bulv. 17/510; tel. (095) 246-25-06; fax (095) 245-09-98; e-mail site@rentv.dol.ru; internet www.ren-tv.com; f. 1998; network of more than 100 television stations in the Russian Federation and 60 stations in republics of the CIS; Pres. Irena Lesnevskaya; Gen. Man. Dmitrii A. Lesnevskii.

STS—Network of Television Stations: 123298 Moscow, ul. 3-aya Khoroshevskaya 12; tel. (095) 797-41-73; fax (095) 797-41-01; e-mail www@ctc-tv.ru; internet www.ctc-tv.ru; f. 1996; owned by StoryFirst Communications (USA); broadcasts to 350 cities in Russia; Dir-Gen. Aleksandr Ye. Rodnyanskii.

TNT—Territory of Our Viewers—TV Network: 127427 Moscow, ul. Akademika Koroleva 19; tel. (095) 217-81-88; fax (095) 748-14-90; e-mail info@tnt-tv.ru; internet www.tnt-tv.ru; f. 1997; cable television network broadcasting to 582 cities in Russia; Chief Exec. Aleksandr Dybal.

TVS—The Sixth TV Channel: 103070 Moscow, ul. Ilinka 15/1; tel. and fax (095) 923-17-07; e-mail tvs@tvs.tv; internet www.tvs.tv; f. 2002 to replace TV-6; broadcasts to 403 towns in 66 regions of Russia; Dir-Gen. Ruslan Terekbayev.

TV-Tsentr (TVTs—TV-Centre): 113184 Moscow, ul. B. Tatarskaya 33/1; tel. (095) 959-39-87; fax (095) 959-39-66; e-mail info@tvc.ru; internet www.tvc.ru; f. 1997; broadcasting consortium for terrestrial cable and satellite television; Pres. Oleg M. Poptsov; Dir Pavel V. Kasparov.

Finance

(cap. = capital; res = reserves; dep. = deposits; m. = million; brs = branches; amounts in new roubles, unless otherwise stated)

BANKING

Following the dissolution of the USSR in 1991, the majority of state-owned banks were privatized and the establishment of private banks was permitted. The Central Bank of the Russian Federation, founded in 1991, replaced the Gosbank (State Bank). Under the 1993 Constitution, responsibility for bank licensing, regulation and supervision was accorded to the Central Bank.

The number of commercial banks increased considerably in the early 1990s, reaching more than 2,500 in 1994. Consolidation of the banking sector, begun in 1995, meant that there were some 1,641 private banks registered in April 1998; by 1 January 2001 there were reported to be 1,311 credit institutions in Russia.

Central Bank

Bank Rossii—Central Bank of the Russian Federation: 103016 Moscow, ul. Neglinnaya 12; tel. (095) 771-40-46; fax (095) 921-91-47; e-mail webmaster@www.cbr.ru; internet www.cbr.ru; f. 1990; cap. 166,048m., res 192,532m., dep. 201,460m. (Dec. 2001); Chair. Sergei M. Ignatiyev; 78 brs.

State-owned Bank

Vneshtorgbank (Bank for Foreign Trade): 103778 Moscow, Kuznetskii most 16; tel. (095) 101-18-80; fax (095) 258-47-81; e-mail info@vtb.ru; internet www.vtb.ru; f. 1990; cap. US $2,153m., res –

THE RUSSIAN FEDERATION *Directory*

$318m., dep. $2,885m. (Dec. 2001); Chair. and Chief Exec. ANDREI L. KOSTIN; 39 brs.

Major Commercial and Co-operative Banks

AK BARS Bank: 420066 Tatarstan, Kazan, ul. Dekabristov 1; tel. (8432) 19-39-00; fax (8432) 57-83-76; e-mail kanc@akbars.ru; internet www.akbars.ru; f. 1993; cap. 2,015.4m., res 810.2m., dep. 9,421.0m. (Dec. 2001); Chair. and Chief Exec. MOUDARIS IDRISSOV.

Alfa-Bank: 107078 Moscow, ul. M. Poryvayevoi 9; tel. (095) 974-25-15; fax (095) 207-61-36; e-mail mail@alfabank.ru; internet www .alfabank.ru; f. 1991; cap. US $112.8m., res $165.2m., dep. $2,272.9m. (Dec. 2001); Chair. of Bd LEONID VID; Chief Exec. ALEKSANDR KNASTR; 45 brs.

Avtobank: 127055 Moscow, ul. Lesnaya 41; tel. (095) 723-77-77; fax (095) 978-66-23; e-mail info@avtobank.ru; internet www.avtobank .ru; f. 1988; 22.7% owned by Ingosstrakh Insurance Co Ltd; cap. US $43m., res $0.9m., dep. $240m. (Sept. 2002); Chair. LYUDMILA A. SHABALKINA; 25 brs.

Bank MENATEP St Petersburg (MENATEP SPb): 191186 St Petersburg, Nevskii pr. 1; tel. (812) 320-45-14; fax (812) 326-39-11; e-mail finance@menatepspb.com; internet www.menatepspb.com; f. 1995; cap. US $72.4m., res $7.0m., dep. $881.9m. (Dec. 2001); Pres. VITALII SAVELIYEV; Chair. of Bd DMITRII LEBEDEV; 58 brs.

Bank of Khanty-Mansiisk: 628012 Khanty-Mansii AOk, Khanty-Mansiisk, ul. Mira 13; tel. (34671) 302-10; fax (34671) 302-19; e-mail admin@khmb.ru; internet www.khmb.ru; f. 1992; cap. 100.0m., res 176.5m., dep. 8,745.0m. (Dec. 2000); Pres. DMITRII MIZGULIN; 7 brs.

Bank Petrocommerce: 103051 Moscow, ul. Petrovka 24; tel. (095) 200-00-51; fax (095) 923-36-07; e-mail welcome@petrocommerce.ru; internet www.petrocommerce.ru; f. 1992; 77.9% owned by LUKoil; cap. 4,500.0m., res 334.2m., dep. 16,953.8m. (Dec. 2001); Pres. VLADIMIR N. NIKITENKO.

Bank ZENIT: 129100 Moscow, Bannyi per. 9; tel. (095) 937-07-37; fax (095) 937-07-36; e-mail info@zenit.ru; internet www.zenit.ru; f. 1994; 50% owned by Tatneft, 20% owned by Novolipetsk MetKom (New Lipetsk Metallurgical Group); cap. 2,000.0m., res 202.9m., dep. 12,842.9m. (Dec. 2001); Chair. of Bd ALEKSEI A SOKOLOV; 4 brs.

BIN Bank: 121471 Moscow, ul Grodnenskaya 5A; tel. (095) 755-50-60; fax (095) 440-09-75; e-mail binbank@binbank.ru; internet www .binbank.ru; f. 1993; cap. 2,040.0m., res 1,005.8m., dep. 20,919.9m. (Dec. 2001); Chair. of Bd SERGEI YE. YEGOREV; Pres. and Chief Exec. MIKHAIL O. SHISHKHANOV; 19 brs.

Commercial Bank for the Development of Business Activities—Guta Bank LLC: 107078 Moscow, Orlikov per. 5/3; tel. (095) 975-63-00; fax (095) 975-63-33; e-mail post@guta.ru; internet www.guta .ru; f. 1991; wholly state-owned; cap. 6,573.3m., res –1,035.5m., dep. 11,571.6m. (Dec. 2001); Pres. ALEKSANDR PETROV; 30 brs.

Doveritelnyi i Investitsionnyi Bank (Trust and Investment Bank): 113035 Moscow, ul. Sadovnicheskaya 84/3/7; tel. (095) 247-25-83; fax (095) 956-99-65; e-mail office@tibank.ru; internet www .tibank.ru; f. 1994; cap. US $86.4m., res $55.8m., dep. $1,030.6m. (Dec. 2001); Chair. and Chief Exec. ILYA YUROV.

Evrofinance: 121099 Moscow, ul. Novyi Arbat 29; tel. (095) 967-81-82; fax (095) 967-81-33; e-mail info@evrofinance.ru; internet www .evrofinance.ru; f. 1990; 58% owned by Banque Commerciale pour l'Europe du Nord (Eurobank—France); cap. 1,312,0m., res 2,541.6m., dep. 15,142.5m. (Dec. 2001); Pres. and Chair. of Bd VLADIMIR M. STOLYARENKO; 6 brs.

Gazprombank: 117420 Moscow, ul. Nametkina 16/1; tel. (095) 719-17-63; fax (095) 913-73-19; e-mail mailbox@gazprombank.ru; internet www.gazprombank.ru; f. 1990; 87.5% owned by Gazprom; cap. US $872.9m., res $-158.9m., dep. $3,024.5m. (Dec. 2001); Chair. of Bd of Dirs ALEKSEI B. MILLER; Chair. of Man. Bd YURII I. LVOV.

Globex Commercial Bank (GlobexBank): 121069 Moscow, ul. B. Nikitskaya 60/1; tel. (095) 202-24-82; fax (095) 290-56-08; e-mail post@globexbank.ru; internet www.globexbank.ru; f. 1992; cap. 10,084.4m., res –5.3m., dep. 2,114.1m. (Dec. 2001); Chair. ANDREI F. DUNAYEV.

IMPEXBANK (JSC Import-Export Bank IMPEXBANK: 125252 Moscow, ul. Novopeschanaya 20/10/1A; tel. and fax (095) 752-52-52; e-mail mail@impexbank.ru; internet www.impexbank.ru; f. 1993; cap. 2,314.9m., dep. 5,933.6m., total assets 9,209.8m. (Dec. 2001); Chair. of Bd DMITRII P. YEROPKIN.

Industry and Construction Bank (ICB) (Promyshlenno-Stroitelnyi Bank): 191014 St Petersburg, ul. Kovesnkii 17–18; tel. (812) 329-84-51; fax (812) 310-61-73; e-mail lider@icbank.ru; internet www.icbank.ru; f. 1870 as Volga-Kama Bank; present name adopted 1990; cap. 124.7m., res 2,095.6m., dep. 29,396.5m. (Dec. 2001); Chair. ALEKSANDR PUSTOVALOV; 48 brs, 21 sub-brs.

International Moscow Bank: 119034 Moscow, Prechistenskaya nab. 9; tel. (095) 258-72-58; fax (095) 258-72-72; e-mail imbank@

imbank.ru; internet www.imb.ru; f. 1989; 43.2% owned by Bayerische Hypo- und Vereinsbank AG (Germany), 21.6% by Nordian Bank Finland plc, 20% by Banque Commerciale pour l'Europe du Nord—EUROBANK (France); finances joint ventures, investments and projects of domestic and foreign customers and international trade deals; absorbed Bank Austria Creditanstalt (Russia ZAO) in 2001; cap. US $139.5m., res $16.6m., dep. $2,252.5m. (Dec. 2001); Chair. of Bd P. O. KOELLE; Pres. ILKKA SALONEN.

Mezhdunarodnyi Promyshlennyi Bank (International Industrial Bank): 103009 Moscow, ul. B. Dmitrovka 23–8/1–2; tel. (095) 926-44-46; fax (095) 292-82-84; e-mail mail@iib.ru; f. 1992; cap. 25,000m., res 923.4m., dep. 74,582.3m. (Dec. 2001); Pres. SERGEI A. VEREMEYENKO; 5 brs.

Moscow Business World Bank (MDM Bank) (Bank Moskovskii Delovoi Mir): 113035 Moscow, ul. Sadovnicheskaya 3; tel. (095) 797-95-00; fax (095) 797-95-01; e-mail info@mdm.ru; internet www .mdmbank.com; f. 1993; cap. 152.1m., res 2,514.3m., dep. 7,150.0m. (Dec. 1999); total assets US $1,520.7m. (Dec. 2001); Chief Exec. VLADIMIR RASHEVSKII; 70 brs and sub-brs.

Moscow Municipal Bank—Bank of Moscow: 107996 Moscow, ul. Rozhdestvenka 8/15/3; tel. (095) 745-80-00; fax (095) 795-26-00; e-mail info@mmbank.ru; internet www.mmbank.ru; f. 1995; 62.7% owned by Govt of Moscow Federal City; cap. 3,000m., res 905.9m., dep. 62,800m. (Jan. 2002); Pres. and Chief Exec. ANDREI BORODIN; 40 brs.

NIKoil IBG Bank: 119048 Moscow, ul. Yefryemova 8; tel. (095) 705-90-39; fax (095) 705-90-60; e-mail pr@nikoil.ru; internet www.nikoil .ru; f. 1990 as Rodina Joint-Stock Bank; present name adopted 1998; cap. 2,945.2m., res 369.9m., dep. 9,197.0m. (Dec. 2001); Pres. NIKOLAI TSVETKOV; 6 brs.

Novaya Moskva (NOMOS-BANK): 109240 Moscow, ul. V. Radishchevskaya 3/1; tel. (095) 797-32-45; fax (095) 797-32-50; e-mail nmosmail@online.ru; internet www.nomos.ru; f. 1992; cap. 1,185.0m., res 1,768.8m., dep. 10,026.2m. (Dec. 2001); Pres. IGOR FINOGENOV.

Promsvyazbank (Industry and Communications Bank): 109052 Moscow, ul. Smirnovskaya 10/2–3/22; tel. (095) 733-96-20; fax (095) 777-10-21; e-mail postmaster@psbank.ru; internet www.psbank.ru; f. 1995; owned by a consortium of communications cos; cap. 2,684.3m., dep. 12,282.4m. (June 2002); Chair. of Bd DMITRII N. ANANIEV; Pres. ALEKSANDR A. LEVKOVSKII; 11 brs.

Rosbank: 107078 Moscow, ul. M. Poryvayevoi 11, POB 208; tel. (095) 725-05-95; fax (095) 725-05-11; e-mail mailbox@rosbank.ru; internet www.rosbank.ru; f. 1998 by merger of Menatep, Most-Bank and Oneximbank, merged with UNEXIMbank in 2000; owned by Interros; cap. 3,405.3m., res 4,190.3m., dep. 58,410.5m. (Dec. 2001); Chair. of Exec. Bd YEVGENII IVANOV; 11 brs.

Sberbank Rossii—Savings Bank of the Russian Federation (Sberbank): 117997 Moscow, ul. Vavilova 19; tel. (095) 957-57-58; fax (095) 957-57-31; e-mail sbrf@sbrf.ru; internet www.sbrf.ru; f. 1841 as a deposit-taking institution, reorganized as a joint-stock commercial bank in 1991; 60.6% owned by Bank Rossii—Central Bank of the Russian Federation; cap. 1,000m., res 23,167m., dep. 645,145m. (Jan. 2002); Chair. of Bd and Chief Exec. ANDREI I. KAZMIN; 1,233 brs and 18,831 sub-brs.

Sobinbank: 121248 Moscow, pr. Kutuzovskii 17; tel. (095) 725-25-25; fax (095) 777-25-45; e-mail mail@sobin.ru; internet www .sobinbank.ru; f. 1990; cap. 500.0m., res 75.0m., dep. 4,054.5m. (Jan. 2002); Chair. of Bd SERGEI A KIRILENKO; 17 brs.

Surgutneftegazbank (SNGB): 628400 Tyumen obl., Khanty-Mansii AOk, Surgut, ul. Kukuyevitskogo 19; tel. (3462) 39-86-10; fax (3462) 39-87-11; e-mail telex@sngb.ru; internet www.sngb.ru; f. 1965 as a br. of Promstroibank; reorganized as a commercial bank in 1990; 81.2% owned by Surgutneftegaz (SNG) Oil Co; cap. 633.0m., res 30.5m., dep. 59,927.6m. (Dec. 2000); Pres. VLADIMIR BOGDANOV; Chair. of Bd YEVGENIYA NEPOMNYASHIKHA.

TransKreditBank: 121099 Moscow, Novinskii bulv. 3/1; tel. (095) 788-08-80; fax (095) 788-08-79; internet www.tkb.ru; f. 1992; cap. 2,931.0m., res –910.4m., dep. 8,202.2m. (Dec. 2001); Pres. ALEKSANDR B. MASALSKII.

UralSib (Uralo-Siberian Bank): 450000 Bashkortostan, Ufa, ul. Revolutsionnaya 41; tel. (3472) 51-94-85; fax (3472) 51-94-88; e-mail ufa@uralsibbank.ru; internet www.uralsibbank.ru; f. 1993 as Bash-CreditBank, present name adopted 2001; 75% owned by the Government of the Republic of Bashkortostan; cap. 9,583.3m., res –4,855.6m., dep. 20,600.8m. (Dec. 2001); Pres. and Chief Exec. AZAT T. KURMANAYEV; Chair. RAFAEL I. BAIDAVLETOV.

Vneshekonombank (Bank for Foreign Economic Affairs): 103810 Moscow, pr. Sakharova 9; tel. (095) 207-10-37; fax (095) 975-21-43; e-mail postmaster@veb.ru; internet www.veb.ru; f. 1924; total assets US $3,826m. (Dec. 2001); Chair. VLADIMIR A. CHERNUKHIN.

Vozrozhdeniye—V-Bank (Rebirth—Moscow Joint Stock Commercial Bank Vozrozdeniye): 101999 Moscow, per. Luchnikov 7/4/1, POB 9; tel. (095) 929-18-88; fax (095) 929-19-99; e-mail vbank@co.voz.ru; internet www.vbank.ru; f. 1991; cap. 145.4m., res 1,374.0m., dep. 12,727.9m. (July 2002); Pres. DMITRII L. ORLOV; 60 brs.

Foreign Banks

ABN AMRO Bank AO (Netherlands): 103009 Moscow, ul. B. Nikitskaya 17/1; tel. (095) 931-91-41; fax (095) 931-91-40; internet www.abnamro.com; Dir M. SCHWARZ.

Crédit Lyonnais Rusbank (France): 191186 St Petersburg, Nevsky pr. 12, POB 139; tel. (812) 313-31-00; fax (812) 313-33-90; f. 1991; present name adopted 1997; cap. 20.0m., res 1,150.5m., dep. 6,885.4m. (Dec. 2000); Chair. BERNARD MIGNUCCI.

Crédit Suisse First Boston AO (Switzerland): 103009 Moscow, Nikitskii per. 5; tel. (095) 967-82-00; fax (095) 967-82-10; investment bank; cap. 460.0m., res 586.1m., dep. 5,040.0m. (Dec. 2000); Pres. NICHOLAS GORDON-SMITH.

Deutsche Bank Ltd (Germany): 129090 Moscow, ul. Shepkina 4; tel. (095) 797-50-00; fax (095) 797-50-17; f. 1998; cap. 1,237.5m., res 891.4m., dep. 3,378.1m. (Dec. 2000); Chief. Exec. HUBERT ALBERT PANDZA.

Dresdner Bank ZAO (Germany): 190000 St Petersburg, ul. M. Morskaya 23; tel. (812) 118-51-51; fax (812) 324-32-81; e-mail zao@dresdner-bank.com; internet www.dresdner-bank.ru; f. 1993 as BNP-Dresdner Bank (ZAO); present name adopted 2001; cap. 727.3m., res 830.5m., dep. 3,853.8m. (Dec. 2001); Pres. WARNIG MATTHIAS.

ING Bank (Eurasia) ZAO—ING Bank (Netherlands): 123022 Moscow, ul. Krasnaya Presnya 31; tel. (095) 755-54-00; fax (095) 755-54-99; internet www.ing.ru; f. 1993; present name adopted 1997; cap. US $6.6m., res $84.6m., dep. $228.5m. (Dec. 2000); Pres and Dir-Gen. HENDRICK WILLEM TEN BOSCH.

Raiffeisenbank Austria ZAO: 129090 Moscow, ul. Troitskaya 17/1; tel. (095) 721-99-00; fax (095) 721-99-01; e-mail common@raiffeisen.ru; internet www.raiffeisen.ru; f. 1996; cap. 6.175.4m., res –3,475.4m., dep. 21,668.6m. (Dec. 2001); Chair. of Man. Bd MICHEL P. PERHIRIN; 7 brs and sub-brs.

Bankers' Association

Association of Russian Banks: 121069 Moscow, Skatertnyi per. 20/1; tel. and fax (095) 291-80-98; e-mail pr@arb.ru; internet www.arb.ru; f. 1991; unites some 500 private banks; Pres. GAGERIN A. TOSUNYAN.

INSURANCE

Department of Insurance Supervision: 109097 Moscow, ul. Ilinka 9; tel. (095) 748-45-10; fax (095) 748-45-11; e-mail d2400@minfin.ru; Dir KONSTANTIN I. PYLOV.

Agroinvest Insurance Co: 127422 Moscow, ul. Timiryazevskaya 26; tel. (095) 976-94-56; fax (095) 977-05-88; health, life and general insurance services; Pres. YURII I. MORDVINTSEV.

AIG Russia: 103009 Moscow, ul. Tverskaya 16/2; tel. (095) 935-89-50; fax (095) 935-89-52; e-mail aig.russia@aig.com; internet www .aigrussia.ru; f. 1994; mem. of the American International GroupInc. personal and business property insurance, also marine, life, financial etc. Pres. GARY COLEMAN.

Ingosstrakh Insurance Co Ltd: 115998 Moscow, ul. Pyatnitskaya 12/2; tel. (095) 232-32-11; fax (095) 959-45-18; e-mail ingos@ingos .ru; internet www.ingos.ru; f. 1947; undertakes all kinds of insurance and reinsurance; Chair. NATALIYA A. RAYEVSKAYA; Gen. Dir YEVGENII TUMANOV.

Medstrakh—Medical Insurance Fund of the Russian Federation: 107076 Moscow, pl. Preobrazhenskaya 7A /1; tel. (095) 964-84-27; fax (095) 964-84-21; e-mail mz@mcramn.ru; internet www .medstrah.ru; f. 1991; health, life, property, travel, liability; also provides compulsory medical insurance; Pres. PETR KUZNETSOV.

Ost-West Allianz Insurance Co: 127473 Moscow, 3-i Samotechnii per. 3; tel. (095) 937-69-96; fax (095) 937-69-80; e-mail allianz@allianz.ru; internet www.allianz.ru; engineering, professional liability, life, medical, property, marine and private; Man. Dir ERHARD JOERCHEL.

RESO-Garantiya Insurance Co: 125047 Moscow, ul. Gasheka 12/1; tel. (095) 234-18-00; fax (095) 956-25-85; e-mail reso@orc.ru; internet www.reso.ru; f. 1991; Dir-Gen. SERGEI E. SARKISOV.

Rosgosstrakh—Russian State Insurance: 127994 Moscow, ul. Novoslobodskaya 23; tel. (095) 781-24-00; fax (095) 978-27-64; e-mail admin@rgs.ru; internet www.gosstrah.ru; majority state-owned; 49% stake transferred to private ownership in 2001; undertakes domestic insurance; subsidiary cos in 80 federal subjects (territorial

units) of the Russian Federation; Chair. VLADISLAV REZNIK; Gen. Dir RUBEN VARDANIAN.

ROSNO—Russian National Society Insurance Co: 115184 Moscow, Ozerkovskaya nab. 30; tel. (095) 232-33-33; fax (095) 232-00-14; e-mail info@rosno.ru; internet www.rosno.ru; f. 1992; offices in 70 regions of Russia; owned by Sistema; Gen. Man. YEVGENII A. KURGIN.

Russkie Strakhovye Traditsii (Russian Traditions Insurance Co): 129366 Moscow, Raketnyi bulv. 13/2; tel. (095) 283-88-03; fax (095) 283-88-05; e-mail info@rustrad.ru; internet www.rustrad.ru; f. 1992; Pres. IVAN I. DAVYDOV.

SOGAZ—Insurance Co of the Gas Industry: 117997 Moscow, ul. Nametkina 16; tel. (095) 782-09-17; fax (095) 432-90-05; e-mail sogaz@sogaz.ru; internet www.sogaz.ru; f. 1993; owned by gas industry interests; Chair. of Bd Dirs SERGEI A. LUKASH.

Soglasiye (Agreement) Insurance Co: 109017 Moscow, M. Tolmachevskii per. 8–11/3; tel. and fax (095) 959-46-32; e-mail official@soglasie.ru; internet www.soglasie.ru; f. 1993 as Interros-Soglasiye; owned by Interros; Gen. Man. IGOR ZHUK.

STOCK EXCHANGES

Moscow Stock Exchange (MSE): 125047 Moscow, Miusskaya pl. 2/2; tel. (095) 250-20-10; fax (095) 250-17-34; e-mail mse@mse.ru; internet www.mse.ru; f. 1997; Pres. ROMAN N. MYLTSEV.

Moscow International Stock Exchange: 103045 Moscow, Prosvirin per. 4; tel. and fax (095) 923-33-39; f. 1990; Pres. VIKTOR SAKHAROV.

Siberian Stock Exchange: 630104 Novosibirsk, ul. Frunze 5, POB 233; tel. (3832) 21-60-67; fax (3832) 21-06-90; e-mail sibex@sibex.nsk .su; f. 1991; Pres. ALEKSANDR V. NOVIKOV.

COMMODITY EXCHANGES

Asiatic Commodity Exchange: 670000 Buryatiya, Ulan-Ude, ul. Sovetskaya 23/37; tel. and fax (30122) 2-26-81; f. 1991; Chair. ANDREI FIRSOV.

European-Asian Exchange (EAE): 101000 Moscow, ul. Myasnitskaya 26; tel. and fax (095) 787-58-93; e-mail info@eae.ru; internet www.eae.ru; f. 2000; Chair. of Council TATYANA S. SOKOLOVA; Gen. Man. ALEKSANDR B. YEREMIN.

Khabarovsk Commodity Exchange (KHCE): 680037 Khabarovsk, ul. K. Marksa 66; tel. and fax (4212) 33-65-60; f. 1991; Pres. YEVGENII V. PANASENKO.

Komi Commodity Exchange (KOCE): 167610 Komi, Syktyvkar, Oktyabrskii pr. 16; tel. (82122) 2-32-86; fax (82122) 3-84-43; f. 1991; Pres. PETR S. LUCHENKOV.

Kuzbass Commodity and Raw Materials Exchange (KECME): 650090 Kemerovo, ul. Novgradskaya 19; tel. (3842) 23-45-40; fax (3842) 23-49-56; f. 1991; Gen. Man. FEDOR MASENKOV.

Moscow Commodity Exchange (MCE): 129223 Moscow, pr. Mira, Russian Exhibition Centre, Pavilion 69 (4); tel. (095) 187-86-14; fax (095) 187-88-76; f. 1990; organization of exchange trading (cash, stock and futures market); Pres. and Chair. of Bd YURII MILYUKOV.

Petrozavodsk Commodity Exchange (PCE): 185028 Kareliya, Petrozavodsk, ul. Krasnaya 31; tel. and fax (8142) 7-80-57; f. 1991; Gen. Man. VALERII SAKHAROV.

Russian Exchange (RE): 101000 Moscow, ul. Myasnitskaya 26; tel. (095) 787-84-34; fax (095) 262-57-57; e-mail ic@ci.re.ru; internet www.re.ru; f. 1990; Pres. PAVEL PANOV.

Russian Commodity Exchange of the Agro-Industrial Complex (RosAgroBirzha): 125080 Moscow, Volokolamskoye shosse 11; tel. (095) 209-52-25; f. 1990; Chair. of Exchange Cttee ALEKSANDR VASILIYEV.

St Petersburg Exchange: 199026 St Petersburg, Vasilyevskii Ostrov, 26-aya liniya 15; tel. (812) 322-44-11; fax (812) 322-73-90; e-mail spbex@spbex.ru; internet www.spbex.ru; f. 1991; Pres. and Chief Exec. VIKTOR V. NIKOLAYEV.

Surgut Commodity and Raw Materials Exchange (SCME): 626400 Tyumen obl., Khanty-Mansii AOk, Surgut, ul. 30 let Pobedy 32; tel. (34561) 2-05-69; f. 1991.

Udmurt Commodity Universal Exchange (UCUE): 426075 Udmurtiya, Izhevsk, ul. Soyuznaya 107; tel. (3412) 37-08-88; fax (3412) 37-16-57; e-mail iger@udmnet.ru; f. 1991; Pres. N. F. LAZAREV.

Yekaterinburg Commodity Exchange (UCE): 620012 Sverdlovsk obl., Yekaterinburg, pr. Kosmonavtov 23; tel. (3432) 34-43-01; fax (3432) 51-53-64; f. 1991; Chair. of Exchange Cttee KONSTANTIN ZHUZHLOV.

Trade and Industry

GOVERNMENT AGENCY

Russian Federal Property Fund: 119049 Moscow, Leninskii pr. 9; tel. (095) 236-71-15; fax (095) 956-27-80; e-mail rffi@dol.ru; internet www.fpf.ru; f. 1992 to ensure consistency in the privatization process and to implement privatization legislation; Chair. VLADIMIR V. MALIN.

NATIONAL CHAMBER OF COMMERCE

Chamber of Commerce and Industry of the Russian Federation: 109012 Moscow, ul. Ilinka 6; tel. (095) 929-00-09; fax (095) 929-03-60; e-mail dios-inform@tpprf.ru; internet www.tpprf.ru; f. 1991; Pres. YEVGENII M. PRIMAKOV.

REGIONAL CHAMBERS OF COMMERCE

In early 2002 there were a total of 148 regional chambers of commerce in the Russian Federation.

Astrakhan Chamber of Commerce: 414040 Astrakhan, ul. Zhelyabova 50; tel. (8512) 25-58-44; fax (8512) 28-14-42; e-mail cci@mail.astrakhan.ru; internet astrcci.astrakhan.ru; f. 1992; Pres. ALEKSEI D. KANTEMIROV.

Bashkortostan Chamber of Commerce: 450008 Bashkortostan, Ufa, ul. Vorovskogo 22; tel. (3472) 23-23-80; fax (3472) 51-70-79; e-mail tpp@bashnet.ru; internet www.tpprb.ru; f. 1990; Chair. ZINNAT KH. KHAIRULLIN.

Bryansk Chamber of Commerce: 241035 Bryansk, ul. Komsomolskaya 11; tel. (0832) 56-68-06; fax (0832) 56-44-24; e-mail tpp@online.bryansk.ru; internet www.bryansk.ru/btpp; Pres. TATYANA F. SUVOROVA.

Buryat Chamber of Commerce: 670047 Buryatiya, Ulan-Ude, ul. Sakhyanovoi 5, POB 4284; tel. (3012) 37-56-26; fax (3012) 37-34-34; e-mail tpprb@buryatia.ru; f. 1993; Pres. GENNADII M. BERBIDAYEV; 85 mems.

Central-Siberian Chamber of Commerce: 660049 Krasnoyarsk, ul. Kirova 26; tel. (3912) 23-96-13; fax (3912) 23-96-83; e-mail cstp@krasmail.ru; internet www.cstpp.ru; f. 1985; Chair. VALERII A. KOSTIN.

Dagestan Chamber of Commerce: 367012 Dagestan, Makhachkala, pl. Lenina 2; tel. (8722) 67-04-61; fax (8722) 67-87-96; e-mail tpprd@dagestan.ru; f. 1991; Pres. SAID G. GAZIYEV.

Eastern Siberian Chamber of Commerce: 664003 Irkutsk, ul. Sukhe-Batora 16; tel. (3952) 33-50-60; fax (3952) 33-50-66; e-mail info@ccies.ru; internet www.ccies.ru; f. 1974; Pres. KONSTANTIN S. SHAVRIN.

Far East Chamber of Commerce: 680670 Khabarovsk, ul. Sheronova 113; tel. (4210) 30-47-70; fax (4210) 30-54-58; e-mail dvtpp@fecci.khv.ru; f. 1970; Pres. MIKHAIL V. KRUGLIKOV.

Kaliningrad Chamber of Commerce: 236010 Kaliningrad, ul. Vatutina 20; tel. (0112) 55-58-81; fax (0112) 21-87-15; e-mail kaliningrad_cci@baltnet.ru; internet www.kaliningrad-cci.ru; f. 1990; Pres. IGOR V. TSARKOV.

Kamchatka Chamber of Commerce: 683000 Kamchatka obl., Petropavlovsk-Kamchatskii, ul. Leninskaya 38/208; tel. and fax (4152) 12-35-10; e-mail kamtpp@iks.ru; Pres. ALLA V. PARKHOMCHUK.

Krasnodar Chamber of Commerce: 350063 Krasnodar, ul. Kommunarov 8; tel. and fax (8612) 68-22-13; e-mail tppkk@tppkuban.ru; internet www.tppkuban.ru; f. 1969; Chair. YURII N. TKACHENKO.

Kursk Chamber of Commerce: 305000 Kursk, ul. Kirova 7; tel. (0712) 56-24-69; fax (0712) 56-24-62; e-mail info@kcci.ru; internet www.kcci.ru; f. 1994; Pres. VALENTINA G. ORDYNETS.

Kuzbass Chamber of Commerce: 650099 Kemerovo, pr. Sovetskii 63/407; tel. and fax (3842) 58-77-64; e-mail ktpp@mail.kuzbass.net; internet city.info.kuzbass.net/ktpp; f. 1991; Pres. TATYANA O. IVLEVA.

Lipetsk Chamber of Commerce: 398019 Lipetsk, ul. Skorokhodova 2; tel. (0742) 45-60-04; fax (0742) 72-05-04; e-mail star@cci.lipetsk.su; internet lcci.lipetsk.ru; f. 1992; Pres. LILIYA D. POGUDINA.

Magnitogorsk Chamber of Commerce: 455002 Chelyabinsk obl., Magnitogorsk, ul. Kirova 70; tel. (3519) 24-82-16; fax (3519) 24-82-17; e-mail mtpp@mdv.ru; Pres. GERMAN I. ZAPYANTSEV.

Maritime (Primorskii) Krai Chamber of Commerce: 690600 Maritime Krai, Vladivostok, Okeanskii pr. 13A; tel. (4232) 26-96-30; fax (4232) 22-72-26; e-mail palata@online.vladivostok.ru; internet www.ptpp.com.ru; f. 1964; Pres. VLADIMIR B. BREZHNEV.

Moscow Chamber of Commerce: 117393 Moscow, ul. Akademika Pilyugina 22; tel. (095) 132-75-10; fax (095) 132-00-29; e-mail mtpp@mtpp.org; internet www.mtpp.org; f. 1991; Chair. YURII I. KOTOV; Pres. LEONID V. GOVOROV.

Naberezhnye Chelny Chamber of Commerce: 423826 Tatarstan, Naberezhnye Chelny, ul. Sh. Usmanova 122; tel. (8552) 54-79-08; fax (8552) 54-76-31; e-mail tpp@tpp.chelny.ru; f. 1994; Pres. VALERII P. SOTSKII.

Nizhnii Novgorod Chamber of Commerce: 603005 Nizhnii Novgorod, pl. Oktyabrskaya 1; tel. (8312) 19-42-10; fax (8312) 19-40-09; e-mail tpp@rda.nnov.ru; internet www.tpp.nnov.ru; f. 1990; Pres. GENNADII M. KHODYRYEV.

North Osetiya—Alaniya Chamber of Commerce: 362002 North Osetiya—Alaniya, Vladikavkaz, ul. Avgustovskikh sobytii 10; tel. (8672) 53-15-84; fax (8672) 54-21-61; e-mail tpprso-a@osetia.ru; f. 1993; Pres. KAZBEK KH. TUGANOV.

Northern Chamber of Commerce: 183766 Murmansk, per. Rusanova 10; tel. (8152) 47-29-99; fax (8152) 47-39-78; e-mail ncci@online.ru; internet www.ncci.ru; f. 1990; Chair. ANATOLII M. GLUSHKOV.

Novgorod Chamber of Commerce: 173002 Velikii Novgorod, ul. Germana 1; tel. (8162) 13-69-00; fax (8162) 13-20-46; e-mail ncci@ncci.novline.ru; internet nbp.natm.ru/~ncci; Pres. VIKTOR A. BYKOV.

Novosibirsk Chamber of Commerce: 630064 Novosibirsk, pr. K. Marksa 1; tel. and fax (3832) 46-41-50; e-mail main@sbcnet.ru; internet www.sbcnet.ru; f. 1991; Chair. BORIS V. BRUSILOVSKII; 315 mems (2002).

Omsk Chamber of Commerce: 644099 Omsk, ul. Krasnyi Put 18; tel. (3812) 23-05-23; fax (3812) 23-52-48; e-mail omtpp@omsknet.ru; internet www.omsknet.ru/cci; f. 1992; Pres. TATYANA A. KHOROSHAVINA.

Orenburg Chamber of Commerce: 460356 Orenburg, Parkovyi pr. 6; tel. and fax (3532) 77-73-29; e-mail cci@orenburg-cci.ru; internet www.orenburg-cci.ru; f. 1995; Pres. VIKTOR A. SYTYEZHEV.

Perm Chamber of Commerce: 614000 Perm, ul. Sovetskaya 24B; tel. (3422) 12-28-11; fax (3422) 12-41-12; e-mail permttp@permttp.ru; internet www.permtpp.ru; f. 1991; Pres. VIKTOR A. ZAMARAYEV.

Rostov Chamber of Commerce: 344022 Rostov-on-Don, ul. Pushkinskaya 176; tel. and fax (8362) 64-45-47; e-mail tpp@rost.ru; internet www.tpp.tis.ru; f. 1992; Pres. NIKOLAI I. PRISYAZHNYUK.

Ryazan Chamber of Commerce: 390023 Ryazan, ul. Gorkovo 14; tel. (0912) 77-20-67; fax (0912) 28-99-02; e-mail ryazancci@rtpp.ryazan.su; f. 1993; Pres. TATYANA V. GUSEVA; 44 mems.

Sakha (Yakutiya) Chamber of Commerce: 677000 Sakha (Yakutiya), Yakutsk, ul. Lenina 22/214; tel. (4112) 26-64-96; e-mail palata91@mail.ru; f. 1991; Chair. SERGEI G. BAKULIN.

Samara Chamber of Commerce: 443034 Samara, ul. A. Tolstogo 6; tel. (8462) 32-11-59; fax (8462) 70-48-96; e-mail ccisr@samara.ru; internet www.cci.samara.ru; f. 1989; Pres. BORIS V. ARDALIN.

Saratov Gubernskaya Chamber of Commerce: 410600 Saratov, ul. B. Kazachya 30; tel. (8452) 24-76-10; fax (8452) 24-72-31; e-mail iao@sgtpp.renet..ru; internet www.sgtpp.renet.ru; f. 1986; Pres. VLADIMIR V. DAVYDOV.

Smolensk Chamber of Commerce: 214000 Smolensk, ul. K. Marksa 12; tel. (0812) 55-41-42; fax (08122) 3-74-50; e-mail smolcci@keytown.com; internet www.keytown.com/users/Torgpal; f. 1993; Pres. OLEG V. LUKIRICH.

South Urals Chamber of Commerce: 454080 Chelyabinsk, ul. Vasenko 63; tel. (3512) 66-52-18; fax (3512) 66-52-32; e-mail mail@tpp.chelreg.ru; internet www.tpp.chelreg.ru; f. 1992; Pres. FEDOR L. DEGTYAREV; 365 mems.

St Petersburg Chamber of Commerce: 191194 St Petersburg, ul. Chaikovskogo 46–48; tel. (812) 273-48-96; fax (812) 272-64-06; e-mail spbcci@spbcci.ru; internet www.spbcci.ru; f. 1921; Pres. TATYANA S. AVETIKYAN (acting).

Stavropol Chamber of Commerce: 355034 Stavropol, ul. Lenina 384; tel. (8652) 94-53-34; fax (8652) 34-05-10; e-mail infostcci@yandex.ru; internet www.ccistavropol.best-business.biz; f. 1991; Pres. VITALII S. NABATNIKOV.

Tatarstan Chamber of Commerce: 420503 Tatarstan, Kazan, ul. Pushkina 18; tel. (8432) 38-24-76; fax (8432) 36-09-66; e-mail tpp@radiotelcom.ru; f. 1992; Gen. Dir SHAMIL R. AGEYEV; 160 mems.

Tolyatti Chamber of Commerce: 445009 Samara obl., Tolyatti, ul. Pobedy 19A; tel. (8482) 22-46-21; fax (8482) 22-47-45; e-mail tpp@infopac.ru; internet www.ccitogliatti.ru; Pres. VLADIMIR A. ZHUKOV.

Tula Chamber of Commerce: 300600 Tula, Krasnoarmeiskii pr. 25/1001–1007; tel. (0872) 31-17-28; fax (0872) 36-02-16; e-mail tulacci@tula.net; internet www.ccitula.ru; f. 1993; Pres. YURII M. AGAFONOV.

Udmurtiya Chamber of Commerce: 426034 Udmurtiya, Izhevsk, ul. Udmurtskaya 251A; tel. (3412) 43-82-81; fax (3412) 43-11-76; e-mail postmaster@izhtpp.udm.ru; internet izhtpp.udmweb.ru; f. 1993; Pres. YEVGENII YU. VYLYEGZHANIN.

Ulyanovsk Chamber of Commerce: 432600 Ulyanovsk, ul. Engelsa 19; tel. (8422) 31-45-23; fax (8422) 32-93-73; e-mail ultpp@mv.ru; f. 1992; Pres. YEVGENII S. BALANDIN.

Urals Chamber of Commerce: 620027 Sverdlovsk obl., Yekaterinburg, ul. Vostochnaya 6, POB 822; tel. (3432) 53-04-49; fax (3432) 53-58-63; e-mail ucci@dialup.mplik.ru; internet ucci.ur.ru; f. 1959; Pres. YURII P. MATUSHKIN.

Volgograd Chamber of Commerce: 400005 Volgograd, ul. 7-aya Gvardeiskaya 2; tel. (8442) 34-41-78; fax (8442) 34-22-02; e-mail cci@volgogradcci.ru; internet www.volgogradcci.ru; f. 1990; Pres. ALEKSANDR D. BELITSKII.

Vologda Chamber of Commerce and Industry: 160600 Vologda, ul. Lermontova 15; tel. (8172) 72-14-80; fax (8172) 72-32-58; e-mail grant@vologda.ru; f. 1992; Pres. GALINA D. TELEGINA.

Voronezh Chamber of Commerce: 394030 Voronezh, 'Voronezhvnesh-servis', POB 63; tel. and fax (0732) 52-49-38; e-mail mail@oootpp.vm.ru; f. 1991; fmrly Central-Black Earth Chamber of Commerce and Industry; Pres. VYACHESLAV A. KONDRATYEV.

Vyatka (Kirov) Chamber of Commerce: 610000 Kirov, ul. Gertsena 37; tel. and fax (8332) 67-93-43; e-mail iac@vtpp.kirov.ru; internet www.vtpp.kirov.ru; f. 1993; Pres. NIKOLAI M. LIPATNIKOV.

Yaroslavl Chamber of Commerce: 150000 Yaroslavl, Sovetskaya pl. 1/19; tel. (0852) 32-87-98; fax (0852) 32-88-85; e-mail tpp@adm.yar.ru; internet yartpp.ru; f. 1992; Pres. VALERII A. LAVROV.

EMPLOYERS' ORGANIZATIONS

Co-ordinating Council of Employers' Unions of Russia (Koordinatsionnyi Sovet Obyedinenii Rabotodatelei Rossii—KSORR): 109017 Moscow, per. M. Tolmachevskii 8–11/3; tel. (095) 232-55-77; fax (095) 232-39-13; e-mail official@ksorr.ru; internet www.ksorr.ru; f. 1994; Chair. ARKADII I. VOLSKII; Gen. Dir OLEG V. YEREMEYEV; unites 29 major employers' unions, including the following:

Agro-Industrial Union of Russia: 107139 Moscow, B-139; tel. (095) 204-41-04; fax (095) 207-83-62; e-mail sva@gvs.aris.ru; internet www.aris.ru/GALLERY/ROS/INF/AGROSZ; Pres. VASILII A. STARODUBTSEV.

Russian Union of Industrialists and Entrepreneurs (Employers) (RSPPR): 103070 Moscow, Staraya pl. 10/4; tel. (095) 748-42-37; fax (095) 206-11-29; e-mail info@rsppr.ru; internet www.rsppr.ru; f. 1991; Pres. ARKADII I. VOLSKII.

Union of Russian Shipowners (SOROSS): 121002 Moscow, per. Sivtsev brazhek 44/28/10; tel. (095) 241-56-75; fax (095) 248-29-66; e-mail murashovaiv@morflot.ru; internet www.morflot.ru/info/soross.asp; Pres. MIKHAIL A. ROMANOVSKII.

UTILITIES

Electricity

Federal Energy Commission: 103074 Moscow, Kitaigorodskii proyezd 7; tel. (095) 220-40-15; fax (095) 206-81-08; e-mail fecrf@orc.ru; regulatory authority for natural energy monopolies; sole responsibility for establishing tariff rates for energy, transportation, shipping, postal and telecommunications industries in the Russian Federation from Sept. 2001; Chair. ANDREI ZADERNYUK.

Irkutskenergo—Irkutsk Energy Co: 664000 Irkutsk, ul. Sukhe-Batora 3; tel. (3952) 21-73-00; fax (3952) 21-78-89; e-mail web@irkutskenergo.ru; internet www.irkutskenergo.ru; f. 1954; generation and transmission of electrical and thermal energy; Dir-Gen. VLADIMIR V. KOLMOGOROV.

Mosenergo (Moscow Energy Co): 113035 Moscow, Raushskaya nab. 8; tel. (095) 957-35-30; fax (095) 957-34-70; e-mail press-centre@mosenergo.ru; internet www.mosenergo.ru; f. 1887; power generator and distributor; Gen. Man. ARKADII V. YEVSTAFYEV.

Rosenergoatom (Russian Atomic Energy Concern): 101000 Moscow, POB 912; tel. (095) 239-47-40; fax (095) 239-27-24; e-mail info@rosatom.ru; internet www.rosatom.ru; f. 1992; electricity generating co; Pres. OLEG SARAYEV.

Sverdlovenergo (Sverdlovsk Energy Co): 620219 Sverdlovsk obl., Yekaterinburg, pr. Lenina 38; tel. (3432) 59-13-99; fax (3432) 59-12-22; e-mail post@energo.pssr.ru; internet www.po.pssr.ru; f. 1942; Chair. of Bd MIKHAIL A. ABYZOV; Gen. Man. VALERII N. RODIN.

Unified Energy System of Russia (RAO EES Rossii): 109526 Moscow, pr. Vernadskogo 101/3; tel. (095) 220-40-01; fax (095) 927-30-07; e-mail rao@elektra.ru; internet www.rao-ees.ru; f. 1992; operates national electricity grid; 52% state-owned; controls about 43,220 km of transmission lines, 32 power plants and majority stakes in 72 regional power cos, including Mosenergo and Lenenergo, accounting for more than 80% of Russia's electricity output; restructuring pending in 2003; Chair. ALEKSANDR S. VOLOSHIN; Chief Exec. ANATOLII B. CHUBAIS.

Uralenergo (Ural Energy): 620219 Yekaterinburg, ul. Tomalcheva 5; tel. (3432) 59-89-22; fax (3432) 56-36-30; manages 22 joint-stock cos; oversees 55 thermal power stations and 6 hydroelectric stations; total installed capacity of over 28,500m. kW.

Gas

Gazprom: 117997 Moscow, ul. Nametkina 16; tel. (095) 719-30-01; fax (095) 719-83-33; e-mail webmaster@gazprom.ru; internet www.gazprom.ru; f. 1989 from assets of Soviet Ministry of Oil and Gas; became independent joint-stock co in 1992, privatized in 1994; Russia's biggest co and world's largest natural gas producer, owning 30% of global natural gas reserves (14,000m. barrels); 38.4% state-owned; Chair. ALEKSEI B. MILLER.

Mezhregiongaz (Inter-Regional Gas Co): 113324 Moscow, ul. Sadovnicheskaya 46/1; tel. and fax (095) 953-08-24; internet www.mrg.ru; f. 1997; gas marketing co, founded by Gazprom; brs in more than 60 federal subjects; Dir-Gen. NIKOLAI GORNOVSKII.

Water

MosVodoKanal: 107005 Moscow, per. Pleteshkovskii 2; tel. (095) 742-96-96; e-mail webmaster@mosvodokanal.ru; internet www.mosvodokanal.ru; provides water and sewerage services to Moscow and the surrounding region; Gen. Man. STANISLAV KHRAMENKOV.

Vodokanal: 193015 St Petersburg, ul. Kavalergardskaya 42; tel. (812) 326-51-44; fax (812) 274-13-61; e-mail office@vodokanal.spb.ru; internet www.vodokanal.spb.ru; water and sewerage utility; Gen. Man. FELIKS V. KARMAZINOV.

TRADE UNIONS

In 1990, in response to the growing independent labour movement, several branch unions of the All-Union Central Council of Trade Unions (ACCTU) established the Federation of Independent Trade Unions of the Russian Federation (FITUR), which took control of part of the property and other assets of the ACCTU. The ACCTU was re-formed as the General Confederation of Trade Unions of the USSR, which was, in turn, renamed the General Confederation of Trade Unions—International Organization in 1992. In November of that year, in an attempt to challenge the influence of the FITUR, the ITUM and several other independent trade unions established a consultative council to co-ordinate their activities.

All-Russian Labour Confederation: 103031 Moscow, ul. Rozhdestvenka 5/7; tel. (095) 785-21-30; fax (095) 915-83-67; e-mail vktrussia@online.ru; internet www.trud.org/guide/VKT.htm; f. 1995; unites five national trade unions and 40 regional orgs with 1,270,900 mems; Pres. ALEKSANDR N. BUGAYEV.

General Confederation of Trade Unions (VKP): 117119 Moscow, Leninskii pr. 42; tel. (095) 938-82-22; fax (095) 938-21-55; e-mail mail@vkp.ru; internet www.vkp.ru; f. 1992; fmrly the General Confederation of Trade Unions of the USSR; co-ordinating body for trade unions in CIS member states; unites nine national trade unions and 47 regional orgs with 85m. mems; publishes *Profsoyuzy* (Trade Unions), weekly, *Vestnik profsoyuzov* (Herald of the Trade Unions), every two weeks, and *Inform-Contact*, in English and French, quarterly; Pres. VLADIMIR P. SHCHERBAKOV.

Federation of Independent Trade Unions of the Russian Federation (FITUR): 117119 Moscow, Leninskii pr. 42; tel. (095) 938-73-12; fax (095) 137-06-94; e-mail korneev@fnpr.ru; internet www.fnpr.ru; f. 1990; Gen. Sec. MIKHAIL V. SHMAKOV; unites 48 national trade unions and 78 regional orgs (with c. 40m. mems), including the following:

All-Russian 'Electroprofsoyuz': 117119 Moscow, Leninskii pr. 42, kor. 3; tel. (095) 938-83-78; fax (095) 930-98-62; f. 1990; electrical workers; Pres. VALERII P. KUZICHEV.

Automobile and Farm Machinery Construction Industries Workers' Union: 117119 Moscow, Leninskii pr. 42/3; tel. (095) 938-76-13; fax (095) 938-86-15; Pres. YULII G. NOVIKOV.

Automobile Transport and Road Workers' Union of the Russian Federation: 117218 Moscow, ul. Krzhizhanovskogo 20/30/5; tel. (095) 125-23-30; fax (095) 125-07-98; f. 1990; Pres. VIKTOR I. MOKHNACHEV.

Civil Aviation Workers' Union: 117218 Moscow, ul. Krzhizhanovskogo 20/30/5; tel. and fax (095) 125-18-39; Pres. BORIS A. KREMNEV.

Communication Workers' Union of Russia: 117119 Moscow, Leninskii pr. 42/3; tel. (095) 938-72-06; fax (095) 930-22-86; f. 1905; Pres. ANATOLII G. NAZEIKIN.

Construction and Building Materials Industry Workers' Union of the Russian Federation: 117119 Moscow, Leninskii pr. 42/1; tel. (095) 930-71-74; fax (095) 952-55-47; f. 1991; Pres. BORIS A. SOSHENKO.

Timber Industry Workers' Union of the Russian Federation: 117119 Moscow, Leninskii pr. 42/1; tel. (095) 938-89-03; fax (095) 137-06-81; Pres. Valerii N. Ochekurov.

Geological, Survey and Cartographical Workers' Union of the Russian Federation: 117119 Moscow, Leninskii pr. 42/5; tel. (095) 938-87-20; Pres. Nikolai K. Popkov.

Health Workers' Union of the Russian Federation: 117119 Moscow, Leninskii pr. 42/3; tel. (095) 938-84-43; fax (095) 938-81-34; e-mail ckprz@online.ru; f. 1990; Chair. Mikhail M. Kuzmenko.

Moscow Federation of Trade Unions: 121205 Moscow, ul. Novyi Arbat 36; tel. (095) 290-82-62; fax (095) 202-92-70; e-mail mfpmskru@cityline.ru; f. 1990; largest regional branch of FITUR; Chair. Mikhail D. Nagaitsev; 3.2m. mems.

National Educational and Scientific Workers' Union of the Russian Federation: 117119 Moscow, Leninskii pr. 42/3; tel. (095) 938-87-77; fax (095) 930-68-15; f. 1990; Pres. Vladimir M. Yakovlev.

Oil, Gas and Construction Workers' Union: 119119 Moscow, Leninskii pr. 42/4; tel. (095) 930-69-74; fax (095) 930-11-24; e-mail rogwu@rogwu.ru; internet www.rogwu.ru; f. 1990; Pres. Lev A. Mironov.

Russian Chemical Industry Workers' Union: 117119 Moscow, Leninskii pr. 42/ 3; tel. (095) 930-99-18; fax (095) 938-21-55; f. 1990; Pres. Boris S. Popenko (acting).

Russian Fishing Industry Workers' Union: 117119 Moscow, Leninskii pr. 42/3; tel. (095) 938-77-82; fax (095) 930-77-26; e-mail bfish@fnpr.ru; f. 1991; Pres. Yurii V. Shalonin.

Russian Independent Trade Union of Coal-industry Workers: 109004 Moscow, ul. Zemlyanoi val 64/1; tel. (095) 915-28-52; fax (095) 915-01-02; Chair. Ivan I. Mokhnachuk.

Russian Radio and Electronics Industry Workers Union: 109180 Moscow, 1-i Golutvinskii per. 3; tel. (095) 238-08-02; fax (095) 238-17-31; Pres. Valerii Ye. Markov.

Russian Textiles and Light Industry Workers' Union: 117119 Moscow, Leninskii pr. 42/3; tel. (095) 938-78-24; fax (095) 938-84-05; f. 1990; Pres. Tatyana I. Sosnina.

Russian Trade Union of Railwaymen and Transport Construction Workers (Rosprofzhel): 103064 Moscow, ul. Staraya Basmannaya 11; tel. (095) 262-58-73; fax (095) 923-88-31; e-mail iturr@orc.ru; Pres. Anatolii B. Vasiliyev.

Russian Union of Aviation Engineering Workers: Moscow; tel. and fax (095) 938-81-07; f. 1934; Pres. Anatolii F. Breusov.

Russian Union of Cultural Workers: 109004 Moscow, ul. Zemlyanoi val 64/1; tel. (095) 915-06-30; fax (095) 915-09-43; Pres. Gennadii P. Paroshin.

Russian Union of Workers in Small and Entrepreneurial Enterprises: 117119 Moscow, Leninskii pr. 42/1; tel. (095) 930-67-71; fax (095) 938-75-85; Pres. Vladimir I. Kuznetsov.

Shipbuilding Workers' Union: 117119 Moscow, Leninskii pr. 42/5; tel. (095) 938-88-72; fax (095) 938-84-74; Pres. Vladimir Ye. Makavchik.

Union of Agro-industrial Workers of the Russian Federation: 117119 Moscow, Leninskii pr. 42/3; tel. (095) 938-77-35; fax (095) 930-68-27; f. 1919; Pres. Aleksandr S. Davydov; 37m. mems.

Union of Engineering Workers of the Russian Federation: 127486 Moscow, ul. Deguninskaya 1/2; tel. (095) 487-3507; fax (095) 487-56-37; Pres. Yurii S. Spichenok.

Union of Food Industry and Production Co-operative Workers of the Russian Federation: 117119 Moscow, Leninskii pr. 42/3; tel. (095) 938-75-03; fax (095) 930-10-56; Pres. Valerii K. Zhovterik.

Union of Security Services Workers of the Russian Federation: 101000 Moscow-Tsentr, ul. Malaya Lubyanka 5/12; tel. (095) 928-99-76; fax (095) 923-72-36; Pres. Yurii N. Sireshchikov.

Union of State and Community Service Workers of the Russian Federation: 117119 Moscow, Leninskii pr. 42/2; tel. (095) 938-74-44; fax (095) 952-56-24; Pres. Vladimir P. Savchenko.

Union of Workers in Enterprises with Foreign Investment of the Russian Federation: 117119 Moscow, Leninskii pr. 42/1; tel. (095) 938-84-62; fax (095) 938-81-95; Pres. Vladimir F. Bazayev.

Independent Trade Unions

Federation of Air Traffic Controllers' Unions of Russia (FPAR): 125993 Moscow, Leningradskii pr. 37/472, POB 3; tel. (095) 155-57-01; fax (095) 155-59-17; e-mail postmaster@fatcurus.ru; internet www.fatcurus.ru; f. 1989; Pres. Sergei A. Kovalev.

Metallurgical Industry Workers' Union: Moscow, ul. Pushkinskaya 5/6; left the FITUR in 1992 to form independent organization; Pres. Boris Misnik.

Transport

RAILWAYS

In 2000 the total length of railway track in use was 86,660 km, of which 40,800 km were electrified. The railway network is of great importance in the Russian Federation, owing to the poor road system, and the relatively few private vehicles outside the major cities. The Trans-Siberian Railway, the electrification of which began in 1998, provides the main route connecting European Russia with Siberia and the Far East. There were plans for the large-scale reform of the railways system.

Russian Railways: 107174 Moscow, ul. Novobasmannaya 2; tel. (095) 262-16-28; fax (095) 975-24-11; internet www.mps.ru; originally comprising 17 of the 32 regional divisions of the former Soviet Railways, in 1992 these were reorganized into 19 operating divisions; additional restructuring, announced in 1996, was to create eight regional divisions; further structural reform was being undertaken in 2002–05; Gen. Mans V. S. Sakharenko, V. N. Shatayev.

City Underground Railways

Moscow Metro: 129110 Moscow, pr. Mira 41/2; tel. (095) 222-10-01; fax (095) 971-37-44; e-mail info@mosmetro.ru; f. 1935; 11 lines (266 km) with 164 stations; suburban light railway extension scheduled to open in late 2003; Gen. Man. Dmitrii V. Gayev.

Nizhnii Novgorod Metro: 603002 Nizhnii Novgorod, pl. Revolutsii 7; tel. (8312) 44-17-60; fax (8312) 44-20-86; e-mail metro@sandy.ru; f. 1985; 15 km with 13 stations; Gen. Man. A. Kuzmin.

Novosibirsk Metro: 630099 Novosibirsk, ul. Serebrennikovskaya 34; tel. (3832) 90-81-10; fax (3832) 46-56-82; e-mail nsk@metro.snt.su; internet www.nsk.su/~metro; f. 1986; 2 lines (13.2 km) with 11 stations, and a further 6 km under construction; Gen. Man. V. I. Demin.

St Petersburg Metro: 198013 St Petersburg, Moskovskii pr. 28; tel. (812) 251-66-68; fax (812) 316-14-41; f. 1955; 4 lines (103 km) with 58 stations; Gen. Man. V. A. Garyugin.

Short underground railways began to operate in Samara and Yekaterinburg in 1987 and 1991, respectively. In 2002 construction of underground railways was under way in Chelyabinsk, Kazan, Krasnoyarsk and Omsk.

ROADS

In 2000 the total length of roads was 532,393 km (45,978 km of highways and 486,415 km of other roads); 67.4% of roads were paved in 1999. The road network is of most importance in European Russia; in Siberia and the Far East there are few roads, and they are often impassable in winter. In 1999 the World Bank granted Russia a loan of US $400m. to finance the construction and repair of roads in Siberia and the Far East of Russia. A new highway, linking Vladivostok with St Petersburg, was due for completion in 2004.

SHIPPING

The seaports of the Russian Federation provide access to the Pacific Ocean, in the east, the Baltic Sea and the Atlantic Ocean, in the west, and the Black Sea, in the south. Major eastern ports are at Vladivostok, Nakhodka, Vostochnyi, Magadan and Petropavlovsk. In the west St Petersburg and Kaliningrad provide access to the Baltic Sea, and the northern ports of Murmansk and Archangel (Arkhangelsk) have access to the Atlantic Ocean, via the Barents Sea. Novorossiisk and Sochi are the principal Russian ports on the Black Sea.

Principal Shipowning Companies

Baltic Shipping Co: 198035 St Petersburg, Mezhevoi kanal 5; tel. (812) 251-33-97; fax (812) 186-85-44; freight and passenger services; Chair. Mikhail A. Romanovskii.

Baltic Transport Systems: 199106 St Petersburg, pl. Morskoi Slavy 1; tel. (812) 303-99-14; fax (812) 380-34-76; e-mail bts@baltics.ru; internet www.baltics.ru; f. 1994; freight and passenger services; Gen. Dir Aleksei E. Shukletsov.

Far Eastern Shipping Co: 690019 Maritime (Primorskii) Krai, Vladivostok, ul. Aleutskaya 15; tel. (4232) 41-14-32; fax (4232) 52-15-51; e-mail 41401@41.fesco.ru; internet www.fesco.ru; f. 1880; Gen. Man. YEVGENII N. AMBROSOV.

Kamchatka Shipping Co: 683600 Kamchatka obl., Petropavlovsk-Kamchatskii, ul. Radiosvyazi 65; tel. (41522) 2-82-21; fax (41522) 2-19-60; f. 1949; freight services; Pres. NIKOLAI M. ZABLOTSKII.

Murmansk Shipping Co: 183038 Murmansk, ul. Kominterna 15; tel. (8152) 48-10-48; fax (8152) 48-11-48; e-mail postmaster@msco.ru; f. 1939; shipping and icebreaking services; Gen. Dir VYACHESLAV RUKSHA.

Novorossiisk Shipping Co: 353900 Krasnodar Krai, Novorossiisk, ul. Svobody 1; tel. (8617) 25-31-26; fax (8617) 25-11-43; e-mail novoship@novoship.ru; internet www.novoship.ru; f. 1992; Chair. V. I. YAKUNIN.

NSC Northern Maritime Steamships-Arkhangelsk: 163000 Archangel, nab. Sev. Dviny 36; tel. (8182) 63-71-06; fax (8182) 65-53-09; e-mail pan@ansc.ru; internet www.ansc.ru; f. 1870; dry cargo shipping, liner services; Gen. Dir VLADIMIR G. UROSHNIKOV.

Primorsk Shipping Corpn: 692904 Maritime (Primorskii) Krai, Nakhodka, Administrativnyi Gorodok; tel. (4236) 69-45-05; fax (4236) 69-45-75; e-mail psc@prisco.ru; internet www.prisco.ru; f. 1972, tanker shipowner; Dir-Gen. ALEKSANDR D. KIRILICHEV.

Sakhalin Shipping Co: 694620 Sakhalin obl., Kholmsk, ul. Pobedy 16; tel. (42433) 6-62-07; fax (42433) 6-60-66; Pres. YAKUB ZH. ALE-GEDPINOV.

Sovfrakht JSC: 127944 Moscow, Rakhmanovskii per. 4, Morskoi Dom; tel. (095) 258-27-41; fax (095) 230-26-40; e-mail general@sovfracht.ru; internet www.sovfracht.ru; f. 1929; chartering and broking of tanker, cargo and other ships; forwarding and booking agency; ship management; Dir-Gen. A. I. KOLTYPIN; 60 employees.

White Sea and Onega Shipping Co: 185005 Kareliya, Petrozavodsk, ul. Rigachina 7; tel. (8142) 71-12-33; fax (8142) 71-12-67; e-mail dir@bpo.onego.ru; f. 1940; cargo shipping, cargo-ship construction and repair; Gen. Dir NIKOLAI GRACHOV.

CIVIL AVIATION

Until 1991 Aeroflot—Soviet Airlines was the only airline operating on domestic routes in the former USSR. In 1992–94 some 300 different independent airlines emerged on the basis of Aeroflot's former regional directorates. Several small private airlines were also established. In 1992 Aeroflot—Soviet Airlines became a joint-stock company, Aeroflot—Russian Airlines. The Government retained 51% of the shares, and company personnel own 49%. A reorganization of Russia's civil aviation industry was proposed in 1998. It was envisaged that, following restructuring, the number of airlines (then 315) would be reduced to some 105, through the creation of alliances and mergers. By 2002 there were 496 airports in Russia, compared with 1,302 in 1992.

Aeroflot—Russian Airlines: 125167 Moscow, Leningradskii pr. 37/9; tel. and fax (095) 155-66-43; internet www.aeroflot.ru; f. 1923; 51% state-owned; operates flights to 108 destinations in 54 countries, and to 26 destinations in Russia; Gen. Dir VALERII M. OKULOV.

Bashkir Airlines (BAL): 450056 Bashkortostan, Ufa, Ufa Airport; tel. (3472) 22-75-12; fax (3472) 23-37-36; e-mail interdep@airbal.ufanet.ru; internet www.bal.ufanet.ru; f. 1933; flights between Ufa and 24 destinations in Russia, and to the countries of the CIS and Turkey; Dir-Gen. VINER V. SHAKIROV.

Domodedova Airlines: 142045 Moscow, Domodedova Airport; tel. (095) 504-03-00; fax (095) 787-86-18; e-mail ak_e3@tch.ru; internet www.dmo.tch.ru; f. 1964; scheduled passenger flights to domestic and CIS destinations; chartered passenger and freight flights to domestic, CIS and international destinations; Gen. Dir ANDREI MASLOV.

Pulkovo Airlines: 196210 St Petersburg, ul. Pilotov 18/4; tel. (812) 324-36-34; fax (812) 104-37-02; internet www.pulkovo.ru; operates regular, direct flights from St Petersburg to 26 destinations in Russia and 10 further destinations in the CIS, as well as destinations in the Middle East; Gen. Dir B. G. DEMCHENKO.

Sibir Airlines: 633104 Novosibirsk obl., gorod Ob; tel. (3832) 59-90-11; fax (3832) 59-90-64; e-mail pr@s7.ru; internet www.s7.ru; scheduled and charter flights to domestic, CIS, European and Middle Eastern destinations; Gen. Dir VLADISLAV FILEV.

Transaero Airlines: 121099 Moscow, 2-i Smolenskii per. 3/4; tel. (095) 937-84-77; fax (095) 578-86-88; e-mail info@transaero.ru; internet www.transaero.ru; f. 1991; Russia's largest privately owned airline; operates scheduled and charter passenger services to the CIS, Europe and Central Asia; Chief Exec. ALEKSANDR PLESHAKOV.

Tsentr-Avia: 140150 Moscow obl., pos. Bykovo, ul. Sovetskaya 19; tel. (095) 558-44-07; fax (095) 501-13-66; e-mail pr@centreavia.ru; internet www.centreavia.ru; f. 1999; flights from Moscow to domestic destinations, and to Austria and Germany.

Ural Airlines: 620910 Sverdlovsk obl., Yekaterinburg, ul. Sputnikov 6; tel. and fax (3432) 26-64-16; e-mail sale@uralairlines.ru; internet www.uralairlines.ru; f. 1993; flights from Yekaterinburg to 17 destinations in Russia, and to destinations in the CIS, Europe and the Middle East.

Vladivostok Avia: 692800 Maritime (Primorskii) Krai, Artem, ul. Portovaya 41, Vladivostok Airport; tel. (4232) 30-71-46; fax (4232) 30-77-00; e-mail support@vladavia.ru; internet www.vladavia.ru; f. 1994; freight and scheduled passenger services to 10 destinations in Russia, and to the People's Republic of China, Japan and the Republic of Korea; Gen. Dir VLADIMIR SAIBEL.

Tourism

In 2000 there were 21,169,100 tourist arrivals in Russia, and in 1999 receipts from tourism totalled US $7,510m.

Intourist Holding Co: 127015 Moscow, ul. Vyatskaya 70; tel. and fax (095) 234-55-49; e-mail intourholding@mtu-net.ru; f. 1992; travel and tourism investment co; owns tour-operating subsidiary; publishing; Gen. Man. SERGEI I. KRUCHEK.

Intourist: 101990 Moscow, Milyutinskii per. 13/1; tel. (095) 956-44-99; fax (095) 956-42-02; e-mail info@intourist.ru; internet www.intourist.ru; f. 1929; brs throughout Russia and abroad; Pres. ABBAS ALIYEV.

RWANDA

Introductory Survey

Location, Climate, Language, Religion, Flag, Capital

The Rwandan Republic is a land-locked country in eastern central Africa, just south of the Equator, bounded by the Democratic Republic of the Congo to the west, by Uganda to the north, by Tanzania to the east and by Burundi to the south. The climate is tropical, although tempered by altitude. It is hot and humid in the lowlands, but cooler in the highlands. The average annual rainfall is 785 mm (31 ins). The main rainy season is from February to May. The population is composed of three ethnic groups: Hutu (85%), Tutsi (14%) and Twa (1%). French, English and Kinyarwanda, the native language, are all in official use, and Kiswahili is widely spoken. About one-half of the population adhere to animist beliefs. Most of the remainder are Christians, mainly Roman Catholics. There are Protestant and Muslim minorities. The national flag (proportions 1 by 2) has three unequal horizontal stripes, of blue, yellow and green, with a blue-ringed yellow disc (framed by 24 yellow rays) depicted near the fly end of the top stripe. The capital is Kigali.

Recent History

Rwanda, with the neighbouring state of Burundi, became part of German East Africa in 1899. In 1916, during the First World War, it was occupied by Belgian forces from the Congo. From 1920 Rwanda was part of Ruanda-Urundi, administered by Belgium under a League of Nations mandate and later as a UN Trust Territory. Dissension between the majority Hutu tribe and their former overlords, the Tutsi, has existed for many years, and in 1959 led to a rebellion and the proclamation of a state of emergency. In September 1961 it was decided by referendum to abolish the monarchy and to establish a republic. Full independence followed on 1 July 1962. Serious tribal conflict erupted in December 1963, and massacres (estimated at 20,000 deaths) were perpetrated by the Hutu against the Tutsi. During 1964–65 large numbers of displaced Rwandans were resettled in neighbouring countries. In 1969 Grégoire Kayibanda, the new Republic's first President, was re-elected, and all 47 seats in the legislature were retained by the governing party, the Mouvement démocratique républicain (MDR), also known as the Parti de l'émancipation du peuple Hutu (Parmehutu).

Tension between Hutu and Tutsi escalated again at the end of 1972 and continued throughout February 1973. In July the Minister of Defence and head of the National Guard, Maj.-Gen. Juvénal Habyarimana, led a bloodless coup against President Kayibanda, proclaimed a Second Republic and established a military administration. In August a new Council of Ministers, with Habyarimana as President, was formed. All political activity was banned until July 1975, when a new ruling party, the Mouvement révolutionnaire national pour le développement (MRND), was formed.

A national referendum in December 1978 approved a new Constitution, which was intended to return the country to democratically elected government (in accordance with an undertaking made by Habyarimana in 1973 to end the military regime within five years). Elections to the legislature, the Conseil national de développement (CND), took place in December 1981 and in December 1983; also in December 1983 Habyarimana was re-elected President. In December 1988 Habyarimana was again elected (unopposed) to the presidency, securing 99.98% of the votes cast. Elections to the CND were conducted in the same month.

In September 1990 a Commission nationale de synthèse was appointed to compile recommendations for a draft national charter, which was to provide for the establishment of a multi-party system. In April 1991, following the CND's revision of the Commission's proposals, the provisions of a draft constitution were presented to an extraordinary congress of the MRND, at which the party was renamed the Mouvement républicain national pour la démocratie et le développement (MRNDD). On 10 June the reforms were promulgated by Habyarimana, and legislation regulating the formation of political parties was adopted; parties were to be non-tribal and independent, while members of the security forces and the judiciary were to be banned from political activity. (By June 1992 15 parties, among

them the MRNDD and a revived MDR, had officially registered.) In October 1991 Sylvestre Nsanzimana, hitherto Minister of Justice, was appointed to the new post of Prime Minister, and in December he formed a transitional Government, in which all but two portfolios (assigned to the Parti démocratique chrétien—PDC) were allocated to members of the MRNDD. Opposition parties, which had been excluded from participation in the transitional Government for their insistence on a non-MRNDD Prime Minister, organized anti-Government demonstrations in late 1991 and early 1992, demanding the removal of the Prime Minister and the convening of a national conference. A series of negotiations between the Government and the major opposition parties was initiated in February 1992, and in April a protocol agreement was signed, providing for the installation of a new transitional administration, with Dismas Nsengiyaremye of the MDR as Prime Minister. Habyarimana announced that multi-party elections would be conducted within one year of the installation of the new Government.

Relations with neighbouring Uganda were frequently strained, owing mainly to the presence of some 250,000 Rwandan refugees in Uganda (mainly members of Rwanda's Tutsi minority), who had fled their homeland following successive outbreaks of persecution by the Hutu regime in 1959, 1963 and 1973. In October 1990 rebel forces, based in Uganda, invaded northern Rwanda, occupying several towns. The 4,000-strong rebel army, known as the Front patriotique rwandais (FPR), which mainly comprised Rwandan Tutsi refugees, aimed to overthrow the Habyarimana regime and secure the repatriation of all Rwandan refugees. The Rwandan Government accused the Ugandan leadership of supporting the rebel forces (many of whom had served in the Ugandan armed forces), although this accusation was strenuously denied. With the assistance of French, Belgian and Zairean troops, the Rwandan army succeeded in repelling the FPR before it could reach Kigali. In late October the Government declared a cease-fire, although hostilities continued in northern Rwanda. The FPR made further incursions into Rwanda in late 1990 and in early 1991, but was repulsed by the Rwandan armed forces on each occasion.

Unsuccessful negotiations took place during 1991 and early 1992, but further talks held in Arusha, Tanzania, in July resulted in an agreement on the implementation of a new cease-fire, effective from the end of that month, and the creation of a military observer group (GOM), sponsored by the Organization of African Unity (OAU—now the African Union, see p. 130), to comprise representatives from both sides, together with officers from the armed forces of Nigeria, Senegal, Zimbabwe and Mali. However, subsequent negotiations failed to resolve outstanding problems concerning the creation of a proposed 'neutral zone' between the Rwandan armed forces and the FPR, the incorporation of the FPR in a future combined Rwandan national force, the repatriation of refugees, and FPR demands for full participation in a transitional government and legislature.

A resurgence in violence followed the breakdown of negotiations in February 1993. An estimated 1m. civilians fled southwards and into neighbouring Uganda and Tanzania, to escape the fighting as the FPR advanced as far as Ruhengeri and seemed, for a time, poised to occupy Kigali. The actions of the FPR were denounced by Belgium, France and the USA. France dispatched reinforcements to join a small military contingent that had been stationed in Kigali since October 1990 to protect French nationals. Meanwhile, the commander of the 50-member GOM declared that the group had inadequate manpower and resources to contain the FPR, and requested the deployment of an additional 400 troops from the OAU. In late February 1993 the Government accepted FPR terms for a cease-fire, in return for an end to attacks against FPR positions and Tutsi communities, and the withdrawal of foreign troops. Although fighting continued with varying intensity, fresh peace negotiations were convened in Arusha in March, and France subsequently began to withdraw its troops. Negotiations conducted during April failed to produce a solution to the crucial issue of the structure of a future single armed Rwandan force. In the same month the five participating parties in the ruling coalition agreed to a three-month extension of the Government's mandate, in order to facilitate the successful conclusion of a peace accord. Significant progress was made during renewed talks between the Government and the FPR during May, when a timetable for the demobilization of the 19,000-strong security forces was agreed. In June the UN Security Council approved the creation of the UN Observer Mission Uganda-Rwanda (UNOMUR), to be deployed on the Ugandan side of the border, for an initial period of six months, in order to prevent the maintenance of a military supply line for the FPR.

In July 1993 President Habyarimana met with delegates from those political parties represented in the Government to seek a further extension of the coalition's mandate. However, the Prime Minister's insistence that the FPR should be represented in any new government exacerbated existing divisions within the MDR, prompting Habyarimana to conclude the agreement with a conciliatory group of MDR dissidents, including the Minister of Education, Agathe Uwilingiyimana, who was elected to the premiership.

In August 1993 a peace accord was formally signed in Arusha by Habyarimana and Col Alex Kanyarengwe of the FPR. A new transitional government, to be headed by a mutually approved Prime Minister, would be installed by 10 September, and multi-party elections would be conducted after a 22-month period. Failure to establish the transitional institutions by the stipulated deadline was attributed by the Government and the FPR to an increasingly precarious national security situation, and both sides urged the prompt dispatch of a neutral UN force to facilitate the implementation of the accord. In October the UN Security Council adopted Resolution 872, providing for the establishment of the UN Assistance Mission to Rwanda (UNAMIR), to be deployed in Rwanda for an initial period of six months, with a mandate to monitor observance of the cease-fire, to contribute to the security of the capital and to facilitate the repatriation of refugees. UNAMIR, which was to incorporate UNOMUR and GOM, was formally inaugurated on 1 November, and was planned to comprise some 2,500 personnel when fully operational. In December the UN expressed the opinion that conditions had been sufficiently fulfilled to allow the inauguration of the transitional institutions. In late December a 600-strong FPR battalion was escorted to the capital by UNAMIR officials, in order to ensure the safety of FPR representatives selected to participate in the transitional government and legislature.

On 5 January 1994 Juvénal Habyarimana was invested as President of a transitional administration, for a 22-month period, under the terms of the Arusha accord. The inauguration of the transitional government and legislature was, however, repeatedly delayed, owing to political opposition to the proposed Council of Ministers, and to the insistence of Habyarimana that the list of proposed legislative deputies, presented in March, should be modified to include representatives of additional political parties, including the reactionary Coalition pour la défense de la République (CDR). Meanwhile, political frustration had erupted into violence in February, with the murder of the Minister of Public Works and Energy, Félicien Gatabazi of the Parti social-démocrate (PSD), who had been a prominent supporter of the Arusha accord and of the transitional administration. Within hours the CDR leader, Martin Bucyana, was killed in a retaliatory attack by PSD supporters; an ensuing series of violent confrontations resulted in a further 30–40 deaths.

On 6 April 1994 the presidential aircraft, returning from a regional summit meeting in Dar es Salaam, Tanzania, was fired on, above Kigali airport, and exploded, killing all 10 passengers, including Habyarimana. (The President of Burundi, Cyprien Ntaryamira, two Burundian cabinet ministers and the Chief of Staff of the Rwandan armed forces were among the other victims.) In Kigali the presidential guard immediately initiated a campaign of retributive violence against Habyarimana's political opponents, although it remained unclear who had been responsible for the attack on the aircraft, and UNAMIR officials attempting to investigate the site of the crash were obstructed by the presidential guard. As politicians and civilians fled the capital, the brutality of the political assassinations was compounded by attacks on the clergy, UNAMIR personnel and members of the Tutsi tribe. Many Hutu civilians were reportedly forced to murder their Tutsi neighbours, and the mobilization of the Interahamwe unofficial militias (allegedly affiliated to the MRNDD and the CDR), seemingly committed to the massacre of Tutsi civilians and opponents of the Government, was encour-

aged by the presidential guard (with support from some factions of the armed forces) and by inflammatory broadcasts from Radio-Télévision Libre des Mille Collines in Kigali. The Prime Minister, the President of the Constitutional Court, the Ministers of Labour and Social Affairs and of Information, and the Chairman of the PSD were among the prominent politicians murdered (or declared missing and presumed dead) within hours of Habyarimana's death. On 8 April the Speaker of the CND, Dr Théodore Sindikubwabo, announced that he had assumed the office of interim President of the Republic, in accordance with the provisions of the 1991 Constitution. The five remaining participating political parties and factions of the Government selected a new Prime Minister, Jean Kambanda, and a new Council of Ministers (drawn largely from the MRNDD) from among their ranks. The legality of the new administration was immediately challenged by the FPR, which claimed that the terms of the Constitution regarding succession had been superseded by the terms of the Arusha accord. The legitimacy of the Government (which had fled south to Gitarama to escape escalating violence in the capital) was subsequently rejected by several political parties and factions.

In mid-April 1994 the FPR resumed operations from its northern stronghold, with the stated aim of relieving its beleaguered battalion in Kigali, restoring order there and halting the massacre of civilians. The UN mediated a fragile 60-hour cease-fire, during which small evacuation forces from several countries escorted foreign nationals out of Rwanda. Belgium's UNAMIR contingent of more than 400 troops was also withdrawn, having encountered increasing hostility as a result of persistent rumours of Belgian complicity in the attack on President Habyarimana's aircraft, and accusations that Belgian troops were providing logistical support to the FPR.

Members of the Rwandan Government embarked on a diplomatic offensive throughout Europe and Africa, seeking to enhance the credibility of the administration through international recognition of its legal status. However, this initiative achieved only limited success, and the FPR's refusal to enter into dialogue with the 'illegal' administration proved a major obstacle to attempts, undertaken by the UN and the Presidents of Tanzania and of Zaire, to sponsor a new cease-fire agreement in late April and early May 1994.

As the violent campaign initiated by the presidential guard and the Interahamwe (estimated at some 30,000-strong) gathered national momentum, the militia's identification of all Tutsi as political opponents of the State provoked tribal polarization and an effective pogrom. Reports of mass Tutsi graves and of unprovoked attacks on fleeing Tutsi refugees and those seeking refuge in schools, hospitals and churches provoked unqualified international outrage, and promises were made of financial and logistical aid for an estimated 2m. displaced Rwandans who were threatened by famine and disease in makeshift camps. By late May attempts to assess the full scale of the humanitarian catastrophe in Rwanda were complicated by reports that the FPR (who claimed to control more than one-half of the territory) was perpetrating retaliatory atrocities against Hutu civilians.

In view of the deteriorating security situation, in late April 1994 the UN Security Council approved a resolution to reduce UNAMIR to just 270 personnel. This was condemned by the Rwandan authorities and internationally, and in mid-May, following intense international pressure and the disclosure of the vast scale of the humanitarian crisis in the region, the Security Council approved Resolution 917, providing for the eventual deployment of some 5,500 UN troops with a revised mandate, including the protection of refugees in designated 'safe areas'. Further UN-sponsored attempts to negotiate a cease-fire failed in late May and early June, and the FPR made significant territorial gains in southern Rwanda, forcing the Government to flee Gitarama and seek refuge in the western town of Kibuye. In early June the UN Security Council extended the mandate of what was designated UNAMIR II until December. However, the UN Secretary-General continued to encounter considerable difficulty in securing equipment and armaments requested by those countries that had agreed to participate.

By mid-June 1994 the emergence of confirmed reports of retributive murders committed by FPR members (among the victims were 22 clergymen, including the Roman Catholic Archbishop of Kigali), and the collapse of an OAU-brokered truce prompted the French Government to announce its willingness to lead an armed police action, endorsed by the UN, in Rwanda. Despite French insistence that its force (expected to total 2,000 troops) would maintain strict political neutrality, and operate, from the border regions, in a purely humanitarian capacity pending the arrival of a multinational UN force, the FPR was vehemently opposed to its deployment, citing the French Government's maintenance of high-level contacts with representatives of the self-proclaimed Rwandan Government as an indication of political bias. The UN Secretary-General welcomed the French initiative; however, the OAU expressed serious reservations as to the appropriateness of the action. In late June a first contingent of 150 French marine commandos launched 'Operation Turquoise', entering the western town of Cyangugu, in preparation for a large-scale operation to protect refugees in the area. By mid-July the French had relieved several beleaguered Tutsi communities, and had established a temporary 'safe haven' for the displaced population in the south-west, through which a massive exodus of Hutu refugees began to flow, prompted by reports (disseminated by supporters of the defeated interim government) that the advancing FPR forces were seeking violent retribution against the Hutu. An estimated 1m. Rwandans sought refuge in the Zairean border town of Goma, while a similar number attempted to cross the border elsewhere in the south-west. The FPR, meanwhile, swiftly secured all major cities and strategic territorial positions, but halted its advance several kilometres from the boundaries of the French-controlled neutral zone, requesting the apprehension and return for trial of those responsible for the recent atrocities. (At the end of June the first report of the recently appointed UN Special Rapporteur on Human Rights in Rwanda confirmed that as many as 500,000 Rwandans had been killed since April, and urged the establishment of an international tribunal to investigate allegations of genocide; in early July the UN announced the creation of a commission of inquiry for this purpose.)

On 19 July 1994 Pasteur Bizimungu, a Hutu, was inaugurated as President for a five-year term. On the same day the FPR announced the composition of a new Government of National Unity, with the leader of the MDR moderate faction, Faustin Twagiramungu, as Prime Minister. The majority of cabinet posts were assigned to FPR members (including the FPR military chief, Maj.-Gen. Paul Kagame, who became Minister of Defence and also assumed the newly created post of Vice-President), while the remainder were divided among the MDR, the PSD, the Parti libéral (PL) and the Parti démocratique chrétien (PDC). The new administration urged all refugees to return to Rwanda, and issued assurances that civilian Hutus could return safely to their homes. Identity cards bearing details of ethnic origin were to be abolished forthwith. The new Government declared its intention to honour the terms of the Arusha accord within the context of an extended period of transition. In August, however, Twagiramungu declared the country to be effectively bankrupt, claiming that members of the former Government, who had fled abroad, had appropriated all exchange reserves. The claims to legitimacy of the exiled former administration were seriously undermined by recognition by the European Union (EU, see p. 199) of the new Government of National Unity in September.

Amid persistent rumours that the Rwandan armed forces were attempting to regroup and rearm in Zaire, in preparation for a counter-offensive against the FPR, in late August 1994 the UN initiated the deployment of some 2,500 UNAMIR II forces, largely drawn from Ghana and Ethiopia, in the security zone (redesignated 'zone four'). French troops began to withdraw from the area (the final contingent departed in late September), prompting hundreds of thousands of internally displaced Hutu refugees within the zone to move to Zairean border areas. An estimated 500,000 refugees remained at camps in the former security zone at the end of August, as the first Rwandan government officials were assigned to customs and immigration and army recruitment duties in the region. The UNAMIR II mandate was extended for a further six months. (In June 1995, at the request of the Rwandan Government, the six-month mandate of the force, which was reduced from 5,586 to 2,330 personnel, was again renewed.)

In November 1994 a number of amendments to the terms of the August 1993 Arusha accord were adopted under a multiparty protocol of understanding. The most notable of the new provisions was the exclusion from the legislative process of those parties implicated in alleged acts of genocide during 1994. A 70-member National Transitional Assembly was formally inaugurated in December, with a composition including five representatives of the armed forces and one member of the national police force. On 5 May 1995 this legislature adopted a new Constitution, which was based on selected articles of the 1991 Constitution, the terms of the Arusha accord, the FPR's victory declaration of July 1994 and the November multi-party protocol.

A political crisis emerged in August 1995, after the Prime Minister expressed dissatisfaction with the Government's lack of adherence to the provisions of the Arusha accord regarding power-sharing, and with the security forces' repeated recourse to violence in their management of the refugee crisis. Twagiramungu and four other disaffected ministers were subsequently replaced. Pierre Célestin Rwigyema of the MDR, also Hutu and the former Minister of Primary and Secondary Education, was named as the new Prime Minister at the end of the month. The new Council of Ministers included representatives of both major ethnic groups and four political parties.

In late 1994 Hutu refugees within Rwanda and in neighbouring countries were continuing to resist the exhortations of the UN and the new Rwandan administration to return to their homes, despite the deteriorating security situation in many camps (which had, moreover, forced the withdrawal of a number of relief agencies). Hutu militias were reported to have assumed control of several camps, notably Katale in Zaire and Benaco in Tanzania. Reports also emerged that Hutu civilians intending to return to their homes had been subjected to violent intimidation by the Interahamwe. It was further alleged that male Hutu refugees were being forced to undergo military training in preparation for a renewed military conflict. The reluctance of many refugees to return to their homes was also attributed to persistent allegations that the Tutsi-dominated FPR armed forces (the Armée patriotique rwandaise—APR) were conducting a systematic campaign of reprisal attacks against returning Hutus.

International scepticism regarding the Government's programme of refugee resettlement increased in early 1995, following a series of uncompromising initiatives to encourage the return of internally displaced Rwandans (including the interruption of food supplies to refugee camps), culminating in the forcible closure of the camps through military intervention. An attempt in April to dismantle the Kibeho camp in southern Rwanda provoked widespread international condemnation, after APR troops opened fire on refugees, amid confusion arising from the actions of some hostile elements within the camp and a sudden attempt by large numbers of anxious refugees to break the military cordon; independent sources estimated as many as 5,000 fatalities.

In August 1995, in response to requests made by the Rwandan Government, the UN Security Council voted to suspend the arms embargo to Rwanda (imposed in May 1994) for one year, in order to allow the Government to safeguard against the threat of a military offensive by Hutu extremists encamped in neighbouring countries. Meanwhile, the security situation in refugee camps along the Zairean border had deteriorated to such an extent that the Zairean Government initiated a programme of forcible repatriation, attracting widespread international concern. Despite a formal agreement between the office of the UN High Commissioner for Refugees (UNHCR) and the Zairean Government for a more regulated approach to the refugee crisis, APR attacks near the border with Zaire further deterred refugees. At a conference of the Great Lakes countries, convened in Cairo, Egypt, in late November, and attended by the Presidents of Burundi, Rwanda, Uganda and Zaire and by a Tanzanian presidential envoy, President Mobutu of Zaire indicated that the forcible return of remaining refugees in early 1996 was no longer a realistic objective. The conference also accepted the Rwandan President's assertion that the participation of UNAMIR forces in peace-keeping operations in Rwanda was no longer necessary, but urged the Rwandan Government to accept the extension of a revised, three-month mandate for the forces to provide assistance in the refugee repatriation process. (A three-month mandate for a 1,200-strong force was thus renewed in December 1995, and the mission was formally terminated in April 1996.)

In February 1995 the UN Security Council adopted Resolution 977, whereby Arusha was designated the seat for the International Criminal Tribunal for Rwanda (ICTR). The six-member Tribunal, to be headed by a Senegalese lawyer, Laïty Kama, was inaugurated in June for a four-year term. It was reported that the ICTR intended to investigate allegations made against some 400 individuals (many of them by this time resident outside Rwanda) of direct involvement in the planning and execution of crimes against humanity perpetrated in Rwanda during 1994. In October 1995 a Supreme Court was established by the Transitional National Assembly.

The ICTR began formal proceedings in November 1995. The first court session of the ICTR was convened in September 1996, but hearings concerning the first two (of 21) individuals indicted on charges of crimes against humanity were almost immediately postponed. Tribunal officials attributed the virtual collapse of proceedings to the escalating conflict in eastern Zaire, but widespread concern was expressed at the high number of administrative errors committed. In contrast, in January 1997 regional courts within Rwanda passed death sentences on five individuals accused of acts of genocide. (Whereas capital punishment would not be invoked by the ICTR, legislation published by the Rwandan authorities in September 1996 regarding penalties for crimes committed during 1994 made provision for the application of the death penalty, and encouraged the use of plea-bargain.) In February 1997 the report of an internal UN investigation of the ICTR was highly critical of many aspects of administrative structure and procedure, prompting the resignation of two senior Tribunal officials. In July seven suspects in the 1994 genocide were arrested in Kenya and transferred for trial to Arusha. Among those arrested were former Prime Minister Jean Kambanda, two senior armed forces officers and a former government minister. Later in July a Belgian journalist, who had worked for the extremist Radio-Télévision Libre des Mille Collines at the time of the massacres, was arrested by the Kenyan authorities and similarly transferred for trial (becoming the first foreign national to be indicted by the ICTR).

Meanwhile, some 300 genocide suspects were tried by Rwandan courts during 1997, and an estimated 125,000 defendants were in detention awaiting trial; arrests reportedly continued at a rate of 1,000 per month. In an attempt to address the problem of severe overcrowding in prisons, in late 1997 the release was authorized of elderly, infirm or juvenile detainees. (This policy was denounced by organizations representing survivors of the 1994 massacres, and there were reports of attacks on freed genocide suspects.) The announcement that 23 people convicted of acts of genocide were to be publicly executed provoked international condemnation. Amnesty International and other human rights organizations expressed serious concerns that those convicted had been denied adequate opportunity to prepare a defence. The Rwandan authorities refuted such claims, and dismissed pleas for clemency. The public executions proceeded in April 1998.

In August 1996, during a visit to Kigali by the Zairean Prime Minister, a bilateral agreement for the organized and unconditional repatriation of all Rwandan refugees in Zaire was concluded (without the participation of UNHCR officials). During September, however, relations between the two countries were placed under renewed strain, when the attempts of the Interahamwe and the Zairean armed forces to displace large numbers of Zairean Banyamulenge (ethnic Tutsis) from eastern Zaire encountered large-scale armed resistance from the Banyamulenge, resulting in Zairean accusations of Rwandan support for the Banyamulenge, and culminating in a cross-border exchange of fire later that month. Throughout October, as the rebels made significant gains in the region, the Rwandan Government continued to deny Zairean allegations of its involvement in the Banyamulenge insurrection, and at the end of the month admitted that Rwandan troops had been deployed in eastern Zaire in response to an artillery attack on the Rwandan town of Cyangugu, allegedly made by the Zairean armed forces.

Meanwhile, there was renewed international concern for the estimated 1m. refugees previously encamped in eastern Zaire, following reports that the regional conflict had resulted in the sudden exodus of some 250,000 refugees, and the interruption of food aid distribution. The rebel army in Zaire (known as the Alliance des forces démocratiques pour la libération du Congo-Zaïre—AFDL) declared a cease-fire for returning refugees, and later in the month announced the creation of a humanitarian corridor to the Rwandan border, with the intention that the estimated 700,000 Rwandan refugees now seeking shelter at the Mugunga camp, west of Goma, would return to Rwanda. The large-scale return of refugees was finally prompted by an AFDL attack on Interahamwe units operating from the camp. In April 1997 the AFDL leader, Laurent-Désiré Kabila, demanded that the UN complete full repatriation of the refugees within 60 days, after which time their return would be undertaken unilaterally by the rebels. The Rwandan authorities, meanwhile, expressed concern that the UN was delaying the rapid repatriation of refugees from eastern Zaire. (By the end of May the AFDL had gained control of most of Zaire, which was renamed the Democratic Republic of Congo—DRC, and Kabila assumed power as

Head of State.) Continuing ethnic unrest and violence, particularly in north-west Rwanda, throughout 1997 were exacerbated by the return from the DRC of large numbers of Hutus (see also the chapter on the DRC). Both the office of the UN High Commissioner for Human Rights and Amnesty International published reports in August, alleging that as many as 3,000 civilians had been killed by government troops in counter-insurgency operations since May. The Government denied having perpetrated massacres of civilians, and claimed that those killed had been Interahamwe militia. An extensive demobilization programme was undertaken from September, with the aim of reintegrating former combatants into civil society; some 57,500 personnel were to be demobilized over a three-year period.

By late 1997 there was evidence that Hutu rebel forces, estimated to number some 10,000–15,000 Interahamwe and former soldiers, were becoming increasingly confident of their military potential, as a series of raids was launched to free prisoners awaiting trial on genocide charges. More than 300 deaths were reported in an abortive attack by 1,200 rebels on a prison in the north-west in November. In early December, however, rebels successfully released more than 500 inmates from a prison in central Rwanda. Genocide survivors and students' groups organized demonstrations in several towns in late 1997 and early 1998 to protest against the Government's failure to suppress the militias and prevent what they regarded as the continuation of the genocide. A further 80 detainees escaped in March 1998, when rebels stormed a prison in central Gitarama.

Violence and ethnic unrest continued throughout 1998, predominantly in the north-west of the country, where the Government continued operations against the Hutu rebels. In March Amnesty International issued a report alleging that both rebels and security forces had been responsible for the massacre of hundreds of unarmed civilians during January and February. The Government claimed several successes in its offensive in the north-west during the year, including the capture of rebel leaders and the discovery of the rebel headquarters. In June, however, 6,000 displaced Tutsis were massacred by Hutu rebels during an attack on a refugee camp. In July the UN Human Rights Field Force in Rwanda announced that it was to withdraw from the country, in protest at the Government's refusal to allow observers to monitor and report human rights abuses.

The trial of genocide suspects continued in 1998 both in Rwanda and at the ICTR, and in early September the ICTR reached its first verdict. A former mayor of Taba, Jean-Paul Akayesu, was convicted and sentenced to life imprisonment; Kambanda, who had pleaded guilty to six charges of genocide and crimes against humanity, was also given a life sentence. Both appealed against their sentences, and Akayesu later began a hunger strike, claiming he had been denied the lawyer of his choice; a further 25 detainees joined his protest. Rwandan courts, meanwhile, convicted and sentenced some 1,000 genocide suspects during 1998 (the authorities had aimed to hear 5,000 cases during the year). By June about 5,000 suspects in Rwandan prisons had pleaded guilty to acts of genocide in order to lessen their sentences, apparently in response to the public executions in April. In June Maj. Augustine Cyiza, the Vice-President of the Supreme Court and President of the Court of Cassation, resigned (he had been suspended for misconduct in March), and in October some controversy was caused by the decision to release at least 10,000 genocide suspects owing to lack of evidence against them. It was announced in November that 34,000 suspects had been freed since 1994.

In October 1998 the Transitional National Assembly approved the establishment of a fund to assist survivors of the genocide, and in the following month the Council of Ministers approved the establishment of two commissions, for human rights and for unity and reconciliation (both had been established by mid-1999). Between February and May 1999 some 16 deputies resigned, or were expelled, from the Transitional National Assembly for misconduct, incompetence or allegations of involvement in the genocide. In June the period of political transition, originally set at five years in 1994, was extended by a further four years, following agreement between the major political parties.

In January 1999 the Minister of Justice resigned his portfolio and left the country. In a reorganization in the following month the Government was expanded to comprise 21 ministers (compared with the previous 17). New ministers included Jean de Dieu Mucyo (the first Tutsi to be appointed Minister for Justice since 1994). Voting in local elections (the first elections to be held since 1988) were conducted on a non-party basis on 29–31 March 1999. Voter participation was estimated to have been 95%, and at the end of the month the EU special envoy to the Great Lakes region commended the manner in which the elections were conducted. In June the Transitional National Assembly approved draft legislation establishing a commission that was to prepare a new constitution. In July the Minister of Foreign Affairs, Amri Sued, was removed from his post, reportedly for dereliction of duty and embezzlement; he was replaced by the Minister of Information, and that ministry was subsequently dissolved. Legislation establishing a national police force (which was to unify the existing national gendarmerie, and the communal and judicial police) was adopted in August.

In September 1999 a parliamentary investigation implicated Marc Rugenera, Charles Ntakirutinka and Anastase Gasana (the Ministers of Institutional Affairs, of Social Affairs and of Commerce, Industry and Tourism, respectively) in severe malpractice concerning the issuing of government contracts. Ntakirutinka and Gasana were censured by the Transitional National Assembly in a vote of 'no confidence' in early October, and subsequently resigned. (Rugenera won a motion demanding his resignation by one vote.) In November a commission responsible for investigating all cases of alleged corruption issued a report implicating the Prime Minister in the misuse of funds, donated by the World Bank, for the reconstruction of the education sector. In December both the Prime Minister and the Minister of Education survived a motion of censure in the Assembly, although a minister of state resigned shortly before being questioned on his involvement in the affair. Plans for the establishment of a permanent national anti-corruption commission were announced in January 2000.

During 1999 a number of prominent Hutu, including three former government ministers, were arrested on suspicion of involvement in the 1994 genocide and extradited to the ICTR. Also in April the Vatican expressed consternation at the arrest of the Roman Catholic Bishop of the southern diocese of Gikongoro, on charges of complicity in the massacre of Tutsi children. (In June 2000, however, the Bishop was acquitted of all charges.) In May a former Rwandan mayor (the first Rwandan to be tried abroad for genocide) was convicted by a Swiss court on charges of inciting the killing of Tutsi civilians, and sentenced to life imprisonment. In June Navanethem Pillay succeeded Kama as President of the ICTR, and in September Carla del Ponte became UN Chief Prosecutor. In November the Rwandan Government suspended co-operation with the ICTR, following the Tribunal's decision to release Jean Bosco Barayagwiza, a former government official who was accused of participation in the genocide, owing to his prolonged detention without trial. The Minister of Justice later refused del Ponte authorization to enter Rwanda, and the newly appointed Rwandan representative to the ICTR announced he would not assume his office until the issue had been resolved. In December the Government announced that it would allow del Ponte to enter Rwanda, following her official request for a review of the decision to release Barayagwiza. Full co-operation was resumed with the ICTR in February 2000, after a three-month suspension, and in March, following the examination of fresh evidence, the Appeals Chamber of the ICTR announced its decision that Barayagwiza should stand trial. Further arrests were made in early 2000. In February legislation introducing a traditional system of justice, known as *gacaca* (grassroots), was adopted; certain categories of genocide crimes were to be tried under this system (by council in local communities), while the most serious genocide crimes would continue to be tried under the existing judicial system. It was hoped that the creation of the *gacaca* courts would alleviate the large number of cases awaiting trial and aid the process of national reconciliation.

In February 2000 the National Assembly voted in favour of investigating alleged abuses of power by Rwigyema. On 28 February he resigned from the office of Prime Minister, citing differences with the legislature. Bernard Makuza, hitherto the Rwandan ambassador in Germany, was appointed Prime Minister in March, and subsequently announced a government reorganization, in which six ministers were replaced. The new Government was the first since 1994 in which the parties were not represented in accordance with the 1993 Arusha peace accords. At its inauguration, Kagame (who remained Vice-President and Minister of Defence and National Security) failed to swear allegiance to the President. On 23 March Bizimungu resigned from office, owing to disagreement over the composition of the new Government, in particular the exclusion of

Mazimhaka. Kagame was subsequently appointed interim President by the Supreme Court. On 17 April he was formally elected President of Rwanda by members of the Transitional National Assembly and the Government, securing 81 of 86 votes cast. He was inaugurated on 22 April (becoming the first Tutsi Head of State since 1959).

At the end of July 2000 Rwigyema was removed from the leadership of the MDR by the party's political bureau, which accused him of acting contrary to its interests; he subsequently left the country. In September the trial of three journalists, on charges of publicly inciting the Hutu civilian population to perpetrate massacres of Tutsi, was repeatedly adjourned after the accused refused to appear before the ICTR. In early October the High Court of the United Kingdom announced that a former officer of the Rwandan armed forces, who had been charged with participation in the genocide of 1994, would be extradited for trial at the ICTR. Later that month the International Court of Justice (ICJ) at The Hague, Netherlands, upheld the life sentence imposed on Kambanda by the ICTR in 1998. In December 2000 del Ponte announced that the Tribunal was to commence investigations into members of the FPR for involvement in massacres of Hutu (having previously only instigated proceedings against Hutu supporters who had participated in the 1994 genocide of Tutsi). In January 2001 the Government announced that former members of the armed forces, who surrendered to the authorities and had not participated in the genocide of Tutsi, would be permitted to rejoin the armed forces. In April elections to municipal councils were conducted on a non-party basis throughout the country, prior to the general election, scheduled to take place in 2003. Human Rights Watch subsequently criticized the manner in which the local government elections were conducted, however, claiming that only one candidate contested the poll in nearly half of the municipalities.

In April 2001 an international warrant was issued for the arrest of Rwigyema, who had taken refuge in the USA, on suspicion of participating in the genocide of 1994. The trial of four Hutus (including two nuns), on charges of complicity in massacres in the southern Butare prefecture, commenced in Belgium later that month (under Belgian legislation permitting foreign nationals to be arraigned there for war crimes). In early June all four were sentenced to terms of imprisonment. Also in early June a former mayor became the first defendant to be acquitted by the ICTR (which at this time had convicted eight people on charges of involvement in the genocide). In July four Hutus, including a relative of former President Habyarimana, were arrested in western Europe and subsequently transferred to the ICTR (increasing the number of suspects held in detention there to more than 50). At that time four former ICTR investigators were also under suspicion of involvement in the genocide. In the same month a Tribunal of First Instance officially banned the MRNDD and CDR for inciting violence in 1994. In September 2001 the trial of a senior Hutu pastor, who had been extradited from the USA, and his son commenced at the ICTR; they were charged with genocide and crimes against humanity, in connection with having allegedly assisted in the massacre of Tutsi.

On 4 October 2001 some 250,000 judges for the *gacaca* courts were elected in a national ballot. With the number of prisoners awaiting trial having increased to some 115,000, those suspected of lesser crimes relating to the genocide were henceforth to be tried by the *gacaca* system. In December a new national flag, emblem and anthem officially replaced those adopted at independence in 1962. In February 2002 a Hutu Roman Catholic priest, who was accused of participating in the 1994 genocide (by inciting the destruction of a church, in which some 2,000 Tutsis had taken refuge), surrendered to the ICTR. (He had resided for several years under the protection of the Vatican in Italy, until the ICTR placed increasing pressure on the Italian authorities.) In early April the trial of Col Theoneste Bagosora, who was considered to be the principal perpetrator of the genocide (the killing of an estimated 80,000 Tutsi and moderate Hutu in early 1994), commenced at the ICTR. Bagosora, who had been in custody since his arrest in Cameroon in 1996, had allegedly organized the militia to massacre Tutsi civilians and had personally ordered the assassination of prominent politicians. He, and a further three former senior army officers on trial, refused to attend the initial session of the ICTR, on the grounds that their right to defence had been violated. Later in April security forces arrested former President Bizimungu (who had attempted to form an opposition political party in May 2001), and searched his residence. The authorities subsequently announced that Bizimungu had continued to engage in illegal political activity, and would be charged with endangering state security. (In early 2003 he remained in detention, awaiting trial.)

In early August 2002 Gen. Augustin Bizimungu, the army Chief of Staff in 1994, who had been indicted by the ICTR jointly with four other former military commanders, was arrested in Angola and transferred to the Tribunal. Later that month he pleaded not guilty to 10 charges, including that of genocide. In November trials by the *gacaca* court system officially commenced throughout the country. In the same month several principal ministers, including those responsible for the portfolios of foreign affairs and defence, were replaced in a government reorganization. In December the UN Security Council adopted a resolution nominating 23 permanent ICTR judges to the UN General Assembly.

In January 2003, in an effort to reduce numbers in prisons, Kagame issued a decree providing for the provisional release of some 40,000 of those held in detention, including many who had pleaded guilty to charges related to the 1994 genocide. Although the Ministry of Justice maintained that legal proceedings against the released prisoners would continue, organizations representing survivors of the genocide criticized the measure. Most of the prisoners due for release were to be dispatched to 'solidarity camps', where they were to be prepared for reintegration into society. The first 2,000 of these were released later in January. In February an elderly pastor and his son were convicted by the ICTR of active participation in the massacre of Tutsis in the west of the country in 1994; they were sentenced to 10 and 25 years' imprisonment, respectively.

On 23 April 2003 the Transitional National Assembly adopted a new Constitution, which was expected to enter into effect in July, subject to approval at a national referendum (scheduled for 26 May). The draft Constitution, which was largely based on the Arusha peace accords, provided for the establishment of a bicameral legislature, which for the first time since 1994 would be elected by universal suffrage. Following the endorsement of the new Constitution, the presidential and legislative elections were scheduled to take place in July. Kagame was to seek re-election to the presidency, while former Prime Minister Twagiramungu announced his intention to return to Rwanda from Belgium in order to contest the election on behalf of the MDR. In mid-May the former Minister of Information in the Government of April 1994, Eliézer Niyitegeka, was sentenced to life imprisonment by the ICTR, after being convicted on six charges of involvement in the genocide.

At the end of July 1998 Laurent-Désiré Kabila (the President of the DRC since 31 May 1997) announced that military co-operation with both Rwanda and Uganda was to end, and demanded that all foreign forces leave the DRC. Relations between Rwanda and the DRC subsequently deteriorated. Kabila claimed that a rebellion, which commenced in the east of the DRC in August, constituted a Rwandan invasion; the Rwandan Government denied any involvement, but in late 1998 conceded that Rwandan troops were present in the DRC to provide logistical support to the rebel-led action. The Rwandan Government participated in a series of regional peace negotiations, at which Kabila refused to negotiate directly with the rebels. Rwanda later denied reports that it was maintaining a joint military command with Uganda in the DRC (see also the chapter on the DRC).

Rwandan action in the DRC continued in 1999, although Rwanda's alliance with Uganda became increasingly unstable during that year. At the end of April Uganda temporarily recalled its ambassador to Rwanda, following an incident in the DRC, in which Rwandan troops killed a number of members of the Ugandan armed forces. A split within the rebel movement in the DRC, the Rassemblement congolais pour la démocratie (RCD), resulted in the creation of two factions, one supported by Rwanda and one by Uganda. Following further clashes in the DRC between Rwandan and Ugandan troops in Kisangani in August, both armies agreed to leave the city. In June the DRC instituted proceedings against Burundi, Rwanda and Uganda at the ICJ, accusing these countries of acts of armed aggression. (In early February 2001, however, the DRC abandoned proceedings against Burundi and Rwanda.)

In May 2000 Rwandan and Ugandan forces again clashed in the town of Kisangani (despite a cease-fire agreement, which had been reached by all forces involved in the conflict in April). After meeting a UN Security Council delegation, the Rwandan and Ugandan contingents agreed to the demilitarization of the

town, and its transfer to the control of the Mission des nations unies en République démocratique du Congo (MONUC, see p. 66) deployed in the country. Despite further fighting, it was confirmed at the end of June that all Rwandan and Ugandan forces had withdrawn from Kisangani. In December, however, the principal RCD faction, supported by Rwandan troops, succeeded in gaining control of the south-eastern town of Pweto. The Rwandan Government denied any involvement in the assassination of Kabila in January 2001 (see the chapter on the DRC). In February Kagame met the new DRC President, Joseph Kabila (the son of Laurent-Désiré), in Washington, DC, USA, to discuss the ongoing conflict. Later that month the groups involved in the conflict, under the aegis of the UN Security Council, agreed to a disengagement of their forces by mid-March, followed by a complete withdrawal of foreign troops from the DRC by mid-May. Although some military disengagement of forces took place accordingly in March, factions subsequently refused to continued until MONUC guaranteed security in the region. In April the Governments of Burundi, Rwanda and Uganda rejected the claims of a UN report that the forces of these countries had exploited the natural resources of the DRC. In June it was reported that Interahamwe militia, led by former members of the Rwandan army, had intensified incursions into north-western Rwanda from the DRC. Despite continued pressure from the UN Security Council, in August Kagame insisted that Kabila fulfil pledges to demobilize the Interahamwe (who were supporting DRC government forces), as a precondition to the withdrawal of Rwandan forces from the DRC.

At the end of July 2002, after further discussions mediated by the South African Government, a peace agreement was signed by Kabila and Kagame in Pretoria. Under the accord, Kabila pledged to arrest and disarm the Interahamwe militia in the DRC, while the Rwandan Government agreed to withdraw all troops from the country. In October the Rwandan Government announced that all forces had been withdrawn from the DRC. Following further hostilities in eastern DRC involving the remaining Ugandan troops, however, the Rwandan legislature approved the redeployment of forces in the country in March 2003. It was reported that Rwandan troops had entered the DRC at the end of that month, and had subsequently regained control of territory in the north-east.

In November 2001 Kagame and the Ugandan Head of State, Lt-Gen. Yoweri Kaguta Museveni, met in London, United Kingdom, in an effort to resolve the increasing tension between the two nations, following the repeated clashes in the DRC. The Ugandan Government had accused Rwanda of supporting dissidents who intended to overthrow Museveni's administration, while Kagame claimed that Ugandan troops were amassing on the joint border between the two countries. In February 2002 further discussions between Kagame and Museveni, with mediation by the British Secretary of State for International Development, were conducted in Uganda. It was agreed that both Governments would urge the dissidents based in their respective countries to take refuge elsewhere, and the adoption of a mutual extradition treaty was envisaged. In April 2003 increasing tension between Rwandan and Ugandan troops in the DRC (see above) was reported, prompting fears of direct military confrontations.

Since 1994 the role of the international community in failing to avert the genocide has come under frequent scrutiny. In late 1997 the report of a Belgian Senate investigation concluded that the international community, and more specifically the UN and the Belgian authorities, was directly or indirectly responsible for certain aspects of the developments arising from the political violence from April 1994. Testifying before the ICTR in February 1998, the former UNAMIR commander stated that he had warned the UN in early 1994 of the impending ethnic catastrophe in Rwanda, but that the international community had lacked the will to intervene adequately. Suggestions that Kofi Annan, the head of UN peace-keeping operations at the time of the conflict, had failed to respond to such warnings prompted tensions between the UN Secretary-General (as Annan had subsequently become) and the Rwandan authorities in May 1998, as government officials refused to receive the Secretary-General in the course of a visit to Rwanda, and announced a two-week suspension of activities of the UN human rights mission in Rwanda (although the suspension was withdrawn after one week). Meanwhile, in February the OAU announced the establishment of a committee to investigate the genocide; the committee held its first meeting in October. In December a French parliamentary committee, established in March, presented its

Rwanda has traditionally relied heavily on foreign aid, owing to an economic development impeded by ethnic and political unrest. Agricultural production in many areas of Rwanda declined, owing to erosion and over-intensive farming methods. The genocide of early 1994 (see Recent History) resulted in the destruction of the country's economic base and of prospects of attracting private and external investment. With assistance from the international financial community, the new Government, which was established in July, initiated measures to resettle more than 2m. displaced civilians and to reconstruct the economy. In 1998 a three-year Enhanced Structural Adjustment Facility was approved by the IMF. By the end of 1999 Rwanda had made considerable progress in rehabilitating and stabilizing the economy; government revenue (negligible in 1994) had recovered, and a reduced rate of inflation had been sustained, while an extensive privatization programme had been initiated with the support of the World Bank. In late 2000, following a meeting with international financial donor institutions, Rwanda qualified for debt relief, under the Heavily Indebted Poor Countries initiative of the IMF and World Bank. In October 2001 the IMF approved further credit to Rwanda, under a Poverty Reduction and Growth Facility (PRGF). Although the economy was adversely affected by a severe decline in the international price of coffee (the country's principal export crop), which increased the already high trade deficit, continued strong economic growth, low inflation and a rise in foreign exchange reserves were recorded at the end of 2001. Also in that year the Government initiated a number of structural reforms, including the introduction of value-added tax, the privatization of some 12 state-owned enterprises, and improvements in civil administration. In August 2002 the IMF approved a further three-year credit arrangement under the PRGF, and extended additional assistance to enable the Government to meet its debt-servicing obligations. The authorities, in consultation with the World Bank, were to proceed with privatization, notably of the state telecommunications enterprise and tea factories. Exceptional government spending in 2002, in accordance with the poverty reduction strategy, included outlays for the reintegration of former combatants, assistance for genocide victims, and jurisdiction of trials of war crime suspects, and was offset by revenue-related measures, such as an increase in value-added tax.

Improvements in fiscal stability were expected to result in an increase in private-sector confidence. Growth in GDP increased in 2002, and an international investment conference was scheduled to take place in the country in May 2003.

Education

Primary education, beginning at seven years of age and lasting for seven years, is officially compulsory. Secondary education, which is not compulsory, begins at the age of 14 and lasts for a further six years. Schools are administered by the state and by Christian missions. In 1999/2000 97.3% of children in the relevant age-group (males 97.1%, females 97.5%) were enrolled in primary schools, according to UNESCO estimates, while secondary enrolment was equivalent to only 12.1% of children in the appropriate age-group (males 12.4%, females 11.8%). Rwanda has a university, with campuses at Butare and Ruhengeri, and several other institutions of higher education, but some students attend universities abroad, particularly in Belgium, France or Germany. The estimated number of students enrolled in higher education in 2000 was 7,000. Of estimated total expenditure by the central Government in 2001, 29,800m. Rwanda francs (18.9%) were allocated to education.

Public Holidays

2003: 1 January (New Year), 28 January (Democracy Day), 7 April (National Mourning Day), 21 April (Easter Monday), 1 May (Labour Day), 29 May (Ascension Day), 9 June (Whit Monday), 1 July (Independence Day), 15 August (Assumption), 25 September (Kamarampaka Day, anniversary of 1961 referendum), 1 October (Armed Forces Day), 1 November (All Saints' Day), 25 December (Christmas).

2004: 1 January (New Year), 28 January (Democracy Day), 7 April (National Mourning Day), 12 April (Easter Monday), 1 May (Labour Day), 20 May (Ascension Day), 31 May (Whit Monday), 1 July (Independence Day), 15 August (Assumption), 25 September (Kamarampaka Day, anniversary of 1961 referendum), 1 October (Armed Forces Day), 1 November (All Saints' Day), 25 December (Christmas).

Weights and Measures

The metric system is in force.

Statistical Survey

Source (unless otherwise stated): Office rwandais d'information, BP 83, Kigali; tel. 75724.

Area and Population

AREA, POPULATION AND DENSITY

Area (sq km)	26,338*
Population (census results)	
15–16 August 1978	4,830,984
15 August 1991†	
Males	3,487,189
Females.	3,677,805
Total	7,164,994
Population (UN estimates at mid-year)‡	
1999	7,087,000
2000	7,609,000
2001	7,949,000
Density (per sq km) at mid-2001	301.8

* 10,169 sq miles.

† Provisional results. The revised total is 7,142,755.

‡ Source: UN, *World Population Prospects: The 2000 Revision; Population and Vital Statistics Report.*

PREFECTURES
(1991 census)

	Area (sq km)	Population*	Density (per sq km)
Butare	1,830	765,910	418.5
Byumba	4,987	779,365	159.2
Cyangugu	2,226	517,550	232.5
Gikongoro	2,192	462,635	211.1
Gisenyi	2,395	728,365	304.1
Gitarama	2,241	849,285	379.0
Kibungo	4,134	647,175	156.5
Kibuye	1,320	472,525	358.0
Kigali	} 3,251 {	921,050 }	355.2
Kigali-Ville		233,640 }	
Ruhengeri	1,762	765,255	434.3
Total	26,338	7,142,755	271.2

* Source: UN, *Demographic Yearbook.*

PRINCIPAL TOWNS
(population at 1978 census)

Kigali (capital) . .	117,749	Ruhengeri. . . .	16,025
Butare	21,691	Gisenyi	12,436

Mid-2001 (UN estimate, incl. suburbs): Kigali 412,000 (Source: UN, *World Urbanization Prospects: The 2001 Revision*).

BIRTHS AND DEATHS
(UN estimates, annual averages)

	1985–90	1990–95	1995–2000
Birth rate (per 1,000)	44.1	43.1	42.4
Death rate (per 1,000)	17.8	45.5	21.7

Source: UN, *World Population Prospects: The 2000 Revision*.

Expectation of life (WHO estimates, years at birth): 40.7 (males 38.9; females 42.8) in 2001 (Source: WHO, *World Health Report*).

ECONOMICALLY ACTIVE POPULATION
(persons aged 14 years and over, official estimates at January 1989)

	Males	Females	Total
Agriculture, hunting, forestry and fishing	1,219,586	1,612,972	2,832,558
Mining and quarrying . . .	4,652	40	4,692
Manufacturing	32,605	12,483	45,088
Electricity, gas and water . . .	2,445	116	2,561
Construction	37,674	563	38,237
Trade, restaurants and hotels . .	61,169	18,857	80,026
Transport, storage and communications	6,796	536	7,332
Financing, insurance, real estate and business services	2,202	926	3,128
Community, social and personal services	89,484	30,537	120,021
Activities not adequately defined .	5,392	4,021	9,413
Total employed.	1,462,005	1,681,051	3,143,056

Source: ILO, *Yearbook of Labour Statistics*.

Mid-2001 (estimates, '000 persons): Agriculture, etc. 3,897; Total labour force 4,321 (Source: FAO).

Health and Welfare

KEY INDICATORS

Total fertility rate (children per woman, 2001).	5.9
Under-5 mortality rate (per 1,000 live births, 2001) . . .	183
HIV/AIDS (% of persons aged 15–49, 2001).	8.88
Hospital beds (per 1,000 head, 1990)	1.65
Health expenditure (2000): US $ per head (PPP)	40
Health expenditure (2000): % of GDP	5.2
Health expenditure (2000): public (% of total)	51.3
Access to water (% of persons, 1999).	41
Access to sanitation (% of persons, 1999)	8
Human Development Index (2000): ranking	162
Human Development Index (2000): value	0.403

For sources and definitions, see explanatory note on p. vi.

Agriculture

PRINCIPAL CROPS
('000 metric tons)

	1999	2000	2001
Maize	54.9	62.5	92.2
Sorghum	107.6	155.1	175.1
Potatoes	175.9	957.2	989.0
Sweet potatoes	862.6	1,032.9	1,137.2
Cassava (Manioc)	316.9	799.8	688.0
Taro (Coco yam)	90.2	90.9	101.4
Sugar cane	40.0	40.0*	40.0*
Dry beans	140.4	215.3	290.7
Dry peas	8.9	15.3	16.0
Groundnuts (in shell)	8.1	15.3	6.6
Pumpkins, squash and gourds . .	100.0*	205.7	205.0*
Plantains	2,897.4	2,212.3	1,572.7
Coffee (green).	18.8	16.1	18.0†
Tea (made)	13.0	14.5	15.0*

* FAO estimate.
† Unofficial figure.

Source: FAO.

LIVESTOCK
('000 head, year ending September)

	1999	2000	2001*
Cattle	749.0	732.1	800.0
Pigs	159.6	177.2	180.0
Sheep	278.0	254.4	260.0
Goats	634.0	750.4	700.0
Rabbits	229	339	340
Chickens	2,043	1,090	1,200

* FAO estimates.

Source: FAO.

LIVESTOCK PRODUCTS
(FAO estimates, '000 metric tons)

	1999	2000	2001
Beef and veal	17.7	17.2	19.2
Goat meat	3.9	4.4	4.4
Pig meat	2.9	3.3	3.3
Poultry meat	2.2	1.2	1.4
Game meat	7.0	7.0	7.0
Other meat	1.4	1.6	1.7
Cows' milk	86.0	85.0	85.0
Sheep's milk	1.3	1.3	1.3
Goats' milk	14.0	14.0	14.0
Poultry eggs	2.1	2.2	2.3
Cattle hides	2.6	2.5	2.8

Source: FAO.

Forestry

ROUNDWOOD REMOVALS
('000 cubic metres, excluding bark)

	1997	1998	1999
Sawlogs, veneer logs and logs for sleepers	79	84	86
Other industrial wood . . .	236	242	250
Fuel wood	7,100	7,200	7,500
Total	7,415	7,526	7,836

Source: FAO.

2000–01: FAO estimates as for 1999.

SAWNWOOD PRODUCTION
('000 cubic metres, including railway sleepers)

	1997	1998	1999
Coniferous (softwood)	20	21	22
Non-coniferous (hardwood) . .	54	55	57
Total	74	76	79

Source: FAO.

2000–01: FAO estimates as for 1999.

Fishing

(metric tons, live weight)

	1998	1999	2000
Capture	6,641	6,433	6,726
Nile tilapia	2,233	2,640	2,646
Aquaculture	128	300	270
Nile tilapia	120	241	252
Total catch	6,769	6,733	6,996

Source: FAO, *Yearbook of Fishery Statistics*.

Mining

(metric tons, unless otherwise indicated)

	1998	1999	2000
Tin concentrates*	260	243	344
Tungsten concentrates*	149	97	130
Columbo-tantalite†	224	122	83
Gold (kilograms)*	17	10	10

* Figures refer to the metal content of ores and concentrates.
† Figures refer to the estimated production of mineral concentrates. The
  metal content (estimates, metric tons) was: Niobium (Columbium) 76 in
  1998, 42 in 1999, 28 in 2000; Tantalum 60 in 1998, 33 in 1999, 22 in 2000.

Source: US Geological Survey.

Natural gas (million cu m): 0.9 in 1998; 1.4 in 1999; 1.4 in 2000 (Source:
IMF, *Rwanda: Statistical Annex*, August 2002).

Industry

SELECTED PRODUCTS

	1999	2000	2001*
Beer ('000 hectolitres)	599	442	479
Soft drinks ('000 hectolitres)	221	207	228
Cigarettes (million)	217	327	278
Soap (metric tons)	6,431	5,867	7,056
Cement (metric tons)	66,291	70,716	83,024
Electric energy (million kWh)	127.3	110.8	89.3

* Estimates.

Source: IMF, *Rwanda: Statistical Annex* (August 2002).

Finance

CURRENCY AND EXCHANGE RATES

Monetary Units
  100 centimes = 1 franc rwandais (Rwanda franc)

Sterling, Dollar and Euro Equivalents (31 December 2002)
  £1 sterling = 825.0 Rwanda francs
  US $1 = 511.9 Rwanda francs
  €1 = 536.8 Rwanda francs
  1,000 Rwanda francs = £1.212 = $1.954 = €1.863

Average Exchange Rate (Rwanda francs per US $)
  2000   389.70
  2001   442.99
  2002   475.37

Note: Since September 1983 the currency has been linked to the IMF
special drawing right (SDR). Until November 1990 the mid-point exchange
rate was SDR 1 = 102.71 Rwanda francs. In November 1990 a new rate of
SDR 1 = 171.18 Rwanda francs was established. This remained in effect
until June 1992, when the rate was adjusted to SDR 1 = 201.39 Rwanda
francs. The latter parity was maintained until February 1994, since when
the rate has been frequently adjusted. In March 1995 the Government
introduced a market-determined exchange rate system.

BUDGET

('000 million Rwanda francs)

Revenue*	1999	2000	2001†
Tax revenue	60.4	65.3	79.5
Taxes on income and profits	15.2	17.9	23.9
Company profits tax	7.4	10.0	14.4
Individual income tax	6.1	7.5	9.0
Domestic taxes on goods and			
services	33.6	35.2	41.0
Excise taxes	17.9	18.8	14.2
Turnover tax	12.9	13.8	24.2
Road fund	2.7	2.5	2.6
Taxes on international trade	11.0	11.6	14.0
Import taxes	8.4	9.3	11.1
Non-tax revenue	3.2	3.3	6.7
Total	63.6	68.7	86.2

Expenditure‡	1999	2000	2001†
Current expenditure	86.0	89.2	107.4
General public services	31.5	35.7	53.7
Defence	27.0	25.8	28.6
Social services	21.9	30.5	36.2
Education	17.2	24.0	29.8
Health	3.3	3.8	5.1
Economic services	2.6	2.1	4.9
Energy and public works	0.7	0.4	2.3
Interest on public debt	4.0	1.8	2.8
Adjustment	−1.1	−6.7	−18.8
Capital expenditure	40.8	42.0	50.0
Sub-total	126.8	131.2	157.5
Adjustment for payment arrears§	2.0	−1.2	31.7
Total	128.8	130.0	189.2

* Excluding grants received ('000 million Rwandan francs): 38.5 in 1999;
  63.7 in 2000; 63.3†in 2001.
† Estimates.
‡ Excluding lending minus repayments ('000 million Rwanda francs): −0.4
  in 1999; 0.5 in 2000; 0.6 in 2001†.
§ Minus sign indicates increase in arrears.

Source: IMF, *Rwanda: Statistical Annex* (August 2002).

INTERNATIONAL BANK RESERVES

(US $ million at 31 December)

	2000	2001	2002
IMF special drawing rights	1.14	12.34	10.17
Foreign exchange	189.50	199.77	233.55
Total	190.64	212.11	243.73

Source: IMF, *International Financial Statistics*.

MONEY SUPPLY

(million Rwanda francs at 31 December)

	1999	2000	2001
Currency outside banks	21,501	24,609	24,380
Demand deposits at deposit money			
banks	37,009	37,575	38,410
Total money (incl. others)	59,172	63,110	63,606

Source: IMF, *International Financial Statistics*.

COST OF LIVING

(Consumer Price Index for Kigali; base: 1995 = 100)

	2000	2001	2002
All items	129.6	133.9	136.6

Source: IMF, *International Financial Statistics*.

NATIONAL ACCOUNTS

(million Rwanda francs at current prices)

Expenditure on the Gross Domestic Product

	1998	1999	2000
Government final consumption			
expenditure	54,453	61,237	60,945
Private final consumption			
expenditure	577,656	572,280	601,237
Increase in stocks			
Gross fixed capital formation	91,999	109,372	120,607
Total domestic expenditure	724,108	742,888	782,788
Exports of goods and services	34,685	37,769	49,858
Less Imports of goods and			
services	131,486	147,892	150,123
GDP in purchasers' values	627,307	632,765	682,523
GDP at constant 1995 prices	478,220	507,163	537,405

Source: Banque Nationale du Rwanda, Kigali.

Gross Domestic Product by Economic Activity

	1998	1999	2000
Agriculture, hunting, forestry and fishing	282,893	256,915	277,462
Mining and quarrying	1,311	785	1,733
Manufacturing	68,762	67,814	68,660
Electricity, gas and water	4,548	4,231	3,745
Construction	41,522	50,449	58,706
Trade, restaurants and hotels	63,330	72,167	78,436
Transport, storage and communications	28,486	36,311	40,155
Finance, insurance and real estate	17,256	20,657	23,395
Public administration	41,656	47,178	52,784
Other community, social and personal services	63,937	66,872	68,348
Private non-profit services	7,601	7,512	7,346
Sub-total	621,303	630,891	680,770
Taxes on imports	14,953	11,270	11,619
Less Imputed bank service charges	8,949	9,396	9,866
GDP in purchasers' values	627,307	632,765	682,523

Source: Banque Nationale du Rwanda, Kigali.

BALANCE OF PAYMENTS
(US $ million)

	1999	2000	2001
Exports of goods f.o.b.	62.3	69.1	93.3
Imports of goods f.o.b.	−249.7	−225.3	−245.1
Trade balance	−187.5	−156.2	−151.8
Exports of services	51.3	40.6	50.2
Imports of services	−195.5	−202.1	−189.1
Balance on goods and services	−331.7	−317.7	−290.7
Other income received	7.9	13.9	14.1
Other income paid	−18.7	−28.7	−34.0
Balance on goods, services and income	−342.5	−332.4	−310.7
Current transfers received	212.3	235.1	210.4
Current transfers paid	−12.8	−17.2	−17.9
Current balance	−143.0	−114.5	−118.2
Direct investment from abroad	1.7	8.4	4.6
Portfolio investment assets	0.8	0.1	—
Other investment assets	−10.4	23.4	−0.5
Other investment liabilities	−25.7	−21.0	−48.2
Net errors and omissions	33.0	−91.1	41.7
Overall balance	−72.6	−132.1	−120.6

Source: IMF, *International Financial Statistics*.

External Trade

PRINCIPAL COMMODITIES
(million Rwanda francs)

Imports c.i.f.	1999	2000	2001*
Consumer goods	45,353	63,080	75,543
Capital goods	15,009	15,179	13,531
Intermediate goods	13,039	19,909	19,267
Fuels and lubricants	11,107	28,488	17,257
Total	84,508	126,656	125,598

Exports f.o.b.†	1998	1999	2000
Coffee	8,101	8,875	8,783
Tea	7,154	5,881	9,470
Columbo-tantalite	774	1,552	4,427
Hides and skins	630	181	168
Total (incl. others)	19,480	18,097	24,048

* Provisional.

† Excluding re-exports (million Rwanda francs): 672 in 1998; 2,693 in 1999; 3,878 in 2000. Also excluded are travellers' personal effects (million Rwanda francs): 367 in 1998; 1,028 in 2000.

Source: Banque Nationale du Rwanda, Kigali.

PRINCIPAL TRADING PARTNERS
(US $ million)

Imports	1997	1998	1999
Belgium-Luxembourg	44.6	88.3	30.9*
France	13.8	15.0	5.5
Germany	19.9	12.9	12.2
Italy	5.2	9.5	4.8
Japan	49.5	30.6	31.5
Kenya	47.5	36.1	30.0
Saudi Arabia	11.7	13.3	19.2
Southern African Customs Union	4.6	8.5	7.3
Tanzania	7.7	7.0	4.2
UAE	12.1	10.2	11.1
United Kingdom	10.1	6.4	2.8
USA	9.4	7.1	7.9
Total (incl. others)	339.9	331.2	240.2

Exports	1997	1998	1999
Bahrain	0.7	0.0	0.0
Belgium-Luxembourg	2.7	2.0	3.5*
Burundi	1.0	0.9	0.8
Germany	3.1	0.3	4.3
Italy	0.6	0.2	0.1
Japan	0.1	0.1	0.0
Kenya	37.6	25.6	34.0
Netherlands	1.5	0.4	0.1
Southern African Customs Union	0.1	0.5	0.1
Switzerland	0.3	0.9	0.3
Tanzania	0.0	1.3	7.6
Uganda	0.6	0.7	0.2
United Kingdom	1.8	0.6	0.0
USA	0.0	0.1	0.0
Total (incl. others)	55.8	35.2	54.5

* Belgium only.

Source: UN, *International Trade Statistics Yearbook*.

Transport

ROAD TRAFFIC
(estimates, motor vehicles in use at 31 December)

	1995	1996
Passenger cars	12,000	13,000
Lorries and vans	16,000	17,100

Source: IRF, *World Road Statistics*.

CIVIL AVIATION
(traffic on scheduled services)

	1992	1993	1994
Passengers carried ('000)	9	9	9
Passenger-km (million)	2	2	2

Source: UN, *Statistical Yearbook*.

Tourism

	1996	1997	1998
Tourist arrivals ('000)	1	1	2
Tourism receipts (US $ million)	4	17	19

1999 (US $ million): Tourism receipts 17.

Source: World Tourism Organization, mainly *Yearbook of Tourism Statistics*.

Communications Media

	1999	2000	2001
Telephones ('000 main lines in use)	12.7	17.6	21.5
Mobile cellular telephones ('000 subscribers).	11	39	65
Internet users ('000)	5	5	20

Source: International Telecommunication Union.

Radio receivers ('000 in use): 601 in 1997.

Facsimile machines (number in use): 900 in 1998.

Daily newspapers: 1 in 1996.

Sources: UN, *Statistical Yearbook*; UNESCO, *Statistical Yearbook*.

Education

(1998, unless otherwise indicated)

	Institutions	Teachers	Pupils/Students		
			Males	Females	Total
Primary . . .	1,710*	23,730	644,835	643,834	1,288,669
Secondary:					
general . . .	n.a.	} 3,413	39,088	38,337	77,425
technical and vocational. .	n.a.		6,859	6,935	13,794
Tertiary . . .	n.a.	412	n.a.	n.a.	5,678

* Figure refers to 1991/92.

Source: mainly UNESCO Institute for Statistics.

Adult literacy rate (UNESCO estimates): 66.8% (males 73.7%; females 60.2%) in 2000 (Source: UN Development Programme, *Human Development Report*).

Directory

The Constitution

On 10 June 1991 a series of amendments to the Constitution in force since 19 December 1978 received presidential assent. The document, as amended, provided, *inter alia*, for a multi-party political system, the separation of the functions of the executive, judiciary and legislature, the limitation of presidential tenure to a maximum of two consecutive five-year terms of office, the establishment of the office of Prime Minister, freedom of the press, and the right of workers to withdraw their labour. On 5 May 1995 the Transitional National Assembly introduced a new Constitution based on selected articles of the 1991 Constitution, the August 1993 Arusha peace accord, the FPR victory declaration of July 1994 and the multi-party protocol of understanding concluded in November 1994.

On 23 April 2003 the Transitional National Assembly adopted a draft Constitution, which was expected to enter into effect in July of that year, subject to approval at a national referendum (scheduled for 26 May). The new Constitution, which was largely based on the Arusha peace accords and the 1991 Constitution, provided for the establishment of a bicameral legislature (comprising an 80-member National Assembly and a 24-member Senate), which for the first time since 1994 would be elected by universal suffrage, for a term of five years. The President was to be eligible for election for two terms of seven years. (The transitional period was to end with presidential and legislative elections, which were scheduled to take place in July 2003.)

The Government

HEAD OF STATE

President: Maj.-Gen. PAUL KAGAME (took office 22 April 2000).

COUNCIL OF MINISTERS
(April 2003)

A coalition Government of National Unity, comprising the Mouvement démocratique républicain, the Front patriotique rwandais, the Parti social-démocrate, the Parti libéral, the Parti démocrate chrétien and the Parti démocratique islamique.

Prime Minister: BERNARD MAKUZA.

Minister of Defence: Maj.-Gen. MARCEL GATSINZI.

Minister of Local Government, Information and Social Affairs: CHRISTOPHE BAZIVAMO.

Minister of Internal Affairs: JEAN DE DIEU NTIRUHUNGWA.

Minister of Foreign Affairs and Regional Co-operation: Dr CHARLES MURIGANDE.

Minister of Finance and Economic Planning: Dr DONALD KABERUKA.

Minister of Agriculture, Livestock and Forestry: Dr EPHREM KABAIJA.

Minister of Education, Science, Technology and Research: Prof. ROMAIN MURENZI.

Minister of Infrastructure: J. DAMASCENE NTAWUKURIRYAYO.

Minister of Commerce, Industry, Investment Promotion, Tourism and Co-operation: Dr ALEXANDRE LYAMBABAJE.

Minister of Lands, Human Resettlement and Environment: Prof. LAURENT NKUSI.

Minister of Justice: JEAN DE DIEU MUCYO.

Minister of Public Service, Skills Development, Vocational Training and Labour: ANDRÉ HABIB BUMAYA.

Minister of Health: Dr ABEL DUSHIMIYIMANA.

Minister of Gender and the Promotion of Women: MARIE MUKANTABANA.

Minister of Youth, Sports and Culture: ROBERT BAYIGAMA.

Minister in the Office of the President: SOLINA NYIRAHABIMANA.

Minister of State for Primary and Secondary Education: EUGÈNE MUNYAKAYANZA.

Minister of State for Economic Planning: CÉLESTIN KABANDA.

Minister of State for Good Governance: PROTAIS MUSONI.

Minister of State for Energy and Communications: SAM NKUSI.

Minister of State for Social Affairs: ODETTE NYIRAMIRIMO.

Minister of State for Water and Natural Resources: Prof. BIKORO MUNYANGANIZI.

Minister of State for Forestry: DROCELLA MUGOREWERA.

Minister of State for Investment Promotion, Tourism and Co-operatives: Dr PATRICK HABAMENSHI.

Minister of State for HIV/AIDS and other Infectious Diseases: Dr INNOCENT NYARUHIRIRA.

Minister of State for Skills Development, Vocational Training and Labour: ANGELINA MUGANZA.

MINISTRIES

All ministries are based in Kigali.

Office of the President: BP 15, Kigali; tel. 84085; fax 83714; e-mail presirep@rwanda1.com.

Ministry of Agriculture, Livestock and Forestry: BP 621, Kigali; tel. 85008; fax 85057.

Ministry of Commerce, Industry, Investment Promotion, Tourism and Co-operation: BP 2378, Kigali; tel. 574725; tel. 574734; fax 575465.

Ministry of Education, Science, Technology and Research: BP 622, Kigali; tel. 83051; fax 82162; e-mail mineducs@aru.org.

Ministry of Finance and Economic Planning: BP 158, Kigali; tel. 575756; fax 575719.

Ministry of Foreign Affairs and Regional Co-operation: blvd de la Révolution, BP 179, Kigali; tel. 574522; fax 572904.

Ministry of Health: BP 84, Kigali; tel. 573481; e-mail sgsante@rwandatel.com.

Ministry of Internal Affairs: BP 446, Kigali; tel. 86708.

Ministry of Justice: BP 160, Kigali; tel. 86561; fax 87051.

Ministry of Local Government, Information and Social Affairs: BP 790, Kigali; tel. 85406; fax 82228.

Ministry of Public Service, Skills Development, Vocational Training and Labour: BP 403, Kigali; tel. 85714; fax 83374.

Ministry of Youth, Sports and Culture: BP 1044, Kigali; tel. 83527; fax 83518.

President and Legislature

PRESIDENT

On 17 April 2000 an electoral college, comprising members of the legislature and the Government, appointed the Chairman of the Front patriotique rwandais, Maj.-Gen. Paul Kagame, as President by 81 votes; his only opponent, Charles Murigande, received five votes.

LEGISLATURE

The multi-party protocol of understanding in November 1994 agreed to a number of amendments to the August 1993 Arusha accord relating to the establishment of a transitional legislature. The new provisions excluded from all legislative processes members of those parties implicated in alleged acts of genocide during 1994.

A 70-member Transitional National Assembly was installed on 12 December 1994. In 2000 the membership of the Transitional National Assembly was increased to 74. A new Constitution, which was expected to enter into effect in July 2003, provided for the election of a bicameral legislature in that month (see The Constitution).

Speaker of the Transitional National Assembly: Dr VINCENT BIRUTA.

Political Organizations

Coalition pour la défense de la République (CDR): Kigali; f. 1992; operates an unofficial Hutu militia known as Impuzamugambi; prohibited by FPR in 1994 from participation in transitional Govt and legislature; banned in 2001.

Front patriotique rwandais (FPR): f. 1990; also known as Inkotanyi; comprises mainly Tutsi exiles, but claims multi-ethnic support; commenced armed invasion of Rwanda from Uganda in Oct. 1990; took control of Rwanda in July 1994; Chair. Maj.-Gen. PAUL KAGAME; Vice-Chair. CHRISTOPHE BAZIVAMO; Sec.-Gen. CHARLES MURIGANDE.

Mouvement démocratique républicain (MDR): Kigali; banned 1973–91; fmrly also known as Parti de l'émancipation du peuple Hutu (Parmehutu), dominant party 1962–73; Chair. CÉLESTIN KABANDA (acting); Exec. Sec. Dr CHRISTIAN MARARA.

Mouvement républicain national pour la démocratie et le développement (MRNDD): BP 1055, Kigali; f. 1975 as the Mouvement révolutionnaire national pour le développement (MRND); sole legal party until 1991; adopted present name in April 1991; draws support from hard-line Hutu elements; Chair. MATHIEU NGIRUMPATSE; operates unofficial militia known as Interahamwe; Leader ROBERT KADJUGA; prohibited by FPR in 1994 from participation in transitional Govt and legislature; banned in 2001.

Parti démocrate chrétien (PDC): BP 2348, Kigali; tel. 76542; fax 72237; f. 1990; Leader JEAN NEPOMUCÈNE NAYINZIRA.

Parti démocratique islamique (PDI): Kigali; f. 1991.

Parti démocratique rwandais (Pader): Kigali; f. 1992; Sec. JEAN NTAGUNGIRA.

Parti libéral (PL): BP 1304, Kigali; tel. 77916; fax 77838; f. 1991; split into two factions in late 1993–early 1994: pro-MRNDD faction (led by JUSTIN MUGENZI and AGNÈS NTAMBYARIRO; anti-MRNDD faction (led by PROSPER HIGIRO JOSEPH MUSENGIMANA and ESDRA KAYIRANGA).

Parti progressiste de la jeunesse rwandaise (PPJR): Kigali; f. 1991; Leader ANDRÉ HAKIZIMANA.

Parti républicain rwandais (Parerwa): Kigali; f. 1992; Leader AUGUSTIN MUTAMBA.

Parti social-démocrate (PSD): Kigali; f. 1991 by a breakaway faction of the MRND.

Parti socialiste rwandais (PSR): BP 827, Kigali; tel. 76658; fax 83975; f. 1991; workers' rights.

Le Peuple en Armes pour Libérer le Rwanda (Palir): Kigali; opposition grouping; in existence since 1996; armed wing L'Armée de Libération du Rwanda (Alir).

Rassemblement travailliste pour la démocratie (RTD): BP 1894, Kigali; tel. 75622; fax 76574; f. 1991; Leader EMMANUEL NIZEYIMANA.

Union démocratique du peuple rwandais (UDPR): Kigali; f. 1992; Pres. VINCENT GWABUKWISI; Vice-Pres. SYLVESTRE HUBI.

Other political organizations have been formed by exiled Rwandans and operate principally from abroad; these include:

Forces de résistance pour la démocratie (FRD): Brussels, Belgium; f. 1996 by moderate Hutu exiles; seeks return of Rwanda to UN Trust Territory status; Leader FAUSTIN TWAGIRAMUNGU.

Rassemblement pour le retour des réfugiés et la démocratie au Rwanda (RDR): Mandenmakerstraat 14, 3841 Harderwijk, Netherlands; fax (32) 10455111; e-mail info@rdrwanda.org; f. 1995 by fmr supporters of Pres. Habyarimana; prin. org. representing Hutu refugees; Chair. FRANÇOIS NSABAHIMANA.

Union du peuple rwandais (UPR): Brussels, Belgium; f. 1990; Hutu-led; Pres. SILAS MAJYAMBERE; Sec.-Gen. EMMANUEL TWAGILIMANA.

Diplomatic Representation

EMBASSIES IN RWANDA

Belgium: rue Nyarugenge, BP 81, Kigali; tel. 75554; fax 73995; Ambassador MARC GEDOPT.

Burundi: rue de Ntaruka, BP 714, Kigali; tel. 75010; Chargé d'affaires a.i. CHARLES NSABIMANA.

Canada: rue Akagera, BP 1177, Kigali; tel. 73210; fax 72719; Ambassador BERNARD DUSSAULT.

Congo, Democratic Republic: 504 rue Longue, BP 169, Kigali; tel. 75289; Ambassador (vacant).

Egypt: BP 1069, Kigali; tel. 82686; fax 82686; Ambassador SAMEH SAMY DARWISH.

Germany: 8 rue de Bugarama, BP 355, Kigali; tel. 75222; fax 77267; Ambassador JOHANNA KÖNIG.

Holy See: 49 ave Paul VI, BP 261, Kigali (Apostolic Nunciature); tel. 75293; fax 75181; e-mail nuntrw@rwandatel1.rwanda1.com; Apostolic Nuncio Most Rev. SALVATORE PENNACCHIO (Titular Archbishop of Montemarano).

Kenya: BP 1215, Kigali; tel. 82774; Ambassador PETER KIHARA MATHANJUKI.

Korea, Democratic People's Republic: Kigali; Ambassador KIM PONG GI.

Libya: BP 1152, Kigali; tel. 76470; Secretary of the People's Bureau MOUSTAPHA MASAND EL-GHAILUSHI.

Russia: 19 ave de l'Armée, BP 40, Kigali; tel. 75286; fax 74818; e-mail ambruss@rwandatel1.rwanda1.com; Ambassador STANISLAV AKHMEDOV.

South Africa: 1370 blvd de l'Umuganda, POB 6563, Kacyiru-Sud, Kigali; tel. 583185; fax 511760; e-mail saemkgl@rwanda1.com; internet www.saembassy-kigali.org.rw; Ambassador Dr A. M. MBERE.

United Kingdom: Parcelle 1131, Blvd de l'Umuganda, Kacyiru, BP 576, Kigali; tel. 84098; fax 82044; e-mail britemb@rwanda1.com; Ambassador SUE HOGWOOD.

USA: blvd de la Révolution, BP 28, Kigali; tel. 505601; fax 72128; e-mail amembkigali@hotmail.com; Ambassador MARGARET K. MCMILLION.

Judicial System

The judicial system comprises a Supreme Court, 12 Tribunals of First Instance and 143 Provincial Tribunals. Each type of court has a Public Prosecutor's Office. As well as these ordinary courts, specialized courts, such as military courts, can be created by law. The Supreme Court directs and co-ordinates the activities of all the Courts and Tribunals. It is divided into five sections, each of which is headed by a Vice-President, who, with the President of the Court, constitute its directorate.

In early 2000 a system of *gacaca* (grassroots) justice was established as a sixth section of the Supreme Court. Trials for categories of lesser genocide crimes were to be conducted by councils in the communities in which they were committed, with the aim of alleviating pressure on the existing judicial system. On 4 October 2001 some 250,000 judges for the *gacaca* courts were elected in a national ballot.

SUPREME COURT

Chair. of the Supreme Court: SIMEON RWAGASORE.

Prosecutor-General: GERALD GAHIMA.

Religion

AFRICAN RELIGIONS

About one-half of the population hold traditional beliefs.

CHRISTIANITY

Union des Eglises Rwandaises: BP 79, Kigali; tel. 85825; fax 83554; f. 1963; fmrly Conseil Protestant du Rwanda.

The Roman Catholic Church

Rwanda comprises one archdiocese and eight dioceses. At 31 December 2000 the estimated number of adherents represented about 46.9% of the total population.

Bishops' Conference

Conférence Episcopale du Rwanda, BP 357, Kigali; tel. 75439; fax 78080; e-mail cerwanda@rwanda1.com.

f. 1980; Pres. Most Rev. THADDÉE NTIHINYURWA (Archbishop of Kigali).

Archbishop of Kigali: Most Rev. THADDÉE NTIHINYURWA, Archevêché, BP 715, Kigali; tel. 75769; fax 72274.

The Anglican Communion

The Church of the Province of Rwanda, established in 1992, has nine dioceses.

Archbishop of the Province and Bishop of Kigali: Most Rev. EMMANUEL MUSABA KOLINI, BP 61, Kigali; tel. and fax 73213; e-mail sonja914@compuserve.com.

Provincial Secretary: Rt Rev. JOSIAS SENDEGEYA (Bishop of Kigali), BP 2487, Kigali; tel. and fax 514160; e-mail peer@rwandatel1 .rwanda1.

Other Protestant Churches

Eglise Baptiste: Nyantanga, BP 59, Butare; Pres. Rev. DAVID BAZIGA; Gen. Sec. ELEAZAR ZIHERAMBERE.

There are about 250,000 other Protestants, including a substantial minority of Seventh-day Adventists.

BAHÁ'Í FAITH

National Spiritual Assembly: BP 652, Kigali; tel. 75982.

ISLAM

There is a small Islamic community.

The Press

Bulletin Agricole du Rwanda: OCIR—Café, BP 104, Kigali-Gikondo; f. 1968; quarterly; French; Pres. of Editorial Bd Dr AUGUSTIN NZINDUKIYIMANA; circ. 800.

L'Ere de Liberté: BP 1755, Kigali; fortnightly.

Etudes Rwandaises: Université Nationale du Rwanda, Rectorat, BP 56, Butare; tel. 30302; f. 1977; quarterly; pure and applied science, literature, human sciences; French; Pres. of Editorial Bd CHARLES NTAKIRUTINKA; circ. 1,000.

Hobe: BP 761, Kigali; f. 1955; monthly; children's interest; circ. 95,000.

Inkingi: BP 969, Kigali; tel. 77626; fax 77543; monthly.

Inkoramutima: Union des Eglises Rwandaises, BP 79, Kigali; tel. 85825; fax 83554; quarterly; religious; circ. 5,000.

Kinyamateka: 5 blvd de l'OUA, BP 761, Kigali; tel. 76164; f. 1933; fortnightly; economics; circ. 11,000.

La Lettre du Cladho: BP 3060, Kigali; tel. 74292; monthly.

The New: BP 635, Kigali; tel. 73409; fax 74166; monthly.

Nouvelles du Rwanda: Université Nationale du Rwanda, BP 117, Butare; every 2 months.

Nyabarongo—Le Canard Déchaîné: BP 1585, Kigali; tel. 76674; monthly.

Le Partisan: BP 1805, Kigali; tel. 73923; fortnightly.

La Patrie—Urwatubyaye: BP 3125, Kigali; tel. 72552; monthly.

La Relève: Office Rwandais d'Information, BP 83, Kigali; tel. 75665; f. 1976; monthly; politics, economics, culture; French; Dir CHRISTOPHE MFIZI; circ. 1,700.

Revue Dialogue: BP 572, Kigali; tel. 74178; f. 1967; bi-monthly; Christian issues; Belgian-owned; circ. 2,500.

Revue Médicale Rwandaise: Ministry of Health, BP 84, Kigali; tel. 76681; f. 1968; quarterly; French.

Revue Pédagogique: Ministry of Education, Technology and Scientific Research, BP 622, Kigali; tel. 85697; quarterly; French.

Rwanda Libération: BP 398, Kigali; tel. 77710; monthly; Dir and Editor-in-Chief ANTOINE KAPITENI.

Rwanda Renaître: BP 426, Butare; fortnightly.

Rwanda Rushya: BP 83, Kigali; tel. 72276; fortnightly.

Le Tribun du Peuple: BP 1960, Kigali; tel. 82035; bi-monthly; Owner JEAN-PIERRE MUGABE.

Ukuri Gacaca: BP 3170, Kigali; tel. 73327; monthly.

Umucunguzi: Gisenyi; f. 1998; organ of Palir; Kinyarwanda and French; Chief Editor EMILE NKUMBUYE.

Umuhinzi-Mworozi: OCIR—Thé, BP 1334, Kigali; tel. 514797; fax 514796; f. 1975; monthly; circ. 1,500.

Umusemburo—Le Levain: BP 117, Butare; monthly.

Urunana: Grand Séminaire de Nyakibanda, BP 85, Butare; tel. 530793; e-mail wellamahoro@yahoo.fr; f. 1967; 3 a year; religious; Pres. PASCAL NIZEYIMANA; Editor-in-Chief CHARLES HAKORIMANA.

NEWS AGENCIES

Agence Rwandaise de Presse (ARP): 27 ave du Commerce, BP 83, Kigali; tel. 75735; f. 1975.

Office Rwandais d'Information (Orinfor): BP 83, Kigali; tel. 75724; Dir JOSEPH BIDERI.

Foreign Bureau

Agence France-Presse (AFP): BP 83, Kigali; tel. 72997; Correspondent MARIE-GORETTI UWIBAMBE.

Publishers

Editions Rwandaises: Caritas Rwanda, BP 124, Kigali; tel. 5786; Man. Dir Abbé CYRIAQUE MUNYANSANGA; Editorial Dir ALBERT NAMBAJE.

Implico: BP 721, Kigali; tel. 73771.

Imprimerie de Kabgayi: BP 66, Gitarama; tel. 62252; fax 62254; f. 1932; Dir THOMAS HABIMANA.

Imprimerie de Kigali, SARL: 1 Blvd de l'Umuganda, BP 956, Kigali; tel. 82032; fax 84047; e-mail impkig@rwandatel1.rwanda1 .com; f. 1980; Dir DENIS MASONGA.

Imprimerie URWEGO: BP 762, Kigali; tel. 86027; Dir JEAN NSENGIYUNVA.

Pallotti-Presse: BP 863, Kigali; tel. 74084.

Government Publishing Houses

Imprimerie Nationale du Rwanda: BP 351, Kigali; tel. 76214; fax 75820; f. 1967; Dir JUVÉNAL NDISANZE.

Régie de l'Imprimerie Scolaire: BP 1347, Kigali; tel. 85818; fax 85695; e-mail imprisco@rwandatel1.rwanda1.com; f. 1985; Dir JEAN DE DIEU GAKWANDI.

Broadcasting and Communications

TELECOMMUNICATIONS

Rwandatel: Kigali; provides national telecommunications service.

MTN Rwandacell: Telecom House, Blvd de l'Umuganda, Kigali; f. 1998; provides mobile cellular telephone services; CEO FRANÇOIS DU PLESSIS.

BROADCASTING

Radio

Radio Rwanda: BP 83, Kigali; tel. 75665; fax 76185; f. 1961; state-controlled; daily broadcasts in Kinyarwanda, Swahili, French and English; Dir of Programmes DAVID KABUYE.

Deutsche Welle Relay Station Africa: Kigali; daily broadcasts in German, English, French, Hausa, Swahili, Portuguese and Amharic.

Television

Télévision rwandaise (TVR): Kigali; fax 75024; transmissions reach more than 60% of national territory.

Finance

(cap. = capital; res = reserves; dep. = deposits; m. = million; brs = branches; amounts in Rwanda francs)

BANKING

Central Bank

Banque Nationale du Rwanda: BP 531, Kigali; tel. 75249; fax 72551; e-mail nbank@rwandatel1.rwanda1.com; f. 1964; bank of issue; cap. 2,000m., res 4,322.9m., dep. 36,039.5m. (Dec. 2000); Gov. FRANÇOIS MUTEMBEREZI; Vice-Gov. FRANÇOIS KANIMBA.

Commercial Banks

Banque de Commerce, de Développement et d'Industrie (BCDI): BP 3268, Kigali; tel. 74143; fax 73790; e-mail bcdinfo@rwandatel1.rwanda1.com; internet www.bcdinfo.rwandatel1; cap. 1.1m., res 217.6m., dep. 22.3m. (Dec. 2000); Pres. and Dir-Gen. ALFRED KALISA.

Banque Commerciale du Rwanda, SA: BP 354, Kigali; tel. 75591; fax 73395; e-mail bcr@rwandatel1.rwanda1.com; internet www.bc-rwanda.com; f. 1963; 49.4% state-owned; cap. 2,000m., res 881.2m., dep. 31,151.6m. (Dec. 2000); Pres. THACIEN MUNYANEZA; Gen. Man. JOHN MADDER; 5 brs.

Banque à la Confiance d'Or (BANCOR): ave du Commerce, BP 2509, Kigali; tel. and fax 75761; cap. 300m., total assets 1,538.4m. (Dec. 1999); Pres. ABID ALAM; Gen. Man. MANZUR ALAM.

Banque Continentale Africaine (Rwanda), SA (BACAR): 20 blvd de la Révolution, BP 331, Kigali; tel. 74456; fax 73486; e-mail bacar@rwandatel1.rwanda1.com; f. 1983; cap. 700m., res 463.6m., dep. 7,942.4m. (Dec. 1999); Pres. VALENS KAJEGUHAKWA; Dir-Gen. JÉRÔME BISSAY; 3 brs.

Banque de Kigali, SA: 63 ave du Commerce, BP 175, Kigali; tel. 76931; fax 73461; e-mail bkig10@calva.com; f. 1966; cap. 1,500.0m., res 1,185.7m., dep. 34,822.7m. (Dec. 2000); Pres. PIUS NDAYAMBAJE; Gen. Man. MICHEL DEUCUYPER; 6 brs.

Caisse Hypothécaire du Rwanda (CHR): BP 1034, Kigali; tel. and fax 76796; cap. 237.5m., total assets 1,187.8m. (Dec. 1999); Pres. FRANÇOIS RUTISHASHA; Gen. Man. FRANÇOIS NDUWUMWE.

Compagnie Générale de Banque: blvd de l'Umuganda, BP 5230, Kigali; tel. 86975; fax 86876; e-mail cogebank@rwandatel1.rwanda1.com; cap. 611.2m., total assets 2,029.7m. (June 2000); Pres. JOSEPH MUGENGA; Dir-Gen. NARCISSE KALINIJABO.

Development Banks

Banque Rwandaise de Développement, SA (BRD): BP 1341, Kigali; tel. 75079; fax 73569; e-mail jbrd@rwandatel1.rwanda1.com; f. 1967; 56% state-owned; cap. 1,484m., total assets 7,410.5m. (Dec. 1999); Pres. EDITH GASANA.

Union des Banques Populaires du Rwanda (Banki z'Abaturage mu Rwanda): BP 1348, Kigali; tel. 73559; fax 73579; e-mail ubpr@rwandatel1.rwanda1.com; f. 1975; cap. 370m., dep. 9,133m. (Dec. 1999); Pres. INNOCENT KAYITARE; 145 brs.

INSURANCE

Société Nationale d'Assurances du Rwanda (SONARWA): BP 1035, Kigali; tel. 73350; fax 72052; e-mail sonarwa@rwandatel1.rwanda1.com; f. 1975; cap. 500m; Pres. FRANÇOIS NGARAMBE; Dir-Gen. HOPE MURERA.

Société Rwandaise d'Assurances, SA (SORAS): BP 924, Kigali; tel. 73716; fax 73362; e-mail sorasinfo@rwandatel1.rwanda1.com; f. 1984; cap. 300m; Pres. FÉLICIEN MUTALIKANWA; Dir-Gen. (Admin.) CHARLES MHORANYI.

Trade and Industry

GOVERNMENT AGENCIES

Central Tender Board: Kigali; f. 1998 to promote effective and efficient procurement.

Centre for Investment Promotion: Kigali; f. 1998.

Rwanda Revenue Authority: Kigali; f. 1998 to maximize revenue collection; Commissioner-Gen. EDWARD LARBI SIAW.

DEVELOPMENT ORGANIZATIONS

Coopérative de Promotion de l'Industrie Minière et Artisanale au Rwanda (COOPIMAR): BP 1139, Kigali; tel. 82127; fax 72128; Dir DANY NZARAMBA.

Institut de Recherches Scientifiques et Technologiques (IRST): BP 227, Butare; tel. 30396; fax 30939; Dir-Gen. CHRYSOLOGUE KARANGWA.

Institut des Sciences Agronomiques du Rwanda (ISAR): BP 138, Butare; tel. 30642; fax 30644; for the development of subsistence and export agriculture; Dir MUNYANGANIZI BIKORO; 12 centres.

Office des Cultures Industrielles du Rwanda—Café (OCIR—Café): BP 104, Kigali; tel. 75600; fax 73992; e-mail ocircafe@rwandatel1.rwanda1.com; f. 1978; development of coffee and other new agronomic industries; operates a coffee stabilization fund; Dir ANASTASE NZIRASANAHO.

Office des Cultures Industrielles du Rwanda—Thé (OCIR—Thé): BP 1344, Kigali; tel. 514797; fax 514796; e-mail ocirthé@rwanda1.com; development and marketing of tea; Dir CÉLESTIN KAYITARE.

Office National pour le Développement de la Commercialisation des Produits Vivriers et des Produits Animaux (OPROVIA): BP 953, Kigali; tel. 82946; fax 82945; privatization pending; Dir DISMAS SEZIBERA.

Office du Pyrèthre du Rwanda (OPYRWA): BP 79, Ruhengeri; tel. 46306; fax 46364; f. 1978; cultivation and processing of pyrethrum; post-war activities resumed in Oct. 1994; current production estimated at 30% pre-war capacity; Dir SYLVAIN NZABAGAMBA.

Régie d'Exploitation et de Développement des Mines (REDEMI): BP 2195, Kigali; tel. 73632; fax 73625; e-mail ruzredem@yahoo.fr; f. 1988 as Régie des Mines du Rwanda; privatized in 2000; state org. for mining tin, columbo-tantalite and wolfram; Man. Dir JEAN RUZINDANA MUNANA.

CHAMBER OF COMMERCE

Chambre de Commerce et d'Industrie de Rwanda: rue de l'Umuganda, POB 319, Kigali; tel. 83534; fax 83532; Pres. T. RUJUGIRO.

INDUSTRIAL ASSOCIATIONS

Association des Industriels du Rwanda: BP 39, Kigali; tel. and fax 75430; Pres. YVES LAFAGE; Exec. Sec. MUGUNGA NDOBA.

Federation of the Rwandan Private Sector Associations: POB 319, Kigali; tel. 83538; fax 83532; e-mail frsp@rwanda1.com; f. 1999 to represent interests of private sector; Exec. Sec. EUGÈNE BITWAYIKI.

UTILITIES

Electrogaz: POB 537, Kigali; tel. 72392; fax 73802; state-owned water, electricity and gas supplier; Dir JOSEPH MUJENGA.

TRADE UNIONS

Centrale d'Education et de Coopération des Travailleurs pour le Développement/Alliance Coopérative au Rwanda (CECOTRAD/ACORWA): BP 295, Kigali; f. 1984; Pres. ELIE KATABARWA.

Centrale Syndicale des Travailleurs du Rwanda: BP 1645, Kigali; tel. 85658; fax 84012; e-mail cestrav@rwandatel1.rwanda1.com; Sec.-Gen. FRANÇOIS MURANGIRA.

Transport

RAILWAYS

There are no railways in Rwanda, although plans exist for the eventual construction of a line passing through Uganda, Rwanda and Burundi, to connect with the Kigoma–Dar es Salaam line in Tanzania. Rwanda has access by road to the Tanzanian railways system.

ROADS

In 1999 there were an estimated 12,000 km of roads, of which 996 km were paved. There are road links with Uganda, Tanzania, Burundi and the Democratic Republic of the Congo. Internal conflict during 1994 caused considerable damage to the road system, and to the destruction of several important bridges. In 1997 Rwanda received a US $45m. loan to be used for road improvement.

Office National des Transports en Commun (ONATRACOM): BP 609, Kigali; tel. 75564; Dir (vacant).

INLAND WATERWAYS

There are services on Lake Kivu between Cyangugu, Gisenyi and Kibuye, including two vessels operated by ONATRACOM.

CIVIL AVIATION

The Kanombe international airport at Kigali can process up to 500,000 passengers annually. There is a second international airport at Kamembe, near the border with the Democratic Republic of the Congo. There are airfields at Butare, Gabiro, Ruhengeri and Gisenyi, servicing internal flights.

Alliance Express Rwanda (ALEX): BP 1440, Kigali; tel. 82409; fax 82417; e-mail aev@aev.com.rw; fax 72562; f. 1998 to succeed fmr Air Rwanda as national carrier; 51% owned by Alliance Air (jtly owned by Govts of Uganda and South Africa and by South African

Airways), 49% state-owned; domestic and regional passenger and cargo services; Chair. GERALD ZIRIMWABAGABO.

Rwanda Airlines: BP 3246, Kigali; tel. 77564; fax 77669; f. 1998; privately-owned; operates one passenger aircraft; Chair. CHARLES NGARAMBE.

Tourism

Attractions for tourists include the flora and fauna of the national parks, Lake Kivu and fine mountain scenery. The genocide of 1994 had a severely negative impact on Rwanda's long-term prospects for tourism. In 1998 there were an estimated 2,000 foreign visitors to Rwanda. Total receipts from tourism were estimated at US $17m. in 1999.

Office rwandais du tourisme et des parcs nationaux (ORTPN): BP 905, Kigali; tel. 76515; fax 76512; f. 1973; govt agency.

SAINT CHRISTOPHER* AND NEVIS

Introductory Survey

Location, Climate, Language, Religion, Flag, Capital

The Federation of Saint Christopher and Nevis is situated at the northern end of the Leeward Islands chain of the West Indies, with Saba and St Eustatius (both in the Netherlands Antilles) to the north-west, Barbuda to the north-east and Antigua to the south-east. Nevis lies about 3 km (2 miles) to the south-east of Saint Christopher, separated by a narrow strait. The tropical heat, varying between 17°C (62°F) and 33°C (92°F), is tempered by constant sea winds, and annual rainfall averages 1,400 mm (55 ins) on Saint Christopher and 1,220 mm (48 ins) on Nevis. English is the official language. The majority of the population are Christians of the Anglican Communion, and other Christian denominations are represented. The national flag (proportions 2 by 3) comprises two triangles, one of green (with its base at the hoist and its apex in the upper fly) and the other of red (with its base in the fly and its apex in the lower hoist), separated by a broad, yellow-edged black diagonal stripe (from the lower hoist to the upper fly) bearing two five-pointed white stars. The capital is Basseterre, on Saint Christopher.

Recent History

Saint Christopher, settled in 1623, was Britain's first colony in the West Indies. The French settled part of the island a year later, and conflict over possession continued until 1783, when Saint Christopher was eventually ceded to Britain under the Treaty of Versailles. Nevis was settled by the British in 1628, and remained one of the most prosperous of the Antilles until the middle of the 19th century. The island of Anguilla was first joined to the territory in 1816. The St Kitts-Nevis-Anguilla Labour Party, formed in 1932, campaigned for independence for the islands. In 1958 Saint Christopher-Nevis-Anguilla became a member of the West Indies Federation, remaining so until the Federation's dissolution in 1962. A new Constitution, granted to each of the British territories in the Leeward Islands in 1960, provided for government through an Administrator and an enlarged Legislative Council. After an abortive attempt to form a smaller East Caribbean Federation, Saint Christopher-Nevis-Anguilla attained Associated Statehood in February 1967, as part of an arrangement that gave five of the colonies full internal autonomy, while the United Kingdom retained responsibility for defence and foreign relations. The House of Assembly replaced the Legislative Council, the Administrator became Governor, and the Chief Minister, Robert Bradshaw, leader of the Labour Party, became the state's first Premier. Three months later Anguilla rebelled against government from Saint Christopher, and in 1971 reverted to being a *de facto* British dependency. Anguilla was formally separated from the other islands in 1980.

General elections in 1971 returned Robert Bradshaw to the premiership. In the 1975 elections the Labour Party again won the largest number of seats, while the Nevis Reformation Party (NRP) again took both the Nevis seats. Bradshaw died in May 1978 and was succeeded as Premier by Paul Southwell, hitherto Deputy Premier (and a former Chief Minister). Southwell died in May 1979, and was replaced by the party's leader, Lee L. Moore (hitherto the Attorney-General).

In February 1980 the Labour Party was removed from government for the first time in nearly 30 years: the Labour Party secured four seats in the legislative elections, while the People's Action Movement (PAM) took three and the NRP retained the two Nevis seats. Although the Labour Party had won 58% of the popular vote, a PAM-NRP coalition Government was formed under PAM leader, Dr Kennedy A. Simmonds. The change of government led to the suspension of a timetable for independence, which had been scheduled for June 1980. In 1982 proposals for a greater degree of autonomy for Nevis and for independence for the whole state were approved by the House of Assembly, although the Labour Party opposed the plans, arguing that the coalition Government did not have a mandate for its independence policy. Disagreements concerning the content of the proposed independence Constitution led to civil

disturbances in 1982 and 1983. Nevertheless, Saint Christopher and Nevis became an independent state, under a federal Constitution, on 19 September 1983. The Labour Party denounced the special provisions for Nevis in the Constitution (see below) as giving the island a powerful role in government that was disproportionate to its size and population. Elections to the Nevis Island Assembly were held in August, at which the NRP, led by Simeon Daniel, won all five elective seats. Upon independence Saint Christopher and Nevis became a full member of the Commonwealth (see p. 164).

Early elections to an enlarged National Assembly (now with 11 elective seats) took place in June 1984, at which the ruling PAM-NRP coalition was returned to power. The Labour Party took only two seats on Saint Christopher, and did not contest the three Nevis seats, which were won by the NRP. The PAM, which won a clear majority of the popular vote on Saint Christopher, secured six seats, while the NRP no longer held the balance of power in the National Assembly.

At an election to the Nevis Island Assembly in December 1987, the NRP retained four seats and the Concerned Citizens' Movement (CCM) secured one. At the general election of March 1989, however, the CCM took one of the three Nevis seats from the NRP. The PAM retained six seats, and the Labour Party its two. Moore resigned as leader of the Labour Party and was succeeded by Denzil Douglas. The electoral success of the coalition Government under the leadership of Simmonds was attributed to its economic policies, and was achieved despite persistent rumours of official connivance in drugs-trafficking activities on the islands.

The CCM secured a majority in the Nevis Island Assembly at an election in June 1992, with three seats, while the NRP retained two. The leader of the CCM, Vance Amory, became Premier of the Nevis Island Administration. Within days of swearing in the new Assembly, the Deputy Governor-General (the Governor-General's representative on Nevis), Weston Parris, was found dead at sea in suspicious circumstances.

At a general election in November 1993 neither the PAM nor the Labour Party managed to secure a majority in the National Assembly, with both parties winning four seats. On Nevis the CCM secured two seats, and the NRP one. Following the refusal of Amory to form a coalition government with either the PAM or the Labour Party, the Governor-General, Sir Clement Arrindell, invited Simmonds to form a minority government with the support of the NRP. Douglas protested against the decision and appealed for a general strike to support his demands for a further general election. Serious disturbances ensued, and in early December the Governor-General declared a 21-day state of emergency. Meanwhile, Simmonds withdrew from negotiations with Douglas, although an initial agreement to hold a further general election had been reached, in protest at Douglas's premature public revelation of the agreement.

An escalation in violent crime in late 1994 prompted renewed concern that drugs-trafficking operations were being conducted on the islands. In October six people were charged in connection with the murder, in Basseterre, of the head of the Saint Christopher special investigations police unit, Jude Matthew, who had been conducting an investigation into the recent disappearances of William Herbert, the country's Permanent Representative to the UN, and Vincent Morris, a son of the Deputy Prime Minister (Sidney Morris). Preliminary investigations suggested that these events were connected to the discovery, at the same time as Morris's disappearance, of a large consignment of cocaine in Saint Christopher. In November Sidney Morris resigned, following the arrest of two other sons on charges related to drugs and firearms offences.

A 'forum for national unity' was convened in November 1994, at which representatives of all political parties, church organizations and tourism, trade, labour and law associations agreed to seek closer political co-operation in the months preceding an early general election, in order to halt the advance of drugs-related crime and the attendant erosion of local- and foreign-investor confidence in the islands. None the less, fierce electoral campaigning culminated, in June 1995, in a violent clash

---

* While this island is officially called Saint Christopher as part of the state, the name is usually abbreviated to St Kitts.

between rival PAM and Labour Party supporters, which resulted in a number of serious injuries. The general election, conducted on 3 July, was won decisively by the Labour Party, which secured seven of the elective seats in the National Assembly, and Denzil Douglas became Prime Minister. The CCM won two seats, while the PAM and the NRP each won one. Simmonds was among prominent PAM politicians who lost their seats. Douglas resolved to address promptly the problems of increasingly violent crime and of deteriorating prison conditions. Douglas also announced plans to draft proposals for constitutional reform that would provide for the establishment of separate governments for the two islands.

On 1 January 1996 Sir Cuthbert Montroville Sebastian succeeded Sir Clement Arrindell as Governor-General.

In July 1997 the National Assembly approved legislation to restore a full-time defence force, to include the coastguard, with the principal aim of strengthening the islands' anti-drugs operations. (The Simmonds administration had disbanded the army in 1981.) The Nevis administration and the PAM accused the Labour Government of seeking to enhance its authority by recruiting party loyalists to the force. In July 1998 a convicted murderer was executed—the first implementation of the death penalty in the country since 1985. The Attorney-General, Delano Bart, defended the reintroduction of capital punishment, against criticism from the Roman Catholic Church and the human rights organization Amnesty International, as part of the Government's strategy to reduce crime rates.

The Government established a commission of inquiry in July 1997 to investigate allegations of corruption within the PAM during its period in government. Simmonds and Hugh Heyliger (the former agriculture minister, who had succeeded Morris as Deputy Prime Minister, now the sole PAM member of, and Leader of the Opposition in, the National Assembly) were summoned to answer charges of financial impropriety. Both former ministers denied the allegations. In September Simmonds appealed to the High Court to declare the commission invalid. In December Heyliger was charged (and subsequently released on bail) with contempt of court, after failing to testify before the commission. The High Court dismissed applications made by former members of the PAM administration in 1998 and 1999 to have the commission terminated on the grounds of political bias. In July 1999 concerns were expressed by the High Court that the commission of inquiry might have been unduly influenced against Simmonds by his efforts to have the inquiry terminated. The Government therefore established a second commission, to be chaired by a prominent British jurist, Sir Louis Blom-Cooper, which was specifically to investigate allegations against Simmonds, while the initial commission was to continue to investigate general allegations of corruption relating to his administration. The Blom-Cooper commission focused in particular on an agreement signed by Simmonds in 1986, which guaranteed a loan to a company intending to run hydrofoil services between Saint Christopher and St Maarten, in the Netherlands Antilles. It was revealed in the course of the investigations that the amount of that loan, which had been made without any public discussion or feasibility studies, was equivalent to one-third of the Government's domestic expenditure. The commission's report, published in February 2000, made 10 specific accusations of negligence, improper behaviour and irresponsible action against Simmonds, who was described as having failed 'to achieve the standards required' of a Prime Minister of a sovereign state. Simmonds, however, vehemently rejected the commission's conclusions; he noted that the treasury had not suffered, as the loan had not been honoured, nor had any member of his Government benefited from the agreement.

In June 1996 Amory announced that the Nevis Island Assembly was initiating proceedings (as detailed in the Constitution—see below) for the secession of Nevis from the federation with Saint Christopher. The announcement was made as plans proceeded for the establishment of a federal government office on Nevis (which Amory considered to be unconstitutional) and as the National Assembly considered a financial services bill that proposed referring all potential investors in Nevis to the federal administration for approval. The Nevis Island Assembly was reported to have interpreted both measures as serious infringements of its administrative rights. Despite the prompt intervention of a number of regional diplomatic initiatives to preserve the Federation, a secession bill for Nevis received its preliminary reading in the National Assembly in July. In October the NRP, while supportive of the right to secede, expressed concern at the precipitant nature of Amory's secession

timetable, and in November the NRP representative in the National Assembly boycotted a second reading of the bill, forcing a postponement of the debate.

At elections to the Nevis Island Assembly, conducted on 24 February 1997, Amory's CCM retained three of the five elective seats, while the NRP retained the remaining two. In October the Nevis Assembly voted unanimously in favour of secession; a referendum on the issue was to follow. In December Douglas appointed a constitutional review commission, with a view to improving relations between Kittitians and Nevisians; however, the review would not affect the constitutional process in Nevis. In late 1997 the Caribbean Community and Common Market (CARICOM, see p. 155) also appointed a constitutional commission, chaired by Sir Fred Phillips (a former Governor of the islands), to draw up a report on the implications of secession. In July 1998 the Nevis Island Assembly announced that a referendum would be held on 10 August. The NRP protested at the short notice given for the referendum, as did Prime Minister Douglas, who noted that the vote had been scheduled to take place during the annual Culturama festival on Nevis, when many Nevisians resident abroad would return to the island. At the referendum 61.7%, less than the two-thirds' majority required by the Constitution, voted for secession. The leaders of the two islands immediately announced that they would work to improve relations, and Douglas pledged to implement the principal recommendations of the Phillips Commission. In September a CARICOM mission, led by the Prime Ministers of Dominica and Saint Vincent and the Grenadines, visited Saint Christopher and Nevis as part of a regional initiative to find a lasting solution to the secession issue.

In March 1999 a Constitutional Task Force, also chaired by Sir Fred Phillips, began work on the drafting of a new constitution, based on Phillips' previous recommendations and public consultations. In August the Task Force submitted its report to the Prime Minister, who appointed a seven-member select committee, comprising representatives of all the major parties, to review its recommendations and to draft proposals for constitutional change.

'Hurricane Georges' struck Saint Christopher and Nevis in September 1998, causing great destruction to the islands' infrastructure. Ports and airports were also severely damaged. Nevis was less severely damaged, although there was an estimated EC $5m. damage to the tourism infrastructure and the agricultural sector was devastated. A state of emergency and a curfew were imposed in Saint Christopher.

In February 2000 Douglas announced that the general election, due in July, was to be brought forward. It was widely believed that the Prime Minister intended to capitalize on the embarrassment caused to the PAM by the publication of the Blom-Cooper report into the allegations of corruption in the Simmonds administration (see above). At the election, held on 6 March, the Labour Party won all eight seats available on Saint Christopher (with 64.5% of the votes cast), gaining the seat previously held by the PAM, which won 35.5% of the votes. There was no change in the position on Nevis, where the CCM retained its two seats and the NRP its one. Turn-out was reported to have been 63.9% of the registered electorate (66.8% on Saint Christopher and 52.6% on Nevis). The PAM subsequently accused the Government of widespread electoral fraud, and announced that the party would not contest any future elections until the electoral register had been revised and voter identification cards issued. Shortly after the election Douglas announced a redistribution of portfolios among members of the previous Cabinet; one new appointment was made, that of Jacinth Lorna Henry-Martin as Minister of Information, Youth, Sports and Culture. In October Lindsay Grant, a lawyer, was elected the new leader of the PAM, replacing Simmonds.

The Government sought to address the increasing crime rate on the islands in 2001, which was affecting the tourist industry. In February a 10pm government curfew for all children under 15 was introduced in an effort to reduce youth crime, and in June the Government sought to persuade the US Navy to relocate one of its bases to Saint Christopher. Douglas stated his hope that the country would derive 'economic, social and financial' benefits from the US presence.

In August 2001 Douglas announced a small cabinet reshuffle. The only new appointment was that of Halva Hendrickson, to the post of Minister of Public Works, Utilities, Transport and Post. In elections to the Nevis Island Assembly in September the CCM, led by Amory, strengthened its control of the legislature, gaining a total of four elective seats. The NRP, under the leadership of Joseph Parry, took the remaining one seat.

In October 2002 Douglas, pronouncing on the recurring issue of greater autonomy for Nevis, said that, while he supported the constitutional right of Nevis to secede from the federation, the federal Government was willing to discuss ways to increase the autonomy of the Nevis Island Administration and Assembly. Amory, however, remained convinced that full autonomy and separate membership of the Organisation of Eastern Caribbean States (OECS, see p. 341) would be a better option for Nevis. To underline Nevis' intention to pursue independence, in October Amory visited Montserrat and the US Virgin Islands to discuss joint tourism marketing initiatives. Douglas insisted that Amory's concerns could be addressed through constitutional reform, which, he said, would be given greater priority in 2003. Nevertheless, in February 2003 Nevis' political parties, the CCM and the NRP, announced they would not participate in future federal elections and would campaign for autonomy from Saint Christopher.

Saint Christopher and Nevis is a member of CARICOM and of the OECS. In the late 1980s regional discussions were held on the issue of political unity in the East Caribbean. Saint Christopher and Nevis expressed interest in political unity only if the proposed merger included its Leeward Island neighbours and the Virgin Islands, where an estimated 10,000 Kittitians and Nevisians reside. From January 1990 the OECS agreed to relax restrictions on travel between member states. Moreover, in February 2002 it was agreed, with effect from March, to allow nationals of member states to travel freely within the OECS area and to remain in the territory of any other member state for up to six months. An OECS passport was scheduled to be introduced by January 2003. Nevertheless, following expressions of reluctance by Antigua and Barbuda and Montserrat, Saint Christopher and Nevis was unlikely to participate in any future political union of OECS member states.

Government

Saint Christopher and Nevis is a constitutional monarchy. Executive power is vested in the British monarch, as Head of State, and is exercised locally by the monarch's personal representative, the Governor-General, who acts in accordance with the advice of the Cabinet. Legislative power is vested in Parliament, comprising the monarch and the National Assembly. The National Assembly is composed of the Speaker, three (or, if a nominated member is Attorney-General, four) nominated members, known as Senators (two appointed on the advice of the Premier and one appointed on the advice of the Leader of the Opposition), and 11 elected members (Representatives), who are chosen from single-member constituencies for up to five years by universal adult suffrage. The Cabinet comprises the Prime Minister, who must be able to command the support of the majority of the members of the National Assembly, the Attorney-General (*ex officio*) and four other ministers. The Prime Minister and the Cabinet are responsible to Parliament.

The Nevis Island legislature comprises the Nevis Island Assembly and the Nevis Island Administration, headed by the British monarch (who is represented on the island by the Deputy Governor-General). It operates similarly to the Saint Christopher and Nevis legislature but has power to secede from the Federation, subject to certain restrictions (see Constitution, below).

Defence

The small army was disbanded by the Government in 1981, and its duties were absorbed by the Volunteer Defence Force and a special tactical unit of the police. In July 1997 the National Assembly approved legislation to re-establish a full-time defence force. Coastguard operations were to be brought under military command; the defence force was also to include cadet and reserve forces. St Christopher and Nevis participates in the US-sponsored Regional Security System, comprising police, coastguards and army units, which was established by independent East Caribbean states in 1982. Budgetary expenditure on national security in 1998 was approximately EC $23.8m.

Economic Affairs

In 2001, according to estimates by the World Bank, Saint Christopher and Nevis's gross national income (GNI), measured at average 1999–2001 prices, was US $283m., equivalent to US $6,880 per head (or $11,730 per head on an international purchasing-power parity basis). During 1990–2001 the population declined by an average of 0.2% per year, largely as a

result of emigration, while over the same period, it was estimated, gross domestic product (GDP) per head increased, in real terms, at an average annual rate of 4.2%. Overall GDP increased, in real terms, by an average of 4.0% annually in 1990–2001; growth was estimated at 2.1% in 2001.

Agriculture (including forestry and fishing) contributed an estimated 2.6% of GDP in 2000. Some 14.7% of the working population were employed in the agriculture sector (including sugar manufacturing) in 1994. Major crops include coconuts and sea-island cotton, although some vegetables are also exported. The principal cash crop is sugar cane. Sugar and sugar products accounted for an estimated 20% of total export earnings in 2000. The cane harvest increased by 49.8% in 1997, owing to favourable weather, increased land under cultivation, and more efficient methods of cultivation and harvesting. Unfavourable weather conditions and a decrease in acreage under cultivation contributed, however, to a decline of 21.3% in 1998, and by 2000 production had fallen further, to 188,373 metric tons, remaining at the same level in 2001. According to early reports, production decreased further in 2002. In spite of a guaranteed European Union (EU) sugar price, which is well above world market levels, the sugar industry survives only as a result of government subsidies, which were equivalent to 3.5% of GDP in 2001. Large areas formerly used for sugar are now designated for tourism, and the Government is expected to announce the closure of the industry within the next few years, making provision for retraining of sugar industry employees. Diversification in agriculture, the principal productive sector of the economy, has been encouraged in order to reduce the economy's vulnerability to fluctuations in the world price of sugar. Important crops include yams, sweet potatoes, groundnuts, onions, sweet peppers, cabbages, carrots and bananas. Fishing is an increasingly important commercial activity. Agricultural GDP increased by an annual average of 1.1% in 1990–2000. According to the Eastern Caribbean Central Bank (ECCB, see p. 343), the real value of agricultural GDP decreased by 9.1% in 1999 and 8.5% in 2000, owing to hurricane damage and the decline in production in the sugar cane sector, but increased by an estimated 11.1% in 2001.

Industry (including mining, manufacturing, construction and public utilities) provided an estimated 27.1% of GDP in 2000. Excluding sugar manufacturing, the sector employed 21.0% of the working population in 1994. Activity is mainly connected with the construction industry (the real GDP of which expanded by 29.2% in 2000 and by a estimated 4.3% in 2001). Real industrial GDP increased by an annual average of 5.8% in 1990–2000. In 1999 the GDP of the sector expanded by 6.9%, and in 2000 by 24.2%.

Manufacturing provided an estimated 9.8% of GDP in 2000, and non-sugar manufacturing employed 7.8% of the working population in 1994. Apart from the sugar industry (the production of raw sugar and ethyl alcohol), the principal manufactured products are garments, electrical components, food products, beer and other beverages. The sector recorded average annual growth of 3.8% during 1990–2000. In 2000, according to the ECCB, real manufacturing GDP increased by 11.3% but, in 2001, was estimated to decreased by 8.9%.

The islands are dependent upon imports of fuel and energy (7.6% of total imports in 2000) for their energy requirements.

The services sector contributed an estimated 70.3% of GDP in 2000, and employed 64.4% of the working population in 1994. Tourism is a major contributor to the economy and some 12.8% of the employed population were engaged in tourism-related activities in 1994. None the less, in 1999 the number of yacht and cruise-ship visitors decreased by 13.2%, to 143,800, while the number of stop-over tourists decreased by 11.0%, to 84,000. In 2000, although there was a 14.1% growth in the number of cruise-ship passengers, the number of stop-over tourists continued to decrease, totalling 73,100, a decline of 13.0%. Furthermore, tourist revenues declined by 11.0% in 1999 and by a further 13.6% in 2000. However, the industry recovered slightly in 2001: revenues increased by 5.8% and the number of stop-over arrivals (70,600) and cruise-ship visitors (167,200) remained relatively stable. Data for the first six months of 2002 indicated that the number of cruise-ship and stop-over visitors would decline slightly that year. In March 2003 a new 900-room resort at Frigate Bay, Saint Christopher opened, increasing the number of hotel rooms on the island by some 60%. The real GDP of the services sector increased at an average annual rate of 4.2% in 1990–2000; growth was 2.0% in 1999 and 3.2% in 2000.

In 2001 Saint Christopher and Nevis recorded a visible trade deficit of EC $111.6m. and there was a deficit of EC $96.5m. on the current account of the balance of payments. The USA was the islands' principal trading partner in 2001, supplying 46.2% of imports and purchasing 72.4% of exports. Trade with the United Kingdom and with other Caribbean states is also important. The sugar industry is the country's leading exporter (accounting for an estimated 20% of total export revenues in 2000), and the principal imports are machinery and transport equipment, basic manufactures and food and live animals.

In 2001 the central Government of Saint Christopher and Nevis recorded an estimated budgetary deficit of EC $135.6m., equivalent to 17.0% of GDP. The country's total external debt was estimated to be US $140.1m. at the end of 2000, of which US $135.8m. was long-term public debt. In that year the cost of debt-servicing was equivalent to 12.3% of the value of exports of goods and services. The annual rate of inflation averaged 3.3% in 1990–2000; consumer prices increased by 3.4% in 1999 and by 2.1% in 2000. There is, however, a recurring problem of labour shortages in the agricultural sector (notably the sugar industry) and the construction industry, and the rate of unemployment (reported to be around 10% in early 2003) is mitigated by mass emigration, particularly from Nevis: remittances from abroad provide an important source of revenue.

Saint Christopher and Nevis is a member of the Caribbean Community and Common Market (CARICOM, see p. 155), and of the Organisation of Eastern Caribbean States (OECS, see p. 341). The ECCB is based in Basseterre. In 2001 a regional stock exchange, the Eastern Caribbean Securities Exchange, opened in Basseterre. Saint Christopher and Nevis is a party to the Cotonou Agreement (see p. 234), the successor agreement to the Lomé Convention, signed in June 2000 between the EU and a group of developing countries.

Successive Governments have attempted to reduce economic dependence on the cultivation and processing of sugar cane, the traditional industry of the islands. The most rapidly developing industry has been tourism, while the development of light manufacturing, particularly of electronic components and textiles, has also helped to broaden the islands' economic base. It is also hoped that an information technology industry can be established. The economic upturn in 1999 was, to a significant extent, the result of increased investment in reconstruction following the damage caused by 'Hurricane Georges' in September 1998, although increased imports of construction materials were expected, in combination with the decline in sugar exports and in electronic components, to contribute to the further deterioration of the trade deficit. The growth in the construction sector was sustained in 2000 and was continued in 2001, albeit at a lower level. In May 2000 the Financial Stability Forum categorized Saint Christopher and Nevis's banking supervision in the lowest group. In June the Organisation for Economic Co-operation and Development (OECD) included the country in a list of tax 'havens' and in the same month it was also included on a list of 'non-co-operative' governments in attempts to combat money-laundering by the Financial Action Task Force (FATF, based in the OECD Secretariat). In an attempt to ensure the country's removal from the list, Prime Minister Douglas had announced a series of financial reforms and as a result of these measures, in June 2002 the FATF removed Saint Christopher and Nevis from the list. In April 2003 a report indicated that the islands' offshore banking operations had been halved as a result of the FATF action and the subsequent financial reforms. In his December 2002 budget speech the Prime Minister announced that, given the debilitating effect of interest payments upon the Government's fiscal position, a reduction in external debt would be a priority over the forthcoming years. In common with similar countries in the region, Saint Christopher and Nevis experienced a sharp economic slowdown in 2002, with real GDP decreasing by an estimated 1.7%. It was feared that the US-led military campaign to remove the regime of Saddam Hussein in Iraq could contribute to a further decline in GDP in 2003.

Education

Education is compulsory for 12 years between five and 17 years of age. Primary education begins at the age of five, and lasts for seven years. Secondary education, from the age of 12, generally comprises a first cycle of four years, followed by a second cycle of two years. In 1993 enrolment at all levels of education was estimated to be equivalent to 78% of the school-age population. There are 30 state, eight private and five denominational schools. There is also a technical college. Budgetary expenditure on education by the central Government in 1998 was projected to be EC $25m. (6.7% of total government expenditure). In September 2000 a privately financed offshore medical college, the Medical University of the Americas, opened in Nevis with 40 students registered.

Public Holidays

2003: 1 January (New Year's Day), 2 January (Carnival Last Lap), 18 April (Good Friday), 21 April (Easter Monday), 5 May (May Day), 9 June (Whit Monday), 14 June (Queen's Official Birthday), 4 August (August Monday), 5 August (Nevis only: Culturama Last Lap), 16 September (Heroes Day), 19 September (Independence Day), 25–26 December (Christmas).

2004: 1 January (New Year's Day), 2 January (Carnival Last Lap), 9 April (Good Friday), 12 April (Easter Monday), 3 May (May Day), 31 May (Whit Monday), 12 June (Queen's Official Birthday), 2 August (August Monday), 3 August (Nevis only: Culturama Last Lap), 16 September (Heroes Day), 19 September (Independence Day), 25–26 December (Christmas).

Weights and Measures

The imperial system is used.

Statistical Survey

Source (unless otherwise stated): St Kitts and Nevis Information Service, Ministry of Information, Culture, Youth and Sport, Church St, POB 186, Basseterre; tel. 465-2521; fax 466-4504; e-mail skninfo@caribsurf.com; internet www.stkittsnevis.net.

AREA AND POPULATION

Area (sq km): 269.4 (St Christopher 176.1, Nevis 93.3).

Population: 40,618 (males 19,933; females 20,685) at census of 12 May 1991; 45,841 (males 22,784; females 23,057) at census of 14 May 2001 (provisional results). Source: partly UN, *Population and Vital Statistics Report*.

Density (May 2001): 170.2 per sq km.

Principal Town (estimated population, 2001): Basseterre (capital) 12,605.

Births and Deaths (2000): Registered live births 838 (estimated birth rate 20.7 per 1,000); Registered deaths 356 (estimated death rate 8.8 per 1,000).

Expectation of life (years at birth): 70.9 (males 69.0; females 72.8) in 2001. Source: WHO, *World Health Report*.

Employment (labour force survey, 1994): Sugar cane production/manufacturing 1,525; Non-sugar agriculture 914; Mining and quarrying 29; Manufacturing (excl. sugar) 1,290; Electricity, gas and water 416; Construction 1,745; Trade (except tourism) 1,249; Tourism 2,118; Transport and communications 534; Business and general services 3,708; Government services 2,738; Other statutory bodies 342; Total 16,608 (Saint Christopher 12,516, Nevis 4,092). Source: IMF, *St Kitts and Nevis: Recent Economic Developments* (August 1997).

HEALTH AND WELFARE

Key Indicators

Total Fertility Rate (children per woman, 2001): 2.4.

Under-5 Mortality Rate (per 1,000 live births, 2001): 24.

Physicians (per 1,000 head, 1996): 1.17.

Hospital Beds (per 1,000 head, 1996): 6.36.

Health Expenditure (2000): US $ per head (PPP): 658.

Health Expenditure (2000): % of GDP: 5.2.

Health Expenditure (2000): public (% of total): 59.2.

Access to Water (% of persons, 2000): 98.

Access to Sanitation (% of persons, 2000): 96.

Human Development Index (2000): ranking: 44.

Human Development Index (2000): value: 0.814.
For sources and definitions, see explanatory note on p. vi.

AGRICULTURE, ETC.

Principal Crops ('000 metric tons, 2001): Roots and tubers 1 (FAO estimate); Sugar cane 188; Coconuts 1; Vegetables and melons 1; Fruits and berries 1 (FAO estimate). Source: FAO.

Livestock (FAO estimates, '000 head, year ending September 2001): Cattle 3.6; Sheep 7.4; Goats 14.5; Pigs 3.0. Source: FAO.

Livestock Products (FAO estimates, '000 metric tons, 2001): Beef and veal 0.1; Pig meat 0.3; Poultry meat 0.1; Hen eggs 0.2. Source: FAO.

Fishing (metric tons, live weight, 2000): Capture 257 (Snappers 21, Needlefishes, etc. 66, Flyingfishes 24, Bigeye scad 35, Common dolphinfish 29, Stromboid conchs 34); Aquaculture 5 (FAO estimate); Total catch 262. Source: FAO, *Yearbook of Fishery Statistics*.

INDUSTRY

Raw Sugar (2000): 18,051 metric tons.

Electric Energy (1999): 96.7 million kWh.

FINANCE

Currency and Exchange Rates: 100 cents = 1 Eastern Caribbean dollar (EC $). *Sterling, US Dollar and Euro Equivalents* (31 December 2002): £1 sterling = EC $4.352; US $1 = EC $2.700; €1 = EC $2.831; EC $100 = £22.985 = US $37.04 = €35.32. *Exchange Rate:* Fixed at US $1 = EC $2.70 since July 1976.

Budget (preliminary, EC $ million, 2001): *Revenue:* Revenue from taxation 194.6 (of which, Taxes on income and profits 57.7, Taxes on domestic goods and services 38.2, Taxes on international trade and transactions 94.2); Other current revenue 67.5; Capital revenue 3.7; Foreign grants 4.6; Total 270.1. *Expenditure:* Current expenditure 307.0 (Personal emoluments 140.3; Goods and services 79.5; Public debt charges 52.4; Transfers 34.7); Capital expenditure and net lending 99.0; Total 406.0. Source: Eastern Caribbean Central Bank, *Report and Statement of Accounts*.

International Reserves (US $ million at 31 December 2002): Reserve position in IMF 0.11; Foreign exchange 65.64; Total 65.75. Source: IMF, *International Financial Statistics*.

Money Supply (EC $ million at 31 December 2002): Currency outside banks 37.690; Demand deposits at deposit money banks 88.58; Total money (incl. others) 127.30. Source: IMF, *International Financial Statistics*.

Cost of Living (Consumer price index; base: 1990 = 100): 131.0 in 1998; 135.4 in 1999; 138.3 in 2000. Source: ILO.

Gross Domestic Product (EC $ million at current factor cost): 693.3 in 1999; 766.5 in 2000; 796.3 in 2001. Source: Eastern Caribbean Central Bank, *Report and Statement of Accounts*.

Expenditure on the Gross Domestic Product (EC $ million, 2001): Government final consumption expenditure 184.1; Private final consumption expenditure 456.9; Gross fixed capital formation 528.6; *Total domestic expenditure* 1,169.6; Exports of goods and services 418.0; *Less* Imports of goods and services 660.1; *GDP in purchasers' values* 927.5. Source: IMF, *International Financial Statistics*.

Gross Domestic Product by Economic Activity (EC $ million at current factor cost, 2000): Agriculture, hunting, forestry and fishing 21.0; Mining and quarrying 2.8; Manufacturing 79.9; Electricity and water 13.9; Construction 124.6; Wholesale and retail trade 115.7; Restaurants and hotels 50.2; Transport 52.9; Communications 45.6; Finance and insurance 108.2; Real estate and housing 20.3; Government services 148.4; Other community, social and personal services 32.9; Sub-total 816.2; *Less* Imputed bank service charge 53.2; Total 763.0.

Balance of Payments (US $ million, 2001): Exports of goods f.o.b. 55.04; Imports of goods f.o.b. –166.67; *Trade balance* –111.63; Exports of services 104.70; Imports of services –71.19; *Balance on goods and services* –78.12; Other income received (net) –36.73; *Balance on goods, services and income* –114.85; Current transfers received (net) 18.32; *Current balance* –96.53; Capital account (net) 10.27; Direct investment from abroad (net) 88.03; Portfolio investment (net) 33.91; Other investment (net) –23.48; Net errors and omissions –1.04; *Overall balance* 11.15. Source: IMF, *International Financial Statistics*.

EXTERNAL TRADE

Principal Commodities (EC $ million, 2000): *Imports c.i.f.:* Food and live animals 82.3; Beverages and tobacco 15.8; Crude materials (inedible) except fuels 14.4; Mineral fuels, lubricants, etc. 40.2; Chemicals 39.7; Basic manufactures 103.2; Machinery and transport equipment 148.3; Total (incl. others) 529.1. *Exports f.o.b.:* Food and live animals 18.3 (Sugar preparations and honey 15.8); Machinery and transport equipment 54.8; Total (incl. others) 78.8.

Principal Trading Partners (EC $ million, 2001): *Imports*: Canada 58.4; Japan 12.8; Puerto Rico 21.0; Trinidad and Tobago 63.2; United Kingdom 42.2; USA 235.9; Total (incl. others) 510.8. *Exports* (excl. re-exports): Dominica 1.0; United Kingdom 17.6; USA 56.1; Total (incl. others) 77.5.

TRANSPORT

Road Traffic (registered motor vehicles): 11,352 in 1998; 12,432 in 1999; 12,917 in 2000.

Shipping: Arrivals (2000): 1,981. *International Freight Traffic* ('000 metric tons, 2000): Goods loaded 24.7; Goods unloaded 234.2.

Civil Aviation (aircraft arrivals): 24,800 in 1998; 23,500 in 1999; 19,400 in 2000.

TOURISM

Tourist Arrivals ('000): 194.3 (88.3 stop-over visitors, 102.7 yacht and cruise-ship passengers, 3.3 excursionists) in 1997; 258.9 (93.2 stop-over visitors, 162.8 yacht and cruise-ship passengers, 2.9 excursionists) in 1998; 230.8 (84.0 stop-over visitors, 143.8 yacht and cruise-ship passengers, 3.0 excursionists) in 1999. *2000* ('000): 73.1 stop-over visitors; 164.1 cruise-ship passengers. *2001* ('000): 70.6 stop-over visitors; 167.2 cruise-ship passengers. Source: mainly Caribbean Development Bank, *Social and Economic Indicators 2001*.

Visitor Expenditure (EC $ million): 182.7 in 1999; 157.8 in 2000; 167.0 in 2001 (preliminary). Source: Eastern Caribbean Central Bank, *Report and Statement of Accounts*.

COMMUNICATIONS MEDIA

Radio Receivers ('000 in use, 1997): 28.

Television Receivers ('000 in use, 1999): 10.

Telephones ('000 main lines in use, 2000): 21.9.

Facsimile Machines (1996): 450.

Mobile Cellular Telephones (subscribers, 2000): 1,200.

Personal Computers ('000 in use, 2001): 8.

Internet Users ('000, 2000): 2.

Non-daily Newspapers (2000): Titles 4; Circulation 34,000 (1996). Sources: mainly UNESCO, *Statistical Yearbook*; UN, *Statistical Yearbook*; International Telecommunication Union.

EDUCATION

Pre-primary (2000/01): 77 schools; 170 teachers; 2,819 pupils.

Primary (2000/01): 23 schools; 302 teachers; 5,835 pupils.

Secondary (2000/01): 7 schools; 365 teachers; 4,493 pupils.

Tertiary (2000/01): 1 institution; 64 teachers (1999/2000); 1,235 students.

Adult Literacy Rate: 97.8% in 2000 (Source: UN Development Programme, *Human Development Report*).

Directory

The Constitution

The Constitution of the Federation of Saint Christopher and Nevis took effect from 19 September 1983, when the territory achieved independence. Its main provisions are summarized below

FUNDAMENTAL RIGHTS AND FREEDOMS

Regardless of race, place of origin, political opinion, colour, creed or sex, but subject to respect for the rights and freedoms of others and for the public interest, every person in Saint Christopher and Nevis is entitled to the rights of life, liberty, security of person, equality before the law and the protection of the law. Freedom of conscience, of expression, of assembly and association is guaranteed, and the inviolability of personal privacy, family life and property is maintained. Protection is afforded from slavery, forced labour, torture and inhuman treatment.

THE GOVERNOR-GENERAL

The Governor-General is appointed by the British monarch, whom the Governor-General represents locally. The Governor-General must be a citizen of Saint Christopher and Nevis, and must appoint a Deputy Governor-General, in accordance with the wishes of the Premier of Nevis, to represent the Governor-General on that island.

PARLIAMENT

Parliament consists of the British monarch, represented by the Governor-General, and the National Assembly, which includes a Speaker, three (or, if a nominated member is Attorney-General, four) nominated members (Senators) and 11 elected members (Representatives). Senators are appointed by the Governor-General; one on the advice of the Leader of the Opposition, and the other two in accordance with the wishes of the Prime Minister. The Representatives are elected by universal suffrage, one from each of the 11 single-member constituencies.

Every citizen over the age of 18 years is eligible to vote. Parliament may alter any of the provisions of the Constitution.

THE EXECUTIVE

Executive authority is vested in the British monarch, as Head of State, and is exercised on the monarch's behalf by the Governor-General, either directly or through subordinate officers. The Governor-General appoints as Prime Minister that Representative who, in the Governor-General's opinion, appears to be best able to command the support of the majority of the Representatives. Other ministerial appointments are made by the Governor-General, in consultation with the Prime Minister, from among the members of the National Assembly. The Governor-General may remove the Prime Minister from office if a resolution of 'no confidence' in the Government is passed by the National Assembly and if the Prime Minister does not resign within three days or advise the Governor-General to dissolve Parliament.

The Cabinet consists of the Prime Minister and other Ministers. When the office of Attorney-General is a public office, the Attorney-General shall, by virtue of holding that office, be a member of the Cabinet in addition to the other Ministers. The Governor-General appoints as Leader of the Opposition in the National Assembly that Representative who, in the Governor-General's opinion, appears to be best able to command the support of the majority of the Representatives who do not support the Government.

CITIZENSHIP

All persons born in Saint Christopher and Nevis before independence who, immediately before independence, were citizens of the United Kingdom and Colonies automatically become citizens of Saint Christopher and Nevis. All persons born in Saint Christopher and Nevis after independence automatically acquire citizenship, as do those born outside Saint Christopher and Nevis after independence to a parent possessing citizenship. There are provisions for the acquisition of citizenship by those to whom it is not automatically granted.

THE ISLAND OF NEVIS

There is a Legislature for the island of Nevis which consists of the British monarch, represented by the Governor-General, and the Nevis Island Assembly. The Assembly consists of three nominated members (one appointed by the Governor-General in accordance with the advice of the Leader of the Opposition in the Assembly, and two appointed by the Governor-General in accordance with the advice of the Premier) and such number of elected members as corresponds directly with the number of electoral districts on the island.

There is a Nevis Island Administration, consisting of a premier and two other members who are appointed by the Governor-General. The Governor-General appoints the Premier as the person who, in the Governor-General's opinion, is best able to command the support of the majority of the elected members of the Assembly. The other members of the Administration are appointed by the Governor-General, acting in accordance with the wishes of the Premier. The Administration has exclusive responsibility for administration within the island of Nevis, in accordance with the provisions of any relevant laws.

The Nevis Island Legislature may provide that the island of Nevis is to cease to belong to the Federation of Saint Christopher and Nevis, in which case this Constitution would cease to have effect in the island of Nevis. Provisions for the possible secession of the island contain the following requirements: that the island must give full and detailed proposals for the future Constitution of the island of Nevis, which must be laid before the Assembly for a period of at least six months prior to the proposed date of secession; that a two-thirds majority has been gained in a referendum which is to be held after the Assembly has passed the motion.

The Government

Head of State: HM Queen ELIZABETH II.

Governor-General: Sir CUTHBERT MONTROVILLE SEBASTIAN (took office 1 January 1996).

CABINET
(April 2003)

Prime Minister and Minister of Finance, Development, Planning and National Security: Dr DENZIL LLEWELLYN DOUGLAS.

Deputy Prime Minister and Minister of International Trade, Labour, Social Security, CARICOM Affairs and Telecommunications and Technology: SAM TERRENCE CONDOR.

Minister of Tourism, Commerce and Consumer Affairs: G.A. DWYER ASTAPHAN.

Minister of Health and the Environment: Dr EARL ASIM MARTIN.

Minister of Agriculture, Fisheries, Co-operatives, Lands and Housing: CEDRIC ROY LIBURD.

Minister of Information, Culture, Youth and Sport: JACINTH LORNA HENRY-MARTIN.

Minister of Public Works, Utilities, Transport and Posts: HALVA HENDRICKSON.

Minister of Social Development, Community and Gender Affairs: RUPERT EMANUEL HERBERT.

Minister of Education and Foreign Affairs: TIMOTHY SYLVESTER HARRIS.

Attorney-General and Minister of Justice and Legal Affairs: DELANO BART.

MINISTRIES

Office of the Governor-General: Government House, Basseterre; tel. 465-2315.

Government Headquarters: Church St, POB 186, Basseterre; tel. 465-2521; fax 465-1001; internet www.stkittsnevis.net.

Prime Minister's Office and Ministry of Finance, Development, Planning and National Security: Church St, POB 186, Basseterre; tel. 465-2521; fax 465-1001; e-mail sknpmoffice@caribsurf.com; internet www.fsd.gov.kn.

Attorney-General's Office and Ministry of Justice and Legal Affairs: Church St, POB 186, Basseterre; tel. 465-2521; fax 465-5040; e-mail attnygenskn@caribsurf.com.

Ministry of Agriculture, Fisheries, Co-operatives, Lands and Housing: Church St, POB 186, Basseterre; tel. 465-2521; fax 465-2635; e-mail minafclh@caribsurf.com.

Ministry of Education and Foreign Affairs: Church St, POB 186, Basseterre; tel. 465-2521; fax 465-2556; e-mail minelsc@caribsurf.com.

Ministry of Health and the Environment: Church St, POB 186, Basseterre; tel. 465-2521; fax 465-1316; e-mail minhwa@caribsurf.com.

Ministry of Information, Culture, Youth and Sport: Church St, POB 186, Basseterre; tel. 465-2521; fax 465-7075; e-mail culture@caribsurf.com.

Ministry of International Trade, Labour, Social Security, (CARICOM) Affairs and Telecommunications and Technology: Church St, POB 186, Basseterre; tel. 465-2521; fax 465-1778; e-mail mintica@thecable.net.

Ministry of Public Works, Utilities, Transport and Posts: Church St, POB 186, Basseterre; tel. 466-7032; fax 465-9475.

Ministry of Social Development, Community and Gender Affairs: Church St, POB 186, Basseterre; tel. 465-2521; fax 465-8244; e-mail mwaskn@caribsurf.com.

Ministry of Tourism, Commerce and Consumer Affairs: Pelican Mall, Bay Rd, POB 132, Basseterre; tel. 465-4040; fax 465-8794; e-mail mintcande@caribsurf.com.

NEVIS ISLAND ADMINISTRATION

Premier: Vance W. Amory.

There are also two appointed members.

Administrative Centre: Administration Bldg, Main St, Charlestown, Nevis; tel. 469-5221; fax 469-1207; e-mail nevisinfo@nevisweb.kn; internet www.nevisweb.kn.

Legislature

NATIONAL ASSEMBLY

Speaker: Walford Gumbs.

Elected members: 11. Nominated members: 3. Ex-officio members: 1.

Election, 6 March 2000

Party	Votes	Seats
St Kitts-Nevis Labour Party	11,762	8
Concerned Citizens' Movement . . .	1,901	2
Nevis Reformation Party	1,710	1
People's Action Movement	6,468	—
Total	21,841	11

NEVIS ISLAND ASSEMBLY

Elected members: 5. Nominated members: 3.

Elections to the Nevis Island Assembly took place in September 2001. The Concerned Citizens' Movement took four seats, and the Nevis Reformation Party retained one seat.

Political Organizations

Concerned Citizens' Movement (CCM): Charlestown, Nevis; alliance of four parties; Leader Vance W. Amory.

Nevis Reformation Party (NRP): Government Rd, POB 480, Charlestown, Nevis; tel. 469-0630; f. 1970; Leader Joseph Parry; Sec. Levi Morton.

People's Action Movement (PAM): Basseterre; e-mail exec@pamskb.com; internet www.pamskb.com; f. 1965; Leader Lindsay Grant.

St Kitts-Nevis Labour Party (SKNLP): Masses House, Church St, POB 239, Basseterre; tel. 465-5347; fax 465-8328; internet www.sknlabourparty.org; f. 1932; socialist party; Chair. Timothy Harris; Leader Dr Denzil Llewellyn Douglas.

United People's Party (UPP): Basseterre; f. 1993; Leader Michael Powell.

Diplomatic Representation

EMBASSIES IN SAINT CHRISTOPHER AND NEVIS

China (Taiwan): Taylor's Range, POB 119, Basseterre; tel. 465-2421; fax 465-7921; e-mail rocemb@caribsurf.com; Ambassador Katharine Chang.

Venezuela: Delisle St, POB 435, Basseterre; tel. 465-2073; fax 465-5452; Ambassador Miriam Troconis Luzardo.

Diplomatic relations with other countries are maintained at consular level, or with ambassadors and high commissioners resident in other countries of the region, or directly with the other country.

Judicial System

Justice is administered by the Eastern Caribbean Supreme Court, based in Saint Lucia and consisting of a Court of Appeal and a High Court. One of the nine puisne judges of the High Court is responsible for Saint Christopher and Nevis and presides over the Court of Summary Jurisdiction. The Magistrates' Courts deal with summary offences and civil offences involving sums of not more than EC $5,000. In 1998 the death penalty was employed in Saint Christopher and Nevis for the first time since 1985.

Puisne Judge: Neville Smith.

Magistrates' Office: Losack Rd, Basseterre; tel. 465-2926.

Religion

CHRISTIANITY

St Kitts Christian Council: Victoria Rd, POB 48, Basseterre; tel. 465-2504; Chair. Rev. Charles Seaton.

St Kitts Evangelical Association: Princess St, POB 773, Basseterre.

The Anglican Communion

Anglicans in Saint Christopher and Nevis are adherents of the Church in the Province of the West Indies. The islands form part of the diocese of the North Eastern Caribbean and Aruba. The Bishop is resident in The Valley, Anguilla.

The Roman Catholic Church

The diocese of Saint John's-Basseterre, suffragan to the archdiocese of Castries (Saint Lucia), includes Anguilla, Antigua and Barbuda, the British Virgin Islands, Montserrat and Saint Christopher and Nevis. At 31 December 2001 the diocese contained an estimated 15,233 adherents. The Bishop participates in the Antilles Episcopal Conference (currently based in Port of Spain, Trinidad and Tobago).

Bishop of Saint John's-Basseterre: Rt Rev. Donald James Reece (resident in St John's, Antigua).

Other Churches

There are also communities of Methodists, Moravians, Seventh-day Adventists, Baptists, Pilgrim Holiness, the Church of God, Apostolic Faith and Plymouth Brethren.

The Press

The Democrat: Cayon St, POB 30, Basseterre; tel. 465-2091; fax 465-0857; internet www.pamskb.com/democrat; f. 1948; weekly on Saturdays; organ of PAM; Dir Capt. J. L. Wigley; Editor Fitzroy P. Jones; circ. 3,000.

The Labour Spokesman: Masses House, Church St, POB 239, Basseterre; tel. 465-2229; fax 466-9866; e-mail skn.union@caribsurf.com; internet www.sknlabourparty.org/spokesman; f. 1957; Wednesdays and Saturdays; organ of St Kitts-Nevis Trades and Labour Union; Editor Dawud Byron; Man. Walford Gumbs; circ. 6,000.

The Leeward Times: Old Hospital Rd, Charlestown, POB 535, Nevis; tel. 469-1409; fax 469-0662; e-mail hbramble@caribsurf.com; Editor Howell Bramble.

The St Kitts and Nevis Observer: Lozack Rd, Basseterre; tel. 466-4994; fax 466-4995; e-mail observsk@caribsurf.com; weekly; Bureau Chief John Perker.

FOREIGN NEWS AGENCIES

Associated Press (USA) and Inter Press Service (IPS) (Italy) are represented in Basseterre.

Publishers

Caribbean Publishing Co (St Kitts-Nevis) Ltd: Dr William Herbert Complex, Frigate Bay Rd, POB 745, Basseterre; tel. 465-5178; fax 466-0307; e-mail lsk-sales@caribsurf.com.

MacPennies Publishing Co: 10A Cayon St East, POB 318, Basseterre; tel. 465-2274; fax 465-8668.

Broadcasting and Communications

TELECOMMUNICATIONS

Regulatory Authority

Eastern Caribbean Telecommunications Authority: based on Castries, Saint Lucia; f. 2000 to regulate telecommunications in Saint Christopher and Nevis, Dominica, Grenada, Saint Lucia and Saint Vincent and the Grenadines.

Service Providers

Cable: Basseterre; f. 1983; granted licence in May 2002 to provide fixed public telecommunications network and services.

Cable & Wireless St Kitts and Nevis: Cayon St, POB 86, Basseterre; tel. 465-1000; fax 465-1106; internet www.candw.kn; f. 1985; fmrly St Kitts and Nevis Telecommunications Co Ltd (SKANTEL); 65% owned by Cable & Wireless plc; 17% state-owned; Chair. LEE L. MOORE; Gen. Man. K. C. RICKY WENT.

Cariglobe: Basseterre; granted licence in May 2002 to provide mobile telecommunications network.

BROADCASTING

Radio

Choice FM: Wellington Rd, Needsmust, Basseterre; tel. 466-1891; fax 466-1892; e-mail choicefm@caribsurf.com; Man. VINCENT HERBERT.

Goodwill Radio FM 104.5: POB 98, Lodge Project; tel. 465-7795; fax 465-9556; Gen. Man. DENNIS HUGGINS-NELSON.

Radio One (SKNBC): Bakers Corner, POB 1773, Basseterre; tel. 465-1141; fax 466-6728; e-mail housecaribbean@hotmail.com; Man. PATRICK QUEELEY.

Radio Paradise: Bath Plain, POB 423, Nevis; tel. 469-1994; fax 469-1642; owned by US co (POB A, Santa Ana, CA 92711); religious; Man. ARTHUR GILBERT.

Sugar City Rock FM: Greenlands, Basseterre; tel. 466-1113; e-mail sugarcityrock@hotmail.com; Gen. Man. VAL THOMAS.

Trinity Broadcasting Ltd: Bath Plain Rd, Charlestown, Nevis; tel. 469-0285; fax 469-1723; Dir ARTHUR GILBERT.

Voice of Nevis (VON) Radio 895 AM: Bath Plain, Bath Village, POB 195, Charlestown, Nevis; tel. 469-1616; fax 469-5329; e-mail vonradio@caribsurf.com; internet www.skbee.com/vonlive.html.

ZIZ Radio and Television: Springfield, POB 331, Basseterre; tel. 465-2622; fax 465-5624; e-mail zbc@caribsurf.com; internet www .zizonline.com; f. 1961; television from 1972; commercial; govt-owned; Gen. Man. WINSTON McMAHON.

Television

ZIZ Radio and Television: see Radio.

Finance

BANKING

Central Bank

Eastern Caribbean Central Bank (ECCB): Headquarters Bldg, Bird Rock, POB 89, Basseterre; tel. 465-2537; fax 465-5615; e-mail eccberu@caribsurf.com; internet www.eccb-centralbank.org; f. 1965 as East Caribbean Currency Authority; expanded responsibilities and changed name 1983; responsible for issue of currency in Anguilla, Antigua and Barbuda, Dominica, Grenada, Montserrat, Saint Christopher and Nevis, Saint Lucia and Saint Vincent and the Grenadines; res EC $109.0m., dep. EC $35.1m., total assets EC $1,188.9m. (March 2000); Gov. and Chair. K. DWIGHT VENNER.

Local Banks

Bank of Nevis Ltd: Main St, POB 450, Charlestown, Nevis; tel. 469-5564; fax 469-5798; e-mail bon@caribsurf.com; internet www .bankofnevis.com.

Caribbean Banking Corporation (SKN) Ltd: Chapel St, POB 60, Charlestown; tel. 469-5277; fax 469-5795.

Nevis Co-operative Banking Co Ltd: Chapel St, POB 60, Charlestown, Nevis; tel. 469-5277; fax 469-1493; f. 1955; Man. Dir I. WALWYN.

St Kitts-Nevis Anguilla National Bank Ltd: Central St, POB 343, Basseterre; tel. 465-2204; fax 466-1050; e-mail administrator@

sknanb.com; internet www.sknanb.com; f. 1971; total assets EC $572.5m. (June 1999); Chair. RUBLIN AUDAIN; Man. Dir EDWIN W. LAWRENCE; 5 brs.

Foreign Banks

Bank of Nova Scotia: Fort St, POB 433, Basseterre; tel. 465-4141; fax 465-8600; Man. W. A. CHRISTIE.

FirstCaribbean International Bank: Basseterre; internet www .firstcaribbeaninternational.com; f. 2002 following merger of Caribbean operations of Barclays Bank PLC and CIBC; Exec. Chair MICHAEL MANSOOR; CEO CHARLES PINK.

Royal Bank of Canada: cnr Bay and Fort St, POB 91, Basseterre; tel. 465-2259; fax 465-1040.

Development Bank

Development Bank of St Kitts and Nevis: Church St, POB 249, Basseterre; tel. 465-2288; fax 465-4016; e-mail dbskskn@caribsurf .com; f. 1981; cap. EC $8.0m., res EC $1.8m., dep. EC$2.5m. Gen. Man. AUCKLAND HECTOR.

STOCK EXCHANGE

Eastern Caribbean Securities Exchange: Bird Rock, POB 94, Basseterre; tel. 466-7192; fax 465-3798; e-mail info@ecseonline.com; internet www.ecseonline.com; f. 2001; regional securities market designed to facilitate the buying and selling of financial products for the eight member territories—Anguilla, Antigua and Barbuda, Dominica, Grenada, Montserrat, Saint Christopher and Nevis, Saint Lucia and Saint Vincent and the Grenadines; Gen. Man. BALJIT VOHRA.

INSURANCE

National Caribbean Insurance Co Ltd: Central St, POB 374, Basseterre; tel. 465-2694; fax 465-3659; subsidiary of St Kitts-Nevis Anguilla National Bank Ltd.

St Kitts-Nevis Insurance Co Ltd: Central St, POB 142, Basseterre; tel. 465-2845; fax 465-5410.

Several foreign companies also have offices in Saint Christopher and Nevis.

Trade and Industry

GOVERNMENT AGENCIES

Central Marketing Corpn (CEMACO): Pond's Pastire, Basseterre; tel. 465-2326; fax 465-2326; Man. MAXWELL GRIFFIN.

The Department of Planning and Development: The Cotton House, Market St, Charlestown, Nevis; tel. 469-5521; fax 469-1273; e-mail planevis@caribsurf.com.

Frigate Bay Development Corporation: Frigate Bay, POB 315, Basseterre; tel. 465-8339; fax 465-4463; promotes tourist and residential developments.

Investment Promotion Agency: Investment Promotion Division, Ministry of Trade and Industry, Church St, POB 186, Basseterre; tel. 465-4106; fax 465-1778; f. 1987.

St Kitts Sugar Manufacturing Corpn: St Kitts Sugar Factory, POB 96, Basseterre; tel. 466-8503; merged with National Agricultural Corpn in 1986; Gen. Man. J. E. S. ALFRED.

Social Security Board: Bay Rd, POB 79, Basseterre; tel. 465-6000; fax 465-5051; e-mail ssbdirof@caribsurf.com; f. 1977; Dir SEPHLIN LAWRENCE.

CHAMBER OF COMMERCE

St Kitts-Nevis Chamber of Industry and Commerce: South Independence Sq. St, POB 332, Basseterre; tel. 465-2980; fax 465-4490; e-mail sknchamber@caribsurf.com; incorporated 1949; 120 mems; Pres. CAROL EVELYN; Exec. Dir WENDY PHIPPS.

EMPLOYERS' ORGANIZATIONS

Building Contractors' Association: Anthony Evelyn Business Complex, Paul Southwell Industrial Park, POB 1046, Basseterre; tel. 465-6897; fax 465-5623; e-mail SKNBCA@caribsurf.com; Pres. ANTHONY E. EVELYN.

Nevis Cotton Growers' Association Ltd: Charlestown, Nevis; Pres. IVOR STEVENS.

Small Business Association: Anthony Evelyn Business Complex, Paul Southwell Industrial Park, POB 367, Basseterre; tel. 465-8630; fax 465-6661; e-mail SB-Association@caribsurf.com; Pres. EUSTACE WARNER.

UTILITIES

Nevis Electricity Company Ltd (Nevlec): Charlestown, Nevis; Gen. Man. EDGAR WIGGINS.

TRADE UNIONS

St Kitts-Nevis Trades and Labour Union: Masses House, Church St, POB 239, Basseterre; tel. 465-2229; fax 466-9866; f. 1940; affiliated to Caribbean Maritime and Aviation Council, Caribbean Congress of Labour, International Federation of Plantation, Agricultural and Allied Workers and International Confederation of Free Trade Unions; associated with St Kitts-Nevis Labour Party; Pres. LEE L. MOORE; Gen. Sec. STANLEY R. FRANKS; about 3,000 mems.

United Workers' Union (UWU): Market St, Basseterre; tel. 465-4130; associated with People's Action Movement.

Transport

RAILWAYS

There are 58 km (36 miles) of narrow-gauge light railway on Saint Christopher, serving the sugar plantations. The railway, complete with new trains and carriages, was restored and developed for tourist excursions, and opened in late 2002.

St Kitts Scenic Railway: Basseterre; tel. 465-7263; e-mail scenicreservations@caribsurf.com; internet www .stkittsscenicrailway.com; f. 2002.

St Kitts Sugar Railway: St Kitts Sugar Manufacturing Corpn, POB 96, Basseterre; tel. 465-8099; fax 465-1059; e-mail agronomy@caribsurf.com; Gen. Man. J. E. S. ALFRED.

ROADS

In 1999 there were 320 km (199 miles) of road in Saint Christopher and Nevis, of which approximately 136 km (84 miles) are paved. In July 2001 the Caribbean Development Bank loaned US $3.75m. to the Nevis Government for a road improvement scheme.

SHIPPING

The Government maintains a commercial motor boat service between the islands, and numerous regional and international shipping lines call at the islands. A deep-water port, Port Zante, was opened at Basseterre in 1981. Work is ongoing on port development projects to improve facilities for cargo ships and cruise ships in Basseterre and to repair the ports of Charlestown and Long Point on Nevis, which were damaged in 1999 by Hurricane Lenny.

St Kitts Air and Sea Ports Authority: Administration Bldg, Deep Water Port, Bird Rock, Basseterre; tel. 465-8121; fax 465-8124; f. 1993; combining St Kitts Port Authority and Airports Authority; Gen. Man. SIDNEY OSBORNE; Airport Man. EDWARD HUGHES; Sea Port Man. CARL BRAZIER-CLARKE.

Shipping Companies

Delisle Walwyn and Co Ltd: Liverpool Row, POB 44, Basseterre; tel. 465-2631; fax 465-1125; e-mail delwal@caribsurf.com; internet www.delisleco.com.

Sea Atlantic Cargo Shipping Corpn: Main St, POB 556, Charlestown, Nevis.

Tony's Ltd: Main St, POB 564, Charlestown, Nevis; tel. 469-5953; fax 469-5413.

CIVIL AVIATION

Robert Llewellyn Bradshaw (formerly Golden Rock) International Airport, 4 km (2½ miles) from Basseterre, is equipped to handle jet aircraft and is served by scheduled links with most Caribbean destinations, the United Kingdom, the USA and Canada. Saint Christopher and Nevis is a shareholder in the regional airline, LIAT (see chapter on Antigua and Barbuda). Vance W. Amory International Airport (formerly Newcastle Airfield), 11 km (7 miles) from Charlestown, Nevis, has regular scheduled services to St Kitts and other islands in the region. A new airport, Castle Airport, was opened on Nevis in 1998. In September 2002 a US $5.9m. project to construct a new passenger terminal at Vance W. Amory Airport was completed.

St Kitts Air and Sea Ports Authority: see Shipping.

Private Airlines

Air St Kitts-Nevis: Vance W. Amory International Airport, Newcastle, Nevis; tel. 469-9241; fax 469-9018.

Caribbean Star Airlines: Robert Llewellyn Bradshaw International Airport; f. 2000; relocated from Antigua in 2003; operates regional services; Pres. and CEO PAUL MOREIRA.

Nevis Express Ltd: Vance W. Amory International Airport, Newcastle, Nevis; tel. 469-9756; fax 469-9751; e-mail reservations@nevisexpress.com; internet www.nevisexpress.com; passenger and cargo charter services to all Caribbean destinations; St Kitts-Nevis shuttle service.

Tourism

The introduction of regular air services to Miami and New York has opened up the islands as a tourist destination. Visitors are attracted by the excellent beaches on Saint Christopher and the spectacular mountain scenery of Nevis, the historical Brimstone Hill Fortress National Park on Saint Christopher and the islands' associations with Lord Nelson and Alexander Hamilton. In 1999 there were 230,800 visitors, of whom 143,800 were yacht and cruise-ship passengers. In 2001 there were an estimated 167,200 cruise-ship passengers and 70,600 stop-over visitors. Receipts from tourism were estimated at EC $167.0m. in 2001. There were 1,508 rooms in hotels and guest houses in Saint Christopher and Nevis in 1999.

Nevis Tourism Authority: Main St, POB 917, Charlestown; tel. 469-7550; fax 469-7551; e-mail nta2001@caribsurf.com; internet www.nevisisland.com; Dir HELEN KIDD.

St Kitts-Nevis Department of Tourism: Pelican Mall, Bay Rd, POB 132, Basseterre; tel. 465-4040; fax 465-8794; e-mail mintitcc@stkittstourism.kn; internet www.stkitts-nevis.com; Permanent Sec. HILARY WATTLEY.

St Kitts-Nevis Hotel and Tourism Association: Liverpool Row, POB 438, Basseterre; tel. 465-5304; fax 465-7746; e-mail stkitnevhta@caribsurf.com; internet www.stkittsnevishta.org; f. 1972; Pres. SAM NG'ALLA; Exec. Dir VAL HENRY.

SAINT LUCIA

Introductory Survey

Location, Climate, Language, Religion, Flag, Capital

Saint Lucia is the second largest of the Windward Islands group of the West Indies, lying 40 km (25 miles) to the south of Martinique and 32 km (20 miles) to the north-east of Saint Vincent, in the Caribbean Sea. The island is volcanic, with spectacular mountain scenery. The average annual temperature is 26°C (79°F), with a dry season from January to April, followed by a rainy season from May to August. The average annual rainfall is 1,500 mm (60 ins) in the low-lying areas, and 3,500 mm (138 ins) in the mountains. The official language is English, although a large proportion of the population speak a French-based patois. Almost all of the island's inhabitants profess Christianity, and 79% are adherents of the Roman Catholic Church. The national flag (proportions 1 by 2) is blue, bearing in its centre a white-edged black triangle partly covered by a gold triangle rising from a common base. The capital is Castries.

Recent History

British settlers made an unsuccessful attempt to colonize the island (originally inhabited by a Carib people) in 1605. A further British party arrived in 1638 but were killed by the indigenous Carib population. France claimed sovereignty in 1642, and fighting between French and Caribs continued until 1660, when a peace treaty was signed. Control of Saint Lucia was transferred 14 times before it was ceded by the French and became a British colony in 1814. It remained under British rule for the next 165 years.

Representative government was introduced in 1924. The colony was a member of the Windward Islands, under a federal system, until December 1959. It joined the newly-formed West Indies Federation in January 1958, and remained a member until the Federation's dissolution in May 1962. From January 1960 Saint Lucia, in common with other British territories in the Windward Islands, was given a new Constitution, with its own Administrator and an enlarged Legislative Council.

In 1951 the first elections under adult suffrage were won by the Saint Lucia Labour Party (SLP), which retained power until 1964, when John (later Sir John) Compton, of the newly-formed conservative United Workers' Party (UWP), became Chief Minister. In March 1967 Saint Lucia became one of the West Indies Associated States, gaining full autonomy in internal affairs, with the United Kingdom retaining responsibility for defence and foreign relations only. The Legislative Council was replaced by a House of Assembly, the Administrator was designated Governor, and the Chief Minister became Premier.

In 1975 the Associated States agreed that they would seek independence individually. After three years of negotiations, Saint Lucia became independent on 22 February 1979, remaining within the Commonwealth. Compton became the country's first Prime Minister.

A general election in July 1979 returned the SLP to government with a clear majority, and its leader, Allan Louisy, succeeded Compton as Prime Minister. In February 1980 a new Governor-General, Boswell Williams, was appointed. This led to disputes within the Government and contributed to a split in the SLP. Louisy's resignation was demanded by 12 SLP members of the House of Assembly, who favoured his replacement by George Odlum, the Deputy Prime Minister. The controversy continued until April 1981, when Odlum and three other SLP members of the House voted with the opposition against the Government's budget, and Louisy was forced to resign. In May Winston Cenac, the Attorney-General in the Louisy Government, took office as Prime Minister, with a parliamentary majority of one. (Odlum and two other SLP members had broken away to form the Progressive Labour Party—PLP.) In September the Cenac administration defeated by one vote a motion of 'no confidence', introduced jointly by UWP and PLP members of the House, who accused the Government of political and economic mismanagement. In January 1982 a government proposal to alter legislation regarding the expenses of members of Parliament produced widespread accusations of corruption and provoked a series of strikes. Demands for the Government's resignation increased from all sectors of the community, culminating in a

general strike. Cenac resigned, and an all-party interim administration was formed, under the deputy leader of the PLP, Michael Pilgrim, pending a general election that was scheduled for May. At the election the UWP was returned to power, obtaining 56% of the votes cast and winning 14 of the 17 seats in the House of Assembly. John Compton was therefore re-elected Prime Minister, and stated that his immediate objective was renewed economic growth. In December Sir Allen Lewis was reappointed Governor-General, following the dismissal of Boswell Williams because of his previous close association with the SLP.

In 1984 the opposition parties began to reorganize in order to present a more effective opposition to the UWP Government. At a general election to the 17-member House of Assembly in early April 1987, the UWP secured nine seats and the SLP eight. A further election took place at the end of the month, in the hope of a more decisive result. As before, the UWP obtained about 53% of the votes, and the distribution of seats remained unchanged. In June the UWP's majority in the House was increased to three seats, when Cenac defected from the SLP. He was subsequently appointed Minister of Foreign Affairs.

In late October 1988 the Government introduced legislation whereby it assumed control of the banana industry for one year. Subsequently, the 1988 annual convention of the Saint Lucia Banana Growers' Association (SLBGA) was cancelled, and the Government dismissed the association's board of directors. The opposition parties alleged that these actions had been motivated by the fact that prominent supporters of the ruling UWP were the SLBGA's principal debtors. Despite continued protests, particularly by banana producers and the SLP, Government control was extended until July 1990.

Legislation against the trade in illicit drugs was enacted in November 1988, following an inquiry into police corruption and inefficacy. The inquiry also resulted in the dismissal of the police Commissioner and two other senior officers. In October 1990 the Government announced the creation of a special force to combat drugs-trafficking, and plans to intensify co-operation on the issue with Saint Vincent and the Grenadines and Martinique were also defined.

At a general election in April 1992 the UWP won 56.3% of the votes cast and secured 11 seats; the SLP, with 43.5% of the votes, took the remaining six. The SLP attributed its defeat largely to a redefinition of constituency boundaries by the Government prior to the election. In October 1993 a three-day strike was organized by a new pressure group, the Banana Salvation Committee (BSC), in support of demands for an increase in the minimum price paid to local producers for bananas and for the dismissal of the board of directors of the SLBGA. Following recommendations made by a government appointed committee, the Government implemented price increases and dismissed the board of directors of the SLBGA, who were replaced by an interim board including representatives of the BSC. An announcement by the Government, in January 1994, that the SLBGA was to be placed into receivership provoked a strike by the BSC in March. The BSC organized further strikes by banana farmers in December and in February and July 1995, in support of demands for an extraordinary meeting of the SLBGA, and for an inquiry into the deaths of two demonstrators during the October 1993 strike. Further industrial action was undertaken by the BSC in February 1996, in protest at the monopoly on banana exports exercised by the state-run Windward Islands Banana Development and Exporting Co (Wibdeco), in the context of higher prices for produce being offered to banana growers by a US distributor. In September the House of Assembly approved a bill to revise the selection procedure for members of the SLBGA and the responsibilities of its general manager. The new legislation effectively transferred control of the Association from the Government to the banana growers, who would henceforth elect six members of the board of directors (while the Government would continue to nominate the remaining five). In October the BSC co-ordinated industrial action by banana growers in support of renewed demands for an end to the Wibdeco monopoly, and for reform of the industry's management and payment systems. Attempts by a number of farmers who opposed the strike to transport produce to ports resulted in violent clashes. Subsequent negotiations with a parliamentary review committee and with the Government (which promised to transfer some responsibility for the industry to the private sector) failed to appease the farmers. At the end of the month six BSC members were elected to the new SLBGA board.

Following strike action by public sector workers in support of pay claims in June 1995, the Government offered of an 8% increase in salary arrears. This was accepted by six trade unions representing public employees in October, but was rejected by the Civil Service Association. In August the report of a commission of inquiry into allegations of the Government's involvement in the misappropriation, for electoral purposes, of some US $100,000 in UN contributions concluded that the former Permanent Representative to the UN, Charles Flemming, had been the sole perpetrator of the fraud. Flemming, who insisted that he had acted with the knowledge and endorsement of senior members of the UWP (including the Prime Minister), failed to return from a visit to the USA undertaken during the commission's hearings. The Minister of State with Responsibility for Financial Services and the National Development Corporation, Rufus Bousquet (who claimed to have been an unwitting recipient of the funds), had been dismissed in May, after he publicly questioned whether it was appropriate that the Government remain in office pending investigation of the affair.

A UWP party conference, convened in January 1996, endorsed the appointment of Vaughan Lewis, the former Director-General of the Organisation of Eastern Caribbean States (OECS, see p. 341), to the vacancy created by the Prime Minister's retirement from the party leadership. Lewis contested and won the Central Castries parliamentary by-election in February, and was subsequently appointed Minister without Portfolio. SLP leader Julian Hunte resigned later in the month, following criticism of the party's poor performance at the by-election; Kenny Anthony, a former SLP education and culture minister, replaced him. In late March Compton resigned the premiership, and was succeeded in early April by Lewis. An expanded Cabinet was named, in which Compton was to occupy the new post of Senior Minister for the duration of the current parliamentary session (although he would not attend cabinet meetings).

A general election on 23 May 1997 was won decisively by the SLP, which was returned to power after 15 years, securing 16 of the 17 seats in the House of Assembly (with 61.3% of the votes cast). Louis George, the Deputy Prime Minister and Minister of Education in the outgoing administration, was the only UWP candidate to retain his seat. (The party took 36.6% of the votes.) Kenny Anthony was sworn in as the new Prime Minister the following day. Among the nine ministers in his first Cabinet was George Odlum (as Minister of Foreign Affairs and International Trade), who had rejoined the SLP in July 1996. Following his electoral defeat, Lewis announced his intention to resign the leadership of the UWP; Sir John Compton (as he had become), the former UWP leader and former Prime Minister, replaced him in June 1998.

In August 1997 the Governor-General, Sir George Mallet resigned. His appointment, in June 1996, had been opposed by the SLP, on the grounds that the post's tradition of neutrality would be compromised—Mallet had previously been Deputy Prime Minister, and his portfolio had included several influential ministries. Saint Lucia's first female Governor-General, Dr Pearlette Louisy, was appointed in mid-September 1997.

In December 1997, in an attempt to address the proliferation in violent crime, the House of Assembly approved an amendment to the Firearms Act whereby persons in possession of unlicensed guns or ammunition would be liable to up to five years' imprisonment. (An ammunitions amnesty during October had proved largely unsuccessful.) In March 1998 Anthony announced further measures to ensure public security, including the recruitment of additional police-officers and the denial of bail to suspects in cases involving firearms.

In September 1997 the inquiry into allegations of corruption under the UWP, which had been promised by the SLP Government after its election, began, but hearings were effectively stalled in subsequent months by complaints by lawyers representing Sir John Compton and Vaughan Lewis that the sole commissioner, Monica Joseph, would not be impartial in her judgment. Despite a high court ruling in November that Joseph was competent to judge, further legal challenges were initiated, and Joseph finally withdrew from the inquiry in March 1998, stating that she did not wish her involvement to be the cause of

any further delay. Sir Louis Blom-Cooper, a prominent British jurist, was appointed in her place. Hearings were concluded in September, and in August 1999 Blom-Cooper submitted his report to the Government. The report cleared Compton and Lewis of corruption, but noted instances of impropriety and a 'high degree of maladministration' in their Governments.

In mid-September 1997 the directors of the SLBGA resigned, at Anthony's request: the Government was reportedly concerned that divisions at boardroom level were damaging the association's operations. Such divisions became increasingly pronounced as plans proceeded for the privatization of the SLBGA, one of the stated aims of the SLP Government. The Concerned Farmers Group (CFG), formed in December and led by the ousted Chairman, Rupert Gajadhar, which grouped larger farmers, expressed concern that the more numerous smaller producers in the BSC (whose secretary, Patrick Joseph, was also a government senator) would unduly dominate the new company, since decision-making was to be on the basis of one-member-one-vote. Members of the CFG threatened to establish their own company unless their concerns were addressed.

In July 1998 the SLBGA was privatized and the Saint Lucia Banana Corpn (SLBC) was created in its place. The Government agreed to assume the debts incurred by the dissolved SLBGA, equivalent to EC $44m. The CFG, which had refused to participate in the process, subsequently established a rival company, the Tropical Quality Fruit Co (TQF). In October 1998 a court judgment ruled that the SLBC did not enjoy monopoly rights in the banana trade. This ruling followed complaints from the TQF that Wibdeco had been refusing to accept its fruit for shipment. The TQF alleged that this refusal was due to pressure exerted by the SLBC Chairman, Patrick Joseph, in his capacity as a member of the Wibdeco board.

In January 1999 the SLBC announced that it had incurred losses of EC $6m. in 1998 and would therefore be forced to reduce the price paid to farmers. The SLBC blamed its operating deficit primarily on the fact that, because banana production had been underestimated, Wibdeco had failed to obtain sufficient European Union (EU, see p. 199) licences, meaning that much of the fruit produced did not reach high-paying markets. The TQF also announced a deficit, but claimed that its lower operating costs had reduced its losses. The TQF further suggested that the SLBC had damaged its own profitability by keeping prices deliberately high in an attempt to force the TQF out of business.

In July 1999 the Government founded a Banana Industry Trust, which was to oversee the improvement of farming practices in the banana sector and manage the financial resources available to the industry, including EC $21m. in funds provided by the EU. In the same month the Government announced that it was to make official loans of $7m. to the SLBC and $1.9m. to the TQF. However, falling prices and the ongoing lack of confidence among growers led the Government to announce that it was to hold senior-level talks with representatives of Wibdeco and Geest Bananas in order to discuss future pricing arrangements, while the Chairman of the SLBC urged Wibdeco and Geest to release money from their emergency funds to farmers threatened with bankruptcy. In August Wibdeco agreed to finance a temporary subsidy on prices in order to alleviate hardship among growers. In late 1999, however, the company encountered increasing pressure from the SLBC and from the Government to deliver increased returns to farmers, and in January 2000, following the expiry of its agreement to sell through Wibdeco, the SLBC announced plans to sell directly to Geest, despite criticism from its other regional partners in Wibdeco. In March Wibdeco announced that it would not contest the SLBC's decision, although it suggested that it might itself bypass the SLBC by buying directly from farmers.

Disbursement of a £1m. bonus fund to banana growers became the centre of a dispute between Wibdeco and the SLBC in April 2000, when the SLBC refused to submit a list of its banana growers and suppliers to Wibdeco, stating instead that it would provide a breakdown of the total payments from either Wibdeco or Geest to the individual growers. SLBC accused Wibdeco of attempting to use SLBC's money to compete directly with growers aligned to the Corporation by making payments directly to the growers. In late May the dispute was resolved when Wibdeco decided to pay the monies to the growers through the local banana associations in the four Windward Islands to whom the growers had sold their bananas in 1999. In October Patrick Joseph resigned as chairman of the SLBC, stating that differences had arisen between himself and the SLBC board.

The Corporation's chief accountant, Dean Nicholas, was reported to have accused Joseph of fraud and of seizing documents relating to the corporation's finances. In the following month the SLBC board of directors was dismissed and a three-member management committee was instituted to run the Corporation until the election of a new board. The committee consisted of Dean Nicholas, Freemont Lawrence, the company secretary, and Ben Emmanuel.

In early October 2000 Vaughan Lewis unexpectedly announced his resignation as leader of the UWP, stating as his reason commitments to his overseas employment at the University of the West Indies. Morella Joseph, one of the party's two deputy leaders, became interim leader before being elected unopposed to the position at the annual party convention later in the month. Eldridge Stephens, a former junior minister, was elected to succeed Romanus Lansiquot as UWP chairman.

In January 2001, following an increase in tourist cancellations, Prime Minister Anthony announced a series of measures intended to reduce the crime rate in Saint Lucia. These included the establishment of a National Anti-Crime Commission, the creation of a 10-member police 'rapid response unit', a review of the penal code, and reforms to the police service. In June Anthony announced the creation of four more rapid response units, a special task force to target known criminals, plans for more severe penalties for gun crimes, an increase in police patrols and an amnesty for holders of illegal firearms. A special joint session of Parliament was due to convene in the following month to debate the increase in violent crime.

In March 2001 the Minister of Foreign Affairs and International Trade, George Odlum, left the Government and the SLP to join a new opposition grouping, the National Alliance (NA). The former premier, Sir John Compton, and the UWP leader, Morella Joseph, founded the NA, in advance of legislative elections, due in 2002, but widely expected to be held in late 2001. Prime Minister Anthony stated that he had dismissed Odlum from his ministerial post, although Odlum himself claimed that he had resigned from the Government. Julian Hunte, a former Permanent Representative to the UN, replaced Odlum as foreign minister.

In October 2001 the NA's assembly elected Compton to head the party. However, Odlum rejected the decision and claimed the voting process was flawed. Later the same month the UWP pulled out of the Alliance and announced it would contest the elections as a single party. Odlum chose to retain the National Alliance name for his group. In November Prime Minister Anthony confirmed that the general election would take place on 3 December.

As expected, the ruling SLP achieved another convincing victory at the December 2001 general election, winning 14 of the 17 parliamentary seats (and 54.2% of the valid votes cast). The remaining seats were taken by the UWP (which received 36.6% of the ballot). Joseph and Odlum, leader of the UWP and the NA, respectively, both lost their seats. Nevertheless, the UWP regained two seats in the troubled 'banana belt' region, including that previously held by the Minister of Agriculture, Forestry and Fisheries, Cassius Elias. Voter turn-out rate decreased to 53%, from 67% in the 1997 election. Following the heavy electoral defeat of the UWP, Joseph resigned as the party's leader. Marius Wilson became the new leader of the opposition in December 2001. Meanwhile, in the same month, Prime Minister Anthony announced the membership of the new 15-member cabinet. Among several changes, Elias was replaced by Calixte George at the Ministry of Agriculture, Forestry and Fisheries and Phillip J. Pierre gained the tourism portfolio. Menissa Rambally, formerly Minister of Tourism and Civil Aviation, became Minister of Social Transformation, Culture and Local Government.

In January 2003 the UWP replaced Wilson as party leader with Arsen James. In the light of the decision, Wilson, whose 18-month tenure as opposition leader was blighted by controversy and allegations of improper conduct, announced his intention to resign from the party and take up a new position as an independent member of parliament.

Responding to the threat of war in the Middle East, widespread concerns about international terrorism and an increase in the number of people applying for visas to enter Saint Lucia, in March 2003 the Government introduced stricter controls on the processing of passports and visas, and strengthened security measures at air and sea ports.

The Speaker of the House of Assembly, Matthew Roberts, resigned in March 2003 in order to prepare a libel lawsuit against a local newspaper, which had published an article containing allegations about Roberts' personal life. He was replaced by Joseph Baden Allain in early April.

Saint Lucia's most important export market is the United Kingdom, which receives most of the banana crop under the terms of the Cotonou Agreement (see p. 234), the successor agreement to the Lomé Convention, which expired in 2000. In July 1993 new regulations came into effect governing the level of imports of bananas by the European Community (now EU, of which the United Kingdom is a member). The regulations were introduced to protect traditional producers covered by the Lomé Convention from competition from the expanding Latin American producers. At the instigation of the Latin American producers, consecutive dispute panels were appointed by the General Agreement on Tariffs and Trade (see World Trade Organization—WTO, see p. 323) to rule on whether the EU's actions contravened GATT rules. Although the dispute panels ruled in favour of the Latin American producers, the rulings were not enforceable. In February 1996, with support from Ecuador, Guatemala, Mexico and Honduras, the USA renewed consultations, begun in September 1995, with the WTO (the successor organization to GATT) concerning the EU's banana import quota regime. In March 1997 a WTO interim report appeared to uphold many of the charges of unfair discrimination brought by the plaintiffs. The WTO Appellate Body rejected representations by the EU against the ruling in September, and the EU was informed that it must formulate a new system for banana imports by early 1998. This ruling was accepted by the EU, which in January 1998 proposed new arrangements under which it would apply a system of quotas and tariffs to both groups of producers, while retaining an import-licensing system.

The EU's new banana import regime was implemented on 1 January 1999 in compliance with the WTO ruling, though the USA criticized the reforms as negligible. Further discussions on the issue broke down in late January 1999 when Saint Lucia, backed by other countries, objected to any discussion of US demands for sanctions on EU goods. On 1 February the USA introduced punitive import duties on various EU goods, and in March the WTO disputes panel was asked to consider whether the EU had done enough to amend its import regime and whether the USA could legally impose retaliatory import tariffs of up to 100% on certain EU goods. In retaliation against this move, the banana-exporting countries threatened to withdraw their co-operation with the US campaign against drugs-trafficking, while banana-producers warned that they might switch to growing marijuana if they were forced out of business. On 6 April WTO arbitrators awarded damages against the EU, although at a lower level than the USA had been claiming. On 12 April the WTO again delivered a ruling criticizing aspects of the EU banana-importing regime, and which gave the USA permission to impose retaliatory tariffs on certain European goods. In April 2001 the USA agreed to suspend these sanctions from 1 July, after the dispute was resolved: following a transition period, a new, tariff-only regime was to be introduced from 2006.

Saint Lucia is a member of the OECS, and, since May 1987, has been a prominent advocate of the creation of a unitary East Caribbean state. In 1988 however, Antigua and Barbuda expressed opposition to political union, thereby discouraging any participation by Montserrat or Saint Christopher and Nevis. The four English-speaking Windward Islands countries (Saint Lucia, Dominica, Grenada and Saint Vincent and the Grenadines) thus announced plans to proceed independently towards a more limited union. In 1990 the leaders of the four countries established a Regional Constituent Assembly. Following a series of discussions, the Assembly issued its final report in late 1992, in which it stated that the four countries were committed to the establishment of economic and political union under a federal system.

The new Government effected a significant reorientation in foreign policy in August 1997, when it was announced that diplomatic relations were to be established with the People's Republic of China; it was reported that China was to provide educational materials valued at US $1m. immediately, and was to finance the construction of a new national sports stadium, a cultural centre, a new highway and a free-trade zone. Taiwan subsequently severed relations with Saint Lucia. In January 2002 China contributed US $35m. towards the construction of the new national stadium. In addition, in January 2003 China agreed to provide technical assistance to help boost agricultural production and some EC $2m. to help fund the construction of a new psychiatric hospital. A technical and economic co-operation agreement was also reached with Cuba in January 1999.

Government

Saint Lucia is a constitutional monarchy. Executive power is vested in the British monarch, as Head of State, and is exercisable by the Governor-General, who represents the monarchy and is appointed on the advice of the Prime Minister. Legislative power is vested in Parliament, comprising the monarch, the 17-member House of Assembly, elected from single-member constituencies for up to five years by universal adult suffrage, and the Senate, composed of 11 members appointed by the Governor-General, including six appointed on the advice of the Prime Minister and three on the advice of the Leader of the Opposition. Government is effectively by the Cabinet. The Governor-General appoints the Prime Minister and, on the latter's recommendation, the other Ministers. The Prime Minister must have majority support in the House, to which the Cabinet is responsible.

Defence

The Royal Saint Lucia Police Force, which numbers about 300 men, includes a Special Service Unit for purposes of defence. Saint Lucia participates in the US-sponsored Regional Security System, comprising police, coastguards and army units, which was established by independent East Caribbean states in 1982. There are also two patrol vessels for coastguard duties.

Economic Affairs

In 2001, according to estimates by the World Bank, Saint Lucia's gross national income (GNI), measured at average 1999–2001 prices, was US $628m., equivalent to $6,880 per head (or $5,200 per head on an international purchasing-power parity basis). During 1990–2001, it was estimated, the population increased by an annual average rate of 1.5%, while gross domestic product (GDP) per head increased, in real terms, by an average rate of 0.5% per year. Overall GDP increased, in real terms, at an average annual rate of 2.0% in 1990–2001; real GDP decreased by an estimated 3.4% in 2001.

In 2001 agriculture (including hunting, forestry and fishing) accounted for 5.8% of GDP and employed some 19.5% of the active working population in 2000. Despite the decline in banana industry, the fruit remains Saint Lucia's principal cash crop, and in 2001 accounted for 33.5% of the total value of domestic merchandise exports (compared with 66.3% in 1996). Other important crops include coconuts, mangoes, citrus fruit, cocoa and spices. Commercial fishing is being developed and in August 2001 Japan granted US $10.6m. towards the rehabilitation and improvement of fishery facilities in the Choiseul and Soufrière districts. During 1990–2001 real agricultural GDP decreased by an estimated annual average of 6.7%, largely as a result of a 12.1% decline in the banana sector. The sector's real GDP decreased by 15.5% in 2000 and by an estimated 24.4% in 2001.

Industry (including mining, manufacturing, public utilities and construction) accounted for 17.4% of GDP in 2001 and the sector engaged an estimated 21.1% of the active working population in 2000. During 1990–2001 industrial GDP increased by an estimated annual average of 2.7%. In 2000 the sector's real GDP decreased by 1.0%, and in 2001 by an estimated 3.5%. Construction contributed 7.8% to GDP in 2001. The sector demonstrated strong growth in the 1990s (average annual growth of 6.7% in 1990–99), but the construction sector's real GDP decreased by 4.6% in 2000 and by an estimated 5.0% in 2001.

Manufacturing accounted for an estimated 4.5% of GDP in 2001, and employed 10.3% of the employed population in 2000. The principal manufacturing industries, which have been encouraged by the establishment of 'free zones', include the processing of agricultural products, the assembly of electronic components and the production of garments, plastics, paper and packaging (associated with banana production), beer, rum and other beverages. During 1990–2001 the sector's real GDP decreased by an estimated annual average of 1.3%. Real manufacturing GDP decreased by some 4.2% in 2001.

Energy is traditionally derived from imported hydrocarbon fuels (mineral fuels and lubricants comprised 12.8% of total imports in 2001). There is a petroleum storage and transhipment terminal on the island.

The services sector contributed an estimated 76.8% of GDP in 2001 and engaged an estimated 56.9% of those employed in 2000. Tourism is the most important of the service industries,

and in 2001 tourist receipts of EC $695.9m. were equivalent to 72.1% of the value of total exports of goods and services. In 2001 tourist arrivals increased by 2.1%, but a decrease of 8.1% was recorded in 2002 as the sector suffered from the effects of the global economic slowdown and the terrorist attacks on the USA in September 2001. The hotels and restaurant sector declined by an estimated 14.1% in 2001. During 1990–2001 the real GDP of the services sector increased by an annual average of 2.4%. The sector grew by 0.8% in 2000, but decreased by an estimated 3.3% in 2001.

In 2001 Saint Lucia recorded a visible trade deficit of US $206.93m., and a deficit of US $37.74m. on the current account of the balance of payments. The principal source of imports in 2000 was the USA (37.5% of the total); other important markets in that year were Trinidad and Tobago (14.4%) and the United Kingdom (8.5%). The principal market for exports is the United Kingdom, which received 55.7% of total exports in 2000; other major export markets were the USA (14.8%) and Barbados (10.3%). The Caribbean Community and Common Market (CARICOM, see p. 155) member states accounted for 21.7% of imports and 26.6% of exports in 2000. Food and live animals (comprised mainly of bananas sent to the United Kingdom) are the principal export commodity, ahead of beverages and tobacco and miscellaneous manufactured articles. The principal imports are foodstuffs, machinery and transport equipment and basic manufactures.

In 2001 there was an estimated overall budgetary deficit of EC $68.0m., equivalent to an estimated 3.83% of GDP. Saint Lucia's total external debt at the end of 2000 was US $237.0m., of which US $169.2m. was long-term public debt. In that year the cost of debt-servicing was equivalent to 9.6% of the value of exports of goods and services. The annual rate of inflation averaged 3.1% in 1990–2001; inflation averaged 3.8% in 20009 and 0.1% in 2001. In 2001 the average rate of unemployment was 18.9%.

Saint Lucia is a member of CARICOM, the Eastern Caribbean Central Bank (ECCB, see p. 343), and of the Organisation of Eastern Caribbean States (OECS, see p. 341). Saint Lucia is also a member of the regional stock exchange, the Eastern Caribbean Securities Exchange (based in Saint Christopher and Nevis), established in 2001. Saint Lucia has been a strong advocate of closer political and economic integration within the Caribbean region. Saint Lucia is party to the Caribbean Basin Initiative (CBI) and to the Lomé Convention and its successor Cotonou Agreement (see p. 234).

The Saint Lucian economy, which traditionally relied on the production of bananas for export, underwent considerable structural change at the end of the 20th century, with the emergence of services industries as the most important sector of the economy, while investment in the islands' infrastructure has also benefited the tourism industry, which is now the island's principal source of foreign exchange. The economy remains, however, heavily influenced by the agricultural sector, which is a significant source of employment, and is thus vulnerable to adverse climatic conditions and to fluctuations in prices, while the erosion of Saint Lucia's preferential access to European markets is also of considerable concern. Banana production declined dramatically in the 1990s, from 135,291 metric tons in 1992 to an estimated 74,000 tons in 2001, as a result of poor climatic conditions and the retrenchments in the industry caused by increased international competition and lower market prices. Output was estimated to have increased slightly in the first half of 2002; however, in September 'Hurricane Lili' destroyed about 50% of Saint Lucia's banana crop. The positive economic growth achieved during the 1990s was primarily attributed to the expansion in the tourism and construction sectors. As part of its attempts to diversity the economy, the Government also intended to establish Saint Lucia as a centre for international financial services; the necessary legislation was approved in late 1999 and Saint Lucia's first 'offshore' bank opened in 2001. Following widely publicized accounting scandals in the USA and elsewhere in 2001 and 2002, the Government tightened regulation of the sector in November 2002. The 2001/02 budget, announced in April 2001, included several tax measures, including the introduction of a foreign tax credit for businesses in the financial services sector. In April 2002 Prime Minister Anthony warned of the possible implementation of restrictive financial measures following the collapse of banana exports and an estimated 13.3% decrease in tourism revenue in 2001. In particular, with over one-third of its visitor arrivals coming from North America, Saint Lucia was badly affected by the repercussions of the terrorist attacks in the USA in September 2001. In 2001 an estimated economic decline of 3.4% was recorded and a further fall in real GDP was expected in 2002. In November 2002 Saint Lucia received two grants to help the embattled banana industry, worth a total of US $8.5m., from the Caribbean Development Bank. In addition, in the same month the EU provided a $1.5m. loan to help banana farmers affected by Hurricane Lili.

Education

Education is compulsory for 10 years between five and 15 years of age. Primary education begins at the age of five and lasts for seven years. Secondary education, beginning at 12 years of age, lasts for five years, comprising a first cycle of three years and a second cycle of two years. Free education is provided in more than 90 government-assisted schools. Facilities for industrial, technical and teacher-training are available at the Sir Arthur Lewis Community College at Morne Fortune, which also houses an extra-mural branch of the University of the West Indies. EC $21.5m. was allocated to education in the 2000/2001 budget. In May 2002 it was announced that an additional US $19m. will be invested in the education system during September 2002–

September 2006. The project, to build two new secondary schools and renovate existing ones, will be partially funded by the World Bank and UNESCO.

Public Holidays

2003: 1–2 January (New Year), 22 February (Independence Day), 18 April (Good Friday), 21 April (Easter Monday), 1 May (Labour Day), 9 June (Whit Monday), 19 June (Corpus Christi), 1 August (Emancipation Day), 3 October (Thanksgiving Day), 1 November (All Saints' Day), 2 November (All Souls' Day), 22 November (Feast of St Cecilia), 13 December (Saint Lucia Day), 25–26 December (Christmas).

2004: 1–2 January (New Year), 22 February (Independence Day), 9 April (Good Friday), 12 April (Easter Monday), 1 May (Labour Day), 31 May (Whit Monday), 10 June (Corpus Christi), 6 August (Emancipation Day), 1 October (Thanksgiving Day), 1 November (All Saints' Day), 2 November (All Souls' Day), 22 November (Feast of St Cecilia), 13 December (Saint Lucia Day), 25–26 December (Christmas).

Weights and Measures

The imperial system is in use.

Statistical Survey

Source (unless otherwise indicated): St Lucian Government Statistics Department, Block A, Government Bldgs, Castries Waterfront, Castries; tel. 452-6653; fax 451-8254; e-mail statsdept@candw.lc; internet www.stats.gov.lc.

AREA AND POPULATION

Area: 616.3 sq km (238 sq miles).

Population: 120,300 at census of 12 May 1980; 135,685 (males 65,988; females 69,697) at census of 12 May 1991; 158,018 (official estimate) at mid-2001. *By District* (official estimates, 2000): Castries 62,967; Anse La Raye 6,356; Canaries 1,935; Soufrière 9,075; Choiseul 7,323; Laborie 8,861; Vieux-Fort 14,833; Micoud 17,708; Dennery 12,966; Gros Islet 13,972; Total 155,996.

Density (mid-2001): 256.4 per sq km.

Principal Town (estimated population incl. suburbs, mid-2001): Castries (capital) 57,000. Source: UN, *World Urbanization Prospects: The 2001 Revision*.

Births, Marriages and Deaths (2001): Registered live births 2,729 (birth rate 17.3 per 1,000); Registered marriages 449 (marriage rate 2.8 per 1,000); Registered deaths 980 (death rate 6.2 per 1,000).

Expectation of Life (years at birth): 71.3 (males 69.5; females 73.0) in 2001. Source: WHO, *World Health Report*.

Economically Active Population (persons aged 15 years and over, labour survey for July–December 2000): Agriculture, hunting and forestry 11,660; Fishing 900; Manufacturing 6,610; Electricity, gas and water 530; Construction 6,460; Wholesale and retail trade; repair of motor vehicles, motorcycles and personal and household goods 11,090; Hotels and restaurants 6,140; Transport, storage and communications 4,540; Financial intermediation 870; Real estate, renting and business activities 1,450; Public administration and defence; compulsory social security 8,180; Education 1,390; Health and social work 450; Other community, social and personal service activities 1,130; Private households with employed persons 1,390; Activities not adequately defined 1,580; Total employed 64,370 (males 35,620, females 28,750); Unemployed 13,630; Total labour force 78,000.

HEALTH AND WELFARE

Key Indicators

Total Fertility Rate (children per woman, 2001): 2.6.

Under-5 Mortality Rate (per 1,000 live births, 2001): 19.

Physicians (per 1,000 head, 1997): 0.47.

Hospital Beds (per 1,000 head, 1996): 3.38.

Health Expenditure (2000): US $ per head (PPP): 272.

Health Expenditure (2000): % of GDP: 4.3.

Health Expenditure (2000): public (% of total): 62.1.

Access to Water (% of persons, 1999): 98.

Human Development Index (2000): ranking: 66.

Human Development Index (2000): value: 0.772.

For sources and definitions, see explanatory note on p. vi.

AGRICULTURE, ETC.

Principal Crops (FAO estimates, '000 metric tons, 2001): Cassava 1; Yams 5; Other roots and tubers 5; Coconuts 12; Vegetables 1; Bananas 74; Plantains 1; Oranges 1; Grapefruit 1; Mangoes 28. Source: FAO.

Livestock (FAO estimates, '000 head, year ending September 2001): Cattle 12; Sheep 13; Goats 10; Pigs 15; Horses 1; Asses 1; Mules 1. Source: FAO.

Livestock Products (FAO estimates, '000 metric tons, 2001): Beef and veal 1; Pig meat 1; Poultry meat 1; Cows' milk 1; Hen eggs 1. Source: FAO.

Fishing (metric tons, live weight, 2000): Capture 1,759 (Snappers 68, Wahoo 243, Skipjack tuna 175, Yellowfin tuna 123, Flyingfishes 99, Common dolphinfish 552); Aquaculture 1; Total catch 1,760. Figures exclude aquatic plants and mammals. Source: FAO, *Yearbook of Fishery Statistics*.

INDUSTRY

Production (estimates, 1998): Electric energy 284.7 million kWh (2001); Copra 2,400 metric tons (2001); Coconut oil (unrefined) 292,000 litres; Coconut oil (refined) 194,000 litres; Coconut meal 558,000 kg; Rum 328,600 gallons (1997). Sources: mainly IMF, *St Lucia: Statistical Annex* (May 1999), and FAO.

FINANCE

Currency and Exchange Rates: 100 cents = 1 Eastern Caribbean dollar (EC $). *Sterling, US Dollar and Euro Equivalents* (31 December 2002): £1 sterling = EC $4.352; US $1 = EC $2.700; €1 = EC $2.831; EC $100 = £22.98 = US $37.04 = €35.32. *Exchange Rate:* Fixed at US $1 = EC $2.70 since July 1976.

Budget (EC $ million, 2001): *Revenue:* Tax revenue 397.2 (Taxes on income and profits 133.7, Taxes on domestic goods and services 70.9, Taxes on international trade and transactions 191.3); Other current revenue 44.7; Capital revenue 1.3; Grants 17.5; Total 460.9. *Expenditure:* Current expenditure 405.9 (Personal emoluments 215.3, Goods and services 73.8, Interest payments 45.8, Transfers 71.0); Capital expenditure and net lending 122.9; Total 528.8. Source: Eastern Caribbean Central Bank, *Report and Statement of Accounts*.

International Reserves (US $ million at 31 December 2002): IMF special drawing rights 2.01; Foreign exchange 91.88; Total 93.89. Source: IMF, *International Financial Statistics*.

Money Supply (EC $ million at 31 December 2002): Currency outside banks 83.59; Demand deposits at deposit money banks 233.12; Total money (incl. others) 316.72. Source: IMF, *International Financial Statistics*.

Cost of Living (Consumer Price Index; base: 1995 = 100): 107.7 in 1999; 111.8 in 2000; 111.9 in 2001. Source: IMF, *International Financial Statistics*.

Expenditure on the Gross Domestic Product (EC $ million at current prices, 2001): Government final consumption expenditure 489.5; Private final consumption expenditure 938.9; Gross capital formation 449.0; *Total domestic expenditure* 1,877.4; Exports of goods and services 942.4; *Less* Imports of goods and services 1,036.8; *GDP at market prices* 1,782.9. Source: IMF, *International Financial Statistics.*

Gross Domestic Product by Economic Activity (EC $ million at current factor cost, provisional, 2001): Agriculture, hunting, forestry and fishing 94.04; Mining and quarrying 6.08; Manufacturing 73.14; Electricity and water 76.16; Construction 125.08; Wholesale and retail trade 176.23; Restaurants and hotels 199.80; Transport 189.31; Communications 122.40; Banking and insurance 153.34; Real estate and housing 96.01; Government services 222.82; Other services 78.54; Sub-total 1,612.95; *Less* Imputed bank service charge 124.10; Total 1,488.85.

Balance of Payments (US $ million, 2001): Exports of goods f.o.b. 51.81; Imports of goods f.o.b. –258.74; *Trade balance* –206.93; Exports of services 305.51; Imports of services –108.88; *Balance on goods and services* –10.30; Other income received (net) –41.09; *Balance on goods, services and income* –51.39; Current transfers received 27.02; Current transfers paid –13.37; *Current balance* –37.74; Capital account (net) 26.40; Direct investment from abroad (net) 22.37; Portfolio investment (net) –0.30; Other investment (net) 12.33; Net errors and omissions –11.21; *Overall balance* 11.85. Source: IMF, *International Financial Statistics.*

EXTERNAL TRADE

Principal Commodities (EC $ million, 2001): *Imports c.i.f.:* Food and live animals 186.4; Beverages and tobacco 31.7; Mineral fuels, lubricants, etc. 107.0; Chemicals and related products 70.3; Basic manufactures 150.3; Machinery and transport equipment 165.2; Miscellaneous manufactured articles 99.1; Total (incl. others) 834.8. *Exports f.o.b.:* Food and live animals 45.5; Beverages and tobacco 28.3; Basic manufactures 7.7; Machinery and transport equipment 17.4; Miscellaneous manufactured articles 16.7; Total (incl. others) 119.6 (excl. re-exports 10.8).

Principal Trading Partners (EC $ million, 2000): *Imports c.i.f.:* Barbados 27.2; Canada 36.9; China, People's Republic 21.9; Finland 17.6; France 19.5; Japan 43.2; Netherlands 10.9; Saint Vincent and the Grenadines 12.0; Trinidad and Tobago 138.3; United Kingdom 81.4; USA 359.5; US Virgin Islands 27.1; Total (incl. others) 958.7. *Exports f.o.b.:* Antigua and Barbuda 5.1; Barbados 10.9; Dominica 3.0; Grenada 3.2; Saint Vincent and the Grenadines 1.1; Trinidad and Tobago 1.9; United Kingdom 59.4; USA 15.7; Total (incl. others) 106.3.

TRANSPORT

Road Traffic (registered motor vehicles, 2001): Goods vehicles 8,972; Taxis and hired vehicles 1,894; Motorcycles 757; Private vehicles 22,453; Passenger vans 3,387; Total (incl. others) 39,416.

Shipping: *Arrivals* (1999): 2,328 vessels. *International Freight Traffic* ('000 metric tons, 1999): Goods loaded 117; Goods unloaded 666.

Civil Aviation (aircraft movements): 41,702 in 1996; 41,160 in 1997; 42,040 in 1998.

TOURISM

Tourist Arrivals ('000): 731.1 (285.4 visitor arrivals, 445.7 cruise-ship passengers) in 2000; 746.5 (256.6 visitors arrivals, 489.9 cruise-ship passengers) in 2001; 684.8 (260.4 visitor arrivals, 424.5 cruise-ship passengers) in 2002.

Tourist Receipts (EC $ million, estimates): 752.1 in 1999; 802.9 in 2000; 695.9 in 2001 (preliminary).
Source: Eastern Caribbean Central Bank, *Report and Statement of Accounts.*

COMMUNICATIONS MEDIA

Radio Receivers ('000 in use, 1997): 111.

Television Receivers ('000 in use, 1999): 56.

Telephones ('000 main lines in use, 2000): 44.9.

Mobile Cellular Telephones (subscribers, 2000): 2,500.

Personal Computers ('000 in use, 1999): 21.

Internet Users ('000, 2000): 3.

Non-daily Newspapers (1996): Titles 5; Circulation 34,000.
Sources: UN, *Statistical Yearbook*; UNESCO, *Statistical Yearbook*; International Telecommunication Union.

EDUCATION

Pre-primary (state institutions only, 2000/01): 106 schools; 359 teachers; 4,275 pupils.

Primary (state institutions only, 2000/01): 82 schools; 1,052 teachers; 28,618 pupils.

General Secondary (state institutions only, 2000/01): 18 schools; 678 teachers; 12,865 pupils.

Special Education (state institutions only, 2000/01): 5 schools; 39 teachers; 227 students.

Adult Education (state institutions only, 2000/01): 19 centres; 80 facilitators; 729 learners.

Tertiary (state institutions, including part-time, 2000/01): 127 teachers; 1,403 students.

Adult Literacy Rate: 90.2% in 2000 (Source: UN Development Programme, *Human Development Report*).

Directory

The Constitution

The Constitution came into force at the independence of Saint Lucia on 22 February 1979. Its main provisions are summarized below:

FUNDAMENTAL RIGHTS AND FREEDOMS

Regardless of race, place of origin, political opinion, colour, creed or sex but subject to respect for the rights and freedoms of others and for the public interest, every person in Saint Lucia is entitled to the rights of life, liberty, security of the person, equality before the law and the protection of the law. Freedom of conscience, of expression, of assembly and association is guaranteed and the inviolability of personal privacy, family life and property is maintained. Protection is afforded from slavery, forced labour, torture and inhuman treatment.

THE GOVERNOR-GENERAL

The British monarch, as Head of State, is represented in Saint Lucia by the Governor-General.

PARLIAMENT

Parliament consists of the British monarch, represented by the Governor-General, the 11-member Senate and the House of Assembly, composed of 17 elected Representatives. Senators are appointed by the Governor-General: six on the advice of the Prime

Minister, three on the advice of the Leader of the Opposition and two acting on his own deliberate judgement. The life of Parliament is five years.

Each constituency returns one Representative to the House who is directly elected in accordance with the Constitution.

At a time when the office of Attorney-General is a public office, the Attorney-General is an *ex-officio* member of the House.

Every citizen over the age of 21 is eligible to vote.

Parliament may alter any of the provisions of the Constitution.

THE EXECUTIVE

Executive authority is vested in the British monarch and exercisable by the Governor-General. The Governor-General appoints as Prime Minister that member of the House who, in the Governor-General's view, is best able to command the support of the majority of the members of the House, and other Ministers on the advice of the Prime Minister. The Governor-General may remove the Prime Minister from office if the House approves a resolution expressing no confidence in the Government, and if the Prime Minister does not resign within three days or advise the Governor-General to dissolve Parliament.

The Cabinet consists of the Prime Minister and other Ministers, and the Attorney-General as an *ex-officio* member at a time when the office of Attorney-General is a public office.

The Leader of the Opposition is appointed by the Governor-General as that member of the House who, in the Governor-General's view, is best able to command the support of a majority of members of the house who do not support the Government.

CITIZENSHIP

All persons born in Saint Lucia before independence who immediately prior to independence were citizens of the United Kingdom and Colonies automatically become citizens of Saint Lucia. All persons born in Saint Lucia after independence automatically acquire Saint Lucian citizenship, as do those born outside Saint Lucia after independence to a parent possessing Saint Lucian citizenship. Provision is made for the acquisition of citizenship by those to whom it is not automatically granted.

The Government

Head of State: HM Queen ELIZABETH II.

Governor-General: Dame PEARLETTE LOUISY (took office 17 September 1997).

CABINET
(April 2003)

Prime Minister, Minister of Finance, Economic Planning, International Financial Services, Economic Affairs and Information: Dr KENNY DAVIS ANTHONY.

Deputy Prime Minister and Minister of Education, Human Resource Development, Youth and Sports: MARIO F. MICHEL.

Minister of Commerce, Tourism, Investment and Consumer Affairs: PHILLIP J. PIERRE.

Minister of Agriculture, Forestry and Fisheries: Sen. CALIXTE GEORGE.

Minister of Health, Human Services and Family Affairs: DAMIAN E. GREAVES.

Minister of Physical Planning: IGNATIUS JEAN.

Minister of Communications, Works, Transport and Public Utilities: FELIX FINNISTERRE.

Minister of Labour Relations, Public Service and Co-operatives: VELON L. JOHN.

Minister of Home Affairs and Gender Relations: SARAH FLOOD-BEAUBRUN.

Minister of Foreign Affairs, International Trade and Civil Aviation: Sen. JULIAN HUNTE.

Minister of Social Transformation, Culture and Local Government: MENISSA RAMBALLY.

Attorney-General and Minister of Justice: Sen. PETRUS COMPTON.

MINISTRIES

Office of the Prime Minister: 5th Floor, Greaham Louisy Administrative Bldg, Waterfront, Castries; tel. 468-2111; fax 453-7352; e-mail pmoffice@candw.lc; internet www.stlucia.gov.lc.

Ministry of Agriculture, Forestry and Fisheries: 5th Floor, NIS Bldg, Waterfront, Castries; tel. 468-4210; fax 453-6314; e-mail admin@candw.lc; internet www.slumaffe.org.

Ministry of Commerce, Tourism, Investment and Consumer Affairs: 4th Floor, Ives Heraldine Rock Bldg, Block B, Waterfront, Castries; tel. 468-4202; fax 451-6986; e-mail mitandt@candw.lc; internet www.commerce.gov.lc.

Ministry of Communications, Works, Transport and Public Utilities: Williams Bldg, Bridge St, Castries; tel. 468-4300; fax 453-2769; e-mail min_com@candw.lc.

Ministry of Education, Human Resource Development, Youth and Sports: Francis Compton Bldg, Waterfront, Castries; tel. 468-5203; fax 453-2299; e-mail mineduc@candw.lc; internet www.education.gov.lc.

Ministry of Finance, Economic Planning, International Financial Services and Economic Affairs: Financial Centre, Bridge St, Castries; tel. 468-4410; fax 452-2506.

Ministry of Foreign Affairs, International Trade and Civil Aviation: Conway Business Centre, Waterfront, Castries; tel. 468-4501; fax 452-7427; e-mail foreign@candw.lc.

Ministry of Health, Human Services and Family Affairs: Chaussee Rd, Castries; tel. 452-2859; fax 452-5655; e-mail health@candw.lc.

Ministry of Home Affairs and Gender Relations: Erdiston's Pl., Manoel St, Castries; tel. 452-3772; fax 453-6315.

Ministry of Labour Relations, Public Service and Co-operatives: 2nd Floor, Greaham Louisy Administrative Bldg, Waterfront, Castries; tel. 468-2202; fax 453-1305.

Ministry of Physical Planning: 3rd Floor, Greaham Louisy Administrative Bldg, Waterfront, Castries; tel. 468-4402; fax 452-2506; e-mail sde@planning.gov.lc.

Ministry of Social Transformation, Culture and Local Government: 4th Floor, Greaham Louisy Administrative Bldg, Waterfront, Castries; tel. 468-5101; fax 453-7921.

Attorney-General's Office and Ministry of Justice: Francis Compton Bldg, Waterfront, Castries; tel. 468-3200; fax 453-6315; e-mail atgen@candw.lc.

Legislature

PARLIAMENT

Senate

The Senate has nine nominated members and two independent members.

President: HILFORD DETERVILLE.

House of Assembly

Speaker: JOSEPH BADEN ALLAIN.

Clerk: DORIS BAILEY.

Election, 3 December 2001

Party	% of votes	Seats
Saint Lucia Labour Party	54.2	14
United Workers' Party	36.6	3
National Alliance	3.5	—
Others	5.7	—
Total	**100.0**	**17**

Political Organizations

National Alliance (NA): Castries; f. 2001; opposition electoral alliance; Pres. Sir JOHN COMPTON; Political Leader GEORGE ODLUM.

Saint Lucia Freedom Party: Castries; f. 1999; campaigns against the political establishment; Spokesman MARTINUS FRANÇOIS.

Saint Lucia Labour Party (SLP): 2nd Floor, Tom Walcott Bldg, Jeremie St, POB 427, Castries; tel. 451-8446; fax 451-9389; e-mail slp@candw.lc; internet www.geocities.com/~slp; f. 1946; socialist party; Leader Dr KENNY DAVIS ANTHONY.

STAFF Party: Castries; Leader CHRISTOPHER HUNTE.

United Workers' Party (UWP): John Compton Highway, Sans Souci, POB 1550, Castries; tel. 451-9103; fax 451-9207; e-mail unitworkers@netscape.net; f. 1964; right-wing party; Chair. STEPHENSON KING; Leader Dr VAUGHAN A. LEWIS; Parliamentary Leader ARSEN JAMES.

Diplomatic Representation

EMBASSIES AND HIGH COMMISSION IN SAINT LUCIA

China, People's Republic: Cap Estate, Gros Islet, POB GM 999, Castries; tel. 452-0903; fax 452-9495; Ambassador GU HUAMING.

France: French Embassy to the OECS, Vigie, Castries; tel. 452-2462; fax 452-7899; e-mail frenchembassy@candw.lc; Ambassador HENRI VIDAL.

United Kingdom: Francis Compton Bldg, Waterfront, POB 227, Castries; tel. 452-2484; fax 453-1543; e-mail britishhc@candw.lc; High Commissioner resident in Barbados; Resident High Commissioner DOUGLAS RICE.

Venezuela: Vigie, BOP 494, Castries; tel. 452-4033; fax 453-6747; Ambassador MAIGUALIDA APONTE.

Judicial System

SUPREME COURT

Eastern Caribbean Supreme Court: Waterfront, Government Bldgs, POB 1093, Castries; tel. 452-2574; fax 452-5475; e-mail appeal@candw.lc; the West Indies Associated States Supreme Court was established in 1967 and was known as the Supreme Court of Grenada and the West Indies Associated States from 1974 until 1979, when it became the Eastern Caribbean Supreme Court. Its jurisdiction extends to Anguilla, Antigua and Barbuda, the British Virgin Islands, Dominica, Grenada (which rejoined in 1991), Montserrat, Saint Christopher and Nevis, Saint Lucia and Saint Vincent and the Grenadines. It is composed of the High Court of Justice and the Court of Appeal. The High Court is composed of the Chief Justice and 13 High Court Judges. The Court of Appeal is presided over by the Chief Justice and includes three other Justices of Appeal. Jurisdiction of the High Court includes fundamental rights and freedoms, membership of the parliaments, and matters concerning the interpretation of constitutions. Appeals from the Court of Appeal lie to the Judicial Committee of the Privy Council, based in the United Kingdom.

Chief Justice: C. M. DENNIS BYRON.

Attorney-General: Sen. PETRUS COMPTON.

Religion

CHRISTIANITY

The Roman Catholic Church

Saint Lucia forms a single archdiocese. The Archbishop participates in the Antilles Episcopal Conference (currently based in Port of Spain, Trinidad and Tobago). At 31 December 2001 there were an estimated 100,243 adherents, equivalent to some 64% of the population.

Archbishop of Castries: KELVIN EDWARD FELIX, Archbishop's Office, POB 267, Castries; tel. 452-2416; fax 452-3697; e-mail archbishop@candw.lc.

The Anglican Communion

Anglicans in Saint Lucia are adherents of the Church in the Province of the West Indies, comprising eight dioceses. The Archbishop of the West Indies is the Bishop of Nassau and the Bahamas. Saint Lucia forms part of the diocese of the Windward Islands (the Bishop is resident in Kingstown, Saint Vincent).

Other Christian Churches

Seventh-day Adventist Church: St Louis St, POB 117, Castries; tel. 452-4408; e-mail adventist@candw.lc; Pastor THEODORE JARIA.

Trinity Evangelical Lutheran Church: Gablewoods, POB GM 858, Castries; tel. 450-1484; fax 450-3382; e-mail jaegerj@candw.lc; Pastor J. JAEGER.

Baptist, Christian Science, Methodist, Pentecostal and other churches are also represented in Saint Lucia.

The Press

The Catholic Chronicle: POB 778, Castries; f. 1957; monthly; Editor Rev. PATRICK A. B. ANTHONY; circ. 3,000.

The Crusader: 19 St Louis St, Castries; tel. 452-2203; fax 452-1986; f. 1934; weekly; Editor GEORGE ODLUM; circ. 4,000.

The Mirror: Bisee Industrial Estate, Castries; tel. 451-6181; fax 451-6197; e-mail mirror@cabdw.lc; internet www.stluciamirroronline.com; f. 1994; weekly on Fridays; Man. Editor GUY ELLIS.

One Caribbean: POB 852, Castries; e-mail dabread@candw.lc; internet www.onecaribbean.com; Editor D. SINCLAIR DABREO.

The Star: Rodney Bay Industrial Estate, Gros Islet, POB 1146, Castries; tel. 450-7827; fax 450-8694; e-mail starpub@candw.lc; internet www.stluciastar.com; weekly; Propr RICK WAYNE.

The Vanguard: Hospital Rd, Castries; fortnightly; Editor ANDREW SEALY; circ. 2,000.

Visions of St Lucia Tourist Guide: POB 947, Castries; tel. 453-0427; fax 452-1522; e-mail visions@candw.lc; internet www.stlucia.com/visions; f. 1989; official tourist guide; published by Island Visions Ltd; annual; circ. 100,000.

The Voice of St Lucia: Odessa Bldg, Darling Rd, POB 104, Castries; tel. 452-2590; fax 453-1453; f. 1885; 2 a week; circ. 8,000.

The Weekend Voice: Odessa Bldg, Darling Rd, POB 104, Castries; tel. 452-2590; fax 453-1453; weekly on Saturdays; circ. 8,000.

NEWS AGENCY

Caribbean Media Corporation: Bisee Rd, Castries; tel. 453-7162; f. by merger of Caribbean News Agency and Caribbean Broadcasting Union.

FOREIGN NEWS AGENCY

Inter Press Service (IPS) (Italy): Hospital Rd, Castries; tel. 452-2770.

Publishers

Caribbean Publishing Co Ltd: American Drywall Bldg, Vide Boutielle Highway, POB 104, Castries; tel. 452-3188; fax 452-3181; e-mail publish@candw.lc; f. 1978; publishes telephone directories and magazines.

Crusader Publishing Co Ltd: 19 St Louis St, Castries; tel. 452-2203; fax 452-1986.

Island Visions: Sans Soucis, POB 947, Castries; tel. 453-0427; fax 452-1522; e-mail visions@candw.lc; internet www.sluonestop.com/visions.

Mirror Publishing Co Ltd: POB 1782, Bisee Industrial Estate, Castries; tel. 451-6181; fax 451-6503; e-mail mirror@candw.lc; internet www.stluciamirroronline.com; Man. Editor GUY ELLIS.

Star Publishing Co: Massade Industrial Park, Gros Islet, POB 1146, Castries; tel. 450-7827; fax 450-8694; e-mail starpub@candw.lc.

Voice Publishing Co Ltd: Odessa Bldg, Darling Rd, POB 104, Castries; tel. 452-2590; fax 453-1453.

Broadcasting and Communications

TELECOMMUNICATIONS

Regulatory Authority

Eastern Caribbean Telecommunications Authority: Castries; f. 2000 to regulate telecommunications in Saint Lucia, Dominica, Grenada, Saint Christopher and Nevis and Saint Vincent and the Grenadines.

Major Service Providers

Cable & Wireless (St Lucia) Ltd: Bridge St, POB 111, Castries; tel. 453-9000; fax 453-9700; e-mail talk2us@candw.lc; internet www.candw.lc; also operates a mobile cellular telephone service; Gen. Man. DAVID MORGAN; in February 2001 Cable & Wireless announced it was to cease operations in Saint Lucia when its current licence expired and relocate its regional call centres to Barbados and Anguilla.

Digicel: Castries; f. 2003; mobile cellular phone operator, owned by an Irish consortium.

St Lucia Boatphone Ltd: POB 2136, Gros Islet; tel. 452-0361; fax 452-0394; e-mail boatphone@candw.lc.

BROADCASTING

Radio

Gem Radio Network: POB 1146, Castries; tel. 459-0609.

Radio Caribbean International: 11 Mongiraud St, POB 121, Castries; tel. 452-2636; fax 452-2637; e-mail rci@candw.lc; internet www.candw.lc/homepage/rci.htm; operates Radio Caraïbes; English and Creole services; broadcasts 24 hrs; Pres. H. COQUERELLE; Station Man. WINSTON FOSTER.

Radyo Koulibwi: POB 20, Morne Du Don, Castries; tel. 451-7814; fax 453-1983; f. 1990.

Saint Lucia Broadcasting Corporation: Morne Fortune, POB 660, Castries; tel. 452-2337; fax 453-1568; govt-owned; Man. KEITH WEEKES.

Radio 100-Helen FM: Morne Fortune, POB 621, Castries; tel. 451-7260; fax 453-1737.

Radio Saint Lucia (RSL): Morne Fortune, POB 660, Castries; tel. 452-7415; fax 453-1568; English and Creole services; Chair. Vaughn Louis Fernand; Man. Keith Weekes.

Trinity Broadcasting Network: Plateau Castries; tel. 450-5979.

Television

Cablevision: George Gordon Bldg, Bridge St, POB 111, Castries; tel. 452-3301; fax 453-2544.

Catholic TV Broadcasting Service: Micoud St, Castries; tel. 452-7050.

Daher Broadcasting Service Ltd: Vigie, POB 1623, Castries; tel. 453-2705; fax 452-3544; Man. Dir Linda Daher.

Helen Television System (HTS): National Television Service of St Lucia, POB 621, The Morne, Castries; tel. 452-2693; fax 454-1737; e-mail hts@candw.lc; internet www.htsstlucia.com; f. 1967; commercial station; Man. Dir Linford Fevriere; Prog. Dir Valerie Albert.

National Television Network (NTN): Castries; f. 2001; operated by the Government Information Service; provides information on the operations of the public sector.

Finance

(cap. = capital; m. = million; br. = branch)

BANKING

The Eastern Caribbean Central Bank (see p. 343), based in Saint Christopher, is the central issuing and monetary authority for Saint Lucia.

Local Banks

Caribbean Banking Corporation Ltd: Gobblewoods Mall, POB 1531, Castries; tel. 451-7469; fax 451-1668; f. 1985; owned by Royal Bank of Trinidad and Tobago Ltd; Chair. Peter July; 4 brs.

East Caribbean Financial Holding Co Ltd: 5th Floor, Financial Centre, Bridge St, POB 1860, Castries; tel. 456-6000; fax 456-6702; e-mail ecfh@candw.lc; f. 1981; fmrly National Commercial Bank of St Lucia Ltd; dep. EC $480.6m., total assets EC $556.4m. (Dec. 2000); 40% state-owned; Chair. Victor A. Eudoxie; Man. Dir Marius St Rose; 7 brs.

Saint Lucia Co-operative Bank Ltd: 21 Bridge St, POB 168, Castries; tel. 452-2880; fax 453-1630; e-mail coopbank@candw.lc; internet www.coopbank.com; incorporated 1937; commercial bank; share cap. EC $4.2m., total assets EC $154.4m. (Dec. 1999); Pres. Ferrel Charles; Man. Dir C. Carlton Glasgow; 3 brs.

Development Bank

Saint Lucia Development Bank: Financial Centre, 1 Bridge St, POB 368, Castries; tel. 457-7532; fax 457-7299; f. 1981; merged with former Agricultural and Industrial Development Bank; provides credit for agriculture, industry, tourism, housing and workforce training; Man. Dir Daniel Girard.

Foreign Banks

Bank of Nova Scotia Ltd (Canada): 6 William Peter Blvd, POB 301, Castries; tel. 456-2100; fax 456-2130; e-mail bns@candw.lc; Man. S. Cozier; 3 brs.

FirstCaribbean International Bank Ltd: Castries; internet www.firstcaribbeaninternational.com; f. 2002 following merger of Caribbean operations of Barclays Bank PLC and CIBC; Exec. Chair. Michael Mansoor; CEO Charles Pink.

Royal Bank of Canada: Laborie St and William Peter Blvd, POB 280, Castries; tel. 452-2245; fax 452-7855; Man. John Miller.

'Offshore' Bank

Bank Crozier International Ltd: Crozier Bldg, Brazil St, Castries; e-mail p.johansson@bankcrozier.com; internet www.bankcrozier.com; f. 2001; CEO Peter Johansson.

STOCK EXCHANGE

Eastern Caribbean Securities Exchange: based in Basseterre, Saint Christopher and Nevis; e-mail info@ecseonline.com; internet www.ecseonline.com; f. 2001; regional securities market designed to facilitate the buying and selling of financial products for the eight member territories—Anguilla, Antigua and Barbuda, Dominica, Grenada, Montserrat, Saint Christopher and Nevis, Saint Lucia and Saint Vincent and the Grenadines; Gen. Man. Baljit Vohra.

INSURANCE

Local companies include the following:

Caribbean General Insurance Ltd: Laborie St, POB 290, Castries; tel. 452-2410; fax 452-3649.

Eastern Caribbean Insurance Ltd: Laborie St, POB 290, Castries; tel. 452-2410; fax 452-3649; e-mail gci.ltd@candw.lc.

Saint Lucia Insurances Ltd: 48 Micoud St, POB 1084, Castries; tel. 452-3240; fax 452-2240.

Saint Lucia Motor and General Insurance Co Ltd: 38 Micoud St, POB 767, Castries; tel. 452-3323; fax 452-6072.

Trade and Industry

DEVELOPMENT ORGANIZATION

National Development Corporation (NDC): Block B, 1st Floor, Govt Bldgs, The Waterfront, POB 495, Castries; tel. 452-3614; fax 452-1841; e-mail devcorp@candw.lc; internet www.stluciandc.com; f. 1971 to promote the economic development of Saint Lucia; owns and manages four industrial estates; br. in New York, USA; Chair. Matthew Beaubrun; Gen. Man. Jacqueline Emmanuel-Albertinie.

CHAMBER OF COMMERCE

Saint Lucia Chamber of Commerce, Industry and Agriculture: Vide Bouteille, POB 482, Castries; tel. 452-3165; fax 453-6907; e-mail chamber@candw.lc; internet www.sluchamber.com.lc; f. 1884; 150 mems; Pres. Guy Mayers.

INDUSTRIAL AND TRADE ASSOCIATIONS

Saint Lucia Banana Corporation (SLBC): Castries; f. 1998 following privatization of Saint Lucia Banana Growers' Asscn (f. 1967); Chair. Eustace Monrose; Sec. Freemont Lawrence.

Saint Lucia Industrial and Small Business Association: 2nd Floor, Ivy Crick Memorial Bldg, POB 312, Castries; tel. 453-1392; Pres. Leo Clarke; Exec. Dir Dr Urban Seraphine.

EMPLOYERS' ASSOCIATIONS

Saint Lucia Agriculturists' Association Ltd: Mongiraud St, POB 153, Castries; tel. 452-2494; Chair. and Man. Dir C. Alcindor; Sec. R. Raveneau.

Saint Lucia Coconut Growers' Association Ltd: Manoel St, POB 259, Castries; tel. 452-2360; fax 453-1499; Chair. Johannes Leonce; Man. N. E. Edmunds.

Saint Lucia Employers' Federation: Morgan's Bldg, Maurice Mason Ave, POB 160, Castries; tel. 452-2190; fax 452-7335.

Saint Lucia Fish Marketing Corpn: Castries; tel. 452-1341; fax 451-7073.

Saint Lucia Marketing Board: Conway, POB 441, Castries; tel. 452-3214; fax 453-1424; Chair. David Demaque; Man. Michael Williams.

Windward Islands Banana Development and Exporting Co (Wibdeco): POB 115, Castries; tel. 452-2651; f. 1994; in succession to the Windward Islands Banana Growers' Association (WINBAN); regional organization dealing with banana development and marketing; jointly owned by the Windward governments and island banana associations; Chair. V. Charles.

UTILITIES

Electricity

Caribbean Electric Utility Services Corpn (CARILEC): 16–19 Orange Park Centre, POB 2056, Bois D'Orange, Gros Islet; tel. 452-0140; fax 452-0142; e-mail admin@carilec.org; internet www.carilec.org.

St Lucia Electricity Services Ltd (LUCELEC): Lucelec Bldg, John Compton Highway, POB 230, Castries; tel. 452-2324; fax 452-1127; e-mail lucelec@candw.lc; internet www.lucelec.com; f. 1964; Chair. Marius St Rose; Man. Dir B. C. Theobalds.

Water

Water and Sewerage Co Inc: L'Anse Rd, POB 1481, Castries; tel. 452-5344; fax 452-6844; e-mail wasco@candw.lc; f. 1999; Chair. Gordon Charles; Man. Dir John C. Joseph.

TRADE UNIONS

Farmers' and Farm Workers' Union: St Louis St, Castries; Pres. Senator FRANCES MICHEL; Sec. CATHERINE BURT; 3,500 mems.

National Workers' Union: POB 713, Castries; tel. 452-3664; represents daily-paid workers; affiliated to World Federation of Trade Unions; Pres. TYRONE MAYNARD; Gen. Sec. GEORGE GODDARD; 3,000 mems (1996).

Saint Lucia Civil Service Association: POB 244, Castries; tel. 452-3903; fax 453-6061; e-mail csa@candw.lc; f. 1951; Pres. DWIGHT LAY; Gen. Sec. LAWRENCE POYOTTE; 1,950 mems.

Saint Lucia Media Workers' Association: Castries; provides training for media workers in partnership with the Government.

Saint Lucia Nurses' Association: POB 819, Castries; tel. 452-1403; fax 453-0960; f. 1947; Pres. LILIA HARRACKSINGH; Gen. Sec. ESTHER FELIX.

Saint Lucia Seamen, Waterfront and General Workers' Trade Union: 24 Chaussee Rd, POB 166, Castries; tel. 452-1669; fax 452-5452; f. 1945; affiliated to International Confederation of Free Trade Unions (ICFTU), International Transport Federation (ITF) and Caribbean Congress of Labour; Pres. MICHAEL HIPPOLYTE; Sec. CRESCENTIA PHILLIPS; 1,000 mems.

Saint Lucia Teachers' Union: POB 821, Castries; tel. 452-4469; fax 453-6668; e-mail sltu@candw.lc; internet www.findsltu.org; f. 1934; Pres. URBAN DOLOR; Gen.-Sec. KENTRY D. J. PIERRE.

Saint Lucia Workers' Union: Reclamation Grounds, Conway, Castries; tel. 452-2620; f. 1939; affiliated to ICFTU; Pres. GEORGE LOUIS; Sec. TITUS FRANCIS; 1,000 mems.

Vieux Fort General and Dock Workers' Union: New Dock Rd, POB 224, Vieux Fort; tel. 454-6193; fax 454-5128; f. 1954; Pres. JOSEPH GRIFFITH; 846 mems (1996).

Transport

RAILWAYS
There are no railways in Saint Lucia.

ROADS
In 2000 there was an estimated total road network of 910 km, of which 150 km were main road and 127 km were secondary roads. In that year only 5.2% of roads were paved. The main highway passes through every town and village on the island. A construction project of a coastal highway, to link Castries with Cul de Sac Bay, was completed in February 2000. Internal transport is handled by private concerns and controlled by Government. A major five-year road maintenance programme was due to commence in 2000 to rehabilitate the estimated 60% of roads which were on the point of collapse. The programme was to be partially funded by the Caribbean Development Bank. In May 2002 it was announced that Agence Française de Développement will provide US $18.5m. to repair 20 km of tertiary and agricultural roads.

SHIPPING
The ports at Castries and Vieux Fort have been fully mechanized. Castries has six berths with a total length of 2,470 ft (753 metres). The two dolphin berths at the Pointe Seraphine cruise-ship terminal have been upgraded to a solid berth of 1000 ft (305 metres) and one of 850 ft (259 metres). A project to upgrade the port at Vieux Fort to a full deep-water container port was completed in 1993. The port of Soufrière has a deep-water anchorage, but no alongside berth for ocean-going vessels. There is a petroleum transhipment terminal at Cul de Sac Bay. In 2002 an estimated 424,500 cruise-ship passengers called at Saint Lucia. Regular services are provided by a number of shipping lines, including ferry services to neighbouring islands.

Saint Lucia Air and Sea Ports Authority: Manoel St, POB 651, Castries; tel. 452-2893; fax 452-2062; e-mail slaspa@candw.lc; Chair. BERNARD LA CORBINIÈRE; Gen. Man. VINCENT HIPPOLYTE.

St Lucia Marine Terminals Ltd: POB 355, Vieux Fort; tel. 454-8742; fax 454-8745; e-mail slumarterm@candw.lc; f. 1995; private port management co.

CIVIL AVIATION
There are two airports in use: Hewanorra International (formerly Beane Field near Vieux Fort), 64 km (40 miles) from Castries, which is equipped to handle large jet aircraft; and George F. L. Charles Airport, which is at Vigie, in Castries, and which is capable of handling medium-range jets. Saint Lucia is served by scheduled flights to the USA, Canada, Europe and most destinations in the Caribbean. The country is a shareholder in the regional airline LIAT (see chapter on Antigua and Barbuda). A US $1.7m. flood-protection project for Hewanorra International, part of the wider Emergency Recovery and Disaster Project, which is funded by the Government and the World Bank, was due to commence in 2002.

Saint Lucia Air and Sea Ports Authority: see Shipping.

Air Antilles: Laborie St, POB 1065, Castries; f. 1985; designated as national carrier of Grenada in 1987; flights to destinations in the Caribbean, the United Kingdom and North America; charter co.

Caribbean Air Transport: POB 253, Castries; f. 1975 as Saint Lucia Airways; local shuttle service, charter flights.

Eagle Air Services Ltd: Vigie Airport, POB 838, Castries; tel. 452-1900; fax 452-9683; e-mail eagleairslu@candw.lc; internet www.eagleairslu.com; charter flights; Man. Dir Capt. EWART F. HINKSON.

Helenair Corpn Ltd: POB 253, Castries; tel. 452-1958; fax 451-7360; e-mail helenair@candw.lc; internet www.stluciatravel.com.lc/helenair.htm; f. 1987; charter and scheduled flights to major Caribbean destinations; Man. ARTHUR NEPTUNE.

Tourism

Saint Lucia possesses spectacular mountain scenery, a tropical climate and sandy beaches. Historical sites, rich birdlife and the sulphur baths at Soufrière are other attractions. Tourist arrivals totalled 648,800 in 2002. Estimated tourist receipts in 2001 were an estimated EC $695.9m. The USA is the principal market (31.5% of total stop-over visitors in 1999, according to preliminary figures), followed by the United Kingdom and Canada. There were an estimated 3,760 hotel rooms in 1997, although expansion of hotel capacity remains a government priority, and it was hoped that 5,000 rooms would be available by the early 21st century.

Saint Lucia Tourist Board: Top Floor, Sureline Bldg, Vide Bouteille, POB 221, Castries; tel. 454-5968; fax 453-1121; e-mail slutour@candw.lc; internet www.stlucia.org; 2 brs overseas; Chair. DESMOND SKEETE; Dir HILARY MODESTE.

Saint Lucia Hotel and Tourism Association (SLHTA): POB 545, Castries; tel. 452-5978; fax 452-7967; e-mail slhta@candw.lc; internet www.stluciatravel.com.lc; f. 1962; Pres. BERTHIA PARLE; Exec. Vice-Pres. HILARY MODESTE.

SAINT VINCENT AND THE GRENADINES

Introductory Survey

Location, Climate, Language, Religion, Flag, Capital

Saint Vincent and the Grenadines is situated in the Windward Islands group, approximately 160 km (100 miles) west of Barbados, in the West Indies. The nearest neighbouring countries are Saint Lucia, some 34 km (21 miles) to the north-east, and Grenada, to the south. As well as the main volcanic island of Saint Vincent, the state includes the 32 smaller islands and cayes known as the Saint Vincent Grenadines, the northerly part of an island chain stretching between Saint Vincent and Grenada. The principal islands in that part of the group are Bequia, Canouan, Mustique, Mayreau, Isle D'Quatre and Union Island. The climate is tropical, with average temperatures of between 18°C and 32°C (64°F–90°F). Annual rainfall ranges from 1,500 mm (60 ins) in the extreme south, to 3,750 mm (150 ins) in the mountainous interior of the main island. English is the official language. Most of the inhabitants profess Christianity and are adherents of the Anglican, Methodist or Roman Catholic Churches. The national flag (proportions 2 by 3) has three unequal vertical stripes, of blue (at the hoist), yellow and green (at the fly), with three lozenges in green, in a 'V' formation, superimposed on the broad central yellow stripe. The capital is Kingstown, on the island of Saint Vincent.

Recent History

The islands were first settled by an Arawak people, who were subsequently conquered by the Caribs. The arrival of shipwrecked and escaped African slaves resulted in the increase of a so-called 'Black Carib' population, some of whose descendants still remain. Under the collective name of Saint Vincent, and despite the opposition of the French and the indigenous population, the islands finally became a British possession during the 18th century. With other nearby British territories, the Governor of the Windward Islands administered Saint Vincent, under a federal system, until December 1959. The first elections under universal adult suffrage took place in 1951. The islands participated in the West Indies Federation from its foundation in January 1958 until its dissolution in May 1962. From January 1960, St Vincent, in common with the other Windward Islands, had a new Constitution, with its own Administrator and an enlarged Legislative Council.

After the failure of negotiations to form a smaller East Caribbean Federation, most of the British colonies in the Leeward and Windward Islands became Associated States, with full internal self-government, in 1967. This change of status was delayed in St Vincent because of local political differences. At controversial elections to the Legislative Council in 1966, the ruling People's Political Party (PPP) was returned with a majority of only one seat. Further elections took place in May 1967, when the Saint Vincent Labour Party (SVLP) secured six of the nine seats in the Council. Milton Cato, leader of the SVLP, became Chief Minister, in succession to Ebenezer Joshua of the PPP. On 27 October 1969, despite objections from the PPP, Saint Vincent became an Associated State, with the United Kingdom retaining responsibility for defence and foreign relations only. The Legislative Council was renamed the House of Assembly, the Administrator was designated Governor, and the Chief Minister became Premier.

Elections were held in April 1972 for an enlarged, 13-seat House of Assembly. The PPP and the SVLP each obtained six seats, while James Mitchell, formerly a minister in the SVLP Government and standing as an independent, secured the remaining one. The PPP agreed to form a Government with Mitchell as Premier and Joshua as Deputy Premier and Minister of Finance. In September 1974 Joshua resigned after policy disagreements with the Premier. A motion expressing 'no confidence' in Mitchell's Government was approved, and the House was dissolved. In the ensuing elections, which took place in December, the PPP and SVLP campaigned in a 'unity agreement'. The SVLP secured 10 of the 13 seats, and the PPP two.

(Mitchell was again elected as an independent.) Cato became Premier again, at the head of a coalition with the PPP, and committed his Government to attaining full independence from the United Kingdom.

After a constitutional conference in September 1978, the colony became fully independent, within the Commonwealth, as Saint Vincent and the Grenadines, on 27 October 1979. The Governor became Governor-General, while Cato took office as the country's first Prime Minister.

Cato's position was reinforced in the general election of December 1979, when the SVLP obtained 11 of the 13 elective seats in the 19-member House of Assembly. In 1982 the leader of the opposition United People's Movement (UPM), Dr Ralph Gonsalves, resigned, accusing the UPM of harbouring Marxist tendencies, and founded a new party, the Movement for National Unity (MNU). In June 1984 Cato announced an early general election, hoping to take advantage of divisions within the opposition. However, the repercussions of scandals surrounding the Cato Government, and the economic and taxation policies of the SVLP, contributed to an unexpected victory for the centrist New Democratic Party (NDP) at the election in July. The NDP (formed in 1975 by James Mitchell) won nine of the 13 elective seats in the House of Assembly, and Mitchell became Prime Minister. Cato subsequently retired from politics, and, in the ensuing by-election, the NDP gained another seat. Hudson Tannis replaced Cato as leader of the SVLP in January 1985; Vincent Beache succeeded him as party leader in August 1986.

At a general election conducted in May 1989 the NDP obtained more than 66% of the valid votes cast, and won all 15 elective seats in the newly-enlarged House of Assembly. Mitchell remained as Prime Minister and formed a new Cabinet.

The NDP secured its third consecutive term of office at a general election in February 1994, obtaining 12 seats in the House of Assembly. An electoral alliance formed by the SVLP and the MNU and headed by Vincent Beache won the three remaining elective seats. Beache was confirmed as the official Leader of the Opposition, and in September 1994 the MNU and the SVLP announced their formal merger as the Unity Labour Party (ULP).

Opposition charges that the Government had failed to address problems presented by a marked decline in banana production, a crisis in the health and education sectors and persistent allegations that drugs-related activities were being conducted on the islands culminated in the defeat, by 10 votes to three, of a motion of 'no confidence' in the Government, brought by the opposition in August 1994. The execution, by hanging, of three convicted murderers in February 1995 provoked outrage from international human rights organizations, who expressed concern at the alacrity and secrecy with which the sentences had been implemented.

At the end of September 1995 Parnell R. Campbell, who had occupied a number of cabinet positions including Deputy Prime Minister, Attorney-General and Minister of Justice, resigned, following allegations of financial impropriety. Carlyle Dougan was appointed to the posts of Attorney-General and Minister of Justice but no new appointment was made to the deputy premiership. Campbell's former responsibilities for Information and for Ecclesiastical Affairs were allocated to the Foreign Affairs and Tourism and to the Education, Culture and Women's Affairs portfolios, respectively. Campbell, who had survived a parliamentary motion of 'no confidence' brought against him by the ULP in August, strenuously denied any wrongdoing.

A minor financial scandal in mid-1996, in which the National Commercial Bank accepted and cleared a fraudulent cheque deposit of more than US $400,000, presented by Bienvenido Bencosome, a national of the Dominican Republic, resulted in the resignation of Dougan as Attorney-General and Minister of Justice, following revelations that $30,000 of $372,950 in local payments subsequently made by Bencosome were paid to

Dougan and his wife, as part of a land-purchase agreement. Carl Joseph replaced Dougan in the Government in August. In late August 1997, the House of Assembly endorsed legislation prescribing a maximum prison sentence of 20 years and fines of as much as EC \$0.5m. for persons convicted of money-laundering and organized fraud.

In May 1998, to the surprise of many observers, Mitchell called a general election for June 1998, almost a year before one was due. Mitchell reportedly hoped to take advantage of perceived divisions in the leadership of the opposition ULP to strengthen the position of the NDP in the House of Assembly. However, at the general election of 15 June the NDP lost four seats, retaining eight, while the ULP obtained the remaining seven. The reverse sustained by the NDP was attributed to voter dissatisfaction with the state of the economy. Although the ULP had actually obtained around 54.6% of the vote, Mitchell claimed that the result was a mandate for his Government to undertake a record fourth term of office. The ULP leader, Vincent Beache, called on the NDP to hold fresh elections within nine months, and not to govern on the basis of a minority vote. The ULP also claimed to have obtained evidence of irregularities during the elections, particularly in the four seats won by the NDP with margins of between 27 and 109 votes. The ULP alleged that the margins of victory in all four cases were less than the number of votes lost by fraud, intimidation and corruption. A number of affidavits were obtained by the ULP, and a formal petition of electoral fraud was to be instigated after the completion of inquiries. Mitchell rejected the ULP accusations, accusing his opponents of attempting to disguise the shortcomings of their campaign.

A new Cabinet was sworn in on 18 June 1998, which included two ministers who had been defeated at the elections. On 9 July, at the opening of the first session of the House of Assembly, several hundred protesters demonstrated against the new Government. Two ministers, Arnhim Eustace, the Minister of Finance and Public Services, and Monty Roberts, the Minister of Housing, Youth, Sports, Local Government and Community Development, were attacked as they tried to drive through the crowd. The ULP refused to acknowledge the appointment of an NDP member, Nolwyn McDowall, as Speaker, as McDowall had been an unsuccessful candidate at the general election.

In September 1998 Mitchell invited the ULP for talks on a proposed commission to reform the Constitution. The principal focus of discussion was to be electoral reform. In January 1999 Mitchell suggested that Saint Vincent and the Grenadines might adopt an electoral system based on a combination of first-past-the-post and proportional representation. He further advocated the introduction of a presidential system, with the president to be directly elected by a simple majority.

In mid-November 1998 members of the public and of the opposition demonstrated outside government offices to call for the resignation of Mitchell and Arnhim Eustace, the Minister of Finance and Public Services. The protests followed the announcement of the details of an agreement reached by the Government of Saint Vincent and the Grenadines with the Italian Government and a consortium of European financial institutions on the repayment of US \$67m., incurred because the Government had guaranteed a loan of \$50m. made to a company of Italian developers that subsequently went into liquidation. The loan had been made to finance the failed Ottley Hall marina and shipyard project, valued at only \$5m. The new agreement stipulated that the shipyard should be sold and that repayments of \$32m. of debt should begin immediately, with the remaining \$30m. to be set aside.

In December 1998 Dr Ralph Gonsalves, the deputy leader of the ULP, was elected leader at the ULP party congress, following the resignation of Vincent Beache, who was to remain leader of the opposition in the House of Assembly. Ken Boyea was elected deputy party leader.

In late November 1998 marijuana growers demonstrated outside the Prime Minister's office against plans to use regional and US troops to destroy the marijuana crop in the highlands of Saint Vincent. Mitchell refused to meet representatives of the protesters, telling them to take advantage of government schemes to promote economic diversification. In December US marines and troops provided by the Regional Security System destroyed crops during a two-week operation, despite opposition from growers. Mitchell subsequently warned the USA that, if Saint Vincent's banana producers were bankrupted by the US initiative to challenge the preferential treatment accorded by the European Union (EU, see p. 199) to banana exports from

Caribbean and African states, it was likely that producers would turn instead to the cultivation of marijuana. In March 1999 Saint Vincent and the Grenadines was one of a number of Caribbean states to warn that, if the USA continued to threaten their economic stability by pursuing its case against the EU banana import regime at the World Trade Organization (see p. 323), they would withdraw co-operation with US-sponsored anti-drugs initiatives. (See the Recent History of Saint Lucia for further details of the trade dispute over bananas between the USA and the EU.) In December, however, a large-scale marijuana eradication exercise took place in Saint Vincent with backing from US marines.

In December 1999 a committee chaired by Dwight Venner, the Governor of the Eastern Caribbean Central Bank, recommended that members of the House of Assembly should receive increased salaries. The committee, however, suggested that the increases should not be awarded until legislation on political integrity had been implemented, and reforms of the public sector had been effected. The proposed increases were opposed by the ULP, which in late January 2000 threatened to introduce a motion of 'no confidence' in the Government, accusing it of corruption, excessive expenditure on development projects, a failure to reduce crime levels and of neglecting education. The Government's subsequent introduction in April of legislation increasing the salaries and benefits of members of the House of Assembly provoked protests throughout the islands, which were directed by the ULP and by public-sector trade unions, who accused the Government of 'disregard and contempt' for ordinary workers. Members of the Saint Vincent Union of Teachers undertook industrial action in protest at the Government's behaviour and to demand wage increases, while the protesters, who were grouped under an 'umbrella' Organization in Defence of Democracy (ODD), demanded the resignation of the Government and fresh elections. Despite appeals for dialogue from the Government, employers' associations and the Chamber of Industry and Commerce, the ODD undertook several days of public demonstrations at the end of April, culminating in a mass rally in Kingstown, addressed by Dr Ralph Gonsalves of the ULP and by leaders of public-sector trade unions. Mediation between the Government and the ODD, undertaken by the Chamber of Industry and Commerce, failed to reach an agreement, while concessions offered to the protesters by Mitchell were denounced by the ULP as unconstitutional and as exceeding his authority. In early May, however, the Government and the ODD reached an agreement, known as the Grand Beach accord, whereby fresh legislative elections were to be called before March 2001; the accord also allowed for a national dialogue on constitutional reform.

In August 2000 Mitchell relinquished the post of NDP President in favour of the Minister of Finance and Public Services, Arnhim Eustace, who defeated Jeremiah Scott, the Minister of Agriculture and Labour, in a leadership election. On 27 October Eustace also succeeded Mitchell as Prime Minister, following the latter's retirement as Head of Government. Mitchell stayed on in the Cabinet as Senior Minister.

Parliament was dissolved on 5 March 2001 in preparation for the general election that was scheduled to be held on 28 March. Prime Minister Eustace and ULP leader Gonsalves called for a peaceful campaign after a ULP supporter was shot and wounded by an NDP supporter. However, in mid-March the ULP accused the NDP of trying to create a situation in which a national emergency could be declared, so that the elections could be postponed. At the election the ULP secured an overwhelming victory, winning 12 of the 15 parliamentary seats and 57% of the votes cast. The NDP, which had been in power since 1984, secured 40.9% of the votes cast and the remaining three House of Assembly seats. Eustace only narrowly avoided losing his own seat. The People's Progressive Movement (formed in 2000 by two former ULP members) secured only 2.1% of the ballot and failed to win any seats. Voter turn-out was 68.7%. The new Government took office in mid-April, led by Gonsalves. The new Prime Minister stated that his Government's priorities would be job creation, education and health.

In June 2001 Gonsalves announced his attention to establish a commission to review the Constitution. Among the issues to be addressed were local government organization and finance, civil service reform and the electoral system. In November opposition politicians accused the Government of failing to prevent the escape from the country of Thierry Nano, a French-Vincentian banker, after the USA issued a warrant for his arrest on money-laundering charges. In February 2002 Eustace criticized the

Government's decision to take control of the two banks owned by Nano, instead of liquidating them.

In June 2002 the Governor-General, Sir Charles Antrobus, died. Sir Frederick Ballantyne was appointed as his successor in September.

Saint Vincent and the Grenadines is a member of the Caribbean Community and Common Market (CARICOM, see p. 155), of the Organisation of Eastern Caribbean States (OECS, see p. 341), and is a signatory of the Cotonou Agreement (see p. 234), the successor agreement to the Lomé Convention. During the late 1980s Mitchell's Government was one of the principal advocates of East Caribbean unity, claiming that only a unitary state could develop a strong and indigenous economy for the island countries of the region. Moreover, the country played a major role in the decision, in 1988, by the Prime Ministers of the four English-speaking Windward Islands countries (Saint Vincent and the Grenadines, Dominica, Grenada and Saint Lucia) to proceed with plans towards a more limited union, following the reluctance of other OECS members to pursue such a project. In 1990 the leaders of the four countries accordingly created a new body, the Regional Constituent Assembly. The Assembly issued its final report in 1992, in which it stated that the four countries were committed to the establishment of economic and political union under a federal system. In September 2001 Gonsalves appointed Joseph Bonadie, an NDP senator, as his advisor on issues related to further OECS integration and in February 2003 proposed that a union of Caribbean states should take the form of a confederal political arrangement similiar to that of the EU. In February 2002 the OECS countries agreed to allow nationals of member states to travel freely within the OECS area and to remain in a foreign territory within the area for up to six months. It was also planned to introduce a common OECS passport by 2003.

In November 2001 Saint Vincent and the Grenadines signed an agreement with Venezuela which would enable it to purchase Venezuelan petroleum at preferential rates. In 1992 the islands established diplomatic relations with Cuba. The two countries signed accords pledging further co-operation in a number of areas, including health and education, in September 2001 and November 2002. Diplomatic relations are maintained with the Republic of China (Taiwan).

In 2001 Libya granted the islands, in common with other eastern Caribbean countries, access to a US $2,000m. development fund. It was also reported in September that Libya had agreed to provide Saint Vincent and the Grenadines with a grant of US $4.5m. (including an immediate disbursement of $1.5m), following Gonsalves' controversial visit to the Libyan capital, Tripoli, earlier in the month.

In February 2003 Saint Vincent and the Grenadines was admitted to the 114-member Non-Aligned Movement.

Government

Saint Vincent and the Grenadines is a constitutional monarchy. Executive power is vested in the British monarch, as Head of State, and is exercisable by the Governor-General, who represents the British monarch locally and who is appointed on the advice of the Prime Minister. Legislative power is vested in Parliament, comprising the Governor-General and the House of Assembly (composed of 21 members: six nominated Senators and 15 Representatives, elected for up to five years by universal adult suffrage). Senators are appointed by the Governor-General: four on the advice of the Prime Minister and two on the advice of the Leader of the Opposition. Government is effectively by the Cabinet. The Governor-General appoints the Prime Minister and, on the latter's recommendation, selects the other Ministers. The Prime Minister must be able to command the support of the majority of the House, to which the Cabinet is responsible.

Defence

Saint Vincent and the Grenadines participates in the US-sponsored Regional Security System, comprising police, coastguards and army units, which was established by independent East Caribbean states in 1982. Since 1984, however, the paramilitary Special Service Unit has had strictly limited deployment. Government current expenditure on public order and safety was estimated at EC $20.8m. (10.2% of total current expenditure) in 1998.

Economic Affairs

In 2001, according to estimates by the World Bank, Saint Vincent and the Grenadines' gross national income (GNI), meas-

ured at average 1999–2001 prices, was US $312m., equivalent to $2,690 per head (or $5,250 per head on an international purchasing-power parity basis). During 1990–2001, it was estimated, the population increased by an annual average rate of 0.7%, while gross domestic product (GDP) per head increased, in real terms, by an average of 2.1% per year. Overall GDP increased, in real terms, by an average annual rate of 2.9% in 1990–2001; according to the IMF, real GDP increased by 0.2% in 2001.

Agriculture (including forestry and fishing) contributed an estimated 9.9% of GDP in 2002. The sector employed 25.1% of the working population at the census of 1991, and agricultural products account for the largest share of export revenue, although Vincentian crops were badly affected by mealybug infestation, which led to the suspension of some exports from 1996 to March 1999. The principal cash crop is bananas, which contributed an estimated 30.6% of the value of total domestic exports in 2002. Other important crops are arrowroot, sweet potatoes, tannias, taro, plantains and coconuts. According to Eastern Caribbean Central Bank (ECCB, see p. 343) data, during 1994–2000 agricultural GDP (growth of which is heavily reliant on weather conditions and banana production) increased by an annual average of 4.3%. A decline of 7.2% was recorded in 2001, followed by an estimated increase of 2.9% in 2002.

Industry (including mining, manufacturing, electricity, water and construction) employed 21.1% of the working population in 1991, and contributed an estimated 23.5% of GDP in 2002. During 1994–2000 industrial GDP increased by an annual average of 1.2%. however, real industrial GDP decreased by 0.1% in 1999 and by a further 7.1% in 2000.

The manufacturing sector contributed an estimated 4.9% of GDP in 2002, and engaged 8.5% of the employed labour force in 1991. Apart from a garment industry and the assembling of electrical components, the most important activities involve the processing of agricultural products, including flour- and rice-milling, brewing, rum distillation, and processing dairy products. During 1994–2000 real manufacturing GDP decreased by an annual average of 2.9%. Real manufacturing GDP decreased by 1.8% in 2001 and by an estimated 8.0% in 2002.

Energy is derived principally from the use of hydrocarbon fuels (mineral fuels and lubricants accounted for an estimated 9.5% of total imports in 2002). The islands imported most of their energy requirements. There is, however, an important hydroelectric plant in Cumberland.

The services sector contributed an estimated 66.6% of GDP in 2002 and engaged 53.8% of the employed population at the time of the 1991 census. Tourism is the most important activity within the sector, but is smaller in scale than in most other Caribbean islands; tourist receipts were equivalent to some 21.8% of GDP in 2002. Tourist activity remains concentrated in the Grenadines and caters for the luxury market. Visitors aboard yachts have traditionally been the most important sector, although the numbers of stop-over and cruise-ship visitors have increased in recent years. In 2000 the total number of visitors increased by 14.7%; however, in 2001 visitor arrivals declined by 0.8%, partly as a result of repercussions of the terrorist attacks on the USA in September of that year. In response to the downturn, the Hotel and Tourism Association announced, in October, that room rates would be reduced by 33%. None the less, the estimated number of visitor arrivals decreased by a further 3.3% in 2002. Aside from tourism, a small 'offshore' financial sector also contributes to the services sector. During 1994–2000 the real GDP of the services sector as a whole increased by an annual average of 5.4%; growth was 7.9% in 1999 and 4.9% in 2000.

In 2002 Saint Vincent and the Grenadines recorded an estimated visible trade deficit of US $110.3m., while there was a deficit of US $42.5m. on the current account of the balance of payments. The principal source of imports is the USA (accounting for an estimated 38.0% of the total in 2002). Other important suppliers in that year were Trinidad and Tobago (20.9%) and the United Kingdom (8.6%). The United Kingdom is the principal market for exports (accounting for an estimated 40.0% of total exports in 2002). Other important markets in that year were Trinidad and Tobago (10.2%), Saint Lucia (8.8%) and Barbados (8.5%). The principal exports in 2002 were bananas (accounting for an estimated 30.6% of exports), flour (16.1%) and rice (10.7%), while the principal imports were food and live animals (24.0%), machinery and transport equipment (19.1%) and basic manufactures (19.1%).

In 2002 there was an estimated overall budget deficit of EC \$36m., equivalent to 3.7% of GDP. Saint Vincent and the Grenadines' total external debt was US \$192.4m. at the end of 2000, of which US \$161.0m. was long-term public debt. In 2002, according to the IMF, the cost of debt-servicing was equivalent to an estimated 6.6% of the value of exports of goods and services. The average annual rate of inflation was 1.45% in 1995–2002, and consumer prices increased by an estimated average of 0.8% in 2001 and 2002. At the 1991 census 20.0% of the labour force were unemployed. In February 2002 the IMF estimated that the rate of unemployment remained at a similar level.

In May 2000 the Financial Stability Forum categorized Saint Vincent and the Grenadines' banking supervision in the lowest group. In June the Organisation for Economic Co-operation and Development (OECD) included Saint Vincent and the Grenadines in a report on countries with harmful tax policies and in the same month it was also included on a list of 'non-co-operative' governments in the fight against money-laundering, by the Financial Action Task Force (FATF—based at the OECD Secretariat). In July the Offshore Finance Authority revoked the licences of six 'offshore' banks in an immediate response to an advisory by the US Department of the Treasury. The Government also announced that it would take further steps to improve its regulatory and advisory mechanisms and in September 2001 it was announced that the ECCB had agreed to supervise these improvements. Nevertheless, Saint Vincent and the Grenadines was not removed from the OECD's harmful tax policy list until February 2002, at which time it was decided the country had made sufficient commitments to improve the transparency of its tax and regulatory systems. In May 2002 the Government established a Financial Intelligence Unit to counter money-laundering; however, in February 2003 Saint Vincent and the Grenadines remained on an updated FATF blacklist. It was believed that the authorities would first have to establish a track record of successful implementation of its new financial regime before the country would removed from the list.

Saint Vincent and the Grenadines is a member of the ECCB, the Caribbean Community and Common Market (CARICOM, see p. 155), which seeks to encourage regional development, particularly by increasing trade between member states, and of the Organisation of Eastern Caribbean States (OECS, see p. 341). The country is also a member of the regional stock exchange, the Eastern Caribbean Securities Exchange (based in Saint Christopher and Nevis), established in 2001.

Agriculture is the dominant sector of the economy and, although the introduction of other crops has reduced dependence on the vulnerable banana harvest, performance is significantly affected by weather conditions. The erosion of the islands' preferential access to European markets, together with lower prices and poor climatic conditions, contributed to a decline in banana production from 1992 onwards. In addition, exports of bananas declined to just 30.6% of the total value of merchandise exports in 2002 (compared with 52.2% in 1990). In 2002 significant grant aid from the EU was made available for irrigation and technical support, as well as for economic diversification and social support. None the less, the continued decline of the banana industry, and a related increase in unemployment and poverty, appeared inevitable. The prospects for long-term growth remain dependent on economic diversification and a recovery in tourism, while state investment in infrastructure is still dependent to a great extent on development assistance, particularly from the EU. In February 2003 the IMF commended the Government for achieving economic growth in 2001 (0.2%) and 2002 (an estimated 0.6%), improving public-sector savings, strengthening the financial sector, restructuring the banana sector and adopting measures to avoid recession and mitigate further unemployment. However, the Fund emphasized the need for the Government to improve the operations of public enterprises and to bring the fiscal deficit under control. In October 2002 Prime Minister Gonsalves announced that 'Hurricane Lili' had cost the country's economy some EC \$50m, destroying an estimated 45% of the banana crop. The 2002/03 budget, announced in December 2002, allocated extra funds to agriculture in the light of the tropical-storm damage. It was also announced that a medium-term plan to strengthen the agricultural diversification process would be introduced in mid-2003.

Education

Free primary education, beginning at five years of age and lasting for seven years, is available to all children in government schools, although it is not compulsory and attendance is low. There are 60 government, and five private, primary schools. Secondary education, beginning at 12 years of age, comprises a first cycle of five years and a second, two-year cycle. However, government facilities at this level are limited, and much secondary education is provided in schools administered by religious organizations, with government assistance. There are also a number of junior secondary schools. There is a teacher-training college and a technical college. In 1994/95 76% and 24% of children in the relevant age-groups were attending primary and secondary schools, respectively. Current expenditure on education by the central Government was a projected EC \$46.4m. in 1998 (22.7% of total current expenditure).

Public Holidays

2003: 1 January (New Year's Day), 18 April (Good Friday), 21 April (Easter Monday), 5 May (Labour Day/Fisherman's Day), 9 June (Whit Monday), 1 July (Carnival Tuesday), 7 July (CARICOM Day), 4 August (Emancipation Day), 27 October (Independence Day), 25–26 December (Christmas).

2004: 1 January (New Year's Day), 9 April (Good Friday), 12 April (Easter Monday), 3 May (Labour Day/Fisherman's Day), 31 May (Whit Monday), 5 July (CARICOM Day), 6 July (Carnival Tuesday), 2 August (Emancipation Day), 27 October (Independence Day), 25–26 December (Christmas).

Weights and Measures

The imperial system is used.

Statistical Survey

Sources (unless otherwise stated): Statistical Office, Ministry of Finance and Planning, Government Bldgs, Kingstown; tel. 456-1111; e-mail statssvg@vincysurf.com.

AREA, POPULATION AND DENSITY

Area: 389.3 sq km (150.3 sq miles). The island of Saint Vincent covers 344 sq km (133 sq miles).

Population: 97,845 at census of 12 May 1980; 106,499 (males 53,165; females 53,334) at census of 12 May 1991; 109,022 at preliminary census count of May 2001.

Density (May 2001): 280.0 per sq km.

Principal Town: Kingstown (capital), population 13,526 at preliminary census count of May 2001.

Births and Deaths (registrations, 2000): Live births 2,149 (birth rate 19.2 per 1,000); Deaths 698 (death rate 6.2 per 1,000).

Expectation of Life (years at birth): 70.0 (males 67.7; females 72.5) in 2001. Source: WHO, *World Health Report*.

Economically Active Population (persons aged 15 years and over, 1991 census): Agriculture, hunting, forestry and fishing 8,377; Mining and quarrying 98; Manufacturing 2,822; Electricity, gas and water 586; Construction 3,535; Trade, restaurants and hotels 6,544; Transport, storage and communications 2,279; Financing, insurance, real estate and business services 1,418; Community, social and personal services 7,696; Total employed 33,355 (males 21,656; females 11,699); Unemployed 8,327 (males 5,078, females 3,249); Total labour force 41,682 (males 26,734, females 14,948). Source: ILO, *Yearbook of Labour Statistics*.

HEALTH AND WELFARE

Key Indicators

Total Fertility Rate (children per woman, 2001): 1.9.

Under-5 Mortality Rate (per 1,000 live births, 2001): 25.

Physicians (per 1,000 head, 1997): 0.88.

Hospital Beds (per 1,000 head, 1996): 1.85.

Health Expenditure (2000): US $ per head (PPP): 374.

Health Expenditure (2000): % of GDP: 6.3.

Health Expenditure (2000): public (% of total): 65.4.

Access to Water (% of persons, 2000): 93.

Access to Sanitation (% of persons, 2000): 96.

Human Development Index (2000): ranking: 91.

Human Development Index (2000): value: 0.733.

For sources and definitions, see explanatory note on p. vi.

AGRICULTURE, ETC.

Principal Crops (metric tons, 1994): Nutmeg and mace 104; Arrowroot starch 115; Ginger 489; Taro (Dasheen, Eddo) 2,591; Tannias 270.

2001 (FAO estimates, '000 metric tons): Maize 2; Sweet potatoes 2; Yams 1; Other roots and tubers 9; Sugar cane 20; Coconuts 24; Vegetables 4; Bananas 43; Plaintains 2; Oranges 1; Lemons and limes 1; Apples 1; Mangoes 1. Source: FAO.

Livestock (FAO estimates, '000 head, year ending September 2001): Cattle 6; Sheep 13; Goats 6; Pigs 10; Asses 1. Source: FAO.

Livestock Products (FAO estimates, '000 metric tons, 2001): Pig meat 1; Cows' milk 1; Hen eggs 1. Source: FAO.

Fishing (metric tons, live weight, 2000): Total catch 7,294 (Albacore 2,819, Yellowfin tuna 1,994, Bigeye tuna 1,215, Marlins, sailfishes, etc. 343). Source: FAO, *Yearbook of Fishery Statistics*.

INDUSTRY

Selected Products ('000 metric tons, 2000, unless otherwise indicated): Copra 2 (FAO estimate); Raw sugar 2 (FAO estimate); Rum 217,000 proof gallons; Electric energy 47.8 million kWh (IMF estimate, 2001). Source: partly FAO.

FINANCE

Currency and Exchange Rates: 100 cents = 1 Eastern Caribbean dollar (EC $). *Sterling, US Dollar and Euro Equivalents* (31 December 2002): £1 sterling = EC $4.352; US $1 = EC $2.700; €1 = EC $2.831; EC $100 = £22.98 = US $37.04 = €35.32. *Exchange rate:* Fixed at US $1 = EC $2.70 since July 1976.

Budget (estimates, EC $ million, 2002): *Revenue:* Revenue from taxation 252 (Taxes on income 80, Taxes on goods and services 49, Taxes on international trade and transactions 121); Other current revenue 43; Capital revenue 1; Foreign grants 16; Total 312. *Expenditure:* Personal emoluments 146; Other goods and services 59; Interest payments 28; Transfers and subsidies 49; Capital expenditure and net lending 65; Total 348. Source: IMF, *St Vincent and the Grenadines: Statistical Appendix* (February 2003).

International Reserves (US $ million at 31 December 2002): IMF special drawing rights 0.02; Reserve position in IMF 0.68; Foreign exchange 52.49; Total 53.19. Source: IMF, *International Financial Statistics*.

Money Supply (EC $ million at 31 December 2002): Currency outside banks 54.02; Demand deposits 210.214; Total money 264.23. Source: IMF, *International Financial Statistics*.

Cost of Living (Consumer Price Index; base: 1995 = 100): 108.4 in 2000; 109.3 in 2001; 110.2 in 2002. Source: IMF, *International Financial Statistics*.

Gross Domestic Product (EC $ million at current prices): 906.0 in 2000; 941.0 in 2001 (provisional); 973.5 (estimate). Source: IMF, *St Vincent and the Grenadines: Statistical Appendix* (February 2003).

Expenditure on the Gross Domestic Product (estimates, EC $ million at current prices, 2003): Government final consumption expenditure 208; Private final consumption expenditure 583; Gross fixed capital formation 292; *Total domestic expenditure* 1,083; Exports of goods and services 463; *Less* Imports of goods and services 572; *Gross domestic product in purchasers' values* 974. Source: IMF, *St Vincent and the Grenadines: Statistical Appendix* (February 2003).

Gross Domestic Product by Economic Activity (estimates, EC $ million at current prices, 2002): Agriculture, hunting, forestry and fishing 84.6; Mining and quarrying 2.0; Manufacturing 42.3; Electricity and water 58.4; Construction 99.5; Wholesale and retail trade 149.5; Hotels and restaurants 15.8; Transport 103.7; Communications 43.2; Banks and insurance 67.2; Real estate and housing 19.3; Government services 156.6; Other community, social and personal services 16.5; *Sub-total* 858.6; *Less* Imputed bank service charge 55.1; *GDP at factor cost* 803.5; Indirect taxes, *less* subsidies 170.1; *GDP in purchasers' values* 973.5. Source: IMF, *St Vincent and the Grenadines: Statistical Appendix* (February 2003).

Balance of Payments (estimates, US $ million, 2002): Exports of goods f.o.b. 42.2; Imports of goods f.o.b. −152.5; *Trade balance* −110.3; Exports of services 129.5; Imports of services −59.5; *Balance on goods and services* −40.3; Other income received 2.4; Other income paid −20.3; *Balance on goods, services and income* −58.2; Current transfers (net) 15.7; *Current balance* −42.5; Capital account (net) 7.3; Financial account 27.1; Net errors and omissions 0.0; *Overall balance* −8.0. Source: IMF, *St Vincent and the Grenadines: Statistical Appendix* (February 2003).

EXTERNAL TRADE

Principal Commodities (estimates, US $ million, 2002): *Imports:* Food and live animals 43.6; Mineral fuels, lubricants, etc. 17.3; Chemicals and related products 18.2; Basic manufactures 34.7; Machinery and transport equipment 34.8; Total (incl. others) 181.9. *Exports:* Bananas 12.9; Eddoes and dasheens 1.8; Flour 6.8; Rice 4.5; Total domestic exports (incl. others) 40.4; Re-exports 1.8; Total 42.2. Source: IMF, *St Vincent and the Grenadines: Statistical Appendix* (February 2003).

Principal Trading Partners (estimates, US $ million, 2002): *Imports:* Barbados 8.1; Canada 5.3; Germany 1.9; Guyana 4.1; Japan 6.7; Netherlands 2.2; Trinidad and Tobago 38.1; United Kingdom 15.6; USA 69.1; Total (incl. others) 181.9. *Exports:* Antigua and Barbuda 2.8; Barbados 3.6; Dominica 1.5; Jamaica 1.3; Saint Lucia 3.7; Trinidad and Tobago 4.3; United Kingdom 16.9; USA 1.4; Total (incl. others) 42.2. Source: IMF, *St Vincent and the Grenadines: Statistical Appendix* (February 2003).

TRANSPORT

Road Traffic (motor vehicles in use, 1998): Passenger cars 6,602; Commercial vehicles 7,276.

Shipping: *Arrivals* (2000): Vessels 1,007. *International Freight Traffic* ('000 metric tons, 2000): Goods loaded 54; Goods unloaded 156. *Merchant Fleet* (vessels registered at 31 December 2001): Number 1,318; Total displacement 7,072,895 grt (Source: Lloyd's Register-Fairplay, *World Fleet Statistics*).

Civil Aviation (visitor arrivals): 94,030 in 2000; 85,735 in 2001 (preliminary); in 2002 (estimate). Source: IMF, *St Vincent and the Grenadines: Statistical Appendix* (February 2003).

TOURISM

Visitor Arrivals: 256,040 (72,895 stop-over arrivals, 21,135 excursionists, 86,247 cruise-ship passengers, 75,763 visitors aboard yachts) in 2000; 254,091 (70,686 stop-over arrivals, 15,049 excursionists, 76,494 cruise-ship passengers, 91,862 visitors aboard yachts) in 2001 (provisional); 245,767 (77,783 stop-over arrivals, 13,096 excursionists, 70,375 cruise-ship passengers, 84,513 visitors aboard yachts) in 2002 (estimates). Source: IMF, *St Vincent and the Grenadines: Statistical Appendix* (February 2003).

Hotel Rooms: 1,762 in 2001.

Tourist Receipts (EC $ million): 203 in 2000; 216 in 2001 (provisional); 212 in 2002 (estimate). Source: IMF, *St Vincent and the Grenadines: Statistical Appendix* (February 2003).

COMMUNICATIONS MEDIA

Radio Receivers ('000 in use, 2000): 100.

Television Receivers ('000 in use, 2000): 50.

Telephones ('000 main lines in use, 2001): 26.

Facsimile Machines (1996): 1,500.

Mobile Cellular Telephones (subscribers, 2000): 2,475.

Personal Computers ('000 in use, 1999): 11.

Internet Users ('000, 2000): 3.5.

Non-daily Newspapers (2000): Titles 8; Circulation 50,000. Sources: mainly UNESCO, *Statistical Yearbook*; UN, *Statistical Yearbook*; and International Telecommunication Union.

EDUCATION

Pre-primary (1993/94): 97 schools; 175 teachers; 2,500 pupils.

Primary (2000): 60 schools; 987 teachers; 20,530 pupils.

Secondary (2000): 21 schools; 406 teachers; 7,939 pupils.

Teacher Training (2000): 1 institution; 10 teachers; 107 students.

Technical College (2000): 1 institution; 19 teachers; 187 students.

Community College (2000): 1 institution; 13 teachers; 550 students.

Nursing College (2000): 1 institution; 6 teachers; 60 students.

Adult Literacy Rate: 88.9% in 2000 (Source: UN Development Programme, *Human Development Report*).

Directory

The Constitution

The Constitution came into force at the independence of Saint Vincent and the Grenadines on 27 October 1979. The following is a summary of its main provisions

FUNDAMENTAL RIGHTS AND FREEDOMS

Regardless of race, place of origin, political opinion, colour, creed or sex, but subject to respect for the rights and freedoms of others and for the public interest, every person in Saint Vincent and the Grenadines is entitled to the rights of life, liberty, security of the person and the protection of the law. Freedom of conscience, of expression, of assembly and association is guaranteed and the inviolability of a person's home and other property is maintained. Protection is afforded from slavery, forced labour, torture and inhuman treatment.

THE GOVERNOR-GENERAL

The British Monarch is represented in Saint Vincent and the Grenadines by the Governor-General.

PARLIAMENT

Parliament consists of the British monarch, represented by the Governor-General, and the House of Assembly, comprising 15 elected Representatives (increased from 13 under the provisions of an amendment approved in 1986) and six Senators. Senators are appointed by the Governor-General—four on the advice of the Prime Minister and two on the advice of the Leader of the Opposition. The life of Parliament is five years. Each constituency returns one Representative to the House who is directly elected in accordance with the Constitution. The Attorney-General is an *ex-officio* member of the House. Every citizen over the age of 18 is eligible to vote. Parliament may alter any of the provisions of the Constitution.

THE EXECUTIVE

Executive authority is vested in the British monarch and is exercisable by the Governor-General. The Governor-General appoints as Prime Minister that member of the House who, in the Governor-General's view, is the best able to command the support of the majority of the members of the House, and selects other Ministers on the advice of the Prime Minister. The Governor-General may remove the Prime Minister from office if a resolution of no confidence in the Government is passed by the House and the Prime Minister does not either resign within three days or advise the Governor-General to dissolve Parliament.

The Cabinet consists of the Prime Minister and other Ministers and the Attorney-General as an *ex-officio* member. The Leader of the Opposition is appointed by the Governor-General as that member of the House who, in the Governor-General's view, is best able to command the support of a majority of members of the House who do not support the Government.

CITIZENSHIP

All persons born in Saint Vincent and the Grenadines before independence who, immediately prior to independence, were citizens of the United Kingdom and Colonies automatically become citizens of Saint Vincent and the Grenadines. All persons born outside the country after independence to a parent possessing citizenship of Saint Vincent and the Grenadines automatically acquire citizenship, as do those born in the country after independence. Citizenship can be acquired by those to whom it would not automatically be granted.

The Government

Head of State: HM Queen ELIZABETH II.

Governor-General: Sir FREDERICK BALLANTYNE (took office 2 September 2002).

CABINET
(April 2003)

Prime Minister and Minister of Finance, Planning, Economic Development, Labour and Information: Dr RALPH GONSALVES.

Deputy Prime Minister and Minister of Foreign Affairs, Commerce and Trade: LOUIS STRAKER.

Minister of National Security, the Public Service, Seaports and Airports and Air Development: VINCENT BEACHE.

Minister of Education, Youth Affairs and Sports: MIKE BROWN.

Minister of Social Development, the Family, Gender Affairs and Ecclesiastical Affairs: GIRLYN MIGUEL.

Minister of Agriculture, Land and Fisheries: SELMON WALTERS.

Minister of Tourism and Culture: RENÉ BAPTISTE.

Minister of Health and the Environment: Dr DOUGLAS SLATER.

Minister of Telecommunications, Science, Technology and Industry: Dr JERROL THOMPSON.

Minister of Transport, Works and Housing: JULIAN FRANCIS.

Attorney-General: JUDITH JONES-MORGAN.

MINISTRIES

Office of the Governor-General: Government Bldgs, Kingstown; tel. 456-1401.

Office of the Prime Minister: Administrative Centre, Kingstown; tel. 456-1703; fax 457-2152; e-mail pmosvg@caribsurf.com.

Office of the Attorney-General: Government Bldgs, Kingstown; tel. 457-2807.

Ministry of Agriculture, Land and Fisheries: Government Bldgs, Kingstown; tel. 457-1380; fax 457-1688.

Ministry of Commerce and Trade: Government Bldgs, Kingstown; tel. 456-1223; fax 457-2880; e-mail mtrade@caribsurf.com.

Ministry of Education, Youth Affairs and Sports: Government Bldgs, Kingstown; tel. 457-1104; e-mail mined@caribsurf.com.

Ministry of Finance, Planning, Economic Development, Labour and Information: Government Bldgs, Kingstown; tel. 456-1111.

Ministry of Foreign Affairs: Administrative Centre, Kingstown; tel. 456-2060; fax 456-2610; e-mail svgforeign@caribsurf.com.

Ministry of Health and the Environment: Government Bldgs, Kingstown; tel. 457-2586; fax 457-2684.

Ministry of National Security, the Public Service, Seaports and Airports and Air Development: Government Bldgs, Kingstown.

Ministry of Social Development, the Family, Gender Affairs and Ecclesiastical Affairs: Government Bldgs, Kingstown; tel. 426-2949.

Ministry of Telecommunications, Science, Technology and Industry: Government Bldgs, Kingstown; tel. 457-2039.

Ministry of Tourism and Culture: Government Bldgs, Kingstown; tel. 457-1502; fax 451-2425; e-mail tourism@caribsurf.com.

Ministry of Transport, Works and Housing: Government Bldgs, Kingstown.

Legislature

HOUSE OF ASSEMBLY

Senators: 6.

Elected Members: 15.

Election, 28 March 2001

Party	% of votes	Seats
Unity Labour Party (ULP)	57.0	12
New Democratic Party (NDP)	40.9	3
People's Progressive Movement (PPM). . . .	2.1	—
Total	100.0	15

Political Organizations

Canouan Progressive Movement: Kingstown; Leader TERRY BYNOE.

New Democratic Party (NDP): Murray Rd, POB 1300, Kingstown; tel. 457-2647; f. 1975; democratic party supporting political unity in the Caribbean, social development and free enterprise; Pres. ARNHIM EUSTACE; Sec.-Gen. STUART NANTON; 7,000 mems.

People's Progressive Movement (PPM): Kingstown; f. 2000 following split from ULP; Leader KEN BOYEA.

People's Working Party: Kingstown; Leader BURTON WILLIAMS.

Unity Labour Party (ULP): Beachmont, Kingstown; tel. 457-2761; fax 456-2811; e-mail ulpweb@aol.com; internet www.ulp.org; f. 1994 by merger of Movement for National Unity and the Saint Vincent Labour Party; moderate, social-democratic party; Leader Dr RALPH E. GONSALVES.

In 2000 the **Organization in Defence of Democracy** (ODD), an umbrella group of trade unions and non-governmental organizations, was formed to protest against government policy.

Diplomatic Representation

EMBASSIES AND HIGH COMMISSION IN SAINT VINCENT AND THE GRENADINES

China (Taiwan): Murray Rd, POB 878, Kingstown; tel. 456-2431; fax 456-2913; Chargé d'affaires a.i. ROGER LUO.

United Kingdom: Granby St, POB 132, Kingstown; tel. 457-1701; fax 456-2750; High Commissioner resident in Barbados; Resident Acting High Commissioner TERENCE KNIGHT.

Venezuela: Baynes Bros Bldg, Granby St, POB 852, Kingstown; tel. 456-1374; fax 457-1934; e-mail lvccsvg@caribsurf.com; Ambassador TIBISAY URDANETA.

Judicial System

Justice is administered by the Eastern Caribbean Supreme Court, based in Saint Lucia and consisting of a Court of Appeal and a High Court. Two Puisne Judges are resident in Saint Vincent. There are five Magistrates, including the Registrar of the Supreme Court, who acts as an additional Magistrate.

Puisne Judges: ODEL ADAMS, IAN DONALDSON MITCHELL.

Office of the Registrar of the Supreme Court
Registry Dept, Court House, Kingstown; tel. 457-1220; fax 457-1888. Registrar JUDITH S. JONES-MORGAN.

Chief Magistrate: BRIDGET NURSE.

Magistrates: ERROL MOUNSEY, SIMONE CHURUMAN, REGINALD JAMES.

Director of Public Prosecutions: HAYMANT BALROOP.

Religion

CHRISTIANITY

Saint Vincent Christian Council: Melville St, POB 445, Kingstown; tel. 456-1408; f. 1969; four mem. churches; Chair. Mgr RENISON HOWELL.

The Anglican Communion
Anglicans in Saint Vincent and the Grenadines are adherents of the Church in the Province of the West Indies, comprising eight dioceses. The Archbishop of the West Indies is the Bishop of Nassau and the Bahamas, and is resident in Nassau. The diocese of the Windward Islands includes Grenada, Saint Lucia and Saint Vincent and the Grenadines.

Bishop of the Windward Islands: Rt Rev. SEHON GOODRIDGE, Bishop's Court, POB 502, Kingstown; tel. 456-1895; fax 456-2591; e-mail diocesewi@vincysurf.com.

The Roman Catholic Church
Saint Vincent and the Grenadines comprises a single diocese (formed when the diocese of Bridgetown-Kingstown was divided in October 1989), which is suffragan to the archdiocese of Castries (Saint Lucia). The Bishop participates in the Antilles Episcopal Conference, currently based in Port of Spain, Trinidad and Tobago. At 31 December 2001 there were an estimated 10,000 adherents in the diocese, comprising about 9% of the population.

Bishop of Kingstown: Rt Rev. ROBERT RIVAS, Bishop's Office, POB 862, Edinboro, Kingstown; tel. 457-2363; fax 457-1903; e-mail rcdok@caribsurf.com.

Other Christian Churches
The Methodists, Seventh-day Adventists, Baptists and other denominations also have places of worship.

BAHÁ'Í FAITH
National Spiritual Assembly: POB 1043, Kingstown; tel. 456-4717.

The Press

DAILY
The Herald: Blue Caribbean Bldg, Kingstown; tel. 456-1242; fax 456-1046; e-mail herald@caribsurf.com; internet www.heraldsvg.com; daily; internationally distributed.

SELECTED WEEKLIES
The Independent Weekly: 85 Sharpe St, Kingstown; tel. 457-2866; Man. Editor CONLEY ROSE.

Justice: Kingstown; weekly; organ of the United People's Movement; Editor RENWICK ROSE.

The New Times: POB 1300, Kingstown; f. 1984; Thursdays; organ of the New Democratic Party.

The News: McCoy St, POB 1078, Kingstown; tel. 456-2942; fax 456-2941; e-mail thenews@caribsurf.com; weekly.

Searchlight: Cnr Bay and Egmont St, POB 152, Kingstown; tel. 456-1558; fax 457-2250; e-mail search@caribsurf.com; weekly on Fridays.

The Star: POB 854, Kingstown.

The Vincentian: Paul's Ave, POB 592, Kingstown; tel. 457-7430; f. 1919; weekly; owned by the Vincentian Publishing Co; Man. Dir EGERTON M. RICHARDS; Editor-in-Chief TERRANCE PARRIS; circ. 6,000.

The Westindian Crusader: Kingstown; tel. 456-9315; fax 456-9315; e-mail crusader@caribsurf.com; weekly.

SELECTED PERIODICALS
Caribbean Compass: POB 175, Bequia; tel. 457-3409; fax 457-3410; e-mail compass@caribsurf.com; internet www.caribbeancompass.com; marine news; monthly; free distribution in Caribbean from Puerto Rico to Panama; circ. 12,000.

Government Bulletin: Government Information Service, Kingstown; tel. 456-3410; circ. 300.

Government Gazette: POB 12, Kingstown; tel. 457-1840; f. 1868; Govt Printer HAROLD LLEWELLYN; circ. 492.

Unity: Middle and Melville St, POB 854, Kingstown; tel. 456-1049; fortnightly; organ of the United Labour Party.

Publishers

CJW Communications: Frenches Gate, Kingstown; tel. 456-2942; fax 456-2941.

Great Works Depot: Commission A Bldg, Granby St, POB 1849, Kingstown; tel. 456-2057; fax 457-2055; e-mail gwd@caribsurf.com.

The Vincentian Publishing Co Ltd: St George's Place; POB 592, Kingstown; tel. 456-1123; Man. Dir EGERTON M. RICHARDS.

Broadcasting and Communications

TELECOMMUNICATIONS

Regulatory Authority
Eastern Caribbean Telecommunications Authority: based in Castries, Saint Lucia; f. 2000 to regulate telecommunications in Saint Vincent and the Grenadines, Dominica, Grenada, Saint Christopher and Nevis and Saint Lucia.

Major Service Providers
Cable & Wireless (WI) Ltd: Halifax St, POB 103, Kingstown; tel. 457-1901; fax 457-2777; e-mail svdinfo@caribsurf.com; Man. IAN KYLE.

Cable & Wireless Caribbean Cellular: Halifax St, Kingstown; tel. 457-4600; fax 457-4940; cellular telephone service.

BROADCASTING

National Broadcasting Corporation of Saint Vincent and the Grenadines: Dorsetshire Hill, POB 617, Kingstown; tel. 456-1078; fax 456-1015; e-mail svgbc@caribsurf.com; internet www.nbcsvg .com; govt-owned; Chair. ST CLAIR LEACOCK.

Radio

Radio 705: National Broadcasting Corpn, Richmond Hill, POB 705, Kingstown; tel. 457-1111; fax 456-2749; e-mail nbcsvg@caribsurf .com; internet www.nbcsvg.com; commercial; broadcasts BBC World Service (United Kingdom) and local programmes.

Television

National Broadcasting Corporation of Saint Vincent and the Grenadines: see Broadcasting.

SVG Television: Dorsetshire Hill, POB 617, Kingstown; tel. 456-1078; fax 456-1015; e-mail svgbc@caribsurf.com; broadcasts US and local programmes; Chief Engineer R. P. MACLEISH.

Television services from Barbados can be received in parts of the islands.

Finance

(cap. = capital; res = reserves; dep. = deposits; m. = million; br. = branch)

BANKING

The Eastern Caribbean Central Bank (see p. 343), based in Saint Christopher, is the central issuing and monetary authority for Saint Vincent and the Grenadines.

Regulatory Authority

Financial Intelligence Unit (FIU): Kingstown; f. 2003; Dir SHARDA BOLLERS.

Principal Banks

Caribbean Banking Corporation Ltd: 81 South River Rd, POB 118, Kingstown; tel. 456-1501; fax 456-2141; e-mail askerrette@ vincysurf.com; f. 1985; cap. EC $17.4m., res EC $3.3m. (Oct. 2000); Chair. PETER J. JULY; Gen. Man. FRANCIS V. BOWMAN; Country Man. ALPHIE SKERRETTE; 2 brs.

First Saint Vincent Bank Ltd: Lot 112, Granby St, POB 154, Kingstown; tel. 456-1873; fax 456-2675; f. 1988; fmrly Saint Vincent Agricultural Credit and Loan Bank; Man. Dir O. R. SYLVESTER.

National Commercial Bank (SVG) Ltd: Bedford St, POB 880, Kingstown; tel. 457-1844; fax 456-2612; e-mail info@ncbsvg.com; internet www.ncbsvg.com; f. 1977; govt-owned; share cap. EC $14.0m., dep. EC $338.4m., total assets EC $366.4m. (June 2000); Chair. RICHARD JOACHIM; Man. DIGBY AMBRIS; 8 brs.

New Bank Ltd: 16 South River Rd and Bay St, POB 1628, Kingstown; tel. 457-1411; fax 457-1357; e-mail nbl.adnw@caribsurf.com; internet www.nbltd.com; under government control following the disappearance of its owner, Thierry Nano, after a warrant for his arrest on money-laundering charges was issued by a US court in 2001.

Owens Bank Ltd: Blue Caribbean Bldg, Bay St, POB 1045, Kingstown; tel. 457-1230; fax 457-2610; f. 1926.

Saint Vincent Co-operative Bank: Cnr Long Lane (Upper) and South River Rd, POB 886, Kingstown; tel. 456-1894; fax 457-2183.

Foreign Banks

Bank of Nova Scotia Ltd (Canada): 76 Halifax St, POB 237, Kingstown; tel. 457-1601; fax 457-2623; Man. S. K. SUBRAMANIAM.

FirstCaribbean International Bank Ltd: Kingstown; internet www.firstcaribbeaninternational.com; f. 2002 following merger of Caribbean operations of Barclays Bank PLC and CIBC; Exec. Chair. MICHAEL MANSOOR; CEO CHARLES PINK.

STOCK EXCHANGE

Eastern Caribbean Securities Exchange: e-mail info@ ecseonline.com; internet www.ecseonline.com; based in Basseterre, Saint Christopher and Nevis; f. 2001; regional securities market designed to facilitate the buying and selling of financial products for the eight member territories—Anguilla, Antigua and Barbuda, Dominica, Grenada, Montserrat, Saint Christopher and Nevis, Saint Lucia and Saint Vincent and the Grenadines; Gen. Man. BALJIT VOHRA.

INSURANCE

A number of foreign insurance companies have offices in Kingstown. Local companies include the following:

Abbott's Insurance Co: Cnr Sharpe and Bay St, POB 124, Kingstown; tel. 456-1511; fax 456-2462.

BMC Agencies Ltd: Sharpe St, POB 1436, Kingstown; tel. 457-2041; fax 457-2103.

Durrant Insurance Services: South River Rd, Kingstown; tel. 457-2426.

Haydock Insurances Ltd: Granby St, POB 1179, Kingstown; tel. 457-2903; fax 456-2952.

Metrocint General Insurance Co Ltd: St George's Place, POB 692, Kingstown; tel. 456-1821.

Saint Hill Insurance Co Ltd: Bay St, POB 1741, Kingstown; tel. 457-1227; fax 456-2374.

Saint Vincent Insurances Ltd: Lot 69, Grenville St, POB 210, Kingstown; tel. 456-1733; fax 456-2225; e-mail vinsure@caribsurf .com.

'OFFSHORE' FINANCIAL SECTOR

Legislation permitting the development of an 'offshore' financial sector was introduced in 1976 and revised in 1996 and 1998. International banks are required to have a place of business on the islands and to designate a licensed registered agent. International business companies registered in Saint Vincent and the Grenadines are exempt from taxation for 25 years. Legislation also guarantees total confidentiality. By December 2001 the offshore financial centre comprised 10,075 international business corporations, 896 trusts, 38 banks, 35 registered agents, five mutual funds and one insurance company.

Saint Vincent and the Grenadines Offshore Finance Authority: Administrative Center, POB 356, Kingstown; tel. 456-2577; fax 457-2568; e-mail ofsh.fin@caribsurf.com; internet www .stvincentoffshore.com.

Saint Vincent Trust Service: Trust House, 112 Bonadie St, POB 613, Kingstown; tel. 457-1027; fax 457-1961; e-mail trusthouse@ saint-vincent-trust.com; internet www.saint-vincent-trust.com; br. in Liechtenstein; Pres. BRYAN JEEVES.

Trade and Industry

DEVELOPMENT ORGANIZATION

Saint Vincent Development Corporation (Devco): Grenville St, POB 841, Kingstown; tel. 457-1358; fax 457-2838; f. 1970; finances industry, agriculture, fisheries, tourism; Chair. SAMUEL GOODLUCK; Man. CLAUDE M. LEACH.

CHAMBER OF COMMERCE

Saint Vincent and the Grenadines Chamber of Industry and Commerce (Inc): Hillsboro St, POB 134, Kingstown; tel. 457-1464; fax 456-2944; e-mail svgcic@caribsurf.com; internet www.svgcic .com; f. 1925; Pres. MARTIN LABORDE; Exec. Dir LEROY ROSE.

INDUSTRIAL AND TRADE ASSOCIATION

Saint Vincent Marketing Corporation: Upper Bay St, POB 872, Kingstown; tel. 457-1603; fax 456-2673; f. 1959; Man. M. DE FREITAS.

EMPLOYERS' ORGANIZATIONS

Saint Vincent Arrowroot Industry Association: Upper Bay St, Kingstown; tel. 457-1511; f. 1930; producers, manufacturers and sellers; 186 mems; Chair. GEORGE O. WALKER.

Saint Vincent Banana Growers' Association: Sharpe St, POB 10, Kingstown; tel. 457-1605; fax 456-2585; f. 1955; over 7,000 mems; Chair. LESLINE BEST; Gen. Man. HENRY KEIZER.

Saint Vincent Employers' Federation: Halifax St, POB 348, Kingstown; tel. 456-1269; Dir ST CLAIR LEACOCK.

UTILITIES

Saint Vincent Electricity Services Ltd (VINLEC): Paul's Ave, POB 856, Kingstown; tel. 456-1701; fax 456-2436.

Water

Central Water and Sewerage Authority (CWSA): New Montrose, POB 363, Kingstown; tel. 456-2946; fax 456-2552; e-mail cwsa@caribsurf.com; internet www.vinlec.com; f. 1961; CEO JOEL HUGGINS.

CO-OPERATIVES

There are 26 Agricultural Credit Societies, which receive loans from the Government, and five Registered Co-operative Societies.

TRADE UNIONS

Commercial, Technical and Allied Workers' Union (CTAWU): Lower Middle St, POB 245, Kingstown; tel. 456-1525; fax 457-1676; f. 1962; affiliated to CCL, ICFTU and other international workers' organizations; Pres. ALICE MANDEVILLE; Gen. Sec. LLOYD SMALL; 2,500 mems.

National Labour Congress: POB 1290, Kingstown; tel. 457-1950; five affiliated unions; Chair. FITZ JONES.

National Workers' Movement: Grenville St, POB 1290, Kingstown; tel. 457-1950; fax 456-2858; e-mail natwok@caribsurf.com; Gen. Sec. NOEL C. JACKSON.

Public Services Union of Saint Vincent and the Grenadines: McKies Hill, POB 875, Kingstown; tel. 457-1950; fax 456-2858; f. 1943; Pres. CONRAD SAYERS; Exec. Sec. ROBERT I. SAMUEL; 738 mems.

Saint Vincent Union of Teachers: POB 304, Kingstown; tel. 457-1062; f. 1952; members of Caribbean Union of Teachers affiliated to FISE; Pres. TYRONE BURKE; 1,250 mems.

Transport

RAILWAYS

There are no railways in the islands.

ROADS

In 1999 there was an estimated total road network of 1,040 km (646 miles), of which 319 km (198 miles) was paved.

SHIPPING

The deep-water harbour at Kingstown can accommodate two ocean-going vessels and about five motor vessels. There are regular motor-vessel services between the Grenadines and Saint Vincent. Geest Industries, formerly the major banana purchaser, operated a weekly service to the United Kingdom. Numerous shipping lines also call at Kingstown harbour. Some exports are flown to Barbados to link up with international shipping lines. A new marina and shipyard complex at Ottley Hall, Kingstown, was completed during 1995. A new container port at Campden Park, near Kingstown, was opened in the same year. A new dedicated Cruise Terminal was scheduled to open in 1999, which would permit two cruise ships to berth at the same time.

Saint Vincent and the Grenadines Port Authority: POB 1237, Kingstown; tel. 456-1830; fax 456-2732; e-mail svgport@caribsurf.com.

CIVIL AVIATION

There is a civilian airport, E. T. Joshua Airport, at Arnos Vale, situated about 3 km (2 miles) south-east of Kingstown. The islands of Mustique and Canouan have landing strips for light aircraft only, although a project to upgrade Canouan Airport began in May 1997. In late 1999 the Government began the process of raising finance for the extension of E. T. Joshua Airport in order to permit the use of long-haul jet aircraft. It was hoped to complete the project by 2003. In April 2002 Kuwait provided a US $8m. loan for the expansion of the islands' international airport facilities.

American Eagle: POB 1232, E. T. Joshua Airport, Arnos Vale; tel. 456-5555; fax 456-5616.

Mustique Airways: POB 1232, E. T. Joshua Airport, Arnos Vale; tel. 456-4380; fax 456-4586; e-mail info@mustique.com; internet mustique.com; f. 1979; charter flights; Chair. JONATHAN PALMER.

Saint Vincent and the Grenadines Air (1990) Ltd (SVG Air): POB 39, E. T. Joshua Airport, Arnos Vale; tel. 457-5124; fax 457-5077; e-mail info@svgair.com; internet www.svgair.com; f. 1990; charter and scheduled flights; CEO J. E. BARNARD.

Tourism

The island chain of the Grenadines is the country's main tourist asset. There are superior yachting facilities, but the lack of major air links with countries outside the region has resulted in a relatively slow development for tourism. In 2002 Saint Vincent and the Grenadines received an estimated 245,767 tourists (including 70,375 cruise-ship passengers and 84,513 visitors aboard yachts). Tourist receipts were estimated to total EC $212m. in 2002.

Department of Tourism: Cruise Ship Terminal, POB 834, Kingstown; tel. 457-1502; fax 451-2425; e-mail tourism@caribsurf.com; internet www.svgtourism.com; Dir VERA-ANN BRERETON.

Saint Vincent and the Grenadines Hotel and Tourism Association: E. T. Joshua Airport; tel. 458-4379; fax 456-4456; e-mail office@svghotels.com; internet www.svghotel.com; Exec. Dir DAWN SMITH.

SAMOA

Introductory Survey

Location, Climate, Language, Religion, Flag, Capital

The Independent State of Samoa (formerly Western Samoa) lies in the southern Pacific Ocean, about 2,400 km (1,500 miles) north of New Zealand. Its nearest neighbour is American Samoa, to the east. The country comprises two large and seven small islands, of which five are uninhabited. The climate is tropical, with temperatures generally between 23°C (73°F) and 30°C (86°F). The rainy season is from November to April. The languages spoken are Samoan (a Polynesian language) and English. Almost all of the inhabitants profess Christianity, and the major denominations are the Congregational, Roman Catholic and Methodist Churches. The national flag (proportions 1 by 2) is red, with a rectangular dark blue canton, containing five differently-sized white five-pointed stars in the form of the Southern Cross constellation, in the upper hoist. The capital is Apia.

Recent History

The islands became a German protectorate in 1899. During the First World War (1914–18) they were occupied by New Zealand forces, who overthrew the German administration. In 1919 New Zealand was granted a League of Nations mandate to govern the islands. In 1946 Western Samoa (as it was known until July 1997) was made a UN Trust Territory, with New Zealand continuing as the administering power. From 1954 measures of internal self-government were gradually introduced, culminating in the adoption of an independence Constitution in October 1960. This was approved by a UN-supervised plebiscite in May 1961, and the islands became independent on 1 January 1962. The office of Head of State was held jointly by two traditional rulers but, upon the death of his colleague in April 1963, Malietoa Tanumafili II became sole Head of State for life, performing the duties of a constitutional monarch.

Fiame Mata'afa Mulinu'u, Prime Minister since 1959, lost the general election in 1970, and a new Cabinet, led by Tupua Tamasese Lealofi, was formed. Mata'afa regained power in 1973, following another general election, and remained in office until his death in May 1975. He was again succeeded by Tamasese, who, in turn, lost the general election in March 1976 to his cousin, Tupuola Taisi Efi. The previously unorganized opposition members formed the Human Rights Protection Party (HRPP) in 1979, and won the elections in February 1982, with 24 of the 47 seats in the Fono (Legislative Assembly). Va'ai Kolone was appointed Prime Minister, but in September he was removed from office as a result of past electoral malpractice. His successor, Tupuola Efi, with much popular support, sought to nullify an earlier agreement between Kolone and the New Zealand Government which, in defiance of a ruling by the British Privy Council, denied automatic New Zealand citizenship to all Western Samoans except those already living in New Zealand. However, Tupuola Efi resigned in December 1982, after the Fono had rejected his budget, and was replaced by the new HRPP leader, Tofilau Eti Alesana. At elections in February 1985 the HRPP won 31 of the 47 seats, increasing its majority in the Fono from one to 15 seats; the newly-formed Christian Democratic Party (CDP), led by Tupuola Efi, obtained the remaining 16 seats. In December Tofilau Eti resigned, following the rejection of the proposed budget by the Fono and the Head of State's refusal to call another general election. Va'ai Kolone, with the support of a number of CDP members and HRPP defectors, was appointed Prime Minister of a coalition Government in January 1986.

At the February 1988 general election the HRPP and an alliance composed of independents and the CDP (later known as the Samoa National Development Party—SNDP) both initially gained 23 seats, with votes in the remaining constituency being tied. After two recounts proved inconclusive, a judge from New Zealand presided over a third and declared the CDP candidate the winner. However, before a new government could be formed, a newly-elected member of the Legislative Assembly defected from the SNDP alliance to the HRPP. In April Tofilau Eti was re-elected Prime Minister, and a new Government, composed of HRPP members, was appointed.

Legislation proposed in early 1990 which would permit local village councils to fine or to impose forced labour or exile on individuals accused of offending communal rules was widely perceived as an attempt by the Government to ensure the support of the Matai (elected clan chiefs) at the next general election. Of the 47 seats in the Fono, 45 were traditionally elected by holders of Matai titles. However, the political importance of the Matai had been increasingly diminished by the procurement of Matai titles by people seeking to be elected to the Fono. This practice was believed to have undermined the system of chief leadership to such an extent that universal suffrage would have to be introduced to decide all of the seats in the Fono. A referendum was conducted in October 1990, at which voters narrowly accepted government proposals for the introduction of universal suffrage. A second proposal, to create an upper legislative chamber composed of the Matai, was rejected. A bill to implement universal adult suffrage was approved by the Fono in December 1990, despite strong opposition from the SNDP.

A general election was held in April 1991 (the election had been postponed from February, owing to the need to register an estimated 80,000 newly-enfranchised voters). In the following weeks petitions were filed with the Supreme Court against 11 newly-elected members of the Fono who were accused of corrupt or illegal electoral practices. Moreover, subsequent political manoeuvring resulted in the HRPP increasing its parliamentary representation from an initial 26 to 30 seats, while the SNDP ultimately secured only 16 seats in the Fono, and the remaining seat was retained by an independent. At the first meeting of the new Fono, convened in early May, Tofilau Eti was re-elected for what, he later announced, would be his final term of office as Prime Minister.

In November 1991 the Fono approved legislation to increase the parliamentary term from three to five years and to create an additional two seats in the Fono. These seats were contested in early 1992 and won by the HRPP.

The introduction of a value-added tax on goods and services in January 1994 (which greatly increased the price of food and fuel in the country) provoked a series of demonstrations and protest rallies, as well as demands for the resignation of the Prime Minister. As a result of overwhelming opposition to the new regulations, the Government agreed, in March, to amend the most controversial aspects of the tax. Meanwhile, four members of the Fono (including three recently-expelled HRPP members), who had opposed the financial reforms, established a new political organization, the Samoa Liberal Party, under the leadership of the former Speaker, Nonumalo Leulumoega Sofara.

In May 1994 treasury officials warned the Government that a financial crisis at the national air carrier, Polynesian Airlines, was threatening the country's economic stability. It was estimated that the company's debts totalled more than 45m. tala. A report by the Chief Auditor, Tom Overhoff, accused the Government of serious financial mismanagement relating to a series of decisions to commit public funds to the airline, and charged seven cabinet ministers with fraud and negligence in their handling of government resources. An inquiry into the allegations conducted in late 1994 cleared the ministers in question of all the charges, although its findings were harshly criticized by Overhoff, who claimed that the inquiry had been neither independent nor impartial.

Protests against the value-added tax on goods and services continued in early 1995, following the Government's decision to charge two prominent members of the Tumua ma Pule group of traditional leaders and former members of the Fono, with sedition, for organizing demonstrations against the tax during 1994. In March 1995 3,000 people delivered a petition to the Prime Minister, bearing the signatures of 120,000 people (some 75% of the population), that demanded that the tax be revoked. The Prime Minister questioned the authenticity of the signatures and appointed a 14-member committee to investigate the matter. In late June the case against the two members of Tumua ma Pule, which had attracted attention from several international non-governmental organizations (including the

World Council of Churches and Amnesty International) was dismissed on the grounds of insufficient evidence.

The announcement in mid-1995 by the French Government that it was to resume nuclear-weapons testing in the South Pacific provoked large-scale demonstrations in Apia and statements of condemnation by the Government, which imposed an indefinite ban on visits to Western Samoa by French warships and aircraft. The tests were concluded in January 1996.

In December 1995 the HRPP unanimously re-elected Tofilau Eti as the leader of the party, despite concern over the Prime Minister's deteriorating health, as well as a previous declaration that he would retire from politics upon completion of his current term in office.

In March 1996 one of the two female members of the Fono, Matatumua Naimoaga, left the HRPP in order to form the Samoa All-People's Party. The formation of the new party, in preparation for the forthcoming general election, was reportedly a result of dissatisfaction with the Government's alleged mismanagement of public assets together with concern over corruption. Legislation was introduced in April, which attempted to distinguish between the traditional Samoan practice of exchanging gifts and acts of bribery, amid numerous reports that voters were demanding gifts and favours from electoral candidates in return for their support.

A general election took place on 26 April 1996. The opposition was highly critical of the delay in the counting of votes (which took some three weeks in total), claiming that the length of time involved allowed the HRPP to recruit successful independent candidates in an attempt to gain a majority of seats in the Fono. It was eventually announced in mid-May that the HRPP had secured a total of 28 seats (with the recruitment of several independent members to their ranks), the SNDP had won 14 seats and independent candidates had secured seven. Tofilau Eti was subsequently re-elected as Prime Minister, defeating the Leader of the Opposition, Tuiatua Tupua Tamasese, with 34 votes to 14.

The issue of government involvement in the media became prominent in early 1997, following Tuiatua Tupua Tamasese's decision to be interviewed on Australian radio. In the interview he urged overseas donors to withhold aid from Western Samoa, alleging widespread mismanagement and corrupt practice within the Government. The opposition leader responded to criticism of his action by denouncing the government policy that denies opposition politicians access to the state-controlled media, and by urging New Zealand to persuade the Western Samoan Government to reform the system. The New Zealand Minister of Foreign Affairs, however, declined to intervene, reminding Tamasese that his own administration had applied the same policy when in power.

The strength of traditional religious beliefs among Samoans and resistance to foreign influences on their culture was illustrated in early 1997. In March a member of the Church of Jesus Christ of Latter-day Saints (Mormon—the fastest-growing denomination in the country) was tied to a stake surrounded by kindling when he refused to obey a banishment order for criticizing the village council's decision to prevent the construction of a Mormon church in the village. The intended victim was rescued by police-officers and church leaders, who negotiated his release from the villagers. A request by the Samoa Council of Churches to impose a ban on the establishment of new churches in the country was refused by the Government as incompatible with the principle of freedom of religion, as guaranteed in the Constitution. The organization was also highly critical of a US religious television channel due to begin operating in the islands in April, claiming that the evangelical style of religion depicted would undermine traditional Samoan Christianity.

In May 1997 the Prime Minister proposed a constitutional amendment in the Fono to change the country's name to Samoa. (The country has been known simply as Samoa at the UN since its admission to the organization in 1976.) On 3 July the Fono voted by 41 votes to one to approve the change, which came into effect on the next day when the legislation was signed by the Head of State. The neighbouring US territory of American Samoa, however, expressed dissatisfaction with the change (which was believed to undermine the Samoan identity of its islands and inhabitants), and in September introduced legislation to prohibit recognition of the new name within the territory. In March 1998 the House of Representatives in American Samoa voted against legislation that proposed not to recognize Samoan passports (thereby preventing Samoans from travelling

to the territory), but decided to continue to refer to the country as Western Samoa and to its inhabitants as Western Samoans. Nevertheless, in January 2000 Samoa and American Samoa signed a memorandum of understanding, increasing co-operation in areas including health, trade and education.

A series of reports in *The Samoa Observer* in mid-1997 alleged that a serious financial scandal involving the disappearance of some 500 blank passports, and their subsequent sale to Hong Kong Chinese for up to US $26,000 each, had occurred. The Government refused to comment on the newspaper's allegations, stating only that several senior immigration officials had been suspended pending the outcome of an investigation into the affair. Moreover, the Government subsequently brought charges of defamatory libel against the editor, Savea Sano Malifa, for publishing a letter criticizing the Prime Minister (who was reported to have told the Fono of his intention to change legislation governing business licences, such that publications could have their licences withdrawn for publishing dissenting material). The regional Pacific Islands News Association also condemned the Prime Minister's comments as an attack on freedom of information and expression. The continued existence of the newspaper was placed in jeopardy when Savea Sano Malifa was found guilty of defaming the Prime Minister in two libel cases in July and September 1998, and was ordered to pay a total of some US $17,000 in costs. The newspaper had alleged that public funds had been used to construct a hotel owned by the Prime Minister and had criticized the allocation of $0.25m. in the 1998 budget to Tofilau Eti's legal costs. The Government's increasingly autocratic style, its apparent intolerance of dissent and the perceived lack of accountability of its members, coupled with its poor economic record, resulted in frequent expressions of popular discontent during 1997. These culminated in a series of protest marches in late 1997 and early 1998, organized by the Tumua ma Pule group of chiefs and attended by several thousand people, which aimed to increase pressure on the Prime Minister to resign.

A long-standing dispute over land rights near Faleolo airport appeared to be the cause of violent activity in June 1998, when villagers shot a government official, burnt buildings and slaughtered or stole hundreds of cattle on a government estate. It was subsequently revealed, however, that the incidents had been perpetrated by members of a gang styling themselves as Japanese Ninja warriors, who were believed to be involved in the cultivation of marijuana and cattle theft. Some 38 men, thought to be members of the gang, were later arrested. The dispute, which originated in a land survey carried out in 1871, re-emerged in January 2003 when villagers presented the Government with a petition and a list of demands relating to land rights and revenue from the airport.

In November 1998 Tofilau Eti Alesana resigned as Prime Minister, owing to ill health. He was replaced by the Deputy Prime Minister, Tuila'epa Sailele Malielegaoi, and, at the same time, the Cabinet was reshuffled. Tofilau Eti Alesana died in March 1999.

In July 1999 the Minister of Public Works, Luagalau Levaula Kamu, was shot dead while attending an event commemorating the 20th anniversary of the foundation of the ruling HRPP. Speculation followed that the killer's intended target had been the Prime Minister, but this was denied both by Tuila'epa Sailele and by the New Zealand police officers sent to the island to assist in the investigation. A man identified as Eletise Leafa Vitale (son of the Minister of Women's Affairs, Leafa Vitale) was arrested and charged with the murder. Eletise Leafa Vitale was later convicted of the murder and sentenced to death (subsequently commuted to a life sentence). Leafa Vitale was subsequently also charged with the murder of Luagalau, together with the former Minister for Telecommunications, Toi Akuso, who faced additional charges of inciting others to murder Luagalau and the Prime Minister, Tuila'epa Sailele. In mid-April 2000 the two former ministers were found guilty of murdering Luagalau and were sentenced to death (which was similarly commuted to life imprisonment; no death sentence had been carried out since Samoa's independence). It subsequently emerged that Luagalau had been killed in an attempt to prevent him from uncovering incidences of corruption and bribery in which the two ministers had become involved.

Meanwhile, in November 1999 the ruling HRPP increased its number of seats in the Fono to 34 (out of a possible 49) following the defection of an independent candidate to the HRPP. By-elections for the two imprisoned former ministers' seats were held in June 2000, and HRPP candidates were successful in both constituencies.

In August 2000 a supreme court ruling ordered the Government to allow opposition politicians access to the state-controlled media. For several years the opposition had been denied free access to the media (see above).

At a general election on 2 March 2001 the HRPP won 22 seats, the SNDP won 13 seats and independent candidates secured 14 seats. On 16 March Tuila'epa Sailele won 28 votes in the Fono, after securing the support of six independents, to be re-elected Prime Minister. However, the opposition mounted a number of legal challenges to his election. In August eight elected members of Parliament, including the Deputy Prime Minister, the Minister of Health and the Minister of Internal Affairs, Women's Affairs and Broadcasting, faced charges of electoral malpractice in the Supreme Court. None of the Cabinet Ministers was found guilty, and by-elections for the vacant parliamentary seats were held in October and November. The HRPP won all four contested seats.

An Electoral Commission, established shortly after the March elections, published its recommendations in October 2001, urging the replacement of the two Individual Voters Roll seats with two Urban Seats and that government employees who wished to stand for Parliament should first be obliged to resign from their offices.

Despite independence, Samoa maintains strong links with New Zealand, where many Samoans live and many more receive secondary and tertiary education. In June 2002 New Zealand formally apologized for injustices it had committed against its former colony during its administration between 1914 and 1962. These included carelessness in allowing the 1918 influenza pandemic to kill 22% of Samoa's population (the virus having been brought in on a ship from New Zealand); the murder of a Samoan paramount chief and independence leader, Tupua Tamasese Lealofi III, and the killing of nine other supporters of the pacifist Mau movement during a non-violent protest in 1929; and the banishment of native leaders, who were also stripped of their chiefly titles. The apology, while accepted, attracted mixed reactions from Samoans, many of whom were more concerned with the issue of the restoration of their rights to New Zealand citizenship (which had been severely curtailed by the Citizenship Western Samoa Act of 1982). Moreover, in March 2003 large protest marches took place in Samoa and New Zealand demanding the repeal of the 1982 law, which ended Samoans' automatic right to New Zealand citizenship.

In March 2003, in common with many other island nations in the region, large demonstrations were organized in Samoa to protest against the US-led military assault against Iraq. The Samoan Government expressed support for the demonstrations, which were attended by some 2,000 people.

Government

The Constitution provides for the Head of State to be elected by the Legislative Assembly for a term of five years. The present Head of State, however, holds the office for life. The Legislative Assembly is composed of 49 members, all of whom are elected by universal suffrage. A total of 47 members are elected from among holders of Matai titles (elected clan chiefs), and two are selected from non-Samoan candidates. Members hold office for five years. Executive power is held by the Cabinet, comprising the Prime Minister and other selected members of the Assembly. The Prime Minister is appointed by the Head of State with the necessary approval of the Assembly.

Defence

In August 1962 Western Samoa and New Zealand signed a Treaty of Friendship, whereby the New Zealand Government, on request, acts as the sole agent of the Western Samoan Government in its dealings with other countries and international organizations.

Economic Affairs

In 2001, according to estimates by the World Bank, Samoa's gross national income (GNI), measured at average 1999–2001 prices, was US $260m., equivalent to US $1,520 per head (or $5,450 per head on an international purchasing-power parity basis). During 1990–2001, it was estimated, the population increased at an average annual rate of 0.6%, while gross domestic product (GDP) per head increased, in real terms, by an average of 2.2% per year. Overall GDP increased, in real terms, by an average annual rate of 2.8% in 1990–2001; growth in 2001 was 10.0%.

Agriculture (including hunting, forestry and fishing) accounted for some 14.2% of GDP in 2001. The principal cash crops are coconuts (in total, coconut oil, cream and copra accounted for 7.9% of total exports in 2001, compared with 15.0% in 2000) and taro (also the country's primary staple food). Sales of taro provided 58% of all domestic export earnings in 1993, but an outbreak of taro leaf blight devastated the crop in 1994 and reduced exports to almost nil in that year and subsequently. A campaign to revive the taro industry was launched in mid-2000; exports of taro in 2001 accounted for 1.6% of total exports. Breadfruit, yams, maize, passion fruit and mangoes are also cultivated as food crops. Exports of breadfruit and papaya were expected to increase significantly following the installation in early 2003 of a treatment facility to eradicate fruit fly from the produce. Pigs, cattle, poultry and goats are raised, mainly for local consumption. Some 1,800 head of cattle were brought to Samoa from Australia in early 2003, in an attempt to boost stocks and increase beef production. The country's commercial fishing industry expanded considerably in the late 1990s, with export revenues rising from some US $4.8m. in 1997 (33.0% of domestic export earnings) to $24.7m. (55.2%) in 2000. Output in the fishing sub-sector contributed 7.6% of GDP in 2000. Significant reductions in fishing taxes announced by the Government in March 2003 were expected to stimulate the country's fishing industry. Between 1994 and 2001, according to figures from the Asian Development Bank (ADB), the GDP of the entire agricultural sector increased, in real terms, at an average annual rate of 0.5%. In real terms, compared with the previous year, agricultural GDP rose by 0.3% in 2000, before decreasing by 4.6% in 2001.

Industry (comprising manufacturing, mining, construction and power) employed 5.5% of the labour force in 1986 and provided 25.9% of GDP in 2001. According to ADB figures, between 1994 and 2001 industrial GDP increased, in real terms, at an average annual rate of 2.6%. The GDP of the industrial sector expanded by 11.3% in 2000 and by 11.1% in 2001.

Manufacturing provided 16.0% of GDP in 2001 and, together with mining, employed 3.5% of the labour force in 1986. Until recently, the main products of the sector were beverages (beer—which accounted for 5.8% of exports in 2001—and soft drinks), coconut-based products and cigarettes. (The coconut oil mill, however, remained closed for much of 2000.) The sector expanded considerably following the opening, in early 1995, of a Japanese-owned factory manufacturing motor-car parts, which employed more than 2,500 workers by 1996 (the largest private-sector employer in the islands). Shipments from the factory are generally excluded from official statistics for visible (merchandise) exports. Instead, the value added by the plant is recorded as part of 'invisible' trade, in the services account of the balance of payments. However, in 1997 the factory's operations were restructured, with output subsequently reduced. The clothing industry has also expanded, and in 2001 garments accounted for 10.4% of total export earnings. Between 1994 and 2001, according to ADB figures, manufacturing GDP increased, in real terms, at an average annual rate of 0.6%, expanding by 7.3% in 2000 and by 13.4% in 2001.

Energy is derived principally from hydroelectric power and thermal power stations. A grant of US $0.3m. was received from the ADB in early 2003 to establish a hydroelectric project on Savai'i island. Imports of petroleum accounted for 12.4% of the value of total imports in 2001.

The services sector provided 59.9% of GDP in 2001. Between 1994 and 2001, according to ADB figures, the sector's GDP increased at an average annual rate of 7.4%. Compared with the previous year, the GDP of the services sector expanded by 7.6% in 2000 and by 8.4% in 2001. Tourism makes a significant contribution to the economy, and tourist revenues, including the proportion of international travel credited to carriers based in Samoa, totalled an estimated 133.07m. tala in 2000, compared with 125.80m. tala in 1999. 'Offshore' banking was introduced to the islands in 1989, and by July of that year more than 30 companies had registered in Apia. A large proportion of the islands' revenue is provided by remittances from nationals working abroad, estimated at 150.7m. tala in 2000 and equivalent to some 19.5% of GDP in that year (more than three times the value of merchandise exports and, for the first time, exceeding tourist remittances). Aid from Australia and New Zealand is also a major source of revenue. Australia provided $A15.8m. in assistance in 2002/03. Aid from New Zealand totalled $NZ7.7m. in that year.

In 2000 the country recorded a visible trade deficit of US $73.4m., and a surplus of US $8.9m. on the current account of the balance of payments. In 2001 Australia was Samoa's principal trading partner, providing an estimated 21.6% of imports and purchasing an estimated 64.7% of exports, while the USA provided 26.6% of imports and purchased 11.7% of exports. Other important trading partners are New Zealand, Fiji and Japan. The principal exports are fish, garments, coconut cream, copra and beer. The main imports are food and beverages, (which accounted for about 34% of total import costs in 1996), industrial supplies and fuels.

In the year ending 30 June 2001 there was an overall budget deficit of 19.2m. tala (equivalent to 2.3% of GDP), reflecting an increase in development spending financed by external borrowing and a decrease in lending to the domestic banking system. At the end of 2000 the country's total external debt was US $197.2m., of which $147.0m. was long-term public debt. In that year the cost of debt-servicing was equivalent to 10.8% of total revenue from exports of goods and services. In 1990–2000 the annual rate of inflation averaged 3.3%. The ADB estimated that consumer prices increased by 4.0% in 2001.

Samoa is a member of the Pacific Islands Forum (see p. 306), the Pacific Community (see p. 304), the Asian Development Bank (ADB, see p. 143) and the UN Economic and Social Commission for Asia and the Pacific (ESCAP, see p. 28), and is a signatory to the Lomé Conventions and the successor Cotonou Agreement with the EU (see p. 235).

In 1998 the UN Committee for Development Planning recommended that Samoa should be removed from the UN's list of the world's least developed countries (LDCs) and recategorized as a developing country. It appeared likely, however, that Samoa would seek to persuade the UN to defer any decision until a full evaluation of the economy had been carried out. In the early 1990s economic development was adversely affected by cyclones, limited agricultural exports and inadequate transport facilities. Strong growth characterized the economy during the mid-1990s, but this slowed considerably in 1997 and 1998, owing to the completion of cyclone reconstruction projects and drought. Nevertheless, by the end of 1998 inflation had been reduced, while foreign reserves had increased. In May 1999 it was announced that Samoa's Post and Telecommunications Department was to be privatized as part of a public-sector reform programme. In December 1999 a report published by the Central Bank of Samoa revealed that it was likely to exceed its objectives for monetary policy in that year, which had included limiting inflation to below 3%, promoting economic growth of 2%–3% and maintaining the competitiveness of the tala to encourage exports, import substitution and tourism. In 2000–01 high rates of GDP growth were maintained (with the construction sector recording particularly strong expansion), while the Samoan currency continued to depreciate against the US dollar. In 2001, however, the increase in consumer prices exceeded the central bank's target of a maximum of 3%. The Government maintained its commitment to private-sector development, including the transfer of the assets of several public enterprises to the corporate and private sectors. The IMF commended the transferral of government-owned land to freehold use in 2001. During 2001 various items of legislation were approved, aiming to raise standards of fiscal and corporate governance and to improve regulation and supervision in the financial sector. The tourism sector, meanwhile, continued to perform well, following the completion of new facilities, and was also well placed to benefit from the political instability in neighbouring Fiji and Solomon Islands. Although the number of arrivals was briefly affected by the repercussions of the terrorist attacks on the USA in September 2001, gross receipts from tourism increased owing to higher individual levels of spending. The Government continued its implementation of the programme of economic and public-sector reform in 2001 and reaffirmed its policies in the Strategy for the Development of Samoa 2002–2004. In April 2003 the number of government departments and ministries was reduced from 27 to 14 (largely through mergers) as part of the reforms. The document stressed the importance of opportunities for all through sustained economic growth and improvements in health and education. The ADB envisaged GDP growth rates of 5.0% in 2002 and 2003.

Education

The education system is based on that of New Zealand. About 97% of the adult population are literate in Samoan. In 1988 a national university was established, with an initial intake of 328 students. Faculties of arts and commerce, science, nursing and education exist. A project to upgrade the university campus was completed in early 1997. In 1992 the Government decided to reintroduce bonds for students awarded government scholarships for overseas study. Expenditure on education by the central Government in 1999 was an estimated 35.1m. tala (21.4% of total budgetary expenditure).

Public Holidays

2003: 1 January (Independence Day), 2 January (for New Year), 4 January (Head of State's birthday), 18–21 April (Easter), 25 April (ANZAC Day), 1–3 June (Independence Celebrations), 9 June (Whit Monday), 14 October (White Monday), 1 November (Arbor Day), 19 November (National Women's Day), 25 December (Christmas Day), 26 December (Boxing Day).

2004: 1 January (Independence Day), 2 January (for New Year), 4 January (Head of State's birthday), 9–12 April (Easter), 25 April (ANZAC Day), 31 May (Whit Monday), 1–3 June (Independence Celebrations), 14 October (White Monday), 1 November (Arbor Day), 19 November (National Women's Day), 25 December (Christmas Day), 26 December (Boxing Day).

Statistical Survey

AREA AND POPULATION

Area: Savai'i and adjacent small islands 1,708 sq km, Upolu and adjacent small islands 1,123 sq km; Total 2,831 sq km (1,093 sq miles).

Population: Savai'i 44,930, Upolu and adjacent small islands 112,228, Total 157,158 at census of 3 November 1986; Savai'i 45,050, Upolu and adjacent small islands 116,248, Total 161,298 (males 84,601; females 76,697) at census of 3 November 1991; Total 176,848 at census of November 2001.

Density (November 2001): 62.5 per sq km.

Principal Town: Apia (capital), population 34,126 at census of 3 November 1991.

Registered Births and Deaths (1996, provisional): Live births 4,966 (birth rate 29.9 per 1,000); Deaths 352 (death rate 2.1 per 1,000). (1998, provisional): Deaths 531 (death rate 3.2 per 1,000). Source: UN, *Population and Vital Statistics Report*.

Expectation of Life (WHO estimates, years at birth): 68.5 (males 67.0; females 69.9) in 2001. Source: WHO, *World Health Report*.

Economically Active Population (census of 3 November 1986): Agriculture, hunting, forestry and fishing 29,023; Manufacturing and mining 1,587; Electricity, gas and water 855; Construction 62; Trade, restaurants and hotels 1,710; Transport, storage and communications 1,491; Financing, insurance, real estate and business services 842; Community, social and personal services 9,436; Activities not adequately defined 629; Total labour force 45,635 (males 37,054; females 8,581). *1991 census* (persons aged 15 years and over, excluding armed forces): Total labour force 57,142 (males 38,839, females 18,303). Source: ILO, *Yearbook of Labour Statistics*.

HEALTH AND WELFARE

Key Indicators

Total Fertility Rate (children per woman, 2001): 4.3.

Under-5 Mortality Rate (per 1,000 live births, 2001): 25.

Physicians (per 1,000 head, 1996): 0.34.

Health Expenditure (2000): US $ per head (PPP): 221.

Health Expenditure (2000): % of GDP: 6.6.

Health Expenditure (2000): public (% of total): 76.2.

Access to Water (% of persons, 2000): 99.

Access to Sanitation (% of persons, 2000): 99.

Human Development Index (2000): ranking 101.

Human Development Index (2000): value 0.715.
For sources and definitions, see explanatory note on p. vi.

AGRICULTURE, ETC.

Principal Crops (FAO estimates, '000 metric tons, 2001): Taro 15; Yams 3; Other roots and tubers 3; Coconuts 140; Copra 11; Bananas 20; Papayas 4; Pineapples 4; Mangoes 3; Avocados 1; Other fruits 9; Cocoa beans 0.5. Source: FAO.

Livestock (FAO estimates, '000 head, year ending September 2001): Pigs 201; Cattle 28; Horses 1.8; Chickens 450. Source: FAO.

Livestock Products (FAO estimates, '000 metric tons, 2000): Beef and veal 1; Pigmeat 4. Source: FAO.

Forestry (roundwood removals, '000 cubic metres): 131 in 1998; 131 in 1999; 131 in 2000. Source: FAO.

Fishing (metric tons, live weight, 2000): Capture 13,004 (Albacore 4,067, Yellowfin tuna 1,120); Total catch 13,004. Source: FAO, *Yearbook of Fishery Statistics*.

INDUSTRY

Electric Energy (million kWh): 85 in 1999; 91 in 2000; 105 in 2001. Source: Asian Development Bank, *Key Indicators of Developing Asian and Pacific Countries*.

FINANCE

Currency and Exchange Rates: 100 sene (cents) = 1 tala (Samoan dollar). *Sterling, US Dollar and Euro Equivalents* (31 December 2002): £1 sterling = 5.184 tala; US $1 = 3.216 tala; €1 = 3.373 tala; 100 tala = £19.29 = US $31.09 = €29.65. *Average Exchange Rate* (US $ per tala): 0.2297 in 2000; 0.2241 in 2001; 0.2287 in 2002.

Budget (provisional, million tala, year ending 30 June 1998): *Revenue:* Tax revenue 138.2 (Income tax 29.5, Excise tax 25.8, Taxes on international trade 47.1, Value-added gross receipts and services tax (VAGST) 32.2, Other taxes 3.6); Other revenue 33.2 (Fees, service charges, etc. 9.7, Departmental enterprises 19.3, Rents, royalties and international investments 4.2); Total 171.4, excl. external grants received (60.5). *Expenditure:* Current expenditure 142.1 (General administration 39.0, Law and order 11.3, Education 32.0, Health 24.8, Social security and pensions 6.8, Agriculture 9.0, Public works 18.6, Land survey 6.2, Other economic services 4.6, Interest on public debt 4.0, Other purposes (residual) –0.7, Sub-total 155.6, *Less* VAGST payable by government 13.5); Development expenditure 71.3; Total 213.4, excl. net lending (8.2). *1998/99* (projections, million tala, incl. supplementary budget proposals): *Revenue:* Tax revenue 155.4; Other revenue 36.4; Total 191.8, excl. external grants (85.1). *Expenditure:* Current expenditure 172.9; Development expenditure 90.4; Total 263.3, excl. net lending (16.1) (Source: IMF, *Samoa: Statistical Appendix* (April 1999)). *2000/01* (provisional, million tala, year ending 30 June): *Revenue:* Tax revenue 174.8; Other revenue 22.5; Total 197.4, excl. external grants received (65.1). *Expenditure:* Current expenditure 164.6; Development expenditure 103.1; Capital and net lending 13.9; Total 281.7 (Source: Treasury Department).

International Reserves (US $ million at 31 December 2002): IMF special drawing rights 2.38; Reserve position in IMF 0.69; Foreign exchange 58.97; Total 63.15. Source: IMF, *International Financial Statistics*.

Money Supply (million tala at 31 December 2002): Currency outside banks 32.57; Demand deposits at banks 63.04; Total money 95.61. Source: IMF, *International Financial Statistics*.

Cost of Living (Consumer Price Index, excluding rent; base: 1995 =100): 115.4 in 1999; 116.5 in 2000; 121.0 in 2001. Source: IMF, *International Financial Statistics*.

Gross Domestic Product by Economic Activity (million tala at current prices, 2001): Agriculture and fishing 121.5; Manufacturing 137.0; Electricity and water 25.5; Construction 59.5; Trade 175.8; Transport and communications 116.8; Finance 59.3; Public administration 69.5; Other services 92.4; Sub-total 857.3; *Less* Imputed bank service charges 5.8; Total 851.5. Source: Asian Development Bank, *Key Indicators of Developing Asian and Pacific Countries*.

Balance of Payments (estimates, US $ million, 2000): Exports of goods f.o.b. 17.0; Imports of goods f.o.b. –90.4; *Trade balance* –73.4; Services and other income (net) 19.3; *Balance on goods, services and income* –54.1; Private remittances (net) 38.6; Official transfers (net) 24.5; *Current balance* 8.9; Capital transactions (incl. net errors and omissions) –14.0; *Overall balance* –5.1. Source: IMF Public Information Notice, *IMF Concludes Article IV Consultation with Samoa* (July 2001).

EXTERNAL TRADE

Principal Commodities (US $ '000, 1990): *Imports c.i.f.:* Food and live animals 19,852; Beverages and tobacco 1,753; Mineral fuels 9,345; Chemicals 3,874; Basic manufactures 15,781; Machinery and transport equipment 23,584; Miscellaneous manufactured articles 4,987; Total (incl. others) 81,742. *Exports f.o.b.* (incl. re-exports): Copra 476; Cocoa 219; Coffee 419; Coconuts 2,519; Taro and taamu 512; Beer 402; Cigarettes and tobacco 275; Palm oil 1,745; Total (incl. others) 8,020.

1991 ('000 tala): *Imports c.i.f.* 225,337; *Exports* Taro 6,878; Total (incl. re-exports) 15,515.

1992 ('000 tala): *Imports c.i.f.* 271,325; *Exports* (incl. re-exports) 14,349.

1993 ('000 tala): *Imports c.i.f.* 269,079; *Exports* (incl. re-exports) 16,522.

1994 ('000 tala): *Imports c.i.f.* 206,347; *Exports* (incl. re-exports) 9,121.

1995 ('000 tala): *Imports c.i.f.* 235,353; *Exports* (incl. re-exports) 21,859.

1996 ('000 tala): *Imports c.i.f.* 247,126; *Exports* (incl. re-exports) 24,868.

1997 ('000 tala): *Imports c.i.f.* 247,377; *Exports* (incl. re-exports) 38,531.

1998 ('000 tala): *Imports c.i.f.* 285,652; *Exports* (incl. re-exports) 43,243.

1999 ('000 tala): *Imports c.i.f.* 346,765; *Exports* (incl. re-exports) 61,695.

2000 ('000 tala): *Imports c.i.f.* 348,610; *Exports* (incl. re-exports) 44,880.
Source (for 1991–2000): IMF, *International Financial Statistics*.

2001 ('000 tala): *Imports c.i.f.:* Petroleum 55,780; Total (incl. others) 449,090. *Exports f.o.b.:* Coconut oil 10; Coconut cream 3,390; Fish 36,010; Copra 780; Kava 500; Beer 3,070; Taro 830; Garments 5,490; Total (incl. others) 52,690. Source: Treasury Department, *Quarterly Review*. Note: The trade data above exclude purchases and sales by the Yazaki car components factory.

Principal Trading Partners (US $ million, 2001): *Imports:* Australia 62.44; Fiji 33.95; Indonesia 4.32; Japan 28.98; Republic of Korea 3.93; New Zealand 46.64; United Kingdom 7.49; USA 77.11; Total (incl. others) 289.52. *Exports:* American Samoa 1.67; Australia 48.35; Germany 1.85; Indonesia 8.90; New Zealand 1.11; USA 8.73; Total (incl. others) 74.78. Source: Asian Development Bank, *Key Indicators of Developing Asian and Pacific Countries*.

TRANSPORT

Road Traffic (motor vehicles in use, 1993): Private cars 5,000; Commercial vehicles 1,800. Source: UN, *Statistical Yearbook for Asia and the Pacific*.

International Shipping (freight traffic, '000 metric tons, 1998): Goods loaded 50; Goods unloaded 140 (Source: UN, *Monthly Bulletin of Statistics*). *Merchant Fleet* (total displacement, '000 grt at 31 December 2001): 9.7; vessels 7 (Source: Lloyd's Register-Fairplay, *World Fleet Statistics*).

Civil Aviation (traffic on scheduled services, 1999): Passengers carried 92,000; Passenger-kilometres 244 million; Total ton-kilometres 23 million. Source: UN, *Statistical Yearbook*.

TOURISM

Visitor Arrivals: 77,926 in 1998; 85,124 in 1999; 87,688 in 2000.

Visitor Arrivals by Country (2000): American Samoa 30,063; Australia 10,954; Fiji 2,032; Germany 1,784; New Zealand 22,818; United Kingdom 2,092; USA 9,032. Source: World Tourism Organization, *Yearbook of Tourism Statistics*.

Tourism Receipts (million tala): 115.2 in 1998; 125.8 in 1999; 133.1 in 2000.

*Includes the proportion of international travel credited to Samoan carriers.

COMMUNICATIONS MEDIA

Telephones (2001): 10,000 main lines in use.

Facsimile Machines (1999): 500 in use.

Personal Computers (2001): 1,000.

Internet Users (2001): 3,000.

Mobile Cellular Telephones (2001): 3,000 subscribers.

Radio Receivers (1997): 410,000 in use.

Television Receivers (1997): 42,000 in use.

Non-daily Newspapers (1988): 5 (estimated circulation 23,000).

* Source: International Telecommunication Union.

† Source: UNESCO, *Statistical Yearbook*.

EDUCATION

Primary (1999): 155 schools (1996); 1,233 teachers; 35,749 pupils.

Intermediate (1983): 8,643 pupils.

General Secondary (1996): 665 teachers; 12,672 pupils.

Universities, etc. (1983): 11 teachers; 136 students.

Other Higher (1996): 71 teachers; 674 students.

Source: partly UNESCO, *Statistical Yearbook*.

Adult Literacy Rate (UNESCO estimates): 80.2% (males 81.2%; females 79.0%) in 2000 (Source: UN Development Programme, *Human Development Report*).

Directory

The Constitution

A new Constitution was adopted by a constitutional convention on 28 October 1960. After being approved by a UN-supervised plebiscite in May 1961, the Constitution came into force on 1 January 1962, when Western Samoa became independent. A constitutional amendment adopted in July 1997, shortened the country's name to Samoa. The main provisions of the Constitution are summarized below:

HEAD OF STATE

The office of Head of State is held (since 5 April 1963, when his co-ruler died) by HH Malietoa Tanumafili II, who will hold this post for life. After that the Head of State will be elected by the Fono (Legislative Assembly) for a term of five years.

EXECUTIVE

Executive power lies with the Cabinet, consisting of the Prime Minister, supported by the majority in the Fono, and ministers selected by the Prime Minister. Cabinet decisions are subject to review by the Executive Council, which is made up of the Head of State and the Cabinet.

LEGISLATURE

The Fono consists of 49 members. It has a five-year term and the Speaker is elected from among the members. Beginning at the election of 5 April 1991, members are elected by universal adult suffrage: 47 members of the Assembly are elected from among the Matai (elected clan leaders) while the remaining two are selected from non-Samoan candidates.

The Government

HEAD OF STATE

O le Ao o le Malo: HH Malietoa Tanumafili II (took office as joint Head of State 1 January 1962; became sole Head of State 5 April 1963).

CABINET
(April 2003)

Prime Minister and Minister of Foreign Affairs: Tuila'epa Sailele Malielegaoi.

Deputy Prime Minister and Minister of Finance: Misa Telefoni.

Minister of Internal Affairs, Women's Affairs and Broadcasting: Tuala Ainiu Iusitino.

Minister of Education: Fiame Naomi Mata'afa.

Minister of Lands, Survey and Environment: Tuala Sale Tagaloa.

Minister of Health and Labour: Mulitalo Siafausa.

Minister of Public Works: Faumui Liuga.

Minister of Agriculture, Forestry, Fisheries and Meteorological Services: Tuisugaletaua Sofara Aveau.

Minister of Trade, Commerce and Industry: Hans Joachim Keil.

Minister of Transport: Palusalue Faapo II.

Minister of Youth, Sports and Culture: Ulu Vaomalo Kini.

Minister for the Legislative Assembly: Tino Gaina.

Minister of Justice: Seumanu Aita Ah Wa.

MINISTRIES AND MINISTERIAL DEPARTMENTS

Prime Minister's Department: POB L 1861, Apia; tel. 63122; fax 21339; e-mail pmdept@ipasifika.net.

Ministry of Agriculture, Forestry, Fisheries and Meteorology: POB 1874, Apia; tel. 22561; fax 24576.

Broadcasting Department: POB 200, Apia; tel. 21420.

Customs Department: POB 44, Apia; tel. 21561.

Economic Affairs Department: POB 862, Apia; tel. 20471.

Education Department: POB 1869, Apia; tel. 21911; fax 21917.

Ministry of Foreign Affairs: POB L 1859, Apia; tel. 25313; fax 21504; e-mail mfa@mfa.gov.ws.

Health Department: Private Bag, Apia; tel. 21212.

Inland Revenue Department: POB 209, Apia; tel. 20411.

Justice Department: POB 49, Apia; tel. 22671; fax 21050.

Lands, Survey and Environment Department: Private Bag, Apia; tel. 22481; fax 23176.

Public Works Department: Private Bag, Apia; tel. 20865; fax 21927; e-mail pwdir@lesamoa.net.

Statistics Department: POB 1151, Apia; tel. 21371; fax 24675.

Department of Trade, Industry and Commerce: POB 862, Apia; tel. 20471; fax 21646; e-mail tipu@tci.gov.ws; internet www.tradeinvestsamoa.ws.

Ministry of Transport: POB 1607, Apia; tel. 23701; fax 21990; e-mail mvnofo@mot.gov.ws.

Treasury Department: Private Bag, Apia; tel. 34333; fax 21312; e-mail treasury@samoa.net.

Ministry of Youth, Sport and Culture: Apia; tel. 23315.

Legislature

FONO
(Legislative Assembly)

The Assembly has 47 Matai members, representing 41 territorial constituencies, and two individual members. Elections are held every five years. At a general election on 2 March 2001, the Human Rights Protection Party (HRPP) won 22 seats, the Samoa National Development Party won 13 seats and independent candidates secured 14 seats. Four by-elections held during October and November 2001 were won by the HRPP.

Speaker: Taleafoa Faisi.

Political Organizations

Human Rights Protection Party (HRPP): c/o The Fono, Apia; f. 1979; Western Samoa's first formal political party; Leader Tuila'epa Sailele Malielegaoi; Gen. Sec. Laulu Dan Stanley.

Samoa All-People's Party: Apia; f. 1996; Leader Matatumua Naimoaga.

Samoa Liberal Party: Apia; f. 1994; Leader Nonumalo Leulumoega Sofara.

Samoa Mo Taeao (Samoans for a Better Tomorrow): Apia; Chair. Tuifa'asisina Meaole Keil.

Samoa National Development Party (SNDP): POB 1233, Apia; tel. 23543; fax 20536; f. 1988 following general election; coalition party comprising the Christian Democratic Party (CDP) and several independents; Leader Hon. LEMAMEA R. MUALIA; Sec. VALASI TAFITO.

Samoa National Party: Apia; f. 2001; Sec. FETU TIATIA.

Diplomatic Representation

EMBASSIES AND HIGH COMMISSIONS IN SAMOA

Australia: Beach Rd, POB 704, Apia; tel. 23411; fax 23159; e-mail peterhooton@dfat.gov.au; High Commissioner PETER HOOTON.

China, People's Republic: Private Bag, Vailima, Apia; tel. 22474; fax 21115; Ambassador GU SICONG.

New Zealand: Beach Rd, POB 1876, Apia; tel. 21711; fax 20086; High Commissioner PENELOPE RIDINGS.

USA: POB 3430, Apia; tel. 21631; fax 22030; e-mail usembassy@samoa.ws; Chargé d'affaires FRANKIE REED CALHOUN.

Judicial System

Attorney-General: BRENDA HEATHER.

The Supreme Court

Is presided over by the Chief Justice. It has full jurisdiction for both criminal and civil cases. Appeals lie with the Court of Appeal.

Chief Justice: TIAVAASUE FALEFATU MAKA SAPOLU.

Secretary for Justice: FAAITAMAI P. F. MEREDITH.

The Court of Appeal: consists of the President (the Chief Justice of the Supreme Court), and of such persons possessing qualifications prescribed by statute as may be appointed by the Head of State. Any three judges of the Court of Appeal may exercise all the powers of the Court.

The District Courts

Replaced the Magistrates' Court in 1998.

Judges: LESATELE RAPI VAAI, TAGALOA ENOKA FERETI PUNI.

The Land and Titles Court

Has jurisdiction in respect of disputes over Samoan titles. It consists of the President (who is also a judge of the Supreme Court) and three Deputy Presidents, assisted by Samoan judges and Assessors.

President of The Land and Titles Court: TIAVAASUE FALEFATU MAKA SAPOLU.

Religion

Almost all of Samoa's inhabitants profess Christianity.

CHRISTIANITY

Fono a Ekalesia i Samoa (Samoa Council of Churches): POB 574, Apia; f. 1967; four mem. churches; Sec. Rev. EFEPAI KOLIA.

The Anglican Communion

Samoa lies within the diocese of Polynesia, part of the Church of the Province of New Zealand. The Bishop of Polynesia is resident in Fiji, while the Archdeacon of Tonga and Samoa is resident in Tonga.

Anglican Church: POB 16, Apia; tel. 20500; fax 24663; Rev. PETER E. BENTLEY.

The Roman Catholic Church

The islands of Samoa constitute the archdiocese of Samoa-Apia. At 31 December 2000 there were an estimated 30,336 adherents in the country. The Archbishop participates in the Catholic Bishops' Conference of the Pacific, based in Fiji.

Archbishop of Samoa-Apia: Cardinal ALAPATI L MATA'ELIGA, Cardinal's Residence, Fetuolemoana, POB 532, Apia; tel. 20400; fax 20402; e-mail archdiocese@samoa.ws.

Other Churches

Church of Jesus Christ of Latter-day Saints (Mormon): Samoa Apia Mission, POB 1865, Apia; tel. 20311; fax 20299; Pres. LINI LYON TO'O; f. 1888; 62,500 mems.

Congregational Christian Church in Samoa: Tamaligi, POB 468, Apia; tel. 22279; fax 20429; e-mail cccsgsec@lesamoa.net; f. 1830; 100,000 mems; Gen. Sec. Rev. MAONE F. LEAUSA.

Congregational Church of Jesus in Samoa: 505 Borie St, Honolulu, HI 96818, USA; Rev. NAITULI MALEPEAI.

Methodist Church in Samoa (Ekalesia Metotisi i Samoa): POB 1867, Apia; tel. 22282; f. 1828; 36,000 mems; Pres. Rev. SIATUA LEULUAIALII; Sec. Rev. FAATOESE AUVAA.

Seventh-day Adventist Church: POB 600, Apia; tel. 20451; f. 1895; covers Samoa and American Samoa; 5,000 mems; Pres. Pastor SAMUELU AFAMASAGA; Sec. UILI SOLOFA.

BAHÁ'Í FAITH

National Spiritual Assembly: POB 1117, Apia; tel. 23348; fax 21363.

The Press

Newsline: POB 2441, Apia; tel. 24216; fax 23623; twice a week.

Samoa News: POB 1160, Apia; daily; merged with the weekly *Samoa Times* (f. 1967) in Sept. 1994; Publr LEWIS WOLMAN.

The Samoa Observer: POB 1572, Apia; tel. 21099; fax 21195; f. 1979; five times a week; independent; English and Samoan; Editor AUMA'AGAOLU ROPETA'ALI; circ. 4,500.

Samoa Weekly: Saleufi, Apia; f. 1977; weekly; independent; bilingual; Editor (vacant); circ. 4,000.

Savali: POB L1861, Apia; publ. of Lands and Titles Court; monthly; govt-owned; Samoan edn f. 1904; Editor FALESEU L. FUA; circ. 6,000; English edn f. 1977; circ. 500; bilingual commercial edn f. 1993; circ. 1,500; Man. Editor (vacant).

South Seas Star: POB 800, Apia; tel. 23684; weekly.

Broadcasting and Communications

TELECOMMUNICATIONS

Samoa Communications Ltd: Apia; tel. 23456; fax 24000; corporatized in July 1999; telecommunications and postal services provider; CEO MARK YEOMAN.

BROADCASTING

Radio

Samoa Broadcasting Service: Broadcasting Department, POB 1868, Apia; tel. 21420; fax 21072; f. 1948; govt-controlled with commercial sponsorship; operates Radio 2AP; broadcasts on two channels in English and Samoan for 24 hours daily; Dir J. K. BROWN.

Magik 98 FM: POB 762, Apia; tel. 25149; fax 25147; e-mail magic98fm@samoa.net; f. 1989; privately-owned; operates on FM wavelengths 98.1 and 99.9 MHz; Man. COREY KEIL.

Radio Graceland: Apia; broadcasts gospel music.

Television

Televise Samoa Corporation: POB 3691, Apia; tel. 26641; fax 24789; e-mail ceotvsamoa@samoa.net; f. 1993; govt-owned national television broadcasting service; locally-produced programmes and programmes supplied by Australian Television (ATV); CEO LEOTA UELESE PETAIA.

Finance

(cap. = capital; res = reserves; dep. = deposits; m. = million; brs = branches; amounts in tala, unless otherwise indicated)

BANKING

Central Bank

Central Bank of Samoa: Private Bag, Apia; tel. 34100; fax 20293; e-mail cbs@lesamoa.net; internet www.cbs.gov.ws; f. 1984; cap. 10.0m., res 15.8m., dep. 40.1m. (Dec. 2001); Gov. and Chair. PAPALI'I TOMMY SCANLAN.

Commercial Banks

ANZ Bank (Samoa) Ltd: Beach Rd, POB L 1885, Apia; tel. 22422; fax 24595; e-mail anz@samoa.ws; internet www.anz.com/samoa; f. 1959 as Bank of Western Samoa, name changed 1997; owned by ANZ Banking Group Ltd; cap. 1.5m., res 22.8m., dep. 139.2m. (Sept. 1998); Dir R. G. LYON; Man. Dir G. R. TUNSTALL; 1 br.

Industrial Bank Inc: POB 3271, Lotemau Centre, Vaea St, Apia; tel. 21878; fax 21869; f. 1995; owned by Industrial Pacific Investments Ltd; cap. US \$0.3m., res US \$1.9m. (1995); Chair. and Pres. IAN BYSTROV.

International Business Bank Corporation Ltd: Chandra House, Convent St, Apia; tel. 20660; fax 23253; e-mail ibb@samoa .net; f. 1991; 46.7% owned by ELECS Investment Ltd, 22.5% by Tidal Funds Co Ltd; cap. US \$25.5m., res US \$0.8m., dep. US \$22.2m. (Jan. 1997); Chair. ILIA KARAS; Exec. Dir SERGUEI GREBELSKI.

National Bank of Samoa: POB 3047L, Apia; tel. 26766; fax 23477; e-mail info@nationalbanksamoa.com; internet www .nationalbanksamoa.com; f. 1995; owned by consortium of private interests in Samoa, American Samoa and the USA; Chair. TERENCE BETHAM; CEO ANNE BONISCH; 5 agencies; 1 sub-br.

Samoa Commercial Bank: Apia; f. 2003; CEO RAY AH LIKI.

Westpac Bank Samoa Ltd: Beach Rd, POB 1860, Apia; tel. 20000; fax 22848; e-mail samoa@westpac.com.ws; f. 1977 as Pacific Commercial Bank Ltd, current name adopted 2001; first independent bank; 93.5% owned by Westpac Banking Corpn (Australia); cap. 8.2m., dep. 91.0m. (Sept. 2001); Chair. ALAN WALTER; Gen. Man. STEVE BAKER; 3 brs.

Development Bank

Development Bank of Samoa: POB 1232, Apia; tel. 22861; fax 23888; f. 1974 by Govt to foster economic and social development; cap. 12.9m. (1992); Gen. Man. FALEFA LIMA.

INSURANCE

National Pacific Insurance Ltd: NPF Bldg, Private Bag, Apia; tel. 20481; fax 23374; f. 1977; 30% govt-owned; Gen. Man. RICKY WELCH.

Progressive Insurance Company: POB 620, Lotemau Centre, Apia; tel. 26110; fax 26112; e-mail progins@samoa.ws; f. 1993; Gen. Man. I. O. FILEMU.

Western Samoa Life Assurance Corporation: POB 494, Apia; tel. 23360; fax 23024; f. 1977; Gen. Man. A. S. CHAN TING.

Trade and Industry

CHAMBER OF COMMERCE

Chamber of Commerce and Industry: Level one, Lotemau Centre, Convent St, POB 2014, Apia; tel. 31090; fax 31089; e-mail info@samoachamber.com; internet www.samoachamber.com; f. 1938; Pres. NORMAN WETZELL; Vice-Pres. SALA EPA'TUIOTI; Sec. JOHN F. BOYLE.

INDUSTRIAL AND TRADE ASSOCIATIONS

Samoa Coconut Products: Apia.

Samoa Forest Corporation: Apia.

UTILITIES

Electricity

Electric Power Corporation: POB 2011, Apia; tel. 22261; fax 23748; e-mail epcgm@samoa.ws.

Water

Western Samoa Water Authority: POB 245, Apia; tel. 20409; fax 20376; e-mail swalatu@samoa.ws; Gen. Man. LATU SAUILE TOGA KUPA.

TRADE UNIONS

Journalists' Association of Samoa: Apia; Pres. APULU LANCE POLU.

Samoa Manufacturers' Association (SMA): Apia; Pres. EDDIE WILSON.

Samoa Nurses' Association (SNA): POB 3491, Apia; Pres. FAAMANATU NIELSEN; 252 mems.

Samoa Trade Union Congress (STUC): POB 1515, Apia; tel. 24134; fax 20014; f. 1981; affiliate of ICFTU; Pres. FALEFATA TUANIU PETAIA; Dir MATAFEO R. MATAFEO; 5,000 mems.

Transport

Public Works Department: see under The Government; Dir of Works ISIKUKI PUNIVALU.

ROADS

In 1983 there were 396 km of main roads on the islands, of which 267 km were bitumen surfaced; 69 km of urban roads, of which 32 km were bitumen surfaced; 440 km of unsealed secondary roads and about 1,180 km of plantation roads. The upgrading and expansion of the road network was a priority of the Government during the late 1980s.

SHIPPING

There are deep-water wharves at Apia and Asau. A programme of improvements to port facilities at Apia funded by Japanese aid, was completed in 1991. Regular cargo services link Samoa with Australia, New Zealand, American Samoa, Fiji, New Caledonia, Solomon Islands, Tonga, US Pacific coast ports and various ports in Europe.

Samoa Ports Authority: POB 2279, Apia; tel. 23552; fax 25870; e-mail spa@lesamoa.net; f. 1999.

Samoa Shipping Services Ltd: POB 1884, Apia; tel. 20790; fax 20026.

Samoa Shipping Corporation Ltd: Private Bag, Shipping House Matautu-tai, Apia; tel. 20935; fax 22352; e-mail ssc@samoa.net; internet www.samoashippingcorporation.com; Gen. Man. OLOIALII KOKI TUALA.

CIVIL AVIATION

There is an international airport at Faleolo, about 35 km from Apia and an airstrip at Fagali'i, 4 km east of Apia Wharf, which receives light aircraft from American Samoa. In mid-1999 US \$19.4m. was allocated by the World Bank to improve facilities at Faleolo airport.

Polynesian Airlines (Holdings) Ltd: NPF Bldg, Beach Rd, POB 599, Apia; tel. 21261; fax 20023; e-mail enquiries@ polynesianairlines.co.nz; internet www.polynesianairlines.co.nz; f. 1959; govt-owned and -operated; international services to American Samoa, Rarotonga (Cook Islands), Nadi (Fiji), Tonga, Sydney and Melbourne (Australia), Auckland and Wellington (New Zealand) and Hawaii and Los Angeles (USA); domestic services between islands of Upolu and Savai'i; Chair. TUILA'EPA SAILELE MALIELEGAOI; CEO JOHN FITZGERALD.

Samoa Air: tel. 22901; operates local shuttle services between Pago Pago and Apia.

Tourism

Samoa has traditionally maintained a cautious attitude towards tourism, fearing that the Samoan way of life might be disrupted by an influx of foreign visitors. The importance of income from tourism has, however, led to some development, including the expansion of hotel facilities and improvements to the road network and airport. Some 87,688 tourists arrived in 2000, and revenue from the tourist industry totalled 133.1m. tala in that year. In 2000 34.3% of tourists came from American Samoa, 26.0% from New Zealand, 12.5% from Australia and 10.3% from the USA. The principal attractions are the scenery and the pleasant climate.

Samoa Visitors' Bureau: POB 2272, Apia; tel. 26500; fax 20886; e-mail samoa@samoa.net; internet www.samoa.co.nz; f. 1986; Gen. Man. SONJA HUNTER; Marketing Man. ALISE FAULALO-STUNNENBERG.

SAN MARINO

Introductory Survey

Location, Climate, Language, Religion, Flag, Capital

The Republic of San Marino lies in southern Europe. The country is situated on the slopes of Mount Titano, in the Apennines, bordered by the central Italian region of Emilia-Romagna to the north, and the Marches region to the south. San Marino has cool winters and warm summers, with temperatures generally between –2°C (28°F) and 30°C (86°F). Average annual rainfall totals 880 mm (35 ins). The language is Italian. Almost all of the inhabitants profess Christianity, and the state religion is Roman Catholicism. The civil flag (proportions 3 by 4) has two equal horizontal stripes, of white and light blue. The state flag has, in addition, the national coat of arms (a shield, framed by a yellow cartouche, bearing three green mountains—each with a white tower, surmounted by a stylized ostrich feather, at the summit—the shield being surmounted by a bejewelled crown and framed by branches of laurel and oak, and surmounting a white ribbon bearing, in black, the word 'libertas') in the centre. The capital is San Marino.

Recent History

San Marino evolved as a city-state in the early Middle Ages and is the sole survivor of the numerous independent states that existed in Italy prior to its unification in the 19th century. A treaty of friendship and co-operation with Italy was signed in 1862, renewed in March 1939 and revised in September 1971.

From 1945 to 1957 San Marino was ruled by a left-wing coalition of the Partito Comunista Sammarinese (PCS) and the Partito Socialista Sammarinese (PSS). Defections from the PCS in 1957 led to a bloodless revolution, after which a coalition of the Partito Democratico Cristiano Sammarinese (PDCS) and the Partito di Democrazia Socialista (PDS) came to power. In early 1973 an internal dispute over economic policy led to the resignation of the Government, and a new Government was formed by an alliance between the PDCS and the PSS. The PSS withdrew from the coalition in November 1975, resulting in the collapse of the Government. The Captains-Regent took over the administration until March 1976, when a new coalition between the PDCS and the PSS was formed. This Government collapsed in late 1977 but continued in an interim capacity until a new administration was formed. Attempts by the PCS to form a government were frustrated by the lack of a clear majority in the unicameral legislature, the Consiglio Grande e Generale (Great and General Council). Eventually the Consiglio agreed to a dissolution and elections were held in May 1978, when the PDCS secured 26 of the 60 seats. However, they were still unable to form an administration and the three left-wing parties, the PCS, PSS and the Partito Socialista Unitario (PSU), which together held 31 seats, agreed to form a coalition Government led by the PCS. San Marino thus became the only Western European country with a communist-led government. A left-wing coalition again formed the administration following the May 1983 elections.

In 1986 a political crisis, resulting from a financial scandal which allegedly involved several prominent PSS members, led to the formation of a new coalition Government, the first to be composed of the PDCS and the PCS. At the general election of May 1988, the PDCS and the PCS obtained 27 and 18 seats respectively, and in June the two parties agreed to form a coalition Government. In 1990 the PCS was renamed the Partito Progressista Democratico Sammarinese (PPDS). In 1992 the PDCS negotiated the formation of a coalition Government with the PSS. The PDCS, with the majority of government members, had decided not to maintain an alliance with the PPDS in view of the demise of communism in Europe.

At the general election of May 1993 the PDCS and the PSS obtained 26 and 14 seats, respectively. The election was regarded as a defeat for the PPDS, which secured only 11 seats, and was also notable for the success of three recently formed parties, the Alleanza Popolare dei Democratici Sammarinese (APDS), the Movimento Democratico and the Rifondazione Comunista Sammarinese (RCS). In June the PDCS and the PSS agreed to form a coalition Government. The PDCS and the PSS were again dominant at the general election of 31 May 1998,

winning 25 and 14 seats, respectively. The PPDS won 11 seats, the APDS six, and the RCS two. The remaining two seats were secured by a new grouping, Socialisti per le Riforme, which had been founded in 1997. A coalition Government was formed by the PDCS and the PSS in July 1998. In February 2000 the PSS left the Government, and in March a new coalition Government was formed, with six members of the PDCS, three members of the PPDS and one member of the Socialisti per le Riforme; it also had parliamentary support from Idee in Movimento (as the Movimento Democratico had been renamed in 1998). A number of minor changes were also made to the portfolios at that time. In March 2001 the Partito dei Democratici Sammarinese (PdD) was formed, following an alliance between Idee in Movimento, the PPDS and the Socialisti per le Riforme; the PPDS Secretary-General, Claudio Felici, was appointed as the PdD's Secretary-General.

At legislative elections, held on 10 June 2001, the PDCS secured 25 seats and 41.5% of the votes cast, and the PSS obtained 15 seats and 24.2% of the votes. The two parties subsequently formed a coalition Government. The PdD won 12 seats (with 20.8% of the votes), while the APDS secured five seats (8%), the RCS two seats (3.4%) and the Alleanza Nazionale Sammarinese one seat (1.9%). Antonio Volpinari of the PSS and Francesco Ugolini of the PDCS were elected as Captains-Regent from April 2002.

In June 2002 the PDCS-PSS coalition Government collapsed after the PSS withdrew its support, ending the long-term domination of Sammarinese politics by the PDCS. A new coalition Government was formed on 25 June, incorporating five members of the PSS, three of the PdD and two members of the APDS. Ugolini served out his mandate as Captain-Regent although his party was no longer represented in the Government, and in October, Captains-Regent from the PSS and PdD were elected.

By December 2002, however, the alliance between the PSS and the PDCS had been renewed, and a new coalition Government was instituted on 17 December with 5 members from each party. From April the new Captains-Regent, Pier Marino Menicucci and Giovanni Giannoni, represented the reinstated PDCS-PSS governing coalition.

San Marino became a member of the UN in 1992.

Government

San Marino is divided into nine 'Castles' (Castelli) corresponding to the original parishes of the Republic. Each 'Castle' is governed by a Castle-Captain (Capitano di Castello), who holds office for two years, and a Castle Board (Giunte di Castello), which holds office for five years.

Legislative power is vested in the unicameral Consiglio Grande e Generale (Great and General Council), with 60 members elected by universal adult suffrage, under a system of proportional representation, for five years (subject to dissolution). The Consiglio elects two of its members to act jointly as Captains-Regent (Capitani Reggenti), with the functions of Head of State and Government, for six months at a time (ending in March and September). Executive power is held by the Congress of State (Congresso di Stato), with 10 members elected by the Council for the duration of its term. The Congresso is presided over by the Captains-Regent.

Defence

There are combined Voluntary Military Forces. There is no obligatory military service but citizens between 16 and 55 years may be enlisted, in certain circumstances, to defend the state.

Economic Affairs

According to IMF estimates, San Marino's gross domestic product (GDP) in 1999 was US $853m., approximately equivalent to $23,390 per head. The IMF estimated average annual GDP growth at 7.1%, in real terms, during 1992–99. Real GDP increased by 7.5% in 1998 and by 9.0% in 1999.

Agriculture engaged 1.3% of the employed population in 2000. The principal crops are wheat, barley, maize, olives and grapes. Livestock-rearing and dairy farming are also important. Olive oil and wine are produced for export.

Industry (including manufacturing and construction) engaged 41.5% of the employed population in 2000. Stone-quarrying is the only mining activity in San Marino, and is an important export industry. Manufacturing engaged 32.9% of the employed population in 2000. The most important branches are the production of cement, synthetic rubber, leather, textiles and ceramics. The sector is largely export orientated, owing to integration with firms in Italy.

Energy is derived principally from gas (more than 75%). San Marino is dependent on the Italian state energy companies for much of its energy requirements.

The services sector engaged an estimated 57.2% of the employed population in 2000. Tourism is the main source of income, contributing about 60% of government revenue. In 2000 the number of visitor arrivals was estimated at 3.1m. In 1997, of an estimated 3,307,983 visitor arrivals, only 27,618 stayed at least one night in the country. Receipts from tourism were estimated at US $252.5m. in 1994, equivalent to 41.6% of GDP in that year. The sale of coins and postage stamps, mainly to foreign collectors, is also a significant source of foreign exchange. San Marino, along with the Vatican and Monaco, was granted special dispensation to mint its own euro coins in 2002, with a view to providing for this specialist market.

In 1996, according to IMF estimates, San Marino recorded a trade surplus of US $22.6m., and there was a surplus of $10.7m. on the current account of the balance of payments. Data concerning imports and exports are included in those of Italy, with which San Marino maintains a customs union. (Customs union is also maintained with the European Union—EU, see p. 199.) The principal source of imports (estimated at 87%) is Italy, upon which the country is dependent for its supply of raw materials. The major exports are wine, woollen goods, furniture, ceramics, building stone and artisan- and hand-made goods.

San Marino receives a subsidy from the Italian Government, under the *Canone Doganale*, amounting to about 9,000m. lire annually, in exchange for the Republic's acceptance of Italian rules concerning exchange controls and the renunciation of customs duties.

No consolidated general government accounts are published by San Marino, and separate accounts and budgets are prepared by the central administration, the Social Security Institute, and each of the public enterprises, on an accrual basis. Figures published by the IMF, on a cash basis, for the consolidated operations of the general account budget (including the central administration and the nine 'Castles') and the Social Security Institute indicated a deficit of 28,000m. lire for 1997 (approximately equivalent to some 2.1% of GDP). The annual rate of inflation averaged 4.4% in 1990–99; consumer prices increased by an average of 2.3% in 1998 and by 3.2% in 1999. In December 2001 2.6% of the total labour force were unemployed. An increasingly large proportion of the labour force (24.5% in 2000, compared with 10.8% in 1991) are cross-border workers, mainly Italians from the surrounding regions.

Tourism has become increasingly important to San Marino's economy since the 1960s, when an increase in tourist activity in nearby Italian resorts resulted in the arrival of large numbers of excursionists. San Marino is currently dependent on the revenues generated by more than 3m. visitors each year, although the expansion of light industries, based on imported materials from Italy, has been encouraged in order to reduce this dependence. In the 1990s political uncertainty in Italy, together with alternative taxation and regulation structures available in San Marino, resulted in the inflow to the banking sector of a large amount of non-resident deposits, and the development of dynamic financial and commercial sectors, which contributed to remarkable economic growth. Although San Marino has traditionally recorded a budget surplus, high levels of government employment, capital spending and subsidies, combined with low income from indirect taxes, resulted in budget deficits in 1996 and 1997. In an effort to reverse this trend, the Government halted all recruitment and implemented a 5% reduction in discretionary current expenditure in the 1999 budget. A review of public-sector activities was also initiated, with a view to reforming the structure of government employment. In January 1999 San Marino adopted the euro, which became the sole currency in circulation at the start of 2002. According to the IMF, GDP was projected to increase by more than 7% in both 2000 and 2001, and the rate of unemployment was expected to remain low, at less than 3%. However, in 1999–2000 the budget deficit of the central administration increased to an estimated 2.75% of GDP, compared with an average of some 1% of GDP during the 1990s.

Education

Education is compulsory for 10 years between the ages of six and 16 years. Primary education begins at six years of age and lasts for five years. Secondary education begins at the age of 11 and may last for up to eight years: a first cycle of three years, a second of two years and a third non-compulsory cycle of three years. A state-administered university, with some 50 students, was inaugurated in 1987. Government expenditure on education was 35,990m. lire in 1994. In early 2001 plans to introduce a single cycle of seven years (incorporating primary education and three years of secondary education), followed by five years of non-compulsory secondary education, were announced.

Public Holidays

2003: 1 January (New Year's Day), 6 January (Epiphany), 5 February (Liberation Day and St Agatha's Day), 19 March (St Joseph's Day), 25 March (Anniversary of the Arengo), 1 April (Investiture of the new Captains-Regent), 21 April (Easter Monday), 1 May (Labour Day), 19 June (Corpus Christi), 28 July (Fall of Fascism), 15 August (Assumption of the Virgin), 3 September (San Marino Day and Republic Day), 1 October (Investiture of the new Captains-Regent), 1 November (All Saints' Day), 2 November (Commemoration of the Dead), 8 December (Immaculate Conception), 25 December (Christmas), 26 December (St Stephen's Day).

2004: 1 January (New Year's Day), 6 January (Epiphany), 5 February (Liberation Day and St Agatha's Day), 19 March (St Joseph's Day), 25 March (Anniversary of the Arengo), 1 April (Investiture of the new Captains-Regent), 12 April (Easter Monday), 1 May (Labour Day), 10 June (Corpus Christi), 28 July (Fall of Fascism), 15 August (Assumption of the Virgin), 3 September (San Marino Day and Republic Day), 1 October (Investiture of the new Captains-Regent), 1 November (All Saints' Day), 2 November (Commemoration of the Dead), 8 December (Immaculate Conception), 25 December (Christmas), 26 December (St Stephen's Day).

Weights and Measures

The metric system is in force.

Statistical Survey

Source (unless otherwise stated): Ufficio di Stato per il Turismo, Contrada Omagnano 20, 47890 San Marino; tel. 0549 882435; fax 0549 882575; e-mail statoturismo@omniway.sm; internet www.omniway.sm.

AREA AND POPULATION

Area: 61.2 sq km (23.6 sq miles).

Population: 19,149 (males 9,654; females 9,495) at census of 30 November 1976; 26,941 at December 2000.

Density (2000): 440 per sq km.

Principal Towns (population at 31 December 1996): Serravalle/Dogano 4,802; Borgo Maggiore 2,394; San Marino (capital) 2,294. Source: Thomas Brinkhoff, *City Population* (internet www.citypopulation.de).

Births, Marriages and Deaths (registrations, 2000): Live births 290 (birth rate 10.8 per 1,000); Marriages (1997) 233 (marriage rate 9.0 per 1,000); Deaths 188 (death rate 7.0 per 1,000). Source: UN, mainly *Population and Vital Statistics Report.*

Expectation of Life (WHO estimates, years at birth): 80.8 (males 77.61; females 83.9) in 2001. Source: WHO, *World Health Report.*

Economically Active Population (2000): Agriculture 244; Manufacturing 6,132; Construction 1,603; Commerce 3,278; Transport 435; Banking and insurance 574; Services 2,223; Government 3,228; Public corporations 927; Total employed 18,644 (including 4,680 cross-border workers); Unemployed 428; Total labour force 19,072. Source: IMF, *Republic of San Marino: Selected Issues and Statistical Appendix* (December 2001).

HEALTH AND WELFARE

Key Indicators

Total Fertility Rate (children per woman, 2001): 1.3.

Under-5 Mortality Rate (per 1,000 live births, 2001): 6.

Physicians (per 1,000 head, 1990): 2.52.

Health Expenditure (2000): US $ per head (PPP): 2,805.

Health Expenditure (2000): % of GDP: 11.7.

Health Expenditure (2000): public (% of total): 85.7.
For sources and definitions, see explanatory note on p. vi.

FINANCE

Currency and Exchange Rates: Italian currency: 100 cent = 1 euro. *Sterling and Dollar Equivalents* (31 December 2002): £1 sterling = 1.5370 euros; US $1 = 0.9536 euros; 100 euros = £65.06 = $104.87. *Average Exchange Rates* (euros per US $): 1.0854 in 2000; 1.1175 in 2001; 1.0626 in 2002. Note: The local currency was formerly the Italian lira (plural = lire). From the introduction of the euro, with Italian participation, on 1 January 1999, a fixed exchange rate of €1 = 1,936.27 lire was in operation. Euro notes and coins were introduced on 1 January 2002. The euro and local currency circulated alongside each other until 28 February, after which the euro became the sole legal tender. Some of the figures in this Survey are still in terms of Italian lire.

Cash Balance of Central Administration (adjusted for contributions collected on behalf of the Social Security Institute, '000 million lire, 1997): *Revenue:* Tax revenue 365 (Taxation on income, profits, etc. 130; Social security contributions 81; Domestic taxes on goods and services 153); Other current revenue 43; Capital revenue 4; Total revenue 411, excl. grants received (9). *Expenditure:* Goods and services 184 (Wages and salaries 140); Interest payments 5; Subsidies and other current transfers 216 (Subsidies 14; Transfers to non-profit-making institutions 14); Other current expenditure 2; Capital expenditure 31 (Capital transfers 23); Unclassified expenditures 8; Total expenditure 448. Source: IMF, *San Marino: Recent Economic Developments* (April 1999).

Money Supply ('000 million lire, at December 1997): Demand deposits at banks 421; Total money (incl. others) 442. Source: IMF, *San Marino: Recent Economic Developments* (April 1999).

Cost of Living (Consumer Price Index; base: 1990 = 100): 143.0 in 1998; 147.6 in 1999; 152.5 in 2000. Source: ILO.

Expenditure on the Gross Domestic Product (estimates, '000 million lire at current prices, 1999): Government final consumption expenditure 254; Private final consumption expenditure 620; Increase in stocks 83; Gross fixed capital formation 642; *Total domestic expenditure* 1,602; Exports of goods and services 3,051; *Less* Imports of goods and services 3,102; *GDP in purchasers' values* 1,551. Source: IMF, *San Marino: Selected Issues and Statistical Appendix* (December 2001).

Balance of Payments (estimates, US $ million, 1996): Merchandise exports f.o.b. 1,741,9; Merchandise imports c.i.f. –1,719.3; *Trade balance* 22.6; Exports of services 120.4; Imports of services –102.2; *Balance on goods and services* 40.9; Interest payments 63.5; Net labour income –57.9; Other capital income –45.5; *Balance on goods, services and income* 1.0; Net transfers 9.7; *Current balance* 10.7; Capital account (net) 218.5; Errors and omissions –219.8; *Overall balance* 9.4. Source: IMF, *San Marino: Recent Economic Developments* (April 1999).

EXTERNAL TRADE

Data concerning imports and exports are included in those of Italy, with which San Marino maintains a customs union.

TOURISM

Visitor Arrivals (incl. excursionists): 3.3m. in 1998; 3.1m. in 1999; 3.1m. in 2000.

Tourist Arrivals (staying at least one night): 27,592 in 1995; 30,178 in 1996; 27,618 in 1997.

COMMUNICATIONS MEDIA

Radio Receivers (1998): 35,100 in use.

Television Receivers (1998): 22,500 in use.

Telephones (2000): 20,302 main lines in use.

Facsimile Machines (1998): 5,800 in use.

Mobile Cellular Telephones (subscribers, 2000): 14,503.
Sources: Direzione Generale Poste e Telecomunicazioni; International Telecommunication Union.

EDUCATION

Pre-primary (1997/98): 14 schools, 97 teachers, 890 pupils.

Primary (1997/98): 14 schools, 225 teachers, 1,211 pupils.

Secondary (Scuola Media) (1997/98): 3 schools, 148 teachers, 703 pupils.

Secondary (Scuola Secondaria Superiore) (1997/98): 1 school, 109 pupils.
There is also a technical institute (19 pupils 2001/02), and a vocational training school (12 pupils 2001/02): total teachers (1993) 44.
* 1999/2000 figure.
† 2001/02 figure.

Directory

The Government

(April 2003)

HEADS OF STATE

Capitani-Reggenti (Captains-Regent): PIER MARINO MENICUCCI I, GIOVANNI GIANNONI I (April 2003–October 2003).

CONGRESSO DI STATO
(Congress of State)

A coalition of the Partito Democratico Cristiano Sammarinese (PDCS) and the Partito Socialista Sammarinese (PSS).

Secretary of State for Foreign and Political Affairs, Planning and Economic Co-operation: FIORENZO STOLFI (PSS).

Secretary of State for Home Affairs and Civil Defence: LORIS FRANCINI (PDCS).

Secretary of State for Budget, Finance, Post and Telecommunications, and Relations with the Azienda Autonoma di Stato Filatelica e Numismatica (AASFN): PIER MARINO MULARONI (PDCS).

Secretary of State for Industry, Handicrafts and Relations with the Azienda Autonoma di Stato per i Servizi Pubblici (AASS): MAURIZIO RATTINI (PSS).

Secretary of State for Territory, Environment, Agriculture and Relations with the Azienda Autonoma di Stato di Produzione (AASP): FABIO BERARDI (PSS).

Secretary of State for Tourism, Commerce, Sport and Transport: PARIDE ANDREOLI (PSS).

Secretary of State for Health and Social Security: ROSA ZAFFERANI (PDCS).

Secretary of State for Public Education, Universities, Culture and Social Affairs: PASQUALE VALENTINI (PDCS).

Secretary of State for Labour and Co-operation: GIAN CARLO VENTURINI (PDCS).

Secretary of State for Justice, Relations with the Castle Boards and Information: ALBERTO CECCHETTI (PSS).

MINISTRIES

Secretariat of State for Budget, Finance, Relations with the Azienda Autonoma di Stato Filatelica e Numismatica (AASFN) and Post and Telecommunications: Palazzo Begni, Contrada Omerelli, 47890 San Marino; tel. 0549 882242; fax 0549 882244; e-mail segr.finanze@omniway.sm.

Secretariat of State for Foreign and Political Affairs, Planning and Economic Co-operation: Palazzo Begni, Contrada Omerelli, 47890 San Marino; tel. 0549 882293; fax 0549 882814; e-mail segretariadistato@esteri.sm; internet www.esteri.sm.

Secretariat of State for Health and Social Security: Via V. Scialoia, 47895 Cailungo; tel. 0549 994438; fax 0549 903967; e-mail dic.sanita@omniway.sm; internet www.sanita.segreteria.sm.

Secretariat of State for Home Affairs and Civil Defence: Parva Domus, Piazza Libertà; tel. 0549 882196; fax 0549 882261; e-mail affariinterni@omniway.sm; internet www.interni.segreteria.sm.

Secretariat of State for Industry, Handicrafts and Relations with the Azienda Autonoma di Stato per i Servizi Publici: Palazzo Mercuri, Contrada del Collegio, 47890 San Marino; tel. 0549 882528; fax 0549 882529; e-mail dic.industria@omniway.sm.

Secretariat of State for Justice, Relations with the Castle Boards and Information: Via A. Superchio 16, 47895 Cailungo; tel. 0549 882522; fax 0549 882524; e-mail segr.giunte-castello@omniway.sm; internet www.giunteaziende.segreteria.sm.

Secretariat of State for Labour and Co-operation: Palazzo Mercuri, Contrada del Collegio 38, 47890 San Marino; tel. 0549 882532; fax 0549 882535; e-mail segr.lavoro@omniway.sm; internet www.lavoro.segreteria.sm.

Secretariat of State for Public Education, Universities, Culture and Social Affairs: Palazzo Begni, Contrada Omerelli, 47890 San Marino; tel. 0549 882250; fax 0549 882301; e-mail segr.pub-istr@omniway.sm; internet www.educazione.sm.

Secretariat of State for Territory, Environment, Agriculture and Relations with the Azienda Autonoma di Stato di Produzione: Contrada Omerelli, 47890 San Marino; tel. 0549 882470; fax 0549 882473; e-mail segr.territorio@omniway.sm.

Secretariat of State for Tourism, Commerce, Sport and Transport: Palazzo del Turismo, Contrada Omagnano, 47890 San Marino; tel. 0549 885397; fax 0549 885399; e-mail segr.turismo@omniway.sm.

Legislature

CONSIGLIO GRANDE E GENERALE
(Great and General Council)

Palazzo Pubblico, Piazza della Libertà, 47890 San Marino; tel. 0549 882259; fax 0549 882389; e-mail info@consigliograndeegenerale.sm; internet www.consigliograndeegenerale.sm.

Election, 10 June 2001

Party		Votes	%	Seats
PDCS	. . . .	9,031	41.45	25
PSS	. . . .	5,262	24.18	15
PD	. . . .	4,535	20.81	12
APDS	. . . .	1,974	8.23	5
RCS	. . . .	738	3.39	2
ANS	. . . .	421	1.93	1
Total	. . . .	21,961	100.0	60

Political Organizations

Alleanza Nazionale Sammarinese (ANS) (San Marino National Alliance): Via Gino Giacomini 45, 47890 San Marino; tel. 0549 914005; fax 0549 913676; internet www.alleanzanazionalersm.org; Pres. VITTORIO ENNIO PELLANDRA; Sec. LORENZ BERTI.

Alleanza Popolare dei Democratici Sammarinese (APDS) (Popular Alliance of San Marino Democrats): Via Luigi Cibrario 25, 47893 Cailungo; tel. 0549 907080; fax 0549 907082; e-mail info@alleanzapopolare.net; internet www.alleanzapopolare.net; advocates a constitution and institutional reform; Leader ROBERTO GIORGETTI.

Partito dei Democratici (PD) (Democrats' Party): San Marino; e-mail info@democratici.sm; internet www.democratici.sm; f. 2001 by an alliance of Idee in Movimento, PPDS and Socialisti per le Riforme; Pres. EMMA ROSSI; Gen. Sec. CLAUDIO FELICI.

Partito Democratico Cristiano Sammarinese (PDCS) (San Marino Christian Democrat Party): Via delle Scalette 6, 47890 San Marino; tel. 0549 991193; fax 0549 992694; e-mail pdcs@omniway.sm; internet www.pdcs.sm; f. 1948; Sec.-Gen. GIOVANNI LONFERNINI; 2,400 mems.

Partito Progressista Democratico Sammarinese (PPDS) ((San Marino Progressive Democratic Party)): e-mail info@ppds.sm; internet www.ppds.sm; Pres. CLAUDIO FELICI; Sec.-Gen. MAURIZIO TOMASSONI.

Partito Socialista Sammarinese (PSS) (San Marino Socialist Party): Via G. Ordelaffi 46, 47890 San Marino; tel. 0549 902016; fax 0549 906438; e-mail pss@omniway.sm; internet www.pss.sm; in 1990 merged with Partito Socialista Unitario; f. 1975; Sec.-Gen. AUGUSTO CASALI.

Rifondazione Comunista Sammarinese (RCS) (Sammarinese Reconstructed Communism): Via Ca' dei Lunghi 70/A, 47893 Borgo Maggiore, San Marino; tel. and fax 0549 906682; e-mail rcs@omniway.sm; internet www.rifondazionecomunista-rsm.org; f. 1992; communist; Leader IVAN FOSCHI.

Diplomatic Representation

EMBASSY IN SAN MARINO

Italy: Via del Voltone 55, 47890, San Marino; tel. 0549 991146; fax 0549 992229; e-mail ambsmar@omniway.sm; Ambassador ALESSIO CARISSIMO.

Judicial System

The administration of justice is entrusted to foreign judges, with the exception of the Justice of the Peace, who must be of San Marino nationality, and who judges minor civil suits. The major legislative institutions are as follows:

Civil and Criminal Commissionary Tribunal (Tribunale Commissariale Civile e Penale): Salita alla Rocca 44, San Marino; tel. 0549 882626; fax 0549 8825980; e-mail tribunale@omniway.sm.

Law Commissioner (Commissario della Legge): deals with civil and criminal cases where the sentence does not exceed three years' imprisonment.

Criminal Judge of the Primary Court of Claims: deals with criminal cases that are above the competence of the Law Commissioner.

Court of Appeal: two judges, who deal with civil and criminal proceedings.

Council of Twelve (Consiglio dei XII): has authority as a Supreme Court of Appeal, for civil proceedings only.

Religion

CHRISTIANITY

The Roman Catholic Church

Roman Catholicism is the official state religion of San Marino. The Republic forms part of the diocese of San Marino-Montefeltro (comprising mainly Italian territory), suffragan to the archdiocese of Ravenna-Cervia.

Bishop of San Marino-Montefeltro: Rt Rev. Paolo Rabitti, Curia Vescovile, Via del Seminario 5, 61016 Pennabilli, Italy; tel. (0541) 928415; fax (0541) 928766.

The Press

There are four daily newspapers and several periodicals, mainly published by the political organizations.

Argomenti: c/o CSdL, Via Cinque Febbraio 17, Fiorina C-3, 47895, Domagnano; tel. (0549) 962060; fax (0549) 962075; organ of the Confederazione Sammarinese del Lavoro (CSdL); periodical; Dir Andrea Leardini; circ. 5,000.

Fixing: Via G. Giacomini 37, 47890 San Marino; e-mail fixing@omniway.sm; periodical.

Nuovo Corriere di Informazione Sammarinese: Via Piana, 47890 San Marino; tel. 0549 995147; fax 0549 879021; e-mail corriere@rimini.com; daily.

Il nuovo Titano: Via G. Ordelaffi 46, 47890 San Marino; tel. 0549 902016; fax 0549 906438; organ of the PSS; periodical; Dir Verter Casali; circ. 1,300.

San Marino: Via delle Scalette 6, 47890 San Marino; tel. 0549 991193; fax 0549 992694; periodical; organ of the PDCS.

San Marino Oggi: Fiorentino; tel. 0549 878290; fax 0549 878949; e-mail sanmarinooggi@omniway.sm; daily.

La Tribuna Sammarinese: Via Gino Giacomini 86/A, 47890 San Marino; tel. 0549 990420; fax 0549 990398; e-mail info@latribunasammarinese.net; internet www.latribunasammarinese.net; daily; Dir Davide Graziosi.

Publishers

AIEP Editore: Via Gino Giacomini 86A, 47890 San Marino; tel. 0549 992590; fax 0549 990398; e-mail aiep@omniway.sm; internet www.aiepeditore.com; f. 1986; general book publishing; Man. Giuseppe Maria Morganti.

Edinter Editore Internazionali: Via Ca' Giello 6, 47890 San Marino; tel. and fax 0549 991672; newspapers; Dir Monica Goracci.

Edizioni del Titano: Via Istriani 94, 47890 San Marino; tel. 0549 995144; fax 0549 990454; e-mail edititano@omniway.sm; internet www.edizionititano.sm; f. 1991; book publishing; Man. Dir Pier Paolo Guardigli.

Broadcasting and Communications

TELECOMMUNICATIONS

Direzione Generale Poste e Telecomunicazioni: Contrada Omerelli 17, 47890 San Marino; tel. 0549 882555; fax 0549 992760; e-mail dirposte@omniway.sm; state body responsible for telecommunications; Dir-Gen. Rosa Zafferani.

The national telecommunications network is provided by Telecom Italia (see the chapter on Italy).

Intelcom San Marino, SpA: Strada degli Angariari 3, 47891 Falciano; tel. 0549 886111; fax 0549 908654; e-mail secretary@intelcom.sm; internet www.intelcom.sm; f. 1992; provides international telecommunications services; Pres. and CEO Andrea Cendali Pignatelli.

BROADCASTING

In 1987 a 1939 co-operation agreement with Italy, preventing San Marino from operating its own broadcasting services, was abrogated, and a joint venture between San Marino and the Italian state-owned radio and television corporation, Radiotelevisione Italiana, (RAI), was established in order to operate an independent broadcasting station for 15 years. RAI (see the chapter on Italy) broadcasts a daily information bulletin about the Republic under the title 'Notizie di San Marino'. San Marino RTV, established in 1991, began broadcasting in mid-1993. There is one private radio station.

Radio

San Marino RTV (Radiotelevisione): Viale Kennedy 13, 47890 San Marino; tel. 0549 882000; fax 0549 882060; e-mail rtv-red@omniway.sm; internet www.tradecenter.sm/rtv/; f. 1991; Pres. Dott. Dennis Guerra; Dir Aldo Bello.

Radio Titano: Via delle Carrare 35, Frazione Murata, 47890 San Marino; tel. 0549 997251; Dir P. Faetanini.

Television

San Marino RTV (Radiotelevisione): (see Radio).

Finance

(cap. = capital; res = reserves; dep. = deposits; m. = million; brs = branches; amounts in Italian lire or euros (€))

BANKING

Central Bank

Istituto di Credito Sammarinese: Via del Voltone 120, 47890 San Marino; tel. 0549 882325; fax 0549 882328; e-mail ics@omniway.sm; internet www.ics.sm; f. 1986; manages both state and public-sector deposits; res €7.9m. dep. €126.9m. (Dec. 2001); Pres. Dott. Antonio Valentini; Deputy Gen. Mans Daniele Bernardi, Patrizio Toaiar.

Commercial Banks

Banca Agricola Commerciale della Repubblica di San Marino SA: Piazza Marino Tini 26, 47891 Dogana; tel. 0549 871111; fax 0549 871222; internet www.bac.sm; f. 1920; cap. €16,820,697, res €65,677,119; Pres. Luigi Lonfernini; Dir Pier Paolo Fabbri; 6 brs.

Banca di San Marino, SpA: Strada della Croce 39, 47896 Faetano; tel. 0549 873411; fax 0549 873401; e-mail info@bsm.sm; internet www.bsm.sm; f. 1920 as Cassa Rurale Depositi e Prestiti di Faetano, Scrl; changed name as above in 2001; cap. 183.3m. lire, res 174,604.5m. lire, dep.1,677,622.3m. lire (Dec. 2000); Chair. Piero Natalino Mularoni; Gen. Man. Paolo Mariani; 8 brs.

Cassa di Risparmio della Repubblica di San Marino: Strada V. Gualdaria 101, Cà Rigo, 47893 Borgo Maggiore; tel. 0549 872330; fax 0549 872710; e-mail info@carisp.sm; internet www.carisp.sm; f. 1882; cap. €389m., dep. €737m. (Dec. 2000); Pres. Dott. Gilberto Ghiotti; Dir Mario Fantini; 16 brs.

Credito Industriale Sammarinese: Piazza Bertoldi 8, 47899 Serravalle; tel. 0549 900726; fax 0549 901513; e-mail cis@omniway.sm; f. 1933; cap. 17,500.0m. lire, res 76,126.0m. lire, dep. 723,290.1m. lire (Dec. 2000); Chair. Aniceto Vittorio Ranieri; Man. Dir Giovanni Paccapelo; 2 brs.

INSURANCE

Several major Italian insurance companies have agencies in San Marino.

Trade and Industry

GOVERNMENT AGENCIES

Azienda Autonoma di Stato Filatelica e Numismatica (AASFN): Piazza Garibaldi 5, 47890 San Marino; tel. 0549 882370; fax 0549 882363; e-mail aasfn@omniway.sm; internet www.aasfn .sm; autonomous public enterprise; responsible for production and distribution of postage stamps and coins; Pres. CORRADO CARATTONI; Dir MARINO ZANOTTI.

Azienda Autonoma di Stato di Produzione (AASP): Via Ventotto Luglio 50, 47031 Borgo Maggiore; tel. 0549 883111; fax 0549 883600; e-mail aasp@omniway.sm; civil engineering works, road works, land reclamation; Pres. Ing. PAOLO RONDELLI; Dir FABIO BERARDI.

Azienda Autonoma di Stato per la gestione della Centrale del Latte: Strada Genghe di Atto 71, 47031 Acquaviva; tel. 0549 999207; fax 0549 999606; operates state monopoly in production and distribution of dairy products; Pres. TIZIANO CANINI; Dir PAOLO MUSCI.

INDUSTRIAL AND TRADE ASSOCIATIONS

Associazione Nazionale dell'Industria Sammarinese (ANIS) (National Association for Industry): Via Gino Giacomini 39, 47890 San Marino; tel. 0549 991128; fax 0549 992832; e-mail anis@ omniway.sm; internet www.anis.sm; Pres. Ing. FRANCO CAPICCHIONI.

Associazione Sammarinese Coltivatori Diretti, Affituari e Mezzadri (ASCDAM): San Marino; tel. 0549 998222; farmers' association.

Associazione Sammarinese Produttori Agricoli (ASPA): Serrabolino 42, 47893 Borgo Maggiore; tel. 0549 902617; agricultural producers' association.

Consorzio San Marino 2000: Contrada Omagnano 20, 47890 San Marino; tel. 0549 885431; fax 0549 885433; e-mail sanmarino2000@ omniway.sm; internet www.sanmarino2000.sm; fmrly Unione Sammarinese Operatori Turistici (USOT); tourism operators' association.

Organizzazione Sammarinese degli Imprendituri (OSLA): Via N. Bonaparte 75, 47890 San Marino; tel. 0549 992885; fax 0549 992620; e-mail osla@sanmarinosite.com; internet www.osla.sm; f. 1985; organization for the self-employed; Pres. PARIDE BUGLI.

Unione Nazionale Artigiani di San Marino (UNAS): Piazzale M. Giangi 2, San Marino; tel. 0549 992148; e-mail unas@omniway .sm; internet sistematica.sm.unas; artisans' association; Pres. GIANFRANCO TERENZI.

Unione Sammarinese Commercianti (USC): Via Piana 111, San Marino; tel. 0549 992892; shopkeepers' association.

UTILITIES

All utilities are imported from Italy.

Azienda Autonoma di Stato per i Servizi Pubblici (AASS): Via A. Superchio 16, Cailungo, 47031 San Marino; tel. 0549 903891; fax 0549 902312; e-mail aass@omniway.sm; internet www.tradecenter .sm/aass; f. 1981; autonomous state service company; distributes electricity, gas and water within San Marino; Pres. GIUSEPPE ROSSI; Dir Ing. MARINO MAIANI.

TRADE UNIONS

Centrale Sindacale Unitaria: Via Napoleone Bonaparte 75, 47031 San Marino.

Confederazione Democratica dei Lavoratori Sammarinesi (CDLS): Via Cinque Febbraio 17, Domagnano, 47895 San Marino; tel. 0549 962011; fax 0549 962095; e-mail cdls2@omniway.sm; internet www.cdls.sm; f. 1957; affiliated to ICFTU; Sec.-Gen. MARCO BECCARI; 4,593 mems.

Confederazione Sammarinese del Lavoro (CSdL): Via Cinque Febbraio 17, Fiorina C-3, 47895 Domagnano; tel. 0549 962060; fax 0549 962075; e-mail csdl@omniway.sm; internet www .tradecenter.sm/csdl; f. 1943; Sec.-Gen. GIOVANNI GHIOTTI; 3,600 mems.

Transport

The capital, San Marino, is connected with Borgo Maggiore, about 1.5 km away, by funicular. There is also a bus service, and a highway down to the Italian coast at Rimini, about 24 km away. San Marino has an estimated 104 km of motorways. The nearest airport to the Republic is at Rimini. There are no frontier or customs formalities.

Azienda Autonoma di Stato per i Servizi Pubblici (AASS): (see Utilities, above); numerous responsibilities include public transport and funicular railway.

Tourism

The mild climate attracts many visitors to San Marino each year. The contrasting scenery and well-preserved medieval architecture are also attractions. In 2000 San Marino received 3.1m. visitors.

Ufficio di Stato per il Turismo (State Tourist Board): Contrada Omagnano 20, 47890 San Marino; tel. 0549 882998; fax 0549 882575; e-mail statoturismo@omniway.sm; internet www.omniway .sm; Dir ANTONIO MACINA.

SÃO TOMÉ AND PRÍNCIPE

Introductory Survey

Location, Climate, Language, Religion, Flag, Capital

The Democratic Republic of São Tomé and Príncipe lies in the Gulf of Guinea, off the west coast of Africa. There are two main islands, São Tomé and Príncipe, and the country also includes the rocky islets of Caroço, Pedras and Tinhosas, off Príncipe, and Rôlas, off São Tomé. The climate is warm and humid, with average temperatures ranging between 22°C (72°F) and 30°C (86°F). The rainy season extends from October to May, and average annual rainfall varies from 500 mm (20 ins) in the southern highlands to 1,000 mm (39 ins) in the northern lowlands. Portuguese is the official language, and native dialects are widely spoken. Almost all of the inhabitants profess Christianity, and the overwhelming majority (some 83%) are adherents of the Roman Catholic Church. The national flag (proportions 1 by 2) has three horizontal stripes, of green, yellow (one-half of the depth) and green, with a red triangle at the hoist and two five-pointed black stars on the yellow stripe. The capital is the town of São Tomé, on São Tomé island.

Recent History

A former Portuguese colony, São Tomé and Príncipe became an overseas province of Portugal in 1951 and received local autonomy in 1973. A nationalist group, the Comissão de Libertação de São Tomé e Príncipe, was formed in 1960 and became the Movimento de Libertação de São Tomé e Príncipe (MLSTP) in 1972, under the leadership of Dr Manuel Pinto da Costa. Based in Libreville, Gabon, the MLSTP was recognized by the Organization of African Unity (now the African Union, see p. 130) in 1973.

Following the military coup in Portugal in April 1974, the Portuguese Government recognized the right of the islands to independence. Negotiations began in November, at which Portugal recognized the MLSTP as the sole representative of the people. On 12 July 1975 independence was achieved, with da Costa as the country's first President and Miguel dos Anjos da Cunha Lisboa Trovoada as Prime Minister. In December a legislative Assembléia Popular Nacional (National People's Assembly) was elected.

In March 1978 the Prime Minister stated that an attempted coup by foreign mercenaries, orchestrated from Gabon by Carlos Alberto Monteiro Dias da Graça, an exiled former Minister of Health, had been suppressed. Angolan troops were called in to support the Government, and in March 1979 the alleged conspirators were sentenced to terms of imprisonment. President da Costa took over the post of Prime Minister, and Trovoada was arrested in September and charged with complicity in the coup attempt. He was released and allowed to go into exile in 1981. Another alleged coup attempt was forestalled in November 1980.

In March 1986 two opposition groups based outside the country, the União Democrática Independente de São Tomé e Príncipe and da Graça's more radical Frente de Resistência Nacional de São Tomé e Príncipe (FRNSTP), announced that they had formed a coalition and demanded the holding of democratic elections. In May da Graça resigned as President of the FRNSTP and expressed his willingness to co-operate with the Government.

Worsening economic conditions, following a severe drought in 1982, prompted the Government to review the country's close ties with communist regimes and its consequent isolation from major Western aid sources. In late 1984 da Costa declared São Tomé and Príncipe to be politically non-aligned, and in early 1985 the pro-Soviet Ministers of Foreign Affairs and of Planning were dismissed. The number of Angolan, Cuban and Soviet military personnel was reduced, and the responsibilities of Eastern bloc advisers in government departments were substantially curtailed. However, in January 1987 the Minister of Planning and Commerce, who had been largely responsible for the programme (which involved considerable lessening of state controls), was dismissed, and the Minister of Foreign Affairs and Co-operation, who had also been prominent in negotiations with donor agencies, was deprived of the foreign affairs portfolio.

In October 1987 the Central Committee of the MLSTP announced major constitutional reforms, including the election by universal adult suffrage of the President of the Republic and of members of the Assembléia Popular Nacional. The amended Constitution also allowed 'independent' candidates to contest legislative elections, although the President of the MLSTP, chosen by the MLSTP Congress from two candidates proposed by the Central Committee, would continue to be the sole candidate for the presidency of the Republic. In January 1988 the premiership was restored, and Celestino Rochas da Costa, hitherto Minister of Education, Labour and Social Security, was appointed as Prime Minister. Rochas da Costa formed a new Council of Ministers, appointing da Graça as Minister of Foreign Affairs.

In March 1988 armed men landed on São Tomé island and attempted to seize the police headquarters outside the capital. Security forces killed two of the men and captured the others. The attack was led by Afonso dos Santos, the leader of a dissident faction of the FRNSTP, who apparently intended to depose President da Costa. The FRNSTP leadership condemned the attempted coup and denied the Government's claim that the group was responsible for the venture. In September 1989 dos Santos was sentenced to 22 years' imprisonment, while 38 other defendants were also given custodial sentences.

In March 1990 a joint meeting of the Assembléia Popular Nacional and the MLSTP Central Committee approved a new draft Constitution, which provided for the establishment of a multi-party system, limited the President's tenure of office to two five-year terms, and permitted independent candidates to participate in legislative elections. In April dos Santos and his accomplices in the 1988 coup attempt were granted an amnesty by presidential decree. In May 1990 Trovoada returned from exile to contest the forthcoming presidential election. On 22 August, in a national referendum, 90.7% of participating voters (72% of the electorate) endorsed the new Constitution. In the following month new legislation on the formation of political parties came into effect. Delegates to the MLSTP Congress in October voted to replace da Costa as party President, appointing da Graça to the new post of Secretary-General. The party's name was amended to the Movimento de Libertação de São Tomé e Príncipe—Partido Social Democrata (MLSTP—PSD). In November da Graça resigned the foreign affairs portfolio. In the same month impatience at successive postponements of the legislative and presidential elections resulted in public demonstrations. Several thousands took part in a demonstration led by the newly registered opposition parties, notably the Partido de Convergência Democrática—Grupo de Reflexão (PCD—GR).

On 20 January 1991 elections to the new Assembléia Nacional resulted in defeat for the MLSTP—PSD, which secured only 30.5% of the votes cast and 21 seats in the 55-member legislature, while the PCD—GR won 54% of the votes and 33 seats. The Partido Democrático de São Tomé e Príncipe—Coligação Democrático da Oposição (PDSTP—CODO), with 5% of the votes, took the remaining seat. In February a transitional Government, headed by the Secretary-General of the PCD—GR, Daniel Lima dos Santos Daio, was installed. In the same month President da Costa announced that he would not be contesting the presidential election, to be held in March. The MLSTP—PSD did not present an alternative candidate. In late February two of the three remaining presidential candidates withdrew from the election. Miguel Trovoada, who stood as an independent candidate (with the support of the PCD—GR), was thus the sole contender, and on 3 March he was elected President with the support of 81% of those who voted. He took office on 3 April. The transitional Government resigned in mid-April, and was reappointed shortly afterwards.

In April 1992 more than 1,000 people joined a demonstration to demand the resignation of the Daio Government; the imposition of stringent austerity measures had precipitated widespread popular dissatisfaction. Some 7,000 people were reported to have attended a further demonstration later in April, and on the following day Trovoada dismissed the Daio administration. The PCD—GR, which had denounced Trovoada's action as an 'institutional coup', was invited to designate a new Prime Minister, and in May Norberto Costa Alegre (hitherto Minister of Economy and Finance) was chosen as Prime Minister. A new Government was named shortly afterwards.

At the first local elections since independence, held in December 1992, the PCD—GR suffered a considerable reverse, failing to secure control of any of the seven districts. Conversely, the opposition MLSTP—PSD gained control of five districts. In February 1993 Daio resigned as Secretary-General of the PCD—GR; he was succeeded by the more moderate João do Sacramento Bonfim.

In April 1994 the Assembléia Nacional adopted legislation, drafted by the MLSTP—PSD, reinforcing the rights of the parliamentary opposition. All opposition parties represented in the legislature were to be consulted on major political issues, including defence, foreign policy and the budget. In the same month deputies began discussion of a draft bill providing for a degree of autonomy for the island of Príncipe, to include the creation of a regional council. The proposed legislation was prompted by concern among inhabitants of Príncipe that the island had been neglected by the central administration.

Meanwhile, relations between the Government and the presidency deteriorated, and in April 1994 Trovoada publicly dissociated himself from government policy. Political tension increased in June, when the PCD—GR accused Trovoada of systematic obstruction of the government programme. In that month opposition parties petitioned the President to dismiss the Government, conduct early legislative elections and appoint foreign auditors to investigate the management of public finances under the PCD—GR administration. In July Trovoada dismissed the Alegre Government, citing 'institutional conflict' as justification for his action, following a dispute concerning the control of the budget. Trovoada appointed Evaristo do Espírito Santo de Carvalho (the Minister of Defence and Security in the outgoing administration) as Prime Minister. The PCD—GR, refusing to participate in an administration formed on presidential initiative, subsequently expelled Carvalho from the party. An interim Government, comprising principally technocrats and senior civil servants, was appointed. Shortly afterwards Trovoada dissolved the Assembléia Nacional, thus preventing the PCD—GR from using its parliamentary majority to declare the new Government unconstitutional.

Legislative elections were held on 2 October 1994, at which the MLSTP—PSD secured 27 seats, one short of an absolute majority. The PCD—GR and Acção Democrática Independente (ADI) each obtained 14 seats; da Graça was subsequently appointed Prime Minister. Despite initial efforts to involve opposition parties in a government of national unity, his Council of Ministers was dominated by members of the MLSTP—PSD. In December da Graça dismissed a number of senior civil servants, including the administrative heads of all public enterprises, notably the Governor of the Central Bank, who was accused of misappropriation of funds.

In March 1995 the first elections to a new seven-member regional assembly and five-member regional government were conducted on Príncipe, which had been granted local autonomy by the Assembléia Nacional in 1994. The elections resulted in an absolute majority for the MLSTP—PSD; the ADI and the PCD—GR did not present candidates, supporting instead a local opposition group. The new regional Government began functioning in April 1995.

In February 1995 the Government announced a general salary increase of 64%–90% in an effort to assuage increasing social tension caused by the high rate of inflation. In June the police took control of the national radio station, following several days of strike action by employees who were demanding salary increases of as much as 300%. Shortly afterwards the Government suspended a 350% salary increase previously awarded to bank employees, and established a commission to review state administration salaries. In June the Minister of Planning and Finance, Carlos Quaresma Batista da Sousa, left the Government to assume fully the position of Governor of the Central Bank (which he had held in an acting capacity since December 1994).

On 15 August 1995 a group of some 30 soldiers, led by five junior officers, seized control of the presidential palace in a bloodless coup. Trovoada was detained at the headquarters of the armed forces, and da Graça was placed under house arrest. The legislature was disbanded, the Constitution suspended and a curfew imposed. Following talks mediated by an Angolan delegation, on 21 August the insurgents and the Government signed a 'memorandum of understanding', providing for the reinstatement of Trovoada and the restoration of constitutional order. In return, the Government gave an undertaking to restructure the armed forces, and the Assembléia Nacional granted a general amnesty to all those involved in the coup. The Minister of Defence and Internal Security, Alberto Paulino, was dismissed and replaced by Capt. Carlos Carneiro Paquete da Silva. In September, however, da Silva's appointment as Commander-in-Chief of the Army prompted a protest by the officers responsible for the coup, who considered it contrary to the 'memorandum of understanding'.

At the end of December 1995 Armindo Vaz d'Almeida was appointed Prime Minister, by presidential decree, to head a Government of National Unity. The new administration included six members of the MLSTP—PSD, four members of the ADI and one of the PDSTP—CODO. The three parties had signed a political pact, with the aim of ensuring political stability. The PCD—GR refused to participate in the new Government. In February 1996, at the request of the national electoral commission, the forthcoming presidential election, which had been set for March, was postponed, pending the satisfactory completion of the electoral rolls. The date of the election was subsequently rescheduled for 30 June. At the Congress of the MLSTP—PSD, held in March, Pinto da Costa was selected as the party's presidential candidate, while Francisco Fortunato Pires was appointed Secretary-General of the party, replacing the more moderate da Graça. In April Trovoada declared his candidacy for the presidential election, supported by the ADI and the PDSTP—CODO.

At the presidential election of 30 June 1996 no candidate secured an absolute majority. The two leading candidates thus proceeded to a second round of voting on 21 July, at which Trovoada won 52.74% of the votes, defeating Pinto da Costa. In late July da Costa, who had initially acknowledged Trovoada's victory, claimed that irregularities had occurred in the registration process. In early August the Supreme Court declared that it was unable to adjudicate on the appeal made by da Costa, and recommended that the Government seek international legal arbitration. However, on 20 August da Costa withdrew his challenge, and Trovoada was confirmed as President. Although he did not command majority support in the Assembléia Nacional, Trovoada dismissed the possibility of new legislative elections, announcing instead his intention to seek a broadly based government of national consensus. In September the Vaz d'Almeida administration was dissolved, following its defeat in a confidence motion in the Assembléia Nacional. The motion had been proposed by Vaz d'Almeida's own party, the MLSTP—PSD, which accused the Government of inefficiency and corruption, and had received the support of the PCD—GR. However, a period of two months elapsed before the legislature was able to agree on the nomination of a successor to Vaz d'Almeida, who remained as Prime Minister in an interim capacity. In November Raul Wagner da Conceição Bragança Neto, Assistant Secretary-General of the MLSTP—PSD, was appointed Prime Minister. A new coalition Government, including five members of the MLSTP—PSD, three members of the PCD—GR and one independent, was inaugurated later that month. (The ADI had refused to participate in the new administration.)

In April 1997, in view of the continuing political struggle between the Government and the presidency, Trovoada held discussions with former President Pinto da Costa, at which he proposed the creation of a 'unity forum for national reconciliation' to debate the country's problems. In that month there were violent protests in the capital, following the introduction of a 140% increase in fuel prices. Demonstrators blocked roads, and security forces were deployed to quell rioting.

In July 1997, as a consequence of Trovoada's unilateral decision, two months previously, to establish diplomatic relations with Taiwan, the People's Republic of China suspended diplomatic relations with São Tomé and demanded the repayment, within 90 days, of bilateral debts amounting to US $17m. In exchange for diplomatic recognition, Trovoada had reportedly secured development aid from Taiwan totalling some $30m. The Government, however, criticized Trovoada's decision, maintaining that the promised aid could not compensate for the loss of the long-standing co-operation enjoyed, since 1975, with the People's Republic of China. Consequently, the Government refused to accept $4.3m. in aid offered by Taiwan and prohibited its officials from receiving the four high-ranking diplomats appointed to represent Taiwan in São Tomé. In October, in order to avoid further conflict with Trovoada, the Government withdrew its opposition to the diplomatic recognition of Taiwan and subsequently accepted the Taiwanese development aid.

At an extraordinary congress of the MLSTP—PSD conducted in May 1998, Pinto da Costa was elected unopposed as President of the party. (The ruling party of Angola, the Movimento Popular de Libertação de Angola (MPLA), had made the resumption of financial support for the MLSTP—PSD conditional on da Costa's election; following his defeat in the 1996 presidential election, the MPLA had ceased payments, creating serious problems for the MLSTP—PSD). New party statutes were approved, creating the position of party President, together with three vice-presidential posts. The former Secretary-General of the party, Francisco Fortunato Pires, refused to assume any leading position within the party and declared the new leadership structure to be unsuitable.

At legislative elections held on 8 November 1998 (postponed from October owing to delays in the electoral process), the MLSTP—PSD secured a majority, with 31 seats, while the ADI won 16 seats and the PCD—GR obtained the remaining eight seats. In December Guilherme Pósser da Costa (a Vice-President of the MLSTP—PSD and former Minister of Foreign Affairs and Co-operation) was appointed Prime Minister. However, the MLSTP—PSD accused Trovoada of interfering in areas outside his jurisdiction when, later that month, he vetoed Pósser da Costa's initial nominations for the Council of Ministers. A revised Council of Ministers was finally installed on 5 January 1999.

In March 1999 the Governor of the Central Bank, Carlos Quaresma, was dismissed for his alleged involvement in corrupt financial practices. The accusations arose following the detention in Brussels, Belgium, two months earlier of three men who had attempted to sell falsified Santomean treasury bonds worth US $500m. The bonds bore the signature of Quaresma, who was alleged to have links with the men concerned. The Government subsequently appointed a commission to conduct an inquiry into the case; its report, released in mid-March, concluded that the bonds had been issued illegally, and the case was referred to the Attorney-General for investigation. Quaresma, meanwhile, denied all allegations of corruption and declared that the deal had been intended to finance development projects in the country and that former Prime Ministers Vaz d'Almeida and Bragança, as well as President Trovoada, had been completely aware of the proceedings. Trovoada denied these allegations. In late March the Minister of Planning, Finance and Co-operation, Afonso da Graça Varela da Silva, resigned, reportedly as a result of the ongoing investigation. In April the Belgian authorities issued an international arrest warrant for Quaresma. In the following month the Assembléia Nacional suspended Quaresma's parliamentary immunity to allow him to be questioned by the Office of the Attorney-General. Quaresma was detained in October 1999. However, in March 2000, Quaresma was released, following the discovery of a document signed by Vaz d'Almeida, ordering the treasury bonds to be issued. Vaz d'Almeida denied any involvement, claiming that the documents had been falsified.

In January 2000 some 3,500 civil servants and public-sector workers demanded a 1,400% increase in the minimum wage. The increase proposed by the Government earlier that month, considered to be insufficient, had been in accordance with IMF recommendations not to increase expenditure on salaries by more than 7%. Despite a reduction in demands by the public-sector unions, talks broke off without an agreement. In April, however, a government proposal to increase the minimum wage by 325% was accepted by the unions, and both parties agreed to resume wage negotiations later that year. Discontent was expressed by the civil servants' trade union in September at significant increases in fuel prices throughout the second half of the year; the union stated its intention to demand further salary rises to compensate for the escalating fuel costs. In mid-October the teachers' union initiated strike action in support of its demands for higher salaries and improved working conditions. Later that month the health workers' union also went on strike demanding wage increases. Both unions called for rises equivalent to that agreed with the civil servants in April. The strike in the health sector ended after 10 days, when the Government agreed to raise the minimum salary by 275%. The teachers' strike lasted until late November, when a number of demands were satisfied.

Meanwhile, in April 2000 Joaquim Rafael Branco, the former Deputy Secretary of the Comunidade dos Países de Língua Portuguesa (CPLP, see p. 349), was appointed as Minister of Foreign Affairs and Co-operation, replacing Paulo Jorge do Espírito Santo, who had resigned, following rumours of disagreements with President Trovoada. The Minister of Justice, Alberto Paulino, assumed responsibility for public administration and labour, while the youth and sports portfolios were integrated into the Ministries of Education and Health, respectively. A further cabinet reshuffle was effected in May.

In August 2000 the parliamentary leader of the PCD—GR, Sebastião Santos, accused Prime Minister Pósser da Costa of giving preferential treatment to a construction company, Solar Construções, that had been awarded a public tender for road repairs. Santos revealed that da Costa owned 5% of the company's shares, and a parliamentary inquiry into the affair was instigated. However, when the results of the inquiry were presented to the Assembléia Nacional in January 2001, the MLSTP—PSD members of the commission refused to sign the document, rejecting the conclusion that the Prime Minister had acted improperly.

A presidential election took place on 29 July 2001. Among the five candidates hoping to succeed Trovoada were former President Manuel Pinto da Costa, the leader of the MLSTP—PSD, and Fradique de Menezes, a businessman standing for the ADI. In the event, de Menezes was elected to the presidency, winning 56.31% of the votes cast, while da Costa secured 38.73% and the remaining three candidates each gained less than 5%. De Menezes was inaugurated as President on 3 September. Following the dissolution by de Menezes of Pósser da Costa's administration (owing to disagreements over the distribution of ministerial positions), a new Government of 'presidential initiative', which did not include any members of the MLSTP—PSD, was appointed in late September. The new Council of Ministers, led by Evaristo de Carvalho as Prime Minister, was composed of members of the ADI, the PCD (which had voted to remove the suffix Grupo de Reflexão from its official name at a recent congress) and one independent. In early December de Menezes dissolved the Assembléia Nacional and announced that legislative elections would be held in March 2002, after which a new, more broadly based Government would be formed, according to an agreement reportedly signed by the President and representatives of political parties. In January 2002 the PCD formed an electoral alliance with the Movimento Democrático Força da Mudança (MDFM), which had been created in December by supporters of de Menezes. A number of prominent members of the ADI had reportedly defected to the MDFM since its establishment.

In February 2002 Patrício Trovoada, the son of former President Miguel Trovoada and a member of the ADI, resigned as Minister of Foreign Affairs, Co-operation and Communities, stating that he had lost confidence in President de Menezes and criticizing de Menezes' recent attempts to distance himself and the MDFM from Miguel Trovoada and the ADI. The Minister of Public Works, Infrastructure and Natural Resources, Mateus Rita, assumed the additional portfolios.

At legislative elections, held on 3 March 2002, no party obtained an absolute majority in the Assembléia Nacional. Provisional results indicated that the MLSTP—PSD and the MDFM-PCD alliance had each secured 23 of the 55 seats, while the remaining nine seats had been won by Uê Kédadji (UK), an alliance of the ADI and four minor parties. However, following a rerun of voting in one small district, the MLSTP—PSD secured an extra seat, to the cost of the UK alliance, and was proclaimed victorious. Gabriel da Costa, the former ambassador to Portugal, was subsequently appointed as the nominally independent Prime Minister, and in April a new coalition Government of National Unity, which included representatives of the MLSTP—PSD, the MDFM-PCD and the UK, as well as a number of independents, was installed.

In late September 2002 the controversial promotion of the Minister of Defence and Internal Affairs, Victor Tavares Monteiro, to the rank of Lt-Col by President de Menezes was quickly followed by Monteiro's resignation over personal differences with the President. Da Costa's Government was subsequently dismissed by de Menezes, who appointed Maria das Neves de Souza, of the MLSTP—PSD, hitherto Minister of Trade, Industry and Tourism, as Prime Minister in early October. A new Government of National Unity, with six representatives from the MLSTP—PSD, five from the MDFM-PCD alliance, two from the UK alliance and one independent, was formed. Dismissed Prime Minister da Costa accused de Menezes of acting unconstitutionally, particularly in his assumption of control over petroleum affairs. Da Costa was subsequently sentenced to

30 days' imprisonment for defamation of the President. In December the first MDFM congress elected Tomé Vera Cruz as Secretary-General of the party.

Meanwhile, in November 2002 the Assembléia Nacional approved a resolution for constitutional reform, altering the structure of the semi-presidential system to reduce presidential power. However, the draft revisions caused a political crisis over President de Menezes' delays in their promulgation and his repeated threats to veto them, according to powers vested in him by the Constitution of 1990; de Menezes also threatened to dismiss the Government if limitations were imposed on presidential power. An apparent consensus was reached in December 2002, but the situation deteriorated further in early 2003, and in mid-January the President vetoed the new draft constitution, on the grounds that it should be endorsed by public referendum before coming into force. De Menezes dissolved the Assembléia Nacional by presidential decree later that month and called early elections for 13 April. However, Prime Minister das Neves vowed to continue working and transferred the Government of National Unity to the island of Príncipe. Following swift negotiations between the Government and the President, de Menezes reversed his decree, reinstating the Government, and a 'memorandum of understanding' was signed by de Menezes and the Assembléia Nacional, which provided for the immediate promulgation of the new Constitution, but called for a referendum to take place in March–April 2006 on the system of government. The President's actions did, however, concern the MLSTP—PSD, as the Assembléia was now legitimized only by his decree and not by popular mandate.

The new Constitution, which took effect in March 2003, provided for the establishment of an advisory Council of State and a Constitutional Tribunal, with jurisdiction over issues of constitutionality. The President's right to veto constitutional amendments was removed. The changes were regarded as significantly reducing the executive power of the President, although maintaining a semi-presidential system pending the referendum of 2006.

São Tomé and Príncipe maintains cordial relations with the other former Portuguese African colonies and with Portugal. In July 1996 São Tomé and Príncipe was among the five lusophone African countries that, together with Portugal and Brazil, formed the CPLP, a Portuguese-speaking commonwealth seeking to achieve collective benefits from co-operation in technical, cultural and social matters. In December 2002 Angola, another CPLP member, agreed to provide São Tomé with assistance in the development of its petroleum reserves and the establishment of a national petroleum company.

São Tomé and Príncipe has important trade links with the nearby mainland states of Gabon, Cameroon and Equatorial Guinea. In November 1999 São Tomé and Príncipe was a founder of the seven-member Gulf of Guinea Commission; it was hoped that the commission would assist in solving inter-state conflicts within the region. In August 2000 São Tomé and Príncipe and Nigeria reached an agreement on the delimitations of their common maritime border (the border had been in contention for a number of years, particularly because of disputes regarding access to the Gulf of Guinea's significant petroleum reserves). Moreover, the two countries agreed to establish a joint development zone (JDZ) for the exploitation of petroleum resources. A further accord, on the joint exploitation of a variety of mineral resources, was signed in February 2001; Nigeria was to receive 60% of revenues and Sao Tomé and Príncipe 40%. In January 2002 the Presidents of both countries inaugurated a development authority to oversee the affairs of the JDZ. Disagreements developed during 2002, however, over Nigeria's commitment to provide São Tomé and Príncipe with 60,000 barrels of petroleum per day (reduced to 40,000 in September, and to 10,000 in October), and the relative lack of Santomean representation in the development authority. In November de Menezes refused to continue with the proposed sale of oil blocs until the issue was resolved; he was supported in this by a report from the World Bank, which suggested that the division of profits was unfair to São Tomé and Príncipe. By early 2003, however, issues had been resolved sufficiently for the first licensing round to commence in mid-April.

Government

Under the 2003 Constitution, legislative power is vested in the Assembléia Nacional, which comprises 55 members, elected by universal adult suffrage for a term of four years. No limit is placed on the number of political parties permitted to operate. Executive power is vested in the President of the Republic, who is Head of State, and who governs with the assistance of an appointed Council of Ministers, led by the Prime Minister. The Council of State acts as an advisory body to the President, who is elected by universal suffrage for a term of five years. The President's tenure of office is limited to two successive terms. The Prime Minister, who is appointed by the President, is, in theory, nominated by the deputies of the Assembléia Nacional.

In 1994 the Assembléia Nacional granted political and administrative autonomy to the island of Príncipe. Legislation was adopted establishing a seven-member regional assembly and a five-member regional government; both are accountable to the Government of São Tomé and Príncipe.

Defence

In 1992 a reorganization was initiated of the islands' armed forces (estimated to comprise some 600 men in 1995) and the police into two separate police forces, one for public order and another for criminal investigation. In the budget for 2000 current expenditure on defence amounted to 1,100m. dobras.

Economic Affairs

In 2001, according to estimates by the World Bank, São Tomé and Príncipe's gross national product (GNI), measured at average 1999–2001 prices, was US $43m., equivalent to $280 per head. During 1990–2001, it was estimated, the population increased at an average annual rate of 2.5%, while gross domestic product (GDP) per head declined, in real terms, by an average of 0.5% per year. Overall GDP increased, in real terms, at an average annual rate of 2.0% in 1990–2001; growth in 2001 was 3.0%.

Agriculture (including fishing) contributed an estimated 20.0% of GDP in 2001, and employed 31.5% of the employed population in that year. The principal cash crop is cocoa, which accounted for 93.0% of export earnings in 2000. Secondary cash crops include coconuts and coffee. Staple crops for local consumption include bananas, taro, tomatoes and cassava. Agricultural production is principally concentrated on export commodities, although smallholder agriculture has become increasingly important. An agricultural policy charter, the Carta de Política e Desenvolvimento Rural, which was introduced in 2000, aimed to emphasize private sector-involvement and diversification into areas such as ylang-ylang, pepper, vanilla, fruits, vegetables and flowers. Fishing is also a significant activity. The sale of fishing licences to foreign fleets is an important source of income. According to the World Bank, agricultural GDP increased at an average annual rate of 3.8% in 1990–2001; growth in 2001 was 2.7%.

Industry (including manufacturing, construction and power) contributed an estimated 17.0% of GDP in 2001, and employed 17.0% of the employed population in that year. According to the World Bank, industrial GDP increased by an average of 1.8% per year in 1990–2001; growth in 2001 was 4.2%.

There are no mineral resources on the islands, but offshore prospecting for hydrocarbons resulted in the discovery of significant quantities of petroleum in 1998, including an estimated 4,000m. barrels in the joint development zone with Nigeria (see Recent History), as well as higher-risk resources in São Tomé's exclusive economic zone. However, these resources were not likely to contribute fully to the economy until 2006/07.

The manufacturing sector consists solely of small processing factories, producing soap, soft drinks, textiles and beer. Manufacturing contributed an estimated 4.2% of GDP in 2001. According to the World Bank, manufacturing GDP increased at an average annual rate of 1.5% in 1990–2001; growth in 2001 was 2.7%.

In 2000 some 74% of electricity generation was derived from thermal sources, and 26% from hydroelectric sources. Imports of petroleum products comprised 10.8% of the value of merchandise imports in 2000.

The services sector contributed an estimated 63.0% of GDP in 2001, and engaged 51.5% of the employed population in that year. According to the World Bank, the GDP of the services sector increased by an average of 1.0% per year in 1990–2001; growth in 2001 was 2.8%.

In 2001 São Tomé and Príncipe recorded a trade deficit of US $21.2m., and a deficit of $21.4m. on the current account of the balance of payments. In 2000 the principal source of imports (41.7%) was Portugal, and the principal market for exports (56.3%) was the Netherlands. Other major trading partners were Angola, Japan, Belgium and France. The principal export in 2000 was cocoa. The principal imports in that year were capital goods, foodstuffs, and petroleum and petroleum products.

In 2001 there was a budgetary deficit of 76,500m. dobras (equivalent to 18.1% of GDP). São Tomé's total external debt was US $315.9m. at the end of 2000, of which $294.4m. was long-term public debt. In that year the cost of debt-servicing was equivalent to 31.7% of the total value of exports of goods and services. Annual inflation averaged 28.1% in 1996–2000. Consumer prices increased by 9.6% in 2000 and by an estimated 9.4% in 2001. According to official figures, 27.4% of the labour force were unemployed in 1993.

São Tomé and Príncipe is a member of the International Cocoa Organization (see p. 336) and of the Communauté économique des états de l'Afrique centrale (see p. 339).

São Tomé and Príncipe's economy is dominated by cocoa production, and is therefore vulnerable to adverse weather conditions and to fluctuations in international prices for cocoa. In April 2000 funding of some US $8.9m. was approved by the IMF under its Poverty Reduction and Growth Facility (PRGF). The funding was conditional on the Government successfully implementing a three-year programme, aimed principally at reducing poverty levels. In May the 'Paris Club' group of donors agreed to reduce the interest on São Tomé and Príncipe's external debt by 95% until 2003, which was worth an estimated $26m. Moreover, in December 2000 a comprehensive debt-reduction programme, worth an estimated $200m., was agreed by the World Bank and the IMF, under the Heavily Indebted Poor Countries initiative. It was hoped that this would allow government expenditure to be invested in education, health and poverty reduction programmes. According to the IMF, however, in 2000 and 2001 the Government failed to meet a number of the performance criteria stipulated in its PRGF-supported programme. Moreover, the negotiation of an agreement with Nigeria on the joint exploration of petroleum was criticized for its lack of transparency. Consequently, in early 2002 a six-month supervised programme was negotiated with the IMF, under which the Government agreed to reform the civil service, to reduce the current-account deficit to less than 1% of GDP in 2002, and to achieve a budget surplus. GDP growth of some 5% was projected for that year. None the less, the Government was praised for stabilizing inflation, and for increasing government revenue through improvements in tax collection. However, progress by mid-2002 was disappointing, with an increase in the fiscal deficit to 3.2% of GDP, owing to high wage demands by trade unions and expenditure on legislative elections in March of that year, and the failure to approve a 2002 budget until July. The supervised programme was extended to December 2002, in the hope of containing inflation to 9% and narrowing the external current-account deficit (excluding official transfers) to 10% of GDP in 2002; the deficit was forecast to increase to 380% of GDP by 2005, reflecting increased imports associated with investment in petroleum exploration and development. As part of a structural adjustment programme, funds generated by offshore petroleum exploration were to be administered by the World Bank and the IMF, to be spent on projects aimed at balancing out the loss of revenues caused by dependence on cocoa and by mismanagement of state finances.

Education

Primary education is officially compulsory for a period of four years between six and 14 years of age. Secondary education lasts for a further seven years, comprising a first cycle of four years and a second, pre-university cycle of three years. In 2001 the country had 73 primary schools, with a total enrolment of 20,858 pupils. There were 13 secondary schools (including two devoted to vocational training) in that year, with a total enrolment of 13,874 pupils. There was one polytechnic institute (with an enrolment of 117 in 2000/01). In 2000 public investment in education (including culture and sport) amounted to US $1.3m., equivalent to 6.7% of total public investment.

Public Holidays

2003: 1 January (New Year), 3 February (Martyrs' Day), 1 May (Labour Day), 12 July (Independence Day), 6 September (Armed Forces Day), 30 September (Agricultural Reform Day), 21 December (São Tomé Day), 25 December (Christmas Day).

2004: 1 January (New Year), 3 February (Martyrs' Day), 3 May (for Labour Day), 12 July (Independence Day), 6 September (Armed Forces Day), 30 September (Agricultural Reform Day), 21 December (São Tomé Day), 25 December (Christmas Day).

Weights and Measures

The metric system is in force.

Statistical Survey

Source (unless otherwise stated): Instituto Nacional de Estatística, CP 256, São Tomé; tel. 21982.

AREA AND POPULATION

Area: 1,001 sq km (386.5 sq miles); São Tomé 859 sq km (331.7 sq miles), Príncipe 142 sq km (54.8 sq miles).

Population: 117,504 (males 58,040; females 59,464) at census of 4 August 1991; 137,599 (males 68,236; females 69,363) at census of September 2001.

Density (census of 2001): 137.5 per sq km.

Population by District (census of 2001): Água-Grande 51,886, Mé-Zochi 35,105, Cantagolo 13,258, Caué 5,501, Lembá 10,696, Lobata 15,157, Príncipe 5,966; Total 137,599.

Principal Towns (population at census of 1991): São Tomé (capital) 42,300; Trindade 11,400; Santana 6,200; Santo Amaro 5,900; Neves 5,900. Source: Stefan Helders, *World Gazetteer* (internet www.world-gazetteer.com).

Births, Marriages and Deaths (2000): Registered live births 4,078 (birth rate 29.20 per 1,000); Registered marriages 210 (marriage rate 1.5 per 1,000); Registered deaths 1,030 (death rate 7.51 per 1,000). *2001:* Birth rate 35.3 per 1,000; Death rate 8.3 per 1,000.

Expectation of Life (years at birth, estimates): 63.9 (males 61.3; females 66.5) in 2001.

Economically Active Population (census of 2001): Agriculture and fishing 13,518; Industry, electricity, gas and water 2,893; Public works and civil construction 4,403; Trade, restaurants and hotels 8,787; Transport, storage and communications 792; Public administration 3,307; Health 776; Education 1,373; Other activities 7,088; Total employed 42,937.

HEALTH AND WELFARE

Key Indicators

Total Fertility Rate (children per woman, 2001): 6.0.

Under-5 Mortality Rate (per 1,000 live births, 2001): 74.

Physicians (per 1,000 head, 1996): 0.47.

Hospital Beds (per 1,000 head, 1991): 4.74.

Health Expenditure (2000): US $ per head (PPP): 23.

Health Expenditure (2000): % of GDP: 2.3.

Health Expenditure (2000): public (% of total): 67.8.

Human Development Index (2000): ranking: 119.

Human Development Index (2000): value: 0.632.

For sources and definitions, see explanatory note on p. vi.

AGRICULTURE, ETC.

Principal Crops (FAO estimates, metric tons, 2001): Bananas 20,000; Maize 2,230; Taro 24,605; Yams 1,300; ; Cocoa 3,418; Coconuts 25,500; Copra 200; Coffee (green) 18; Cinnamon 30. Source: FAO.

Livestock (FAO estimates, head, 2001): Cattle 4,100; Sheep 2,600; Goats 4,800; Pigs 2,200; Poultry 381,000. Source: FAO.

Livestock Products (FAO estimates, metric tons, 2001): Beef and veal 108; Pig meat 80; Sheep and goat meat 24; Poultry meat 592; Hen eggs 385; Cows' milk 141. Source: FAO.

Forestry ('000 cubic metres, 1988): Roundwood removals 9; Sawnwood production 5. *1989–2001:* Annual output assumed to be unchanged since 1988. Source: FAO.

Fishing (FAO estimates, metric tons, live weight, 2000): Total catch 3,500 (Halfbeaks 150, Flyingfishes 1,000, Jacks and crevalles 150, Sharks, rays and skates 180). Source: FAO, *Yearbook of Fishery Statistics*.

INDUSTRY

Production (metric tons, unless otherwise indicated, 2000): Bread and biscuits 3,768 (1995); Soap 261.1 (1995); Beer (litres) 529,400 (1995); Palm oil 446.2; Electric energy (million kWh) 26.1 (Source: mainly IMF, *São Tomé and Príncipe: Statistical Appendix* (September 1998), and IMF, *São Tomé and Príncipe: Statistical Appendix* (February 2002)). *2001* (FAO estimate, metric tons): Palm oil 2,025.

FINANCE

Currency and Exchange Rates: 100 cêntimos = 1 dobra (Db). *Sterling, Dollar and Euro Equivalents* (31 December 2002): £1 sterling = 14,815.4 dobras; US $1 = 9,191.8 dobras; €1 = 9,639.5 dobras; 100,000 dobras = £6.750 = $10.879 = €10.374. *Average Exchange Rate* (dobras per US $): 7,978.2 in 2000; 8,842.1 in 2001; 9,088.3 in 2002.

Budget ('000 million dobras, 2001): *Revenue:* Taxation 78.6 ; Other current revenue 17.1; Total 95.6, excl. grants (178.4). *Expenditure:* Current expenditure 124.3 (Personnel costs 40.5; Goods and services 18.8; Interest on external debt 31.1; Interest on internal debt 1.1; Transfers 13.1; Other current expenditure 17.0; Redeployment fund 2.8); Capital 180.3; Net lending 0.0; Total 323.6. Note: Expenditure excludes adjustment for net change in arrears (26,900m. dobras). Source: IMF, *São Tomé and Príncipe: Review of Performance Under a Staff-Monitored Program* (December 2002).

International Reserves (US $ million at 31 December 2002): IMF special drawing rights 0.01; Foreign exchange 17.34; Total 17.35. Source: IMF, *International Financial Statistics*.

Money Supply (million dobras at 31 December 2002): Currency outside banks 39,424; Demand deposits at commercial banks 69,112; Total money (incl. others) 108,597. Source: IMF, *International Financial Statistics*.

Cost of Living (Consumer Price Index; base: 1996 = 100): 277.7 in 1998; 305.3 in 1999; 301.6 in 2000.

Gross Domestic Product by Economic Activity (estimates, '000 million dobras at current prices, 2000): Agriculture and fishing 74.3; Manufacturing, electricity, gas and water 20.3; Construction 43.7; Trade and transport 85.7; Public administration 84.8; Financial institutions 32.1; Other services 28.8; *Total* 369.5. Source: IMF, *São Tomé and Príncipe: Statistical Appendix* (February 2002).

Balance of Payments (US $ million, 2001): Exports of goods f.o.b. 3.3; Imports of goods f.o.b. −24.4; *Trade balance* −21.2; Exports of services 13.6; Imports of services −15.2; *Balance on goods and services* −22.8; Other income (net) −3.7; *Balance on goods, services and income* −26.5; Current transfers (net) 5.1; *Current balance* −21.4; Capital account (net) 11.4; Direct investment (net) 5.5; Other investment liabilities (net) 3.4; Net errors and omissions 3.7; *Overall balance* 2.6. Source: IMF, *International Finance Statistics*.

EXTERNAL TRADE

Principal Commodities (million dobras, 2000): *Imports c.i.f.:* Foodstuffs 64,225.7; Petroleum and petroleum products 23,146.5; Capital goods 45,564.3; Total (incl. others) 215,123.7. *Exports f.o.b.:* Cocoa 18,491.8; Total (incl. others) 19,883.3.

Principal Trading Partners (US $ million, 2000): *Imports c.i.f.:* Angola 2.9; Belgium 1.9; France 1.7; Gabon 0.7; Germany 0.1; Japan 2.4; Portugal 9.3; Total (incl. others) 22.3. *Exports f.o.b.:* Netherlands 1.8; Portugal 0.3; Total (incl. others) 3.2. Source: IMF, *São Tomé and Príncipe: Statistical Appendix* (February 2002).

TRANSPORT

Road Traffic (registered vehicles, 1996, estimates): Passenger cars 4,000; Lorries and vans 1,540. Source: International Road Federation, *World Road Statistics*.

Shipping: *International Freight Traffic* (estimates, metric tons, 1992): Goods loaded 16,000; Goods unloaded 45,000. *Merchant Fleet* (registered at 31 December 2001): Number of vessels 64; Total displacement 190,428 grt. (Source: Lloyd's Register-Fairplay, *World Fleet Statistics*).

Civil Aviation (traffic on scheduled services, 1998): Passengers carried ('000) 24; Passenger-km (million) 9; Total ton-km (million) 1. Source: UN, *Statistical Yearbook*.

TOURISM

Foreign Tourist Arrivals: 5,584 in 1998; 5,710 in 1999; 7,137 in 2000. Source: Tourism and Hotels Bureau.

Arrivals by Country of Residence (1997): Angola 336; Cape Verde 110; France 996; Gabon 289; Germany 165; Portugal 1,706; Spain 238; USA 103; Total (incl. others) 4,924. Source: World Tourism Organization, *Yearbook of Tourism Statistics*.

Tourism Receipts (US $ million): 2 in 1995; 2 in 1996; 2 in 1997. Source: World Tourism Organization, *Yearbook of Tourism Statistics*.

COMMUNICATIONS MEDIA

Radio Receivers (1997): 38,000 in use. Source: UNESCO, *Statistical Yearbook*.

Television Receivers (1997): 23,000 in use. Source: UNESCO, *Statistical Yearbook*.

Newspapers and Periodicals (2000): Titles 14 (1997); Average circulation 18,500 copies.

Telephones ('000 main lines, 2001): 5.4 in use. Source: International Telecommunication Union.

Facsimile Machines (2000): 372 in use.

Internet Users ('000): 9.0 in 2001. Source: International Telecommunication Union.

EDUCATION

Pre-primary (2001): 18 schools; 2,376 pupils.

Primary (2001): 73 schools; 623 teachers; 20,858 pupils.

General Secondary and Pre-university (2001): 11 schools; 630 teachers; 13,874 (including vocational education) pupils. There are also 2 vocational secondary schools.

Tertiary (2000/01): 1 polytechnic; 29 teachers; 117 pupils.

Adult Literacy Rate (official estimate, 2000): 83.1% (Source: UN Development Programme, *Human Development Report*).

Source: mostly *Carta Escolar de São Tomé e Príncipe,* Ministério de Educação de Portugal.

Directory

The Constitution

A new Constitution came into force on 4 March 2003, after the promulgation by the President of a draft approved by the Assembléia Nacional in December 2002. A 'memorandum of understanding', which was signed in January 2003 by the President and the Assembléia Nacional, provided for the scheduling of a referendum on the system of governance for March–April 2006, to coincide with the expiry of the current presidential mandate and with legislative elections. The following is a summary of the main provisions of the Constitution:

The Democratic Republic of São Tomé and Príncipe is a sovereign, independent, unitary and democratic state. Sovereignty resides in the people, who exercise it through universal, equal, direct and secret vote, according to the terms of the Constitution. There shall be complete separation between Church and State. There shall be freedom of thought, expression and information and a free and independent press, within the terms of the law.

Executive power is vested in the President of the Republic, who is elected for a period of five years by universal adult suffrage. The President's tenure of office is limited to two successive terms. He is the Supreme Commander of the Armed Forces and is accountable to the Assembléia Nacional. In the event of the President's death, permanent incapacity or resignation, his functions shall be assumed by the President of the Assembléia Nacional until a new President is elected.

The Council of State acts as an advisory body to the President and comprises the President of the Assembléia Nacional, the Prime Minister, the President of the Constitutional Tribunal, the Attorney-General, the President of the Regional Government of Príncipe, former Presidents of the Republic who have not been dismissed from their positions, three citizens of merit nominated by the President and three elected by the Assembléia Nacional. Its meetings are closed and do not serve a legislative function.

Legislative power is vested in the Assembléia Nacional, which comprises 55 members elected by universal adult suffrage. The Assembléia Nacional is elected for four years and meets in ordinary session twice a year. It may meet in extraordinary session on the proposal of the President, the Council of Ministers or two-thirds of its members. The Assembléia Nacional elects its own President. In the period between ordinary sessions of the Assembléia Nacional its functions are assumed by a permanent commission elected from among its members.

The Government is the executive and administrative organ of State. The Prime Minister is the Head of Government and is appointed by the President. Other ministers are appointed by the President on the proposal of the Prime Minister. The Government is responsible to the President and the Assembléia Nacional.

Judicial power is exercised by the Supreme Court and all other competent tribunals and courts. The Supreme Court is the supreme judicial authority, and is accountable only to the Assembléia Nacional. Its members are appointed by the Assembléia Nacional. The right to a defence is guaranteed.

The Constitutional Tribunal, comprising five judges with a mandate of five years, is responsible for jurisdiction on matters of constitutionality. During periods prior to, or between, the installation of the Constutional Tribunal, its function is assumed by the Supreme Court. The Constitution may be revised only by the Assembléia Nacional on the proposal of at least three-quarters of its members. Any amendment must be approved by a two-thirds' majority of the Assembléia Nacional. The President does not have right of veto over constitutional changes.

Note: In 1994 the Assembléia Nacional granted political and administrative autonomy to the island of Príncipe. Legislation was adopted establishing a seven-member Regional Assembly and a five-member Regional Government; both are accountable to the Government of São Tomé and Príncipe

The Government

HEAD OF STATE

President and Commander-in-Chief of the Armed Forces: FRADIQUE DE MENEZES (took office 3 September 2001).

COUNCIL OF MINISTERS
(April 2003)

A coalition Government of National Unity, comprising the Movimento de Libertação de São Tomé e Príncipe—Partido Social Democrata (MLSTP—PSD), the Movimento Democrático Força da Mudança-Partido de Convergência Democrática (MDFM-PCD) alliance, the Uê Kédadji (UK) alliance and one independent.

Prime Minister: MARIA DAS NEVES CEITA BATISTA DE SOUSA (MLSTP—PSD).

Minister of Foreign Affairs and Co-operation: MATEUS MEIRA RITA (MDFM-PCD).

Minister of Defence and Internal Affairs: Maj. FERNANDO DA TRINIDADE DANQUÁ (Ind.).

Minister of Justice, State Reform and Public Administration: JUSTINO TAVARES VIEGAS (MDFM-PCD).

Minister of Planning and Finance: MARIA DOS SANTOS TEBÚS TORRES (MDFM-PCD).

Minister of Trade, Industry and Tourism: ARZEMIRO DOS PRAZERES (MDFM-PCD).

Minister of Public Works, Infrastructure, Natural Resources and the Environment: JOAQUIM RAFAEL BRANCO (MLSTP—PSD).

Minister of Agriculture, Fisheries and Rural Development: JÚLIO LOPES LIMA DA SILVA (UK).

Minister of Health: CLAUDINA AUGUSTO CRUZ (MLSTP—PSD).

Minister of Education and Culture: MARIA FERNANDA PONTÍFICE DE JESUS BONFIM (MDFM-PCD).

Minister of Labour, Employment and Solidarity: DAMIÃO VAZ DE ALMEIDA (MLSTP—PSD).

Minister of Youth, Sports and Parliamentary Affairs: JOSÉ DA GRAÇA VIEGAS SANTIAGO (MLSTP—PSD).

In addition, there are two Secretaries of State.

Government of the Autonomous Region of Príncipe
(April 2003)

President and Secretary for Social Affairs: ZEFERINO VAZ DOS SANTOS DOS PRAZERES.

Secretary for Infrastructure and Environment: OSÓRIO UMBELINA.

Secretary for Economic Affairs and Finance: SILVESTRE UMBELINA.

MINISTRIES

Office of the Prime Minister: Rua do Município, CP 302, São Tomé; tel. 223913; fax 224679; e-mail gpm@cstome.net.

Ministry of Agriculture, Fisheries and Rural Development: Avda Marginal 12 de Julho, Edifício Ministério da Agricultura, 1° andar, São Tomé; tel. 222714.

Ministry of Defence and Internal Affairs: Avda 12 de Julho, CP 427, São Tomé; tel. 222041; e-mail midefesa@cstome.net.

Ministry of Education and Culture: Rua Misericórdia, CP 41, São Tomé; tel. 222861; fax 221466; e-mail mineducal@cstome.net.

Ministry of Foreign Affairs and Co-operation: Avda 12 de Julho, CP 111, São Tomé; tel. 221017; fax 222597; e-mail minecoop@cstome.net; internet 212.54.130.168/sites/gabinetepm/minecoop.htm.

Ministry of Health: Avda Patrice Lumumba, CP 23, São Tomé; tel. 241200; fax 221306; e-mail msaude@cstome.net.

Ministry of Justice, State Reform and Public Administration: Avda 12 de Julho, CP 4, São Tomé; tel. 222318; fax 222256; e-mail emilioma@cstome.net.

Ministry of Labour, Emploment and Solidarity: Rua Município, Edifício Ministério do Trabalho, São Tomé; tel. 221466.

Ministry of Planning and Finance: Largo Alfândega, CP 168, São Tomé; tel. 224173; fax 222683; e-mail mpfc@cstome.net.

Ministry of Public Works, Infrastructure, Natural Resources and the Environment: Avda 12 de Julho, CP 47, São Tomé; tel. 221631; fax 222347; e-mail mirna@cstome.net.

Ministry of Trade, Industry and Tourism: Largo Alfândegas, São Tomé; tel. 224657.

Ministry of Youth, Sports and Parliamentary Affairs: Rua Misericórdia, CP 41, São Tomé; tel. 222861; fax 221466.

President and Legislature

PRESIDENT

Presidential Election, 29 July 2001

Candidate	Votes	% of votes
Fradique de Menezes	21,149	56.31
Manuel Pinto da Costa	14,544	38.73
Carlos Tiny	1,237	3.29
Victor Monteiro	381	1.02
Francisco Fortunato Pires	244	0.65
Total	**37,555**	**100.00**

ASSEMBLÉIA NACIONAL

Assembléia Nacional: Palácio dos Congressos, CP 191, São Tomé; tel. 222986; fax 222835; e-mail sganstp@cstome.net; internet www.parlamento.st/home.

President: DIONÍSIO TOMÉ DIAS.

General Election, 3 March 2002

	Seats
Movimento de Libertação de São Tomé e Príncipe—Partido Social Democrata	24
Movimento Democrático Força da Mudança-Partido de Convergência Democrática	23
Uê Kédadji*	8
Total	**55**

* A coalition of the Acção Democrática Independente, the Partido de Coligação Democrática, the Partido Popular do Progresso, the Partido de Renovação Democrática and the União Nacional para Democracia e Progresso.

Political Organizations

Acção Democrática Independente (ADI): Avda Marginal 12 de Julho, Edificio C. Cassandra, São Tomé; tel. 222201; f. 1992; Leader José Fret Lau Chong.

Frente Democrata Cristã—Partido Social da Unidade (FDC—PSU): São Tomé; f. 1990; Pres. (vacant); Vice-Pres. Sabino dos Santos.

Movimento Democrático Força da Mudança (MDFM): São Tomé; f. 2001; Sec.-Gen. Tomé Vera Cruz.

Movimento de Libertação de São Tomé e Príncipe—Partido Social Democrata (MLSTP—PSD): Estrada Riboque, Edificio Sede do MLSTP, São Tomé; tel. 222253; f. 1972 as MLSTP; adopted present name in 1990; sole legal party 1972–90; Pres. Manuel Pinto da Costa.

Partido de Convergência Democrática (PCD): Avda 12 de Julho, São Tomé; tel. 225583; fax 223257; f. 1990 as Partido de Convergência—Grupo de Reflexão; Pres. Arzemiro dos Prazeres.

Partido de Coligação Democrática (CÓDÓ): São Tomé; f. 1990 as Partido Democrático de São Tomé e Príncipe—Coligação Democrática da Oposição; renamed as above June 1998; Leader Manuel Neves e Silva.

Partido Popular do Progresso (PPP): São Tomé; f. 1998; Leader Francisco Silva.

Partido de Renovação Democrática (PRD): São Tomé; f. 2001; Pres. Armindo Graça.

Partido Trabalhista Santomense (PTS): CP 254, São Tomé; tel. 223338; fax 223255; e-mail pascoal@cstome.net; f. 1993 as Aliança Popular; Leader Anacleto Rolin.

União Nacional para Democracia e Progresso (UNDP): São Tomé; f. 1998; Leader Paixão Lima.

Diplomatic Representation

EMBASSIES IN SÃO TOMÉ AND PRÍNCIPE

Angola: Avda Kwame Nkrumah 45, CP 133, São Tomé; tel. 222376; fax 221562; Ambassador Pedro Fernando Mavunza.

China (Taiwan): Avda Marginal de 12 de Julho, CP 839, São Tomé; tel. 223529; fax 221376; e-mail rocstp@cstome.net; Ambassador Jaison Ko.

Equatorial Guinea: Travessa Imprensa, São Tomé; tel. 224658.

Gabon: Rua Damão, CP 394, São Tomé; tel. 224434; fax 223531; Ambassador Emmanuel Mba Allo.

Nigeria: Avda Nações Unidas; tel. 225404; fax 225406; e-mail nigeria@cstome.net.

Portugal: Avda Marginal de 12 de Julho, CP 173, São Tomé; tel. 222470; fax 221190; e-mail eporstp@sol.stome.telepac.net; Ambassador Mário de Jesus Santos.

Judicial System

Judicial power is exercised by the Supreme Court of Justice and the Courts of Primary Instance. The Supreme Court is the ultimate judicial authority.

Supreme Court: Avda Marginal de 12 de Julho, São Tomé; tel. and fax 222329; Pres. Alice Vera Cruz.

Religion

According to the 2001 census 77% of the population are Christians, almost all of whom are Roman Catholics.

CHRISTIANITY

The Roman Catholic Church

São Tomé and Príncipe comprises a single diocese, directly responsible to the Holy See. At the census of 2001 there were 96,684 adherents in the country, representing 70.3% of the population. The bishop participates in the Episcopal Conference of Angola and São Tomé (based in Luanda, Angola).

Bishop of São Tomé e Príncipe: Rt Rev. Abílio Rodas de Sousa Ribas, Centro Diocesano, CP 104, São Tomé; tel. and fax 223455; e-mail diocese@cstome.net.

BAHÁ'Í FAITH

National Spiritual Assembly: Estrada São João, Edificio Centro Nacional Bahá'í, São Tomé; tel. 223264.

The Press

Diário da República: Cooperativa de Artes Gráficas, Rua João Devs, CP 28, São Tomé; tel. 222661; f. 1836; official gazette; Dir Oscar Ferreira.

Jornal Vitrina: Avda Independência, Edificio Cosme Rita, CP 490, São Tomé; tel. 224568; fax 221666; f. 1999; Dir Manuel Barros.

Notícias: Avda 12 de Julho, CP 112, São Tomé; tel. 222087; fax 221973; f. 1991; state-owned; Dir Ricardo Neto.

O País: Avda Amílcar Cabral, CP 361, São Tomé; tel. 223833; fax 221989; e-mail iucai@cstome.net; f. 1998; Dir Francisco Pinto da Silveira Rita.

O Parvo: CP 535, São Tomé; tel. 221031; f. 1994; Editor Armindo Cardoso.

Téla Non: e-mail diario_digital@cstome.net; internet www.cstome.net; f. 2000; provides online daily news service.

Tribuna: Praça Yon Gato, CP 19, São Tomé; tel. and fax 223295; e-mail tribuna@clix.pt; f. 1998; Dir Nelson Mendes.

NEWS AGENCY

STP-Press: Avda Marginal de 12 de Julho, CP 112, São Tomé; tel. 223431; fax 221365; e-mail stp_press@cstome.net; f. 1985; operated by the radio station in asscn with the Angolan news agency ANGOP; Dir Manuel Dênde.

Broadcasting and Communications

TELECOMMUNICATIONS

Companhia Santomense de Telecomunicações, SARL (CST): CP 141, São Tomé; tel. 222226; fax 222500; e-mail cst@cstome.net; internet www.cstome.net; f. 1989 by Govt of São Tomé (49%) and Rádio Marconi SA (Portugal 51%) to facilitate increased telecommunications links and television reception via satellite; in March 1997 CST introduced internet services; Rádio Marconi's shares subsequently assumed by Portugal Telecom SA; introduced mobile cellular telephone service in the capital and its outskirts in April 2001; Pres. of Admin. Bd José Manuel Briosa e Gala; Administrator-Delegate Manuel Joaquim Capitão Amaro.

BROADCASTING

Portuguese technical and financial assistance in the establishment of a television service was announced in May 1989. Transmissions commenced in 1992, and the service currently broadcasts seven days a week. In 1995 Radio France Internationale and Rádio Televisão Portuguesa Internacional began relaying radio and television broadcasts, respectively, to the archipelago. In 1997 Voice of America, which had been broadcasting throughout Africa since 1993 from a relay station installed on São Tomé, began local transmissions on FM.

Radio

Rádio Nacional de São Tomé e Príncipe: Avda Marginal de 12 de Julho, CP 44, São Tomé; tel. 223293; fax 221973; e-mail rnstp@cstome.net; f. 1958; state-controlled; home service in Portuguese and Creole; Dir Maximino Carlos.

Television

Televisão Santomense (TVS): Bairro Quinta de Santo António, CP 393, São Tomé; tel. 221041; fax 221942; state-controlled; Dir Manuel Barros.

Finance

(cap. = capital; m. = million)

BANKING

Central Bank

Banco Central de São Tomé e Príncipe (BCSTP): Praça da Independência, CP 13, São Tomé; tel. 221269; fax 222777; e-mail bcentral@cstome.net; f. 1992 to succeed fmr Banco Nacional de São

Tomé e Príncipe; bank of issue; Gov. MARIA DO CARMO TROVOADA SILVEIRA.

Commercial Bank

Banco Internacional de São Tomé e Príncipe (BISTP): Praça da Independência, CP 536, São Tomé; tel. 221445; fax 222427; e-mail bistp@cstome.net; f. 1993; 48% govt-owned, 30% owned by Banco Totta e Açores, SA (Portugal), 22% by Caixa Geral de Depósitos (Portugal); cap. US $1.8m. (1998); Pres. JOSÉ CARLOS AFONSO PROENÇA.

INSURANCE

Instituto de Segurança Social: Rua Soldado Paulo Ferreira, São Tomé; tel. 221382; e-mail inss@cstome.net; f. as Caixa de Previdência dos Funcionários Públicos, adopted present name 1994; insurance fund for civil servants; Pres. of Admin. Bd ALBINO GRAÇA DA FONSECA; Dir JUVENAL DO ESPÍRITO SANTO.

Trade and Industry

DEVELOPMENT ORGANIZATION

Instituto para o Desenvolvimento Económico e Social (INDES): Travessa do Pelourinho, CP 408, São Tomé; tel. 222491; fax 221931; e-mail indes@cstome.net; f. 1989 as Fundo Social e de Infrastructuras, adopted present name 1994; channels foreign funds to local economy; Dir HOMERO JERÓNIMO SALVATERRA.

CHAMBER OF COMMERCE

Câmara do Comércio da Indústria e Agricultura (CCIA): CP 31, Largo Bom Despacho 1, São Tomé; tel. 222992; fax 221365; Pres. ANTONIO DE BARROS AMARAL AGUIAR.

UTILITIES

Electricity and Water

Empresa de Água e Electricidade (EMAE): Avda Água Grande, CP 46, São Tomé; tel. 222096; fax 222488; e-mail emae@cstome.net; f. 1979; state electricity and water co; privatization scheduled for 2003; Dir JOSÉ GOMES BARBOSA.

TRADE UNIONS

Organizacão Nacional de Trabalhadores de São Tomé e Príncipe (ONTSTP): Rua Cabo Verde, São Tomé; tel. 222431; Sec.-Gen. JOÃO TAVARES.

União Geral dos Trabalhadores de São Tomé e Príncipe (UGSTP): Avda Kwame Nkrumah, São Tomé; tel. 222443; Sec.-Gen. COSTA CARLOS.

Transport

RAILWAYS

There are no railways in São Tomé and Príncipe.

ROADS

In 1999 there were an estimated 320 km of roads, of which 218 km were asphalted.

SHIPPING

The principal ports are at São Tomé city and at Neves on São Tomé island. In 2000 plans to construct a deep-water port at Agulhas Bay on Príncipe island were abandoned.

Agência de Navegação e Turismo, Lda (AGENTUR): Rua Cabo Verde, São Tomé; tel. 224866; fax 221894.

Companhia Santomense de Navegação, SA (CSN): CP 49, São Tomé; tel. 222657; fax 221311; e-mail csn@setgrcop.com; internet www.navegor.pt; shipping and freight forwarding.

Empresa Nacional de Administração dos Portos (ENAPORT): Largo das Alfândegas, São Tomé; tel. 221841; fax 224949; e-mail enaport@cstome.net; Dir-Gen. CELESTINO ANDRADE.

Navetur-Equatour, Navegação e Turismo, Lda: Rua Viriato da Curz, CP 398, São Tomé; tel. 223781; fax 221748; e-mail equatour@cstome.net.

Transportes e Serviços, Lda (TURIMAR): Rua Patrice Lumumba, CP 48, São Tomé; tel. 221869; fax 222162; e-mail turimar@cstome.net.

CIVIL AVIATION

The international airport is at São Tomé.

Air São Tomé e Príncipe: Avda Marginal de 12 de Julho, CP 45, São Tomé; tel. 221976; fax 221375; e-mail astp@cstome.net; f. 1993; owned by Govt of São Tomé (35%), TAP-Air Portugal, SA (40%), Golfe International Air Service (France) (24%) and Mistral Voyages (France) (1%); operates domestic service between the islands of São Tomé and Príncipe and international connection to Libreville (Gabon); Pres. RAÚL BRAGANÇA WAGNER NETO; Chair. and Man. Dir FELISBERTO NETO.

Empresa Nacional de Aeroportos e Segurança Aérea (ENASA): São Tomé; tel. 221877; fax 221154; e-mail enasa@cstome.net.

Linhas Aéreas São-tomenses (LAS): São Tomé; f. 2002.

Tourism

The islands benefit from spectacular mountain scenery, unspoilt beaches and unique species of flora and wildlife. Although still largely undeveloped, tourism is currently the sector of the islands' economy attracting the highest level of foreign investment. However, the high level of rainfall during most of the year limits the duration of the tourist season, and the expense of reaching the islands by air is also an inhibiting factor. There were 7,137 tourist arrivals in 2000, when receipts totalled some US $9.9m. In that year there were seven hotels, seven boarding houses (pensões) and four guest houses (residências), with a total of 495 beds.

SAUDI ARABIA

Introductory Survey

Location, Climate, Language, Religion, Flag, Capital

The Kingdom of Saudi Arabia occupies about four-fifths of the Arabian peninsula, in south-western Asia. It is bordered by Jordan, Iraq and Kuwait to the north, by Yemen to the south, by Oman to the south and east, and by Qatar and the United Arab Emirates to the north-east. Saudi Arabia has a long western coastline on the Red Sea, facing Egypt, Sudan and Eritrea, and a shorter coastline (between Kuwait and Qatar) on the Persian (Arabian) Gulf, with the Bahrain archipelago just off shore and Iran on the opposite coast. Much of the country is arid desert, and some places are without rain for years. In summer average temperatures in coastal regions range from 38°C to 49°C, and humidity is high. Temperatures sometimes reach 54°C in the interior. Winters are mild, except in the mountains. Annual rainfall averages between 100 mm and 200 mm in the north, and is even lower in the south. The official language is Arabic, which is spoken by almost all of the population. Except for the expatriate community (estimated to represent some 27% of the total population at the time of the 1992 census), virtually all of the inhabitants are adherents of Islam, the official religion. About 85% of the population are Sunni Muslims, and most of the indigenous inhabitants belong to the strictly orthodox Wahhabi sect. About 15% of the population are Shi'a Muslims, principally in the east of the country. The national flag (proportions 2 by 3) is green and bears, in white, an Arabic inscription ('There is no God but Allah and Muhammad is the Prophet of Allah') above a white sabre. The capital is Riyadh.

Recent History

The whole of the Arabian peninsula became part of Turkey's Ottoman Empire in the 16th century. Under the suzerainty of the Ottoman Sultan, the local tribal rulers enjoyed varying degrees of autonomy. The Wahhabi movement, dedicated to the reform of Islam, was launched in the Najd (Nejd) region of central Arabia in the 18th century. A Wahhabi kingdom, ruled by the House of Sa'ud from its capital at Riyadh, quickly expanded into the Hejaz region on the west coast of Arabia. In 1890 the rival Rashidi family seized control of Riyadh, but in 1902 a member of the deposed Sa'udi family, Abd al-Aziz ibn Abd ar-Rahman, expelled the Rashidi dynasty and proclaimed himself ruler of Najd. In subsequent years he recovered and consolidated the outlying provinces of the kingdom, defeating Turkish attempts to subjugate him. Having restored the House of Sa'ud as a ruling dynasty, Abd al-Aziz became known as Ibn Sa'ud. In order to strengthen his position, he instituted the formation of Wahhabi colonies, known as Ikhwan ('Brethren'), throughout the territory under his control.

During the First World War, in which Turkey was allied with Germany, the Arabs under Ottoman rule rebelled. In 1915 the United Kingdom signed a treaty of friendship with Ibn Sa'ud, who was then master of central Arabia, securing his co-operation against Turkey. Relations subsequently deteriorated as a result of the British Government's decision to support Hussein ibn Ali, who proclaimed himself King of the Hejaz in 1916, as its principal ally in Arabia. Hussein was also Sharif of Mecca (the holiest city of Islam), which had been governed since the 11th century by his Hashimi (Hashemite) family, rivals of the House of Sa'ud. At the end of the war, following Turkey's defeat, the Ottoman Empire was dissolved. Continuing his conquests, Ibn Sa'ud successfully campaigned against the rulers of four Arabian states (the Hejaz, Asir, Hayil and Jauf) between 1919 and 1925. In September 1924 his forces captured Mecca, forcing Hussein to abdicate, and in 1925 they overran the whole of the Hejaz. In January 1926 Ibn Sa'ud was proclaimed King of the Hejaz and Sultan of Najd. On 23 September 1932 the dual monarchy ended when the two areas were merged as the unified Kingdom of Saudi Arabia.

Commercially exploitable deposits of petroleum (the basis of Saudi Arabia's modern prosperity) were discovered in the Eastern Province in 1938, and large-scale exploitation of the kingdom's huge reserves of petroleum began after the Second World War. Petroleum royalties were used to develop and modernize the country's infrastructure and services.

Ibn Sa'ud remained in power until his death in November 1953; all subsequent rulers of Saudi Arabia have been sons of Ibn Sa'ud. The kingdom has remained an absolute monarchy and a traditional Islamic society. The King is the supreme religious leader as well as the Head of State, and governs by royal decree. In foreign affairs, Saudi Arabia has historically allied itself with the USA and other Western countries.

Ibn Sa'ud was succeeded by the Crown Prince, Sa'ud ibn Abd al-Aziz. Another of the late King's sons, Faisal ibn Abd al-Aziz, replaced Sa'ud as Crown Prince and Prime Minister. In 1958, bowing to pressure from the royal family, King Sa'ud conferred on Crown Prince Faisal full powers over foreign, internal and economic affairs. In March 1964 King Sa'ud relinquished power to Crown Prince Faisal, and in November was forced by the royal family to abdicate in his favour. The new King Faisal retained the post of Prime Minister, and appointed his half-brother, Khalid ibn Abd al-Aziz, to be Crown Prince in 1965. In the Six-Day War of June 1967 Saudi Arabian forces collaborated with Iraqi and Jordanian troops in action against Israel. As a result of the Arab–Israeli war of October 1973, Saudi Arabia led a movement by Arab petroleum producers to exert pressure on Western countries by reducing supplies of crude oil.

In March 1975 King Faisal was assassinated by one of his nephews, and was immediately succeeded by Crown Prince Khalid. The new King also became Prime Minister, and appointed his brother, Fahd ibn Abd al-Aziz (Minister of the Interior since 1962), as Crown Prince and First Deputy Prime Minister.

The religious fervour that the Middle East experienced in the wake of the Iranian Revolution also arose in Saudi Arabia in late 1979, when an armed group of about 250 Sunni Muslim extremists attacked and occupied the Grand Mosque in Mecca, the most important centre of pilgrimage for Muslims. There was also a riot by Shi'a Muslims in the Eastern Province. In response to the unrest, Crown Prince Fahd announced in early 1980 that a consultative assembly would be formed to act as an advisory body, although the assembly was not inaugurated until December 1993 (see below).

King Khalid died in June 1982 and was succeeded by Crown Prince Fahd, who, following precedent, became Prime Minister and appointed a half-brother, Abdullah ibn Abd al-Aziz (Commander of the National Guard since 1962), to be Crown Prince and First Deputy Prime Minister.

As a result of its position as the world's leading exporter of petroleum, Saudi Arabia is a dominant member of the Organization of the Petroleum Exporting Countries (OPEC, see p. 298) and one of the most influential countries in the Arab world. In May 1981 the kingdom joined five neighbouring states in establishing the Co-operation Council for the Arab States of the Gulf (the Gulf Co-operation Council—GCC, see p. 175). In August Crown Prince (subsequently King) Fahd announced an eight-point plan for the settlement of the Arab–Israeli conflict. His proposals, by implication, recognized Israel as a legitimate state. At a summit conference of Arab states in September 1982, the so-called 'Fahd Plan' formed the basis of an agreed proposal for the achievement of peace in the Middle East, and during 1983 Saudi Arabia sponsored repeated diplomatic initiatives within the region. In November 1987 Saudi Arabia resumed full diplomatic relations with Egypt. Relations had been severed in 1979, following the signing of the peace treaty between Egypt and Israel.

Relations with Iran, already strained as a result of Saudi Arabia's support for Iraq in the Iran–Iraq war, deteriorated further in July 1987 following fierce clashes between Iranian pilgrims and Saudi security forces during the *Hajj*, in which 402 people, including 275 Iranians, were killed. Mass demonstrations took place in Tehran, where the Saudi Arabian embassy was sacked, and Iranian leaders vowed to avenge the pilgrims' deaths by overthrowing the Saudi ruling family. In March 1988 the Government announced its intention to limit the number of foreign pilgrims during the *Hajj* season by allocating national quotas. Saudi Arabia severed diplomatic relations with Iran, which subsequently refused to send pilgrims on that year's *Hajj*.

In July 1988, after the US Congress had refused to sanction an agreement to supply military equipment to Saudi Arabia (following the delivery of an unspecified number of medium-range missiles from the People's Republic of China to Saudi Arabia earlier that year), the Government signed a large-scale defence procurement agreement with the United Kingdom, which as a result superseded the USA as Saudi Arabia's main supplier of military equipment.

Widely held misgivings regarding national defence capabilities, and fears of Iraqi expansionist policy (a pact of non-aggression was signed with Iraq in March 1989), were exacerbated in August 1990, when Iraq invaded and annexed Kuwait and proceeded to deploy armed forces along the Kuwaiti–Saudi Arabian border. King Fahd requested that US forces be deployed in Saudi Arabia, as part of a multinational force, in order to deter a possible attack by Iraq. The dispatch of US combat troops and aircraft to Saudi Arabia signified the beginning of 'Operation Desert Shield' for the defence of Saudi Arabia, in accordance with Article 51 of the UN Charter. By the beginning of 1991 some 30 countries had contributed ground troops, aircraft and warships to the US-led multinational force based in Saudi Arabia and the Gulf region. The entire Saudi Arabian armed forces (numbering about 67,500 men) were mobilized. In January, following the failure of international diplomatic efforts to secure Iraq's withdrawal from Kuwait, the multinational force launched a military campaign ('Operation Desert Storm') to liberate Kuwait. As part of its response to the initial aerial bombardment, Iraq launched *Scud* missiles against targets in Saudi Arabia. However, fighting on Saudi Arabian territory was confined to a few minor incidents. In February Iraq formally severed diplomatic relations with Saudi Arabia.

Following the liberation of Kuwait in February 1991, the ministers responsible for foreign affairs of the GCC met their Syrian and Egyptian counterparts in Damascus, Syria, in March in order to discuss regional security issues. The formation of an Arab peace-keeping force, comprising mainly Egyptian and Syrian troops, was subsequently announced. In May, however, following the endorsement by the GCC member states of US proposals for an increased Western military presence in the Gulf region, Egypt announced its decision to withdraw all of its forces from the region, casting doubt on the future of joint Arab regional security arrangements. Diplomatic relations between Saudi Arabia and Iran were re-established in March, and Iranian pilgrims resumed attendance of the *Hajj*, their numbers regulated in accordance with the quota system.

In March 1992 King Fahd announced by royal decree the imminent creation of an advisory Consultative Council (Majlis ash-Shoura), with 60 members to be selected by the King every four years. Two further decrees provided for the establishment of regional authorities, and a 'basic law of government', equivalent to a written constitution. In September Sheikh Muhammad al-Jubair, hitherto Minister of Justice, was appointed Chairman of the Majlis. In November a major reorganization of the 18-member Council of Ulema (Saudi Arabia's most senior Islamic authority) was instigated by royal decree. Among 10 new members appointed by the King was the new Minister of Justice, Abdullah ibn Muhammad ash-Sheikh. The Majlis was inaugurated by King Fahd at the end of 1993. (Its membership was increased to 90 in July 1997, and to 120 in May 2001.)

In September 1992 Qatar accused a Saudi force of attacking a Qatari border post, killing two border guards and capturing a third. As a result, Qatar suspended a 1965 border agreement with Saudi Arabia, which had never been fully ratified. In December 1992, following mediation by President Hosni Mubarak of Egypt, the Qatari Amir, Sheikh Khalifa, signed an agreement in Medina with King Fahd to establish a committee to demarcate the disputed border. In June 1999 officials of the two countries met in Riyadh to sign the maps defining their joint border, and a final land and maritime demarcation agreement was signed in Doha, Qatar, in March 2001. The border agreement provided for a joint Saudi-Qatari committee, charged with ensuring full implementation of the 1965 accord. In October 2002 the Saudi Ambassador to Qatar returned to Riyadh for unspecified 'consultations', apparently following broadcasts by the Qatari television news channel Al-Jazeera that were deemed to be critical of the Saudi regime. Saudi-Qatar relations were also reported to be strained over competition to influence the USA in its plans to attack the regime of Saddam Hussein in Iraq.

In May 1993 the Saudi authorities disbanded the Committee for the Defence of Legitimate Rights (CDLR), recently established by a group of six prominent Islamist scholars and lawyers. The organization's founders were also dismissed from their positions, and their spokesman, Muhammad al-Masari, arrested. In April 1994 it was reported that members of the CDLR, including al-Masari (who had recently been released from custody), had relocated their organization to the United Kingdom. In January 1996 the British authorities ordered the deportation of al-Masari to Dominica: prominent British defence and aerospace companies were believed to have exerted pressure on their Government to concede to Saudi Arabia's demands that al-Masari be expelled in order to secure the continuation of lucrative trade agreements with Saudi Arabia. However, the Chief Immigration Adjudicator in the United Kingdom rejected the deportation order, recommending that the Government should reconsider al-Masari's application for political asylum, and in April al-Masari was granted exceptional leave to remain in the United Kingdom for a period of at least four years, although he was not granted asylum.

In September 1994 the CDLR was among organizations to report the arrest of more than 1,000 people, including clerics and academics, most of whom had attended a demonstration in Buraidah, north-west of Riyadh, to protest at the arrest of two religious leaders who had allegedly been agitating for the stricter enforcement of *Shari'a* (Islamic) law. The Government announced in October that 130 of the 157 people arrested in September had since been released. Also in October the King approved the creation of a Higher Council for Islamic Affairs, under the chairmanship of Prince Sultan ibn Abd al-Aziz, the Second Deputy Prime Minister and Minister of Defence and Civil Aviation, in a measure apparently aimed at limiting the influence of militant clerics and at diminishing the authority of the powerful Council of Ulema. In mid-1995 King Fahd replaced six of the seven University chancellors and more than one-half of the members of the Council of Ulema, in an attempt to counter the perceived spread of Islamist fundamentalism.

In June 1995 an opposition activist, Abdullah Abd ar-Rahman al-Hudaif, was sentenced to 20 years' imprisonment for his part in an attack on a security officer and for maintaining links with the CDLR in the United Kingdom. In August al-Hudaif was reported to have been executed; no explanation was given for the alteration of his sentence, nor were details of his trial revealed. A further nine opposition activists reportedly received prison sentences ranging from three to 18 years; according to a prominent human rights organization, Amnesty International, as many as 200 'political suspects' remained in detention in Saudi Arabia.

In August 1995 the King announced the most far-reaching reorganization of the Council of Ministers for two decades, although no changes were made to the portfolios held by members of the royal family. The strategic portfolios of finance and national economy and of petroleum and mineral resources were allocated to younger, though highly experienced, officials. The new Minister of Finance and National Economy resigned in October, citing ill health, and in January 1996 the economy portfolio was conferred on Dr Ibrahim Abd al-Aziz al-Assaf (hitherto Minister of State).

A Supreme Economic Council, established by royal decree, convened for the first time in October 1997 under the chairmanship of the Crown Prince. A Supreme Petroleum and Minerals Council was established by royal decree in January 2000. In April the Cabinet approved broad guide-lines for the issuing of tourist visas, and the creation of a supreme commission to promote foreign tourism in Saudi Arabia was announced. The Government declared in May that ministers were to lose their right to hold company posts while in office, with the exception of employees of the state-owned Saudi Aramco petroleum corporation. In June the inaugural session was held of the newly formed Royal Family Council, an officially apolitical body to be chaired by Crown Prince Abdullah. In late August 2001 King Fahd appointed Prince Nawaf ibn Abd al-Aziz to replace Prince Turki al-Faisal ibn Abd al-Aziz as the head of the intelligence services. Prince Nawaf was known to be a close associate of Crown Prince Abdullah, prompting speculation that his appointment was the result of a power struggle within the Saudi royal family.

It was announced in mid-September 2002 that the Ministry of Agriculture and Water had been divided into two ministries; the former Saudi ambassador to the United Kingdom, Ghazi al-

Gosaibi, was named as the new Minister of Water and Electricity.

King Fahd announced a restructured 27-member Cabinet at the end of April 2003; this was only the third reorganization of the Council of Ministers in almost 30 years. Reformists were disappointed that most of the key positions were unchanged, and that all the senior ministers belonging to the ruling as-Sa'ud family remained in post. Among the most significant changes were the transfer of the national economy portfolio to the Ministry of Planning, and the rebranding of the Ministry of Posts, Telegraphs and Telecommunications as the Ministry of Communications and Information Technology. In addition, responsibility for industry was assigned to the Minister of Commerce, the electricity portfolio was merged with Ministry of Water, and a new culture portfolio was added to responsibilities of the Minister of Information.

Saudi Arabia's human rights record has for many years been the focus of international scrutiny. Concern was again raised in 2000 regarding the use of public beheading in the Saudi judicial system. By the end of September at least 104 people had been executed, compared with some 103 during 1999. It was reported that 81 people were executed in 2001. A report issued by Amnesty International in March 2000 alleged that Saudi Arabia was guilty of widespread human rights abuses, including use of torture and refusal to allow prisoners access to family members and lawyers. In April it was announced that the Government had invited the UN Special Rapporteur of the Commission on Human Rights on the independence of judges and lawyers to study the Saudi justice system, although no date was arranged for the visit. A document published by Amnesty International in September accused the Saudi authorities of widespread discrimination against women and cited serious abuses of their human rights, including arbitrary detention and torture. The organization also reiterated its criticism of the Saudi judiciary for failing to conduct trials in compliance with internationally recognized standards. However, it was reported in late 2000 that Saudi Arabia had agreed to sign the UN Convention on the Elimination of All Forms of Discrimination against Women, although it stated that it would lodge reservations regarding any section deemed to contravene *Shari'a* law. In October a Saudi Arabian woman, Thuraya Ahmad Obeid, had been appointed Director of the UN Fund for Population Activities. In December 2001 identity cards were issued to women (showing them with unveiled faces) for the first time, in an effort to prevent people from claiming false identities. In March 2002 King Fahd issued a royal decree merging the authority responsible for female education with the Ministry of Education after 14 female students died in a fire at a girls' school in Mecca. The department responsible for female education was under the jurisdiction of the religious establishment, and thus the merger was interpreted as a step towards reform of the education system.

In November 1995 a car bomb exploded outside the offices of the Saudi Arabian National Guard in Riyadh, which was being used by US civilian contractors to train Saudi personnel. Seven foreign nationals (including five US citizens) were killed in the explosion, and a further 60 were injured. Responsibility for the bomb was claimed by several organizations, including the Islamic Movement for Change, which earlier in the year had warned that it would initiate attacks if non-Muslim Western forces did not withdraw from the Gulf region. In April 1996 four Saudi nationals were arrested in connection with the attack; they were executed at the end of May.

In June 1996 19 US military personnel were killed, and as many as 400 others (including 147 Saudi, 118 Bangladeshi and 109 US citizens) were injured, when an explosive device attached to a petroleum tanker was detonated outside a military housing complex in al-Khobar, near Dhahran. Saudi officials pledged increased security measures, and offered a substantial reward for information leading to the arrest and prosecution of those responsible for the explosion. (Earlier in the year US officials had reportedly been critical of the Saudi authorities' investigation of the November 1995 bombing, and of the swift execution of the alleged perpetrators.) By late 1996 there was speculation that the investigating authorities were holding Saudi Shi'a groups with possible links to Iran responsible for the atrocity, rather than the same Sunni extremist factions that were widely blamed for the 1995 explosion. The Iranian Government, however, repeatedly denied any involvement in the incident. In March 1997 the Canadian intelligence service announced the detention, in Ottawa, of Hani Abd ar-Rahim as-Sayegh, a Saudi Shi'a Muslim implicated in the al-Khobar attack and who was alleged to have links with the militant Hezbollah. In June as-Sayegh was extradited from Canada to stand trial in the USA, but in September US officials announced that there was insufficient evidence to secure a conviction and that as-Sayegh would not be tried in the USA. Saudi Arabia subsequently applied for as-Sayegh's extradition. In May 1998 Saudi Arabia's Minister of the Interior stated that there was no indication of a foreign role in the bombing, despite continuing US assertions of Iranian involvement. There were reports in June that US investigations into the bombing had collapsed and that the USA had withdrawn the majority of its investigators from Saudi Arabia. In October 1999, however, as-Sayegh was extradited from the USA to Saudi Arabia, shortly after the Saudi Minister of the Interior stated that the country's security services possessed information regarding as-Sayegh's involvement in the bombing. Several Saudi nationals were arrested in January 2001 in connection with the bombing. In June US investigators indicted 14 individuals on charges relating to the explosion, although three of them remained at large in June 2002 when the Saudi authorities announced that sentences had been imposed on a number of the detainees. Meanwhile, as-Sayegh remained in custody in Saudi Arabia.

In October 2000 a Saudi Arabian Airlines passenger flight, *en route* from Jeddah to the United Kingdom and carrying some 40 British citizens, was hijacked by two armed Saudi nationals. The aircraft finally landed in the Iraqi capital, Baghdad, where the hijackers (who were reportedly protesting against human rights abuses in Saudi Arabia and the presence of US and British troops on Saudi territory) were detained by the Iraqi authorities. Saudi Arabia initially demanded the men's extradition; however, in December Saudi officials announced that they would not be pursuing such a demand. Meanwhile, one British national died and three were injured in November, as a result of two separate car bomb attacks in Riyadh. No group claimed responsibility for the blasts, although they were initially believed to have been perpetrated by militant Islamists in protest at the role of Western states in the Israeli–Palestinian crisis. The Saudi authorities ordered an official inquiry into both explosions. In December it was reported that a US citizen was among several foreign nationals arrested for questioning in relation to the bombings; Saudi officials suggested that the attacks may not have been politically motivated. A third bomb was detonated in al-Khobar in that month, injuring one Briton. In February 2001 three expatriates (a British national, a Canadian and a Belgian) were detained by the Saudi authorities. Saudi television subsequently broadcast alleged confessions by the three men relating to their involvement in the November bomb explosions, an admission punishable by the death penalty. In March a minor explosion was reported in Riyadh, although it was unclear whether it was linked to the recent bombings there. In May a US national was injured in a further bomb attack in al-Khobar. In August three more expatriates (all Britons) were detained and their alleged confessions were broadcast on Saudi television. However, the confessions were later withdrawn amid allegations that the accused had been tortured. A US national was killed in another bomb attack in al-Khobar in October 2001, though this was later attributed to a Palestinian suicide bomber. In December 2002 one of four British nationals who had in December 2000 been sentenced to 12 years' imprisonment for the al-Khobar bombing admitted responsibility for the attack as part of a wider bombing campaign, which was said to be related to gang warfare over illegal trade in alcohol. However, the man's family claimed that his confession had been extracted under torture and that Islamist dissidents were responsible for the bombings. A total of seven Britons were convicted in connection with the bombing campaign (two of whom were sentenced to death), although in February 2003 a report by the Special Rapporteur of the UN Commission on Human Rights on the independence of judges and lawyers, which cited 'substantial procedural irregularities' and noted that the men's descriptions of torture were 'consistent', cast considerable doubt on the validity of their trials. (In May one of the men was released from his eight-year sentence.) Meanwhile, another Briton was detained in November 2002 for the murder of a German national who died in a car bomb attack in September. Fears of intensified attacks against Westerners grew in early 2003 following the murders of a British defence contractor in February and of two North Americans in March.

In late 1997, as the crisis developed regarding access to sites in Iraq by weapons inspectors of the UN Special Commission

(UNSCOM, see p. 14), Saudi Arabia firmly advocated a diplomatic solution. In February 1998 Saudi Arabia stated that it would not allow the USA to use Saudi territory as a base for air-strikes against Iraq, and reiterated its desire for a diplomatic solution. As relations deteriorated between Iraq and UNSCOM in late 1998, Saudi Arabia again refused to allow its territory to be used as a base for US-led air-strikes against Iraq, although it was later claimed that discreet support had been given which included the use of its bases. In September 2000 Iraq accused Saudi Arabia and Kuwait of inflicting (through the maintenance of the sanctions regime) suffering on the Iraqi population, and alleged that Saudi Arabia was appropriating Iraqi petroleum transported under the oil-for-food programme. Saudi Arabia, encouraged by the mediation of the League of Arab States (the Arab League, see p. 260), indicated at the beginning of 2002 that it was ready for cautious *rapprochement* with Iraq. In October the border crossing from Saudi Arabia to Iraq was to be re-opened, providing a fifth land route for Iraqi trade under the UN oil-for-food arrangement. In the same month it was reported that the Saudi authorities were considering the negotiation of a free-trade agreement with Iraq.

Relations between Saudi Arabia and Iran, which were particularly strained by suspicions of Iranian involvement in the 1996 al-Khobar bombing, improved considerably following the election of Muhammad Khatami to the Iranian presidency in 1997. Co-operation was notably strengthened following the September 2001 attacks on New York and Washington, DC, for which the USA held the al-Qa'ida (Base) organization of the Saudi-born militant Islamist Osama bin Laden to be principally responsible, as Saudi Arabia and Iran sought to counter the emergence of anti-Islamc sentiment in the West.

In December 1994 Yemen accused Saudi Arabia of erecting monitoring posts and constructing roads on Yemeni territory. Relations had been strained as a result of Saudi Arabia's apparent support for secessionist forces in Yemen earlier in the year (q.v.). There was a further deterioration in January 1995, when the two countries failed to renew the 1934 Ta'if agreement (renewable every 20 years), delineating their *de facto* frontier. Following military clashes between Saudi and Yemeni forces, and intense mediation by Syria, a joint statement was issued in mid-January 1995 in which the two sides undertook to halt all military activity in the disputed border area; it was subsequently agreed to pursue demarcation of the border by a joint committee. In February the Saudi and Yemeni Governments signed a memorandum of understanding that reaffirmed their commitment to the legitimacy of the Ta'if agreement and provided for the establishment of six joint committees to delineate the land and sea borders and to develop economic and commercial ties. The new Saudi-Yemeni military committee held its first meeting in Riyadh in March. In June President Ali Abdullah Saleh of Yemen led a high-level delegation to the kingdom. The two countries signed a border security agreement in July 1996. In November 1997, however, armed clashes on the border led to the deaths of three Saudis and one Yemeni border guard. Bilateral contacts continued, and in May 1998 Saudi Arabia began issuing visas to Yemeni workers, following a seven-year suspension. At the end of the month, however, Saudi Arabia invaded the disputed island of Huraym in the Red Sea. Saudi Arabia was reported to have sent a memorandum to the UN stating that it did not recognize the 1992 border agreement between Yemen and Oman, claiming that parts of the area involved were Saudi Arabian territory. The Saudi objection to the accord was widely believed to be related to its attempts to gain land access to the Arabian Sea, via a corridor between Yemen and Oman, which it had thus far been denied in its negotiations with Yemen. In July 1998 Yemen submitted a memorandum to the Arab League, refuting the Saudi claim to the land and stating that the Saudi protests contravened the Ta'if agreement signed by that country. Further clashes were reported close to the land and sea border between Yemen and Saudi Arabia in June, and in July three Yemeni troops were killed during fighting with a Saudi border patrol on the disputed island of Duwaima in the Red Sea; Saudi Arabia claimed its actions there were in self-defence and that, under the Ta'if agreement, three-quarters of the island was Saudi territory. The Saudi Minister of Foreign Affairs visited Yemen at the end of July to discuss the conflict. Meetings of the joint committees continued in 1998 and 1999, although little substantive progress was made. In January 2000 both countries denied reports of armed confrontations in the border area, and a meeting of the joint military committee began in San'a in February. Talks on

the border issue continued meanwhile, and in June, during a visit to Saudi Arabia by President Saleh, a final agreement delineating land and sea borders was signed. As part of the accord, which incorporated the 1934 Ta'if agreement and much of the 1995 memorandum of understanding, both sides agreed to promote economic, commercial and cultural relations, and each undertook not to permit on its territory activities against the other by opposition groups. The agreement did not demarcate sections of the eastern border, and in August 2000 three Saudi border guards and one Yemeni soldier were reportedly killed in border clashes. Nevertheless, the first meeting of the Saudi-Yemen Co-operation Council for more than a decade took place in December; a further meeting followed in June 2001. Meanwhile, it was reported that the withdrawal from the border region of troops of both countries, in accordance with the border agreement, was almost complete.

In July 1995 officials from Saudi Arabia and Oman signed documents to demarcate their joint border. In March 1999 Saudi Arabia held talks with Iran in an effort to mediate in its dispute with the United Arab Emirates (UAE) over the Tunb islands. Following a statement by the GCC condemning both Iran's recent military exercises near the islands and its claim to them and emphasizing UAE sovereignty of the islands, the Iranian President cancelled a planned visit to Saudi Arabia (the visit proceeded in May). Saudi Arabia's *rapprochement* with Iran had resulted in a deterioration in its relations with the UAE, and in March the UAE boycotted a meeting of GCC ministers responsible for petroleum production in protest at Saudi exploration of an oilfield in disputed territory prior to an agreement being reached. In September 2000 the Saudi Government approved an agreement, signed in July, which ended the long-standing dispute with Kuwait regarding their mutual sea border. Final maps delineating that border were signed by officials from both sides in January 2001.

In January 1994 the Chairman of the Palestine Liberation Organization (PLO), Yasser Arafat, visited Riyadh to discuss the Middle East peace settlement with King Fahd. This meeting represented a significant *rapprochement* between Saudi Arabia and the PLO in the aftermath of the 1990–91 Gulf crisis. In January 1995 King Fahd and Arafat held talks in Mecca, and in April Saudi Arabia became the first Arab country to recognize passports issued by the Palestinian (National) Authority (PA). In June the Council of Ministers approved the import of goods made within the area controlled by the PA. Jordan's Minister of Foreign Affairs met his Saudi counterpart in Riyadh in the following month; this was the first senior-level visit made by a Jordanian official since the Gulf crisis. The normalization of relations began in November with the appointment of a Saudi ambassador to Jordan, and was consolidated in February and August 1996, when King Hussein of Jordan met Crown Prince Abdullah in Saudi Arabia.

In early January 2001 Saudi Arabia signed a major defence agreement with the USA: the deal, worth some US $2,000m., included the purchase of US military equipment and a project to modernize the Saudi National Guard.

Saudi Arabia severed diplomatic relations with the Taliban regime in Afghanistan in late September 2001, in response to the suicide attacks on the mainland USA. Saudi Arabia was only one of three countries (along with Pakistan and the UAE) ever to have recognized the Taliban administration in Afghanistan. Although the USA's principal suspect in the attacks, the Afghan-based Osama bin Laden, was born to a wealthy Saudi Arabian family, the Saudi authorities emphasized that bin Laden had been exiled since 1991 and his nationality revoked because of his subversive activities against the royal family. It was later revealed that 15 of the 19 hijackers were also of Saudi descent (although many of the identities were forged or stolen). Visiting Washington shortly after the attacks, Saudi Arabia's Minister of Foreign Affairs stated that he had conveyed to the US Secretary of State, Colin Powell, the support of the Saudi people for efforts to eliminate terrorism. Saudi Arabia also agreed to investigate alleged Saudi funding of bin Laden's al-Qa'ida (Base) organization, said to be raised through certain charitable organizations and individual donations. However, the Saudi regime, under pressure from internal Islamist groups implacably opposed to the US military presence on Saudi territory and to any military action against another Islamic state, subsequently refused permission for the use of its airbases for military action against Afghanistan (although an air 'command and control' base in the kingdom was made available to support the military operation). Following the launch of military attacks against Afghanistan by the US-led 'coalition against terror' in October, the USA briefly closed its embassy in Saudi Arabia because of fear of reprisals. Later that month Crown Prince Abdullah accused the US media of conspiring to damage Saudi Arabia's reputation following the publication of articles highly critical of Saudi Arabia's perceived lack of co-operation after the September attacks. Although official statements by the US Administration continued to praise the Saudi regime, rumours of a deterioration in the relationship between the two countries persisted, and in January 2002 there was speculation that Saudi Arabia was considering demanding the withdrawal of all US forces from its territory. Both governments denied that a formal request had been issued. In the same month the Saudi authorities asked for the return of all Saudi citizens (reported to number more than 100 detainees), captured in Afghanistan while apparently fighting for the Taliban, who were imprisoned at Camp X-Ray, Guantánamo Bay (Cuba). This request was denied by the US authorities, but in June 2002 a delegation of officials of the Saudi Ministries of the Interior and of Foreign Affairs was reported to have been allowed access to the Saudi prisoners. In January 2002 it was announced that the Saudi Arabian Monetary Agency had been tasked with drafting legislation to combat the 'laundering' of illicit funds through the country's banking system.

Relations between Saudi Arabia and the USA were placed under renewed strain in August 2002 after a group representing 900 relatives of victims of the September 2001 attacks filed a civil suit in Washington, DC, against senior Saudi ministers and institutions (and the Government of Sudan) seeking compensation amounting to US $1,000,000m. for their alleged funding of al-Qa'ida activities. Saudi investors reacted angrily to the suit, threatening in response to withdraw from the USA some $750,000m. in Saudi investments. In late 2002 Saudi Arabia was criticized by the USA for ignoring the funding of alleged terrorist organizations by Saudi nationals, and in November US media reports claimed that a charitable donation from the Saudi royal family had assisted two hijackers responsible for the suicide attacks on the USA in 2001. The allegations were strenuously denied by the Saudi authorities, and the US Administration quickly moved to defend the role Saudi Arabia had played in President George W. Bush's 'war against terror'. Nevertheless, in the same month a senior US presidential spokesman asserted that Saudi Arabia 'could do more' to fight terrorism, and it emerged that US authorities were investigating the affairs of a number of wealthy Saudis in connection with alleged sponsorship of Islamist extremists, including al-Qa'ida. Saudi Arabia countered that it was being unfairly maligned, reiterating that it had begun auditing all charitable organizations operating in the country and that it had frozen three bank accounts allegedly linked to radical Islamist groups. Also in November the Saudi authorities, hitherto reluctant to admit to an al-Qa'ida presence in the country, conceded that some 100 Saudis had been detained under suspicion of involvement with the organization and that a further 700 people had been questioned. The Minister of the Interior, Prince Nayef ibn Abd al-Aziz as-Sa'ud, subsequently confirmed that 90 suspects were referred for trial in February 2003, while 250 people remained under investigation in that month; he added that some 150 Saudis had been released after investigations proved they had no links with al-Qa'ida.

Despite the tensions between Saudi Arabia and the USA, in September 2002, following intense pressure from the USA and the United Kingdom, the Saudi Minister of Foreign Affairs indicated that Saudi Arabia might be prepared to approve the use of military bases in Saudi Arabia for a future US-led attack on the regime of Saddam Hussein in Iraq. However, he emphasized that Saudi co-operation would only be forthcoming if the Iraqi authorities continued to reject UN resolutions demanding the unconditional return of weapons inspectors to Iraq and if such a military undertaking was to be conducted under UN auspices. In late December it was reported that the USA would be allowed to use Saudi airbases. It was later established that the highly equipped Prince Sultan airbase would be made available to the US military, and, although combat aircraft would not be allowed to fly offensive missions from the base with the primary aim of bombing Iraqi targets, aircraft launched from Iraqi soil would be permitted to open fire or release bombs in self-defence. In January 2003 Saudi Arabia attempted to secure support for a plan to persuade Saddam Hussein to relinquish power and go into exile in order to avert a US-led war to oust his regime. In the following month, however, as conflict

appeared increasingly inevitable, the Saudi authorities deployed warships, troops and military helicopters to Kuwait, in order to strengthen the emirate's defences. In late April 2003, after most of the main US military objectives in Iraq had been achieved, it was announced that US troops would be withdrawn from Saudi Arabia by the end of August.

In mid-May 2003 suicide bomb attacks on three expatriate residential compounds in Riyadh killed 34 people. The Minister of Foreign Affairs indicated that 19 people, including 17 Saudis, were believed to have been responsible for the attacks. The bombings, widely held to be the work of al-Qa'ida, provoked further US criticism of Saudi security measures.

Meanwhile, in March 2003 Libya recalled its ambassador to Riyadh. At a summit meeting of the Arab League Council held earlier in the month, Libya had been particularly critical of Saudi Arabia for hosting US forces on its territory.

In February 2002 Crown Prince Abdullah put forward a proposal, based on the 1981 'Fahd Plan', to end the escalating conflict between Israel and the Palestinians based on the principle of 'land-for-peace'. In return for a collective Arab recognition of the State of Israel, the plan insisted on Israel's complete withdrawal from Arab territories occupied since 1967. The Crown Prince also urged the US Administration to exert pressure on Israel to withdraw its forces from the West Bank. The Saudi peace initiative was unanimously endorsed at a summit conference of the Arab League Council held in late March 2002 in Beirut (see the Recent History of Lebanon), but was categorically rejected by Israel. During a summit meeting with US President George W. Bush in Crawford, Texas, in late April, Crown Prince Abdullah reiterated his call for the USA to restrain Israel's actions against the Palestinians.

Government

Saudi Arabia is an absolute monarchy, with no legislature or political parties. Constitutionally, the King rules in accordance with the *Shari'a*, the sacred law of Islam. He appoints and leads a Council of Ministers, which serves as the instrument of royal authority in both legislative and executive matters. Decisions of the Council are reached by majority vote, but require royal sanction. A Consultative Council (Majlis ash-Shoura) was officially inaugurated in December 1993. Members of the Majlis are chosen by the King. The membership of the Majlis was increased in number from 60 to 90 in July 1997, at the beginning of the council's second four-year term, and to 120 in May 2001.

The organs of local government are the General Municipal Councils and the tribal and village councils. A General Municipal Council is established in the towns of Mecca, Medina and Jeddah. Its members are proposed by the inhabitants and must be approved by the King. Functioning concurrently with each General Municipal Council is a General Administration Committee, which investigates ways and means of executing resolutions passed by the Council. Every village and tribe has a council composed of the sheikh, who presides, his legal advisers and two other prominent personages. These councils have power to enforce regulations. A system of provincial government was announced in late 1993 by royal decree. The decree defined the nature of government for 13 newly-created regions, as well as the rights and responsibilities of their governors, and appointed councils of prominent citizens for each region to monitor development and advise the government. Each council is to meet four times a year under the chairmanship of a governor, who will be an emir with ministerial rank. A royal decree, issued in April 1994, further divided the 13 regions into 103 governorates.

Defence

In August 2002 the active armed forces totalled an estimated 124,500 men: army 75,000, air force 18,000, navy 15,500 (including 3,000 marines); air defence forces 16,000. There were also paramilitary forces totalling more than 15,500 men, which included a frontier force of 10,500 and a 4,500-strong coastguard. There was a National Guard with 75,000 active personnel and 25,000 tribal levies. The GCC's Peninsula Shield Force, based in Saudi Arabia, comprised some 7,000 troops. Military service is voluntary. The allocation for defence and security in the budget for 2002 was SR 80,100m., equivalent to 36.7% of total expenditure for that year.

Economic Affairs

In 2000, according to estimates by the World Bank, Saudi Arabia's gross national income (GNI), measured at average 1998–2000 prices, was US $149,932m., equivalent to $7,230 per head (or $11,390 per head on an international purchasing-power parity basis). During 1990–2001, it was estimated, the population increased by an average annual rate of 2.8%, while gross domestic product (GDP) per head decreased, in real terms, by an average of 0.5% per year in 1990–2000. Overall GDP increased, in real terms, at an average annual rate of 2.2% in 1990–2000; growth in 2001 was an estimated 1.2%.

Agriculture (including forestry and fishing) contributed an estimated 5.1% of GDP in 2001, and employed an estimated 7.8% of the economically active population in the same year. The principal crop is wheat; from the late 1980s a large wheat surplus was exported. Barley, dates, tomatoes, potatoes and watermelons are also significant crops. Saudi Arabia is self-sufficient in many dairy products, and in eggs and broiler chickens. Agricultural GDP increased by an average of 0.9% per year in 1990–2000; the sector's real GDP increased by 0.8% in 2001, according to provisional estimates.

Industry (including mining, manufacturing, construction and power) employed some 25.7% of the labour force in 2001, and provided an estimated 51.2% of GDP in 2001. During 1990–2000, it was estimated, industrial GDP increased at an average annual rate of 3.1%.

Mining and quarrying engaged only 1.6% of the employed population in 2001, but contributed an estimated 34.5% of GDP in 2000. The sector is dominated by petroleum and natural gas, which provided an estimated 41.6% of GDP in that year. Saudi Arabia remained the largest petroleum producer in the world in 2001, and petroleum and petroleum products provided an estimated 88.6% of total export revenue in 2001. At the end of 2001 Saudi Arabia's proven recoverable reserves of petroleum were 261,800m. barrels, sufficient to maintain production at 2001 levels for 85 years, and equivalent to about one-quarter of the world's proven oil reserves. Crude petroleum production averaged 8.8m. barrels per day (b/d) in 2001, although the kingdom has a production capacity of some 10m. b/d. With effect from February 2003, Saudi Arabia's production quota within the Organization of the Petroleum Exporting Countries (OPEC, see p. 298) was 8.0m. b/d. Gas reserves, mostly associated with petroleum, totalled 6,220,000m. cu m at the end of 2001. Other minerals produced include limestone, gypsum, marble, clay and salt, while there are substantial deposits of phosphates, bauxite, gold and other metals. The GDP of the mining sector increased at an average annual rate of 2.9% in 1990–2000.

Manufacturing contributed an estimated 10.0% of GDP in 2001, and provided 8.4% of employment in 2001. The most important activity is the refining of petroleum. The production of petrochemicals, fertilizers, construction materials (particularly steel and cement), and food- and drink-processing are also important activities. Manufacturing GDP increased by an estimated average of 4.0% per year in 1990–2000.

Electrical energy is generated by thermal power stations, using Saudi Arabia's own petroleum resources, although an increasing amount of electricity is now produced in association with sea-water desalination. Electricity expansion projects were planned in the early part of the 21st century to satisfy increased demand.

The services sector contributed an estimated 43.7% of GDP in 2001, and engaged 66.5% of the employed labour force in 2001. The GDP of the services sector increased by an estimated average of 0.9% per year in 1990–2000.

In 2001 Saudi Arabia recorded a visible trade surplus of US $44,387m., and a surplus of $14,502m. on the current account of the balance of payments. In 2001 the principal source of imports (17.8%) was the USA; other important suppliers were Japan, Germany, the United Kingdom, Australia and Italy. The USA was also the principal market for exports (20.2%) in 2000; other major markets were Japan, the Republic of Korea and Singapore. In 2000 the dominant exports were crude and refined petroleum, and construction materials. The principal imports in 2001 were machinery and electrical equipment, chemicals and chemical products, base metals and metal manufactures, vegetable products, and textiles and clothing.

A balanced budget was forecast for 2001; however, revised figures indicated a deficit of SR 25,000m. A deficit of SR 45,000m. was forecast for 2002. Consumer prices increased by an annual average of 0.7% in 1990–2001; consumer prices decreased by 0.8% in 2000 and by 0.6% in 2001. Unemployment was estimated to be 15%–20% among Saudi nationals in early 2002. In 2001 non-Saudi nationals comprised 52.1% of the labour force.

In addition to its membership of OPEC, Saudi Arabia is a member of the Islamic Development Bank (see p. 257), and the Organization of Arab Petroleum Exporting Countries (OAPEC, see p. 292). Saudi Arabia is the major aid donor in the region, disbursing loans to developing countries through the Arab Fund for Economic and Social Development (AFESD, see p. 136), the Arab Bank for Economic Development in Africa (BADEA, see p. 261) and other organizations. Negotiations regarding entry to the World Trade Organization (WTO, see p. 323) were in progress in 2002. Saudi Arabia is also a member of the Co-operation Council for the Arab States of the Gulf (GCC, see p. 175), which created a unified regional customs tariff in January 2003, and has undertaken to establish a single market and currency no later than January 2010.

Saudi Arabia's prosperity is based on exploitation of its petroleum reserves. Although the country remained the world's largest oil producer at the beginning of the 21st century, and continued to play a crucial role in determining OPEC production levels and thus world prices, the decline in the price of petroleum in the early 1990s caused the Government subsequently to seek alternative sources of revenue. The 2000–05 economic plan aimed to increase private investment and growth in the private and non-oil sectors, and envisaged the provision of 817,300 (mainly private-sector) jobs for the rapidly expanding Saudi population. The Manpower Development Fund, partly financed by more expensive expatriate work permits and visas, was launched in April 2002 to subsidize skills training for Saudi nationals and to promote the 'Saudiization' of the work-force. The anticipated involvement of international companies in Saudi hydrocarbons and utilities industries was expected to contribute to private-sector growth. In October 2002 the world's largest natural gas plant was opened at Hawiya; the plant, which was the first Saudi project for gas not associated with petroleum, was expected to increase the country's gas production by more than 30%. Further non-associated gas reserves are yet to be fully exploited. As part of a process of structural and administrative reform, two new policy-making bodies, the Supreme Economic Council and the Supreme Petroleum and Minerals Council, have been established (the latter accompanied by the creation of the Saudi Electricity Company and a new tariff structure), and, as part of the deregulation process, two independent supervisory authorities for the electricity and telecommunications sectors were created in 2001. A successful public offering of 20% of the Saudi Telecommunications Company in January 2001 was likely to lead to liberalization of the telecommunications sector in 2004. In November 2002 the Government announced plans to privatize a further 20 sectors. Saudi Arabia failed to achieve a planned balanced budget for 2001 (after an unexpected budgetary surplus of SR 22,743m. in 2000) because of the sharp fall in world petroleum prices following the September attacks on the USA and the resulting fears of a global recession. Strict spending limits were prescribed for the 2002 and 2003 budgets, but as petroleum prices rallied it was expected that the budgetary deficit would narrow.

Education

Elementary, secondary and higher education are available free of charge, but education is not compulsory. Primary education begins at six years of age and lasts for six years. From the age of 12 there are three years of intermediate education, followed by three years of secondary schooling. Primary enrolment included 61% of children in the relevant age-group (boys 63%; girls 60%) in 1996. In that year enrolment at intermediate and secondary schools was equivalent to 61% of children (boys 65%; girls 57%). The proportion of females enrolled in Saudi Arabian schools increased from 25% of the total number of pupils in 1970 to 47.5% in 2001. In the 2001/02 academic year some 397,000 students were enrolled in higher education. Tertiary institutions in 1999/2000 included 75 university colleges and 72 colleges exclusively for women. Construction of the first private university, in partnership with a US technology institute, was scheduled to begin in late 2002. Government expenditure on education in 2002 was provisionally estimated at SR 47,037m., equivalent to 23% of total expenditure.

Public Holidays

2003: 7–15 February (Id al-Adha, Feast of the Sacrifice), 20–30 November (Id al-Fitr, end of Ramadan).

2004: 28 January–5 February (Id al-Adha, Feast of the Sacrifice), 31 October–10 November (Id al-Fitr, end of Ramadan).

These holidays are dependent on the Islamic lunar calendar and may vary by one or two days from the dates given.

Weights and Measures

The metric system is in force.

Statistical Survey

Sources (unless otherwise indicated): Kingdom of Saudi Arabia, *Statistical Yearbook*; Saudi Arabian Monetary Agency, *Annual Report* and *Statistical Summary*.

Area and Population

AREA, POPULATION AND DENSITY

Area (sq km)	2,240,000*
Population (census results)	
9–14 September 1974	7,012,642
27 September 1992†	
Males	9,479,973
Females.	7,468,415
Total	16,948,388
Population (official estimates at mid-year)	
1999	21,334,000
2000	22,010,000
2001	20,690,000
Density (per sq km) at mid-2001	10.1

* 864,869 sq miles.

† Of the total population at the 1992 census, 12,310,100 (males 50.5%; females 49.5%) were nationals of Saudi Arabia, while 4,638,300 (males 70.4%; females 29.6%) were foreign nationals.

SAUDI ARABIA-IRAQ NEUTRAL ZONE: The Najdi (Saudi Arabian) frontier with Iraq was defined in the Treaty of Mohammara in May 1922. Later a Neutral Zone of 7,044 sq km was established adjacent to the western tip of the Kuwait frontier. No military or permanent buildings were to be erected in the zone and the nomads of both countries were to have unimpeded access to its pastures and wells. A further agreement concerning the administration of this zone was signed between Iraq and Saudi Arabia in May 1938. In July 1975 Iraq and Saudi Arabia signed an agreement providing for an equal division of the diamond-shaped zone between the two countries, with the border following a straight line through the zone.

SAUDI ARABIA-KUWAIT NEUTRAL ZONE: A Convention signed at Uqair in December 1922 fixed the Najdi (Saudi Arabian) boundary with Kuwait. The Convention also established a Neutral Zone of 5,770 sq km immediately to the south of Kuwait in which Saudi Arabia and Kuwait held equal rights. The final agreement on this matter was signed in 1963. Since 1966 the Neutral Zone, or Partitioned Zone as it is sometimes known, has been divided between the two countries and each administers its own half, in practice as an integral part of the State. However, the petroleum deposits in the Zone remain undivided and production from the onshore oil concessions in the Zone is shared equally between the two states' concessionaires.

PRINCIPAL TOWNS
(population at 1992 census)

Riyadh (royal		Khamis-Mushait. .	217,870
capital) . . .	2,776,096	Ha'il (Hayil) . . .	176,757
Jeddah		Al-Kharj	152,071
(administrative		Al-Khubar . . .	141,683
capital) . . .	2,046,251	Jubail	140,828
Makkah (Mecca) . .	965,697	Hafar al-Batin . .	137,793
Al-Madinah		Yanbo	119,819
(Medina) . .	608,295	Abha	112,316
Dammam . . .	482,321	Ar Ar	108,055
At-Ta'if . . .	416,121	Al-Qatif	98,920
Tabouk . . .	292,555		
Buraidah . . .	248,636		
Hufuf . . .	225,847		
Al-Mobarraz . . .	219,123		

2000: (UN estimates, incl. suburbs) Jeddah 3,192,000; Mecca 1,335,000; Medina 891,000; Dammam 764,000 (Source: UN, *World Urbanization Prospects: The 2001 Revision*).

2001: (UN estimates, incl. suburbs) Riyadh 4,761,000 (Source: UN, *World Urbanization Prospects: The 2001 Revision*).

BIRTHS AND DEATHS
(UN estimates, annual averages)

	1985–90	1990–95	1995–2000
Birth rate (per 1,000)	40.2	37.5	34.9
Death rate (per 1,000)	6.0	5.0	4.4

Source: UN, *World Population Prospects: The 2000 Revision*.

Expectation of life (WHO estimates, years at birth): 70.5 (males 68.4; females 73.5) in 2001 (Source: WHO, *World Health Report*).

EMPLOYMENT
('000 persons)

	2001
Agriculture, hunting, forestry and fishing	567.5
Mining and quarrying	113.3
Manufacturing	616.8
Electricity, gas and water	96.6
Construction.	1,051.5
Trade, restaurants and hotels.	1,050.3
Transport and communications	303.5
Finance and real estate services	350.5
Government services	922.6
Other community and personal services.	2,232.9
Total	**7,304.9**
Saudi nationals	3,496.2
Non-Saudi nationals	3,808.8

Health and Welfare

KEY INDICATORS

Total fertility rate (children per woman, 2001). . . .	5.7
Under-5 mortality rate (per 1,000 live births, 2001) . .	28
Physicians (per 1,000 head, 1997)	1.66
Hospital beds (per 1,000 head, 1997)	2.3
Health expenditure (2000): US $ per head (PPP) . . .	448
Health expenditure (2000): % of GDP	5.3
Health expenditure (2000): public (% of total) . . .	79.1
Access to water (% of persons, 2000).	95
Access to sanitation (% of persons, 2000)	100
Human Development Index (2000): ranking	71
Human Development Index (2000): value	0.759

For sources and definitions, see explanatory note on p. vi.

Agriculture

PRINCIPAL CROPS
('000 metric tons)

	1999	2000	2001
Wheat	2,046	1,787	1,780†
Barley	192	118	100†
Millet	7	8	7*
Sorghum	205	212	200†
Potatoes	394	380	380*
Tomatoes	277	310	310*
Pumpkins, squash and gourds . .	79	78	78*
Cucumbers and gherkins . . .	133	136	136*
Aubergines (Eggplants)	60	65	65*
Dry onions	95	95	95*
Carrots	65	68	68*
Okra	50	52	52*
Other vegetables	360	362	362*
Citrus fruit	119	125	125*
Grapes	116	117	117*
Watermelons	262	275	275*
Cantaloupes and other melons . .	100	105	105*
Dates	712	735	735*
Other fruits	206	212	212*

* FAO estimate.
† Unofficial figure.

Source: FAO.

LIVESTOCK
('000 head, year ending September)

	1999	2000	2001*
Asses*	100	100	100
Camels	410†	415†	415
Cattle	297	307	307
Sheep	7,554†	7,931†	7,931
Goats	4,305	4,529†	4,529
Poultry*	139,000	160,000	160,000

* FAO estimates.
† Unofficial figure.

Source: FAO.

LIVESTOCK PRODUCTS
('000 metric tons)

	1999	2000	2001*
Beef and veal	19	20*	20
Mutton and lamb	66†	67†	67
Goat meat	21	22†	22
Poultry meat	419	484	484
Camel meat*	52	53	53
Cows' milk	601	709	709
Sheep's milk*	75	79	79
Goats' milk*	71	75	75
Camels' milk*	88	89	89
Hen eggs	136	129	129*
Wool: greasy*	10	10	10
Cattle hides (fresh)*	3	3	3
Sheepskins (fresh)*	11	11	11
Goatskins (fresh)*	4	4	4

* FAO estimate(s).
† Unofficial figure.

Source: FAO.

Fishing

(metric tons, live weight)

	1998	1999	2000
Capture	51,206	46,618	49,650
Groupers and seabasses . .	5,053	5,430	5,402
Snappers and jobfishes . .	2,302	2,022	1,647
Emperors (Scavengers) . .	6,796	7,233	7,078
Porgies and seabreams . .	2,822	2,771	2,488
Spinefeet (Rabbitfishes) . .	1,761	1,691	1,832
Narrow-barred Spanish mackerel . .	6,722	6,032	6,057
Carangids	4,795	5,534	6,612
Indian mackerel	2,072	1,979	1,525
Penaeus shrimps	7,812	3,612	5,639
Aquaculture	5,101	5,052	6,004
Nile tilapia	3,212	3,631	3,885
Giant tiger prawn	1,681	1,300	1,961
Total catch	**56,307**	**51,670**	**55,654**

Source: FAO, *Yearbook of Fishery Statistics*.

Mining

('000 metric tons, unless otherwise indicated)

	1999	2000	2001§
Crude petroleum (million barrels)*	2,651	2,847	2,763
Natural gas (million cu metres)* †	46,200§	58,870	54,900
Silver (kilograms)‡	10,470	9,300§	15,000
Gold (kilograms)‡	4,570	3,800§	5,000
Salt (unrefined)§	200	200	200
Gypsum (crude)	380	400	450
Pozzolan§	140	150	150

* Including 50% of the total output of the Neutral or Partitioned Zone, shared with Kuwait.
† On a dry basis.
‡ Figures refer to the metal content of concentrate and bullion.
§ Estimate(s).
Source: US Geological Survey.

Industry

SELECTED PRODUCTS
(including 50% of the total output of the Neutral Zone; '000 barrels, unless otherwise indicated)

	1999	2000	2001
Phosphatic fertilizers*	145	147†	150†
Motor spirit (petrol)	99,540	100,370	98,890
Naphtha ('000 barrels)	49,320	55,030	53,340
Kerosene ('000 barrels)	60,640	66,920	60,050
Gas-diesel (distillate fuel) oils ('000 barrels)	188,850	198,180	193,770
Residual fuel oils ('000 barrels)	164,030	163,940	169,530
Petroleum bitumen (asphalt, '000 barrels)	6,620	8,080	8,650
Liquefied petroleum gas ('000 barrels)	12,530	9,630	13,230†
Cement	16,460	18,232	20,994
Crude steel	2,610	2,973	3,400†

* Production in terms of phosphoric acid.
† Provisional or estimated figure.

Source: partly US Geological Survey.

Nitrogenous fertilizers (estimates, production in terms of nitrogen): 981 in 1997; 1,080 in 1998; 1,064 in 1999.

Jet fuel (estimates): 2,900 in 1996; 2,770 in 1997; 2,440 in 1998.

Lubricating oils (estimates): 750 in 1996; 752 in 1997; 755 in 1998.

Electric energy (million kWh): 103,353 in 1996; 107,289 in 1997; 112,691 in 1998 (estimate).

Source: UN, *Industrial Commodity Statistics Yearbook*.

Finance

CURRENCY AND EXCHANGE RATES

Monetary Units
100 halalah = 20 qurush = 1 Saudi riyal (SR).

Sterling, Dollar and Euro Equivalents (31 December 2002)
£1 sterling = 6.036 riyals
US $1 = 3.745 riyals
€1 = 3.927 riyals
100 Saudi riyals = £16.57 = $26.70 = €25.46.

Exchange Rate: Since June 1986 the official mid-point rate has been fixed at US $1 = 3.745 riyals.

BUDGET ESTIMATES
(million riyals)

Revenue	1999	2000	2001
Petroleum revenues	75,881	117,895	169,000
Other revenues	45,119	39,105	46,000
Total	121,000	157,000	215,000

Expenditure	1999	2000	2001
Human resource development	42,792	49,284	53,010
Transport and communications	5,197	5,534	5,732
Economic resource development	4,418	5,955	5,629
Health and social development	15,152	16,381	18,089
Infrastructure development	1,707	2,067	2,532
Municipal services	5,400	5,710	7,224
Defence and security	68,700	74,866	78,850
Public administration and other government spending	16,458	19,277	37,372
Government lending institutions*	420	436	411
Local subsidies	4,756	5,490	6,151
Total	165,000	185,000	215,000

* Including transfers to the Saudi Fund for Development (SFD).

1999 (revised figures, million riyals): Total revenue 147,454; Total expenditure 183,841.

2000 (revised figures, million riyals): Total revenue 258,065; Total expenditure 235,322.

2001 (revised figures, million riyals): Total revenue 230,000; Total expenditure 255,000.

2002 (estimates, million riyals): Total revenue 157,000; Total expenditure 202,000.

INTERNATIONAL RESERVES
(US $ million in December)

	2000	2001	2002
Gold*	210	202	219
IMF special drawing rights	191	242	332
Reserve position in IMF	1,359	2,558	3,564
Foreign exchange	18,036	14,796	16,715
Total	19,796	17,798	20,830

* Valued at SDR 35 per troy ounce.

Source: IMF, *International Financial Statistics*.

MONEY SUPPLY
('000 million riyals in December)

	2000	2001	2002
Currency outside banks	51.02	49.25	52.33
Demand deposits at commercial banks	114.69	130.45	150.24
Total money	165.71	179.70	202.57

Source: IMF, *International Financial Statistics*.

COST OF LIVING
(Consumer Price Index for all cities; base: 1988 = 100)

	2000	2001	2002
Food, drink and tobacco	117.5	118.2	117.5
Housing	122.8	122.8	122.8
Textiles and clothing	83.4	81.2	79.9
House furnishing	99.1	97.7	96.9
Medical care	103.6	103.5	103.4
Transport and communications	131.0	126.8	124.6
Entertainment and education	101.5	100.7	99.6
All items (incl. others)	112.6	111.7	111.0

NATIONAL ACCOUNTS
(million riyals at current prices)

Expenditure on the Gross Domestic Product

	1999	2000	2001*
Government final consumption expenditure	154,094	183,804	188,695
Private final consumption expenditure	252,217	258,126	255,784
Increase in stocks	9,421	8,903	5,135
Gross fixed capital formation	118,196	123,324	126,609
Total domestic expenditure	533,928	574,157	576,223
Exports of goods and services	210,231	308,473	292,913
Less Imports of goods and services	140,570	175,973	170,733
GDP in purchasers' values	603,589	706,657	698,403
GDP at constant 1999 prices	603,589	632,906	640,413

* Preliminary figures.

Gross Domestic Product by Economic Activity

	1999	2000	2001*
Agriculture, forestry and fishing	34,443	34,973	35,708
Mining and quarrying:			
crude petroleum and natural gas	173,102	259,847	238,492
other	2,464	2,552	2,650
Manufacturing:			
petroleum refining	18,021	21,084	20,671
other	44,779	47,206	49,425
Electricity, gas and water	2,899	3,015	3,152
Construction	39,437	41,724	43,018
Trade, restaurants and hotels	45,992	47,832	49,506
Transport, storage and communications	27,893	29,103	30,500
Finance, insurance, real estate and business services:			
ownership of dwellings	42,221	43,056	43,835
other	31,603	33,073	34,462
Government services	116,789	119,123	123,753
Other community, social and personal services	21,377	22,176	23,130
Sub-total	601,020	704,764	698,302
Import duties	9,634	9,650	8,077
Less Imputed bank service charge	7,065	7,758	7,976
GDP in purchasers' values	603,589	706,656	698,403

* Preliminary figures.

BALANCE OF PAYMENTS
(US $ million)

	1999	2000	2001
Exports of goods f.o.b.	50,757	77,584	73,032
Imports of goods f.o.b.	−25,717	−27,741	−28,645
Trade balance	25,039	49,843	44,387
Exports of services	5,380	4,785	5,182
Imports of services	−18,855	−25,262	−19,307
Balance on goods and services	11,564	29,367	30,262
Other income received	5,811	3,349	4,130
Other income paid	−2,887	−2,869	−4,650
Balance on goods, services and income	14,489	29,847	29,742
Current transfers paid	−14,077	−15,511	−15,240
Current balance	412	14,336	14,502
Direct investment from abroad	−780	−1,884	20
Portfolio investment assets	11,712	−9,394	−2,798
Other investment assets	−10,678	−3,943	−12,343
Other investment liabilities	2,149	3,549	−1,289
Overall balance	2,815	2,665	−1,909

Source: IMF, *International Financial Statistics*.

External Trade

PRINCIPAL COMMODITIES
(million riyals)

Imports c.i.f.	1999	2000	2001*
Live animals and animal products	5,313	5,675	5,137
Vegetable products	7,637	8,268	6,588
Prepared foodstuffs, beverages, spirits, vinegar and tobacco	4,192	5,531	5,630
Products of chemical or allied industries	9,494	9,5125	9,864
Plastics, rubber and articles thereof	3,488	4,141	4,255
Textiles and textile articles	6,494	6,674	6,557
Pearls, precious or semi-precious stones, precious metals, etc.	5,113	4,574	3,563
Base metals and articles of base metal	8,808	8,895	9,535
Machinery and mechanical appliances; electrical equipment; sound and television apparatus	25,187	24,982	24,062
Vehicles, aircraft, vessels and associated transport equipment	15,201	19,995	25,356
Total (incl. others)	104,980	113,2470	116,931

Exports†	1999	2000	2001*
Mineral products	168,298	265,747	242,306
Crude petroleum	136,321	232,211	211,728
Refined petroleum products	31,977	33,536	30,578
Petrochemicals	9,189	12,125	13,451
Construction materials	2,808	2,712	2,779
Agricultural, animal and food products	1,768	1,700	1,542
Total (incl. others)	190,084	290,553	273,505

* Provisional, preliminary or estimated figures.
† Including re-exports (million riyals): 1,869 in 1999; 1,886 in 2000; 3,635 in 2001 (provisional).

PRINCIPAL TRADING PARTNERS
(million riyals)

Imports c.i.f.	1999	2000	2001*
Australia	2,273	2,907	4,733
Belgium	1,558	1,707	1,892
Brazil	1,650	2,314	2,431
Canada	1,321	1,082	1,408
France	4,421	4,675	4,473
Germany	7,648	9,164	9,395
India	2,770	3,132	2,811
Indonesia	1,508	1,699	1,407
Italy	4,424	4,698	4,543
Japan	9,650	11,837	13,039
Korea, Republic	3,801	3,846	3,831
Malaysia	890	1,152	1,140
Netherlands	1,971	2,387	2,190
Spain	1,962	1,607	1,666
Sweden	1,441	1,813	1,646
Switzerland	3,523	3,694	2,832
Syria	1,325	757	1,019
Taiwan	1,258	1,158	1,187
Turkey	985	833	1,324
United Arab Emirates	2,213	2,206	2,375
United Kingdom	8,456	7,3080	8,037
USA	19,882	21,802	20,768
Total (incl. others)	107,674	113,240	116,931

Exports (incl. re-exports)	1998	1999	2000*
Bahrain	4,387	5,560	7,158
Brazil	2,210	2,216	3,505
France	5,456	7,469	10,910
Germany	1,514	1,886	3,056
Greece	2,128	2,321	3,964
India	6,083	8,175	12,823
Indonesia	2,280	3,318	4,071
Italy	4,908	4,428	6,971
Japan	21,668	28,496	46,074
Korea, Republic	13,886	20,429	31,273
Kuwait	1,887	1,783	1,802
Netherlands	6,043	7,845	11,592
Pakistan	1,520	2,562	4,766
Philippines	2,021	2,828	4,023
Singapore	8,697	11,107	14,632
Spain	3,048	3,388	5,013
Taiwan	3,476	4,185	7,742
Thailand	1,607	2,100	3,578
Turkey	2,320	1,944	3,248
United Arab Emirates	4,912	4,710	5,886
United Kingdom	1,258	1,637	3,223
USA	23,695	37,185	58,832
Total (incl. others)	145,388	190,084	290,553

* Provisional.

Transport

RAILWAYS
(traffic)

	1999	2000	2001
Passenger journeys ('000)	770.4	853.8	790.4
Freight carried ('000 metric tons)	1,800.0	1,600.0	1,500.0

ROAD TRAFFIC
(motor vehicles in use at 31 December)

	1989	1990	1991
Passenger cars	2,550,465	2,664,028	2,762,132
Buses and coaches	50,856	52,136	54,089
Goods vehicles	2,153,297	2,220,658	2,286,541
Total	4,754,618	4,936,822	5,103,205

1996 (estimates): Passenger cars 1,744,000; Buses and coaches 23,040; Goods vehicles 1,169,000; Total 2,935,000.

Source: IRF, *World Road Statistics*.

SHIPPING

Merchant Fleet
(vessels registered at 31 December)

	1999	2000	2001
Oil tankers:			
vessels	25	24	26
displacement ('000 grt)	218	219	224
Others:			
vessels	247	252	248
displacement ('000 grt)	989	1,041	909
Total vessels	272	276	274
Total displacement ('000 grt)	1,208	1,260	1,133

Source: Lloyd's Register-Fairplay, *World Fleet Statistics*.

International Sea-borne Freight Traffic
('000 metric tons)*

	1988	1989	1990
Goods loaded	161,666	165,989	214,070
Goods unloaded	42,546	42,470	46,437

* Including Saudi Arabia's share of traffic in the Neutral or Partitioned Zone.

Source: UN, *Monthly Bulletin of Statistics*.

2001 ('000 metric tons, excluding crude oil): Goods loaded 68,894; Goods unloaded 31,668.

CIVIL AVIATION
(traffic on scheduled services)

	1997	1998	1999
Kilometres flown (million)	68	71	76
Passengers carried ('000)	3,895	3,895	4,074
Passenger-kilometres (million)	13,061	12,875	13,357
Total ton-km (million)	2,038	2,030	2,138

Source: UN, *Statistical Yearbook*.

2001: 27.8m. passengers carried; 440,400 metric tons of cargo carried.

Tourism

	1996	1997	1998
Tourist arrivals ('000)	3,458	3,594	3,700
Tourist receipts (US $ million)	1,308	1,420	1,462

Source: World Tourism Organization, *Yearbook of Tourism Statistics*.

1999: 4.8m. tourist arrivals.

2000: 6,750m. riyals in tourism receipts.

PILGRIMS TO MECCA FROM ABROAD*

	1990/91	1991/92	1992/93
Total	720,102	1,015,664	992,813

* Figures relate to Islamic lunar years. The equivalent dates in the Gregorian calendar are: 23 July 1990 to 11 July 1991; 12 July 1991 to 30 June 1992; 1 July 1992 to 19 June 1993.

2000/01 (5 April 2000 to 24 March 2001): 1,363,992 pilgrims.

Communications Media

	1999	2000	2001
Television receivers ('000 in use)	5,500	5,700	n.a.
Telephones ('000 main lines in use)	2,706.2	2,964.7	3,232.9
Mobile cellular telephones ('000 subscribers)	836.6	1,375.9	2,528.6
Personal computers ('000 in use)	1,200	1,300	1,400
Internet users ('000 in use)	100	200	300

1995 (estimate): 150,000 facsimile machines in use.

1996: 13 daily newspapers; 185 non-daily newspapers.

1997: 6,250,000 radio receivers in use.

Sources: UNESCO, *Statistical Yearbook*; International Telecommunication Union.

Education

(2000/2001)

	Institutions	Teachers	Students
Pre-primary*	893	7,703	85,484
Primary	12,585	195,201	2,308,460
Intermediate	6,320	91,592	1,083,935
Secondary (general)	3,454	60,259	794,179
Teacher training†	18	1,807	24,655
Technical and vocational	77	5,221	56,522
University colleges†	75	10,554	190,478

* Figures refer to 1996/97 (Source: UNESCO, *Statistical Yearbook*).
† Figures refer to 1999/2000.

Adult literacy rate (UNESCO estimates): 76.3% (males 83.1%; females 66.9%) in 2000 (Source: UNDP, *Human Development Report*).

Directory

The Constitution

The Basic Law of Government was introduced by royal decree in 1992.

Chapter 1 defines Saudi Arabia as a sovereign Arab, Islamic state. Article 1 defines God's Book and the Sunnah of his prophet as the constitution of Saudi Arabia. The official language is Arabic. The official holidays are Id al-Fitr and Id al-Adha. The calendar is the Hegira calendar.

Chapter 2 concerns the system of government, which is defined as a monarchy, hereditary in the male descendants of Abd al-Aziz ibn Abd ar-Rahman al-Faisal as-Sa'ud. It outlines the duties of the Heir Apparent. The principles of government are justice, consultation and equality in accordance with Islamic law (*Shari'a*).

Chapter 3 concerns the family. The State is to aspire to strengthen family ties and to maintain its Arab and Islamic values. Article 11 states that 'Saudi society will be based on the principle of adherence to God's command, on mutual co-operation in good deeds and piety and mutual support and inseparability'. Education aims to instil the Islamic faith.

Chapter 4 defines the economic principles of the State. All natural resources are the property of the State. The State protects public money and freedom of property. Taxation is only to be imposed on a just basis.

Chapter 5 concerns rights and duties. The State is to protect Islam and to implement the *Shari'a* law. The State protects human rights in accordance with the *Shari'a*. The State is to provide public services and security for all citizens. Punishment is to be in accordance with the *Shari'a*. The Royal Courts are open to all citizens.

Chapter 6 defines the authorities of the State as the judiciary, the executive and the regulatory authority. The judiciary is independent, and acts in accordance with *Shari'a* law. The King is head of the Council of Ministers and Commander-in-Chief of the Armed Forces. The Prime Minister and other ministers are appointed by the King. It provides for the establishment of a Consultative Council (Majlis ash-Shoura).

Chapter 7 concerns financial affairs. It provides for the annual presentation of a state budget. Corporate budgets are subject to the same provisions.

Chapter 8 concerns control bodies. Control bodies will be established to ensure good financial and administrative management of state assets.

Chapter 9 defines the general provisions pertaining to the application of the Basic Law of Government.

The Government

HEAD OF STATE

King: FAHD IBN ABD AL-AZIZ AS-SA'UD (acceded to the throne 13 June 1982).

Crown Prince: ABDULLAH IBN ABD AL-AZIZ AS-SA'UD.

COUNCIL OF MINISTERS
(April 2003)

Prime Minister: King FAHD IBN ABD AL-AZIZ AS-SA'UD.

First Deputy Prime Minister and Commander of the National Guard: Crown Prince ABDULLAH IBN ABD AL-AZIZ AS-SA'UD.

Second Deputy Prime Minister, Minister of Defence and Civil Aviation and Inspector General: Prince SULTAN IBN ABD AL-AZIZ AS-SA'UD.

Minister of Municipal and Rural Affairs: Prince MUTAIB IBN ABD AL-AZIZ AS-SA'UD.

Minister of the Interior: Prince NAYEF IBN ABD AL-AZIZ AS-SA'UD.

Minister of Foreign Affairs: Prince SA'UD AL-FAISAL AS-SA'UD.

Minister of Petroleum and Mineral Resources: Eng. ALI IBN IBRAHIM AN-NUAIMI.

Minister of Labour and Social Affairs: ALI IBN IBRAHIM AN-NAMLA.

Minister of Agriculture: Dr FAHD IBN ABD AR-RAHMAN IBN SULAIMAN BALGHUNAIM.

Minister of Water and Electricity: GHAZI AL-GOSAIBI.

Minister of Education: Dr MUHAMMAD IBN AHMAD AR-RASHID.

Minister of Higher Education: Dr KHALID IBN MUHAMMAD AL-ANGARI.

Minister of Communications and Information Technology: MUHAMMAD IBN JABIL IBN AHMAD MULLA.

Minister of Finance: Dr IBRAHIM IBN ABD AL-AZIZ AL-ASSAF.

Minister of Planning and National Economy: KHALED IBN MUHAMMAD AL-QUSAIBI.

Minister of Information and Culture: Dr FOUAD IBN ABD AS-SALAM IBN MUHAMMAD FARSI.

Minister of Commerce and Industry: Dr HASHEM IBN ABDULLAH YAMANI.

Minister of Justice: Dr ABDULLAH IBN MUHAMMAD IBN IBRAHIM ASH-SHEIKH.

Minister of Pilgrimage (Hajj) Affairs: IYAD IBN AMIN MADANI.

Minister of Awqaf (Religious Endowments), Dawa, Mosques and Guidance Affairs: SALEH IBN ABD AL-AZIZ MUHAMMAD IBN IBRAHIM ASH-SHEIKH.

Minister of Health: Dr HAMAD IBN ABDULLAH AL-MANE.

Minister of the Civil Service: MUHAMMAD IBN ALI AL-FAYEZ.

Minister of Transport: Dr JUBARAH IBN EID AS-SURAISERI.

Ministers of State: Dr MUTLIB IBN ABDULLAH AN-NAFISA, Dr MUSAID IBN MUHAMMAD AL-AYBAN, Dr ABD AL-AZIZ AL-ABDULLAH AL-KHUWAITER, Prince ABD AL-AZIZ IBN FAHD AS-SA'UD, ABDULLAH IBN AHMAD IBN YUSUF ZAINAL.

MINISTRIES

Most ministries have regional offices in Jeddah.

Council of Ministers: Murabba, Riyadh 11121; tel. (1) 488-2444.

Ministry of Agriculture: Airport Rd, Riyadh 11195; tel. (1) 401-6666; fax (1) 404-4592; e-mail info@agrwat.gov.sa; internet www.agrwat.gov.sa.

Ministry of Awqaf (Religious Endowments) Dawa, Mosques and Guidance Affairs: Riyadh 11232; tel. (1) 473-0401; internet www.islam.org.sa.

Ministry of the Civil Service: POB 18367, Riyadh 11114; tel. (1)402-6900; fax (1) 403-4998; internet www.mcs.gov.sa.

Ministry of Commerce and Industry: POB 1774, Airport Rd, Riyadh 11162; tel. (1) 401-2222; fax (1) 403-8421.

Ministry of Communications and Information Technology: Airport Rd, Riyadh 11178; tel. (1) 404-3000; fax (1) 403-1401.

Ministry of Defence and Civil Aviation: POB 26731, Airport Rd, Riyadh 11165; tel. (1) 476-9000; fax (1) 405-5500; internet www.pca.gov.sa.

Ministry of Education: POB 3734, Airport Rd, Riyadh 11481; tel. (1) 402-9500; fax (1) 404-1391; e-mail webmaster@moe.gov.sa; internet www.moe.gov.sa.

Ministry of Finance: Airport Rd, Riyadh 11177; tel. (1) 405-0000; fax (1) 401-0583; internet www.mof.gov.sa.

Ministry of Foreign Affairs: Nasseriya St, Riyadh 11124; tel. (1) 401-5000; fax (1) 403-0159; internet www.mofa.gov.sa.

Ministry of Health: Airport Rd, Riyadh 11176; tel. (1) 401-5555; fax (1) 402-9876; internet www.moh.gov.sa.

Ministry of Higher Education: King Faisal Hospital St, Riyadh 11153; tel. (1) 441-9849; fax (1) 441-9004; internet www.mohe.gov.sa.

Ministry of Information and Culture: POB 570, Nasseriya St, Riyadh 11161; tel. (1) 406-8888; fax (1) 404-4192; internet www.saudinf.com.

Ministry of the Interior: POB 2933, Airport Rd, Riyadh 11134; tel. (1) 401-1111; fax (1) 403-1185.

Ministry of Justice: University St, Riyadh 11137; tel. (1) 405-7777.

Ministry of Labour and Social Affairs: Omar bin al-Khatab St, Riyadh 11157; tel. (1) 477-8888; fax (1) 478-9175; internet www.mol.gov.sa.

Ministry of Municipal and Rural Affairs: Nasseriya St, Riyadh 11136; tel. (1) 441-8888; fax (1) 441-7368; internet www.momra.gov.sa.

Ministry of Petroleum and Mineral Resources: POB 247, King Abd al-Aziz Rd, Riyadh 11191; tel. (1) 478-1661; fax (1) 478-1980; internet www.mopm.gov.sa.

Ministry of Pilgrimage (Hajj) Affaris: Omar bin al-Khatab St, Riyadh 11183; tel. (1) 404-3003; fax (1) 402-2555.

Ministry of Planning and National Economy: POB 358, University St, Riyadh 11182; tel. (1) 401-3333; fax (1) 404-9300; e-mail info@planning.gov.sa; internet www.planning.gov.sa.

Ministry of Transport: Riyadh.

Ministry of Water and Electricity: Riyadh.

MAJLIS ASH-SHOURA
(Consultative Council)

In March 1992 King Fahd issued a decree to establish a Consultative Council of 60 members, whose powers include the right to summon and question ministers. The composition of the Council was announced by King Fahd in August 1993, and it was officially inaugurated in December of that year. Each member is to serve for four years. The Council's membership was increased to 90 when its second term began in July 1997; it was increased further, to 120, in May 2001.

Chairman: SALIH IBN HUMAYD.

Vice-Chairman: ABDULLAH IBN UMAR IBN MUHAMMAD IBN NASIF.

Secretary-General: HAMOUD IBN ABD AL-AZIZ AL-BADR.

Diplomatic Representation

EMBASSIES IN SAUDI ARABIA

Algeria: POB 94388, Riyadh 11693; tel. (1) 488-7171; fax (1) 482-1703; Ambassador ABD AL-KARIM GHARIB.

Argentina: POB 94369, Riyadh 11693; tel. (1) 465-2600; fax (1) 465-3057; e-mail earab@nesma.net.sa; Ambassador LUIS DOMINGO MENDIOLA.

Australia: POB 94400, Riyadh 11693; tel. (1) 488-7788; fax (1) 488-7973; Ambassador ROBERT J. TYSON.

Austria: POB 94373, Riyadh 11693; tel. (1) 480-1217; fax (1) 480-1526; e-mail riyadh-ob@bmaa.gov.at; Ambassador Dr HARALD WIESNER.

Bahrain: POB 94371, Riyadh 11693; tel. (1) 488-0044; fax (1) 488-0208; Ambassador Issa Muhammad al-Khalifa.

Bangladesh: POB 94395, Riyadh 11693; tel. (1) 419-6665; fax (1) 419-3555; e-mail bdootriyadh@zajil.net; Ambassador Mahboob Alam.

Belgium: POB 94396, Riyadh 11693; tel. (1) 488-2888; fax (1) 488-2033; e-mail ambelgium@saudionline.com.sa; Ambassador Franz Michils.

Bosnia and Herzegovina: POB 94301, Riyadh 11693; tel. (1) 456-7914; fax (1) 454-4360; Ambassador Senahid Bistrić.

Brazil: POB 94348, Riyadh 11693; tel. (1) 488-0018; fax (1) 488-1073; e-mail arabras@nesma.net.sa; Ambassador Luís Sérgio Gama Figueira.

Burkina Faso: POB 94330, Riyadh 11693; tel. (1) 465-2244; fax (1) 465-3397; e-mail burkinafaso.ksa@arab.net.sa; Ambassador Oumar Diawara.

Cameroon: POB 94336, Riyadh 11693; tel. (1) 488-0022; fax (1) 488-1463; e-mail ambacamriyad@ifrance.com; Ambassador Mohamadou Labarang.

Canada: POB 94321, Riyadh 11693; tel. (1) 488-2288; fax (1) 488-1997; Ambassador Melvyn L. MacDonald.

Chad: POB 94374, Riyadh 11693; tel. and fax (1) 465-7702; Ambassador al-Hajji Djime Tougou.

China, People's Republic: POB 75231, Riyadh 11578; tel. (1) 482-4246; fax (1) 482-1123; Ambassador Yu Xingzhi.

Côte d'Ivoire: POB 94303, Riyadh 11693; tel. (1) 482-5582; fax (1) 482-9629; e-mail ambciryd@digi.net.sa; Ambassador Lancina Dosso.

Denmark: POB 94398, Riyadh 11693; tel. (1) 488-0101; fax (1) 488-1366; e-mail ruhamb@um.dk; internet www.dkembassyriyadh.dk; Ambassador Sven Erik Nordberg.

Djibouti: POB 94340, Riyadh 11693; tel. (1) 454-3182; fax (1) 456-9168; Ambassador Idriss Ahmad Chirwa.

Egypt: POB 94333, Riyadh 11693; tel. (1) 465-8425; fax (1) 465-2800; Ambassador Fathy ash-Shazly.

Ethiopia: POB 94341, Riyadh 11693; tel. (1) 477-5285; fax (1) 476-8020; e-mail ethembsa@shabakah.net.sa; Ambassador: Ato Muhammad Ali.

Finland: POB 94363, Riyadh 11693; tel. (1) 488-1515; fax (1) 488-2520; Ambassador Heikki Puurunen.

France: POB 94009, Riyadh 11693; tel. (1) 488-1255; fax (1) 488-2882; e-mail diplomatie@ambafrance.org.sa; internet www .ambafrance.org.sa; Ambassador Bernard Poletti.

Gabon: POB 94325, Riyadh 11693; tel. (1) 456-7173; fax (1) 470-0669; Ambassador Nabil Koussou Inama.

Gambia: POB 94322, Riyadh 11693; tel. (1) 465-1320; fax (1) 462-1481; e-mail gamextriyadh@yahoo.com; Ambassador Dr Mangom M. Ceesay.

Germany: POB 94001, Riyadh 11693; tel. (1) 488-0700; fax (1) 488-0660; Ambassador Dr Harald Kindermann.

Ghana: POB 94339, Riyadh 11693; tel. (1) 454-5122; fax 450-9819; e-mail ghanaemb@naseej.com; Ambassador Abd ar-Razaq Muyhideen Hassan Tahir.

Greece: POB 94375, Riyadh 11693; tel. (1) 480-1975; fax (1) 480-1969; Ambassador Paul Apostolides.

Guinea: POB 94326, Riyadh 11693; tel. (1) 488-1101; fax (1) 482-6757; Ambassador el-Hadj Aboul Karim Dioubatè.

Hungary: POB 94014, al-Waha District, Ahmad Tonsy St 23, Riyadh 11693; tel. (1) 454-6707; fax (1) 456-0834; e-mail huemb .ryd@nournet.com.sa; Ambassador Tamás Varga.

India: POB 94387, Riyadh 11693; tel. (1) 488-4144; fax (1) 488-4750; e-mail ieriyadh@shabakah.net.sa; Ambassador Talmiz Ahmad.

Indonesia: POB 94343, Riyadh 11693; tel. (1) 488-2800; fax (1) 488-2966; Ambassador Dr Ismail Suny.

Iran: POB 94394, Riyadh 11693; tel. (1) 488-1916; fax (1) 488-1890; Ambassador Muhammad Reza Nuri-Sharudi.

Ireland: POB 94349, Riyadh 11693; tel. (1) 488-2300; fax (1) 488-0927; Ambassador Michael Collins.

Italy: POB 94389, Riyadh 11693; tel. (1) 488-1212; fax (1) 488-1951; e-mail info@italia-as.org; internet www.italia-as.org; Ambassador Torquato Cardilli.

Japan: POB 4095, Riyadh 11491; tel. (1) 488-1100; fax (1) 488-0189; Ambassador Minoro Tamba.

Jordan: POB 94316, Riyadh 11693; tel. (1) 488-0051; fax (1) 488-0072; Ambassador Hani Khalifah.

Kazakhstan: POB 94012, Riyadh 11693; tel. (1) 470-1839; fax (1) 454-7781; e-mail kazruh@ae.net.sa; Ambassador Baghdad Amreyev.

Kenya: POB 94358, Riyadh 11693; tel. (1) 488-1238; fax (1) 488-2629; Ambassador Ali Muhammad Abdi.

Korea, Republic: POB 94399, Riyadh 11693; tel. (1) 488-2211; fax (1) 488-1317; Ambassador Kim Chung-Ki.

Kuwait: POB 94304, Riyadh 11693; tel. (1) 488-3401; fax (1) 488-3682; Ambassador Abd ar-Rahman Ahmad al-Bakr.

Lebanon: POB 94350, Riyadh 11693; tel. (1) 419-7000; fax (1) 419-2767; Ambassador Zouheir Hamdan.

Libya: POB 94365, Riyadh 11693; tel. (1) 454-4511; fax (1) 456-7513; Ambassador Muhammad Sa'id al-Qashshat.

Malaysia: POB 94335, Riyadh 11693; tel. (1) 488-7100; fax (1) 482-4177; Ambassador Datuk Haji Mokhtar bin Haji Ahmad.

Mali: POB 94331, Riyadh 11693; tel. (1) 464-5640; fax (1) 419-5016.

Malta: POB 94361, Riyadh 11693; tel. (1) 463-2345; fax (1) 463-3993; e-mail maltaemb@shabakah.net.sa; Ambassador Saviour P. Gauci.

Mauritania: POB 94354, Riyadh 11693; tel. (1) 464-6749; fax (1) 465-8355; Ambassador Baba Ould Muhammad Abdullah.

Mexico: POB 94391, Riyadh 11693; tel. (1) 482-8218; fax (1) 482-8379; e-mail embamex@embamex.org.sa; Ambassador Edgardo Flores Rivas.

Morocco: POB 94392, Riyadh 11693; tel. (1) 481-1858; fax (1) 482-7016; Ambassador Abd al-Krim Semmar.

Nepal: POB 94384, Riyadh 11693; tel. (1) 461-1108; fax (1) 464-0690; e-mail rneksa@zajil.net; Ambassador Badri P. Khanal.

Netherlands: POB 94307, Riyadh 11693; tel. (1) 488-0011; fax (1) 488-0544; internet www.holland.org.sa; Ambassador P. Lagendijk.

New Zealand: POB 94397, Riyadh 11693; tel. (1) 488-7988; fax (1) 488-7912; Ambassador James Howell.

Niger: POB 94334, Riyadh 11693; tel. and fax (1) 464-2931.

Nigeria: POB 94386, Riyadh 11693; tel. (1) 482-3024; fax (1) 480-1828; e-mail nigeriaryd@zajil.net; Ambassador Alhaji Ahmad al-Gazali.

Norway: POB 94380, Riyadh 11693; tel. (1) 488-1904; fax (1) 488-0854; e-mail emb.riyadh@mfa.no; Ambassador Svein Andreassen.

Oman: POB 94381, Riyadh 11693; tel. (1) 482-3120; fax (1) 482-3738; Ambassador Hamad H. al-Mo'amary.

Pakistan: POB 94007, Riyadh 11693; tel. (1) 488-7272; fax (1) 488-7953; Ambassador Admiral (retd) Adul Aziz Mirza.

Philippines: POB 94366, Riyadh 11693; tel. (1) 488-0835; fax (1) 488-3945; Ambassador Romulo M. Espaldon.

Portugal: POB 94328, Riyadh 11693; tel. (1) 462-2115; fax (1) 462-3365; Ambassador José Manuel Waddington Matos Parreira.

Qatar: POB 94353, Riyadh 11461; tel. (1) 482-5544; fax (1) 482-5394; Ambassador M. Ali al-Ansari.

Russia: POB 94308, Riyadh 11693; tel. (1) 481-1875; fax (1) 481-1890; Ambassador Igor A. Melikhov.

Rwanda: POB 94383, Riyadh 11693; tel. (1) 454-0808; fax (1) 456-1769; Ambassador Simon Insonere.

Senegal: POB 94352, Riyadh 11693; tel. (1) 454-2144; fax (1) 264-7675; Ambassador Modou Dia.

Sierra Leone: POB 94329, Riyadh 11693; tel. (1) 464-3982; fax (1) 464-3662; e-mail slembrdh@zajil.net; Ambassador Alhaji Amadu Deen Tejan-Sie.

Singapore: POB 94378, Riyadh 11693; tel. (1) 465-7007; fax (1) 465-2224; Chargé d'affaires a.i. Anthony Chng.

Somalia: POB 94372, Riyadh 11693; tel. (1) 464-3456; fax (1) 464-9705; Ambassador Abd ar-Rahman A. Hussein.

South Africa: POB 94006, Riyadh 11693; tel. (1) 456-2982; fax (1) 454-3727; e-mail embriyad@ogertel.com; Ambassador (vacant).

Spain: POB 94347, Riyadh 11693; tel. (1) 488-0606; fax 488-0420; e-mail embespsa@mail.mae.es; Ambassador Ramón Ansoáin Garraza.

Sri Lanka: POB 94360, Riyadh 11693; tel. (1) 454-2368; fax (1) 454-9748; e-mail lankaemb@shabakah.net.sa; Ambassador Nowfel Saly Jabir.

Sudan: POB 94337, Riyadh 11693; tel. (1) 488-7979; fax (1) 488-7729; Ambassador Dr Attalla H. Bashir.

Sweden: POB 94382, Riyadh 11693; tel. (1) 488-3100; fax (1) 488-0604; e-mail ambassaden.riyadh@foreign.ministry.se; internet www .swedemb.org.sa; Ambassador Åke Karlsson.

Switzerland: POB 94311, Riyadh 11693; tel. (1) 488-1291; fax (1) 488-0632; Ambassador Dominik M. Alder.

Syria: POB 94323, Riyadh 11693; tel. (1) 482-6191; fax (1) 482-6196; Ambassador MUHAMMAD KHALID AT-TALL.

Tanzania: POB 94320, Riyadh 11693; tel. (1) 454-2839; fax (1) 454-9660; Ambassador Prof. A. A. SHAREEF.

Thailand: POB 94359, Riyadh 11693; tel. (1) 488-1174; fax 488-1179; e-mail thaiemry@awalnet.net.sa; Chargé d'affaires SOMSAKDI SURIYAWONGSE.

Tunisia: POB 94368, Riyadh 11693; tel. (1) 488-7900; fax (1) 488-7641; Ambassador KACEM BOUSNINA.

Turkey: POB 94390, Riyadh 11693; tel. (1) 482-0101; fax (1) 488-7823; e-mail turkemb@concept.net.sa; Ambassador TÜRKEKUL KURT-TEKIN.

Uganda: POB 94344, Riyadh 11693; tel. (1) 454-4910; fax (1) 454-9264; e-mail ugariyadh@arab.net.sa; Ambassador Dr MOHAMMED AHMED KISUULE.

United Arab Emirates: POB 94385, Riyadh 11693; tel. (1) 482-9652; fax (1) 482-7504; Ambassador ISSA K. AL-HURAIMIL.

United Kingdom: POB 94351, Riyadh 11693; tel. (1) 488-0077; fax (1) 488-2373; e-mail Information.Riyadh@fco.gov.uk; internet www.ukm.org.sa; Ambassador Sir DEREK PLUMBLY.

USA: POB 94309, Riyadh 11693; tel. (1) 488-3800; fax (1) 488-7360; e-mail usisriyadh@yahoo.com; internet www.usembassy.state.gov/riyadh/; Ambassador ROBERT W. JORDAN.

Uruguay: POB 94346, Riyadh 11693; tel. (1) 462-0739; fax (1) 462-0648; e-mail ururia@mcimail.com; Ambassador CARLOS A. CLULOW.

Uzbekistan: Riyadh; Ambassador ULUGBEK ISROILOV.

Venezuela: POB 94364, Riyadh 11693; tel. (1) 476-7867; fax (1) 476-8200; Ambassador NORMAN PINO.

Yemen: POB 94356, Riyadh 11693; tel. (1) 488-1769; fax (1) 488-1562; Ambassador KHALED ISMAIL AL-AKWA'A.

Judicial System

Judges are independent and governed by the rules of Islamic *Shari'a*. The following courts operate:

Supreme Council of Justice: consists of 11 members and supervises work of the courts; reviews legal questions referred to it by the Minister of Justice and expresses opinions on judicial questions; reviews sentences of death, cutting and stoning; Chair. Sheikh SALIH AL-LIHAYDAN.

Court of Cassation: consists of Chief Justice and an adequate number of judges; includes department for penal suits, department for personal status and department for other suits.

General (Public) Courts: consist of one or more judges; sentences are issued by a single judge, with the exception of death, stoning and cutting, which require the decision of three judges.

Summary Courts: consist of one or more judges; sentences are issued by a single judge.

Specialized Courts: Article 26 of the judicial system stipulates that the setting up of specialized courts is permissible by Royal Decree on a proposal from the Supreme Council of Justice.

Religion

ISLAM

Arabia is the centre of the Islamic faith, and Saudi Arabia includes the holy cities of Mecca and Medina. Except in the Eastern Province, where a large number of people follow Shi'a rites, the majority of the population are Sunni Muslims, and most of the indigenous inhabitants belong to the strictly orthodox Wahhabi sect. The Wahhabis originated in the 18th century but first became unified and influential under Abd al-Aziz (Ibn Sa'ud), who became the first King of Saudi Arabia. They are now the keepers of the holy places and control the pilgrimage to Mecca. In 1986 King Fahd adopted the title of Custodian of the Two Holy Mosques. The country's most senior Islamic authority is the Council of Ulema.

Mecca: Birthplace of the Prophet Muhammad, seat of the Great Mosque and Shrine of Ka'ba, visited by 1,363,992 Muslims in the Islamic year 1421 (2000/2001).

Medina: Burial place of Muhammad, second sacred city of Islam.

Grand Mufti and Chairman of Council of Ulema: Sheikh ABD AL-AZIZ IBN ABDULLAH ASH-SHEIKH.

CHRISTIANITY

The Roman Catholic Church

A small number of adherents, mainly expatriates, form part of the Apostolic Vicariate of Arabia. The Vicar Apostolic is resident in the United Arab Emirates

The Anglican Communion

Within the Episcopal Church in Jerusalem and the Middle East, Saudi Arabia forms part of the diocese of Cyprus and the Gulf. The Anglican congregations in the country are entirely expatriate. The Bishop in Cyprus and the Gulf is resident in Cyprus, while the Archdeacon in the Gulf is resident in Qatar.

Other Denominations

The Greek Orthodox Church is also represented.

The Press

Since 1964 most newspapers and periodicals have been published by press organizations, administered by boards of directors with full autonomous powers, in accordance with the provisions of the Press Law. These organizations, which took over from small private firms, are privately owned by groups of individuals experienced in newspaper publishing and administration (see Publishers).

There are also a number of popular periodicals published by the Government and by the Saudi Arabian Oil Co, and distributed free of charge. The press is subject to no legal restriction affecting freedom of expression or the coverage of news.

DAILIES

Arab News: POB 10452, Jeddah 21433; tel. (2) 639-1888; fax (2) 639-3223; e-mail editorial1@arabnews.com; f. 1975; English; publ. by Saudi Research and Marketing Co; Editor-in-Chief KHALED AL-MAEENA; circ. 110,000.

Al-Bilad (The Country): POB 6340, Jeddah 21442; tel. (2) 672-3000; fax (2) 671-2545; f. 1934; Arabic; publ. by Al-Bilad Publishing Organization; Editor-in-Chief QUINAN AL-GHOMDI; circ. 66,210.

Al-Jazirah (The Peninsula): POB 354, Riyadh 11411; tel. (1) 487-0000; fax (1) 487-1201; e-mail chief@al-jazirah.com; internet www.al-jazirah.com; Arabic; Gen. Man. ABD AR-RAHMAN BIN FAHD AR-RASHAD; Editor-in-Chief KHALID IBN HAMAD AL-MALIK; circ. 94,000.

Al-Madina al-Munawara (Medina—The Enlightened City): POB 807, Makkah Rd, Jeddah 21421; tel. (2) 671-2100; fax (2) 671-1877; internet www.almadinah.com; f. 1937; Arabic; publ. by Al-Madina Press Est; Chief Editor USAMA AS-SIBA'IE; circ. 46,370.

An-Nadwah (The Council): Jarwal Sheikh Sayed Halabi Bldg, POB 5803, Mecca; tel. (2) 520-0111; fax (2) 520-3055; f. 1958; Arabic; publ. by Mecca Printing and Information Establishment; Editor Dr ABD AR-RAHMAN AL-HARTHI; circ. 35,000.

Okaz: POB 1508, Seaport Rd, Jeddah 21441; tel. (2) 672-2630; fax (2) 672-4297; e-mail 104127.266@compuserve.com; f. 1960; Arabic; Editor-in-Chief HASHIM ABDU HASHIM; circ. 107,614.

Ar-Riyadh: POB 2943, Riyadh 11476; tel. (1) 442-0000; fax (1) 441-7417; internet www.alriyadh.com.sa; f. 1965; Arabic; publ. by Al-Yamama Publishing Establishment; Editor TURKI A. AS-SUDARI; circ. 150,000 (Sat.–Thurs.), 90,000 (Friday).

Riyadh Daily NP: POB 2943, Riyadh 11476; tel. (1) 441-7544; fax (1) 441-7116; English; publ. by Yamama Publishing Establishment; Editor-in-Chief TALA'T WARFA.

Saudi Gazette: POB 5576, Jeddah 21432; tel. (2) 676-0000; fax (2) 672-7621; e-mail news@saudigazette.com.sa; internet www.saudigazette.com.sa; f. 1976; English; publ. by Okaz Organization for Press and Publication; Editor-in-Chief Dr AHMAD AL-YUSUF; circ. 60,000.

Al-Watan: POB 15156, Airport Road, Abha; tel. (7) 227-3333; fax (7) 227-3590; internet www.alwatan.com.sa; f. 1998; publ. by Assir Establishment for Press and Publishing; Asst Man. Dir Dr MAMDOUH A. BA-OWAIDAN; Editor JAMAL KHASHOGGI.

Al-Yaum (Today): POB 565, Dammam 31421; tel. (3) 858-0800; fax (3) 858-8777; e-mail admin@alyaum.com; internet www.alyaum.com; f. 1965; Editor-in-Chief MUHAMMAD AL-WAEEL; circ. 80,000.

WEEKLIES

Al-Muslimoon (The Muslims): POB 13195, Jeddah 21493; tel. (2) 669-1888; fax (2) 669-5549; f. 1985; Arabic; cultural and religious affairs; publ. by Saudi Research and Marketing Co; Editor-in-Chief Dr ABDULLAH AR-RIFA'E; circ. 68,665.

Saudi Arabia Business Week: POB 2894, Riyadh; English; trade and commerce.

Saudi Economic Survey: POB 1989, Jeddah 21441; tel. (2) 651-4952; fax (2) 652-2680; e-mail walid@saudieconomicsurvey.com; internet www.saudieconomicsurvey.com; f. 1967; English; a weekly review of Saudi Arabian economic and business activity; Publr S. A. Ashoor; Gen. Man. Walid S. Ashoor; circ. 4,500.

Sayidati (My Lady): POB 4556, Madina Rd, Jeddah 21412; tel. (2) 639-1888; fax (2) 669-5549; Arabic; women's magazine; publ. by Saudi Research and Marketing Co; Editor-in-Chief Matar al-Ahmadi.

Al-Yamama: POB 851, Riyadh 11421; tel. (1) 442-0000; fax (1) 441-7114; f. 1952; Editor-in-Chief Abdullah al-Jahlan; circ. 35,000.

OTHER PERIODICALS

Ahlan Wasahlan (Welcome): POB 8013, Jeddah 21482; tel. (2) 686-2349; fax (2) 686-2006; monthly; flight journal of Saudi Arabian Airlines; Gen. Man. and Editor-in-Chief Yarub A. Balkhair; circ. 150,000.

Al-Faysal: POB 3, Riyadh 11411; tel. (1) 465-3027; fax (1) 464-7851; monthly; f. 1976; Arabic; culture, education, health, interviews; Editor-in-Chief Dr Yahya Mahmoud ibn Junaid.

Al-Manhal (The Spring): POB 2925, Jeddah; tel. (2) 643-2124; fax (2) 642-8853; f. 1937; monthly; Arabic; cultural, literary, political and scientific; Editor Nabih Abd al-Qudous Ansari.

Majallat al-Iqtisad wal-Idara (Journal of Economics and Administration): King Abd al-Aziz University, POB 9031, Jeddah 21413; twice a year; Chief Editor Prof. Abd al-Aziz A. Diyab.

The MWL Journal: Press and Publications Department, Rabitat al-Alam al-Islami, POB 537, Mecca; fax 544-1622; monthly; English; Dir Murad Sulaiman Irqisous.

Ar-Rabita: POB 537, Mecca; tel. 543-3583; fax 543-1488; Arabic; Man. Editor Muhammad al-Asad.

Saudi Review: POB 4288, Jeddah 21491; tel. (2) 651-7442; fax (2) 653-0693; f. 1966; English; monthly; newsletter from Saudi newspapers and broadcasting service; publ. by International Communications Co; Chief Editor Saad al-Mabrouk; circ. 5,000.

Ash-Sharkiah-Elle (Oriental Elle): POB 6, Riyadh; monthly; Arabic; women's magazine; Editor Samira M. Khashaggi.

As-Soqoor (Falcons): POB 2973, Riyadh 11461; tel. (1) 476-6566; f. 1978; 2 a year; air-force journal; cultural activities; Editor Hamad A. as-Saleh.

At-Tadhamon al-Islami (Islamic Solidarity): Ministry of Pilgrimage (*Hajj*) Affairs, Omar bin al-Khatab St, Riyadh 11183; monthly; Editor Dr Mustafa Abd al-Wahid.

At-Tijarah (Commerce): POB 1264, Jeddah 21431; tel. (2) 651-5111; fax (2) 651-7373; e-mail jcci@mail.gcc.com.bh; f. 1960; monthly; publ. by Jeddah Chamber of Commerce and Industry; Chair. Sheikh Ismail Abu Daud; circ. 8,000.

NEWS AGENCIES

International Islamic News Agency (IINA): POB 5054, Jeddah 21422; tel. (2) 665-2056; fax (2) 665-9358; e-mail iina@sps.net.sa; internet www.islamicnews.org; f. 1972; operates under OIC auspices; Dir Gen. Abd al-Wahab Kashif.

Islamic Republic News Agency (IRNA) (Iran): Riyadh; f. 2001; Dir-Gen. Abdollah Nasiri.

Saudi Press Agency: c/o Ministry of Information, POB 7186, Riyadh 11171; tel. (1) 462-3333; fax (1) 462-6747; e-mail wass@spa.gov.sa; internet www.spa.gov.sa; f. 1970; Dir-Gen. Badi Kuiayyem.

Publishers

Assir Establishment for Press and Publishing: POB 15156, Abha; tel. (7) 227-3333; fax (7) 227-3590; f. 1998; publishes *Al-Watan*; cap. 200m. Chair. and Acting Dir-Gen. Fahd al-Harithi.

Al-Bilad Publishing Organization: POB 6340, As-Sahafa St, Jeddah 21442; tel. (2) 672-3000; fax (2) 671-2545; publishes *Al-Bilad* and *Iqra'a*; Dir-Gen. Amin Abdullah al-Qarqouri.

Dar ash-Shareff for Publishing and Distribution: POB 58287, Riyadh 11594; tel. (1) 403-4931; fax (1) 405-2234; f. 1992; fiction, religion, science and social sciences; Pres. Ibrahim al-Hazemi.

Dar al-Yaum Press, Printing and Publishing Ltd: POB 565, Dammam 31421; tel. (3) 858-0800; fax (3) 858-8777; e-mail salhumaidan@alyaum.com; f. 1964; publishes *Al-Yaum*.

International Publications Agency (IPA): POB 70, Dhahran 31942; tel. (3) 895-4925; fax (3) 895-4925; publishes material of local interest; Man. Said Salah.

Al-Jazirah Corpn for Press, Printing and Publishing: POB 354, Riyadh 11411; tel. (1) 441-9999; fax (1) 441-2536; e-mail marketing@al-jazirah.com; f. 1964; 42 mems; publishes *Al-Jazirah* and *Al-Masaeyah* (both dailies); Dir-Gen. Salah al-Ajroush; Editor-in-Chief Khalid el-Malek.

Al-Madina Press Establishment: POB 807, Jeddah 21421; tel. (2) 671-2100; fax (2) 671-1877; f. 1937; publishes *Al-Madina al-Munawara*; Gen. Man. Ahmed Salah Jamjoum.

Makkah Printing and Information Establishment: POB 5803, Jarwal Sheikh Sayed Halabi Bldg, Mecca; tel. (2) 542-7868; publishes *An-Nadwah* daily newspaper.

Okaz Organization for Press and Publication: POB 1508, Jeddah 21441; tel. (2) 672-2630; fax (2) 672-8150; publishes *Okaz*, *Saudi Gazette* and *Child*.

Saudi Publishing and Distributing House: Umm Aslam District, nr Muslaq, POB 2043, Jeddah 21451; tel. (2) 629-4278; fax (2) 629-4290; f. 1966; publishers, importers and distributors of English and Arabic books; Chair. Muhammad Salahuddin.

Saudi Research and Publishing Co: POB 4556, Jeddah 21412; tel. (2) 669-1888; fax (2) 669-5549; e-mail arabnews@arabnews.com; internet www.arabnews.com; publishes 17 titles incl. *Arab News*, *Asharq al-Awsat*, *Al-Majalla*, *Al-Muslimoon* and *Sayidati*; Chair. Prince Ahmad ibn Salman.

Yamama Publishing Establishment: POB 2943, Riyadh 11476; tel. (1) 442-0000; fax (1) 441-7116; publishes *Ar-Riyadh* and *Al-Yamama*; Dir-Gen. Sakhal Maidan.

Broadcasting and Communications

TELECOMMUNICATIONS

Saudi Communications Commission (SCC): Riyadh; f. 2001; ind. regulatory authority; Gov. Muhammad Jamil Mulla.

Saudi Telecommunications Co: Riyadh; internet www.stct.com.sa; f. 1998; provides telecommunications services in Saudi Arabia; partially privatized in January 2001; cap. 12,000m. riyals; Pres. Khaled al-Molhem.

BROADCASTING

Radio

Saudi Arabian Broadcasting Service: c/o Ministry of Information, POB 60059, Riyadh 11545; tel. (1) 401-4440; fax (1) 403-8177; 24 medium- and short-wave stations, including Jeddah, Riyadh, Dammam and Abha, broadcast programmes in Arabic and English; 23 FM stations; overseas service in Bengali, English, Farsi, French, Hausa, Indonesian, Somali, Swahili, Turkestani, Turkish and Urdu; Dir-Gen. Muhammad al-Mansoor.

Saudi Aramco FM Radio: Bldg 3030 LIP, Dhahran 31311; tel. (3) 876-1845; fax (3) 876-1608; f. 1948; English; private; for employees of Saudi Aramco; Man. Essam Z. Tawfiq.

Television

Saudi Arabian Government Television Service: POB 7971, Riyadh 11472; tel. (1) 401-4440; fax (1) 404-4192; began transmission 1965; 112 stations, incl. six main stations at Riyadh, Jeddah, Medina, Dammam, Qassim, Abha, transmit programmes in Arabic and English; Dir-Gen. Abd al-Aziz al-Hassan (Channel 1).

Saudi Arabian Government Television Service Channel 2: POB 7959, Riyadh 11472; tel. (1) 442-8400; fax (1) 403-3826; began transmission 1983; Dir-Gen. Abd al-Aziz S. Abu Annaja.

Finance

(cap. = capital; res = reserves; dep. = deposits; m. = million; brs = branches; amounts in Saudi riyals unless otherwise stated)

BANKING

At the end of 2001 the Saudi Arabian banking system consisted of: the Saudi Arabian Monetary Agency, as central note-issuing and regulatory body; 11 commercial banks (three national and eight foreign banks); and five specialist banks. There is a policy of 'Saudi-ization' of the foreign banks.

Central Bank

Saudi Arabian Monetary Agency (SAMA): POB 2992, Riyadh 11169; tel. (1) 463-3000; fax (1) 466-2963; e-mail info@sama.ksa.org; internet www.sama.gov.sa; f. 1952; functions include stabilization of currency, administration of monetary reserves, regulation of banking and issue of notes and coins; res 2,103.7m., dep. 61,843.7m., total assets 154,301.8m. (June 2001); Gov. Sheikh HAMAD SA'UD AS-SAYARI; 10 brs.

National Banks

National Commercial Bank (NCB): POB 3555, King Abd al-Aziz St, Jeddah 21481; tel. (2) 649-3333; fax (2) 644-6468; e-mail contact@alahli.com; internet www.alahli.com; f. 1950; cap. 6,000m., res 2,051m., dep. 88,757m. (Dec. 2001); Chair. and Man. Dir Sheikh ABDULLAH SALIM BAHAMDAN; Gen. Man. ABD AL-HADI ALI SHAYIF; 258 brs.

Ar-Rajhi Banking and Investment Corpn (ARABIC): POB 28, Riyadh 11411; tel. (1) 460-1000; fax (1) 460-0922; e-mail contactus@alrajhibank.com.sa; internet www.alrajhibank.com.sa; f. 1988; operates according to Islamic financial principles; cap. 2,250.0m., res 3,189.4m., dep. 40,625.6m. (Dec. 2001); Chair. and Man. Dir Sheikh SULAYMAN BIN ABD AL-AZIZ AR-RAJHI; 362 brs.

Riyad Bank Ltd: POB 22601, King Abd al-Aziz St, Riyadh 11416; tel. (1) 401-3030; fax (1) 404-2707; internet www.riyadbank.com.sa; f. 1957; cap. 4,000m., res 4,195m., dep. 55,161m. (Dec. 2001); Chair. RASHED A. AR-RASHED; Pres. and CEO TALAL I. AL-QUDAIBI; 180 brs.

Specialist Bank

Arab Investment Co SAA (TAIC): POB 4009, King Abd al-Aziz St, Riyadh 11491; tel. (1) 476-0601; fax (1) 476-0514; e-mail taic@taic.com; internet www.taic.com; f. 1974 by 17 Arab countries for investment and banking; cap. US $400.0m., res $47.9m., dep. $1,414.2m. (Dec. 2001); Chair. Dr MUHAMMAD SULAYMAN AL-JASSER; Dir-Gen. Dr SALIH AL-HUMAIDAN; 1 br, 3 offices throughout Middle East.

Banks with Foreign Interests

Al-Bank as-Saudi al-Fransi (Saudi French Bank): POB 56006, Riyadh 11554; tel. (1) 404-2222; fax (1) 404-2311; e-mail communications@alfransi.com; internet www.alfransi.com; f. 1977; Saudi shareholders 68.9%, Crédit Agricole Indosuez 31.1%; cap. 1,800.0m., res 2,223.0m., dep. 34,087.7m. (Dec. 2001); Chair. IBRAHIM A. AT-TOUQ; Man. Dir BERTRAND P. VIRIOT; 57 brs.

Arab National Bank (ANB): POB 56921, Riyadh 11564; tel. (1) 402-9000; fax (1) 402-7747; e-mail marketing@anb.com.sa; internet www.anb.com.sa; f. 1980; Arab Bank plc, Jordan, 40%, Saudi shareholders 60%; cap. 1,500.0m., res 1,843.7m., dep. 34,442.1m. (Dec. 2001); Chair. ABD H. AL-JABR; Man. Dir and CEO NEMEH SABBAGH; 117 brs.

Bank al-Jazira: POB 6277, Jeddah 21442; tel. (2) 651-8070; fax (2) 653-2478; e-mail info@baj.com.sa; internet www.baj.com.sa; 94.17% Saudi-owned; cap. 600.0m., res 80.0m. dep. 4,322.9m. (Dec. 2001); Chair. ADEL MUHAMMAD FAKEIH; Gen. Man. and CEO MISHARI I. AL-MISHARI; 13 brs.

Gulf International Bank (Bahrain): POB 93413, Riyadh 11673; tel. (1) 218-0888; fax (1) 218-0088; f. 2000; Man. ZAFER AL-KALALI.

Saudi American Bank (SAMBA): POB 833, Riyadh 11421; tel. and fax (1) 477-4770; internet www.samba.com.sa; 74% owned by Saudi nationals, 23% by Citibank NA, USA, 2% by Banque du Caire, Egypt, 1% by Bank Melli Iran; merged with United Saudi Bank in 1999; cap. 4,000.0m., res 4,309.2m., dep. 65,986.4m. (Dec. 2001); Chair. ABD AL-AZIZ IBN HAMAD AL-GOSAIBI; Man. Dir ARTHUR M. DE GRAFFANRIED; 43 brs.

Saudi British Bank: POB 9084, Riyadh 11413; tel. (1) 405-0677; fax (1) 405-0660; e-mail pr@sabb.com.sa; internet www.sabb.com.sa; 60% owned by Saudi nationals, 40% by HSBC Holdings BV; f. 1978; cap. 2,000.0m., res 1,879.5m., dep. 36,332.0m. (Dec. 2001); Chair. Sheikh ABDULLAH MUHAMMAD AL-HUGAIL; Man. Dir DAVID HODGKINSON; 78 brs.

Saudi Hollandi Bank (Saudi Dutch Bank): POB 1467, Riyadh 11431; tel. (1) 401-0288; fax (1) 403-1104; e-mail csc@shb.com.sa; internet www.saudihollandibank.com; a joint-stock co; f. 1977 to assume activities of Algemene Bank Nederland NV in Saudi Arabia; ABN AMRO Bank (Netherlands) 40%, Saudi citizens 60%; cap. 630.0m., res 1,421.6m., dep. 22,015.6m. (Dec. 2001); Chair. Sheikh SULEYMAN A. R. AS-SUHAIMI; Man. Dir PETER PAUL M. BALTUSSEN; 40 brs.

Saudi Investment Bank (SAIB): POB 3533, Riyadh 11481; tel. (1) 477-8433; fax (1) 477-6781; internet www.saib.com.sa; f. 1976; provides a comprehensive range of traditional and specialized banking services; cap. 1,100.0m., res 885.1m., dep. 12,512.1m. (Dec 2001);

Chair. Dr ABD AL-AZIZ O'HALI; Pres. and Gen. Man. SA'UD AS-SALEH; 13 brs.

Government Specialized Credit Institutions

Real Estate Development Fund (REDF): POB 5591, Riyadh 11139; tel. (1) 479-2222; fax (1) 479-0148; f. 1974; provides interest-free loans to Saudi individuals and cos for private or commercial housing projects; cap. 70,841 (1993); loans granted amounted to 1,900m. in 2000; Gen. Dir AHMAD AL-AKEIL; 25 brs.

Saudi Arabian Agricultural Bank (SAAB): POB 1811, Riyadh 11126; tel. (1) 402-3911; fax (1) 402-2359; f. 1963; cap. 10,000m. (1982); loans disbursed amounted to 803.9m. in 2000; Controller-Gen. ABDULLAH SAAD AL-MENGASH; Gen. Man. ABD AL-AZIZ MUHAMMAD AL-MANQUR; 70 brs.

Saudi Credit Bank: POB 3401, Riyadh 11471; tel. (1) 402-9128; f. 1973; provides interest-free loans for specific purposes to Saudi citizens of moderate means; loans disbursed amounted to 321.3m. in 2000; Chair. SAID IBN SAIED; Dir-Gen. MUHAMMAD AD-DRIES; 24 brs.

STOCK EXCHANGE

The Saudi Arabian Monetary Agency (see Central Bank, above) operates the Electronic Securities Information System. In March 2003 shares in 79 companies were being traded. In 2001 691m. shares amounting to 83,602m. riyals were traded.

INSURANCE COMPANIES

In 2000 there were 99 insurance companies, agencies and brokerage offices operating in Saudi Arabia.

Amana Gulf Insurance Co (E.C.): POB 6559, Jeddah 21452; tel. and fax (2) 665-5692.

Arabia Ace Insurance Co Ltd (E.C.): POB 276, Dammam 31411; tel. (3) 832-4441; fax (3) 834-9389; internet www.khereiji.com; cap. US $1m. Chair. Sheikh ABD AL-KARIM AL-KHEREIJI; Man. Dir TAJUDDIN HASSAN.

Independent Insurance Co of Saudi Arabia Ltd: POB 1178, Jeddah 21431; tel. (2) 651-7732; fax (2) 651-1968; f. 1977; all classes of insurance; cap. US $1m. Pres. KHALID TAHER; Man. JULIAN D. SHARPE.

Insaudi Insurance Co (E.C.): POB 3984, Riyadh 11481; tel. (1) 476-7711; fax (1) 476-1213.

Islamic Arab Insurance Co: POB 430, Jeddah; tel. (2) 671-0000; fax (2) 617-1027; e-mail iaic@dallah.com.

Al-Jazira Insurance Co Ltd: POB 153, al-Khobar 31952; tel. and fax (3) 895-3445.

National Company for Co-operative Insurance (NCCI): POB 86959, Riyadh 11632; tel. (1) 218-0100; fax (1) 218-0102; e-mail ncci@ncci.com.sa; internet www.ncci.com.sa; f. 1985 by royal decree; owned by three govt agencies; auth. cap. 500m. Chair. SULAYMAN AL-HUMMAYYD; Man. Dir and Gen. Man. MOUSA AR-RUBAIAN; 13 brs and sales offices.

Ar-Rajhi Insurance Co: POB 22073, Jeddah 21495; tel. (2) 651-1017; fax (2) 651-1797.

Ar-Rajhi Islamic Co for Co-operative Insurance: POB 42220, Jeddah 21541; tel. (2) 651-4514; fax (2) 651-3185.

Red Sea Insurance Group of Cos: POB 5627, Jeddah 21432; tel. (2) 660-3538; fax (2) 665-5418; e-mail redsea@anet.net.sa; internet www.redsains.com; f. 1974; insurance, development, and reinsurance; cap. US $9m. (1998); Chair. KHALDOUN B. BARAKAT.

Royal & Sun Alliance Insurance (Middle East) Ltd (E.C.): POB 2374, Jeddah 21451; tel. (2) 671-8851; fax (2) 671-1377; e-mail alalamiya@dmp.net.sa; managed by Royal & Sun Alliance Insurance Group, London; total assets US $51m. (2000); Chair. WAHIB S. BIN-ZAGR; Man. Dir P. W. HEAD.

Saudi Continental Insurance Co: POB 2940, Riyadh; tel. (1) 479-2141; fax (1) 476-9310; f. 1983; all classes of insurance; cap. US $3m. Chair. OMAR A. AGGAD; Gen. Man. J.A. McROBBIE.

Saudi National Insurance Co EC: POB 5832, Jeddah 21432; tel. (2) 660-6200; fax (2) 667-4530; Gen. Man. OMAR S. BILANI.

Saudi Union National Insurance Corpn: POB 2357, Jeddah 21451; tel. (2) 667-0648; fax (2) 667-2084.

Saudi United Insurance Co Ltd: POB 933, al-Khobar 31952; tel. (3) 894-9090; fax (3) 894-9428; f. 1976; all classes of insurance and reinsurance except life; cap. US $5m. majority shareholding held by Ahmad Hamad al-Gosaibi & Bros; Chair. and Man. Dir Sheikh ABD AL-AZIZ HAMAD AL-GOSAIBI; Dir and Gen. Man. ABD AL-MOHSIN AL-GOSAIBI; 6 brs.

U.C.A. Insurance Co (E.C.): POB 5019, Jeddah 21422; tel. (2) 653-0068; fax (2) 651-1936; e-mail ucajed@hotmail.com; f. 1974 as United

Commercial Agencies Ltd; all classes of insurance; cap. US $8m. Chair. Dr GHAITH R. PHARAON; Senior Vice-Pres. MACHAAL A. KARAM.

Al-Yamamah Insurance Co Ltd: POB 41522, Riyadh 11531; tel. (1) 477-4498; fax (1) 477-4497.

Trade and Industry

DEVELOPMENT ORGANIZATIONS

Arab Petroleum Investments Corpn: POB 1547, al-Khobar 31932; tel. (3) 887-0555; fax (3) 887-0404; f. 1975; affiliated to the Organization of Arab Petroleum Exporting Countries; specializes in financing petroleum and petrochemical projects and related industries in the Arab world and in other developing countries; shareholders: Kuwait, Saudi Arabia and the United Arab Emirates (17% each), Libya (15%), Iraq and Qatar (10% each), Algeria (5%), Bahrain, Egypt and Syria (3% each); authorized cap. US $1,200m. subscribed cap. $460m. (Dec. 1996); Chair. ABDULLAH A. AZ-ZAID; Gen. Man. RASHEED AL-MARAJ.

General Investment Fund: c/o Ministry of Finance and National Economy, Airport Rd, Riyadh 11177; tel. (1) 405-0000; f. 1970; provides government's share of capital to mixed capital cos; 100% state-owned; cap. 1,000m. riyals; Chair. Minister of Finance; Sec.-Gen. SULAYMAN MANDIL.

National Agricultural Development Co (NADEC): POB 2557, Riyadh 11461; tel. (1) 404-0000; fax (1) 405-5522; e-mail info@nadec-sa.com; internet www.nadec-sa.com; f. 1981; interests include 4 dairy farms, 40,000 ha for cultivation of wheat, barley, forage and vegetables and processing of dates; the govt has a 20% share; chief agency for agricultural development; cap. 400m. riyals; Chair. Minister of Agriculture; Dir MUHAMMAD AL-BUBTAIN.

National Industrialization Co (NIC): POB 26707, Riyadh 11496; tel. (1) 476-7166; fax (1) 477-0898; e-mail general@nic.com.sa; internet www.nic.com.sa; f. 1985 to promote and establish industrial projects in Saudi Arabia; cap. 600m. riyals; 100% owned by Saudi nationals; CEO MOAYYED AL-QURTAS.

Saudi Arabian General Investment Authority (SAGIA): POB 1267, Riyadh 11431; tel. 448-4533; fax 448-1234; e-mail alshareef@sagia.org; internet www.sagia.org; f. 2000 to promote foreign investment; Gov. Prince TURKI IBN ABD AL-AZIZ AS-SA'UD.

Saudi Fund for Development (SFD): POB 50483, Riyadh 11523; tel. (1) 464-0292; fax (1) 464-7450; e-mail info@sfd.gov.sa; internet www.sfd.gov.sa; f. 1974 to help finance projects in developing countries; cap. 31,000m. riyals (1991); had financed 344 projects by 2002; total commitments amounted to 23,150.6m. riyals; Chair. Minister of Finance; Vice-Chair. and Man. Dir E. YOUSEF I. AL-BASSAM.

Saudi Industrial Development Fund (SIDF): POB 4143, Riyadh 11149; tel. (1) 477-4002; fax (1) 479-0165; f. 1974; supports and promotes local industrial development, providing medium-term interest-free loans; also offers marketing, technical, financial and administrative advice; cap. 7,000m. riyals (1996); loans disbursed amounted to 1,100m. riyals in 2000; Chair. HAMAD BIN SAUD AS-SAYYARI; Dir-Gen. SALEH ABDULLAH AN-NAIM.

CHAMBERS OF COMMERCE

Council of Saudi Chambers of Commerce and Industry: POB 16683, Riyadh 11474; tel. (1) 405-3200; fax (1) 402-4747; e-mail council@saudichambers.org.sa; internet www.saudichambers.org.sa; comprises one delegate from each of the chambers of commerce in the kingdom; Chair. ABD AR- RAHMAN ALI AL-JERAISY; Sec.-Gen. Dr FAHD AS-SULTAN.

Abha Chamber of Commerce and Industry: POB 722, Abha; tel. (7) 227-1818; fax (7) 227-1919; e-mail Abhachamber@arab.net.sa; Pres. ABDULLAH SAEED AL-MOBTY; Sec.-Gen. HAMDI ALI M. AL-MALIKI.

Al-Ahsa Chamber of Commerce and Industry: POB 1519, al-Ahsa 31982; tel. (3) 852-0458; fax (3) 857-5274; Pres. ABD AL-AZIZ SULAYMAN AL-AFALIQ.

Ar'ar Chamber of Commerce and Industry: POB 440, Ar'ar; tel. (4) 662-6544; fax (4) 662-4581; Sec.-Gen. MATAB MOZIL AS-SARRAH.

Al-Baha Chamber of Commerce and Industry: POB 311, al-Baha; tel. (7) 727-0291; fax (7) 828-0146; Pres. SAID ALI AL-ANGARI; Sec.-Gen. YAHYA AZ-ZAHRANI.

Eastern Province Chamber of Commerce and Industry: POB 719, Dammam 31421; tel. (3) 857-1111; fax (3) 857-0607; e-mail info@chamber.org.sa; internet www.chamber.org.sa; f. 1952; Chair. ABD AR-RAHMAN RASHID AR-RASHID; Sec.-Gen. IBRAHIM ABDULLAH AL-OLAYAN.

Federation of Gulf Co-operation Council Chambers (FGCCC): POB 2198, Dammam 31451; tel. (3) 826-5943; fax (3) 826-

6794; e-mail fgccc@zajil.net; Pres. SALIM H. ALKHALILI; Sec.-Gen. MUHAMMAD A. AL-MULLA.

Ha'il Chamber of Commerce and Industry: POB 1291, Ha'il; tel. (6) 532-1060; fax (6) 533-1366; e-mail info@hail_chamber.org.sa; internet www.hail_chamber.org.sa; Pres. MANSOUR AGEEL AL-AMAR; Sec.-Gen. MUSA SALEH AZ-ZURAIGY.

Jeddah Chamber of Commerce and Industry: POB 1264, Jeddah 21431; tel. (2) 651-5111; fax (2) 651-7373; e-mail customerservice@jcci.org.sa; internet www.jcci.org.sa; f. 1946; 26,000 mems; Chair. ABD AHMAD ZEINAL ALIREZA; Sec.-Gen. Dr MAJED A. AL-KASSABI.

Jizan Chamber of Commerce and Industry: POB 201, Jizan; tel. (7) 322-5155; fax (7) 322-3635; Pres. Dr SALEH AZ-ZAIDAN.

Al-Jouf Chamber of Commerce and Industry: POB 585, al-Jouf; tel. (4) 624-9060; fax (4) 624-0108; Pres. MA'ASHI DUKAN AL-ATTIYEH; Sec.-Gen. AHMAD KHALIFA AL-MUSALLAM.

Al-Majma' Chamber of Commerce and Industry: POB 165, al-Majma' 11952; tel. (6) 432-0268; fax (6) 432-2655; Pres. FAHD MUHAMMAD AR-RABIAH; Sec.-Gen. ABDULLAH IBRAHIM AL-JAAWAN.

Mecca Chamber of Commerce and Industry: POB 1086, Mecca; tel. (2) 534-3838; fax (2) 534-2904; f. 1947; Pres. ADEL ABDULLAH KA'AKI; Sec.-Gen. ABDULLAH ABD AL-GAFOOR TOUJAR-ALSHAHI.

Medina Chamber of Commerce and Industry: POB 443, King Abd al-Aziz Rd, Medina; tel. (4) 838-8909; fax (4) 838-8905; Sec.-Gen. Dr SALEH D. AL-HARTI.

Najran Chamber of Commerce and Industry: POB 1138, Najran; tel. (7) 522-2216; fax (7) 522-3926; Sec.-Gen. MAKHFOOR ABDULLAH AL-BISHER.

Al-Qassim Chamber of Commerce and Industry: POB 444, Buraydah, Qassim; tel. (6) 381-4000; fax (6) 381-2231.

Al-Qurayat Chamber of Commerce and Industry: POB 416, al-Qurayat; tel. (4) 642-6200; fax (4) 642-3172; Pres. OTHMAN ABDULLAH AL-YOUSEF; Sec.-Gen. JAMAL ALI AL-GHAMDI.

Riyadh Chamber of Commerce and Industry: POB 596, Riyadh 11421; tel. (1) 404-0044; fax (1) 402-1103; e-mail rdchamber@rdcci.org.sa; f. 1961; acts as arbitrator in business disputes, information centre; Chair. Sheikh ABD AR-RAHMAN AL-JERAISY; Sec.-Gen. HUSSEIN ABD AR-RAHMAN AL-AZAL; 23,000 mems.

Tabouk Chamber of Commerce and Industry: POB 567, Tabouk; tel. (4) 422-2736; fax (4) 422-7387; Pres. ABD AL-AZIZ M. OWADEH; Sec.-Gen. AWADH AL-BALAWI.

Ta'if Chamber of Commerce and Industry: POB 1005, Ta'if; tel. (2) 736-6800; fax (2) 738-0040; Pres. IBRAHIM ABDULLAH KAMAL; Sec.-Gen. Eng. YOUSUF MUHAMMAD ASH-SHAFI.

Yanbu Chamber of Commerce and Industry: POB 58, Yanbu; tel. (4) 322-7878; fax (4) 322-6800; f. 1979; produces quarterly magazine; 5,000 members; Pres. Dr TALAL ALI ASH-SHAIR; Sec.-Gen. OSMAN NAIM AL-MUFTI.

STATE HYDROCARBONS COMPANIES

General Petroleum and Mineral Organization (PETROMIN JET): POB 7550, 21472 Jeddah; tel. (2) 685-7666; fax (2) 685-7545; works in conjunction with the Ministry of Petroleum and Mineral Resources to oversee petroleum industry; Chair. and Exec. Asst ABDULLAH O. ATTAS (acting).

Arabian Drilling Co: POB 708, Dammam 31421; tel. (3) 887-2020; fax (3) 882-6588; e-mail adcgen@al-khobar.oilfield.slb.com; f. 1964; PETROMIN shareholding 51%, remainder French private cap. undertakes contract drilling for oil (on shore and off shore), minerals and water both inside and outside Saudi Arabia; Chair. SULAYMAN J. AL-HERBISH; Man. Dir SAAD ABDULLAH SAAB.

Arabian Geophysical and Surveying Co (ARGAS): POB 535, al-Khobar 31952; tel. (3) 882-9122; fax (3) 882-9060; f. 1966; with the General Petroleum and Mineral Organization (PETROMIN) having a shareholding of 51%; remainder provided by Cie Générale de Géophysique; geophysical exploration for petroleum, other minerals and groundwater, as well as all types of land, airborne and marine surveys; Chair. AHMAD MUHAMMAD GHAZZAWI; Man. Dir HABIB M. MERGHELANI.

Petromin Marketing (PETMARK): POB 50, Dhahran Airport 31932; tel. (3) 890-3883; f. 1967; operates the installations and facilities for the distribution of petroleum products in the Eastern, Central, Southern and Northern provinces of Saudi Arabia; Pres. and CEO HUSSEIN A. LINJAWI.

Saudi Arabian Oil Co (Saudi Aramco): POB 5000, Dhahran 31311; tel. (3) 875-4915; fax (3) 873-8490; e-mail webmaster@aramco.com.sa; internet www.saudiaramco.com; f. 1933; previously known as Arabian-American Oil Co (Aramco); in 1993 incorporated the Saudi Arabian Marketing and Refining Co (SAMAREC, f. 1988) by

SAUDI ARABIA   *Directory*

merger of operations; holds the principal working concessions in Saudi Arabia; operates five wholly-owned refineries (at Jeddah, Rabigh, Ras Tanura, Riyadh and Yanbu) with total capacity of more than 1m. barrels per day; Pres. and CEO ABDULLAH S. JAMA'AH; Exec. Vice-Pres. (Exploration and Production) SADAD AL-HUSSEINI.

Saudi Arabian Lubricating Oil Co (PETROLUBE): POB 1432, Jeddah 21431; tel. (2) 661-3333; fax (2) 661-3322; f. 1968; 71% owned by Saudi Aramco, 29% by Mobil; for the manufacture and marketing of lubricating oils and other related products; production 199m. litres (1988); cap. 110m. Pres. KHALID M. ALAGIL.

Saudi Aramco Lubricating Oil Refining Co (LUBEREF): POB 5518, Jeddah 21432; tel. (2) 638-5040; fax (2) 636-6932; f. 1975; owned 70% by Saudi Aramco and 30% by Mobil; production 3,800,000 barrels; Chair. SALIM S. AL-AYDH; Pres. and CEO MUHAMMAD ALI AL-HARAZY.

Saudi Aramco Mobil Refinery Co Ltd (SAMREF): POB 30078, Yanbu; tel. (4) 396-4000; fax (4) 396-0942; f. 1981; operated by Saudi Aramco and Mobil, capacity 360,000 b/d; Pres. and CEO MUHAMMAD A. MISFER.

Saudi Aramco Shell Refinery Co (SASREF): POB 10088, Jubail 31961; tel. (3) 357-2000; fax (3) 358-9667; e-mail k .al-buainain@pr.sasrefalj.simis.com; internet www.shell.com; operated by Saudi Aramco and Shell; capacity 300,000 b/d; exports began in 1985; Chair. ABD AL-AZIZ M. AL-HOKAIL.

Saudi Basic Industries Corpn (SABIC): POB 5101, Riyadh 11422; tel. (1) 401-2033; fax (1) 401-2045; internet www.sabic.com; f. 1976 to foster the petrochemical industry and other hydrocarbon-based industries through jt ventures with foreign partners, and to market their products; 70% state-owned; production 35m. tons (2001); Vice-Chair. and CEO MUHAMMAD AL-MADY.

Projects include:

Al-Jubail Petrochemical Co (Kemya): POB 10084, Jubail 31961; tel. (3) 357-6000; fax (3) 358-7858; f. 1980; began production of linear low-density polyethylene in 1984, of high-density polyethylene in 1985, and of high alfa olefins in 1986, capacity of 330,000 tons per year of polyethylene; jt venture with Exxon Corpn (USA) and SABIC; Pres. ABD AL-AZIZ I. AL-AUDAH; Exec. Vice-Pres. CLAY LEWIS.

Arabian Petrochemical Co (Petrokemya): POB 10002, Jubail 31961; tel. (3) 358-7000; fax (3) 358-4480; e-mail otaibifr@ petrokemya.sabic.com; produced 2.4m. tons of ethylene, 135,000 tons of polystyrene, 100,000 tons of butene-1; 570,000 tons of propylene, 100,000 tons of butadiene and 150,000 tons of benzene in 2001; wholly-owned subsidiary of SABIC; owns 50% interest in ethylene glycol plant producing 610,000 tons per year of monoethylene glycol, 65,000 tons per year of diethylene glycol and 3,900 tons per year of triethylene glycol; Chair. HOMOOD AT-TUWAIJRI; Pres. KHALID S. AR-RAWAF.

Eastern Petrochemical Co (Sharq): POB 10035, Jubail 31961; tel. (3) 357-5000; fax (3) 358-0383; f. 1981 to produce linear low-density polyethylene, ethylene glycol; total capacity 660,000 tons of ethylene glycol and 280,000 tons of polyethylene per year; a SABIC jt venture; Pres. IBRAHIM S. ASH-SHEWEIR.

National Industrial Gases Co (Gas): POB 10110, Jubail 31961; tel. (3) 357-5700; fax (3) 358-5542; total capacity of 876,000 tons of oxygen and 492,750 tons of nitrogen per year; jt venture with Saudi private sector; Pres. ABDULLAH MUJBEL AL-JALAWI.

National Plastic Co (Ibn Hayyan): POB 10002, Jubail 31961; tel. (3) 358-7000; fax (3) 358-4736; f. 1984; produces 390,000 tons per year of vinylchloride monomer and 324,000 tons per year of polyvinylchloride; jt venture with Lucky Group (Republic of Korea), SABIC and three other cos; Pres. KHALED AR-RAWAF.

Saudi-European Petrochemical Co (Ibn Zahr): POB 10330, Jubail 31961; tel. (3) 341-5060; fax (3) 341-2966; f. 1985; annual capacity 1.4m. tons of methyl-tertiary-butyl ether (MTBE), 0.3m. tons of propylene; SABIC has a 70% share, Ecofuel, Nesté Corpn and APICORP each have 10%; Pres. SAMI AS-SUWAIGH.

Saudi Methanol Co (ar-Razi): POB 10065, Jubail Industrial City 31961; tel. (3) 357-7820; fax (3) 358-0838; e-mail emt@arrazi.com; f. 1979; capacity of 3,158,000 tons per year of chemical-grade methanol; total methanol exports in 2001 were 3,248,000 tons; jt venture with a consortium of Japanese cos; Pres. NABIL A. MANSOURI; Exec. Vice-Pres. H. MIZUNO.

Saudi Petrochemical Co (Sadaf): POB 10025, Jubail 31961; tel. (3) 357-3000; fax (3) 357-3142; f. 1980 to produce ethylene, ethylene dichloride, styrene, crude industrial ethanol, caustic soda and methyl-tertiary-butyl-ether (MTBE); total capacity of 4,710,000 tons per year; Shell (Pecten) has a 50% share; Pres. MOSAED S. AL-OHALI.

Saudi Yanbu Petrochemical Co (Yanpet): POB 30139, Yanbu; tel. (4) 396-5000; fax (4) 396-5006; f. 1980; to produce 820,000 tons per year of ethylene, 600,000 tons per year of high-density polyethylene and 340,000 tons per year of ethylene glycol; total capacity

1,692,200 tons per year by 1990; Mobil and SABIC each have a 50% share; Pres. ALI AL-KHURAIMI; Exec. CEO P. J. FOLEY.

Foreign Concessionaires

Arabian Oil Co Ltd (AOC): POB 256, Ras al-Khafji 31971; tel. (3) 766-0555; fax (3) 766-2001; f. 1958; holds concession (2,200 sq km at Dec. 1987) for offshore exploitation of Saudi Arabia's half-interest in the Kuwait-Saudi Arabia Neutral Zone; Pres. KEIICHI KONAGA; Chief Exec. General Affairs. AHMAD IBRAHIM AL-ASFOUR.

Saudi Arabian Texaco Inc: POB 363, Riyadh; tel. (1) 462-7274; fax (1) 464-1992; also office in Kuwait; f. 1928; fmrly Getty Oil Co; holds concession (5,200 sq km at Dec. 1987) for exploitation of Saudi Arabia's half-interest in the Saudi Arabia-Kuwait Neutral Zone.

UTILITIES

Utilities Co (Uco): Jubail; f. 1999; owned equally by Royal Commission for Jubail and Yanbu, Public Investment Fund, Saudi Aramco and SABIC; cap. 2,000m. riyals; to provide utilities in industrial cities of Jubail and Yanbu.

Electricity

Electricity Services Regulatory Authority (ESRA): Riyadh; f. 2001 to regulate the power industry and to recommend tariffs for the sector; Gov. FAREED ZEDAN.

Saudi Electricity Co (SEC): POB 57, Riyadh 11411; tel. (1) 403-2222; fax (1) 405-1191; f. 2000; following merger of 10 regional companies; joint-stock co; cap. 33,758m. to organize the generation, transmission and distribution of electricity into separate operating companies; Chair. Minister of Water and Electricity; CEO SULAYMAN A. AL-QADI.

Water

Saline Water Conversion Corpn (SWCC): POB 4931, 21412 Jeddah; tel. (2) 682-1240; fax (2) 682-0415; provides desalinated water; 24 plants; capacity 2m. cu m per day (1994); Dir-Gen. ABD AL-AZIZ OMAR NASSIEF.

TRADE UNIONS

Trade unions are illegal in Saudi Arabia.

Transport

RAILWAYS

Saudi Arabia has the only rail system in the Arabian peninsula. The Saudi Government Railroad comprises 719 km of single and 157 km of double track. In addition, the total length of spur lines and sidings is 348 km. The main line, which was opened in 1951, is 578 km in length; it connects Dammam port, on the Gulf coast, with Riyadh, and passes Dhahran, Abqaiq, Hufuf, Harad and al-Kharj. A 310-km line, linking Hufuf and Riyadh, was inaugurated in May 1985. A new 2,000-km network, linking Riyadh to the north of the kingdom and connecting Jubail to Dammam, was under consideration in early 2003. A total of 790,400 passengers travelled by rail in the kingdom in 2000, and 1.5m. metric tons of freight was carried by the railways in the same year.

Saudi Railways Organization: POB 36, Dammam 31241; tel. (3) 871-5151; fax (3) 833-6337; Pres. K. H. AL-YAHYA.

ROADS

Asphalted roads link Jeddah to Mecca, Jeddah to Medina, Medina to Yanbu, Ta'if to Mecca, Riyadh to al-Kharj, and Dammam to Hufuf as well as the principal communities and certain outlying points in Aramco's area of operations. During the 1980s the construction of other roads was undertaken, including one extending from Riyadh to Medina. The trans-Arabian highway, linking Dammam, Riyadh, Ta'if, Mecca and Jeddah, was completed in 1967. A causeway linking Saudi Arabia with Bahrain was opened in November 1986. A 317-km highway linking Riyadh to Qassim was completed in the late 1980s. The construction of a 810–km road connecting Al-Qasim, Al-Madinah, Yanbo, Rabigh and Thuwal, at a cost of some SR 5,350m., was underway in 2003. At the end of 2001 there were 156,949.8 km of roads, of which 13,865.8 km were main roads (including motorways), 8,602.7 km were secondary roads and 22,710.9 km were asphalted agricultural roads. Metalled roads link all the main population centres.

Saudi Public Transport Co (SAPTCO): POB 10667, Riyadh 11443; tel. (1) 454-5000; fax (1) 454-2100; f. 1979; operates a public bus service throughout the country and to neighbouring countries; the Govt holds a 30% share; Chair. Dr NASIR AS-SALOOM; CEO Dr ABD AL-AZIZ AL-OHALY.

National Transport Co of Saudi Arabia: Queen's Bldg, POB 7280, Jeddah 21462; tel. (2) 643-4561; specializes in inward clearance, freight forwarding, general and heavy road haulage, re-export, charter air freight and exhibitions; Man. Dir A. D. BLACKSTOCK; Operations Man. I. CROXSON.

SHIPPING

Responsibility for the management, operation and maintenance of the commercial ports of Jeddah, Dammam, Yanbu, Dhiba and Jizan, the King Fahd Industrial Ports of Jubail and Yanbu, and the oil port of Ras Tanura, as well as a number of minor ports, began to be transferred to the private sector after 1997, but all ports remain subject to regulation and scrutiny by the Ports Authority. Some 95% of Saudi Arabia's imports and exports pass through the country's sea ports. An estimated 12,000 vessels visit annually. In 2002 there were 183 mechanized and organized berths. In 2001 the total cargo handled by Saudi Arabian ports, excluding crude petroleum, was 100.6m. metric tons, compared with 68.2m. tons in 1990/91. Some 1.8m. passengers were also embarked and disembarked in 2001.

Jeddah is the principal commercial port and the main point of entry for pilgrims bound for Mecca. It has berths for general cargo, container traffic, 'roll on, roll off' (ro-ro) traffic, livestock and bulk grain shipments, with draughts ranging from 8 m to 16 m. The port also has a 200-ton floating crane, cold storage facilities and a fully-equipped ship-repair yard. In 1997 a total of 4,515 vessels called at Jeddah Islamic Port. Some19.7m. tons of cargo, excluding crude petroleum, were handled and 1.1m. passengers were processed in 2001.

Dammam is the second largest commercial port and has general cargo, container, ro-ro, dangerous cargo and bulk grain berths. Draughts at this port range from 8 m to 13.5 m. It has a 200-ton floating crane and a fully-equipped ship-repair yard. In 1997 a total of 2,430 vessels called at King Abd al-Aziz Port in Dammam. 12.1m. tons of cargo, excluding crude petroleum, were handled in 2001.

Jubail has one commercial and one industrial port. The commercial port has general cargo, bulk grain and container berths with ro-ro facilities, and a floating crane. Draughts at this port range from 12 m to 14 m. In 1997 a total of 183 vessels called at Jubail Commercial Port, and 1.9m. tons of goods, excluding crude petroleum, were handled in 2001. The industrial port has bulk cargo, refined and petrochemical and ro-ro berths, and an open sea tanker terminal suitable for vessels up to 300,000 dwt. Draughts range from 6 m to 30 m. In 1997 a total of 1,032 vessels called at King Fahd Industrial Port in Jubail; 35.6m. tons of cargo, excluding crude petroleum, were handled in 2001.

Yanbu, which comprises one commercial and one industrial port, is Saudi Arabia's nearest major port to Europe and North America, and is the focal point of the most rapidly growing area, in the west of Saudi Arabia. The commercial port has general cargo, ro-ro and bulk grain berths, with draughts ranging from 10 m to 12 m. It also has a floating crane, and is equipped to handle minor ship repairs. In 1997 a total of 77 vessels called at Yanbu Commercial Port, and less than 1.7m. tons of cargo, excluding crude petroleum, were handled in 2001. The industrial port has berths for general cargo, containers, ro-ro traffic, bulk cargo, crude petroleum, refined and petrochemical products and natural gas liquids, and a tanker terminal on the open sea. In 1997 a total of 1,388 vessels called at King Fahd Industrial Port in Yanbu; the port handled 27.8m. tons of cargo, excluding crude petroleum, in 2001.

Jizan is the main port for the southern part of the country. It has general cargo, ro-ro, bulk grain and container berths, with draughts ranging from 8 m to 11 m. It also has a 200-ton floating crane. In 1997 a total of 752 vessels called at Gizan Port, and 1.5m. tons of cargo, excluding crude petroleum, were handled in 2001.

Dhiba port, on the northern Red Sea coast, serves the Tabouk region. It has three general cargo berths with a ro-ro ramp, and passenger-handling facilities. Maximum draught is 10.5m. In 1997 a total of 490 vessels called at Dhiba, and 0.3m. tons of cargo, excluding crude petroleum, were handled in 2001.

In addition to these major ports, there are a number of minor ports suitable only for small craft, including Khuraiba, Haql, al-Wajh, Umlujj, Rabigh, al-Lith, Qunfoudah, Farasan and al-Qahma on the Red Sea coast and al-Khobar, Qatif, Uqair, Darin and Ras al-Khafji on the Gulf coast. Ras Mishab, on the Gulf coast, is operated by the Ministry of Defence and Civil Aviation.

Saudi Ports Authority: POB 5162, Riyadh 11422; tel. (1) 405-0005; fax (1) 405-3508; internet www.ports.gov.sa; f. 1976; regulatory authority; Chair. Dr FAYEZ I. BADR; Vice-Chair. and Dir-Gen. MUHAMMAD IBN ABD AL-KARIM BAKR.

Dammam: POB 28062, Dammam 31188; tel. (3) 833-2500; fax (3) 857-1727; Dir-Gen. NAEEM IBRAHIM AN-NAEEM.

Dhiba: POB 190, Dhiba; tel. (4) 432-1060; fax (4) 432-2679; Dir-Gen MUHAMMAD ASH-SHAREEF.

Jeddah: POB 9285, Jeddah 21188; tel. (2) 647-1200; fax (2) 647-7411; Dir-Gen. MUHAMMAD AL-GHAITHI.

Jizan: POB 16, Jizan; tel. (7) 317-1000; fax (7) 317-0777; Dir-Gen. ALI HAMOUD BAKRI.

Jubail: POB 547, Jubail 31951; tel. (3) 357-8000; fax (3) 357-8011; Dir-Gen. MUTHANNA ISA AL-QURTAS.

Yanbu: POB 30325, Yanbu; tel. (4) 396-7000; fax (4) 396-7037; Dir-Gen. Dr HUMOOD SAADI.

Arabian Petroleum Supply Co Ltd: POB 1408, Al-Qurayat St, Jeddah 21431; tel. (2) 637-1120; fax (2) 636-2366; Chair. Sheikh MUHAMMAD YOUSSUF ALI REZA; Gen. Man. E. D. CONNOLLY.

Baaboud Trading and Shipping Agencies: POB 7262, Jeddah 21462; tel. (2) 642-1468; fax (2) 644-0912; Chair. AHMAD M. BAABOUD; Man. Dir ABOUD M. BAABOUD.

Bakry Navigation Co Ltd: POB 3757, Jeddah 21481; tel. (2) 651-9995; fax (2) 651-2908; Chair. Sheikh A. K. AL-BAKRY; Man. Dir G. A. K. AL-BAKRY.

National Shipping Co of Saudi Arabia (NSCSA): POB 8931, Riyadh 11492; tel. (1) 478-5454; fax (1) 477-8036; e-mail prmail@nscsa.com.sa; internet www.nscsa.com; f. 1979; transportation of crude petroleum and petrochemical products; routes through Red Sea and Mediterranean to USA and Canada; Chair. SULEIMAN J. AL-HERBISH; CEO ZIYAD FAHAD AD-DUGAITHER.

Saudi Lines: POB 66, Jeddah 21411; tel. (2) 642-3051; regular cargo and passenger services between Red Sea and Indian Ocean ports; Pres. M. A. BAKHASHAB PASHA; Man. Dir A. M. BAKHASHAB.

Saudi Shipping and Maritime Services Co Ltd (TRANSHIP): POB 7522, Jeddah 21472; tel. (2) 642-4255; fax (2) 643-2821; e-mail tranship@dmp.net.sa; Chair. Prince SA'UD IBN NAYEF IBN ABD AL-AZIZ; Man. Dir Capt. MUSTAFA T. AWARA.

Shipping Corpn of Saudi Arabia Ltd: POB 1691, Arab Maritime Center, Malik Khalid St, Jeddah 21441; tel. (2) 647-1137; fax (2) 647-8222; Pres. and Man. Dir ABD AL-AZIZ AHMAD ARAB.

CIVIL AVIATION

King Abd al-Aziz International Airport, which was opened in 1981, has three terminals, one of which is specifically designed to cope with the needs of the many thousands of pilgrims who visit Mecca and Medina each year. The airport handled 12.1m. passengers in 2001. King Khalid International Airport, at Riyadh, opened in 1983 with four terminals. It handled 8.7m. passengers in 2001. A third major airport, King Fahd International Airport (with an initial handling capacity of 5.2m. passengers per year), opened in the Eastern Province in 1994. Some 2.7m. passengers used the airport in 2001. Overall, the country's airports were used by 27.8m. passengers in 2001. There are 25 commercial airports in the kingdom.

Presidency of Civil Aviation (PCA): POB 887, Jeddah 21165; tel. (2) 640-5000; fax (2) 640-2444; internet www.pca.gov.sa; Pres. Dr ALI ABD AR-RAHMAN AL-KHALAF.

National Air Services Co: Riyadh; f. 1998; privately-owned; cap. SR60m. Chair. YOUSUF AL-MAIMANI.

Saudi Arabian Airlines: POB 620, Jeddah 21231; tel. (2) 686-0000; fax (2) 686-4552; internet www.saudiairlines.com; f. 1945; began operations in 1947; in 1999 carried 13.3m. passengers, its fleet numbering 126 aircraft; regular services to 25 domestic and 52 international destinations; scheduled for privatization; Chair. Prince SULTAN IBN ABD AL-AZIZ; Dir-Gen. KHALED A. IBN AL-BAKR; Exec. Vice-Pres. (operations) ADNAN AD-DABBAGH.

Tourism

All devout Muslims try to make at least one visit to the holy cities of Medina, the burial place of Muhammad, and Mecca, his birthplace. In 2000 there were 518 hotels in the kingdom, with a total of more than 50,000 rooms. Tourist numbers increased to 4.8m. in 1999 and receipts from tourism amounted to 6,750m. riyals in 2000. A total of 1,363,992 foreign pilgrims visited Mecca in the Islamic year ending in March 2001.

In 2000 the Government decided to issue tourist visas for the first time. A Supreme Commission for Tourism, to develop the tourist industry in Saudi Arabia, was subsequently established.

Saudi Hotels and Resort Areas Co (SHARACO): POB 5500, Riyadh 11422; tel. (1) 481-6666; fax (1) 480-1666; f. 1975; Saudi Govt has 40% interest; cap. SR500m. Chair. MUSAAD AS-SENANY; Dir-Gen. ABD AL-AZIZ AL-AMBAR.

SENEGAL

Introductory Survey

Location, Climate, Language, Religion, Flag, Capital

The Republic of Senegal lies on the west coast of Africa, bordered to the north by Mauritania, to the east by Mali, and to the south by Guinea and Guinea-Bissau. In the southern part of the country The Gambia forms a narrow enclave extending some 320 km (200 miles) inland. The climate is tropical, with a long dry season followed by a short wet season—from June to September in the north, and from June to October in the south. Average annual temperatures range from 22°C (72°F) to 28°C (82°F). French is the official language; the most widely spoken national languages at the time of the 1988 census were Wolof (spoken by 49.2% of the population), Peul (22.2%), Serer (12.8%) and Diola (5.1%). At the 1988 census almost 94% of the population were Muslims, and some 4% Christians, mostly Roman Catholics; a small number followed traditional beliefs. The national flag (proportions 2 by 3) has three equal vertical stripes, of green, yellow and red, with a five-pointed green star in the centre of the yellow stripe. The capital is Dakar. In December 2002 the Government announced that a new administrative capital, Mékhé-Pékesse, was to be developed east of Dakar.

Recent History

After 300 years as a French colony, Senegal became a self-governing member of the French Community in November 1958. The formation in April 1959 of the Mali Federation, linking Senegal with Soudan (later the Republic of Mali), had only two months of independence before being dissolved when Senegal seceded, to become a separate independent state, on 20 August 1960. The Republic of Senegal was proclaimed on 5 September, with Léopold Sédar Senghor, leader of the Union progressiste sénégalaise (UPS), as the country's first President.

In late 1962, following the discovery of a coup attempt led by the Prime Minister, Mamadou Dia, Senghor assumed the premiership. Following the victory of the UPS at elections to the Assemblée nationale in 1963, other political parties were gradually absorbed into it or outlawed, effectively creating a one-party state by 1966. In 1970 the office of Prime Minister was restored and assigned to a provincial administrator, Abdou Diouf, who in 1976 was made Senghor's constitutional successor. In 1973 Senghor, the sole candidate, was re-elected President.

Senghor amended the Constitution in March 1976 to allow three parties to contest elections—the UPS, renamed the Parti socialiste (PS), the Parti démocratique sénégalais (PDS) and the Parti africain de l'indépendance (PAI). The first national elections under the three-party system took place in February 1978; the PS won 83 of the 100 seats in the Assemblée nationale, the remainder being won by the PDS. In the concurrent presidential election, Senghor overwhelmingly defeated the leader of the PDS, Abdoulaye Wade.

Senghor retired in December 1980, and was succeeded as President by Diouf in January 1981. An amnesty was declared for political dissidents, and the Constitution was amended to allow the existence of more than four political parties (a fourth party, the Mouvement républicain sénégalais, had been legalized in December 1978). At elections in February 1983 Diouf received 83.5% of the presidential vote (compared with 14.8% for his nearest rival, Wade), while in legislative elections the PS won 111 of the 120 seats. Disputing the results, the opposition boycotted the Assemblée nationale for several months. In April Diouf abolished the post of Prime Minister, which had latterly been held by Habib Thiam.

When preliminary results of the February 1988 presidential and legislative elections indicated clear victories for both Diouf and the PS, opposition parties alleged fraud on the part of the ruling party, and, following the outbreak of rioting in Dakar, a state of emergency was imposed. Various opposition members, including Wade and Amath Dansokho, the leader of the Parti de l'indépendance et du travail (PIT), were arrested. According to the official results of the presidential election, contested by four candidates, Diouf obtained 73.2% of the votes cast, and Wade 25.8%. In the legislative elections, the PS won 103 seats, and the PDS the remaining 17. Wade, Dansokho and other opposition activists were tried on charges of incitement to violence and attacks on the internal security of the State; Dansokho and five others were acquitted, but in May Wade received a one-year suspended prison sentence. Later in the month, however, Diouf announced an amnesty for all those who had been condemned in the aftermath of the elections.

In October 1989 changes to the electoral code were approved by PS representatives in the Assemblée nationale (PDS deputies had begun a boycott of legislative sessions in mid-1989, in protest against what they perceived as the unsatisfactory media coverage of parliamentary debates); a partial system of proportional representation was to be introduced for legislative elections, and access to the state-owned media was to be granted to opposition parties. The legislature also approved a 'National Democratic Charter', which provided for the dissolution of any political party that did not abide by the Constitution, or by the principles of democracy, or that received subsidies from abroad. The opposition boycotted municipal and rural elections in November 1990, claiming that the modified electoral code permitted widespread electoral malpractice.

In March 1991 the legislature approved several amendments to the Constitution, notably the restoration of the post of Prime Minister. It was also agreed that opposition parties would, henceforth, be allowed to participate in government. In April Thiam was again named Prime Minister. Thiam's Government included four representatives of the PDS (including Wade, who was designated Minister of State, effectively the most senior post in the Government other than the Prime Minister); Dansokho, the PIT leader, became Minister of Town Planning and Housing. In September 1991 the Assemblée nationale adopted amendments to the electoral code. Presidential elections would henceforth take place, in two rounds if necessary (to ensure that the President would be elected by at least one-quarter of registered voters, and by an absolute majority of votes cast), every seven years, with a mandate that would be renewable only once. Legislative voting would, however, continue to take place at five-yearly intervals.

In October 1992 Wade and his three PDS colleagues resigned from the Council of Ministers, protesting that they had been excluded from the governmental process. Eight candidates contested the presidential election, which took place on 21 February 1993. Despite some irregularities, voting was reported to be orderly in most areas, except the Casamance region (see below). The opposition denounced the preliminary results, which indicated that Diouf had won a clear majority. Disagreements within the electoral commission resulted in considerable delay in determining the official result, and eventually prompted the resignation of the President of the Constitutional Council. On 13 March the Council announced that Diouf had been re-elected with 58.4% of the votes cast (51.6% of the electorate had voted); Wade secured 32.0% of the votes.

Elections to the Assemblée nationale took place on 9 May 1993, in which the PS won 84 of the legislature's 120 seats; the PDS took 27 seats. The rate of participation by voters was 40.7%. Shortly after the announcement of the results the Vice-President of the Constitutional Council, Babacar Sèye, was assassinated. Wade and three other PDS leaders were detained for three days in connection with the killing. Thiam formed a new Government in June 1993. Dansokho, who had supported Diouf's presidential campaign, retained his portfolio, while Abdoulaye Bathily, the leader of the Ligue démocratique—Mouvement pour le parti du travail (LD—MPT), who had also contested the presidency, received a ministerial post.

In October 1993 Wade was charged with complicity in the assassination of Sèye; Wade's wife and a PDS deputy were also charged with 'complicity in a breach of state security'. Although none was detained, five people remained in custody in connection with the murder. In November Ousmane Ngom, the PDS parliamentary leader and Landing Savané, the leader of And Jëf—Parti africain pour la démocratie et le socialisme (AJ—PADS), were among those detained following a protest in Dakar to demand the cancellation of austerity measures. Ngom, Savané and some 87 others were convicted of participating in an unauthorized demonstration, and received suspended prison sentences.

Following the devaluation of the CFA franc, in January 1994, emergency measures were adopted to offset the immediate adverse economic effects and consequent hardship. In February a demonstration in Dakar to denounce the devaluation, degenerated into serious rioting, as a result of which eight people were killed. The Government stated that it regarded the opposition Coordination des forces démocratiques, which had organized the demonstration, as responsible for the unrest. Wade and Savané were among those subsequently charged with attacks on state security.

Charges against Wade and his opposition associates in connection with the murder of Sèye were dismissed in May 1994, on the grounds of insufficient evidence, although Wade and Savané, awaiting trial in connection with the post-devaluation violence, were not released from custody until July. Later in July legal proceedings against them and 140 others implicated in the February riots were dismissed, again on the grounds of insufficient evidence. In October three of Sèye's alleged assassins were convicted and sentenced to 18–20 years' imprisonment.

In a new Council of Ministers named in March 1995, Wade was appointed as Minister of State at the Presidency, while four other PDS members were also appointed to the new administration. Djibo Kâ, a long-serving government member who, as Minister of the Interior, had been associated with the legal proceedings against Wade and other opposition leaders, left the Government. In August it was announced that municipal and rural elections, scheduled for November, were to be postponed by one year. In September Dansokho and another PIT member were dismissed from the Council of Ministers. In March 1996 a PS congress elected Diouf to the new post of party Chairman, in place of the abolished position of Secretary-General; a new position of Executive Secretary was created, to which post Ousmane Tanor Dieng was elected.

In January 1996 Diouf announced that a second legislative chamber, the Sénat, was to be established. The abolition of independent candidatures for municipal, rural and regional elections prompted widespread criticism. Within the Government there was marked antipathy between the PS and the PDS and LD—MPT, prompting Dieng, in October, to warn Wade and Bathily either to cease their criticism or resign their posts.

Voting for regional, municipal and rural councillors took place on 24 November 1996. Logistical and administrative difficulties were widespread, and necessitated a subsequent rerun of the elections at certain polling stations, which led opposition parties to demand that the elections be annulled. The PS won control of all 10 regions, all the main towns and the vast majority of rural communities. None the less, the PDS resolved, at an extraordinary session in February 1997, to remain in the Government, and was among 19 opposition groups to join the PS in a commission to examine the possibility of the establishment of an independent electoral body. However, in March the PS issued writs for defamation against the representatives of 12 parties (including the PDS and LD—MPT), in respect of allegations that the success of the PS in the local elections was attributable to official complicity and to the misappropriation of foreign aid. In May the opposition withdrew from the commission. In August, however, Diouf proposed the creation of an independent electoral verification body, which would be responsible for ensuring the conduct of the elections in accordance with the law. The new Observatoire national des élections (ONEL) would be composed of nine presidential appointees. Legislation to amend the electoral law was approved by the Assemblée nationale at the end of August. The PIT and AJ—PADS opposed the legislation, on the grounds that the Ministry of the Interior was to remain responsible for the organization of elections.

Meanwhile, rumours of divisions within the PS were apparently confirmed in late 1997, when Kâ led a number of senior members who urged radical reforms of the party. Although Kâ insisted that he remained loyal to Diouf, 11 leading members of the group were suspended from the PS for a period of three months in November 1997. In January 1998 Maj.-Gen. Lamine Cissé retired as the armed forces Chief of Staff, prior to his appointment as Minister of the Interior. In February Wade appealed to the Constitutional Council to reject an amendment to the electoral code whereby the number of deputies in the Assemblée nationale was to be increased to 140; later in the month the Council annulled the proposed increase, the first

occasion on which the Council had ruled against a decision of the legislature. In March, however, the Assemblée nationale again voted to increase the number of deputies. In early April Wade, stating that he was no longer a member of the Government, refused an invitation to the presidential palace to meet President Bill Clinton of the USA. At the same time Kâ resigned from the PS to present his own list of candidates: the Union pour le renouveau démocratique (URD) was to present candidates in each of Senegal's 31 departments, with its national list to be headed by Kâ himself. Kâ subsequently denounced what he alleged was corruption and electoral fraud by the PS.

A total of 18 parties and coalitions contested the legislative elections on 24 May 1998. Outwith Casamance, voting was reported to have taken place generally in an atmosphere of calm. The PS retained 93 seats in the enlarged assembly (including 58 elected on the basis of majority voting within departments), with 50.19% of the valid votes cast, while the number of PDS deputies was reduced to 23 (including 10 elected by majority voting within departments); Kâ's URD, in alliance with the Alliance pour le progrès et la justice—Jëf-Jël (APJ—JJ), secured 11 seats (including two elected by majority voting within departments). Eight further groups won representation on the basis of national lists. The rate of participation by voters was 39% of the registered electorate.

Following the elections, the LD—MPT, which had held two portfolios in the previous Government, announced that it was to form a parliamentary alliance with the URD and that it would not participate in the new administration. In early July 1998 Thiam resigned as Prime Minister, and was replaced by Mamadou Lamine Loum. A new Council of Ministers was named shortly afterwards, in which most ministers in the outgoing administration, with the notable exception of Moustapha Niasse, hitherto Minister of Foreign Affairs and Senegalese Abroad, retained their portfolios. Serigne Diop, the leader of the Parti démocratique sénégalais—Rénovation (which had broken away from the PDS in 1997) was the only non-PS member of the Government.

In late August 1998 the Assemblée nationale voted to revise the Constitution to remove the clause restricting the Head of State to a maximum of two terms of office, thus permitting Diouf to contest the next presidential election, in 2000. The requirement that the President be elected by more than 25% of all registered voters was also abandoned. The opposition parties, condemning the amendments as a 'constitutional *coup d'état*', boycotted the vote. In October Diouf became the first Head of State from sub-Saharan Africa to address the French Assemblée nationale. The leaders of seven opposition groups sent a delegation to Paris to protest against what they regarded as Diouf's manipulation of the Constitution. Speaking in the French capital, Wade denounced the infringement by the PS of the Constitution, widespread electoral fraud, increasingly authoritarian government, and the handling of the conflict in Casamance.

Elections to the newly created Sénat took place in January 1999. An electoral college of deputies, local, municipal and regional councillors was to elect 45 of its 60 members; 12 senators were to be chosen by the President of the Republic, and three were to be elected by Senegalese resident abroad. Only the PS, the Parti libéral du Sénégal (PLS—formed in mid-1998 by Ngom, leading a breakaway movement from the PDS), and a coalition of the PIT and AJ—PADS contested the elections. The PDS and other opposition parties had urged a boycott of the elections, describing the new chamber (which the Government claimed would complete a policy of decentralization, improving the representation of local government areas) as unnecessary. The PS won all 45 of the elective seats. The 12 senators nominated by Diouf included two opposition figures, Marcel Bassene of the PLS and Majmout Diop of the PAI. The first session of the Sénat began on 15 February; Abdoulaye Diack, a prominent member of the PS and a senator nominated by the President, was elected President of the new body; Majmout Diop was elected First Vice-President.

In March 1999 an alliance of AJ—PADS, the PIT, the PDS and the LD—MPT agreed to nominate Wade, who had resigned from the Assemblée nationale in mid-1998, as their joint candidate in the presidential election scheduled for 2000. Also in March 1999 Talla Sylla, the leader of the APJ—JJ, was sentenced to six months' imprisonment for having denounced the Head of State at an unauthorized rally held in October 1998. Sylla, who had been planning to stand in the presidential election, was also banned from voting or participating in elections for a period of five years. In late April 1999 the PDS began a boycott of the

Assemblée nationale, accusing the Government of seeking to manipulate the voters' register for the presidential election. The PDS claimed that many of the registers in areas in which it enjoyed strong support had been lost. The Government admitted that about 600 of some 8,400 registers used for the 1998 legislative elections were missing, but offered to reconstitute and update these lists in the presence of the opposition parties.

In June and July 1999 demonstrations took place at the office of ONEL, in protest at the appointment in May of Gen. Amadou Dieng as Chairman. The opposition claimed that Dieng actively supported the re-election of Diouf. Although Dieng denied this charge, he subsequently resigned. Meanwhile, in June Niasse announced his intention of contesting the presidential election, and published a document criticizing the policies of Diouf and the PS, accusing them of corruption; Niasse was consequently expelled from the PS and subsequently formed his own party, the Alliance des forces de progrès (AFP).

In August 1999 PDS activists in Thiès alleged that members of the PS had been gathering false administrative papers in order to apply for identity cards, and subsequently for voter cards. ONEL upheld the complaint, although the fraud was blamed on uncoordinated individual action. In January 2000 a collective of 20 opposition parties accused the Government of having supplementary voter cards printed in Israel, without having informed ONEL. The Government stated that the cards had been produced abroad and in secret for security reasons and to reduce the risk of fraud. The PS also announced that it was to sue Wade and Niasse over their claims that the party had financed the printing of the voter cards, and that the electoral register had been altered. In early February the collective held a public demonstration in Dakar to demand the printing of new cards. However, Wade's calls for the armed forces to guarantee the legality of the election and, if necessary, to intervene, were rejected by other opposition leaders. In early February the Government announced that disputed voter lists were to be re-examined at local level.

Shortly before the election, which took place on 27 February 2000 and was contested by eight candidates, violent incidents were recorded following visits to Saint-Louis by Diouf and Wade, in which 10 people were injured in clashes and the headquarters of two parties loyal to Diouf were set on fire, while in the town of Ndofane, in the Kaolack region, two people were reportedly killed, and others injured, during clashes between supporters of the PS and of the opposition. Although Diouf won the largest proportion of votes cast (41.3%), his failure to secure an absolute majority of votes cast meant that a second round of voting, between Diouf and Wade (who had secured 31.0% of votes cast), would be necessary. Of the remaining candidates, Niasse received 16.8% of votes cast, while Kâ took 7.1%. Overall turn-out was estimated at 61.0%.

Prior to the second round of voting, Wade received the endorsement of Niasse, and of the majority of the candidates defeated in the first round, with the notable exception of Kâ, who defied the wishes of his party and gave public support to Diouf, who pledged to accelerate the process of reform. At the second round of voting, on 19 March 2000, Wade won 58.5% of the total votes cast, thus taking the presidency from the PS for the first time. Turn-out was estimated at 60.1%.

Wade was sworn in as President on 1 April 2000, at a public ceremony attended by seven African Heads of State. In early April Wade announced the composition of his 27-member Council of Ministers, although two further ministers were appointed in mid-April. Niasse was named Prime Minister, and several other opposition leaders, including Savané of AJ—PADS and Bathily of the LD—MPT, received ministerial portfolios, while several members of civil society were also appointed to the Government. Niasse subsequently instigated an audit of the operations of the State, and announced that senior officials of the previous Government had been temporarily prohibited from leaving the country. Wade announced that he did not envisage governing alongside an Assemblée nationale dominated by the PS, and that he therefore intended to hold fresh legislative elections, following a constitutional referendum initially scheduled for 27 November 2000. Among the proposed changes, the President would gain the power to dissolve the Assemblée nationale, while other presidential powers would be transferred to the Prime Minister, and the presidential mandate would again be reduced from seven to five years, renewable only once. Furthermore, the abolition of the Sénat, the recently created second legislative chamber, was envisaged. Wade was widely

applauded for his appointment of Diouf as his representative at the Europe-Africa summit held in mid-April in Cairo, Egypt.

Following the resignation from the URD of a number of the party's deputies, who had opposed Kâ's support for Diouf, controversy was provoked by the PS in effect 'lending' the URD a number of deputies, in order that the party could remain registered as a parliamentary group. (A parliamentary group was required to include a minimum of 12 deputies.) In July 2000, in turn, a number of PS deputies defected to the PDS. The most senior figure to transfer political allegiance in this way was the President of the Sénat, Diack, pre-empting reports that his defection would delay the abolition of the second legislative chamber. Minor ministerial reshuffles were effected in November.

In mid-December 2000 it was announced that the constitutional referendum, which had been postponed on several occasions, was to be held on 7 January 2001. In late December the PS, in common with almost all other opposition parties, announced its support for the referendum, and Dieng emphasized that the party would not introduce a 'no confidence' motion against the Government. While the draft Constitution was generally regarded as increasing and rationalizing the powers of the Assemblée nationale, three small opposition parties rejected it, on the grounds that it would increase the prerogatives of the President, and consequently urged their supporters to boycott the referendum. In the referendum, which was duly held on 7 January, some 94.0% of votes cast supported the new Constitution; some 65.8% of the registered electorate voted. Most provisions of the Constitution, including the abolition of the Sénat and the Economic and Social Council, took immediate effect, following its promulgation by the President, with only those sections relating to the legislature necessitating new elections before their implementation. Future presidential mandates would be reduced from seven to five years, and the number of deputies in the Assemblée nationale was reduced from 140 to 120.

In February 2001, following student disorder, in which one student had died in clashes with police, a new Minister of Higher Education was appointed. The President dissolved the Assemblée nationale in mid-February and announced that the new legislature, which was to be elected in April, would consist of 65 seats to be elected by majority voting in departments, and 55 on a basis of proportional representation using national lists.

In March 2001 Wade appointed Mame Madior Boye, a magistrate and member of no political party, and hitherto Minister of Justice, as Prime Minister. In the ensuing reshuffle Niasse and other members of the AFP were removed from office, in what was regarded as an attempt by Wade to create a more unified Government, which incorporated greater representation for the PDS and its allies, prior to the legislative elections. Notably, members of two small parties supportive of Wade were appointed to ministerial positions.

In March 2001 it was announced that a number of senior PS current and former officials, including Diack (now a member of the PDS) and Dieng, were being investigated in connection with allegations that the PS had misappropriated funds related to an international sports contest in 1992. Also in March a prominent PS member and former Chairman of the national railway company, Abdou Diouf, was charged with fraud and imprisoned. Senegalese human rights activists criticized the conduct of these investigations into the leading opposition party one month prior to legislative elections. Meanwhile, a ruling by the Constitutional Council forbade the use of Wade's photograph, or the acronym WAD (Wacco ak Alternance ak Democratie—Fight for Change and Democracy), in view of Wade's position as Head of State, in campaign material for the legislative elections. The pro-Wade coalition, led by the PDS and headed by that party's Deputy-General, Idrissa Seck, thus adopted the name Sopi (Change), and, citing a provision of the new Constitution that entitled the Head of State to hold office in a political party, used a silhouette image of the President in campaign material; despite criticism, notably from the PS, that the President should remain outside party politics, Wade actively participated in the coalition's campaign. The campaign proceeded largely without incident, except in Casamance, and in the central city of Kaolack, where a number of violent incidents were reported.

The legislative elections duly took place on 29 April 2001, in conditions that were widely praised for their democracy and transparency; outbreaks of violence in Casamance were none the less reported. Apart from the Sopi coalition (which included some 40 parties), a further 24 parties contested the polls. The

Sopi coalition won 49.59% of votes cast, and 89 of the 120 seats in the Assemblée nationale, including 62 of the 65 seats elected by majority voting within departments. The AFP obtained 11 seats, including two elected by majority voting, with 16.14% of the vote. The PS, despite receiving a slightly larger share of the vote than the AFP (17.36%), secured only 10 seats, and failed to win any departmental seats. The URD won the remaining majority seat, in addition to two national-list seats. AJ—PADS received two seats, while five other small parties each received one seat. The rate of electoral participation was 67.53%, and observers from the Organization of African Unity (OAU, now the African Union, see p. 130) and La Francophonie (see p. 349) praised the fair conduct of the elections. Boye was reappointed as Prime Minister on 10 May. The new 24-member Government comprised 11 members of the PDS (who obtained most principal posts), nine representatives of civil society, and two members each of AJ—PADS and the LD—MPT.

Following the elections, nine parties, including the AFP, the APJ—JJ and the URD, announced that they were to join the PS in an informal opposition alliance. In late May 2001 the Minister of the Economy and Finance, Mamadou Seck, resigned and was replaced by Abdoulaye Diop. Seck's resignation followed reports, which he denied, that he had previously received a suspended prison sentence on charges of embezzlement. In August 2001 some 25 parties, led by the PDS, formed an pro-presidential electoral alliance, the Convergence des actions autour du Président en perspective du 21ième siècle (CAP-21), in advance of local and municipal elections (initially scheduled for November, but subsequently postponed); meanwhile, opposition groups also formed an electoral alliance, the Cadre permanent de concertation. In late February 2002 the three men convicted of the assassination of Babacar Sèye in 1993 were granted presidential pardons and subsequently released from prison, provoking renewed controversy about the case, as the three recipients of the pardon continued to protest their innocence. In the delayed local and municipal elections, which were eventually held on 12 May 2002, CAP-21 won control of nine of the 11 regional governments, as well as a majority of municipal and communal seats. Some 26 parties and alliances contested the elections, although turn-out was reportedly low, and isolated violent incidents, which resulted in at least one death, were reported in the Kolda region, neighbouring Casamance. In mid-June Youssou Diagne tendered his resignation as President of the Assemblée nationale, and from his position of a deputy; he was subsequently appointed as Ambassador to the Republic of China (Taiwan). Meanwhile, Pape Diop, a PDS deputy who had recently been elected as Mayor of Dakar, was elected as the new President of the legislature. In mid-October Diouf resigned from the chairmanship of the PS, in order to assume the elected position of Secretary-General of La Francophonie.

The sinking of a state-owned passenger ferry, the MV *Joola*, in late September 2002, en route from Ziguinchor, the principal city of Casamance, to Dakar led to a national political crisis, even before the final death toll of the accident, subsequently enumerated at more than 1,800 people, became apparent. In early October the Minister of Equipment and Transport, Youssouph Sakho, and the Minister of the Armed Forces, Yoba Sambou, resigned in response to the tragedy, as it became clear that the vessel, which was licensed to carry 550 people and was maintained by the navy, had been severely overloaded; only 64 survivors were reported. Later in the month the head of the navy was dismissed, and Wade announced that the Government accepted responsibility for the disaster. In early November Wade dismissed Boye and her Government; although no official reason for the dismissal was given, it was widely believed to have been prompted by the Government's response to the disaster. Shortly after Boye's dismissal, an inquiry into the incident found that safety regulations had been widely violated on the *Joola*, and that the dispatch of rescue equipment and staff to the ship by the armed forces had been inexplicibly delayed. Idrissa Seck, the Mayor of Thiès, a close ally of Wade and previously a senior official in the PDS, was appointed as the new Prime Minister; several principal posts in the new Government remained unchanged. In mid-December the Government announced that a new capital city was to be constructed at Mékhé-Pékesse, 120 km from Dakar.

Long-standing resentment against the Government of Senegal in the southern province of Casamance (which is virtually cut off from the rest of the country by the enclave of The Gambia) was embodied from the early 1980s by the separatist Mouvement des forces démocratiques de la Casamance (MFDC). The MFDC initiated a new offensive from April 1990. The Senegalese Government dispatched military reinforcements, and in September 1990 a military governor was appointed for Casamance. By April 1991 at least 100 people had reportedly died as a result of violence in the region, while more than 300 Casamançais were awaiting trial for sedition. The announcement in May 1991 of the imminent release of more than 340 detainees (including the Secretary-General and executive leader of the MFDC, Fr Augustin Diamacouné Senghor) who had been arrested in connection with unrest in Casamance facilitated the conclusion, shortly afterwards in Guinea-Bissau, of a cease-fire agreement by representatives of the Senegalese Government and of the MFDC. In June the region's military Governor was replaced by a civilian. An amnesty was approved by the Assemblée nationale later in June, and some 400 detainees were released. A period of relative calm ensued.

In January 1992 a peace commission (the Comité de gestion de la paix en Casamance), comprising government representatives and members of the MFDC, was established, with mediation by Guinea-Bissau. A resurgence of violence in Casamance from July prompted the Government to redeploy armed forces in the region, giving rise to MFDC protests that the 'remilitarization' of Casamance contravened the truce. In August some 50 rebels and two members of the armed forces were reportedly killed in a violent clash near the regional capital, Ziguinchor. Contradictory statements made by MFDC leaders regarding their commitment to the peace accord evidenced a split within the movement. The 'Front nord' and the MFDC Vice-President, Sidi Badji, appealed to the rebels to lay down their arms; meanwhile, the 'Front sud', led by Diamacouné Senghor (who was now based in Guinea-Bissau), appeared determined to continue the armed struggle. In October 32 people were killed when rebels attacked a fishing village, causing local residents and tourists to flee the region. Following further attacks in November and December, the army instigated a major security operation, launching air attacks on supposed rebel bases along the border with Guinea-Bissau.

About 30 people were reported to have been killed in rebel attacks on voters participating in the presidential election in February 1993. Army reinforcements were dispatched to Casamance in March, in response to renewed clashes. Diamacouné Senghor, who had returned to Ziguinchor in March, having seemingly been expelled from Guinea-Bissau, reportedly appealed for a cease-fire in April, and expressed willingness to negotiate with the Senegalese Government. Shortly afterwards, however, at least 100 rebels and three members of the armed forces were reportedly killed in a further clash. In July the Government and Diamacouné Senghor signed a cease-fire agreement. The accord, for which Guinea-Bissau was to act as a guarantor, envisaged the release of MFDC prisoners, and made provision for the return of those who had fled the region. Some 256 Casamançais were subsequently released from detention. It was estimated that, in the year preceding the new accord, up to 1,000 people had been killed, many hundreds injured, and that 25,000–30,000 had fled the region. In December, in response to a request from the MFDC for historical arbitration, the French Government ruled that Casamance had not existed as an autonomous territory prior to the colonial period, and that independence for the region had been neither demanded nor considered at the time of decolonization.

From early 1995, renewed violence indicated a re-emergence of divisions between the two factions of the MFDC. Rebels in the south accused the Senegalese armed forces of violating the provisions of the 1993 cease-fire accord. At least 20 soldiers were reported to have been killed in southern Casamance between January and May 1995; there were believed to have been heavy casualties among the rebels and the civilian population. A major military operation was instigated following the disappearance, in April, of four French tourists in Basse-Casamance. More than 1,000 élite Senegalese troops were assisted in their search by French reconnaissance aircraft; although they failed to locate the missing tourists, the aim of the operation appeared increasingly to be to dislodge MFDC dissidents from the border region. Although both factions of the MFDC denied any involvement in the apparent kidnap of the tourists, who were never found, Diamacouné Senghor was placed under house arrest in late April, and the other members of the MFDC 'political bureau' were detained. In June MFDC rebels announced an end to the cease-fire, again accusing government forces of having violated the 1993 accord. Although Diamacouné Senghor appealed to the rebels not to break the truce, renewed violence in the south-west resulted in some 60 deaths.

In September 1995 a Commission nationale de paix (CNP) was established, headed by a Casamance-born former Minister of State for Foreign Affairs (in 1973–78), Assane Seck. Members of the commission reportedly sought a dialogue with Diamacouné Senghor and the MFDC's four other political leaders (all of whom remained under house arrest). During October, renewed rebel attacks on government forces were accompanied by a major army offensive in the south-west. By the end of the November it was reported that about 150 separatists and 15 members of the armed forces had been killed in clashes.

In November 1995 the MFDC's representative in Europe, Mamadou N'Krumah Sané, indicated the organization's willingness to enter negotiations with the Government if Diamacouné Senghor and his associates were released from house arrest. In December Diamacouné Senghor made a televised appeal to the rebels to lay down their arms. He proposed that preliminary talks between the MFDC and the CNP take place in January 1996, to be followed by peace negotiations, in a neutral country, three months later. The members of the MFDC 'political bureau' were released from house arrest at the end of December 1995; it was also reported that the CNP had secured the release of 50 of some 150 suspected separatists detained in recent months. Peace talks, scheduled to begin in Ziguinchor in April, were postponed indefinitely, following the refusal of Diamacouné Senghor and other MFDC leaders to attend, citing the failure of the Government to meet a number of their conditions, and renewed violence was reported in the region. During a visit to Ziguinchor in May, Diouf expressed his commitment to the pursuit of peace, stating that the ongoing process of administrative decentralization would afford greater autonomy to the region, but as an integral part of Senegal.

There was renewed optimism regarding the possible resumption of negotiations between a united MFDC and the authorities, following discussions in July 1996 between Diamacouné Senghor and Diouf's personal Chief of Staff in Ziguinchor. However, in March 1997 more than 40 rebels and two members of the armed forces were killed in clashes near the border with Guinea-Bissau. The MFDC denied that it had ended its cease-fire, stating that it would investigate these incidents. In that month four representatives of the MFDC had been permitted to travel to France, where they had spent three weeks meeting with representatives of the movement based in Europe.

While both the Senegalese authorities and the MFDC leadership appeared committed to reviving the peace process, the deaths of 25 soldiers in August 1997 near Ziguinchor prompted fears of a revival of the conflict. In September the armed forces launched a new offensive, in which rebel forces were reported to have sustained heavy losses. A further armed forces offensive in October, the largest such operation in Casamance since the 1995 cease-fire, involved as many as 3,000 soldiers and resulted in the deaths of 12 soldiers and 80 rebels in clashes near the border with Guinea-Bissau, according to Senegalese military sources. Salif Sadio, the MFDC's military leader, stated that the organization remained committed to the peace process, but maintained that its forces were justified in defending themselves against armed attack.

The violence in the south was reported to have caused more than 20,000 people to flee to Guinea-Bissau or to The Gambia between October 1997 and the end of the year. In January 1998 the MFDC alleged that some 3,000 members of Guinea-Bissau's armed forces were massing along the border in preparation for an attack on rebel bases in Casamance, in a joint operation with 4,000 Senegalese soldiers. Both Senegal and Guinea-Bissau denied these allegations, although the Guinea-Bissau Government acknowledged the dispatch of military reinforcements to the border region to protect its citizens and territorial integrity. None the less, it was subsequently reported that 10 alleged rebels had been killed, and 40 captured, by the Guinea-Bissau armed forces in an operation (conducted in accordance with a security agreement reached by the military chiefs of Senegal, Guinea-Bissau and The Gambia in October 1997) against rebels suspected of hiding in refugee camps.

In mid-January 1998 Diamacouné Senghor appealed for a cease-fire, indicating that his organization would be prepared to abandon its demand for independence, subject to the Government instituting measures to ensure greater economic and social development in Casamance. Security operations in advance of the legislative elections resulted in the deaths of some 30 rebels in May, and six civilians were killed by separa-

tists on the day before the election. There was further violence as voting proceeded, and two soldiers who were transporting voting results were reportedly killed. In August the Senegalese army bombarded rebel positions on both sides of the border with Guinea-Bissau. The armed forces reported that seven soldiers and 43 rebels had been killed in the clashes, although the MFDC claimed that the majority of the victims were civilians. Rebel violence continued intermittently throughout the second half of 1998.

In January 1999 Diouf visited Ziguinchor, where he again urged a restoration of peace in the region, and held talks with Diamacouné Senghor. In February the Senegalese authorities released 123 rebels from prison, and in March serious fighting took place between security forces and rebels believed to have crossed into Casamance from Guinea-Bissau. In late April a delegation of the various factions of the MFDC, led by Diamacouné Senghor, met in Banjul, The Gambia, in an attempt to arrive at a common stance in preparation for negotiations with the Senegalese Government. In May Diamacouné Senghor called upon members of the MFDC to respect the peace process, while the Government promised to increase investment in Casamance. However, from late May dissident elements within the MFDC elements, whom Diamacouné Senghor accused of seeking to sabotage the peace process, launched a series of attacks near Ziguinchor.

In June 1999 talks between several MFDC factions began in Banjul, sponsored by President Yahya Jammeh of The Gambia. Some 50 observers attended the talks, including Gen. Ansumane Mané, the leader of the rebels in Guinea-Bissau, and two Senegalese ministers. The Senegalese authorities subsequently acceded to the MFDC's demand that Diamacouné Senghor be released from house arrest; his movements were, however, to remain restricted. Despite this apparent progress towards reconciliation, further incidents occurred between late July and September, including kidnappings and clashes between the armed forces and dissident groups of MFDC fighters, who rejected the peace process.

In November 1999 Diamacouné Senghor agreed to recommence negotiations with the Senegalese Government, demanding, however, that the safety of MFDC negotiators be guaranteed, and that representatives of Casamançais civil society be included in the negotiations. At the meeting, held in Banjul in late December, the Senegalese Government and the MFDC agreed to an immediate cease-fire and to create the conditions necessary to bring about lasting peace; the Governments of The Gambia and of Guinea-Bissau were to monitor the situation in the region. Although sporadic fighting continued in early January 2000, the MFDC and the Senegalese Government met again in Banjul later that month. The Government agreed to recognize the MFDC as its interlocutor in discussions on the future of Casamance, and to lift its ban on MFDC activities. Both sides agreed to withdraw their armed forces from all places occupied during the conflict, and to establish a joint monitoring body. Both sides also resolved to issue a joint call for assistance from the international community in order to facilitate the resolution of a number of issues, including the return of refugees and the clearing of landmines. Following the meeting, the MFDC also announced that Sané, who was now outspokenly opposed to the peace process, had been expelled from the organization. President Diouf, meanwhile, announced the release of some 40 MFDC prisoners.

In early February 2000 a joint mission of the Senegalese Government and the MFDC was established to oversee the cease-fire. Despite the presence of the mission and of increased security designed to prevent the disturbance of the Senegalese presidential election, violent incidents, in which three soldiers and two civilians were killed, were reported in February. Following his election as President in early March, Abdoulaye Wade announced that he was to continue the process of negotiations, but that his preference was to conduct direct dialogue with the MFDC, without the mediation of the 'peace commissions', which were to be dissolved. Wade further announced that Diamacouné Senghor would be permitted total freedom of movement. However renewed clashes were subsequently reported. The Gambian Government suspended its mediation in the conflict for several weeks, in protest against Wade's denunciation, in late May, of the reputed supply of arms from Libya to The Gambia and Guinea-Bissau. In mid-August two civilians were killed in an attack, reportedly committed by members of the MFDC near to Ziguinchor. In late August Senegal and Guinea-Bissau announced that they would undertake joint military border patrols in order to restrict rebel activities in the region. In September MFDC rebels launched an attack using rocket-propelled grenades on a military unit west of Ziguinchor, injuring at least seven soldiers.

In November 2000 members of a peace commission, headed by the Minister of the Interior, Maj.-Gen. Mamadou Niang, and by Diamacouné Senghor, signed a joint statement that envisaged a series of official meetings between the Senegalese Government and the MFDC, the first of which would convene on 16 December. The Government simultaneously warned that full legal action would be taken against any person promoting or distributing speeches in favour of separatism. The discussions in mid-December were boycotted by representatives of the 'Front sud' of the MFDC, led by Ali Badji, in protest at the decision to hold the negotiations in Ziguinchor, rather than upon neutral territory. However, a senior MFDC official present at the onset of negotiations, Alexandre Djiba (who had long been resident outside Senegal), subsequently reportedly met Ali Badji's representatives in Guinea-Bissau. The Senegalese Minister of the Armed Forces, Yoba Sambou, himself a native of Casamance, meanwhile stated that the Government preferred the rebels to unite into a single faction, so that more militant factions within the MFDC would not dispute the peace talks. In December at least sixteen people were reportedly killed in clashes around Ziguinchor, near to the border with Guinea-Bissau and to the north of Bignona, a region that had hitherto been calm for some 10 years. As a result of the renewed unrest, the MFDC postponed a proposed meeting in Banjul, to be held in January 2001, which had been intended to establish a common position between its various factions.

The overwhelming support in Casamance for the new Constitution, which was endorsed by 96% of voters in the region at the referendum in January 2001, prompted Wade to announce that Casamance had definitively voted to remain part of Senegal. In mid-January the Guinea-Bissau armed forces reportedly destroyed all the Casamance rebel bases in that country, in response to clashes between rival MFDC factions there. In early February the Senegalese armed forces began a new operation intended to pacify the region to the south-west of Ziguinchor. The continued unrest further delayed the signature of a cease-fire agreement, originally intended to take place at the meeting of mid-December, which had been rescheduled to occur in Dakar in early February

In mid-February 2001 Diamacouné Senghor announced that, in order to accelerate the peace process in Casamance, several senior members of the MFDC, including Sidi Badji and Djiba, had been removed from their positions, and that Sané would henceforth serve as First Deputy Secretary General of the movement, while remaining in France. However, Sidi Badji, who had served as Military Affairs Adviser to Diamacouné Senghor, rejected the legitimacy of his dismissal. Also in mid-February, in what was reportedly the most serious attack on civilian targets in Casamance for several years, separatist rebels killed some 13 civilians in an ambush. Both Sidi Badji and Diamacouné Senghor denied any knowledge of their supporters' involvement and condemned the attack, into which Wade announced the opening of a judicial inquiry. Later in February a Senegalese soldier was killed in an attack on an army supply convoy, and two people were killed and 13 others injured in two further ambushes, attributed to separatist rebels, in late February and early March. In early March Diamacouné Senghor accused Sadio of being implicated in the recent killings of civilians; in mid-March the Senegalese Government issued an international arrest warrant for Sadio, who had recently been removed from Guinea-Bissau, and announced that a reward of some US $200,000 would be paid for his capture.

In mid-March 2001 Niang and Diamacouné Senghor signed a cease-fire agreement at a meeting in Ziguinchor, which provided for the release of detainees, the return of refugees, the removal of landmines (which had been utilized in the region since 1998) and for economic aid to reintegrate rebels and to ameliorate the infrastructure of Casamance. Some 16 prisoners were released several days after the accord was signed. The Gambian Government issued a communiqué in mid-March, in which it promised to prevent armed rebel groups from operating on Gambian territory; it was suspected that the renewed violence had been co-ordinated by groups based in The Gambia. Later in March Niang and Diamacouné Senghor signed a further agreement, which provided for the disarmament of rebel groups and the confinement to barracks of military forces in Casamance. In April Wade and Sambou participated in negotiations with Dia-

macouné Senghor, at which other MFDC leaders, including Sidi Badji, were also present. Attacks on security personnel in Casamance were reported to have caused minor disruption to the conduct of the Senegalese legislative elections on 29 April. In early May fighting was reported on the border with Guinea-Bissau between separatist forces and troops from Guinea-Bissau, reportedly in response to MFDC raids on villages in the region.

As a result of the renewed conflict, Diamacouné Senghor announced, in late May 2001, that a proposed reconciliation forum, intended to unite the various factions of the MFDC, had been postponed indefinitely, and a number of members of the movement, including Djiba, were reportedly expelled. None the less, Diamacouné Senghor and Sidi Badji attended a meeting convened by the Gambian Government in Banjul in early June, in an attempt to overcome the impasse. As tensions between factions within the MFDC intensified, with further clashes reported in June and July, Diamacouné Senghor was removed from the position of Secretary-General of the MFDC in August, at the much-delayed reconciliation forum, and appointed as honorary President. Jean-Marie François Biagui, who had previously been involved in the French-based section of the MFDC, became Secretary-General and *de facto* leader. Sidi Badji, who continued to question the tactics of Diamacouné Senghor, was appointed as the organization's head of military affairs.

Despite these personnel changes within the MFDC, President Wade met Diamacouné Senghor at the presidential palace in Dakar in September 2001; both leaders reiterated the importance of implementing the cease-fire agreement signed in March. In response to this meeting, it was reported that the new leadership of the MFDC had suspended all further negotiations with the Government. Following further attacks by rebels, Biagui resigned as Secretary-General in early November. Sidi Badji was announced as Biagui's successor, in an acting capacity, although Diamacouné Senghor rejected this appointment. In November MFDC rebels launched numerous attacks on civilians in Casamance. Diamacouné Senghor led a rally in Ziguinchor in mid-November to demand an immediate cease-fire; the rally was boycotted by supporters of Sidi Badji. Violence in the province intensified in December; several civilians were killed during attacks on villages. In an attempt to quell the rebellion, Diamacouné Senghor appointed an envoy, his nephew, Laurent Diamacouné, to seek negotiations with Sidi Badji, but with only limited success. In mid-December Diamacouné Senghor's position was further undermined, when an episcopal conference declared that his leadership of a movement that was using armed struggle to attain its ends was incompatible with his role as a Roman Catholic priest. Meanwhile, it was suggested that the upsurge in banditry by MFDC rebels was attributable to the increasingly dire financial situation of the organization.

In mid-January 2002 Niang held talks with Diamacouné Senghor and Sidi Badji, although no date for the resumption of peace negotiations with the Government was forthcoming. In March further incidents of looting and robbery by MFDC militants were reported, with several attacks notably occurring in the hitherto largely peaceful region around Bignona, where Sadio was now believed to be based. In late March mediators from The Gambia and Guinea-Bissau met with MFDC representatives, with the intention of establishing a timetable for the resumption of peace talks. Representatives of the Senegalese Government also attended the meeting, but only in the capacity of observers. At the end of the month five civilians were killed during an attack by 200 MFDC fighters in the coastal resort of Kafoutine, and a further attack by rebels, at the end of April, resulted in seven deaths near Bignona. Following continued fighting, some 9,000 Casamançais were reported to have fled to The Gambia by the end of June.

In late July 2002 Djiba, who had returned to Senegal in May, wrote to President Wade, proposing the resumption of negotiations between the Government and the MFDC. In late August, following a joint declaration signed by Diamacouné Senghor and Sidi Badji urging the resumption of peace talks between the rebels and the Government, Wade appointed an official delegation, chaired by the Second Vice-President of the Assemblée nationale and President of Ziguinchor Regional Council, Abdoulaye Faye, and including among its membership Niang and Sambou, to undertake negotiations with the MFDC. Although the inclusion of Sambou was reportedly in response to a request by the MFDC leaders, the organization expressed concern that other members of the government commission were unfamiliar with conditions in Casamance. Meanwhile, the holding of an intra-Casamance conference, in early September, appeared to indicate a decline in support for separatist aspirations, as the conference produced a declaration, signed by representatives of 10 ethnic groups resident in the region, in favour of a 'definitive peace in Casamance', and which referred to the region as 'belonging to the great and single territory of Senegal'. Moreover, the absence from the meeting of the MFDC faction loyal to Sidi Badji appeared to refute reports that the various wings of the MFDC had effectively reunited. In mid-September a further meeting between Faye and Niang, representing the Government, and Diamacouné Senghor and Sidi Badji, for the MFDC, was held in Ziguinchor. In late September five civilians, including the brother of Sambou, were killed in an attack attributed to separatist rebels near Bono, north of Ziguinchor. The internal disunity of the MFDC was emphasized in mid-October, when Biagui publicly demanded forgiveness from the people of Casamance and Senegal for the actions of the organization, and acknowledged that the MFDC was responsible for causing suffering to the populace; this statement was emphatically rejected by Sidi Badji. In spite of further discussions between the government commission and Diamacouné Senghor and Sidi Badji in January 2003, intermittent conflict and banditry continued to be reported in Casamance in early 2003.

From 1989 Senegal's regional relations underwent a period of considerable strain. A long-standing border dispute with Mauritania, which also involved ethnic and economic rivalries, was exacerbated by the deaths, in April of that year, of two Senegalese farmers, who had been involved in a dispute regarding grazing rights with Mauritanian livestock-breeders. Mauritanian nationals residing in Senegal were attacked, and their businesses looted, while Senegalese nationals in Mauritania suffered similar aggression. By early May it was believed that several hundred people, mostly Senegalese, had been killed. Operations to repatriate nationals of both countries commenced, with international assistance. Diplomatic relations, which had been suspended in August 1989, were fully restored in April 1992, and the process of reopening the border began in May, although the contentious issues that had hitherto impeded the normalization of relations remained largely unresolved. In December 1994, however, the Governments of Senegal and Mauritania agreed new co-operation measures, including efforts to facilitate the free movement of goods and people between the two countries.

In January 1995 the Governments of Senegal, Mauritania and Mali undertook to co-operate in resolving joint border issues and in combating extremism, arms-smuggling and drugs-trafficking. In July the office of the UN High Commissioner for Refugees (UNHCR) began a census of Mauritanian refugees in Senegal (estimated to number some 66,000), as part of initiatives for their eventual repatriation. In June 1996 the repatriation of a group of 4,000 refugees was postponed, apparently as a result of logistical difficulties. In May 1998 the Ministers of the Interior of Mauritania, Mali and Senegal met to discuss border security, following reports of increased cross-border banditry, particularly in eastern Senegal. The unrest in the region was blamed by the Senegalese press on the continued presence there of Mauritanian refugees; in September it was reported that the Senegalese authorities had ceased to issue the refugees with travel documents. In May 1999 the two countries signed a further agreement on the joint exploitation of fisheries. In mid-2000, however, a dispute over water rights resulted in a period of substantial tension between Senegal and Mauritania. Reports that Mauritanian coastguards had killed a Senegalese fisherman found illegally in Mauritanian maritime territory in February 2001 further increased tensions between the countries. However, following renewed negotiations, the visit of President Taya of Mauritania to Dakar in April, as the guest of honour at a ceremony to commemorate the 41st anniversary of the independence of Senegal, was widely regarded as indicating an improvement in relations between the countries.

Relations with Guinea-Bissau were strained in late 1992. In December an offensive by the Senegalese armed forces against MFDC strongholds close to the border resulted in the deaths of two nationals of Guinea-Bissau. The Government of President Commdr João Vieira formally protested at Senegalese violations of Guinea-Bissau's airspace, and reiterated that it was not assisting the rebels. Guinea-Bissau sought to facilitate the new cease-fire agreement between the Senegalese Government and the MFDC of mid-1993; in October the two countries signed an agreement regarding the joint exploitation and management of

fishing and petroleum resources in their maritime zones. This treaty was ratified in December 1995, to the effect that fishing resources were to be shared equally between the two countries, while Senegal was to benefit from an 85% share of revenue obtained from petroleum deposits. During bilateral contacts in 1995–97 Senegal and Guinea-Bissau pledged co-operation in matters of joint defence and security. It was hoped that the movement of refugees from the conflict in Casamance to Guinea-Bissau, which began, under the auspices of UNHCR, in February 1996, would expedite efforts to restore security in the border region between the countries. In January 1998 it was announced that the authorities in Guinea-Bissau had intercepted a consignment of armaments destined for MFDC rebels, and that some 15 officers of the Guinea-Bissau armed forces had been arrested and suspended from duty, including the head of the armed forces, Brig. (later Gen.) Ansumane Mané. The Government of Guinea-Bissau reiterated that the country was not assisting rebels in Casamance, but stated that it would not participate in joint operations in Casamance with the Senegalese armed forces, although Vieira again expressed his willingness to mediate between the Senegalese Government and the MFDC. In June, however, troops loyal to Mané rebelled against Vieira, and civil war broke out in Guinea-Bissau. Senegalese troops intervened in support of the armed forces loyal to Vieira. By the end of the month refugees from the conflict were crossing into Casamance, exacerbating security concerns in the province, while it was also reported that members of the MFDC were fighting alongside the rebels against the Government of Guinea-Bissau and Senegalese forces. From December, as a result of a peace-keeping agreement brokered by the Economic Community of West African States (ECOWAS, see p. 187), Senegalese troops began to depart from Guinea-Bissau, but strengthened their presence in the border area, while the ECOWAS peace-keeping force, ECOMOG (see p. 191), assumed positions on the Guinea-Bissau side of the frontier with Casamance.

In May 1999 fighting again broke out in Guinea-Bissau, and Vieira was overthrown. Tensions between the two countries resurfaced in April 2000, when an armed group, reportedly composed of members of the MFDC operating from within Guinea-Bissau, attacked a Senegalese border post, killing three soldiers, and later that month the border between the two countries was temporarily closed. In August the terms of the agreement concerning the joint exploitation of maritime resources by the two countries was revised; henceforth, Guinea-Bissau was to receive 20% rather than 15% of the revenue generated from petroleum deposits. In early September, following clashes near the border in Guinea-Bissau, attributed to an armed faction of the MFDC, the Senegalese Government closed all border posts between the two countries. Following the killing of Mané in November 2000, during an attempted *coup d'état*, relations between Senegal and Guinea-Bissau improved significantly. In January 2001 Guinea-Bissau forces launched a new offensive against MFDC rebel bases, while heightened security in the border regions during 2001 was regarded as a significant factor in restricting rebel activity and funding.

In August 1989 Diouf announced the withdrawal of Senegalese troops from The Gambia, in protest at a request by President Jawara of that country that The Gambia be accorded more power within the confederal agreement of Senegambia that had been formed by the two countries in 1982. Diouf subsequently stated that, in view of The Gambia's reluctance to proceed towards full political and economic integration with Senegal, the functions of the Confederation would be suspended. The Confederation was dissolved in September. In January 1991 the two countries signed a bilateral treaty of friendship and co-operation. Senegal's abrupt decision to close the Senegalese–Gambian border in September 1993, apparently to reduce smuggling between the two countries, again strained relations, although subsequent negotiations sought to minimize the adverse effects of the closure on The Gambia's regional trading links. Since the *coup d'état* in The Gambia in July 1994 Senegal has fostered cordial relations with the Government of President Jammeh. In January 1996 the two countries signed an agreement aimed at increasing bilateral trade and at minimizing cross-border smuggling. A further agreement was concluded in April 1997, designed to facilitate the trans-border movement of goods destined for re-export. In June the two countries agreed to take joint measures to combat insecurity, illegal immigration, arms-trafficking and drugs-smuggling. In early 1998 Jammeh offered to act as a mediator between the Senegalese Government and the MFDC, and subsequently held regular meetings with MFDC representatives. None the less, intermittent disputes relating to transportation issues between the two countries have occured, and in July 2002 the Gambian Secretary of State for Foreign Affairs, Blaise Baboucar Jagne, was prevented from entering Senegal by demonstrators protesting at the recent increase in fees for the transportation of foreign-registered vehicles on the ferry across the Gambia river, a principal trade route from the south of Senegal; the increase was revoked later in the month, following a meeting between Senegalese and Gambian officials.

Since his election in March 2000, President Wade has on several occasions promoted greater democratization in other West African countries and encouraged an expansion in the international political engagement of African countries. Notably, Wade's well-publicized condemnation, at an international conference on racism and xenophobia held under the auspices of the office of the UN High Commissioner for Human Rights in Dakar in January 2001, of the increasing importance of ethnically-based politics in Côte d'Ivoire prompted violent anti-Senegalese demonstrations in Abidjan and across Côte d'Ivoire. At the UN World Conference against Racism, Racial Discrimination, Xenophobia and Related Intolerance, held in Durban, South Africa, in August–September, Wade, notably among African leaders, condemned the notion that reparations should be paid by Western nations to the descendants of slaves. Following the disputed presidential election in Madagascar in December 2001, Wade hosted peace talks between the two rival candidates in Dakar, which led to the signing of an accord, in April 2002, between the two parties. Further negotiations, which ended without a resolution of the dispute, were held in Dakar in June, and in July Senegal recognized Marc Ravalomanana as President of Madagascar, to which position he had been inaugurated in early May, in spite of objections by the OAU and other African states.

President Wade was one of the four African leaders most closely involved in the initial development of the New Partnership for Africa's Development (NEPAD, see p. 133), a long-term plan for socio-economic recovery in Africa that was launched in October 2001 in accordance with a decision of the OAU summit of heads of state and government held in Lusaka, Zambia, in July of that year. In February 2002 the Prime Minister of the United Kingdom, Anthony (Tony) Blair, became the first British leader to make an official visit to Senegal; Blair and Wade held discussions on NEPAD, which were also attended by the President of Ghana, John Kufuor, and the Deputy President of South Africa, Jacob Zuma, among others. Meanwhile, in April Senegal hosted a fund-raising conference for NEPAD, which was attended by more than 900 delegates, including the leaders of some 20 African countries.

Relations with France have remained particularly strong since independence, and the existing defence arrangements between France and Senegal have remained substantially unaltered during the major restructuring of the French armed forces undertaken by the administration of Jacques Chirac in the late 1990s and early 2000s.

Senegal is an active participant in regional and international peace-keeping operations. In February 1998 Senegal, with Mali and Mauritania, was among the principal participants in multinational military exercises conducted in eastern Senegal under the auspices of the UN and the OAU, as part of efforts to establish a regional crisis-intervention force. The exercise was organized by France and involved almost 3,500 troops from eight West African countries, as well as units from the USA, the United Kingdom and Belgium. Senegal is a member of the Accord de Non-agression et d'assistance en matière de défense, which in April 1999 adopted a draft protocol on the setting up of a peace-keeping force in the region. In September 1999 a Senegalese contingent joined the international peace-keeping operation in the Kosovo and Metohija province of Yugoslavia (now Serbia and Montenegro). In early April 2001 260 Senegalese soldiers joined the UN Observation Mission in Kananga, the Democratic Republic of the Congo (DRC), while a further 280 were dispatched to Mbandaka, the DRC, later in the month. In early 2003 it was announced that Senegal was to contribute some 650 troops to the ECOWAS peace-keeping force in Côte d'Ivoire, ECOMICI; more than 200 Senegalese troops had arrived in Côte d'Ivoire by mid-January.

Government

Under the terms of the Constitution, approved by popular referendum in January 2001, executive power is held by the President, who is directly elected for a mandate of five years, which is renewable only once. (President Wade will, however, complete the seven-year mandate to which he was elected in March 2000 by the terms of the former Constitution). Legislative power rests with the Assemblée nationale, with 120 members elected for five years by universal adult suffrage. There is no restriction on the number of political parties, although the formation of parties on an ethnic, religious or geographical basis is prohibited. The President appoints the Prime Minister, who, in consultation with the President, appoints the Council of Ministers. Senegal comprises 10 regions, each with an appointed governor, an elected local assembly and a separate budget.

Defence

In August 2002 Senegal's active armed forces totalled 9,400 men: army 8,000 (including an estimated 3,500 conscripts), navy 600, air force 800. There was also a 5,800-strong paramilitary gendarmerie. Military service is by selective conscription and lasts for two years. France and the USA provide technical and material aid, and in August 2002 there were 1,150 French troops stationed in Senegal. The defence budget for 2002 was 48,000m. francs CFA.

Economic Affairs

In 2001, according to estimates by the World Bank, Senegal's gross national income (GNI), measured at average 1999–2001 prices, was US $4,726m., equivalent to $480 per head (or $1,560 on an international purchasing-power parity basis). During 1990–2001, it was estimated, the population increased at an average annual rate of 2.6%, while gross domestic product (GDP) per head increased by an average of 0.9% per year. Overall GDP increased, in real terms, at an average annual rate of 3.6% per year in 1990–2001; growth in 2001 was 5.7%.

Agriculture (including forestry and fishing) contributed 17.9% of GDP in 2001, when 73.4% of the labour force were engaged in the sector. The principal cash crops are groundnuts (exports of groundnut oil contributed 9.7% of total export earnings in 2000) and cotton. In the late 1990s Senegal began to export mangoes, melons, asparagus and green beans to European markets. Groundnuts, millet, sorghum, rice, maize and vegetables are produced for domestic consumption. Senegal has yet to achieve self-sufficiency in basic foodstuffs. In August 2002 President Wade apologized for an announcement, issued by the Government in the previous month, that the country was facing a drought-induced famine, stating that there was no threat of hunger; an emergency appeal for US $23m. in aid was also withdrawn. Among the principal economic measures proposed for 2003 was the strengthening and diversification of the agricultural sector. The fishing sector makes an important contribution to both the domestic food supply and export revenue: fish and fish products had become Senegal's principal export commodity by the mid-1980s, and provided 37.9% of export earnings in 2000. The sale of fishing licences to the European Union (EU) was an important source of revenue from the late 1990s. However, following the expiry of the fishing agreement with the EU in December 2001, negotiations on a new arrangement were suspended in March 2002. In June agreement was reached with the EU; under the new arrangement, the EU was to pay €16m. annually for fishing licences (compared with €12m under the previous agreement), and the proportion of Senegalese fishermen working on EU-registered vessels in Senegalese waters was to increase from one-third to one-half. Senegalese concerns at the dwindling fish stocks in its waters were also to be addressed, with an annual two-month moratorium on fishing. According to the World Bank, during 1990–2001 agricultural GDP increased by an average of 2.4% per year; growth in 2001 was 6.8%.

Industry (including mining, manufacturing, construction and power) contributed 26.9% of GDP in 2001. The principal activities are the processing of fish and agricultural products and of phosphates, while the production of cement is of increasing importance. According to the World Bank, during 1990–2001 industrial GDP increased at an average annual rate of 4.7%. Industrial GDP increased by 6.8% in 2001.

Mining contributed only 1.1% of GDP in 2000. The principal mining activity is the extraction of calcium phosphates (aluminium phosphates are also mined in smaller quantities). Deposits of salt, fuller's earth (attapulgite), clinker and natural gas are also exploited, and there are currently investigations under way into the feasibility of mining copper, alluvial diamonds and iron ore. Explorations at Sabodala have revealed gold reserves estimated at 30 metric tons. Offshore deposits of petroleum are also to be developed, in co-operation with Guinea-Bissau. According to IMF estimates, the GDP of the mining sector declined by an average of 4.0% per year in 1992–99; the GDP of the sector fell by 2.0% in 1998, but increased by 20.8% in 1999.

Manufacturing contributed 17.6% of GDP in 2001. The most important manufacturing activities are food-processing (notably fish, groundnuts and sugar), chemicals, textiles and petroleum-refining (using imported crude petroleum). According to the World Bank, manufacturing GDP increased at an average annual rate of 3.6% in 1990–2001; growth in 2001 was 4.8%.

Electrical energy is almost wholly derived from petroleum, which provided 98.5% of total electricity production in 1999. The Manantali hydroelectric power installation (constructed under the auspices of the Organisation pour la Mise en Valeur du Fleuve Sénégal—OMVS) commenced operations in December 2001; it was anticipated that Senegal would receive approximately one-third of the energy generated by the installation. Imports of mineral fuels and lubricants (including petroleum for refining) accounted for 22.6% of the value of merchandise imports in 2000.

The services sector contributed 55.2% of GDP in 2001. Tourism is a major source of foreign exchange, generating some 96,800m. francs CFA in receipts in 2000. In 1995 the tourism sector contributed almost 3% of GDP; about 4,500 people are directly employed (and some 15,000 indirectly employed) in the sector. The tourism sector is, however, vulnerable to domestic political developments (such as separatist unrest in Casamance), as well as to external economic conditions. Dakar's port is of considerable importance as a centre for regional trade. According to the World Bank, the GDP of the services sector increased by an average of 3.7% per year in 1990–2001. The GDP of the sector increased by 3.4% in 2000 and by 5.0% in 2001.

In 2001 Senegal recorded a visible trade deficit of 286,700m. francs CFA, while there was a deficit of 183,100m. francs CFA on the current account of the balance of payments. In 2000 the principal source of imports (27.4%) was France; other major suppliers were Nigeria and Thailand. France was the principal market for exports in that year (taking 18.4% of the total); India and Italy were also important purchasers. The principal exports in 2000 were fish, refined petroleum products, groundnut products and phosphoric acid. The principal imports in that year were machinery and transport equipment, petroleum and petroleum products, food and live animals, basic manufactures, and chemicals and related products.

Senegal's overall budget deficit in 2000 was 35,900m. francs CFA (equivalent to 1.2% of GDP). In 2001 a budget deficit of 69,200m. francs CFA was recorded. Total external debt was US $3,372m. at the end of 2000, of which $2,971m. was long-term public debt. In that year the cost of debt-servicing was equivalent to 14.4% of the value of exports of goods and services. In 1990–93 consumer prices declined by an annual average of 0.8%. However, following the 50% devaluation of the CFA franc, inflation averaged 32.3% in 1994; inflation subsequently slowed to an annual average of 1.8% in 1995–2002. Consumer prices increased by an average of 2.3% in 2002. In early 1999 157,063 people were registered as unemployed.

Senegal is a member of the Economic Community of West African States (see p. 187), of the West African organs of the Franc Zone (see p. 238), of the African Groundnut Council (see p. 335), of the West Africa Rice Development Association (see p. 338), of the Gambia River Basin Development Organization (see p. 340) and of the OMVS (see p. 341).

The attainment of sustained economic growth has been impeded by Senegal's dependence on revenue from a narrow export base, and by its consequent vulnerability to fluctuations in international prices for its principal commodities. Several important state-owned companies were privatized in the late 1990s, although attempts to transfer the groundnut-oil production company, the Société Nationale de Commercialisation des Oléagineux du Sénégal, to private ownership failed in both 1997 and 1999, while the perceived under-performance of the electricity company, the Société Nationale d'Electricité, led to the Government, in 2001, reacquiring those shares in the com-

pany that had previously been sold to private investors, prior to the instigation of a new round of privatization; it was intended that both of these companies would be transferred to the private sector in 2003. Proposed fiscal reforms aimed at promoting greater transparency, including the introduction of a flat-rate of value-added tax, were implemented only partially and intermittently in the late 1990s and early 2000s. None the less, Senegal has generally enjoyed good relations with the IMF, which approved a new three-year Enhanced Structural Adjustment Facility (subsequently renamed Poverty Reduction and Growth Facility—PRGF) in April 1998; this Facility was subsequently extended for a further year, until 2002. In 2000 Senegal was declared eligible for assistance under the Heavily Indebted Poor Countries initiative. Strong economic growth was recorded from 1998, in spite of the frequent shortages of electricity experienced during 1999, the rise in the world price of petroleum, one of Senegal's principal imports, in 2000, and a relatively poor harvest in 2002. Since taking office in March 2000, President Wade, has sought to utilize Senegal's strategic geographic location to establish it as a centre for international trade between Africa, America and Europe. Furthermore, Wade's involvement in the creation and promotion of the New Partnership for Africa's Development, has served to increase Senegal's international profile as a country committed to thorough economic reform and transparency. A priority in the early 2000s was to be the development of the social sector, including health, education, improvements in the provision of drinking water and communications. Provisional figures indicated GDP growth of 4.8% in 2002.

Education

Primary education, which usually begins at seven years of age, lasts for six years and is officially compulsory. In 1999/2000 primary enrolment included 61.7% of children in the relevant age-group (males 65.6%; females 57.8%), according to UNESCO estimates. The 1995–2008 Educational and Training Plan places special emphasis on increasing levels of female enrolment, and is intended to raise overall levels of pupil enrolment by 5% annually. Secondary education usually begins at the age of 13, and comprises a first cycle of four years (also referred to as 'middle school') and a further cycle of three years. In 1998/99 secondary enrolment was equivalent to only 19.5% of children in the relevant age-group (males 23.7%; females 15.3%). There are two universities in Senegal, the Université Cheikh Anta Diop in Dakar and the Université Gaston Berger in Saint-Louis. Since 1981 the reading and writing of national languages has been actively promoted, and is expressly encouraged in the 2001 Constitution. Current government expenditure on education in 2000 was some 100,400m. francs CFA (representing 24.4% of total current expenditure).

Public Holidays

2003: 1 January (New Year's Day), 12 February* (Tabaski, Feast of the Sacrifice), 14 March* (Ashoura), 4 April (National Day), 18 April (Good Friday), 21 April (Easter Monday), 1 May (Labour Day), 14 May* (Mouloud, Birth of the Prophet), 29 May (Ascension Day), 9 June (Whit Monday), 14 July (Day of Association), 15 August (Assumption), 1 November (All Saints' Day), 26 November* (Korité, end of Ramadan), 25 December (Christmas).

2004: 1 January (New Year's Day), 2 February* (Tabaski, Feast of the Sacrifice), 2 March* (Ashoura), 4 April (National Day), 9 April (Good Friday), 12 April (Easter Monday), 1 May (Labour Day), 2 May* (Mouloud, Birth of the Prophet), 20 May (Ascension Day), 31 May (Whit Monday), 14 July (Day of Association), 15 August (Assumption), 1 November (All Saints' Day), 14 November* (Korité, end of Ramadan), 25 December (Christmas).

* These holidays are determined by the Islamic lunar calendar and may vary by one or two days from the dates given.

Weights and Measures

The metric system is in force.

Statistical Survey

Source (unless otherwise stated): Direction de la Prévision et de la Statistique, Ministère de l'Economie et des Finances, rue René Ndiaye, BP 4017, Dakar; tel. 821-96-99; fax 822-41-95.

Area and Population

AREA, POPULATION AND DENSITY

Area (sq km)	196,722*
Population (census results)†	
16 April 1976	5,085,388
27 May 1988	
Males	3,353,599
Females	3,543,209
Total	6,896,808
Population (official estimates at mid-year)	
1998	9,037,906
1999	9,278,617
2000	9,524,000
Density (per sq km) at mid-2000	48.4

* 75,955 sq miles.

† Figures refer to the *de jure* population. The *de facto* population at the 1976 census was 4,907,507, and at the 1988 census was 6,773,417.

POPULATION BY ETHNIC GROUP
(at 1988 census)

Ethnic group	Number	%
Wolof	2,890,402	42.67
Serere	1,009,921	14.91
Peul	978,366	14.44
Toucouleur	631,892	9.33
Diola	357,672	5.28
Mandingue	245,651	3.63
Rural-Rurale	113,184	1.67
Bambara	91,071	1.34
Maure	67,726	1.00
Manjaag	66,605	0.98
Others	320,927	4.74
Total	**6,773,417**	**100.00**

Source: UN, *Demographic Yearbook*.

REGIONS
(1988 census)

	Area (sq km)	Population (*de jure*)	Density (per sq km)	Population of capital*
Dakar (capital) .	550	1,488,941	2,707.2	1,375,067
Diourbel . . .	4,359	619,245	142.1	76,548
Fatick . . .	7,935	509,702	64.2	18,416
Kaolack . . .	16,010	811,258	50.7	150,961
Kolda . . .	21,011	591,833	28.2	34,337
Louga . . .	29,188	490,077	16.8	52,057
Saint-Louis .	44,127	660,282	15.0	113,917
Tambacounda . .	59,602	385,982	6.5	41,885
Thiès . . .	6,601	941,151	142.6	175,465
Ziguinchor . .	7,339	398,337	54.3	124,283
Total . . .	**196,722**	**6,896,808**	**35.1**	

* Each region has the same name as its capital.

Mid-1999 (official estimates, rounded figures): Dakar 1,976,500; Thiès 256,100; Kaolack 227,900.

PRINCIPAL TOWNS
(estimated population at mid-1996)

Dakar (capital)* . .	1,770,068	Mbour	109,317
Thiès	228,017	Diourbel . . .	99,437
Kaolack . . .	199,023	Louga	59,745
Rufisque† . . .	185,142	Tambacounda . .	56,173
Ziguinchor . . .	180,555	Richard Toll . . .	53,105
Saint-Louis . .	132,425	Mbacké . . .	51,859

* Including Pikine and Guediaway.

† Including Bargny.

BIRTHS AND DEATHS
(UN estimates, annual averages)

	1985–90	1990–95	1995–2000
Birth rate (per 1,000) . . .	49.5	49.5	49.5
Death rate (per 1,000) . . .	17.7	14.8	13.0

Source: UN, *World Population Prospects: The 2000 Revision*.

Expectation of life (WHO estimates, years at birth): 55.8 (males 54.4; females 57.2) in 2001 (Source: WHO, *World Health Report*).

ECONOMICALLY ACTIVE POPULATION
('000 persons, ILO estimates, 1990)

	Males	Females	Total
Agriculture, hunting, forestry and fishing . . .	1,319	1,190	2,508
Industry	195	51	246
Manufacturing . . .	177	50	227
Services	370	145	516
Total	**1,884**	**1,386**	**3,269**

Source: ILO.

Mid-2001 (estimates in '000): Agriculture, etc. 3,151; Total labour force 4,294 (Source: FAO).

Unemployed (general survey, February–March 1999): 157,063 (males 99,892; females 57,171).

Health and Welfare

KEY INDICATORS

Total fertility rate (children per woman, 2001)	5.2
Under-5 mortality rate (per 1,000 live births, 2001) . . .	138
HIV/AIDS (% of persons aged 15–49, 2001)	0.50
Physicians (per 1,000 head, 1995)	0.08
Hospital beds (per 1,000 head, 1998)	0.4
Health expenditure (2000): US $ per head (PPP)	56
Health expenditure (2000): % of GDP	4.6
Health expenditure (2000): public (% of total)	56.6
Access to water (% of persons, 2000)	78
Access to sanitation (% of persons, 2000)	70
Human Development Index (2000): ranking	154
Human Development Index (2000): value	0.431

For sources and definitions, see explanatory note on p. vi.

Agriculture

PRINCIPAL CROPS
('000 metric tons)

	1999	2000	2001
Rice (paddy)	239.8	202.3	243.9
Maize	66.1	78.6	106.4
Millet	675.0	600.2	470.1
Sorghum	147.4	143.8	140.5
Cassava (Manioc)	104.0	132.9	137.9
Sugar cane*	889	850	850
Pulses*	68.3	47.6	47.6
Cashew nuts*	15.0	0.5	0.5
Groundnuts (in shell)	1,014.3	1,061.5	959.9
Oil palm fruit*	64	65	65
Cotton seed*	8.1	11.4	20.0
Tomatoes	17.7	15.5	13.2
Dry onions*	65*	50	50
Other vegetables*	51.4	50.9	50.9
Oranges*	28	31	31
Watermelons	283.2	110.5	127.3
Mangoes	75.2†	70.0*	70.0*
Other fruit*	27.5	28.0	28.0
Cotton (lint)	6.4†	8.9†	15.0*

* FAO estimate(s).
† Unofficial figure.

Source: FAO.

LIVESTOCK
('000 head, year ending September)

	1999	2000	2001
Cattle	2,927	3,073	3,227*
Sheep	4,497	4,542	4,818*
Goats	3,833	3,879	3,995
Pigs	240	269	280*
Horses	446	471	492*
Asses	377	399	410†
Camels	4	4	4†
Poultry†	45,000	45,000	45,000

* Unofficial figure.
† FAO estimate(s).

Source: FAO.

LIVESTOCK PRODUCTS
(FAO estimates, '000 metric tons)

	1999	2000	2001
Beef and veal	47.6	49.9	52.5
Mutton and lamb	15.1	15.3	16.2
Goat meat	16.1	16.3	16.8
Pig meat	6.1	6.9	7.1
Horse meat	6.1	6.5	6.8
Poultry meat	64.1	64.1	64.1
Other meat	6.0	6.2	6.2
Cows' milk	105.0	110.6	116.2
Sheep's milk	14.8	15.6	16.6
Goats' milk	15.1	16.3	16.8
Poultry eggs	33	33	33
Cattle hides	9.5	10.0	10.5

Source: FAO.

Forestry

ROUNDWOOD REMOVALS
(FAO estimates, '000 cubic metres, excl. bark)

	1999	2000	2001
Sawlogs, veneer logs and logs for sleepers*	40	40	40
Other industrial wood	754	754	754
Fuel wood	5,083	5,114	5,145
Total	5,877	5,908	5,939

* Annual output assumed to be unchanged since 1986.

Source: FAO.

SAWNWOOD PRODUCTION
('000 cubic metres, incl. railway sleepers)

	1989	1990	1991
Total (all broadleaved)	15	22	23

1992–2001: Annual production as in 1991 (FAO estimates).

Source: FAO.

Fishing

('000 metric tons, live weight)

	1998	1999	2000
Capture	403.9	412.1	402.0
Freshwater fishes	22.3*	35.4*	24.1
Round sardinella	129.4	93.5	113.0
Madeiran sardinella	103.4	105.1	114.7
Bonga shad	16.5	29.5	22.0
Octopuses	5.5	37.3	6.1
Aquaculture	0.0*	0.2	0.2*
Total catch	403.9	412.2	402.2

* FAO estimate.

Source: FAO, *Yearbook of Fishery Statistics*.

Mining

('000 metric tons, estimates)

	1999	2000	2001
Calcium phosphates	1,646	1,845	1,708
Aluminium phosphates*	31	182	n.a.
Fuller's earth (attapulgite)*	136	131	n.a.
Salt (unrefined)	145	124	141

* Estimates from US Geological Survey.

Source: Banque centrale des états de l'Afrique de l'ouest.

Industry

PETROLEUM PRODUCTS
('000 metric tons, estimates)

	1996	1997	1998
Jet fuels	93	94	94
Motor gasoline (petrol)	120	120	120
Kerosene	18	20	20
Gas-diesel (distillate fuel) oils	296	298	299
Residual fuel oils	227	227	229
Lubricating oils	3	3	3
Liquefied petroleum gas	3	3	3

Refinery products (estimates, million barrels): 2.5 in 1996; 6 per year in 1997–2000 (Source: US Geological Survey).

Source: UN, *Industrial Commodity Statistics Yearbook*.

SELECTED OTHER PRODUCTS
('000 metric tons, unless otherwise indicated)

	1998	1999	2000
Sugar cubes	42.2	46.6	36.3
Tobacco products (tons)	1,816	1,846	2,195
Groundnut oil—crude	49.8	71.7	132.6
Vegetable oil—refined	103.4	81.4	76.2
Canned tuna	18.7	14.4	11.9
Footwear (million pairs)	0.7	0.6	0.6
Cotton yarn (tons)	1,107	814	635
Soap	38.6	40.9	43.3
Paints and varnishes	2.9	3.9	4.6
Cement	846.5	898.4	1,340.5
Metal cans (million)	149.9	105.0	127.4
Electricity (million kWh)	1,304.1	1,348.0	1,365.3

Nitrogenous fertilizers (nitrogen content, '000 metric tons, unofficial figures): 38.8 in 1998; 24.5 in 1999; 19.4 in 2000 (Source: FAO).

Phosphate fertilizers (phosphoric acid content, '000 metric tons, unofficial figures): 67.5 in 1998; 45.0 in 1999; 32.4 in 2000 (Source: FAO).

Source: IMF, *Senegal: Selected Issues* (October 2001).

Finance

CURRENCY AND EXCHANGE RATES

Monetary Units
100 centimes = 1 franc de la Communauté financière africaine (CFA)

Sterling, Dollar and Euro Equivalents (31 December 2002)
£1 sterling = 1,008.17 francs CFA
US $1 = 625.50 francs CFA
€1 = 655.96 francs CFA
10,000 francs CFA = £9.919 = $15.987 = €15.245

Average Exchange Rate (francs CFA per US $)
2000   711.98
2001   733.04
2002   696.99

Note: An exchange rate of 1 French franc = 50 francs CFA, established in 1948, remained in force until January 1994, when the CFA franc was devalued by 50%, with the exchange rate adjusted to 1 French franc = 100 francs CFA. This relationship to French currency remained in effect with the introduction of the euro on 1 January 1999. From that date, accordingly, a fixed exchange rate of €1 = 655.957 francs CFA has been in operation.

BUDGET
('000 million francs CFA)

Current revenue*	1999	2000	2001
Tax revenue	491.2	537.4	576.2
Taxes on income, profits and capital gains	107.5	130.1	131.3
Individual	55.3	63.1	63.3
Corporate	39.1	50.1	48.1
Domestic taxes on goods and services (excl. petroleum)	179.7	206.4	200.0
Taxes on international trade and transactions	185.1	180.9	219.8
Other current revenue	15.6	24.9	25.9
Total	506.8	562.3	602.1

Expenditure†	1999	2000	2001
Current expenditure	351.1	411.1	516.6
Goods and services	259.3	286.3	307.6
Wages and salaries	166.6	175.8	177.3
Interest payments	42.5	45.3	30.3
Subsidies and other current transfers	49.3	79.5	178.7
Transfers to other levels of national Government	35.9	66.0	64.5
Capital expenditure	234.5	216.1	217.2
Total	596.8	641.2	737.6

* Excluding grants received ('000 million francs (CFA): 61.6 in 1999; 49.9 in 2000; 61.7 in 2001.

† Excluding net lending ('000 million francs (CFA): 5.3 in 1999; 6.9 in 2000; −4.6 in 2001.

Source: IMF, *Government Finance Statistics Yearbook*.

INTERNATIONAL RESERVES
(excluding gold, US $ million at 31 December)

	2000	2001	2002
IMF special drawing rights	0.9	7.5	9.1
Reserve position in IMF	1.8	1.8	2.0
Foreign exchange	381.2	438.0	626.3
Total	383.9	447.3	637.4

Source: IMF, *International Financial Statistics*.

MONEY SUPPLY
(million francs CFA at 31 December)

	1999	2000	2001
Currency outside banks	179,358	171,545	211,684
Demand deposits at deposit money banks	255,883	287,715	315,317
Checking deposits at post office	3,914	4,069	4,662
Total money (incl. others)	439,757	464,046	532,973

Source: IMF, *International Financial Statistics*.

COST OF LIVING
(Consumer price index, Dakar; base: 1996 = 100)

	2000	2001	2002
Food, beverages and tobacco	103.4	108.5	113.9
Clothing	96.8	94.4	92.1
Housing, water, electricity and gas	110.1	113.1	114.7
All items (incl. others)	104.4	107.5	110.0

Source: Banque centrale des états de l'Afrique de l'ouest.

NATIONAL ACCOUNTS
('000 million francs CFA at current prices)

Expenditure on the Gross Domestic Product

	1998	1999	2000
Government final consumption expenditure	324.7	370.2	435.9
Private final consumption expenditure	2,073.3	2,172.5	2,271.0
Gross fixed capital formation	486.3	572.7	539.1
Total domestic expenditure	2,884.3	3,115.4	3,246.0
Exports of goods and services	821.9	888.6	924.5
Less Imports of goods and services	1,016.7	1,110.3	1,231.8
GDP in purchasers' values*	2,746.7	2,925.0	3,114.0
GDP at constant 1987 prices	1,871.1	1,964.6	2,073.8

* Including adjustment.

Source: UN, *National Accounts Statistics*.

Gross Domestic Product by Economic Activity

	1998	1999	2000
Agriculture, hunting, forestry and fishing	492.8	543.7	603.9
Mining and quarrying	28.8	31.8	33.1
Manufacturing	337.1	353.1	372.6
Electricity, gas and water	61.9	63.6	68.6
Construction	111.2	128.9	134.9
Trade, restaurants and hotels	754.2	789.1	800.2
Transport, storage and communications	305.1	330.3	369.1
Financial intermediation; real estate; renting and business activities	389.3	400.5	419.1
Public adminstration and defence; compulsory social security	212.0	225.5	241.1
Private households with employed persons	33.0	34.4	35.8
GDP in purchasers' values*	2,746.0	2,925.0	3,114.0

* Including adjustment.

Source: UN, *National Accounts Statistics*.

BALANCE OF PAYMENTS

('000 million francs CFA)

	1999	2000	2001
Exports of goods f.o.b.	632.4	654.9	708.3
Imports of goods f.o.b.	−845.3	−951.6	−995.0
Trade balance	−212.9	−296.7	−286.7
Services (net)	−8.7	−12.9	−11.1
Balance on goods and services	−221.6	−309.6	−297.8
Other income (net)	−73.4	−79.3	−64.6
Balance on goods, services and income	−295.0	−388.9	−362.4
Private unrequited transfers (net)	50.7	100.1	132.6
Public unrequited transfers (net)	47.2	52.2	46.7
Current balance	−197.1	−236.6	−183.1
Capital account (net)	60.7	59.4	80.5
Direct investment (net)	87.5	44.3	25.7
Portfolio investment (net)	−10.2	9.8	−5.5
Other investment (net)	99.1	120.9	153.0
Net errors and omissions	4.8	−6.3	—
Overall balance	44.8	−8.5	70.6

Source: Banque centrale des états de l'Afrique de l'ouest.

External Trade

PRINCIPAL COMMODITIES

(distribution by SITC, US $ million)

Imports c.i.f.	1998	1999	2000
Food and live animals	366.1	361.4	289.7
Cereals and cereal preparations	226.5	225.3	170.1
Rice, semi-milled or wholly milled	146.4	158.9	109.4
Rice, broken	145.2	158.1	108.8
Crude materials (inedible) except fuels	53.3	51.3	41.7
Mineral fuels, lubricants, etc.	132.7	163.4	350.2
Petroleum, petroleum products, etc.	132.4	153.4	338.0
Crude petroleum oils, etc.	102.0	112.1	292.6
Animal and vegetable oils, fats and waxes	86.2	76.6	44.9
Fixed vegetable oils and fats	72.9	64.7	39.0
Fixed vegetable oils, 'soft', crude, refined or purified	68.2	61.0	32.0
Soya bean oil	65.1	55.6	28.7
Chemicals and related products	185.8	188.8	160.5
Medicinal and pharmaceutical products	51.1	59.6	44.4
Medicaments (incl. veterinary)	45.0	48.3	39.5
Basic manufactures	275.7	247.0	215.3
Iron and steel	110.2	57.3	52.3
Machinery and transport equipment	375.3	414.9	353.3
Power generating machinery and equipment	30.3	49.5	39.6
Machinery specialized for particular industries	47.4	43.7	42.2
General industrial machinery, equipment and parts	60.8	93.9	79.2
Electrical machinery, apparatus, etc.	42.1	50.7	50.3
Road vehicles and parts (excl. tyres, engines and electrical parts)	113.2	105.5	93.5
Passenger motor cars (excl. buses)	48.2	51.7	47.9
Miscellaneous manufactured articles	75.7	80.0	70.1
Total (incl. others)	1,573.9	1,604.4	1,552.8

Exports f.o.b.	1998	1999	2000
Food and live animals	27.0	27.7	290.6
Fish, crustaceans and molluscs, and preparations thereof	1.3	0.7	262.5
Fish, fresh, chilled or frozen	0.2	0.1	96.1
Fish, fresh or chilled, excl. fillets	0.1	0.1	32.1
Fish, frozen, excl. fillets	—	—	29.6
Fish fillets, frozen	0.1	—	28.4
Crustaceans and molluscs, fresh, chilled, frozen, salted, etc.	0.3	—	139.0
Vegetables and fruit	8.1	15.0	5.6
Crude materials (inedible) except fuels	73.1	61.3	45.7
Textile fibres (excl. wool tops) and wastes	23.4	7.8	6.9
Cotton	22.2	6.2	6.1
Raw cotton (excl. linters)	22.2	1.3	0.3
Crude fertilizers and crude minerals	38.4	43.1	28.5
Natural calcium phosphates, etc.	30.5	35.1	16.5
Minerals fuels, lubricants, etc.	93.3	81.0	97.2
Petroleum, petroleum products, etc.	92.5	80.2	96.4
Refined petroleum products	91.9	78.7	79.3
Kerosene (incl. kerosene-type jet fuel)	0.0	25.2	0.0
Gas oils (distillate fuels)	0.0	36.6	0.0
Animal and vegetable oils, fats and waxes	45.1	24.7	68.3
Fixed vegetable oils and fats	44.3	23.5	68.1
Fixed vegetable oils, 'soft', crude, refined or purified	43.2	22.2	67.8
Groundnut (peanut) oil	42.9	21.5	67.0
Chemicals and related products	210.0	169.4	119.7
Inorganic chemicals	109.5	88.2	67.2
Phosphorus pentoxide and phosphoric acids	108.5	87.4	66.7
Oils and perfume materials; toilet and cleansing preparations	16.0	21.6	16.8
Manufactured fertilizers	52.0	34.8	14.5
Basic manufactures	27.4	30.5	30.6
Machinery and transport equipment	23.5	51.2	23.9
Road vehicles	8.0	15.2	4.4
Aircraft and associated equipment and parts	0.9	24.2	2.0
Helicopters	—	17.4	0.3
Total (incl. others)	517.4	471.3	693.0

Source: UN, *International Trade Statistics Yearbook*.

2001 ('000 million francs CFA): Total imports c.i.f. 1,129.8; Total exports f.o.b. 731.5 (Source: IMF, *International Financial Statistics*).

PRINCIPAL TRADING PARTNERS

(US $ million)*

Imports c.i.f.	1998	1999	2000
Argentina	16.8	12.5	6.5
Belgium	59.6†	48.1	44.3
Brazil	16.3	15.0	13.5
Canada	15.9	20.5	21.7
China, People's Republic	28.7	42.5	41.5
Côte d'Ivoire	39.6	50.0	40.7
France (incl. Monaco)	537.7	484.0	425.2
Germany	67.5	68.8	54.8
India	49.4	56.3	24.9
Ireland	16.5	17.1	23.3
Italy	56.2	95.3	48.4
Japan	51.3	53.8	39.9
Netherlands	42.3	40.4	46.7
Nigeria	92.0	113.2	293.4
Portugal	10.0	8.2	n.a.
Russia	32.0	24.8	22.3
Spain	56.8	64.3	52.5
Thailand	83.6	83.8	82.7
United Kingdom	31.5	33.0	30.8
USA	86.3	65.2	56.5
Viet Nam	12.6	35.5	30.6
Total (incl. others)	1,573.9	1,604.4	1,552.8

Exports f.o.b.	1998	1999	2000
Belgium	n.a.	3.3	7.7
Benin	15.0	19.9	7.0
Cameroon	6.5	6.1	9.2
Chad	6.0	1.6	n.a.
China, People's Republic . . .	—	0.1	12.7
Côte d'Ivoire	19.4	19.1	14.9
France (incl. Monaco)	56.7	69.9	127.6
Gambia	16.0	19.0	33.1
Germany	2.6	2.0	10.6
Greece	—	—	17.3
Guinea	11.8	9.3	11.0
Guinea-Bissau	8.3	10.8	11.7
India	142.9	131.6	84.9
Italy	14.9	11.0	76.5
Japan	0.7	0.5	8.6
Mali	42.5	42.7	42.7
Mauritania	21.3	24.5	17.7
Netherlands	10.6	3.0	17.0
Portugal	12.4	3.6	12.6
Spain	3.5	1.5	43.5
Togo	5.2	5.4	6.9
United Kingdom	2.5	4.8	8.4
Total (incl. others)	517.4	471.3	693.0

* Imports by country of production; exports by country of last consignment.
† Including trade with Luxembourg.

Source: UN, *International Trade Statistics Yearbook*.

Transport

RAILWAYS
(traffic)

	1997	1998	1999
Passengers ('000)	5,065	4,029	4,789
Freight carried ('000 metric tons)	2,088	1,992	2,017
Passenger-km (million)	78.3	63.4	n.a.
Freight ton-km (million) . . .	446.4	435.2	n.a.

ROAD TRAFFIC
(motor vehicles in use)

	1997	1998	1999
Passenger cars	76,971	85,805	98,260
Buses and coaches	9,236	9,974	10,477
Lorries and vans	21,693	23,851	25,276
Road tractors	2,110	2,278	2,458
Motorcycles and mopeds . . .	3,624	4,155	4,515

Source: IRF, *World Road Statistics*.

SHIPPING

Merchant Fleet
(vessels registered at 31 December)

	1999	2000	2001
Number of vessels	194	200	188
Total displacement ('000 grt) . .	47.6	50.0	48.0

Source: Lloyd's Register-Fairplay, *World Fleet Statistics*.

International Sea-borne Freight Traffic
('000 metric tons)

	1997	1998	1999
Goods loaded	4,062.5	4,544.9	4,951.0
Goods unloaded	2,064.1	1,854.0	2,242.0

Source: Port Autonome de Dakar.

CIVIL AVIATION
(traffic on scheduled services)*

	1997	1998	1999
Kilometres flown (million) . . .	4	3	3
Passengers carried ('000) . . .	166	121	103
Passenger-km (million)	265	267	241
Total ton-km (million)	40	39	37

* Including an apportionment of the traffic of Air Afrique.

Source: UN, *Statistical Yearbook*.

Tourism

	1998	1999	2000
Tourist arrivals ('000)	392.5	420.0	442.7
Tourism receipts ('000 million CFA francs)	100.1	101.4	96.8

Source: IMF, *Senegal: Selected Issues* (October 2001).

Communications Media

	1999	2000	2001
Television receivers ('000 in use)	375	380	n.a.
Telephones ('000 main lines in use)	165.9	208.6	237.2
Mobile cellular telephones ('000 subscribers)	87.9	250.3	390.8
Personal computers ('000 in use) .	140	160	180
Internet users ('000)	30	40	100

Radio receivers: ('000 in use) 1,240 in 1997.

Daily newspapers: 1 (average circulation 45,000 copies) in 1996.

Non-daily newspapers: 6 (average circulation 37,000 copies) in 1995.

Source: mainly International Telecommunication Union; UNESCO, *Statistical Yearbook*.

Education

(1999/2000)

	Institutions	Teachers	Males	Females	Total
			Students		
Pre-primary . . .	356	1,357	12,458	12,934	25,392
Primary	4,751	23,198	598,191	509,251	1,107,712
Middle	455	6,883	112,230	73,908	186,138
Secondary:					
general	111	3,187	36,586	22,397	58,983
technical	12	384	2,795	1,630	4,425

Source: Ministère de l'Education, Dakar.

Tertiary: 29,303 students in 1998/99 (Source: UNESCO Institute for Statistics).

Adult literacy rate (UNESCO estimates): 37.3% (males 47.3%; females 27.6%) in 2000 (Source: UN Development Programme, *Human Development Report*).

Directory

The Constitution

The Constitution of the Republic of Senegal was promulgated following its approval by popular referendum on 7 January 2001, and entered into force thereafter, with the exception of those sections relating to the Assemblée nationale and the relations between the executive and legislative powers (articles 59–87), which took effect following legislative elections on 29 April 2001. The main provisions are summarized below:

PREAMBLE

The people of Senegal, recognizing their common destiny, and aware of the need to consolidate the fundaments of the Nation and the State, and supporting the ideals of African unity and human rights, proclaim the principle of national territorial integrity and a national unity respecting the diverse cultures of the Nation, reject all forms of injustice, inequality and discrimination, and proclaim the will of Senegal to be a modern democratic State.

THE STATE AND SOVEREIGNTY

Articles 1–6: Senegal is a secular, democratic Republic, in which all people are equal before the law, without distinction of origin, race, sex or religion. The official language of the Republic is French; the national languages are Diola, Malinké, Pular, Sérère, Soninké, Wolof and any other national language that may be so defined. The principle of the Republic is 'government of the people, by the people and for the people'. National sovereignty belongs to the people who exercise it, through their representatives or in referenda. Suffrage may be direct or indirect, and is always universal, equal and secret. Political parties and coalitions of political parties are obliged to observe the Constitution and the principles of national sovereignty and democracy, and are forbidden from identifying with one race, one ethnic group, one sex, one religion, one sect, one language or one region. All acts of racial, ethnic or religious discrimination, including regionalist propaganda liable to undermine the security or territorial integrity of the State are punishable by law. The institutions of the Republic are the President of the Republic, the Assemblée nationale, the Government and the Constitutional Council, the Council of State, the Final Court of Appeal (Cour de Cassation), the Revenue Court (Cour de Comptes), and Courts and Tribunals.

PUBLIC LIBERTIES AND THE HUMAN PERSON; ECONOMIC AND SOCIAL RIGHTS AND COLLECTIVE RIGHTS

Articles 7–25: The inviolable and inalienable rights of man are recognized as the base of all human communities, of peace and justice in the world, and are protected by the State. All humans are equal before the law. The Republic protects, within the rule of law, the right to free opinion, free expression, a free press, freedom of association and of movement, cultural, religious and philosophical freedoms, the right to organize trade unions and businesses, the right to education and literacy, the right to own property, to work, to health, to a clean environment, and to diverse sources of information. No prior authorization is required for the formation of an organ of the press. Men and women are guaranteed equal rights to possess property.

Marriage and the family constitute the natural and moral base of the human community, and are protected by the State. The State is obliged to protect the physical and moral health of the family, in particular of the elderly and the handicapped, and guarantees to alleviate the conditions of life of women, particularly in rural areas. Forced marriages are forbidden as a violation of individual liberty. The State protects youth from exploitation, from drugs, and from delinquency.

All children in the Republic have the right to receive schooling, from public schools, or from institutions of religious or non-religious communities. All national educational institutions, public or private, are obliged to participate in the growth of literacy in one of the national languages. Private schools may be opened with the authorization of, and under the control of, the State.

Freedom of conscience is guaranteed. Religious communities and institutions are separate from the State.

All discrimination against workers on grounds of origins, sex, political opinions or beliefs are forbidden. All workers have the right to join or form trade or professional associations. The right to strike is recognized, under legal conditions, as long as the freedom to work is not impeded, and the enterprise is not placed in peril. The State guarantees sanitary and human conditions in places of work.

THE PRESIDENT OF THE REPUBLIC

Articles 26–52: The President of the Republic is elected, for a term of five years, by universal direct suffrage. The mandate may be renewed once. Candidates for the presidency must be of solely Senegalese nationality, enjoy full civil and political rights, be aged 35 years or more on the day of elections, and must be able to write, read and speak the official language fluently. All candidates must be presented by a political party or a legally-constituted coalition of political parties, or be accompanied by a petition signed by at least 10,000 electors, including at least 500 electors in each of six administrative regions. Candidates may not campaign predominately on ethnic or regional grounds. Each political party or coalition of political parties may present only one candidate. If no candidate receives an absolute majority of votes cast in the first round, representing the support of at least one-quarter of the electorate, a second round of elections is held between the two highest-placed candidates in the first round. In the case of incapacity, death or resignation, the President's position is assumed by the President of the Assemblée nationale, and in the case of his or her incapacity, by one of the Vice-Presidents of the Assemblée nationale, in all cases subject to the same terms of eligibility that apply to the President. The President presides over the Council of Ministers, the Higher Council of National Defence, and the National Security Council, and is the Supreme Chief of the Armed Forces. The President appoints a Prime Minister, and appoints ministers on the recommendation of the Prime Minister.

THE GOVERNMENT

Articles 53–57: The head of the Government is the Prime Minister. In the event of the resignation or removal from office of a Prime Minister, the entire Government is obliged to resign.

THE OPPOSITION

Article 58: The Constitution guarantees the right to oppose to political parties that are opposed to Government policy, and recognizes the existence of a parliamentary opposition.

THE ASSEMBLÉE NATIONALE

Article 59–66: Deputies of the Assemblée nationale are elected by universal direct suffrage, for a five-year mandate, subject only to the dissolution of the Assemblée nationale. Any serving deputy who resigns from his or her party shall have his or her mandate removed. Deputies enjoy immunity from criminal proceedings, except with the authorization of the bureau of the Assemblée nationale. The Assemblée nationale votes on the budget. Deputies vote as individuals and must not be obligated to vote in a certain way. Except in exceptional and limited circumstances, sessions of the Assemblée nationale are public.

RELATIONS BETWEEN THE EXECUTIVE AND LEGISLATIVE POWERS

Articles 67–87: The Assemblée nationale is the sole holder of legislative power, votes on the budget and authorizes a declaration of war. The President of the Republic may, having received the opinion of the Prime Minister and the President of the Assemblée nationale, pronounce by decree the dissolution of the Assemblée nationale, except during the first two years of any Assemblée.

INTERNATIONAL TREATIES

Articles: 88–91: The President of the Republic negotiates international engagements, and ratifies or approves them with the authorization of the Assemblée nationale. The Republic of Senegal may conclude agreements with any African State that would comprise a partial or total abandonment of national sovereignty in order to achieve African unity.

JUDICIAL POWER

Articles 92–98: The judiciary is independent of the legislature and the executive power. The judiciary consists of the Constitutional Council, the Council of State, the Court of Final Appeal, the Revenue Court and Courts and Tribunals. The Constitutional Council comprises five members, including a President, a Vice-President and three judges. Each member serves for a mandate of six years (which may not be renewed) with partial renewals occurring every two years. The President of the Republic appoints members of the Constitutional Council, whose decisions are irreversible.

President and Legislature

PRESIDENT

Presidential Election, First Ballot, 27 February 2000

Candidate	Votes	% of votes
Abdou Diouf (PS)	690,886	41.33
Abdoulaye Wade (PDS)	517,642	30.97
Moustapha Niasse (AFP)	280,085	16.76
Djibo Kâ (URD)	118,487	7.09
Iba Der Thiam (CDP)	20,133	1.20
Ousseynou Fall (Parti républicain sénégalais)	18,676	1.12
Others	25,534	1.53
Total	**1,671,443**	**100.00**

Second Ballot, 19 March 2000

Candidate	Votes	% of votes
Abdoulaye Wade (PDS)	969,332	58.49
Abdou Diouf (PS)	687,969	41.51
Total	**1,657,301**	**100.00**

ASSEMBLÉE NATIONALE

Assemblée nationale: BP 86, Dakar; tel. 823-10-99; fax 823-94-02; e-mail assnat@gouv.sn.

President: PAPE DIOP.

General Election, 29 April 2001

Party	Votes	% of votes	Seats
Sopi Coalition*	931,144	49.59	89†
Alliance des forces de progrès (AFP)	303,012	16.14	11‡
Parti socialiste du Sénégal (PS)	325,979	17.36	10
Union pour le renouveau démocratique (URD)	68,956	3.67	3§
And Jëf—Parti africain pour la démocratie et le socialisme (AJ—PADS)	76,083	4.05	2
Parti libéral sénégalais (PLS)	17,232	0.92	1
Parti pour le progrès et la citoyenneté (PPC)	17,119	0.91	1
Alliance pour le progrès et la justice—Jëf-Jël (APJ—JJ)	15,041	0.80	1
Rassemblement national démocratique (RND)	13,279	0.71	1
Parti de l'indépendance et du travail (PIT)	10,854	0.58	1
Others	99,137	5.28	—
Total	**1,877,836**	**100.00**	**120**

* A coalition of some 40 parties and movements, led by the PDS.
† Including 62 seats won by majority voting within departments.
‡ Including two seats won by majority voting within departments.
§ Including one seat won by majority voting within departments.

Political Organizations

In mid-2001 there were 64 political parties registered in Senegal. The following parties were among the most prominent at the time of the 2001 legislative elections

Alliance des forces de progrès (AFP): rue 1, angle rue A, point E, BP 5825, Dakar; tel. 825-40-21; fax 825-77-70; e-mail admin@afp-senegal.org; internet www.afp-senegal.org; f. 1999; mem. of opposition Cadre permanent de concertation (f. 2001); Sec.-Gen. MOUSTAPHA NIASSE.

Alliance pour le progrès et la justice—Jëf-Jël (APJ—JJ): Quartier Ablaye Niakheit, BP 581, Thiès; tel. 825-44-09; mem. of opposition Cadre permanent de concertation (f. 2001); Pres. TALLA SYLLA.

And Jëf—Parti africain pour la démocratie et le socialisme (AJ—PADS): BP 12025, Dakar; tel. 822-54-63; e-mail ajsavmar@telecomplus.sn; internet www.ajpads.org; f. 1992; Sec.-Gen. LANDING SAVANÉ.

Bloc des centristes Gaïndé (BCG): Villa no 734, Sicap Baobabs, Dakar; tel. 825-37-64; e-mail jpdias@sentoo.sn; f. 1996; Pres. and First Sec. JEAN PAUL DIAS.

Convention des démocrates et des patriotes—Garap Gui (CDP): 96 rue 7, Bopp, Dakar; f. 1992; Sec.-Gen. Prof. IBA DER THIAM.

Front pour le socialisme et la démocratie—Benno Jubël (FSD—BJ): Villa no 3G, Résidence Front de Terre, BP 17614, Dakar; tel. and fax 827-97-53; e-mail cheikhdieye@sentoo.sn; f. 1996; Sec.-Gen. CHEIKH ABDOULAYE DIÈYE BAMBA.

Ligue démocratique–Mouvement pour le parti du travail (LD—MPT): BP 10172, Dakar Liberté; tel. 825-67-06; fax 827-43-00; regd 1981; social-democrat; Sec.-Gen. ABDOULAYE BATHILY.

Mouvement pour la démocratie et le socialisme—Naxx Jarinu (MDS—NJ): Unité 20, Parcelles Assainies, Villa no 528, Dakar; tel. 869-50-49; f. 2000; Leader OUMAR KHASSIMOU DAI.

Mouvement de la réforme pour le développement social (MRDS): HLM 4, Villa no 858, Dakar; tel. 644-31-70; f. 2000; Pres. IBRAHIMA DIENG; Sec.-Gen. Imam BABACAR NIANG.

Mouvement pour le socialisme et l'unité (MSU): Dakar; tel. 825-85-44; f. 1981 as Mouvement démocratique populaire; mem. of opposition Cadre permanent de concertation (f. 2001); Sec.-Gen. BAMBA N'DIAYE.

Mouvement républicain sénégalais (MRS): BP 4193, Dakar; tel. 822-03-19; fax 822-07-00; Leader and Sec.-Gen. DEMBA BA.

Parti africain de l'indépendance (PAI): BP 820, Maison du Peuple Guediewaye, Dakar; tel. 837-01-36; f. 1957; reorg. 1976; Marxist; Sec.-Gen. MAJMOUT DIOP.

Parti démocratique sénégalais (PDS): ave Gen. de Gaulle, Dakar; tel. 825-61-77; fax 824-47-00; e-mail boromnaas@aol.com; internet www.sopionline.com; f. 1974; liberal democratic; Sec.-Gen. Me ABDOULAYE WADE; Dep. Sec.-Gen. IDRISSA SECK.

Parti de l'indépendance et du travail (PIT): BP 2678, Dakar Fann; e-mail contact@pit-senegal.com; internet www.pit-senegal .com; regd 1981; Marxist-Leninist; mem. of opposition Cadre permanent de concertation (f. 2001); Sec.-Gen. AMATH DANSOKHO.

Parti libéral sénégalais (PLS): 13 ave Malick Sy, Dakar; tel. and fax 823-51-60; f. 1998 by breakaway faction of PDS; Leader Me OUSMANE NGOM.

Parti populaire sénégalais (PPS): Dakar; regd 1981; populist; mem. of opposition Cadre permanent de concertation (f. 2001); Sec.-Gen. Dr OUMAR WANE.

Parti pour le progrès et la citoyenneté (PPC): Quartier Merina, Rufique; tel. 836-18-68; absorbed Rassemblement pour le progrès, la justice et le socialisme in 2000; Sec.-Gen. Me MBAYE JACQUES DIOP.

Parti pour la renaissance africaine—Sénégal (PARENA): Sicap Dieuppeul, Villa no 2685/B, Dakar; f. 2000; Sec.-Gen. MARIAM MAMADOU WANE LY.

Parti de la renaissance et de la citoyenneté: Liberté 6, Villa no 7909, Dakar; tel. 827-85-68; f. 2000; supports Pres. Wade; Sec.-Gen. SAMBA DIOULDÉ THIAM.

Parti socialiste du Sénégal (PS): Maison du Parti, Colobane, BP 12010, Dakar; tel. 824-06-73; fax 825-50-54; e-mail ps@telecomplus .sn; internet www.telecomplus.sn/ps; f. 1958 as Union progressiste sénégalaise, reorg. 1978; democratic socialist; mem. of opposition Cadre permanent de concertation (f. 2001); Chair. (vacant); Exec. Sec. OUSMANE TANOR DIENG.

Rassemblement des ecologistes du Sénégal—Les verts (RES): BP 3308, Dakar RP; tel. 821-18-05; Sec.-Gen. OUSMANE SOW HUCHARD.

Rassemblement national démocratique (RND): Sacré-Coeur III, Villa no 972, Dakar; tel. 827-50-72; e-mail wourydiouf@hotmail .com; f. 1976; legalized 1981; mem. of opposition Cadre permanent de concertation (f. 2001); Sec.-Gen. MADIOR DIOUF.

Rassemblement des travailleurs africains—Sénégal (RTA): Villa no 999, HLM Grand, Yoff, Dakar; tel. 827-16-79; Co-ordinator El Hadj MOMAR SAMB.

Union pour le renouveau démocratique (URD): Bopp Villa no 234, rue 7, Dakar; tel. 824-54-54; fax 820-73-17; f. 1998 by break-away faction of PS; mem. of opposition Cadre permanent de concertation (f. 2001); Sec.-Gen. DJIBO LEITY KÂ.

In August 2001 some 25 pro-Government parties, which were formerly members of the Sopi (Change) Coalition that contested the legislative elections in April 2001, formed an electoral alliance, the **Convergence des actions autour du Président en perspective du 21ième siècle (CAP-21),** to contest municipal and local elections in May 2002. In May 2001 several opposition parties (numbering 16 in January 2002 and led by the AFP) formed an opposition consultative framework, the **Cadre permanent de concertation (CPC),** which was also to operate an an electoral alliance in the municipal and local elections.

The **Mouvement des forces démocratiques de la Casamance (MFDC)** was founded in 1947; it has paramilitary and political wings and seeks the independence of the Casamance region of southern Senegal. The MFDC is not officially recognized as a political party (the Constitution of 2001 forbids the formation of parties on a geographic basis) and has waged a campaign of guerrilla warfare in the region since the early 1980s. None the less, representatives of the MFDC have participated in extensive negotiations with the Senegalese Government on the restoration of peace and the granting of greater autonomy to Casamance; its Honorary President and former leader is Fr AUGUSTIN DIAMACOUNÉ SENGHOR, while its Secretary-General (in an acting capacity) is SIDI BADJI.

Diplomatic Representation

EMBASSIES IN SENEGAL

Algeria: 5 rue Mermoz, Plateau, Dakar; tel. 822-35-09; fax 821-16-84; Ambassador Dr BOUALEM BOUGUETAIA.

Austria: 18 rue Emile Zola, Dakar; tel. 849-40-00; fax 849-43-70; e-mail ambaut@sentoo.sn; Ambassador GERHARD WEINBERGER.

Belgium: route de la Corniche-Est, BP 524, Dakar; tel. 821-25-24; fax 821-63-45; e-mail dakar@diplobel.org; Ambassador PHILIPPE DE CLERK.

Brazil: Immeuble Fondation Fahd, 4e étage, blvd Djily Mbaye, angle rue Macodou Ndiaye, BP 136, Dakar; tel. 823-14-92; fax 823-71-81; e-mail embdakar@sentoo.sn; Ambassador RICARDO CARVAHLO DO NASCIMENTO BORGES.

Burkina Faso: Immeuble Résidence Excellence, 4 ave Léopold Sédar Senghor, BP 11601, Dakar; tel. 822-77-10; fax 822-77-11; e-mail ambabf@sentoo.sn; Ambassador SALAMATA SAWADOGO.

Cameroon: 157–9 rue Joseph Gomis, BP 4165, Dakar; tel. 849-02-92; fax 823-33-96; Ambassador EMMANUEL MBONJO-EJANGUE.

Canada: 45–47 blvd de la République, BP 3373, Dakar; tel. 823-92-90; fax 823-87-49; e-mail dakar-td@dfait-maeci.gc.ca; internet www.dfait-maeci.gc.ca/dakar; Ambassador DENIS THIBAULT.

Cape Verde: 3 blvd El-Hadji Djilly M'Baye, BP 11269, Dakar; tel. 821-18-73; fax 821-06-97; e-mail ambcvsen@sentoo.sn; Ambassador RAÚL JORGE VERA CRUZ BARBOSA.

China (Taiwan): 30 ave Nelson Mandela, BP 4164, Dakar; tel. 821-98-19; fax 821-98-21; Ambassador HUANG YUN-CHEH.

Congo, Democratic Republic: Fenêtre Mermoz, Dakar; tel. 825-12-80; Chargé d'affaires FATAKI NICOLAS LUNGUELE MUSAMBYA.

Congo, Republic: Statut Mermoz, BP 5243, Dakar; tel. 824-83-98; fax 824-89-60; Chargé d'affaires a.i. JOSEPH NGOUBELI.

Côte d'Ivoire: ave Birago Diop, BP 359, Dakar; tel. 869-02-70; fax 825-21-15; e-mail cmrci@ambaci-dakar.org; internet www.ambaci-dakar.org; Ambassador FATIMATA TANOE TOURÉ.

Cuba: 43 rue Aimé Césaire, BP 4510, Dakar-Fann; tel. 864-10-32; fax 864-10-63; Ambassador LUIS CASTILLO CAMPOS.

Czech Republic: rue Aimé Césaire, Fann Résidence, BP 3253, Dakar; tel. 825-77-82; fax 824-14-06; e-mail dakar@embassy.mzv.cz; internet www.mzv.cz/dakar; Chargé d'affaires JAN PROKOPEC.

Egypt: 45 blvd de la République, BP 474, Dakar; tel. 821-24-75; fax 821-89-93; e-mail ambegydk@telecomplus.sn; Ambassador ALAA EL-DIN ELLEISSY.

Ethiopia: 18 blvd de la République, BP 379, Dakar; tel. 821-98-96; fax 821-98-95; e-mail ethembas@telecomplus.sn; Chargé d'affaires a.i. BEKELE GEMU HECHAMO.

France: 1 rue Amadou Assane Ndoye, BP 4035, Dakar; tel. 839-51-00; fax 839-51-81; Ambassador JEAN DE GLINIASTY.

Gabon: 12 ave Albert Sarraut, BP 436, Dakar; tel. 865-28-34; fax 864-31-45; Ambassador PATRICE TONDA.

Gambia: 11 rue de Thiong, BP 3248, Dakar; tel. 821-44-16; fax 821-62-79; Ambassador BAI OUSMANE SECKA.

Germany: 6 ave Pasteur, BP 2100, Dakar; tel. 823-48-84; fax 822-52-99; internet www.ambassade-allemagne.sn; Ambassador Dr REINALD STECK.

Guinea: rue 7, angle B&D, point E, BP 7123, Dakar; tel. 824-86-06; fax 82-55-94; Chargé d'affaires AMIR SAMPIL.

Guinea-Bissau: rue 6, angle B, point E, BP 2319, Dakar; tel. 823-00-59; fax 825-29-46; Ambassador LANSANA TOURÉ.

Holy See: rue Aimé Césaire, angle Corniche-Ouest, Fann Résidence, BP 5076, Dakar; tel. 824-26-74; fax 824-19-31; e-mail vatemb@sentoo.sn; Apostolic Nuncio Most Rev. GIUSEPPE PINTO (Titular Archbishop of Anglona).

India: 5 rue Carde, BP 398, Dakar; tel. 822-58-75; fax 822-35-85; Ambassador BALKRISHNA SHETTY.

Indonesia: 126 ave Cheikh Anta Diop, BP 5859, Dakar; tel. 825-73-16; fax 825-58-96; Ambassador YAHYA RIDWAN.

Iran: 17 ave des Ambassadeurs, BP 735, Dakar; tel. 825-25-28; fax 824-23-14; Ambassador SEYED MOUHAMED HOSSEINI.

Israel: ave Roume, Immeuble SDIH, BP 2096, Dakar; tel. 823-79-65; fax 823-64-90; e-mail amisrael@sentoo.sn; Ambassador SHLOMO MORGAN.

Italy: rue El Hadj Seydou Nourou Tall, BP 348, Dakar; tel. 822-05-78; fax 821-75-80; e-mail ambitsen@sentoo.sn; internet www.ambitaliadakar.sn; Ambassador ALAIN GIORGIO MARIA ECONOMIDES.

Japan: blvd Martin Luther King, Corniche-Ouest, BP 3140, Dakar; tel. 823-85-03; fax 849-55-55; Ambassador AKIHIKO FURUYA.

Korea, Republic: rue Amadou Assande Ndoye, BP 3338, Dakar; tel. 822-58-22; fax 822-32-99; Ambassador CHO IL-HWAN.

Kuwait: blvd Martin Luther King, Dakar; tel. 824-17-23; fax 825-58-99; Ambassador ABDUL HAMID ALY.

Lebanon: 56 ave Jean XXIII, BP 234, Dakar; tel. 822-09-20; fax 823-58-99; e-mail ambaliban@sentoo.sn; Ambassador MICHEL HADDAD.

Libya: route de Ouakam, Dakar; tel. 824-57-10; fax 824-57-22; Ambassador AL HADY SALEM HAMMAD.

Madagascar: rue 2, angle Ellipse, Point E, Daka r; tel. and fax 825-26-66; Ambassador RATSIFANDRIHAMANANA LILA HANITRA.

Malaysia: 7 (VDN) Fann Mermoz, BP 15057, Dakar; tel. 825-89-35; fax 825-47-19; e-mail mwdakar@telecomplus.sn; Ambassador Dato' IDRISS BIN ZAINUDDIN.

Mali: Fann Résidence, Corniche-Ouest, rue 23, BP 478, Dakar; tel. 824-62-52; fax 825-94-71; e-mail ambamali@sentoo.sn; Ambassador FATOUMATA DIALL.

Mauritania: 37 blvd Charles de Gaulle, Dakar; tel. 823-53-44; fax 823-53-11; Ambassador MOHAMED ABDERRAHMAN OULD MOINE.

Morocco: 73 ave André Peytavin, BP 3871, Dakar; tel. 823-96-45; fax 821-20-56; e-mail toua@sentoo.sn; Ambassador ABDELLAH TOUARSA.

Netherlands: 37 rue Kléber, BP 3262, Dakar; tel. 849-03-580; fax 821-70-84; e-mail dak@minbuza.nl; internet www.nlambassadedakar.org; Ambassador ADRIANNUS H. F. VAN AGGELEN.

Nigeria: 8 ave Cheikh Anta Diop, BP 3129, Dakar; tel. 824-43-97; fax 825-81-36; Ambassador SULÉ BUBA.

Pakistan: Stèle Mermoz, Villa no 7602, BP 2635, Dakar; tel. 824-61-35; fax 824-61-36; e-mail parepdkr@telecomplus.sn; Ambassador (vacant).

Poland: Fann Résidence, angle Corniche-Ouest, BP 343, Dakar; tel. 824-23-54; fax 824-95-26; Ambassador TOMASZ NIEGOSZISZ.

Portugal: 6 ave des Ambassadeurs, BP 281, Dakar; tel. 823-58-22; fax 864-03-22; e-mail amb.portugal.dakar@telecomplus.sn; Ambassador JOÃO LUÍS NIZA PINHEIRO.

Qatar: 52 blvd Martin Luther King, Dakar; tel. 864-38-08; fax 869-10-12; Ambassador YOUSSEF BIN KHALIFI AL-SAADA.

Romania: blvd de l'Est, Point E, BP 3171, Dakar; tel. and fax 825-20-68; e-mail romania@arc.sn; Ambassador (vacant).

Russia: ave Jean Jaurès, angle rue Carnot, BP 3180, Dakar; tel. 822-48-21; fax 821-13-72; e-mail ambrus@telecomplus.sn; Ambassador ALEKSANDR ROMANOV.

Saudi Arabia: Route Corniche-Ouest, face Olympique Club,BP 3109, Dakar; tel. 864-01-41; fax 864-01-30; e-mail snemb@mofa.gov.sa; Ambassador AHMED BIN MOHAMED BAYARI.

South Africa: Memoz SUD, Lotissement Ecole de Police, BP 21010, Dakar-Ponty; tel. 865-19-59; fax 864-23-59; e-mail ambafsud@sentoo.sn; Ambassador O. RANTOBENG WILLIAM MOKOU.

Spain: 18–20 ave Nelson Mandela, BP 2091, Dakar; tel. 821-11-78; fax 821-68-45; e-mail ambespsn@mail.mae.es; Ambassador JACOBO GONZÁLES ARNAO CAMPOS.

Sudan: 31 route de la Pyrotechnie, Mermoz, Dakar; tel. 824-98-53; fax 824-98-52; e-mail sudembse@sentoo.sn; Ambassador BÉCHIR ABDALLAH ABUSSITA.

Sweden: 18 rue Emile Zola, BP 6087, Dakar; tel. 849-03-33; fax 849-03-40; e-mail ambassaden.dakar@foreign.ministry.se; Ambassador BO LENNHARD WILÉN.

Switzerland: rue René N'Diaye, BP 1772, Dakar; tel. 823-05-90; fax 822-36-57; e-mail swiemdkr@metissacana.sn; Ambassador INGRID APELBAUM-PIDOUX.

Syria: rue 1, point E, angle blvd de l'Est, BP 498, Dakar; tel. 824-62-77; fax 825-17-55; Chargé d'affaires NADIM JABAR.

Thailand: 10 rue Léon Gontran Damas, BP 3721, Dakar; tel. 824-30-76; fax 824-84-58; e-mail thaidkr@telcomplus.sn; Ambassador POJ INDUWONGSE.

Tunisia: rue El Hadj Seydou Nourou Tall, BP 3127, Dakar; tel. 823-47-47; fax 823-72-04; Ambassador ISMAËL LEJRI.

Turkey: Villa 'La Corne d'Or', ave des Ambassadeurs, Fann Résidence, BP 6060, Etoile, Dakar; tel. 824-58-11; fax 825-69-77; Ambassador YALÇIN KAYA ENENSOY.

United Kingdom: 20 rue du Dr Guillet, BP 6025, Dakar; tel. 823-73-92; fax 823-27-66; e-mail britemb@telecomplus.sn; Ambassador E. ALAN BURNER.

USA: ave Jean XXIII, angle rue Kleber, BP 49, Dakar; tel. 823-42-96; fax 823-51-63; e-mail thpdakar@pd.state.gov; internet usembassy.state.gov/dakar; Ambassador RICHARD ALLAN ROTH.

Judicial System

In 1992 the Supreme Court was replaced by three judicial bodies. The Constitutional Council verifies that legislation and international agreements are in accordance with the Constitution. It decides disputes between the Executive and the Legislature, and determines the relative jurisdictions of the Council of State and the Court of Cassation. The Council of State judges complaints brought against the Executive. It also resolves electoral disputes. The Court of Cassation is the highest court of appeal, and regulates the activities of subordinate courts and tribunals. The Revenue Court supervises the public accounts.

Constitutional Council: Fann Résidence, Ex-Musée Dynamique, Dakar; tel. 822-52-52; 5 mems; Pres. YOUSSOU NDIAYE.

Council of State: rue Béranger, Ferraut, Dakar; tel. 822-47-86; Pres. ABDOU AZIZ BA.

Court of Cassation: Fann Résidence, Ex-Musée Dynamique, Dakar; tel. 822-37-53; internet www.gouv.sn/institutions/cour_cassation.html; Procurator-Gen. ANDRÉSIA VAZ; Sec.-Gen. MOUSTAPHA TOURÉ.

Revenue Court: 15 ave Franklin Roosevelt, BP 9097, Peytavin, Dakar; tel. 849-40-01; fax 849-43-62; internet www.courdescomptes.sn; Pres. ABDOU BAME GUEYE; Sec.-Gen. El Hadj MALICK KONTE.

Religion

At the time of the 1988 census almost 94% of the population were Muslims, while some 4% professed Christianity (the dominant faith being Roman Catholicism); a small number, mostly in the south, followed traditional beliefs.

ISLAM

There are four main Islamic brotherhoods active in Senegal: the Tidjanes, the Mourides, the Layennes and the Qadiriyas.

Association pour la coopération islamique (ACIS): Dakar; f. 1988; Pres. Dr THIERNAO KÁ.

Grande Mosquée de Dakar: Dakar; tel. 822-56-48; Grand Imam El Hadj BAYE DAME DIÈNE.

CHRISTIANITY

The Roman Catholic Church

Senegal comprises one archdiocese and six dioceses. At 31 December 2000 there were an estimated 482,946 adherents of the Roman Catholic Church, representing about 5.0% of the total population.

Bishops' Conference

Conférence des Evêques du Sénégal, de la Mauritanie, du Cap-Vert et de Guinée-Bissau, BP 941, Dakar; tel. 836-33-09; fax 836-16-17; e-mail archevchedkr@sentoo.sn.

f. 1973; Pres. Most Rev. THÉODORE-ADRIEN SARR (Archbishop of Dakar).

Archbishop of Dakar: Most Rev. THÉODORE-ADRIEN SARR, Archevêché, ave Jean XXIII, BP 1908, Dakar; tel. 823-69-18.

The Anglican Communion

The Anglican diocese of The Gambia, part of the Church of the Province of West Africa, includes Senegal and Cape Verde. The Bishop is resident in Banjul, The Gambia.

Protestant Church

Eglise Protestante du Senegal: 65 rue Wagane Diouf, BP 22390, Dakar; tel. 821-55-64; fax 821-71-32; f. 1862; Pastor ETITI YOMO DJERIWO.

BAHÁ'Í FAITH

National Spiritual Assembly: BP 1662, Dakar; tel. 824-23-59; e-mail asl_Dakar@yahoo.fr; regd 1975.

The Press

DAILY NEWSPAPERS

L'Actuel: route du Front de Terre, angle ave Bourguiba, Immeuble Dramé, BP 11874, Dakar; tel. 864-26-01; fax 864-26-02; e-mail lactuel@sentoo.sn.

Dakar Soir: BP 21548, Dakar-Ponty; tel. and fax 832-10-93; e-mail dakar-soir@telecomplus.sn; f. 2000.

Dekeu Bi: quartier Casier, Thiès; tel. 557-29-15.

L'Evénement du Soir: Fann Résidence, rue A, angle rue 4, point E, BP 16060, Dakar; tel. 864-34-30; fax 864-36-00; evenings.

Frasques Quotidiennes: 51 rue du Docteur Thèze, BP 879, Dakar; tel. 842-42-26; fax 842-42-77; e-mail frasques@arc.sm.

L'Info 7: Sicap rue 10, BP 11357, Dakar; tel. and fax 864-26-58; e-mail comsept@sentoo.sn; f. 1999.

Le Matin: route de l'Aéroport Léopold Sédar Senghor, BP 6472, Dakar; tel. 825-73-59; fax 825-73-58; e-mail lematin@metissacana.sn; daily; independent; Dir MAME LESS CAMARA; Editor-in-Chief ALIOUNE FALL.

La Pointe: Dakar; tel. 820-50-35; fax 820-50-43.

Le Populaire: 114 ave Peytavin, Immeuble Serigne Massamba Mbacké, Dakar; tel. 822-79-77; fax 822-79-27; e-mail populaire@sentoo.sn; f. 2000; Editor-in-Chief MAMADOU THIERNO TALLA.

Scoop: route du Service Géographique, BP 92, Dakar; tel. 859-59-59; fax 859-60-50.

Le Soleil: Société sénégalaise de presse et de publications, route du Service géographique, Hann, BP 92, Dakar; tel. 859-59-59; fax 859-60-50; e-mail lesoleil@lesoleil.sn; internet www.lesoleil.sn; f. 1970; Man. Dir El Hadj KASSÉ; Editor IBRAHIMA GAYE; circ. 45,000.

Sud Quotidien: Immeuble Fahd, BP 4130, Dakar; tel. 821-33-38; fax 822-52-90; e-mail info@sudonline.sn; internet www.sudonline.sn; independent; Dir ABDOULAYE NDIAGA SYLLA; circ. 30,000.

Tract: 13 rue de Thann, BP 3683, Dakar; tel. and fax 823-47-25; e-mail tract.sn@laposte.net; f. 2000.

Le Volcan: Dakar; tel. 820-50-35; fax 820-50-43.

Wal Fadjri/L'Aurore (The Dawn): Sicap Sacré-Coeur no 8542, BP 576, Dakar; tel. 824-23-43; fax 824-23-46; e-mail walf@walf.sn; internet www.walf.sn; f. 1984; Islamic; Exec. Dir MBAYE SIDY MBAYE; circ. 15,000.

PERIODICALS

Afrique Médicale: 10 rue Abdou Karim Bourgi, BP 1826, Dakar; tel. 823-48-80; fax 822-56-30; f. 1960; 11 a year; review of tropical medicine; Editor P. CORREA; circ. 7,000.

Afrique Nouvelle: 9 rue Paul Holle, BP 283, Dakar; tel. 822-51-22; f. 1947; weekly; development issues; Roman Catholic; Dir RENÉ ODOUN; circ. 15,000.

Afrique Tribune: BP 10340, Dakar; tel. and fax 821-15-92; monthly.

Amina: BP 2120, Dakar; e-mail amina@calva.net; monthly; women's magazine.

Le Cafard Libéré: 10 rue Tolbiac, angle Autoroute, BP 7292, Dakar; tel. 822-84-43; fax 822-08-91; e-mail caflibere@sentoo.sn; f. 1987; weekly; satirical; Editor PAPE SAMBA KANE; circ. 12,000.

Construire l'Afrique: Dakar; tel. 823-07-90; fax 824-19-61; f. 1985; six a year; African business; Dir and Chief Editor CHEIKH OUSMANE DIALLO.

Le Courrier du Sud: BP 190, Ziguinchor; tel. 991-11-66; weekly.

Démocratie: Liberté V, 5375 M, 71 rue du rond-point Liberté V et VI; tel. 824-86-69; fax 825-18-79.

Eco Hebdo: 22 x 19 rue Médina, BP 11451, Dakar; tel. and fax 837-14-14; weekly.

L'Equipe Sénégal: Dakar; tel. 824-00-13; e-mail lequipesenegal@yahoo.fr; weekly; sports.

Ethiopiques: BP 2035, Dakar; tel. and fax 821-53-55; f. 1974; literary and philosophical review; publ. by Fondation Léopold Sédar Senghor.

Le Journal de l'Economie: 15 rue Jules Ferry, BP 2851, Dakar; tel. 823-87-33; fax 823-60-07; weekly.

Journal Officiel de la République du Sénégal: Rufisque; f. 1856; weekly; govt journal.

Momsareew: BP 820, Dakar; f. 1958; monthly; publ. by PAI; Editor-in-Chief MALAMINE BADJI; circ. 2,000.

Nord Ouest: Immeuble Lonase, BP 459, Louga; tel. 680-79-43; e-mail lenordouest@yahoo.fr; regional monthly; Dir MOMAR CISSÉ.

Nouvel Horizon: Dakar; tel. and fax 822-74-14; weekly.

Nuit et Jour: Rocade Fann Bel-Air, Immeuble Seynabou Cissé, Dakar; tel. 832-15-70; weekly.

Le Politicien: 8123 Terminus Liberté VI, BP 11018, Dakar; tel. and fax 827-63-96; f. 1977; weekly; satirical.

Promotion: BP 1676, Dakar; tel. 825-69-69; fax 825-69-50; e-mail giepromo@telecomplus.sn; f. 1972; fortnightly; Dir BOUBACAR DIOP; circ. 5,000.

République: BP 21740, Dakar; tel. 822-73-73; fax 822-50-39; e-mail republike@yahoo.fr; f. 1994.

Sénégal d'Aujourd'hui: 58 blvd de la République, BP 4027, Dakar; monthly; publ. by Ministry of Culture; circ. 5,000.

Sopi (Change): 5 blvd Dial Diop, Dakar; tel. 824-49-50; fax 824-47-00; f. 1988; weekly; publ. by PDS; Dir of Publishing JOSEPH NDONG; Editor CHEIKH KOUREYSSI BA.

Le Témoin: Gibraltar II, Villa no 310, Dakar; tel. 822-32-69; fax 821-78-38; f. 1990; weekly; Editor-in-Chief MAMADOU OUMAR NDIAYE; circ. 5,000.

Unir Cinéma: 1 rue Neuville, BP 160, Saint Louis; tel. 861-10-27; fax 861-24-08; f. 1973; quarterly African cinema review; Editor PIERRE SAGNA.

Vive La République: Sicap Amitié III, Villa no 4057, Dakar; tel. 864-06-31; weekly.

Xareli (Struggle): BP 12136, Dakar; tel. 822-54-63; fortnightly; publ. by AJ—PADS; circ. 7,000.

NEWS AGENCIES

Agence Panafricaine d'Information—PANA-Presse SA: BP 4056, Dakar; tel. 824-13-95; fax 824-13-90; e-mail panapress@panapress.com; internet www.panapress.com; f. 1979; as Pan-African News Agency, restructured as majority privately-owned (75%) co in 1997; operates under AU auspices providing news service to 130 countries; Co-ordinator-Gen. BABACAR FALL.

Agence de Presse Sénégalaise: 58 blvd de la République, BP 117, Dakar; tel. 823-16-67; fax 822-07-67; e-mail aps@primature.sn; internet www.aps.sn; f. 1959; govt-controlled; Dir AMADOU DIENG.

Foreign Bureaux

Agence France-Presse (AFP): Immeuble Maginot, 7e étage, BP 363, Dakar; tel. 823-21-92; fax 822-16-07.

Xinhua (New China) News Agency (People's Republic of China): Villa no 1, 2 route de la Pyrotechnie, Stele Mernoz, BP 426, Dakar; tel. 823-05-38.

ANSA (Italy), ITAR—TASS (Russia) and UPI (USA) are also represented in Dakar.

PRESS ORGANIZATION

Syndicat des Professionnels de l'Information et de la Communication du Sénégal (SYNPICS): BP 21722, Dakar; tel. 822-36-25; fax 822-17-61.

Publishers

Africa Editions: BP 1826, Dakar; tel. 823-48-80; fax 822-56-30; f. 1958; general, reference; Man. Dir JOËL DECUPPER.

Agence de Distribution de Presse: km 2.5, blvd du Centenaire de la Commune de Dakar, BP 374, Dakar; tel. 832-02-78; fax 832-49-15; e-mail adpresse@telecomplus.sn; f. 1943; general, reference; Man. Dir PHILIPPE SCHORP.

Centre Africain d'Animation et d'Echanges Culturels Editions Khoudia: BP 5332, Dakar-Fann; tel. 21-10-23; fax 21-51-09; f. 1989; fiction, education, anthropology; Dir AISSATOU DIA.

Editions Clairafrique: 2 rue El Hadji Mbaye Guèye, BP 2005, Dakar; tel. 822-21-69; fax 821-84-09; e-mail clairafrique@le-senegal .com; internet www.le-senegal.com/clairafrique; f. 1951; politics, law, sociology, anthropology, literature, economics, development, religion, school books.

Editions des Ecoles Nouvelles Africaines: ave Cheikh Anta Diop, angle rue Pyrotechnie, Stèle Mermoz, BP 581, Dakar; tel. 864-

05-44; fax 864-13-52; e-mail eenas@sentoo.sn; youth and adult education, in French.

Editions Juridiques Africaines (EDJA): 18 rue Raffenel, BP 22420, Dakar-Ponty; tel. 821-66-89; fax 823-27-53; e-mail edja.ed@sentoo.sn; f. 1986; law; Dir SALIMATA NGOM DIOP.

Editions des Trois Fleuves: blvd de l'Est, angle Cheikh Anta Diop, BP 123, Dakar; tel. 825-79-23; fax 825-59-37; f. 1972; general non-fiction; luxury edns; Dir GÉRARD RAZIMOWSKY; Gen. Man. BERTRAND DE BOISTEL.

Enda—Tiers Monde Editions (Environmental Development Action in the Third World): 54 rue Carnot, BP 3370, Dakar; tel. 822-98-90; fax 823-51-57; e-mail editions@enda.sn; internet www.enda .sn; f. 1972; third-world environment and development; Dir GIDEON PRISLER OMOLU; Exec. Sec. JACQUES BUGNICOURT.

Goorgoorlou: BP 21636, Dakar-Ponty; tel. 834-92-52; e-mail goorgoorlou@yahoo.fr; internet www.goorgoorlou.com; f. 1991; illustrated satire; Dir T. T. FONS.

Grande imprimerie africaine (GIA): 9 rue Amadou Assane Ndoye, Dakar; tel. 822-14-08; fax 822-39-27; f. 1917; law, administration; Man. Dir CHEIKH ALIMA TOURÉ.

Institut fondamental d'Afrique noire (IFAN)—Cheikh Anta Diop: BP 206, Campus universitaire, Dakar; tel. 825-98-90; fax 824-49-18; e-mail bifan@telecomplus.sn; internet www.refer.sn/sngal_ct/rec/ifan/accueil.htm; f. 1936; scientific and humanistic studies of black Africa, for specialist and general public.

Nouvelles éditions africaines du Sénégal (NEAS): 10 rue Amadou Assane Ndoye, BP 260, Dakar; tel. 822-15-80; fax 822-36-04; e-mail neas@telecomplus.sn; f. 1972; literary fiction, school-books; Dir-Gen. FRANÇOIS BOIROT.

Per Ankh: BP 2, Popenguine; history.

Société africaine d'édition: 16 bis rue de Thiong, BP 1877, Dakar; tel. 821-79-77; f. 1961; African politics and economics; Man. Dir PIERRE BIARNES.

Société d'édition 'Afrique Nouvelle': 9 rue Paul Holle, BP 283, Dakar; tel. 822-38-25; f. 1947; information, statistics and analyses of African affairs; Man. Dir ATHANASE NDONG.

Société nationale de Presse, d'édition et de publicité (SONA-PRESS): Dakar; f. 1972; Pres. OBEYE DIOP.

Sud-Communication: BP 4100, Dakar; operated by a journalists' co-operative; periodicals.

Xamal, SA: BP 380, Saint-Louis; tel. 961-17-22; fax 961-15-19; e-mail xamal@sentoo.sn; general literature, social sciences, in national languages and in French; Dir ABOUBAKAR DIOP.

Government Publishing House

Société sénégalaise de presse et de publications (SSPP): route du Service géographique, BP 92, Dakar; tel. 832-46-92; fax 832-03-81; f. 1970; 62% govt-owned; Pres. and Man. Dir ALIOUNE DRAME.

Broadcasting and Communications

Excaf Telecom: Domaine Industriel SODIDA, rue 14 Prolongée, BP 1656, Dakar; tel. 824-24-24; fax 824-21-91.

Sentel Sénégal GSM: ave Nelson Mandela angle ave Moussé Diop. BP 146, Dakar; tel. 675-42-02; fax 823-18-73; mobile cellular telephone operator in Dakar, most western regions, and in selected localities nation-wide; 75% owned by Millicom International Cellular (Luxembourg), 25% by Senegalese private investors; Gen. Man. YOUVAL ROSH.

Société Nationale des Télécommunications du Sénégal (SONATEL): BP 69, Dakar; tel. 839-12-00; fax 839-12-12; e-mail webmaster@sonatel.sn; internet www.sonatel.sn; f. 1985; 42% owned by France Câbles et Radio; Pres. MICHEL HIRSCH; Man. Dir CHEIKH TIDIANE MBAYE; 2,000 employees (2000).

Alizé: 46 blvd de la République, BP 2352, Dakar; tel. 839-17-00; fax 839-17-54; e-mail webmaster@alize.sn; internet www.alize.sn; f. 1996 as Sonatel Mobiles.

Télécom Plus SARL: 20 rue Amadou Assane Ndoye, BP 21100, Dakar; tel. 839-97-00; fax 823-46-32; telecommunications products and services.

BROADCASTING

Regulatory Authority

Haut Conseil de l'Audiovisuel: Immeuble Fahd, Dakar; tel. and fax 823-47-84; f. 1991; Pres. AMINATA CISSÉ NIANG.

Radio

Radiodiffusion-Télévision Sénégalaise (RTS): Triangle sud, angle ave El Hadj Malick Sy, BP 1765, Dakar; tel. 849-12-12; fax 822-34-90; e-mail rts@primature.sn; internet www.rts.sn; f. 1992; state broadcasting co; broadcasts two national and eight regional stations; Man. Dir (vacant).

Radio Sénégal International: Triangle sud, angle ave El Hadj Malick Sy, BP 1765, Dakar; tel. 849-12-12; fax 822-34-90; f. 2001; broadcasts news and information programmes in French, English, Arabic, Portuguese, Spanish, Italian, Soninké, Pulaar and Wolof from 14 transmitters across Senegal and on cable; Dir CHÉRIF THIAM.

RST1: Triangle sud, angle ave El Hadj Malick Sy, BP 1765, Dakar; tel. 849-12-12; fax 822-34-90; f. 1992; broadcasts in French, Arabic and six vernacular languages from 16 transmitters across Senegal; Dir MANSOUR SOW.

JDP FM (Jeunesse, Développement, Paix): BP 17040, Dakar; tel. 827-20-97; fax 824-07-41; e-mail sarrabdou@sentoo.sn.

Radio Nostalgie Dakar: BP 21021, Dakar; tel. 821-21-21; fax 822-22-22; e-mail nostafric@globeaccess.net; internet www.metissacana .sn/nostalgie; f. 1995; music; broadcasts in French and Wolof; Gen. Man. SAUL SAVÎOTE.

Oxy-Jeunes: Fojes BP 18303, Pikine, Dakar; tel. 834-49-19; fax 827-32-15; e-mail cheikh_seck@eudoramail.com; f. 1999; youth and community radio station supported by the World Assn of Community Radio Stations and the Catholic Organization for Development and Peace.

Radio PENC-MI: BP 51, Khombole; tel. 957-91-03; fax 824-58-98; e-mail rdoucoure@oxfam.org.uk.

Radio Rurale FM Awagna de Bignona: BP 72, Ziginchor; tel. 994-10-21; fax 991-22-20; e-mail sudinfo@telecomplus.sn.

Sud FM: Immeuble Fahd, 5e étage, BP 4130, Dakar; tel. 822-53-93; fax 822-52-90; e-mail info@sudonline.sn; internet www.sudonline .sn; f. 1994; operated by Sud-Communication; regional stations in Saint-Louis, Kaolack, Louga, Thiès, Ziguinchor and Diourbel; Man. Dir CHERIF EL-WAHIB SEYE.

Wal Fadjri FM: Sicap Sacré-Coeur no 8542, BP 576, Dakar; tel. 824-23-43; fax 824-23-46; e-mail walf@walf.sn; internet www.walf .sn; f. 1997; Islamic broadcaster; Exec. Dir MBAYE SIDY MBAYE.

Broadcasts by the Gabonese-based Africa No. 1, the British Broadcasting Corporation and Radio France International are received in Dakar.

Television

Radiodiffusion-Télévision Sénégálaise (RTS): see Radio; Dir of Television DAOUDA NDIAYE.

Canal Horizons Sénégal: 31 ave Albert Sarrault, BP 1390, Dakar; tel. 823-25-25; fax 823-30-30; e-mail canalh@sonatel.sn; internet www.canalhorizons.com; f. 1990; private encrypted channel; 18.8% owned by RTS and Société Nationale des Télécommunications du Sénégal, 15% by Canal Horizons (France); Man. Dir JACQUES BARBIER DE CROZES.

Réseau MMDS-EXCAF Télécom: rue 14 prolongée, HLM 1, Domaine Industriel SODIDA, BP 1656, Dakar; tel. 824-24-24; fax 824-21-91; broadcasts selection of African, US, European and Saudi Arabian channels.

The French television stations, France–2, France–5 and Arte France, are also broadcast to Senegal.

Finance

(cap. = capital; res = reserves; dep = deposits; m. = million; brs = branches; amounts in francs CFA)

BANKING

Central Bank

Banque Centrale des Etats de l'Afrique de l'Ouest (BCEAO): National HQ: blvd du Général de Gaulle, angle Triangle Sud, BP 3159, Dakar; tel. 823-53-84; fax 823-57-57; e-mail akangni@bceao .int; internet www.bceao.int; f. 1962; bank of issue for mem. states of the Union économique et monétaire ouest africaine (UEMOA, comprising Benin, Burkina Faso, Côte d'Ivoire, Guinea-Bissau, Mali, Niger, Senegal and Togo); cap. and res 850,500m., total assets 5,157,700m. (Dec. 2001); Gov. CHARLES KONAN BANNY; Dir in Senegal SEYNI NDIAYE; brs at Kaolack and Ziguinchor.

Commercial Banks

Bank of Africa Sénégal: 4 ave Léopold Sédar Senghor, Dakar; f. 2001; cap. 1,500m. (Jan. 2001); Pres. MAMADOU AMADOU AW; Dir-Gen. CHRISTIAN F. N. CONIL.

Banque Internationale pour le Commerce et l'Industrie du Sénégal (BICIS): 2 ave Léopold Sédar Senghor, BP 392, Dakar; tel. 839-03-90; fax 823-37-07; e-mail bicis@bicis.sn; internet www.bicis .sn; f. 1962; 28% owned by Société Financière pour les Pays d'Outre-Mer, 25% state-owned, 22% owned by BNP Paribas (France); cap. 5,000m., dep. 145,883m. (Dec. 2001); Pres. SERIGNE LAMINE DIOP; Dir-Gen. AMADOU KANE; 17 brs.

Compagnie Bancaire de l'Afrique Occidentale (CBAO): 2 place de l'Indépendance, BP 129, Dakar; tel. 839-96-96; fax 823-20-05; e-mail cbaonet@telecomplus.sn; f. 1853; 65% owned by Groupe Mimran; cap. 7,920m., res 2,575m., dep. 115,206m. (Dec. 2000); Pres. JEAN-CLAUDE MIMRAN; Dir-Gen. BERNARD DE LA VALLÉE; 8 brs.

Compagnie Ouest Africaine de Crédit Bail (LOCAFRIQUE): 11 rue Galandou Diouf, BP 292, Dakar; tel. 822-06-47; fax 822-08-94; e-mail cfoa.senegal@ns.arc.sn; cap and res 1,481m., total assets 1,780m. (Dec. 1999); Pres. ANDRÉ BOURUET-AUBERTOT; Dir-Gen. PATRICK BOLZER.

Crédit Lyonnais Sénégal (CLS): blvd El Hadji Djily Mbaye, angle rue Huart, BP 56, Dakar; tel. 849-00-00; fax 823-84-30; e-mail cl_senegal@creditlyonnais.fr; f. 1989; 95% owned by Crédit Lyonnais (France); 5% state-owned; cap. 2,000m., res 4,736m, dep. 89,477m. (Dec. 2001); Pres. and Chair. BERNARD NORMAND; 1 br.

Crédit National du Sénégal (CNS): 7 ave Léopold Sédar Senghor, BP 319, Dakar; tel. 823-34-86; fax 823-72-92; f. 1990 by merger; 87% state-owned; cap. 1,900m., total assets 2,032m. (Dec. 1996); Pres. ABDOU NDIAYE.

Ecobank Sénégal: 8 ave Léopold Sédar Senghor, BP 9095 CD, Dakar; tel. 849-20-00; fax 823-47-07; e-mail ecobank@sentoo.sn; internet www.ecobank.com; cap. and res 1,500m., total assets 26,654m. (Dec. 1999); Pres. MAHENTA BIRIMA FALL; Dir-Gen. EVELYNE TALL.

Société Générale de Banques au Sénégal SA (SGBS): 19 ave Léopold Sédar Senghor, BP 323, Dakar; tel. 839-55-00; fax 823-90-36; e-mail sgbs@sgbs.sn; internet www.sgbs.sn; f. 1962; 51% owned by Société Générale (France); 38% owned by private Senegalese investors; cap. 4,528m., res 9,374m., dep. 184,867m. (Dec. 2000); Pres. PAPA DEMBA DIALLO; Dir-Gen. BERNARD LABADENS; 14 brs.

Development Banks

Banque de l'Habitat du Sénégal (BHS): 69 blvd du Général de Gaulle, BP 229, Dakar; tel. 839-33-33; fax 823-80-43; e-mail bhsdaf@ sentoo.sn; internet www.earth2000.com/BHS; f. 1979; cap. 1,650m., res 4,757m., total assets 102,641m. (Dec. 2000); Pres. ISDY MOCTAR KOUNDOUL; Man. Dir ABDOUL KADER SOW; 1 br.

Banque Sénégalo-Tunisienne (BST): Immeuble Kebe, 97 ave Peytavin, BP 4111, Dakar; tel. 849-60-60; fax 823-82-38; e-mail bst@ bst.sn; internet www.bst.sn; f. 1986; 54.9% owned by Compagnie Africaine pour l'Investissement; cap. 2,100m., res 932m., dep. 43,050m. (Dec. 2001); Pres. and Chair. MAMADOU TOURÉ; Dir-Gen. ABDOUL MBAYE; 3 brs.

Caisse Nationale de Crédit Agricole du Sénégal (CNCAS): 45 ave Albert Sarrault, BP 3890, Dakar; tel. 839-36-36; fax 821-26-06; e-mail cncas@telecomplus.sn; f. 1984; 24% state-owned; cap. and res 11,017m. total assets 56,132m. (Dec. 1999); Pres. OUSMANE NOËL MBAYE; Dir-Gen. ARFANG BOUBACAR DAFFE; 4 brs.

Société Financière d'Equipement (SFE): 2e étage, Immeuble Sokhna Anta, rue Dr Thèze, BP 252, Dakar; tel. 823-66-26; fax 823-43-37; e-mail sfe@telecomplus.sn; 59% owned by Compagnie Bancaire de l'Afrique Occidentale; cap. and res 388m., total assets 6,653m. (Dec. 1999); Pres. ARISTIDE ORSET ALCANTARA; Dir-Gen. MOHAMED A. WILSON.

Islamic Bank

Banque Islamique du Senegal (BIS): Immeuble Faycal, angle rue Huad et rue Amadou Ndoye, BP 3381, Dakar; tel. 823-99-20; fax 822-49-48; e-mail bis@telecomplus.sn; internet www.senegal-online .com/bis; f. 1983; 44.5% owned by Dar al-Maal al-Islami (Switzerland), 33.3% by Islamic Development Bank (Saudi Arabia), 22.2% state-owned; cap. and res 1,360.2m., dep. 9,587.9m. (Dec. 2000); Pres. ABDERRAOUF BENESSAÏAH; Dir-Gen. JUNAID IQBAL.

Banking Association

Association Professionnelle des Banques et des Etablissements Financiers du Sénégal (APBEF): c/o CBAO, 2 place de l'Indépendance, BP 129, Dakar; tel. 823-10-00; Pres. AMADOU KANE.

STOCK EXCHANGE

Bourse Régionale des Valeurs Mobilières (BRVM): BP 22500, Dakar; tel. 821-15-18; fax 821-15-06; e-mail osane@brvm.org; internet www.brvm.org; f. 1998; national branch of BRVM (regional stock exchange based in Abidjan, Côte d'Ivoire, serving the member states of UEMOA); Man. OUSMANE SANE.

INSURANCE

Les Assurances Conseils Dakarois A. Gueye et cie: 20 rue Mohamed V, BP 2345, Dakar; tel. 822-69-97; fax 822-86-80.

Assurances Générales Sénégalaises (AGS): 43 ave Albert Sarraut, BP 225, Dakar; tel. 839-36-00; fax 823-37-01; e-mail ags@metissacana.sn; f. 1977; cap. 2,990m. Dir-Gen. IBRAHIM GUEYE.

AXA Assurances Sénégal: 5 place de l'Indépendance, BP 182, Dakar; tel. 849-10-10; fax 823-46-72; e-mail axasene@sentoo.sn; f. 1977; cap. 945m. (Dec. 1998); Pres. IBRAHIM NDIAYE.

Compagnie d'Assurances-Vie et de Capitalisation (La Nationale d'Assurances-Vie): 7 blvd de la République, BP 3853, Dakar; tel. 822-11-81; fax 821-28-20; f. 1982; cap. 80m. Pres. MOUSSA DIOUF; Man. Dir BASSIROU DIOP.

Compagnie Sénégalaise d'Assurances et de Réassurances (CSAR): 5 place de l'Indépendance, BP 182, Dakar; tel. 823-27-76; fax 823-46-72; f. 1972; cap. 945m. 49.8% state-owned; Pres. MOUSTAPHA CISSÉ; Man. Dir MAMADOU ABBAS BA.

V. Capillon Assurances: BP 425, Dakar; tel. 821-13-77; fax 822-24-35; f. 1951; cap. 10m. Pres. and Man. Dir GILLES DE MONTALEMBERT.

Gras Savoye Sénégal: 15 blvd de la République, BP 9, Dakar; tel. 823-01-00; fax 823-44-72; correspondent co of the Forbes Group; Dir MAURICE MOYAL.

Intercontinental Life Insurance Co (ILICO): BP 1359, Dakar; tel. 821-75-20; fax 822-04-49; f. 1993; life insurance; fmrly American Life Insurance Co; Pres. and Dir-Gen. MAGATTE DIOP.

Mutuelles Sénégalaises d'Assurance et de Transport (MSAT): 2 rue Malenfant, BP 370, Dakar; tel. 822-29-38; fax 823-42-47; f. 1981; all branches; Dir MOR ATJ.

La Nationale d'Assurances: 5 ave Albert Sarrault, BP 3328, Dakar; tel. 822-10-27; fax 821-28-20; f. 1976; fire, marine, travel and accident insurance; privately owned; Pres. AMSATA DIOUF; also **La Nationale d'Assurances–Vie;** life insurance.

La Sécurité Sénégalaise (ASS): BP 2623, Dakar; tel. 849-05-99; e-mail ass.dk@sentoo.sn; f. 1984; cap. 500m. (2002); Pres. MOUSSA SOW; Man. Dir MBACKE SENE.

Société Africaine d'Assurances: ave Léopold Sédar Senghor, angle Victor Hugo, BP 508, Dakar; tel. 823-64-75; fax 823-44-72; f. 1945; cap. 9m. Dir CLAUDE GERMAIN.

Société Nationale d'Assurances Mutuelles (SONAM): 6 ave Léopold Sédar Senghor, BP 210, Dakar; tel. 823-10-03; fax 820-70-25; f. 1973; cap. 1,464m. Pres. ABDOULAYE FOFANA; Man. Dir DIOULDÉ NIANE.

Société Nouvelle d'Assurances du Sénégal (SNAS): rue de Thann, BP 2610, Dakar; tel. 823-41-76; fax 823-10-78; e-mail snas@telecomplus.sn; Dir-Gen. FRANÇOIS BURGUIERRE.

Société Sénégalaise de Courtage et d'Assurances (SOSECODA): 16 ave Léopold Sédar Senghor, BP 9, Dakar; tel. 823-54-81; fax 821-54-62; f. 1963; cap. 10m. 55% owned by SONAM; Man. Dir A. AZIZ NDAW.

Société Sénégalaise de Réassurances SA (SENRE): 6 ave Léopold Sédar Senghor, angle Carnot, BP 386, Dakar; tel. 822-80-89; fax 821-56-52; cap. 600m.

Insurance Association

Syndicat Professionel des Agents Généraux d'Assurances du Sénégal: 43 ave Albert Sarraut, BP 1766, Dakar; Pres. URBAIN ALEXANDRE DIAGNE; Sec. JEAN-PIERRE CAIRO.

Trade and Industry

GOVERNMENT AGENCIES

Agence nationale pour la promotion des investissements et des grands travaux (APIX): BP 430, 52–54 rue Mohamed V, Dakar; tel. 823-94-75; fax 823-94-89; e-mail apix@sentoo.sn; internet www.apix.sn; promotes investment and major projects; f. 2000; Dir-Gen. AMINATA NIANE.

Société de Développement Agricole et Industriel (SODAGRI): BP 222, Dakar; tel. 821-04-26; fax 822-54-06; cap. 120m. francs CFA;

agricultural and industrial projects; Pres. and Dir-Gen. AMADOU TIDIANE WANE.

Société de Développement des Fibres Textiles (SODEFITEX): BP 3216, Dakar; tel. 832-47-80; fax 832-06-75; e-mail dg@sodefitex.sn; f. 1974; 77.5% state-owned, 20% owned by Dagris (France); responsible for planning and development of cotton industry; cap. 750m. francs CFA; Pres. YOUSSOU DAOU; Dir-Gen. AHMED BACHIR DIOP.

Société d'Exploitation des Ressources Animales du Sénégal (SERAS): BP 14, Dakar; tel. 832-31-78; fax 832-06-90; f. 1962; cap. 619.2m. francs CFA; 28% state-owned; livestock farming; Dir-Gen. SOW SADIO.

Société Nationale d'Aménagement et d'Exploitation des Terres du Delta du Fleuve Sénégal et des Vallées du Fleuve Sénégal et de la Falémé (SAED): route de Khor, BP 74, Saint-Louis; tel. 961-13-33; fax 961-14-63; e-mail saed@metissacana.sn; f. 1965; cap. 2,500m. francs CFA; 28% state-owned; controls the agricultural development of 30,000 ha around the Senegal river delta; Pres. and Man. Dir SIDY MOCTAR KEITA.

Société Nationale d'Etudes et de Promotion Industrielle (SONEPI): Domaine Industriel SODIDA, BP 100, Dakar; tel. 825-21-30; fax 824-654-65; f. 1969; cap. 150m. francs CFA; 28% state-owned; promotion of small- and medium-sized enterprises; Chair. and Man. Dir HADY MAMADOU LY.

Société Nouvelle des Etudes de Développement en Afrique (SONED–AFRIQUE): 22 rue Moussé Diop, BP 2084, Dakar; tel. 823-94-57; fax 823-42-31; e-mail sonedaf@telecomplus.sn; f. 1974; cap. 150m. francs CFA; Pres. ABDOU WAHAH TALLA; Man. Dir El Hadj AMADOU WONE.

DEVELOPMENT ORGANIZATIONS

Agence Française de Développement (AFD): 15 ave Mandela, BP 475, Dakar; tel. 823-11-88; fax 823-40-10; e-mail afddkn@telecomplus.sn; Dir in Senegal ALAIN CÉLESTE.

Association Française des Volontaires du Progrès (AFVP): BP 1010, route de la VDN, Sacré coeur 3, Villa no 9364, Dakar; tel. 827-40-75; fax 827-40-74; e-mail afvp@telecomplus.sn; internet www.afvp.org; f. 1972; Regional Delegate for Senegal, Cape Verde, Guinea, Guinea-Bissau, Mali and Mauritania JEAN-LOUP CAPDEVILLE; Nat. Delegate KARIM DOUMBIA.

Centre International du Commerce Extérieur du Sénégal: route de l'Aéroport, BP 8166, Dakar-Yoff, Dakar; tel. 827-54-66; fax 827-52-75; e-mail cices@metissacana.sn; Sec.-Gen. AMADOU SY.

Service de Coopération et d'Action Culturelle: BP 2014, Dakar; tel. 839-53-05; administers bilateral aid from France; fmrly Mission Française de Coopération et d'Action Culturelle; Dir XAVIN ROZE.

CHAMBERS OF COMMERCE

Chambre de Commerce, d'Industrie et d'Agriculture de la Région de Dakar: 1 place de l'Indépendance, BP 118, Dakar; tel. 823-71-89; fax 823-93-63; e-mail cciad@telecomplus.sn; internet www.tpsnet.org/cciad; f. 1888; Pres. MAMADOU LAMINE NIANG; Sec.-Gen. AMATH BENOÎT GAYE.

Chambre de Commerce, d'Industrie et d'Agriculture de la Région de Diourbel: BP 7, Diourbel; tel. 971-12-03; fax 971-38-49; e-mail ccdiour@cyg.sn; f. 1969; Pres. ALIOU DIOP; Sec.-Gen. MAMADOU NDIAYE.

Chambre de Commerce de la Région de Fatick: BP 66, Fatick; tel. 949-51-27; Sec.-Gen. SEYDOU NOUROU LY.

Chambre de Commerce et d'Industrie de la Région du Kaolack: BP 203, Kaolack; tel. 941-20-52; Pres. IDRISSA GUÈYE; Sec.-Gen. AROHA TRAORÉ.

Chambre de Commerce d'Industrie et d'Agriculture de la Région de Kolda: BP 23, Kolda; tel. 996-12-30; fax 996-10-68; Sec.-Gen. YAYA CAMARA.

Chambre de Commerce de la Région de Louga: BP 26, Louga; tel. 967-11-14; Pres. El Hadj AMADOU BAMBA SOURANG; Sec.-Gen. SOULEYMANE N'DIAYE.

Chambre de Commerce, d'Industrie et d'Agriculture de la Région de Saint-Louis: rue Bisson Nord, BP 19, Saint-Louis; tel. 961-10-88; f. 1879; Pres. El Hadj MOMAR SOURANG; Sec.-Gen. MASSAMBA DIOP.

Chambre de Commerce, d'Industrie et d'Agriculture de la Région de Tambacounda: BP 127, Tambacounda; tel. 981-10-14; fax 981-29-95; e-mail cham.comm.tamba@sentoo.sn; Pres. DJIBY CISSÉ; Sec.-Gen. TENGUELLA BA.

Chambre de Commerce, d'Industrie et d'Agriculture de la Région de Thiès: ave Lamine-Guèye, BP 3020, Thiès; tel. 951-10-02; f. 1883; 38 mems; Pres. El Hadj ALIOUNE PALLA M'BAYE; Sec.-Gen. ABDOUL KHADRE CAMARA.

Chambre de Commerce, d'Industrie et d'Artisanat de la Région de Ziguinchor: BP 26, Ziguinchor; tel. 991-13-10; f. 1908; Pres. YOUSSOUF SEYDI; Sec.-Gen. MAMADI DIATTA.

EMPLOYERS' ASSOCIATIONS

Chambre des Métiers de Dakar: route de la Corniche-Ouest, Soumbedioune, Dakar; tel. 821-79-08; Sec.-Gen. MBAYE GAYE.

Confédération Nationale des Employeurs du Sénégal: Dakar; tel. 821-76-62; fax 822-96-58; e-mail cnes@sentoo.sn; Pres. MANSOUR CAMA.

Conseil National du Patronat du Sénégal (CNP): 70 rue Jean Mermoz, BP 3537, Dakar; tel. 821-58-03; fax 822-28-42; e-mail cnp@sentoo.sn; Pres. YOUSSOUPHA WADE; Sec.-Gen. MABOUSSO THIAM.

Groupement Professionnel de l'Industrie du Pétrole du Sénégal (GPP): rue 6, km 4.5, blvd du Centenaire de la Commune de Dakar, BP 479, Dakar; tel. and fax 832-52-12; e-mail noeljp@sentoo.sn; Sec.-Gen. JEAN-PIERRE NOËL.

Organisation des Commerçants, Agriculteurs, Artisans et Industriels: Dakar; tel. 823-67-94.

Rassemblement des Opérateurs Economiques du Sénégal (ROES): Dakar; tel. 825-57-17; fax 825-57-13.

Syndicat des Commerçants Importateurs, Prestataires de Services et Exportateurs de la République du Sénégal (SCIMPEX): 2 rue Parent, angle ave Abdoulaye Fadiga, BP 806, Dakar; tel. and fax 821-36-62; e-mail scimpex@sentoo.sn; f. 1943; Pres. PAPE ALSASSANE DIENG.

Syndicat Patronal de l'Ouest Africain des Petites et Moyennes Entreprises et des Petites et Moyennes Industries: Dakar; tel. 821-35-10; fax 823-37-32; f. 1937; Pres. BABACAR SEYE; Sec.-Gen. MOCTAR NIANG.

Syndicat Professionnel des Entrepreneurs de Bâtiments et de Travaux Publics du Sénégal: ave Abdoulaye Fadiga, BP 593, Dakar; tel. 823-43-73; f. 1930; 130 mems; Pres. CHRISTIAN VIRMAUD.

Syndicat Professionnel des Industries du Sénégal (SPIDS): BP 593, Dakar; tel. 823-43-24; fax 822-08-84; e-mail spids@syfed.refer.sn; internet www.refer.sn/spids/spids1.htm; f. 1944; 110 mems; Pres. DONALD BARON; Sec.-Gen. PHILIPPE BARRY.

Union des Entreprises du Domaine Industriel de Dakar: Dakar; tel. 825-67-39.

Union Nationale des Chambres de Métiers: Domaine Industriel SODIDA, ave Bourguiba, BP 30040, Dakar; tel. 825-05-88; fax 824-54-32; f. 1981; Pres. El Hadj SEYNI SECK; Sec.-Gen. BABOUCAR DIOUF.

Union Nationale des Commerçants et Industriels du Sénégal (UNACOIS): BP 11542, 3 rue Valmy, Dakar; tel. 826-15-19.

UTILITIES

Electricity

Société Nationale d'Electricité (SENELEC): 28 rue Vincent, BP 93, Dakar; tel. 839-30-00; fax 823-82-46; e-mail senelec@senelec.sn; internet www.senelec.sn; f. 1983; state-owned; transfer to majority private ownership pending in 2003; Chair. ABDOU AZIZ NDAO; Man. Dir ABDOURAHMANE NDIR.

Gas

Société Sénégalaise des Gaz: BP 2062, Dakar; tel. 832-82-12; fax 823-59-74.

Water

Société Nationale des Eaux du Sénégal (SONES): Route de Front de Terre, BP 400, Dakar; tel. 839-78-00; fax 832-20-38; f. 1995; water works and supply; state-owned; Pres. LAMINE DIACK; Man. Dir BABACAR DIENG.

Sénégalaise des Eaux (SDE): BP 224, Dakar; tel. 839-37-37; fax 839-37-05; e-mail bdtt@sde.sn; f. 1996; water distribution services; Pres. ABDOULAYE BOUNA FALL; Dir-Gen. BERNARD DEBENEST.

TRADE UNIONS

Confédération Nationale des Travailleurs du Sénégal (CNTS): 7 ave du Président Laminé Gueye, BP 937, Dakar; tel. 821-04-91; fax 821-77-71; e-mail cnts@sentoo.sn; f. 1969; affiliated to PS; Sec.-Gen. MODY GUIRO.

Confédération Nationale des Travailleurs du Sénégal—Forces de Changement (CNTS—FC): Dakar; f. 2002 following split from CNTS; Sec.-Gen CHEIKH DIOP; 31 affiliated asscns.

Confédération des Syndicats Autonomes (CSA): Dakar; organization of independent trade unions; Sec.-Gen. IBA NDIAYE DIADJI.

Union Démocratique des Travailleurs du Sénégal (UDTS): BP 7124, Médina, Dakar; tel. 835-38-97; fax 854-10-70; 18 affiliated unions; Sec.-Gen. ALIOUNE SOW.

Union Nationale des Syndicats Autonomes du Sénégal (UNSAS): BP 10841, HLM, Dakar; fax 824-80-13; Sec.-Gen. MADEMBA SOCK.

Transport

RAILWAYS

There are 922 km of main line including 70 km of double track. One line runs from Dakar north to Saint-Louis (262 km), and the main line runs to Bamako (Mali). All the locomotives are diesel-driven. In late 1995 the Governments of Senegal and Mali agreed to establish a joint company to operate the Dakar–Bamako line. Tenders were invited from private interests to operate the company in early 2001.

Société Nationale des Chemins de Fer du Sénégal (SNCS): BP 175A, Thiès; tel. 951-10-13; fax 951-13-93; e-mail siamoncs@telecomplus.sn; f. 1905; state-owned; privatization pending; Pres. DRAME ALIA DIENE; Man. Dir DIOUF MBAYE.

ROADS

In 1996 there were 14,576 km of roads, of which 3,361 km were main roads and 1,194 km were secondary roads. Some 4,265 km of the network were paved. A 162.5 km road between Dialakoto and Kédougou, the construction of which (at a cost of some 23,000m. francs CFA) was largely financed by regional donor organizations, was inaugurated in March 1996. The road is to form part of an eventual transcontinental highway linking Cairo (Egypt) with the Atlantic coast, via N'Djamena (Chad), Bamako (Mali) and Dakar. In 1999 new highways were completed in the east of Senegal, linking Tambacounda, Kidira and Bakel.

Comité Executif des Transports Urbains de Dakar (CETUD): Résidence Fann, route du Front de Terre, Dakar; tel. 832-47-42; fax 832-47-44; e-mail cetud@telecomplus.sn; f. 1997; regulates the provision of urban transport in Dakar; Pres. OUSMANE THIAM.

Dakar-Bus: Dakar; f. 1999; operates public transport services within the city of Dakar; owned by RATP (France), Transdev (France), Eurafric-Equipment (Senegal), Mboup Travel (Senegal) and Senegal Tours (Senegal).

INLAND WATERWAYS

Senegal has three navigable rivers: the Senegal, navigable for three months of the year as far as Kayes (Mali), for six months as far as Kaédi (Mauritania) and all year as far as Rosso and Podor, and the Saloun and Casamance. Senegal is a member of the Organisation de mise en valeur du fleuve Gambie and of the Organisation pour la mise en valeur du fleuve Sénégal, both based in Dakar. These organizations aim to develop navigational facilities, irrigation and hydroelectric power in the basins of the Gambia and Senegal rivers respectively.

SHIPPING

The port of Dakar is the second largest in West Africa, after Abidjan (Côte d'Ivoire), and the largest deep sea port in the region, serving Senegal, Mauritania, The Gambia and Mali. It handled more than 7m. metric tons of international freight in 1999. The port's facilities include 40 berths, 10 km of quays, and also 53,000 sq m of warehousing and 65,000 sq m of open stocking areas. There is also a container terminal with facilities for vessels with a draught of up to 11 m. In September 1998 the World Bank agreed to finance improvements to the secondary regional ports of Senegal.

Compagnie Sénégalaise de Navigation Maritime (COSENAM): rue le Dantec, angle Huart, BP 683, Dakar; tel. 821-57-66; fax 821-08-95; f. 1979; 26.1% state-owned, 65.9% owned by private Senegalese interests, 8.0% by private French, German and Belgian interests; river and ocean freight transport; Pres. ABDOURAHIM AGNE; Man. Dir SIMON BOISSY.

Conseil Sénégalais des Chargeurs (COSEC): BP 1423, Dakar; tel. 849-07-07; fax 823-11-44; e-mail cosec@cyg.sn; Dir-Gen. SALIOU SARR.

Dakar-marine: Dakar; tel. 823-82-16; fax 823-83-99; e-mail dakarnav@sentoo.sn; internet www.dakarnave.sn; responsible for Senegalese shipyards; owned by Chantier Navals de Dakar, SA (Dakarnave), a subsidiary of Lisnave International, Portugal; Dir-Gen. CARLOS PIMPÃO.

Maersk Sénégal: route de Rufisque, BP 3836, Dakar; tel. 859-11-11; fax 832-13-31; e-mail dkrmkt@maersk.com; internet www.maersksealand.com/senegal; f. 1986.

SDV Sénégal: 47 ave Albert Sarrault, BP 233, Dakar; tel. 839-00-00; fax 839-00-69; e-mail sdvdir@sentoo.sn; f. 1936; fmrly Union Sénégalaise d'Industries Maritimes; shipping agents, warehousing; Pres. ANDRÉ GUILLABERT; Dir-Gen. BERNARD FRAUD.

Société pour le Développement de l'Infrastructure de Chantiers Maritimes du Port de Dakar (Dakar-Marine): Dakar; tel. 823-36-88; fax 823-83-99; f. 1981; privately-controlled; operates facilities for the repair and maintenance of supertankers and other large vessels; Man. YORO KANTE.

Société Maritime Casamançaise (SOMARCA): Dakar; tel. 821-52-19.

Société Nationale de Port Autonome de Dakar (PAD): BP 3195, Dakar; tel. 823-45-45; fax 823-36-06; e-mail pad@sonatel.senet.net; internet www.portdakar.sn; f. 1865; state-operated port authority; Dir-Gen. PATHÉ NDIAYE.

SOCOPAO-Sénégal: BP 233, Dakar; tel. 823-10-01; fax 823-56-14; f. 1926; warehousing, shipping agents, sea and air freight transport; Man. Dir GILLES CUCHE.

TransSene: 1 blvd de l'Arsenal, face à la gare ferroviaire, Dakar; tel. 821-81-81; e-mail transsen@telecomplus.sn; internet www.transsene.sn.

Yenco Shipping: Fondation Fahd, blvd Djily Mbaye, Dakar; tel. 821-27-26.

CIVIL AVIATION

The international airport is Dakar-Léopold Sédar Senghor. There are other major airports at Saint-Louis, Ziguinchor and Tambacounda, in addition to about 15 smaller airfields. Facilities at Ziguinchor and Cap-Skirring were upgraded during the mid-1990s, with the aim of improving direct access to the Casamance region. In 1998 the Islamic Development Bank agreed to fund a new international airport at Tobor, Casamance. In 2000 work began to extend the runway at Saint-Louis in order to accommodate larger aircraft. The construction of a new international airport, at Ndiass, to serve both Dakar and the proposed future capital city, Mékhé-Pékesse, commenced in 2003.

Direction de l'aviation civile (DAC): BP 8184, Dakar; fax 820-39-67; civil aviation authority; Dir ABABACAR DIOP.

Aeroservices: Dakar; f. 1996; charter flights; Sec.-Gen. El Hadj OMAR BA.

African West Air: Dakar; tel. 822-45-38; fax 822-46-10; f. 1993; services to western Europe and Brazil; Man. Dir J. P. PIEDADE.

Air Sénégal International (ASI): 45 ave Albert Sarraut, Dakar; tel. 842-41-00; e-mail siege@airsenegalinternational.sn; internet www.air-senegal-international.com; f. 2001 to replace Air Sénégal; 51% owned by Royal Air Maroc, 49% state-owned; domestic, regional and international services; Chief Exec. MOHAMED ZOUHAIR EL-AOUFIR.

Tourism

Senegal's attractions for tourists include six national parks (one of which, Djoudj, is listed by UNESCO as a World Heritage Site) and its fine beaches. The island of Gorée, near Dakar, is of considerable historic interest as a former centre for the slave-trade. In 1993 the number of foreign tourist arrivals declined dramatically, largely as a result of the suspension of tourist activity in the Casamance region in that year. The sector recovered strongly from 1995 onwards, and in 2000 visitor arrivals of 442,700 were recorded; receipts from tourism in that year were 96,800m. francs CFA. Senegal has announced its intention of attracting 1m. tourists per year by 2005.

Ministry of Tourism: rue Calmette, BP 4049, Dakar; tel. 821-11-26.

SERBIA AND MONTENEGRO

Introductory Survey

Location, Climate, Language, Religion, Flag, Capital

The union of Serbia and Montenegro (reconstituted from the Federal Republic of Yugoslavia), lies in south-eastern Europe. Serbia and Montenegro is bordered to the north by Hungary, to the east by Romania and Bulgaria, and by the former Yugoslav republic of Macedonia and Albania to the south; Montenegro, in the south-west, has a coastline on the Adriatic Sea, and the union's inland western border is with Bosnia and Herzegovina and with Croatia. The climate is continental in the hilly interior and Mediterranean on the coast, with steady rainfall throughout the year. The average summer temperature in Belgrade is 22°C (71°F), the winter average being 0°C (32°F). The principal language is Serbo-Croat in its Serbian form (written in Cyrillic script). Orthodox Christianity is predominant, the Serbian Orthodox Church being the largest denomination. There is a significant Muslim population, principally in the south of the country, and Roman Catholicism is especially strong in the Vojvodina province of Serbia. There is a small Jewish community. The national flag (proportions 1 by 2) has three equal horizontal stripes, of blue, white and red. The capital is Belgrade (Beograd).

Recent History

A movement for the union of the South Slav peoples, despite long-standing ethnic rivalries and cultural diversity, began in the early 19th century. However, it was not until the end of the First World War, and the collapse of the Austro-Hungarian empire (which ruled Croatia, Slovenia and Bosnia and Herzegovina), that the project for a Yugoslav ('south Slav') state could be realized. A pact between Serbia (which was under Ottoman Turkish rule until the 19th century) and the other South Slavs was signed in July 1917, declaring the intention to merge all the territories in a unitary state under the Serbian monarchy. Accordingly, when the First World War ended and Austria-Hungary was dissolved, the Kingdom of Serbs, Croats and Slovenes was proclaimed on 4 December 1918.

Prince Alexander, Regent of Serbia since 1914, accepted the regency of the new state, becoming King in August 1921. Following bitter disputes between Serbs and Croats, King Alexander assumed dictatorial powers in January 1929. He formally changed the country's name to Yugoslavia in October. Alexander's regime was Serb-dominated, and in October 1934 he was assassinated in France by Croatian extremists. His brother, Prince Paul, assumed power as Regent on behalf of King Peter II. Paul's regime retained power with the support of the armed forces, despite internal unrest, particularly in Croatia (which was granted internal autonomy in 1939). Among the anti-Government groups was the Communist Party of Yugoslavia (CPY), which had been officially banned in 1921, but continued to operate clandestinely. In 1937 the CPY appointed a new General Secretary, Josip Broz (Tito).

In March 1941 the increasingly pro-German regime of Prince Paul was overthrown in a coup, and a Government that supported the Allied Powers was installed, with King Peter as Head of State. In April, however, German and Italian forces invaded, forcing the royal family and Government into exile. Resistance to the occupation forces was initially divided between two rival groups. The Yugoslav Army of the Fatherland (chetniks) operated mainly in Serbia and represented the exiled Government, while the National Liberation Army (partisans), led by the CPY, under Gen. (later Marshal) Tito, recruited supporters from Bosnia, Croatia, Montenegro and Slovenia. Rivalry between the two groups led to civil war, eventually won by the communist partisans. On 29 November 1943 the partisans proclaimed their own government in liberated areas. Attempts to reconcile the Tito regime with the exiled Government proved unsuccessful, and King Peter II was deposed in 1944.

After the war ended, elections were held, under communist supervision, for a Provisional Assembly. The Federative People's Republic of Yugoslavia was proclaimed on 29 November 1945, with Tito as Prime Minister. A Soviet-type Constitution, establishing a federation of six republics (Serbia, Montenegro, Croatia, Slovenia, Macedonia, and Bosnia and Herzegovina) and two autonomous regions, was adopted in January 1946.

The independent socialist policies of Tito led to tension in relations with the USSR, and in 1948 Yugoslavia was expelled from the Soviet-dominated Cominform. The CPY was renamed the League of Communists of Yugoslavia (LCY) in November 1952, by which time it had established exclusive political control. A new Constitution was adopted in January 1953, with Tito becoming President of the Republic. Another Constitution, promulgated in April 1963, changed the country's name to Socialist Federal Republic of Yugoslavia (SFRY). Links with the USSR were resumed in 1955, but Yugoslavia largely pursued a policy of non-alignment, the first conference of the Non-aligned Movement (see p. 350) being held in the Serbian and federal capital, Belgrade, in 1961.

In July 1971 President Tito introduced a system of collective leadership and regular rotation of personnel between posts, in an attempt to unify the various nationalities. A collective State Presidency, headed by Tito, was established. A new Constitution, introduced in February 1974, granted Tito the presidency for an unlimited term of office, and in May he became Life President of the LCY. Tito died in 1980, and his responsibilities were transferred to the collective State Presidency and to the Presidium of the LCY.

Following the death of Tito, inter-ethnic tensions, largely suppressed during his period in power, became evident. In early 1981 there were widespread demonstrations in Kosovo (an autonomous province in Serbia, where ethnic Albanians accounted for about 90% of the population) by Albanian nationalists, demanding that the province receive full republican status. A state of emergency was declared, and the riots resulted in several deaths and many injuries. Further demonstrations took place in March 1982, and hundreds of Albanian nationalists were convicted and imprisoned. Tensions were exacerbated in April 1987, when thousands of Serbs and Montenegrins gathered at Kosovo Polje (the site of a famous battle between the Serbs and Ottoman Turks in 1389) to protest at alleged harassment by the Albanian majority population clashed violently with the security forces. In June Serbs and Montenegrins staged a further mass protest in Belgrade, and demonstrations continued in Kosovo. The perceived failure of the Serbian and federal leadership to curb Albanian nationalism led to the dismissal in September of the First Secretary of the LCS, Ivan Stambolić, and his replacement by Slobodan Milošević. Milošević had denounced the Serbian leadership's policy on Kosovo and promised to reverse the emigration of Serbs from the area and halt the activities of Albanian nationalists.

During 1988 and 1989 ethnic unrest increased in Serbia, particularly in the autonomous provinces of Kosovo and Vojvodina. (The latter, in north-east Serbia, has a large Hungarian minority.) Proposals to amend the Serbian Constitution to reduce the level of autonomy of the two regions (providing Serbia with more direct control over security, financial and social policy in the two provinces) were supported by regular demonstrations by Serbs, especially those from Kosovo. Demonstrations, organized by Milošević and his supporters, were also staged in Vojvodina, directed against the local party leadership. In October 1988 protests by some 100,000 demonstrators in Novy Sad, the administrative centre of Vojvodina, forced the resignation of the Presidium of the League of Communists of Vojvodina, which had opposed some of the proposed constitutional amendments. Tension between the respective party leaderships of Kosovo and Serbia increased, and in November, following the resignation of several members of the Kosovo leadership, some 100,000 ethnic Albanians demonstrated in Priština (the administrative capital of Kosovo) to demand their reinstatement. In Belgrade a further mass rally was staged by Serbs in protest at alleged discrimination by the Albanian population in Kosovo. Public demonstrations in Kosovo were banned in late November. In Montenegro continuing unrest resulted in the resignations of the members of the Montenegrin Presidency and of the republican party leadership in January

1989, and their replacement by leaders more sympathetic to Milošević.

In February 1989 the dismissal from the LCY Central Committee of Azem Vlasi, a popular Kosovar Albanian, and the adoption by the Assembly of the Serbian Republic of the constitutional amendments limiting provincial autonomy, led to renewed unrest in Kosovo. A hunger strike by some 13,000 miners, supported by general strike action in the province, was ended when federal troops intervened. However, further rioting was precipitated by the arrest of Vlasi in early March, and the approval of the new constitutional arrangements by the Kosovo Provincial Assembly later that month. Unrest persisted throughout the year, and protests escalated again in January 1990. The situation was further exacerbated when Milošević (who had been elected President of the Serbian State Presidency in May 1989) urged the Serbs to begin a campaign of mass settlement in Kosovo (some 50,000 Serbs and Montenegrins were reported to have left the province since 1981). A curfew was imposed in Priština, and units of the federal army were deployed to quell the disturbances. In April 1990 the state of emergency was ended, and Vlasi and other defendants were acquitted and released. In May, however, the Serbian leadership announced new proposals for constitutional amendments that would end Kosovo's autonomy.

In May 1988 an emergency conference of the LCY took place. Radical economic and political reforms, including the separation of the powers of the LCY and the State, and greater democracy within the LCY, were proposed. At the end of December, having been defeated in a vote of 'no confidence' (based on the Government's economic policy), Branko Mikulić, the President of the Federal Executive Council (Prime Minister), and his Government were obliged to resign. In January 1989 Ante Marković, a member of the Croatian Presidency, was appointed to head a new Government. In September the Slovene Assembly voted to adopt radical amendments to the Constitution of Slovenia, affirming its sovereignty and its right to secede from Yugoslavia. Relations with the leadership of Serbia and the other constituent republics deteriorated sharply, and in Serbia and Montenegro demonstrations were staged in response to the perceived threat to the unity of Yugoslavia. In early December Serbia imposed economic sanctions on Slovenia. At an Extraordinary Congress of the LCY in January 1990, the abolition of the LCY's constitutional monopoly of power and the introduction of a multi-party system were formally approved, but a proposal by Slovenia to award greater autonomy to the republican branches of the LCY was overwhelmingly defeated. As a result, the Slovene delegation left the Congress, which was then adjourned. It resumed its work in May, but was not attended by delegations from Croatia, Slovenia or Macedonia, where the local communist parties had effectively seceded from the LCY. The LCY was reconstituted in November as the League of Communists—Movement for Yugoslavia.

Multi-party elections took place in Slovenia and Croatia in April and May 1990, respectively. In Slovenia the Democratic Opposition of Slovenia (DEMOS) secured the highest number of seats in the Assembly, while Milan Kučan, the candidate of the Party of Democratic Reform (the former Slovene League of Communists), but an outspoken opponent of President Milošević, was elected President of the republican presidency. In Croatia the nationalist Croatian Democratic Union obtained almost two-thirds of the seats in the Assembly, and its leader, Franjo Tudjman, won the presidential election.

In May 1990, under the system of rotating leadership, Dr Borisav Jović of Serbia replaced Janez Drnovšek of Slovenia as President of the Federal Presidency. Jović promised to uphold national integrity and advocated the introduction of a stronger federal constitution. In early July a referendum in Serbia resulted in approval for proposed amendments to the republic's Constitution, effectively removing the autonomous status of the provinces of Kosovo and Vojvodina. The Kosovo Provincial Assembly and Government were dissolved by the Serbian authorities. In response, a group of 114 ethnic Albanian deputies to the Assembly attempted to declare Kosovo's independence from Serbia. Unrest continued, and in September a general strike was organized to protest against the mass dismissals of ethnic Albanian officials by the Serbian authorities. Criminal charges were brought against more than 100 members of the Provincial Assembly who attempted to re-establish the body, and several former ministers in the Government of Kosovo were charged with establishing an illegal separatist organization.

During November and December 1990 multi-party elections were held in four republics. In Bosnia and Herzegovina (where tension between Muslims and Serbs had led to clashes) and in Macedonia the nationalist parties were successful. In Montenegro the League of Communists was able to retain the Presidency and secure a majority of seats in the Assembly. In Serbia, amid allegations of widespread irregularities, Milošević was re-elected President, overcoming a challenge by Vuk Drašković of the nationalist and anti-communist Serbian Renewal Movement (SRM). In the Serbian Assembly 194 of the 250 seats were won by the Socialist Party of Serbia (SPS—led by Milošević), which had been formed in July 1990 by a merger of the Serbian Socialist Alliance of Working People and the League of Socialists (the Serbian branch of the LCY).

In October 1990 Croatia and Slovenia had proposed the transformation of the Yugoslav federation into a looser confederation, in which constituent republics would have the right to maintain armed forces and enter into diplomatic relations with other states. Serbia and Montenegro, however, advocated a centralized federal system, while Macedonia and Bosnia and Herzegovina supported the concept of a federation of sovereign states, based on the model of the European Community (EC), later known as the European Union (EU, see p. 199). Tension increased in December, when Croatia adopted a new Constitution, giving the republic the right to secede from Yugoslavia, while in Slovenia an overwhelming majority voted in favour of secession at a referendum. In January 1991 Macedonia declared its sovereignty and right to secede from the SFRY.

A crisis developed in March 1991, when mass demonstrations, led by Drašković's SRM, demanding the resignation of Milošević, were violently suppressed by the security forces. Jović resigned as President of the Federal Presidency, following his failure to secure approval from other members of the Presidency for emergency measures, requested by the security forces, to allow the deployment of federal troops. Following an appeal from the Serbian Assembly, Jović withdrew his resignation.

In February 1991 Slovenia formally initiated its process of 'dissociation' from Yugoslavia, and Croatia asserted the primacy of its Constitution and laws over those of the federation; both Republics declared their willingness to engage in negotiations. Later that month the self-proclaimed 'Serb Autonomous Region (SAR) of Krajina' declared its separation from Croatia and aim to unite with Serbia. In Croatia an overwhelming majority voted in favour of independence at a referendum in May. The referendum was largely boycotted by the Serbian minority in Croatia, and armed clashes between Serbs and Croats in the republic intensified. Relations between Serbia and Croatia deteriorated further in that month, when Serbian representatives in the Federal Presidency refused to sanction the scheduled transfer of the Presidency to Stipe Mesić of Croatia. In early June the leaders of the six republics met to consider a compromise plan, which would transform the country into an alliance of sovereign states. However, on 25 June, following the failure of the talks, Slovenia and Croatia declared independence, thereby formally beginning the process of dissociation from the federation. In response, federal troops (largely Serb-dominated) took retaliatory action, bombarding a number of targets in Slovenia, including Ljubljana airport. A cease-fire agreement, sponsored by the EC, resulted in Serbia's acceptance of Mesić as President of the Federal Presidency. In July agreement was reached on the immediate cessation of hostilities and on a three-month suspension in the implementation of dissociation by Croatia and Slovenia. The withdrawal of federal troops from Slovenia began almost immediately, but fighting intensified in Croatia, where federal troops increasingly identified openly with local Serb nationalist forces. By September Serb forces controlled almost one-third of Croatia's territory, and successive cease-fire agreements failed to end the conflict. In the same month, at a referendum in Macedonia, voters approved the establishment of an independent and sovereign republic.

In late September 1991 the UN Security Council adopted Resolution 713, which imposed an armaments embargo on Yugoslavia and urged that all hostilities end immediately. However, sporadic fighting continued in Croatia. In October Croatia and Slovenia formally ended their association with Yugoslavia, the moratoriums on independence (agreed in July) having expired. In the same month the Assembly of Bosnia and Herzegovina declared the republic's sovereignty, despite the objections of ethnic Serb deputies. The EC continued its negotiation efforts, and the UN also become directly involved, but several proposed cease-fires failed to end the hostilities. In Belgrade the

Federal Prime Minister, Ante Marković, resigned, having been defeated in a vote of 'no confidence' in the Federal Assembly. In December, declaring that Yugoslavia had ceased to exist, Stipe Mesić resigned as President of the Federal Presidency. In January 1992 Slovenia and Croatia were recognized as independent states by the EC; numerous other countries followed. The deployment in Croatia of a UN contingent of 14,000 peace-keeping troops (agreed by the Federal Presidency in December 1991) commenced in March 1992.

Following the recognition of the independence of Croatia and Slovenia by the international community, Serbia and Montenegro agreed to uphold the Yugoslav state, the Montenegrin commitment being overwhelmingly endorsed in a referendum, held in March 1992 (although boycotted by the ethnic Albanian and Muslim minorities). Macedonia's representative to the Federal Presidency had resigned in January, but EC recognition of Macedonian independence was delayed, owing to opposition from Greece, which was concerned for the territorial integrity of its northern territory of the same name. In March Bosnia and Herzegovina also declared its independence from the Yugoslav Federation, the decision having been approved by the electorate in a referendum. Later that month the 'Serb Republic of Bosnia and Herzegovina' was proclaimed, and a severe escalation in the Bosnian conflict ensued.

In April 1992 the Federal Assembly adopted a new Constitution, formally establishing the Federal Republic of Yugoslavia (FRY), which comprised Serbia (including the provinces of Kosovo, now officially known as Kosovo and Metohija, and Vojvodina) and Montenegro, thereby effectively acknowledging the secession of the other four republics. In late May elections to the Federal Assembly were held in Serbia and Montenegro, the SPS enjoying considerable success as a result of an opposition boycott of the elections. In June Dobrica Ćosić became President of the FRY, and the collective Federal Presidency ceased to exist. Meanwhile, in May large anti-war demonstrations, organized by the opposition, were staged in Belgrade. In that month an alliance of opposition parties formed the Democratic Movement of Serbia (Depos), led by Drašković, and further mass anti-Milošević demonstrations took place at the end of June. Internal disagreements threatened to split the Serbian Government in June, but the administration survived a vote of 'no confidence' submitted by the opposition parties.

In May 1992 elections, declared to be illegal by the Serbian authorities, were held in Kosovo to establish a 130-member provincial Assembly. The Democratic Alliance of Kosovo (DAK) secured most seats in the elections, and the movement's leader, Dr Ibrahim Rugova, was elected 'President' of the self-proclaimed 'Republic of Kosovo'. In July Milan Panić was elected Federal Prime Minister by a joint session of the Federal Assembly. Following a visit to Albania in August (the first by a Yugoslav leader since 1948), Panić revoked the state of emergency in Kosovo, which had been in effect since the unrest of 1989–90. In October 1992 Panić attended talks in Priština with Cyrus Vance and Lord Owen (co-Chairmen of the joint UN-EC negotiating initiative on the former Yugoslavia) to discuss the situation in Kosovo. However, the arrest of two deputies of the 'Kosovo Assembly' and the banning of the Albanian newspaper exacerbated tensions, and there were further disturbances in the province in October and November.

At the conference on the former Yugoslavia, which took place in London, United Kingdom, in August 1992, Panić condemned the policy of 'ethnic cleansing', following the discovery of Serb concentration camps in Bosnia and Herzegovina, and reiterated the claim that there was no federal military involvement in the republic. Tension between the strongly nationalist Milošević, whose policies were denounced by his opponents as repressive, and the more moderate Panić was evident at the conference. In early September Panić survived a vote of 'no confidence', proposed in the Federal Assembly by supporters of Milošević. In an attempt to force Milošević's removal from office, presidential and legislative elections were scheduled for December 1992, and Ćosić and Panić urged Milošević to resign. In October Milošević retaliated by using Serbian police forces to seize control of the federal police headquarters in Belgrade, blockading the building for several weeks. In November Panić survived a further vote in the Federal Assembly, expressing 'no confidence' in his premiership, by one vote. The Federal Minister of Foreign Affairs resigned in September, claiming that Panić's policies were 'against the interests of Serbia'; in November three more federal ministers resigned.

Presidential and parliamentary elections, at both federal and republican levels, took place on 20 December 1992. Ćosić was re-elected Federal President, with some 85% of the votes cast. Milošević was re-elected President of Serbia, receiving 57.5% of the votes cast, and the SPS secured 47 of the 138 seats in the Federal Assembly. Panić, who contested the Serbian presidency, winning some 35% of the votes, subsequently demanded that new elections be held, alleging widespread electoral malpractice on the part of the SPS. However, he was removed from the office of Federal Prime Minister on 29 December, after losing a vote of 'no confidence' in the Federal Assembly. The SPS won 101 seats in the elections to the 250-member Serbian Assembly, while the extreme nationalist Serbian Radical Party (SRP) secured 73. In early February 1993 a new Federal Government, comprising the SPS and the DPMS, was established, with Radoje Kontić as Federal Prime Minister. In the same month the SPS formed a new Serbian Government, headed by Nikola Šainović. Depos, which had obtained 49 seats in the Serbian Assembly, commenced a legislative boycott (following strenuous claims by Drašković that the elections had been fraudulent). In Montenegro Momir Bulatović of the ruling Democratic Party of Montenegrin Socialists (DPMS—the former League of Communists of Montenegro) failed to win an overall majority in the first round of the presidential election. He was re-elected President in a second round of voting on 10 January 1993, defeating his nationalist rival, Branko Kostić, by a substantial margin. A new coalition Government, headed by Milo Djukanović, was established in Montenegro in March.

On 1 June 1993 Ćosić (who was accused of conspiring with army generals to overthrow Milošević) was removed from office by a vote of 'no confidence' at an emergency debate of the Federal Assembly; the motion had been initiated by deputies of the SPS and the SRP, in what was widely regarded as an attempt by Milošević to consolidate his power. Ćosić's dismissal was followed by a large anti-Government demonstration in Belgrade, at which Drašković and his wife were arrested; they were both released in July. In late June the Federal Assembly appointed Zoran Lilić of the SPS (recently the Chairman of the Serbian Assembly) as Federal President. Lilić was generally regarded as sympathetic to Milošević, and a reorganization of the Serbian Government in July was believed to have further strengthened Milošević's position. A new Commander-in-Chief of the Yugoslav Army was appointed in late August. It was also announced that the Supreme Defence Council was to assume responsibility for all military and defence duties, and that the republican defence ministries were to be abolished (a measure that was opposed by the Montenegrin Government).

By the second half of 1993 it appeared that the co-operation between Milošević and the SRP had ended: in October an attempt by the SRP to force a parliamentary vote expressing 'no confidence' in the Šainović Government prompted Milošević to dissolve the Serbian Assembly, scheduling new elections for December. In response to SRP allegations that the Serbian leadership was betraying national interests by its involvement in attempts to end the conflict in Bosnia and Herzegovina, a campaign of denigration (believed to have been orchestrated by Milošević) against the SRP began. The party's leader, Dr Vojislav Šešelj, and his associates were accused of involvement in atrocities committed in the former Yugoslavia, and prominent members of the party associated with its paramilitary wing (styled 'chetniks') were arrested. (In April 1994 it was reported that the SRP had abolished the 'chetnik' movement.)

In the elections to the 250-member Serbian National Assembly, which took place on 19 December 1993, the SPS increased its representation to 123 deputies, winning 36.7% of the votes cast. Depos secured 45 seats (with 16.6% of the votes), and the SRP took 39 (with 13.9%). Despite its increased level of representation, the SPS failed to achieve an outright majority in the legislature, and was therefore forced to seek the support of another party in order to form a government. Prolonged negotiations between the SPS and opposition parties ensued, and in late February 1994 a new Serbian Government was formed, with the support of the six members of the New Democracy (ND) party, which had campaigned in the elections as a member of the Depos coalition. Mirko Marjanović, a pro-Milošević business executive, who had not previously held a political post, was appointed Prime Minister, replacing Šainović, who became a Deputy Prime Minister in the Federal Government. The new Government was approved by the Serbian Assembly in mid-March. In September a smaller, 14-member Federal Government, which included six new ministers, was appointed. Radoje Kontić retained the post of Federal Prime Minister.

The results of the December 1993 elections in Serbia and the defection of the ND to the Government permitted Milošević to distance himself further from his erstwhile allies in the nationalist opposition, notably Šešelj's SRP, and to consolidate his political control in Yugoslavia. The campaign of denigration by the government-controlled media against Šešelj and the SRP continued in 1994, and Šešelj's personal position was discredited, when he was sentenced to a short term of imprisonment in late September for assaulting the parliamentary Speaker. Milošević also strengthened his control over the media during 1994.

In late August 1994, in a controversial vote that was boycotted by the opposition, the Serbian Assembly endorsed a peace plan, sponsored by the five-nation 'Contact Group' on the Bosnian conflict, that the Bosnian Serbs had rejected earlier in the month. The SRP, the Democratic Party (DP) and the Democratic Party of Serbia (DPS) continued to oppose the peace proposals. A decision by the Serbian leadership to impose a blockade on the Bosnian Serbs in September was strongly opposed by the SRP (which retained close links with the leadership of the Bosnian Serbs) and other opposition movements.

In early August 1995, in an unexpected military offensive, Croatian troops took control of the RSK, prompting a mass exodus of ethnic Serbs from the region. The Yugoslav leadership protested strongly against the Croatian action, demanding UN intervention and a withdrawal of Croatian troops from the area. However, President Milošević also blamed the leadership of the RSK, accusing it of intransigence, and criticizing its reluctance to comply with international peace proposals. Some opposition groups, notably the SRP, condemned the Yugoslav leadership for failing to provide military support for the Serbs in Croatia, and organized protest rallies in Belgrade. The Croatian offensive against the RSK resulted in the exodus of some 160,000 Serb refugees to Yugoslavia. Many were settled in Vojvodina, prompting protests from ethnic Hungarians in that region.

In early November 1995 peace negotiations were convened in Dayton, Ohio, USA, with the aim of resolving the conflict in the former Yugoslavia. The conference, at which Milošević represented not only Yugoslavia, but also the self-proclaimed 'Serbian Republic', resulted in an agreement on the future territorial and constitutional structure of Bosnia and Herzegovina. In response to Yugoslav acceptance of the plan, all UN sanctions against Yugoslavia were revoked in late November. The SRP denounced the Dayton agreement, which was also criticized by the DP, the DPS and the increasingly nationalist leadership of the Serbian Orthodox Church. However, the SRM, while remaining critical of the President's domestic policies, supported the agreement. In late November Milošević dismissed several leading members of the SPS, who were known to be critical of the Dayton accord and supportive of militant factions among the Bosnian Serbs.

There was further evidence of opposition to Milošević's regime in April 1996, when Dragoslav Avramović, the Governor of the National Bank of Yugoslavia, strongly criticized the economic policies of the Federal Government, in particular its insistence that the IMF agree to recognize Yugoslavia as the successor to the SFRY, with full rights to the assets of the former Yugoslavia. In late April Avramović was dismissed as the Government's chief negotiator with the IMF. His dismissal coincided with an escalation of industrial unrest and strike action in demand of unpaid wages. Despite public support, in mid-May Avramović was dismissed from his post as Governor of the National Bank. In early June the Serbian Government was reorganized. All the new ministers appointed were members of the increasingly influential Yugoslav United Left (YUL), led by the wife of President Milošević, Mirjana Marković.

In August 1996 Rugova announced that ethnic Albanians in Kosovo would boycott federal parliamentary elections, which were scheduled for 3 November (when elections to the Montenegrin Republican Assembly and municipal elections were also to take place). Later that month the Federal Assembly approved a decision by the Government (in a reversal of its previous stance) to accede to IMF terms for the restoration of membership of the organization. Prior to the elections, a number of new coalitions were formed, notably a grouping known as Zajedno, which comprised the SRM, the DP, the DPS and the Civic Alliance of Serbia. Zajedno nominated Avramović to contest the elections on behalf of the coalition; in October, however, he withdrew his candidacy on grounds of ill health. The SPS established an alliance with the YUL and the ND, which became known as the United List.

On 3 November 1996 elections to the Federal Chamber of Citizens, the Montenegrin Republican Assembly and the municipal assemblies of Serbia and Montenegro took place. At the elections to the Chamber of Citizens, the United List secured 64 seats, while Zajedno took 22, the DPMS 20 and the SRP 16 seats; of the 138 elected deputies, 108 were from Serbia and 30 from Montenegro. At the concurrent elections to the Republican Assembly of Montenegro, the DPMS won 45 seats (with the total number of seats reduced from 85 to 71). The DPMS also gained control of the majority of the municipal assemblies in Montenegro. Following a number of inconclusive results in the Serbian municipal elections, a second round of voting was scheduled for 17 November. Provisional results subsequently indicated that Zajedno had gained control of 14 principal towns in Serbia, including Belgrade. After the SPS challenged the results, however, most of the opposition victories were annulled by (SPS-dominated) municipal courts and electoral commissions. Mass demonstrations in protest at the Government's refusal to recognize the results of the municipal elections were subsequently staged by students and other Zajedno supporters in Belgrade. In early December the Serbian Supreme Court rejected opposition appeals against the annulment of the election results in a number of the municipal seats under review.

In December 1996 opposition supporters continued to organize daily demonstrations (which had developed into general protests against the Milošević Government) in Belgrade and other towns. The Serbian Minister of Information (a former journalist) resigned in protest at the Government's temporary closure of two independent radio stations, which had reported the demonstrations. Milošević denied government involvement in electoral malpractice and condemned the protests. In late December the demonstrations (which had hitherto had been peaceful) degenerated into violent clashes between protesters and members of the security forces in Belgrade; it was reported that two people had been killed and a further 58 injured. The Ministry of Internal Affairs subsequently ordered a ban on demonstrations, which the security forces attempted to enforce; nevertheless, anti-Government rallies continued. At the end of December a delegation from the Organization for Security and Co-operation in Europe (OSCE, see p. 283), which earlier that month had been invited by the Federal Minister of Foreign Affairs to visit Serbia, issued a report upholding the results of the municipal elections that had been invalidated. The Permanent Council of the OSCE subsequently confirmed the findings of the delegation, and demanded complete official recognition of the opposition victories. The international community consequently increased pressure on Milošević to comply with the OSCE ruling.

In early February 1997 the violent suppression by security forces of anti-Government demonstrations attracted further criticism from the international community. Shortly afterwards Milošević publicly instructed Majanović to prepare emergency legislation providing for the official recognition of the results of the municipal elections, in accordance with the OSCE ruling. However, the leader of the DP, Zoran Djindjić, urged his supporters to continue protests until the election results were officially verified, further demanding that the electoral code and legislation governing the media be reformed and that members of the security forces involved in the violence earlier that month be charged. On 11 February the Serbian legislature voted in favour of reinstating the annulled results by 128 of the 130 votes cast (with deputies from the opposition and extreme nationalist parties boycotting the session); Zajedno consequently gained control of the municipal assemblies in Belgrade and a further 13 towns. At the same time seven ministers were replaced in a reorganization of the Serbian Cabinet. Later in February Djindjić was elected Mayor of Belgrade by Zajedno members, who controlled 69 of the 110 seats in the city's municipal council. Zajedno leaders subsequently suspended the daily protests.

In February 1997 a published interview with Milo Djukanović, in which he pronounced Milošević to be unfit to hold public office, prompted retaliatory criticism from the Serbian state-owned press, and resulted in division between himself and Bulatović. In March Djukanović was obliged to resign from the post of Deputy Chairman of the DPMS, owing to opposition within the party, while it was reported that he had refused to comply with instructions from Bulatović to reorganize the Montenegrin Cabinet (thereby removing ministers considered to be hostile towards Milošević). Meanwhile, a number of additional

DPMS representatives were included in the Federal Government, following a ministerial reorganization (in which the Serbian Minister of Internal Affairs was appointed to the equivalent federal post). In April Bulatović indicated that the DPMS would support the nomination of Milošević to the federal presidency, following the expiry of Lilić's mandate on 25 June (thereby enabling Milošević to secure a majority of votes in the Federal Assembly for his election to the presidency). Also in April Zajedno announced that Drašković was to contest the Serb presidential election on behalf of the opposition alliance. However, dissent between the opposition leaders subsequently emerged over the nomination of a joint candidate for the Serb presidency. In June it was announced that the SRM had withdrawn from Zajedno. Later that month one of Montenegro's Deputy Prime Ministers, Slavko Drljević, was obliged to resign, after stating that a separate Montenegrin currency might be introduced in the event of further hyperinflation in the FRY.

In June 1997 the SPS nominated Milošević as a candidate for the federal presidency, and also proposed constitutional amendments for the direct election of the President. Later that month a DPMS committee declared its support for Milošević's candidature (which was, however, strongly opposed by elements within the party, including Djukanović), but rejected the proposed constitutional amendments. On 25 June Lilić relinquished office; the Speaker of the federal Chamber of Republics, Srdjan Bozović, was to act as interim President for one month, pending an election.

In early July 1997 Dušan Vlatković, hitherto the Serbian Minister of Finance, was appointed to the post of Governor of the National Bank of Yugoslavia. In the same month supporters of Djukanović within the DPMS voted to remove Bulatović from the leadership of the party, on the grounds that he was too closely associated with the Serbian Government. In mid-July Milošević was elected to the federal presidency by the Federal Assembly (having arranged for the parliamentary session to take place earlier than scheduled, owing to concern that the division within the DPMS would undermine his support). Opposition deputies boycotted the vote in the federal Chamber of Citizens, which they subsequently declared to be invalid. On 23 July Milošević formally resigned from the office of President of Serbia and was inaugurated as Federal President. Later in July the SPS nominated Lilić to contest the Serbian presidential election, which, together with elections to the Serbian National Assembly, were scheduled to take place on 21 September. In August supporters of Bulatović organized a DPMS congress at which he was re-elected Chairman of the party. Later that month, however, the Montenegrin Constitutional Court ruled against Bulatović's candidacy in the forthcoming Montenegrin presidential election (which was scheduled to take place on 5 October), after both he and Djukanović were nominated by factions of the DPMS. Following an appeal by supporters of Bulatović, however, the federal Constitutional Court abrogated legislation in force in Montenegro, which had stipulated that a political party was entitled to nominate only one presidential candidate (consequently allowing Bulatović to stand for re-election).

In September 1997 students demonstrated in Belgrade in support of Djindjić, who, following the dissolution of Zajedno, urged a boycott of the Serbian presidential and legislative elections, on the grounds that they would be biased in favour of the incumbent administration. At the elections to the Serbian National Assembly, which took place on 21 September, the United List coalition won 110 seats (thereby failing to secure an outright majority); the SRP increased its representation in the chamber to 82 seats and the SRM obtained 45 seats. In the concurrent presidential election, which was contested by 17 candidates, Lilić (the candidate of the United List) received 35.7% of the votes cast, while Šešelj, who contested the poll on behalf of the SRP, won 27.3% and Drašković 20.6% of the votes. Despite the boycott implemented by supporters of a number of opposition parties and ethnic Albanians in Kosovo, some 62% of the electorate participated in the poll. Since none of the candidates had secured the requisite majority of more than one-half of the votes cast, a second round was scheduled to take place on 5 October. In early October SPS and SRP councillors in the Belgrade municipal assembly voted in support of an SRM initiative to remove Djindjić from the office of Mayor of Belgrade. Security forces subsequently suppressed protests in Belgrade by supporters of the DP, who demanded that further legislative and municipal elections be conducted. In the second round of voting in the Serbian presidential election on 5 October Šešelj won

49.1% and Lilić 47.9% of the votes cast. However, owing, in part, to the electoral boycott organized by Djindjić, less than 50% of the electorate participated in the poll, which consequently, under the terms of the Constitution, was declared to be invalid, requiring the first round to be repeated. The Serbian authorities subsequently announced that a further presidential election was to take place on 7 December.

The electoral campaign in Montenegro was dominated by acrimony between Bulatović and Djukanović, who were to contest the presidency on behalf of opposing factions of the DPMS. In the first round of the presidential election, which was contested by a total of eight candidates on 5 October 1997, Bulatović secured 48.2% of votes cast, narrowly defeating Djukanović, with 47.4%, but failed to obtain the requisite majority of the votes. At a second round of voting, conducted on 19 October, Djukanović was elected to the Montenegrin presidency, with 50.8% of the votes cast. Although the OSCE declared the conduct of the elections to be generally satisfactory, Bulatović subsequently claimed that Djukanović's supporters had falsified voting lists prior to the second round. Later in October, however, the Montenegrin Constitutional Court rejected an appeal by Bulatović that the results of the presidential election be annulled on the grounds of electoral malpractice.

Following his appointment as a Federal Deputy Prime Minister in November 1997, Lilić withdrew his candidacy to the Serbian presidency. In a further Serbian presidential election, which was contested by seven candidates on 7 December, the United List coalition was represented by the Federal Minister of Foreign Affairs, Milan Milutinović, who secured 43.7% of the votes cast, with Šešelj receiving 32.2% of the votes. In the ensuing second round, which took place on 21 December, Milutinović won 59.2% of the votes cast, while Šešelj obtained 37.5% of the votes. The Serbian electoral commission announced that about 50.1% of the electorate had participated in the poll, which was consequently pronounced to be valid. However, Šešelj claimed that the Serbian authorities had perpetrated electoral malpractice, particularly in Kosovo, where ethnic Albanians had continued to boycott the polls. Later in December OSCE observers who had monitored the elections issued a report indicating that severe irregularities had taken place. On 29 December Milutinović was inaugurated as President of Serbia.

In January 1998 protests by supporters of Bulatović against the election of Djukanović to the Montenegrin presidency resulted in increasing violence. Two members of the security forces were killed in clashes with demonstrators, who had attempted to seize government buildings in Podgorica. Nevertheless, Djukanović was inaugurated as President of Montenegro in mid-January. Following continued violent protests, the Montenegrin authorities prohibited further demonstrations. Later that month a number of minor bomb attacks in Podgorica were generally attributed to supporters of Bulatović. Following mediation by the Federal Prime Minister, Radoje Kontić, however, the authorities agreed that further legislative elections would take place in Montenegro in May, while supporters of Bulatović were to refrain from staging further protests. In early February the Montenegrin Republican Assembly approved the establishment of a transitional Government, pending legislative elections (which were scheduled for 31 May). The new transitional administration comprised 17 representatives of Djukanović's faction of the DPMS, seven members of opposition parties and four ministers without party affiliation. (Bulatović's faction of the DPMS and the Liberal Alliance of Montenegro refused to participate in the new Government.) It was announced that criminal proceedings were to be initiated against Bulatović and three of his prominent supporters, who were accused of inciting the unrest in January. Later in February the Republican Assembly adopted new electoral legislation, which, among other amendments, increased the number of seats in the chamber to 78 (of which five were to be allocated to representatives of the ethnic Albanian minority).

In February 1998 Milutinović reappointed Marjanović to the office of Serbian Prime Minister. Following protracted negotiations, the SPS formed an alliance with the SRP in March. Marjanović subsequently formed a new coalition Government, comprising 15 representatives of the SRP (including Šešelj, who became a Deputy Prime Minister), 13 representatives of the SPS, and four of the YUL. In May the Federal Assembly adopted a motion expressing 'no confidence' in Kontić, which had apparently been initiated by DPMS deputies. Milošević's subsequent nomination of Bulatović to the office of Federal Prime Minister was approved by the Federal Assembly, and a new Federal

Government was established. Djukanović, however, announced his opposition to the installation of the Federal Government headed by Bulatović, which he declared to be illegitimate. At the legislative elections in Montenegro, which took place on 31 May, a coalition (known as 'For a Better Life'), headed by Djukanović, secured 42 seats in the Republican Assembly, while the Socialist People's Party of Montenegro (Socijalistička Narodna Partija Crne Gore—SNP), led by Bulatović, obtained 29 seats. In June the new Republican Assembly withdrew the 20 Montenegrin deputies from the federal Chamber of Republics and replaced them with members of Djukanović's coalition, to ensure that Milošević would not command the requisite two-thirds' majority for constitutional amendments. (Milošević, however, refused to allow deputies from Djukanović's coalition to assume seats in the Chamber of Republics.) In July a new Montenegrin Government, headed by a Deputy Chairman of the DPMS, Filip Vujanović, was installed. In early August the Montenegrin administration announced that it had suspended links with the Federal Government until Bulatović agreed to resign from the office of Federal Prime Minister in favour of a supporter of Djukanović.

In May 1999 the International Criminal Tribunal for the former Yugoslavia (ICTY, see p. 15) indicted Milošević, together with Milutinović, the former Yugoslav Deputy Prime Minister, Nikola Sainović, the former Serbian Minister of the Interior, Vlajko Stojiljković, and the Yugoslav Army Chief of Staff, Gen. Dragoljub Ojdanić, for crimes against humanity. In June SRP ministers and legislative deputies temporarily suspended participation in the Serbian Government, in protest at Milošević's acceptance of the peace plan for Kosovo (whereby NATO forces were deployed in the province under a peace-keeping mandate). During July a series of demonstrations were conducted by a loose grouping of opposition associations, known as Alliance for Change, in support of Milošević's resignation, and the establishment of a transitional government. In early August Milošević reorganized the Federal Government. A mass opposition gathering was staged in Belgrade later that month, but was undermined by continuing dissent between the principal opposition leaders, Djindjić and Drašković. Also in August the Montenegrin Government presented proposals for the dissolution of the Yugoslav Federation, and its replacement with an 'Association of States of Serbia and Montenegro', and announced that a referendum on independence for the republic would be conducted if Milošević failed to agree to the demands. In September the Alliance for Change initiated a joint campaign against Milošević; however, Drašković, who had publicly criticized the strategy adopted by the other parties of the opposition grouping, refused to participate in the protest rallies. In early October Drašković declared an automobile collision (in which he was injured, and a further four SRM officials killed) to have been a deliberate attempt to kill him; a previously unknown organization, the Serbian Liberation Army, subsequently claimed responsibility for the incident. Later that month the SRM conducted discussions with the other parties belonging to the Alliance for Change, in an effort to co-ordinate opposition demands for democratic elections. In January 2000 opposition leaders presented unified demands for elections to be conducted in Serbia by the end of April.

In mid-January 2000 a notorious Serbian paramilitary leader and war crime suspect, Zeljko Raznatović (known as Arkan), was shot and killed in Belgrade. Amid much speculation regarding the motives of the killing, it was suggested that, following his indictment by the ICTY in 1997, he had been prepared to implicate Milošević in war crimes. In early February 2000 the Federal Minister of Defence, Pavle Bulatović, was also killed. Milošević subsequently appointed Gen. Ojdanić to the post. Later in February the SPS re-elected Milošević as the party's President. Meanwhile, the Serbian authorities continued to oppose efforts by the Montenegrin Government to pursue independence. In December 1999 federal Yugoslav troops temporarily seized control of Montenegro's principal airport at Podgorica, prompting increasing concern that a coup attempt would be staged in the republic. In January 2000 the federal Constitutional Court ruled Montenegro's adoption of the Deutsche Mark as its official currency to be illegal.

In May 2000 the Federal Government accused opposition groups of involvement in the killing of a senior SPS official in Novi Sad. Serbian security forces subsequently seized control of the opposition-owned television station, Studio B, and two independent radio stations, and arrested a number of opposition activists. However, opposition parties continued to conduct daily rallies in the principal Serbian towns. In May opposition parties organized a protest rally in Belgrade, following the Serbian Government's decision to close several independent newspapers and television stations. In June Drašković was shot and injured in Montenegro; he claimed that Serbian security agents were responsible for the attack.

In early July 2000 the federal legislature approved constitutional amendments removing limits on the President's tenure of office, providing for direct election to the presidency and the federal Chamber of Republics, and reducing Montenegro's status within the FRY. The amendments, which allowed Milošević to seek a second term, attracted immediate criticism from Serbian opposition parties and the international community. The Montenegrin legislature subsequently voted to reject the amendments, which Vujanović condemned as an attempt by Milošević to retain power. At the end of July Milošević announced that federal presidential and legislative elections were to take place on 24 September. The Montenegrin Government announced that the republic would not participate in the forthcoming elections, in protest at the amendments. In early August an alliance of 18 opposition parties, known as the Democratic Opposition of Serbia (DOS), presented the leader of the DPS, Dr Vojislav Koštunica, as their joint candidate to oppose Milošević in the presidential election. During the pre-election period supporters of Milošević carried out a campaign of harassment against Koštunica.

Numerous allegations of electoral malpractice and intimidation emerged, following the voting to the federal presidency and legislature on 24 September 2000. Preliminary results, released by the Federal Election Commission, indicated that Koštunica had won about 48% of the votes cast, compared with the 40% of the votes received by Milošević, and thereby failed to obtain the 50% majority required to secure the presidency. Milošević subsequently insisted that a second round of voting be conducted on 8 October, while Koštunica rejected the results of the Commission as fraudulent, and claimed to have won the election outright. The international community declared its support for Koštunica and urged Milošević to accept defeat. The Yugoslav army announced that it would not intervene on Milošević's behalf, while the SRP and Serbian parties in Montenegro also acknowledged Koštunica's victory. Opposition supporters commenced a campaign of peaceful protest in Serbia (including a widely observed general strike from the beginning of October), in an effort to compel Milošević to resign. On 5 October protesters, who had gathered to stage a mass rally in Belgrade, overpowered security forces and seized control of the parliament building, the state television station and the official news agency, subsequently declaring Koštunica to be the elected President. On the following day, amid increasing international pressure, Milošević finally relinquished the presidency. Koštunica was officially inaugurated as President on 7 October. According to the final official results, Koštunica received about 51.7% of the votes cast and Milošević 38.2%; in the concurrent legislative election, the DOS secured 58 seats in the 138-member Chamber of Citizens, and the SPS 44. Despite continued hostility from supporters of Milošević, the DOS negotiated an agreement with the SPS in mid-October; the Serbian legislature was to be dissolved, and a transitional cabinet installed, pending elections to the Serbian National Assembly, which were scheduled to take place on 23 December. The new transitional Serbian Government, in which the SPS retained the premiership, was installed later that month. Since only about 30% of the Montenegrin electorate had participated in the elections, as a result of Djukanović's boycott, Koštunica was obliged to form a federal government with the SNP (the only Montenegrin party to be represented in the legislature). A member of that party, Zoran Žižić, was nominated to the post of Prime Minister, and a new Government, comprising representatives of the DOS and the Socialist People's Party, was established in early November. In December Koštunica reorganized the armed forces, removing officers loyal to Milošević.

In the elections to the 250-member Serbian National Assembly, which took place on 23 December 2000, the DOS secured a substantial majority, with 176 seats, while the SPS won 37 seats and the SRP 23 seats. Later that month Djukanović announced proposals that the Yugoslav federation become a loose union of two internationally recognized, separate states. At the end of December the People's Party of Montenegro, which supported a continued federation, withdrew from the governing coalition. Djukanović subsequently announced that elections to the Montenegrin Republican Assembly would take place in April

3626   www.europaworldonline.com

2001. In January Djindjić was elected to the Serbian premiership, and a new Government, comprising members of the DOS, was installed later that month.

In early 2001 the new Federal Government came under increasing pressure from the EU and USA to arrest Milošević and other war crime suspects (following their indictment in May 1999); Koštunica maintained that their extradition would contravene the Constitution. In February a former head of the secret service, Radovan Marković, was detained in connection with the assassination attempt against Vuk Drašković in October 1999. (In July 2001 Marković was sentenced to a custodial term of one year on charges of revealing classified state information, after a trial that been conducted largely in secret.) Following a warning by the US Government that it would end financial aid to the FRY unless the new administration fully co-operated with the ICTY by the end of March 2001, Milošević was finally taken into custody on 1 April. The federal Public Prosecutor issued a series of charges against Milošević for abuses of power during his term of office (principally extensive embezzlement from state funds, and involvement in political assassinations, electoral malpractice and organized crime). Later that month Milošević, who was in detention in Belgrade, was personally delivered the ICTY indictment. At the end of April Serbian courts authorized the extension of Milošević's period of detention for a further two months, despite an appeal that he be released on grounds of ill health. Koštunica, however, refused to comply with international demands that Milošević be dispatched for trial at the ICTY (apparently owing to concern that his extradition might prompt political unrest), and insisted that he face legal proceedings in the FRY for the charges of abuse of power.

Meanwhile, elections to the 78-member Montenegrin Republican Assembly were conducted on 22 April 2001. The pro-independence alliance, led by the DPMS, won 36 seats, while the coalition opposing independence, led by the SNP, won 33 seats, and the Liberal Alliance of Montenegro (LAM) six seats. Despite having failed to secure a decisive majority in the legislature, Djukanović announced that he would continue to pursue his aim of organizing a referendum on independence. In May an agreement was signed between the DPMS, the Social-Democratic Party of Montenegro (SDP) and the LAM, whereby a LAM representative was also to become Speaker of the Republican Assembly. In late June Vujanović (who had been reappointed Prime Minister) formed a new coalition Government, comprising representatives of the DPMS, the SDP and a junior member of the DPMS alliance, the Democratic Union of Albanians.

In late June 2001, following continued international pressure for the authorities to co-operate with the ICTY, the Serbian Government approved a decree, providing for the extradition of Milošević and other indicted war criminals to the ICTY. Supporters of Milošević subsequently staged a large demonstration in Belgrade, in protest at his proposed extradition. The Serbian Government refused to comply with a ruling by the federal Constitutional Court that the decree was invalid, and on 29 June (shortly before an important international donor conference was to take place) Milošević was extradited to the ICTY. On the following day Zizić resigned from the office of Federal Prime Minister, in protest at Milošević's extradition (which had been strongly opposed by the SNP). In July Koštunica appointed Dragiša Pešić, also a member of the SNP and hitherto Federal Minister of Finance, to the post. Later that month a reorganized Federal Government, proposed by Pešić, was approved in the legislature.

In August 2001 the division between Koštunica and Djindjić, resulting from the Serbian Government's decision to extradite Milošević, was further exacerbated by the killing in Belgrade of a security agent, who had reportedly been investigating alleged connections of prominent state officials to organized crime. Koštunica accused Djindjić's administration of failing to address widespread crime, and withdrew the DPS ministers from the Government (although the party officially remained within the DOS coalition). At the end of August a district court in The Hague dismissed a legal challenge by Milošević against his detention and arraignment at the ICTY, on the grounds that the Dutch judiciary had no jurisdiction over the Tribunal.

In October 2001 the initial indictment against Milošević relating to Kosovo was amended, henceforth alleging that he had organized security-force operations against Kosovar Albanians, which had resulted in the expulsion of 80,000 civilians from the province. (In September investigators announced that

five mass graves, containing remains of civilians killed during the conflict in Kosovo, had been discovered.) Also in October Milošević was further indicted in connection with war crimes perpetrated in Croatia in 1991–92; he was accused of ordering the forcible removal of the majority of the non-Serb population from one-third of the territory of Croatia, with the aim of incorporating the region into a Serb-dominated state. Four former naval officers were also indicted for participation in an offensive by the Yugoslav People's Army against the Dubrovnik region of Croatia in 1991. The former Commander of the Yugoslav Navy, Pavle Strugar, surrendered to the ICTY later in October 2001, and a further senior officer travelled voluntarily to the Hague in early November. Later in November Milošević (hitherto indicted for crimes against humanity, breaches of the 1949 Geneva Convention, and violations of the laws or customs of war) was charged, for the first time, with genocide, in connection with the atrocities perpetrated by Serbian forces during the planned removal of Muslims and Croats from large areas of Bosnia and Herzegovina in 1992–95. He continued to refuse to recognize the authority of the ICTY, and 'not guilty' pleas were submitted on his behalf for all three indictments. In December the European Court of Human Rights announced that Milošević had initiated a further challenge to the legality of his detention and trial in the Netherlands. Milošević's trial officially commenced on 12 February 2002 (with testimony on the charges relating to Kosovo), and was expected to continue for at least two years. Milošević, who had decided to conduct his own defence, continued to deny all charges, and strongly condemned the NATO bombardment of Serbia in 1999 (see below).

In December 2001 the Speaker of the Serbian National Assembly, who was the deputy leader of the DPS and a close associate of Koštunica, was obliged to resign from the post, after accusing parties belonging to the DOS coalition of electoral malpractice. In January 2002 the Federal Minister of Finance, who had opposed a decision by the National Bank of Yugoslavia to declare four Serbian banks insolvent (in accordance with structural reforms), also tendered his resignation. In March one of the Serbian Deputy Prime Ministers, Momčilo Perišić, was arrested, and subsequently resigned, after military intelligence sources claimed to have evidence that he had given classified information to a US diplomat. Djindjić rejected demands by Koštunica that he also submit his resignation over the issue, and requested the dismissal of the head of the military security service responsible for Perišić's arrest. Perišić claimed that the charges had been fabricated, in an attempt to cause the dissolution of Djindjić's Government. In June the DPS withdrew from the Serbian National Assembly, in protest at the expulsion of 21 DPS deputies. The Serbian Government was reorganized in the same month.

Following protracted negotiations on the issue of Montenegro's independence (which were mediated by the EU from November 2001), the government leaders of the FRY and the two entities signed a framework agreement on 14 March 2002, providing for the establishment of a state union (to be known as 'Serbia and Montenegro'). Under the accord, the two republics were to maintain separate economies, but have joint foreign and defence ministries, and elect a new, joint presidency and legislature. (However, Montenegro was to retain the right to refer the issue of independence to a referendum after a period of three years.) It was envisaged that, following endorsement of the agreement by the Federal Assembly and the legislatures of the two republics, a new constitution would be adopted, and elections to the new joint parliament would take place later that year. Later in March the LAM withdrew from Djukanović's coalition (thereby ending its narrow majority in the Republican Assembly), in protest at the agreement, which prompted widespread criticism from pro-independence supporters. In early April the legislatures of Serbia and Montenegro both approved the accord, which was submitted for ratification in the Federal Assembly. However, four principal pro-independence ministers, belonging to the LAM and the SDP, subsequently resigned from the Montenegrin Government. On 19 April Vujanović submitted his resignation. He was subsequently reappointed to office by Djukanović, but proved unable to secure majority support in the legislature for a new government. Djukanović was to announce early elections to the Republican Assembly by the end of July, in accordance with the Constitution.

Meanwhile, the USA renewed pressure on the Federal Government to demonstrate co-operation with the ICTY. Following the expiry of a deadline for Yugoslav compliance with these demands, economic aid to the FRY was suspended at the end of

March 2002. On 11 April the Federal Assembly finally approved legislation providing for the extradition of indicted war crime suspects, and the issue of arrest warrants for those who did not surrender to the ICTY. Shortly afterwards the former Serbian Minister of the Interior, Vlajko Stojiljković (who had been indicted in May 1999) committed suicide, in protest at the adoption of the legislation. Of 10 former Yugoslav state officials indicted, six (including Gen. Ojdanić and Sainović) agreed to surrender to the Tribunal. In early May 2002 a former Yugoslav Deputy Prime Minister, Nikola Sainović, who had been indicted in May 1999, was voluntarily transferred to the ICTY.

On 31 May 2002 the Federal Assembly officially approved the agreement on the creation of a joint state (which had been ratified by the legislatures of both entities in April). In June a reorganization of the Serbian Government was approved in the National Assembly. Later that month President Koštunica replaced the Chief of General Staff of the Yugoslav Army, Col-Gen. Nebojsa Pavković, who initially refused to accept his dismissal. In July the former Yugoslav President, Zoran Lilić, was arrested and extradited to the ICTY, having been subpoenaed as a prosecution witness in the trial of Milošević. He refused to testify unless he was himself guaranteed immunity from prosecution. It was announced that presidential elections in Serbia would be brought forward to 29 September, to allow the extradition of Milutinović (who had been indicted in 1999) to the ICTY. On 19 July, following the failure of Vujanović to secure majority support for a new government, the Republican Assembly was dissolved and further legislative elections in Montenegro were scheduled for 6 October. Later that month the ruling Serbian DOS coalition formally expelled the DPS. (DPS deputies had withdrawn from the National Assembly in June.)

In August 2002 Koštunica announced that he intended to seek election to the Serbian presidency in September (since the office of Federal President was no longer to exist under the agreement for the creation of a joint state). The other most prominent presidential candidate was Miroljub Labus, the incumbent Federal Deputy Prime Minister and Minister of Foreign Trade, who was supported by Djindjić. In the same month Milošević, from The Hague, appointed Bogoljub Bjelica as leader of the SPS (rejecting the candidate nominated by the party). At the Serbian presidential election, which was conducted on 29 September, Koštunica won some 30.9% of the votes cast, while Labus received 27.4% and Šešelj 23.2% of the votes; the rate of participation was 55.5% of the registered electorate. Since no candidate had secured an outright majority of votes, a second round between Koštunica and Labus was scheduled for 13 October. However, this second ballot, at which Koštunica secured some 68.4% of the votes cast, was declared invalid, owing to participation of only 44.0% of the electorate (lower than the required minimum level of 50%). (Šešelj had urged his supporters not to participate in the poll, while it was reported that Djindjić had also unofficially supported a boycott.)

Elections to the Montenegrin Republic Assembly took place on 20 October 2002: Djukanović's pro-independence coalition, now known as Democratic List for a European Montenegro, secured 39 of the 75 seats, with the SNP-led Together for Change coalition, which had opposed the planned creation of a looser union with Serbia, receiving 30 seats. In November Djukanović resigned from the office of President (prior to becoming the new Prime Minister), and a presidential election in Montenegro was scheduled for 22 December. On 6 December a 27-member commission on constitutional reform, comprising representatives of the principal parties of the two entities, submitted a draft of the new Constitutional Charter for the proposed state of Serbia and Montenegro. A third presidential poll in Serbia on 8 December was again annulled, owing to a voter turnout of only about 45.0% of the registered electorate; Koštunica had won 57.7% of votes cast. On 30 December Milutinović was replaced, on an interim basis, by the Speaker of the Serbian National Assembly, Nataša Micić. The presidential election in Montenegro on 22 December was also invalidated by a participation level of 45.9%, following a boycott organized by the SNP and the LAM; Vujanović (representing the Democratic List for European Montenegro) had consequently secured 83.7% of votes cast in the ballot, which was contested by 11 candidates. It was subsequently announced that a further election to the Montenegrin presidency would take place on 9 February 2003. Following protracted disagreement in the Republican Assembly between the DPMS and the allied SDP over the allocation of ministerial portfolios, a new Cabinet, headed by Djukanović, was finally approved by the legislature on 8 January 2003.

On 20 January 2003 Milutinović was voluntarily transferred to the ICTY, where he subsequently pleaded not guilty to charges relating to crimes perpetrated during the 1999 conflict in Kosovo. The new Constitutional Charter, which provided for the creation of the state union of Serbia and Montenegro, was approved by the Serbian National Assembly on 27 January and by the Montenegrin Republican Assembly on 29 January. At the end of January Marković was sentenced to a further seven years' imprisonment, after he was convicted for concealing evidence in connection with the assassination attempt against Drašković in October 1999 (which was attributed to members of a paramilitary group).

On 4 February 2003 both chambers of the Federal Assembly approved the Constitutional Charter, thereby officially replacing the FRY with the state union of Serbia and Montenegro. (A new flag, national symbols and anthem were expected to be adopted by the end of 2003.) Ethnic Albanians in Kosovo voiced their opposition to the province's inclusion in the new union as part of Serbia, and continued to demand independence. The presidential ballot in Montenegro on 9 February (at which Vujanović secured 82.0% of votes cast) was again declared invalid, with a rate of participation of 46.6% of the registered electorate. The Montenegrin authorities announced that electoral regulations would be amended to abolish the legal minimum requirement of 50% voter participation, and a third round was scheduled for 11 May. Later in February Šešelj surrendered to the ICTY, where he was charged on several counts in connection with the forcible removal of the non-Serb population from parts of the former Yugoslavia in 1991–95. On 25 February 2003, in accordance with the Constitutional Charter, the existing federal and entity legislatures elected a 126-member Assembly of Serbia and Montenegro, comprising 91 Serbian and 35 Montenegrin deputies. On 7 March a former Speaker of the Republican Assembly, Svetozar Marović, was elected unopposed as President of Serbia and Montenegro by the new Assembly. Marović also became Prime Minister, heading a five-member Cabinet, which was approved by the Assembly on 18 March.

On 12 March 2003 Djindjić, having survived an apparent assassination attempt in February, was shot dead by an unknown assailant outside government buildings in Belgrade. Micić immediately imposed a state of emergency in Serbia, and some 1,200 suspects, including a former Serbian Minister of Security, were arrested in connection with the assassination. The former Federal Minister of Internal Affairs, Zoran Živković, was nominated by the DP to replace Djindjić, and was approved by the Assembly as the new Serbian Prime Minister on 18 March. At the end of March security forces discovered the remains of Ivan Stambolić, who had been abducted in August 2000. The Serbian authorities issued an international arrest warrant for Mirjana Marković and her son (who were in hiding in Russia), in connection with the killing of Stambolić; Milošević (who had become hostile to Stambolić in the 1980s) was subsequently also charged. In mid-April the Assembly of Serbia and Montenegro voted in favour of extending the state's co-operation with the ICTY, ending a stipulation that all war crime suspects indicted by the Tribunal from that month be tried by domestic courts. Later that month the state of emergency in Serbia was ended and some 45 suspects, including Šešelj, were charged with alleged involvement in the assassination of Djindjić. Two former senior security advisers of Koštunica were also charged with conspiring to overthrow the Government in a coup, which, according to the Serbian authorities, was to have followed Djindjić's killing, with the aim of reinstating an administration opposed to co-operation with the ICTY. In early May two former Serbian heads of security and close associates of Milošević, already in detention in Belgrade in connection with Djindjić's assassination, were also indicted by the ICTY for war crimes perpetrated against Croats and Muslims.

At the third poll in Montenegro on 11 May 2003, Vujanović was elected to the presidency, with 63.3% of the votes cast. (Although only about 48% of the electorate had participated in the ballot, regulations had been amended to end the 50% minimum requirement.) Vujanović subsequently pledged that a referendum on the issue of independence would be conducted in Montenegro within three years.

With the imposition by the UN, from May 1992, of economic sanctions against the FRY, in an attempt to force Serbia to exert its influence to bring about an end to the conflict in Bosnia and Herzegovina, and the FRY's exclusion from the UN and other major multilateral organizations, Yugoslavia was largely isolated from the international community. In September 1994, after the Yugoslav Government imposed an embargo against Bosnia and Herzegovina in response to Bosnian Serb opposition to a peace plan, the UN suspended certain sanctions against the FRY. All UN sanctions against the FRY were suspended in November 1995, and the Yugoslav authorities ended the blockade of Bosnian Serb territories in February 1996. In early April Yugoslavia and the former Yugoslav republic of Macedonia (FYRM) signed an agreement on mutual diplomatic recognition. This was one of the major conditions imposed by the EU for wider recognition of Yugoslavia, and during April most EU countries proceeded to recognize the FRY as one of the successor states of the SFRY, and to upgrade their diplomatic relations to ambassadorial level. In August the FRY and Croatia signed a treaty of mutual recognition, providing for the establishment of full diplomatic relations; remaining issues of contention, notably the territorial dispute over the Prevlaka Peninsula (which Yugoslavia insisted was to be ceded to Montenegro under the terms of the Dayton agreement), on the Adriatic coast, were to be resolved by further negotiations. In October the UN Security Council officially ended sanctions against the FRY; however, some punitive measures imposed by the USA remained in place, effectively preventing the FRY Government access to the international financial institutions. Following the election of a new Federal Government in September 2000 (see above), the normalization of relations between the FRY and the international community proceeded rapidly. In October the EU ended the embargo on the export of petroleum products to the FRY, and also removed all financial and travel restrictions against Serbs (with the exception of Milošević and his relatives). At the end of October the US Government approved a programme of financial aid to the FRY, which was, however, conditional on the new administration's co-operation with the ICTY. The FRY was admitted to the UN on 1 November, and diplomatic relations were restored with a number of western European nations later that month.

In October 1997 students demonstrated in Priština in support of demands that the Serbian authorities implement an agreement, reached in 1996, which provided for the restoration of an Albanian language curriculum in the education system in the province. (Ethnic Albanians had initiated a boycott of the state school system imposed in the province, following the closure in 1990 of schools in which the Albanian language was used.) In late December the Serbian security forces violently suppressed further student protests in the province, injuring a large number of demonstrators. In early January 1998 the Kosovo Liberation Army (KLA—Ushtria Clirimtare e Kosoves), a paramilitary movement that had claimed responsibility for a number of attacks against members of the Serbian security forces in 1997, announced its intention to achieve separatism for the province through armed resistance against the Serbian authorities. Later in January 1998 special Serbian security forces were dispatched to Kosovo with the aim of quelling KLA activity. In late February four members of the Serbian security forces were killed by KLA troops, prompting a retaliatory operation by Serbian security forces, which killed some 24 ethnic Albanians in villages in central Kosovo. Although the Serbian authorities claimed that those killed had been members of the KLA, they were accused of instigating massacres of civilians. In early March Serbian security forces staged an offensive against KLA bases in central Kosovo, subsequently claiming to have killed the movement's leader and capturing a number of its troops. Ethnic Albanians staged a number of mass protests in response to the violence in the province. Despite international condemnation (see below), the Serbian security forces continued to instigate reprisals for KLA attacks; by the end of March it was reported that about 80 ethnic Albanians had been killed. The UN Preventive Deployment Force in Macedonia (UNPREDEP) increased its presence at the border with the FRY, amid international concern that the violence would escalate into a large-scale regional conflict.

In early March 1998 a Serbian government delegation was dispatched to Priština to enter into discussions with the DAK 'government', headed by Ibrahim Rugova (which supported the achievement of autonomy for the province through peaceful means). However, Rugova rejected the offer of negotiations, on the grounds that it had been made in an effort to reduce international pressure on the FRY Government. Elections to the 'Kosovo Assembly' took place later in March, while Rugova was elected 'President' with more than 90% of the votes cast. (The Serbian authorities again declared the elections to be illegal.) In early April Milošević announced that a referendum was to be

conducted in Serbia to determine whether the authorities should accept the mediation urged by the international community to resolve the conflict in Kosovo; at the referendum, which took place later that month, his refusal of mediation was endorsed by 94.7% of votes cast. In May the Serbian authorities (which continued to refuse international mediation) dispatched large numbers of security forces to western Kosovo, following reports that the KLA was receiving illicit supplies of armaments from Albania.

In February 1998 the US Government announced a relaxation of its remaining sanctions against the FRY, in response to Milošević's support for the Bosnian peace process. In early March, however, the USA and EU issued statements condemning the violent measures taken by the Serbian security forces to suppress the activities of the KLA in Kosovo (while also criticizing the violence employed by the KLA in support of separatism). The US Government announced that it was to withdraw the concessions that it had granted to the FRY in February, and threatened possible military intervention in Kosovo. The 'Contact Group', which had been established in response to the Bosnian conflict, was convened in London; member nations envisaged the imposition of further sanctions against the FRY, including an embargo on armaments, unless the Serbian authorities acceded to a number of demands, including the withdrawal of security forces from Kosovo and the initiation of negotiations regarding the future status of the province. The British Government subsequently submitted a draft resolution to the UN Security Council for the imposition of an embargo on armaments against the FRY. Following a further meeting of the 'Contact Group', which took place in Bonn, Germany, later in March a statement was issued conceding that the Serbian authorities had achieved progress in reaching an agreement on education (see above), but continued to demand that they engage in negotiations regarding the future status of Kosovo. At the end of March the UN Security Council officially imposed an embargo on armaments against the FRY; of the member nations of the Council, only the People's Republic of China failed to endorse the resolution. The members of the 'Contact Group' (apart from Russia) announced in April that Yugoslav assets abroad were to be 'frozen' and in May imposed a ban on foreign investment in Serbia.

In early July 1998 Milošević agreed that diplomatic observers from the EU, the USA and Russia would be allowed access to all regions of Kosovo to report on the activities of Serbian security forces. The 'Contact Group', which met in Bonn to discuss a peace settlement for Kosovo, recognized for the first time that it would be necessary to include KLA representatives in future negotiations on the status of the province. Meanwhile, Serbian security forces continued to initiate attacks against the KLA in Kosovo. At the end of July, following discussions with a visiting EU delegation, Milošević apparently agreed to suspend the military action by the Serbian security forces. However, violence in the province continued during August, with further Serbian offensives against the KLA and killings of ethnic Albanian civilians (including a massacre at the southern town of Orahovac).

In September 1998 the UN Security Council adopted Resolution 1199 (with the People's Republic of China abstaining), which demanded the immediate cessation of hostilities in Kosovo, the withdrawal of Serbian forces from the province, unrestricted access for humanitarian aid organizations, and the continuation of negotiations to determine the status of the province. NATO subsequently authorized its Supreme Allied Commander, Gen. Wesley Clark, to request member states to provide forces for possible military intervention. Despite an announcement by Marjanović at the end of September that Serbian security forces had suspended hostilities against the KLA, intensive fighting south of Priština was reported. In early October the 'Contact Group' reiterated the demands of the UN Security Council. (Russia continued to oppose military intervention against the FRY and had indicated that it would veto a further UN Security Council resolution authorizing such action.) NATO officially approved air bombardments against the FRY, and issued an ultimatum to Milošević that attacks would commence unless he complied with UN demands by a stipulated date later that month. Following intensive discussions with the US special envoy, Richard Holbrooke, Milošević agreed to the presence in Kosovo of a 2,000-member OSCE 'verification force' (to be known as the Kosovo Diplomatic Observer Mission), and to NATO surveillance flights in FRY airspace, to monitor the implementation of the UN Security Council's demands. Serbian leaders in Kosovo criticized Milošević's acceptance of the peace settlement, while the KLA considered the deployment of the OSCE monitors to be inadequate and continued to urge NATO military intervention. It was subsequently reported that the majority of federal army units had been withdrawn from Kosovo, but that some 11,600 members of the special Serbian security forces remained in the province. NATO urged further progress in the withdrawal of Serbian forces from Kosovo, but at the end of October suspended indefinitely the implementation of military action against the FRY.

In November 1998 the deployment of OSCE observers in Kosovo commenced; however, intermittent violations of the cease-fire were reported. Following the outbreak of heavy fighting between the KLA and Serbian forces in northern Kosovo in December, it became evident that the OSCE monitoring force was inadequate for peace-keeping operations (for which it had no mandate). A 2,300-member NATO 'extraction force' was deployed in the FYRM, near the border with Kosovo, to effect the evacuation of the OSCE monitors in the event of attacks against them. In early January 1999 further clashes between Serbian and KLA forces were reported. In mid-January the discovery that some 45 ethnic Albanian civilians had been killed at the village of Racak, 30 km south-west of Priština, prompted international condemnation of the Serbian authorities. OSCE observers dismissed claims by the Federal Government that those killed had been members of the KLA. At the end of January the 'Contact Group', meeting in London, decided that a peace conference should be convened at the French town of Rambouillet in early February. The British Secretary of State for Foreign and Commonwealth Affairs, Robin Cook, visited Belgrade to present the demands of the 'Contact Group' (which he chaired) that Serbian, DAK and KLA leaders attend the negotiations on a draft peace agreement, based on Hill's earlier proposals. Following international pressure, the KLA agreed that representatives of the movement would attend the conference, while in early February the Serbian legislature voted in favour of participation.

In early February 1999 the peace conference was convened in Rambouillet, as scheduled. Under the proposed peace plan, which was presented by the 'Contact Group' to the delegations, the Serbian authorities would be required to withdraw most of the 14,000 armed and security forces in Kosovo, while the KLA would disarm within a period of three months. It was envisaged that NATO troops would be deployed in Kosovo to enforce the peace agreement. Negotiations at Rambouillet were extended, owing to the opposition of the Serbian delegation to the proposed deployment of the NATO force, and to the reluctance of elements of the KLA to accept the provisions in the agreement for disarmament. At the end of February, however, the ethnic Albanian delegation, including the KLA representatives, agreed, in principle, to accept the peace plan. Meanwhile, in early March it was reported that Serbian troops had forced several thousand ethnic Albanian civilians to flee from southern Kosovo, amid continued heavy fighting in the province. The peace conference was reconvened at Rambouillet in mid-March. The ethnic Albanian representatives signed the agreement; however, the Serbian delegation continued to present objections and proposed amendments to the peace plan, which were rejected by the 'Contact Group'. It was subsequently reported that the Federal Government had deployed a further 30,000 Serbian forces in, or near, Kosovo. NATO reiterated threats of imminent air bombardments, despite continued opposition from the Russian Government, which attempted unsuccessfully to persuade Milošević to accept the peace plan. In the absence of a negotiated settlement to the conflict, the NATO Secretary-General ordered the commencement of air attacks against the FRY, in a campaign, codenamed Operation Allied Force, which was designed to force Milošević's capitulation to the demands of the 'Contact Group'.

On 24 March 1999 NATO forces commenced an aerial bombardment of air defences and military installations, notably in Belgrade, Novi Sad, Priština and Podgorica. The Federal Government declared a state of war (which, however, the Montenegrin administration refused to recognize), suspended diplomatic relations with the USA, France, Germany and the United Kingdom (the countries directly involved in the attacks), and ordered foreign journalists to leave the country. China and Russia immediately condemned the air offensive (which NATO justified on humanitarian grounds, despite the lack of endorsement by a UN Security Council resolution), while the Italian and Greek Governments expressed reservations, and urged further diplomatic efforts. Serbian security forces in Kosovo subse-

quently intensified the campaign of mass expulsions and large-scale massacres of the ethnic Albanian civilian population (which was condemned by the international community as genocidal), precipitating a continued exodus of refugees from the province. By early April some 140,000 ethnic Albanians had fled to the FYRM, 300,000 to Albania, and 32,000 to Montenegro. Some 12,000 NATO troops were stationed at the FYRM border with Kosovo, after the reinforcement of the 'extraction force' in preparation for possible Serbian counter-attacks.

During April 1999 the NATO air offensive intensified, with the extension of legitimate targets to include those of political and economic significance; the bombardment of the Serbian state television station attracted particular criticism. The increasing number of civilian casualties was condemned by opponents of the air offensive; notably, NATO aircraft bombarded a convoy of ethnic Albanian refugees in Kosovo in mid-April, killing about 64, apparently owing to confusion over Serbian military targets. NATO imposed an embargo on the export of petroleum to the FRY (which, however, Russia strongly opposed), with the aim of increasing the effects of the destruction of the country's petroleum refineries. Djukanović refused to comply with an order from Milošević to place Montenegrin security forces under federal military command (following warnings by NATO that Milošević intended to overthrow the Montenegrin Government). In late April Drašković was removed from his office of Federal Deputy Prime Minister, after he publicly opposed Milošević's refusal to comply with NATO demands.

From April 1999 the Russian special envoy to the Balkans, Viktor Chernomyrdin, was engaged in intensive mediation effort with the Federal Government, but urged a suspension of the NATO air offensive. NATO, however, continued to demand the full withdrawal of Serbian forces from Kosovo, and the return of refugees with an international military presence, as a precondition to the suspension of air attacks. In early May the Group of Eight (G-8—comprising the seven Western industrialized nations and Russia), meeting in Bonn, agreed on general principles for a political solution to the conflict (which was referred to the UN Security Council), although differences over the composition of the international military force for Kosovo remained. Shortly afterwards, apparently owing to faulty military information, NATO forces bombarded the embassy of the People's Republic of China in Belgrade. Violent anti-NATO protests ensued in the Chinese capital, Beijing, and the Chinese Government, supported by Russia, demanded a cessation of the air offensive and Milošević's agreement to peace proposals as a precondition to the discussion of the settlement at the UN Security Council. The Federal Government protested to the International Court of Justice (ICJ) that the NATO air offensive was an illegal act of aggression, on the grounds that it had not received UN authorization. (The ICJ subsequently rejected the legal appeal.) At mid-May it was estimated that the NATO air campaign had resulted in the deaths of 1,200 civilians; about 600,000 ethnic Albanian refugees from Kosovo had fled to neighbouring countries. (A proportion of the refugees were provisionally resettled in Canada, the USA and EU member nations.)

At the beginning of June 1999 the Federal Government announced that it had accepted the G-8 principles for a solution to the conflict. On 3 June, following mediation by the President of Finland, Martti Ahtisaari, the Serbian National Assembly formally approved a peace plan presented to the Federal Government by EU and Russian envoys. The peace agreement provided for the withdrawal of Serbian forces from Kosovo, and the deployment of a joint NATO-Russian peace-keeping force of about 50,000 personnel. Ethnic Albanian refugees were to be allowed to return to Kosovo, and the province was to be granted some autonomy under an interim administration. On 9 June, following discussions between NATO and Yugoslav military commanders, which were conducted in the FYRM, a Military Technical Agreement, providing for the complete withdrawal of Serbian forces within 11 days, was signed. On the following day the UN Security Council adopted Resolution 1244 (with the People's Republic of China abstaining) approving the peace plan for Kosovo, and NATO announced the suspension of the air offensive, after it had been verified that the withdrawal of Serbian forces had commenced. NATO formally approved the establishment of the Kosovo Force (KFOR), and divided the province into five sectors (which were to be under the respective control of the United Kingdom, Germany, France, the USA and Italy). Shortly before NATO troops commenced deployment in Kosovo, however, about 200 Russian forces unexpectedly entered the province, and assumed control of the airport at Priština (resulting in NATO personnel in the FYRM being placed on alert). Following discussions between the US Secretary of Defense, William Cohen, and his Russian counterpart, Igor Sergeyev, an agreement was reached whereby a Russian contingent, numbering about 3,600, would participate in KFOR (without controlling a separate sector as the Russian Government had previously demanded). Under the terms of the UN Resolution, the UN Interim Administration Mission in Kosovo (UNMIK, see p. 62) was established as the supreme legal and executive authority in Kosovo, with responsibility for civil administration, and for facilitating the reconstruction of the province as an autonomous region. A 3,100-member international police unit (which constituted part of UNMIK) was to supervise the creation of a new security force in Kosovo. The OSCE was allocated primary responsibility for installing democratic institutions, organizing elections in 2000 and monitoring human rights in the province. On 20 June NATO announced that the air campaign had officially ended, following the completion of the withdrawal of Serbian forces from Kosovo in accordance with the peace plan. The KLA subsequently signed an agreement with NATO, whereby the paramilitary organization was to disarm within a period of 90 days. On 24 June the Serbian National Assembly formally ended the state of war in the FRY. Meanwhile, following the deployment of KFOR troops, nearly one-half of the ethnic Albanian refugees in neighbouring countries had returned to Kosovo by the end of the month, while an estimated 70,000 Serbian civilians had fled from the province, following reprisal attacks from KLA forces and members of the returning Albanian community. Investigators from the ICTY discovered increasing forensic evidence of large-scale massacres perpetrated by the Serbian forces against ethnic Albanian civilians during the conflict.

In early July 1999 the UN Secretary-General appointed Bernard Kouchner, the French Secretary of State for Health, as his permanent Special Representative to head UNMIK. Later that month the Kosovo Transitional Council (KTC), comprising representatives of the principal political parties and ethnic groups in Kosovo, was created as a consultative body to UNMIK. In August Rugova, who had initially boycotted the KTC, owing to the exclusion of other parties formerly represented in the DAK 'government' of Kosovo, agreed to join the Council (which also included four members of the KLA). Meanwhile, despite the efforts of the KFOR troops to enforce order in Kosovo, the increasing incidence of retaliatory bomb attacks and killings of Serbian civilians, particularly in Priština, prompted most of the remaining Serbian residents to flee from the capital. In September attempts to resettle ethnic Albanian refugees in the province were impeded by increased violence, with armed clashes between Serbs and Albanians, in which KFOR troops also became involved. Later that month, following protracted negotiations prior to the expiry of the stipulated date for the disarmament of the KLA, NATO acceded to demands that the paramilitary organization be reconstituted as a 5,000-member civil emergency security force, the Kosovo Protection Corps. The Serbian representatives in the KTC subsequently withdrew from the Council in protest at the agreement.

In October 1999 KFOR troops intervened to suppress violent rioting by ethnic Albanians in the northern town of Titova Mitrovica (which, following the conflict, had become divided into separate ethnic Albanian and Serbian regions). In the same month a UN official was killed in Priština by ethnic Albanians, who reportedly believed him to be a local Serb. Later that month the UN Secretary-General recommended that the Security Council increase the strength of the UNMIK police force to 4,718, in response to a request from Kouchner. However, KFOR and UNMIK forces attracted increasing criticism for failing to protect the Serbian minority in Kosovo. In February 2000 five ethnic Albanians were killed in clashes with KFOR troops in Titova Mitrovica. Additional peace-keeping forces were dispatched to the town, and later that month NATO approved a reinforcement of KFOR (which at that time numbered 30,000). In the same month the 'Republic of Kosovo' was dissolved, and Rugova established the Democratic League of Kosovo (DLK) as a successor organization to the DAK. In April Serbian representatives announced that they were to resume participation in the KTC and another multi-ethnic body established by UNMIK. (At the end of April some 200,000 Serbs were estimated to have fled from Kosovo in response to numerous retaliatory attacks by KLA supporters, while about 822,000 of the estimated 900,000 ethnic Albanian refugees had returned to the province.)

Following the completion of a voter registration process, local government elections took place in Kosovo on 28 October 2000. Rugova's DLK secured 58% of the votes cast to 30 municipal councils, while the Democratic Party of Kosovo (DPK), led by a former KLA Commander, Hashim Thaçi, won 27% of the votes. In late November members of an ethnic Albanian separatist movement, the Army of Preševo, Medvedja and Bujanovac (believed to be related to the former KLA) launched an offensive in the Preševo region in southern Serbia, near the border with Kosovo. Attacks against a number of local government officials in Priština were also reported. Serbian authorities threatened to dispatch troops to the region (which formed part of the demilitarized zone under the June 1999 agreement), if KFOR troops failed to suppress the rebel activity. In January 2001 the Danish Minister of Defence, Hans Hækkerup, was nominated by the UN to replace Bernard Kouchner as head of UNMIK. In the same month the UN announced that it had discovered evidence of radioactivity in Kosovo, as a result of depleted uranium from ammunition used by NATO during its air bombardment. Violence continued in the province between the KFOR and ethnic Albanian separatists, who staged numerous attacks against Serbian civilians. In early March the ethnic Albanian rebels signed a cease-fire agreement, after NATO agreed for the first time to allow Serbian forces to enter the demilitarized zone; the troops were to provide support to KFOR in suppressing separatist activity in the province and to deter infiltration into Macedonia by ethnic Albanian militants (see the chapter on the FYRM). In September the UN Security Council finally ended the embargo on armaments that had been imposed against the FRY in March 1998.

In May 2001 UNMIK presented a plan granting provisional self-government for Kosovo, and announced that elections to a legislative assembly would take place in the province on 17 November. (However, the head of UNMIK was to retain ultimate executive authority, and control over the province's finances and judiciary.) Elections to 100 seats of the 120-member Kosovo Assembly were conducted peacefully, as scheduled. (The remaining 20 seats were allocated proportionally to Serbs and other ethnic groups.) Rugova's DLK secured 47 seats, while the DPK won 26 seats and a coalition of Serbian parties, known as Povratak (Return), 22 seats. A seven-member presidency for the legislature was established in December. However, repeated attempts to elect Rugova as President of Kosovo proved unsuccessful, owing to a boycott of the vote by the other parties represented in the legislature. In January 2002 the Serbian National Assembly voted in favour of restoring the autonomy of Vojvodina. In the same month a German diplomat, Michael Steiner, replaced Hækkerup as head of UNMIK. On 4 March, following protracted inter-party discussions, Rugova was finally elected President of Kosovo, after it was agreed that a member of the DPK, Bajram Rexhepi, would become Prime Minister. A 10-member Cabinet (in which the LDK held four and the DPK two portfolios) was subsequently established. In April the Povratak coalition finally agreed to join the Government. On 28 July, under an agreement reached by the Serbian authorities and ethnic Albanian separatists, elections to new multi-ethnic local governments in the municipalities of Preševo, Medvedija and Bujanovac were conducted peacefully. In August KFOR troops arrested a former KLA commander, Rustem Mustafa; he and a further three KLA members were subsequently charged with war crimes perpetrated against ethnic Albanians who had been perceived as co-operating with the Serbian authorities. The LDK won control of most municipalities at local government elections in Kosovo, which were conducted on 26 October. In February 2003 KFOR forces arrested three prominent members of the KLA, who were subsequently extradited to the ICTY and charged with crimes committed at a detention camp during the Kosovo conflict.

Government

On 4 February 2003 the legislature of the Federal Republic of Yugoslavia (FRY—comprising the two republics of Serbia and Montenegro) approved a Constitutional Charter, thereby officially reconstituting the FRY as the state union of Serbia and Montenegro. On 25 February, in accordance with the Constitutional Charter, the existing federal and republican legislatures elected a 126-member Assembly of Serbia and Montenegro, comprising 91 Serbian and 35 Montenegrin deputies, for a four-year term. On 7 March the Assembly elected a joint President of Serbia and Montenegro, who was also the Prime Minister of the union, for a four-year term. A five-member joint Cabinet was approved by the Assembly on 18 March. At republican level legislative power continued to be vested, respectively, in the 250-member National Assembly of Serbia and the 75-member Republican Assembly of Montenegro, both of which were directly elected. Each member state had its own elected President and Government. Under the Constitutional Charter, the armed forces of Serbia and Montenegro were under the command of the Supreme Defence Council, which comprised the three Presidents.

In June 1999 the UN Interim Administration Mission in Kosovo (UNMIK, see p. 62) was established as the supreme executive and legal authority in the province of Kosovo and Metohija (see Recent History). (Kosovo remained part of Serbia under the Constitutional Charter of February 2003.) Elections to 30 municipal councils in Kosovo took place in October 2000. Elections to 100 seats of a 120-member Kosovo Assembly were conducted on 17 November 2001. (The remaining 20 seats were allocated proportionally to Serbs and other ethnic groups.) A seven-member presidency for the legislature was subsequently established. In March 2002 the Assembly elected a President, and a 10-member Cabinet, headed by a Prime Minister, for the province.

Defence

Military service is compulsory for men, and lasts for 12–15 months. Voluntary military service for women was introduced in 1983. In August 2002 the estimated total strength of the armed forces was 74,500 (of whom 60,000 were conscripts), including an army of 60,000, a navy of 3,500 and an air force of 11,000. Projected budgetary expenditure on defence by the Government in 2001 was 32,100m. dinars. Under an agreement between NATO and the Federal Government, reached in June 1999 (see Recent History), and a subsequent UN resolution, the Kosovo Force (KFOR), led by NATO, was deployed in the province of Kosovo and Metohija. The UN Security Council established the UN Interim Administration Mission in Kosovo (UNMIK, see p. 62) as the supreme legal and executive authority in the province. KFOR comprised its maximum authorized strength of 50,000 personnel, of whom 42,500 (contributed by more than 30 nations) were deployed in Kosovo, and a further 7,500 in neighbouring countries. At January 2003 UNMIK comprised 4,446 civilian police officers, 39 military personnel, and an additional 1,022 international civilian personnel and 3,243 local civilian personnel. In September 1999, following the disarmament of the insurgent paramilitary organization, the Kosovo Liberation Army, the movement became reconstituted as a 5,000-member civil emergency security force, known as the Kosovo Protection Corps.

Economic Affairs

In 2000, according to estimates by the World Bank, the gross national income (GNI) of the Federal Republic of Yugoslavia (FRY—comprising the two republics of Serbia and Montenegro —reconstituted as Serbia and Montenegro in February 2003), was US $10,080m. (measured at 1998–2000 prices). (GNI per head in 1999 was $1,060.) During 1990–2000, it was estimated, the population increased by an annual average of 0.1%, while gross domestic product (GDP) per head increased, in real terms, by 1.8% during 1995–2001. Overall GDP increased, in real terms, at an average annual rate of 2.0% in 1995–2001; growth in 2000 and in 2001 was 5.0%.

Agriculture (including forestry and fishing) contributed an estimated 23.3% of GDP in 2001. In 2002 an estimated 4.0% of the total employed labour force were engaged in the sector. The FRY's principal crops are maize, wheat, sugar beet and potatoes. The cultivation of fruit and vegetables is also important. In 1990–95 agricultural GDP declined, in real terms, by 6.2%. Agricultural production in the FRY increased by 1.3% in 1996, and by 7.2% in 1997, but declined by 4.0% in 1998, by 0.9% in 1999 and by an estimated 19.7% in 2000.

Industry (including mining, manufacturing and power) contributed an estimated 37.1% of GDP in the FRY in 2001, with construction accounting for a further 6.2%. Including construction, the sector engaged an estimated 35.5% of the employed labour force in 2002. In 1990–95 industrial GDP (excluding construction) declined, in real terms, by 58.0%. Industrial production increased by an estimated 18.9% in 1996–2000 (declining by 24.4% in 1999, but increasing by an estimated 11.1% in 2000, according to the IMF).

In 2002 the mining and quarrying sector engaged 1.8% of the employed labour force. The principal minerals extracted in the FRY are coal (mainly brown coal), copper ore and bauxite. Iron ore, crude petroleum, lead and zinc ore and natural gas are also produced. Mining has been less severely affected in recent years than other sectors.

In 2002 the manufacturing sector engaged 26.9% of the employed labour force. In that year the principal branches of manufacturing were building materials, metalworking and electrical equipment, chemicals and paper, textiles, leather and rubber, woodworking, and food products and tobacco. In 1996–2000, according to official estimates, production of capital goods increased by 6.8% and intermediate goods by 1.1%.

Energy in the FRY is derived principally from thermal power stations (providing about 68% of total electricity generated in 1994) and hydroelectric power (32%). Imports of mineral fuels accounted for about 20.7% of the value of total imports in 2001.

Services contributed an estimated 33.4% of GDP in the FRY in 2001. Some 60.6% of the employed labour force were employed in the sector in 2002. In 1990–95 GDP in the transport and communications sector declined, in real terms, by 68.2%; GDP in commerce declined by 42.0%, and GDP in the catering and tourist trades by 24.6%. Total foreign tourist arrivals increased from 151,650 in 1999 to 238,957 in 2000.

In 2000 the FRY recorded a visible trade deficit of US $1,988m., and there was a deficit of $1,298m. on the current account of the balance of payments. In 2001 the principal source of imports (14.2%) was Russia; other major sources were Germany, Italy and Greece. The principal market for exports in that year was Italy (16.4%); other important purchasers were Bosnia and Herzegovina, Germany, the FYRM, and Switzerland and Liechtenstein. The main exports from the FRY in 2001 were basic manufactures (principally non-ferrous metals, and iron and steel), miscellaneous manufactured articles (notably articles of clothing), foodstuffs, machinery and transport equipment, and chemicals. The principal imports in that year were machinery and transport equipment, mineral fuels, basic manufactures, chemicals, and foodstuffs.

In 2001 the overall budgetary deficit was equivalent to 5.7% of GDP. At the end of 2000 total external debt of the former Yugoslavia was US $11,960m., of which $6,074m. was long-term public debt. In 1991–2001 the rate of inflation increased by an annual average of 11.5%. Consumer prices increased by 88.9% in 2001. The rate of unemployment was estimated at 29.6% of the labour force in 2002.

Owing to armed conflict in parts of the former SFRY and the imposition by the UN of sanctions on the FRY in May 1992, the country's membership of numerous international organizations was suspended. Following the political changes in the FRY in September 2000, the country was readmitted to the UN on 1 November. It was readmitted to the Organization for Security and Co-operation in Europe (OSCE, see p. 283) later in November, to the IMF in December and to the World Bank in May 2001. Serbia and Montenegro officially became a member of the Council of Europe (see p. 181) in April 2003.

Since its constitution in April 1992 the FRY has experienced severe economic deterioration, as a result of regional conflict, international isolation and lack of structural reform and investment. In July 1998 the Montenegrin Government announced that it had assumed full control of the republic's economy, owing to the adverse effects of international sanctions and the pressures of federal government economic policy. The NATO bombing offensive of the FRY in March–June 1999 (see Recent History) resulted in extensive damage to infrastructure and severe economic hardship in Serbia. Following the election of a new Federal Government in September 2000, however, the FRY's integration into international institutions progressed rapidly. In October the European Union (EU, see p. 199) ended all sanctions against the FRY (including the damaging embargo on petroleum exports, imposed in April 1999), and it was agreed that the country would receive aid under the EU's programme for Balkan reconstruction, development and stabilization. In December the FRY was readmitted to the IMF, and was granted emergency post-conflict assistance. The US Government officially ended economic sanctions against the FRY in January 2001; however, subsequent financial support from the USA was made conditional on the Yugoslav authorities' co-operation with the International Criminal Tribunal for the former Yugoslavia (ICTY). The new Federal Government implemented a short-term stabilization programme, which involved a managed flotation of the currency. In June an international donor conference pledged further funds to support the FRY's economic recovery. Economic activity continued to increase from very low levels, but real GDP remained at less than one-half of its 1989 total. In

November 2001 the 'Paris Club' of creditor Governments agreed to cancel two-thirds of the FRY's outstanding debt, conditional on the authorities reaching a further agreement with the IMF. In April 2002, following renewed US pressure on the Government to demonstrate full co-operation with the ICTY, the Federal Assembly finally approved legislation providing for the extradition of war crime suspects. In May the IMF approved an extended credit arrangement to support the Government's economic programme for 2002–05. Further stabilization efforts resulted in a reduced rate of inflation and strengthening of foreign reserves in 2002. Serbia's economy had recovered significantly, although illicit activity continued to account for 40%–50% of GDP and living standards remained low. Principal objectives included further liberalization of the foreign-exchange market, strengthening of the banking system, and restructuring and privatization of state-owned enterprises. It was hoped that the establishment of the state union of Serbia and Montenegro in February 2003 would further the normalization of economic relations between the two entities, with the harmonization of trade, customs and tax systems in accordance with EU standards. It was reported, however, that the two republics had failed to reach agreement on the harmonization of trade regulations by a stipulated date at the end of April, thereby possibly delaying consideration of Serbia and Montenegro for eventual EU membership.

Education

The educational system of Serbia and Montenegro is organized at republican level. Elementary education is free and compulsory for all children between the ages of seven and 15, when children attend the 'eight-year school'. Various types of secondary education are available to all who qualify, but the vocational and technical schools are the most popular. Alternatively, children may attend a general secondary school (gymnasium) where they follow a four-year course, prior to university entrance. At the secondary level there are also a number of art schools, apprentice schools and teacher-training schools. In 1996 primary enrolment was equivalent to 71% of children in the appropriate age-group (boys 71%; girls 72%), while the comparable ratio for secondary education was 64% (boys 62%; girls 66%). In 2000/01 there were 4,087 primary schools, attended by 787,423 students, 518 secondary schools, attended by 355,424 students, 51 post-secondary schools, and 87 institutes of higher education (including six universities) in the country.

Public Holidays

2003: 1–2 January (New Year), 7–8 January (Christmas), 25–28 April (Orthodox Easter), 27 April (Statehood Day), 1–2 May (Labour Days), 29–30 November (Republic Days).

2004: 1–2 January (New Year), 7–8 January (Christmas), 9–12 April (Orthodox Easter), 27 April (Statehood Day), 1–2 May (Labour Days), 29–30 November (Republic Days).

In addition, Montenegro observes a holiday on 13 July, and Serbia observes 7 July as a public holiday.

Weights and Measures

The metric system is in force.

Statistical Survey

Sources: Savezni zavod za statistiku (Federal Statistical Office), 11000 Belgrade, Kneza Miloša 20; tel. (11) 681999; fax (11) 642368; internet www.szs.sv .gov.yu ; National Bank of Yugoslavia, 11000 Belgrade, bul. Revolucije 15; tel. (11) 3248841; internet www.nbj.yu.
Note: Unless otherwise indicated, figures in this Survey refer to the territory of the Federal Republic of Yugoslavia (FRY), comprising the two republics of Serbia and Montenegro (now the union of Serbia and Montenegro). Where data for the FRY are not available, the Survey has retained tables relating to the former Socialist Federal Republic of Yugoslavia (SFRY), which comprised six republics. Such tables are indicated by the phrase 'former SFRY' after the heading.

Area and Population

AREA, POPULATION AND DENSITY

Area (sq km)	102,173*
Population (census results)	
31 March 1981	9,897,986
31 March 1991	
Males	5,157,120
Females	5,236,906
Total	10,394,026
Population (official estimates at mid-year)	
2000	10,633,500
2001	10,651,600
2002	10,664,300
Density (per sq km) at mid-2002	104.4

* 39,449 sq miles.

REPUBLICS

(census of 31 March 1991)

Republic	Area (sq km)	Population	Density (per sq km)	Capital (with population)
Serbia . .	88,361	9,778,991	111	Belgrade (1,168,454)
Vojvodina* . .	21,506	2,013,889	94	Novi Sad (179,626)
Kosovo and				
Metohija* .	10,887	1,956,196	180	Priština (155,499)
Montenegro . .	13,812	615,035	45	Podgorica† (117,875)
Total . .	102,173	10,394,026	102	—

* Provinces within Serbia.

† Formerly Titograd.

PRINCIPAL TOWNS

(population at 1991 census)

Beograd (Belgrade, the capital) . .	1,168,454	Podgorica* . . .	117,875
Novi Sad . . .	179,626	Subotica	100,386
Niš	175,391	Zrenjanin . . .	81,316
Kragujevac . . .	147,305	Pančevo	72,793
Priština	155,409	Čačak	71,550

* Formerly Titograd.

Mid-2001 (UN estimate, incl. suburbs): Belgrade 1,687,000 (Source: UN, *World Urbanization Prospects: The 2001 Revision*).

POPULATION BY ETHNIC GROUP

(1991 census)

Ethnic group	Population ('000)	%
Serbs	6,504	62.6
Albanians	1,715	16.5
Montenegrins	520	5.0
Yugoslavs	350	3.4
Hungarians	344	3.3
Muslims	336	3.2
Total (incl. others)	10,394	100.0

BIRTHS, MARRIAGES AND DEATHS

	Registered live births Number	Rate (per 1,000)	Registered marriages Number	Rate (per 1,000)	Registered deaths Number	Rate (per 1,000)
1995	140,504	13.3	60,325	5.7	107,535	10.2
1996	137,312	13.0	56,719	5.4	111,146	10.5
1997*	131,400	12.4	56,200	5.3	111,800	10.5
1998*	128,500	12.1	54,800	5.3	113,300	10.5
1999*	124,000	11.7	53,000	5.0	115,500	10.9
2000*	125,900	11.8	58,300	5.5	118,100	11.1
2001*	130,200	12.2	57,200	5.4	113,100	10.6
2002*	132,200	12.4	57,800	5.4	119,100	11.2

* Rounded figures. Data for Kosovo and Metohija are estimates (Source: Federal Statistical Office, Belgrade).

Source: UN, *Demographic Yearbook*.

Expectation of life (WHO estimates, years at birth): 72.2 (males 69.7; females 74.8) in 2001 (Source: WHO, *World Health Report*).

ECONOMICALLY ACTIVE POPULATION
('000 employees, average at 30 September)

	2000	2001	2002*
Agriculture, forestry, fishing and water works	95	90	87
Mining and quarrying	43	41	40
Manufacturing	668	643	591
Public utilities	54	55	53
Construction	111	104	97
Wholesale and retail trade	235	226	226
Hotels and restaurants	44	44	41
Transport, storage and communications	143	140	138
Financial intermediation	49	45	35
Real estate and property	50	56	52
Public administration and social security	70	73	72
Education	129	134	139
Health and social care	170	173	174
Other community, social and personal services	55	55	55
Private shop workers and owners	322	361	401
Total employed	2,237	2,241	2,201
Unemployed	806	850	924
Total labour force	3,043	3,091	3,125

* Estimates.

Health and Welfare

KEY INDICATORS

Total fertility rate (children per woman, 2001)	1.6
Under-5 mortality rate (per 1,000 live births, 2001)	19
HIV/AIDS (% of persons aged 15–49, 2001)	0.19
Physicians (per 1,000 head, 1998)	2.04
Hospital beds (per 1,000 head, 1995)	5.31
Health expenditure (2000): US $ per head (PPP)	237
Health expenditure (2000): % of GDP	5.6
Health expenditure (2000): public (% of total)	51

For sources and definitions, see explanatory note on p. vi.

Agriculture

PRINCIPAL CROPS
('000 metric tons)

	1999	2000	2001
Wheat	2,035.0	2,056.0	2,529.9
Barley	300.0	252.2	423.5
Maize	6,140.0	2,968.0	5,930.9
Oats	122.0	96.2	126.2
Sugar beet	2,427.6	1,070.0	1,806.4
Potatoes	865.0	690.4	1,015.0
Dry beans	73.0	33.9	31.6
Other pulses†	65.0	71.0	71.5
Walnuts	21.5	23.8	23.6†
Soybeans	294.0	170.6	207.1
Sunflower seed	273.0*	223.0*	317.9
Cabbages	282.0	285.3	283.9
Tomatoes	176.6	180.0†	175.2
Cucumbers and gherkins†	34.8	34.8	34.8
Chillies and green peppers	131.0	131.0†	132.5
Dry onions	120.0	120.0†	137.0
Garlic	36.5*	36.5†	28.2
Carrots	58.0†	60.0†	63.6
Apples	98.0	105.0†	197.5
Pears	70.0	60.0†	43.4
Cherries (incl. sour)	99.0	81.5	73.0
Peaches and nectarines	44.0	41.6	41.7
Plums	380.0	370.0	333.1
Strawberries	23.5†	25.1	34.7
Raspberries	60.0*	56.1	77.8
Grapes	213.0	362.6	380.8
Watermelons and melons	285.0*	244.4	253.9
Tobacco (leaves)	14.5	11.3	16.6

* Unofficial figure.
† FAO estimate(s).

Source: FAO.

LIVESTOCK
('000 head, year ending 30 September)

	1999	2000	2001
Horses	76	49	49*
Cattle	1,831	1,452	1,831*
Buffaloes	21	29	29*
Pigs	4,372	4,087	3,578
Sheep	2,195	1,917	1,448
Goats	326	241	164
Chickens	26,492†	21,118†	21,100*

* FAO estimate.
† Unofficial figure.

Source: FAO.

LIVESTOCK PRODUCTS
('000 metric tons)

	1999	2000	2001
Beef and veal	104.0	98.2	92.5
Mutton and lamb	22.0	22.0*	17.2
Pig meat	640.0†	655.4*	590.0*
Poultry meat	93.6	88.6*	82.8
Cows' milk	1,825.0	1,830.0*	1,625.3
Sheep's milk	34.0	26.0*	18.0
Cheese	12.7	12.0*	13.8
Butter	2.2	2.2*	2.3
Hen eggs	76.3	72.0	67.7
Honey	2.5	2.5*	2.3
Wool: greasy	3.0	3.0*	2.2
Wool: scoured	1.8	1.8*	1.8*
Cattle hides*	20.1	20.0	20.0
Sheep skins*	4.3	4.3	4.3

* FAO estimate(s).
† Unofficial figure.

Source: FAO.

Forestry

ROUNDWOOD REMOVALS

('000 cubic metres, excl. bark)

	1999	2000	2001
Sawlogs, veneer logs and logs for sleepers	972	1,266	1,006
Pulpwood	103	189	140
Fuel wood	1,282	1,772	1,277
Total	2,357	3,227	2,423

Source: FAO, *Yearbook of Forest Products*.

SAWNWOOD PRODUCTION

('000 cubic metres, incl. railway sleepers)

	1999	2000	2001
Coniferous (softwood)	94	106	95
Non-coniferous (hardwood)	270	398	297
Total	364	504	391

Source: FAO.

Fishing

('000 metric tons, live weight)

	1998	1999	2000
Capture	2.6*	1.3	1.1
Freshwater fishes	2.2*	0.8	0.7
Aquaculture	6.6	3.4	2.8
Rainbow trout	6.6	3.4	2.8
Total catch	9.2	4.7	3.9

* FAO estimate.

Source: FAO, *Yearbook of Fishery Statistics*.

Mining

('000 metric tons, unless otherwise indicated)

	1998	1999	2000
Coal	44,072	31,429	34,124
Crude petroleum	913	705	805
Lead and zinc ore*	1,249	349	602
Bauxite	226	500	630
Natural gas (million cubic metres)	731	679	729

* Figures refer to gross weight of ores extracted. In the former Socialist Federal Republic of Yugoslavia lead and zinc ore contained 2.7% lead and 2.3% zinc in 1989 and 1990.

Source: US Geological Survey.

Industry

SELECTED PRODUCTS

('000 metric tons, unless otherwise indicated)

	1997	1998	1999
Wine*	402.5	257.7	136.6
Edible vegetable oils*	122.9	130.3	132.6
Oil of sunflower seed*	89.9	96.5	77.0
Beer of barley*	610.6	662.8	682.5
Cotton yarn ('000 metric tons)	8.6	9.8	8.5
Wool yarn	5.6	6.7	4.8
Woven fabrics of cellulose fibres (million sq metres)	1.2	0.8	0.2
Footwear (excl. rubber) ('000 pairs)	6,848	6,976	3,892
Cement	2,011	2,253	1,575
Sulphuric acid	177	211	30
Motor spirit (petrol)	470	n.a.	n.a.
Residual fuel oil	959	584	n.a.
Pig-iron	907	792	128
Crude steel	979	948	226
Aluminium—unwrought	67.2	61.2	73.4
Refined copper—unwrought	106.6	94.4	50.1
Refined lead—unwrought	23.6	23.8	n.a.
Zinc—unwrought	31.4	15.6	0.8
Television receivers ('000 units)	25	30	13
Tractors (number)	4,099	3,530	1,867
Lorries (number)	1,278	1,139	407
Motor cars ('000)	10	12	8
Bicycles ('000)	37	50	18
Electric energy (million kWh)†	40,312	40,651	n.a.

* FAO figures, referring to production during crop year ending 30 September.
† Estimates.

Source: mainly UN, *Industrial Commodity Statistics Yearbook*.

Wine ('000 metric tons): 197.3 in 2000; 198.0 in 2001.

Edible vegetable oils ('000 metric tons): 128.5 in 2000.

Oil of sunflower seed ('000 metric tons): 70.1 in 2000; 84.2 in 2001.

Beer of barley ('000 metric tons): 680 in 2000–2001.

Pig-iron ('000 metric tons): 563 in 2000.

Crude steel ('000 metric tons): 682 in 2000.

Sources: FAO; US Geological Survey.

Finance

CURRENCY AND EXCHANGE RATES

Monetary Units
100 para = 1 Yugoslav dinar

Sterling, Dollar and Euro Equivalents (31 December 2002)
£1 sterling = 98.00 dinars
US $1 = 60.80 dinars
€1 = 63.76 dinars
1,000 Yugoslav dinars = £10.204 = $16.447 = €15.684

Average Exchange Rate (new dinars per US $)
1989   2.876
1990   11.318
1991   19.638

Note: On 1 January 1990 the new dinar, equivalent to 10,000 old dinars, was introduced in the Socialist Federal Republic of Yugoslavia (SFRY). After the disintegration of the SFRY, the Federal Republic of Yugoslavia (FRY) continued to use the Yugoslav dinar as its currency. Meanwhile, the other republics of the former SFRY introduced their own currencies to replace (initially at par) the Yugoslav dinar. As a result of rapid inflation in the FRY, the value of the Yugoslav dinar depreciated sharply. By the end of May 1993 the exchange rate was about 89,000 dinars per US dollar. After further devaluations, the currency was redenominated from 1 October, with the introduction of another new dinar, worth 1,000,000 of the former units. However, the depreciation of the currency continued, and on 30 December the new dinar was replaced by a further dinar, worth 1,000 million of its predecessors. In January 1994 there was another currency reform, with the establishment of a dinar officially valued at 1 Deutsche Mark (DM, equivalent to 13 million former dinars). In November 1999 Montenegro, one of the two constituent republics of the FRY, announced the introduction of the DM as its official currency. In September of that year the UN had decided to adopt the DM as the currency for official transactions in the Serbian province of Kosovo and Metohija. Euro notes and coins were introduced on 1 January 2002, replacing the DM, at an exchange rate of €1 = 1.95583 DM.

CONSOLIDATED BUDGET*
('000 million dinars)

Revenue†	2000	2001‡	2002§
Current revenue	140.2	300.5	419.8
Tax revenue	126.4	273.8	385.3
Personal income tax	12.7	36.2	52.8
Social security contributions	44.8	85.5	112.9
Retail sales tax	32.9	75.8	110.5
Excises	10.7	28.4	50.3
Taxes on international trade and operations	10.3	16.0	23.9
Other current revenue	13.8	26.6	34.6
Capital revenue	—	—	1.2
Total	140.2	300.5	421.0

Expenditure‖	2000	2001‡	2002§
Current expenditure	131.2	292.6	435.9
Expenditure on goods and services	66.4	134.5	178.9
Wages and salaries	36.0	73.0	98.6
Subsidies and other current transfers	62.5	152.4	239.0
Transfers to households	54.5	126.5	197.0
Capital expenditure	11.8	10.0	30.5
Total	143.0	310.2	477.0

* Comprising a consolidation of the Federal Budget, and the budgets of the Republic of Serbia and the Republic of Montenegro.
† Excluding grants received ('000 million dinars): 2.8 in 2000; 6.4 in 2001.
‡ Preliminary figures.
§ Projected figures.
‖ Excluding lending minus repayments ('000 million dinars): 0.3 in 2000; 9.6 in 2001.

Source: IMF, *Federal Republic of Yugoslavia: Selected Issues and Statistical Appendix* (May 2002).

INTERNATIONAL RESERVES
(former SFRY, US $ million at 31 December)

	1989	1990	1991
Gold*	80	81	81
IMF special drawing rights	—	13	
Foreign exchange	4,136	5,461	2,682
Total	4,216	5,555	2,763

* Valued at US $42.22 per troy ounce.

Source: IMF, *International Financial Statistics*.

Foreign exchange (FRY, US $ million at 31 December): 663.0 in 1999; 890.0 in 2000; 1,808.6 in 2001.

MONEY SUPPLY
(million dinars at 31 December)

	1999	2000	2001
Currency in circulation	6,688	10,932	25,273
Demand deposits	7,864	14,848	31,259
Total money (incl. others)	14,552	25,780	56,532

Source: IMF, *Federal Republic of Yugoslavia: Selected Issues and Statistical Appendix* (May 2002).

COST OF LIVING
(Consumer Price Index; base: previous year = 100)

	2000	2001	2002
Food	205	188	107
Clothing and footwear	171	184	117
Housing	145	227	146
Fuel and light	147	220	152
All items (incl. others)	186	189	117

NATIONAL ACCOUNTS

Gross Domestic Product by Economic Activity
(million dinars at current prices)*

	1997	1998	1999
Agriculture, hunting, forestry and fishing	19,875	25,274	37,331
Mining and quarrying	5,671	6,845	7,144
Manufacturing	23,555	32,934	42,958
Electricity, gas and water	4,900	6,030	7,879
Construction	5,460	7,170	8,220
Wholesale and retail trade	7,249	11,637	15,588
Restaurants and hotels	1,459	1,962	2,081
Transport, storage and communications	8,832	13,709	16,439
Financial intermediation	5,281	7,477	10,815
Real estate, renting and business activities	3,599	4,228	6,097
Public administration and defence; compulsory social security	5,016	6,033	10,274
Education	3,595	4,371	4,753
Health and social work	5,129	6,230	6,780
Other	3,539	4,949	5,600
GDP at factor cost	103,160	138,849	181,959
Indirect taxes, *less* subsidies	9,196	13,402	14,557
GDP in purchasers' values	112,355	152,251	196,516

2000: GDP in purchasers' values 358,056*.
* Foreign trade transactions at official exchange rates, and Federal Statistics Office estimates of change in stocks; excluding Kosovo and Metohija.

Source: IMF, *Federal Republic of Yugoslavia: Selected Issues and Statistical Appendix* (May 2002).

BALANCE OF PAYMENTS
(US $ million)

	1998	1999	2000
Exports of goods f.o.b.	2,858	1,498	1,723
Imports of goods c.i.f.	−4,849	−3,296	−3,711
Trade balance	−1,991	−1,798	−1,988
Exports of services	914	471	624
Imports of services	−421	−243	−293
Balance on goods and services	−1,498	−1,570	−1,657
Other income received	57	43	53
Other income paid	−49	−35	−42
Balance on goods, services and income	−1,490	−1,562	−1,646
Private transfers received	688	501	632
Private transfers paid	−378	−280	−284
Current balance	−1,180	−1,341	−1,298
Foreign direct investment (net)	113	112	25
Medium- and short-term loans: disbursements	50	29	377
Medium- and short-term loans: amortization	−25	−17	−143
Short-term loans and deposits (net)	−35	−37	−33
Other capital inflows	78	30	92
Net errors and omissions	884	1,113	1,207
Overall balance	−115	−111	227

External Trade

PRINCIPAL COMMODITY GROUPS
(distribution by SITC, US $ million)

Imports c.i.f.	1999	2000	2001
Food and live animals	279	279	441
Crude materials (inedible) except fuels	231	221	188
Mineral fuels, lubricants, etc.	588	745	1,001
Chemicals and related products	519	556	698
Basic manufactures	677	772	948
Machinery and transport equipment	714	820	1,029
Miscellaneous manufactured articles	213	237	356
Total (incl. others)	3,296	3,711	4,837

Exports f.o.b.	1999	2000	2001
Food and live animals	291	255	275
Crude materials (inedible) except fuels	82	123	102
Chemicals and related products	145	145	132
Basic manufactures	465	632	653
Machinery and transport equipment	184	215	243
Miscellaneous manufactured articles	221	270	363
Total (incl. others)	1,498	1,723	1,903

Source: IMF, *Federal Republic of Yugoslavia: Selected Issues and Statistical Appendix* (May 2002).

PRINCIPAL TRADING PARTNERS
(US $ million)*

Imports c.i.f.	1999	2000	2001
Austria	114	114	147
Bosnia and Herzegovina	187	174	135
Bulgaria	149	324	153
Germany	404	479	589
Greece	147	132	218
Hungary	101	123	194
Italy	333	390	500
Romania	108	145	175
Russia	274	319	685
Slovenia	24	35	145
Total (incl. others)	3,296	3,711	4,837

Exports f.o.b.	1999	2000	2001
Bosnia and Herzegovina	303	254	249
France	41	43	43
Germany	175	177	231
Greece	74	75	63
Hungary	32	62	63
Italy	167	223	312
Macedonia, former Yugoslav republic	157	210	176
Russia	77	86	80
Switzerland	106	107	160
United Kingdom	42	34	56
Total (incl. others)	1,497	1,723	1,903

* Imports by country of origins; exports by country of destination.

Source: IMF, *Federal Republic of Yugoslavia: Selected Issues and Statistical Appendix* (May 2002).

Transport

RAILWAYS
(traffic)

	1999	2000	2001*
Passengers carried ('000)	9,904	12,221	11,423
Passenger-kilometres (million)	860	1,436	1,292
Freight carried ('000 metric tons)	6,657	9,278	9,159
Freight ton-kilometres (million)	1,308	1,970	2,027

* Estimates.

ROAD TRAFFIC
(motor vehicles in use at 30 June)

	1997	1998	1999
Passenger cars	1,500,888	1,598,262	1,593,183
Buses and coaches	11,640	11,857	11,181
Goods vehicles	125,144	131,893	130,026
Motorcycles and mopeds	39,585	40,048	35,547

Source: IRF, *World Road Statistics*.

INLAND WATERWAYS

Fleet
(number of vessels)

	1994
Tugs	143
Motor barges	67
Barges	421
Tankers	100
Passenger vessels	8

Traffic
('000 metric tons)

	1992	1993	1994
Goods unloaded	9,777	2,270	2,776

SHIPPING

Merchant Fleet
(registered at 31 December)

	1999	2000	2001
Number of vessels	8	8	7
Displacement ('000 gross registered tons)	4.4	4.4	3.5

Source: Lloyd's Register-Fairplay, *World Fleet Statistics*.

International Sea-borne Freight Traffic
('000 metric tons, unless otherwise indicated)

	1998	1999	2000
Goods loaded	40	30	16
Goods unloaded	61	81	94

CIVIL AVIATION
(traffic)

	1999	2000	2001
Passengers carried ('000)	489	1,122	1,211
Passenger-kilometres (million)	332	978	997
Cargo carried ('000 tons)	1,091	3,053	3,773
Ton-kilometres (million)	1.6	7.6	4.2

Tourism

FOREIGN TOURIST ARRIVALS
(at accommodation establishments)

Country of origin	1998	1999	2000
Austria	7,019	2,933	5,189
Bosnia and Herzegovina	71,080	58,447	75,902
Bulgaria	10,523	5,946	8,605
Croatia	4,977	3,585	7,920
Czech Republic and Slovakia	6,891	3,057	8,668
Germany	13,033	3,907	8,327
Hungary	6,851	2,477	4,808
Italy	20,404	8,133	12,605
Macedonia, former Yugoslav republic	21,462	11,787	19,484
Romania	8,243	4,309	7,611
Russia	24,189	6,946	14,025
Slovenia	7,479	3,131	7,336
United Kingdom	6,838	2,171	3,225
USA	8,807	2,148	2,740
Total (incl. others)	282,639	151,650	238,957

Tourism Receipts (US $ million): 42 in 1997; 35 in 1998; 17 in 1999.

Source: mainly World Tourism Organization, *Yearbook of Tourism Statistics*.

Communications Media

	1999	2000	2001
Television receivers ('000 in use)	2,950	3,000	n.a.
Telephones ('000 main lines in use)	2,280.7	2,406.2	2,443.9
Mobile cellular telephones ('000 subscribers)	605.7	1,303.6	1,977.8
Facsimile machines (number in use)	19,860	n.a.	n.a.
Personal computers ('000 in use)	220	250	250
Internet users ('000)	80	400	600

Radio receivers ('000 in use): 3,150 in 1997.

Books (titles published): 5,367 in 1996.

Daily newspapers: 18 in 1996 (average circulation 1,128,000).

Non-daily newspapers: 602 in 1996 (average ciculation 3,935,000).

Periodicals: 411 in 1994 (average annual circulation 3,191,000).

Source: partly International Telecommunication Union.

Education

(1996/97, unless otherwise indicated)

	Institu- tions	Teachers	Students		
			Males	Females	Total
Pre-primary	1,748	17,198	94,139	87,986	182,125
Primary	4,436*	21,368†	224,887	212,893	437,780
Secondary . . .	2,284‡	55,745†	410,416	404,416	815,029
General	n.a.	n.a.	270,947	278,947	548,953
Teacher training . .	n.a.	n.a.	88	239	327
Vocational	n.a.	n.a.	140,322	125,427	265,749
Higher	145‡	12,273	79,616	92,697	172,313

* 1995/96 figure.
† 1992/93 figure.
‡ 1991/92 figure.

Source: mainly UNESCO, *Statistical Yearbook*.

Adult literacy rate: 93.3% (males 97.6%; females 89.2%) in 1991 (Source: UNESCO, *Statistical Yearbook*).

Directory

The Constitution*

The Constitution of the Federal Republic of Yugoslavia, comprising Serbia and Montenegro, was adopted on 27 April 1992. Its main provisions are summarized below:

The Federal Republic of Yugoslavia (FRY) is a sovereign federal state, based on the principle of equality of its citizens and its member republics. The FRY comprises the Republic of Serbia and the Republic of Montenegro, and there are constitutional provisions for it to be joined by other republics. The FRY covers a unified territory consisting of the territories of the member republics. The FRY borders are inviolable.

Each member republic will have sovereignty over issues which, under the Federal Constitution, do not come within the competence of the FRY. In the FRY, power is in the hands of citizens, who exercise it either directly or through their freely-elected representatives. The FRY is based on the rule of law. The FRY recognizes and guarantees human liberties and citizens' rights as recognized by international law. The FRY recognizes and guarantees the rights of national minorities to preserve, develop and express their ethnic, cultural, linguistic and other characteristics, and their right to use their own national symbols in accordance with international law.

Authority in the FRY is shared between legislative, executive and judicial organs of state. Under the Constitution, the FRY is a single economic space with a single market. Political pluralism is a condition for, and a guarantee of, a democratic political system in the FRY.

In the FRY all citizens are equal before the law, regardless of their national affiliation, race, sex, language, religion, political or other convictions, education, social origin, property status and any other personal characteristic. Each citizen has a duty to respect the freedoms and rights of others and will be accountable for it.

The freedom of work and enterprise is guaranteed in the FRY. The right to private ownership is guaranteed. Nobody can be deprived of property, nor can it be limited (except when general interests require, as envisaged by the law and provided that compensation not lower than the market value of the property is paid to the owner). A foreigner assumes the right to private ownership and the right to enterprise under the conditions of reciprocity.

The FRY establishes policies, adopts and implements federal laws, other regulations and general documents, and secures constitutional and judicial protection in the following areas: human liberties, citizens' rights and duties as laid down in the Federal Constitution, the single market, the development of the FRY, communications and technical and technological systems, safety in all types of transport, the health service, international relations, and the defence and security of the FRY.

Bodies of the FRY are: the Federal Assembly, the President of the Republic, the Federal Government, the Federal Court, the Federal Public Prosecutor and the National Bank of Yugoslavia. Provision is made for the power and composition of the Federal Constitutional Court.

The FRY has an army which protects its sovereignty, territory, independence and constitutional system. The Yugoslav Army has both active and reserve staff. The active staff comprises professional soldiers and conscripts engaged in national service. The President of the Republic commands the Army both in time of peace and in time of war, in accordance with decisions of the Supreme Defence Council. The Supreme Defence Council consists of the President of the Republic and presidents of member republics. The FRY President is the president of the Supreme Defence Council. National service in the FRY is compulsory. A citizen who does not wish to perform regular military service on account of religious or other conscientious objections can participate in national service in the Yugoslav Army without weapons or in civilian service.

* On 4 February 2003 the legislature of the Federal Republic of Yugoslavia (FRY—comprising the two republics of Serbia and Montenegro) approved a Constitutional Charter, thereby officially reconstituting the FRY as the state union of Serbia and Montenegro. Under the Constitutional Charter, a 126-member Assembly of Serbia and Montenegro, comprising 91 Serbian and 35 Montenegrin deputies, is directly elected for a four-year term. The Assembly elects a joint President of Serbia and Montenegro, who is also the Prime Minister of the union, for a four-year term. A five-member joint Cabinet is approved by the Assembly. At republican level legislative power continues to be vested, respectively, in the National Assembly of Serbia and the Republican Assembly of Montenegro, both of which are directly elected. Each republic has its own President and Government. The member states of Serbia and Montenegro are to amend their respective Constitutions in accordance with the Constitutional Charter.

The Government

HEAD OF STATE

President of the Republic: SVETOZAR MAROVIĆ (elected 7 March 2003).

COUNCIL OF MINISTERS
(April 2003)

Prime Minister: SVETOZAR MAROVIĆ.

Minister of Foreign Economic Relations: BRANKO LUKOVAC.

Minister of Foreign Affairs: GORAN SVILANOVIĆ.

Minister of Defence: BORIS TADIĆ.

Minister of Internal Economic Relations: AMIR NURKOVIĆ.

Minister of Human and Minority Rights: RASIM LJAJIĆ.

MINISTRIES

Office of the Prime Minister: Belgrade; tel. (11) 334281.

Ministry of Defence: 11000 Belgrade, Kneza Miloša 37; tel. (11) 656122.

Ministry of Foreign Affairs: 11000 Belgrade, Kneza Miloša 24; tel. (11) 682555; fax (11) 682668; e-mail smip@smip.sv.gov.yu; internet www.mfa.gov.yu.

Ministry of Foreign Economic Relations: Belgrade.

Ministry of Internal Economic Relations: 11070 Belgrade, Bulevar Lenjina 2; tel. (11) 2223550; fax (11) 195244.

Ministry of Human and Minority Rights: Belgrade.

The Republican Governments

MONTENEGRO

STATE PRESIDENT

President of the Republic: FILIP VUJANOVIĆ.

MINISTERS
(April 2003)

A coalition of the Democratic Party of Montenegrin Socialists (DPMS), the Social-Democratic Party of Montenegro (SDP) and the Democratic Union of Albanians (DUA).

Prime Minister: MILO DJUKANOVIĆ (DPMS).

Deputy Prime Minister, with responsibility for the Political System and Internal Affairs: DRAGAN DJUROVIĆ (DPMS).

Deputy Prime Minister, with responsibility for the Financial System and Public Spending: JUSUF KALOMPEROVIĆ (SDP).

Deputy Prime Minister, with responsibility for Economic Policy and Economic Development: BRANIMIR GVOZDENOVIĆ (DPMS).

Minister of Justice: ZELJKO STURANOVIĆ (DPMS).

Minister of Internal Affairs: MILAN FILIPOVIĆ (Ind.).

Minister of Finance: MIROSLAV IVANISEVIĆ (DPMS).

Minister of Foreign Affairs: DRAGIŠA BURZAN (SDP).

Minister of Education and Science: SLOBODAN BACKOVIĆ (DPMS).

Minister of Culture: VESNA KILIBARDA (Ind.).

Minister of Economic Affairs: DARKO USKOKOVIĆ (DPMS).

Minister of Maritime Industry and Transport: ANDRIJA LOMPAR (SDP).

Minister of Agriculture, Forestry and Water Management: MILUTIN SIMOVIĆ (DPMS).

Minister of Tourism: PREDRAG NENEZIĆ (DPMS).

Minister of Trade: SLAVICA MILACIĆ (DPMS).

Minister of the Environment and Town Planning: RANKO RADOVIĆ (Ind.).

Minister of Health: MIODRAG PAVLICIĆ (SDP).

Minister of Labour and Social Welfare: SLAVOLJUB STILJEPOVIĆ (DPMS).

Minister for the Protection of Human Rights of Ethnic Groups and National Minorities: JEZIM HAJDINAGA (DUA).

Minister without Portfolio: SUAD NUMANOVIĆ (DPMS).

MINISTRIES

Office of the President: Podgorica; fax (81) 42329.

Office of the Prime Minister: Podgorica, Jovana Tomaševića bb; tel. (81) 52833; fax (81) 52246.

Ministry of Agriculture, Forestry and Water Management: 81000 Podgorica, Stanka Dragojevića 2; tel. (81) 242106; fax (81) 246553.

Ministry of Culture: 81000 Podgorica, Njegoševa 2; tel. (81) 225408; fax (81) 224878.

Ministry of Education and Science: 81000 Podgorica, Vuka Karadžića 3; tel. (81) 612999; fax (81) 612996.

Ministry of the Environment and Town Planning: Podgorica.

Ministry of Finance: 81000 Podgorica, Stanka Dragojevića 2; tel. (81) 242835; fax (81) 224450.

Ministry of Foreign Affairs: 81000 Podgorica, Stanka Dragojevića 2; tel. (81) 246357; fax (81) 224609; e-mail mip@cg.yu.

Ministry of Health: 81000 Podgorica, Trg. 'Vektra' b.b. tel. (81) 242276; fax (81) 242762.

Ministry of Internal Affairs: Podgorica, Lenjina 6; tel. (81) 5223; fax (81) 52919.

Ministry of Justice: Podgorica, Vuka Karadžića 3; tel. (81) 51355; fax (81) 612780.

Ministry of Labour and Social Welfare: 81000 Podgorica, Vuka Karadžić 3; tel. and fax (81) 612986.

Ministry of Maritime Industry and Transport: 81000 Podgorica, Stanka Dragojevića 2; tel. (81) 245720; fax (81) 243081.

Ministry for the Protection of Human Rights of Ethnic Groups and National Minorities: Podgorica.

Ministry of Religious Affairs: Podgorica.

Ministry of Tourism: 81000 Podgorica, Cetinjski Put bb, Poslovna Zgrada 'Vektra'; tel. (81) 234116; fax (81) 234168; e-mail ministarstvo.turizma@mn.yu; internet www.mturizma.cg.yu.

Ministry of Trade: Podgorica.

SERBIA

STATE PRESIDENT

President of the Republic: NATAŠA MIĆIĆ (acting).

MINISTERS
(April 2003)

Prime Minister: ZORAN ŽIVKOVIĆ.

Deputy Prime Minister and Minister of Internal Affairs: DUŠAN MIHAJLOVIĆ.

Deputy Prime Ministers: NEBOJSA COVIĆ, ŽARKO KORAĆ, JOŽEF KASA, CEDOMIR JOVANOVIĆ.

Minister of Finance and Economy: BOZIDAR DJELIĆ.

Minister of Energy and Mining: GORAN NOVAKOVIĆI.

Minister of Religious Affairs: VOJISLAV MILOVANOVIĆ.

Minister of Foreign Trade Relations: GORAN PITIĆ.

Minister of Economic Affairs and Privatization: ALEKSANDAR VLAHOVIĆ.

Minister of Transport and Telecommunications: MARIJA RAŠETA VUKOSAVLJEVIĆ.

Minister of Sport and Education: GAŠO KNEŽEVIĆ.

Minister of Social Welfare: GORDANA MATKOVIĆ.

Minister of Science, Technology and Development: DRAGAN DOMAZET.

Minister of Construction and Town Planning: DRAGOSLAV ŠUMARAĆ.

Minister of Health and Environmental Protection: TOMICA MILOSAVLJEVIĆ.

Minister of Culture: BRANISLAV LEČIĆ.

Minister of Justice and Local Authority: VLADAN BATIĆ.

Minister of Labour and Employment: DRAGAN MILOVANOVIĆ.

Minister of Agriculture, Forestry and Waterpower Engineering: DRAGAN VESELINOV.

Minister of Trade, Tourism and Services: SLOBODAN MILOSAVLJEVIĆ.

MINISTRIES

Office of the President: 11000 Belgrade, Andrićev venac 1; tel. (11) 3030866; fax (11) 3030868; e-mail kprsa.ptt.yu.

Office of the Prime Minister: 11000 Belgrade, Nemanjina 11; tel. (11) 3617719; fax (11) 3617609.

Ministry of Agriculture, Forestry and Waterpower Engineering: 11000 Belgrade, Nemanjina 26; tel. (11) 3616271; fax (11) 3616272.

Ministry of Construction and Town Planning: 11000 Belgrade, Nemanjina 22–26; tel. (11) 3614652; fax (11) 3614653; e-mail murgs@eunet.yu.

Ministry of Culture: 11000 Belgrade, 11 Nikola Pasic Sq; tel. (11) 3346330; fax (11) 3346100; e-mail kabinet@min-cul.sr.gov.yu; internet www.min-cul.sr.gov.yu.

Ministry of Economic Affairs and Privatization: Belgrade, Srpskih vladara 16; tel. tel. (11) 3617599; fax (11) 3617640; e-mail officemprov@mpriv.sr.gov.yu; internet www.mpriv.sr.gov.yu.

Ministry of Energy and Mining: 11000 Belgrade, 36 Kralja Milana (Srpskih vladara) St; tel. (11) 3346755; fax 3616603; e-mail ljubica.todorovic@mem.sr.gov.yu; internet www.mem.sr.gov.yu.

Ministry of Finance and Economy: 11000 Belgrade, Nemanjina 22–26; tel. (11) 3616361; fax (11) 3616535; e-mail bdjelsc@mfin.sr.gov.yu; internet www.mfin.sr.gov.yu.

Ministry of Foreign Trade Relations: 11000 Belgrade, Gračanička 8; tel. (11) 3617628; fax (11) 3633142; e-mail office@mier.sr.gov.yu.

Ministry of Health and Environmental Protection: 11000 Belgrade, Nemanjina 22–26; tel. (11) 3616298; fax (11) 3616596; e-mail minzdr1@eunet.yu.

Ministry of Internal Affairs: 11000 Belgrade, Kneza Miloša 103; tel. (11) 3612589; fax (11) 3617814; e-mail muprs@mup.sr.gov.yu; internet www.mup.sr.gov.yu.

Ministry of Justice and Local Authority: 11000 Belgrade, Nemanjina 26; tel. (11) 3616548; fax (11) 3616419; e-mail ksenija@mpravde.sr.gov.yu.

Ministry of Labour and Employment: 11000 Belgrade, Nemanjina 22; tel. (11) 3616253; fax (11) 3617498; e-mail mrz@mrz.sr.gov.yu; internet www.mrz.sr.gov.yu.

Ministry of Religious Affairs: 11000 Belgrade, Nusiceva St. 4; tel. (11) 3346649; fax (11) 3617595; e-mail min_vera@uzzpro.sr.gov.yu.

Ministry of Science, Technology and Development: 11000 Belgrade, Nemanjina 22–26; tel. (11) 3616516; fax (11) 3616584; e-mail administrator@mnt.bg.ac.yu; internet www.nauka.ac.yu.

Ministry of Social Welfare: 11000 Belgrade, Nemanjina 22–26; tel. (11) 3616294; fax (11) 3616259; e-mail goga@msoc.sr.gov.yu; internet www.msoc.sr.gov.yu.

Ministry of Sport and Education: 11000 Belgrade, Nemanjina 22–26; tel. (11) 3616489; fax (11) 3616491; e-mail min.edu.sr@yubc.net.

Ministry of Trade, Tourism and Services: 11000 Belgrade, Nemanjina 22–26; tel. (11) 3631136; fax (11) 3610258.

Ministry of Transport and Telecommunications: 11000 Belgrade, Nemanjina 22–26; tel. (11) 3616426; fax (11) 3617486; e-mail info@msaotel.sr.gov.yu; internet www.msaotel.sr.gov.yu.

President and Legislature

PRESIDENT

The President of Serbia and Montenegro is elected for a four-year term by the Assembly.

SKUPŠTINA SRBIJE I CRNE GORE
(Assembly of Serbia and Montenegro)

The Assembly of Serbia and Montenegro comprises 126 deputies, who are directly elected for a four-year term (91 from Serbia and 35 from Montenegro). the first Assembly was elected on 25 February by the existing federal and republican legislatures.

Speaker: Dragoljub Micunović.

Election, 25 February 2003

Party	Seats
Democratic Opposition of Serbia*	37
Democratic List for European Montenegro†	19
Democratic Party	17
Together for Changes‡	14
Socialist Party of Serbia	12
Serbian Radical Party	8
Social Democratic Party of Montenegro	5
Party of Serbian Unity	5
Christian Democratic Party of Serbia	2
Democratic Alternative	2
Others	5
Total	**126**

* Alliance of 18 political parties.
† Coalition, principally comprising the Democratic Party of Montenegrin Socialists, the Social-Democratic Party of Montenegro and the Citizens' Party of Montenegro.
‡ Coalition, comprising the Socialist People's Party of Montenegro, the Serbian People's Party of Montenegro and the People's Party of Montenegro.

Republican Presidents and Legislatures

MONTENEGRO

REPUBLICAN PRESIDENT

The presidential elections of 22 December 2002 and 9 February 2003 had a participation rate of 45.9% and 46.6%, respectively, and were consequently declared invalid (under electoral regulations requiring a minimum voter turnout of 50%).

Presidential Election, First Ballot, 22 December 2002

Candidate	Votes	% of votes
Filip Vujanović (Democratic List for European Montenegro) *	175,328	83.7
Dragan Hajduković (Independent)	12,319	5.9
Aleksandar Vasiljević (Serbian Radical Party)	6,448	3.1
Milan Milo Radulović (Party of Natural Law)	3,115	1.5
Others	7,294	3.4
Total †	**204,504**	**100.00**

* Coalition, principally comprising the Democratic Party of Montenegrin Socialists, the Social-Democratic Party of Montenegro and the Citizens' Party of Montenegro.
† Excluding 5,094 invalid votes. Percentage of votes is based on total votes cast.

Second Ballot, 9 February 2003

Candidate	Votes	% of votes
Filip Vujanović (Democratic List for European Montenegro) *	174,536	82.0
Dragan Hajduković (Independent)	14,556	6.8
Aleksandar Vasiljević (Serbian Radical Party)	8,734	4.1
Milan Milo Radulović (Party of Natural Law)	3,218	1.5
Others	4,727	5.6
Total †	**205,771**	**100.00**

* Coalition, principally comprising the Democratic Party of Montenegrin Socialists, the Social-Democratic Party of Montenegro and the Citizens' Party of Montenegro.
† Excluding 7,001 invalid votes. Percentage of votes is based on total votes cast.

Third Ballot, 11 May 2003

Candidate	Votes	% of votes
Filip Vujanović (Democratic List for European Montenegro)†	141,000	63.3
Dragan Hajduković (Independent)	69,000	30.8
Miodrag Zivković (Liberal Alliance of Montenegro)	8,000	3.9
Total‡	**218,000**	**100.0**

* Estimated number of votes cast.
† Coalition, principally comprising the Democratic Party of Montenegrin Socialists, the Social-Democratic Party of Montenegro and the Citizens' Party of Montenegro.
‡ Total excludes an estimated 4,500 invalid votes. Percentage of votes is based on total votes cast.

REPUBLICAN ASSEMBLY

Election, 20 October 2002

Party	Votes	% of votes	Seats
Democratic List for European Montenegro*	167,166	47.97	39
Together for Changes†	133,900	38.43	30
Liberal Alliance of Montenegro	20,365	5.83	4
Albanians Together‡	8,498	2.44	2
Total (incl. others)	**330,199**	**100.00**	**75**

* Coalition, principally comprising the Democratic Party of Montenegrin Socialists, the Social-Democratic Party of Montenegro and the Citizens' Party of Montenegro.
† Coalition, comprisingthe Socialist People's Party of Montenegro, the Serbian People's Party of Montenegro and the People's Party of Montenegro.
‡ Coalition, principally comprising the Democratic Union of Albanians and the Democratic Alliance of Albanians in Montenegro.
§ Excluding 9,851 invalid votes.

SERBIA

REPUBLICAN PRESIDENT

The second and third rounds of the presidential election, on 13 October and 8 December 2002, had a participation rate of 44.0% and

45.0%, respectively, and were consequently declared invalid (under electoral regulations requiring a minimum voter turnout of 50%).

Presidential Election, First Ballot, 29 September 2002

Candidate	Votes	% of votes
Vojislav Koštunica (Democratic Party of Serbia)	1,123,420	30.89
Mirolujub Labus (Independent) .	995,200	27.36
Dr Vojislav Šešelj (Serbian Radical Party) .	845,308	23.24
Vuk Drašković (Serbian Renewal Movement)	159,959	4.40
Borislav Pelević (Party of Serbian Unity) .	139,047	3.82
Velimir Zivojinović (Socialist Party of Serbia)	119,052	3.27
Nebojsa Pavković (Independent)	75,662	2.08
Others	179,394	4.93
Total*	3,637,042	100.00

* Excluding invalid votes.

Second Ballot, 13 October 2002

Candidate	Votes	% of votes
Vojislav Koštunica (Democratic Party of Serbia)	1,974,450	68.40
Mirolujub Labus (Indpendent) .	911,567	31.60
Total*	2,886,017	100.00

* Excluding invalid votes.

Third Ballot, 8 December 2002

Candidate	Votes	% of votes
Vojislav Koštunica (Democratic Party of Serbia)	1,699,098	57.66
Vojislav Šešelj (Serbian Radical Party) . .	1,063,296	36.08
Borislav Pelević (Party of Serbian Unity) .	103,926	3.53
Total*	2,866,320	100.00

* Excluding 80,396 invalid votes. Percentage of votes is based on total votes cast.

NATIONAL ASSEMBLY

President: NATAŠA MICIĆ.

Election, 23 December 2000

Party	Votes	% of votes	Seats
Democratic Opposition of Serbia* .	2,402,387	64.1	176
Socialist Party of Serbia	515,845	13.8	37
Serbian Radical Party	322,333	8.6	23
Party of Serbian Unity†	199,847	5.3	14
Others	n.a.	8.2	—
Total	n.a.	100.00	250

* Alliance of 18 political parties.

† Coalition of Party of Serbian Progress, Party of Serbian Union, Peasants' Party of Serbia and United Pensioners' Party.

Provinces of Serbia

Kosovo and Metohija

Until 1990 Kosovo (now Kosovo and Metohija) was an autonomous province within Serbia, with its own provincial assembly and government; following the adoption of amendments to the Yugoslav Constitution, the province's autonomous status was removed, and the provincial assembly and government dissolved. Most ethnic Albanian deputies in the assembly opposed its dissolution, and formed a 'Kosovo assembly-in-exile', which proclaimed Kosovo a 'republic'. They also established an interim 'government', based in Zagreb, Croatia, which organized a referendum among the ethnic Albanian population in September 1991, which was overwhelmingly in favour of Kosovo's becoming a sovereign republic. The Assembly-in-Exile also arranged elections to a new 130-seat provincial assembly on 24 May 1992 (the Democratic Alliance of Kosovo won the most seats and its leader, Dr IBRAHIM RUGOVA, was declared the President of the 'Republic of Kosovo'). The referendum and the elections were declared illegal by the Serbian and federal authorities. Further presidential and legislative elections, again declared illegal, took place in the province in March 1998. In May 2001 the UN Interim Administration Mission in Kosovo agreed to grant the province provisional self-government. Elections to a new, 120-seat legislative assembly took place on 17 November (20 seats were

allocated proportionally to Serbs and other ethnic groups). Rugova's Democratic League of Kosovo secured 47 seats, the Democratic Party of Kosovo won 26 seats, and a Serbian coalition, Povratak (Return), won 22 seats. On 4 March 2002 Rugova was elected President of Kosovo.

Vojvodina

The Province of Vojvodina has an elected Provincial Assembly, based at Novi Sad. Elections to the Provincial Assembly took place on 24 September and 8 October 2000. The President of the Provincial Assembly is NENAD CEMAK. The President of the Provincial Government is DAMNJAN RADENKOVIĆ. The Prime Minister is KOVILJKO LOVRE. In January 2002 the Serbian National Assembly voted in favour of restoring the autonomy of Vojvodina.

Political Organizations

Alliance of Peasants of Serbia Party: Belgrade; tel. (11) 789235; f. 1990 as Peasants' Party of Serbia; Pres. MILOMIR BABIĆ.

Citizens' Party of Montenegro (Gradanska Partija Crne Gore): Podgorica; mem. of Democratic List for European Montenegro electoral coalition.

Democratic Alliance of Albanians in Montenegro (Demokratski Savez U Crnoj Gori—DSCG): Podgorica; mem. of Albanians Together electoral coalition; Chair. MEHMED BARDHI.

Democratic Community of Vojvodina Hungarians (Demokratska zajednica vojvodjanskih Madjara—DZVM): tel. (24) 852248; f. 1990; supports interests of ethnic Hungarian minority in Vojvodina; c. 20,000 mems; Chair. SANDOR PAL.

Democratic League of Kosovo: Priština; f. 2000 as successor to the Democratic Alliance of Kosovo; ethnic Albanian grouping; party with largest representation in Kosovo Assembly after Nov. 2001 elections; Chair. Dr IBRAHIM RUGOVA.

Democratic League of Montenegro: Podgorica; Leader MEHNED BARDHI.

Democratic League of Vojvodina (Liga Socijaldemokrata Vojvodine—LSV): Novi Sad, Trg Mladenaca 10; tel. and fax (21) 29139; internet www.lsv.org.yu; Pres. NENAD ČANAK.

Democratic Party of Kosovo: Priština; fmrly Party for the Democratic Party of Kosovo; represented in Kosovo Assembly after Nov. 2001 elections; Chair. HASHIM THAÇI.

Democratic Opposition of Serbia (DOS) (Demokratska Opozicija Srbije): 11000 Belgrade, Brace Jugovica 2a; tel. and fax (11) 3340620; e-mail info@dos.org.yu; internet www.dos.org.yu; alliance of 18 political parties, which secured a majority in legislative elections in December 2000; Leader ZORAN ŽIVKOVIĆ.

Alliance of Vojvodina's Hungarians: 24000 Subotica, Age Mamuzica 13; tel. (24) 553801; e-mail office@vmsz.org.yu; internet www.vmsz.org.yu; f. 1993; supports autonomous status for Vojvodina; Chair. JOŽEF KASA.

Christian Democratic Party of Serbia: 11000 Belgrade, Hadži Nikole Živkovića 2-II; tel. and fax (11) 3284695; e-mail dhss@net .yu; internet www.dhss.org.yu; Pres. Dr VLADAN BATIĆ.

Civic Alliance of Serbia: 11000 Belgrade, Terazije 3; tel. and fax (11) 3341696; e-mail gss@gradjanskisavez.org.yu; internet www .gradjanskisavez.org.yu; Pres. GORAN SVILANOVIĆ.

Coalition Sumadija: 34000 Kragujevac, ul. Branka Radicevića; tel. and fax (34) 67973; e-mail sumadija@infosky.net; internet www.sumadija.org.yu; Pres. BRANISLAV KOVACEVIĆ.

Coalition Vojvodina: Panačevo, Trg Slobode 3; tel. and fax (13) 353629; e-mail info@koalicijavojvodina.org.yu; internet www .koalicijavojvodina.org.yu; Pres. DRAGAN VESELINOV.

Democratic Alternative: Belgrade, Makedonska 5; tel. and fax (11) 3343471; e-mail da@da.org.yu; internet www.da.org.yu; Pres. NEBOJSA COVIĆ.

Democratic Centre: Belgrade, Terazije 3; tel. (11) 3229925; e-mail centar@idc.org.yu; internet www.dc.org.yu; Pres. DRAGOLJUB MICUNOVIĆ.

Democratic Party (DP) (Demokratska Stranka): 11000 Belgrade, Krunska 69; tel. and fax (11) 3443003; e-mail info@ds.org .yu; internet www.ds.org.yu; f. 1990; Pres. ZORAN ŽIVKOVIĆ.

League of Social-Democrats of Vojvodina: 21000 Novi Sad, trg Mladenaca 10/II; tel. (21) 29139; e-mail office@lsv.org.yu; internet www.lsv.org.yu; Pres. NENAD CANAK.

Movement for Democratic Serbia: Belgrade, Francuska 12; tel. (11) 3229821; fax (11) 3234730; e-mail pokret@pokret.org.yu; internet www.pokret.org.yu; Pres. MOMČILO PERISIĆ.

New Democracy: Belgrade, Proleterskih brigada 76; tel. (11) 4440677; fax (11) 3444230; e-mail izv.odbor@novademokratija.org .yu; internet www.novademokratija.org.yu; f. 1990 as New Democracy–Movement for Serbia; Chair. DUŠAN MIHAILOVIĆ; Sec.-Gen. TAHIR HASANOVIĆ.

New Serbia: 11000 Belgrade, Dragoslava Jovanovića 7; tel. and fax (11) 3238225; e-mail info@nova-srbija.org.yu; internet www .nova-srbija.org.yu; Pres. VELIMIR ILIĆ, MIHAJLO MARKOVIĆ.

Party of Democratic Action: 36300 Novi Pazar, Poštanskifah 101; tel. (20) 311454; Pres. RASIM LJAJIĆ.

Reform Democratic Party of Vojvodina: 21000 Novi Sad, Ilje Ognjanovića 10/II; tel. (21) 29561; e-mail rdsv@eunet.yu; internet www.rdsv.org.yu; f. 1992; Pres. MIODRAG ISAKOV.

Serb Resistance Movement–Democratic Movement: Priština; Pres. MOMČILO TRAJKOVIĆ.

Social-Democracy: 11000 Belgrade, Kralja Milana 23/I; tel. (11) 3342753; fax (11) 3343792; e-mail info@socijaldemokratija.org.yu; internet www.socijaldemokratija.org.yu; Pres. VUK OBRADOVIĆ.

Social-Democratic Union: 11000 Belgrade, Beogradska 8/II; tel. and fax (11) 434107; e-mail info@sdu.org.yu; internet www .sdu.org.yu; Pres. ZARKO KORAC.

Democratic Party of Montenegrin Socialists (DPMS) (Demokratska Partija Socijalista): 81000 Podgorica, Jovana Tomaśevića 33; tel. (81) 225830; fax (81) 242101; e-mail dps4@mn.yu; internet www.dps.cg.yu; name changed from League of Communists of Montenegro in 1991; supports the independence of Montenegro; division within the party emerged in mid-1997; Chair. MILO DJUKANOVIĆ.

Democratic Party of Serbia (DPS) (Demokratska stranka Srbije): Belgrade, Braće Jugovića 2A; tel. and fax (11) 3282886; e-mail info@dss.org.yu; internet www.dss.org.yu; f. 1992 following split from Democratic Party; withdrew from Govt in Aug. 2001, although officially remained in Democratic Opposition of Serbia; Leader Dr VOJISLAV KOŠTUNICA.

Democratic Reform Party of Muslims (Demokratska reformska stranka Muslimana): 38400 Prizren, Koritnik 3; tel. (29) 22322; party of ethnic Muslims; left-wing; Pres. AZAR ZULJI.

Democratic Union of Albanians (DUA) (Demokratska partija Albanaca): Preševo, Selami Halaci bb; f. 1990; Pres. FUAD NIMANI.

League of Communists—Movement for Yugoslavia of Montenegro: Podgorica; Chair. RADE LAKUSIĆ.

Liberal Alliance of Montenegro (LAM): Podgorica; e-mail webmaster@lscg.cmagora.com; internet www.lscg.cmagora.com; pro-independence; Leader MIODRAG ZIVKOVIĆ.

Liberal Party (Liberalna Stranka): Valjevo, Dr Pantića 70; tel. (14) 222659; f. 1989; favours a free-market economy; Leader PREDRAG M. VULETIĆ.

Party of Democratic Action of Kosovo and Metohija (PDA-KM): Vitomirića; party of ethnic Muslims; affiliated to the PDA of Bosnia and Herzegovina; Chair. NUMAN BALIĆ.

Party of Democratic Action—Montenegro: Rozaj; Slav Muslim party, affiliated to PDA of Bosnia and Herzegovina; Leader HARUN HADŽIĆ.

Party of Democratic Action of Sandžak (PDA-S): 36300 Novi Pazar, trg Maršala Tita 2; tel. (20) 25667; f. 1990; party of ethnic Muslims of Sandžak; affiliated to the PDA of Bosnia and Herzegovina; advocates autonomy for the Sandžak region; Chair. Dr SULEJMAN UGLJANIN.

Party of Natural Law: Belgrade; Leader MILAN MILO RADULOVIĆ.

Party of Serbian Unity: coalition, comprising Party of Serbian Progress, Party of Serbian Unity, Peasants' Party of Serbia and United Pensioners' Party; Leader ZELJKO RAZNJATOVIĆ.

People's Assembly Party (Narodna saborna stranka): 11040 Belgrade, Masarikova 5/VIII; tel. (11) 685490; fax (11) 656818; f. 1992 as Democratic Movement of Serbia (Depos), a coalition of four parties and a party faction; reconstituted as a political party and renamed in 1995; Pres. SLOBODAN RAKITIĆ.

People's Party of Montenegro (Narodna Stranka Crne Gore): 11000 Belgrade, Srpskih Vladara 14; e-mail narodna@cg.yu; internet www.narodnastranka.cg.yu; Chair. DRAGAN SOC.

People's Socialist Party of Montenegro: Podgorica; Leader DUSKO JOVANOVIĆ.

Povratak (Return): Priština; Serbian coalition with representation in Kosovo Assembly after Nov. 2001 elections.

Radical Party of the Left 'Nikola Pasić': Belgrade.

Regeneration of Serbia (Preporod Srbije): Belgrade; f. 2000; Leader MILOVAN DRECUN.

Serbian People's Party of Montenegro (Srpska Narodna Stranka Crne Gore): 81000 Podgorica, Bratstva i jedinstva 53; tel. (81) 620324; e-mail sns@cg.yu; internet www.sns.cg.yu.

Serbian Popular Party: Belgrade; Leader ŽELIDRAG NIKČEVIĆ.

Serbian Radical Party (SRP) (Srpska Radikalna Stranka—SRS): 11000 Belgrade, Ohridska 1; tel. (11) 457745; f. 1991; extreme nationalist; advocates a 'Greater Serbian' state; Leader Dr VOJISLAV ŠEŠELJ; Gen. Sec. ALEKSANDAR VUCIĆ.

Serbian Renewal Movement (SRM) (Srpski pokret obnove—SPO): Belgrade, Krez Mihajlovna 48; tel. (11) 635281; fax (11) 628170; internet www.spo.org.yu; f. 1990; right-wing; nationalist; Pres. VUK DRAŠKOVIĆ.

Serb National Council: Priština; Leader RADA TRAJKOVIĆ.

Social-Democratic Party of Montenegro (SDP): 81000 Podgorica, Jovana Tomaśevića bb; tel. (81) 248648; fax (81) 612133; e-mail sdp@cg.yu; internet www.sdp.cg.yu; Pres. RANKO KRIVOKAPIĆ.

Socialist People's Party of Montenegro (Socijalistička Narodna Partija Crne Gore—SNP): Podgorica; e-mail admin@snp.cg.yu; internet www.snp.cg.yu; Leader MOMIR BULATOVIĆ.

Socialist Party of Serbia (SPS) (Socijalistička partija Srbije): 11000 Belgrade, bul. Lenjina 6; tel. (11) 634921; fax (11) 628642; internet www.sps.org.yu; f. 1990 by merger of League of Communists of Serbia and Socialist Alliance of Working People (SAWP) of Serbia; Pres. BOGOLJUB BJELICA; Gen. Sec. ZORAN ANDJELKOVIĆ.

United Democratic Movement: Priština; f. 1998 by fmr mems of the Democratic Alliance of Kosovo; ethnic Albanian party; Chair. REXHEP QOSJA.

United Radical Party of Serbia: Belgrade; Leader SLOBODAN JOVIĆ.

Vojvodina Democratic Opposition: Novi Sad; f. 2000.

Yugoslav Green Party: Belgrade, Mutapova 12; tel. (11) 4447030; f. 1990; open to all citizens regardless of national, religious or racial affiliation; Pres. DRAGAN JOVANOVIĆ.

Yugoslav United Left: Belgrade; internet www.jul.org.yu; f. 1994; alliance of 23 left-wing organizations; Pres. MIRJANA MARKOVIĆ.

Diplomatic Representation

EMBASSIES IN SERBIA AND MONTENEGRO

Albania: 11000 Belgrade, Bulevar Mira 25A; tel. (11) 3065350; fax (11) 665439; Chargé d'affaires EDMOND HAXHINASTO.

Algeria: 11000 Belgrade, Maglajska 26B; tel. (11) 668211; Ambassador MOULOUD HAMAI.

Angola: 11000 Belgrade, Vase Pelagića 32 51; tel. (11) 3690241; fax (11) 3690191; Ambassador FILIPE FELISBERTO MONIMAMBU.

Argentina: 11000 Belgrade, Knez Mihajlova 24/I; tel. (11) 623569; fax (11) 622630; Ambassador CARLOS ABEL MARTESE.

Australia: 11000 Belgrade, Čika Ljubina 13; tel. (11) 624655; fax (11) 624029; e-mail austemba@eunet.yu; internet www.australia .org.eu; Ambassador JOHN OLIVER.

Austria: 11000 Belgrade, Kneza Sime Markovića 2; tel. (11) 635955; fax (11) 635500; Ambassador HANNES PORIAS.

Belarus: 11000 Belgrade, Deligradska 13; tel. (11) 3616836; fax (11) 3616938; e-mail bvalerij@eunet.yu; Ambassador VLADIMIR MATSKEVICH.

Belgium: 11000 Belgrade, Krunska 18; tel. (11) 3230016; fax (11) 3244394; e-mail embassy@belgium.org.yu; Ambassador WILFRIED NARTUS.

Bosnia and Herzegovina: Milana Tankosića 8; tel. (11) 3291277; fax (11) 766507; Ambassador ŽELJKO KOMŠIĆ.

Brazil: 11000 Belgrade, Krunska 14; tel. (11) 3239781; fax (11) 3230653; e-mail brasbeig@eunet.yu; Ambassador RUBEM AMARAL JUNIOR.

Bulgaria: 11000 Belgrade, Birčaninova 26; tel. (11) 3613980; fax 3611136; Ambassador YANI MILCHAKOV.

Canada: 11000 Belgrade, Kneza Miloša 75; tel. (11) 3063000; fax (11) 3063042; e-mail bgrad@dfait-maeci.gc.ca; internet www.canada .org.yu; Ambassador DONALD P. MCLENNAN.

Chile: 11000 Belgrade, Cakorska 3; tel. (11) 3670403; fax (11) 3670405; Ambassador AGUSTÍN PÍO GARCÍA.

China, People's Republic: 11000 Belgrade, Lackovićeva 6; tel. (11) 662737; fax (11) 653538; Ambassador WEN XIGUI.

Congo, Democratic Republic: 11000 Belgrade, Diplomatska kolonija 3; tel. (11) 664131; Chargé d'affaires a.i. PAUL EMILE TSHINGA AHUKA.

Croatia: 11000 Belgrade, Kneza Miloša 62; tel. (11) 3610535; fax (11) 3610032; e-mail croambg@eunet.yu; Ambassador DAVOR BOŽINOVIĆ.

Cuba: 11000 Belgrade, Vasilija Gaćeše 9b; tel. (11) 3692441; fax (11) 647858; Ambassador JUAN SANCHEZ MONROE.

Cyprus: 11040 Belgrade, Diplomatska Kolonija 9; tel. (11) 3672725; fax (11) 3671348; e-mail cyprus@eunet.yu; Ambassador STAVROS AMVROSIOU.

Czech Republic: 11000 Belgrade, bul. Kralja Aleksandra 22; tel. (11) 3230133; fax (11) 3230134; e-mail belgrade@embassy.mzv.cz; Ambassador JUDITA ŠTOURAČOVÁ.

Denmark: 11040 Belgrade, Neznanog Junaka 9A; tel. (11) 3670443; fax (11) 660759; e-mail ambadane@eunet.yu; Chargé d'affaires JÖRGEN V. ANDERSEN.

Egypt: 11000 Belgrade, Andre Nikolića 12; tel. (11) 651225; fax (11) 652036; Ambassador AMR KHODEIR YEHYA MOSTAFA KHODEIR.

Finland: 11000 Belgrade, Birčaninova 29; tel. (11) 3065400; fax (11) 3065375; e-mail finembas@eunet.yu; Ambassador HANNU MÄNTYVAARA.

France: 11000 Belgrade, Pariska 11; tel. (11) 636200; fax (11) 636274; e-mail amba_fr@eunet.yu; Ambassador GABRIEL KELLER.

Germany: 11000 Belgrade, Kneza Miloša 74–76; tel. (11) 3064300; fax (11) 3064303; e-mail germemba@eunet.yu; Ambassador KURT LEONBERGER.

Ghana: 11000 Belgrade, Ognjena Price 50; tel. (11) 3440856; fax (11) 3440071; e-mail ghana@eunet.yu; Chargé d'affaires KARK ASMAH.

Greece: 11000 Belgrade, Francuska 33; tel. (11) 3226523; fax 3344746; e-mail office@greekemb.co.yu; Ambassador MICHELL SPINELLIS.

Guinea: 11000 Belgrade, Ohridska 4; tel. (11) 431830; fax (11) 451391; Ambassador Dr FARA MILLIMONO.

Holy See: 11000 Belgrade, Svetog Save 24; tel. (11) 3085356; fax (11) 3085216; Apostolic Nuncio Most Rev. EUGENIO SBARBARO (Archbishop of Tiddi).

Hungary: 11000 Belgrade, Proleterskih brigada 72; tel. (11) 4440472; fax (11) 4445708; e-mail hunemblg@eunet.yu; Ambassador JÓZSEF PANDUR.

India: 11000 Belgrade, Generala Hanrisa 37; tel. (11) 466192; fax (11) 465043; Ambassador ARUN KUMAR.

Indonesia: 11000 Belgrade, bul. Mira 18; tel. (11) 3674062; fax (11) 3672984; Chargé d'affaires a.i. ALOYSIUS BOENTARMAN.

Iran: 11000 Belgrade, Proleterskih brigada 9; tel. (11) 338782; fax (11) 3223676; Ambassador ALI ABOLHASSANI SHAHREZA.

Iraq: 11000 Belgrade, Teodora Drajzera 38; tel. (11) 3671580; fax (11) 3671590; Ambassador Dr SAMI SAOUN KHATI AL-KINANI.

Israel: 11000 Belgrade, bul. Mira 47; tel. (11) 3672400; fax (11) 3670304; Ambassador YORAM SHANI.

Italy: 11000 Belgrade, Birčaninova 11; tel. (11) 3066100; fax (11) 3249413; e-mail italbelg@eunet.yu; internet www.italy.org.yu; Ambassador GIOVANNI CARACCIOLO DI VIETRI.

Japan: 11070 Novi Belgrade, Vladimira Popovica 6; tel. (11) 3012800; fax (11) 3118258; Ambassador YOSHIKI MINE.

Korea, Republic: 11070 Belgrade, Hyatt Regency, Milentija Popovića 5; tel. (11) 3011194; fax (11) 3011195; Chargé d'affaires a.i. LEE SOK-BAE.

Lebanon: 11000 Belgrade, Vase Pelagića 38; tel. (11) 3691178; fax (11) 3693108; e-mail ambaleb@eunet.yu; Chargé d'affaires a.i. NIDAL YEHYA.

Libya: 11000 Belgrade, Mirka Tomića 6; tel. (11) 663445; fax (11) 3670805; e-mail libyaamb@eunet.yu; Chargé d'affaires AISHA MOKHTAR TRHUNI.

Macedonia, former Yugoslav republic: 11000 Belgrade, Gospodar Jevremova 34; tel. (11) 633348; fax (11) 182287; Ambassador VIKTOR DIMOVSKI.

Mexico: 11000 Belgrade, Cara Dušana 58/V; tel. (11) 638111; fax (11) 629566; e-mail embamex@net.yu; Ambassador CARLOS ALEJANDRO RODRIGUEZ Y QUEZADA.

Morocco: 11000 Belgrade, Sanje Živanović 4; tel. (11) 651775; Chargé d'affaires a.i. KAMAL FAQIR BENAISSA.

Myanmar: 11000 Belgrade, Kneza Miloša 72; tel. (11) 645420; fax (11) 3614968; e-mail mebel@eunet.yu; Ambassador U KYAR NYO CHIT PE.

Netherlands: 11000 Belgrade, Simina 29; tel. (11) 3282332; fax (11) 628986; e-mail nlgovbel@eunet.yu; Ambassador KEES J. R. KLOMPENHOUWER.

Nigeria: 1100 Belgrade, Geršićeva 14A; tel. (11) 413411; fax (11) 401305; e-mail nigeria@bits.net; Ambassador MOHAMMED BUBA AHMED.

Norway: 11000 Belgrade, Kablarska 30; tel. (11) 3690154; fax (11) 3690158; Ambassador HANS OLA URSTAD.

Pakistan: 11000 Belgrade, bul. Mira 62; tel. (11) 661676; fax (11) 661667; Chargé d'affaires a.i. ARSHED SAUD KHOSA.

Peru: 11000 Belgrade, Terazije 1/II; tel. (11) 3221197; fax (11) 3228694; Chargé d'affaires a.i. HÉCTOR FRANCSICO MATALLANA MARTINEZ.

Poland: 11000 Belgrade, Kneza Miloša 38; tel. (11) 3615287; fax (11) 3616939; e-mail ambrpfrj@eunet.yu; Chargé d'affaires a.i. TADEUSZ DIEM.

Portugal: 11000 Belgrade, Vladimira Gaćinovića 4; tel. (11) 662895; fax (11) 662892; e-mail embporbg@yubc.net; Ambassador AGUSTO RUSSO DIAS.

Romania: 11000 Belgrade, Kneza Miloša 70; tel. (11) 3618327; fax (11) 3618339; Ambassador STEFAN GLAVAN.

Russia: 11000 Belgrade, Deligradska 32; tel. (11) 657533; fax (11) 657845; Ambassador VLADIMIR IVANOVSKI.

Slovakia: 11070 Belgrade, bul. Umetvosti 18; tel. (11) 3010000; fax (11) 3010020; Ambassador MIROSLAV LAJČÁK.

Slovenia: Belgrade, Zmaj Jovina 33a; tel. (11) 3284458; fax (11) 625884; Ambassador BORUT ŠUKLJE.

Spain: 11000 Belgrade, Prote Mateje 45; tel. (11) 3440231; fax (11) 3444203; e-mail embajada@sezampro.yu; Ambassador MARIANO GARCÍA MUNOZ.

Sweden: 11000 Belgrade, Pariska 7; tel. (11) 3031600; fax (11) 3031601; e-mail swedeemb@eunet.yu; Ambassador MICHAEL SAHLIN.

Switzerland: 11000 Belgrade, Birčaninova 27; tel. (11) 3065820; fax (11) 657253; Ambassador GAUDENZ B. RUF.

Syria: 11000 Belgrade, Mlade Bosne 31; tel. (11) 3443671; fax (11) 3440121; Chargé d'affaires MOHAMAD ALI OBEID.

Tunisia: 11000 Belgrade, Vase Pelagića 19; tel. (11) 3691961; fax (11) 3690642; e-mail at.belgr@eunet.yu; Ambassador RIDHA TNANI.

Turkey: 11000 Belgrade, Krunska 1; tel. (11) 3235431; fax (11) 3235433; e-mail turem@eunet.yu; Ambassador HASAN SERVET ÖKTEM.

Ukraine: 11000 Belgrade, Josipa Slavenskog 27; tel. (11) 3671516; fax (11) 36781; Ambassador ANATOLY SHOSTAK.

United Kingdom: 11000 Belgrade, Generala Ždanova 46; tel. (11) 645055; fax (11) 659651; e-mail britemb@eunet.yu; Ambassador CHARLES CRAWFORD.

USA: 11000 Belgrade, Kneza Miloša 50; tel. (11) 3619344; fax (11) 3615489; e-mail billmont@aol.com; Ambassador WILLIAM D. MONTGOMERY.

Zimbabwe: 11000 Belgrade, Tolstojeva 51; tel. (11) 3672996; fax (11) 3671218; e-mail zimbegd@eunet.yu; Ambassador LLOYD GUNDU.

Judicial System

Judicial functions are to be discharged within a uniform system, and the jurisdiction of the courts shall be established and altered only by law. In general, court proceedings are conducted in public (exceptionally the public may be excluded to preserve professional secrets, public order or morals) in the national language of the region in which the court is situated. Citizens who do not know the language in which the proceedings are being conducted may use their own language.

The judicial system comprises courts of general jurisdiction, i.e. communal courts, county courts, republican supreme courts and the Federal Court. The courts of general jurisdiction are organized in accordance with individual republican legislation. In general, the courts are entitled to proceed in criminal, civil and administrative matters. Military courts, headed by the Supreme Military Court, proceed in criminal and administrative matters connected with military service or national defence. Economic or trade matters are under the jurisdiction of economic courts. They proceed also in penal-economic matters. Judges are elected or replaced by the republican assemblies or the Assembly of Serbia and Montenegro (see below).

The Federal Court and federal Constitutional Court were to continue functioning under the Constitutional Charter, adopted on 4 February 2003, until otherwise specified by this law. The Assembly of Serbia and Montenegro, which was established on 25 February, approved legislation providing for the creation of the Court of Serbia and Montenegro. Unfinished cases before the existing federal Constitutional Court and Federal Court within the remit of the Court of Serbia and Montenegro on the basis of the Constitutional Charter were to be transferred to that Court. The Court of Serbia and Montenegro was to have constitutional court and administrative court functions, and was to decide on the harmonization of court practice between the member states. The administrative court function was to be exercised in relation with administrative acts of the joint Council of Ministers. The Court of Serbia and Montenegro has an equal number of judges from the member states, who are elected by the Assembly of Serbia and Montenegro.

THE JUDICIARY OF SERBIA AND MONTENEGRO

Constitutional Court

This court decides on the conformity of the Constitutions of the member republics with the state Constitution. The court has seven judges, who elect the President of the Court from among themselves.

President of the Constitutional Court: MILOVAN BUZADZIĆ.

Federal Court

This is the highest organ of justice. The Federal Court comprises 11 judges who are elected and replaced by the Assembly of Serbia and Montenegro. The judges of the Federal Court elect the President of the Court from among themselves.

President of the Federal Court: Dr RAFAEL CIJAN, 11000 Belgrade, Svetozara Markovića 21; tel. (11) 3242547.

THE REPUBLICAN JUDICIARIES

Montenegro

The courts in Montenegro are supervised by the republican Ministry of Justice. The highest courts in the republican judicial system are the Supreme Court and the Constitutional Court.

Constitutional Court of the Republic of Montenegro: 81000 Podgorica, Lenjina 3; tel. (81) 41846; Pres. NIKOLA VUJANOVIĆ.

Supreme Court: 81000 Podgorica, Njegoševa 6; tel. (81) 43070; Pres. STEVAN DAMJANOVIĆ.

Office of the Public Prosecutor: 81000 Podgorica, Njegoševa 6; tel. (81) 43053; Public Prosecutor VLADIMIR ŠUŠOVIĆ.

Serbia

All courts in Serbia are within the jurisdiction of the republican Ministry of Justice. The Supreme Court and the Constitutional Court are the highest courts in the republican judicial system.

Constitutional Court of the Republic of Serbia: 11000 Belgrade, Nemanjina 22–26; tel. (11) 658755; Pres. Dr BALŠA SPADIJER.

Supreme Court of Serbia: 11000 Belgrade, Nemanjina 22–26; tel. (11) 658755; Pres. LEPOSAVA KARAMARKOVIĆ.

Office of the Public Prosecutor of the Republic of Serbia: 11000 Belgrade, Nemanjina 22–26; tel. (11) 658755; Public Prosecutor MILOMIR JAKOVLJEVIĆ.

Provincial Secretariat of Justice for the Province of Kosovo and Metohija: Zejnel Salihu br. 4; fax (38) 31929.

Provincial Secretariat for National Minorities, Administration and Regulations for the Province of Vojvodina: 21000 Novi Sad, bul. Mihaila Pupina 16; tel. (21) 56170; fax (21) 56137.

Religion

Most of the inhabitants of Serbia and Montenegro are, at least nominally, Christian, but there is a significant Muslim minority. The main Christian denomination is Eastern Orthodox, but there is a strong Roman Catholic presence. There are also small minorities of Old Catholics, Protestants and Jews.

CHRISTIANITY

The Eastern Orthodox Church

Serbian Orthodox Church: Headquarters: 11001 Belgrade, Kralja Petra 5, POB 182; tel. (11) 638161; fax (11) 182780; e-mail pravoslavlje@spc.yu; internet www.spc.yu; 11m. adherents; mainly in Yugoslavia; Patriarch of Serbia His Holiness PAVLE (Archbishop of Peć and Metropolitan of Belgrade-Karlovci); Sec. Archdeacon MOMIR LEĆIĆ.

Head of the Orthodox Church in Montenegro: Cetinje; acknowledges the jurisdiction of the Patriarch of Serbia and commands the allegiance of most of the Orthodox in Montenegro; AMFILOHIJE RADOVIĆ (Metropolitan of Crna Gora and Primorje).

Montenegrin Orthodox Church: Cetinje; autocephalous until 1920, when it was dissolved against the Constitution and canon law and annexed to the Serbian Orthodox Church; restored 1993 by the Committee of the Restoration of the Autocephaly of the Montenegrin Orthodox Church; Patriarch of Montenegro His Excellency MIHAILO DEDEIĆ (Metropolitan of Montenegro).

The Roman Catholic Church

Serbia and Montenegro, and the former Yugoslav republic of Macedonia together comprise two archdioceses (including one, Bar, directly responsible to the Holy See) and four dioceses. At 31 December 2000 the estimated number of adherents was equivalent to 4.0% of the total population.

Archbishop of Bar: Most Rev. JOSIP ZEF GASHI, Nadbiskupski Ordinarijat, 85000 Bar, Popovići 98; tel. (85) 313863; fax (85) 313817.

Archbishop of Belgrade: Most Rev. STANISLAV HOČEVAR, Nadbiskupski Ordinarijat, 11000 Belgrade, Svetozara Markovića 20; tel. (11) 3234846; fax (11) 3344613; e-mail nadbisbg@eunet.yu.

Old Catholic Church

Old Catholic Church in Serbia and Vojvodina: 11000 Belgrade; Dir of Bishop's Diocese JOVAN AJHINGER.

Protestant Churches

Christian Assemblies—Church of Christ's Brethren: 21470 Bački Petrovac, Janka Kralja 4; tel. (21) 780153; Pres. of Elders SAMUEL RYBAR.

Christian Church Jehovah's Witnesses: 11000 Belgrade, Milorada Mitrovića 4; tel. (11) 450383.

Christian Nazarene Community: Hrišćanska nazarenska zajednica, 21000 Novi Sad, Vodnikova br. 12; tel. (21) 401049; Pres. KAROL HRUBIK VLADIMIR.

Christian Reformed Church: 24323 Feketic, Bratsva 26; tel. and fax (24) 738070; f. 1919; 22,000 mems; Bishop ISTVAN CSETE-SZEMISI.

Evangelical Christian Church of the Augsburg Confession in Serbia-Vojvodina: 24000 Subotica, Brace Radiča 17; tel. and fax (24) 721048; e-mail dolinski@suonline.net; Superintendent DOLINSKY ÁRPÁD.

Evangelical Church of Republic of Croatia, Republic of Bosnia and Herzegovina and Vojvodina: 10000 Zagreb, Gundulićeva 28; tel. (48) 55622; fax (48) 54289; e-mail evang.lut.c.o.zg@email.hinet.hr; 7,500 mems; Pres. Dr VLADO L. DEUTSCH.

Seventh-Day Adventist Church: Hrišćanska adventistička crkva, 11000 Belgrade, Božidara Adzije 4; tel. (11) 453842; fax (11) 3442631; e-mail rantic@eunet.yu; Pres. RADIŠA ANTIĆ; Sec. JOVAN MIHALJĆIĆ.

Slovak Evangelical Church of the Augsburg Confession: 21000 Novi Sad, Karadžićeva 2; tel. (21) 611882; Lutheran; 51,500 mems (1990); Bishop Dr ANDREJ BEREDI.

Union of Baptist Churches in Serbia: 11000 Belgrade, Slobodanke D. Savic 33; tel. and fax (11) 410964; f. 1992; Gen. Sec. Rev. AVRAM DEGA.

United Methodist Church: 21000 Novi Sad, L. Mušičkoga 7; tel. and fax (21) 613122; e-mail emc@eunet.yu; f. 1898; 3,000 mems; Superintendent MARTIN HOVAN.

ISLAM

Almost 20% of the Montenegrin population profess Islam as their faith, many being ethnic Muslims of the Sandžak region (which was partitioned between Montenegro and Serbia in 1913). Most Muslims in Serbia are ethnic Albanians, mainly resident in the Province of Kosovo and Metohija, but there are also ethnic Slav Muslims in the part of Sandžak located in south-west Serbia. Serbian Islam is predominantly Sunni, although a Dervish sect, introduced in 1974, is popular among the Albanians (some 50,000 adherents, mainly in Kosovo and Metohija).

Islamic Community in the Republic of Serbia: 38000 Priština; Pres. of the Mesihat Dr REDZEP BOJE.

JUDAISM

Federation of Jewish Communities in Yugoslavia: Belgrade, Kralja Petra 71A /III, POB 512; tel. (11) 621837; fax (11) 626674; e-mail savezjev@infosky.net; f. 1919, revived 1944; Pres. ACA SINGER.

www.europaworldonline.com

The Press

In 2000 some 629 newspapers and 564 periodicals were published in the then FRY (of which 583 newspapers and 539 periodicals were published in Serbia).

PRINCIPAL DAILIES
(In Serbo-Croat, except where otherwise stated)

Belgrade

Blic: 11000 Belgrade, Masarikova 5; tel. (11) 3619148; fax (11) 3619271; e-mail sveseline@yahoo.com; internet www.blic.com; f. 1996; Editor-in-Chief Veslin Simonović; circ. 230,000.

Borba: 11000 Belgrade, trg Marksa i Engelsa 7; tel. (11) 334531; fax (11) 344913; f. 1922; morning; taken under govt control in 1994; Editor-in-Chief Zarko Obradović; circ. 46,000.

Danas: 11000 Belgrade, Alekse Nenadovica 19–23 V; tel. and fax (11) 3441186; e-mail danas@eunet.yu; internet www.danas.co.yu; banned Oct. 1998; independent; Dir Dusan Mitrović; Editor Grujica Spašović.

Dnevni Telegraf: 11000 Belgrade, trg Nikole Pašić 7; tel. (11) 334531; fax (11) 344913; morning; banned Oct. 1998; independent; Editor-in-Chief (vacant).

Nacional: Belgrade; f. 2000; Editor-in-Chief Predrag Popović.

Naša Borba: Belgrade, 29 Novembar 68B; tel. (11) 3020000; fax (11) 753734; e-mail nasa_borba@yurope.com; f. 1995 by journalists from *Borba* who rejected imposition of govt control, banned Oct. 1998; independent; Editor-in-Chief Mihal Ramać; circ. 35,000.

Newsday: 11001 Belgrade, Obiličev Venac 2, POB 439; f. 1983; Mon.–Fri; published in English by Tanjug and *Privredni Pregled*.

Politika: 11000 Belgrade, Makedonska 29; tel. (11) 3221836; fax (11) 3248768; f. 1904; Dir-Gen. and Editor-in-Chief Hadži Dragan Antić; circ. 300,000.

Politika Ekspres: 11000 Belgrade, Makedonska 29; tel. (11) 325630; evening; Editor-in-Chief Mile Kordić; circ. 76,000.

Privredni Pregled: 11000 Belgrade, Marsala. Birjuzova 3; tel. (11) 182888; fax (11) 627591; f. 1950; business and economics; Dir and Chief Editor Dušan Djordjević; circ. 14,000.

Sport: 11000 Belgrade, trg Marksa i Engelsa 7/III; tel. (11) 33451; fax (11) 344913; e-mail jslsport@bits.net.yu; internet www.jsl-sport .co.yu; f. 1945; Editor Zoran Milović; circ. 50,000.

Večernje novosti: 11000 Belgrade, trg Nikole Pašića 7; tel. (11) 334531; fax (11) 344913; e-mail vnovosti@eunet.yu; f. 1953; evening; Chief and Executive Editor Radisav Brajović; circ. 270,000.

Niš

Narodne Novine: 18000 Niš, Vojvode Gojka 14; morning; Chief Editor Ljubiša Sokolović (acting); circ. 7,210.

Novi Sad

Dnevnik: 21000 Novi Sad, 23; internet www.dnevnik.co.yu; f. 1942 as *Slobodna Vojvodina*; morning; Editor-in-Chief Dragan Radević; circ. 61,000.

Magyar Szó: 21000 Novi Sad, V. Mišića 1; f. 1944; morning; in Hungarian; Editor-in-Chief (vacant); circ. 25,590.

Podgorica

Pobjeda: Podgorica, Bulevar Revolucije 11; tel. (81) 246701; fax (81) 244475; e-mail pobjeda@cg.yu; internet www.pobjeda.co.yu; morning; Editor-in-Chief Vidoje Kontar (acting); circ. 17,959.

Publika: Podgorica, Crnogorskih serdara 8; tel. (81) 601430; fax (81) 625123; e-mail info.publika@cg.yu; internet www.publika.co.yu.

Priština

Bujku: Priština; in Albanian; banned by Serbian authorities October 1992; Editor-in-Chief Binak Kelmendi.

Jedinstvo: 38000 Priština, Srpskih Vladara 41; morning; Editor-in-Chief Dragan Malović; circ. 2,465.

Koha Ditore: Priština; published in Albanian; Editor Veton Surroi.

PERIODICALS

Belgrade

4. Jul.: Belgrade, trg Bratstva i Jedinstva 9/III–IV; weekly; organ of Federation of Veterans of the People's Liberation War of Yugoslavia; Dir and Editor-in-Chief Rajko Pavićević; circ. 10,000.

Duga (Rainbow): Belgrade; 2 a month; news magazine; Editor-in-Chief Ilija Repaić.

Ekonomist: Belgrade; f. 1948; quarterly; journal of the Yugoslav Association of Economists; Editor Dr Hasan Hadžiomerović.

Ekonomska Politika: 11000 Belgrade, trg Nikole Pašića 7; tel. (11) 3398298; f. 1952; weekly; Man. Pretplate Radojka Kolarović.

Evropljanin: Belgrade; current affairs; weekly; Publr Ivan Tadić.

Finansije: Belgrade, Jovana Ristića 1; f. 1945; 6 a year; Editor Bogoljub Lazarević.

Front: Belgrade, Proleterskih brigada 13; f. 1945; fortnightly; illustrated review; Editor-in-Chief Stevan Korda; circ. 263,000.

Ilustrovana Politika: 11000 Belgrade, Macetenska 39; tel. (11) 326938; fax (11) 32255602; f. 1958; weekly illustrated review; Editor-in-Chief Jevern Damnjanović; circ. 90,000.

Jisa Info: 11000 Belgrade, Zmaj Jovina 4; tel. (11) 3282447; fax (11) 626576; e-mail jisa@yubc.net; internet www.jisa.org.yu; Editor Dubravka Djurić.

Književne Novine: Belgrade, Francuska 7; f. 1948; fortnightly; review of literature, arts and social studies; Editor-in-Chief (vacant); circ. 7,500.

Književnost: Belgrade, Čika Ljubina 1; tel. (11) 620130; fax (11) 627465; f. 1946; monthly; literary review; Editor Vuk Krnjević; circ. 1,800.

Medjunarodna Politika (Review of International Affairs): Belgrade, Nemanjina 34, POB 413; e-mail intenaff@eunet.yu; f. 1950 by the Federation of Yugoslav Journalists; monthly; published in English and Serbian; Editor-in-Chief Dr Ranko Petković; Gen. Man. Milivoje Obradović.

Medjunarodni Problemi: Belgrade, Makedonska 25; tel. (11) 3221433; fax (11) 3224013; e-mail branam@eunet.yu; f. 1949; quarterly; review of the Institute of International Politics and Economics; Editor B. Marković; circ. 1,000.

Mikro/PC World: 11030 Belgrade, Pozeska 81a; tel. (11) 5447971; fax (11) 542397; e-mail pisma@mikro.co.yu; internet www.mikro.co .yu; f. 1997; 11 a year; computing; Editor Milenko Vasić; circ. 23,000.

NIN (Nedeljne informativne novine): Belgrade, Cetinjska 1, POB 208; tel. (11) 3224410; fax (11) 3221272; e-mail nin@eunet.yu; f. 1935; weekly; Editor-in-Chief Milivoje Glišić; Gen. Man. Tomislav Dzadzić; circ. 35,000.

Novi Glasnik: Belgrade; f. 1993; 6 a year; military magazine; Editor-in-Chief Col Mile Susnjar.

Official Gazette of the Federal Republic of Yugoslavia: 11000 Belgrade, Jovana Ristića 1; f. 1945; editions in Serbo-Croat, Slovene, Albanian, Hungarian and Macedonian; Dir Veljko Tadić; circ. 73,000.

Ošišiani Jež: 11000 Belgrade, Generala Ždanova 28/IV; tel. (11) 3232211; fax (11) 3232423; f. 1935; fortnightly; humour and satire; Editor Radivoje Bojičić; circ. 50,000.

Politikin Zabavnik: Belgrade, Makedonska 29; f. 1939; weekly; comic; Editor Radomir Soškić; circ. 41,000.

Pravoslavlje: 11000 Belgrade, Kralja Petra 5; tel. (11) 3282596; fax (11) 630865; e-mail pravoslavlje@spc.yu; f. 1967; fortnightly; religious; published by the Serbian Orthodox Church; Publr Radomir Rakić; circ. 7,600.

Rad: Belgrade, trg Nikole Pašića 5; tel. (11) 330927; weekly; organ of the Confederation of Trade Unions; Dir Radoslav Roso; Editor-in-Chief Stanislav Marinković; circ. 70,000.

Svet Kompjutera: 11000 Belgrade, Makedonska 29; tel. and fax (11) 3373181; e-mail editors@sk.co.yu; internet sk.beograd.com; f. 1984; monthly; computing; Editor Zorán Mosorinski; circ. 26,000.

Tehničke novine: 11000 Belgrade, Hajduk Veljkov venac 12; tel. (11) 657415; e-mail ivladan@net.yu; internet solair.eunet.yu/ _ivladan; monthly; technical; Chief Editor Saša Imperl; circ. 75,000.

Viva: 11000 Belgrade, Cetinjska 1V; tel. (11) 3220132; fax (11) 3220552; e-mail viva@politika.co.uk; internet www.politika.co.yu; monthly; health; Editor Dragutin Gregorić; circ. 25,000.

Vojska: Belgrade, Proleterskih brig. 13; f. 1945; weekly; Yugoslav Army organ; Dir Milan Kavgić; Editor-in-Chief Col Milorad Pantelić.

Yugoslav Journal of Operations Research: 11000 Belgrade, Faculty of Organizational Sciences, University of Belgrade, Jove Ilica 154; tel. (11) 3972383; fax (11) 461221; e-mail yujor@fon.fonbg .ac.yu; internet jujor.fon.bg.ac.yu; 2 a year; systems science and management science; Editor Radivoj Petrović; circ. 700.

Yugoslav Law (1975–): Belgrade, Terazije 41; tel. and fax (11) 3233213; 3 a year; in English and French; publ. by the Institute of Comparative Law and the Union of Jurists' Asscn; Editor Dr Oliver Antić.

Yugoslav Survey: Belgrade, Moše Pijade 8/1, POB 677; tel. (11) 3233610; fax (11) 3240291; f. 1960; quarterly; general reference publication of basic documentary information about Yugoslavia in English; Dir ILE KOVAČEVIĆ; Editor-in-Chief TOMO KOSOVIĆ (acting); circ. 3,000.

Niš

Bratstvo: Niš; Bulgarian-language magazine; Dir VENKO DIMITROV.

Novi Sad

Letopis Matice Srpske: Novi Sad, Matice srpske 1; f. 1824; monthly; literary review; Editor Dr SLAVKO GORDÍC.

Podgorica

Koha (Time): Podgorica; f. 1978; Albanian-language magazine; circ. 2,000 (estimated).

Stvaranje: Podgorica, Revolucije 78; f. 1946; monthly; literary review; publ. by the Literary Asscn of Montenegro; Man. RANKO JOVOVIĆ.

Priština

Koha (Time): Priština; f. 1994; Albanian-language magazine; Editor-in-Chief VETON SUROI.

Zeri: Priština; political weekly; in Albanian; Editor-in-Chief BLERIM SHALA.

NEWS AGENCY

Novinska Agencija Tanjug: 11001 Belgrade, Obilićev Venac 2, POB 439; tel. (11) 332230; f. 1943; 90 correspondents in Serbia and Montenegro and 30 offices abroad; press and information agency governed by self-management; news service for domestic press, radio and television; news and features service for abroad in English, French and Spanish; photo and telephoto service; economic and financial services for home and abroad; publishes EITI, service for trade, industry and banking in Serbo-Croat, English and French; computerized commodity service for domestic businesses and banks; Dir and Editor-in-Chief DUŠAN DJORDJEVIĆ.

Foreign Bureaux

Agence France-Presse (AFP) (France): 11000 Belgrade, trg Nikole Pasica 2; tel. (11) 3232622; fax (11) 620638; e-mail afpbgd@eunet.yu; Bureau Chief JEAN-EUDES BARBIER.

Agenzia Nazionale Stampa Associata (ANSA) (Italy): 11000 Belgrade, Braće Jugovića 5; tel. (11) 620221; fax (11) 628225; Bureau Chief LUCIANO CAUSA.

Allgemeiner Deutscher Nachrichtendienst (ADN) (Germany): 11000 Belgrade, Šiva Stena 1A; tel. (11) 461752; Correspondent Dr WILLFRIED MUCH.

Associated Press (AP) (USA): 11000 Belgrade, Dositejeva 12; tel. (11) 631553; Correspondent IVAN STEFANOVIĆ.

Bulgarska Telegrafna Agentsia (BTA) (Bulgaria): Belgrade; tel. (11) 636361; fax (11) 636361; Correspondent NIKOLA KITSEVSKI.

Česká tisková kancelář (ČTK) (Czech Republic): 11070 Belgrade, 190/Stan. 6/III, Blok 37; tel. (11) 134892; Correspondent MIROSLAV JILEK.

Informatsionnoye Telegrafnoye Agentstvo Rossii—Telegrafnoye Agentstvo Suverennykh Stran (ITAR—TASS) (Russia): Belgrade, Ognjena Price 17; tel. (11) 4446928; Correspondent MIKHAIL ABELEV.

Korean Central News Agency (KCNA) (Democratic People's Republic of Korea): Belgrade, Dr Milutina Ivkovića 9; tel. (11) 668426; Bureau Chief KIM JONG SE.

Magyar Távirati Iroda (MTI) (Hungary): 11030 Belgrade, Vladimira Rolovica 176; tel. (11) 506508; Correspondent GYÖRGY WALKO.

Rossiiskoye Informatsionnoye Agentstvo—Novosti (RIA—Novosti) (Russia): Belgrade, Strahinjića Bana 50; tel. (11) 629419; Bureau Chief SERGEI GRIZUNOV.

United Press International (UPI) (USA): 11000 Belgrade, Generala Zdanova 19; tel. (11) 342490; Correspondent NESHO DJURIĆ.

Xinhua (New China) News Agency (People's Republic of China): Belgrade; tel. (11) 493789; Correspondent YANG DAZHOU.

PRESS ASSOCIATIONS

Federation of Yugoslav Journalists (Savez Novinara Jugoslavije): Belgrade, trg Republike 5/III; tel. (11) 624993; f. 1945; 11,500 mems; Pres. MILISAV MILIĆ.

Independent Association of Journalists of Serbia: Belgrade; f. 1994; Pres. DRAGAN NIKITOVIĆ.

Yugoslav Newspaper Publishers' Association: Belgrade; Dir RASTKO GUZINA.

There is also an **Association of Professional Journalists of Montenegro**

Publishers

Alfa-Narodna knjiga: 11000 Belgrade, Šafarikova 11; tel. (11) 3227426; fax (11) 3227946; e-mail tea@eunet.yu; internet www .narodnaknjiga.co.yu; f. 1950; fiction, non-fiction, children's books and dictionaries; Gen. Man. MILIČKO MIJOVIĆ.

BIGZ (Beogradski izdavačko-grafički zavod): 11000 Belgrade, bul. vojvode Mišića 17/VI; tel. (11) 650627; fax (11) 648626; f. 1831; literature and criticism, children's books, pocket books, popular science, philosophy, politics; Dir SNEŽANA KNEŽEVIĆ.

Dečje novine: 32300 Gornji Milanovac, T. Matijevića 4; tel. (32) 711195; fax (32) 711248; general literature, children's books, science, science fiction, textbooks; Gen. Dir MIROSLAV PETROVIĆ.

Forum: Novinsko-izdavačka i štamparska radna organizacija, 21000 Novi Sad, Vojvode Mišića 1, POB 200; tel. (21) 611300; f. 1957; newspapers, periodicals and books in Hungarian; Dir GYULA GOBBY.

Gradjevinska Knjiga: 11000 Belgrade, trg Nikole Pašića 8/II; tel. (11) 3233565; fax (11) 3233563; f. 1948; technical, scientific and educational textbooks; Dir LJUBINKO ANDELIĆ.

IP Matice srpske: 21000 Novi Sad, trg Toze Markovića 2; tel. (21) 420199; fax (21) 27281; e-mail m.grujic@sezampro.yu; f. 1826; Yugoslav and foreign fiction and humanities; Man. Dir MILORAD GRUJIĆ.

Jedinstvo: 38000 Priština, Dom štampe bb, POB 81; tel. (38) 27549; fax (38) 29809; poetry, novels, general literature, science, children's books; Dir JORDAN RISTIĆ.

Jugoslovenska knjiga: 11000 Belgrade, trg Republike 5/VIII, POB 36; tel. (11) 621992; fax (11) 625970; art, economics and culture; Dir ZORAN NIKODIJEVIĆ.

Medicinska knjiga: 11001 Belgrade, Mata Vidakovića 24–26; tel. (11) 458165; f. 1947; medicine, pharmacology, stomatology, veterinary; Dir MILE MEDIĆ.

Minerva: Izdavačko-štamparsko preduzeće, 24000 Subotica, trg 29 novembra 3; tel. (24) 25712; fax (24) 23208; novels and general; Dir LADISLAV ŠEBEK.

Naučna knjiga: 11000 Belgrade, Uzun Mirkova 5; tel. (11) 637220; f. 1947; school, college and university textbooks, publications of scientific bodies; Dir Dr BLAŽO PEROVIĆ.

Nolit: 11000 Belgrade, Terazije 27/II; tel. (11) 3245017; fax (11) 627285; f. 1928; Yugoslav and other belles-lettres, philosophy and fine art; scientific and popular literature; Dir-Gen. RADIVOJE NESIĆ; Editor-in-Chief RADIVOJE MIKIĆ.

Obod: 81250 Cetinje, Njegoševa 3; tel. (86) 21331; fax (86) 21953; general literature; Dir VASKO JANKOVIĆ.

Panorama: Priština; f. 1994; publishes newspapers and journals in Serbian, Albanian and Turkish; Dir JORDAN RISTIĆ.

Pobjeda: 81000 Podgorica, Južni bb; tel. (81) 44433; f. 1974; poetry, fiction, lexicography and scientific works.

Proex Commerce: 11000 Belgrade, Terazije 16; tel. (11) 686978; fax (11) 641052; e-mail gbproex@eunet.yu; internet www.proex.co .yu; editorial and typographic co-productions; export and import of books and periodicals.

Prosveta: 11000 Belgrade, Čika Ljubina 1/I; tel. (11) 629843; fax (11) 182581; f. 1944; general literature, art books, dictionaries, encyclopaedias, science, music; Dir BUDIMIR RUDOVIĆ.

Rad: 11000 Belgrade, Dečanska 12; tel. (11) 3239998; fax (11) 3230923; e-mail rad@radbooks.co.yu; internet www.radbooks.co.yu; f. 1949; politics, economics, sociology, psychology, literature, biographies; Man. Dir SIMON SIMONOVIĆ; Editor-in-Chief NOVICA TADIĆ.

Rilindja: 38000 Priština, Dom štampe bb; tel. (38) 23868; popular science, literature, children's fiction and travel books, textbooks in Albanian; Dir NAZMI RRAHMANI.

Savremena administracija: 11000 Belgrade, Crnotravska 7–9; tel. (11) 667633; fax (11) 667277; f. 1954; economy, law, science university textbooks; Dir TOMISLAV JOVIĆ.

Sportska knjiga: 11000 Belgrade, Makedonska 19; tel. (11) 320226; f. 1949; sport, chess, hobbies; Dir BORISLAV PETROVIĆ.

Srpska književna zadruga: 11000 Belgrade, Srpskih Vladara 19/I; tel. (11) 330305; fax (11) 626224; f. 1892; works of classical and modern Yugoslav writers, and translations of works of foreign writers; Pres. RADOVAN SAMARDŽIĆ; Editor RADOMIR RADOVANAĆ.

Svetovi: 21000 Novi Sad, Arse Teodorovića 11; tel. (21) 28032; fax (21) 28036; general; Dir JOVAN ZIVLAK.

Tehnička Knjiga: 11000 Belgrade, Vojvode Stepe 89; tel. (11) 468596; fax (11) 473442; f. 1948; technical works, popular science, reference books, 'how to' books, hobbies; Dir RADIVOJE GRBOVIĆ.

Vuk Karadžič: 11000 Belgrade, Kraljevića Marka 9, POB 762; tel. (11) 628066; fax (11) 623150; scientific literature, popular science, children's books, general; Gen. Man. VOJIN ANČIĆ.

Zavod za udžbenike i nastavna sredstva: 11000 Belgrade, Obilićev Venac 5; tel. (11) 637426; e-mail zavodudz@eunet.yu; internet www.zavod.co.yu; fax (11) 630014; f. 1957; textbooks and teaching aids; Dir RADOSLAV PETKOVIĆ.

PUBLISHERS' ASSOCIATION

Association of Yugoslav Publishers and Booksellers (Udruženje izdavača i knjižara Jugoslavije): 11000 Belgrade, Kneza Miloša 25, POB 570; tel. (11) 642533; fax (11) 646339; e-mail ognjenl@eunet.yu; f. 1954; organizes Belgrade International Book Fair; Dir OGNJEN LAKIĆEVIĆ; 116 mem. organizations.

Broadcasting and Communications

TELECOMMUNICATIONS

Telecom Serbia: 11000 Belgrade, Takovska 2; tel. (11) 3234414; fax (11) 3232141; e-mail drasko.Petrovic@telekom.yu; 49% transferred to Hellenic Telecommunications Organization and Telecom Italia SpA in 1997; Dir-Gen. DRAŠKO PETROVIĆ.

BROADCASTING

Jugoslovenska Radiotelevizija (JRT) (Association of Yugoslav Radio and Television Organizations): 11000 Belgrade, Generala Ždanova 28; tel. (11) 3230194; fax (11) 434023; f. 1952; Exec. Dir NIKOLIĆ VJERA.

Radio

Radio D: Podgorica; f. 2000; independent radio station.

Radio Jugoslavija: 11000 Belgrade, Hilandarska 2/IV, POB 200; tel. (11) 346884; fax (11) 332014; e-mail radioyu@bitsyu.net; internet www.radioyu.org; f. 1951; foreign service; broadcasts in Serbo-Croat, Arabic, English, French, German, Russian and Spanish; Dir Dr DRAGAN MARKOVIĆ.

Radiotelevizija Crne Gore: 81000 Podgorica, Cetinjski put bb; tel. (81) 41800; fax (81) 43640; f. 1944; 2 radio programmes; broadcasts in Serbo-Croat; Dir-Gen. ZORAN JOCOVIĆ.

Radiotelevizija Srbije (RTS): 11000 Belgrade, Takovska 10; tel. (11) 3229780; fax (11) 3229788; f. 1929; five radio programmes; Dir-Gen. DRAGOLJUB MILANOVIĆ; Asst Dir-Gen. MILIVOJE PAPLOVIĆ; comprises.

Radiotelevizija Beograd: 11000 Belgrade, Hilandarska 2; tel. (11) 346801; fax (11) 326768; f. 1929; 5 radio programmes; Dir-Gen. DOBROSAV BJELETIĆ; Dir of Radio DRAGOSLAV NIKITOVIĆ (acting).

Radiotelevizija Novi Sad: 21000 Novi Sad, Ignata Pavlasa 3Ž; tel. (21) 611588; fax (21) 26624; f. 1949; 7 radio programmes; broadcasts in Serbo-Croat, Slovak, Romanian, Hungarian and Ruthenian; Gen. Man. PETAR JOVANOVIĆ.

Radiotelevizija Priština: 38000 Priština, Marsala Tita bb; tel. (38) 26255; fax (38) 25355; f. 1944; 3 radio programmes; broadcasts in Serbo-Croat, Romany and Turkish; Dir-Gen. RICHARD LUCAS; Dir of Radio MILORAD VUJOVIĆ.

B92: Belgrade, Makedonska 22; tel. (11) 3248577; fax (11) 3248075; f. 1989; independent radio station; Editor-in-Chief VERAN MATIĆ.

Mir: Tuza; tel. (81) 875305; e-mail dino@co.yu; f. 1998; independent Albanian-language station; Chair. DINO RAMOVIĆ.

Radio TV Bajina Basta: 31250 Bajina Basta, Svetosavska 34; tel. (31) 851688; fax (31) 853162; e-mail office@bajinabasta.org; internet www.bajinabasta.org; f. 1986; independent radio and television station; Dir BOBAN TOMIĆ.

Television

Radiotelevizija Crne Gore: 81000 Podgorica; f. 1971; 2 television programmes; Dir of Television MILUTIN RADULOVIĆ (acting).

Radiotelevizija Srbije: see Radio.

Radiotelevizija Beograd: 11000 Belgrade, Takovska 10; tel. (11) 342001; fax (11) 543178; f. 1958; 3 television programmes; in Serbo-Croat; Dir of Television SLOBODAN IGNJATOVIĆ.

Radiotelevizija Novi Sad: 21000 Novi Sad, Sutjeska 1; tel. (21) 615144; fax (21) 613959; f. 1975; two television programmes; broadcast in eight languages; Gen. Man. PETAR JOVANOVIĆ.

Radiotelevizija Priština: 38000 Priština, Zejnel Ajdini 12; tel. (38) 31211; fax (38) 32073; f. 1975; 1 television programme; Dir of Television NIKOLA SARIĆ.

RTV BK Television: 1070 Belgrade, Nikole Tesle 42a; tel. (11) 3013555; fax (11) 3013526; e-mail info@bkt.com; internet www.bktv.com; f. 1994; independent television station; Dir-Gen. Dr TIMOHIR SIMIĆ; Editor-in-Chief MILOMIR MARIĆ.

Kosava Television: Belgrade; f. 1998; Dir MARIJA MILOŠEVIĆ.

Studio B: Belgrade; Editor-in-chief LJUBISLAV ALEKSIĆ.

TV Srbijasume 92: Belgrade; f. 2000; state-sponsored youth television station.

Uzice Television S: Uzice; f. 2000.

Finance

(cap. = capital; res = reserves; dep. = deposits; m. = million; amounts in convertible Yugoslav dinars unless otherwise stated; br. = branch)

BANKING

Central Banking System

The National Bank of Serbia and Montenegro is the country's central bank, its powers and obligations being determined by law. Its functions include the issue of money, provision of credit to banks and government authorities, control of credits and bank activities, recommendation of legislation relating to the activities, recommendation of legislation relating to the foreign exchange system and its implementation, management of gold and foreign exchange reserves, control of foreign exchange operations and other special activities.

National Bank of Serbia and Montengro (Narodna banka Srbije i Crne Gore): 11000 Belgrade, Kralja Petra 12, POB 1010; tel. (11) 3027100; fax (11) 3027113; e-mail kabinet@nbj.sv.gov.yu; internet www.nbj.yu; f. 1884, restructured 1963; cap. and res 2,391.9m., dep. 16,120.0m. (Dec. 1999); total assets 147,883m. (Dec. 2001); Gov. MLADJAN DINKIĆ; 4 brs.

National Bank of Montenegro: 81000 Podgorica, Blaža Jovanovića 7; tel. (81) 43381; Gov. KRUNISLAV VUKČEVIĆ.

National Bank of Serbia: 11000 Belgrade, 7 jula 12; tel. (11) 625555; Gov. BORISLAV ATANACKOVIĆ.

Bank for International Economic Co-operation

Jugoslovenska Banka Za Medjunarodnu Ekonomsku Saradnju (Yugoslav Bank for International Economic Co-operation): Head Office: 11000 Belgrade, Srpskih vladara 5, POB 219; tel. (11) 3239012; fax (11) 3244114; e-mail jubmes@jubmes.co.yu; f. 1979; focuses on the financing of export-orientated and development projects; total assets US $61.3m. (2000); Pres. ZORAN STANKOVIĆ; Exec. Vice-Pres. PREDRAG KAPOR.

Other Banks

Alco Banka: 11000 Belgrade, Požeška 65b; tel. (11) 3050300; fax (11) 3540930; e-mail banka@alcoyu.co.yu; f. 1996; cap. 277.1m., res 2.9m., dep. 369.2m. (2000); Chair. MIROLJUB ALEKSIĆ.

Delta Banka a.d. Beograd: 11070 Belgrade, Narodnih heroja 43; tel. (11) 3113850; fax (11) 693808; e-mail dbanka@deltabanka.co.yu; internet www.deltabanka.co.yu; f. 1991; cap. 1,636.9m., res 561.3m., dep. 3,475.5m. (Dec. 2000); Pres. MIROSLAV MIŠKOVIĆ; Dir-Gen. VLADAN DJORDJEVIĆ; 34 brs.

Jubanka a.d. Beograd: 11000 Belgrade, Kralja Milana 11; tel. (11) 3234931; fax (11) 3246840; e-mail jubanka@jubanka.com; internet www.jubanka.com; f. 1956; cap. 1,625.5m., res 1,737.2m., dep. 32,012.8m. (2000); Dir-Gen. BORISLAV DJOKIĆ; 14 brs.

Komercijalna Banka a.d. Beograd: 11000 Belgrade, Svetog Save 14; tel. (11) 3080100; fax (11) 3442372; e-mail posta@kombank.com; internet www.kombank.com; cap. 1,445.8m., res 271.6m., dep. 12,803.1m. (2001); Pres. LJUBOMIR MIHAJLOVIĆ.

Yu Garant Banka a.d.: 11000 Beograd, 25 Slobodana Penezica; tel. (11) 656999; fax (11) 644854; internet www.yugb.co.yu; cap. 1,115.1m., res 203.2m., dep. 4.165.2m. (Dec. 2000); Gen. Man. Dr VUK OBRADOVIĆ.

Zepter Banka a.d. Beograd: 11070 Belgrade, Bulevar Lenjina 117; tel. (11) 3113233; fax (11) 138603; e-mail zepterb@bitsyu.net; internet www.banka.zepter.co.yu; cap. 404.0m., res 147.2m., dep. 635.4m. (2000); Pres. PHILIP ZEPTER.

Vojvodina

Metals Banka a.d. Novi Sad: 21000 Novi Sad, Bulevar Cara Lazara 7A; tel. (21) 450695; fax (21) 350611; f. 1990; cap. 300.7m., dep. 327.6m. (2000); Gen. Man. ANANIJE PAVIĆEVIĆ.

Panonska Banka a.d.: 21001 Novi Sad, 76 Bulevar Oslobodjenja, POB 351; tel. (21) 612444; fax (21) 613939; e-mail office@panban.co .uk; internet www.panban.co.yu; f. 1974 as branch of Vojvodjanska Banka-Centrala; cap. and res 972m., dep. 2,217m. (Nov. 2001); Gen. Man. RAŠKO BOŽOVIĆ; 8 brs.

Vojvodjanska Banka, a.d.: 21001 Novi Sad, POB 391, Trg Slobode 7; tel. (21) 421077; fax (21) 624859; internet www.voban.co.yu; f. 1962; cap. 5,130.6m., res 667.6m., dep. 11,709.6m. (Dec. 2000); Pres. ŽIVOTA MIHAJLOVIĆ; 275 brs.

Banking Association

Association of Banks of Serbia and Montenegro (Udruženje banaka Srbije i Crne Gore): 11001 Belgrade, Bulevar Aleksandra 86; tel. (11) 3020760; fax (11) 3370179; e-mail ubj@fimmet.co .yu; f. 1955; association of business banks; works on improving interbank co-operation, organizes agreements of mutual interest for banks, gives expert assistance, establishes co-operation with foreign banks, other financial institutions and their associations, represents banks in relations with the Government and the National Bank of Serbia and Montenegro; Pres. Prof. VOJIN BJELICA; Sec.-Gen. MILETA BABOVIĆ.

STOCK EXCHANGE

Belgrade Stock Exchange: 11070 Belgrade, Omladinskih brigada 1, POB 214; tel. (11) 3117297; fax (11) 138242; e-mail marketing@ belex.co.yu; internet www.belex.co.yu; f. 1894.

INSURANCE

Kompanija 'Dunav Osiguranje' (Dunav Insurance Company): 11001 Belgrade, Makedonska 4, POB 624; tel. (11) 3224001; fax (11) 624652; f. 1974; all types of insurance.

Trade and Industry

GOVERNMENT AGENCY

Foreign Trade Institute (Institut za Spoljnu Trgovinu): 11000 Belgrade, Moše Pijade 8; tel. (11) 339041; Dir Dr SLOBODAN MRKŠA.

CHAMBERS OF COMMERCE

Chamber of Commerce and Industry of Serbia and Montenegro (Privredna Komora Srbije i Crne Gore): 11000 Belgrade, Terazije 23, POB 1003; tel. (11) 3248123; fax (11) 3248754; e-mail info@pkj.co.yu; internet www.pkj.co.yu; f. 1990; independent organization affiliating all domestic economic organizations; promotes economic and commercial relations with foreign countries; Pres. Dr SLOBODAN KORAĆ.

Chamber of Commerce of Montenegro (Privredna Komora Crne Gore): 81000 Podgorica, Novaka Miloševa 29/II; tel. (81) 31071; fax (81) 34926; Pres. VOJIN DJUKANOVIĆ.

Chamber of Commerce of Serbia (Privredna Komora Srbije): 11000 Belgrade, Gen. Zdanova 13–15; tel. (11) 3240611; fax (11) 3230949; e-mail pksrbije@pks.co.yu; internet www.pks.co.yu; Pres. RADOSLAV VESELINOVIĆ.

UTILITIES

Electricity

Elektroprivreda Crne Gore (Elektroprivreda Montenegro): 81400 Nicšić, Vuka Karadžića 2; tel. (83) 212177; production, transmission and distribution of electric power; 3,480 employees.

Elektroprivreda Srbije (Elektroprivreda Serbia): 11000 Belgrade, Balkanska 7; tel. (11) 620921; fax (11) 629489; state-owned; Pres. DRAGAN KOSTIĆ; 528 employees.

Gas

Naftna Industrija Srbije (NIS) (Serbian Oil Industry): 21000 Novi Sad, Sutjeska 1; tel. (21) 615144; fax (21) 25037; f. 1990 as Naftagas-Hip-Jugopetrol by merger of 42 social enterprises, previously affiliated to 3 composite orgs of associated labour; petroleum and natural gas exploration and production in Yugoslavia and abroad; refines crude petroleum and natural gas, producing a variety of petroleum derivatives and associated products, incl. mineral fertilizers and synthetic rubber; also operates petro-chemical and chemical plants; Pres. ARVO SUPPI; 18,694 employers.

TRADE UNIONS

Association of Free and Independent Trade Unions: 11000 Belgrade, Karadjordjeva 50; tel. and fax (11) 623671; e-mail asns@ asns.org.yu; internet www.asns.org.yu; mem. of the Democratic Opposition of Serbia alliance which won Sept. 2000 elections; Pres. DRAGAN MILOVANOVIĆ.

Confederation of Autonomous Trade Unions of Serbia and Montenegro (Savez Samostalnih Sindikata Srbije i Crne Gore): 11000 Belgrade, trg Nikola Pašić 5; tel. (11) 3230922; fax (11) 3241911; 1.9m. mems.

Trade unions comprising the Confederation of Autonomous Trade Unions of Serbia and Montenegro:

Agricultural, Food and Tobacco Industry Workers' Union (Sindikat radnika poljprivrede, prehrambene i duvanske industrije): Pres. Federal Cttee ERNE KIČI.

Building Workers' Union (Sindikat radnika gradjevinarstva): Pres. Federal Cttee MILOŠ ŽORIĆ.

Catering and Tourism Workers' Union (Sindikat radnika u ugostiteljstvu i turizmu): Pres. Federal Cttee MILAN FRKOVIĆ.

Chemistry and Non-Metallic Industry Workers' Union (Sindikat radnika hemije i nemetala): Pres. Federal Cttee STOJMIR DOMAZETOVSKI.

Commerce Workers' Union (Sindikat radnika u trgovini): Pres. Federal Cttee LJUBICA BRAČKO.

Education, Science and Culture Workers' Union (Sindikat radnika delatnosti vaspitanja, obrazovanja, nauke i kulture): Pres. Federal Cttee BORIS LIPUŽIĆ.

Energy Workers' Union (Sindikat radnika energetike): Pres. Federal Cttee VASKRSIJE SAVIĆIĆ.

Forestry and Wood Industry Workers' Union (Sindikat radnika šumarstva i prerade drveta): Pres. Federal Cttee DRAGOLJUB OBRADOVIĆ.

Health and Social Care Workers' Union (Sindikat radnika delatnosti zdravstva i socijalne zaštite): Pres. Federal Cttee LJILJANA MILOŠEVIĆ.

Metal Production and Manufacturing Workers' Union (Sindikat radnika proizvodnje i prerade metala): Pres. Federal Cttee SLAVKO URŠIĆ.

Public Utilities and Handicrafts Workers' Union (Sindikat radnika u komunalnoj privredi i zanatstvu): Pres. Federal Cttee JOSIP KOLAR.

Printing, Newspaper, Publishing and Information Workers' Union (Sindikat radnika grafičke, novinsko-izdavačke i informativne delatnosti): Pres. Federal Cttee BORIS BIŠĆAN.

State Administration and Finance Workers' Union (Sindikat radnika državne uprave i finansijskih organa): Pres. Federal Cttee RAM BUĆAJ.

Textile, Leather, and Footwear Workers' Union (Sindikat radnika industrije tekstila, kože i obuće): Pres. Federal Cttee JOZEFINA MUSA.

Transport and Communications Workers' Union (Sindikat radnika saobraćaja i veza): Belgrade; tel. (11) 646321; Pres. Federal Cttee HASAN HRNJIĆ.

Transport

Much international transport activity to or from the FRY was halted in 1992–94 as a result of UN sanctions. In 2000 it was announced that the FRY was to receive aid from the Stability Pact for South Eastern Europe for transport projects. The construction of the road and railway bridge across the River Danube in Novi Sad was completed in May. Work on the construction of the Belgrade–Novi Sad highway began in June.

RAILWAYS

In 2000 there were 4,058 km of railway track in use, of which 1,364 km were electrified. In March 2002 the Government signed an agreement with the European Union on an €80m. loan for the reconstruction of the major rail route.

Zajednica Jugoslovenskih Železnica (Yugoslav Railways): 11000 Belgrade, Nemanjina 6, POB 553; tel. (11) 3616722; fax (11) 3616797; Gen. Man. SVETOLIK KOSTADINOVIĆ.

ROADS

In 2000 there were an estimated 44,777 km of roads, of which 28,061 km were paved.

INLAND WATERWAYS

About 3.7m. metric tons of freight were carried on inland water transport in 2000.

SHIPPING

With the dissolution of the SFRY, Yugoslavia lost much of its access to the sea; the principal coastal outlet is the Montenegrin port of Bar, which is linked to Bari (Italy) by a regular ferry service. In 1992–95 many Yugoslav vessels were impounded abroad, as a result of UN sanctions. In 1996 the maritime fleet resumed operations.

Jugoslovenska Oceanska Plovidba (Yugoslav Ocean Lines): 85330 Kotor; tel. (82) 25011; Pres. ANTON MOŠKOV.

Jugoslovenska Pomorska Agencija (Yugoslav Shipping Agency): 11070 Belgrade, bul. Mihaila Pupina 165A , POB 210; tel. (11) 3115994; fax (11) 3112070; e-mail jugentyu@eunet.yu; f. 1947; charter services, liner and container transport, port agency, passenger service, air cargo service; Gen. Man. MIROSLAV PAVLIČIĆ.

CIVIL AVIATION

There are international airports at Belgrade and Podgorica, as well as several domestic airports.

Jugoslovenski Aerotransport (JAT) (Yugoslav Airlines): 11070 Belgrade, Bulevar umetnosti 16; tel. (11) 3114222; fax (11) 3112853; e-mail pr@jat.com; internet www.jat.com; f. 1947; 51% owned by Govt of Serbia; re-establishing former network of commercial flights following the lifting of the ban by the EU in February 2000; renewed regular flights to Lebanon, Saudi Arabia and Syria in July; operates two domestic routes; Dir-Gen. PREDRAG VUJOVIC.

Smaller operators included:

Air Jugoslavia: 11000 Belgrade, Bul Utmetnosti 16; tel. (11) 2221454; fax (11) 327832; f. 1969; wholly-owned subsidiary of JAT; Gen. Man. NEOLO LOZIĆ.

Air Montenegro: 81000 Podgorica, Airport Podgorica, POB 073; tel. (81)230641; fax (81) 623762; e-mail contact@mgr.cg.yu; internet www.montenegro-airlines.com; f. 1991; operations commenced 1997; regular domestic and international charter services; Pres. ZORAN DURIJIĆ.

Aviogenex: 11070 Belgrade, Vladimira Popovića 8; tel. (11) 3119385; fax (11) 3111017; e-mail agxdir@icg.co.yu; f. 1968; passenger flights within Europe; Man. Dir BRATISLAV PEJKOVIĆ.

Tourism

Prior to the disintegration of the SFRY, tourism was a major source of foreign exchange (receipts were estimated at US $2,700m. in 1990); most foreign tourists were, however, attracted to Croatia and Slovenia. The great lake of Scutari, in Montenegro, is a notable tourist attraction, as is Montenegro's Adriatic coastline. The Yugoslav tourist industry was adversely affected by the imposition of UN sanctions, in May 1992. Although some recovery in the tourism industry was subsequently achieved, the NATO air offensive against the FRY, which commenced in March–June 1999, resulted in the suspension of tourist activity. In that year the number of tourist arrivals declined to 151,650, compared with 282,639 in 1998. Tourist arrivals recovered to 238,957 in 2000.

National Tourism Organization of Montenegro: 81000 Podgorica, Omladinskih brigada 7; tel. (81) 230959; fax (81) 230979; e-mail tourism@cg.yu; internet www.visit-montenegro.com; Man. Dir PREDRAG JELUSIĆ.

National Tourism Organization of Serbia (Turistička Organizacija Srbije): 11000 Belgrade, POB 433, Dobrinska 11; tel. (11) 3612754; fax (11) 686804; e-mail ntos@eunet.yu; internet www .serbia-info.com/ntos; f. 1953; produces information and conducts market research and promotion in the field of tourism; Dir JOVAN POPESKU.

Yugotours: 11000 Belgrade, Zmaj Jovina 4; tel. (11) 626163; fax (11) 625380; f. 1957; organizes travel and accommodation arrangements for foreign and domestic tourists; 3 branch offices, 2 European; Man. Dir SLOBODAN ŠĆEPANOVIĆ.

SEYCHELLES

Introductory Survey

Location, Climate, Language, Religion, Flag, Capital

The Republic of Seychelles comprises about 115 islands, widely scattered over the western Indian Ocean. Apart from the Seychelles archipelago, the country includes several other island groups, the southernmost being about 210 km (130 miles) north of Madagascar. The climate is tropical, with small seasonal variations in temperature and rainfall. The average temperature in Victoria is nearly 27°C (80°F) and average annual rainfall 236 cm (93 ins). In 1981 Seselwa, a creole spoken by virtually all Seychellois, replaced English and French as the official language. Almost all of the inhabitants are Christians, of whom more than 90% belong to the Roman Catholic Church. The national flag (proportions 1 by 2) has five rays, extending from the lower hoist corner, of blue, yellow, red, white and green. The capital is Victoria, on the island of Mahé.

Recent History

Seychelles was uninhabited until colonized by France in 1770. It was ceded to the United Kingdom in 1814 and administered as a dependency of Mauritius until 1903, when it became a Crown Colony.

During the 1960s political activity was focused on the centre-right Seychelles Democratic Party (SDP), led by James (later Sir James) Mancham, and the socialist-orientated Seychelles People's United Party (SPUP), led by Albert René. A ministerial system of government was introduced in 1970, and Seychelles proceeded to full independence, as a sovereign republic within the Commonwealth, on 29 June 1976, under a coalition Government with Mancham as President and René as Prime Minister. Under the independence agreement, the United Kingdom returned to Seychelles the islands of Aldabra, Farquhar and Desroches, detached in 1965 to form part of the British Indian Ocean Territory (q.v.) and subsequently leased to the USA. In 1982 the Aldabra group, which (including its lagoon) represents about one-third of Seychelles' total area, was designated by UNESCO as a world heritage site.

In June 1977 the SPUP staged an armed coup while Mancham was absent from the islands. René was declared President, the National Assembly was dissolved and the Constitution suspended. In May 1978 the SPUP was renamed the Seychelles People's Progressive Front (SPPF). A new Constitution, proclaimed in March 1979, established a one-party state. In June elections for a new National Assembly were held. René was the sole candidate in the concurrent presidential election and was re-elected in June 1984 and, again in 1989 as sole candidate, for a third term of office, the maximum period permitted under the 1979 Constitution. During this period opponents of René's socialist Government made a number of attempts to overthrow the regime, with the use of foreign-backed mercenaries. The most serious assault took place in November 1981, when about 50 mercenaries, mainly South Africans posing as tourists, flew to join insurgents already on the islands. When the rebellion collapsed, most of the mercenaries escaped to South Africa, where several of their number were later tried and imprisoned. Further plots, discovered in October 1982 and November 1983, were ascribed to the same Seychellois exiles who had planned the 1981 coup attempt. In November 1985 Gérard Hoareau, the leader of an exiled opposition group, was shot dead in the United Kingdom. The incident formed one of a series of attacks on, and disappearances of, anti-René activists. In September 1986 it was reported that the Minister of Youth and Defence, Col Ogilvy Berlouis, had been asked to resign, together with three senior army officers, following an unsuccessful attempt to overthrow the Government. In the same month President René reorganized the Council of Ministers, assuming the post of Minister of Defence himself, and several ministries were restructured. In July 1987 a plot against the Seychelles Government was discovered by police in the United Kingdom, along with details of a plan to abduct leading members of the African National Congress of South Africa, who were based in London, United Kingdom. Criminal proceedings against four men accused of conspiracy were later withdrawn, on the grounds of insufficient evidence.

Until the early 1990s exiled opposition to René remained split among a number of small groups based principally in London. In July 1991 five of these parties formed a coalition, the United Democratic Movement (UDM), under the leadership of Dr Maxime Ferrari, a former political associate of René, while ex-President Mancham established a 'Crusade for Democracy'. René, meanwhile, came under increasing pressure from France and the United Kingdom, the islands' principal aid donors, to restore a democratic political system. Internally, open opposition to the SPPF was fostered by the newly formed Parti Seselwa, or Parti Seychellois (PS), led by an Anglican clergyman, Wavel Ramkalawan. In August 1991 Ferrari returned from exile to organize support for the UDM, and in November the Government invited all political dissidents to return to the islands. In the following month the Minister of Tourism and Transport, Jacques Hodoul, left the Government; he subsequently formed the Seychelles Movement for Democracy.

In December 1991 the SPPF agreed to surrender the party's monopoly of power. It was announced that, from January 1992, political groups numbering at least 100 members would be granted official registration, and that multi-party elections would take place in July for a constituent assembly, whose proposals for constitutional reform would be submitted to a national referendum, with a view to holding multi-party parliamentary elections before the end of 1992. In April Mancham returned from exile to lead the New Democratic Party (NDP). At the July elections for the 20-seat constitutional commission, the SPPF won 58.4% of the votes, while the NDP received 33.7%. The PS, which took 4.4% of the votes, was the only other political party to obtain representation on the commission.

The commission, which comprised 11 representatives from the SPPF, eight from the NDP (now renamed the Democratic Party—DP) and one from the PS, completed its work in October 1992. In the previous month, however, the DP withdrew its delegation, on the grounds that the SPPF had allegedly refused to permit a full debate of reform proposals. The DP also expressed objections that the commission's meetings had been closed to the public and news media. Following publication of the draft Constitution, the DP challenged the proposed voting arrangements for a new National Assembly, whose members were to be elected on a basis of one-half by direct vote and one-half by proportional representation. The latter formula was to reflect the percentage of votes obtained by the successful candidate in presidential election, and was intended to ensure a legislative majority for the President's party. Other sections of the proposed Constitution, relating to social issues, were strongly opposed by the Roman Catholic Church, to which more than 90% of the islanders belong.

The draft Constitution, which required the approval of at least 60% of voters, was endorsed by only 53.7% and opposed by 44.6% at a referendum held in November 1992. A second constitutional commission, whose meetings were opened to the public, began work in January 1993 on proposals for submission to a further referendum, and in May the second commission unanimously agreed on a new draft Constitution, in which a compromise plan was reached on the electoral formula for a new National Assembly. With the joint endorsement of René and Mancham, the draft document was submitted to a national referendum in June, at which voters approved the constitutional plan by 73.9% to 24.0%. Opponents of the new constitutional arrangements comprised the PS, the Seychelles National Movement (SNM) and the National Alliance Party (NAP). At the presidential and legislative elections that followed in July, René received 59.5% of the vote, against 36.7% for Mancham and 3.8% for Philippe Boullé, the candidate representing an electoral alliance of the PS, the Seychelles Christian Democrat Party (SCDP), the SNM and the NAP. In the legislative elections, the SPPF secured 21 of the 22 seats elected by direct vote, and the DP one seat. Of the 11 additional seats allocated on a proportional basis, the SPPF received a further seven seats, the DP three seats and the PS one seat. Immediately following the elections, René, whose decisive victory was widely attributed to his promise of increased expenditure on social programmes, extensively reshuffled the Council of Ministers.

Following the 1993 elections, however, the Government began to promote a gradual transition from socialism to free-market policies, aimed at maximizing the country's potential as an 'offshore' financial and business centre. State-owned port facilities were transferred to private ownership in 1994, when plans were also announced for the creation of a duty-free International Trade Zone to provide transhipment facilities. Measures were introduced to implement the privatization of government activities in tourism, agriculture and tuna-processing. The economic liberalization, accompanied by diminished levels of aid and the consequent pressure to reduce budgetary deficits, led the Government to announce, in February 1995, that some state-funded welfare services were to be reduced.

In early 1995 tensions developed within the opposition DP, whose only directly elected MP, Christopher Gill, sought to remove Mancham from the party leadership on the grounds that the former President was insufficiently vigorous in opposing the policies of the René Government. Gill was suspended from the DP in June, and subsequently formed a breakaway 'New Democratic Party' with the aim of restructuring the DP under a new leader. The official registration of active political organizations, affording them corporate status, led to the formal amalgamation of the PS, the SNM, the SCDP and the NAP as a single party, the United Opposition (UO), under the leadership of Ramkalawan.

In the furtherance of its efforts to promote Seychelles as an international 'offshore' financial centre, the Government introduced, in November 1995, an Economic Development Act (EDA), under whose provisions investors of a minimum US $10m. would receive immunity in Seychelles from extradition or seizure of assets. It was feared in international financial circles, however, that the operation of the EDA would make Seychelles a refuge for the proceeds of drugs-trafficking and other crimes. Protest was led by the United Kingdom, France and the USA, and in February 1996 the EDA was described by the Financial Action Task Force on Money Laundering (see p. 343), established in 1989 on the recommendation of the Group of Seven industrialized nations, as a 'serious threat to world financial systems.' The Government, while refusing to rescind the EDA, established an Economic Development Board under the chairmanship of René, to vet potential EDA investors. In April 1996 the Government introduced legislation aimed at preventing the use of the EDA for 'laundering' illicit funds. Following reports critical of Seychelles' financial sector from two international organizations, the EDA was finally repealed in July 2000.

In July 1996 the SPPF introduced a series of constitutional amendments, creating the post of Vice-President, to which James Michel, the Minister of Finance, Communications and Defence and a long-standing political associate of René, was appointed in the following month. The constitutional changes also provided for revisions in constituency boundaries, which were generally interpreted as favouring SPPF candidates in future parliamentary elections. Measures were also implemented whereby the number of seats in the National Assembly was to be increased (see Government).

Following the 1993 elections, effective opposition to the Government came increasingly to be led by Ramkalawan's UO, as the DP opted to pursue a policy of 'reconciliation' and 'non-confrontation' with the SPPF. In November 1997, ahead of the presidential and legislative elections due to take place by mid-1998, Mancham rejected proposals by Ramkalawan for the creation of an electoral alliance.

In January 1998 René announced that the elections would be held in March, and that he was to seek the second of a maximum of three consecutive five-year terms as president permitted under the 1993 Constitution. The outcome of the elections provided the SPPF with a decisive victory. René obtained 66.7% of the presidential ballot (compared with 59.5% in the previous election), while his party secured 30 of the 34 seats in the enlarged National Assembly. Ramkalawan, with 19.5% of the presidential vote (compared with 3.8% for the UO candidate in the 1993 election), substantially exceeded support for Mancham, who received 13.8% (as against 36.7% in 1993). In the National Assembly the UO increased its representation from one seat to three seats, with the DP losing three of the four seats previously held. Mancham, who lost his parliamentary seat, subsequently announced his temporary withdrawal from active politics. The UO, which consequently emerged as the principal parliamentary opponent of the SPPF, boycotted a number of debates during 1998 in protest at allegedly partisan coverage of legislative proceedings by the Seychelles Broadcasting Corporation, and accused the Speaker of the National Assembly of authoritarian conduct. In mid-1998 the UO changed its name to the Seychelles National Party (SNP). Further criticism of the Government's alleged intolerance of political opposition was voiced in July by the Anglican Bishop of Seychelles, who claimed that local administrations controlled by the SPPF neglected the needs of inhabitants who did not support the Government. In December 1999 a reallocation of cabinet portfolios was announced, although it brought no new ministers into the administration. Proposals to amend the 1993 Constitution were being finalized in April 2000 by René, under which the President would be empowered to declare a presidential election at any time following the completion of one year in office. This proposal was interpreted by some observers as an attempt by René to ensure the eventual succession to a candidate of his own choice.

The President faced international criticism in 2001 over freedom of the press, following his pursuit of defamation suits against the island's only independent newspaper, *Regar*, and the opposition SNP's newsletter, *Nuovo Vizyon*. Were René to be successful in these cases, both publications would be bankrupted by the individual SR 9m. compensation claims, and the free press would effectively be silenced. The defendants argued that the trials would not be fair, owing to the fact that the President appoints the judiciary and that he cannot legally be countersued. At the Government's request, the trials were postponed until 2002. In March 2002 the international press freedom group Reporters sans frontières protested about another libel suit against *Regar*, which had been brought by Vice-President Michel.

In July 2001 René declared a presidential election almost two years early, claiming that this was in order to reassure investors about the long-term stability of the country. The election was postponed from its scheduled date of 12 August until 31 August–2 September, in order to allow the opposition sufficient time to prepare. René was re-elected as President, but with the smallest mandate of his career, securing 54.19% of the valid votes cast. Wavel Ramkalawan, the SNP candidate, won 44.95% of the votes, but refused to accept the result, claiming serious irregularities in the electoral process, and subsequently filed a formal complaint with the Constitutional Court. Philippe Boullé, the first independent candidate in the country's history (who had contested the presidential election in July 1993 for an opposition alliance), secured only 0.86% of the votes. Legislative elections, which were due in 2003, took place early, on 4–6 December 2002. The SPPF retained its majority in the National Assembly, but with a reduced margin, securing 23 of the 34 seats, while the SNP won the remaining 11 seats. In March 2003 René indicated during the congress of the SPPF that he would progressively relinquish control of certain presidential duties to Vice-President Michel, who was also designated as the party's candidate for the next presidential election; there was some speculation that René might resign prior to the end of his term, owing to ill health, and this was the first official recognition of Michel as his preferred successor.

Seychelles has traditionally pursued a policy of non-alignment in international affairs, and supports movements for the creation of a 'zone of peace' in the Indian Ocean area. Until 1983 all naval warships wishing to dock at Seychelles had to provide a guarantee that they were not carrying nuclear weapons. The United Kingdom and US Governments refused to agree to this condition, and their respective naval fleets were therefore effectively banned from using Seychelles port facilities. This requirement was withdrawn in September 1983, although Seychelles continued, in theory, to refuse entry to ships carrying nuclear weapons. In 1986 Seychelles and the USA renegotiated an agreement, signed in 1976 and renewed in 1981, which allowed the USA to maintain a satellite-tracking station on Mahé. This installation, however, was closed, simultaneously with the US diplomatic mission, in 1996, as part of cost-reduction measures by the US Government in its defence expenditure; the USA finally agreed to dismantle the structure in July 2000. Since the late 1980s Seychelles has expanded the scope of its formal diplomatic contacts. Relations have been established with the Comoros and with Mauritius, and agreements have been made with the latter for co-operation in health and economic development matters. In 1989 diplomatic relations were established with Morocco, Madagascar and Côte d'Ivoire, and in 1990 with Kenya. During 1992 formal relations were established with Israel and South Africa, and in 1998 Seychelles proposed to establish a diplomatic mission in Malaysia to expand its relations in Asia and Oceania. Libya opened a diplomatic mission in Seychelles in January 2000, and diplomatic ties were established with Sudan in October. Following years of minimal interaction between France and Seychelles, owing to Seychelles' accumulated debt to the Agence Française de Développement, the French Minister for Co-operation was the first minister in over four years to visit Seychelles in February 2001. It was hoped that a resolution to the situation could be found and a new schedule for repayments negotiated. In 2001 relations were restored with Japan, which granted a subsidy for fishery development to Seychelles; this was said to be a consequence of the reversal of Seychelles' whaling policy.

Government

Under the 1993 Constitution, executive power is vested in the President, who is Head of State and Commander-in-Chief of the Armed Forces. The President, who is elected by direct popular vote, appoints and leads the Council of Ministers, which acts in an advisory capacity to him. The President also appoints the holders of certain public offices and the judiciary. The President may hold office for a maximum period of three five-year terms. The legislature is the unicameral National Assembly, presently comprising 34 members, of whom 25 are directly elected for five years and nine allocated on a proportional basis. Constitutional changes, introduced in July 1996, provide for an enlargement to 35 members: 25 directly elected and a maximum of 10 allocated on a proportional basis.

Defence

At August 2002 the army numbered 450 men, including a coastguard of 200. Paramilitary forces comprised a 250-strong national guard. Government expenditure on defence was SR 66m. in 2002.

Economic Affairs

In 2000, according to estimates by the World Bank, Seychelles' gross national income (GNI), measured at average 1998–2000 prices, was US $573m., equivalent to $7,050 per head. During 1990–2000, it was estimated, the population increased at an average annual rate of 1.5%, while gross domestic product (GDP) per head increased, in real terms, by an average of 1.1% per year. Overall GDP increased, in real terms, at an average annual rate of 2.6% in 1990–2000. Real GDP declined by 3.0% in 1999, but increased by 1.2% in 2000.

Agriculture (including hunting, forestry and fishing) contributed 3.0% of GDP in 2000, and accounted for 7.5% of total employment in 1999. Much of Seychelles' production of coconuts has traditionally been exported in the form of copra, but there were no exports of copra in 1996–1999. Other cash crops include cinnamon bark, tea, patchouli, vanilla and limes. Tea, sweet potatoes, cassava, yams, sugar cane, bananas, eggs and poultry meat are produced for local consumption. However, imports of food and live animals constituted 24.0% of the value of total imports in 1999. Fishing became increasingly important in the 1980s, and exports of fish (mainly canned tuna) contributed 96.2% of the value of total domestic exports in 1999, despite the adverse effects of the El Niño weather phenomenon on fish migration. Licence fees from foreign fishing vessels, allowed to operate in Seychelles' waters, contribute significantly to foreign exchange. A three-year fishing protocol, worth €3.48m., was signed with the European Union in 2001. Agricultural GDP declined at an average annual rate of 1.6% during 1990–2000, according to the World Bank. Agricultural GDP increased by 4.5% in 2000.

Industry (including mining, manufacturing, construction and power) contributed 21.6% of GDP in 2000, and manufacturing and construction accounted for 23.6% of total employment in 1999. Industrial GDP increased at an average annual rate of 8.5% during 1990–2000, according to the World Bank; growth in 2000 was 2.5%.

The mining sector is small; the sole mineral export is guano (of which 6,000 metric tons was exported in 1990, although consistent output was discontinued in the mid-1980s). Mineral production consists mainly of quantities of construction materials, such as clay, coral, stone and sand. There are deposits of natural gas, and during the 1980s concessions were sold to several foreign companies, allowing exploration for petroleum. Exploratory drilling has so far proved unsuccessful. A survey of offshore areas, initiated in 1980, revealed the presence of nodules, containing deposits of various metals, on the sea-bed. The possibility of renewed commercial exploitation of Seychelles'

granite reserves is under investigation and the future development of offshore petroleum reserves is a possibility.

Manufacturing contributed 12.5% of GDP in 2000. Apart from a tuna-canning plant (opened in 1987), the manufacturing sector consists mainly of small-scale activities, including boat-building, printing and furniture-making. According to the World Bank, manufacturing GDP increased at an average annual rate of 7.1% during 1990–2000. Manufacturing GDP increased by 3.1% in 2000.

Energy is derived principally from oil-fired power stations. In 1999 mineral fuels accounted for 10.0% of the value of total imports. However, the vast majority of fuel imports are re-exported, mainly as bunker sales to visiting ships and aircraft—exports of refined petroleum products contributed 30.0% of total export earnings in that year. In 2000 Seychelles generated SR 357m. from petroleum re-exports, and it was anticipated that by the end of 2003 the proceeds from re-exports would fully fund fuel imports.

Services accounted for 69.0% of total employment in 1999, and provided 75.4% of GDP in 2000. In 1997 tourism generated 33.6% of total earnings from exports of goods and services. Tourist arrivals totalled some 132,246 in 2002; income from that source amounted to US $110m in 2000. The majority of visitors were from western Europe, notably from France, Germany, Italy and the United Kingdom. The GDP of the services sector increased at an average annual rate of 1.1% during 1990–2000, according to the World Bank. Services GDP declined by 5.0% in 1999, but increased by 0.5% in 2000.

In 2001 Seychelles recorded a visible trade deficit of US $171.7m. In the same year there was a deficit of $100.1m. on the current account of the balance of payments. The principal source of imports (13.3%) in 1999 was Italy; other important suppliers were the Southern African Customs Union (comprising Botswana, Lesotho, Namibia, South Africa and Swaziland), Finland, France and Saudi Arabia. The principal market for exports in 1998 was the United Kingdom (23.1%); other significant purchasers were Yemen, Germany, France and Italy. The principal export in 1999 was canned tuna, following the expansion of the Indian Ocean Tuna Company in 1995 and increasing production thereafter. The main imports in 1999 were machinery and transport equipment, food and live animals, and basic manufactures.

In 1999 Seychelles recorded a budgetary deficit of SR 347.9m. (equivalent to 11.0% of GDP). Seychelles' total external debt was US $163.2m. at the end of 2000, of which $124.4m. was long-term public debt. In that year the cost of debt-servicing was equivalent to 3.4% of the value of exports of goods and services. The annual rate of inflation averaged 2.6% in 1990–2001; consumer prices increased by an average of 6.1% in 2001 and 0.2% in 2002. Some 8.3% of the labour force were registered as unemployed in 1993.

Seychelles is a member of the African Development Bank (see p. 128), of the Common Market for Eastern and Southern Africa (see p. 162), of the Southern African Development Community (see p. 311) and of the Indian Ocean Commission (see p. 340), which aims to promote co-operation in the region. It was announced in December 1996 that Seychelles was to provide the headquarters of the Indian Ocean Tuna Commission.

Since the early 1970s tourism has been the mainstay of the Seychelles economy. Development of agriculture is impeded by the lack of cultivable land. Income from fisheries expanded greatly after the commissioning of a tuna-canning plant in 1987 and the establishment of a prawn farm in the early 1990s. Manufacturing growth is inhibited, however, by the lack of natural resources, although since 1988 the Government has offered incentives for new manufacturing enterprises. Measures were introduced in 1995 to develop Seychelles as an 'offshore' financial services centre (see Recent History), and to establish the islands as a centre for transhipment and air freight in the Indian Ocean area. An export-processing zone has been established, and most state-owned enterprises, with the exception of public utilities and transport, have been transferred to private-sector ownership. In an effort to increase inflows of foreign exchange, with effect from May 1999 visitors to Seychelles were to be required to pay hotel accounts in foreign currency. However, the continuing dependence of the economy on tourism leaves the country highly vulnerable to outside economic influences, while the cost of servicing the external debt remains a major impediment to balanced growth. A deceleration in overall output in 1998–99 was attributed to a decline in tourist arrivals, an increased shortage of foreign exchange and the effects of adverse global weather phenomena. In the IMF's assessment, at February 2001, the country was in danger of losing its status as offering one of the highest standards of living in Africa, as real GDP had remained unchanged for two years, inflation was rising (above 10% for the first time in over a decade) and the balance of payments demonstrated serious problems. The organization strongly recommended less government intervention in the economy, including over price-controls, foreign-exchange allocation, import licensing and monopolies in manufacturing and distribution. However, in mid-2001 the Government imposed further measures to control the urgent foreign-exchange situation, caused by the country's dependence on imports, requiring tourists also to pay for services and merchandise in foreign currency and prohibiting Seychellois from holding unauthorized currency. According to the Government, this resulted in an increase of up to 40% in the amount of foreign currency within the banking system. In 2001 the Government refused to follow the advice of the IMF and the World Bank to devalue the artificially high Seychelles rupee and remained in arrears in the repayment of its external debts.

Education

In 1979 free and compulsory primary education was introduced for children between six and 16 years of age. A programme of educational reform, based on the British comprehensive schools system, was introduced in 1980. The language of instruction in primary schools is English. The duration of primary education is six years, while that of general secondary education is five years (of which the first four years are compulsory), beginning at 12 years of age. Pre-primary and special education facilities are also available. Seychelles Polytechnic had 1,847 students in 1999. A number of students study abroad, principally in the United Kingdom. Government expenditure on education in 1998 was SR 164.9m., or about 8.6% of total expenditure.

Public Holidays

2003: 1–2 January (New Year), 18–19 April (Easter), 1 May (Labour Day), 5 June (Liberation Day, anniversary of 1977 coup), 18 June (National Day), 19 June (Corpus Christi), 29 June (Independence Day), 15 August (Assumption), 1 November (All Saints' Day), 8 December (Immaculate Conception), 25 December (Christmas Day).

2004: 1–2 January (New Year), 9–10 April (Easter), 1 May (Labour Day), 5 June (Liberation Day, anniversary of 1977 coup), 10 June (Corpus Christi), 18 June (National Day), 29 June (Independence Day), 15 August (Assumption), 1 November (All Saints' Day), 8 December (Immaculate Conception), 25 December (Christmas Day).

Weights and Measures

The imperial system is being replaced by the metric system.

Statistical Survey

Source (unless otherwise stated): Statistics and Database Administration Section, Management and Information Systems Division, POB 206, Victoria; e-mail misdstat@seychelles.net; internet www.seychelles.net/misdstat.

AREA AND POPULATION

Area: 455.3 sq km (175.8 sq miles), incl. Aldabra lagoon (145 sq km).

Population: 74,331 at census of 26 August 1994; 75,876 (males 37,589, females 38,287) at census of 29 August 1997; 80,410 (official estimate) at mid-1999.

Density (mid-1999): 176.6 per sq km.

Principal Town: Victoria (capital), estimated population 60,000 (incl. suburbs) in 1994.

Births and Deaths (registered in 1999): Live births 1,460 (birth rate 18.2 per 1,000); Deaths 560 (death rate 7.0 per 1,000).

Expectation of Life (WHO estimates, years at birth): 71.1 (males 66.7; females 76.5) in 2001. Source: WHO, *World Health Report*.

Economically Active Population: 1987 census (persons aged 12 years and over): Employed 24,293; Unemployed 4,442; Total labour force 28,735 (Source: UN, *Demographic Yearbook*). June 1989 (persons aged 15 years and over): Total labour force 29,494 (males 16,964, females 12,530).

Employment (1999): Agriculture, hunting, forestry and fishing 2,301; Manufacturing and construction 7,251; Restaurants and hotels 3,829; Transport, distribution and communications 5,968; Other services 11,437; Total 30,786. Figures exclude self-employed persons, unpaid family workers and employees in private domestic services.

HEALTH AND WELFARE

Key Indicators

Total Fertility Rate (children per woman, 2001): 1.8.

Under-5 Mortality Rate (per 1,000 live births, 2001): 17.

Physicians (per 1,000 head, 1998): 1.32.

Hospital Beds (per 1,000 head, 1995): 6.28.

Health Expenditure (2000): US $ per head (PPP): 758.

Health Expenditure (2000): % of GDP: 6.2.

Health Expenditure (2000): public (% of total): 66.9.

Human Development Index (2000): ranking: 47.

Human Development Index (2000): value: 0.811.

For sources and definitions, see explanatory note on p. vi.

AGRICULTURE, ETC.

Principal Crops (FAO estimates, metric tons, 2001): Coconuts 3,200; Vegetables 1,940; Bananas 1,970; Other fruit 505; Tea (green leaf) 231; Cinnamon 400. Source: FAO.

Livestock (FAO estimates, '000 head, 2001): Cattle 2; Pigs 18; Goats 5. Source: FAO.

Livestock Products ('000 metric tons, 2001): Pig meat 1; Poultry meat 1; Hen eggs 2*.
*FAO estimate. Source: FAO.

Fishing ('000 metric tons, live weight, 2000): Capture 40.2 (Snappers and jobfishes 0.6, Carangids 1.8, Skipjack tuna 11.5, Yellowfin tuna 11.6, Bigeye tuna 11.9); Aquaculture 0.4 (Giant tiger prawn 0.4); Total catch 40.6. Source: FAO, *Yearbook of Fishery Statistics*.

MINING AND INDUSTRY

Industrial Production (provisional figures, 1999): Canned tuna 33,234 metric tons; Beer 6,768,000 litres; Soft drinks 10,561,000 litres; Cigarettes 60 million; Electric energy 170 million kWh. Source: IMF, *Seychelles: Recent Economic Developments* (December 2000).

FINANCE

Currency and Exchange Rates: 100 cents = 1 Seychelles rupee (SR). *Sterling, Dollar and Euro Equivalents* (31 December 2002): £1 sterling = 8.148 rupees; US $1 = 5.055 rupees; €1 = 5.301 rupees; 1,000 Seychelles rupees = £122.73 = $197.82 = €188.64. *Average Exchange Rate* (Seychelles rupees per US $): 5.7138 in 2000; 5.8575 in 2001; 5.4800 in 2002. Note: In November 1979 the value of the Seychelles rupee was linked to the IMF's special drawing right (SDR). In March 1981 the mid-point exchange rate was set at SDR 1 = 7.2345 rupees. This remained in effect until February 1997, when the fixed link with the SDR was ended.

Budget (SR million, 1998): *Revenue:* Taxation 966.2 (Taxes on income, etc. 164.9, Social security contributions 119.9, Domestic taxes on goods and services 92.2, Import duties 575.0); Other current revenue 413.4 (Entrepreneurial and property income 202.1, Administrative fees and charges, non-industrial and incidental sales 162.4); Capital revenue 41.2; Total 1,420.8, excl. grants received (24.8). *Expenditure:* General public services 272.0; Defence 55.5; Public order and safety 68.1; Education 164.9; Health 141.3; Social security and welfare 267.2; Housing and community amenities 6.2; Recreational, cultural and religious affairs and services 18.3; Economic affairs and services 116.7 (Agriculture, forestry, fishing and hunting 29.7, Transport and communications 34.6); Other purposes 814.4 (Interest payments 288.9); Total 1,924.6 (Current 1,509.9, Capital 414.7), excl. lending minus repayments (−517.6). Note: Figures represent the consolidated accounts of the central Government, covering the operations of the Recurrent and Capital Budgets and of the Social Security Fund. Source: IMF, *Government Finance Statistics Yearbook*.

International Reserves (US $ million at 31 December 2002): IMF special drawing rights 0.01; Foreign exchange 69.78; Total 69.79. Source: IMF, *International Financial Statistics*.

Money Supply (SR million at 31 December 2002): Currency outside banks 301.0; Demand deposits at commercial banks 1,275.9; Total money (incl. others) 1,577.8. Source: IMF, *International Financial Statistics*.

Cost of Living (Consumer Price Index; base: 1990 = 100): All items 117.6 in 1999; 124.9 in 2000; 132.5 in 2001. Source: UN, *Monthly Bulletin of Statistics*.

Expenditure on the Gross Domestic Product (SR million at current prices, 1998): Government final consumption expenditure 847.0; Private final consumption expenditure 1,603.9; Increase in stocks 56.0; Gross fixed capital formation 1,100.0; *Total domestic expenditure* 3,607.0; Exports of goods and services 2,045.5; *Less* Imports of goods and services 2,525.8; *GDP in purchasers' values* 3,126.7. Source: IMF, *International Financial Statistics*.

Gross Domestic Product by Economic Activity (preliminary figures, SR million at current prices, 1999): Agriculture, hunting, forestry and fishing 99.8; Manufacturing 489.0; Electricity and water 96.6; Building and construction 345.6; Restaurants and hotels 257.8; Transport, distribution and communications 994.7; Finance, insurance, real estate and business services 315.7; Government services 434.0; Other services 72.9; *Sub-total* 3,106.1; Import duties 330.7; *Less* Imputed bank service charge 141.7; Statistical discrepancy−20.1; *GDP in purchasers' values* 3,275.0. Source: IMF, *Seychelles: Recent Economic Developments* (December 2000).

Balance of Payments (US $ million, 2001): Exports of goods f.o.b. 215.26; Imports of goods f.o.b. −386.94; *Trade balance* −171.68; Exports of services 283.19; Imports of services −192.88; *Balance on goods and services* −81.36; Other income received 8.93; Other income paid −27.98; *Balance on goods, services and income* −100.41; Current transfers received 10.52; Current transfers paid −10.16; *Current balance* −100.06; Capital account (net) 9.39; Direct investment abroad −11.10; Direct investment from abroad 59.43; Portfolio investment assets −0.07; Portfolio investment liabilities 1.09; Other investment assets −8.76; Other investment liabilities 84.56; Net errors and omissions −12.62; *Overall balance* 21.86. Source: IMF, *International Financial Statistics*.

EXTERNAL TRADE

Principal Commodities (distribution by SITC): *Imports c.i.f.* (SR million, 1999): Food and live animals 477.5; Beverages and tobacco 22.9; Minerals, fuels, lubricants etc. 198.4; Chemicals and related products 102.1; Basic manufactures 427.2; Machinery and transport equipment 553.2; Miscellaneous manufactured articles 156.0; Total (incl. others) 1,989.6. Source: IMF, *Seychelles: Recent Economic Developments* (December 2000). *Exports f.o.b.* (US $ million, 1998): Food and live animals 90.1 (Fish, crustaceans and molluscs, fresh, chilled or frozen 9.0; Fish, prepared or preserved 78.5); Mineral fuels, lubricants, etc. 26.6 (Refined petroleum products 26.6); Machinery and transport equipment 2.7; Total (incl. others) 121.4 (Source: UN, *International Trade Statistics Yearbook*). *1999 (Exports f.o.b., SR million):* Canned tuna 531.9; Fresh and frozen fish 15.0; Frozen prawns 7.2; Cinnamon bark 2.2; Other 12.4; Total 568.8. Figures exclude re-exports (SR 15.7 million) and bunkers and stores for ships and aircraft (SR 178.3 million) (Source: IMF, *Seychelles: Recent Economic Developments* (December 2000)).

Principal Trading Partners (US $ million): *Imports c.i.f.* (1999): Finland 43.7; France 42.4; Italy 57.1; Saudi Arabia 39.4; Singapore 32.9; Southern African Customs Union* 45.8; Spain 27.0; United Kingdom 34.1; Total (incl. others) 428.5. *Exports f.o.b.* (1998): France 16.0; Germany 23.6; Italy 15.7; Japan 4.4; United Kingdom 28.0; Yemen 25.7; Total (incl. others) 121.4.

* Comprising Botswana, Lesotho, Namibia, South Africa, Swaziland. (Source: UN, *International Trade Statistics Yearbook*).

TRANSPORT

Road Traffic (estimates, motor vehicles in use, 1996): Passenger cars 7,120; Lorries and vans 1,980. Source: International Road Federation, *World Road Statistics*.

Shipping: *Merchant Fleet* (registered at 31 December 2001): Vessels 25; Total displacement 33,971 grt (Source: Lloyd's Register-Fairplay, *World Fleet Statistics*); *Sea-borne Freight Traffic* (2000): Freight ('000 metric tons): Loaded 74; Unloaded 493.

Civil Aviation (traffic on scheduled services, 1998): Kilometres flown 9 million; Passengers carried 369,000; Passenger-km 755 million; Total ton-km 84 million. Source: UN, *Statistical Yearbook*.

TOURISM

Foreign Tourist Arrivals: 128,258 in 1998; 124,865 in 1999; 130,046 in 2000.

Arrivals by Country of Residence (2000): France 28,282; Germany 17,720; Italy 19,951; Mauritius 3,068; Réunion 2,842; South Africa 4,260; Switzerland 5,001; United Kingdom 16,117; USA 4,746; Total (incl. others) 130,046.

Tourism Receipts (US $ million): 111 in 1998; 112 in 1999; 110 in 2000.
Source: World Tourism Organization, mainly *Yearbook of Tourism Statistics*.

COMMUNICATIONS MEDIA

Radio Receivers (1997): 42,000 in use. Source: UNESCO, *Statistical Yearbook*.

Television Receivers (2000): 16,500 in use. Source: International Telecommunication Union.

Telephones (2001): 21,400 main lines in use. Source: International Telecommunication Union.

Facsimile Machines (1999): 581 in use.

Mobile Cellular Telephones (2001): 44,100 subscribers. Source: International Telecommunication Union.

Personal Computers (2001): 12,000 in use. Source: International Telecommunication Union.

Internet Users (2001): 9,000. Source: International Telecommunication Union.

Book Production (1980): 33 titles (2 books, 31 pamphlets).

Daily Newspapers (1996): 1 (average circulation 3,000 copies). Source: UNESCO, *Statistical Yearbook*.

Non-daily Newspapers (1996): 3 (average circulation 7,000 copies). Source: UNESCO, *Statistical Yearbook*.

EDUCATION

Pre-primary (2000): 35 schools*; 206 teachers; 3,065 pupils.

Primary (2000): 26 schools*; 708 teachers; 10,026 pupils.

Secondary (2000): 535 teachers; 7,742 pupils.

Post-secondary (2000): 219 teachers; 1,818 pupils.
* 1996 figure.

Adult Literacy Rate: 88.0% (males 87.2%; females 88.7%) in 1994 (Source: UNESCO, *Statistical Yearbook*).

Directory

The Constitution

The independence Constitution of 1976 was suspended after the coup in June 1977 but reintroduced in July with substantial modifications. A successor Constitution, which entered into force in March 1979, was superseded by a new Constitution, approved by national referendum on 18 June 1993.

The President is elected by popular vote simultaneously with elections for the National Assembly. The President fulfils the functions of Head of State and Commander-in-Chief of the armed forces

and may hold office for a maximum period of three consecutive five-year terms. The Assembly, elected for a term of five years, consists of 34 seats, of which 25 are filled by direct election and nine are allocated on a proportional basis. Constitutional amendments, introduced in July 1996, provided for an Assembly of 25 directly elected seats and a maximum of 10 proportionally allocated seats. There is provision for an appointed Vice-President. The Council of Ministers is appointed by the President and acts in an advisory capacity to him. The President also appoints the holders of certain public offices and the judiciary.

The Government

HEAD OF STATE

President: FRANCE ALBERT RENÉ (assumed power 5 June 1977; elected President 26 June 1979, re-elected 18 June 1984, 12 June 1989, 23 July 1993, 22 March 1998 and 31 August–2 September 2001).

Vice-President: JAMES MICHEL.

COUNCIL OF MINISTERS
(April 2003)

President and Minister of Internal Affairs, Defence and Legal Affairs: FRANCE ALBERT RENÉ.

Vice-President and Minister of Finance, Economic Planning, Information Technology and Communications: JAMES MICHEL.

Minister of Foreign Affairs: JÉRÉMIE BONNELAME.

Minister of Industry and International Trade: JACQUELIN DUGASSE.

Minister of Local Government, Sport and Culture: SYLVETTE POOL.

Minister of Health: PATRICK PILLAY.

Minister of Land Use and Habitat: JOSEPH BELMONT.

Minister of Tourism and Transport: SIMONE DE COMARMOND.

Minister of Social Affairs and Employment: DOLOR ERNESTA.

Minister of the Environment: RONNY JUMEAU.

Minister of Education and Youth: DANNY FAURE.

Minister of Agriculture and Marine Resources: WILLIAM HERMINIE.

Minister of Administration and Manpower Development: NOELLIE ALEXANDER.

MINISTRIES

Office of the President: State House, Victoria; tel. 224391; fax 224200.

Ministry of Administration and Manpower Development: National House, POB 56, Victoria; tel. 383000; fax 224936; e-mail psadmin@seychelles.net.

Ministry of Agriculture and Marine Resources: Independence House, POB 166, Victoria; tel. 224030; fax 225245; internet www.agricta.org/partners/mamr.

Ministry of Education and Youth: POB 48, Mont Fleuri; tel. 224777; fax 224859; e-mail edups@seychelles.net.

Ministry of the Environment: Victoria.

Ministry of Finance, Economic Planning, Information Technology and Communications: Central Bank Bldg, POB 313, Victoria; tel. 225252; fax 225265.

Ministry of Foreign Affairs: POB 656, Mont Fleuri; tel. 224688; fax 224845; e-mail mfapesey@seychelles.net.

Ministry of Health: POB 52, Victoria; tel. 388000; fax 224792; e-mail mohprs@seychelles.net.

Ministry of Industry and International Trade: International Conference Centre, POB 648, Victoria; tel. 225060; fax 225086; e-mail minind@seychelles.net.

Ministry of Land Use and Habitat: Independence House, Victoria; tel. 284444; fax 235197; e-mail mluh@seychelles.net.

Ministry of Local Government, Sport and Culture: Oceangate House, Victoria; tel. 225477; fax 225262.

Ministry of Social Affairs and Employment: Unity House, POB 190, Victoria; tel. 281500; fax 321880; e-mail psmsamd@seychelles.net.

Ministry of Tourism and Transport: Independence House, Independence Ave, POB 92, Victoria; tel. 225313; fax 224035; e-mail mtca@seychelles.net.

President and Legislature

PRESIDENT

Election, 31 August–2 September 2001

Candidate	Votes	% of votes
France Albert René (SPPF)	27,223	54.19
Wavel Ramkalawan (SNP)	22,581	44.95
Philippe Boullé (Independent)	434	0.86
Total	50,238	100.00

NATIONAL ASSEMBLY

Speaker: FRANCIS MACGREGOR.

Election, 4–6 December 2002

Party	Votes	% of votes	Seats*
Seychelles People's Progressive Front	28,075	54.3	23
Seychelles National Party	22,030	42.6	11
Democratic Party	1,605	3.1	0
Total	51,710	100.0	34

*Of the Assembly's 34 seats, 25 were filled by direct election and nine by allocation on a proportional basis.

Political Organizations

Democratic Party (DP): POB 169, Mont Fleuri; tel. 224916; fax 224302; internet www.framework.co.za/dua/seychelles/dp.html; f. 1992; successor to the Seychelles Democratic Party (governing party 1970–77); Leader JAMES MANCHAM; Sec.-Gen. DANIEL BELLE.

Mouvement Seychellois pour la Démocratie: Mont Fleuri; tel. 224322; fax 224460; f. 1992; Leader JACQUES HODOUL.

Seychelles National Party (SNP): Arpent Vert, Mont Fleuri, POB 81, Victoria; tel. 224124; fax 225151; e-mail snp2003@hotmail.com; internet www.seychelles.net/snp; f. 1995 as the United Opposition, comprising the fmr mem. parties of a coalition formed to contest the 1993 elections; adopted present name in 1998; Leader Rev. WAVEL RAMKALAWAN; Sec. ROGER MANCIENNE.

Seychelles People's Progressive Front (SPPF): POB 91, Victoria; tel. 224455; fax 225351; fmrly the Seychelles People's United Party (f. 1964), which assumed power in 1977; renamed in 1978; sole legal party 1978–91; Pres. FRANCE ALBERT RENÉ; Sec.-Gen. JAMES MICHEL.

Diplomatic Representation

EMBASSIES AND HIGH COMMISSIONS IN SEYCHELLES

China, People's Republic: POB 680, St Louis; tel. 266808; fax 266866; e-mail china@seychelles.net; Ambassador CHEN MEIFEN.

France: Immeuble Arpent Vert, Mont Fleuri, POB 478, Victoria; tel. 224523; fax 225248; Ambassador MARCEL SURBIGUET.

India: Le Chantier, POB 488, Victoria; tel. 224489; fax 224810; e-mail hicomind@seychelles.net; internet www.seychelles.net/hicomind; High Commissioner R. O. WALLANG.

Libya: Victoria.

Russia: Le Niol, POB 632, Victoria; tel. 266590; fax 266653; Ambassador GENNADII I. FEDOSOV.

South Africa: British-American Insurance Bldg, 4th Floor, Pope Hennessy St, POB 908, Victoria; tel. 226925; fax 226936.

United Kingdom: 3rd floor, Oliaji Trade Centre, POB 161, Victoria; tel. 225225; fax 225127; e-mail bhcsey@seychelles.net; High Commissioner JOHN PRICE.

Judicial System

The legal system is derived from English Common Law and the French Code Napoléon. There are three Courts, the Court of Appeal, the Supreme Court and the Magistrates' Courts. The Court of Appeal hears appeals from the Supreme Court in both civil and criminal cases. The Supreme Court is also a Court of Appeal from the Magistrates' Courts as well as having jurisdiction at first instance. The Constitutional Court, a division of the Supreme Court, determines matters of a constitutional nature, and considers cases bearing on civil liberties. There is also an industrial court and a rent tribunal.

Chief Justice: VIVEKANAND ALLEEAR.

President of the Court of Appeal: EMMANUEL AYOOLA.

Justices of Appeal: ANNEL SILUNGWE, A. PILLAY, G. P. S. DE SILVA, K. P. MATADEEN.

Puisne Judges: RANJAN PERERA, D. KARUNAKARAN, N. JUDDOO.

Attorney-General: ANTHONY F. FERNANDO.

Religion

Almost all of the inhabitants are Christians, of whom more than 90% are Roman Catholics and about 8% Anglicans.

CHRISTIANITY

The Anglican Communion

The Church of the Province of the Indian Ocean comprises six dioceses: four in Madagascar, one in Mauritius and one in Seychelles. The Archbishop of the Province is the Bishop of Antananarivo, Madagascar.

Bishop of Seychelles: Rt Rev. FRENCH CHANG-HIM, POB 44, Victoria; tel. 224242; fax 224296; e-mail angdio@seychelles.net.

The Roman Catholic Church

Seychelles comprises a single diocese, directly responsible to the Holy See. At 31 December 2000 there were an estimated 69,020 adherents in the country, representing 85% of the total population.

Bishop of Port Victoria: Rt Rev. XAVIER BARONNET, Bishop's House-Evêché, Olivier Maradan St, POB 43, Victoria; tel. 322152; fax 324045; e-mail rcchurch@seychelles.net.

The Press

L'Echo des Iles: POB 138, Victoria; tel. 322620; monthly; French, Creole and English; Roman Catholic; Editor P. SYMPHORIEN; circ. 2,800.

The People: Maison du Peuple, Revolution Ave, Victoria; tel. 224455; owned by the SPPF; monthly; Creole, French and English; circ. 1,000.

Popsport: Premier Bldgs, POB 485, Victoria; tel. 323158.

Regar: Arpent Vert, Victoria; tel. 224507; fax 224987; opposition political weekly.

Seychelles Nation: Information Technology and Communication Division, POB 800, Victoria; tel. 225775; fax 321006; e-mail seynat@seychelles.net; internet www.seychelles-online.com.sc; govt-owned; Mon.–Sat. English, French and Creole; Dir DENIS ROSE; circ. 3,500.

Seychelles Review: POB 29, Victoria; tel. 323700; monthly.

Seychellois: POB 32, Victoria; f. 1928; publ. by Seychelles Farmers Asscn; quarterly; circ. 1,800.

NEWS AGENCY

Seychelles Agence de Presse (SAP): Victoria Rd, POB 321, Victoria; tel. 224161; fax 226006.

Broadcasting and Communications

TELECOMMUNICATIONS

Cable and Wireless (Seychelles) Ltd: Mercury House, Francis Rachel St, POB 4, Victoria; tel. 284000; fax 322777; e-mail cws@seychelles.net; internet www.cws.seychelles.net; f. 1990; CEOs GEOFF HOUSTON, CYRIL BONNELAME.

Seychelles Telecom: Victoria; 80% owned by private investors, 10% by Govt of Seychelles; provides fixed-line and satellite telephone and internet services.

BROADCASTING

Radio

Seychelles Broadcasting Corpn (SBC): Hermitage, POB 321, Victoria; tel. 224161; fax 225641; e-mail sbcradtv@seychelles.sc; f. 1983; reorg. as independent corpn in 1992; programmes in Creole, English and French; Man. Dir IBRAHIM AFIF.

FEBA Radio: POB 234, Mahé; tel. 282000; fax 242146; e-mail reception@feba.org.sc; Christian programmes; Dir HUGH BARTON.

SBC Radio: Union Vale, POB 321, Victoria; tel. 224161; fax 324015; e-mail sbcradtv@seychelles.sc; f. 1941; programmes in Creole, English and French; Programme Man. MARGUERITE HERMITTE.

Television

Seychelles Broadcasting Corpn (SBC): see Radio.

SBC TV: Hermitage, POB 321, Mahé; tel. 224161; fax 225641; e-mail sbcradtv@seychelles.sc; f. 1983; programmes in Creole, English and French; Head of Production PATRICK MATHIOT.

Finance

(cap. = capital; res = reserves; dep. = deposits; m. = million; brs = branches; amounts in Seychelles rupees)

BANKING

Central Bank

Central Bank of Seychelles (CBS): Independence Ave, POB 701, Victoria; tel. 225200; fax 224958; e-mail cbs@seychelles.net; internet www.cbs.sc; f. 1984; bank of issue; cap. 1.0m., res 38.9m., dep. 268.0m. (Dec. 2000); Gov. FRANCIS CHANG-LENG; Gen. Man. Dr PETER LAROSE.

National Banks

Development Bank of Seychelles: Independence Ave, POB 217, Victoria; tel. 224471; fax 224274; e-mail dbs.md@seychelles.net; f. 1978; 55.5% state-owned; cap. 39.2m., res 43.7m., dep. 11.5m. (Dec. 2000); Chair. ANTONIO LUCAS; Man. Dir R. TOUSSAINT.

Seychelles International Mercantile Banking Corporation Ltd (Nouvobanq): Victoria House, State House Ave, POB 241, Victoria; tel. 225011; fax 224670; e-mail simbc@seychelles.net; f. 1991; 78% state-owned, 22% by Standard Chartered Bank (UK); cap. 50.0m., res 50.0m., dep. 1,095.3m. (Dec. 2001); Chair. CONRAD BENOÎTON; Pres. AHMED SAEED; 1 br.

Seychelles Savings Bank Ltd: Kingsgate House, POB 531, Victoria; tel. 225251; fax 224713; e-mail savbank@seychelles.net; f. 1902; state-owned; term deposits, savings and current accounts; cap. and res 7.8m. (Dec. 1992), dep. 356.4m. (1999); Chair. JOSEPH NOURRICE; 4 brs.

Foreign Banks

Bank of Baroda (India): Trinity House, Albert St, POB 124, Victoria; tel. 323038; fax 324057; e-mail baroda@seychelles.net; f. 1978; Man. M. M. PRASAD.

Banque Française Commerciale Océan Indien (BFCOI) (France): POB 122, Albert St, Victoria; tel. 284555; fax 322676; e-mail bfcoi@seychelles.net; f. 1976; Man. Dir DENIS MOTET; 5 brs.

Barclays Bank PLC (United Kingdom): Independence Ave, POB 167, Victoria; tel. 224101; fax 224678; f. 1959; Seychelles Dir M. P. LANDON; 3 brs and 4 agencies.

Habib Bank Ltd (Pakistan): Frances Rachel St, POB 702, Victoria; tel. 224371; fax 225614; e-mail habibsez@seychelles.net; f. 1976; Vice-Pres. and Chief Man. SOHAIL ANWAR.

INSURANCE

H. Savy Insurance Co Ltd: Maison de la Rosière, 2nd Floor, POB 20; Victoria; tel. 322272; fax 321666; all classes; Man. Dir GUY SAVY.

State Assurance Corporation of Seychelles (SACOS): Pirate's Arms Bldg, POB 636, Victoria; tel. 225000; fax 224495; e-mail sacos@seychelles.net; f. 1980; state-owned; all classes of insurance; Exec. Chair. ANTONIO LUCAS.

Trade and Industry

GOVERNMENT AGENCIES

Seychelles Fishing Authority: POB 449, Fishing Port, Victoria; tel. 224597; fax 224508; e-mail management@sfa.sc; Man. Dir PHILIPPE MICHAUD.

Seychelles Marketing Board (SMB): Latanier Rd, POB 634, Victoria; tel. 285000; fax 224735; e-mail mail@smb.sc; internet www.smb.sc; f. 1984; manufacturing and marketing of products, retailing, trade; Chair. FRANCE ALBERT RENÉ; CEO MUKESH VALABHJI.

DEVELOPMENT ORGANIZATIONS

Seychelles Agricultural Development Co Ltd (SADECO): POB 172, Victoria; tel. 375888; f. 1980; Gen. Man. LESLIE PRÉA (acting).

Seychelles Industrial Development Corporation (SIDEC): POB 537, Victoria; tel. 323151; fax 324121; promotes industrial development and manages leased industrial sites; CEO MAXWELL JULIE.

Seychelles International Business Authority (SIBA): POB 991, Victoria; tel. 380800; fax 380888; e-mail siba@seychelles.net; internet www.siba.net; f. 1995 to supervise registration of companies, transhipment and 'offshore' financial services in an international free trade zone covering an area of 23 ha near Mahé International Airport; Man. Dir CONRAD BENOITON.

CHAMBER OF COMMERCE

Seychelles Chamber of Commerce and Industry: Ebrahim Bldg, 2nd Floor, POB 1399, Victoria; tel. 323812; fax 321422; e-mail scci@seychelles.net; Chair. BERNARD POOL; Sec.-Gen. NICOLE TIRANT-GHERARDI.

EMPLOYERS' ORGANIZATION

Federation of Employers' Associations of Seychelles: POB 214, Victoria; tel. 224710; Chair. BASIL SOUNDY.

UTILITIES

Electricity

Public Utilities Corporation (Electricity Division): Unity House, POB 34, Victoria; tel. 322444; fax 321020; Man. Dir PHILLIP MORIN.

Water

Public Utilities Corporation (Water and Sewerage Division): Unity House, POB 34, Victoria; tel. 322444; fax 325612; Man. Dir STEPHEN ROUSSEAU.

TRADE UNION

Seychelles Federation of Workers' Unions: Maison du Peuple, Latanier Rd, POB 154, Victoria; tel. 224455; fax 225351; f. 1978 to amalgamate all existing trade unions; affiliated to the Seychelles People's Progressive Front; 25,200 mems; Pres. OLIVIER CHARLES; Gen. Sec. BERNARD ADONIS.

Transport

RAILWAYS

There are no railways in Seychelles.

ROADS

In 1999 there were 397 km of roads, of which 343 km were tarmac roads. Most surfaced roads are on Mahé and Praslin.

SHIPPING

Privately-owned ferry services connect Victoria, on Mahé, with the islands of Praslin and La Digue. At 31 December 2001 Seychelles' merchant fleet numbered 25 vessels, totalling 33,971 grt.

Port and Marine Services Division, Ministry of Tourism and Transport: POB 47, Mahé Quay, Victoria; tel. 224701; fax 224004; e-mail ports@seychelles.net; Dir-Gen. (Port of Victoria) SAM ANDRADE.

Allied Agencies Ltd: POB 345, Victoria; tel. 224441; fax 224226; shipping agents.

Aquarius Shipping Agency Ltd: POB 865, Victoria; tel. 225050; fax 225043; e-mail aqua@seychelles.net; Gen. Man. ANTHONY SAVY.

Hunt, Deltel and Co Ltd: Victoria House, POB 14, Victoria; tel. 380300; fax 225367; e-mail hundel@seychelles.net; Man. Dir E. HOUAREAU.

Mahé Shipping Co Ltd: Maritime House, POB 336, Victoria; tel. 380500; fax 380538; e-mail maheship@seychelles.net; shipping agents; Chair. Capt. G. C. C. ADAM.

Harry Savy & Co Ltd: POB 20, Victoria; tel. 322120; fax 321421; e-mail hsavyco@seychelles.net; shipping agents; Man. Dir GUY SAVY.

Seychelles Shipping Line Ltd: POB 977, Providence, Victoria; tel. 373655; fax 373185; e-mail gondwana@seychelles.net; f. 1994; operates freight services between Seychelles and Durban, South Africa; Chair. SELWYN GENDRON; Man. Dir HASSAN OMAR.

Union Trading Co Ltd: POB 475, Victoria; tel. 322708.

CIVIL AVIATION

The international airport is located at Pointe Larue, 10 km from Victoria. There are airstrips on several outlying islands.

Air Seychelles: Victoria House, POB 386, Victoria; tel. 381000; fax 224305; e-mail airseymd@seychelles.net; internet www.airseychelles.com; f. 1979; operates scheduled internal flights from Mahé to Praslin; also charter services to Bird, Desroches and Denis Islands and to outlying islands of the Amirantes group; international services to Europe, Far East, East and South Africa; Chief Exec. Capt. DAVID SAVY.

Tourism

Seychelles enjoys an equable climate, and is renowned for its fine beaches and attractive scenery. There are more than 500 varieties of flora and many rare species of birds. Most tourist activity is concentrated on the islands of Mahé, Praslin and La Digue, although the potential for ecological tourism of the outlying islands received increased attention in the late 1990s. It is government policy that the development of tourism should not blight the environment, and strict laws govern the location and construction of hotels. In 1998 the Government indicated that up to 200,000 visitors (although not more than 4,000 at any one time) could be accommodated annually without detriment to environmental quality. Receipts from tourism totalled an estimated US $110m. in 2000, when there were 130,046 tourist and business arrivals; most visitors (80.4% in 2000) are from Europe; in 1999 there were 4,780 hotel beds. By 2002 the number of tourist arrivals had increased to 132,246.

Compagnie Seychelloise de Promotion Hotelière Ltd: POB 683, Victoria; tel. 224694; fax 225291; e-mail cosproh@seychelles.net; promotes govt-owned hotels.

Seychelles Tourism Marketing Authority: POB 1262, Victoria; tel. 620000; fax 620620; e-mail seychelles@aspureasitgets.com; internet www.aspureasitgets.com; Chair. FRANCIS SAVY.

Seychelles Tourist Office: POB 92, Victoria; tel. 225313; fax 225131; internet www.webltd.com/webxs/seychelles/tourism/html.

SIERRA LEONE

Introductory Survey

Location, Climate, Language, Religion, Flag, Capital

The Republic of Sierra Leone lies on the west coast of Africa, with Guinea to the north and east, and Liberia to the south. The climate is hot and humid, with an average annual temperature of 27°C (80°F). The rainy season lasts from May to October. The average annual rainfall is about 3,436 mm (13.5 ins). English is the official language, while Krio (Creole), Mende, Limba and Temne are also widely spoken. The majority of the population follow animist beliefs, but there are significant numbers of Islamic and Christian adherents. The national flag (proportions 2 by 3) has three equal horizontal stripes, of green, white and blue. The capital is Freetown.

Recent History

Sierra Leone was formerly a British colony and protectorate. A new Constitution, which provided for universal adult suffrage, was introduced in 1951. In that year the Sierra Leone People's Party (SLPP) won the majority of votes in elections. The leader of the SLPP, Dr (later Sir) Milton Margai, became Chief Minister in 1953 and Prime Minister in 1958. On 27 April 1961 Sierra Leone achieved independence as a constitutional monarchy within the Commonwealth. The SLPP retained its majority at elections in May 1962. Margai died in April 1964 and was succeeded as Prime Minister by his half-brother, Dr (later Sir) Albert Margai, previously the Minister of Finance.

Following disputed elections in March 1967, the army assumed control and established a ruling body, the National Reformation Council. The Governor-General was subsequently forced to leave the country. In December a commission of inquiry announced that the All-People's Congress (APC) had won the elections in March. In April 1968 a further coup was staged by army officers, and power was subsequently transferred to a civilian Government; Dr Siaka Stevens, the leader of the APC, was elected as Prime Minister. In April 1971 a republican Constitution was introduced and Stevens became executive President.

The general election in May 1973 was not contested by the SLPP, and in 1976 Stevens, the sole candidate, was unanimously re-elected to the presidency for a second five-year term of office. In May 1977 the APC won the majority of votes in legislative elections, which were contested by the SLPP; however, outbreaks of violence and allegations of corruption and intimidation were reported. In July the House of Representatives ruled that the SLPP was no longer the official opposition party, on the grounds that it was incapable of undertaking government administration. A new Constitution, which provided for a one-party system, was promulgated in May 1978, approved in a national referendum and adopted by the House of Representatives in June. The APC thus became the sole legitimate political organization. Stevens was inaugurated as President for a seven-year term on 14 June 1978. He subsequently released political detainees and allocated ministerial posts to several former SLPP members (who had joined the APC).

The Government faced increasing opposition in 1981, following a scandal involving government officials and several cabinet ministers in the misappropriation of public funds. Legislative elections took place in May 1982, amid serious incidents of violence. Civil unrest, prompted by economic hardship, subsequently increased. In April 1985 Stevens announced that (contrary to earlier indications) he would not seek re-election to the presidency upon the expiry, in June, of his existing mandate. Stevens' term of office was subsequently extended for six months, to allow time for registration of voters and the nomination of a presidential candidate. At a conference of the APC in August, Maj.-Gen. Joseph Momoh, a cabinet minister and the Commander of the Army, was the sole candidate for the leadership of the party and for the presidential nomination. Momoh was elected to the national presidency in October, with 99% of the votes cast, and was inaugurated on 28 November. Although retaining his military status, Momoh appointed a civilian Cabinet, which included several members of the previous administration. Elections to the House of Representatives took place in

May 1986. In 1987 Momoh initiated an extensive campaign against financial malpractice in the public sector.

Momoh's administration failed to improve the serious economic situation, however, and his popularity declined. In March 1987 the Government announced that it had suppressed an attempted coup; more than 60 people were subsequently arrested, including the First Vice-President, Francis Minah. In October Minah and 15 other defendants were sentenced to death for plotting to assassinate Momoh and to overthrow the Government, and two defendants received custodial sentences for misprision of treason. In October 1989 Minah and five others were executed, despite international appeals for clemency.

Following the outbreak of civil conflict in Liberia in December 1989, an estimated 125,000 Liberians took refuge in Sierra Leone. The Sierra Leonean Government contributed troops to the cease-fire monitoring group (ECOMOG) of the Economic Community of West African States (ECOWAS, see p. 187), which was dispatched to Liberia in August 1990. In November of that year Charles Taylor, the leader of the principal Liberian rebel faction, the National Patriotic Front of Liberia (NPFL), threatened to attack Freetown International Airport (alleged to be a base for ECOMOG offensives against rebel strongholds). In early April 1991, following repeated border incursions by members of the NPFL, which resulted in the deaths of several Sierra Leoneans, government forces entered Liberian territory and launched a retaliatory attack against NPFL bases. By the end of that month, however, NPFL forces had advanced 150 km within Sierra Leone. The Momoh Government alleged that the rebel offensive had been instigated by Taylor, in an attempt to force Sierra Leone's withdrawal from ECOMOG, and also accused the Government of Burkina Faso of actively assisting the rebels. It was reported, however, that members of a Sierra Leonean resistance movement, known as the Revolutionary United Front (RUF), had joined the NPFL in attacks against government forces. In mid-1991 government troops, with the assistance of military units from Nigeria and Guinea, initiated a counteroffensive against the rebels, and succeeded in recapturing several towns in the east and south of the country.

In August 1990, at a session of the Central Committee of the APC, Momoh (who had hitherto made clear his opposition to the establishment of a multi-party political system) conceded the necessity of electoral reforms, and announced an extensive review of the Constitution. Momoh subsequently appointed a 30-member National Constitutional Review Commission, which was to revise the Constitution. In March 1991 the Commission submitted a draft Constitution, which provided for the adoption of a multi-party system, for consideration by the Government. The new Constitution stipulated that the President, who was to appoint the Cabinet, was to be elected by a majority of votes cast nationally and by at least 25% of the votes cast in more than one-half of the electoral districts. Members of the legislature were to be elected by universal adult suffrage for a term of five years. The Government subsequently accepted the majority of the Commission's recommendations. In June the Government presented the draft Constitution to the House of Representatives, and announced that the parliamentary term, which was due to end that month, was to be extended until May 1992 to allow time for the transition to a multi-party system.

In early August 1991 the House of Representatives formally approved the new Constitution, and at a national referendum, which was conducted later in August, the new Constitution was endorsed by 60% of voters, with 75% of the electorate participating. On 3 September the Government formally adopted the new Constitution. In the same month six newly created political associations formed an alliance, known as the United Front of Political Movements (UNIFOM), which subsequently demanded that the forthcoming elections be monitored by international observers, and that the incumbent Government be dissolved and an interim administration established. On 23 September, following the resignation of the First Vice-President and Second Vice-President from both the APC and the Government, Momoh announced the formation of a new 18-member Cabinet, which retained only seven members of the previous Government. Later that month legislation that formally permitted the formation of political associations was introduced; several organizations were subsequently granted legal recognition. In December, following discussions between Momoh and leaders of the other registered political parties, the opposition movements pledged to co-operate in the establishment of a multi-party system.

On 29 April 1992 members of the armed forces, led by a five-member military junta, seized a radio station in Freetown and broadcast demands for improvements in conditions in the armed forces. The rebel troops later occupied the presidential offices, and the leader of the military junta, Capt. Valentine E. M. Strasser, announced that the Government had been overthrown. On the following day Momoh fled to Guinea, and Strasser announced the establishment of a governing council, to be known as the National Provisional Ruling Council (NPRC). Strasser affirmed the NPRC's commitment to the introduction of a multi-party system, and pledged to end the conflict in the country. On the same day the Constitution was suspended, the House of Representatives was dissolved and a state of emergency, which included a curfew, was imposed. On 1 May the NPRC (which principally comprised military officers), chaired by Strasser, was formed. Shortly afterwards a new 19-member Cabinet, which included a number of members of the NPRC, was appointed, and the Commander of the Armed Forces and the head of the security forces were replaced. On 6 May Strasser was inaugurated as Head of State.

In July 1992 Strasser replaced three members of the NPRC in the Cabinet with civilians, and removed all civilian cabinet ministers from the NPRC. Later that month he announced extensive structural changes, which were designed to reduce the direct involvement of the NPRC in government administration: the NPRC was officially designated the Supreme Council of State, while the Cabinet was reconstituted as the Council of Secretaries (headed by the Chief Secretary of State), which was to be responsible for government administration, subject to the authority of the NPRC. The three members of the NPRC who had been removed from the Cabinet earlier that month were appointed Principal Liaison Officers, with responsibility for the supervision of government administration in a number of ministries (henceforth known as departments). In the same month the Government introduced legislation that imposed severe restrictions on the media.

In September 1992 the Deputy Chairman of the NPRC, Capt. Solomon A. J. Musa, temporarily assumed the office of Head of State during a visit by Strasser to the USA. In that month Musa suspended a number of senior army officers and members of the security forces. In November some 30 people, who were alleged to be supporters of Momoh, were arrested by the security forces and charged with involvement in subversive activities. In early December Strasser announced a reorganization of the Council of Secretaries, in which the two remaining members of the Momoh administration were replaced. In the same month Musa became Chief Secretary of State. Later in December, in an apparent attempt to regain public support, the Government established a 19-member National Advisory Council, comprising representatives of various non-governmental organizations, which was to draft a programme for transition to civilian rule.

At the end of December 1992 the Government announced that the security forces had suppressed a coup attempt by a group known as the Anti-Corruption Revolutionary Movement (which included former members of the army and security forces). Shortly afterwards nine of those accused of involvement in the attempted coup were convicted by a special military tribunal, and, together with 17 prisoners who had been convicted in November on charges of treason, were summarily executed. Human rights organizations subsequently contested the Government's statement that a coup attempt had been staged, and condemned the trial by special military tribunal. In January 1993 the United Kingdom announced the suspension of economic aid to Sierra Leone in protest at the executions. Later that month, in an apparent response to criticism from foreign Governments, several former members of the Momoh administration, who had been detained in May 1992, were released.

In April 1993 Strasser announced that a programme providing for a transition to civilian rule within a period of three years was to be adopted; in addition, all political prisoners were to be released, press restrictions would be relaxed, and the function of special military tribunals was to be reviewed. In July Musa was replaced as Deputy Chairman of the NPRC and Chief Secretary of State by Capt. Julius Maada Bio, ostensibly on the grounds that false allegations against him had proved detri-

mental to the stability of the administration. Musa (who was widely believed to be responsible for the repressive measures undertaken by the Government) took refuge in the Nigerian high commission in Freetown, amid widespread speculation regarding his dismissal, and subsequently emigrated to the United Kingdom.

At the end of November 1993 Strasser announced the details of a two-year transitional programme, which provided for the installation of a civilian government by January 1996. The registration of political parties was to take place in June 1995, prior to a presidential election in November and legislative elections in December of that year. In December a five-member Interim National Electoral Commission was established to organize the registration of voters and the demarcation of constituency boundaries, in preparation for forthcoming local government elections. In the same month the National Advisory Council submitted constitutional proposals (which included a number of similar provisions to the 1991 Constitution), stipulating that: executive power was to be vested in the President, who was to be required to consult with the Cabinet, and was to be restricted to a tenure of two four-year terms of office; only Sierra Leonean nationals of more than 40 years of age were to qualify to contest a presidential election (thereby precluding Strasser and the majority of NPRC members, on the grounds of age); the legislature was to comprise a House of Representatives, which was to be elected by universal adult suffrage for a term of five years, and a 30-member upper chamber, the Senate.

At the end of December 1993 the Government ended the state of emergency that had been imposed in April 1992 (although additional security measures remained in force). In April 1994 13 senior members of the armed forces were dismissed, following widespread criticism of the Government's failure to end continued conflict in the south-east of the country with the RUF, led by Foday Sankoh, which, in 1991, had joined Liberian rebels in attacks against government forces. In July a National Security Council, chaired by Strasser, was established to co-ordinate the operations of the armed forces. Later that month it was reported that the RUF (which had been joined by disaffected members of the armed forces) had besieged the principal town of Kenema, near the border with Liberia, and was exploiting diamond reserves in the region.

In October 1994 a draft Constitution was submitted to the NPRC. However, an increase in rebel activity in many parts of the country, with widespread looting and killing by armed groups, prevented the organization of district council elections, which had been scheduled to take place later that month. In January 1995 the RUF gained control of the mining installations owned by the Sierra Leone Ore and Metal Company (SIEROMCO) and Sierra Rutile Ltd, and seized a number of employees of the two enterprises, including eight foreign nationals. Later in January seven Roman Catholic nuns, together with a number of Sierra Leonean citizens, were abducted, following an attack by the RUF against the north-western town of Kambia. In the same month the RUF threatened to kill the British hostages if the Sierra Leonean authorities executed an officer, who had been convicted by military tribunal of collaborating with the rebels. In February the RUF rejected appeals by the UN and the Organization of African Unity (OAU, now the African Union, see p. 130) that peace negotiations be initiated, and demanded that all troops that had been dispatched by foreign Governments to assist the Strasser administration be withdrawn as a precondition to discussions. In mid-February government forces (which had succeeded in recapturing the mining installations owned by Sierra Rutile) launched an offensive against a principal rebel base in the Kangari region, east of Freetown. Meanwhile, continued atrocities perpetrated against civilians were increasingly attributed to disaffected members of the armed forces.

In February 1995 the military administration engaged 58 Gurkha mercenaries, who had previously served in the British army, prompting further concern regarding the safety of the British hostages in Sierra Leone. In March government forces regained control of the mining installations owned by SIEROMCO and the principal town of Moyamba, 100 km south-east of Freetown (which had been captured by the RUF earlier that month). Later that month the rebels released the seven nuns who had been abducted in January. Despite the successful counter-offensives by government forces, by April the RUF had advanced towards Freetown and had initiated a series of attacks against towns in the vicinity (including Songo, which was situated only 35 km east of Freetown), apparently prior to besieging the capital. Later in April the remaining foreign nationals who had been seized by the RUF were released.

In March 1995 the Council of Secretaries was reorganized to allow principal military officials in the Government to assume active functions within the armed forces (following the advance of RUF forces towards Freetown); Lt-Col Akim Gibril became Chief Secretary of State, replacing Bio, who was appointed Chief of Defence Staff. At the end of April, on the anniversary of the NPRC's assumption of power, Strasser formally announced that the ban on political activity was to be rescinded, and that a National Consultative Conference was to be convened to discuss the transitional process; he further indicated that elections were to take place by the end of that year, prior to the installation of a civilian government in January 1996, in accordance with the transitional programme. The ban on political activity was formally ended on 21 June; some 15 parties were subsequently granted registration (although the RUF failed to respond to government efforts to include the movement in the electoral process). Later in June 56 former government officials, including Momoh, were prohibited from assuming public office for a period of 10 years (and thereby precluded from contesting the elections), after the government commissions of inquiry concluded that they had misused public funds.

In May 1995 government forces initiated a number of counter-attacks against the RUF, and succeeded in recapturing Songo. The Governments of Guinea and Nigeria dispatched additional troops to Sierra Leone, while it was reported that mercenaries recruited via a private South African concern were assisting the authorities with military training and logistics. By the end of June government forces had regained control of significant diamond-mining regions in the eastern Kono District, and part of Bo District, in a successful counter-offensive, which was generally attributed to the assistance of the mercenaries. In September, however, the RUF launched further offensives in Bo District, while increasing reports of massacres and other violations of human rights perpetrated by the rebels against the civilian population emerged.

In October 1995, while Strasser was abroad, a coup attempt was suppressed by government forces; seven military officers were subsequently arrested on suspicion of attempting to overthrow the Government. In December it was announced that the presidential and legislative elections were to take place concurrently on 26 February 1996. In January 1996, however, Strasser was deposed by military officers, led by Bio, in a bloodless coup. Bio, who assumed the office of Head of State, announced that the coup had been instigated in response to efforts by Strasser to remain in power. (It was reported that Strasser had indicated that he intended to amend restrictions on the age of prospective candidates to enable himself to contest the elections.) Strasser (who had been expelled to Guinea) claimed, however, that the new military administration planned to delay the transition to civilian government. A reconstituted Supreme Council of State and Council of Secretaries were formed, and, following a meeting of the new military leadership, the political parties and INEC, it was announced that the elections were to take place as scheduled. The RUF indicated that it was prepared to enter into negotiations with the new Government, and declared a temporary cease-fire to allow voter registration to proceed throughout the country; however, it urged a postponement of the elections, pending a peace settlement that would allow the movement to participate in the democratic process. However, delegates at the National Consultative Conference, which was convened by INEC in early February, voted in favour of adherence to the scheduled date. The RUF subsequently abandoned the cease-fire and launched a series of attacks in various parts of the country, in an apparent attempt to undermine the electoral process.

On 26 February 1996 presidential and legislative elections, which were contested by 13 political parties and were monitored by international observers, took place as scheduled. However, some 27 people were killed in attacks by armed groups, particularly in Bo and parts of Freetown, which were generally attributed to the RUF; voting was consequently extended for a further day. The reconstituted SLPP secured 36.1% of votes cast in the legislative elections, while its presidential candidate, Ahmed Tejan Kabbah, also received most support, with 35.8% of votes. Seven of the political parties demanded that the results be annulled, owing to the disruption of the elections in several regions caused by the civil violence. Since none of the candidates had achieved the requisite majority of 55% of the votes, a second round of the presidential election, which took place on 15 March,

was contested by Kabbah and the candidate of the United National People's Party (UNPP), John Karefa-Smart (who had obtained 22.6% of votes cast in the first round): Kabbah was elected President by 59.5% of the votes. Later in March seats in the new 80-member Parliament were allocated on a basis of proportional representation, with the SLPP securing 27, the UNPP 17, the People's Democratic Party 12 and the reconstituted APC only five seats; the 12 provincial districts were represented in the legislature by Paramount Chiefs. Kabbah was inaugurated on 29 March, when the military Government officially relinquished power to the new civilian administration. In April Kabbah appointed a new Cabinet, which was subsequently approved by the new Parliament.

Following the elections, the Government announced in March 1996 that the RUF had agreed to a cease-fire; at a meeting between Sankoh and Bio in Yamoussoukro, Côte d'Ivoire, later that month, the RUF undertook to observe the cease-fire for a period of two months and to continue negotiations with the newly elected civilian Government. Following discussions between Sankoh and Kabbah in April, the Government and RUF reaffirmed their commitment to a permanent cessation of hostilities, and announced the establishment of three joint committees, which would consider issues regarding the demobilization of rebel forces. However, Sankoh continued to refuse to recognize the legitimacy of the new Government, and demanded that a transitional administration be installed pending further elections. At continuing negotiations in May, agreement was reached on a number of issues, although the RUF demanded that the mercenaries be withdrawn from the country as a precondition to the demobilization of its forces. Despite the official cease-fire, sporadic attacks by the RUF were subsequently reported. Additional clashes occurred later that year between government forces and the Kamajors (traditional fighters reconstituted as an auxiliary defence force).

In July 1996 the Parliament adopted legislation that formally reinstated the Constitution of 1991. In September 1996 Kabbah ordered the compulsory retirement of some 20 officers, including Strasser and Bio, from the armed forces. Shortly afterwards it was reported that a conspiracy to overthrow the Government had been thwarted by senior military officers. About 17 members of the armed forces were arrested, of whom nine were subsequently charged with involvement in the conspiracy. In November Kabbah effected a government reorganization, in which a number of ministries were amalgamated. Following reports of a further conspiracy to overthrow the Government in January 1997, Kabbah announced that an investigative mission from Nigeria had concluded that former members of the NPRC administration had instigated the coup attempt of September 1996.

In November 1996 Kabbah demanded that the RUF relinquish armaments within a period of two weeks, threatening that government forces would resume military operations. At the end of that month Kabbah and Sankoh signed a peace agreement in Abidjan, Côte d'Ivoire, whereby RUF forces were to be demobilized and the movement was to be reconstituted as a political organization, while all foreign troops were to be withdrawn from the country and replaced with foreign observers. A National Commission for the Consolidation of Peace was subsequently established to monitor the peace settlement. By February 1997 all foreign mercenaries had left Sierra Leone in accordance with the agreement, while the repatriation of Sierra Leonean refugees from Liberia had commenced. However, at the end of that month (when the implementation of the peace agreement was scheduled for completion) it was reported that members of the RUF had repeatedly violated the peace agreement and had failed to report to designated centres for disarmament. In March numbers of the political wing of the RUF issued a declaration that Sankoh had been removed as leader of the organization, owing to his failure to implement the peace accord. Later that month, however, RUF forces loyal to Sankoh kidnapped members of the movement who had supported his replacement, together with the Sierra Leonean ambassador to Guinea; the faction issued demands for the release of Sankoh, who had been detained in Nigeria earlier that month (being reportedly in possession of armaments).

On 25 May 1997 dissident members of the armed forces, led by Maj. Johnny Paul Koroma, seized power, deposing Kabbah, who fled to Guinea. Koroma claimed that the coup, which was condemned internationally, was in response to the Government's failure to implement the peace agreement with the RUF. (The coup leaders were believed to have connections with members of the NPRC administration, many of whom, it was reported, planned to return to Sierra Leone.) The Nigerian Government demanded that the junta relinquish power, and increased its military strength in Freetown to about 3,000 troops. The new authorities imposed a curfew in Freetown, following widespread violent looting by armed factions; most foreign nationals were evacuated. In early June Nigerian forces initiated a naval bombardment of Freetown in an effort to force the new military leaders to resign. However, forces loyal to the coup leaders, assisted by RUF members, succeeded in repelling Nigerian attacks. Koroma announced the establishment of a 20-member Armed Forces Revolutionary Council (AFRC), with himself as Chairman and Sankoh (who remained in detention in Nigeria) as Vice-Chairman; the AFRC (which was not internationally recognized as the legitimate Government) included a further three members of the RUF and several civilians. All political activity, the existing Constitution and government bodies were suspended, although Koroma pledged that democratic rule would be restored. Nigeria reiterated that it intended to reinstate the ousted Government with the support of ECOWAS, and a further two Nigerian warships were dispatched to the region; further clashes between Nigerian troops, who had been serving under the mandate of ECOMOG in neighbouring Liberia (q.v.), and supporters of the new military leaders occurred at the international airport at Lungi. In mid-June the AFRC announced that it had suppressed a coup attempt, following the arrest of 15 people, including several senior military officers. In the same month it was reported that troops supporting the junta had repulsed an attack by Kamajors (who remained loyal to Kabbah) at the town of Zimmi, 250 km southeast of Freetown. On 17 June Koroma was formally inaugurated as the self-proclaimed Head of State. However, despite appeals from Koroma, civilians continued to observe a campaign of civil disobedience, which had been organized by the labour congress in protest at the coup.

By early July 1997 the new military Government had been completely isolated by the international community. The Commonwealth Ministerial Action Group (CMAG—which had been established to ensure adherence to the principles of democracy by member states) suspended Sierra Leone from meetings of the Commonwealth, pending the restoration of constitutional order and the reinstatement of a democratically elected government. The UN Security Council also condemned the coup, and expressed support for ECOWAS efforts to resolve the situation. Meanwhile, a four-member ministerial committee, comprising representatives of Nigeria, Côte d'Ivoire, Guinea and Ghana, which had been established by ECOWAS, urged the Government to relinquish power during a series of negotiations with an AFRC delegation.

In mid-July 1997 Koroma formed a cabinet, known as the Council of Secretaries, comprising representatives of the RUF and the army, together with a number of civilians. Later that month, following further reports of clashes between Kamajors and forces loyal to the junta in the south of the country, AFRC representatives and the ECOWAS committee, meeting in Abidjan, agreed to an immediate cease-fire; negotiations were to continue, with the aim of restoring constitutional order. However, Nigeria subsequently accused the AFRC of violating the cease-fire, while further clashes between the Kamajors and the AFRC forces were reported at Zimmi. Renewed skirmishes between Nigerian and AFRC troops also occurred at Lungi airport. At the end of July continuing discussions between the ECOWAS committee and AFRC representatives in Abidjan were abandoned, after Koroma insisted that he retain power for a tenure of four years, and refused to restore the Constitution and to end the ban on political activity. Consequently, in late August an ECOWAS conference, which was convened at Abuja, Nigeria, officially endorsed the imposition of sanctions against Sierra Leone, with the aim of obliging the AFRC to relinquish power; however, the conference rejected demands by Kabbah, which were supported by the Nigerian Government, for military intervention to reinstate his administration. ECOMOG was granted a mandate to monitor the cease-fire and to enforce the economic embargo (which excluded essential humanitarian supplies); it was also agreed that the ECOWAS monitoring committee would henceforth include Liberia (following the election of a democratic Government in that country).

In September 1997 ECOMOG troops stationed at the airport at Lungi bombarded container vessels that were suspected of attempting to violate the sanctions, and staged aerial attacks against commercial and military targets in Freetown, killing about 50 civilians. In the same month CMAG voted in support of the decision of the ECOWAS committee to effect the reinstatement of the Kabbah administration. In early October the UN Security Council imposed sanctions on the import of armaments and petroleum products to Sierra Leone. Following further aerial bombardments of Freetown by ECOMOG troops (in which large numbers of civilians were killed), a mass demonstration was held in the capital to demand that the Nigerian Government withdraw its troops from Sierra Leone. Negotiations between the AFRC and the five-member committee continued, however, and later in October an agreement, which was signed in Conakry, Guinea, provided for an immediate cease-fire, and the reinstatement of Kabbah's Government by April 1998, together with immunity from prosecution for AFRC members; all troops loyal to the incumbent military administration and RUF members were to be demobilized, under the supervision of a disarmament committee, comprising representatives of the AFRC, ECOMOG and local forces loyal to Kabbah. In November 10 people, including a senior RUF official, were arrested in connection with an alleged conspiracy to overthrow the military junta. In January 1998 ECOMOG forces again bombarded the port at Freetown (for the first time since the peace agreement in October), apparently with the aim of preventing merchant vessels from contravening the sanctions. Meanwhile, later that month Kamajors gained control of the town of Tongofield (where principal reserves of diamonds were located), 240 km east of Freetown, and in early February were reported to have captured the town of Bo.

In early February 1998 further clashes erupted near Freetown between ECOMOG troops and supporters of the military junta. Nigerian troops belonging to ECOMOG subsequently launched an intensive bombardment against Freetown and succeeded in gaining control of the capital, after senior members of the AFRC, including Koroma, fled into hiding, or surrendered to the ECOMOG forces; some 100 civilians were killed in the fighting, while more than 3,000 took refuge in Guinea. About 50 members of the military junta were arrested at James Spriggs Payne Airport at Monrovia, Liberia, prompting protests from the Liberian Government regarding the Nigerian military intervention. It was announced that the Government that had been ousted on 25 May 1997 was to be reinstated, and that all subsequent appointments were to be considered invalid. ECOMOG forces were to remain in the country to assist in the restructuring of the armed forces. Meanwhile, following reports that troops loyal to the former military junta, with the assistance of the RUF, had recaptured Bo, ECOMOG forces were deployed in the region to support the Kamajors, and rapidly succeeded in regaining control of most of the region (prompting speculation that the Nigerian military initiative had been undertaken with the aim of gaining access to Sierra Leone's mineral resources).

On 10 March 1998 Kabbah returned from exile and was officially reinstated as President; he subsequently appointed a Cabinet (which included a number of members of his previous administration). The new Government declared a state of emergency under which members of the former military junta could be detained for a maximum of 30 days without being formally charged. It was announced that some 1,500 civilians and members of the armed forces (including Momoh) had been placed in detention and were to be charged for their alleged connections with the former military junta. Also in March the UN Security Council voted to end its embargo on imports of petroleum products to Sierra Leone (which had resulted in severe fuel shortages), although an embargo on the supply of armaments was maintained. It was reported that ECOMOG forces had launched an offensive in the east of the country, in an effort to eradicate the remaining forces loyal to the former military junta and members of the RUF. In May the British High Commissioner in Sierra Leone, Peter Penfold, was temporarily withdrawn from the country, following investigations into allegations that a British company had supplied armaments, in contravention of the UN embargo, for the offensive to reinstate Kabbah's Government. In July the UN Security Council adopted a resolution establishing a UN Observer Mission in Sierra Leone (UNOMSIL), comprising 70 military observers, with an initial six-month mandate to monitor the security situation, supervise the disarmament of former combatants, and advise the authorities on the restructuring of the security forces. In the same month it was announced that the national army had been dissolved; the establishment of a new, 5,000-member force was envisaged.

In late July 1998 the Nigerian Government returned Foday Sankoh (who had been in detention in Nigeria since early 1997) to Sierra Leone, where he was charged with treason following his support for the military coup of May 1997. In August 16 civilians, including five journalists, were sentenced to death, after being convicted of supporting the former military junta. In October 24 army officers were publicly executed, following their conviction for involvement with the military junta, provoking condemnation from many foreign Governments and human rights organizations, which had appealed for clemency. Death penalties imposed against a further 10 officers were commuted to terms of life imprisonment. In November a further 15 civilians, including several ministers who had served in the AFRC Government, were sentenced to death for their part in the May 1997 coup; Momoh received a custodial term of 10 years for colluding with the military junta.

Meanwhile, ECOMOG continued efforts to suppress rebel activity, particularly in the north and east of the country, and in October 1998 transferred its operational headquarters from the Liberian capital, Monrovia, to Freetown. In that month the RUF intensified hostilities, after it was announced that Sankoh had been sentenced to death by the High Court on charges of treason. In November ECOMOG forces commenced aerial bombardments of rebel bases. By late December, however, RUF forces, together with supporters of the former military junta, had advanced towards Freetown—amid reports of large-scale atrocities perpetrated against the civilian population—and had seized control of the principal town of Makeni, 140 km northeast of Freetown. The Governments of Nigeria and Ghana dispatched additional troops to reinforce the ECOMOG contingent (which henceforth numbered about 15,000). At the end of December the acting Commander of the RUF, Sam Bockarie, rejected a government invitation to enter into peace negotiations, and ECOMOG forces, supported by Kamajors, attempted to repulse rebel attacks in the outskirts of Freetown.

On 6 January 1999 rebel forces attacked Freetown (where thousands of civilians from the surrounding area had taken refuge), releasing a number of supporters of the former junta from the capital's prison and seizing the Nigerian High Commission and government offices; Kabbah and a number of cabinet ministers were obliged to flee to ECOMOG headquarters. (It was subsequently discovered that two ministers had been killed by the rebels.) Bockarie announced that Freetown was under the control of the RUF, and demanded that Sankoh be released from detention. However, he rejected a subsequent offer by Kabbah to release Sankoh on condition that the rebels comply with the November 1996 peace agreement. ECOMOG troops initiated a counter-offensive, with an aerial bombardment of Freetown, forcing the rebels to retreat to the outskirts of the capital. It was estimated that about 3,000 people had been killed during the RUF occupation of the capital, and further large numbers of civilians were maimed by the rebels. The rebel forces had taken hostage the Roman Catholic Archbishop, Joseph Ganda, and about 11 European priests and nuns; Ganda and five priests were rescued by ECOMOG troops, but it was subsequently reported that some of the nuns had been killed. By late January ECOMOG forces claimed to have regained control of Freetown, and a cease-fire was agreed, pending peace negotiations, which were convened in Conakry, with mediation by the Governments of Guinea, Côte d'Ivoire and Togo. It was reported that Sankoh (who had been allowed by the Sierra Leonean authorities to attend the peace discussions) demanded his release and the official recognition of the RUF as a political movement as preconditions to the cessation of hostilities. Some 100 members of ECOMOG were arrested, following claims by a UN report (which were denied by ECOMOG) that suspected rebels had been summarily executed; the Kamajors were also implicated in summary killings. In late January the Government of Mali dispatched some 500 troops to join the ECOMOG contingent.

Following the rebel offensive in January 1999, a number of West African Governments, particularly those of Nigeria and Ghana, reiterated claims that the Liberian Government was supporting the RUF with mercenaries and illicit exports of armaments in exchange for diamonds. ECOMOG also accused Burkina Faso and Libya of assisting rebel operations. Charles Taylor (now the Liberian President) denied any connections with the RUF, dismissing the allegations as an attempt to destabilize his administration. Following further economic hardship in Nigeria (owing principally to a decline in the international price for petroleum), domestic opposition to the presence of the Nigerian contingent in Sierra Leone had increased. In early 1999 the Nigerian Government announced that it intended to withdraw its forces from Sierra Leone prior to the transition to civilian rule in Nigeria, which was scheduled to take place at the end of May. In April, however, the Nigerian President-elect, Olusegun Obasanjo, announced that the Nigerian contingent (then numbering nearly 15,000) would remain in Sierra Leone until peace was restored, apparently in response to the influence of the international community; however, a gradual withdrawal of ECOMOG troops, to be completed by early 2000, was envisaged. Meanwhile, Kabbah authorized discussions between Sankoh and active RUF leaders to clarify RUF demands, and, following pressure from the Nigerian, US and British Governments, agreed to conduct formal peace negotiations with the rebels. In late April, following discussions between RUF leaders, formal negotiations between the RUF and a government delegation commenced in the Togolese capital, Lomé, with mediation by President Gnassingbé Eyadéma of Togo. In early May the Government and the RUF signed a cease-fire agreement, which came into effect later that month. Continuing negotiations on the proposed participation of the RUF in a coalition transitional administration, as part of a wider peace settlement, followed. In early July the Government and the RUF reached a power-sharing agreement, after government negotiators acceded to rebel demands that Sankoh be granted vice-presidential powers, with responsibility for the mineral resources industry, and the RUF be allocated a number of cabinet posts. The accord provided for the release of civilians who had been abducted by the rebels, and the disarmament and reintegration into the armed forces of former combatants; the RUF was to be reconstituted as a political organization. Following the completion of disarmament, legislative and presidential elections were to take place by February 2001. The office of the UN High Commissioner for Human Rights and other human rights organizations objected to a general amnesty for perpetrators of human rights violations allowed under the provisions of the peace agreement. (Atrocities committed by the rebels against the civilian population, including mass amputations, had attracted international condemnation.)

In early August 1999 former supporters of the AFRC junta kidnapped some 32 members of ECOMOG and UNOMSIL (including five British nationals) who had been abducted by the rebels, after attempting to negotiate the release of about 200 civilians, principally minors, held by the rebels. The dissidents issued demands for the extension of the amnesty to supporters of the former junta, and the release of Koroma, who, they believed, had been detained by the RUF. Koroma was transported by the UN to Monrovia, where he urged his supporters to free the hostages. Following negotiations between the Sierra Leonean authorities and the rebels, with the assistance of British mediators, the ECOMOG and UNOMSIL hostages were subsequently released.

In early October 1999 Sankoh (who had been conducting discussions with Taylor) and Koroma returned to Freetown from Monrovia, and pledged to co-operate with Kabbah in the implementation of the Lomé peace accord. Later that month the UN Security Council adopted Resolution 1270, establishing a 6,000-member force, the UN Mission in Sierra Leone (UNAMSIL, see p. 66), which was granted a six-month mandate to supervise the implementation of the peace agreement, and to assist in a programme for the disarmament and reintegration of the former rebel factions; at the same time the mandate of UNOMSIL was terminated. The withdrawal of the ECOMOG contingent was to be completed following the deployment of UNAMSIL, although, in effect, the new peace-keeping force (which was to comprise 4,000 Nigerian troops and 2,000 principally Kenyan and Indian troops) would incorporate a number of the Nigerian forces belonging to ECOMOG. On 2 November a new coalition Cabinet was officially installed; four former members of the RUF and AFRC junta were allocated ministerial posts (but failed to secure any principal portfolios). Sankoh became Chairman of a commission supervising the reconstruction of the mineral resources industry, with vice-presidential status, while Koroma was nominated Chairman of the Commission for the Consolidation of Peace. In the same month the Government announced the establishment of a Truth and Reconciliation Commission, which was to make recommendations regarding compensation for victims of human rights violations. However, reports of atrocities perpetrated against the civilian population by rebels continued, and in November division between the AFRC and RUF leadership emerged, apparently as a result of the former junta's dissatisfaction with its cabinet posts. Fighting between the former allied factions was reported in northern Sierra Leone, with RUF forces ousting Koroma's supporters from the town of Makeni. The arrival of UNAMSIL troops in Sierra Leone commenced at the end of November.

In early 2000 reports emerged of RUF forces in the Kailahun District of eastern Sierra Leone (where illegal diamond-mining continued) resisting disarmament and the deployment of UNAMSIL troops. In February the UN Security Council adopted a resolution in favour of expanding UNAMSIL to number 11,100, and extended its mandate for a further six months; further African states, including Zambia, Ghana and Guinea, were to contribute troops. In March Kabbah established a commission to supervise the elections, which, under the terms of the peace agreement, were to take place following the disarmament of the former rebel factions. By the end of that month, however, only about 17,000 of the 45,000 former combatants had been disarmed.

In April 2000 UNAMSIL troops stationed in the eastern town of Kenema repulsed attacks from rebel forces. In early May, following a further dispute over disarmament, RUF forces attacked UNAMSIL troops in Makeni and the neighbouring town of Magburaka, killing at least four Kenyan members of the contingent, and seizing a number of UN personnel as hostages. Six civilian UN observers were subsequently released, following intervention by Taylor. However, rebel forces continued to hold about 300 members of UNAMSIL (principally Zambians) hostage at the towns of Makeni and Kailahun, while a further Zambian contingent of the peace-keeping force, numbering about 200, was reported missing (and was subsequently believed to have also been captured). The UN Secretary-General urged West African Heads of State, notably Obasanjo, to increase pressure on Sankoh to order the release of the hostages. Following a reported advance on Freetown by RUF forces, foreign nationals were advised to leave the country. The British Government dispatched a military task force to the region (stationing troops at the airport at Lungi, and in Senegal), which evacuated most European and Commonwealth nationals. RUF supporters guarding Sankoh's residence in Freetown fired on civilian demonstrators, who were demanding that Sankoh comply with the peace agreement; some 20 protesters were killed. (UN officials were subsequently unable to contact Sankoh, who had fled from Freetown.) Sierra Leonean government forces, led by Koroma (who continued to support the Kabbah administration), were deployed to halt rebel advances, and claimed to have recaptured territory from the RUF. At an ECOWAS summit meeting in Abuja, Taylor was authorized to negotiate with the RUF regarding their release of the hostages; the redeployment of Nigerian troops under an ECOMOG mandate was considered. In late May Sankoh was arrested in Freetown by troops loyal to Kabbah. By the end of that month, following mediation by Taylor, the hostages held by the RUF were released. In early June, however, 21 Indian members of UNAMSIL were seized by the RUF at the eastern town of Pendembu, while a further 233 peace-keeping troops were surrounded by rebels at nearby Kailahun. By mid-June most of the British forces had withdrawn (with about 250 troops remaining in the country to train new members of the Sierra Leone armed forces, and to assist in establishing the operations of a British military advisory team). At that time UNAMSIL was reinforced to number some 12,061 military personnel, following a further resolution by the UN Security Council on 19 May, which increased the maximum authorized strength of the force to about 13,000.

In early July 2000 the UN Security Council adopted a resolution, proposed by the British Government, imposing an international embargo on the purchase of unauthenticated diamonds (in an effort to prevent illicit trade from RUF-held regions, thereby ending the rebels' principal source of funding for armaments); the Sierra Leonean Government was to implement a system whereby officially mined diamonds would be granted certification. In the same month government forces clashed with one of the most notorious militia groups, the West Side Boys (WSB—reported to number about 300), which had hitherto supported the former AFRC junta. In mid-July the battalion of (principally Indian) peace-keeping personnel, who had been besieged by the RUF at Kailahun, were rescued in a military operation by UNAMSIL; one member of the contingent was killed during the offensive. In early August the UN Security Council approved the establishment of an international tribunal, where Sankoh and others responsible for atrocities committed during the civil conflict would be placed on trial. The

RUF leadership announced the nomination of Gen. Issa Sesay (who was reported to be a more moderate commander) to replace Sankoh. Later in August the WSB abducted 11 British military personnel and one member of the Sierra Leonean armed forces, subsequently issuing a number of demands as a precondition to releasing the hostages. Five of the British personnel were freed after negotiations, but additional British troops were dispatched to Sierra Leone, following the failure of government officials to secure an agreement on the remaining hostages. In early September about 150 British troops attacked the main WSB base, 48 km east of Freetown, and succeeded in rescuing the other seven hostages. One member of the British armed forces died during the military operation, while 25 members of the WSB were killed, and a further 18 (including the movement's leader, Foday Kallay) were captured.

In September 2000 the Indian Commander of UNAMSIL, Maj.-Gen. Vijay Jetley, accused Nigeria (which contributed about 3,025 troops to UNAMSIL) of perpetuating the conflict in order to continue the illicit trade in diamonds in collusion with the RUF. The Nigerian authorities denied the allegations, and demanded Jetley's resignation. Later that month the Indian Government announced that it was to withdraw its contingent (then numbering 3,073 troops) from UNAMSIL, despite a proposal by the UN Secretary-General that the peace-keeping force be increased in size to number 20,500. In October several nations, notably Bangladesh, Ghana and Kenya, pledged to dispatch additional troops to replace those of India, which had agreed to postpone the withdrawal of its forces until February 2001 to allow for their replacement. The Jordanian Government had also announced the withdrawal of its troops by the end of 2000, on the grounds that it had no regional interests in Sierra Leone. In early November the Kenyan Deputy Chief of Staff, Lieut-Gen. Daniel Opande, replaced Jetley as Commander of UNAMSIL. The number of British troops in the country had been increased to 400, while a 500-member naval task force was deployed off Freetown to provide additional support to the UN peace-keeping operations. (The British Government had also undertaken to dispatch as many as 5,000 troops to Sierra Leone in the event of a crisis.) On 10 November, following further negotiations mediated by ECOWAS, the Government and the RUF signed a cease-fire agreement in Abuja, providing for the demobilization and disarmament of all militia forces, and the deployment of UNAMSIL throughout the country.

Meanwhile, civilians continued to flee from the country, and by August 2000 some 331,000 Sierra Leonean refugees were registered in Guinea. In September the Guinean President, Gen. Lansana Conté, claimed that Liberian and Sierra Leonean refugees were supporting the activity of rebels attempting to overthrow his Government (see the chapter on Guinea), and ordered them to leave the country. Following clashes on Guinea's border with Liberia, tripartite discussions between Guinea, Liberia and Sierra Leone, commenced in October. At an ECOWAS summit meeting, which was convened in Abuja at the end of December, the deployment of a contingent of West African troops along Guinea's borders with Liberia and Sierra Leone was proposed. (Owing to the difficulties in securing further military support, however, the force was not established.) In March Taylor expelled the ambassadors of Guinea and Sierra Leone from Liberia, on the stated grounds that they had been engaged in activity incompatible with their office. Kabbah retaliated by ordering the Liberian Chargé d'affaires to leave the country, and announced the closure of the joint border with Liberia. Large numbers of the refugees in Guinea, prompted by the continued violence and the hostility of the Guinean authorities, began to return to Sierra Leone.

In February 2001 the National Assembly unanimously approved a proposal by Kabbah that presidential and legislative elections, scheduled to take place in February and March, respectively, be postponed for six months, owing to the continued civil unrest in the country. Following the extension of the mandate of the Government, Kabbah reorganized the Cabinet in early March. At the end of that month the UN Security Council adopted a resolution increasing the strength of UNAMSIL (which numbered 9,500, following the withdrawal of the Indian and Jordanian peace-keepers) to 17,500 troops. Some 650 British troops stationed in Sierra Leone were engaged in the continued training of the armed forces, and were to remain in the country until the end of the year. In April UNAMSIL began to deploy troops in northern regions of the country, including the towns of Lunsar and Makeni, formerly held by the RUF. In early May, however, it was reported that the pro-Government

Kamajor militia, now known as the Civil Defence Forces (CDF), had attacked RUF positions in eastern towns. UNAMSIL accused the CDF, which had advanced within RUF-held territory, of instigating the hostilities. In mid-May the RUF and CDF signed an agreement, providing for the immediate cessation of hostilities and resumption of disarmament for both forces. In June UNAMSIL and (British-trained) government forces regained control of part of the significant diamond-mining regions and the eastern border with Guinea and Sierra Leone (thereby forestalling renewed rebel activity originating from the neighbouring countries). Further clashes between the RUF and CDF continued to impede the disarmament process, and in mid-July discussions regarding the implementation of the peace agreement were conducted at Bo; the Government, the RUF and UNAMSIL agreed to a ban on diamond-mining in eastern regions still controlled by the rebels, in order to facilitate the demobilization of combatants.

In early September 2001 the Government announced that presidential and legislative elections would take place, under the aegis of the UN, on 14 May 2002 (after a further postponement, owing to the continued uncertainty of the security situation). A number of political prisoners, including senior RUF members, were released from detention. The RUF, however, protested at the delay and threatened to withdraw from the peace process unless an interim coalition administration replaced the incumbent Government. Later in September the UN Security Council adopted a resolution extending the mandate of UNAMSIL for a further six months. In response to the progress made in the peace process, the United Kingdom reduced its military presence in Sierra Leone, although some 335 British troops remained in the country to support UNAMSIL and to continue with the reorganization of the armed forces. In November representatives of the Government, the RUF and civil society agreed that parliamentary deputies in the forthcoming elections were to be elected by district (rather than under the previous system of proportional representation). Meanwhile, the Sierra Leonean authorities reacted with consternation to US media claims that the al-Qa'ida (Base) organization (suspected of responsibility for the terrorist attacks against the USA on 11 September) had benefited from the purchase of illicitly mined diamonds from the RUF, in exchange for armaments. In December the UN Security Council extended its ban on trade in unauthenticated diamonds for a further 11 months (effective from 5 January 2002).

In preparation for the forthcoming elections, a three-week process of voter registration commenced in mid-January 2002. The disarmament of the estimated 45,000 former combatants was officially completed on 18 January, with a symbolic ceremony. Later that month the UN and the Government reached agreement on the establishment of a war crimes tribunal, to be known as the Special Court, which was to be based in Sierra Leone; the Special Court had a three-year mandate to prosecute crimes perpetrated from the end of November 1996. (Eight UN and local judges to the Special Court were inaugurated in December 2002.) Meanwhile, the continuing rebel insurgency in northern Liberia, which had advanced rapidly towards Monrovia by early 2002, prompted concern that the resumption of civil conflict there would cause further instability in Sierra Leone. Despite UN pressure on the Liberian Government to end assistance for the RUF, it was reported that Bockarie, supported by 4,000 rebel forces, continued to be based in Liberia.

Following the completion of disarmament, the RUF announced its reconstitution as a political organization, the Revolutionary United Front Party (RUFP), with the aim of contesting the elections. In early March 2002, however, Sankoh (who remained titular leader of the RUFP) was formally charged with murder, in connection with the killing of some 20 civilian protesters by his supporters in May 2000. (The trial of Sankoh, together with a further 49 former RUF members, commenced later in March.) In mid-March Kabbah was elected unopposed as the presidential candidate of the SLPP. A total of 24 political parties had officially registered by this time, notably the Peace and Liberation Party (PLP), led by Koroma. However, after the collapse of an opposition alliance, which had been established in late 2001, no serious challenge to the SLPP had emerged. In early April, after the authorities announced that Sankoh would not be permitted to contest the elections on behalf of the RUFP, the party's Secretary-General, Pallo Bangura, was nominated as its presidential candidate. By the end of that month an estimated 60,000 of the 150,000 Sierra Leonean refugees in Guinea

and Liberia had returned voluntarily in order to participate in the elections (which were to be supervised by UNAMSIL).

Presidential and legislative elections took place peacefully on 14 May 2002. Kabbah was elected to a second term in office by 70.1% of the votes cast, while Ernest Bai Koroma of the APC received 22.4% of the votes. The SLPP also secured an outright majority in the expanded 124-member Parliament, with 83 seats, while the APC won 27 seats and the PLP two. Later that month Solomon Berewa (hitherto Minister of Justice) became the new Vice-President, and a reorganized Cabinet was installed.

In July 2002 the authorities announced that a seven-member Truth and Reconciliation Commission had been established. At the end of that month the British military presence in Sierra Leone was reduced to number some 100 military officers, who were to continue the reorganization and training of the armed forces. In August Pallo Bangura resigned his RUFP office, having secured less than 2% of votes cast in the presidential election. In September the UN Security Council adopted a resolution extending the mandate of UNAMSIL for a further six months, but also advocating that the contingent be reduced in size. In December the UN embargo on illicit trade in diamonds was renewed for a further six months. In February 2003 a further 300 British troops were deployed in Sierra Leone, owing to concern that the intensification of hostilities between government and rebel Liberians United for Reconciliation and Democracy (LURD) forces in Liberia (see chapter on Liberia) might cause destabilization in Sierra Leone.

In March 2003 the Special Court approved indictments for war crimes against seven former faction leaders, notably Sankoh, Koroma, the former RUF Commanders, Bockarie and Sesay, and the incumbent Minister of the Interior (and Kamajor leader), Sam Hinga Norman. Five of those indicted, including Hinga Norman, were taken into custody. Koroma went into hiding, following an attempt by the authorities to arrest him, while it was reported that Bockarie was supporting Liberian government forces against the LURD. In April Hinga Norman pleaded not guilty at the Special Court to charges relating to atrocities perpetrated during the civil war. Public hearings before the Truth and Reconciliation Commission commenced in mid-April. In early May the Liberian authorities announced that Bockarie had been killed near the border with Côte d'Ivoire, after clashing with Liberian troops attempting to arrest him, and ordered an investigation into the incident.

Government

Under the terms of the Constitution of 1991, executive power is vested in the President, who is directly elected by universal adult suffrage. The President appoints the Cabinet (subject to approval by the legislature). The maximum duration of the President's tenure of office is limited to two five-year terms. Legislative power is vested in a unicameral Parliament, which is elected for a four-year term and comprises 112 members elected by a system of proportional representation, in 14 constituencies, and 12 Paramount Chiefs, who represent the provincial districts.

The country is divided into four regions: the Northern, Eastern and Southern Provinces, and the Western Area, which comprise 12 districts. There are 147 chiefdoms, each controlled by a Paramount Chief and a Council of Elders, known as the Tribal Authority.

Defence

In August 2002 active members of the armed forces of the Republic of Sierra Leone numbered about 13,000–14,000, with a navy of 200. In October 1999 the UN Security Council adopted a resolution (No. 1270) establishing the UN Mission in Sierra Leone (UNAMSIL, see p. 66), which was to supervise the implementation of a peace agreement between the Government and rebel forces, signed in July of that year. Following the completion of disarmament in January 2002, a new army, restructured with British military assistance, was established. Some 100 British troops remained in the country to support peacekeeping operations and to continue reorganization of the Sierra Leone armed forces. In early 2003 a further 300 British troops were deployed in Sierra Leone, in response to increased hostilities in neighbouring Liberia. At the end of March UNAMSIL numbered 14,549 troops and 259 military observers; the contingent had a maximum authorized strength of 17,500. Expenditure on defence in 2002 was forecast at Le 36,803m. (equivalent to 5.2% of total expenditure).

Economic Affairs

In 2001, according to the World Bank, Sierra Leone's gross national income (GNI), measured at average 1999–2001 prices, was US $726m., equivalent to $140 per head (or $480 per head on an international purchasing-power parity basis). During 1990–2001, it was estimated, the population increased at an average annual rate of 2.3%, while gross domestic product (GDP) per head declined, in real terms, by an average of 4.7% per year. Overall GDP declined, in real terms, at an average annual rate of 2.5% in 1990–2001; however, growth in 2001 was 5.4%.

Agriculture (including forestry and fishing) contributed 48.7% of GDP in 2001. About 61.6% of the labour force were employed in the sector in that year. The principal cash crops are cocoa beans and coffee. Staple food crops include cassava, rice and bananas. Cattle, sheep and poultry are the principal livestock. During 1990–2001 the GDP of the agricultural sector declined at an average annual rate of 6.3%; however, growth in agricultural GDP was 3.9% in 2001.

Industry (including mining, manufacturing, construction and power) contributed 30.5% of GDP in 2001, and employed an estimated 17.1% of the labour force in 1996/97. The GDP of the industrial sector declined by an average of 4.7% per year in 1990–2001; however, industrial GDP increased by 5.7% in 2001.

Mining and quarrying contributed 17.5% of GDP in 1994/95. The principal mineral exports are diamonds (which, according to the Bank of Sierra Leone, accounted for 89.9% of total export earnings in 2001), rutile (titanium dioxide), bauxite and gold. The production of iron ore, previously an important mineral export, was suspended in 1985. In 1995 increased rebel activity effectively suspended official mining operations (although illicit exports of diamonds by rebel forces continued). In June 2000 a UN embargo was imposed on the purchase of unauthenticated diamonds from Sierra Leone, in an effort to prevent widespread illicit trade (which had continued to finance rebel activities). In October official exports of diamonds were resumed under a certification scheme.

Manufacturing contributed 4.9% of GDP in 2001. The manufacturing sector consists mainly of the production of palm oil and other agro-based industries, textiles and furniture-making. During 1990–96 the GDP of the manufacturing sector increased at an average annual rate of 2.5%. Manufacturing GDP declined by 9.9% in 1995, but increased by 1.7% in 1996.

Energy is derived principally from oil-fired thermal power stations. The use of solar energy for domestic purposes was introduced in 1990. Imports of mineral fuels comprised 23.4% of the value of total imports in 2001.

The services sector contributed 20.8% of GDP in 2001, and employed 22.1% of the labour force in 1996/97. The GDP of the services sector increased by an average of 15.1% per year in 1990–2001, rising by 5.1% in 2001.

In 1999 Sierra Leone recorded a trade deficit of US $69m., and there was a deficit of $30m. on the current account of the balance of payments. In 1994 the principal source of imports (42.7%) was the USA; other major suppliers were the Netherlands and the United Kingdom. The USA was also the principal market for exports (taking 44.8% of the total); other significant purchasers were the United Kingdom and Belgium. The principal export in 2001 was diamonds. The principal imports in that year were food and live animals, mineral fuels and lubricants, machinery and transport equipment, and basic manufactures.

In the financial year ending 31 December 2000 the overall budget deficit was Le 124,064m. (equivalent to 9.3% of GDP). In the year ending 31 December 2001 the budget deficit was Le 159,634m. Sierra Leone's external debt totalled US $1,273m. at the end of 2000, of which $969m. was long-term public debt. In that year the cost of debt-servicing was equivalent to 48.0% of the value of exports of goods and services. The annual rate of inflation averaged 29.2% in 1990–2001. Consumer prices increased by 2.1% in 2001, but declined by 3.3% in 2002. An estimated 50% of the labour force were unemployed in early 1990.

Sierra Leone is a member of the Economic Community of West African States (see p. 187) and of the Mano River Union (see p. 341), which aims to promote economic co-operation with Guinea and Liberia.

The civil conflict, which commenced in 1991, resulted in the progressive destruction of Sierra Leone's infrastructure, and severe disruption, or complete suspension, of traditional economic activities. In March 1994 the IMF declared Sierra Leone to be eligible to receive new credit, following its payment of accumulated debt arrears. However, a military coup in May 1997 resulted in the suspension of reforms, and further economic deterioration. The elected Government was reinstated in March 1998, but reform efforts were impeded by continued violence and political instability. Following a peace agreement between the Government and the rebels, which was signed in July 1999, a new coalition administration was installed, and a recovery and rehabilitation programme was adopted. Subsequent improvements in fiscal control and considerable post-conflict support from the international financial institutions resulted in some progress in reconstruction. Under a further cease-fire agreement, signed in November 2000 (see Recent History), the disarmament of rebel forces was completed in January 2002, and presidential and legislative elections were conducted in May. The reorganized Government's priorities were to alleviate widespread poverty, resettle displaced civilians (amounting to nearly one-half of the population at the end of 2001), reintegrate disarmed former combatants, reconstruct the country's infrastructure, and reduce dramatically high debt levels. In March 2002 the IMF, which had approved a further three-year credit arrangement in September 2001, commended the Government's progress in advancing the peace process and the country's improved economic and financial performance (demonstrated by significant GDP growth and continued restraint of the rate of inflation in 2001). In response to the implementation of structural reforms, the IMF and World Bank pledged debt relief to Sierra Leone under concessionary terms (conditional on the Government complying with the stipulated measures of fiscal control). Economic recovery continued in 2002, with increased GDP growth and continued low inflation; however, unemployment remained at a very high level. The IMF approved further disbursements to Sierra Leone in September 2002 and April 2003, under the existing Poverty Reduction and Growth Facility. The Fund advocated an accelerated implementation of structural reforms, including the privatization of state-owned enterprises, and measures to improve governance, and the legal and judicial systems (with the aim of encouraging private investment). Despite sustained peace in Sierra Leone, reinforced by the resettlement of displaced civilians, reintegration of former combatants, and continuing assistance to former war victims, regional stability was threatened by an increase in hostilities in Liberia in early 2003.

Education

Primary education in Sierra Leone begins at six years of age and lasts for six years. Secondary education, beginning at the age of 12, lasts for a further six years, comprising two three-year cycles. In 1999/2000 primary enrolment included 65.2% of children in the relevant age-group (males 67.8%; females 62.7%), while the comparable ratio for secondary enrolment was 23.9% (boys 26.4%; girls 21.6%). There is one university, which comprises six colleges; in 1995 some 1,463 full-time undergraduate students were enrolled at the university. Following the onset of the civil conflict in 1991, large numbers of children were forced to join rebel militia, and to participate in atrocities. After peace was largely restored in July 1999, the reintegration of young former combatants into the community was a priority for the new administration. At the end of 2001 school enrolment continued to be affected, as a result of the large displacement of civilians, and the destruction of school facilities. Education was allocated Le 30,700m. in the 2001 budget, increasing to a forecast Le 36,400m. in 2002, equivalent to 5.2% of total expenditure.

Public Holidays

2003: 1 January (New Year's Day), 12 February* (Id al-Adha, Feast of the Sacrifice), 18–21 April (Easter), 27 April (Independence Day), 14 May* (Mouloud, Birth of the Prophet), 26 November* (Id al-Fitr, end of Ramadan), 25–26 December (Christmas and Boxing Day).

2004: 1 January (New Year's Day), 2 February* (Id al-Adha, Feast of the Sacrifice), 9–12 April (Easter), 27 April (Independence Day), 2 May* (Mouloud, Birth of the Prophet), 14 November* (Id al-Fitr, end of Ramadan), 25–26 December (Christmas and Boxing Day).

*Islamic religious holidays, dependent on the lunar calendar, may vary by one or two days from the dates given.

Weights and Measures

The metric system is in force.

Statistical Survey

Source (unless otherwise stated): Central Statistics Office, PMB 595, Tower Hill, Freetown; tel. (22) 223287; fax (22) 223897; internet www.sierra-leone .org/cso.html,www.statistics-sierra-leone.org.

Area and Population

AREA, POPULATION AND DENSITY

Area (sq km)	71,740*
Population (census results)†	
8 December 1974.	2,735,159
14 December 1985	
Males	1,746,055
Females.	1,769,757
Total	3,515,812
Population (UN estimates at mid-year)‡	
1999	4,272,000
2000	4,405,000
2001	4,587,000
Density (per sq km) at mid-2001	63.9

* 27,699 sq miles.
† Excluding adjustment for underenumeration, estimated to have been 10% in 1974 and 9% in 1985. The adjusted total for 1974 (based on a provisional total of 2,729,479 enumerated) is 3,002,426.
‡ Source: UN, *World Population Prospects: The 2000 Revision*.

PRINCIPAL TOWNS
(population at 1985 census)

Freetown (capital) .	384,499	Kenema	52,473
Koindu . . .	82,474	Makeni	49,474
Bo	59,768		

2001 (UN estimate, including suburbs): Freetown 837,000 (Source: UN, *World Urbanization Prospects: The 2001 Revision*).

BIRTHS AND DEATHS
(UN estimates, annual averages)

	1985-90	1990–95	1995–2000
Birth rate (per 1,000)	49.1	49.5	49.5
Death rate (per 1,000)	27.4	29.8	26.4

Source: UN, *World Population Prospects: The 2000 Revision*.

Expectation of life (WHO estimates, years at birth): 34.2 (males 32.7; females 35.9) in 2001 (Source: WHO, *World Health Report*).

ECONOMICALLY ACTIVE POPULATION
(% of labour force)

	1994/95	1995/96	1996/97
Agriculture, etc.	61.08	60.96	60.83
Industry	16.99	17.04	17.10
Services	21.93	22.00	22.07

Mid-2001 (estimates in '000): Agriculture, etc. 1,046; Total 1,697 (Source: FAO).

Health and Welfare

KEY INDICATORS

Total fertility rate (children per woman, 2001)	6.5
Under-5 mortality rate (per 1,000 live births, 2001) . . .	316
HIV/AIDS (% of persons aged 15–49, 2001). . . .	7.00
Physicians (per 1,000 head, 1996)	0.07
Health expenditure (2000): US $ per head (PPP) . . .	28
Health expenditure (2000): % of GDP	4.3
Health expenditure (2000): public (% of total) . . .	60.0
Access to water (% of persons, 2000).	28
Access to sanitation (% of persons, 2000)	28
Human Development Index (2000): ranking	173
Human Development Index (2000): value	0.275

For sources and definitions, see explanatory note on p. vi.

Agriculture

PRINCIPAL CROPS
('000 metric tons)

	1998	1999	2000
Rice (paddy)	328	247	199
Millet	17	5	4
Sorghum	18	17	8
Sweet potatoes	42	20	28
Cassava (Manioc) . . .	289	240	241
Sugar cane*	21	21	21
Pulses*	49	52	52
Groundnuts (in shell) . .	35	29	15
Oil palm fruit*	200	175	175
Tomatoes*.	27	25	12
Other vegetables* . . .	160	170	170
Plantains*.	27	28	28
Citrus fruit*	77	80	80
Mangoes	10*	7	7*
Other fruit*	47	48	48
Coffee (green).	26*	15	15*
Cocoa beans	13*	11	11*

* FAO estimate(s).

Source: FAO.

LIVESTOCK
(FAO estimates, '000 head, year ending September)

	1999	2000	2001
Cattle	420	420	400
Pigs	52	52	52
Sheep	365	365	365
Goats	200	200	200
Chickens	6,000	6,000	6,000
Ducks	65	65	65

Source: FAO.

LIVESTOCK PRODUCTS
(FAO estimates, '000 metric tons)

	1998	1999	2000
Beef and veal	6	7	7
Poultry meat	9	9	9
Other meat	7	8	8
Cows' milk	21	21	21
Poultry eggs	7	7	8

Source: FAO.

Forestry

ROUNDWOOD REMOVALS
(FAO estimates, '000 cubic metres, excl. bark)

	1999	2000	2001
Sawlogs, veneer logs and logs for sleepers*	4	4	4
Other industrial wood† . . .	120	120	120
Fuel wood	5,215	5,358	5,364
Total	5,339	5,482	5,488

* Annual output assumed to be unchanged since 1993.
† Annual output assumed to be unchanged since 1980.

Source: FAO.

SAWNWOOD PRODUCTION
('000 cubic metres, incl. railway sleepers)

	1991	1992	1993
Total (all broadleaved) . . .	9	9*	5

1994–2001: Annual production as in 1993 (FAO estimates).

* Estimate.

Source: FAO.

Fishing

('000 metric tons, live weight of capture)

	1998	1999	2000
West African ilisha	3.1	—	3.0
Tonguefishes	0.2	0.7	2.3
Snappers	—	1.7	0.3
Bobo croaker	0.4	0.4	4.0
Royal threadfin	1.7	1.8	1.8
Sardinellas	7.5	7.9	7.6
Bonga shad	21.8	22.4	21.6
Tuna-like fishes	5.0	2.2	0.7
Penaeus shrimps	1.7	2.2	1.7
Total catch (incl. others) . .	63.1	59.4	74.7

Source: FAO, *Yearbook of Fishery Statistics*.

Mining

(estimates, '000 metric tons, unless otherwise indicated)

	1999	2000	2001
Gold (kilograms)	30	30	30
Gypsum	4	4	4
Diamonds ('000 metric carats) . .	600	600	600

Source: US Geological Survey.

Industry

SELECTED PRODUCTS
(estimates, '000 metric tons, unless otherwise indicated)

	1996	1997	1998
Jet fuels	17	17	17
Motor spirit (petrol)	28	28	29
Kerosene	8	8	8
Distillate fuel oils	68	70	70
Residual fuel oils	53	54	54
Electric energy (million kWh) . .	241	242	242

Source: UN, *Industrial Commodity Statistics Yearbook*.

2000: Beer and stout ('000 cartons) 305.97; Soft drinks ('000 crates) 1,429.41; Cement ('000 metric tons) 73.40; Plastic footwear ('000 pairs) 1,436.84; Wheat flour ('000 metric tons) 17.81 (Source: Bank of Sierra Leone, *Annual Report*).

2001: Beer and stout ('000 cartons) 770.43; Soft drinks ('000 crates) 1,701.18; Cement ('000 metric tons) 113.27; Plastic footwear ('000 pairs) 1,419.63; Wheat flour ('000 metric tons) 13.34 (Source: Bank of Sierra Leone, *Annual Report*).

Finance

CURRENCY AND EXCHANGE RATES

Monetary Units
100 cents = 1 leone (Le)

Sterling, Dollar and Euro Equivalents (31 December 2002)
£1 sterling = 3,532.6 leones
US \$1 = 2,191.7 leones
€1 = 2,298.5 leones
10,000 leones = £2.830 = \$4.563 = €4.351

Average Exchange Rate (leones per US \$)
2000   2,092.12
2001   1,986.15
2002   2,099.03

BUDGET
(Le million)

Revenue†	2000	2001	2002*
Income tax department . . .	39,742	52,134	59,999
Customs and excise department .	95,424	136,987	153,139
Other departments	12,368	8,929	10,683
Road user charges	4,641	6,648	6,531
Social security contributions . .	0	0	9,073
Total	152,175	204,698	239,425

Expenditure†	2000	2001	2002‡
Recurrent expenditure . . .	301,831	363,363	456,787
Wages and salaries . . .	89,495	111,583	132,002
Goods and services . . .	56,879	79,742	90,700
Security-related expenditures .	53,101	71,950	91,173
Defence	28,636	32,270	36,803
Democratization and DDR§	13,730	22,993	36,265
Grants to educational institutions	11,475	12,997	14,710
Interest payments	83,915	76,047	66,253
Possible HIPC-financed expenditures	0	0	47,000
Development expenditure . .	68,864	92,370	235,942
Total	370,696	455,733	701,834¶

* Excluding grants received (Le million): 106,107 in 2000; 94,394 in 2001; 162,745 (forecast) in 2002.

† Forecasts.

‡ Excluding lending minus repayments (Le million): 11,648 in 2000; 2,993 in 2001; 600 (forecast) in 2002.

§ Disarmament, demobilization and reintegration.

¶ Including (Le million): social security expenditures 7,605; contingency expenditures 1,500.

Source: IMF and International Development Association, *Sierra Leone, Enhanced Heavily Indebted Poor Countries Initiative Decision Point Document* (February 2002).

INTERNATIONAL RESERVES
(US \$ million at 31 December)

	2000	2001	2002
IMF special drawing rights . .	5.2	0.4	24.0
Foreign exchange	43.9	50.9	60.6
Total	49.2	51..3	84.7

Source: IMF, *International Financial Statistics*.

MONEY SUPPLY
(Le million at 31 December)

	2000	2001	2002
Currency outside banks . . .	88,854	116,153	148,015
Demand deposits at commercial banks	48,447	67,452	90,808
Total money (incl. others) . . .	139,957	189,437	247,478

Source: IMF, *International Financial Statistics*.

COST OF LIVING
(Consumer Price Index for Freetown; base: 1995 = 100)

	2000	2001	2002
All items .	255.1	260.4	251.8

Source: IMF, *International Financial Statistics*.

NATIONAL ACCOUNTS
(Le million at current prices)

National Income and Product
(year ending 30 June)

	1992/93	1993/94	1994/95*
Compensation of employees . .	86,503.1	107,650.3	138,658.6
Operating surplus	313,873.8	352,605.6	467,380.1
Domestic factor incomes . .	400,376.9	460,255.8	606,038.7
Consumption of fixed capital .	30,097.2	35,104.2	41,907.3
Gross domestic product (GDP) at factor cost . .	430,474.1	495,360.0	647,946.1
Indirect taxes, *less* subsidies .	36,713.4	48,351.0	62,443.2
GDP in purchasers' values .	467,187.5	543,711.0	710,389.3
Factor income received from abroad.	−66,914.8	−70,237.5	−84,216.0
Less Factor income paid abroad .			
Gross national product (GNP)	400,272.7	473,473.5	626,173.3
Less Consumption of fixed capital	30,097.2	35,104.2	41,907.3
National income in market prices.	370,175.5	438,369.3	584,265.9
Other current transfers received from abroad	11,483.0	12,438.6	15,067.8
Less Other current transfers paid abroad. . . .			
National disposable income .	381,658.5	450,807.9	599,333.7

* Provisional figures.

Expenditure on the Gross Domestic Product

	1998	1999	2000
Government final consumption expenditure.	107,236	119,746	134,374
Private final consumption expenditure.	887,613	1,040,868	1,142,681
Increase in stocks	−1,427	−10,856	1,143
Gross fixed capital formation . .	59,204	52,885	84,761
Total domestic expenditure.	1,052,626	1,202,643	1,362,959
Exports of goods and services . .	203,345	225,868	230,179
Less Imports of goods and services	−206,062	−229,815	−261,561
Statistical discrepancy . . .	1,427	10,856	−1,144
GDP in purchasers' values .	1,051,336	1,209,552	1,330,433
GDP at constant 1989/90 prices	64,629	59,407	61,670

Source: IMF, *International Financial Statistics*.

Gross Domestic Product by Economic Activity
(year ending 30 June)

	1992/93	1993/94	1994/95*
Agriculture, hunting, forestry and fishing	162,194.6	188,884.1	275,327.5
Mining and quarrying	98,615.8	96,748.8	119,229.2
Manufacturing	39,567.0	47,816.7	61,475.3
Electricity, gas and water . . .	469.8	757.3	2,816.8
Construction	4,655.4	12,544.4	15,788.2
Trade, restaurants and hotels . .	69,139.9	77,251.0	98,270.1
Transport, storage and communications	37,056.5	50,047.1	61,267.5
Finance, insurance, real estate and business services . . .	15,947.0	17,988.0	14,732.2
Government services. . . .	14,500.0	17,884.0	19,844.9
Other community, social and personal services . . .	8,998.3	9,769.0	12,308.9
Sub-total	451,144.3	519,690.4	681,060.6
Import duties	18,994.0	27,410.0	32,942.0
Less Imputed bank service charge .	2,950.8	3,389.8	3,612.3
GDP in purchasers' values . .	467,187.5	543,711.0	710,389.3

* Provisional figures.

BALANCE OF PAYMENTS
(US $ million)

	1997	1998	1999
Exports of goods f.o.b.	16	32	6
Imports of goods f.o.b.	−72	−89	−75
Trade balance	−56	−57	−69
Services and other income (net)	−29	−41	−40
Balance on goods, services and income	−85	−98	−109
Private unrequited transfers (net)	6	20	24
Government unrequited transfers (net)	19	44	55
Current balance	−60	−33	−30
Long-term official loans (net) . .	22	48	15
Other official capital (net) . . .	−8	−6	−5
Private capital (net)	−106	−88	−56
Net errors and omissions . . .	68	−26	−135
Overall balance	−84	−105	−210

Source: Bank of Sierra Leone.

External Trade

PRINCIPAL COMMODITIES
(Le million)

Imports c.i.f.	1999	2000	2001
Food and live animals	52,801.8	95,823.1	104,757.2
Beverages and tobacco . . .	7,759.1	10,052.0	9,616.3
Crude materials (inedible) except fuels	5,468.5	9,851.0	11,562.8
Mineral fuels, lubricants, etc. .	37,404.7	84,135.1	86,875.9
Animal and vegetable oils and fats	2,035.1	4,762.7	3,219.3
Chemicals	16,203.1	26,943.4	17,831.4
Basic manufactures	11,258.6	27,832.9	43,910.4
Machinery and transport equipment	14,565.3	38,727.2	75,584.8
Miscellaneous manufactured articles	6,359.2	10,294.0	18,148.3
Total (incl. others)	153,855.4	308,421.4	371,506.4

Exports f.o.b.	1999	2000	2001
Coffee	1,342.7	1,464.2	48.2
Cocoa beans	1,070.5	679.7	573.3
Diamonds	2,454.9	20,600.6	52,073.0
Rutile	2,065.1	—	—
Re-exports	3,001.5	2,010.3	1,587.9
Total (incl. others) . . .	11,347.2	26,770.8	57,898.0

Source: Bank of Sierra Leone.

PRINCIPAL TRADING PARTNERS
(Le million)

Imports	1992	1993	1994
Belgium	5,828	5,889	4,377
China, People's Repub. . . .	4,986	8,160	4,794
Côte d'Ivoire	1,315	1,762	4,026
France	2,440	14,639	2,525
Germany	8,750	19,564	5,578
Hong Kong	325	7,465	5,536
Indonesia	261	4,377	6,838
Italy	8,896	4,618	2,019
Japan	6,256	6,521	3,715
Netherlands	6,015	40,506	26,050
Pakistan	2,678	1,719	1,626
Switzerland	881	9,647	855
United Kingdom	6,809	43,680	10,453
USA	23,295	19,960	78,288
Total (incl. others) . . .	101,672	222,697	183,550

Exports	1992	1993	1994
Belgium	25,770	54	11,412
Germany	1,060	2,486	1,328
Guinea	1,315	817	1,331
Netherlands	5,307	1,201	2,815
Switzerland	7,546	486	215
United Kingdom	5,567	5,988	11,767
USA	13,832	17,564	30,431
Total (incl. others)	75,034	67,077	67,930

Transport

ROAD TRAFFIC

(motor vehicles in use at 31 December)

	1994	1995	1996*
Passenger cars	34,288	20,860	17,640
Buses and coaches	1,103	933	890
Goods vehicles	11,201	10,081	10,000
Motorcycles	10,977	9,879	10,120

1999* Passenger cars 8,138; Buses and coaches 1,838; Lorries and vans 2,717.

* Estimates.

Source: International Road Federation, *World Road Statistics*.

SHIPPING

Merchant Fleet

(registered at 31 December)

	1999	2000	2001
Number of vessels	47	47	41
Displacement (gross registered tons)	17,306	16,729	13,148

Source: Lloyd's Register-Fairplay, *World Fleet Statistics*.

International Sea-borne Freight Traffic

(estimates, '000 metric tons)

	1991	1992	1993
Goods loaded	1,930	2,190	2,310
Goods unloaded	562	579	589

Source: UN Economic Commission for Africa, *African Statistical Yearbook*.

CIVIL AVIATION

(traffic on scheduled services)

	1994	1995	1996
Passengers carried ('000) . . .	14	14	15
Passenger-km (million)	23	23	24
Total ton-km (million)	2	2	2

Source: UN, *Statistical Yearbook*.

1999: Passengers carried ('000) 19; Passenger-km (million) 30; Total ton-km (million) 3.

Tourism

	1998	1999	2000*
Tourist arrivals ('000)	6	6	10
Tourism receipts (US $ million) .	8	8	12

* Preliminary data.

Source: World Tourism Organization, mainly *Yearbook of Tourism Statistics*.

Communications Media

	1998	1999	2000
Television receivers ('000 in use) .	60	62	64
Telephones ('000 main lines in use)	17.4	18.2	19.0
Facsimile machines ('000 in use)*	2.5	n.a.	n.a.
Mobile cellular telephones ('000 subscribers)	n.a.	n.a.	11.9
Internet users ('000)	0.6	2.0	5.0

2001: Mobile cellular telephones ('000 subscribers) 26.9; Internet users ('000) 7.0.

Radio receivers ('000 in use): 1,120 in 1997.

Daily newspapers: 1 (average circulation 20,000) in 1996.

* Twelve months beginning 1 April of year stated.

Sources: UNESCO, *Statistical Yearbook*; UN, *Statistical Yearbook*; and International Telecommunication Union.

Education

(pupils/students, 2000/01, projections)

	Males	Females	Total
Primary	428,300	301,300	729,600
Secondary	434,700	260,400	695,100
University*	1,163	300	1,463

* Full-time undergraduate students in 1995.

Adult literacy rate (UNESCO estimates): 31.5% (males 45.4%; females 18.2%) in 1995 (Source: UNESCO, *Statistical Yearbook*).

Directory

The Constitution

Following the transfer of power to a democratically elected civilian administration on 29 March 1996, the Constitution of 1991 (which had been suspended since April 1992) was reinstated. The Constitution provided for the establishment of a multi-party system, and vested executive power in the President, who was to be elected by the majority of votes cast nationally and by at least 25% of the votes cast in each of the four provinces. The maximum duration of the President's tenure of office was limited to two five-year terms. Legislative power was vested in a unicameral 80-member Parliament, elected by universal adult suffrage for a five-year term. The President was to appoint the Cabinet, subject to approval by the Parliament. From the general election of May 2002 the Parliament was elected for a four-year term and comprised 124 members, 112 of whom were elected by a system of proportional representation, in 14 constituencies, while 12 Paramount Chiefs also represented the provincial districts in the legislature. Members of the Parliament were not permitted concurrently to hold office in the Cabinet.

The Government

HEAD OF STATE

President and Commander-in-Chief of the Armed Forces: Alhaji Ahmed Tejan Kabbah (took office 29 March 1996; reinstated 10 March 1998; re-elected 14 May 2002).

Vice-President: Solomon Berewa.

CABINET
(April 2003)

Minister of Foreign Affairs and International Co-operation: Momodu Koroma.

Minister of Finance: Joseph B. Dauda.

Minister of Development and Economic Planning: Mohamed B. Daramy.

Minister of Trade and Industry: Dr Kadi Sesay.

Minister of Transport and Communications: Dr Prince A. Harding.

Minister of Marine Resources: Okere Adams.

Minister of Health and Sanitation: Dr Agnes Taylor-Lewis.

Minister of Education, Science and Technology: Dr Alpha T. Wurie.

Minister of Mineral Resources: Alhaji Mohamed Swarray Deen.

Minister of Local Government and Community Development: Sidike Brima.

Minister of Tourism and Culture: Chernoh Jalloh.

Minister of Lands, Housing, Country Planning, Forestry and the Environment: Dr Alfred Bobson Sesay.

Minister of Information and Broadcasting: Prof. Septimus Kaikai.

Minister of Works, Housing and Technical Maintenance: Dr Caiser J. Boima.

Minister of Labour and Industrial Relations, and Social Security: Alpha O. Timbo.

Minister of Social Welfare, Gender and Children's Affairs: Shirley Gbujama.

Minister of Justice and Attorney-General: Eke A. Holloway.

Minister of Internal Affairs: George Banda Thomas (acting).

Minister of Youth and Sports: Dr Dennis Bright.

Minister of Energy and Power: Emmanuel O. Grant.

Minister of Agriculture and Food Security: Dr Sama S. Mondeh.

Minister of Political and Parliamentary Affairs: George Banda Thomas.

Minister of State of Presidential Affairs: Mohamed Foday Yumkella.

Minister of the Northern Region: Alex Alie Kargbo.

Minister of the Southern Region: Dr S. U. M. Jah.

Minister of the Eastern Region: Sahr Randolph Fillie-Faboe.

MINISTRIES

Ministry of Agriculture and Food Security: Youyi Bldg, Freetown; tel. (22) 222242; fax (22) 241613.

Ministry of Defence: State Ave, Freetown; tel. (22) 227369; fax (22) 229380.

Ministry of Development and Economic Planning: Youyi Bldg, Freetown; tel. (22) 225236; fax (22) 241599.

Ministry of Education, Science and Technology: New England, Freetown; tel. (22) 240881; fax (22) 240137.

Ministry of Energy and Power: Electricity House, Siaka Stevens St, Freetown; tel. (22) 226566; fax (22) 228199.

Ministry of Finance: Secretariat Bldg, George St, Freetown; tel. (22) 225612; fax (2) 228472.

Ministry of Foreign Affairs and International Co-operation: Gloucester St, Freetown; tel. (22) 224778; fax (22) 225615.

Ministry of Health and Sanitation: Youyi Bldg, 4th Floor, Brookfields, Freetown; tel. (22) 240427; fax (22) 241613.

Ministry of Information and Broadcasting: Youyi Bldg, 8th Floor, Brookfields, Freetown; tel. (22) 240339; fax (22) 241757.

Ministry of Internal Affairs: Liverpool St, Freetown; tel. (22) 226979; fax (22) 227727.

Ministry of Justice: Guma Bldg, Lamina Sankoh St, Freetown; tel. (22) 227444; fax (22) 229366.

Ministry of Labour and Industrial Relations, and Social Security: New England, Freetown; tel. (22) 241947.

Ministry of Lands, Housing, Country Planning, Forestry and the Environment: Youyi Bldg, 4th Floor, Brookfields, Freetown; tel. (22) 242013.

Ministry of Local Government and Community Development: New England, Freetown; tel. (22) 226589; fax (22) 222409.

Ministry of Marine Resources: Freetown.

Ministry of Mineral Resources: Youyi Bldg, 5th Floor, Brookfields, Freetown; tel. (22) 240142; fax (22) 241757.

Ministry of Political and Parliamentary Affairs: State House, State Ave, Freetown; tel. (22) 228698; fax (22) 222781.

Ministry of Presidential Affairs: State House, State Ave, Freetown; tel. (22) 229728; fax (22) 229799.

Ministry of Social Welfare, Gender and Children's Affairs: New England, Freetown; tel. (22) 241256; fax (22) 242076.

Ministry of Trade and Industry: Ministerial Bldg, George St, Freetown; tel. (22) 225211.

Ministry of Transport and Communications: Ministerial Bldg, George St, Freetown; tel. (22) 221245; fax (22) 227337.

Ministry of Tourism and Culture: Ministerial Bldg, George St, Freetown; tel. (22) 222588.

Ministry of Works, Housing and Technical Maintenance: New England, Freetown; tel. (22) 240937; fax (22) 240018.

Ministry of Youth and Sports: Freetown.

President and Legislature

PRESIDENT

Presidential Election, 14 May 2002

Candidate	% of votes
Ahmed Tejan Kabbah (SLPP)	70.06
Ernest Bai Koroma (APC)	22.35
Johnny Paul Koroma (PLP)	3.00
Pallo Bangura (RUFP)	1.73
Dr John Karefa-Smart (APC)	1.04
Dr Raymond Kamara (GAP)	0.59
Zainab Hawa Bangura (MOP)	0.55
Bamidele Thompson (CUPP)	0.47
Andrew Turay (YPP)	0.20
Total	**100.00**

PARLIAMENT

Speaker: Justice E. K. Cowan.

General Election, 14 May 2002

Party	Seats
Sierra Leone People's Party (SLPP)	83
All-People's Congress (APC)	27
Peace and Liberation Party (PLP)	2
Total	**112**

*A further 12 seats were allocated to Paramount Chiefs, who represented the 12 provincial districts.

Political Organizations

A ban on political activity was rescinded in June 1995. Numerous political parties were officially granted registration, prior to elections in May 2002.

All-People's Congress (APC): 39 Siaka Stevens St, Freetown; e-mail info@new-apc.org; internet www.new-apc.org; f. 1960; sole authorized political party 1978–91; merged with the Democratic People's Party in 1992; reconstituted in 1995; Leader Ernest Bai Koroma.

Citizens United for Peace and Progress (CUPP): e-mail info@cupp.org; internet www.cupp.org; f. 2002; Chair. Abubakarr Yanssaneh.

Grand Alliance Party (GAP): Freetown; f. 2002; Pres. Dr Raymond Kamara.

Movement for Progress (MOP): Freetown; f. 2002; Pres. Zainab Hawa Bangura.

National Alliance Democratic Party (NADP): Leader Mohamed Yahya Sillah.

National Democratic Alliance (NDA): Leader Amadu M.B. Jalloh.

National Unity Movement (NUM): Leader Desmond Luke.

National Unity Party (NUP): e-mail johnben@nupsl.org; internet www.nupsl.org; Leader JOHN OPONJO BENJAMIN (acting).

Peace and Liberation Party (PLP): Freetown; f. 2002; Leader JOHNNY PAUL KOROMA.

People's Democratic Party (PDP): Freetown; supported Sierra Leone People's Party in May 2002 elections; Leader OSMAN KAMARA.

People's National Convention (PNC): Leader EDWARD JOHN KARGBO.

People's Progressive Party (PPP): Leader ABASS CHERNOR BUNDU.

Revolutionary United Front Party (RUFP): 15 Charlotte St, Freetown; tel. (22) 231624; fax (22) 232329; e-mail info@rufp.org; internet www.rufp.org; f. 1991 as rebel movement in conflict with govt forces; after disarmament in Jan. 2002, reconstituted as political party; Leader Gen. ISSA HASSAN SESAY (acting); Sec.-Gen. PALLO BANGURA.

Sierra Leone People's Party (SLPP): 29 Rawdon St, Freetown; tel. and fax (22) 228222; e-mail sq-slpp@hotmail.com; internet www.slpp.ws; largest parl. party, following elections in Feb. 1996; Leader Alhaji AHMED TEJAN KABBAH; Sec.-Gen. Dr PRINCE A. HARDING.

Social Democratic Party (SDP): Leader ANDREW VICTOR LUNGAY.

United National People's Party (UNPP): Leader Dr JOHN KAREFA-SMART.

Young People's Party (YPP): 19 Lewis St, Freetown; tel. (22) 232907; e-mail info@yppsl.org; internet www.yppsl.org; f. 2002; Leader SYLVIA BLYDEN; Sec.-Gen. ABDUL RAHMAN YILLA.

Diplomatic Representation

EMBASSIES AND HIGH COMMISSIONS IN SIERRA LEONE

China, People's Republic: 29 Wilberforce Loop, Freetown; tel. (22) 231797; Ambassador YU WUZHEN.

Egypt: 174C Wilkinson Rd, POB 652, Freetown; tel. (22) 231245; fax (22) 272231; Ambassador TAREK ABDEL MONEM GHONEIM.

Gambia: 6 Wilberforce St, Freetown; tel. (22) 225191; High Commissioner CRISPIN GREY-JOHNSON.

Ghana: 16 Percival St, Freetown; tel. (22) 223461; fax (22) 227043; High Commissioner EBENEZER ANKU TSEDE.

Guinea: 6 Wilkinson Rd, Freetown; tel. (22) 223080; Ambassador MOHAMED LAMIN SOMPARE.

Lebanon: 22 Wilberforce St, POB 727, Freetown; tel. (22) 222513; Chargé d'affaires a.i. IBRAHIM ASSAF.

Liberia: 10 Motor Rd, Brookfields, POB 276, Freetown; tel. (22) 230991; Chargé d'affaires a.i. SAMUEL PETERS.

Nigeria: 37 Siaka Stevens St, Freetown; tel. (22) 224202; fax (22) 224219; High Commissioner POLYCAP AZIGE.

United Kingdom: 6 Spur Rd, Wilberforce, Freetown; tel. (22) 232563; fax (22) 228169; e-mail bhc@sierratel.sl; High Commissioner DAVID ALAN JONES.

USA: Walpole and Siaka Stevens Sts, Freetown; tel. (22) 226481; fax (22) 225471; Ambassador PETER R. CHAVEAS.

Judicial System

The Supreme Court
The ultimate court of appeal in both civil and criminal cases. In addition to its appellate jurisdiction, the Court has supervisory jurisdiction over all other courts and over any adjudicating authority in Sierra Leone, and also original jurisdiction in constitutional issues.

Chief Justice: DESMOND LUKE.

Supreme Court Justices: C. A. HARDING, AGNES AWUNOR-RENNER.

The Court of Appeal
The Court of Appeal has jurisdiction to hear and determine appeals from decisions of the High Court in both criminal and civil matters, and also from certain statutory tribunals. Appeals against its decisions may be made to the Supreme Court.

Justices of Appeal: S. C. E. WARNE, C. S. DAVIES, S. T. NAVO, M. S. TURAY, E. C. THOMPSON-DAVIS, M. O. TAJU-DEEN, M. O. ADOPHY, GEORGE GELAGA KING, Dr A. B. Y. TIMBO, VIRGINIA A. WRIGHT.

High Court
The High Court has unlimited original jurisdiction in all criminal and civil matters. It also has appellate jurisdiction against decisions of Magistrates' Courts.

Judges: FRANCIS C. GBOW, EBUN THOMAS, D. E. M. WILLIAMS, LAURA MARCUS-JONES, L. B. O. NYLANDER, A. M. B. TARAWALLIE, O. H. ALGHALLI, W. A. O. JOHNSON, N. D. ALHADI, R. J. BANKOLE THOMPSON, M. E. T. THOMPSON, C. J. W. ATERE-ROBERTS (acting).

Magistrates' Courts: In criminal cases the jurisdiction of the Magistrates' Courts is limited to summary cases and to preliminary investigations to determine whether a person charged with an offence should be committed for trial.

Local Courts have jurisdiction, according to native law and custom, in matters that are outside the jurisdiction of other courts.

Religion

A large proportion of the population holds animist beliefs, although there are significant numbers of Islamic and Christian adherents.

ISLAM
In 1990 Islamic adherents represented an estimated 30% of the total population.

Ahmadiyya Muslim Mission: 15 Bath St, Brookfields, POB 353, Freetown; Emir and Chief Missionary KHALIL A. MOBASHIR.

Kankaylay (Sierra Leone Muslim Men and Women's Association): 15 Blackhall Rd, Kissy, POB 1168, Freetown; tel. (22) 250931; f. 1972; 500,000 mems; Pres. Alhaji IBRAHIM BEMBA TURAY; Lady Pres. Haja ISATA KEBE; Vice-Pres. Haja SERAY SILLAH.

Sierra Leone Muslim Congress: POB 875, Freetown; Pres. Alhaji MUHAMMAD SANUSI MUSTAPHA.

CHRISTIANITY
Council of Churches in Sierra Leone: 4A King Harman Rd, Brookfields, POB 404, Freetown; tel. (22) 240568; fax (22) 241109; e-mail ccsl@sierratel.sl; f. 1924; 17 mem. churches; Pres. Rev. MOSES B. KHANU; Gen. Sec. ALIMAMY P. KOROMA.

The Anglican Communion
Anglicans in Sierra Leone are adherents of the Church of the Province of West Africa, comprising 12 dioceses, of which two are in Sierra Leone. The Archbishop of the Province is the Bishop of Koforidua, Ghana.

Bishop of Bo: Rt Rev. SAMUEL SAO GBONDA, MacRobert St, POB 21, Bo, Southern Province.

Bishop of Freetown: Rt Rev. JULIUS O. PRINCE LYNCH, Bishopscourt, Fourah Bay Rd, POB 537, Freetown.

Baptist Churches
Sierra Leone Baptist Convention: POB 64, Lunsar; Pres. Rev. JOSEPH S. MANS; Sec. Rev. N. T. DIXON.

The Nigerian Baptist Convention is also active.

Methodist Churches
Methodist Church Sierra Leone: Wesley House, George St, POB 64, Freetown; tel. (22) 222216; autonomous since 1967; Pres. of Conf. Rev. GERSHON F. H. ANDERSON; Sec. Rev. CHRISTIAN V. A. PEACOCK; 26,421 mems.

United Methodist Church: Freetown; Presiding Bishop T. S. BANGURA; 36,857 mems.

Other active Methodist bodies include the African Methodist Episcopal Church, the Wesleyan Church of Sierra Leone, the Countess of Huntingdon's Connexion and the West African Methodist Church.

The Roman Catholic Church
Sierra Leone comprises one archdiocese and two dioceses. At 31 December 2000 there were an estimated 71,623 adherents in the country, representing about 1.2% of the total population.

Inter-territorial Catholic Bishops' Conference of The Gambia and Sierra Leone
Santanno House, POB 893, Freetown; tel. (22) 228240; fax (22) 228252.

f. 1971; Pres. Most Rev. JOSEPH HENRY GANDA (Archbishop of Freetown and Bo).

Archbishop of Freetown and Bo: Most Rev. JOSEPH HENRY GANDA, Santanno House, POB 893, Freetown; tel. (22) 224590; fax (22) 224075; e-mail archbis@hotmail.com.

Other Christian Churches

The following are represented: the Christ Apostolic Church, the Church of the Lord (Aladura), the Evangelical Church, the Missionary Church of Africa, the Sierra Leone Church and the United Brethren in Christ.

AFRICAN RELIGIONS

There is a diverse range of beliefs, rites and practices, varying between ethnic and kinship groups.

The Press

DAILY

Daily Mail: 29–31 Rawdon St, POB 53, Freetown; tel. (22) 223191; f. 1931; state-owned; Editor AIAH MARTIN MONDEH; circ. 10,000.

PERIODICALS

African Crescent: 15 Bath St, POB 353, Brookfields, Freetown; Editor MAULANA-KHALIL A. MOBASHIR.

The Catalyst: Christian Literature Crusade Bookshop, 35 Circular Rd, POB 1465, Freetown; tel. (22) 224382; Editor Dr LEOPOLD FOULLAH.

Concord Times: 139 Pademba Rd, Freetown; 3 a week; Editor DOROTHY GORDON.

Leonean Sun: 49 Main Rd, Wellington, Freetown; tel. (22) 223363; f. 1974; monthly; Editor ROWLAND MARTYN.

Liberty Voice: 139 Pademba Rd, Freetown; tel. (22) 242100; Editor A. MAHDIEU SAVAGE.

New Breed: Freetown; weekly; independent; Man. Editor (vacant).

New Citizen: 5 Hanna Benka-Coker St, Freetown; tel. (22) 241795; Editor I. BEN KARGBO.

The New Globe: 49 Bathurst St, Freetown; tel. (22) 228245; weekly; Man. Editor SAM TUMOE; circ. 4,000.

The New Shaft: 60 Old Railway Line, Brookfields, Freetown; tel. (22) 241093; 2 a week; independent; Editor FRANKLIN BUNTING-DAVIES; circ. 10,000.

The Pool Newspaper: 1 Short St, 5th Floor, Freetown; tel. and fax (22) 220102; e-mail pool@justice.com; internet www.poolnewspaper .tripod.com; f. 1992; 3 a week; independent; Man. Dir CHERNOR OJUKU SESAY; circ. 3,000.

Progress: 1 Short St, Freetown; tel. (22) 223588; weekly; independent; Editor FODE KANDEH; circ. 7,000.

Sierra Leone Chamber of Commerce Journal: Sierra Leone Chamber of Commerce, Industry and Agriculture, Guma Bldg, 5th Floor, Lamina Sankoh St, POB 502, Freetown; tel. (22) 226305; fax (22) 228005; monthly.

Unity Now: 82 Pademba Rd, Freetown; tel. (22) 227466; Editor FRANK KPOSOWA.

The Vision: 60 Old Railway Line, Brookfields; tel. (22) 241273; Editor SIAKA MASSAQUOI.

Weekend Spark: 7 Lamina Sankoh St, Freetown; tel. (22) 223397; f. 1983; weekly; independent; Editor ROWLAND MARTYN; circ. 20,000.

Weekly Democrat: Freetown; Editor JON FORAY.

NEWS AGENCY

Sierra Leone News Agency (SLENA): 15 Wallace Johnson St, PMB 445, Freetown; tel. (22) 224921; fax (22) 224439; f. 1980; Man. Dir ABDUL KARIM JALLOH (acting).

Publishers

Njala University Publishing Centre: Njala University College, PMB, Freetown; science and technology, university textbooks.

Sierra Leone University Press: Fourah Bay College, POB 87, Freetown; tel. (22) 22491; fax (22) 224439; f. 1965; biography, history, Africana, religion, social science, university textbooks; Chair. Prof. ERNEST H. WRIGHT.

United Christian Council Literature Bureau: Bunumbu Press, POB 28, Bo; tel. (32) 462; books in Mende, Temne, Susu; Man. Dir ROBERT SAM-KPAKRA.

Broadcasting and Communications

TELECOMMUNICATIONS

Sierra Leone Telecommunications Co (SIERRATEL): 7 Wallace Johnson St, POB 80, Freetown; tel. (22) 222804; fax (22) 224439.

BROADCASTING

Sierra Leone Broadcasting Service: New England, Freetown; tel. (22) 240403; f. 1934; state-controlled; programmes mainly in English and the four main Sierra Leonean vernaculars, Mende, Limba, Temne and Krio; weekly broadcast in French; television service established 1963; Dir-Gen. JEANA BANDATOMO.

Finance

(cap. = capital; res = reserves; dep. = deposits; m. = million; brs = branches; amounts in leones)

BANKING

Central Bank

Bank of Sierra Leone: Siaka Stevens St, POB 30, Freetown; tel. (22) 226501; fax (22) 224764; e-mail coposafe@sierratel.sl; f. 1964; cap. and res 50,899.6m., dep. 28,621.5m. (Dec. 2000); Gov. SANPHA KOROMA; Dep. Gov. MELVIN TUCKER; 1 br.

Other Banks

First Merchant Bank of Sierra Leone: Sparta Bldg, 12 Wilberforce St, Freetown; tel. (22) 228493; fax (22) 228318; e-mail fmb@ sierratel.sl; cap. 3,313.7m., total assets 4,434.4m. (Dec. 1999); Chair. ADEKOYA OTUSANYA.

National Development Bank Ltd: Leone House, 6th Floor, 21–23 Siaka Stevens St, Freetown; tel. (22) 226792; fax (22) 224468; f. 1968; 99% state-owned; provides medium- and long-term finance and tech. assistance to devt-orientated enterprises; cap. 1,604.3m., total assets 1,844.5m. (Jan. 1998); Chair. MURRAY E. S. LAMIN; Man. Dir MOHAMED M. TURAY; 3 brs.

Rokel Commercial Bank of Sierra Leone Ltd: 25–27 Siaka Stevens St, POB 12, Freetown; tel. (22) 222501; fax (22) 222563; e-mail rokelsl@sierratel.sl; f. 1971; cap. 1,119.7m., res 11,955.7m., dep. 46,027.1m. (Dec. 2001); 51% govt-owned; Chair. AUGUSTUS D. A. M'CORMACK; Man. Dir CHRISTOPHER J. WALTON; 6 brs.

Sierra Leone Commercial Bank Ltd: 29–31 Siaka Stevens St, Freetown; tel. (22) 225264; fax (22) 225292; e-mail slcb@sierratel.sl; f. 1973; state-owned; cap. 600m., res 10,428.0m., dep. 48,799.6m. (Dec. 2000); Chair. I. I. MAY-PARKER; Man. Dir A. KAKAY; 7 brs.

Standard Chartered Bank Sierra Leone Ltd: 9 and 11 Lightfoot-Boston St, POB 1155, Freetown; tel. (22) 225022; fax (22) 225760; e-mail scbsl@sierratel.sl; f. 1971; cap. 813m., total assets 60,812m. (Dec. 2000); Chair. LLOYD A. DURING; Man. Dir SIMON J. MILLETT; 12 brs.

Union Trust Bank Ltd: Lightfoot Boston St, PMB 1237, Freetown; tel. (22) 226954; fax (22) 226214; e-mail utb@sierratel.sl; fmrly Meridien BIAO Bank Sierra Leone Ltd; adopted present name in 1995; cap. 672.4m., total assets 12,922.8m. (Dec. 1999); Chair. S. B. NICOL-COLE; Man. Dir J. D. OKRAFO-SMART.

INSURANCE

Aureol Insurance Co Ltd: Kissy House, 54 Siaka Stevens St, POB 647, Freetown; tel. (22) 223435; fax (22) 229336; f. 1987; Chair. LLOYD A. DURING; Man. Dir S. G. BENJAMIN.

National Insurance Co Ltd: 18–20 Walpole St, PMB 84, Freetown; tel. (22) 224328; fax (22) 226097; e-mail nic@sierratel.sl; f. 1972; state-owned; Chair. S. MACAULEY; CEO A. N. YASKEY.

New India Assurance Co Ltd: 18 Wilberforce St, POB 340, Freetown; tel. (22) 226453; fax (22) 222494; Man. Dir A. CHOPRA.

Reliance Insurance Trust Corpn Ltd: 24 Siaka Stevens St, Freetown; tel. (22) 225115; fax (22) 228051; f. 1985; Chair. MOHAMED B. COLE; Man. Dir ALICE M. ONOMAKE.

Sierra Leone Insurance Co Ltd: 31 Lightfoot Boston St, POB 836, Freetown; tel. (22) 224920; fax (22) 222115; Man. Dir IDRISSE YILLE.

Trade and Industry

GOVERNMENT AGENCY

Government Gold and Diamond Office (GGDO): c/o Bank of Sierra Leone, Siaka Stevens St, Freetown; tel. (22) 222600; fax (22) 229064; f. 1985; govt regulatory agency for diamonds and gold; combats illicit trade; Chair. Alhaji M. S. DEEN.

CHAMBER OF COMMERCE

Sierra Leone Chamber of Commerce, Industry and Agriculture: Guma Bldg, 5th Floor, Lamina Sankoh St, POB 502, Freetown; tel. (22) 226305; fax (22) 228005; f. 1961; 215 mems; Pres. Alhaji MOHAMED MUSA KING.

TRADE AND INDUSTRIAL ASSOCIATIONS

Sierra Leone Export Development and Investment Corpn (SLEDIC): 18–20 Walpole St, PMB 6, Freetown; tel. (22) 227604; fax (22) 229097; e-mail sledic@sierratel.sl; f. 1993; Man. Dir CHRIS JASABE.

Small-Medium Scale Businesses Association (Sierra Leone): O.A.U. Drive, Tower Hill, PMB 575, Freetown; tel. (22) 222617; fax (22) 224439; Dir ABU CONTEH.

EMPLOYERS' ORGANIZATIONS

Sierra Leone Employers' Federation: POB 562, Freetown; Chair. AMADU B. NDOEKA; Exec. Officer L. E. JOHNSON.

Sierra Leone Chamber of Mines: POB 456, Freetown; tel. (22) 226082; f. 1965; mems comprise the principal mining concerns; Pres. D. J. S. FRASER; Exec. Officer N. H. T. BOSTON.

UTILITIES

Electricity

Sierra Leone Electricity Corpn: Freetown; supplies all electricity in Sierra Leone.

Water

Guma Valley Water Co: Guma Bldg, 13/14 Lamina Sankoh St, POB 700, Freetown; tel. 25887; f. 1961; responsible for all existing water supplies in Freetown and surrounding villages, including the Guma dam and associated works.

TRADE UNIONS

Artisans', Ministry of Works Employees' and General Workers' Union: 4 Pultney St, Freetown; f. 1946; 14,500 mems; Pres. IBRAHIM LANGLEY; Gen. Sec. TEJAN A. KASSIM.

Sierra Leone Labour Congress: 35 Wallace Johnson St, POB 1333, Freetown; tel. (22) 226869; f. 1966; c. 51,000 mems in 19 affiliated unions; Pres. H. M. BARRIE; Sec.-Gen. KANDEH YILLA.

Principal affiliated unions:

Clerical, Mercantile and General Workers' Union: 35 Wallace Johnson St, Freetown; f. 1945; 3,600 mems; Pres. M. D. BENJAMIN; Gen. Sec. M. B. WILLIAMS.

Sierra Leone Association of Journalists: Freetown; Pres. SIAKA MASSAQUOI.

Sierra Leone Dockworkers' Union: 165 Fourah Bay Rd, Freetown; f. 1962; 2,650 mems; Pres. D. F. KANU; Gen. Sec. A. C. CONTEH.

Sierra Leone Motor Drivers' Union: 10 Charlotte St, Freetown; f. 1960; 1,900 mems; Pres. A. W. HASSAN; Gen. Sec. ALPHA KAMARA.

Sierra Leone Teachers' Union: Regaland House, Lowcost Step —Kissy, POB 477, Freetown; f. 1951; 18,500 mems; Pres. FESTUS E. MINAH; Sec.-Gen. A. O. TIMBO.

Sierra Leone Transport, Agricultural and General Workers' Union: 4 Pultney St, Freetown; f. 1946; 1,600 mems; Pres. S. O. SAWYERR-MANLEY; Gen. Sec. S. D. KARGBO.

United Mineworkers' Union: 35 Wallace Johnson St, Freetown; f. 1944; 6,500 mems; Pres. H. M. BARRIE; Gen. Sec. S. D. GBENDA.

Also affiliated to the Sierra Leone Labour Congress: **General Construction Workers' Union**, **Municipal and Local Government Employees' Union**, **Sierra Leone National Seamen's Union**.

Transport

RAILWAYS

There are no passenger railways in Sierra Leone.

Marampa Mineral Railway: Delco House, POB 735, Freetown; tel. (22) 222556; 84 km of track linking iron ore mines at Marampa (inactive since 1985) with Pepel port; Gen. Man. SYL KHANU.

ROADS

In 1999 there were an estimated 11,330 km of classified roads, including 4,000 km of main roads and 4,152 km of secondary roads; about 895 km of the total network was paved. In 1993 the Government announced a seven-year road rehabilitation programme, which, at an estimated cost of US $100m., was to be financed by the World Bank.

Sierra Leone Road Transport Corpn: Blackhall Rd, POB 1008, Freetown; tel. (22) 250442; fax (22) 250000; f. 1965; state-owned; operates transport services throughout the country; Gen. Man. DANIEL R. W. FAUX.

INLAND WATERWAYS

Established routes for launches, which include the coastal routes from Freetown northward to the Great and Little Scarcies rivers and southward to Bonthe, total almost 800 km. Although some of the upper reaches of the rivers are navigable only between July and September, there is a considerable volume of river traffic.

SHIPPING

Freetown, the principal port, has full facilities for ocean-going vessels.

Sierra Leone National Shipping Co Ltd: 45 Cline St, POB 935, Freetown; tel. (22) 250881; fax (22) 223222; e-mail nsc@sierratel.sl; f. 1972; state-owned; shipping, clearing and forwarding agency; representatives for foreign lines; Chair. K. A. I. FODAY.

Sierra Leone Ports Authority: Queen Elizabeth II Quay, PMB 386, Cline Town, Freetown; tel. (22) 226480; fax (22) 226443; f. 1965; parastatal body, supervised by the Ministry of Transport and Communications; operates the port of Freetown; Gen. Man. Capt. P. E. M. KEMOKAI.

Sierra Leone Shipping Agencies Ltd: Deep Water Quay, Clinetown, POB 74, Freetown; tel. (22) 250882; fax (22) 250400; f. 1949; Man. Dir I. HEDEMANN.

Silver Star Shipping Agency Ltd: PMB 1023, Freetown; tel. (22) 221035; fax (22) 226653; e-mail silver2_star@hotmail.com; Dir Capt. H. A. BLOOMER.

CIVIL AVIATION

There is an international airport at Lungi.

Directorate of Civil Aviation: Dept of Transport and Communications, Ministerial Bldg, 5th Floor, George St, Freetown; tel. (22) 222106; Dir T. T. A. VANDY.

Sierra National Airlines: Leone House, 25 Pultney St, POB 285, Freetown; tel. (22) 222075; fax (22) 222026; e-mail alpha@kanu; f. 1982; state-owned; operates domestic and regional services, and a weekly flight to Paris, France; operations resumed, following civil conflict, in Nov. 2000; Chair. TAMBA MATTURI; Man. Dir JOSEPH KAMANDA.

Tourism

The main attractions for tourists are the coastline, the mountains and the game reserves. However, civil conflict throughout most of the 1990s effectively suspended tourist activity. In 2000, according to preliminary figures, tourist arrivals recovered slightly, to 10,000, compared with 6,000 in 1999. Receipts from tourism totalled US $12m. in 2000.

National Tourist Board: Cape Sierra Hotel, Room 100, Aberdeen Hill, POB 1435, Freetown; tel. (22) 272520; fax (22) 272197; e-mail ntb@sierratel.com; f. 1990; Gen. Man. CECIL J. WILLIAMS.

SINGAPORE

Introductory Survey

Location, Climate, Language, Religion, Flag, Capital

The Republic of Singapore lies in South-East Asia. The country comprises one main island and some 64 offshore islands, situated approximately 137 km (85 miles) north of the Equator, off the southernmost tip of the Malay Peninsula, to which it is linked by a causeway. The climate is equatorial, with a uniformly high daily and annual temperature varying between 24°C and 27°C (75°F–80°F). Relative humidity is high (often exceeding 90%), and the average annual rainfall is 235 cm (93 ins). There are four official languages—Malay (the national language), Chinese (Mandarin), Tamil and English. The language of administration is English. Chinese dialects were spoken as a first language by 24% of the population in 2000. The principal religions are Daoism, Buddhism, Islam, Christianity and Hinduism. The national flag (proportions 2 by 3) has two equal horizontal stripes of red and white, with a white crescent moon and five white stars, arranged in a pentagram, in the upper hoist. The capital is Singapore City.

Recent History

In 1826 the East India Company formed the Straits Settlements by the union of Singapore and the dependencies of Penang and Malacca on the Malay Peninsula. They came under British rule in 1867 as a crown colony. Singapore was occupied by Japan for three years during the Second World War. At the end of the war, following Japan's defeat, Singapore was governed by a British military administration. When civil rule was restored in 1946, Singapore was detached from the other Straits Settlements and became a separate crown colony. A new Constitution, adopted in February 1955, introduced some measure of self-government, and in June 1959 the state achieved complete internal self-government, with Lee Kuan Yew as Prime Minister. The Federation of Malaysia came into being in September 1963, with Singapore as a constituent state. On 9 August 1965, following irreconcilable differences with the central Government in Malaysia, Singapore seceded from the federation and became an independent country. Singapore joined the UN in September and became a member of the Commonwealth in October. In December Singapore was proclaimed a republic, with a President as constitutional Head of State. In May 1973 the last major ties with Malaysia, concerning currency and finance, were renounced. In September 1972 Lee Kuan Yew's ruling People's Action Party (PAP) won all 65 parliamentary seats in a general election.

After independence the Government supported a strong US military presence in South-East Asia. However, with the collapse of US influence in the area during 1974–1975, Singapore adopted a conciliatory attitude towards the People's Republic of China and its communist neighbours. The Government called for the removal of foreign bases from member states of the Association of South East Asian Nations (ASEAN, see p. 146), and advocated a policy of neutrality. Singapore sought to consolidate its trade links with China, although diplomatic relations were not established until 1982.

At general elections in December 1976 and again in December 1980, the PAP won all 69 seats in the enlarged Parliament. The PAP's monopoly ended in October 1981, however, when the Secretary-General of the opposition Workers' Party, J. B. Jeyaretnam, won a by-election. This posed no direct threat, but, in order to reassert its authority, the Government increased its control over trade unions and restructured the ownership of major newspapers. The PAP was again returned to power in December 1984 with a large majority in Parliament (now enlarged to 79 seats), but the party lost two seats to opposition parties, and its share of the total votes was reduced to 62.9% from 75% in 1980. A constitutional amendment approved in July 1984 provided for up to three 'non-constituency' parliamentary seats for the opposition (with restricted voting rights) if none was won in the election. One extra seat was subsequently offered to the losing opposition candidate with the highest percentage of votes. However, this seat was refused by the Workers' Party in January 1985. In March the state President, Devan Nair, resigned. A new President, Wee Kim Wee (hitherto

the Chairman of the Singapore Broadcasting Corporation), was elected by Parliament in August.

During 1986 the Government exhibited signs of increasing intolerance towards its critics. In August amendments to the Parliament (Privileges, Immunities and Powers) Act were hurriedly adopted, enabling Parliament to fine, expel or imprison members who were deemed to have abused their parliamentary privileges. In the same month Parliament also approved a Newspaper and Printing Presses (Amendment) Act, which empowered the Government to restrict the distribution of foreign publications deemed to be interfering in domestic political affairs; the circulation of several foreign periodicals was subsequently restricted.

In November 1986 Jeyaretnam (one of the two opposition members of Parliament) was sentenced to one month's imprisonment and fined S $5,000 (enough, according to the Constitution, to deprive him of his parliamentary seat and prevent him from standing for election for five years), when the Supreme Court upheld a conviction for perjury in connection with bankruptcy proceedings brought against the Workers' Party four years previously. In February 1987 Jeyaretnam was also fined by a parliamentary committee for abuse of privilege, having made allegations of government interference in the judiciary; further fines were imposed on him for publishing 'distorted' accounts of an earlier hearing of the committee, and (in May) for alleged contempt of Parliament and abuse of parliamentary privilege. In October Jeyaretnam's removal from the Law Society register was ordered by a three-judge court. An appeal to the Judicial Committee of the Privy Council in the United Kingdom (then the highest court of appeal for Singapore) resulted, in October 1988, in his reinstatement as a practising lawyer. During the course of the appeal, investigations into Jeyaretnam's previous convictions found that they had been 'fatally flawed'. However, since the criminal case had been considered in the District Court, where there was no right of appeal to the Privy Council, the original convictions prevented Jeyaretnam from re-entering Parliament without a presidential pardon. This was refused by Wee Kim Wee in May 1989.

In May and June 1987 the Government detained 22 people (including 10 Roman Catholic church workers and four members of the Workers' Party) without trial, under the Internal Security Act, for alleged involvement in a 'Marxist conspiracy' to subvert state organizations. The arrests were denounced by Jeyaretnam, who claimed that the Government wished to intimidate Singaporeans so that they would not support opposition parties. In November the Government was also criticized by international human rights groups, including Amnesty International, for its refusal to present evidence of such a conspiracy in court. By December most of the alleged conspirators had been released, but eight of them were rearrested in April 1988, after complaining that they had been tortured while in detention. Four prisoners were released by June, and in December a further four detainees were released in accordance with a ruling by the Court of Appeal, based on a fault in their detention orders. They were immediately rearrested. The trial had, however, established a precedent for the judicial review of cases brought under the Internal Security Act, including the acceptability to the courts of evidence used in warrants for the arrest of suspects. In January 1989 Parliament approved legislation ensuring that the judiciary could examine such detentions only on technical grounds, and abolishing the right of appeal to the Privy Council in cases brought under the Internal Security Act. In March three detainees were released. The two remaining prisoners (of the original 22) remained in detention until June 1990.

A general election was held in September 1988. The electoral system was altered so that 39 of the existing 79 constituencies were replaced by 13 'group representation constituencies', to be contested by teams of three representatives for each party, at least one of whom was to be a member of an ethnic minority (i.e. non-Chinese). The declared aim was to ensure the presence of racial minorities in Parliament; in practice, however, opposition parties with few resources were handicapped by the difficulty of presenting three candidates. The PAP won 80 of the elective seats (which now totalled 81); one was taken by the leader of the Singapore Democratic Party (SDP), Chiam See Tong. Two 'non-constituency' seats were offered to Francis Seow (Workers' Party) and Lee Siew Choh (Socialist Front). In December, however, while Seow (who had already been detained in May under the Internal Security Act for organizing a meeting between a US diplomat and lawyers critical of the Government) was undergoing medical treatment in the USA, he was convicted *in absentia* for tax evasion and fined S $19,000: he was thus debarred from taking his seat in Parliament.

In January 1989 Lee began his eighth term as Prime Minister, and announced that he would retire from the premiership before the expiry of the term. This announcement was followed by a statement from the First Deputy Prime Minister, Goh Chok Tong (Lee's chosen successor), that Lee was adopting a secondary and more advisory role in the government of the country. In August Parliament unanimously re-elected Wee Kim Wee for a further four-year term as President. In early 1990 Parliament approved legislation enabling the Government to nominate as many as six unelected MPs. The politically-neutral nominated MPs would be appointed for two years, and would be able to vote on all legislative proposals except those concerning financial and constitutional affairs.

On 28 November 1990 Lee was duly replaced as Prime Minister by Goh Chok Tong. Lee remained in the Cabinet as Senior Minister in the Prime Minister's Office, and retained the position of Secretary-General of the PAP, while Lee's son, Brig.-Gen. Lee Hsien Loong, was appointed as a Deputy Prime Minister.

In January 1991 the Constitution was amended to provide for a popularly-elected presidency with extensive powers of veto on proposed financial legislation, a role as final arbiter in cases of detention for reasons of national security, and influence in civil and military appointments. The changes to the (hitherto highly ceremonial) functions of the President were initially proposed by Lee in 1984, and were criticized by members of opposition parties as being intended to accommodate the former Prime Minister. Under the amendment, Wee Kim Wee was to continue in office until October 1993. Legislation empowering him with the authority of an elected president took effect from 30 November 1991. Candidates for the presidency were limited to those who had held the post of a minister, chief justice or senior civil servant or were at the head of a large company. The candidates were to be scrutinized by a new presidential election committee, which was to comprise the head of the Society of Accountants, the Chairman of the Public Service Commission and a member of the Presidential Council of Human Rights. The last two officials were appointed by the Government, prompting fears that the selected candidates would be those favoured by the PAP. The constitutional amendment also included a clause increasing the number of candidates required to contest a 'group representation constituency' in a general election to a minimum of three and a maximum of four, one of whom was to be a member of an ethnic minority.

In early 1991 the Government promoted the acceptance of five 'shared values', based on Confucian philosophy, as the basis of a national ideology. Critics alleged that the ideology would be used to reinforce support for the PAP and to obviate opposition challenges. Goh attempted, in principle, to introduce a more 'open', consultative form of government. He instituted an extensive programme of community visits to assess popular opinion, showing solicitude for the views of the minority Malay and Indian communities. Although film censorship was relaxed, the Internal Security Act and restrictions on the foreign press remained in force. In early August, seeking a popular mandate for his style of government, Goh announced that there would be a general election at the end of the month. Under a plan conceived by Chiam, the opposition parties contested only 40 of the 81 seats, thus guaranteeing an absolute majority for the incumbent PAP. Chiam issued an appeal to the electorate to take the opportunity to elect a strong opposition. Goh indicated that a failure to receive a popular endorsement would result in a return to a more authoritarian and paternalistic form of government. At the election, held on 31 August, the PAP's share of the vote was 61.0% (compared with 63.2% in 1988), and the party won 77 seats (compared with 80 in 1988). Chiam's SDP secured three seats, and the Workers' Party one seat. Jeyaretnam was unable to contest the election, as his disqualification remained in force until the beginning of November 1991. In response to Jeyaretnam's accusations that he had been deliberately excluded from the election, and also because the election

schedule had prevented the PAP from presenting enough new candidates, Goh had announced, prior to the polls, that he would organize by-elections within 12–18 months of the general election.

In October 1991 Seow, who had remained in exile in the USA since 1988, was convicted *in absentia* of a further 60 offences involving tax evasion, rendering him ineligible to contest any potential by-election. Later that month Jeyaretnam paid S $392,838 in legal costs to Lee, thus avoiding bankruptcy, which would have prevented his candidacy. Lee had instituted a successful defamation suit against Jeyaretnam in 1990, over remarks made by Jeyaretnam at a 1988 election rally.

Following the general election, Lee, who had temporarily withdrawn from public attention after Goh's accession to the premiership, resumed a prominent role in domestic politics. He attributed the decline in PAP support to neglect of the Mandarin-educated ethnic Chinese majority, and advocated a greater emphasis on Chinese culture and language. In April 1991 Goh announced that the level of electoral support among residents would be one of the criteria used to determine the order in which refurbishments would be undertaken in public housing estates. Since about 86% of Singaporeans lived in public housing, this was widely interpreted as a warning against voting for the opposition in the forthcoming by-elections.

Prior to the convening of Parliament in September 1992 the Government appointed the maximum of six nominated MPs. This was widely regarded as an attempt to discourage support for opposition candidates in the impending by-elections. In October the implementation of legislation prohibiting MPs from using the ground floors of public housing blocks as office space adversely affected all four opposition MPs, who, because of a shortage of party funds, were unable to afford commercial rents.

In November 1992 Goh announced to the Central Executive Committee of the PAP that the renewal of national leadership was the party's most urgent consideration. This statement was followed two days later by the public disclosure that both Deputy Prime Ministers, Lee Hsien Loong and Ong Teng Cheong, had been diagnosed as suffering from cancer. The revelation strengthened Goh's position as Prime Minister, since many had previously regarded his incumbency as an interim arrangement prior to Lee Hsien Loong's assumption of the premiership. In December Goh was unanimously elected to replace Lee Kuan Yew (who proposed his candidacy) as Secretary-General of the PAP.

In December 1992 Goh resigned his parliamentary seat (which formed part of a four-member 'group representation constituency') in order to contest a by-election. Jeyaretnam was unable to contest the by-election as only three candidates from the Workers' Party registered with the authorities. The results of the by-election were regarded as an endorsement of Goh's leadership, as the four PAP candidates received 72.9% of the votes cast, while the opposition SDP secured 24.5%.

In March 1993 Chee Soon Juan, who contested the December by-election as a candidate for the SDP, was dismissed from his post as a lecturer at the National University of Singapore for 'dishonest conduct'. The Government denied that the dismissal was politically motivated, and defamation proceedings were initiated by university officials against Chee. In June, following a rejection by the SDP Central Committee of a motion of censure proposed by Chiam against Chee for bringing the party into disrepute, Chiam resigned as Secretary-General of the party. Chee replaced him as acting Secretary-General, pending party elections in early 1995. In August 1993 the SDP expelled Chiam for alleged indiscipline; however, a High Court ruling in December declared the expulsion 'illegal and invalid'. (This enabled Chiam to retain his seat in Parliament: under the Constitution a member of the legislature is obliged to relinquish his seat if he resigns or is expelled from the party he has been elected to represent.) The following month, under a judicial ruling, a 'breakaway' central executive committee, formed in 1993 by a faction of the SDP that remained loyal to Chiam, was declared void. Chee subsequently published a book entitled *Dare to Change*, which demanded greater democracy and was adopted as official party policy by the SDP in June 1994. Chee was formally elected Secretary-General of the SDP in January 1995.

Meanwhile, in August 1993 Ong Teng Cheong was elected President with 58.7% of the votes cast. Contrary to expectation, however, the only other candidate, Chua Kim Yeow, a former government official, who adopted an apolitical position, secured a substantial proportion (41.3%) of the vote. The candidacies of both Jeyaretnam and Tan Soo Phuan, another member of the

Workers' Party, were rejected by the Presidential Election Committee on the grounds that they were unsuitable 'in regard to integrity, good character and reputation'.

In July 1995 Lee Kuan Yew, Lee Hsien Loong and Goh were awarded record damages by the Supreme Court in Singapore following a successful defamation suit, in January, against the US-owned *International Herald Tribune*. The newspaper had published an article in the previous year implying that Lee Hsien Loong's position had been attained through nepotism and that the Singapore Government suppressed democratic activity by using a compliant judiciary to bankrupt political opponents through defamation suits. Lee revived the libel suit in March 1996, and in April was awarded further damages for which the author of the article in question was to be liable. In November 1995 Lee Kuan Yew received further damages from the newspaper following its publication of an article referring to intolerant regimes in the region.

In late October 1996 Parliament approved amendments to the Constitution that redefined the role of the President and partially reformed the voting system. The President's powers were restricted by new provisions empowering the Government to call a referendum if the President vetoed certain constitutional amendments, and also enabling Parliament to overturn (by a two-thirds' majority) a presidential veto on key civil service appointments. A further amendment expanded the number of 'group representation constituencies' and increased the maximum number of group candidates from four to six. The electoral reforms were opposed by the opposition parties on the grounds that the amendments favoured large, well-established parties such as the PAP, while smaller parties would have difficulty both in finding and funding large numbers of candidates.

In November 1996 the parliamentary privileges committee found Chee guilty of contempt, fining him S $25,000, in respect of a document submitted to Parliament earlier in the year in which it was stated that government subsidies for health-care had decreased from 40% in 1970 to 5% in 1990: the latter statistic was actually 25%. Chee claimed that the published figure was the result of a typing error. Three of his party colleagues received lesser fines, having been found to have attempted to mislead Parliament.

Prior to the general election, which took place on 2 January 1997, the success of the PAP was predetermined by the opposition parties' decision to contest only 36 of the 83 seats. Nevertheless, the PAP conducted a rigorous campaign in an effort to ensure that the party received two-thirds of the total votes cast, a margin regarded as sufficient endorsement of Goh and his administration. During the campaign, it was again announced that public housing improvements would be prioritized according to levels of electoral support for the PAP. The party secured a resounding victory, winning 65% of the votes and 81 seats (including all nine single-member constituencies). The remaining two elective seats were won by Chiam See Tong of the Singapore People's Party (for the fourth time, although previously he had been elected as a representative of the SDP) and Low Thia Khiang of the Workers' Party (for a second time). The Workers' Party, as the opposition party with the most votes but less than three seats, was also allocated a non-constituency seat; this was accepted by Jeyaretnam. The SDP lost the three seats it had previously held.

Seemingly a particular focus for attack by the PAP during the election campaign was Tang Liang Hong, a candidate of the Workers' Party. The PAP accused Tang of being anti-Christian, of promoting Chinese interests over those of Singapore's ethnic minorities and of attempting to foment discontent amongst the ethnic Chinese community. Tang, standing in the same 'group representation constituency' as Jeyaretnam, failed to secure election. (Goh, unopposed in a single-member constituency, personally campaigned against Tang in the group constituency.) Tang's public rebuttal of the accusations of the PAP leaders prompted them to issue writs against him for defamation. Tang fled to Malaysia in January 1997, claiming to have received anonymous death threats. Tang was found guilty of defamation by the High Court in March, as he failed to attend the trial and provide a defence, and was ordered in May to pay a record sum of S $8m. in libel damages to Goh and 10 senior PAP leaders. Tang appealed against the judgment in September on the grounds that it contained legal errors and that the cases had been brought for political motives. The Court of Appeal ruled in November that the damages awarded against Tang were disproportionate to the injury caused, and reduced the sum to S $4.53m. In February 1998, despite this concession, Tang,

against whom a warrant for arrest had been issued on 33 counts of tax evasion, was declared bankrupt.

Goh and 10 senior PAP members also sued Jeyaretnam for alleged defamation following remarks made at an election rally concerning two police reports submitted by Tang accusing the PAP leadership of criminal conspiracy and lying. In September 1997 Jeyaretnam was ordered to pay damages of S $20,000; the award was, however, only one-tenth of the amount sought by the PAP leadership, and the judge, who criticized Goh's lawyers for their handling of the case, ordered that Jeyaretnam pay only 60% of the legal costs. During the trial Goh admitted under cross-examination that he had authorized the unofficial disclosure of the police reports to the press, and it was put to him that the legal suits were an attempt to bankrupt Jeyaretnam and thus disqualify him from Parliament. However, the Court of Appeal dismissed an appeal by Jeyaretnam in July 1998, increasing the damages to S $100,000, and awarding full costs against him. It was subsequently agreed, however, that Jeyaretnam would be permitted to pay the damages in five instalments, thereby enabling him to avoid bankruptcy proceedings and to continue as a legislator.

On 26 November 1998 the Government revoked the remaining restrictions on the activities of the political activist Chia Thye Poh. Chia had been arrested in 1966, imprisoned for more than 22 years without trial under the Internal Security Act, confined to a fortress on an island off the coast of Singapore for a further three years, then permitted to reside in Singapore from 1992, although prohibited from taking part in any political activity. Despite this concession to Chia, government suppression of expressions of opposition continued. In January 1999 Chee was charged twice under the Public Entertainment Act for making unlicensed public speeches in December 1998 and January 1999. Chee had deliberately refused to apply for licences to make the two public speeches, in which he criticized government policy, on the grounds that freedom of expression was guaranteed under the Constitution. During the first trial Chee was represented by Jeyaretnam, who attempted to expose the alleged use of the above Act to restrict political opposition. However, Chee was found guilty at the beginning of February, and was sentenced to seven days' imprisonment, owing to his refusal to pay a fine of S $1,400. Following his release, Chee appeared in court for a second time in February, and was sentenced, with the Assistant Secretary-General of the SDP, Wong Hong Toy, who had reportedly assisted Chee at the speech, to 12 days' imprisonment after Chee and Wong refused to pay respective fines of S $2,500 and S $2,400. The level of the fines automatically disqualified both men from seeking political office for five years; however, following an appeal, the two had their fines reduced to S $1,900 each, below the level that would have rendered them ineligible to stand for election. For its part, the Government maintained that opposition politicians had adequate opportunity to expound their views in Parliament or in the media (although in February 1998 the Government had banned political parties from producing videos and from promoting their opinions on television). In April 1999 it was reported that, subsequent to his release from prison after serving his second term of imprisonment, Chee had been fined S $600 for illegal sales of a book he had produced on Asian opposition leaders. In March members of the PAP filed a petition to close the Workers' Party, owing to its inability to pay more than S $280,000 in damages and costs awarded against it in a defamation case. The party's closure would force the resignation of its two parliamentary representatives. In May it was reported that the party had lost a judicial appeal against the award.

On 5 May 2000 Jeyaretnam was declared bankrupt by the High Court after he failed to make payments of S $30,000 in libel damages arising from a lawsuit concerning an article that appeared in the Workers' Party newspaper, *The Hammer*, in 1995. The bankruptcy ruling would have disqualified Jeyaretnam from serving in Parliament, but on 11 May the orders were set aside after the outstanding debt was paid, and he was authorized to retain his non-constituency seat. In January 2001, however, Jeyaretnam was once again declared bankrupt by the High Court, with a S $235,000 debt as a result of a defamation claim against a Workers' Party newsletter. The appeal against the bankruptcy ruling was dismissed in February. In May Jeyaretnam was replaced as Secretary-General of the Workers' Party by Low Thia Khiang. In July he finally lost his seat in Parliament when the Court of Appeals confirmed that it would not overturn the bankruptcy ruling against him.

Meanwhile, legislation introduced in May 1997 increased the number of nominated MPs from six to nine; the Constitution was amended accordingly in September. During the year nine Community Development Councils (CDCs) were formed. The CDCs encompassed all constituencies, including the two opposition wards, which, despite election campaign threats, were to receive the same services as other constituencies, although opposition representatives would not be permitted to stand as council chairmen and would have no power to disburse funds.

During 1999 Lee Hsien Loong, who had been appointed Chairman of the Monetary Authority of Singapore in December 1997, began to assume a more prominent political role. Goh acknowledged that Lee's succession to the premiership was likely to take place after the next election. George Yeo, hitherto the Minister of Information and the Arts, also gained prominence following his promotion to the trade and industry portfolio in a minor cabinet reorganization in June 1999. Singapore's second presidential election was scheduled to take place in August 1999. President Ong, despite his PAP affiliation, had proved an independent President, whose determination to exercise the full powers of the elected presidency had resulted in strained relations with his former government colleagues. His allegations of government obstruction of his efforts to establish the details of the Republic's financial reserves (in order to fulfil his role of guardian of those reserves as specified in the constitutional amendments of 1991) had led to a rare display of disunity amongst senior PAP officials, involving public disputes with both Goh and Lee. Despite a medical report confirming that Ong was in complete remission from a cancer diagnosed in 1992, the PAP announced that, on the grounds of health, they would not support his candidacy should he choose to seek a second term of office. Ong, who was widely believed to command sufficient popular support to secure the presidency without a government endorsement, informed Goh that his candidacy remained a personal decision. He finally announced his decision not to contest the election in July, but unexpectedly proceeded to enumerate his political difficulties while in office. Despite Goh's expressed support for a more consultative style of governance, in mid-August a government-appointed committee declared that only one of three potential presidential candidates, S. R. Nathan (a former Singaporean ambassador to the USA whose presidential candidature was supported by the Cabinet), had fulfilled the criteria set by the committee; Nathan was subsequently nominated as the new President of Singapore on 18 August, and was formally appointed to the position on 1 September, prompting criticism of the Government's autocratic approach.

In September 2000 the Government appeared to have relaxed its tight control over public speaking, with the opening of a 'Speakers' Corner', theoretically allowing a forum for any citizen to air issues of concern. In practice, however, speakers were obliged to register with the police beforehand, and to refrain from speaking on certain racial issues. The opportunity to speak was taken up by members of two Singaporean policy centres, after they were refused a permit to organize a marathon run to protest against the Internal Security Act in December. The gathering of around 50 people was not dispersed, but a report on the event broadcast by the Radio Corporation of Singapore was later edited at the request of the management, and the presenter who publicized the re-editing was dismissed. In April 2001 the Government permitted a rare opposition political rally. It was the first authorized protest to be openly critical of the Government since independence. The rally, intended as a pro-democracy fund-raising event for Jeyaretnam, was attended by over 1,000 people, the permit having been issued after organizers assured police that security guards would be hired to prevent disturbances. It was suspected that there was substantial government surveillance of the rally.

In July 2001 four opposition parties—the Singapore People's Party, the Singapore Malay National Organization, the National Solidarity Party and the Singapore Justice Party—formed the Singapore Democratic Alliance (SDA). The new coalition was chaired by Chiam See Tong, and it was hoped that its formation would strengthen the fragmented political opposition to the PAP in the forthcoming general election. In October President Nathan unexpectedly dissolved Parliament and announced that a general election was to be held on 3 November 2001, significantly in advance of the August 2002 deadline. During the campaign the Government declared that the allocation of priority to public housing improvements would again be affected by levels of electoral support. Electoral boundaries were also redrawn, leading to the enlargement of 14 multi-member

constituencies and to an increase in the number of parliamentary seats to 84, in order to accommodate a rise in the number of registered voters. The opposition protested that it had been disadvantaged by the rearrangements. When nominations closed in late October PAP candidates were unopposed in 55 of the 84 seats available. The Government thus secured victory by default before the polls opened. The Prime Minister, however, urged voters to turn out on election day to decide the outcome of the contests for the remaining 29 seats, warning that Singapore faced its 'gravest challenge since independence'. He also officially announced that he would leave office upon the conclusion of his next term.

The elections were held on 3 November 2001. The level of voter participation was low, owing to the large number of uncontested seats. Despite speculation that the PAP would lose some ground in the election because of the deterioration in the economy (see Economic Affairs), it succeeded in winning 82 seats and increasing its share of the votes cast to 75.3%. The remaining two seats went to Chiam See Tong, Chairman of the SDA, and Low Thia Khiang of the Workers' Party. Steve Chia of the SDA was awarded a non-constituency seat.

Shortly after the election it was reported that Lee and Goh were suing Chee Soon Juan of the SDP for defamation. Chee had alleged that the Government had lent more than S \$17,000m. of public money to the Suharto administration in Indonesia during the 1997–98 financial crisis. He had issued a public apology for the comments soon afterwards and admitted fabricating the accusation, but had later retracted his statement, claiming that it had been made under duress. Goh claimed that, while the loan had been offered to the Suharto administration, it had never been disbursed. In February 2002 Chee faced further legal action after contravening the rule banning the discussion of racial and religious issues in 'Speakers' Corner'. He had criticized the Government's policy of banning Muslim girls from wearing headscarves in public schools and called for the promotion of cultural diversity. His comments came after three Muslim girls were suspended from school for wearing headscarves.

In April 2002 Jeyaretnam made a public apology in the High Court in an attempt to bring to an end the series of defamation suits that had been brought against him by the Government; seven outstanding lawsuits were subsequently abandoned. In the same month Chee stated that he intended to defend the lawsuits against him. In May Chee and the vice-chairman of the SDP, Ghandi Ambalam, led an unauthorized rally outside the presidential palace demanding workers' rights. Following the rally, Chee and Ambalam were both sentenced to brief prison terms, having elected not to pay the fines imposed upon them. However, Ambalan's family subsequently paid his fine, in order to enable his release from prison on the grounds of ill health. In August the High Court ordered Chee to pay damages to Lee and Goh, after his request for a trial was rejected; Chee appealed against the verdict. Meanwhile, a constitutional amendment was passed stipulating that any member of Parliament declared bankrupt or found guilty of a crime would be banned from speaking or voting in Parliament for the duration of any appeal. In February 2003 Ambalam's appeal against his fine (which was sufficient to prohibit him from standing for political office for five years) was rejected by the Chief Justice.

In late April 2003 Prime Minister Goh announced a cabinet reshuffle. The acting Minister of Information, Communications and the Arts, David Lim Tik En, resigned and was replaced by Dr Lee Boon Yang, the former Minister of Manpower, who was succeeded by Dr Ng Eng Hen. Khaw Boon Wan was appointed to be acting Minister of Health, replacing Lim Hng Kiang, who became a Minister in the Prime Minister's Office. Meanwhile, Deputy Prime Minister and former Minister of Defence Dr Tony Tan Keng Yam was appointed to the newly created position of Co-ordinating Minister of Security and Defence in the Prime Minister's Office (effective from August 2003). The defence portfolio was allocated to the former Minister of Education, Teo Chee Hean, who was to be succeeded in an acting capacity by Tharman Shanmugaratnam.

Singapore's foreign policy is dominated by its membership of the regional grouping, ASEAN (which comprised all 10 South-East Asian nations by mid-1999), although it has also maintained strong political and military links with more distant allies, including the USA.

In November 2000 the fourth informal summit meeting of the ASEAN + 3 group of leaders was convened in Singapore. The summit comprised the leaders of all 10 ASEAN members, as well as those of the People's Republic of China, Japan and the Republic of Korea. An outcome of the meeting was the commissioning of an East Asia Study Group to report on the feasibility of a larger East Asia political and economic grouping and free trade area.

Singapore's relations with Indonesia improved in the late 1980s: the process of establishing joint military training facilities with Indonesia, which had begun in 1986, was accomplished in February and March 1989 by the signing of two agreements. In January 1995 the two countries launched a bilateral Defence Forum and signed a Defence Co-operation Pact. In June 1996 Singapore and Indonesia jointly opened the Bintan tourist resort in the Riau Islands. Following the resignation of President Suharto in May 1998, relations deteriorated, in part owing to Lee's criticism of the new President, Prof. Dr. Ir B. J. Habibie. In February 1999 Habibie accused Singapore of racism for allegedly discriminating against its Malay minority. The principal problem was, however, Singapore's refusal to meet Indonesia's high expectations of aid from Singapore in response to the regional economic crisis. In March the Singaporean Minister of Foreign Affairs, Shanmugam Jayakumar, defused tensions in relations between Singapore and Indonesia by declaring in Parliament that Singapore had a vested interest in the economic and political stability of the Indonesian archipelago and pledging the Singaporean Government's intention to co-operate with the Indonesian administration. Relations improved temporarily following Habibie's replacement as President by Abdurrahman Wahid in October 1999. In November 2000, however, Wahid jeopardized the relationship by accusing Singapore of discriminating against Malays, after Singapore rejected certain motions proposed by its neighbour at the ASEAN summit. Nevertheless, Singapore subsequently concluded an agreement with Indonesia to supply the city-state with natural gas for the next 22 years. In February 2002 bilateral relations deteriorated again following the publication of an article in *The Straits Times* in which Lee Kwan Yew remarked that Singapore's national security was being compromised by the fact that terrorists remained at large in Indonesia. In response, the Indonesian Government summoned the Singaporean envoy to Jakarta and lodged an objection to the accusations, claiming that they were provocative and unsubstantiated. Meanwhile, Indonesian Islamic groups held protests outside Singapore's embassy in Jakarta. The situation was further exacerbated by the suspension of three Muslim schoolgirls in Singapore for wearing headscarves while at school. In March 2002 Abu Bakar Bashir, an Indonesian cleric accused of being linked to the international terrorist al-Qa'ida (Base) network, issued a writ of defamation against Lee in relation to his comments.

In September 1994 Singapore and Malaysia agreed to settle their long-standing dispute over the ownership of Pedra Branca Island (Batu Putih) by referring the case to the International Court of Justice in The Hague, the Netherlands. An agreement on the referral was finally signed in early 2003. In August Singapore and Malaysia agreed on the permanent boundary of their territorial waters following 15 years of negotiations. In March 1997 Lee Kuan Yew provoked tension between the two countries by making disparaging comments about security in the Malaysian State of Johore. Lee subsequently made an apology to Malaysia, which was accepted. In April 1999 Singapore and Malaysia undertook joint defence exercises within the context of the regional Five-Power Defence Arrangements; Malaysia had withdrawn from similar exercises in 1998, citing tensions between the two countries as well as economic difficulties.

In February 1998 Goh made an official visit to Malaysia. In the latter half of 1998, however, relations between the two countries deteriorated as a result of conflict over a number of issues. In early August the Malaysian Prime Minister condemned Singapore for requesting that Malaysia move its customs, immigration and quarantine facilities from Tanjung Pagar, a railway station in central Singapore situated on land owned by the Malaysian Government; Malaysia subsequently decided to continue using its facilities at Tanjung Pagar, while Singapore moved its customs office to a new location. In September Malaysia announced its decision to insist on prior clearance for Singaporean military aircraft wishing to enter its airspace; combined operations and exercises between the two countries' air forces were also terminated. In the same month the publication of the memoirs of Lee Kuan Yew, which referred to the events surrounding the secession of Singapore from the Federation of Malaysia, exacerbated tensions in bilateral rela-

tions. However, an improvement in relations between the two countries was perceived in November, when Goh visited Malaysia at the invitation of Mahathir. Lee Kuan Yew further angered Malaysian politicians in August 2000, however, when he publicly criticized Mahathir over his handling of the dismissal and detention of Malaysia's former Deputy Prime Minister, Anwar Ibrahim.

In September 2001 Lee Kuan Yew visited Malaysia and held talks with Mahathir to address the outstanding issues affecting the relationship between the two countries. A framework agreement was subsequently signed under which Malaysia agreed to relocate its facilities at Tanjung Pagar in return for Singapore's agreement to construct a railway tunnel under the strait. Lee also reported that the two countries would work together to construct a suspension bridge, which would enable the demolition of the causeway linking the two countries. However, in January 2002 the Malaysian Government denied the existence of such an agreement and proposed that Malaysia should build a suspension bridge and a railway swing bridge to replace its half of the road link, enabling the Malaysian half of the causeway to be demolished without Singapore's co-operation. Tension was also promoted by the ongoing renegotiation of the terms upon which Malaysia would continue to supply water to Singapore (based upon an agreement originally concluded in 1961 and due to expire in 2061). While an agreement had provisionally been reached in September, the Malaysian Government was dissatisfied with its terms and continued to increase its demands. In March 2002 relations were further strained when Malaysia claimed that reclamation work being carried out by Singapore in the Tebrau Straits was too close to its border and was obstructing ships sailing into ports in Johore. The issue was among those discussed when Deputy Prime Minister Lee Hsien Loong visited Malaysia in the same month. In July the two countries held talks in an attempt to find a solution to the ongoing water supply problem; further negotiations over the issue also took place in September and October of that year. Whilst the Government wished to link resolution of the matter to other issues it considered to be a cause of tension in the bilateral relationship, Malaysia threatened to take Singapore to an international court of arbitration to seek a solution. In February 2003 Mahathir pledged that his country would continue to supply water to Singapore indefinitely. However, he stated that Malaysia would cease its provision of untreated water to the city state upon the termination of an existing agreement in 2011 and provide filtered water instead, at what it considered to be a reasonable price. Singapore continued to insist that any proposed price was too high and that it received too little for the treated water that it supplied to Malaysia in return.

In November 1990 representatives of the Governments of the USA and Singapore signed an agreement providing the US navy and air force with increased access to existing bases in Singapore following the planned US withdrawal from military installations in the Philippines. In January 1992 the two countries reached an agreement, in principle, on the relocation of a naval logistic command headquarters from Subic Bay, in the Philippines. However, relations with the USA were occasionally strained by attacks on the authoritarian style of government in Singapore by the liberal US media. Following the terrorist attacks on the USA in September 2001 (see the chapter on the USA), Singapore affirmed its support for the US-led alliance against terrorism. In January 2002 it was reported that 15 people had been arrested in December 2001 under the Internal Security Act for allegedly participating in terrorist activities. The suspects were believed to be linked to terrorist organizations in Malaysia and Indonesia and to the international terrorist organization, al-Qa'ida. Several of those detained were junior national servicemen, prompting concerns about security in the country, particularly in the aftermath of the September attacks. Shortly afterwards the Government declared that the arrests had dismantled a network of militants plotting to blow up the US embassy and US businesses in Singapore. In order to address the ensuing national security concerns, the Government announced the establishment of a national security secretariat within the Ministry of Defence intended to strengthen co-ordination between the security services.

In September 2002 it was announced that 21 people had been detained in August on suspicion of engaging in terrorist activities. Of those arrested, 19 were believed to be members of the regional terrorist organization, Jemaah Islamiah. In March 2003 the Government announced its support for the US-led military campaign to oust the regime of Saddam Hussein in Iraq. Security measures within Singapore were strengthened subsequently, as the conflict was perceived to have raised the level of the terrorist threat to the country.

Despite the establishment of important economic links during the 1980s, Singapore's relations with the People's Republic of China were adversely affected by the perceived threat of Chinese domination, owing to the preponderance of ethnic Chinese in Singapore (76.8% in 2000). Relations were also strained by Singapore's close military and economic ties with Taiwan. In October 1990, however, Singapore and the People's Republic of China established diplomatic relations at ambassadorial level. This development was prompted mainly by the resumption of diplomatic relations between the People's Republic of China and Indonesia, and followed a visit by the Chinese Premier, Li Peng, to Singapore in August. Singapore's relations with Taiwan were apparently unaffected by these events, and Goh made his first official visit to that country in October 1993. In October 1996 Singapore and Australia issued a joint communiqué urging the integration of the People's Republic of China into the Asian regional security structure, and reaffirming their commitment to a co-operative dialogue with the People's Republic. However, a private visit to Singapore in January 1998 by the Taiwanese Vice-President, Lien Chan, during which he met with Goh and with Singaporean cabinet ministers, provoked the disapproval of the People's Republic, as did a visit by Lee Kuan Yew to Taiwan in September 2000. In November 1998 Goh made an official visit to the People's Republic, and in November 1999 the Chinese Premier, Zhu Rongji, made a reciprocal visit to Singapore.

Government

Legislative power is vested in the unicameral Parliament, with 84 members who are elected by universal adult suffrage for five years (subject to dissolution—within three months of which a general election must be held) in single-member and multi-member constituencies. As many as three additional 'non-constituency' seats may be offered to opposition parties, and up to nine non-elected, neutral MPs may be nominated: all have restricted voting rights. The President is directly elected by universal adult suffrage for a six-year term as a constitutional Head of State, vested with limited powers of veto in financial matters, public appointments and detentions for reasons of national security. Effective executive authority rests with the Cabinet, led by the Prime Minister, which is appointed by the President and responsible to Parliament.

Defence

In August 2002 the Singapore armed forces had an estimated total active strength of 60,500 troops (including 39,800 conscripts): 50,000 in the army, an estimated 4,500 in the navy and 6,000 in the air force. Military service is compulsory for between 24 and 30 months. Paramilitary forces comprised a civil defence force (numbering an estimated 84,300) and a police force. Singapore is a participant in the Five-Power Defence Arrangements (with Australia, Malaysia, New Zealand and the United Kingdom). Government expenditure on internal security and defence for the financial year 2000/01 was S $7,800m. In 2001/02 the Government budgeted S $8,200m. for defence.

Economic Affairs

In 2000, according to estimates by the World Bank, Singapore's gross national income (GNI), measured at average 1998–2000 prices, was US $99,404m., equivalent to $24,740 per head (or $24,910 per head on an international purchasing-power parity basis). During 1990–2001, it was estimated, the population increased at an annual average rate of 2.7%, while gross domestic product (GDP) per head increased, in real terms, at an average rate of 4.8% per year in 1990–2000. According to official figures, overall GDP increased, in real terms, at an average annual rate of 6.3% in 1990–2002. GDP contracted by 2.4% in 2001 but expanded by an estimated 2.2% in 2002.

Agriculture (including hunting, forestry and fishing) and quarrying contributed an estimated 0.1% of GDP in 2002, and accounted for 0.3% of the employed labour force in 2001. Vegetables, plants and orchid flowers are the principal crops. During 1990–2001, according to the Asian Development Bank (ADB), agricultural GDP (including mining) declined at an average annual rate of 2.8%; agricultural GDP declined by 5.9% in 2001 and by an estimated 6.0% in 2002.

Industry (including manufacturing, construction and power) contributed an estimated 33.5% of GDP in 2002, and engaged 25.4% of the employed labour force in 2001. During 1990–2001, according to the ADB, industrial GDP increased at an average annual rate of 6.3%. The GDP of the sector contracted by 9.2% in 2001 but expanded by an estimated 4.0% in 2002.

Mining (chiefly the quarrying of granite) accounted for only an estimated 0.01% of GDP in 1998 and 0.03% of employment in 2001. According to the ADB, the GDP of the mining sector declined at an average annual rate of 17.4% in 1990–98; it declined by 22.4% in 1998.

Manufacturing contributed an estimated 26.4% of GDP in 2002, and engaged 18.8% of the employed labour force in 2001. The principal branches of manufacturing in 1998 (measured in terms of the value of output) were electronic products and components (which accounted for 52.2% of total manufacturing production), refined petroleum products, chemicals and chemical products, non-electrical machinery and equipment, fabricated metal products, and transport equipment (especially shipbuilding). According to the ADB, manufacturing GDP increased at an average annual rate of 5.6% in 1990–2001. Manufacturing GDP contracted by 11.5% in 2001, but increased by an estimated 8.3% in 2002.

Singapore relies on imports of hydrocarbons to fuel its three thermal power stations. In 2002 imports of mineral fuels accounted for 13.1% of merchandise imports.

The services sector contributed an estimated 62.8% of GDP in 2002, and engaged 74.2% of the employed labour force in 2001. Finance and business services provided an estimated 24.4% of GDP in 2002, and engaged 17.2% of the employed labour force in 2001. The GDP of the financial and business services sector increased by 3.3% in 2001 but decreased by 1.9% in 2002. Singapore is an important foreign-exchange dealing centre in Asia and the Pacific. Banking is also a significant sector, with a total of 117 commercial banks in operation in April 2003. Tourism is an important source of foreign exchange, and receipts from tourism amounted to US $6,370m. in 2000. In 2002 the number of tourist arrivals exceeded 7.5m. In 2002 transport and communications contributed an estimated 11.5% of GDP. Growth in the GDP of the transport and communications sector measured 2.6% in 2001 and an estimated 5.0% in 2002. Singapore is the world's busiest port in tonnage terms and has one of the largest merchant shipping registers in the world. According to the ADB, the GDP of the services sector increased at an average annual rate of 7.3% in 1990–2001. Growth in the sector was 2.0% in 2001 and an estimated 1.5% in 2002.

In 2001 Singapore recorded a visible trade surplus of US $12,872m., and there was a surplus of $17,884m. on the current account of the balance of payments. In 2002 the principal sources of imports were Malaysia (18.2%), the USA (14.2%) and Japan (12.5%); other major suppliers were the People's Republic of China and Thailand. The principal markets for exports were Malaysia (17.4%) and the USA (14.7%); other major purchasers were Hong Kong, Japan and China. Principal imports in 2002 included machinery and equipment, electronic components and parts, mineral fuels, miscellaneous manufactured articles, basic manufactures and chemicals. Principal exports included machinery and equipment (notably electronic components and parts), mineral fuels, chemicals and miscellaneous manufactured articles. Singapore is an important entrepôt, and re-exports accounted for 42.8% of total exports in 2000.

In 2001, according to the IMF, there was a budgetary deficit of S $467m. (equivalent to 0.003% of GDP) and in 2002 there was a deficit of S $1,901m. At 31 December 2000 Singapore had no external government debt. The annual rate of inflation averaged 1.5% in 1990–2002; consumer prices increased by 1.0% in 2001, but decreased by 0.4% in 2002. In September 2002 the rate of unemployment was 4.8%. It was expected to rise to an estimated 5.5% in the first half of 2003.

Singapore is a member of the Asian Development Bank (see p. 143), of the Association of South East Asian Nations (ASEAN, see p. 146), of the Asia-Pacific Economic Co-operation (APEC, see p. 139), and of the Colombo Plan (see p. 339). As a member of ASEAN, Singapore signed an accord in January 1992 pledging the creation of a free-trade zone to be known as the ASEAN Free Trade Area (AFTA). A reduction of tariffs to between 0% and 5% was originally envisaged to be completed by 2008 but this was subsequently advanced to 2002, when AFTA was formally implemented. However, Malaysia applied for an extension of this date for its automotive industry, fearing direct competition. Target dates for the removal of all tariffs were brought forward from 2015 to 2010 in November 1999.

Singapore's economic success is based largely on its central location in the region, efficient planning, advanced infrastructure and highly-skilled work-force, which encouraged international investment. In the late 1980s and early 1990s many state-owned corporations were transferred to the private sector, and the Government encouraged companies to transfer labour-intensive operations to neighbouring low-cost countries. Singapore was less affected than its neighbours by the regional financial crisis, which began in July 1997, owing to its high savings and investment rates, negligible debt and massive foreign-exchange reserves. It proceeded to take advantage of the instability of neighbouring countries to secure its own position as a financial and trading centre through the reform of the financial services sector. The comprehensive deregulation of the telecommunications industry was effected in April 2000 (eliminating limits on the foreign ownership of service providers and allowing international companies to offer a range of new services), and plans were announced for the deregulation of the power and insurance sectors. Both the public and private sectors attempted to become more competitive globally. In April 2001 Singapore's largest telecommunications company, SingTel, in response to greater competition in the deregulated sector, concluded an agreement to buy Australia's second largest telecommunications company, Optus, from Cable & Wireless. Simultaneously, the Government announced that it was to reduce its share in SingTel from 78% to 68%. Further expansionary measures were taken by the Government in a series of free trade agreement (FTA) initiatives, as it became clearer that Singapore might be constrained by ASEAN, with political and economic uncertainty in the face of strong pressure from North Asia. In November 2000 an FTA was signed with New Zealand and, in January 2002, with Japan. In June 2002 an FTA was also concluded with the European Free Trade Association (EFTA, see p. 195), and in November with Australia. In early 2003 negotiations for a similar bilateral trade relationship with the USA had been concluded, while discussions were in progress with India, the Republic of Korea, Canada and Mexico. The global economic downturn, particularly in the electronics sector, exacerbated by the effects of the September 2001 terrorist attacks on the USA (a major export market), had a particularly damaging effect upon Singapore's export-driven economy. In 2001 GDP contracted by 2.4%, as Singapore experienced its worst recession since independence in 1965. In May 2002 the Government announced that it intended to implement significant reductions in personal and corporate tax rates, in an attempt to improve Singapore's economic competitiveness, while increasing the tax on goods and services from 3% to 5% in order to offset any subsequent shortfall in revenue. In December it was announced that the proposed rise in taxation on goods and services would be implemented in stages, owing to concerns about its effect on consumer confidence. Largely as a result of high levels of government spending, the economy avoided a further recession in 2002, when GDP expanded by an estimated 2.2%. Unemployment levels, however, remained high. The 2003/04 budget introduced several important tax exemptions and rebates, as well as 'freezing' the level of compulsory contributions to the government-administered pension scheme, in an attempt to stimulate economic growth. However, in February 2003 the Government attracted criticism when it announced that it intended to postpone indefinitely the tax reductions that it had proposed in 2002. In March the US-led military campaign to bring about regime change in Iraq was expected to cause some disruption to international trade and, thus, to affect further Singapore's export sector. National security concerns, owing to an increasing number of incidents of terrorism in the region in 2002 (including the bomb attack on Bali, Indonesia, in October), also threatened to deter overseas investors. In an attempt to stimulate foreign investment, the Government announced in January 2003 that it intended to offer preferential tax rates over a three-year period to companies that established regional headquarters in Singapore. Official forecasts predicted GDP growth of 2%–5% in 2003; a stronger performance was expected in the second half of the year to compensate for slow growth in the first six months. However, the extent of the economic threat posed by the epidemic of Severe Acute Respiratory Syndrome (SARS) in the region in early 2003, which by the end of April had killed 24 people in Singapore alone, remained unclear.

Education

Primary and secondary education is available in the four official languages of Malay, Chinese, Tamil and English. In 1978, as part of a policy of bilingualism, examinations in English and Mandarin Chinese became compulsory for pupils seeking to enter secondary education. In 1987 English became the medium of instruction in all schools. Primary education begins at six years of age and lasts for six years. Secondary education lasts for four or five years from the age of 12. Post-secondary education lasts for two or three years and provides pre-university instruction. Outside the school system there are several higher education centres and vocational institutes, providing craft and industrial training, and technical institutes providing advanced craft training. According to UNESCO, in 1996 total enrolment in tertiary-level education was equivalent to 38.5% of those in the relevant age-group (males 41.5%; females 35.3%). Adult education courses are conducted by a statutory board. Education is not compulsory, but in 1996 the number of children attending primary schools was equivalent to 94% of children in the relevant age-group (males 95%; females 93%) and secondary school enrolment was equivalent to 74% of children in the relevant age-group. Expenditure on education by the central Government in the financial year 2002/03 was S $4,768.1m. (14.3% of total spending).

Public Holidays

2003: 1 January (New Year's Day), 1–2 February (Chinese New Year), 12 February* (Hari Raya Haji, Feast of the Sacrifice), 18 April (Good Friday), 1 May (Labour Day), 15 May (Vesak Day), 9 August (National Day), 25 October (Deepavali), 26 November* (Hari Raya Puasa, end of Ramadan), 25 December (Christmas Day).

2004: 1 January (New Year's Day), 22–23 January (Chinese New Year), 2 February* (Hari Raya Haji, Feast of the Sacrifice), 9 April (Good Friday), 1 May (Labour Day), 2 June (Vesak Day), 9 August (National Day), 12 November (Deepavali), 14 November* (Hari Raya Puasa, end of Ramadan), 25 December (Christmas Day).

*These holidays are dependent on the Islamic lunar calendar and may vary by one or two days from the dates given.

Weights and Measures

The metric system is in force, but the following local units are also used:

Weight
1 tahil = 11/3 oz (37.8 grams).
16 tahils = 1 kati = 11/3 lb (604.8 grams).
100 katis = 1 picul = 1331/3 lb (60.48 kg).
40 piculs = 1 koyan = 5,3331/3 lb (2,419.2 kg).

Capacity
1 chupak = 1 quart (1.1365 litres).
1 gantang = 1 gallon (4.5461 litres).

Statistical Survey

Source (unless otherwise stated): Department of Statistics, 100 High St, 05-01 The Treasury, Singapore 179434; tel. 63327686; fax 63327689; e-mail info@singstat.gov.sg; internet www.singstat.gov.sg.

Area and Population

AREA, POPULATION AND DENSITY

Area (sq km)	659.9*
Population (census results)†	
30 June 1990	3,047,132‡
30 June 2000	
Males	2,061,800§
Females	1,955,900§
Total	4,017,733
Population (official estimates at mid-year)	
2001	4,131,200
2002	4,163,700
Density (per sq km) at mid-2002	6,309.6

* 254.8 sq miles.
† Includes non-residents, totalling 311,264 in 1990 and 754,524 in 2000.
‡ Includes resident population temporarily residing overseas.
§ Provisional.

ETHNIC GROUPS

(at census of 30 June 2000)*

	Males	Females	Total
Chinese	1,245,782	1,259,597	2,505,379
Malays	228,174	225,459	453,633
Indians	134,544	123,247	257,791
Others	21,793	24,613	46,406
Total	**1,630,293**	**1,632,916**	**3,263,209**

* Figures refer to the resident population of Singapore.

BIRTHS, MARRIAGES AND DEATHS*

	Registered live births		Registered Marriages		Registered deaths	
	Number	Rate (per 1,000)	Number	Rate (per 1,000)†	Number	Rate (per 1,000)
1993 . .	50,225	15.4	25,298	7.8	14,461	4.4
1994 . .	49,554	14.7	24,662	7.3	14,946	4.4
1995 . .	48,635	14.0	24,974	7.2	15,569	4.5
1996 . .	48,577	13.2	24,111	6.6	15,590	4.2
1997 . .	47,333	12.5	25,667	6.8	15,307	4.0
1998 . .	43,838	11.2	23,106	5.9	15,657	4.0
1999 . .	43,336	11.0	25,648†	6.5	15,516	3.9
2000† . .	46,631	11.3	22,566	5.5	15,692	3.8

* Data are tabulated by year of registration, rather than by year of occurrence.
† Provisional.

Source: mainly UN, *Demographic Yearbook*.

Expectation of life (WHO estimates, years at birth): 78.8 (males 76.5; females 81.1) in 2001 (Source: WHO, *World Health Report*).

ECONOMICALLY ACTIVE POPULATION

('000 persons aged 15 years and over, at June of each year)

	1999	2000*	2001
Agriculture, hunting, forestry and fishing	5.5	5.1	6.3
Mining and quarrying	1.4	0.7	0.6
Manufacturing	395.6	434.9	384.0
Electricity, gas and water supply .	8.9	7.1	10.4
Construction	130.7	274.0	124.9
Wholesale and retail trade; repair of motor vehicles, motorcycles and personal and household goods	278.9	286.8	303.6
Hotels and restaurants . . .	121.2	114.5	128.3
Transport, storage and communications	203.7	196.5	228.2
Financial intermediation . . .	104.6	96.3	108.7
Real estate, renting and business activities	196.8	226.2	243.1
Public administration and defence; compulsory social security . .	121.9	105.9	133.9
Education, health and social work	142.0	127.4	159.9
Other community, social and personal service activities; private households with employed persons	172.4	217.3	212.4
Extra-territorial organizations and bodies	2.3	2.1	2.4
Total employed	**1,885.9**	**2,094.8**	**2,046.7**
Unemployed	90.1	97.5	72.9
Total labour force	**1,976.0**	**2,192.3**	**2,119.7**
Males	1,138.6	1,324.3	1,190.4
Females	837.3	868.0	929.2

* Figures at census of 30 June 2000.

Source: ILO.

Health and Welfare

KEY INDICATORS

Total fertility rate (children per woman, 2001)	1.5
Under-5 mortality rate (per 1,000 live births, 2001) . . .	4
HIV/AIDS (% of persons aged 15–49, 2001)	0.20
Physicians (per 1,000 head, 1998)	1.63
Hospital beds (per 1,000 head, 1994)	3.05
Health expenditure (2000): US $ per head (PPP)	913
Health expenditure (2000): % of GDP	3.5
Health expenditure (2000): public (% of total)	35.7
Access to water (% of persons, 2000)	100
Access to sanitation (% of persons, 2000)	100
Human Development Index (2000): ranking	25
Human Development Index (2000): value	0.885

For sources and definitions, see explanatory note on p. vi.

Agriculture

PRINCIPAL CROPS

(FAO estimates, '000 metric tons)

	1999	2000	2001
Vegetables	4.8	4.8	4.8

Source: FAO.

LIVESTOCK
(FAO estimates, '000 head, year ending September)

	1999	2000	2001
Pigs	190	190	190
Chickens	2,000	2,000	2,000
Ducks	600	600	600

Source: FAO.

LIVESTOCK PRODUCTS
('000 metric tons)

	1999	2000	2001
Pig meat	50.0	50.0*	50.0
Poultry meat*	69.6	69.6	69.6
Hen eggs	16.0	16.0*	16.0*

* FAO estimate(s).

Source: FAO.

Forestry

SAWNWOOD PRODUCTION
(FAO estimates, '000 cubic metres, incl. railway sleepers)

	1990	1991	1992
Coniferous (softwood)	5	10	5
Broadleaved (hardwood)	50	20	20
Total	55	30	25

1993–2001: Annual production as in 1992 (FAO estimates).

Source: FAO.

Fishing

(metric tons, live weight)

	1998	1999	2000
Capture	7,733	6,489	5,371
Sea catfishes	358	241	141
Shrimps and prawns	621	522	422
Common squids	462	376	348
Aquaculture	3,706	4,029	5,112
Indonesian snakehead	200	380	500
Milkfish	148	378	676
Green mussel	2,640	2,358	2,898
Total catch	11,439	10,518	10,483

Note: Figures exclude crocodiles, recorded by number rather than by weight. The number of estuarine crocodiles caught was: 416 in 1998; 350 in 1999; 481 in 2000.

Source: FAO, *Yearbook of Fishery Statistics*.

Industry

PETROLEUM PRODUCTS
('000 metric tons)

	1996	1997	1998*
Liquefied petroleum gas	875	965	965
Naphtha*	5,850	5,100	5,200
Motor spirit (petrol)	5,231	5,032	4,920
Kerosene	3,025*	3,100*	3,250
Jet fuel	9,029	7,995	6,463
Gas-diesel (distillate fuel) oils	19,200*	19,500*	19,650
Residual fuel oil	16,200*	17,000*	17,800
Lubricating oils	648*	849*	849
Petroleum bitumen (asphalt)	1,132*	1,480*	1,480

* Estimate(s).

Source: UN, *Industrial Commodity Statistics Yearbook*.

SELECTED OTHER PRODUCTS

	1988	1989	1990
Paints ('000 litres)	48,103.6	52,746.9	58,245.9
Broken granite ('000 metric tons)	6,914.0	7,007.5	6,371.7
Bricks ('000 units)	103,136	116,906	128,386
Soft drinks ('000 litres)	269,689.4	252,977.6	243,175.1
Plywood, plain and printed ('000 sq m)	31,307.0	28,871.3	26,106.9
Vegetable cooking oil (metric tons)	75,022	103,003	102,854
Animal fodder (metric tons)	110,106	115,341	104,541
Electricity (million kWh)	13,017.5	14,039.0	15,617.6
Gas (million kWh)	681.1	722.4	807.1
Cassette tape recorders ('000 sets)	15,450	14,006	18,059

Source: UN, *Industrial Commodity Statistics Yearbook*.

Plywood ('000 cu m, estimates): 280 per year in 1991–2000 (Source: FAO).

Electricity (million kWh): 29,520 in 1999; 31,665 in 2000; 33,089 in 2001 (Source: Asian Development Bank, *Key Indicators of Developing Asian and Pacific Countries*).

Finance

CURRENCY AND EXCHANGE RATES

Monetary Units
100 cents = 1 Singapore dollar (S $)

Sterling, US Dollar and Euro Equivalents (31 December 2002)
£1 sterling = S $2.7989
US $1 = S $1.7365
€1 = S $1.8211
S $100 = £35.73 = US $57.59 = €54.91

Average Exchange Rate (Singapore dollars per US $)
2000   1.7240
2001   1.7917
2002   1.7906

BUDGET
(S $ million)

Revenue*	2000	2001	2002†
Tax revenue	25,277.4	25,108.8	21,484.0
Income tax	13,422.9	13,463.8	11,550.0
Corporate and personal income tax	12,230.5	12,601.6	10,926.2
Contributions by statutory board	1,192.4	862.2	623.8
Assets taxes	1,484.7	1,694.2	1,241.9
Taxes on motor vehicles	2,179.7	2,473.5	1,559.2
Customs and excise duties	1,766.2	1,840.2	1,696.5
Betting taxes	1,452.2	1,573.5	1,523.0
Stamp duty	1,380.0	834.9	700.0
Goods and services tax	2,244.0	2,013.0	2,097.9
Others	1,347.7	1,215.9	1,115.6
Fees and charges	5,572.3	4,946.6	3,751.2
Total (incl. others)	31,090.9	30,265.7	25,401.2

* Figures refer to operating revenue only. The data exclude investment income and capital revenue.

† Preliminary figures.

Expenditure	2000	2001	2002*
Operating expenditure	18,896.9	17,845.5	19,243.9
Security and external relations .	9,043.7	8,890.0	9,361.5
Social development . . .	6,180.0	7,093.5	7,978.6
Education	3,901.9	4,366.2	4,768.1
Health	990.2	1,203.9	1,624.5
Community development and			
sports	386.4	515.4	525.8
Environment.	357.2	413.3	468.7
Economic development . .	2,920.3	1,053.2	1,104.8
Communications and			
information technology† . .	2,427.8	386.2	—
Trade and industry . . .	391.3	484.1	535.4
Transport†	—	69.0	378.6
Government administration . .	752.9	808.8	799.0
Development expenditure . . .	9,077.6	9,998.6	7,877.1
Total	27,974.5	27,844.1	27,121.0

* Preliminary figures.
† The Ministry of Communications and Information Technology was renamed the Ministry of Transport in November 2001. Its portfolio of information technology and telecommunications was transferred to the Ministry of Information, Communications and the Arts.

INTERNATIONAL RESERVES
(US $ million at 31 December)

	2000	2001	2002
Gold and foreign exchange . .	79,685	74,851	81,367
IMF special drawing rights . .	137	150	177
Reserve position in the IMF . .	310	374	478
Total	80,132	75,375	82,021

Source: IMF, *International Financial Statistics*.

MONEY SUPPLY
(S $ million at 31 December)

	2000	2001	2002
Currency outside banks . . .	11,289	11,868	12,358
Demand deposits at commercial			
banks	21,973	24,215	23,468
Total money	33,262	36,083	35,826

Source: IMF, *International Financial Statistics*.

COST OF LIVING
(National Consumer Price Index; base: year ending October 1998 = 100)

	2000	2001	2002
Food	101.4	101.9	101.9
Transport and communication . .	100.7	99.4	98.4
Clothing	97.1	97.5	97.8
Housing	100.6	101.8	99.6
Education	102.9	105.1	106.6
Health	102.3	105.7	109.1
All items (incl. others) . . .	101.1	102.1	101.7

NATIONAL ACCOUNTS
(S $ million at current prices)

National Income and Product

	1998	1999	2000
Gross domestic product (GDP) in			
market prices	137,464.0	142,111.0	159,042.0
Primary incomes received from			
abroad.	21,705.0	25,382.0	26,295.0
Less Primary incomes paid			
abroad.	13,126.0	14,024.0	15,740.0
Gross national income (GNI) . .	146,043.0	153,469.0	169,597.0
Less Consumption of fixed capital .	19,173.0	20,254.0	20,920.0
Net national income . . .	126,870.0	133,215.0	148,676.0
Current transfers from abroad .}			
Less Current transfers paid }	−1,837.0	−1,972.0	−2,342.0
abroad. . . . . . .}			
Net national disposable			
income	125,033.0	131,243.0	146,334.0

Source: UN, *National Accounts Statistics*.

Expenditure on the Gross Domestic Product

	2000	2001	2002*
Government final consumption			
expenditure.	17,298.1	19,370.2	20,058.4
Private final consumption			
expenditure.	64,808.6	66,432.0	66,896.5
Increase in stocks	3,612.4	−7,991.0	−7,960.9
Gross fixed capital formation . .	47,290.9	44,843.0	40,064.3
Statistical discrepancy	−236.1	−576.8	−849.6
Total domestic expenditure. .	132,773.9	122,077.4	118,208.7
Trade in goods and services (net) .	24,926.3	29,988.1	37,517.9
GDP in purchasers' values . .	157,700.2	152,065.5	155,726.6
GDP at constant 1995 prices .	161,142.8	157,318.5	160,853.4

* Preliminary figures.

Gross Domestic Product by Economic Activity

	2000	2001	2002*
Agriculture, fishing and quarrying	189.3	177.5	166.1
Manufacturing	42,077.9	36,548.4	41,204.3
Electricity, gas and water . . .	2,329.4	2,835.6	2,763.0
Construction	9,853.2	9,280.0	8,375.6
Wholesale and retail trade . .	19,971.8	19,440.6	19,884.0
Hotels and restaurants . . .	3,593.9	3,607.9	3,471.7
Transport and communications .	17,840.2	17,439.9	17,943.8
Financial services	17,250.8	17,863.7	17,449.6
Business services.	20,511.8	21,343.2	20,689.0
Other services	16,254.0	17,632.7	18,654.4
Owner-occupied dwellings . . .	5,337.4	5,610.4	5,641.5
Sub-total	155,209.7	151,779.9	156,243.0
Taxes on products	11,230.8	9,955.8	9,214.3
Less Financial intermediation			
services indirectly measured .	8,740.3	9,670.2	9,730.7
GDP in purchasers' values . .	157,700.2	152,065.5	155,726.6

* Preliminary figures.

BALANCE OF PAYMENTS
(US $ million)

	1999	2000	2001
Exports of goods f.o.b. . . .	115,514	139,054	122,478
Imports of goods f.o.b. . . .	−104,287	−127,483	−109,605
Trade balance	11,227	11,571	12,872
Exports of services	23,690	26,761	26,168
Imports of services	−19,235	−21,694	−20,443
Balance on goods and services.	15,682	16,639	18,598
Other income received . . .	16,184	16,295	14,920
Other income paid	−14,156	−15,700	−14,257
Balance on goods, services and			
income	17,710	17,234	19,262
Current transfers received . . .	134	127	123
Current transfers paid . . .	−1,317	−1,441	−1,501
Current balance	16,527	15,921	17,884
Capital account (net)	−191	−163	−161
Direct investment abroad . . .	−4,277	−4,966	−10,216
Direct investment from abroad. .	11,803	5,407	8,609
Portfolio investment assets . . .	−7,938	−7,867	−5,256
Portfolio investment liabilities . .	2,311	−2,034	720
Other investment assets . . .	−20,002	−5,974	−15,472
Other investment liabilities . .	6,743	4,598	2,847
Net errors and omissions . . .	−783	1,884	184
Overall balance	4,194	6,806	−861

Source: IMF, *International Financial Statistics*.

External Trade

PRINCIPAL COMMODITIES
(distribution by SITC, S $ million)

Imports c.i.f.	2000	2001	2002
Mineral fuels, lubricants, etc.	27,987.3	26,119.3	27,199.2
Crude petroleum	15,077.8	13,589.0	13,204.0
Chemicals and related			
products	13,282.5	12,181.4	12,990.0
Basic manufactures	16,359.4	15,249.0	15,350.9
Machinery and equipment	141,067.5	123,932.5	122,632.4
Electric generators	10,933.5	8,826.4	8,542.1
Electronic components and parts	55,723.0	43,555.7	44,913.8
Aircraft and vessels	3,186.2	7,170.2	6,068.7
Miscellaneous manufactured			
articles	21,693.9	18,521.5	18,370.9
Total (incl. others)	232,175.1	207,692.1	208,311.9

Exports f.o.b.	2000	2001	2002
Mineral fuels, lubricants, etc.	23,061.5	22,472.8	23,250.7
Petroleum products	17,054.0	16,043.9	16,993.8
Chemicals and related			
products	16,488.0	17,631.7	20,816.5
Basic manufactures	9,016.7	8,429.6	8,776.2
Machinery and equipment	160,402.2	140,620.3	142,318.3
Electronic components and parts	62,457.5	51,127.8	54,587.2
Miscellaneous manufactured			
articles	19,381.6	19,040.4	19,066.1
Total (incl. others)	237,826.3	218,026.3	223,901.4

Source: International Enterprise Singapore.

PRINCIPAL TRADING PARTNERS
(S $ million)

Imports c.i.f.	2000	2001	2002
Australia	3,965.5	4,305.6	3,863.2
China, People's Republic	12,278.7	12,900.3	15,853.4
France	3,773.5	3,719.3	3,791.8
Germany	7,304.1	6,861.5	7,077.6
Hong Kong	6,058.8	4,985.6	5,073.1
Italy	2,869.0	2,350.4	2,321.2
Japan	39,955.0	28,794.1	26,079.8
Korea, Republic	8,308.7	6,842.7	7,690.7
Kuwait	2,614.2	2,431.8	3,118.0
Malaysia	39,399.4	35,974.6	37,950.8
Netherlands	2,294.4	2,047.3	2,324.8
Philippines	5,793.5	4,572.6	4,480.6
Saudi Arabia	7,477.7	7,557.7	6,828.8
Switzerland	3,927.7	3,501.7	3,322.1
Taiwan	10,296.3	8,830.6	9,530.1
Thailand	10,008.7	9,242.6	9,676.7
United Arab Emirates	2,595.7	2,440.1	2,816.1
United Kingdom	4,721.6	4,372.9	4,212.1
USA	34,717.8	34,137.0	29,515.2
Total (incl. others)	232,175.1	207,692.1	208,311.9

Exports f.o.b.	2000	2001	2002
Australia	5,534.5	5,658.9	6,029.1
China, People's Republic	9,285.0	9,545.0	12,268.1
France	3,684.1	2,850.8	2,614.3
Germany	7,378.2	7,690.9	7,257.2
Hong Kong	18,704.9	19,373.7	20,492.1
India	4,803.7	4,872.8	4,717.7
Japan	17,948.7	16,712.3	15,990.2
Korea, Republic	8,478.9	8,391.7	9,316.5
Malaysia	43,189.8	37,821.5	39,002.9
Netherlands	7,051.8	7,225.6	7,691.1
Philippines	5,838.5	5,516.1	5,438.0
Taiwan	14,195.5	11,219.5	11,086.7
Thailand	10,121.7	9,486.6	10,214.2
United Kingdom	6,127.2	5,102.5	4,631.5
USA	41,188.9	33,533.6	32,935.3
Viet Nam	3,610.5	3,769.3	3,729.2
Total (incl. others)	237,826.3	218,026.3	223,901.4

Source: International Enterprise Singapore.

Transport

ROAD TRAFFIC
(registered vehicles)

	2000	2001	2002
Cars*	392,961	405,354	404,274
Motorcycles and scooters	130,964	130,910	131,437
Motor buses	12,300	12,624	12,707
Taxis	18,327	18,798	19,106
Goods vehicles (incl. private)	124,854	127,273	125,931
Others	13,401	13,411	13,501
Total	692,807	708,370	706,956

* Including private, company, tuition and private hire cars.

SHIPPING

Merchant Fleet
(at 31 December)

	1999	2000	2001
Number of vessels	1,736	1,728	1,729
Displacement (grt)	21,780,112	21,491,085	21,022,604

Source: Lloyd's Register-Fairplay, *World Fleet Statistics*.

International Sea-borne Shipping
(vessels of over 75 net registered tons)

	1995	1996	1997
Vessels:			
entered	104,014	117,723	130,333
cleared	104,123	117,662	130,237
Cargo ('000 freight tons):			
loaded	130,224.3	134,592	159,272
unloaded	175,259.7	179,572	188,234

Note: One freight ton equals 40 cubic feet (1.133 cubic metres) of cargo.

1998: Vessels entered 140,922; Vessels cleared 140,838.

1999: Vessels entered 141,523; Vessels cleared 141,745.

2000: Vessels entered 145,383; Vessels cleared 145,415.

Source: mainly UN, *Statistical Yearbook*.

CIVIL AVIATION

	1995	1996	1997
Passengers:			
arrived	10,919,739	11,587,394	11,915,969
departed	10,823,457	11,542,408	11,883,259
in transit	1,453,046	1,384,446	1,375,116
Mail (metric tons):			
landed	9,521	10,572	10,813
dispatched	9,543	10,380	10,978
Freight (metric tons):			
landed	577,749	622,019	696,710
dispatched	528,024	568,438	639,544

Source: Civil Aviation Authority of Singapore.

1998: Kilometres flown (million) 293; Passengers carried ('000) 13,316; Passenger-km (million) 58,174; Total ton-km (million) 10,381 (Source: UN, *Statistical Yearbook*).

1999: Kilometres flown (million) 326; Passengers carried ('000) 15,283; Passenger-km (million) 65,471; Total ton-km (million) 11,824 (Source: UN, *Statistical Yearbook*).

Tourism

FOREIGN VISITOR ARRIVALS

('000, incl. excursionists)

Country of nationality	2000†	2001	2002
Australia	484.6	550.7	538.4
China, People's Republic	440.0	497.4	670.1
Germany	184.6	167.0	157.5
Hong Kong	160.5	276.2	265.9
India	410.0	339.8	375.6
Indonesia	1,293.2	n.a.	1,392.9
Japan	978.8	755.8	723.4
Korea, Republic	365.0	359.1	371.0
Malaysia*	459.6	n.a.	548.5
Philippines	185.2	n.a.	n.a.
Taiwan	292.8	222.1	209.3
Thailand	222.7	n.a.	263.8
United Kingdom	559.9	460.0	458.5
USA	406.1	343.8	327.6
Total (incl. others)*	7,691.4	7,522.2	7,566.2

* Figures exclude arrivals of Malaysians by land.

† Source: World Tourism Organization, *Yearbook of Tourism Statistics*.

Source: Singapore Tourism Board.

Tourism receipts (US $ million): 5,402 in 1998; 5,974 in 1999; 6,370 in 2000 (Source: World Tourism Organization).

Communications Media

(at 31 December)

	1999	2000	2001
Television receivers ('000 in use)	1,200	1,200	n.a.
Telephones ('000 main lines in use)	1,876.6	1,946.5	1,948.5
Mobile cellular telephones ('000 subscribers)	1,630.8	2,747.4	2,858.8
Personal computers ('000 in use)	1,700	1,941	2,100
Internet users ('000)	950	1,200	1,500

Sources: International Telecommunication Union; UN, *Statistical Yearbook*.

Radio receivers ('000 in use): 2,550 in 1997.

Facsimile machines ('000 in use, estimate): 100 in 1998.

Daily newspapers: 8 (with average circulation of 1,095,000 copies) in 1996.

Non-daily newspapers: 2 in 1996.

Sources: mainly UNESCO, *Statistical Yearbook*; UN, *Statistical Yearbook*.

Education

(June 2000)

	Institutions	Students	Teachers
Primary	201	305,992	12,287
Secondary	163	176,132	9,462
Centralized Institutes } Junior Colleges	17	24,975	1,878
Institute of Technical Education	10	15,974	1,257
Polytechnics	4	58,374	3,931
National Institute of Education	1	3,308	561
Universities	3	49,856	2,826
Total	399	634,611	32,202

Adult literacy rate (UNESCO estimates): 92.3% (males 96.3%; females 88.4%) in 2000 (Source: UN Development Programme, *Human Development Report*).

Directory

The Constitution

A new Constitution came into force on 3 June 1959, with the establishment of the self-governing State of Singapore. This was subsequently amended as a consequence of Singapore's affiliation to Malaysia (September 1963 to August 1965) and as a result of its adoption of republican status on 22 December 1965. The Constitution was also amended in January 1991 to provide for the election of a President by universal adult suffrage, and to extend the responsibilities of the presidency, which had previously been a largely ceremonial office. A constitutional amendment in October 1996 placed restrictions on the presidential right of veto. The main provisions of the Constitution are summarized below:

HEAD OF STATE

The Head of State is the President, elected by universal adult suffrage for a six-year term. He normally acts on the advice of the Cabinet, but is vested with certain functions and powers for the purpose of safeguarding the financial reserves of Singapore and the integrity of the Public Services.

THE CABINET

The Cabinet, headed by the Prime Minister, is appointed by the President and is responsible to Parliament.

THE LEGISLATURE

The Legislature consists of a Parliament of 84 elected members, presided over by a Speaker who may be elected from the members of Parliament themselves or appointed by Parliament although he may not be a member of Parliament. Members of Parliament are elected by universal adult suffrage for five years (subject to dissolution) in single-member and multi-member constituencies.* Additionally, up to three 'non-constituency' seats may be offered to opposition parties, in accordance with a constitutional amendment approved in 1984, while legislation approved in 1990, and amended in 1997, enables the Government to nominate up to nine additional, politically-neutral members for a term of two years; these members have restricted voting rights.

A 21-member Presidential Council, chaired by the Chief Justice, examines material of racial or religious significance, including legislation, to see whether it differentiates between racial or religious communities or contains provisions inconsistent with the fundamental liberties of Singapore citizens.

CITIZENSHIP

Under the Constitution, Singapore citizenship may be acquired either by birth, descent or registration. Persons born when Singapore was a constituent State of Malaysia could also acquire Singapore citizenship by enrolment or naturalization under the Constitution of Malaysia.

* A constitutional amendment was introduced in May 1988, whereby 39 constituencies were merged to form 13 'group representation constituencies' which would return 'teams' of three Members of Parliament. At least one member of each team was to be of minority (non-Chinese) racial origin. In January 1991 the Constitution was further amended, stipulating that the number of candidates contesting 'group representation constituencies' should be a minimum of three and a maximum of four. The maximum was increased to six by constitutional amendment in October 1996.

The Government

HEAD OF STATE

President: SELLAPAN RAMANATHAN (S. R.) NATHAN (took office 1 September 1999).

THE CABINET
(May 2003)

Prime Minister: GOH CHOK TONG.

Senior Minister in the Prime Minister's Office: LEE KUAN YEW.

Deputy Prime Minister and Minister of Finance: Brig.-Gen. (retd) LEE HSIEN LOONG.

Deputy Prime Minister and Minister of Defence: Dr TONY TAN KENG YAM.

Minister of Law and of Foreign Affairs: Prof. SHANMUGAM JAYA-KUMAR.

Minister of Trade and Industry: Brig.-Gen. (retd) GEORGE YONG BOON YEO.

Minister of Home Affairs: WONG KAN SENG.

Minister of Health and Second Minister of State for Finance: LIM HNG KIANG.

Minister of Information, Communications and the Arts: Dr LEE BOON YANG.

Acting Minister of Manpower: Dr NG ENG HEN.

Minister of Transport: YEO CHEOW TONG.

Minister in the Prime Minister's Office and Second Minister of Foreign Affairs: LEE YOCK SUAN.

Minister in the Prime Minister's Office: LIM BOON HENG.

Minister of National Development: MAH BOW TAN.

Minister of Community Development and Sports: Dr YAACOB IBRAHIM.

Minister of Education and Second Minister of Defence: Rear-Adm. (retd) TEO CHEE HEAN.

Minister of the Environment: LIM SWEE SAY.

MINISTRIES

Office of the President: The Istana, Orchard Rd, Singapore 238823; internet www.istana.gov.sg.

Office of the Prime Minister: Orchard Rd, Istana Annexe, Istana, Singapore 238823; tel. 62358577; fax 67324627; e-mail goh_chok_tong@pmo.gov.sg; internet www.pmo.gov.sg.

Ministry of Community Development and Sports: 512 Thomson Rd, MCD Bldg, Singapore 298136; tel. 62589595; fax 63548324; e-mail mcds_home@mcds.gov.sg; internet www.mcds.gov.sg.

Ministry of Defence: Gombak Drive, off Upper Bukit Timah Rd, Mindef Bldg, Singapore 669645; tel. 67608844; fax 67646119; e-mail mfu@starnet.gov.sg; internet www.mindef.gov.sg.

Ministry of Education: 1 North Buona Vista Drive, MOE Bldg, Singapore 138675; tel. 68721110; fax 67755826; e-mail contact@moe.edu.sg; internet www.moe.gov.sg.

Ministry of the Environment: 40 Scotts Rd, Environment Bldg, 22nd Floor, Singapore 228231; tel. 67327733; fax 67319456; e-mail contact_env@env.gov.sg; internet www.env.gov.sg.

Ministry of Finance: 100 High St, 06-03 The Treasury, Singapore 179434; tel. 62259911; fax 63327435; e-mail mof_qsm@mof.gov.sg; internet www.mof.gov.sg.

Ministry of Foreign Affairs: Tanglin, Singapore 248163; tel. 63798000; fax 64747885; e-mail mfa@mfa.gov.sg; internet www.mfa.gov.sg.

Ministry of Health: 16 College Rd, College of Medicine Bldg, Singapore 169854; tel. 63259220; fax 62241677; e-mail moh_info@moh.gov.sg; internet www.moh.gov.sg.

Ministry of Home Affairs: New Phoenix Park, 28 Irrawaddy Rd, Singapore 329560; tel. 62359111; fax 62546250; e-mail mha_feedback@mha.gov.sg; internet www.mha.gov.sg.

Ministry of Information, Communications and the Arts: 140 Hill St, 02-02 MITA Bldg, Singapore 179369; tel. 62707988; fax 68379480; e-mail mita_pa@mita.gov.sg; internet www.mita.gov.sg.

Ministry of Law: 100 High St, 08-02 The Treasury, Singapore 179434; tel. 63328840; fax 63328842; e-mail mlaw_enquiry@minlaw.gov.sg; internet www.minlaw.gov.sg.

Ministry of Manpower: 18 Havelock Rd, 07-01, Singapore 059764; tel. 65341511; fax 65344840; e-mail mom_hq@mom.gov.sg; internet www.mom.gov.sg.

Ministry of National Development: 5 Maxwell Rd, 21/22-00, Tower Block, MND Complex, Singapore 069110; tel. 62221211; fax 63257254; e-mail mnd_hq@mnd.gov.sg; internet www.mnd.gov.sg.

Ministry of Trade and Industry: 100 High St, 09-01 The Treasury, Singapore 179434; tel. 62259911; fax 63327260; e-mail mti_email@mti.gov.sg; internet www.mti.gov.sg.

Ministry of Transport: 460 Alexandra Rd, 39-00 PSA Bldg, Singapore 119963; tel. 62707988; fax 63757734; e-mail mot@mot.gov.sg; internet www.mot.gov.sg.

President and Legislature

PRESIDENT

On 18 August 1999 SELLAPAN RAMANATHAN (S. R.) NATHAN was nominated as President by a state-appointed committee. S. R. Nathan was the sole candidate for the Presidency, following the rejection by the committee of the only two other potential candidates, and was officially appointed to the post on 1 September.

PARLIAMENT

Parliament House

1 Parliament Place, Singapore 178880; tel. 63326666; fax 63325526; e-mail parl@parl.gov.sg; internet www.gov.sg/parliament/.

Speaker: ABDULLAH TARMUGI.

General Election, 3 November 2001

	Seats
People's Action Party	82*
Workers' Party	1
Singapore Democratic Alliance	1
Total	**84**

*55 seats were unopposed.

Political Organizations

Angkatan Islam (Singapore Muslim Movement): Singapore; f. 1958; Pres. MOHAMED BIN OMAR; Sec.-Gen. IBRAHIM BIN ABDUL GHANI.

National Solidarity Party: Blk 531, Upper Cross St, Hong Lim Complex, 03-30, Singapore 050531; fax 65366388; e-mail nsp@nsp-singapore.org; internet www.nsp-singapore.org; f. 1987; joined Singapore Democratic Alliance (SDA) in July 2001; Pres. YIP YEW WENG; Sec.-Gen. STEVE CHIA.

People's Action Party (PAP): Blk 57B, PCF Bldg, 01-1402 New Upper Changi Rd, Singapore 463057; tel. 62444600; fax 62430114; e-mail paphq@pap.org.sg; internet www.pap.org.sg; f. 1954; governing party since 1959; 12-member Cen. Exec. Cttee; Chair. Dr TONY TAN KENG YAM; Sec.-Gen. GOH CHOK TONG.

Pertubuhan Kebangsaan Melayu Singapura (PKMS) (Singapore Malay National Organization): 218F Changi Rd, 4th Floor, PKM Bldg, Singapore 1441; tel. 64470468; fax 63458724; f. in 1950 as the United Malay National Organization (UMNO) of Malaysia; renamed as UMNO Singapore in 1954 and as PKMS in 1967; seeks to advance the implementation of the special rights of Malays in Singapore, as stated in the Constitution, to safeguard and promote the advancement of Islam and to encourage racial harmony and goodwill in Singapore; joined Singapore Democratic Alliance (SDA) in July 2001; Pres. Haji BORHAN ARIFFIN; Sec.-Gen. MOHD RAHIZAN YAACOB.

Singapore Democratic Alliance (SDA): Singapore; f. 2001 to contest 2001 general election; coalition of Pertubuhan Kebangsaan Melayu Singapura (PKMS), Singapore People's Party (SPP), National Solidarity Party and the Singapore Justice Party; Chair. CHIAM SEE TONG.

Singapore Democratic Party (SDP): 1357A Serangoon Rd, Singapore 328240; tel. and fax 63981675; e-mail speakup@singaporedemocrats.org; internet www.singaporedemocrats.org; f. 1980; 12-mem. Cen. Cttee; Chair. LING HOW DOONG; Sec.-Gen. CHEE SOON JUAN.

Singapore Justice Party: Singapore; f. 1972; joined Singapore Democratic Alliance (SDA) in July 2001; Pres. A. R. SUIB; Sec.-Gen. MUTHUSAMY RAMASAMY.

Singapore People's Party (SPP): Singapore; f. 1993; a breakaway faction of the SDP, espousing more moderate policies; joined Singapore Democratic Alliance (SDA) in July 2001; 12-mem. Cen. Exec. Cttee; Chair. Sin Kek Tong; Sec.-Gen. Chiam See Tong.

Workers' Party: 411B Jalan Besar, Singapore 209014; tel. 62984765; fax 64544404; e-mail wp@wp.org.sg; internet www.wp .org.sg; f. 1961; active as opposition party in Singapore since 1957, merged with Barisan Sosialis (Socialist Front) in 1988; seeks to establish a democratic socialist govt with a constitution guaranteeing fundamental citizens' rights; Chair. Dr Tan Bin Seng; Sec.-Gen. Low Thia Khiang.

Other parties are the Alliance Party Singapura, Barisan Sosialis (Socialist Front), the Democratic People's Party, the Democratic Progressive Party, the National Party of Singapore, the Partai Rakyat, the People's Front, the Parti Kesatuan Ra'ayat (United Democratic Party), the People's Republican Party, the Persatuan Melayu Singapura, the Singapore Chinese Party, the Singapore Indian Congress, the Singapore National Front, the United National Front, the United People's Front and the United People's Party.

Diplomatic Representation

EMBASSIES AND HIGH COMMISSIONS IN SINGAPORE

Argentina: 9 Temasek Blvd, 44-03 Suntec Tower 2, Singapore 038989; tel. 68830415; fax 68830410; e-mail eargsing@pacific.net.sg; internet www.ar.c-d.org/sg/; Ambassador Alfredo Raúl Morelli.

Australia: 25 Napier Rd, Singapore 258507; tel. 68364100; fax 67337134; e-mail public-affairs-sing@dfat.gov.au; internet www .singapore.embassy.gov.au; High Commissioner Gary Quinlan.

Austria: 600 North Bridge Rd, 24-04/05 Parkview Sq., Singapore 188778; tel. 63966350; fax 63966340; e-mail embassy@austria.org .sg; internet www.austria.org.sg; Chargé d'affaires a.i. Wolfgang Mayerhofer.

Bangladesh: 101 Thomson Rd, 05-04 United Sq., Singapore 307591; tel. 62550075; fax 62551824; e-mail bdoot@singnet.com.sg; internet www.bangladesh.org.sg; High Commissioner Ruhul Alam Siddique (acting).

Belgium: 8 Shenton Way, 14-01 Temasek Tower, Singapore 068811; tel. 62207677; fax 62226976; e-mail singapore@diplobel.org; internet www.embelsing.org.sg; Ambassador Philippe Kridelka.

Brazil: 101 Thomson Rd, 10-05 United Sq., Singapore 307591; tel. 62566001; fax 62566619; e-mail cinbrem@singnet.com.sg; internet web.singnet.com.sg/~cinbrem; Ambassador Paulo Dyrceu Pinheiro.

Brunei: 325 Tanglin Rd, Singapore 247955; tel. 67339055; fax 67375275; High Commissioner Haji Adnan Haji Zainal.

Cambodia: 152 Beach Rd, 11-05 Gateway East, Singapore 189721; tel. 62993028; fax 62993622; e-mail cambodiaembasy@pacific.net .sg.

Canada: 80 Anson Rd, 14-00 and 15-01/02 IBM Towers, Singapore 079907; tel. 63253200; fax 63253297; e-mail echiesg@pacific.net.sg; internet www.dfait-maeci.gc.ca/singapore; High Commissioner Doreen Steidle.

Chile: 105 Cecil St, 25-00 The Octagon, Singapore 069534; tel. 62238577; fax 62250677; e-mail echilesg@pacific.net.sg; internet www.conchile.org.sg; Ambassador Juan Scaff Martabit.

China, People's Republic: 150 Tanglin Rd, Singapore 247969; tel. 64180246; fax 67344737; e-mail emprc@singnet.com.sg; Ambassador Zhang Jiuhuan.

Czech Republic: 7 Temasek Blvd, 18-02 Suntec Tower 1, Singapore 038987; tel. 63322378; fax 63322372; e-mail singapore@embassy .mzv.cz; internet www.mfa.cz/singapore; Chargé d'affaires Rudolf Hykl.

Denmark: 101 Thomson Rd, 13-01/02 United Sq., Singapore 307591; tel. 63555010; fax 62533764; e-mail sinamb@um.dk; internet www.denmark.com.sg; Ambassador Jørgen Ørstrøm Møller.

Egypt: 75 Grange Rd, Singapore 249579; tel. 67371811; fax 67323422; Ambassador Nadia Kafafi.

Finland: 101 Thomson Rd, 21-03 United Sq., Singapore 307591; tel. 62544042; fax 62534101; e-mail sanomat.sin@formin.fi; Ambassador Yrjö Kim David Luotonen.

France: 101–103 Cluny Park Rd, Singapore 259595; tel. 68807800; fax 68807801; e-mail ambassadeur@france.org.sg; internet www .france.org.sg; Ambassador Michel Filhol.

Germany: 545 Orchard Rd, 14-00 Far East Shopping Centre, Singapore 238882; tel. 67371355; fax 67372653; e-mail germany@singnet .com.sg; internet www.germanembassy-singapore.org.sg; Ambassador Andreas Michaelis.

Greece: 61B Duxton Rd, Singapore 089525; tel. and fax 62212364.

Holy See: 55 Waterloo St 6, Singapore 187954 (Apostolic Nunciature); tel. 63372466; fax 63372466; Apostolic Nuncio Most Rev. Adriano Bernardini (Titular Archbishop of Faleri).

Hungary: 250 North Bridge Rd, 29-01 Raffles City Tower, Singapore 179101; tel. 68830882; fax 68830177; e-mail humemsin@ singnet.com.sg; Ambassador Dr György Nanovfszky.

India: 31 Grange Rd, India House, Singapore 239702; tel. 67376777; fax 67326909; e-mail indiahc@pacific.net.sg; internet www .embassyofindia.com; High Commissioner P. P. Shukla.

Indonesia: 7 Chatsworth Rd, Singapore 249761; tel. 67377422; fax 67375037; Ambassador (vacant).

Ireland: Ireland House, 541 Orchard Rd, 8th Floor, Liat Towers, Singapore 238881; tel. 62387616; fax 62387615; e-mail ireland@ magix.com.sg; Ambassador Hugh Swift.

Israel: 58 Dalvey Rd, Singapore 259463; tel. 68349200; fax 67337008; e-mail singapor@israel.org; internet www.israelbiz.org .sg; Ambassador Itzhak Shoham.

Italy: 101 Thomson Rd, 27-02 United Sq., Singapore 307591; tel. 62506022; fax 62533301; e-mail ambitaly@italyemb.org.sg; internet www.italyemb.org.sg; Ambassador Guido Scalici.

Japan: 16 Nassim Rd, Singapore 258390; tel. 62358855; fax 67331039; e-mail eojs04@singnet.com.sg; internet www.sg .emb-japan.go.jp; Ambassador Kunihiko Makita.

Korea, Democratic People's Republic: 7500A Beach Rd, 09-320 The Plaza, Singapore 199591; tel. 64403498; fax 63482026; Ambassador Yu Jae Han.

Korea, Republic: 47 Scotts Rd, 08-00 Goldbell Towers, Singapore 228233; tel. 62561188; fax 62543191; e-mail info@koreaembassy.org .sg; internet www.koreaembassy.org.sg; Ambassador Hahm Myung-Chul.

Laos: 101 Thomson Rd, 05-03A United Sq., Singapore 307591; tel. 62506044; fax 62506014; e-mail laoembsg@singnet.com.sg; Ambassador Leuane Sombounkhan.

Malaysia: 30 Hill St, 02-01, Singapore 179360; tel. 62350111; fax 67336135; e-mail mwspore@mbox3.singnet.com.sg; High Commissioner Hamidon Ali.

Mexico: 152 Beach Rd, 06-07/08, 6th Floor, Gateway East Tower, Singapore 189721; tel. 62982678; fax 62933484; e-mail embamexsing@embamexsing.org.sg; internet www.embamexsing .org.sg; Ambassador Andrés Carral Cuevas.

Myanmar: 15 St Martin's Drive, Singapore 257996; tel. 67350209; fax 67356236; e-mail ambassador@mesingapore.org.sg; Ambassador U Hla Than.

Netherlands: 541 Orchard Rd, 13-01 Liat Towers, Singapore 238881; tel. 67371155; fax 67371940; e-mail nlgovsin@singnet.com .sg; internet www.nethemb.org.sg; Ambassador H. J. Van Pesch.

New Zealand: 391A Orchard Rd, 15-06/10 Ngee Ann City, Singapore 238873; tel. 62359966; fax 67339924; e-mail enquiries@ nz-high-com.org.sg; internet www.nz-high-com.org.sg; High Commissioner Nigel Moore.

Nigeria: 350 Orchard Rd, 16-09/10 Shaw House, Singapore 238868; tel. 67321741; fax 67321742; High Commissioner Alex Chike Aniegbo.

Norway: 16 Raffles Quay, 44-01 Hong Leong Bldg, Singapore 048581; tel. 62207122; fax 62202191; e-mail emb.singapore@mfa.no; Ambassador Enok Nygaard.

Pakistan: 1 Scotts Rd, 24-02/04 Shaw Centre, Singapore 228208; tel. 67376988; fax 67374096; e-mail parep@singnet.com.sg; internet www.parep.org.sg; High Commissioner Abdul Moiz Bokhari.

Panama: 16 Raffles Quay, 41-06 Hong Leong Bldg, Singapore 048581; tel. 62218677; fax 62240892; e-mail pacosin@pacific.net.sg; Ambassador Ricardo A. Aragon.

Peru: 390 Orchard Rd, 12-03 Palais Renaissance, Singapore 238871; tel. 67388595; fax 67388601; e-mail embperu@pacific.net .sg; Ambassador Juan Carlos Capunay.

Philippines: 20 Nassim Rd, Singapore 258395; tel. 67373977; fax 67339544; e-mail php@pacific.net.sg; internet www.rpsing.org; Ambassador Jesus I. Yabes.

Poland: 435 Orchard Rd, 10-01/02 Wisma Atria, Singapore 238877; tel. 67340466; fax 67346129; e-mail polish_embassy@pacific.net.sg; Chargé d'affaires a.i. Włodzimierz Pacześny (acting).

Portugal: 55 Waterloo St, 09-03A, Singapore 187954; tel. 63341231; fax 65334943.

Romania: 48 Jalan Harom Setangkai, Singapore 258827; tel. 64683424; fax 64683425; e-mail comofrom@starhub.net.sg; Chargé d'affaires a.i. SEVER COTU.

Russia: 51 Nassim Rd, Singapore 258439; tel. 62351834; fax 67334780; e-mail rosposol@pacific.net.sg; internet www.singapore .mid.ru; Ambassador SERGEI B. KISELEV.

Saudi Arabia: 40 Nassim Rd, Singapore 258449; tel. 67345878; fax 67385291; Chargé d'affaires MOHAMMAD A. AL-HAMDAN.

South Africa: 331 North Bridge Rd, 15/01-06 Odeon Towers, Singapore 188720; tel. 63393319; fax 63396658; e-mail sahcp@singnet .com.sg; internet www.southafricahc.org.sg; High Commissioner S. J. SCHOEMAN.

Sri Lanka: 13-07/12 Goldhill Plaza, 51 Newton Rd, Singapore 308900; tel. 62544595; fax 62507201; e-mail slhcs@lanka.com.sg; internet www.lanka.com.sg; High Commissioner AJIT JAYARATNE.

Sweden: 111 Somerset Rd, 05-01 Power Bldg, Singapore 238164; tel. 64159720; fax 64159747; e-mail swedemb@singnet.com.sg; internet www.swedemb.org.sg; Ambassador TEPPO TAURIAINEN.

Switzerland: 1 Swiss Club Link, Singapore 288162; tel. 64685788; fax 64668245; e-mail vertretung@sin.rep.admin.ch; internet www .eda.admin.ch/singapore_emb/e/home.html; Ambassador DANIEL WOKER.

Thailand: 370 Orchard Rd, Singapore 238870; tel. 67372158; fax 67320778; e-mail thaisgp@singnet.com.sg; internet www .thaiembsingapore.org; Ambassador THAKUR PHANIT.

Turkey: 20B Nassim Rd, Singapore 258397; tel. 67329211; fax 67381786; e-mail turksin@cyberway.com.sg; Ambassador HAYRI EROL.

United Kingdom: 100 Tanglin Rd, Singapore 247919; tel. 64244200; fax 64244218; e-mail brit–1>hc@pacific.net.sg; internet www.britain.org.sg; High Commissioner ALAN COLLINS.

USA: 27 Napier Rd, Singapore 258508; tel. 64769100; fax 64769340; internet singapore.usembassy.gov; Ambassador FRANKLIN L. LAVIN.

Viet Nam: 10 Leedon Park, Singapore 267887; tel. 64625938; fax 64625936; e-mail vnemb@singnet.com.sg; Ambassador DO CONG MINH.

Judicial System

Supreme Court: St Andrew's Rd, Singapore 178957; tel. 63381034; fax 63379450; e-mail supcourt_qsm@supcourt.gov.sg; internet www .supcourt.gov.sg.

The judicial power of Singapore is vested in the Supreme Court and in the Subordinate Courts. The Judiciary administers the law with complete independence from the executive and legislative branches of the Government; this independence is safeguarded by the Constitution. The Supreme Court consists of the High Court and the Court of Appeal. The Chief Justice is appointed by the President if the latter, acting at his discretion, concurs with the advice of the Prime Minister. The other judges of the Supreme Court are appointed in the same way, in consultation with the Chief Justice. At 1 April 2003 there were two judges of appeal, including the Chief Justice, and 11 judges in the Supreme Court. Under a 1979 constitutional amendment, the position of judicial commissioner of the Supreme Court was created 'to facilitate the disposal of business in the Supreme Court'. A judicial commissioner has the powers and functions of a judge, and is appointed for such period as the President thinks fit. At 1 April 2003 there were no judicial commissioners in the Supreme Court.

The Subordinate Courts consist of District Courts and Magistrates' Courts. In addition, there are also specialized courts such as the Coroner's Court, Family Court, Juvenile Court, Mentions Court, Night Court, Sentencing Courts and Filter Courts. The Primary Dispute Resolution Centre and the Small Claims Tribunals are also managed by the Subordinate Courts. The Subordinate Courts have also established the Multi-Door Courthouse, which serves as a one-stop centre for the screening and channelling of any cases to the most appropriate forum for dispute resolution.

District Courts and Magistrates' Courts have original criminal and civil jurisdiction. District Courts try offences for which the maximum penalty does not exceed 10 years of imprisonment and in civil cases where the amount claimed does not exceed S $250,000. Magistrates' Courts try offences for which the maximum term of imprisonment does not exceed three years. The jurisdiction of Magistrates' Courts in civil cases is limited to claims not exceeding S $60,000. The Coroners' Court conducts inquests. The Small Claims Tribunal has jurisdiction over claims relating to a dispute arising from any contract for the sale of goods or the provision of services and any claim in tort in respect of damage caused to any property involving an amount that does not exceed S $10,000. The

Juvenile Court deals with offences committed by young persons aged under 16 years.

The High Court has unlimited original jurisdiction in criminal and civil cases. In its appellate jurisdiction it hears criminal and civil appeals from the District Courts and Magistrates' Courts. The Court of Appeal hears appeals against the decisions of the High Court in both criminal and civil matters. In criminal matters, the Court of Appeal hears appeals against decisions made by the High Court in the exercise of its original criminal jurisdiction. In civil matters, the Court of Appeal hears appeals against decisions made by the High Court in the exercise of both its original and appellate jurisdiction.

With the enactment of the Judicial Committee (Repeal) Act 1994 in April of that year, the right of appeal from the Court of Appeal to the Judicial Committee of the Privy Council in the United Kingdom was abolished. The Court of Appeal is now the final appellate court in the Singapore legal system.

Attorney-General: CHAN SEK KEONG.

Chief Justice: YONG PUNG HOW.

Judge of Appeal: CHAO HICK TIN.

Judges of the High Court: LAI KEW CHAI, S. RAJENDRAN, M. P. H. RUBIN, KAN TING CHIU, LAI SIU CHIU, JUDITH PRAKASH, TAN LEE MENG, CHOO HAN TECK, BELINDA ANG, WOO BIH LI, TAY YONG KWANG.

Religion

According to the 2000 census, 64.4% of ethnic Chinese, who constituted 76.8% of the population, professed either Buddhism or Daoism (including followers of Confucius, Mencius and Lao Zi) and 16.5% of Chinese adhered to Christianity. Malays, who made up 13.9% of the population, were 99.6% Muslim. Among Indians, who constituted 7.9% of the population, 55.4% were Hindus, 25.6% Muslims, 12.1% Christians and 6.3% Sikhs, Jains or adherents of other faiths. There are small communities of Zoroastrians and Jews. Freedom of worship is guaranteed by the Constitution.

BAHÁ'Í FAITH

National Spiritual Assembly: 110D Wishart Rd, Singapore 098733; tel. 62733023; fax 62732497; e-mail secretariat@bahai.org .sg; internet www.bahai.org.sg.

BUDDHISM

Buddhist Union: 28 Jalan Senyum, Singapore 418152; tel. 64435959; fax 64443280.

Singapore Buddhist Federation: 12 Ubi Ave 1, Singapore 408932; tel. 67444635; fax 67473618; e-mail buddhist@singnet.com .sg; internet www.buddhist.org.sg; f. 1948.

Singapore Buddhist Sangha Organization: 88 Bright Hill Drive, Singapore 579644.

Evangelical Fellowship of Singapore (EFOS): Singapore; f. 1980.

CHRISTIANITY

National Council of Churches: 6 Mt Sophia, Singapore 228457; tel. 63372150; fax 63360368; e-mail nccs@cyberway.com.sg; f. 1948; six mem. churches, six assoc. mems; Pres. Bishop JOHN TAN; Gen. Sec. Rev. Canon Dr JAMES WONG.

Singapore Council of Christian Churches (SCCC): Singapore; f. 1956.

The Anglican Communion

The Anglican diocese of Singapore (also including Indonesia, Laos, Thailand, Viet Nam and Cambodia) is part of the Province of the Anglican Church in South-East Asia.

Bishop of Singapore: The Rt Rev. Dr JOHN HIANG CHEA CHEW, 4 Bishopsgate, Singapore 249970; tel. 64741661; fax 64791054; e-mail bpoffice@anglican.org.sg.

Orthodox Churches

The Orthodox Syrian Church and the Mar Thoma Syrian Church are both active in Singapore.

The Roman Catholic Church

Singapore comprises a single archdiocese, directly responsible to the Holy See. In December 2000 there were an estimated 151,655 adherents in the country, representing 3.8% of the total population.

Archbishop of Singapore: Most Rev. NICHOLAS CHIA, Archbishop's House, 31 Victoria St, Singapore 187997; tel. 63378818; fax 63334725; e-mail nc@veritas.org.sg.

Other Christian Churches

Brethren Assemblies: Bethesda Hall (Ang Mo Kio), 601 Ang Mo Kio Ave 4, Singapore 569898; tel. 64587474; fax 64566771; e-mail bethesda@pacific.net.sg; f. 1864; Hon. Sec. WONG TUCK KEONG.

Methodist Church in Singapore: 2 Cluny Rd, 02–00, Singapore 259570; tel. 64715665; fax 64736754; e-mail mcsbp@cyberway.com .sg; internet www.methodist.org.sg; f. 1885; 30,393 mems (July 2000); Bishop Dr ROBERT SOLOMON.

Presbyterian Church: 3 Orchard Rd, cnr Penang Rd, Singapore 238825; tel. 63376681; fax 63391979; e-mail orpcenglish@orpc.org .sg; f. 1856; services in English, Chinese (Mandarin), Indonesian and German; 2,000 mems; Chair. Rev. DAVID BURKE.

Singapore Baptist Convention: 01 Goldhill Plaza, 03–19 Podium Blk, Singapore 308899; tel. 62538004; fax 62538214; e-mail sbcnet@ singnet.com.sg; internet www.baptistconvention.org.sg; Chair. Rev. M. S. SONG; Sec. RUSSELL MORRIS.

Other denominations active in Singapore include the Lutheran Church and the Evangelical Lutheran Church.

HINDUISM

Hindu Advisory Board: c/o 397 Serangoon Rd, Singapore 218123; tel. 62963469; fax 62929766; e-mail heb@pacific.net.sg; Chair. AJAIB HARI DASS; Sec. E. SANMUGAM.

Hindu Endowments Board: 397 Serangoon Rd, Singapore 218123; tel. 62963469; fax 62929766; e-mail heb@pacific.net.sg; internet www.gov.sg/heb; Chair. V. R. NATHAN; Sec. SATISH APPOO.

ISLAM

Majlis Ugama Islam Singapura (MUIS) (Islamic Religious Council of Singapore): Islamic Centre of Singapore, 273 Braddell Rd, Singapore 579702; tel. 62568188; fax 62537572; e-mail maarof@ muis.gov.sg; internet www.muis.gov.sg; f. 1968; Pres. Haji MAAROF Haji SALLEH.

Muslim Missionary Society Singapore (JAMIYAH): 31 Lorong, 12 Geylang Rd, Singapore 399006; tel. 67431211; fax 67450610; e-mail info@jamiyah.org.sg; internet www.jamiyah.org.sg; Pres. Haji ABU BAKAR MAIDIN; Sec.-Gen. ISMAIL ROZIZ.

SIKHISM

Sikh Ad: c/o 2 Towner Rd, 03-01, Singapore 327804; tel. and fax 62996440; Chair. BHAJAN SINGH.

The Press

Compulsory government scrutiny of newspaper management has been in operation since 1974. All newspaper enterprises must be public companies. In August 1986 there were more than 3,700 foreign publications circulating in Singapore. The Newspaper and Printing Presses (Amendment) Act 1986 empowers the Government to restrict the circulation of foreign periodicals that are deemed to exert influence over readers on domestic political issues. An amendment to the Newspaper and Printing Presses Act was promulgated in October 1990. Under this amendment, all publications of which the 'contents and editorial policy were determined outside Singapore' and which dealt with politics and current events in South-East Asia would be required to obtain a ministerial licence, renewable annually. The permit would limit the number of copies sold and require a deposit in case of legal proceedings involving the publication. Permits could be refused or revoked without any reason being given. In November, however, a statement was issued exempting 14 of the 17 foreign publications affected by the amendment, which came into effect in December.

DAILIES

English Language

Business Times: 1000 Toa Payoh North, Singapore 318994; tel. 63196319; fax 63198277; e-mail btnews@sph.com.sg; internet www .business-times.asia1.com.sg; f. 1976; morning; Editor PATRICK DANIEL; circ. 36,000 (Singapore only).

The New Paper: 1000 Toa Payoh North, Annexe Blk, Level 6, Singapore 318994; tel. 63196319; fax 63198266; e-mail tnp@sph.com .sg; internet www.newpaper.asia1.com.sg; f. 1988; afternoon tabloid; Editor IVAN FERNANDEZ; circ. 121,000 (Singapore only).

Streats: 1000 Toa Payoh North, Podium Blk, Level 1, Singapore 318994; tel. 63192421; fax 63198191; e-mail streats@sph.com.sg; Editor KEN JALLEH, Jr.

The Straits Times: 1000 Toa Payoh North, Singapore 318994; tel. 63196319; fax 67320131; e-mail stlocal@sph.com.sg; internet www

.straitstimes.asia1.com.sg; f. 1845; morning; Editor HAN FOK KWANG; circ. 392,611 (Singapore only).

Chinese Language

Lianhe Wanbao: 1000 Toa Payoh North, Podium Blk, Level 4, Singapore 318994; tel. 63196319; fax 63198133; e-mail wanbao@sph .com.sg; f. 1983; evening; Editor KOH LIN HOE; circ. 127,656 (week), 123,283 (weekend) in Feb. 2001.

Lianhe Zaobao: 1000 Toa Payoh North, Podium Blk, Level 4, Singapore 318994; tel. 63196319; fax 63198199; e-mail zaobao@ zaobao.com.sg; internet www.zaobao.com.sg; f. 1923; Editor LIM JIM KOON; circ. 200,761.

Shin Min Daily News (S) Ltd: 1000 Toa Payoh North, Podium Blk, Level 4, Singapore 318994; tel. 63196319; fax 63198166; e-mail shinmin@sph.com.sg; f. 1967; evening; Editor TOH LAM HHAT; circ. 128,383.

Malay Language

Berita Harian: 1000 Toa Payoh North, Singapore 318994; tel. 63196319; fax 63198255; e-mail aadeska@sph.com.sg; internet www .cyberita.asia1.com.sg; f. 1957; morning; Editor MOHD GUNTOR SADALI; circ. 68,000 (Singapore only).

Tamil Language

Tamil Murasu: 151 Chin Swee Rd, 01-52 Manhattan House, Singapore 169876; tel. 67366077; fax 67366033; e-mail murasu4@ cyberway.co.sg; internet www.tamilmurasu.asia1.com.sg; f. 1935; Editor CHITRA RAJARAM; circ. 14,000 (daily), 23,000 (Sunday).

WEEKLIES

English Language

Sunday Times: 1000 Toa Payoh North, Singapore 318994; tel. 63195397; fax 67320131; e-mail stlocal@sph.com.sg; internet www .straitstimes.asia1.com.sg; f. 1845; Editor-in-Chief CHEONG YIP SENG; circ. 387,000 (Singapore only).

Malay Language

Berita Minggu: 1000 Toa Payoh North, Singapore 318994; tel. 63196319; fax 63198255; e-mail aadeska@sph.com.sg; internet www .cyberita.asia1.com.sg; f. 1957; Sunday; Editor MOHD GUNTOR SADALI; circ. 73,500 (Singapore only).

SELECTED PERIODICALS

English Language

Accent: Accent Communications, 215 Intrepid Warehouse Complex, 4 Ubi Ave, Singapore 1440; tel. 67478088; fax 67472811; f. 1983; monthly; lifestyle; Senior Editor DORA TAY; circ. 65,000.

Cherie Magazine: 12 Everton Rd, Singapore 0208; tel. 62229733; fax 62843859; f. 1983; bimonthly; women's; Editor JOSEPHINE NG; circ. 20,000.

8 Days: 298 Tiong Bahru Rd, 19-01/06 Tiong Bahru Plaza, Singapore 168730; tel. 62789822; fax 62724800; e-mail feedback@ 8daysonline.com; internet www.8days.mediacorppublishing.com; f. 1990; weekly; Editor-in-Chief TAN LEE SUN; circ. 113,258.

Go Flirt: Times Periodicals Pte Ltd, 422 Thomson Rd, Singapore 298131; tel. 62550011; fax 62568016; e-mail tpgo@cyberway.com.sg; f. 1980; monthly; women's; Editor LYNN LEE; circ. 29,632.

Her World: Times Periodicals Pte Ltd, 422 Thomson Rd, Singapore 298131; tel. 62550011; fax 62568016; e-mail herworld@cyberway .com.sg; internet www.herworld.asiaone.com.sg; f. 1960; monthly; women's; Editor CAROLINE NGUI; circ. 64,042.

Home and Decor: Times Periodicals Pte Ltd, 422 Thomson Rd, Singapore 298131; tel. 62550011; fax 62568016; e-mail hdecor@ cyberway.com.sg; f. 1981; 6 a year; home-owners; Editor SOPHIE KHO; circ. 25,385.

LIME: 65 Io Ang Mo Kio St, 01-06/08 Techpoint, Singapore 569059; tel. 64837118; fax 64837286; f. 1996; Editor PAMELA QUEK; circ. 34,947.

Man—Life & Style: 55 Cuppage Rd, 08-06 Cuppage Centre, Singapore 0922; tel. 67386166; fax 67386122; f. 1986; monthly; men's; Editor SU MANN ONG; circ. 130,000.

Mondial Collections: Singapore; f. 1990; bimonthly; arts; Chair. CHRIS CHENEY; circ. 100,000.

NSman: Times Periodicals Pte Ltd, 422 Thomson Rd, Singapore 298131; tel. 62550011; fax 62568016; e-mail timesp@cyberway.com .sg; f. 1973; bimonthly; publication of the SAF National Service; Editor KOH BOON PIN; circ. 130,705.

Republic of Singapore Government Gazette: Singapore National Printers Ltd, 1 Kim Seng Promenade, 18-01 Great World City East Tower, Singapore 237994; tel. 68338680; fax 67321866; e-mail egazinfo@snp.com.sg; internet www.egazette.com.sg; weekly; Friday.

Reservist: 5200 Jalan Bukit Merah, Singapore 0315; tel. 62786011; fax 6273441; f. 1973; bimonthly; men's; Editor SAMUEL EE; circ. 130,000.

Singapore Medical Journal: Singapore Medical Association, Level 2, Alumni Medical Centre, 2 College Rd, Singapore 169850; tel. 62231264; fax 62247827; e-mail smj@sma.org.sg; internet www .sma.org.sg/smj; monthly; Editor Dr C. RAJASOORYA.

Times Guide to Computers: 1 New Industrial Rd, Times Centre, Singapore 536196; tel. 62848844; fax 62850161; e-mail ttd@corp.tpl .com.sg; internet www.tpl.com.sg; f. 1986; annually; computing and communications; Vice-Pres. LESLIE LIM; circ. 30,000.

Visage: Ubi Ave 1, 02-169 Blk 305, Singapore 1440; tel. 67478088; fax 67472811; f. 1984; monthly; Editor-in-Chief TENG JUAT LENG; circ. 63,000.

WEEKENDeast: 82 Genting Lane, News Centre, Singapore 349567; tel. 67401200; fax 67451022; e-mail focuspub@cyberway .com.sg; f. 1986; Editor VICTOR SOH; circ. 75,000.

Woman's Affair: 140 Paya Lebar Rd, 04-10 A-Z Bldg, Singapore 1440; tel. 67478088; fax 67479119; f. 1988; 2 a month; Editor DORA TAY; circ. 38,000.

Young Parents: Times Periodicals Pte Ltd, 422 Thomson Rd, Singapore 298131; tel. 62550011; fax 62568016; e-mail yparents@ cyberway.com.sg; f. 1986; monthly; family; Editor GLORIA CHAN (acting); circ. 10,725.

Chinese Language

Characters: 1 Kallang Sector, 04-04/04-05 Kolam Ayer Industrial Park, Singapore 349276; tel. 67458733; fax 67458213; f. 1987; monthly; television and entertainment; Editor SAM NG; circ. 45,000.

The Citizen: People's Association, 9 Stadium Link, Singapore 397750; tel. 63405138; fax 63468657; monthly; English, Chinese, Tamil and Malay; Man. Editor OOI HUI MEI.

i-weekly: 298 Tiong Bahru Rd, 19-01/06 Tiong Bahru Plaza, Singapore 168730; tel. 62789822; fax 62724811; f. 1981; weekly; radio and television; Editor-in-Chief LOKE TAI TAY; circ. 113,000.

Punters' Way: 4 Ubi View (off Ubi Rd 3), Pioneers and Leaders Centre, Singapore 408557; tel. 67458733; fax 67458213; e-mail pnlhldg@pcl.com.sg; f. 1977; biweekly; English and Chinese; sport; Editor T. S. PHAN; circ. 90,000.

Racing Guide: 1 New Industrial Rd, Times Centre, Singapore 1953; tel. 62848844; fax 62881186; f. 1987; 2 a week; English and Chinese; sport; Editorial Consultant BENNY ORTEGA; Chinese Editor KUEK CHIEW TEONG; circ. 20,000.

Singapore Literature: Singapore Literature Society, 122B Sims Ave, Singapore 1438; quarterly; Pres. YAP KOON CHAN; Editor LUO-MING.

Tune Monthly Magazine: Henderson Rd 06-04, Blk 203A, Henderson Industrial Park, Singapore 0315; tel. 62733000; fax 62749538; f. 1988; monthly; women's and fashion; Editor CHAN ENG; circ. 25,000.

Young Generation: SNP Media Asia Pte Ltd, 97 Ubi Avenue 4, SNP Building, Singapore 408754; tel. 67412500; fax 68463890; e-mail yg@snp.com.sg; internet www.snp.com.sg; monthly; children's; Editor EVELYN TANG; circ. 80,000.

NEWS AGENCIES

Foreign Bureaux

Agence France-Presse (AFP): 10 Hoe Chiang Rd, 07-03 Keppel Towers, Singapore 089315; tel. 62228581; fax 62247465; e-mail afpsin@afp.com; Bureau Chief ROBERTO Z. COLOMA.

Agenzia Nazionale Stampa Associata (ANSA) (Italy): Blk 628, 8 Hougang Ave, 04-94, Singapore 530628; tel. 63855514; fax 63855279; e-mail kuttynng@pacific.net.sg; Correspondent N. G. KUTTY.

Associated Press (AP) (USA): 10 Anson Rd, 32-11 International Plaza, Singapore 079903; tel. 62201849; fax 62212753; e-mail sgutkin@ap.org; Chief of South-East Asian Services STEVEN GUTKIN.

Central News Agency Inc (CNA) (Taiwan): 78A Lorong N, Telok Kurau, Ocean Apartments, Singapore 425223; tel. 63445746; fax 63467645; e-mail cnanews@signet.com.sg; South-East Asia Correspondent SHERMAN SHEAN-SHEN WU.

Inter Press Service (IPS) (Italy): Marine Parade Rd, 10-42 Lagoon View, Singapore 1544; tel. 64490432; Correspondent SURYA GANG-ADHARAN.

Jiji Tsushin (Jiji Press) (Japan): 10 Anson Rd, 24-16A International Plaza, Singapore 079903; tel. 62244212; fax 62240711; e-mail jijisp@jiji.com.sg; internet www.jiji.com; Bureau Chief AMANO KAZU-TOSHI.

Kyodo News (Japan): 138 Cecil St, Cecil Court, Singapore; tel. 62233371; fax 62249208; e-mail goinrk@kyodonews.or.jp; Chief NORIKO GOI.

Reuters Singapore Pte Ltd: 18 Science Park Drive, Singapore 118229; tel. 68703080; fax 67768112; e-mail singapore.newsroom@ reuters.com; Bureau Chief RICHARD HUBBARD.

Rossiiskoye Informatsionnoye Agentstvo—Vesti (RIA—Vesti) (Russia): 8 Namly Grove, Singapore 1026; tel. 64667998; fax 64690784; Correspondent MIKHAIL I. IDAMKIN.

United Press International (UPI) (USA): Singapore; tel. 63373715; fax 63389867; Man. DEAN VISSER.

Bernama (Malaysia), United News (India) and Xinhua (People's Republic of China) are also represented.

Publishers

ENGLISH LANGUAGE

Addison-Wesley (S) Pte Ltd: 25 First Lok Yang Rd, Jurong City, Singapore 629734; tel. 62682666; fax 62641740; e-mail enquiry@awl .com.sg; educational, computing and professional books; Gen. Man. CHWEE LEONG LOW.

Butterworths Asia: 1 Temasek Ave, 17-01 Millenia Tower, Singapore 039192; tel. 63369661; fax 63369662; e-mail sales@ butterworths.com.sg; internet www.lexisnexis.com.sg/ butterworths-online; f. 1932; law texts and journals; Man. Dir GRAHAM J. MARSHALL.

Caldecott Publishing Pte Ltd: 10 Ang Mo Kio St 65, 01-06/08 Techpoint, Singapore 569059; tel. 64837118; fax 64837286; f. 1990; CEO MICHAEL CHIANG; Editor-in-Chief TAN LEE SUN.

EPB Publishers Pte Ltd: Blk 162, 04-3545 Bukit Merah Central, Singapore 150162; tel. 62780881; fax 62782456; e-mail epb@sbg.com .sg; fmrly Educational Publications Bureau Pte Ltd; textbooks and supplementary materials, general, reference and magazines; English and Chinese; Gen. Man. ROGER PHUA.

FEP International Pte Ltd: 11 Arnsal Chetty Rd 03-02, Singapore 239949; tel. 67331178; fax 67375561; f. 1960; textbooks, reference, children's and dictionaries; Gen. Man. RICHARD TOH.

Flame of the Forest Publishing Pte Ltd: Blk 5, Ang Mo Kio Industrial Park 2A, 07-22/23, AMK Tech II, Singapore 567760; tel. 64848887; fax 64842208; e-mail editor@flameoftheforest.com; internet www.flameoftheforest.com; Man. Dir ALEX CHACKO.

Graham Brash Pte Ltd: 45 Kian Teck Drive, Blk 1, Level 2, Singapore 628859; tel. 62624843; fax 62621519; e-mail graham_brash@giro.com.sg; internet www.grahambrash.com.sg; f. 1947; general, academic, educational; English, Chinese and Malay; CEO CHUAN I. CAMPBELL; Dir HELENE CAMPBELL.

HarperCollins, Asia Pte Ltd: 970 Toa Payoh North, 04-24/26, Singapore 1231; tel. 62501985; fax 62501360; f. 1983; educational, trade, reference and general; Man. Dir FRANK FOLEY.

Institute of Southeast Asian Studies: 30 Heng Mui Keng Terrace, Pasir Panjang Rd, Singapore 119614; tel. 67780955; fax 67781735; e-mail publish@iseas.edu.sg; internet www.iseas.edu.sg; f. 1968; scholarly works on contemporary South-East Asia and the Asia-Pacific; Dir Prof. CHIA SIOW YUE.

Intellectual Publishing Co: 113 Eunos Ave 3, 04-08 Gordon Industrial Bldg, Singapore 1440; tel. 67466025; fax 67489108; f. 1971; Man. POH BE LECK.

Pearson Education Asia Pte Ltd: 23/25 First Lok Yang Rd, Jurong Town, Singapore 629733; tel. 63199388; fax 62641740; educational; Pres. WONG WEE WOON.

Simon & Schuster Asia Pte Ltd: 317 Alexandra Rd, 04-01 Ikea Bldg, Singapore 159965; tel. 64764688; fax 63780370; e-mail prenhall@signet.com.sg; f. 1975; educational; Man. Dir GUNAWAN HADI.

Singapore University Press Pte Ltd: National University of Singapore, 31 Lower Kent Ridge Rd, Singapore 119078; tel. 67761148; fax 67740652; e-mail supbooks@nus.edu.sg; internet www.nus.edu.sg/SUP; f. 1971; scholarly; Editor and Man. PATRICIA TAY.

Stamford College Publishers: Colombo Court 05-11A, Singapore 0617; tel. 63343378; fax 63343080; f. 1970; general, educational and journals; Man. LAWRENCE THOMAS.

Times Editions Pte Ltd: Times Centre, 1 New Industrial Rd, Singapore 536196; tel. 62139288; fax 62844733; e-mail tpl@tpl.com .sg; internet www.tpl.com.sg; f. 1978; political, social and cultural books, general works on Asia; Chair. LIM KIM SAN; Pres. and CEO LAI SECK KHUI.

Times Media Pte Ltd (Education Division): Times Centre, 1 New Industrial Rd, Singapore 536196; tel. 62139463; fax 62889254; e-mail tmesales@tpl.com.sg; internet www.timesone.com.sg/fpl; f. 1957; educational, children's, general and reference books; Vice-Pres. and Gen. Man. JUNE OEI.

World Scientific Publishing Co Pte Ltd: 5 Toh Tuck Link, Singapore 596224; tel. 64665775; fax 64677667; e-mail wspc@wspc .com.sg; internet www.worldscientific.com; f. 1981; academic texts and science journals; Man. Dir DOREEN LIU.

MALAY LANGUAGE

Malaysia Press Sdn Bhd (Pustaka Melayu): Singapore; tel. 62933454; fax 62911858; f. 1962; textbooks and educational; Man. Dir ABU TALIB BIN ALLY.

Pustaka Nasional Pte Ltd: 2 Joo Chiat Rd, 05-1125 Joo Chiat Complex, Singapore 420002; tel. 67454321; fax 67452417; e-mail webmaster@pustaka.com.sg; internet www.pustaka.com.sg; f. 1965; Malay and Islamic religious books and CD-Roms; Man. Dir SYED AHMAD BIN MUHAMMED.

CHINESE LANGUAGE

Shanghai Book Co (Pte) Ltd: 231 Bain St, 02-73 Bras Basah Complex, Singapore 180231; tel. 63360144; fax 63360490; e-mail shanghaibook@pacific.net.sg; f. 1925; educational and general; Man. Dir MA JI LIN.

Shing Lee Publishers Pte Ltd: 120 Hillview Ave, 05-06/07 Kewalram Hillview, Singapore 2366; tel. 67601388; fax 67625684; e-mail shingleebook@sbg.com.sg; f. 1935; educational and general; Man. PEH CHIN HUA.

Union Book Co (Pte) Ltd: 231 Bain St 03-01, Bras Basah Complex, Singapore 0718; tel. 63380696; fax 63386306; general and reference; Gen. Man. CHOW LI-LIANG.

TAMIL LANGUAGE

EVS Enterprises: Singapore; tel. 62830002; f. 1967; children's books, religion and general; Man. E. V. SINGHAN.

Government Publishing House

SNP Corpn Ltd: 1 Kim Seng Promenade, 18-01 Great World City East Tower, Singapore 237994; tel. 68269600; fax 68203341; e-mail btsypang@snpcorp.com; internet www.snpcorp.com; f. 1973; printers and publishers; Pres. and CEO YEO CHEE TONG.

PUBLISHERS' ORGANIZATIONS

National Book Development Council of Singapore (NBDCS): Singapore; promotes reading and jtly organizes the annual Singapore Book Fair with the Singapore Book Publishers' Association.

Singapore Book Publishers' Association: c/o Chopmen Publrs, 865 Mountbatten Rd, 05-28 Katong Shopping Centre, Singapore 1543; tel. 63441495; fax 63440180; Pres. N. T. S. CHOPRA.

Broadcasting and Communications

TELECOMMUNICATIONS

Infocomm Development Authority of Singapore: 8 Temasek Blvd, 14-00 Suntec Tower Three, Singapore 038988; tel. 62110888; fax 62112222; e-mail info@ida.gov.sg; internet www.ida.gov.sg; f. 1999 as result of merger of National Computer Board and Telecommunication Authority of Singapore; the national policy maker, regulator and promoter of telecommunications in Singapore; CEO LEONG KENG THAI (acting).

Netrust: 10 Collyer Quay, 09-05/06 Ocean Bldg, Singapore 049315; tel. 62121388; fax 62121366; e-mail infoline@netrust.net; internet www.netrust.net; f. 1997; the first Internet Certification Authority (CA), jtly formed by the National Computer Board and the Network for Electronic Transfers; the authority verifies the identity of parties doing business or communicating in cyberspace through the issuing of electronic identification certificates.

Singapore Telecommunications Ltd (SingTel): Comcentre, 31 Exeter Rd, Singapore 239732; tel. 68383388; fax 67383769; e-mail contact@singtel.com; internet www.singtel.com; f. 1992; a postal and telecommunications service operator and a holding company for a number of subsidiaries; 68%-owned by Temasek Holdings (Private) Ltd (a government holding company), 32% transferred to the private sector; Chair. ANG KONG HUA; Pres. and CEO LEE HSIEN YANG.

StarHub Pte Ltd: Head Office, 51 Cuppage Rd, 07-00 StarHub Centre, Singapore 229469; tel. 68255000; fax 67215000; e-mail customercare@starhub.com.sg; internet www.starhub.com.sg; f. 2000; telecommunications service provider; consortium includes Singapore Technologies Telemedia Pte Ltd, Singapore Power Ltd, Nippon Telegraph and Telephone Corpn (NTT) and British Telecom (BT); CEO and Pres. TERRY CLONTZ.

Singapore Technologies Telemedia: 51 Cuppage Rd, 10-11/17, Starhub Centre, Singapore 229469; tel. 67238777; fax 67207277; e-mail contactus@stt.st.com.sg; internet www.stt.st.com.sg; Pres. LEE THENG KIAT.

BROADCASTING

Regulatory Authority

Media Development Authority (MDA): MITA Bldg 04-01, 140 Hill St, Singapore 179369; tel. 68379973; fax 63368023; internet www.mda.gov.sg; f. 1994; fmrly Singapore Broadcasting Authority, name changed as above in Jan. 2003; licenses and regulates the media industry in Singapore; encourages, promotes and facilitates the development of media industries in Singapore, ensures the provision of an adequate range of media services to serve the interests of the general public, maintains fair and efficient market conduct and effective competition in the media industry, ensures the maintenance of a high standard of media services, regulates public service broadcasting; Chair. TAN CHIN NAM; CEO LIM HOCK CHUAN.

Radio

Far East Broadcasting Associates: 30 Lorong Ampas, 07-01 Skywaves Industrial Bldg, Singapore 328783; tel. 62508577; fax 62508422; e-mail febadmin@febasgp.com; f. 1960; Chair. GOH EWE KHENG; Exec. Dir Rev. JOHN CHANG.

Media Corporation of Singapore: Caldecott Broadcast Centre, Andrew Rd, Singapore 299939; tel. 63333888; fax 62515628; e-mail cherfern@mediacorpradio.com; internet www.mediacorpsingapore .com; f. 1994 as Singapore International Media (SIM), following the corporatization of the Singapore Broadcasting Corpn; holding co for seven operating cos—Television Corpn of Singapore (TCS), Singapore Television Twelve (STV12), Radio Corpn of Singapore (RCS), MediaCorp Studios, MediaCorp News, MediaCorp Interactive and MediaCorp Publishing; Chair. CHENG WAI KEUNG.

Radio Corpn of Singapore Pte Ltd (RCS): Caldecott Broadcast Centre, Radio Bldg, Andrew Rd, Singapore 299939; tel. 62518622; fax 62569533; e-mail feedback@rcs.com.sg; internet www .mediacorpradio.com; f. 1936; operates 12 domestic services—in English (five), Chinese (Mandarin) (three), Malay (two), Tamil (one) and foreign language (one)—and three international radio stations (manages Radio Singapore International (RSI)—services in English, Mandarin and Malay for three hours daily and service in Bahasa Indonesia for one hour daily); Chief Operating Officer CHUA FOO YONG.

Radio Heart: Singapore; internet www.heart913.org.sg; f. 1991; first private radio station; broadcasts in English, Chinese (Mandarin), Malay and Tamil; 2 channels broadcasting a total of 280 hours.

Rediffusion (Singapore) Pte Ltd: 6 Harper Rd, 04-01/08 Leong Huat Bldg, Singapore 369674; tel. 63832633; fax 63832622; e-mail md@rediffusion.com.sg; internet www.rediffusion.com.sg; f. 1949; commercial audio wired broadcasting service and wireless digital audio broadcasting service; broadcasts two programmes in Mandarin (18 hours daily) and English (24 hours daily); Man. Dir WONG BAN KUAN.

SAFRA Radio: Defence Technology Towers, Tower B, 5 Depot Rd, 12–04, Singapore; tel. 63731924; fax 62783039; e-mail power98@ pacific.net.sg; internet www.power98.com.sg/; f. 1994; broadcasts in Chinese (Mandarin) and English.

Television

CNBC Asia Business News (S) Pte Ltd: 10 Anson Rd, 06-01 International Plaza, Singapore 079903; tel. 63230488; fax 63230788; e-mail talk2us@cnbcasia.com; internet www.cnbcasia.com.sg; f. 1998; cable and satellite broadcaster of global business and financial news; US controlled; broadcasts in English (24 hours daily) and Mandarin; Pres. PAUL FRANCE.

Media Corporation of Singapore: see Radio.

Singapore CableVision: Singapore; internet www.scv.com.sg; f. 1992; broadcasting and communications co, subscription television service; three channels; launched cable service with 33 channels in June 1995; offers broadband access services.

Singapore Television Twelve Pte Ltd (STV12): 12 Prince Edward Rd, 05-00 Bestway Bldg, Singapore 079212; tel. 62258133; fax 62203881; internet www.stv12.com.sg; f. 1994; terrestrial television station; 2 channels—Suria (Malay, 58 hours weekly) and Central (110.5 hours weekly); Chief Operating Officer WOON TAI HO.

Television Corpn of Singapore (TCS): Caldecott Broadcast Centre, Andrew Rd, Singapore 299939; tel. 62560401; fax 62538119; e-mail webmaster@mediacorptv.com; internet www.mediacorptv.com; f. 1994 following the corporatization of Singapore Broadcasting Corpn; four channels—TCS 5 (English), TCS 8 (Mandarin), Suria (Malay) and Central; teletext service on two channels; also owns TVMobile, Singapore's first digital television channel, and Digital TV; Chair. CHENG WAI KEUNG; CEO LIM HUP SENG.

Finance

(cap. = capital; res = reserves; dep. = deposits; m. = million; brs = branches; amounts in Singapore dollars)

BANKING

The Singapore monetary system is regulated by the Monetary Authority of Singapore (MAS) and the Ministry of Finance. The MAS performs all the functions of a central bank, except the issuing of currency, a function which is carried out by the Board of Commissioners of Currency. In April 2003 there were 117 commercial banks (5 local, 112 foreign) and 51 representative offices in Singapore. Of the foreign banks, 22 had full licences, 31 had wholesale licences and 59 foreign banks had 'offshore' banking licences.

Government Financial Institutions

Board of Commissioners of Currency, Singapore: 109 Pasir Panjang Rd, Singapore 118536; tel. 63776868; fax 63776800; e-mail currency@bccs.gov.sg; internet www.singaporecurrency.gov.sg; Chair. Brig.-Gen. (retd) LEE HSIEN LOONG; Dep. Chair. LIM SIONG GUAN.

Monetary Authority of Singapore (MAS): 10 Shenton Way, MAS Bldg, Singapore 079117; tel. 62255577; fax 62299229; e-mail webmaster@mas.gov.sg; internet www.mas.gov.sg; cap. 100m., res 13,857m., dep. 78,004m. (Dec. 2001); Chair. Brig.-Gen. (retd) LEE HSIEN LOONG; Man. Dir KOH YONG GUAN.

Domestic Full Commercial Banks

Bank of Singapore Ltd: 55 Market St, 13-00 Sinsov Bldg, Singapore 048941; tel. 63893000; fax 63893016; internet www.bankofsingapore.com; f. 1954; subsidiary of Oversea-Chinese Banking Corpn Ltd; cap. 50m., res 207m., dep. 2,984.5m. (Dec. 1997); Chair. DAVID PHILBRICK CONNER; CEO TAN NGIAP JOO.

DBS Bank (Development Bank of Singapore Ltd): 6 Shenton Way, DBS Bldg, Tower One, Singapore 068809; tel. 68788888; fax 64451267; e-mail dbs@dbs.com; internet www.dbs.com; f. 1968; 29% govt-owned; merged with Post Office Savings Bank in 1998; cap. 1,307m., res 9,187.5m., dep. 93,422.7m. (Dec. 2000); Chair. S. DHANABALAN; Pres. JACKSON TAI; 100 local brs, 14 overseas brs.

Far Eastern Bank Ltd: 156 Cecil St, 01-00 FEB Bldg, Singapore 069544; tel. 62219055; fax 62242263; internet www.uobgroup.com; f. 1959; subsidiary of United Overseas Bank Ltd; cap. 24.4m., res 53m., dep. 577.0m. (Dec. 2000); Chair. and CEO WEE CHO YAW; Pres. WEE EE CHEONG; 4 brs.

Oversea-Chinese Banking Corpn (OCBC) Ltd: 65 Chulia St, 08-00 OCBC Centre, Singapore 049513; tel. 65357222; fax 65337955; e-mail info@obc.com.sg; internet www.ocbc.com; f. 1932; merged with Keppel TatLee Bank Ltd in Aug. 2001; cap. 1,286m., res 4,348.8m., dep. 41,715.2m. (Dec. 2000); Chair. LEE SENG WEE; Vice-Chair. and CEO ALEXANDER AU SIU KEE; 37 local brs, 44 overseas brs.

United Overseas Bank Ltd: 80 Raffles Place, UOB Plaza, Singapore 048624; tel. 65339898; fax 65342334; internet www.uobgroup.com; f. 1935; merged with Overseas Union Bank Ltd in Jan. 2002; cap. 1,052.5m., res 4,004.8m., dep. 46,718.0m. (Dec. 2000); Chair. and CEO WEE CHO YAW; Pres. WEE EE CHEONG; 49 local brs, 15 overseas brs.

Foreign Banks

Full Commercial Banks

ABN AMRO Asia Pacific Pte Ltd (Netherlands): 63 Chulia St, Singapore 049514; tel. 62318888; fax 65323108; Country Rep. DAVID WONG SEE HONG; Country Admin. Officer ROBERT DAVIS.

Bangkok Bank Public Co Ltd (Thailand): 180 Cecil St, Bangkok Bank Bldg, Singapore 069546; tel. 62219400; fax 62255852; Sr Vice-Pres. and Gen. Man. TORPHONG CHARUNGCHAREONVEJI.

Bank of America NA (USA): 9 Raffles Place, 18-00 Republic Plaza Tower 1, Singapore 048619; tel. 62393888; fax 62393188; CEO ALAN KOH; Man. Dir GOETZ EGGELHOEFER.

Bank of China (People's Republic of China): 4 Battery Rd, Bank of China Bldg, Singapore 049908; tel. 65352411; fax 65343401; Gen. Man. ZHU HUA.

Bank of East Asia Ltd (Hong Kong): 137 Market St, Bank of East Asia Bldg, Singapore 048943; tel. 62241334; fax 62251805; Gen. Man. KHOO KEE CHEOK.

Bank of India (India): 01-01, 02-01, 03-01, Hong Leong Centre, 138 Robinson Rd, Singapore 068906; tel. 62220011; fax 62254407; Chief Exec. B. R. PARTHASARATHI; Gen. Man. RAJIV KUMAR BAKSHI.

PT Bank Negara Indonesia (Persero) Tbk (Indonesia): 158 Cecil St, 01-00 to 04-00 Dapenso Bldg, Singapore 069545; tel. 62257755; fax 62254757; e-mail ptbni@starhub.net.sg; Gen. Man. SUWOKO SINGOASTRO.

Bank of Tokyo-Mitsubishi Ltd (Japan): 9 Raffles Place, 01-01 Republic Plaza, Singapore 048619; tel. 65383388; fax 65388083; Gen. Man. HISAO SAKASHITA; Dep. Gen. Man. KAZUAKI IWAMOTO.

BNP Paribas (France): 20 Collyer Quay, 18-01 Tung Centre, Singapore 049319; tel. 62103888; fax 62103671; internet www.bnpparibas.com.sg; CEO SERGE FORTI.

Citibank NA (USA): 3 Temasek Ave, 12-00 Centennial Tower, Singapore 039190; tel. 62242611; fax 6325880; internet www.citibank.com.sg; Country Corporate Officer SUNIL SREENIVASAN.

Crédit Agricole Indosuez (France): 6 Raffles Quay, 17-00 John Hancock Tower, Singapore 048580; tel. 65354988; fax 65322422; e-mail cai.singapore@sg.ca-indosuez.com; internet www.ca-indosuez.com; f. 1905; Senior Country Man. JEAN-FRANCOIS CAHET.

HL Bank (Malaysia): 20 Collyer Quay, 01-02 and 02-02 Tung Centre, Singapore 049319; tel. 65352466; fax 65339340; Country Head GAN HUI TIN.

Hongkong and Shanghai Banking Corpn Ltd (Hong Kong): 14-01 HSBC Bldg, 21 Collyer Quay, Singapore 049320; tel. 65305000; fax 62250663; e-mail HSBC@hsbc.com.sg; internet www.hsbc.com.sg; CEO (Singapore) ERIC W. GILL.

Indian Bank (India): 3 Raffles Place, Bharat Bldg, Singapore 048617; tel. 65343511; fax 65331651; e-mail ceibsing@mbox3.singnet.com.sg; Chief Exec. V. SRINIVASAN.

Indian Overseas Bank (India): POB 792, 64 Cecil St, IOB Bldg, Singapore 049711; tel. 62251100; fax 62244490; Chief Exec. A. C. KHER.

JP Morgan Chase Bank (USA): 168 Robinson Rd, 17th Floor, 14-01 Capital Tower, Singapore 068912; tel. 68822888; fax 68821756; Senior Country Officer JEANETTE WONG KAI YUAN.

Maybank (Malaysia): Maybank Chambers, 2 Battery Rd 01-00, Singapore 049907; tel. 65352266; fax 65327909; internet www.maybank2u.com.sg; Sr Gen. Man. SPENCER LEE TIEN CHYE.

RHB Bank Bhd (Malaysia): 90 Cecil St 01-00, Singapore 069531; tel. 62253111; fax 62273805; Asst Gen. Man. (Head of Singapore Operations) ANTHONY YEO.

Southern Bank Bhd (Malaysia): 39 Robinson Rd, 01-02 Robinson Point, Singapore 068911; tel. 65321318; fax 65355366; Dir YEAP LAM YANG.

Standard Chartered Bank (UK): 6 Battery Rd, Singapore 049909; tel. 62258888; fax 64230965; internet www.standardchartered.com.sg; Group Exec. Dirs MIKE DENOMA, KAI NARGOLWALA; Chief Exec. (Singapore) EULEEN GOH.

Sumitomo Mitsui Banking Corpn (Japan): 3 Temasek Ave, 06-01 Centennial Tower, Singapore 039190; tel. 68820001; fax 68870330; Gen. Man. HITOSHI YOSHIMATSU.

UCO Bank (India): 3 Raffles Place, 01-01 Bharat Bldg, Singapore 048617; tel. 65325944; fax 65325044; e-mail general@ucobank.com.sg; Chief Exec. R. K. MUKHERJEE.

Wholesale Banks

American Express Bank Ltd (USA): 16 Collyer Quay, Hitachi Tower, Singapore 049318; tel. 65384833; fax 65343022; Sr Country Exec. S. LACHLAN HOUGH.

Australia and New Zealand Banking Group Ltd (Australia): 10 Collyer Quay, 17-01/07 Ocean Bldg, Singapore 049315; tel. 65358355; fax 65396111; Regional Gen. Man. JOHN WINDERS.

Bank of Nova Scotia (Canada): 10 Collyer Quay, 15-01/09 Ocean Bldg, Singapore 049315; tel. 65358688; fax 65363325; Country Head, Vice-Pres. and Man. SEONG KOON WAH SUN.

Barclays Bank plc (UK): 23 Church St, 13-08 Capital Sq., Singapore 049481; tel. 63953000; fax 63953139; Regional Head JAMES LOH; Country Man. QUEK SUAN KIAT.

Bayerische Landesbank Girozentrale (Germany): 300 Beach Rd, 37-01 The Concourse, Singapore 199555; tel. 62933822; fax 62932151; e-mail sgblb@blb.de; Gen. Man. and Sr Vice-Pres. MANFRED WOLF; Exec. Vice-Pres. HEINZ HOFFMANN.

BNP Paribas Private Bank (France): 20 Collyer Quay, 18-01 Tung Centre, Singapore 049319; tel. 62101037; fax 62103671; internet www.bnpparibas.com.sg; CEO SERGE FORTI.

Chiao Tung Bank Co Ltd (Taiwan): 80 Raffles Place, 23-20 UOB Plaza II, Singapore 048624; tel. 65366311; fax 65360680; Sr Vice-Pres. and Gen. Man. FRANK WEI KUANG HUA.

Commerzbank AG (Germany): 8 Shenton Way, 41-01 Temasek Tower, Singapore 068811; tel. 63110000; fax 62253943; Gen. Man. MICHAEL OLIVER.

Crédit Lyonnais (France): 3 Temasek Ave, 11-01 Centennial Tower, Singapore 039190; tel. 63336331; fax 63336332; Gen. Man. PIERRE EYMERY.

Crédit Suisse (Switzerland): 1 Raffles Link, 05-02, Singapore 039393; tel. 62126000; fax 62126200; internet www.cspb.com.sg; Br. Man. PIERRE-FRANCOIS BAER.

Crédit Suisse First Boston (Switzerland): 1 Raffles Link, 03/04-01 South Lobby, Singapore 039393; tel. 62122000; fax 62123100; Br. Man. ERIC M. VARVEL.

Deutsche Bank AG (Germany): 6 Shenton Way, 15-08 DBS Bldg, Tower Two, Singapore 068809; tel. 64238001; fax 62259442; Gen. Man. RONNY TAN CHONG TEE.

Dresdner Bank AG (Germany): 20 Collyer Quay, 22-00 Tung Centre, Singapore 049319; tel. 62228080; fax 62244008; Man. Dirs PHILIP DEFORD, RAYMOND B. T. KOH, LEE SIEW CHIANG; CEO BAUDOUIN GROONENBERGHS.

First Commercial Bank (Taiwan): 76 Shenton Way, 01-02 ONG Bldg, Singapore 079119; tel. 62215755; fax 62251905; e-mail fcbsin@singnet.com.sg; Vice-Pres. and Gen. Man. YANG TAY-PYNG.

Habib Bank Ltd (Pakistan): 3 Phillip St, 01-03 Commerce Pt, Singapore 048693; tel. 64380055; fax 64380644; e-mail gmhbl@singnet.com.sg; Regional Gen. Man. ASHRAF MAHMOOD WATHRA.

ING Bank NV (Netherlands): 9 Raffles Place, 19-02 Republic Plaza, Singapore 048619; tel. 65353688; fax 65338329; Country Head J. KESTEMONT.

IntesaBci SpA (Italy): 9 Raffles Place, 51-01/02 and 52-02 Republic Plaza, Singapore 048619; tel. 62201333; fax 62271619; e-mail singapore@intesabci.com.sg; Gen. Man. GIORGIO MARIA ROSICA.

KBC Bank NV (Belgium): 30 Cecil St, 12-01/08 Prudential Tower, Singapore 049712; tel. 63952828; fax 65342929; Gen. Man. YIN MIN YONG.

Korea Exchange Bank (Republic of Korea): 30 Cecil St, 24-03/08 Prudential Tower, Singapore 049712; tel. 65361633; fax 65382522; e-mail kebspore@singnet.com.sg; Gen. Man. KIM SEONG JUNG.

Mizuho Corporate Bank Ltd (Japan): 168 Robinson Rd, 13-00 Capital Tower, Singapore 068912; tel. 6420330; fax 64230012; Gen. Man. FUSATO SUZUKI.

Moscow Narodny Bank Ltd (UK): 50 Robinson Rd, MNB Bldg, Singapore 068882; tel. 62209422; fax 62250140; Man. Dir EVGENY MIKHAILOVICH GREVTSEV.

National Australia Bank Ltd (Australia): 5 Temasek Blvd, 15-01 Suntec City Tower Five, Singapore 038985; tel. 63380038; fax 63380039; Gen. Man. VICTOR CHUA BENG KHOON.

Norddeutsche Landesbank Girozentrale (Germany): 6 Shenton Way, 16-08 DBS Bldg Tower Two, Singapore 068809; tel. 63231223; fax 63230223; e-mail nordlb.singapore@nordlb.com; Gen. Man. and Regional Head Asia/Pacific HEINZ WERNER FRINGS.

Northern Trust Company (USA): 80 Raffles Place, 46th Floor, UOB Plaza 1, Singapore 048624; tel. 64376666; fax 64376609; e-mail hynl@ntrs.com; Sr Vice-Pres. LAWRENCE AU.

Rabobank International (Netherlands): 77 Robinson Rd, 09-00 SIA Bldg, Singapore 068896; tel. 65363363; fax 65363236; Exec. Vice-Pres. CHRISTIAN H. A. M. MOL.

San Paolo IMI SpA (Italy): 6 Temasek Blvd, 42/04-05 Suntec Tower Four, Singapore 038986; tel. 63338270; fax 63338252; e-mail singapore.sg@sanpaoloimi.com; Gen. Man. GUIDO IMBIMBO.

Societé Generale (France): 80 Robinson Rd, 25-00, Singapore 068898; tel. 62227122; fax 62252609; CEO and Country Man. DANIEL MOLLE.

UBS AG (Switzerland): 5 Temasek Blvd, 18-00 Suntec City Tower, Singapore 038985; tel. 64318000; fax 64318188; e-mail rolf-w

.gerber@wdr.com; Man. Dir and Head of Br. (Singapore) ROLF GERBER.

UFJ Bank Ltd (Japan): 6 Raffles Quay, 24-01 John Hancock Tower, Singapore 048580; tel. 65384838; fax 65384636; Gen. Man. GEN TOMII.

UniCredito Italiano SpA (Italy): 80 Raffles Place, 51-01 UOB Plaza 1, Singapore 048624; tel. 62325728; fax 65344300; e-mail singaporebranch@gruppocredit.it; Gen. Man. GIANNI FRANCO PAPA.

WestLB AG (Germany): 3 Temasek Ave, 33-00 Centennial Tower, Singapore 039190; tel. 63332388; fax 63332399; Gen. Man. TEO EE-NGOH.

'Offshore' Banks

ABSA Bank Ltd (South Africa): 9 Temasek Blvd, 40-01 Suntec Tower Two, Singapore 038989; tel. 63331033; fax 63331066; Gen. Man. DAVID MEADOWS.

Agricultural Bank of China (People's Republic of China): 80 Raffles Place, 27-20 UOB Plaza 2, Singapore 048624; tel. 65355255; fax 65387960; e-mail aboc@abchina.com.sg; Gen. Man. WANG GANG.

Arab Bank PLC (Jordan): 80 Raffles Place, 32-20 UOB Plaza 2, Singapore 048624; tel. 65330055; fax 65322150; e-mail abplc@pacific.net.com.sg; Exec. Vice-Pres. and Area Exec. Asia Pacific KIM EUN-YOUNG.

Arab Banking Corpn (BSC) (Bahrain): 9 Raffles Place, 35-01 Republic Plaza, Singapore 048619; tel. 65359339; fax 65326288; Gen. Man. JOHN MEADS.

Banca Monte dei Paschi di Siena SpA (Italy): 10 Collyer Quay, 13-01 Ocean Bldg, Singapore 0104; tel. 65352533; fax 65327996; Gen. Man. GIUSEPPE DE GIOSA.

Banca Nazionale del Lavoro SpA (Italy): 9 Raffles Place, 50-01 Republic Plaza, Singapore 048619; tel. 65366063; fax 65365213; e-mail bnlsing@pacific.net.sg; Sen. Vice-Pres. and Gen. Man. FRANCO UNGARO.

Banca di Roma (Italy): 9 Raffles Place, 20-20 Republic Plaza II, Singapore 048619; tel. 64387509; fax 65352267; e-mail bdrsi@singnet.com.sg; Gen. Man. MARIO FATTORUSSO.

Bank of Communications (People's Republic of China): 50 Raffles Place, 26-04 Singapore Land Tower, Singapore 048623; tel. 65320335; fax 65320339; Gen. Man. DU PING.

PT Bank Mandiri (Persero) (Indonesia): 16 Collyer Quay, 28-00 Hitachi Tower, Singapore 049318; tel. 65320200; fax 65320206; Gen. Man. ERWIN ALIMUDIN.

Bank of New York (USA): 1 Temasek Ave, 02-01 Millenia Tower, Singapore 039192; tel. 64320222; fax 63374302; Sr Vice-Pres. and Man. Dir JAI ARYA.

Bank of New Zealand (New Zealand): 5 Temasek Blvd, 15-01 Suntec City Tower, Singapore 038985; tel. 63322990; fax 63322991; Gen. Man. VICTOR CHUA BENG KHOON.

Bank of Scotland (UK): 50 Raffles Place, 16-06 Singapore Land Tower, Singapore 048623; tel. 64382721; fax 64382706; Regional Dir and CEO ADAM R. ION.

Bank of Taiwan (Taiwan): 80 Raffles Place, 28-20 UOB Plaza 2, Singapore 048624; tel. 65365536; fax 65368203; Vice-Pres. and Gen. Man. CHANG SHOU-HSING.

Bayerische Hypo- und Vereinsbank AG (Germany): 30 Cecil St, 26-01 Prudential Tower, Singapore 049712; tel. 64133688; fax 65368591; Gen. Man. PETER NG POH LIAN.

Bumiputra Commerce Bank Bhd (Malaysia): 7 Temasek Blvd, 37-01/02/03 Suntec Tower One, Singapore 038987; tel. 63375115; fax 63371335; e-mail bpsp3700@pacific.net.sg; Gen. Man. Raja SULONG AHMAD BIN Raja ABDUL RAZAK.

Canadian Imperial Bank of Commerce (Canada): 16 Collyer Quay, 04-02 Hitachi Tower, Singapore 049318; tel. 65352323; fax 65357565; Br. Man. NORMAN SIM CHEE BENG.

Chang Hwa Commercial Bank Ltd (China): 1 Finlayson Green, 08-00, Singapore 049246; tel. 65320820; fax 65320374; Gen. Man. YANG JIH-CHENG.

China Construction Bank (China): 9 Raffles Place, 33-01/02 Republic Plaza, Singapore 048619; tel. 65358133; fax 65386616; Gen. Man. KONG YONG XIN.

Chohung Bank (Republic of Korea): 50 Raffles Place, 04-02/03 Singapore Land Tower, Singapore 048623; tel. 65361144; fax 65331244; Gen. Man. HA-WOOK PARK.

Commonwealth Bank of Australia (Australia): 50 Raffles Place, 22-02 Singapore Land Tower, Singapore 048623; tel. 62243877; fax 62245812; Gen. Man. ROBERT LEWIS BUCHAN.

Crédit Industriel et Commercial (France): 9 Raffles Place, 23-01/02 Republic Plaza, Singapore 048619; tel. 65366008; fax 65367008; internet www.cic.com.sg; Gen. Man. JEAN-LUC ANGLADA.

Dexia Banque Internationale à Luxembourg (Luxembourg): 9 Raffles Place, 42-01 Republic Plaza, Singapore 048619; tel. 62227622; fax 65360201; Gen. Man. ALEXANDRE JOSSET.

DZ Bank AG Deutsche Zentral (Germany): 50 Raffles Place, 40-01 Singapore Land Tower, Singapore 048623; tel. 64380082; fax 62230082; Gen. Man. KLAUS GERHARD BORIG.

Fleet National Bank (USA): 150 Beach Rd, 07-00 Gateway West, Singapore 189720; tel. 62962366; fax 62960998; Regional Man. ANTHONY LOH.

Fortis Bank SA/NV (Belgium/Netherlands): 30 Raffles Place, 18-00 Caltex House, Singapore 048622; tel. 65394988; fax 65394933; Gen. Man. GIJSBERT SCHOT.

Hamburgische Landesbank Girozentrale (Germany): 3 Temasek Ave, 32-03 Centennial Tower, Singapore 039190; tel. 65509000; fax 65509003; e-mail info@hamburglb.com.sg; Gen. Man. and Exec. Dir DETLEV REHMKE.

Hana Bank (Republic of Korea): 8 Cross St, 23-06 PWC Bldg, Singapore 048424; tel. 64384100; fax 64384200; Gen. Man. SHIN JOON-SANG.

Hang Seng Bank Ltd (Hong Kong): 21 Collyer Quay, 14-01 HSBC Bldg, Singapore 049320; tel. 65363118; fax 65363148; e-mail sgp@hangseng.com; Country Man. ALEX CHEN CHARNG-TERK (acting).

HSBC Bank USA: 21-00 HSBC Bldg, 21 Collyer Quay, Singapore 049320; tel. 62240077; fax 62255769; Man. Dir and Country Chief JOHN C. HANSON.

HSBC Republic Bank (Suisse) SA (Switzerland): 21 Collyer Quay, 21-01 HSBC Bldg, Singapore 049320; tel. 62248080; fax 62237146; CEO KENNETH SIT YIU SUN.

Hua Nan Commercial Bank Ltd (Taiwan): 80 Robinson Rd, 14-03, Singapore 068898; tel. 63242566; fax 63242155; Gen. Man. GEENG JENG FANG.

Industrial and Commercial Bank of China (People's Republic of China): 6 Raffles Quay, 12-01 John Hancock Tower, Singapore 048580; tel. 65381066; fax 65381370; e-mail icbcsg@singnet.com.sg; Gen. Man. SHI QILU.

International Commercial Bank of China (Taiwan): 6 Battery Rd, 39-03, Singapore 049909; tel. 62277667; fax 62271858; Vice-Pres. and Gen. Man. YEN-PING HSIANG.

Korea Development Bank (Republic of Korea): 8 Shenton Way, 07-01 Temasek Tower, Singapore 068811; tel. 62248188; fax 62256540; Gen. Man. KIM KI CHEOL.

Krung Thai Bank Public Co Ltd (Thailand): 65 Chulia St, 32-05/08 OCBC Centre, Singapore 049513; tel. 65336691; fax 65330930; e-mail ktbs@pacific.net.sg; Gen. Man. PERMPOM SITTIPIYASAKUL.

Land Bank of Taiwan: UOB Plaza 1, 34-01 Raffles Place, Singapore 048624; tel. 63494555; fax 63494545; Gen. Man. WILSON W. B. LIN.

Landesbank Baden-Württemberg (Germany): 25 International Business Park, 01-72 German Centre, Singapore 609916; tel. 65627722; fax 65627729; Man. Dr WOLFHART AUER VON HERREN-KIRCHEN.

Lloyds TSB Bank PLC (UK): 3 Temasek Ave 19-01, Centennial Tower, Singapore 039190; tel. 65341191; fax 65322493; e-mail mktg@lloydstsb.com.sg; Country Head BARRY LEA.

Mitsubishi Trust and Banking Corpn (Japan): 50 Raffles Place, 42-01/06 Singapore Land Tower, Singapore 048623; tel. 62259155; fax 62241857; Gen. Man. MIKIO KOBAYASHI.

Natexis Banques Populaires (France): 50 Raffles Place, 41-01, Singapore Land Tower, Singapore 048623; tel. 62241455; fax 62248651; Gen. Man. PHILIPPE PETITGAS.

National Bank of Kuwait SAK (Kuwait): 20 Collyer Quay, 20-00 Tung Centre, Singapore 049319; tel. 62225348; fax 62245438; Gen. Man. R. J. MCKEGNEY.

Nedcor Bank Ltd (South Africa): 30 Cecil St, 10-05 Prudential Tower, Singapore 049712; tel. 64169438; fax 64388350; e-mail nedsing@nedcor.com; Gen. Man. BRIAN SHEGAR.

Nordea Bank Finland Plc (Finland): 50 Raffles Place, 15-01 Singapore Land Tower, Singapore 048623; tel. 62258211; fax 62255469; e-mail singapore@nordea.com; Gen. Man. PETRI SANDELL.

Norinchukin Bank (Japan): 80 Raffles Place, 53-01 UOB Plaza 1, Singapore 048624; tel. 65351011; fax 65352883; Gen. Man. JUNICHI KOBAYASHI.

Den norske Bank ASA (Norway): 8 Shenton Way, 48-02 Temasek Tower, Singapore 068811; tel. 62206144; fax 62249743; e-mail dnb .singapore@dnb.no; Gen. Man. PÅL SKOE.

Philippine National Bank (Philippines): 96 Somerset Rd, 04-01/04 UOL Bldg, Singapore 238183; tel. 67374646; fax 67374224; e-mail singapore@pnb.com.ph; Vice-Pres. and Gen. Man. RODELO G. FRANCO.

Raiffeisen Zentralbank Oesterreich Aktiengesellschaft (Austria): 50 Raffles Place, 45-01 Singapore Land Tower, Singapore 048623; tel. 62259578; fax 62253973; Gen. Man. RAINER SILHAVY.

Royal Bank of Canada (Canada): 20 Raffles Place, 27-03/08 Ocean Towers, Singapore 048620; tel. 65369206; fax 65322804; Gen. Man. LARRY YAN KING NAM.

Royal Bank of Scotland PLC (UK): 50 Raffles Place, 08-00 Singapore Land Tower, Singapore 048623; tel. 64168600; fax 62259827; Gen. Man. ROBERT I. GARDEN.

Skandinaviska Enskilda Banken AB Publ (Sweden): 50 Raffles Place, 36-01 Singapore Land Tower, Singapore 048623; tel. 62235644; fax 62253047; Gen. Man. PER ENGSTRÖM.

Siam Commercial Bank Public Company Ltd (Thailand): 16 Collyer Quay, 25-01 Hitachi Tower, Singapore 049318; tel. 65364338; fax 65364728; Vice-Pres. and Gen. Man. NATTAPONG SAMIT AMPAIPISARN.

State Bank of India (India): 6 Shenton Way, 22-08 DBS Bldg Tower Two, Singapore 068809; tel. 62222033; fax 62253348; e-mail sbinsgsg@pacific.net.sg; CEO PADMA RAMASUBBAN.

State Street Bank and Trust Co (USA): 8 Shenton Way, 33-03 Temasek Tower, Singapore 068811; tel. 63299600; fax 62259377; Br. Man. LEE YOW FEE.

Sumitomo Trust & Banking Co Ltd (Japan): 8 Shenton Way, 45-01 Temasek Tower, Singapore 068811; tel. 62249055; fax 62242873; Gen. Man. HIDEHIKO ASAI.

Svenska Handelsbanken AB (publ) (Sweden): 65 Chulia St, 21-01/04 OCBC Centre, Singapore 049513; tel. 65323800; fax 65344909; Gen. Man. MAJ-LISS OLSSON.

Toronto-Dominion (South East Asia) Ltd (Canada): 15-02 Millenia Tower, 1 Temasek Ave, Singapore 039192; tel. 64346000; fax 63369500; Man. Dir HENRY SCHINDELE.

Union de Banques Arabes et Françaises (UBAF) (France): 6 Temasek Blvd, 25-04-05 Suntec Tower Four, Singapore 038986; tel. 63336188; fax 63336789; e-mail ubafsg@singnet.com.sg; Gen. Man. BENOIT GUEROULT.

Westpac Banking Corpn (Australia): 77 Robinson Rd, 19-00 SIA Bldg, Singapore 068896; tel. 65309898; fax 65326781; e-mail yhlee@westpac.wm.au; Gen. Man. LEE YEW HUAT.

Woori Bank (Republic of Korea): 5 Shenton Way, 17-03 UIC Bldg, Singapore 068808; tel. 62235855; fax 62259530; e-mail combksp@singnet.com.sg; Gen. Man. PARK DONG YOUNG.

Association

Association of Banks in Singapore: 10 Shenton Way, 12-08 MAS Bldg, Singapore 079117; tel. 62244300; fax 62241785; e-mail banks@abs.org.sg; internet www.abs.org.sg; Dir ONG-ANG AI BOON.

STOCK EXCHANGE

Singapore Exchange Limited (SGX): 2 Shenton Way, 19-00 SGX Centre One, Singapore 068804; tel. 62368888; fax 65356994; e-mail webmaster@sgx.com; internet www.sgx.com; f. 1999 as a result of the merger of the Stock Exchange of Singapore (SES, f. 1930) and the Singapore International Monetary Exchange Ltd (SIMEX, f. 1984); Chair. J. Y. PILLAY; CEO TOM KLOET; Pres. ANG SWEE TIAN.

INSURANCE

The insurance industry is supervised by the Monetary Authority of Singapore (see Banking). In April 2003 there were 150 insurance companies, comprising 61 direct insurers (seven life insurance, 47 general insurance, seven composite insurers), 38 professional reinsurers (one life reinsurer, 27 general reinsurers, 10 composite reinsurers) and 51 captive insurers.

Domestic Companies

Life Insurance

Asia Life Assurance Society Ltd: 2 Finlayson Green, 05-00 Asia Insurance Bldg, Singapore 049247; tel. 62243181; fax 62239120; e-mail asialife@asialife.com.sg; internet www.asialife.com.sg; f. 1948; Chair. TAN ENG HENG.

John Hancock Life Assurance Co Ltd: 6 Raffles Quay, 21-00 John Hancock Tower, Singapore 048580; tel. 65383333; fax 65383233; internet www.jhancock.com.sg; f. 1954; Pres. MALCOLM J. J. ARNEY.

OUB Manulife Pte Ltd: 491B River Valley Rd, 07-00 Valley Pt, Singapore 248373; tel. 67371221; fax 67378488; e-mail custrve@

oubmanulife.com.sg; internet www.oubmanulife.com.sg; Pres. KEITH WEAVER.

Prudential Assurance Co Singapore (Pte) Ltd: 30 Cecil St, 30-01 Prudential Tower, Singapore 049712; tel. 65358988; fax 65354043; e-mail customer.service@prudential.com.sg; internet www.prudential.com.sg; CEO TAN SUEE CHIEH.

UOB Life Assurance Ltd: 156 Cecil St, 10-01 Far Eastern Bank Bldg, Singapore 069544; tel. 62278477; fax 62243012; internet www.uob.com.sg; Man. Dir RAYMOND KWOK CHONG SEE.

General Insurance

Allianz Insurance Company of Singapore Pte Ltd: 3 Temasek Ave, 03-01 Centennial Tower, Singapore 039190; tel. 62972529; fax 62971956; e-mail askme@allianz.com.sg; internet www.allianz.com.sg; formed by merger between Allianz Insurance (Singapore) Pte Ltd and AGF Insurance (Singapore) Pte Ltd; Man. Dir NEIL BASSETT EMERY.

Asia Insurance Co Ltd: 2 Finlayson Green, 03-00 Asia Insurance Bldg, Singapore 049247; tel. 62243181; fax 62214355; e-mail asiains@asiainsurance.com.sg; internet www.asiainsurance.com.sg; f. 1923; cap. p.u. S $75m. Chair. TAN ENG HENG; Man. Dir LOO SUN MUN.

Asian Securitization and Infrastructure Assurance (Pte) Ltd: 9 Temasek Blvd, 38-01 Suntec Tower 2, Singapore 038989; tel. 63342555; fax 63342777; e-mail general@asialtd.com; Dir ELEANOR L. LIPSEY.

Axa Insurance Singapore Pte Ltd: 143 Cecil St, 01-01 GB Bldg, Singapore 069542; tel. 63387288; fax 63382522; e-mail customer.service@axa-insurance.com.sg; internet www.axainsurance.com.sg; fmrly East West-USI Insurance Pte Ltd; Pres. and CEO CLAUDE MARX.

Cigna Insurance Singapore Ltd: 152 Beach Rd, 25-05 Gateway East, Singapore 189721; tel. 63910501; fax 62981323; Prin. Officer PAUL HARTLEY.

Cosmic Insurance Corpn Ltd: 410 North Bridge Rd, 04-01 Cosmic Insurance Bldg, Singapore 188726; tel. 63387633; fax 63397805; internet www.cosmic.com.sg; f. 1971; Gen. Man. TEO LIP MOH.

ECICS-COFACE Guarantee Co (Singapore) Ltd: 7 Temasek Blvd, 11-01 Suntec City Tower 1, Singapore 038987; tel. 63374779; fax 63389267; e-mail ecics@ecics.com.sg; internet www.ecics.com.sg; Chair. KWAH THIAM HOCK; Asst Vice-Pres. JONATHAN TANG.

First Capital Insurance Ltd: 80 Robinson Rd, 09-02/03, Singapore 068898; tel. 62222311; fax 62223547; e-mail enquiry@fcc.com.sg; internet www.first-insurance.com.sg; Gen. Man. TAN THIAM SENG.

India International Insurance Pte Ltd: 64 Cecil St, 04-00/05-00 IOB Bldg, Singapore 049711; tel. 62238122; fax 62244174; e-mail insure@iii.com.sg; internet www.iii.com.sg; f. 1987; all non-life insurance; CEO R. ATHAPPAN.

Kemper International Insurance Co (Pte) Ltd: 3 Shenton Way, 22-09 Shenton House, Singapore 068805; tel. 68369120; fax 68369121; e-mail vchia@kemper.com.sg; internet www.kemper.com.sg; Gen. Man. VIOLET CHIA.

Liberty Citystate Insurance Pte Ltd: 51 Club St, 03-00 Singapore 069428; tel. 62218611; fax 62263360; e-mail koh.peter@libertycitystate.com.sg; internet www.libertycitystate.com.sg; fmrly Citystate Insurance Pte Ltd; Man. Dir PETER KOH TIEN HOE.

Mitsui Sumitomo Insurance (Singapore) Pte Ltd: 16 Raffles Quay, 24-01 Hong Leong Bldg, Singapore 048581; tel. 62209644; fax 62256371; internet www.ms-ins.com.sg; fmrly Mitsui Marine and Fire Insurance (Asia) Private Ltd; merged with The Sumitomo Marine and Fire Insurance Co Ltd and name changed as above; Man. Dir YOSHIO IIJIMA; Dep. Gen. Man. NOBORI OMORI.

The Nanyang Insurance Co Ltd: 302 Orchard Rd, 09-01 Tong Bldg, Singapore 238862; tel. 67388211; fax 67388133; e-mail tnicl@nanyanginsurance.com.sg; f. 1956; Dir and Principal Officer FREDDIE YEO.

Overseas Union Insurance Ltd: 50 Collyer Quay, 02-02 Overseas Union House, Singapore 049321; tel. 62251133; fax 62246307; internet www.oub.com.sg; f. 1956; Gen. Man. PETER YAP KIM KEE; Asst Gen. Man. YEO TIAN CHU.

Royal & Sun Alliance Insurance (Singapore) Ltd: 77 Robinson Rd, 18-00 SIA Bldg, Singapore 068896; tel. 62201188; fax 64230798; e-mail rsail-sg@sg.royalsun.com; internet www.royalsunalliance.com.sg; Man. Dir and CEO EDMUND LIM.

Singapore Aviation and General Insurance Co (Pte) Ltd: 25 Airline Rd, 06-A Airline House, Singapore 819829; tel. 65423333; fax 65450221; f. 1976; Man. AMARJIT KAUR SIDHU.

Standard Steamship Owners' Protection and Indemnity Association (Asia) Ltd: 140 Cecil St, 10-02 PIL Bldg, Singapore 069540; tel. 62211060; fax 62211082; e-mail central@ctg-ap.com; internet www.standard-club.com; Prin. Officer DAVID ALWYN.

Tenet Insurance Co Ltd: 10 Collyer Quay, 04-01 Ocean Bldg, Singapore 049315; tel. 65326022; fax 65333871; Chair. ONG CHOO ENG.

The Tokio Marine & Fire Insurance Co (Singapore) Pte Ltd: 6 Shenton Way, 23-08 DBS Bldg Tower Two, Singapore 068809; tel. 62216111; fax 62240895; Man. Dir KYOZO HANAJIMA.

United Overseas Insurance Ltd: 156 Cecil St, 09-01 Far Eastern Bank Bldg, Singapore 069544; tel. 62227733; fax 62242718; internet www.uoi.com.sg; Man. Dir DAVID CHAN MUN WAI.

Winterthur Insurance (Far East) Pte Ltd: 5 Shenton Way, 06-01 UIC Bldg, Singapore 068808; tel. 65368669; fax 65368870; Man. Dir ANG YEW LEE.

Yasuda Fire and Marine Insurance Co (Asia) Pte Ltd: 50 Raffles Place, 03-03 Singapore Land Tower, Singapore 048623; tel. 62235293; fax 62257947; e-mail yasudaqa@yasudaasia.com; internet www.yasudaasia.com; f. 1989; Man. Dir and Gen. Man. KOJI OTSUKA.

Zürich Insurance (Singapore) Pte Ltd: 78 Shenton Way, 06-01, Singapore 079120; tel. 62202466; fax 62255749; Prin. Officer and Man. Dir RONALD CHENG JUE SENG.

Composite Insurance

Great Eastern Life Assurance Co Ltd: 1 Pickering St, 13-01 Great Eastern Centre, Singapore 048659; tel. 62482000; fax 65322214; e-mail wecare@lifeisgreat.com.sg; internet www.lifeisgreat.com.sg; f. 1908; Dir and CEO TAN BENG LEE.

Insurance Corpn of Singapore Ltd: 4 Shenton Way, 23-01 SGX Centre Two, Singapore 068807; tel. 68277988; fax 68277900; e-mail prd_div@cguasia.com; internet www.icsinsurance.com.sg; f. 1969; Prin. Officer KEITH PERKINS.

Keppel Insurance Pte Ltd: 10 Hoe Chiang Rd, 13-00 Keppel Towers, Singapore 089315; tel. 62256111; fax 62212188; internet www.keppelinsurance.com.sg; Prin. Officer ALBERT KOH.

NTUC Income Insurance Co-operative Ltd: 75 Bras Basah Rd, NTUC Income Centre, Singapore 189557; tel. 63363322; fax 63381500; e-mail inbox@income.wm.sg; internet www.income.com.sg; CEO TAN KIN LIAN; Gen. Man. ALOYSIUS TEO SENG LEE.

Overseas Assurance Corpn Ltd: 1 Pickering St, 13-01 Great Eastern Centre, Singapore 048659; tel. 62482000; fax 65322214; e-mail general@oac.com.sg; internet www.oac.com.sg; f. 1920; Chair. MICHAEL WONG PAKSHONG.

Associations

General Insurance Association of Singapore: 103 Amoy St, Singapore 069923; tel. 62218788; fax 62272051; internet www.gia.org.sg; f. 1965; Pres. LAW SONG KENG; Vice-Pres. DAVID CHAN.

Life Insurance Association: 20 Cross St, 02-07/08 China Court, China Sq. Central, Singapore 048422; tel. 64388900; fax 64386989; e-mail lia@lia.org.sg; internet www.lia.org.sg; f. 1967; Pres. RAYMOND KWOK.

Reinsurance Brokers' Association: c/o Ins Communications Pte, 55–58 Amoy St, Singapore 069881; tel. 62245583; fax 62241091; e-mail rbas@asiainsurancereview.com; internet www.rbas.org.sg; Chair. RICHARD AUSTEN.

Singapore Insurance Brokers' Association: 138 Cecil St, 15-00 Cecil Court, Singapore 069538; tel. 62227777; fax 62220022; Pres. ANTHONY LIM; Vice-Pres. DAVID LUM.

Singapore Reinsurers' Association: 85 Amoy St, Singapore 069904; tel. 63247388; fax 62248910; e-mail secretariat@sraweb.org.sg; internet www.sraweb.org.sg; f. 1979; Chair. PHUA KIA TING.

Trade and Industry

GOVERNMENT AGENCIES

Housing and Development Board: 3541 Bukit Merah Rd, HDB Centre, Singapore 159459; tel. 62739090; fax 62780144; e-mail hdbmailbox@hdb.gov.sg; internet www.hdb.gov.sg; f. 1960; public housing authority; Chair. NGIAM TONG DOW.

Urban Redevelopment Authority (URA): 45 Maxwell Rd, URA Centre, Singapore 069118; tel. 62216666; fax 62263549; e-mail ura_main_registry@ura.gov.sg; internet www.ura.gov.sg; statutory board; responsible for national planning.

DEVELOPMENT ORGANIZATIONS

Applied Research Corpn (ARC): independent non-profit-making research and consultancy org. aiming to facilitate and enhance the use of technology and expertise from the tertiary institutions to benefit industry, businesses and joint institutions.

Asian Infrastructure Fund (AIF): Singapore; f. 1994; promotes and directs investment into regional projects; Chair. MOEEN QURESHI.

Economic Development Board (EDB): 250 North Bridge Rd, 24-00 Raffles City Tower, Singapore 179101; tel. 63362288; fax 63396077; e-mail webmaster@edb.gov.sg; internet www.sedb.com.sg; f. 1961; statutory body for industrial planning, development and promotion of investments in manufacturing, services and local business; Chair. TEO MING KIAN; Man. Dir LIEW HENG SAN.

Government of Singapore Investment Corp Pte Ltd (GSIC): 250 North Bridge Rd, 38-00 Raffles City Tower, Singapore 179101; tel. 63363366; fax 63308722; internet www.gic.com.sg; f. 1981; Chair. LEE KUAN YEW; Man. Dir LEE EK TIENG.

Jurong Town Corpn: 8 Jurong Town Hall Rd, Singapore 609434; tel. 65600056; fax 65655301; e-mail askjtc@jtc.gov.sg; internet www.jtc.gov.sg; f. 1968; statutory body responsible for developing and maintaining industrial estates; Chair. LIM NEO CHIAN; CEO CHONG LIT CHEONG.

Infocomm Development Authority of Singapore (IDA): see under Telecommunications.

Agency for Science, Technology and Research (A*STAR): 10 Science Park Rd, 01/01-03 The Alpha, Singapore Science Park II, Singapore 117684; tel. 67797066; fax 67771711; e-mail astar_contact@a-star.gov.sg; internet www.a-star.gov.sg; f. 1990; fmrly National Science and Technology Board; statutory board; responsible for the development of science and technology; Chair. PHILIP YEO; Man. Dir BOON SWAN FOO.

Singapore Productivity and Standards Board (PSB): PSB Bldg, 2 Bukit Merah Central, Singapore 159835; tel. 62786666; fax 62786667; e-mail queries@psb.gov.sg; internet www.psb.gov.sg; f. 1996; merger of Singapore Institute of Standards and Industrial Research and the National Productivity Board; carries out activities in areas including workforce development, training, productivity and innovation promotion, standards development, ISO certification, quality programmes and consultancy, technology application, product and process development, system and process automation services, testing services, patent information, development assistance for small and medium-sized enterprises; Chief Exec. LEE SUAN HIANG.

Trade Development Board: 230 Victoria St, 07-00 Bugis Junction Office Tower, Singapore 188024; tel. 63376628; fax 63376898; e-mail enquiry@tdb.gov.sg; internet www.tdb.gov.sg; f. 1983 to develop and expand international trade; due to be renamed International Enterprise Singapore in 2002; statutory body; Chair. STEPHEN LEE; CEO LEE YI SHYAN.

CHAMBERS OF COMMERCE

Singapore Federation of Chambers of Commerce and Industry: 47 Hill St, 03-01 Chinese Chamber of Commerce Bldg, Singapore 179365; tel. 63389761; fax 63395630; e-mail sfcci@singnet.com.sg; f. 1978; Pres. KWEK LENG JOO; Hon. Sec.-Gen. LIM SAH SOON; mems comprise the following:

   Singapore Chinese Chamber of Commerce and Industry: 47 Hill St, 09-00 Singapore 179365; tel. 63378381; fax 63390605; e-mail corporate@sccci.org.sg; internet www.sccci.org.sg; f. 1906; promotes trade and industry and economic development of Singapore.

   Singapore Confederation of Industries: The Enterprise 02-02, 1 Science Centre Rd, Singapore 609077; tel. 68263000; fax 68228828; e-mail scihq@sci.org.sg; internet www.sci.org.sg; f. 1932; Pres. ROBIN LAU CHUNG KEONG; Sec.-Gen. THAM HOCK CHEE.

   Singapore Indian Chamber of Commerce and Industry: 101 Cecil St, 23-01/04 Tong Eng Bldg, Singapore 069533; tel. 62222855; fax 62231707; e-mail sicci@singnet.com.sg; internet www.sicci.com.

   Singapore International Chamber of Commerce: 6 Raffles Quay, 10-01 John Hancock Tower, Singapore 048580; tel. 62241255; fax 62242785; e-mail general@sicc.com; internet www.sicc.com.sg; f. 1837.

   Singapore Malay Chamber of Commerce: 72A Bussorah St, Singapore 199485; tel. 62979296; fax 63924527; e-mail smcci@singnet.com.sg.

INDUSTRIAL AND TRADE ASSOCIATIONS

Association of Singapore Marine Industries (ASMI): 1 Maritime Sq., 10–32 World Trade Centre, Singapore 099253; tel. 62704730; fax 62731867; e-mail asmi@pacific.net.sg; internet www.asmi.com; f. 1968; 12 hon. mems, 67 assoc. mems, 51 ord. mems (2001); Pres. HENG CHIANG GNEE; Exec. Dir WINNIE LOW.

Singapore Commodity Exchange (SICOM): 111 North Bridge Rd, 23-04/05 Peninsula Plaza, Singapore 179098; tel. 63385600; fax 63389116; e-mail marketing@sicom.com.sg; internet www.sicom.com.sg; f. 1968 as Rubber Association of Singapore, adopted present name 1994; to regulate, promote, develop and supervise commodity futures trading in Singapore, including the establishment and dissemination of official prices for various grades and types of rubber; provides clearing facilities; endorses certificates of origin and licences for packers, shippers and mfrs; Chair. VICTOR LIEW CHENG SAN; Gen. Man. LIM TOH ENG.

EMPLOYERS' ORGANIZATION

Singapore National Employers' Federation: 19 Tanglin Rd, 10-01/07 Tanglin Shopping Centre, Singapore 247909; tel. 68276827; fax 68276800; e-mail webmaster@snef.org.sg; internet www.sgemployers.com; f. 1948; Pres. STEPHEN LEE; Vice-Pres ALEX CHAN, BOB TAN BENG HAI.

UTILITIES

Electricity and Gas

Singapore Power Ltd: 111 Somerset Rd 16-01, Singapore Power Bldg, Singapore 238164; tel. 68238888; fax 68238188; e-mail prdiv@spower.com.sg; internet www.spower.com.sg; incorporated in 1995 to take over the piped gas and electricity utility operations of the Public Utilities Board (see Water) which now acts as a regulatory authority for the privately-owned cos; 100% owned by government holding company, Temasek Holdings Pte Ltd; subsidiaries include PowerGrid, PowerGas, Power Supply, Singapore Power International, Development Resources, Power Automation, SP E-Services, SP Systems, Singapore District Cooling and SP Telecommunications; Chair. NG KEE CHOE; Pres. and CEO KWEK SIEW JIN.

Water

Public Utilities Board: 111 Somerset Rd 15-01, Singapore 238164; tel. 62358888; fax 67313020; e-mail pub_pr@pub.gov.sg; internet www.pub.gov.sg; statutory board responsible for water supply; manages Singapore's water system to optimize use of water resources, develops additional water sources; Chair. TAN GEE PAW.

TRADE UNIONS

In 1998 there were 86 registered trade unions and associations with 287,062 members, and three employer unions.

In December 1998 the largest private-sector union, the United Workers of Electronics and Electrical Industries, had 40,433 members, while the largest public-sector union, the Amalgamated Union of Public Employees, had 20,872 members.

National Trades Union Congress (NTUC): NTUC Trade Union House, 73 Bras Basah Rd, Singapore 189556; tel. 62226555; fax 63343373; internet www.ntuc.org.sg; f. 1961; 65 affiliated unions and 6 affiliated associates, 383,621 mems (Oct. 2002); Pres. JOHN DE PAYVA; Sec.-Gen. LIM BOON HENG.

Transport

RAILWAYS

In 1993 there was 26 km of 1-m gauge railway, linked with the Malaysian railway system and owned by the Malayan Railway Pentadbiran Keretapi Tanah Melayu—KTM. The main line crosses the Johore causeway (1.2 km) and terminates near Keppel Harbour. Branch lines link it with the industrial estate at Jurong.

Construction began in 1983 on the Mass Rapid Transit (MRT) system. The first section was completed in 1987, and the remaining sections by 1990. The system extends for 83 km and consists of two lines with 48 stations (32 elevated, 15 under ground and one at ground level). The construction of a further 20-km line, the North–East Line, began in 1997; the line has 16 stations and one depot, and was completed in 2002. In 2002 the extension of the East–West line to Changi Airport was completed; the Changi Airport Line (CAL) has one underground and one elevated station. In 2001 construction was under way on the Circle Line, a 34-km orbital line running entirely under ground which was to link all the radial lines into the city. The line was to start at Dhoby Ghaut and terminate at Harbour Front and was to be implemented in five stages, the last of which was scheduled for completion in 2010.

Singapore's first Light Rapid Transit (LRT) system, the Bukit Panjang LRT (a 7.8-km line with 14 stations), was completed in April 1998. Work on two further LRT lines, in Sengkang and

Punggol, was also under way, and these lines were expected to be completed in 2002 and 2004 respectively.

Land Transport Authority: 460 Alexandra Rd, 28-00 PSA Bldg, Singapore 119963; tel. 63757100; fax 63757200; internet www.lta .gov.sg; Chair. FOCK SIEW WAH; Chief Exec. Maj.-Gen. HAN ENG JUAN.

ROADS

In 1999 Singapore had a total of 3,066 km of roads, of which 150 km were motorway; in that year 100% of the road network was paved. In 1990 the Government introduced a quota system to control the number of vehicles using the roads. A manual road-pricing system was introduced on one expressway in June 1996 and extended to two further expressways in May 1997. It was replaced by a system of Electronic Road Pricing (ERP) in 1998, whereby each vehicle was charged according to road use in congested areas. The ERP was first introduced on one expressway in April 1998, and was subsequently extended to include two other expressways and the Area Licensing Scheme gantry areas by early September of that year. In 2002 construction of the 12-km Kallang–Paya Lebar expressway began; an estimated 9 km of the expressway was to be underground. It was scheduled for completion in 2007.

SHIPPING

The Port of Singapore is the world's busiest in tonnage terms; Singapore handled an estimated 146,265 vessels with a total displacement of 960.1m. grt in 2001.

The Port of Singapore Authority operates six cargo terminals: Tanjong Pagar Terminal, Keppel Terminal, Brani Terminal, Pasir Panjang Terminal, Sembawang Terminal and Jurong Port.

Tanjong Pagar Terminal and Keppel Terminal have the capacity to handle 10.7m. 20-foot equivalent units (TEUs).

The third container terminal, Brani, built on an offshore island connected to the mainland by a causeway, has a capacity of 5.5m. TEUs.

Pasir Panjang Terminal, Singapore's main gateway for conventional cargo (particularly timber and rubber), has five deep-water berths and eight coastal berths and 17 lighter berths.

Sembawang Terminal has three deep-water berths and one coastal berth. This terminal is the main gateway for car carriers as well as handling steel and timber products.

Jurong Port (which handles general and dry-bulk cargo, is situated in south-western Singapore, and serves the Jurong Industrial Estate) has 20 deep-water berths and one coastal berth.

A new container terminal at Pasir Panjang was under construction in the late 1990s. Upon completion, the terminal, which was to be built in four phases, was to have 49 berths and a handling capacity of 36m. TEUs.

Maritime and Port Authority of Singapore: 460 Alexandra Rd, 18-00 PSA Bldg, Singapore 119963; tel. 63751600; fax 62759247; internet www.mpa.gov.sg; f. 1996; regulatory body responsible for promotion and development of the port, overseeing all port and maritime matters in Singapore.

Port of Singapore Authority: 460 Alexandra Rd, PSA Bldg, Singapore 119963; tel. 63751600; fax 62759247; internet www.psa .gov.sg; f. 1964 as a statutory board under the Ministry of Communications; made a corporate entity in 1997 in preparation for privatization; responsible for the provision and maintenance of port facilities and services; Chair. Dr YEO NING HONG; Pres. KHOO TENG CHYE.

Major Shipping Companies

American President Lines Ltd (APL): 456 Alexandra Rd, 08-00 NOL Bldg, Singapore 119962; tel. 62789000; fax 62742113; e-mail hung-song-goh@apl.com; internet www.apl.com; container services to North and South Asia, the USA, the Middle East, India and Pakistan; Chief Operating Officer ED ALDRIDGE.

Glory Ship Management Private Ltd: 24 Raffles Place 17-01/02, Clifford Centre, Singapore 048621; tel. 65361986; fax 65361987; e-mail gene@gloryship.com.sg.

Guan Guan Shipping Pte Ltd: 2 Finlayson Green, 13-05 Asia Insurance Bldg, Singapore 049247; tel. 65343988; fax 62276776; e-mail golden@golden.com.sg; f. 1955; shipowners and agents; cargo services to East and West Malaysia, Indonesia, Pakistan, Sri Lanka, Bengal Bay ports, Persian (Arabian) Gulf ports, Hong Kong and China; Man. Dir RICHARD THIO.

IMC Shipping Co Pte Ltd: 5 Temasek Blvd, 12-01 Suntec City Tower, Singapore 038985; tel. 63362233; fax 63379715; e-mail commercial@imcshipping.com.sg; internet www.imcshipping.com; Man. Dir PETER CHEW.

Nedlloyd Lines Singapore Pte Ltd: 138 Robinson Rd, 01-00 Hong Leong Centre, Singapore 068906; tel. 62218989; fax 62255267; f. 1963; Gen. Man. F. C. SCHUCHARD.

Neptune Orient Lines Ltd: 456 Alexandra Rd, 05-00 NOL Bldg, Singapore 119962; tel. 63715300; fax 63716489; e-mail shirley_ting@ccgate.apl.com; internet www.nol.com.sg; f. 1968; liner containerized services on the Far East/Europe, Far East/North America, Straits/Australia, South Asia/Europe and South-East Asia, Far East/Mediterranean routes; tankers, bulk carriers and dry cargo vessels on charter; 36% govt-owned; Chair. LUA CHENG ENG; CEO RON WIDDOWS (acting).

New Straits Shipping Co Pte Ltd: 51 Anson Rd, 09-53 Anson Centre, Singapore 0207; tel. 62201007; fax 62240785.

Ocean Tankers (Pte) Ltd: 41 Tuas Rd, Singapore 638497; tel. 68632202; fax 68639480; e-mail admin@oceantankers.com.sg; Marine Supt V. LIM.

Osprey Maritime Ltd: 8 Cross St, 24-02/03 PWC Bldg, Singapore 048424; tel. 62129722; fax 65570450; internet www.ospreymaritime .com; CEO PETER GEORGE COSTALAS.

Pacific International Lines (Pte) Ltd: 140 Cecil St, 03-00 PIL Bldg, POB 3206, Singapore 069540; tel. 62218133; fax 62273933; e-mail sherry.chua@sgp.pilship.com; shipowners, agents and managers; liner services to South-East Asia, the Far East, India, the Red Sea, the Persian (Arabian) Gulf, West and East Africa; container services to South-East Asia; world-wide chartering, freight forwarding, container manufacturing, depot operators, container freight station operator; Exec. Chair. Y. C. CHANG; Man. Dir S. S. TEO.

Petroships Private Ltd: 460 Alexandra Rd, 25-04 PSA Bldg, Singapore 119963; tel. 62731122; fax 62732200; e-mail gen@ petroships.com.sg; Man. Dir KENNETH KEE.

Singa Ship Management Private Ltd: 78 Shenton Way 16-02, Singapore 079120; tel. 62244308; fax 62235848; e-mail agency@ singaship.com.sg; Chair. OLE HEGLAND; Man. Dir EILEEN LEONG.

Syabas Tankers Pte Ltd: 10 Anson Rd, 34-10 International Plaza, Singapore 0207; tel. 62259522.

Tanker Pacific Management (Singapore) Private Ltd: 1 Temasek Ave, 38-01 Millenia Tower, Singapore; tel. 63365211; fax 63375570; Man. Dir HUGH HUNG.

CIVIL AVIATION

Singapore's international airport at Changi was opened in 1981. Construction on a third terminal at Changi began in October 2000, and was scheduled to be completed in 2006, increasing the airport's total capacity to 64m. passengers a year. A second airport at Seletar operates as a base for charter and training flights.

Civil Aviation Authority of Singapore: Singapore Changi Airport, POB 1, Singapore 918141; tel. 65412222; fax 65421231; e-mail thennarasee_R@caas.gov.sg; internet www.caas.gov.sg; responsible for regulatory and advisory services, air services development, airport management and development and airspace management and organization; Chair. TJONG YIK MIN; Dir-Gen. WONG WOON LIONG.

SilkAir: Singapore Airlines Superhub, Airfreight Terminal 5, Core L, 5th Storey, 30 Airline Rd, Singapore 819830; tel. 65428111; fax 65426286; internet www.silkair.net; f. 1975; fmrly Tradewinds Private; wholly-owned subsidiary of Singapore Airlines Ltd; began scheduled services in 1989; Chair. CHEW CHOON SENG; Gen. Man. PAUL TAN.

Singapore Airlines Ltd (SIA): Airline House, 25 Airline Rd, Singapore 819829; tel. 65415880; fax 65456083; e-mail publicaffairs@singaporeair.com.sg; internet www.singaporeair.com; f. 1972; passenger services to 88 destinations in 42 countries; Chair. MICHAEL FAM; CEO CHEW CHOON SENG (from June 2003).

Tourism

Singapore's tourist attractions include a blend of cultures and excellent shopping facilities. Tourist arrivals totalled 7,566,237 in 2002. Receipts from tourism totalled an estimated US $6,370m. in 2000.

Singapore Tourism Board: Tourism Court, 1 Orchard Spring Lane, Singapore 247729; tel. 67366622; fax 67369423; e-mail feedback@stb.com.sg; internet www.stb.com.sg; f. 1964; Chair. WEE EE-CHAO; Chief Exec. YEO KHEE LENG.

SLOVAKIA

Introductory Survey

Location, Climate, Language, Religion, Flag, Capital

The Slovak Republic (formerly a constituent republic of the Czech and Slovak Federative Republic, or Czechoslovakia) is a land-locked state located in central Europe, bordered to the north by Poland, to the east by Ukraine, to the south by Hungary, to the west by Austria and to the north-west by the Czech Republic. The climate is typically continental, with cold, dry winters and hot, humid summers. Average temperatures in Bratislava range from $-0.7°C$ ($30.7°F$) in January to $21.1°C$ ($70.0°F$) in July. Average annual rainfall in the capital is 649 mm (26 ins). The official language is Slovak, although Hungarian, Czech and the languages of other ethnic minorities living in Slovakia are also spoken. The major religion is Christianity, the Roman Catholic Church being the largest denomination, followed by the Evangelical Church of the Augsburg Confession. The national flag (proportions 2 by 3) consists of three equal horizontal stripes, of white, blue and red; in the centre hoist there is a white-rimmed red shield containing a silver archiepiscopal (double-barred) cross surmounted on the central (and highest) of three blue hillocks. The capital is Bratislava.

Recent History

Slovaks and Czechs (who are closely related members of the western Slavic peoples) were first united in the ninth century AD, in the Great Moravian Empire, but were divided following the Empire's dissolution in 907. While the Slovaks came under Hungarian rule (which was to last, in different forms, until the early 20th century), the Czechs established a kingdom that remained an important political force until the incorporation of the Czech Lands into the Habsburg Empire in the 16th and 17th centuries.

A movement of nationalist revival, closely linked with a similar movement in the Czech Lands, evolved in Slovakia in the late 18th and 19th centuries. During the First World War (1914–18) Slovaks joined with Czechs in campaigning for an independent state, which would be composed of the Czech Lands and Slovakia. The Republic of Czechoslovakia was established on 28 October 1918, as one of the successor states to the Austro-Hungarian Empire. The country's boundaries were defined by the Treaty of Trianon of 1920, under which a large Hungarian minority was incorporated into Slovakia. Czechoslovakia's first Constitution, promulgated in 1920, made no provision for a proper federal system, and Slovak proposals for self-government were rejected by the central authorities in the capital, Prague. A further cause of Slovak disaffection was the fact that the Czech Lands were the focus of the country's economic development, while Slovakia remained comparatively undeveloped. There was also an ideological divide between the two parts of the country: while the majority of Slovaks were strict Roman Catholics, the central Government in Prague was professedly anticlerical.

In October 1938, following the Munich Agreement of 29 September (whereby the predominantly German-populated areas of Czechoslovakia were ceded to Germany), Slovak nationalists declared Slovak autonomy. On 14 March 1939, one day before Nazi armed forces occupied the Czech Lands, Hitler agreed to the establishment of a separate Slovak state, under the pro-Nazi 'puppet' regime of Fr Jozef Tiso. Under the wartime Slovak state any opposition to the Tiso regime was ruthlessly suppressed, and the treatment of Jews, especially after the adoption of the Jewish Code in 1941, was particularly severe. In August 1944 an armed resistance (the Slovak National Uprising) against Tiso's regime was begun, but it was suppressed within two months by German troops.

Following the restoration of the Czechoslovak state in 1945, at the end of the Second World War, certain concessions were made to Slovak demands for autonomy, including the establishment of a regional legislature with restricted powers (the Slovak National Council) and an executive, both in Bratislava, the Slovak capital. However, this limited progress towards a federal system was largely negated by the seizure of power by the Communists (led by Gustav Husák) in Slovakia in late 1947, and in the whole of the country in 1948. In May 1948 a new

Constitution was approved, which declared Czechoslovakia to be a 'people's democracy'. The Communists' consolidation of power was completed in the following month with the election to the post of President of Klement Gottwald, a Czech and the leader of the Communist Party of Czechoslovakia (CPCz), who had been Prime Minister since 1946.

In the first years of Communist rule there was widespread repression, not only of political opponents of the CPCz, but also of party members. Expressions of Slovak nationalism were harshly suppressed, and in 1954 Husák and other Slovaks were imprisoned on charges of separatism. The new Constitution of 1960 restricted Slovak autonomy: the executive in Bratislava was dissolved and legislative authority was removed from the Slovak National Council.

It was not until the 1960s, when reformist policies began to be adopted within the CPCz, that the issue of Slovak autonomy re-emerged in public debate. In January 1968 Alexander Dubček (a Slovak and hitherto the leader of the Communist Party of Slovakia, CPS) was appointed First Secretary of the CPCz. The wide-ranging political and economic reforms introduced by Dubček and the new Government included plans for the creation of a federal system of two equal republics. This period of political tolerance and freedom of expression (subsequently known as the 'Prague Spring') was abruptly ended in August 1968 by the armed intervention of some 600,000 troops of the USSR and its allies. Dubček was replaced by Husák as First (subsequently General) Secretary of the CPCz, and there was a severe purge of party members, in particular reformists and associates of Dubček. Nevertheless, the federal system was realized in January 1969: separate Czech and Slovak Socialist Republics were established, each with its own government and legislature (National Council). Supreme legislative and executive power, meanwhile, were vested, respectively, in the Federal Assembly and the Federal Government. However, the reimposition of centralized Communist rule, under the leadership of Husák, left the new regional institutions largely powerless.

In 1975 Husák was appointed President of Czechoslovakia. He remained General Secretary of the CPCz until December 1987, when he was replaced in the latter post by Miloš Jakeš, a Czech member of the CPCz Presidium. Although the new administration publicly avowed its commitment to introduce political and economic reforms similar to those taking place in the USSR under Mikhail Gorbachev, political liberalization was not forthcoming. The Government continued its repressive treatment of both the Roman Catholic Church and the several dissident groups that had been established since the late 1970s (the most important being Charter 77). Nevertheless, the dissident movement was instrumental in organizing a series of anti-Government demonstrations, beginning in 1988, which were to culminate in the anti-Communist revolution of late 1989 (see chapter on the Czech Republic).

Elections to the Federal Assembly and to the Czech and Slovak National Councils on 8–9 June 1990 were the first to be held freely since 1946. Of the Slovak parties and movements, Public Against Violence (PAV), which, with its Czech counterpart, Civic Forum, had been the principal force in effecting the end of Communist rule, emerged with the largest representation at both federal and republican level. A coalition Slovak Government, dominated by PAV, was subsequently formed, with Vladimír Mečiar as Prime Minister.

The future of Czech-Slovak relations emerged in the latter half of 1990 as the dominant topic of political debate. While most Czech and Slovak citizens appeared to favour the preservation of a common state, there was increasing support in Slovakia for a more decentralized form of the existing federation. Among the Slovak political parties, the Christian Democratic Movement (CDM), which formed part of the Slovak coalition Government, advocated greater Slovak autonomy within a common state; however, more radical parties—most notably the Slovak National Party (SNP), which held seats in both the federal and republican legislatures—advocated the complete secession of Slovakia from the federation. The debate over the future of the country (which since April 1990 had been officially known as the

Czech and Slovak Federative Republic) led to increasing political turmoil in Slovakia during 1991. In March Mečiar was forced to resign as Slovak Prime Minister, accused of harming Czech-Slovak relations by his increasingly strident advocacy of full autonomy for Slovakia. Mečiar left PAV and formed a new party, the Movement for a Democratic Slovakia (MDS). He was replaced as Prime Minister by Ján Čarnogurský, the leader of the CDM. Proposals by the Czechoslovak President, Václav Havel, for a referendum to determine the country's future were repeatedly rejected by the Federal Assembly.

Following elections to the federal and republican legislatures on 5–6 June 1992, the MDS emerged clearly as the dominant Slovak party both in the Federal Assembly and the Slovak National Council. In the latter body the MDS won 74 of the total 150 seats, compared with only 18 won by the CDM and 15 by the SNP. The Party of the Democratic Left (PDL—the successor to the CPS) won the second largest representation in the Council (29 seats). A coalition of Hungarian national parties obtained the remaining 14 seats. In late June Mečiar was reinstated as Prime Minister, at the head of a new, MDS-dominated Slovak Government.

On 17 July 1992 the Slovak National Council overwhelmingly approved a declaration of Slovak sovereignty, as a result of which the dismantling of the Czechoslovak federation appeared inevitable. In late July Mečiar and his Czech counterpart, Václav Klaus, reached agreement on the necessary measures to permit the separation of the two republics. On 1 September the new Slovak Constitution was adopted by the Slovak National Council. In November the Federal Assembly finally approved (albeit at the third attempt and by a margin of only three votes) legislation to permit the constitutional dissolution (to be effected on 1 January 1993) of Czechoslovakia.

During the remainder of 1992 there was an acceleration of the process of dividing federal assets and liabilities, as well as the armed forces, between the Czech and Slovak Republics. In late December the two republics signed a co-operation agreement, and subsequently established formal diplomatic relations. With the dissolution of all federal structures at midnight on 31 December, the Czech Republic and the Slovak Republic came into existence. Recognition was quickly accorded to the new countries by all those states that had maintained relations with Czechoslovakia, as well as by various international bodies. The entirely peaceful nature of the dissolution of Czechoslovakia (notably at the time of the conflict in the former Yugoslavia) was believed to have contributed to the rapid international recognition of both republics.

Slovakia's existing MDS-dominated Government remained in place, and the National Council was retained as the republic's legislature. In January 1993 the National Council held two rounds of voting to elect Slovakia's President; however, none of the four candidates (representing the leading parties in the legislature, the MDS, the PDL, the CDM and the SNP) received the required three-fifths' majority. In a subsequent round of voting in February, the sole candidate, Michal Kováč, the Deputy Chairman of the MDS and the former Chairman of Czechoslovakia's Federal Assembly, was appointed President. (Prior to his death, in November 1992, it had been considered probable that Alexander Dubček would be elected Slovakia's first President.) The presidential election campaign was conducted against a background of growing internal divisions within the MDS, which culminated in March 1993 with the dismissal of Milan Kňažko, the strongest critic of Mečiar within the MDS, from his post of Deputy Prime Minister and Minister of Foreign Affairs. Kňažko subsequently formed a liberal party, the Alliance of Democrats of the Slovak Republic (ADSR), in opposition to Mečiar's Government. Also in March the SNP leader, Ľudovít Černák, resigned as Minister of the Economy, leaving the Government (with the exception of two independent ministers), composed exclusively of members of the MDS. However, as a result of several defections, the party (plus affiliates) lost its majority in the legislature. Following negotiations between the MDS and the SNP in the latter half of 1993, a new coalition Government, in which the SNP held several principal portfolios, was formed in November. One of Mečiar's ministerial nominees was rejected by Kováč, who had by this time become severely critical of the Prime Minister's outspoken opinions. In December Mečiar ignored a demand by the President for his resignation.

Mečiar's position was again undermined in early 1994 by further resignations and defections. In February six SNP deputies left the party to form what became the National Democratic

Party—New Alternative (NDP—NA), led by Černák. In the same month the Minister of Foreign Affairs, Jozef Moravčík, and the Deputy Prime Minister, Roman Kováč, resigned from the Government, subsequently establishing another new opposition party, the Democratic Union of Slovakia (DUS). In March the National Council approved a motion expressing 'no confidence' in Mečiar's Government by 78 votes to two (the MDS and SNP both abstained from voting). Following the resignation of Mečiar's administration, a new, five-party coalition was hastily agreed, and installed in mid-March. The new Government, with Moravčík as Prime Minister, comprised members of the CDM and the PDL, as well as the three new formations: the NDP—NA, the DUS and the ADSR (the last was subsequently absorbed into the DUS). This Government was to act in an interim capacity, pending early legislative elections in September. The new administration adopted a policy of closer integration with western European states and successfully improved relations with Hungary, giving assurances that the rights of Slovakia's Hungarian minority would be respected.

Despite the achievements of Moravčík's coalition Government, the MDS again emerged as the leading party at elections to the National Council, held on 30 September and 1 October 1994 (with the participation of some 76% of the electorate). The renewed success of the MDS (which, in alliance with the smaller Farmers' Party of Slovakia, secured 35.0% of the total votes cast and 61 seats in the Council) was attributed to the highly populist character of Mečiar's election campaign. The Common Choice bloc (an alliance of left-wing parties, led by the PDL) won 10.4% of the votes and 18 seats (fewer than had been expected), followed by a coalition of Hungarian parties (17) and the CDM (also 17). The remaining seats were taken by the DUS (15), the Association of Workers of Slovakia (AWS—formed earlier in the year, following a split in the PDL—13 seats) and the SNP (nine seats).

Inter-party negotiations ensued, with the aim of establishing a new coalition, but proved inconclusive. Thus, in late October 1994 Kováč requested that Mečiar form a new Government. Finally, in mid-December a coalition of the MDS, the SNP and the AWS was announced. The new Government immediately used its majority in the National Council to annul all decisions on privatization that had been made by the previous administration in January 1995. Kováč refused his assent to the legislation, but the Council overturned his veto. Opposition deputies then submitted the controversial legislation to the Constitutional Court, which in May declared the suspension of the privatization programme to have been illegal. The personal enmity between Mečiar and Kováč culminated in an unsuccessful vote by the National Council on a motion of 'no confidence' in the President, following allegations that the Slovak Intelligence Service (SIS, which had been under presidential control until April, when it came under the control of the Government) had provided Kováč with confidential information concerning the activities of political parties, in particular the MDS, and of state officials.

In August 1995 one of Kováč's sons (also called Michal) was abducted from Bratislava by unknown assailants and taken to the Austrian border town of Hainburg, where he was detained by Austrian police on an international arrest warrant issued by a court in Munich, Germany, in connection with allegations of embezzlement. In February 1996 Austrian prosecutors decided not to extradite him to Germany, and he was permitted to return to Slovakia. In the same month President Kováč claimed that there was evidence to suggest that the SIS had been responsible for his son's abduction. The Director of the SIS, Ivan Lexa, responded by accusing Kováč of libel. Mečiar, meanwhile, alleged that the President, too, had been involved in the embezzlement affair, and that his son had himself organized the abduction in order to divert attention from the financial scandal; President Kováč subsequently filed libel charges against Mečiar. However, investigations into both the abduction of Kováč's son and Kováč's libel suit were adjourned in May and August, respectively, owing to lack of evidence.

The episode was regarded by many observers as a further attempt to discredit the President, and strengthened the belief that democratic processes in Slovakia were under threat. Indeed, during 1995 there was increased international criticism of Slovakia's respect for human rights, with allegations of intimidation of political opponents of the Government, growing authoritarianism on the part of Mečiar, as well as insufficient protection of ethnic minorities' rights. In March 1996 international censure was prompted by the National Council's approval of a new anti-subversion law, under which, opposition parties argued, freedom of expression and public assembly could potentially be curbed. In the following month Kováč refused to endorse the legislation, and returned it to the National Council for reconsideration.

The stability of the Government appeared to be threatened in mid-1996, when Mečiar accused the SNP and the AWS of violating the provisions of the coalition agreement and of failing to support government policies. The Ministers of the Economy, Foreign Affairs and the Interior were replaced in August, in what was interpreted by some observers as an attempt to address the increasing international concern at Slovakia's apparent lack of commitment to democratic reform. Discussion of the anti-subversion law continued throughout 1996; having been returned to the legislature by the President for a third time, the amendment was finally, in a rare political reverse for Mečiar, rejected by the National Council in February 1997. The increasing concern over the Government's anti-democratic stance was reflected in the establishment of a civic movement, Charter 97, in January, to monitor observance of the Constitution and of civil rights. Opposition deputies, meanwhile, were campaigning for a referendum to be held on their proposals for a new system for the presidential elections, whereby the Head of State would be elected by direct popular vote, rather than chosen by the National Council. Sufficient signatures for the plebiscite to proceed were collected in a petition and, as a result, President Kováč scheduled a referendum for 23–24 May 1997. The ballot was to decide on Slovakia's proposed membership of NATO, as well as the issue of the nature of presidential elections. The Government, which had already accused the President of acting in an undemocratic manner, submitted a petition to the Constitutional Court concerning the legitimacy of the opposition's referendum question—specifically, whether the Constitution could be amended by means of a referendum. The Constitutional Court ruled that the Government had no authority to participate in constitutional disputes concerning the calling of a referendum. However, despite this ruling, when the referendum took place, as scheduled, the question on presidential elections was omitted from the ballot papers, on the orders of Gustáv Krajči, the Minister of the Interior. The majority of voters boycotted the referendum, angered by the Government's decision to delete the question, and the rate of electoral participation (less than 10%) was consequently too low to render the vote valid. The Minister of Foreign Affairs, Pavol Hamžík, resigned in protest at what he regarded as the Government's manipulation of the democratic process. In early June several thousand people attended a rally organized by the opposition to protest against the Government's intervention in the referendum. In mid-June opposition attempts to vote on a motion of 'no confidence' in Krajči were frustrated on two occasions, when deputies from the governing coalition refused to participate. In a secret ballot later that month, however, Krajči survived a vote of 'no confidence' in the National Council.

Discussions held in early July 1997 between representatives of the ruling coalition and eight opposition parties failed to produce any agreement on presidential elections, or on the implementation of the recommendations of the joint parliamentary committee of the European Union (EU, see p. 199) and Slovakia, which had insisted on the need to approve a law on minority languages and the participation of opposition representatives in parliamentary committees responsible for overseeing the SIS. The opposition declared that it would not participate in further talks. Later in July both the President and opposition parties blamed the Government for Slovakia's exclusion from the first group of countries invited to join NATO, and also from a list of countries recommended by the European Commission for early negotiations on membership of the EU. The Slovak Democratic Coalition (SDC), a new grouping of five opposition parties (including the CDM and the DUS), demanded Mečiar's resignation, accusing his administration of endangering Slovakia's political and economic future. Ongoing tension between the President and the Prime Minister intensified; an appeal from the former for early elections prompted the MDS to demand his resignation.

At the end of September 1997 the National Council voted against an opposition motion to reinstate František Gaulieder (a former MDS deputy whose parliamentary mandate had been revoked in December 1996, following his resignation from the MDS), in defiance of a Constitutional Court ruling that Gaulieder's expulsion from the National Council should be reversed. The National Council's decision was severely criticized by Kováč

and the EU. In mid-October, amid increasing concerns regarding the country's image abroad, Kováč and Mečiar united to issue a joint statement affirming Slovakia's firm commitment to future membership of the EU and other international organizations. None the less, later that month the European Parliament adopted a resolution appealing to the National Council to restore Gaulieder's mandate and emphasizing the need to convince Slovakia's leaders to respect democracy and minority rights; the MDS rejected the resolution. At the end of the month Mečiar appealed to the Gypsy (Roma) population (unofficially estimated at some 400,000—the Gypsy population was officially enumerated at 86,383 at the end of 1996) not to seek asylum abroad, after a number of Roma were repatriated from the United Kingdom.

In early December 1997 an opposition motion proposing direct presidential elections was rejected by the National Council. Later that month the Constitutional Court settled a protracted dispute between Mečiar and Kováč, when it ruled that the President's term of office would end five years after his inauguration (on 2 March 1998), rather than five years after his election, as Mečiar had claimed. Also that month Kováč pardoned all those involved in the embezzlement case in which his son had been implicated in 1994–95.

During January–March 1998 several attempts to elect a new President failed in the National Council, when candidates were unable to secure the required three-fifths' majority. The MDS had not contested these first rounds of elections, seemingly confirming opposition fears that Mečiar was attempting to ensure that the presidency remained vacant when Kováč left office, enabling him to assume a number of presidential powers. In mid-February, meanwhile, following a ruling by the Constitutional Court that Krajči had violated citizens' rights to vote in the May 1997 referendum, and in response to appeals from the opposition, Kováč announced that a further referendum would be held in April 1998.

On 2 March 1998 Kováč's term expired and a number of presidential powers were transferred to the Government, in accordance with the Constitution. Mečiar immediately cancelled the referendum scheduled by Kováč for April and announced the dismissal of some 28 of Slovakia's ambassadors abroad. He also granted an amnesty to various prisoners, including those suspected of abducting Kováč's son in 1995, and halted all criminal proceedings relating to the May 1997 referendum. The Prime Minister's actions prompted a series of widely-supported protest rallies organized by opposition parties, and were strongly criticized by the EU and the USA. A further round of voting in the presidential election on 16 April was contested for the first time by an MDS candidate; however, the National Council again failed to elect a new Head of State. Subsequent attempts in May and July were also unsuccessful, and two further rounds, scheduled for August and September, had to be cancelled, when no nominations were forthcoming.

At the end of May 1998, in preparation for legislative elections scheduled for September, the National Council approved controversial amendments to the electoral law, including a stipulation that all individual political parties (including those belonging to coalitions) obtain at least 5% of the votes cast in order to secure parliamentary representation. Also approved was legislation that restricted pre-election campaigning to the state-run media. In June three ethnic Hungarian parties formally merged to create the Party of the Hungarian Coalition (PHC) and the SDC also registered officially as a single party. In July a constitutional amendment, providing for the transfer of a number of presidential powers to the Chairman of the National Council, in the event of the presidency becoming vacant, was supported by deputies from all parties.

The election campaign was marked by disagreements over access to the media, with the SDC accusing Slovak Television of bias towards the MDS. A dispute over the ownership of Slovakia's principal independent television channel, Markíza TV, culminated in the dismissal of its Director-General, Pavol Rusko, in what was claimed by opposition parties to be politically motivated, and thousands of opposition supporters reportedly participated in demonstrations. (Rusko was reappointed in October 1998.) The elections to the National Council were held, as scheduled, on 25–26 September, with the participation of 84.2% of the electorate. The ruling MDS narrowly retained its position as the strongest party in the legislature, winning 43 seats (with 27.0% of the votes cast), but was unable to form a government, with its only possible ally, the SNP, holding 14 seats. The SDC performed well, with 42 seats (26.3% of the votes), while three other opposition parties also secured representation. The PDL won 23 seats (14.7%), the PHC took 15 seats and the Party of Civic Understanding (PCU—formed earlier that year) won 13 seats. The 11 remaining parties that contested the elections failed to attain the 5% threshold. With a combined total of 93 seats, the SDC, the PDL, the PHC and the PCU agreed to attempt to form a new administration. Negotiations took place throughout October, and a new coalition Government, headed by Mikuláš Dzurinda, the leader of the SDC, was finally appointed at the end of the month. Jozef Migaš, the leader of the PDL, was elected Chairman of the National Council.

The opposition's victory was welcomed both by Western institutions and by neighbouring countries, which hoped the change of government would result in improved relations with Slovakia. In his policy statement to the National Council in mid-November 1998, Dzurinda emphasized the new Government's intention to pursue early membership of the EU and NATO, pledged to combat organized crime, and outlined measures to improve Slovakia's economic situation. In December the European Parliament adopted a resolution on Slovakia's application for membership of the EU, insisting that the European Commission consider initiating entry talks in 1999.

In January 1999 the National Council approved a government-sponsored constitutional amendment providing for the introduction of direct presidential elections. The ruling coalition nominated Rudolf Schuster, the Chairman of the PCU, as its presidential candidate, and Kováč announced his intention to stand for re-election. Also that month, Ján Ducký, a former Minister of the Economy and former head of the Slovak Gas Company (SGC), was found shot dead; Ducký had recently come under investigation for his alleged involvement in illegal activities at the SGC. In March tension within the ruling coalition led to a two-day parliamentary boycott by the PHC, which claimed that the PDL was breaching the coalition agreement over funding for minority culture.

Nine candidates contested the first round of the presidential election, which was held on 15 May 1999. Rudolf Schuster, the candidate of the ruling coalition, won 47.4% of the votes cast, while Mečiar, who had reversed an earlier decision to retire from public life, gained 37.2%. Michal Kováč had withdrawn his candidature prior to the first round, in favour of Schuster. Schuster defeated Mečiar in a second round of voting on 29 May, with 57.2% of the votes cast, and was duly inaugurated as President on 15 June, having resigned the chairmanship of the PCU.

Investigations into the circumstances surrounding the abduction of Kováč's son in August 1995 and the failed referendum of May 1997 resumed in early 1999, following Dzurinda's cancellation of amnesties granted by Mečiar in March 1998. In February 1999 the National Council revoked the parliamentary immunity of Gustáv Krajči, and in June he was charged with sabotaging the referendum and abusing public office. In April Ivan Lexa, the former head of the SIS, was also deprived of his immunity from prosecution and arrested in connection with Michal Kováč's abduction and other offences alleged to have been committed by the SIS under his leadership. The prosecution of Krajči and Lexa was effectively halted in July, however, when the Constitutional Court ruled that Dzurinda had not been entitled to revoke the amnesties granted by Mečiar to those involved in the kidnapping. (In December 2002, however, Lexa was arrested and charged with having organized the murder of a former police officer in 1996, in an attempt to obstruct the investigation into the kidnapping of Michal Kováč.)

In September 1999 a large demonstration was staged in Bratislava to protest against rising unemployment and declining living standards, resulting from a series of austerity measures implemented by the Government. In October L'udovít Černák, the Minister of the Economy, who had been criticized in connection with the measures, resigned from the Government and the National Council; his ministerial post was assumed by L'ubomír Harach, the Chairman of the DUS. In January 2000, following several weeks of disputes over the future structure of the SDC, during which he had failed to consolidate the unity of the party (many of whose members favoured a return to a less rigid five-party coalition), Dzurinda announced plans to form a new centre-right party, the Slovak Democratic and Christian Union (SDCU), in preparation for the next legislative elections, due in 2002. The SDCU, which was to be temporarily inactive, was officially registered in mid-February 2000, and was joined by several government ministers. Further SDC deputies subsequently resigned from the CDM and the DUS to join the

SDCU, while retaining membership of the SDC. In April the MDS announced its intention to propose legislation, aimed at SDC members that had joined the SDCU, to prohibit membership of more than one political party. Following Dzurinda's election as SDCU Chairman at the party's opening congress in November, the SDC became effectively defunct.

In April 2000 Mečiar was arrested on charges of abuse of power and fraud, in connection with allegations that he had illegally paid bonuses to government ministers while serving as Prime Minister. He was fined for refusing to answer questions related to the abduction of Kováč's son and later released. (In October 2001 it was announced that the charges against him had been abandoned, on the grounds that the bonuses had been paid under the terms of a cabinet resolution.)

In mid-June 2000 Schuster underwent emergency surgery, and later that month was airlifted to Austria for medical treatment. In July the Minister of Health, Tibor Sagat, resigned his portfolio, following criticism of the medical attention received by Schuster in Slovakia. In August a criminal investigation was initiated into the treatment received by Schuster (who claimed that it had resulted in potentially fatal complications). Schuster resumed office in mid-August.

In early September 2000 Schuster announced that a referendum on the issue of early legislative elections was to be conducted on 11 November, after the MDS submitted a petition of some 600,000 signatures in support of the proposal. At the referendum 92.4% of votes were cast in favour of early elections; however, the results were subsequently declared to be invalid, since the participation rate of 20.3% of registered voters failed to meet the requisite level. In December the Minister of Defence, Paval Konis, resigned, after attracting criticism for appointing former Communists to influential posts within his ministry, and for allegedly using public funds for the construction of a luxury private residence.

In early 2001 discussions commenced in the National Council regarding proposed revisions to the Constitution, which would provide for the reform of public administration and the judiciary, and allow the Government to proceed with other restructuring measures essential for Slovakia's admission to the EU. The constitutional amendments, although opposed by the MDS and SNP, were adopted by a narrow majority in the legislature in late February. The revisions to the Constitution (which officially entered into effect on 1 July) redefined the relationship between national and international law, thereby facilitating the process of joining foreign alliances, strengthened the powers of the Constitutional Court, granted greater independence to the judiciary and provided for public administration reform. In March the National Council voted in favour of Slovakia joining NATO. In April 2001 the EU suspended all payments for development programmes in Slovakia, in response to the alleged embezzlement of EU funds by a government official. In early May Schuster replaced Pavol Hamzik, the Deputy Prime Minister for European Integration, owing to his responsibility for the misuse of the donations. In the same month the Minister of the Interior tendered his resignation, following increasing criticism over his investigation into the mismanagement of the Mečiar administration. Schuster subsequently appointed a member of the SDCU to the cabinet post, despite protests from the CDM that it was entitled to the portfolio. Later in May opposition parties strongly criticized the Deputy Prime Minister for the Economy, Ivan Mikloš, for lack of progress in economic and public administration reform. However, a motion expressing 'no confidence' in him was defeated in the legislature, after Dzurinda indicated that he would resign if Mikloš was removed. The Government subsequently announced the adoption of a programme of extensive economic reforms.

In July 2001 the Government pledged to introduce measures to restore public confidence in the security forces, after the death of a Roma in police custody prompted widespread criticism and further controversy regarding treatment of the ethnic group. In the same month dissension increased between the government coalition parties over the issue of local government reform. The PHC, which opposed new legislation providing for the establishment of a higher level of regional self-administration, announced that it intended to withdraw from the coalition (thereby reducing its majority in the National Council). The PHC leadership subsequently agreed to remain in the coalition, in exchange for the amendment of the proposed legislation. Following the adoption of the reforms, which provided for the creation of eight 'higher territorial units' (rather than 12, as originally proposed), local government elections took place, in two rounds, on 1 and 15 December. In a reflection of increasing popular support for the party, MDS representatives secured 146 of the 401 seats in the regional councils and six of the eight gubernatorial posts. (However, voter participation in the second round was estimated at only 22% of the registered electorate.)

In January 2002 the PDL demanded the resignation of the Minister of Finance, Brigita Schmögnerová (who was a member of that party), after she allegedly withheld information regarding the privatization programme. (The opposition of the PDL leadership reflected dissent with her reformist stance.) Although Dzurinda initially refused to dismiss her, PDL threats to withdraw from the coalition finally resulted in her replacement. Schmögnerová subsequently left the PDL and formed a new political party, the Social Democratic Alternative (SDA). In February the collapse of 'pyramid' financial investment schemes, resulting in huge losses of individual savings, provoked further political controversy and criticism of the Government. Despite considerable popular pressure, Dzurinda refused to compensate investors and claimed that Mečiar's administration was responsible for the establishment of the enterprises. In mid-February Mikloš (who was principally responsible for the programme of structural reforms) survived a further motion of 'no confidence' in the National Council. In early March Dzurinda announced that he was to contest forthcoming legislative elections, which were scheduled for 20–21 September, as the SDCU candidate. In April the Minister of Education, Milan Ftáčnik, defected from the PDL to the SDA, of which he was elected Chairman; he subsequently resigned his ministerial post.

In July 2002 disaffected members of the MDS, who had not been selected by the party to contest the legislative elections, established a breakaway party, known as the Movement for Democracy. At the elections to the National Council on 20–21 September, the MDS, despite obtaining the highest proportion of the votes cast, with 19.5%, failed to secure an overall majority; Mečiar's party won 36 of the 150 seats in the Council (seven fewer than in the 1998 elections). The SDCU received 15.1% of the votes cast and 28 seats, a centre-right party, known as Direction (Smĕr), 13.5% and 25 seats, the PHC 11.2% and 20 seats, and the CDM 8.3% and 15 seats. The New Citizens' Alliance (NCA), established in 2001, won 8.0% of the votes and 15 seats, while the Slovak Communist Party (SCP) significantly increased its share, securing 6.3% and 11 seats. Mečiar subsequently proved unable to negotiate alliances with other parties, in order to form a coalition government, however, and in late September Schuster invited Dzurinda to establish a new administration. Following brief inter-party negotiations, a coalition agreement was signed in early October by four reformist parties (the SDCU, the PHC, the CDM and the NCA), which together commanded a narrow majority of 78 of the 150 seats in the National Council. On 16 October Schuster formally appointed a new coalition Government, comprising representatives of the four parties (while the leader of the Democratic Party, which had supported the SDCU in the elections, was also allocated a portfolio). Mikloš was retained in the administration as the new Minister of Finance. The adoption of an austerity budget in November prompted further popular protests, and the MDS urged deputies in the National Council to reverse the legislation. In early December five opposition parties, which had failed to secure seats in the legislative elections, announced their intention to amalgamate. Local government elections took place on 6–7 December; mayoral offices were equally divided between the government coalition parties and the MDS.

Slovakia is a member, together with the Czech Republic, Hungary and Poland, of the Visegrad Group, which promotes economic and other integration in the Central European region. Relations with the Czech Republic were strained in early 1997 after claims that the Czech President, Václav Havel, had made insulting remarks about Mečiar during a dispute over Czech membership of NATO. Slovakia, in an apparent attempt to obstruct the issuing of a formal invitation to the Czech Republic to join NATO, claimed that the Czech leadership was failing to discuss several issues concerning federal property that had arisen following the division of the two countries; the Slovak ambassador was subsequently temporarily recalled from Prague. Relations appeared to have improved to some extent in October of that year, when Mečiar and Václav Klaus, the Czech Prime Minister, held their first official meeting since the division of Czechoslovakia. It was reported that some progress had been made regarding former federal property, including the return of Slovak gold held by the Czech Republic. In December, however, further tension arose, when Mečiar refused to apolo-

gize for offensive remarks he had apparently made about Havel, and announced that he would not negotiate with the new Czech Government. In September 1998, however, following talks between Mečiar and Miloš Zeman, the Czech Prime Minister, it was announced that a joint Czech-Slovak committee was to meet in an attempt to further discussions on unresolved issues, including the exchange of bank shares between the two countries. The success of opposition parties in the Slovak election later that month, and the subsequent change of government, led to a further improvement in bilateral relations. Measures providing for dual Czech-Slovak citizenship became fully effective in October 1999, and in November an agreement on the division of former federal property was signed in Bratislava by Zeman and Dzurinda. The agreement provided for the exchange of shares between the Czech Republic's Komerční banka and Slovakia's Všeobecná úverová banka and the return to Slovakia of gold reserves (which had been held by the Czech central bank as collateral for debts owed by Slovakia to the Czech Republic). The Czech Government consequently opted effectively to relieve Slovakia of its debts by buying the central bank's claim for the sum of one koruna. Following the ratification of the agreement by both countries' legislatures in early 2000, the final settlement of the property dispute was confirmed in May, during a visit by Dzurinda to Prague.

Slovakia's relations with Hungary have been strained by the issue of the large Hungarian minority (numbering almost 570,000 at the end of 1996) resident in Slovakia, who are campaigning for cultural and educational autonomy. The two countries are also involved in a dispute over the Gabčíkovo-Nagymaros hydroelectric project, a scheme initiated by the Governments of Czechoslovakia and Hungary in 1978, which involved the construction of two dams and the diversion of the River Danube. Despite Hungary's decision in 1989 to abandon the project (following pressure by environmentalist groups), the Czechoslovak Government announced that it would proceed unilaterally with its part of the construction (which was nearing completion in late 1992). In March 1993 Slovakia and Hungary agreed to forward the dispute to the International Court of Justice (ICJ) in The Hague, the Netherlands. In March 1995, none the less, an historic bilateral Treaty of Friendship and Co-operation was signed. The treaty notably guaranteed the rights of ethnic minorities in each republic, while confirming the existing state border. However, the language law approved by the Slovak legislature in November, declaring Slovak the only official language and thereby potentially restricting the use of minority languages, was criticized both by Hungarian residents of Slovakia, and also by the Hungarian Government, as a violation of the treaty. In June 1997 the first of a series of rallies was held in Slovakia to protest against measures restricting the use of minority languages in the education system. At a meeting in August Gyula Horn, the Hungarian Prime Minister, and Mečiar agreed on the establishment of a joint commission to assess the implementation of the 1995 treaty, although there was subsequently disagreement over its composition. Hungary also insisted on the need for a Slovak law on the use of minority languages.

In September 1997 relations became tense, after it emerged that Mečiar had proposed the initiation of a voluntary repatriation programme for the ethnic minorities of both countries. Later in September the ICJ pronounced its judgment on the Gabčíkovo-Nagymaros hydroelectric project, ruling that both countries had breached international law: Hungary was not justified in suspending work on the project, while the former Czechoslovakia should not have proceeded unilaterally. Both countries were to pay compensation for damages, and to negotiate regarding the realization of the original agreement. At the end of February 1998 the Slovak and Hungarian delegations presented a draft framework agreement on the hydroelectric project. Tension resurfaced in March, however, following the Hungarian Government's decision to await the results of environmental and feasibility studies before signing the agreement. Furthermore, in July a new Hungarian Government announced the draft agreement to be invalid. Meanwhile, the participation of the PHC in the new Slovak Government appointed in October improved prospects for the protection of minority rights. In February 1999, after a delay of some four years, the first meeting of the joint minorities commission to monitor the implementation of the 1995 treaty was held in Budapest, Hungary. In July 1999 the Slovak National Council approved legislation that provided for the use of an ethnic minority language in towns where the minority accounted for at least 20% of the population, despite the opposition of PHC deputies, who had favoured a limit of 10%. In December Hungary renounced any claim to a share of the hydroelectric energy produced by the dam project, but requested an increase in the common flow of water along the Danube, for ecological reasons. In February 2001 Slovakia accepted that it had no legal means to compel Hungary to complete the project, but stated that it was to seek compensation from the Hungarian Government. In early 2002 relations between Slovakia and Hungary again became acrimonious, following Hungary's adoption of legislation that granted ethnic Hungarians resident in six neighbouring states, including Slovakia, education, employment and medical benefits from January of that year. The Slovak Government protested that the new legislation violated Slovakia's sovereignty over its own citizens, and demanded that it be cancelled or amended. In early March 2003 Hungary agreed to suspend the application of the law in Slovakia.

Relations with neighbouring Austria were strained by the issue of the partially-constructed, Soviet-designed nuclear power station at Mochovce (north-east of Bratislava), the completion of which was opposed by the Austrian Government, owing to safety concerns. In April 1995 the European Bank for Reconstruction and Development (EBRD, see p. 193) pledged funds to Slovakia to help complete the station's construction. However, in September the Slovak Government rejected the EBRD's offer, as it had been conditional on the closure of Slovakia's existing nuclear power plant at Jaslovské-Bohunice, which the Bank deemed to be a safety hazard. An agreement on completion of the project was signed in April 1996, with western European, Russian and Czech companies, according to which the first reactor would be commissioned by July 1998 and the second by March 1999. Tension increased in June 1998, when the first reactor was activated, despite a request from the Austrian Government that Slovakia delay the opening of the plant until an international team of inspectors, who had visited Mochovce in May, had submitted a final report on the plant's safety. In late 1999 the Slovakian Government announced its decision to close the two reactors at Jaslovské-Bohunice between 2006 and 2008, further antagonizing Austria, which had favoured closure by 2000.

Slovakia's Roma continued to seek political asylum abroad during 1999 and early 2000 (largely unsuccessfully), prompting several countries to introduce mandatory visa requirements, on a temporary basis, for Slovak citizens. In February 1994 Slovakia joined NATO's 'Partnership for Peace' (see p. 273) programme, with the eventual aim of full membership of NATO. In December 1999 Slovakia was among six countries formally invited to commence talks on accession to the EU; entry negotiations opened in February 2000, when the Government expressed its aim of achieving membership by 2004. In December 2001 the EU officially included Slovakia in the first group of applicant states, which were expected to join the organization in 2004. At a NATO summit meeting in Prague at the end of November 2002, Slovakia (together with Bulgaria, Latvia, Lithuania, Poland, Romania, and Slovenia) were formally invited to join the organization by 2004. Following the return to power of a reformist coalition Government in October 2002 (see above), Slovakia was, at an EU summit meeting held in Copenhagen, Denmark, in December, one of 10 nations invited to become members in the 2004 enlargement. At a national referendum, which was conducted on 16–17 May 2003, 93.7% of votes cast were in favour of Slovakia becoming a member of the EU; some 52% of the electorate participated in the ballot.

Government

Supreme legislative power is vested in the National Council of the Slovak Republic, the 150 members of which are elected for a term of four years by universal adult suffrage. The President of the Republic (Head of State) is directly elected by universal adult suffrage for a five-year term. The President, who is restricted to two consecutive terms of office, appoints the Prime Minister and, on the latter's recommendation, the other members of the Government (the supreme body of executive power). For administrative purposes, Slovakia is divided into eight 'higher territorial units', each with a regional council (together totalling 401 seats), and 79 electoral districts.

Defence

In August 2002 the total active strength of Slovakia's armed forces was 26,200: army 13,000, air force 10,200, with some 3,000 centrally controlled personnel, and logistical and support staff. Paramilitary forces numbered 4,700, including 1,700 internal security forces and 1,350 civil defence troops. Military service is compulsory and lasts for 12 months. The Government planned to modernize the military industry by 2004, when the country was scheduled to be granted membership of NATO. The 2001 Slovak budget allocated 18,200m. koruny to defence.

Economic Affairs

In 2001, according to the World Bank, Slovakia's gross national income (GNI), measured at average 1999–2001 prices, was US $20,028m., equivalent to $3,700 per head (or $11,610 per head on an international purchasing-power parity basis). During 1990–2001, it was estimated, the population increased at an annual average rate of 0.2%, while gross domestic product (GDP) per head increased, in real terms, by an average of 0.5% per year. Overall GDP increased, in real terms, at an annual average of 0.7% in 1990–2001; growth was 2.2% in 2000 and 3.3% in 2001.

In 2001 the agricultural sector (including forestry and fishing) contributed 4.2% of GDP, according to IMF estimates. The sector employed an estimated 6.2% of the employed labour force in 2002. The principal crops are wheat and other grains, sugar beet, potatoes and other vegetables. Livestock breeding is also important. During 1990–2001, according to the World Bank, the GDP of the agricultural sector increased, in real terms, by an annual average of 0.1%. Agricultural GDP increased by 3.1% in 2000 and by 2.0% in 2001.

Industry (including mining, manufacturing, construction and power) contributed 29.7% of GDP in 2001 (according to IMF estimates), and engaged 38.4% of the employed labour force in 2002. According to the World Bank, the GDP of the industrial sector declined, in real terms, by an annual average of 4.6% during 1990–2001. However, industrial GDP increased by 0.4% in 2000 and by 5.5% in 2001.

Mining and quarrying contributed 0.7% of GDP (according to IMF estimates) in 2001, and engaged 1.2% of the employed labour force in 2000. The principal minerals extracted include brown coal and lignite, copper, zinc, lead, iron ore and magnesite. There are also deposits of crude petroleum, natural gas and mercury, as well as materials used in construction (including limestone, gravel and brick loam). According to IMF estimates, the GDP of the mining and quarrying sector increased by an annual average of 2.5% in 1995–2001. Mining GDP declined by 9.2% in 2001.

The manufacturing sector contributed 21.8% of GDP (according to IMF estimates) in 2001, and engaged 25.7% of the employed labour force in 2000. From 1989 the dominance of the armaments industry has been considerably reduced, in favour of the light manufacturing sector. The metallurgical, engineering and chemicals industries have also expanded considerably. The GDP of the manufacturing sector increased by an annual average of 4.5% in 1995–2001. Manufacturing GDP increased by 5.5% in 2000 and by 6.0% in 2001.

Energy is derived principally from nuclear power, which provided some 47.7% of electricity generated in 1999, while coal supplied 23.4% and hydroelectric power 16.5% in that year. A large-scale nuclear power station at Jaslovské-Bohunice has been in operation since the early 1980s. In July 1998 the first block of a new nuclear power installation, at Mochovce, commenced operations. Slovakia has been heavily dependent on imported fuel and energy products. Mineral fuels and lubricants accounted for 17.5% of the value of total merchandise imports in 2000.

The services sector contributed 66.0% of GDP in 2001, and engaged 55.4% of the employed labour force in 2002. During 1990–2001, according to the World Bank, the GDP of the services sector increased, in real terms, by an annual average of 6.0%, rising by 3.0% in 2000 and by 2.3% in 2001.

In 2000 Slovakia recorded a trade deficit of US $895m., while there was a deficit of $694m. on the current account of the balance of payments. In 2002 the principal source of imports was Germany, which accounted for 22.6% of the total; other major suppliers were the Czech Republic, Russia and Italy. Germany was also the principal market for exports in that year (26.0%); other important purchasers were the Czech Republic, Italy, Austria, Hungary and Poland. The main exports in 2000 were machinery and transport equipment, basic manufactures, miscellaneous manufactured articles, and chemical products. The principal imports were machinery and transport equipment, basic manufactures, mineral fuels and lubricants, and chemical products.

Slovakia's overall budgetary deficit for 2001 was 32,012m. koruny, equivalent to 3.2% of GDP. Slovakia's total external debt (including commitments to the Czech Republic) at the end of 2000 was US $9,462m., of which $4,883m. was long-term public debt. In that year the cost of debt-servicing was equivalent to 18.0% of the value of exports of goods and services. The annual rate of inflation averaged 10.4% in 1991–2001; consumer prices increased by 7.4% in 2001 and by 3.3% in 2002. At the end of 2002 the rate of unemployment was estimated at 18%.

Slovakia is a member of the IMF and the World Bank, as well as of the European Bank for Reconstruction and Development (see p. 193), as a 'Country of Operations'. It is also a member of the Central European Free Trade Association, and in late 2000 was admitted to the Organisation for Economic Co-operation and Development (see p. 277). In October 1993 Slovakia signed an association agreement with the European Community (now European Union—EU, see p. 199).

Following Slovakia's independence in 1993, sustained economic growth was achieved (despite political instability under the Governments of Vladimír Mečiar in 1993–98). The economy successfully shifted from its traditional reliance on industry to services, and from state to private ownership. Nevertheless, the monetary deficits and foreign debt burden had increased substantially by 1998. In October the new reformist Government introduced a number of austerity measures, while the Central Bank introduced a 'floating' exchange rate. Some reduction in the fiscal deficit was achieved in 1999; however, the austerity measures also resulted in a sharp increase in the rate of unemployment. Extension of the privatization programme included the divestment of the state-owned telecommunications company in mid-2000. In May the Government finally agreed a 14-year enterprise and financial sector adjustment loan with the World Bank, which committed the administration to a programme of measures supported by the Bretton Woods institutions, including continued bank restructuring and privatization, and reform of the financial sector. Government revenue benefited from the completion of the privatization of the major gas distributor in 2002. Priorities of a new, strongly reformist Government, which was established in October, were to reduce the budgetary deficit, reduce the exceptionally high level of unemployment (particularly in the east of the country), reform the judiciary system and address corruption. In November the legislature approved an extensive austerity budget, which was to be sustained by tax increases and delays in wage rises. (The planned reductions in public expenditure prompted popular protests.) Extensive structural changes to public expenditure were to be introduced in 2004; these included greater private contributions to the health and welfare systems, the establishment of a funded pension system and welfare reforms (which were to contribute to lowering the rate of unemployment). In late 2002 Slovakia was among the first group of applicant states invited to join the EU in its planned enlargement in 2004. Foreign direct investment, which had hitherto remained limited, was immediately stimulated by the return to power of a reformist administration and confirmation of the country's scheduled entry into the EU.

Education

Education in Slovakia is provided free of charge at all levels in state-controlled and church-affiliated schools. Children between the ages of three and six may attend kindergarten (materská škola). Compulsory education begins at six years of age, when children enter basic school (základná škola), which takes nine years to complete (although the ninth year is optional). In the 2000/01 academic year 650,966 pupils were enrolled at primary schools. There are three types of secondary school: the grammar school (gymnázium), which prepares students for higher education, and of which there were 212 in the 2000/01 academic year, secondary specialized school (stredná odborná škola, 372) and secondary vocational school (stredné odborné učilište, 368), with a total enrolment of 297,576 students. In 2001/01 secondary enrolment was equivalent to 86.6% of children in the relevant age-group (males 85.8%; females 87.4%). In the same year there were 20 institutions of higher education, with a total enrolment of 125,896 students. Children who, owing to disabilities, cannot attend regular schools may receive instruction at special schools. There are also private schools (basic and secondary). Of total estimated government expenditure (excluding wages) in 2001, 1,800m. koruny (0.5%) was allocated to education.

Public Holidays

2003: 1 January (Anniversary of the Slovak Republic), 6 January (Epiphany, Orthodox Christmas Day), 18 April (Good Friday), 21 April (Easter Monday), 1 May (Labour Day), 8 May (Anniversary of Liberation), 5 July (Day of the Slav Apostles, Cyril and Methodius), 29 August (National Day, Anniversary of the Slovak National Uprising), 1 September (Constitution Day), 15 September (Our Lady of Seven Sorrows), 1 November (All Saints' Day), 24–26 December (Christmas).

2004: 1 January (Anniversary of the Slovak Republic), 6 January (Epiphany, Orthodox Christmas Day), 9 April (Good Friday), 12 April (Easter Monday), 1 May (Labour Day), 8 May (Anniversary of Liberation), 5 July (Day of the Slav Apostles, Cyril and Methodius), 29 August (National Day, Anniversary of the Slovak National Uprising), 1 September (Constitution Day), 15 September (Our Lady of Seven Sorrows), 1 November (All Saints' Day), 24–26 December (Christmas).

Weights and Measures

The metric system is in force.

Statistical Survey

Source: Statistical Office of the Slovak Republic, Miletičova 3, 824 67 Bratislava; tel. (7) 5023-6340; fax (7) 5556-1361; e-mail agnesa.kralikova@statistics .sk; internet www.statistics.sk.

Area and Population

AREA, POPULATION AND DENSITY

Area (sq km)	49,033*
Population (census results)	
3 March 1991	5,274,335
26 May 2001	
Males	2,612,515
Females	2,766,940
Total	5,379,455
Population (official estimates at mid-year)	
1999	5,395,324
2000	5,400,679
2001	5,379,780
Density (per sq km) at mid-2001	109.7

* 18,932 sq miles.

POPULATION BY NATIONALITY

(at 2001 census)

	Number	%
Slovak	4,614,854	85.79
Hungarian	520,528	9.68
Gypsy	89,920	1.67
Czech, Moravian, Silesian	46,968	0.87
Ruthenian and Ukrainian	35,015	0.65
German	5,405	0.10
Polish	2,602	0.05
Russian	1,590	0.03
Others (incl. undeclared)	62,573	1.16
Total	**5,379,455**	**100.00**

REGIONS
(at 2001 census)

	Area (sq km)	Population	Density (per sq km)
Bratislava	2,053	599,015	292
Trnava	4,148	551,003	133
Trenčín	4,501	605,582	135
Nitra	6,343	713,422	112
Žilina	6,788	692,332	102
Banská Bystrica . . .	9,455	662,121	70
Prešov	8,993	789,968	88
Košice	6,753	766,012	113
Total	49,034	5,379,455	110

PRINCIPAL TOWNS
(estimated population at 31 December 2001)

Bratislava (capital) .	428,094	Trnava	70,189
Košice	236,036	Martin	60,055
Prešov	92,720	Trenčín	57,813
Nitra	87,308	Poprad	56,241
Žilina	85,384	Prievidza . . .	52,947
Banská Bystrica .	82,961	Zvolen	43,796

BIRTHS, MARRIAGES AND DEATHS

	Registered live births		Registered marriages		Registered deaths	
	Number	Rate (per 1,000)	Number	Rate (per 1,000)	Number	Rate (per 1,000)
1994 . .	66,370	12.4	28,155	5.3	51,386	9.6
1995 . .	61,427	11.4	27,489	5.1	52,686	9.8
1996 . .	60,123	11.2	27,484	5.1	51,236	9.5
1997 . .	59,111	11.0	27,955	5.2	52,124	9.7
1998 . .	57,582	10.7	27,494	5.1	53,156	9.9
1999 . .	56,223	10.4	27,340	5.1	54,402	9.8
2000 . .	55,151	10.2	25,903	4.8	52,724	9.8
2001 . .	51,136	9.5	23,795	4.4	51,980	9.7

Expectation of life (WHO estimates, years at birth): 73.1 (males 69.3; females 77.4) in 2001 (Source: WHO, *World Health Report*).

EMPLOYMENT
(labour force surveys, '000 persons)

	2000	2001	2002
Agriculture, hunting, forestry and fishing	139.8	130.6	131.4
Mining and quarrying . . .	24.8 ⎫		
Manufacturing	540.4 ⎬	628.8	640.9
Electricity, gas and water . .	50.1 ⎭		
Construction	167.7	169.5	176.0
Wholesale and retail trade; repair of motor vehicles, motorcycles and personal and household goods	324.9	327.3	340.0
Hotels and restaurants . . .			
Transport, storage and communications	167.1	162.1	154.4
Financial intermediation . .	37.1	38.3	39.8
Real estate, renting and business services	90.8	104.3	103.3
Public administration and defence; compulsory social security	158.3	157.8	149.7
Education	161.6	168.9	162.8
Health and social work . . .	147.9	143.6	141.5
Other community, social and personal service activities .	86.6	87.0	79.1
Private households with employed persons	3.9	4.7	7.9
Activities not adequately defined	0.8	1.0	0.6
Total	2,101.7	2,123.7	2,127.0
Males	1,137.3	n.a.	n.a.
Females	964.4	n.a.	n.a.

Registered unemployed (annual averages, '000 persons): 482.2 in 2000; 508.0 in 2001.

Health and Welfare

KEY INDICATORS

Total fertility rate (children per woman, 2001)	1.3
Under-5 mortality rate (per 1,000 live births, 2001) . . .	9
HIV/AIDS (% of persons aged 15–49, 2001)	<0.10
Physicians (per 1,000 head, 1998)	3.53
Hospital beds (per 1,000 head, 1996)	7.48
Health expenditure (2000): US $ per head (PPP)	690
Health expenditure (2000): % of GDP	5.9
Health expenditure (2000): public (% of total)	89.6
Access to water (% of persons, 2000)	100
Access to sanitation (% of persons, 2000)	100
Human Development Index (2000): ranking	36
Human Development Index (2000): value	0.835

For sources and definitions, see explanatory note on p. vi.

Agriculture

PRINCIPAL CROPS
('000 metric tons)

	1999	2000	2001
Wheat	1,187.3	1,254.3	1,894.1
Barley	723.7	396.7	685.2
Maize	779.3	440.4	616.0
Rye	69.6	64.2	118.6
Oats	48.4	25.0	35.6
Triticale	—	19.3	33.4
Potatoes	384.4	418.8	387.3
Sugar beet	1,404.9	961.5	1,286.2
Dry peas	48.0	18.2	23.0
Sunflower seed	125.1	117.3	118.4
Rapeseed	237.1	113.8	240.3
Cabbages (white)	198.5	98.6	30.9
Tomatoes	70.4	73.0	35.0
Chillies and green peppers	40.4	35.4	36.0*
Cucumbers and gherkins	40.7	44.7	44.0*
Onions	50.1	26.3	15.8
Carrots	74.6	51.2	14.1
Apples	68.3	81.5	50.2
Grapes	61.2	61.1	71.6
Watermelons	41.2	29.2	28.0*
Other fruit*	146.6	142.3	120.9
Tobacco (leaves)	1.3	1.9	2.0

* FAO estimate(s).

Source: FAO.

LIVESTOCK
('000 head, year ending 30 September)

	1999	2000	2001
Cattle	705	664	645
Pigs	1,593	1,562	1,488
Sheep	326	348	358
Goats	51	51	51
Horses	10	9	9*
Chickens†	12,644	14,036	14,621

* FAO estimate.
† Unofficial figures.

Source: FAO.

LIVESTOCK PRODUCTS
('000 metric tons, unless otherwise indicated)

	1999	2000	2001
Beef and veal	50.2	48.0	38.2
Pig meat	175.5	163.6	153.0
Poultry meat	82.7	89.9	91.7
Cows' milk	1,162.6	1,067.0	1,147.2
Goats' milk	13.2	13.2	13.3
Butter	16.1	16.1	17.0
Cheese	55.0	54.5	58.1
Hen eggs	64.8	60.8	64.3
Other poultry eggs*	10	10	10
Cattle hides (fresh)*	5.4	4.8	0.0

* FAO estimates.

Source: FAO.

Forestry

ROUNDWOOD REMOVALS
('000 cubic metres, excl. bark)

	1998	1999	2000
Sawlogs, veneer logs and logs for sleepers	2,176	2,303	2,396
Pulpwood	2,890	2,717	2,613
Other industrial wood	60	55	37
Fuel wood	404	193	167
Total	5,530	5,268	5,213

Source: FAO.

2001: Figures assumed to be unchanged from 2000, except for fuel wood (194,000 cubic metres).

SAWNWOOD PRODUCTION
('000 cubic metres, incl. railway sleepers)

	1997	1998	1999
Coniferous (softwood)	501	845	541
Broadleaved (hardwood)	266	420	203
Total	767	1,265	744

2000: Production as in 1999 (FAO estimates).

Source: FAO.

Fishing

(metric tons, live weight)

	1998	1999	2000
Capture	1,414	1,391	2,255
Common carp	778	822	928
Rainbow trout	17	16	771
Northern pike	68	69	77
Breams	99	98	94
Aquaculture	648	872	887
Common carp	63	157	74
Rainbow trout	487	630	752
Total catch (incl. others)	2,062	2,263	3,142

Source: FAO, *Yearbook of Fishery Statistics*.

Mining

('000 metric tons, unless otherwise indicated)

	1998	1999	2000
Brown coal	2,764.9	2,513.0	2,485.5
Lignite	1,200.0	1,211.3	1,101.3
Iron ore	41.7	40.0	32.1
Crude petroleum	54.0	32.4	29.9
Natural gas (million cu metres)	257.0	409.6	358.8
Limestone	3,291.5	3,158.9	3,841.4
Natural sands	608.8	507.5	421.9
Gravel	4,750.4	2,633.6	2,572.5

Industry

SELECTED PRODUCTS
('000 metric tons, unless otherwise indicated)

	1998	1999	2000
Wheat flour	349.6	319.4	327.0
Bread	124.7	125.5	124.3
Sugar	211.8	197.0	122.9
Pasta	19.0	17.9	20.8
Beer ('000 hectolitres)	4,477.8	4,473.2	4,491.4
Wine ('000 hectolitres)	514.4	544.9	476.4
Spirits and distillates (million litres)	39	34	35
Cotton yarn	5.2	3.7	3.3
Footwear ('000 pairs)	11,630	9,426	10,069
Paper and paperboard	625.6	646.5	703.7
Paints and enamels	30.2	31.0	32.6
Chemical fibres	63.3	73.2	65.5
Black-coal coke	1,515	1,615	1,705
Engine and petrochemical petrol	1,520	1,120	1,473
Gas-diesel (distillate fuel) oil	1,900	1,445	880
Cement*	4,705.0	4,717.9	4,509.9
Pig-iron	2,797	2,987	3,166
Crude steel	3,179	3,419	3,520
Aluminium	229.0	239.8	251.2
Household refrigerators and freezers (number)	257,178	240,122	198,948
Passenger motor cars (number)	125,467	126,561	180,804
Lorries and vans (number)	312	76	40
Motorcycles	7,011	4,106	2,196
Colour television receivers	304,127	311,294	431,177
Electric energy (million kWh)	26,308.8	27,746.2	30,607.4

* Including cement clinker.

Finance

CURRENCY AND EXCHANGE RATES

Monetary Units

100 halierov (singular: halier) = 1 Slovenská koruna (Slovak crown or Sk; plural: koruny)

Sterling, Dollar and Euro Equivalents (31 December 2002)

£1 sterling = 64.53 koruny
US $1 = 40.04 koruny
€1 = 41.99 koruny
1,000 koruny = £15.50 = $24.98 = €23.82

Average Exchange Rate (koruny per US $)

2000	46.035
2001	48.355
2002	45.327

Note: In February 1993 Slovakia introduced its own currency, the Slovak koruna, to replace (at par) the Czechoslovak koruna.

STATE BUDGET
('000 million koruny)

Revenue	1999	2000	2001*
Tax revenue	274.6	303.9	298.8
Personal income tax	46.1	41.3	44.2
Corporate income tax	23.0	26.4	21.7
Value-added tax	58.9	70.6	73.6
Excise taxes	25.2	28.5	28.4
Custom duties and import surcharge	12.5	13.2	3.9
Other taxes	7.6	8.3	9.2
Social security contributions	101.3	115.7	117.9
Total	339.5	347.6	351.8

Expenditure	1999	2000	2001*
Current expenditure	311.1	338.8	347.9
Wages	55.8	59.7	63.3
Education†	2.5	2.0	1.8
Health	43.6	48.8	51.3
Other consumption	42.2	46.0	50.9
Subsidies to enterprises	26.3	35.3	25.9
Interest payments	23.5	23.7	23.7
Social expenditure	117.2	123.3	131.0
Investment expenditure	30.8	34.5	37.2
Net lending	25.6	5.8	6.2
Total	367.5	379.1	391.4

* Estimates.
† Excluding wages.

Source: IMF, *Slovak Republic: Selected Issues and Statistical Appendix* (September 2002).

INTERNATIONAL RESERVES
(US $ million at 31 December)

	2000	2001	2002
Gold*	53	45.3	54.8
IMF special drawing rights	0.49	0.66	1.15
Foreign exchange	4,022	4,140	8,808
Total	4,075	4,186	8,863

* National valuation.

Source: IMF, *International Financial Statistics*.

MONEY SUPPLY
(million koruny at 31 December)

	2000	2001	2002
Currency outside banks	67,048	80,963	84,211
Demand deposits at commercial banks	118,916	144,603	160,560
Total money	185,964	225,566	244,771

Source: IMF, *International Financial Statistics*.

COST OF LIVING
(Consumer Price Index; base December 1995 = 100))

	1999	2000	2001
Foodstuffs and non-alcoholic beverages	116.5	122.7	129.5
Alcoholic beverages and tobacco	123.9	135.8	140.2
Clothing and footwear	129.0	133.0	136.2
Housing, water, electricity, gas and other fuels	151.7	201.0	235.5
All items (incl. others)	128.6	144.0	154.6

Source: IMF, *Slovak Republic: Selected Issues and Statistical Appendix* (September 2002).

NATIONAL ACCOUNTS

Expenditure on the Gross Domestic Product
(million koruny at current prices, provisional figures)

	2000	2001	2002
Government final consumption expenditure	180,330	197,580	214,050
Private final consumption expenditure	510,680	560,240	603,880
Increase in stocks	−22,080	7,180	14,980
Gross fixed capital formation	267,930	309,610	319,750
Total domestic expenditure	936,860	1,074,610	1,152,660
Exports of goods and services	652,430	732,350	781,410
Less Imports of goods and services	674,490	816,040	857,930
GDP in purchasers' values	908,800	989,300	1,073,610

Source: IMF, *International Financial Statistics*.

Gross Domestic Product by Economic Activity

('000 million koruny, current prices)

	1999	2000	2001
Agriculture and forestry	33.2	36.0	40.6
Industry*	215.6	233.1	241.3
Construction	42.4	42.3	45.6
Market services	343.3	388.2	437.5
Communications	23.6	23.6	27.6
Transport	57.8	66.5	83.3
Wholesale and retail trade	114.1	134.2	144.9
Other market services	147.7	163.9	181.6
Non-market services	101.7	106.1	113.8
Total	815.3	887.2	964.6

* Principally mining, manufacturing, electricity, water and gas.

Source: IMF, *Slovak Republic: Selected Issues and Statistical Appendix* (September 2002).

BALANCE OF PAYMENTS

(US $ million)

	1998	1999	2000
Exports of goods f.o.b.	10,720	10,201	11,896
Imports of goods f.o.b.	−13,071	−11,310	−12,791
Trade balance	−2,351	−1,109	−895
Exports of services	2,292	1,899	2,241
Imports of services	−2,276	−1,844	−1,805
Balance on goods and services	−2,334	−1,054	−459
Other income received	437	268	268
Other income paid	−595	−568	−623
Balance on goods, services and income	−2,492	−1,353	−814
Current transfers received	645	466	344
Current transfers paid	−279	−268	−224
Current balance	−2,126	−1,155	−694
Capital account (net)	70	158	91
Direct investment abroad	−145	376	−22
Direct investment from abroad	562	354	2,052
Portfolio investment assets	−57	247	−195
Portfolio investment liabilities	841	405	1,016
Other investment assets	190	1,713	−973
Other investment liabilities	520	−1,307	−407
Net errors and omissions	−333	−14	51
Overall balance	−478	777	920

Source: IMF, *International Financial Statistics*.

External Trade

COMMODITY GROUPS

(distribution by SITC, million koruny)

Imports f.o.b.	1998	1999	2000
Food and live animals	24,249	24,121	26,468
Crude materials (inedible) except fuels	17,669	17,894	22,907
Mineral fuels, lubricants, etc.	50,291	60,665	103,321
Chemicals and related products	48,843	52,869	64,669
Basic manufactures	82,984	85,765	104,187
Machinery and transport equipment	185,625	176,935	210,535
Miscellaneous manufactured articles	45,758	44,480	51,807
Total (incl. others)	460,736	468,892	590,275

Exports f.o.b.	1998	1999	2000
Food and live animals	12,144	12,849	13,874
Crude materials (inedible) except fuels	13,565	16,276	17,814
Mineral fuels, lubricants, etc.	13,235	20,126	38,376
Chemicals and related products	33,579	33,417	43,519
Basic manufactures	113,284	116,385	146,618
Machinery and transport equipment	141,144	166,899	216,836
Miscellaneous manufactured articles	47,967	54,543	68,193
Total (incl. others)	377,807	423,648	548,527

2001 (million koruny): *Imports f.o.b.:* Prepared foodstuffs, beverages and tobacco, 22,779; Mineral products 117,890; Products of the chemical or allied industries 61,769; Rubber and plastics, and articles thereof 37,035; Wood pulp, cellulose and paper, and articles thereof 20,882; Textiles and textile articles 40,625; Base metals and articles of base metal 59,533; Machinery and electrical equipment 180,458; Vehicles, aircraft, vessels and transport equipment 89,858; Optical, photographic, measuring and medical apparatus; clocks and watches; musical instruments 16,715; Total (incl. others) 713,898. *Exports f.o.b.:* Mineral products 47,519; Products of the chemical or allied industries 30,126; Rubber and plastics, and articles thereof 32,499; Wood and articles of wood 14,848; Wood pulp, cellulose and paper, and articles thereof 31,376; Textiles and textile articles 41,578; Articles of stone, plaster, cement, asbestos, mica; ceramic products; glass 14,365; Base metals and articles of base metal 92,402; Machinery and electrical equipment 114,424; Vehicles, aircraft, vessels and transport equipment 126,077; Total (incl. others) 611,325.

2002 (million koruny): *Imports f.o.b.:* Prepared foodstuffs, beverages and tobacco, 24,959; Mineral products 109,175; Products of the chemical or allied industries 65,650; Rubber and plastics, and articles thereof 45,560; Wood pulp, cellulose and paper, and articles thereof 22,472; Textiles and textile articles 41,993; Base metals and articles of base metal 66,886; Machinery and electrical equipment 191,471; Vehicles, aircraft, vessels and transport equipment 95,423; Optical, photographic, measuring and medical apparatus; clocks and watches; musical instruments 17,807; Total (incl. others) 714,071. *Exports f.o.b.:* Mineral products 46,618; Products of the chemical or allied industries 31,023; Rubber and plastics, and articles thereof 37,854; Wood and articles of wood 15,249; Wood pulp, cellulose and paper, and articles thereof 31,692; Textiles and textile articles 43,297; Articles of stone, plaster, cement, asbestos, mica; ceramic products; glass 15,534; Base metals and articles of base metal 93,481; Machinery and electrical equipment 122,763; Vehicles, aircraft, vessels and transport equipment 137,560; Total (incl. others) 651,256.

PRINCIPAL TRADING PARTNERS

(million koruny)

Imports f.o.b.	2000	2001	2002
Austria	23,248	29,608	31,480
Belgium	9,399	11,927	13,501
Czech Republic	86,852	107,622	113,290
France	19,759	27,577	32,960
Germany	147,867	176,187	169,188
Hungary	12,401	18,227	20,423
Italy	36,449	45,579	51,529
Japan	9,955	11,466	13,873
Netherlands	9,107	10,512	13,143
Poland	18,046	23,175	24,088
Russia	100,577	105,433	93,848
Switzerland	7,374	9,178	10,169
Ukraine	8,737	9,387	8,473
United Kingdom	14,293	18,158	18,957
USA	12,223	13,797	15,961
Total (incl. others)	590,275	714,071	747,883

Exports f.o.b.	2000	2001	2002
Austria.	45,885	49,651	50,053
Belgium	11,467	14,699	13,531
Czech Republic	95,414	101,576	99,023
France.	25,427	24,102	27,202
Germany	146,856	165,525	169,200
Hungary	26,700	32,855	35,528
Italy	50,334	54,015	69,916
Netherlands	14,560	17,209	19,806
Poland	32,095	35,598	34,761
Russia.	4,917	6,306	6,494
Switzerland	9,411	9,371	8,155
Ukraine	6,796	7,037	7,064
United Kingdom.	10,366	15,030	15,457
USA	7,776	7,837	9,387
Total (incl. others)	548,527	611,325	651,256

Transport

	1999	2000	2001
Railway transport:			
freight ('000 tons)	49,115	54,177	53,588
passengers (million)	69	67	63
Public road transport:			
freight ('000 tons)*	33,920	39,680	34,773
passengers (million)	622	604	566
Waterway transport: freight ('000			
tons).	1,507	1,607	1,551

* Road transport for transport organizations including non-incorporated tradesmen.

ROAD TRAFFIC
(motor vehicles in use at 31 December)

	1998	1999	2000
Passenger cars	1,196,109	1,236,396	1,274,244
Buses and coaches	11,293	11,101	10,920
Goods vehicles	111,081	115,981	110,714
Motorcycles*	100,891	44,215	45,647

* Excluding scooters.

CIVIL AVIATION
(traffic on scheduled services)

	1998	1999	2000
Passengers carried ('000)	232.6	168.4	158.9
Freight carried (metric tons)	637	776	697
Passenger-km (million)	316.0	260.5	250.9
Freight ton-km ('000)	338	262	220

Tourism

FOREIGN TOURIST ARRIVALS
(visitors at accommodation facilities)

Country of origin	1998	1999	2000
Austria.	31,832	32,643	36,779
Czech Republic	244,454	275,031	277,401
France.	14,633	14,833	16,015
Germany	141,373	137,964	155,129
Hungary	49,423	53,057	59,322
Italy	24,968	27,076	28,097
Netherlands	15,911	16,540	18,772
Poland.	132,047	173,135	201,082
Russia.	27,313	22,361	30,861
Ukraine	37,725	31,732	24,212
USA	23,736	23,310	28,851
Total (incl. others)	896,100	975,105	1,045,614

Receipts from tourism (US $ million): 489 in 1999; 461 in 2000 (Source: World Bank).

Communications Media

	1998	1999	2000
Radio receivers (licensed)	1,255,624	1,368,863	1,347,477
Television receivers (licensed)	1,392,883	1,241,663	1,211,773
Telephones in use	1,539,283	1,655,380	1,697,982
Telefax stations (registered)	54,037	n.a.	n.a.
Mobile cellular telephones			
(subscribers)	493,868	662,511	1,109,888
Personal computers ('000 in use)*	470	590	n.a.
Internet users ('000)*	500	600	650
Newspapers and periodicals: titles	1,269	1,290	1,465

2001*: Main telephone lines in use 1,556,300; Personal computers in use 800,000.
* Source: International Telecommunication Union.

Book production (1996): 3,800 titles (Source: UNESCO, *Statistical Yearbook*).

Education

(2000/01)

	Institutions	Teachers	Students
Kindergarten	3,263	15,229	154,232
Primary (basic)	2,447	39,745	650,966
Secondary: grammar	212	6,259	82,147
Secondary: specialized.	372	9,882	104,301
Secondary: vocational	368	11,255	111,128
Higher*	20	9,047	125,896

* Full-time study only.

Directory

The Constitution*

On 1 September 1992 the Slovak National Council adopted the Constitution of the Slovak Republic (which entered into force on 1 January 1993), the main provisions of which, as amended in January 1999, are summarized below:

FUNDAMENTAL PROVISIONS

The Slovak Republic is a democratic and sovereign state, ruled by law. It is bound neither to an ideology, nor to a religion. State power belongs to the people, who exercise it either through their representatives or directly. The state authorities shall act only on the basis of the Constitution and to the extent and in the manner stipulated by law.

The territory of the Slovak Republic is integral and indivisible. The conditions for naturalization or deprival of state citizenship of the Slovak Republic are regulated by law. No person may be deprived of citizenship against his/her will. The Slovak language is the state language in the republic. The use of languages other than the state language in administrative relations is regulated by law. The capital of the republic is Bratislava.

BASIC RIGHTS AND FREEDOMS

The people are free and equal, and the rights and freedoms of every citizen are guaranteed, irrespective of sex, race, colour, language, faith, political or other conviction, national or social origin, nationality or ethnic origin. No person may be tortured, nor be subjected to cruel, inhuman or humiliating treatment or punishment. Capital punishment is not practised.

Every person has the right to own property. The place of abode is inviolable. The freedom of migration and the freedom of domicile are guaranteed.

The freedom of expression and the right to information are guaranteed. Censorship is prohibited. The right to assemble peacefully is guaranteed. Every person has the right to be a member of a union, community, society or any other association. Citizens have the right to found political parties and movements. Such parties and movements, as well as other associations, are separate from the state.

The citizens have the right to participate in the administration of public affairs, either directly or through the free election of their representatives. The right to vote is universal, direct and equal and is exercised by secret ballot.

The universal advancement of citizens who are members of national minorities and ethnic groups is guaranteed, above all the right to develop their own culture, to broadcast and receive information in their mother tongue, to join national associations and to found and maintain educational and cultural institutions. The languages of national minorities may also be used in administrative relations.

Every person has the right to the free choice of profession and vocational training as well as to do business and to perform other commercial activities. Employees are entitled to fair and satisfactory working conditions. Citizens may form free associations to protect their economic and social interests. Trade unions are independent of the state. The right to strike is guaranteed.

Every citizen is entitled to adequate old-age and disability benefits; widow's allowances; free health care; family support; and education.

NATIONAL COUNCIL OF THE SLOVAK REPUBLIC

Supreme legislative power is vested in the National Council of the Slovak Republic, which has 150 deputies, elected for a four-year term. The deputies represent the citizens and are elected by them in general, equal and direct elections, by secret ballot.

The National Council has the power to: adopt the Constitution, constitutional and other laws and supervise their execution; elect and recall the President of the Slovak Republic by secret ballot; decide on proposals to call a referendum; prior to their ratification, give consent to international political, economic or other agreements; establish ministries and other bodies of state administration; supervise the activities of the Government and pass a vote of confidence or censure on the Government or its members; approve the state budget and supervise its execution; elect judges, including the Chairman and Vice-Chairmen of the Supreme Court and of the Constitutional Court; adopt a resolution to declare war if the Slovak Republic is attacked, or if such a declaration ensues from the obligations of international treaties.

THE PRESIDENT OF THE REPUBLIC

The President is the Head of State of the Slovak Republic. He/she is directly elected by universal adult suffrage for a five-year term. The President is responsible to the National Council. He/she may not be elected for more than two consecutive terms.

The President represents the Slovak Republic internationally; negotiates and ratifies international agreements; receives and gives credentials to envoys; convenes constituent sessions of the National Council; may dissolve the National Council; signs laws; appoints and recalls the Prime Minister and other members of the Government and receives their resignation; grants amnesty, pardons and commutes sentences imposed by courts; may declare a state of emergency on the basis of constitutional law; may declare a referendum.

THE GOVERNMENT

The Government of the Slovak Republic is the highest organ of executive power. It is composed of the Prime Minister and Ministers. The Prime Minister is appointed by the President of the Republic. On the Prime Minister's recommendation, the President appoints and recalls the members of the Government and puts them in charge of their ministries. For the execution of office, the Government is responsible to the National Council.

The Government has the power to prepare bills; issue decrees; adopt fundamental provisions for economic and social policy; authorize drafts for the state budget and closing account of the year; decide international agreements; decide principal questions of internal and international policy; submit bills to the National Council; request the legislature for a vote of confidence.

*Further revisions to the Constitution were approved in February 2001 and officially entered into effect on 1 July. The amendments redefined the relationship between national and international law, incorporated Slovakia's aim of joining foreign alliances, strengthened the powers of the Constitutional Court, granted greater independence to the judiciary (by the establishment of a new judicial council), and provided for public administration reform, with the creation of a higher level of regional self-government.

The Government

HEAD OF STATE

President of the Republic: RUDOLF SCHUSTER (inaugurated 15 June 1999).

GOVERNMENT
(May 2003)

The Government comprises members of the Slovak Democratic and Christian Union (SDCU), the Christian Democratic Movement (CDM), the Party of the Hungarian Coalition (PHC), the New Civic Alliance (NCA) and the Democratic Party (DP).

Prime Minister: MIKULÁŠ DZURINDA (SDCU).

Deputy Prime Minister for European Integration, Human Rights and Minorities: PÁL CSÁKY (PHC).

Deputy Prime Minister and Minister of Finance: IVAN MIKLOŠ (SDCU).

Deputy Prime Minister and Minister of Justice: DANIEL LIPŠIĆ (CDM).

Deputy Prime Minister, and Minister of the Economy, and Administration and Privatization of National Property: ROBERT NEMCSICS (NCA).

Minister of Foreign Affairs: EDUARD KUKAN (SDCU).

Minister of Defence: IVAN ŠIMKO (SDCU).

Minister of the Environment: LÁSZLÓ MIKLÓS (PHC).

Minister of the Interior: VLADIMIR PALKO (CDM).

Minister of Labour, Social Affairs and the Family: L'UDOVÍT KANÍK (DP).

Minister of Culture: RUDOLF CHMEL (NCA).

Minister of Education: MARTIN FRONC (CDM).

Minister of Health: RUDOLF ZAJAC (ANC).

Minister of Agriculture: SIMON ZSOLT (PHC).

Minister of Transport, Posts and Telecommunications: PAVOL PROKOPOVIĆ (SDCU).

Minister of Construction and Public Works: ISTVÁN HARNA (PHC).

MINISTRIES

Office of the Government of the Slovak Republic: nám. Slobody 1, 813 70 Bratislava; tel. (2) 5729-5111; fax (2) 5249-7603; e-mail tio@government.gov.sk; internet www.government.gov.sk.

Ministry of Agriculture: Dobrovičova 12, 812 66 Bratislava; tel. (2) 5296-6111; fax (2) 5296-1834; e-mail majkut@mpsr.sanet.sk; internet www.mpsr.sk.

Ministry of Construction and Public Works: Špitálska 8, 816 44 Bratislava; tel. (2) 5975-1111; fax (2) 5293-1203; e-mail informacie@build.gov.sk; internet www.build.gov.sk.

Ministry of Culture: nám. SNP, 81101 Bratislava; tel. (2) 5939-1111; fax (2) 5926-6457; e-mail webmaster@culture.gov.sk; internet www.culture.gov.sk.

Ministry of Defence: Kutuzovova 7, 832 28 Bratislava; tel. (2) 4425-0320; fax (2) 4425-3242; e-mail linka.dovery@mod.gov.sk; internet www.mod.gov.sk.

Ministry of the Economy, and Administration and Privatization of National Property: Mierová 19, 827 15 Bratislava; tel. (2) 4854-1111; fax (2) 4333-7827; e-mail icom@economy.gov.sk; internet www.economy.gov.sk.

Ministry of Education: Stromová 1, 813 30 Bratislava; tel. (2) 5937-4315; fax (2) 5477-3766; e-mail kancmin@education.gov.sk; internet www.education.gov.sk.

Ministry of the Environment: nám. L'. Štúra 1, 812 35 Bratislava; tel. (2) 5956-1111; fax (2) 5956-2031; e-mail info@lifeenv.gov.sk; internet www.lifeenv.gov.sk.

Ministry of Finance: Štefanovičova 5, 817 82 Bratislava; tel. (2) 5958-1111; fax (2) 5249-8042; e-mail inform@mfsr.sk; internet www.finance.gov.sk.

Ministry of Foreign Affairs: Hlboká cesta 2, 833 36 Bratislava; tel. (2) 5978-1111; fax (2) 5978-2213; internet www.foreign.gov.sk.

Ministry of Health: Limbová 2, 831 05 Bratislava; tel. (2) 5937-3111; fax (2) 5477-7983; e-mail office@health.gov.sk; internet www.health.gov.sk.

Ministry of the Interior: Pribinova 2, 812 72 Bratislava; tel. (2) 5091-1111; fax (2) 5094-4017; e-mail www@minv.sk; internet www.minv.sk.

Ministry of Justice: Župné nám. 13, 813 11 Bratislava; tel. (2) 5935-3111; fax (2) 5441-5952; e-mail tlacove@justice.gov.sk; internet www.justice.gov.sk.

Ministry of Labour, Social Affairs and the Family: Špitálska 4–6, 816 43 Bratislava; tel. (2) 5975-1111; fax (2) 5292-1258; internet www.employment.gov.sk.

Ministry of Transport, Posts and Telecommunications: nám. Slobody 6, 810 05 Bratislava; tel. (2) 5949-4111; fax (2) 5249-4794; e-mail info@telecom.gov.sk; internet www.telecom.gov.sk.

President

Presidential Election, 15 and 29 May 1999

Candidates	First ballot votes cast %	Second ballot votes cast Number	%
Rudolf Schuster	47.38	1,727,398	57.18
Vladimír Mečiar	37.24	1,293,642	42.82
Magda Vášáryová	6.60	—	—
Ivan Mjartan	3.59	—	—
Ján Slota	2.50	—	—
Others	2.69	—	—
Total	100.00	3,021,040	100.00

Legislature

NATIONAL COUNCIL OF THE SLOVAK REPUBLIC

Chairman: PAVOL HRUŠOVSKÝ.

Deputy Chairmen: ZUZANA MARTINÁKOVÁ, BÉLA BUGÁR, Dr PAVOL RUSKO, VILIAM VETEŠKA.

General Election, 20–21 September 2002

Party	Votes	% of votes	Seats
Movement for a Democratic Slovakia	560,691	19.50	36
Slovak Democratic and Christian Union	433,953	15.09	28
Direction (Směr)	387,100	13.46	25
Party of the Hungarian Coalition	321,069	11.16	20
Christian Democratic Movement	237,202	8.25	15
New Civic Alliance	230,309	8.01	15
Communist Party of Slovakia	181,872	6.32	11
Others	522,885	18.19	—
Total*	2,875,081	100.00	150

* Excluding 34,917 invalid votes.

Political Organizations

Association of Workers of Slovakia (AWS) (Združenie robotníkov Slovenska): Horná 83, 974 01 Banská Bystrica; tel. (88) 742-703; f. 1994; Chair. JÁN ĽUPTÁK.

Christian Democratic Movement (CDM) (Kresťansko-demokratické hnutie): Žabotova 2, 811 04 Bratislava; tel. (2) 396-308; fax (2) 396-313; e-mail kdh@kdh.sk; internet www.kdh.sk; f. 1990; Chair. PAVOL HRUŠOVSKY.

Civic Conservative Party: Bratislava; f. Dec. 2001 by breakaway mems of the Democratic Party; Chair. PETER TATAR.

Communist Party of Slovakia (Komunistická strana Slovenska—KSS): 83103 Bratislava, Hattalova 12A; tel. and fax (2) 4437-2540; e-mail sekr@kss.sk; internet www.kss.sk; Pres. JOZEFA ŠEVCA.

Democratic Party (Demokratická strana): Šancová 70, 813 47 Bratislava; tel. (2) 5249-6927; fax (2) 5249-5893; e-mail secret@demstrana.sl; internet www.demstrana.sk; f. 1944; in 1994 absorbed the Civic Democratic Union, Civic Democratic Party of Slovakia, Democrats '92, Czech-Slovak Understanding and the Green League; conservative; breakaway faction (Leader FRANTIŠEK SEBEJ), f. Feb. 2001; Chair. LUDOVIT KANIK; 3,000 mems.

Democratic Union of Slovakia (DUS) (Demokratická únia Slovenska): Medená 10, 811 04 Bratislava; tel. and fax (2) 361-637; internet www.demunia.sk; f. 1994; by former members of the Movement for a Democratic Slovakia; in 1995 absorbed the National Democratic Party—New Alternative; splinter group, Liberal Demo-

cratic Union, f. in 2000; Chair. ĽUBOMÍR HARACH; First Dep. Chair. MILAN KŇAŽKO.

Direction (Směr): Sumračna 27, 821 02 Bratislava; tel. and fax (2) 4342-6297; e-mail kancelaria@asistent.sk; internet www.strana-smer.sk; f. 1999; absorbed the Party of Civic Understanding in 2003; centre-right, pro-EU, pro-NATO; Chair. ROBERT FICO.

Green Party in Slovakia (Strana zelených na Slovensku): Palisády 56, 811 06 Bratislava; tel. (2) 323-231; fax (2) 364-848; f. 1989; Chair. LADISLAV AMBROS.

Movement for a Democratic Slovakia (MDS) (Hnutie za demokratické Slovensko): Tomášikova 32A, 830 00 Bratislava; tel. (2) 4329-3800; fax (2) 4341-0225; e-mail webmaster@hzds.sk; internet www.hzds.sk; f. 1991; Chair. VLADIMÍR MEČIAR.

Movement for Democracy: Bratislava; f. 2002 by former members of the MDS (q.v.); Chair. IVAN GASPAROVIC.

New Agrarian Party: Bratislava; f. 1997; coalition of the Farmers' Movement of Slovakia and the Farmers' Party of Slovakia; Chair. PAVEL DELINGA.

Farmers' Movement of Slovakia (Hnutie poľnohospodárov Slovenska): Sama Chalúpku 18, 071 01 Bratislava; tel. (2) 215-291; Chair. JOZEF KLEIN.

Farmers' Party of Slovakia (Roľnícka strana Slovenska): Trenčianska 55, 821 09 Bratislava; tel. (2) 215-800; Chair. PAVEL DELINGA.

New Civic Alliance (Aliancia Nového Občana—ANO): 84101 Bratislava, Drobného 27; tel. (2) 6920-2919; fax (2) 6920-2920; e-mail ano@ano-aliancia.sk; internet www.ano-aliancia.sk; f. April 2001; centre-right, pro-reform; Dir PAVOL RUŠKO.

Party of the Democratic Centre (Strana demokratického stredu): Kopčianska 94A, 851 01 Bratislava; tel. (2) 6828-7291; fax (2) 6383-0572; e-mail strana@sds.sk; internet www.sds.sk; f. 1999; Chair. IVAN MJARTAN.

Party of the Democratic Left (PDL) (Strana demokratickej ľavice): Gunduličova 12, 811 05 Bratislava; tel. (2) 5443-3617; fax (2) 5443-5574; e-mail hovorca@sdl.sk; internet www.sdl.sk; f. 1991 by mems of the fmr Communist Party of Slovakia; Chair. PAVEL KONCOŠ.

Party of the Hungarian Coalition (PHC) (Strana madarskej koalicie): Žabotova 2, 811 04 Bratislava; tel. (2) 5249-7684; fax (2) 5249-5791; e-mail smk@smk.sk; internet www.mkp.sk; f. 1998 by Coexistence, the Hungarian Christian Democratic Movement and the Hungarian Civic Party to contest the 1998 parliamentary elections as a single party; Chair. BÉLA BUGÁR.

Coexistence (Spolužitie/Együttélés): Pražská 7, POB 44, 814 09 Bratislava; tel. and fax (2) 497-877; represents ethnic Hungarian interests; Leader MIKLÓS DURAY.

Hungarian Christian Democratic Movement: Žabotova 2, Bratislava; tel. (2) 395-164; fax (2) 395-264; e-mail bugar@nciz.tsa .de; Pres. BÉLA BUGÁR; Vice-Pres. PÁL CSÁKY.

Hungarian Civic Party: Žabotova 2, 811 04 Bratislava; tel. (2) 397-684; fax (2) 395-791; Chair. LÁSZLÓ A. NAGY.

Party of Labour and Development (Strana prace a rozvoja): Bratislava; f. 2000; left-wing; Chair. JAN KALEJA.

Romany Civic Initiative: represents interests of Romany population; Chair. GEJZA ADAM.

Slovak Democratic and Christian Union (SDCU) (Slovenská Demokratická a Krestanská Unia): Ružinovska 28, 821 03 Bratislava; tel. (2) 4341-4102; fax (2) 4341-4106; e-mail sdku@sdkuonline.sk; internet www.sdkuonline.sk; f. 2000 to contest legislative elections in 2002; Leader MIKULÁŠ DZURINDA; Gen. Sec. IVAN HARMAN.

Slovak National Party (SNP) (Slovenská národná strana): Šafárikovo nám. 3, 814 99 Bratislava; tel. (2) 5292-4260; fax (2) 5296-6188; e-mail sns@isnet.sk; internet www.sns.sk; Chair. ANNA MALIKOVA.

Slovak Social Democratic Union: f. 1997 by former members of the Social Democratic Party of Slovakia; left-wing; Chair. JOZEF SKULTETY.

Social Democratic Alternative (Sociálnodemokratická alternatíva—SDA): 81107 Bratislava, Karadžičova 41; tel. and fax (2) 5564-8627; e-mail sda@sdalternativa.sk; f. Feb. 2002 by breakaway mems of Party of the Democratic Left; Chair. MILAN FTÁČNIK.

Social Democratic Party of Slovakia (Sociálno-demokratická strana Slovenska): Žabotova 2, 811 04 Bratislava; tel. and fax (2) 5249-4621; e-mail sdss@ba.psg.sk; internet www.sdss.sk; re-established 1990; Chair. JAROSLAV VOLF.

Diplomatic Representation

EMBASSIES IN SLOVAKIA

Angola: Jančova 8, BII/4, 811 02 Bratislava; tel. (2) 6280-3373; fax (2) 6280-3364; e-mail embangol@netax.sk; Ambassador MANUEL QUARTA 'PUNZA'.

Austria: Venturska 10, 811 01 Bratislava; tel. (2) 5443-2985; fax (2) 5443-2486; e-mail ambasada@austria.isternet.sk; Ambassador GABRIELE MATZNER-HOLZER.

Belgium: Fraňa kráľa 5, 811 05 Bratislava; tel. (2) 5249-1338; fax (2) 5249-4296; e-mail ambabelbratis@gtinet.sk; Ambassador FRANÇOIS DEL MARMOL.

Bulgaria: Kuzmányho 1, 811 06 Bratislava; tel. (2) 5441-5308; fax (2) 5441-2404; e-mail bulembassy@stonline.sk; internet www.stonline.sk/bg_embassy/; Ambassador JANI MILČAKOV.

China, People's Republic: Údolná 7, 811 06 Bratislava; tel. (2) 5441-5304; fax (2) 5441-6551; Ambassador TAO MIAOFA.

Croatia: Mišikova 21, 811 06 Bratislava; tel. (2) 5443-3647; fax (2) 5443-5365; Ambassador GJURO DEŽELIĆ.

Cuba: Somolického 1, 811, 05 Bratislava; tel. (2) 5249-2777; fax (2) 5249-4200; e-mail embacuba@zutom.sk; Chargé d'affaires a.i. LAUREANO CARDOSO TOLEDO.

Czech Republic: 29 Augusta 5, 810 00 Bratislava; tel. (2) 5293-1204; fax (2) 5293-1209; e-mail bratislava@embassy.mzv.cz; Ambassador RUDOLF SLANSKY.

France: Hlavné nám. 7, 811 01 Bratislava; tel. (2) 5934-7111; fax (2) 5934-7199; e-mail diplo@france.sk; internet www.france.sk; Ambassador GEORGES VAUGIER.

Germany: Hviezdoslavovo nám. 10, 813 03 Bratislava; tel. (2) 5290-4400; fax (2) 5443–1480; e-mail info@germanembassy.sk; internet www.germanembassy.sk; Ambassador Dr UTA MAYER-SCHALBURG.

Greece: Hlavné nám. 4, 811 01 Bratislava; tel. (2) 5443-9841; fax (2) 5443-9854; e-mail embassy@greece.sk; internet www.greece.sk; Ambassador VASSILIOS IKOSSIPENTARCHOS.

Holy See: Nekrasovova 17, 811 04 Bratislava (Apostolic Nunciature); tel. (2) 5479-3528; fax (2) 5479-3529; Apostolic Nuncio Most Rev. HENRYK JÓZEF NOWACKI (Titular Archbishop of Blera).

Hungary: Sedlárska 3, 814 25 Bratislava; tel. (2) 5443-0541; fax (2) 5443-5484; Ambassador MIKLÓS BOROS.

India: Radlinkkého 2, 811 02 Bratislava; tel. (2) 5293-1700; fax (2) 5293-1690; e-mail india@indembassy.sk; internet www.eindia.sk; Ambassador UPENDRA CHANDRA.

Indonesia: Mudroňova 51, 811 02 Bratislava; tel. (2) 5441-9886; fax (2) 5441-9890; e-mail indonesia@indonesia.sk; internet www.indonesia.sk; Ambassador MALIKUS SUAMIN.

Italy: Červeňova 19, 811 03 Bratislava; tel. (2) 5441-2585; fax (2) 5441-3202; e-mail amb@ambitaba.sk; internet www.caambitaba.sk; Ambassador EGONE RATZENBERGER.

Netherlands: Fraňa Kral'a 5, 811 05 Bratislava; tel. (2) 5262–5081; fax (2) 5249-1075; e-mail hollandembassy@internet.sk; internet www.netherlandsembassy.sk; Ambassador L. L. STOKVIS.

Poland: ul. Zelena 6, 814 26 Bratislava; tel. (2) 5443-2744; fax (2) 5443-2007; e-mail polskyobchradca@brh.sk; internet www.polskyobchracdca.sk; Ambassador JAN KOMORNICKI.

Romania: Fraňa Kráľa 11, 811 05 Bratislava; tel. (2) 5249-1665; fax (2) 5244-4056; e-mail ro-embassy@ba.sknet.sk; Chargé d'affaires a.i. GHEORGHE LUPES.

Russia: Godrova 4, 811 06 Bratislava; tel. (2) 5441-5823; fax (2) 5443-4910; e-mail embrus@gtinet.sk; Ambassador ALEKSANDR AKSENYONOK.

Serbia and Montenegro: Búdková 38, 811 04 Bratislava; tel. (2) 5443-1927; fax (2) 5443-1933; e-mail embas_yu@isternet.sk; Ambassador VELJKO ČURČIĆ.

Slovenia: Moyzesova 4, 813 15 Bratislava; tel. (2) 5245-0005; fax (2) 5245-0009; Ambassador ROBERT KOKALJ.

Spain: Prepoštská, 811 01 Bratislava; tel. (2) 5441-5724; fax (2) 5441-7565; e-mail embespsk@mail.mae.es; Ambassador ESTANISLAO DE GRANDES PASCUAL.

Turkey: Holubyho 11, 811 03 Bratislava; tel. (2) 5441-5504; fax (2) 5441-3145; e-mail testta@nextra.sk; Ambassador INCI TÜMAY.

Ukraine: Radvaňská 35, 811 01 Bratislava; tel. (2) 5443-1672; fax (2) 5441-2651; Ambassador JURIJ RYLACH.

United Kingdom: Panská 16, 811 01 Bratislava; tel. (2) 5441-9632; fax (2) 5441-0002; e-mail bebra@internet.sk; internet www.britemb.sk; Ambassador RIC TODD.

USA: Hviezdoslavovo nám. 4, 811 02 Bratislava; tel. (2) 5443-3338; fax (2) 5443-0096; e-mail hengeldc@state.gov; internet www.usis.sk; Ambassador RONALD WEISER.

Judicial System

Justice in Slovakia is the responsibility of the district courts (first level), county courts (second level) and the Supreme Court of the Slovak Republic. The Constitutional Court was restored in 1993.

Chairman of the Supreme Court: ŠTEFAN HARABÍN.

Prosecutor-General: MICHAL HANZEL.

Chairman of the Constitutional Court: JÁN MAZÁK.

Religion

The principal religion in Slovakia is Christianity, of which the largest denomination (representing some 69% of the total population according to the census of May 2001) is the Roman Catholic Church. About 10% of the population profess no religious belief.

CHRISTIANITY

The Roman Catholic Church

Slovakia consists of two archdioceses and five dioceses, including one (directly responsible to the Holy See) for Catholics of the Slovak (Byzantine) rite, also known as 'Greek' Catholics or Uniates. At 31 December 2000 the estimated number of adherents represented about 67.2% of the total population.

Bishops' Conference: Konferencia biskupov Slovenska, Kapitulská 11, 81499 Bratislava; tel. (2) 5443-5234; fax (2) 5443-5913; e-mail kbs@kbs.sk; internet www.rcc.sk; f. 1993; Pres. Rt Rev. FRANTIŠEK TONDRA (Bishop of Spiš).

Latin Rite

Archbishop of Bratislava-Trnava: Most Rev. JÁN SOKOL, Arcibiskupský úrad, Hollého 10, 917 66 Trnava; tel. (33) 591-2111; fax (33) 551-1224; e-mail abu@abu.sk.

Archbishop of Košice: Most Rev. ALOJZ TKÁČ, Arcibiskupský úrad, Hlavná 28, 041 83 Košice; tel. (55) 682-8111; fax (55) 622-1034; e-mail abukosica@kbs.sk.

Slovak Rite

Bishop of Prešov: Rt Rev. JÁN HIRKA, Gréckokatolícky biskupský úrad, Hlavná ul. 1, 081 35 Prešov; tel. (51) 772-2814; fax (51) 772-2723; e-mail grkbupo@nextra.sk; internet www.home.nextra.sk/greckoka; 175,000 adherents, 199 parishes (Dec. 1999).

The Orthodox Church

Orthodox Church of the Czech Lands and Slovakia Theological Faculty of Prešov University, Masaryková 15, Prešov, 080 80 Slovakia; POB 655, 111 21 Prague 1, Czech Republic; tel. (2) 431-5015.

Divided into four eparchies in the former Czechoslovakia: Prague and Olomouc (Czech Republic), Prešov and Michalovce (Slovakia); Archbishop of Prague and Metropolitan of the Czech Lands and Slovakia DOROTHEOS; 53,613 mems (March 1991); 127 parishes; Theological Faculty in Charles University, Prague, Czech Republic.

Archbishop of Prešov: Rev. NIKOLAJ, Budovatelská 1, 080 01 Prešov; e-mail mrpc@orthodox.sk.

Bishop of Michalovce: Rev. JOHN, Štefánikova, 071 44 Michalovce.

Protestant Churches

Baptist Union of Slovakia: Súl'ovská 2, 821 05 Bratislava; tel. and fax (2) 4342-1145; e-mail jozef-kulacik@computel.sk; f. 1994; 2,038 mems (April 2000); Pres. Rev. TOMÁŠ KRIŠKA; Gen. Sec. Rev. Dr JOZEF KULAČÍK.

Evangelical Church of the Augsburg Confession in Slovakia (Lutheran Church): Palisády 46, POB 289, 811 00 Bratislava; tel. (2) 5443-2842; fax (2) 5443-2940; e-mail tlac@ecav.sk; internet www.ecav.sk; presided over by the Bishop-General and Inspector-General; 327 parishes in 14 seniorates and two districts; 374,000 mems (Nov. 2001); Bishop-Gen. JÚLIUS FILO; Inspector-Gen. JÁN HOLČÍK.

Reformed Christian Church of Slovakia: Jókaiho 34, 945 01 Komárno; tel. (35) 770-1826; fax (35) 770-1827; e-mail rkc@freemail.hu; 109,735 mems and 325 parishes (2001); Bishop Dr GÉZA ERDÉLYI; Dir Mgr MIHÁLY TÓTH.

United Methodist Church in Slovakia: Panenská 10, 811 03 Bratislava; tel. and fax (2) 5441-4468; e-mail ecmrso@ba.psg.sk; internet www.slovaknet.sk/cirkev-metodisticka; 400 mems and 7 parishes; Superintendent PAVEL PROCHÁZKA.

Other Christian Churches

Apostolic Church: Sreznevského 2, 831 03 Bratislava; tel. and fax (2) 4425-0913; e-mail acs@gtinet.sk; internet www.acs-net.sk; f. 1956; 4,000 mems; Pres. JÁN LACHO.

JUDAISM

Union of the Jewish Religious Communities in the Slovak Republic (Ústredný zväz židovských náboženských obcí v Slovenskej republike): Kozia ul. 21/II, 814 47 Bratislava; tel. (2) 5441-2167; fax (2) 5441-1106; e-mail uzzno@netax.sk; 3,300 mems; Hon. Pres. Prof. PAVEL TRAUBNER; Exec. Chair. FERO ALEXANDER; Rabbi BARUCH MYERS.

The Press

In 2000 there were 1,465 newspapers and periodicals published in Slovakia, of which 16 were daily newspapers. In 1998 there were 39 titles published in Hungarian, seven in German, four in Ukrainian and two in Ruthenian.

The publications listed below are in Slovak, unless otherwise indicated.

PRINCIPAL DAILIES

Banská Bystrica

Smer dnes (Direct Today): Čs. armády 26, 974 01 Banská Bystrica; tel. (48) 433-43; fax (48) 433-41; f. 1948; independent; Editor-in-Chief JURAJ KUČERA; circ. 20,000.

Večerník (Evening Paper): nám. SNP 3, 974 00 Banská Bystrica; tel. (48) 539-01; fax (48) 526-03; Editor-in-Chief EVA BENČÍKOVÁ; circ. 5,000.

Bratislava

Hospodárske noviny (Economic News): Pribinova 25, 810 11 Bratislava; tel. (2) 5063-3627; fax (2) 5063-4724; e-mail hn@hnx.sk; morning; Editor-in-Chief SLAVOMÍR MALIČKAY; circ. 40,000.

Národná obroda (National Renewal): Mickiewiczova 1, 810 05 Bratislava; tel. (2) 323-973; fax (2) 323-983; e-mail extro@savba.sk; f. 1990; independent; economic; Editor-in-Chief ŠTEFAN MESÁROŠ; circ. 28,000 (March 1998).

Nový čas (New Time): Gorkého 5, 812 78 Bratislava; tel. (2) 363-070; fax (2) 363-104; f. 1991; morning; Editor-in-Chief ZUZANA RAČKOVÁ; circ. 230,000.

Práca (Labour): Odborárske nám. 3, 814 99 Bratislava; tel. (2) 5023-9316; fax (2) 5542-2985; e-mail marketing@praca.sk; internet www.praca.sk; f. 1946; publ. by the Confederation of Trade Unions of the Slovak Republic; Editor-in-Chief (vacant); circ. 80,000.

Pravda (Truth): Pribinova 25, 810 11 Bratislava; tel. (2) 367-503; fax (2) 210-4759; f. 1920; independent; left-wing; Editor-in-Chief PAVOL MINARIK; circ. 165,000.

Roľnícke noviny (Agricultural News): Dobrovičova 12, 813 78 Bratislava; tel. (2) 368-449; fax (2) 321-282; f. 1946; Editor-in-Chief JURAJ ŠESTÁK; circ. 20,000.

Slovenská republika (Slovak Republic): Ružová dolina 6, 824 70 Bratislava; tel. (2) 5022-1505; fax (2) 5022-1500; e-mail redakcia@republika.sk; Editor-in-Chief EDUARD FAŠUNG; circ 78,000.

Sme (We Are): Mytná 33, 810 05 Bratislava; tel. (2) 498-726; fax (2) 498-306; f. 1993; Editor-in-Chief MARTIN SIMECKA; circ. 50,000.

Šport (Sport): Svätoplukova 2, 819 23 Bratislava; tel. (2) 600-53; fax (2) 211-380; Editor-in-Chief ZDENO SIMONIDES; circ. 85,000.

Új szó (New Word): Prievozská 14A, 820 06 Bratislava; tel. (2) 523-8320; fax (2) 523-8321; f. 1948; midday; Hungarian-language paper; Editor-in-Chief ATTILA LOVÁSZ; circ. 42,000.

Večerník (Evening Paper): Pribinova 25, 819 16 Bratislava; tel. (2) 325-085; fax (2) 210-4521; f. 1956; evening; Editor-in-Chief MARTIN PODSTUPKA; circ. 30,000.

Košice

Košický večer (Košice Evening): tr. SNP 24, 042 97 Košice; tel. (55) 429-820; fax (55) 421-214; f. 1990; Editor-in-Chief MIKULÁŠ JESENSKÝ; circ. 25,000.

Lúč (Ray): B. Němcovej 32, 042 62 Košice; tel. (55) 633-2117; fax (55) 359-090; f. 1992; Editor-in-Chief EDITA PAČAJOVÁ-KARDOŠOVÁ; circ. 15,000.

Slovenský východ (Slovak East): Letná 45, 042 66 Košice; tel. (55) 539-79; fax (55) 539-50; Editor-in-Chief DUŠAN KLINGER; circ. 30,000.

Prešov

Prešovský večerník (Prešov Evening Paper): Jarkova 4, 080 01 Prešov; tel. (51) 724-563; fax (51) 723-398; f. 1990; Editor-in-Chief PETER LIČÁK; circ. 13,000.

PRINCIPAL PERIODICALS

A Het (The Week): Bratislava; weekly; Hungarian-language magazine; Editor-in-Chief ATTILA LOVÁSZ.

Deák–Avízo: Pribišova 19A, 841 05 Bratislava; tel. (2) 722-485; fax (2) 714-655; 3 a week; advertising and information; Dir ERNEST DEAK; circ. 70,000.

Dievča (Girl): Mudroňova 12, 815 05 Bratislava; tel. (2) 311-920; monthly; publ. by the Slovak Union of Women; Editor-in-Chief DANA VIESTOVÁ; circ. 18,000.

Domino Efekt: Hlavná 68, 040 01 Košice; tel. and fax (55) 622-7692; f. 1992; weekly; Editor-in-Chief ANDREJ HRICO; circ. 20,000.

Elektrón + Zenit: Pražská 11, 812 84 Bratislava; tel. (2) 417-225; fax (2) 493-385; monthly; science and technology for young people; Editor-in-Chief LADISLAV GYORFFY; circ. 22,000.

Eurotelevízia (Eurotelevision): Pribinova 25, 819 14 Bratislava; tel. (2) 5063-4194; fax (2) 5063-4152; e-mail etv@euroskopringier.sk; weekly; Editor-in-Chief TAŇA LUCKÁ; circ. 290,000.

Eva: Pribinova 25, 819 39 Bratislava; tel. (2) 5063-3340; fax (2) 5063-4128; e-mail eva@euroskop.sk; internet www.euroskop.riniger.sk; monthly; magazine for women; Editor-in-Chief KATARINA PATVAROŠOVÁ; circ. 120,000.

International: Štúrova 4, 815 80 Bratislava; tel. (2) 367-808; fax (2) 326-685; weekly; current affairs; Editor-in-Chief TATIANA JAGLOVÁ; circ. 60,000.

Kamarát (Friend): POB 73, 820 14 Bratislava; tel. and fax (2) 240-8777; f. 1950; fortnightly; magazine for teenagers; Editor-in-Chief VLADIMÍR TOPERCER; circ. 30,000.

Katolícke noviny (Catholic News): Kapitulská 20, 815 21 Bratislava; tel. (2) 533-1790; fax (2) 533-3178; f. 1849; weekly; Editor-in-Chief MÁRIA KOTESOVÁ; circ. 116,000.

Krásy Slovenska (Beauty of Slovakia): Vajnorská 100A, 832 58 Bratislava; tel. (2) 279-0641; fax (2) 279-0587; illustrated bimonthly; Editor-in-Chief MILAN KUBIŠ; circ. 10,000.

Línia: Pribišova 19A, 841 05 Bratislava; tel. (2) 6025-1123; fax (2) 6025-1130; monthly; life-style; Editor-in-Chief JÁN HANUŠKA; circ. 25,000.

Móda (Fashion): Štefánikova 4, 812 64 Bratislava; tel. (2) 765-704; fax (2) 491-191; quarterly; Editor-in-Chief DANA LAPŠANSKÁ; circ. 20,000.

Ohník (Little Flame): Pražská 11, 812 84 Bratislava; tel. (2) 417-233; monthly; youth; Editor-in-Chief STANISLAV BEBJAK; circ. 35,000.

Plus 7 dní: Ružová dolina 27, 825 06 Bratislava; tel. (2) 656-83; fax (2) 201-6309; weekly; social magazine; Editor-in-Chief MILOŠ LUKNÁR; circ. 60,000.

Poradca podnikateľa (Entrepreneurs' Adviser): Národná 13, POB 29, 010 01 Žilina; tel. (89) 734-1112; fax (89) 734-1180; e-mail mesticka@pp_holding.sk; internet www.pp_holding.sk; f. 1993; monthly; Gen. Dir ZOJA ŽIDEKOVÁ; Editor-in-Chief MÁRIA MESTICKÁ; circ. 70,000.

Rodina (Family): Pribinova 25, POB 122, 810 11 Bratislava; tel. (2) 210-4027; monthly; family magazine; Editor-in-Chief M. VÁROŠ; circ. 145,000.

Romano ľil nevo: Jarková 4, 080 01 Prešov; tel. (41) 772-5238; fax (41) 773-3439; e-mail romskylist@vadium.sk; internet www.rnj.vadium.sk; f. 1991; in Romany and Slovak; publ. by the Association Jekhetane-Spolu-Together; Editor-in-Chief DANIELA HIVEŠOVÁ-ŠILANOVÁ; circ. 8,500.

Slovenka (Slovak Woman): Jaskový rad 5, 833 80 Bratislava; tel. (2) 5478-9652; fax (2) 5477-6118; e-mail slovenka@slovenka.sk; f. 1948; weekly; illustrated magazine; Editor-in-Chief ZUZANA KRÚTKA; circ. 220,000.

Slovenské národné noviny (Slovak National News): Matica slovenská, Mudroňová 1, 036 52 Martin; tel. and fax (43) 345-35; f. 1845; weekly; organ of Matica slovenská cultural organization; Editor-in-Chief PETER MIŠÁK; circ. 7,000.

Slovenský profit: Pribinova 25, 810 11 Bratislava; tel. (2) 563-3817; fax (2) 563-4581; economic weekly; Editor-in-Chief IVETA SEI-FERTOVÁ; circ. 25,000.

Stop: Exnárova 57, 820 12 Bratislava; tel. (2) 522-5052; fax (2) 522-0554; fortnightly; motoring; Editor-in-Chief L'UBOŠ KRÍŽ; circ. 47,000.

Szabad újság (Free Journal): Michalská 9, 814 99 Bratislava; tel. (2) 333-012; fax (2) 330-519; f. 1991; Hungarian-language economic weekly; Editor-in-Chief GÉZA SZABÓ; circ. 40,000.

Trend: Rezedova 5, POB 31, 820 07 Bratislava; tel. (2) 4341-1652; fax (2) 4333-1336; e-mail redakcia@trend.sk; internet www.trend.sk; f. 1991; weekly; for entrepreneurs; publ. by Trendy Ltd; Editor-in-Chief JAROSLAV MATYAS; circ. 25,000.

Vasárnap (Sunday): Pribinova 25, 819 15 Bratislava; tel. (2) 323-220; fax (2) 364-529; f. 1948; weekly; independent Hungarian-language magazine; Editor-in-Chief JÓZSEF SZILVÁSSY; circ. 97,000.

Výber (Digest): Kominárska 2, 832 03 Bratislava; tel. (2) 203-4486; fax (2) 203-4521; f. 1968; weekly; digest of home and foreign press; Editor-in-Chief MIROSLAVA AVRAMOVOVÁ; circ. 15,000.

Život (Life): Pribinova 25, 819 37 Bratislava; tel. (2) 210-4135; fax (2) 210-4145; f. 1951; illustrated family weekly; Editor-in-Chief MILAN VÁROŠ; circ. 255,000.

Zmena (Change): Sabinovská 14, 821 02 Bratislava; tel. (2) 237-758; fax (2) 522-6420; f. 1989; weekly; independent; Editor-in-Chief VLA-DIMÍR MOHORITA; circ. 20,000.

NEWS AGENCIES

SITA: internet www.sita.sk; f. 1997; independent; Dir-Gen. PAVOL MUDRY.

Tlačová agentúra Slovenskej republiky (TASR) (News Agency of the Slovak Republic): Pribinova 23, 819 28 Bratislava; tel. (2) 5921-0152; fax (2) 5296-2468; e-mail market@tasr.sk; internet www.tasr.sk; f. 1992; has overseas bureaux in Russia, Germany, Czech Republic and Belgium; Dir PETER NEDAVSKA.

Foreign Bureaux

Česká tisková kancelář (ČTK) (Czech Republic): Pribinova 25, 819 02 Bratislava; tel. (2) 210-4633; fax (2) 210-4605.

Informatsionnoye Telegrafnoye Agentstvo Rossii– Telegrafnoye Agentstvo Suverennykh Stran (ITAR—TASS) (Russia): Jancova 8A, 811 01 Bratislava; tel. (2) 315-797; Correspondent VALERII I. RZHEVSKII.

The following news agencies are also represented in Slovakia: Reuters (UK), Deutsche Presse-Agentur (Germany), Austria Presse-Agentur (Austria), Agence France-Presse (France), Magyar Távirati Iroda (Hungary), RIA—Novosti (Russia), Polska Agencja Prasowa (Poland), Agenzia Nazionale Stampa Associata (Italy), Novinska Agencija Tanjug (Yugoslavia) and Viet Nam News Agency (Viet Nam).

PRESS ASSOCIATIONS

Slovenský syndikát novinárov (Slovak Syndicate of Journalists): Župné nám. 7, 815 68 Bratislava; tel. (2) 5443-5071; fax (2) 5443-4534; e-mail ssn@internet.sk; internet www.ssn.sk; f. 1968; reorganized 1990; 2,600 mems; Chair. STANISLAVA BENICKA.

Združenie slovenských novinárov (Association of Slovak Journalists): Šafárikovo nám. 4, 811 02 Bratislava; tel. and fax (2) 363-184; f. 1992; 700 mems; Chair. JÁN SMOLEC.

Publishers

Alfa-press: Križkova 9, 811 04 Bratislava; tel. and fax (2) 399-837; technical and economic literature, dictionaries; Dir JOZEF BEDNÁRIK.

Matica slovenská: J. C. Hronského, 036 52 Martin; tel. (43) 413-2454; fax (43) 413-3188; e-mail sprava@matica.sk; internet www.matica.sk; f. 1863; literary science, bibliography, biography and librarianship; literary archives and museums; Man. Ing. JOZEF MARKUŠ, Dr MIROSLAV BIELIK.

Mladé letá (Young Years): Sasinkova 5; tel. (2) 5556-4293; fax (2) 5542-5714; e-mail mleda@medlab.sk; f. 1950; literature for children and young people; Dir Ing. JAROSLAV JANKOVIĆ.

Obzor (Horizon): Špitálska 35, 815 85 Bratislava; tel. (2) 361-015; fax (2) 361-237; f. 1953; educational encyclopaedias, popular scientific, fiction, textbooks, law; Editor-in-Chief MARGITA SVITKOVÁ.

Osveta (Education): Osloboditel'ov 21, 036 54 Martin; tel. (43) 341-21; fax (43) 350-60; f. 1953; medical, health, photographic, fiction; Gen. Dir Ing. MARTIN FARKAŠ.

Práca (Labour): Štefánikova 19, 812 71 Bratislava; tel. (2) 333-779; fax (2) 330-046; f. 1946; law, guides, cookery, fiction, etc.; Dir MIROSLAV BERNÁTH.

Príroda a.s. (Nature): Križkova 9, 811 04 Bratislava; tel. (2) 396-335; fax (2) 397-564; e-mail priroda@priroda.bts.sk; f. 1949; school textbooks, encyclopaedias, reference books, etc. for children and youth; Chair. Ing. EMILIA JANKOVITSOVÁ.

Slovenské pedagogické nakladatel'stvo: Sasinkova 5, 815 19 Bratislava; tel. (2) 5557–2454; fax (2) 5557-1894; e-mail spn@slovanet.sk; internet www.spn.sk; f. 1920; pedagogical literature, educational, school texts, dictionaries; Dir MÁRIA SEDLÁKOVÁ.

Slovenský spisovatel a.s. (Slovak Writer): A. Pla'vku 12, 813 67 Bratislava; tel. (2) 399-734; fax (2) 399-736; fiction, poetry; Dir MARTIN CHOVANEC.

Smena (Change): Pražská 11, 812 84 Bratislava; tel. (2) 498-018; fax (2) 493-305; f. 1949; fiction, literature for young people, newspapers and magazines; Dir Ing. JAROSLAV ŠIŠOLÁK.

Šport: Vajnorská 100/A, 832 58 Bratislava; tel. (2) 691-95; sport, physical culture, guide books, periodicals; Dir Dr BOHUMIL GOLIAN.

Tatran: Michalská 9, 815 82 Bratislava; tel. (2) 5443-5849; fax (2) 5443-5777; f. 1949; fiction, art books, children's books, literary theory; Dir Dr EVA MLÁDEKOVÁ.

Veda (Science): Bradáčova 7, 852 86 Bratislava; tel. (2) 832-254; fax (2) 832-254; f. 1953; publishing house of the Slovak Academy of Sciences; scientific and popular scientific books and periodicals; Man. EVA MAJESKÁ.

PUBLISHERS' ASSOCIATION

Združenie vydavatel'ov a kníhkupcov Slovenskej republiky (Publishers' and Booksellers' Asscn of Slovakia): Gregorovej 8, 821 03 Bratislava; tel. and fax (2) 4333-6700; e-mail austo@post.sk; Pres. Dr ALEX AUST.

WRITERS' UNION

Asociácia organizácií spisovatel'ov Slovenska (Asscn of Writers' Organizations in Slovakia): Laurinská 2, 815 08 Bratislava; tel. (2) 5443-5368; fax (2) 5443-4117; e-mail aoss@nextra.sk; f. 1949; reorganized 1990; 330 mems; Pres. VASIL DACEJ.

Broadcasting and Communications

TELECOMMUNICATIONS

Regulatory Authority

Telecommunications Office of the Slovak Republic: Jarošova 1, POB 76, 830 08 Bratislava 38; tel. (2) 4425-4328; fax (2) 4425-9577; e-mail roman.vavro@teleoff.gov.sk; internet www.teleoff.gov.sk; Chair. MILAN LUKNÁR.

Major Service Providers

Eurotel: f. 1997; 60% owned by Slovak Telecom; operates mobile cellular telephone network; Chair. and CEO ARTUR BOBOVNICKY.

Globtel: Prievozská 6, 821 09 Bratislava; f. 1997; operates mobile cellular telephone network; Gen. Man. BRUNO DUTHOIT.

Slovak Telecom (Slovenské Telekomunikácie): nám. Slobody 6, 817 62 Bratislava; tel. (2) 5249-2324; fax (2) 5249-2492; e-mail sekr.gr@st.sk; internet www.telecom.sk; scheduled for privatization in 2000; Dir-Gen. EMIL HUBINÁK.

BROADCASTING

Slovak Radio (Slovenský rozhlas): Mýtna 1, POB 55, 817 55 Bratislava; tel. (2) 5727-3560; fax (2) 5249-8923; e-mail interrel@slovakradio.sk; internet www.slovakradio.sk; f. 1926; Dir-Gen. JAROSLAV REZNÍK.

Television

Slovenská televízia (STV) (Slovak Television): Mlynská dolina 28, 845 45 Bratislava; tel. (2) 6542-3001; fax (2) 6542-2341; internet www.stv.sk; f. 1956; public broadcasting co; Chair. of Council JAROSLAV FRANEK; Dir RICHARD RYBNIČEK.

Slovenska Televizna Spolocnost: Palisady 39, 811 06 Bratislava; tel. (2) 531-6610; fax (2) 531-4061; f. 1996; broadcasts as Markiza TV; first privately owned television channel; owned by Central European Media Enterprises; Dir-Gen. PAVOL RUSKO.

TA3: Gagarinova 12, POB 31, 820 15 Bratislava; e-mail web@ta3.com; internet www.ta3.com; f. 2001; privately owned; Dir-Gen. MARTIN LENGYEL; Editor-in-Chief ZDENEK SAMAL.

TV Joj: Grešákova 10, 040 01 Kosiče; tel. (55) 622-2664; fax (55) 6221-027; e-mail joj@joj.sk; internet www.joj.sk; f. 2002; privately owned subsidiary of Nova TV (Czech Republic); Dir-Gen. VLADIMÍR ŽELEZNÝ; Dir MILAN KNAŽKO.

Finance

(cap. = capital; res = reserves; dep. = deposits; m. = million; brs = branches; amounts in Slovak koruny)

BANKING

Central Bank

National Bank of Slovakia (Národná banka Slovenska): Štúrova 2, 813 25 Bratislava; tel. (2) 5953-1111; fax (2) 5413-1167; internet www.nbs.sk; f. 1993; total assets 257,530.0m. (Dec. 2000); determines monetary policy, issues banknotes and coins, controls circulation of money, co-ordinates payments and settlements between banks, supervises the performance of banking activities; Gov. MARIÁN JUSKO; Vice-Govs ELENA KOHÚTIKOVÁ, JOZEF MUDRÍK.

Commercial Banks

Banka Slovakia, a.s.: Janka Krála, POB 76, 974 01 Banská Bystrica; tel. (48) 431-7111; fax (48) 413-2222; e-mail sekretar@basl.sk; internet www.basl.sk; f. 1996; cap. 756.9m., res 35.7m., dep. 3,261.5m. (Dec. 2000); Pres. ALENA LONGAUEROVÁ.

Citibank (Slovakia), a.s.: Viedenská cesta 5, 851 01 Bratislava; tel. (2) 6827-8111; fax (2) 6827-8200; e-mail citibank.slovakia@citibank.com; internet www.citibank.sk; f. 1995; cap. 1,650m., res 772.2m., dep. 21,880.8m. (Dec. 2000); Gen. Dir TIRAD MAHMOUD.

Crédit Lyonnais Bank Slovakia, a.s.: Klemensova 2A, POB 70, 811 09 Bratislava; tel. (2) 5926-2111; fax (2) 5926-2248; f. 1994; cap. 500.0m., res 64.4m., dep. 5,532.7m. (Dec. 2000); Dir-Gen. JEAN-MICHEL GIOVANNETTI.

Devín banka, a.s.: Františkánske nám. 8, 813 10 Bratislava; tel. (2) 5936-6102; fax (2) 5443-2311; e-mail devinbanka@devinbanka.sk; f. 1992; total assets 13,177m. cap. 993.5m., dep. 10,891m. (Dec. 1999); Gen. Dir PAVEL RUSNAK; 26 brs.

HVB Bank Slovakia, a.s.: Mostovà 6, 814 16 Bratislava; tel. (2) 5969-1111; fax (2) 5969-9406; e-mail infobacask@sk.bacai.com; internet www.hvb-bank.sk; f. Sept. 2001 by merger of Bank Austria Creditanstalt Slovakia and HypoVereinsbank Slovakia; Chair. CHRISTIAN SUPPANZ.

Investičná a rozyojová banka, a.s. (Investment and Development Bank, Inc.): Štúrová 5, 813 54 Bratislava; tel. (2) 5979-1111; fax (2) 5296-3484; e-mail info@irb.sk; internet www.irb.sk; f. 1992; 95.7% of shares divested to NSB Ltd (Hungary) in April 2002; cap. 8.7m., res 9.1m., dep. 23.2m. (Dec. 1999); Pres. ADAM CELUŠÁK; 41 brs.

Istrobanka, a.s.: Laurinská 1, POB 109, 811 00 Bratislava; tel. (2) 5939-7111; fax (2) 5443-1744; e-mail info@istrobanka.et.sk; internet www.istrobanka.sk; f. 1992; cap. 1,300m., res 555m., dep. 15,465m. (Dec. 2000); Chair. and Dir-Gen. MIROSLAV PAULEN; 11 brs.

Komerční Banka Bratislava, a.s.: Medená 6, 810 00 Bratislava; tel. (2) 5293-2153; fax (2) 5296-4801; e-mail koba@koba.sk; internet www.koba.sk; f. 1995; cap. 500.0m., res 0.3m., dep. 5,670.6m. (Dec. 2000); Chair. IVAN DUDA.

L'udová banka, a.s. (People's Bank, Inc.): Vysoká 9, POB 81, 810 00 Bratislava; tel. (2) 5965-1111; fax (2) 5441-2453; e-mail market@luba.sk; internet www.luba.sk; f. 1992; cap. 670.0m., res 848.9m., dep. 22,521.7m. (Dec. 2000); Chair. JOZEF KOLLÁR; 12 brs.

Pol'nobanka, a.s.: Vajnorská 21, 832 65 Bratislava; tel. (2) 4437-3964; fax (2) 4437-3975; e-mail mail@polnobanka.sk; internet www.polnobanka.sk; f. 1990; cap. 717.6m., res 1.9m., dep. 28,044.6m. (Dec. 2000); Chair. of Bd FRANTIŠEK PALIČ; 16 brs.

Poštová banka, a.s. (Postal Bank, Inc.): Gorkého 3, POB 149, 814 99 Bratislava; tel. (2) 5960-3333; fax (2) 5960-3344; e-mail silvia_valekova@pabk.sk; internet www.pabk.sk; f. 1993; scheduled for privatization; cap. 2,269.6m., res 55.2m., dep. 18,302.0m. (Dec. 2001); Pres. and Chair. LIBOR CHRÁST; 24 brs.

Prvá komunálna banka, a.s. (First Municipal Bank, Inc.): Hodžova 11, 010 11 Žilina; tel. (41) 511-1101; fax (41) 562-4129; e-mail webinfo@pkb.sk; internet www.pkb.sk; f. 1993; cap. 1,002.0m., res 95.5m., dep. 18,166.5m. (Dec. 2000); Pres. JOZEF MIHALIK; 45 brs.

Tatra banka, a.s.: Vajanského nábr. 5, POB 50, 810 11 Bratislava; tel. (2) 6865-1111; fax (2) 5292-4760; e-mail info@tatrabanka.sk; internet www.tatrabanka.sk; f. 1990; cap. 1,044.3m., res 2,539.5m., dep. 51,606.5m. (Dec. 1999); Chair. and Gen. Man. RAINER FRANZ; 30 brs.

Všeobecná úverová banka, a.s. (General Credit Bank, Inc.): Mlynské Nivy 1, POB 90, 829 90 Bratislava 25; tel. (2) 5055-1111; fax (2) 5556-6650; e-mail webmaster@vub.sk; internet www.vub.sk; f. 1990; sold to Banka Intesa (Italy) in 2001; cap. 12,978.0m., res 7,754.0m., dep. 142,939.0m. (Dec. 2000); Pres. VILIAM VAŠKOVIČ; 40 brs.

Savings Banks

Prvá stavebná sporiteľňa, a.s.: Bajkalská 30, POB 48, 829 48 Bratislava; tel. (2) 5823-1111; fax (2) 5341-1131; f. 1992; cap. 1,000m. Chair. of Bd JÁN ROLAND BURGER.

Slovenská sporiteľňa, a.s. (Slovak Savings Bank): Suché mýto 4, 816 07 Bratislava; tel. (2) 5957-4500; fax (2) 5957-4503; e-mail postmaster@slsp.sk; internet www.slsp.sk; f. 1969; fmrly state-owned; absorbed operations of Priemyselná banka (Industrial Bank) in 1999; privatized in 2000, majority stake bought by Erste Bank (Austria); cap. 6,374.2m., res 175.1m., dep. 152,699.1m. (Dec. 1999); Chair. REGINA OVENSKY-STRAKA; 638 brs and agencies.

COMMODITY AND STOCK EXCHANGES

Bratislava Commodity Exchange (Komoditná burza Bratislava): Ul. 29 Augusta 2, 811 07 Bratislava; tel. (2) 5293-1010; fax (2) 5293-1007; e-mail burza@kbb.sk; internet www.kbb.sk; Gen. Sec. IGOR KREJČÍ.

Bratislava Stock Exchange (Burza cenných papierov v Bratislave a.s.): Vysoká 17, POB 151, 814 99 Bratislava; tel. (2) 4923-6111; fax (2) 4923-6102; e-mail info@bsse.sk; internet www.bsse.sk; Dir-Gen. MÁRIA HURAJOVÁ.

INSURANCE

Slovak Insurance Co (Slovenská poisťovňa, a.s.): Strakova 1, 815 74 Bratislava; tel. (2) 533-2949; fax (2) 533-1272; majority stake divested to Allianz (Germany) in Dec. 2001; Chair. and Pres. RUDOLF JANAC.

Trade and Industry

GOVERNMENT AGENCIES

National Property Fund: Drieňová 27, 821 01 Bratislava; tel. (2) 4827-1448; fax (2) 4827-1289; e-mail fnm@natfund.gov.sk; internet www.natfund.gov.sk/index.htm; f. 1993; supervises the privatization process; Pres. JOZEF KOJDA; Vice-Pres. PAVOL HULÍK.

Slovak Investment and Trade Development Agency: Martinekova 17, 821 01 Bratislava; tel. (2) 5810-0310; fax (2) 5819–0319; e-mail sario@sario.sk; internet www.sario.sk; f. 1991; Gen. Dir ARTUR BOBOVNICKÝ.

CHAMBERS OF COMMERCE

Slovak Chamber of Commerce and Industry (Slovenská obchodná a priemyselná komora): Gorkého 9, 816 03 Bratislava; tel. (2) 5443-3291; fax (2) 5413-1159; e-mail sopkurad@scci.sk; internet www.scci.sk; Pres. Prof. PETER MIHÓK.

Banská Bystrica Chamber of Commerce and Industry: Svermeva 43, 974 01 Banská Bystrica; tel. (48) 345-057; fax (48) 363-88; e-mail sopkrbb@sopk.sk; internet www.bb.scci.sk.

Košice Chamber of Commerce and Industry: Južna Trieda 2A, 040 01 Košice; tel. (45) 641-9477; fax (45) 641-9470; e-mail sopkrkke@scci.sk; internet www.sopk.sk/ko/; Dir STEFAN KARAŠ.

Trenčin Chamber of Commerce and Industry: Jilemnickeho St 2, 911 01 Trenčín; tel. (32) 652-3834; fax (32) 652-1023; e-mail sopkrktn@scci.sk; internet www.commerce-and-industry.com.

Žilina Chamber of Commerce and Industry: Vysokoskolakov 4, 010 08 Žilina; tel. (41) 459-59; fax (41) 451-82; e-mail sopkrkza@scci.sk; internet www.sopk.sk/za/an/; Dir JAN MISURA.

UTILITIES

Electricity

Slovenské electrárne (SE): Hraničná 12, 827 36 Bratislava; tel. (2) 5069-1111; fax (2) 5341-7533; e-mail valovic_jozef@hq.seas.sk; internet www.seas.sk; largest state-owned utility; External Relations Dir JOZEF VALOVIC.

Gas

Nafta a.s.: Naftárska 965, 908 45 Gbely; tel. (34) 921-500; fax (34) 921-103; f. 1918; privatized 1996, renationalized 1999; gas exploration and production; Chair. JURAJ GREBÁČ; 2,588 employees.

Slovenský Plynárenský Priemysel (SPP) (Slovak Gas Company): Mlynské nivy 44A, 825 11 Bratislava; tel. (2) 5869-2111; fax (2) 5341-5590; e-mail spp@spp.sk; internet www.spp.sk; scheduled for partial privatization in 2002; Gen. Dir JÁN DUCKÝ.

TRADE UNIONS

Confederation of Trade Unions of the Slovak Republic (Konfederácia odborových zväzov Slovenskej republiky): Odborárské nám. 3, 815 70 Bratislava; tel. (2) 622-65; fax (2) 213-303; e-mail press@kozsr.sk; internet www.internet.sk/kozsr/; Pres. IVAN SAKTOR; 1.1m. members; affiliated unions include.

Metalworkers' Federation: Miletičova 24, 815 70 Bratislava; tel. (2) 5556-5383; fax (2) 5556-5387; e-mail oskovo@kovo.sk; Pres. EMIL MACHYNA.

Trade Union of Workers in Agriculture: Vajnorská 1, 815 70 Bratislava; tel. (2) 542-4186; fax (2) 542-1673; Pres. SVETOZÁR KORBEL'.

Trade Union of Workers in the Chemical Industry: Osadná 6, 831 03 Bratislava; tel. (2) 273-527; fax (2) 273-538; Pres. JURAJ BLAHÁK.

Trade Union of Workers in Construction and Construction Materials: Vajnorská 1, 815 70 Bratislava; tel. (2) 5542-4180; fax (2) 5542-2764; e-mail stavba@nextra.sk; Pres. DUŠAN BARČÍK.

Trade Union of Workers in Cultural and Social Organizations: Vajnorská 1, 815 70 Bratislava 1; tel. and fax (2) 5542-3760; e-mail sozkaso@nextra.sk; Pres. MÁRIA KRIŠTOFIČOVÁ.

Trade Union of Workers in Energy: Vajnorská 1, 815 70 Bratislava; tel. and fax (2) 542-1622; f. 1992; Pres. VLADIMÍR MOJŠ.

Trade Union of Workers in the Food-processing Industry: Vajnorská 1, 815 70 Bratislava; tel. (2) 5542-1575; fax (2) 566-2506; e-mail ozp@isnet.sk; Pres. MAGDALENA MELLENOVA.

Trade Union of Workers in the Glass Industry: ul. Matice Slovenskej 19, 911 05 Trenčín; tel. (32) 743-7200; Pres. MIROSLAV BUČEK.

Trade Union of Workers in the Health and Social Services: Vajnorská 1, 815 70 Bratislava 3; tel. (2) 5542-3965; fax (2) 5542-5330; Pres. ANDREJ KUČINSKÝ.

Trade Union of Workers in Radio, Television and Newspapers: Vajnorská 1, 815 70 Bratislava; tel. (2) 211-844; Pres. PETER JÁCHIN.

Trade Union of Workers in the Textile, Clothing and Leather Industry: Vajnorská 1, 815 70 Bratislava; tel. (2) 213-389; fax (2) 526-2570; Pres. Ing. KONŠTANTÍN BALÁŽ.

Trade Union of Workers in the Wood-working, Furniture and Paper Industries: Vajnorská 1, 815 70 Bratislava; tel. (2) 213-660; fax (2) 213-163; Pres. BORISLAV MAJTÁN.

Transport

RAILWAYS

In early 2001 the total length of railways in Slovakia was estimated at 3,600 km, of which 1,400 km were electrified.

Železnost Spolocnost: Bratislava; f. 2001; state-owned co established in 2001 to operate passenger and freight services and maintain rolling stock.

Železnice Slovenskej republiky (Slovak State Railways): Klemensova 8, 813 61 Bratislava; tel. (2) 5058-7007; fax (2) 5296-2296; e-mail gr@zsr.sk; internet www.zsr.sk; f. 1993; became a joint-stock co with responsibility for management of rail infrastructure in 2001, when responsibility for operations was transferred to the newly established state-owned concern, Železnica Spolocnost; Dir-Gen. ANDREJ EGYED.

Dopravný podnik Bratislava, a.s. (Bratislava Transport): Olejkárska 1, 814 52 Bratislava; tel. (2) 5950-1111; fax (2) 5950-1400; e-mail zad@dpb.sk; internet www.dpb.sk; tramway being upgraded to light-rail system; 11 routes with 154 stops; Dir-Gen. J. ZACHAR.

ROADS

In early 2001 the total road system (including motorways) was estimated at 17,880 km.

Slovenská správa ciest (Slovak Road Administration): Mileticová 19, 826 19 Bratislava; tel. (2) 5556-8008; fax (2) 5556-8011; internet www.ssc.sk; Dir DUŠAN FAKTOR.

INLAND WATERWAYS

The total length of navigable waterways in Slovakia (on the River Danube) is 172 km. The Danube provides a link with Germany, Austria, Hungary, Yugoslavia, Bulgaria, Romania and the Black Sea, although it was closed to traffic in the Federal Republic of Yugoslavia after damage caused during the conflict in that country in 1999. The main river ports are Bratislava and Komárno.

Štátna plavebná správa (State Shipping Authority): ul. Prístavná 10, 810 11 Bratislava; tel. (2) 5556-6336; fax (2) 5556-6335; internet www.sps.sk; Dir Ing. JÁN JURIA.

Slovenská plavba a prístavy (Slovak Shipping and Ports): Pribinova 24, 815 24 Bratislava; tel. (2) 5292-5798; fax (2) 5296-3002; e-mail spap@spap.sk; internet www.spap.sk; Gen. Man. OLDŘICH STRUMINSKÝ.

CIVIL AVIATION

There are five international airports in Slovakia: Bratislava (M. R. Štefánik Airport), Košice, Piešťany, Poprad and Sliač. Until Slovak Airlines, the national carrier, began operations in March 1998, ČSA (Czech Airlines) provided air transport services for both Slovakia and the Czech Republic.

Air Slovakia: M. R. Štefánik Airport, 823 11 Bratislava; tel. (2) 4342-2742; fax (2) 4342-2742; internet www.airslovakia.sk; f. 1993; scheduled passenger flights to Israel, Kuwait, Bulgaria, Cyprus, Greece and Spain; charter and cargo services; Gen. Dir AUGUSTIN BERNAT.

SkyEurope Airlines: Ivanská 26, 821 04 Bratislava; tel. (2) 4850-1111; fax (2) 4850-1000; internet www.skyeurope.com; f. 2001; first budget airline in Central Europe; joint venture with Spanish and Belgian interests; scheduled and charter passenger and cargo services; domestic and international services; Chief Execs CHRISTIAN MANDL, ALAIN SKOWRONEK.

Slovak Airlines: Trnavská cesta 56, 821 02 Bratislava; tel. (2) 4445-0096; fax (2) 4445-0097; e-mail sll@sll.sk; internet www.sll.sk; f. 1995; 34% state-owned; scheduled and charter passenger and cargo services; domestic services to Košice; international charter services to Russia, Spain, Italy, Bulgaria, Cyprus, Turkey, Greece and Tunisia; Chair. and Gen. Dir PAVOL MLADY.

Slovenská správa letísk (Slovak Airports Authority): M. R. Štefánik Airport, 823 11 Bratislava; tel. (2) 4342-4633; fax (2) 4342-2146; e-mail saa@ssl.sk; Dir-Gen. JAN KASSAK.

Tatra Air, a.s.: M. R. Štefánik Airport, 823 14 Bratislava; tel. (2) 292-318; fax (2) 294-259; f. 1990; joint-stock airline co; Exec. Dir BOHUŠ HURAJ.

Tourism

Slovakia's tourist attractions include ski resorts in the High and Low Tatras and other mountain ranges, more than 20 spa resorts (with thermal and mineral springs), numerous castles and mansions, and historic towns, including Bratislava, Košice, Nitra, Bardejov, Kežmarok and Levoča. In 2000 1,045,614 foreign tourists visited Slovakia; revenue from tourism was US $461m.

Slovak Tourist Board: Namestie L. Stura 1, POB 35, 974 05 Banska Bystrica; tel. (48) 413-6146; fax (48) 413-6149; e-mail sacr@sacr.sk; internet www.slovakiatourism.sk.

SATUR: Bratislava; f. 1993; from the former Czechoslovak state travel agency, Čedok; has 52 brs throughout Slovakia.

Slovakoturist: Volgogradská 1, Bratislava; tel. (2) 552-47.

Tatratour: Bajkalská 25, 827 27 Bratislava; tel. (2) 521-4826; fax (2) 521-2722.

SLOVENIA

Introductory Survey

Location, Climate, Language, Religion, Flag, Capital

The Republic of Slovenia (formerly the Socialist Republic of Slovenia, a constituent republic of the Socialist Federal Republic of Yugoslavia) is situated in south-central Europe. It is bounded by Austria to the north, Hungary to the north-east, Croatia to the south and east and by Italy to the west, and it has a short (40-km—25-mile) western coastline on the Adriatic Sea. The climate is Alpine in the mountainous areas, Mediterranean along the coast and continental in the interior. Average temperatures range from between 0°C (32°F) and 22°C (71.6°F) inland, and between 2°C (35.6°F) and 24°C (75.2°F) on the coast. Average annual rainfall ranges from 800 mm (31.5 ins) in the east to 3,000 mm (118.1 ins) in the north-west. The official language is Slovene, and in ethnically-mixed regions also Hungarian and Italian. The majority religion in Slovenia is Roman Catholicism, although there are small communities of other Christian (in particular Eastern Orthodox) denominations and of Muslims and Jews. The national flag (proportions 2 by 3) consists of three horizontal stripes of white, blue and red, with a shield in the upper hoist depicting a white three-peaked mountain (the Triglav), below which are two horizontal wavy blue lines and above which are three six-pointed yellow stars. The capital is Ljubljana.

Recent History

Following the collapse of the Austro-Hungarian empire, the Kingdom of Serbs, Croats and Slovenes was proclaimed on 4 December 1918. (The territory of Slovenia was formally ceded by Austria by the Treaty of Saint-Germain in 1919.) In 1929 the name of the country was changed to Yugoslavia. Yugoslavia collapsed under German attack in 1941 and, during the Second World War, Germany annexed lower Styria and Yugoslav Carinthia, while Italy annexed Istria and the territory around Ljubljana. (There was a continuing dispute with Italy over Istria; in 1954 Italy was awarded the city of Trieste, and Yugoslavia the remainder of the territory, giving Slovenia access to the sea.) Hungary occupied the plains along the Mura in north-eastern Slovenia.

The Slovene Liberation Front, formed in 1941, joined with the Communist-led all-Yugoslav Partisan Army of Josep Broz (Tito), which was eventually recognized as an ally by the British and US. Following the post-war proclamation of the Federal People's Republic of Yugoslavia (from 1963 the Socialist Federal Republic of Yugoslavia—SFRY), Slovenia became the most prosperous of the Yugoslav republics, but was increasingly suspicious of Serb domination. On 27 September 1989 the Slovene Assembly voted in favour of radical amendments to the Constitution of Slovenia, confirming Slovenia's sovereignty and its right to secede from the SFRY. The organization of multi-party elections was envisaged, and the establishment of opposition parties (the local League of Communists of Slovenia—LCS—having hitherto been the only legal party) was formally authorized. Slovenia was warned that the amendments contravened the Federal Constitution, and the Serbian leader, Slobodan Milošević, attempted to arrange protests in Slovenia against the Slovene leadership; the planned demonstrations, were, however, banned in November. Milošević subsequently instructed all Serbian enterprises to sever links with Slovenia, which retaliated by closing its border with Serbia and by imposing reciprocal economic sanctions. Thousands of demonstrators in Montenegro and Serbia protested against the perceived threat to the unity of the SFRY, and relations between Slovenia and the other republics deteriorated sharply.

In January 1990 the Slovenian delegation withdrew from the 14th (Extraordinary) Congress of the League of Communists of Yugoslavia (LCY), following the overwhelming rejection of their proposals to reform the federal party and to give greater autonomy to the respective Leagues of Communists of the republics. The LCY suffered a further reverse in February, when its Central Committee was unable to secure the quorum necessary to set a date for the reconvening of the Congress. A boycott by the entire Slovene contingent was supported by members of the Leagues of Communists of Croatia and Macedonia. The LCS

suspended its links with the LCY, and changed its name to the Party of Democratic Reform (Stranka democratskih reformi—PDR). In that month Stefan Korosec of Slovenia was removed from the position of Secretary of the Presidium of the LCY Central Committee, in advance of the expiry of his mandate, and was replaced by a Serb. In March Slovenia was redesignated the Republic of Slovenia. Meanwhile, opposition parties had been formed, and in December 1989 six of the main parties formed a coalition, the Democratic Opposition of Slovenia (DEMOS). In multi-party elections, held in April 1990, DEMOS won a majority in the republican parliament, and subsequently formed a Government under Lojze Peterle, the leader of the Slovenian Christian Democrats (Slovenski krščanski demokrati—S CD). However, the leader of the PDR, Milan Kučan (an outspoken opponent of Milošević), was elected President of the State Presidency (defeating Peterle in the second round of voting) and the PDR remained the largest single party in the legislature.

On 2 July 1990 the Slovenian legislature declared the sovereignty of the Republic and resolved that republican laws should take precedence over federal laws. This was confirmed by an amendment to the republican Constitution, approved by the legislature on 27 September. The Republic also assumed control over the local territorial defence force, thereby bringing Slovenia into direct confrontation with the Serb-dominated federal army, which attempted to reassert its authority by confiscating weapons and seizing the headquarters of the republican force. Slovenian and Croatian proposals to reform the Yugoslav Federation were rejected, and Serbia imposed economic sanctions on imports from the secessionist states. None the less, in a referendum held in Slovenia on 23 December 1990, some 89% of those who voted (about 94% of the electorate) endorsed Slovenian independence.

Relations between Slovenia and the SFRY deteriorated further in January 1991, when the Slovenian authorities refused to implement an order by the SFRY Presidency to disarm all paramilitary groups. In the same month Slovenia and Croatia signed friendship and military co-operation agreements. Although the Slovenian Government approved a programme for Slovenian dissociation from the SFRY in February, both Slovenia and Croatia remained willing to consider a federation of sovereign states. However, following the Serbian-led crisis in the Federal State Presidency in March (see the Recent History of Serbia and Montenegro), the Slovenian Government became more resolved to withdraw from the federation. In May Slovenia declared its intention to secede before the end of June, and legislation was adopted that would enable eventual independence, including the establishment of a Slovenian army. Tensions with the federal authorities were exacerbated when Slovenia attempted to take control of the collection of customs duties.

Slovenia and Croatia declared their independence from the SFRY on 25 June 1991. In response, Serbian-dominated federal troops were mobilized on 27 June, and tanks were dispatched from Belgrade. Sporadic fighting ensued and, despite attempts by the European Community (EC—now European Union—EU, see p. 199) to arrange a cease-fire, there was an aerial bombardment of Ljubljana on 2 July (the first of a European city since the Second World War). On the same day, however, the Slovenian Government agreed to the implementation of an EC-brokered cease-fire, and the federal army began its withdrawal from Slovenia on 3 July. On 8 October (following the expiry of a three-month moratorium on dissociation, agreed as part of the EC cease-fire accord) Slovenia proclaimed its full independence, introduced its own currency (the tolar), and recalled all its citizens serving in federal institutions. All federal army units had withdrawn from Slovenia by 26 October. A new Slovenian Constitution, providing for a bicameral legislature, was promulgated on 23 December. Slovenia was recognized by the EC in January 1992. The USA recognized the country in April, and withdrew sanctions against Slovenia (previously imposed on all of the former Yugoslavia) in August. Slovenia was admitted to the UN in May.

Peterle's administration experienced increasing difficulties, as the struggle for independence became less of a unifying factor. In October 1991 the Slovenian Democratic Union, one of the larger and most influential of the DEMOS parties, split into two factions, both of which remained in the coalition. A minority liberal wing formed the Democratic Party (Demokratska stranka—DP) under the Minister of Foreign Affairs, Dr Dmitrij Rupel, while the majority of the party's parliamentary delegates supported a more right-wing programme and formed the National Democratic Party (Narodni demokrati stranka), led by the Minister of Justice and Administration, Dr Rajko Pirnat. DEMOS, undermined by such factionalism, was dissolved in December, although it was envisaged that the Peterle administration would remain in power pending the organization of elections (to take place under the terms of the new Constitution). However, the Government lost a parliamentary motion of 'no confidence' in April 1992, and Peterle resigned. He was replaced by Dr Janez Drnovšek, the leader of the Liberal Democratic Party (Liberalno demokratska stranka—LDP) and a former President of the SFRY Presidency.

Parliamentary and presidential elections took place on 6 December 1992. About 85% of the registered electorate participated in elections to the Državni Zbor (National Assembly). Although the LDP returned the greatest number of deputies (22) to the 90-member body, it failed to secure a majority of seats in the legislature. Among the groupings that enjoyed considerable success were the SCD, with a total of 15 seats, the United List (Združena lista—a four-party electoral alliance), with 14 seats, and the extreme right-wing Slovenian National Party (Slovenska nacionalna stranka—SNP), which won 12 seats. In the presidential election Kučan (standing as an independent candidate) was re-elected to what had become, under the terms of the 1991 Constitution, a largely ceremonial post, obtaining 63.9% of the votes cast. His nearest rival, Ivan Bizjak of the SCD, secured 21.1% of the votes. Voting was held concurrently for the 22 directly-elected members of the advisory Državni Svet (National Council); its remaining 18 members were chosen by an electoral college shortly afterwards.

In January 1993 Drnovšek formed a coalition Government, comprising members of the LDP, the SCD, the United List (later renamed the United List of Social Democrats—Združena lista socialnih demokratov—ULSD), the Greens of Slovenia (Zeleni Slovenije) and the Social Democratic Party of Slovenia (Social-demokratska stranka Slovenije—SDPS). Peterle was appointed Minister of Foreign Affairs, and Bizjak Minister of Internal Affairs.

In July 1993 the Minister of Defence, Janez Janša, was among senior politicians implicated in a scandal involving the sale of armaments to Bosnian Muslims, in contravention of the UN embargo on the transfer of military equipment between the former Yugoslav republics. Earlier in the year Janša (the President of the SDPS) had accused Kučan of protecting former officials of the communist regime. Janša was dismissed from the Government in March 1994, after a ministerial commission found that security forces under the command of the Ministry of Defence had ill-treated a former ministry employee. The SDPS withdrew from the Government, protesting that the coalition agreement had been breached. In addition, the party cited as its reasons for leaving the Government continuing high-level corruption and the change in the coalition's structure, following the merger in March of the LDP with three other organizations to form a new party, Liberal Democracy of Slovenia (Liberalna demokracija Slovenije—LDS). The LDS, led by Drnovšek, also included the DP and the Greens of Slovenia—Eco-Social Party (comprising the parliamentary members of the Greens of Slovenia, which had divided into two factions), and numbered 30 deputies in the Državni Zbor. Drnovšek subsequently formed a new coalition Government with the SCD and the ULSD. However, Bizjak resigned as Minister of Internal Affairs in May, following allegations that security forces controlled by his ministry had been involved in criminal activities in Austria. Revelations of irregularities in the allocation of government housing loans resulted in the resignation of the Minister of Justice in the following month. In September the appointment of an LDS member, Jožef Školjč, to the presidency of the Državni Zbor prompted Peterle's resignation from the Government, in protest at what he regarded as the excessive concentration of authority in the hands of the LDS. Although the SCD remained within the government coalition, Drnovšek refused to accede to the party's demand that Peterle's successor should also be a member of the SCD. In January 1995 an agreement was finally reached whereby Zoran Thaler of the LDS was appointed Minister of Foreign Affairs, while Janko Deželak of the SCD assumed the

post of Minister of Economic Relations and Development (a portfolio hitherto held by the LDS).

In January 1996 the ULSD withdrew from the governing coalition, following the Prime Minister's proposal to replace the ULSD Minister of Economic Affairs, Dr Maks Tajnikar, which, they claimed, violated the coalition agreement. Tajnikar was subsequently replaced by an independent deputy, Metod Dragonja, and the three other positions left vacant by the ULSD withdrawal were allocated to one member of the LDS and two of the SCD. The coalition, which had lost its overall majority in the Državni Zbor (it now controlled 45 of the 90 seats), was subsequently placed under pressure to relax its economic austerity measures by a series of public sector strikes for wage increases. The forthcoming general election apparently prompted the Government to agree to the demands of certain groups. In May Thaler was defeated in a motion of 'no confidence', prompted by his acceptance of a compromise solution to a dispute with Italy (which had prevented Slovenia's accession to associate membership of the EU—see below), after the SCD voted against the minister. Thaler remained in office as acting Minister of Foreign Affairs.

At the elections to the Državni Zbor, which took place on 10 November 1996, the LDS returned 25 deputies to the 90-member assembly, and subsequently increased its overall strength to 45 seats, having gained the support of the ULSD, the Democratic Party of Pensioners of Slovenia (DESUS), the SNP and the representatives of the Hungarian and Italian minorities (see Government, below). A newly formed opposition alliance, Slovenian Spring, comprising the Slovenian People's Party (Slovenska ljudska stranka—SPP), the SCD and the SDPS, also held 45 seats in the Državni Zbor. Consequently, Kučan's nomination that Drnovšek be returned to the office of Prime Minister failed to obtain the requisite majority of more than one-half of the deputies. Following a protracted delay, an SCD deputy announced his withdrawal from the party to become an independent deputy, and agreed to support Drnovšek's candidacy, and in January 1997 Drnovšek was re-elected to the office of Prime Minister. However, the continued absence of a majority in the Državni Zbor impeded the formation of a new government, with the parties belonging to Slovenian Spring refusing to accept an administration headed by Drnovšek. Drnovšek consequently failed to gain sufficient support for his proposed new coalition government, which was to include representatives of all the political parties in the legislature. In late February the SPP (which held 19 seats in the Državni Zbor) finally agreed to join a coalition government with the LDS and DESUS, which was subsequently approved by 52 votes in the Državni Zbor.

Accession to the EU and to NATO was a priority for the new Government. Although it was announced at the NATO summit in Madrid, Spain, in early July 1997, that only the Czech Republic, Hungary and Poland had been successful in their bids to join the alliance, the Slovenian Government none the less expressed its commitment to fulfilling the requisite defence obligations to achieve membership at a second round of expansion. Following an agreement earlier in the month by parliamentary party leaders to co-operate over the country's bid to join the EU, in July a two-thirds' majority of the Državni Zbor voted to amend the Constitution, to allow foreigners to purchase land in Slovenia, thereby meeting the requirements for ratification of the EU association agreement (Europe Agreement). Despite opposition claims that Slovenia would be entering the EU under less favourable conditions than other states, the agreement was ratified by parliament the following day. The European Commission subsequently recommended that the EU begin membership negotiations with Slovenia in 1998. Despite this positive development, in late July 1997 Zoran Thaler resigned as Minister of Foreign Affairs, reportedly as the result of disunity on the issue of Slovenia's accession. His post remained vacant until the appointment of Boris Frlec in September.

A presidential election took place on 23 November 1997. Kučan won a second (and final) term of office by a convincing majority, with 55.6% of the votes cast. His nearest rival, the President of the Državni Zbor, Janez Podobnik, secured 18.4% of the votes. Indirect elections to the Državni Svet followed on 26 November.

In February 1998 the Minister of Defence, Tit Turnšek, formally tendered his resignation, after two Slovenian military intelligence agents were arrested in early January, after having crossed into Croatian territory with electronic surveillance equipment. (They were later released.) Also in February Frlec presented the Government's NATO membership strategy to the

Državni Zbor; the strategy was presented to the NATO Council in March 1998. In April the Government announced plans to establish a National Security Council to co-ordinate the work of the defence, security and emergency services. In October the Minister of Defence, Alojz Krapež, resigned, following allegations against him of corruption. Franci Demšar, a member of the SPP, was approved as Krapež's successor by the Državni Zbor in February 1999. In the same month the Minister of Internal Affairs, Mirko Bandelj, lost a vote of confidence in the Državni Zbor and was dismissed; Borut Šuklje was subsequently appointed as his successor.

In January 2000 Frlec tendered his resignation as Minister of Foreign Affairs, following criticism of his failure to resolve long-standing disputes between the Governments of Slovenia and Croatia (particularly regarding the joint sea border between the two countries and over the Krško nuclear power station—see below). He was replaced in early February by Dr Dmitrij Rupel. In March it was announced that, following lengthy negotiations between the SPP and the SCD, the two parties were to amalgamate in the following month, and that the nine ministers belonging to the SPP would resign from the Government. In early April Drnovšek attempted to form a new government, nominating eight independents to the vacant portfolios. However, the proposed Government was rejected by the Državni Zbor, and Drnovšek (who no longer commanded a parliamentary majority following the departure of the SPP from the government coalition) was obliged to resign. The SPP and SCD merged as planned in mid-April, and subsequently formed a new alliance, Coalition Slovenia, with the SDPS. Coalition Slovenia nominated Andrej Bajuk as a candidate for the premiership, and in early May, after having twice been narrowly rejected by the Državni Zbor, Bajuk was endorsed as Prime Minister by 46 of the 90 votes cast in the legislature. The Government, which was endorsed in the Državni Zbor in early June, notably included Lojze Peterle as Minister of Foreign Affairs and Janez Janša as Minister of Defence.

In late July 2000 the approval by 70 of the 90 deputies in the Državni Zbor of constitutional amendments, providing for the introduction of a system of proportional representation in the forthcoming elections, resulted in division within the SPP. Bajuk (who had opposed the new legislation and favoured a majority electoral system) announced his resignation from the reconstituted SPP, and his intention of establishing a new breakaway party. Kučan subsequently declared that the legislative elections would take place on 15 October; Bajuk's administration was to remain in office until then, despite the collapse of the government coalition. In early August Bajuk was elected Chairman of the newly formed New Slovenia—Christian People's Party (NSi), which was also joined by Peterle. The elections to the Državni Zbor on 15 October were conducted under the new system, whereby 40 deputies were directly elected, while the remaining 50 were elected on a proportional basis by the parties represented in the chamber (which held the requisite minimum of 3% of votes cast). The LDS secured 34 seats (an increase of nine seats compared with 1996), while the SDPS won 14 seats, the ULSD 11 seats, the SPP nine seats, and the NSi eight seats. Consequently, Drnovšek was re-elected to the premiership by the Državni Zbor in early November. Following inter-party negotiations, a coalition agreement was reached by the LDS, the ULSD, the SPP and DESUS. A new Government, which included several prominent members of Drnovšek's previous administrations, was endorsed by the legislature at the end of November; the Cabinet comprised eight representatives of the LDS, three of the ULSD and three of the SPP. Drnovšek undertook to expedite administrative reforms essential to EU requirements. In March 2001 a member of the LDS, Mitja Gaspari, was appointed Governor of the National Bank. In January 2002 Janez Potocnik, previously in charge of negotiations on Slovenia's accession to the EU, became Minister without Portfolio, responsible for European Affairs.

The presidential election on 10 November 2002 was contested by Drnovšek and Barbara Brezigar, a state prosecutor, who was supported by the SDPS and the NSi, together with a further seven candidates. (Kučan was prohibited, under the terms of the Constitution, from seeking election for a third term.) Drnovšek won the highest number of votes, with 44.4%, but failed to secure an outright majority; a second round between him and Brezigar (who had received 30.8% of the votes) was scheduled for 1 December. At this second ballot Drnovšek was elected to the presidency, with 56.5% of the votes cast. Anton Rop, also a member of the LDS and hitherto Minister of Finance, was

nominated to replace Drnovšek as Prime Minister, and on 19 December a new Government was approved by the Državni Zbor. Drnovšek was inaugurated as President on 22 December.

Areas of disputed border territory with Croatia, most notably the Bay of Piran in Istria, undermined otherwise harmonious relations between the two countries following independence. In July 1993 tensions between the two countries prevented the signing of agreements on friendship and co-operation and on the regulation of bilateral payments (although protocols governing other issues, including trade and economic relations, were concluded). In November Slovenian proposals to decommission the country's nuclear power plant, at Krško (constructed by the former federal authorities to supply energy to both Slovenia and Croatia), prompted protests by Croatia, which was reliant on the installation for one-quarter of its energy requirements. Little progress was achieved during 1994 in efforts to delineate the joint border, and the resumed construction by Croatia of border facilities on Slovenian territory provoked renewed protests by the Slovenian Government. In October the Croatian Government submitted a formal protest to Slovenia, following the approval of legislation providing for a reorganization of local government boundaries in Slovenia, as part of which four villages in the disputed area were to be included within the Slovenian municipality of Piran. A subsequent proposal by the Slovenian Government to revise the law to exclude the villages was rejected by parliament, although deputies agreed to delay implementation of the law (and thus the holding of elections) in three villages, pending a resolution of the border issue. In February 1995 a meeting of the Slovenian-Croatian joint border commission agreed that, since the process of delineating the border would be lengthy, this should be pursued separately from other bilateral concerns. In March Slovenia and Croatia agreed to divide ownership of the Krško nuclear station equally between the two countries.

By mid-June 1995 some 98% of the two countries' land and sea borders were agreed, although the Croatian Government remained opposed to any formal agreement pending the resolution of a dispute concerning outstanding debts owed to Croatian citizens by Ljubljanska Banka. Negotiations concerning mutual borders and the repayment of Ljubljanska Banka debts resumed in September, although Slovenia's repeated demands for direct access to the sea remained an obstacle to agreement.

In December 1997 Drnovšek strongly criticized the removal from the Croatian Constitution of Slovenes as a recognized minority. Tension between the two countries escalated in early 1998, with the arrest in January of two Slovenian intelligence agents (see above). Negotiations on border issues and other areas of contention continued, none the less, and in March the Slovenian Minister of Foreign Affairs met with his Austrian and Croatian counterparts in Split, Croatia, with the aim of developing trilateral links within the framework of the Central European Initiative (see p. 349).

In July 1998 Slovenia ceased distributing electricity generated at the Krško nuclear power plant to Croatia, claiming that it had failed to pay for power, valued at some US $14m., already supplied. In the same month Slovenia privatized the Krško power plant. Croatia was reported to have resumed payments to Slovenia in August, and subsequently the transfer of electricity was restored. In November it was announced that the dispute over the Krško nuclear power plant would be resolved on the basis of co-ownership. Following the election of a new Government in Croatia in early 2000, bilateral relations improved significantly. After lengthy negotiations between Drnovšek and the Croatian Prime Minister, Ivica Račan, an agreement resolving the outstanding issues of contention between Slovenia and Croatia was signed in July 2001. The accord (which required endorsement by the legislatures of the two countries) granted Slovenia access to the Adriatic Sea through the Bay of Piran, and provided for continued joint management of the Krško nuclear installation; the four disputed border villages were to remain under Croatian sovereignty.

Slovenia and Croatia are united in their opposition to movements for Istrian autonomy and to any revision to their detriment of the 1975 Treaty of Osimo, which had defined the borders between the SFRY and Italy, and had provided for the payment by the SFRY of compensation for Italian property transferred to Yugoslav sovereignty after 1947. Although Slovenia asserted that its debt in this matter (in accordance with the Treaty of Osimo and the 1983 Treaty of Rome) had been discharged in full, in 1993 some 35,000 Italians were reported to be demanding compensation for, or the restitution of, property in Slovenia. In

July 1994 the Italian Government of Silvio Berlusconi stated that until the Slovenian authorities agreed to compensate Italian nationals who had fled after 1947 from territory now held by Slovenia, and whose property had been confiscated under communist rule, Italy would block efforts by Slovenia to achieve further integration with western Europe. Italy thus prevented scheduled negotiations on an association agreement between Slovenia and the EU until March 1995, when the new Italian Government of Lamberto Dini withdrew the veto. Preliminary agreement on trade and political co-operation was reached in June. However, it was not until May 1996 that Slovenia and Italy agreed to a compromise solution proposed by Spain, whereby Slovenia was to allow EU nationals to purchase property in Slovenia, on a reciprocal basis, within four years of the association agreement's ratification, and EU citizens who had previously permanently resided in Slovenia for a period of three years (thus including Italian nationals who had fled after the Second World War) would be permitted to buy immediately. In June Slovenia finally signed an association agreement with the EU, and simultaneously applied for full membership of the organization. At the beginning of July 1997 it was announced that Italy was to begin ratification of the agreement brokered by Spain as soon as the Slovenian parliament had approved the Europe Agreement (see above).

In April 1993 Slovenia was the first former Yugoslav republic to sign a trade and economic co-operation accord with the EC, and it achieved associate membership of the EU in June 1996 (see above). Slovenia joined the Council of Europe (see p. 181) in May 1993, and in December was granted observer status at the Western European Union (see p. 318) conference in Paris, France. In March 1994 it was announced that Slovenia was to join NATO's 'Partnership for Peace' programme. In January 1996 Slovenia was admitted to the Central European Free Trade Agreement (now Association). Formal accession negotiations to the EU commenced in November 1998. At a summit meeting in Prague in November 2002, Slovenia was formally invited to join the organization in 2004. In December, at a summit meeting in Copenhagen, Denmark, Slovenia was one of 10 nations officially invited to become members of the EU in 2004. A national referendum on the issue of joining both organizations was conducted on 23 March 2003; some 89.6% of voters endorsed membership of the EU, and 66.0% membership of NATO. The referendum was the first to determine public opinion in any of the Central European nations included in the planned EU enlargement in 2004.

In November 1995, following the Dayton agreement (see the chapter on Bosnia and Herzegovina), Slovenia recognized the Federal Republic of Yugoslavia (FRY—comprising Serbia and Montenegro) and proposed the establishment of diplomatic relations between the two countries. In March 1996 the FRY began legal action in the United Kingdom in an attempt to block an agreement between Slovenia and the 'London Club' of commercial creditors, whereby Slovenia assumed responsibility for 18% of the debt incurred by the SFRY. The FRY claimed that the agreement was in breach of the 1988 New Financing Agreement, whereby 10 banks (two from Slovenia) were liable for the whole debt. The FRY's principal concern was the effect of the agreement on the issue of succession to the SFRY. The FRY maintained that the other former members of the SFRY had seceded illegally and therefore forfeited their right to a share of the SFRY's assets, which remained 'frozen' pending the settlement of the succession issue. Slovenia, Croatia, Bosnia and Herzegovina and the former Yugoslav republic of Macedonia were meanwhile co-operating in efforts to secure international recognition as successor states to the SFRY. At discussions on this issue in Brussels, Belgium, in February 1998, Slovenia rejected the claim by the FRY to gold reserves of US $859m. from the assets of the SFRY (reputedly the sum that Serbia had brought to the Kingdom of Serbs, Croats and Slovenes in 1918). In December 2000 the Ministers of Foreign Affairs of Slovenia and Yugoslavia formally signed an agreement establishing diplomatic relations between the two countries.

Government

Under the terms of the 1991 Constitution, legislative power is vested in the 90-member Državni Zbor (National Assembly). Of the 90 deputies, who serve a term of four years, 40 are directly elected, while 50 are elected on a proportional basis by the parties represented in the chamber; two members are representatives of the Hungarian and Italian minorities. The Državni Svet (National Council), which is elected for five years, comprises 22 directly-elected members, and 18 members chosen by an electoral college to represent various social, economic, trading, political and local interest groups; the Council's role is mainly advisory, but it is empowered to veto decisions of the Državni Zbor. The Prime Minister, who is elected by the Državni Zbor, nominates the Government (subject to the approval of the legislature). The President of the Republic has largely ceremonial powers, and is directly elected for a maximum of two five-year terms. For administrative purposes, Slovenia is divided into 148 municipalities, 11 of which are urban.

Defence

Military service is compulsory and lasts for seven months. In August 2002 the active Slovenian armed forces numbered 9,000; reserve forces totalled 20,000. There was a paramilitary police force of 4,500 (with 5,000 reserves). The estimated defence budget for 2001 was SIT 66,700m.

Economic Affairs

In 2001, according to the World Bank, Slovenia's gross national income (GNI), measured at average 1999–2001 prices, was US $19,447m., equivalent to $9,780 per head (or $18,160 per head on an international purchasing-power parity basis). During 1990–2001, it was estimated, the population decreased at an average annual rate of 0.04%, while gross domestic product (GDP) per head increased, in real terms, by an average of 2.0% per year. Overall GDP increased, in real terms, at an average annual rate of 2.0% per year in 1990–2001. Growth was 4.6% in 2000 and 3.0% in 2001.

Agriculture (including hunting, forestry and fishing) contributed 3.1% of GDP in 2001. In that year the sector engaged 9.8% of the employed labour force. The principal crops are cereals (particularly maize and wheat), potatoes, sugar beet and fruits (especially grapes and apples). Slovenia's forests, which cover about one-half of the country, are an important natural resource. According to the IMF, agricultural GDP decreased at an average rate of 0.4% per year during 1995–2000, and declined by 2.1% in 2001.

Industry (including mining, manufacturing, construction and power) contributed 36.8% of GDP in 2001. In that year the industrial sector engaged 38.1% of the employed labour force. Industrial GDP increased at an average rate of 5.1% per year in 1995–2000. Growth in the industrial sector was 7.1% in 2000 and 2.9% in 2001.

Mining and quarrying contributed 0.9% of GDP and engaged 0.5% of the employed labour force in 2001. The principal activity is coal-mining; lead and zinc are also extracted, together with relatively small amounts of natural gas, petroleum and salt. Slovenia also has small deposits of uranium. The GDP of the mining sector increased at an average rate of 0.9% per year in 1995–2000. Mining GDP declined by 7.3% in 2000.

Manufacturing contributed 26.8% of GDP and engaged 30.3% of the employed labour force in 2001. The principal branches of the sector in 1997, measured by the value of output, were base metals and metal products (accounting for 13.3% of the total), food products, beverages and tobacco (12.5%), electrical machinery (10.2%), chemicals, other machinery and transport equipment. Manufacturing GDP increased at an average rate of 4.9% per year in 1995–2000. Growth in the manufacturing sector was 4.3% in 2001.

A nuclear power station was constructed in Slovenia by the former Yugoslav authorities to provide energy for both Slovenia and Croatia (see Recent History). Imports of fuel products comprised 8.1% of the value of merchandise imports in 2001. In 1999 nuclear power stations provided 35.4% of energy requirements, coal-fired electricity generating stations provided 33.8%, and hydroelectric power stations provided 28.2%.

The services sector contributed 60.1% of GDP and engaged 52.1% of the employed labour force in 2001. Tourism is a significant source of revenue; tourist activity was adversely affected by the political instability of 1991, but the number of arrivals subsequently recovered, reaching 1,218,700 in 2001. The GDP of the services sector increased at an average rate of 4.1% per year in 1995–2000. Growth in the services sector was 3.6% in 2001.

In 2002 Slovenia recorded a visible trade deficit of US $243.0m., while there was a surplus of $374.8m. on the current account of the balance of payments. In 2001 Slovenia's principal source of imports was Germany (accounting for 19.2% of the total); other major suppliers were Italy, France and Austria. Germany was also the principal market for exports (taking 26.2% of the total in that year); Italy, Croatia and Austria were also significant purchasers. The major imports in

2001 were machinery and transport equipment (particularly road vehicles and parts), basic manufactures, chemical products, miscellaneous manufactured articles, and mineral fuels. The principal exports in that year were machinery and transport equipment (particularly electrical machinery and road vehicles and parts), basic manufactures, miscellaneous manufactured articles (particularly furniture and clothing) and chemicals.

Slovenia's provisional overall budget deficit for 2002 was US $48,100m. In 2002 (according to the IMF) total external debt amounted to $8,799m (of which $3,238m. was medium- and long-term public debt), and the cost of debt-servicing was equivalent to 14.3% of the value of exports of goods and services. The annual rate of inflation averaged 22.5% in 1991–2001. Consumer prices increased by 8.1% in 2001 and by 7.5% in 2002. An estimated 6.3% of the total labour force were unemployed at September 2002.

Slovenia has joined several international organizations, including the IMF, the World Bank and (as a 'Country of Operations') the European Bank for Reconstruction and Development (see p. 193). Slovenia concluded an association agreement with the European Union (EU, see p. 199) in June 1996, and applied, simultaneously, for full membership of the organization. Formal accession negotiations began in November 1998. The country became a full member of the World Trade Organization (see p. 323) in July 1995. Slovenia is also a member of the Central European Free Trade Association.

Slovenia's economy was severely disrupted by secession from the Yugoslav Federation, and by the international economic blockade of Serbia and Montenegro, together with the conflicts in Croatia and in Bosnia and Herzegovina. By the mid-1990s this disruption had been largely overcome, and important advances in the transformation of the economy (such as the full convertibility of the tolar) had allowed Slovenia to gain a favourable position among the five countries of Eastern Europe chosen to participate in negotiations to join the EU. In 1998 agreement was also reached on the issue of the reform of the state pension system (which had proved an increasingly heavy burden on public finances). Value-added tax was introduced in July 1999, while progress was made during that year in the privatization of the banking sector, as part of efforts to fulfil EU criteria. However, the Government remained reluctant to implement extensive liberalization measures, and foreign direct investment remained relatively low. A new administration, which was installed in November 2000, undertook to expedite public administration reform and the standardization of legislation in accordance with EU requirements. Although economic growth slowed in 2001–02, following a weakening of external demand, the country's exports remained competitive and the external current account moved into surplus. However, year-on-year inflation was the highest of any of the 10 countries due to join the EU in the 2004 enlargement. In early 2002 all remaining restrictions to foreign investment in Slovenia were removed. However, in April the IMF (while commending liberalization measures) observed that progress in the transfer of two large state-owned banks to the private sector was slow, and that considerable opposition remained to foreign participation in the privatization process. Slovenia's scheduled accession to the EU was officially announced in December 2002 (and endorsed by national referendum in March 2003). At April 2003 Slovenia had achieved sustained convergence in per head income to about 70% of the EU average; however, efforts to reduce the rate of inflation (which had remained at about 7%–8% since 1997) had resulted in little progress (owing, in part, to large increases in indirect taxes and in the international price of petroleum). The IMF welcomed a government agreement linking public- and private-sector wages to the average EU inflation rate. Stronger growth was projected by 2004, based on expected recovery in the EU and a rise in private consumption.

Education

Primary education is free and compulsory for all children between the ages of six and 15, as is a one-year pre-primary programme. In ethnically-mixed regions, two methods of schooling have been developed: bilingual or with instruction in the minority languages. Various types of secondary education, beginning at 15 and lasting between two and five years, are also available. In 1998/99 93.9% of children in the relevant age-group (males 94.3%; females 93.4%) were enrolled at primary schools, while the equivalent rate for secondary education was 89.5% of children of the appropriate age-group (males 88.0%; females 91.1%). Slovenia's two universities are situated in Ljubljana and Maribor, with 54,312 and 28,082 students, respectively, in 2001/02. Expenditure on education by all levels of government in 1995 was SIT 128,657m., representing 12.6% of total government spending.

Public Holidays

2003: 1–2 January (New Year), 8 February (Prešeren Day, National Day of Culture), 18–21 April (Easter), 27 April (Resistance Day), 1–2 May (Labour Days), 25 June (National Statehood Day), 15 August (Assumption), 31 October (Reformation Day), 1 November (All Saints' Day), 25 December (Christmas Day), 26 December (Independence Day).

2004: 1–2 January (New Year), 8 February (Prešeren Day, National Day of Culture), 9–12 April (Easter), 27 April (Resistance Day), 1–2 May (Labour Days), 25 June (National Statehood Day), 15 August (Assumption), 31 October (Reformation Day), 1 November (All Saints' Day), 25 December (Christmas Day), 26 December (Independence Day).

Weights and Measures

The metric system is in force.

Statistical Survey

Source (unless otherwise indicated): Statistični letopis (Statistical Yearbook), published by Statistical Office of the Republic of Slovenia, 1000 Ljubljana, Vožarski pot 12; tel. (61) 1255322; fax (61) 216932; e-mail indok@gov.si; internet www.sigov.si/zrs.

Area and Population

AREA, POPULATION AND DENSITY

Area (sq km)	20,273*
Population (census results)	
31 March 1991	1,913,355
31 March 2002	
Males	958,576
Females	1,005,460
Total	1,964,036
Population (official estimates at 31 December)	
1999	1,987,755
2000	1,990,094
2001	1,994,026
Density (per sq km) at 31 March 2002	96.1

* 7,827 sq miles.

POPULATION BY ETHNIC GROUP
(2002 census)

Ethnic group	Number	%
Slovenes	1,631,363	83.1
Serbs	38,964	2.0
Croats	35,642	1.8
Bosniacs	21,542	1.1
Muslims*	10,467	0.5
Hungarians	6,243	0.3
Albanians	6,186	0.3
Macedonians	3,972	0.2
Montenegrins	2,667	0.1
Italians	2,258	0.1
Total (incl. others)	1,964,036	100.0

* Including persons claiming Muslim ethnicity rather than religious adherence.

PRINCIPAL TOWNS
(population at 2002 census)

Ljubljana (capital) .	265,881	Koper (Capodistria) .	47,539
Maribor	110,668	Novo mesto . . .	40,925
Kranj	51,225	Nova gorica . . .	35,640
Celje	48,081		

BIRTHS, MARRIAGES AND DEATHS

	Registered live births		Registered marriages		Registered deaths	
	Number	Rate (per 1,000)	Number	Rate (per 1,000)	Number	Rate (per 1,000)
1994 . .	19,463	9.8	8,314	4.2	19,359	9.7
1995 . .	18,980	9.5	8,245	4.2	18,968	9.5
1996 . .	18,788	9.5	7,555	3.8	18,620	9.4
1997 . .	18,165	9.1	7,500	3.8	18,928	9.5
1998 . .	17,856	9.0	7,528	3.8	19,039	9.6
1999 . .	17,533	8.8	7,716	3.9	18,885	9.5
2000 . .	18,180	9.1	7,201	3.6	18,588	9.3
2001 . .	17,477	8.8	6,935	3.5	18,508	9.3

Expectation of life (years at birth): 75.9 (males 72.1; females 79.5) in 2001 (Source: WHO, *World Health Report*).

ECONOMICALLY ACTIVE POPULATION
('000 persons aged 15 years and over, at May each year)

	1999	2000	2001
Agriculture, hunting, forestry and fishing	96	85	90
Mining and quarrying . . .	6	7	5
Manufacturing	278	269	277
Electricity, gas and water supply .	8	10	11
Construction	45	48	55
Wholesale and retail trade; repair of motor vehicles, motorcycles and personal and household goods	109	119	113
Hotels and restaurants . . .	34	34	34
Transport, storage and communications	54	60	57
Financial intermediation . . .	21	22	24
Real estate, renting and business activities	49	43	45
Public administration and defence; compulsory social security . .	49	53	48
Education	60	57	62
Health and social work . . .	45	46	47
Other social and personal services	36	34	33
Private households with employed persons	—	—	1
Activities not adequately defined	3	6	12
Total employed	892	894	914
Unemployed	71	69	57
Total labour force	963	963	972
Males	519	517	527
Females	444	446	445

Health and Welfare

KEY INDICATORS

Total fertility rate (children per woman, 2001)	1.2
Under-5 mortality rate (per 1,000 live births, 2001) . .	5
HIV/AIDS (% of persons aged 15–49, 2001)	<0.10
Physicians (per 1,000 head, 1998)	2.28
Health expenditure (2000): US $ per head (PPP) . . .	1,462
Health expenditure (2000): % of GDP	8.6
Health expenditure (2000): public (% of total)	78.9
Access to water (% of persons, 2000)	100
Human Development Index (2000): ranking	29
Human Development Index (2000): value	0.879

For sources and definitions, see explanatory note on p. vi.

Agriculture

PRINCIPAL CROPS
('000 metric tons)

	1999	2000	2001
Wheat	117.3	162.6	180.4
Barley	33.1	38.2	43.2
Maize	308.0	282.4	257.5
Rye	2.6	1.8	2.3
Oats	5.6	5.4	4.7
Mixed grain	1.4	3.2	3.6*
Potatoes	194.2	186.2	148.3
Sugar beet	467.1	349.1	185.7
Dry beans	3.0*	5.8	0.5
Walnuts	1.6	2.9	2.3
Cabbages	45.2*	27.0	17.2
Tomatoes	9.4*	3.4	3.1
Dry onions	1.1*	6.3	5.4
Garlic	1.4*	0.1	0.1
Carrots	5.6*	2.8	2.3
Apples	81.2	129.7	76.9
Pears	9.0	15.4	8.8
Cherries	2.4	3.3	2.2
Peaches and nectarines . . .	9.7	12.2	5.3
Plums	3.8	6.3	6.0
Grapes	98.3	126.7	126.8*
Hops	2.7	2.0	2.0*

* FAO estimate.

Source: FAO.

LIVESTOCK
('000 head)

	1999	2000	2001
Cattle	453.1	471.4	493.7
Pigs	592.4	558.5	603.6
Sheep	72.5	72.5	96.2
Goats	16.8	14.6	22.0
Horses	12.1	14.3	14.6*
Chickens*	7.2	7.2	7.2

* FAO estimate(s).

Source: FAO.

LIVESTOCK PRODUCTS
('000 metric tons)

	1999	2000	2001*
Beef and veal	43.1	42.2	42.2
Pig meat	67.3	58.5	60.0
Chicken meat	54.5	54.5*	54.5
Cows' milk	634.4	649.3	649.3
Cheese	21.0	21.7	22.0
Butter	4.3	3.5	3.5
Hen eggs	23.4	22.7	22.9

* FAO estimate(s).

Source: FAO.

Forestry

ROUNDWOOD REMOVALS
('000 cubic metres, excl. bark)

	1999	2000	2001
Sawlogs, veneer logs and logs for sleepers	992	1,120	1,144
Pulpwood	434	396	410
Other industrial wood . . .	137	205	408
Fuel wood	505	532	295
Total	2,068	2,253	2,257

SAWNWOOD PRODUCTION
('000 cubic metres, incl. railway sleepers)

	1999	2000	2001
Coniferous (softwood) . . .	338	300	302
Broadleaved (hardwood). . .	117*	139	157
Total	455	439	459

* FAO estimate.
Source: FAO.

Fishing

(metric tons, live weight)

	1999	2000	2001
Freshwater fishes	1,330	1,313	1,314
Marine fishes	1,885	1,746	1,774
Crustaceans and molluscs . .	65	77	226
Total catch	3,215	3,039	3,088

Mining

('000 metric tons, unless otherwise indicated)

	1998	1999	2000
Brown coal	1,277	1,163	1,175
Lignite	4,122	3,726	3,718
Natural gas (million cubic metres)	16.1	18.4	n.a.
Crude petroleum	900	100	100
Aluminium	73.8	77.2	100.0
Kaolin	10	10	10
Gypsum	10	10	10*
Pumice*	40	40	40
Salt	5	5*	2*

* Estimate(s).
Source: partly US Geological Survey.

Industry

SELECTED PRODUCTS
('000 metric tons, unless otherwise indicated)

	1997	1998	1999
Wine ('000 hectolitres)	501	466	365
Beer ('000 hectolitres)	2,138	2,000	2,022
Cigarettes (million)	5,767	7,555	8,032
Wool yarn	n.a.	1.1	1.0
Cotton yarn	16.8	n.a.	7.2
Woven cotton fabrics (million sq metres)	16.8	n.a.	n.a.
Woven woollen fabrics (million sq metres)	n.a.	n.a.	1.2
Footwear (excl. rubber) ('000 pairs)	5,976	5,641	4,779
Veneer sheets ('000 cubic metres)	18	22	22
Plywood ('000 cubic metres) . .	24	32	32
Mechanical wood pulp	28	30	30
Chemical wood pulp	105	112	112
Newsprint	49	68	68
Other printing and writing paper	183	240	240
Household and sanitary paper . .	56	52	52
Wrapping and packaging paper and paperboard	133	120	120
Hydrochloric acid	20.6	22.1	6.6
Sulphuric acid	109	128	126
Rubber tyres ('000)*	6,472	6,320	4,924
Roofing tiles (million)	16	17	12
Cement	1,113	1,149	1,222
Crude steel	97	95	76
Aluminium	9.1	10.2	9.0
Refined lead	6.0	7.3	8.2
Refrigerators for household use ('000)	692	756	780
Washing machines (household) ('000)	405	474	447
Television receivers ('000) . . .	—	231	244
Passenger motor cars ('000) . .	n.a.	n.a.	119
Bicycles ('000)	69	61	99
Electric energy (million kWh) . .	13,166	13,718	13,142

* Tyres for road motor vehicles only.

Source: UN, *Industrial Commodity Statistics Yearbook* and *Monthly Bulletin of Statistics*.

2000: Passenger motor cars (number) 124,843; Electric energy (million kWh) 13,624.

Finance

CURRENCY AND EXCHANGE RATES

Monetary Units
  100 stotins = 1 tolar (SIT)

Sterling, Dollar and Euro Equivalents (31 December 2002)
  £1 sterling = 356.3 tolars
  US $1 = 221.1 tolars
  €1 = 231.8 tolars
  1,000 tolars = £2.806 = $4.523 = €4.313

Average Exchange Rate (tolars per US $)
  2000   222.66
  2001   242.75
  2002   240.25

Note: The tolar was introduced in October 1991, replacing (initially at par) the Yugoslav dinar.

BUDGET
('000 million tolars)*

Revenue	1999	2000	2001
Tax revenue	1,499	1,600	1,798
Taxes on income and profits . .	274	311	358
Taxes on payroll, property etc.	82	95	116
Social security contributions . .	496	553	621
Domestic taxes on goods and services	601	603	673
Value-added tax	207	399	439
Excises	70	134	166
Taxes on international trade and transactions	46	38	30
Other current revenue	80	95	139
Capital revenue and grants . . .	11	17	21
Total	1,590	1,727	1,968

Expenditure†	1999	2000	2001
Current expenditure (excl. transfers)	708	797	924
Wages and salaries . . .	351	388	456
Expenditure on goods and services	296	336	386
Interest payments	51	61	73
Current transfers	738	813	908
Subsidies	63	59	63
Transfers to households . .	648	731	817
Capital expenditure (excl. transfers)	109	111	128
Capital transfers	58	60	71
Total	1,613	1,781	2,031

* Figures represent a consolidation of the accounts of the central Government (State Budget, Pension Fund and Health Insurance Fund) and local administrative authorities.

† Excluding net lending.

INTERNATIONAL RESERVES
(US $ million at 31 December)

	2000	2001	2002
Gold*	0.09	67.22	83.25
IMF special drawing rights . . .	3.69	5.03	6.98
Reserve position in IMF	82.33	80.63	120.69
Foreign exchange	3,110.00	4,244.33	6,852.57
Total	3,196.01	4,397.21	7,063.48

* Valued at market-related prices.

Source: IMF, *International Financial Statistics*.

MONEY SUPPLY
(million tolars at 31 December)

	2000	2001	2002
Currency outside banks	119,818	142,110	143,054
Demand deposits at commercial banks	263,472	317,305	378,220
Total money (incl. others) . .	385,881	462,532	526,100

Source: IMF, *International Financial Statistics*.

COST OF LIVING
(Consumer Price Index for urban areas; base: 1990 = 100)

	1999	2000	2001
Food (incl. beverages) . . .	1,554.5	1,639.6	1,793.5
Fuel and light	1,879.7	2,340.5	2,585.1
Clothing (incl. footwear) . . .	1,539.6	1,644.8	1,679.2
Rent	3,366.9	3,555.4	4,043.9
All items (incl. others) . . .	1,647.0	1,793.4	1,939.2

Source: ILO.

NATIONAL ACCOUNTS
(million tolars at current prices)

National Income and Product

	1998	1999	2000
Compensation of employees . . .	1,700,323	1,889,714	2,122,115
Operating surplus	472,084	535,628	586,717
Domestic factor incomes . .	2,172,407	2,425,342	2,708,832
Consumption of fixed capital . .	580,989	634,144	706,093
Gross domestic product (GDP) at factor cost	2,753,396	3,059,486	3,414,925
Indirect taxes	572,126	668,115	697,701
Less Subsidies	71,771	79,200	77,108
GDP in purchasers' values . .	3,253,751	3,648,401	4,035,518
Factor income from abroad . . .	69,279	74,352	87,689
Less Factor income paid abroad	64,230	80,602	102,630
Gross national product . . .	3,258,799	3,642,151	4,020,577
Less Consumption of fixed capital	580,989	634,144	706,093
National income in market prices	2,677,810	3,008,007	3,314,484
Other current transfers from abroad	54,842	63,756	79,018
Less Other current transfers paid abroad	34,141	40,866	51,209
National disposable income	2,698,511	3,030,897	3,342,294

Expenditure on the Gross Domestic Product

	1999	2000	2001
Government final consumption expenditure	738,388	841,108	974,047
Private final consumption expenditure	2,034,015	2,216,174	2,447,405
Increase in stocks	38,128	44,810	23,407
Gross fixed capital formation . .	999,183	1,076,840	1,138,673
Total domestic expenditure . .	3,809,714	4,178,932	4,583,532
Exports of goods and services . .	1,916,217	2,386,009	2,743,370
Less Imports of goods and services	2,077,530	2,529,423	2,760,711
GDP in purchasers' values . .	3,648,401	4,035,518	4,566,191
GDP at constant 1995 prices	2,625,942	2,747,021	2,828,409

Gross Domestic Product by Economic Activity

	1999	2000	2001
Agriculture, hunting and forestry	114,552	115,101	124,161
Fishing	520	534	460
Mining and quarrying	36,825	36,763	36,393
Manufacturing	859,603	970,014	1,082,244
Electricity, gas and water supply	98,108	112,768	134,556
Construction	195,879	214,935	236,420
Wholesale and retail trade; repair of motor vehicles, motorcycles and personal and household goods	365,101	403,227	460,079
Hotels and restaurants . . .	94,979	111,721	131,266
Transport, storage and communications	259,090	282,646	313,330
Financial intermediation . . .	134,177	156,326	176,644
Real estate, renting and business activities	380,744	421,884	489,887
Public administration and defence; compulsory social security	178,540	203,034	236,766
Education	177,098	205,041	240,022
Health and social work . . .	169,420	195,243	227,855
Other community, social and personal services	115,126	133,145	153,066
Sub-total	3,179,760	3,562,382	4,043,150
Less Imputed bank service charge	69,351	77,324	79,058
GDP at basic prices . . .	3,110,409	3,485,059	3,964,092
Taxes on products	591,242	602,030	602,099
Less Subsidies on products . .	53,250	51,570	602,099
GDP in purchasers' values	3,648,401	4,035,518	4,566,191

BALANCE OF PAYMENTS
(US $ million)

	2000	2001	2002
Exports of goods f.o.b.	8,807.9	9,342.8	10,472.6
Imports of goods f.o.b.	−9,946.9	−9,962.3	−10,715.7
Trade balance	−1,138.9	−619.5	−243.0
Exports of services	1,887.6	1,959.6	2,291.5
Imports of services	−1,437.9	−1,457.5	−1,736.1
Balance on goods and services	−689.2	−117.4	312.4
Other income received	434.0	462.6	487.8
Other income paid	−407.8	−443.4	−559.1
Balance on goods, services and income	−663.0	−98.2	241.1
Current transfers received	340.8	390.0	451.4
Current transfers paid	−225.4	−260.8	−317.7
Current balance	−547.6	31.0	374.8
Capital account (net)	3.5	−3.6	1.6
Direct investment abroad	−65.3	−132.8	−117.0
Direct investment from abroad	135.9	503.3	1,865.3
Portfolio investment assets	−58.4	−107.5	−94.1
Portfolio investment liabilities	246.0	188.9	27.0
Other investment assets	−519.2	206.6	−887.2
Other investment liabilities	941.3	545.7	662.8
Net errors and omissions	42.1	53.0	33.6
Overall balance	178.3	1,284.6	1,866.9

Source: IMF, *International Financial Statistics*.

External Trade

PRINCIPAL COMMODITIES
(distribution by SITC, million euros)

Imports c.i.f.	1999	2000	2001
Food and live animals	507.4	558.1	603.7
Crude materials (inedible) except fuels	444.9	593.9	568.0
Mineral fuels, lubricants, etc.	605.8	997.4	916.3
Petroleum, petroleum products, etc.	445.5	776.5	663.0
Chemicals and related products	1,112.9	1,361.0	1,442.0
Basic manufactures	2,042.2	2,405.5	2,597.7
Textile yarn, fabrics, etc.	330.8	375.1	407.9
Iron and steel	393.6	477.7	491.3
Non-ferrous metals	276.3	384.8	424.0
Other metal manufactures	365.8	406.2	414.6
Machinery and transport equipment	3,501.8	3,748.2	3,815.5
Power-generating machinery and equipment	263.7	267.3	290.6
Machinery specialized for particular industries	327.3	319.9	334.0
General industrial machinery equipment and parts	453.9	531.2	502.2
Electrical machinery, apparatus etc.	548.5	689.5	728.2
Road vehicles (incl. air-cushion vehicles) and parts (excl. tyres engines and electrical parts)	1,284.0	1,190.7	1,212.1
Miscellaneous manufactured articles	1,158.3	1,210.2	1,292.6
Clothing and accessories (excl. footwear)	373.6	385.7	391.8
Total (incl. others)	9,477.6	10,984.2	11,344.4

Exports f.o.b.	1999	2000	2001
Chemicals and related products	880.3	1,062.9	1,968.0
Medicinal and pharmaceutical products	358.2	432.9	524.9
Basic manufactures	2,102.4	2,590.4	2,768.7
Paper, paperboard and articles thereof	319.5	431.2	431.5
Textile yarn, fabrics, etc.	268.3	310.9	367.9
Iron and steel	233.6	296.4	298.4
Non-ferrous metals	277.0	361.5	399.5
Other metal manufactures	347.2	430.7	462.2
Machinery and transport equipment	2,849.9	3,411.3	3,738.4
General industrial machinery equipment and parts	357.3	409.1	467.2
Electrical machinery, apparatus etc.	867.1	1,065.3	1,149.3
Road vehicles (incl. air-cushion vehicles) and parts (excl. tyres engines and electrical parts)	1,037.3	1,157.6	1,196.6
Miscellaneous manufactured articles	1,686.9	1,830.6	1,978.8
Furniture and parts; bedding mattresses, etc.	576.6	636.7	713.3
Clothing and accessories (excl. footwear)	431.9	421.2	421.2
Total (incl. others)	8,030.8	9,491.6	10,346.8

PRINCIPAL TRADING PARTNERS
(million euros)*

Imports c.i.f.	1999	2000	2001
Austria	757.3	905.7	943.8
Belgium	140.2	159.0	176.4
China, People's Republic	127.2	148.6	176.8
Croatia	417.9	486.6	451.2
Czech Republic	264.2	273.5	278.0
France	1,032.5	1,127.4	1,204.6
Germany	1,945.4	2,082.4	2,178.3
Hungary	251.9	320.0	352.4
Italy	1,586.2	1,916.8	2,004.0
Japan	179.5	180.5	162.6
Korea, Republic	97.2	78.1	70.3
Netherlands	195.4	230.1	219.5
Poland	104.0	149.8	160.7
Russia	149.6	250.8	314.8
Slovakia	85.7	143.7	159.6
Spain	219.3	286.2	295.3
Sweden	174.7	179.7	114.8
Switzerland	203.4	175.3	170.4
United Kingdom	289.7	336.9	292.2
USA	274.7	325.1	332.8
Total (incl. others)	9,477.6	10,984.2	11,344.5

Exports f.o.b.	1999	2000	2001
Austria	584.0	713.8	773.3
Belgium	125.3	106.3	111.9
Bosnia and Herzegovina	341.8	408.3	444.8
Croatia	631.3	749.5	894.4
Czech Republic	149.3	164.5	187.9
France	459.6	671.7	702.2
Germany	2,465.9	2,574.5	2,714.6
Hungary	136.0	183.3	174.9
Italy	1,101.8	1,288.7	1,289.7
Macedonia, former Yugoslav republic	166.8	171.4	147.1
Netherlands	134.9	163.6	172.4
Poland	178.7	245.2	271.1
Russia	121.8	209.9	315.4
Switzerland	84.0	110.8	108.3
United Kingdom	160.1	202.6	289.6
USA	243.1	293.5	272.7
Yugoslavia	80.5	156.7	263.6
Total (incl. others)	8,030.8	9,491.6	10,346.8

* Imports by country of origin; exports by country of destination.

Transport

RAILWAYS
(traffic)

	1999	2000	2001
Passenger journeys ('000) . . .	13,756	15,010	14,484
Passenger-kilometres (million). .	623	705	715
Freight carried ('000 metric tons) .	14,226	15,064	14,919
Freight ton-kilometres (million) .	2,784	2,857	2,837

ROAD TRAFFIC
(registered motor vehicles at 31 December)

	1999	2000	2001
Motorcycles and mopeds . . .	9,978	11,308	11,723
Passenger cars	829,674	847,941	862,648
Buses and coaches	2,319	2,257	2,212
Lorries	42,088	44,251	45,811
Agricultural tractors. . . .	61,312	64,028	66,088

SHIPPING

Merchant Fleet
(at 31 December)

	1999	2000	2001
Number of vessels	10	10	10
Displacement (gross registered tons).	1,767	1,767	1,891

Source: Lloyd's Register-Fairplay, *World Fleet Statistics*.

International Sea-borne Freight Traffic
('000 metric tons)

	1999	2000	2001
Goods loaded	189	184	180
Goods unloaded	2,760	2,679	2,791

CIVIL AVIATION
(traffic)

	1999	2000	2001
Kilometres flown ('000) . . .	12,841	13,661	12,836
Passengers carried ('000) . .	780	866	801
Passenger-kilometres (million). .	832	866	790
Freight carried (metric tons) . .	4,147	4,556	4,173
Freight ton-kilometres ('000) . .	4,160	4,495	4,108

Tourism

FOREIGN TOURIST ARRIVALS
('000)*

Country of origin	1999	2000	2001
Austria.	126.4	150.3	174.4
Bosnia and Herzegovina . . .	26.3	28.9	27.9
Croatia.	82.0	91.3	95.5
Czech Republic	22.6	26.7	29.0
France	17.9	22.2	23.5
Germany	157.5	204.0	234.2
Hungary	25.1	30.4	32.6
Italy	207.2	256.2	269.3
Netherlands	21.0	31.5	34.8
Russia	10.4	12.1	15.5
United Kingdom	23.7	31.2	40.4
USA	18.9	25.4	28.3
Total (incl. others)	884.0	1,089.5	1,218.7

* Figures refer to arrivals at accommodation establishments.

Tourism receipts (US $ million): 1,088 in 1998; 954 in 1999; 961 in 2000.

Communications Media

	1999	2000	2001
Telephone subscribers ('000) . .	786.2	808.8	945.3
Facsimile machines (subscribers)	18,290	19,739	11,072
Mobile cellular telephones (subscribers)	325,048	468,351	662,619
Radio licences ('000)	533.1	n.a.	n.a.
Television licences ('000) . . .	471.3	n.a.	n.a.
Personal computers ('000 in use)	500	548	550
Internet users ('000)	250	300	600
Book production (titles published)*	3,976	3,917	3,598
Daily newspapers	5	5	6
Non-daily newspapers . . .	221	200	227
Other periodicals.	1,332	1,296	1,515

* Including pamphlets.
Sources: partly UNESCO, *Statistical Yearbook*; UN, *Statistical Yearbook*; and International Telecommunication Union.

Education

(1999/00, unless otherwise indicated)

	Institutions	Teachers	Students		
			Males	Females	Total
Pre-primary . . .	806	7,329	33,512	30,639	64,151
Elementary*† . . .	476	15,489	98,294	93,407	191,701
Upper secondary† . .	275	13,043	60,829	61,589	122,418
Higher education . .	37‡	4,666	36,300§	51,800§	88,100§

* 1998/99.
† Including education of adults.
‡ 1995/96.
§ Excluding post-graduate students, 2000/01 figures.

Pre-primary: Students 63,328 in 2000/01 (Source: Ministry of Education, Science and Sport).

Adult literacy rate (UNESCO estimates): 99.6% (males 99.7%; females 99.6%) in 2000 (Source: UN Development Programme, *Human Development Report*).

Directory

The Constitution

The Constitution of the Republic of Slovenia was enacted on 23 December 1991. Its provisions for the independence and sovereignty of Slovenia had been endorsed by a plebiscite held on 23 December 1990. The following is a summary of the Constitution's main articles:

INTRODUCTION

Slovenia is a democratic republic, governed by the rule of law. Slovenia is a territorially indivisible state. Human rights and fundamental freedom—including the rights of the autochthonous Italian and Hungarian ethnic communities—are protected. Slovenia attends to the welfare of the autochthonous Slovenian minorities in neighbouring countries and of Slovenian emigrants and migrant workers abroad.

The separation of church and state is guaranteed. Religious groups enjoy equal rights under the law and are guaranteed freedom of activity.

The autonomy of local government in Slovenia is guaranteed. The capital of the republic is Ljubljana. The official language of Slovenia is Slovene. In those areas where Italian or Hungarian ethnic communities reside, the official language is also Italian or Hungarian.

HUMAN RIGHTS AND FUNDAMENTAL FREEDOMS

All persons are guaranteed equal human rights and fundamental freedoms, irrespective of national origin, race, sex, language, religion, political or other beliefs, financial status, birth, education or social status, and all persons are equal before the law. Human life is inviolable, and there is no capital punishment. No person may be subjected to torture, inhuman or humiliating punishment or treatment. The right of each individual to personal liberty is guaranteed.

Respect for the humanity and dignity of the individual is guaranteed in all criminal or other proceedings. The use of violence of any sort on any person whose liberty has been restricted in any way is forbidden. Except for certain situations (as determined by statute), all court proceedings are conducted in public and all judgments are delivered in open court. Each person is guaranteed the right of appeal. Any person charged with a criminal offence is presumed innocent until proven guilty by due process of the law.

Each person has the right to freedom of movement, to choose his place of residence, to leave the country and to return at any time he wishes. The right to own and to inherit property is guaranteed. The dwellings of all persons are inviolable, and the protection of personal data relating to the individual is guaranteed. Freedom of expression of thought, freedom of speech and freedom to associate in public, together with freedom of the press and of other forms of public communication and expression, are guaranteed. The right to vote is universal and equal. Each citizen who has attained the age of 18 years is eligible both to vote and to stand for election.

The freedom of work is guaranteed. Each person may freely choose his employment. Forced labour is forbidden. All citizens who fulfil such conditions as are laid down by statute, have the right to social security. The State regulates compulsory health, pension, disability and other social insurance, and ensures the proper administration thereof. Education is free, and the State provides the opportunity for all citizens to obtain a proper education.

Each person is entitled freely to identify with his national grouping or ethnic community, to foster and give expression to his culture and to use his own language and script. All incitement to ethnic, racial, religious or other discrimination, as well as the inflaming of ethnic, racial, religious or other hatred or intolerance, is unconstitutional, as is incitement to violence or to war. The autochthonous Italian and Hungarian ethnic communities are guaranteed the right freely to use their national symbols and to establish organizations, to foster economic, cultural, scientific and research activities, as well as activities associated with the mass media and publishing. These two communities have the right to education and schooling in their own languages. They are also entitled to establish autonomous organizations in order to exercise their rights. The Italian and Hungarian communities are directly represented both at the local level and in the National Assembly (Državni Zbor). The status and special rights of Gypsy communities living in Slovenia are determined by statute.

ECONOMIC AND SOCIAL RELATIONS

The State is responsible for the creation of opportunities for employment. Each person has the right to a healthy environment, and the State is responsible for such an environment. The protection of animals from cruelty is regulated by statute. State and local government bodies are responsible for the preservation of the natural and cultural heritage.

Free enterprise is guaranteed. The establishment of trade unions, and the operation and membership thereof, is free. Workers enjoy the right to strike. The State creates the conditions necessary to enable each citizen to obtain proper housing.

ADMINISTRATION OF THE STATE

The National Assembly (Državni Zbor)

The Državni Zbor consists of 90 deputies, who serve a four-year term; 40 deputies are directly elected, while 50 are elected on a proportional basis by the parties represented in the chamber (which are required to hold a minimum of 3% of the votes). The Italian and Hungarian ethnic communities are entitled to elect one deputy each to the Državni Zbor. The President of the Državni Zbor (Speaker) is elected by a majority vote of all elected deputies.

The Državni Zbor enacts laws; makes other decisions; authorizes adherence to international agreements; may call a referendum; may proclaim a state of war or a state of emergency, at the initiative of the Government; may establish parliamentary inquiries with respect to matters of public importance.

The National Council (Državni Svet)

The Državni Svet represents social, economic, trade and professional and local interests. It is composed of 40 councillors: four representing employers; four representing employees; four representing farmers, small business persons and independent professional persons; six representing non-profit-making organizations; and 22 representing local interests. Councillors are elected for a five-year term.

The Državni Svet may: propose the enactment of statutes by the Državni Zbor; demand that the Državni Zbor reconsider statutes prior to their proclamation; demand the holding of a referendum; and demand the establishment of a parliamentary inquiry. The Državni Zbor may require the Državni Svet to provide its opinions on specific matters. A councillor of the Državni Svet may not be simultaneously a deputy of the Državni Zbor.

The President of the Republic

The President of the Republic of Slovenia is Head of State and Commander-in-Chief of the Defence Forces. The President is elected on the basis of universal, equal and direct suffrage by secret ballot. The President's term of office is five years (with a maximum of two consecutive terms). Only a citizen of Slovenia may be elected President of the Republic. Presidential elections are called by the President of the Državni Zbor. The office of President of the Republic is incompatible with other public offices or other employment. In the event that the President of the Republic is permanently incapacitated, dies, resigns or is otherwise permanently unable to perform his functions, the President of the Državni Zbor temporarily occupies the office of the President of the Republic until such time as a replacement is elected.

The President of the Republic is empowered to: call elections to the Državni Zbor; proclaim statutes; appoint state officers and functionaries; accredit, and revoke the accreditation of, Slovenian ambassadors to foreign states, and to accept the credentials of foreign diplomatic representatives; grant amnesties; and confer state honours, decorations and honorary titles.

If, in the course of carrying out his office, the President of the Republic acts in a manner contrary to the Constitution or commits a serious breach of the law, he may be brought before the Constitutional Court upon the request of the Državni Zbor. The President may be dismissed from office upon the vote of no less than two-thirds of all of the judges of the Constitutional Court.

The Government

The Government is composed of the Prime Minister and ministers. The Government is independent, and individual ministers are independent within their own particular portfolios. Ministers are accountable to the Državni Zbor. After consultations with the leaders of the various political groups within the Državni Zbor, the President of the Republic proposes to the Državni Zbor a candidate for the office of Prime Minister. The Prime Minister is elected by the Državni Zbor by a majority vote. Ministers in the Government are appointed or dismissed by the Državni Zbor, upon the proposal of the Prime Minister. The Prime Minister is responsible for the political unity, direction and administrative programme of the Government and for the co-ordination of the work of the various ministers. The Državni Zbor may, upon the motion of no fewer than 10 deputies and by a majority vote, elect a new Prime Minister (such a vote is deemed a vote of 'no confidence' in the Government). Furthermore, the Državni Zbor may bring the Prime Minister or any minister before the Constitutional Court to answer charges relating to breaches of the Constitution.

The Judiciary

Judges independently exercise their duties and functions in accordance with the Constitution and with the law. The Supreme Court is the highest court for civil and criminal cases in the republic. The Državni Zbor elects judges upon the recommendation of the Judicial Council, which is composed of 11 members. The office of a judge is incompatible with office in any other state body, local government body or organ of any political party.

The Office of the Public Prosecutor

The Public Prosecutor is responsible for the preferment of criminal charges, for prosecuting criminal matters in court and for the performance of such other duties as are prescribed by statute.

LOCAL SELF-GOVERNMENT

Slovenians exercise local government powers and functions through self-governing municipalities and other local government organizations. A municipality may comprise a single community or a number of communities, whose inhabitants are bound together by common needs and interests. The State supervises the proper and

SLOVENIA   *Directory*

efficient performance of municipalities and wider self-governing local administrative bodies. Municipalities raise their own revenue. Municipalities are at liberty to join other municipalities in establishing wider self-governing local administrative bodies or regional local government bodies to exercise administrative powers and to deal with matters of wider common interest. Citizens may join together and form self-governing local bodies to further their common interests.

PUBLIC FINANCE

The State and local government bodies fund the performance of their respective duties and functions from taxes and other mandatory charges levied by them and from such other income as they may derive from their assets. All revenues raised, and all monies expended, for public purposes by the State and by local government bodies must be accounted for in their respective budgets.

The Auditor General's office is the body with ultimate responsibility for auditing state finances, the state budget and monies expended for public purposes. The Auditor General's office is independent in the performance of its functions. Officers of the Auditor General's office are appointed by the Državni Zbor.

The Bank of Slovenia is the central bank. It is independent in its operations and accountable to the Državni Zbor. The Governor of the Bank of Slovenia is appointed by the Državni Zbor.

THE CONSTITUTIONAL COURT

The Constitutional Court is composed of nine judges, elected by the Državni Zbor, upon the nomination of the President of the Republic, for a term (non-extendable) of nine years. The President of the Constitutional Court is elected by the judges from amongst their own number to hold office for a period of three years.

The Constitutional Court is empowered to decide upon matters relating to: the conformity of statutes with the Constitution and with international agreements; complaints of breaches of the Constitution involving individual acts infringing human rights and fundamental freedoms; juridical disputes between the state and local government bodies or among such local government bodies; juridical disputes between the Državni Zbor, the President of the Republic and the Government; and unconstitutional acts or activities of political parties.

The Government

HEAD OF STATE

President: Dr JANEZ DRNOVŠEK (elected 1 December 2002; inaugurated 22 December 2002).

GOVERNMENT
(May 2003)

A coalition of the Liberal Democracy of Slovenia, the United List of Social Democrats and the Slovenian People's Party.

Prime Minister: Dr ANTON ROP.

Minister of Finance: Dr DUŠAN MRAMOR.

Minister of Internal Affairs: Dr RADO BOHINC.

Minister of Foreign Affairs: Dr DIMITRIJ RUPEL.

Minister of Justice: IVAN BIZJAK.

Minister of Defence: Dr ANTON GRIZOLD.

Minister of Labour, Family and Social Affairs: Dr VLADO DIMOVSKI.

Minister of the Economy: Dr TEA PETRIN.

Minister of Agriculture, Forestry and Food: FRANC BUT.

Minister of Culture: ANDREJA RIHTER.

Minister of the Environment, Physical Planning and Energy: JANEZ KOPAČ.

Minister of Transport: JAKOB PRESEČNIK.

Minister of Education, Science and Sport: Dr SLAVKO GABER.

Minister of Health: Dr DUŠAN KEBER.

Minister of the Information Society: Dr PAVEL GANTAR.

Minister without Portfolio, responsible for European Affairs: JANEZ POTOČNIK.

Minister without Portfolio, responsible for Regional Development: ZDENKA KOVAČ.

MINISTRIES

Office of the President: 1000 Ljubljana, Erjavčeva 17; tel. (1) 4781205; fax (1) 4781357; internet www.sigov.si/up-rs.

Office of the Prime Minister: 1000 Ljubljana, Gregorčičeva 20; tel. (1) 4781000; fax (1) 4781607; e-mail gp.upv@gov.si; internet www.sigov.si/pv.

Ministry of Agriculture, Forestry and Food: 1000 Ljubljana, Dunajska 56–58; tel. (1) 1789103; fax (1) 4789013; e-mail franc.but@gov.si; internet www.sigov.si/mkgp.

Ministry of Culture: 1000 Ljubljana, Cankarjeva 5; tel. (1) 4785900; fax (1) 4785901; e-mail mkinfo@gov.si; internet www.sigov.si/mk.

Ministry of Defence: 1000 Ljubljana, Kardeljeva ploščad 25; tel. (1) 1331111; fax (1) 1318164; e-mail soi@oub.mo-rs.si; internet www.mo-rs.si.

Ministry of the Economy: 1000 Ljubljana, Kotnikova 5; tel. (1) 4783600; fax (1) 4331031; e-mail kabinet@gov.si; internet www2.gov.si/mg/mgslo.nsf.

Ministry of Education, Science and Sport: 1000 Ljubljana, Župančičeva 6; tel. (1) 4784600; fax (1) 4784719; e-mail vprasajte.mszs@gov.si; internet www.mszs.si.

Ministry of the Environment, Physical Planning and Energy: 1000 Ljubljana, Dunajska c. 48; tel. (1) 4787400; fax (1) 4787422; e-mail info.mop@gov.si; internet www.sigov.si/mop.

Ministry of Finance: 1502 Ljubljana, Župančičeva 3; tel. (1) 4785211; fax (1) 4785655; internet www.gov.si/mf.

Ministry of Foreign Affairs: 1000 Ljubljana, Prešernova 25; tel. (1) 4782294; fax (1) 4782340; e-mail info.mzz@gov.si; internet www.sigov.si/mzz.

Ministry of Health: 1000 Ljubljana, Štefanova 5; tel. (1) 4786001; fax (1) 4786058; e-mail ministrstvo.zdravje@gov.si; internet www.gov.si/mz.

Ministry of the Information Society: 1508 Ljubljana, Langusova 4; tel. (1) 4788000; fax (1) 4788375; e-mail mid@gov.si; internet www.gov.si/mid.

Ministry of Internal Affairs: 1501 Ljubljana, Štefanova 2; tel. (1) 4325125; fax (1) 1214330; e-mail ssj@mnz.si; internet www.mnz.si.

Ministry of Justice: 1000 Ljubljana, Župančičeva 3; tel. (1) 3695200; fax (1) 3695519; internet www.sigov.si/mp.

Ministry of Labour, Family and Social Affairs: 1000 Ljubljana, Kotnikova 5; tel. (1) 4783450; fax (1) 4783456; e-mail vlado.dimovski@gov.si; internet www.sigov.si/mddsz.

Ministry of Transport: 1535 Ljubljana, Langusova ul. 4; tel. (1) 4788000; fax (1) 4788139; e-mail mpz.info@gov.si; internet www.sigov.si/mpz.

President and Legislature

PRESIDENT

Presidential Election, First Ballot, 10 November 2002

Candidate	Votes	% of votes
Janez Drnovšek (Liberal Democracy of Slovenia)	506,800	44.40
Barbara Brezigar (Independent)	351,049	30.76
Zmago Jelinèiè Plemeniti (Slovenian National Party)	97,103	8.51
France Arhar (Independent)	86,678	7.60
Franc Bucar (Independent)	36,989	3.24
Lev Kreft (United List of Social Democrats)	25,655	2.25
Anton Bebler (Independent)	21,096	1.85
Gorazd Drevensek (New Party)	9,772	0.86
Jure Cekuta (Independent)	6,188	0.54
Total*	1,141,330	100.00

* Excluding 15,019 invalid votes.

Second Ballot, 1 December 2002

Candidate	Votes	% of votes
Janez Drnovšek (Liberal Democracy of Slovenia)	583,570	56.54
Barbara Brezigar (Independent)	448,482	43.46
Total*	1,032,052	100.00

* Excluding 13,803 invalid votes.

www.europaworldonline.com

DRŽAVNI ZBOR
(National Assembly)

President: BORUT PAHOR, 1000 Ljubljana, Šubičeva 4; tel. (1) 4789400; fax (1) 4789845; e-mail borut.pahor@dz-rs.si; internet www.dz-rs.si.

General Election, 15 October 2000

	Votes	% of votes	Seats
Liberal Democracy of Slovenia .	389,485	36.26	34
Social Democratic Party of Slovenia	169,957	15.82	14
United List of Social Democrats	129,749	12.10	11
Slovenian People's Party . .	102,550	9.55	9
New Slovenia—Christian People's Party	92,823	8.64	8
Democratic Party of Pensioners of Slovenia	55,468	5.16	4
Slovenian National Party . .	47,095	4.38	4
Youth Party of Slovenia . . .	46,594	4.34	4
Others*	40,311	3.75	2
Total †	1,074,032	100.00	90

*Two of the 90 seats in the National Assembly are reserved for representatives of the Italian and Hungarian minorities.
† Excluding 36,813 invalid votes.

DRŽAVNI SVET
(National Council)

President: TONE HROVAT, 1000 Ljubljana, Šubičeva 4; tel. (1) 4789802; fax (1) 4789851; e-mail tone.hrovat@ds-rs.si; internet www.ds-rs.si.

There are 40 councillors in the Državni Svet, who are indirectly elected for a five-year term by an electoral college.

Political Organizations

Christian Social Union: 1000 Ljubljana; f. 1995; Pres. FRANC MIKLAVIČ; Sec.-Gen. IVAN KEPIČ.

Democratic Party of Pensioners of Slovenia (DESUS): 1000 Ljubljana, Kersnikova 6; tel. (1) 324171; fax (1) 1314113; internet www.desus.si; Pres. JANKO KUSAR.

Democratic Party of Slovenia: 1000 Ljubljana, Tomšičeva 5; tel. (1) 1261073; fax (1) 1255077; f. 1994 by mems of Democratic Party who opted not to join the LDS (see below); Pres. ANTON PERŠAK; 2,200 mems.

Greens of Slovenia (Zeleni Slovenije): 1000 Ljubljana; f. 1989; in 1993 the party split into two factions, one retaining the original name, the other, more radical wing adopting the title, Greens of Slovenia—Eco-Social Party; Leader VANE GOŠNIK.

Liberal Democracy of Slovenia (LDS) (Liberalna demokracija Slovenije): 1000 Ljubljana, Republike trg 3; tel. (1) 2000310; fax (1) 1256150; e-mail lds@lds.si; internet www.lds.si; f. 1994 by a merger of the Liberal Democratic Party, the Greens of Slovenia—Eco-Social Party, the Democratic Party and the Socialist Party of Slovenia; Pres. Dr JANEZ DRNOVŠEK; Gen. Sec. GREGOR GOLOBIČ; 18,000 mems.

National Democratic Party (NDP) (Narodni demokratska stranka): 1000 Ljubljana; withdrew from SCD 1994; Pres. MARJAN VIDMAR.

New Party (Nova Stranka): 1000 Ljubljana, Linhartova cesta 13; tel. (1) 3063995; fax (1) 2310567; e-mail info@nova-stranka.si; internet www.nova-stranka.si; Pres. Dr GORAZD DREVENŠEK.

New Slovenia—Christian People's Party (Nova Slovenija—Krščanska Ljudska Stranka—NSi): 1000 Ljubljana; tel. (1) 5004180; fax (1) 5004190; e-mail tajnistvo@nsi.si; internet www.nsi.si; f. Aug. 2000 by disaffected mems of the Slovenian People's Party; Pres. Dr ANDREJ BAJUK.

Party of Albanian Democratic Union: Ljubljana; f. 2000; Chair. BESNIK TALLAJ.

Slovenian National Party (SNP) (Slovenska nacionalna stranka—SNS): 1000 Ljubljana, Tivolska 13; tel. and fax (1) 4325207; internet www.sns.si; f. 1991; right-wing nationalist party; Pres. ZMAGO JELINČIČ; Vice-Pres. SAŠO PEČE; Sec.-Gen. MIŠA GLAŽAR; 5,500 mems.

Slovenian National Right (SNR) (Slovenska nacionalna desnica): f. 1993 by a 'breakaway' faction of the SNP; Pres. SAŠO LAP.

Slovenian People's Party (SPP) (Slovenska ljudska stranka—SLS): 1000 Ljubljana, Zarnikova 3; tel. (1) 301891; fax (1) 301871; internet www.sls.si; f. 1989 as the Slovenian Farmers' Association;

conservative; merged with the Slovenian Christian Democrats—SCD in April 2000; Pres. FRANC ZAGOZEN; Chair. JOŽE ZUPANCIC.

Social Democratic Party of Slovenia (SDPS) (Socialdemokratska stranka Slovenije—SDS): 1000 Ljubljana, Komenskega 11; tel. (1) 4345450; fax (1) 4345452; e-mail tajnistvo@sds.si; internet www.sds.si; f. 1989; centre-right; mem. of European People's Party; Pres. JANEZ JANŠA; Sec.-Gen. DUŠAN STRNAD; Parl. Group Leader ANDREJ VIZJAK; 20,000 mems.

United List of Social Democrats (ULSD) (Združena lista socialnih demokratov—ZLSD): 1000 Ljubljana, Levstikova 15; tel. (1) 2515897; fax (1) 4261170; e-mail info@zlsd.si; internet www.zlsd.si; f. 1992 as the United List, an electoral alliance of the Democratic Party of Pensioners, the Party of Democratic Reform of Slovenia, the Social Democratic Union and the Workers' Party of Slovenia; in 1993 it became a single party and adopted its current name; Pres. BORUT PAHOR; Gen. Sec. DUSAN KUMER; 23,000 mems.

Youth Party of Slovenia (Stranka Mladih Slovenije—SMS): 1000 Ljubljana, Rimska cesta 8; tel. (1) 4211400; e-mail info@sms.si; internet www.sms.si; Pres. DOMINIK S. ČERNJAK.

Diplomatic Representation

EMBASSIES IN SLOVENIA

Albania: 1000 Ljubljana, Ob Ljubljanici 12; tel. (1) 4322324; fax (1) 4322053; e-mail albania@siol.net; Ambassador DAUT GUMENI.

Austria: 1000 Ljubljana, Prešernova cesta 23; tel. (1) 4790700; fax (1) 2521717; e-mail laibach-ob@bmaa.gv.at; Ambassador Dr FERDINAND MAYRHOFER-GRUNBUHEL.

Belgium: 1000 Ljubljana, Republike trg 3/IX; tel. (1) 2006010; fax (1) 4266395; e-mail ljubljana@si-diplobel.org; Ambassador GEORGES GODART.

Bosnia and Herzegovina: 1000 Ljubljana, Korlajeva 26; tel. (1) 4324042; fax (1) 4322230; Ambassador MLADEN BOSIĆ.

Bulgaria: 1000 Ljubljana, Stari trg 1; tel. (1) 4265744; fax (1) 4258845; Chargé d'affaires a.i. Dr TODOR DRAZHEV.

China, People's Republic: 1111 Ljubljana, Legatova ul. 2; tel. (1) 2005810; fax (1) 2005832; Ambassador YANG HEXIONG.

Croatia: 1000 Ljubljana, Gruberjevo nabrežje 6; tel. (1) 4256220; fax (1) 4258106; e-mail croemb.slovenia@siol.net; Ambassador CELESTIN SARDELIĆ.

Czech Republic: 1000 Ljubljana, Riharjeva 1; tel. (1) 4202450; fax (1) 2839259; e-mail ljubljana@embassy.mzv.cz; Ambassador TOMÁŠ SZUNYOG.

Denmark: 1000 Ljubljana, Tivolska 48; tel. (1) 4380800; fax (1) 4317417; e-mail ljuamb@danish-embassy.si; Ambassador LARS MØLLER.

France: 1109 Ljubljana, Barjanska 1; tel. (1) 4264525; fax (1) 4250465; e-mail info@ambafrance.si; internet www.ambafrance.si; Ambassador OLIVIER DE LA BAUME.

Germany: 1000 Ljubljana, Prešernova cesta 27; tel. (1) 2516166; fax (1) 4250899; e-mail germanembassy-slovenia@siol.net; Ambassador HEIKE ZENKER.

Greece: 1000 Ljubljana, Mestni trg 8; tel. (1) 4201400; fax (1) 2811114; e-mail emb.gr.slo@siol.net; Ambassador GEORGE NICOLAIDIS.

Holy See: 1000 Ljubljana, Krekov trg 1; tel. (1) 4339204; fax (1) 4315130; e-mail nun-slo@siol.net; Apostolic Nuncio Most Rev. MARIAN OLEŠ (Titular Archbishop of Ratiaria).

Hungary: 1210 Ljubljana, Konrada Babnika 5; tel. (1) 5121882; fax (1) 5121878; e-mail huemblju@siol.net; Ambassador GÁBOR BAGI.

Italy: 1000 Ljubljana, Snežniška 8; tel. (1) 4262194; fax (1) 4253302; e-mail amblubiana@siol.net; Ambassador NORBERTO CAPPELLO.

Macedonia, former Yugoslav republic: 1000 Ljubljana, Dunajska 104; tel. (1) 5684454; fax (1) 5685181; Ambassador ILJAZ SABRIU.

Netherlands: 1000 Ljubljana, Palača Kapitelj, Polijanski nasip 6; tel. (1) 4201462; fax (1) 4201417; Ambassador JAN C. HENNEMAN.

Poland: 1000 Ljubljana, Rožna dolina XV, št. 18; tel. (1) 4232882; fax (1) 4232881; e-mail ambpol.slo@siol.net; internet www.poland-embassy.si; Ambassador MACIEJ SZYMANSKI.

Romania: 1000 Ljubljana, Podlimbarskega 43; tel. (1) 5058294; fax (1) 5055432; e-mail embassy.of.romania@siol.net; Ambassador VICTOR CHIUJDEA.

Russia: 1000 Ljubljana, Tomšičeva 9; tel. (1) 4256875; fax (1) 4256878; e-mail ambrus.slo@siol.net; Ambassador VYACHESLAV IVANOVICH DOLGOV.

Serbia and Montenegro: 1000 Ljubljana, Vogelna ul. 8; tel. and fax (1) 4380110; Ambassador Dr IVO VISKOVIĆ.

Slovakia: 1000 Ljubljana, Tivolska cesta 4; tel. and fax (1) 4255425; e-mail velepos.slovakia@siol.net; Ambassador Dr ROMAN PALDAN.

Spain: 1000 Ljubljana, Trnovski pristan 24; tel. (1) 4202330; fax (1) 4202333; Ambassador LUIS FELIPE FERNÁNDEZ DE LA PEÑA.

Sweden: 1000 Ljubljana, Ajdovščina 4/8; tel. (1) 3000270; fax (1) 3000271; Ambassador JOHN-CHRISTER AHLANDER.

Switzerland: 1000 Ljubljana, Republike trg 3/VI; tel. (1) 2008640; fax (1) 2008669; Ambassador PAUL KOLLER.

Turkey: 1000 Ljubljana, Livarska 4; tel. (1) 4368149; fax (1) 4368148; e-mail vrtucije@siol.net; Ambassador HALIL AKINCI.

United Kingdom: 1000 Ljubljana, Republike trg 3/IV; tel. (1) 2003910; fax (1) 4250174; e-mail info@british-embassy.si; internet www.british-embassy.si; Ambassador HUGH ROGER MORTIMER.

USA: 1000 Ljubljana, Presernova cesta 31; tel. (1) 2005500; fax (1) 2005555; e-mail Email@usembassy.si; internet www.usembassy.si; Ambassador JOHNNY YOUNG.

Judicial System

The Slovenian Constitution guarantees the independence of the judiciary.

The 44 district courts decide minor cases (criminal acts incurring a maximum sentence of three years' imprisonment, property disputes where the value of the disputed property is not more than SIT 2m., and certain other civil cases). The 11 regional courts act as courts of the first instance in all cases other than those for which the district courts have jurisdiction. Four regional courts act as courts of the second instance. There are, in addition, labour courts, which have jurisdiction in labour disputes, and social courts, which adjudicate in disputes over pensions, welfare allocations and other social benefits. A higher labour and social court has jurisdiction in the second instance. The Supreme Court is the highest authority for civil and criminal law. There is also a Constitutional Court, composed of nine judges, each elected for a single term of nine years, which determines, *inter alia*, the conformity of national legislation and all other regulations with the Constitution.

Constitutional Court of the Republic of Slovenia: 1000 Ljubljana, Beethovnova 10; tel. (1) 4776400; fax (1) 2510451; e-mail info@us-rs.si; internet www.us-rs.si; Pres. DRAGICA WEDAM-LUKIĆ.

Supreme Court: 1000 Ljubljana, Tavčarjeva 9; tel. (1) 3005310; fax (1) 3005318; e-mail mitja.deisinger@sodisce.si; internet www.sodisce.si; Pres. MITJA DEISINGER.

Office of the Public Prosecutor: 1511 Ljubljana, Dunajska 22; tel. (1) 2320396; fax (1) 4310381; e-mail sebastijan.rakovec@dt-rs.si; Public Prosecutor ZDENKA CERAR.

Office of the Public Attorney: 1000 Ljubljana, Cankarjeva 5; Public Attorney JOŽE GREGORIČ.

Religion

Most of the population are Christian, predominantly adherents of the Roman Catholic Church. The Archbishop of Ljubljana is the most senior Roman Catholic prelate in Slovenia. There is also a Slovene Old Catholic Church. There are few Protestant Christians, despite the importance of a Calvinist sect (the Church of Carniola) to the development of Slovene literature in the 16th century. There are some members of the Eastern Orthodox Church, some Muslims and a small Jewish community.

CHRISTIANITY

The Roman Catholic Church

The Roman Catholic Church in Slovenia comprises one archdiocese and two dioceses. At 31 December 2000 there were an estimated 1,620,968 adherents (equivalent to about 81.3% of the total population).

Bishops' Conference

Slovenska Škofovska Konferenca, 1000 Ljubljana, p.p. 121/III, Ciril Metodov trg 4; tel. (1) 2342600; fax (1) 2342612.

f. 1993; Pres. Most Rev. FRANC RODÉ (Archbishop of Ljubljana).

Archbishop of Ljubljana: Most Rev. FRANC RODÉ, 1001 Ljubljana, p.p. 1990, Ciril Metodov trg 4; tel. (1) 2342600; fax (1) 2314169; e-mail nadskofija.lubljana@rkc.si.

Old Catholic Church

Slovene Old Catholic Church: 1000 Ljubljana; Maribor, Vita Kraigherja 2; f. 1948; Bishop Rev. JOSIP KVOČIĆ.

The Protestant Church

Evangelical Lutheran Church of Slovenia: 9226 Moravske Toplice, 11 Levstikova; tel. (2) 5381323; fax (2) 5381324; e-mail evang.cerkev.si@siol.nt; f. 1561; 20,000 mems; Chair. GEZA ERNIŠA.

JUDAISM

Jewish Community of Slovenia: 1000 Ljubljana, Trzaska 2, POB 37; tel. and fax (1) 2521836; e-mail jss@siol.net; Pres. ANDREJ KOŽAR BECK.

The Press

The publications listed below are in Slovene, unless otherwise indicated.

PRINCIPAL DAILIES

Delo: 1509 Ljubljana, Dunajska 5; tel. (1) 4727402; fax (1) 4737406; e-mail webmaster@delo.si; internet www.delo.si; f. 1959; morning; Editor-in-Chief MITJA MERŠOL; circ. 93,781.

Dnevnik: 1510 Ljubljana, Kopitarjeva 2; tel. (1) 3082100; fax (1) 3082189; e-mail info@dnevnik.si; internet www.dnevnik.si; f. 1951; evening; independent; Man. Dir BRANKO BERGANT; Editor-in-Chief ZLATKO SETINC; circ. 63,000.

Slovenske novice: 1509 Ljubljana, Dunajska 5; tel. (1) 1737700; fax (1) 1737352; f. 1991; Editor-in-Chief MARJAN BAUER; Man. Editor TIT DOBERSEK; circ. 80,000.

Večer: 2000 Maribor, Svetozarevska 14; tel. (2) 2353500; fax (2) 2353368; e-mail desk@vecer.com; internet www.vecer.si; f. 1945; Man. Dir BOŽO ZORKO; Editor-in-Chief MILAN PREDAN; circ. 70,000.

PERIODICALS

Antena: 1000 Ljubljana, Slovenska 15; tel. (1) 1253418; fax (1) 1253367; f. 1965; weekly; youth magazine concerned with popular culture; Editor-in-Chief JASMIN PETAN MALACHOVSKY; circ. 20,000.

Ars Vivendi: 1000 Ljubljana, Poljanska 6; tel. and fax (1) 317058; f. 1987; quarterly; visual arts and design; publ. in Slovene and English; Editor-in-Chief SONJA TOMAŽIČ; circ. 10,000.

Avto magazin: 1000 Ljubljana, Dunajska 5; tel. (1) 1738251; fax (1) 1738220; f. 1967; fortnightly; cars, motorcycles and sports; Editor BOŠTJAN JEVŠEK; circ. 16,000.

Delavska enotnost: 1000 Ljubljana, Dalmatinova 4; tel. (1) 1310033; fax (1) 1313942; f. 1942; weekly; trade union issues; Dir and Editor-in-Chief MARJAN HORVAT; circ. 16,000.

Dolenjski List: 8000 Novo Mesto, Glavni trg 24; tel. (7) 3323606; fax (7) 3322898; f. 1950; weekly; general and local information; Editor-in-Chief MARJAN LEGAN; circ. 24,000.

Družina: 1000 Ljubljana, Krekov trg 1; tel. (1) 1316202; fax (1) 1316152; e-mail druzina@siol.net; f. 1952; Christian; Editor-in-Chief JANEZ GRIL; circ. 70,000.

Finance: 1509 Ljubljana, Dunajska 5; tel. (1) 1330137; fax (1) 1312223; internet www.finance-on.net; f. 1992; 2 a week; Editor-in-Chief JOŽE PETROVČIČ; circ. 8,500.

Flaneur: 1000 Ljubljana, Šaranovičeva 12; f. 1992; bi-monthly; English; politics, economy, culture and leisure; Editor-in-Chief TADEJ ČATER; circ. 2,500.

Gea: 1536 Ljubljana, Slovenska 29; tel. (1) 2413230; fax (1) 1252836; e-mail gea@mkz-lj.si; internet www.mkz-lj.si; f. 1990; monthly; popular science; Editor-in-Chief JANA LESKOVEC; circ. 23,000.

Gorenjski glas: 4000 Kranj, Zoisova ul. 1; tel. (4) 2014200; fax (4) 2014213; f. 1947; 2 a week; general and regional information; Editor-in-Chief MARIJA VOLEJAK; circ. 23,300.

Gospodarski vestnik: 1509 Ljubljana, Dunajska 5; tel. (1) 3091700; fax (1) 3091705; e-mail gvrevija@gvestnik.si; internet www.gvestnik.si; f. 1952; weekly; business; Editor-in-Chief JOŽE PETROVČIČ; circ. 9,500.

Jana: 1509 Ljubljana, Dunajska 5; tel. (1) 319260; fax (1) 1334320; f. 1972; weekly; women's interest; Editor-in-Chief BERNARDA JEKLIN; circ. 62,000.

Kaj: 62000 Maribor, Svetozarevska 14; tel. (2) 26951; fax (2) 227736; f. 1984; weekly; popular; Editor-in-Chief MILAN PREDAN; circ. 16,500.

Kmečki glas: 1000 Ljubljana, p.p. 47, Železna 14; tel. (1) 1735350; fax (1) 1735376; weekly; general and agricultural news; Dir BORIS DOLNIČAR; circ. 38,000.

Lipov List: 1000 Ljubljana, Miklosičeva 38/6; tel. (1) 312087; fax (1) 1332338; e-mail tzs@siol.net; monthly; Editor-in-Chief MARJETICA NOVAK.

Mag: 1000 Ljubljana, Njegoševa 14; tel. (1) 319480; fax (1) 1329158; f. 1995; weekly; news and politics; Editor-in-Chief DANILO SLIVNIK.

Manager: 1000 Ljubljana, Dunajska 5; tel. (1) 3091990; fax (1) 3091705; internet www.gvrevija.com/manager; f. 1990; monthly; business management; Editor-in-Chief JOŽE PETROVČIČ; circ. 3,000.

Mladina: 1000 Ljubljana, Resljeva 16; tel. (1) 1328175; fax (1) 1331329; f. 1942; weekly; news magazine; Editor-in-Chief JANI SEVER; circ. 30,000.

Moj mikro: 1509 Ljubljana, Dunajska 5; tel. (1) 4738261; fax (1) 4738109; e-mail marjan.kodelja@delo-revije.si; internet www .delo-revije.si; monthly; personal computers; Editor-in-Chief MARJAN KODELJA.

Muska: 1000 Ljubljana, Kersnikova 4; tel. (1) 1317039; fax (1) 322570; e-mail kaja.sivic@kiss.uni_lj.si; monthly; music; Editor-in-Chief KAJA SIVIČ.

Naš Caš (Our Time): 63320 Velenje, Foltova 10; tel. (3) 855450; fax (3) 851990; f. 1956; weekly; general and regional information; Editor-in-Chief STANE VOVK; circ. 6,250.

Nedeljski Dnevnik: 1000 Ljubljana, Kopitarieva 2; tel. (1) 1325261; fax (1) 1321020; f. 1961; weekly; popular; Editor-in-Chief ZLATKO ŠETINC; circ. 171,000.

Novi Tednik (New Weekly): 3000 Celje, Prešernova 19; tel. (3) 442500; fax (3) 441032; f. 1945; weekly; general and local information; Editor-in-Chief BRANE STAMEJČIĆ; circ. 16,980.

Obrtnik: 1000 Ljubljana, Celovška 71; tel. (1) 5830507; fax (1) 5193496; e-mail revija.obrtnik@ozs.si; internet www.ozs.si; f. 1971; monthly; small businesses; Editor-in-Chief MIRAN JAREC; circ. 60,000.

Pavliha: 1000 Ljubljana, Slovenska 15; tel. (1) 221661; monthly; satire; Editor-in-Chief JOZE PETELIN.

PIL: 1000 Ljubljana, Nazorjeva 1; tel. (1) 2413220; fax (1) 4252836; e-mail pil@mkz-lj.si; internet www.mkz-lj.si; teenagers' interest; Editor-in-Chief YANA ZIZKELBACH; circ. 30,000.

Podjetnik: 1000 Ljubljana, Dunajska 51; tel. (1) 1330102; fax (1) 1330450; f. 1992; monthly; business and management; Editor-in-Chief JOŽE VILFAN; circ. 8,500.

Primorske Novice: 6000 Koper, OF ul. 12; tel. (5) 6648100; fax (5) 6272350; e-mail editors@prim-nov.si; internet www.prim-nov.si; f. 1947; 3 a week; general and regional information; Editor-in-Chief ROBERT MECILOŠEK; circ. 28,000.

Profit: 1000 Ljubljana, Dunajska 7; tel. (1) 4304310; fax (1) 2318940; e-mail profit.uredmistvo@sid.net; 2 a month; business; Editor-in-Chief JOŽE SIMČIČ.

Rodna Gruda: 1000 Ljubljana, Cankarjeva 1/II; tel. (1) 2410286; fax (1) 1251673; e-mail rodna.gruda@zdruzenje-sim.si; internet www.zdruzenje-sim.si; f. 1951; monthly; ethnic issues and news; Editor-in-Chief JOŽE PREŠEREN; circ. 4,000.

7D: 2000 Maribor, Svetozarevska 14; tel. (2) 224221; fax (2) 211264; f. 1972; weekly; general, travel; Man. Dir BOŽO ZORKA; Editor-in-Chief MILAN PREDAN; circ. 20,000.

Slovenia Weekly: 1000 Ljubljana, Hradeckega 38; tel. (1) 4261412; fax (1) 5402027; e-mail marketing@vitrum.si; internet weekly .vitrum.si; f. 1994; weekly; politics and business; Editor-in-Chief TOMAŽ GERDINA; circ. 3,000.

Slovenian Business Report: 1000 Ljubljana, Dunajska 5; tel. (1) 3091924; fax (1) 3091705; f. 1991; monthly; in English; economic affairs; Editor-in-Chief JOŽE PETROVČIĆ; circ. 4,000.

Slovenija: 1000 Ljubljana, Cankarjeva 1; tel. (1) 210716; fax (1) 1251673; e-mail sim@siol.net; internet www.zdruzenje.si; f. 1987; quarterly; in English; ethnic issues and news; Man. Editor JOŽE PREŠEREN; circ. 3,500.

Slovenske brazde: 1000 Ljubljana, Zarnikova 3; tel. (1) 301891; fax (1) 301871; f. 1990; weekly; Man. Editor NACE POTOCNIK.

Stop: 1000 Ljubljana, Dunajska 5; tel. (1) 319190; fax (1) 1330403; f. 1967; weekly; leisure, film, theatre, pop music, radio and television programmes; Editor IGOR SAVIČ; circ. 44,600.

Tednik: 2250 Ptuj, Raičeva 6; tel. (2) 7493410; fax (2) 7493435; e-mail tednik@radio-tednik.si; internet www.radio-tednik.si; f. 1948; weekly; politics, local information; Editor-in-Chief JOŽE ŠMIGOC; circ. 12,000.

Tretji Dan (Third Day): 1000 Ljubljana, Jurčičev trg 2; tel. (1) 1263071; fax (1) 223864; weekly; Editor-in-Chief Dr TONE JAMNIK.

Tribuna: 1000 Ljubljana, Kersnikova 4; tel. (1) 319496; fax (1) 319448; 3 a week; student newspaper; Editor-in-Chief BOJAN KORENINI.

Vestnik Murska Sobota: 9000 Murska Sobota, Arhitekta Novaka ul. 13; tel. (2) 5311960; fax (2) 5321175; e-mail vestnik@eunet.si; internet www.p-inf.si; f. 1949; weekly; popular; Editor-in-Chief JANEZ VOTEK; circ. 20,000.

Zdravje (Health): 1000 Ljubljana, Cigaletova 5; tel. (1) 2319360; e-mail gasamil@k2.net; monthly; Editor-in-Chief GASA MILIVOJEVIČ.

PRESS AGENCIES

Morel: 1000 Ljubljana, Reboljeva 13, statti Parmova 41-45; tel. (1) 4361222; fax (1) 4361223; e-mail morel@si21.com; internet www .morel.si; f. 1993; Dir and Chief Editor EMIL LUKANČIČ-MORI.

Slovenska Tiskovna Agencija (STA): 1000 Ljubljana, Cankarjeva 5, p.p. 145; tel. (1) 2410100; fax (1) 4266050; e-mail desk@sta.si; internet www.sta.si; f. 1991; Dir-Gen. IGOR VEZOVNIK; Editor-in-Chief TADEJA ŠERGAN.

Publishers

Cankarjeva Založba: 1512 Ljubljana, Kopitarjeva 2; tel. (1) 1323144; fax (1) 318782; e-mail import.books@cankarjeva-z.si; internet www.cankarjeva-z.si; f. 1945; philosophy, science and popular science; dictionaries and reference books; Slovenian and translated literature; import and export; international co-productions; Dir-Gen. JOŽE KORINŠEK.

DZS d.d.: 1000 Ljubljana, Mali trg 6; tel. (1) 1252040; fax (1) 1254329; e-mail irenajunkar@dzs.si; f. 1945; Slovenian textbooks, manuals, world classics, natural sciences, art books, encyclopaedias, dictionaries, educational CD-ROMS; import and export; Mans IRENA JUNKAR, MIMA ŠUŠTARŠIČ HVASTIJA.

Mladinska Knjiga Založba d.d.: 1000 Ljubljana, Slovenska 29; tel. (1) 2413288; fax (1) 4252294; e-mail intsales@mkz-lj.si; f. 1945; books for youth and children, including general, fiction, science, travel and school books, language courses, magazines and videos; international co-operation; Dir MILAN MATOS.

Slovenské Matica: 1000 Ljubljana, Kongresni trg 8; tel. and fax (1) 2514200; e-mail drago.jancar@siol.net; f. 1864; poetry, science, philosophy; Pres. Prof. Dr JOŽA MAHNIČ.

Založba Obzorja: 2000 Maribor, Partizanska 3–5; tel. (2) 25681; fax (2) 225875; f. 1950; popular science, general literature, periodicals, etc. Man. Dir PAVLA PEČE.

Zdo Založba Lipa Koper: 66000 Koper, Muzejski trg 7; tel. (5) 23291; fax (5) 23293; fiction; Dir Prof. JOŽE A. HOČEVAR.

Broadcasting and Communications

TELECOMMUNICATIONS

Telecommunications Agency (Agencija za telekomunikacije, radiodifuzijo in pošto Republike Slovenije—ATRP): 1000 Ljubljana, Kotnikova 19A; tel. (1) 4734900; fax (1) 4328036; e-mail urst.box@gov .si; internet www.atrp.si; Dir JOŽE KLEŠNIK (acting).

MOBITEL: 1537 Ljubljana, Vilharjeva 23; tel. (1) 4722200; fax (1) 4722950; e-mail ma@mobitel.si; internet www.mobitel.si; f. 1991; Dir ANTON MAJZELJ; 700 employees.

SI.MOBIL d.d.: 1000 Ljubljana, Šmartinska cesta 134B; tel. (1) 5440000; fax (1) 5440099; e-mail info@simobil.si; internet www .simobil.com; f. 1999; shares acquired by Mobilkom Austria in Feb. 2001; Chair. of Bd BOJAN DREMELJ.

Telekom Slovenije: 1000 Ljubljana, Cigaletova 15; tel. (1) 4334111; fax (1) 4322013; internet www.telekom.si; f. 1949; scheduled for privatization; Chief Exec. (acting) and Chair. of Bd PETER GRAŠEK; 3,350 employees.

BROADCASTING

Regulatory Authority

Slovenian Broadcasting Council: 1000 Ljubljana, Parmova 53; tel. (1) 1363596; fax (1) 1363595; e-mail info.srdf@srd.gov.si; internet www.sigov.si/srd; f. 1994; nine mems; protects independence of radio and television programmes; supervises the activities of broadcasting and cable operators.

Radio

In 1996 49 regional and local radio stations were operating in Slovenia.

Radiotelevizija Slovenija (RTV Slo): 1550 Ljubljana, Kolodvorska 2; tel. (1) 4752154; fax (1) 4752150; e-mail webmaster@rtvslo.si; internet www.rtvslo.si/html/radio-slo; f. 1928; 3 radio programmes nationally; broadcasts in Slovene, Hungarian and Italian; Gen. Man. ALEKS ŠTAKUL.

Radio Koper Capodistria: 6000 Koper, OF ul. 15; tel. (5) 485483; fax (5) 485488; e-mail leon.horvatic@rtvslo.si; internet www.rtvslo.si; Editor LEON HORVATIČ.

Radio Maribor: 2000 Maribor, Ilichova 33; tel. (2) 4299132; fax (2) 4299215; e-mail srecko.trglec@rtvslo.si; internet www.rtvslo.si; Editor SREČKO TRGLEC.

Radio Murski val: 9000 Murska Sobota, Arhitekta Novaka ul. 13; tel. (2) 5311960; fax (2) 5321175; e-mail radio-murski.val@siol.net; internet www.p-inf.si; f. 1958; Editor-in-Chief MARJAN DORA.

Radio Ptuj: 2250 Ptuj, Raiceva 6; tel. (2) 7493410; fax (2) 7493435; e-mail nabiralnik@radio-tednik.si; internet www.radio-teknik.si.

Television

In 1996 42 regional television stations were operating as part of Televizija Slovenia. Three private television stations and more than 20 local cable television stations were also broadcasting in Slovenia.

Radiotelevizija Slovenija (RTV Slo): 1550 Ljubljana, Kolodvorska 2; tel. (1) 4752154; fax (1) 4752150; e-mail webmaster@rtvslo.si; internet www.rtvslo.si/html/radio-slo; f. 1928; 2 television programmes (TV1 and TV2) nationally; broadcasts in Slovene, Hungarian and Italian; Gen. Man. ALEKS ŠTAKUL.

Kanal A: 1000 Ljubljana, Tivolska 50; tel. (1) 1334133; fax (1) 1334222; Pres. DOUGLAS FULTON.

Pop TV: 1000 Ljubljana, Kranjčeva 26; tel. (1) 1893200; fax (1) 1612222; Editor TOMAŽ PEROVIČ.

TV 3: 1210 Ljubljana, Štula 23; tel. (1) 1831200; fax (1) 1521512; Editor-in-Chief MLADEN SICHROVSKY.

Finance

BANKS

(cap. = capital; res = reserves; dep. = deposits; m. = million; amounts in Slovene tolars unless otherwise stated; brs = branches)

The Slovenian banking sector is currently undergoing a rationalization process, involving a conversion to commercial banking (new regulations took effect in January 1995) and the merging of smaller banks.

National Bank

Banka Slovenije (Bank of Slovenia): 1505 Ljubljana, Slovenska 35; tel. (1) 4719000; fax (1) 2515516; e-mail bsl@bsi.si; internet www.bsi.si; formerly National Bank of Slovenia, as part of the Yugoslav banking system; assumed central bank functions in 1991; bank of issue since Oct. 1991; res 199,911.7m., dep. 1,202,090.6m., total assets 1,594,811.6m. (Dec. 2002); Gov. MITJA GASPARI.

Selected Banks

Abanka d.d. Ljubljana (Abanka Joint-Stock Company): 1517 Ljubljana, Slovenska 58, POB 368; tel. (1) 1718100; fax (1) 4325165; e-mail info@abanka.si; internet www.abanka.si; f. 1955 as Ljubljana Branch of Yugoslav Bank for Foreign Trade, adopted current name 1989; cap. 5,156.7m., res 7,977.7m., dep. 133,646.0m. (Dec. 2000); Pres. and Chief Exec. ALJOŠA TOMAŽ; 32 brs.

Bank Austria Creditanstalt d.d. Ljubljana: 1000 Ljubljana, Smartinska 140; tel. (1) 5876600; fax (1) 5411860; e-mail info@si.bacai.com; internet www.ba-ca.si; f. 1991; cap. 3,101.4m., res 6,669.2m., dep. 79,057.6m. (Dec. 2000); Chair. JOACHIM REITMEIER.

Banka Celje d.d.: 3000 Celje, Vodnikova 2, POB 431; tel. (3) 5431000; fax (3) 5483511; e-mail info@banka-celje.si; internet www.banka-celje.si; cap. 6,131.9m., res 14,602.1m., dep. 134,946.8m. (Dec. 2000); Pres. NIKO KAČ; 16 brs.

Banka Koper d.d.: 6502 Koper, Pristaniška 14; tel. (5) 6651100; fax (5) 6397472; e-mail info@banka-koper.si; internet www.banka-koper.si; f. 1955; cap. 5,313.6m., res 13,999.6m., dep. 158,127.6m. (Dec. 2000); Man. Dir VOJKO ČOK; 9 brs.

Banka Vipa d.d.: POB 52, 5000 Nova Gorica, Erjavceva ul. 2; tel. (5) 3385000; fax (5) 3028506; e-mail int@banka-vipa.si; f. 1992; cap. 1,895.8m., res 3,289.4m., dep. 45,863.0m. (Dec. 2000); Chair. EGIDIJ BIRSA.

Factor Banka: 1000 Ljubljana, Železna cesta 16; tel. (1) 4311136; fax (1) 4328066; e-mail info@factorb.si; internet www.factorb.si; f. 1993; cap. 1,452.5m., res 384.6m., dep. 17,182.4m. (Dec. 2000); Chair. BORIS PESJAK.

Gorenjska Banka d.d. Kranj: 4000 Kranj, Bleiweisova cesta 1, POB 147; tel. (4) 2084000; fax (4) 2021718; e-mail info@gbkr.si; internet www.gbkr.si; f. 1955; cap. 3,779.2m., res 21,347.8m., dep. 99,560.6m. (Dec. 2000); Man. Dir ZLATKO KAVČIČ; 5 brs.

Nova Kreditna Banka Maribor d.d. (NKBM): 2505 Maribor, Vita Kraigherja 4; tel. (2) 2292290; fax (2) 2524333; e-mail info@nkbm.si; internet www.nkbm.si; f. 1955; adopted present name 1994; scheduled for partial privatization; cap. 5,600m., res 29,699m., dep. 285,443m. (Dec. 2000); Pres. and Chief Exec. Dr JOŽE GLOGOVŠEK; 81 brs and sub-brs.

Nova Ljubljanska Banka d.d. (NLB): 1520 Ljubljana, Republike trg 2; tel. (1) 4250155; fax (1) 4250331; e-mail info@nlb.si; internet www.nlb.si; f. 1994; commercial, investment and savings bank; 34% of shares divested to KBC Bank NV (Belgium) in May 2002; cap. 13,800m., res 25,790m., dep. 794,574m. (Dec. 2000); Pres. and Chief Exec. MARKO VOLJC; 16 brs.

Raiffeisen Krekova Banka d.d.: 2000 Maribor, Slomškov trg 18; tel. (2) 2293100; fax (2) 223502; e-mail info@r-kb.si; internet www.r-kb.si; f. 1992; cap. 2,058.0m., res 4,233.4m., dep. 55,602.8m. (Dec. 2000); Chair. ALEŠ ŽAJDELA; 14 brs.

SKB Banka d.d.: 1000 Ljubljana, Ajdovščina 4; tel. (1) 4715918; fax (1) 4715757; e-mail info@skb.si; internet www.skb.si; f. 1978; shares acquired by Société Générale in May 2001; cap. 16,499.3m., res 6,509.1m., dep. 213,298.7m. (Dec. 2000); Pres. and Chief Exec. JEAN-LOUIS MATTEI.

Slovenska Zadružna Kmetijska Banka d.d. Ljubljana: 1000 Ljubljana, Kolodvorska 9; tel. (1) 4727100; fax (1) 4727411; e-mail info@szkbanka.si; internet www.szkbanka.si; f. 1990; cap. 1,759.2m., res 4,379.0m., dep. 39,321.9m. (Dec. 2000); Man. Dir MILAN KNEŽEVIČ; 5 brs.

STOCK EXCHANGE

Ljubljana Stock Exchange d.d.: 1000 Ljubljana, Slovenska 56; tel. (1) 4710211; fax (1) 4710213; e-mail info@ljse.si; internet www.ljse.si; f. 1989; operative 1990; Pres. and Chief Exec. Dr DRAŠKO VESELINOVIČ.

INSURANCE

Adriatic Insurance Co d.d.: 6503 Koper, Ljubljanska C.3A; tel. (5) 443100; fax (5) 443482; e-mail info@adriatic.si; internet www.adriatic.si; f. 1990.

Grawe Zavarovalnica d.d.: 2000 Maribor, Gregorčičeva 39; tel. (2) 2285500; fax (2) 2285526; e-mail prima@prima.si.

Maribor Insurance Co d.d.: 2507 Maribor, Cankarjeva 3; tel. (2) 224111.

Merkur Insurance Co d.d.: 1000 Ljubljana, Dunajska 58; tel. (1) 3005450; fax (1) 4361092; e-mail info@merkur-zav.si; internet www.merkur-zav.si; f. 1992; Gen. Man. DENIS STROLIGO; Marketing Man. ANDREJ OSTERC; Financial Man. MOJCA ANDROJNA.

Triglav Insurance Co d.d.: 1000 Ljubljana, Miklošičeva 19; tel. (1) 1747200.

Trade and Industry

GOVERNMENT AGENCY

Agency of the Republic of Slovenia for Restructuring and Privatization: 1000 Ljubljana, Kotnikova 28; tel. (1) 1316030; fax (1) 1316011; e-mail webmaster@arspip.si; internet www.arspip.si; Dir MIRA PUC.

DEVELOPMENT ORGANIZATION

Development Corporation of Slovenia: 1000 Ljubljana, Dunajska 160; tel. (1) 1894800; fax (1) 1894819; e-mail jana.bogdanovski@srd.si; Pres. BOGDAN TOPIČ; Chair. MARJAN REKAR.

CHAMBERS OF COMMERCE

Chamber of Commerce and Industry of Slovenia: 1504 Ljubljana, Dimičeva 13; tel. (1) 5898313; fax (1) 5898317; e-mail irma.butina@gzs.si; internet www.gzs.si; Pres. MARTA TURK; Sec.-Gen. IRMA BUTINA; 55,000 mems.

Slovene Businessmen's Association: 1504 Ljubljana, Dimičeva 13; tel. (1) 1898312; fax (1) 1898317; e-mail romana.tomc@gzs.si; internet www.gzs.si; f. 1994 as autonomous part of Chamber of Economy of Slovenia; Pres. MARTA TURK; Sec.-Gen. ROMANA TOMC LAMPIČ; 48,000 mems.

Chamber of Small Businesses of Slovenia: 1000 Ljubljana, Celovška 71; tel. (1) 1593241; fax (1) 559270; Pres. MIHA GRAH; Sec. ANTON FILIPIČ; 50,000 mems.

UTILITIES

Electricity

Elektro-Slovenija d.o.o. (ELES): 1000 Ljubljana, Hajdrihova 2; tel. (1) 1301440; fax (1) 1250333; e-mail info@eles.si; internet www .eles.si; national electricity distributor; Chief Exec. VEKOSLAV KOROŠEC; 530 employees.

Nuklearna Elektrarna p.o.: 8270 Krško, Vrbina 12; tel. (608) 21621; fax (608) 21528; f. 1974; jtly owned by Slovenia and Croatia, pending privatization; production and distribution of electricity; Man. Dir STANE ROŽMAN; 610 employees.

Gas

GEO PLIN d.o.o.: 1000 Ljubljana, Ljubljanska brigade 11; tel. (1) 5820600; fax (1) 5820601; e-mail info@geoplin.si; internet www .geoplin.si; f. 1975; nat. gas co; Gen. Man. JANEZ MOŽINA; 145 employees.

TRADE UNIONS

The Association of Independent Trade Unions of Slovenia: 1000 Ljubljana, Dalmatinova 4; tel. (1) 317983; fax (1) 318294; Pres. DUŠAN SEMOLIČ.

Independence—Confederation of New Trade Unions of Slovenia: 1000 Ljubljana, Linhartova 13; tel. (1) 1329141; fax (1) 302868; Pres. FRANCE TOMŠIČ.

Transport

RAILWAYS

The rail link between western Europe and Greece, Turkey and the Near and Middle East runs through Slovenia. In 1999 there were 1,201 km of railway lines in Slovenia, of which 499 km were electrified.

Slovenske Železnice (SŽ) (Slovenian Railways): 1506 Ljubljana, Kolodvorska 11; tel. (1) 2912100; fax (1) 2914813; e-mail info@ slo-zeleznice.si; internet www.slo-zeleznice.si; Chief Exec. BLAŽ MIKLAVČIČ.

ROADS

In 2000 the country had 20,177 km of roads, of which 427 km were motorways, 1,112 km were highways, main or national roads and 4,733 km were secondary or regional roads. An 84-km motorway links Ljubljana, Postojna and Sežana with the coastal region in the south-west, and a 25-km motorway connects the capital with Kranj and the Gorenjska region in the north-east. A motorway construction programme was approved by the Government in January 1998. The plan envisaged the completion of 519 km of motorway sections by 2004.

Directorate of the Republic of Slovenia for Roads: Ministry of Transport, 1535 Ljubljana, Langusova ul. 4; tel. (1) 1788000; fax (1) 1788139; e-mail drsc-info@gov.si.

SHIPPING

Slovenia's principal international trading port, at Koper, handles some 6m. tons of freight annually, and has terminals for general, bulk and liquid cargo, containers and 'roll on, roll off' traffic, as well as warehousing facilities. The port is a duty-free zone. There are also major ports at Portorož and Izola.

Luka Koper d.d.: 6501 Koper, Vojkovo nabrežje 38; tel. (5) 6656100; fax (5) 6395020; e-mail portkoper@luka-kp.si; internet www.luka-kp.si; f. 1957; Chief Exec. BRUNO KORELIČ.

Principal Shipping Company

Splošna Plovba Ltd: 6320 Portorož, Obala 55, POB 60; tel. (5) 6766000; fax (5) 6766130; e-mail plovba@5-plovba.si; transport of all types of cargo; regular liner service; Man. Dir ALDO KREJAČIČ.

CIVIL AVIATION

There are three international airports in Slovenia, at Brnik (Ljubljana), Maribor and Portorož.

Adria Airways: 1000 Ljubljana, Kuzmičeva 7; tel. (1) 3691000; fax (1) 4369233; e-mail info@adria.si; internet www.adria.si; f. 1961; operates international scheduled services to destinations in Europe and the Near and Middle East; Pres. BRANKO LUCOVNIK.

Tourism

Slovenia offers a variety of tourist attractions, including Mediterranean beaches to the west, the Alps to the north and the 'karst' limestone regions, with more than 6,000 caves. The number of foreign tourist arrivals has increased steadily from the mid-1990s, reaching 1,218,700 in 2001. Tourism receipts totalled US $961m. in 2000.

Slovenian Tourist Board: 1000 Ljubljana, Dunajska 156; tel. (1) 5891840; fax (1) 5891841; e-mail info@slovenia-tourism.si; internet www.slovenia-tourism.si; Exec. Man. BOJAN MEDEN.

SOLOMON ISLANDS

Introductory Survey

Location, Climate, Language, Religion, Flag, Capital

Solomon Islands is a scattered Melanesian archipelago in the south-western Pacific Ocean, east of Papua New Guinea. The country includes most of the Solomon Islands (those to the north-west being part of Papua New Guinea), Ontong Java Islands (Lord Howe Atoll), Rennell Island and the Santa Cruz Islands, about 500 km (300 miles) to the east. The climate is equatorial, with small seasonal variations, governed by the trade winds. In Honiara the average temperature is about 27°C (81°F) and the average annual rainfall about 2,160 mm (85 ins). The official language is standard English, although pidgin English is more widely used and understood. More than 80 different local languages exist, and no vernacular is common to the whole country. More than 95% of the inhabitants profess Christianity, and most of the remainder follow traditional beliefs. The national flag (proportions 1 by 2) comprises two triangles, one of blue (with its base at the hoist and its apex in the upper fly) and one of dark green (with its base in the fly and its apex in the lower hoist), separated by a narrow yellow diagonal stripe (from lower hoist to upper fly), with five white five-pointed stars (arranged to form a diagonal cross) in the upper hoist. The capital is Honiara, on the island of Guadalcanal.

Recent History

The northern Solomon Islands became a German protectorate in 1885 and the southern Solomons a British protectorate in 1893. Rennell Island and the Santa Cruz Islands were added to the British protectorate in 1898 and 1899. Germany ceded most of the northern Solomons and Ontong Java Islands to the United Kingdom between 1898 and 1900. The whole territory, known as the British Solomon Islands Protectorate, was placed under the jurisdiction of the Western Pacific High Commission (WPHC), with its headquarters in Fiji.

The Solomon Islands were invaded by Japan in 1942, but, after a fierce battle on Guadalcanal, most of the islands were recaptured by US forces in 1943. After the Second World War the protectorate's capital was moved from Tulagi Island to Honiara. In January 1953 the headquarters of the WPHC also moved to Honiara. Meanwhile, elected local councils were established on most of the islands, and by 1966 almost the whole territory was covered by such councils.

Under a new Constitution, introduced in October 1960, a Legislative Council and an Executive Council were established for the protectorate's central administration. Initially, all members of both bodies were appointed, but from 1964 the Legislative Council included elected members, and the elective element was gradually increased. Another Constitution, introduced in March 1970, established a single Governing Council of 17 elected members, three ex-officio members and (until the end of 1971) up to six public service members. A new Governing Council of 24 directly elected members was formed in 1973, when a ministerial system was introduced.

A further new Constitution, adopted in April 1974, instituted a single Legislative Assembly, containing 24 members who chose a Chief Minister with the right to appoint his own Council of Ministers. A new office of Governor of the Protectorate was also created, to assume almost all of the functions previously exercised in the territory by the High Commissioner for the Western Pacific. Solomon Mamaloni, leader of the newly-founded People's Progressive Party (PPP), was appointed the first Chief Minister in August 1974. The territory was officially renamed the Solomon Islands in June 1975, although it retained protectorate status.

In January 1976 the Solomon Islands received internal self-government, with the Chief Minister presiding over the Council of Ministers in place of the Governor. In June elections were held for an enlarged Legislative Assembly, and in July the Assembly elected one of its new members, Peter Kenilorea, to the position of Chief Minister. Solomon Islands (as it was restyled) became an independent state, within the Commonwealth, on 7 July 1978. The Legislative Assembly became the National Parliament and designated Kenilorea the first Prime Minister. The main political issue confronting the new nation was the proposed decentralization of authority to the regions, support for which was particularly strong in the Western District, the most commercially developed part of the country. The first general election since independence took place in August 1980. Independent candidates won more seats than any of the three parties. Parliament again elected Kenilorea Prime Minister by an overwhelming majority. In August 1981, however, Parliament approved a motion expressing 'no confidence' in Kenilorea, and chose Mamaloni, who now led the People's Alliance Party (PAP) following the merger of the PPP with the Rural Alliance Party in 1979, to succeed him as Prime Minister.

After legislative elections in October 1984, Sir Peter Kenilorea (as he had become) was again elected as Prime Minister. The new Government consisted of a coalition of nine members of Kenilorea's Solomon Islands United Party (SIUPA), three members of the newly formed Solomone Ano Sagufenua (SAS) party and three independents. The five provincial ministries, established by Mamaloni, were abolished, in accordance with Kenilorea's declared policy of restoring to central government control some of the powers held by the provincial governments.

In October 1985 a new political party, which sought a resolution of ongoing land disputes, the Nationalist Front for Progress (NFP), was formed, under the leadership of Andrew Nori. The SAS subsequently withdrew from the coalition, and Kenilorea formed a new Cabinet, comprising nine members of the SIUPA, three of the NFP and three independents. Kenilorea resigned following the approval of a motion of 'no confidence' (two others having previously been defeated); in December Ezekiel Alebua, the former Deputy Prime Minister assumed the premiership.

A report by a specially-commissioned constitutional review committee, chaired by Mamaloni, was published in March 1988, and proposed that Solomon Islands become a federal republic within the Commonwealth, and that the President of the Republic be a native of the territory. In January 1989 the PAP announced that Solomon Islands would be declared a republic if the party won the next general election, scheduled to take place in February. At the election the PAP won 11 of the 38 seats, the largest representation obtained by any party, while Alebua's party, the United Party, won only four seats. In March Mamaloni was elected Prime Minister. His Cabinet included the former Governor-General of Solomon Islands, Sir Baddeley Devesi, and was described as the first since independence to comprise the members of a single party.

In October 1990 Mamaloni resigned as leader of the PAP, one week before Parliament was due to vote on another motion of 'no confidence' in his premiership, declaring that he would remain as an independent Prime Minister. He dismissed five members of the Cabinet, replacing them with four members of the opposition and a PAP back-bencher. The Prime Minister defied persistent demands for his resignation by a majority of the members of Parliament. The remaining 10 ministers of the PAP were expelled from the party in February 1991, following their refusal to resign from their posts in the interests of party unity. Later that year, as a result of continuing economic decline, the Solomon Islands Council of Trade Unions issued an ultimatum demanding Mamaloni's resignation.

At elections to the recently-enlarged National Parliament in May 1993 the Group for National Unity and Reconciliation (GNUR), led by Mamaloni, won 21 of the 47 seats. However, a newly-formed coalition of opposition parties and independents, the National Coalition Partners (NCP), was successful in electing an independent member, Francis Billy Hilly, to the premiership in June. Hilly defeated Mamaloni by a single vote.

In October 1994 a constitutional crisis arose, following attempts by the Governor-General, Moses (later Sir Moses) Pitakaka, to dismiss Hilly on the grounds that he no longer held a parliamentary majority. Hilly remained in office, however, with the support of a High Court ruling, and confusion intensified when Pitakaka appointed the opposition leader, Mamaloni, to the position of Prime Minister. Hilly finally resigned on 31 October, and the post was declared vacant. In a parliamentary election to the premiership on 8 November, Mamaloni defeated the former Governor-General, Devesi, by 29 votes to 18.

In late 1995 and early 1996 Mamaloni's Government suffered a series of allegations of corruption and misconduct, particularly in relation to allegations that seven ministers had received payments from foreign logging companies between 1993 and 1995, although in February 1996 all seven were acquitted.

Controversy arose in July 1996 when it was reported that members of the National Parliament had begun to present gifts to their constituencies in preparation for the general election scheduled for 1997. This followed the reinstatement of the controversial Constituency Development Fund, which entitled each member to US $66,000, and which had been widely used by members at the previous general election to secure re-election by purchasing gifts for voters. In September the regional trades union organization, SPOCTU, cited the prevalence of corruption as the greatest obstacle to the islands' development, and stated that, in consequence, investors and aid donors would remain reluctant to make financial commitments to Solomon Islands.

In early August 1996 the National Parliament approved legislation to reform the provincial government system, which the Government claimed was inefficient and costly to maintain. Under the new system, the legislative and administrative powers of the nine provincial governments were to be transferred to 75 area assemblies and councils, with financial control vested wholly in the central Government. In February 1997, however, the legislation, which had been vehemently opposed by the larger provinces, was declared invalid by the High Court.

In May 1997 Mamaloni announced his intention to hold an early general election, following which he would resign as leader of the GNUR. Meanwhile, Alebua resigned from the leadership of the NCP, following accusations of misconduct, and was replaced by Edward Hunuehu. A general election took place on 6 August to a legislature that had recently been enlarged to 50 seats. The GNUR won 24 seats and a coalition grouping, Alliance for Change, secured the remainder. A period of intense political manoeuvring followed the election, in attempts to form a parliamentary majority. On 27 August Bartholomew Ulufa'alu was elected Prime Minister, defeating the newly-elected leader of the GNUR, Danny Philip, by 26 votes to 22. The new Government announced a programme of extensive structural reforms, including a rationalization of the public sector, a reduction in the number of ministerial portfolios (from 16 to 10), and measures to expand the private sector and to encourage greater participation of non-governmental organizations in the country's socio-economic development. The measures aimed to restore a degree of economic stability to Solomon Islands and to attract increased foreign investment. Legislation proposing that a politician seeking to change party allegiance would automatically lose his or her seat and be subject to a by-election was similarly intended to increase political stability.

In early 1998 a shipment of weapons (including a helicopter gunship, two military aircraft and smaller armaments) ordered by the previous administration for use in defending the maritime border with Papua New Guinea, arrived in the country from the USA. Ulufa'alu requested assistance from Australia in impounding the weapons, following widespread concern that unofficial organizations (particularly the Bougainville secessionist rebels within Papua New Guinea) might intercept the shipment. A dispute subsequently arose between Ulufa'alu and the former Prime Minister, Solomon Mamaloni, who had ordered the weapons. Mamaloni accused Ulufa'alu of treason for surrendering sovereign property to a foreign government, while the Prime Minister claimed that serious irregularities had occurred in procuring the arms, citing missing files and apparent overpayment.

In April 1998 Job Dudley Tausinga, whose Coalition for National Advancement (CNA) constituted the largest group outside the Government, was appointed Leader of the Opposition. Following the defection of six government members in July–August 1998, the opposition claimed to hold a parliamentary majority (with 25 of the 49 sitting members), and consequently sought to introduce a motion of 'no confidence' in the Prime Minister. A vote eventually took place on 18 September, after the failure of an attempt by the Government to declare the vote unlawful in the High Court, but was deemed to have been defeated as an equal number of votes were cast for and against the motion. Three opposition members subsequently defected to the Government, thus increasing its representation to 27 members. The climate of ongoing political instability prompted the Government to reiterate its proposal for

legislation to restrict the rights of elected members of the National Parliament to change party allegiance. In late September Solomon Mamaloni was elected Leader of the Opposition. Mamaloni died in January 2000 and was succeeded by Manasseh Sogavare, under whose leadership the CNA subsequently reverted to its original name of the PPP.

From April 1998 violent unrest in Honiara was attributed to ethnic tensions, mainly between the inhabitants of Guadalcanal and Malaita provinces. One underlying cause of the disturbances was the alienation of land by the Government since independence. Title to some land thus expropriated had been returned to Guadalcanal in late November, but this had not allayed a widespread feeling of resentment in the province at the financial burden imposed by hosting the capital. It was reported that a group styling itself the 'Guadalcanal Revolutionary Army' (GRA) had begun a campaign of militancy to force the Government to relocate the capital. The unrest intensified in early 1999, prompting the Government to establish a peace committee for the province. In mid-1999 talks between the Premier of Guadalcanal Province, Ezekiel Alebua, and the Solomon Islands Prime Minister failed to alleviate inter-ethnic tensions in the province. Riots broke out in Honiara, and some 80 Malaitan immigrants were evacuated following threats by armed GRA militants. Following Ulufa'alu's demands that peace be restored to the province before the implementation of any further measures, the GRA ordered an immediate halt to its activities. The Guadalcanal Provincial Assembly subsequently declared that it had accepted an initial payment of SI $500,000 in compensation for accommodating the national capital. A reconciliation ceremony was held between the two parties, during which Alebua appealed to the GRA to lay down its arms. However, the Malaitans subsequently demanded that they too be compensated, to the sum of US $600,000, for damage to their property by the GRA militants.

Following an increase in violence during which three Malaitan immigrants were reported to have been killed, and an estimated 10,000 forced to flee their villages, in mid-June 1999 a state of emergency was declared in Guadalcanal. A leader of the Isatambu Freedom Movement (IFM, formerly the GRA, and also known in 1999 as the Isatambu Freedom Fighters—IFF), Andrew Te'e, announced that the movement was willing to surrender in return for a full amnesty for the militants; however, this was rejected by Ulufa'alu. The former Prime Minister of Fiji, Sitiveni Rabuka, was appointed Commonwealth Special Envoy, following a request for assistance by Ulufa'alu. After meeting with the parties concerned, Rabuka announced on 28 June that a peace agreement had been reached, and a UN delegation and police officers from Fiji and Vanuatu were dispatched to help implement the peace plan. As part of the Honiara Peace Accord, the Solomon Islands Government agreed to pay SI $2.5m. into a Reconciliation Trust Fund, which was to be jointly administered by Guadalcanal Province and the national Government, to compensate the victims of the unrest. In return, the IFM agreed to disarm and to abandon their demands for a full amnesty for their supporters. In early August, however, Rabuka and the UN monitoring team returned to the province, after four members of the IFM were reported to have been shot by police near Honiara. On 12 August, however, a new peace agreement was signed by Rabuka, Alebua and others. The agreement, known as the Panatina Agreement, allowed for a reduction in police activity in the province followed by the eventual revocation of the state of emergency, in return for the surrender of weapons by the IFM. Despite the extension of the disarmament deadline into September, the state of emergency was ended in mid-October and, following negotiations in Honiara and the signing of an agreement in Fiji, a multinational peace-monitoring group from Fiji and Vanuatu, jointly funded by Australia and New Zealand, arrived in Guadalcanal late in October. In early December the peace-keeping force's mandate was extended into January 2000, and subsequently further extended by three months, following renewed outbreaks of violence and the emergence of a new guerrilla group, the Malaita Eagle Force (MEF), demanding US $40m. in compensation payments for loss of property incurred by Malaitans as a result of the conflict. Among their spokesmen was the former Minister of Finance, Andrew Nori.

Following further outbreaks of violence in the province that led to the death of four people, including two policemen, in February 2000, the Governor-General issued a decree outlawing membership of both the IFM and the MEF. Further clashes between the two rebel groups were reported in early March, and later that month riots took place in Honiara during which Malaitan immigrants stoned the headquarters of the Guadalcanal provincial government. Peace talks took place in May without members of the IFM and the MEF, both of which refused to attend in protest at the decision to outlaw them. However, a document, known as the Buala Peace Communiqué, was issued as the outcome of these talks on 5 May. Later that month the order that outlawed the groups was suspended. On 5 June members of the MEF, armed with weapons obtained in raids on police armouries, seized control of Honiara, placing Ulufa'alu under house arrest. The rebels demanded the immediate resignation of the Prime Minister, claiming that he, himself an ethnic Malaitan, had failed to compensate displaced Malaitans within the established deadline (allegedly set for that day) and also demanded the appointment of a new Commissioner of Police, the *de facto* head of national security. In renewed outbreaks of violence, up to 100 people were reportedly killed. The MEF, meanwhile, claimed to have gained control of the Police Force, 98% of the military-style weapons in the territory, broadcasting services and the telecommunications infrastructure. Ulufa'alu was released after four days, following an agreement between the MEF and government negotiators that a special parliamentary sitting would be convened during which Ulufa'alu would be subject to a motion of 'no confidence'. A 14-day cease-fire was called to guarantee the safe passage of a Commonwealth monitoring team. On 14 June Ulufa'alu resigned, one day before the scheduled 'no confidence' vote; he would, however, remain as 'caretaker' Prime Minister for a 14-day transitional period during which negotiations between the MEF, the IFM and a Commonwealth Special Envoy, Prof. Ade Adefuye of Nigeria, were to take place. However, negotiations collapsed following the MEF's refusal to hand over its weapons, pending the appointment of a new Prime Minister, which was to occur in an extraordinary parliamentary session on 28 June. As this session failed to raise the necessary quorum, the election of a new Prime Minister was delayed until 30 June, when Sogavare, the leader of the opposition, defeated Rev. Leslie Boseto, incumbent Minister for Lands and Housing, by 23 votes to 21. (The third candidate, Hilly, withdrew in support of Boseto.) Sogavare declared that he would seek to establish peace without making significant changes to the policy of the previous Government. None the less, Sogavare announced a comprehensive reallocation of ministerial posts and restructuring of ministries. A new Ministry for National Unity, Reconciliation and Peace was established, and plans to create a Solomon Islands Defence Force and Ministry of Defence were announced. (Previously defence issues had fallen within the remit of the police service, which had become compromised because of alleged MEF infiltration, and by allegations that about 75% of officers were ethnic Malaitans.)

New cease-fire negotiations in August 2000 resulted in the declaration of a 90-day cease-fire between the IFM and the MEF, although intermittent violent disorder continued in Guadalcanal. In late August IFM dissidents kidnapped the brother of Deputy Prime Minister Allan Kemakeza, demanding that SI $6.5m. in compensation be paid to the displaced persons of Guadalcanal. Kemakeza was released unharmed after 10 days without the payment of a ransom. Logistical problems delayed the onset of further peace talks until early September, when a further communiqué concerning potential methods of advancing the peace process was issued. In mid-September a breakaway group from the IFM, which had reverted to the former name of the GRA under the leadership of Harold Keke, held an airline pilot hostage with a demand for SI $2m.; he was released unharmed without the demands being acceded to, although Keke later claimed that the Government had paid him US $200,000.

A further round of peace talks in Queensland, Australia, led to the signing on 15 October 2000 of a peace treaty known as the Townsville Agreement, by the MEF, the IFM, the Solomon Islands Government and the Provincial Governments of Malaita and Guadalcanal. An amnesty for all those involved in crimes associated with the ethnic conflict would be granted, subject to the surrender of all weaponry within 30 days. The agreement also envisaged the creation of an international peace-monitoring team, and the repatriation to their home villages of all MEF and IFM soldiers at the expense of the Solomon Islands Government. Infrastructure and service in the two provinces would also be restored and developed, while the two provinces would also be granted a greater degree of administrative autonomy. Malaita Province was to receive additional funding to reflect the de-

mands placed on the region by the influx of 20,000 displaced persons from Guadalcanal. Public displays of forgiveness, reconciliation and confession were organized, and a Peace and Reconciliation Committee was to be established.

The implementation of the peace process, overseen by monitors from Australia and New Zealand, was threatened in mid-November 2000, when four people were killed in a shooting in Gizo, Western Province. Among the dead were two members of Papua New Guinea's Bougainville Revolutionary Army. Moreover, delays in the disarmament process involving the MEF and the IFM caused the deadline for the surrender of arms to be extended from 15 November until the end of that month, and then further until 15 December. In mid-November, following an announcement that the Guadalcanal Provincial Government headquarters, which had been occupied by members of the MEF since June, was to be rehabilitated as a symbol of national unity, arsonists, believed to be linked with the MEF, attacked the building. Despite a series of ceremonies in late November and early December, in which members of the IMF and MEF surrendered weapons, it was believed that at least 400 illegally-held weapons remained in circulation at the end of December. The legislation granting immunity to those who had committed crimes during the conflict was passed by Parliament in mid-December, and was criticized by the prominent human rights organization, Amnesty International. In late December one man was wounded in an attack on a motel, in Honiara, in which disarmed former IFM rebels recruited to join the police were resident. Responsibility for the attack was attributed to a group calling itself the Marau Eagle Force, from the eastern Marau region of Guadalcanal, which was subject to separate peace negotiations. The breakaway GLF led by Harold Keke also announced that it had not accepted the cease-fire. In early January 2001 concerns were expressed that, as a result of the ongoing economic crisis and a larger number of rebels having opted to join the police than had been anticipated, the Government might be unable to pay the former rebels, thus precipitating further concerns about security.

In early December 2000 new legislation had permitted the appointment of two further ministers, a Minister of Rehabilitation, Reconstruction and Redirection, and a Minister of Economic Reform and Structural Adjustment. In early January 2001 it was reported that the Government was contemplating an extension of the amnesty. Further violence broke out between Guadalcanal militants and members of the Marau Eagle Force. A peace agreement between the group and the IFM was signed in early February, although the Peace Monitoring Council observed that the infrastructure of the Marau region had been almost entirely destroyed since 1998 and that there was little immediate prospect of recovery. In early March 2001 peace in the Marau region appeared to be threatened following an incident in which police officers, in connection with a drink-driving charge, opened fire on a vehicle owned by a former commander of the Marau Eagle Force. It was also reported that two other former Marau commanders had demanded SI $100,000 from the Government, and that other Marau militants would refuse to surrender their arms, in conformity with the agreement signed in February, unless the GLF were also disarmed. In mid-March tensions heightened following a security operation against the GLF leader, Keke, in which a government patrol boat fired at villages on the western coast of Guadalcanal. In the same month police disarmed and arrested a group of villagers from Munda, Western Province. Further incidents in early April, in which a boat fired at coastal targets in southern Guadalcanal, led the international peace monitoring force from Australia to state that the cease-fire arrangement reached under the Townsville Agreement might have been breached. The Assistant Commissioner of Police Operations protested that the Townsville Agreement did not require the police to surrender their guns, although a report published in April claimed that some of the weapons used in the security operation should have been surrendered the previous year. In June the Premier of Guadalcanal, Ezekiel Alebua, was shot and seriously injured in an assassination attempt, apparently carried out on the orders of former leaders of the IFM. Harold Keke met the Deputy Prime Minister and the secretary of the Peace Monitoring Council in June and, in October, he voiced his support for the imminent general elections. However, the failure of former militia groups to surrender their guns was the main obstacle to a lasting peace throughout 2001, and officials estimated that there remained some 500 high-powered weapons in the community, in addition to hand-made weapons. The Government declared an 'arms amnesty' in

April 2002. Militants surrendered some 2,000 guns with impunity. Weapons disposal began in June, coinciding with the International Peace Monitoring Team's departure from the country.

In the second half of 2000 Western, Choiseul, and Temutu provinces all declared themselves to be semi-autonomous states within Solomon Islands; on 1 September the legislature of the latter, representing 20,000 inhabitants, approved a bill allowing for a referendum on the province's proposed independence; the worsening economic situation caused by the conflict in Guadalcanal was believed to be a determining factor; additionally, movements in Guadalcanal and Makira provinces demanding greater autonomy were reported to have gained strength at this time. In late November the Minister of Provincial Government and Rural Development Nathaniel Waena announced that legislation to amend the Constitution would be submitted in 2001, in order to institute a federal system of government. Controversy arose following an announcement by the Government, in mid-March 2001, that it intended to introduce legislation to extend the life of Parliament for a further year, to expire in August 2002, stating that the social and economic position of the Islands would not facilitate the holding of elections as scheduled in August 2001. This proposal attracted widespread opposition, including that of churches, trade unions, all provincial premiers, and the principal overseas aid donors to Solomon Islands. When it became apparent that he would not possess a parliamentary majority to support the legislation, Sogavare withdrew the bill from Parliament in early May; later that month it was announced that the elections would be held, as scheduled, funded wholly from overseas. In September the National Parliament approved a bill to increase national general election registration fees by 150%; Walter Folotalu, former member of the National Parliament for Baegu, successfully challenged the proposed legislation in the High Court in October. In the same month the High Court also began hearing the case brought by former Prime Minister Bartholomew Ulufa'alu; he had challenged the legality of the Government, seeking a ruling that the coup and subsequent election that ousted him were unconstitutional (he lost the case in November 2001).

In October 2001 public services deteriorated as nation-wide power cuts resulted from the Solomon Islands Electricity Authority's inability to pay for its supplies of diesel fuel. The Government announced the introduction of health charges in order to maintain medical services, and was forced to appeal to Australia and New Zealand for assistance in policing, as violent crime was becoming endemic. A storage container holding weapons relinquished under the Townsville peace agreement was broken into and, in November, the revelation that compensation totalling SI $17.4m. had been paid to former members of the MEF for alleged property damage precipitated a violent demonstration by protesters demanding similar recompense. The Prime Minister was prevented from leaving his office (to attend a session of the UN General Assembly in New York), while the house of the Deputy Prime Minister was vandalized.

Accusations and rumours of bribery and intimidation were rife during the campaigning that preceded the general election, held on 5 December 2001. The electoral coalition of the Solomon Islands Alliance for Change Coalition (SIACC) won 12 seats, the PAP secured nine and the PPP six, while 22 seats were won by independent candidates. In the absence of a clear SIACC leader, 11 elected members of the coalition convened with 11 elected independents to decide upon a satisfactory premier. Following various shifts in allegiances, Sir Allan Kemakeza (as he had become), leader of the PAP and former Deputy Prime Minister, was declared Prime Minister. Despite having been previously accused of misappropriating state funds, the former Minister of Finance, Snyder Rini, was appointed Deputy Prime Minister and Minister of National Planning.

The new Government, however, was unable to improve the increasingly desperate political and economic situation on the islands. A peace summit, organized by the Peace Monitoring Council, scheduled to be held in March 2002 was postponed until June, and, as the security situation in the country deteriorated further, numerous international peace monitors began withdrawing from the islands. Later in March the New Zealand Deputy High Commissioner to Solomon Islands, Bridget Nichols, was discovered at her home suffering from severe knife wounds, and died shortly afterwards in hospital, in what was initially believed to have been an incident linked to the recent escalation in violence. However, subsequent investigations by both the New Zealand and Solomon Islands authorities con-

cluded that the diplomat's death had been an accident. Also in March Kemakeza dismissed Michael Maina, the Minister of Finance, after Maina failed to consult the Cabinet prior to announcing a number of drastic budgetary measures, the most significant of which was his decision to devalue the national currency by 25%. Maina was replaced by Laurie Chan, who in early April revised the devaluation.

There were reports of further disturbances on the western coast of Guadalcanal in early June 2002 during which it was claimed that 11 Malaitans, who were part of a force attempting to capture the GLF leader, Harold Keke, had been killed. In mid-July water and electricity supplies to the capital were interrupted after the SIEA was once again unable to purchase fuel to power its generators, and the Solomon Islands Water Authority had failed to pay rental arrears to the landowners of the Kongulai water source. The country was further adversely affected by a series of strikes in mid-August by public-sector workers in protest at the non-payment of their salaries. Later that month the Minister for Youth and Sports and Women's Affairs, Rev. Augustin Greve, was assassinated. It was subsequently reported that Harold Keke had claimed responsibility for the murder. In September a church deacon was found beheaded on a beach on Guadalcanal's southern coast, an area considered to be a stronghold of the GLF. In a separate incident in the same month a woman and three children were shot dead and 11 others wounded in an assault which local chiefs attributed to Keke's organization. In late September Kemakeza made a formal request to the UN for a peace-keeping force to address the increasing state of lawlessness in the country and in the following month a delegation of four UN officials visited the islands to assess the situation.

In mid-October 2002 the Cabinet approved the establishment of the National Peace Council, an interim body, to replace the Peace Monitoring Council, the mandate of which expired on 15 October under the terms of the Townsville Peace Agreement. A permanent body was to be established after 16 January 2003. It was confirmed, however, in the same month that more weapons were in circulation in the country than when the peace agreement was signed in October 2000. The National Peace Council expressed a belief that many of the weapons surrendered under the arms amnesty of April 2002 had been removed for use by police officers in their campaign to capture Keke.

In mid-December 2002 the Minister of Finance, Laurie Chan, resigned. The Government claimed that this action was in response to criticism of his budget, which had recently been approved by the Cabinet. However, Radio New Zealand reported that his resignation was in protest at the Government's decision to pay unscheduled allowances to the 'special constables' (former militants from the ethnic conflict who were allowed to join the police force as part of the peace agreement) who had demanded the payments with threats and violence. The latter had included an incident in which gunshots were fired at the Prime Minister's residence by a group of 'special constables' believed to include members of the Marau Eagle Force. The Government faced a serious challenge in mid-December when six independent members of Parliament resigned because of what they described as a 'leadership problem' within the coalition. However, the Government defeated an opposition motion of 'no confidence' by 28 votes to 17. Meanwhile, several financial advisers fled the country, reportedly as a result of threats they had received.

In late December 2002 the remote islands of Tikopia and Anuta in the province of Temotu were struck by Cyclone Zoe and lost contact with the rest of the country. The islands suffered widespread devastation with the loss of all crops, buildings and water supplies, and heavy casualties were feared. The dispatch of a boat containing relief supplies was delayed by several days because of the Government's inability to pay for a crew or fuel for the vessel. When aid finally reached the islands, it was found that, contrary to all expectations, there had been no fatalities among the combined population of some 4,000, despite the severity of the storms. Islanders were believed to have used their knowledge of tunnels and caves on the islands to shelter from the cyclone.

The country's precarious peace process suffered a major reversal in February 2003 when a leading member of the National Peace Council, Sir Frederick Soaki, was assassinated. The motive for the killing was not immediately apparent, although there was speculation that it might have been connected to his involvement in a 'demobilization' programme for 'special constables'. A report by the human rights organization, Amnesty International, in March 2003 claimed that the country's 'special constables' had tortured and killed numerous people in the operation against Harold Keke along the southern coast of Guadalcanal. In April three of Keke's close associates deserted him and reported that they had witnessed him carry out nine murders in recent weeks. The killings were mostly thought to have involved his own supporters whom he had suspected of collaborating with the police. In May it was reported that Keke had taken six missionaries hostage in southern Guadalcanal. In a separate incident on Mailita, in the same month, an Australian missionary was beheaded.

In 1990 relations between Papua New Guinea and Solomon Islands deteriorated, following allegations by the Solomon Islands' Government that patrol boats from Papua New Guinea were interfering with the traditional crossing between Bougainville Island (Papua New Guinea) and the Shortland Islands, while the Papua New Guinea Government accused Solomon Islands of harbouring members of the rebel Bougainville Revolutionary Army (BRA) and of providing them with supplies. Despite the signing that year of an agreement on joint border surveillance and arrangements to host peace negotiations between the BRA and the Papua New Guinea Government, relations worsened considerably in 1992 when Papua New Guinea forces carried out several unauthorized incursions into the Shortland Islands, in which a fuel depot was destroyed and two Solomon Islanders were killed. Alleging Australian involvement in the incursions, Mamaloni suspended surveillance flights by the Australian air force over its territory, and relations between the two countries deteriorated significantly. Despite the initiation of discussions between Solomon Islands and Papua New Guinea in January 1993, further incursions were reported in April. Following the election of a new Government in May in Solomon Islands, however, relations appeared to improve, and subsequent negotiations between the two countries resulted in an agreement to close the BRA office in Honiara. Tensions with Papua New Guinea, however, increased in 1996 as violence on Bougainville intensified. Numerous incursions by Papua New Guinea defence forces into Solomon Islands' waters were reported, while the Papua New Guinea Government repeated accusations that Solomon Islands was harbouring BRA activists. However, in June 1997 Papua New Guinea and Solomon Islands concluded a maritime border agreement, following several years of negotiations. The purpose of the agreement was not only to delineate the sea boundary between the two countries but also to provide a framework for co-operation in matters of security, natural disaster, customs, quarantine, immigration and conservation. In December 1997 the Prime Ministers of the two countries paid an extended visit to Bougainville to express support for the recently-established truce agreement. Furthermore, the Governor of Bougainville was sympathetic to the problem of increasing numbers of Solomon Islanders from the Western Province crossing to Bougainville in late 2001. Many were trading goods in Bougainville in exchange for food and services. Discussions regarding the border of Papua New Guinea were held in April 2002; both Governments were concerned about the increase of weapons trafficking from Bougainville to the Western Province.

In March 1988 Solomon Islands signed an agreement with Vanuatu and Papua New Guinea to form the 'Melanesian Spearhead Group' (MSG). The new group regarded as its principal aims the preservation of Melanesian cultural traditions and the attainment of independence by the French Overseas Territory of New Caledonia. In March 1990 the MSG admitted the FLNKS (the main Kanak, or Melanesian, political group in New Caledonia). In mid-1994 the group concluded an agreement regarded as the first step towards the establishment of a free-trade area by the three countries. Fiji was admitted to the group in mid-1996. Solomon Islands announced its commitment to further economic integration between the MSG countries in late 1997. In October 1995 Solomon Islands became a signatory of the Federated States of Micronesia Agreement on Regional Fisheries Access. In early 1997 Solomon Islands and Vanuatu agreed to undertake negotiations on the maritime boundaries between the two countries in an attempt to clarify uncertainty regarding fishing rights.

Relations with Australia, which is one of the principal sources of overseas assistance to Solomon Islands, became increasingly strained in the aftermath of the coup of June 2000. The Australian Minister for Foreign Affairs, Alexander Downer, was notably critical of proposals of Solomon Islands to establish its own defence force. Sogavare, in turn, stated that he regarded the funding of the Solomon Islands peace process by Australia as an attempt by that country to interfere in Solomon Islands' internal affairs, and also accused Australia of failing to alleviate ethnic tensions on Guadalcanal.

Government

Under the 1978 Constitution, executive authority is vested in the British monarch, as Head of State, and is exercisable by the monarch's representative, the Governor-General, who is appointed on the advice of Parliament and acts on the advice of the Cabinet. Legislative power is vested in the unicameral National Parliament, with 47 members elected by universal adult suffrage for four years (subject to dissolution) in single-member constituencies. The Cabinet is composed of the Prime Minister, elected by Parliament, and other ministers appointed by the Governor-General on the Prime Minister's recommendation. The Cabinet is responsible to Parliament. The country comprises four Districts, within which there are nine local government councils, elected by universal adult suffrage. The Constitution provides for further devolution of power to provincial authorities.

Defence

Prior to the coup of June 2000, a unit within the Police Force, the Police Field Force, received technical training and logistical support from Australia and New Zealand. The Force latterly had two patrol boats and undertook surveillance activities in Solomon Islands' maritime economic zone. The Solomon Islands Peace Plan, signed in July 2000, provided for the establishment of a Ministry of Defence that would be independent of the Ministry of Police, Justice and Legal Affairs. The Ministry of Defence would, as one of its first tasks, introduce legislation that would permit the establishment of a Solomon Islands Defence Force. A national reconnaissance and surveillance force was founded in 1995, and was also to become answerable to the new ministry.

Economic Affairs

In 2001, according to estimates by the World Bank, Solomon Islands' gross national income (GNI), measured at average 1999–2001 prices, was US $253m., equivalent to US $580 per head (or $1,680 on an international purchasing-power parity basis). During 1990–2001, it was estimated, the population increased at an average annual rate of 2.8%, while gross domestic product (GDP) per head decreased, in real terms, at an average annual rate of 2.2%. Overall GDP increased, in real terms, an average annual rate of 0.6% in 1990–2001; GDP contracted by 9.0% in 2001.

Agriculture (including hunting, forestry and fishing) contributed 42.1% of GDP (measured at constant 1985 prices) in 2000. In 2000 an estimated 73.1% of the working population were involved in agriculture. The principal cash crops have traditionally included coconuts, cocoa, rice and oil palm. However, the palm oil business was seriously affected by the closure in June 1999 of the islands' largest agricultural enterprise, Solomon Islands Plantations Ltd, as a result of the civil unrest. Moreover, earnings from copra (which was for many years the country's main export) declined from SI $34.7m. in 2000 to SI $0.4m. in 2001. High prices on the world market for cocoa in the early 2000s, however, increased the value of exports of that commodity, and in April 2003 the Government announced plans to reopen the palm oil plant. Spices are cultivated for export on a small scale, while in the 1990s the production of honey became increasingly important. The main subsistence crops are root crops, garden vegetables and fruit. Pigs and cattle are also reared. Seaweed farming has been introduced, and sea-shells are exported. Giant-clam farming became an important activity in the mid-1990s, and by 1996 a ban on the sale and export of giant clams had been introduced in an attempt to conserve stocks. Fish accounted for 15.0% of export earnings in 2001. The forestry sector is an extremely important source of revenue, timber exports accounting for 76.6% of total export receipts in 2001. A dramatic increase in the production of timber in the early 1990s prompted several international organizations, including the World Bank, to express alarm at the rate of logging in the country. None the less, by the late 1990s Solomon Islands was one of the few remaining countries in the world to allow the export of round logs. However, a dramatic decline in the price of timber on the international market led to a crisis in the industry in 1997, which the recently elected Government aimed to address with a new logging policy (including a moratorium on new licences, introduced in April 1998). According to the Asian Development Bank (ADB), agricultural GDP increased by an annual average of less than 0.1% in 1990–2000. The ADB estimated that agricultural GDP decreased by 12.0% in 1999 and by 26.4% in 2000.

Industry (including mining, manufacturing, construction and power) contributed 12.1% of GDP in 2000 (at 1985 prices), and employed 13.7% of wage-earners in 1993. The GDP of the industrial sector expanded by an average annual rate of 5.0% in 1990–2000. The ADB estimated that industrial GDP declined by 3.9% in 1999 and 25.9% in 2000.

Mining employed 0.5% of the working population in 1988. The mining sector's share of real GDP was an estimated 3.1% in 2000. During 1990–97, however, the sector made a negative contribution to GDP. Compared with the previous year, the mining sector's GDP increased by 181.0% in 1999, but declined by 51.4% in 2000. Gold is the sole mineral export, but revenue from this source declined from SI $1.3m. (from exports of 50 kg) in 1991 to only SI $57,000 (from 2 kg) in 1997. The Gold Ridge gold-mining project in central Guadalcanal was suspended in June 2000, partly owing to the civil unrest in Guadalcanal and partly owing to the legal challenges brought by landowners seeking compensation for alleged environmental damage caused by the mine. However, in April 2003 the Government announced plans to reopen the site. Other (undeveloped) mineral resources include deposits of copper, lead, zinc, silver, cobalt, asbestos, phosphates, nickel and high-grade bauxite. The Government planned to auction nickel deposits of some 43m. metric tons of ore on San Jorge Island, Isabel province, in 2001.

Manufacturing contributed 4.9% of GDP (at 1985 prices) in 2000, and employed 15.6% of wage-earners in 1995. The most important branches are food-processing (particularly fish-canning), coconut-based products, brewing, saw-milling, logging and handicrafts. Manufacturing GDP increased by an annual average of 3.8% in 1990–2000. Compared with the previous year, however, there was no discernible growth in 1999, and in 2000 the manufacturing sector's GDP contracted by 19.8%.

Energy is derived principally from hydroelectric power. Mineral fuels accounted for 17.5% of the total value of imports in 2001. In 1992 exploratory projects revealed several potential petroleum-producing areas in the islands.

Service industries contributed 45.8% of GDP (at 1985 prices) in 2000 and engaged 58.8% of wage-earners in 1993. Tourism was encouraged by a 10-year development plan, announced in 1989. In 2000 some 25,127 people visited Solomon Islands. Earnings from the sector were estimated at some US $13m. in 1998. The trade, restaurants and hotels sector engaged 11.5% of wage-earners in 1993. The ADB estimated that the GDP of the services sector contracted by 2.0% in 1999, but expanded by 0.8% in 2000.

In 2000 Solomon Islands recorded a visible trade deficit of SI $223.6m., and a deficit of SI $329.9m. on the current account of the balance of payments. In 2001 the principal sources of imports were Australia (29.3%) and Singapore (18.3%), while the principal markets for exports were Japan (19.8%) and the Republic of Korea (17.8%). Other major trading partners are the United Kingdom, Thailand, the Philippines, New Zealand and the People's Republic of China. The principal exports in 2001 were timber, fish and other marine products, and cocoa. The principal imports were machinery and transport equipment, basic manufactures, foodstuffs and mineral fuels.

In 2000 a budgetary surplus of SI $35.4m. was recorded. In 2001, however, a fiscal deficit equivalent to 8% of GDP was anticipated. Budgetary expenditure of SI $468m. was approved for 2003. In 2000 official development assistance totalled US $68.4m., of which US $22.1m. was bilateral aid. Aid from Australia totalled $A36.2m. in 2002/2003. In the same year financial assistance from New Zealand totalled $NZ8.0m. Solomon Islands' external debt totalled US $155.4m. in 2000. In that year the cost of debt-servicing was equivalent to 6.7% of the value of exports of goods and services. The average annual rate of inflation in 1990–99 was 10.9%. Compared with the previous year, the rate of inflation was estimated by the ADB at 4.8% in 2000 and at 1.8% in 2001.

Solomon Islands is a member of the Pacific Community (see p. 304), the Pacific Islands Forum (see p. 306), the Asian Development Bank (see p. 143) and the UN Economic and Social Commission for Asia and the Pacific (ESCAP, see p. 28), and is a signatory to the Lomé Conventions and the successor Cotonou Agreement (see p. 235) with the EU.

During the 1990s Solomon Islands' economic development was adversely affected by inadequate transport facilities, inclement weather and by fluctuations in prices on the international market for the country's major agricultural exports. Successive budget deficits and a substantial current-account deficit were financed by heavy borrowing and foreign aid. Increasing environmental concern over the exploitation of the country's natural resources and its vulnerability to unscrupulous foreign operators continued to threaten the islands' economic stability. The economy was severely affected by ethnic unrest in Guadalcanal. Furthermore, subsequent housing and welfare payments to displaced victims of the unrest became a severe drain on domestic finance, forcing the Government into increased foreign borrowing and unsustainable drawdowns from the Central Bank of Solomon Islands. In mid-2000 government revenue was reported to be declining sharply. Government revenue in 2000 fell short of budget projections by more than 30%. During 2000 a total of 8,000 workers, or 15% of the formal sector's total labour force, were made redundant or dispatched on unpaid leave. Youth unemployment, meanwhile, remained a particular problem. In February 2001 the Central Bank of Solomon Islands reportedly declared that the country faced economic and social disaster, stating that the country's GDP had contracted by 19% in one year, and that exports had declined by 40% in six months, while domestic borrowing, particularly by the Government, had notably increased. The fiscal position deteriorated sharply in 2001. Payments to public servants, along with the transfer of funds to provincial health and education services, were delayed. Furthermore, the Government defaulted on various external and domestic debts held by commercial banks and the National Provident Fund (no employee contributions having been made to the latter in 2001). Merchandise trade showed no signs of recovery in 2001; the country's dependence upon forestry—logging being the prime constituent of both taxation and export revenues—rendered the economy vulnerable to the low international prices for round logs prevailing in 2001. Economic recovery appeared likely to be dependent upon the maintenance of prolonged political stability, necessitating improved inter-ethnic relations, in addition to a settlement of the demands for increased devolution from the provinces. Furthermore, the dramatic rise in crime, which in part had occurred as a result of the alleged infiltration of the police force by rebel groups (see Recent History), appeared to be a deterrent to growth and investment. Among the most serious problems facing the new Government that took office in December 2001 were ongoing security concerns, the need to control expenditure (partly through further reductions in the numbers of public servants) and the restoration of the country's industrial capacity and infrastructure, particularly in the export sector. In January 2002 the Central Bank announced that the country's total debt amounted to some US $200m., while its foreign reserves had fallen to below US $18m. The Government subsequently announced plans to reduce expenditure by up to 50%, which would reportedly result in about one-third of employees losing their jobs. In October the Government reduced the number of ministries from 20 to 10. The ADB envisaged that GDP would decline by 5.0% in 2002 and subsequently remain stagnant, prior to any recovery in growth.

Education

Education is not compulsory in Solomon Islands. Primary education generally begins at six years of age and lasts for six years. Secondary education, normally beginning at the age of 12, lasts for up to five years. In 1994 an estimated 97% of children (104% of boys; 90% of girls) in the relevant age-group were enrolled in primary education, while 17% of children (21% of boys; 14% of girls) in the relevant age-group attended secondary schools. In 1993 there were 523 primary schools, with a total of 60,493 pupils in 1994, while in 1993 there were 23 secondary schools, with a total of 7,981 pupils in 1995. In 1993 10 of the country's secondary schools were national secondary schools, which are run either by the Government or by one of the churches, and the remaining 13 were provincial secondary schools, which are run by provincial assemblies and provide courses of a practical nature, mainly in agriculture and development studies. There are two teacher-training schools and a technical institute. Scholarships are available for higher education at various universities overseas, which in 1987 were attended by 413 students from Solomon Islands. In 1977 the Solomon Islands Centre of the University of the Pacific opened in Honiara. Government expenditure on education was SI $51m. (9.7% of total spending) in 1998.

Public Holidays

2003: 1 January (New Year's Day), 18–21 April (Easter), 2 June (Queen's Official Birthday), 9 June (Whit Monday), 7 July (Independence Day), 25 December (Christmas Day), 26 December (Boxing Day).

2004: 1 January (New Year's Day), 9–12 April (Easter), 31 May (Whit Monday), 1 June (Queen's Official Birthday), 7 July (Independence Day), 25 December (Christmas Day), 26 December (Boxing Day).

Statistical Survey

Source (unless otherwise stated): Statistics Office, POB G6, Honiara; tel. 23700; fax 20392.

AREA AND POPULATION

Area: 27,556 sq km (10,639 sq miles).

Population: 285,176 at census of 23–24 November 1986; 409,042 (males 211,381; females 197,661) at census of 21–22 November 1999; mid-year 2001 estimate 463,000 (Source: UN *Population and Vital Statistics Report*).

Density (mid-2001): 16.8per sq km.

Ethnic Groups (census of November 1986): Melanesians 268,536; Polynesians 10,661; Micronesians 3,929; Europeans 1,107; Chinese 379; Others 564.

Principal Towns (population in '000, 2000): Honiara (capital) 50.1; Gizo 7.0; Auki 5.0. Source: Stefan Helders, *World Gazetteer* (internet www.world-gazetteer.com).

Births and Deaths (2000): Birth rate 34.8 per 1,000; Death rate 4.4 per 1,000. Source: UN, *Statistical Yearbook for Asia and the Pacific*.

Expectation of Life (WHO estimates, years at birth): 66.4 (males 64.7; females 68.4) in 2001 Source: WHO, *World Health Report*.

Employment (employees only, June 1993): Agriculture, hunting, forestry and fishing 8,106; Manufacturing (incl. mining and quarrying) 2,844; Electricity and water 245; Construction 977; Trade, restaurants and hotels 3,390; Transport, storage and communications 1,723; Finance, insurance, real estate and business services 1,144; Community, social and personal services 11,148; Total 29,577 (Source: UN, *Statistical Yearbook for Asia and the Pacific*). *1996*: Total employed 34,200 In 1993 some 72% of the employed labour force were males.

HEALTH AND WELFARE

Key Indicators

Total Fertility Rate (children per woman, 2001): 5.4.

Under-5 Mortality Rate (per 1,000 live births, 2001): 24.

Physicians (per 1,000 head, 1995): 0.14.

Hospital Beds (per 1,000 head, 1992): 2.75.

Health Expenditure (2000): US $ per head (PPP): 97.

Health Expenditure (2000): % of GDP: 5.9.

Health Expenditure (2000): public (% of total): 94.5.

Access to Water (% of persons, 2000): 71.

Access to Sanitation (% of persons, 2000): 34.

Human Development Index (2000): ranking: 121.

Human Development Index (2000): value: 0.622.
For sources and definitions, see explanatory note on p. vi.

AGRICULTURE, ETC.

Principal Crops (FAO estimates, metric tons, 2001): Coconuts 330,000; Oil palm fruit128,000; Rice 4,800; Cocoa beans 3,000; Sweet potatoes 79,000; Yams 29,500; Taro 34,000; Vegetables and melons 6,950; Fruit 16,890. Source: FAO.

Livestock (FAO estimates, '000 head, year ending September 2001): Cattle 13; Pigs 67. Source: FAO.

Livestock Products (FAO estimates, '000 metric tons, 2001): Beef and veal 0.6; Pig meat 2.0. Source: FAO.

Forestry (roundwood removals, '000 cu m): Industrial wood 734 per year in 1996–2000, 554 in 2001; Fuel wood 138 per year in 1996–2001. Source: FAO.

Fishing (FAO estimates, metric tons, live weight, 2000): Capture 23,443(Skipjack tuna 8,276, Yellowfin tuna 3,035); Aquaculture 15; Total catch 23,458. Source: FAO, *Yearbook of Fishery Statistics*.

MINING

Production (kilograms, 2000): Gold 338; Silver 200 (estimate). Source: US Geological Survey.

INDUSTRY

Production (metric tons, 2001, unless otherwise stated): Copra 2,000 (2001); Coconut oil 11,500; Palm oil 30,000 (FAO estimates); Frozen fish 23,100 (1996); Electric energy 32 million kWh (1998).

FINANCE

Currency and Exchange Rates: 100 cents = 1 Solomon Islands dollar (SI $). *Sterling, US Dollar and Euro Equivalents* (31 October 2001): £1 sterling = SI $7.898; US $1 = SI $5.426; €1 = SI $4.906; SI $100 = £12.66 = US $18.43 = €20.38. *Average Exchange Rate* (SI $ per US $): 4.8156 in 1998; 4.8381 in 1999; 5.0889 in 2000.

Budget (SI $ million, 2000): *Revenue*: Taxes 258.8; Other current revenue 18.6; Capital revenue 35.3; Total 312.7; *Expenditure*: Total 277.3 (Current 254.8; Capital 22.5). Source: Asian Development Bank, *Key Indicators of Developing Asian and Pacific Countries*.

Development Expenditure (estimates, SI $ '000, 1990): Human resources and community development 28,125; Natural resources 30,442; Commerce, industry and finance 13,375; Physical infrastructure 18,981; Government and security 6,691; Total 97,614. *2000* (SI $ million): Total 30 (Source: Central Bank of Solomon Islands, *Quarterly Review* (June 2001)).

Overseas Aid (external grants, US $ million, 1994): Australia 8.5; EU 6.6; Japan 20.5; New Zealand 2.9; Taiwan 2.7; United Kingdom 3.4; USA 0.6; World Health Organization 0.5; Total (incl. others) 54.4.

International Reserves (US $ million at 31 December 2000): IMF special drawing rights 0.002; Reserve position in IMF 0.71; Foreign exchange 31.34; Total 32.05. Source: IMF, *International Financial Statistics*.

Money Supply (SI $ million at 31 December 2000): Currency outside banks 88.27; Demand deposits at deposit money banks 159.35; Total money (incl. others) 248.29. Source: Central Bank of Solomon Islands, *Quarterly Review* (June 2001).

Cost of Living (Consumer Price Index for Honiara; base: 1995 = 100): 120.8 in 1997; 135.7 in 1998; 146.9 in 1999. Source: IMF, *International Financial Statistics*.

Gross Domestic Product by Economic Activity (official estimates, SI $ million at constant 1985 market prices, 2000): Agriculture 116.0; Mining 8.6; Manufacturing 13.4; Electricity, gas and water 3.6; Construction 7.6; Trade 29.7; Transport and communications 15.5; Finance 12.9; Other services 68.0; GDP at factor cost 275.3. Source: Asian Development Bank, *Key Indicators of Developing Asian and Pacific Countries*.

Balance of Payments (US $ million, 1999): Exports of goods f.o.b. 164.57; Imports of goods f.o.b. –110.04. *Trade balance* 54.53; Exports of services 56.30; Imports of services –87.49; *Balance on goods and services* 23.34; Other income received 5.46; Other income paid–22.38; *Balance on goods, services and income* 6.41; Current transfers received 41.54; Current transfers paid –26.48; *Current balance* 21.48; Capital account (net) 9.16; Direct investment from abroad 9.90; Other investment assets 0.04; Other investment liabilities –43.72; Net errors and omissions –1.58; *Overall balance* –4.72. Source: IMF, *International Financial Statistics*.

EXTERNAL TRADE

Principal Commodities (SI $ '000, 2001): *Imports c.i.f.*: Food and live animals 108,448; Beverages and tobacco 9,298; Crude materials (inedible) except fuels, mineral fuels, lubricants, etc., and animal and vegetable oils and fats 75,750; Chemicals 13,745; Basic manufactures 22,577; Machinery and transport equipment 53,320; Miscellaneous manufactured articles and other commodities and transactions 148,799; Total 431,937. *Exports f.o.b.*: Fish 37,336; Copra 432; Timber 190,457; Cocoa 4,536; Palm oil 237; Total (incl. others) 248,685.

Principal Trading Partners (US $ million, 2001): *Imports*: Australia 30.6; Fiji 3.9; Hong Kong 2.6; Japan 3.5; New Zealand 5.1; Papua New Guinea 3.9; Singapore 19.1; Thailand 2.8; USA 7.4; Total (incl. others) 104.3. *Exports*: Australia 1.5; China, People's Republic 8.3; Japan 17.1; Korea, Republic 15.4; Malaysia 1.3; Philippines 9.8; Singapore 0.9; Thailand 7.4; United Kingdom 1.0; Total (incl. others) 86.4.
Source: Asian Development Bank, *Key Indicators of Developing Asian and Pacific Countries*.

TRANSPORT

Road Traffic (motor vehicles in use at 30 June 1986): Passenger cars 1,350; Commercial vehicles 2,026.

Shipping (international traffic, '000 metric tons, 1990): Goods loaded 278; Goods unloaded 349 (Source: UN, *Monthly Bulletin of Statistics*). *Merchant Fleet* (registered at 31 December 2001): Vessels 28; Total displacement ('000 grt) 8.4 (Source: Lloyd's Register-Fairplay, *World Fleet Statistics*).

Civil Aviation (traffic on scheduled services, 1999): Passengers carried 98,000; Passenger-km 80 million. Source: UN, *Statistical Yearbook*.

TOURISM

Foreign Tourist Arrivals: 13,229 in 1998; 21,318 in 1999; 25,127 in 2000.

Tourist Arrivals by Country (1999): Australia 4,979; China, People's Republic 1,347; Fiji 729; Japan 887; Korea, Republic 1,237; New Zealand 925; Papua New Guinea 1,457; Philippines 2,102; Taiwan 478; United Kingdom 893; USA 1,589; Total (incl. others) 21,318. Source: World Tourism Organization, *Yearbook of Tourism Statistics*.

Tourism Receipts (US $ million): 14 in 1996; 16 in 1997; 13 in 1998. Source: World Bank.

COMMUNICATIONS MEDIA

Non-daily Newspapers (1996): 3; estimated circulation 9,000.

Radio Receivers (1997): 57,000 in use.

Television Receivers (2000): 10,000 in use.

Telephones (2001): 7,400 main lines in use.

Mobile Cellular Telephones (2001): 1,000 subscribers.

Personal Computers (2001): 22,000 in use.

Internet Users (2001): 2,000.

Facsimile Machines (1999): 764 in use.
Sources: UNESCO, *Statistical Yearbook*; International Telecommunication Union.

EDUCATION

Pre-primary (1994): 12,627 pupils.

Primary (1994): 523 schools (1993); 2,514 teachers; 60,493 pupils.

Secondary: 23 schools (1993); 618 teachers (1994); 7,981 pupils (1995).

Overseas Centres (1988): 405 students.
Source: mainly UNESCO, *Statistical Yearbook*.

Adult Literacy Rate: 76.6% in 2000 (Source: UN Development Programme, *Human Development Report*).

Directory

The Constitution

A new Constitution came into effect at independence on 7 July 1978.

The main provisions are that Solomon Islands is a constitutional monarchy with the British sovereign (represented locally by a Governor-General, who must be a Solomon Islands citizen) as Head of State, while legislative power is vested in the unicameral National Parliament composed of 50 members (increased from 47 in 1997), elected by universal adult suffrage for four years (subject to dissolution), and executive authority is exercised by the Cabinet, led by the Prime Minister. The Governor-General is appointed for up to five years, on the advice of Parliament, and acts in almost all matters on the advice of the Cabinet. The Prime Minister is elected by and from members of Parliament. Other ministers are appointed by the Governor-General, on the Prime Minister's recommendation, from members of Parliament. The Cabinet is responsible to Parliament. Emphasis is laid on the devolution of power, and traditional chiefs and leaders have a special role within these arrangements. Legislation approved in August 1996 provided for the abolition of the provincial government system and the transfer of legislative and administrative powers from the nine provincial governments to 75 area assemblies and councils controlled by central Government.

The Constitution contains comprehensive guarantees of fundamental human rights and freedoms, and provides for the introduction of a 'leadership code' and the appointment of an Ombudsman and a Public Solicitor. It also provides for 'the establishment of the underlying law, based on the customary law and concepts of the Solomon Islands people'. Solomon Islands citizenship was automatically conferred on the indigenous people of the islands and on other residents with close ties with the islands upon independence. The acquisition of land is reserved for indigenous inhabitants or their descendants.

In mid-1999 it was announced that two review committees had been established to amend the Constitution. They were expected to examine ways in which the traditions of the various ethnic groups could be better accommodated.

The Government

HEAD OF STATE

Monarch: HM Queen Elizabeth II.

Governor-General: Fr Sir John Ini Lapli (sworn in 7 July 1999).

THE CABINET
(April 2003)

Prime Minister: Sir Allan Kemakeza.

Deputy Prime Minister and Minister for National Planning and Human Resource Development: Snyder Rini.

Minister for Agriculture and Livestock: Edward Hunuehu.

Minister for Commerce, Employment and Trade: Trevor Olavae.

Minister for Economic Reform and Structural Adjustment: Daniel Fa'afunua.

Minister for Education and Training: Mathias Taro.

Minister for Finance: Laurie Chan.

Minister for Fisheries and Marine Resources: Nelson Kile.

Minister for Foreign Affairs and Trade Relations: Nollen Leni.

Minister for Forestry, Environment and Conservation: David Holisivi.

Minister for Health and Medical Services: Benjamin Una.

Minister for Home Affairs: Clement Rojumana.

Minister for Lands and Surveys: Siriako Usa.

Minister for Mines and Energy: Stephen Paeni.

Minister for National Unity, Reconciliation and Peace: Nathaniel Waena.

Minister for Police, Justice and National Security: Augustine Taneko.

Minister for Provincial Government and Rural Development: Walton Naezon.

Minister for Tourism and Aviation: Alex Bartlett.

Minister for Transport, Works and Communication: Bernard Giro.

Minister for Youth and Sports and Women's Affairs: (vacant).

MINISTRIES

In October 2002 it was announced that the number of ministries would be reduced from 20 to 10.

Office of the Prime Minister: POB G1, Honiara; tel. 21867; fax 26088.

Ministry of Agriculture and Lands: POB G13, Honiara; tel. 21327; fax 21955; e-mail drsteve@solomon.com.sb.

Ministry of Education and Human Resources Development: POB G28, Honiara; tel. 23900; fax 20485.

Ministry of Finance and Treasury: POB 26, Honiara; tel. 22535; fax 20392; e-mail finance@welkam.solomon.com.sb.

Ministry of Foreign Affairs Commerce and Tourism: POB G10, Honiara; tel. 2476; fax 20351; e-mail commerce@commerce.gov .sb; internet www.commerce.gov.sb.

Ministry of Health and Medical Services: POB 349, Honiara; tel. 20830; fax 20085.

Ministry of Infrastructure Development: POB G30, Honiara; tel. 38255; fax 38259; e-mail kudu@mnpd.gov.sb.

Ministry of Natural Resorces: POB G24, Honiara; tel. 25848; fax 21245; e-mail kdfmp@welkam.solomon.com.sb.

Ministry of Police, National Security and Justice: POB 1723/404, Honiara; tel. 22208; fax 25949.

Ministry of Provincial Government, Home Affairs, National Reconciliation and Peace: POB G35, Honiara; tel. 21140; fax 21289.

Legislature

NATIONAL PARLIAMENT
POB G19, Honiara; tel. 21751; fax 23866.

Speaker: PAUL TOVUA.

General Election, 5 December 2001

Party	Seats
Solomon Islands Alliance for Change	12
People's Alliance Party	9
People's Progressive Party	6
Labour Party	1
Independents	22
Total	**50**

Political Organizations

Parties in the National Parliament can have a fluctuating membership and an influence disproportionate to their representation. There is a significant number of independents who are loosely associated in the amorphous, but often decisive, 'Independent Group'. The following parties represent the main groupings:

National Action Party of Solomon Islands (NAPSI): Honiara; f. 1993; Leader FRANCIS SAEMALA.

National Party: Honiara; f. 1996; Pres. EZEKIEL ALEBUA.

People's Alliance Party (PAP): Honiara; f. 1979 by a merger of the People's Progressive Party (f. 1973) and the Rural Alliance Party (f. 1977); advocates the establishment of a federal republic; Leader Sir ALLAN KEMAKEZA; Sec. EDWARD KINGMELE.

People's Progressive Party (PPP): Honiara; f. 1973; latterly Coalition for National Advancement, reverted to original name in January 2000; Leader MANASSEH SOGAVARE; Pres. JOB DUDLEY TAUSINGA.

Solomon Islands Alliance for Change Coalition (SIACC): Honiara; f. 1997; formed from the previous Solomon Islands Alliance for Change (SIAC); Co-Leaders PATTERSON OTI, FRANCIS BILLY HILLY.

Solomon Islands Labour Party: Honiara; f. 1988; formed from the Solomon Islands Trade Union movement; Leader JOSES TUHANUKU; Gen. Sec. TONY KAGOVAI.

Solomon Islands Liberal Party (SILP): Honiara; f. 1976 as the National Democratic Party (NADEPA); present name adopted in 1986; Leader BARTHOLOMEW ULUFA'ALU.

United Democratic Party (UDP): f. 1980; fmrly United Solomon Islands Party; present name adopted in 2000; Pres. PETER KENILOREA; Chair. JOHN MAETIO.

Diplomatic Representation

EMBASSIES AND HIGH COMMISSIONS IN SOLOMON ISLANDS

Australia: Hibiscus Ave, POB 589, Honiara; tel. 21561; fax 23691; High Commissioner ROBERT DAVIS.

China (Taiwan): Pantina Plaza, POB 586, Honiara; tel. 38050; fax 38060; Ambassador PEI Y. TENG.

Japan: National Provident Fund Bldg, Mendana Ave, POB 560, Honiara; tel. 22953; fax 21006; Chargé d'affaires YUTAKA HIRATA.

New Zealand: Mendana Ave, POB 697, Honiara; tel. 21502; fax 22377; e-mail nzhicom@.solomon.com.sb; High Commissioner HEATHER RIDDELL.

Papua New Guinea: POB 1109, Honiara; tel. 20561; fax 20562; High Commissioner PONABE YUWA.

United Kingdom: Telekom House, Mendana Ave, POB 676, Honiara; tel. 21705; fax 21549; e-mail bhc@solomon.com.sb; High Commissioner BRIAN BALDWIN.

Judicial System

The High Court is a Superior Court of Record with unlimited original jurisdiction and powers (except over customary land) as prescribed by the Solomon Islands Constitution or by any law for the time being in force in Solomon Islands. The Judges of the High Court are the Chief Justice, resident in Solomon Islands and employed by its Government, and the Puisne Judges (of whom there are usually three). Appeals from this Court go to the Court of Appeal, the members of which are senior judges from Australia, New Zealand and Papua New Guinea. The Chief Justice and judges of the High Court are *ex officio* members of the Court of Appeal.

In addition there are Magistrates' Courts staffed by qualified and lay magistrates exercising limited jurisdiction in both civil and criminal matters. There are also Local Courts staffed by elders of the local communities, which have jurisdiction in the areas of established native custom, petty crime and local government by-laws. In 1975 Customary Land Appeal Courts were established to hear land appeal cases from Local Courts, which have exclusive original jurisdiction over customary land cases.

Office of the Registrar
High Court and Court of Appeal, POB G21, Honiara; tel. 21632; fax 22702; e-mail chetwynd@welkam.solomon.com.sb.

President of the Court of Appeal: Sir ANTHONY MASON.

Chief Justice of the High Court: Sir JOHN BAPTIST MURIA.

Puisne Judges: ALBERT ROCKY PALMER, SAM LUNGOLE AWICH, FRANK KABUI.

Registrar and Commissioner of the High Court: DAVID CHETWYND.

Chief Magistrate: DAVID CHETWYND (acting).

Attorney-General: PRIMO AFEAU.

Director of Public Prosecutions: FRANCIS MWANESALUA.

Solicitor-General: RANJIT HEWEGAMA.

Auditor-General: ISAAC VALU.

Public Solicitor: PATRICK LAVERY.

Chair of Law Reform Commission: (vacant).

Religion

More than 95% of the population profess Christianity, and the remainder follow traditional beliefs. According to the census of 1976, about 34% of the population adhered to the Church of Melanesia (Anglican), 19% were Roman Catholics, 17% belonged to the South Seas Evangelical Church, 11% to the United Church (Methodist) and 10% were Seventh-day Adventists. Most denominations are affiliated to the Solomon Islands Christian Association. In many areas Christianity is practised alongside traditional beliefs, especially ancestor worship.

CHRISTIANITY

Solomon Islands Christian Association: POB 1335, Honiara; tel. 23350; fax 26150; e-mail vepsica@welkam.solomon.com.sb; f. 1967; four full mems, one assoc. mem. and eight mem. orgs; Chair. Most Rev. ELLISON L. PAGE; Exec. Sec. PHILIP SOLODIA FUNIFAKA.

The Anglican Communion

Anglicans in Solomon Islands are adherents of the Church of the Province of Melanesia, comprising eight dioceses: six in Solomon Islands (Central Melanesia, Malaita, Temotu, Ysabel, Hanuato'o and Central Solomons, which was established in May 1997) and two in Vanuatu (one of which also includes New Caledonia). The Archbishop is also Bishop of Central Melanesia and is based in Honiara. The Church had an estimated 180,000 members in 1988.

Archbishop of the Province of Melanesia: Most Rev. Sir ELLISON POGO, Archbishop's House, POB 19, Honiara; tel. 21892; fax 21098; e-mail epogo@comphq.org.sb.

General Secretary: GEORGE KIRIAU, Provincial Headquarters, POB 19, Honiara; tel. 21892; fax 21098; e-mail gkiriau@comphq.oeg.sb.

The Roman Catholic Church

For ecclesiastical purposes, Solomon Islands comprises one archdiocese and two dioceses. At 31 December 2000 there were an estimated 83,115 adherents in the country. The Bishops participate in the Bishops' Conference of Papua New Guinea and Solomon Islands (based in Papua New Guinea).

Archbishop of Honiara: Most Rev. ADRIAN THOMAS SMITH, Holy Cross, POB 237, Honiara; tel. 21943; fax 26426; e-mail ahonccsi@solomon.com.sb.

Other Christian Churches

Assembly of God: POB 928, Honiara; tel. and fax 25512; f. 1971; Gen. Supt Rev. JERIEL OTASUI.

Christian Fellowship Church: Church, Paradise, Munda, Western Province; f. 1960; over 5,000 mems in 24 villages; runs 12 primary schools in Western Province.

Seventh-day Adventist Mission: POB 63, Honiara; tel. 21191; over 9,000 mems on Guadalcanal and over 6,800 on Malaita (Oct. 2000); Pres. of Western Pacific Region NEIL WATTS; Sec. Pastor J. PIUKI TASA.

South Seas Evangelical Church: POB 16, Honiara; tel. 22388; fax 20302; Pres. ERIC TAKILA; Gen. Sec. CHARLES J. RAFEASI.

United Church in Solomon Islands: POB 82, Munda, Western Province; tel. 61125; fax 61265; e-mail ucsihq@solomon.com.sb; a Methodist church; Bishop of Solomon Islands Region Rev. PHILEMON RITI; Gen. Sec. Rev. ESAU TUZA.

BAHÁ'Í FAITH

National Spiritual Assembly: POB 245, Honiara; tel. 22475; fax 25368; e-mail bahainsa@welkam.solomon.com.sb.

ISLAM

Solomon Islands Muslim League: Honiara; Gen. Sec. Dr MUSTAPHA RAMO; 66 mems; In mid-1997 the organization was still awaiting official registration as a religious group in Solomon Islands.

The Press

Agrikalsa Nius (Agriculture News): POB G13, Honiara; tel. 21211; fax 21955; f. 1986; monthly; Editor ALFRED MAESULIA; circ. 1,000.

Citizens' Press: Honiara; monthly.

Link: Solomon Islands Development Trust, POB 147, Honiara; tel. 21130; fax 21131; pidgin and English; 3 or 4 per year.

Solomon Nius: POB 718, Honiara; tel. 22031; fax 26401; monthly; Dept of Information publication; Editor-in-Chief THOMAS KIVO; monthly; circ. 2,000.

Solomon Star: POB 255, Honiara; tel. 22913; fax 21572; f. 1982; daily; English; Dir JOHN W. LAMANI; Editor OFANI EREMAI (acting); circ. 4,000.

Solomon Times: POB 212, Honiara; tel. 39197; fax 39197; weekly; Chief Editor and Man. Dir EDWARD KINGMELE.

Solomon Voice: POB 1235, Honiara; tel. 20116; fax 20090; f. 1992; daily; circ. 3,000; Editor CAROL COLVILLE.

Broadcasting and Communications

TELECOMMUNICATIONS

Telekom (Solomon Telekom Company Ltd): POB 148, Honiara; tel. 21576; fax 23642; e-mail sales@telekom.com.sb; internet www.solomon.com.sb; 51% owned by Solomon Islands National Provident Fund, 41.9% by Cable and Wireless plc., 7.1% by Govt; operates national and international telecommunications links; Chair. JOHN BEVERLY; Gen. Man. MARTYN ROBINSON.

BROADCASTING

Radio

Solomon Islands Broadcasting Corporation: POB 654, Honiara; tel. 20051; fax 23159; e-mail sibcnews@solomon.com.sb;

internet www.sibconline.com; f. 1976; daily transmissions in English and Pidgin; broadcasts total 112 hours per week; Chair. DICKSON WARAKOHIA; Programme Dir DAVID PALAPU; Gen. Man. JOHNSON HONIMAE; Editor WALTER NALANGU.

Finance

The financial system is regulated and monitored by the Central Bank of Solomon Islands. There are three commercial banks and a development bank. Financial statutory corporations include the Home Finance Corpn (which took over from the Housing Authority in 1990), the Investment Corporation of Solomon Islands (the state holding company) and the National Provident Fund. At the end of 1996 there were 142 credit unions, with some 17,000 members and total assets estimated at SI $18m.

BANKING

(cap. = capital; res = reserves; dep. = deposits; brs = branches; amounts in Solomon Islands dollars)

Central Bank

Central Bank of Solomon Islands: POB 634, Honiara; tel. 21791; fax 23513; e-mail cbsi-it@welkam.solomon.com.sb; f. 1983; sole bank of issue; cap. 2.6m., res 93.5m., dep. 26.9m. (Dec. 1997); Gov. RICK HOUWENIPWELA; Deputy Gov. JOHN KAITU.

Development Bank

Development Bank of Solomon Islands: POB 911, Honiara; tel. 21595; fax 23715; e-mail dbsi@welkam.solomon.com.sb; f. 1978; cap. 8.6m., res 4.6m. (Dec. 1998); Chair. JOHN MICHAEL ASIPARA; Man. Dir LUKE LAYMAN ETA; 4 brs; 5 sub-brs.

Commercial Banks

Australia and New Zealand Banking Group Ltd (Australia): Mendana Ave, POB 10, Honiara; tel. 21835; fax 22957; Gen. Man. CECIL BROWNE.

National Bank of Solomon Islands Ltd: Mendana Ave, POB 37, Honiara; tel. 21874; fax 24358; e-mail nbsi@welkam.solomon.com.sb; f. 1982; 51% owned by the Bank of Hawaii; 49% owned by Solomon Islands National Provident Fund; cap. 2.0m., res 20.0m., dep. 221.3m. (Dec. 1999); Chair. W. M. ORD; Gen. Man. E. MURRAY; 11 brs and 6 agencies.

Westpac Banking Corporation (Australia): 721 Mendana Ave, POB 466, Honiara; tel. 21222; fax 23419; e-mail gtaviani@westpac.com.au; Man. GIAN TAVIANI.

INSURANCE

About 10 major British insurance companies maintain agencies in Solomon Islands. In mid-1995 the Government announced a joint venture with an Australian insurance company to establish the Solomon Islands Insurance Company.

Trade and Industry

GOVERNMENT AGENCY

Investment Corporation of Solomon Islands: POB 570, Honiara; tel. 22511; holding company through which the Government retains equity stakes in a number of corporations; Chair. FRANCIS BILLY HILLY.

DEVELOPMENT ORGANIZATIONS

Solomon Islands Development Trust (SIDT): POB 147, Honiara; tel. 21130; fax 21331; e-mail sidt@welkam.solomon.com.sb; f. 1982; development org; Chief Officer ABRAHAM BALANISIA.

CHAMBER OF COMMERCE

Solomon Islands Chamber of Commerce and Employers: POB 650, Honiara; tel. 22643; fax 22907; e-mail chamberc@welkam.solomon.com.sb; 116 member cos (Sept. 2000); Chair. DAVID QUAN; Gen. Sec. HILDA TANGO.

INDUSTRIAL AND TRADE ASSOCIATIONS

Association of Mining and Exploration Companies: c/o POB G24, Honiara; f. 1988; Pres. NELSON GREG YOUNG.

Commodities Export Marketing Authority: POB 54, Honiara; tel. 22528; fax 21262; e-mail cema@solomon.com.sb; sole exporter of copra; agencies at Honiara and Yandina; Chair. HUGO RAGOSO; Gen. Man. MOSES PELOMO.

Livestock Development Authority: Honiara; tel. 29649; fax 29214; f. 1977; privatized 1996; Man. Dir WARREN TUCKER.

Solomon Islands Business Enterprise Centre: POB 972, Honiara; tel. 26651; fax 26650; e-mail simbec@solomon.com.sb.

Solomon Islands Forest Industries Association: POB 1617, Honiara; tel. 26026; fax 20267; Chair. and Sec. KAIPUA TOHI.

EMPLOYERS' ORGANIZATIONS

Chinese Association: POB 1209, Honiara; tel. 22351; fax 23480; asscn of businessmen from the ethnic Chinese community.

Federation of Solomon Islands Business: POB 320, Honiara; tel. 22902; fax 21477.

Solomon Islands Farmers' Association: POB 113, Honiara; tel. 27508; fax 27509; founded a credit union in 1990; Technical Adviser. SRI RAMON JUN QUITALES.

Solomon Islands Chamber of Commerce and Employers: See above.

UTILITIES

Electricity

Solomon Islands Electricity Authority (SIEA): POB 6, Honiara; tel. 21711; fax 21467; e-mail mike@siea.com.sb; f. 1961; Chair. DANNY BULA; CEO M. L. NATION.

Water

Solomon Islands Water Authority (SIWA): POB 1407; Honiara; tel. 23985; fax 20723; f. 1994; Gen. Man. DONALD MAKINI.

CO-OPERATIVE SOCIETIES

In 1986 there were 156 primary co-operative societies, working mostly outside the capital. There are two associations running and aiding co-operative societies in Solomon Islands:

Central Co-operative Association (CCA): Honiara.

Salu Fishing Cooperative Association: POB 1041, Honiara; tel. 26550.

Solomon Islands Consumers Co-operative Society Ltd: Honiara; tel. 21798; fax 23640.

Solomon Islands Farmers and Producers Cooperative Association Ltd: Honiara; tel. 30908.

Western General Co-operative Association (WGCA): Gizo, Western Province.

TRADE UNIONS

There are 14 registered trade unions in Solomon Islands.

Solomon Islands Council of Trade Unions (SICTU): National Centre for Trade Unions, POB 271, Honiara; tel. 22566; fax 23171; f. 1986; Pres. DAVID P. TUHANUKU; Sec. BENEDICT ESIBAEA; the principal affiliated unions are:

Solomon Islands Media Association: POB 654, Honiara; tel. 20051; fax 23300; e-mail sibcnews@welkam.solomon.com.sb; Pres. GEORGE ATKIN.

Solomon Islands Medical Association: Honiara.

Solomon Islands National Teachers' Association (SINTA): POB 967, Honiara; f. 1985; Pres. K. SANGA; Gen. Sec. BENEDICT ESIBAEA.

Solomon Islands National Union of Workers (SINUW): POB 14, Honiara; tel. 22629; Pres. DAVID P. TUHANUKU.

Solomon Islands Post and Telecommunications Union: Honiara; tel. 21821; fax 20440; Gen. Man. SAMUEL SIVE.

Solomon Islands Public Employees' Union (SIPEU): POB 360, Honiara; tel. 21967; fax 23110; Pres. MARTIN KARANI; Sec.-Gen. CLEMENT WAIWORI.

Solomon Islands Seamen's Association: POB G32, Honiara; tel. 24942; fax 23798.

Transport

ROADS

There are about 1,300 km of roads maintained by the central and provincial governments; in 1976 main roads covered 455 km. In addition, there are 800 km of privately maintained roads mainly for plantation use. Road construction and maintenance is difficult because of the nature of the country, and what roads there are serve as feeder roads to the main town of an island.

Honiara has a main road running about 65 km each side of it along the north coast of Guadalcanal, and Malaita has a road 157 km long running north of Auki and around the northern end of the island to the Lau Lagoon, where canoe transport takes over; and one running south for 35 km to Masa. On Makira a road links Kira Kira and Kakoranga, a distance of 35 km. Before it abandoned mining investigations in 1977, the Mitsui Mining and Smelting Co built 40 km of road on Rennell Island.

SHIPPING

Regular shipping services (mainly cargo) exist between Solomon Islands and Australia, New Zealand, Hong Kong, Japan, Singapore, Taiwan and European ports. In 1994 internal shipping was provided by 93 passenger/cargo ships, 13 passenger-only ships, 61 fishing vessels and 17 tugs. The four main ports are at Honiara, Yandina, Noro and Gizo. The international seaports of Honiara and Noro are controlled by the Solomon Islands Ports Authority.

Solomon Islands Ports Authority: POB 307, Honiara; tel. 22646; fax 23994; e-mail ports@solomon.com.sb; f. 1956; responsible for the ports of Honiara and Noro; Chair. NELSON BOSO; Gen. Man. N. B. KABUI.

Sullivans (SI) Ltd: POB 3, Honiara; tel. 21643; fax 23889; e-mail shipserv@solomon.com.sb; shipping agents, importers, wholesalers.

National Shipping Service of Solomon Islands (NSSI): Honiara; f. 1994; Gen. Man. NELSON KABUI.

Tradco Shipping Ltd: POB 114, Honiara; tel. 22588; fax 23887; e-mail tradco@solomon.com.sb; f. 1984; shipping agents, agents for Lloyd's; Man. Dir GERALD STENZEL.

CIVIL AVIATION

Two airports are open to international traffic and a further 25 serve internal flights. Air Niugini (Papua New Guinea), Air Nauru and Qantas (Australia) fly to the principal airport of Henderson, 13 km from Honiara. In March 1998 a new terminal building, built with US $15.5m. of funds from Japan, was opened at Henderson airport.

Director of Civil Aviation: DEMETRIUS T. PIZIKI.

Solomon Airlines Limited: POB 23, Honiara; tel. 20031; fax 20232; e-mail gzoleveke@solair.com.sb; internet solomonairlines .com.au; f. 1968; govt-owned; international and domestic operator; scheduled services between Honiara and Port Moresby (Papua New Guinea), Nadi (Fiji), Brisbane (Australia) and Port Vila (Vanuatu); Chair. STEPHEN TONAFALEA; Gen. Man. GIDEON ZOLEVEKE Jr.

Tourism

Tourism is hindered by the relative inaccessibility of the islands and the inadequacy of tourist facilities. In 2000 tourist arrivals totalled 25,127. The industry earned US $13m. in 1998.

Solomon Islands Visitors Bureau: POB 321, Honiara; tel. 22442; fax 23986; e-mail visitors@solomon.com.sb; internet www.commerce .gov.sb/tourism/index.htm; f. 1980; Gen. Man. MORRIS OTTO NAMOGA; Marketing Man. ANDREW NIHOPARA.

SOMALIA

Introductory Survey

Location, Climate, Language, Religion, Flag, Capital

The Somali Democratic Republic lies on the east coast of Africa, with Ethiopia to the north-west and Kenya to the west. There is a short frontier with Djibouti to the north-west. Somalia has a long coastline on the Indian Ocean and the Gulf of Aden, forming the 'Horn of Africa'. The climate is generally hot and dry, with an average annual temperature of 27°C (80°F). It is hotter in the interior and on the Gulf of Aden, but cooler on the Indian Ocean coast. Average annual rainfall is less than 430 mm (17 ins). The national language is Somali, but Arabic is also in official use. English and Italian are widely spoken. The state religion is Islam, and the majority of Somalis are Sunni Muslims. There is a small Christian community, mostly Roman Catholics. The national flag (proportions 2 by 3) is pale blue, with a large five-pointed white star in the centre. The capital is Mogadishu.

Recent History

Somalia was formed by a merger of two former colonial territories: British Somaliland, in the north, and its larger and more populous neighbour, Italian Somaliland. The United Kingdom established a protectorate in British Somaliland in 1886. Italian Somaliland originated in 1889, when Italy concluded agreements with two local rulers, who placed their territories under Italian protection. Italy's occupation of the region was subsequently extended along the coast and inland, and Italian control was completed in 1927. Italian forces in Somaliland and Eritrea invaded and occupied neighbouring Abyssinia (Ethiopia) in 1935–36. During the Second World War British Somaliland was conquered temporarily by Italian troops, but in 1941 it was recaptured by a British counter-offensive, which also forced the Italians to withdraw from Eritrea, Italian Somaliland and Ethiopia. A British military administration was then established in British and Italian Somaliland.

Under the provisions of the post-war peace treaty of February 1947, Italy renounced all rights to Italian Somaliland. In December 1950, however, the pre-war colony became the UN Trust Territory of Somalia, with Italy returning as the administering power for a 10-year transitional period, prior to independence. The territory's first general election on the basis of universal adult suffrage was held in March 1959, when 83 of the 90 seats in the Legislative Assembly were won by the Somali Youth League (SYL), a pro-Western party led by the Prime Minister, Seyyid Abdullah Issa.

British Somaliland reverted to civilian rule in 1948. The British colonial authorities prepared the territory for self-government, and the first general election took place in March 1959. Fresh elections, for a new legislative council, were held in February 1960, with all parties in favour of early independence and the unification of all Somali territories. Representatives of British Somaliland and the Trust Territory of Somalia met in April and agreed on a merger of the two territories in an independent republic. British Somaliland was granted independence on 26 June 1960, and the merger received unanimous approval by the legislature on the following day.

Accordingly, the union of former British and Italian Somaliland took effect on 1 July 1960, when the independent Somali Republic was proclaimed. Dr Aden Abdullah Osman, hitherto President of the legislature of the southern territory, was elected to be the first President of the new Republic, and the legislatures of the two Somali regions merged to create a single National Assembly. The two dominant parties in former British Somaliland joined with the SYL to form a tripartite coalition government. Dr Abd ar-Rashid Ali Shermarke of the SYL became Prime Minister. In June 1964 Shermarke resigned as Prime Minister and was replaced by Abd ar-Razak Hussein, who formed a cabinet exclusively from members of the SYL. In June 1967, however, Shermarke was elected by the National Assembly to replace President Osman. He appointed a new Cabinet, led by Mohamed Ibrahim Egal, the former Prime Minister of British Somaliland.

On 15 October 1969 President Shermarke was assassinated. Six days later the army seized control in a coup on the eve of a planned presidential election. Power was assumed by the armed forces Commander-in-Chief, Maj.-Gen. Mohamed Siad Barre. The 1960 Constitution was suspended, political parties were abolished and the National Assembly was dissolved. A new Government was formed by the Supreme Revolutionary Council (SRC), chaired by Siad Barre, which proclaimed the Somali Democratic Republic. In October 1970 Siad Barre declared Somalia a socialist state and began a revolutionary programme of national unification and social and economic reform. In July 1976 the SRC dissolved itself, and power was transferred to the newly formed Somali Revolutionary Socialist Party (SRSP), with Siad Barre as Secretary-General.

A new Constitution came into force in September 1979. Elections were held in December for a new legislature, the People's Assembly, which, in January 1980, elected Siad Barre as President of the Republic. A government reshuffle in March 1982 was notable for the increasing influence of Siad Barre's Marehan clan at the expense of the northern Majerteen and Isaaq clans, from which the main insurgent opposition groups drew their support. Constitutional amendments, approved by the Assembly in November 1984, effectively transferred all powers of government to the President. Despite continuing internal unrest, at elections to the Assembly, in December, a single list of SRSP candidates was reportedly endorsed by 99.9% of voters.

A presidential election, at which Siad Barre was the sole candidate, took place in December 1986, confirming his presidency for a further seven-year term by 99.9% of a reported 4.9m. votes cast. Although Lt-Gen. Mohamed Ali Samater was appointed to the newly created post of Prime Minister in February 1987, the President continued to dominate Somalia's political life.

In October 1981 the Somali Salvation Front formed the Democratic Front for the Salvation of Somalia (DFSS, later renamed the Somali Salvation Democratic Front—SSDF) with two other opposition groups. Together with another group founded in 1981, the Somali National Movement (SNM), and with substantial Ethiopian military support, DFSS guerrillas invaded the central border area of Somalia in July 1982. The invasion was contained by the Somali national forces but, despite US and Italian military aid, they failed to expel the rebel troops from the country. Following a meeting between Siad Barre and Lt-Col Mengistu, the Ethiopian leader, in January 1986, Ethiopian military support for the insurgent groups was reduced, particularly in respect of the DFSS.

Anti-Government demonstrations in Mogadishu in July 1989, in protest at the arrest of several leading Muslim clerics, were violently suppressed by the armed forces, resulting in the deaths of more than 400 demonstrators. Two recently created opposition groups, the United Somali Congress (USC—composed of Hawiye clan intellectuals) and the National United Front of Somalia (allegedly dominated by disaffected army officers), were thought to have orchestrated the demonstrations. Two government ministers were dismissed subsequently, accused of threatening state security. In August, amid reports that the ruling Marehan clan had lost the crucial support of the Ogadeni clan, the President offered to relinquish power and announced that the next elections would take place in the context of a multiparty system. At the same time there were reports of fighting between government troops and members of the Ogadeni clan in southern Somalia, and Western sources claimed that the only areas of the country that remained under government control were Mogadishu, parts of Hargeysa and Berbera. In September it was reported that Ogadeni deserters from the army had formed two new opposition groupings: the Somali Patriotic Movement (SPM) in the south and the Somali National Army in central Somalia.

Meanwhile, the USC gained support in the south, where its forces were fighting alongside those of the SPM. In the north the emergence of the Somali Democratic Alliance (SDA), led by Mohamed Farah Abdullah, intensified the challenge to Siad Barre's authority. The President responded to these pressures by dismissing the Government in January 1990 and offering posts (which were refused) in a successor administration to prominent opposition leaders. A new Government, headed by Samater, took office in February.

In July 1990 the Council of Ministers endorsed the proposals of August 1989 for the democratization of Somalia's political system. It was decided that, following a review by the People's Assembly, a new constitution would be submitted to a national referendum in October, and that multi-party legislative and local government elections would be held in February 1991. In August 1990 the USC, the SNM and the SPM agreed to co-ordinate their separate military campaigns to overthrow Siad Barre. In September the President appointed a new Government, led by Mohamed Hawadle Madar, a member of the Isaaq clan. In October the Government announced the immediate introduction of the new Constitution and a new electoral code. Siad Barre relinquished the post of Secretary-General of the SRSP, in accordance with the Constitution, which stipulated that the President should hold no responsibilities other than those of the presidency. Despite the apparent readiness of the new Government to hasten the process of political reform, the principal insurgent groups showed no signs of relaxing their military campaigns, and in November SPM forces seized control of Kismayu, in southern Somalia. On 25 December legislation was introduced to permit the establishment of political parties opposed to the Government.

On 1 January 1991 the USC announced that it had captured most areas of Mogadishu and that it had besieged the home of Siad Barre. It rejected offers by Egypt and Italy to mediate in the conflict. On 27 January Siad Barre was reported to have fled the capital with those forces remaining loyal to him, and the USC took power. It immediately invited all former opposition groups to participate in a national conference to discuss the democratization of Somalia. On 29 January the USC appointed Ali Mahdi Mohamed (a government minister in the 1960s) as President, in a temporary capacity, and he, in turn, invited Umar Arteh Ghalib (a former foreign affairs minister) to form a government that would prepare the country for democracy. The provisional Government was approved by the President on 2 February. However, both the SNM and the SPM opposed the appointment of Ali Mahdi as interim President.

The USC emphasized that it did not intend to form a permanent government independently of the other insurgent movements that had collaborated in the overthrow of Siad Barre; however, by mid-March 1991 Somalia was close to anarchy. A consolidation of the divisions between the various Somali clans was taking place, while Siad Barre was reported to have re-located to his native region of Gedo, near the border with Kenya, accompanied by loyal armed forces. Opposition movements rejected the USC's invitation to take part in a national conference, and the SNM was reported to have formed an 11-member administration and a legislature to govern the former territory of British Somaliland.

In May 1991 the SNM announced its official support for the secession of the former territory of British Somaliland, which the leaders of the northern-based clans were demanding. Later in the month the SNM Central Committee elected Abd ar-Rahman Ahmed Ali 'Tur' as President of the self-proclaimed 'Republic of Somaliland'. In June the Committee approved a 17-member government to administer the territory for a period of two years, after which free elections were to be held.

The SNM declined an invitation issued by the USC to participate in a conference of national reconciliation in June 1991, stating that it did not concern 'Somaliland'. The conference, convened in Djibouti, was attended by representatives of the USC, the Somali Democratic Movement (SDM), the SPM and the DFSS, and was chaired by former President Osman. The conference mandated delegates from the four organizations to travel to 'Somaliland' to persuade the SNM to abandon its declaration of independence. The SNM insisted, however, that the secession of 'Somaliland' from Somalia was irreversible. At a second reconciliation conference, held in Djibouti in July, the four groups that had met in June were joined by the United Somali Front (USF) and the SDA. The leaders of the six groups signed a manifesto, which, *inter alia*, committed them to defeat the forces of Siad Barre (which had regrouped as the Somali National Front—SNF), to readopt the 1960 Constitution, which Barre had suspended in 1969, and to implement a general cease-fire. The manifesto also confirmed Ali Mahdi in his position as Somalia's President for a period of two years pending free elections. The participants in the conference agreed that a transitional government was to be formed, in which each of the groups would be represented, with an equitable distribution of

major posts and portfolios. Ali Mahdi was sworn in as President on 18 August 1991, and in September he reappointed Umar Arteh Ghalib as Prime Minister; in October the latter announced the formation of a newly expanded Government, comprising 72 ministers and deputy ministers, in order to ensure equal representation for the six participating groups.

In June 1991 a major rift developed within the USC, and supporters of President Ali Mahdi clashed with those of the USC's military commander, Gen. Mohamed Farah Aidid, in Mogadishu. Aidid objected to Ali Mahdi's assumption of the presidency, since he had commanded the military campaign to overthrow Siad Barre. Moreover, the rival factions represented two 'sub-clans' of the Hawiye tribal grouping: although there was no tradition of enmity between the two sub-clans, rivalry was now fostered by the leaders, and clan loyalty quickly became entrenched. In July Aidid was elected Chairman of the USC. The internal conflict appeared to have abated following Ali Mahdi's inauguration as President in August: Aidid pledged to support the new President, and the two signed a co-operation agreement. However, in October Aidid rejected the legitimacy of the Government appointed earlier that month, and in November his faction launched a major offensive on the President's positions in the capital (which largely represented the extent of Ali Mahdi's control of the country), capturing most of the city and forcing Ali Mahdi to flee. Aidid claimed to have overthrown the President, but by late November Ali Mahdi appeared to have regained control of much of the north of Mogadishu. The fighting subsequently intensified, and in December Ali Mahdi appealed to the UN to send a peace-keeping force to intervene in the conflict. The UN responded by sending a special envoy to Mogadishu in January 1992. However, the envoy's attempts to negotiate a cease-fire were thwarted by Aidid's refusal to agree to UN involvement in Somalia's internal affairs, and the mission was followed by an escalation in violence. In mid-January Aidid appointed his own, 21-member administration. By the end of March it was estimated that 14,000 people (mostly civilians) had been killed and 27,000 wounded in the hostilities in Mogadishu.

In January 1992 the UN imposed an embargo on the sale of armaments to Somalia. In the following month the UN, the Organization of African Unity (now the African Union, see p. 130), the League of Arab States (the Arab League, see p. 260) and the Organization of the Islamic Conference (OIC, see p. 295) issued a joint appeal for a cease-fire, stating that it was a prerequisite for the granting of humanitarian aid to Somalia. Representatives from the rival factions in Mogadishu subsequently joined the conference and agreed to the terms of a cease-fire accord devised by the international organizations. In March, in discussions with a joint mission of the UN, the OAU, the OIC and the Arab League in Mogadishu, Aidid agreed to some form of monitoring of the cease-fire by a foreign observer mission. The terms of the cease-fire accord (signed by both Aidid and Ali Mahdi) provided for a visit, in late March, by a UN technical team, to survey the situation in Mogadishu, in advance of the dispatch of an unarmed observer mission. In April the UN Security Council approved the establishment of a 'UN Operation in Somalia' (UNOSOM), to comprise a 50-strong observer mission to monitor the cease-fire, while it also agreed, in principle, to the dispatch of a peace-keeping force to protect UN personnel and supplies at Mogadishu's port, and to escort food supplies to distribution points. However, the Security Council needed to obtain consent for the peace-keeping force from both parties involved in the conflict, and Aidid was opposed to the deployment of foreign military personnel in Somalia. In late April the UN Secretary-General appointed a special representative to Somalia to oversee UN activities.

In April 1992 the SNF advanced on Mogadishu, with Siad Barre apparently intent on recapturing the capital. Forces of the SNF came to within 40 km of the capital, but Gen. Aidid's militias decisively repelled them, pursuing them to the south of the country. At the end of April the USC captured the town of Garba Harre, in the south-west, which had served as Siad Barre's base since his overthrow. Siad Barre fled, with some 200 supporters, to Kenya. (Siad Barre was refused political asylum in Kenya, and in May he moved to Nigeria, where he died in exile in January 1995.) In May Aidid's forces and those of the SPM, the SDM and the Southern Somali National Movement (SSNM), with which he had formed a military alliance known as the Somali Liberation Army (SLA), captured Kismayu, which had been held by the SNF, a rival faction of the SPM and the SSDF. By June the SLA was in control of the majority of central and southern Somalia, making Aidid the most powerful of the country's warlords. In late June the UN secured agreement from the principal factions in Mogadishu for the deployment of the 50-strong observer mission envisaged in the March cease-fire accord. In August, after much prevarication, Aidid agreed to the deployment of 500 UN troops entrusted with escorting food aid from Mogadishu's port and airport to distribution points. By late September the armed UN group had arrived, but were yet to be deployed. Meanwhile, in August the UN Security Council approved the dispatch of a further 3,000 troops to Somalia, although this was opposed by Aidid.

Also in August 1992 the coalition of Gen. Aidid's faction of the USC with the SPM, the SDM and the SSNM was consolidated with the formation of the Somali National Alliance (SNA), of which Aidid was the leader. Meanwhile, Ali Mahdi strengthened ties with other armed groups hostile to Aidid, notably the SSDF and a faction of the SPM, and forged links with the SNA's main opponent in the south, Gen. Mohamed Siad Hersi 'Morgan' (who had led the SNF since the departure of his father-in-law, Siad Barre). In October forces loyal to Gen. 'Morgan' temporarily ousted those of the SNA from Bardera, which had served as Aidid's headquarters in that part of the country. Kismayu subsequently became the focus for hostilities between the SNF and the SNA (the SNA faction of the SPM holding control of the town).

In September 1992 'Somaliland' stated its categorical opposition to the deployment of UN troops within its borders. By early November UNOSOM's 500 armed troops still had not been deployed: Gen. Aidid placed conditions on their deployment in Mogadishu's port that were unacceptable to the UN. Later in the month UNOSOM secured Mogadishu's airport with the agreement of the clan controlling it; however, the 3,000 additional UN troops were not dispatched. The USA subsequently offered to lead a military operation in the country, with a US contingent of up to 30,000 men. The proposed US operation was sanctioned by the Security Council in early December. Shortly afterwards an advance contingent of 1,800 US marines landed on the beaches of Mogadishu and took control of the port and airport. Aidid and Ali Mahdi had instructed their supporters that the US forces were amicable, and consequently they encountered little resistance. The arrival of the foreign force, however, provoked fierce fighting in Kismayu, Baidoa and the north-east, with rival factions attempting to gain territory before the expected imposition of a cease-fire. The US members of the Unified Task Force (UNITAF) were reinforced subsequently by troops from 21 other countries.

Shortly after the arrival of UNITAF, Gen. Aidid and Ali Mahdi signed a peace agreement (at talks chaired by the US Special Envoy to Somalia), providing for an end to hostilities between the two USC factions. Aidid and Ali Mahdi subsequently met again and agreed to implement fully their initial peace accord, which had been flouted by both sides. A peace demonstration organized by the two leaders, in which about 10,000 people participated, followed this new agreement. However, shortly afterwards heavy fighting was reported between the SNA and militants of the Murusade clan in north-west Mogadishu.

In January 1993 14 of Somalia's political organizations attended peace negotiations in Addis Ababa, Ethiopia, held under the auspices of the UN. The talks resulted in agreements on an immediate cease-fire, disarmament under UN supervision and the holding of a conference of national reconciliation in March. Despite the cease-fire agreement, hostilities were resumed in various parts of the country almost immediately. Fighting was reported between the SNA and SSDF in the northeast, and the SNF continued its campaign to wrest control of the south from the SNA. In February 1993 UNITAF repulsed attacks on Kismayu, launched by Gen. 'Morgan', but later in the month the SNF made gains in the city, prompting violent anti-UNITAF demonstrations by SNA supporters in Mogadishu, who accused UNITAF of assisting Gen. 'Morgan'. Fighting between UNITAF troops and armed Somali youths continued in the capital for several days: at least seven Somalis were shot dead by the international force. In the battle for Kismayu more than 100 people were killed in late February. Gen. 'Morgan' finally yielded to demands by UNITAF to withdraw from the city at the end of the month, and in early March both the SNF and SNA surrendered heavy weapons to UNITAF. In mid-March the national reconciliation conference opened in Addis Ababa, but proceedings were adjourned almost immediately, when Aidid withdrew in protest at a renewed SNF attack on Kismayu. Discussions subsequently resumed, and in late March the

leaders agreed to an accord providing for the establishment of a Transitional National Council as the supreme authority in Somalia, with a mandate to hold elections within two years. The Council was to comprise 74 members: one from each of the 15 organizations represented at the conference, three from each of the 18 proposed administrative regions (inclusive of 'Somaliland') and five from Mogadishu.

Agreement on the future government of Somalia was reached hours after the UN Security Council approved the establishment of UNOSOM II, which was to take over responsibility for maintaining security from UNITAF by 1 May 1993. UNOSOM II was to be the UN's largest ever peace-keeping operation, comprising 28,000 military personnel and 2,800 civilian staff, and its first where peace-enforcement without consent from parties within the country was authorized. UNOSOM II was, in addition, to be responsible for overseeing the rehabilitation of the country and the repatriation of Somali refugees. In January 1993 US forces had begun to be redeployed, and were replaced by military personnel from other countries; however, the USA was expected to maintain a contingent of 5,000 in UNOSOM II. Hostilities in and around Kismayu continued after the national reconciliation conference, although none of the parties involved threatened to withdraw from the agreement. By April Gen. 'Morgan' appeared to be in control of the city, with the SNA accusing UNITAF of supporting the SNF by failing to oppose its advances (a claim that was not wholly refuted by the Belgian forces responsible for Kismayu). In May the USA transferred responsibility for international efforts in Somalia to UNOSOM II; shortly afterwards Belgian troops (under UN command) were involved in an armed confrontation with SPM forces attempting to enter Kismayu. In June 24 Pakistani members of UNOSOM II were killed, and more than 50 injured, when they were attacked by supporters of Gen. Aidid while attempting to inspect a weapons cache belonging to the SNA; 23 Somali fighters were killed in the confrontation. The Security Council adopted a resolution that condemned the attack on UN forces and sought to bring to justice those responsible. UNOSOM forces embarked on a series of armed initiatives, including air strikes, against suspected strategic positions of the SNA. An exchange of gunfire between Pakistani troops and Somali militiamen, during a demonstration against the intensification of the UN's campaign of enforced disarmament, resulted in the deaths of more than 20 civilians. Despite the increased scale of UNOSOM operations, Aidid avoided injury or capture during June, prompting the Security Council to issue a formal warrant for his arrest. The violent deaths of three Italian UNOSOM soldiers in July provoked Italian media claims that the military emphasis of the mission, promoted by the USA in pursuit of Aidid, was threatening the security of UN personnel and jeopardizing diplomatic initiatives undertaken by the Italian Government. The situation was exacerbated by a US helicopter attack on a suspected pro-Aidid command centre, which resulted in the deaths of 50–100 Somalis, and the murder, in retaliation, of four foreign journalists by enraged Somali crowds.

The allegedly belligerent methods employed by the UN in Somalia were subject to renewed scrutiny following sustained hostilities between UNOSOM forces and Somali militia during August 1993 (resulting in fatalities on both sides), culminating in a major embarrassment for the USA, when, owing to inaccurate intelligence reports, the first operation involving US Ranger élite forces resulted in the forced occupation of the offices of a French humanitarian aid organization and the building being used by the UN Development Programme (eight of whose employees were temporarily taken captive by the US force). Further misgivings were expressed in September, following the deaths of an estimated 200 Somalis, after the armed intervention of a US helicopter in support of UN forces under fire in the midst of a crowd of civilians, in the capital. The UN Secretary-General attributed the tragedy to the Somali militia's practice of sheltering behind civilians while firing.

Uncompromising media coverage of the aftermath of the deaths of three US soldiers in September 1993, and a violent exchange in the capital in October (which resulted in the deaths of some 300 Somalis, 18 US servicemen and the capture, by local militiamen, of a US helicopter pilot and a Nigerian soldier), prompted widespread public outrage in the USA and encouraged US congressional demands for a reassessment of the US role in Somalia. The US President, Bill Clinton, subsequently indicated a shift in US policy toward fostering multilateral political contacts in Somalia and announced that all US troops were to be withdrawn by the end of March 1994, regardless of the outcome of attempts to negotiate a political settlement to the conflict by that date. (In the mean time the US military presence was to be increased significantly.) Clinton's decision, announced in October, to withdraw the Ranger forces (which had actively sought to apprehend Aidid) prompted speculation that the release of the US pilot and the Nigerian soldier, secured in mid-October following lengthy discussions between representatives of the US Government and Aidid, had been achieved as part of an undisclosed bilateral agreement. Despite Aidid's declaration of a unilateral cease-fire prior to the talks, and subsequent indications of his willingness to enter into negotiations with the USA (in preference to the UN), fighting between pro-Aidid and pro-Mahdi factions escalated. In November, responding to US pressure to sponsor Aidid's participation in the pursuit of a politically negotiated peace, the UN Security Council adopted a resolution providing for the establishment of a commission of inquiry to investigate attacks on UNOSOM personnel, but suspending actions to apprehend further suspects (including Aidid). In December Aidid and Ali Mahdi (who in November reportedly assumed the leadership of the Somali Salvation Alliance—SSA, a coalition of 12 factions opposed to Aidid) attended negotiations in Addis Ababa, but discussions disintegrated with little progress.

In February 1994, in the context of the imminent withdrawal of UNOSOM contingents from the USA and several other Western nations, the UN Security Council revised UNOSOM's mandate, reducing the troop strength of the mission to a maximum of 22,000. In March, following protracted negotiations, initiated by the UN, an agreement on the restoration of peace was signed by Aidid and Ali Mahdi (on behalf of the SSA) in Nairobi, Kenya, committing both sides to a cease-fire, disarmament and the organization of a conference of national reconciliation in May to elect a president, vice-presidents and a prime minister. (A similar agreement, concluded in Nairobi days later between community leaders from the lower Juba region, sought to restore order to the port of Kismayu, where fighting between factions had intensified in February.) Electoral procedures and a future legislative structure were to be decided at a meeting of all signatories to the 1993 Addis Ababa agreement and the SNM, to be convened in April. By mid-1994, however, no such meeting had taken place, with accusations of failure to adhere to the terms of the Nairobi agreement proceeding from both Aidid and the SSA. Prospects for the successful organization of the meeting were further complicated by serious divisions within the SNM, arising from a declaration made by Ahmed Ali 'Tur', the former head of the self-proclaimed 'Republic of Somaliland', that the region should seek reintegration within a reconciled national territory of Somalia (an opinion that was strenuously opposed by Egal, the territory's new President—see below).

In June 1994 the UN Security Council agreed to renew UNOSOM's mandate by four months; in November it extended the mandate to a final date of 31 March 1995. In October 1994 fierce fighting erupted in Mogadishu between Ali Mahdi's Abgal clan and the Murusade clan. Hostilities continued sporadically into January 1995 (resulting in as many as 200 fatalities), in which month the two clans brokered a peace agreement. As the deadline for UNOSOM's departure approached, the competition for control of installations currently held by the UN, in particular the port and airport, became the focus of factional hostility.

In November 1994 UN forces began to withdraw from positions outside Mogadishu in the first stages of UNOSOM's departure. In December Harti and Marehan clansmen fought for control of Kismayu port in the wake of the UN's withdrawal from that town. 'Operation United Shield', to ensure the safe evacuation of the UN troops and civilian personnel, as well as most of the equipment brought in under UNOSOM, was organized and led by the USA. The USA stationed several thousand marines in warships off the Somali coast in December, and in early 1995 they were joined by a multinational force of naval and air force units (comprising some 10,000 armed personnel) in order to protect departing UN employees (by early 1995 some 136 members of UNOSOM had been killed since the beginning of the operation).

In early February 1995 UN troops left their compound in Mogadishu, which had served as UNOSOM's headquarters, and withdrew to positions in the port and airport. In mid-February thousands of SNA supporters demonstrated against the return of US forces, although Aidid gave assurances that they would not be attacked. Although Aidid and Ali Mahdi reached agreement on joint management of the port and airport, as well as a cessation of hostilities, including the removal of weapons from the streets of the capital during the UN withdrawal, in late February fighting was reported around both the port and airport areas. At the end of February 1,800 US and 400 Italian marines landed on Mogadishu's beaches, and command of the remaining 2,400 UN troops and of the whole operation was passed from the UN to the US commander. The marines secured the port and airport, and evacuated the remaining UN soldiers. The departure of the last UN personnel on 2 March (almost one month ahead of schedule) was closely followed by that of the US and Italian marines themselves. Somali looters overran the airport, but armoured cars from Aidid's faction, reportedly accompanied by UN-trained police-officers, took control of the area. Ali Mahdi's Abgal clansmen gained control of the eastern section of the airport, and skirmishes were reported between the two sides. Aidid and Ali Mahdi subsequently agreed on the reopening of the port and set out detailed terms for the 'technical peace committee' that was to administer the port and airport; however, the terms of the agreement were promptly violated by both sides, and fighting for control of the crucial sites resumed.

Significant divisions within the SNA became more apparent in June 1995, following an attempt by disaffected members to replace Aidid with his former aide, Osman Hassan Ali 'Ato', as Chairman of the party. SNA members loyal to Aidid immediately rejected the legitimacy of the actions of the Ali 'Ato' faction and announced the expulsion of the faction from the SNA. In mid-June a conference of reconciliation, convened in southern Mogadishu by representatives of 15 pro-Aidid factions, elected Aidid President of the Republic of Somalia for a three-year term. Five Vice-Presidents, representing the interests of distinct clans, were also elected, and the composition of a comprehensive cabinet was subsequently announced. However, Aidid's presidency and mandate to govern were immediately rejected in a joint statement issued by Ali Mahdi and Ali 'Ato'.

Tensions among opposing factions in the capital were exacerbated by the Aidid 'administration's' attempts at forcible disarmament of civilians and at tax collection. Moreover, in September 1995 Aidid's forces seized Baidoa. In October a joint committee representing the interests of supporters of Ali Mahdi and those of Ali 'Ato' was established to consider the future of banana exports (a crucial source of revenue) in the context of Aidid's increasingly effective stranglehold on all operations at the port of Mogadishu. (Some goods were being imported through the neighbouring natural harbour at Ceel Macaan.) The committee announced that it would extend a ban on all banana exports from the port of Mogadishu for as long as all revenues were diverted into Aidid's war efforts. Ships attempting to dock at the port were subsequently shelled by the committee's supporters, while Aidid's gunboats returned fire in an attempt to secure the safe passage of merchant vessels.

Fighting between Gen. Aidid's supporters and those loyal to Ali 'Ato' intensified in early 1996, resulting in Aidid's capture of the town of Hoddur in January and the deaths of more than 120 people in Mogadishu and southern Somalia in April alone. In July pro-Aidid factions clashed with supporters of Ali Mahdi in Mogadishu, resulting in some 90 fatalities. Aidid was wounded during the skirmishes, and on 1 August he died as a result of his injuries. Despite initial hopes that Aidid's death might result in a cessation of hostilities and the resumption of peace negotiations, on 4 August one of his sons, Hussein Mohamed Aidid (a former US marine and hitherto Aidid's chief of security), was appointed interim President by the SNA leadership council. Hussein Aidid (who was subsequently elected Chairman of the SNA) vowed to continue his father's struggle, and factional fighting quickly resumed.

In October 1996, during negotiations in Nairobi, Ali 'Ato', Hussein Aidid and Ali Mahdi agreed to a series of measures, including the cessation of hostilities; however, fighting resumed in late October and intensified in the following months. In December representatives of some 26 Somali factions (notably excluding the SNA) held protracted talks in Sodere, Ethiopia, under the auspices of the Ethiopian Government and the Intergovernmental Authority on Development (IGAD). The conference culminated in January 1997 in the formation of a 41-member National Salvation Council (NSC), with an 11-member executive committee and a five-member joint chairmanship committee, to act as an interim government charged with drafting a transitional charter and holding a national reconciliation conference. Aidid condemned the establishment of the NSC and accused the Ethiopian authorities of interfering in Somali affairs. (He was also critical of attacks launched by Ethiopian forces in August 1996 and January 1997 in Somalia's

Gedo region on alleged bases of al-Ittihad al-Islam, a radical Islamist organization fighting to create an independent homeland in eastern Ethiopia.)

International mediation efforts continued, and in March 1997 representatives of Somali factions participated in talks in Cairo, Egypt, under the auspices of the Egyptian Government and the Arab League. In May Ali 'Ato' and Hussein Aidid were reported to have reaffirmed their commitment to the Nairobi agreement, during a meeting held in San'a, Yemen. Later in the month Aidid and Ali Mahdi signed a reconciliation agreement in Cairo. In December, moreover, at the culmination of negotiations that began in November, 26 Somali faction leaders (including Aidid and Ali Mahdi) signed an accord in Cairo, establishing an end to all hostilities and providing for the eventual formation of a transitional government, charged with holding a general election within three years. A condition of the accord was that a national reconciliation conference be held in Baidoa in February 1998 in order to elect a 13-member presidential council (three representatives from each of Somalia's four principal clans and one from a minority group), a prime minister and a 189-seat legislature. The conference was later postponed on two occasions, not least because troops loyal to Aidid remained stationed in Baidoa. In April, at a meeting with the Kenyan President, Daniel arap Moi, in Kenya, Aidid, Ali Mahdi and Ali 'Ato' publicly appealed for international financial assistance to fund the conference, which subsequently failed to take place in May.

In October 1997 the Rahanwin Resistance Army (RRA), which had launched sporadic attacks on Hussein Aidid's militias during the year, claimed to have taken control of Baidoa. The SNA subsequently recaptured the town, and clashes between the SNA and the RRA continued in early 1998. In February 1998 as many as 37 people were killed in Hoddur and Baidoa during fighting between followers of the two groups, and in June there were at least 40 fatalities when the RRA once again attempted to capture Baidoa. In October the RRA succeeded in wresting control of Hoddur from the SNA, prompting the return to the town of thousands of refugees. Clashes between SNA and RRA militias continued in Baidoa in late 1998 and early 1999.

In July 1998, after Libyan mediation, Mogadishu's principal faction leaders (including Hussein Aidid, Ali Mahdi, Ali 'Ato' and Mohammed Qanyareh Afrah) issued a seven-point peace agreement on the creation of an administration for the Banaadir region (Mogadishu and its environs); Aidid and Ali Mahdi were designated as its two Chairmen, and Ali 'Ato' and Qanyareh Afrah as its Vice-Chairmen. Later that month the faction leaders agreed to establish a technical committee to address the capital's various problems, including the circulation of multiple currencies. In early August the Banaadir administration was inaugurated, despite opposition from Ali 'Ato', who appealed to the international community not to recognize it. It was subsequently announced that Islamic (*Shari'a*) law would be applied in the Banaadir region, and Mogadishu's port and airport were officially reopened. Muse Sudi Yalahow (a faction leader opposed to the new administration) warned that his forces would attack ships or aircraft that sought to use the capital's port and airport, and in September hostile militias fired at a vessel attempting to dock at Mogadishu. During late 1998 the Banaadir administration received financial aid from several Arab states. The region's police force, which was deployed in December, initially comprised some 3,000 former militiamen and police-officers; an additional 3,000 members were recruited in early 1999. However, within months the police force had disbanded as a result of the Banaadir administration's failure to pay them.

In June 1999 it was reported that Islamic militias operating under the auspices of self-appointed Islamic courts and financed by local businesses had closed down hundreds of checkpoints set up by warring factions. In September the UN Secretary-General, Kofi Annan, announced that the UN Security Council was to consider a solution to the Somalia problem, following a proposal made by the Somali Peace Alliance (under the chairmanship of 'Puntland' Leader Abdullahi Yussuf) that central authority in Somalia be gradually rebuilt, beginning with regionally based administrations. This proposal was, however, immediately rejected by the Mogadishu faction leaders and President Egal of 'Somaliland'. In October IGAD delegates met in Addis Ababa to discuss President Gelleh of Djibouti's proposed peace plan for Somalia. They agreed to refer the proposal, which included the involvement of clan elders, religious leaders, non-governmental organizations and the business community in the peace discussions, to an IGAD summit conference to be held

in Nairobi in November. Gelleh's peace proposals immediately drew a positive response from Ethiopia and Libya; however, the proposals were rejected by the Mogadishu faction leaders and by Egal. In February 2000 IGAD member states finally endorsed Gelleh's peace plan for Somalia, which envisaged the staging of a Somali national reconciliation conference in Djibouti in late April and early May, to be attended by up to 1,500 delegates from various cross-sections of Somali society. Under the plan they would elect members to a new national legislature to be based in Mogadishu, which would, in turn, elect a President. The President would be responsible for choosing a Prime Minister, subject to the approval of the legislature, who would lead a transitional government for a period of no longer than two years, during which time a national constitution would be drafted and a date for elections would be selected. However, although the peace plan was unanimously approved by OAU foreign ministers in March, and also won the approval of the UN and the USA, Egal announced that 'Somaliland' would go to war if attempts were made to unite it with Somalia. The 'Somaliland' parliament subsequently issued a decree, which stated it would be an act of treason to attend the Djibouti peace conference. A preliminary peace conference meeting scheduled for mid-March was postponed, owing to the absence of the majority of the participants, although in mid-April 'Puntland' delegates agreed to participate in the conference in Djibouti, provided the conference acknowledge the legitimacy of the 'Puntland' administration.

Following a short postponement, the Somali national reconciliation conference opened in Arta, Djibouti, on 2 May 2000, with some 400 delegates, representing various Somali clans and political and armed groups, in attendance. By mid-June the number of delegates attending the discussions had risen to around 900, although notably only one of the principal Somali faction leaders, Ali Mahdi Mohamed, was present. Later that month it was reported that the 'Puntland' administration had announced its rejection of the peace conference initiatives and stated that it would not recognize the outcome of the conference. In early July the conference produced a draft national charter, which envisaged the Somali Republic adopting a federal system of government, after a three-year interim period, comprising 18 regional administrations. Mogadishu was to remain the capital of the country. Futhermore, it provided for the creation of the Somali Transitional National Assembly (TNA), which would consist of 225 members, of whom 25 would be women. In mid-July the Charter was approved by 638 votes to four and the process of electing members to the TNA began. The Charter, which was to serve as the Somali constitution for the three-year interim period, guaranteed freedom of expression and association for all Somali citizens, as well as free access to health and education services. The Charter also distinctly separated the executive, legislative and judiciary and guaranteed the independence of the latter. By late July the commission appointed by the peace conference participants to apportion the parliamentary seats among the various Somali clans had submitted its report. Each of the four major Somali clans (Dir, Hawiye, Darod and Oigil and Mirifle) was allocated 44 seats, and an alliance of small clans was to receive 24 seats; the remaining 25 seats were reserved for women from the four major clans and the alliance of small clans, each of which would receive five seats. However, disagreements between clans and sub-clans over the distribution of seats ensued, and in early August President Gelleh intervened, suggesting the appointment of a further 20 members to the assembly, thus increasing the total number to 245. Gelleh's proposal was accepted, and on 13 August the TNA held its inaugural session in Arta, which was attended by 166 members. On 26 August it was announced that Abdulkasim Salad Hasan, a member of the Hawiye clan, who had held several ministerial positions in the Siad Barre administration, had been elected President of Somalia by the members of the TNA. Hasan obtained 145 of the 245 votes, comfortably defeating his nearest rival, Abdallah Ahmed Addow, who gained 92. Hasan was sworn in as President on the following day at a ceremony in Arta, attended by numerous regional leaders, including the Ethiopian Prime Minister, Meles Zenawi, and the Sudanese President, Omar Hassan Ahmad al-Bashir.

On 30 August 2000 President Hasan returned to Mogadishu, where he was greeted by tens of thousands of Somalis who had gathered at the city's stadium. At the same time several Mogadishu faction leaders opposed to the outcome of the Djibouti conference, including Hussein Aidid, Ali 'Ato' and Hussein Haji Bod, met in San'a for talks with Yemeni President Ali Abdullah

Saleh, who attempted to persuade them to lend their support to Hasan's administration. However, on his return to Somalia, Aidid implored the international community not to recognise the legitimacy of Hasan's appointment. Furthermore, the authorities of both 'Somaliland' and 'Puntland' subsequently issued directives ordering the immediate arrest of those elected to the TNA should they enter either territory. In early September at least 25 people were killed, and numerous others injured, in clashes between two rival clans in southern Somalia, and later that month fighting again erupted in Mogadishu between supporters of Aidid and Ali Mahdi. In late September the Libyan leader, Col Muammar al-Qaddafi, hosted talks between Hasan and Aidid and other leaders of the SNA in Sirte, Libya, at which the SNA leaders expressed their commitment to the principle of national reconciliation, and Hasan emphasized the need for the SNA's participation in the new legislative and executive bodies. Aidid, however, subsequently denied press reports that an agreement had been reached between the SNA and Hasan.

On 8 October 2000 President Hasan appointed Ali Khalif Galaydh, a former Minister of Industry in the Siad Barre regime, to the post of Prime Minister; later that month Galaydh announced a 32-member Cabinet. Hussein Aidid immediately expressed his dissatisfaction at the appointment of Galaydh, and Ali 'Ato' and another Mogadishu faction leader, Musa Sudi Yalahow, both publicly stated that the members of the new Government would not be welcome in the areas under their control. Galaydh's appointment was also rejected by the 'Somaliland' and 'Puntland' authorities. Furthermore, the Chairman of the RRA, Mohamed Hasan Nur, announced that he had withdrawn his support for the TNA.

Throughout late 2000 and early 2001 Hasan and Galaydh made numerous visits abroad, as they attempted to consolidate foreign support for the new Somali administration. However, most notably, relations between Somalia and Ethiopia deteriorated in January 2001, after Galaydh accused Ethiopia of providing arms to factions opposed to the Transitional National Government (TNG). Relations between the two countries were further strained in March, when the Ethiopian authorities allowed several Somali faction leaders (including Gen. 'Morgan', Aidid, Ali 'Ato', Yahalow, Hasan Nur and the 'Puntland' President, Abdullahi Yussuf) to convene in Addis Ababa for a series of meetings, which resulted in the creation of the Somali Reconciliation and Restoration Council (SRRC), headed by Aidid. The following month the SRRC announced its intention to form a national government in direct opposition to the TNG within six months. Meanwhile, in late March members of the faction loyal to Yalahow attacked a compound of the French relief agency Médecins sans frontières (MSF) in Mogadishu. According to reports, 14 people were killed, and 40 others injured, in exchanges between security forces and faction members, and nine foreign aid workers (including four UN representatives) were taken hostage by the faction, in what it maintained was a demonstration of the lack of security in Mogadishu. By early April all nine had been released. Nevertheless, MSF subsequently suspended all operations in the Somali capital until further notice.

In early May 2001 Galaydh appointed 25 members to a Peace and Reconciliation Committee (PRC), chaired by former Prime Minister Abdirazzaq Hajj Hussein, which was charged with obtaining recommendations from a cross-section of Somali factions for ways of accelerating the reconciliation process, defining the most suitable means of establishing a federal system in the country and addressing property and land issues. Later that month at least 50 people were killed in heavy fighting in Mogadishu between pro-Government militia and members of Aidid's faction. In mid-June Mohamed Abdi Gas, a member of the TNA, was kidnapped in Mogadishu. This followed the abduction earlier in the year of another member of the TNA, Abdirahman Du'ale Ali. The two incidents were believed to be linked to the failure of the deputies to repay debts owed to militia groups. Gas was released in September, but Ali remained in captivity. Meanwhile, in mid-July violent clashes were again reported to have taken place in Mogadishu between followers of Aidid and Ali 'Ato' and troops loyal to the TNG, resulting in numerous fatalities. In late July the new administration suffered a further major set-back after Hajj Hussein resigned as Chairman of the PRC, claiming that Galaydh had demonstrated a lack of co-operation with the committee and had failed actively to support its work. Abdiqadir Muhammad Adan Zope was subsequently appointed acting Chairman of the PRC.

In mid-October 2001 a group of dissatisfied TNA members proposed a motion of 'no confidence' in the TNG, citing the administration's failure to promote the reconciliation process and its lack of progress regarding the constitution of regional administrations; it was also alleged that corruption was widespread among the members of the Government. Later that month 141 of the 174 TNA members participating in the vote approved the motion to dismiss the Galaydh administration, with just 29 deputies indicating their support for the TNG; four members abstained. Galaydh's deputy, Uthman Jama' Ali, became acting Prime Minister. In early November talks, sponsored by President Moi of Kenya, took place in Nairobi between a delegation of TNA members, headed by President Hasan, and moderate members of the SRRC. Aidid declined to attend. Nevertheless, following the conclusion of discussions, both sides reported that some progress had been made and agreed to meet again to continue the *rapprochement* process.

On 12 November 2001 President Hasan appointed Col Hassan Abshir Farah, hitherto Minister of Water and Mineral Resources, as Prime Minister. Abshir Farah announced that his first priority was to implement a programme of national reconciliation, and thus the appointment of a new cabinet was delayed until after the conclusion of further peace talks between the SRRC and members of the TNA, which were scheduled to take place in Nairobi later that month. Although the talks were subsequently delayed until mid-December, they were attended by senior members of the SNA (again with the notable exception of Aidid) and representatives of several other Mogadishu faction leaders. On 24 December, in the Kenyan town of Nakura, Abshir Farah, on behalf of the TNA, and Mowlid Ma'aneh Mohamed, the Secretary-General of the SRRC, signed a peace agreement, which provided for the formation of an 'all-inclusive government' to ensure equitable power-sharing among all Somali clans and the establishment of a Nairobi-based secretariat to oversee the implementation of the Somali peace process and to solicit funds for it. The parties also agreed to propose an increase in the number of members appointed to both the TNA and the Cabinet. Furthermore, the signatories appealed to those groups currently outside the peace process to join it. However, it was subsequently reported that Aidid had announced his rejection of the agreement.

In mid-February 2002 Abshir Farah formed a new 31-member Cabinet, which notably included Dr Hussein Mohamed Usman Jimbir, a former senior member of the SRRC, as Minister of Education. However, several members of factions that had signed the Nakura peace agreement in December 2001, who were expected to be represented in the new administration, were reported to have requested to be excluded from the new Government until a parliamentary committee established to investigate the proposed increase in the number of parliamentary seats had released its recommendations. The reconciliation process in Somalia was further endangered in early April 2002, when the RRA announced that it had established a new autonomous region in south-western Somalia, based in Baidoa, to be known as the 'State of South-western Somalia'. The Chairman of the RRA, Mohamed Hasan Nur, was elected as 'President' of the new region for a four-year period and stated his intention to appoint a 19-member cabinet later that month.

In early May 2002 the UN announced the suspension of all activities in Mogadishu, following the abduction of a member of its staff. The abductee was released later that month; however, a number of similar incidents occurred during the year. Later in May heavy fighting was reported in Mogadishu between forces loyal to Yalahow and those of the TNG; some 60 people were believed to have been killed in the clashes, with hundreds more wounded.

In late June 2002 the TNG confirmed that it would attend an IGAD-sponsored reconciliation conference scheduled to be held in Kenya in July. The conference was subsequently postponed until September, and early that month the authorities in 'Somaliland' announced that they would not attend the talks. Following a further postponement, the conference, which was expected to continue for several months, opened in the Kenyan town of Eldoret in mid-October in the presence of representatives of the Governments of Ethiopia, Kenya, Uganda, Sudan, Djibouti and Eritrea. Some 350 delegates from various Somali factions attended the opening sessions, including a delegation from the TNG led by Abshir Farah. The conference was to be conducted in three phases and in late October, following the conclusion of the first phase, the TNG and a number of Somali factions signed a temporary cease-fire and agreed to abide by the final outcome of the conference; to establish an all-inclusive federal system of government; to combat terrorism; and to enhance the safety of aid workers in the country. Further progress was slowed by continuing deadlock over the allocation of seats to the plenary session of the conference. However, by early December it appeared that the impasse had been overcome, and the TNG and Mogadishu-based faction leaders Aidid, Qanyareh Afreh, Yalahow and Ali 'Ato' signed a declaration committing themselves to ending violence in the Somali capital. The conference was adjourned in late December, until after the Kenyan legislative elections, and upon its resumption Yalahow announced that he would no longer participate in the talks. Yalahow's departure followed the earlier withdrawal of Qanyareh Afreh from the proceedings. In February 2003 the conference was moved to Nairobi, and, despite a number of cease-fire violations, in the following month the TNG and the remaining faction leaders provisionally agreed on the formation of an administration for Mogadishu and further measures to bring peace to the capital. Six committees had also been created, which were responsible for federalism and a provisional federal charter; demobilization, disarmament and reintegration; land and property rights; economic institution-building and resource mobilization; regional and international relations; and conflict resolution and reconciliation. In early April a Harmonization Council was established to co-ordinate the work of the six committees and to produce a report into their findings. Its creation was criticized by the SRRC.

In May 1993 Egal, who had been Somalia's Prime Minister in 1967–69, was elected as the new President of 'Somaliland'. In June Egal announced the composition of a 14-member council of ministers for 'Somaliland'. By late September a two-year transitional programme for reconstruction had been approved by a 47-member bicameral parliament (comprising a council of elders and a council of representatives). The administration's hopes that the prevailing atmosphere of peace in the north-western region would inspire the international community's prompt recognition of 'Somaliland' were largely frustrated, in October, by the OAU Secretary-General's rejection of the territory's independent status. Relations between the Egal administration and UNOSOM officials improved in late 1993, following the assurances of the UN Secretary-General that the mission would not interfere in the region's affairs but would provide funding for reconstruction and the rehabilitation of the police force. Nevertheless, in August 1994 Egal expelled UN representatives from 'Somaliland', accusing them of interfering in internal affairs. This was apparently precipitated by talks between the new UN Special Representative to Somalia, James Victor Gbeho (appointed in July), and Ahmed Ali 'Tur', who was courted by both the UN and Gen. Aidid following his disavowal of secession for 'Somaliland'. In October the rift between Egal and Ahmed Ali 'Tur' culminated in violent confrontations in Hargeysa between military units remaining loyal to Egal and those defecting to support Ahmed Ali 'Tur'. By mid-December it was estimated that three-quarters of the population of Hargeysa had fled, many thousands of them seeking refuge in Ethiopia (see below). The rebel militias continued launching attacks on government positions in Hargeysa during 1995. Fighting spread to other parts of 'Somaliland', and in April government forces were in conflict with fighters from the Garhadji clan who had recently formed an alliance with Issa militiamen belonging to the antisecessionist USF. Despite Egal's weakened position, he persevered with the introduction of a new currency for the territory, the 'Somaliland shilling'.

In August 1995 four sub-committees were established to draft a new constitution for 'Somaliland'. A provisional document was published in March 1996. Peace talks between the territory's warring factions were conducted in December 1995, and in May 1996 it was reported that rebel armed forces had surrendered their weapons at an official disarmament ceremony in Hargeysa. In February 1997, shortly after it was announced that the constitution had become effective for a three-year interim period, Egal was re-elected (by an electoral college) President of 'Somaliland' for a five-year term. In October Egal appointed a new Minister of the Interior, and in December, in an apparent attempt to rally support, Egal offered his resignation to parliament, citing lack of co-operation from government ministers. Parliament rejected the resignation offer. In May 1999 Egal reorganized the 'Somaliland' government. In September Egal reiterated that 'Somaliland' would never reunite with Somalia, and in October Egal visited the USA in an attempt to persuade

the UN to confer observer status on 'Somaliland' and to gain US support for the idea of a peace conference.

At a referendum held in late May 2001, according to official results, 91.7% of the voters in 'Somaliland' approved a new constitution for the territory, which contained a clause confirming the self-declared state's independence. However, the outcome appeared unlikely to persuade the international community to grant recognition to 'Somaliland'. In mid-January 2002 Egal's term of office, which had been due to expire at the end of February, prior to scheduled presidential and parliamentary elections, was extended for one year by the council of elders. A legal challenge to the extension was mounted by several opposition figures and potential presidential candidates, who alleged that the move was unconstitutional; however, the challenge was rejected, and it was anticipated that Egal would use the extension to delay the elections until a later date. In early May, however, Egal died from complications following surgery at a military hospital in South Africa; a seven-day period of national mourning was declared, and the Vice-President, Dahir Riyale Kahin, was inaugurated as President of 'Somaliland'. Kahin appointed Ahmed Yusuf Yassin as Vice-President later that month, and in July Kahin announced that a presidential election would be held in January 2003. The election was delayed on a number of occasions, although it finally took place in mid-April. According to the Somaliland Election Commission, Kahin was re-elected to the presidency, with 42.1% of the votes cast, although the opposition rejected this result.

In July 1998 Col Abdullahi Yussuf Ahmed, a former leader of the SSDF, announced the formation of 'Puntland', a new autonomous administration in north-eastern Somalia. In August Abdullahi Yussuf, as 'President' of the new administration, appointed a cabinet, which was subsequently approved by the recently inaugurated 69-member parliament (empowered to act as the legislature for a three-year transitional period, prior to the holding of regional elections). A charter for 'Puntland', released shortly afterwards, precluded 'Puntland' from seceding from Somalia, while it envisaged the adoption of a federal system of national government, with similar regional governments emerging around the country. Hussein Aidid declared his opposition to the administration, accusing the Ethiopian authorities of encouraging 'Puntland' to secede. In late June 2001 Yussuf's mandate was controversially extended for a further three years by the 'Puntland' parliament, at the behest of clan elders. The constitutionality of the decision was challenged by several opposition figures, and the 'Puntland' High Court issued a decree, effective from 1 July, placing all security services and other government institutions under the its supervision. The Chief Justice of 'Puntland', Yussuf Haji Nur, subsequently proclaimed himself 'President' of the territory; senior clan elders subsequently confirmed Haji Nur as 'acting President' until 31 August. However, Yussuf rejected this decision, and heavy fighting ensued between followers of Yussuf and Haji Nur. In late August a general congress, attended by representatives of all major 'Puntland' clans, opened in Garowe, the region's capital, to elect a new 'President' and 'Vice-President', as well as members to a new 'Puntland' assembly, and in mid-November Jama Ali Jama and Ahmad Mahmud Gunle were sworn in as 'President' and 'Vice-President', respectively. Just days later violent clashes were reported to have taken place in Garowe between troops loyal to Yussuf and Ali Jama. In April 2002 Yussuf and Ali Jama met for talks in Ethiopia, but no agreement was reached. Fighting continued in 'Puntland' during 2002 and early 2003, with numerous casualties reported on both sides.

The departure of Western UN contingents by mid-1994 prompted international reappraisal and renewed criticism of UN operations in Somalia, despite the organization's promotion of its success in containing the humanitarian crisis and rehabilitating local administration, the judiciary and the police force. In March it was revealed that the unpublished report of an internal commission of inquiry, appointed by the UN in November 1993, was highly critical of several aspects of UN operations in the country, recommending that financial compensation should be considered for innocent Somali victims of UN peace-enforcement actions, and questioning the appropriateness, within the UN mandate, of some actions undertaken by US forces. Several Canadian servicemen and a Belgian soldier were subsequently sentenced to terms of imprisonment for their involvement in the murder of Somali civilians while serving with UNOSOM. An official inquiry launched in Italy to investigate alleged atrocities committed by the Folgore Paratroop Regiment prompted the resignation of two senior Italian officers in 1997. In late September 2001 the UN announced the withdrawal of its entire international staff from Somalia after it was unable to obtain insurance cover for flights to the country in the aftermath of the suicide attacks on the USA on 11 September.

In 1992 severe drought, combined with the disruption to agriculture and relief efforts caused by conflict in many parts of the country, resulted in the deaths from starvation and famine-related diseases of some 500,000 people. UNITAF's operations greatly increased the amount of food reaching people in need, and by February 1993 deaths from starvation had been virtually eliminated. As a result of good rains, harvests were much better in 1993–94 than in previous years, and the country was expected to become self-sufficient in food once again. There remained, however, much to do in the rehabilitation of infrastructure and health care in many parts of Somalia. During 1994 the incidence of attacks on foreign aid workers increased, and, in anticipation of the departure of UNOSOM, which had provided a measure of protection, aid organizations withdrew many of their personnel from Somalia, thus impeding many relief and rehabilitation projects. In June 1995 the UN disclosed that of the US $70.3m. requested by the organization for emergency relief and short-term rehabilitation projects in Somalia, only $13.1m. had been contributed to date. In July 1999 the US Agency for International Development announced that, effective from October, it would no longer be disbursing aid to Somalia. In September the UN Children's Fund (UNICEF) suspended its operations in southern Somalia, following the murder of its highest-ranking health officer and the wounding of five other UNICEF workers during a robbery attempt in Dibi Arab in central Somalia.

The escalation of hostilities between the Siad Barre Government and the rebel forces increased the flow of refugees from Somalia to Ethiopia and Kenya. Following the SNM's assumption of control in northern Somalia in early 1991, thousands of refugees returned from Ethiopia. Many more returned to their home territory in 'Somaliland' in late 1991 and early 1992, as a result of the ethnic conflict in south-western Ethiopia. The intensification of hostilities in the south of Somalia from April 1992 precipitated a huge movement of refugees: by the end of 1992 there were approximately 400,000 Somali refugees in Kenya, more than 300,000 in Ethiopia, up to 100,000 in Yemen, and hundreds of thousands in the Persian (Arabian) Gulf region, in Europe and North America. In early 1993 the International Committee of the Red Cross estimated that three-quarters of Somalia's population had been internally displaced by the civil conflict, although by late 1994 many thousands had returned to their villages. However, in November some 30,000 civilians fled to Ethiopia to escape fighting in Hargeysa, 'Somaliland'. It was estimated in 2000 that some 350,000 Somalis were internally displaced, and, according to the office of the UN High Commissioner for Refugees, at the end of 2001 there were 144,300 Somali refugees in Kenya, 67,500 in Yemen and 67,100 in Ethiopia. In 2000 UNHCR repatriated 43,467 refugees to north-western Somalia, bringing the number of Somali returnees since 1997 to 125,572. In 2001 UNHCR repatriated 50,200 Somalian refugees from Ethiopia.

In April 1988 a decade of hostile relations between Somalia and Ethiopia, following the war in 1977–78 over the Ogaden area of Ethiopia (which is inhabited by ethnic Somalis), ended with a peace accord. It was agreed to re-establish diplomatic relations, to withdraw troops from border areas and to exchange prisoners of war. Following the overthrow of the Mengistu regime in May 1991, the new Government in Ethiopia declared itself neutral with regard to the factions fighting for control of Somalia. Ethiopia hosted peace conferences for the warring Somali factions in 1993, 1996 and 1997. The Egyptian, Kenyan and Libyan authorities also fostered peace initiatives for Somalia in the late 1990s.

In March 1998 Ethiopian troops reportedly occupied several towns in Somalia's Gedo region, following the capture of the SNF-controlled town of Elwak (in Kenya) by al-Ittihad. In April 1999 the Ethiopian Government denied reports that its forces were occupying two districts in western Somalia, while Hussein Aidid and Ali Mahdi reiterated their claims that Ethiopia was encouraging the division of Somalia by providing armaments and ammunition to autonomous administrations in the country.

In 1999 the security situation along the Somali–Kenyan border deteriorated after both Ethiopia and Eritrea began sending arms to opposing Somali factions. In June around 400 Somali militiamen loyal to the pro-Aidid SNF faction attacked a small patrol base at Amuma and stole rifles, ammunition and communications equipment. Kenyan military presence in the area was increased, and President Moi warned the raiders that they would face military action if the stolen equipment was not returned. The commander of the SNF faction, Gen. Omari Haji Mohamed, unconditionally returned all the stolen items and claimed that his troops had mistaken the Kenyans for an opposing SNF faction. Nevertheless, Kenya subsequently closed its border with Somalia to prevent the further influx of Somali refugees and defeated militiamen. Five Kenyan navy ships were also deployed to patrol the border area following the Somali attack. In April 2000 the border between the two countries was reopened. In July 2001 Kenya again closed the border after numerous clashes were reported on the Somali side, which threatened to spill over into Kenya. However, Moi agreed to reopen the border in November.

Following the outbreak of the Eritrean–Ethiopian border conflict in mid-1998, rival Somali factions were the recipients of increasingly large consignments of weapons from the two warring countries, which sought to secure Somali allegiance to their causes. Growing concern about the activities of Eritrean-supported Somali militias prompted Ethiopia to launch cross-border raids into Somalia against warlords, and in June 1999 the RRA, assisted by some 3,000 Ethiopian troops, captured the town of Baidoa from Aidid's SNA. Aidid's continuing support of the Eritrean Government and Ethiopian insurgent groups led neutral observers to believe that the conflict was in danger of spreading elsewhere in the Horn of Africa. The Ethiopian Government claimed, however, that its actions were merely attempts to protect the border from attacks initiated by Somali-based rebel opposition groups. In September Ali 'Ato' and Aidid attended a meeting with the Ethiopian Minister of Foreign Affairs, Seyoum Mesfin, in Libya where an agreement was reached whereby Aidid would withdraw support for Ethiopian Oromo rebels in return for Ethiopian disengagement from Somalia. In November the SNA announced that it had disarmed several hundred Oromo Liberation Front (OLF) rebels living in Somalia, had closed down their offices and had asked the OLF leaders to leave the country. It was, however, reported that Ethiopian incursions into Somalia continued in early 2000. During late 2000 and early 2001 relations between the two countries deteriorated after the Hasan administration accused Ethiopia of offering support to faction leaders hostile to the TNA (see above). Relations between the two countries improved following the visit of a Somali government delegation to Ethiopia in June 2001. However, in September it was reported that Ethiopia had ordered the closure of the common border, fearing an increase in terrorist activity in Somalia after the events of 11 September. In November the Prime Ministers of the two countries met for talks in Addis Ababa, at which Ethiopia reiterated its concern over the suspected presence of Islamist terrorist elements in Somalia. Nevertheless, both sides pledged to improve bilateral relations, and Ethiopia affirmed its support for a comprehensive reconciliation process in Somalia. In February 2003 relations between the two countries were again strained after the Ethiopian Prime Minister admitted sending Ethiopian troops into Somali territory in pursuit of members of the Islamist, Somali-based al-Ittihad al-Islam.

Following the suicide attacks on New York and Washington, DC, on 11 September 2001, for which the USA held the al-Qa'ida (Base) organization of Osama bin Laden responsible, the USA froze the foreign assets of Somalia's al-Barakat bank, as it suspected that much of the estimated US $500m. remitted from Somalis abroad to the bank was being funnelled to terrorist organizations. Furthermore, al-Ittihad al-Islam was among 27 groups designated as foreign terrorist organizations in September by the US Government, which believed that al-Ittihad had links to al-Qa'ida. In November the new Somali Prime Minister, Hassan Abshir Farah, denied that his Government had any links to al-Ittihad or to al-Qa'ida and stated that he would not object to the deployment of US troops inside Somalia to monitor and detect alleged terrorist activities. In the following month US officials were reported to have held talks with several Somali faction leaders regarding the possible existence of al-Qa'ida camps in areas under their control. However, despite much speculation that US attacks on suspected terrorist camps in Somalia were imminent, by mid-2003 no official missions had been carried out. US special forces did, however, raid a Mogadishu hospital in March of that year and seized a suspected al-Qa'ida operative, who was believed to have been involved in the bombing of an Israeli-owned hotel in Mombasa, Kenya, in November 2002, which resulted in the deaths of 18 people.

Government

In July 2000 a Somali national reconciliation conference, sponsored by President Gelleh of Djibouti, approved a national Charter, which envisaged the Somali Republic adopting a federal system of government, comprising 18 regional administrations, after a three-year interim period. The Charter provided for the creation of a Transitional National Assembly (TNA), which was to exercise legislative power in Somalia during the interim period. The 245-member TNA, comprising members of the four major clans and of an alliance of smaller clans, as well as 20 influential Somalis, was inaugurated in August and elected a President of Somalia. In October the President nominated a Prime Minister, who formed a Cabinet.

Defence

Of total armed forces of 64,500 in June 1990, the army numbered 60,000, the navy 2,000 and the air force 2,500. In addition, there were 29,500 members of paramilitary forces, including 20,000 members of the People's Militia. Following the overthrow of the Siad Barre regime in January 1991, there were no national armed forces. Somalia was divided into areas controlled by different armed groups, which were based on clan, or sub-clan, membership. In March 1994 the UN announced that 8,000 former Somali police-officers had been rehabilitated throughout the country, receiving vehicles and uniforms from the UN. Following the UN withdrawal from Somalia in early 1995, these police-officers ceased receiving payment and their future and their hitherto neutral stance appeared uncertain. In December 1998 a 3,000-strong police force was established for the Banaadir region (Mogadishu and its environs). An additional 3,000 members (comprising former militiamen and police-officers) were recruited to the force in early 1999; however, the force was disbanded within months. Following his election to the presidency in August 2000, Abdulkasim Salad Hasan announced his intention to recruit former militiamen into a new national force: by December some 5,000 Somalis had begun training under the supervision of Mogadishu's Islamic courts. In August 2002 the total armed forces of the self-proclaimed 'Republic of Somaliland' were estimated to number 7,000.

Economic Affairs

In 1990, according to estimates by the World Bank, Somalia's gross national income (GNI), measured at average 1988–90 prices, was US $946m., equivalent to $150 per head. According to UN figures, in 1999 gross domestic product (GDP) was US $2,020m., equivalent to $240 per head. During 1990–2001, it was estimated, the population increased at an average annual rate of 2.2%. GDP declined, in real terms, at an average annual rate of 3.3% in 1990–99; however, growth of 2.1% was recorded in 1999.

Agriculture (including forestry and fishing) contributed 66% of GDP in 1990. An estimated 70.7% of the working population were employed in agriculture in 2001. Agriculture is based on the breeding of livestock, which accounted for 49% of GDP in 1989 and 38.4% of the total value of exports in 1988. Bananas are the principal cash crop, accounting for 40.3% of export earnings in 1988. The GDP of the agricultural sector declined by an average of 5.7% per year in 1990–98; agricultural GDP declined by 0.4% in 1997, but increased by 1.7% in 1998. Although crop production in 1996 was reported to have increased by 50% compared with the previous year, output was still some 37% lower than it had been prior to the civil war. Severe flooding in southern Somalia during 1997 led to widespread crop failure and resulted in the loss of as many as 30,000 cattle. Total cereals production was 207,800 metric tons in 1999, the lowest annual yield since 1993, but recovered to 312,900 in 2000.

Industry (including mining, manufacturing, construction and power) contributed 8.6% of GDP in 1988, and employed an estimated 10.5% of the working population in 1991. The combined GDP of the mining, manufacturing and power sectors increased by an average of 1.1% per year in 1990–98; growth in 1998 was 9.1%. The GDP of the construction sector declined at an average annual rate of 0.8% in 1990–98; growth of 3.8% was recorded in 1998.

Mining contributed 0.3% of GDP in 1988. Somalia's mineral resources include salt, limestone, gypsum, gold, silver, nickel, copper, zinc, lead, manganese, uranium and iron ore. Deposits of petroleum and natural gas have been discovered, but remain unexploited: US petroleum companies were granted exploration rights covering two-thirds of the country by Siad Barre, and were expected to start investigations once there was a durable

peace. There were reports in late 1998 that US companies had begun prospecting for petroleum around Boorama in north-western Somalia. In February 2001 it was reported that the French petroleum company TotalFinaElf had signed an agreement with the transitional Somali Government to carry out oil exploration in the south of the country.

Manufacturing contributed almost 5% of GDP in 1988. The most important sectors are food-processing, especially sugar-refining, the processing of hides and skins, and the refining of petroleum. Manufacturing GDP increased by an average of 0.3% per year in 1990–98; growth in 1998 was 8.8%.

Energy is derived principally from oil-fired generators. Imports of fuel products comprised 14% of the value of merchandise imports in 1990.

The services sector contributed 24.6% of GDP in 1988, and engaged an estimated 18.8% of the employed labour force in 1991. Tourism accounted for some 9.3% of GDP in 1988.

In 1989 Somalia recorded a visible trade deficit of US $278.6m., and there was a deficit of $156.7m. on the current account of the balance of payments. In 1982 the principal source of imports (34.4%) was Italy, while Saudi Arabia was the principal market for exports (86.5%). Other major trading partners in that year were the United Kingdom, the Federal Republic of Germany and Kenya. The principal exports in 1988 were live-stock and bananas. The principal imports were petroleum, fertilizers, foodstuffs and machinery. Livestock and bananas remained the principal exports in the late 1990s, while the United Arab Emirates emerged as Somalia's main trading partner.

In 1988 Somalia recorded a budget deficit of 10,009.4m. Somali shillings. A provisional budget for 1991 was projected to balance at 268,283.2m. Somali shillings. Somalia's total external debt was US $2,562m. at the end of 2000, of which $1,825m. was long-term public debt. In 1990 the cost of debt-servicing was equivalent to 11.7% of the value of exports of goods and services. In 1990–99 the average annual rate of inflation was 22.7%. Consumer prices increased by 16.3% in 1998 and by 12.0% in 1999.

Somalia is a member of the African Development Bank (see p. 128) and the Islamic Development Bank (see p. 257).

Somalia's long history of civil unrest, together with unreliable climatic conditions, have undermined the traditional agricultural base of the economy. By the mid-1990s a significant recovery had been recorded in livestock numbers, sorghum output and exports of bananas, although the production and export of the last exacerbated factional fighting, with rival clansmen competing for control of the industry in order to fund their war efforts. The relative stability of the self-proclaimed 'Republic of Somaliland' (following its secession in 1991) contributed to an improvement in the economy of that territory, with an estimated increase of GNI per head of 20% in 1991–94, largely fuelled by exports of livestock to the states of the Persian (Arabian) Gulf region. Following the establishment of the Transitional National Assembly in August 2000, it was hoped that the Somali economy would make some progress towards recovery. On his appointment, President Hasan appealed for foreign donors to provide assistance with the rehabilitation of basic infrastructures and to finance development projects. However, the Government's attempts to establish control over the economy by issuing large quantities of currency notes resulted in a rapid rise in the rate of inflation and a further depreciation in the value of the shilling. Although the economy subsequently began to show signs of a recovery, in December 2001 the UN announced that Somalia was on the verge of an economic collapse unparalleled in modern history. This was attributed largely to the US administration's decision to enforce the closure of the al-Barakat banking and telecommunications organization (see Recent History), owing to its suspected links to terrorist organizations, thus severing the remittance process on which so much of the country is heavily dependent. In mid-2002 the European Union agreed to grant the country aid worth some €200m. over five years; however, it stated that assistance would be concentrated on infrastructural projects in 'Somaliland' and 'Puntland', as security fears prevented aid workers from commencing rehabilitation work in the more dangerous areas of the country.

Education

All private schools were nationalized in 1972, and education is now provided free of charge. Primary education, lasting for eight years, is officially compulsory for children aged six to 14 years. However, the total enrolment at primary schools of children in this age-group declined from 14% (boys 18%; girls 10%) in 1980 to only 8% (boys 11%; girls 6%) in 1985. Secondary education, beginning at the age of 14, lasts for four years but is not compulsory. In 1985 the enrolment at secondary schools included 3% of children (boys 4%; girls 2%) in the relevant age-group. In 1985 enrolment at primary and secondary schools was equivalent to 10% of the school-age population (boys 13%; girls 7%). Current expenditure on education in the Government's 1988 budget was 478.1m. Somali shillings (equivalent to 1.9% of total current spending). Following the overthrow of Siad Barre's Government in January 1991 and the descent of the country into anarchy, Somalia's education system collapsed. In January 1993 a primary school was opened in the building of Somalia's sole university, the Somali National University in Mogadishu (which had been closed in early 1991). The only other schools operating in the country were a number run by Islamist groups and some that had been reopened in 'Somaliland' in mid-1991.

Public Holidays

2003: 1 January (New Year's Day), 12 February* (Id al-Adha, Feast of the Sacrifice), 14 March* (Ashoura), 1 May (Labour Day), 14 May* (Mouloud, Birth of the Prophet), 26 June (Independence Day), 1 July (Foundation of the Republic), 26 November* (Id al-Fitr, end of Ramadan).

2004: 1 January (New Year's Day), 2 February* (Id al-Adha, Feast of the Sacrifice), 2 March* (Ashoura), 1 May (Labour Day), 2 May* (Mouloud, Birth of the Prophet), 26 June (Independence Day), 1 July (Foundation of the Republic), 14 November* (Id al-Fitr, end of Ramadan).

*These holidays are dependent on the Islamic lunar calendar and may vary by one or two days from the dates given.

Weights and Measures

The metric and imperial systems are both used.

Statistical Survey

Sources (unless otherwise stated): Economic Research and Statistics Dept, Central Bank of Somalia, Mogadishu, and Central Statistical Dept, State Planning Commission, POB 1742, Mogadishu; tel. (1) 80385.

Area and Population

AREA, POPULATION AND DENSITY

Area (sq km)	637,657*
Population (census results)†	
7 February 1975	3,253,024
February 1986 (provisional)	
Males	3,741,664
Females.	3,372,767
Total	7,114,431
Population (UN estimates at mid-year)‡	
1999	8,418,000
2000	8,778,000
2001	9,157,000
Density (per sq km) at mid-2001	14.4

* 246,201 sq miles.

† Excluding adjustment for underenumeration.

‡ Source: UN, *World Population Prospects: The 2000 Revision, Population and Vital Statistics Report*.

PRINCIPAL TOWNS

(estimated population in 1981)

Mogadishu (capital) .	500,000	Berbera	65,000
Hargeysa	70,000	Merca	60,000
Kismayu	70,000		

Mid-2000 (UN projection, including suburbs): Mogadishu 1,219,000 (Source: UN, *World Urbanization Prospects: The 1999 Revision*).

BIRTHS AND DEATHS

(UN estimates, annual averages)

	1985–90	1990–95	1995–2000
Birth rate (per 1,000)	51.7	52.0	52.3
Death rate (per 1,000)	20.3	25.1	18.5

Source: UN, *World Population Prospects: The 2000 Revision*.

Expectation of life (WHO estimates, years at birth): 43.1 (males 41.0; females 45.4) in 2001 (Source: WHO, *World Health Report*).

ECONOMICALLY ACTIVE POPULATION

(estimates, '000 persons, 1991)

	Males	Females	Total
Agriculture, etc.	1,157	1,118	2,275
Industry	290	46	336
Services	466	138	604
Total labour force	1,913	1,302	3,215

Source: UN Economic Commission for Africa, *African Statistical Yearbook*.

Mid-2001 (estimates in '000): Agriculture, etc. 2,762; Total labour force 3,906 (Source: FAO).

Health and Welfare

KEY INDICATORS

Total fertility rate (children per woman, 2001). . . .	7.3
Under-5 mortality rate (per 1,000 live births, 2001) . . .	225
HIV/AIDS (% of persons aged 15–49, 2001).	1.00
Physicians (per 1,000 head, 1997)	0.04
Hospital beds (per 1,000 head, 1997)	0.75
Health expenditure (2000): US $ per head (PPP) . . .	7
Health expenditure (2000): % of GDP	1.3
Health expenditure (2000): public (% of total)	71.4

For sources and definitions, see explanatory note on p. vi.

Agriculture

PRINCIPAL CROPS
('000 metric tons)

	1999	2000	2001*
Rice (paddy)	2†	2†	2
Maize*	143	210	210
Sorghum*	62	100	100
Sweet potatoes*	5	6	6
Cassava (Manioc)*	65	70	70
Sugar cane*	210	220	220
Pulses*	14	15	15
Groundnuts (in shell)* . . .	3	3	3
Sesame seed*	22	23	23
Vegetables*	46	47	47
Grapefruit and pomelos* . .	18	19	19
Bananas*	50	55	55
Oranges*	8	8	8
Lemons and limes*	3	3	3
Watermelons*	25	26	26
Dates*	10	10	10

* FAO estimates.
† Unofficial figure.

Source: FAO.

LIVESTOCK
(FAO estimates, '000 head, year ending September)

	1999	2000	2001
Cattle	5,000	5,100	5,300
Sheep	13,000	13,100	13,200
Goats	12,000	12,300	12,500
Pigs	4	4	4
Asses	19	20	20
Mules	18	19	19
Camels	6,000	6,100	6,200
Chickens	3,100	3,200	3,300

Source: FAO.

LIVESTOCK PRODUCTS
(FAO estimates, '000 metric tons)

	1999	2000	2001
Cows' milk	520	530	530
Goats' milk	380	390	390
Sheep's milk	420	430	430
Beef and veal	58	59	61
Mutton and lamb	36	38	38
Goat meat	36	38	38
Hen eggs	2	3	3
Cattle hides	11	11	11
Sheepskins	7	7	7
Goatskins	6	6	6

Source: FAO.

Forestry

ROUNDWOOD REMOVALS
(FAO estimates, '000 cubic metres, excl. bark)

	1999	2000	2001
Sawlogs, veneer logs and logs for sleepers*	28	28	28
Other industrial wood . . .	82	82	82
Fuel wood	8,874	9,228	9,522
Total	8,984	9,338	9,632

* Annual output assumed to be unchanged since 1975.

Source: FAO.

SAWNWOOD PRODUCTION
('000 cubic metres, incl. railway sleepers)

	1973	1974	1975
Total (all broadleaved)	15*	10	14

* FAO estimate.

1976–2001: Annual production as in 1975 (FAO estimates).

Source: FAO.

Fishing

(FAO estimates, '000 metric tons, live weight)

	1998	1999	2000
Marine fishes	21.1	19.1	19.1
Marine molluscs	0.5	0.5	0.5
Total catch (incl. others) . . .	22.3	20.3	20.2

Source: FAO, *Yearbook of Fishery Statistics*.

Mining

(Estimates, '000 metric tons)

	1999	2000	2001
Salt	1	1	1
Gypsum	2	2	2

Source: US Geological Survey.

Industry

SELECTED PRODUCTS
('000 metric tons, unless otherwise indicated)

	1986	1987	1988
Sugar*	30.0	43.3	41.2
Canned meat (million tins) . . .	1.0	—	—
Canned fish	0.1	—	—
Pasta and flour	15.6	4.3	—
Textiles (million yards)	5.5	3.0	6.3
Boxes and bags	15.0	12.0	5.0
Cigarettes and matches	0.3	0.2	0.1
Petroleum products	128	44	30
Electric energy (million kWh)† . .	253	255‡	257‡

Sugar (unofficial estimates, '000 metric tons)* 21 in 1996; 18 in 1997; 19 in 1998.

Electric energy (million kWh)† 271 in 1994‡; 272 in 1995‡; 275 in 1996.

* Data from FAO.
† Source: UN, *Industrial Commodity Statistics Yearbook*.
‡ Provisional figure.

Finance

CURRENCY AND EXCHANGE RATES

Monetary Units
100 cents = 1 Somali shilling (So. sh.)

Sterling, Dollar and Euro Equivalents (31 December 2002)
£1 sterling = 29,663.6 Somali shillings
US $1 = 18,404.0 Somali shillings
€1 = 19,300.3 Somali shillings
100,000 Somali shillings = £3.371 = $5.433 = €5.181

Average Exchange Rate (Somali shillings per US $)

1987	105.18
1988	170.45
1989	490.68

Note: A separate currency, the 'Somaliland shilling', was introduced in the 'Republic of Somaliland' in January 1995. The exchange rate was reported to be US $1 = 2,750 'Somaliland shillings' in March 2000.

CURRENT BUDGET
(million Somali shillings)

Revenue	1986	1987	1988
Total tax revenue	8,516.4	8,622.4	12,528.1
Taxes on income and profits	1,014.8	889.7	1,431.0
Income tax	380.5	538.8	914.8
Profit tax	634.3	350.9	516.2
Taxes on production, consumption and domestic transactions	1,410.4	1,274.2	2,336.4
Taxes on international transactions	6,091.2	6,458.5	8,760.6
Import duties	4,633.2	4,835.2	6,712.1
Total non-tax revenue	6,375.2	8,220.4	7,623.4
Fees and service charges	274.1	576.1	828.8
Income from government property	633.4	656.4	2,418.9
Other revenue	5,467.2	6,987.9	4,375.7
Total	14,891.6	16,842.8	20,151.5

Expenditure	1986	1987	1988
Total general services	11,997.7	19,636.7	24,213.6
Defence	2,615.9	3,145.0	8,093.9
Interior and police	605.0	560.7	715.4
Finance and central services	7,588.3	14,017.8	12,515.6
Foreign affairs	633.0	1,413.9	2,153.1
Justice and religious affairs	248.5	290.2	447.0
Presidency and general administration	93.0	148.0	217.4
Planning	189.0	24.9	24.3
National Assembly	25.0	36.2	46.9
Total economic services	1,927.6	554.1	600.3
Transportation	122.2	95.2	94.5
Posts and telecommunications	94.3	76.7	75.6
Public works	153.9	57.5	69.8
Agriculture	547.2	59.4	55.3
Livestock and forestry	459.0	89.5	109.9
Mineral and water resources	318.8	85.2	93.1
Industry and commerce	131.0	45.1	43.9
Fisheries	101.2	45.5	58.2
Total social services	1,050.5	900.1	930.8
Education	501.6	403.0	478.1
Health	213.8	203.5	255.2
Information	111.5	135.0	145.8
Labour, sports and tourism	139.6	49.3	51.7
Other	84.0	109.3	—
Total	14,975.8	21,091.0	25,744.7

1989 (estimates): Budget to balance at 32,429m. Somali shillings.

1990 (estimates): Budget to balance at 86,012.0m. Somali shillings.

1991 (estimates): Budget to balance at 268,283.2m. Somali shillings.

CENTRAL BANK RESERVES
(US $ million at 31 December)

	1987	1988	1989
Gold*	8.3	7.0	6.9
Foreign exchange	7.3	15.3	15.4
Total	15.6	22.3	22.3

* Valued at market-related prices.

Source: IMF, *International Financial Statistics*.

MONEY SUPPLY
(million Somali shillings at 31 December)

	1987	1988	1989
Currency outside banks	12,327	21,033	70,789
Private-sector deposits at central bank	1,771	1,555	5,067
Demand deposits at commercial banks	15,948	22,848	63,971
Total money	30,046	45,436	139,827

Source: IMF, *International Financial Statistics*.

COST OF LIVING
(Consumer Price Index; base: 1995 = 100)

	1997	1998	1999
All items	133.0	154.7	173.3

Source: African Development Bank.

NATIONAL ACCOUNTS

Expenditure on the Gross Domestic Product*
(estimates, million Somali shillings at current prices)

	1988	1989	1990
Government final consumption expenditure	33,220	58,530	104,760
Private final consumption expenditure	240,950	481,680	894,790
Increase in stocks	14,770	n.a.	n.a.
Gross fixed capital formation	44,780	134,150	240,030
Total domestic expenditure	333,720	674,360	1,239,580
Exports of goods and services	7,630	8,890	8,660
Less Imports of goods and services	49,430	57,660	58,460
GDP in purchasers' values	291,920	625,580	1,189,780

* Figures are rounded to the nearest 10m. Somali shillings.

Source: UN Economic Commission for Africa, *African Statistical Yearbook*.

Gross Domestic Product by Economic Activity
(million Somali shillings at constant 1985 prices)

	1986	1987	1988
Agriculture, hunting, forestry and fishing	54,868	59,378	61,613
Mining and quarrying	291	291	291
Manufacturing	4,596	4,821	4,580
Electricity, gas and water	77	62	57
Construction	3,289	3,486	2,963
Trade, restaurants and hotels	8,587	9,929	8,599
Transport, storage and communications	6,020	6,153	5,873
Finance, insurance, real estate and business services	3,743	4,095	3,890
Government services	1,631	1,530	1,404
Other community, social and personal services	2,698	2,779	2,863
Sub-total	85,800	92,524	92,133
Less Imputed bank service charges	737	748	748
GDP at factor cost	85,064	91,776	91,385
Indirect taxes, *less* subsidies	5,301	4,250	3,262
GDP in purchasers' values	90,365	96,026	94,647

GDP at factor cost (estimates, million Somali shillings at current prices): 249,380 in 1988; 500,130 in 1989; 923,970 in 1990 (Source: UN Economic Commission for Africa, *African Statistical Yearbook*).

BALANCE OF PAYMENTS
(US $ million)

	1987	1988	1989
Exports of goods f.o.b.	94.0	58.4	67.7
Imports of goods f.o.b.	−358.5	−216.0	−346.3
Trade balance	−264.5	−157.6	−278.6
Imports of services	−127.7	−104.0	−122.0
Balance on goods and services	−392.2	−261.6	−400.6
Other income paid	−52.0	−60.6	−84.4
Balance on goods, services and income	−444.2	−322.2	−485.0
Current transfers received	343.3	223.7	331.2
Current transfers paid	−13.1	—	−2.9
Current balance	−114.0	−98.5	−156.7
Investment liabilities	−22.8	−105.5	−32.6
Net errors and omissions	39.0	22.4	−0.8
Overall balance	−97.9	−181.7	−190.0

Source: IMF, *International Financial Statistics*.

External Trade

PRINCIPAL COMMODITIES
(million Somali shillings)

Imports*	1986	1987	1988
Foodstuffs	1,783.3	3,703.6	1,216.1
Beverages and tobacco	298.1	183.6	6.2
Manufacturing raw materials	230.0	626.9	661.4
Fertilizers	1.8	238.0	2,411.4
Petroleum	2,051.0	3,604.2	3,815.9
Construction materials	981.4	2,001.9	307.8
Machinery and parts	1,098.3	1,203.6	957.1
Transport equipment	1,133.8	1,027.6	195.2
Total (incl. others)	8,443.4	13,913.7	11,545.5

* Figures cover only imports made against payments of foreign currencies.
The total value of imports in 1986 was 20,474 million Somali shillings.

Exports	1986	1987	1988
Livestock	4,420.3	7,300.0	3,806.5
Bananas	1,207.2	2,468.8	3,992.3
Hides and skins	294.0	705.2	492.0
Total (incl. others)	6,372.5	10,899.9	9,914.1

1992 (estimates, US $ million): Imports 150; Exports 80.

PRINCIPAL TRADING PARTNERS
('000 Somali shillings)

Imports	1980	1981	1982
China, People's Repub.	46,959	40,962	89,772
Ethiopia	43,743	146,853	155,775
Germany, Fed. Repub.	104,117	430,548	214,873
Hong Kong	5,351	13,862	3,972
India	41,467	19,638	4,801
Iraq	2,812	67,746	402
Italy	756,800	662,839	1,221,146
Japan	28,900	54,789	48,371
Kenya	86,515	105,627	198,064
Saudi Arabia	120,208	160,583	82,879
Singapore	18,569	15,592	73,652
Thailand	19,296	40,527	106,474
United Kingdom	172,613	935,900	238,371
USA	201,662	141,823	154,082
Total (incl. others)	2,190,627	3,221,715	3,548,805

Exports	1980	1981	1982
Djibouti	6,640	3,209	2,458
Germany, Fed. Repub.	11,376	1,956	20,086
Italy	107,661	58,975	77,870
Kenya	2,425	6,929	4,211
Saudi Arabia	583,768	803,631	1,852,936
United Kingdom	1,233	—	3,169
USA	1,301	—	6,970
Yemen, People's Dem. Repub.	3,182	—	—
Total (incl. others)	844,012	960,050	2,142,585

Source: the former Ministry of Planning, Mogadishu.

1986: *Imports* (estimates, million Somali shillings) USA 1,816; Japan 836; China, People's Repub. 553; United Kingdom 773; France 341; Germany, Fed. Repub. 1,481; Total (incl. others) 8,443; *Exports* (estimates, million Somali shillings) USA 5; China, People's Repub. 4; United Kingdom 31; France 27; Germany, Fed. Repub. 11; Total (incl. others) 6,373 (Source: UN Economic Commission for Africa, *African Statistical Yearbook*).

Transport

ROAD TRAFFIC
(estimates, '000 motor vehicles in use)

	1994	1995	1996
Passenger cars	2.8	2.0	1.0
Commercial vehicles	7.4	7.3	6.4

Source: International Road Federation, *World Road Statistics*.

SHIPPING
Merchant Fleet
(registered at 31 December)

	1999	2000	2001
Number of vessels	17	17	17
Total displacement ('000 grt)	6.3	6.6	6.3

Source: Lloyd's Register-Fairplay, *World Fleet Statistics*.

International Sea-borne Freight Traffic
('000 metric tons)

	1989	1990	1991
Goods loaded	325	324	n.a.
Goods unloaded	1,252*	1,118	1,007*

* Estimate.

Source: UN Economic Commission for Africa, *African Statistical Yearbook*.

CIVIL AVIATION
(traffic on scheduled services)

	1989	1990	1991
Kilometres flown (million)	3	3	1
Passengers carried ('000)	89	88	46
Passenger-km (million)	248	255	131
Freight ton-km (million)	8	9	5

Source: UN, *Statistical Yearbook*.

Tourism

	1996	1997	1998
Tourist arrivals ('000)	10	10	10

Source: World Bank.

Communications Media

	1995	1996	1997
Radio receivers ('000 in use)	400	450	470
Television receivers ('000 in use)	124	129	135
Telephones ('000 main lines in use)*	15	15	15
Daily newspapers	1	2	n.a.

* Estimates.

Telephones (estimates, '000 main lines in use): 15 per year in 1998–2000.

Sources: UNESCO, *Statistical Yearbook*; International Telecommunication Union.

Education

(1985)

	Institutions	Teachers	Pupils
Pre-primary	16	133	1,558
Primary	1,224	10,338	196,496
Secondary:			
general	n.a.	2,149	39,753
teacher training	n.a.	30*	613*
vocational	n.a.	637	5,933
Higher	n.a.	817†	15,672†

* Figure refers to 1984.
† Figure refers to 1986.

Source: UNESCO, *Statistical Yearbook*.

1990 (UN estimates): 377,000 primary-level pupils; 44,000 secondary-level pupils; 10,400 higher-level pupils.

1991: University teachers 549; University students 4,640.

Adult literacy rate (UNESCO estimates): 24.1% (males 36.1%; females 14.0%) in 1990 (Source: UNESCO, *Statistical Yearbook*).

Directory

The Constitution

The Constitution promulgated in 1979 and amended in 1990 was revoked following the overthrow of President Siad Barre in January 1991. In July 2000 delegates at the Somali national reconciliation conference in Arta, Djibouti, overwhelmingly approved a national Charter, which was to serve as Somalia's constitution for an interim period of three years. The Charter, which is divided into six main parts, guarantees Somali citizens the freedoms of expression, association and human rights, and distinctly separates the executive, the legislature and the judiciary, as well as guaranteeing the independence of the latter.

The Government

HEAD OF STATE

President: ABDULKASIM SALAD HASAN (took office 27 August 2000).

CABINET
(April 2003)

Prime Minister: Col HASSAN ABSHIR FARAH.

Deputy Prime Minister: OSMAN JAMA ALI.

Minister of Justice and Religious Affairs: MAHMUD UMAR FARAH INDHABUR.

Minister of Internal Affairs and Rural Development: DAHIR SHAYKH MOHAMED.

Minister of Foreign Affairs: YUSUF HASAN IBRAHIM.

Minister of Defence: Gen. ABDIWAHAB MOHAMED HUSSEIN.

Minister of Finance: HUSSEIN MAHMUD SHAYKH HUSSEIN.

Minister of International Co-operation: Dr HUSSEIN EELABE FAHIYE.

Minister of Livestock and Animal Husbandry: Dr SAYID AHMED SHAYKH DAHIR.

Minister of Industry: Dr YUSSUF MA'ALIN AMIN.

Minister of Minerals and Water Resources: Dr AHMED MOHAMED HANDULLE.

Minister of Public Works: Dr MOHAMED WARSAME ALI.

Minister of Air and Land Transport: Dr ABDIGULED MOHAMED.

Minister of Ports and Shipping: Dr ABDIWELI JAMA' WARSAME.

Minister of Science and Technology: Eng. ABDI'AZIZ SHAYKH MUKHTAR.

Minister of Information: Prof. ABDIRAHMAN ADAN IBRAHIM IBBI.

Minister of Health: Dr MOHAMED NURANI BAKAR.

Minister of Education: Dr HUSSEIN MOHAMED USMAN JIMBIR.

Minister of Higher Education: Dr ZAKARIYA MAHMUD HAJI ABDI.

Minister of Labour: ABDULLAHI MOHAMMED SHIRWA.

Minister of Sports and Youth Affairs: ABDI'AZIZ MUQTAR QARIDI.

Minister of Local Government: Dr MOHAMED NUR JILEY.

Minister of Tourism and Wildlife: HASAN FARAH HUJALE.

Minister of Monetary Affairs: UMAR HASHI ADAN.

Minister of Reconciliation and Conflict Resolution: Dr MOHAMED MEYDANE BURALE.

Minister of the Constitution and Federalism: (vacant).

Minister of Environment: Dr ABUBAKR ABDI USMAN.

Minister of Women's and Family Affairs: Dr SAYNAB AWAYS HUSSEIN.

Minister of Culture and Heritage: ALI MURSAL MOHAMED.

Minister of Reconstruction and Resettlement: Dr ABDIQADIR AW-YUSUF MOHAMED.

Minister of the Disabled and Rehabilitation: Dr ABDIQADIR MOHAMED ABDULLE MADAHE.

Minister of Energy: (vacant).

Minister of the Diaspora and Refugee Affairs: AHMED ABDULLAHI JAMA.

MINISTRIES

Office of the President: People's Palace, Mogadishu; tel. (1) 723.

Ministry of Air and Land Transport: Mogadishu.

Ministry of the Constitution and Federalism: Mogadishu.

Ministry of Culture and Heritage: Mogadishu.

Ministry of Defence: Mogadishu; tel. (1) 710.

Ministry of the Diaspora and Refugee Affairs: Mogadishu.

Ministry of the Disabled and Rehabilitation: Mogadishu.

Ministry of Education: Mogadishu.

Ministry of Environment: Mogadishu.

Ministry of Energy: Mogadishu.

Ministry of Finance: Mogadishu; tel. (1) 33090.

Ministry of Foreign Affairs: Mogadishu; tel. (1) 721.

Ministry of Health: Mogadishu; tel. (1) 31055.

Ministry of Higher Education: POB 1182, Mogadishu; tel. (1) 35042.

Ministry of Industry: Mogadishu.

Ministry of Information: POB 1748, Mogadishu; tel. (1) 999621.

Ministry of Internal Affairs and Rural Development: Mogadishu.

Ministry of International Co-operation: Mogadishu.

Ministry of Justice and Religious Affairs: Mogadishu; tel. (1) 36062.

Ministry of Labour: Mogadishu; tel. (1) 33086.

Ministry of Livestock and Animal Husbandry: Mogadishu.

Ministry of Local Government: Mogadishu.

Ministry of Minerals and Water Resources: Mogadishu.

Ministry of Monetary Affairs: Mogadishu.

Ministry of Ports and Shipping: Mogadishu.

Ministry of Public Works: Mogadishu; tel. (1) 21051.

Ministry of Reconciliation and Conflict Resolution: Mogadishu.

Ministry of Reconstruction and Resettlement: Mogadishu.

Ministry of Science and Technology: Mogadishu.

Ministry of Sports and Youth Affairs: Mogadishu.

Ministry of Tourism and Wildlife: Mogadishu.

Legislature

TRANSITIONAL NATIONAL ASSEMBLY

Speaker: ABDULLAH DEEROW ISA.

Deputy Speakers: MOHAMED ABDI YUSUF, AHMAD ABARONE AMIN.

In August 2000, following the successful completion of the Somali national reconciliation conference, which commenced in Arta, Djibouti, in May, a Transitional National Assembly, comprising 245 members, was established. Each of the four major clans (Dir, Hawiye, Darod and Oigil and Mirifleh) received 44 seats in the Assembly; an alliance of minority tribes and clans was allocated 24 seats and 25 seats were reserved for women from the four major clans and the alliance, each of which would receive five seats. The remaining 20 seats were distributed among influential Somalis. It was proposed that following a three-year interim period the Somali Republic would adopt a federal system of government, which would comprise 18 regional administrations.

Political Organizations

The majority of Somalia's political organizations have split into two factions, with one aligned to the Somali National Alliance (SNA) and the other to the Somali Salvation Alliance (SSA).

Alliance Party: Hargeysa; f. 2001; Chair. SULAYMAN MAHMUD ADAN.

Islamic Party (Hizb al-Islam): radical Islamist party; Chair. Sheikh AHMAD QASIM.

Islamic Union Party (al-Ittihad al-Islam): aims to unite ethnic Somalis from Somalia, Ethiopia, Kenya and Djibouti in an Islamic state.

Northern Somali Alliance (NSA): f. 1997 as alliance between the United Somali Front and the United Somali Party.

United Somali Front (USF): f. 1989; represents Issas in the north-west of the country; Chair. ABD AR-RAHMAN DUALEH ALI; Sec.-Gen. MOHAMED OSMAN ALI.

United Somali Party (USP): opposes the SNM's declaration of the independent 'Republic of Somaliland'; Leader MOHAMED ABDI HASHI.

Peace and Development Party: Mogadishu; f. 2002; Chair. ABDULLAHI HASAN AFRAH.

Rahanwin Resistance Army: guerrilla force active around Baidoa; Chair. MOHAMED HASAN NUR.

Somali Democratic Alliance (SDA): f. 1989; represents the Gadabursi ethnic grouping in the north-west; opposes the Isaaq-dominated SNM and its declaration of an independent 'Republic of Somaliland'; Leader MOHAMED FARAH ABDULLAH.

Somali Democratic Movement (SDM): represents the Rahanwin clan; movement split in early 1992, with this faction in alliance with Ali Mahdi Mohamed; Leader ABDULKADIR MOHAMED ADAN.

Somali Eastern and Central Front (SECF): f. 1991; opposes the SNM's declaration of the independent 'Republic of Somaliland'; Chair. HIRSI ISMAIL MOHAMED.

Somali National Alliance (SNA): f. 1992 as alliance between the Southern Somali National Movement (which withdrew in 1993) and the factions of the United Somali Congress, Somali Democratic Movement and Somali Patriotic Movement given below; Chair. HUSSEIN MOHAMED AIDID.

Somali Democratic Movement (SDM): represents the Rahanwin clan; Chair. ADAM UTHMAN ABDI; Sec.-Gen. Dr YASIN MA'ALIM ABDULLAHI.

Somali Patriotic Movement (SPM): f. 1989; represents Ogadenis (of the southern Darod clan); Chair. GEDI UGAS MADHAR.

United Somali Congress (USC): f. 1989; overthrew Siad Barre in 1991; party split in mid-1991, and again in mid-1995; Chair. OSMAN HASSAN ALI 'ATO'.

Somali National Front (SNF): f. 1991; guerrilla force active in southern Somalia, promoting Darod clan interests and seeking restoration of SRSP Govt; a rival faction (led by Omar Haji Masaleh) is active in southern Somalia; Leader Gen. MOHAMED SIAD HERSI 'MORGAN'.

Somali Patriotic Movement (SPM): f. 1989; in southern Somalia; represents Ogadenis (of the Darod clan) in southern Somalia; this faction of the SPM has allied with the SNF in opposing the SNA; Chair. Gen. ADEN ABDULLAHI NOOR ('Gabio').

Somali Peace Loving Party: Mogadishu; f. 2002; Dr KHALID UMAR ALI.

Somali People's Democratic Union (SPDU): f. 1997; breakaway group from the SSDF; Chair. Gen. MOHAMED JIBRIL MUSEH.

Somali Reconciliation and Restoration Council (SRRC): f. 2001 by faction leaders opposed to the establishment of the Hasan administration; aims to establish a rival national government; Co-Chair. HUSSEIN MOHAMED AIDID, HILOWLE IMAN UMAR, ADEN ABDULLAHI NOOR, HASAN MOHAMED NUR, ABDULLAHI SHAYKH ISMA'IL; Sec.-Gen. MOWLID MA'ANEH MOHAMED.

Somali Revolutionary Socialist Party (SRSP): f. 1976 as the sole legal party; overthrown in Jan. 1991; conducts guerrilla operations in Gedo region, near border with Kenya; Sec.-Gen. (vacant); Asst Sec.-Gen. AHMED SULEIMAN ABDULLAH.

Somali Salvation Democratic Front (SSDF): f. 1981 as the Democratic Front for the Salvation of Somalia (DFSS), as a coalition of the Somali Salvation Front, the Somali Workers' Party and the Democratic Front for the Liberation of Somalia; operates in cen. Somalia, although a smaller group has opposed the SNA around Kismayu in alliance with the SNF; Chair. MOHAMED ABSHIR MONSA.

Somali Solidarity Party: Mogadishu; f. 1999; Chair. ABD AR-RAHMAN MUSA MOHAMED; Sec.-Gen. SA'ID ISA MOHAMED.

Southern Somali National Movement (SSNM): based on coast in southern Somalia; Chair. ABDI WARSEMEH ISAR.

United Somali Congress (USC): f. 1989; in cen. Somalia; overthrew Siad Barre in Jan. 1991; party split in 1991, with this faction dominated by the Abgal sub-clan of the Hawiye clan, Somalia's largest ethnic group; Leader ABDULLAHI MA'ALIN; Sec.-Gen. MUSA NUR AMIN.

United Somali Congress—Somali National Alliance (USC—SNA): f. 1995 by dissident mems of the SNA's USC faction; represents the Habr Gidir sub-clan of the Hawiye; Leader OSMAN HASSAN ALI 'ATO'.

United Somali Congress—Somali Salvation Alliance (USC—SSA): Leader MUSE SUDI YALAHOW.

Unity for the Somali Republic Party (USRP): f. 1999; the first independent party to be established in Somalia since 1969; Leader ABDI NUR DARMAN.

In November 1993 interim President Ali Mahdi Mohamed was reported to have assumed the leadership of the **Somali Salvation Alliance (SSA)**, a new coalition of 12 factions opposed to Gen. Aidid, including the Somali African Muki Organization (SAMO), the Somali National Union (SNU), the USF, the SDA, the SDM, the SPM, the USC (pro-Mahdi faction), the SSDF, the Somali National Democratic Union (SNDU), the SNF and the SSNM. In May 1994 the SNU announced its intention to leave the alliance and join the SNA.

Diplomatic Representation

EMBASSIES IN SOMALIA

Note: Following the overthrow of Siad Barre in January 1991, all foreign embassies in Somalia were closed and all diplomatic personnel left the country. Some embassies were reopened, including those of France, Sudan and the USA, following the arrival of the US-led Unified Task Force (UNITAF) in December 1992; however, nearly all foreign diplomats left Somalia in anticipation of the withdrawal of the UN peace-keeping force, UNOSOM, in early 1995.

Algeria: POB 2850, Mogadishu; tel. (1) 81696.

Bulgaria: Hodan District, Km 5, off Via Afgoi, POB 1736, Mogadishu; tel. (1) 81820.

China, People's Republic: POB 548, Mogadishu; tel. (1) 20805.

Cuba: Mogadishu.

Djibouti: Mogadishu.

Egypt: Via Maka al-Mukarama Km 4, POB 76, Mogadishu; tel. (1) 80781; Ambassador Dr SALIH HALIM.

Ethiopia: POB 368, Mogadishu.

France: Corso Primo Luglio, POB 13, Mogadishu; tel. (1) 21715.

Germany: Via Mahamoud Harbi, POB 17, Mogadishu; tel. (1) 20547.

India: Via Jigjiga, Shingani, POB 955, Mogadishu; tel. (1) 21262.

Iran: Via Maka al-Mukarama, POB 1166, Mogadishu; tel. (1) 80881.

Iraq: Via Maka al-Mukarama, POB 641, Mogadishu; tel. (1) 80821.

Italy: Via Alto Giuba, POB 6, Mogadishu; tel. (1) 20544; Ambassador FRANCESCO SCIORTINO.

Kenya: Via Mecca, POB 618, Mogadishu; tel. (1) 80857.

Korea, Democratic People's Republic: Via Km 5, Mogadishu; Ambassador KIM RYONG SU.

Kuwait: First Medina Rd, Km 5, POB 1348, Mogadishu.

Libya: Via Medina, POB 125, Mogadishu; Ambassador MOHAMED ZUBEYD.

Nigeria: Via Km 5, Mogadishu; tel. (1) 81362.

Oman: Via Afgoi, POB 2992, Mogadishu; tel. (1) 81658.

Pakistan: Via Afgoi, Km 5, POB 339, Mogadishu; tel. (1) 80856.

Qatar: Via Km 4, POB 1744, Mogadishu; tel. (1) 80746.

Romania: Via Lido, POB 651, Mogadishu.

Saudi Arabia: Via Benadir, POB 603, Mogadishu; tel. (1) 22087.

Serbia and Montenegro: Via Mecca, POB 952, Mogadishu; tel. (1) 81729.

Sudan: Via Maka al-Mukarama, POB 552, Mogadishu; Chargé d'affaires a.i. ALI HASSAN ALI.

Syria: Via Medina, POB 986, Mogadishu.

Turkey: Via Km 6, POB 2833, Mogadishu; tel. (1) 81975.

United Arab Emirates: Via Afgoi, Km 5, Mogadishu; tel. (1) 23178.

United Kingdom: Waddada Xasan Geedd Abtoow 7/8, POB 1036, Mogadishu; tel. (1) 20288.

USA: Via Afgoi, Km 5, POB 574, Mogadishu; tel. (1) 39971.

Yemen: Via Km 5, POB 493, Mogadishu.

Zimbabwe: Mogadishu.

Judicial System

Constitutional arrangements in operation until 1991 provided for the Judiciary to be independent of the executive and legislative powers. Laws and acts having the force of law were required to conform to the provisions of the Constitution and to the general principles of Islam.

Attorney-General: AYDID ABDULLAHI.

Supreme Court: Mogadishu; the court of final instance in civil, criminal, administrative and auditing matters; Chair. Sheikh AHMAD HASAN.

Military Supreme Court: Mogadishu; f. 1970; tried mems of the armed forces.

National Security Court: Mogadishu; heard cases of treason.

Courts of Appeal: Mogadishu; sat at Mogadishu and Hargeysa, with two sections, General and Assize.

Regional Courts: There were eight Regional Courts, with two sections, General and Assize.

District Courts: There were 84 District Courts, with Civil and Criminal Divisions. The Civil Division had jurisdiction over all controversies where the cause of action had arisen under *Shari'a* (Islamic) Law or Customary Law and any other Civil controversies where the matter in dispute did not involve more than 3,000 shillings. The Criminal Division had jurisdiction with respect to offences punishable with imprisonment not exceeding three years, or fines not exceeding 3,000 shillings, or both.

Qadis: Districts Courts of civil jurisdiction under Islamic Law.

In September 1993, in accordance with Resolution 865 of the UN Security Council, a judiciary re-establishment council, composed of Somalis, was created in Mogadishu to rehabilitate the judicial and penal systems.

Judiciary Re-establishment Council (JRC): Mogadishu; Chair. Dr ABD AL-RAHMAN HAJI GA'AL.

Following the withdrawal of the UN peace-keeping force, UNOSOM, in early 1995, most regions outside of Mogadishu reverted to clan-based fiefdoms where Islamic (*Shari'a*) law (comprising an Islamic Supreme Council and local Islamic high courts) prevailed. In October 1996 Ali Mahdi Mohamed endorsed a new Islamic judicial system under which appeals could be lodged on all sentences passed by Islamic courts, and no sentence imposed by the courts could be implemented prior to an appeal court ruling. In August 1998 the Governor of the Banaadir administration announced the application of *Shari'a* law in Mogadishu and its environs thenceforth.

Religion

ISLAM

Islam is the state religion. Most Somalis are Sunni Muslims.

Imam: Gen. MOHAMED ABSHIR.

CHRISTIANITY

The Roman Catholic Church

Somalia comprises a single diocese, directly responsible to the Holy See. At 31 December 2000 there were an estimated 100 adherents.

Bishop of Mogadishu: (vacant), POB 273, Ahmed bin Idris, Mogadishu; tel. (1) 20184.

The Anglican Communion

Within the Episcopal Church in Jerusalem and the Middle East, the Bishop in Egypt has jurisdiction over Somalia.

The Press

The Country: POB 1178, Mogadishu; tel. (1) 21206; f. 1991; daily.

Dalka: POB 388, Mogadishu; f. 1967; current affairs; weekly.

Heegan (Vigilance): POB 1178, Mogadishu; tel. (1) 21206; f. 1978; weekly; English; Editor MOHAMOUD M. AFRAH.

Horseed: POB 1178, Mogadishu; tel. (1) 21206; weekly; in Italian and Arabic.

Huuriya (Liberty): Hargeysa; daily.

Jamhuuriya (The Republic): Hargeysa; independent; daily; Editor-in-Chief MAHMOUD ABDI SHIDE; circ. 2,500.

Al Mujeehid: Hargeysa; weekly.

New Era: POB 1178, Mogadishu; tel. (1) 21206; quarterly; in English, Somali and Arabic.

Qaran (Nation): Mogadishu; financial information; daily; in Somali; Editor ABDULAHI AHMED ALI; circ. 2,000.

Riyaaq (Happiness): Boosaaso.

Sahan (Pioneer): Boosaaso; Editor MUHAMMAD DEEQ.

Somalia in Figures: Ministry of National Planning, POB 1742, Mogadishu; tel. (1) 80384; govt statistical publ. 3 a year; in English.

Xiddigta Oktobar (October Star): POB 1178, Mogadishu; tel. (1) 21206; in Somali; daily.

NEWS AGENCIES

Horn of Africa News Agency: Mogadishu; f. 1990.

Somali National News Agency (SONNA): POB 1748, Mogadishu; tel. (1) 24058; Dir MUHAMMAD HASAN KAHIN.

Foreign Bureaux

Agence France-Presse (AFP) (France): POB 1178, Mogadishu; Rep. MOHAMED ROBLE NOOR.

Agenzia Nazionale Stampa Associata (ANSA) (Italy): POB 1399, Mogadishu; tel. (1) 20626; Rep. ABDULKADIR MOHAMOUD WALAYO.

Publishers

Government Printer: POB 1743, Mogadishu.

Somalia d'Oggi: Piazzale della Garesa, POB 315, Mogadishu; law, economics and reference.

Broadcasting and Communications

TELECOMMUNICATIONS

Ministry of Information: POB 1748, Mogadishu; tel. (1) 999621; Dir-Gen. A. ALI ASKAR.

Somali Telecom (Olympic Telecommunications): Mogadishu.

Somaliland Telecommunications Corpn: Hargeysa; Dir MOHAMED ARWO.

BROADCASTING

Radio

Holy Koran Radio: Mogadishu; f. 1996; religious broadcasts in Somali.

Radio Awdal: Boorama, 'Somaliland'; operated by the Gadabursi clan.

Radio Banaadir: Mogadishu; f. 2000; serves Mogadishu and its environs.

Radio Free Somalia: f. 1993; operates from Galacaio in north-eastern Somalia; relays humanitarian and educational programmes.

Radio Gaalkayco: operates from 'Puntland'.

Radio Hargeysa, the Voice of the 'Republic of Somaliland': POB 14, Hargeysa; tel. 155; serves the northern region ('Somaliland'); broadcasts in Somali, and relays Somali and Amharic transmission from Radio Mogadishu; Dir of Radio IDRIS EGAL NUR.

Radio HornAfrique: Mogadishu; f. 1999; commercial independent station broadcasting music and programmes on social issues; Dir AHMAD ABDI SALAN HAJI ADAN.

Radio Mogadishu, Voice of the Masses of the Somali Republic: southern Mogadishu; f. 1993 by supporters of Gen. Aidid after the facilities of the fmr state-controlled radio station, Radio Mogadishu (of which Gen. Aidid's faction took control in 1991), were destroyed by UNOSOM; broadcasts in Somali, Amharic, Arabic, English and Swahili; Chair. FARAH HASAN AYOBOQORE.

Radio Mogadishu, Voice of Somali Pacification: Mogadishu; f. 1995 by supporters of Osman Hassan Ali 'Ato'; broadcasts in Somali, English and Arabic; Dir-Gen. MUHAMMAD DIRIYEH ILMI.

Radio Mogadishu, Voice of the Somali Republic: northern Mogadishu; f. 1992 by supporters of Ali Mahdi Mohamed; Chair. FARAH HASSAN AYOBOQORE.

Voice of Peace: POB 1631, Addis Ababa, Ethiopia; f. 1993; aims to promote peace and reconstruction in Somalia; receives support from UNICEF and the AU.

Some radio receivers are used for public address purposes in small towns and villages.

Television

A television service, financed by Kuwait and the United Arab Emirates, was inaugurated in 1983. Programmes in Somali and Arabic are broadcast for three hours daily, extended to four hours on Fridays and public holidays. Reception is limited to a 30-km radius of Mogadishu.

Somali Television Network (STN): Mogadishu; f. 1999; broadcasts 22 channels in Somali, English, French, Indian, Italian and Arabic; Man. Dir ABURAHMAN ROBLEY ULAYEREH.

Television HornAfrique: Mogadishu; f. 1999; broadcasts 6 channels in Somali and Arabic; CEO ALI IMAN SHARMARKEH.

Finance

(cap. = capital; res = reserves; m. = million; brs = branches; amounts in Somali shillings unless otherwise stated)

BANKING

Central Bank

Central Bank of Somalia (Bankiga Dhexe ee Soomaaliya): Corso Somalia 55, POB 11, Mogadishu; tel. (1) 657733; f. 1960; bank of issue; cap. and res 132.5m. (Sept. 1985); Gov. MAHMOUD MOHAMED ULUSOW; Gen. Mans MOHAMED MOHAMED NUR, BASHIR ISSE ALI.

A central bank (with 10 branches) is also in operation in Hargeysa (in the self-proclaimed 'Republic of Somaliland').

Commercial Bank

Commercial Bank of Somalia: Via Primo Luglio, POB 203, Mogadishu; tel. (1) 22861; f. 1990 to succeed the Commercial and Savings Bank of Somalia; state-owned; cap. 1,000m. (May 1990); 33 brs.

Universal Bank of Somalia: Mogadishu; f. 2002; cap. US $10m; Gen. Man. MAHAD ADAN BARKHADLE (acting).

Private Banks

Somali-Malaysian Commercial Bank: Mogadishu; f. 1997; cap. US $4m.

Development Bank

Somali Development Bank: Via Primo Luglio, POB 1079, Mogadishu; tel. (1) 21800; f. 1968; state-owned; cap. and res 2,612.7m. (Dec. 1988); Pres. MOHAMED MOHAMED NUR; 4 brs.

INSURANCE

Cassa per le Assicurazioni Sociali della Somalia: POB 123, Mogadishu; f. 1950; workers' compensation; Dir-Gen. HASSAN MOHAMED JAMA; 9 brs.

State Insurance Co of Somalia: POB 992, Mogadishu; f. 1974; Gen. Man. ABDULLAHI GA'AL; brs throughout Somalia.

Trade and Industry

DEVELOPMENT ORGANIZATIONS

Agricultural Development Corpn: POB 930, Mogadishu; f. 1971; by merger of fmr agricultural and machinery agencies and grain marketing board; supplies farmers with equipment and materials and purchases growers' cereal and oil seed crops; Dir-Gen. MOHAMED FARAH ANSHUR.

Livestock Development Agency: POB 1759, Mogadishu; Dir-Gen. HASSAN WELI SCEK HUSSEN; brs throughout Somalia.

Somali Co-operative Movement: Mogadishu; Chair. HASSAN HAWADLE MADAR.

Somali Oil Refinery: POB 1241, Mogadishu; Chair. NUR AHMED DARAWISH.

Water Development Agency: POB 525, Mogadishu; Dir-Gen. KHALIF HAJI FARAH.

CHAMBER OF COMMERCE

Chamber of Commerce, Industry and Agriculture: Via Asha, POB 27, Mogadishu; tel. (1) 3209; Chair. MOHAMED IBRAHIM HAJI EGAL.

TRADE ASSOCIATION

National Agency of Foreign Trade: POB 602, Mogadishu; major foreign trade agency; state-owned; brs in Berbera and over 150 centres throughout Somalia; Dir-Gen. JAMA AW MUSE.

UTILITIES

Water Development Agency: POB 525, Mogadishu; Dir-Gen. KHALIF HAJI FARAH.

TRADE UNION

General Federation of Somali Trade Unions: POB 1179, Mogadishu; Chair. MOHAMED FARAH ISSA GASHAN.

Transport

RAILWAYS

There are no railways in Somalia.

ROADS

In 1999 there were an estimated 22,100 km of roads, of which some 11.8% were paved.

SHIPPING

Merca, Berbera, Mogadishu and Kismayu are the chief ports. An EU-sponsored development project for the port of Berbera (in 'Somaliland') was announced in February 1996. It was reported that the port of Mogadishu, which had been largely closed since 1995, was reopened in early 2000.

Somali Ports Authority: POB 935, Mogadishu; tel. (1) 30081; Port Dir MOHAMED JUMA FURAH.

Juba Enterprises Beder & Sons Ltd: POB 549, Mogadishu; privately-owned.

National Shipping Line: POB 588, Mogadishu; tel. (1) 23021; state-owned; Gen. Man. Dr ABDULLAHI MOHAMED SALAD.

Puntland Shipping Service: Boosaaso.

Shosman Commercial Co Ltd: North-Eastern Pasaso; privately-owned.

Somali Shipping Corpn: POB 2775, Mogadishu; state-owned.

CIVIL AVIATION

Mogadishu has an international airport. There are airports at Hargeysa and Baidoa and six other airfields. It was reported that a daily service had been inaugurated in April 1994 between Hargeysa (in the self-declared 'Republic of Somaliland') and Nairobi, Kenya. Mogadishu international airport (closed since 1995) was officially reopened in mid-1998, but continuing civil unrest limited services significantly.

Air Somalia: Mogadishu; f. 2001; operates internal passenger services and international services to destinations in Africa and the Middle East; Chair. ALI FARAH ABDULLEH.

SOUTH AFRICA

Introductory Survey

Location, Climate, Language, Religion, Flag, Capital

The Republic of South Africa occupies the southern extremity of the African mainland. It is bordered by Namibia to the north-west, by Botswana and Zimbabwe to the north, by Mozambique to the north-east, and by Swaziland to the east. Lesotho is completely surrounded by South African territory. The climate is generally sub-tropical, but with considerable regional variations. Temperatures in Cape Town, on the south-west coast, vary from 7°C (45°F) to 26°C (79°F), with an annual average of about 17°C (63°F). Annual rainfall averages 510 mm (20 ins) at Cape Town, and 1,101 mm (43 ins) at Durban, on the east coast. The official languages are Sepedi, Sesotho, Setswana, siSwati, Tshivenda, Xitsonga, Afrikaans, English, isiNdebele, isiXhosa and isiZulu. About 77.8% of the population are black, 10.2% are white, 8.7% are Coloured (of mixed race), and 2.5% are Asian (mainly of Indian origin). Most of the inhabitants profess Christianity, although traditional African religions are still adhered to. There are also small minorities of Hindus (nearly all Asians) and Muslims (mainly Coloureds and Asians). The national flag (proportions 2 by 3) has a green 'Y' shape extending from the upper and lower hoist corners to the centre of the fly end, bordered in white on its outer edges, and in light orange on its inner edges near the hoist; the areas above and below the horizontal band of the 'Y' are red and blue respectively, with a black triangle at the hoist. The administrative capital is Pretoria, the legislative capital is Cape Town, and the judicial capital is Bloemfontein.

Recent History

On 31 May 1910 four British dependencies were merged to form the Union of South Africa, a dominion under the British Crown. In 1931 the British Parliament recognized the Union as an independent country within the Commonwealth. From the establishment of South Africa until 1984, national administration was the exclusive preserve of the white population.

The National Party (NP), which acceded to power in 1948, introduced the doctrine of apartheid (in theory the separate, but equal, development of all racial groups, in practice leading to white, particularly Afrikaner, supremacy). The principal opposition to government policy during the 1950s took the form of a campaign of civil disobedience, led by the multiracial African National Congress of South Africa (ANC). In 1959 some members of the ANC formed the exclusively black Pan-Africanist Congress (PAC). In 1960 the ANC and the PAC conducted opposition to the 'pass laws' (which required blacks to be in possession of special documentation in designated white urban areas); at one demonstration, in Sharpeville, 67 blacks were killed by security forces, prompting international outrage, and further demonstrations within South Africa, as a result of which the ANC and the PAC were declared illegal. Both movements subsequently formed military wings, based outside South Africa, to conduct campaigns of sabotage. An influential leader of the ANC, Nelson Mandela, was detained in 1962 and sentenced to life imprisonment on a charge of sabotage in 1964, but remained a focus for opposition to apartheid.

On 31 May 1961, following a referendum among white voters in October 1960, South Africa became a republic, and left the Commonwealth. Dr Hendrik Verwoerd was Prime Minister from 1958 until his assassination in September 1966. He was succeeded by the former Minister of Justice, Balthazar Johannes (B. J.) Vorster.

As an integral part of the policy of apartheid, the territorial segregation of African ethnic groups was enforced, on the grounds that the Native Reserves (comprising only 13% of national territory) constituted the historic 'homelands' (Bantustans) of different African nations. In 1963 Transkei was accorded 'self-governing' status, with an Executive Council, headed by a Chief Minister, to be elected by a Legislative Assembly. Bophuthatswana (June 1972), Ciskei (August 1972), Lebowa (October 1972), Gazankulu (February 1973), KwaZulu (April 1973), Qwaqwa (November 1974), KwaNdebele (October 1977), and KaNgwane (August 1984) were subsequently granted 'self-government'. Transkei was declared 'independent'

in October 1976, Bophuthatswana in December 1977, Venda in September 1979 and Ciskei in December 1981. The population of the 'independent homelands' was not entitled to South African citizenship. The 'independent homelands' were not recognized by any government other than that of South Africa.

The numerous discriminatory laws regulating the lives of the country's black, 'Coloured' (a term used to denote people of mixed race) and 'Indian' (Asian) populations, combined with stringent security legislation, led to the detention without trial of many of the Government's opponents, the banning of black political organizations outside the 'homelands', and the forced removal of hundreds of thousands of blacks in accordance with the provisions of the Group Areas Act of 1966 (which imposed residential segregation of the races) and the 'homelands' policy. In June 1976 violent riots occurred in Soweto (South-Western Townships), near Johannesburg, and rapidly spread to other black urban areas. Vorster used the executive's virtually limitless powers, conferred by the newly adopted Internal Security Act, to suppress riots and strikes. Several hundred people died in confrontations with the security forces, and many more were detained without trial. Allegations of human rights violations by security forces culminated in international indignation at the death in detention of a black community leader, Steve Biko, in September 1977. In 1978 black, Coloured and Indian activists founded the Azanian People's Organization (AZAPO).

The parliamentary majority of the NP was considerably strengthened at the November 1977 general election. In September 1978 Vorster resigned as Prime Minister, and was succeeded by Pieter Willem (P. W.) Botha, hitherto the Minister of Defence. In 1979, following the disclosure of corruption and misappropriation of public funds, Vorster resigned from the largely honorary post of State President. In February 1981 a new, 60-member advisory body, the President's Council, comprising representatives of the white, Coloured and Indian population, was formed to consider constitutional reform. Its recommendations to include Coloureds and Indians (but not blacks) in a three-chamber Parliament, with a multiracial government (led by an executive President), exacerbated inter-party differences: the 'verligte' (liberal) wing of the NP, led by Botha, advocated the establishment of a confederation of South Africa and the 'homelands', with separate citizenships but a common South African nationality, and was strongly opposed by the 'verkrampte' (uncompromising) wing of the party. In March 1982 16 extreme right-wing parliamentary deputies who had opposed the constitutional recommendations were expelled from the NP; they subsequently formed the Conservative Party of South Africa (CP), in conjunction with other right-wing elements.

Throughout 1983 and 1984, despite opposition from both the CP and the Progressive Federal Party (PFP), Botha pursued his policy of constitutional reform. The majority vote of the Coloured Labour Party (LP) in 1983 to participate in the reform programme caused divisions within the party. The constitutional body representing the Indian population, the South African Indian Council (SAIC), provisionally agreed to the proposals, subject to approval by an Indian community referendum. This decision was, however, opposed by the Transvaal Anti-SAIC Committee, an organization that had been formed in 1981 in protest at participation in elections to the SAIC. In August 1983 the Committee established the United Democratic Front (UDF), to organize resistance on a national scale to Indian and Coloured participation in the constitutional reforms. The UDF rapidly became the principal legal opposition movement.

The constitutional reforms were approved by the House of Assembly in September 1983, and by about 66% of voters in an all-white referendum in November. In the same month the PFP decided to take part in the reformed system. However, six 'homeland' leaders, including Chief Mangosuthu Gatsha Buthelezi, the Chief Minister of KwaZulu (who had consistently opposed the 'homelands' policy), rejected the constitutional reforms on the grounds that blacks remained excluded from participation in the central Government. Despite a previous pledge by the Prime Minister to assess Coloured and Indian opinion on the reforms, elections to the Coloured and Indian chambers of the new Parliament, known as the House of Representatives and the House of Delegates respectively, took place in August 1984, without prior referendums. As a result, the boycott that had been organized by the UDF was widely observed: about 18% of the eligible Coloured population voted in the elections to the House of Representatives, with the LP winning 76 of the 80 directly elected seats, while only 16.6% of eligible Indian voters participated in the elections to the House of Delegates, with the National People's Party (NPP) winning 18 and the Solidarity Party 17 of the 40 directly elected seats. (The House of Assembly, as elected in 1981, remained in office.)

The new Constitution came into effect in September 1984. Under the terms of the Constitution, legislative power was vested in the State President and the tricameral Parliament, comprising the 178-member House of Assembly (for the representation of whites), the 85-member House of Representatives (for Coloureds) and the 45-member House of Delegates (for Indians). Following the adoption of the Constitution in September, the post of Prime Minister was abolished, and Botha was unanimously elected to the new office of State President (which combined the powers of Head of State and Prime Minister) by an electoral college, comprising members of all three parliamentary chambers. A President's Council, a new Cabinet and three Ministers' Councils (one for each population group) were subsequently established. The Cabinet comprised only two non-white members, the Chairmen of the Indian and Coloured Ministers' Councils, neither of whom was given a portfolio.

During 1985–86 a number of the laws on which apartheid was based were modified or repealed, prompting strong right-wing opposition. The Immorality Act (1927) and the Prohibition of Mixed Marriages Act (1949), which banned sexual relations and marriage between members of different races, were repealed in April 1985, and in the following month it was announced that the Prohibition of Political Interference Act (1967), prohibiting members of different racial groups from belonging to the same political party, was to be abrogated. In April 1986 the Government promulgated legislation that provided for the removal of a number of restrictions on the movement, residence and employment of blacks in white urban areas. On 1 July the 'pass laws' were officially repealed, with the introduction of uniform identity documents for all South African citizens. On the same day reforms concerning the structure of local and provincial government were implemented, and legislation granting blacks limited rights to own property in black urban areas entered into force. In the same month it was announced that citizens of the four 'independent homelands' who were residing and working permanently in South Africa were to regain South African citizenship; in effect, however, only a small proportion of the population of the 'homelands' was eligible. Following discussions, initiated by Buthelezi in April 1986, regarding the establishment of a joint authority for his 'homeland', KwaZulu, and the province of Natal, the Government agreed to the formation of an administrative body, the Joint Executive Authority (which was installed in November 1987).

The introduction of the new Constitution in September 1984 prompted severe rioting in the black townships, which was violently repressed by the security forces. Violence took place within the black community, directed at those who were regarded as collaborators with the Government; factional clashes also occurred, notably between supporters of the ANC and of the Inkatha Movement, a Zulu organization led by Buthelezi. In July 1985 the Government declared a state of emergency in 36 districts; by March 1986 it was estimated that 757 people had been killed, and almost 8,000 arrested. In June of that year Botha declared a nationwide state of emergency, on the grounds that national security was endangered by subversive elements. Press censorship subsequently became progressively stricter, and the powers of the security forces were extended. Opposition to the Government emerged from the Congress of South African Trade Unions (COSATU), an influential federation of trade unions.

At a general election to the House of Assembly in May 1987, the NP was returned to power, winning 123 of the 166 directly-elective seats. The CP increased its representation from 17 to 22 elective seats, thereby replacing the PFP as the official opposition. In June the Government renewed the state of emergency, and further stringent press restrictions were imposed. In August the Rev. Allan Hendrickse (the leader of the LP) resigned as the sole Coloured minister in the Cabinet, owing to his disagreement with certain cabinet decisions.

In February 1988, following the involvement of trade unionists in allegedly subversive activities, the Government restricted the activities of COSATU to purely trade union affairs. In June legislation was approved that provided for the establishment of a multiracial consultative body, which was to include black members. In March 1989 the Group Areas Act was amended to permit some racially mixed residential areas. Nevertheless, the suppression of dissidents increased. The state of emergency was renewed for a further 12 months in June 1988, and strict limitations on strike action came into effect from September. During 1988 the Government proscribed more than 30 organizations, including the UDF and AZAPO (thereby effectively banning almost all peaceful extra-parliamentary opposition to apartheid).

In January 1989 Botha withdrew from his official duties, owing to ill health; in February he resigned as leader of the NP, and was succeeded by Frederik Willem (F. W.) de Klerk, hitherto Minister of National Education. Despite almost unanimous demands from the party that he should share power with de Klerk before retiring at the next general election, Botha refused to allow his power as State President to be eroded, and in March he resumed his official duties. In April the PFP, the Independent Party (which had been formed by one of a number of 'verligte' defectors from the NP in 1988) and the National Democratic Movement (established by dissident PFP members in late 1987) merged to form the Democratic Party (DP).

The state of emergency was extended for a further 12 months in June 1989. In August Botha claimed that members of his Cabinet had omitted to inform him of a prospective visit by de Klerk to Zambia to meet with President Kenneth Kaunda (which he opposed, owing to Kaunda's support for the ANC). Following a confrontation with the Cabinet, Botha resigned as State President. Shortly afterwards de Klerk was appointed acting President.

Elections to the three Houses of Parliament took place in September 1989. The NP won 93 of the 166 elective seats in the House of Assembly, while the CP secured 39 seats, and the DP 33 seats. Less than 12% of the Coloured electorate voted in the general election to the House of Representatives, at which the LP won 69 of the 80 directly-elective seats. Some 20% of the Indian electorate voted in the general election to the House of Delegates: the Solidarity Party secured 16 of the 40 directly-elective seats, while the NPP won nine. In mid-September, following his inauguration as State President, de Klerk stated that the implementation of constitutional reforms was his highest priority.

On 2 February 1990 de Klerk announced several radical reforms, including the legalization of the ANC, the PAC, the South African Communist Party (SACP), the UDF and more than 30 other banned political organizations. Nelson Mandela and a further 120 political prisoners were to be released unconditionally. In addition, most emergency regulations restricting the media were to be removed, as were repressive measures imposed on former political detainees; detention without trial was to be limited to a maximum of six months. De Klerk confirmed that the Government intended to initiate negotiations with the black opposition, with the aim of drafting a new democratic constitution. Leaders of the extreme right-wing parties reacted to de Klerk's reforms with threats of violence.

Mandela's release from prison, on 11 February 1990, received much international attention. In March he was elected Deputy President of the ANC. In spite of appeals by Mandela for reconciliation between rival factions within the black community, the continuing violence in Natal between supporters of the Inkatha Movement and mainly Xhosa-speaking supporters of the ANC intensified in March and April, and unrest erupted in several black townships. The first formal discussions between the ANC and the de Klerk Government took place in early May. In mid-May legislation was introduced that granted temporary immunity from prosecution to political exiles, including leaders of the ANC, who had committed crimes. In June de Klerk repealed the state of emergency in all provinces except Natal. In July Buthelezi reconstituted the Inkatha Movement as the Inkatha Freedom Party (IFP), in order to participate in future constitutional negotiations. At a second series of discussions in August, the ANC and the Government reached an agreement whereby, in preparation for constitutional negotiations, the ANC was to suspend its guerrilla activities, and the Government was to release more than 3,000 political prisoners and to facilitate the return to South Africa of an estimated 40,000 exiles. However, the ANC subsequently continued to train recruits for

SOUTH AFRICA

its military wing (known as Umkhonto we Sizwe—MK) and to stockpile ammunition, thereby contravening the terms of its cease-fire and causing the Government to delay the release of political prisoners and the repatriation of exiles.

During August 1990 factional fighting between supporters of the IFP and of the ANC, which was no longer confined to Natal, escalated in the black townships surrounding Johannesburg; more than 500 people were reported to have been killed by the end of that month. Intense fighting continued during September, when temporary curfews were imposed in several districts. Nevertheless, in the following month the state of emergency was revoked in Natal. In October the Separate Amenities Act of 1953 (which had imposed racial segregation with regard to public amenities) was repealed, prompting right-wing protests, particularly from the Afrikaanse Weerstandsbeweging (AWB), a paramilitary organization that had been formed in 1973 under the leadership of Eugene Terre'Blanche. During October the NP opened its membership to all races. In December Oliver Tambo, the President of the ANC, returned after more than 30 years in exile.

In January 1991 Mandela and Buthelezi held a meeting, at which both leaders appealed to their respective followers to end hostilities. In February de Klerk announced that he was to introduce draft legislation to repeal the principal remaining apartheid laws: the Land Acts of 1913 and 1936 (which stipulated that the black population was entitled to own only 13.6% of the land), the Group Areas Act, the Black Communities Act of 1984 (which enforced the separate status of black townships) and the Population Registration Act of 1950 (which decreed that all South Africans should be registered at birth according to race) were subsequently abolished. In the same month the Government agreed to assume joint administrative powers in Ciskei, following increasing pressure within the 'independent homeland' for its reincorporation into South Africa and for the resignation of its military ruler. In mid-February the Government and the ANC reached agreement on a wide range of issues, including the release of political prisoners, the return of exiles and the curtailment of activities by the MK. However, increasing township violence continued to impede constitutional negotiations. In May Winnie Mandela, the wife of Nelson Mandela, was found guilty of assaulting and kidnapping a young ANC activist, Stompie Moeketsi Seipei, in 1988, and was sentenced to six years' imprisonment, causing considerable embarrassment for the ANC. (Winnie Mandela, who became separated from Nelson Mandela in 1992, remained at liberty, pending an appeal against the verdict; in June 1993 the conviction for assault was overturned, and her sentence was commuted to a fine and a suspended term of imprisonment.) In July 1991, at a national congress of the ANC, Nelson Mandela was elected as its President and Cyril Ramaphosa, hitherto leader of the National Union of Mineworkers, was elected Secretary-General of the organization.

In July 1991, amid intense speculation that Inkatha was supported by the security forces, the Government admitted that it had made secret payments to the IFP in 1989 and 1990; however, de Klerk and Buthelezi maintained that they had not known about the covert transfer of funds. Shortly afterwards, in response to renewed pressure from the ANC, compounded by international outrage at the affair, de Klerk announced the demotion of the Ministers of Defence and of Law and Order to minor cabinet posts. In August 1991 the Government declared an amnesty for all political exiles. During that month the UDF was dissolved. In September the Government, the ANC, the IFP and 23 other political organizations signed a national peace accord, in an attempt to end township violence; however, unrest continued to escalate. In October a judicial commission of inquiry was established to assess the causes of civil violence.

A multi-party conference on South Africa's future, known as the Convention for a Democratic South Africa (CODESA), was convened in December 1991. CODESA was attended by the Government and 18 political organizations, including the ANC, NP, DP, LP, NPP, New Solidarity (formerly the Solidarity Party) and representatives of the 'homelands' (including the IFP, which represented KwaZulu); the conference was boycotted by the PAC, AZAPO and the CP. The negotiating body's stated aim to create an undivided South Africa was rejected by the IFP, which favoured the concept of a South African federation of independent states, and by the Bophuthatswana administration, which demanded total independence from South Africa.

In March 1992 a referendum of the white population, aimed at determining the level of support for the negotiation of a demo-cratic constitution, resulted in an overwhelming mandate for the continuation of the process of reform. In May, however, constitutional negotiations were suspended, owing to the Government's insistence on having a majority vote in CODESA. The ANC subsequently organized a campaign of mass protests. In June several residents of Boipatong, a black township, were massacred, apparently by Inkatha supporters and allegedly with the complicity of the security forces. Following a visit to the township by de Klerk, 30 demonstrators were killed as the security forces suppressed an anti-Government protest. The ANC subsequently withdrew from all bilateral discussions with the Government, pending the latter's agreement to a number of demands, including the immediate release of all remaining political prisoners and effective action to curtail township violence. In August the ANC, SACP and COSATU intensified their campaign of anti-Government protests. In the same month several parliamentary deputies belonging to the CP defected to form a new extreme right-wing party, the Afrikaner Volksunie (AVU).

In mid-1992 the ANC announced that it was to organize a series of demonstrations in protest against 'homeland' leaders who wished their territories (Bophuthatswana, Ciskei, Kwa-Zulu and Qwaqwa) to retain a strong measure of autonomy in the future South Africa. In September Ciskei security forces killed 28 ANC demonstrators, and injured about 200, prompting international outrage. The ANC accused the South African security forces (some of whose members had been seconded to Ciskei) of complicity in the incident. In mid-September de Klerk announced that measures to reduce the 'independence' of the 'homelands' would be implemented. In late 1992 the leaders of Bophuthatswana, Ciskei and KwaZulu, in conjunction with the IFP, the AVU and the CP, formed a pressure group (the Concerned South Africans Group—COSAG) to campaign for a maximum degree of regional autonomy.

In late September 1992, following intense negotiations, a peace summit was held, at which the Government accepted the ANC's preconditions for the resumption of constitutional negotiations. A 'record of understanding' was signed, which stated that the new Constitution would be drafted by an elected constitutional assembly and that there would be a non-racial elected interim government. In October the Constitution was amended to permit blacks to serve in the Cabinet. Later in that month legislation was approved that granted immunity from prosecution to perpetrators of politically motivated offences committed prior to 8 October 1990. In December Buthelezi published a draft constitution for a planned state comprising the KwaZulu 'homeland' and the province of Natal, which would retain a strong measure of autonomy within a future South African federation.

In February 1993 the ANC and the Government agreed to the immediate resumption of multi-party discussions. In March, at a meeting between the Government and 25 delegations from national political parties (including the formerly unco-operative PAC, IFP and CP) and the 'homeland' Governments, it was decided that CODESA was to be reconstituted, with the PAC, the IFP and the CP granted equal status with the other representatives. In April, shortly after the recommencement of constitutional negotiations, Chris Hani, the General Secretary of the SACP and the former leader of the MK, was assassinated by a white right-wing extremist; three members of the CP were subsequently charged in connection with the murder, which appeared to be part of a right-wing plot to disrupt the negotiations. (In October two of the alleged conspirators received the death sentence, which was subsequently commuted to life imprisonment, while the remaining defendant was acquitted.) The assassination precipitated widespread violent unrest, which was suppressed by the security forces. The ANC, SACP and COSATU organized a national strike on the day of Hani's funeral, and announced that a period of mass action would ensue in support of demands for the swift agreement of a date for multi-party elections and the immediate introduction of multi-party control of the army and security forces. In May an informal alliance was established of 21 right-wing organizations (including the AVU, the CP and the AWB), known as the Afrikaner Volksfront (AVF), to co-ordinate opposition to the negotiating process.

In June 1993 legislation providing for the abolition of the President's Council was approved by Parliament. Shortly before the date of the elections was due to be confirmed, armed right-wing extremists, many of whom were members of the AWB, staged a violent protest at the negotiating centre in support of demands for the establishment of a separate Afrikaner state. The ANC subsequently criticized the failure of the security forces to prevent the attack; some 25 members of the AWB were later detained.

In July 1993 the negotiating forum confirmed that the elections would take place on 27 April 1994, despite continuing opposition from COSAG. The IFP, CP and KwaZulu delegations subsequently withdrew from the negotiations, while the remaining representatives in the forum continued discussions on the precepts of a multiracial interim constitution, which was to remain in force pending the preparation and adoption of a permanent constitution. The confirmation of the election date prompted increased clashes between supporters of the IFP and those of the ANC, while there was increased speculation regarding the existence of a 'third force', an unidentified group that appeared to be inciting factional violence in order to undermine the negotiating process. At the end of July a draft interim Constitution was promulgated. The interim Constitution entrenched equal rights for citizens regardless of race, and vested executive power in a President and a Cabinet, which was to comprise representatives of the political parties that held a stipulated number of seats in the legislature. Legislative authority was vested in a bicameral Parliament, comprising a 400-member National Assembly (to be elected by proportional representation) and a Senate (with 10 members elected by each regional legislature. The National Assembly and Senate were together to form a 'constitution-making body' (later designated the Constitutional Assembly), which was to draft a new constitution, with adherence to the principles stipulated by the negotiating forum. Failure to adopt the draft by a majority of two-thirds within a period of two years would require the new document to be submitted for approval at a national referendum. Although the interim Constitution included provisions for the establishment of regional legislatures, it was rejected by COSAG (while the IFP, KwaZulu and CP delegations continued to boycott negotiations).

In early September 1993 the negotiating forum approved legislation providing for the establishment of a multiracial Transitional Executive Council (TEC), which was to rule in conjunction with the existing Government pending the elections, thereby allowing blacks to participate in central government for the first time. The TEC was to comprise representatives of the groups involved in the negotiating process; however, the IFP, the CP, the governments of Bophuthatswana, Ciskei and KwaZulu, and the PAC refused to participate. Later in September Parliament adopted legislation providing for the installation of the TEC, and the establishment of an Independent Electoral Commission (IEC), and an independent media commission and broadcasting authority.

In October 1993 the constituent members of COSAG, together with the AVF, formed the Freedom Alliance (FA), with the stated objective of negotiating concessions regarding regional autonomy. The Bophuthatswana and Ciskei delegations subsequently withdrew from the negotiating forum. In November the negotiating forum repealed legislation providing for detention without trial. Later that month agreement was reached regarding the establishment of a new security force, which was to be under the control of both central and provincial government, and a reconstituted national defence force, which was to comprise members of the existing armed forces of South Africa and the 'independent homelands', and the military wings of political organizations.

On 18 November 1993, following intensive discussions, 19 of the 21 delegations remaining in the negotiating forum approved the interim Constitution, which incorporated several amendments to the draft promulgated in July. A number of significant compromises between the Government and the ANC had been achieved: the Government abandoned its demand that cabinet decisions require a two-thirds' majority (thereby accepting that power-sharing would not be constitutionally entrenched), while the ANC agreed to a fixed five-year period for transition to majority rule. The President was to be elected by the National Assembly, and was to exercise executive power in consultation with at least two Deputy Presidents, who were to be nominated by parties with a minimum of 80 seats in the National Assembly (equivalent to 20% of the national vote). A Constitutional Court was to be appointed by the President from a list of candidates nominated by an independent judicial commission. As a concession to the FA, the interim Constitution included a provision that entitled the legislatures of the nine redesignated provinces to draft their own constitutions, subject to the principles governing the national Constitution. Nevertheless, the FA, together with the PAC, rejected the interim Constitution.

In early December 1993 the the negotiating forum reached agreement on the reincorporation of the four 'independent homelands' into South Africa on 27 April 1994, when the interim Constitution was to enter into force. On 1 January South African citizenship was to be restored to the population of the 'homelands', who would be entitled to vote in the elections. However, the governments of Bophuthatswana and Ciskei refused to recognize the decision. On 7 December 1993 the TEC commenced sessions, but was, as expected, boycotted by a number of delegations. In mid-December the IEC was established. On 22 December Parliament ratified the interim Constitution, thereby effecting its own dissolution as an organ of the apartheid regime.

In December 1993 the judicial commission of inquiry into political violence that had been established in October 1991 announced that several members of the KwaZulu security forces, who had been trained by the South African armed forces, had killed ANC members in Natal (apparently with the aim of inciting unrest). In January 1994 the military wing of the PAC, the Azanian People's Liberation Army (APLA), was implicated in further indiscriminate killings of civilians; the PAC, however, denied responsibility for the violence and announced that it had suspended the activities of the APLA. In January the Ciskei government decided to join the TEC and subsequently withdrew from the FA.

In February 1994, in accordance with a decision by the TEC, de Klerk announced that the elections, which were to be monitored by international observers, would take place between 26 and 28 April. Nineteen political parties had registered to contest the elections by the stipulated date on 12 February (which was subsequently extended to March). The ANC's list of candidates incorporated members of the SACP, COSATU, the 'homeland' governments and parties representing the Indian and Coloured communities; the inclusion of Winnie Mandela (who had been elected President of the ANC's Women's League in December 1993) attracted widespread criticism. The IFP confirmed that it intended to boycott the elections, after the Zulu tribal monarch, King Goodwill Zwelithini (who was Buthelezi's nephew), rejected the interim Constitution and declared sovereignty over the territory traditionally owned by the Zulus, prompting increased fears of civil conflict. In mid-February Nelson Mandela announced a number of proposed amendments to the interim Constitution, in an effort to comply with the demands of the IFP and the AVF. The proposed constitutional amendments recognized the right to regional self-determination, including the concept of a separate Afrikaner state, provided for a 'double-ballot system', whereby the electorate was to vote separately for national and provincial candidates, allowed each province to determine its legislative and executive structure, and redesignated Natal as KwaZulu/Natal. The FA, however, rejected the concessions, on the grounds that the powers of regional government remained inadequate, and refused to attend discussions on the proposed amendments, which were, nevertheless, adopted by the negotiating forum. During that month a series of bomb attacks, which were attributed to right-wing extremists, took place in Orange Free State and Transvaal. In early March, after the ANC and IFP agreed to accept international mediation regarding the issue of regional autonomy, Buthelezi announced that he was to register the IFP provisionally to contest the elections. The leader of the AVU, Gen. (retd) Constand Viljoen (who had increasingly dissociated himself from extreme right-wing elements in the AVF) also provisionally registered a new party, the Freedom Front (FF). Despite the insistence of the AVF that its constituent groups were to boycott the elections, the FF subsequently submitted a list of candidates, which included several prominent members of the CP. The IFP, however, failed to present a list of candidates by the stipulated date, while Zwelithini continued to urge his followers to boycott the elections.

In March 1994 the President of Bophuthatswana, Lucas Mangope (a member of the FA), announced that the population of the 'homeland' would not participate in the elections. Following subsequent widespread protests in Bophuthatswana, Mangope fled from the capital, Mmabatho, after disaffected members of the security forces demanded that he allow participation in the elections and refused to take action against the demonstrators. At the apparent instigation of the AVF, some 5,000 armed right-wing extremists, principally members of the AWB, entered Bophuthatswana and occupied Mmabatho, with the aim of reinstating Mangope. Shortly afterwards the Government dispatched some 2,000 members of the armed forces to Bophuthatswana, which, together with disaffected local troops, regained control of the 'homeland'. The Government and the TEC formally deposed Mangope, whose removal signified the effective dissolution of the FA. Later in March members of the armed forces were deployed in Ciskei to maintain civil order, following the resignation of the 'homeland's' military ruler in response to a strike by reformist members of the security forces. (The TEC and the Government assumed joint responsibility for administration in Bophuthatswana and Ciskei pending the elections.) In the same month de Klerk announced the conclusions of a report by the judicial commission of inquiry into political violence, which implicated three senior officials in the security forces and prominent members of the IFP in a conspiracy to organize political assassinations, with the aim of undermining national stability prior to the elections (apparently confirming suspicions regarding the existence of the 'third force'). The security forces and the IFP denied the accusations. De Klerk subsequently stated that the allegations would be investigated by an international task force and suspended a number of members of the security forces, including the three officials.

Following renewed clashes between members of the IFP and the ANC in KwaZulu/Natal in March 1994, the ANC urged the Government to dispatch troops to the region. Later that month about 53 people were killed after a demonstration by Zulus in support of the demands of Zwelithini culminated in violent clashes with security forces at ANC headquarters in Johannesburg. At the end of March de Klerk, with the approval of the ANC, imposed a state of emergency in KwaZulu/Natal; some 3,000 troops were subsequently deployed in the province to maintain civil order during the election period, but political violence continued. In April, following protracted negotiations between the Government, the ANC and the IFP, with the assistance of international mediators, an agreement was reached whereby the IFP was to participate in the elections, in exchange for guarantees that the institutions of the Zulu monarch and kingdom were to be recognized in the interim Constitution. Under the terms of a proposed draft constitution for KwaZulu/Natal, the Zulu monarch was to be granted additional territorial powers and sovereignty with regard to traditional law and custom. However, the AVF announced that it would continue to boycott the elections. At the end of April about 32 members of the AWB, including prominent party officials, were arrested in connection with a bombing offensive conducted during that month, in which a total of 21 people were killed. Terre'Blanche subsequently threatened that the campaign would continue unless the Government acceded to demands for Afrikaner self-determination. Under the terms of an accord between the Government, the ANC and the FF earlier in April, the level of support for the FF in the elections was to be used to determine whether a separate Afrikaner state might be established in any region with the approval of the majority of the resident population. Prior to the elections, the Government also reached an agreement with the PAC, which provided for the inclusion of members of the APLA in the new national defence force, in exchange for a guaranteed cessation of hostilities.

On 27 April 1994 the interim Constitution came into force, with voting commencing on the previous day, as scheduled. However, a number of logistical difficulties led to widespread delays. On 28 April voting was extended by one day in KwaZulu/Natal and other regions affected by administrative confusion. A number of reports of electoral malpractice emerged; notably, the ANC accused the IFP of assuming control of polling stations in KwaZulu/Natal. Nevertheless, the IEC declared that the elections had been free and fair. The promulgation of the official results was delayed, owing, in part, to disputed ballots in KwaZulu/Natal; following negotiations between the IFP and the ANC, it was agreed that the IFP would be allocated 50.3% of the vote in the province, thereby allowing it a majority of one seat in the regional legislature. On 2 May, after partial results indicated a substantial majority in favour of the ANC, de Klerk conceded defeat, prompting widespread jubilation. Shortly afterwards it was announced that the ANC had secured 62.65% of votes cast, while the NP had won 20.39%, the IFP 10.54% and the FF 2.17%. Consequently, the ANC narrowly failed to obtain a parliamentary majority of two-thirds, which, under the terms of the interim Constitution, would have allowed its members to draft and adopt the new constitution without consulting other parties. The NP, which secured a majority in the province of Northern Cape, received the stipulated percentage of the national vote entitling it to nominate a Deputy President. Mandela subsequently appointed a senior official of the ANC, Thabo Mbeki, as First Deputy President, while de Klerk was nominated as Second Deputy President.

Mandela was officially elected as President by the National Assembly on 9 May 1994, and was inaugurated on the following day at a ceremony that was attended by a large number of international heads of state. A Cabinet of National Unity, comprising 18 representatives of the ANC, six of the NP and three of the IFP, was subsequently formed, with Buthelezi allocated the portfolio of home affairs. The appointment of Winnie Mandela as a deputy minister was widely interpreted as an attempt to prevent her from criticizing the new administration. Later in May the provincial legislatures elected a 90-member Senate, comprising 60 representatives of the ANC, 17 of the NP, five of the IFP and FF respectively, and three of the DP. The ANC consequently held a slightly higher majority in the Constitutional Assembly than in the National Assembly, but failed, nevertheless, to obtain a two-thirds' majority. The Secretary-General of the ANC, Cyril Ramaphosa, was subsequently elected Chairman of the Constitutional Assembly.

The new Government adopted a Reconstruction and Development Programme (RDP), which comprised extensive measures for social and economic development, including the reform of the education and health services. The Government also announced plans to establish a 'Truth and Reconciliation Commission' (TRC), composed of eminent citizens, which would investigate violations of human rights perpetrated under the apartheid regime; the TRC was to be empowered to grant indemnity to individuals who confessed to politically motivated crimes committed before 5 December 1993 (when the TEC was effectively installed). Although the FF had failed to obtain the level of support in the elections stipulated as a precondition to the consideration of its demands, the Government subsequently agreed to the establishment of a 'volkstaat council', in which Viljoen and other right-wing Afrikaners were to debate the issue of self-determination. Meanwhile, it was disclosed that de Klerk had authorized the transfer of state-owned land (comprising one-third of the territory of KwaZulu/Natal) to Zwelithini shortly before the elections. The ANC denied knowledge of the agreement, which, it was speculated, had been designed to prevent attempts to include the territory in the ANC's land reform programme (whereby communities or individuals were entitled to claim restitution for land dispossessed under regional legislation from 1913).

In June 1994 it was announced that the new South African National Defence Force (SANDF) was to be constituted over a period of three years (to allow the integration of former members of the MK and APLA). In mid-June a cabinet committee decided that Zwelithini was to remain the statutory trustee of the territory in KwaZulu/Natal that had been transferred to his control prior to the elections. At the end of June nine former MK officials were allocated prominent positions within the SANDF. (The commander of the former defence forces, Gen. George Meiring, had been reappointed Chief of the SANDF in May.) In early September the Government officially ended the state of emergency in KwaZulu/Natal that had been imposed in March.

In October 1994 Joe Modise, the Minister of Defence, announced that some 7,500 former members of the MK and APLA had absconded from the SANDF and had refused to resume duties unless the Government addressed grievances regarding the protracted process of their integration into the SANDF and alleged discrimination against them. Mandela subsequently announced that any members of the SANDF who failed to report for duty within seven days would be regarded as deserters and consequently dismissed. In the same month the Minister of Justice, Abdullah Mohammed Omar, submitted draft legislation providing for the establishment of the TRC. In late October the IFP majority in the provincial legislature of KwaZulu/Natal adopted legislation that provided for the establishment of an advisory council of Zulu chiefs, the House of Traditional Leaders, in which Zwelithini would be equal in status to other chiefs (including Buthelezi). In November the Government dismissed more than 2,000 members of the SANDF, who had failed to return to base by the stipulated date.

In November 1994 the Government adopted legislation that formally restored the rights of land ownership to members of the black population who had been dispossessed following the introduction of discriminatory legislation beginning in 1913; the Restitution of Land Rights Act provided for the establishment of a special commission and court to investigate and arbitrate claims. At a national conference of the ANC in December,

Mandela and Ramaphosa were returned unopposed as party President and Secretary-General, respectively; Jacob Zuma, the leader of the ANC in KwaZulu/Natal, was elected Chairman, replacing Mbeki, who became Vice-President.

In January 1995 the National Intelligence Service (NIS) was replaced with two new bodies, incorporating elements of the ANC's security department and agencies of the former 'homelands': the South African Secret Service, under the command of the former head of the NIS, was to control international intelligence, while the National Intelligence Agency (NIA), headed by a former ANC security official, was to be responsible for internal intelligence. In the same month, amid reports of increasing political violence between ANC and IFP supporters in KwaZulu/Natal, Buthelezi was elected Chairman of the House of Traditional Leaders.

In accordance with the interim Constitution, an 11-member Constitutional Court was installed in February 1995; the Court was to ensure that the executive, legislative and judicial organs of government adhered to the principles entrenched in the interim Constitution, and was to endorse a final constitutional text with respect to these principles. In the same month Mandela confirmed that he would not contest the elections in 1999. Meanwhile, Dr Allan Boesak, a prominent former anti-apartheid activist, was obliged to resign as the South African permanent representative at the UN, after it was alleged that he had misappropriated donations to the Foundation for Peace and Justice, a charity that he administered. The activities of Winnie Mandela also attracted increasingly adverse publicity: following rumours in December that she had been involved in a clandestine business transaction with the Angolan Head of State, she was accused by senior members of the ANC Women's League of misappropriating funds that the Pakistani Prime Minister, Benazir Bhutto, had donated to the League in 1994. After publicly denouncing the Government for concentrating on the appeasement of the white population while failing to address the continuing hardship of the black majority, she was threatened with dismissal from the Cabinet and forced to apologize.

In February 1995 Buthelezi claimed that the ANC and NP had reneged on a pledge (which had been made shortly before the elections in April 1994) to invite international mediators to arbitrate on IFP demands for the devolution of power to KwaZulu/Natal, and announced that IFP deputies were consequently to suspend participation in Parliament and the Constitutional Assembly. At a special party congress, which took place in March, the IFP agreed to resume participation in Parliament and in the Constitutional Assembly, but issued a resolution to the effect that IFP deputies would resume the boycott of the Constitutional Assembly if Mandela failed to invite international mediators for negotiations on the issue of regional autonomy. In mid-March Mandela announced that local government elections would take place on 1 November. Buthelezi had previously indicated that the IFP's participation in the elections remained conditional on the Government's acceptance of demands for regional autonomy. Meanwhile, Winnie Mandela's position in the Cabinet appeared to be increasingly untenable, as a result of her continued autocratic behaviour. In late March Mandela finally removed her from the Cabinet, after she publicly criticized government expenditure on the visit to South Africa of the British monarch.

At a party conference on constitutional policy in April 1995, the ANC rejected NP proposals that the principle of power-sharing be entrenched in the final constitution, thereby extending the tenure of the coalition Government. The conference also failed to accept IFP demands for international mediation on regional autonomy, and adopted constitutional proposals that provided for a Senate comprising members of provincial legislatures, which would be empowered to veto provincial legislation. Buthelezi implemented his threat to suspend IFP participation in the Constitutional Assembly, and indicated that the IFP would not accept a constitution that had been drafted by the remaining parties in the Assembly.

In May 1995, following reports that factional hostilities in KwaZulu/Natal had increased, Mandela accused Buthelezi of inciting political violence and threatened to suspend government funds to the province. None the less, it was announced shortly afterwards that Mandela and Buthelezi had agreed to resolve their differences and to negotiate regarding the issue of international mediation. Later in May Mandela consented to foreign mediation on constitutional discussions. In the same month the National Assembly approved draft legislation pro-

viding for the establishment of the TRC; only the FF deputies opposed the enactment of the legislation.

In September 1995 the Constitutional Court ruled that Mandela had exceeded his presidential powers in overruling electoral boundaries that had been determined by the Western Cape Provincial Government prior to the local elections in November. The Court declared an amendment to the Local Government Transition Act (which had granted the President authority to issue decrees regarding the local elections) to be unconstitutional; the legislation was amended accordingly at an emergency session of Parliament in October. Elections in KwaZulu/Natal were postponed until March 1996, owing to continuing violence in the region. Voting took place in some parts of Western Cape, but not in the metropolitan area of Cape Town, nor in some rural areas of the province, as a result of delays in the demarcation of electoral boundaries. At the local elections, which took part in most parts of the country on 1 November 1995, the ANC secured 66.37% of the votes cast and the majority of the seats on the local councils, while the NP won 16.22% and the FF 4.03%.

In November 1995 Gen. Magnus Malan, the Minister of Defence in 1980–91, and a further 10 prominent officials in the former armed forces were arrested on charges relating to the killing of 13 people in KwaMakutha (south of Durban) in 1987; they were accused of involvement in the establishment in 1985 of a military camp in Namibia where IFP commandos were trained to perpetrate attacks on prominent ANC supporters. The arrest and subsequent indictment of Gen. Malan and the other former officers provoked great controversy; Mandela was accused by members of the NP and FF of political bias in his refusal to grant temporary indemnity to the accused until their cases could be heard by the TRC, which was to commence sessions in April 1996. (In late November 1995 Archbishop Desmond Tutu was appointed as Chairman of the Commission.) Buthelezi was cited in the indictment as having in 1985 requested the assistance of the security forces in creating paramilitary units to combat the ANC.

A renewed increase in violence in KwaZulu/Natal in December 1995 culminated in an attack by some 600 IFP supporters against the village of Shobashobane, an ANC enclave in the south of the province, in which some 19 people were killed. In early February 1996 the NP Minister of Provincial Affairs and Constitutional Development, Roelf Meyer, announced that he was to resign from the Government and would assume the new post of Secretary-General of the NP. Later in the month Abraham Williams, also of the NP, resigned from the post of Minister of Welfare and Population Development, following allegations that he had defrauded social security funds. In March Mandela was granted a divorce from Winnie Mandela (who subsequently became known as Winnie Madikizela-Mandela). Later that month, in a cabinet reorganization, Mandela appointed Trevor Manuel, hitherto the Minister of Trade and Industry, to the finance portfolio. The NP protested at the appointment of an ANC member to the ministry, claiming that it breached an agreement reserving the position for a nominee without political affiliations.

The trial of Gen. Malan and his 19 co-defendants began in Durban in early March 1996. (In May charges were abandoned against three of the former security force commanders, owing to insufficient evidence.) In mid-March the Government withdrew indemnity from prosecution that had been granted by de Klerk's Government to 73 ANC members, including Mbeki and Modise. In April the TRC, comprising Archbishop Tutu (who retired from the archbishopric in June) and 16 other members drawn from all racial groups and a variety of professions, commenced hearings, which were to continue for up to two years. The Commission was empowered to grant judicial amnesties to perpetrators of human rights violations committed during the apartheid era, if it were satisfied that a full disclosure had been made and that the crime in question had been politically motivated, also depending on the gravity of the crime. The TRC was also to advise on appropriate reparations to the victims (or to their families) of crimes committed.

On 8 May 1996 Parliament approved the final version of the Constitution, with the NP voting in favour, in spite of its reservations over some provisions. The IFP maintained its boycott of the Constitutional Assembly, while the 10 FF deputies abstained; only the two deputies of the African Christian Democratic Party (ACDP) voted against the adoption of the Constitution. The new Constitution incorporated an extensive Bill of Rights, and provided for the establishment of a commission to guarantee the rights of the white minority. A National Council of Provinces was to replace the existing Senate, and was designed to increase the influence of the provinces on the policy of the central Government (although falling short of the provincial powers demanded by the IFP). De Klerk subsequently announced that the NP was to withdraw from the Government of National Unity (with effect from 30 June), attributing the decision (which was taken in spite of the dissent of a significant number of NP deputies) to the diminishing influence of his party on government policy, the refusal of the ANC to include power-sharing arrangements in the new Constitution, and the necessity, in the interests of democracy, for an effective opposition. The NP later withdrew from all the Provincial Governments except for that of Western Cape (where it was in the majority). Mandela appointed members of his own party to the ministerial portfolios vacated by NP members and abolished the position of Second Deputy President.

Local elections in KwaZulu/Natal had been postponed from March 1996 until 29 May; however, renewed violence in the province, which was regarded as threatening the democratic process, prompted the Government to postpone the elections still further. However, elections took place on 29 May in Cape Town and the remaining areas of Western Cape province where elections had not been held in November 1995: the NP increased its share of the votes cast compared with the general election in 1994, and secured control of the majority of the local councils in the areas in which polling took place. Following negotiations between the province's political leaders, the local elections in KwaZulu/Natal took place on 26 June, amid relative calm. The IFP won the largest share (44.5%) of the votes cast.

In late August 1996 Mbeki made a statement to the TRC regarding violations of human rights perpetrated during the apartheid era, including the execution of 34 people at the ANC's camps in Angola, asserting that these were justified in the context of the struggle against apartheid. De Klerk apologized before the TRC for the suffering that the apartheid policies of the NP had caused, but denied that any violations of human rights had been authorized during his time in government. Also in late August Eugene de Kock, a former commander of the notorious counter-insurgency 'hit squad', the Vlakplaas, was convicted of 89 charges relating to the activities of the unit, including six charges of murder. In September de Kock detailed to the Supreme Court his involvement in the apartheid regime's campaign against its opponents, claiming that de Klerk and Botha had both had full knowledge of these operations, which included assassinations.

In early September 1996 the Constitutional Court ruled that the new Constitution failed to adhere to the principles enshrined in the interim Constitution in a number of respects, notably with regard to the powers of the provinces, which the Court deemed insufficient. The Constitutional Assembly was to amend the document accordingly within a period of 90 days. In a separate ruling the Court rejected an alternative constitution that had been drafted by Buthelezi, stating that the proposed constitution attempted to encroach on the powers of national goverment. The IFP (which had boycotted the Constitutional Assembly in the negotiations resulting in the adoption of the national Constitution) rejoined the negotiations in early October, but withdrew shortly afterwards. (The IFP had argued for a greater role for traditional leaders in regional and local government than the other parties would accept.) The amended Constitution was approved by both chambers of Parliament on 11 October, with the ANC and the NP having negotiated a slight increase in the powers of the provinces. The new Constitution was returned to the Constitutional Court for final endorsement, and was promulgated by the President at a ceremony in Sharpeville on 10 December.

In mid-October 1996 Gen. Malan and his co-defendants were acquitted of all charges in connection with the massacre in Kwa-Makutha. Although it was accepted that the killings had been committed by IFP supporters who had been trained by the former armed forces, the prosecution failed to prove that the attack had been authorized by military or political leaders. The judgment was regarded as a reverse for the TRC, with Gen. Malan urging former members of the armed forces not to seek amnesties from the TRC, but to submit to trial in the courts if charged (thus discouraging potential confessions to the Commission). Later in October the TRC proposed that the final date for indemnity be extended from 6 December 1993 to 10 May 1994 (the date of Mandela's inauguration as President). Shortly afterwards a former police commissioner submitted evidence to the TRC implicating Botha in an attack against the head-

quarters of the South African Council of Churches in 1988. Botha declared that he would not submit evidence to the Commission and denied involvement in any crimes for which he needed to apply for amnesty. Following discussions with Tutu, however, he agreed to co-operate with the TRC by means of correspondence. In late October Tutu criticized the ANC for failing to submit amnesty applications from its members, and subsequently threatened to resign from the TRC if such applications were not made. The ANC responded by assuring the TRC that applications by its members would be made where necessary.

On 13 December 1996 (the eve of the deadline for applications for amnesty from the TRC) Mandela announced that the final date for the period in which crimes had been committed and the deadline for the receipt of amnesty applications were to be extended, to 10 May 1994 and 10 May 1997 respectively. The ANC confirmed that some 360 of its members, including three cabinet ministers, had applied for amnesty. In late December four people were killed in a bomb attack at a shopping centre in Worcester, near Cape Town. The incident was attributed to members of the AWB who had escaped from prison earlier in the year, after being convicted of conducting a bombing campaign prior to the 1994 general election. In the same month more than 35 people were killed in factional violence in Northwest Province, while some 26 people were killed in continuing violence in KwaZulu/Natal.

From January 1997 South Africa's main political parties conducted discussions regarding possible inter-party co-operation. Mandela issued invitations to both the DP and the PAC to participate in the Government of National Unity (which, however, both parties subsequently declined). In late January the IFP appeared to be in crisis, following the resignations of the KwaZulu/Natal Premier, Frank Mdlalose, the IFP Secretary-General and the Chairman of the IFP in Gauteng. Although ill health was the stated reason for Mdlalose's departure, it was reported that he had become disaffected following continual interference from Buthelezi in the affairs of the provincial administration. The new Constitution entered into force on 4 February 1997. On 6 February the inaugural session of the new National Council of Provinces, which replaced the Senate as the second chamber of Parliament, was held. In mid-March some 10,000 IFP supporters commemorated the massacre of the IFP protesters outside the ANC headquarters in 1994; three people were killed in violence related to the demonstration. An inquest into the deaths of the IFP supporters began in April 1997.

In April 1997 the ANC leader in Natal Midlands was expelled on the grounds that he had acted as an informer for the apartheid regime. (In March, under pressure from the President, the TRC had reversed a previous decision that the names of ANC informants disclosed to the Commission be kept secret.) Also in April the ANC appealed to the NP, including de Klerk, to make full revelations regarding the NP Government's involvement in 'third force' activity. Later in the month Mandela inaugurated the national Council for Traditional Leaders, as provided for in the new Constitution. In early May Tutu appealed for amnesty applications to be submitted to the TRC before 10 May; nearly 8,000 applications had been received by that date. In mid-May Meyer resigned from the NP and from the National Assembly, following opposition from within the NP to his proposal that the party be reconstituted in order to attract black support. Meyer, in alliance with Bantu Holomisa, the former ruler of Transkei (who, in 1996, had been dismissed from the Government and expelled from the ANC for indiscipline, in connection with allegations he had made at a hearing of the TRC), subsequently established a new political movement, the United Democratic Movement (UDM), with the intention of contesting the elections in 1999. Also in May 1997 de Klerk made a second appearance before the TRC; his continued insistence that he had been unaware of the violations of human rights perpetrated during the period of apartheid prompted an angry response from Tutu, who accused de Klerk of being responsible for abuses. The NP subsequently suspended co-operation with the TRC, and initiated legal action against the TRC on the grounds of political bias.

In June 1997 the leader of the AWB, Eugene Terre'Blanche, received a custodial term of six years for the attempted murder of a black employee, and a further one-year sentence for assault; he was released on bail pending an appeal against his conviction. In the same month Buthelezi invited the ANC to enter into negotiations with the aim of reaching an agreement to end political violence in KwaZulu/Natal. However, in July the killing of five ANC members, including two newly elected municipal councillors, in KwaZulu/Natal reflected the continuing political tensions in the province; Mandela subsequently claimed that members of the local security forces had been involved in the incident. In early August the IFP withdrew from the peace discussions, after it was alleged during hearings of the TRC that Buthelezi had been aware of political killings perpetrated by supporters of the IFP during apartheid. At the end of August de Klerk resigned from the leadership of the NP (thereby retiring from active politics), on the grounds that the party would benefit from a break with past associations; he was subsequently replaced by Marthinus van Schalkwyk. It was reported that de Klerk's resignation from the NP had been influenced by his dispute with the TRC in May, and by the defection of large numbers of liberals, including Meyer, from the party.

In September 1997 five members of the former security forces appeared before the TRC to apply for amnesty for the killing of Steve Biko in 1977; it was admitted during the hearing that some of the evidence presented at the inquest into Biko's death had been fabricated. In the same month the publication of a book, based on statements by a former bodyguard of Winnie Madikizela-Mandela, Katiza Cebekhulu, attracted considerable publicity; Cebekhulu alleged that Winnie Madikizela-Mandela had been actively involved in the killing of Stompie Moeketsi Seipei in 1988, and that she had subsequently ordered that a physician who had examined the victim prior to his death be killed. Nevertheless, Madikizela-Mandela continued to receive widespread public support, and was nominated for the post of Deputy President of the ANC by the party's Women's League prior to the ANC's December 1997 congress. Later in September Madikizela-Mandela appeared before the TRC, having been implicated by previous applicants for amnesty in 18 incidences of human rights violations, including eight killings. The TRC subsequently acceded to Madikizela-Mandela's request that hearings of her testimony be conducted in public. In October four former NP ministers, including the former Minister of Foreign Affairs, Roelof ('Pik') Botha, denied that they had authorized the killing of political opponents during the apartheid period. In November representatives of the business community (principally state corporations and banks) applied for amnesty for their involvement with the apartheid system; however, Tutu criticized the failure of much of the private business sector, including three multinational petroleum companies, to participate in the TRC. During hearings of the TRC regarding the allegations against Madikizela-Mandela later that month, a number of witnesses testified that she had assaulted and killed several people. Cebekhulu appeared before the TRC to reiterate the claims that had been published in September 1997. Madikizela-Mandela subsequently denied involvement in any violations of human rights, and initiated legal action against Cebekhulu for libel.

In December 1997 the inquest into the deaths of IFP demonstrators outside the ANC headquarters in March 1994 ruled their killing to have been unlawful, but indicated that there was insufficient evidence for the criminal prosecution of those involved. At the ANC congress later that month Mandela resigned from the presidency of the party, as anticipated, and was succeeded by Mbeki, who was elected unopposed. (Mandela's refusal to be re-elected to the party's National Executive Committee (NEC) further confirmed his stated intention to retire from active politics in May 1999.) Jacob Zuma was elected Deputy President of the party. Winnie Madikizela-Mandela, who had refused her nomination to contest the post of Deputy President, was, however, elected to the National Executive Committee.

In March 1998 Mandela was subpoenaed to testify at the Pretoria High Court, after the South African Rugby Football Union (SARFU) protested at the establishment of a judicial commission of inquiry into allegations of racism and corruption within the organization. In April the Pretoria High Court ruled in favour of SARFU's legal challenge to Mandela's decision to establish the commission of inquiry. Nevertheless, in May the President of SARFU, Louis Luyt, submitted his resignation, following pressure from the government-supported National Sports Council. (Luyt subsequently established a new political organization, the Federal Alliance—FA, to contest the elections in 1999.) Also in May 1998 the DP defeated the NP in three municipal by-elections (in constituencies hitherto held by the NP), reflecting a decline in white support for the former ruling party.

In May 1998 the Cape High Court upheld an application by the TRC to reconsider amnesties granted to 37 prominent ANC officials, including Mbeki. During June a number of former government scientists submitted evidence to the TRC regarding studies conducted by the apartheid administration into chemical and biological means of suppressing black opposition. Terre' Blanche conceded responsibility to the TRC for the bombing campaign prior to the 1994 elections, in which 21 people had been killed. In July the former NP Minister of Law and Order, Adriaan Vlok (who had applied for amnesty), admitted before the TRC that he had ordered a number of bomb attacks in the 1980s against institutions opposed to the apartheid Government, including COSATU headquarters in 1987 and the offices of the South African Council of Churches in 1988. The TRC's period of gathering evidence of human rights violations was concluded at the end of July 1998.

In August 1998, following considerable delays, Botha, who had failed to comply with three subpoenas ordering him to testify at the TRC regarding his enforcement of apartheid through emergency rule in the 1980s, was convicted of being in contempt of the TRC, receiving a fine of R 10,000 and a one-year suspended sentence (which could be brought into effect if he failed to comply with a further TRC subpoena). In the same month Boesak pleaded not guilty at Cape Town Supreme Court to a number of charges of fraud and theft in connection with his alleged misappropriation of foreign charitable donations. In September Parliament adopted legislation (which was strongly opposed by the FF) guaranteeing employment equity, whereby corporations were required to employ a certain proportion of blacks, women and disabled people.

In October 1998 the TRC commenced reparation payments to victims of human rights violations under the apartheid system. Shortly before the TRC was due to release the report of its findings, de Klerk appealed to the Cape Town High Court to prevent the publication of sections alleging that he had prior knowledge of the bomb attacks against anti-apartheid bodies in the 1980s. The TRC agreed to remove provisionally the sections concerned, which were, however, to be contested at the High Court in early 1999. However, the Cape Town High Court dismissed a legal challenge by the ANC to the publication of findings that it had perpetrated human rights violations in armed opposition to apartheid, on the grounds that it had failed to appeal against previous drafts of the report. Tutu condemned the ANC's efforts to prevent the release of part of the report, which had been opposed by Mandela and had resulted in division within the party. At the end of October 1998 Tutu presented to Mandela the TRC's final comprehensive report detailing human rights violations committed in 1960–64, based on statements from some 21,000 victims of abuses and about 7,000 amnesty applicants. The report concluded that the apartheid system constituted a crime against humanity; it was alleged that, while the State was primarily accountable for violations of human rights, the ANC had also committed abuses in its legitimate struggle against apartheid (notably in the MK's torture and execution of suspected dissidents in detention camps outside South Africa). Botha, as President of the State Security Council in 1978–89, was considered to be responsible for an increase in killings of government opponents and to have ordered the bomb attacks by state agents in the 1980s. Buthelezi was deemed accountable for human rights violations perpetrated by the IFP (which was responsible for the highest proportion of killings in 1990–94). The report also cited Viljoen, Terre'Blanche, and Winnie Madikizela-Mandela (who was implicated in some 12 incidences of assault, abduction and murder) as being responsible for serious violations of human rights. It was stated that the South African business community had benefited from the apartheid system, and the introduction of a 'wealth tax' to assist in social reconstruction was proposed. The prosecution of those responsible for human rights violations who had not applied for amnesty, or who had been denied amnesty, was recommended. Buthelezi and Viljoen dismissed the findings of the report as reflecting pro-ANC bias in the TRC, and Buthelezi subsequently threatened to prosecute the Commission, particularly with regard to the report's allegation that the IFP had colluded with the apartheid regime. In November 1998 one of the members of the security forces implicated in the 1977 killing of Steve Biko was refused amnesty, on the grounds that the killing was not politically motivated. (The amnesty applications of the remaining four members of the security forces involved in the incident were rejected in early 1999.) In December 1998 Mandela confirmed that perpetrators of crimes committed under the apartheid regime would not be granted a general amnesty, which had been urged by the NP, IFP and some members of the ANC. Under TRC regulations, applicants would only be granted amnesty after submitting a full confession and evidence that the crime was politically motivated.

In January 1999 the Secretary-General of the UDM, Sifiso Nkabinde, was assassinated (apparently by ANC supporters) in the town of Richmond, in KwaZulu/Natal. Some 11 ANC members were killed in a retaliatory attack by armed assailants. Further clashes between UDM and ANC supporters around Richmond were reported. Also in January a bomb attack at the principal police station in Cape Town was widely attributed to an Islamist group, People Against Gangsterism and Drugs (PAGAD). Meanwhile, an increasing number of attacks against farmers by organized armed groups were reported. The South African Agricultural Union claimed that the attacks (in which more than 550 members of the farming community had been killed in 1994–98) were part of a campaign to force farmers to abandon their land.

In March 1998 the TRC rejected the amnesty applications of the 37 senior members of the ANC, including Mbeki, whose amnesties had been revoked in May 1998. Later in March Boesak was sentenced to a custodial term of six years for misappropriation of donor funds, despite an appeal for clemency from Tutu. In early April the TRC rejected the amnesty applications of the right-wing extremists implicated in the killing of Chris Hani in 1993. Also in April 1999 a further 79 ANC supporters were refused amnesty by the TRC. In May the ANC and IFP signed an agreement to end hostilities between their supporters in KwaZulu/Natal during the forthcoming electoral period.

More than 16m. voters participated in legislative elections, which took place peacefully, at national and provincial level, on 2 June 1999. Some 32 political parties had registered to contest the elections. The ANC secured 266 of the 400 seats in the National Assembly, with 66.4% of votes cast; the DP increased its representation in the Assembly from seven to 38 seats, while the IFP won 34, and the New National Party (NNP, as the NP had been reconstituted), which had lost much support to the DP only 28 seats. The ANC subsequently formed a coalition with an Indian party, the Minority Front, thereby securing a two-thirds' majority in the National Assembly. The IFP reached a coalition agreement with the ANC in KwaZulu/Natal, where the IFP Premier retained his post. In Western Cape no party won a majority of seats in the provincial legislature, and, after intensive negotiations, the NPP and DP established a coalition Government to prevent the ANC, which had obtained the highest number of votes, from gaining power. On 16 June Mbeki was inaugurated as President, in a ceremony that also marked the formal retirement of Mandela. The IFP joined the ANC in a further coalition Government, in which Buthelezi remained Minister of Home Affairs. Zuma became Deputy President, while a number of ANC ministers retained their portfolios in the expanded Cabinet.

In June 1999 Botha's appeal against his conviction was upheld, on the technical grounds that the TRC's subpoena was invalid since its mandate had temporarily expired. In July the TRC released a report containing evidence from former members of the security forces that implicated Botha in the killing of eight anti-apartheid activists in 1988. In August the TRC granted amnesty to Vlok, the former Commissioner of Police, Gen. Johan van der Merwe, de Kock, and a further 14 members of the former security forces, in respect of ordering the bombing of the offices of the South African Council of Churches in 1988. In September the Minister of Justice announced the closure of the commission investigating incidences of public-sector corruption, following disagreements between the head of the commission and the Government over financing; further cases were to be submitted to judges specially nominated by Mbeki. In the same month a PAC deputy submitted a motion urging a judicial inquiry into allegations that senior ANC officials had accepted bribes from armaments traders. In October the trial of Wouter Basson, the head of the apartheid regime's chemical and biological armaments programme in 1982–92, on 64 charges (including responsibility for the killing of 200 members of the South West Africa People's Organisation of Namibia—SWAPO), commenced at the High Court in Pretoria. He was acquitted of 15 charges in June 2001, and the remaining charges in April 2002. Later in October 1999 the TRC granted amnesty to nine former members of the security forces, including de Kock, who had provided evidence regarding the bombing of the ANC offices

in London in 1982. In December 1999 10 members of the AWB were granted amnesty for the bombing campaign in 1994. At the end of December four members of PAGAD were arrested in connection with more than 80 bombing incidents in the region of Cape Town (including one bomb explosion in a restaurant in November, in which some 46 people were killed).

In January 2000 the National Assembly adopted extensive legislation prohibiting discrimination on any grounds, and the use of racist terms in language. Meanwhile, the principal opposition parties (the DP, NNP, UDM and the FA) announced their intention to form an alliance prior to local government elections due in November; the DP also signed an electoral agreement with the smaller ACDP. In February, however, seven senior UDM officials left the party to join the ANC (increasing the total number of defections from the UDM since late 1999 to 34). In March, following the rejection of an appeal in October 1999, Terre'Blanche was ordered by the Pretoria High Court to surrender to the authorities to serve the one-year sentence he had received for assault, pending a further appeal against his six-year sentence. He was subsequently released on parole from the shorter sentence, but the longer sentence was confirmed on appeal in March 2001. In May 2000 the Supreme Court of Appeal reduced Boesak's six-year sentence, imposed in March 1999, to three years. Boesak was released from prison in May 2001. In June 2000 it was announced that the NNP and DP were to form a new coalition, known as the Democratic Alliance (DA), to contest the local government elections.

President Mbeki was criticized by many observers, including religious leaders, trade-union officials and prominent ANC members, as a result of statements he made throughout 2000, questioning the causal link between HIV and AIDS, and asserting that poverty could also cause the disease. Responsibility for policy on HIV/AIDS was subsequently transferred to a newly created cabinet committee. In April 2001 a court began hearing a petition, made by a group of 39 pharmaceutical manufacturers, to invalidate legislation, passed in 1997 (but suspended following an interim court ruling in the companies' favour in 1998), that enabled South Africa to purchase less expensive generic versions of patented anti-AIDS drugs from third parties. However, following international criticism, the companies abandoned the action unconditionally before the conclusion of the hearing. In September 2001 the South African Medical Research Council reported that HIV/AIDS was the largest single cause of death in South Africa, responsible for approximately 40% of adult deaths, and estimated that, without effective treatment, up to 7m. people could die from the disease by 2010. Mbeki had attracted further criticism in August 2001 after urging the Minister of Health to reduce the budget for HIV/AIDS treatment, citing mortality figures from 1995 (when the disease accounted for only 2.2% of deaths). In December the Ministry of Health lost a case brought by the Treatment Action Campaign (TAC), a group of AIDS activists, when the High Court in Pretoria ordered it to provide antiretroviral drugs to all pregnant women infected with HIV to reduce the chance of transmission to their children; the Government had argued that the drugs were toxic and excessively expensive to administer. (The Government lost its appeal against the ruling in April 2002.) In February 2002 Buthelezi, as Minister of Home Affairs, ordered the distribution of antiretroviral drugs in Kwazulu/Natal, in contravention of official government policy, and in March the High Court upheld the ruling that ordered state provision of antiretroviral drugs. The Government sought leave to appeal the ruling, but it was overturned by the Constitutional Court in July; in October the Government announced that it would investigate means of providing antiretroviral drugs through the public health system. Meanwhile, in November 2001 the trial of six men in the Northern Cape on charges of raping a nine-month-old baby was extensively covered by the international media. It emerged that many young girls in rural areas had been raped because of a belief that sexual intercourse with a virgin could cure HIV infection; some 32,000 cases of sexual assault on children were reported in 2000–01. In September 2002 the TAC commenced legal action against two large European pharmaceutical companies, claiming that they had taken advantage of patent protection on their AIDS durgs and charged excessive prices for them.

Meanwhile, municipal elections were held throughout the country in December 2000, including in the newly created urban regions around South Africa's six largest cities (the so-called 'megacities'), which generally merged the city proper and the surrounding townships into one administrative unit. Nationally, the ANC won approximately 60% of the votes cast, and gained control of five of the six conurbations, the DA winning control of Cape Town.

In January 2001 allegations of corruption were made against senior politicians, including ministers, regarding the award of weapons contracts, with an estimated combined value of R 43,000m. The Minister of Justice, Penuell Maduana, and President Mbeki were criticized for rejecting a demand from the National Assembly that a judge specializing in the investigation of corruption allegations join the inquiry into the issue. The Government was cleared of all charges when the inquiry report was published in November, although opposition parties accused the ANC of manipulating the investigations and suppressing parts of the report. The ANC chief whip, Tony Yengeni, resigned in October after being charged with corruption, forgery and perjury, following allegations that he had received favours from a weapons manufacturer while chairman of the parliamentary defence committee. He pleaded guilty to charges of defrauding the Government in February 2003, and was sentenced to four years' imprisonment in March.

In April 2001 Steve Tshwete, the Minister of Safety and Security, announced that three prominent businessmen and members of the ANC, Ramaphosa, Matthews Phosa, the former Premier of Mpumalanga, and Tokyo Sexwale, the former Premier of Gauteng, were being investigated regarding their alleged involvement in a conspiracy to discredit Mbeki and occasion his removal from the leadership of the party and the presidency; they had allegedly claimed that Mbeki had been involved in the killing of Hani in 1993. All three denied the allegations, which were widely criticized within South Africa and abroad. In December Tshwete exonerated the three men. Mbeki's critics suggested that the episode had been an exercise in discrediting potential challengers.

In early July 2001 the PAC drew attention to what it considered the Government's inadequate housing and land redistribution policies, by seizing land belonging to farmers and the Provincial Government in east Johannesburg and inviting thousands of homeless people to settle there; many constructed shacks, believing that they were part of a resettlement scheme. Within two weeks the Government had forced the estimated 7,000 squatters off the land, using armed police-officers. COSATU and affiliated unions organized a two-day general strike in August in protest at the proposed privatization of public assets, which, it claimed, would result in large-scale redundancies. COSATU estimated that 4m. workers had participated in the strike, a figure that the Government described as exaggerated. Violence erupted in a squatter camp in Johannesburg in October, directed principally at Zimbabweans (with dual South African nationality) and women who lived with Zimbabwean men; it was reported that the attacks were economically motivated, despite the fact that most of the Zimbabweans in the camp were unemployed. More than 70 shacks were burned down, and a further 100 were looted, while hundreds of people were forced to seek refuge at a local police station.

In August 2001 Agri South Africa, an organization representing commercial farmers (mainly white) and 'emerging' black farmers, reported that there had been more than 6,000 attacks on South African farms since 1991, resulting in the deaths of more than 1,000 people; it was widely feared that the motivation for the attacks was land redistribution, as had been the case in Zimbabwe since the late 1990s. The South African Government declared land seizures illegal in August, and the Department of Safety and Security established a committee of inquiry to determine the reasons for the attacks.

The leader of the NNP, van Schalkwyk, announced in October 2001 that the party was suspending its participation in the DA, following differences with the DP; the DP had dismissed the mayor of Cape Town, a prominent figure in the NNP, while the DP suspected the NNP of attempting to increase membership in an attempt to take overall control of the DA. Van Schalkwyk announced that the NNP would seek an accommodation with the ANC, as the IFP had done, retaining its independence, but holding positions in the Cabinet. In late November the ANC and NNP announced a power-sharing agreement in the Western Cape (the only province not previously under ANC control), and the NNP also took seats in seven of the eight other Provincial Governments (all except Kwazulu/Natal, where the ANC had an agreement with the IFP). Discord within the NNP emerged when Gerald Morkel resigned as Premier of the Western Cape in November, after publicly refusing to support closer co-operation with the ANC; he was replaced by Peter Marais. Meanwhile, in October COSATU accused the ANC of attempting to discredit it and suppress criticism of the Government, after a leaked report from the ANC national executive suggested that COSATU intended to establish a rival, extreme left-wing party. In early May 2002 Mbeki appointed Charles Nqakula, the Chairman of the SACP, as Minister of Safety and Security, following the death of Steve Tshwete. Marais resigned in May over allegations of sexual harassment and was replaced by van Schalkwyk.

In October 2002 one person was killed and a mosque was damaged in a series of nine bomb explosions in Soweto. A further explosion took place near a Buddhist temple in Pretoria. A right-wing extremist group, the Warriors of the Boer Nation, admitted responsibility in the following month, claiming that it was seeking the downfall of the ANC Government and the release of fellow right-wing extremists from prison. In December the police claimed to have dismantled the Boeremag (Boer Force), which had also been implicated in the attacks. At the ANC conference in that month, Mbeki was elected unopposed to serve a second five-year term as President of the party. Meanwhile, human rights groups brought legal action in the USA against a number of multinational companies, whom they accused of encouraging human rights abuses while operating under the apartheid regime; the groups sought financial reparations, although they did not cite a specific figure. The Government refused to support the action, claiming that it would damage foreign investment in South Africa.

A ruling by the Constitutional Court in late 2002, allowing national and provincial deputies to change parties without losing their seats, led to significant changes in the political landscape: in April 2003 the ANC increased its share of parliamentary seats to over two-thirds, which would allow it to change the Constitution, when members of the UDM and the NNP defected to it, while the FA and the Afrikaner Eenheidsbeweging lost all their seats. At provincial level, members of the IFP defected to the ANC in KwaZulu/Natal and assumed further positions in the Cabinet, although the premiership of the province remained under IFP control. In April 2003 Madikizela-Mandela, who had been re-elected to the NEC of the ANC in December, was convicted of fraud and theft for obtaining bank loans using the fabricated names of employees of the ANC Women's League, and sentenced to five years' imprisonment.

South Africa became increasingly isolated politically in southern Africa after Zimbabwe (formerly Rhodesia) underwent the transition to independence in April 1980. During the 1980s South Africa's continued occupation of Namibia resulted in frequent clashes between SWAPO guerrillas and South African troops (see chapter on Namibia). In 1971 the International Court of Justice had declared South Africa's presence in Namibia to be illegal and the UN had, in 1973, recognized SWAPO as the 'authentic representative of the Namibian people'. Following the collapse of the semi-autonomous internal administration, South Africa resumed direct rule of Namibia in January 1983. In February 1984 South Africa and Angola agreed on a cease-fire along the Angola–Namibia border, and established a joint commission to monitor the withdrawal of South African troops from Angola. In May 1988 negotiations began between Angola, Cuba and South Africa, with the USA acting as mediator. On 22 December Angola, Cuba and South Africa signed a formal treaty designating 1 April 1989 as the commencement date for the process leading to Namibian independence, as well as a treaty requiring all 50,000 Cuban troops to be withdrawn from Angola by July 1991. Elections were held in Namibia in November 1989, and independence for the former South African territory was achieved on 21 March 1990, under a SWAPO-controlled Government. The strategic port of Walvis Bay and 12 offshore islands, to which Namibia laid claim, remained under South African jurisdiction until September 1991, when the two countries agreed to administer the disputed territories jointly. In August 1993 South Africa relinquished sovereignty over Walvis Bay and the 12 islands, which were officially transferred to Namibia in March 1994. In August 2001 the South African and Namibian foreign ministers met to discuss the issue of their joint border on the Orange river; Namibia claimed the border extended to the middle of the river, while South Africa claimed it lay on the northern bank, provoking differences over mineral and fishing rights.

In 1984 South Africa signed a mutual non-aggression pact with Mozambique (the Nkomati accord), which implied that South Africa would withdraw its covert support for the Resistência Nacional Moçambicana (Renamo), while Mozambique would prevent the ANC from using its territory as a base for attacks on South Africa. In September 1985 the South African Government conceded that there had been 'technical' violations of the accord. In May 1988 Mozambican and South African officials agreed to reactivate the Nkomati accord, and in September President Botha visited President Joaquim Chissano of Mozambique, his first state visit to a black African nation. Following his election as President, Mandela made an official visit to Mozambique in July 1994. In August of that year South Africa, Mozambique and Swaziland signed a security co-operation accord, in an effort to combat the continuing illicit transport of armaments. In February 1997 South Africa appealed to the Government of Swaziland to release Swazi trade union leaders from detention. The Swazi Government protested at action mounted by COSATU in support of its Swazi counterparts, stating that it represented interference in the internal affairs of Swaziland.

In 1979 the Southern African Development Co-ordination Conference (SADCC) was established by southern African countries, to work towards a reduction of their economic dependence on South Africa. The SADCC reformed in August 1992 as the Southern African Development Community (SADC, see p. 311), which aimed to achieve closer economic integration between its member states. South Africa was admitted to the SADC in August 1994. In April 1997 members of the South African armed forces participated in military training exercises in Zimbabwe, as part of a nascent SADC regional peace-keeping force. In September 1998 about 600 South African and 200 Botswanan troops were dispatched to restore order in the Lesotho capital, Maseru, under the aegis of the SADC, following a coup attempt by junior military officers. The rebels subsequently withdrew from the capital, after fighting in which about 66 people were killed. About 750 South African troops, together with some 350 Botswanan troops, remained in Lesotho to maintain civil order, before their withdrawal in May 2000.

In April 2000 Mbeki, together with the Presidents of Namibia and Mozambique, visited Zimbabwe to increase pressure on President Robert Mugabe to prevent the illegal occupation of white-owned farmland (see chapter on Zimbabwe). Despite international condemnation of Mugabe and requests by a number of countries, most notably the United Kingdom, for more unequivocal criticism of President Mugabe's actions from South Africa, President Mbeki attempted to maintain 'constructive engagement' towards Zimbabwe. Relations with the United Kingdom were strained in January 2001, when a British government minister openly criticized South African policy on the issue. Following Mugabe's re-election as President in March 2002, the ANC issued a statement endorsing the ballot, despite allegations that Mugabe's party, the Zimbabwe African National Union—Patriotic Front, had intimidated voters and engaged in electoral fraud. The South African Government's position strained relations with the United Kingdom and the USA, and the latter threatened to withdraw support for the New Partnership for Africa's Development (NEPAD, see below) if the Government did not condemn Mugabe. However, later in March Mbeki was part of a Commonwealth troika (also comprising the President of Nigeria and the Prime Minister of Australia) that decided to suspend Zimbabwe from meetings of that organization for a period of one year. Mbeki had previously ignored pleas from Morgan Tsvangirai, the leader of the main opposition party in Zimbabwe, the Movement for Democratic Change, to impose sanctions on Zimbabwe prior to the election. In March 2003 Donald (Don) McKinnon, the Secretary-General of the Commonwealth, stated that the troika had concluded that Zimbabwe's suspension from the organization's meetings should remain in force for a further nine months, pending consideration by the next summit of heads of government, scheduled to be held in December, in Abuja, Nigeria. However, South Africa subsequently denied that it had agreed to the extension of the suspension.

In November 1996 South Africa was criticized for its approval of a substantial sale of weapons to Rwanda, which was believed to be providing military support to rebels in eastern Zaire who were engaged in conflict with the Zairean army. In response to international pressure, the South African Government subsequently decided to suspend the sale of armaments to Rwanda. During 1996 South Africa supported efforts to achieve reconciliation in Angola and in early 1997 was involved in intensive diplomatic activity, along with other African countries, with the aim of negotiating an end to the civil war in Zaire. Following the assumption of power by Alliance des forces démocratiques pour la libération du Congo-Zaïre, led by Laurent-Désiré Kabila, in

May, South Africa became the first foreign government to recognize the new regime and pledged to assist in reconstruction efforts and in the holding of elections in the renamed Democratic Republic of the Congo. In October 2001 South African soldiers were dispatched to Burundi (q.v.) as part of a proposed 700-member peace-keeping mission, in an effort to enforce national security and to support the formation of a multi-ethnic transitional government. Mandela had been instrumental in negotiating a peace accord (signed in August 2000), whereby the Hutu and Tutsi ethnic groups, which had been engaged in civil conflict since 1993, were each to hold the presidency for 18 months during a three-year transitional period.

During the 1980s, despite appeals by anti-apartheid groups within and outside the country for the imposition of economic sanctions, South Africa retained vital trading links with many Western countries, and its economy was supported by considerable foreign investment. Nevertheless, following the violent events of 1984–85, the UN Security Council imposed a number of economic sanctions and restrictions on sport and cultural relations. The US Government (which had hitherto maintained a policy of 'constructive engagement' with South Africa) imposed a series of limited economic sanctions, as did members of the European Community (EC, now European Union—EU, see p. 199) and Nordic countries. In 1986 the Heads of Government of seven Commonwealth countries agreed (with the exception of the United Kingdom) to adopt wide-ranging sanctions.

Following the implementation of political reforms in South Africa from February 1990, international sanctions were reviewed. During 1991 South Africa was readmitted to international sporting competition, after many years of exclusion. In July the USA officially withdrew sanctions (which were, however, retained by a number of US states and cities). In October Commonwealth Heads of Government endorsed the withdrawal of cultural sanctions against South Africa; however, sanctions on finance, arms and trade and investment remained. Japan ended all its sanctions during that month. In 1992 the EC withdrew a number of sanctions against South Africa. In September 1993, following the adoption of legislation providing for the installation of a multiracial transitional administration (see above), the international community ended the remaining economic sanctions against South Africa. The UN Security Council ended its mandatory embargo on armaments, following the establishment of an interim Government of National Unity in May 1994; South Africa subsequently established diplomatic relations with more than 165 countries. South Africa became a member of the Commonwealth on 1 June, and joined the Organization of African Unity (OAU—now the African Union, see p. 130) later that month. The People's Republic of China refused to establish formal diplomatic links while South Africa maintained relations with Taiwan. In November 1996 President Mandela announced that South Africa's diplomatic relations with Taiwan were to be severed in favour of the People's Republic of China, with effect from the end of 1997. In response, Taiwan withdrew its ambassador indefinitely and announced that the majority of its aid projects in South Africa would be suspended.

Despite the ANC Government's commitment to an independent foreign policy and consequent good relations with regimes that are unpopular with Western nations, including Cuba, Iran and Libya, South Africa's relations with the USA were considerably strengthened following the transition to multiracial, democratic rule. In December 1995 a joint US-South African commission was established, chaired by Mbeki and the US Vice-President, Al Gore. In February 1998 it was announced that South Africa and the USA were to normalize their defence trade agreement, thereby allowing South African armaments companies to trade with their US counterparts for the first time. In August 1998 two people were killed, and about 27 injured, in a bomb attack on a US restaurant in Cape Town. A supporter of an organization styled Muslims Against Global Oppression (MAGO) claimed to have perpetrated the bombing, apparently in retaliation for US air attacks on Sudan and Afghanistan (although MAGO officially denied responsibility for the incident). Several members of PAGAD were subsequently arrested in connection with the bombing. A series of further bombings in the Cape Town area, and the killing of a local magistrate in July 2000, were also attributed by the authorities to PAGAD.

South Africa hosted the UN World Conference against Racism, Racial Discrimination, Xenophobia and Related Intolerance in August–September 2001, which was widely regarded as a failure. Many African nations demanded reparations and an apology from European nations and the USA for colonization and slavery, while South Africa made more moderate calls for an expression of 'regret' and indirect reparations in the form of debt relief and aid. The conference finished acrimoniously (after the US and Israeli delegations walked out in protest at calls from Arab nations to equate Zionism with racism and apartheid), with European countries expressing regret but offering no apology for slavery (for fear of potential legal claims for compensation from the descendants of slaves) and refusing to consider it as a crime against humanity; limited commitments were made to increase aid to African countries. In August–September 2002 South Africa hosted the UN World Summit on Sustainable Development in Johannesburg, which sought to address issues of poverty and environmental degradation; the summit was criticized for broadly failing to establish substantive targets for poverty reduction and for apparent intransigence on the part of certain developed nations.

In March 1998, following four years of negotiations, the EU approved the terms for a comprehensive free-trade agreement with South Africa. The agreement provisionally came into force on 1 January 2000; a continuing dispute with the Governments of Italy, Spain, Portugal and Greece, which had refused to sign the accord on wines and spirits, was resolved after South Africa agreed to discontinue the use of traditional European names for alcoholic drinks within five years. In December 2000 a framework agreement was reached on a free-trade accord with the Southern Common Market (known as Mercosur—Mercado Común del Sur, comprising Argentina, Brazil, Paraguay and Uruguay); Mercosur was scheduled to conduct a trade mission to South Africa in June 2002.

In October 2001 NEPAD (see p. 133) was launched, as part of a long-term strategy for socio-economic recovery in Africa, in accordance with a decision taken at the OAU summit held in Lusaka, Zambia, in July. Mbeki formulated NEPAD's founding documents, in conjunction with the heads of state of Algeria, Egypt, Nigeria and Senegal, and South Africa was to host the Secretariat. Broad support was promised by the EU and the G-8 group of industrialized nations, although no financial assistance had been agreed by March 2002.

Government

Under the terms of the Constitution, which was adopted on 8 May 1996 and entered into force on 4 February 1997, legislative power is vested in a bicameral Parliament, comprising a National Assembly and a National Council of Provinces (formerly the Senate). The National Assembly is elected by universal adult suffrage under a system of proportional representation and has between 350 and 400 members. The 90-member National Council of Provinces comprises six permanent delegates and four special delegates from each of the provincial legislatures (see below). The President, who is elected by the National Assembly from among its members, exercises executive power in consultation with the other members of the Cabinet. Any party that holds a minimum of 80 seats in the National Assembly (equivalent to 20% of the national vote) is entitled to nominate an Executive Deputy President. A Constitutional Court ensures that the executive, legislative and judicial organs of government adhere to the provisions of the interim Constitution.

Each of the nine provinces has a legislature, which is elected under a system of proportional representation. Each legislature is entitled to draft a constitution for the province, subject to the principles governing the national Constitution, and to elect a Premier, who heads an Executive Council. Parties that hold a minimum of 10% of seats in the provincial legislature are entitled to a proportional number of portfolios in the Executive Council.

Defence

In August 2002 the South African National Defence Force (SANDF) totalled about 60,000: army 40,250, navy 5,000, air force 9,250 and a medical corps numbering 5,500. The SANDF comprised members of the former South African armed forces, together with personnel from the former military wings of the ANC and the Pan-Africanist Congress, and the former 'homelands'. Revised estimates of budget expenditure in 2001/02 indicated that R 16,053.0m. (6.1% of total expenditure) was allocated to defence. The numbers of military personnel were significantly reduced in the late 1990s. Voluntary military service for school leavers was to be introduced in January 2003.

Economic Affairs

In 2001, according to estimates by the World Bank, South Africa's gross national income (GNI), measured at average 1999–2001 prices, was US $125,486m., equivalent to $2,900 per head (or $9,510 per head on an international purchasing-power parity basis). During 1990–2001, it was estimated, the population increased at an average annual rate of 1.9%, while gross domestic product (GDP) per head decreased, in real terms, by an average of 0.1% per year. Overall GDP increased, in real terms, at an average annual rate of 1.8% in 1990–2001, according to the World Bank. Growth was 2.8% in 2001 and 3.0% in 2002, according to official figures.

Agriculture (including forestry and fishing) contributed 3.8% of GDP in 2002. Some 9.7% of the employed labour force were engaged in the sector at September 2001. Maize (also the principal subsistence crop), fruit and sugar are exported, and livestock-rearing is also important: wool is another significant export. The GDP of the agricultural sector increased by an average of 0.3% per year in 1990–2001, according to the World Bank. Agricultural GDP increased by 1.0% in 2001.

Industry (including mining, manufacturing, construction and power) contributed 32.1% of GDP in 2002, and engaged 25.7% of the employed labour force at September 2001. Industrial GDP increased at an average annual rate of 0.6% in 1990–2001, according to the World Bank. Industrial GDP increased by 2.0% in 2001.

Mining contributed 8.1% of GDP in 2002, and engaged 4.4% of the employed labour force at September 2001. South Africa is the world's leading producer of gold, which is the major mineral export, accounting for about 30% of total world production. Coal, platinum, iron ore, diamonds, chromium, manganese, vanadium, vermiculite, antimony, limestone, asbestos, fluorspar, uranium, copper, lead and zinc are also important mineral exports. There are reserves of petroleum, natural gas, sillimanite, titanium and zirconium. The GDP of the mining sector declined by an average of 1.4% per year in 1997–2001. Mining GDP declined by 1.5% in 2001.

Manufacturing contributed 18.8% of GDP in 2002, and engaged 14.8% of the employed labour force at September 2001. The GDP of the manufacturing sector increased at an average annual rate of 0.8% in 1990–2001, according to the World Bank. Manufacturing GDP increased by 2.0% in 2001.

Energy is derived principally from coal-based electricity; this is supplemented by nuclear power and by hydroelectric power. The construction of a plant to convert natural gas into liquid fuel was completed in 1992. Exploitation of petroleum reserves in oilfields located 140 km south-west of the Southern Cape commenced in 1997. In 2001 substantial reserves of natural gas were discovered off the Western Cape. Imports of mineral fuels and lubricants comprised 14.4% of the value of total imports in 2000.

The services sector contributed an estimated 64.1% of GDP in 2002, and engaged 64.2% of the employed labour force at September 2001. The real GDP of the services sector increased by an average of 2.5% per year in 1990–2001, according to the World Bank. Services GDP increased by 3.6% in 2001.

In 2001 South Africa recorded a visible trade surplus of US $4,966m., while there was a deficit of $166m. on the current account of the balance of payments. In 2000 the principal source of imports for the Southern African Customs Union (SACU, see below) was Germany (an estimated 13.2%); other major suppliers of imports were the USA, the United Kingdom, Japan, Saudi Arabia, Iran and France. The principal market for exports in that year was the USA (9.2%); other important purchasers were the United Kingdom, Germany, Japan and the Netherlands. The principal exports in 2000 were basic manufactures (particularly iron and steel, and diamonds), machinery and transport equipment, mineral fuels, crude materials, chemical products, and food and live animals. The principal imports were machinery and transport equipment (notably telecommunications and sound equipment), mineral fuels (particularly petroleum), basic manufactures and chemical products.

In 2002 South Africa recorded a budgetary deficit of R 6,031m., equivalent to 0.5% of GDP. At the end of 2000 the total external debt was US $24,861m., of which $15,308m. was long-term public debt. The cost of debt-servicing in that year was equivalent to 10.0% of the value of exports of goods and services. The annual rate of inflation averaged 8.6% in 1990–2001; consumer prices increased by 4.8% in 2001. According to official figures, 29.5% of the labour force were unemployed at September 2001.

South Africa is a member of SACU (with Botswana, Lesotho, Namibia and Swaziland), of the Southern African Development Community (SADC, see p. 311) and of the African Development Bank (see p. 128). The Secretariat of the New Partnership for Africa's Development (see p. 133) is located in South Africa.

Despite South Africa's mineral wealth and highly-developed manufacturing sector, economic progress was hindered during the 1980s following the imposition of economic sanctions by the international community in protest at apartheid (see Recent History). In late 1993, in response to the Government's adoption of political reforms, the remaining economic sanctions were ended, relations with international financial institutions were normalized, and an agreement with foreign creditor banks regarding the country's outstanding debt was reached. Following democratic elections in April 1994, foreign Governments pledged considerable financial assistance to South Africa. The new Government initiated a Reconstruction and Development Programme; however, subsequent progress in social and economic development was impeded by the necessity for fiscal restraint. Plans to commence the partial transfer to the private sector of state-owned companies were announced in 1995. In mid-1996 the Government announced its long-term strategy for 'growth, employment and redistribution' (GEAR), which placed emphasis on continued fiscal discipline, reductions in the budgetary deficit and the removal of exchange controls. By 1999 financial market conditions had improved considerably, resulting in lower inflation, increased real GDP and an increase in investor confidence. Progress had also been achieved in privatization, with the sale of a 20% share in South African Airways (SAA) to Swissair in mid-1999. However, the Government was forced to buy back the share in SAA in late 2001, when Swissair went bankrupt, and the partial privatization of the telecommunications company, Telkom SA Ltd, which had been scheduled for 2002, was postponed in late 2001. GDP growth slowed to 2.8% in 2001, owing to a world economic slowdown, which was compounded by high interest rates and a shortage of skilled labour. It increased to 3.0% in 2002, and was forecast to increase further, to 3.3%, in 2003. Meanwhile, the IMF urged the Government to accelerate the implementation of the structural reforms of the GEAR strategy, particularly the reduction of unemployment (which remained critically high), trade liberalization and privatization. Political violence in Zimbabwe (see Recent History) contributed to a dramatic reduction in the value of the rand in 2000–01, and prompted concern that the South African economy (particularly with regard to foreign investment) might be adversely affected. The rand reached an all-time low against the US dollar in 2001, partly as a result of South Africa's reliance on exports at a time when global economic activity was slowing down. The mining sector, one of the most significant in the South African economy, underwent significant rationalization and consolidation in the late 1990s, and in June 2002 the National Assembly approved legislation transferring the control of mineral rights from private companies to the Government, which would then lease them. In September 2001 South Africa was the first country to implement the SADC Free Trade Protocol: tariffs were removed on 76% of goods traded with member countries, a figure expected to rise to 97% by 2006. The rand strengthened against the US dollar in 2002, partly owing to higher interest rates in South Africa. The budget for 2003 included commitments to reduce levels of taxation for individuals and small businesses, and to increase spending on social security, health and infrastructure.

Education

School attendance is compulsory for children of all population groups between the ages of seven and 16 years. From 1991 state schools were permitted to admit pupils of all races, and in 1995 the right to free state education for all was introduced. In 1998/99 the total enrolment at primary schools included 95.2% of pupils in the relevant age-group (males 94.9%; females 95.5%), while in 1999/2000 secondary enrolment was equivalent to 90.2% of pupils in the relevant age-group (males 85.8%; females 94.7%). During the 1980s universities, which were formerly racially segregated, began to admit students of all races. In 1999 there were 21 universities and 15 'technikons' (tertiary education institutions offering technological and commercial vocational training); in 2002 it was announced that the number of universities was to be reduced to 11, the number of technikons reduced to six, and that four comprehensive institutions and two national higher education institutes would be created. Revised budget estimates for 2001/02 indicated the allocation of R 7,819.6m. (3.0% of total expenditure) to education.

Public Holidays

2003: 1 January (New Year's Day), 21 March (Human Rights Day), 18 April (Good Friday), 21 April (Family Day), 28 April (Freedom Day), 1 May (Workers' Day), 16 June (Youth Day), 9 August (National Women's Day), 24 September (Heritage Day), 16 December (Day of Reconciliation), 25 December (Christmas Day), 26 December (Day of Goodwill).

2004: 1 January (New Year's Day), 22 March (for Human Rights Day), 9 April (Good Friday), 12 April (Family Day), 27 April (Freedom Day), 1 May (Workers' Day), 16 June (Youth Day), 9 August (National Women's Day), 24 September (Heritage Day), 16 December (Day of Reconciliation), 25 December (Christmas Day), 26 December (Day of Goodwill).

Weights and Measures

The metric system is in use.

Statistical Survey

Source (unless otherwise indicated): Statistics South Africa, Private Bag X44, Pretoria 0001; tel. (12) 3108911; fax (12) 3108500; e-mail info@statssa.pwv.gov.za; internet www.statssa.gov.za.

Area and Population

AREA, POPULATION AND DENSITY*

Area (sq km)	1,219,090†
Population (census results)	
7 March 1991	37,944,018
9 October 1996	
Males	19,520,887
Females	21,062,685
Total	40,583,573
Population (official estimates at mid-year)	
2000	43,291,441‡
2001	44,560,644‡
2002	45,454,211
Density (per sq km) at mid-2002	37.3

* Excluding data for Walvis Bay (area 1,124 sq km or 434 sq miles, population 22,999 in 1991), sovereignty over which was transferred from South Africa to Namibia on 1 March 1994.

† 470,693 sq miles.

‡ Figures exclude the effect of additional deaths caused by HIV/AIDS.

ETHNIC GROUPS
(estimates, 30 June 2002)*

	Number	% of total
Africans (Blacks)	35,474,192	78.04
Europeans (Whites)	4,555,289	10.02
Coloureds	3,918,048	8.62
Asians	1,121,815	2.47
Other and unspecified	384,867	0.85
Total	**45,454,211**	**100.00**

* Figures exclude the effect of additional deaths caused by HIV/AIDS.

PROVINCES

(30 June 2002)

	Area (sq km)	Population (estimates)	Density (per sq km)	Capital
KwaZulu/Natal . .	92,100	9,212,123	100.0	Pietermaritzburg
Gauteng* . . .	17,010	8,106,190	476.6	Johannesburg
Eastern Cape . .	169,580	7,132,141	42.1	Bisho
Limpopo† . . .	123,910	5,843,851	47.2	Pietersburg
Western Cape . .	129,370	4,313,959	33.3	Cape Town
North-West . .	116,320	3,659,902	31.5	Mmabatho
Mpumalanga‡ . .	79,490	3,156,272	39.7	Nelspruit
Free State§ . . .	129,480	2,859,081	22.1	Bloemfontein
Northern Cape . .	361,830	888,390	2.5	Kimberley
Total . . .	1,219,090	45,171,908	37.1	

* Formerly Pretoria-Witwatersrand-Vereeniging.

† Known as Northern Province (formerly Northern Transvaal) until February 2002.

‡ Formerly Eastern Transvaal.

§ Formerly the Orange Free State.

PRINCIPAL TOWNS

(Metropolitan areas, population at 1996 census)

Cape Town* . .	2,415,408	Uitenhage . . .	192,120
Durban . . .	2,117,650	Mdantsane . .	182,998
Johannesburg .	1,480,530	Botshabelo . .	177,971
Pretoria* . .	1,104,479	Brakpan . . .	171,359
Soweto . . .	1,098,094	Kimberley . . .	170,432
Port Elizabeth . .	749,921	Witbank . . .	167,183
Pietermaritzburg .	378,126	Carletonville . .	164,367
Benoni . . .	365,467	Springs . . .	160,795
Vereeniging . .	346,780	Alberton . . .	147,948
Bloemfontein* . .	333,769	Klerksdorp . .	137,318
Tembisa . . .	282,272	Midrand . . .	126,400
Boksburg . . .	260,905	Verwoerdburg . .	114,575
Vanderbijlpark . .	253,335	Westonaria . .	113,932
Newcastle . .	219,682	Somerset West . .	112,489
East London . .	212,323	Rustenburg . .	104,537
Welkom . . .	203,296	Potchefstroom . .	101,682
Krugersdorp . .	203,168		

* Pretoria is the administrative capital, Cape Town the legislative capital and Bloemfontein the judicial capital.

Source: Thomas Brinkoff, *City Population* (internet www.citypopulation.de).

BIRTHS AND DEATHS

(UN estimates, annual averages)

	1985–90	1990–95	1995–2000
Birth rate (per 1,000)	30.3	27.0	26.7
Death rate (per 1,000)	9.7	8.7	10.8

Source: UN, *World Population Prospects: The 2000 Revision*.

Expectation of life (WHO estimates, years at birth): 49.0 (males 47.7; females 50.3) in 2001 (Source: WHO, *World Health Report*).

IMMIGRATION AND EMIGRATION

	1999	2000	2001
Immigrants:			
Africa	1,054	831	1,450
Europe	1,213	978	1,714
Asia	693	991	1,398
Americas	131	133	213
Oceania	40	33	51
Total (incl. others and unspecified)	3,669	3,053	4,832
Emigrants:			
Africa	1,106	1,655	1,710
Europe	3,054	3,811	5,316
Asia	181	198	506
Americas	1,196	1,645	1,713
Oceania	2,488	2,441	2,912
Total (incl. others and unspecified)	8,402	10,262	12,260

ECONOMICALLY ACTIVE POPULATION

(household survey, '000 persons aged 15 to 65 years, September 2001)*

	Males	Females	Total
Agriculture, hunting, forestry and fishing . . .	727	324	1,051
Mining and quarrying	470	17	487
Manufacturing	1,004	602	1,605
Electricity, gas and water . . .	80	15	95
Construction	534	60	594
Trade, restaurants and hotels . .	1,186	1,212	2,397
Transport, storage and communications	448	94	543
Financing, insurance, real estate and business services	547	428	975
Community, social and personal services	878	1,110	1,988
Private households	150	905	1,055
Total employed (incl. others) . .	6,049	4,783	10,833
Unemployed†	2,139	2,386	4,525
Total labour force	8,188	7,169	15,358

* Figures have been assessed independently, so that totals are not always the sum of the component parts.

† Based on the official definition. According to the expanded definition, the number of unemployed (in '000) was 7,698 (males 3,280, females 4,418).

Health and Welfare

KEY INDICATORS

Total fertility rate (children per woman, 2001)	2.9
Under-5 mortality rate (per 1,000 live births, 2001) . . .	71
HIV/AIDS (% of persons aged 15–49, 2001)	20.10
Physicians (per 1,000 head, 1993)	0.56
Health expenditure (2000): US $ per head (PPP)	663
Health expenditure (2000): % of GDP	8.8
Health expenditure (2000): public (% of total)	42.2
Access to water (% of persons, 2000)	86
Access to sanitation (% of persons, 2000)	86
Human Development Index (2000): ranking	107
Human Development Index (2000): value	0.695

For sources and definitions, see explanatory note on p. vi.

Agriculture

PRINCIPAL CROPS

('000 metric tons)

	1999	2000	2001
Maize .	7,946	11,536	8,045
Sorghum .	223	473	211
Wheat .	1,733	2,342	2,342
Barley .	267	93	115
Oats .	22	33	33
Dry beans .	93	87	111
Sugar cane .	21,228	24,008	n.a.
Tobacco (leaves) .	30	31	n.a.
Potatoes .	1,674	1,588	1,681
Sweet potatoes .	52	52	54
Soybeans .	175	149	n.a.
Groundnuts (in shell) .	138	136	204
Sunflower seed .	1,212	567	677
Cabbages .	199	191	183
Lettuce .	34	31	30
Tomatoes .	431	403	489
Pumpkins, squash and gourds .	337	329	335
Onions (dry) .	398	298	332
Green beans .	30	36	34
Carrots .	101	96	101
Green corn (maize) .	299	298	230
Watermelons .	72	61	55
Apples .	618	578	561
Grapefruit and pomelo .	213	288	433
Grapes .	1,554	1,455	1,332
Lemons and limes .	102	119	144
Oranges .	1,156	1,118	1,086
Tangerines, mandarins, clementines and satsumas .	127	98	87
Peaches and nectarines .	213	221	165
Plums .	47	34	39
Pears .	289	304	250
Bananas .	255	252	273
Mangoes .	46	44	46
Avocados .	56	82	54
Apricots .	53	57	59
Pineapples .	150	169	137
Cotton (lint) .	44	23	32

Source: Department of Agriculture, Pretoria.

LIVESTOCK

('000 head, year ending September)

	1999	2000	2001
Cattle .	13,565	13,461	13,506
Pigs .	1,531	1,556	1,592
Sheep .	28,680	28,551	28,786
Goats .	6,457	6,706	6,809
Horses .	258	255	n.a.
Mules .	14	14	n.a.
Asses .	210	210	n.a.
Chickens .	60,000	61,000	n.a.

Source: Department of Agriculture, Pretoria.

LIVESTOCK PRODUCTS

('000 metric tons)

	1999	2000	2001
Beef and veal .	553	580	568
Mutton and lamb .	112	98	95
Goat meat .	36	8	8
Pig meat .	117	113	111
Poultry meat .	452	796	900
Cows' milk .	2,667	3,532	2,532
Butter .	19	9	9
Cheese .	36	35	35
Hen eggs .	334	318	329
Wool greasy .	56	53	n.a.
Cattle hides (fresh) .	83	54	n.a.
Sheepskins (fresh) .	18	18	n.a.

Source: Department of Agriculture, Pretoria.

Forestry

(including Namibia)

ROUNDWOOD REMOVALS

('000 cubic metres, excl. bark)

	1997	1998	1999
Sawlogs, veneer logs and logs for sleepers .	4,775	6,002	6,002
Pulpwood .	10,166	9,223	9,223
Other industrial wood .	3,630	3,391	3,391
Fuel wood .	14,600	12,000	12,000
Total .	33,171	30,616	30,616

2001: Annual production as in 1998–99.

Source: FAO.

SAWNWOOD PRODUCTION

('000 cubic metres, incl. railway sleepers)

	1997	1998	1999
Coniferous (softwood) .	1,439	1,396	1,396
Broadleaved (hardwood) .	135	102	102
Total .	1,574	1,498	1,498

2001: Annual production as in 1998–99.

Source: FAO.

Fishing

('000 metric tons, live weight)

	1998	1999	2000
Capture .	559.4	588.6	643.8
Cape hakes (*Stokvisse*) .	151.3	141.2	135.0
Cape horse mackerel (*Maasbanker*) .	46.4	18.0	16.0
Southern African pilchard .	128.0	131.3	136.1
Whitehead's round herring .	52.5	58.9	37.8
Southern African anchovy .	107.5	180.5	267.8
Aquaculture .	5.1	4.1	4.0
Total catch* .	563.9	592.1	647.8

* Excluding aquatic plants ('000 metric tons): 6.1 in 1998; 6.1 in 1999; 6.2 in 2000. Also excluded are crocodiles. The number of Nile crocodiles captured was: 8,863 in 1998; 27,631 in 1999; 29,942 in 2000.

Source: FAO, *Yearbook of Fishery Statistics*.

Mining

('000 metric tons, unless otherwise indicated)

	1998	1999	2000
Hard coal	224,385	223,357	224,834
Crude petroleum ('000 barrels). .	6,549	5,493	6,606
Natural gas	1,486.1	1,616.5	1,513.4
Iron ore: gross weight . .	32,965	29,517	33,707
Iron ore: metal content*[1] . .	20,400	18,442	20,898
Copper ore (metric tons)[1,2] . .	164,000	144,263	137,092
Nickel ore (metric tons)[1,3] . .	36,679	36,200	36,616
Lead concentrates (metric tons)[1,2] .	84,128	80,191	75,262
Zinc ore (metric tons)[1,2] . .	69,630	69,733	62,703
Manganese ore: gross weight . .	3,044	3,122	3,635
Manganese ore: metal content*[1] .	1,300	1,340	1,545
Chromium ore: gross weight[1] .	6,480	6,817	6,621
Vanadium ore (metric tons)*[1,2] .	18,954	17,612	18,021
Zirconium concentrates (metric tons)*[1]	300,000	400,000	379,394
Antimony concentrates (metric tons)*[1,2]	4,243	6,000	6,347
Cobalt ore (metric tons)[2] . .	296.4	305.8	n.a.
Silver ore (kilograms)[2] . .	144,482	151,960	144,100
Uranium ore (metric tons)[2,4] .	962	981	861
Gold (kilograms)[2]	464,216	451,184	430,816
Platinum-group metals (kilograms)[2,5]	200,143	216,478	206,770
Kaolin	138	122	89.0
Magnesite—crude[1] . . .	65	64	63
Natural phosphates	2,739	2,900	2,796
Fluorspar—Fluorite[6]	228.6	217.5	215.7
Salt—unrefined	356.1	358.6	345.6
Diamonds ('000 metric carats)[7] .	10,756	10,022	10,805
Gypsum—crude[1]	485.7	513.8	413.1
Asbestos	27.2	18.7	18.8
Mica (metric tons)	1,558	1,010	475
Talc (metric tons)[1]	11,300	7,900	5,600

* Provisional or estimated figures.
[1] Data from the US Geological Survey.
[2] Figures relate to the metal content of ores or concentrates.
[3] Nickel content of matte and refined nickel.
[4] Data from the Uranium Institute (London).
[5] Comprising platinum, palladium, rhodium, ruthenium, iridium and osmium. Individual metal data, 2000 (kg): Platinum 114,459; Palladium 55,818; Rhodium 12,067; others 24,426.
[6] Acid, metallurgical and ceramic grade.
[7] According to the US Geological Survey, production in 2000 comprised 6.06 million carats of industrial diamonds and 4.75 million carats of gem diamonds.

Source (unless otherwise indicated): Department of Minerals and Energy, Pretoria.

Industry

SELECTED PRODUCTS
('000 metric tons, unless otherwise indicated)

	1998	1999	2000
Wheat flour	1,905	1,798	1,837
Sugar—refined	1,151	1,034	1,148
Wine ('000 hectolitres)[1] . . .	218	203	187
Cotton yarn—incl. mixed . . .	74.1	76.0	79.2
Woven cotton fabrics (million sq metres)	223	224	219
Footwear ('000 pairs)	29,581	24,257	20,195
Mechanical wood pulp[2] . . .	270	270*	270*
Chemical wood pulp[2]	1,478	1,372	1,372*
Newsprint paper	347	328	328*
Other printing and writing paper	479	506	506*
Other paper and paperboard[2] . .	1,279	1,207	1,207
Synthetic rubber	62.9	52.4	65.5
Rubber tyres ('000)	9,853	10,524	11,862
Nitrogenous fertilizers . . .	1,839	1,026	694
Phosphate fertilizers. . . .	557	663	370
Motor spirit—petrol (million litres)[3]	10,042	10,248	10,013
Kerosene (million litres)[3] . .	1,214	1,150	1,017
Jet fuel (million litres)[3] . . .	2,156	2,561	2,586
Distillate fuel oils (million litres)[3]	6,550	7,178	7,228
Lubricating oils (million litres)[3] .	310	253	277
Petroleum bitumen—asphalt* . .	242	233	237
Cement	7,620	8,211	8,715
Pig-iron[4]	5,650	4,587	4,573
Crude steel[4]	7,506	6,830	7,019
Refined copper—unwrought[4] . .	125.6	116.4	100.5*
Colour television receivers ('000)	273	273	290
Passenger motor cars—assembled ('000)	216.9	242.0	266.0
Lorries—assembled ('000) . . .	117.1	113.3	130.6
Electric energy (million kWh)[5] .	205,428	200,292	210,684

* Estimate(s).
[1] Natural and sparkling wines.
[2] Including data for Namibia.
[3] Excluding data for Transkei, Bophuthatswana, Venda and Ciskei.
[4] Source: US Geological Survey.
[5] Electricity available for distribution.

Sources: partly UN, *Monthly Bulletin of Statistics* ; FAO.

Finance

CURRENCY AND EXCHANGE RATES

Monetary Units
100 cents = 1 rand (R)

Sterling, Dollar and Euro Equivalents (31 December 2002)
£1 sterling = 13.9260 rand
US $1 = 8.6400 rand
€1 = 9.0608 rand
1,000 rand = £71.81 = $115.74 = €110.37

Average Exchange Rate (rand per US $)
2000   6.93983
2001   8.60918
2002   10.5407

BUDGET
(million rand, year ending 31 March)

Revenue*	1999/2000	2000/01†	2001/02‡
Tax revenue (gross)	200,640.7	220,273.5	252,205.5
Taxes on incomes and profits	116,148.9	126,145.2	149,600.0
Individuals	85,883.9	86,478.0	91,000.0
Companies	20,971.6	29,491.8	44,000.0
Retirement funds . . .	5,330.4	5,219.8	6,500.0
Domestic taxes on goods and			
services	72,286.4	79,103.9	84,342.5
Value-added tax . . .	48,376.8	54,455.2	58,600.0
Excise duties. . . .	8,886.1	9,126.6	9,561.0
Levies on fuel	14,289.8	14,495.3	14,988.0
Taxes on international trade and			
transactions	6,778.1	8,226.6	9,211.0
Customs duties on imports	6,517.8	7,853.6	9,000.0
Other current revenue . . .	4,603.2	3,592.1	4,323.4
Capital revenue	41.7	10.0	30.0
Recoveries of loans and repayments	74.1	112.3	93.3
Sub-total	205,359.7	223,987.9	256,652.2
Less SACU payments§ . . .	7,197.3	8,396.1	8,205.0
Total	198,162.4	215,591.8	248,447.2

Expenditure‖	1999/2000	2000/01†	2001/02‡
National allocations	65,673.5	73,101.9	87,016.4
Central government			
administration	3,331.3	3,751.6	3,912.3
Public works	2,803.1	3,195.9	3,320.5
Financial and administrative			
services	5,494.3	5,904.1	7,374.5
National treasury . . .	5,092.0	5,452.7	6,084.3
Social services	9,594.7	9,713.5	10,439.7
Education	6,919.6	7,327.0	7,819.6
Justice and protection services	33,251.4	37,917.2	43,872.3
Correctional services . .	5,145.4	5,474.9	6,534.0
Defence	10,717.3	13,932.1	16,053.0
Safety and security . . .	14,572.5	15,597.4	17,620.4
Economic services and			
infrastructure development	11,198.7	12,619.6	18,097.1
Transport	4,031.5	4,077.4	4,926.4
Interest on debt	44,289.7	46,320.9	47,515.1
Transfers to provinces . . .	99,262.4	108,904.1	121,206.0
Transfers to local governments	4,626.9	5,575.9	6,552.5
Umsobomvu fund	855.0	—	—
Standing appropriations . .	42.6	39.2	300.0
Total¶	214,749.9	233,941.9	262,589.8

* Excluding proceeds from sales of state assets, fuel stocks and strategic supplies (million rand); 7,476.9 in 1999/2000; 3,451.9 (preliminary) in 2000/01; 5,784.1 (revised estimate) in 2001/02.

† Preliminary figures.

‡ Revised estimates.

§ Payments to Botswana, Lesotho, Namibia and Swaziland, in accordance with Southern African Customs Union agreements.

‖ Excluding extraordinary transfers (million rand): 1,485.4 (preliminary) in 1999/2000; 2,297.2 (preliminary) in 2000/01; 2,075.0 in 2001/02 (revised estimate).

¶ Based on unrounded data.

Source: National Treasury, Pretoria.

INTERNATIONAL RESERVES
(US $ million at 31 December)

	1999	2000	2001
Gold*	1,020	1,451	1,427
IMF special drawing rights . .	288	290	280
Foreign exchange.	6,065	5,793	5,765
Total	7,373	7,534	7,472

* National valuation, based on market prices.

Source: IMF, *International Financial Statistics.*

MONEY SUPPLY
(million rand at 31 December)

	2000	2001	2002
Currency outside banks	23,724	25,286	29,219
Demand deposits at deposit money			
banks	242,244	286,776	320,496
Total (incl. others)	266,185	312,364	349,920

Source: IMF, *International Financial Statistics.*

COST OF LIVING
(Consumer Price Index; base: 1995 = 100)

	1997	1998	1999
Food	116.1	123.3	129.3
Housing	121.3	130.7	131.9
All items (incl. others)	116.6	124.6	131.1

2000: All items 138.1.

2001 (base: 2000 = 100): All items 105.7.

2002 (base: 2000 = 100): All items 116.4.

NATIONAL ACCOUNTS
(million rand at current prices)

National Income and Product
(provisional figures)

	2000	2001	2002
Compensation of employees . .	424,958	458,415	497,843
Operating surplus	244,453	282,566	325,892
Domestic factor incomes . .	669,411	740,981	823,735
Consumption of fixed capital . .	118,641	129,508	145,169
Gross domestic product			
(GDP) at factor cost . . .	788,052	870,489	968,904
Indirect taxes . . . . . }	100,005	112,455	129,810
Less Subsidies . . . . . }			
GDP in purchasers' values .	888,057	982,944	1,098,714
Factor income received from			
abroad.	15,701	19,246	18,913
Less Factor income paid abroad .	37,418	51,093	47,201
Gross national income . .	866,340	951,097	1,070,426
Less Consumption of fixed capital	118,641	129,508	145,169
National income in market			
prices.	747,699	821,589	925,257
Current transfers received from			
abroad.	741	1,103	1,462
Current transfers paid abroad .	−7,163	−7,360	−7,305
National disposable income	859,918	944,840	1,064,583

Expenditure on the Gross Domestic Product

	2000	2001	2002
Government final consumption			
expenditure.	166,330	185,348	211,443
Private final consumption			
expenditure.	556,652	608,646	682,374
Increase in stocks	6,419	3,995	7,574
Gross fixed capital formation . .	138,267	148,424	173,934
Total domestic expenditure	863,571	947,656	1,061,303
Exports of goods and services . .	253,956	301,258	373,035
Less Imports of goods and services	229,470	265,970	335,624
GDP in purchasers' values . .	888,057	982,944	1,098,714
GDP at constant 1995 prices .	624,379	642,038	661,147

Gross Domestic Product by Economic Activity

	2000	2001	2002
Agriculture, forestry and fishing .	26,060	31,060	37,674
Mining and quarrying	54,951	67,161	80,586
Manufacturing	150,198	166,415	188,182
Electricity, gas and water . .	22,657	22,630	23,905
Construction (contractors) . .	23,843	25,532	27,545
Wholesale and retail trade, catering and accommodation. .	107,299	118,737	132,691
Transport, storage and communication.	80,799	88,161	96,086
Finance, insurance, real estate and business services	160,936	177,217	194,591
Government services. . . .	132,519	142,974	157,936
Other community, social and personal services	24,049	27,551	31,066
Other producers (non-profit institutions and domestic servants)	24,930	27,463	28,592
GDP at basic prices . . .	808,241	894,901	998,854
Taxes on products	83,268	91,293	103,714
Less Subsidies on products . .	3,452	3,250	3,854
GDP in purchasers' values . .	888,057	982,944	1,098,714

Source: Reserve Bank of South Africa.

BALANCE OF PAYMENTS

(US $ million)

	1999	2000	2001
Exports of goods f.o.b.	28,627	31,636	30,693
Imports of goods f.o.b.	−24,554	−27,320	−25,677
Trade balance	4,073	4,316	4,966
Exports of services	5,074	4,895	4,662
Imports of services	−5,707	−5,719	−5,208
Balance on goods and services	3,440	3,492	4,419
Other income received . . .	1,568	2,260	2,168
Other income paid	−4,721	−5,401	−6,014
Balance on goods, services and income	287	351	573
Current transfers received . .	66	106	126
Current transfers paid . . .	−993	−1,033	−865
Current balance	−640	−575	−166
Capital account (net)	−62	−52	−32
Direct investment abroad . .	−1,584	−277	3,686
Direct investment from abroad. .	1,503	969	7,162
Portfolio investment assets . .	−5,113	−3,672	−5,331
Portfolio investment liabilities .	13,799	1,807	−2,971
Financial derivatives assets .	−46	−144	—
Financial derivatives liabilities	−76	2	—
Other investment assets . .	−1,644	59	−1,432
Other investment liabilities . .	−1,535	1,354	−614
Net errors and omissions . .	−389	928	1,855
Overall balance	4,215	400	2,158

Source: IMF, *International Financial Statistics*.

External Trade

Figures refer to the Southern African Customs Union, comprising South Africa, Namibia, Botswana, Lesotho and Swaziland. Trade between the component territories is excluded.

PRINCIPAL COMMODITIES
(distribution by SITC, US $ million)

Imports c.i.f.	1998	1999	2000
Food and live animals . . .	945.4	860.2	910.3
Crude materials (inedible) except fuels	840.9	710.3	869.1
Mineral fuels, lubricants, etc.	2,245.2	2,452.4	3,840.6
Petroleum, petroleum products, etc. .	2,095.0	2,349.7	3,748.9
Crude petroleum oils, etc. .	1,810.7	2,089.2	3,486.8
Chemicals and related products	2,864.1	2,950.2	3,055.7
Basic manufactures . . .	3,188.1	3,178.4	3,292.9
Non-metallic mineral manufactures	671.6	798.5	860.3
Machinery and transport equipment.	10,318.5	9,199.6	9,823.8
Machinery specialized for particular industries . . .	1,294.8	1,185.8	1,128.9
General industrial machinery, equipment and parts . . .	1,728.3	1,429.7	1,383.7
Office machines and automatic data-processing equipment . .	1,242.0	1,314.8	1,204.8
Telecommunications and sound equipment	2,378.8	1,694.2	1,858.6
Telecommunication equipment; parts and accessories, etc. . .	2,118.0	1,455.2	1,602.0
Other electrical machinery, apparatus, etc.	1,296.4	1,229.5	1,333.5
Road vehicles	947.3	969.4	1,448.5
Miscellaneous manufactured articles.	2,264.8	2,235.1	2,348.2
Total (incl. others)	26,624.1	24,092.5	26,606.7

Exports f.o.b.	1998	1999	2000
Food and live animals . . .	1,947.9	1,900.3	1,730.5
Vegetables and fruit	907.5	977.7	818.6
Fresh and dried fruits and nuts	645.4	714.7	569.6
Crude materials (inedible) except fuels	2,291.8	2,378.4	2,604.9
Metalliferous ores and metal scrap	1,250.7	1,324.8	1,382.8
Mineral fuels, lubricants, etc.	1,501.4	2,282.4	2,667.3
Coal, lignite and peat . . .	1,403.5	1,381.3	1,326.4
Petroleum, petroleum products, etc.	90.7	890.6	1,164.3
Chemicals and related products	1,754.3	1,853.5	2,035.4
Basic manufactures . . .	4,777.2	9,044.9	7,568.6
Non-metallic mineral manufactures	1,410.8	1,779.2	1,969.0
Pearl, precious and semi-precious stones, unworked or worked	1,225.0	1,576.3	1,756.9
Diamonds (non-industrial), not mounted or set	1,220.4	1,560.1	1,750.6
Iron and steel.	1,392.8	2,325.2	2,768.9
Pig-iron, etc.	99.9	1,166.9	1,304.3
Ferro-alloys	—	1,068.4	1,219.1
Non-ferrous metals	422.5	3,417.0	1,209.0
Metals of the platinum group, unwrought, unworked, or semi-manufactured	1.0	2,181.1	—
Platinum, etc., alloys, semi-manufactured	—	1,097.3	—
Aluminium	54.5	821.4	867.1
Aluminium and aluminium alloys, unwrought . . .	—	751.3	725.2
Machinery and transport equipment.	3,330.6	4,052.0	4,551.5
Road vehicles and parts . . .	1,113.1	1,734.3	1,816.4
Passenger motor cars (excl. buses).	283.3	872.3	1,041.6
Miscellaneous manufactured articles.	1,001.9	1,085.3	1,098.2
Total (incl. others)	19,586.1	23,188.6	26,075.3

Source: UN, *International Trade Statistics Yearbook*.

PRINCIPAL TRADING PARTNERS
(US $ million)*

Imports f.o.b.	1998	1999	2000
Australia	593.2	531.4	661.6
Belgium-Luxembourg	416.9	—	409.7
Brazil	202.9	202.9	294.4
China, People's Repub.	733.9	820.4	995.9
Finland	267.4	277.8	368.1
France (incl. Monaco)	1,068.3	955.2	1,138.0
Germany	3,589.5	3,533.4	3,523.8
Hong Kong	301.3	281.8	278.6
India	279.2	244.9	253.4
Iran	10.9	665.2	1,163.8
Ireland	342.3	369.4	339.2
Italy	996.6	892.9	894.0
Japan	1,954.3	1,873.3	2,131.2
Korea, Repub.	458.7	458.9	506.5
Malaysia	320.1	290.8	297.3
Netherlands	610.2	564.2	513.2
Saudi Arabia	27.6	986.6	2,020.5
Singapore	284.1	223.8	205.3
Spain	397.4	275.0	297.8
Sweden	431.8	353.3	417.2
Switzerland-Liechtenstein	630.8	622.2	652.3
Thailand	232.5	245.0	264.6
United Kingdom	2,427.7	2,286.8	2,251.0
USA	3,316.9	3,319.8	3,187.0
Zimbabwe	177.6	195.0	—
Total (incl. others)	26,624.1	24,092.5	26,606.7

Exports f.o.b.	1998	1999	2000
Australia	325.0	433.1	480.2
Belgium-Luxembourg	562.0	—	965.3
Canada	213.0	219.5	219.4
China, People's Repub.	160.6	271.1	335.2
France (incl. Monaco)	450.8	565.4	564.2
Germany	1,665.4	2,192.7	1,900.0
Hong Kong	270.6	383.2	326.4
Israel	217.5	490.2	511.8
Italy	633.2	710.6	838.3
Japan	1,486.2	1,841.5	1,354.6
Kenya	222.6	207.1	219.2
Korea, Repub.	271.4	702.6	594.4
Malawi	216.8	234.6	235.1
Mauritius	164.3	200.0	294.9
Mozambique	393.3	655.3	708.6
Netherlands	862.3	1,015.6	1,010.4
Spain	415.3	509.9	494.3
Switzerland-Liechtenstein	284.5	312.8	316.7
United Kingdom	1,530.0	2,531.2	2,288.0
USA	2,418.2	2,792.9	2,409.2
Zambia	369.5	392.3	645.5
Zimbabwe	877.0	838.6	683.9
Total (incl. others)	19,586.1	23,188.6	26,075.3

* Imports by country of origin; exports by country of destination.

Source: UN, *International Trade Statistics Yearbook*.

Transport

RAILWAYS
(traffic, year ending 31 March)*

	1997/98	1998/99	1999/2000
Passenger-km (million)	1,775	1,794	3,930
Net ton-km (million)	103,866	102,777	106,786

* Including Namibia.

Source: UN, *Statistical Yearbook*.

ROAD TRAFFIC
(registered motor vehicles)

	2002
Heavy load vehicles	326,798
Heavy passenger motor vehicles	164,369
Light load vehicles	1,875,234
Light passenger motor vehicles	4,135,037
Motorcycles	159,266
Special vehicles	296518
Other vehicles	17,955
Total (incl. others)	6,975,177

SHIPPING

Merchant Fleet
(vessels registered at 31 December)

	1999	2000	2001
Number of vessels	192	198	197
Displacement ('000 grt)	379.3	379.8	381.9

Source: Lloyd's Register-Fairplay, *World Fleet Statistics*.

International Sea-borne Freight Traffic
(metric tons)*

	1999	2000	2001
Goods loaded	125,984,474	133,727,037	136,137,592
Goods unloaded	21,685,792	25,980,142	23,326,603

* Excluding petroleum products.

Source: National Ports Authority of South Africa, Johannesburg.

CIVIL AVIATION
(traffic on scheduled services)

	1997	1998	1999
Kilometres flown (million)	69	75	84
Passengers carried ('000)	1,808	1,913	2,189
Passenger-km (million)	11,928	12,869	14,247
Total ton-km (million)	1,449	1,636	1,904

Source: UN, *Statistical Yearbook*.

Tourism

FOREIGN VISITOR ARRIVALS*

Country of origin	1999	2000	2001
Botswana	554,923	563,365	644,253
Germany	211,052	215,011	207,511
Lesotho	1,588,365	1,559,422	1,288,160
Mozambique	473,939	491,526	506,077
Namibia	201,685	206,022	203,667
Swaziland	785,062	742,621	751,538
United Kingdom	343,934	358,072	363,825
USA	173,533	181,632	176,412
Zimbabwe	494,530	477,380	501,698
Total (incl. others and unspecified)	6,026,086	6,000,538	5,908,024

* Figures include same-day visitors (excursionists), but exclude arrivals of South African nationals resident abroad. Border crossings by contract workers are also excluded.

Communications Media

	1999	2000	2001
Radio receivers ('000 in use) . .	10,555	11,655	11,696
Television receivers ('000 in use)	6,623	7,589	7,708
Telephones ('000 main lines in use)	5,492.8	4,961.7	4,969.0
Mobile cellular telephones ('000 subscribers). . . .	5,269	8,308	9,197
Internet users ('000)	1,820	2,400	3,068
Daily newspapers: number . . .	20	18	21
Daily newspapers: average circulation ('000)	1,343.8	1,254.3	1,233.4

Facsimile machines (number in use): 150,000 in 1997.

Book production: 5,418 titles in 1995.

Sources: partly UNESCO, *Statistical Yearbook*; UN, *Statistical Yearbook*; International Telecommunication Union.

Education

(2000)*

	Institutions	Teachers	Students
Primary	17,213	183,639	6,266,223
Secondary	5,790	114,996	3,559,295
Combined	3,975	50,601	1,662,521
Intermediate and middle . . .	782	11,487	367,050
ABET centres†	2,318	18,447	439,185
ELSEN centres‡	390	7,419	76,123
Colleges of education	72	2,623	32,696
Technical colleges	153	7,036	271,900
Universities§	21	n.a.	330,100
Technikons§	15	n.a.	190,120

* Figures for public and independent institutions.
† Adult basic education and training.
‡ Education for learners with special needs.
§ Figures refer to 1999.

Adult literacy rate (UNESCO estimates): 85.3% (males 86.0%; females 84.6%) in 2000 (Source: UN Development Programme, *Human Development Report*).

Directory

The Constitution

The Constitution was adopted by the Constitutional Assembly (comprising the National Assembly and the Senate) on 8 May 1996, and entered into force on 4 February 1997. Its main provisions are summarized below:

FOUNDING PROVISIONS

The Republic of South Africa is one sovereign democratic state founded on the following values: human dignity, the achievement of equality and advancement of human rights and freedoms; non-racialism and non-sexism; supremacy of the Constitution and the rule of law; universal adult suffrage, a national common voters' roll, regular elections, and a multi-party system of democratic government, to ensure accountability, responsiveness and openness. There is common South African citizenship, all citizens being equally entitled to the rights, privileges and benefits, and equally subject to the duties and responsibilities of citizenship.

BILL OF RIGHTS

Everyone is equal before the law and has the right to equal protection and benefit of the law. The state may not unfairly discriminate directly or indirectly against anyone on one or more grounds, including race, gender, sex, pregnancy, marital status, ethnic or social origin, colour, sexual orientation, age, disability, religion, conscience, belief, culture, language and birth. The rights that are enshrined include: protection against detention without trial, torture or any inhuman form of treatment or punishment; the right to privacy; freedom of conscience; freedom of expression; freedom of assembly; political freedom; freedom of movement and residence; the right to join or form a trade union or employers' organization; the right to a healthy and sustainable environment; the right to property, except in the case of the Government's programme of land reform and redistribution, and taking into account the claims of people who were dispossessed of property after 19 June 1913; the right to adequate housing; the right to health care, food and water and social security assistance, if needed; the rights of children; the right to education in the official language of one's choice, where this is reasonably practicable; the right to use the language and to participate in the cultural life of one's choice, but not in a manner inconsistent with any provision of this Bill of Rights; access to state information; access to the courts; the rights of people who have been arrested or detained; and the right to a fair trial.

CO-OPERATIVE GOVERNMENT

Government is constituted as national, provincial and local spheres of government, which are distinctive, interdependent and interrelated. All spheres of government and all organs of state within each sphere must preserve the peace, national unity and indivisibility of the Republic; secure the well-being of the people of the Republic; implement effective, transparent, accountable and coherent government for the Republic as a whole; respect the constitutional status, institutions, powers and functions of government in the other spheres; not assume any power or function except those conferred on them in terms of the Constitution.

PARLIAMENT

Legislative power is vested in a bicameral Parliament, comprising a National Assembly and a National Council of Provinces. The National Assembly has between 350 and 400 members and is elected, in general, by proportional representation. National and provincial legislatures are elected separately, under a 'double-ballot' electoral system. Each provincial legislature appoints six permanent delegates and nominates four special delegates to the 90-member National Council of Provinces, which is headed by a Chairperson, who is elected by the Council and has a five-year term of office. Parliamentary decisions are generally reached by a simple majority, although constitutional amendments require a majority of two-thirds.

THE NATIONAL EXECUTIVE

The Head of State is the President, who is elected by the National Assembly from among its members, and exercises executive power in consultation with the other members of the Cabinet. No person may hold office as President for more than two terms. Any party that holds a minimum of 80 seats in the National Assembly (equivalent to 20% of the national vote) is entitled to nominate an Executive Deputy President. If no party, or only one party, secures 80 or more seats, the party holding the largest number of seats and the party holding the second largest number of seats in the National Assembly are each entitled to designate one Executive Deputy President from among the members of the Assembly. The President may be removed by a motion of no-confidence or by impeachment. The Cabinet comprises a maximum of 27 ministers. Each party with a minimum of 20 seats in the National Assembly (equivalent to 5% of the national vote) is entitled to a proportional number of ministerial portfolios. The President allocates cabinet portfolios in consultation with party leaders, who are entitled to request the replacement of ministers. Cabinet decisions are reached by consensus.

JUDICIAL AUTHORITY

The judicial authority of the Republic is vested in the courts, which comprise the Constitutional Court; the Supreme Court of Appeal; the High Courts; the Magistrates' Courts; and any other court established or recognized by an Act of Parliament. (See Judicial System.)

PROVINCIAL GOVERNMENT

There are nine provinces: Eastern Cape, Free State (formerly Orange Free State), Gauteng (formerly Pretoria-Witwatersrand-Vereeniging), KwaZulu/Natal, Limpopo (formerly Northern Transvaal, subsequently Northern Province), Mpumalanga (formerly Eastern Transvaal), Northern Cape, North-West and Western Cape. Each province is entitled to determine its legislative and executive structure. Each province has a legislature, comprising between 30 and 80 members (depending on the size of the local electorate), who are elected by proportional representation. Each legislature is entitled to draft a constitution for the province, subject to the principles governing the national Constitution, and elects a Premier, who heads a Cabinet. Parties that hold a minimum of 10% of seats in the legislature are entitled to a proportional number of portfolios in the

Cabinet. Provincial legislatures are allowed primary responsibility for a number of areas of government, and joint powers with central government in the principal administrative areas.

LOCAL GOVERNMENT

The local sphere of government consists of municipalities, with executive and legislative authority vested in the Municipal Council. The objectives of local government are to provide democratic and accountable government for local communities; to ensure the provision of services to communities; to promote social and economic development, and a safe and healthy environment; and to encourage the involvement of communities and community organizations in the matters of local government. The National Assembly is to determine the different categories of municipality that may be established, and appropriate fiscal powers and functions for each category. Provincial Governments have the task of establishing municipalities, and of providing for the monitoring and support of local government in each province.

STATE INSTITUTIONS SUPPORTING CONSTITUTIONAL DEMOCRACY

The following state institutions are designed to strengthen constitutional democracy: the Public Protector (whose task is to investigate any conduct in state affairs, or in the public administration in any sphere of government, that is alleged or suspected to be improper); the Human Rights Commission; the Commission for the Protection and Promotion of the Rights of Cultural, Religious and Linguistic Communities; the Commission for Gender Equality; the Auditor-General; and the Electoral Commission.

TRADITIONAL LEADERS

The institution, status and role of traditional leadership, according to customary law, are recognized, subject to the Constitution. A traditional authority that observes a system of customary law may function subject to any applicable legislation and customs. National and provincial legislation may provide for the establishment of local or provincial houses of traditional leaders; the National Assembly may establish a national council of traditional leaders.

The Government

HEAD OF STATE

President: Thabo Mbeki (inaugurated 16 June 1999).
Deputy President: Jacob Zuma.

CABINET
(April 2003)

The Government comprises representatives of the African National Congress of South Africa (ANC), the Inkatha Freedom Party (IFP) and the South African Communist Party (SACP).

Minister of Agriculture and Land Affairs: Thoko Didiza (ANC).
Minister of Arts, Culture, Science and Technology: Ben Ngubane (IFP).
Minister of Communications: Ivy Matsepe-Casaburri (ANC).
Minister of Correctional Services: Ben Skosana (IFP).
Minister of Defence: Mosiuoa Lekota (ANC).
Minister of Education: Kader Asmal (ANC).
Minister of Environmental Affairs and Tourism: Mohammed Valli Moosa (ANC).
Minister of Finance: Trevor Manuel (ANC).
Minister of Foreign Affairs: Nkosazana Dlamini-Zuma (ANC).
Minister of Health: Manto Tshabalala-Msimang (ANC).
Minister of Home Affairs: Mangosuthu Buthelezi (IFP).
Minister of Housing: Brigitte Mabandla (ANC).
Minister of Intelligence: Lindiwe Nonceba Sisulu (ANC).
Minister of Justice and Constitutional Development: Penuell Maduna (ANC).
Minister of Labour: Membathisi Mdladlana (ANC).
Minister of Minerals and Energy: Phumzile Mlambo-Ngcuka (ANC).
Minister of Provincial and Local Government: Sydney Mufamadi (ANC).
Minister of Public Enterprises: Jeff Radebe (ANC).
Minister of Public Service and Administration: Geraldine Fraser-Moleketi (ANC).

Minister of Public Works: Stella Sigcau (ANC).
Minister of Safety and Security: Charles Nqakula (SACP).
Minister of Social Development: Zola Skweyiya (ANC).
Minister of Sport and Recreation: Ngconde Balfour (ANC).
Minister of Trade and Industry: Alec Erwin (ANC).
Minister of Transport: Dullah Omar (ANC).
Minister of Water Affairs and Forestry: Ronnie Kasrils (ANC).
Minister at the Presidency: Essop Pahad (ANC).

MINISTRIES

The Presidency: Union Bldgs, West Wing, Government Ave, Pretoria 0001; Private Bag X1000, Pretoria 0001; tel. (12) 3005200; fax (12) 3238246; e-mail president@po.gov.za; internet www.gov.za/president/index.html.

Ministry of Agriculture and Land Affairs: Agriculture Bldg, Block Da, Ground Floor, Room 10, cnr Beatrix St and Soutpansberg Rd, Pretoria 0002; Private Bag X250, Pretoria 0001; tel. (12) 3196000; fax (12) 3253618; e-mail sanitag@nda.agric.za; internet www.nda.agric.za.

Ministry of Arts, Culture, Science and Technology: Oranje Nassau Bldg, 188 Schoeman St, Pretoria 0002; Private Bag X894, Pretoria 0001; tel. (12) 3378000; fax (12) 3232720; e-mail frans@dacsts.pwv.gov.za; internet www.dacst.gov.za.

Ministry of Communications: Nkululeko House, Iparioli Office Park, 399 Duncan St, 0083 Hatfield, Pretoria; Private Bag X860, Pretoria 0001; tel. (12) 4278000; fax (12) 4278026; e-mail nowjoan@doc.org.za; internet www.doc.gov.za/index.html.

Ministry of Correctional Services: Poyntons Bldg, West Block, cnr Church and Schubart Sts, Pretoria 0002; Private Bag X853, Pretoria 0001; tel. (12) 3072000; fax (12) 3286149; internet www.dcs.gov.za.

Ministry of Defence: Armscor Bldg, Block 5, Nossob St, Erasmusrand 0181; Private Bag X910, Pretoria 0001; tel. (12) 3556000; fax (12) 3470118; e-mail webmaster@mil.za; internet www.mil.za.

Ministry of Education: Sol Plaatje House, 123 Schoeman St, Pretoria 0002; Private Bag X895, Pretoria 0001; tel. (12) 3125911; fax (12) 3216770; e-mail webmaster@educ.pwv.gov.za; internet www.education.pwv.gov.za.

Ministry of Environmental Affairs and Tourism: Fedsure Forum Bldg, North Tower, cnr Van der Walt and Pretorius Sts, Private Bag X447, Pretoria 0001; tel. (12) 3103911; fax (12) 3222682; e-mail vmoosa@ozone.pwv.gov.za; internet www.environment.gov.za.

Ministry of Foreign Affairs: Union Bldgs, East Wing, Government Ave, Pretoria 0002; Private Bag X152, Pretoria 0001; tel. (12) 3511000; fax (12) 3510257; internet www.dfa.gov.za.

Ministry of Health: 2027 Civitas Bldg, cnr Andries and Struben Sts, Pretoria 0002; Private Bag X828, Pretoria 0001; tel. (12) 3120000; fax (12) 3255706; e-mail mnwbd@hltrsa2.pwv.gov.za; internet www.health.gov.za.

Ministry of Home Affairs: 1005 Civitas Bldg, cnr Andries and Struben Sts, Pretoria 0002; Private Bag X741, Pretoria 0001; tel. (12) 3268081; fax (12) 3216491; e-mail dha@dbs1.pwv.gov.za; internet www.home-affairs.gov.za.

Ministry of Housing: 240 Walker St, Sunnyside, Pretoria 0002; Private Bag X644, Pretoria 0001; tel. (12) 4211311; fax (12) 3412998; internet www.housing.gov.za.

Ministry of Intelligence: Embassy House, Third Floor, cnr Edmund St and Bailey Crescent, Arcadia, Pretoria 0083; POB 56450, Arcadia 0007; tel. (12) 3236738; fax (12) 3230718.

Ministry of Justice and Constitutional Development: Presidia Bldg, 8th Floor, cnr Pretorius and Paul Kruger Sts, Pretoria 0002; Private Bag X81, Pretoria 0001; tel. (12) 3151111; fax (12) 3231846; internet www.doj.gov.za.

Ministry of Labour: Laboria House, Schoeman St, Pretoria 0002; Private Bag X117, Pretoria 0001; tel. (12) 3094000; fax (12) 3201942; internet www.labour.gov.za.

Ministry of Minerals and Energy: Mineralia Centre, cnr Andries and Visagie Sts, Pretoria 0002; Private Bag X59, Pretoria 0001; tel. (12) 3179000; fax (12) 3223416; e-mail estha@mepar.pwv.gov.za; internet www.dme.gov.za.

Ministry of Provincial and Local Government: cnr Hamilton and Proes Sts, Arcadia, Pretoria 0083; Private Bag X804, Pretoria 0001; tel. (12) 3340600; fax (12) 3340603; e-mail editor@dso.pwv.gov.za; internet www.dplg.gov.za.

Ministry of Public Enterprises: Infotech Bldg Suite 401, 1090 Arcadia St, Hatfield, Pretoria 0083; Private Bag X15, Hatfield 0028;

tel. (12) 4311000; fax (12) 3427224; e-mail info@dpe.gov.za; internet www.dpe.gov.za.

Ministry of Public Service and Administration: Transvaal House, cnr Vermeulen and van der Walts Sts, Pretoria 0002; Private Bag X916, Pretoria 0001; tel. (12) 3147911; fax (12) 3232386; e-mail info@dpsa.pwv.gov.za; internet www.dpsa.gov.za.

Ministry of Public Works: Central Government Bldg, cnr Bosman and Vermeulen Sts, Pretoria 0002; Private Bag X65, Pretoria 0001; tel. (12) 3372000; fax (12) 3252856; e-mail imochaliban@pwdmail .pwv.gov.za; internet www.publicworks.gov.za.

Ministry of Safety and Security: Van Erkom Bldg, 7th Floor, 217 Pretorius St, Pretoria 0002; Private Bag X922, Pretoria 0001; tel. (12) 33925500; fax (12) 3392536; internet www.gcis.gov.za/sss.

Ministry of Social Development: HSRC Bldg, North Wing, Pretorius St, Pretoria 0002; Private Bag X9153, Pretoria 0001; tel. (12) 3127696; fax (12) 3257071; e-mail welso57@welspta.pwv.gov.sa; internet www.welfare.gov.za.

Ministry of Sport and Recreation: Oranje Nassau Bldg, 3rd Floor, 188 Schoeman St, Pretoria; Private Bag X896, Pretoria 0001; tel. (12) 3343100; fax (12) 3216187; e-mail sandra@sport1.pwv.gov .za; internet www.dsr.gov.za.

Ministry of Trade and Industry: House of Trade and Industry, 11th Floor, cnr Prinsloo and Pretorius Sts, Pretoria 0002; Private Bag X84, Pretoria 0001; tel. (12) 3109791; fax (12) 3222701; e-mail alec@dti.pwv.gov.za; internet www.dti.gov.za.

Ministry of Transport: Forum Bldg, cnr Struben and Bosman Sts, Pretoria 0002; Private Bag X193, Pretoria 0001; tel. (12) 3093000; fax (12) 3285271; e-mail mabasam@ndot.pwv.gov.za; internet www .transport.gov.za.

Ministry of Water Affairs and Forestry: Sidibeng Bldg, 185 Schoeman St, Pretoria 0002; Private Bag X313, Pretoria 0001; tel. (12) 3367500; fax (12) 3262715; e-mail zan@dwaf-par.wcape.gov.za; internet www.dwaf.pwv.gov.za.

National Treasury: 40 Church Sq., Private Bag X115, Pretoria 0001; tel. (12) 315 5111; fax (12) 315 5234; internet www.treasury .gov.za.

Legislature

PARLIAMENT

National Council of Provinces

Chairman: MOSIUOA LEKOTA.

The National Council of Provinces (NCOP), which replaced the Senate under the new Constitution, was inaugurated on 6 February 1997. The NCOP comprises 90 members, with six permanent delegates and four special delegates from each of the nine provinces.

National Assembly

Speaker: Dr FRENE NOSHIR GINWALA.

General Election, 2 June 1999

Party	Votes	% of votes	Seats
African National Congress	10,600,838	66.36	266
Democratic Party	1,526,244	9.55	38
Inkatha Freedom Party	1,371,436	8.58	34
New National Party	1,097,998	6.87	28
United Democratic Movement	546,705	3.42	14
African Christian Democratic Party	228,908	1.43	6
Freedom Front	127,188	0.80	3
United Christian Democratic Party	125,273	0.78	3
Pan-Africanist Congress of Azania	113,114	0.71	3
Federal Alliance	86,672	0.54	2
Minority Front	48,276	0.30	1
Afrikaner Eenheidsbeweging	46,286	0.29	1
Azanian People's Organization	27,255	0.17	1
Abolition of Income Tax and Usury Party	10,611	0.07	—
Government by the People Green Party	9,188	0.06	—
Socialist Party of Azania	9,060	0.06	—
Total	**15,975,052**	**100.00**	**400**

Provincial Governments

(April 2003)

EASTERN CAPE

Premier: Rev. MAKENKHESI STOFILE (ANC).
Speaker of the Legislature: MKHANGELI MATOMELA (ANC).

FREE STATE

Premier: ISABELLA WINKIE DIREKO (ANC).
Speaker of the Legislature: JANI MOHAPI (ANC).

GAUTENG

Premier: MBHAZIMA SHILOWA (ANC).
Speaker of the Legislature: FIROZ CACHALIA (ANC).

KWAZULU/NATAL

Premier: LIONEL MTSHALI (IFP).
Speaker of the Legislature: Chief BONGA MDLETSHE (IFP).

LIMPOPO

Premier: NGOAKO RAMATHLODI (ANC).
Speaker of the Legislature: ROBERT MALAVI (ANC).

MPUMALANGA

Premier: NDAWENI MAHLANGU (ANC).
Speaker of the Legislature: S. W. LUBISI (ANC).

NORTHERN CAPE

Premier: MANNE DIPICO (ANC).
Speaker of the Legislature: ETHNE PAPENFUS (DP).

NORTH-WEST

Premier: POPO MOLEFE (ANC).
Speaker of the Legislature: JOHANNES SELAPEDI (ANC).

WESTERN CAPE

Premier: MARTHINUS VAN SCHALKWYK (NNP).
Speaker of the Legislature: WILLEM DOMAN (NNP).

Political Organizations

African Christian Democratic Party (ACDP): Alberton; tel. (11) 8693941; fax (11) 8693942; e-mail acdpwebmaster@mweb.co.za; internet www.acdp.org.za; f. 1993; Leader Rev. KENNETH MESHOE.

African National Congress of South Africa (ANC): 54 Sauer St, Johannesburg 2001; POB 61884, Marshalltown 2107; tel. (11) 3761000; fax (11) 3761134; e-mail info@anc.org.za; internet www .anc.org.za; f. 1912; in alliance with the South African Communist Party (SACP) and the Congress of South African Trade Unions (COSATU); governing party since April 1994; Pres. THABO MBEKI; Deputy Pres. JACOB ZUMA; Sec.-Gen. KGALEMA MOTLANTHE.

Afrikaner Eenheidsbeweging (AEB) (Unity Movement): Pretoria; right-wing movement; Leader CASPERUS AUCAMP.

Afrikaner Weerstandsbeweging (AWB) (Afrikaner Resistance Movement): POB 274, Ventersdorp 2710; tel. (18) 2642005; fax (18) 2642032; e-mail awb@awb.co.za; internet www.awb.co.za; f. 1973; extreme right-wing paramilitary group; Leader EUGENE TERRE' BLANCHE; Sec.-Gen. PIET 'SKIET' RUDOLPH.

Azanian People's Organization (AZAPO): Kopanong Centre 3, cnr Luthuli and Main Rds, Dobsonville; POB 4230, Johannesburg 2000; tel. (11) 9881255; fax (11) 9883925; e-mail azapo@sn.apc.za; internet www.azapo.org.za; f. 1978 to seek the establishment of a unitary, democratic, socialist republic; excludes white mems; Pres. MOSIBUDI MANGENA; Nat. Chair. NKOSI MOLALA; Sec.-Gen. JAIRUS KGOKONG.

Blanke Bevrydingsbeweging (BBB) (White Protection Movement): f. 1987; extreme right-wing activist group; Leader Prof. JOHAN SCHABORT.

Boerestaat Party (Boer State Party): POB 3456, Randburg 2125; tel. and fax (11) 7081988; f. 1988; seeks the reinstatement of the Boer Republics in a consolidated Boerestaat; Leader COEN VERMAAK.

Cape Democrats: f. 1988; white support; liberal.

Conservative Party of South Africa (CPSA): 203 Soutpansberg Rd, Rietondale, Pretoria; Private Bag X847, Pretoria 0001; tel. (12) 3291220; fax (12) 3291229; e-mail info@kpvansa.co.za; internet www .kpvansa.co.za; f. 1982 by fmr mems of the National Party; seeks the establishment of a separate Afrikaner state as part of a South African confed. Leader Dr FERDINAND HARTZENBERG; Dep. Leader Dr WILLIE SNYMAN.

Democratic Alliance (DA): POB 1475, Cape Town 8000; e-mail headoffice@da.org.za; internet www.da.org.za; f. 2000 by opposition parties, including the Democratic Party and the Federal Alliance, to contest that year's municipal elections; Leader ANTHONY (TONY) LEON; Chair. JOE SEREMANE.

Democratic Party (DP): 123 Louis Botha Ave, Fellside, Johannesburg; POB 46400, Orange Grove 2119; tel. (11) 4832743; fax (21) 4615276; e-mail democrat@dp.org.za; internet www.dp.org.za; f. 1989 by merger; mem. of DA; supports the implementation of a democratic, multiracial society by peaceful means; Leader ANTHONY (TONY) LEON; Exec. Dir GREG KRUMBOCK.

Democratic Reform Party (DRP): f. 1988; Coloured support; Leader CARTER EBRAHIM.

Democratic Workers' Party (DWP): Cape Town; f. 1984 by breakaway faction of the People's Congress Party; mainly Coloured support; Leader DENNIS DE LA CRUZ.

Federal Alliance: POB 767, Saxonwold 2132, Johannesburg; tel. (11) 4824691; fax (11) 4822180; e-mail media@federalalliance.org .za; internet www.federalalliance.org.za; f. Sept. 1998 by fmr Pres. of the South African Rugby Football Union; mem. of DA; Pres. LOUIS LUYT.

Federal Independent Democratic Alliance (FIDA): POB 10528, Johannesburg 2000; tel. (11) 4034268; fax (11) 4031557; f. 1987; black support; centrist; Leader JOHN GOGOTYA.

Freedom Front (FF/VF): Agri SA Bldg, cnr Schoeman and Andries Sts, Pretoria; POB 74693, Lynnwood Ridge 0040; tel. (12) 3227141; fax (12) 3227144; e-mail info@vf.co.za; internet www.vf.co.za; f. 1994 as a right-wing electoral alliance; included some mems of the CPSA; Leader Dr P. W. A. MULDER; Chief Sec. PIET UYS.

Freedom Party: Coloured support; Leader ARTHUR BOOYSEN.

Herstigte Nasionale Party (HNP) (Reconstituted National Party): 1043 Pretorius St, Hatfield, POB 1888, Pretoria 0001; tel. (12) 3423410; fax (12) 3423417; e-mail info@hnp.org.za; internet www.hnp.org.za; f. 1969 by fmr mems of the National Party; advocates 'Christian Nationalism'; Leader WILLEM MARAIS; Gen. Sec. L. J. VAN DER SCHYFF.

Inkatha Freedom Party (IFP): Albany House North, 4th Floor, Albany Grove, POB 4432, Durban 4000; tel. (31) 3074962; fax (31) 3074964; internet www.ifp.org.za; f. as Inkatha Movement, a liberation movement with mainly Zulu support; reorg. in 1990 as a multiracial political party; represented in Govt; Leader Chief MANGOSUTHU GATSHA BUTHELEZI; Nat. Chair. L. P. H. M. MTSHALI; Sec.-Gen. ZAKHELE KHUMALO.

Justice and Freedom Alliance (JAFA): ME Store Bldg, 4th Floor, 155 Smit St; Private Bag X49, Johannesburg; tel. (11) 3397129; fax (11) 3396982; f. 1997; CEO BARRY NILSSON; Sec.-Gen. A. DLOMO.

Minority Front: Durban; Indian support; formed political alliance with ANC in June 1999; Leader AMICHAND RAJBANSI.

National People's Party: Private Bag X54330, Durban 4000; Indian support; Leader AMICHAND RAJBANSI.

New Freedom Party of Southern Africa: 15 Eendrag St, Bellville 7530; Coloured support.

New National Party (NNP): POB 1698, Cape Town 8000; tel. (21) 4615833; fax (21) 4615329; e-mail info@natweb.co.za; internet www .natweb.co.za; f. 1912 as National Party; ruling party 1948–94; opened membership to all racial groups in 1990; represented in interim Govt of Nat. Unity, following 1994 elections, withdrew in June 1996 to form the official opposition; adopted present name in 1999; joined the DA in 2000; withdrew from the DA in late 2001; Leader MARTHINUS VAN SCHALKWYK; Sec.-Gen DARYL SWANEPOEL.

New Solidarity: POB 48687, Qualbert 4078; tel. (11) 3055692; fax 3011077; f. 1989; Indian support; Leader Dr J. N. REDDY.

Die Oranjewerkers: POB 74550, Lynwoodrif 0040; tel. and fax (12) 3485607; seeks to establish several small, self-governing white states; Leader HENDRIK FRENSCH VERWOERD.

Pan-Africanist Congress of Azania (PAC): SAAU/SALU Bldg, 15th Floor, 316 Andries St, Pretoria 0001; POB 13412, The Tramshed 0126; tel. (12) 3206243; fax (12) 3201509; e-mail azania@ pac.org.za; internet www.paca.org.za; f. 1959; Pres. Rev. STANLEY MOGOBA; Sec.-Gen. THAMI PLAATJIE.

Progressive Independent Party (PIP): Indian support; Leader FAIZ KHAN.

South African Communist Party (SACP): Cosatu House, 3rd Floor, 1 Leyds St, Braamfontein; POB 1027, Johannesburg 2000; tel. (11) 3393633; fax (11) 3396880; e-mail info@sacp.org.za; internet www.sacp.org.za; f. 1921; reorg. 1953; supports ANC; Chair. CHARLES NQAKULA; Gen. Sec. BLADE NZIMANDE.

Transvaal Indian Congress: f. 1902; reactivated 1983; Pres. Dr ESSOP JASSAT.

United Christian Democratic Party: Johannesburg; f. 1986; multiracial; Pres. LUCAS MANGOPE.

United Democratic Movement: Tomkor Bldg, 2nd Floor, cnr Vermeulen and Du Toit Sts, Pretoria; POB 26290, Arcadia 0007; tel. (12) 3210010; fax (12) 3210014; e-mail info@udm.org.za; internet www.udm.org.za; f. 1997; multiracial support; demands effective measures for enforcement of law and order; Pres. BANTU HOLOMISA; Deputy Pres. GERHARD KOORNHOF.

United Democratic Reform Party: POB 14048, Reigerpark 1466; f. 1987 by merger; mainly Coloured and Indian support; Leader JAKOBUS (JAC) ALBERT RABIE; Nat. Chair. NASH PARMANAND.

Workers' Organization for Socialist Action (WOSA): Cape Town; e-mail 155VAS@mentor.edcm.wits.ac.za; f. 1990; Chair. Dr NEVILLE ALEXANDER; Gen. Sec. C. BRECHER.

Other political parties that contested the 1999 elections included the Abolition of Income Tax and Usury Party, the Government by the People Green Party and the Socialist Party of Azania.

Diplomatic Representation

EMBASSIES AND HIGH COMMISSIONS IN SOUTH AFRICA

Algeria: 950 Arcadia St, POB 57480, Hatfield, Pretoria 0083; tel. (12) 3425074; fax (12) 3426479; Ambassador SAÏD KITOUNI.

Angola: 1030 Schoeman St, POB 8685, Hatfield, Pretoria 0001; tel. (12) 3420049; fax (12) 3427039; Ambassador M. A. DUARTE RODRIGUES.

Argentina: 200 Standard Plaza, 440 Hilda St, POB 11125, Hatfield, Pretoria 0083; tel. (12) 433527; fax (12) 433521; Ambassador PEDRO R. HERRERA.

Australia: 292 Orient St, Arcadia, Pretoria 0083; Private Bag X150, Pretoria 0001; tel. (12) 3423740; fax (12) 3428442; e-mail ian .wilcock@dfat.gov.au; internet www.australia.co.za; High Commissioner IAN WILCOCK.

Austria: 1109 Duncan St, Brooklyn 0181; POB 95572, Waterkloof 0145; tel. (12) 4529155; fax (12) 4601151; e-mail pretoria-ob@bmaa .gv.za; Ambassador Dr KURT SPALLINGER.

Bangladesh: 410 Farenden St, Sunnyside, Pretoria 0002; tel. (12) 3432105; fax (12) 3435222; e-mail bangladoot@global.co.za; High Commissioner A. T. KARIM.

Belgium: 625 Leyds St, Muckleneuk, Pretoria 0002; tel. (12) 4403201; fax (12) 4403216; Ambassador L. TEIRLINCK.

Benin: 900 Park St, cnr Orient St, Arcadia 0083, Pretoria 26484; tel. (12) 3426978; fax (12) 3421823; e-mail embbenin@yebo.cp.za; Ambassador JEAN-PIERRE ADÉLUI EDON.

Botswana: 24 Amos St, Colbyn, POB 57035, Arcadia 0007; tel. (12) 3424761; fax (12) 3421845; High Commissioner O. J. TEBAPE.

Brazil: 201 Leyds St, Arcadia 0083; POB 3269, Pretoria 0009; tel. (12) 3411712; fax (12) 3417547; e-mail braspret@cis.co.za; internet www.brazil.co.za; Ambassador JÓRIO SALGADO GAMA.

Bulgaria: 1071 Church St, Hatfield 0083; POB 26296, Arcadia 0007; tel. (12) 3423720; fax (12) 3423721; Ambassador PETKO DRAGANOV.

Burundi: 1090 Arcadia St, POB 12914, Hatfield, Pretoria 0083; tel. (12) 3424881; fax (12) 3424885; e-mail ambabusa@mweb.co.za; Ambassador G. MAGETE.

Canada: 1103 Arcadia St, cnr Hilda St, Hatfield, Pretoria 0028; tel. (12) 4223000; fax (12) 4223052; e-mail lizette.vanniekerk@ dfait-maeci.gc.ca; internet www.dfait-maeci.gc.ca/southafrica/ menu-en.asp; High Commissioner LUCIE EDWARDS.

Chile: Campus Centre 1102, 5th Floor, Burnett St, Hatfield 0083; POB 12672, Pretoria 0028; tel. (12) 3421511; fax (12) 3421658; e-mail chile@iafrica.com; Ambassador BORIS HERRERA.

China, People's Republic: 972 Pretorius St, Arcadia 0083, Pretoria; tel. (12) 3424194; fax (12) 3424244; e-mail info@ chinese-embassy.co.za; internet www.chinese-embassy.co.za; Ambassador LIN GUIJIN.

Colombia: First National Bank Bldg, 3rd Floor, 1105 Park St, Pretoria 0083; tel. (12) 3420211; fax (12) 3420216; e-mail emcolsf@ mweb.co.za; Ambassador Fred Erik Jacobsen.

Congo, Democratic Republic: 791 Schoeman St, POB 28795, Sunnyside 0132, Arcadia 0083; tel. (12) 3441478; fax (12) 3441510; Ambassador Emmanuel Dungia.

Congo, Republic: 960 Arcadia St, Arcadia, Pretoria; POB 40427, Arcadia 0007; tel. (12) 3425508; fax (12) 3425510; Ambassador Anatole Kondho.

Côte d'Ivoire: 795 Government Ave, POB 13510, Hatfield, Arcadia 0083; tel. (12) 3426913; fax (12) 3426713; Ambassador K. Ballou.

Croatia: 1160 Church St, Colbyn, Pretoria 0083; POB 11335, Hatfield 0028; tel. (12) 3421206; fax (12) 3421819; e-mail vrhjar@iafrica .com; Ambassador Matko Zupanić.

Cuba: 45 Mackenzie St, Brooklyn 0181; POB 11605, Hatfield 0028; tel. (12) 3462215; fax (12) 3462216; e-mail sudafri@iafrica.com; Ambassador Marcos Rodríguez.

Czech Republic: 936 Pretorius St, Arcadia 0083; POB 3326, Pretoria 0001; tel. (12) 433601; fax (12) 432033; e-mail pretoria@ embassy.mzv.cz; internet www.icon.co.za; Ambassador Jaroslav Siro.

Denmark: iParioli Office Park, Block B2, Ground Floor, 1166 Park Street, POB 11439, Hatfield, Pretoria 0028; tel. (12) 4309340; fax (12) 3427620; e-mail pryamb@um.dk; internet www.denmark.co.za; Ambassador Torben Brylle.

Egypt: 270 Bourke St, Muckleneuk 0002; POB 30025, Sunnyside 0132; tel. (12) 3431590; fax (12) 3431082; Ambassador Naéla Gabr.

Eritrea: 1281 Cobham Rd, POB 11371, Queenswood 0121; tel. (12) 3331302; fax (12) 3332330; Chargé d'affaires a.i. Tekeste G. Zemuy.

Estonia: 16 Hofmeyer St, Cape Town 7530; tel. (21) 9133850.

Ethiopia: 47 Charles St, Bailey's Muckleneuk, Brooklyn 0181; POB 11469, Hatfield 0028; tel. (12) 3463542; fax (12) 3463687; Ambassador Aman Hassen.

Finland: 628 Leyds St, Muckleneuk, Pretoria 0002; POB 443, Pretoria 0001; tel. (12) 3430275; fax (12) 3433095; e-mail sanomat .pre@forming.fi; Ambassador Kirsti Lintonen.

France: 807 George Ave, Arcadia 0083; tel. (12) 4297000; fax (12) 4297029; e-mail france@ambafrance-za.org; internet www .ambafrance-za.org; Ambassador Jean Cadet.

Gabon: Southern Life Plaza, cnr Festival and Schoeman Sts, POB 9222, Hatfield, Pretoria 0083; tel. (12) 3424376; fax (12) 3424375; Ambassador J. Ehoumba.

Germany: 180 Blackwood St, Arcadia 0083; POB 2023, Pretoria 0001; tel. (12) 4278900; fax (12) 3439401; e-mail germanembassy .pretoria@gonet.co.za; Ambassador Anna-Margareta Peters.

Ghana: 1038 Arcadia St, POB 12537, Hatfield, Pretoria; tel. (12) 3425847; fax (12) 3425863; e-mail ghcom27@icon.co.za; High Commissioner Ellen S. Nee-Whang.

Greece: 1003 Church St, Arcadia, Pretoria 0083; tel. (12) 437351; fax (12) 434313; Ambassador I. Theophanopoulos.

Guinea: 336 Orient St, POB 13523, Arcadia, Pretoria 0083; tel. (12) 3428465; fax (12) 3428467; Ambassador Dr O. Sylla.

Holy See: 800 Pretorius St, Arcadia, Pretoria 0083; tel. (12) 3443815; fax (12) 3443595; e-mail nunziosa@iafrica.com; Apostolic Nuncio Most Rev. Blasco Francisco Collaço.

Hungary: 959 Arcadia St, Hatfield, Pretoria 0083; POB 27077, Sunnyside 0132; tel. (12) 433030; fax (12) 433029; e-mail hunem@cis .co.za; Ambassador Dr László Pordány.

India: 852 Schoeman St, Arcadia 0083; POB 40216, Arcadia 0007; tel. (12) 3425392; fax (12) 3425310; e-mail hcipta@iafrica.com; High Commissioner Harsh K. Bhasin.

Indonesia: 949 Schoeman St, Arcadia 0083; POB 13155, Hatfield 0028; tel. (12) 3423350; fax (12) 3423369; e-mail indonemb@lantic.co .za; Ambassador R. Iskandar.

Iran: 1002 Schoeman St, Hatfield 0083; POB 12546, Hatfield 0028; tel. (12) 3425880; fax (12) 3421878; e-mail Office@Iranembassy-sa .org.za; Ambassador Javid Ghorbanoghli.

Ireland: Southern Life Plaza, 1st Floor, 1059 Schoeman St, POB 4174, Arcadia, Pretoria 0001; tel. (12) 3425062; fax (12) 3424752; e-mail pretoria@iveagh.irlgov.ie; internet www.embassyireland.org .za; Ambassador Gerard Corr.

Israel: 3rd Floor, 339 Hilda St, Hatfield, Pretoria 0083; POB 3726, Pretoria 0001; tel. (12) 3422693; fax (12) 3421442; e-mail embofisr@ iafrica.com; Ambassador U. Oren.

Italy: 796 George Ave, Arcadia, Pretoria 0083; tel. (12) 435541; fax (12) 435547; e-mail ambpret@iafrica.com; Ambassador Renato Volpini.

Japan: Sanlam Bldg, 2nd Floor, 353 Festival St, Hatfield 0083; POB 11434, Hatfield 0028; tel. (12) 3422100; fax (12) 433922; Ambassador A. Hatakenaka.

Jordan: 209 Festival St, Hatfield 0083; POB 55755, Arcadia 0007; tel. (12) 3428026; fax (12) 3427847; e-mail embjord@embjord.co.za; internet www.embjord.co.za; Ambassador S. Bak.

Kenya: 302 Brooks St, Menlo Park 0081; POB 35954, Menlo Park 0102; tel. (12) 3622249; fax (12) 3622252; e-mail kenrep@mweb.co .za; High Commissioner Prof. Ciarunji Chesaina.

Korea, Democratic People's Republic: Ambassador Pak Kun Gwang.

Korea, Republic: Greenpark Estates, Block 3, 27 George Storrar Dr., Groenkloof 0181; POB 939, Groenkloof 0027; tel. (12) 462508; fax (12) 461158; Ambassador Y. S. Kim.

Kuwait: 890 Arcadia St, Pretoria 0001; Private Bag X920, Arcadia 0083; tel. (12) 3420877; fax (12) 3420876; e-mail safarku@global.co .za; Ambassador Dhari al-Ajran.

Lebanon: 7 Sixteenth Ave, POB 2150, Lower Houghton, Johannesburg 2198; tel. (11) 4831106; fax (11) 4831810; Chargé d'affaires a.i. Charbel Stephan.

Lesotho: West Tower Momentum Centre, 6th Floor, 343 Pretorius St, POB 55817, Pretoria 0002; tel. (12) 3226090; fax (12) 3220376; High Commissioner L. R. Mokose.

Libya: 900 Church St, Arcadia, POB 40388, Pretoria 0083; tel. (12) 3423902; fax (12) 3423904; Ambassador Dr. A. A. al-Zubedi.

Malawi: 770 Government Ave, Arcadia, Pretoria 0083; POB 11172, Hatfield 0028; tel. and fax (12) 3420146; e-mail mhc@easun.co.za; High Commissioner J. J. Chikago.

Malaysia: 1007 Schoeman St, Arcadia, Pretoria 0083; POB 11673, Hatfield 0028; tel. (12) 3425990; fax (12) 437773; High Commissioner A. K. B. M. Deen.

Mali: 876 Pretorius St, Block B, Arcadia 0083; tel. (12) 3427464; fax (12) 3420670; e-mail malipta@iafrica.com; Ambassador L. M. J. Bastide.

Mauritius: 1163 Pretorius St, Hatfield, Pretoria 0083; tel. (12) 3421283; fax (12) 3421286; e-mail mhcpta@mweb.co.za; High Commissioner John Harold Dacruz.

Mexico: 1 Hatfield Sq., 3rd Floor, 1101 Burnett St, POB 9077, Hatfield, Pretoria 0083; tel. (12) 3622822; fax (12) 3621380; e-mail embamexza@mweb.co.za; Ambassador Ignacio Villaseñor.

Morocco: 799 Schoeman St, POB 12382, Arcadia, Pretoria 0083; tel. (12) 3430230; fax (12) 3430613; Ambassador Saïd Benryane.

Mozambique: 529 Edmond St, Arcadia, Pretoria 0083; POB 57465, Pretoria 0001; tel. (12) 4010300; fax (12) 3266388; e-mail highcommin@iafrica.com; High Commissioner Lt-Gen. (retd) Armando Alexandre Panguene.

Myanmar: 23 Amos St, Colbyn, Pretoria 0083; tel. (12) 3420706; fax (12) 3422039; e-mail euompta@global.co.za; Ambassador U Hla Myint Oo.

Namibia: 702 Church St, Pretoria 0083; tel. (12) 3445992; fax (12) 3445998; High Commissioner S. N. Kaukungua.

Netherlands: 825 Arcadia St, Pretoria; POB 117, Pretoria 0001; tel. (12) 3443910; fax (12) 3439950; e-mail nlgovpre@mweb.co.za; internet www.dutchembassy.co.za; Ambassador Laetitia van den Assum.

New Zealand: Block C, Hatfield Gardens, 1110 Arcadia St, Hatfield, Pretoria 0083; Private Bag X17, Hatfield 0028; tel. (12) 3428656; fax (12) 3428640; e-mail nzhc@global.co.za; High Commissioner Warren Searell.

Nigeria: 971 Schoeman St, Arcadia, Pretoria 0083; tel. (12) 3420805; fax (12) 3420718; e-mail nhcp@iafrica.com; High Commissioner Dr T. Olagunju.

Norway: iParioli Bldg, A2, 1166 Park St, Hatfield 0083; POB 9843, Pretoria 0001; tel. (12) 3426100; fax (12) 3426099; e-mail embpta@ noramb.co.za; Ambassador Jon D. Bech.

Pakistan: 97 Charles St, Brooklyn, Pretoria 0181; tel. (12) 3464605; fax (12) 467824; e-mail pakistan@icon.co.za; High Commissioner Shafkat Saeed.

Paraguay: 189 Strelitzia Rd, POB 95774, Waterkloof Heights, Pretoria 0181; tel. (12) 3471047; fax (12) 3470403; Ambassador: Chargé d'affaires a.i. Víctor Aquino Fornera.

Peru: Infotech Bldg, Suite 202, 1090 Arcadia St, Hatfield, Pretoria 0083; tel. (12) 3422390; fax (12) 3424944; e-mail emperu@iafrica .com; Ambassador Juan José Meier.

Philippines: 54 Nicolson St, Muckleneuk 0181, Pretoria 0083; tel. (12) 3460451; fax (12) 3460454; e-mail pretoriape@mweb.co.za;

internet mzone.mweb.co.za/residents/philemb/index.html; Ambassador ALADIN G. VILLACORTE.

Poland: 14 Amos St, Colbyn, Pretoria 0083; tel. (12) 4302631; fax (12) 4302608; e-mail amb.pol@pixie.co.za; Ambassador KRZYSZTOF ŚLIWIŃSKI.

Portugal: 599 Leyds St, Muckleneuk, Pretoria 0002; POB 27102, Sunnyside 0132; tel. (12) 3412340; fax (12) 3413975; e-mail portemb@satin.co.za; Ambassador FERNANDES PEREIRA.

Romania: 117 Charles St, Brooklyn 0181; POB 11295, Pretoria 0011; tel. (12) 4606941; fax (12) 4606947; e-mail romembsa@global .co.za; Ambassador RADU GABRIEL MATEESCU.

Russia: Butano Bldg, 316 Brooks St, Menlo Park 0081; POB 6743, Pretoria 0001; tel. (12) 3621337; fax (12) 3620116; e-mail ruspospr@ mweb.co.za; internet www.russianembassy.org.za; Ambassador ANDREI KUSHAKOV.

Rwanda: 35 Marais St, Brooklyn, POB 55224, Pretoria 0181; tel. (12) 460709; fax (12) 460708; Ambassador Dr B. KARENZI.

Saudi Arabia: 711 Duncan St, Pretoria 0083; POB 13930, Hatfield 0028; tel. (12) 3624230; fax (12) 3624239; Ambassador Dr S. M. ZEDAN.

Serbia and Montenegro: 163 Marais St, Brooklyn, Pretoria; POB 13026, Hatfield 0028; tel. (12) 465626; fax (12) 4660023; Chargé d'affaires a.i. O. DŽUVEROVIĆ.

Seychelles: Pretoria; High Commissioner PETER SINON.

Singapore: 173 Beckett St, Arcadia, Pretoria 0083; POB 11809, Hatfield 0028; tel. (12) 3434371; fax (12) 3433083; High Commissioner H. HOCHSTADT.

Slovakia: 930 Arcadia St, Pretoria 0083; POB 12736, Hatfield 0028; tel. (12) 3422051; fax (12) 3423688; e-mail slovakemb@mweb.co.za; Ambassador FRANTISZK HUDÁK.

Spain: 169 Pine St, POB 1633, Arcadia, Pretoria 0083; tel. (12) 3443875; fax (12) 3434891; Ambassador MIGUEL ANGEL CARRIEDO MONPIN.

Sri Lanka: 410 Alexander St, Brooklyn, Pretoria 0181; tel. (12) 4607690; fax (12) 4607702; e-mail srilanka@global.co.za; internet www.srilanka.co.za; High Commissioner GAMINI MUNASINGHE.

Sudan: 1203 Pretorius St, Hatfield, Pretoria 0083; POB 25513, Monumentpark 0105; tel. (12) 3424538; fax (12) 3424539; e-mail sudani@pop.co.za; internet www.sudani.co.za; Ambassador N. A. M. IDRIS.

Swaziland: 715 Government Ave, POB 14294, Arcadia, Pretoria 0007; tel. (12) 3441910; fax (12) 3430455; High Commissioner M. J. N. HLOPHE.

Sweden: iParioli Bldg, 1166 Park St, POB 13477, Hatfield 0028; tel. (12) 4266400; fax (12) 4266464; e-mail sweden@iafrica.com; Ambassador B. HEINEBÄCK.

Switzerland: 818 George Ave, Arcadia, Pretoria 0083; POB 2289, Pretoria 0001; tel. (12) 4306707; fax (12) 4306771; e-mail vertretung@pre.rep.admin.ch; Ambassador RUDOLF SCHALLER.

Tanzania: 822 George Ave, Arcadia, Pretoria 0083; POB 56572, Arcadia 0007; tel. (12) 3424393; fax (12) 4304383; e-mail tanzania@ cis.co.za; High Commissioner EMMANUEL A. MWAMBULUKUTU.

Thailand: 840 Church St, Eastwood, Pretoria 0083; POB 12080, Hatfield 0028; tel. (12) 3425470; fax (12) 3424805; Ambassador B. SOTIPALALIT.

Tunisia: 850 Church St, Arcadia, Pretoria; POB 56535, Arcadia 0007; tel. (12) 3425282; fax (12) 3426284; Ambassador MONCEF BENATTIA.

Turkey: 1067 Church St, Hatfield, Pretoria 0083; POB 56014, Arcadia 0007; tel. (12) 3426053; fax (12) 3426052; Ambassador K. ÖZGÜVENÇ.

Uganda: 882 Church St, Pretoria 0083; POB 12442, Hatfield 0083; tel. (12) 3426031; fax (12) 3426206; High Commissioner Prof. E. RUGUMAYO.

Ukraine: 398 Marais St, Brooklyn, Pretoria 0181; POB 57291, Arcadia 0007; tel. (12) 461946; fax (12) 461944; Ambassador L. M. GURYANOV.

United Arab Emirates: 980 Park St, Arcadia, Pretoria 0083; POB 57090, Arcadia 0007; tel. (12) 3427736; fax (12) 3427738; Ambassador ALI T. AL-SUWAIDI.

United Kingdom: 255 Hill St, Arcadia, Pretoria 0083; tel. (12) 4831200; fax (12) 4831302; e-mail britain@icon.co.za; internet www .britain.org.za; High Commissioner ANN GRANT.

USA: 877 Pretorius St, Pretoria 0083; POB 9536, Pretoria 0001; tel. (12) 3421048; fax (12) 3422244; internet www.usembassy.state.gov/ southafrica; Ambassador CAMERON R. HUME.

Venezeula: 474 Hatfield Gables South, Hilda St, Pretoria 0083; POB 11821, Hatfield 0028; tel. (12) 3626593; fax (12) 3626591; Ambassador Dr VICENTE VALLENILLA.

Yemen: 1063 Pretorius St, Hatfield, Pretoria 0083; POB 13343, Hatfield 0028; tel. (12) 3428650; fax (12) 3428653; e-mail ghamdan@ tta.lia.net; Chargé d'affaires a.i. ALI MOHAMED AL-THAUR.

Zambia: 570 Ziervogel St, Arcadia, POB 12234, Pretoria 0083; tel. (12) 3421541; fax (12) 3424963; e-mail zahpta@mweb.co.za; High Commissioner J. M. KABINGA.

Zimbabwe: 798 Merton St, Arcadia, Pretoria 0083; POB 55140, Arcadia 0007; tel. (12) 3425125; fax (12) 3425126; High Commissioner S. K. MOYO.

Judicial System

The common law of the Republic of South Africa is the Roman-Dutch law, the uncodified law of Holland as it was at the time of the secession of the Cape of Good Hope in 1806. The law of England is not recognized as authoritative, though the principles of English law have been introduced in relation to civil and criminal procedure, evidence and mercantile matters.

The Constitutional Court consists of a President, Deputy President and nine other judges. Its task is to ensure that the executive, legislative and judicial organs of government adhere to the provisions of the Constitution. It has the power to reverse legislation that has been adopted by Parliament. The Supreme Court of Appeal comprises a Chief Justice, Deputy Chief Justice and a number of judges of appeal, and is the highest court of appeal in all but constitutional matters. There are also High Courts and Magistrates' Courts. A National Director of Public Prosecutions is the head of the prosecuting authority and is appointed by the President of the Republic. A Judicial Service Commission makes recommendations regarding the appointment of judges and advises central and provincial government on all matters relating to the judiciary.

THE SUPREME COURT

Chief Justice: J. J. F. HEFER (acting).

THE CONSTITUTIONAL COURT

President: ARTHUR CHASKALSON.

Religion

Some 80% of the population profess the Christian faith. Other religions that are represented are Hinduism, Islam, Judaism and traditional African religions.

CHRISTIANITY

South African Council of Churches: POB 62098, Marshalltown 2107; tel. (11) 4921380; fax (11) 4921448; e-mail info@sacc.org.za; internet www.sacc.org.za; f. 1936; 26 mem. churches; Pres. Dr K. MGOJO; Gen. Sec. Rev. Dr MOLEFE TSELE.

The Anglican Communion

Most Anglicans in South Africa are adherents of the Church of the Province of Southern Africa, comprising 23 dioceses (including Lesotho, Namibia, St Helena, Swaziland and two dioceses in Mozambique). The Church had more than 2m. members in 1988.

Archbishop of Cape Town and Metropolitan of the Province of Southern Africa: Most Rev. NJONGONKULU WINSTON HUGH NDUNGANE, 16–20 Bishopscourt Dr., Cape Town 7708; tel. (21) 7612531; fax (21) 7614193; e-mail archbish@bishopscourt-cpsa.org.za; internet www.cpsa.org.za.

The Dutch Reformed Church (Nederduitse Gereformeerde Kerk–NGK)

In 1996 the Dutch Reformed Churches in South Africa consisted of the Dutch Reformed Church with 1,288,837 (mainly white) mems, the Uniting Reformed Church with 1,216,252 (mainly Coloured and black) mems, and the Reformed Church in Africa with 2,386 Indian mems. All congregations were desegregated in 1986.

General Synod: POB 4445, Pretoria 0001; tel. (12) 3228900; fax (12) 3223803; e-mail ngkdrc@mweb.co.za; Moderator Dr C. BURGER; Scribe Rev. J. C. CARSTENS; CEO Dr W. J. BOTHA.

The Lutheran Churches

Lutheran Communion in Southern Africa (LUCSA): POB 7170, Bonaero Park 1622; tel. (11) 9731873; fax (11) 3951615; e-mail lucsa@iafrica.com; f. 1991; co-ordinating org. for the Lutheran churches in southern Africa, incl. Angola, Botswana, Malawi, Mozambique, Namibia, South Africa, Swaziland, Zambia and Zimbabwe; 1,618,720 (1999); Pres. Bishop P. J. ROBINSON; Exec. Dir Bishop Dr A. MOYO.

Evangelical Lutheran Church in Southern Africa (ELCSA): POB 7231, 1622 Bonaero Park; tel. (11) 9731853; fax (11) 3951888; f. 1975; by merger of four non-white churches; the largest Lutheran church in southern Africa; Pres. Bishop LOUIS SIBIYA; Gen. Sec. Rev. T. MAKGATO; 624,567 mems.

Evangelical Lutheran Church in Southern Africa (Cape Church): 240 Long St, Cape Town 8001; tel. (21) 4244932; fax (21) 4249618; e-mail rohwernj@iafrica.com; Pres. Bishop NILS ROHWER; 4,239 mems.

Evangelical Lutheran Church in Southern Africa (Natal–Transvaal): POB 7095, Bonaero Park 1622; tel. (11) 9731851; fax (11) 3951862; e-mail elksant@elksant.co.za; internet www.elcsant.org.za; Pres. Bishop D. R. LILJE.

Moravian Church in Southern Africa: POB 24111, Lansdowne 7779; tel. (21) 7614030; fax (21) 7614046; e-mail mcsa@iafrica.com; f. 1737; Pres. A. H. SWART; 100,000 mems (2002).

The Roman Catholic Church

South Africa comprises four archdioceses, 21 dioceses and one Apostolic Prefecture. At 31 December 2000 there were an estimated 3,059,275 adherents in the country, representing about 6.6% of the total population.

Southern African Catholic Bishops' Conference (SACBC) Khanya House, 140 Visagie St, Pretoria 0002; POB 941, Pretoria 0001; tel. (12) 3236458; fax (12) 3266218; e-mail sacbelib@wn.apc.org; internet www.sacbc.org.za.
f. 1951; mems representing South Africa, Botswana and Swaziland; Pres. Rt Rev. LOUIS NDLOVU (Bishop of Manzini (Swaziland)).

Archbishop of Bloemfontein: Most Rev. BUTI JOSEPH TLHAGALE, Archbishop's House, 7A Whites Rd, Bloemfontein 9300; POB 362, Bloemfontein 9300; tel. (51) 4481658; fax (51) 4472420; e-mail bfnarch@mweb.co.za.

Archbishop of Cape Town: Most Rev. LAWRENCE HENRY, Cathedral Place, 12 Bouquet St, Cape Town 8001; POB 2910, Cape Town 8000; tel. (21) 4622417; fax (21) 4619330; e-mail archbish@bishopscourt-cpsa.org.za; internet www.catholic-ct.co.za.

Archbishop of Durban: Cardinal WILFRID NAPIER, Archbishop's House, 154 Gordon Rd, Durban 4001; POB 47489, Greyville 4023; tel. (31) 3031417; fax (31) 231848; e-mail chancery@durban-archdiocese.co.za.

Archbishop of Pretoria: Most Rev. GEORGE DANIEL, Archbishop's House, 125 Main St, Waterkloof 0181; POB 17245, Groenkloof, Pretoria 0027; tel. (12) 4602048; fax (12) 4602452; e-mail ptadiocese@freemail.absa.co.za.

Other Christian Churches

In addition to the following Churches, there are a large number of Pentecostalist groups, and more than 4,000 independent African Churches (with 8,563,000 members in 1994).

African Gospel Church: POB 32312, 4060 Mobeni; tel. (31) 9074377; Moderator Rev. F. D. MKHIZE; Gen. Sec. O. MTOLO; 100,000 mems.

Afrikaanse Protestantse Kerk (Afrikaans Protestant Church): POB 11488, Hatfield 0028; tel. (12) 3621390; fax (12) 3622023; e-mail apkskkan@lantic.net; f. 1987 by fmr mems of the Dutch Reformed Church (Nederduitse Gereformeerde Kerk) in protest at the desegregation of church congregations; c. 48,500 mems.

Apostolic Faith Mission of South Africa: POB 890197, 2106 Lyndhurst; tel. (11) 7868550; fax (11) 8871182; e-mail afmgens@mweb.co.za; f. 1908; Gen. Sec. Pastor M. G. MAHLABO; 136,000 mems.

Assemblies of God: POB 51065, Musgrave 4062; tel. (31) 231341; fax (31) 231342; f. 1915; Chair. Rev. ISAAC HLETA; Gen. Sec. Rev. C. P. WATT; 300,000 mems.

Baptist Union of Southern Africa: Private Bag X45, Wilropark 1731; tel. (11) 7685980; fax (11) 7685983; e-mail bapunion@telkomsa.net; f. 1877; Pres. Rev. Dr M. H. POHLMANN; Gen. Sec. Rev. N. J. COERTZE SCHEEPERS; 49,565 mems; (2001).

Black Dutch Reformed Church: POB 137, Bergvlei 2012; Leader Rev. SAM BUTI; c. 1m. mems.

Church of England in South Africa: POB 185, Gillitts 3603; tel. (31) 7652876; fax (31) 7655150; e-mail noel.wright@pixie.co.za; internet www.cesa.org.za; 207 churches; Bishop Rt Rev. F. RETIEF (presiding), Bishop Rt Rev. M. MORRISON, Bishop Rt Rev. Dr W. COLE-EDWARDES, Bishop Rt Rev. M. NDLOVU.

Evangelical Presbyterian Church in South Africa: POB 31961, Braamfontein 2017; tel. (11) 3391044; Gen. Sec. Rev. S. NGOBE; Gen. Sec. Rev. J. S. NGOBE; Treas. Rev. H. D. MASANGU; 60,000 mems.

The Methodist Church of Southern Africa: Methodist Connexional Office, POB 50216, Musgrave 4062; tel. (31) 2024214; fax (31) 2017674; e-mail methodist@mweb.co.za; internet www.users.club.co.za/mco; f. 1883; Pres. Bishop H. M. DANDALA; Sec. Rev. ROSS A. J. OLIVER; 696,353 mems.

Nederduitsch Hervormde Kerk van Afrika: POB 2368, Pretoria 0001; tel. (12) 3228885; fax (12) 3227907; e-mail fanie@nhk.co.za; Chair. Prof. T. F. J. DREYER; Gen. Sec. Dr S. P. PRETORIUS; 193,561 mems.

Nederduitse Gereformeerde Kerk in Afrika: Portland Place, 37 Jorissen St, 2017 Johannesburg; tel. (11) 4031027; 6 synods (incl. 1 in Swaziland); Moderator Rev. S. P. E. BUTI; Gen. Sec. W. RAATH; 350,370 mems.

Presbyterian Church of Africa: POB 54840, Umlazi 4031; tel. (31) 9072366; f. 1898; 8 presbyteries (incl. 1 in Malawi and 1 in Zimbabwe); Chief Clerk Rev. S. A. KHUMALO; 1,231,000 mems.

Reformed Church in South Africa (Die Gereformeerde Kerke): POB 20004, Noordbrug 2522, Potchefstroom; tel. (148) 2973986; fax (148) 2931042; f. 1859; Prin. Officer H. S. J. VORSTER; 158,973 mems.

Seventh-day Adventist Church: POB 468, Bloemfontein 9300; tel. (51) 4478271; fax (41) 4488059; Pres. Pastor V. S. WAKABA; Sec. Pastor B. H. PARKERSON; 150,000 mems.

United Congregational Church of Southern Africa: POB 61305, Marshalltown 2107; tel. (11) 8366537; fax (11) 8369249; f. 1799; Gen. Sec. Rev. S. M. ARENDS; 234,451 mems.

Uniting Presbyterian Church in Southern Africa: POB 96188, Brixton 2019; tel. (11) 8371258; fax (11) 8371653; e-mail gensec@presbyterian.org.za; f. 1999; Moderator Rt Rev. M. K. BOSHOMANE; Gen. Sec. and Clerk of the Assembly Rev. A. RODGER; 130,000 mems.

Zion Christian Church: Zion City, Moria; f. 1910; South Africa's largest black religious group, with c. 4m. mems; Leader Bishop BARNABAS LEKGANYANE.

JUDAISM

There are about 100,000 Jews in South Africa, and about 200 organized Jewish communities.

South African Jewish Board of Deputies: POB 87557, Houghton 2041; tel. (11) 6452523; fax (11) 6452559; e-mail sajbod@iafrica.com; internet www.jewish.org.za; f. 1903; the representative institution of South African Jewry; Pres. MARLENE BETHLEHEM; Chair. RUSSELL GADDIN; Nat. Dir YEHUDA KAY.

BAHÁ'Í FAITH

National Spiritual Assembly: 10 Acorn Lane, Houghton Estate, Houghton 2198; POB 2142, Houghton 2041; tel. (11) 4872077; fax (11) 4871809; e-mail nsa.sec@bahai.org.za; internet www.bahai.org.za; f. 1956; 11,000 mems resident in 320 localities; Sec. SHOHREH RAWHANI.

The Press

In December 1993 legislation was adopted that provided for the establishment of an Independent Media Commission, which was to ensure the impartiality of the press.

Government Communication and Information System (GCIS): Midtown Bldg, cnr Vermeulen and Prinsloo Sts, Pretoria; Private Bag X745, Pretoria 0001; tel. (12) 3142911; fax (12) 3233831; e-mail govcom@gcis.pwv.gov.za; internet www.gcis.gov.za; govt agency; CEO JOEL NETSHITENZHE.

Press Ombudsman of South Africa: POB 47221; tel. (11) 7884837; fax (11) 7884990; e-mail pressombudsman@ombudsman.org.za; Ombudsman E. H. LINNINGTON.

DAILIES

Eastern Cape

Die Burger (Oos-Kaap): 52 Cawood St, POB 525, Port Elizabeth 6001; tel. (41) 5036111; fax (41) 5036138; e-mail dbokaap@burger.naspers.co.za; f. 1937; morning; Afrikaans; Editor LEON VAN DER VYVER; circ. 23,849.

Cape Times: Newspaper House, 122 St George's St, POB 56, Cape Town 8000; tel. (21) 4884911; fax (21) 4884762; internet www.iol.co.za; f. 1876; morning; English; Editor JOHN SCOTT; circ. 45,594.

Daily Dispatch: 35 Caxton St, POB 131, East London 5200; tel. (43) 7022000; fax (43) 7435159; e-mail gavinst@dispatch.co.za; internet www.dispatch.co.za; f. 1872; morning; English; Editor Prof. G. STEWART; circ. 70,486.

Eastern Province Herald: Newspaper House, 19 Baakens St, POB 1117, Port Elizabeth 6000; tel. (41) 5047911; fax (41) 554966; f. 1845; morning; English; Editor Ric Wilson; circ. 30,000 (Mon.–Fri.), 25,000 (Sat.).

Evening Post: Newspaper House, 19 Baakens St, POB 1121, Port Elizabeth 6000; tel. (41) 5047911; fax (41) 554966; f. 1950; evening; English; Editor Neville Woudberg; circ. 19,000.

Free State

Die Volksblad: 79 Voortrekker St, POB 267, Bloemfontein 9300; tel. (51) 4047600; fax (51) 4306949; e-mail nuus@volksblad.com; internet www.naspers.com; f. 1904; morning; Afrikaans; Editor Paul Marais; circ. 28,000 (Mon.–Fri.), 23,000 (Sat.).

Gauteng

Beeld: 32 Miller St, POB 5425, Johannesburg 2000; tel. (11) 4064600; fax (11) 4064643; f. 1974; morning; Afrikaans; Editor Willie Kühn; circ. 111,958 (Mon.–Fri.), 81,000 (Sat.).

Business Day: POB 1745, Saxonwold 2132; tel. (11) 2803000; fax (11) 2805505; e-mail busday@tml.co.za; internet www.bday.co.za; f. 1985; morning; English; financial; Editor Jim Jones; circ. 44,000.

The Citizen: POB 7712, Johannesburg 2000; tel. (11) 4022900; fax (11) 4026862; f. 1976; morning; English; Editor M. A. Johnson; circ. 14,000 (Mon.–Fri.), 108,000 (Sat.).

The Pretoria News: 216 Vermeulen St, Pretoria 0002; tel. (12) 3255382; fax (12) 3257300; e-mail ptanews@ptn.independent.co.za; f. 1898; morning; English; Editor A. Dunn; circ. 25,500 (Mon.–Fri.), 14,000 (Sat.).

Sowetan: 61 Commando Rd, Industria West, POB 6663, Johannesburg 2000; tel. (11) 4714000; fax (11) 4748834; e-mail swtnedit@sowetan.co.za; internet sowetan.co.za; f. 1981; Mon.–Fri. English; Editor Z. Aggrey Klaaste; circ. 225,000.

The Star: 47 Sauer St, POB 1014, Johannesburg 2000; tel. (11) 6332334; fax (11) 8366186; e-mail webmaster@star.co.za; f. 1887; English; Editor Peter J. Sullivan; circ. 162,316 (Mon.–Fri.), 135,203 (Sat.).

Transvaaler: 28 Height St, Doornfontein, POB 845, Johannesburg 2000; tel. (11) 7769111; fax (11) 4020037; afternoon; Afrikaans; Editor G. Johnson; circ. 40,000.

KwaZulu/Natal

The Daily News: 18 Osborne St, Greyville 4001, POB 47549, Greyville 4023; tel. (31) 3082355; fax (31) 3082715; internet www.iol.co.za; f. 1878; Mon.-Fri., afternoon; English; Editor D. Pather; circ. 50,000.

Mercury: 18 Osborne St, Greyville, POB 47549, Greyville 4023; tel. (31) 3082911; fax (31) 3082555; e-mail mercnews@nn.independent.co.za; internet www.inkinc.co.za; f. 1852; morning; English; Editor D. Canning; circ. 40,000.

Natal Witness: 244 Longmarket St, POB 362, Pietermaritzburg 3200; tel. (33) 3551111; fax (33) 3551122; e-mail newsed@witness.co.za; internet www.witness.co.za; f. 1846; morning; English; Editor J. Conyngham; circ. 26,000.

Northern Cape

Diamond Fields Advertiser: POB 1014, cnr Bean and Villiers Sts, Kimberley 8300; tel. (53) 6339111; fax (53) 8368398; e-mail johandp@dfa.independent.co.za; morning; English; Editor Kevin Ritchie; circ. 8,149.

North-West

Rustenburg Herald: 28 Steen St, POB 2043, Rustenburg 0300; tel. (14) 5928329; fax (14) 5921869; e-mail mailbag@rtbherald.co.za; f. 1924; English and Afrikaans; Editor P. J. Theron; circ. 16,500.

Western Cape

Die Burger: 40 Heerengracht, POB 692, Cape Town 8000; tel. (21) 4062222; fax (21) 4062913; e-mail webred@burger.naspers.co.za; f. 1915; morning; Afrikaans; Editor E. Dommisse; circ. 105,841 (Mon.–Fri.), 97,881 (Sat.).

Cape Argus: 122 St George's St, POB 56, Cape Town 8000; tel. (21) 4884911; fax (21) 4884075; f. 1857; English; independent; Editor Moegsien Williams; circ. 85,000.

WEEKLIES AND FORTNIGHTLIES

Eastern Cape

Imvo Zabantsundu (Black Opinion): 35 Edes St, POB 190, King William's Town 5600; tel. (433) 23550; fax (433) 33865; f. 1884; weekly; English and Xhosa; Editor W. Mnyikizo; Gen. Man. Will Ferreira; circ. 31,000.

Weekend Post: POB 1141, Port Elizabeth 6000; tel. (41) 5047911; fax (41) 554966; English; Editor N. M. Woudberg; circ. 38,000.

Free State

Vista: POB 1027, Welkom 9460; tel. (57) 3571304; fax (57) 3532427; e-mail avaneck@volksblad.com; internet www.perskorfs.co.za; f. 1971; 2 a week; English and Afrikaans; Editor P. Gouws; circ. 34,368 (Tues. and Thurs.).

Gauteng

African Jewish Newspaper: Johannesburg 2000; tel. (11) 6468292; f. 1931; weekly; Yiddish; Editor Levi Shalit.

Die Afrikaner: POB 1888, Pretoria 0001; tel. (12) 3423410; fax (12) 3423417; f. 1970; Wednesday; organ of Herstigte Nasionale Party; Editors Dr J. L. Basson, J. J. Venter; circ. 10,000.

Benoni City Times en Oosrandse Nuus: 28 Woburn Ave, POB 494, Benoni 1500; tel. (11) 8451680; fax (11) 4224796; English and Afrikaans; Editor Hilary Green; circ. 32,000.

City Press: POB 3413, Johannesburg 2000; tel. (11) 4021632; fax (11) 4026662; f. 1983; weekly; English; Editor-in-Chief Khulu Sibiya; circ. 251,748.

Finance Week: Private Bag 78816, Sandton 2146; tel. (11) 4440555; fax (11) 4440424; f. 1979; Editor S. Murray; circ. 15,000.

Financial Mail: POB 1746, Saxenwold 2132; tel. (11) 2805808; fax (11) 2805800; e-mail fmmail@tml.co.uk; internet www.fm.co.za; weekly; English; Editor Peter Bruce; circ. 33,000.

The Herald Times: POB 31015, Braamfontein 2017; tel. (11) 8876500; weekly; Jewish interest; Man. Dir R. Shapiro; circ. 5,000.

Mail and Guardian: POB 32362, Braamfontein 2017; tel. (11) 4037111; fax (11) 4031025; e-mail newsdesk@nmail.misnet.org; CEO Govin Reddy; Editor Philip van Niekerk; circ. 33,023.

Mining Week: Johannesburg; tel. (11) 7892144; f. 1979; fortnightly; Editor Val Pienaar; circ. 10,000.

Die Noord-Transvaler: POB 220, Ladanna, Pietersburg 0704; tel. (152) 931831; fax (152) 932586; weekly; Afrikaans; Editor A. Buys; circ. 12,000.

Noordwes Gazette: POB 515, Potchefstroom 2520; tel. (18) 2930750; e-mail potchherald@media24.com; weekly; English and Afrikaans; Editor H. Stander; circ. 35,000.

Northern Review: 16 Grobler St, POB 45, Pietersburg 0700; tel. (152) 2959167; fax (152) 2915148; weekly; English and Afrikaans; Editor R. S. de Jager; circ. 10,300.

Potchefstroom and Ventersdorp Herald: POB 515, Potchefstroom 2520; tel. (18) 2930750; fax (18) 2930759; e-mail potchherald@media24.com; f. 1908; 1 a week; English and Afrikaans; Editor H. Stander; Man. Dirk Uys; circ. 6,000 (Fri.).

Rapport: POB 8422, Johannesburg 2000; tel. (11) 4022620; fax (11) 4026163; internet www.naspers.co.za/rapport; weekly; Afrikaans; Editor Izak de Villiers; circ. 353,000.

South African Industrial Week: Johannesburg; Man. Editor W. Mastingle; circ. 19,000.

Springs and Brakpan Advertiser: POB 138, Springs 1560; tel. (11) 8121600; fax (11) 8121908; f. 1916; English and Afrikaans; Editor Cathy Grosvenor; circ. 13,000.

Sunday Times: POB 1742, Saxonwold 2132; tel. (11) 2805102; fax (11) 2805111; internet www.suntimes.co.za; English; Editor Mike Robertson; circ. 508,000.

Vaalweekblad: 27 Ekspa Bldg, D.F. Malan St, POB 351, Vanderbijlpark 1900; tel. (16) 817010; fax (16) 810604; weekly; Afrikaans and English; Editor W. J. Buys; circ. 16,000.

Vrye Weekblad: 153 Bree St, Newtown, Johannesburg 2001; tel. (11) 8362151; fax (11) 8385901; f. 1988; weekly; Afrikaans; Editor Max du Preez; circ. 13,000.

KwaZulu/Natal

Farmers' Weekly: POB 1797, Pinegowrie 2123; tel. (11) 8890836; fax (11) 8890862; e-mail maddys@caxton.co.za; f. 1911; weekly; agriculture and horticulture; Editor M. Fisher; circ. 17,000.

Ilanga: 128 Umgeni Rd, POB 2159, Durban 4000; tel. (31) 3094350; fax (31) 3093489; e-mail edilanga@nn.independent.co.za; f. 1903; 2 a week; Zulu; Editor S. Ngobese; circ. 117,000.

Independent On Saturday: 18 Osborne St, Greyville 4001, POB 47549, Greyville 4023; tel. (31) 3082500; fax (31) 3082355; e-mail satmail@nn.independent.co.za; internet www.nn.independent.co.za; f. 1878; English; Editor D. Reynolds (acting); circ. 77,500.

Keur: POB 32083, Mobeni 4060; tel. (31) 422041; fax (31) 426068; f. 1967; Afrikaans; Editor Carl Steyn; circ. 69,496.

Ladysmith Gazette: POB 10019, Ladysmith 3370; tel. (36) 6376801; fax (36) 6372283; f. 1902; weekly; English, Afrikaans and Zulu; Editor Diana Procter; circ. 7,000.

Post: 18 Osborne St, Greyville 4000, POB 733, Durban 4000; tel. (31) 3082400; fax (31) 3082427; e-mail post@nn.independent.co.za; internet www.nn.independent.co.za; f. 1935; weekly; English; general; Editor Briglall Ramguthee; circ. 45,000.

Sunday Tribune: 18 Osborne St, POB 47549, Greyville 4023; tel. (31) 3082911; fax (31) 3082355; e-mail tribnews@nn.independent.co.za; internet www.iol.co.za; f. 1937; English; weekly; Editor S. Harichunder; (acting); circ. 114,304.

Umafrika: POB 11002, Mariannhill 3601; tel. (31) 7006116; fax (31) 7006115; e-mail editor@umafrika.co.za; f. 1911; weekly; Zulu and English; Editor Cyril Madlala; circ. 50,000.

Northern Cape

Die Gemsbok: POB 60, Upington 8800; tel. 27017; fax 24055; English and Afrikaans; Editor D. Jones; circ. 8,000.

Western Cape

Eikestadnuus: 44 Alexander St, POB 28, Stellenbosch 7600; tel. (2231) 72840; fax (2231) 99538; weekly; English and Afrikaans; Editor R. Gerber; circ. 7,000.

Fair Lady: Naspers Bldg, 9th Floor, 40 Heerengracht, Foreshore, Cape Town, POB 1802, Cape Town 8000; tel. (21) 4062204; fax (21) 4062930; e-mail flmag@fairlady.com; fortnightly; English; Editor Alice Bell; circ. 100,952.

Huisgenoot: 40 Heerengracht, POB 1802, Cape Town 8000; tel. (21) 4062115; fax (21) 4063316; e-mail eweidema@huisgenoot.com; f. 1916; weekly; Afrikaans; Editor Esmaré Weideman; circ. 358,000.

Sarie: 40 Heerengracht, Cape Town 8000; tel. and fax (21) 4062203; fax (21) 4062513; e-mail sarie@sarie.com; internet www.sarie.com; fortnightly; Afrikaans; women's interest; Editor Michelle van Breda; circ. 165,589.

South: 6 Russel St, Castle Mews, Woodstock 7925; POB 13094, Sir Lowry Rd 7900; tel. (21) 4622012; fax (21) 4615407; weekly; black interest; Editor Dr Guy Berger; circ. 25,000.

The Southern Cross: POB 2372, Cape Town 8000; tel. (21) 4655007; fax (21) 4653850; f. 1920; weekly; English; Roman Catholic; Editor Gunther Simmermacher; circ. 10,104.

Tyger-Burger: 40 Heerengracht, POB 2271, Cape Town 8000; tel. (21) 4062121; fax (21) 4062913; weekly; Afrikaans and English; Editor Abie von Zyl.

Weekend Argus: 122 St George's Mall, POB 56, Cape Town 8000; tel. (21) 4884911; fax (21) 4884762; internet www.iol.co.za; f. 1857; Sat. and Sun. English; Editor Chris Whitfield; circ. 108,294.

You Magazine: 40 Heerengracht, Cape Town 8000; tel. (21) 4062366; fax (21) 4063289; f. 1987; weekly; English; Editor-in-Chief Andries van Wyk; circ. 258,138.

MONTHLIES

Free State

Wamba: POB 1097, Bloemfontein; educational; publ. in seven vernacular languages; Editor C. P. Senyatsi.

Gauteng

Centre News: Johannesburg; tel. (11) 5591781; English; publ. by R.J.J. Publications; circ. 30,000.

The Mail of Rosebank News: Johannesburg; tel. (11) 3391781; English; publ. by R. J. J. Publications; circ. 40,000.

Nursing News: POB 1280, Pretoria 0001; tel. (12) 3432315; fax (12) 3440750; f. 1978; magazine of the Democratic Nursing Org. English and Afrikaans; circ. 76,000.

Pace: POB 48985, Roosevelt Park 2129; tel. (11) 8890600; fax (11) 8805942; Man. Editor Force Koshani; circ. 131,000.

Postal and Telkom Herald: POB 9186, Johannesburg 2000; tel. (11) 7255422; fax (11) 7256540; f. 1903; English and Afrikaans; Staff Assen (Workers' Union); Editor F. A. Gerber; circ. 13,000.

Technobrief: POB 395, Pretoria 0001; tel. (12) 8413887; fax (12) 8413924; e-mail bvrooyen@csir.co.za; internet www.csir.co.za; f. 1991; publ. by the Council for Scientific and Industrial Research (CSIR); Editors D. Lötter, B. van Rooyen; circ. 6,000.

Telescope: POB 925, Pretoria 0001; tel. (12) 3217121; fax (12) 3114031; e-mail mudzwim@telkom.co.za; f. 1970; English, Afrikaans and vernacular languages; telecom staff journal; Editor Moses Mudzwiti; circ. 60,000.

KwaZulu/Natal

Bona: POB 32083, Mobeni 4060; tel. (31) 422041; fax (31) 426068; f. 1956; English, Sotho, Xhosa and Zulu; Editor Daizer Mqhaba; circ. 256,631.

Living and Loving: POB 32083, Mobeni 4060; tel. (31) 422041; fax (31) 426068; English; Editor Fiona Wayman; circ. 89,268.

Rooi Rose: POB 412982, Craighall 2024; tel. (31) 422041; fax (31) 426068; e-mail rooirose@caxton.co.za; internet www.rooirose.co.za; Afrikaans; women's interest; Editor Joan Kruger; circ. 159,223.

Tempo: POB 16, Pinetown 3600; tel. (31) 7013225; fax (31) 7012166; f. 1984; weekly; Afrikaans; Editor Dr Hilda Grobler; circ. 7,000.

World Airnews: POB 35082, Northway 4065; tel. (31) 5641319; fax (31) 5637115; e-mail tom@airnews.co.za; internet www.airnews.co.za; f. 1973; aviation news; Editor T. Chalmers; circ. 13,632.

Your Family: POB 473016, Parklands 2121; tel. (11) 8890749; fax (11) 8890642; e-mail yourfamily@caxton.co.za; f. 1973; English; cooking, crafts, DIY; Editor Patti Garlick; circ. 216,000.

Western Cape

Boxing World: 4 Constantia Rd, Wynberg, Cape Town, POB 364, Plumstead 7801; tel. (21) 7978500; fax (21) 7976465; e-mail info@boxingworld.co.za; f. 1976; Editor Bert Blewett; circ. 10,000.

Car: POB 180, Howard Place 7450; tel. (21) 5303333; fax (21) 5322698; e-mail anne@rsp.co.za; internet www.cartoday.com; Editor J. Wright; circ. 114,404.

Drum: POB 1802, Cape Town 8000; tel. (21) 4062120; fax (21) 4062924; e-mail rvermeul@cmags.naspers.co.za; internet www.natmags.com; f. 1951; English; Editor Reg Vermenen; circ. 137,035 in southern Africa.

Femina: 21 St. John's St, POB 3647, Cape Town 8000; tel. (21) 4623070; fax (21) 4612500; e-mail femina@assocmags.co.za; Editor Jane Raphaely; circ. 88,442.

Finance Week: POB 1802, Cape Town 8000; tel. (21) 4062366; fax (21) 2805800; e-mail fmmail@tml.co.uk; internet www.fm.co.za; Afrikaans and English; Publisher G. L. Marais; circ. 21,910.

Learning Roots: POB 1161, Cape Town 8000; tel. (21) 6968414; fax (21) 6968346; f. 1980; newsletter for black schools in the Western Cape; circ. 50,000.

Nursing RSA Verpleging: Private Bag XI, Pinelands 7430; tel. (21) 5312691; fax (21) 5314126; f. 1986; professional nursing journal; Editor Lillian Medlin; circ. 10,000.

Reader's Digest (South African Edition): Hercol House, 10 Mill St, Newlands, Cape Town 7708; tel. (21) 6706000; fax (21) 6706206; internet www.readersdigest.co.za; f. 1948; English; Editor-in-Chief Anthony Johnson; circ. 125,307.

South African Medical Journal: MASA House, Central House, Pinelands 7430; tel. (21) 5313081; fax (21) 5314126; e-mail publishing@samedical.co.za; f. 1884; publ. by the South African Medical Assen; Editor N. C. Lee; circ. 20,000.

Die Unie: POB 196, Cape Town 8000; tel. (21) 4616340; fax (21) 4619238; e-mail saou@jaywalk.com; f. 1905; educational; publ. by the South African Teachers' Union; Editor H. M. Nel; circ. 7,200.

Die Voorligter: Private Bag, Tyger Valley 7536; tel. (21) 9177000; fax (21) 9141333; e-mail lig@cnw-inter.net; internet www.christene.co.za; f. 1937; journal of the Dutch Reformed Church of South Africa; Editor Dr F. M. Gaum; circ. 50,000.

Woman's Value: 40 Heerengracht, Cape Town 8001; tel. (21) 4062366; e-mail adonald@womansvalue.com; internet www.natmags.com; English; Editor Ann Donald; circ. 134,749.

Wineland Magazine: Wijngaard, POB 1411, Suider-Paarl 7646; tel. (21) 8073267; fax (21) 8631562; e-mail in@wineland.co.za; internet www.wineland.com; f. 1931; viticulture and the wine and spirit industry; Editor Cassie du Plessis; circ. 10,000.

QUARTERLIES

Gauteng

The Motorist/Die Motoris: POB 31015, Braamfontein 2017; tel. (11) 8876500; fax (11) 8876551; f. 1966; journal of the Automobile Asscn of SA; Editor MICHAEL WANG; circ. 184,000.

South African Journal of Economics: 4-44 EBW Bldg, University of Pretoria, Pretoria 0002; tel. (12) 4203525; fax (12) 3625266; e-mail saje@hakuna.up.ac.za; internet www.essa.org.za; f. 1933; English and Afrikaans; Man. Editor Prof. D. J. J. BOTHA.

Western Cape

New Era: Cape Town 8000; tel. (2721) 7975101; fax (2721) 7627424; f. 1884; Editor ELLISON KAHN; circ. 3,000.

South African Law Journal: POB 14373, Kenwyn 7790; tel. (21) 7975101; fax (21) 7970121; e-mail law@juta.co.za; f. 1884; Editor C. H. LEWIS; circ. 1,100.

NEWS AGENCIES

South African Press Association: Kine Centre, Commissioner St, POB 7766, Johannesburg 2000; tel. (11) 7821600; fax (11) 7821591; internet www.sapa.org.za; f. 1938; 40 mems; Chair. S. P. JORDAAN; Man. W. J. H. VAN GILS; Editor MARK A. VAN DER VELDEN.

Foreign Bureaux

Agence France-Presse (AFP): Nixdorf Centre, 6th Floor, 37 Stanley Ave, Milpark; POB 3462, Johannesburg 2000; tel. (11) 4822170; fax (11) 7268756; Bureau Chief MARC HUTTEN.

Agenzia Nazionale Stampa Associata (ANSA) (Italy): POB 32312, Camps Bay, Cape Town 8040; tel. (21) 7903991; fax (21) 7904444; Correspondent LICINIO GERMINI.

Associated Press (AP) (USA): 15 Napier St, Richmond, Johannesburg 2092; tel. (11) 7267022; fax (11) 7267834; Bureau Chief JOHN DANISZEWSKI.

Central News Agency (Taiwan): Kine Centre, 1st Floor, 141 Commissioner St, Johannesburg 2001; tel. (11) 3316654; fax (11) 3319463; Chief CHANG JER SHONG.

Deutsche Presse-Agentur (dpa) (Germany): 96 Jorrisen St, POB 32521, Braamfontein 2017; tel. (11) 4033926; fax (11) 4032849; Chief Dr ARNO MAYER.

Informatsionnoye Telegrafnoye Agentstvo Rossii—Telegrafnoye Agentstvo Suverennykh Stran (ITAR—TASS) (Russia): 1261 Park St, Atfield, Pretoria; tel. (12) 436677; fax (12) 3425017; Bureau Chief YURII K. PICHUGIN.

Inter-Press Service (IPS) (Italy): POB 30764, Braamfontein 2017, Johannesburg; tel. (11) 4034967; fax (11) 4032516; e-mail ipsjnb@wn.apc.org; Correspondent GUMISAI MUTUME.

Kyodo News (Japan): Sandton Office Towers, 6th Floor, cnr Rivonia and 5th Sts, Sandton 2196; tel. (11) 8834995; fax (11) 8834996; e-mail nako@kyodo.co.jp; Rep. DAI KANEKO.

Reuters Ltd (UK): Surrey House, 7th and 8th Floors, 35 Rissik St, Johannesburg; Man. CHRIS INWOOD.

United Press International (UPI) (USA): Nedbank Centre, 2nd Floor, POB 32661, Braamfontein 2017; tel. (11) 4033910; fax (11) 4033914; Bureau Chief PATRICK COLLINS.

Agencia EFE (Spain) is also represented.

PRESS ASSOCIATIONS

Newspaper Association of Southern Africa: Nedbank Gardens, 5th Floor, 33 Bath Ave, Rosebank 2196, Johannesburg; POB 47180, Parklands 2121; tel. (11) 4471264; fax (11) 4471289; e-mail na@printmedia.org.za; f. 1882; represents 28 urban daily, weekly and independent nat. newspapers; Chair. C. MOLUSI.

Print Media SA: North Wing, Nedbank Gardens, 5th Floor, 33 Bath Ave, Rosebank 2196, Johannesburg; POB 47180, Parklands 2121; tel. (11) 4471264; fax (11) 4471289; e-mail printmediasa@printmedia.org.za; f. 1995 following the restructuring of the Newspaper Press Union of Southern Africa; represents all aspects of the print media (newspapers and magazines); 680 mems; CEO (vacant).

Publishers

Acorn Books: POB 4845, Randburg 2125; tel. (11) 8805768; fax (11) 8805768; e-mail acorbook@iafrica.com; f. 1985; Africana, general, natural history.

Albertyn Publishers (Pty) Ltd: Andmar Bldg, Van Ryneveld St, Stellenbosch 7600; tel. (21) 8871202; fax (21) 8871292; f. 1971; encyclopaedias; Editorial Man. S. CARSTENS.

BLAC Publishing House: POB 17, Athlone, Cape Town; f. 1974; general fiction, poetry; Man. Dir JAMES MATTHEWS.

Jonathan Ball Publishers: POB 33977, Jeppestown 2043; tel. (11) 6222900; fax (11) 6223553; fiction, reference, bibles, textbooks, general.

A. Donker (Pty) Ltd: POB 33977, Jeppestown 2043; tel. (11) 6222900; fax (11) 6223553; Africana, literature, South African history, general non-fiction.

Bible Society of South Africa: POB 6215, Roggebaai 8012; tel. (21) 4212040; fax (21) 4194846; f. 1820; Gen. Sec. Rev. G. S. KRITZINGER.

Book Promotions (Pty) Ltd: POB 5, Plumstead 7800; tel. (21) 7060949; fax (21) 7060940; e-mail enquiries@bookpro.co.za; internet www.bookpro.co.za; Man. Dir. R. MANSELL.

Book Studio (Pty) Ltd: POB 121, Hout Bay 7872.

Books of Africa (Pty) Ltd: POB 10, Muizenberg 7950; tel. (21) 888316; f. 1947; biography, history, Africana, art; Man. Dir T. V. BULPIN.

Brenthurst Press (Pty) Ltd: POB 87184, Houghton 2041; tel. (11) 6466024; fax (11) 4861651; e-mail orders@brenthurst.co.za; internet www.brenthurst.org.za; f. 1974; Southern African history.

Clever Books: POB 13186, Hatfield 0028; tel. (12) 3423263; fax (12) 432376; e-mail inl0631@mweb.co.za; f. 1981; Propr J. STEENHUISEN.

College of Careers/Faircare Books: POB 10207, Caledon Sq., Cape Town 7905; tel. (21) 4614411; f. 1946; general, educational; Man. Dir MICHAEL IRVING.

CUM Books: POB 1599, Vereeniging 1930; tel. (16) 4214781; fax (16) 4211748; e-mail Cabooks@cum.co.za; internet www.cum.co.za.

Da Gama Publishers (Pty) Ltd: MWU Bldg, 6th Floor, 19 Melle St, Braamfontein 2017; tel. (11) 4033763; fax (11) 4031263; travel; Publr DERMOT SWAINE.

Digma Publications: POB 95466, Waterkloof 0145; tel. (11) 3463840; fax (11) 3463845.

Dreyer Printers and Publishers: POB 286, Bloemfontein 9300; tel. (51) 4479001; fax (51) 4471281.

Educum Publishers: POB 3068, Halfway House 1685.

Eksamenhulp: POB 55555, Arcadia 0007.

Fisichem Publishers: Private Bag X3, Matieland 7602; tel. (21) 8870900; fax (21) 8839635; e-mail fisichem@iafrica.com.

Flesch Publications: 11 Peninsula Rd, Zeekoevlei, Cape Town 7941; POB 31353, Grassy Park 7888; tel. (21) 7054317; fax (21) 7060766; e-mail sflesch@iafrica.com; f. 1954; Prin. Officer S. FLESCH.

Fortress Books: POB 2475, Knysna 6570; tel. and fax (44) 3826805; fax (44) 3826848; e-mail fortress@iafrica.com; f. 1973; military history, biographies, financial; Man. Dir I. UYS.

F. J. N. Harman Publishers: Menlo Park; tel. (12) 469575; f. 1981; educational; Man. Dir F. J. N. HARMAN.

HAUM: Prima Park 4 and 6, cnr Klosser and King Edward Rds, Porow 7500; tel. (21) 926123; f. 1894; Man. C. J. HAGE.

Kagiso Publishers: POB 629, Pretoria 0001; tel. (12) 3284620; fax (12) 3284705; school textbooks and other materials for schools and tertiary institutions in all 11 official South African languages; Man. Dir L. M. MABANDLA.

University Publishers & Booksellers (Pty) Ltd: POB 29, Stellenbosch 7599; tel. (21) 8870337; fax (21) 8832975; f. 1947; educational; Man. Dir B. B. LIEBENBERG.

Heinemann Publishers (Pty) Ltd: POB 781940, Sandown, Sandton 2146; tel. (11) 3228600; fax (11) 3228715; internet www.heinemann.co.za; educational; incl. imprints Lexicon, Isando and Centaur; Man. Dir O. KRUT.

Home Economics Publishers: POB 7091, Stellenbosch 7599; tel. (21) 8864722; fax (21) 8864722; e-mail MCV1@SUN.ac.za.

Human and Rousseau (Pty) Ltd: POB 5050, Cape Town 8000; tel. (21) 4233911; fax (21) 4265744; e-mail humanhk@humanrousseau.com; internet www.humanrousseau.com; f. 1959; English, Afrikaans, Xhosa and Zulu; general adult and children's trade books; Gen. Man. C. T. BREYTENBACH.

Incipit Publishers: POB 28754, Sunnyside, Pretoria 0132; tel. and fax (12) 463802; f. 1987; music; Man. MARIANNE FEENSTRA.

Juta and Co Ltd: POB 14373, Kenwyn 7790, Cape Town; tel. (11) 7975101; fax (11) 7627424; e-mail books@juta.co.za; internet www.juta.co.za; f. 1853; academic, educational, law, electronic; CEO R. J. WILSON.

Klipbok Publishers: POB 170, Durbanville 7550; tel. and fax (21) 9762293; f. 1979; prose, poetry, drama.

Knowledge Unlimited (Pty) Ltd: POB 781337; Sandton 2146; tel. (11) 6521800; fax (11) 3142984; children's fiction, educational; Man. Dir MIKE JACKLIN.

Konsensus Publishers: 213 Orion St, Waterkloof 0180.

Lemur Books (Pty) Ltd: POB 1645, Alberton 1450; tel. (11) 9072029; fax (11) 8690890; e-mail lemur@mweb.co.za; internet www .galago.co.za; military, political, history, hunting, general; Man. Dir F. STIFF.

Lexis Nexis Butterworths SA: POB 792, Durban 4000; tel. (31) 2683266; fax (31) 2683109; e-mail liane.mulholland@lexisnexis.co .za; internet www.lexisnexis.co.za; law, tax, accountancy; Man. Dir WILLIAM J. LAST.

LMA (Pty) Ltd: 341 West St, Durban 4001; tel. (31) 3048571; primary school educational.

Lovedale Press: Private Bag X1346, Alice; tel. (040) 6531135; fax (040) 6531871; f. 1841; Gen. Man. Rev. B. NTISANA.

Lux Verbi: POB 1822, Cape Town 8000; tel. (21) 4215540; fax (21) 4191865; e-mail luxverbi.publ@kingsley.co.za; religion; CEO H. S. SPIES; Editor-in-Chief D. FOURIE.

Macdonald Purnell (Pty) Ltd: POB 51401, Randburg 2125; tel. (11) 7875830; South African flora, fauna, geography and history; Man. Dir E. ANDERSON.

Marler Publications (Pty) Ltd: POB 27815, Sunnyside, Pretoria 0132; tel. (12) 573770; f. 1987; educational; Man. Dir C. J. MULLER.

Maskew Miller Longman (Pty) Ltd: cnr Forest Dr. and Logan Way, Pinelands 7405, POB 396, Cape Town 8000; tel. (21) 5317750; fax (21) 5314049; e-mail webmaster@mml.co.za; internet mml.co.za; f. 1983; educational and general.

Methodist Publishing House: POB 13128, Woodstock, Cape Town 7915; tel. (21) 4483640; fax (21) 4483716; e-mail methpub@ iafrica.com; internet www.methodist.org.za; religion and theology; Gen. Man. D. R. LEVERTON.

Nasionale Boekhandel: POB 122, Parow 7500; tel. (21) 5911131; fiction, general, educational, academic; English, Afrikaans and several African languages; Man. Dir P. J. BOTMA.

Nasou—Via Afrika: POB 5197, Cape Town 8000; tel. (21) 4063313; fax (21) 4062922; e-mail nasouhk@nasou.com; educational; Gen. Man. D. H. SCHROEDER.

New Holland Publishing (South Africa) (Pty) Ltd: POB 1144, Cape Town 8000; tel. (21) 4624360; fax (21) 4619378; Dir S. CONNOLLY, P. C. DESAI, F. M. LEE, A. C. B. MOLUSI, L. O'BRIEN, S. RYLANDS, R. P. WILKINSON, B. D. WOOTTON.

Oudiovista Productions (Pty) Ltd: Parow; tel. (21) 5911131; Man. Dir P. J. BOTMA.

Oxford University Press: POB 12119, N1 City, Cape Town 7463; tel. (21) 5954400; fax (21) 5954430; e-mail oxford@oup.com; internet www.oup.com/za; f. 1914; Man. Dir KATE MCCALLUM.

Perskor Publishers: POB 3068, Halfway House 1685; tel. (11) 3153647; fax (11) 3152757; e-mail vlacberg@icon.co.za; f. 1940; general and educational; Sr Gen. Man. G. DE BEER.

David Philip Publishers (Pty) Ltd: POB 23408, Claremont 7735; tel. (21) 6744136; fax (21) 6743358; e-mail info@dpp.co.za; f. 1971; general, academic, literature, reference, fiction; Man. Dir BRIAN WAFOWAROWA.

Pretoria Boekhandel: POB 23334, Innesdale, Pretoria 0031; tel. (12) 761531; f. 1971; Prin. Officer L. S. VAN DER WALT.

Random House SA (Pty) Ltd: POB 2263, Parklands 2121; tel. (11) 4843538; fax (11) 4846180; e-mail mail@randomhouse.co.za; f. 1966; Man. Dir S. JOHNSON.

Ravan Press (Pty) Ltd: POB 145, Randburg 2125; tel. (11) 7897636; fax (11) 7897653; e-mail ipuseng@hodder.co.za; f. 1972; political, sociological, fiction, business studies, gender, history, autobiography, biography, educational; Man. Dir DAVID LEA.

Saayman and Weber (Pty) Ltd: POB 673, Cape Town 8000; f. 1980.

Sasavona Publishers and Booksellers: Private Bag X8, Braamfontein 2017; tel. (11) 4032502; fax (11) 3397274; Northern Sotho, Tshwa, Tsonga, Tswana, Venda and Zulu; Man. A. E. KALTENRIEDER.

Shuter and Shooter (Pty) Ltd: 230 Church St, Pietermaritzburg 3201; POB 109, Pietermaritzburg 3200; tel. (33) 3946830; fax (33) 3427419; e-mail dryder@shuter.co.za; internet www.shuter.co.za; f. 1921; educational, general and African languages; Man. Dir D. F. RYDER.

Study Aids Ltd: 13 Darrock Ave, Albemarle Park, Germiston 1401; study aids.

Hans Strydom Publishers: Private Bag 10, Mellville 2109.

Sunray Publishers: 96 Queen St, Durban 4001; tel. (31) 3052543.

Tafelberg Publishers Ltd: 28 Wale St, POB 879, Cape Town 8000; tel. (21) 4241320; fax (21) 4242510; e-mail tafelbrg@tafelberg.com; internet www.tafelberg.com; f. 1950; juvenile, fiction and non-fiction, arts and crafts, nature and tourism; Gen. Man. J. P. VAN ZYL.

Thomson Publications: Johannesburg 2123; tel. (11) 7892144; fax (11) 7893196; f. 1948; trade and technical; Man. Dir JOE M. BRADY.

UCCSA Publications Dept: POB 31083, Braamfontein 2017; tel. (11) 8360065; f. 1946; Gen. Man. W. WESTENBORG.

University of Natal Press: Private Bag X01, Scottsville 3209; tel. (33) 2605226; fax (33) 2605801; e-mail books@press.unp.ac.za; internet www.unpress.co.za; Publr GLENN COWLEY.

Van der Walt and Son, J. P. (Pty) Ltd: POB 123, Pretoria 0001; tel. (12) 3252100; fax (12) 3255498; f. 1947; general; Man. Dir C. J. STEENKAMP.

Chris van Rensburg Publications (Pty) Ltd: POB 29159, Mellville 2109; tel. (31) 7264350; yearbooks, general; Man. Dir. C. C. VAN RENSBURG.

Van Schaik, J. L. Publishers: POB 12681, Hatfield 0028; tel. (12) 3422765; fax (12) 4303563; e-mail dventer@vanscaiknet.com; f. 1914; educational, academic; English, Afrikaans and vernaculars; Gen. Man. E. WESSELS.

Waterkant Publishers: POB 4539, Cape Town 8000; tel. (21) 215540; fax (21) 4191865; f. 1980; Exec. Chair. W. J. VAN ZIJL.

Witwatersrand University Press: PO Wits, Johannesburg 2050; tel. (11) 4845910; fax (11) 4845971; e-mail klippv@wup.wits.ac.za; internet witspress.ac.za; f. 1922; academic; Head VERONICA KLIPP.

PUBLISHERS' ASSOCIATION

Publishers' Association of South Africa: 7 Warwick House, 150 Main Rd, Fish Hoek, Cape Town; POB 22640, Fish Hoek, Cape Town 7974; tel. (21) 7827677; fax (21) 7827679; e-mail pasa@publisha.co .za; internet www.publishsa.co.za; f. 1992; Nat. Man. LOUISE GAIN; Nat. Admin. DESIREE MURDOCH.

Broadcasting and Communications

TELECOMMUNICATIONS

South African Telecommunications Regulatory Authority (SATRA): 164 Katherine St, Sandton 2146; Private Bag X1, Marlboro 2063; tel. (11) 3218200; fax (11) 3218551; e-mail estag@satra .gov.za; internet www.satra.gov.za.

Mobile Telephone Network: PMB 9955, Sandton 2146; tel. (11) 3016000; fax (11) 3016111; internet www.mtn.co.za.

Telkom SA Ltd: Private Bag X74, Pretoria 0001; tel. (12) 3111028; fax (12) 3114031; internet www.telkom.co.za; f. 1991; in process of being privatized in 2003; Chair. E. D. MOSENEKE; CEO SIZWE NXASANA.

BROADCASTING

Regulatory Authority

Independent Broadcasting Authority: Pinmill Farm, 164 Katherine St, Sandton 2146; tel. (22) 7220000; fax (11) 4441919; e-mail info@theiba.org.za; internet www.iba.org.za; f. 1993; Chair. MANDLA LANGA.

RADIO

South African Broadcasting Corpn (SABC)—Radio: Private Bag X1, Auckland Park 2006; tel. (11) 7143407; fax (11) 7142635; e-mail info@sabc.co.za; internet www.sabc.co.za; Chair. Prof. PAULUS ZULU; CEO CHARLOTTE MAMPANE.

Domestic Services

Radio South Africa; Afrikaans Stereo; Radio 5; Radio 2000; Highveld Stereo; Good Hope Stereo; Radio Kontrei; RPN Stereo; Jacaranda Stereo; Radio Algoa (regional services); Radio Lotus (Indian service in English); Radio Metro (African service in English); Radio Lebowa; Radio Ndebele; Radio Sesotho; Setswana Stereo; Radio Swazi; Radio Tsonga; Radio Xhosa; Radio Zulu.

External Service

Channel Africa Radio: POB 91313, Auckland Park 2006; tel. (11) 7142255; fax (11) 7142546; e-mail africancan@channel.africa.org; internet www.channelafrica.org.za; f. 1966; SABC's external service; broadcasts 217 hours per week in English, French, Kiswahili, Portuguese and several African languages; Exec. Editor Hans-Dieter Winkens.

TELEVISION

South African Broadcasting Corpn (SABC)—Television: Private Bag X41, Auckland Park 2006; tel. (11) 7149111; fax (11) 7145055; e-mail info@sabc.co.za; internet www.sabc.co.za; transmissions began in 1976; operates television services in seven languages over three channels; English and Afrikaans programmes on Channel one (TV1); Channel two (CCV-TV) broadcasts in English, Northern and Southern Sotho, Tswana, Xhosa and Zulu; Channel three (NNTV) broadcasts documentaries, educational programmes and sport; Chair. Prof. Paulus Zulu; CEO Molefe Mokgatle.

Finance

(cap. = capital; auth. = authorized; res = reserves; dep. = deposits; m. = million; brs = branches; amounts in rand)

BANKING

Central Bank

South African Reserve Bank: 370 Church St, POB 427, Pretoria 0001; tel. (12) 3133911; fax (12) 3133197; e-mail info@gwise.resbank .co.za; internet www.resbank.co.za; f. 1921; cap. and res 3,730.5m., dep. 44,426.2m. (March 2001); Gov. Tito Mboweni; Sen. Dep. Gov. X. P. Guma; 7 brs.

Commercial Banks

ABSA Bank Ltd: ABSA Towers, 3rd Floor, 160 Main St, Johannesburg 2001; tel. (11) 3504000; fax (11) 3503768; e-mail absa@absa.co .za; internet www.absa.co.za; cap. and res 10,046m., dep. 200,906m. (March 2002); Chair. Dr Danie Cronje; Man. Dir E. R. Bosman; 726 brs.

African Bank Ltd: Block D1, Old Mutual Business Park, Gewel St, Isando, POB 700, Kempton Park 1620; tel. (11) 9741156; fax (11) 9741100; e-mail linette@altfin.co.za; internet www.abil.co.za; f. 1975; cap. 1,600.0m., res 1,116.7m. (Dec. 1998); Man. Dir L. Kirkinis; 268 brs.

Albaraka Bank Ltd: POB 4395, Durban 4000, KwaZulu/Natal; tel. (31) 3072972; fax (31) 3052631; e-mail albaraka@icon.co.za; f. 1989; cap. and res 31.4m., dep. 249.2m. (June 1997); Chair. A. A. Sabbahi; CEO E. E. Vawda.

Boundary Financing Ltd: Sunnyside Ridge Bldg, 3rd Floor, 32 Princess of Wales Terrace, Parktown, Johannesburg 2193, Gauteng; tel. (11) 6443300; fax (11) 6431122; e-mail bsa@internationalbank.co .za; f. 1990 as Commercial Bank of Namibia S.A. cap. 64.1m., dep. 1,906.4m. (Dec. 1999); Chair. Guentar Zeno Steffens; Man. Dir Nigel Ernest Palmer.

FirstRand Bank Ltd: 1 First Place, 6th Floor, BankCity, Johannesburg 2001; POB 1153, Johannesburg 2000; tel. (11) 3712111; fax (11) 3712257; internet www.fnb.co.za; First National Bank of Southern Africa and Rand Merchant Bank merged July 1999; f. 1971; cap. 3,500m., res 5,087.1m., dep. 86,767.8m. (Sept. 1998); Chair. T. N. Chapman; Man. Dir V. W. Bartlett; 1,360 brs.

Habib Overseas Bank Ltd: Oriental Plaza, Fordsburg 2092; tel. (11) 8347441; fax (11) 8347446; e-mail habib@global.co.za; internet www.habibsons.com; f. 1990; cap. 11m., dep. 186.7m. (Dec. 2001); Chair. Mohammad Hassan Habib; Man. Dir Anjum Zaheer; 4 brs.

Investec Bank Ltd: 100 Grayston Dr., Sandown, Sandton 2196; tel. (11) 2867000; fax (11) 2867777; internet www.investec.com; f. 1974; cap. 14m., res 5,419m., dep. 156,168m. (March 2000); Chair. Hugh Herman.

Meeg Bank Ltd: POB 232, Bank of Transkei Bldg, 60 Sutherland St, Umtata; tel. (471) 311367; fax (471) 22546; f. 1977; cap. and res 34.8m., dep. 392.6m. (March 1996); formerly Bank of Transkei; name changed Oct. 1998; Chair. E. R. Bosman; Man. Dir. E. G. Kaltenbrünn; 5 brs.

Mercantile Bank Ltd: Mercantile Lisbon House, 142 West St, Sandown, Gauteng 2196; tel. (11) 3020477; fax (11) 8837756; e-mail fcoelho@mercantile.co.za; internet www.mercantile.co.za; f. 1965; cap. and res 816.3m. dep. 3,141.2m. (March 2001); Chair. J. A. S. de Andrade Campos; Man. Dir R. J. Symmonds.

Nedcor Bank: 135 Rivonia Road, Sandown, Sandton, Johannesburg 2001; tel. (11) 2944444; fax (11) 2955555; e-mail nedcorir@icon .co.za; internet www.nedcor.co.za; f. 1988; cap. and res 11,429m., dep. 141,420m. (Dec. 2001); Chair. C. F. Liebenberg; CEO Richard C. M. Laubscher; 242 brs.

South African Bank of Athens Ltd: Bank of Athens Bldg, 116 Marshall St, Johannesburg 2001; POB 7781, Johannesburg 2000; tel. (11) 8321211; fax (11) 8381001; e-mail sabafmad@mweb.co.za; f. 1947; associated with National Bank of Greece; cap. 4.1m., res 26.6m., dep. 345.3m. (Dec. 2001); Chair. G. Lanaras; Man. Dir N. E. Palmer; 14 brs.

Standard Bank South Africa Ltd: Standard Bank Centre, 5 Simmonds St, Johannesburg, Gauteng 2000; tel. (11) 6369111; fax (11) 6365617; internet www.standardbank.co.za; f. 1862; cap. 4,995.0m., res 6,393.0m., dep. 155,335.0m. (Dec. 2001); Chair. D. E. Cooper; CEO Jacko H. Maree; 997 brs.

Merchant Bank

UAL Merchant Bank Ltd: UAL Gardens, 1 Newton Ave, Killarney, Johannesburg; tel. (11) 4801000; fax (11) 4801525; cap. 6.0m., total assets 5,830.1m. (Sept. 1997); Chair. R. C. M. Laubscher.

Savings Banks

British Kaffrarian Savings Bank Society: POB 1432, King William's Town 5600; tel. (433) 21478; f. 1860; dep. 28.8m. CEO D. E. Daubermann.

Pretoria Bank Ltd: Woltemade Bldg, POB 1393, Pretoria; cap. 601,250; dep. 7.6m. Chair. M. D. Marais; Gen. Man. I. W. Ferreira.

Staalwerkerssparbank: 417 Church St, POB 1747, Pretoria; cap. 240,630; dep. 2.5m. Chair. and Man. Dir L. J. van den Berg.

Investment Banks

Investec Bank Ltd: 100 Grayston Dr., Sandton City 2146; tel. (11) 2867000; fax (11) 2867777; e-mail crosenberg@investec.co.za; internet www.investec.com; f. 1974; cap. 14m., res 5,419m., dep. 156,168m. (March 2000); Chair. H. S. Herman; CEO S. Koseff; 5 brs.

Nedcor Investment Bank Ltd: 1 Newtown Ave, Killarney 2193; POB 582, Johannesburg 2000; tel. (11) 4801000; fax (11) 4801525; internet www.nib.co.uk; f. 1955 as Union Acceptances Ltd; total assets 24,948.5m. (Dec. 2001); Chair. Prof. M. M. Katz; 2 brs.

Development Bank

Development Bank of Southern Africa (DBSA): 1258 Lever Rd, Midrand, POB 1234, Halfway House 1685; tel. (11) 3133911; fax (11) 3133086; e-mail thandim@dbsa.org; internet www.dbsa.org; cap. and res 4,069.8m., dep. 1,024.4m. (March 2001); f. 1983; Chair. Jayaseelan Naidoo; CEO Mandla Gantsho.

Discount Houses

Discount House Merchant Bank Ltd: 66 Marshall St, Johannesburg 2001; POB 61574, Marshalltown 2107; tel. (11) 8367451; fax (11) 8369636; f. 1957; cap. 18.8m. Exec. Chair. C. J. H. Dunn; Man. Dir M. R. Thompson.

Interbank Ltd: 108 Fox St, POB 6035, Johannesburg; tel. (11) 8344831; fax (11) 8345357; f. 1971; cap. 15.5m., dep. 564m. (1990); Chair. A. Kelly; Man. Dir M. Swart.

The National Discount House of South Africa Ltd: Loveday House, 1st Floor, 15 Loveday St, Johannesburg; tel. (11) 8323151; f. 1961; auth. cap. 10m., dep. 357.1m. (1987); Chair. M. MacDonald; Man. Dir G. G. Lund.

Bankers' Association

Banking Council of South Africa: 17 Harrison St, 10th Floor, POB 61674, Marshalltown 2107; tel. (11) 3703500; fax (11) 8365509; e-mail banking@banking.org.za; internet www.banking.org.za; f. 1993; 15,000 mems; CEO R. S. K. Tucker.

STOCK EXCHANGE

Johannesburg Stock Exchange: 17 Diagonal St, POB 1174, Johannesburg 2000; tel. (11) 3772200; fax (11) 8387106; e-mail pr@ jse.co.za; internet www.jse.co.za; f. 1887; in late 1995 legislation was enacted providing for the deregulation of the Stock Exchange; automated trading commenced in June 1996; Exec. Pres. R. M. Loubser.

INSURANCE

ACA Insurers Ltd: 35 Symons Rd, Auckland Park; tel. (11) 7268900; f. 1948; Man. Dir L. G. Y. Nemorin.

Aegis Insurance Co Ltd: Aegis Insurance House, 91 Commissioner St, Johannesburg; tel. (11) 8367621; fax (11) 8384559; Man. Dir B. H. Seach.

African Mutual Trust & Assurance Co Ltd: 34 Church St, POB 27, Malmesbury; f. 1900; Chief Gen. Man. R. A. L. Cuthbert.

Allianz Insurance Ltd: Allianz House, 13 Fraser St, Johannesburg 2001; POB 62228, Marshalltown 2107; tel. (11) 2804300; fax (11) 2804309; Chair. D. du Preez; Man. Dir Dr U. F. Delius.

Anglo American Life Assurance Co Ltd: Life Centre, 45 Commissioner St, POB 6946, Johannesburg 2000; Exec. Chair. Dr Z. J. DE BEER; Man. Dir Dr M. BERNSTEIN.

Credit Guarantee Insurance Corpn of Africa Ltd: 31 Dover St, POB 125, Randburg 2125; tel. (11) 8897000; fax (11) 8861027; e-mail info@cgic.co.za; internet www.creditguarantee.co.za; f. 1956; Chair. K. T. M. SAGGERS; Man. Dir M. C. TRUTER.

Fedsure Life Assurance Ltd: Fedsure House, 1 de Villiers St, POB 666, Johannesburg 2000; tel. (11) 3326500; fax (11) 4921102; e-mail fedsure@fedsure.co.za; internet www.fedsure.co.za; f. 1944; Chair. J. A. BARROW; Man. Dir MORRIS BERNSTEIN.

I. G. I. Insurance Co Ltd: 162 Anderson St, POB 8199, Johannesburg 2000; tel. (11) 3351911; fax (11) 290491; f. 1954; Chair. I. M. A. LEWIS; Man. Dir P. S. DENNISS.

Liberty Group Ltd (LGL): Liberty Life Centre, 1 Ameshoff St, Johannesburg 2001; POB 10499, Johannesburg 2000; tel. (11) 4083911; fax (11) 4082109; e-mail info@liberty.co.za; internet www.liberty.co.za; f. 1959; Chair. D. E. COOPER; CEO ROY ANDERSEN.

Metropolitan Life Ltd: 7 Coen Steytler Ave, Foreshore, Cape Town; POB 2212, Bellville 7535; tel. (21) 9405911; fax (21) 9405730; internet www.metropolitan.co.za; Chair. D. E. MOSENEKE; Man. Dir P. R. DOYLE.

Momentum Life Assurers Ltd: Momentum Park, 267B West Ave, Centurion 0157; POB 7400, Centurion 0046; tel. (12) 6718911; fax (12) 6636288; internet www.momentum.co.za; f. 1967; Chair. LAURIE DIPPENAAR; Man. Dir HILLIE P. MEYER.

Mutual & Federal Insurance Co Ltd: Mutual Federal Centre, 75 President St, POB 1120, Johannesburg 2000; tel. (11) 3749111; fax (11) 3742652; internet www.mf.co.uk; f. 1970; Chair. K. T. M. SAGGERS; Man. Dir B. CAMPBELL.

Old Mutual (South African Mutual Life Assurance Society): Mutualpark, Jan Smuts Dr., POB 66, Cape Town 8001; tel. (21) 5099111; fax (21) 5094444; internet www.oldmutual.com; f. 1845; Chair. MICHAEL J. LEVETT; CEO JAMES SUTCLIFFE.

Protea Assurance Co Ltd: Protea Assurance Bldg, Greenmarket Sq., POB 646, Cape Town 8000; tel. (21) 4887911; fax (21) 4887110; Man. Dir A. L. TAINTON.

The Rand Mutual Assurance Co Ltd: POB 61413, Marshalltown 2107; tel. (11) 4976600; fax (11) 8344150; f. 1894; Chair. P. J. EUSTACE; Man. Dir A. J. E. FIVAZ.

Santam Ltd: Santam Head Office, 1 Sportica Crescent, Bellville 7530, POB 3881, Tyger Valley 7536; tel. (21) 9157000; fax (21) 9140700; internet www.santam.co.za; f. 1918; Chair. M. H. DALING; Man. Dir L. VERMAAK.

South African Eagle Insurance Co Ltd: SA Eagle House, The Braes, 193 Bryanston Dr., Bryanston 2021, POB 61489, Marshalltown 2107; tel. (11) 5404000; fax (11) 5404444; internet www.saeagle.co.za; Chair. P. J. O'SULLIVAN; CEO N. V. BEYERS.

South African National Life Assurance Co Ltd (SANLAM): 2 Strand Rd, Bellville, POB 1, Sanlamhof 7532; tel. (21) 9479111; fax (21) 9478066; e-mail chairman@sanlam.co.za; f. 1918; Chair. MARINUS DALING.

South African Trade Union Assurance Society Ltd: Capital Alliance Life Ltd, 162 Anderson St, Johannesburg 2000; tel. (11) 3301000; fax (11) 3301013; f. 1941; Chair. E. VAN TONDER; Gen. Man. A. SUMNER.

Standard General Insurance Co Ltd: Standard General House, 12 Harrison St, POB 4352, Johannesburg 2000; tel. (11) 8362723; fax (11) 8344935; f. 1943; Man. Dir Dr M. DEYSEL.

Swiss Re Southern Africa Ltd: Swiss Park, 10 Queens Rd, Parktown, POB 7049, Johannesburg 2000; tel. (11) 4895600; fax (11) 4844448; f. 1950; Chair. and Man. Dir L. KEEL.

UBS Insurance Co Ltd: United Bldgs, 6th Floor, cnr Fox and Eloff Sts, Johannesburg; Chair. P. W. SCEALES; Gen. Man. J. L. S. HEFER.

Westchester Insurance Co (Pty) Ltd: Mobil Court, POB 747, Cape Town 8000; tel. (21) 4034000.

Association

South African Insurance Asscn: POB 30619, Braamfontein 2017; tel. (11) 7265381; fax (11) 7265351; e-mail info@sainsurance.co.za; internet www.sainsurance.co.za; f. 1973; represents short-term insurers; CEO BARRY SCOTT.

Trade and Industry

DEVELOPMENT ORGANIZATIONS

Industrial Development Corpn of South Africa Ltd (IDC): 19 Fredman Dr., POB 784055, Sandton 2146; tel. (11) 2693000; fax (11) 2693116; e-mail idc@idc.co.za; internet www.idc.co.za; f. 1940; Chair. Dr D. MJI; CEO K. NGQULA.

The Independent Development Trust: 129 Bree St, Cape Town 8001, POB 16114, Vlaeberg 8018; tel. (21) 238030; fax (21) 238401; f. 1990; finances health and rural devt, housing and urban devt, micro-enterprises, education, school and clinic-building projects; Chair. Dr MAMPHELA RAMPHELE.

National Productivity Institute: POB 3971, Pretoria 0001; tel. (12) 3411470; fax (12) 441866; e-mail npiinfo@cis.co.za; internet www.npi.co.za; f. 1968; Exec. Dir Dr Y. DLADLA.

CHAMBER OF COMMERCE

South African Chamber of Business (SACOB): JCC House, 3rd Floor, Empire Rd, Milpark, Johannesburg; POB 91267, Auckland Park 2006; tel. (11) 3589743; fax (11) 3589773; e-mail econo@sacob.co.za; internet www.sacob.co.za; f. 1990 by merger of Asscn of Chambers of Commerce and Industry and South African Federated Chamber of Industries; 70 chambers of commerce and industry are mems; Pres. HUMPHREY KHOZA; Dir-Gen. R. W. K. PARSONS; CEO KEVIN WAKEFORD.

CHAMBERS OF INDUSTRIES

Bloemfontein Chamber of Trade and Industry: POB 87, Kellner Heights, Bloemfontein 9300; tel. (51) 473368; fax (51) 475064.

Cape Chamber of Commerce and Industry: Cape Chamber House, 19 Louis Gradner St, Foreshore, Cape Town 8001; tel. (21) 4184300; fax (21) 4181800; f. 1994; Pres. DENIS SKEATE; 3,800 mems.

Durban Chamber of Commerce and Industry: POB 1506, Durban 4000; tel. (31) 3351000; fax (31) 3321288; e-mail chambers@durbanchamber.co.za; internet www.durbanchamber.co.za; CEO Dr J. WILSON; 5,500 mems.

Johannesburg Chamber of Commerce and Industry: JCC House, 6th Floor, Empire Road, Milpark; Private Bag 34, Auckland Park 2006; tel. (11) 7265300; fax (11) 4822000; e-mail info@jcci.co.za; internet www.jcci.co.za; Pres. R. NTULI; 3,800 mems.

Pietermaritzburg Chamber of Industries: POB 637, Pietermaritzburg 3200; tel. (331) 452747; fax (331) 944151; f. 1910; Dir R. J. ALLEN; 300 mems.

Port Elizabeth Regional Chamber of Commerce and Industry: Chamber House, 22 Grahamstown Rd, Port Elizabeth 6001, POB 2221, North End 6056; tel. (41) 4844430; fax (41) 4871851; e-mail info@pechamber.org.za; internet www.pechamber.org.za; f. 1995; CEO A. DA COSTA; 1,100 mems.

Pretoria Business and Agricultural Centre: Showground Office, Soutter St, Pretoria 0183; POB 933, Pretoria 0001; tel. (12) 3271487; fax (12) 3271501; e-mail info@comsa.com; f. 1929; Exec. Dir R. A. BUITENDAG; 310 mems.

Wesvaal Chamber of Business: POB 7, Klerksdorp 2570; tel. (18) 4627401; fax (18) 4627402; e-mail chamber@gds.co.za; Pres. K. LE ROUX.

INDUSTRIAL AND TRADE ORGANIZATIONS

Association of Cementitious Material Producers: POB 10181, Centurion 0046; tel. (12) 6635146; fax (12) 6636036; e-mail naudek.ACMP@mweb.co.za.

Building Industries Federation South Africa: POB 1619, Halfway House 1685; tel. (11) 3151010; fax (11) 3151644; e-mail bifsa@bifsa.org.za; internet www.bifsa.org.za; f. 1904; 5,000 mems.

Chamber of Mines of South Africa: Chamber of Mines Bldg, 5 Hollard St, POB 61809, Marshalltown 2107; tel. (11) 4987100; fax (11) 8341884; e-mail webmaster@bullion.org.za; internet www.bullion.org.za; f. 1889; Pres. RICK MENELL.

Clothing Federation of South Africa: 35 Siemers Rd, 6th Floor, Doornfontein, POB 2303, Johannesburg 2000; tel. (11) 4020664; fax (11) 4020667; e-mail clofed@clofed.co.za; internet www.clofed.co.za; Dir P. L. THERON.

FOSKOR Ltd: POB 1, Phalaborwa 1390; tel. (15) 7892910; fax (15) 7892070; e-mail foskor.msmail@foskor.co.za; Man. Dir P. J. GREYLING.

Grain Milling Federation: Johannesburg; f. 1944; Sec. J. BARENDSE.

Industrial Rubber Manufacturers' Association of South Africa: POB 91267, Auckland Park 2006; tel. (11) 4822524; fax (11) 7261344; f. 1978; Chair. Dr D. DUNCAN.

Master Diamond Cutters' Association of South Africa: S.A. Diamond Centre, Suite 310, 240 Commissioner St, Johannesburg 2001; tel. (11) 3341930; fax (11) 3341933; e-mail diam@pixie.co.za; f. 1928; 76 mems.

National Association of Automobile Manufacturers of South Africa: Nedbank Plaza, 1st Floor, cnr Church and Beatrix Sts, Pretoria 0002; POB 40611, Arcadia 0007; tel. (12) 3232003; fax (12) 3263232; e-mail naamsa@iafrica.com; f. 1935; Dir N. M. W. VERMEULEN.

National Chamber of Milling, Inc: Braamfontein; tel. (11) 4033739; f. 1936; Dir Dr J. B. DE SWARDT.

National Textile Manufacturers' Association: POB 1506, Durban 4000; tel. (31) 3013692; fax (31) 3045255; f. 1947; Sec. PETER McGREGOR; 9 mems.

Plastics Federation of South Africa: 18 Gazelle Rd, Corporate Park, Old Pretoria Rd, Midrand, Private Bag X68, Halfway House 1685; tel. (11) 3144021; fax (11) 3143764; f. 1979; Exec. Dir W. NAUDÉ; 3 mems.

Printing Industries Federation of South Africa: Printech Ave, Laser Park, POB 1084, Honeydew 2040; tel. (11) 7943810; fax (11) 7943964; e-mail pifsa@pifsa.org; internet www.pifsa.org; f. 1916; CEO C. W. J. SYKES.

Retail Motor Industry Organization (RMI): POB 2940, Randburg 2125; tel. (11) 8866300; fax (11) 7894525; e-mail rmi@rmi.org.za; internet www.rmi.org.za; Dir JEFF OSBORNE.

SOEKOR E and P (Pty) Ltd: POB 307, Parow 7499; tel. (21) 9383911; fax (21) 9383144; e-mail soekor@soekor.co.za; internet www.soekor.co.za; f. 1965; responsible for all offshore petroleum and natural gas prospecting in South Africa; CEO M. J. HEÜSER.

South African Dairy Foundation: POB 72300, Lynnwood Ridge 0040; tel. (2712) 3485345; fax (2712) 3486284; f. 1980; Sec. S. L. VAN COLLER; 59 mems.

South African Federation of Civil Engineering Contractors: POB 644, Bedfordview 2008; tel. (11) 4551700; fax (11) 4501715; e-mail contract@safcec.org.za; internet www.safcec.org.za; f. 1939; Exec. Dir H. P. LANGENHOVEN; 310 mems.

South African Foreign Trade Organization (SAFTO): POB 782706, Sandton 2146; tel. (11) 8833737; fax (11) 8836569; e-mail safto@apollo.is.co.za; f. 1963; Chair. W. C. VAN DER MERWE; CEO J. J. SCHEEPERS; 1,500 mems.

South African Fruit and Vegetable Canners' Association (Pty) Ltd: Canning Fruit Board Bldg, 258 Main St, POB 6175, Paarl 7622; tel. (21) 8711308; fax (21) 8725930; e-mail safvpa@mweb.co.za; f. 1953; Gen. Man. T. R. M. MALONE; 9 mems.

South African Inshore Fishing Industry Association (Pty) Ltd: POB 2066, Cape Town 8000; tel. (21) 251500; f. 1953; Chair. W. A. LEWIS; Man. S. J. MALHERBE; 4 mems.

South African Lumber Millers' Association: Private Bag X686, Isando 1600; tel. (11) 9741061; fax (11) 9749779; e-mail jmort@salma.org.za; internet www.salma.org.za; f. 1941; Exec. Dir J. H. MORTIMER; 88 mems.

South African Oil Expressers' Association: Cereal Centre, 6th Floor, 11 Leyds St, Braamfontein 2017; tel. (11) 7251280; f. 1937; Sec. Dr R. DU TOIT; 14 mems.

South African Paint Manufacturers' Association: POB 751605, Gardenview, Johannesburg 2047; tel. (11) 4552503; fax (11) 4552502; e-mail sapma@sapma.org.za; internet www.sapma.org.za.

South African Petroleum Industry Association (SAPIA): Cape Town; represents South Africa's six principal petroleum cos; Chair. FRED PHASWANA.

South African Sugar Association: 170 Flanders Dr., POB 700, Mount Edgecombe 4300; tel. (31) 5087000; fax (31) 5087199; e-mail sugarmail@sasa.org.za; internet www.sugar.org.za; Exec. Dir M. K. TRIKAM.

South African Wool Board: POB 2191, Port Elizabeth 6056; tel. (41) 544301; fax (41) 546760; f. 1946; 12 mems: nine appointed by wool-growers and three by the Minister of Agriculture and Land Affairs; Chair. H. F. PRINSLOO; CEO Dr J. W. GIESELBACH.

South African Wool Textile Council: POB 2201, North End, Port Elizabeth 6056; tel. (41) 4845252; fax (41) 4845629; e-mail woolexsa@iafrica.com; Sec. BEATTY-ANNE STARKEY.

Steel and Engineering Industries Federation of South Africa (SEIFSA): POB 1338, Johannesburg 2000; tel. (11) 8336033; fax (11) 8381522; e-mail angelique@seifsa.co.za; internet www.seifsa.co.za; f. 1943; Exec. Dir. B. ANGUS; 40 affiliated trade asscns representing 2,443 mems.

Sugar Manufacturing and Refining Employers' Association: 170 Flanders Dr., POB 1000, Mount Edgecombe 4300; tel. (31) 5087300; fax (31) 5087310; e-mail sasmal@sasa.org.za; f. 1947; Chair. M. M. KUMALO.

UTILITIES

Electricity

Electricity Supply Commission (ESKOM): POB 1091, Johannesburg 2000; tel. (11) 8008111; fax (11) 8004390; internet www.eskom.co.za; f. 1923; state-controlled; CEO A. J. MORGAN.

Gas

SASOL Gas: POB 4211, Randburg 2125; tel. (11) 8897600; fax (11) 8897955; internet www.sasol.com/gas; f. 1964; Man. Dir HANS NAUDÉ.

Water

Umgeni Water: 310 Burger St, Pietermaritzburg 3201; tel. (331) 3411111; fax (331) 3411167; internet www.umgeni.co.za/contact.html.

Water Research Commission: Private Bag X03, Gezina 0031; tel. (12) 3300342; fax (12) 3312565; e-mail orders@wrc.org.za; internet www.wrc.org.za.

TRADE UNIONS

In 1994 the number of registered unions totalled 213, with a membership that represented about 24% of the economically active population. In addition there were an estimated 65 unregistered unions, with a membership of about 510,000.

Trade Union Federations

Congress of South African Trade Unions (COSATU): COSATU House, 4th Floor, 1–5 Leyds St, Braamfontein, POB 1019, Johannesburg 2000; tel. (11) 3394911; fax (11) 3396940; e-mail cosatu@wn.apc.org; internet www.cosatu.org.za; f. 1985; 19 trade union affiliates representing c. 1.8m. mems; Pres. WILLIE MADISHA; Gen. Sec. JOSEPH NKOSI.

Principal affiliates include:

Chemical Workers' Industrial Union: Dalbridge 4014; tel. (11) 259510; fax (11) 256680; Pres. D. GUMEDE; Gen. Sec. R. CROMPTON.

Construction and Allied Workers' Union: POB 1962, Johannesburg 2000; tel. (11) 294321; fax (11) 3371578; Pres. D. NGCOBO; Gen. Sec. L. MADUMA.

Food and Allied Workers' Union: POB 234, Salt River 7925; tel. (21) 6379040; fax (21) 6383761; Pres. ERNEST THERON; Gen. Sec. MANDLA GXANYANA.

Health and Allied Workers' Union: POB 47011, Greyville 4023; tel. (11) 3063993; Gen. Sec. S. NGCOBO.

National Education, Health and Allied Workers' Union: 56 Marshall St, Marshalltown, POB 10812, Johannesburg 2000; tel. (11) 8332902; fax (11) 8343416; e-mail nehawu@wn.apc.org; Pres. VUSI NHLAPO; Gen. Sec. FIKILE MAJOLE.

National Union of Metalworkers of South Africa (NUMSA): 153 Bree St, Newtown, POB 260483, Johannesburg 2001; tel. (11) 8322031; fax (11) 8384092; e-mail dumisan@numsa.org.za; internet www.numsa.org.za; Pres. M. TOM; Gen. Sec. SILUMKO NONDWANGU; 232,000 mems (2000).

National Union of Mineworkers: POB 2424, Johannesburg 2000; tel. (11) 8337012; e-mail jmotlatsi@num.org.za; internet www.num.org.za; Pres. SENZENI ZOKWANA; Gen. Sec. GWEDE MANTASHE; 350,000 mems.

Paper, Printing, Wood and Allied Workers' Union: POB 3528, Johannesburg 2000; tel. (11) 3317721; fax (11) 3313750; e-mail ppwawu@wn.apc.oyg; Pres. P. DYANI; Gen. Sec. B. MTHOMBENI.

Post and Telecommunications Workers' Association: POB 260100, Excom 2023; tel. (11) 234351; Pres. K. MOSUNKULU; Gen. Sec. V. A. KHUMALO.

Southern African Clothing and Textile Workers' Union (SACTWU): POB 203, Woodstock 7915; tel. (21) 4474570; fax (21) 4472194; e-mail lynnt@sactwu.co.za; Pres. A. NTULI; Gen. Sec. EBRAHIM PATEL; 110,000 mems.

South African Railways and Harbours Workers' Union: POB 8059, Johannesburg 2000; tel. (11) 8343251; fax (11) 8344664; Pres. J. LANGA; Gen. Sec. M. SEBEKOANE.

South African Transport and Allied Workers' Union: POB 9451, Johannesburg 2000; tel. (11) 3319321; fax (11) 3315418; Pres. EZROM MABYANA; Gen. Sec. R. HOWARD.

Federation of Unions of South Africa (FEDUSA): POB 2096, Northcliff 2115, Johannesburg; tel. (11) 4765188; fax (11) 4765131; e-mail fedusa@fedusa.org.za; internet www.fedusa.org.za; Gen. Sec. CHEZ MILANI.

National Council of Trade Unions (NACTU): Lekton House, 7th Floor, 5 Wanderers St, POB 10928, Johannesburg 2000; tel. (11) 3368031; fax (11) 3337625; f. 1986; fed. of 22 African trade unions; Pres. JAMES MDLALOSE; Gen. Sec. CUNNINGHAM McGUKAMU.

Principal affiliates include:

Building, Construction and Allied Workers' Union: POB 96, Johannesburg 2000; tel. (11) 236311; Pres. J. SEISA; Gen. Sec. V. THUSI.

Hotel, Liquor and Catering Trade Employees' Union: POB 1409, Johannesburg 2000; tel. (11) 234039; Pres. E. NKOSI (acting); Gen. Sec. K. KEELE (acting).

Metal and Electrical Workers' Union of South Africa: POB 3669, Johannesburg 2000; tel. (11) 8369051; fax (11) 8369002; e-mail mewusa@cis.co.za; f. 1989; Pres. RUSSELL SABOR; Gen. Sec. ZITHULELE CINDI.

National Union of Farm Workers: POB 10928, Johannesburg 2000; tel. (11) 333054; fax (11) 337625; Pres. E. MUSEKWA; Gen. Sec. T. MOLETSANE.

National Union of Food, Beverage, Wine, Spirits and Allied Workers: POB 5718, Johannesburg 2000; tel. (11) 3335561; fax (1) 3333480; Pres. M. L. KWELEMTINI; Gen. Sec. L. SIKHAKHANE.

National Union of Public Service Workers: POB 10928, Johannesburg 2000; tel. (11) 232812; Pres. K. NTHUTE; Gen. Sec. S. RADEBE.

South African Chemical Workers' Union: POB 236, Johannesburg 2000; tel. (11) 8386581; fax (11) 8386622; Pres. W. THUTHANI; Gen. Sec. O. H. NDABA.

Steel, Engineering and Allied Workers' Union of South Africa: POB 4283, Johannesburg 2001; tel. (11) 3364865; fax (11) 294869; Pres. G. MABIDIKAMA; Gen. Sec. N. RAMAEMA.

South African Confederation of Labour: POB 19299, Pretoria West 0117; tel. (12) 793271; 7 mems; Pres. I. J. ELS; Sec. L. N. CELLIERS.

South African Independent Trade Unions Confederation (SAITUCO): f. 1995 by 14 independent trade unions that opposed the new draft legislation on labour relations; Pres. PIET SKHOSANA; Gen. Sec. THEMBA NCALO.

Transport

Most of South Africa's railway network and the harbours and airways are administered by the state-owned Transnet Ltd. There are no navigable rivers. Private bus services are regulated to complement the railways.

Transnet Ltd: 8 Hillside Rd, Parktown, Johannesburg; POB 72501, Parkview 2122; tel. (11) 4887055; fax (11) 4887511; e-mail sakim@transnet.co.za; internet www.tnet.co.za; Chair. Prof. LOUISE A. TAGER; Man. Dir SAKI MACOZOMA.

RAILWAYS

With the exception of commuter services, the South African railways system is operated by Spoornet Ltd (the rail division of Transnet). The network comprised 31,400 track-km in 1996, of which 16,946 km was electrified. Extensive rail links connect Spoornet with the rail networks of neighbouring countries.

Spoornet: Paul Kruger Bldg, 30 Wolmarans St, Private Bag X47, Johannesburg 2001; tel. (11) 7735090; fax (11) 7733033; internet www.spoornet.co.za; CEO ZANDILE JAKARULA.

ROADS

In 1999 there were an estimated 534,131 km of classified roads, including 2,032 km of motorways.

South African National Roads Agency Ltd: POB 415, Pretoria 0001; tel. (12) 4266000; fax (12) 3421320; internet www.nra.co.za; f. 1998; responsible for design, construction, management and maintenance of national road network; CEO NAZIR ALLI.

SHIPPING

The principal harbours are at Richards Bay, Cape Town, Port Elizabeth, East London, Durban and Saldanha Bay. The deep-water port at Richards Bay has been extended and its facilities upgraded. Both Richards Bay and Saldanha Bay are major bulk-handling ports, while Saldanha Bay also has an important fishing fleet.

More than 30 shipping lines serve South African ports. At the end of 2001 South Africa's merchant fleet had a total displacement of 381,868 grt.

PORTNET: POB 72501, Johannesburg; tel. (11) 2424019; fax (11) 2424027; e-mail webmaster@portnet.co.za; internet www.portnet.co .za; manages all seven commercial ports; Gen. Mans GERT DE BEER, PUMI SITHOLE, SYLVESTER HAANYAMA.

South African Maritime Safety Authority: SAMSA, POB 13186, Hatfield 0028; tel. (12) 3423049; fax (12) 3423160; e-mail samsa@iafrica.com; advises the Govt on matters connected with sea transport to, from or between South Africa's ports, incl. safety at sea, and prevention of pollution by petroleum; CEO Capt. B. R. WATT.

CIVIL AVIATION

Civil aviation is controlled by the Minister of Transport. The Chief Directorate: Civil Aviation Authority at the Department of Transport is responsible for licensing and control of domestic and international air services. The Airports Co owns and operates South Africa's nine principal airports, of which three (at Johannesburg, Cape Town and Durban) are classified as international airports.

Civil Aviation Authority (CAA): 281 Middle St, Nieu Muckleneuk, Pretoria; tel. (12) 3465566; fax (12) 3465979; e-mail mail@caa .co.za; internet www.caa.gov.za; CEO TREVOR ABRAHAMS.

South African Airways (SAA): Airways Park, Jones Rd, Private Bag X13, Johannesburg 1627; tel. (11) 9781111; fax (11) 9781106; internet www.flysaa.com; f. 1934; state-owned; internal passenger services linking all the principal towns; international services to Africa, Europe, N and S America and Asia; CEO and Pres. ANDRÉ VILJOEN.

Air Cape (Pty) Ltd: POB D. F. Malan Airport, Cape Town 7525; tel. (21) 9340344; fax (21) 9348379; scheduled internal passenger services and charters, engineering services and aerial surveys; Chair. Dr P. VAN ASWEGEN; Gen. Man. G. A. NORTJE.

Airlink Airline: POB 7529, Bonaero Park 1622; tel. (11) 3953333; fax (11) 3951076; f. 1992; internal and external scheduled services and charters; flights; Man. Dirs RODGER FOSTER, BARRIE WEBB.

COMAIR Ltd: POB 7015, Bonaero Park 1622; tel. (11) 9210111; fax (11) 9733913; e-mail comair.co.za; internet www.comair.co.za; f. 1946; scheduled domestic, regional and international services; Chair. D. NOVICK; Man. Dir P. VAN HOVEN.

Safair (Pty) Ltd: POB 938, Kempton Park 1620; tel. 9280000; fax 3951314; internet www.safair.co.za; f. 1965; subsidiary of Safmarine Aircraft Charters and Leasing; aircraft charters, leasing, engineering and maintenance services; Chair. W. G. LYNCH; CEO BRIAN FRANKEL.

Tourism

Tourism is an important part of South Africa's economy. The chief attractions for visitors are the climate, scenery and wildlife reserves. Tourist receipts provided an estimated US $2,738m. in foreign exchange in 1998. In 2001 5,908,024 tourists visited South Africa.

South African Tourism Board (SATOUR): 442 Rigel Ave South, Erasmusrand 0181, Private Bag X164, Pretoria 0001; tel. (12) 4826200; fax (12) 3478753; e-mail jhb@satour.com; internet www.za .satour.com; f. 1947; 13 overseas brs; Exec. Dir STELLA DU PLESSIS.

South African Tourism: Private Bag X10012, Sandton 2146; tel. (11) 7788000; fax (11) 7788001; e-mail info@satour.co.za; internet www.southafrica.net.

SPAIN

Introductory Survey

Location, Climate, Language, Religion, Flag, Capital

The Kingdom of Spain, in south-western Europe, forms more than four-fifths of the Iberian peninsula. The country also includes the Balearic Islands in the Mediterranean Sea, the Canary Islands in the Atlantic Ocean and a few small enclaves in Morocco. Mainland Spain is bounded to the north by France and to the west by Portugal. To the east is the Mediterranean Sea, and Morocco lies 30 km to the south. The climate is less temperate than in most of western Europe, with hot summers and, in the hilly interior, cold winters. The principal language is Castilian Spanish. Catalan is widely spoken in the north-east, Basque in the north and Galician in the north-west. The overwhelming majority of the population are Roman Catholics, but the 1978 Constitution laid down that Spain had no official state religion. The national flag (proportions 2 by 3) carries three horizontal stripes, of red, yellow (half the depth) and red. The state flag carries, in addition, the national coat of arms. The capital is Madrid.

Recent History

After winning the civil war of 1936–39, the Nationalist forces, led by Gen. Francisco Franco y Bahamonde, established an authoritarian rule which provided peace and stability, while restricting individual liberties and severely repressing challenges to its power. In 1942 Gen. Franco revived the traditional legislative assembly, the Cortes ('Courts'), with limited powers. After keeping Spain neutral in the Second World War, Gen. Franco announced in 1947 that the monarchy (abolished in 1931) would be restored after his death or retirement. In 1967, in the first elections since the civil war, a portion of the Cortes was directly elected under a limited franchise. In July 1969 Gen. Franco nominated Prince Juan Carlos de Borbón (grandson of the last reigning monarch, King Alfonso XIII) as his successor, and in June 1973 relinquished the post of President of the Council of Ministers to Adm. Luis Carrero Blanco, who was killed in December. Responsibility for the assassination was claimed by Euskadi ta Askatasuna (ETA), the Basque separatist organization. Carlos Arias Navarro became Prime Minister in January 1974.

Gen. Franco died in November 1975. He was succeeded as Head of State by King Juan Carlos, and in December a more liberal Council of Ministers was formed. In 1976 restrictions on political activity were lifted, but the slow progress of the reforms resulted in widespread demonstrations. In July Arias Navarro resigned at the King's request, and was replaced by Adolfo Suárez González. The introduction of democratic government then proceeded rapidly. Political reforms included the establishment of an elected bicameral legislature. Most of the numerous *de facto* political parties were able to take part in the general elections for the Cortes, held in June 1977. An overall majority was won by the Unión de Centro Democrático (UCD), a coalition party headed by the Prime Minister. In December 1978 a new Constitution was endorsed by referendum and ratified by the King. It confirmed Spain as a parliamentary monarchy, with freedom for political parties, and guaranteed the right of Spain's 'nationalities and regions' to autonomy.

A general election was held in March 1979, resulting in little change in the distribution of seats in the Cortes, although there was stronger support for the regionalist parties. The new Government was again headed by Suárez. Basque and Catalan autonomous parliaments were established in March 1980 and, in both elections, the UCD was heavily defeated by the moderate regionalist parties. Confidence in Suárez diminished and in January 1981, as a result of growing opposition from right-wing factions within the UCD, he unexpectedly resigned. Leopoldo Calvo Sotelo, hitherto the Deputy Prime Minister, succeeded him.

In February 1981 a group of armed civil guards, led by Lt-Col Antonio Tejero Molina, stormed into the Cortes, taking hostage 350 Deputies. The military commander of Valencia, Lt-Gen. Jaime Milans del Bosch, declared a state of emergency in that region and sent tanks on to the streets of the city of Valencia. King Juan Carlos acted swiftly to secure the loyalty of other military commanders, and by the following morning had been able to persuade Lt-Gen. Milans himself to stand down. Lt-Col Tejero surrendered, and the Deputies were released unharmed. More than 30 military officers were subsequently brought to trial, and both Lt-Col Tejero and Lt-Gen. Milans received lengthy prison sentences. Lt-Gen. Milans was released in mid-1990, and Lt-Col Tejero was released in December 1996.

Immediately after the attempted coup, Calvo Sotelo formed a new Council of Ministers, resisting pressure to establish a coalition government. The Prime Minister addressed various contentious issues during his term of office, including his decision to take Spain into the North Atlantic Treaty Organization (NATO, see p. 271). At the election for the first Galician Parliament, held in October 1981, the Alianza Popular (AP) won two seats more than the UCD. The overwhelming Socialist victory at the election for the Parliament of Andalucía in May 1982 was a grave set-back for the central Government. Following Calvo Sotelo's replacement as party leader by Landelino Lavilla Alsina in July, Suárez defected to found a rival party, the Centro Democrático y Social (CDS). Desertion from the UCD continued and by August the party no longer commanded a workable majority, and an early general election was called. In October, however, shortly before the election, a right-wing plot to stage a pre-emptive military coup was uncovered. Four colonels were arrested (three of whom were subsequently sentenced to prison terms), and Lt-Gen. Milans was also implicated. The election resulted in a decisive victory for the Partido Socialista Obrero Español (PSOE—Socialist Workers' Party), led by Felipe González Márquez, who formed a new Council of Ministers in December 1982.

One of the most serious problems facing the new Government was the continuing tension in the Basque region (see below). The Government's proposals for the rationalization of Spain's industry and bureaucracy, instigated in 1983, met with strong opposition from the trade unions. Further public demonstrations were held against a new education law, imposing stricter controls over privately-run schools in receipt of state subsidies, against the Government's restructuring policies, and against the lack of new jobs. In June 1985 hundreds of thousands of workers, motivated by the Unión General de Trabajadores (UGT —the socialist trade union) and supported by the Confederación Sindical de Comisiones Obreras (CCOO—the left-wing trade union), took to the streets to protest against proposed reforms in the social security system and consequent reductions in pension rights. Following large-scale demonstrations against Spain's continued membership of NATO, in March 1986 the long-awaited referendum on the question of Spain's membership of NATO was held. Contrary to expectations, the Spanish people voted to remain within the alliance, following Prime Minister González's reversal on the issue and an extensive pro-NATO campaign by the Government.

In an early general election held in June 1986 the PSOE was returned to power, winning 184 of the 350 seats in the Congreso de los Diputados (Congress of Deputies) (18 fewer than at the 1982 election), while the conservative Coalición Popular (CP), which incorporated the AP, the Partido Demócrata Popular (subsequently Democracia Cristiana) and the Partido Liberal, won 105 seats. The new Council of Ministers was appointed in late July, again led by González.

Following its defeat in the general election of mid-1986, the CP fell into disarray and in December Manuel Fraga, the leader of the AP, the principal component of the conservative grouping, resigned. Industrial unrest continued with frequent strikes against the Government's economic policies, notably its commitment to pay restraint; the public transport sector was particularly badly affected. At Reinosa (Cantabria) steelworkers protesting against the Government's rationalization programme were repeatedly involved in violent clashes with the police.

In June 1987 the results of the elections for the European Parliament, for 13 of the 17 regional parliaments and for the municipal governments confirmed the continuing decline in support for the PSOE. The AP also sustained losses, while the centre-left CDS was able to strengthen its position. The growing rift between the Prime Minister and the UGT, the socialist trade union, became increasingly evident during 1987, and in October Nicolás Redondo, the UGT leader, and a union colleague resigned from their seats as PSOE deputies in the Cortes, in protest against the Government's economic policies. The UGT and the left-wing CCOO then combined forces to organize a new campaign of protests against the Government, which continued throughout 1988. Intermittent strike action by teachers, in support of their demands for higher salaries, lasted for several months. Protests by civil servants, miners, farmers and workers in the transport, health and industrial sectors also took place. In northern Spain in May redundant shipyard workers became involved in violent confrontations with the security forces. In December 1988 the country was paralysed by a one-day general strike (the first since 1934), which was supported by almost 8m. workers. In April 1989 Madrid was brought to a halt by strikers demanding pay increases of up to 8%, action by transport workers again being particularly effective. Similar strikes elsewhere in Spain followed.

In January 1989 Fraga returned to the leadership of the AP, which was relaunched as the Partido Popular (PP) and was subsequently joined by Democracia Cristiana and the Partido Liberal. The unity of the PSOE was undermined by the establishment of a dissident faction and by the defection to the Izquierda Unida (IU, an alliance comprising the Partido Comunista de España (PCE) and other left-wing parties) of 100 PSOE members. Nevertheless, at the general election, held eight months early, in late October 1989, the PSOE was returned to power on a provisional basis, pending investigations into allegations of polling irregularities. After several months of controversy, the PSOE's final representation in the Congreso de los Diputados was reduced to 175 of the 350 seats, the PP holding 107 seats. The PSOE, however, was able to retain a majority by subsequently entering into a tactical alliance with the CDS, the Catalan Convergència i Unió (CiU) and the Partido Nacionalista Vasco (PNV, also known as Euzko Alderdi Jeltzalea—Basque Nationalist Party).

In April 1990 a corruption scandal involving the financing of the opposition PP was revealed. Rosendo Naseiro, the party treasurer, together with a number of other party officials and business executives, was arrested in connection with allegations of bribery. It was alleged that the PP had received funds from companies that were seeking planning permission or hoping to win municipal contracts. The allegations were substantiated by the publication of transcripts of recorded telephone conversations between PP officials. Furthermore, it was suggested that both José María Aznar, the new leader of the PP, and Fraga, his predecessor, had been aware of these illegal activities. The integrity of the PP, and indeed of other political parties, was therefore questioned. Many observers believed that parties were deriving a substantial portion of their income in this way. In December 1994, during the course of a congressional inquiry into the financing of political parties, Naseiro strenuously denied the allegations against him. Discrepancies in the PP's accounts, however, appeared to confirm suggestions that Fraga had received 363m. pesetas from Naseiro (to finance the former's Galician presidential campaign) of which only 199m. had been declared.

Following the revelation of a scandal involving his brother, in January 1991 the Deputy Prime Minister, Alfonso Guerra, resigned. He was replaced by Narcís Serra, hitherto Minister of Defence. An extensive government reorganization followed in March. Local elections were held in May, to coincide with elections to the regional parliaments. Although remaining the most widely-supported party, the PSOE lost control of several major cities. The CDS suffered heavy losses, as a result of which Suárez, the party leader and former Prime Minister, resigned.

In June 1991 Carlos Navarro, a senior PSOE treasurer, was obliged to resign, following the exposure of a scandal concerning alleged illicit donations to the ruling party. In January 1992, as labour unrest and protests against the Government's programme of industrial restructuring and attendant job losses continued, a fresh scandal arose, leading to the resignation of the Minister of Health and Consumer Affairs, Julián García Valverde. It was alleged that in 1990, while head of RENFE (the state railways organization), García Valverde had been responsible for fraudulent land purchases. Public concern at apparent widespread corruption increased further in February, when a new financial scandal was revealed, this time involving the Governor of the Central Bank, Mariano Rubio, who was accused of irregularities relating to his personal investments.

In early 1993 the PSOE's reputation was further damaged by new revelations concerning the party's financing. Having refused to permit inspection of its accounts, in late 1992 the PSOE headquarters had been forcibly searched on the orders of the judge investigating the allegations. The 'Filesa case', as the principal scandal became known, was named after a bogus Barcelona holding company which, it was claimed, had been administered by senior PSOE officials, including Navarro. It was alleged that during 1989–91 illicit contributions, totalling an estimated 1,000m. pesetas, had been made to Filesa by both private companies and public corporations, in return for fictitious consultancy work. Following a Supreme Court inquiry into the affair, PSOE officials, business executives and bankers were charged; the trial of 12 defendants, including Navarro, opened in July 1997. In September González, the previous Prime Minister, and Guerra, his former deputy, were obliged to give evidence in court. In late October Navarro was sentenced to a total of 11 years' imprisonment. Seven other defendants were sentenced to terms of imprisonment, including former Senator Josep Maria Sala who received three years. In December 1997, however, Sala was released pending an appeal. (The sentences of Navarro and the remaining defendants had also been suspended by July 2001.) In May 1993 the ruling party's difficulties were compounded by fresh allegations of misconduct, this time concerning the funding in 1986 of the campaign for the referendum to remain in NATO and for the legislative elections of that year.

At the general election in June 1993 the PSOE failed to obtain an absolute majority in the Congreso de los Diputados, where its strength declined to 159 of the 350 seats. The PP increased its representation to 141 seats, while the IU won 18 seats, the CiU 17 and the PNV five. The CDS lost all of its seats. The PSOE's negotiations with the CiU (which insisted upon greater control over taxes in return for support) and with the PNV failed to result in the conclusion of a formal coalition agreement. In July, therefore, González commenced his fourth term as Prime Minister, at the head of a minority administration.

With the Spanish economy in recession the Prime Minister appealed for support for drastic measures to address the economic crisis. In November 1993, however, thousands of protesters demonstrated against the Government's economic policies. Controversial labour legislation, as amended to comply with CiU requests, was approved by the Congreso de los Diputados in late March 1994.

In November 1993 the Government was embarrassed by the discovery of an illegal telephone 'tapping' network, centred on a respected Barcelona newspaper. The existence of a complex espionage and extortion operation was subsequently revealed, in which former agents of the country's military intelligence service, Centro Superior de Información de la Defensa (CESID), were implicated. In late June 1995 González accepted the resignations of Serra, the former Minister of Defence and current Deputy Prime Minister, and of Julián García Vargas, Serra's successor as Minister of Defence, following the exposure of the operation. In May 1999 Lt-Gen. Emilio Alonso Manglano, the former director of CESID, and Col Juan Alberto Perote, the intelligence service's former head of operations, both received a six-month prison sentence and were barred from public office for eight years for their part in the illegal recording of private telephone conversations during 1984–91, victims having included King Juan Carlos and senior politicians. Manglano and Perote were both pardoned in May 2001.

In April 1994 fresh accusations of tax evasion and 'insider' stock trading were made against Rubio, the former Governor of the central bank. In May he was arrested and imprisoned, along with Manuel de la Concha, a former chairman of the Madrid stock exchange.

Meanwhile, in April 1994 another government appointee, Luis Roldán, the former head of the paramilitary civil guard, absconded while under investigation on charges of tax fraud and embezzlement of government funds. It was alleged that Roldán's substantial personal wealth was derived from the misappropriation of the Ministry of the Interior's covert-operations reserves (notably for the financing of GAL—see below). Antoni Asunción, appointed Minister of the Interior in November 1993, was obliged to resign. In February 1995 Roldán was captured in Laos and promptly extradited via Thailand. The case against him, however, was jeopardized by the Laotian authorities' disclosure that Roldán's extradition documents had been forged. The Spanish Government was further embarrassed when, at a court hearing in March, Roldán accused the Deputy Prime Minister, among others, of corruption. Roldán was formally charged in July 1995, and brought to trial in June 1997. In February 1998, having been found guilty of fraud, embezzlement and tax evasion, Roldán was sentenced to a total of 28 years' imprisonment. (In December 1999 his sentence was increased to 31 years.) An associate received a nine-year sentence (subsequently increased to 12 years), while Roldán's wife was sentenced to four years. Five other defendants were acquitted. (In May 1996 Roldán also became implicated in the murders of José Antonio Lasa and José Ignacio Zabala—see below.)

In May 1994 the Minister of Agriculture resigned, following an admission of his failure, 10 years previously, to fulfil tax obligations on personal investments also handled by Manuel de la Concha. Furthermore, a number of former government ministers, including Carlos Solchaga, Minister of Finance during Rubio's tenure of office and a close associate of González, announced their intention to relinquish their seats in the Cortes.

Following the failure in December 1993 of the Banco Español de Crédito (Banesto), and the revelation of its huge debts and of irregularities, in June 1994 Mario Conde, the bank's former head, was accused of having conducted fraudulent operations. He was formally charged in November 1994, along with several other former executives of the bank. In March 1997 Conde received a six-year prison sentence, was fined 18m. pesetas and was ordered to pay 600m. pesetas in compensation to Banesto, the latter amount representing the sum illegally transferred in 1990 from the bank to an account of the Argentia Trust, based in Switzerland. Conde remained on bail, pending an appeal. At the opening in December 1997 of a new trial on other charges of fraud and embezzlement, Conde reappeared in court along with 10 former associates. In February 1998, the Supreme Court having confirmed a prison sentence of four-and-a-half years (instead of the original six years), Conde was returned to prison. In March 1998 the former banker claimed that in 1989, in exchange for favourable treatment, he had donated 300m. pesetas to the CDS. Testifying in court in October 1998, the former leader of that political party, Suárez, again denied that he had received the money in question. Conde was released in August 1999; in March 2000 he was sentenced to 10 years' imprisonment upon conviction of charges of fraud and misappropriation during his chairmanship of Banesto.

Confidence in the country's financial system was further undermined by the arrest in October 1994 of Javier de la Rosa, the prominent Barcelona financier, pending the investigation of charges of fraud and misappropriation of funds, brought in the United Kingdom by the Kuwait Investment Office (KIO). In July 1997, furthermore, it was reported that (during the campaign for elections to the Catalan Parliament in 1991) de la Rosa had made a substantial contribution to PP funds. Appearing in court in November 1997, de la Rosa confirmed the donation. In November 2002 de la Rosa was sentenced to 20 months' imprisonment.

Meanwhile, in mid-1988 the PSOE Government had been embarrassed by suggestions that it had been involved in the establishment of the counter-terrorist grouping, Grupos Antiterroristas de Liberación (GAL), which had been formed in 1983 with the aim of combating ETA. It was alleged that members of the Ertzaintza (Basque police force) had given support to these death squads, which were suspected of responsibility for the murders of numerous ETA members exiled in France. The Ministry of the Interior in Madrid was also implicated in the scandal. In July 1988 a senior police-officer in Bilbao, José Amedo Fouce, and an accomplice, Michel Domínguez, were formally charged with organizing the groups of mercenaries. Their trial concluded in mid-1991, both defendants receiving long prison sentences. In December 1994, following further questioning of the pair and the reopening of the case, Julián Sancristóbal, a former director-general of state security in the Ministry of the Interior, was arrested on suspicion of financing and assisting GAL. The Prime Minister denied that the Government had been connected in any way with the so-called 'dirty war' against ETA. At the end of the month the Minister of Justice and the Interior was obliged to appear before a congressional commission of inquiry.

In January 1995 the investigating judge, Baltasar Garzón, ordered the arrest of the former personal assistant of Rafael Vera, ex-Secretary of State for Security, on suspicion of embezzlement. Vera himself was detained in the following month, accused of involvement in the kidnapping in 1983 of Segundo Marey, a French business executive mistaken for an ETA

member, and of misappropriation of public funds. In early 1995 the Prime Minister came under increasing pressure over the GAL affair. In March the remains of José Antonio Lasa and José Ignacio Zabala, two ETA members apparently tortured before being murdered by GAL in 1983, were identified by forensic scientists. An inquiry into their fate had been closed in 1988, ostensibly owing to lack of evidence. A new inquiry into their deaths was instigated. In April 1995, concluding that GAL had been established and financed by the Ministry of the Interior, Judge Garzón indicted a total of 14 former officials, including Vera and Sancristóbal, both of whom were subsequently released on bail.

Despite the gravity of the latest scandals and the PSOE's heavy losses at the municipal and regional elections of May, the Prime Minister continued to reject demands for his resignation. In July, however, he announced that a general election would be held in early 1996. At the end of July Judge Garzón submitted to the Supreme Court a report of his investigations into the origins and financing of GAL: his findings implicated González personally; Serra, the former Deputy Prime Minister and Minister of Defence; José Barrionuevo, Minister of the Interior during 1982–88; the Basque socialist leader, Txiki Benegas; and other PSOE officials. In a separate development, it was reported that, prior to their murders in 1983, Lasa and Zabala had been abducted by a group of civil guards and detained in San Sebastián in a building owned by the Ministry of the Interior. In August 1995, appearing before Judge Garzón, Lt-Gen. Manglano, who in June had resigned as director of CESID prior to being formally charged, denied the existence of secret service documents relating to GAL.

In September 1995, shortly after the Supreme Court's appointment of Judge Eduardo Móner to examine the allegations against the Prime Minister and the other senior politicians, the CiU formally withdrew its support for the ruling party. In the same month the Prime Minister's claim that there existed a plot to discredit his administration appeared to assume some credibility when it was reported that Conde, the disgraced banker, had attempted to blackmail the Government by threatening to release stolen CESID documents relating to GAL, if the legal action against him were not withdrawn and compensation paid. In June 1997 Conde admitted to having used the stolen documents in his blackmail attempts. (In July 1997 Col Perote, the former head of operations at CESID, was sentenced by a military court to seven years' imprisonment for the theft of the documents; he was released in April 1999.) In a magazine interview in February 1998, Luis María Anson, former director of *ABC* (the conservative newspaper), disclosed that he had been a member of a media group that had indeed conspired to bring down the Government of González. The PP was also implicated in the affair.

Also in September 1995 Sancristóbal declared before Judge Móner that the abduction of Marey in 1983 had been approved by both Barrionuevo and Vera. In October 1995 José Luis Corcuera (who had succeeded Barrionuevo as Minister of the Interior), Sancristóbal and Vera were charged with misuse of public funds.

In January 1996, his parliamentary immunity having been removed, Barrionuevo was indicted by the Supreme Court. His alleged involvement in the 'dirty war' of the 1980s related to three charges: illegal detention (the abduction of Marey); misuse of public funds; and association with an armed group. In April Judge Móner reported that he had found no evidence linking González to the activities of the death squads, believed to be responsible for the murders of 27 ETA members. Serra and Benegas were also exonerated. In May further arrests in connection with the GAL inquiry were made. Several members of the Civil Guard, including Gen. Enrique Rodríguez Galindo and two other senior generals, were detained. Charges included involvement in the murders of Lasa and Zabala. In June 1996 Vera was charged with concealing these two murders, while the former Governor of Guipúzcoa, Julen Elgorriaga, was also imprisoned in connection with the case.

In August 1996 the Government approved draft legislation clarifying the regulations on official secrets. In late August, however, the investigating judge, Javier Gómez de Liaño, accused the Government of obstructing his inquiry by refusing to declassify CESID documents relating to the 'dirty war'. The matter was referred to the Supreme Court. In November 1996 the Supreme Court voted not to pursue the case against González, Serra and Benegas, as there was insufficient evidence to connect the former Prime Minister and his colleagues to the activities of GAL. (In November 1999 the Supreme Court refused a further request for an investigation into González's alleged involvement in the events of the 'dirty war'.)

In December 1996 the General Council of Judicial Power ordered an investigation into the release to the press (and their publication in two daily newspapers) of the CESID documents in question. In March 1997 the Supreme Court ordered the declassification of 13 of the 16 CESID documents, thereby permitting their use as evidence in court. In April Judge Móner concluded his inquiry into the abduction of Marey. In September the Supreme Court confirmed that 12 defendants were to stand trial: Barrionuevo, former Minister of the Interior; Vera, former Secretary of State for Security; Ricardo García Damborenea, a former PSOE official; Sancristóbal, Amedo and Domínguez, the former civil guards; and six others. In April 1998 the Supreme Court ruled that González, the former Prime Minister, and Francisco Álvarez-Cascos, the current Deputy Prime Minister, were to give evidence in court in relation to the abduction of Marey. The trial concluded in July 1998. Barrionuevo, Vera and Sancristóbal were found guilty of kidnapping and misappropriation of public funds, each receiving a prison sentence of 10 years. The sentences of the other nine defendants ranged from two to nine years. The 12 defendants were also ordered to pay 30m. pesetas in compensation to Marey. During September the immediate commencement of the prison terms of Barrionuevo and Vera (the pair having refused to request a pardon) and of the other defendants was ordered. By the end of December, however, 11 of the prisoners had been set free, their sentences having been suspended, while the 12th was released in June 2000. In March 2001 the Constitutional Court rejected Barrionuevo and Vera's appeal against the ruling, and in late May they returned to prison, together with seven others, to complete their terms. A further trial began in September, with González among some 100 witnesses called to testify. In January 2002 Barrionuevo and Corcuera were absolved of the charges of misappropriation of funds. However, Vera was sentenced to seven years' imprisonment and barred from holding public office for 18 years. The former Chief of the National Police, José Maria Rodriguez Colorado, received a six-year sentence, Sancristóbal one of four years and Álvarez-Cascos one of 11 months.

At the general election, held 15 months early, in March 1996, and in which 78% of the electorate participated, the PP took 156 of the 350 seats in the Congreso de los Diputados, thus falling short of an outright majority. The PSOE won 141 seats, the IU 21 and the CiU 16. In the Senado (Senate) the PP received 132 of the 256 seats (winning 111 by direct election), while the PSOE took 96 (81 by direct election). The King invited José María Aznar of the PP to form a government. After protracted negotiations, the PP and the CiU reached agreement on a pact enabling Aznar to take office. Having also secured the support of the five PNV deputies and of the four representatives of Coalición Canaria (CC), the new Prime Minister's investiture finally took place in early May. The incoming Government included three independent ministers.

One of the new administration's main priorities was the reduction of the budget deficit. Several aspects of the Government's policies, however, aroused intense opposition. In mid-October 1996 and again in late November thousands of public-sector workers attended demonstrations to protest against the Government's imposition of a pay 'freeze'. In December a 24-hour strike by civil servants took place, demonstrators being joined by students and teachers protesting against reductions in the education budget. A two-week strike by truck drivers, in support of improved working conditions, caused severe disruption and led to the closure of the country's road borders in February 1997. In early 1998 one miner died during violent protests in northern Spain, where the coal-miners of Asturias were demonstrating against proposed job losses (the Government having been obliged to plan decreases in coal output in order to comply with European Union (EU, see p. 199) directives regarding reductions in subsidies to state-owned industries). At the end of January, after a month-long strike that attracted much public sympathy, agreement was reached when the Government granted concessions on the terms of early retirement for miners.

Public concern regarding the functioning of the country's judicial system was aroused in October 1996 when Miguel Moreiras, a National Court judge, was removed from office as a result of having disclosed to a newspaper (in October 1995) confidential information relating to his handling of the cases against the disgraced Conde (see above). Furthermore, in December 1996 the General Prosecutor ordered the removal of José Aranda, chief prosecutor of the National Court, and the instigation of disciplinary proceedings against four of its judges. The General Council of Judicial Power warned the judges of the National Court that it would not tolerate 'excesses', a reference to the judges' perceived disregard for the law and for the Constitution; many observers were critical of the judges' wide-ranging powers. In May 1997, after only eight months in office, the General Prosecutor himself, Juan Ortiz Urculo, was abruptly dismissed by the Government. He was replaced by Jesús Cardenal. The crisis surrounding the National Court worsened in June when, despite the rejection of his nomination by prosecutors of the Supreme Court, the Government appointed Eduardo Fungairiño to replace Aranda.

In May 1997 the Prime Minister announced that CESID was to be reformed and that responsibility for the secret service was to be transferred from the Ministry of Defence to his own office, under the direct supervision of the Deputy Prime Minister. In April 1998, however, the Government was embarrassed by the revelation that surveillance devices, which lacked the requisite legal authorization, had been found in the headquarters of Herri Batasuna (HB, the political wing of ETA) in Vitoria and that, moreover, this operation by CESID had been approved, inter alia, by the Minister of Defence in March 1997. (Devices in numerous other HB offices had apparently been dismantled by the PSOE administration in late 1995, following the exposure of the scandal relating to stolen CESID documents.) In May 2001 the Government implemented the reforms and for the first time CESID was directed by a civilian. Additionally, new legislation was to be introduced to supervise intelligence operations more closely.

At the PSOE congress in June 1997, after leading the party for 23 years, González unexpectedly announced his resignation as Secretary-General. Joaquín Almunia, hitherto the party's parliamentary spokesman and a loyal associate of González, was chosen to succeed him. In April 1998, in a new procedure that required the holding of primary elections in the contest for the selection of the PSOE's next prime ministerial candidate, Almunia was defeated by Josep Borrell, a former member of the Council of Ministers. The former's offer of resignation from the party leadership was rejected. In November, in a bid to restore party unity, the PSOE designated Borrell as party leader and sole spokesman, while Almunia was to remain responsible for political affairs, at the head of the party's federal executive committee.

In September 1997, as a result of a regional financing dispute, the PNV declared that it considered the pact with the PP to have ended. Nevertheless, Xabier Arzallus, the PNV leader, expressed his willingness to co-operate with the Government on individual issues. In late 1997 PP-CiU relations were strained by a disagreement relating to the introduction of a new national curriculum for the teaching of history in schools (the Government being obliged to withdraw its proposals) and by the Catalan Parliament's approval in December of a law, presented by the CiU, to promote the Catalan language. In January 1998, however, the CiU formally renewed its collaboration agreement with the PP until the end of the current legislature. The CC gave a similar undertaking in April.

In April 1998, meanwhile, after an inquiry lasting three years, Judge Gómez de Liaño concluded his investigation into the fate of Lasa and Zabala, the two ETA activists allegedly killed by GAL members during the 'dirty war'. Criminal proceedings were instigated against seven suspects, including Vera, Elgorriaga (former Governor of Guipúzcoa) and Gen. Rodríguez Galindo. In April 2000 Galindo and Elgorriaga were found guilty of involvement in the abduction and murder in 1983 of Lasa and Zabala. Both were sentenced to 71 years' imprisonment.

In December 1998 Francisco Frutos replaced Julio Anguita as Secretary-General of the PCE, Anguita retaining his leadership of the IU. At the PP congress in January 1999 Javier Arenas, hitherto Minister of Labour and Social Affairs, succeeded Álvarez-Cascos as the ruling party's Secretary-General. The opposition was thrown into disarray in May by the abrupt resignation of Borrell, the PSOE prime ministerial candidate, following the revelation of a financial scandal, involving allegations of malpractice by two former colleagues during the 1980s.

In June 1999, at elections for the European Parliament, for 13 of Spain's 17 regional Parliaments and for municipal councils, the ruling PP maintained its level of support, while the PSOE increased its share of the vote, mainly at the expense of the left-wing IU (which lost five of its nine seats in Strasbourg). In July

Almunia, the PSOE Secretary-General, was selected unopposed as the party's prime ministerial candidate. In early December, owing to the deteriorating situation in the Basque region (see below), the five PNV members of the Chamber of Deputies finally withdrew their support for the minority Government.

In December 1999 the Chamber of Deputies approved controversial new legislation relating to the residency rights of immigrants; under the legislation, which was liberal by EU standards, more than 70,000 illegal immigrants in Spain would be able to obtain residence permits and their dependants would be allowed to join them. The Government was subsequently defeated in its attempt to secure approval for its proposed amendments to the legislation, following reservations expressed by the Ministry of the Interior.

In February 2000, only three weeks before the forthcoming general election, Manuel Pimentel, the Minister of Labour and Social Affairs, abruptly resigned, owing to allegations of departmental corruption in relation to the allocation of state contracts. In the same month the opposition PSOE and IU agreed to conduct a joint electoral campaign aimed at increasing their representation in the Senado.

The ruling party's strong performance at the legislative election held on 12 March 2000 was largely attributed to the Government's record of economic success (in particular its reduction of the unemployment rate). In the lower house the PP won 183 of the 350 seats, thus unexpectedly securing an absolute majority. The PSOE's representation was reduced to 125 seats, while the moderate regional parties, the CiU and the PNV, took 15 and seven seats respectively. The IU suffered a sharp decline in support, the communist-led coalition losing 13 of its 21 seats in the Chamber of Deputies. In the Senado the PP increased its strength to 127 of the 208 directly-elective seats, whereas the PSOE's representation decreased to 61 seats. The level of voter participation was less than 70%. Almunia immediately conceded defeat and resigned as leader of the PSOE. At the party congress in July José Luis Rodríguez Zapatero, a lawyer, was unexpectedly elected to the leadership of the PSOE, defeating the more experienced José Bono Martínez, the President of the Government of Castilla-La Mancha. Zapatero, who excluded left-wingers from the new national executive committee, declared his intention to modernize the party in order to form an effective opposition.

At the end of April 2000, with the support of the 15 CiU and four CC deputies, Aznar, who expressed a desire to govern largely by consensus, was sworn in for a second term of office. The Prime Minister announced the composition of the new Council of Ministers on the following day. Mariano Rajoy, hitherto Minister of Education, was appointed Deputy Prime Minister. Rodrigo Rato also remained a Deputy Prime Minister, retaining the economy portfolio, while that of finance was allocated to Cristóbal Montoro. Josep Piqué (who had joined the PP only in January 1999 and, as Minister of Industry, Energy and Tourism, had subsequently been accused by the opposition of irregularities with regard to his allocation of subsidies to Spanish businesses) became Minister of Foreign Affairs. Other changes included the establishment of a new Ministry of Science and Technology, headed by Anna Birulés. There was also a reorganization of the administrative structure of the state secretariats and directorate-generals. The incoming Government's programme included the reduction of taxes, reforms in the financing of the autonomous regions and improvements in the judicial system.

In mid-September 2000 farmers, fishermen and lorry drivers demonstrated over the increase in fuel prices. Despite government promises of tax rebates to cushion the impact of higher fuel prices, there was a three day strike on 2–4 October. However, an agreement was signed soon afterwards.

The first case of bovine spongiform encephalopathy (BSE) in Spanish cattle was detected in November 2000; the disease subsequently spread rapidly and by April 2001 there were some 40 known cases. Amid growing national alarm the Government proposed the testing of animals and introduced a special tax on all meat products to cover the cost of dealing with the disease. In January 2001 a special committee was established to monitor the cases. However, there was a difference of opinion between the Government and the agricultural sector regarding the financial and organizational co-ordination and resolution of the crisis. In protest at government handling of the crisis, farmers blockaded slaughterhouses and meat-packing plants across Spain. In mid-January the Minister of Agriculture in Galicia was dismissed, after ordering the illegal burial of cattle and animal-based feed in a disused mine shaft.

In the late 1990s there was growing concern over the increasing number of illegal immigrants entering Spain, mostly from Latin America and North Africa. In 2000 some 14,893 people were apprehended, compared with 3,569 in the previous year. The influx of illegal immigrants had resulted in social unrest in some areas, with anti-immigration protests and violent attacks against the immigrant population. Despite intense opposition from the other parties in the Congreso, in July 2000 the Government announced proposals for the reform of the immigration law (adopted by the Congreso de los Diputados in December 1999), introducing severe penalties for illegal immigrants, and for traffickers and employers of illegal immigrants. Those entering the country illegally could be deported within 48 hours. Illegal workers would be deprived of the right to strike and to join a trade union, and their use of public services would be limited. They would gain the right to remain in the country only after five years of employment, rather than the two years previously specified. The reforms entered into force on 23 January 2001, at which time there were an estimated 200,000 illegal immigrants in Spain. Demonstrations were staged all across the country, and in Barcelona 300 illegal immigrants locked themselves into the Santa Maria Pi Church and declared a hunger strike. In June 2001 the Government agreed to grant the protesters legal status. Owing to the large number of Ecuadorian illegal immigrants in Spain, the Government arranged to finance a limited voluntary return system, whereby some 1,210 Ecuadorians would return to Ecuador and then apply to enter the country legally. The first returning Ecuadorians arrived in March. The authorities estimated in mid-2001 that there had been a 10% increase in illegal immigration compared with the previous year, and in August there were further protests in Barcelona when police arrested some 100 African illegal immigrants who had established a camp in one of the city's parks. Despite criticism from the opposition, amendments to the electoral legislation received parliamentary approval in late July: these specified modalities whereby immigrants who could prove that they had been working in Spain since January 2001 could obtain residency, but otherwise imposed a strict quota system linked to the needs of the labour market. In March 2002 the US human rights organization Human Rights Watch accused the Spanish authorities of routinely subjecting illegal immigrants to abuse in detention centres.

On 13 January 2001 a new juvenile criminal law, principally with regard to terrorist crimes, entered into force. The age of imprisonment was increased from 16 to 18 years; new forms of alternative punishment and varying imprisonment levels denoting different degrees of freedom were introduced. In 2001 a number of proposed changes to the justice system were under consideration, including a return to the former system whereby 12 of the 20 members of the General Council of Judicial Power were selected by the judicial associations, rather than by the Congreso and Senado.

In February 2001 Jaime Mayor resigned as Minister of the Interior to run as the PP candidate for Lehendakari (President of the Basque Government) in the Basque regional election. He was replaced by Rajoy, the former Minister of the Presidency, who was in turn replaced by Juan José Lucas.

During 2001 the Government suffered from the alleged involvement of several PP members in corruption cases. In mid-June the Supreme Court decided to proceed with an investigation into the role of the Minister of Foreign Affairs, Josep Piqué, in the fraudulent sale of Ertoil, a subsidiary of the Spanish fuel company Ercros, of whose board Piqué was a member, to the French company Elf Aquitaine. Aznar announced that he would wait for the results of the investigation before reviewing Piqué's position in the Council of Ministers. The Government's reputation was further undermined by the collapse of the Antonio Camacho Gescartera stockbroking company in mid-2001, as a result of which several prominent charities and organizations lost significant sums of money. The Secretary of State for Finance, Enrique Gimenez-Reyna, was forced to resign in July when it became known that his sister had been a manager at the company. In September the President of the National Securities and Exchange Commission (Comisión Nacional del Mercado de Valores—CNMV), Pilar Valiente, was remanded in custody following the publication of her personal diaries, in which it was revealed that she had long been aware of discrepancies in the stockbroker's accounts. Since Valiente had been appointed by the Deputy Prime Minister and

Minister of the Economy, Rodrigo Rato, his position also came under scrutiny and a full reorganization of the CNMV was ordered in early 2002, following the implication of several more of its members in the case. In November 2002 a €2.1m. fine was imposed on the Spanish arm of the HSBC Bank, for its role in laundering Gescartera funds worth some €100m. in 138 numbered accounts.

Following the terrorist attacks in the USA on 11 September 2001, it was reported that 16 Islamist activists had been arrested in Spain in late 2001. They were accused of belonging to the al-Qa'ida (Base) organization of Osama bin Laden, the Saudi-born militant Islamist held principally responsible for the attacks, and charged with terrorist activities. Further arrests were made during April and June 2002. In January 2003 16 North Africans, mostly from Algeria, were arrested near Barcelona and Girona following the discovery of a cache of chemicals and explosives, which were purportedly to be used in terrorist attacks around Europe.

In January 2002 the PP re-elected Aznar as its President, but he made clear his intention not to seek a third term as Prime Minister in 2006. The national executive committee of the PP was also enlarged, from 30 to 35 members.

In May 2002, after the trial of Arnaldo Otegi of HB was shelved by the Supreme Court, a request by Aznar for reconsideration was strongly criticized by the judiciary as misplaced government intervention. Also in May the first general strike since 1988 was called for 20 June by the CCOO and the UGT in protest at proposed government reforms to unemployment subsidies. The reforms were approved by the PP in the Senado on 13 June, with all other parties abstaining. The general strike proceeded one week later, with the UGT claiming a rate of participation of 80%. The largest demonstrations took place in Sevilla on the eve of the EU summit to conclude Spain's presidency of the Union. The Sevilla summit itself, at Spain's instigation, was dominated by the issue of illegal immigration, including the proposition of more extensive visa restrictions. In January 2003, however, changes to immigration legislation, allowing South Americans of Spanish ancestry to apply for Spanish citizenship, were expected to lead to some 1m. applications. At the same time, greater strictures were placed on applications from other non-EU countries.

In June 2002 disagreements between Aznar and Jordi Pujol i Soley, the President of the CiU, (Aznar accused the latter of disloyalty to the Government and support for the general strike) led to a 'freezing' of relations between the PP and the CiU for a 'period of reflection'. Instability in the PP following the strike lead to a major ministerial reshuffle by Aznar in mid-July; notably, the Minister of Foreign Affairs, Josep Piqué i Camps, was transferred to the Ministry of Science and Technology and was replaced by Ana Palacio, while Mariano Rajoy was promoted from the position of Minister of the Interior to that of Deputy Prime Minister and was replaced by Angel Acebes. Divisions within the party were not entirely resolved, however, since the appointment of the Secretary-General of the PP, Javier Arenas, to the post of Minister of Public Administration was questioned by the Minister of Public Works, Francisco Álvarez-Cascos Fernández, who contested that Arenas could not hold both positions simultaneously.

In mid-November 2002 the Aznar Government was faced with a serious crisis following the sinking of the Liberian-registered, Greek-owned oil tanker *Prestige* 240 km off the coast of Galicia. The vessel, which had reported to the authorities on 13 November that its hull had ruptured and that it was leaking oil, had been refused landfall and had been towed out to sea, where it split in two and sank on 19 November. An estimated 12,000 metric tons of the vessel's 77,000-ton capacity was believed to have been released into the sea in the first slick, around one-half of which soon reached the Galician Costa da Morte, requiring the imposition of a fishing ban between Finisterre and A Coruña. On 27 November Deputy Prime Minister Mariano Rajoy refuted claims by French and Portuguese investigators that the wreck was still issuing oil and that a second leak was possible. However, it was subsequently revealed that the oil remaining in the wreck had not completely solidified and was indeed still leaking (in early January 2003 the total amount of spillage was revised to 25,000 tons). The Spanish Minister of Foreign Affairs, Ana Palacio, accused Gibraltar of failing properly to report the vessel's condition, and named the British territory as the intended destination of the *Prestige*, thus precipitating a minor diplomatic fracas. The British Government immediately denied her claim, claiming that the ship had last

docked near Gibraltar in June, but that an inspection had not been required as the vessel had not entered the port, and affirmed that the ship's actual destination in November had been Singapore. Massive clean-up operations were launched, mostly by environmental groups and by the local population; there was a significant lack of aid from the Spanish military, a fact that aroused widespread public discontent. Demonstrations attended by some 150,000 people in Santiago de Compostela in December and by around 100,000 people in Vigo in January 2003 protested at the perceived mishandling of the disaster by both the regional and national PP authorities and demanded the resignation of Aznar: the protesters highlighted the fact that neither the Prime Minister nor the President of the Galician Regional Government, Manuel Fraga Iribarne, had visited Galicia following the disaster, which some observers compared to the sinking of the *Exxon Valdez* in Alaska, in the USA, in 1989. The PSOE demanded a commission of inquiry into the Government's handling of the situation. However, a local commission launched by the Regional Government of Galicia met with obstruction from the central Government, which also delayed the setting up of a national investigation. Meanwhile, the oil slicks spread to the Basque region, incurring €6m. worth of damages, and also reached the coastlines of France and Portugal. The total cost of the cleaning-up process to the Spanish Government was projected at more than €1,000m.

In December 2002 the President of the Council of State, Íñigo Cavero Lataillade, died, and was replaced the following month by former Minister of Health José Manuel Romay Beccaría. In January 2003 Ana Botella, the wife of José Aznar, announced her intention to represent the PP in the municipal elections in Madrid in May, with the support of her husband.

Amid the increasing likelihood of US-led military action against the Iraqi regime of Saddam Hussain in early 2003, Aznar was one of eight European leaders to sign a declaration at the end of January in support of US moves towards an ultimatum. Public opinion, however, already swayed against the PP by the Government's handling of the *Prestige* disaster, was, in general, strongly against military action, with 3m. people participating in anti-war demonstrations in mid-February, and opinion polls suggesting that at least 80% of the population were against the launching of armed conflict in Iraq. None the less, in late February Aznar expressed his support for US-led military action with a UN mandate, although he remained guarded as to the line Spain would adopt should a UN resolution not be achieved. As the US intention to commence armed intervention with or without UN approval became clear, Aznar assured the Spanish people that Spain would not contribute to any military coalition. A summit meeting hosted in the Azores in March led to a joint declaration by Aznar, Prime Minister Anthony (Tony) Blair of the United Kingdom and President George W. Bush of the USA, condemning the regime of Saddam Hussain and expressing support for necessary military actions. Aznar publicly maintained the importance of continuing attempts to secure UN-backing for military action; however, the subsequent announcement by the USA of its intention to act, if need be, without international ratification received the PP Government's concerted support, which aroused strong criticism from the national media. Although the PP Government strongly supported Aznar's policy on Iraq, by 1 April six parliamentary motions rejecting war had been proposed by opposition parties, and on 29 March a number of non-governmental organizations filed charges against Aznar before the Supreme Court, accusing him of exceeding his authorities. Public demonstrations continued in March and April, with a march in Madrid on 6 April supported by Spain's most respected judge, Balthasar Garzón, and another comprising up to 200,000 protesters in Barcelona on 12 April. In April seven diplomatic staff at the Iraqi embassy in Madrid were expelled at the request of the USA, ostensibly on the grounds of alleged espionage, while the dispatch of 900 Spanish non-combative troops to Iraq aroused specific anger among protesters. After the apparent fall of Saddam Hussain's regime in mid-April, Spain pledged forces for peace-keeping duties and humanitarian activities in Iraq, while the Minister of Foreign Affairs, Ana Palacio, emphasized the importance of UN involvement in Iraq's reconstruction.

The scale of public protest against the Iraqi conflict prompted the drafting of legislation by the PP in April 2003 that would extend the jurisdiction of military courts to include trial (with a maximum sentence of six years) for acts of protest staged to discredit Spain's participation in international armed conflict; the proposed legislation, which was the first of its kind since the reintroduction of democracy in 1975, was accused of being reactionary and a threat to civil rights.

Autonomous parliaments were established in the Basque Country and in Cataluña in 1980; elections were held in March. The parliaments of Galicia and Andalucía were established in October 1981 and May 1982 respectively, and the remaining 13 Legislative Assemblies were elected in May 1983. At elections to the Galician Legislative Assembly which took place in October 1997, the PP Government of the former Minister of Information in Franco's Government, Manuel Fraga Iribarne, was returned to office. At elections for 13 of the 17 regional parliaments in June 1999, the PP retained control of nine autonomous regions. At elections to the Catalan Parliament in October 1999, Jordi Pujol i Soley of the CiU was returned to office for a sixth consecutive term, again heading a minority Government. Elections to the Parliament of Andalucía took place in March 2000. The PSOE, led by Manuel Chaves González, retained power. At elections to the Basque Parliament which took place on 13 May 2001, Juan José Ibarretxe Markuartu of the PNV/EA electoral coalition was returned to office. In October Manuel Fraga won a fourth consecutive term as President of the Galician Assembly. In 2001 proposals were announced to complete the development process of the autonomous communities with a policy of co-operation between the communities, through meetings and conferences. The presidents of each autonomous community were to be incorporated into the Senado, thus making it more representative of Spain as a whole. (See Legislative Assemblies of the Autonomous Regions (see p. 3817) for details of most recent elections to all regional parliaments.)

In the Basque region, meanwhile, terrorist activity by the separatist organization, ETA, founded in 1959, continued. Having claimed its first victim in 1961, between 1978 and 1992 alone a total of 711 murders was attributed to the group. Despite bomb attacks in Bilbao in February 1983 and Madrid in July 1986, the central Government maintained its offer of social reintegration, instigated in mid-1984, to former ETA members. The explosion in June 1987 of a bomb beneath a crowded Barcelona supermarket, which killed 21 and injured 45, was the most devastating ETA attack ever, prompting HB's first condemnation of a terrorist attack. Co-operation with the authorities of France and Algeria (where numerous ETA members were discovered to be living) was strengthened, and in October the French police arrested 67 Basque suspects. In December five children were among the 12 killed in a bomb attack on the married quarters of a civil guard barracks in Zaragoza, which provoked a further public outcry. In January 1988, after protracted negotiations, six Basque parties (excluding HB) signed the Ajuria Enea Pact, rejecting terrorism as a means of determining the region's future.

In January 1989 a unilateral truce was declared by ETA, in an effort to reopen negotiations with the Government, broken off in early 1988. Secret discussions between representatives of the Government and of ETA commenced in Algeria, but collapsed in April 1989, and violent action recommenced, resulting in reprisals by GAL in which a HB deputy-elect, Josu Muguruza, was murdered. In February 1990 a resolution declaring the right of the Basque people to self-determination was approved by the Basque Parliament.

The authorities continued to make arrests and to convict members of ETA, including José Javier Zabaleta Elósegui ('Waldo'), alleged to be ETA's second-in-command, who was sentenced to 57 years' imprisonment for three attempted murders. Nevertheless, ETA's campaign of violence continued during the 1990s. In December 1991, following an apparent rift within ETA over the organization's future policy, the central Government denied that it was planning to resume direct negotiations with the terrorists. The capture near Biarritz in March of Francisco Múgika Garmendia ('Pakito'), ETA's military leader, along with other senior commanders, represented a particular achievement in the Government's increasingly successful anti-terrorist campaign. Between mid-1992 and early 1993 more than 500 ETA suspects were arrested. In July 1992 ETA's offer of a truce (to coincide with the forthcoming Olympic Games in Barcelona), in return for the reopening of dialogue, was rebuffed by the Government, which continued to insist upon the group's permanent renunciation of violence. Hopes that ETA's campaign might be ended were raised in February 1993, upon the discovery of a major arsenal in France and the capture of Rafael Caride, thought to be ETA's operational head. In June, however, following the conclusion of the trial in Paris of six ETA

members, two car bombs exploded in Madrid, one of which killed seven people, including five senior military officers.

The Basque people's growing revulsion at ETA's actions, demonstrated by HB's loss of two of its four seats in the Congreso de los Diputados at the general election, was intensified by the abduction in July 1993 of industrialist Julio Iglesias Zamora, leading to a resurgence of the peace movement within the region. He was released in October, reportedly upon the payment of a large ransom. In August there were violent clashes in San Sebastián and Bilbao between peace demonstrators and supporters of ETA. In September there was renewed unrest in the Basque region, following the deaths in custody of two ETA suspects and the disclosure of medical evidence suggesting violent treatment of a third detainee. Detentions in Spain of terrorist suspects totalled 127 in 1993, including eight suspects believed to be part of an extortion network responsible for the attempted blackmailing of numerous Basque enterprises.

In January 1994, in response to an offer to HB by Basque socialist leaders of negotiations in return for an ETA truce, the Minister of the Interior reiterated the central Government's commitment to its anti-terrorist policy and declined the Basque invitation. In March Henri Parot, a French member of ETA, was sentenced to a total of 1,802 years' imprisonment for the bomb attack on the Zaragoza barracks in 1987. Both attacks by ETA and arrests by the authorities continued in 1994; Pedro Picabea Ugalde ('Kepa'), believed to be responsible for 24 murders and for the abduction of Iglesias Zamora, and Idoia López Riaño ('Margarita' or 'La Tigresa') were arrested in France in July and August. At the end of August the ETA leadership ordered its imprisoned members to embark upon a hunger strike, in an attempt to reassert its authority and to obstruct the process of 'reinsertion' into society. About 100 of the 600 ETA prisoners had expressed an interest in the Government's offer of reintegration, in return for the renunciation of violence. In September the all-party anti-terrorist pact was jeopardized by the PP's opposition to the Government's new partial-parole initiative for selected ETA prisoners.

The results of the election to the Basque Parliament in October 1994 demonstrated the continuing decline in support for HB. ETA suffered a major reverse in mid-November, when several activists were arrested, including José Luis Martín Carmona ('Koldo'), believed to be the head of the notorious Vizcaya unit, who was captured near Bilbao, and Félix Alberto López de la Calle Gauna ('Mobutu'), the terrorist group's alleged second-in-command, who was detained in the French city of Toulon.

In January 1995, as attacks on police-officers continued, Gregorio Ordóñez, a member of the Basque Parliament and the PP candidate for the mayoralty of San Sebastián at the forthcoming municipal elections, was shot dead, the first politician since 1992 to be murdered by ETA. Thousands of Basque citizens took to the streets of San Sebastián and Bilbao to protest against the assassination. In April Aznar, leader of the then opposition PP, narrowly survived a car-bomb attempt on his life in Madrid, which injured 19 others. ETA warned that its campaign of violence would continue if the Basque country were not granted self-determination. Upon his renunciation of violence and subsequent extradition from the Dominican Republic in July, Juan Manuel Soares Gamboa confessed to his involvement in a total of 29 murders. In April 2000 he received a prison sentence of 1,401 years for the murder of the 12 civil guards in 1986.

In August 1995 it was revealed that, with assistance from the French authorities, a plot to assassinate King Juan Carlos had been foiled; 18 ETA suspects were arrested, and three were later convicted in 1997, receiving sentences of 35–37 years. In February 1996 the shooting dead in San Sebastián of Fernando Múgica Herzog, a Basque socialist leader, followed by the murder of Francisco Tomás y Valiente, a former President of the Constitutional Court and a close associate of the then Prime Minister, González, provoked a public outcry. Some 1m. citizens, including González and many other political leaders, attended an anti-ETA march in Madrid. As the general election approached, Jon Idígoras, the veteran HB leader, was arrested, amidst controversy arising from a campaign video that apparently supported the activities of ETA. The arrest of Valentín Lasarte, believed to be responsible for the murders of Ordóñez and of Múgica Herzog, led to the discovery of a large bomb-making factory near San Sebastián. (In May 1998 Lasarte, who had previously received three prison sentences of 30 years, including one in January 1995 for the murder of Ordóñez, was sentenced to a further 82 years' imprisonment for the murder of Múgica Herzog.)

In July 1996, following a brief truce and the PP Government's conditional offer of dialogue in the previous month, ETA renewed its bombing campaign, this time targeting the tourism industry. In January 1997 Jesús Arkautz Arana ('Josu de Mondragón'), a senior ETA member detained in 1991, was expelled from France and handed over to the Spanish authorities (In June 1998 he received a prison sentence of 83 years.) This expulsion was followed by the capture near Bordeaux of José Luis Urrusolo Sistiaga, sought by the authorities for 15 years and believed to be responsible for 16 murders.

A resurgence of violence in 1997 culminated in the abduction in July of Miguel Angel Blanco, a young PP councillor in the Basque town of Ermua. ETA issued an ultimatum that prisoners belonging to the separatist organization be transferred to gaols in the Basque region. Despite numerous appeals, including a message from the Pope, Blanco was duly shot upon the expiry of ETA's 48-hour deadline. His death provoked an unprecedented display of public outrage, which united most of the country against ETA. In the largest demonstration since the attempted military coup of 1981, millions of Spaniards took to the streets, including the Prime Minister, who led a protest march in Madrid. In response to public feeling, the Prime Minister vowed to intensify the Government's campaign against ETA, while urging (along with the moderate Basque parties) the isolation of HB

ETA's suspected head of intelligence, Igor Urrestarazu Garijo, was arrested in southern France in early August 1997. Following the deportation of Eugenio Etxebeste Arizcuren ('Antxon') and two other ETA exiles from the Dominican Republic to Spain, the Dominican Government indicated that it would not extradite any further ETA members. Etxebeste Arizcuren was sentenced to 10 years' imprisonment in April 2001.

In September 1997 the Government confirmed that more than 100 businesses in Navarra had received letters of extortion from ETA, in which sums of between 5m. and 40m. pesetas had been demanded. In the same month, following the death of two alleged leaders of the Vizcaya unit in an exchange of gunfire with the Civil Guard in Bilbao, 12 suspected ETA collaborators were detained and a large arsenal was discovered. In October an attempt to plant remote-controlled grenades outside the new Guggenheim Museum in Bilbao, which was due to be inaugurated by the King, was thwarted by the police, but resulted in the death of one officer.

Their trial on charges of collaborating with an armed group having opened in the Supreme Court in October 1997, in early December the 23 members of the collective leadership of HB were each sentenced to seven years' imprisonment. In a significant development, for the first time the direct relationship between ETA and HB, which continued to claim to be independent of the terrorist organization, was recognized by the judiciary. The members of the collective leadership were released in July 1999, when their imprisonment was ruled unconstitutional.

In January 1998, as ETA continued its attacks against local councillors belonging to the PP, Alberto Jiménez Becerril and his wife were shot in Sevilla, provoking renewed outrage. The murder of Jiménez Becerril was the first of a PP councillor outside the Basque region. In February a dispute arose between the President of the Basque regional Government, which administered its own police force, and the central Government, following the disclosure that national forces had been clandestinely deployed in the Basque region. At a meeting in early 1998 HB elected a new collective leadership, which pledged to continue the policies of its predecessor.

In May 1998 the terrorist organization continued its campaign against local councillors with the murder of Tomás Caballero, spokesman for the Unión del Pueblo Navarro (UPN), in Pamplona. The capture of several ETA activists in San Sebastián, as they prepared to launch mortar bombs at a police barracks, resulted in the discovery of another plot to assassinate King Juan Carlos.

Following a dispute relating to a proposal to oblige all members of the Basque Parliament to accord formal recognition to the Spanish Constitution in late June 1998, after 12 years of co-operation, the Partido Socialista de Euskadi-Euskadiko Ezkerra (PSE-EE) announced its withdrawal from the Basque coalition Government. In July Judge Garzón, who was investigating ETA's fund-raising activities, ordered the closure of *Egin*, a radical Basque newspaper, and that of an associated radio

station, on the grounds of their connections to ETA. A series of fire-bomb attacks on Basque media groups followed.

In early September 1998, apparently attempting to pre-empt any ban on its activities and while still declining to renounce the use of violence, HB announced that it was to contest the forthcoming elections to the Basque Parliament as the newly-formed Euskal Herritarrok (EH). In mid-September both the PP and the opposition PSOE expressed reservations at the conclusion of an agreement (the 'Lizarra Pact') by the PNV, Eusko Alkartasuna (EA), HB and IU on proposals for unconditional discussions with ETA. Nevertheless, following several months of secret talks between representatives of the PNV and HB, on 16 September ETA declared an indefinite truce. In response, the central Government urged the separatist organization to disarm and to respect the results of the forthcoming elections to the Basque Legislative Assembly. In a conciliatory gesture, the Prime Minister indicated his willingness to transfer a number of ETA convicts to prisons in the Basque country.

At the Basque elections, held in October 1998, the PNV again received the greatest support, while the PP supplanted the PSE-EE as the party with the second largest representation in the regional parliament. The EH improved the position previously held by HB, again at the expense of the minor parties. At the end of October it was announced that the State was to assume responsibility for compensation of the victims of ETA, the total sum in question now estimated at 60,000m. pesetas. However, the Government refused to compensate members of GAL. The Prime Minister also stated that, while being required to renounce the use of violence, ETA would not be obliged to relinquish all its weapons. In November the central Government announced the inauguration of direct contact with representatives of ETA, the separatist organization reaffirming its commitment to the cease-fire. In December, with the support of EH, an entirely nationalist Basque Government was established; the coalition was headed by Ibarretxe of the PNV. In the same month, as transfers of ETA convicts to prisons located in the Basque region continued, the Prime Minister invited EH to join discussions on the region's future. In January 1999, however, EH refused to attend the inauguration ceremony of the Basque region's new President. As street disturbances and arson attacks began to escalate in early 1999, in January thousands of Basques participated in a march to demonstrate support for the transfer of ETA inmates to prisons nearer their homes.

In February 1999, in France, the first arrest since the cease-fire of an ETA suspect was made. The failure of EH categorically to condemn the continuing street violence further hindered the faltering peace process. In March the police arrested six ETA activists, including José Javier Arizkuren Ruiz ('Kantauri'), the alleged head of ETA's military wing, who was believed to have been involved in 20 murders and also the 1995 plot to kill King Juan Carlos; he was convicted in April 2002.

In May 1999 the Spanish Government announced that 304 (of an estimated 550) exiles, who had been obliged to leave Spain on account of their alleged connections to ETA, were to be permitted to return to their homeland. In early June the Prime Minister admitted that direct talks between government representatives and members of ETA had taken place in the previous month, the first such official acknowledgement since 1989. In late June a newly-elected deputy to the parliament of Navarra and member of ETA, José Luis Barrios, was sentenced to 60 years' imprisonment, along with an accomplice, upon conviction for the murder in 1998 of the PP councillor Jiménez Becerril and his wife.

In July 1999, for the first time, EH joined other Basque parties in signing a declaration rejecting the use of violence. In August ETA stated that dialogue with the Government was being suspended, owing to the latter's perceived attempt to gain political advantage from the peace process. The Government reiterated its willingness to resume contact. In early September, as the first anniversary of the truce approached, it was revealed that a total of 180 ETA prisoners had been released within the last year. At the end of September, following the theft of a substantial quantity of industrial dynamite from a depot in Britanny (and only a few days prior to an official visit to Spain by the French President, Jacques Chirac), the French authorities arrested three ETA suspects, including Jon Bienzobas Arreche ('Karaka'), alleged to be responsible for the murder in 1996 of Tomás y Valiente.

In October 1999 ETA's proposals for the resumption of direct peace talks were rejected by the central Government on the grounds that the release of hundreds of ETA prisoners, as urged by the terrorist organization, was not negotiable. At the end of October ETA members exiled overseas were reported to be returning to Europe and regrouping in France. On 28 November, on the eve of the opening in Paris of the trial of Arizkuren Ruiz and 12 other ETA defendants, the terrorist organization announced the end of the 14-month cease-fire. Thousands of dismayed citizens took to the streets to urge that the truce be maintained. Hours before the expiry of the truce on 3 December, the PNV, along with other members of the Lizarra Pact, invited HB to sign a document demanding full sovereignty for the Basque region and criticizing the policies of both the Spanish and French Governments.

Despite the authorities' recent interception of vehicles laden with explosives, and the detention of three ETA suspects belonging to the Vizcaya unit, in January 2000, nevertheless, ETA successfully exploded two car-bombs in Madrid, one of which killed an army officer. More than 1m. people, led by the Prime Minister, participated in a protest march in the capital. At the end of the month it was reported that ETA's international network, responsible for the co-ordination of financial and logistical support, had been dismantled. In February, in Vitoria, a Basque socialist politician, Fernando Bueso, and his bodyguard died in a bomb attack, prompting Ibarretxe to sever all links with EH. In April it was reported that, since July 1999, the PNV had been attempting unsuccessfully to hold direct discussions with ETA. EH subsequently announced that it was withdrawing from the Basque Parliament.

In early May 2000 the central Government discounted the possibility of renewed contact with ETA unless a cease-fire were reinstated. Also in May the Spanish and French Governments determined to intensify collaboration to combat terrorism. In June a PP politician, Jesús María Pedrosa Urquiza, was assassinated in Durango, resulting in the abolition of local government pacts between the PNV and EH. In July three members of the Andalucía unit were sentenced to 36 years' imprisonment each for various terrorist actions and murders. In the same month the interior ministries of Madrid and the Basque Country established a joint co-ordinating committee to share and assess intelligence regarding ETA. Attacks in July and August claimed the lives of six people, including a former socialist governor. In September 20 financial and political organizers of EKIN, ETA's fund-raising wing, were arrested. Seven of these were convicted in April 2001, on the same day that Judge Garzón pronounced EKIN illegal, owing to its associations with ETA. On 15 September 2000 the French authorities arrested the suspected former leader of ETA, Ignacio Gracia Arregui ('Iñaki de Rentería') on charges of terrorism and attempting to assassinate the King in 1995. In December he was sentenced to five years' imprisonment, added to a previous sentence of 11 years. In retaliation for Arregui's arrest, José Luis Ruiz Casado, a PP politician, was assassinated in Barcelona. On the following day some 100,000 Catalans, led by Prime Minister Aznar, demonstrated in Barcelona.

In September 2000 the EH abandoned the ruling coalition, leaving the PNV without a majority in the Basque Government. In October Ibon Muñoa, a former HB politician, was convicted of providing ETA with information to aid the assassination of Blanco. In the same month a public prosecutor in Andalucía, Luis Portero, and Lt-Col Antonio Muñoz Cariñanos were assassinated, and five people were killed by car-bombs. Demonstrations were held in Madrid and in the Basque Country. In November a former socialist health minister, Ernest Lluch, was assassinated in Barcelona, and in the following month a PP politician, Francisco Cano Consuegra, was killed in a car-bomb. At the end of December the Basque regional television station controversially refused to broadcast King Juan Carlos's Christmas speech, owing to his references to ETA. During 2000 some 100 members or collaborators of ETA were detained following covert civil guard operations; six command units were dismantled; and 12 members of ETA were successfully extradited. However, street disturbances in Basque cities continued to escalate, many caused by the youth wing of ETA, and there were 23 fatalities resultant from ETA attacks.

In January 2001 José Benigno Rey ('Pepe Rei'), editor of the magazine *Ardi Beltza* (Black Sheep), was convicted for collaboration with ETA. Judge Garzón subsequently announced his intention to suspend the magazine's publication. In the same month, in an attempted car-bomb attack on Princess Alexia of Greece, one man was killed. In February French police arrested a key ETA leader, Francisco Javier García Gaztelu ('Txapote'), and the Spanish Civil Guard arrested 10 members of the

Donosti unit. On 20 February the Lehendakari (President of the Basque Government) announced that Basque regional elections would be held early, on 13 May. The PP and PSOE had proposed an all-party anti-terrorist pact to follow the elections, and a co-ordinating committee was established to form anti-terrorist policy. In March 16 people, who were believed to be leaders of Haika (Rise Up), the youth wing of ETA, were arrested; in May Judge Garzón pronounced Haika illegal. Following retaliatory attacks throughout March, ETA warned that it was to target holiday resorts.

Elections to the Basque Parliament took place on 13 May 2001. The PNV/EA electoral coalition, led by Ibarretxe, retained power, taking 33 of the 75 seats. The PP retained its position as the party with the second largest representation, gaining 19 seats, while the PSE-EE won 13 seats, the EH seven seats and the IU-EB three. The PNV/EA now controlled more seats than the combined forces of the PP and the PSOE.

As the violence continued throughout April and May 2001, with a number of attempted bombings, Ibarretxe reiterated his refusal to allow EH to attend peace talks owing to its support for ETA. Attacks during May included the assassination of the financial director of the regional newspaper *El Diario Vasco*, and the fire-bombing of a civil guard barracks in Vizcaya; there were a number of arrests in June, and in July a court case against 33 members of EKIN opened. Garzón had announced earlier in the month that he would investigate members of ETA who had been interviewed by the newspapers *Gara* and *Euskaldunon Egunkaria*. In late June a parcel-bomb in Madrid injured 20 people, including Brig.-Gen. Justo Oreja Pedraza, who died a month later. Earlier bomb attacks in Logrono, San Sebastián and a conspiracy to bomb a ferry en route to Plymouth, United Kingdom, had failed. Following its losses in the elections of 13 May, HB elected new members to its leadership and declared that henceforth it wished to be known as Batasuna (Unity).

On 2 July 2001 Spain secured an agreement with Mexico for the extradition of 20 suspected ETA members and further co-operation against ETA. On 14 July the inauguration of Ibarretxe as Lehendakari was accompanied by ETA action in Tolosa, where a member of the Ertzaintza was assassinated, and in Leitxa, Navarra, where a local councillor was killed in a bomb attack. Two days later 50,000 people demonstrated on the streets of Pamplona in protest at the violence. In late July it became apparent that ETA had planned a series of bomb attacks on Spain's holiday resorts to coincide with the summer tourist season. A car-bomb at Málaga airport was defused on 26 July and a series of co-ordinated bomb attacks took place in towns across the Basque country. The following day, a bomb injured three people in Barcelona. On 30 July the National High Court in Madrid sentenced two former leading ETA members, Francisco Mujika Garmendia ('Pakito') and José Maria Arregi Erostarbe ('Fiti'), to 1,128 years' imprisonment for various crimes, including 46 counts of murder. ETA's campaign of violence and bombing continued throughout August. At the end of the month it was estimated that, so far in 2001, some 51 arrests of alleged ETA members had been made.

There was a brief interlude in ETA violence during September 2001. Nevertheless, the Minister of the Interior reported that month that police had discovered a list, compiled by ETA, of potential targets, which included more than 2,000 politicians, police and military personnel. In late September police in France captured the alleged chief of ETA logistics, Asier Oiartzabal Txapartegi ('Baltza') and four other suspects. In early October Ibarretxe warned that he was determined to hold a referendum on self-determination for the Basque country, should the Government in Madrid continue to reject dialogue and ETA continue its campaign of violence. However, Prime Minister Aznar condemned the proposal as unconstitutional, and the violence resumed with the bombing of a courthouse in Vitoria. On 12 October a car-bomb exploded in Madrid, injuring 17 people. It was later reported that the bomb had been intended to be detonated at a military parade earlier in the day, at which members of the royal family were present, to commemorate National Day. On 26 October the French courts confirmed the expulsion of 17 Basques resident in France, who were suspected of links with ETA. In the same month police also carried out operations against the ETA prisoners' support group, Gestoras Pro Amnista, which the Minister of the Interior accused of inciting violence.

On 17 November 2001 some 35,000 people marched through Bilbao to demand the right for self-determination for the region. This followed two high-profile bomb attacks on Madrid earlier that month, of which one took place during the city's 'rush hour' and injured 95 people. On the same day, two ETA gunmen assassinated a judge, José Maria Lidon, who had presided over the regional court of Vizcaya. Members of Ertzainta again became the targets of ETA when two were shot dead in Guipuzcoa province on 23 November. On the same day it was reported that Pedro José Pikabea Ugalde had been convicted in France in connection with a plot to assassinate King Juan Carlos. In December seven people were arrested in the Urretxe and Zumarraga provinces in connection with the summer bombing campaign on tourist resorts. In late December the Secretary General of the PSE-EE, Nicolas Redondo Terreros, resigned. Since the party's poor performance in the regional elections in May, disputes had developed over the party's approach to self-determination and a perceived lack of support from the leadership of the PSOE in Madrid. Redondo was replaced by Paxti Lopez.

Basque groups took advantage of the beginning of Spain's presidency of the EU in January 2002 to demand greater representation in the European Parliament. The central Government, however, welcomed the introduction of an EU-wide arrest warrant, which it hoped would help capture ETA suspects, due to come into effect in 2004. ETA claimed responsibility for several terrorist attacks in March 2002. In the following month a demand from independent, left-wing Basque parties for a cease-fire was denounced by Batasuna and ETA. A total of 122 arrests of ETA members were carried out during 2002 as part of a crack-down on the organization. In May the trial of Arnaldo Otegi of Batasuna for vocal support of ETA was dismissed by the Supreme Court, to the consternation of the Government which attempted to intervene. After a number of ETA actions during the EU summit in Sevilla in June, however, the Senado approved measures to outlaw political parties deemed to support terrorist organizations. The legislation was widely seen as targeting Batasuna, and, indeed, in August a parliamentary vote outlawed the party, while a separate Supreme Court order enforced the closure of party offices and a three-year suspension of party activities. Subsequently, in March 2003, the Supreme Court officially outlawed Batasuna. Meanwhile, ETA declared its intention to attack the political offices of the PP and PSOE, and a number of violent actions were attempted in late 2002, including a thwarted attack on shopping centres in Madrid with five linked bombs in late December. In September ETA leaders Olarra Guridi and Ainhoa Mújika were arrested; this was followed in December by the arrest, in France, of their successors, one of whom, Ibon Fernandez de Iradi ('Susper'), subsequently escaped from custody. In November Judge Garzón accused 20 Batasuna leaders of membership of ETA, while in December an attempt to circumvent the illegalization of the party led Batasuna to establish another organization, the Sozialsta Abertzaleak (Patriotic Socialists), in the hope of contesting regional elections in May 2003. On 22 December 2002 a silent rally in Bilbao organized by Lehendakari Juan Ibarretxe, who had put forward a set of proposals for the establishment of an independent Basque state in October, protested against ETA's political use of violence. As part of a global crackdown on terrorism, an anti-terrorist bill was passed by the national legislature in January 2003, raising the maximum sentence for terrorist activities from 30 to 40 years, and in February the Basque-language newspaper, *Euskaldunon Egunkari*, was shut down, on the grounds of its alleged links with ETA. Aznar's hope for external support in the eradication of ETA was widely believed to have been one of the reasons for his backing of US-led military action in Iraq during 2003 (see above). Prior to regional and municipal elections in May 2003, the central Government banned some 1,500 candidates from standing on the grounds of their alleged links with ETA. In response, ETA urged the lodging of protest votes in support of the banned politicians.

Catalan and Galician nationalist groups, meanwhile, had continued their terrorist activities, the Catalan organization, Terra Lliure, claiming its first victim in September 1987 and the Galician Exército Guerrilheiro do Pobo Galego Ceibe (EGPGC) carrying out its first murder, of a civil guard, in February 1989. In mid-1989 the Catalan Government was reported to be negotiating with Terra Lliure. In July 1991 the dissolution of Terra Lliure was announced, following the group's renunciation of the use of violence. In mid-1992, however, a dissident faction planted several bombs. The trial of 24 alleged members of Terra Lliure concluded in July 1995, 18 being found guilty; 15 were pardoned in June 1996. The EGPGC's campaign continued intermittently. In September 1991 the alleged leader of the

group was apprehended by the authorities and, upon the arrest in November of eight suspected EGPGC members, it was believed that the organization had been annihilated. In June 1994 six EGPGC activists received prison sentences, while two others were acquitted. In September 1998 proceedings for the extradition of an EGPGC suspect from Mexico were instigated.

In January 1985 the police arrested 17 members of Grupos de Resistencia Antifascista Primero de Octubre—GRAPO, an extreme left-wing organization. Detainees included the alleged leader of GRAPO, Mercedes Padrós Corominas. After a period of inactivity, GRAPO resumed its guerrilla campaign in 1988. In December 1989 GRAPO announced an intensification of its activities, shooting dead two civil guards shortly afterwards. In January 1990, as a hunger strike by more than 50 GRAPO prisoners progressed, the Minister of Justice confirmed that the Government would not negotiate with the terrorist organization. In September GRAPO claimed responsibility for various bomb attacks, targets including the stock exchange and the Ministry of Finance in Madrid and the PSC-PSOE headquarters in Barcelona. Two further bombs at government offices in Barcelona in November again caused extensive damage. GRAPO remained active in 1992, the bombing of a gas pipeline in Zaragoza in February being attributed to the grouping. Between its foundation in 1975 and 1992, GRAPO was believed to have been responsible for a total of 70 murders. In December 1992 Laureano Ortega and two other leaders of the grouping were captured in Santander. In March 1993, however, three bombs planted by GRAPO exploded at offices in Madrid. Similar bomb attacks were carried out in May and in January 1994. At the end of the latter month four GRAPO suspects were arrested. Several members of GRAPO, including Ortega, received long prison sentences upon the conclusion of their trial in June 1995. Responsibility for the abduction later that month of Publio Cordón, a Zaragoza business executive, was claimed by GRAPO. In November more than 20 suspects were detained. Judicial proceedings against four GRAPO members, who claimed to have released Cordón in August 1995 upon receipt of a ransom, began in August 1996. Reports that the Government was negotiating with GRAPO prisoners, regarding the group's dissolution in return for certain concessions, were denied by José María Sánchez Casas, co-founder of GRAPO, upon his release from prison in July 1997. Having been imprisoned in October 1979 on various charges, including murder, Sánchez Casas vowed to resume the armed struggle. Also in July 1997 another GRAPO leader, Olegario Sánchez, was released after serving 20 years' imprisonment. Resuming its campaign, GRAPO detonated several devices in Madrid during 1998. In November three members of GRAPO were sentenced to 27 years' imprisonment for the abduction in 1995 of Cordón, the fate of the businessman remaining unknown. In April 1999 GRAPO claimed responsibility for an explosion at the tomb of Gen. Franco. In June GRAPO was linked to the bombing of a PP office in Carabanchel, and in May 2000 GRAPO claimed responsibility for an attack in Vigo on an armoured vehicle transporting 390m. pesetas, in which two security guards were killed. In June and September a number of bombs exploded, targeting locations in Seville, Valencia and Vigo. Later in the month bombs were found in Madrid and in the *El Mundo* office in Barcelona, both of which were attributed to GRAPO. In November an alleged leader, Manuel Perez, and a further six members of GRAPO were arrested in Paris, France. In retaliation for their arrest, Francisco Javier Sanz Morales, a civil guard, was assassinated in Madrid. In July 2002 14 GRAPO members were arrested in police operations in Paris, Madrid and Vitoria, including suspected leader Hierro Txomon; this was followed by a second series of arrests in November. In December proceedings were instigated for the extradition of Manuel Perez from France.

In foreign relations, in December 1988 Spain and the USA renewed their bilateral defence agreement, permitting the USA's use of bases in Spain, for a further eight years from May 1989. In late 1996 the accord was extended until May 1998. In November 1999 the US Government requested permission to establish their principal base in southern Europe, in Cádiz. Spain was admitted to Western European Union (WEU, see p. 318) in November 1988. In November 1992 Spain dispatched a substantial contingent of troops to Bosnia and Herzegovina, the first Spanish soldiers to serve in a UN peace-keeping operation. Continuing to assume a greater international role, Spain contributed troops to the multinational force deployed in Albania in April 1997, and again in April 1999 during the NATO offensive against Yugoslavia. The Spanish Government also offered temporary accommodation to as many as 10,000 refugees from the Yugoslav province of Kosovo. Spain committed 1,200 ground troops to the international peace-keeping force deployed in Kosovo in June 1999. In November 2000 the EU announced plans for a rapid reaction force with the ability to deploy 60,000 troops in 60 days. Spain pledged some 6,000 troops to the force, which was expected to be fully established by 2003.

In the late 1990s criminal proceedings continued in Spain against former Argentine and Chilean officials of the military dictatorships of Argentina (1976–83) and of Chile (1979–90), during which numerous Spanish citizens had been killed. In November 1999 the investigating judge, Garzón, issued international arrest warrants for 98 citizens of Argentina. In January 2000, however, the judge's request for the extradition of 48 Argentines, accused of various atrocities, was refused. In August 2000 Ricardo Cavallo, a naval officer during Argentina's 'dirty war', was extradited from Mexico on charges of human rights abuses. He was indicted on 1 September. In November 1998, following the arrest in the United Kingdom of Gen. Augusto Pinochet and the instigation by Spain of extradition proceedings against the former Chilean President, Chile's ambassador to Madrid was recalled for consultations. In October 1999 a British judge ruled that the former Chilean President could be extradited to Spain to answer 35 charges of torture and conspiracy. In March 2000, however, Pinochet was permitted to return to Chile from the United Kingdom, where he had remained under house arrest, extradition proceedings having been abandoned on medical grounds.

Spanish ratification of the Maastricht Treaty on European Union was completed in November 1992. The dispute between Spain and the United Kingdom over the sovereignty of the neighbouring British dependent territory of Gibraltar remained unresolved. In May 1991 the Prime Minister, González, was reported to have put forward proposals for nominal joint Spanish-British sovereignty of the territory, whereby Gibraltar would be granted effective autonomy. Negotiations were resumed in March 1993. Relations between Spain and the United Kingdom were strained in early 1995 by British support for Canada in that country's dispute with the EU over North Atlantic fishing rights. The situation deteriorated further upon Spain's announcement that, in protest at the apparent inadequacy of British efforts, it was to implement stricter border controls to combat the problem of drugs- and tobacco-smuggling from Gibraltar. In May 1996, upon the election of a new Government in the territory, border controls were further strengthened by the Spanish authorities, leading to even greater delays for travellers and to renewed protests from the British Government. In 1997 the United Kingdom rejected Spanish initiatives entailing joint sovereignty for up to 100 years prior to the eventual transfer of power to Spain. In December Spanish proposals that, following a period of joint sovereignty, Gibraltar became an autonomous community were similarly rebuffed by the British Government. In 1998 tension was renewed over the issue of access to fishing grounds. The seizure of a Spanish fishing vessel in early 1999 led to a serious escalation of the dispute and the imposition of new border controls and travel restrictions by Spain. In September 1996, meanwhile, it was announced that Gibmed, the NATO base in Gibraltar, was to be phased out, thus facilitating Spain's full integration into the alliance's military structure. In July 1998 Spain and the United Kingdom were reported to have reached agreement regarding the removal of restrictions on the use of Gibraltar as a communications centre during NATO exercises. In April 2000 Spain and the United Kingdom signed an agreement relating to the administrative status of Gibraltar. The territory's identity cards would henceforth be accepted by Spain as valid for travel within the EU. While emphasizing that the accord did not alter its claim to Gibraltar, Spain was expected to co-operate more fully with the territory's police force. Furthermore, the agreement permitted the implementation of numerous EU directives, long obstructed by Spain, which had refused to recognize the Government of Gibraltar as a 'competent authority' in EU affairs. It was also agreed that Spain and Gibraltar would communicate indirectly through a facility, based in London, provided by the British authorities. In March 2001 Spain condemned plans by the political parties of Gibraltar to request reforms to the 1969 Constitution, allowing self-determination, and to hold a referendum on decolonization. Following a meeting between Spanish and British officials in Brussels in mid-2001, the Minister of Foreign Affairs, Josep Piqué, and his British counterpart, Jack Straw, held discussions in October, at which they agreed to work

towards solving the dispute by December 2002. The issue of the right of Gibraltarians to vote on any agreement reached by the two Governments continued to impede the progress of the discussions, Piqué warning the British Government that Spain would not accept the results of such a referendum. At further talks in November, however, Piqué announced plans to increase the number of telephone lines available to Gibraltar, from 35,000 to 100,000, and provide access to Spanish health care for the inhabitants of the territory. The deadline for achieving a solution was also brought forward to September 2002. In January 2002 it was reported that the Spanish Government had agreed to modify its demand for outright sovereignty over the territory and reconsider the option of sharing sovereignty over the territory with the United Kingdom for an indefinite period. In an open letter published in the Gibraltan press, Piqué attempted to persuade the citizens of Gibraltar of the advantages of Spanish sovereignty and urged its Chief Minister, Peter Caruana, to join the discussions; Caruana had hitherto boycotted the negotiations. At a meeting in March, the Spanish and British Governments agreed to seek EU funding for proposals for the development of Gibraltar's port, airport and other infrastructure. During May, however, Aznar announced that Spain would never withdraw its territorial claim to the British enclave. Negotiations progressed in mid-2002, although a stalemate emerged when Spain disagreed with the British conditions for joint sovereignty — that it be permanent, that the military base would remain under British control, and that all changes be approved by a referendum put to the people of Gibraltar. In a referendum organized by the local administration of Gibraltar in November, which was not, however, recognized by the Spanish or British Government, the electorate voted overwhelmingly (by 99%, of a turn-out of 87.9%) against joint sovereignty with Spain. Further discussions were scheduled for 2003.

Relations with Portugal, traditionally tense, improved throughout the 1980s, culminating in 1989 when King Juan Carlos became the first Spanish monarch to address the Portuguese parliament. In the mid-1990s the principal bilateral issue between the two countries was the division of water resources; an accord over the sharing over river resources was reached in 1998. During 1997 relations were strained by Portugal's refusal to extradite an ETA terrorist. In 2002 tensions rose again, firstly over a border incident in which two Portuguese MPs were refused entry into Spain in July, then, later in the year, over mutual accusations of responsibility for the *Prestige* disaster (see above). In early January 2003 a clash between Portuguese maritime police and Spanish fishermen accused of using illegal fishing nets in Portuguese territorial waters led to the instigation of legal proceedings by Portugal, souring relations further between the two countries.

Relations with Morocco have been dominated by the issues of sovereignty of the enclaves of Ceuta and Melilla, illegal immigration and drugs-trafficking, and by disputes over fishing rights. Following his investiture as Prime Minister in May 1996, Aznar's first overseas visit was to Morocco. In February 2000 the Moroccan Government lodged an official protest following an outbreak of unprecedented racial violence in the southern Spanish town of El Ejido, where three recent murders had allegedly been committed by Moroccan immigrants. The majority of the 50 injured in the ensuing unrest were of Moroccan origin. By early 2000 the problems of illegal immigration (not only via Spanish North Africa but increasingly via the Canary Islands) had become a major political issue. In May, during a visit to Morocco, the Spanish Prime Minister confirmed that the recently implemented immigration law, one of the most liberal within the EU, was to be reformed (see above). Since its entry into force earlier in the year, the new legislation had encouraged more than 82,000 immigrants to apply for Spanish residency permits. Protests against the reforms were staged in Spanish North Africa as well as in Spain. Negotiations on the renewal of the fishing agreement between Morocco and the EU, permitting Spanish vessels access to Moroccan waters, commenced in mid-September 1999. The agreement expired at the end of November and Morocco indicated that the accord would not be renewed. Spanish vessels were once again required to withdraw from Moroccan waters and more than 4,000 Spanish fishermen remained without work. Despite extensive negotiations, by early 2001 the EU had failed to reach an agreement with Morocco, and Aznar announced that the consequences would be felt in the relations between the two countries. Relations began to deteriorate in August, when the Spanish Minister of Foreign Affairs expressed his concern at the number of illegal immigrants arriving in Spain via Morocco. In October the Moroccan Government recalled its ambassador to Spain at short notice after declaring that it was dissatisfied with the level of bilateral relations following the failure of the EU negotiations. In the following month a Spanish fishing vessel was apprehended by the Moroccan authorities and charged with fishing without a licence. In early April 2002, however, it was reported that the two Governments were preparing to reinstate their respective ambassadors. Relations were threatened again in mid-July, following the occupation of a small islet near Ceuta, the Isla de Perejil, by 12 Moroccan soldiers. Spain lodged a formal protest against this action on 12 July, but Morocco refused to withdraw its men, claiming that Perejil (known as Laila by the Moroccans) had been a part of Morocco since independence in 1956. Four Spanish gunboats were dispatched to patrol the locality and Spanish soldiers reoccupied the island on 17 July. A subsequent US-mediated agreement between Spain and Morocco left the island unoccupied. Issues over the sovereignty of Ceuta and Melilla continued to be problematic, however, especially in relation to negotiations on Gibraltar, and in September Morocco accused Spain of repeated violations of its airspace and territorial waters and reasserted its claims over the enclaves before the UN. Relations improved somewhat in November, however, when Morocco offered the temporary use of its territorial waters to 64 Spanish fishing boats after the *Prestige* oil disaster. Meetings in December 2002 and January 2003 contributed to the re-establishment of diplomatic relations between the two countries in February 2003.

Government

Under the Constitution approved in 1978, Spain is an hereditary monarchy, with the King as Head of State. He appoints the President of the Government (Prime Minister) and, on the latter's recommendation, other members of the Council of Ministers. Legislation is initiated for discussion in the Cortes (national assembly) in Madrid, in the Parliaments of the Autonomous Communities, or by popular petition. The King's actions in state affairs must receive the prior approval of the Cortes, to which the Government is responsible. The Council of State is the supreme consultative organ and comprises 23 members.

Legislative power is vested in the Cortes Generales, comprising two Houses, elected by direct universal adult suffrage for four years (subject to dissolution). The Congreso de los Diputados (Congress of Deputies) has 350 members, elected by proportional representation, and the Senado has 208 directly-elected members, plus 51 regional representatives, elected by the autonomous parliaments. A party can gain representation only if it obtains at least 3% of the votes.

The process of regional self-government was initiated in 1967. In October 1979 the statutes of the first of 17 Autonomous Communities were approved by referendum. The first Legislative Assemblies (Basque and Catalan) were elected in March 1980. The Galician Legislative Assembly was elected in October 1981, and that of Andalucía in May 1982. The remaining 13 were constituted in May 1983, thus completing the process of devolution. The regions possess varying degrees of autonomy. Each Legislative Assembly is elected for four years.

Spain comprises 50 provinces, each with its own Council (Diputación Provincial). The system of Civil Governors was replaced (by royal decree) in April 1997: a government sub-delegate is appointed by each autonomous region's government delegate.

Defence

It was announced in May 2001 that military service (of nine months) was to remain compulsory in Spain until December 2002. Exemption may be granted on family, medical and other grounds, and legislation relating to conscientious objection was approved in 1984. Plans for the gradual abolition of military service and for the establishment of professional armed forces were announced in early 1996; conscription was abolished in 2000, while the final stages of professionalization were due for completion in 2003. In August 2002 the total strength of the armed forces was 177,950 (including 9,450 not identified by service), comprising: army 118,800, navy 26,950 (including 5,600 marines), and air force 22,750. The paramilitary Guardia Civil (Civil Guard) numbered 72,600. Spain became a member of NATO (see p. 271) in May 1982. In December 1997 Spain's full integration into the military structure of NATO (with effect from January 1999) was approved by the alliance. Spain joined Western European Union (WEU, see p. 318) in November 1988.

The US military presence in Spain totalled 2,190, including a naval force of 1,760 and an air force of 260, in mid-2002. In November 2000 the EU announced plans for a rapid reaction force with the ability to deploy 60,000 troops in 60 days. Spain pledged some 6,000 troops to the force, which was intended to be fully established by 2003. The 2002 defence budget was €8,200m. Legislation to permit the entry of women to all sections of the armed forces took effect in early 1989.

Economic Affairs

In 2001, according to estimates by the World Bank, Spain's gross national income (GNI), measured at average 1999–2001 prices, was US \$586,874m., equivalent to US \$14,860 per head (or \$20,150 per head on an international purchasing-power parity basis). During 1990–2001, it was estimated, the population increased at an average annual rate of 0.2% per year, while gross domestic product (GDP) per head increased, in real terms, by an average of 2.4% per year. Overall GDP increased, in real terms, at an average annual rate of 2.5% in 1990–2001; growth in 2001 was 2.8%, according to official estimates.

Agriculture (including forestry and fishing) contributed an estimated 3.2% of GDP in 2001 and engaged 6.4% of the employed labour force. The principal crops are barley, wheat, sugar beet, vegetables, citrus fruits, grapes and olives; wine and olive oil are important products. In the late 1990s farmers were encouraged to grow sunflowers. Farmers were seriously affected by the infection of cattle with both bovine spongiform encephalopathy (BSE) and foot and mouth disease during 2000–01. According to the World Bank, agricultural GDP decreased at an average annual rate of 0.5% in 1990–2000; it declined by 3.1% in 1999, but grew by 1.5% in 2000. The fishing industry is significant. The Spanish fishing fleet is one of the largest in the world, and has been involved in various international disputes. In December 2000 the EU proposed a dramatic reduction in fishing levels, in an attempt to address the over-fishing of certain species.

Industry (including mining, manufacturing, utilities and construction) contributed an estimated 27.1% of GDP in 2001 and engaged 31.5% of the employed labour force. According to the World Bank, industrial GDP increased at an average annual rate of 2.3% in 1990–2000; it increased by 4.4% in 1999 and by 5.4% in 2000.

The mining and quarrying industry provided less than 1.0% of GDP in 2000, and engaged 0.4% of the employed labour force in 2001. Hard coal and brown coal are the principal minerals extracted, although production fell in the late 1990s owing to environmental standards imposed by the European Union (EU, see p. 3808). There are small reserves of petroleum. Some natural gas requirements are obtained from the Bay of Biscay, the remainder being imported by pipeline from Algeria.

Manufacturing contributed 15.9% of GDP in 2001 and engaged 18.8% of the employed labour force. Spain is one of the world's largest exporters of passenger cars. In 2001 production of passenger vehicles was 2.34m. units, of which more than 80% were exported. Other important industries are shipbuilding, chemicals, steel, textiles and footwear; some of these sectors underwent a process of rationalization in the 1980s. Investment is being made in new manufacturing industries, such as information technology and telecommunications equipment. According to the World Bank, manufacturing GDP decreased at an average annual rate of 0.3% in 1989–99; the rate of growth was 5.3% in 1998.

Energy contributed 2.6% of GDP in 2000 and employed 0.6% of the labour force in 2001. Energy is derived principally from petroleum, most of which is imported. In 1998 imports of mineral fuels and petroleum products accounted for 6.4% of total import costs. However, natural gas became an increasingly important fuel source in the late 1990s. Nuclear energy supplied 31.0% of total electricity production in 1999. In 2001 the electricity sector underwent major restructuring. The Government of Valencia has invested €2.6m. to build 40 wind farms in the region by 2003.

In 2001 the services sector accounted for 64.2% of GDP and engaged 62.1% of the employed labour force. The tourism industry makes an important contribution to the Spanish economy. In 1999 the number of tourist arrivals approached 51.8m., and receipts from tourism reached US \$32,913m.; however, tourist arrivals declined to 47.9m. in 2000. In 2002 there were 48.7m. tourist arrivals. In April 2001 several areas, including the Balearic Islands, introduced an environmental tourist tax, included in the cost of tourist accommodation, to protect the environment and repair the damage caused by the annual influx of tourists. Remittances from emigrants are also significant. According to the World Bank, the GDP of the services sector increased at an average annual rate of 2.8% in 1990–2000; services GDP increased by 4.0% in 1999 and by 3.6% in 2000.

In 2001 Spain recorded a visible trade deficit of US $31,500m., and there was a deficit of US $15,082m. on the current account of the balance of payments. In 2000 the principal sources of imports were France (17.1%) and Germany (14.8%), while the former was the main export market, purchasing 19.4%, followed by Germany (12.3%). Italy, the United Kingdom and other EU countries, and the USA, are also important trading partners. The principal imports in 2000 were machinery, electrical equipment, vehicles, mineral fuels and petroleum products, and chemical products. The main exports were motor cars, machinery, metals and their manufactures, and chemical products.

The 2002 draft budget envisaged a deficit of €3,762m., equivalent to 0.5% of GDP (compared with 0.3% in 2001). Compared with the previous year, government expenditure was projected to decrease by 2.3%. At December 1995 the external debt of the central Government totalled 6,153,200m. pesetas. In 1997–2000 the annual rate of inflation averaged 2.4%; consumer prices increased by an average of 3.4% in 2000 and by 3.6% in 2001. In 2000 the number of unemployed continued to decline, reaching a 20-year low in September of 1,501,442, equivalent to 8.9% of the labour force. By November 2001, however, unemployment had increased to 1,540,030, equivalent to 9.2% of the labour force.

Spain became a member of the EU in January 1986, and joined the exchange rate mechanism of the European Monetary System in June 1989. For the period 2000–06 the EU allocated €8,159m. annually in structural and cohesion funds towards projects in Spain. Spain is also a member of the Organisation for Economic Co-operation and Development (OECD, see p. 277).

Upon taking office in May 1996, the PP Government declared its commitment to European economic and monetary union (as agreed by EU members at Maastricht in December 1991). In order to meet the EU convergence criteria, Spain's budget deficit was duly reduced to the equivalent of below 3.0% of GDP by 1997. Spain was thus able to qualify for membership of the single European currency, introduced in January 1999. As a direct consequence of entering the single European currency, from early 1999 there was a sudden and sustained rise in inflation. Annual average inflation in 2000–01 was substantially higher than the average rate prevailing in most other member countries of the single European currency. In addition to high consumer demand, the introduction of the euro also encouraged stronger GDP growth. Following its re-election to office in March 2000, the PP Government confirmed its intention to eliminate the public deficit in 2001, to reduce taxes, to increase investment, with particular emphasis on regional development, and to implement minor pension reforms. Although declining, the level of unemployment (by far the highest rate within the EU) remained a serious economic and social problem. In April 2000 the Government announced that it aimed to achieve a target of full employment within 10 years. In a renewed attempt to contain inflationary pressures, in May 2000 the Government announced various economic liberalization measures, including the opening of local telephone services to greater competition. The Government also planned to raise substantial revenue through its acceleration of the country's programme to transfer the assets of state-owned companies to the private sector. Major disposals were to be made in the energy and telecommunications sectors. In May 2000 Telefónica negotiated a merger with KPN Telekom of the Netherlands. However, owing to the stakes held in the companies by their respective Governments, the deal had to be abandoned. In July the European Commission condemned the Spanish Government's use of its stake in a company to prevent foreign takeovers of Spanish businesses. However, Spain claimed that it would only block a bid from a company under foreign state control. In May Unión Fenosa announced its acquisition of Hidroeléctrica del Cantabria, but again the deal was blocked by the Government, to safeguard competition. In June the gas supply monopoly of Gas Natural was ended, when the Government awarded 12 licences to gas companies. In July 2000 the Government announced an investment plan, valued at 3,000m. pesetas, for the water system. Water was to be piped from the Ebro river in the north, to the arid south-east of the country. Proposals also included improvement to city water supplies, reforestation and recycling projects, a reduction in water prices, the modernization of irrigation methods for agriculture, and the implementa-

tion of a quality control and monitoring system of the water supply. However, there was strong opposition to the plan, and in March 2001 some 120,000 people protested in Madrid. The plan was submitted to the Congreso in mid-April 2001 and approved by the Senado in June. In early 2001 the Spanish companies Airtel, Euskaltel Menta, Desarrollo de Cable and Retecal, together with a group of international operators, announced their intention to construct a fibre optic cable network across Spain, along the road network. Following criticism over the Government's sale of third-generation mobile telephone licences at too low a price, the Government announced that it would sell two further licences in 2001, in order to create greater competition. However, the original operators protested against the plan and presented a case before the Administrative Economic Tribunal in April. Spain is the largest investor in Argentina, after the USA, and many of its banks and other companies suffered substantial losses as a result of the worsening debt crisis there and the devaluation of the national currency, the peso, in mid-2001.

Having narrowly missed its target of a balanced budget in 2002, partly as a result of fiscal deficits in the autonomous regions, Spain presented a balanced budget in 2003, aided by €16,000m. in EU donations (equivalent to 2% of GDP). An IMF report in December 2002 praised Spain for sound fiscal policies, which had helped it to achieve a predicted GDP growth of 2.0% for 2002; GDP was expected to rise by 2.5% in 2003 despite a regional slow-down. Concern was expressed, however, over continuing high unemployment and inflation, the latter being projected to reach 4% in 2002. The Spanish energy market entered its final stages of liberalization in early 2003, although deficits in the sector as a result of the fixing of a low price ceiling led to a government promise of a reimbursement of €1,600m. in December 2002. In February 2003 the European Commission's advocate-general, Damaso Ruiz-Jarabo, provoked controversy by expressing approval of the Spanish Government's possession of so-called 'golden shares' (which allow governmental control of private entities) in companies such as Telefónica and Repsol; the Commission had previously expressed concern at the Government's use of these stakes (see above) and a European Court of Justice decision on the matter was expected during 2003.

Education

In 2001/02 some 1.21m. children were attending pre-school institutions. In that year 2.48m. children were enrolled at primary schools and a total of 3.13m. in some form of secondary education. Under reforms implemented in 1991, basic education is compulsory, and available free of charge, from the ages of six to 16 years. It comprises primary education, which begins at six years of age and lasts for six years, and secondary education, composed of two two-year cycles, followed between the ages of 12 and 16. Thereafter, students may take either a vocational training course, lasting one or two years, or the two-year Bachillerato course, in preparation for university entrance. Private schools, many of which are administered by the Roman Catholic Church, are responsible for the education of more than 30% of Spanish children. In autonomous communities the teaching of languages other than Spanish (such as Catalan) is regulated by decree. In 2001 enrolment at primary schools and in the first cycle of obligatory secondary education (ages 6–13) was equivalent to 108.7% of children in the relevant age-group, while enrolment at secondary schools (ages 14–18) in that year was equivalent to 94.5% of children in the appropriate age-group. In November 2000 the Government announced a four-year reform of the secondary education system, improving mathematics, languages and philosophy; offering new subjects, including Greek, classics and technical drawing; and expanding information technology.

Some 1.59m. students were attending university in 2001/02. In 1996/97 there were about 50 universities, including the open university (UNED, established in 1972—which had 128,820 students). There are three cycles within university education. The first cycle lasts for three years and leads to the degree of Diplomatura. The second cycle lasts for two or three years and leads to the degree of Licenciatura. The degree of Doctor is awarded upon completion of the two-year third cycle and the writing of a thesis. Higher Technical studies in engineering and architecture are followed at Escuelas Técnicas de Grado Medio and Escuelas Técnicas de Grado Superior. In 2001 a number of proposed changes to the higher education system were under consideration, for implementation in 2003–04. The changes were to affect the direction and administration of the universities, and the selection process of the students. The 2002 draft budget allocated €2,091.0m. (1.9% of total expenditure) to education, culture and sport.

Public Holidays

2003: 1 January (New Year's Day), 6 January (Epiphany), 17 April (Maundy Thursday), 18 April (Good Friday), 21 April (Easter Monday), 1 May (Labour Day), 15 August (Assumption), 12 October (National Day, anniversary of the discovery of America), 1 November (All Saints' Day), 6 December (Constitution Day), 8 December (Immaculate Conception), 25 December (Christmas Day).

2004: 1 January (New Year's Day), 6 January (Epiphany), 8 April (Maundy Thursday), 9 April (Good Friday), 12 April (Easter Monday), 1 May (Labour Day), 15 August (Assumption), 12 October (National Day, anniversary of the discovery of America), 1 November (All Saints' Day), 6 December (Constitution Day), 8 December (Immaculate Conception), 25 December (Christmas Day).

In addition, various regional holidays are observed.

Weights and Measures

The metric system is in force.

Statistical Survey

Source (unless otherwise stated): Instituto Nacional de Estadística, Paseo de la Castellana 183, 28046 Madrid; tel. (91) 5839301; fax (91) 5839086; e-mail info@ine.es; internet www.ine.es.

Area and Population

AREA, POPULATION AND DENSITY

Area (sq km)	
Land	499,542
Inland water	5,240
Total	504,782*
Population (census results)	
1 March 1991	38,872,268
1 November 2001	
Males	20,021,850
Females	20,825,521
Total	40,847,371
Population (official estimates at 1 January)†	
2000	40,499,791
2001	41,116,842
2002	41,692,558
Density (per sq km) at 1 November 2001	80.9

* 194,897 sq miles.

† Not revised to take account of the November 2001 census results.

PROVINCES

(population at 1 January 2002)*†

Alava	291,860	Lugo	361,782
Albacete	371,787	Madrid	5,527,152
Alicante	1,557,968	Málaga	1,330,010
Almería	546,498	Murcia	1,226,993
Avila	165,138	Navarra	569,628
Badajoz	662,808	Ourense	343,768
Illes Balears (Balearic Is)	916,968	Oviedo (Principado de Asturias)	1,073,971
Barcelona	4,906,117	Palencia	176,125
Burgos	352,723	Las Palmas	951,037
Cáceres	410,242	Pontevedra	919,934
Cádiz	1,140,793	Salamanca	347,120
Castellón (Castelló) de la Plana	501,237	Santa Cruz de Tenerife	892,718
Ciudad Real	484,338	Santander (Cantabria)	542,275
Córdoba	771,131	Segovia	148,286
A Coruña	1,111,886	Sevilla	1,758,720
Cuenca	201,614	Soria	91,487
Girona (Gerona)	598,112	Tarragona	631,156
Granada	818,959	Teruel	137,342
Guadalajara	177,761	Toledo	546,538
Guipúzcoa	682,977	Valencia	2,267,503
Huelva	464,934	Valladolid	501,157
Huesca	208,963	Vizcaya	1,133,444
Jaén	647,387	Zamora	200,678
La Rioja	281,614	Zaragoza	871,209
León	496,655	**Total**	41,692,558
Lleida (Lérida)	371,055		

* Excluding Spanish North Africa (area 32 sq km), an integral part of Spain. Ceuta had a population of 76,152 on 1 January 2002, while Melilla's population was 69,184.

† Including residents temporarily abroad.

PRINCIPAL TOWNS*

(population at 1 January 2002)

Madrid (capital)	3,016,788	Vitoria-Gasteiz	221,270
Barcelona	1,527,190	Santa Cruz de Tenerife	217,415
Valencia	791,871	Badalona	210,370
Sevilla (Seville)	704,114	Oviedo	202,938
Zaragoza	620,419	Elche	201,731
Málaga	535,686	Móstoles	198,819
Murcia	377,888	Pamplona (Iruña)	189,364
Las Palmas de Gran Canaria	370,649	Cartagena	188,003
Palma de Mallorca	358,462	Sabadell	187,201
Bilbao	353,950	Jerez de la Frontera	187,087
Valladolid	318,576	Santander	184,661
Córdoba	314,805	Donostia-San Sebastián	181,700
Alicante (Alacant)	293,629	Fuenlabrada	179,735
Vigo	288,324	Alcalá de Henares	179,602
Gijón	270,211	Terrassa	179,300
Hospitalet de Llobregat	244,523	Leganés	174,436
(A) Coruña	242,458	Almería	173,338
Granada	240,522	Burgos	167,962

* Population figures refer to *municipios*, each of which may contain some rural area as well as the urban centre.

BIRTHS, MARRIAGES AND DEATHS

	Registered live births		Registered marriages		Registered deaths	
	Number	Rate (per 1,000)	Number	Rate (per 1,000)	Number	Rate (per 1,000)
1994	370,148	9.5	199,731	5.1	338,242	8.6
1995	363,469	9.3	200,688	5.1	346,227	8.8
1996	362,626	9.2	194,084	4.9	351,449	8.9
1997	369,035	9.4	196,499	5.0	349,521	8.9
1998	365,193	9.3	207,041	5.3	360,511	9.2
1999	377,809	9.6	206,048	5.2	370,423	9.4
2000	395,756	9.9	209,854	5.3	359,148	9.0
2001*	403,859	9.9	206,254	5.0	358,856	8.7

* Provisional figures.

Expectation of life (WHO estimates, years at birth): 78.9 (males 75.3, females 82.6) in 2001 (Source: WHO, *World Health Report*).

ECONOMICALLY ACTIVE POPULATION
(average of quarterly sample surveys, '000 persons aged 16 years and over)

	1999	2000	2001
Agriculture, hunting and forestry	958.5	927.2	954.5
Fishing	56.4	61.8	64.7
Mining and quarrying	63.1	60.6	63.3
Manufacturing	2,634.5	2,725.5	3,005.6
Electricity, gas and water supply	86.3	92.8	98.8
Construction	1,463.7	1,591.8	1,850.2
Wholesale and retail trade; repair of motor vehicles, motorcycles and personal and household goods	2,265.8	2,452.4	2,555.9
Hotels and restaurants	848.7	904.9	970.3
Transport, storage and communications	805.9	863.0	965.2
Financial intermediation	363.0	383.2	392.1
Real estate, renting and business activities	931.0	1,036.6	1,238.3
Public administration and defence; compulsory social security	887.6	927.6	1,008.1
Education	801.9	806.1	888.8
Health and social work	743.5	789.3	852.8
Other community, social and personal service activities	516.0	559.3	616.3
Private households with employed persons	390.0	390.0	418.0
Extra-territorial organizations and bodies	1.5	1.6	2.9
Total employed	13,817.4	14,473.7	15,945.6
Total unemployed	2,605.5	2,370.4	1,869.0
Total labour force	16,422.9	16,844.1	17,814.6
Males	9,892.8	10,067.3	10,837.1
Females	6,530.1	6,776.8	6,977.6

Health and Welfare

KEY INDICATORS

Total fertility rate (children per woman, 2001)	1.1
Under-5 mortality rate (per 1,000 live births, 2001)	6
HIV/AIDS (% of persons aged 15–49, 2001)	0.50
Physicians (per 1,000 head, 1997)	4.24
Hospital beds (per 1,000 head, 1995)	3.9
Health expenditure (2000): US $ per head (PPP)	1,539
Health expenditure (2000): % of GDP	7.7
Health expenditure (2000): public (% of total)	69.9
Human Development Index (2000): ranking	21
Human Development Index (2000): value	0.913

For sources and definitions, see explanatory note on p. vi.

Agriculture

PRINCIPAL CROPS
('000 metric tons)

	1999	2000	2001
Wheat	5,084	7,333	4,938
Rice (paddy)	845	798	888
Barley	7,434	11,283	6,245
Maize	3,769	3,867	4,957
Oats	531	952	659
Potatoes	3,367	3,138	2,957
Sugar cane	80	80*	110*
Sugar beet	8,162	8,232	6,775
Olives	3,395	4,944	6,780
Sunflower seed	644	848	871
Lettuce	1,007	991	973
Tomatoes	3,865	3,583	3,730
Chillies and green peppers	924	939	965
Dry onions	1,005	1,014	1,104
Other vegetables	3,024	3,352	3,222*
Oranges	2,828	2,687	2,822
Tangerines, mandarins, clementines and satsumas	2,071	1,780	1,655
Lemons and limes	892	905	1,037
Apples	922	755	962
Pears	731	673	720
Peaches and nectarines	987	1,127	1,031
Grapes	5,421	6,641	5,111
Watermelons	704	723	618
Cantaloupes and other melons	1,184	1,007	984

* FAO estimate.

Source: FAO.

LIVESTOCK
('000 head, year ending September)

	1999	2000	2001
Horses	248	248*	248*
Mules	117	117	115*
Asses	140	140*	140*
Cattle	5,951	6,291	6,164
Pigs	21,668	21,526	23,348
Sheep	24,190	23,965	24,400
Goats	2,779	2,627	2,830
Chickens*	127,000	128,000	128,000

* FAO estimate(s).

Source: FAO.

LIVESTOCK PRODUCTS
('000 metric tons)

	1999	2000	2001
Beef and veal	678	632	642
Mutton and lamb	221	232	236
Goat meat	17	19	17
Pig meat	2,893	2,912	2,993
Horse meat	6	7	7
Rabbit meat	101	114	115
Poultry meat	1,002*	987	1,031
Cows' milk	6,300	6,047*	6,294*
Sheep's milk	305	306*	306†
Goats' milk	317	320*	320†
Butter	36	39	32
Cheese	175	180	181
Hen eggs	640	522*	560*
Other poultry eggs	2	4	4
Honey	32	32†	32†
Wool: (greasy)	31	31†	31†
Wool: (scoured)†	18	18	18
Cattle hides†	51	48	47
Sheepskins†	21	23	23

* Unofficial figure.
† FAO estimate(s).

Source: FAO.

Forestry

ROUNDWOOD REMOVALS
('000 cubic metres, excl. bark)

	1998	1999	2000*
Sawlogs, veneer logs and logs for sleepers	5,732	5,690	5,690
Pulpwood	6,702	6,790	6,790
Other industrial wood	730	680	680
Fuel wood	1,710	1,650	1,650
Total	14,874	14,810	14,810

* FAO estimates.

Source: FAO.

SAWNWOOD PRODUCTION
('000 cubic metres, incl. railway sleepers)

	1998	1999	2000*
Coniferous (softwood)	2,437	2,437	2,437
Broadleaved (hardwood)	741	741	741
Total	3,178	3,178	3,178

* FAO estimates.

Source: FAO.

Fishing

('000 metric tons, live weight)

	1998	1999	2000
Capture	1,263.0	1,190.0	976.9
European pilchard (sardine)	195.3	128.2	81.0
Skipjack tuna	114.8	167.8	95.9
Yellowfin tuna	75.8	88.3	57.2
Bigeye tuna	23.4	44.8	39.5
Jack and horse mackerels	36.9	43.8	44.5
Aquaculture	313.5	317.8	312.2
Blue mussel	261.1	262.0	247.7
Total catch	1,529.2	1,485.0	1,289.1

Note: Figures exclude aquatic plants ('000 metric tons, capture only): 14.9 in 1998; 14.8 in 1999; 14.2 in 2000. Also excluded are Sardinia coral (metric tons):2.5 in 1998; 6.9 in 1999; 7.3 in 2000. Also excluded are sponges (FAO estimates, metric tons): 0.8 in 1998; 0.8 in 1999; 0.7 in 2000.

Source: FAO, *Yearbook of Fishery Statistics*.

Mining

('000 metric tons, unless otherwise indicated)

	1999	2000	2001†
Anthracite	5,436	4,651	4,694‡
Lignite	12,535	12,153	12,193‡
Crude petroleum ('000 barrels)	2,295	1,648	2,505‡
Natural gas (million cubic metres)	143	179	180
Copper*	1.7	23.3	9.7
Lead*	41.8	40.3	49.5‡
Zinc*	154.1	201.3	164.9‡
Kaolin	320.0	353.4	400.0
Potash salts (crude)	549.0	646.3	569.1‡
Pyrites	733.0	205.0	152.0‡
Sepiolite	800.0	794.1	897.0‡
Dolomite	9,080.0	8,752.0‡	9,628.0‡
Fluorspar*	133.0	132.7	126.5‡
Salt (unrefined)	3,600.0	3,869.0	4,100.0
Gypsum (crude)	9,450.0	9,929.0	10,900.0

* Figures refer to the metal content of ores.

† Provisional figures.

‡ Reported figure.

Source: US Geological Survey.

Industry

SELECTED PRODUCTS
('000 metric tons, unless otherwise indicated)

	1997	1998	1999
Wine ('000 hectolitres)	20,892	n.a.	n.a.
Aluminium (primary)	359.9*	360.4*	363.9†
Refined copper (primary)	268.0*	239.6†	250.8†
Pig-iron	3,927‡	4,236‡	4,059†
Cement (Portland)	27,860	27,943†	30,800†
Sulphuric acid	2,817	3,134‡	n.a.
Caustic soda	660	689	788
Motorcycles ('000)	38	57	68
Passenger cars ('000)	2,278	2,469	2,473
Merchant ships launched ('000 gross tons)§	167	556	247
Electricity (million kWh)	190,201‡	n.a.	n.a.

* Data from *World Metal Statistics* (London).

† Data from the US Geological Survey.

‡ Data from the UN Economic Commission for Europe.

§ Data from Lloyd's Register of Shipping (London).

Source: mainly UN, *Industrial Commodity Statistics Yearbook*.

2000 (units): Motorcycles 70,657; Passenger cars 2,366,334.

2001 (units): Motorcycles 75,029; Passenger cars 2,210,428.

Finance

CURRENCY AND EXCHANGE RATES

Monetary Units
100 cent = 1 euro (€)

Sterling and Dollar Equivalents (31 December 2002)
£1 sterling = 1.5370 euros
US $1 = 0.9536 euros
100 euros = £65.06.00 = $104.87

Average Exchange Rate (euros per US $)
2000	1.0854
2001	1.1175
2002	1.0626

Note: The national currency was formerly the peseta. From the introduction of the euro, with Spanish participation, on 1 January 1999, a fixed exchange rate of €1 = 166.386 pesetas was in operation. Euro notes and coins were introduced on 1 January 2002. The euro and local currency circulated alongside each other until 28 February, after which the euro became the sole legal tender. Some of the figures in this Survey are still in terms of pesetas.

BUDGET
('000 million pesetas, provisional)

Revenue	2000	2001	2002*
Direct taxation	8,401.0	8,940.9	50,673.1
Personal income tax	5,308.7	5,599.6	29,556.6
Corporate tax	2,787.4	3,024.7	18,982.4
Indirect taxation	8,638.2	9,168.3	45,488.8
Value-added tax	5,648.2	6,076.9	30,266.4
Special taxes	2,685.6	2,774.3	13,170.4
Rates and other revenue	336.5	457.5	2,517.6
Current transfers	971.4	955.3	4,173.0
Estate taxes	583.6	594.3	4,418.8
Transfer of real investments	10.2	11.0	108.2
Capital transfers	291.6	256.1	1,444.7
Total	19,232.5	20,383.4	108,824.3

Expenditure	2000	2001	2002*
Pensions	990.4	1,027.0	6,413.0
Interior	714.4	728.3	4,582.6
Justice	158.5	171.6	1,076.5
Defence	965.0	1,008.4	6,320.2
Public works	941.1	970.8	447.7
Environment	253.4	264.9	1,670.4
Education, culture and sport	646.3	323.2	2,091.0
Agriculture, fisheries and food	203.3	195.2	1,297.3
Science and technology†	274.1	224.5	1,457.2
Health and consumer affairs	4,271.7	4,537.8	11,018.6
Labour and social affairs	845.2	821.5	4,478.1
Economy and finance	309.7	544.9	3,833.3
Territorial bodies	4,528.7	5,058.9	31,822.2
EU contributions	1,133.2	1,233.6	8,086.6
Public debt	2,805.0	2,835.0	17,729.9
Total (incl. others)	19,769.5	20,661.5	112,586.9

* In terms of million euros. Figures are provisional.

† In 2000 the Ministry of Industry and Energy was replaced by the Ministry of Science and Technology.

INTERNATIONAL RESERVES
(US $ million at 31 December)

	2000	2001	2002
Gold*	4,588	4,653	5,768
IMF special drawing rights	290	351	354
Reserve position in IMF	1,182	1,326	1,592
Foreign exchange*	29,516	27,905	32,590
Total	35,577	34,235	40,303

* Figures for gold and foreign exchange exclude deposits made with the European Monetary Institute (now the European Central Bank). Gold is valued at market-related prices.

Source: IMF, *International Financial Statistics*.

MONEY SUPPLY
(million euros at 31 December)

	2000	2001	2002
Currency issued	59,793	48,749	40,500*
Demand deposits at banking institutions	147,564	170,189	175,190

* Currency put into circulation by the Banco de España was 59,085 million euros.

Source: IMF, *International Financial Statistics*.

COST OF LIVING
(Consumer Price Index. Base: 1990 = 100)

	1999	2000	2001
Food (incl. beverages and tobacco)	116.2	118.6	125.7
Fuel and light	129.5	137.0	138.1
Clothing (incl. footwear)	133.4	136.2	139.9
Rent	166.8	173.2	180.5
All items (incl. others)	141.6	146.4	151.7

Source: ILO, *Yearbook of Labour Statistics*.

NATIONAL ACCOUNTS
(estimates, million euros at current prices)

National Income and Product

	1999	2000	2001
Gross domestic product (GDP) in market prices	565,199	609,319	651,641
Primary incomes recieved from abroad.			
Less Primary incomes paid abroad.	−6,106	−6,360	−8,839
Gross national income	559,093	602,959	642,802
Less Consumption of fixed capital	74,393	83,428	90,631
Net national income	484,700	519,531	552,171
Current transfers from abroad			
Less Current transfers paid abroad.	1,428	266	23
Net national disposable income	486,128	519,797	552,194

Expenditure on the Gross Domestic Product

	1999	2000	2001
Final consumption expenditure	433,832	466,714	494,717
Households	331,290	355,213	376,199
Non-profit institutions serving households	3,956	4,278	4,491
General government	98,586	107,223	114,027
Gross capital formation	138,733	156,467	167,586
Gross fixed capital formation	136,128	154,305	165,634
Changes in inventories	2,605	2,162	1,952
Total domestic expenditure	572,565	623,191	662,303
Exports of goods and services	155,477	183,647	194,952
Less Imports of goods and services	162,843	197,509	205,614
GDP in market prices	565,199	609,319	651,641

Gross Domestic Product by Economic Activity

	1999	2000	2001
Agriculture, hunting and forestry	18,488	18,833	21,001
Fishing	1,429	1,287	
Mining and quarrying	2,272	2,455	19,221
Electricity, gas and water supply	14,833	15,618	
Manufacturing	94,380	100,064	103,511
Construction	41,693	48,172	53,673
Commercial sector services:			
Wholesale and retail trade; repair of motor vehicles, motorcycles and personal and household goods	61,040	64,543	
Hotels and restaurants	41,770	46,473	
Transport, storage and communications	43,574	46,148	
Financial intermediation	26,584	29,950	330,938
Real estate, renting and business activities	74,160	80,083	
Education	7,662	8,191	
Health and social work	10,961	12,054	
Other social and service activities	14,251	15,355	
Non-commercial sector services:			
Public administration and defence; compulsory social security	32,581	35,176	
Education	17,698	18,902	
Health and social work	17,935	19,061	87,298
Other community, social and personal service activities	2,570	2,743	
Private households with employed persons	5,999	6,284	
Sub-total	529,880	571,392	615,642
Less Financial intermediation services indirectly measured	19,050	21,269	25,994
Gross value added in basic prices	510,830	550,123	589,648
Taxes, *less* subsidies, on products	54,369	59,196	61,993
GDP in market prices	565,199	609,139	651,641

BALANCE OF PAYMENTS
(US $ million)

	1999	2000	2001
Exports of goods f.o.b.	112,664	116,205	117,561
Imports of goods f.o.b.	−143,002	−151,025	−149,061
Trade balance	−30,339	−34,820	−31,500
Exports of services	53,418	53,540	57,775
Imports of services	−30,532	−31,283	−33,516
Balance on goods and services.	−7,452	−12,564	−7,242
Other income received . . .	12,636	15,017	19,796
Other income paid	−22,087	−23,268	−29,342
Balance on goods, services and			
income	−16,903	−20,815	−16,787
Current transfers received . .	13,435	11,629	12,567
Current transfers paid . . .	−10,292	−10,050	−10,862
Current balance	−13,761	−19,237	−15,082
Capital account (net)	6,967	4,792	4,960
Direct investment abroad . .	−41,754	−53,865	−27,704
Direct investment from abroad	15,541	36,931	21,540
Portfolio investment assets . .	−47,397	−59,320	−43,528
Portfolio investment liabilities .	45,549	58,146	27,569
Financial derivatives liabilities	260	2,025	47
Other investment assets . .	−24,624	−18,640	10,196
Other investment liabilities . .	41,427	51,666	27,766
Net errors and omissions . .	−5,059	−5,379	−7,104
Overall balance	−22,850	−2,881	−1,340

Source: IMF, *International Financial Statistics*.

External Trade

PRINCIPAL COMMODITIES
('000 euros)

Imports c.i.f.	1998	1999	2000
Live animals and animal			
products	5,064,585	5,023,372	5,785,927
Vegetable products . . .	4,278,194	4,209,684	4,165,778
Products of the food industries,			
drinks and tobacco . . .	4,795,182	5,215,084	5,647,770
Mineral products	9,388,678	11,555,208	22,393,981
Mineral fuels and petroleum			
products.	7,832,468	9,950,768	20,435,9935
Products of the chemical			
industries and related			
industries	11,747,291	12,433,390	14,740,988
Artificial plastic materials,			
rubber and their			
manufactures	6,051,775	6,530,410	7,267,525
Artificial plastic materials and			
their manufactures . . .	4,113,304	4,559,372	5,264,668
Textiles and their			
manufactures	6,260,544	6,743,483	7,825,700
Base metals and their			
manufactures	9,502,194	9,742,139	11,756,516
Cast iron, iron and steel . .	4,382,145	4,185,242	5,170,580
Machines and apparatus,			
electrical equipment . .	28,762,809	32,844,793	37,776,797
Nuclear reactors, boilers,			
mechanical machines, apparatus			
and appliances	17,518,156	19,254,124	21,117,247
Electrical machines and apparatus	11,244,653	13,590,669	16,659,550
Transport equipment. . .	21,152,733	27,281,765	31,373,935
Motor cars, tractors, mopeds, etc.	19,363,489	23,997,353	27,323,085
Optical, photographic and			
cinematographic, precision			
instruments and apparatus .	3,815,382	4,251,927	4,580,989
Total (incl. others)	122,856,110	139,093,706	169,468,101

Exports f.o.b.	1998	1999	2000
Vegetable products	6,895,833	6,745,728	7,189,825
Edible fruits, citrus and melon peel	3,543,849	3,375,986	3,560,187
Products of the food industries,			
drinks and tobacco	4,807,237	4,980,150	5,428,356
Mineral products	2,859,400	3,191,518	5,564,970
Mineral fuels and petroleum			
products.	2,063,276	2,302,239	4,576,909
Products of the chemical			
industries and related			
industries	6,459,257	7,254,434	8,823,964
Artificial plastic materials,			
rubber and their			
manufactures	4,856,059	5,220,121	6,321,445
Artificial plastic materials and			
their manufactures	3,020,472	3,269,666	4,198,146
Paper and related			
manufactured products . .	2,703,333	2,842,580	3,731,850
Textiles and their			
manufactures	4,629,278	4,863,355	5,540,763
Manufactures of stone, cement,			
etc., ceramics, glass and its			
manufactures	3,306,038	3,442,726	3,903,649
Base metals and their			
manufactures	7,224,157	7,165,093	9,099,065
Machines and apparatus,			
electrical equipment . .	16,824,171	17,964,505	20,349,658
Nuclear reactors, boilers,			
mechanical machines, apparatus			
and appliances	9,775,365	10,238,063	11,555,084
Electrical machines and apparatus	7,048,806	7,726,443	8,794,574
Transport equipment. . . .	25,935,755	27,593,773	32,146,015
Motor cars, tractors, mopeds, etc.	23,628,683	24,656,300	28,929,596
Total (incl. others)	99,849,458	104,788,627	124,177,336

PRINCIPAL TRADING PARTNERS*
('000 euros)

Imports c.i.f.	1998	1999	2000
Algeria	1,180,673	1,411,315	3,093,843
Austria	1,339,720	1,725,002	1,801,542
Belgium-Luxembourg-			
Netherlands	9,655,669	10,702,349	12,093,929
France	22,572,417	24,886,345	29,001,687
Germany	19,006,095	21,933,756	25,152,981
Ireland	1,717,940	2,017,375	2,424,702
Italy	12,180,715	12,999,077	15,127,330
Japan	3,689,952	4,399,540	4,831,226
Libya	763,356	1,074,754	2,030,720
Portugal	3,439,728	3,858,258	4,609,075
Russia.	991,274	1,267,519	2,446,225
Saudi Arabia	855,512	785,204	1,715,204
Sweden	1,790,393	2,690,833	2,638,849
Switzerland	1,569,692	1,581,331	2,030,905
United Kingdom	9,460,952	10,387,851	12,059,557
USA	7,025,843	7,653,731	8,758,315
Total (incl. others)	122,856,110	139,093,706	169,468,101

Exports f.o.b.	1998	1999	2000
Argentina.	1,146,417	949,019	946,328
Belgium-Luxembourg-			
Netherlands	6,246,048	6,952,936	8,098,390
Brazil	1,228,074	1,293,723	1,256,791
France	19,434,710	20,438,501	24,129,123
Germany	13,607,734	13,765,121	15,324,986
Greece.	948,059	1,089,737	1,315,358
Italy	9,228,578	9,426,605	10,855,203
Japan	916,810	1,098,985	1,214,989
Mexico	1,070,248	1,140,396	1,509,702
Morocco	968,411	1,105,738	1,370,896
Portugal	9,407,381	10,495,543	11,854,776
Sweden	1,109,870	1,224,060	1,251,335
Switzerland	1,087,757	1,083,071	1,206,674
Turkey	1,149,932	1,248,371	2,117,089
United Kingdom	8,408,183	8,747,652	10,198,907
USA	4,187,146	4,598,668	6,051,668
Total (incl. others) . . .	99,849,458	104,788,627	124,177,336

* Imports by country of production; exports by country of last consignment. For exports the distribution by country excludes stores and bunkers for ships and aircraft.

Transport

RAILWAYS
(RENFE only)

	1999	2000	2001
Number of passengers ('000) . .	418,900	438,870	466,790
Passenger-kilometres (million). .	18,143	18,571	19,190
Freight ('000 metric tons) . .	25,330	25,789	25,640
Freight ton-kilometres (million)	11,4865	11,621	11,750

Source: RENFE, Madrid.

ROAD TRAFFIC
(motor vehicles in use at 31 December)

	1999	2000	2001
Passenger cars	16,847,300	17,449,200	18,150,900
Buses	53,500	54,700	56,100
Lorries.	3,605,000	3,780,200	3,949,000
Motorcycles	1,403,800	1,445,600	1,483,400

SHIPPING

Merchant Fleet
(registered at 31 December)

	1999	2000	2001
Number of vessels	1,562	1,554	1,545
Displacement (grt)	1,903,081	2,030,088	2,147,545

Source: Lloyd's Register-Fairplay, *World Fleet Statistics*.

International Sea-borne Freight Traffic
('000 metric tons)

	1999	2000	2001
Goods loaded	56,820	56,264	59,297
Goods unloaded	n.a.	193,427	198,696

Source: UN, *Monthly Bulletin of Statistics*.

CIVIL AVIATION
(domestic and international traffic on scheduled services)

	1996	1997	1998
Kilometres flown (million) . .	285	305	331
Passengers carried ('000) . .	27,759	30,316	31,594
Passenger-km (million) . .	34,102	37,240	40,042
Total metric ton-km (million) . .	3,807	4,093	4,378

Source: UN, *Statistical Yearbook*.

Tourism

FOREIGN TOURIST ARRIVALS
(incl. Spaniards resident abroad)

Country of residence	2000	2001	2002
Belgium	1,679,874	1,651,914	1,656,100
France	5,680,578	6,668,709	7,546,400
Germany	11,171,050	10,563,015	9,528,600
Italy	2,097,666	2,184,085	2,349,800
Netherlands	1,968,010	2,178,577	2,255,000
Portugal	1,489,856	1,472,663	1,608,900
Sweden	1,209,675	1,202,490	1,064,500
Switzerland	1,198,479	1,169,838	1,140,400
United Kingdom	13,238,973	14,065,359	13,715,800
USA	1,145,629	907,161	879,600
Total (incl. others)	47,897,915	49,519,408	48,734,600

Source: Instituto de Estudios Turísticos, Madrid.

Receipts from tourism (million euros): 30,482 in 1999; 33,711 in 2000; 36,705 in 2001 (Source: Banco de España).

Communications Media

	1999	2000	2001
Television receivers ('000 in use) .	22,000	24,000	n.a.
Telephones ('000 main lines in use)	16,480.4	17,101.7	17,427.0
Mobile cellular telephones ('000 subscribers).	12,300.3	24,736.0	26,494.2
Personal computers ('000 in use) .	4,800	5,800	6,800
Internet users ('000)	2,830.0	5,387.8	7,388

Facsimile machines (1996): 700,000 in use (estimate).

Radio receivers ('000 in use, 1997): 13,100.

Book production (2000): titles ('000) 62.0; copies (million) 233.2.

Daily newspapers (1996): 87 (with combined average circulation of 3,931,000 copies per issue).

Weekly newspapers (1996): 12 (with combined average circulation of 4,850,000).

Source: UN, *Statistical Yearbook*; UNESCO, *Statistical Yearbook* and International Telecommunication Union.

Education

(2001/02, estimated)

	Institutions	Teachers	Pupils/Students
Pre-primary	2,670	} 244,483	{ 1,211,826
Primary	8,547*		2,475,027
Secondary: general . . . }	4,319	264,434	{ 2,618,552
Secondary: vocational . . }			501,818
Higher: universities, etc. . .	1,263	91,606†	1,590,667
Higher: other	511	6,961	27,241

* Excluding institutions providing primary education and the first cycle of secondary education (3,837 in 2001/02), or institutions providing both primary and secondary education (1,285 in 2001/02).
† 1999/2000 figure.

Source: Ministerio de Educación, Cultura y Deporte, Madrid.

Adult literacy rate (UNESCO estimates): 97.6% (males 98.6%; females 96.8%) in 2000 (Source: UN Development Programme *Human Development Report*).

Directory

The Constitution

The Constitution of the Kingdom of Spain was approved by popular referendum on 6 December 1978, and promulgated on 29 December 1978.

According to the final provisions, all the fundamental laws of the Franco regime are repealed, together with all measures incompatible with the Constitution.

The following is a summary of the main provisions:

PRELIMINARY PROVISIONS

Spain is established as a social and democratic State whose supreme values are freedom, justice, equality and political pluralism. National sovereignty and power reside with the Spanish people, the political form of the State being a parliamentary Monarchy.

The Constitution is based on the indissoluble unity of the Spanish nation, and recognizes and guarantees the right to autonomy of the nationalities and regions.

FUNDAMENTAL RIGHTS, DUTIES AND FREEDOMS

Standards concerning fundamental rights and freedoms recognized in the Constitution are to be interpreted in accordance with the Universal Declaration of Human Rights and other international treaties and agreements of a similar nature ratified by Spain.

All Spaniards are equal under the law and no Spaniard by birth may be deprived of his nationality. The age of majority is 18, suffrage is free and universal and every person has a right to public service.

The main freedoms listed are described below, bearing in mind that the Constitution contains the proviso that no person, group or action pose a threat to public order and safety. Free entry to and exit from Spain, freedom of thought, belief and expression are guaranteed, as is the right of access to state and public communications media by significant social and political groups and to administrative archives and registers by individuals, except in matters concerning state security and defence, and the private life and home of the individual, which are inviolable.

The Constitution states that there is no state religion but that it will maintain co-operation with the Roman Catholic Church and other religious groups.

Freedom of association is guaranteed, except for criminal, paramilitary and secret associations, all associations being bound to inscribe themselves in a public register; the right to form trade unions and to strike is also guaranteed, military personnel being subject to special laws in these cases.

Every person has a right to work for a just remuneration, including paid holiday, under conditions of safety, hygiene and a healthy environment. The State is to be run on the principles of a market economy. Taxation is determined according to means and consumer protection is encouraged by the State. Social-security payments are provided for and it is stipulated that special care be taken of the handicapped and the elderly.

In criminal matters, the death penalty is abolished except under military criminal law in time of war. Extradition functions on the principle of reciprocity but the terms do not apply to political crimes, acts of terrorism, however, not being considered as such. All persons are presumed innocent before trial, and a *habeas corpus* clause provides for a detainee to be freed within 72 hours of arrest or to be brought before a court.

THE CROWN

The King is the Head of State, the symbol of its unity and permanence, and the highest representative of the Spanish State in international relations. The person of the King is inviolable. His decisions and acts must be approved by the Government, without which they are deemed invalid, and responsibility for the King's actions is borne by those who approve them. The Crown is hereditary descending to the sons of the Sovereign in order of seniority or, if there are no sons, to the daughters. Persons marrying against the wishes of the King or Cortes (national assembly) are excluded from the succession. The Constitution lays down the procedure for establishing the Regency.

The King's duties are as follows:

to approve and promulgate laws;

to convene and dissolve the Cortes Generales and to call elections and referendums (according to the Constitution);

to propose a candidate for the presidency of the Cortes and dismiss him;

to appoint the members of the Cortes on the proposal of the President;

to issue decrees approved by the Council of Ministers, and to confer civil and military posts and grant honours and distinctions in accordance with the laws;

to be informed of the affairs of State, and to preside over the Council of Ministers when he deems it necessary on the request of the President of the Government;

to command the Armed Forces;

to grant mercy according to the law (which may not authorize general pardons);

to accredit ambassadors and other diplomatic representatives;

to express the State's assent to bind itself to international treaties;

to declare war and peace on the prior authorization of the Cortes.

THE CORTES GENERALES
(National Assembly)

The Cortes represent the Spanish people and comprise the Congress of Deputies (Congreso de los Diputados—Lower House) and the Senate (Senado—Upper House).

The Congreso has a minimum of 300 deputies and a maximum of 400, elected by universal, free, equal, direct and secret suffrage. Each province forms one constituency, the number of deputies in each one being determined according to population and elected by proportional representation for four years, Ceuta and Melilla having one deputy each. Elections must be held between 30 and 60 days after the end of each parliamentary mandate, and the Congreso convened within 25 days of the elections.

The Senado is based on territorial representation. Each province elects four senators for four years. Each island or group of islands forms one constituency. Gran Canaria, Mallorca and Tenerife return three senators each, the others one each. The Autonomous Communities return, in addition, one senator, plus one more for each million inhabitants, appointed by the legislative assembly of the community.

Each House lays down its own rules of procedure and elects its own president and governing body. Each year there are two ordinary sessions of the Cortes, of four and five months each, and a standing committee of 21 members in each House looks after affairs while the Cortes is in recess or during electoral periods. Plenary sessions are normally public. Measures are adopted by a majority in both Houses providing that a majority of the members is present. If agreement is not reached between the Congreso and the Senado, a joint committee must attempt to solve the differences by drawing up a text to be voted on again by both Houses. In the case of further non-agreement, the issue is decided by an absolute majority vote in the Congreso. Members may not vote by proxy.

LEGISLATION

Laws may not be retroactive.

Organic laws concern the development of fundamental rights and public freedoms, the approval of statutes of autonomy, the general electoral system, and other matters specified in the Constitution. Any approval, modification or repeal of these laws requires an absolute majority in the Congreso. The Cortes may delegate the power to issue measures called Legislative Decrees with the status of law to a governmental legislative body. In urgent cases the Government may issue provisional measures in the form of Decree-Laws not affecting the fundamental laws and rights of the nation, which must be voted upon by the Cortes within 30 days.

All laws must be sanctioned by the King within 15 days of their approval by the Cortes.

Provision is made for the popular presentation of bills if they are supported by 500,000 reputable signatures. Petitions to the Cortes by public demonstration are prohibited.

THE GOVERNMENT

The Government is the executive power and is composed of a President proposed by the King on the Cortes' approval and voted into office by the Congreso by absolute majority. If no President is elected within two months, the King will dissolve the Cortes and convene new elections with the approval of the President of the Congreso. The President of the Government designates the Ministers.

The Council of State is the supreme consultative organ of the Government. (An Organic law will regulate its composition.)

Further articles provide for the procedure for declaring a state of alarm, emergency or siege.

THE JUDICIARY

Justice derives from the people and is administered in the name of the King by judges and magistrates subject only to the law. The principle of jurisdictional unity is the basis of the organization and functioning of the Courts, which are established in an Organic Law of judicial power. Emergency courts are prohibited.

The Judiciary is governed by the General Council of Judicial Power (Consejo General del Poder Judicial), presided over by the President of the Supreme Court and made up of 20 members appointed by the King for five years, of whom 12 are judges or magistrates, four are nominated by the Congreso and four by the Senado, these eight being elected by a three-fifths majority from lawyers and jurists of more than 15 years' professional service.

The Attorney-General is appointed by the King on the Government's approval. Citizens may act on juries.

TERRITORIAL ORGANIZATION

The State is organized into municipalities, provinces and Autonomous Communities, all of which have local autonomy. The Constitution states that the differences between the Statutes of the Autonomous Communities shall not imply economic or social privileges.

THE AUTONOMOUS COMMUNITIES

The peripheral provinces, with their own historical, cultural and economic characteristics, are entitled to accede to self-government, but the Constitution states that in no case will the federation of the Autonomous Communities be permitted.

Article 148 lists the matters in which the Communities may assume competence, among which are: land use and building, public works and transport, ports, agriculture, environment, minerals, economic development, culture, tourism, social aid, health and local policing, all within the framework of national laws and policy and as long as nothing outside the regional boundaries is involved. Areas solely under state control are listed in article 149. In the specific case of financial autonomy, revenue proceeds from the State and from each Autonomous Community's own taxes, and a State Compensation Fund acts to correct any imbalances between the Communities. State competence will always prevail over regional competence should conflict arise over matters not under the exclusive control of the Autonomous Communities.

Although the State will delegate state power wherever possible, legislative measures must always be guided by state law. The State, in the general public interest, may pass laws by absolute majority to establish the principles for the harmonization of measures taken by the Autonomous Communities, even concerning matters directly under their authority.

The institutional organization of the Communities is based on a Legislative Assembly elected by universal suffrage and proportional representation, a Governing Council with executive and administrative functions, and a President elected by the Assembly from its members and appointed by the King to be the supreme representative of the Community to the State, and the ordinary representative of the State in the Community, and finally a High Court of Justice, inferior only to the Supreme Court.

THE CONSTITUTIONAL COURT

This court monitors observance of the Constitution and comprises 12 members appointed by the King, of whom four are elected by the Congreso and four by the Senado by three-fifths majority, two on the proposal of the Government and two on the proposal of the General Council of Judicial Power. The members must satisfy the conditions for membership of the aforesaid Council. They are appointed for nine years, with three members resigning every three years.

Three further articles establish the procedure for constitutional reform.

The Government

HEAD OF STATE

King of Spain, Head of State, Commander-in-Chief of the Armed Forces and Head of the Supreme Council of Defence: HRH King JUAN CARLOS (succeeded to the Throne, 22 November 1975).

COUNCIL OF MINISTERS
(April 2003)

Prime Minister and President of the Council: JOSÉ MARÍA AZNAR LÓPEZ.

Deputy Prime Minister, Minister of the Presidency and Government Spokesman: MARIANO RAJOY BREY.

Deputy Prime Minister and Minister of the Economy: RODRIGO DE RATO Y FIGAREDO.

Minister of the Interior: ÁNGEL ACEBES PANIAGUA.

Minister of Foreign Affairs: ANA PALACIO VALLELERSUNDI.

Minister of Justice: JOSÉ MARIA MICHAVILA NÚÑEZ.

Minister of Defence: FEDERICO TRILLO-FIGUEROA Y MARTÍNEZ-CONDE.

Minister of Finance: CRISTÓBAL RICARDO MONTORO ROMERO.

Minister of Public Works: FRANCISCO ÁLVAREZ-CASCOS FERNÁNDEZ.

Minister of Education, Culture and Sport: PILAR DEL CASTILLO VERA.

Minister of Labour and Social Affairs: EDUARDO ZAPLANA HERNÁNDEZ-SORO.

Minister of Science and Technology: JOSEP PIQUÉ I CAMPS.

Minister of Agriculture, Fisheries and Food: MIGUEL ARIAS CAÑETE.

Minister of Public Administration: JAVIER ARENAS BOCANEGRA.

Minister of Health and Consumer Affairs: ANA MARÍA PASTOR JULIÁN.

Minister of Environment: ELVIRA RODRÍGUEZ HERRER.

MINISTRIES

Prime Minister's Chancellery and Ministry of the Presidency: Complejo de la Moncloa, 28071 Madrid; tel. (91) 3353535; fax (91) 5492739; internet www.mpr.es.

Ministry of Agriculture, Fisheries and Food: Paseo Infanta Isabel 1, 28071 Madrid; tel. (91) 3475000; fax (91) 4686888; internet www.mapya.es.

Ministry of Defence: Paseo de la Castellana 109, 28071 Madrid; tel. (91) 3955000; fax (91) 5563958; e-mail infodefensa@mde.es; internet www.mde.es.

Ministry of the Economy: Alcalá 9, 28071 Madrid; tel. (91) 5837400; fax (91) 5830010; e-mail informacion.castellana@sgt.meh .es; internet www.mineco.es.

Ministry of Education, Culture and Sport: Alcalá 34, 28071 Madrid; tel. (91) 7018000; fax (91) 7018600; internet www.mec.es.

Ministry of Environment: Nuevos Ministerios, Plaza San Juan de la Cruz s/n, 28071 Madrid; tel. (91) 5976000; fax (91) 5976020; internet www.mma.es.

Ministry of Finance: Alcalá 9, 28071 Madrid; tel. (91) 5958000; fax (91) 5958000; e-mail informacion.alcala@sgt.minhac.es; internet www.minhac.es.

Ministry of Foreign Affairs: Plaza Marqués de Salamanca 8, 28071 Madrid; tel. (91) 3798300; fax (91) 3667098; internet www .mae.es.

Ministry of Health and Consumer Affairs: Paseo del Prado 18–20, 28071 Madrid; tel. (91) 5961000; fax (91) 5961547; internet www .msc.es.

Ministry of the Interior: Paseo de la Castellana 5, 28071 Madrid; tel. (91) 5371000; fax (91) 5371177; internet www.mir.es.

Ministry of Justice: San Bernardo 45, 28017 Madrid; tel. (91) 3902000; fax (91) 3902054; e-mail registrogeneral@sb.mju.es; internet www.mju.es.

Ministry of Labour and Social Affairs: Nuevos Ministerios, Agustín de Bethencourt 4, 28071 Madrid; tel. (91) 3630000; fax (91) 5534033; internet www.mtas.es.

Ministry of Public Administration: Paseo de la Castellana 3, 28071 Madrid; tel. (91) 5861000; fax (91) 3192448; e-mail cia .difusion@igsap.map.es; internet www.map.es.

Ministry of Public Works: Nuevos Ministerios, Paseo de la Castellana 67, 28071 Madrid; tel. (91) 5977000; fax (91) 5978542; internet www.mfom.es.

Ministry of Science and Technology: Paseo de la Castellana 160, 28071 Madrid; tel. (91) 3494000; fax (91) 4578066; e-mail info@mcyt .es; internet www.mcyt.es.

COUNCIL OF STATE

The Council of State has 29 Members.

President: JOSÉ MANUEL ROMAY BECCARÍA.

Legislature

LAS CORTES GENERALES

Congreso de los Diputados
(Congress of Deputies)

Carrera de San Jerónimo s/n, 28071 Madrid; tel. (91) 3906000; fax (91) 4298707; internet www.congreso.es.

President: Luisa Fernanda Rudi Údeba.

First Vice-President: Margarita Mariscal de Gante y Mirón.

General Election, 12 March 2000

	% of votes	Seats
Partido Popular (PP)	46.6	183
Partido Socialista Obrero Español (PSOE)	34.1	125
Convergència i Unió (CiU)	4.2	15
Izquierda Unida (IU)	5.5	8
Euzko Alderdi Jeltzalea (EAJ)/Partido Nacionalista Vasco (PNV)	1.5	7
Coalición Canaria (CC)	1.1	4
Bloque Nacionalista Galego (BNG)	1.3	3
Partido Andalucista (PA)	0.9	1
Esquerra Republicana de Catalunya (ERC)	0.8	1
Iniciativa per Catalunya-Los Verdes (IC-LV)	0.5	1
Eusko Alkartasuna (EA)	0.4	1
Chunta Aragonista (ChA)	0.3	1
Total	100.0	350

Senado:

Senado
(Senate)

Plaza de la Marina Española 8, 28071 Madrid; tel. (91) 5381000; fax (91) 5381007; internet www.senado.es.

The Senate comprises 259 members, 208 of whom are directly elected, the remaining 51 regional representatives being chosen by the assemblies of the autonomous regions.

President: Juan José Lucas Jiménez.

General Election, 12 March 2000

	Seats
Partido Popular (PP)	127
Partido Socialista Obrero Español (PSOE)	61
Convergència i Unió (CiU)	8
Euzko Alderdi Jeltzalea (EAJ)/Partido Nacionalista Vasco (PNV)	6
Coalición Canaria (CC)	5
Partido Independiente de Lanzarote (PIL)	1
Total	208

Legislative Assemblies of the Autonomous Regions

(For full names of political parties, see pp. 3819–20)

ANDALUCÍA (ANDALUSIA)

President of the Government: Manuel Chaves González (PSOE).

President of the Parliament: Javier Torres Vela (PSOE).

Election, 12 March 2000

	Seats
PSOE	52
PP	46
IU-LV-CA*	6
PA	5
Total	109

*Convocatoria por Andalucía.

ARAGÓN

President of the Government: Marcelino Iglesias Ricou (PSOE).

President of the Parliament: Benjamín Blasco Segura.

Election, 13 June 1999

	Seats
PP	28
PSOE	23
PAR	10
ChA	5
IU	1
Total	67

ASTURIAS

President of the Government: Vicente Alvarez Areces (PSOE).

President of the Parliament: Julio Alberto García Lagares.

Election, 13 June 1999

	Seats
PSOE	24
PP	15
IU	3
URAS	3
Total	45

BALEARES (BALEARIC ISLANDS)

President of the Government: Francesc Antich i Oliver (PSOE).

President of the Parliament: Carlo Maximillà Morales i Gómez (UM).

Election, 13 June 1999

	Seats
PP	28
PSOE	13
PSM-NM*	5
IU	3
UM	3
Others	7
Total	59

* Nacionalistes de Mallorca.

BASQUE COUNTRY (see EUSKADI)

CANARIAS (CANARY ISLANDS)

President of the Government: Román Rodríguez Rodríguez (CC/AIC).

President of the Parliament: José Miguel Bravo de Laguna (PP).

Election, 13 June 1999

	Seats
CC	25
PSOE	19
PP	14
AHI	2
Total	60

CANTABRIA

President of the Government: Juan Joaquín Martínez Sieso (PP).

President of the Parliament: Rafael de la Sierra González (PRC).

Election, 13 June 1999

	Seats
PP	19
PSOE	14
PRC	6
Total	39

CASTILLA Y LEÓN (CASTILLE AND LEON)

President of the Government: Juan Vicente Herrera Campo (PP).

President of the Parliament: Manuel Estella Hoyos (PP).

Election, 13 June 1999

	Seats
PP.	48
PSOE.	30
UPL.	3
IU.	1
Other.	1
Total.	**83**

CASTILLA-LA MANCHA

President of the Government: José Bono Martínez (PSOE).

President of the Parliament: Antonio Marco Martínez (PSOE).

Election, 13 June 1999

	Seats
PSOE.	26
PP.	21
Total.	**47**

CATALUÑA/CATALUNYA (CATALONIA)

President of the Government: Jordi Pujol i Soley (CiU).

President of the Parliament: Joan Rigol i Roig (CiU).

Election, 17 October 1999

	Seats
CiU	56
PSC	52
PP.	12
ERC.	12
IC-EV*	3
Total.	**135**

* Els Verds (Greens).

EUSKADI (BASQUE COUNTRY)

President (Lehendakari) of the Government: Juan José Ibarretxe Markuartu (PNV).

President of the Parliament: Juan María Atutxa Mendiola (PNV).

Election, 13 May 2001

	Seats
PNV*/EA.	33
PP/UA	19
PSE-EE	13
EH.	7
IU-EB†	3
Total.	**75**

* Also known as Euzko Alderdi Jeltzalea (EAJ).
† Ezker Batua.

EXTREMADURA

President of the Government: Juan Carlos Rodríguez Ibarra (PSOE).

President of the Parliament: Manuel Veiga López (PSOE).

Election, 13 June 1999

	Seats
PSOE.	34
PP.	28
IU.	3
Total.	**65**

GALICIA/GALIZA

President of the Government (Xunta): Manuel Fraga Iribarne (PP).

President of the Parliament: José María García Leira (PP).

Election, 21 October 2001

	Seats
PP.	41
BNG.	17
PS de G-PSOE;.	17
Total.	**75**

MADRID

President of the Government: Alberto Ruiz-Gallardón Jiménez (PP).

President of the Parliament: Jesús Pedroche Nieto (PP).

Election, 13 June 1999

	Seats
PP.	55
PSOE.	39
IU.	8
Total.	**102**

MURCIA

President of the Government: Ramón Luis Valcárcel Siso (PP).

President of the Parliament: Francisco Celdrán Vidal (PP).

Election, 13 June 1999

	Seats
PP.	27
PSOE.	17
IU.	1
Total.	**45**

NAVARRA (NAVARRE)

President of the Government: Miguel Sanz Sesma (UPN).

President of the Parliament: José Luis Castejón Garrués (PSN-PSOE).

Election, 13 June 1999

	Seats
UPN	22
PSN-PSOE	11
EH	8
EA.	3
CDN	3
IU-EB*	3
Total.	**50**

* Ezker Batua.

LA RIOJA

President of the Government: Pedro María Sanz Alonso (PP).

President of the Parliament: José Ignacio Ceniceros González (PP).

Election, 13 June 1999

	Seats
PP.	18
PSOE.	13
PR.	2
Total.	**33**

VALENCIA

President of the Government: José Luis Olivas Martínez (PP).

President of the Parliament: Marcela Miró Pérez (PP).

Election, 13 June 1999

	Seats
PP.	49
PSPV-PSOE.	35
EU-PV.	5
Total.	**89**

Political Organizations

In mid-1994 more than 1,000 political parties were officially registered.

PRINCIPAL NATIONAL PARTIES

Izquierda Unida (IU): Olimpo 35, 28043 Madrid; tel. (91) 7227500; fax (91) 3880405; e-mail gabinete.prensa@izquierda-unida.es; internet www.izquierda-unida.es; Co-ordinator-Gen. GASPAR LLAMA-ZARES TRIGO; f. 1989 by left-wing parties to contest elections; includes:

Candidatura Unitaria de Trabajadores (CUT): Miguel del Cid 34, 41002 Sevilla; tel. 4903336; Co-ordinator JUAN MANUEL SÁNCHEZ GORDILLO.

Izquierda Republicana (IR): Meléndez Valdés 33, 1° Derecha, 28006 Madrid; tel. (91) 5436930; fax (91) 5437649; e-mail ir@bitmailer.net; internet www.izqrepublicana.es; f. 1935; running independently in regional elections of 2003; Sec.-Gen. ISABELO HERREROS MARTÍN MAESTRO.

Partido de Acción Socialista (PASOC): Calle Espoz y Mina, 1° Izda, 28012 Madrid; tel. (91) 5311988; fax (91) 5313299; e-mail pasoc.madrid@izquierda-unida.es; internet www.nodo50.org/pasoc-madrid; f. 1879; took present name 1982; fmrly Partido Socialista Obrero Español—Histórico (PSOE(h), Partido Socialista); Pres. PABLO CASTELLANO; Sec.-Gen. ALONSO PUERTA.

Partido Comunista de España (PCE): Olimpo 35, 28043 Madrid; tel. (91) 3004969; fax (91) 3004744; e-mail administracion@pce.es; internet www.pce.es; f. 1922; Euro-communist; absorbed Partido Comunista Obrero Español (PCOE) in 1986, and most of Partido Comunista de los Pueblos de España (PCPE) in Jan. 1989; Sec.-Gen. FRANCISCO FRUTOS.

Partido Democrático de la Nueva Izquierda (PDNI): San Bernardo 23, 4°, 28015 Madrid; tel. (91) 5595893; fax (91) 5473867; e-mail pdni@nuevaizquierda.es; internet www.nuevaizquierda.es; f. 1996 by dissident mems of IU; Pres. CRISTINA ALMEIDA CASTRO; Sec.-Gen. DIEGO LÓPEZ GARRIDO.

Partido Popular (PP): Génova 13, 28004 Madrid; tel. (91) 5577300; fax (91) 3085587; e-mail atencion@pp.es; internet www.pp.es; f. 1976; fmrly Alianza Popular, name changed Jan. 1989; absorbed Democracia Cristiana (fmrly Partido Demócrata Popular) and Partido Liberal in early 1989; centre-right, Christian Democrat; 600,000 mems (Feb. 2000); Pres. JOSÉ MARÍA AZNAR; Sec.-Gen. JAVIER ARENAS BOCANEGRA.

Partido Socialista Obrero Español (PSOE): Ferraz 68 y 70, 28008 Madrid; tel. (91) 5820444; fax (91) 5820422; internet www.psoe.es; f. 1879; socialist workers' party; affiliated to the Socialist International; merged with the Partido Socialista Popular in 1978; joined by Partido de los Trabajadores de España-Unidad Comunista (PTE-UC) in 1991 and Partido de Nueva Izquierda (PDNI) in 2001; 366,000 mems (1996); Sec.-Gen. JOSÉ LUIS RODRÍGUEZ ZAPATERO.

Los Verdes (LV): Navellos 9, 2°, 46003 Valencia; tel. (96) 2817581; fax (96) 3921314; e-mail verdes@verdes.es; internet www.verdes.es; f. 1984; green party; confederation of 9 national and regional parties, and 6 observers.

REGIONAL PARTIES

There are branches of the main national parties in most Spanish regions, and numerous regional parties including the following:

Agrupación Herreña Independiente (AHI): La Constitución 4, 38900 Valverde, El Hierro, Santa Cruz de Tenerife; tel. (922) 551134; fax (922) 551224; Canary Islands group; Pres. TOMÁS PADRÓN HERNÁNDEZ.

Bloque Nacionalista Galego (BNG): Avda Rodríguez de Viguri 16, Baixo, 15702 Santiago de Compostela; tel. (981) 555850; fax (981) 555851; e-mail sedenacional@bng-galiza.org; internet www.bng-galiza.org; f. 1982; Galician nationalist organization; Leader XOSÉ MANUEL BEIRAS.

Chunta Aragonesista (ChA): Conde de Aranda 14–16, 1°, 50003 Zaragoza; tel. (976) 284242; fax (976) 281311; e-mail sedenacional@chunta.com; internet www.chunta.com; left-wing regional party of Aragón; Pres. BIZÉN FUSTER.

Coalición Canaria (CC): Buenos Aires 24, 35002 Las Palmas, Gran Canaria; tel. (928) 363142; internet www.coalicioncanaria.es; Canary Islands coalition; Pres. PAULINO RIVERO BAUTE; coalition includes:

Agrupaciones Independientes de Canarias (AIC): Galcerán 7–9, 1°, Edif. El Drago, 38003 Santa Cruz de Tenerife; tel. (922) 279702; fax (922) 7; e-mail agrupacion-ati@jet.es; federation of Canary Island groupings (incl. Agrupación Tinerfeña de Independientes—ATI; Pres. Manuel Hermoso Rojas; Sec.-Gen. Paulino Rivero); Pres. VICTORIANO RÍOS.

Asamblea Majorera (AM): La Venta 4 y 6, Apdo 195, 35600 Puerto del Rosario, Fuerteventura; tel. (928) 850798; fax (928) 531591; e-mail asamblea@majorero.com; internet www.majorero.com/asamblea; f. 1977; progressive, left-wing Canary Islands nationalist party; Gen. Co-ordinator MARIO CABRERA GONZÁLEZ; Sec.-Gen. JOSÉ MIGUEL BARRAGÁN CABRERA.

Centro Canario Nacionalista (CCN): Juan de Quesada 20, 35001 Las Palmas de Gran Canaria; tel. (928) 331162; fax (928) 332350; Pres. LUIS HERNÁNDEZ PÉREZ.

Iniciativa Canaria (I.CAN): Buenos Aires 24, 35002 Las Palmas de Gran Canaria; tel. (928) 363142; fax (928) 380356; f. 1991 as Canary Islands grouping of Communists and left-wing nationalists; Co-ordinators JOSÉ CARLOS, MAURICIO RODRÍGUEZ.

Partido Nacionalista Canario (PNC): Sagasta 492, 35008 Las Palmas de Gran Canaria; tel. and fax (928) 221736; f. 1977 as Canary Islands nationalist group; National Pres. JUAN MANUEL GARCÍA RAMOS; National Sec.-Gen. GUSTAVO DAVILA DE LEÓN.

Convergencia de Demócratas de Navarra (CDN): San Ignacio 12, 1°, 31002 Pamplona; tel. (948) 228185; fax (948) 227336; e-mail cdn@cdn.es; internet www.cdn.es; f. 1995 as progressive centre party; social-Christian ideology; Pres. JUAN CRUZ ALLI; Sec. CARLOS PÉREZ-NIEVAS.

Convergència i Unió (CiU): internet www.convergencia-i-unio.org; f. 1979 as an electoral coalition; became confederation of parties in March 2001; Pres. JORDI PUJOL I SOLEY; Sec.-Gen. JOSEP ANTONI DURAN I LLEIDA; an alliance of the following two parties:

Convergència Democràtica de Catalunya (CDC): Córcega 331–333, 08037 Barcelona; tel. (93) 2363100; fax (93) 2363120; e-mail cdc@convergencia.org; internet www.convergencia.org; f. 1974; f. 1977; Catalan nationalist; centre; 45,523 mems (2000); Pres. JORDI PUJOL I SOLEY; Sec.-Gen. ARTUR MAS I GAVARRÓ.

Unió Democràtica de Catalunya (UDC): Travessera de Gràcia 17–21, àtic, 08021 Barcelona; tel. (93) 2402200; fax (93) 2402201; e-mail info@uniodemocratica.org; internet www.uniodemocratica.org; f. 1931; 34,255 mems (1998); Pres. of National Council NÚRIA GISPERT I CATALÀ; Pres. of Exec. Cttee JOSEP ANTONI DURAN I LLEIDA.

Esquerda Galega Unida (EGU): Calle San Lazaro, 95°C, 15700 Santiago de Compostela; left-wing Galician party; Co-ordinator ANXO GUERRERO.

Esquerra Republicana de Catalunya (ERC) (Republican Left of Catalonia): Carrer Villarroel 45, 08011 Barcelona; tel. (93) 4536005; fax (93) 3237122; e-mail info@esquerra.org; internet www.esquerra.org; f. 1931; advocates independence for Catalonia within European context, a just society and national solidarity of Catalan people; Pres. JORDI CARBONELL; Sec.-Gen. JOSEP-LLUÍS CAROD-ROVIRA.

Esquerra Unida (EU): Las Cortes Valencianas, Palau de les Corts Valencianes, Plaza San Lorenzo 4, 46003 Valencia; e-mail esquerra4.gp@cortes.m400.gra.es; left-wing; Pres. JOAN RIBÓ CANUT.

Euskal Herritarrok (EH): Parlamento Vasco, Becerro de Bengoa s/n, 01005 Vitoria-Gasteiz (Alava); internet www.euskal-herritarrok.org; left-wing; supports independence for Basque country and right to self-determination; political wing of Euskadi ta Askatasuna (Basque Homeland and Liberty—ETA); f. 1998; Leader ARNALDO OTEGI MONDRAGÓN.

Batasuna (Unity): Astarloa 8, 3°, 48001 Bilbao; tel. (94) 4240799; fax (94) 4235932; internet www.batasuna.org; f. 1978 as Herri Batasuna (HB—People's Unity); achieved legal recognition in 1986; changed name as above in 2001, on 26 August 2002 the party was suspended from carrying out political activity for three years owing to its links with the separatist group ETA (see p. 3820); the party's headquarters were closed by the authorities; in March 2003, the party was banned by the Supreme Court; Spokesman ARNALDO OTEGI MONDRAGÓN; Co-ordinator JOSEBA PERMACH.

Eusko Alkartasuna (EA) (Basque Solidarity): Camino de Portuetxe 23, 1°, 20009 San Sebastián; tel. (943) 311377; fax (943) 311361; internet www.euskoalkartasuna.es; f. 1985; (as Eusko Abertzaleak—Basque Nationalists) by dissident group of progressive PNV mems; 15,000 mems; Pres. BEGOÑA ERRAZTI ESNAL; Sec.-Gen. GORKA KNÖRR BORRAS.

Euzko Alderdi Jeltzalea/Partido Nacionalista Vasco (EAJ/PNV): Ibáñez de Bilbao 16 (Sabin Etxea), 48001 Bilbao; tel. (94) 4039400; fax (94) 4039412; e-mail prensa@eaj-pnv.com; internet www.eaj-pnv.com; f. 1895; Basque nationalist; seeks to achieve autonomous region through peaceful means; 31,000 mems (1998); Pres. XABIER ARZALLUZ ANTÍA; Sec. JOSUNE ARIZTONDO.

Iniciativa per Catalunya–Verds (IC-V): Ciutat 7, 08002 Barcelona; tel. (93) 3010612; fax (93) 4124252; e-mail iniciativa@ic-v.org; internet www.ic-v.org; f. 1987 as Iniciativa per Catalunya, a left-wing alliance comprising the Partit Socialista Unificat de Catalunya PSUC, see below, Entesa des Nacionalistes d'Esquerra (ENE); in

1995 formed a coalition with the above name, incl. Els Verds, L'Espai roig-verd-violeta, and individual citizens; Pres. JOAN SAURA LAPORTA.

Partit Socialista Unificat de Catalunya (PSUC): Ciutat 7, 08002 Barcelona; tel. 3010612; fax 4124252; f. 1936; Communist; Sec.-Gen. RAFAEL RIBÓ MASSÓ.

Partido Andalucista (PA): Vidrio 32, 41003 Sevilla; tel. (95) 4502157; fax (95) 4210446; e-mail prensa@partidoandalucista.org; internet www.partidoandalucista.org; f. 1977; Pres. ALEJANDRO ROJAS-MARCOS; Sec.-Gen. ANTONIO ORTEGA.

Partido Aragonés (PAR): Coso 87, 50001 Zaragoza; tel. (976) 200616; fax (976) 200987; f. 1977; fmrly Partido Aragonés Regionalista; Pres. JOSÉ MARÍA MUR BERNAD; Sec.-Gen. EMILIO EIROA GARCÍA.

Partido Nacionalista Vasco (PNV): see Euzko Alderdi Jeltzalea.

Partido Regionalista de Cantabria (PRC): Calle Amos de Escalante 3, 2°, 39002 Santander; internet www.prc.es; centre-right party of Cantabria Region; Sec.-Gen. MIGUEL ANGEL REVILLA.

Partido Riojano (PR): Portales 17, 1°, 26001 Logroño; tel. (941) 238199; fax (941) 254396; e-mail partidoriojano@partidoriojano.es; internet www.partidoriojano.es; Pres. MIGUEL GONZÁLEZ DE LEGARRA; Sec.-Gen. ALEJANDRO FERNÁNDEZ DE LA PRADILLA.

Partido Socialista de Euskadi-Euskadiko Ezkerra (PSE-EE) (Basque Socialist Party-Basque Left): Alameda de Recalde 27, 4°, Bilbao 9; tel. (94) 4241606; internet www.pse-ee.psoe.es/pse-docs/; f. 1993 by merger of PSE-PSOE and EE; Pres. JESÚS EGUIGUREN; Sec.-Gen. PAXTI LÓPEZ.

Partido Socialista de Navarra (PSN): c/o Parlamento de Navarra, Pamplona; internet www.cin.es/psn-psoe; Pres. VÍCTOR MANUEL ARBELOA; Sec.-Gen. JUAN JOSÉ LIZARBE.

Partido dos Socialistas de Galicia (PS de G-PSOE) (Galician Socialist Party): Pino 1–9, 15704 Santiago de Compostela; tel. (981) 552030; fax (981) 588708; e-mail ceng@psdeg-psoe.org; internet www.psdeg-psoe.org; Sec.-Gen. EMILIO PÉREZ TOURIÑO.

Partido Socialista del País Valenciano (PSPV-PSOE) (Valencian Socialist Party): Las Cortes Valencianas, Palau de les Corts Valencianes, Plaza San Lorenzo 4, 46003 Valencia; internet www.pspv-psoe.org; Leader JUANA SERNA.

Partit Socialista de Mallorca—Nacionalistes de Mallorca (PSM—NM): Parlamento de les Illes Balears, Palau Reial 16, 07012 Palma de Mallorca; Sec.-Gen. MATEU MORRO.

Partit dels Socialistes de Catalunya (PSC-PSOE): Nicaragua 75, 08029 Barcelona; tel. (93) 4955400; fax (93) 4955435; e-mail psc@psc.es; internet www.psc.es; f. 1978 by merger of various Catalan parties of socialist ideology; Pres. JOSÉ MONTILLA.

Unidad Alavesa (UA): Calle San Antonio 27, 1°, 01005 Vitoria-Gasteiz; e-mail uaforal@unidadalavesa.es; internet www.unidadalavesa.es; f. 1989; splinter group of PP; supports rights of province of Alava, within Basque Country; Pres. JOSÉ LUIS AÑÚA AJURIA; Sec.-Gen. PABLO MOSQUERA.

Unió Mallorquina (UM): Via Sindicat 21, 07002 Palma de Mallorca; tel. (971) 726336; fax (971) 728116; e-mail um@ctv.es; internet www.unio-mallorquina.com; f. 1982; liberal party; Pres. MARÍA ANTÒNIA MUNAR; Sec.-Gen. BARTOMEU VICENS.

Unión del Pueblo Leonés (UPL): Ordoño II 20, 24001 León; León separatist party.

Unión del Pueblo Navarro (UPN): Plaza Príncipe de Viana 1, 4° Dcha, 31002 Pamplona; tel. (948) 227211; fax (948) 210810; e-mail info@upn.org; internet www.upn.org; f. 1979; social Christian; Pres. MIGUEL SANZ SESMA; Sec.-Gen. ALBERTO CATALÁN HIGUERAS.

Unión Renovadora Asturiana (URAS): Palacio de la Junta General, Fruela 17, 33071 Oviedo; internet www.uras.org; f. 1998 following split in PP of Asturias; Leader SERGIO MARQUÉS FERNÁNDEZ.

OTHER ORGANIZATIONS

Illegal terrorist organizations include the Basque separatist Euskadi ta Askatasuna (ETA, Basque Homeland and Liberty, f. 1959); and the extreme left-wing Grupos de Resistencia Antifascista Primero de Octubre (GRAPO, First of October Anti-Fascist Resistance Groups, f. 1975). The Grupos Antiterroristas de Liberación (GAL) were formed in 1983 to oppose ETA, and were subsequently revealed to have received government funding. Catalan nationalist movements have included the right-wing anti-separatist Milicia Catalana (f. 1986 to oppose Terra Lliure), Moviment de Defensa de la Terra (MDT) and Ejército Rojo Catalán de Liberación (ERCA); Terra Lliure (Free Land, f. 1975), which had links with ETA, was dissolved in July 1991, but a dissident faction subsequently became active. A Galician nationalist movement, Exército Guerrilheiro do Pobo Galego Ceibe (EGPGC), was active between 1987 and 1991.

Diplomatic Representation

EMBASSIES IN SPAIN

Albania: María de Molina 64, 5°B, 28006 Madrid; tel. (91) 5612118; fax (91) 5613775; e-mail albania@nauta.es; Ambassador ANILA BITRI LANI.

Algeria: General Oráa 12, Apdo 6025, 28006 Madrid; tel. (91) 5629705; fax (91) 5629877; e-mail embargel@tsai.es; Ambassador (vacant).

Andorra: Alcalá 73, 28009 Madrid; tel. (91) 4317453; fax (91) 5776341; Ambassador VICENÇ MATEU-ZAMORA.

Angola: Serrano 64, 3°, 28001 Madrid; tel. (91) 4356430; fax (91) 5779010; e-mail gabinete@embajadadeangola.com; internet www.embajadadeangola.com; Ambassador PEDRO SEBASTIÃO.

Argentina: Pedro de Valdivia 21, 28006 Madrid; tel. (91) 5622800; fax (91) 5635185; e-mail embajada@portalargentino.net; internet www.portalargentino.net; Ambassador ABEL PARENTINI POSSE.

Australia: Plaza del Descubridor Diego de Ordás 3, 2° (Edif. Santa Engracia 120), 28003 Madrid; tel. (91) 4416025; fax (91) 4425362; e-mail information@embaustralia.es; internet www.embaustralia.es; Ambassador TIMOTHY SPENCER GEORGE.

Austria: Paseo de la Castellana 91, 9°, 28046 Madrid; tel. (91) 5565315; fax (91) 5973579; e-mail madrid-ob@bmaa.gv.at; Ambassador MANFRED KIEPACH.

Bangladesh: Diego de León 69, 2°D, 28006 Madrid; tel. (91) 4019932; fax (91) 4029564; e-mail bangladesh.embassy@mad.servicom.es; Ambassador SHAHED AKHTAR.

Belgium: Paseo de la Castellana 18, 6°, 28046 Madrid; tel. (91) 5776300; fax (91) 4318166; Ambassador CLAUDE MISSON.

Bolivia: Velázquez 26, 3°, 28001 Madrid; tel. (91) 5780835; fax (91) 5773946; e-mail embolivia-madrid@rree.gov.bo; Ambassador GUILLERMO BEDREGAL GUTIÉRREZ.

Bosnia and Herzegovina: Lagasca 24, 2° Izqda, 28001 Madrid; tel. (91) 5750870; fax (91) 4355056; e-mail ambasada@ctv.es; Ambassador DARIA KRSTICEVIĆ.

Brazil: Fernando el Santo 6, 28010 Madrid; tel. (91) 7004650; fax (91) 7004660; e-mail chancelaria@embajadabrasil.es; Ambassador CARLOS MOREIRA-GARCIA.

Bulgaria: Santa María Magdalena 15, 28016 Madrid; tel. (91) 3456761; fax (91) 3591201; e-mail embulmad@teleline.es; Ambassador VASSILIY CHRISTOV TAKEV.

Cameroon: Rosario Pino 3, 28020 Madrid; tel. (91) 5711160; fax (91) 5712504; Ambassador PHILIPPE MATAGA.

Canada: Núñez de Balboa 35, Edif. Goya, 28001 Madrid; tel. (91) 4233250; fax (91) 4233251; e-mail mdrid-gr@dfait-maeci.gc.ca; internet www.canada-es.org; Ambassador ALAIN DUDOIT.

Chile: Lagasca 88, 6°, 28001 Madrid; tel. (91) 4319160; fax (91) 5775560; e-mail echilees@tsai.es; Ambassador ENRIQUE KRAUSS RUSQUE.

China, People's Republic: Arturo Soria 113, 28043 Madrid; tel. (91) 5194242; fax (91) 5192035; e-mail embchina@dominios.es; Ambassador XIAOQI QIU.

Colombia: General Martínez Campos 48, 28010 Madrid; tel. (91) 7004770; fax (91) 3102869; e-mail embcol.mad@retemail.es; Ambassador MARTHA NOEMÍ SANÍN POSADA.

Congo, Democratic Republic: Paseo de la Castellana 255, 1°, 28046 Madrid; tel. (91) 7332647; fax (91) 3231575; Ambassador (vacant).

Costa Rica: Paseo de la Castellana 164, 17°, 28046 Madrid; tel. (91) 3459622; fax (91) 3533709; e-mail embajada.costarica@anit.es; Ambassador MARIA ELENA POZUELO PAGÉS.

Côte d'Ivoire: Serrano 154, 28006 Madrid; tel. (91) 5626916; fax (91) 5622193; e-mail costamarfil@ic1.inycom.es; Ambassador TUAN YAO MATHIEU.

Croatia: Claudio Coello 78, 2°, 28001 Madrid; tel. (91) 5776881; fax (91) 5776905; e-mail cromad@terra.es; Ambassador (vacant).

Cuba: Paseo de la Habana 194, 28036 Madrid; tel. (91) 3592500; fax (91) 3596145; Ambassador ISABEL ALLENDE KARAM.

Cyprus: Serrano 23, 2°, 28001 Madrid; tel. (91) 5783114; fax (91) 5782189; e-mail cyembassy@mx4.redestb.es; Ambassador ATHENA MAVRONICOLA.

Czech Republic: Avda de Pío XII 22–24, 28016 Madrid; tel. (91) 3531880; fax (91) 3531885; e-mail madrid@embassy.mzv.cz; internet www.mfa.cz/Madrid; Ambassador MARTIN POVEJSIL.

Denmark: Claudio Coello 91, 4°, 28006 Madrid; tel. (91) 4318445; fax (91) 4319168; e-mail madamb@.um.dk; internet www .embajadadinamarca.es; Ambassador CHRISTOPHER BO BRAMSEN.

Dominican Republic: Paseo de la Castellana 30, 1° Dcha, 28046 Madrid; tel. (91) 4315395; fax (91) 4358139; e-mail embrdes@ infomegocio.com; Ambassador JOSÉ AUGUSTO VEGA IMBERT.

Ecuador: Velázquez 114, 2°, 28006 Madrid; tel. (91) 5627215; fax (91) 7450244; e-mail mecuador@embajada.e.telfonica.net; Ambassador FRANCISCO CARRIÓN MENA.

Egypt: Velázquez 69, 28006 Madrid; tel. (91) 5776308; fax (91) 5781732; internet www.sis.gov.eg; Ambassador MOHAMED EL AMIR KHALIL.

El Salvador: Serrano 114, 2° Izqda, 28006 Madrid; tel. (91) 5628002; fax (91) 5630584; Ambassador MIGUEL ANGEL SALAVERRIA ALCAINE.

Equatorial Guinea: Claudio Coello 91, 5°, 28006 Madrid; tel. (91) 5782616; Ambassador JOSÉ ELA EBANG.

Estonia: Claudio Coello 91, 1° Dcha, 28006 Madrid; tel. (91) 4261671; fax (91) 4261672; e-mail embassy.madrid@mfa.ee; Ambassador ANDRÉS TOMASBERG.

Finland: Paseo de la Castellana 15, 4°, 28046 Madrid; tel. (91) 3196172; fax (91) 3083901; e-mail finlandia@mundivia.es; internet www.finlandia.org; Ambassador CHARLES MURTO.

France: Salustiano Olózaga 9, 28001 Madrid; tel. (91) 4238900; fax (91) 4238901; e-mail chancellerie@ctv.es; internet www.ambafrance .es; Ambassador OLIVIER SCHRAMECK.

Gabon: Angel de Diego Roldán 14–16, 28016 Madrid; tel. (91) 4138211; fax (91) 4131153; e-mail emb-gabon-es@nemo.es; Ambassador NOËL BAIOT.

Germany: Fortuny 8, 28010 Madrid; tel. (91) 5579000; fax (91) 3102104; internet www.embajada-alemania.es; Ambassador GEORG BOOMGAARDEN.

Greece: Avda del Dr Arce 24, 28002 Madrid; tel. (91) 5644653; fax (91) 5644668; internet www.greekembassy.org; Ambassador PETROS ANGHELAKIS.

Guatemala: Rafael Salgado 3, 10° Dcha, 28036 Madrid; tel. (91) 3440347; fax (91) 4587894; e-mail embaguat@accesnet.es; Ambassador JOSÉ ALBERTO SANDOVAL COJULUN.

Haiti: Marques del Duero 3, 1°, 28001 Madrid; tel. (91) 5752624; fax (91) 4314600; e-mail embhaiti@ctv.es; Ambassador ANTONIO RODRIGUE.

Holy See: Avda de Pío XII 46, 28016 Madrid (Apostolic Nunciature); tel. (91) 7668311; fax (91) 7667085; e-mail nunap@planalfa.es; Apostolic Nuncio MANUEL MONTEIRO DE CASTRO.

Honduras: Rosario Pino 6, 4°, 28020, Madrid; tel. (91) 5790251; fax (91) 5721319; e-mail e7610193@teleline.es; Ambassador LEILA AMALIA ODEH DE SCOTT.

Hungary: Angel de Diego Roldán 21, 28016 Madrid; tel. (91) 4137011; fax (91) 4134138; e-mail info@embajada-hungria.org; internet www.embajada-hungria.org; Ambassador (vacant).

India: Avda de Pío XII 30–32, 28016 Madrid; tel. (91) 3450406; fax (91) 3451112; e-mail amb.madrid@mad.servicom.es; internet www .visualware.es; Ambassador DILIP LAHIRI.

Indonesia: Agastia 65, 28043 Madrid; tel. (91) 4130394; fax (91) 4138994; e-mail kbrimadrid@cempresarial.com; Ambassador RAMCHAT RANUDIWIJAYA.

Iran: Jerez 5, Villa El Altozano (Chamartín), 28016 Madrid; tel. (91) 3450112; fax (91) 3451190; Ambassador SAYED HASSAN SHAFTI.

Iraq: Ronda de Sobradiel 67 (Parque Conde de Orgaz), 28043 Madrid; tel. (91) 7591282; fax (91) 7593180; Ambassador (vacant).

Ireland: Paseo de la Castellana 46, 4°, 28046 Madrid; tel. (91) 4364093; fax (91) 4351677; e-mail embajada.irlanda@terra.es; Ambassador DECLAN O'DONOVAN.

Israel: Velázquez 150, 7°, 28002 Madrid; tel. (91) 4111357; fax (91) 5645974; e-mail embajada@embajada-israel.es; internet www .embajada-israel.es; Ambassador HERZL INBAR.

Italy: Lagasca 98, 28006 Madrid; tel. (91) 4233300; fax (91) 5757776; e-mail ambitalsp@cempresarial.com; internet www .ambitaliamadrid.org; Ambassador AMEDEO DE FRANCIS.

Japan: Serrano 109, 28006 Madrid; tel. (91) 5907612; fax (91) 5901336; e-mail embjapon@embjapon.es; internet www.es .emb-japon.go.jp; Ambassador KATSUYUKI TANAKA.

Jordan: General Martínez Campos 41, 5°, 28010 Madrid; tel. (91) 3191100; fax (91) 3082536; Ambassador ABDULLAH ABDUL HAMID SIRAJ.

Kazakhstan: Cascanueces 25, Parque Conde de Orgaz, 28043 Madrid; tel. (91) 7216290; fax (91) 7219374; e-mail kazakhstan@ entorno.es; Ambassador ALMAZ KHAMZAYEV.

Korea, Republic: González Amigó 15, 28033 Madrid; tel. (91) 3532000; fax (91) 3532001; e-mail embcorea@embcorea.com; internet www.embcorea.com; Ambassador JANG HEE HONG.

Kuwait: Paseo de la Castellana 141, 16°, 28046 Madrid; tel. (91) 5792467; fax (91) 5702109; Ambassador Dr SUHAIL KHALIL SHOHAIBAR.

Latvia: Alfonso XII 52-1, 28014 Madrid; tel. (91) 5631745; fax (91) 4110418; e-mail letspan@telefonica.net; Ambassador ALJA ODINA.

Lebanon: Paseo de la Castellana 178, 3° Izqda, 28046 Madrid; tel. (91) 3451368; fax (91) 3455631; e-mail leem_e@teleline.es; Ambassador SAMIR MOUBARAK.

Libya: Pisuerga 12, 28002 Madrid; tel. (91) 5635753; fax (91) 5643986; Head of People's Bureau KASEM MOHAMED SHERLALA.

Lithuania: Fortuny 19, 1° Izqda, 28010 Madrid; tel. (91) 3102075; fax (91) 3104018; e-mail embajada.@emblituania.es; internet www .emblituania.es; Ambassador VYTAUTAS ANTANAS DAMBRAVA.

Luxembourg: Claudio Coello 78, 1°, 28001 Madrid; tel. (91) 4359164; fax (91) 5774826; Ambassador JEAN A. WELTER.

Malaysia: Paseo de la Castellana 91, 5°, 28046 Madrid; tel. (91) 5550684; fax (91) 5555208; e-mail mwmadrid@adv.es; Ambassador Dato' SHAARANI BIN IBRAHIM.

Malta: Paseo de la Castellana 45, 6° Dcha, 28046 Madrid; tel. (91) 3913061; fax (91) 3913066; e-mail maltaembassy.madrid@gov.mt; Ambassador CECILIA ATTARD-PIROTTA.

Mauritania: Velázquez 90, 3°, 28006 Madrid; tel. (91) 5757006; fax (91) 4359531; Ambassador SALEM OULD MEMMOU.

Mexico: Carrera de San Jerónimo 46, 28014 Madrid; tel. (91) 3692814; fax (91) 4202292; e-mail embamex@embamex.es; internet www.embamex.es; Ambassador GABRIEL JIMÉNEZ REMUS.

Monaco: Villanueva 12, 28001 Madrid; tel. (91) 5782048; fax (91) 4357132; e-mail ambmonacomad@hotmail.com; Ambassador (vacant).

Morocco: Serrano 179, 28002 Madrid; tel. (91) 5631090; fax (91) 5617887; Ambassador ABDESALAM BARAKA.

Mozambique: Goya 67, 1° Izqda, 28001 Madrid; tel. (91) 5773682; fax (91) 5776705; e-mail dionikule@hotmail.com; Ambassador (vacant).

Netherlands: Avda del Comandante Franco 32, 28016 Madrid; tel. (91) 3537500; fax (91) 3537565; e-mail nlgovmad@ctv.es; internet internet www.embaijadapaisesbajas.es; Ambassador Baron S. VAN HEEMSTRA.

New Zealand: Plaza de la Lealtad 2, 3°, 28014 Madrid; tel. (91) 5230226; fax (91) 5230171; e-mail nzembmad@santandersupernet .com; Ambassador CHRISTINE BOGLE.

Nicaragua: Paseo de la Castellana 127, 1°B, 28046 Madrid; tel. (91) 5555510; fax (91) 4555737; e-mail embanic@tsai.es; Ambassador JORGE SALAVERRY ROMERO.

Nigeria: Segre 23, 28002 Madrid; tel. (91) 5630911; fax (91) 5636320; e-mail nigerian-emb-sp@jet.es; Ambassador SAMUEL ADELANA OTUYELU.

Norway: Paseo de la Castellana 31, 9°, 28046 Madrid; tel. (91) 3103116; fax (91) 3190969; e-mail emb.madrid@mfa.no; internet www.emb-noruega.es; Ambassador KJELL MARTIN FREDERIKSEN.

Pakistan: Avda de Pio XII 11, 28016 Madrid; tel. (91) 3458995; fax (91) 3458158; e-mail pakistan@teleline.es; internet www .parepmadrid.topcities.com; Ambassador AFTAB HUSSAIN SYED.

Panama: Claudio Coello 86, 1° Dcha, 28006 Madrid; tel. (91) 5765001; fax (91) 5767161; Ambassador VICENTINA RODRÍGUEZ DE FERNÁNDEZ-FIGARES.

Paraguay: Eduardo Dato 21, 4° Izqda, 28010 Madrid; tel. (91) 3082746; fax (91) 3084905; e-mail embapar@arrakis.es; Ambassador JULIO CÉSAR FRUTOS CORONEL.

Peru: Príncipe de Vergara 36, 5° Dcha, 28001 Madrid; tel. (91) 4314242; fax (91) 5776861; e-mail lepru@embajadaperu.es; Ambassador FERNANDO OLIVEIRA VEGA.

Philippines: Eresma 2, 28002 Madrid; tel. (91) 7823830; fax (91) 4116606; e-mail philmadrid@compuserve.com; Ambassador JOSEPH DELANO M. BERNARDO.

Poland: Guisando 23 bis, 28035 Madrid; tel. (91) 3736605; fax (91) 3736624; e-mail madryt@embajada-polonia.org; internet www .embajada-polonia.org; Ambassador GRAZYNA BERNATOWICZ.

Portugal: Calle Pinar 1, 28006 Madrid; tel. (91) 7824960; fax (91) 7824972; e-mail embajadaportugal@madrid.cempresarial.com; Ambassador JOÃO ROSA LÃ.

Romania: Alfonso XIII 157, 28016 Madrid; tel. (91) 3504436; fax (91) 3452917; e-mail roembmad@wol.es; Ambassador STELIAN OANCEA.

Russia: Velázquez 155, 28002 Madrid; tel. (91) 4110807; fax (91) 5629712; e-mail embrues@infonegocio.com; internet www.spain.mid.ru; Ambassador MIHAIL L. KAMYNIN.

San Marino: Padre de Jesús Ordóñez 18, 3°, 28002 Madrid; tel. (91) 5639000; fax (91) 5631931; e-mail rsm_madridaccessnet.es; Ambassador ENRICO MARAÍA PASQUINI.

Saudi Arabia: Dr Alvarez Sierra 3, 28033 Madrid; tel. (91) 3834300; fax (91) 3021212; Ambassador (vacant).

Senegal: Príncipe de Vergara 90, 1° A y B, 28006 Madrid; tel. (91) 7451003; fax (91) 7451148; e-mail senegal@repsenmadrid.e.telefonica.net; Ambassador ABAS NDIOUR.

Serbia and Montenegro: Velázquez 162, 28002 Madrid; tel. (91) 5635045; fax (91) 5630440; Ambassador TRIVO INDIĆ.

Slovakia: Pinar 20, 28006 Madrid; tel. (91) 5903861; fax (91) 5903868; e-mail re-emb@dimasoft.es; Ambassador JÁN VODERADSKÝ.

Slovenia: Hermanos Bécquer 7, 2°, 28006 Madrid; tel. (91) 4116893; fax (91) 5646057; e-mail vma@mzz-dkp.gov.si; Ambassador TOMAZ LOVRENCIĆ.

South Africa: Claudio Coello 91, 6° y 7°, 28006 Madrid; tel. (91) 4363780; fax (91) 5777414; e-mail embassy@sudafrica.com; internet www.sudafrica.com; Ambassador GERT G. GROBLER.

Sudan: Paseo de la Castellana 115, 11 Izqda, 28046 Madrid; tel. (91) 5972516; fax (91) 4174904; e-mail sudani49@hotmail.com; Chargé d'affaires a.i. ABD-ALLAH AHMED HASSAN SALIM.

Sweden: Caracas 25, 28010 Madrid; tel. (91) 7022000; fax (91) 7022040; e-mail ambassaden.madrid@foreign.ministry.se; internet www.embajadasuecia.es; Ambassador LARS ARNE GRUNDBERG.

Switzerland: Núñez de Balboa 35, 7°, 28001 Madrid; tel. (91) 4363960; fax (91) 4363980; e-mail vertretung@mad.rep.admin.ch; internet www.eda.admin.ch/madrid; Ambassador JOSEF DOSWALD.

Syria: Plaza de Platería Martínez 1, 1°, 28014 Madrid; tel. (91) 4203946; fax (91) 4202681; Ambassador MOHSEN BILAL.

Thailand: Joaquín Costa 29, 28002 Madrid; tel. (91) 5632903; fax (91) 5640033; e-mail madthai@wanadoo.es; internet www.mfa.go.th; Ambassador RAVEE HONGSAPRABHAS.

Tunisia: Plaza de Alonso Martínez 3, 28004 Madrid; tel. (91) 4473508; fax (91) 5938416; Ambassador MOHAMED SAHBI BASLY.

Turkey: Rafael Calvo 18, 2°, 28010 Madrid; tel. (91) 3198064; fax (91) 3086602; e-mail info@tcmadridbe.org; internet www.tcmadridbe.org; Ambassador VOLKAN VURAL.

Ukraine: Ronda de Abubilla 52, 28043 Madrid; tel. (91) 7489360; fax (91) 3887178; e-mail ukr-emb@arrakis.es; Ambassador OLEXANDER TARANENKO.

United Arab Emirates: Capitán Haya 40, 28020 Madrid; tel. (91) 5701003; fax (91) 5715176; Ambassador RASHID SULTAN AL-KAITUD.

United Kingdom: Fernando el Santo 16, 28010 Madrid; tel. (91) 7008200; fax (91) 7008272; e-mail webmaster@ukinspain.com; internet www.ukinspain.com; Ambassador STEPHEN WRIGHT.

USA: Serrano 75, 28006 Madrid; tel. (91) 5872200; fax (91) 5872303; internet www.embusa.es; Ambassador GEORGE L. ARGYROS.

Uruguay: Paseo del Pintor Rosales 32, 1° Dcha, 28008 Madrid; tel. (91) 7580475; fax (91) 5428177; e-mail urumatri@teleline.es; Ambassador JOSÉ MARÍA ARANEO GALLART.

Venezuela: Avda Capitán Haya 1, 13°, Edif. Eurocentro, 28020 Madrid; tel. (91) 5981200; fax (91) 5971583; e-mail embvenez@teleline.es; Ambassador GLADIS GUTIÉRREZ ALVARADO.

Vietnam: Arturo Soria 201, 1°A-B, 28043 Madrid; tel. (91) 5102867; fax (91) 4157004; Ambassador NGUYEN XUAN PHONG.

Yemen: Paseo de la Castellana 114, 3° esc.1–n°1, 28046 Madrid; tel. (91) 4119950; fax (91) 5623865; internet www.embajadayemen.es; Ambassador OMER HUSSEIN THEBT SAB'A.

Judicial System

Consejo General del Poder Judicial (CGPJ)
(General Council of Judicial Power)

Marqués de la Ensenada 8, 28071 Madrid; tel. (91) 7006100; fax (91) 7006358; e-mail josemaria.marquez@cgpj.es; internet www.poderjudicial.es.

The highest governing body of the judiciary; comprises the President of the Supreme Court, 20 members elected by the Cortes and appointed by the King for a five-year term (10 by the Congress of Deputies and 10 by the Senate); supervises the judicial system; independent of the Ministry of Justice; Pres. FRANCISCO JOSÉ HERNANDO SANTIAGO.

General Prosecutor: JESÚS CARDENAL FERNÁNDEZ.

SUPREME COURT

Tribunal Supremo

Palacio de Justicia, Plaza de la Villa de París s/n, 28071 Madrid; tel. (91) 3971200; internet www.poderjudicial.es/tribunalsupremo.

Is composed of five courts, each with its president and its respective judges.

President: FRANCISCO JOSÉ HERNANDO SANTIAGO.

First Court
Civil; President and 9 judges; Pres. IGNACIO SIERRA GIL DE LA CUESTA.

Second Court
Criminal; President and 14 judges; Pres. LUIS-ROMÁN PUERTA LUIS.

Third Court
Litigation; President and 32 judges; Pres. ANGEL RODRÍGUEZ GARCÍA.

Fourth Court
Company; President and 12 judges; Pres. LUIS GIL SUÁREZ.

Fifth Court
Military; President and 7 judges; Pres. JOSÉ MARÍA RUIZ-JARABO FERRÁN.

HIGH COURTS

Audiencia Nacional (National Court): García Gutiérrez 1, 28004 Madrid; tel. (91) 3973339; fax (91) 3973306; established in 1977; consists of three divisions—**Penal, Social and Contencioso-Administrativo,** each with its president and respective judges; attached to Second Court of Supreme Court; deals primarily with crimes associated with a modern industrial society, such as corruption, forgery, drugs-trafficking and also terrorism; Pres. CARLOS DIVAR.

Tribunales Superiores de Justicia de las Comunidades Autónomas (Autonomous Communities' Superior Courts of Justice): consist of civil and criminal division, administrative division and labour division.

Audiencias Provinciales (Provincial Courts): hear oral public proceedings, in single instance, for prosecutions of offences punishable by major prison terms, and appeals against decisions, sentences and judgments of lower courts.

OTHER COURTS

Lower courts are the Criminal, Administrative, Labour, Juvenile and Prison Supervisory Courts of First Instance and Trial Courts. In municipalities where there are no Courts of First Instance and Trial, there is a Magistrates' Court.

Religion

CHRISTIANITY

About 90% of Spain's inhabitants profess adherence to Roman Catholicism, and the country contains some 61,000 churches, with about 500 persons in each parish. Opus Dei, which seeks to integrate religious faith and professional work, plays an important role in Spanish society. There are some 30,000 Protestants in Spain.

The Roman Catholic Church

For ecclesiastical purposes, Spain (including Spanish North Africa) comprises 14 archdioceses and 53 dioceses. The archdiocese of Barcelona is directly responsible to the Holy See, while the remaining 13 are metropolitan sees. Each diocese is suffragan to a metropolitan see. At 31 December 2000 there were an estimated 38,775,057 adherents in the country, equivalent to some 98.3% of the population.

Bishops' Conference

Conferencia Episcopal Española, Añastro 1, 28033 Madrid; tel. (91) 3439600; fax (91) 3439602; e-mail conferenciaepiscopal@planalfa.es; internet www.conferenciaepiscopal.es.

f. 1977; Pres. Cardinal Antonio María Rouco Varela (Archbishop of Madrid).

Archbishop of Tarragona and Primate of Spain: Lluís Martínez Sistach, Arzobispado, Apdo 458, Pla de Palau 2, 43003 Tarragona; tel. (977) 233412; fax (977) 251847; e-mail arqtarragona@planalfa .es; internet www.fut.es/~arqbt.

Archbishop of Barcelona: Cardinal Ricardo María Carles Gordó.

Archbishop of Burgos: Francisco Gil Hellín.

Archbishop of Granada: Francisco Javier Martínez Fernández.

Archbishop of Madrid: Cardinal Antonio María Rouco Varela.

Archbishop of Mérida-Badajoz: Antonio Montero Moreno.

Archbishop of Oviedo: Carlos Osoro Sierra.

Archbishop of Pamplona y Tudela: Fernando Sebastián Aguilar.

Archbishop of Santiago de Compostela: Julián Barrio Barrio.

Archbishop of Sevilla: Carlos Amigo Vallejo.

Archbishop of Toledo: Antonio Cañizares Llovera.

Archbishop of Valencia: Augustín García-Gasco Vicente.

Archbishop of Valladolid: Braulio Rodríguez Plaza.

Archbishop of Zaragoza: Elías Yanes Alvarez.

The Anglican Communion

Anglicans in Spain are adherents of the Spanish Reformed Episcopal Church (Iglesia Española Reformada Episcopal), founded in 1869. The Church had 17 congregations, with a total of about 2,510 members, in 1994.

Bishop: Rt Rev. Carlos López, Beneficencia 18, 28004 Madrid; tel. (91) 4452560; fax (91) 5944572; e-mail eclesiae@arrakis.es; f. 1869.

Other Christian Churches

Baptist Evangelical Union of Spain: Salvador F. Luna 45, 26°, 46018 Valencia; tel. (96) 3591633; fax (96) 3134581; e-mail secretaria@uebe.org; internet www.uebe.org; Gen. Sec. Manuel Sarrias; Pres. Rev. José A. Cuenca.

Iglesia Evangélica Española (Spanish Evangelical Church): Noviciado 5, 08015 Madrid; tel. (91) 5313947; fax (91) 5234137; f. 1869 by merger of Presbyterians, Methodists, Congregationalists and Lutherans; 3,000 mems (1994); Pres. Enrique Capó; Sec. Alfredo Abad.

Iglesia Ortodoxa Griega (Greek Orthodox Church): Nicaragua 12, 28016 Madrid; tel. (91) 3454085; fax (91) 3509374; internet iglesiaortodoxa.net; Rector Arcipreste Dimitri Tsiamparlis.

ISLAM

In the early 1990s there were an estimated 300,000 Muslims in Spain.

Centro Islámico: Alfonso Cano 3, 28010 Madrid; tel. (91) 4480554.

Comisión Islámica de España: Anastasio Herrero 5, 28020 Madrid; tel. (91) 5714040; fax (91) 5708889; e-mail cie@teleline.es; Sec.-Gen. Riay Tatary Bakry.

Comunidad Ahmadía del Islam en España: La Mezquita Basharat, 14630 Pedro Abad (Córdoba); tel. (957) 186203; fax (957) 186300; e-mail ahmadiat_islam@teleline.es; internet www.alislam .org; Pres. Abdur Razzak Shahid.

JUDAISM

There are an estimated 15,000 Jews in Spain.

Comunidad Judía (Jewish Community): Balmes 3, 28010 Madrid; tel. (91) 5913131; fax (91) 5941517; e-mail cjmsecretaria@terra.es.

Federación de Communidades Israelitas de España: Avda 24, 08021 Barcelona; tel. (93) 2008513; fax (93) 2006148.

OTHER RELIGIOUS GROUPS

There are minorities of Bahá'ís (2,000 adherents), Buddhists and Jehovah's Witnesses.

The Press

There are four national newspapers: *ABC*, *Marca*, *El Mundo* and *El País*. Others, such as *As*, *El Correo*, *El Periódico de Catalunya* and *La Vanguardia*, may readily be obtained outside the region in which they are published. In 1996, according to UNESCO, there were 87 daily newspapers in Spain, with a total daily circulation estimated at 3.9m.

PRINCIPAL NEWSPAPERS

(arranged alphabetically by province)

Alava

El Periódico de Alava—Arabako Egunkaria: General Alava 5, interior, 01005 Vitoria; tel. (945) 230032; fax (945) 133086; e-mail prensa@elperiodicodealava.com; f. 1996; daily; Dir Iñigo Muñoz Trigo; circ. 15,000.

Albacete

La Tribuna de Albacete: Paseo de la Cuba 14, 02005 Albacete; tel. (967) 191000; fax (967) 240386; e-mail redaccion@ latribunadealbacete.es; internet www.latribunadealbacete.es; daily; Dir Dimas Cuevas Cuerda.

La Verdad de Albacete: Plaza Catedral 6, 02005 Albacete; tel. (967) 219311; fax (967) 210781; Dir Eduardo San Martín Montilla.

Alicante

Ciudad de Alcoy: Avda Puente San Jorge 8 y 10, 03803 Alcoy; tel. (96) 6521548; fax (96) 6521551; e-mail ciudaddealcoy@elperiodico .com; internet www.ciudaddealcoy.com; daily; Dir José Vicente Botella.

Información: Avda Dr Rico 17, Apdo 214, 03005 Alicante; tel. (96) 5989100; fax (96) 5989165; e-mail redaccion@epi.es; internet www .diarioinformacion.com; f. 1941; morning; Dir-Gen. Jesús Prado Sánchez; circ. 21,269.

La Verdad de Alicante: Avda Oscar Esplá 4, Bajo 5, 03003 Alicante; tel. (96) 5921950; fax (96) 5922248; e-mail alicante@ la-verdad.com; internet www.la-verdad.com; Dir Eduardo San Martín Montilla.

Almería

La Voz de Almería: Avda Mediterráneo, 1° planta, Edif. Cadena Ser n° 159, 04007 Almería; tel. (950) 280036; fax (950) 256458; e-mail lavoz@lavozdealmeria.com; internet www.lavozdealmeria .com; morning; Dir Pedro Manuel de la Cruz Alonso; circ. 7,737.

Asturias—see Oviedo

Avila

El Diario de Ávila: Plaza del Ejército 8 (sótano), Antigua de Gracia, s/n, 05001 Ávila; tel. (920) 351852; fax (920) 351853; e-mail info@ diariodeavila.com; f. 1888; morning; Dir Juan Carlos Fernandez Aganzo; circ. 8,000.

Badajoz

Diario Badajoz: López Prudencio 25 (Plaza Cervantes), 06002 Badajoz; tel. and fax (924) 224408; Dir Roberto Pérez Sagols.

Hoy—Diario de Extremadura: Crtra Madrid–Lisboa 22, 06008 Badajoz; tel. (924) 252511; fax (924) 205297; e-mail hoyredaccion@ hoy.es; internet www.hoy.es; f. 1933; morning; Catholic; Badajoz and Cáceres editions; Dir Teresiano Rodríguez Núñez; circ. 21,815.

Barcelona

Avui: Consell de Cent 425, 08009 Barcelona; tel. (93) 3163900; fax (93) 3163936; e-mail info@avui.com; internet www.avui.es; f. 1976; morning; in Catalan; Dir Vicent Sanchis Llàcer; circ. 50,000.

Diari de Sabadell: Sant Quirze 37–41, 2°, 08201 Sabadell; tel. (93) 7261100; fax (93) 7270865; e-mail redaccion@diarisabadell.es; f. 1977; 5 a week; Dir Ramón Rodríguez Zorrilla; circ. 7,164.

Diari de Terrassa: Vinyals 61, 08221 Terrassa; tel. (93) 7283700; fax (93) 7283719; e-mail opinion@diariterrasa.net; f. 1977; daily; Dir Ana Muñoz Núñez; circ. 5,590.

Metro Directo: Torre Central Cerdá, General Almirante 2 y 6, 8°, 08014, Barcelona; tel. (93) 3903500; fax (93) 3903595; e-mail trafico .bcn@metrospain.com; internet www.metropoint.com; free daily;; partly in Catalan; Dir Ramón Pedrós.

Mundo Deportivo: Tallers 62–64, 4°, 08001 Barcelona; tel. (93) 3444100; fax (93) 3444250; e-mail cd@elmundodeportivo.es; internet www.elmundodeportivo.es; f. 1906; morning; sport; Dir Santi Nolla Zayas; circ. 102,480.

El 9 Punt: Sardà 1, baixos, 08203 Sabadell; tel. (93) 7209990; fax (93) 7121025; Dir Jaume Espuny.

El País: Consell de Cent 341, 08007 Barcelona; tel. (93) 4010500; fax (93) 4010631; internet www.elpais.es; daily; f. 1982; Assistant Editor-in-Chief Xavier Vidal-Folch; circ. 80,000 (Sun. 143,000).

El Periódico de Catalunya: Consell de Cent 425–427, 08009 Barcelona; tel. (93) 2655353; fax (93) 4846512; e-mail redaccion@ elperiodico.com; internet www.elperiodico.com; daily; f. 1978; Dir Antonio Franco Estadella; circ. 210,000, (Sun. 380,000).

Regió 7 Informatiu Intercomarcal: Sant Antoni M. Claret 32, 08240 Manresa; tel. (93) 8772233; fax (93) 8740352; e-mail regio7@ regio7.com; internet www.regio7.com; f. 1978; 6 a week; Dir GONÇAL MAZCUŃÁN BOIX; circ. 9,261 (Sat. 12,337).

Sport: Valencia 49–51, 08015 Barcelona; tel. (93) 2279400; fax (93) 2279410; e-mail redaccion@diariosport.com; internet www .diariosport.com; daily; Editor JOSÉ MARIA CASANOVAS; Dir JOSÉ PRATS FIOL; circ. 130,000.

La Vanguardia: Pelayo 28, 08001 Barcelona; tel. (93) 4812200; fax (93) 3185587; e-mail lavanguardia@lavanguardia.es; internet www .lavanguardia.es; f. 1881; morning; Dir JOSÉ ANTICH; circ. 210,153; (Sun. 339,528).

20 Minutos: Plaça Universitat 3, 7°, 3A, 08007 Barcelona; tel. (93) 4706250; fax (93) 4706257; e-mail noesven@20minutos.es; internet www.20minutos.es; free daily; ; partly in Catalan; Dir ARSENIO ESCOLAR.

Burgos

Diario de Burgos: San Pedro de Cardeña 34, Apdo 46, 09002 Burgos; tel. (947) 267280; fax (947) 268003; e-mail redaccion@ diariodeburgos.es; internet www.diariodeburgos.es; f. 1891; morning; Catholic; independent; Dir VICENTE RUIZ DE MENCÍA; circ. 15,028 (Sun. 21,600).

Cáceres

El Periodico de Extremadura: Doctor Marañón 2, Local 7, 10002 Cáceres; tel. (927) 620600; fax (927) 620626; e-mail epextremadura@ elperiodico.es; internet www.elperiodico.es/extremadura; f. 1926; morning; Dir JULIÁN RODRÍGUEZ MOSCOSO; circ. 12,000.

Cádiz

Area: Gibraltar 13–15, Apdo 15, 11300 La Línea de la Concepción; tel. (956) 171450; fax (956) 763050; e-mail diario_area@gra; morning; Dir JOSÉ ANTONIO GÓMEZ AMADO; circ. 2,601.

Diario de Cádiz: Ceballos 1, Apdo 57, 11003 Cádiz; tel. (956) 297900; fax (956) 224883; e-mail redaccion@diariodecadiz.es; internet www.diariodecadiz.es; f. 1867; morning; independent; Dir MANUEL DE LA PEŃA MUŃOZ; circ. 32,120.

Diario de Jerez: Patricio Garvey s/n, Apdo 316, 11402 Jerez de la Frontera; tel. (956) 321411; fax (956) 349904; e-mail redaccion@ diariojerez.es; internet www.diariodejerez.com; f. 1984; Dir RAFAEL NAVAS RENEDO; circ. 10,265.

Europa Sur: Muro 3, 11201 Algeciras; tel. (956) 568250; fax (956) 631167; f. 1989; daily; Dir JORGE BEZARES BERMÚDEZ; circ. 6,485.

Información Jerez: Oso s/n, 11405 Jerez de la Frontera; Edif. Melkart, Of. 1 Izqda, 11011 Cádiz; tel. (956) 319833; fax (956) 307912; tel. (956) 262415; fax (956) 290737; Dir JUAN MANUEL GARRO REMENTERÍA; Cádiz edn: *Información Jerez*; Dir JOAQUÍN LADRÓN DE GUEVARA.

Cantabria (Santander)

Alerta de Cantabria: 1 de Mayo s/n, Barrio San Martín, 39011 Peñacastillo; tel. (942) 320033; fax (942) 322046; e-mail alerta@ cantabria.org; f. 1937; morning; Dir CIRIACO DÍAZ PORRAS; circ. 30,619.

El Diario Montañés: La Prensa s/n, La Albericia, 39012 Santander; tel. (942) 354000; fax (942) 341806; internet www .eldiariomontanes.es; f. 1902; morning; independent; Dir MANUEL ANGEL CASTAŃEDA PÉREZ; circ. 40,610 (Sun. 56,409).

Castellón

Mediterráneo: Carretera de Almassora s/n, 12005 Castellón de la Plana; tel. (964) 349500; fax (964) 349505; e-mail mediterraneo@ elperiodico.com; internet www.elperiodicomediterraneo.com; f. 1938; morning; Dir JESÚS MONTESINOS CERVERA; circ. 15,000.

Ciudad Real

Canfali: Plaza España 8, 1°, Edif. Mercado de Abastos, 13600 Alcazar de San Juan; tel. (926) 550940; fax (926) 550944; Dir MANUEL ESQUEMBRE BAŃULS.

El Día de Ciudad Real: Toledo 8, Edif. Miró, 3°, 12001 Ciudad Real; tel. (926) 223040; fax (926) 227150; e-mail redaccion@ eldiaciudadreal.com; Dir SANTIAGO MATEO SAHUQUILLO.

Lanza—Ciudad Real: Ronda del Carmen s/n (antiguo Hospital provincial), 13002 Ciudad Real; tel. (926) 274690; fax (926) 274746; e-mail redaccion@lanzadigital.com; internet www.lanzadigital.com; morning; Dir LAURA ESPINAR SÁNCHEZ; circ. 5,000.

La Tribuna de Ciudad Real: Juan II 7, 1°, 13001 Ciudad Real; tel. (926) 215301; fax (926) 215306; e-mail redaccion@diariolatribuna .com; Dir MARISA GARCÍA CARRETERO.

Córdoba

Córdoba: Ing. Juan de la Cierva 18 (Polígono Industrial de la Torrecilla), Apdo 2, 14013 Córdoba; tel. (957) 420302; fax (957) 204648; e-mail cordoba@elperiodico.es; f. 1941; morning; Dir ANTONIO GALÁN ORTIZ; circ. 18,660.

El Día de Córdoba: Avda Gran Capitán 23, 2°, 14008 Córdoba; tel. (957) 222050; fax (957) 222072; e-mail eldia@eldiadecordoba.com; internet www.eldiadecordoba.com; Dir ALFREDO MARTÍNEZ PÉREZ.

A Coruña

El Correo Gallego: Preguntoiro 29, 15704 Santiago de Compostela; tel. (981) 543700; fax (981) 543701; e-mail grupocorreogallego@ elcorreogallego.es; internet www.elcorreogallego.es; morning; Dir JOSÉ MANUEL REY NÓVOA; circ. 18,238.

O Correo Galego: f. 1994; Galician edn of above; circ. 10,000.

Deporte Campeón: Polígono de Pocomaco, C12, 2°, 15190 Mesoiro; tel. (981) 138586; fax (981) 138575; e-mail dxt@deportecampeon .com; f. 1995; daily; sport; Dir JUAN CARLOS BOGA SÁNCHEZ.

El Ideal Gallego: Polígono de Pocomaco Parcela C-12, 15190 Mesoiro; tel. (981) 173040; fax (981) 299327; e-mail elidealgallego@ elidealgallego.com; internet www.elidealgallego.com; f. 1917; morning; Dir JUAN RAMÓN DÍAZ GARCÍA; circ. 10,803.

La Voz de Galicia: Avda de la Prensa 84–85, Polígono de Sabón, 15142 Arteixo; tel. (981) 180180; fax (981) 180410; e-mail redac@ lavoz.com; internet www.lavozdegalicia.com; f. 1882; morning; commercial; Dir BIEITO RUBIDO RAMONDE; circ. 131,544 (Sun. 177,474).

Cuenca

El Día de Cuenca: Polígono 'El Cantorral' 13, 16004 Cuenca; tel. (969) 240423; fax (969) 225351; f. 1984; Dir SANTIAGO MATEO SAHUQUILLO; circ. 5,500.

Girona

Diari de Girona: Passeig General Mendoza 2, 17002 Girona; tel. (972) 202066; fax (972) 202005; e-mail diariegirona@epi-es; internet www.diaridegirona.es; f. 1891; morning; Dir JORDI XARGAYO I TEIXIDOR; circ. 6,208.

El Punt: Santa Eugènia 42, 17005 Girona; tel. (972) 186400; fax (972) 186420; e-mail elpunt@elpunt.com; internet www.elpunt.com; f. 1979; Dir JOAN VALL I CLARA; circ. 23,131.

Granada

Ideal: Huelva 2, Polígono 'La Unidad' de Asegra, 18210 Peligros; tel. (958) 809809; fax (958) 405072; e-mail ideal@ideal.es; internet www .ideal.es; f. 1932; morning; Dir EDUARDO PERALTA DE ANA; circ. 40,000; edns also in Jaén and Almería.

Guipúzcoa

El Diario Vasco: Camino de Portuetxe 2, Barrio de Ibaeta, Apdo 201, 20018 San Sebastián; tel. (943) 410700; fax (943) 410814; internet www.diariovasco.com; f. 1934; morning; liberal; Dir JOSE GAVRIEL MUGICA; circ. 103,000 (125,000 Sat./Sun.).

Euskaldunon Egunkaria: Gudarien Etorbidea Z/G, 20140 Andoain; tel. (943) 300222; fax (943) 300707; e-mail egunkaria@ egunkaria.com; internet www.egunkaria.com; f. 1990; daily; entirely in Basque; shut down by Government in February 2002; Dir MARTXELO OTAMENDI; circ. 15,000.

Gara: Camino Portuetxe 23, 2°, 20018 San Sebastián; tel. (943) 316999; fax (943) 316998; internet www.gara.net; Dir MERTXE AIZPURUA.

Huelva

Huelva Información: Plaza San Pedro 7, Apdo 176, 21004 Huelva; tel. (959) 541150; fax (959) 260608; e-mail redaccion@ huelvainformacion.es; internet www.huelvainformacion.es; Dir MANUEL CAPELO HERNÁNDEZ; circ. 7,047.

Huesca

Diario del Altoaragón: Ronda Estación 4, 22005 Huesca; tel. (974) 215656; fax (974) 215658; e-mail redaccion@diariodelaltoaragon.es; internet www.diariodelaltoaragon.es; fmrly *Nueva España*; morning; Dir ANTONIO ANGULO ARAGUÁS.

Heraldo de Huesca: Coso Bajo 28, 22001 Huesca; tel. (974) 239000; fax (974) 239005; e-mail huescaredaccion@heraldo.es; Dir GUILLERMO FATÁS CABEZA.

Jaén

Diario Jaén: Torredonjimeno 1, Polígono los Olivares, 23009 Jaén; tel. (953) 221810; fax (953) 280207; e-mail diariojaen@diariojaen.es;

internet www.diariojaen.es; f. 1941; morning; Dir JUAN ESPEJO GON-ZÁLEZ; circ. 7,466.

León

La Crónica/El Mundo de León: Moisés de León, Bloque 49, Bajo, 24006 León; tel. (987) 212512; fax (987) 213152; e-mail la-cronica@alehep.com; f. 1986; daily; Dir JOSÉ LUIS ESTRADA LIÉBANA; circ. 9,800.

Diario de León: Crtra de León-Astorga, Km 4–6, 24010 León; tel. (987) 840300; fax (987) 840340; e-mail diarioleon@diarioleon.com; internet www.diarioleon.com; morning; Dir FERNANDO ALLER GON-ZÁLEZ; circ. 18,366.

El Faro Astorgano: Manuel Gullón 5, 24700 Astorga; tel. (987) 617012; fax (987) 617025; e-mail alberto@astorga.com; internet www.astorga.com; f. 1980; 5 a week; Dir ALBERTO MATÍAS GARCÍA ALVAREZ; circ. 2,250.

Lleida (Lérida)

La Mañana-Diari de Ponent: Polígono Industrial El Segre 118, Apdo 11, 25080 Lérida; tel. (973) 204600; fax (973) 201646; e-mail manyana@lamanyana.es; internet www.lamanyana.es; f. 1938; morning; Dir JORDI PÉREZ ANSÓTEGUI; circ. 7,510.

Segre: Riu 6, Apdo 543, 25007 Lérida; tel. (973) 248000; fax (973) 246031; e-mail redaccio@diarisegre.com; internet www.diarisegre.com; f. 1982; morning; Dir JUAN CAL SÁNCHEZ; circ. 17,000 (Sun. 21,000).

Lugo

El Progreso: Ribadeo 5, 27002 Lugo; tel. (982) 298100; fax (982) 298102; e-mail correo@elprogreso.es; f. 1908; morning; independent; Dir LUIS RODRÍGUEZ GARCÍA; circ. 13,177.

Madrid

ABC: Juan Ignacio Luca de Tena 7, 28027 Madrid; tel. (91) 3399000; fax (91) 3203680; e-mail info@abc.es; internet www.abc.es; f. 1905; morning; Monarchist, independent; Dir JOSÉ ANTONIO ZARZALEJOS; circ. 334,696 (Sun. 765,668).

As: Albasanz 14, 4°, 28037 Madrid; tel. (91) 3752500; fax (91) 3752558; e-mail diarioas@diarioas.es; internet www.as.com; f. 1967; morning, sporting paper; Dir ALFREDO RELAÑO ESTAPÉ; circ. 162,420.

El Boletín de la Tarde: Bárbara de Braganza 11, 1°, 28004 Madrid; tel. (91) 3197000; fax (91) 3195831; e-mail redaccion@elboletin.com; internet www.elboletin.com; Dir CARLOS HUMANES FERNÁNDEZ.

Cinco Días: Gran Vía 32, 2°, 28013 Madrid; tel. (91) 5386100; fax (91) 5231128; e-mail redaccion@cincodias.es; internet www.cincodias.es; f. 1978; morning, incl. Sat. and Sun. economic; Dir FÉLIX MONTEIRA; Gen. Man. JUAN JOSÉ MANCEBO ZAFORAS; circ. 21,011.

Diario de Alcalá: Plaza de Navarra 1° C y D, 28804 Alcalá de Henares; tel. (91) 8894162; fax (91) 8895115; e-mail diarioalcala@tsai.es; Dir ANTONIO NARANJO.

Expansión: Paseo de la Castellana 66, 3°, 28046 Madrid; tel. (91) 3373220; fax (91) 3373245; e-mail expansion@recoletos.es; internet www.expansion.es; daily; Dir MIGUEL ANGEL BELLOSO BLÁZQUEZ; circ. 49,000.

La Gaceta de los Negocios: Pantoja 14, 28002 Madrid; tel. (91) 4327600; fax (91) 4327733; e-mail jpv@negocios.com; internet www.negocios.com; f. 1989; daily; business and finance; Dir JUAN PABLO DE VILLANUEVA; circ. 35,000.

Marca Deportivo: Paseo de la Castellana 66, 2°, 28046 Madrid; tel. (91) 3373220; fax (91) 3373276; e-mail marca@recoletos.es; internet www.marca.com; f. 1938 as weekly in San Sebastián, 1942 as daily in Madrid; morning; sports; Editor LUIS INFANTE BRAVO; Dir ELIAS ISRAEL; circ. 474,405.

Metro Directo: Caleruega 102–4, 5°, 28033 Madrid; tel. (91) 1318800; fax (91) 1318809; e-mail trafico.mdr@metrospain.com; free daily; Dir RAMÓN PEDRÓS.

El Mundo (del Siglo Veintiuno): Pradillo 42, 28002 Madrid; tel. (91) 5864800; fax (91) 5864848; internet www.elmundo.es; f. 1989; daily; Dir PEDRO J. RAMÍREZ CODINA; circ. 230,000 (Sun. 215,000).

El País: Miguel Yuste 40, 28037 Madrid; tel. (91) 3378200; fax (91) 3048766; e-mail marketing@elpais.es; internet www.elpais.es; f. 1976; morning; Dir JESÚS CEBERIO; Dir-Gen. PEDRO GARCÍA GUILLÉN; circ. 578,499 (Sun. 1,040,808); various regional and international edns.

La Razón: Josefa Valcárcel 42, 28027 Madrid; tel. (91) 3247000; fax (91) 7423604; internet www.larazon.es; f. 1998; Pres. LUIS MARÍA ANSÓN; Dir JOSÉ ANTONIO VERA.

20 Minutos: Palacio de la Prensa, Plaza del Callao 4, 2°, 28013 Madrid; tel. (91) 7015600; fax (91) 7015660; e-mail nosevende@20minutos; internet www.20minutos.es; f. 2000; free daily; Dir ARSENIO ESCOLAR.

Málaga

Diario Málaga-Costa del Sol: Avda García Morato 50, 29004 Málaga; tel. (95) 2244353; fax (95) 2245540; e-mail redaccion@diariomalaga.com; internet www.diariomalaga.com; Dir JAVIER CHECA.

La Opinión de Málaga: Granada 42, 29015 Málaga; tel. (95) 2126200; fax (95) 2126255; e-mail secretaria@epi.es; internet www.laopiniondemalaga.es; Dir JOAQUÍN MARÍN ALARCÓN.

Sur: Avda Dr Marañón 48, 29009 Málaga; tel. (95) 2649600; fax (95) 2279508; e-mail redaccion.su@diariosur.es; internet www.diariosur.es; f. 1937; morning; Dir JOSÉ ANTONIO FRÍAS RUIZ; circ. 60,000; also publishes free English weekly; circ. 42,975.

Murcia

La Opinión de Murcia: Plaza Condestable 3, 30009 Murcia; tel. (968) 281888; fax (968) 281417; f. 1988; Dir PALOMA REVERTE DE LUIS; circ. 8,415.

La Verdad de Murcia: Camino Viejo de Monteagudo s/n, 30160 Murcia; tel. (968) 369100; fax (968) 369147; internet www.laverdad.es; f. 1903; morning; independent; Dir EDUARDO SAN MARTÍN MONTILLA; circ. 42,724.

Navarra

Diario de Navarra: Zapatería 49, Apdo 5, 31001 Pamplona; tel. (948) 236050; fax (948) 237940; internet www.diariodenavarra.es; f. 1903; morning; independent; Dir JULIO MARTÍNEZ TORRES; circ. 64,406.

Diario de Noticias: Polígono Areta Huarte s/n, 31620 Huarte; tel. (948) 332533; fax (948) 332518; e-mail redacción@noticiasdenavarra.com; internet www.noticiasdenavarra.com; f. 1994; daily; Dir PABLO MUÑOZ PEÑA; circ. 17,000.

Ourense

La Región (Ourense): Polígono Industrial de San Ciprián de Viñas C/4, 32091 Orense; tel. (988) 383838; fax (988) 244449; e-mail laregion@laregion.net; internet www.lri.laregion.net; f. 1910; morning; Dir ALFONSO SÁNCHEZ IZQUIERDO; circ. 12,273 (international edn (weekly); f. 1966; circ. 44,259).

Oviedo (Asturias)

El Comercio: Calle del Diario El Comercio 1, 33207 Gijón; tel. (98) 5179800; fax (98) 5340955; e-mail elcomercio@elcomercio-sa.es; internet www.elcomerciodigital.com; f. 1878; morning; Dir JUAN CARLOS MARTÍNEZ GAUNA; circ. 27,483.

La Nueva España: Calvo Sotelo 7, Edif. Sedes, 33007 Oviedo; tel. (98) 5279700; fax (98) 5279711; internet www.lanuevaespaña.es; f. 1937; morning; Dir ISIDORO NICIEZA; circ. 57,561.

El Periódico-La Voz de Asturias: Polígono Puente Nora 4, 33420 Lugones-Siero; tel. (98) 5101500; fax (98) 5101505; e-mail vozredaccion@elperiodico.com; internet www.lavozdeasturias.es; f. 1923; morning; independent; Dir RODRIGO CAPEDA FERNÁNDEZ-MIRANDA; circ. 23,500.

La Voz de Avilés: La Camara 47, 33402 Avilés; tel. (98) 5522456; fax (98) 5569899; internet www.elcomerciodigital.com/lavozdeaviles; morning; Dir JUAN MANUEL WES LÓPEZ; circ. 3,541.

Palencia

Diario Palentino-El Día de Palencia: Mayor Principal 67, Apdo 17, 34001 Palencia; tel. (979) 744822; fax (979) 743360; e-mail redaccion@diariopalentino.es; internet www.diariopalentino.es; f. 1882; morning; independent; Dir CARLOS MARTÍN SANTOYO; circ. 10,000.

Pontevedra

Atlántico Diario: Camelias 104, 36211 Vigo; tel. (986) 208686; fax (986) 201269; e-mail atlantico@atlantico.net; f. 1987; daily; Dir FERNANDO R. OJEA; circ. 5,470.

Diario de Pontevedra: Lepanto 5, 36002 Pontevedra; tel. (986) 011100; fax (986) 011142; morning; Dir ANTÓN GALOCHA LÓPEZ; circ. 3,903.

Faro de Vigo: Colón 30, Apdo 91, 36201 Vigo; tel. (986) 814600; fax (986) 814615; e-mail redaccion@farodevigo.es; internet www.farodevigo.es; f. 1853; morning; Dir PEDRO PABLO ALONSO GARCÍA; circ. 36,862.

Terceiro Tempo: Rúa Barcelona 33, entresuelo, 36205 Vigo; tel. and fax (986) 410706; e-mail tvision@teleline.es; internet www.agexre.com; Dir DANIEL SOTO RODRIGO.

La Rioja (Logroño)

La Rioja: Vara del Rey 74, Apdo 28, 26002 Logroño; tel. (941) 279107; fax (941) 279106; e-mail director@larioja.com; internet www.diariolarioja.com; f. 1889; morning; Dir JOSÉ MARÍA ESTEBAN IBÁÑEZ; circ. 15,043.

Salamanca

El Adelanto: Gran Vía 56, 37001 Salamanca; tel. (923) 280228; fax (923) 280260; e-mail eladelanto@elperiodico.com; internet www.eladelanto.com; f. 1883; morning; independent; Dir NUNCHI PRIETO GARCÍA; circ. 6,100.

La Gaceta Regional de Salamanca: Avda de los Cipreses 81, 37004 Salamanca; tel. (923) 252020; fax (923) 256155; e-mail opinion@lagacetadesalamanca.com; f. 1920; morning; Dir IÑIGO DOMINGUÉZ DE CALATAYUD; circ. 13,740 (Sun. 25,377).

Tribuna de Salamanca: Cañón de Riolobos 14 (Polígono Montalvo II), 37008 Salamanca; tel. (923) 191111; fax (923) 191152; e-mail info@tribuna.net; internet www.tribuna.net; Dir-Gen. ÁNGEL LUIS HERNÁNDEZ SÁNCHEZ.

Santander—see Cantabria

Segovia

El Adelantado de Segovia: Peñalara 3 (Polígono Industrial El Cerro), 40006 Segovia; tel. (921) 437261; fax (921) 442432; e-mail adelantado@eladelantado.com; internet www.eladelantado.com; f. 1901; evening; Dir CARLOS HERRANZ CANO; circ. 5,000.

Sevilla

ABC: Albert Einstein s/n, Isla de la Cartuja, 41092 Sevilla; tel. (95) 4488600; fax (95) 4488601; f. 1929; morning; monarchist; independent; Dir ALVARO YBARRA PACHECO; circ. 59,874; see also under Madrid.

El Correo de Andalucía: Avda de la Prensa 1, Polígono Carretera Amarilla, 41007 Sevilla; tel. (95) 4999251; fax (95) 4517635; e-mail redaccion@correodeandalucia.es; internet www.correodeandalucia.es; f. 1899; morning; independent; Dir FERNANDO ORGAMBIDES; circ. 27,204.

Diario de Andalucía: Sevilla; e-mail diarioandalucia@arrakis.es; Dir JUAN EMILIO BALLESTEROS.

Diario de Sevilla: Rioja 13, pasaje, 41001 Sevilla; tel. (95) 4506200; fax (95) 4506222; e-mail secretaria@diariodesevilla.es; internet www.diariodesevilla.es; Dir MANUEL JESÚS FLORENCIO.

Estadio Deportivo: Avda San Francisco Javier, Edif. Sevilla 2, 11°, 41018 Sevilla; tel. (95) 4933940; fax (95) 4637839; e-mail estadio@estadio-deportivo.com; internet www.estadio-deportivo.com; ; sport; Dir JOSÉ DAVID MARTÍN LAÍNEZ.

El País: Cardenal Bueno Monreal s/n, Edif. Columbus, 41013 Sevilla; tel. (95) 4246100; fax (95) 4246124; f. 1986; regional edition of the Madrid daily; Dir ROMÁN OROZCO; circ. 74,000.

Sevilla Información: Ediciones Culturales Andaluzas, SA, Avda de la República Argentina 21, ACC, 1° modulo 8, Sevilla; tel. (95) 5051000; fax (95) 5051008; e-mail sevillainformacion@sevillainformacion.com; internet www.sevillainformacion-ed.es; Pres. JAVIER GALLARDO; Dir ANTONIO L. SOMOZA.

Soria

Diario de Soria: Morales Contreras 2, bajo, 42003 Soria; tel. (975) 212063; fax (975) 221504; e-mail diariosoria@maptel.es; internet www.gumaro.com/diariosoria; daily; Dir PATXI VERAMENDI MORENO.

Heraldo Soria 7 Días: El Collado 17, 1° A–C, 42001 Soria; tel. (975) 233607; fax (975) 229211; e-mail soriaredaccion@heraldo.es; internet www.heraldo.es; Dir ESTHER GUERRERO GIJÓN; circ. 5,000.

Tarragona

Diari de Tarragona: Domènech Guansé 2, 43005 Tarragona; tel. (977) 299700; fax (977) 223013; e-mail diari@diaridetarragona.com; internet www.diaridetarragona.com; f. 1808; morning; Dir ANTONIO COLL I GILABERT; circ. 12,302.

Teruel

Diario de Teruel: Avda de Sagunto 27, 44002 Teruel; tel. (978) 617086; fax (978) 600682; e-mail redaccion@diariodeteruel.net; internet www.diariodeteruel.net; evening; Dir JULIO ZAPATER GARCÍA; circ. 2,853.

Toledo

El Día de Toledo: Cuesta de Carlos V 4, 3° Izqda, 45001 Toledo; tel. (925) 221170; fax (925) 214065; e-mail diadetoledo@ticom.es;

internet www.eldia-digital.com; f. 1987; daily; Dir SANTIAGO MATEO SAHUQUILLO; circ. 3,500.

Valencia

Levante—El Mercantil Valenciano: Traginers 7, 46014 Valencia; tel. (96) 3992200; fax (96) 3992276; e-mail levante-emv@epi.es; internet www.levante-emv.es; f. 1872; morning; Dir PEDRO MUELAS NAVARRETE; circ. 54,860, Sunday 86,779.

Mini Diario de la Comunidad Valenciana: Avda Campanar 33, 1°, 46009 Valencia; tel. (96) 3462624; fax (96) 3173140; e-mail valencia@minidiario.com; internet www.minidiario.com; f. 1992; ; free daily; Dir NACHO SAPENA ESCUDERO; circ. 55,000.

El País: Poeta Querol 11, 1°, 46002 Valencia; tel. (96) 3981150; fax (96) 3511731; e-mail valencia@elpais.es; internet www.elpais.es; Dir JOSEP TORRENT; f. 1986; regional edn of national daily.

Las Provincias: Polígono Industrial Vara de Quart, Gremis 4, 46014 Valencia; tel. (96) 3502211; fax (96) 3590188; e-mail lasprovincias@lasprovincias.es; internet www.lasprovincias.es; f. 1866; morning; rightist, independent; Dir PEDRO ORTIZ SIMARRO; circ. 59,370, (Sun. 85,084).

The Spanish World: Irlanda 1, 46901 Vedat de Torrent; tel. (96) 1553799; fax (96) 1561583; e-mail spia@spia.com; internet www.thespanishworld.com; Dir PATRICIA MURRAY.

Super Deporte: Avda de Aragón 2, Entresuelo, 46021 Valencia; tel. (96) 3371818; fax (96) 3372045; e-mail super@superdeporte.es; sport; Dir VICENTE BAU MIQUEL.

Valladolid

El Norte de Castilla: Vázquez de Menchaca 10 (Polígono de Argales), 47008 Valladolid; tel. (983) 412100; fax (983) 412111; internet www.nortecastilla.es; f. 1854; morning; agricultural and economic interests; Dir CARLOS ROLDÁN SAN JUAN; circ. 34,111 (Sun. 45,522).

El Día de Valladolid: Pasaje Marquesina 5, 47004 Valladolid; tel. (983) 215000; fax (983) 303564; e-mail redaccion@diavalladolid.es; f. 2000; Dir RICARDO ARQUES.

Vizcaya

El Correo Español-El Pueblo Vasco: Pintor Losada 7, Apdo 205, 48004 Bilbao; tel. (94) 4870100; fax (94) 4870111; e-mail info@diario-elcorreo.es; internet www.elcorreodigital.com; f. 1910; morning; independent; Dir ÁNGEL ARNEDO GIL; circ. 133,032.

Deia: Crta Bilbao Galdácano 8 (Bolueta), 48004 Bilbao; tel. (94) 4599100; fax (94) 4599120; internet www.deia.com; f. 1997; morning; Basque; Dir JUAN JOSÉ BAÑOS LOINAZ; circ. 50,690.

Diario El Boletín de Bolsa, Economía y Finanzas: Alameda de Mazarredo 31, 3° Izqda, 48009 Bilbao; tel. (94) 4235504; fax (94) 4248394; e-mail redaccion@elboletin.net; internet www.elboletin.net; f. 1987; daily; finance; Dir FERNANDO MATA IRIONDO; circ. 10,500.

El País: Epalza 8, 7°, 48007 Bilbao; tel. (94) 4132300; regional edn of Madrid daily; Dir ANDER LANDÁBURU.

Zamora

La Opinión-El Correo de Zamora: Rua de los Francos 20, 49001 Zamora; tel. (988) 534759; fax (988) 513552; internet www.laopiniondezamora.es; f. 1896; morning; Dir FRANCISCO GARCÍA ALONSO; circ. 6,404.

Zaragoza

Equipo: Plaza Mariano Arregui 15–16, 50005 Zaragoza; tel. (976) 700440; fax (976) 700449; internet www.diarioequipo.com; Dir MANUEL DE MIGUEL GUILLÉN.

Heraldo de Aragón: Plaza de la Independencia 29, Apdo 175, 50001 Zaragoza; tel. (976) 765000; fax (976) 765001; e-mail redaccion1@heraldo.es; internet www.heraldo.es; f. 1895; morning; independent; Dir GUILLERMO FATÁS CABEZA; circ. 62,262.

El Periódico de Aragón: Hernán Cortés 37, bajo, 50005 Zaragoza; tel. (976) 700400; fax (976) 700458; e-mail eparagon@elperiodico.es; internet www.elperiodicodearagon.com; f. 1990; Dir MIGUEL ANGEL LISO TEJADA; circ. 14,446.

Balearic Islands

Diari de Balears: Paseo Mallorca, 9°A, 07011 Palma de Mallorca; tel. (971) 788322; fax (971) 455740; e-mail mc.dbalears@bitel.es; internet www.diaridebalears.com; f. 1939; fmrly *Baleares*; morning; in Catalan; Dir MIGUEL SERRA MAGRANER; circ. 11,777.

Diario de Ibiza: Fray Vicente Nicolás 27, 07800 Ibiza; tel. (971) 190000; fax (971) 190322; e-mail diariodeibiza@epi.es; internet www.diariodeibiza.es; morning; Dir JOAN SERRA TUR; circ. 6,496.

Diario de Mallorca: Puerto Rico 15, Polígono de Levante, 07007 Palma de Mallorca; tel. (971) 170300; fax (971) 170301; e-mail diariomallorca@diariodemallorca.es; internet www .diariodemallorca.es; f. 1953; morning; Dir José Eduardo Iglesias Barca; circ. 22,414.

Majorca Daily Bulletin: Paseo Mallorca 9A, Palau de la Premsa, Apdo 304, 07011 Palma de Mallorca; tel. (971) 788400; fax (971) 719706; e-mail editorial@majorcadailybulletin.es; internet www .majorcadailybulletin.es; f. 1962; 6 a week; English language; Dir Jason Moore; circ. 5,300.

Menorca, Diario Insular: Cap de Cavalleria 5, 07714 Mahón, Menorca; tel. (971) 351600; fax (971) 351983; e-mail redaccion@ menora.info; internet www.menora.info; f. 1941; morning; Dir Joan Bosco Marquès Bosch; circ. 5,499.

El Mundo/El Día de Baleares: 16 de Julio 75, Polígono de Son Castelló, 07009 Palma de Mallorca; tel. (971) 767600; fax (971) 767656; e-mail eldia.redaccion@el-mundo.es; internet www .elmundo-eldia.com; f. 1981; daily; Dir Luis Fidalgo Hortelano; circ. 18,000.

Última Hora: Edif. Palacio de la Prensa, Paseo de Mallorca 9ºA, 07011 Palma de Mallorca; tel. (971) 788333; fax (971) 454190; internet www.ultimahora.es; f. 1893; morning; Dir Pedro Comas Barceló; circ. 33,100.

Canary Islands—Lanzarote

La Voz Diario de Lanzarote: Canalejas 2, 2° Izqda, 35500 Arrecife, Lanzarote; tel. (928) 803949; fax (928) 814225; Dir Francisca Trujillo Eugenio.

Canary Islands—Las Palmas

Canarias 7: Profesor Lozano 7, Urbanización El Sebadal, 35008 Las Palmas; tel. (928) 301300; fax (928) 301434; e-mail infocan@ canarias7.es; internet www.canarias7.es; f. 1982; daily; Dir Francisco Suárez Álamo; circ. 36,227.

La Provincia—Diario de las Palmas: Alcalde Ramírez Bethencourt 8, 35003 Las Palmas; tel. (928) 479410; fax (928) 479401; e-mail laprovincia@editorialprensacanaria.es; internet www .la-provincia.com; La Provincia; f. 1911; Diario de las Palmas; f. 1895; morning; independent; Dir Julio Puente; circ. 40,316.

Canary Islands—Santa Cruz de Tenerife

El Día: Avda de Buenos Aires 71, Apdo 97, 38005 Santa Cruz; tel. (922) 238300; fax (922) 214247; e-mail redaccioneldia@eldia.es; internet www.eldia.es; f. 1910; morning; Dir José E. Rodríguez Ramírez; circ. 25,437.

Diario de Avisos: Salamanca 5, 38006 Santa Cruz; tel. (922) 272350; fax (922) 241039; e-mail redaccion@diariodeavisos.com; internet www.diariodeavisos.com; f. 1890; re-f. 1976; morning; Dir Leopoldo Fernández Cabeza de Vaca; circ. 12,293.

La Gaceta de Canarias: Polígono Industrial Los Majuelos, Fernando Díaz Cutillas s/n, 38108 La Laguna; tel. (922) 821555; fax (922) 821460; e-mail lagaceta@teide.net; f. 1989; Dir Andrés González de Chaves y Sotomayor; circ. 11,407.

Jornada Deportiva: Avda Buenos Aires 71, Apdo 714, 38005 Santa Cruz; tel. (922) 238300; fax (922) 213834; f. 1953; morning; general information; Gen. Man. José E. Rodríguez Ramírez; circ. 10,000 (Tue.–Sat.), 26,000 (Mon.).

La Opinión de Tenerife: Plaza Santa Cruz de la Sierra 2, 38003 Santa Cruz; tel. (922) 471800; fax (922) 471801; e-mail lectores@ la-opinion.com; internet www.la-opinion.com; Dir Francisco Pomares.

GENERAL INTEREST PERIODICALS

A Nosa Terra: Rúa Príncipe 22, 36202 Vigo; tel. (986) 222405; fax (986) 223101; e-mail info@anosaterra.com; internet www.anosaterra .com; f. 1907; weekly; in Gallego; Dir Alfonso Eiré López.

Aceprensa: Núñez de Balboa 125, 28006 Madrid; tel. (91) 5158975; fax (91) 5631243; e-mail redaccion@aceprensa.com; internet www .aceprensa.com; f. 1973; weekly; news and features; Dir Ignacio Aréchaga; circ. 4,000.

Cambio 16: Ramón Pérez de Ayala 88, local comercial, 28038 Madrid; tel. (91) 44201199; fax (91) 3601302; e-mail cambio16@ cambio16.info; internet www.cambio16.info; f. 1972; weekly (Wed.); general; Dir Francisco Caparros.

El Ciervo: Calvet 56, 08021 Barcelona; tel. (93) 2005145; fax (93) 2011015; e-mail elciervo96@elciervo.es; internet www.elciervo.es; f. 1951; monthly; Dir Lorenzo Gomis Sanahuja; circ. 5,000.

Ciudad Nueva: José Picón 28, 28028 Madrid; tel. (91) 7259530; fax (91) 7130452; e-mail revista@ciudadnueva.com; internet www .ciudadnueva.com; f. 1958; monthly; Dir Javier Rubio; circ. 7,000.

Ciudadano: Silva 6, 4°, 28013 Madrid; tel. (91) 5484045; fax (91) 5480010; e-mail ciudadano@teleline.es; internet www.uce.org; f. 1975; monthly; consumer news; Dir Antonio B. Cazorla; Editors Julio Ruiz Herreras, Francisco González Patón; circ. 70,000.

La Clave: Avda de Argón 336, 28022 Madrid; tel. (91) 8373131; e-mail redaccion@laclave.com; internet www.laclave.com; weekly; news magazine; Dir José Luis Balbin.

Diez Minutos: Avda Cardenal Herrera Oria 3, 28034 Madrid; tel. (91) 7287000; fax (91) 7289132; e-mail diezminutos@hachette.es; internet www.diezminutos.es; f. 1951; weekly; Dir Cristina Acebal; circ. 209,208.

El Empresario: Diego de León 50, 3°, 28006 Madrid; tel. (91) 4116161; fax (91) 5645269; e-mail elempresario@cepyme.es; internet www.cepyme.es; monthly; Dir Carlota Domínguez Núñez; circ. 15,000.

Época: Mesena 83, Edif. Epoca, 28033 Madrid; tel. (91) 5109100; fax (91) 5109149; e-mail epoca@epoca.es; internet www.epoca.es; weekly; Dir Rafael Miner Guerrero.

Gaceta Internacional: Alonso Cano 66, 1°B, 28003 Madrid; tel. (91) 5547354; fax (91) 5534800; e-mail info@aphis.org; internet aphis .org/gaceta; monthly; ; international magazine produced by the Associacíon de la Prensa Hispanamerica; Dir Armando Restrepo Bretón; circ. 16,500 in Spain; 150,000 internationally.

Geo: Marqués de Villamagna 4, 28001 Madrid; tel. (91) 4369800; fax (91) 5759128; e-mail geo@gyj.es; internet www.gyj.es; f. 1987; monthly; Dir David Corral; circ. 61,427.

Guía del Ocio—Barcelona y Area Metropolitana: Muntaner 492 bajos, 08022 Barcelona; tel. (93) 4185005; fax (93) 4179471; e-mail redaccion@guiadelociobcn.com; internet www.guiadelociobcn .com; f. 1977; weekly; Dir Xavier Muniesa Calderó; circ. 50,000.

Guía del Ocio—La Semana de Madrid: Alcalá 106, 3°, 28009 Madrid; tel. (91) 4316080; fax (91) 5769307; e-mail p.javaloyes@ guiadelocio.mad.com; weekly; Dir-Gen. Juan Miguel Alonso Seco.

¡Hola!: Miguel Angel 1, 4°, 28010 Madrid; tel. (91) 7021300; fax (91) 3196444; f. 1944; weekly; general illustrated; Dir Eduardo Sánchez Junco; circ. 582,778.

Insula: Carretera de Irún, Km 12,200 (Variante de Fuencarral), 28049 Madrid; tel. (91) 3589689; fax (91) 3589505; e-mail insula@ espasa.es; f. 1946; monthly; literature and social sciences; Dir Víctor García de la Concha; circ. 6,000.

Interviú: O'Donnell 12, 5°, 28009 Madrid; tel. (91) 5863300; fax (91) 5863555; e-mail interviu@grupozeta.es; internet www.zetainterviu .com; f. 1976; weekly; Dir Teresa Viejo; circ. 494,347.

El Jueves: Avda Diagonal 468, 5°, 08006 Barcelona; tel. (93) 2922217; fax (93) 2375824; e-mail redaccion@eljveves.es; internet www.eljueves.es; f. 1977; weekly; satirical; Dir Manuel Fontdevila; circ. 130,000.

Muy Interesante: Marqués de Villamagna 4, 28001 Madrid; tel. (91) 4369800; fax (91) 5759128; e-mail publicidad@gyj.es; internet www.muyinteresante.es; f. 1981; monthly; Dir José Pardina Cancer; circ. 283,690.

Natura: Islas Marquesas 28B, 28035 Madrid; tel. (91) 3865152; fax (91) 3860265; e-mail redaccion@mundonatura.es; f. 1983; bimonthly; wildlife, archaeology, research, travel, food; Dir Jesús Iniesta; circ. 69,913.

El Nuevo Lunes de la Economía y la Sociedad: Plaza de España 18, 7°, Of. 3, 28008 Madrid; tel. (91) 5160803; fax (91) 5160819; e-mail nuevolunes@elnvevolunes.com; internet www.elnuevolunes .com; weekly; Dir Rosa del Río Cabrerizo.

Nuevo Vale: Gran Vía de Carlos III 124, 5°, 08034 Barcelona; tel. (93) 2061540; fax (93) 2805555; e-mail buzon@publicacionesheres .com; weekly; Dir Esther Giralt; circ. 200,000.

Pronto: Gran Vía de Carlos III 124, 5°, 08034 Barcelona; tel. (93) 2061540; fax (93) 2805555; e-mail pronto@publicacionesheres.com; f. 1972; weekly; general information; Dir Antonio Gómez Abad; circ. 960,000.

Semana: Cuesta de San Vicente 28, 28008 Madrid; tel. (91) 5472300; fax (91) 5414488; e-mail redaccion@semana.es; internet www.semana.es; f. 1942; weekly; general, illustrated; Pres. Vicente Montiel y Rodríguez de la Encina; Dir Rosario Montiel Armada; circ. 340,590.

El Socialista: Gobelas 31, 28023 Madrid; tel. (91) 5820044; fax (91) 5820045; e-mail elsocialista@elsocialista.es; internet www .elsocialista.es; f. 1866; monthly; general information; Dir Joaquín Tagar; circ. 185,000.

Super Pop: Gran Vía Carlos III 124, 5°, 08034 Barcelona; tel. (93) 2061540; fax (93) 2805555; e-mail superpop@publicacionesheres .com; f. 1976; fortnightly; teenage magazine; Dir Carmen Grasa; circ. 125,000.

Supertele: Cardenal Herrera Oria 3, 28034 Madrid; tel. (91) 7287000; fax (91) 7289129; e-mail supertele@hachette.es; internet www.supertele.es; f. 1992; weekly; TV magazine; Dir AGUSTÍN DE TENA.

Tele Digital: San Bernardo 82, 28015 Madrid; tel. (91) 4451950; fax (91) 4450621; e-mail teledigital@grupotsp.com; internet www.telesatellite.com; Dir JOSÉ DA CUNHA.

Tele Indiscreta: Cardenal Herrera Oria 3, 28034 Madrid; tel. (91) 7287000; fax (91) 7289142; e-mail teleindiscreta@hachette.es; internet www.teleindiscreta.es; weekly; popular illustrated; TV programmes; Dir PURIFICACIÓN BLANCO; circ. 700,000.

Telenovela: Cardenal Herrera Oria 3, 28034 Madrid; tel. (91) 7287051; fax (91) 7289142; e-mail telenovela@hachette.es; internet www.tele-novela.com; f. 1993; TV series; Dir IRENE GONZÁLEZ; circ. 200,000.

El Temps: Avinguda del Baró de Càrcer 40, 13°, 46001 Valencia; tel. (96) 3535100; fax (96) 3534569; e-mail eltemps@eltemps.com; internet www.eltemps.com; f. 1984; weekly; general information; Dir JORDI FORTUNY I BATALLA; circ. 25,000.

Tiempo de Hoy: O' Donnell 12, 3°, 28009 Madrid; tel. (91) 5863300; fax (91) 5863346; e-mail tiempo@grupozeta.es; internet www.tiempodehoy.es; weekly; Dir JESÚS RIVASÉS.

TP Teleprograma: Avda Cardenal Herrera Oria 3, 28034 Madrid; tel. (91) 7287000; fax (91) 7289141; e-mail tp@hachette.es; internet www.t-p.es; f. 1966; weekly; TV, cinema and video; Dir AGUSTÍN DE TENA; circ. 300,000.

Viajar: O'Donnell 12, 2°, 28009 Madrid; tel. (91) 5863630; fax (91) 5869780; e-mail viajar@grupozeta.es; f. 1978; monthly; travel magazine; Dir JESÚS RIVASÉS; circ. 75,000.

Vida Nueva: Agastia 80, 28043 Madrid; tel. (91) 7444551; fax (91) 7444891; e-mail vidanueva@ppc-editorial.com; f. 1958; weekly; Dir NINFA WATT; circ. 20,000.

SPECIALIZED PUBLICATIONS

Arts, Literature, etc.

Amadeus: RBA Revistas, SA, Pérez Galdós 36 bis., 08012 Barcelona; tel. (93) 4157374; fax (93) 2177378; e-mail amadeus@rba.es; internet www.rba.es; monthly; classical music; Editorial Dir JOSÉ LUIS CÓRDOBA DEL ÁGUILA.

Arquitectura y Diseño: RBA Revistas, SA, Pérez Galdós 36 bis., 08012 Barcelona; internet www.rba.es; monthly; architecture and design.

Claves de Razón Práctica: Fuencarral 6, 2°, 28004 Madrid; tel. (91) 5386100; fax (91) 5222291; e-mail claves@progresa.es; monthly; books and culture; Dirs JAVIER PRADERA, FERNANDO SAVATER.

Clio: Gran Vía de les Corts Catalanes 133, 2A, 08014 Barcelona; tel. (93) 2230353; fax (93) 4322907; e-mail clio@hachette.es; internet www.cliorevista.com; monthly; history; Editorial Dir ELISENDA NADAL.

El Croquis: Avda de los Reyes Católicos 9, El Escorial, 28280 Madrid; tel. (91) 8969410; tel. (91) 8969411; e-mail elcroquis@infornet.es; internet www.elcroquis.net; six a year; architecture, in Spanish and English.

Experimenta: Churucca 27, 4° drcha, 28004 Madrid; tel. (91) 5214049; fax (91) 5213212; e-mail publi@revistaexperimenta.com; internet www.revistaexperimenta.com; design; Dir PIERLUIGI CATTERMOLE FIORAVANTI.

Historia 16: Rufino González 23 bis, 28037 Madrid; tel. (91) 3271171; fax (91) 3271220; e-mail h16redaccion@terra.es; f. 1976; monthly; history; Dir MARÍA ALDAVE; circ. 25,000.

Letra Internacional: Monte Esquinza 30, 2° drcha, 28010 Madrid; tel. (91) 3104313; fax (91) 3194585; e-mail redaccion@fpabloiglesias.es; internet www.fpabloiglesias.es; quarterly; culture; Dir SALVADOR CLOTAS I CIERCO.

Matador: Alameda 9, 28014 Madrid; tel. (91) 3601320; fax (91) 3601322; e-mail matador@lafabrica.com; internet www.lafabrica.com; annual; art; Dir ALBERTO ARNAUT.

Ritmo: Isabel Colbrand 10, 4°, Oficina 95, 28050 Madrid; tel. (91) 3588945; fax (91) 3588944; e-mail correo@ritmo.es; internet www.ritmo.es; classical music; Dir ANTONIO RODRÍGUEZ MORENO.

Qué Leer: Gran Vía de les Corts Catalanes 133, 2°, 08014 Barcelona; tel. (93) 2232136; fax (93) 4322907; e-mail queleer@hachette.es; internet www.que-leer.com; f. 1996; monthly; book news, etc. Dir JORGE DE COMINGES; circ. 80,000.

Finance

Actualidad Económica: Paseo de la Castellana 66, 3°, 28046 Madrid; tel. (91) 3373220; fax (91) 5628415; e-mail aeconomica@recoletos.es; internet www.recoletos.es/económica; f. 1958; Mon. Dir JAIME VELASCO KINDELAN; circ. 39,497.

Dinero: Pantoja 14, 28002 Madrid; tel. (91) 4327600; fax (91) 4327765; e-mail pmonsalve@negocios.com; internet www.negocios.com/dinero; weekly; business and finance; Dir MIGUEL ORMAETXEA ARROYO; circ. 35,000.

El Economista: Bárbara de Braganza 11, 1° Izqda, 28004 Madrid; tel. (91) 3197000; fax (91) 3195831; e-mail eleconomista@tsai.es; internet www.semanarioeleconomista.com; f. 1886; weekly; Dir CARLOS HUMANES FERNÁNDEZ.

Información Comercial Española—Revista de Economía: Paseo de la Castellana 162, 5°, 28046 Madrid; tel. (91) 3493627; fax (91) 3493634; 8 a year; published by Ministry of the Economy; Dir ENRIQUE VERDEGUER PUIG.

Inversión y Capital: Fuencarral 121, 6°, 28010 Madrid; tel. (91) 4442300; fax (91) 4475765; e-mail r.rubio@inverca.com; internet www.inverca.com; Dir RAFAEL RUBIO GÓMEZ-CAMINERO.

El Mundo Financiero: Peña Sacra 1, 28260 Madrid; tel. and fax (91) 8583547; e-mail mundofinanciero@nauta.es; internet www.nauta.es/mundof/; f. 1946; monthly; Dir JOSÉ LUIS BARCELÓ MEZQUITA; circ. 15,000.

Politics, Sociology, Religion, etc.

Ecclesia: Alfonso XI 4, 28014 Madrid; tel. (91) 5315400; fax (91) 5225561; e-mail ecclesia@planalfa.es; weekly; f. 1941; Dir JOSÉ ANTONIO CARRO CELADA; Propr Conferencia Episcopal Española; circ. 24,000.

Iniciativa i Treball: Gutat 7, 08002 Barcelona; tel. (93) 3010612; fax (93) 4124252; e-mail publicacions@ic-v.org; f. 1991; fortnightly; organ of Iniciativa per Catalunya–Verds; Dir JOSEP VENDRELL; circ. 6,000.

Mundo Cristiano: Paseo de la Castellana 210, 2°B, 28046 Madrid; tel. (91) 3459855; fax (91) 3590230; e-mail mundoc@edicionespalabra.es; f. 1963; monthly; Dir DARIO CHIMENO CANO; circ. 46,852.

El Nuevo Lunes de la Economía y la Sociedad: Plaza de España 18 (Torre de Madrid), 3/11, 28008 Madrid; tel. (91) 5160803; fax (91) 5160819; e-mail nuevolunes@elnuevolunes.com; internet www.elnuevolunes.com; Editor JOSÉ GARCÍA ABAD.

Política—Revista Republicana: Meléndez Valdés 33, 1°, 28015 Madrid; tel. (91) 5436930; fax (91) 5437649; e-mail ir@bitmailer.net; f. 1935; bimonthly; organ of the Izquierda Republicana; Dir PEDRO LÓPEZ ARRIBA.

Nueva Revista: Javier Ferrero 2, 28002 Madrid; tel. (91) 5199756; fax (91) 4151254; e-mail nuevarevista@tst.es; internet www.nuevarevista.net; f. 1990; 6 a year; politics, culture, art; Pres. ANTONIO FONTÁN PÉREZ.

Revista de Estudios Políticos: Plaza de la Marina Española 9, 28071 Madrid; tel. (91) 5401950; fax (91) 5419574; e-mail public@cepc.es; f. 1941; quarterly; Dirs PEDRO DE VEGA, JUAN J. SOLOZÁBAL; publ. by Centro de Estudios Politicos y Constitucionales; circ. 1,000.

Science and Medicine

Arbor: Vitruvio 8, 28006 Madrid; tel. (91) 5616651; fax (91) 5855326; e-mail arbor@csic.es; internet www.csic.es/arbor; f. 1944; monthly; science, thought and culture; publ. by Consejo Superior de Investigaciones Científicas (CSIC); Dir PEDRO GARCÍA BARRENO.

El Ecologista: Marqués de Laganés 12, 28004 Madrid; tel. (91) 5312389; fax (91) 5312611; e-mail comunicacion@ecologistasenaccion.org; internet www.ecologistasenaccion.org; quarterly; ecological issues; Dir JOSÉ LUIS GARCÍA CANO; circ. 5,000.

Gaceta Médica de Bilbao: Lersundi 9, Apdo 5073, 48080 Bilbao; tel. (94) 4233768; fax (94) 4230111; f. 1894; quarterly; official publication of the academy of medical sciences; Dir Prof. Dr. JOSÉ MARÍA SÁNCHEZ FERNÁNDEZ; circ. 5,000.

Investigación y Ciencia: Muntaner 339, Pral 1°, 08021 Barcelona; tel. (93) 4143344; fax (93) 4145413; e-mail precisa@investigacionyciencia.es; internet www.investigacionyciencia.es; f. 1976; monthly; Dir JOSÉ MARIA VADERAS GALLARDO; circ. 38,000.

Mundo Cientifico: Pérez Galdós 36, 08012 Barcelona; tel. (93) 4157374; fax (93) 2177378; monthly; Editorial Dir JOSÉ LUIS CÓRDOBA DE ÁGUILA.

Tiempos Médicos: Editores Médicos, SA, Gabriela Mistral 2, 28035 Madrid; tel. (91) 3768140; fax (91) 3739907; e-mail edimsa@edimsa.es; 10 issues per year; Dir Dr A. CHICHARRO PAPIRI; circ. 10,000.

Women's Magazines

Clara: Muntaner 40–42, 08011 Barcelona; tel. (93) 4541004; fax (93) 4545949; e-mail clara@hymsa.com; internet www.hymsa.com; f. 1992; monthly; Dir ASSUMPTA SORIA BADIA; circ. 292,990.

Cosmopolitan: Marqués de Villamagna 4, 28001 Madrid; tel. (91) 4369820; fax (91) 4358701; e-mail cosmopolitan@gyj.es; internet www.cosmopolitan.es; monthly; Dir SARAH GLATTSTEIN FRANCO; circ. 175,594.

Elle: Avda Cardenal Herrera Oria 3, 28034 Madrid; tel. (91) 7287000; fax (91) 7289135; e-mail elle@hachett.es; internet www .elle.navegalia.com; f. 1986; monthly; Dir SUSANA MARTÍNEZ VIDAL; circ. 180,000.

Elle Decoración: Avda Cardenal Herrera Oria 3, 28034 Madrid; tel. (91) 7287000; fax (91) 7289144; e-mail malvari@hachette.es; 5 a year; Dir MILAGROS ALVAREZ GORTARI.

Labores del Hogar: Muntaner 40–42, 08011 Barcelona; tel. (93) 5087000; fax (93) 4540551; e-mail labores@hymsa.com; f. 1925; monthly; home textile crafts; Dir EULALIA UBACH; circ. 96,627.

Lecturas: Muntaner 40–42, 08011 Barcelona; tel. (93) 5087000; fax (93) 4541322; e-mail lecturas@hymsa.com; f. 1921; Fri. Dir CATALINA VIDAL SERRA; Man. XAVIER ELIES; circ. 339,028.

Marie Claire: Marqués de Villamagna 4, 28001 Madrid; tel. (91) 4369800; fax (91) 5751392; e-mail cblanchuelo@gyj.es; f. 1987; monthly; Dir JOANA BONET CAMPRUBÍ; circ. 118,243.

Mía: Marqués de Villamagna 4, 28001 Madrid; tel. (91) 4369889; fax (91) 5758880; e-mail mia@gyj.es; internet www.miarevista.es; f. 1986; weekly; Dir KETTY RICO OLIVER; circ. 257,222.

Telva: Paseo de la Castellana 66, 28046 Madrid; tel. (91) 3373220; fax (91) 3373143; e-mail telva@recoletos.es; internet www.recoletos .es/telva; f. 1963; beauty, fashion, weddings, interviews, cookery and fitness; monthly; Dir NIEVES FONTANA LÍBANO; circ. 125,000.

Vogue España: Paseo de la Castellana 9–11, 28046 Madrid; tel. (91) 7004170; fax (91) 3199325; e-mail vogue@condenast.es; internet www.vogue.es; f. 1988; monthly; Dir YOLANDA SACRISTÁN; circ. 117,515.

Woman: Bailén 84, 2°, 08009 Barcelona; tel. (93) 4846600; fax (93) 2324630; e-mail woman@grupozeta.es; f. 1992; monthly; Dir INMA SEBASTIA; circ. 125,000.

Miscellaneous

Automóvil: Ancora 40, 28045 Madrid; tel. (91) 3470100; fax (91) 3470204; e-mail pubautos@mpib.es; internet www .motorpress-iberica.es; monthly; motoring; Dir FERNANDO GÓMEZ BLANCO; circ. 88,000.

Autopista: Ancora 40, 28045 Madrid; tel. (91) 3470100; fax (91) 3470135; e-mail autopista@mpib.es; internet www .motorpress-iberica.es; weekly; motoring; Dir ALBERTO MALLO; circ. 65,088.

Avión Revue: Ancora 40, 28045 Madrid; tel. (91) 3470100; fax (91) 3470152; e-mail pubavion@mpib.es; f. 1982; monthly; aeroplanes; Dir JOSÉ MARÍA PARÉS; circ. 30,000.

Boletín Oficial del Estado: Avda Manoteras 54, 28050 Madrid; tel. (91) 3841500; fax (91) 5382121; internet www.boe.es; f. 1936; successor of *Gaceta de Madrid*, f. 1661; daily except Sundays; laws, decrees, orders, etc. Dir-Gen. JULIO SEAGE MARIÑO; circ. 60,000.

Cinemanía: Progresa (Grupo Prisa) Fuencarral, 6, 3A planta, 28004 Madrid; tel. (91) 5386140; fax (91) 5222291; e-mail cinemania@ progresa.es; f. 1995; monthly; films; Dir JAVIER ANGULO; circ. 125,000.

Coche Actual: Ancora 40, 28045 Madrid; tel. (91) 3470100; fax (91) 3470119; e-mail cocheactual@mpib.es; internet www .motorpress-iberica.es; weekly; cars; Dir ARANCHA PATO; circ. 65,394.

Computerworld: Fortuny 18, 4°, 28010 Madrid; tel. (91) 3496600; fax (91) 3196104; e-mail computerworld@idg.es; internet www.idg .es/computerworld; f. 1981; weekly; also available: PCWorld, Comunicaciones World, MacWorld, Dealer World, iWorld, Lideres.com; Editor-in-Chief CARLOS DE LA IGLESIA; circ. 10,327.

Don Balón: Avda Diagonal 435, 1–2°, 08036 Barcelona; tel. (93) 2092000; fax (93) 2412358; e-mail info@donbalon.org; internet www .donbalon.com; f. 1975; weekly; sport; Dir ANTONIO CASALS (acting).

Fotogramas & Video: Gran Vía de les Corts Catalanes 133, 2°, 08014 Barcelona; tel. (93) 2232790; fax (93) 4322907; e-mail fotogramas@hachette.es; internet www.fotogramas.es; f. 1946; monthly; cinema and video; Dir ELISENDA NADAL GAÑÁN; circ. 144,000.

GQ: Paseo de la Castellana 9–11, 28046 Madrid; tel. (91) 7004170; fax (91) 3199325; e-mail gq@condenast.es; internet www.revistagq .com; monthly; men's magazine; Dir MIGUEL DE SANTOS.

El Magisterio Español: Javier Ferrero 2, 28002 Madrid; tel. (91) 5199131; fax (91) 4151124; e-mail jmoya@magisnet.com; internet

www.magisnet.com; f. 1866; Wed. education; Dir JOSÉ MARÍA DE MOYA ANEGÓN; circ. 24,200.

Man: Consejo de Ciento 425, 5°, 08009 Barcelona; tel. (93) 4846600; fax (93) 2324542; monthly; men's fashion, etc. Dir JUAN CARLOS DE LAIGLESIA GONZÁLEZ; circ. 95,782.

Motociclismo: Ancora 40, 28045 Madrid; tel. (91) 3470100; fax (91) 3470119; e-mail pubmotos@mpib.es; f. 1951; weekly; motorcycling; Dir AUGUSTO MORENO DE CARLOS; Editor MAXIMO SANT; circ. 110,000.

Nuevo Estilo: Grupo Axel Springer, Los Vascos 17, 28040 Madrid; tel. (91) 5140600; fax (91) 5140625; e-mail nuevoestilo@axelspringer .es; internet www.axelspringer.es; f. 1977; monthly; home decoration; Dir BLANCA MIQUEL; circ. 172,000.

PC Actual: San Sotero 8, 4° planta, 28037 Madrid; tel. (91) 3137900; fax (91) 3273704; e-mail fercla@bpe.es; internet www.pc-actual.com; Dir FERNANDO CLAVER.

PC World: Fortuny 18, 4°, 28010 Madrid; tel. (91) 3496600; fax (91) 3496796; e-mail pcworld@idg.es; internet www.idg.es/pcworld; f. 1988; monthly; for users of personal computers; Dir MARÍA ISABEL CAMPO.

Ser Padres Hoy: Marqués de Villamagna 4, 28001 Madrid; tel. (91) 4369800; fax (91) 5767881; e-mail publicidad@gyj.es; f. 1974; monthly; for parents; Dir JAVIER J. GARCÍA GONZÁLEZ; circ. 60,577.

Sport Life: Ancora 40, 28045 Madrid; tel. (91) 3470100; fax (91) 3470204; e-mail pubsportlife@mpib.es; internet www .motorpress-iberica.es; monthly; Editor MONTSE SALA.

Tu Bebé: Muntaner 40–42, 08011 Barcelona; tel. (93) 5087000; fax (93) 4545949; e-mail tu_bebe@hymsa.com; f. 1993; monthly; for parents; Dir PEDRO RIAÑO MARTÍNEZ; circ. 60,000.

Vinos de España: Islas Marquesas 28B, 28035 Madrid; tel. (91) 3865152; fax (91) 3860265; e-mail vinos@mundonatura.es; f. 1996; wines and viniculture; bimonthly; also trimonthly in German; Dir ALBERTO HUERTA; circ. 30,000.

NEWS AGENCIES

Agencia EFE, SA: Espronceda 32, 28003 Madrid; tel. (91) 3467100; fax (91) 3467134; e-mail efe@efe.es; internet www.efe.es; f. 1939; national and international news; 140 bureaux and correspondents abroad; sports, features, radio and television, and photographic branches; Pres. and Dir-Gen. MIGUEL ANGEL GOZALO.

Colpisa: José Abascal 56, 1°, 28003 Madrid; tel. (91) 4564600; fax (91) 4564701; f. 1972; Pres. JOSÉ MARÍA BERGARECHE; Dir ROGELIO RODRÍGUEZ.

Europa Press Noticias: Paseo de la Castellana 210, 3°, 28046 Madrid; tel. (91) 3592600; fax (91) 3503251; e-mail noticias@ europapress.es; internet www.europapress.es; Dir ANGEL EXPÓSITO MORA.

Iberia Press: Velázquez 46, 1°, 28001 Madrid; tel. and fax (91) 8155319; e-mail press-bulletin@jet.es; f. 1977; Dir JOSÉ RAMÓN ALONSO.

Mencheta: Cea Bermúdez 24, 1°, 28003 Madrid; tel. (91) 5539949; fax (91) 5340769; e-mail mencheta@jet.es; Pres. L. ENRIQUE PERÍS-MENCHETA Y RÍOS-MELIDA; Dir ARTURO MÁRMOL PERÍS MENCHETA.

Foreign Bureaux

Agence France-Presse: Paseo de Recoletos 18, 28001 Madrid; tel. (91) 4358740; fax (91) 5755380; e-mail afp.madrid@afp.com; Chief Correspondent XAVIER BARON.

Agência Lusa de Informação (Portugal): Espronceda 32, 6°, 28003 Madrid; tel. (91) 4424308; fax (91) 4421938; e-mail manuel .lopes@teleline.es; Correspondent MANUEL JOSÉ LOPES.

Agenzia Nazionale Stampa Associata (ANSA) (Italy): Vergara, 1°, 28013 Madrid; tel. (91) 5488867; fax (91) 5488989; Chief Correspondent JAVIER FERNÁNDEZ BONELLI.

AICA (Argentina): Toledo 109, 5°D, 28005 Madrid; tel. and fax (91) 3661827; e-mail arp41228@wanadoo.es; f. 1947; Correspondent ARMANDO PUENTE.

Algerie Presse Service (APS): Madrid; Correspondent YACINE SEMCH-EDDINE BENTAHAR.

Associated Press (AP) (USA): Espronceda 32, 5°, 28003 Madrid; tel. (91) 3958110; fax (91) 4423612; internet www.ap.org; Chief of Iberian services KERNAN TURNER.

Bulgarska Telegrafna Agentsia (BTA) (Bulgaria): Fernando Garrido 4, 2°B, 28015 Madrid; tel. and fax (91) 5940203; Correspondent IOSSIF DAVIDOV SOLOMONOV.

Ceibo Producciones (Chile): Cuchilleros 10, 4°B, 28005 Madrid; tel. (91) 3650210; e-mail andreapacheco@worldonline.es; Correspondent ANDREA PAOLA PACHECO GONZÁLEZ.

Deutsche Presse-Agentur (dpa) (Germany): Capitán Haya 56, 8°, 28020 Madrid; tel. (91) 5718481; fax (91) 5712192; Chief Correspondent HUBERT KAHL.

Informatsionnoye Telegrafnoye Agentstvo Rossii— Telegrafnoye Agentstvo Suverennykh Stran (ITAR—TASS) (Russia): Príncipe de Vergara 133, 2°C, 28002 Madrid; tel. and fax (91) 5632774; e-mail medved@arrakis.es; Correspondent SERGEY SEREDA.

IRNA (Iran): Padre Damián 40, 28036 Madrid; tel. (91) 4570434; fax (91) 4570414; e-mail aajavan321@hotmail.com; Correspondent ALI AKBAR JAVANFEKER.

Maghreb Arabe Presse (Morocco): Espronceda 32, 6°, 28003 Madrid; tel. (91 3467616; fax (91) 3467615; e-mail mapmad@wanadoo.es; Chief Correspondent MOHAMED BOUNDI.

Magyar Távirati Iroda (MTI) (Hungary): Taibilla 1, 4° Izqda, 03130 Santa Pola, Alicante; tel. and fax (96) 6696959; e-mail xantus@ciberia.es; Correspondent JUDIT XANTUS SZARVAS.

Notimex (Mexico): San Bernardo 63, 3°B, 28015 Madrid; tel. (91) 5214022; fax (91) 5317699; e-mail notimex@telefónica.net; internet www.notimex.com.mx; Chief Correspondent LUIS CASTRO OBREGÓN.

Prensa Latina (Cuba): Perú 23, 4°, 28820 Coslada, Madrid; tel. (91) 2318387; e-mail plmadrid@mi.madritel.es; Correspondent RAFAEL JUSTO CALCINES ARMAS.

Reuters (United Kingdom): Paseo de la Castellana 36–38, 5°, 28046 Madrid; tel. (91) 5852100; fax (91) 4359666; e-mail madrid .newsroom@reuters.com; Chief Correspondent PETER ALEXANDER SMITH.

Septimus International (Egypt): Julio Palacios 2, portal 3, 9°, 28029 Madrid; tel. and fax (91) 5721179; Correspondent ELMEHDI KAJIJI.

Tanjug (Serbia and Montenegro): Madrid; Correspondent SVETLANA BOSCOVIĆ.

Xinhua (New China) News Agency (People's Republic of China): Arturo Soria 154, Bloque 3, 1°F, 28043 Madrid; tel. (91) 4131620; fax (91) 4168543; e-mail guojibu@jet.es; Correspondent RUICHANG LIU.

PRESS ASSOCIATIONS

National Organizations

Asociación de Editores de Diarios Españoles (AEDE): Madrid; e-mail aede@idecnet.com; f. 1978; 31 mems, representing 82 daily newspapers; Pres. JESUS FERNÁNDEZ-MIRANDA Y LOZANA; Dir-Gen. IGNACIO M. BENITO GARCÍA.

Federación de Asociaciones de la Prensa de España (FAPE): Plaza del Callao 4, 7°C, 28013 Madrid; tel. (91) 5221950; fax (91) 5211573; e-mail fape@infonegocío.com; f. 1922; Pres. ALEJANDRO FERNÁNDEZ POMBO; Sec.-Gen. JOSÉ M. TORRE CERVIGNON; mems: 6,040 journalists in 45 associations.

Unión de Escritores e Periodistas Españoles: Madrid; f. 1978; journalists' asscn; Pres. ANTONIO ARIAS PIQUERAS; Sec.-Gen. ELOY S. CASTAÑARES; 4,000 mems.

Asociación de Corresponsales de Prensa Extranjera (ACPE): Monte Esquinza 41, 1°, 28010 Madrid; tel. (91) 3101433; fax (91) 3080950; e-mail acpe@nexo.es; f. 1923; foreign correspondents' asscn; Pres. MASAKO ISHIBASHI; Sec.-Gen. ANTÓN ALONSO; 150 mems.

Provincial Organizations

Barcelona

Centre Internacional de Premsa de Barcelona: Rambla de Catalunya 10, 1°, 08007 Barcelona; tel. (93) 4121111; fax (93) 3178386; e-mail cipb@periodistes.org; internet www.periodistes.org; f. 1988; Pres. CARLES SENTÍS I ANFRUNS; Sec. MONICA VIÑAS.

Bilbao

Centro Internacional de Prensa de Bilbao: Dr Achucarro 10, 1°, 48011 Bilbao; tel. and fax (94) 4168748; Pres. JOSÉ MANUEL ALONSO; Sec. BLANCA GARCÍA-EGOCHEAGA.

Madrid

Asociación de la Prensa de Madrid: Juan Bravo 6, 28006 Madrid; tel. (91) 5850010; fax (91) 5850040; f. 1895; Pres. ALEJANDRO FERNÁNDEZ POMBO; 3,130 mems.

Centro de Prensa de Madrid: Claudio Coello 98, 28006 Madrid; tel. (91) 5850052; fax (91) 5850020; Sec.-Gen. JOSÉ MARÍA LORENTE TORIBIO.

Sevilla

Asociación de la Prensa de Sevilla: Plaza de San Francisco 9, 1°, 41004 Sevilla; tel. (95) 4500468; fax (95) 4225299; e-mail aps@

asociacionprensa.org; internet www.asociacionprensa.org; f. 1909; Pres. SANTIAGO SÁNCHEZ TRAVER; Sec.-Gen. FRANCISCO GIL CHAPARRO.

Zaragoza

Centro de Prensa de Zaragoza: Cinco de Marzo 9, 50004 Zaragoza; tel. (976) 223210; fax (976) 222963; e-mail aparagon@aparagon.es; Pres. RAMÓN J. BUETAS CORONAS; Sec. ROBERTO GARCÍA BERMEJO.

Publishers

Madrid

Aguilar, SA de Ediciones: Torrelaguna 60, 28043 Madrid; tel. (91) 7449060; fax (91) 7449224; internet www.gruposantillana.com/general2.htm; f. 1923; world classics, literature, reference books, law, history, geography, cartography, political and social economics, science, medicine, psychology, technical, art, children's books, education, etc. Pres. JESÚS DE POLENCO; Dir ANA ROSA SEMPRÚN.

Alfaguara Global: Torrelaguna 60, 28043 Madrid; tel. (91) 7449060; fax (91) 7449224; internet www.alfaguara.santillana.es; f. 1960; language and literature reference; Editorial Dir AMAYA ELEZCANO.

Alianza Editorial, SA: Juan Ignacio Luca de Tena 15, 28027 Madrid; tel. (91) 3938888; fax (91) 7414343; e-mail alianza@anaya .es; internet www.alianzaeditorial.es; f. 1959; part of Grupo Anaya; advanced textbooks, fiction, general non-fiction, reference, paperbacks; Pres. JOSÉ MANUEL GÓMEZ; Gen. Man. VALERIA CIOMPI.

Ediciones Cátedra: Juan Ignacio Luca de Tena 15, 28027 Madrid; tel. (91) 3938600; fax (91) 3209129; e-mail catedra@catedra.com; internet www.catedra.com; f. 1973; part of Grupo Anaya; literature, literary criticism, history, humanities, linguistics, arts, cinema, music, feminism; Pres. JOSÉ MANUEL GÓMEZ; Man. Dir GUSTAVO DOMÍNGUEZ.

Ediciones de Cultura Hispánica: Avda de los Reyes Católicos 4, 28040 Madrid; tel. (91) 5838249; fax (91) 5838311; internet www.aea .es; f. 1943; arts, law, history, economics for circulation in Latin America; Literary and Artistic Dir ANTONIO PAPELL.

Ediciones Encuentro: Cadaceros 3, 2°, 28014 Madrid; tel. (91) 5322607; fax (91) 5322346; e-mail encuentro@ediciones-encuentro .es; internet www.ediciones-encuentro.es; f. 1978; theology, philosophy, art, history, literature.

Ediciones Morata, SL: Mejía Lequerica 12, 28004 Madrid; tel. (91) 4480926; fax (91) 4480925; e-mail morata@infornet.es; internet www.edmorata.es; f. 1920; psychology, psychiatry, pedagogics, sociology; Dir FLORENTINA GÓMEZ MORATA.

Ediciones Pirámide, SA: Juan Ignacio Luca de Tena 15, 28027 Madrid; tel. (91) 3938989; fax (91) 7423661; e-mail piramide@anaya .es; internet www.edicionespiramide.es; f. 1973; part of Grupo Anaya; scientific and technical books (business, economics and psychology; Pres. JOSÉ MANUEL GÓMEZ; Man. Dir GUILLERMO DE TOCA.

Ediciones Siruela, SA: Plaza de Manuel Becerra 15, 28028 Madrid; tel. (91) 3555720; internet www.siruela.com; f. 1982; history, literature, art, children's books, translations; Dir JACOBO FITZJAMES STUART.

Editorial Biblioteca Nueva, SL: Almagro 38, 28010 Madrid; tel. (91) 3100436; fax (91) 3198235; e-mail editorial@bibliotecanueva .com; f. 1920; literature, essays, poetry, history, psychiatry, psychology, philosophy, economy, law; Dir ANTONIO ROCHE.

Editorial Castalia: Zurbano 39, 28010 Madrid; tel. (91) 3195857; fax (91) 3102442; e-mail castalia@infornet.es; internet www.castalia .es; f. 1945; classics, literature; Pres. AMPARO SOLER GIMENO; Dir FEDERICO IBAÑEZ SOLER.

Editorial Edaf, SA: Jorge Juan 30, 1°, 28001 Madrid; tel. (91) 4358260; fax (91) 4315281; e-mail edaf@edaf.net; internet www.edaf .net; f. 1967; literature, dictionaries, occult, natural health, paperbacks; Dir-Gen. JOSÉ ANTONIO FOSSATI SEDDON.

Editorial Gredos, SA: Sánchez Pacheco 85, 28002 Madrid; tel. (91) 7444920; fax (91) 5192033; e-mail comercial@editorialgredos.com; internet www.editorialgredos.com; f. 1944; linguistics, philology, humanities, art, literature, dictionaries; Dir MANUEL OLIVEIRA CALVET.

Editorial Paraninfo, SA: Magallanes 25, 28015 Madrid; tel. (91) 4463350; fax (91) 4456218; e-mail clientes@paraninfo.es; internet www.paraninfo.es; f. 1946; technical, reference and educational; Man. MIGUEL MANGADA FERBER.

Editorial Reus, SA: Preciados 23, 28013 Madrid; tel. (91) 5213619; fax (91) 5312408; e-mail reus@editorialreus.es; internet www

.editorialreus.es; f. 1852; law, literature; Pres. Jesús M. Pinto Varela.

Editorial Tecnos, SA: Juan Ignacio Luca de Tena 15, 28027 Madrid; tel. (91) 3938550; fax (91) 7426631; e-mail mmoreno@anaya.es; f. 1947; law, social and political science, philosophy and economics; Pres. José Manuel Gómez; Man. Manuel González Moreno.

La Esfera de los Libros, SL: Avda de Alfonso XIII 1, bajos, 28002 Madrid; tel. (91) 2960200; fax (91) 2960206; e-mail laesfera@esferalibros.com; internet www.esferalibros.com; history, journalism, biography; Dir José María Calvín.

Espasa-Calpe, SA: Carretera de Irún, Km 12, 200, Apdo 547, 28049 Madrid; tel. (91) 3589689; fax (91) 3589505; internet www.espasa.com; f. 1926; part of Grupo Planeta; encyclopaedias, history, dictionaries, literature, biographies, paperbacks, etc. Dir-Gen. Jorge Hernández Aliques.

Fondo de Cultura Económica de España, SA de CV: Sede Editorial, Librería México, Fernando el Católico 86, 28015 Madrid; tel. (91) 5432960; fax (91) 5498652; e-mail jglopezfce@terra.es; f. 1974; pocket collections, sciences, literature, children's books, history; Dir Juan Guillermo López.

Grupo Anaya, SA: Juan Ignacio Luca de Tena 15, 28027 Madrid; tel. (91) 3938600; fax (91) 7426631; e-mail cga@cga.es; internet www.anaya.es; f. 1959; reference, sciences, arts, literature, education; Pres. José Manuel Gómez.

Grupo Editorial Bruño: Maestro Alonso 21, 28028 Madrid; tel. (91) 3610448; fax (91) 3613133; e-mail info@editorial-bruno.es; internet www.editorial-bruno.es; f. 1897; education, children's books; Dir-Gen. José Antonio Camacho.

Grupo Editorial Luis Vives: Xauduró 25, 28034 Madrid; tel. (91) 3344883; fax (91) 3344882; internet www.grupoeditorialluisvives.com; children's books, textbooks, reference under the imprints Edelvives, Baula (Catalan), Alhucema, Ibaizabal (Basque) and Tambre (Galician).

Iberoamericana de Libros y Ediciones, SL: Amor de Dios 1, E-28014 Madrid; tel. (91) 4293522; fax (91) 4295397; e-mail info@iberoamericanalibros.com; internet www.ibero-americana.net; f. 1996; owned by Verveut Verlagsgesellschaft (Frankfurt); academic books.

Narcea, SA de Ediciones: Dr Federico Rubio y Galí 9, 28039 Madrid; tel. (91) 5546484; fax (91) 5546487; e-mail narcea@narceaediciones.es; internet www.narceaediciones.es; f. 1968; humanities, pedagogy, psychology, spiritualism and textbooks; Man. Dir Ana María de Miguel Carro.

Nivola Libros y Ediciones, SL: Avda de las Viñuelas 31, 1°B, Tres Cantos, 28760 Madrid; tel. (91) 8045817; fax (91) 8049317; e-mail nivola@nivola.com; internet www.nivola.com; science.

Siglo XXI de España, Editores, SA: Príncipe de Vergara 78, 28006 Madrid; tel. (91) 5623723; fax (91) 5615819; e-mail sigloxxi@sigloxxieditores.com; internet www.sigloxxieditores.com; f. 1967; pocket collections, reference, history, social sciences; Pres. Pablo García-Arenal.

SM Grupo Editorial: Joaquín Turina 39, 28044 Madrid; tel. (91) 4228800; fax (91) 5089927; f. 1939; textbooks, children's, reference, travel, literature; Man. Dir Jorge Delkáder Teig.

Susaeta Ediciones, SA: Campezo s/n, 28022 Madrid; tel. (91) 3009100; fax (91) 3009110; f. 1963; children's books; Dir José Ignacio Susaeta Erburu.

Visor Libros, SL: Isaac Peral 18, 28015 Madrid; tel. (91) 5492655; e-mail visor@visor-libros.com; internet www.visor-libros.com; poetry, linguistics, philology.

Barcelona

Actar: Roca i Batlle 2, 08023 Barcelona; tel. (93) 4187759; fax (93) 4186707; e-mail info@actar-mail.com; internet www.actar.es; architecture, photography, art, design.

Barcino Editorial: Montseny 9, 08012 Barcelona; tel. (93) 2186888; fax (93) 2186888; e-mail ebarcino@editorialbarcino.com; f. 1924; Catalan classics, general; Dir Andreu Morta i Mora.

Carroggio, SA de Ediciones: Pelai 28-30, 08001 Barcelona; tel. (93) 4949922; fax (93) 4949923; e-mail carroggio@carroggio.com; internet www.carroggio.com; f. 1911; art, literature, reference books, multimedia; Man. Dir Santiago Carroggio Guerim.

EDEBE: Paseo San Juan Bosco 62, 08017 Barcelona; tel. (93) 2037408; fax (93) 2054670; e-mail editorial@edebe.com; internet www.edebe.com; f. 1968; children's and educational publications; Man. José Aldunate Jurío.

EDHASA (Editora y Distribuidora Hispano-Americana, SA): Avda Diagonal 519–521, 2°, 08029 Barcelona; tel. (93) 4949720; fax (93) 4194584; e-mail info@edhasa.es; internet www.edhasa.es; f. 1946;

contemporary fiction, non-fiction, pocket books, historical fiction and non-fiction, crime, philosophy; Editorial Dir and Man. Daniel Fernández.

Ediciones Destino, SA: Provenza 260, 5°, 08008 Barcelona; tel. (93) 4967001; fax (93) 4967002; e-mail edicionesdestino@stl.logiccontrol.es; internet www.edestino.es; f. 1942; general fiction, history, art, children's books.

Ediciones Martínez Roca, SA: Provenza 260, 6°, 08008 Barcelona; tel. (93) 4967012; fax (93) 4967014; e-mail dtorello@ediciones-martinez-roca.es; internet www.planeta.es; f. 1965; fiction, New Age, spirituality, sport, how-to books, psychology, psychiatry; Dir Laura Falcó.

Ediciones Obelisco: Pedro IV 78, 4°, 5, 08005 Barcelona; tel. (93) 3098525; fax (93) 3098523; e-mail info@edicionesobelisco.com; internet www.edicionesobelisco.com; f. 1981; general fiction and non-fiction; Dirs Rosa Sallán, Juli Peradejordi.

Ediciones Omega, SA: Platón 26, 08006 Barcelona; tel. (93) 2010599; fax (93) 2097362; e-mail omega@ediciones-omega.es; internet www.ediciones-omega.es; f. 1948; biology, field guides, geography, geology, agriculture, photography; Chair. Antonio Paricio; Mans Antonio; and, Gabriel Paricio.

Ediciones Polígrafa, SA: Crta Nal. 152, Km 22, Can Volart, 08150 Parets del Valles, Barcelona; tel. (93) 4882381; fax (93) 5031097; e-mail poligrafa@cecot.es; f. 1960; arts, leisure; Man. Dir Juan de Muga Dòria.

Editorial Acervo, SL: Ronda General Mitre 200, 08006 Barcelona; tel. (93) 2122664; fax (93) 4174425; e-mail acervo25@hotmail.com; f. 1954; law, literature, history, science fiction; Man. Dir Ana Perales Herrero.

Editorial Aedos, SA: Consejo de Ciento 391, 08009 Barcelona; tel. (93) 4883492; fax (93) 4877659; e-mail barcelona@mundiprensa.es; internet www.mundiprensa.es; f. 1939; agriculture and stock-breeding, veterinary surgery, biography, art and tourism; specialists in Catalan works; Dir Cristina Concellón Rodríguez.

Editorial Anagrama, SA: Pedró de la Creu 58, 08034 Barcelona; tel. (93) 2037652; fax (93) 2037738; e-mail anagrama@anagrama-ed.es; internet www.anagrama-ed.es; f. 1969; foreign literature in translation; Editor and Dir Jorge Herralde.

Editorial Ariel, SA: Avda Diagonal 662–664, 7°, 08034 Barcelona; tel. (93) 4967030; fax (93) 4967032; e-mail editorial@ariel.es; internet www.ariel.es; f. 1942; social and political science, economics, history, sciences and law; Editorial Dir José Luis Castillejo.

Editorial Bosch, SA: Comte d'Urgell 51 bis, Apdo 928, 08011 Barcelona; tel. (93) 4521050; fax (93) 3236736; e-mail bosch@bosch.es; internet www.bosch.es; f. 1934; law, social science, classics; Man. Albert Ferré.

Editorial Casanovas, SA: Montserrat de Casanovas 49, 08032 Barcelona; tel. (93) 4290335; fax (93) 4070479; f. 1956.

Editorial Claret, SA: Roger de Llúria 5, 08010 Barcelona; tel. (93) 3010887; fax (93) 3174830; e-mail editorial@claret.es; internet www.claret.es; f. 1926; Dirs Claretian Fathers; religion, children's books, Catalan grammar and general books, slides, cassettes and videos, *Audio-visuals Claret*.

Editorial Gustavo Gili, SA: Rosellón 87–89, 08029 Barcelona; tel. (93) 3228161; fax (93) 3229205; e-mail info@ggili.com; internet www.ggili.com; f. 1902; photography, art, architecture, design; Dirs Gabriel Gili, Mónica Gili.

Editorial Herder, SA: Provença 388, 08025 Barcelona; tel. (93) 4762626; fax (93) 2073448; e-mail editorialherder@herder-sa.com; internet www.herder-sa.com; f. 1944; literature, language, theology, sociology, psychology.

Editorial Hispano-Europea, SA: Bori y Fontestá 6, 08021 Barcelona; tel. (93) 2018500; fax (93) 4142635; e-mail hispanoeuropea@hispanoeuropea.com; f. 1954; technical, scientific, sport, pet books and reference; Propr and Man. Dir Jorge J. Prat Rosal.

Editorial Juventud, SA: Provenza 101, 08029 Barcelona; tel. (93) 4441800; fax (93) 4441802; e-mail editorialjuventud@retemail.es; internet www.editorialjuventud.es; f. 1923; general fiction, biography, history, art, music, reference, dictionaries, travel books, children's books, paper-backs; Dir Luis Zendrera.

Editorial Molino: Calabria 166, 08015 Barcelona; tel. (93) 2260625; fax (93) 2266998; e-mail molino@menta.net; internet www.editorialmolino.com; f. 1933; crime, children's books, reference books; Dir Luis Antonio del Molino Jover.

Editorial Reverté, SA: Loreto 13–15, Local B, 08029 Barcelona; tel. (93) 4193336; fax (93) 4195189; e-mail j.reverte@teleline.es; internet www.reverte.com; f. 1947; engineering, general science, university and scientific books; Dir Javier Reverte Mascó.

Editorial Seix Barral: Avda Diagonal 662–664, 7°, 08034 Barcelona; e-mail editorial@seix-barral.es; internet www.seix-barral.es; f. 1911; literature.

Editorial Selecta Catalònia: Ronda de Sant Pere 3, 08010 Barcelona; tel. (93) 3172331; fax (93) 3024793; f. 1946; books in Catalan; Man. Sebastià Borràs i Tey.

Editorial Teide, SA: Viladomat 291, 08029 Barcelona; tel. (93) 4104507; fax (93) 3224192; e-mail info@editorialteide.es; internet www.editorialteide.es; f. 1942; educational, scientific, technical and art; Man. Dir Federico Rahola.

Empresa Editorial Herder, SA: Provenza 388, 08025 Barcelona; tel. (93) 4762626; fax (93) 2073448; e-mail editorialherder@herder-sa.com; internet www.herder-sa.com; f. 1943; philosophy, pedagogy, sociology; philology, psychology, theology, history, languages, dictionaries; Dir Dr Raitund Herder.

Grupo Editorial Ceac, SA: Perú 164, 08020 Barcelona; tel. (93) 2660247; fax (93) 3084392; e-mail info@ceacedit.com; internet www.ceacedit.com; f. 1957; textbooks, education, leisure; Man. Jaime Pintanel.

Grupo Planeta, SA: Córcega 273–277, 08008 Barcelona; tel. (93) 2285800; fax (93) 2177140; f. 1948; popular, literature, children's; Pres. José Manuel Lara Hernández.

Grup 62, SA: Peu de la Creu 4, 08001 Barcelona; tel. (93) 4437100; fax (93) 4437130; e-mail correu@grup62.com; internet www.grup62.com; f. 1962; Man. Pere Sureda.

Instituto Gallach de Librería y Ediciones, SL: Milanesat 21–23, 08017 Barcelona; tel. (93) 2802020; fax (93) 2045958; e-mail presid@oceano.com; f. 1924; illustrated and reference books, encyclopaedias; Chair. José Lluis Monreal; Gen. Man. José María Marti Costa.

LEDA (Las Ediciones de Arte): Riera San Miguel 37, 08006 Barcelona; tel. (93) 2379389; fax (93) 2155273; f. 1940; artistic books; Propr and Man. Dir Daniel Basilio Bonet.

Marcombo, SA de Boixareu Editores: Gran Vía de les Corts Catalanes 594, 08007 Barcelona; tel. (93) 3180079; fax (93) 3180508; e-mail jm.boixareu@marcombo.es; internet www.marcombo.es; f. 1945; reference, sciences, textbooks; Pres. and Man. Dir Josep M. Boixareu Vilaplana.

Montagud Editores: Ausiàs Marc 25, 1°, 08010 Barcelona; tel. (93) 3182082; fax (93) 3025083; e-mail montagud@montagud.com; internet www.montagud.com; f. 1906; business; Chair. Francisco Antoja Giralt.

Noguer y Caralt Editores, SA: Santa Amèlia 22, bajos, 08034 Barcelona; tel. (93) 2801399; fax (93) 2801993; e-mail noguer-caralt@mx2.redestb.es; f. 1993; includes Editorial Noguer and Luis de Caralt Editores; dictionaries, children's, philosophy, art; Man. Emilio Ardévol.

Oceáno Grupo Editorial, SA: Milanesat 21–23, 08017 Barcelona; tel. (93) 2802020; fax (93) 2045958; e-mail presid@oceano.com; internet www.oceano.com; f. 1950; general; Chair. José Lluis Monreal; Gen. Man. José María Martí Costa.

Oikos-Tau, SL—Editorial—Gráficas: Barcelona; f. 1963; economics, science, geography, history, marketing, management, agriculture, sociology, urban planning, education, school-books; Man. Jordi García-Jacas.

Plaza y Janés, Editores, SA: Travessera de Gràcia 47–49, 08021 Barcelona; tel. (93) 3660300; fax (93) 2002219; f. 1959; fiction and non-fiction, reference; owned by Mondadori, SA; Dir-Gen. Juan Pascual.

Random House Mondadori, SA: Aragó 385, 08013 Barcelona; tel. (93) 4767100; fax (93) 4767121; e-mail comercial@grijalbo.com; internet www.grijalbo.com; f. 2001 by merger; Gen. Man. Ricardo Cavallero.

Salvat Editores, SA: Mallorca 45, 08029 Barcelona; tel. (93) 4955700; fax (93) 4955710; e-mail infosalvat@salvat.com; internet www.salvat.com; f. 1923; art, history, dictionaries, encyclopaedias, English courses, music; Pres. Jean-Louis Lisimachio.

SPES Editorial, SL: Aribau 197–9, 3°, 08021 Barcelona; tel. (93) 2413505; e-mail spes@speseditorial.com; internet www.vox.es; www.larousse.es; encyclopaedias, dictionaries, atlases, linguistics; f. 2000; by merger of Larousse Editorial and Bibliograf.

Tusquets Editores, SA: Cesare Cantú 8, 08023 Barcelona; tel. (93) 2530400; fax (93) 4176703; internet www.tusquets-editores.es; art, general fiction and non-fiction.

Vicens Vives, SA: Avda Sarriá 130, 08017 Barcelona; tel. (93) 2523700; fax (93) 2523711; e-mail e@vicensvives.es; internet www.vicensvives.es; f. 1961; school and university, educational; Dir Rosario Rahola de Espona.

Other Towns

Ediciones Deusto, SA: Alameda Recalde 27, 7°, 48009 Bilbao; tel. (94) 4356161; fax (94) 4356166; e-mail deustomail@ediciones-deusto.es; internet www.ediciones-deusto.es; f. 1960; diaries, newsletters, management and law books; Man. Dir Enrique Iglesias Montejo.

Durvan, SA de ediciones: Colón de Larreátegui 13–3°, 48001 Bilbao; tel. (94) 4230777; fax (94) 4243832; e-mail editorial@durvan.com; internet www.durvan.com.

Ediciones Mensajero, SAU: Sancho de Azpeitia 2, 48014 Bilbao; tel. (94) 4470358; fax (94) 4472630; e-mail mensajero@mensajero.com; internet www.mensajero.com; f. 1915; arts, biography, theology, psychology, pedagogy, social science and paperbacks; Dir Angel Antonio Pérez Gómez.

Ediciones Universidad de Navarra, SA (EUNSA): Plaza de los Sauces 1 y 2, 31010 Barañain (Navarra); tel. (948) 256850; fax (948) 256854; e-mail eunsa@cin.es; internet www.eunsa.es; f. 1967; architecture, natural sciences, law, history, social sciences, theology, philosophy, medical, engineering, journalism, education, economics and business administration, biology, literature, library science, paperbacks, etc; Chair. Dámaso Rico.

Edicións Xerais de Galicia, SA: Doutor Marañón 12, 36211 Vigo; tel. (986) 214888; fax (986) 201366; e-mail xerais@xerais.es; internet www.xerais.es; f. 1979; literature, education, history and reference books in Galician.

Editorial Aranzadi SA: Ctra Aoiz, Km 3.5, 31486 Elcano; tel. (948) 297297; fax (948) 297200; e-mail clientes@aranzadi.es; internet www.aranzadi.es; f. 1929; law; Dir Juan Carlos Franquet.

Editorial Desclée de Brouwer, SA: Henao 6, 3° Dcha, 48009 Bilbao; tel. (94) 4246843; fax (94) 4237594; e-mail info@desclee.com; internet www.edesclee.com; f. 1945; general non-fiction in Spanish and Basque; Pres. Javier Gogeaskoetxea.

Editorial Everest, SA: Carretera León-Coruña, Km 5, Apdo 339, 24080 León; tel. (987) 844200; fax (987) 844202; e-mail marketing@everest.es; internet www.everest.es; f. 1957; general; Dir-Gen. José Antonio López Martínez.

Editorial Galaxia: Reconquista 1, 36201 Vigo; tel. (986) 432100; fax (986) 223205; e-mail galaxia@editorialgalaxia.es; internet www.editorialgalaxia.es; f. 1950; literary works, reviews, popular, children's, Galician literature; Dir Víctor F. Freixanes.

Editorial Marfil, SA: San Eloy 17, 03804 Alcoy; tel. (96) 5523311; fax (96) 5523496; e-mail editorialmarfil@editorial.marfil.com; internet www.editorialmarfil.com; f. 1947; textbooks, psychology, pedagogy, university texts, literature; Man. Verónica Cantó Doménech.

Editorial Nerea, SA: Juan de Laborda 2, Bajo, 20280 Hondarribia, Guipúzcoa; tel. (943) 645743; fax (943) 646027; e-mail nerea@nerea.net.

PUBLISHERS' ASSOCIATIONS

Federación de Gremios de Editores de España (Federation of Publishers' Associations of Spain): Cea Bermúdez 44, 2° Dcha, 28003 Madrid; tel. (91) 5345195; fax (91) 5352625; e-mail fgee@fge.es; internet www.federacioneditores.org; Pres. Jordi Úbeda; Exec. Dir Antonio Avila.

Associació d'Editors en Llengua Catalana (Association of Publishers in Catalan Language): València 279, 1°, 08009 Barcelona; tel. (93) 2155091; fax (93) 2155273; e-mail associacio.editors@retemail.es; internet www.catalanpublishers.org; Pres. Manuel Sanglas Muchart; Sec.-Gen. Segimon Borràs.

Gremi d'Editors de Catalunya: València 279, 1°, 08009 Barcelona; tel. (93) 2155091; fax (93) 2155273; e-mail info@gremieditorscat.es; internet www.gremieditorscat.es; Pres. Josep M. Puig de la Bellacasa; Sec.-Gen. Segimon Borràs.

Gremio de Editores de Euskadi (Euskadiko Editoreen Elkartea): Bilbao; internet www.editores-euskadi.com; Pres. Javier Gogeascoechea Arrien; Man. Dir Andrés Fernández Seco.

Gremio de Editores de Madrid: Santiago Rusiñol 8, 28040 Madrid; tel. (91) 5544745; fax (91) 5532553; e-mail editoresmadrid@editoresmadrid.org; internet www.editoresmadrid.org; f. 1977; Pres. Juan de Isasa González de Ubieta; Sec.-Gen. Amalia Martín Pereda.

Broadcasting and Communications

TELECOMMUNICATIONS

The telecommunications market was fully deregulated in December 1998.

Airtel: Avda Europa, Parque Empresarial La Moraleja, 28108 Alcobendas (Madrid); internet www.airtel.es; f. 1998; controlled by Vodafone AirTouch; mobile services; Pres. JUAN ABELLÓ.

ALÓ Comunicaciones, SA: Príncipe de Vergara 112, 28002 Madrid; tel. (91) 5634717; internet www.alo.es; f. 1997; Contact ALEJANDRO RIVAS-MICOUD.

BT España: Salvador de Madariaga 1–3, 28027 Madrid; tel. (91) 270800; fax (91) 2708888; internet www.bt.es.

Grupo Auna: Avda Diagonal 579–585, 08014 Barcelona; tel. (93) 5020000; internet www.auna.es; telecommunications group; f. 2000; by merger of Endesa, Unión Fenosa, Telecom Italia and various financial companies; operates: the cable telecommunications providers Aragón de Cable, Cabletelca, Cable i Televisió de Catalunya, Madritel, Supercable de Andalucía, Supercable Sevilla, Supercable Almería; and the broadcasting and telecommunications providers Amena (mobile telecommunications) and Retevisión; Pres. LUIS ALBERTO SALAZAR-SIMPSON BOS; Dir-Gen. MIGUEL IRABURU ELIZONDO.

Jazztel, SA: Avda de Europa 14, La Moraleja, 28108 Alcobendas; tel. (91) 2917200; fax (91) 2917201; e-mail contact@jazztel.com; internet www.jazztel.com; Pres. MASSIMO PRELZ.

Telefónica, SA: Beatriz de Bobadilla 3, 9°, 28040 Madrid; tel. (91) 5849107; fax (91) 5347972; internet www.telefonica.es; f. 1924; privatized in 1997; monopoly on telephone services removed in 1998, announced in 2002 that would it merge its digital services with the television company Sogecable (see below); provides services in 41 countries; Pres. CÉSAR ALIERTA; CEO FERNANDO ABRIL-MARTORELL; comprises the following telecommunications companies:

Atento: call centre company.

Emergia: controlling company of the submarine fibre optic network that connects Latin America and the USA.

Global Terra Networks: global internet company with 122 websites in over 40 countries; includes Terra-Lycos and Terra Mobile.

Telefónica B2B, Inc.: business and e-commerce development.

Telefónica Cable, SA: cable communications company.

Telefónica DataCorp, SAU: corporate services.

Telefónica Internet, SA: internet services.

Telefónica Latinoamericana: Latin American telephone operations company.

Telefónica Media (Admira): production and distribution company; controls Endemol Entertainment, Antena 3, Via Digital and Onda Cero Radio.

Telefónica Móviles: worldwide mobile communications.

Uni 2: José Ortega y Gasset 100, 28006 Madrid; tel. (91) 2521200; internet www.uni2.es; f. 1998; owned by France Télécom; land line telecommunications; Exec. Pres. VICTORIA HERNÁNDEZ VALCÁRCEL.

Xfera Móviles, SA: Ribera del Sena, s/n, Campo de las Naciones, 28042 Madrid; tel. (91) 1315200; fax (91) 1315202; e-mail xferacontact@xfera.com; internet www.xfera.es; began operations 2001; mobile communications.

In March 2000 the Spanish Government awarded 3G ('third generation') licences to the three existing mobile operators, the fourth being granted to the Xfera consortium. The 3G technology, also known as Universal Mobile Telephone Services (UMTS), permits users to receive and deliver internet data and video images on cellular handsets. By mid-2000 there were some 20,025m. mobile telephones in use in Spain. In 2001 the Government issued provisional licences for the resale of mobile telecommunications services to the following companies: Affinalia, Aló Comunicaciones, Aviron, Globatel, Primus, Timón, Vallehermoso Telecom and British Telecom.

Regulatory Authorities

Comisión del Mercado de las Telecomunicaciones (CMT): Alcalá 37, 28014 Madrid; tel. (91) 3724300; fax (91) 3724205; e-mail cmt@cmt.es; internet www.cmt.es; f. 1996; Pres. JOSÉ MARÍA VÁZQUEZ QUINTANA.

Secretaría de Estado de Telecommunicaciones y para la Sociedad de la Información: Palacio de Comunicaciones, Alcalá 50, 28071 Madrid; tel. (91) 3461500; internet www.setsi.mcyt.es.

BROADCASTING

Grupo Radio Televisión Española (RTVE): Edif. Prado del Rey, 28223 Pozuelo de Alarcón, Madrid; tel. (91) 5815461; fax (91) 5815454; e-mail direccion.comunicacion@rtve.es; internet www.rtve.es; state organization; controls and co-ordinates radio and television; incorporates: Televisión Española, Televisión Española Internacional, Televisión Española Temática, Radio Nacional de España, Instituto Oficial de Radio y Televisión and the Orquesta

Sinfónica y Coro; Dir-Gen. JOSÉ ANTONIO SÁNCHEZ DOMÍNGUEZ; Sec.-Gen. MARCELINO ALONSO LÓPEZ.

Independent Companies

Compañía de Radio y Televisión de Galicia (CRTVG): Apdo 707, San Marcos, 15780 Santiago de Compostela; tel. (981) 540640; fax (981) 540619; f. 1985; Galician language station; Dir-Gen. FRANCISCO CAMPOS FREIRE.

Corporació Catalana de Ràdio i Televisió (CCRTV): Avda Dioagonal 477, 7°, 08036 Barcelona; tel. (93) 4444800; fax (93) 4444824; e-mail direccio@ccrtv.es; internet www.ccrtv.es; f. 1983; Catalan language station; three television channels and four radio stations; Dir-Gen. VICENÇ VILLATORIO I LAMOLLA; Sec.-Gen. JOSEP BADIA I SÁNCHEZ.

Euskal Irrati Telebista (EITB)/Radiotelevisión Vasca: 48215 Iurreta (Vizcaya); tel. (94) 6031000; fax (94) 6031095; e-mail info@eitb.com; internet www.eitb.com; f. 1982; Basque station; two television channels, two international television channels and five radio stations; Dir-Gen. ANDONI ORTUZAR ARRUABARRENA.

Onda Regional de Murcia: Avda Libertad 6, Bajo, 30009 Murcia; tel. (968) 200000; fax (968) 230850; e-mail ondaregional,or@carm.es; internet www.ondaregionalmurcia.es; Dir-Gen. JUAN MANUEL MÁIQUEZ ESTÉVEZ.

Ràdiotelevisió Valenciana (RTVV): Polígon Accés Ademús s/n, 46100 Burjassot (Valencia); tel. (96) 3183000; fax (96) 3183001; internet www.rtvv.es; f. 1984; Dir-Gen. JOSÉ VICENTE VILLAESCUSA.

Radio Televisión de Andalucía (RTVA): Crta San Juan de Aznalfarache–Tomares, Km 1.3, 41920 San Juan de Aznalfarache; tel. (95) 5054600; fax (95) 5054937; e-mail comunicacion@rtva.es; internet www.canal.sur.es; Dir-Gen. EDUARDO ABELLÁN GARCÍA.

Radio Televisión Madrid (RTVM): Paseo del Príncipe 3, Ciudad de la Imagen, 28223 Pozuelo de Alarcón (Madrid); tel. (91) 5128200; fax (91) 5128300; Dir-Gen. FRANCISCO GIMÉNEZ-ALEMÁN.

Radiotelevisión Canaria (RTVC): Avda Bravo Murillo 5, Edif. Mapfre, 1°, 38003 Santa Cruz de Tenerife; tel. (922) 470200; fax (922) 273173; internet www.tvcanaria.tv; f. 1997; broadcasts in the Canaries; Dir-Gen. FRANCISCO MORENO GARCÍA.

Radiotelevisión Castilla-La Mancha (RTVCM): Berna 1, 4°, 45005 Toledo; tel. (925) 288600; fax (925) 211429; e-mail comunicacion@rtvcm.es; internet www.rtvcm.es; Dir-Gen. JORDI GARCÍA CANDAU.

Retevisión: Avda Diagonal 579—585, 08014 Barcelona; tel. (93) 5020000; fax (93) 5022850; internet www.retevision.es; privatized in 1997; in 1998 acquired internet providers Redes TB, Servicom and Xarxa Cirnet; services include: cable and digital terrestrial television, radio broadcasting, fixed-line and mobile telephones, satellite communications and the internet; operates digital terrestrial company Onda Digital.

Federation

Federación de Asociaciones de Radio y Televisión de España: Evaristo San Miguel 8, 28008 Madrid; tel. (91) 5481222; fax (91) 5593630; Pres. JUAN VAN HALEN ACEDO; Sec.-Gen. FEDERICO SÁNCHEZ AGUILAR.

RADIO

RNE: Casa de la Radio, Prado del Rey, 28223 Pozuelo de Alarcón (Madrid); tel. (91) 5817000; fax (91) 5183240; e-mail secretario_general.rne@rtve.es; internet www.rtve.es/rne; broadcasts Radio 1, Radio Clásica, Radio 3, Radio 4, Radio 5 Todo Noticias; 17 regional stations; Dir-Gen. JOSÉ ANTONIO SENTÍS CASTAÑO; Man. Dir JULIO BLANCO NOVILLO.

Radio Exterior de España (REE): Apdo 156.202, 28080 Madrid; tel. (91) 3461081; fax (91) 3461815; e-mail dir_radioexterior.rne@rtve.es; overseas service of RNE; broadcasts in 10 languages; includes a world service in Spanish; Dir FRANCISCO JAVIER GARRIGÓS.

Independent Stations

Ambiente Musical, SA: Paseo de la Castellana 210, 10°, 28046 Madrid; tel. (91) 3454000; fax (91) 3591321; e-mail estudio@musicam.net; Dir-Gen. MANEL SALLÉS CARCELLER.

Antena Boreal Radio: Real 8, 28340 Valdemoro (Madrid); tel. (91) 8095321; fax (91) 8082434; e-mail antenaboreal@nsi.es; Dir CRISTINA FONTÁN OÑATE.

Cadena 40 Principales: Gran Vía 32, 8°, 28013 Madrid; tel. (91) 3470705; fax (91) 5317370; internet www.los40.es; Dir JAUME BARÓ GARRIGA.

Cadena 100: Alfonso XI 4, 28014 Madrid; tel. (91) 5951200; fax (91) 5317517; e-mail casoliva@cadena100.es; internet www.cadena100.es; Dir JORDI CASOLIVA.

Cadena M80: Gran Vía 32, 8°, 28013 Madrid; tel. (91) 3470798; fax (91) 5228693; Dir MANUEL DAVILA MORENO.

Cadena Dial: Gran Vía 32, 8°, 28013 Madrid; tel. (91) 3470880; fax (91) 5211753; Dir FRANCISCO HERRERA.

Cadena Europa FM (Medipress, SA): Bueso Pineda 7, 28043 Madrid; tel. (91) 4134361; fax (91) 4137175; e-mail europafm@europafm.com; internet europafm.com; Pres. FRANCISCO GAYA GONZÁLEZ.

Cadena Flaix FM: Passeig de Gràcia 54, 08007 Barcelona; tel. (93) 5055555; fax (93) 4880775; Dirs-Gen. CARLES CUNÍ, MIQUEL CALÇADA.

Cadena Herri Irratia/Radio Popular: Garibai 19, 20004 San Sebastián; tel. (943) 423644; fax (943) 427821; e-mail info@herri-irratia.com; internet herri-irratia.com; Dir GORKA BARAÑANO.

Cadena NGRadio (NGR)/Cadena Nervión-Gorbea-Rabel Radio: Hurtado de Amézaga 27, 17°, 48008 Bilbao (Vizcaya); tel. (94) 4433317; fax (94) 4448302; Dir-Gen. ENRIQUE CAMPOS LED.

Cadena Ona Catalana, SA: Aragón 390–394, 2°, 08013 Barcelona; tel. (93) 2449990; fax (93) 2459459; e-mail onacatalana@onacatalana.com; internet www.onacatalana.com; Dir-Gen. JOSEP PUIGBÓ.

Cadena Ondacero Radio Voz Galicia: Ronda de Outeiro 1, Bajo, 15009 A Coruña; tel. (981) 180600; fax (981) 180477; e-mail mantilla@radiovoz.com; Man. Dir MANUEL MANTILLA FERNÁNDEZ.

Cadena de Ondas Populares Españolas/Radio Popular, SA (COPE): Alfonso XI 4, 3°, 28014 Madrid; tel. (91) 5951200; fax (91) 5322008; e-mail postmaster@cope.es; internet www.cope.es; f. 1959; numerous medium-wave and FM stations; Pres. BERNARDO HERRÁEZ RUBIO; Dir-Gen. JENARO GONZÁLEZ DEL YERRO VALDÉS.

Cadena Radio Club 25: Gütemberg 3–16, 6°, 08224 Terrassa (Barcelona); tel. (93) 7806166; fax (93) 7803358; e-mail radioclub25@radioclub25.com; internet www.radioclub25.com; Dir FRANCISCO JAVIER SALILLAS PINILLOS; Man. Dir JOSÉ MANUEL SALILLAS GARCÍA.

Cadena Radio España/Radio España Madrid: Manuel Silvela 9, 28010 Madrid; tel. (91) 4475300; fax (91) 5938413; internet www.radioes.es; Pres. and Dir-Gén. JOSÉ ANTONIO SÁNCHEZ.

Cadena Radio Estudio: Pasaje de la Radio 1, 28100 Alcobendas (Madrid); tel. (91) 6531199; fax (91) 6533072; e-mail radioestudio@futurnet.es; internet www.radioestudio.com; Dir-Gen. ROMÁN BEITIA ALONSO.

Cadena Radiolé: Gran Vía 32, 8°, 28013 Madrid; tel. (91) 3470886; Dir MANUEL DÁVILA MORENO.

Cadena Sinfo Radio: Gran Vía 32, 8°, 28013 Madrid; tel. (91) 3470808; fax (91) 5228693.

Cadena TOP Radio España: Manuel Silvela 9, 28010 Madrid; tel. (91) 4475300; fax (91) 4477026; internet www.topradio.es; Pres. JOSÉ ANTONIO SÁNCHEZ.

Canal-3 Radio Bilbao: Gordóniz 44, 12°, 48002 Bilbao; tel. (94) 4101156; fax (94) 4444054; e-mail topbilbao@topbilbao.com; internet www.topbilbao.com; Dir RICARDO FONTANES MATO.

Canal 28 Producciones, SL: Sao Paulo 40, 2°, 35008 Las Palmas de Gran Canaria; tel. and fax (928) 475126; e-mail radioeconomia@telecan.es; Pres. JOSÉ MIGUEL GONZALO RODRÍGUEZ.

Catalunya Ràdio, SRG, SA: Avda Diagonal 614–616, 08021 Barcelona; tel. (93) 3069200; fax (93) 3069201; e-mail correo@catradio.com; internet www.catradio.com; f. 1983; run by Catalan autonomous govt; four channels: Catalunya Ràdio, Catalunya Música, Catalunya Informació, Catalunya Cultura; Dir EUGENI CABANES I DURAN.

Compañía de Radiodifusión Intercontinental, SA (INTER): Modesto Lafuente 42, 28003 Madrid; tel. (91) 5544603; fax (91) 5331302; Dir-Gen. FERNANDO SERRANO-SUÑER POLO.

COMRàdio: Pavelló Cambó, Recinte de la Maternitat, Travessera de les Corts 131–159, 08028 Barcelona; tel. (93) 5080600; fax (93) 5080810; e-mail comradio@comradio.com; internet www.comradio.com; Dir-Gen. JORDI LLONCH MASSANÉS; Dir of Programmes JOSEP MARIA FRANCINO.

Eusko Irratia: Miramón Pasealekua 172, 20014 San Sebastián; tel. (943) 012300; fax (943) 012295; e-mail beloki@eitb.com; run by Basque autonomous govt; broadcasts on FM and MW; also stations in Bilbao (Radio Euskadi) and Vitoria (Radio Vitoria); Dir ODILE KRUZETA.

Grupo Pavesa Comunicación, SL—Radio Ondas Riojanas: Sabto Domingo 5, 26580 Arnedo; tel. (941) 383350; fax (941) 383383; e-mail ondarioja@ondarioja.com; internet www.ondarioja.com; Pres. PEDRO VEGA HERNÁNDEZ.

Muinmo, SL: Apolonio Morales 6-8-10, 28036 Madrid; tel. (91) 3536017; fax (91) 3536019; Dir-Gen. MIGUEL ANGEL MONTERO QUEVEDO.

Onda Cero Radio (OCR): José Ortega y Gasset 22–24, 28006 Madrid; tel. (91) 436400; fax (91) 436101; e-mail ondacero@ondacero.es; internet www.ondacero.es; owned by Telefónica, SA; Pres. JAVIER GONZÁLEZ FERRARI; Dir-Gen. JOSÉ LUIS OROSA ROLDAN.

Onda Rambla Catalunya: Diagonal 441, 1°, 08036 Barcelona; tel. (93) 4448000; fax (93) 4106662; e-mail ondarrambla@ondarrambla.es; internet www.ondarrambla.es; Pres. LUIS DEL OLMO MAROTE; Dir-Gen. FRANCESC X. OLONA CABASSÉS.

Radio Autonomía Madrid, SA: Ciudad de la Imagen, Paseo del Príncipe 3, 28223 Pozuelo de Alarcón (Madrid); tel. (91) 5128679; fax (91) 5128670; e-mail telemadrid@telemadrid.com; internet www.telemadrid.es; f. 1985; broadcasts on 101.3 and 106.0 MHz; Dir JOSE ESCALERA TERÁN.

Ràdio Autonomia Valenciana, SA/Ràdio 9: Avda Blasco Ibáñez 136, 46022 Valencia; tel. (96) 3183600; fax (96) 3183601; internet www.rtvv.es; Dir ANACLETO RODRÍGUEZ MOYANO.

Radio ECCA: Avda Mesa y López 38, Apdo 994, 35080 Las Palmas de Gran Canaria; tel. (928) 257400; fax (928) 207395; e-mail info@radioecca.org; internet www.radioecca.org; adult education; Dir-Gen. JUAN LUIS VEZA IGLESIAS.

Radio Galega, SA (RG): San Marcos, 15780 Santiago de Compostela; tel. (981) 540940; fax (981) 540919; internet www.crtvg.es/rtg/hisradio.htm; f. 1985; run by Galician autonomous govt; Man. Dir LUIS PÉREZ FERNÁNDEZ.

Radio Surco-Castilla La Mancha: Concordia 14, Bajo C, 13700 Tomelloso (Ciudad Real); tel. (926) 505959; fax (926) 505961; e-mail r.surco@retemail.es; internet www.surcastv.com; Dir RAFAEL ARROCHA NIZ.

Sociedad Española de Radiodifusión (SER): Gran Vía 32, 28013 Madrid; tel. (91) 3470700; fax (91) 3470709; internet www.cadenaser.es; f. 1924; 235 regional stations; Pres. JESÚS DE POLANCO; Dir-Gen. MANUEL SABIDO DURÁN.

Digital Radio

On 10 March 1999 two digital radio licences were awarded for the frequencies MF-1 and MF-2. MF-1 was controlled by Cope, Intereconomia, Recoletos and El Mundo, while MF-2 was controlled by SER, Onda Rambla-Planeta, Onda Cero, Radio España, Onda Digital and Prensa Española. MF-1 began broadcasting in Madrid and Barcelona on 25 July 2000.

Radio Association

Asociación Española de Radiodifusión Comercial (AERC): Plaza Independencia 2, 4° Dcha, 28001 Madrid; tel. (91) 4357072; fax (91) 4356196; e-mail aerc@retemail.es; groups nearly all commercial radio stations; Pres. IGNACIO BAEZA; Sec.-Gen. JAVIER GONZALEZRUIZ FERRARI.

TELEVISION

Legislation relating to the ending of TVE's monopoly and the regulation of private TV stations was approved in April 1988.

Televisión Española (TVE): Edif. Prado del Rey, Pozuelo de Alarcón, 28223 Madrid; tel. (91) 3464968; fax (91) 3463055; e-mail secretaria_dir.tve@rtve.es; internet www.tve.es; broadcasts on TVE-1 and La 2; production centres in Barcelona and Las Palmas de Gran Canaria and 15 regional centres; broadcasts to Europe and the Americas on Canal Internacional; Dir JUAN MENOR SENDRA; Sec.-Gen. JORDI BOSCH I MOLINET.

Independent Stations

Antena 3 Televisión: Avda de Isla Graciosa s/n, San Sebastian de los Reyes, Madrid; tel. (91) 6230500; fax (91) 6548517; e-mail antena3tv@antena3tv.com; internet www.antena3tv.com; f. 1989; private commercial national network; owned by Telefónica, SA; Pres. LUIS BLASCO BOSQUED; Sec.-Gen. ADOLFO LEFORT.

Canal 9—Televisió Autonómica Valenciana (TVV): Polígon Accés Ademús, 46100 Burjassot (Valencia); tel. (96) 3183000; fax (96) 3183001; e-mail wmaster@rtvv.es; internet www.rtvv.es; commenced regular transmissions Oct. 1989; second channel commenced operations in Oct. 1997; Dir GENOVEVA REIG.

Canal Sur Televisión, SA: Carretera San Juan de Aznalfarache, Apdo 132, 41920 San Juan de Aznalfarache, Sevilla; tel. (95) 5607600; fax (95) 5054740; e-mail csalinas@cica.es; internet www.canalsur.es; commenced transmissions in 1989; regional station for Andalucía; controlled by RTVA; Dir-Gen. RAFAEL CAMACHO.

Euskal Telebista—ETB (TV Vasca): 48215 Iurreta (Vizcaya); tel. (94) 6031000; fax (94) 6031095; e-mail sarasol@eitb.com; internet www.eitb.com; f. 1982; broadcasts in Basque Country in Basque language on ETB-1 and in Spanish on ETB-2; mem. of EITB; Dir BINGEN ZUPIRIA GOROSTIDI; Dir of Programmes PELLO SARASOLA.

Sogecable, SA: Avda de los Artesanos 6, 28760 Tres Cantos, Madrid; tel. (91) 7367000; internet www.sogecable.es; f. 1989; private commercial national network; services include satellite and digital television, film rights production and management, film distribution and exhibition, thematic channels, sports rights production and management, and internet services; operates Canal+, Canal Satélite Digital, CNN+, Compañia Independiente de Televisión, Gestsport, Sogecine, the Plus.es internet portal; announced in 2002 that it would merge with Via Digital (see below); Pres. JESÚS DE POLANCO GUTIÉRREZ; Sec.-Gen. IÑIGO DAGO.

Grupo Telecinco: Crta de Irún, Km 11,700, 28049 Madrid; tel. (91) 155555; e-mail oinf@telecinco.es; internet www.telecinco.es; f. 1990; private commercial national network; joint owned by Grupo Mediaset (Italy), Grupo Correo de Comunicación, Ice Finance (The Netherlands); Pres. ALEJANDRO ECHEVARRÍA.

Televisió de Catalunya, SA: Carrer de la TV3, s/n, 08970 Sant Joan Despi, Barcelona; tel. (93) 4999333; fax (93) 4730671; internet www.tvcatalunya.com; f. 1983; broadcasts on TV-3, Canal 33 and K3 in Catalan over north-eastern Spain; controlled by CCRTV; Dir JOAN OLIVER.

Televisión de Galicia (TVG): Apdo 707, San Marcos, 15820 Santiago de Compostela; tel. (981) 540640; fax (981) 540719; e-mail crtvg@crtvg.es; internet www.crtvg.es; f. 1985; broadcasts in Galician; controlled by CRTVG; Man. Dir ANGEL QUINTANILLA LOUZAO.

Televisión Autonomía Madrid, SA (Telemadrid): Paseo del Príncipe de España 1, 28223 Pozuelo de Alarcón (Madrid); tel. (91) 5128200; fax (91) 5128300; e-mail correo@telemadrid.com; internet www.telemadrid.es; commenced transmissions in 1989; controlled by RTVM; Cultural channel, laOtra, commenced transmission in March 2001; Dir-Gen. FRANCISCO GIMÉNIZ ALEMÁN; Man-Dir FERNANDO JERÉZ.

Other Satellite, Cable and Digital Television

By early 1996 more than 1.1m. Spanish homes were receiving programmes by satellite. These companies used the Hispasat and Astra satellites. Legislation relating to the regulation of cable television received the Government's approval in late 1996. The first licences were awarded during 1997. The country is divided into 43 operating sectors. Each of these is served by Telefónica de España, and 36 sectors are also served by one of the other cable companies operating in Spain, offering television, telephone and internet access. By 2000 more than 2m. Spanish homes and businesses were served by cable telecommunications and some 900,000 received digital television. In 1999 the first licence for a terrestrial digital network was awarded. By 2000 there were more than 100 satellite, cable and digital television broadcasters in Spain. Many of these were operated by existing broadcasting companies. Others include:

Aragón de Cable, SA (Able): Aragón; internet www.able.es; cable; part of Grupo Auna.

Canal Satélite Digital (CSD): Gran Vía 32, 4°, 28013 Madrid; tel. (91) 201515; fax (91) 213121; e-mail abonados@cplus.es; internet www.plus.es; f. 1996; digital and satellite; announced in May 2002 that it would merge with Via Digital (see below); Dir-Gen. SANTIAGO TAPIA.

Euskaltel: Vizcaya; internet www.euskaltel.es; cable; operator for Vizcaya; part of Grupo Auna.

Hispasat: Gobelas 41, 28023 Madrid; tel. (91) 7102540; fax (91) 3729000; e-mail comunicacion@hispasat.es; internet www.hispasat.com; satellite system; part of Grupo Auna, Telefónica, BBVA and Eutelsat; Pres. PEDRO ANTONIO MARTÍN MARÍN; CEO JACINTO GARCÍA PALACIOS.

Madritel: Obenque 4, Madrid; internet www.madritel.es; cable and digital; part of Grupo Auna.

Menta: Barcelona; internet www.menta.net; cable; part of Grupo Auna.

Multicanal: Saturno 1, Pozuelo de Alarcón, 28224 Madrid; tel. (91) 7141080; fax (91) 3515884; e-mail multicanal@multicanaltps.com; internet www.multicanaltps.com; f. 1996; cable; operates five thematic channels.

El Mundo R: Apdo 2096, 15080 A Coruña; fax (981) 911505; e-mail fala-con-R@mundo-R.net; internet www.mundo-r.com; cable; operator for Galicia;; part of Grupo Auna.

Net TV: Madrid; f. 2001; digital.

ONO: Basauri 7–9, Urbanización La Florida, 28023 Madrid; tel. (91) 7089300; fax (91) 7089337; internet www.ono.es; cable Pres. EUGENIO GALDÓN.

Paquete Digital RTVE: Pozelo de Alarcón, 28223 Madrid; tel. (91) 5817000; fax (91) 5815476; e-mail direccion.comunicacion@rtve.es; internet www.rtve.es; digital; operates five thematic channels; part of RTVE.

Retecal: Bajada al Molino 15, 09400 Aranda de Duero (Burgos); tel. (947) 500828; fax (947) 508885; e-mail info-aranda@retecal.es; internet www.retecal.es; cable; operator for Castilla y León.

Retena: Crta Zaragoza Km 3, 31191 Cordovilla (Navarra); tel. (948) 070707; e-mail info@retena.es; internet www.retena.es; cable; operator for Navarra.

Reterioja: Piqueras 38–40, 26006 Logroño (La Rioja); tel. (941) 585858; internet www.reterioja.es; cable; operator for La Rioja.

Retevisión: Avda Diagonal 579–585, 08014 Barcelona; tel. (93) 5020000; fax (93) 5022850; internet www.retevision.es; cable, digital and satellite; operates digital terrestrial company Onda Digital; part of Grupo Auna.

Supercable: Andalucía; e-mail saccliente@supercable.es; internet www.supercable.es; cable; part of Grupo Auna.

Telecable: Marqués de Teverga 20, Oviedo (Asturias); tel. (900) 222111; e-mail info@telecable.es; internet www.telecable.es; cable; operator for Asturias.

Telecom Canarias: internet www.canariastelecom.com; f. 1998 as Cabletelca, SA; cable; part of Grupo Auna.

Telefónica Cable, SA: Calle Virgilio 2, Edif. 2, planta 2°, 28223 Pozuelo de Alarcón (Madrid); tel. (91) 5129510; e-mail cac@tcable.es; internet www.telefonica-cable.com; f. 1997; cable; operates in all sectors.

Veo TV: Madrid; f. 2001; 25.5% owned by Recoletos, 25.5% owned by Unedisa; digital.

Via Digital: Edif. 1, Virgilio 2, Ciudad de la Imagen, Crta de Boadilla del Monte, Km 2, 200, Pozuelo de Alarcón, 28223 Madrid; tel. (91) 5129200; fax (91) 5129262; e-mail viadigital@viadigital.net; internet www.viadigital.net; f. 1997; digital; owned by Telefónica, announced in May 2002 that it would merge with Canal Satélite Digital (see above); Pres. LUIS ABRIL.

Associations

Agrupación de Operadores de Cable (AOC): f. 1998 by CYC Madrid, Retecal, Telecable and Grupo Cable; group of cable telecommunications operators; Dir JESÚS PELEGRÍN.

Promoción e Identificación de Servicios Emergentes de Telecomunicaciones Avanzadas (PISTA): government initiative for the promotion and identification of emerging advanced telecommunications.

Finance

(amounts in pesetas unless stated otherwise; cap. = capital, res = reserves, dep. = deposits, br. = branch, m. = million)

BANKING

Central Bank

Banco de España: Alcalá 50, 28014 Madrid; tel. (91) 3385000; fax (91) 5310059; e-mail bde@bde.es; internet www.bde.es; f. 1829; granted exclusive right of issue in 1874; nationalized 1962; granted a degree of autonomy in 1994; cap. €1.4m., res €10,071.8m., dep. €39,111.5m. (Dec. 2000); Gov. JAIME CARUANA; 52 brs.

Principal Commercial and Development Banks

Altae Banco: Calle Montesquinza, 48, 28010 Madrid; tel. (91) 3915380; fax (91) 3915415; f. 1983 as Banco de Crédito y Ahorro, changed to current name 1995; Pres. MIGUEL BLESA; Gen. Man. JOSÉ IGNACIO AYUSO.

Banca March, SA: Avda Alejandro Rosselló 8, 07002 Palma de Mallorca; tel. (971) 779100; fax (971) 779187; e-mail divinter@bancamarch.es; internet www.bancamarch.es; f. 1926; cap. €29.2m., res €285.9m., dep. €2,933.9m. (Dec. 2001); Pres. JOSÉ CARLOS MARCH DELGADO; Man Dir FRANCISCO VERDÚ PONS; 190 brs.

Banco de Andalucía: Fernández y González 4, 41001 Sevilla; tel. (95) 4594736; fax (95) 4594835; internet www.bancoandalucia.es; f. 1844; cap. €16.3m., res €484.1m., dep. €3,648.0m. (Dec. 2001); Pres. MIGUEL DE SOLÍS Y MARTÍNEZ CAMPOS; Gen. Man. FRANCISCO FERNÁNDEZ DOPICO; 298 brs.

Banco Atlántico: Avda Diagonal 407 bis, Apdo 424, 08008 Barcelona; tel. (93) 4020100; fax (93) 2188317; internet www.batlantico.es; f. 1901 as Banca Nonell; changed name as above in 1946; cap. €125.6m., res €370.1m., dep. €7,977.9m. (Dec. 2001); Chair. ABDULLA S. AL-HUMAIDHI; 284 brs.

Banco Bilbao Vizcaya Argentaria (BBVA): Paseo de la Castellana 81, 28046 Madrid; tel. (91) 3746000; fax (91) 3746202; internet www.bbva.es; f. 1999 through merger; absorbed Banca

Catalana, Banco del Comercio and Banco de Negocios Argentaria in 2000; cap. €1,566.0m., res €13,568.8m., dep. €256,463.1m. (Dec. 2001); Pres. Francisco González Rodríguez; Chief Exec. José Ignacio Goirigolzarri Tellaeche.

Banco de Castilla: Plaza de los Bandos 10, 37002 Salamanca; tel. (923) 290000; fax (923) 211902; f. 1915; cap. €26.0m., res €251.0m., dep.€ 1,775.5m. total assets €2,409.3m. (Dec. 2001); Gen. Man. José Bravo Jiménez; 197 brs.

Banco Cooperativo Español, SA: Virgen de los Peligros 6, 28013 Madrid; tel. (91) 5956700; fax (91) 5956800; internet www.cajarural .com; f. 1990; cap. €72.3m., res €86.0m., dep. €5,547.5m. (Dec. 2001); Chair. Jose Luis Palacios; Gen. Man. Javier Petit Asumendi; 3,671 brs.

Banco Español de Crédito (Banesto): Gran Vía de Hortaleza 3, 28043 Madrid; tel. (91) 3383100; fax (91) 3381883; e-mail uninternac@banesto.es; internet www.banesto.es; f. 1902; cap. €1,335.6m. res €732.8m., dep. €36,542.1m. (Dec. 2001); Chair. Ana Patricia Botín-Sanz de Sautuola y O'Shea; CEO Federico Outon del Moral; 1,909 brs.

Banco de Galicia: Policarpo Sanz 23, 36202 Vigo (Pontevedra); tel. (986) 822100; fax (986) 822101; f. 1918; cap. 1,521m., res 26,436m., dep. 216,872m. (Dec. 1998); total assets 1,990,646m. (Dec. 2001); Gen. Man. Francisco Pardo Martínez; 132 brs.

Banco Guipuzcoano: Avda de la Libertad 21, 20004 San Sebastián; tel. (943) 418100; fax (943) 418337; e-mail bgintnal@bancogui .com; internet www.bancogui.es; f. 1899; cap. €31.2m., res €196.8m., dep. €4,565.4m. (Dec. 2001); Pres. José María Aguirre González; Gen. Man. Juan Luis Arrieta; 209 brs.

Banco Herrero: Fruela 11, 33007 Oviedo; tel. (985) 5968080; fax (985) 5968221; f. 1911; part of Banco Sabadell Group; cap. €23.1m., res €205.2m., dep. €3,423.5m. (Dec. 2001); Chair. Ignacio Herrero Alvarez; Chief Exec. Man. Francisco Vallejo Vallejo; 256 brs.

Banco Luso Español, SA: María de Molina 39, 28006 Madrid; tel. (91) 3099000; fax (91) 5641730; internet www.grupocgde.com; f. 1969; cap. €50.5m., res €5.3m., dep. €2,036. 6m. (Dec. 2001); Chair. Carlos Prieto Traguelho; Man. Dir Mateo Ruiz-Oriol; 21 brs.

Banco Mapfre, SA: Edif. Mapfre, Carretera Pozuelo de Alarcón–Majadahonda s/n, 28220 Majadahonda; tel. (91) 5812500; fax (91) 5812503; f. 1840; cap. 17,253m., res 9,594m., dep. 229,729m. (Dec. 1998); Chair. Luis Leguina Cebreiros; CEO and Gen. Man. José María García Alonso.

Banco Pastor, SA: Edif. Pastor, Cantón Pequeño 1, 15003 La Coruña; tel. (981) 127600; fax (981) 210301; internet www .bancopastor.es; f. 1776; cap. €54.5m., res €423.10m., dep. €8,622.5m. (Dec. 2001); Chair. José Maria Arias Mosquera; Exec. Vice-Chair. Vicente Arias Mosquera; 442 brs.

Banco Popular Español: Velázquez 34 (esquina a Goya), 28001 Madrid; tel. (91) 5207000; fax (91) 5783274; internet www .bancopopular.es; f. 1926; absorbed Banco Popular Industrial (Eurobanco), 1995; cap. €108.6m., res € 1,921.4m., dep. 32,526.8m. (Dec. 2001); Co-Pres Luis Valls Taberner, Javier Valls Taberner; 1,835 brs.

Banco de Sabadell: Plaza de Catalunya 1, 08201 Sabadell; tel. (93) 7289289; fax (93) 7270606; e-mail info@bancsabadell.com; internet www.bancsabadell.com; f. 1881; cap.€102.0m., res €2,232.9m., dep. €22,037.5m. (Dec. 2001); part of Banco Sabadell Group; Chair. and CEO Josep Oliu; Gen. Man. José Permanyer; 910 brs; An online unit, Activobank, was formed with the Portuguese bank, Banco Comercial Portugues, in May 2001.

Banco Urquijo: Príncipe de Vergara 131, 28002 Madrid; tel. (91) 3372000; fax (91) 3372096; internet www.bancourquijo.es; f. 1870; 89.68% owned by Kredietbank SA (Luxembourg); cap. €92.7m., res €130.1m., dep. €4,850.0m. (Dec. 2001); Pres. Ferdinand Verdonck; CEO Alfonso Alvarez Tolcheff; 58 brs.

Banco de Valencia: Pintor Sorolla 2–4, 46002 Valencia; tel. (96) 3984500; fax (96) 3984570; f. 1900; cap. €87.4m., res €238.0m., dep. €5,102.3m. (Dec. 2001); Pres. and Chair. Julio de Miguel Aynat; Gen. Man. Domingo Parra Soria; 253 brs.

Banco Zaragozano: Coso 47–49, 50003 Zaragoza; tel. (976) 470303; fax (976) 470358; internet www.bancozaragozano.es; e-mail ainternational@bancozaragozano.es; f. 1910; cap. €90.0m., res €209.5m., dep. €4,633.6m. (Dec. 2001); Chair. Alberto de Alcocer Torra; Man. Dir Felipe Echeverria Herrerias; 362 brs.

Bankinter, SA: Paseo de la Castellana 29, 28046 Madrid; tel. (91) 3397500; fax (91) 3397540; e-mail international@bankinter.es; internet www.ebankinter.com; f. 1965; finances industrial and business dealings with medium- and long-term loans and investments; cap.€112.9m., res €644.4.4m., dep. €19,015.5m. (Dec. 2001); Pres. Juan Arena de la Mora; 253 brs.

Barclays Bank SA: Plaza de Colón 1, 28046 Madrid; tel. (91) 3361000; fax (91) 3361134; internet www.barclays.es; f. 1979 as

Banco de Valladolid, name changed in 1982; cap. €86.2m., res €178.7m., dep. €6,243.2m. (Dec. 2000); Chair. C. Martínez de Campos; Man. Dir Jacobo Gonzalez-Robatto; 178 brs.

Deutsche Bank SAE: Avda Diagonal 446, 08006 Barcelona; tel. (93) 5818181; fax (93) 5818544; internet www.deutsche-bank.es; f. 1950; cap. €67.4m., res €372.7m., dep. €8,730.5m. (Dec. 2001); Chair. Carl von Boehm-Bezig; Vice-Chair. and CEO Juan Carlos Garay; 277 brs.

Instituto de Crédito Oficial (ICO): Paseo del Prado 4, 28014 Madrid; tel. (91) 5921600; fax (91) 5921700; e-mail ico@ico.es; internet www.ico.es; f. 1971; state credit bank; Pres. Ramón Aguirre.

Santander Central Hispano (BSCH): Plaza de Canalejas 1, 28014 Madrid; tel. (91) 5581111; fax (91) 5219691; internet www .gruposantander.com; f. 1999; through merger as Banco Santander Central Hispano; changed name as above in Sept. 2001; cap. €2,280.1m., res €15,544.3m., dep. €271,731.3m. (2000); acquired Brazilian bank, Banespa, in 2000; Chairs Emilio Botín-Sanz de Sautuola y García de los Ríos, José María Amusátegui; 8,848 brs.

Savings Banks

Bilbao Bizkaia Kutxa: Gran Vía 30–32, 48009 Bilbao; tel. (94) 4017000; fax (94) 4017208; e-mail info@bbk.es; internet www.bbk.es; f. 1907; res €1,478.7m., dep. €11,200.8m. (Dec. 2001); Chair. and CEO José Ignacio Berroeta; 282 brs.

Caixa de Aforros de Vigo, Ourense e Pontevedra (CAIXANOVA): Avda García Barbon 1–3, 36201 Vigo; tel. (986) 282200; fax (986) 828238; e-mail internacionalcx@caixanova.com; internet www.caixanova.com; f. 1929 as Caixa de Vigo e Ourense; merged with Caixa de Pontevedra in 2000 and changed name as above; cap. €0.01m., res €597.3m., dep. €8,025.8m. Pres. and Chair. Ramón Cornejo Molins; 376 brs.

Caixa d'Estalvis de Catalunya: Plaza Antonio Maura 6, 08003 Barcelona; tel. (93) 4845000; fax (93) 4845141; e-mail secretaria .general@caixacatalunya.es; internet www.caixacatalunya.es; f. 1926; res €862.5m., dep. €26,095.0m. (Dec. 2001); Pres. Antoni Serra Ramoneda; Gen. Man. Josep María Loza; 936 brs.

Caixa d'Estalvis de Sabadell: Gràcia 17, 08201 Sabadell (Barcelona); tel. (93) 7286700; fax (93) 7286555; e-mail info@caixasabadell .es; internet www.caixasabadell.com; f. 1859; res €230.0m., dep. €3,574.0m. Pres. Manuel Grau Gasulla; Gen. Man. Pere Rifà Pujol; 222 brs.

Caixa d'Estalvis de Tarragona: Plaza Imperial Tarraco 9–11, 43005 Tarragona; tel. (977) 299200; fax (977) 299250; e-mail butia@ caixatarragona.es; internet www.caixatarragona.es; f. 1949; cap. and res €187,2m., dep. €2,882m. (Dec. 2001); Pres. Gabriel Ferrate Pascual; Gen. Man. Rafael Jene Villagrasa; 277 brs (Dec. 2001).

Caixa d'Estalvis de Terrassa: Ramble d'Ègara 350, Apdo 217, 08221 Terrasa; tel. (93) 7397700; fax (93) 7397777; f. 1877; res €184.8m., dep. €3,163.9m. (Dec. 2001); Pres. Oriol Badia Tobella; Gen. Man. Enric Mata Tarrago; 164 brs.

Caja de Ahorros de Asturias (CAJASTUR): Plaza de la Escandalera 2, 33003 Oviedo; tel. (98) 5102222; fax (98) 5215649; e-mail extranjero@cajastur.es; internet www.cajastur.es; f. 1945; res €435.3m., dep. €5,639.1m. Chair., Pres. and CEO Manuel Menendez Menendez; 211 brs.

Caja de Ahorros de Galicia/Caixa Galicia: Rúa Nueva 30, 15003 A Coruña; tel. (981) 188000; fax (981) 188001; internet www .caixagalicia.es; f. 1978; res €808.0m., dep. €18,872.1m. (Dec. 2001); Pres. José Ramón Docal Labaen; 670 brs.

Caja de Ahorros de la Inmaculada de Aragón: Paseo Independencia 10, 50004 Zaragoza; tel. (976) 718100; fax (976) 718347; e-mail cai@cai.es; internet www.cai.es; f. 1905; cap. 70,936m. (2000); Pres. Fernando Gil Martínez; Gen. Man. Luis Calvera Serrano; 198 brs.

Caja de Ahorros del Mediterráneo (CAM): San Fernando 40, 03007 Alicante; tel. (96) 5905000; fax (96) 5905044; internet www .cam.es; f. 1976; cap. €3.0m., res €974.9m., dep. €16,549.8m. (Dec. 2001); Chair. Vicente Sala Belló; Gen. Man. Roberto López Abad; 803 brs.

Caja de Ahorros y Monte de Piedad de las Baleares 'Sa Nostra': Cl Ter 16, 07001 Palma de Mallorca; tel. (971) 171717; fax (971) 171784; e-mail sanostra@sanostra.es; res 37,354.0m., dep. 624,904.0m. (Dec. 2000); Chair. Miquel Pocovi Juan; Gen. Man. Pedro Batle Mayo; 142 brs.

Caja de Ahorros y Monte de Piedad del Círculo Católico de Obreros de Burgos: Avda de los Reyes Católicos 1, 09005 Burgos; tel. (947) 288200; fax (947) 288210; internet www.cajacirculo.es; f. 1909; res €238.0m., dep. €2,173.6m. (Dec. 2001); Chair. Juan Manuel Velázquez Ruiz; 157 brs.

Caja de Ahorros y Monte de Piedad de Gipuzkoa y San Sebastián/Gipuzkoa eta Donstiako Aurrezki Kutxa: Garibay

15, Apdo 1389, 20004 San Sebastián; tel. (943) 411000; fax (943) 426006; e-mail infokutxa@kutxa.es; internet www.kutxa.es; f. 1896; cap. €180.3m., res €1,042.6m., dep. €7,846.6m. (Dec. 2001); Chair. FERNANDO SPAGNOLO; Gen. Mans JESÚS MARÍA ITURRIOZ, XABIER ALKORTA; 188 brs.

Caja de Ahorros y Monte de Piedad de Madrid: Pz Celenque 2, 28013 Madrid; tel. (91) 3792000; fax (91) 4239454; internet www .cajamadrid.es; f. 1869; res 460,106m., dep. 6,630,412m. (Dec. 1998); Pres. MIGUEL BLESA DE LA PARRA; 1,790 brs.

Caja de Ahorros y Monte de Piedad de Navarra: Avda de Carlos III 8, 25, 31002 Pamplona; tel. (948) 208208; fax (948) 224179; e-mail can@can.es; internet www.can.es; f. 1921 as Caja de Ahorros de Navarra; merged with Caja de Ahorros Municipal de Pamplona in 2000 and changed name as above ; res €581.4m., dep. €5,901.4m. (Dec. 2001); Pres. MIGUEL SANZ SESMA; Gen. Man. ENRIQUE GOÑI BELTRÁN DE GARIZURIETA; 164 brs.

Caja de Ahorros y Monte de Piedad de Zaragoza, Aragón y Rioja 'IBERCAJA': Plaza del Paraíso 2, 50008 Zaragoza; tel. (976) 767718; fax (976) 211847; internet www.ibercaja.es; f. 1876; res 153,662m., dep. 2,244,185m. (Dec. 2001); Chair. MANUEL PIZARRO; Gen. Man. AMADO FRANCO; 765 brs.

Caja de Ahorros de Murcia: Gran Vía Escultor Salzillo 23, 30005 Murcia; tel. (968) 361600; fax (968) 306160; internet www .cajamurcia.es; f. 1965; res 21,635m., dep. 428,538m. (Dec. 1994); Pres. RAMÓN OJEDA VALCARCEL; Gen. Man. CARLOS EGEA KRAUEL; 318 brs.

Caja de Ahorros y Pensiones de Barcelona 'La Caixa': Avda Diagonal 621–629, 08028 Barcelona; tel. (93) 4046000; fax (93) 3395703; internet www.lacaixa.es; f. 1990; res €5,260.8m., dep. €69,078.5m. (Dec. 2001); Chair. JOSEP VILARASAU; Pres. and CEO ISIDRO FAINÉ; 4,524 brs.

Caja de Ahorros de Valencia, Castellón y Alicante/Caixa d'Estalvis de València, Castelló i Alacant (BANCAJA): Pintor Sorolla, 8, 46002 Valencia; tel. (96) 3875500; fax (96) 3527550; internet www.bancaja.es; f. 1878; res €935.8m., dep. €22,507,1m. Chair. JULIO DE MIGUEL AYNAT; Gen. Man. JOSÉ FERNANDO GARCÍA CHECA; 751 brs.

Caja Duero: Plaza de los Bandos 15–17, 37002 Salamanca; tel. (923) 279300; fax (923) 270680; internet www.cajaduero.es; f. 1881 as Caja de Ahorros y Monte Piedad de Salamanca; changed name as above in 1997; res €505.8m., dep. €9,374.0; Pres. and Chair. SEBASTIAN BATTANER; 558 brs.

Caja España: Ordoño II 17, 24001 León; tel. (987) 292500; fax (987) 231026; e-mail buzon@cajaespana.es; internet www.cajaespana.es; f. 1900; cap. 2m. (Dec. 2000), res €711.9m., dep. 10,660.9m. (Dec. 2001); Chair. MARCIAL MANZANO PRESA; Gen. Man. EVARISTO DEL CANTO CANTO; 538 brs.

Caja Laboral Popular (S Coop. de Crédito Ltda): Paseo José María Arizmendiarrieta s/n, Apdo 34, 20500 Mondragón, Guipúzcoa; tel. (943) 719500; fax (943) 719786; e-mail cajalaboral.net@ cajalaboral.es; internet www.cajalaboral.es; f. 1959; cap. €246.2m., res 601.5m., dep 7,292.7m. (Dec. 2001); Pres. JUAN M. OTAEGUI MURUA; Gen. Man. JUAN JOSÉ ARRIETA SUDUPE; 300 brs.

Confederación Española de Cajas de Ahorros (CECA): Alcalá 27, 28014 Madrid; tel. (91) 5965000; fax (91) 5965742; e-mail admin@ceca.es; internet www.ceca.es; f. 1928; national asscn of savings banks; cap. €30.1m., res €293.3m., dep. €7,310.8m. (Dec. 2001); Chair. JUAN RAMÓN QUINTÁS SEOANE; Gen. Man. J. A. OLAVARREITA; 47 affiliates, 19,297 brs.

Montes de Piedad y Caja de Ahorros de Ronda, Cádiz, Almería, Málaga y Antequera (Unicaja): Avda Andalucia 10–12, 29007 Málaga; tel. (952) 138000; fax (952) 611349; e-mail info@ personal.unicaja.es; internet www.unicaja.es; f. 1991; res. 132,534m., dep. 1,627,113m. (Dec. 2000); Pres. BRAULIO MEDEL CAMARA; Gen. Man. MIGUEL ANGEL CABELLO JURADO; 740 brs.

Banking Associations

Asociación Española de Banca Privada (AEB): Velázquez 64–66, 28001 Madrid; tel. (91) 5777015; fax (91) 5777022; f. 1977; Pres. JOSÉ LUIS LEAL MALDONADO; Sec. MANUEL TORRES ROJAS.

Fondo de Garantía de Depósitos (FGD): José Ortega y Gasset 22, Madrid; tel. (91) 4316645; f. 1977; deposit guarantee fund; Pres. GONZALO GIL GARCÍA.

STOCK EXCHANGES

Bolsa de Barcelona: Paseo de Gracia 19, 08007 Barcelona; tel. (93) 4013555; fax (93) 4013525; e-mail estudios@borsabcn.es; internet www.borsabcn.es; f. 1915; Pres. HORTALÀ I ARAU.

Bolsa de Bilbao: José M. Olabarri 1, 48001 Bilbao; tel. (94) 4034400; fax (94) 4034430; e-mail bolsabilbao@bolsabilbao.es; internet www.bolsabilbao.es; f. 1890; Chair. JOSÉ LUIS MARCAIDA; CEO JOSÉ LUIS DAMBORENEA.

Bolsa de Madrid: Plaza de la Lealtad 1, 28014 Madrid; tel. (91) 5891161; fax (91) 5312290; e-mail internacional@bolsamadrid.es; internet www.bolsamadrid.es; f. 1831; 49 mems; Chair. and CEO ANTONIO ZOIDO.

Bolsa de Valores de Valencia: Libreros 2 y 4, 46002 Valencia; tel. (96) 3870100; fax (96) 3870133; e-mail mjose.medialdea@ bolsavalencia.es; internet www.bolsavalencia.es; f. 1980; Vice-Pres. and CEO MANUEL ESCÁMEZ SÁNCHEZ.

Regulatory Authority

Comisión Nacional del Mercado de Valores (CNMV): Paseo de la Castellana 19, 28046 Madrid; tel. (91) 5851500; fax (91) 3193373; e-mail inversores@cnmv.es; internet www.cnmv.es; f. 1988; national securities and exchange commission; Pres. BLAS CALZADA.

INSURANCE

In 1995 total premiums of private companies reached 3,340,000m. pesetas.

Aegon Unión Aseguradora, SA: Príncipe de Vergara 156, 28002 Madrid; tel. (91) 5636222; fax (91) 5639715; f. 1944; merged with Unión Levantina in 1986, Unión Previsora in 1987 and Labor Médica, La Sanitaria and Caja de Previsión y Socorro in 1996; life, property, health and personal insurance and reinsurance; total premiums €289.9m. (2000); also owns Aegon Ahorro, Vida e Inversión and Aegon Money Maxx; Chair. ALEJANDRO ROYO-VILLANOVA PAYÁ; CEO JESÚS QUINTANAL SAN EMETERIO.

AGF Unión Fénix: Paseo Castellana 33, 28046 Madrid; tel. (91) 5960000; fax (91) 5960600; f. 1994; total premiums 86,641m. (1996); Pres. YVES DE GAULLE; Man. Dir LOUIS DE MONTFERRAND.

Asistencia Sanitaria Interprovincial de Seguros, SA (ASISA): Caracas 12, 28010 Madrid; tel. (91) 3190191; fax (91) 4103836; e-mail asisa.informacion@asisa.es; internet www.asisa.es; total premiums 49,340m. (1992); Pres. FRANCISCO CARREÑO CASTILLA.

Axa Seguros: Paseo de la Castellana 79, 28046 Madrid; tel. (91) 5388200; fax (91) 5553197; e-mail webmaster@axa-seguros.es; internet www.axa-seguros.es; total premiums 164,000m. (1998); Pres. EDUARDO DE AGUIRRE ALONSO-ALLENDE.

Banco Vitalicio de España, Compañía Anónima de Seguros: Paseo de Gracia 11, 08007 Barcelona; tel. (93) 4840100; fax (93) 4840226; internet www.vitalicio.es; f. 1880; total premiums 115,415m. (1992); Pres. ALFONSO ESCÁMEZ LÓPEZ; Man. Dir JOSÉ LUIS PÉREZ TORRES.

Bilbao, Cía Anónima de Seguros y Reaseguros: Paseo del Puerto 20, 48990 Neguri-Getxo (Vizcaya); tel. (94) 4898100; fax (94) 4898263; internet www.segurosbilbao.com; f. 1918; total premiums 34,731m. (1998); gen. insurance, represented throughout Spain; Pres. PATRICK DE LA SOTA MACMAHON; Man. Dir IÑAKI ALVARES.

Caja de Seguros Reunidos, Cía de Seguros y Reaseguros, SA (Caser): Plaza de la Lealtad 4, 28014 Madrid; tel. (91) 5955000; fax (91) 5955018; internet www.caser.es; f. 1942; total premiums 134,000m. (2001); represented throughout Spain; Dir-Gen. IGNACIO EYRIES GARCÍA DE VINUESA.

Catalana Occidente, SA de Seguros y Reaseguros: Avda Alcalde Barnils s/n, 08190 Sant Cugat del Vallés (Barcelona); tel. (93) 5820500; fax (93) 5820719; internet www.catalanaoccidente .com; insurance and reinsurance; total premiums €1,117m. (1999); Pres. JESÚS SERRA SANTAMANS.

Crédito y Caución, SA (Compañía Española de Seguros y Reaseguros): Paseo de la Castellana 4, 28046 Madrid; tel. (91) 4326300; fax (91) 4326506; e-mail comunicacion@creditoycaucion.es; internet www.creditoycaucion.com; total premiums 30,086m. (1998); Pres. JOSÉ MARÍA SERRÁ FARRÉ.

La Estrella, SA: Paseo de la Castellana, 130 28046, Madrid; tel. (91) 5905656; fax (91) 3301400; e-mail clientes@laestrella.es; internet www.laestrella.es; f. 1901; all classes of insurance and reinsurance; total premiums 56,500m. (1994); Pres. Duque D. CARLOS ZURITA DELGADO; Man. Dir LUIS ESPACIO CASANOVAS; 124 brs.

Euroseguros, SA: Plaza Marqués de Salamanca 3 y 4, 28006 Madrid; tel. (91) 3747255; total premiums 118,344m. (1996); Pres. ALFONSO BASAGOITI.

Mapfre (Mutualidad de Seguros): Carretera de Pozuelo a Majadahonda, Km 3800, 28820 Majadahonda (Madrid); tel. (91) 6262100; fax (91) 6262308; car insurance; total premiums 98,093m. (1992); Pres. JOSÉ A. REBUELTA GARCÍA.

Mapfre Seguros Generales, SA: Paseo de Recoletos 23, 28004 Madrid; tel. (91) 5816300; fax (91) 5815252; internet www.mapfre .com; total premiums 33,436m. (1992); Pres. RAFAEL GALARRAGA SOLORES.

Mapfre Vida, SA: Avda General Perón 40, 28020 Madrid; tel. (91) 5811400; fax (91) 5811592; internet www.mapfre.com; life and health insurance; total premiums 82,969m. (1996); Pres. José Manuel Martínez Martínez; Man. Dir Sebastian Homet Dupra.

Multinacional Aseguradora, SA: Doctor Ferrán 3 y 5, 08034 Barcelona; tel. (93) 4847000; fax (93) 4847070; internet www .ascat-mna.com; total premiums 27,318m. (1998).

Musini, Sociedad Anónima de Seguros y Reaseguros: Manuel Cortina 2, 6°, 28006 Madrid; tel. (91) 5509090; fax (91) 5509000; internet www.musini.com; f. 1968; total premiums 74,553m. (1997); CEO Alvaro Muñoz López.

Mutua General de Seguros: Diagonal 543, 08029 Barcelona; tel. (93) 3222112; fax (93) 4397046; e-mail mgs@mgs.es; internet www .mgs.es; f. 1907; total premiums 28,007m. (1999); Chair. G. Artiach Meda; Gen. Man. J. M. Sampietro Villacampa; brs throughout Spain.

Mutua Madrileña Automovilista: Almagro 9, 28010 Madrid; tel. (91) 5578200; internet www.mutua-mad.es; f. 1930; total premiums 60,355m. (1992); Pres. Gabriel Gancedo.

Ocaso, SA, Compañía de Seguros y Reaseguros: Princesa 23, 28008 Madrid; tel. (91) 5380100; fax (91) 5418509; e-mail ocaso@ ocaso.es; internet www.ocaso.es; f. 1920; total premiums €513m., cap. €100m. (2002); 370 brs in Spain, 1 in London, 1 in Puerto Rico; Pres. Isabel Castelo d'Ortega; Dir-Gen. D. Antonio Domínguez Cuerdo.

Plus Ultra: Plaza de las Cortes 8, 28014 Madrid; tel. (91) 5899292; fax (91) 4298921; e-mail plus.ultra@plusultra.es; internet www .plusultra.es; life premiums 33,626m., non-life premiums 59,748m. (2000); Pres. Gerardo Aróstegui Gómez.

Sanitas, SA de Seguros: Calle Padilla 1, Madrid; tel. (91) 5852400; fax (91) 4326200; e-mail iferrando@sanitas.es; internet www.sanitas .es; health insurance; total premiums 49,880m. (1997); Pres. Juan José López-Ibor.

Santa Lucía, SA: Plaza de España 15, 28008 Madrid; tel. (91) 5419387; fax (91) 5410133; e-mail atencion@santalucia.es; internet www.santalucia.es; f. 1922; cap., res, etc. €1.106,254m. (2000); Pres. Carlos J. Alvarez Navarro.

Vidacaixa, SA: General Almirante, 6, 08014 Barcelona; tel. (93) 2278700; fax (93) 3324441; internet www.vidacaixa.es; total premiums 421,476m. (2000); Pres. Tomás Muniesa Arantegui.

Winterthur Seguros: Pl. Francesc Macià 10, 08036 Barcelona; tel. (93) 2901090; fax (93) 2901029; internet www.winterthur.es; f. 1996 by merger; Pres. and Dir-Gen. César Bardají.

Zurich: Vía Augusta 192–200, 08021 Barcelona; tel. (93) 2099111; fax (93) 2014849; internet www.zurichspain.com; total premiums 35,406.6m. (1995).

Insurance Associations

Dirección General de Seguros: Paseo de la Castellana 44, 28046 Madrid; tel. (91) 3397000; fax (91) 3397113; e-mail dgsinforma@ seguras.meh.es; internet www.dgseguros.mineco.es; supervisory body; part of Ministry of the Economy; Dir-Gen. María del Pilar González de Frutos.

Comisión Liquidadora de Entidades Aseguradoras (CLEA): Marqués de la Ensenada 16, 2°, 28004 Madrid; tel. (91) 7005500; fax (91) 3195390; e-mail clea@clea.es; internet www.clea.es; f. 1984; empowered to liquidate companies dissolved by the Public Administration; part of Ministry of the Economy; Pres. Concepción Bermúdez Meneses.

Unión Española de Entidades Aseguradoras y Reaseguradoras (UNESPA): Núñez de Balboa 101, 28006 Madrid; tel. (91) 7451530; fax (91) 7451531; internet www.unespa.es; professional association; Pres. Alvaro Muñoz; Sec. Aranzazu del Valle.

Trade and Industry

GOVERNMENT AGENCIES

Secretaria General de Comercio Exterior: Secretaria de Estado de Comercio y Turismo, Paseo de la Castellana 162, 28046 Madrid; e-mail buzon.oficial@secgcomex.sscc.mcx.es; internet www.mcx.es; Sec.-Gen. Francisco Utrera Mora.

Instituto Español de Comercio Exterior (ICEX): Paseo de la Castellana 14, 28046 Madrid; tel. (91) 3496100; fax (91) 4316128; internet www.icex.es; f. 1982; institute for foreign trade; Pres. María Elena Pisonero Ruiz.

DEVELOPMENT ORGANIZATIONS

Instituto Andaluz de la Reforma Agraria (IARA): Avda San Fco Javier s/n, Edif. Sevilla 1, 1°, 41005 Sevilla; tel. (95) 463900; empowered to expropriate land under the agricultural reform programme; Pres. Francisco Vázquez.

Instituto Galego de Promoción Económica (IGAPE): Complexo Administrativo Barrio de San Lázaro, s/n, 15703 Santiago de Compostela; tel. (902) 300903; e-mail igape@igape.es; internet www .igape.es.

Instituto Madrileño de Desarrollo: José Abascal 57, 28003 Madrid; tel. (91) 5802600; fax (91) 5802589; e-mail informacion@ imade.es; internet www.imad.es; f. 1984; public development institution for Madrid region; Man. Rodolfo del Olmo López.

Sociedad de Desarrollo de Navarra (SODENA): Avda Carlos III el Noble, 36, 1° dcha., 31003 Pamplona; tel. (948) 421942; fax (948) 421943; e-mail info@sodena.com; internet www.sodena.com.

Sociedad para el Desarrollo de las Comarcas Mineras (SODECO): La Unión 21, La Felguera, 33930 Langreo, Asturias; tel. (98) 5678116; fax (98) 5678172; internet www.sodeco.es.

Sociedad para el Desarrollo Económico de Canarias, SA: Villalba Hervás 4, 6°, 38002 Santa Cruz de Tenerife; tel. (922) 298020; fax (922) 298131; e-mail sodecantf@sodecan.es; internet www.sodecan.es; Pres. José Carlos Francisco Díaz.

Sociedad para el Desarrollo Industrial de Andalucía (SODIAN): República Argentina 29 accessorio, Sevilla 11; tel. (95) 4278705.

Sociedad para el Desarrollo Industrial de Castilla y León, SA (SODICAL): Doctrinos 6, 4°, 47001 Valladolid; tel. (983) 343811; e-mail sodical@sodical.es; internet www.sodical.es; f. 1982; Dir-Gen. Manuel Fernández Díez.

Sociedad para el Desarrollo Industrial de Extremadura (SODIEX): Doctor Marañon 2, Cáceres; tel. (927) 227700; fax (927) 243304; f. 1977.

Sociedad para el Desarrollo Industrial de Galicia, SA (SODIGA): Orense 6, La Rosaleda, 15701 Santiago de Compostela; tel. (981) 566100; fax (981) 566183.

CHAMBERS OF COMMERCE

Cámara de Comercio Internacional (International Chamber of Commerce): Avda Diagonal 452–4, 08006 Barcelona; tel. (91) 4169300; fax (91) 4169301; e-mail iccspain@cambrabcn.es; f. 1922; Pres. Guillermo de la Dehesa; Sec.-Gen. Luis Solá Vilardell.

Consejo Superior de Cámaras Oficiales de Comercio, Industria y Navegación de España (High Council of Official Chambers of Commerce, Industry, and Navigation of Spain): Velázquez 157, 28002 Madrid; tel. (91) 5906900; fax (91) 5906913; e-mail informacion@cscamaras.es; internet www.camaras.prg; f. 1922; Pres. José Manuel Fernández Norniella; Dir-Gen. Fernando Gómez Aviles-Casco; Sec.-Gen. Fernando Ferrero; comprises 85 Chambers throughout Spain, incl. the following:

Cámara Oficial de Comercio, Industria y Navegación de Bilbao: Alameda Recalde 50, 48008 Bilbao; tel. (94) 172000; fax (94) 4436171; e-mail info@camaranet.com; internet www .camaranet.com.

Cámara Oficial de Comercio e Industria de Madrid: Huertas 13, 28012 Madrid; tel. (91) 5383500; fax (91) 5383677; e-mail camara@camaramadrid.es; f. 1887; Pres. Fernando Fernández-Tapias; Dir José Maria Isardo; 370,000 mems.

Cámara Oficial de Comercio, Industria y Navegación de Sevilla: Plaza de la Contratación 8, 41004 Sevilla; tel. (954) 211204; fax (954) 225619; internet www.ppxc.es.

Cámara Oficial de Comercio, Industria y Navegación de Valencia: Poeta Querol 15, 46002 Valencia; tel. (96) 3511301; fax (96) 3516349; e-mail info@camaravalencia.com; f. 1886; Pres. Arturo Virosque Ruiz; Dir Fernando Zárraga Quintana; Sec.-Gen. Antonio Rico Gil.

Cambra Oficial de Comerç, Indústria i Navegació de Barcelona: Avda Diagonal 452–454, 08006 Barcelona; tel. (93) 4169300; fax (93) 4169301; f. 1886; Pres. Antoni Negre; Dir Carles Castells Oliveres.

Confederación Española de Comercio: Diego de León 50, 28006 Madrid; tel. (91) 4116161; fax (91) 5645269; Pres. Pere Llorens Lorente; Sec.-Gen. Javier Millán-Astray Romero.

INDUSTRIAL AND TRADE ASSOCIATIONS

Agrupación de Exportadores del Centro de España (AGRECE): Plaza de la Independencia 1, 28001 Madrid; tel. (91) 5383500; fax (91) 5383718; e-mail cex2@camaramadrid.es; exporters.

Agrupación de Fabricantes de Cemento de España (OFICEMEN): José Abascal 53, 28003 Madrid; tel. (91) 4411688; fax (91) 4423817; cement manufacturers; Pres. José Antonio Rumeu; Dir-Gen. Rafael Fernández.

Agrupación de Importadores y Exportadores de Productos Agrícolas: Londres 96, 08036 Barcelona; tel. (93) 2093478; agricultural products.

Asociación de Comercio de Cereales y Oleaginosas de España (ACCOE): Doctor Fleming 56, 3°, 28036 Madrid; tel. (91) 3504305; fax (91) 3455009; cereal traders; Pres. PELAYO MORENO SÁNCHEZ; Sec. RICARDO GARCÍA SAN JOSÉ.

Asociación de Criadores Exportadores de Sherry (ACES): Eguiluz 2, 1°, 11402 Jerez de la Frontera; tel. (956) 341046; fax (956) 346081; e-mail fedejerez@fedejerez.com; internet www.fedejerez.com; sherry exporters; Pres. FRANCISCO VALENCIA JAÉN.

Asociación Española de Comercio Exterior (AECE): Madrid; f. 1983; traders' organization; Pres. ANDRÉS MANZANO GARCÍA; Sec. MIGUEL ANGEL JORQUERA FERNÁNDEZ.

Asociación Española de Comercio Exterior de Cereales y Productos Análogos (AECEC): Calle Orense, 85 Edif. Lexington, 28020 Madrid; tel. (91) 678400; fax (91) 5714244; e-mail aecec@arrakis.es; cereal exporters; Pres. J. CORNEJO; Sec.-Gen. GUILLERMO LORENZO ZAMORANO.

Asociación Española de Exportadores de Electrónica e Informática (SECARTYS): Gran Vía de les Corts Catalanes 774, 4°, 08013 Barcelona; tel. (93) 2478560; fax (93) 2478561; e-mail secartys@secartys.org; internet www.secartys.org; f. 1968; electronics exporters; Pres. JOSÉ BELTRÁN; Dir-Gen. IGNACIO TORMO MARXUACH.

Asociación Española de Extractores de Aceite de Orujo de Aceitunas (ANEO): Paseo Reina Cristina 6, 28014 Madrid; tel. (91) 4376585; fax (91) 5515013; olive oil extractors; Pres. ALVARO ESPUNY RODRÍGUEZ; Sec. JUAN JOSÉ VÁZQUEZ CANSINO.

Asociación Española de Fabricantes de Equipos y Componentes para Automoción (SERNAUTO): Castelló 120, 28006 Madrid; tel. (91) 5621041; fax (91) 5618437; e-mail sernauto@sernauto.es; internet www.sernauto.es; association of manufacturers of equipment and components for automobile industry; Pres. JOSÉ MARÍA PUJOL; Gen. Man. JOSÉ A. JIMÉNEZ SACEDA.

Asociación Española de la Industria y Comercio Exportador de Aceite de Oliva (ASOLIVA): José Abascal 40, 2°, 28003 Madrid; tel. (91) 4468812; fax (91) 5931918; e-mail asoliva@ctv.es; olive oil exporters; Pres. FRANCISCO SENSAT ALEMANY.

Asociación Española de Productoras de Fibras Químicas (PROFIBRA): Alta de San Pere 1, 08003 Barcelona; tel. (93) 2682644; fax (93) 2682630; e-mail profibra@profibra.com; internet www.profibra.com; chemical fibre producers; Pres. RAFAEL ESPAÑOL NAVARRO; Sec.-Gen. GUILLERMO GRAELL DENIEL.

Asociación de Exportadores de Pescado y Cefalopodos Congelados (AEPYCC): Diego de León 44, 28006 Madrid; tel. (91) 4112407; fax (91) 5618178; fish exporters; Pres. RAMON MASO; Sec. IGNACIO MONTENEGRO GONZÁLEZ.

Asociación Industrial Textil de Proceso Algodonero (AITPA): Gran Vía de les Corts Catalanes 670, 08010 Barcelona; tel. (93) 3189200; fax (93) 3026235; e-mail aitpa@aitpa.es; internet www.aitpa.es; cotton textile industry; Pres. RAMON MASO; Exec. Vice-Pres. SALVADOR MALUQUER.

Asociación Nacional Española de Fabricantes de Hormigón Preparado (ANEFHOP): Bretón de los Herreros 43 Bajo, 28003 Madrid; tel. (91) 4416834; fax (91) 4418341; e-mail anefhop@nauta.es; internet www.anefhop.com; concrete manufacturers; Pres. MANUEL A. SOBRAL CRUZ; Dir-Gen. FRANCISCO JAVIER MARTÍNEZ DE EULATE.

Asociación Nacional de Fabricantes de Automóviles y Camiones (ANFAC): Fray Bernardino Sahagún 24, 28036 Madrid; tel. (91) 3431343; fax (91) 3594488; e-mail prensa@anfac.com; internet www.anfac.com; car and lorry manufacturers; Pres. JESÚS RUÍZ-BEATO BRAVO; Gen. Sec. LUIS VALERO.

Asociación Nacional de Fabricantes de Pastas Papeleras, Papel y Cartón (ASPAPEL): Alcalá 85, 4°, 28009 Madrid; tel. (91) 5763002; fax (91) 5774710; e-mail c.reinoso@aspapel.es; paper and cardboard manufacturers; Pres. FERNANDO ARRIETA SAN MIGUEL; Dir-Gen. CARLOS REINOSO TORRES.

Asociación Nacional de Industrias Electrónicas y de Telecomunicaciones (ANIEL): Príncipe de Vergara 74, 28006 Madrid; tel. (91) 5902300; fax (91) 4114000; e-mail aniel@aniel.es; internet www.aniel.es; f. 1984; electronic, information and telecommunication industries; Man. Dir GONZALO CARO.

Comité de Gestión de la Exportación de Frutos Cítricos: Monjas de Santa Catalina 8, 4°, 46002 Valencia; tel. (96) 3521102; fax (96) 3510718; citrus fruit exporters; Pres. JULIO DE MIGUEL MARTÍNEZ DE BUJANDA; Sec. RICARDO LLERENA.

Confederación de Cooperativas Agrarias de España (CCAE): Agustín de Bethencourt 17, 4°, 28003 Madrid; tel. (91) 5351035; fax (91) 5540047; e-mail prensa@ccae.es; internet www.ccae.es; Pres. JOSÉ MARÍA LUQUI GARDE.

Confederación Española de Organizaciones Empresariales del Metal (CONFEMETAL): Príncipe de Vergara 74, 5°, 28006 Madrid; tel. (91) 5625590; fax (91) 5628477; metal organizations; Pres. CARLOS PÉREZ DE BRICIO OLARIAGA; Sec.-Gen. ANDRÉS SÁNCHEZ DE APELLANIZ.

Confederación Nacional de la Construcción (CNC): Diego de León 50, 2°, 28006 Madrid; tel. (91) 2619715; fax (91) 2615269; construction industry; Pres. JOSÉ LUIS ALONSO; Sec. Pastor JOSÉ LUIS RODRÍGUEZ-PONGA.

Confederación Nacional de Empresarios de la Minería y de la Metalurgia (CONFEDEM): Núñez de Balboa 37, 28001 Madrid; tel. (91) 4319402; mining and metallurgy; Pres. UBALDO USUNÁRIZ BALANZATEGUI; Sec. ANDRÉS VILLALOBOS BELTRÁN.

Consejo Intertextil Español (CIE): Gran Vía de las Cortes Catalanas 670, 4°, 08010 Barcelona; tel. (93) 3189200; fax (93) 3026235; e-mail intertextil@aitpa.es; textile industry; Pres. JUAN CANALS; Sec. SARA PÉREZ.

CONSTRUNAVES—CNE, SA: Orense 11, 1°, 28020 Madrid; tel. (91) 5560458; fax (91) 5555216; e-mail construnaves@construnaves.es; f. 1959; private shipbuilders' asscn; Man. Dir RAMÓN LÓPEZ-EADY.

Federación Empresarial de la Industria Química Española (FEIQUE): Hermosilla 31, 1°, 28001 Madrid; tel. (91) 4317964; fax (91) 5763381; e-mail info@feique.org; internet www.feique.org; chemical industry; Pres. FRANCISCO BELIL CREIXELL.

Federación Española de Asociaciones de Productores Exportadores de Frutas y Hortalizas (FEPEX): Miguel Angel 13, 4a Pl., 28010 Madrid; tel. (91) 3191050; fax (91) 3103812; e-mail fepex@fepex.es; internet www.fepex.es; fruit and vegetable producers and exporters; Pres. ANDRÉS CUARTERO RUIZ; Dir JOSÉ MARÍA POZANCOS.

Federación Españõla de Exportadores de Frutos Cítricos (FECIT): Valencia; citrus fruit exporters; Pres. ANTONIO PELUFO; Sec. LUIS RIBERA PERIS.

Federación Española de Industrias de la Alimentación y Bebidas (FIAB): Diego de León 44, 1° Izqda, 28006 Madrid; tel. (91) 4117211; fax (91) 4117344; e-mail fiab@fiab.es; internet www.fiab.es; f. 1977; food and drink industries; Pres. ARTURO GIL PÉREZ ANDUJAR; Sec. JORGE JORDANA BUTTICAZ DE POZAS.

Federación de la Industria Textil Lanera: San Quirico 30, 08201 Sabadell; tel. (93) 7450944; fax (93) 7261526; e-mail gremifab@textilespain.com; internet www.gremifab.es; wool industry; Pres. JOSEP ROCA VALLRRIBERA; Sec. BENET ARMENGOL OBRADORS.

Federación de Industrias del Calzado Español (FICE): Núñez de Balboa 116, 3°, Ofs 5 y 6, 28006 Madrid; tel. (91) 5627001; fax (91) 5620094; e-mail fice@inescop.es; internet www.paso-paso.com; footwear; Pres. RAFAEL CALVO RODRÍGUEZ.

Servicio Comercial de la Industria Textil Lanera (SCITL): Rosellón 216, 08008 Barcelona; tel. (93) 2150170; fax (93) 2158463; wool industry; Pres. PEDRO GUITART; Sec. ANTONIO AIZPÚN.

Unión de Empresas Siderúrgicas (UNESID): Castelló 128, 3°, Apdo 13098, 28006 Madrid; tel. (91) 5610369; fax (91) 5626584; e-mail jibartolome@unesid.org; internet www.unesid.org; association of Spanish producers of steel; Pres. GONZALO URQUIJO; Dir-Gen. JUAN I. BARTOLOMÉ.

EMPLOYERS' ORGANIZATIONS

Confederación Española de Organizaciones Empresariales (CEOE) (Spanish Confederation of Employers' Organizations): Diego de León 50, 28006 Madrid; tel. (91) 5663400; fax (91) 5644247; e-mail comunicacion@ceoe.es; internet www.ceoe.es; f. 1977; covers industry, agriculture, commerce and service sectors; comprises 165 orgs; Pres. JOSÉ MARÍA CUEVAS SALVADOR; Sec.-Gen. JUAN JIMÉNEZ AGUILAR.

Círculo de Empresarios: Serrano 1, 4°, 28001 Madrid; tel. (91) 5781472; fax (91) 5774871; e-mail asociacion@circulodeempresarios.org; internet www.circulodeempresarios.org; f. 1977; comprises CEOs of more than 180 major companies; Pres. MANUEL AZPILICUETA FERRER; Sec.-Gen. VICENTE BOCETA ÁLVAREZ.

Confederación Empresarial de Barcelona (CEB): Vía Layetana 32, 08003 Barcelona; tel. (93) 4841200; fax (93) 4841230; e-mail foment@foment.com; internet www.foment.com.

Confederación Empresarial de Madrid: Diego de León 50, 1°, 28006 Madrid; tel. (91) 4115317; fax (91) 5627537; small, medium and large businesses; Pres. FERNANDO FERNÁNDEZ TAPIAS; Sec. AGUSTÍN MASCAREÑAS.

Confederación Empresarial Valenciana (CEV): Plaza Conde de Carlet 3, 46003 Valencia; tel. (96) 3155720; fax (96) 3923199; e-mail cev@cev.es; internet www.cev.es; f. 1977; Pres. RAFAEL FERRANDO; Sec.-Gen. PEDRO COCA.

Confederación Empresarial Vasca (CONFEBASK): Henao 5, 3°, 48009 Bilbao; tel. (94) 4238800; fax (94) 4232311; f. 1983; Pres. BALTASAR ERRAZTI NAVARRO; Sec.-Gen. JOSÉ GUILLERMO ZUBIA GUINEA.

Confederación Española de la Pequeña y Mediana Empresa (CEPYME): Diego de León 50, 3°, 28006 Madrid; tel. (91) 4116161; fax (91) 5645269; e-mail cepyme@cepyme.es; internet www.cepyme.es; small and medium businesses; Pres. ANTONIO MASA GODOY; Sec.-Gen. ELÍAS APARICIO BRAVO.

Fomento del Trabajo Nacional: Vía Layetana 32, 08003 Barcelona; tel. (93) 4841200; fax (93) 4841230; f. 1771; development of national labour; Pres. JUAN ROSELL LASTORTRAS; Sec.-Gen. JUAN PUJOL SEGARRA.

Tribunal de Defensa de la Competencia: Avda Pío XII 17–19, Madrid 16; tel. (91) 3530510; fax (91) 3530590; e-mail secretaria.general@tdcompetencia.org; internet www.tdcompetencia.org; f. 1963; Pres. GONZALO SOLANA GONZÁLEZ; Sec. ANTONIO FERNÁNDEZ FÁBREGA.

UTILITIES

Instituto para la Diversificación y Ahorro de la Energía (IDAE): Paseo de la Castellana 95, 28046 Madrid; tel. (91) 4564900; fax (91) 5551389; internet www.idae.es; Dir-Gen. MARÍA ISABEL MONREAL PALOMINO.

Electricity

Asociación Española de la Industria Eléctrica (UNESA): Francisco Gervás 3, 28020 Madrid; tel. (91) 5674800; fax (91) 5674982; e-mail comunic@unesa.es; internet www.unesa.es; f. 1944; groups principal electricity cos; Pres. JOSÉ MARÍA AMUSÁTEGUI; Dir-Gen. PEDRO RIVERO TORRE.

Comisión Nacional de Energía (CNE): Marqués del Duero 4, 28001 Madrid; tel. (91) 4329600; fax (91) 5776218; internet www.cne.es; Pres. PEDRO MARÍA MEROÑO VÉLEZ.

Red Eléctrica de España (REE): Paseo del Conde de los Gaitanes 177, 28109 La Moraleja (Madrid); tel. (91) 6508500; fax (91) 6504542; internet www.ree.es; manages and operates the national grid; Chair. PEDRO MIELGO ALVAREZ; Dir-Gen. FRANCISCO PEDROSA ORTEGA.

Principal Electricity Companies

Endesa, SA: Príncipe de Vergara 187, 28002 Madrid; tel. (91) 5668525; fax (91) 5668655; internet www.endesa.es; f. 1983; generator, distributor and vendor of electricity; also provides gas; Pres. RODOLFO MARTÍN VILLA; CEO RAFAEL MIRANDA.

Hidroeléctrica del Cantábrico, SA (Hidrocantábrico): Plaza de la Gesta 2, 33007 Oviedo; tel. (98) 5230300; generator, distributor and vendor of electricity; also provides gas; owned by Electricidade de Portugal and Energie Baden-Wuerttemberg (Germany); Pres. (vacant).

Iberdrola, SA: Hermosilla 3, 28001 Madrid; tel. (91) 5776565; fax (91) 5777101; internet www.iberdrola.es; generator, distributor and vendor of electricity; supplies mainly hydroelectric power; also provides gas; Pres. IÑIGO DE ORIOL; CEO JAVIER HERRERO.

Unión Eléctrica Fenosa, SA: Capitán Haya 53, 28020 Madrid; tel. (91) 5676650; fax (91) 5676658; e-mail uef@uef.es; internet www.uef.es; generator, distributor and vendor of electricity; also provides gas; Pres. JOSÉ MARÍA AMUSÁTEGUI; Sec.-Gen. RAMÓN NOVO.

Viesgo: Medio 12, 39003 Santander; tel. (942) 246000; fax (942) 246034; internet www.viesgo.es; f. 1906; 100% owned by Enel SpA (Italy); distributor; Pres. MIGUEL ANTOÑANZAS.

Gas

As a part of the restructuring of the sector, in 2000 the Government awarded 11 licences for the transportation of gas.

Compañía Distribuidora de Gas de Bilbao, SA (Bilbogas): Ledesma 10, Bajos, 48001 Bilbao; tel. (94) 4354960; fax (94) 4239572; distributor of gas; Pres. IBÓN ARESO MENDUGUREN.

Compañía Española de Gas, SA: Grabador Esteve 14, 46004 Valencia; tel. (96) 3537700; distributor of gas; Dir-Gen. PEDRO SÁENZ DE SANTA MARÍA.

Donostigas, SA: Alto de Errondo 2, 20009 San Sebastián; tel. (94) 3445090; distributor of gas; Dir-Gen. GONZALO SUBIJANA.

Endesa Gas, SA: Aznar Molina 2, 50002 Zaragoza; tel. (976) 760000; fax (976) 760044; internet www.endesa.es; distributor of gas; comprises five subsidiaries; also provides electricity; Pres. AMADO FRANCO LAHOZ; Dir-Gen. FERNANDO CORTINA GONZÁLEZ.

Gas Natural SDG, SA: Avda Portal de l'Angel 22, 08002 Barcelona; tel. (93) 4025100; fax (93) 4029317; internet www.gasnatural.com;

distributor of gas; also provides electricity and communications; comprises regional distribution companies; Pres. ANTONIO BRUFAU NIUBÓ.

Sociedad de Gas de Euzkadi, SA: Plaza Pío Baroja 3, 2°, 48001 Bilbao; tel. (94) 4355600; fax (94) 4249733; distributor of gas; Pres. JESÚS GOIRI BASTERRA.

Water

Aguas de Valencia, SA: Gran Vía Marqués del Turia 19, 46005 Valencia; tel. (96) 3860600; internet www.aguasdevalencia.es; water and sewerage services; Chair. V. BOLUDA FOS; Man. Dir AUDREY HERNÁNDEZ MONAR.

Sociedad General de Aguas de Barcelona (AGBAR), SA: Passeig de Sant Joan 39–43, 08009 Barcelona; tel. (93) 3422000; fax (93) 3422670; e-mail comunicacion@agbar.es; internet www.agbar.es; treatment of water and waste liquid; provision of sanitation services; Chair. R. FORNESA RIBÓ.

TRADE UNIONS

Central Sindical Independiente y de Funcionarios (CSI-CSIF): Fernando El Santo 17, 1° y 2°, 28010 Madrid; tel. (91) 7022910; fax (91) 7022919; e-mail presidente@csi-scif.es; internet www.csi-csif.es; Pres. DOMINGO FERNÁNDEZ VEIGUELA; Sec.-Gen. ROBUSTIANO BUENO PUERTA.

Confederación General de Trabajo (CGT) (General Confederation of Labour): Sagunto 15, 28010 Madrid; tel. (91) 4475769; fax (91) 4453132; e-mail spcc.cgt@cgt.es; internet www.cgt.es; Sec.-Gen. ELADIO VILLANUEVA SARAVIA.

Confederación Intersindical Galega (CIG): Rua do Campo do Forno 1, Baixo, Santiago de Compostela, 15703 A Coruña; tel. (986) 262679; fax (986) 262781; e-mail cig.com@teleline.es; internet www.galizacig.com; Galician confederation; Pres. MANUEL MERA SÁNCHEZ; Sec.-Gen. XÉSUS E. SEIXO FERNÁNDEZ.

Confederación Nacional del Trabajo (CNT) (National Confederation of Labour): Secretariado Permanente del Comité Nacional, Plaza Tirso de Molina 5, 6 dcha., 28012 Madrid; tel. (91) 4204015; fax (91) 4202749; e-mail sp_cn@cnt.es; internet www.cnt.es; Sec.-Gen. ANA SIGÜENZA.

Confederación Sindical de Comisiones Obreras (CCOO) (Workers' Commissions): Fernández de la Hoz 12, 28010 Madrid; tel. (91) 7028000; fax (91) 3104804; e-mail ccoo@ccoo.es; internet www.ccoo.es; f. 1956; independent left-wing; Sec.-Gen. JOSÉ MARÍA FIDALGO; 930,000 mems (1994).

Eusko Langilleen Alkartasuna/Solidaridad de Trabajadores Vascos (ELA/STV) (Basque Workers' Solidarity): Barrainkua 15, 48009 Bilbao; tel. (94) 4037700; fax (94) 4037766; e-mail fundm001@sarenet.es; f. 1911; independent; Sec.-Gen. JOSÉ ELORRIETA AURREKOETXEA; 110,000 mems.

Unión General de Trabajadores (UGT) (General Union of Workers): Hortaleza 88, 28004 Madrid; tel. (91) 5897601; fax (91) 5897603; e-mail info@cec.ugt.org; internet www.ugt.es; f. 1888; eight affiliated federations; Sec.-Gen. CÁNDIDO MÉNDEZ; 672,185 mems (1997).

Unión Sindical Obrera (USO) (Workers' Trade Union): Príncipe de Vergara 13, 7°, 28001 Madrid; tel. (91) 5774113; fax (91) 5772959; e-mail uso@uso.es; internet www.uso.es; f. 1960; independent; Sec.-Gen. BENITO LÓPEZ GONZALEZ; 82,000 mems.

Transport

RAILWAYS

In August 2000 it was announced that rail transport was to be liberalized by 2004, with private operators using the state rail infrastructure. In January 2001 Spain and Portugal agreed on the route of a high-speed train to be built, linking the two countries. The infrastructure was to be completed by 2008. A proposal to link the French high-speed train line to Cataluña was announced in 2001.

Red Nacional de los Ferrocarriles Españoles (RENFE) (National System of Spanish Railways): Avda Pío XII 110, 28036 Madrid; tel. (91) 3006251; internet www.renfe.es; operates 12,319 km of wide-gauge track, of which 6,959 km are electrified; the 481-km Madrid–Córdoba–Sevilla high-speed line opened in 1992, forming the first stage of a high-speed network that was to extend northwards via Barcelona to the French border, from Córdoba to Malaga, from Madrid to Valladolid, Valencia and Alicante; Pres. MIGUEL CORSINI FREESE.

Eusko Trenbideak—Ferrocarriles Vascos (ET/FV), SA: Atxuri 6, 48006 Bilbao; tel. (94) 543210; fax (94) 4336009; e-mail attcliente@euskotren.es; internet www.euskotren.es; f. 1982; controlled by the

Basque Government; 202 km of 1,000 mm gauge; passengers carried 43.6m. (1994); Man. Dir ROBERTO OTXANDIO IZAGIRRE.

Ferrocarriles de Vía Estrecha (FEVE) (Narrow Gauge Railways): General Rodrigo 6, 28003 Madrid; tel. (91) 4533800; fax (91) 4533825; e-mail info@feve.es; internet www.feve.es; f. 1965 by integration of private companies; operates mainly in suburban areas of northern cities; 1,267.9 km (2000) of narrow-gauge track (of which 337.0 km were electrified); passengers carried (1999): 212.5m. goods loaded (1999): 442.1m. metric tons net; Pres. EUGENIO DAMBORIENA Y OSA; Dir-Gen. JUAN DE LA CRUZ PACHECO.

Ferrocarrils de la Generalitat de Catalunya (FGC): Pau Casals 24, 8°, 08021 Barcelona; tel. (93) 3663000; fax (93) 3663350; e-mail rrpp@fgc.net; internet www.fgc.net; f. 1979; 197 km, of which 156 km are electrified; Pres. ANTONIO HERCE.

Ferrocarrils de la Generalitat de Valencia (FGV): Partida de Xirivelleta s/n, B. de San Isidro, 46014 Valencia; tel. (96) 3976565; fax (96) 3976580; e-mail metroval@coput.gva.es; internet www.cop .gva.es/serv/fgv/; f. 1986; operates 92.6-km Dénia–Alicante line; operates Metro Valencia, with four lines and 120 km of line; Pres. JOSÉ RAMON GARCÍA ANTÓN; Dir-Gen. JORGE GARCÍA BERNIA.

Metro Bilbao: Navarra 2; tel. (94) 4254025; e-mail metrobilbao@ metrobilbao.net; internet www.metrobilbao.net; f. 1995; Dir-Gen. JOSU SAGASTAGOITIA.

Metro de Madrid: e-mail prensa@metromadrid.es; internet www .metromadrid.es; 11 lines; infrastructure was to be expanded by 2003; Pres. MANUEL MELIS MAYNAR; Dir-Gen. JOSÉ LUIZ ALVAREZ DE FRANCISCO.

Transports Metropolitans de Barcelona (TMB): Carrer 60, 21–31, Sector A. Polígon industrial Zona Franca, 08040 Barcelona; tel. (93) 2987000; e-mail relext@tmb.net; internet www.tmb.net; five lines.

Association

Fundación de los Ferrocarriles Espanoles: Santa Isabel 44, 28012 Madrid; tel. (91) 1511071; fax (91) 1511066; internet www.ffe .es; foundation of Spanish railways; mems: RENFE, Eusko Tren, FEVE, FGC, FGV, GIF, Metro Bilbao, Metro de Madrid and TMB.

ROADS

Total road network at December 1999 was 663,795 km, including 10,317 km of motorway and 24,124 km of main roads.

Dirección General de Carreteras: Paseo de la Castellana 67, 28071 Madrid; tel. (91) 5977000; fax (91) 5978535; Dir-Gen. JUAN FRANCISCO LAZCANO ACEDO.

Empresa Nacional de Autopistas (ENA): Serrano 45, 28001 Madrid; tel. (91) 4310220; fax (91) 4317013; e-mail ena@ena.es; internet www.ena.es; motorway authority; Pres. JOSÉ MIGUEL ORTÍ BORDÁS.

Empresa Nacional de Transportes de Viajeros por Carretera (ENATCAR): Alcalá 478, 28027 Madrid; tel. (91) 7542004; fax (91) 3271445; f. 1985; road transport organization; Pres. FERNANDO PASCUAL BRAVO.

SHIPPING

Spain has many ports. Among the most important are Barcelona, Bilbao, Santa Cruz de Tenerife, Gijón, Las Palmas, Seville and Valencia. The 1,545 ships of the merchant fleet totalled 2,147,545 grt in December 2001.

Asociación de Navieros Españoles (ANAVE): Dr Fleming 11, 1° Dcha, 28036 Madrid; tel. (91) 4580040; fax (91) 4586087; e-mail anave@anave.es; internet www.anave.es; shipowners' asscn; Pres. ALFREDO PARDO BUSTILLO; Dir MANUEL CARLIER DE LAVALLE.

Dirección General de la Marina Mercante: Ruíz de Alarcón 1, 28014 Madrid; tel. (91) 5979118; fax (91) 5979120; Dir-Gen. FERNANDO CASAS BLANCO.

Empresa Naviera Elcano, SA: José Abascal 4°, 28003 Madrid; tel. (91) 5369800; fax (91) 4474275; e-mail elcano@elcano.sa.es; Pres. JOSÉ SILVERA.

Puertos del Estado y Autoridades Portuarias: Avda del Partenón 10, Campo de las Naciones, 28042 Madrid; tel. (91) 5245500; fax (91) 5245502; e-mail mabeal@eppe.portel.es; Pres. FERNANDO OSORIO PÁRAMO; Sec.-Gen. MARIANO NAVAS GUTIÉRREZ.

Principal Shipping Companies

Auxiliar Marítima, SL: Miño 4, 28002 Madrid; tel. (91) 7454300; fax (91) 7454303; e-mail central@auximar.es; f. 1957; ship management, refrigerated cargo vessels, liquefied gas tankers; Dirs IÑIGO DE SENDAGORTA, JAVIER DE SENDAGORTA.

Compañía Remolcadores Ibaizabal, SA: Muelle de Tomás Olabarri 4, 5°, 48930 Las Arenas-Getxo; tel. (94) 4645133; fax (94) 4645565; e-mail ibaizabal@sarenet.es; f. 1906; ocean-going, coastal, harbour, salvage, fire-fighting; Pres. ALEJANDRO AZNAR SAINZ; Man. Dir FRANCISCO GARAYGORDOBIL AMORRORTU.

Compañía Trasmediterránea, SA: Alcalá 61, 28014 Madrid; tel. (91) 4238500; fax (91) 4238555; internet www.transmediterranea.es; f. 1917; Spanish ports, Balearic and Canary Is and Spanish North African ports; Pres. MIGUEL ANGEL FERNÁNDEZ VILLAMANDOS; Dir-Gen. JOSÉ MANUEL FERNÁNDEZ VILLAMANDOS.

Ership: Don Ramón de la Cruz 13, 28001 Madrid; tel. (91) 4355620; fax (91) 5750883; fmrly TAC; Pres. GUILLERMO ZATARAÍN GUTIÉRREZ DE LA CONCHA.

Ibarra y Cía, SA: Menéndez Pelayo 4, Apdo 15, 41004 Sevilla; tel. (95) 4421658; fax (95) 4410112; f. 1881; cargo vessels to South America from Italy, France, Spain and Portugal; Pres. LUIS DE YBARRA YBARRA.

Naviera García Minaur, SA: Bilbao; operates on seven lines between Northern Europe, the United Kingdom, South and Central America, the Mediterranean and West Africa; Pres. ALEJANDRO BARRAZA.

Naviera Pinillos, SA: Capitán Haya 21, 28020 Madrid; tel. (91) 5556711; fax (91) 5569777; e-mail pinillos@pinillos.com; f. 1840; services between Canary Is and other Spanish ports; Pres. VICENTE BOLUDA; Dir ANGEL MATO.

Repsol Naviera Vizcaina, SA: Juan de Aguriaguerra 35, 2°, 48009 Bilbao; tel. (94) 4251100; fax (94) 4251143; f. 1956; world-wide, but particularly Mediterranean, Near East and Persian Gulf to Spain and transatlantic trade; Man. Dir JAVIER GONZÁLEZ JULIÁ.

CIVIL AVIATION

In 1999 there were 42 airports. More than 20 airports are equipped to receive international flights. In 2001 the construction of an airport in Ciudad Real was announced, to be completed by 2004.

Dirección General de Aviación Civil: Paseo de la Castellana 67, 28071 Madrid; tel. (91) 5975356; fax (91) 5975357; Dir-Gen. ENRIQUE SANMARTÍ AULET.

Aeropuertos Españoles y Navegación Aérea (AENA): Arturo Soria 109, 28043 Madrid; tel. (91) 3211000; fax (91) 3212571; internet www.aena.es; f. 1990; network of 42 airports in Spain; Dir-Gen. PEDRO ARGÜELLES SALAVERÍA.

Principal Airlines

Air Europa Líneas Aéreas, SA: Centro Empresarial Globalia, POB 132, Baleares; tel. (971) 178190; fax (971) 178353; internet www.air-europa.com; f. 1986; charter and scheduled services to Canary and Balearic Islands, North Africa, Western and Northern Europe; also Thailand, Egypt, Mexico, USA, Cuba and Dominican Republic; Pres. JUAN JOSÉ HIDALGO ACERA; Dir-Gen. MANUEL PANADERO.

Cygnus Air, SA: Calle Aguetol 7, Barajas, 28042 Madrid; tel. (91) 329 3031; fax (91) 3966899; e-mail cygnus@gestair.es; f. 1998; part of Grupo Gestair; freight services; Pres. JESÚS MACARRÓN; Gen. Man. FRANCISCO BERNALTE.

Gestair Executive Jet, SA: Aguetol 7, Barajas, 28042 Madrid; tel. (91) 3290500; fax (91) 3293323; e-mail infoair@gestair.es; internet www.gestair.es; f. 1977; air-taxi operator, domestic and international services; part of Grupo Gestair; Pres. JESÚS MACARRÓN; Man. Dir JOSÉ M. ESPINOSA JIMÉNEZ.

Grupo Iberia: María de Molina 40, 4°, 28006 Madrid; tel. (91) 5877593; fax (91) 5877949; e-mail igonzalez@retemail.es; internet www.iberia.com; f. 1927; domestic and international passenger and freight services to 99 destinations in 42 countries; partner in airline alliance OneWorld; Chair. and CEO XABIER DE IRALA; Dir-Gen. ANGEL MULLOR PARRONDO.

incorporates:

Binter Canarias, SA: Aeropuerto de Gran Canaria, Parcela 9, del ZIMA Apdo 50 Gran Canaria; tel. (928) 579601; fax (928) 579603; e-mail info@bintercanarias.es; internet www .bintercanarias.com; f. 1988; scheduled services within Canary Islands and to Madeira; Pres. ANGEL MULLOR PARRONDO; Dir-Gen. LUIS GREGORIO GARCIA RUIZ.

Iberia Regional/Air Nostrum: Avda Fco Valldecabres 31, 46940 Valencia; tel. (96) 1960209; fax (96) 1960218; e-mail direccion@ airnostrum.es; internet www.airnostrum.es; f. 1996; domestic scheduled passenger and freight services; Chair. CARLOS BERTOMEU; Pres. EMILIO SERRATOSA.

LTE International Airways, SA: Carrer del Ter 27, 07009 Palma de Mallorca; tel. (971) 475700; fax (971) 478886; e-mail dgeneral@lte .es; f. 1987; charter flights between Spanish islands and Europe; Pres. JOSÉ M. GOYA; Dir CASIMIRO BERMÚEZ.

SPAIN

Directory

Oasis International Airlines: Madrid; f. 1986; fmrly Andalus Air; charter services to Europe, Canary Islands and Caribbean; Pres. and Gen. Man. Antonio Mara.

Pan Air Líneas Aéreas, SA: Edif. TNT, 2°, Centro de Cargo Aérea, Aeropuerto de Madrid-Barajas, 28022 Madrid; tel. (91) 3120422; fax (91) 3120440; f. 1987; international and domestic freight charter; Pres. (vacant).

Spanair: Aeropuerto de Palma, Apdo 50.086, Palma de Mallorca; tel. (971) 745020; fax (971) 492553; e-mail spanair@spanair.es; internet www.spanair.com; f. 1986; passenger scheduled and charter services within Spain, incl. Canary and Balearic Islands and within Europe; owned by Teinver and Scandinavian Airlines System; Pres. Gonzalo Pascual; Dir Gen. Enrique Melía.

Tourism

Spain's tourist attractions include its climate, beaches and historic cities. Since 1985 the Government has aimed at attracting more visitors to the interior and to the north-west of Spain. Hotel bedrooms totalled 1,132,350 in December 1994. Tourism makes an important contribution to the country's economy. In 2002 Spain received some 48.7m. foreign tourists. Receipts from tourism totalled an estimated €36,705m. in 2001.

Instituto de Turismo de España (Turespaña): José Lázaro Galdeano 6, 28071 Madrid; tel. (91) 3433500; fax (91) 3433446; e-mail german.porras@tourspain.es; internet www.tourspain.es; fmrly Inprotur; autonomous organization; Dir Germán Porras Olalla.

Secretaria de Estado de Comercio y Turismo: José Lázaro Galdiano 6, 28071 Madrid; tel. (91) 3493500; fax (91) 3495240; e-mail buzon.oficial@dgturismo.sscc.mcx.es; internet www.mcx.es; Sec.-Gen. D. Juan Costa Climent.

SPANISH EXTERNAL TERRITORIES

SPANISH NORTH AFRICA

Introductory Survey

Location, Climate, Language, Religion

Spanish North Africa comprises mainly two enclaves within Moroccan territory: Ceuta, on the north African coast opposite Gibraltar, the Strait here being about 25 km wide; and Melilla, situated on a small peninsula jutting into the Mediterranean Sea. Attached to Melilla, for administrative purposes, are Peñón de Vélez de la Gomera, a small fort on the Mediterranean coast, and two groups of islands, Peñón de Alhucemas and the Chafarinas. The average temperature is 17°C. Spanish and Arabic are spoken. Most Europeans are Roman Catholic, most North Africans being Muslim. There are small Hindu and Jewish communities.

Recent History

The population of the enclaves is mostly Spanish. The proportion of Arab residents, however, particularly in Melilla, has greatly increased, owing to the large numbers of illegal immigrants from Morocco. Those born in the territories are Spanish citizens and subjects. An ancient port and walled city, Ceuta was retained by Spain upon Moroccan independence from France in 1956. Having developed as a military and administrative centre for the former Spanish Protectorate in Morocco, Ceuta now functions as a bunkering and fishing port. In 1974 the town became the seat of the Capitanía General de Africa. Two-thirds of Ceuta's land area are used exclusively for military purposes.

Melilla was the first Spanish town to rise against the Government of the Popular Front in July 1936, at the beginning of the Spanish Civil War. Like Ceuta, Melilla was retained by Spain when Morocco became independent in 1956. In addition to its function as a port, Melilla now serves as a military base, more than one-half of the enclave's land area being used solely for military purposes.

In October 1978 King Hassan of Morocco attempted to link the question of the sovereignty of Melilla to that of the return of the British dependent territory of Gibraltar to Spain. In November King Hassan stated his country's claim to Ceuta and Melilla. In October 1981 Spain declared before the UN that Ceuta and Melilla were integral parts of Spanish territory. In April 1982 Istiqlal, a Moroccan political party, demanded action to recover the territories from Spain, and in March 1983 the Moroccan Government blocked the passage of goods across the frontiers of Ceuta and Melilla. In August the movement of Moroccan workers to Ceuta, Melilla and also Gibraltar was restricted. Following the opening of the Spanish frontier with Gibraltar in early 1985, Morocco reiterated its claim to Ceuta and Melilla. King Hassan indicated, however, that he desired a political solution to the problem. Spain rejects any comparison between the two enclaves and Gibraltar.

From 1984 there was increasing unease over Spanish North Africa's future. Rioting in Morocco in January 1984 and the signing of the treaty of union between Libya and Morocco in August gave rise to disquiet. In July 1985 the joint Libyan-Moroccan assembly passed a resolution calling for the 'liberation' of Ceuta and Melilla. In July 1985 the leaders of the nationalist parties of both Ceuta and Melilla visited Gibraltar for talks with the Chief Minister, in an effort to secure support for their cause. Details of the enclaves' new draft statutes, envisaging the establishment of two local assemblies, with jurisdiction over such matters as public works, agriculture, tourism, culture and internal trade, were announced in August and approved by the central Government in December 1985. Unlike Spain's other regional assemblies, however, those of Ceuta and Melilla were not to be vested with legislative powers, and this denial of full autonomy was much criticized in the two enclaves.

After negotiations with representatives of the Muslim community, in May 1986 the central Government in Madrid agreed to grant Spanish nationality to more than 2,400 Muslims resident in the enclaves, under the terms of legislation introduced in July 1985 requiring all foreigners resident in Spain to register with the authorities or risk expulsion. (While most Muslims in Ceuta possessed the necessary documentation, in Melilla only some 7,000 of the estimated 27,000-strong Muslim community held Spanish nationality.) In response to protests particularly in Melilla, the central Government had given assurances that it would assist the full integration into Spanish society of Muslims in Ceuta and Melilla, and promised to improve conditions in the territories. By mid-1986, however, the number of Muslims applying for Spanish nationality in Melilla alone had reached several thousand. As a result of the delays in the processing of the applications by the authorities, Aomar Muhammadi Dudú, the leader of the newly founded Muslim Partido de los Demócratas de Melilla (PDM), accused the Government of failing to fulfil its pledge to the Muslim residents.

At the general election of June 1986 the ruling Partido Socialista Obrero Español (PSOE) was successful in Ceuta, but was defeated by the centre-right Coalición Popular (CP) in Melilla, the latter result indicating the strong opposition of the Spanish community in the territories to the Government's plan to integrate the Muslim population. Tight security surrounded the elections in Melilla, where 'parallel elections', resulting in a vote of confidence in the PDM leader, were held by the Muslim community, and polling was accompanied by several days of unrest. In August Juan Díez de la Cortina, Secretary-General of the extreme right-wing Partido Nacionalista (Español) de Melilla, was arrested on suspicion of planning a terrorist attack against the Government Delegate in Melilla. Following talks in Madrid between representatives of the main political parties in Melilla and the Ministry of the Interior, concessions to the enclave included the replacement of Andrés Moreno as Government Delegate by Manuel Céspedes. The Madrid negotiations were denounced by Aomar Muhammadi Dudú, the Muslim leader of Melilla, who nevertheless in September agreed to accept a senior post in the Ministry of the Interior in Madrid, with responsibility for relations with the Muslim communities of Spain.

In October 1986 it was reported that Dudú had travelled to Rabat, Morocco, for secret discussions with the country's Minister of the Interior. In November Muslim leaders in Melilla announced that they wished to establish their own administration in the enclave, in view of the Madrid Government's failure to fulfil its promise of Spanish citizenship for Muslim residents. The Spanish Minister of the Interior reiterated assurances of the Government's commitment to integrating the Muslim community. Later in the month Muslim traders closed their businesses to draw attention to their cause, and thousands of Muslims took part in a peaceful demonstration in support of Dudú, who had resigned his Madrid post after only two months in office. (Dudú subsequently went into exile in Morocco and lost the support of Melilla's Muslim community.) A similar protest, to have taken place in Ceuta in December, was banned by the Spanish authorities.

In January 1987 Spain rejected a proposal by King Hassan to establish a joint commission to seek a solution to the problem of the Spanish enclaves. Police reinforcements were dispatched from Spain in the following month, in response to a serious escalation of inter-racial tensions in Melilla. Numerous demonstrators were detained, and several prominent Muslims were charged with sedition and briefly held in custody on the mainland. King Hassan reaffirmed his support for the Muslims of the Spanish enclaves, and later warned that a serious crisis in relations between Rabat and Madrid would arise if Spain were to grant autonomy to Ceuta and Melilla; he also renewed his proposal for dialogue on the issue of the territories. In April Spanish and Moroccan troops participated in joint manoeuvres on Moroccan territory adjacent to Melilla, as part of a programme of military co-operation. During a visit to Melilla in mid-1987 a senior official of the ruling PSOE emphasized the need for the integration of Christians and Muslims, while asserting that Spanish sovereignty would continue and would form the basis of the territory's future autonomy statute. In July, following a visit to Rabat by the Spanish Minister of Foreign Affairs, King Hassan declared that it had been agreed to hold talks on the question of Ceuta and Melilla; however, the Spanish Government denied the existence of such an agreement, maintaining that the issue was not negotiable.

In February 1988 it was announced that, in accordance with regulations of the European Community (EC, now European Union—EU, see p. 199), to which Spain had acceded in 1986, Moroccan citizens would in due course require visas to enter Spain. Entry to Spanish North Africa, however, was to be exempt from the new ruling.

In March 1988, after several months of negotiations, the central Government and main opposition parties in Madrid reached a broad consensus on draft autonomy statutes for the Spanish External Territories. In July a senior member of the ruling PSOE acknowledged that the party's Programme 2000 contained contradictory proposals regarding Ceuta and Melilla. Although it was envisaged that Spain would retain the territories, the possibility of a negotiated settlement with Morocco was not discounted. In that month, seven years after the enclaves' first official request for autonomy, the central Government announced that the implementation of the territories' autonomy statutes was to be accelerated. Revised draft statutes were submitted by the PSOE to the main opposition parties for consideration. The statutes declared Ceuta and Melilla to be integral parts of Spain and the Spanish Government undertook for the first time to guarantee financial support for the territories. As previously indicated by the Spanish Government, the two Spanish North African assemblies were to be granted 'normative' rather than legislative powers. Each new assembly would elect from among its members a city president. However, it was subsequently revealed that the revised statutes encompassed only the enclaves of Ceuta and Melilla, thus excluding the associated Spanish North African islands—the Chafarinas Islands, the Peñón de Alhucemas, the Peñón de Vélez de la Gomera and the island of Perejil (Spanish sovereignty over the last was uncertain)—which had been erroneously incorporated in the preliminary statutes approved by the Government in 1985. The islands would remain the responsibility of the Spanish Ministry of Defence, and would not form part of any Spanish autonomous region. By December 1988 a total of 5,257 Muslims in Melilla had been granted Spanish citizenship since 1986, and a further 1,126 applications were pending; by 1990 nearly all residents were in possession of an identity card.

Meanwhile, in October 1988 Morocco's Minister of Foreign Affairs formally presented his country's claim to Ceuta and Melilla to the UN General Assembly. An official visit by King Hassan to Spain, scheduled for November, was indefinitely postponed without explanation, and in Melilla a Muslim group acknowledged that it had been in receipt of financial assistance from the Moroccan Government. In May 1989 the Spanish Prime Minister met with King Hassan in Casablanca, Morocco, for discussions on the situation in the Middle East. During an official visit to Spain in September, King Hassan later reiterated his country's claim to Ceuta and Melilla, although, as previously, he discounted the use of force as a means of settling the dispute. Spain and Morocco agreed to hold annual summit meetings in an effort to improve relations.

At the general election held in October 1989 the ruling PSOE retained its Ceuta seats, despite allegations by the opposition PP that many names on the electoral register were duplicated. In Melilla, however, the election results were declared invalid, following the discovery of serious irregularities. At the repeated ballot, in March 1990, both Senate seats and the one Congress seat were won by the PP, the latter result depriving the PSOE of its overall majority in the Madrid lower chamber.

In April 1990 the Spanish Government presented the autonomy statutes for discussion in the territories. It was confirmed that the enclaves were to remain an integral part of Spain, and that they were to be granted self-government at municipal, rather than regional, level. Moroccan political parties were united in their denunciation of what they considered an attempt to legalize Spanish possession of the territories. In August 1990 Spain granted its Government Delegate in Melilla direct powers to expel illegal residents from the territory. In the same month King Hassan and the Spanish Prime Minister met near Rabat for talks. Their discussions focused on the crisis caused by Iraq's recent invasion of Kuwait, and on their bilateral relations, particularly increased co-operation and security. In December 1990 a Spanish delegation, led by the Prime Minister, travelled to Morocco, where the first of the planned regular summit meetings between the Spanish and Moroccan premiers took place. Among the topics discussed was the forthcoming

implementation (from May 1991) of new visa requirements for North Africans entering Spain; special arrangements were to apply to Moroccan citizens who worked in, or travelled regularly to, Ceuta and Melilla. In mid-1991, at the invitation of the Spanish Government, the Moroccan Minister of the Interior, Driss Basri, and a cabinet colleague made an unprecedented visit to Ceuta.

At elections to the municipal councils of Ceuta and Melilla held in May 1991, in each territory the PSOE Mayor was replaced. In Ceuta Francisco Fraiz Armada of the Progreso y Futuro de Ceuta (PFC), became Mayor. In Melilla, where the PP had secured 12 of the 25 seats, Ignacio Velázquez Rivera of the right-wing Partido Nacionalista de Melilla (PNM) was elected Mayor of the enclave.

The draft autonomy statutes of Ceuta and Melilla were submitted to the Congreso de los Diputados (Congress of Deputies) in Madrid for discussion in October 1991. In November thousands of demonstrators, many of whom had travelled from the enclaves, attended a protest march in Madrid (organized by the Governments of Ceuta and Melilla), in support of demands for full autonomy for the territories. In early 1992, however, the central Government confirmed that the assemblies of Ceuta and Melilla were not to be granted full legislative powers. In March 1993, in an attempt to bring about the transfer of powers to the territories, the PP submitted its own draft statute for Melilla to the central Government, which immediately condemned the document as unconstitutional.

At the general election of June 1993 the PSOE of Ceuta lost its one seat in Congress and its two seats in the Senate to the PP. In Melilla the PSOE candidate defeated the incumbent PP Congress member; the PP also lost one of its two seats in the Senate.

The final statutes of autonomy were finally approved by the Spanish Government in September 1994, in preparation for their presentation to the Cortes. The statutes provided for 25-member local assemblies with powers similar to those of the municipal councils of mainland Spain. The proposals for limited self-government were generally acceptable in Melilla but not in Ceuta, where, in October 1994, a general strike received widespread support. An estimated 20,000 residents of Ceuta participated in a demonstration to demand equality with other Spanish regions and full autonomy for the enclave. Earlier in the month, following expressions of concern regarding the territories' protection in the event of Moroccan aggression, the Minister of Defence confirmed that Spain would continue to maintain an appropriate military presence in Ceuta and Melilla. In December more than 2,000 citizens of Ceuta attended a demonstration in Madrid in support of their demands for full autonomy.

Following their approval by the Congress of Deputies in December 1994, the autonomy statutes were ratified by the Senate in February 1995. Approval of the statutes by the Spanish Cortes was denounced by Morocco, which declared that the recovery of Ceuta and Melilla was to be one of its major objectives.

Elections for the new local assemblies were held in May 1995. In Ceuta the PP won nine of the 25 seats, the PFC six, the nationalist Ceuta Unida four and the PSOE three. Basilio Fernández López of the PFC was re-elected Mayor/President, heading a coalition with Ceuta Unida and the PSOE. Mustafa Mizziam Ammar, leader of the Partido Democrático y Social de Ceuta (PDSC), became the first Muslim candidate ever to be elected in the territory. Fewer than 57% of those eligible voted in Ceuta. In Melilla, where the level of participation was less than 62%, the PP won 14 of the 25 seats, the PSOE five seats, Coalición por Melilla (CpM), a new Muslim grouping, four seats and the right-wing Unión del Pueblo Melillense (UPM) two seats. Ignacio Velázquez (PP/PNM) returned to the position of Mayor/President.

In Ceuta concern about the level of illegal immigration from sub-Saharan Africa increased during 1995. In October a police-officer was seriously injured in a violent confrontation involving about 150 Africans and the security forces (the latter had been joined by citizens' vigilante groups). More than 100 illegal immigrants were subsequently transferred to a detention centre on the Spanish mainland, while 15 Africans who were alleged to have led the riot were imprisoned in Ceuta. In an attempt to curtail illegal immigration, Ceuta's frontier with Morocco was strengthened.

At the general election held in March 1996, in Ceuta the three PP delegates to the Cortes in Madrid were re-elected. In Melilla the PSOE lost its seat in the lower house to the PP, which also took both seats in the Senate. Following the installation of the PP administration in Madrid, both Government Delegates in the territories were replaced. In the same month thousands of Muslims took part in a demonstration, organized by Coalición por Melilla, to protest against their position on the margins of society.

In February 1996, meanwhile, the Spanish and Moroccan Prime Ministers met in Rabat for their first summit meeting since December 1993. In May on his first official overseas trip, Prime Minister José María Aznar travelled from Spain to Morocco for discussions with King Hassan.

In July 1996 the Mayor/President of Ceuta, Basilio Fernández López of the PFC, resigned after seven months at the head of a minority administration, and was replaced by Jesús Fortes Ramos of the PP, who urged that the enclave be considered a full autonomous region. In September the Secretary-General of NATO confirmed that Ceuta and Melilla would remain outside the alliance's sphere of protection if Spain were to be fully integrated into NATO's military structure.

In mid-1996 attention focused once again on the issue of illegal immigration from Africa. Both Ceuta and Melilla appealed to the EU for financial assistance to counter the problems arising from the enclaves' attractive location as an entry point to Europe and from the recent implementation of the EU's Schengen Agreement permitting the free movement of persons among the accord's signatory countries. In June, following disturbances involving refugees from Central Africa, more than 100 immigrants were flown from Melilla to detention centres on the Spanish mainland and then swiftly expelled via the Canary Islands to various sub-Saharan countries. The Spanish Government's apparently peremptory procedure and dismissal of requests for asylum not only provoked criticism from humanitarian groups, but also led to demands from senior judges and politicians for clarification of the events. The General Prosecutor of Spain was ordered to initiate an inquiry, and the Spanish Ministry of the Interior, which had admitted that sedative drugs had been administered to the refugees prior to their deportation, also opened an investigation. (The case was closed in July 1998, with no charges brought.) In September 1996 the local organization of the International Committee of the Red Cross declared that its supplies of rations were insufficient to feed the 406 (mainly Moroccan and Algerian) immigrants located at an encampment in Ceuta. Negotiations in Madrid in the following month between the Spanish Minister of the Interior and his Moroccan counterpart resulted in an agreement on the establishment of two joint commissions to address the specific problems of illegal immigration and drugs-trafficking. At further discussions in December, for the first time since the signing of a joint accord in 1992, Morocco agreed to the readmission of illegal immigrants held in the Spanish enclaves.

Between January and December 1996, according to the Spanish Ministry of the Interior, a total of 1,552 illegal Moroccan immigrants were detained in Ceuta, while 2,321 were detained in Melilla. The central Government allocated emergency funding of 28m. pesetas to meet the immediate needs of the immigrants. A sum of 30m. pesetas was granted to the Red Cross. In early 1997, in view of increased concern that much of the illegal immigration from Morocco was being controlled by networks involved in the smuggling of drugs and tobacco, the first joint police operation with Morocco was undertaken against these networks.

In March 1997, in Melilla, a motion of censure against Ignacio Velázquez resulted in the Mayor/President's defeat, owing to the defection to the opposition of two PP councillors, Enrique Palacios and Abdelmalik Tahar. The latter subsequently absconded to the Canary Islands. The opposition then declared Enrique Palacios to be Mayor/President, although the central Government continued to recognize Ignacio Velázquez as the rightful incumbent. In May Enrique Palacios alleged that at the election of May 1995 the PP had employed irregular tactics in its campaign for the support of Muslim voters. Also in May 1997, for the first time, the Mayor/Presidents of Ceuta and Melilla attended a conference of the autonomous regions' presidents, held in Madrid. Despite the attempted 'coup' in Melilla, the territory was represented by Ignacio Velázquez. In November 1997, from Tenerife, Abdelmalik Tahar accused Ignacio Velázquez and five associates of having subjected him to blackmail and threats, as a result of which he had relinquished his seat on the Council, thereby permitting the PP to replace him and to regain its majority. In December 1997 Tahar, who was now

under police protection, declared to the investigating judge that he had been offered 50m. pesetas (of which he had received 3m.) and a monthly sum of 200,000 pesetas. Following an appeal by Enrique Palacios and a judicial ruling leading to the successful revival of the motion of censure against Ignacio Velázquez in February 1998, Palacios took office as Mayor/President of Melilla, accusing his predecessor, furthermore, of serious financial mismanagement. A new motion of censure, presented by the PP urging that (despite the bribery charges against him) Ignacio Velázquez be restored to office, was deemed to be illegal and therefore rejected in a decree issued by Enrique Palacios, who also ordered the temporary closure of the local assembly. In July Enrique Palacios accused the PP of having employed public funds, amounting to more than 200m. pesetas, to secure the votes of some 2,500 Muslims at the 1995 local elections, the bribes reportedly having taken the form of building materials for the purposes of residential repairs. The allegations were denied by the PP.

During 1997 there was increased concern regarding the numbers of illegal immigrants. In June police reinforcements were drafted into Melilla, following renewed disturbances in which one immigrant died. More than 100 illegal immigrants were immediately returned to Morocco as part of a special security operation, and on the same day of action a total of 873 Moroccans were denied entry to Melilla. (More than 10,000 Moroccans continued to cross the border legally each day, in order to work in the enclave.) In August 1997 the Spanish General Prosecutor demanded emergency measures to address the immigration crisis, having already urged the Ministry of the Interior in June to find an immediate solution. In the same month various non-governmental organizations (NGOs) condemned the rudimentary conditions in which more than 900 illegal immigrants, mainly from sub-Saharan Africa and Algeria, were being held in Melilla. By December the number of immigrants in Melilla alone totalled 930. In that month the Spanish Government announced that 1,206 sub-Saharan Africans were to be transferred from Ceuta and Melilla to the mainland. The authorities effected the first transfers to Spain later that month, where the illegal immigrants were received by NGOs.

In January 1998 four members of the security forces were injured in three separate incidents involving carriers of contraband on the border with Morocco. Efforts were subsequently taken to strengthen the territories' borders, and both maritime and street patrols were increased. It was announced that during 1997 4,358 illegal immigrants had been expelled from Ceuta. It was also estimated that since 1990 some 2,000 people had drowned during unsuccessful attempts to cross the Strait of Gibraltar, while about 20,000 illegal immigrants had been arrested by the Spanish authorities.

During a visit by the Spanish Prime Minister to Morocco in April 1998, his Moroccan counterpart requested that Spain review its policy on Ceuta and Melilla. In September the Government of Melilla was the first to reject Morocco's offer of dual nationality for the citizens of the two enclaves, urging the Spanish Government to lodge a protest with the Moroccan authorities.

In January 1999 alone the Ceuta authorities expelled more than 100 Moroccans, including 60 children, all of whom lacked documentation. In March, however, the Spanish General Prosecutor ordered the police force of Ceuta to suspend expulsions of destitute minors.

In January 1999 the PP Senator for Melilla, Aurel-Gheorghe Sava, announced his resignation owing to an internal party dispute. He was replaced by Beatriz Caro. In the same month, after 12 years' exile in Morocco, Aomar Muhammadi Dudú, the former Muslim leader, returned to Melilla, in preparation for the local elections to be held in June. In February, as the internal crisis within the local party grew, the PP lost a motion of censure against Enrique Palacios.

At the elections of June 1999, the most successful party in both Ceuta and Melilla was the Grupo Independiente Liberal (GIL), recently founded by Jesús Gil, the controversial Mayor of Marbella. The GIL secured 12 of the 25 seats in the Assembly of Ceuta and seven of the 25 in Melilla. Antonio Sampietro Casarramona of the GIL replaced Jesús Fortes Ramos of the PP as Mayor/President of Ceuta in August, following the latter's removal from office by a motion of censure supported by a rebel PSOE deputy, Susana Bermúdez. The defection to the GIL of the socialist deputy was ostensibly due to the PSOE's apparent refusal to allocate her the education and culture portfolio, as desired. The authorities subsequently announced that a judicial inquiry into the defection of Bermúdez was to be conducted. Both the PSOE and the PP accused the GIL of having bribed the deputy to transfer her allegiance. In March 2000 Sampietro and Bermúdez were charged with bribery. The accession of the GIL to power in Ceuta, along with the group's increasing influence in Melilla, in September 1999 prompted the central Government to announce changes in the laws relating to town planning in the enclaves.

In Melilla in July 1999 the two newly-elected PSOE councillors defied a central directive to vote with the five PP delegates (in order to obstruct the accession of the GIL to the city presidency), and instead gave their support to Mustafa Aberchán Hamed of the CpM, which had won five seats. The Muslim Aberchán was thus elected to replace Enrique Palacios as Mayor/President of Melilla. In mid-July Aberchán and the GIL agreed to form a minority Government. The two rebel PSOE councillors subsequently relinquished their seats. In August a replacement PSOE delegate claimed that a representative of Aberchán had offered him a bribe of 20m. pesetas in exchange for the renunciation of his seat. The fact that his predecessor had relinquished her seat and then attempted to withdraw her resignation led to intense speculation that she had also been offered a bribe. In September, following a rift between the CpM and the GIL, the Mayor/President of Melilla attempted to form a minority Government with representatives of the Partido Independiente de Melilla (PIM), recently established by Palacios. In October, however, Aberchán reached a broad agreement with members of the PP and UPM, enabling him to remain in office. In November the Melilla branch of the GIL announced that henceforth it was to operate independently of the mainland party. In the same month, a new agreement between Aberchán and the GIL having been concluded, the latter grouping declared its intention to renew its participation in the Government of Melilla. As a result, the socialist councillors withdrew from the administration. In early December the Mayor/President of Melilla announced the composition of a new coalition Government, the post of First Vice-President being allocated to Crispin Lozano, the local leader of the GIL, while Palacios of the PIM became Second Vice-President. In the same month Ignacio Velázquez, the former PP Mayor/President of Melilla, was barred from public office for six years, having been found guilty of neglecting his duty during his tenure of office. The conviction was in respect of an incident in 1992 when Velázquez had convened a session of the Council, which was due to vote on a motion of censure against him, in full knowledge of the fact that at least one member was due to be in Madrid that day, thus rendering any vote invalid. However, he was acquitted of charges of misappropriation of public funds. In May 2000, following the defection to the opposition of two GIL deputies and one UPM representative, Aberchán declared that, despite the Government's loss of its majority, he would not resign. The opposition subsequently announced that they would request a vote of 'no confidence' in Aberchán's government at the earliest opportunity. Later in the month the national leadership of the PP and the PSOE met in Madrid in an attempt to negotiate a solution to the political crisis in Melilla. The two parties agreed that, if Aberchán's Government were removed from office, they would form a coalition government in partnership with the Unión del Pueblo Melillense (UPM), whose leader, Juan José Imbroda Ortiz, would be nominated Mayor/President. In early July the remaining five GIL members left the Government and joined the opposition. The opposition subsequently introduced a motion of censure against Aberchán, whom they accused of nepotism, a lack of transparency and of harassment of the opposition. Aberchán, who described the accusations as being racially motivated, announced that the CpM was to withdraw from the legislature. In mid-July some 2,000 Muslim citizens of Melilla demonstrated in support of Aberchán. At the same time Palacios suspended the motion of censure by decree, reportedly without having consulted Aberchán. (Palacios was subsequently barred from public office for seven years, having been found guilty of perversion of the course of justice.) The opposition later successfully overturned the decree in the courts, and the vote on the motion of censure against Aberchán was therefore able to proceed. The motion was adopted on 17 September, with the support of 16 of the 25 deputies, and Imbroda was elected as Mayor/President. In late 2000 four members of the GIL announced their departure from the party. In January 2002 Velázquez resigned as Councillor of the Presidency, after the Supreme Court upheld his 1999 conviction.

In January 2000, meanwhile, Aznar made a visit to the North African enclaves, the first by a Spanish Prime Minister for 19 years. His decision to visit in his capacity as leader of the PP, however, rather than as head of government, was severely criticized by the Mayor/Presidents of Ceuta and Melilla and by the opposition parties. At the general election held on 12 March 2000, Ceuta's three PP representatives in Madrid, one deputy and two senators, all secured re-election. The PP also retained Melilla's three seats in the Spanish legislature.

In February 1999 it emerged that the two enclaves were being used extensively by drugs-traffickers for the purposes of 'money-laundering' operations. The Ministry of Economy and Finance began an inquiry into these irregular movements of substantial amounts of foreign exchange. In March the Ministry of the Interior initiated an investigation into allegations of corruption in the prison and security services of Ceuta, the accusations again related to the trade in illicit drugs. In July 48 arrests were made in Melilla following a police operation to dismantle an extensive 'money-laundering' network, believed to be responsible for the illegal processing of a total of 1,000m. pesetas derived from drugs-trafficking.

In early 1999 it was conceded that the security barrier on Ceuta's border with Morocco was proving inadequate. The EU-funded project had been initiated five years previously but remained unfinished. Further improvements were undertaken, and were completed in February 2000. Between January and July 1999 alone a total of 21,411 illegal immigrants were apprehended on Ceuta's frontier and returned to Morocco. A new reception centre in Ceuta, to replace the inadequate facilities of the Calamocarro camp, was completed in May 2000. In September 1999, in one of the most serious disturbances to date, damage estimated at 20m. pesetas was caused during rioting at a reception centre in Melilla, where 300 illegal immigrants were accommodated. The inmates alleged that they were being mistreated by the security guards. There were increasing numbers of disturbances at Ceuta reception centres in late 2000 and early 2001.

In November 1999 a battalion of the Spanish Legion commenced duty on Ceuta's frontier with Morocco, reinforcing the 300 civil guards. The implementation in February 2000 of new legislation relating to immigrants' rights obliged the border post at Ceuta to provide legal assistance to those being denied entry to Spain by the police. In February an operation to prevent the entry of 500 sub-Saharan Africans into Ceuta led to violent confrontation between the migrants and the authorities. In May the Government of Ceuta estimated that more than 25,000 potential immigrants, mainly Moroccans, were concentrated on the North African coast, awaiting an opportunity to travel to southern Spain. In May 2000 it was revealed that during 1999 a total of 700,000 illegal immigrants had been refused admission to Spanish North Africa.

In Morocco, meanwhile, King Hassan died in July 1999. In August the Moroccan Prime Minister urged Spain to open negotiations on the future of Ceuta and Melilla. In January 2000 Aznar visited Ceuta and Melilla, describing the enclaves as constant parts of Spain's future. Morocco subsequently cancelled a scheduled official visit of the Spanish Minister of Foreign Affairs (although the official reason given by the Moroccan authorities for the cancellation was that King Muhammad was on holiday). It was announced in March that Spain was to invest 6,725m. pesetas in joint projects to be implemented in Morocco during 2000–02, an increase of 22.6% compared with the previous three-year period. During an official visit to Morocco in May 2000, the Spanish Prime Minister reiterated his concern regarding the growing problem of illegal immigration from North Africa, offering to finance development plans in Morocco in exchange for greater co-operation on the part of the Moroccan authorities in curbing the number of migrants. Aznar also declared that the controversial immigration law, which had taken effect in February, would need to be reviewed, as, since its entry into force, more than 82,000 immigrants had applied for Spanish residency permits. Large numbers of immigrants continued to enter the two enclaves illegally throughout 2000 and clashes between migrants and the security forces continued to be reported. The immigration law reforms entered into force on 23 January 2001, intended to assist those seeking asylum but offering severe penalties to illegal immigrants and to traffickers in and employers of illegal immigrants. Under the law, those entering the country illegally could be deported within 48 hours of apprehension; illegal workers would be deprived of the right to strike and to join a union, and their use of public services would be limited; illegal immigrants would gain the right to remain in the country only after five years of employment, rather than the two years previously specified. Protests against the reforms were staged in Spanish North Africa, as in Spain.

In June 2000, meanwhile, in Melilla, four policemen were arrested for their involvement in one of the principal immigrant trafficking networks. Three organizers of a similar network were detained in Ceuta in November, and two further networks were uncovered there in April 2001. In November 2000 the border guard of the Tarajal frontier between Ceuta and Morocco announced an indefinite strike, protesting against the lack of resources and personnel. In the resulting delays and closures of the border, three policemen were injured when 800 Moroccans attempted to force entrance to Ceuta.

In early September 2000, following a ruling in the Spanish courts that Ceuta and Melilla could not be considered to be autonomous communities, the ruling GIL proposed in the Ceuta Assembly that the Spanish Government grant Ceuta greater autonomy. Discussions on the proposal, which proved highly emotive, led to disturbances within the Assembly. The motion was subsequently carried by a majority vote, despite the opposition of the PP and PSOE and the abstention of the PDSC.

In early January 2001 five Ceuta councillors resigned their posts and announced their departure from the GIL, thus depriving the party of its majority in the Assembly. Former PSOE deputy Bermúdez subsequently withdrew her support for the GIL which had previously enabled the party to assume office. A motion of censure was subsequently brought against Sampietro by the PP, PSOE, PDSC and one of the former GIL councillors, Aída Pietra. The motion was carried on 10 February, with the support of 17 of the 25 deputies, and Juan Jesús Vivas Lara of the PP was appointed Mayor/President of Ceuta. A new Council was subsequently announced, including the five 'rebel' councillors (now members of the Grupo Mixto). Some controversy was caused by the appointment of Bermúdez's husband to a Director-General post. However, he subsequently resigned following protests by the PSOE. There was further controversy in late July when the Vice-President of the Council, Jesús Simarro Marín resigned, ostensibly for personal and political reasons. He was also involved in an investigation into a property development firm which had planned to build a new shopping centre in the town. Cristina Bernal Dúran was subsequently appointed to replace him. In the following four days, the Councillor of Development and the Environment, Tomás Álvarez de Lara, and deputy in the Council of Social Services also resigned.

It was estimated that in late August 2001 some 800 Moroccan immigrants who were attempting to take advantage of a high level of traffic at the Tarajal border crossing in Ceuta during an annual trade fair, were intercepted by police. In September, the Government announced that the identification papers of Moroccans wishing to enter Ceuta and Melilla would be examined more closely and the presence of extra police at the frontiers. Unrest in mid-October, when Moroccan rioters threw stones at frontier posts, prompted the authorities to close the border for several hours. Also in October, two members of the Civil Guard were imprisoned for trafficking in illegal immigrants from Pakistan. Meanwhile, in mid-August the human rights organization Amnesty International accused the Spanish Government of the systematic abuse of the rights of homeless children from Morocco and Algeria, citing Melilla and Ceuta as regions where the worst offences occurred.

Relations with Morocco remained tense in late 2001, especially following that country's abrupt withdrawal of its ambassador from Madrid in October. A confrontation developed between Moroccan and Spanish police at the end of December when the Spanish authorities attempted to seize a vessel, allegedly laden with narcotics, which the Moroccans had already been pursuing through their own waters. In February 2002, the Spanish Ministry of Foreign Affairs again rejected the Moroccan Government's comparison of the status of Ceuta and Melilla with that of Gibraltar, as talks between the Spanish and British governments regarding the British territory progressed. Relations were threatened again in July 2002, after the occupation of a small islet near Ceuta, Perejil, by 12 Moroccan soldiers. Madrid made a formal protest to Rabat 12 July, but Morocco refused to withdraw its men, claiming that Perejil (known as Laila to the Moroccans) had been a part of Morocco since independence in 1956. Four Spanish gunboats were dispatched to patrol the locality and Spanish soldiers re-occupied the island on 17 July. A subsequent US-mediated arrangement resulted in agreement by both countries to leave the islet unoccupied,

although issues regarding the sovereignty of Ceuta and Melilla continued to be problematic. Indeed in September Morocco reasserted its claims to the enclaves at the UN. Later in the month Morocco additionally accused Spain of violating its airspace and territorial waters more than 90 times since July, and cancelled a scheduled meeting with Spain in protest against the alleged landing of a Spanish military helicopter on Perejil; Spain denied the claim. The Spanish Minister of Foreign Affairs, Ana Palacio, reiterated that Spanish possession of Ceuta and Melilla was non-negotiable. In response to several border incidents and in an attempt to halt illegal immigration, Spain ordered the permanent closure of the border with Morocco at Benzu in October 2002; as this border was the principal commercial route from Morocco into Ceuta, there were some local fears that trade would be threatened and that the only official entrance, at Tarajal, would be put under added pressure.

A bilateral immigration accord signed by Spain and Morocco in February 2003 led to the proposed repatriation to Morocco of 200 illegal immigrant minors from Ceuta and Melilla in March. Early 2003 saw in an increase in measures to strenthen border security and in Spain's naval presence, in large part reflecting the increasing likelihood of US-led armed intervention to oust the regime of Saddam Hussain in Iraq. In March 2003 some 700–1,000 Muslim residents of Ceuta protested against the US-led military campaign in Iraq (q.v.).

Government

Following the adoption of statutes of autonomy and the establishment of local assemblies in 1995, Spanish North Africa remains an integral part of Spain, but has greater jurisdiction over matters such as public works, internal trade and tourism. Each enclave has its own Mayor/President. Ceuta, Melilla and the island dependencies are known as plazas de soberanía, fortified enclaves over which Spain has full sovereign rights. In both Ceuta and Melilla civil authority is vested in an official (Delegado del Gobierno) directly responsible to the Ministry of the Interior in Madrid. This official is usually assisted by a government sub-delegate. There is also one delegate from each of the Ministries in Madrid.

Defence

Military authority is vested in a commandant-general. The enclaves are attached to the military region of Sevilla. Spain had 8,100 troops deployed in Spanish North Africa in August 2002.

Economic Affairs

In 2001 the combined gross domestic product (GDP) of Ceuta and Melilla totalled an estimated €1,840.2m., equivalent to €13,343 per head. An unofficial report issued in October 1996 classified Melilla as by far the poorest city in Spain. In 2000 GDP per head was equivalent to 78.44% of the average for Spain in Ceuta and 85.18% of the Spanish average in Melilla. The GDP of Ceuta and Melilla grew by 5.07% in 2000 and by 4.02% in 2001.

Agricultural activity in the territories is negligible, and industry is on a limited scale. There is a local brewery in Ceuta. In 2000 the economically active population of the two enclaves totalled 65,600, of whom 8,400 were unemployed, 4,200 were employed in the construction sector, 2,100 in industry and 300 in agriculture, hunting, forestry and fishing; 36,300 were employed in the services sector. In 1996 the civil service employed 2,904 workers in Ceuta and 2,877 in Melilla. In November 2001 3,374 persons were registered as unemployed in Ceuta, and 3,587 in Melilla.

Most of the population's food is imported, with the exception of fish which is obtained locally. Sardines and anchovies are the most important items. A large proportion of the tinned fish is sold outside Spain. More important to the economies of the cities is the port activity; most of their exports take the form of fuel supplied—at very competitive rates—to ships. Most of the fuel comes from the Spanish refinery in Tenerife. Ceuta's port is the busier, receiving a total of 11,804 ships in 1998. Apart from the ferries from Málaga and Almería in mainland Spain, Melilla's port is not so frequented, and its exports are correspondingly low. Ceuta's main exports are frozen and preserved fish, foodstuffs and beer. Most trade is conducted with other parts of Spain. Tourism previously made a significant contribution to the territories' economies. Almost 1m. tourists visited Ceuta in 1986, attracted by duty-free goods; however, owing to the high ferry-boat fares and the opening of the Spanish border with Gibraltar, tourist numbers gradually declined, totalling 64,684 in 2000. The average annual rate of inflation in the year to December 1999 was 2.2%, rising to 3.8% in 2000.

Upon the accession in January 1986 of Spain to the EC (EU since November 1993), Ceuta and Melilla were considered as Spanish cities and European territory, and joined the organization as part of Spain. They retained their status as free ports. The statutes of autonomy, adopted in early 1995, envisaged the continuation of the territories' fiscal benefits. Euro notes and coins became the sole legal tender in Ceuta and Melilla on 28 February 2002.

In June 1994 the EU announced substantial regional aid: between 1995 and 1999 Ceuta and Melilla were to receive totals of ECU 28m. and ECU 45m., of which ECU 20m. and ECU 18m., respectively, were to be in the form of direct aid. However, the successive enlargements of the EU planned for 2004 and 2007 were to limit Spain's access to EU aid; Ceuta and Melilla would no longer be eligible for support. With assistance from the European Social Fund, a programme of employment and vocational training for Melilla was announced in 1996. In 1997 projected state investment in Ceuta and Melilla was 7,786m. pesetas, compared with 6,363m. pesetas in 1996. Ceuta's budget for 2001 was estimated at 23,172m. pesetas. An Action Plan for Ceuta was launched in late 2002, providing for €71m. in investment by mainland Spain to reduce the enclave's dependence upon Morocco.

Education

The education system is similar to that of mainland Spain. In addition to the conventional Spanish facilities, the Moroccan Government finances a school for 600 Muslim children in Melilla, the languages of instruction being Arabic and Spanish. The curriculum includes Koranic studies. In 1982 only 12% of Muslim children were attending school, but by 1990 the authorities had succeeded in achieving an attendance level of virtually 100%. The open university (UNED) maintains a branch in Melilla.

Statistical Survey

Ceuta

Sources (unless otherwise stated): Administración General del Estado, Beatriz de Silva 4, 51001 Ceuta; tel. (956) 512616; fax (956) 511893; Instituto Nacional de Estadística, Paseo de la Castellana 183, 28046 Madrid; tel. (91) 5839301; fax (91) 5839086; e-mail info@ine.es; internet www.ine.es.

AREA, POPULATION AND DENSITY

Area: 19.7 sq km (7.6 sq miles).

Population (census results): 67,615 at 1 March 1991; 71,505 at 1 November 2001 (males 35,991; females 35,514).

Density (1 November 2001): 3,630 per sq km.

Births, Marriages and Deaths (2001): Live births 996 (birth rate 15.97 per 1,000); Marriages 301 (marriage rate 4.0 per 1,000); Deaths 430 (death rate 6.27 per 1,000).

Expectation of Life (Ceuta and Melilla, years at birth, 1998–99): Males 73.7; Females 80.0.

Immigration and Emigration (1998): Immigrants 2,114; Emigrants 1,695.

Economically Active Population (incl. Melilla, '000 persons, 2000): Agriculture, hunting, forestry and fishing 0.3; Industry 2.1; Construction 4.2; Services 42.2; Total employed 57.2; Unemployed 8.4; Total labour force 65.6. *2001* (Ceuta only, '000 persons): Agriculture, hunting, forestry and fishing 0.3; Industry 1.2; Construction 1.7; Services 21.6; Total employed 24.5; Unemployed 7.4; Total labour force 31.9 (Source: *Ceuta—Memoria de la situación socioeconómica y laboral de la ciudad*).

AGRICULTURE, ETC.

Agriculture (head, 2000): Cattle 110; Sheep 450; Pigs 100; Goats 100.

Fishing (metric tons, live weight): Total catch 231.3 in 1999; 304.8 in 2000; 335.9 in 2001. Source: *Ceuta—Memoria de la situación socioeconómica y laboral de la ciudad*.

FINANCE

Currency and Exchange Rates: 100 cent = 1 euro (€). *Sterling and Dollar Equivalents* (31 December 2002): £1 Sterling = 1.5370 euros; US $1 = 0.9536 euros; 100 euros = £65.06 = $104.87. *Average Exchange Rate* (euros per US $): 1.0854 in 2000; 1.1175 in 2001; 1.0626 in 2002. Note: The local currency was formerly the Spanish peseta. From the introduction of the euro, with Spanish participation, on 1 January 1999, a fixed exchange rate of €1 = 166.386 pesetas was in effect. Euro notes and coins were introduced on 1 January 2002. The euro and local currency circulated alongside each other until 28 February, after which the euro became the sole legal tender. Some of the figures in this Survey are still in terms of pesetas.

Cost of Living (incl. Melilla, Consumer Price Index, annual averages; base: 1992 average = 100): 125.9 in 1999; 130.1 in 2000; 135.1 in 2001.

Gross Domestic Product (estimates, million euros, incl. Melilla): 1,682.5 in 1999; 1,767.8 in 2000; 1,840.2 in 2001.

Gross Domestic Product by Economic Activity (estimates, million euros, incl. Melilla, 2001): Agriculture, hunting, forestry and fishing 2.9; Industry 147.8 (incl. Energy 25.9, Construction 95.6); Services 1,586.0; *Sub-total* 1,736.7; *Less* Imputed bank service charges 68.4; *GDP at basic prices* 1,668.3; Taxes (less subsidies) on products 171.8; *GDP in purchasers' values* 1,840.2.

EXTERNAL TRADE

Principal Commodities: *Imports* (million pesetas, 2001): Fuel and lubricants 13,495; Milk and dairy products 2,630; Textile materials 5,292; Articles of clothing 3,125; Total (incl. others) 40,659. *Exports:* Ceuta supplies fuel and water to ships entering the port. Other exports include frozen and preserved fish, beer and foodstuffs. Total (million pesetas, 2001) 18,337 (Source: *Ceuta—Memoria de la situación socioeconómica y laboral de la ciudad*).

Principal Trading Partners (percentages, 2000): *Imports:* China 22.1; Germany 5.5; Indonesia 4.5; Italy 14.0; Netherlands 10.1; Russia 4.4; South Korea 13.4; United Kingdom 3.65. *Exports:* In 2001, the most important export partners were the Republic of Korea, Morocco, Japan, China and Argentina.

TRANSPORT

Road Traffic (2001): New vehicles registered 3,142 (passenger cars 2,555; lorries 434; motorcycles 423); Vehicles entering 218,419; Vehicles departing 225,159 (Source: *Ceuta—Memoria de la situación socioeconómica y laboral de la ciudad*).

Shipping (2001): Goods loaded 293,858 metric tons, Goods unloaded 1,412,000 metric tons; Passenger arrivals 1,193,000; Passenger departures 1,253,000 (Source: *Ceuta—Memoria de la situación socioeconómica y laboral de la ciudad*).

TOURISM

Visitor Arrivals: 71,448 in 1999; 64,684 in 2000; 95,332 in 2001.

Tourist Nights: 129,841 in 1998; 203,843 in 1999; 158,777 in 2000.

COMMUNICATIONS MEDIA

Telephones (main lines in use, 2001): 18,233 (Source: *Ceuta—Memoria de la situación socioeconómica y laboral de la ciudad*).

EDUCATION

Pre-primary (2001/02): 2,782 students.

Primary (2001/02): 22 schools (incl. pre-primary); 6,147 students; 509 teachers (incl. pre-primary).

Secondary (2001/02): 19 schools serving the first 2-year cycle, of which 6 serve the second 2-year cycle and further general secondary education; 5,471 students; 498 teachers.

Vocational (2001/02): 2 centres; 1,162 students.
Source: Ministerio de Educación, Cultura y Deporte, Madrid.

Melilla

Sources (unless otherwise stated): Instituto Nacional de Estadística, Paseo de la Castellana 183, 28046 Madrid; tel. (91) 5839301; fax (91) 5839086; e-mail info@ine.es; internet www.ine.es.

AREA, POPULATION AND DENSITY

Area: 12.5 sq km. (4.8 sq miles).

Population (census results): 56,600 at 1 March 1991; 66,411 at 1 November 2001 (males 33,224; females 33,187).

Density (1 November 2001): 5,312 per sq km.

Births, Marriages and Deaths (2000): Live births 1,223 (birth rate 18.6 per 1,000); Marriages 503 (marriage rate 7.7 per 1,000); Deaths 438 (marriage rate 6.8 per 1,000).

2001: Live births 1,243; Marriages 404; Deaths 412.

Expectation of Life: see Ceuta.

Immigration and Emigration (1998): Immigrants 2,409; Emigrants 1,948.

Economically Active Population: see Ceuta.

FINANCE

Currency and Exchange Rates: see Ceuta.

Cost of Living: see Ceuta.

Gross Domestic Product: see Ceuta.

EXTERNAL TRADE

Melilla is a duty-free port. Most imports are from Spain but over 90% of exports go to non-Spanish territories. The chief export is fish.

TRANSPORT

Road Traffic: Vehicles registered: (2000): 3,184. Source: Dirección General de Tráfico, Madrid.

Shipping (1999): Goods loaded 145,000 metric tons; Goods unloaded 622,000 metric tons.

Civil Aviation (1999): Passengers transported 260,000; Goods transported 644 metric tons.

EDUCATION

Pre-primary (2001/02): 5 schools; 2,972 students.

Primary (2001/02): 14 schools; 5,863 students; 531 teachers (incl. pre-primary).

Secondary (2001/02): 8 schools; 5,356; 522 teachers.

Vocational (2001/02): 1 centre; 923 students.
Source: Ministerio de Educación, Cultura y Deporte, Madrid.

Directory

Ceuta

GOVERNMENT
(April 2003)

Delegación del Gobierno: Beatriz de Silva 4, 51001 Ceuta; tel. (956) 512523; fax (956) 513671; e-mail roberto@ceuta.map.es; Government Delegate in Ceuta LUIS VICENTE MORO DÍAZ.

Deputy elected to the Congress in Madrid: FRANCISCO ANTONIO GONZÁLEZ PÉREZ (PP).

Representatives to the Senate in Madrid: JOSÉ LUIS MORALES MONTERO (PP), NICOLÁS FERNÁNDEZ CUCURULL (PP).

Commandant-General: FERNANDO LÓPEZ DE OLMEDO.

COUNCIL OF GOVERNMENT

Mayor/President of Ceuta: JUAN JESÚS VIVAS LARA (PP).

Councillor of Development: NICOLÁS FERNÁNDEZ CUCURULL (PP).

Councillor of the Environment: JUAN ANTONIO RODRÍGUEZ FERRÓN.

Councillor of the Economy and Employment: JUAN JOSÉ ROSALES FERNÁNDEZ (GM).

Councillor of Education, Culture and Sport: ADELAIDA ALVAREZ RODRÍGUEZ (PP).

Councillor of Finance: ALFONSO CONEJO RABANEDA (PP).

Councillor of the Presidency and the Interior: EMILIO CARREIRA RUIZ (PP).

Councillor of Public Health and Consumer Affairs: JUSTO OSTALÉ BLANCO (GM).

Councillor of Social Services: MOHAMMADI ANANOU EL FUNTI.

Councillor of Tourism: AIDA PIEDRA RUBIO (GM).

Councillor of Citizen Participation, Youth and Festivals: (vacant).

Presidency of Ceuta: Plaza de Africa s/n, 51001 Ceuta; tel. (956) 528200; fax (956) 514470; internet www.ciceuta.es.

Council of Co-ordination and Communication: Plaza de Africa s/n, 51001 Ceuta; tel. (956) 528200.

Council of Development and the Environment: Plaza de Africa s/n, 51001 Ceuta; tel. (956) 528200; e-mail fomento@ciceuta.es; e-mail medioambiente@ciceuta.es.

Council of the Economy and Employment: Plaza de Africa s/n, 51001 Ceuta; tel. (956) 528200; e-mail economia@ciceuta.es; e-mail presupuestos@ciceuta.es.

Council of Education, Culture and Sport: Plaza de Africa s/n, 51001 Ceuta; tel. (956) 528200; e-mail cultura@ciceuta.es.

Council of Finance: Padilla, Edif. Ceuta Center, 51001 Ceuta; tel. (956) 528200; e-mail hacienda@ciceuta.es.

Council of the Presidency and the Interior: Plaza de Africa s/n, 51001 Ceuta; tel. (956) 528200; e-mail presidencia@ciceuta.es.

Council of Public Health, and Consumer Affairs: Avda Barcelona s/n, 51001 Ceuta; tel. (956) 528200; e-mail sanidad@ciceuta.es.

Council of Public Works: Plaza de Africa s/n, 51001 Ceuta; tel. (956) 528200; e-mail fomento@ciceuta.es.

Council of Social Services: Padilla, Edif. Ceuta Center, 51001 Ceuta; tel. (956) 528200; e-mail bsocial@ciceuta.es.

Council of Tourism: Padilla, Edif. Ceuta Center, 51001 Ceuta; tel. (956) 528200; fax (956) 528247; e-mail turismo@ciceuta.es; internet www.turiceuta.com.

Council of Citizen Participation, Youth and Festivals: Avda de Africa s/n 51001, Ceuta; tel. (956) 510654; e-mail participacion@ciceuta.es.

COUNCIL

Election, 13 June 1999

	Seats
Grupo Independiente Liberal (GIL)*	12
Partido Popular (PP)	8
Partido Socialista Obrero Español (PSOE)	2
Partido Democrático y Social de Ceuta (PDSC)	3
Total	25

*In January 2001, following the resignation of 5 GIL representatives, all 12 GIL councillors and one PSOE councillor joined the Grupo Mixto, forming a new council.

POLITICAL ORGANIZATIONS

Ceuta Unida (CEU): Ceuta; nationalist party; Sec.-Gen. JOSÉ ANTONIO QUEROL.

Grupo Mixto (GM): Ceuta; f. 2001; fmrly Grupo Independiente Liberal; Leader ANTONIO SAMPIETRO CASARRAMONA.

Izquierda Unida: Gral. Yaque, 4-1°, 11701 Ceuta; tel. (956) 513558; fax (956) 513558; left-wing electoral alliance; Leader MUSTAFA HASSEN.

Partido Democrático y Social de Ceuta (PDSC): Bolivia 35, Ceuta; Muslim party; Leader MUSTAFA MIZZIAM AMMAR.

Partido Independiente de Ceuta: B. Príncipe Alfonso, Fuerte 6, 51003 Ceuta; Leader HAMED MOHAMED LIAZID.

Partido Popular (PP): Real 90 Bajo Izquierda, 51001 Ceuta; tel. (956) 518139; fax (956) 511636; e-mail opceuta@pp.es; internet www.pp.es; fmrly Alianza Popular; centre-right; Pres. PEDRO GORDILLO DURÁN.

Partido Socialista Obrero Español (PSOE): Ceuta; socialist workers' party; Leader FRUCTUOSO MIAJA.

Partido Socialista del Pueblo de Ceuta (PSPC): Carretera del Embalse 10, 11704 Ceuta; dissident group of PSOE; Leader JUAN LUIS ARÓSTEGUI.

Progreso y Futuro de Ceuta (PFC): Poligono Virgen de Africa s/n, Ceuta; Leader FRANCISCO FRAIZ ARMADA.

There are branches of the major Spanish parties in Ceuta, and also various civic associations. The **Asociación Ceuta y Melilla (Acyme)** is based in Granada (Pres. Francisco Godino), and is opposed to the limited autonomy of the enclaves. The **Organización 21 de Agosto para la Liberación de los Territorios Marroquíes Usurpados** resumed its activities in 1995.

JUDICIAL SYSTEM

Tribunal Superior de Justicia de Andalucía, Ceuta y Melilla: Plaza Nueva, 10, Palacio de la Real Chancillería, 18071 Granada, Spain; tel. (958) 002600; fax (958) 002720; Pres. AUGUSTO MÉNDEZ DE LUGO Y LÓPEZ DE AYALA.

RELIGION

The majority of the European inhabitants are Christians, almost all being adherents of the Roman Catholic Church. Most Africans are Muslims, totalling about 13,000 in 1991. There were about 500 Hindus in 1995. The Jewish community numbers several hundred.

Christianity

The Roman Catholic Church

Bishop of Cádiz and Ceuta: ANTONIO CEBALLOS ATIENZA (resident in Cádiz), Vicars-General MANUEL DE LA PUENTE SENDÓN, FRANCISCO CORRERO TOCÓN, Plaza de Nuestra Señora de Africa, 11701 Ceuta; tel. (956) 517732; fax (956) 513208; e-mail obispadoceuta@planalfa.es.

THE PRESS

El Faro de Ceuta: Sargento Mena 8, 51001 Ceuta; tel. (956) 524148; fax (956) 524147; e-mail elfaro@retemail.es; f. 1934; morning; Dir CARMEN ETXARRI PIUDO; Editor-in-Chief ROCÍO ABAD DE LOS SANTOS; circ. 5,000.

El Periódico de Ceuta: Ampliación Muelle de Poniente P-104-10, 11701 Ceuta; tel. (956) 513348; fax (956) 513669.

El Pueblo de Ceuta: Independencia 11, 1°, 51001, Ceuta; tel. (956) 514367; fax (956) 517650; e-mail elpueblo_redaccion@teleline.es; daily; Dir and Editor-in-Chief SALVADOR VIVANCOS CANALES.

News Agency

Agencia EFE: Milán Astray 1, 1°, Of. 8, 51001 Ceuta; tel. (956) 517550; Correspondent RAFAEL PEÑA SOLER.

Press Association

Asociación de la Prensa: Sargento Mena 8, 51001 Ceuta; tel. (956) 524148.

BROADCASTING

Radio

Onda Cero Radio Ceuta: Delgado Serrano, 1, 1° Dcha, 51001 Ceuta; tel. (956) 200068; fax (956) 200179; Dir RAFAEL ROMAGUERA MENA.

Radio Ceuta: Real 90, Portón 4, 1° Dcha, 51001 Ceuta; tel. (956) 511820; fax (956) 516820; f. 1934; commercial; owned by Sociedad Española de Radiodifusión (SER); Dir ANTONIO ROSA GUERRERO.

Radio Nacional de España: Real 90, 51001 Ceuta; tel. (956) 524688; fax (956) 519067; Dir EDUARDO SÁNCHEZ DORADO.

Radio Popular de Ceuta/COPE: Sargento Mena 8, 1°, 11701 Ceuta; tel. (956) 524200; fax (956) 524202; Dir DANIEL OLIVA.

Television

Televisión Ceuta: Ceuta; tel. (956) 514417; Dir MANUEL GONZÁLEZ BOLORINO.

FINANCE

Banking

Banco Bilbao Vizcaya Argentaria (BBVA): Plaza de los Reyes s/n, 51001 Ceuta; tel. (956) 511611; 3 brs.

Banco de España: Plaza de España 2, 51001 Ceuta; tel. (956) 511805; fax (956) 513108.

Banco Español de Crédito (Banesto): Camoens 6, 51001 Ceuta; tel. (956) 513009.

Banco Popular Español: Paseo del Revellín 1, 51001 Ceuta; tel. (956) 510740.

Caja de Ahorros y Pensiones de Barcelona 'la Caixa': Ceuta.

Caja Duero: Sargento Coriat 5, 51001 Ceuta; tel. (956) 518040; fax (956) 517019; 1 br.

Caja Madrid: Plaza de los Reyes s/n, 51001 Ceuta; tel. (956) 510942; 6 brs.

Santander Central Hispano (BSCH): Marina Española 10, 51001 Ceuta; tel. (956) 510015; 2 brs.

Insurance

MAPFRE: Cervantes 14, 51001 Ceuta; tel. (956) 519638; fax (956) 513916.

TRADE AND INDUSTRY

Cámara Oficial de Comercio, Industria y Navegación: Muelle Cañonero Dato s/n, 51001 Ceuta; tel. (956) 509590; fax (956) 509589; e-mail sgeneralceuta@camaras.org; internet www.camaraceuta.org;

Pres. LUIS MORENO NARANJO; Sec.-Gen. MARIÁ DEL ROSARIO ESPINOSA SUÁREZ.

Confederación de Empresarios de Ceuta: Teniente Arrabal 2, 51001 Ceuta; tel. (956) 516912; employers' confederation; Pres. MIGUEL ANGEL AZCOITIA LEÓN; Sec.-Gen. EVARISTO RIVERA GÓMEZ.

Utilities

Empresa de Alumbrado Eléctrico de Ceuta SA: Beatriz de Silva 2, Ceuta; generates and transmits electricity; Rep. ALBERTO RAMÓN GAITÁN RODRÍGUEZ.

Trade Union

Confederación Sindical de Comisiones Obreras (CCOO): Alcalde Fructuoso Miaja 1, 11701 Ceuta; tel. (95) 6516243; fax (95) 6516991; e-mail ccooce@ctv.es; internet www.ccoo.es; 1,721 mems (1999); Sec.-Gen. JOSÉ MARIA FIDALGO.

TRANSPORT

Much of the traffic between Spain and Morocco passes through Ceuta; there are ferry services to Algeciras, Melilla, Málaga and Almería. Plans for an airport are under consideration. Helicopter services to Málaga are provided by Helisureste.

Compañía Trasmediterránea: Muelle Canoero Dato 6, 51001 Ceuta; tel. (956) 509532; fax (956) 522239; internet www.trasmediterranea.es.

TOURISM

Visitors are attracted by the historical monuments, the Parque Marítimo and by the museums, as well as by the Shrine of Our Lady of Africa. There were 45,332 visitors to Ceuta in 2001. In 2000 Ceuta had four hotels and 19 hostels.

Oficina Municipal de Turismo: Alcalde Sánchez Prados, 51001 Ceuta; tel. (956) 528146; e-mail turismo@ciceuta.es; internet www.turiceuta.com.

Patronato Municipal de Turismo: Estacion Maritima s/n, 51001 Ceuta; tel. (956) 506275.

Melilla

GOVERNMENT
(April 2003)

Delegación del Gobierno: Avda de la Marina Española 3, 52001 Melilla; tel. (95) 2675840; fax (95) 2672657; e-mail puri@melilla.map.es; Government Delegate in Melilla ARTURO ESTEBAN ALBERT.

Deputy elected to the Congress in Madrid: ANTONIO GUTIÉRREZ MOLINA (PP-UPM).

Representatives to the Senate in Madrid: CARLOS A. BENET CAÑETE (PP-UPM), JUAN JOSÉ IMBRODA ORTIZ (PP-UPM).

Commandant-General: FRANCISCO DÍEZ MORENO.

COUNCIL OF GOVERNMENT

Mayor/President of Melilla: JUAN JOSÉ IMBRODA ORTIZ (UPM).

First Vice-President and Councillor of the Environment: RAFAEL HERNÁNDEZ SOLER (PSOE).

Second Vice-President and Councillor of Culture, Sport, Tourism and Festivals: FRANCISCO JAVIER MARTÍNEZ MONREAL (PP).

Councillor of the Economy, Finance and Heritage: GUILLERMO FRÍAS BARERRAS (PP).

Councillor of Education, Youth and Women: JOAQUÍN GONZÁLEZ MOLERO (PSOE).

Councillor of Labour and Human Resources: INÉS URDIALES MORENO (UPM).

Councillor of the Presidency: ANTONIO MIRANDA MONTILLA (PP).

Councillor of Public Works and Territorial Affairs: ERNESTO RODRÍGUEZ MUÑOZ (PP).

Councillor of Social Welfare and Health: JOSE ANTONIO VALLÉS MUÑOZ (PP).

Presidency of Melilla: Plaza de España 1, 52001 Melilla; tel. (95) 2699100; fax (95) 2674800; internet www.camelilla.es.

Council of Culture, Sport, Tourism and Festivals: Plaza de España 1, 52001 Melilla; tel. (95) 2699193; fax (95) 2674394.

Council of the Economy, Finance and Heritage: Plaza de España 1, 52801 Melilla; tel. (95) 2699219; fax (95) 2699103.

Council of Education, Youth and Women: General Prim 1, 52001 Melilla; tel. (95) 2681950; fax (95) 2264328; e-mail cej01@melilla500.com.

Council of the Environment: Plaza de España 1, 52001 Melilla; tel. (95) 2699134.

Council of Labour and Human Resources: Plaza de España 1, 52001 Melilla; tel. (95) 2699102; fax (95) 2699103.

Council of the Presidency: Plaza de España 1, 52001 Melilla; tel. (95) 2699140.

Council of Public Works and Territorial Affairs: Jiménez Iglesias 30, 52071 Melilla; tel. (95) 2699100; fax (95) 2680255.

Council of Social Welfare and Health: Avda de la Marina Española 12, 52004 Melilla; tel. (95) 2676790; fax (95) 2678080; e-mail cbs01@melilla500.com.

COUNCIL

Election, 13 June 1999

	Seats
Grupo Independiente Liberal (GIL)*	7
Coalición por Melilla (CpM)	5
Partido Popular (PP)	5
Partido Independiente de Melilla (PIM)	3
Unión del Pueblo Melillense (UPM)	3
Partido Socialista Obrero Español (PSOE)	2
Total	**25**

*Reformed in 2001 as Grupo Mixto (GM).

POLITICAL ORGANIZATIONS

Coalición por Melilla (CpM): c/ Querol, 46 Melilla; Leader Mustafa Aberchán Hamed.

Grupo Independiente Hispano Bereber: c/ Garcia Cabrelles 23, Melilla.

Grupo Mixto (GM): Melilla; f. 1999 as Grupo Independiente Liberal (GIL); reformed in 2001; Leader Crispin Lozano.

Partido de los Demócratas de Melilla (PDM): Avda del General Aizpuru 29, Melilla; f. 1985; Muslim party; Leader Abdelkáder Mohamed Alí.

Partido Independiente de Melilla (PIM): Avda Juan Carlos I Rey 23, 1° Izqda, Melilla; f. 1999; Leader Enrique Palacios.

Partido Popular (PP): Roberto Cano 2, 1° Izqda, POB 384, 52001 Melilla; tel. (95) 2681095; fax (95) 2684477; centre-right; Pres. Antonio Gutiérrez Molina.

Partido Social Demócrata de Melilla (PSDM): c/ General O'Donnell, 8-1° Izqda, Melilla; f. 1998.

Partido Socialista de Melilla-Partido Socialista Obrero Español (PSME-PSOE): Cándido Lobera 7-1°, Melilla; tel. (95) 2681820; socialist workers' party; favours self-government but not full autonomy; Leader Javier de Pro.

Unión del Pueblo Melillense (UPM): Ejército Español 7, 1°, Apdo 775, 52001 Melilla; tel. (95) 2681987; fax (95) 2684677; e-mail www .lanzadera.com/melilla; f. 1985; right-wing; Pres. Daniel Conesa Mínguez; Sec.-Gen. Guillermo Merino Barrera.

There are branches of the major Spanish parties in Melilla, and also various civic associations.

RELIGION

As in Ceuta, most Europeans are Roman Catholics. The registered Muslim community numbered 20,800 in 1990. The Jewish community numbered 1,300. There is also a Hindu community.

Islam

Comisión Islámica de Melilla (CIM): c/ Garcia Cabrelles 13, Melilla; Pres. Abderraman Benyahya.

THE PRESS

Diario Sur: Avda Juan Carlos I Rey 19, 1° Izqda, Melilla; tel. (95) 2681854; fax (95) 2683908; Perm. Rep. Avelino Gutiérrez Pérez.

El Faro de Melilla: General Marina 11, 1°, 52001 Melilla; tel. (95) 2690050; fax (95) 2680010; e-mail faromeli@arrakis.es; Dir Juan Antonio Calleja Flórez.

Melilla Hoy: Polígono Industrial SEPES, La Espiga, Naves A-1/A-2, 52006 Melilla; tel. (95) 2690000; fax (95) 2675725; e-mail redaccionmelillahoy@arrakis.es; f. 1985; Dir Irene Flores Sáez; Editor-in-Chief María Angeles Jiménez Padilla; circ. 2,000.

El Telegrama de Melilla: Polígono El Sepes, Calle La Espiga, Nave A-8, 52006 Melilla; tel. (95) 2691443; fax (95) 2691469; e-mail eltelegrama@eltelegrama.com; internet www.eltelegrama.com; Dir Rafael Martos Vilchez.

News Agency

Agencia EFE: Candido Lobera 4, 1° Izqda, 52001 Melilla; tel. (95) 2685235; fax (95) 2680043; Correspondent Pilar Salas Durán.

Press Association

Asociación de la Prensa: Crtra Alfonso XII, Edif. Miguel de Cervantes, Bloque 5 Bajo, 52006 Melilla; tel. (95) 2679121; Pres. Angel Morán Jiménez.

BROADCASTING

Radio

40 Melilla: Muelle Ribera 1°, 29805 Melilla; tel. (95) 2681708; fax (95) 2681573; Dir Antonia Ramos Peláez.

Antena 3: Edif. Melilla, Urbanización Rusadir, 29805 Melilla; tel. (95) 2688840; Dir Toñi Ramos Peláez.

Cadena Rato: Melilla; Dir Angel Valencia.

Dial Melilla: Urbanización Rusadir, Edif. Melilla, 52005 Melilla; tel. (95) 2673333; fax (95) 2678342; Representative Nuria Fernández.

Ingar Radio: Abdelkader 3 bajo, 52000 Melilla; tel. (952) 682100.

Onda Cero Radio Melilla: Músico Granados 2, 52004 Melilla; tel. (95) 2691283; fax (95) 2824209; Dir José Jesús Navajas Trobat.

Radio Melilla: Muelle Ribera 1, 52005 Melilla; tel. (95) 2681708; fax (95) 2681573; commercial; owned by Sociedad Española de Radiodifusión (SER); Dir Antonia Ramos Peláez.

Radio Nacional de España (RNE): Duque de Ahumada 5, 52001, Melilla; tel. (95) 2681907; fax (95) 2683108; state-controlled; Rep. Montserrat Cobos Ruano.

Television

A fibre optic cable linking Melilla with Almería was laid in 1990. From March 1991 Melilla residents were able to receive three private TV channels from mainland Spain: Antena 3, Canal+ and Tele 5.

FINANCE

Banking

The following banks have branches in Melilla: Banco Bilbao Vizcaya Argentaria (2 brs), Banco de España, Banco Español de Crédito (Banesto), Banco Popular Español, Santander Central Hispano and Caja de Ahorros y Pensiones de Barcelona 'la Caixa'.

Insurance

MAPFRE: Avda Democracia 9, 52004 Melilla; tel. (95) 2673189; fax (95) 2674977.

TRADE AND INDUSTRY

Cámara Oficial de Comercio, Industria y Navegación: Cervantes 7, 52001 Melilla; tel. (95) 2684840; fax (95) 2683119; f. 1906; Pres. Margarita López Almendáriz; Sec.-Gen. María Jesús Fernández de Castro y Pedrajas.

Confederación de Empresarios de Melilla: Paseo Marítimo Mir Berlanga 26 Entreplanta, Apdo de Correos 445, 29806 Melilla; tel. (95) 2678295; fax (95) 2676175; f. 1979; employers' confederation; Pres. Margarita López Almendáriz; Sec.-Gen. Jerónimo Pérez Hernández.

Trade Union

Confederación Sindical de Comisiones Obreras (CCOO): Plaza 1° de Mayo s/n, 3°, 29803 Melilla; tel. (95) 2676535; fax (95) 2672571; e-mail orga.melilla@melilla.ccoo.es; internet www.ccoo.es; 1,314 mems (1999); Sec.-Gen. Máximo García Agüera.

TRANSPORT

There is a daily ferry service to Málaga and a service to Almería. Melilla airport, situated 4 km from the town, is served by daily flights to various destinations on the Spanish mainland, operated by Iberia and by Melilla Jet/Pauknair. There are also services to Madrid and Granada.

Compañía Trasmediterránea: Avda General Marina 1, 52001 Melilla; tel. (95) 2681635; fax (95) 2682685; e-mail correom@ trasmediterranea.es; internet www.trasmediterranea.es; operates ferry service between Melilla and mainland Spain.

Empresa C.O.A.: Estación de Autobuses, Melilla; tel. (95) 2672616; operates bus services throughout the city.

TOURISM

There is much of historic interest to the visitor, while Melilla is also celebrated for its modernist architecture. Melilla had 19 hotels in the late 1980s. Further hotels, including a luxury development, were under construction in the 1990s.

Dirección Provincial Comercio y Turismo: Calle Cervantes, 29801 Melilla; tel. (95) 2681906.

Oficina Provincial de Turismo: Pintor Fortuny 21, 52004 Melilla; tel. (95) 2675444; fax (95) 2691232; e-mail cevtt@melilla500.com.

Viceconsejería de Turismo: Calle Pintor Fortuny 20, Palacio de Congresos y Exposiciones, 52004 Melilla; tel. (95) 2675444; fax (95) 2691232; e-mail cevtt@melilla500.com; internet www.camelilla.es; part of Council of Culture; Dir Javier Mateo Figueroa.

The Peñón de Vélez de la Gomera, Peñón de Alhucemas and Chafarinas Islands

These rocky islets, situated respectively just west and east of al-Hocima (Alhucemas) and east of Melilla off the north coast of Morocco, are administered with Melilla. The three Chafarinas Islands lie about 3.5 km off Ras el-Ma (Cabo de Agua). The Peñón de Alhucemas is situated about 300 m from the coast. The Peñón de Vélez de la Gomera is situated about 80 km further west, lying 85 m from the Moroccan shore, to which it is joined by a narrow strip of sand. A small military base is maintained on the Peñón de Vélez, while a military garrison of fewer than 100 men is stationed on the Peñón de Alhucemas, and a garrison of about 100 Spanish soldiers is maintained on the Isla del Congreso, the most westerly of the Chafarinas Islands. A supply ship calls at the various islands every two weeks. Prospective visitors must obtain the necessary military permit in Ceuta or Melilla.

SRI LANKA

Introductory Survey

Location, Climate, Language, Religion, Flag, Capital

The Democratic Socialist Republic of Sri Lanka lies in southern Asia. It comprises one large island and several much smaller ones, situated in the Indian Ocean, about 80 km (50 miles) east of the southern tip of India. The climate is tropical, with an average annual temperature of about 27°C (81°F) in Colombo. There is very little seasonal variation in temperature: the monthly average in Colombo ranges from 25°C (77°F) to 28°C (82°F). The south-western part of the island receives rain from both the south-west and the north-east monsoons: average annual rainfall in Colombo is 2,365 mm (93 ins). Sinhala, Tamil and English are all recognized national languages. One of the official languages, Sinhala, is spoken by more than 70% of the population. Tamil was made the country's second official language in 1988. According to the 2001 census, in 18 out of 25 districts 76.7% of the population are Buddhist, 8.5% are Muslim, 7.9% are Hindu and 6.1% are Roman Catholic. The census results did not cover the Tamil-dominated (and therefore mainly Hindu) northern and eastern districts. The national flag (proportions 1 by 2) consists mainly of a dark crimson rectangular panel, with a yellow border, in the fly. In the centre of the panel is a gold lion, carrying a sword, while in each corner (also in gold) there is a leaf of the bo (bodhi) tree, which is sacred to Buddhists. At the hoist are two vertical stripes, also edged in yellow, to represent Sri Lanka's minorities: one of green (for Muslims) and one of orange (for Tamils). The commercial capital is Colombo. In 1982 the ancient capital of Sri Jayawardenepura (Kotte) became the administrative capital.

Recent History

Sri Lanka, known as Ceylon until 1972, gained its independence from the United Kingdom in February 1948. From then until 1956, for a brief period in 1960 and from 1965 to 1970 the country was ruled, latterly in coalition, by the United National Party (UNP), which was concerned to protect the rights of the Tamils, Hindu members of an ethnic minority (closely linked with the inhabitants of the southern Indian state of Tamil Nadu), who are concentrated in the north (and, to a lesser extent, in the east) of the main island. The socialist Sri Lanka Freedom Party (SLFP), formed in 1951 by Solomon Bandaranaike, emphasized the national heritage, winning the support of groups that advocated the recognition of Sinhala as the official language and the establishment of Buddhism as the predominant religion. The SLFP won the 1956 elections decisively and remained in power, except for a three-month interruption in 1960, until 1965, having formed a coalition Government with the Lanka Sama Samaj Party (LSSP), a Trotskyist group, in 1964. Following the assassination of Solomon Bandaranaike in 1959, his widow, Sirimavo Bandaranaike, assumed the leadership of the SLFP. At the 1970 elections the SLFP became the leading partner of a United Front coalition Government with the LSSP and the Communist Party of Sri Lanka.

In 1971 the United Front Government suppressed an uprising led by the left-wing Janatha Vimukthi Peramuna (JVP—People's Liberation Front). A state of emergency was declared, and the party was banned. In 1976 the main Tamil party, the Federal Party, and other Tamil groups formed the Tamil United Liberation Front (TULF), demanding a separate Tamil state ('Eelam') in the northern and eastern parts of the country.

In December 1976 the communists supported strikes of transport unions, which were initiated by the UNP and the LSSP (which had been expelled from the coalition in 1975). The strikes ended in January 1977, and in February Sirimavo Bandaranaike prorogued the National State Assembly until May. Several members of the SLFP resigned, and seven members of the Communist Party left the coalition Government, forming an independent group within the opposition. In February the state of emergency, which had been imposed in 1971, was lifted and the JVP was legalized again. A general election was held in July 1977, accompanied by widespread violence. The UNP won the election, with an overwhelming majority, and the party's leader, Junius Richard Jayewardene, became Prime Minister. In August riots broke out between the Sinhalese majority and the

Tamil minority. The TULF, which had become the main opposition party, increased its demands for an independent Tamil state. In October a constitutional amendment was passed to establish a presidential system of government, and in February 1978 Jayewardene became the country's first executive President.

Continued violence and pressure from the Tamils during 1978 led the Government to make some concessions, such as the recognition of the Tamil language, in the new Constitution of the Democratic Socialist Republic of Sri Lanka, which came into force in September. In view of this, the Ceylon Workers' Congress (CWC) joined the Government, but the TULF remained undecided, mainly for fear of reprisals by Tamil extremists. Continuing violence prompted the declaration of a state of emergency in July 1979 in the northern district of Jaffna, where the Tamils are in a majority. At the same time, stringent anti-terrorist legislation was passed in Parliament (as the National State Assembly had been renamed in 1978), and a presidential commission was established to study the Tamil problem.

In June 1980 a general strike, called by left-wing trade unions seeking higher wages, led to the declaration of a state of emergency between July and August, and more than 40,000 government workers lost their jobs. In August the TULF agreed to the establishment of District Development Councils, providing for a wide measure of regional autonomy. Elections to these, held in June 1981, were boycotted by the SLFP, the LSSP and the Communist Party, and the UNP won control of 18 of the 24 Councils. Subsequent communal disturbances between Sinhalese and Tamils led to the imposition of a state of emergency in the north for five days in June, and throughout the country from August 1981 to January 1982. Tamil MPs proposed a motion of 'no confidence' in the Government and subsequently boycotted Parliament until November 1981, when a peace initiative to ease racial tension was proposed by the Government.

Meanwhile, in October 1980 the former Prime Minister, Sirimavo Bandaranaike, was found guilty of having abused power by a special presidential commission, which deprived her of all civic rights and effectively prevented her from standing in the next elections.

In August 1982 Parliament approved an amendment to the 1978 Constitution which enabled President Jayewardene to call a presidential election before his term of office expired, i.e. after four years instead of six. Sri Lanka's first presidential election was held in October 1982, and Jayewardene was returned to office with 53% of the votes cast. The SLFP candidate, Hector Kobbekaduwa, polled 39%, despite his party's disarray and Sirimavo Bandaranaike's loss of civic rights.

Following this success, the President announced, with the approval of Parliament and the Supreme Court, that, instead of a general election, a referendum would be held to decide whether to prolong the life of Parliament for a further six years after the session ended in July 1983. A state of emergency was in force between October 1982 and January 1983, and all opposition newspapers were closed by the Government. Sirimavo Bandaranaike was allowed to campaign in the referendum, which took place in December 1982 and resulted in approval of the proposal to prolong Parliament until 1989. On a 71% turnout, 55% (3.1m.) voted in favour, with the dissenting minority of 2.6m. being concentrated mainly in and around Jaffna.

In May 1983 by-elections were held for seats where the UNP had fared badly in both the presidential election and the referendum, and the UNP won 14 of the 18 seats. This was accompanied by success for the UNP in the local government elections, held concurrently, although the TULF was successful in Tamil-speaking areas. The UNP had now defeated its opponents in four polls at national level between October 1982 and June 1983.

A state of emergency was declared in May 1983 to combat mounting terrorism, and in June Tamil terrorist activity led to army reprisals and the worst outbreak of violence for many years, with more than 400 deaths and particularly severe rioting in Jaffna and Colombo. A curfew and press censorship were imposed, and three left-wing parties (including the JVP) were banned. In July the 16 TULF MPs resigned in protest at the extension of Parliament, as approved by the referendum. In August Parliament passed a 'no-separation' amendment to the Constitution, depriving those espousing Tamil separatism of their civic rights. In October the TULF MPs were found to have forfeited their seats because of their parliamentary boycott. After much discussion and with the informal mediation of India, an All-Party Conference (APC) began in January 1984. The APC comprised representatives of the Buddhist, Christian and Muslim faiths as well as political leaders from the Sinhalese and Tamil communities. The Government proposed to establish provincial councils, with some regional autonomy, throughout the country. The TULF, however, demanded regional devolution that would enable the northern province, with its Tamil majority, to amalgamate with the eastern province where the Tamils were in a minority and thus create a Tamil state within the framework of a united Sri Lanka. The Sinhalese and the Muslims were implacably opposed to this proposal. The APC was finally abandoned in December, without agreement on the crucial question of the extent of regional autonomy.

Further violent outbursts in the northern part of the island in November and December 1984 led to the proclamation of another state of emergency. There were widespread accusations of gross military indiscipline, and there was condemnation of government-sponsored settlement of Sinhalese in Tamil areas in the eastern province. A restricted zone was established between Mannar and Mullaitivu, to prevent contact with the Indian state of Tamil Nadu, where many of the Tamil militants were based.

In February 1986 there was a resurgence of violence in the northern and eastern provinces. In May a series of explosions in Colombo was widely believed to have been carried out by Tamil terrorists. In the same month, the Government intensified its campaign against the insurgents by increasing defence expenditure and by launching an offensive against the militant Tamils in the Jaffna peninsula. This offensive made little headway, but the government cause was helped by internecine fighting which broke out between two of the principal Tamil militant groups, the Tamil Eelam Liberation Organization (TELO) and the Liberation Tigers of Tamil Eelam (LTTE—also known as the Tamil Tigers), which, over the year, emerged as the dominant Tamil separatist group under the leadership of Velupillai Prabhakaran. In May Tamil terrorists renewed their attacks on Sinhalese villagers who had been settled by the Government in Tamil-dominated areas in the eastern province. In June the Government presented new devolution proposals to a newly-convened APC, in which the TULF was not invited to participate, while the SLFP boycotted the talks. The proposals again envisaged the formation of provincial councils, but did not satisfy the Tamils' demand for amalgamation of the northern and eastern provinces. The proposals were also rejected by the SLFP, on the grounds that they conceded too much to the Tamils.

In January 1987, in response to an announcement by the LTTE that they intended to seize control of the civil administration of Jaffna, the Government suspended, indefinitely, the distribution of all petroleum products to the peninsula. In the same month all the powers previously vested in the Prime Minister, Ranasinghe Premadasa, as Minister of Emergency Civil Administration were transferred to a new Ministry of National Security, directly supervised by the President. In February the Government launched an offensive against the terrorists in the Batticaloa district of the eastern province. The situation worsened in April, when the LTTE, having rejected an offer of a cease-fire by the Sri Lankan Government, carried out a series of outrages against the civilian population, including a bomb explosion in Colombo's main bus station, which killed more than 100 people. In response, the Government attempted to regain control of the Jaffna peninsula, the stronghold of the LTTE. During the resultant struggle between the LTTE and government forces, India demonstrated its support for the Tamils by violating Sri Lankan airspace to drop food and medical supplies in Jaffna. On 29 July, however, an important breakthrough was made when President Jayewardene and the Indian Prime Minister, Rajiv Gandhi, signed an accord regarding an attempted settlement of the country's ethnic crisis. The main points of this accord were: the provision of an Indian Peace-Keeping Force (IPKF) to oversee its proper implementation; a complete cessation of hostilities, and the surrender of all weapons held by the Tamil militants; the amalgamation of the northern and eastern provinces into one administrative unit, with an elected provincial council (together with the creation of

provincial councils in the seven other provinces); the holding of a referendum in the eastern province at a date to be decided by the Sri Lankan President, to determine whether the mixed population of Tamils, Sinhalese and Muslims supported an official merger with the northern province into a single Tamil-dominated north-east province; a general amnesty for all Tamil militants; the repatriation of some 130,000 Tamil refugees from India to Sri Lanka (by early 1991 the number of Tamil refugees in India had risen to an estimated 210,000, and in early 1992 the Indian Government began to repatriate them, allegedly on a voluntary basis); the prevention of the use of Indian territory by Tamil militants for military or propaganda purposes; the prevention of the military use of Sri Lankan ports by any country in a manner prejudicial to Indian interests; and the provision that Tamil and English should have equal status with Sinhala as official languages. The accord encountered widespread disapproval among the Sinhalese population and from the SLFP, which claimed that it granted too much power to the Tamil minority.

In July and August 1987 more than 7,000 Indian troops were dispatched to Sri Lanka. After a promising start in August, the surrender of arms by the Tamil militant groups became more sporadic in September, and the implementation of the peace accord was impeded by further bitter internecine fighting among the Tamil militias (involving the LTTE in particular), which necessitated direct intervention by the IPKF. Under arrangements reported to have been negotiated in September with the Indian authorities, the LTTE was to be allocated a majority of seats on an interim council, which was to administer the northern and eastern provinces, pending the holding of elections. Despite this concession, the surrender of arms by the LTTE had virtually ceased by early October; the group had resumed its terrorist attacks on Sinhalese citizens, and had declared itself to be firmly opposed to the peace accord. In response to the resurgence in violence, the IPKF launched an offensive against the LTTE stronghold in the Jaffna peninsula in October. The Indian troops encountered fierce and prolonged resistance from the Tamil militants, which necessitated the deployment of thousands of reinforcements. By the end of the month, however, the IPKF had gained control of Jaffna city, while most of the LTTE militants had escaped to establish a new base for guerrilla operations, in the Batticaloa district of the eastern province. Both sides had suffered heavy casualties.

Because of the continuing violence, the Sri Lankan Government abandoned its plan to create an interim administrative council for the northern and eastern provinces. However, in November 1987, despite strong opposition from the SLFP (which vehemently opposed the proposed merger of the northern and eastern provinces), Parliament adopted the legislation establishing provincial councils.

Another major threat to the successful implementation of the peace accord was the re-emergence in 1987 of the outlawed Sinhalese group, the JVP, which had been officially banned in August 1983 and which was based mainly in the south of the island. This group claimed that the accord conceded too much power to the Tamils. As part of its anti-accord campaign, the JVP was widely believed to have been responsible for an assassination attempt on President Jayewardene in August, in which one MP was killed and several cabinet ministers were seriously wounded, and to have murdered more than 200 UNP supporters by February 1988, including the Chairman of the UNP, Harsha Abeywardene, and the leader of the left-wing Sri Lanka Mahajana (People's) Party (SLMP), Vijaya Kumaratunga, who supported the accord. In May 1988 the Government revoked the five-year ban on the JVP in return for an agreement by the party to end its campaign of violence, but JVP leaders disowned the agreement as a hoax. The JVP was believed to be responsible for the murder of the UNP General Secretary, later in the same month.

In February 1988 a new opposition force emerged when an alliance, named the United Socialist Alliance (USA), was formed between the SLMP, the LSSP, the Communist Party of Sri Lanka, the Nava Sama Samaja Party, and (most notably) the Tamil rights group entitled the Eelam People's Revolutionary Liberation Front (EPRLF). Although the USA group, led by Chandrika Bandaranaike Kumaratunga (the widow of the SLMP leader and the daughter of Sirimavo Bandaranaike), comprised opposition parties, it expressed support for the peace accord.

Elections to seven of the new provincial councils were held in April and June 1988 (in defiance of the JVP's threats and violence); elections in the northern and eastern provinces were postponed indefinitely. The UNP won a majority and effective control in all seven (with 57% of the elective seats), while the USA emerged as the main opposition group (with 41% of the seats). The SLFP boycotted the elections, in protest at the continuing presence of the IPKF (which now numbered about 50,000) in Sri Lanka. In September President Jayewardene officially authorized the merger of the northern and eastern provinces into a single north-eastern province, prior to provincial council elections there. The JVP reacted violently, and was widely believed to have been responsible for the murder of the Minister of Rehabilitation and Reconstruction at the end of the month. In protest against the proposed elections in the new north-eastern province and the presidential election (due to be held in December), the JVP organized a series of disruptive strikes and violent demonstrations in the central, western and southern provinces in October. In an effort to curb the increasing violence, the Government applied extensive emergency regulations, imposed curfews in areas of unrest, and deployed armed riot police. Despite boycotts and threats by both the JVP and the LTTE, elections to the new north-eastern provincial council took place in November. The moderate and pro-accord Tamil groups, the EPRLF and the Eelam National Democratic Liberation Front (ENDLF), together with the Sri Lanka Muslim Congress (SLMC), were successful in the elections, while the UNP won only one seat. In early December Parliament unanimously approved a Constitution Amendment Bill to make Tamil one of the country's two official languages (with Sinhala), thus fulfilling one of the major commitments envisaged in the peace accord. On 19 December the presidential election took place, in circumstances of unprecedented disruption, and was boycotted by the LTTE and the JVP. None the less, about 55% of the total electorate was estimated to have voted. The Prime Minister, Ranasinghe Premadasa (the UNP's candidate), won by a narrow margin, with 50.4% of the total votes, while Sirimavo Bandaranaike, the President of the SLFP (whose civil rights had been restored in January 1986), received 44.9%. On the following day, as promised earlier in the month by the Government, Parliament was dissolved in preparation for a general election, which was to be held in February 1989 (six months in advance of the date when it was due).

In early January 1989 Premadasa was sworn in as Sri Lanka's new President, and an interim Cabinet was appointed. In the same month, the Government repealed the state of emergency, which had been in force since May 1983, and abolished the Ministry of National Security. Concurrently, however, special security measures were invoked in an attempt to arrest the escalating violence. Shortly after his inauguration, Premadasa offered to confer with the extremists and invited all groups to take part in the electoral process. The JVP and the LTTE, however, intensified their campaigns of violence in protest at the forthcoming general election. In early February 1989 the moderate, pro-accord Tamil groups, the EPRLF, the ENDLF and the TELO, formed a loose alliance, under the leadership of the TULF, to contest the general election. In the election, which was held on 15 February and which was, again, marred by widespread violence, the UNP won 125 of the 225 contested seats. The new system of proportional representation, which was introduced at this election, was especially advantageous to the SLFP, which became the major opposition force in Parliament, with 67 seats. The comparatively low electoral participation of 64% confirmed, again, that intimidatory tactics, employed by the LTTE and the JVP, had had an effect on the voters. A few days later, President Premadasa installed a new Cabinet, and in March he appointed the Minister of Finance, Dingiri Banda Wijetunga, as the country's new Prime Minister. Although both the LTTE and the JVP rejected a conciliatory offer made by the President in April, in a surprising development, representatives of the LTTE began discussions with government officials in Colombo in the following month.

Between January and April 1989, five battalions of the IPKF left Sri Lanka, and in May the Sri Lankan Government announced that it wanted all Indian troops to have left Sri Lanka by the end of July. In response, Rajiv Gandhi stressed that the timetable for a complete withdrawal would have to be decided mutually, and that, before the Indian forces left, he wanted to ensure the security of the Tamils and the devolution of real power to the elected local government in the north-eastern province. In protest against the continued presence of the IPKF in Sri Lanka, the JVP organized a series of demonstrations and strikes. As a result of the escalating unrest, the Government reimposed a state of emergency on 20 June. In the same month, shortly after the murders of several prominent Tamil leaders, including the Secretary-General of the TULF, Appapillai Amirthalingam, and the leader of the People's Liberation Organization of Tamil Eelam (PLOTE), Kadirkamam Uma Maheswaran, the peace negotiations between the Sri Lankan Government and the LTTE were temporarily discontinued. It was widely believed that the Government had demanded, and had not been given, a categorical denial that the LTTE were involved in the murders. In September the Governments of Sri Lanka and India signed an agreement in Colombo, under which India promised to make 'all efforts' to withdraw its remaining 45,000 troops from Sri Lanka by the end of the year, and the IPKF was to declare an immediate unilateral cease-fire. In turn, the Sri Lankan Government pledged immediately to establish a peace committee for the north-eastern province in an attempt to reconcile the various Tamil groups and to incorporate members of the LTTE into the peaceful administration of the province.

The JVP suffered a very serious set-back when its leader, Rohana Wijeweera, and his principal deputy were shot dead by the security forces in November 1989. In the following month the leader of the military wing of the JVP, Saman Piyasiri Fernando, was killed in an exchange of gunfire in Colombo. Between September 1989 and the end of January 1990 the Sri Lankan security forces effectively destroyed the JVP as a political force, thus substantially transforming the country's political scene. All but one member of the JVP's political bureau and most leaders at district level had been killed. It was estimated, however, that the number of civilians killed in the lengthy struggle between the JVP and the Government might have been as high as 25,000–50,000.

As the Indian troops increased the speed of their withdrawal from Sri Lanka in the latter half of 1989, the LTTE initiated a campaign of violence against its arch-rivals, the more moderate Indian-supported EPRLF, which was mustering a so-called Tamil National Army, with Indian help, in the north-eastern province, to resist the LTTE. The LTTE accused the EPRLF and its allies of forcibly conscripting thousands of Tamil youths into the Tamil army. Following months of peace talks with the Government, however, the political wing of the LTTE was recognized as a political party by the commissioner of elections in December. The LTTE leaders then proclaimed that the newly-recognized party would take part in the democratic process (it demanded immediate fresh elections in the north-eastern province) under the new name of the People's Front of the Liberation Tigers (PFLT). By the end of 1989 the inexperienced and undisciplined Tamil National Army had been virtually destroyed by the LTTE, who now appeared to have the tacit support of the central Government and had taken control of much of the territory in the north-eastern province.

Following further talks between the Governments of Sri Lanka and India, the completion date for the withdrawal of the IPKF was postponed until the end of March 1990. In early March the EPRLF-dominated north-eastern provincial council, under the leadership of Annamalai Varadharajah Perumal, renamed itself the 'National Assembly of the Free and Sovereign Democratic Republic of Eelam' and gave the central Government a one-year ultimatum to fulfil a charter of demands. Two weeks later, however, Perumal was reported to have fled to southern India. The last remaining IPKF troops left Sri Lanka on 24 March, a week ahead of schedule. In the next month the Government eased emergency regulations (including the ban on political rallies) in an effort to restore a degree of normality to the country after years of violence. At the same time, Sri Lanka's security forces, encouraged by the relative lull in violence, halted all military operations against the now much-weakened JVP and the Tamil militant groups. A fragile peace was maintained until June, when the LTTE abandoned its negotiations with the Government and renewed hostilities with surprise attacks on military and police installations in the north and north-east. Consequently, the Sri Lankan security forces were compelled to launch a counter-offensive. In mid-June the Government dissolved the north-eastern provincial council (despite protests by the EPRLF), and the holding of fresh elections in the province was postponed indefinitely pending the LTTE's agreement to participate in them (as earlier promised). In August the LTTE intensified its campaign of violence in the eastern province against the Muslim population, which retaliated with counter-attacks. At the end of August the Government launched a major offensive against the Tamil strongholds in the Jaffna peninsula. In January 1991 the LTTE suffered an apparent set-back when the Indian central Government dismissed the state government in Tamil Nadu, on account of the latter's alleged support for the Tamil militants in Sri Lanka. In March it was widely suspected that the LTTE was responsible for the assassination of a senior cabinet member, the Minister of Plantation Industries and Minister of State for Defence, Ranjan Wijeratne (who had been in charge of both the government forces' successful offensive against the JVP, several years earlier, and the ongoing offensive against the LTTE), and for the bomb attack on an armed-forces building in Colombo in June. More significantly, for its regional implications, the LTTE were believed to have been responsible for the assassination of the former Indian Prime Minister, Rajiv Gandhi, near Madras (now known as Chennai), the state capital of Tamil Nadu, in May. In early 1992 the Indian Government proscribed the LTTE in India and banned its activities on Indian territory. By mid-1992 the fighting between the Sri Lankan army and the LTTE showed no sign of abating, despite several offers of a resumption of talks made by the Government to the Tamil militants.

In May 1991 President Premadasa consolidated his political position when the UNP won a decisive victory in the local government elections. In August, however, the opposition, with the support of a number of UNP parliamentary members, began proceedings for the impeachment of the President. The impeachment motion listed 24 instances of alleged abuse of power, including illegal land deals, improperly aiding Tamil rebels, and failure to consult the Cabinet (thus violating the Constitution). The motion constituted a serious challenge to the authority of Premadasa and to the stability of his Government, but was rejected in October by the Speaker of Parliament on the grounds that some of the signatures on the resolution were invalid. Eight erstwhile UNP parliamentary members, including two former cabinet members, Lalith Athulathmudali and Gamini Dissanayake, who were expelled from the party (thus losing their parliamentary seats as well) by Premadasa for supporting the impeachment motion, formed a new party in December, called the Democratic United National Front (DUNF), to which they hoped to attract dissident members of the UNP.

The security forces suffered a serious reversal in August 1992, when 10 senior officers, including the northern military commander and the Jaffna peninsula commander, were killed in a landmine explosion near Jaffna. Tension between the Muslim and Tamil populations in the north-eastern district of Polonnaruwa drastically increased following the massacre of more than 170 Muslim villagers by suspected LTTE guerrillas in October. In the next month the LTTE were also widely believed to have been responsible for the murder of the naval commander, Vice-Admiral Clancy Fernando, in Colombo. The LTTE themselves lost one of their most senior leaders when Velupillai Prabhakaran's chief deputy was killed at sea in January 1993.

In late April 1993 the opposition DUNF accused Premadasa's Government of having been responsible for the assassination of the party's leader, Lalith Athulathmudali. In response, Premadasa alleged that the perpetrators of the murder had been LTTE terrorists; the LTTE, however, denied any responsibility for the killing. The country was thrown into greater political turmoil on 1 May, when President Premadasa was assassinated in a bomb explosion in Colombo. The LTTE were officially blamed for the murder, although, again, they strenuously denied any involvement. A few days later Parliament unanimously elected the incumbent Prime Minister, Dingiri Banda Wijetunga, to serve the remaining presidential term (expiring in December 1994), and the erstwhile Minister of Industries, Science and Technology, Ranil Wickremasinghe, was appointed to replace him in the premiership. In provincial elections held in mid-May 1993 the UNP won control of four of the seven councils; no polling was carried out in the area covered by the now defunct north-eastern province. Although the ruling party received 47% of the votes, it was the first time since 1977 that its percentage of total votes had fallen below 50%, an indication of an erosion of its support base that became more pronounced in the early part of 1994.

The Sri Lankan forces achieved considerable success in their fight against ethnic violence in the eastern province in 1993, but were forced to abandon a massive military offensive in the Jaffna peninsula in October owing to the ferocity of the LTTE resistance. In the following month both sides suffered heavy casualties in the course of the battle over the military base at Pooneryn on the Jaffna lagoon. As a result of this military

débâcle, in which, according to official figures, more than 600 army and naval personnel were either killed or captured, the Government established a new combined security forces command for the Jaffna and Kilinochchi districts to counter the LTTE threat.

Despite the continuing violence, provincial elections were held in the eastern province and in the northern town of Vavuniya in early March 1994; the UNP secured the greatest number of seats, while independent Tamil groups also performed well. The LTTE and the TULF boycotted the poll. The ruling party suffered its first major electoral reverse for 17 years at the end of the month, however, when an opposition grouping known as the People's Alliance (PA, of which the main constituents were the SLFP and the traditional Marxist left and which was headed by the former leader of the USA group, Chandrika Kumaratunga) won a clear majority in elections to the southern provincial council. In an attempt to regain lost support, the UNP proceeded to reintroduce various populist welfare policies, such as had been adopted by former President Premadasa. In early May Wijetunga's Government defeated a parliamentary motion of 'no confidence' by 111 votes to 71. On 24 June, in an apparent attempt to catch the opposition by surprise, the President dissolved Parliament and announced that early legislative elections were to be held on 16 August, ahead of the presidential election. Wijetunga's ploy failed, however: the PA obtained 48.9% of the votes, thus securing a narrow victory over the UNP, which received 44% of the poll. Under the prevailing system of proportional representation, this translated to 105 seats for the PA and 94 for the UNP in the 225-seat Parliament. The 17-year rule of the UNP had thus come to an end. On 18 August President Wijetunga abandoned hope of forming a UNP minority Government and appointed Kumaratunga as Prime Minister, the PA having secured the support of the SLMC, the TULF, the Democratic People's Liberation Front and a small, regional independent group. A new Cabinet was appointed on the following day, almost all members of which belonged to the SLFP. In line with her electoral pledge to abolish the executive presidency and to establish a parliamentary system in its place, the Prime Minister removed the finance portfolio from the President and assumed responsibility for it herself. Although Wijetunga retained the title of Minister of Defence, actual control of the ministry was expected to be exercised by the Deputy Minister of Defence. The Prime Minister's mother, Sirimavo Bandaranaike, was appointed as Minister without Portfolio. With regard to the Tamil question, overtures were made between the new Government and the LTTE concerning unconditional peace talks (these commenced in mid-October) and at the end of August, as a gesture of goodwill, the Government partially lifted the economic blockade on LTTE-occupied territory. In addition, the Prime Minister created a new Ministry of Ethnic Affairs and National Integration and assumed the portfolio herself, thus revealing her determination to seek an early solution to the civil strife.

In September 1994 Kumaratunga was unanimously elected by the PA as its candidate for the forthcoming presidential poll, while Gamini Dissanayake, the leader of the opposition (who had left the DUNF and returned to the UNP in 1993), was chosen as the UNP's candidate. The election campaign was thrown into confusion, however, on 24 October 1994, when Dissanayake was assassinated by a suspected LTTE suicide bomber in a suburb of Colombo; more than 50 other people, including the General Secretary of the UNP, Gamini Wijesekara, and the leader of the SLMP, Ossie Abeyagoonasekera, were killed in the blast. The Government declared a state of emergency and suspended the ongoing peace talks with the LTTE. Dissanayake had been an outspoken critic of these talks and had been one of the architects of the 1987 Indo-Sri Lankan accord. His widow, Srima Dissanayake, was chosen by the UNP to replace him as the party's presidential candidate. The state of emergency was revoked on 7 November (with the exception of the troubled areas in the north and east) to facilitate the fair and proper conduct of the presidential election, which was held on 9 November. Kumaratunga won the election, with 62.3% of the votes, while Srima Dissanayake obtained 35.9%. The Government viewed the victory as a clear mandate for the peace process initiated earlier that year. Sirimavo Bandaranaike was subsequently appointed Prime Minister, for the third time. The new President pledged to abolish the executive presidency before mid-July 1995, on the grounds that she believed that the post vested too much power in one individual, and promised to initiate a programme of social, economic and constitutional change.

The Government and the LTTE resumed peace talks in early January 1995, which resulted in the drawing up of a preliminary agreement on the cessation of hostilities as a prelude to political negotiations. This important development constituted the first formal truce since fighting was renewed in the north-east in June 1990. In April 1995, however, following several rounds of deadlocked negotiations, with both sides accusing each other of making unreasonable demands and proposals, the LTTE unilaterally ended the truce, withdrew from the peace talks and resumed hostilities against the government forces. (As feared, the LTTE had apparently used the 14-week truce period to fortify and consolidate its strategic positions, notably in the eastern province.) In response, the Government cancelled all the concessions made to the guerrillas during the peace negotiations and placed the security forces on alert. A disturbing escalation in the violence was demonstrated at the end of the month by the LTTE's deployment, for the first time, of surface-to-air missiles.

In mid-1995 Kumaratunga's administration began to prepare a range of constitutional proposals, including a more comprehensive devolution of power to the provinces than the system prevailing. In August an official statement was issued explaining that the proposed new structure was essentially a federal system in which the units were named regions rather than provinces. In the mean time, the Government admitted in July that the abolition of the executive presidency would not be effected by the middle of that month, as earlier pledged.

In July 1995 the Government launched another major offensive in the Jaffna peninsula. As the Government's offensive was intensified in mid-October, tens of thousands of civilians were compelled by the LTTE to flee the area. In retaliation against the army's attack, rather than actively confronting the troops, the LTTE detonated explosives on the country's two largest oil storage facilities near Colombo, which received virtually all of Sri Lanka's imported petroleum. As a result, about 20% of the island's petroleum supply was destroyed. In November two LTTE suicide bombers caused 18 deaths and more than 50 injuries in Colombo. In early December, however, the Sri Lankan army achieved a major victory in capturing the city of Jaffna and subsequently much of the Jaffna peninsula. Although the LTTE's military strength and morale were undermined, the rebels, as expected, reverted to guerrilla warfare and further terrorist activity. The day after the armed forces had raised the national flag above Jaffna, the LTTE rejected the President's offer of an amnesty in exchange for disarmament and announced a new recruitment drive. The Government's short-term strategy with regard to the Jaffna peninsula was to attempt to persuade the tens of thousands of civilians now living in refugee camps to return there and to establish a fully functional civil administration in the region. As widely feared, there was an escalation in LTTE-organized terrorist activity following the recapture of Jaffna; at the end of January 1996 more than 100 people were killed and about 1,400 were injured as a result of a suicide bomb attack on the Central Bank in Colombo. This devastating attack appeared to be the LTTE's response to the Government's release of the legal draft of devolution proposals earlier that month. Against a background of continuing conflict between the Tamil militants and the government forces in the north and east of the country, the President extended the state of emergency to cover the whole country in April (since coming to power in November 1994, the People's Alliance administration had restricted the emergency provisions to the troubled northern and eastern regions and Colombo). In mid-May 1996 the army announced that it now controlled the whole of the Jaffna peninsula and claimed that, of the 300,000 Tamil civilians who had been displaced by the ethnic violence, about 250,000 had returned to the government-held areas. Despite the army's controlling presence in the Jaffna peninsula, the LTTE was, by no means, a spent force. In mid-July the Tamil militants attacked and overran the isolated military base at Mullaitivu on the north-eastern coast of Sri Lanka, inflicting very heavy casualties on the army (according to the LTTE, at least 1,200 government soldiers were killed; according to official figures, the army death toll was about 300). About one week later the LTTE were suspected of planting a bomb on a crowded suburban train near Colombo, which left more than 70 people dead. In September the army seized control of the northern town of Kilinochchi, which had served as the LTTE's new headquarters since April. In the following month Prabhakaran and nine other militants were charged with more than 700 criminal acts of terrorism, including the bombing of the Central Bank in January. This constituted the first occasion that the Government had taken legal action against the LTTE leader. Fierce fighting between the Tamil militants and government troops continued into 1997, both in the north and east of the country; in early March it was estimated that more than 50,000 people had died and about one million people had been displaced as a result of the 14-year civil war.

The Government was given a considerable boost in March 1997, following its overwhelming success in local elections, in which it won more than 80% of the contested bodies (voting did not take place in the troubled northern and eastern provinces). However, although the Government secured control over a majority of the local bodies, its share of the total vote decreased to 48%, compared with the 62% it achieved in the presidential election of November 1994. The UNP obtained nearly 42% of the poll. None the less, the Government viewed the election results as a mandate to continue preparing its devolution plans offering limited autonomy to the Tamil secessionists (plans that had, so far, been blocked by the UNP). In May the Government launched a fresh military offensive against the LTTE, with the aim of gaining control of the 75-km stretch of the A9 highway between Vavuniya and Elephant Pass, which is the point of entry to the Jaffna peninsula. In June the Prime Minister implemented an extensive cabinet reshuffle, including the merger and alteration of various ministries. In late August the Government announced that it would submit its devolution proposals for parliamentary debate in October. In mid-October, however, 18 people were killed and more than 100 injured (including about 35 foreigners) when a bomb exploded in the car park of a Colombo hotel. It was widely believed that the LTTE deliberately targeted foreigners in this attack following the US Government's decision a few days earlier to place the organization on its official proscribed list of international terrorist groups. At the end of the month, despite protests from the UNP, the draft of the proposed constitutional amendments was presented to Parliament. The prospect of peace, however, appeared increasingly remote in late January 1998 when 16 people were killed in a suspected LTTE suicide bombing in Kandy at Sri Lanka's most sacred Buddhist temple, the Dalada Maligawa ('Temple of the Tooth'). The following day the Government retaliated by formally outlawing the LTTE, thus apparently ruling out the prospect of further peace negotiations in the near future and focusing instead on a military solution. The Government suffered another set-back in late January when the UNP effectively rejected the proposed devolution package. The UNP disagreed with the Government's proposal to devolve wide-ranging powers to regional councils—including a Tamil-administered area—and favoured the concept of power-sharing at the centre. Also at the end of January, polls were conducted in Jaffna for the first time in 15 years. The local authority elections, which were monitored by tens of thousands of troops, were contested by a number of moderate Tamil political parties but were, not surprisingly, boycotted by the LTTE. The largest number of seats was won by the Eelam People's Democratic Party, but the turn-out was a mere 28%, owing to LTTE threats to disrupt the voting.

In February–March 1998 nearly 50 people were killed and about 250 were injured as a result of two suicide bomb attacks in Colombo. In mid-May the recently-elected mayor of Jaffna (the first person to hold that position in 14 years), Sarojini Yogeswaran, who was a member of the moderate TULF, was assassinated by two suspected LTTE gunmen after refusing demands by Tamil militants to resign. In September Yogeswaran's replacement, Ponnuthurai Sivapalan, who was also a leading member of TULF, was killed, along with 19 others, in a suspected LTTE bomb explosion in Jaffna city hall.

In early August 1998, following the proclamation of a national state of emergency the previous day (owing to the security situation), the Sri Lankan authorities postponed indefinitely elections to five provincial councils, which had been scheduled to take place at the end of the month. The opposition claimed that the Government had deliberately engineered the postponement of the important polls since it was concerned about performing badly in them.

In early June 1998 the Government imposed an indefinite 'total ban' on news coverage (both local and foreign) of the ongoing civil war. In late September hundreds of troops on both sides were killed when the LTTE recaptured Kilinochchi and the army seized Mankulam, the last major town held by the guerrillas on the vital northern highway. In November Sri Lankan intelligence reports indicated that the LTTE was in the process of acquiring helicopters and military aircraft. By the end of the year, despite fierce fighting and large numbers of casualties on both sides, the army had still failed to capture completely the northern highway, which, if opened, would provide the military with a vital land route to the Jaffna peninsula (hitherto during the civil war, all government troops and supplies had had to be transported by sea or air). In early December the Government announced its decision to cancel the operation to capture the highway, which, since it was launched in May 1997, had cost the lives of more than 3,000 government troops. There were also indications that the army had a serious manpower problem (it needed to recruit 20,000 fresh troops), caused partly by desertions and growing numbers of casualties.

In late January 1999 the ruling PA won the elections to the north-western provincial council by a significant margin, but amid allegations of widespread electoral fraud and violence against opposition activists. A few days later the Supreme Court in Colombo overruled President Kumaratunga's order made in August 1998 postponing elections to five other provincial councils. The Court stated that the presidency had no constitutional right to postpone the elections through the declaration of a state of emergency and asked the election commission to hold the polls within the next three months and to hold all five of them on a single day. In the provincial elections, which were eventually held in early April, the PA won control in four provinces and retained power in the fifth—the polls were very keenly contested, however, with the PA achieving about 43% of the total votes and the UNP obtaining around 41%. Elections to the southern province, which were held in May, also resulted in a PA-led administration. One noteworthy feature of this series of provincial polls was the resurgence of the JVP as a credible political force (it won 8% of the vote in all of the contested provincial councils, and, specifically, as much as 20% in the Hambantota district of the southern province).

Meanwhile, in March 1999 the army launched another offensive against the LTTE in the northern province, the objective of which was to reduce the area under the effective control of the Tamil guerrillas. In mid-June, in an unprecedented order, the President temporarily dissolved the powerful National Security Council and divested the Chief of Defence Staff of sweeping powers. Prospects of achieving a peace settlement in Sri Lanka appeared even more distant in late July, following the assassination by a suspected LTTE suicide bomber in Colombo of the TULF Vice-President, Neelan Tiruchelvam, who was a leading peace campaigner and human rights activist. In the same month Kumaratunga promoted 15 PA members to the position of deputy minister, in a move that was widely interpreted as an attempt to ensure that politicians remained loyal to the alliance prior to and during the forthcoming general election. The promotions were heavily criticized by the opposition as financially profligate.

In October 1999 President Kumaratunga announced the holding of early presidential elections in December (about 11 months ahead of schedule), prompting the opposition to claim that her decision was aimed at bolstering the foundering ruling coalition prior to the legislative elections, which were due to be held in October 2000. In November 1999, however, the Government suffered a debilitating set-back following a rapid series of LTTE victories in the northeastern Wanni region, thus reversing more than two years of territorial gains by the military. Following these demoralizing defeats and amidst reports of a large-scale desertions and mutiny in the army ranks, the Government announced a tightening of existing military censorship on domestic news coverage in an attempt to stem adverse publicity and reorganized the northern military command.

A few days before the presidential election, which was held on 21 December 1999, Kumaratunga survived an assassination attempt by a suspected LTTE suicide bomber in Colombo; the explosion killed more than 20 people and injured more than 100, while the President sustained wounds to her right eye. The election, which was contested by 13 candidates and attracted a 73% turn-out of the electorate, was marred by widespread allegations of vote-rigging, intimidation and violence. Kumaratunga was returned to power by a narrow majority (possibly having garnered a considerable sympathy vote), winning 51% of the total votes, while her main rival, Ranil Wickremasinghe of the UNP, secured 43%. In early January 2000, despite tightened security in the capital, another suspected LTTE suicide bomber killed herself and 12 other people outside the office of Prime

Minister Bandaranaike in Colombo in what police described as a failed assassination attempt.

At the end of January 2000, in a dramatic reversal of policy, Wickremasinghe announced that, in spite of reservations, the UNP would henceforth offer legislative support to the Government's proposed constitutional amendments regarding devolution (first unveiled in 1995), which were designed to prepare the ground for peace talks with the LTTE; the opposition party, however, later appeared to vacillate with regard to their support, following indications that Kumaratunga intended to retain the executive presidency for a further six years. In early 2000 the Government confirmed that, at Kumaratunga's request, the Norwegian Government had agreed to play an intermediary role in any peace negotiations. The Norwegian Minister of Foreign Affairs, Knut Vollebæk, arrived in Colombo in February to discuss with Kumaratunga and Wickremasinghe the modalities for commencing direct peace talks between the Sri Lankan Government and the LTTE. Earlier that month Vollebæk had met a senior LTTE official in London to assess the separatists' opinions regarding peace negotiations. According to commentators, the preconditions of both sides (respectively, the withdrawal of all government troops from Tamil areas and the abandonment by the LTTE of its demand for an independent state) were the most serious obstacles to the commencement of talks.

Despite the steps being taken towards the instigation of peace talks, heavy fighting continued between the army and the LTTE in the north, and another suspected LTTE terrorist killed more than 20 civilians in a bomb explosion in the capital in March 2000. In the same month the Sri Lankan army suffered heavy casualties when the LTTE launched a massive sea and land assault on the Jaffna peninsula. In the following month, after further significant gains, the LTTE announced that it had captured the large military base at Elephant Pass at the strategic entrance point to the peninsula (the garrison had been under government control since the IPKF's withdrawal in 1990). In early May President Kumaratunga came under intense pressure from various quarters to seek Indian assistance in an attempt to halt the rapid LTTE march to recapture Jaffna; the Indian Government firmly ruled out military intervention, but offered to provide humanitarian aid (including mediation and the evacuation of troops). India also announced that it was extending its ban on the outlawed LTTE for a further two years. In response to the escalating military crisis, the Government imposed draconian security measures, banning all activities perceived as a threat to national security and giving extensive powers to the armed forces and police, and renewed press censorship on the foreign media. By mid-May the LTTE claimed to be only 1 km from the administrative centre of Jaffna, and thousands of terrified civilians were reported to be fleeing from the embattled city. In late May, as the army and the LTTE continued to struggle for control of the peninsula, the Government appealed for new army recruits, and Norway launched a fresh diplomatic initiative to find a peaceful solution to the ethnic crisis. Fighting continued during June, with neither side making any significant advances. Meanwhile, in early June the Minister of Industrial Development, Clement V. Gunaratna, and more than 20 others were killed by a suspected LTTE suicide bomber in Colombo. In mid-June the Indian Minister of External Affairs, during his visit to Sri Lanka, reiterated India's support for Sri Lanka's territorial integrity and offered the country a US $100m. credit facility. At the end of the month President Kumaratunga and the leader of the opposition UNP, Ranil Wickremasinghe, began discussions on the draft of the new Constitution designed to resolve the conflict with the LTTE. The LTTE, however, immediately denounced the proposals. At the same time, the Supreme Court ruled that the recently renewed press censorship was illegal as the appointment of the official censor had not been approved by Parliament. Nevertheless, the President reimposed a series of restrictions on the local and foreign press and reappointed the official censor under the same emergency regulations employed in May. The Government and UNP then agreed on a draft constitution, which recommended converting the country into a *de facto* federal state through the establishment of eight semi-autonomous regional councils. However, the Tamil parliamentary parties, the TULF, PLOTE and Eelam People's Democratic Party (EPDP), rejected the proposals as providing inadequate autonomy to the Tamil regions of the country. Senior Buddhist monks rejected the reforms, owing to fears that devolution would threaten the Sinhalese-dominated population and prominence of Buddhism in Sri Lanka. In late July the UNP withdrew its support for the reforms. Street demonstrations were held in protest at the proposals. In August the President indefinitely postponed a parliamentary vote on the issue, and hence any further discussion of the reform programme, once it became clear that the Government would not obtain the two-thirds majority required to secure the passage of the requisite legislation. The LTTE intensified attacks on security forces. On 10 August Sirimavo Bandaranaike announced her resignation as Prime Minister, owing to ill health. She was replaced by Ratnisiri Wickramanayake, the erstwhile Minister of Public Administration, Home Affairs and Plantation Industries. Parliament was dissolved in preparation for a general election.

Meanwhile, a report issued by the University Teachers for Human Rights in mid-July 2000 claimed that there had been a dramatic increase in the number of child soldiers forcibly recruited by the LTTE, in preparation for a major assault on Jaffna city. In September heavy fighting between the LTTE and Sri Lankan army continued; the army reclaimed a naval base and Jaffna's second largest town, Chavakachcheri. By the end of September, however, the LTTE had managed to regain some territory. In the same month the Minister of Shipping and Shipping Development, Mohammad H. M. Ashraff, and the President of the SLMC, along with 14 others were killed, in a helicopter crash in Kegalle District. A high-level investigation into the incident was ordered; there was widespread speculation that the aircraft had been shot down by LTTE guerrillas. At the same time, the Minister of Health, Nirmal Siripala de Silva, escaped a possible assassination attempt in which seven people were killed.

The parliamentary elections of 10 October 2000 were marred by electoral malpractice and systematic violence and intimidation (particularly on the part of the incumbent PA); according to the independent Centre for Monitoring Election Violence, at least 71 people were killed during the five-week election campaign. Nevertheless, the elections attracted a turn-out of 75% of the electorate. Despite the electoral irregularities, neither the PA nor the UNP won an absolute majority (taking 107 and 89 of the 225 parliamentary seats, respectively), but, having gained the support of the EPDP and National Unity Alliance (NUA—primarily a constituent of the SLMC), the PA was able to form a new, expanded coalition under the premiership of Wickramanayake. The former Prime Minister, Sirimavo Bandaranaike, died shortly after casting her vote. On 18 October Parliament elected Anura Bandaranaike, a member of the UNP and the President's estranged brother, as parliamentary speaker; this was the first time in 40 years that the position had been held by a member of the opposition. This development was followed by an agreement between the PA and UNP to preserve the stability of the new Government for the next two years. On 19 October a new Cabinet was announced. In exchange for its support, the NUA established a 100-day deadline for the President to introduce a new constitution and to open negotiations with the LTTE. At the end of the month the JVP announced its willingness to support the Government in order to prevent the NUA from wielding excessive influence. Meanwhile, a group of Sinhalese attacked a detention camp for former LTTE soldiers, killing 29 Tamils. Fighting between the LTTE and army escalated at the end of October but had subsided by mid-November. In November Parliament approved a motion to extend the state of emergency by a further month.

In late October 2000 negotiations between the leader of the LTTE, Velupillai Prabhakaran and the Norwegian peace envoy, Erik Solheim, commenced. Discussions between Solheim and the President were also initiated. In early November Prabhakaran proposed direct peace negotiations with the Government, without any preconditions, but demanded a reduction in fighting and the lifting of an economic embargo on areas controlled by the LTTE to create a suitable atmosphere for talks. The Government did not immediately respond to the offer, although it had made it clear that it was willing to attempt to reach a peace accord. President Kumaratunga later requested the Norwegian envoy to clarify certain issues before the Government made a decision. Prabhakaran publicly confirmed his offer at the end of November. The Prime Minister ruled out an imminent cease-fire, declaring that the army would continue to fight LTTE guerrillas. In mid-December the Government announced that it was prepared to enter immediate peace negotiations, but would not scale down its offensive or lift the embargo until talks were under way. The LTTE rejected peace talks without the prior implementation of a cease-fire and later declared a unilateral

one-month cease-fire, to begin from 24 December, as a 'goodwill gesture' to assist the peace process. Shortly afterwards, however, government troops launched an offensive in the Jaffna peninsula, and violence continued. The Government rejected the cease-fire, dismissing it as a strategic manoeuvre, and insisted that it would not discuss a cease-fire until the two parties entered peace negotiations.

On 23 January 2001, and at regular intervals thereafter, the LTTE extended the cease-fire by one month. The Government refused to reciprocate with a cease-fire. Nevertheless, dialogue between Solheim and representatives of the LTTE and Government, respectively, resumed in late January. In early March both sides appeared to react positively to Solheim's efforts to broker peace; however, in mid-March violence escalated and continued during the rest of the month. In early March the United Kingdom banned the LTTE under its anti-terrorism legislation. In April Parliament agreed to extend the state's emergency powers for another month. Also, the Government effected a partial removal of the embargo on Tamil-controlled areas. On the following day the LTTE demanded legal status as a prerequisite to negotiations, despite the fact that such a concession remained highly improbable. The Government declared a four-day cease-fire and the release of 10 detainees, supposedly LTTE militants, during the Sinhala and Tamil New Year, as a 'gesture of goodwill'. However, one day before the cease-fire was due to end clashes took place between the navy and the LTTE. Violence continued and worsened throughout April. The LTTE decided not to extend the cease-fire. At the end of the month Solheim held negotiations with the President. Talks between Solheim and the Government and the LTTE, respectively, in mid-May ended inconclusively.

In early June 2001 a motion for the impeachment of Chief Justice Sarath Silva, accusing him of misconduct, was submitted to Parliament. Later that month the President dismissed the leader of the SLMC, Abdul Rauf Hakeem, from his position as Minister of Internal and International Trade, Commerce, Muslim Religious Affairs and Shipping Development, later accusing him of making anti-Government statements and refusing to support government policies. The President's strategy foundered, however, when Hakeem and six other members of the SLMC withdrew their support for the ruling PA, thereby reducing the coalition Government to a minority in Parliament. Immediately afterwards, opposition parties challenged the Government with a no-confidence motion. In order to prevent the motion from being debated in Parliament in mid-July, the President suspended the legislature on 10 July until 7 September, and announced that a referendum on a new constitution would take place on 21 August. The rulings, which were undemocratic and unconstitutional, respectively, caused a constitutional crisis. The UNP-led opposition organized a series of demonstrations against the President's decision to prorogue Parliament. The campaign turned violent at times. The President also faced opposition within the Cabinet, particularly to the referendum. As a result, Kumaratunga announced in early August that the referendum would be postponed until mid-October.

In the mean time, in early June 2001 the Norwegian Minister of Foreign Affairs, Thorbjørn Jagland, arrived in Colombo, at the request of the President, in an attempt to bolster the peace initiative. The LTTE, however, protested against this development, claiming that it was an effort to reduce in importance Solheim's position. In early July President Kumaratunga circumvented Parliament and reimposed a state of emergency under anti-terrorist regulations. The President also extended a ban on the LTTE. On 24 July, the 18th anniversary of the start of the LTTE's separatist campaign, Tamil militants attacked the capital's international airport and an adjacent air base. Several hours of shooting between Tamil militants and the army ended with all 13 guerrillas and seven soldiers killed. The LTTE had destroyed eight military aircraft and three civilian aircraft, and damaged others. The attack caused considerable damage to the country's tourist industry and, thus, the economy. The attack on the country's only international airport, renowned for its impenetrable security, adversely affected foreign-visitor confidence and raised questions about the air force and airport's defence system. Following the incident, the army launched a retaliatory air attack on LTTE bases; violence between the army and guerrillas escalated. At the end of August the LTTE rejected the Government's offer of a cease-fire, dismissing it as a strategic manoeuvre.

SRI LANKA

In an attempt to resolve the political crisis, the Prime Minister and senior cabinet members conducted negotiations with the UNP on the possible establishment of a coalition government. The UNP, however, opted to form a UNP-led coalition with other opposition parties. Consequently, the President entered into negotiations with the left-wing, radical JVP. On 5 September 2001 the JVP formally agreed to support the minority Government for one year (but not to join the administration), in return for a set of conditions laid out in a 28-point memorandum of understanding. The JVP's 10 seats in Parliament raised the Government's share to a majority of 119 out of 225 seats. The President had already granted the JVP two of its demands by cancelling the referendum and announcing that Parliament would be reconvened one day earlier. In addition, the President agreed to suspend negotiations with the LTTE for one year and to postpone the privatization programme. According to the JVP's demands, in mid-September the size of the Cabinet was halved to 22 members. However, three senior cabinet members resigned, refusing to participate in an administration supported by the left-wing party. Several members of the PA criticized the pact and doubted its longevity. Later that month Parliament approved an item of legislation to establish a Constitutional Council which would be responsible for removing political influence from major institutions and appointing independent commissions for public service, the judiciary, the police and elections. At the end of September a motion of 'no confidence' in the Government was resubmitted to Parliament. On 8 October the SLFP removed its General Secretary, S. B. Dissanayake. Two days later 13 members of the PA, including several ministers, defected to the opposition, reducing the coalition to a minority. In order to forestall defeat in the vote of 'no confidence' due to take place the next day, President Kumaratunga dissolved Parliament. The opposition condemned the decision, although the dissolution was constitutional (one year after the previous legislative elections had passed). A general election was scheduled to take place on 5 December.

In mid-October 2001 four opposition Tamil parties, the TULF, TELO, EPRLF and All Ceylon Tamil Congress, announced the formation of a Tamil Nationalist Alliance (TNA). In the mean time, violence between the LTTE and the Government continued. In late October the Prime Minister escaped a possible assassination attempt in which three people were killed.

The general election on 5 December 2001, reportedly one of the most violent in Sri Lanka's history, was marred by incidents of vote-rigging and other electoral malpractices. Some 43 people were killed during the election campaign, and another 17 died on the day of the election. Some tens of thousands of Tamil voters were barred from voting after the army prevented them from leaving LTTE-controlled areas to cast their vote. The outgoing Government claimed that the UNP had signed a secret pact with the LTTE, an allegation strongly denied by the opposition. Nevertheless, 72% of the electorate voted. The UNP won 109 of the 225 seats (45.6% of the vote) and the PA received 77 seats (37.2%). The JVP secured 16 seats (9.1%) and the TNA won 15 seats (3.9%). The UNP leader, Ranil Wickremasinghe, formed the United National Front (UNF) with the SLMC to ensure a majority of 114 seats in Parliament. Two days after the election Wickremasinghe was invited to form a government. On 9 December he was sworn in as Prime Minister. For the first time since 1984, the Prime Minister and the President were from two opposing parties; consequently, the relationship between the PA President and the UNF Government proved to be uneasy at times. President Kumaratunga banned live state media coverage of the Prime Minister's inauguration ceremony. The President was also at first reluctant to relinquish her defence and finance portfolios, which she eventually gave up in return for full control over the élite Presidential Security Division that was deployed for her personal protection, and refused initially to allow members of her former administration who had defected to the UNP to join the Government. After long negotiations, a new coalition Government, including the TNA and 12 members of the former PA administration, was sworn in on 12 December. In 2002 the right of the President to dissolve Parliament after one year from the date of the last election loomed over the new Government. In an attempt to curb the President's powers and to ensure stability for the peace process (see below), the Government recommended that parliamentary resolutions determine future elections; however, the President refused to support this suggestion. In September the Government introduced to Parliament a constitutional amendment which would restrict the right of the President to dissolve the legislature when the governing party has a majority in Parliament. In October, however, the Supreme Court ruled that the proposed statute required not only a two-thirds' majority in the legislature, but also endorsement by a national referendum.

The UNP's victory was largely attributed to the party's keenness to resume negotiations with the LTTE; on his accession, the Prime Minister repeated this willingness. Significantly, the TNA was a member of the coalition Government. Although the LTTE launched major attacks against army troops and the police, during which 26 were killed, to mark the inauguration of the new Cabinet, on 19 December the Tamil extremists announced a unilateral one-month cease-fire from 25 December. On 21 December the Government responded with the declaration of a cease-fire as a 'gesture of goodwill'. The Prime Minister also announced that the free movement of food, medicine and other non-military supplies into the Tamil-controlled areas would be allowed; a concession refused, hitherto, by the President. In early January 2002 the Government announced the reduction of economic sanctions on the northern areas controlled by the LTTE. One week later a delegation of Norwegian diplomats, led by Norway's Deputy Minister of Foreign Affairs, Vidar Helgesen, arrived in Colombo to conduct negotiations with the Prime Minister and President, and eventually to facilitate peace talks between the Government and the LTTE. At the end of January both sides extended the cease-fire by one month. At the same time, the LTTE released 10 army and civilian prisoners. As a further confidence-building measure, the Government restored the electricity supply to part of the northern Tamil-controlled Vavuniya district.

In the mean time, in late January 2002 the Supreme Court issued a momentous judgment, which awarded compensation to a Tamil woman for a rape by three soldiers and three policemen. The human rights group, Amnesty International, welcomed the decision, and shortly afterwards published a report on custodial rape by the security forces, recommending the Government to create an independent authority to investigate allegations of torture and rape.

On 22 February 2002 the Government and LTTE signed an agreement on an internationally monitored indefinite cease-fire to take effect the following day. Norway was requested to monitor the cease-fire. It was hoped that this breakthrough would lead to peace negotiations and end years of fighting in which more than 60,000 people had been killed. However, in mid-February there were several reports that the LTTE was continuing forcibly to recruit Tamil children.

Meanwhile, in early February 2002 the Prime Minister avoided a coalition crisis when he convinced two government members, both representatives of the CWC, to withdraw their resignations. The ministers objected to the UNP's removal of CWC candidates to the local elections, which were scheduled for March. Later that month the President's uncle, former Deputy Minister of Defence Gen. Anuruddha Ratwatte, was arrested in connection with the murder of 10 Muslim supporters of the UNP on the day of the December election. In free and fair elections held in March, the UNP acheived victory in 240 out of 247 councils; the PA was spectacularly defeated, winning in only four of the municipal legislatures.

In mid-March 2002 Prime Minister Wickremasinghe visited Jaffna, the first premier to do so since 1982. In early April the Government lifted a six-year ban on domestic flights and allowed commercial airlines to resume flights to Jaffna. A week later an important road linking the Jaffna peninsula with the rest of the country was opened for the first time in 12 years. On 10 April Prabhakaran addressed an international press conference for the first time in more than 10 years. He demanded the lifting of the ban on the LTTE as a prerequisite to negotiations and declared his commitment to peace and full support of the cease-fire. A few days later he signed a pact with the SLMC, allowing the largest Muslim party in Sri Lanka to participate in proposed negotiations with the Government. It was also agreed that nearly 100,000 Muslims expelled from the north by the LTTE about 10 years ago would be allowed to return to their homes. At the end of April the Prime Minister rejected the LTTE's demand for an independent Tamil state, or eelam, raising doubts about resolving the ethnic conflict. A team of US-led experts began removing landmines in the Jaffna peninsula. Meanwhile, Kumaratunga, who had reportedly criticized the Government for making too many concessions to the Tamil militants, expressed her support in late April for a public demonstration against the proposal to grant legal status to the

LTTE. She had already disagreed with some of the terms of the peace agreement.

In May 2002 a Tamil-owned trawler, reported to have been illegally importing weapons, was destroyed by the Sri Lankan navy in an exchange of gunfire off the coast of the eastern Batticaloa district—the first major violation of the cease-fire to have occurred. The LTTE refuted allegations that it had been smuggling arms and accused the army of attacking a civilian fishing boat in an effort to undermine the cease-fire. Later in the month the Norwegian-led Sri Lanka Monitoring Mission issued a statement conveying concern over the increasing number of cases of civilians being harassed by the LTTE. In June incidents of violence between Hindu Tamils and Muslims in eastern Sri Lanka, resulting in eight deaths and several injuries, threatened to jeopardize the peace process. Clashes between Hindus and Muslims in the town of Valaichchenai in Batticaloa in late June prompted the security forces to impose a curfew on the town. It was reported that Muslims were protesting against alleged extortion by the LTTE and Tamil attacks.

Meanwhile, in May 2002 the first direct talks for seven years between the Government and the LTTE took place on the Jaffna peninsula. Formal peace negotiations that were expected to begin in May were moved to June and postponed again to August. The August deadline was not achieved but the cease-fire was maintained. Meanwhile, the Sri Lanka Monitoring Mission reported that breaches of the cease-fire declined by 28% in July and August. According to the office of the UN High Commissioner for Refugees (UNHCR), by mid-August 103,000 displaced families had returned to their homes since the beginning of the cease-fire in February. On 4 September the Government lifted the official ban on the LTTE, a prerequisite to negotiations set by the LTTE. (The President, however, firmly opposed the removal of the ban until the talks were under way.) The first round of negotiations took place on 16–18 September in Thailand. The minister G. L. Peiris was chief negotiator for the Government; Anton Balasingham led negotiations on behalf of the LTTE. The talks were successful: both sides agreed to establish a joint committee to deal with security issues, and a joint task force to concentrate on the reconstruction of areas destroyed by war, the clearing of landmines and the resettling of 800,000 internally displaced people to high-security zones. On the last day of negotiations Balasingham unexpectedly renounced the LTTE's long-standing demand for independence, instead agreeing to consider regional autonomy and self-government. The Government and LTTE agreed to hold the next set of negoiations in October.

In early October 2002 four people were killed and 15 injured in clashes between government and LTTE forces in Ampara district, in one of the most serious violations of the cease-fire to date. On 31 October a Sri Lankan court convicted *in absentia* Prabhakaran for his role in a 1996 truck bombing in Colombo and sentenced him to 200 years' imprisonment. The sentencing did not have an effect on the second round of negotiations which began on 31 October in Thailand. The four-day talks were expected to concentrate mainly on humanitarian issues, but concluded in a breakthrough with both sides agreeing to create a subcommittee to examine a political solution to the conflict. Balasingham announced that the LTTE was willing to participate in democracy, would allow other political parties to operate in the areas under its control and would cease the recruitment of child soldiers. The LTTE also abandoned its demand for an interim government in the north-east. Both sides agreed to establish subcommittees to deal with rehabilitation and military de-escalation. However, while the talks progressed, a curfew was imposed in large parts of Colombo after three days of rioting between the majority Sinhalese and members of the Muslim community. Furthermore, the Prime Minister's cousin was attacked in the capital. Sinhalese nationalists opposed to the peace process questioned the sincerity of the LTTE, dismissing the progress at the negotiations as an attempt to win publicity and international favour. Nevertheless, the peace process gained momentum in late November when Balasingham arrived in Norway to enter negotiations with the Prime Minister on the eve of a one-day international donor conference in support of the peace process. A few days later Prabhakaran confirmed in his annual address that the LTTE was prepared to accept regional autonomy rather than an independent state, but warned that violence would resume if negotiations collapsed.

At the third round of peace talks on 2–5 December 2002 in Oslo, Norway, the two sides agreed on 'internal self-determination' based on a federal system of government within a united Sri Lanka. Peiris and Balasingham described the developments as unprecedented and historic. However, in order to achieve the two thirds' majority required in Parliament to pass a constitutional amendment, the Government needed to secure the support of the President. Although Kumaratunga welcomed the peace agreement, she had repeatedly criticized the Government for making too many concessions during the peace process. In mid-December a close adviser of the President stated that the PA would not support a political solution unless the LTTE disarmed. However, at the fourth round of negotiations, held on 6–9 January 2003 in Thailand, Balasingham refused to yield to pressure to disarm the Tamil guerrillas prior to a political settlement and rejected Kumaratunga's demand that the LTTE's squad of suicide bombers disband. The talks concluded with an agreement to accelerate the rate of return and resettlement of up to 250,000 displaced people. Meanwhile, despite Tamil promises to halt the involuntary recruitment of children, the Sri Lanka Monitoring Mission reported that the LTTE had enlisted hundreds of child soldiers since the beginning of the cease-fire. In late January the President ordered police and military chiefs to curb the recruitment of child soldiers within one week. Representatives of UNICEF conducted training sessions with the Sri Lankan military and talks with the LTTE on the recruitment of child soldiers, as well as issues of child protection and rehabilitation. The fifth round of negotiations, held in Germany in early February, was overshadowed by a serious violation of the cease-fire. On 7 February three LTTE guerrillas committed suicide by setting fire to their trawler after the Sri Lankan navy intercepted the vessel and Norwegian peace monitors discovered arms on board. The two-day negotiations focused on human rights issues; it was agreed that UNICEF would monitor a joint programme to rehabilitate child soldiers.

Meanwhile, the SLMC split in early December 2002 after two members of the party mounted a challenge to Hakeem's leadership. The divisions threatened to weaken the UNF Government and adversely affect the preace process. In January 2003 the Government allowed the LTTE to import the necessary equipment to resume broadcasting of the hitherto banned Voice of Tigers radio station. Peiris declared that both parties should have the opportunity to express their views; however, critics argued that the Voice of Tigers, which began broadcasting in mid-January, would provide the LTTE with a powerful vehicle for propaganda. In early February President Kumaratunga censured the Prime Minister for granting a licence to the LTTE radio station, amid rising tension in the cohabitation Government. Kumaratunga had earlier threatened to dismiss the Government. On 7 February the PA and JVP began negotiations to form a joint front against the UNF Government. The JVP strongly opposed the LTTE and attempted to convince the President to dismiss the governing coalition. Prabhakaran failed to attend a meeting with Norwegian peace mediators in mid-March, reportedly owing to the sinking of a civilian Tamil ship by the Sri Lankan navy several days earlier. The LTTE declared that it was considering abandoning the peace talks as a result of the incident. The sixth round of negotiations on 18–21 March, held in Japan, ended without agreement, amid reports of renewed violence in Sri Lanka. Both sides reaffirmed their commitment to the cease-fire, however, after a Chinese fishing trawler was attacked by suspected LTTE guerrillas off the coast of Sri Lanka. An international donor meeting in Washington, DC, USA to consider aid for Sri Lanka's reconstruction in preparation for a major donor conference to be held in Japan in June, took place in mid-April. The LTTE, however, was not invited: the USA had not yet lifted its ban on the Tamil organization; neither had India, one of the attendees at the meeting. On 21 April the LTTE announced that it was temporarily withdrawing from the peace negotiations and that it would not attend the donor conference in Japan in June because it was excluded from the aid conference in the USA. It was also dissatisfied with the manner in which the cease-fire had been implemented (government troops remained stationed in many parts of the Tamil-controlled areas in a clear violation of the cease-fire) and the way in which the Government was carrying out rehabilitation and relief measures.

In foreign policy, Sri Lanka has adopted a non-aligned role. Sri Lanka is a founder member of the South Asian Association for Regional Co-operation (SAARC, see p. 310), formally established in 1985.

Government

A presidential form of government was adopted in October 1977 and confirmed in the Constitution of September 1978. The Constitution provides for a unicameral Parliament as the supreme legislative body, its members being elected by a system of modified proportional representation. Executive powers are vested in the President, who is Head of State. The President is directly elected for a term of six years and is not accountable to Parliament. The President has the power to appoint or dismiss the Prime Minister and members of the Cabinet; may assume any portfolio; and is empowered to dismiss Parliament. In 1982 the Constitution was amended, allowing the President to call a presidential election before his/her first term of office was completed. In 1983 the Constitution was further amended to include a 'no-separation' clause, making any division of Sri Lanka illegal, and any advocates of separatism liable to lose their civic rights.

Sri Lanka comprises nine provinces and 24 administrative districts, each with an appointed Governor and elected Development Council. In November 1987 a constitutional amendment was adopted, providing for the creation of eight provincial councils (the northern and eastern provinces were to be merged as one administrative unit). A network of 68 Pradeshiya Sabhas (district councils) was inaugurated throughout the country in January 1988.

Defence

In August 2002 the armed forces totalled 157,900 (including recalled reservists): army 118,000, navy 20,600, air force 19,300. There were also paramilitary forces of around 88,600 (including 13,000 Home Guard, an estimated 15,000 National Guard and a 3,000-strong anti-guerrilla unit). Defence expenditure for 2002 was budgeted at Rs 62,000m. Military service is voluntary.

Economic Affairs

In 2001, according to estimates by the World Bank, Sri Lanka's gross national income (GNI), measured at average 1999–2001 prices, was US $16,294m., equivalent to $830 per head (or $3,560 per head on an international purchasing-power parity basis). During 1990–2001, it was estimated, the population increased at an average annual rate of 1.3%, while gross domestic product (GDP) per head increased, in real terms, by an average of 3.6% per year. Overall GDP increased, in real terms, at an average annual rate of 5.0% in 1990–2001. Real GDP grew by 6.0% in 2000, but decreased, in real terms, by 1.4% in 2001. Real GDP increased by 3.0% in 2002.

Agriculture (including hunting, forestry and fishing) contributed 18.8% of GDP in 2001, and in the first quarter of that year 33.0% of the employed labour force were engaged in the sector. The principal cash crops are tea (which accounted for 14.2% of total export earnings in 2002), rubber and coconuts. In 1990 Sri Lanka overtook India as the world's largest tea exporter. Rice production is also important. Cattle, buffaloes, goats and poultry are the principal livestock. During 1990–2000 agricultural GDP increased at an average annual rate of 1.9%. Growth in agricultural output decelerated to an estimated 1.9% in 2000. Agricultural GDP declined by 3.0% in 2001, largely as a result of drought, before increasing by 1.9% in 2002.

Industry (including mining and quarrying, manufacturing, construction and power) contributed 25.8% of GDP in 2001, and engaged 24.4% of the employed labour force (excluding inhabitants of the northern and eastern provinces) in the first quarter of that year. During 1990–2000 industrial GDP increased at an average annual rate of 6.8%. Industrial GDP increased by an estimated 7.5% in 2000, but contracted by about 2% in 2001, mainly owing to a dramatic decrease in export-orientated industries. Industrial output increased by 1.3% in 2002.

Mining and quarrying contributed 1.9% of GDP in 2001, and engaged 1.3% of the employed labour force in 2000. Gemstones are the major mineral export (accounting for an estimated 1.9% of total export earnings in 2002). Another commercially important mineral in Sri Lanka is graphite, and there are also deposits of iron ore, monazite, uranium, ilmenite sands, limestone and clay.

Manufacturing contributed 15.3% of GDP in 2001, and engaged 17.2% of the employed labour force in the first quarter of the same year. In the mid-1990s the principal branches of manufacturing were wearing apparel (excluding footwear), food products, textiles and petroleum and coal products. The garment industry is Sri Lanka's largest earner of foreign exchange, with sales of garments and textiles providing an estimated 51.9% of total export earnings in 2002. During 1990–2000 manufacturing GDP increased by an average of 8.0% per year. The GDP of the manufacturing sector rose by an estimated 8.8% in 2000, but declined by 4.0% in 2001.

Energy is derived principally from hydroelectric power, which accounted for 67.5% of electricity production in 1999. Imports of mineral fuels and lubricants comprised 9.2% of the value of total imports in 2000.

The services sector, which is dominated by tourism, contributed 55.3% of GDP in 2001, and engaged 42.5% of the employed labour force (excluding inhabitants of the northern and eastern provinces) in the first quarter of 2001. During 1990–2000 services GDP increased at an average annual rate of 6.0%. The sector's GDP grew by 7.0% in 2000, before declining by 0.5% in 2001. Growth in the sector reached 4.2% in 2002.

In 2001 Sri Lanka recorded a visible trade deficit of US $553.5m., and there was a deficit of $264.7m. on the current account of the balance of payments. In 2001 the principal source of imports (9.9%) was India, while the USA was the principal market for exports (38.9%). Other major trading partners were Japan, Singapore and the United Kingdom. The principal exports in 2002 were clothing, tea and basic manufactures. The principal imports were textile yarn and fabrics, basic manufactures, machinery and transport equipment, and food and live animals.

The projected budgetary deficit for 2003 totalled Rs 134,000m. (7.5% of GDP). Sri Lanka's total external debt was US $9,066m. at the end of 2000, of which $8,035m. was long-term public debt. In that year the cost of debt-servicing was equivalent to 9.6% of earnings from the exports of goods and services. During 1990–2001 the average annual rate of inflation was 10.1%; the rate declined to 4.7% in 1999, before rising to 6.2% in 2000 and an estimated 14.2% in 2001. The rate of inflation decelerated to 9.6% in 2002. An estimated 8.7% of the labour force were unemployed in the first quarter of 2002.

Sri Lanka is a member of the Asian Development Bank (ADB, see p. 143), a founder member of the South Asian Association for Regional Co-operation (SAARC, see p. 310), which seeks to improve regional co-operation, particularly in economic development, and a founder member of the Colombo Plan (see p. 339), which seeks to promote economic and social development in Asia and the Pacific.

Unemployment, a persistent fiscal deficit and inflation, together with the economic dislocation resulting from the ethnic conflict, are among the country's main economic problems The economy showed encouraging signs of recovery in 1997, despite the continuing ethnic violence; however, economic growth decelerated in 1998, partly owing to weak tea prices, declining exports and low levels of foreign investment. The economy showed signs of recovery in 1999: the tourism industry showed steady growth, and the high fiscal deficit, still a major concern for the Government, decreased to 7.5% of GDP. However, the upsurge in fighting between government forces and Tamil guerrillas from the latter half of 1999 led to a further deterioration of the economic situation in 2000. Lack of confidence in the economy continued to deter foreign investment. Although Sri Lanka's main export markets recovered, the burden of the civil war and the higher cost of petroleum imports resulted in a sharp increase in the external current-account deficit. In April the Government removed the ban on the import of wheat grain and flour. In April 2001 the IMF approved a 14-month stand-by credit worth US $253m. to support the Government's economic programme. Under this programme the Government aimed to lower the fiscal deficit to 8.5% of GDP and to increase official reserves. The economy performed well until mid-2001: the current-account deficit narrowed and the country's foreign-exchange reserves increased. In July the Central Bank 'floated' the rupee and after an initial period of volatility, the currency stabilized. However, the political and economic developments in the latter half of 2001 caused considerable damage to the country's economy. The assault on the international airport in Colombo in July and the attacks on the USA in September adversely affected foreign-investor confidence and led to a sharp decline in tourism. The increase in insurance premiums payable by airlines and ships had a negative impact on the exports market. The global economic slowdown caused a decrease in demand for garments and textiles, and the prolonged drought led to negative growth in agricultural GDP. Consequently, the economy contracted for the first time, the fiscal deficit increased to 10.8% of GDP (from 9.8% in 2001), and public debt stood at 103% of GDP (compared with 96.4% in 2001). The situation was exacerbated by the political crisis, which culminated in a general election in December, only 14 months after the previous poll. The new Government, led by the United National Party, immediately embarked on a peace process to end the civil war that was draining the country's economic resources. One year after the cease-fire between the Government and the LTTE was declared in February 2002, the economy was showing clear signs of recovery. The Government had reduced the fiscal deficit in 2002 to 8.9% of GDP, and increased GDP growth to 3.0%. The export sector improved, with exports of textiles, industrial machinery and agriculture recording strong increases. Growth in imports, partly owing to rising fuel prices, also indicated a strengthening domestic economy. Imports of investment goods increased as a result of the reconstruction efforts under way in the north-east of Sri Lanka. The rate of inflation declined and the rupee stabilized. Furthermore, tourist arrivals increased in the latter half of 2002, contributing to a rise in foreign-exchange reserves; in October SriLankan Airlines made its first profit in flight services since 1985, largely owing to the peace process and internal reforms. A privatization programme was under way in 2002: the insurance, utilities, petroleum and telecommunications sectors were opened to private investment. The 2002/03 budget introduced measures to curb the high public debt and to boost economic growth, employment opportunities and earning capacity. The Government projected GDP growth of 5.5% in 2003 and aimed to reduce fiscal deficit to 7.5% of GDP. A donor conference was scheduled to take place in June with the aim of mobilizing much-needed economic support to rebuild the country's economy and infrastructure, shattered by two decades of war. International financial organizations (such as the IMF) and individual nations (such as the United Kingdom) had already pledged funds for rehabilitation. The prerequisites to the assistance were a serious commitment from the Government to a restructuring programme and a permanent peace agreement between the LTTE and the Government. However, international donors warned that the conference might have to be postponed owing to the LTTE's decision to suspend temporarily peace negotiations with the Government in April.

Education

Education is officially compulsory for 11 years between five and 15 years of age, and it is available free of charge from lower kindergarten to university age. There are three types of school: state-controlled schools (mostly co-educational), denominational schools and Pirivenas (for Buddhist clergy and lay students).

Primary education begins at the age of five and lasts for five years. Secondary education, beginning at 10 years of age, lasts for up to eight years, comprising a first cycle of six years and a second of two years. In 1995 the total enrolment at primary and secondary schools was equivalent to 89% of the school-age population (boys 87%; girls 90%). Primary enrolment in 1996 was equivalent to 109% of children in the relevant age-group (boys 110%; girls 108%); the comparable ratio for secondary enrolment was 75% (boys 72%; girls 78%) in 1995. In 1998 primary enrolment was equivalent to 107% of children in the relevant age-group. There are 26 teacher-training colleges, 13 universities, 13 polytechnic institutes, eight junior technical colleges and an open university. Estimated expenditure on education by the central Government in 2002 was Rs 32,123m. (7.8% of total government spending).

Public Holidays

2003: 14 January (Tamil Thai Pongal Day), 4 February (Independence Commemoration Day), 12 February (Id al-Adha, Hadji Festival Day), 1 March (Maha Sivarathri), 13 April (Sinhala and Tamil New Year's Eve), 14 April (Sinhala and Tamil New Year's Day), 18 April (Good Friday), 1 May (May Day), 14 May (Milad un-Nabi, Birth of the Prophet), 25 October (Diwali—Festival of Lights), 26 November (Id al-Fitr, Ramazan Festival Day), 25 December (Christmas Day), 31 December (Special Bank Holiday).

2004: 14 January (Tamil Thai Pongal Day), 2 February (Id al-Adha, Hadji Festival Day), 4 February (Independence Commemoration Day), 18 February (Maha Sivarathri), 9 April (Good Friday), 13 April (Sinhala and Tamil New Year's Eve), 14 April (Sinhala and Tamil New Year's Day), 1 May (May Day), 2 May (Milad un-Nabi, Birth of the Prophet), 12 November (Diwali—Festival of Lights), 14 November (Id al-Fitr, Ramazan Festival Day), 25 December (Christmas Day), 31 December (Special Bank Holiday).

Note: A number of Hindu, Muslim and Buddhist holidays depend on lunar sightings. There is a holiday every lunar month on the day of the full moon.

Weights and Measures

Legislation passed in 1974 provided for the introduction of the metric system, but imperial units are still used for some purposes.

Statistical Survey

Source (unless otherwise stated): Department of Census and Statistics, 15/12 Maitland Crescent, POB 563, Colombo 7; tel. (1) 682176; fax (1) 697594; e-mail dcensus@lanka.ccom.lk; internet www.statistics.gov.lk.

Area and Population

AREA, POPULATION AND DENSITY

Area (sq km)	65,525*
Population (census results)	
17 March 1981	14,846,750
17 July 2001 (provisional)†	
Males	8,343,964
Females.	8,520,580
Total	16,864,544
Population (official estimates at mid-year)	
1999‡	19,043,000
2000‡	19,359,000
2001	18,700,000
Density (per sq km) at July 2001	286§

* 25,299 sq miles. This figure includes inland water (3,189 sq km).

† Figures refer to 18 out of 25 districts where enumeration was carried out completely. Enumeration was only partially conducted in Mannar, Vavuniya, Batticaloa and Trincomalee districts, owing to security concerns; data from these districts brought the total enumerated population to approximately 17,560,000. The census was not conducted in the districts of Jaffna, Mullaitivu and Kilinochchi, also owing to security concerns. The total estimated population for the entire country at July 2001 was 18,732,255.

‡ Not adjusted to take account of the July 2001 census results.

§ Including adjustment for underenumeration.

ETHNIC GROUPS

(census results)

	1981	2001*†
Sinhalese	10,979,561	13,810,664
Sri Lankan Tamil	1,886,872	736,484
Indian Tamil	818,656	855,888
Sri Lankan Moors	1,046,926	1,349,845
Others	114,735	111,663
Total.	14,846,750	16,864,544

* Provisional.

† Figures refer to 18 out of 25 districts.

DISTRICTS
(population at 2001 census)

	Area (sq km, excl. inland water)*	Population (provisional)	Density (persons per sq km)
Colombo	676	2,234,289	3,305
Gampaha	1,341	2,066,096	1,541
Kalutara	1,576	1,060,800	673
Kandy	1,917	1,272,463	664
Matale	1,952	442,427	227
Nuwara Eliya	1,706	700,083	410
Galle	1,617	990,539	613
Matara	1,270	761,236	599
Hambantota	2,496	525,370	210
Jaffna†	929	490,621	528
Mannar†	1,880	115,577	81
Vavuniya†	1,861	149,835	80
Mullaitivu†	2,415	121,667	49
Kilinochchi†	1,205	127,263	106
Batticaloa†	2,610	486,447	186
Ampara	4,222	589,344	140
Trincomalee†	2,529	340,158	351
Kurunegala	4,624	1,452,369	314
Puttalam	2,882	705,342	245
Anuradhapura	6,664	746,466	112
Polonnaruwa	3,077	359,197	117
Badulla	2,827	774,555	274
Monaragala	5,508	396,173	72
Ratnapura	3,236	1,008,164	312
Kegalle	1,685	779,774	463
Total	62,705	18,732,255	299

* Revised total land area is 62,336 sq km.

† Official estimates where census was not conducted or only partially conducted.

PRINCIPAL TOWNS
(provisional, population at 2001 census)

Colombo (Kolamba) (commercial capital)	642,020	Sri Jayawardenepura (Kotte) (administrative capital)	115,826
Dehiwala-Mount Lavinia	209,787		
Moratuwa	177,190	Kandy (Maha Nuwara)	110,049
Jaffna (Yapanaya)	145,600*	Kalmunai (Galmune)	94,457
Negombo (Migamuwa)	121,933	Galle (Galla)	90,934

* Estimated population at mid-1997 (Source: Provincial Councils, Department of Elections).

Source: Thomas Brinkhoff, *City Population* (internet www.citypopulation.de).

BIRTHS, MARRIAGES AND DEATHS*

	Registered live births		Registered marriages		Registered deaths	
	Number	Rate (per 1,000)	Number	Rate (per 1,000)	Number	Rate (per 1,000)
1992	356,842	20.5	155,345	8.9	98,380	5.6
1993	350,707	19.9	152,423	8.6	96,179	5.5
1994	356,071	19.9	162,489	9.1	100,394	5.6
1995	343,224	18.9	169,220	9.3	104,707	5.8
1996	340,649	18.6	170,444	9.3	122,161	6.7
1997	332,626	17.9	n.a.	n.a.	113,078	6.1
1998†	329,148	17.5	169,209	9.0	112,657	6.0
1999†	329,121	17.3	n.a.	n.a.	114,392	6.0

* Data are tabulated by year of registration, rather than by year of occurrence.

† Provisional.

Source: partly UN, *Demographic Yearbook* and *Population and Vital Statistics Report*.

Expectation of life (WHO estimates, years at birth): 69.9 (males 66.6; females 74.1) in 2001 (Source: WHO, *World Health Report*).

ECONOMICALLY ACTIVE POPULATION*
('000 persons aged 10 years and over, January–March of each year)

	1999	2000	2001
Agriculture, hunting, forestry and fishing	2,536.3	2,290.0	1,992.1
Manufacturing	843.3	1,013.2	1,035.5
Mining and quarrying	68.7	77.8 }	110.0
Electricity, gas and water	31.7	25.0 }	
Construction	279.1	320.6	337.3
Trade, restaurants and hotels	577.8	767.7	820.4
Transport, storage and communications	333.2	278.1	412.0
Financing, insurance, real estate and business services	87.8	122.6	138.4
Community, social and personal services	1,110.6	1,153.7	1,195.0
Activities not adequately defined	290.0	258.5	180.7
Total employed	6,159.0	6,307.7	6,212.4
Unemployed	580.0	546.1	518.3
Total labour force	6,739.1	6,853.8	6,730.7

* Excluding northern and eastern provinces.

2002 ('000 persons aged 10 years and over, January–March): Total employed 6,662.8; Unemployed 632.8; Total labour force 7,295.6.

Health and Welfare

KEY INDICATORS

Total fertility rate (children per woman, 2001)	2.1
Under-5 mortality rate (per 1,000 live births, 2001)	19
HIV/AIDS (% of persons aged 15–49, 2001)	<0.10
Physicians (per 1,000 head, 1999)	0.37
Hospital beds (per 1,000 head, 1990)	2.74
Health expenditure (2000): US $ per head (PPP)	120
Health expenditure (2000): % of GDP	3.6
Health expenditure (2000): public (% of total)	49.0
Access to water (% of persons, 2000)	83
Access to sanitation (% of persons, 2000)	83
Human Development Index (2000): ranking	89
Human Development Index (2000): value	0.741

For sources and definitions, see explanatory note on p. vi.

Agriculture

PRINCIPAL CROPS
('000 metric tons)

	1999	2000	2001
Rice (paddy)	2,857	2,860	2,694
Maize	31	31	29
Potatoes	27	48	58
Sweet potatoes	52	52	49
Cassava (Manioc)	252	249	234
Sugar cane	1,021	1,066	1,006
Dry beans	14	12	12*
Dry cow-peas	12	12	12*
Cashew nuts	5	5	5
Coconuts	2,149	2,353	2,211†
Copra	85	82	113
Cabbages	52	53	54
Tomatoes	40	44	40
Pumpkin, squash and gourds*	170	170	170
Cucumbers and gherkins*	28	28	28
Aubergines (Eggplants)	74	69	69*
Chillies and green peppers	60	56	49
Dry onions	105	79	69
Green beans	32	35	31
Carrots	27	26	28
Other vegetables*	69	69	69
Plantains*	615	615	610
Lemons and limes*	20	21	21
Mangoes	86	86	92
Pineapples	39	42	51
Other fresh fruit*	68	68	68
Coffee (green)	11	10	10
Tea (made)	284	306	295
Pepper	17	17	17*
Cinnamon	12	12	12*
Other spices*	16	14	14
Natural rubber	97	88	86

* FAO estimate(s).
† Unofficial figure.

LIVESTOCK
('000 head, year ending September)

	1999	2000	2001
Buffaloes	728	694	661
Cattle	1,617	1,557	1,565
Sheep	12	11	12
Goats	514	495	493
Pigs	74	71	68
Chickens	9,923	10,622	10,655

LIVESTOCK PRODUCTS
('000 metric tons)

	1999	2000	2001
Beef and veal	23.6	28.7	27.4
Goat meat	1.7	1.7	1.6
Pig meat	1.7	1.8	2.0
Poultry meat	57.0	63.3	82.2
Cows' milk	219.9	221.2	224.4
Buffaloes' milk	69.7	68.1	68.2
Goats' milk*	5.4	5.2	5.3
Hen eggs	50.9	52.3	53.6
Cattle and buffalo hides*	5.9	6.3	5.9

* FAO estimates.
Source: FAO.

Forestry

ROUNDWOOD REMOVALS
('000 cubic metres, excl. bark)

	1999	2000	2001
Sawlogs, veneer logs and logs for sleepers	59*	99	99*
Other industrial wood*	577	577	577
Fuel wood*	5,955	5,907	5,840
Total	6,591	6,583	6,516

* FAO estimate(s).

Source: FAO.

SAWNWOOD PRODUCTION
(FAO estimates, '000 cubic metres, incl. railway sleepers)

	1999	2000	2001
Total	5*	29	29*

* FAO estimate.

Source: FAO.

Fishing

('000 metric tons)*

	1998	1999	2000
Inland waters: freshwater fishes	29.9	31.5	36.7
Indian Ocean: marine fishes	233.5	241.9 ⎫	267.7
other marine animals	6.5	6.5 ⎭	
Total catch	269.9	279.9	304.4

* Excluding (a) quantities landed by Sri Lanka craft in foreign ports, and (b) quantities landed by foreign craft in Sri Lanka ports.

Sources: Ministry of Fisheries and Aquatic Resources Development, Colombo; UN, *Statistical Yearbook for Asia and the Pacific*.

Mining

('000 metric tons, unless otherwise indicated)

	1999	2000	2001
Zirconium concentrates (metric tons)	13,000	n.a.	n.a.
Natural graphite (metric tons)	4,592	5,902	6,585
Salt—unrefined	107	70	130
Kaolin	13	12	9
Natural phosphates	32	34	36

Ilmenite concentrates ('000 metric tons): 34.1.

Sources: US Geological Survey; UN, *Industrial Commodity Statistics Yearbook*.

Industry

SELECTED PRODUCTS
('000 barrels, unless otherwise indicated)

	1999	2000	2001
Raw sugar ('000 metric tons)	66	64	48
Plywood ('000 cu m)	7	n.a.	n.a.
Jet fuel	500	550	600
Motor gasoline—petrol	1,950	2,000	2,000
Kerosene	1,500	1,550	1,500
Distillate fuel oil	4,600	4,700	4,800
Residual fuel oil	5,300	5,300	5,200
Cement ('000 metric tons)	976	1,008	1,010
Electric energy (million kWh)	6,184	6,844	6,602

1997: Naphtha ('000 metric tons) 99.

Sources: US Geological Survey; Asian Development Bank, *Key Indicators of Developing Asian and Pacific Countries*; UN, *Industrial Commodity Statistics Yearbook*.

Finance

CURRENCY AND EXCHANGE RATES

Monetary Units
100 cents = 1 Sri Lanka rupee

Sterling, Dollar and Euro Equivalents (31 December 2002)
£1 sterling = 155.90 rupees
US $1 = 96.73 rupees
€1 = 101.44 rupees
1,000 Sri Lanka rupees = £6.414 = $10.339 = €9.858

Average Exchange Rate (rupees per US $)
2000   77.005
2001   89.383
2002   95.662

BUDGET
(million rupees)

Revenue	2000	2001*	2002†
Taxation	181,657	204,723	237,149
Taxes on income	27,224	34,618	38,992
Taxes on goods and services	44,473	45,603	87,835
National Security levy	34,136	42,939	17,211
Excise levy	41,682	44,911	52,321
Stamp duty	8,564	8,442	3,407
Taxes on international trade	23,444	26,096	29,775
Non-tax revenue	29,464	26,740	41,053
Interest	8,742	6,074	11,203
Sales and charges	6,177	5,938	7,629
Total	211,121	231,463	278,202

Expenditure	2000	2001*	2002†
Current expenditure	254,117	300,440	332,564
General public services	36,610	46,185	46,392
National security and defence	70,773	68,290	64,050
Interest payments	71,200	94,307	117,184
Transfers to other institutions	33,719	39,104	49,467
Provincial councils	23,220	26,405	31,684
Social safety	41,513	51,318	54,700
Pension	21,602	26,325	31,863
Samurdhi	9,661	12,574	9,950
Capital expenditure and net lending	81,545	83,246	81,062
Public investment	80,956	82,743	84,909
Acquisition of fixed assets	32,934	33,414	43,716
Capital transfers	26,617	26,585	21,385
Provincial transfers	8,218	7,844	5,531
On-lending	13,187	14,900	14,277
Other expenditure	589	503	−3,847
Total	335,662	383,686	413,626

* Provisional figures.
† Forecasts.

Source: Central Bank of Sri Lanka, Colombo.

INTERNATIONAL RESERVES
(US $ million at 31 December)

	2000	2001	2002
IMF special drawing rights	—	1	2
Reserve position in IMF	62	60	65
Foreign exchange	976	1,226	1,564
Total (excl. gold)	1,039	1,287	1,631

Source: IMF, *International Financial Statistics*.

MONEY SUPPLY
(million rupees at 31 December)

	1999	2000	2001
Currency outside banks	58,481	62,647	65,536
Demand deposits at commercial banks	50,059	55,788	56,665
Total money (incl. others)	108,554	118,478	122,211

Source: IMF, *International Financial Statistics*.

COST OF LIVING
(Consumer Price Index for Colombo; base: 1990 = 100)

	1999	2000	2001
Food (incl. beverages)	247.1	258.1	297.4
Fuel and light	203.2	241.0	275.5
Clothing (excl. footwear)	141.5	143.1	149.1
Rent	100.0	100.0	100.0
All items (incl. others)	237.2	251.8	287.5

Source: ILO, *Yearbook of Labour Statistics*.

NATIONAL ACCOUNTS
(million rupees at current prices)

Expenditure on the Gross Domestic Product

	2000	2001	2002
Government final consumption expenditure	132,189	141,072	143,021
Private final consumption expenditure	906,186	1,023,990	1,175,245
Increase in stocks	40	40	—
Gross fixed capital formation	352,632	308,473	351,603
Total domestic expenditure	1,391,047	1,473,575	1,669,869
Exports of goods and services	490,676	514,285	561,709
Less Imports of goods and services	624,048	605,673	666,588
Sub-total	1,257,675	1,382,187	1,564,990
Statistical discrepancy*	41	17,930	1
GDP in purchasers' values	1,257,634	1,400,117	1,564,991

* Referring to the difference between the sum of the expenditure components and official estimates of GDP, compiled from the production approach.

Source: IMF, *International Financial Statistics*.

Gross Domestic Product by Economic Activity

	1999	2000	2001
Agriculture, hunting, forestry and fishing	205,599	218,408	242,532
Mining and quarrying	18,322	21,547	23,869
Manufacturing	163,103	189,331	198,073
Construction	75,538	82,684	94,547
Electricity, gas and water	14,425	13,415	16,127
Transport, storage and communications	113,814	131,669	154,595
Wholesale and retail trade, restaurants and hotels	211,376	254,100	274,796
Finance	80,696	91,186	105,496
Public administration	52,412	58,020	69,409
Other services	59,445	64,899	73,301
GDP at factor cost	994,730	1,125,259	1,252,744
Indirect taxes, *less* subsidies	111,234	132,375	147,373
GDP in purchasers' values	1,105,964	1,257,634	1,400,117

Source: Asian Development Bank, *Key Indicators of Developing Asian and Pacific Countries*.

BALANCE OF PAYMENTS
(US $ million)

	1999	2000	2001
Exports of goods f.o.b.	4,596.2	5,439.6	4,821.1
Imports of goods f.o.b.	−5,365.5	−6,483.6	−5,374.6
Trade balance	−769.3	−1,004.0	−553.5
Exports of services	964.3	938.7	1,365.9
Imports of services	−1,413.7	−1,621.4	−1,755.6
Balance on goods and services	−1,218.6	−1,726.7	−943.1
Other income received	166.7	149.0	93.4
Other income paid	−419.3	−448.9	−373.9
Balance on goods, services and income	−1,471.2	−2,026.6	−1,223.6
Current transfers received	1,078.1	1,165.7	1,145.7
Current transfers paid	−168.2	−182.7	−186.8
Current balance	−561.3	−1,043.6	−264.7
Capital account (net)	80.0	49.4	49.1
Direct investment from abroad	176.4	173.0	171.7
Portfolio investment assets	71.8	19.1	23.6
Portfolio investment liabilities	−84.6	−63.4	−34.7
Other investment assets	23.2	−243.7	13.0
Other investment liabilities	226.6	562.3	206.6
Net errors and omissions	−27.3	186.2	164.7
Overall balance	−95.2	−360.8	329.3

Source: IMF, *International Financial Statistics*.

OFFICIAL DEVELOPMENT ASSISTANCE
(US $ million)

	1998	1999	2000
Bilateral donors	296.7	219.9	251.1
Multilateral donors	210.3	43.7	25.2
Total	507.0	263.6	276.3
Grants	195.6	198.4	187.2
Loans	311.4	65.2	89.1
Per caput assistance (US $)	28.3	14.5	15.0

Source: UN, *Statistical Yearbook for Asia and the Pacific*.

External Trade

PRINCIPAL COMMODITIES
(distribution by SITC, million rupees)

Imports c.i.f.	1998	1999	2000
Food and live animals	43,751	43,928	49,127
Beverages and tobacco	7,217	7,149	8,076
Crude materials (inedible) excluding fuels	6,192	5,974	7,359
Mineral fuels, lubricants, etc.	22,698	21,601	44,118
Animal, vegetable oil and fats	4,492	5,033	3,247
Chemicals	17,175	18,276	21,974
Basic manufactures	134,314	140,887	173,888
Machinery and transport equipment	87,688	87,616	106,554
Miscellaneous manufactured articles	44,993	47,543	61,940
Total (incl. others)	369,014	378,509	477,487

Exports f.o.b.	1998	1999	2000
Food and live animals	68,788	63,549	78,240
Tea	50,280	43,728	53,133
Desiccated coconut	2,975	5,095	4,951
Beverages and tobacco	2,904	2,816	3,108
Crude materials (inedible) excluding fuels	549	311	399
Rubber	2,808	2,305	2,179
Copra	458	631	587
Mineral fuels, lubricants, etc.	783	1,364	2,016
Animal, vegetable oil and fats	355	450	525
Coconut oil	199	247	249
Chemicals	2,021	1,869	2,299
Basic manufactures	52,205	51,489	60,736
Machinery and transport equipment	11,147	13,436	17,342
Miscellaneous manufactured articles	160,413	175,211	231,147
Total (incl. others)	305,850	318,810	412,733

Source: Asian Development Bank, *Key Indicators of Developing Asian and Pacific Countries*.

PRINCIPAL TRADING PARTNERS
(US $ million)

Imports c.i.f.	1999	2000	2001
China, People's Republic	161.5	251.1	404.0
Germany	136.0	157.0	174.1
Hong Kong	459.1	515.9	420.1
India	511.6	600.1	660.2
Japan	560.8	646.1	318.5
Korea, Republic	386.8	396.4	368.1
Malaysia	168.4	217.3	207.8
Singapore	451.8	496.0	435.1
United Kingdom	251.1	311.4	233.7
USA	216.2	254.9	215.4
Total (incl. others)	6,255.2	6,688.0	6,672.9

Exports f.o.b.	1999	2000	2001
France	101.7	114.2	140.9
Germany	215.7	230.2	221.5
Italy	64.7	69.1	63.0
Japan	159.1	229.7	203.6
Netherlands	107.5	104.3	75.3
Russia	87.9	109.8	70.1
Turkey	59.8	53.9	59.5
United Arab Emirates	122.2	135.1	134.5
United Kingdom	604.1	736.7	541.6
USA	1,791.8	2,192.6	1,956.6
Total (incl. others)	4,621.8	5,458.8	5,036.2

Source: Asian Development Bank, *Key Indicators of Developing Asian and Pacific Countries*.

Transport

RAILWAYS

	1998	1999	2000*
Passengers (million)	82.0	82.8	84.2
Freight carried ('000 metric tons)	1,051	1,160	1,194

* Provisional.

Source: Sri Lanka Railways.

ROAD TRAFFIC
(motor vehicles in use at 31 December)

	1997	1998	1999
Passenger cars	202,456	208,593	219,125
Buses and coaches	56,751	60,097	62,672
Lorries and vans	273,561	292,391	323,809
Road tractors	93,912	116,901	123,661
Motorcycles and mopeds	909,922	752,009	794,506
Total	1,536,602	1,429,991	1,523,773

Source: International Road Federation, *World Road Statistics*.

SHIPPING
Merchant Fleet
(registered at 31 December)

	1999	2000	2001
Number of vessels	64	65	69
Displacement ('000 grt)	194.6	150.0	153.7

Source: Lloyd's Register-Fairplay, *World Fleet Statistics*.

International Sea-borne Shipping
(freight traffic, '000 metric tons)

	1998	1999	2000
Goods loaded	9,490	9,292	9,192
Goods unloaded	16,633	17,703	18,343

Source: UN, *Statistical Yearbook for Asia and the Pacific*.

CIVIL AVIATION
(traffic on scheduled services)

	1997	1998	1999
Kilometres flown (million) . .	25.2	26.0	31.7
Passengers carried ('000) . . .	1,231.9	1,212.5	1,421.8
Passenger-km (million)	4,249.1	4,136.1	5,156.0
Total ton-km (million)	588.5	553.2	669.7

Tourism

FOREIGN TOURIST ARRIVALS*

Country of residence	1998	1999	2000
Australia	10,329	13,218	16,443
Belgium	4,992	5,643	10,224
France	26,874	34,458	25,992
Germany	74,058	77,259	70,584
India	37,356	42,315	31,860
Italy	15,867	19,815	16,883
Japan	13,785	16,332	10,266
Netherlands	22,977	29,670	22,618
Pakistan	10,782	11,421	10,005
Switzerland	9,048	8,310	8,490
United Kingdom	66,432	80,919	84,693
USA	9,987	10,572	9,816
Total (incl. others)	381,063	436,440	400,414

* Excluding Sri Lanka nationals residing abroad.

Tourist arrivals: 336,794 in 2001.

Tourism receipts (US $ million): 230 in 1998; 275 in 1999; 253 in 2000 (estimate).

Sources: Ceylon Tourist Board; World Tourism Organization.

Communications Media

	1998	1999	2000
Television receivers ('000 in use)	1,800	1,900	2,100
Telephones ('000 main lines in use)	523.5	669.1	767.4
Mobile cellular telephones ('000 subscribers).	174.2	256.7	430.2
Personal computers ('000 in use) .	90	105	135
Internet users ('000)	55	65	121.5
Daily newspapers	181	174	180
Books published: titles	5,839	4,655	1,818
Books published: copies ('000) . .	58,157.5	n.a.	25,459.3

Facsimile machines (in use)* 11,000 in 1994.

Radio receivers ('000 in use): 3,850 in 1997.

2001 ('000): Telephones (main lines in use) 828.0; Mobile cellular telephones (subscribers) 720.0; Personal computers (in use) 150; Internet users 150.0.

* Estimate.

Sources: UN, *Statistical Yearbook*; UNESCO, *Statistical Yearbook*; Telecommunications Regulatory Commission of Sri Lanka and International Telecommunication Union.

Education
(1995)

	Institutions	Teachers	Students
Primary	9,657	70,537	1,962,498
Secondary	5,771*	103,572	2,314,054
Universities and equivalent . .	n.a.	2,344	40,035
Distance learning	n.a.	206	20,601

* 1992 figure.

1996: Primary: 9,554 institutions, 66,339 teachers, 1,843,848 students.

1997: Primary: 60,832 teachers, 1,807,751 students; Secondary: 2,313,511 students.

1998: Primary: 1,798,162 students.

2001 (provisional): Universities: 13 institutions, 3,268 teachers, 48,061 students.

Sources: UNESCO, *Statistical Yearbook*; Ministry of Education, Colombo.

Adult literacy rate (UNESCO estimates): 91.6% (males 94.4%; females 89.0%) in 2000 (Source: UN Development Programme, *Human Development Report*).

Directory

The Constitution

The Constitution of the Democratic Socialist Republic of Sri Lanka was approved by the National State Assembly (renamed Parliament) on 17 August 1978, and promulgated on 7 September 1978. The following is a summary of its main provisions.

FUNDAMENTAL RIGHTS

The Constitution guarantees the fundamental rights and freedoms of all citizens, including freedom of thought, conscience and worship and equal entitlement before the law.

THE PRESIDENT

The President is Head of State, and exercises all executive powers including defence of the Republic. The President is directly elected by the people for a term of six years, and is eligible for re-election. The President's powers include the right to:
 (i) choose to hold any portfolio in the Cabinet;

 (ii) appoint or dismiss the Prime Minister or any other minister;
 (iii) preside at ceremonial sittings of Parliament;
 (iv) dismiss Parliament at will; and
 (v) submit to a national referendum any Bill or matter of national importance which has been rejected by Parliament.

LEGISLATURE

The Parliament is the legislative power of the people. It consists of such number of representatives of the people as a Delimitation Commission shall determine. The members of Parliament are directly elected by a system of modified proportional representation. By-elections are abolished, successors to members of Parliament being appointed by the head of the party which nominated the outgoing member at the previous election. Parliament exercises the judicial power of the people through courts, tribunals and institutions created and established or recognized by the Constitution or established by law. Parliament has control over public finance.

OTHER PROVISIONS

Religion

Buddhism has the foremost place among religions and it is the duty of the State to protect and foster Buddhism, while assuring every citizen the freedom to adopt the religion of their choice.

Language

The Constitution recognizes two official languages, Sinhala and Tamil. Either of the national languages may be used by all citizens in transactions with government institutions.

Amendments

Amendments to the Constitution require endorsement by a two-thirds majority in Parliament. In February 1979 the Constitution was amended by allowing members of Parliament who resigned or were expelled from their party to retain their seats, in certain circumstances. In January 1981 Parliament amended the Constitution to increase its membership from 168 to 169. An amendment enabling the President to seek re-election after four years was approved in August 1982. In February 1983 an amendment providing for by-elections to fill vacant seats in Parliament was approved. An amendment banning parties that advocate separatism was approved by Parliament in August 1983. In November 1987 Parliament adopted an amendment providing for the creation of eight provincial councils (the northern and eastern provinces were to be merged as one administrative unit). In December 1988 Parliament adopted an amendment allowing Tamil the same status as Sinhala, as one of the country's two official languages.

The Government

HEAD OF STATE

President: CHANDRIKA BANDARANAIKE KUMARATUNGA (sworn in 12 November 1994; re-elected 21 December 1999).

CABINET
(April 2003)

Prime Minister and Minister of Policy Development and Implementation: RANIL WICKREMASINGHE.

Minister of Foreign Affairs: TYRONNE FERNANDO.

Minister of Finance: K. N. CHOKSY.

Minister of Interior and Christian Affairs: JOHN AMARATUNGA.

Minister of Home Affairs, Provincial Councils and Local Government: ALICK ALUVIHARE.

Minister of Defence, and of Transport, Highways and Aviation: THILAK MARAPANE.

Minister of Agriculture and Livestock, and of Samurdhi: S. B. DISSANAYAKE.

Minister of Enterprise Development, Industrial Policy and Investment Promotion, and of Constitutional Affairs: Prof. G. L. PEIRIS.

Minister of Women's Affairs: AMARA PIYASEELI RATNAYAKE.

Minister of Justice, Law Reform and National Integration, and of Buddha Sasana: W. J. M. LOKUBANDARA.

Minister of Irrigation and Water Management: GAMINI JAYAWICKRAMA PERERA.

Minister of Environment and Natural Resources: RUKMAN SENANAYAKE.

Minister of Health, Nutrition and Welfare: P. DAYARATNE.

Minister of Power and Energy: KARU JAYUSURIYA.

Minister of Tourism: GAMINI LOKUGE.

Minister of Human Resources Development, Education and Cultural Affairs: Dr KARUNASENA KODITUWAKKU.

Minister of Mass Communication: IMITHIYAS BAKEER MAKAR.

Minister of Employment and Labour: MAHINDA SAMARASINGHE.

Minister of Commerce and Consumer Affairs: RAVI KARUNANAYAKE.

Minister of Economic Reform, Science and Technology: MILINDA MORAGODA.

Minister of Public Administration, Management and Reforms: VAJIRA ABEYWARDENA.

Minister of Housing and Plantation Infrastructure: ARUMUGAN THONDAMAN.

Minister of Plantation Industries: LAKSHMAN KIRIELLA.

Minister of Fisheries and Ocean Resources: MAHINDA WIJESEKERA.

Minister of Lands: RAJITHA SENARATNE.

Minister of Community Development: P. CHANDRASEKARAN.

Minister of Port Development and Shipping, and of Eastern Development and Muslim Religious Affairs: RAUF HAKEEM.

Minister of Southern Region Development: ANANDA KULARATNE.

Minister of Western Region Development: M. H. MOHAMED.

Minister of Central Region Development: TISSA ATTANAYAKE.

Minister of Rural Economy: BANDULA GUNAWARDANE.

Minister of Co-operatives: A. R. M. ABDUL CADER.

MINISTRIES

President's Secretariat: Republic Sq., Colombo 1; tel. (1) 24801; internet www.priu.gov.lk/execpres/presecretariat.html.

Prime Minister's Office: Sir Ernest de Silva Mawatha, Colombo 7; tel. (1) 575317; fax (1) 575454.

Ministry of Agriculture and Livestock: 'Govijana Mandiraya', 82 Rajamalwatta Rd, Battaramulla, Colombo; tel. (1) 868922; fax (1) 863497; e-mail minagr@slt.lk.

Ministry of Buddha Sasana: 135 Anagarika Dharmapala Mawatha, Colombo 7; tel. (1) 326126; fax (1) 437997.

Ministry of Central Region Development: 1120, Getambe, Peradeniya; tel. (8) 385784; fax (8) 385785; e-mail mcrd@kandyan.net.

Ministry of Commerce and Consumer Affairs: Rakshana Mandiraya, 21 Vauxhall St, Colombo 2; tel. (1) 435601; fax (1) 447669.

Ministry of Community Development: 45 St Michael's Rd, Colombo 3; tel. (1) 441849; fax (1) 328117; e-mail secomdev@sltnet.lk.

Ministry of Constitutional Affairs: 44B Horton Place, Colombo 7; tel. (1) 662261; fax (1) 662252; e-mail constaff@sltnet.lk.

Ministry of Co-operative Development: 349 Galle Rd, Colombo 3; tel. (1) 421211; fax (1) 301476; e-mail coopacct@sltnet.lk.

Ministry of Defence: 15/5 Baladaksha Mawatha, POB 572, Colombo 3; tel. (1) 430860; fax (1) 541529.

Ministry of Eastern Development and Muslim Religious Affairs: 45 Leyden Bastian Rd, Colombo 1; tel. (1) 438344; fax (1) 435142; e-mail minpds@slpa.lk.

Ministry of Economic Reform, Science and Technology: 561/3 Etvigala Mawatha, Colombo 5; tel. (1) 554848; fax (1) 554845; e-mail milindamora@sltnet.lk; internet www.most.gov.lk.

Ministry of Employment and Labour: 2nd Floor, Labour Secretariat, Kirula Rd, Narahenpita, Colombo; tel. (1) 581991; fax (1) 582938; e-mail mlabour@slt.lk; internet www.labour.gov.lk.

Ministry of Enterprise Development, Industrial Policy and Investment Promotion: Colombo; internet www.industry.gov.lk.

Ministry of Environment and Natural Resources: 'Sampathpaya', 82 Rajamalwatte Rd, Battaramulla, Colombo.

Ministry of Finance and Planning: Galle Face Secretariat, Colombo 1; tel. (1) 433937; fax (1) 449823; e-mail dst@sltnet.lk; internet www.eureka.gov.lk/fpea.

Ministry of Fisheries and Ocean Resources: Maligawatte, Colombo 10; tel. (1) 446184; fax (1) 541184.

Ministry of Foreign Affairs: Republic Bldg, Colombo 1; tel. (1) 325371; internet www.lanka.net/fm.

Ministry of Health, Nutrition and Welfare: 'Suwasiripaya', 385 Wimalawansha Mawatha, Colombo 10; tel. (1) 698471; fax (1) 693869; internet www.lk/government.html.

Ministry of Home Affairs, Provincial Councils and Local Government: 330 Union Place, Colombo 2.

Ministry of Housing and Plantation Infrastructure: Colombo.

Ministry of Human Resource Development, Education and Cultural Affairs: 'Isurupaya', Sri Jayawardenepura Kotte, Battaramulla, Colombo; tel. (1) 785141; fax (1) 785162; e-mail secedu@sltnet.lk; internet www.mca.gov.lk.

Ministry of Interior: 15/5 Baladaksha Mawatha, Colombo 3; tel. (1) 430860; fax (1) 389021; e-mail interior_1@sltnet.lk.

Ministry of Irrigation and Water Management: 500 T. B. Jayah Mawatha, Colombo 10; tel. (1) 673013; fax (1) 677247.

Ministry of Justice, Law Reform and National Integration: Superior Courts Complex Bldg, Colombo 12; tel. (1) 323022; fax (1) 320785; e-mail justices@sri.lanka.net; internet www.justiceministry.gov.lk.

Ministry of Land: 'Govijana Mandiraya', 80/5 Rajamalwatte Rd, Battaramulla, Colombo.

Ministry of Mass Communication: Level 7&18, West Tower, World Trade Centre, Echelon Sq, Colombo 1.

Ministry of North-West Region Development: Colombo.

Ministry of Plantation Industries: Vauxhall Lane, Colombo 2; tel. (1) 320901; fax (1) 438031.

Ministry of Policy Development and Implementation: Colombo.

Ministry of Port Development and Shipping: 45 Leyden Bastian Rd, Colombo 1; tel. (1) 438344; fax (1) 435142; e-mail minpds@slpa.lk.

Ministry of Power and Energy: 80 Flower Rd, Colombo 7.

Ministry of Public Administration, Management and Reforms: Independence Sq., Colombo 7; tel. (1) 696211; fax (1) 695279; e-mail minister@pubad.gov.lk; internet www.gov.lk/public/index.htm.

Ministry of Rehabilitation, Resettlement and Refugees: 14, BOI Bldg, Sir Baron Jayatilleke Mawatha, Colombo 1; tel. (1) 382069; fax (1) 382066.

Ministry of Rural Economy: Janakala Kendraya, Pelawatte, Battaramulla, Colombo.

Ministry of Samurdhi: 7A Ried Ave, Colombo 7; tel. (1) 689589; fax (1) 688945.

Ministry of Southern Region Development: Colombo.

Ministry of Tourism: 64 Galle Rd, Colombo 3; tel. (1) 385241; fax (1) 441505; internet www.slmts.slt.lk.

Ministry of Transport, Highways and Aviation: 1 D. R. Wijewardene Mawatha, POB 588, Colombo 10; tel. (1) 687212; fax (1) 687284; internet www.transport.gov.lk.

Ministry of Urban Public Utilities: 29 Galle Face Terrace, Colombo 3; tel. (1) 307831; fax (1) 307827; e-mail sec_upu@sltnet.lk.

Ministry of Western Region Development: Colombo.

Ministry of Women's Affairs: 177 Nawala Rd, Narahenpita, Colombo 5; tel. (1) 598371; internet www.womens-affairs.gov.lk.

Ministry of Youth Affairs and Sports: 7A Ried Ave, Colombo 7.

President and Legislature

PRESIDENT

Presidential Election, 21 December 1999

Candidate	Valid votes	% of votes
Chandrika Bandaranaike Kumaratunga (PA)	4,312,157	51.12
Ranil Wickremasinghe (UNP)	3,602,748	42.71
M. D. Nandana Gunathilaka (JVP)	344,173	4.08
Total (incl. others)	8,435,754	100.00

PARLIAMENT

Speaker: JOSEPH MICHAEL PERERA (UNP).

Deputy Speaker: (vacant).

General Election, 5 December 2001

Party	Seats
United National Party (UNP)	109
People's Alliance (PA)	77
Janatha Vimukthi Peramuna (JVP)	16
Tamil National Alliance (TNA)	15
Sri Lanka Muslim Congress (SLMC)	5
Eelam People's Democratic Party (EPDP)	2
Democratic People's Liberation Front (DPLF)	1
Total	225

Notes: Direct elections were held for 196 of the 225 seats on the basis of a proportional representation system involving preferential voting; the remaining 29 were chosen from party lists according to each party's national share of the vote.

Political Organizations

Ceylon Workers' Congress (CWC): 'Savumia Bhavan', 72 Ananda Coomarasamy Mawatha, POB 1294, Colombo 5; tel. (1) 565082; fax (1) 301355; e-mail cwcctuc@slt.lk; f. 1939; represents the interests of workers in the mercantile and local government sectors and of workers (mainly of Indian Tamil origin) on tea plantations; 250,000 mems; Pres. and Gen. Sec. S. R. ARUMUGAN THONDAMAN.

Democratic People's Liberation Front (DPLF): has operated as a national political party since Sept. 1988; political wing of the People's Liberation Organization of Tamil Eelam (PLOTE); Leader DHARMALINGAM SITHADTHAN.

Democratic Workers' Congress (DWC) (Political Wing): 70 Bankshall St, POB 1009, Colombo 11; tel. (1) 439199; fax (1) 435961; f. 1939 as trade union, f. 1978 as political party; aims to eliminate discrimination against the Tamil-speaking Sri Lankans of recent Indian origin; 201,382 mems (1994); Pres. and Gen. Sec. MANO GANESHAN.

Desha Vimukthi Janatha Party (National Liberation People's Party): has operated as a national political party since Sept. 1988.

Deshapriya Janatha Viyaparaya (DJV) (Patriotic People's Movement): militant, Sinhalese group; associated with the JVP.

Eelam National Democratic Liberation Front (ENDLF): Kilinochchi; Tamil; supports 1987 Indo-Sri Lankan peace accord; has operated as a national political party since Sept. 1988; Gen. Sec. G. GNANASEKARAN; Dep. Gen. Sec. P. RAJARATNAM.

Eelam People's Democratic Party (EPDP): 121 Park Rd, Colombo 5; tel. (1) 551015; fax (1) 585255; e-mail epdp@sltnet.lk; internet www.epdpnews.com; Tamil; Sec.-Gen. DOUGLAS DEVANANDA.

Eelavar Democratic Front: fmrly known as Eelam Revolutionary Organization of Students (EROS); Tamil separatist group; Leader VELUPILLAI BALAKUMAR.

Eksath Lanka Jathika Peramuna: f. by fmr mems of the UNP.

Janatha Vimukthi Peramuna (JVP) (People's Liberation Front): 198/19 Panchikawattha Rd, Colombo 10; tel. (1) 822379; fax (1) 819775; e-mail contact@jvpsrilanka.com; internet www.jvpsrilanka.com; f. 1964; banned following a coup attempt in 1971, regained legal status in 1977, banned again in 1983, but regained legal status in 1988; Marxist; Sinhalese support; c. 2,000 mems; Leader TILWIN SILVA.

Liberal Party: Colombo.

Mahajana Eksath Peramuna (MEP) (People's United Front): Gothami Rd, Borella, Colombo 8; tel. (1) 595450; f. 1956; Sinhalese and Buddhist support; left-wing; advocates economic self-reliance; Pres. DINESH C. R. GUNAWARDENA.

Muslim United Liberation Front: has operated a national political party since Sept. 1988.

National Unity Alliance (NUA): affiliate party of the Sri Lanka Muslim Congress; has operated as a national political party since 1986; Leader FARIEL ASHRAFF.

Nava Sama Samaja Party (NSSP) (New Equal Society Party): 17 Barracks Lane, Colombo 2; tel. (1) 324053; fax (1) 305963; e-mail nssp@visual.lk; internet www.nssp.info; f. 1977; Trotskyist; operates under the New Left Front; Gen. Sec. LINUS JAYATILAKE; Presidium Member Dr VICKRAMABAHU KARUNARATHNE.

People's Alliance (PA): f. 1993 as a left-wing alliance, incl. communists and Trotskyists; Leader CHANDRIKA BANDARANAIKE KUMARATUNGA; Gen. Sec. D. M. JAYARATNE.

Communist Party of Sri Lanka (CPSL): 91 Dr N. M. Perera Mawatha, Colombo 8; tel. (1) 694945; fax (1) 691610; f. 1943; advocates establishment of socialist society; seeks broadening of democratic rights and processes, political solution to ethnic problem, defence of social welfare and presses for social justice; supports national sovereignty, territorial integrity and national unity of the country; Chair. PIETER KEUNEMAN; Gen. Sec. RAJA COLLURE.

Democratic United National Front (DUNF): f. 1991 by a dissident group of UNP politicians; 500,000 mems; Leader SRIMANI ATHULATHMUDALI; Gen. Sec. G. M. PREMACHANDRA.

Lanka Sama Samaja Party (LSSP) (Lanka Equal Society Party): 457 Dr Colvin R. de Silva Mawatha, Colombo 2; tel. (1) 679544; f. 1935; Trotskyist; Gen. Sec. BATTY WEERAKOON.

Sri Lanka Freedom Party (SLFP): 301 T. B. Jayah Mawatha, Colombo 10; tel. (1) 696289; internet www.slfp.lk; f. 1951; democratic socialist; advocates a non-aligned foreign policy, industrial development in both the state sector and the private sector, rapid modernization in education and in the economy, and safeguards for minorities; Pres. CHANDRIKA BANDARANAIKE KUMARATUNGA.

Sri Lanka Mahajana (People's) Party (SLMP): Colombo; tel. (1) 696038; f. 1984 by fmr mems of the SLFP; social democrats; Leader SARATH KONGAHAGE; Gen. Sec. PREMASIRI PERERA.

People's Front of the Liberation Tigers (PFLT): f. 1989; political wing of the LTTE (see below); Leader GOPALSWAMY MAHENDRARAJAH ('Mahathya'); Gen. Sec. YOGARATNAM YOGI.

Singhalaye Nithahas Peramuna (Sinhalese Freedom Front): Sri Panchananda Charity Bldg, Kelani Railway Station Rd, Colombo; f. 1994; nationalist, Buddhist; Pres. ARYA SENA TERA; Sec. Prof. NALIN DE SILVA.

Sri Lanka Muslim Congress: Colombo; internet www.slmc.org; Leader RAUF HAKEEM.

Sri Lanka Progressive Front: c/o Parliament, Colombo.

Tamil National Alliance (TNA): c/o Parliament, Colombo; f. 2001; alliance of Tamil parties.

Eelam People's Revolutionary Liberation Front (EPRLF): Tamil rights group; c. 1,000 mems; Leader ANNAMALAI VARADHARAJAH PERUMAL; Gen. Sec. SURESH K. PREMACHANDRAN.

Tamil Eelam Liberation Organization (TELO): supports 1987 Indo-Sri Lankan peace accord; has operated as a national political party since Sept. 1988; Leader Sri SABARATNAM.

Tamil United Liberation Front (TULF): 30/1B Alwis Place, Colombo 3; tel. (1) 347721; fax (1) 384904; f. 1976 following merger of All Ceylon Tamil Congress (f. 1945) and Federal Party (f. 1949); Pres. VEERASINGHAM ANANDASANGAREE; Sec.-Gen. R. SAMPANTHAN.

United National Party (UNP): Sirikotha, 400 Kotte Rd, Sri Jayawaredenepura; tel. (1) 865375; fax (1) 865347; e-mail unpweb@yahoo.com; internet www.unplanka.org; f. 1946; democratic socialist; aims at a non-aligned foreign policy, supports Sinhala and Tamil as the official languages and state aid to denominational schools; Leader RANIL WICKREMASINGHE; Chair. KARU JAYASURIYA; Gen. Sec. GAMINI ATUKORALE.

Up-Country People's Front: represents interests of workers (mainly of Indian Tamil origin) on tea plantations.

Tamil separatist groups also include the Liberation Tigers of Tamil Eelam (LTTE; Leader Velupillai Prabhakaran), the Tamil Eelam Liberation Front (TELF; Gen. Sec. M. K. Eelaventhan), the People's Liberation Organization of Tamil Eelam (PLOTE; Leader Dharmalingam Siddharthan; Vice-Pres. Karuvai A. Srikanthasami), the People's Revolutionary Action Group, the Ellalan Force and the Tamil People's Protection Party.

Diplomatic Representation

EMBASSIES AND HIGH COMMISSIONS IN SRI LANKA

Australia: 3 Cambridge Place, POB 742, Colombo 7; tel. (1) 698767; fax (1) 686939; High Commissioner DAVID ALEXANDER RITCHIE.

Bangladesh: 286 Bauddhaloka Mawatha, Colombo 7; tel. (1) 502198; fax (1) 681309; High Commissioner MASUM AHMED CHOWDHURY.

Canada: 6 Gregory's Rd, Cinnamon Gdns, POB 1006, Colombo 7; tel. (1) 695841; fax (1) 687049; e-mail clmbo@dfait-maeci.gc.ca; High Commissioner VALERIE RAYMOND.

China, People's Republic: 381A Bauddhaloka Mawatha, Colombo 7; tel. (1) 694494; Ambassador JIANG QINZHENG.

Egypt: 39 Dickman's Rd, Colombo 5; tel. (1) 583621; fax (1) 585292; Ambassador RAMZY Y. ALLAM.

Finland: 81 Barnes Place, Colombo 7; tel. (1) 698819.

France: 89 Rosmead Place, POB 880, Colombo 7; tel. (1) 698815; fax (1) 699039; e-mail ambfrclb@sltnet.lk; internet www.ambafrance.lk; Ambassador MARIE-FRANCE PAGNIER.

Germany: 40 Alfred House Ave, POB 658, Colombo 3; tel. (1) 580431; fax (1) 580440; e-mail germaemb@sltnet.lk; internet www.germanyembassy.lk; Ambassador JÜRGEN ELIAS.

Holy See: 220 Bauddhaloka Mawatha, Colombo 7 (Apostolic Nunciature); tel. (1) 582554; fax (1) 580906; e-mail aponun@sri.lanka.net; Apostolic Nuncio Most Rev. Dr THOMAS YEH SHENG-NAN (Titular Archbishop of Leptis Magna).

India: 36–38 Galle Rd, Colombo 3; tel. (1) 421605; fax (1) 446403; High Commissioner GOPALKRISHNA GANDHI.

Indonesia: 400/50 Sarana Rd, off Bauddhaloka Mawatha, Colombo 7; tel. (1) 674337; Ambassador MOHAMMAD SALEH.

Iran: 17 Bullers Lane, Colombo 7; tel. (1) 501137; Ambassador ALIREZA MOTEVALI ALAMUTI.

Iraq: 19 Barnes Place, POB 79, Colombo 7; tel. (1) 698733; fax (1) 697676; e-mail iraqiya@sol.lk; Ambassador AMER NAJI.

Italy: 55 Jawatta Rd, Colombo 5; tel. (1) 588388; fax (74) 712272; e-mail itembgen@lankacom.net; internet www.italianembassy.lk; Ambassador MAURIZIO TEUCCI.

Japan: 20 Gregory's Rd, POB 822, Colombo 7; tel. (1) 393831; fax (1) 698629; Ambassador YOJI SUGIYAMA.

Korea, Democratic People's Republic: Colombo; Ambassador PAK MYONG GU.

Korea, Republic: 98 Dharmapala Mawatha, Colombo 7; tel. (1) 699036; fax (1) 672358; e-mail kesl@koreanembassy.net; Ambassador LEE NAM-SOO.

Libya: 120 Horton Place, POB 155, Colombo 7; tel. (1) 693700; fax (1) 695671; e-mail libya@eureka.lk; Secretary of the People's Bureau ABDUL KARIM ALI ABDUL KARIM.

Malaysia: 47/1 Jawatta Rd, Colombo 5; tel. (1) 508773; fax (1) 508972; High Commissioner SHAMSUDDIN BIN ABDULLAH.

Maldives: 25 Melbourne Ave, Colombo 4; tel. (1) 586762; fax (1) 581200; High Commissioner RASHIDA YOOSUF.

Myanmar: 17 Skeleton Gdns, Colombo 5; tel. (1) 587607; fax (1) 681196; Ambassador U AUNG GYI.

Nepal: 290 R. A. de Mel Mawatha, Colombo 4; tel. (1) 575510; Ambassador NILAMBER ACHARYA.

Netherlands: 25 Torrington Ave, Colombo 7; tel. (1) 596914; fax (1) 502855; e-mail nethemb@sri.lanka.net; Ambassador H. C. R. M. PRINCEN.

Norway: 34 Ward Place, Colombo 7; tel. (1) 469611; fax (1) 695009; e-mail emb.colombo@mfa.no; Ambassador JON WESTBORG.

Pakistan: 211 De Saram Place, Colombo 10; tel. (1) 696301; fax (1) 695780; e-mail hcpak1@sltnet.lk; High Commissioner ASHRAF QURESHI.

Philippines: 10 Gregory's Rd, Colombo 7.

Poland: 120 Park Rd, Colombo 5.

Romania: 6A Samudra Mawatha, Mount Lavinia, Greater Colombo; tel. (1) 203153; fax (1) 723256; e-mail romania1@embassy.org; Chargé d'affaires a.i. CRISTIAN OVIDIU MATEESCU.

Russia: 62 Sir Ernest de Silva Mawatha, Colombo 7; tel. (1) 573555; fax (1) 574957; Ambassador MIKHAIL G. KARPOV.

Sweden: 49 Buller's Lane, POB 1072, Colombo 7; tel. (1) 688452; fax (1) 688455; e-mail sweden@panlanka.net; Chargé d'affaires a.i. ANN MARIE FALLENIUS.

Switzerland: 63 Gregory's Rd, POB 342, Colombo 7; tel. (1) 695117; fax (1) 695176; Ambassador BENARDINO REGAZZONI.

Thailand: 43 Dr C. W. W. Kannangara Mawatha, Colombo 7; tel. (1) 689037; Ambassador SAMROENG LAKSANASUT.

United Kingdom: 190 Galle Rd, Kollupitiya, POB 1433, Colombo 3; tel. (1) 437336; fax (1) 430308; e-mail bhc@eureka.lk; High Commissioner LINDA J. DUFFIELD.

USA: 210 Galle Rd, POB 106, Colombo 3; tel. (1) 448007; fax (1) 437345; e-mail ecpo@eureka.lk; internet www.usia.gov/posts/sri_lanka; Ambassador E. ASHLEY WILLS.

Judicial System

The judicial system consists of the Supreme Court, the Court of Appeal, the High Court, District Courts, Magistrates' Courts and Primary Courts. The last four are Courts of the First Instance and appeals lie from them to the Court of Appeal and from there, on questions of law or by special leave, to the Supreme Court. The High Court deals with all criminal cases and the District Courts with civil cases. There are Labour Tribunals to decide labour disputes.

The Judicial Service Commission comprises the Chief Justice and two judges of the Supreme Court, nominated by the President. All judges of the Courts of First Instance (except High Court Judges) and the staff of all courts are appointed and controlled by the Judicial Service Commission. The Supreme Court consists of the Chief Justice and not fewer than six and not more than 10 other judges. The Court of Appeal consists of the President and not fewer than six and not more than 11 other judges.

Chief Justice of the Supreme Court: G. P. S. DE SILVA.

Attorney-General: TILAK MARAPANA.

Religion

According to the 2001 census, the distribution of the population by religion in 18 out of 25 districts was: Buddhist 76.7%, Muslim 8.5%, Hindu 7.9%, Roman Catholics 6.1%, Other Christians 0.8%. The census results did not cover the Tamil-dominated northern and eastern districts.

BUDDHISM

Theravada Buddhism is the predominant sect. There are an estimated 53,000 Buddhist Bhikkhus (monks), living in about 6,000 temples.

All Ceylon Buddhist Congress: 380 Bauddhaloka Mawatha, Colombo 7; tel. (1) 691695; fax (1) 688517; f. 1919; Pres. MILINA SUMATHIPALA; Jt Secs ANURA SUDHARMAN DE SILVA, Dr SURIYA GUNASEKERA.

Sri Lanka Regional Centre of the World Fellowship of Buddhists: 380 Bauddhaloka Mawatha, Colombo 7; tel. (1) 681886; e-mail palikann@sltnet.lk; Pres. S. PALITHA KANNANGARA; Sec. Dr MALANI DIAS.

HINDUISM

The majority of the Tamil population are Hindus. According to the 2001 census the Hindu population in 18 out of 25 districts was 1,329,020.

CHRISTIANITY

National Christian Council of Sri Lanka: 368/6 Bauddhaloka Mawatha, Colombo 7; tel. (1) 671723; fax (1) 671721; e-mail nccsl@eureka.lk; f. 1945; 13 mem. bodies; Gen. Sec. Rev. W. P. EBENEZER JOSEPH.

The Anglican Communion

The Church of Ceylon (Sri Lanka) comprises two Anglican dioceses. In 1985 there were about 78,000 adherents.

Bishop of Colombo: Rt Rev. DULEEP KAMIL DE CHICKERA, Bishop's House, 358/2 Bauddhaloka Mawatha, Colombo 7; tel. (1) 696208; fax (1) 684811; e-mail bishop@eureka.lk; diocese f. 1845.

Bishop of Kurunegala: Rt Rev. KUMARA BANDARA SAMUEL ILLANGASINGHE, Bishop's House, Kandy Rd, Kurunegala; tel. (37) 22191; fax (37) 26806; e-mail bishopkg@sltnet.lk; diocese f. 1950.

The Roman Catholic Church

For ecclesiastical purposes, Sri Lanka comprises one archdiocese and 10 dioceses. At 31 December 2000 there were an estimated 1,299,935 adherents in the country.

Catholic Bishops' Conference in Sri Lanka

19 Balcombe Place, Cotta Rd, Borella, Colombo 8; tel. (1) 597110; fax (1) 699619; e-mail neildias@rocketmail.com.

f. 1975; Pres. Rt Rev. Dr OSWALD THOMAS COLMAN GOMIS (Archbishop of Colombo); Sec.-Gen. Rt Rev. MARIUS PEIRIS.

Archbishop of Colombo: Most Rev. Dr OSWALD THOMAS COLMAN GOMIS, Archbishop's House, 976 Gnanarthapradeepaya Mawatha, Colombo 8; tel. (1) 695471; fax (1) 692009; e-mail cyrilsp@sltnet.lk; internet www.ceylon.net/catholicchurchcolombo.

The Church of South India

The Church comprises 21 dioceses, including one, Jaffna, in Sri Lanka. The diocese of Jaffna, with an estimated 18,500 adherents in 1997, was formerly part of the South India United Church (a union of churches of the Congregational and Presbyterian/Reformed traditions), which merged with the Methodist Church in South India and the four southern dioceses of the (Anglican) Church of India to form the Church of South India in 1947.

Bishop in Jaffna: Rt Rev. Dr S. JEBANESAN, 41 4th Cross St, Jaffna; tel. (21) 2029; fax (1) 584836; e-mail jdcsiacm@panlanka.net.

Other Christian Churches

Dutch Reformed Church: General Consistory Office, 363 Galle Rd, Colombo 6; tel. (1) 360861; fax (1) 582469; e-mail drc1642@sltnet.lk; f. 1642; Pres. of Gen. Consistory Rev. CHARLES N. JANSZ; Admin. Sec. GODFREY B. EBENEZER.

Methodist Church: Methodist Headquarters, 252 Galle Rd, Colombo 3; tel. (1) 575707; fax (1) 436090; e-mail methhq@sltnet.lk; internet www.gbgm-umc.org/methchsrilan; 30,139 mems (2000); Pres. of Conference Rev. A. NOEL P. FERNANDO; Sec. of Conference Rev. NIMAL L. S. MENDIS.

Other denominations active in the country include the Sri Lanka Baptist Sangamaya.

BAHÁ'Í FAITH

Spiritual Assembly: Bahá'í National Centre, 65 Havelock Rd, Colombo 5; tel. and fax (1) 587360.

The Press

NEWSPAPERS

Newspapers are published in Sinhala, Tamil and English. There are five main newspaper publishing groups:

Associated Newspapers of Ceylon Ltd: Lake House, D. R. Wijewardene Mawatha, POB 248, Colombo 10; tel. (1) 435641; fax (1) 449069; e-mail webmgr@sri.lanka.net; internet www.lanka.net/lakehouse; f. 1926; nationalized 1973; publr of *Daily News*, *Evening Observer*, *Thinakaran*, *Janatha* and *Dinamina* (dailies), three Sunday papers: *Sunday Observer*, *Silumina* and *Thinakaran Vaara Manjari* and 11 periodicals; Chair. ALOY N. RATNAYAKE; Sec. B. A. JINADASA.

Express Newspapers (Ceylon) Ltd: 185 Grandpass Rd, POB 160, Colombo 14; tel. (1) 320881; fax (1) 439987; e-mail kesari10@virakesari.lk; internet www.virakesari.lk; publr of *Virakesari Daily*, *Mithran Varamalar* and *Virakesari Weekly* (Sunday); Man. Dir KUMAR NADESAN; Editor S. NADARAJAH.

Leader Publications (Pvt) Ltd: No. 101, 2nd Floor, Collettes Bldg, D. S. Senanayake Mawatha, Colombo 8; tel. (1) 686047; fax (1) 699968; e-mail leader@sri.lanka.net; internet www.thesundayleader.lk; publr of *The Sunday Leader* and *Irida Peramuna*.

Upali Newspapers Ltd: 223 Bloemendhal Rd, POB 133, Colombo 13; tel. (1) 324001; fax (1) 448103; f. 1981; publr of *The Island*, *Divaina* (dailies), two Sunday papers, *Sunday Island* and *Sunday Divaina*, four weeklies, *Vidusara*, *Navaliya*, *Bindu* and *The Island International* (for sale abroad only), and one bi-weekly, *Vathmana–News Magazine*; English and Sinhala; Editor-in-Chief (vacant); Man. Dir J. H. LANEROLLE.

Wijeya Newspapers Ltd: 8 Hunupitiya Cross Rd, Colombo 2; tel. (1) 441070; fax (1) 449504; f. 1979; publr of *Daily Mirror*, *The Sunday Times*, *Sri Lankadipa*, *Woman's Weekly*, *Men's Weekly*, *Children's Weekly*; Sinhala and English.

Dailies

Daily Mirror: 8 Hunupitiya Cross Rd, Colombo 2; tel. (1) 436998; fax (1) 753308; e-mail mirror@wijeya.lk; internet dailymirror.lk; f. 1996; English and Sinhala; Editor LALITH ALAHAKOON; circ. 45,500.

Daily News: Lake House, D. R. Wijewardene Mawatha, POB 248, Colombo 10; tel. (1) 429429; fax (1) 429210; e-mail editor@dailynews.lk; internet www.dailynews.lk; f. 1918; morning; English; Editor GEOFF WIJEYESINGHE; circ. 65,000.

Dinakara: 95 Maligakanda Rd, Colombo 10; tel. (1) 595754; f. 1978; morning; Sinhala; publ. by Rekana Publrs; Editor MULEN PERERA; circ. 12,000.

Dinamina: Lake House, D. R. Wijewardene Mawatha, POB 248, Colombo 10; tel. (1) 21181; f. 1909; morning; Sinhala; Editor G. S. PERERA; circ. 140,000.

Divaina: 223 Bloemendhal Rd, POB 133, Colombo 13; tel. (1) 24001; fax (1) 448103; internet www.divaina.com; f. 1982; morning and Sunday; Chief Editor UPALI TENNAKOON.

Eelanadu: Jaffna; tel. (21) 22389; f. 1959; morning; Tamil; Chair. S. RAVEENTHIRANATHAN; Editor M. SIVANANTHAM; circ. 15,000.

The Island: 223 Bloemendhal Rd, Colombo 13; tel. (1) 324001; internet www.island.lk; f. 1981; English; Editor GAMINI WEERAKOON; circ. 80,000.

Janatha: Janata Lake House, D. R. Wijewardene Mawatha, Colombo 10; tel. (1) 421181; f. 1953; evening; Sinhala; Editor MOHAN LAL PIYADASA; circ. 15,000.

Lankadeepa: 8 Hunupitiya Cross Rd, Colombo 2; tel. (1) 448321; fax (1) 438039; e-mail siri@wijeya.lk; internet www.lankadeepa.com; f. 1986; Sinhala and English; Editor SIRI RANASINGHE; circ. 160,000.

Evening Observer: Associated Newspapers of Ceylon Ltd, Lake House, D. R. Wijewardene Mawatha, POB 248, Colombo 10; tel. (1) 434544; fax (1) 449069; f. 1834; evening (weekdays) and Sunday morning; Editor AJITH SAMARANAYAKE; circ. 10,000 (evening), 95,000 (Sunday).

Peraliya: 2nd Floor, Borella Supermarket Complex, Colombo 8; Editor SUJEEWA GAMAGE.

Thinakaran: Lake House, D. R. Wijewardene Mawatha, POB 248, Colombo 10; tel. (1) 21181; f. 1932; morning; Tamil; Editor R. SIVAGURUNATHAN; circ. daily 14,000.

Uthayan: Jaffna; internet www.uthayan.com; Tamil; Associate Editor N. VITHIYADHARAN.

Virakesari Daily: 185 Grandpass Rd, POB 160, Colombo 14; tel. (1) 320881; fax (1) 439987; e-mail virakesari@lanka.ccom.lk; internet www.virakesari.lk; f. 1931; morning; Tamil; Man. Dir M. G. WENCE-SLAUS; Editor S. NADARAJAH; circ. 49,500.

Sunday Newspapers

Janasathiya: 47 Jayantha Weerasekara Mawatha, Colombo 10; f. 1965; Sinhala; publ. by Suriya Publishers Ltd; Editor SARATH NAWANA; circ. 50,000.

Mithran Varamalar: 185 Grandpass Rd, Colombo 14; tel. (1) 320881; fax (1) 448205; e-mail virakesari@lanka.ccom.lk; internet www.virakesari.lk; f. 1969; Tamil; Man. Dir M. G. WENCESLAUS; Editor P. SURIYAKUMARY; circ. 29,000.

Silumina: Lake House, 35 D. R. Wijewardene Mawatha, Colombo 10; tel. (1) 324772; fax (1) 449069; f. 1930; Sinhala; Editor NIWAL HORANA; circ. 264,000.

Sunday Island: 223 Bloemendhal Rd, POB 133, Colombo 13; tel. (1) 421599; fax (1) 609198; e-mail manik@unl.upali.lk; f. 1981; English; Editor MANIK DE SILVA; circ. 40,000.

The Sunday Leader: No. 101, 2nd Floor, Collettes Bldg, D. S. Senanayake Mawatha, Colombo 8; tel. (1) 686047; fax (1) 699968; internet www.lanka.net/sundayleader; English; Editor LASANTHA WICKRAMATUNGA.

Sunday Observer: D. R. Wijewardene Mawatha, POB 248, Colombo 10; tel. (1) 429239; fax (1) 429230; e-mail editor@sundayobserver.lk; internet www.sundayobserver.lk; f. 1923; English; Editor H. L. D. MAHINDAPALA.

The Sunday Times: 8 Hunupitiya Cross Rd, Colombo 2; tel. (1) 326247; fax (1) 449504; e-mail editor@suntimes.is.lk; internet www.is.lk/times/index.html; f. 1986; English and Sinhala; Editor SINGHA RATNATUNGA; circ. 116,000.

Thinakaran Vaara Manjari: Lake House, 35 D. R. Wijewardene Mawatha, Colombo 10; tel. (1) 21181; f. 1948; Tamil; Editor R. SRIKANTHAN; circ. 35,000.

Virakesari Weekly: 185 Grandpass Rd, Colombo 14; tel. (1) 320881; fax (1) 448205; e-mail virakesari@lanka.ccom.lk; internet www.virakesari.lk; f. 1931; Tamil; Man. Dir M. G. WENCESLAUS; Editor S. NADARAJAH; circ. 69,000.

The Weekend Express: 185 Grandpass Rd, Colombo 14; tel. (1) 320881; fax (1) 613982; e-mail express@sri.lanka.net; Chief Editor SUKUMAR ROCKWOOD; circ. 27,500.

PERIODICALS
(weekly unless otherwise stated)

Athavan: Colombo; Tamil.

Aththa: 91 Dr N. M. Perera Mawatha, Colombo 8; tel. (1) 691450; fax (1) 691610; f. 1964; Sinhala; publ. by the Communist Party of Sri Lanka; Editor GUNASENA VITHANA; circ. 28,000.

Business Lanka: Trade Information Service, Sri Lanka Export Development Board, Level 7, 42 Navam Mawatha, POB 1872, Colombo 2; tel. (1) 300677; fax (1) 300715; e-mail tisinfo@tradenetsl.lk; f. 1981; quarterly; information for visiting businessmen etc. Editor Mrs S. D. ISAAC.

Ceylon Commerce: The National Chamber of Commerce of Sri Lanka, NCCSL Bldg, 450 D. R. Wijewardene Mawatha, POB 1375, Colombo 10; tel. (1) 689597; fax (1) 689596; e-mail nccsl@slt.lk; internet www.nationalchamberlk.org; monthly.

Ceylon Medical Journal: 6 Wijerama Mawatha, Colombo 7; tel. (1) 693324; fax (1) 698802; e-mail slma@eureka.lk; internet www.medinet.lk/cmj; f. 1887; quarterly; Editors Prof. COLVIN GOONARATNA, Prof. H. JANAKA DE SILVA.

The Economic Times: 146/54, Aramaya Rd, Colombo 9; tel. and fax (1) 610952; f. 1970; Editor THIMSY FAHIM.

The Financial Times: 323 Union Place, POB 330, Colombo 2; tel. (1) 26181; quarterly; commercial and economic affairs; Man. Editor CYRIL GARDINER.

Gnanarthapradeepaya: Colombo Catholic Press, 2 Gnanartha-pradeepaya Mawatha, Borella, Colombo 8; tel. (1) 695984; f. 1866; Sinhala; Roman Catholic; Chief Editor Rev. Fr W. DON BENEDICT JOSEPH; circ. 26,000.

Janakavi: 47 Jayantha Weerasekera Mawatha, Colombo 10; fortnightly; Sinhala; Assoc. Editor KARUNARATNE AMERASINGHE.

Manasa: 150 Dutugemunu St, Dehiwala; tel. (1) 553994; f. 1978; Sinhala; monthly; science of the mind; Editor SUMANADASA SAMARA-SINGHE; circ. 6,000.

Mihira: Lake House, 35 D. R. Wijewardene Mawatha, Colombo 10; tel. (1) 21181; f. 1964; Sinhala children's magazine; Editor M. NEWTON PINTO; circ. 145,000.

Morning Star: 39 Fussels Lane, Colombo 6; tel. (1) 511233; fax (1) 584836; e-mail jdcsiacm@panlanka.net; f. 1841; English and Tamil; publ. by the Jaffna diocese of the Church of South India.

Nava Yugaya: Lake House, 35 D. R. Wijewardene Mawatha, Colombo 10; tel. (1) 21181; f. 1956; literary fortnightly; Sinhala; Editor S. N. SENANAYAKE; circ. 57,000.

Navaliya: 223 Bloemendhal Rd, Colombo 13; tel. (1) 324001; fax (1) 448103; internet www.navaliya.com; Sinhala; women's interest; Editor CHANDANI WIJETUNGE; circ. 148,260.

Pathukavalan: POB 2, Jaffna; tel. (21) 22300; f. 1876; Tamil; publ. by St Joseph's Catholic Press; Editor Rev. Fr RUBAN MARIAMPILLAI; circ. 7,000.

Puthiya Ulaham: 115, 4th Cross St, Jaffna; tel. (21) 22627; f. 1976; Tamil; six a year; publ. by Centre for Better Society; Editor Rev. Dr S. J. EMMANUEL; circ. 1,500.

Ravaya: Colombo; Sinhala; Editor VICTOR IVAN.

Samajawadhaya: 91 Dr N. M. Perera Mawatha, Colombo 8; tel. (1) 595328; monthly; theoretical; publ. by the Communist Party of Sri Lanka.

Sarasaviya: Lake House, 35 D. R. Wijewardene Mawatha, Colombo 10; tel. (1) 21181; f. 1963; Sinhala; films; Editor GRANVILLE SILVA; circ. 56,000.

Sinhala Bauddhaya: Maha Bodhi Mandira, 130 Rev. Hikkaduwe Sri Sumangala Nahimi Mawatha, Colombo 10; tel. (1) 698079; f. 1906; publ. by The Maha Bodi Society of Ceylon; Editor-in-Chief KIRTHI KALAHE; circ. 25,000.

Sri Lanka Government Gazette: Government Press, POB 507, Colombo; tel. (1) 93611; f. 1802; official govt bulletin; circ. 54,000.

Sri Lanka News: Lake House, 35 D. R. Wijewardene Mawatha, Colombo 10; tel. (1) 429429; fax (1) 449069; f. 1938; digest of news and features; printing temporarily suspended from March 2002; Editor RUWAN GODAGE.

Sri Lanka Today: Government Dept of Information, 7 Sir Baron Jayatilaka Mawatha, Colombo 1; tel. (1) 28376; English; quarterly; Editor MANEL ABHAYARATNE.

Subasetha: Lake House, 35 D. R. Wijewardene Mawatha, Colombo 10; tel. (1) 21181; f. 1967; Sinhala; astrology, the occult and indigenous medicine; Editor Capt. K. CHANDRA SRI KULARATNE; circ. 100,000.

Tharunee: Lake House, 35 D. R. Wijewardene Mawatha, Colombo 10; tel. (1) 21181; f. 1969; Sinhala; women's journal; Editor SUMANA SAPRAMADU; circ. 95,000.

Vidusara: 223 Bloemendhal Rd, Colombo 13; tel. (1) 324001; fax (1) 448103; internet www.vidusara.com; Sinhala; Editor ANURA SIRIWARDENA; circ. 103,992.

NEWS AGENCIES

Lankapuvath (National News Agency of Sri Lanka): Transworks House, Lower Chatham St, Colombo 1; tel. (1) 433173; fax (1) 433173; f. 1978; Chair. D. E. W. GUNASEKARA; Editor G. L. W. WIJESINHA.

Press Trust of Ceylon: Negris Bldg, POB 131, Colombo 1; tel. (1) 31174; Chair. R. BODINAGODA; Sec. and Gen. Man. A. W. AMUNUGAMA.

Foreign Bureaux

Agence France-Presse (AFP): Colombo Bureau, 100 Barnes Place, Colombo 7; tel. (1) 694384; fax (1) 694385; Chief of Bureau AMAL JAYASINGHE.

Deutsche Presse-Agentur (dpa) (Germany): Independent Newspapers Ltd, 5 Gunasena Mawatha, Colombo 12; tel. (1) 545327; Correspondent REX DE SILVA.

Iraqi News Agency: Dinakara, 301 Darley Rd, Colombo 10; tel. (1) 595323; Correspondent SARATH COORAY.

Press Trust of India (PTI): Colombo; Correspondent K. DHARMARAJAN.

Reuters (UK): Level 27, East Tower, World Trade Centre, Echelon Sq., Colombo 1; tel. (1) 431187; fax (1) 338302; Sr Co Rep. DION SCHOORMAN.

United Press International (UPI) (USA): 'Jasmin Court', 60/1 Wijerama Lane, Udahamulla, Nugegoda; tel. (1) 853923; fax (1) 856496; Correspondent IQBAL ATHAS.

Xinhua (New China) News Agency (People's Republic of China): 24 Pathiba Rd, Colombo 5; tel. (1) 589092; e-mail xhco@eureka.lk; Chief Correspondent ZHANG YADONG.

Prensa Latina (Cuba) is also represented.

PRESS ASSOCIATIONS

Press Association of Ceylon: Negris Bldg, POB 131, Colombo 1; tel. (1) 31174; Pres. K. SIVAPIRAGASAM; Gen. Sec. U. L. D. CHANDRATILLAKE.

Sri Lanka Foreign Correspondents' Association: 20 1/1 Regent Flats, Sir Chittampalan Gardiner Mawatha, Colombo; tel. (1) 31224.

Publishers

W. E. Bastian and Co (Pvt) Ltd: 23 Canal Row, Fort, Colombo 1; tel. (1) 432752; f. 1904; art, literature, technical; Dirs H. A. MUNIDEVA, K. HEWAGE, N. MUNIDEVA, G. C. BASTIAN.

Buddhist Publication Society Inc.: 54 Sangharaja Mawatha, POB 61, Kandy; tel. (8) 237283; fax (8) 223679; e-mail bps@ids.lk; internet www.lanka.com/dhamma; philosophy, religion and theology; Editor-in-Chief BHIKKHU BODHI.

Colombo Catholic Press: 2 Gnanarthapradeepaya Mawatha, Borella, Colombo 8; tel. (1) 695984; f. 1865; religious; publrs of *The Messenger, Gnanartha Pradeepaya, The Weekly*; Exec. Dir Rev. Fr BERTRAM DABRERA.

M. D. Gunasena and Co Ltd: 217 Olcott Mawatha, POB 246, Colombo 11; tel. (4) 323981; fax (1) 323336; e-mail mdgunasena@mail.ewisl.net; f. 1913; educational and general; Chair M. D. PERCY GUNASENA; Man. Dir M. D. ANANDA GUNASENA.

Lake House Printers and Publishers Ltd: 41 W. A. D. Ramanayake Mawatha, POB 1458, Colombo 2; tel. (1) 433271; fax (1) 449504; e-mail rstimes@lanka.ccom.lk; f. 1965; Chair. R. S. WIJEWARDENE; Sec. D. P. ANURA NISHANTHA KUMARA.

Pradeepa Publishers: 34/34 Lawyers' Office Complex, Colombo 12; tel. (1) 435074; fax (1) 863261; academic and fictional; Propr K. JAYATILAKE.

Saman Publishers Ltd: 49/16 Iceland Bldg, Colombo 3; tel. (1) 23058; fax (1) 447972.

Sarexpo International Ltd: Caves Bookshop, 81 Sir Baron Jayatilleke Mawatha, POB 25, Colombo 1; tel. (1) 422676; fax (1) 447854; f. 1876; history, arts, law, medicine, technical, educational; Man. Dir C. J. S. FERNANDO.

K. V. G. de Silva and Sons (Colombo) Ltd: 49 Abdulgaffor Mawatha, Colombo 3; tel. (1) 301490; fax (1) 588875; f. 1898; art, philosophy, scientific, technical, academic, 'Ceyloniana', fiction; Man. FREDERICK JAYARATNAM.

PUBLISHERS' ASSOCIATION

Sri Lanka Association of Publishers: 112 S. Mahinda Mawatha, Maradana, Colombo 10; tel. (1) 695773; fax (1) 696653; e-mail dayawansajay@hotmail.com; Pres. DAYAWANSA JAYAKODY; Sec.-Gen. GAMINI WIJESURIYA.

Broadcasting and Communications

TELECOMMUNICATIONS

Lanka Communication Services (Pvt) Ltd: 6th Floor, City Bank Bldg, 65c Dharmapala Mawatha, Colombo 7; tel. (1) 437545; fax (1) 537547; Man. Dir D. HANLY.

Lanka Internet Services Ltd: World Trade Center, 24th Floor, Echelon Sq., Colombo 1; tel. (1) 346441; CEO Dr P. SAMARATUNGA.

MTN Networks (Pvt) Ltd: 502 R. A. de Mel Mawatha, Colombo 3; tel. (1) 594329; fax (1) 594337; Chief Exec. H. SURIA.

Sri Lanka Telecom Ltd: Telecom Headquarters, 7th Floor, Lotus Rd, POB 503, Colombo 1; tel. (1) 335010; fax (1) 424800; e-mail md@slt.lk; 35% owned by Nippon Telegraph and Telephone Corpn (Japan), 49.5% by Govt of Sri Lanka and 3.5% by employees; Chair. H. FERNANDO; CEO HIDEAKI KAMITSUMA.

Regulatory Authority

Telecommunications Regulatory Commission of Sri Lanka: 276 Elvitigala Mawatha, Manning Town, Colombo 8; tel. (1) 689345; fax (1) 689341; e-mail dgtsl@slt.lk; internet www.trc.gov.lk; Chair. S. S. EDIRIWEERA; Dir-Gen. R. D. SOMASIRI.

RADIO

Sri Lanka Broadcasting Corpn: Independence Sq., POB 574, Colombo 7; tel. (1) 697491; fax (1) 695488; e-mail slbcweb@srilankanet; f. 1967; under Ministry of Posts, Telecommunications and the Media; controls all broadcasting in Sri Lanka; regional stations at Anuradhapura, Kandy and Matara; transmitting stations at Ambewela, Amparai, Anuradhapura, Diyagama, Ekala, Galle, Kanthalai, Mahiyangana, Maho, Matara, Puttalam, Ratnapura, Seeduwa, Senkadagala, Weeraketiya; home service in Sinhala, Tamil and English; foreign service also in Tamil, English, Sinhala, Hindi, Kannada, Malayalam, Nepali and Telugu; 893 broadcasting hours per week: 686 on domestic services, 182 on external services and 126 on education; Chair. JANADASA PEIRIS; Dir-Gen. ERIC FERNANDO.

Colombo Communications (Pvt) Ltd: 2/9 2nd Floor, Liberty Plaza, 250 R. A. de Mel Mawatha, Colombo 3; tel. (1) 577924; fax (1) 577929; commercial station; three channels broadcast 24 hrs daily in English, Sinhala and Tamil.

Lite FM: No. 52 5th Lane, Colombo 3; tel. (1) 575000; fax (1) 301082; e-mail info@tnlradio.com; internet www.tnlradio.com; commercial station; broadcasts 24 hrs daily in English; Chair. NIRAJ WICKREMESINGHE.

MBC Networks (Pvt) Ltd: Colombo; tel. (1) 689234; commercial station; broadcasts 24 hrs daily in English and Sinhala.

TNL Radio: No. 52, 5th Lane, Colombo 3; tel. (1) 575000; fax (1) 301082; e-mail info@tnlradio.com; internet www.tnlradio.com; commercial station; broadcasts 24 hrs daily in English; Chair. NIRAJ WICKREMESINGHE.

Trans World Radio: 125/3, 3rd Lane, Subadrarama Rd, POB 123, Nugegoda; tel. (75) 559321; fax (1) 817749; e-mail rkoch@twr.org; f. 1978; religious station; broadcasts 3 hours every morning and 7.75 hours each evening to Indian subcontinent; Dir (Finance) ROGER KOCH; Eng. P. VELMURUGAN.

Voice of Tigers: Vanni; internet www.eelam.com/vot; f. 1990 by the LTTE; banned until 2003; broadcasts 8.5 hrs daily in Tamil and Sinhalese.

TELEVISION

Sri Lanka Rupavahini Corpn (SLRC): Independence Sq., POB 2204, Colombo 7; tel. (1) 599506; fax (1) 580929; e-mail dg@rupavahini.lk; internet www.rupavahini.lk; f. 1982; studio at Colombo; transmitting stations at nine locations; broadcasts 18 hrs daily on Channel I, 15 hrs daily on Channel II; Chair. Prof. DAMMIKA GANGANATH DISSANAYAKE; Dir-Gen. NIMAL LAKSHAPATHIARACHCHI.

Independent Television Network (ITN—Sri Lanka): Wickremasinghepura, Battaramulla; tel. (1) 865494; fax (1) 864591; e-mail itnch@slt.lk; internet www.itnsl.lk; broadcasts about 6 hrs daily; Chair. NEWTON GUNARATNE; Gen. Man. S. LOKUGAMAGE.

EAP Network (Pvt) Ltd: 676 Galle Rd, Colombo 3; tel. (1) 503819; fax (1) 503788; e-mail eapnet@slt.lk; Chair. SOMA EDIRISINGHE; Man. Dir JEEVAKA EDIRISINGHE.

MTV Channel (Pvt) Ltd: Araliya Uyana, Depanama, Pannipitiya.

Telshan Network (Pvt) Ltd (TNL): 9D, Tower Bldg, 25 Station Rd, Colombo 4; tel. (1) 501681; fax (1) 501683; Chair. and Man. Dir SHANTILAL NILKANT WICKREMESINGHE.

Finance

(cap. = capital; res = reserves; dep. = deposits; m. = million; brs = branches; amounts in Sri Lanka rupees, unless otherwise indicated)

BANKING

Central Bank

Central Bank of Sri Lanka: 30 Janadhipathi Mawatha, POB 590, Colombo 1; tel. (1) 477000; fax (1) 477677; e-mail cbslgen@sri.lanka.net; internet www.centralbanklanka.org; f. 1950; sole bank of issue; cap. 15m., res 985m., dep. 70,210m. (Dec. 1999); Gov. and Chair. of the Monetary Board A. S. JAYAWARDENA; Dep. Govs P. M. NAGAHAWATTA, W. A. WIJEWARDENA; 3 regional offices.

Commercial Banks

Bank of Ceylon: 4 Bank of Ceylon Mawatha, POB 241, Colombo 1; tel. (1) 446811; fax (1) 447171; e-mail agmint@boc.lanka.net; internet www.bankofceylon.net; f. 1939; 100% state-owned; cap. 2,600m., res 8,512.6m., dep. 131,126.7m. (Dec. 2000); Chair. DESAMANYA K. BALENDRA; Gen. Man. A. SARATH DE SILVA; 296 brs in Sri Lanka, 7 brs abroad.

SRI LANKA

Directory

Commercial Bank of Ceylon Ltd: Commercial House, 21 Bristol St, POB 856, Colombo 1; tel. (1) 430416; fax (1) 449889; e-mail e-mail@combank.net; internet www.combank.net; f. 1969; 29.77% owned by DFCC Bank, 29.91% by govt corpns and 40.32% by public; cap. 1,324.4m., res 5,420.4m., dep. 46,533.5m. (Dec. 2001); Chair. M. J. C. AMARASURIYA; Man. Dir A. L. GOONERATNE; 86 brs.

Hatton National Bank Ltd: 10 R. A. de Mel Mawatha, POB 837, Colombo 3; tel. (1) 421885; fax (1) 434057; e-mail moreinfo@hnb.net; internet www.hnb.net; f. 1970; 15.7% owned by Standard Finance Ltd, 29.9% by public and 54.5% by others; cap. 650m., res 4,897.9m., dep. 62,757.8m. (Dec. 2000); Chair. J. CHRISANTHA R. COORAY; Gen. Man. and CEO RIENZIE T. WIJETILLEKE; 96 brs.

Nations Trust Bank Ltd: 76 York St, Colombo 1; tel. (1) 447655; fax (1) 447659; e-mail bank@nationstrust.lk; internet www.nationstrust.com; f. 1999; privately-owned; cap. 500.0m., res 85.5m., dep. 2,196.2m. (Dec. 2000); Chair. VIVENDRA LINTOTAWELA; CEO MOKSEVI R. PRELIS.

Pan Asia Bank Ltd: 450 Galle Rd, Colombo 3; tel. (1) 565556; fax (1) 565562; e-mail panasia@itmin.com; internet www.pabnk.lk; f. 1995; 100% privately-owned; cap. 445.0m., res 45m., dep. 3,488m. (Dec. 2001); Chair. W. M. ABEYRATNE BANDARA; Gen. Man. and CEO R. NADARAJAH; 13 brs.

People's Bank: 75 Sir Chittampalam A. Gardiner Mawatha, POB 728, Colombo 2; tel. (1) 327841; fax (1) 446407; e-mail info@people.is.lk; internet www.peoplesbank.lk; f. 1961; 92% owned by Govt, 8% by co-operatives; cap. 1,202m., res −7,511.3m., dep. 115,864.7m. (Dec. 2000); Chair. MANO TITTAWELLA; CEO/Gen. Man. DERECK J. KELLY; 323 brs.

Sampath Bank Ltd: 110 Sir James Peiris Mawatha, POB 997, Colombo 2; tel. (1) 300153; fax (1) 300143; e-mail mgr@oper.sampath.lk; internet www.sampath.lk; f. 1987; cap. 442.8m., res 2,090.9m., dep. 29,668.8m. (Dec. 2001); Chair. EDGAR GUNATUNGA; Man. Dir/CEO ANIL AMARASURIYA; 40 brs.

Seylan Bank Ltd: Ceylinco Seylan Towers, 90 Galle Rd, POB 400, Colombo 3; tel. (1) 456789; fax (1) 456456; e-mail info@seylan.lk; internet www.eseylan.com; f. 1988; cap. 446.1m., res 1,791.9m., dep. 47,859.5m. (Dec. 2001); Chair. J. L. B. KOTELAWALA; Gen. Man./CEO/Dir Mrs ROHINI L. NANAYAKKARA; 90 brs.

Union Bank of Colombo Ltd: Level 28, East Tower, World Trade Center, Echelon Sq., POB 348, Colombo 1; tel. (1) 346357; fax (74) 714452; e-mail shan@unionb.com; internet www.unionb.com; f. 1995; cap. 360.0m., res 20.9m., dep. 4,804.0m. (Dec. 1999); Chair. CHANAKA DE SILVA; CEO and Man. Dir SHAN SHANMUGANATHAN.

Development Banks

Agricultural and Industrial Credit Corpn of Ceylon: POB 20, Colombo 3; tel. (1) 23783; f. 1943; loan cap. 30m. Chair. V. P. VITTACHI; Gen. Man. H. S. F. GOONEWARDENA.

DFCC Bank: 73/5 Galle Rd, POB 1397, Colombo 3; tel. (1) 440366; fax (1) 440376; e-mail info@dfccbank.com; internet www.dfccbank.com; f. 1956 as Development Finance Corpn of Ceylon; name changed as above 1997; provides long- and medium-term credit, investment banking and consultancy services; cap. 423.1m., res 6,228.6m. (March 2002); Chair. M. L. MACK; Gen. Man., Dir and CEO N. FONSEKA; 3 brs.

National Development Bank of Sri Lanka: 40 Navam Mawatha, Colombo 2; tel. (1) 437701; fax (1) 440262; e-mail info@ndb.org; internet www.ndb.org; f. 1979; provides long-term finance for projects, equity financing and merchant banking services; cap. 537.5m., res 5,115.5m. (March 2000); Chair. SARATH KUSUM WICKREMESINGHE; Gen. Man. and Chief Exec./Dir RANJIT MICHAEL SAMUEL FERNANDO.

State Mortgage and Investment Bank: 269 Galle Road, POB 156, Colombo 3; tel. (1) 573563; fax (1) 573346; e-mail smibgm@itmin.com; internet www.lanka.net/smib; f. 1979; Chair. Dr GAMINI FERNANDO; Gen. Man. U. H. D. PATHMASIRI.

Merchant Banks

Merchant Bank of Sri Lanka Ltd: Bank of Ceylon Merchant Tower, 28 St. Michael's Rd, POB 1987, Colombo 3; tel. (74) 711711; fax (74) 711743; e-mail mbslbank@mbslbank.com; internet www.mbslbank.com; f. 1982; 53.8% owned by Bank of Ceylon; public ltd liability co; cap. p.u. 500m. (1999), total assets 3,398m. (1994); Chair. SUMI MOONESINGHE; Man. Dir/CEO SUNIL G. WIJESINHA; 3 brs.

People's Merchant Bank Ltd: Level 4, Hemas House, 75 Braybrooke Place, Colombo 2; tel. (1) 300191; fax (1) 300190; e-mail pmbank@sltnet.lk; f. 1983; total assets 610m. (1999); Chair. Dr G. FERNANDO.

Foreign Banks

ABN AMRO Bank NV (Netherlands): 103A Dharmapala Mawatha, Colombo 7; tel. (1) 448448; fax (1) 446986; Gen. Man. MICHAEL MOORMANN.

American Express Bank Ltd (USA): 104 Dharmapala Mawatha, Colombo 7; tel. (1) 682787; fax (1) 682786; Dir of Operations K. BALACHANDRARAJAN.

Citibank NA (USA): 67 Dharmapala Mawatha, POB 888, Colombo 7; tel. (1) 447316; fax (1) 445487; Vice-Pres. KAPILA JAYAWARDENA.

Crédit Agricole Indosuez (France): 1st Floor, Ceylinco House, 69 Janadhipathi Mawatha, POB 303, Colombo 1; tel. (1) 436181; fax (1) 541537; f. 1979; Gen. Man. FRANCIS DUBUS.

Deutsche Bank AG (Germany): 86 Galle Rd, POB 314, Colombo 3; tel. (1) 447062; fax (1) 447067; Gen. Man. MATTHIAS KLUG.

Emirates Bank International Ltd (United Arab Emirates): 64 Lotus Rd, POB 358, Colombo 1; tel. (1) 23467; Gen. Man. N. C. VITARANA.

Habib Bank Ltd (Pakistan): 140–142 Second Cross St, POB 1088, Colombo 11; tel. (1) 326565; fax (1) 447827; e-mail habiblk@serendib.ccom.lk; f. 1941; Sr Vice-Pres. and Gen. Man. MUHAMMAD YOUNUS PINGAL.

Hongkong and Shanghai Banking Corpn Ltd (Hong Kong): 24 Sir Baron Jayatilaka Mawatha, POB 73, Colombo 1; tel. (1) 325435; fax (1) 448388; internet www.asiapacific.hsbc.com; CEO NIK CHERRILL.

Indian Bank (India): 22 & 24 Mudalige Mawatha, POB 624, Colombo 1; tel. (1) 323402; fax (1) 447562; e-mail ibcol@slnet.lk; Chief Exec. C. S. RAMANI.

Indian Overseas Bank (India): 139 Main St, POB 671, Colombo 11; tel. (1) 324422; fax (1) 447900; e-mail iobch@lgo.lk; Country Head K. LAKSHMI NARASIMHAN; 1 br.

Mashreq Bank PSC (United Arab Emirates): 245 Dharmapala Mawatha, Colombo 7; tel. (1) 679000; fax (75) 331849; e-mail mshqgen@sri.lanka.net; Country Man. KHURRAM HUSSAIN.

Overseas Trust Bank Ltd (Hong Kong): YMCA Bldg, 39 Bristol St, POB 835, Colombo 1; tel. (1) 547655.

Public Bank Berhad (Malaysia): Ground and First Floor, Jewelarts Bldg, 324 Galle Rd, Colombo 3; tel. (1) 576289; fax (1) 573958.

Standard Chartered Grindlays Bank Ltd (UK): 37 York St, Colombo 1; tel. (1) 480000; fax (1) 422618; e-mail wasim.saifi-sri-lanka@lk.standardchartered.com; internet www.standardchartered.com; f. 1853; CEO WASIM SAIFI.

State Bank of India: 16 Sir Baron Jayatilleke Mawatha, POB 93, Colombo 1; tel. (1) 26133; fax (1) 547166; f. 1955; Chief Man. B. P. AGRAWAL.

Financial Association

The Finance Houses' Association of Sri Lanka: 84 Ward Place, Colombo 7; tel. (1) 699295; fax (1) 697205; f. 1958; represents the finance cos registered and licensed by the Central Bank of Sri Lanka; Chair. KITHSIRI B. WANIGASEKERA; Sec. M. M. N. DE SILVA.

STOCK EXCHANGE

Colombo Stock Exchange: 04–01, West Block, World Trade Center, Echelon Sq., Colombo 1; tel. (1) 446581; fax (1) 445279; e-mail cse@cse.lk; internet www.cse.lk; f. 1896; stock market; 15 mem firms and 241 listed cos; Chair. AJIT D. GUNEWARDENE; Dir-Gen. HIRAN MENDIS.

INSURANCE

Ceylinco Insurance Co Ltd: Ceylinco House, 4th Floor, 69 Janadhipathi Mawatha, Colombo 1; tel. (1) 485706; fax (1) 485769; e-mail jagath@lanka.ccom.lk; f. 1987; Chair. and Man. Dir J. L. B. KOTELAWALA.

Eagle Insurance Co Ltd: 'Eagle House', 75 Kumaran Ratnam Rd, Colombo 2; tel. (1) 437090; fax (1) 447620; e-mail eaglehouse@eureka.lk; internet www.eagle.com.lk; f. 1988 as CTC Eagle Insurance Co Ltd; general and life insurance; mem. of the Zurich Group; Chair. Dr F. A. SCHNEWLIN; Man. Dir CHANDRA JAYARATNE.

Hayleys Ltd: Hayley Bldg, 400 Deans Rd, Colombo 10; internet www.hayleys.com; f. 1952; Chair. SUNIL MENDIS; Dep. Chair. R. YATAWARA.

National Insurance Corpn Ltd: 47 Muttiah Rd, POB 2202, Colombo 2; tel. (1) 445738; fax (1) 445733; general; Chair. T. M. S. NANAYAKKARA; Sec. A. C. J. DE ALWIS.

Sri Lanka Insurance Corporation Ltd: 'Rakshana Mandiraya', 21 Vauxhall St, POB 1337, Colombo 2; tel. (1) 325311; fax (1) 447742; e-mail jww@eureka.lk; internet www.lk.rakshana; f. 1961; priva-

tized in 2003; all classes of insurance; Chair. Prof. J. W. WICKRAMA-SINGHE; Exec. Dir K. L. SAMARASINGHE.

Union Assurance Ltd: Union Assurance Centre, 20 St. Michael's Rd, Colombo 3; tel. (1) 344171; fax (1) 343065; e-mail info@union-assurance.com; internet www.union-assurance.com; f. 1987; general and life insurance; Chair. KEN BALENDRA; Dep. Chair. R. SIVARATNAM.

Trade and Industry

GOVERNMENT AGENCIES

Board of Investment of Sri Lanka: World Trade Center, West Tower, 24th-26th Floor, Echelon Sq., Colombo 1; tel. (1) 434403; fax (1) 447995; e-mail infoboi@boi.gov.lk; internet www.boisrilanka.org; f. 1978 as the Greater Colombo Economic Commission; promotes foreign direct investment and administers the eight Export Processing Zones at Katunayake, Biyagama, Koggala, Mirigama, Malwatta, Horana, Mawathagama and Polgahawela; also administers industrial township at Watupitiwala and industrial parks at Seetawaka and Kandy; Chair. ARJUNNA MAHENDRAN.

Public Enterprises Reform Commission (PERC): 11–01 West Tower, World Trade Center, Colombo 1; tel. (1) 338756; fax (1) 326116; e-mail dg@perc.gov.lk; internet www.perc.gov.lk; f. 1995 to advise Govt on privatization and restructuring of loss-making state-sector enterprises; Chair. Dr P. B. JAYASUNDERA; Dir-Gen. MANO TITTAWELLA.

Sri Lanka Gem and Jewellery Exchange: Level 4 and 5, East Low Block, World Trade Center, Echelon Sq., Colombo 1; e-mail gemautho@sltnet.lk; f. 1990; testing and certification of gems, trading booths; Dir-Gen. T. PIYADASA; Man.(Export Promotion) AJITH PERERA.

> **National Gem and Jewellery Authority:** 25 Galle Face Terrace, Colombo 3; tel. and fax (1) 329352; e-mail ngja@sltnet.lk; f. 1971 as State Gem Corpn; Chair. Prof. P. G. R. DHARMARATNE; Dir-Gen. T. PIYADASA.

Trade Information Service: Sri Lanka Export Development Board, Colombo Renaissance Hotel Complex, 115 Sir Chittampalam A. Gardiner Mawatha, POB 1872, Colombo 2; tel. (1) 438523; fax (1) 438404; f. 1981 to collect and disseminate commercial information and to provide advisory services to trade circles; Dir Mrs G. I. UNAMBOOWE.

DEVELOPMENT ORGANIZATIONS

Industrial Development Board of Ceylon (IDB): 615 Galle Rd, Katubedda, Moratuwa; tel. 605887; fax 607002; e-mail idbch@sltnet.lk; internet www.nsf.ac.lk/idb; f. 1969; under Ministry of Industrial Development; promotes industrial development through provincial network; Chair. C. T. S. B. PERERA; Gen. Man. CHANDRASIRI KALUPAHNAGE.

> **Centre for Entrepreneurship Development and Consultancy Services:** 615 Galle Rd, Katubedda, Moratuwa; tel. (1) 632156; f. 1989; Dir T. M. KULARATHNE (acting).

> **Centre for Industrial and Technology Information Services (CITIS):** 615 Galle Rd, Katubedda, Moratuwa; tel. (1) 605372; fax (1) 607002; e-mail citis@slt.lk; internet www.nsf.ac.lk/idb; f. 1989; Dir CHANDRASIRI KALUPAHANAGE (acting).

Sri Lanka Export Development Board: Level 7, Trade Information Service, 42 Navam Mawatha, Colombo 2; tel. (1) 300705; fax (1) 300715; e-mail tisinfo@edb.tradenetsl.lk; internet www.tradenetsl.lk; Chair. G. L. J. HEWAWASAM (acting).

Coconut Development Authority: 11 Duke St, POB 386, Colombo 1; tel. (1) 421027; fax (1) 447602; e-mail cocoauth@panlanka.net; internet www.cda.lk; f. 1972; state body; promotes the coconut industry through financial assistance for mfrs of coconut products, market information, consultancy services and quality assurance; Chair. H. A. THILAKARATNE.

Janatha Estates Development Board: 55/75 Vauxhall St, Colombo 2; tel. (1) 320901; fax (1) 446577; f. 1975; manages 18 tea and spice plantations; 10,164 employees; 1 regional office.

CHAMBERS OF COMMERCE

Federation of Chambers of Commerce and Industry of Sri Lanka: 29 Gregory's Rd, Colombo 7; tel. (1) 698225; fax (1) 699530; internet www.fccisl.org; f. 1973; Pres. LAL DE MEL.

All Ceylon Trade Chamber: Colombo; tel. (1) 432428; Pres. MUDLIYAR N. W. J. MUDALIGE; Gen. Sec. Y. P. MUTHUKUMARANA.

Ceylon Chamber of Commerce: 50 Navam Mawatha, POB 274, Colombo 2; tel. (1) 421745; fax (1) 449352; e-mail info@chamber.lk;

internet www.chamber.lk; f. 1839; 517 mems; Chair. TILAK DE ZOYSA; Sec.-Gen. RENTON DE ALWIS.

Ceylon National Chamber of Industries: Galle Face Court 2, Room 20, 1st Floor, POB 1775, Colombo 3; tel. (1) 423734; fax (1) 423734; f. 1960; 300 mems; Chair. LAL DE MEL; Chief Exec. JOE SOTHINATHAN.

International Chamber of Commerce Sri Lanka: 141/7, Vauxhall St, POB 1733, Colombo 2; tel. and fax (1) 307841; e-mail iccsl@sltnet.lk; f. 1955; Chair. M. J. C. AMARASURIYA; CEO GAMINI PEIRIS.

The National Chamber of Commerce of Sri Lanka: NCCSL Bldg, 450 D. R. Wijewardene Mawatha, POB 1375, Colombo 10; tel. (1) 689600; fax (1) 689596; e-mail nccsl@slt.lk; internet www.nationalchamberlk.org; f. 1948; Pres. ASOKA DE Z. GUNASEKERA; Sec.-Gen. NEIL C. SENEVIRATNE.

INDUSTRIAL AND TRADE ASSOCIATIONS

The Association of Computer Training Organizations: 5 Clifford Ave, Colombo 3; tel. (1) 565193; fax (1) 713821; e-mail infotel@sri.lanka.net; internet www.actoslanka.org; f. 1991; 29 mems; Pres. KITHSIRI MANCHANAYAKE.

Ceylon Coir Fibre Exporters' Association: c/o Volanka Ltd, 193 Minuwangoda Rd, Kotugoda; tel. (1) 232938; fax (1) 237365; e-mail volanka@sri.lanka.net; internet www.slcfa.lk; Chair. INDRAJITH PIYASENA.

Ceylon Hardware Merchants' Association: 20B Central Rd, Colombo 12; tel. and fax (1) 435920; Pres. S. THILLAINATHAN.

Ceylon Planters' Society: 40/1 Sri Dharmadara Mawatha, Ratmalana; tel. (1) 715656; fax (1) 716758; e-mail plansoty@sltnet.lk; f. 1936; 1,660 mems (plantation mans); 25 brs and nine regional organizations; Pres. J. W. Y. K. DE SILVA; Sec. D. S. P. HETTIARACHCHI.

Coconut Products Traders' Association: c/o Ceylon Chamber of Commerce, 50 Navam Mawatha, POB 274, Colombo 2; tel. (1) 421745; fax (1) 449352; f. 1925; Chair. N. PIERIS; Sec. C. G. JAYASURIYA.

Colombo Rubber Traders' Association: c/o Ceylon Chamber of Commerce, 50 Navam Mawatha, POB 274, Colombo 2; tel. (1) 380150; fax (1) 449352; e-mail kanchana@chamber.lk; internet www.chamber.lk; f. 1918; Chair. W. T. ELLAWALA; Sec. RENTON DE ALWIS.

Colombo Tea Traders' Association: c/o Ceylon Chamber of Commerce, 50 Navam Mawatha, POB 274, Colombo 2; tel. (1) 380150; fax (1) 449352; e-mail kanchana@chamber.lk; internet www.chamber.lk; f. 1894; 198 mems; Chair. MAHEN DAYANANDA; Sec. RENTON DE ALWIS.

Free Trade Zone Manufacturers' Association: Plaza Complex, Unit 6 (Upper Floor), IPZ, Katunayake; tel. (1) 252813; Administrative Sec. TUWAN SAMAHOON.

The Industrial Association of Sri Lanka: c/o Ceylon Chamber of Commerce, 50 Nawam Mawatha, POB 274, Colombo 2; tel. (1) 422084; e-mail puvi@chamber.lk.

Sea Food Exporters' Association: c/o Andriesz & Co Ltd, 39 Nuge Rd, Peliyagoda; tel. 530021.

Software Exporters' Association: c/o Project Management Division, Sri Lanka Export Development Board, 42 Nawam Mawatha, Colombo 2; e-mail it@eureka.lk; internet www.islandsoftware.org.

Sri Lanka Apparel Exporters' Association: 45 Rosmead Place, Colombo 7; tel. (1) 670778; fax (1) 683118; e-mail srilanka-apparel@eureka.lk; internet www.srilanka-apparel.com; f. 1982; Chair. RANJAN CASIE CHETTY; Sec. HEMAMALI SIRISENA.

Sri Lanka Association of Manufacturers and Exporters of Rubber Products (SLAMERP): 341/12 Kotte Rd, Rajagirya; tel. (1) 863429; fax (74) 410557; e-mail slamerp@panlanka.net; internet www.tradenetsl.lk/slamerp; f. 1984; Chair. ANANDA CALDERA; Sec.-Gen. C. DIAS BANDARANAYAKE.

Sri Lanka Association of Printers: 593 Kularatne Mawatha, Colombo 10; tel. (1) 687557; fax (1) 572875; e-mail christo@itmin.com; f. 1993; Pres. CHRISTOPHER R. DIAS; Sec. KOSALA THILLEKARATNE.

Sri Lanka Chamber of the Pharmaceutical Industry: 15 Tichbourne Passage, Colombo 10; tel. (1) 694823; fax (1) 671877; e-mail nimjay@sltnet.lk; Pres. N. DIAS JAYASINHA; Sec. NAUSHAD ISMAIL.

Sri Lanka Fruit and Vegetables Producers, Processors and Exporters' Association: c/o Sri Lanka Export Development Board, 42 Navam Mawatha, Colombo 2; tel. (1) 300705; fax (1) 300715; e-mail ead@edb.tradenetsl.lk; internet www.tradenetsl.lk; Sec. M. A. JUNAID.

Sri Lanka Importers, Exporters and Manufacturers' Association (SLIEMA): 28 Rajamalwatte Rd, POB 12, Colombo 15; tel. (1) 696321; fax (1) 522524; e-mail sliema@isplanka.lk; f. 1955; Pres. WILLIAM JOHN TERRENCE PERERA.

Sri Lanka Jewellery Manufacturing Exporters' Association: Colombo; tel. (1) 445141; fax (1) 445105; Pres. IFTHIKHAR AZIZ; Sec. CHANAKA ELLAWELA.

Sri Lanka Shippers' Council: c/o Ceylon Chamber of Commerce, 50 Nawam Mawatha, POB 274, Colombo 2; tel. (1) 422156; internet www.slcs.ws.

Sri Lanka Tea Board: 574 Galle Rd, POB 1750, Colombo 3; tel. (1) 582236; fax (1) 589132; e-mail tboard@sri.lanka.net; internet www .pureceylontea.com; f. 1976 for development of tea industry through research and promotion in Sri Lanka and in world markets; Chair. RONNIE WEERAKOON; Dir-Gen. S. WIRITHAMULLA.

Sri Lanka Wooden Furniture and Wood Products Manufacturers' and Exporters' Association: c/o E. H. Cooray & Sons Ltd, 411 Galle Rd, Colombo 3; tel. (1) 509227; fax (1) 575198; Pres. PATRICK AMARASINGHE; Sec. PINSIRI FERNANDO.

Sugar Importers' Association of Sri Lanka: c/o C. W. Mackie & Co Ltd, 36 D. R. Wijewardena Mawatha, POB 89, Colombo 10; tel. (1) 423554; fax (1) 438069; Pres. M. THAVAYOGARAJAH; Sec. C. KAPUWATTA.

EMPLOYERS' ORGANIZATION

Employers' Federation of Ceylon: 385 J3 Old Kotte Rd, Rajagiriya, Colombo; tel. (1) 867966; fax (1) 867942; e-mail gkbd@eureka .lk; internet www.empfed.lk; f. 1928; mem. International Organization of Employers and Confederation of Asian Pacific Employers; 440 mems; Dir-Gen. G. K. B. DASANAYAKA.

UTILITIES

Electricity

Ceylon Electricity Board: 50 Sir Chittampalam A. Gardiner Mawatha, POB 540, Colombo 2; tel. (1) 320953; fax (1) 323935; e-mail chairceb@sri.lanka.net; f. 1969; undergoing privatization in 2003; Chair. ARJUN DERANIYAGALA.

Water

National Water Supply and Drainage Board (NWSDB): Galle Rd, Ratmalana; tel. (1) 638999; fax (1) 636449; e-mail gmswe@sltnet .lk; f. 1975; govt corpn; Gen. Man. S. WEERARATNE.

CO-OPERATIVES

In 2000 there were an estimated 11,793 co-operative societies in Sri Lanka, with membership totalling 17,235,000.

TRADE UNIONS

At the end of 2000 there were 1,588 trade unions functioning in Sri Lanka.

All Ceylon Federation of Free Trade Unions (ACFFTU): 94-1/6 York Bldg, York St, Colombo 1; tel. (1) 431847; fax (1) 470874; e-mail nwccmb@itmin.com; nine affiliated unions; 80,000 mems; Pres. Mrs M. C. RAJAHMONEY; Sec.-Gen. ANTONY LODWICK.

Ceylon Federation of Labour (CFL): 457 Union Place, Colombo 2; tel. (1) 94273; f. 1957; 16 affiliated unions; 155,969 mems; Pres. Dr COLVIN R. DE SILVA; Gen. Sec. R. WEERAKOON.

Ceylon Mercantile, Industrial and General Workers' Union (CMU): Colombo; Sec. G. JAGANATHAN.

Ceylon Trade Union Federation (CTUF): Colombo; tel. (1) 20365; f. 1941; 24 affiliated unions; 35,271 mems; Sec.-Gen. L. W. PANDITHA.

Ceylon Workers' Congress (CWC): 'Savumia Bhavan', 72 Ananda Coomarasamy Mawatha, POB 1294, Colombo 7; tel. (1) 301359; fax (1) 301355; e-mail cwcctuc@slt.lk; f. 1939; represents mainly plantation workers of Indian Tamil origin; 50 district offices and 7 regional offices; 250,000 mems; Pres. and Gen. Sec. S. ARUMUGAN THONDAMAN.

Democratic Workers' Congress (DWC): 70 Bankshall St, POB 1009, Colombo 11; tel. (1) 423746; fax (1) 435961; f. 1939; 201,382 mems (1994); Pres. MANO GANESHAN; Gen. Sec. R. KITNAN.

Government Workers' Trade Union Federation (GWTUF): 457 Union Place, Colombo 2; tel. (1) 95066; 52 affiliated unions; 100,000 mems; Leader P. D. SARANAPALA.

Jathika Sevaka Sangamaya (JSS) (National Employees' Union): 416 Kotte Rd, Pitakotte, Colombo; tel. (1) 565432; f. 1959; 357,000 mems; represents over 70% of unionized manual and clerical workers of Sri Lanka; Pres. W. A. NEVILLE PERERA; Sec. SIRINAL DE MEL.

Lanka Jathika Estate Workers' Union (LJEWU): 60 Bandaranayakepura, Sri Jayawardenepura Mawatha, Welikada, POB 1918, Rajagiriya; tel. (1) 865138; fax (1) 862262; e-mail ctucljew@sri .lanka.net; f. 1958; 350,000 mems; Pres. RANIL WICKREMASINGHE; Gen. Sec. RAJAH SENEVIRATNE.

Public Service Workers' Trade Union Federation (PSWTUF): POB 500, Colombo; tel. (1) 31125; 100 affiliated unions; 100,000 mems.

Sri Lanka Nidahas Sewaka Sangamaya (Sri Lanka Free Workers' Union): 301 T. B. Jayah Mawatha, POB 1241, Colombo 10; tel. and fax (1) 694074; f. 1960; 478 br. unions; 193,011 mems; Gen. Sec. LESLIE DEVENDRA.

Union of Post and Telecommunication Officers: 11/4 Lotus Rd, POB 15, Colombo 1; tel. (1) 350687; fax (1) 341626; f. 1945; Pres. M. A. SHANTHA KUMARA; Sec. K. S. WEERASEKERA.

Transport

RAILWAYS

Sri Lanka Railways (SLR): Olcott Mawatha, POB 355, Colombo 10; tel. (1) 431177; fax (1) 446490; e-mail slrail@itmin-com; internet www.sciencelandlk-railway; f. 1864; under Ministry of Transport and Highways; operates 1,447 track-km; there are 9 railway lines across the country and 164 stations, with 134 sub-stations (1997); Gen. Man. W. K. B. WERAGAMA.

ROADS

In 1999 there were an estimated 96,695 km of roads in Sri Lanka, of which 11,462 km were main roads. In April 2002 a major highway linking the Jaffna peninsula with the rest of the country was opened for the first time in 12 years.

Office of the Minister of Transport and Highways: 1 D. R. Wijewardene Mawatha, POB 588, Colombo 10; tel. (1) 687311; fax (1) 694547; maintains 11,147 km of national highways and 4,441 bridges through the Road Development Authority.

Department of Motor Traffic: 581-341 Elvitigala Mawatha, POB 533, Colombo 5; tel. (1) 694331; fax (1) 694338; e-mail dmtsl@sltnet .lk.

Sri Lanka Central Transport Board: 200 Kirula Rd, POB 1435, Colombo 5; tel. (1) 581121; f. 1958; nationalized organization responsible for road passenger transport services consisting of a central transport board, 11 Cluster Bus Cos and one regional transport board; fleet of 8,900 buses (2001); Chair. THILAK IDDAMALGODA; Sec. R. ARIYAGAMA.

SHIPPING

Colombo is one of the most important ports in Asia and is situated at the junction of the main trade routes. The other main ports of Sri Lanka are Trincomalee, Galle and Jaffna. Trincomalee is the main port for handling tea exports.

Ceylon Association of Ships' Agents (CASA): 56 Ward Place, Colombo 7; tel. (1) 696227; fax (1) 698648; e-mail casa@itmin.com; f. 1966; primarily a consultative organization; represents mems in dealings with govt authorities; 116 mems; Chair. A. R. PERERA; Sec.-Gen. N. K. WARUSAVITHARANA.

Sri Lanka Ports Authority: 19 Church St, POB 595, Colombo 1; tel. (1) 421201; fax (1) 440651; e-mail slpainfo@slpa.lk; internet www .slpa.lk; f. 1976; responsible for all cargo handling operations and harbour development and maintenance in the ports of Colombo, Galle, Kankasanthurai and Trincomalee; Chair. PARAKRAMA DISSANAYAKE; Man. Dir M. COLONNE.

Shipping Companies

Ceylon Ocean Lines Ltd: 'Sayuru Sevana', 46/12 Nawam Mawatha, Colombo 2; tel. (1) 434928; fax (1) 439245; e-mail oceanlines@col.lk; f. 1956; shipping agents, freight forwarders, charterers, container freight station operators and bunkers; Dirs Capt. L. P. WEINMAN, Capt. A. V. RAJENDRA.

Ceylon Shipping Corpn Ltd: 6 Sir Baron Jayatilleke Mawatha, POB 1718, Colombo 1; tel. (1) 328772; fax (1) 449486; e-mail cscemail@sri.lanka.netA21CE846(COMTEXT); f. 1971 as a govt corpn; became govt-owned limited liability co in 1992; operates fully-containerized service to Europe, the Far East, the Mediterranean, USA and Canada (East Coast); Chair. SUNDRA JAYAWARDHANA; Gen. Man. M. S. P. GUNAWARDENA.

Ceylon Shipping Lines Ltd: 450 D.R. Wijewardena Mawatha, POB 891, Colombo 10; tel. (1) 689500; fax (1) 689510; shipping agents, travel agents, off dock terminal operators; Chair. E. A. WIRASINHA; Man. Dir T. D. V. GUNARATNE.

Ceyoceanic Ltd: 80 Reclamation Rd, POB 795, Colombo 11; tel. (1) 36071; Dir M. T. G. ANAAM.

Colombo Dockyard Ltd: Port of Colombo, Graving Docks, POB 906, Colombo 15; tel. (1) 522461; fax (1) 446441; e-mail coldock@cdl .lk; internet www.cdl.lk; f. 1974; 51% owned by Onomichi Dockyard

Co Ltd, Japan, and 49% by Sri Lankan public and government institutions; four dry-docks, seven repair berths (1,200 m), repair of ships up to 125,000 dwt, and builders of steel/aluminium vessels of up to 3,000 dwt; Chair. K. YAMANAKA; Gen. Man. M. P. B. YAPA.

Mercantile Shipping Co Ltd: 108 Aluthmawatha Rd, Colombo 15; tel. 331792; fax (1) 331799.

Sri Lanka Shipping Co Ltd: 46/5 Navam Mawatha, POB 1125, Colombo 2; tel. (1) 336853; fax (1) 437420; e-mail lankaship@slsc.lk; f. 1956.

INLAND WATERWAYS

There are more than 160 km of canals open for traffic.

CIVIL AVIATION

Civil aviation is controlled by the Government's Department of Civil Aviation. There are airports at Batticaloa, Colombo (Bandaranaike for external flights and Ratmalana for internal), Gal Oya, Palali, Jaffna and Trincomalee. In April 2002 the Government lifted a six-year ban on domestic flights and permitted commercial airlines to resume services to Jaffna.

SriLankan Airlines Ltd: 22-01 East Tower, World Trade Center, Echelon Sq., Colombo 1; tel. (1) 735555; fax (1) 735122; e-mail admin@srilankan.lk; internet www.srilankan.lk; f. 1979 as Air Lanka Ltd, name changed as above in 1999; 60% state-owned, 44% owned by Emirates Airline (UAE) and 6% by employees; international services to Europe, the Middle East, Far East and Australasia; Chair. D. PELPOLA; CEO P. M. HILL.

Helitours: Air Headquarters, POB 594, Colombo 2; tel. (1) 508927; fax (1) 20541; e-mail slafgops@slklk.

Lionair (Pvt) Ltd: Asian Aviation Centre, Colombo Airport, Ratmalana, Colombo; tel. (1) 622622; fax (1) 611540; e-mail lionair@sri.lanka.net; f. 1994; scheduled and charter services to eight domestic destinations; Chair. CHANDRAN RUTNAM; Man. Dir ASOKA PERERA.

Sky Cabs: 294 1/1 Union Place, POB 683, Colombo 2; tel. (1) 333105; fax (1) 635575; e-mail skycabs@lanka.com.lk; internet www.skycab.com; f. 1991; commenced operations 1993; privately-owned; scheduled passenger and cargo services to Bahrain, India, Oman, the Maldives and Pakistan; Chair. ALI AKBER S. JEEVUNJEE; Man. Dir SURENDRA DE SILVA.

Tourism

As a stopping place for luxury cruises and by virtue of the spectacle of its Buddhist festivals, ancient monuments and natural scenery, Sri Lanka is one of Asia's most important tourist centres. Good motor roads connect Colombo to the main places of interest.

Owing to the continuing intercommunal violence, tourist arrivals decreased from 403,101 in 1995 to 302,265 in 1996 and tourism receipts fell from US $224m. to $168m. The tourism sector, however, recovered well in 1997; total arrivals rose by 21% to reach 366,165 and receipts increased by 26% to stand at $212m. Tourism receipts in 1999 were estimated at $275m., while arrivals rose by 14.5% compared with 1998 to reach 436,440. At the end of 2000 the industry appeared to be improving, although arrivals decreased to 400,414 in that year. However, the LTTE attack on Colombo's international airport in July 2001 caused severe damage to the tourist industry. One half of Sri Lankan Airlines' fleet was out of service as a result of the raid, and tourists were advised not to visit the country. The industry was also adversely affected by the increased insurance costs payable by airlines. The number of tourist arrivals in 2001 decreased to 336,794.

Ceylon Tourist Board: 80 Galle Rd, Colombo 3; tel. (1) 437059; fax (1) 437953; e-mail tourinfo@sri.lanka.net; internet www.lanka.net/ctb; f. 1966; Chair. H. M. S. SAMARANAYAKE; Dir-Gen. TISSA WARNASURIYA.

SUDAN

Introductory Survey

Location, Climate, Language, Religion, Flag, Capital

The Republic of Sudan lies in north-eastern Africa. It is bordered by Egypt to the north, by the Red Sea, Eritrea and Ethiopia to the east, by the Central African Republic, Chad and Libya to the west, and by Kenya, Uganda and the Democratic Republic of the Congo (formerly Zaire) to the south. The climate shows a marked transition from the desert of the north to the rainy equatorial south. Temperatures vary with altitude and latitude. The annual average for the whole country is about 21°C (70°F). Arabic is the official language, although other languages are spoken and English is widely understood. Most northern Sudanese are Muslims, while in the south most of the inhabitants are animists or Christians. The national flag (proportions 1 by 2) has three equal horizontal stripes, of red, white and black, with a green triangle at the hoist. The capital is Khartoum.

Recent History

The Sudan (as the country was known before 1975) achieved independence as a parliamentary republic on 1 January 1956. After a military coup in November 1958, a Supreme Council of the Armed Forces was established and ruled until October 1964, when it was overthrown in a civilian revolution. In May 1969 power was seized by a group of officers, led by Col Gaafar Muhammad Nimeri. All existing political institutions and organizations were abolished, and the 'Democratic Republic of the Sudan' was proclaimed, with supreme authority in the hands of the Revolutionary Command Council (RCC). In October 1971 a referendum confirmed Nimeri's nomination as President. A new Government was formed, the RCC was dissolved, and the Sudanese Socialist Union (SSU) was recognized as the only political party.

An early problem facing the Nimeri Government concerned the disputed status of the three southern provinces (Bahr al-Ghazal, Equatoria and Upper Nile), whose inhabitants are racially and culturally distinct from most of the country's population. Rebellion against rule from the north had first broken out in 1955, and fighting continued until March 1972, when an agreement to give the three provinces a degree of autonomy was concluded between members of the Government and representatives of the South Sudan Liberation Movement. A High Executive Council (HEC) for the Southern Region was established in April 1972, and Sudan's permanent Constitution was endorsed in April 1973. Elections to the Regional People's Assembly for southern Sudan took place in November 1973, followed by elections to the National People's Assembly in April 1974.

The establishment of a National Assembly and a political party broadened the Government's base of power, although the army continued to play an important role in the country's affairs. Regional and national elections were held in February 1978, with the provision that opposition candidates had to be approved by the SSU. About one-half of the 274 elective seats in the National Assembly were won by SSU candidates. Elections were held in May 1980 for the National and Regional Assemblies, and in October legislative proposals to legalize a regional system of government were approved. The National People's Assembly was dissolved in October 1981. When new elections were held in December, its membership had been reduced from 366 to 151, as many powers had been devolved to the regions. At the same time, the southern HEC was dissolved. The entire Sudanese Government was dismissed in November, although many individuals were later reinstated. In April 1982 a new Southern Region People's Assembly was elected.

In April 1983 President Nimeri was re-elected for a third six-year term. During that year Sudan's north–south conflict escalated, and in June Nimeri finally decided to redivide the south into three smaller regions, each with its own assembly, in an effort to quell the unrest. In September Nimeri suddenly announced the imposition of strict Islamic law (the *Shari'a*), provoking anger in the largely non-Muslim south, and in April 1984 Nimeri proclaimed a state of emergency. The subsequent stringent application of *Shari'a* law aggravated tensions within the country and strained relations between Sudan and its allies, Egypt and the USA.

In May 1984 Nimeri replaced his Council of Ministers with a 64-member Presidential Council, in accordance with the '*Shoura*' (consultation) principle of *Shari'a* law. In July, however, the National People's Assembly rejected his proposed constitutional amendments to make Sudan a formal Islamic state. In October Nimeri ended the state of emergency and offered to revoke the redivision of the south, if a majority of southerners desired it. The situation in the south continued to deteriorate, with the emergence of the Sudan People's Liberation Movement (SPLM), whose armed forces, the Sudan People's Liberation Army (SPLA), rapidly gained military control over large areas of the provinces of Bahr al-Ghazal and Upper Nile.

On 6 April 1985, while Nimeri was visiting the USA, he was deposed in a bloodless military coup. The country's new leader, Gen. Abdel-Rahman Swar ad-Dahab (who had recently been made Minister of Defence and Commander-in-Chief of the army by Nimeri), appointed a Transitional Military Council (TMC) to govern the country, but he pledged a return to civilian rule after a one-year transitional period. The SSU and the National People's Assembly were dissolved, and hundreds of Nimeri's officials were arrested; Nimeri went into exile in Cairo, Egypt. A transitional Constitution was introduced in October 1985 that allowed numerous new political groupings to emerge in preparation for a general election, and in December the name of the country was officially changed to 'the Republic of Sudan'.

In a general election in April 1986 the Umma Party (UP), led by Sadiq al-Mahdi, won 99 of the 264 seats in the new National Assembly, followed by the Democratic Unionist Party (DUP), with 63 seats. A coalition Government was formed by the UP and DUP, with four portfolios in the Council of Ministers allocated to southern parties. Al-Mahdi became Prime Minister and Minister of Defence, and a six-member Supreme Council assumed the functions of Head of State. With these appointments, the TMC was dissolved, signifying a return to civilian rule.

In response to the April 1985 coup, the SPLM initially declared a cease-fire, but presented the new regime with a series of demands concerning the southern region. Despite Swar ad-Dahab's offer of various concessions to the south, the SPLM refused to negotiate with the TMC, and fighting resumed. Following the 1986 election, Col John Garang, the SPLM leader, was offered a place in the Council of Ministers. Although the SPLM announced that it would not recognize, or join, the new Government, negotiations took place during 1986 between the SPLM and the National Alliance for Salvation (NAS), a semi-official group of trade unionists and politicians who supported the Government, and in July al-Mahdi and Garang met in Addis Ababa, Ethiopia. All contacts were discontinued, however, after the SPLM shot down a Sudan Airways aircraft in August.

In May 1987, following increasing instability in the south, a temporary Council for the Southern Sudan (CSS) was established. Its influence on the army and the SPLM, the two contending *de facto* ruling powers that now existed in the south, was, however, negligible. On 14 May al-Mahdi, prompted partly by dissension within the Council of Ministers, dissolved his coalition Government, although the reconstructed Council of Ministers, announced in June, differed little from its predecessor. Al-Mahdi announced that the coalition parties had agreed on guide-lines for the conduct of government policy and that laws based on a 'Sudanese legal heritage' would replace those unacceptable to non-Muslims, who would be exempted from Islamic taxation and special penalties. However, the SPLM continued to demand a total abrogation of Islamic law as a precondition for peace negotiations, while the National Islamic Front (NIF) demanded that the Islamic code be imposed on the whole country. On 25 July the Government imposed a 12-month state of emergency, aimed at bringing under control the worsening economic situation.

In May 1988 a new Government of National Unity, comprising members of the UP, the DUP, the NIF and some southern Sudanese political parties, was formed, following the dissolution of the previous coalition. In November representatives of the

SPLM met senior members of the DUP and reached agreement on proposals to end the civil war. A statement issued by the two sides stipulated that, prior to the convening of a national constitutional conference, the Islamic legal code should be suspended, that military agreements between Sudan and other countries should be abandoned, and that the state of emergency be lifted and a cease-fire implemented in the south. In December, however, a state of emergency was again declared, amid reports that a military coup had been attempted. The DUP withdrew from the Government. The political crisis was caused by al-Mahdi's requesting the National Assembly to convene the national constitutional conference, while refusing to incorporate the agreement between the SPLM and the DUP into his proposal.

In February 1989, in a major cabinet reshuffle, Dr Hassan at-Turabi, the leader of the NIF, was appointed Deputy Prime Minister. In March al-Mahdi agreed to form a new, broad-based government, which would begin negotiations with the SPLM. Although the peace agreement concluded by the DUP and the SPLM in November 1988 had been widely endorsed, the NIF opposed its provision for the suspension of Islamic laws as a prelude to the negotiation of a peace settlement. The NIF was consequently excluded from the new Government formed in March 1989. Peace negotiations between a government delegation and the SPLM commenced in Ethiopia in April, and at the beginning of May Col Garang proclaimed a one-month cease-fire (subsequently extended to 30 June), renewing hopes for peace and aiding the work of famine relief. The negotiations culminated in an agreement to suspend Islamic laws, pending the proposed convening, in September, of a constitutional conference.

On 30 June 1989 a bloodless coup, led by Brig. (later Lt-Gen.) Omar Hassan Ahmad al-Bashir, removed al-Mahdi's Government. Al-Bashir formed a 15-member Revolutionary Command Council for National Salvation (RCC), which declared its primary aim to be the resolution of the southern conflict. Al-Bashir, who became Head of State, Chairman of the RCC, Prime Minister and Minister of Defence, and Commander-in-Chief of the armed forces, abolished the Constitution, the National Assembly and all political parties and trade unions, and declared a state of emergency. Many members of the former Government were detained, although three ex-ministers were included in the new, 21-member Cabinet appointed in early July.

The SPLM's response to the coup was cautious. In early July 1989 Lt-Gen. al-Bashir declared a one-month unilateral cease-fire and offered an amnesty to those opposing the Government 'for political reasons'. In an effort to restart negotiations, al-Bashir requested Ethiopia, Egypt and Kenya to act as mediators. However, the Government's proposals for a national referendum on *Shari'a* law alienated the SPLM, which demanded its suspension as a precondition for talks. Peace negotiations were renewed in Ethiopia in August. By this time the SPLM's terms for a negotiated settlement to the conflict included the immediate resignation of the RCC, prior to the establishment of an interim government, in which the SPLM, the banned political parties and other groupings would be represented. The new regime's proximity to the NIF had become apparent, and the negotiations collapsed immediately over the issue of Islamic law. Hostilities, which had been in abeyance since the beginning of May, resumed at the end of October.

In March 1990 57 people were reported to have been arrested for having attempted to seize control of the Government. A cabinet reshuffle in April was believed to have strengthened the influence of Islamic fundamentalists in Sudanese politics, as two of the new appointees had close links with the NIF. It was claimed that a further military coup was attempted on 23 April, resulting in the execution, on the following day, of 28 army officers. In February 1991 the RCC enacted a decree instituting a new, federal system of government. Sudan was divided into nine states, each of which had its own governor, deputy governor and cabinet of ministers, and assumed responsibility for local administration and the collection of some taxes. The central Government retained control over foreign policy, military affairs, the economy and the other principal areas of administration. This new administrative structure was intended as a step towards ending the civil war in the south, but the SPLM immediately condemned the degree of power retained by the central Government. At the beginning of February it had been announced that a new penal code, based on *Shari'a* law, would take effect in March, but would not apply in the three southern states, pending the establishment there of elected assemblies to resolve the issue. The SPLM nevertheless regarded the application of Islamic law in the northern states as unacceptable, citing the large numbers of non-Muslims resident there.

The overthrow, in May 1991, of the Ethiopian Government, led by Mengistu Haile Mariam, had implications for the SPLA forces, who had previously enjoyed Ethiopian support. In late May armed clashes were reported within Ethiopia between SPLA forces and those of the new Ethiopian Government, and the Sudanese Government declared its recognition of, and support for, the new Ethiopian regime. In June the Ethiopian Government was reported to have presented SPLA fighters in western Ethiopia with a deadline by which they had either to leave the country, to disarm or to accept refugee status. In October Sudan and Ethiopia signed a treaty of friendship and co-operation.

In February 1992 al-Bashir appointed all 300 members of a new transitional National Assembly, which included the entire RCC, all government ministers and the governors of Sudan's nine states. The Assembly was accorded legislative authority, with the power to examine all decrees issued by the RCC, and responsibility for preparing the country for parliamentary elections. In March government forces commenced an offensive in southern Sudan against the SPLA, which had split into two rival factions, and by May they were reported to have recaptured a number of towns. In late May a new round of peace negotiations commenced in Abuja, Nigeria, between a government delegation and two from the SPLA: one representing the faction led by Garang, and one from the dissident group based at Nasir. At the conclusion of the talks in June all parties agreed to continue negotiations at a future date. In July government forces were reported to have captured the town of Torit, near the Ugandan border, which had been the headquarters of Garang's faction of the SPLA. At the start of the rainy season, however, the SPLA, which appeared to have achieved a degree of unity since the Abuja talks, launched a new offensive.

In early 1993 the NIF was reported to be opposed to the continued military character of the Government, and to favour the dissolution of the RCC. Regional councils were in the process of being elected, and the Government had reportedly undertaken, in 1992, to dissolve the RCC once the regional councils were in place. In January 1993 al-Bashir effected an extensive reorganization of the Cabinet, but stated that there would be no change in government policy and that the RCC would not be dissolved. Rather, in 1994 the gradual transfer of power to the regional councils would begin. Further talks between the Government and the SPLA ended inconclusively in January 1993. By this time the SPLA was reported to have split into three rival factions.

Peace talks between the Government and Garang's faction of the SPLA resumed in Abuja in April 1993. Meanwhile, in Nairobi, Kenya, talks were taking place between a government delegation and SPLA-United, an alliance of the Nasir faction, the 'Forces of Unity' and a faction led by Kerubino Kuanyin Bol. The Abuja talks adjourned in mid-May, having made little progress. Although the Government claimed that the talks would resume in June, the SPLA regarded them as having failed. The Nairobi talks resumed in May, and ended with agreement on the concept of a unified federal state and on the rights of state governments to introduce laws supplementary to federal legislation—allowing the implementation of *Shari'a* law in the north, but not in the south.

The collapse of the Abuja negotiations was quickly followed by allegations of cease-fire violations from both the Government and rebel factions, and in July 1993 Garang's faction of the SPLA launched a major offensive after attacks by government troops, aided by rival SPLA factions. The renewed fighting caused the influx of some 100,000 starving people into the area around the southern provincial capital of Malakal. In August the Nuba people were reported to be threatened by government forces in central Sudan. Independent observers urged the UN to establish 'safe havens' for refugees and to extend its Operation Lifeline Sudan to the Nuba Mountains.

On 19 October 1993 al-Bashir announced political reforms in preparation for presidential and legislative elections in 1994 and 1995, respectively. The RCC had been dissolved three days previously—after it had appointed al-Bashir as President and as head of a new civilian Government. Cabinet ministers were requested to remain in office until elections took place. On 20 October al-Bashir appointed a new Minister of Defence—a portfolio that he had formerly held himself—and a new Vice-President. Western observers regarded the dissolution of the RCC as reinforcing the position of the NIF within the Government during the transition to civilian rule.

In January 1994 the two principal rival factions of the SPLA were reported to have agreed on a cease-fire. In February Sudan was redivided into 26 states instead of the nine that had formed the basis of administration since 1991. The executive and legislative powers of each state government were to be expanded, and southern states were expected to be exempted from *Shari'a* law. In March delegations representing the Government and two factions of the SPLA participated in peace talks held in Nairobi under the auspices of the Intergovernmental Authority on Drought and Development (IGADD—superseded in 1996 by the Intergovernmental Authority on Development—IGAD, see p. 242), which in September 1993 had formed a committee on the Sudanese conflict comprising the Heads of State of Kenya, Ethiopia, Uganda and Eritrea. All parties to the talks agreed to allow the free passage of relief supplies to southern Sudan. In April 1994 the Government adopted legislation providing for the appointment, by the President, of an independent commission to supervise legislative elections scheduled to take place in the second half of 1994, and for a constitutional referendum. On 16 May the Government held a conference in Juba province, at the conclusion of which a declaration was issued that urged national unity and appealed to all rebel forces to embrace conventional politics. On 18 May a second round of IGADD-sponsored peace talks commenced in Nairobi, but was adjourned until mid-July two days later, in order to allow the participants time to study a draft declaration of principles on which future negotiations might be based.

In mid-July 1994 a restructuring of the Cabinet was viewed as having strengthened the position of those within the Government who opposed any compromise with the SPLA. A third round of IGADD-sponsored peace negotiations was held in Nairobi on 18–28 July. On 23 July the Government announced a unilateral cease-fire, to which Garang's faction of the SPLA reportedly responded on 28 July with a cease-fire of its own. Negotiations were adjourned until early September; in the interim delegations were to study proposed solutions to the southern conflict. However, when the negotiations resumed, divergent positions on the issues of the governance of the south and the role of religion in government quickly led to deadlock. In late September President al-Bashir announced the creation of an 89-member peace council, which was formally inaugurated in November as the Supreme Council for Peace. The Council was enlarged to 96 members at the end of that month. The severing, in December, of diplomatic relations between Sudan and Eritrea led Sudan to inform the IGADD in early 1995 that it no longer considered Eritrea to be a suitable intermediary in the Sudanese conflict. A cabinet reshuffle in February suggested a reinforcement of the Islamic character of the Government.

In mid-March 1995 Garang announced that his faction of the SPLA was to mount a new northern offensive in collaboration with other northern rebels. This grouping, the New Sudan Brigade, aimed to unite other insurgent groups against the Government, but did not appear to gain the support of rival SPLA factions. In late March it was reported that former US President Jimmy Carter had persuaded the Government to declare a unilateral cease-fire for a period of two months, and to offer rebel groups an amnesty if they surrendered their weapons. The SPLA and the South Sudan Independence Movement (SSIM) responded by also declaring cease-fires. In late May the Government extended its cease-fire for two months. However, it soon became apparent that the army was continuing to conduct military operations. In June a conference of groups and parties opposed to the Sudanese Government commenced in Asmara, Eritrea. The conference, hosted by the Eritrean People's Front for Democracy and Justice and organized by the Asmara-based National Democratic Alliance (NDA), was attended, among others, by representatives of the DUP, the UP and the Sudanese Communist Party. It was agreed that, once the al-Bashir regime had been ousted, religion would be separated from politics and that a referendum would be held regarding the secession of the southern provinces. The conference was also reported to have achieved a *rapprochement* between the SPLA and other opposition groups.

In August 1995 a reshuffle of the Cabinet was announced. The DUP claimed that those ministers who had been dismissed had been involved in the attempted assassination of President Mubarak of Egypt in June (see below). Later in August President al-Bashir announced that legislative and presidential elec-

tions would be held in 1996. At the end of January 1996 the USA announced the withdrawal of all of its diplomatic personnel from Sudan, owing to its doubts about the Government's ability to guarantee their safety. Prior to their withdrawal, the UN Security Council had unanimously adopted Resolution 1044, which accused Sudan of supporting terrorism and condemned its role in the attempted assassination of Mubarak. The resolution also demanded that Sudan immediately extradite three individuals implicated in the attempted assassination.

The first legislative and presidential elections to be held in Sudan since 1989 took place in March 1996. Some 5.5m. of Sudan's 10m. eligible voters were reported to have participated in the election of 275 deputies to a new, 400-seat National Assembly. The remaining 125 deputies had been appointed at a national conference in January. Representatives of opposition groups and parties alleged that electoral malpractice had been widespread. In the presidential election al-Bashir (who was reportedly opposed only by token candidates) obtained 75.7% of the total votes cast, and formally commenced a five-year term of office on 1 April. On the same day Dr Hassan at-Turabi, the Secretary-General of the NIF, was unanimously elected President of the National Assembly.

Rumours of an attempted *coup d'état* in late March 1996 prejudiced the newly constituted regime's claim that the elections signified the beginning of a new period of stability and reconciliation, as did reports of serious unrest in Khartoum in early April and the decision not to appoint a new Cabinet until it became clear whether the UN would impose sanctions on Sudan for its failure to comply with the terms of UN Security Council Resolution 1044. On 10 April, however, a substantial breakthrough in the southern conflict appeared to be achieved through the signing of a 'political charter for peace', by the Government, the SSIM and the SPLA-United, which pledged to preserve Sudan's national unity and to take joint action to develop those areas of the country that had been affected by the civil war. The charter also provided for the holding of a referendum as 'a means of realizing the aspirations of southern citizens' and affirmed that Islamic law would be the basis of future legislation. On 17 April Sudan's First Vice-President was reported to have invited Garang to sign the charter on behalf of his faction of the SPLA, prompting speculation that this was part of an ongoing attempt to form a new government of national unity. However, the new Cabinet, announced on 21 April, retained the military, Islamist cast of its predecessor. On 28 April the UN Security Council adopted Resolution 1054, which imposed diplomatic sanctions on Sudan for its failure to comply with the terms of Resolution 1044. In mid-May a second faction of the SPLA was reported to have concluded a peace agreement with the Government. In October al-Bashir appointed eight deputies to the National Assembly to represent constituencies in the south where, owing to the civil war, it had not been possible to hold elections in March. In December Sadiq al-Mahdi, the leader of the UP and former Prime Minister, fled the country to Eritrea.

In January 1997 the Government was reported to be seeking assistance from Egypt, after its forces suffered a series of defeats by allied rebel forces. Sudan claimed that Ethiopia was lending active support to the rebels and appealed to the UN Security Council to intervene. In April a peace accord, covering major issues such as power-sharing and *Shari'a* law, and promising a referendum on southern secession after a four-year transition period, was signed by six of the rebel groups (two of which later merged). Both the NDA and the SPLA, however, rejected the agreement. In August, in accordance with the terms of the agreement, the Southern States Co-ordination Council (SSCC) was established; Dr Riek Mashar Teny-Dhurgon, the leader of the Southern Sudan Defence Force (SSDF), was sworn in as its Chairman. In June Garang announced that the SPLA had advanced as far as it could in the south; future efforts were to be concentrated in the east. At the beginning of September the SPLA-United declared a cease-fire, and its commander, Dr Lam Akol, returned to Khartoum in the following month. Meanwhile, in June the leader of the DUP, Sharif Zayn al-Abidin al-Hindi, returned to Sudan; shortly afterwards the party announced that he had ceased to be its leader. In July al-Bashir announced his commitment to implementing *Shari'a* law and ruled out a return to multi-party politics. In October a 277-member constitutional committee was established with the task of drafting a new constitution.

In March 1998 al-Bashir announced a government reorganization in which a number of former rebel leaders were appointed to the Cabinet, including Akol as Minister of Transport. In April a new Constitution was endorsed by the National Assembly, and was presented to al-Bashir. The new Constitution was endorsed by 96.7% of voters in a referendum held between 1 and 20 May. Under its terms, executive power would be vested in the Council of Ministers, which would be appointed by the President but responsible to the National Assembly. Legislative power was to be vested in the National Assembly. The Constitution would also guarantee freedoms of thought and religion, and the right to lawful political association.

A further round of IGAD-sponsored peace talks commenced in Nairobi in May 1998, but did not achieve any substantive progress. It was agreed that a further round of talks would be held three months later, in Addis Ababa. In July the SPLA announced a three-month cease-fire in the south, to allow the distribution of food aid; the Government later agreed to observe the cease-fire. The peace talks resumed in Addis Ababa in August, but collapsed without agreement after two days. At that time a northern opposition group, the Sudan Alliance Forces (SAF), launched an attack in Kassala, near the Eritrean border, reportedly taking control of the area.

New legislation approved in November 1998 provided for the establishment of an independent election commission and of a Constitutional Court, and for the legalization of political associations. Registration of political parties began in January 1999; all parties were required to have 100 founding members, none of whom was to have a criminal record. The first registration documents were issued in February. In late January, meanwhile, it was reported that the Government had introduced a new code requiring all women to wear Islamic dress regardless of their religion.

Clashes were reported between government and rebel forces in early January 1999, in which the rebels claimed to have captured seven soldiers and to have killed a further 48. In mid-January it was announced that the Government had agreed to extend the nominal cease-fire for a further three months, although bombing raids were reported in the southern town of Yei at the end of the month. In April three government officials and a Sudanese aid worker were killed by rebel forces; the four had been kidnapped with two Red Cross workers who had subsequently been released. Following this incident, the Government suspended all contacts with the rebels through IGAD. The rebels, however, claimed that the four had been killed in cross-fire during a rescue attempt by government forces, despite ongoing negotiations for their release, and that the Government was, in fact, seeking an alternative mediator to IGAD. Both the Government and the rebels extended the cease-fire for a further three months in April. At that time it was announced that voting for legislative assemblies was to be postponed in the southern states until November, as adverse weather conditions would impede the movement of citizens. Elections in the northern and central states were to be completed in June.

In May 1999 former President Nimeri returned to Sudan after 14 years in exile in Egypt. His return was welcomed by the Government, and he held meetings with both al-Bashir and at-Turabi, although opposition parties demanded his prosecution for crimes he had allegedly committed while President. In the same month at-Turabi held talks in Switzerland with Sadiq al-Mahdi, with the aim of initiating a process of reconciliation; a second round of talks, scheduled for July, was called off at the beginning of that month after al-Mahdi reportedly demanded the abrogation of the Constitution. At the end of May a meeting took place in Kampala, Uganda, between al-Mahdi, Garang and Mubarak al-Mahdi (of the NDA), to discuss several issues regarding their conflict with the Sudanese Government. In June 11 opposition politicians were charged with public order offences following a meeting at which they announced the formation of a new party, the Democratic Forces Front (DFF). All 11 were subsequently acquitted. In July the executive board of the NDA met in Cairo to discuss ways to solve the Sudanese crisis and the role Egypt could play in facilitating a reconciliation within the Government; further NDA talks were held in Libya at the end of the month. A further round of peace talks was held in Nairobi in July. Following a week of talks the Government and the SPLA reached an impasse and failed to renew the cease-fire. While the SPLA offered to extend a cease-fire in Bahr al-Ghazal province, the Government reportedly sought a cease-fire that applied to the whole of the southern region. They did, however, agree to establish a standing committee to conduct peace negotiations, and to appoint a special envoy to conduct indirect talks. It was

also agreed to appoint IGAD observers and to resume negotiations within 60 days.

In August 1999 the Government accepted a Libyan peace initiative, which envisaged a cease-fire, an end to media propaganda, direct talks through a conference of national dialogue and the establishment of a preparatory committee. The peace effort was to be co-ordinated jointly by Egypt and Libya. The Government did, however, express reservations over a number of conditions proposed by the NDA, which included the suspension of articles in the Constitution that restricted public liberty and the release of political prisoners. In September the SPLA stated that it supported the Egyptian-Libyan peace initiative 'in principle', although after a meeting with the US Secretary of State in October (see below) Garang discounted the Egyptian-Libyan initiative in favour of the IGAD-sponsored peace process. Both the Government and the rebels extended the cease-fire for a further three months in October.

In May 1999 a new oil export pipeline, which was to transport oil some 1,600 km from oilfields in southern Sudan to Port Sudan on the Red Sea, had been inaugurated. Despite heavy security, a number of bomb attacks on the pipeline were carried out by rebel fighters during 1999, and in September Sudan formally requested the extradition from Egypt of the deputy commander of the NDA in connection with one of these attacks. The pipeline and the oilfields were operated by Greater Nile Oil, a joint venture that was led by the Canadian firm, Talisman Energy. In early 2000 a Canadian government investigation found that Talisman was contributing to human rights violations in Sudan through its operations the country, although it was later announced that Canada would not take action against the company. In February the USA imposed a ban on trade with Greater Nile Oil.

At an NDA conference, held in Cairo in October 1999, the leaders of the alliance decided to examine ways of combining the peace initiative sponsored by IGAD and the Egyptian-Libyan initiative, in order to unite the parties of the NDA, a number of whom opposed the pursuit of two parallel initiatives. In November al-Bashir chaired the first meeting of the Peace and National Accord Committee. The Committee's work was divided into three areas: peace, working with the political parties and achieving accord with the northern opposition. Shortly afterwards it was reported that some 25 SSDF officers had been killed by the pro-Government United Army during talks held to investigate the prospects for cease-fire between the two groups. In the same month the NDA leader, al-Mirghani, held talks with the Egyptian Minister of Foreign Affairs to discuss the Egyptian-Libyan peace initiative. Al-Mirghani expressed his dissatisfaction at the lack of progress made towards establishing a conference of national dialogue and urged co-ordination with the IGAD peace initiative. Al-Bashir reiterated his offer of a general amnesty for rebel fighters at that time, and the Peace and National Accord Committee announced its decision to pardon all political prisoners, as well as to return confiscated property.

At the end of November 1999 Djibouti hosted a regional IGAD summit meeting, attended by Kenya, Ethiopia and Sudan, to discuss issues related to development and stability in the region. While in Djibouti, President al-Bashir met the UP leader, al-Mahdi, following which the Sudanese Government and the UP signed a declaration of principles, which envisaged a federal system of government and the holding of a referendum within four years to allow southerners to choose between the division of the country or unity with decentralized powers. The agreement was welcomed by many parties; however, the NDA responded by stating that it would escalate the war in the south, not end it. Garang later condemned and disavowed the Djibouti agreement.

During 1999 there were increasing reports of rivalry between al-Bashir and at-Turabi, particularly following the introduction of a bill in the National Assembly that sought to remove the President's power to appoint and dismiss state governors. Consideration of the draft legislation was repeatedly delayed, but a vote was scheduled to be held in mid-December in which the National Assembly was widely expected to approve it. However, on 12 December al-Bashir dissolved the National Assembly and imposed a three-month state of emergency, claiming that he had taken these measures in order to end the 'duality' in the administration. An emergency order suspended some articles of the Constitution, although provincial councils and governors were to continue working. At-Turabi accused al-Bashir of having carried out a *coup d'état*, although a legal challenge, mounted against the measures, was later rejected by the Constitutional

Court. At the end of the month the Cabinet and state governors tendered their resignations; they were to retain their posts pending a reshuffle.

In January 2000 the Libyan and Egyptian foreign ministers visited Sudan and discussed recent developments with al-Bashir; at the end of the meeting they stressed that the Egyptian-Libyan peace initiative would continue. IGAD peace efforts continued in that month with a visit by IGAD officials to southern Sudan, where they held talks with rebel leaders. IGAD-sponsored talks held in Nairobi in January made some progress on the issue of a referendum, and further talks were scheduled for February. The Government extended the cease-fire for a further three months, and the SPLA reportedly agreed to release some 1,000 captive government soldiers. At the end of January al-Bashir appointed a new Cabinet and state governors. In early February al-Bashir stated that the dissolution of the National Assembly was irrevocable and relocated several senior army officers in order to prevent a possible coup. An emergency development programme, formulated by the SSCC, for the southern states was approved by the Government in February. The Chairman of the SSCC, Dr Riek Mashar Teny-Dhurgon, resigned in February in protest at the Government's failure to implement the terms of the peace accords and at al-Bashir's disregard for the Constitution. It was also reported that he had resigned as Chairman of the United Democratic Salvation Front (UDSF, registered in 1999 as the political wing of the SSDF), although he later denied this. In mid-February 2000 Teny-Dhurgon claimed a major victory over government forces and announced the establishment of the Sudan People's Defence Force (SPDF) to replace the UDSF.

In March 2000 the Government extended the state of emergency until the end of the year, and approved a law allowing the formation of political parties (superseding the 1998 law), although this was rejected by the opposition, as it still incorporated provisions to suspend the activities of any party. In the same month the UP announced its decision to suspend its membership of the NDA during a meeting in Asmara. Relations between the UP and the NDA had deteriorated after December 1999, when al-Mahdi initiated independent talks with al-Bashir following the dissolution of the National Assembly. The NDA accused the UP of a lack of co-operation and of violating the NDA's principles, while the UP stated that it advocated co-operation with the Government. In April 2000 it was reported that a presidential election was planned for October; the ruling National Congress (NC) had nominated al-Bashir as its candidate in October 1999. However, most opposition parties, including the UP, indicated that they would not participate in any elections prior to the convening of a national conference to discuss the problems in Sudan.

A meeting between the leaders of Egypt, Sudan and Libya was held in Cairo in April 2000 to discuss the Egyptian-Libyan peace initiative. At that time al-Bashir revealed that discussions were under way for the return of al-Mahdi to Sudan. In May al-Bashir announced the suspension of the secretariat of the NC, including the activities of at-Turabi and his deputies, and affirmed his intention to restructure the party.

IGAD-sponsored peace talks, held in April 2000, ended inconclusively, and in May the SPLA suspended its participation in these peace negotiations in protest at the Government's alleged continued bombing of civilian targets. It reaffirmed its commitment to the unification of the IGAD process and the Egyptian-Libyan initiative, but did not indicate on what conditions it would resume talks. The next round of IGAD-sponsored talks had been scheduled to begin on 17 May. In June the SPLA announced it would rejoin the peace talks, and in that month al-Bashir declared a general amnesty for all opponents of the Government; however, it was rejected by a number of opposition groups, including the SPLA. Later that month at-Turabi announced the formation of a new political party, the Popular National Congress (PNC), whose registration was formally approved in August. In mid-July al-Bashir effected a cabinet reshuffle following the defection of two ministers to the PNC. Also in July it was announced that a preparatory meeting on national reconciliation was to be held in Khartoum in the following month. Invitations were extended to all political parties, both inside and outside Sudan. However, at-Turabi immediately stated that the PNC would boycott the conference.

In September 2000 al-Mahdi confirmed the withdrawal of the UP from the NDA alliance. A further round of IGAD-sponsored talks between the Government and the SPLA commenced in Nairobi on 23 September, but collapsed in early October over the issue of separating religion from state, with little progress having been made. Also in late September al-Bashir visited Asmara, where he met with an NDA delegation led by al-Mirghani. The two parties discussed possible political settlements to the situation in Sudan and agreed to meet for further direct talks, although no firm date for such discussions was set. In October it was reported that al-Bashir had dismissed Maj.-Gen. George Kongor Arop from the post of Second Vice-President. The following month al-Mahdi returned to Sudan from his four-year self-imposed exile in Eritrea and Egypt, but announced that he would not participate in the forthcoming elections.

Presidential and legislative elections were held concurrently over a 10-day period in mid-December 2000, although they were boycotted by the main opposition parties. As expected, al-Bashir was re-elected President, with 86.5% of the votes cast, comfortably defeating his nearest rival, former President Nimeri, who obtained 9.6% of the vote. Voting did not take place in three southern states. The NC secured 355 seats in the new 360-member National Assembly; the remaining five seats were won by small opposition parties. On 3 January 2001 al-Bashir extended the state of emergency for a further year. However, during that month heavy fighting was reported in Upper Nile state between government troops and rebel forces.

On 21 February 2001 at-Turabi was arrested at his home in Khartoum after it was announced that the PNC and the SPLA had signed a memorandum of understanding in Switzerland, which urged the Sudanese people to participate in 'peaceful popular resistance' against the al-Bashir regime. Over the following days some 30 associates of at-Turabi were also taken into police custody, and in early March at-Turabi and several other members of the PNC's leadership council were reported to have been charged with criminal conspiracy, undermining the constitutional order, waging war on the state and calling for violent opposition to public authority. (In late May at-Turabi was released from prison and placed under house arrest.) Meanwhile, the day after at-Turabi's arrest, al-Bashir implemented a major reorganization of the Cabinet and replaced many of the country's state governors. Several new ministries were created, and, although the new, 32-member Cabinet was dominated by NC members, al-Bashir incorporated four members of two minor opposition parties into the Government. Two members of the UDSF retained their positions in the Cabinet, but the UP, despite earlier indications to the contrary, refused to participate in the new administration and officially stated that it would not accept ministerial posts before the holding of free and fair elections in the south of the country and the resolution of the armed conflict in that region. Also in February more than 2,600 child soldiers were handed over to UN aid agencies by southern rebel groups. It was estimated that a further 7,500 children were still serving as soldiers in the various rebel groups operating in the south of the country.

In early May 2001 six Sudanese opposition members, including the Secretary-General of the NDA, Joseph Okela, who had met with a US embassy official in December 2000 (see below) were rearrested and charged with 'waging war against the state' and espionage. They had initially been detained in December, and placed on trial in mid-March 2001, but were released on bail in late April. In late May the Government announced the suspension of air strikes against southern rebel groups, but stated that it reserved the right to protect individuals and lines of supply and to counter any rebel offensives. The cessation proved short-lived, as heavy fighting swiftly broke out, and in early June an SPLA offensive resulted in the capture of the strategically important town of Raga in the Bahr al-Ghazal province. Just days later the Government officially revoked the suspension of air strikes, although it stated that it would attempt to avoid the bombing of densely populated areas. Despite these clashes, in early June al-Bashir and Garang attended an IGAD-sponsored meeting in Nairobi; notably, it was the first time that they had both been present at the same talks since 1997. However, there was no face-to-face meeting between the two, and the negotiations concluded without producing a cease-fire.

During early 2001 several foreign human rights groups and non-governmental organizations vehemently criticized international petroleum companies involved in petroleum exploration and production in Sudan, as well as numerous firms responsible for supplying equipment to those companies, maintaining that they were indirectly aiding the Government with its programme of removing civilians from areas surrounding oilfields, and that government revenue from the sale of petroleum was being channelled into the funding of war efforts against the rebel movement in the south. It was also alleged that several airstrips close to the oilfields, which had been upgraded by foreign petroleum companies, were being used by government forces to launch bombing campaigns against civilian populations in the south. In mid-June Garang declared that he considered petroleum companies operating in Sudan to be legitimate targets, describing them as government mercenaries. Earlier that month the SPLA claimed to have killed 244 government troops after ambushing a convoy that was escorting equipment near oilfields.

In early July 2001 it was reported that the Sudanese Government and the NDA had both provisionally accepted a renewed Libyan-Egyptian peace initiative, which provided for an immediate cease-fire, the establishment of a transitional government and a number of constitutional reforms. Later that month the leadership council of the NC approved the Libyan-Egyptian plan. However, al-Bashir maintained that he would not support any proposals that involved the separation of state and religion or the partition of the country, thus endangering the success of the initiative, as the NDA concurrently reiterated its demand for the right of the southern states to be granted self-determination. In mid-August it was reported that the Sudanese Government had acquired a number of surface-to-surface missiles, which it was using in the conflict with the rebels in the south. Earlier that month the SPLA claimed that it had attacked a petroleum-producing facility at Heglig, owned by Talisman, and inflicted heavy casualties. Representatives of the petroleum company denied that any damage to facilities had occurred, although they did confirm that production had been temporarily suspended. Fierce fighting between government forces and rebels continued during September–October; some 170 government fatalities were reported in late September. In the following month, however, government troops recaptured Raga from the SPLA.

Meanwhile, in late September 2001 the UN Security Council voted to remove the sanctions imposed on Sudan in 1996 (see above) and praised the country's recent efforts to combat terrorism. Notably, the USA, which had previously used its vote to veto the lifting of sanctions, abstained, enabling the motion to be carried. In mid-December the state of emergency was again extended for a further 12 months. In January 2002 Teny-Dhurgon and Garang announced the merger of the SPDF and the SPLA. Teny-Dhurgon had defected from the SPLM/SPLA in 1991 and had signed a peace accord with the Government in 1997 (as leader of the SSDF); however, this agreement had collapsed in early 2001.

In mid-January 2002 talks sponsored jointly by the USA and Switzerland commenced in Buergenstock, Switzerland. Following six days of intensive discussions, the Sudanese Government and the SPLA agreed to observe a six-month cease-fire, to be supervised by a joint military commission, in the central Nuba region in order to facilitate the delivery of vital aid supplies to the area. However, the following month the USA announced that it had suspended discussions with the Sudanese Government, after two separate incidents earlier that month in which Sudanese air force planes had bombed civilians collecting food supplies in the Bahr al-Ghazal province. In the second incident at least 24 civilians were killed when a UN World Food Programme (WFP) relief centre came under fire. Although the Government insisted that the earlier incident, which resulted in the deaths of two children, was accidental, the US Department of State insisted that discussions would not recommence until it had received a full explanation for the attacks from the Sudanese Government. It was anticipated that talks would resume, however, following the issuing of an apology for the attacks by the Sudanese Minister of External Relations and the conclusion, in mid-March, of a US-brokered agreement between the SPLA and the Sudanese Government, which aimed to guarantee the protection of civilians from military attacks; the agreement was to be monitored by two teams of international observers. In early July the cease-fire was extended for a further six months, and in late December it was agreed that it would continue until July 2003.

In May 2002 the Minister of Finance, Adb ar-Rahim Muhammad Hamdi, reportedly resigned owing to ill health. There was, however, speculation that he had been dismissed by al-Bashir following the implementation of several unpopular economic measures. Hamdi was subsequently replaced by Muhammad al-Hasan az-Zubayr. In June three members of the NC, including the Minister of Transport, Dr Lam Akol, resigned

from the party in protest at the increasing dominance of al-Bashir. In mid-August al-Bashir renewed the detention order that had been placed on at-Turabi the previous year for a further 12 months. In September at-Turabi was removed from house arrest and transferred to prison. In the previous month al-Bashir had effected a minor reorganization of the Council of Ministers, and in September al-Bashir dismissed Akol from his ministerial post. Akol was one of a number of former NC members who had, earlier that month, established a new political party, the Justice Party. In November al-Bashir carried out a further reshuffle of the Council of Ministers and created two new ministries. Furthermore, he appointed a dissident member of the DUP to replace Akol. In the following month the state of emergency was once again extended for a further 12 months.

Meanwhile, in mid-June 2002 a new round of IGAD-sponsored peace talks between the Government and the SPLA opened in Machakos, Kenya. Despite the ongoing discussions, fighting between the two sides continued, and there were numerous reports of heavy civilian casualties following bombing raids on southern towns by government forces. Nevertheless, a major breakthrough in the conflict was achieved on 20 July, when delegations from the SPLA and the Government signed an accord, known as the Machakos Protocol, which provided for a six-year period of autonomy for the south, to be followed by an internationally monitored referendum on self-determination. The Protocol also stated that Sudan's Constitution would be rewritten to ensure that *Shari'a* law would not be applied to non-Muslim southerners. Government and SPLA delegations reconvened in Machakos in mid-August for talks. However, further outbreaks of fighting between the two sides were reported, and in early September, in response to the SPLA's capture of the town of Torit, the Government announced that it had suspended talks with the SPLA and launched an offensive to try and reclaim the town. Despite agreeing to cease hostilities and resume peace talks, government forces recaptured Torit in early October. Later that month the two sides reconvened in Machakos and signed a cease-fire agreement for the duration of the ongoing discussions. Both sides subsequently accused each other of breaking the cease-fire, and it was reported that some 300 government troops had been killed by rebel forces just hours after the signing of the accord. Negotiations between the Government and the SPLA were halted in mid-November, after no agreement could be reached on the number of government and civil service posts to be allocated to southerners and the distribution of petroleum revenues. The two sides did, however, agree to extend the cease-fire until the end of March 2003. Talks resumed in Nairobi in mid-January 2003, and in mid-April, following a meeting between Garang and al-Bashir, it was announced that the two sides expected to reach a final peace agreement by June.

In addition to civil war and economic crisis, Sudan has experienced drought and famine, and the problem has been compounded by a very large number of refugees in the southern provinces, mainly from Ethiopia and Chad. International relief operations to provide food aid, in years of drought and failed harvests, have frequently been obstructed by the civil war and by the Government's refusal to recognize the need for them. Even when successful, they have done little to solve the problems of under investment in, and mismanagement of, Sudanese agriculture, and the economic impoverishment that has resulted from drought and famine.

In December 2001, according to the office of the UN High Commissioner for Refugees (UNHCR), there were some 489,500 Sudanese refugees abroad, of whom 176,800 were in Uganda, 80,900 in Ethiopia, 75,000 in the Democratic Republic of the Congo (DRC, formerly Zaire), 69,800 in Kenya, 36,300 in the Central African Republic, 16,400 in the USA and 12,600 in Chad. Sudan was also host to more than 350,000 refugees at that time, of whom 324,500 were originally from Eritrea and 16,100 were from Ethiopia. During 1997 there had been large-scale refugee repatriation, particularly to Ethiopia and the DRC, and during 1998 a further 37,000 refugees arrived in Sudan, including 10,300 from Kenya and 9,500 from Uganda. During 2000 more than 94,000 Eritrean refugees fleeing the border war with Ethiopia entered Sudanese territory; by the end of that year, however, some 68,000 had been repatriated. Furthermore, a report published by the US Committee for Refugees in mid-2001 stated that at the end of 2000 Sudan possessed the largest internally displaced population in the world, officially estimated at 4m. people. In December 2002 the refugee status of Eritreans living in Sudan expired, and in the following month

UNHCR convoys, which would return Eritreans to their country, recommenced. It was reported that since May 2001 more than 100,000 Eritreans had been repatriated.

In June 1997 the Government banned relief flights to the south—an act that caused concern to aid agencies; UNICEF stated that thousands of children were at risk and announced that there had been a rise in the infant mortality rate in that area. By April 1998 many aid agencies were warning of widespread famine in the south if immediate action was not taken. The Government initially refused to act, as it claimed that aid would fall into rebel hands. However, in May, following UN requests, the Government agreed to reopen all relief corridors in the worst affected areas and to allow the aid agencies to operate a total of 22 food distribution sites. It also agreed to increase the frequency of relief flights and to provide some food aid from that year's surplus in the north; it later criticized what it perceived as the tardy international response to UN requests for aid. Relief operations continued throughout mid-1998. In October, however, the Government banned aid agency flights in the country. In November, following two days of negotiations in Rome, Italy, the Government and the rebels signed an agreement to guarantee the safety of aid workers and to facilitate access to the worst affected areas, despite the continuing fighting. In March 1999 further warnings were issued of impending famine. Hostilities again escalated in the south in August 2000, and the Sudanese Government was accused of deliberately bombing relief facilities in that region. In response, the UN announced the suspension of all aid flights under the Operation Lifeline Sudan programme. However, later that month, following personal assurances from al-Bashir that measures were being taken to ensure the safety of all humanitarian workers in the region, the UN agreed to resume relief flights. In February 2001 the WFP launched an appeal for US $135m. of food aid, required to feed the estimated 2.9m. people in Sudan under threat of starvation as a result of the ongoing civil war and severe drought. Appeals for significant humanitarian assistance were repeated in May, as conditions in Sudan reached critical levels. However, in that month the International Committee of the Red Cross temporarily suspended all aid deliveries, after the co-pilot of one of its planes was killed while flying over southern Sudan. Aid flights were subsequently resumed later that month.

Following an unsuccessful coup attempt in 1976, Sudan severed diplomatic relations with Libya and established a mutual defence pact with Egypt. Diplomatic links between Sudan and Libya were restored in 1978, but relations became strained in 1981, during Libya's occupation of Chad, and President Nimeri frequently accused Libya of supporting plots against him. After the 1985 coup, Libya was the first country to recognize the new regime, and relations between the two countries improved significantly. Although Libya's military involvement in Chad declined, some Libyan forces remained in north-western Sudan, despite repeated Sudanese demands for their withdrawal. The regime that took power in Sudan in 1985 adopted a foreign policy of non-alignment, in contrast to Nimeri's strongly pro-Western attitude, and sought improved relations with Ethiopia and the USSR, to the concern of Sudan's former allies, Egypt and the USA. In 1990, after Lt-Gen. al-Bashir had visited Col Qaddafi, the Libyan leader, in Tripoli, Sudan and Libya signed a 'declaration of integration' that envisaged the complete union of the two countries within four years. In 1995 Sudan, Libya and Chad were reported to be discussing integration after eventual legislative elections in Chad. Tension subsequently arose between Libya and Sudan as a result of Libya's expulsion of Sudanese expatriate workers, but did not, apparently, detract from the two countries' commitment to integration, reiterated in 1996.

Relations with Ethiopia have fluctuated since 1987, but, until late 1995, were mostly characterized by harmony and co-operation. In September 1995, however, Ethiopia accused Sudan of harbouring terrorists implicated in the attempted assassination of President Mubarak in June and, in response, announced the closure of some Sudanese diplomatic facilities in the country and of non-governmental organizations connected with Sudan. In April 1996 Sudan claimed that Ethiopian government forces had collaborated with the SPLA in attacks on two towns in southeastern Sudan, while in June Ethiopia accused Sudan of attempting to destabilize the region. In January 1997 relations deteriorated further when, following alleged attacks on Sudan, President al-Bashir declared a *jihad* (holy war) against Ethiopian aggression and ordered a general mobilization. Ethiopia, however, denied any involvement in the attacks. An improvement in relations was reported during 1998, although in December the Ethiopian Minister of Foreign Affairs stated that relations between the two countries would not improve until Sudan handed over those responsible for the attempted assassination of the Egyptian President. One of the suspects was extradited in 1999 (see below), and in November, on his return from a visit to Ethiopia, al-Bashir stated that relations with that country were fully normalized. The common border was reopened in early 2000, and in March the Sudanese and Ethiopian Governments signed a number of agreements, which provided for increased co-operation in political, cultural, commercial and transport sectors. Further agreements regarding border security were signed in the following month. Relations between the two countries were temporarily strained in late April 2001 after an internal Ethiopian flight was hijacked and diverted to Khartoum. Although the incident was brought to a swift conclusion, and all passengers on board the aircraft were released unharmed, the Sudanese authorities refused Ethiopia's request for the hijackers to be extradited to Ethiopia for trial. The following month it was announced that the five were to be tried in Sudan on charges of terrorism and could face the death penalty if found guilty.

Sudan's relations with Eritrea deteriorated after 1991, and in December 1994 Eritrea severed diplomatic relations with Sudan. Eritrea has sponsored meetings of the principal groups opposed to the Sudanese regime, which it accuses of lending support to the insurgent Eritrean Islamic Jihad. In December 1994 Eritrea sponsored a meeting between various Sudanese opposition groups, which resulted in a 'Declaration of Political Agreement'. The signatories included the SPLA, the UP, the DUP and the SAF. In January 1995 Sudan demanded that Eritrea withdraw from the IGADD peace committee (see above), which also included Ethiopia, Kenya, and Uganda. A further deterioration in relations occurred after a conference of the Sudanese opposition, organized by the NDA, was held in Asmara in June (see above). In July 1996 Sudanese government forces claimed that attacks had been launched against them from within Eritrea. In October the National Assembly endorsed a report by the Sudanese Security and National Defence Committee, which recommended—with reference to Eritrea—the strengthening of defence facilities and a firm response to military provocation. Among the conclusions reached at an NDA conference held in Asmara that month was that the al-Bashir regime was responsible for the sanctions imposed on the country by the UN. Attention was also drawn to the threat that Iranian support for the al-Bashir regime allegedly posed to regional stability. In April 1997 Sudan protested to the UN over Eritrean aggression on its territory. In June Sudan denied Eritrean accusations that the Sudanese Government had masterminded a plot to assassinate the Eritrean President. At the end of the month Sudan closed the border with Eritrea and mobilized its forces to maximum levels for fear of a military strike against Sudan. The border was again closed in February 1998 in order to prevent Eritrean troops entering the country following reported border clashes between the two countries. Further attacks were reported in the border area by both Eritrea and Sudan throughout 1998. Following talks held in November 1998, in Qatar, the two sides signed an agreement for the open discussion of bilateral issues. Qatar again acted as mediator at a further meeting, held in Doha, Qatar, in May 1999. This meeting resulted in an accord, signed by the Presidents of Sudan and Eritrea, in which they agreed to restore diplomatic relations, to refrain from hostile propaganda and to establish joint committees, both to implement the terms of the accord and to study any further issues that might arise between the two countries. However, tensions between the two countries remained, and in June Sudan accused Eritrea of violating the Doha agreement, following an NDA conference in Asmara. At that time the two countries established joint committees in accordance with the terms of the Doha agreement. In August it was reported that Eritrea had ordered the Sudanese opposition to cease political activity and to leave the Sudanese embassy, which it had occupied since December 1994. In October 1999 the Sudanese Minister of External Relations stated that relations with Eritrea would not improve until Eritrea stopped aiding the Sudanese opposition, and in November Eritrea denied massing troops near the Sudanese border. A further agreement was signed in Asmara in January 2000, providing for the immediate reopening of the two countries' borders and embassies and the resumption of flights between their airports. In February the Presidents of Eritrea and Sudan held talks in Khartoum, and it was agreed to issue passports to residents in the border area. Furthermore, they declared that they would not allow opposition groups located in their respective countries to launch cross-border raids. However, relations between the two countries deteriorated in July, when the Sudanese Government accused Eritrea of assisting the NDA with a planned offensive in eastern Sudan. In October President Afewerki visited Khartoum, where he held talks with al-Bashir, during which both sides expressed their desire for a fresh beginning to their bilateral relations and agreed to take measures to settle differences between the two countries in a peaceful manner. In July 2001 Eritrea and Sudan signed an agreement on border security, which aimed to eradicate smuggling and illegal infiltration, as well as ensure the safe passage of people and goods. Relations between the two countries deteriorated again in mid-2002, and in October the Sudanese authorities closed the common border, claiming that Eritrea had been involved in an NDA offensive in eastern Sudan.

Sudan and Uganda have accused each other of supporting groups opposed to their respective regimes, and in 1995 Uganda broke off diplomatic relations with Sudan. A further deterioration in relations in December brought the two countries to the brink of open war. In 1996, following mediation by President Rafsanjani of Iran, Sudan and Uganda agreed to restore diplomatic relations, provided that each side undertook to cease its support for rebel factions operating from the other's territory, and to participate in an international committee to monitor the agreement. In February 1997, in response to protests about its deployment of troops on the Sudan–Uganda border, Uganda denied accusations that it intended to invade Sudan. In late April Sudan denied allegations that its forces had invaded northern Uganda and, at the end of the month Dr Riek Mashar Teny-Dhurgon, the Chairman of the SSCC, visited Uganda to discuss relations between the two countries prior to the forthcoming IGAD summit meeting. Talks held in Kenya in May achieved little progress in easing tension, and the planned IGAD summit meeting was later cancelled, owing to a concurrent meeting of leaders of the Organization of African Unity (OAU, now the African Union (see p. 130). In August President Mandela of South Africa hosted talks between the two countries. Mandela later said that the talks had been successful, although he did not reveal what progress had been made. At the end of the year there were reports of Ugandan attacks in the border area; Uganda, however, denied the reports and said that the attacks had been made by the SPLA and had been wrongly attributed to Uganda. Relations with Uganda improved during 1999, and in December, following a meeting in Nairobi, mediated by former US President Jimmy Carter, the two countries signed an accord in which they agreed to restore diplomatic relations and to end support to each other's rebel groups; shortly afterwards it was announced that eight leaders of the Lord's Resistance Army (LRA) were to be relocated from Sudan to a country of their choice in accordance with the agreement. In February 2000, however, Uganda expressed its dissatisfaction with Sudan's implementation of the accord and called for Sudan to disarm the LRA and to disband all LRA camps within Sudan. Sudan reaffirmed its commitment to the agreement. In October it was agreed that Egyptian and Libyan observers would be deployed on the Uganda–Sudan border to prevent any further violations by the SPLA and the LRA. In mid-May 2001 President al-Bashir attended the inauguration of the Ugandan President, Yoweri Museveni, in Kampala, and in the following month the two countries exchanged diplomats. In August the Ugandan embassy in Khartoum reopened, and a chargé d'affaires was appointed. In March 2002 the two countries signed an agreement whereby Sudan temporarily authorized Ugandan troops to pursue LRA rebels within Sudan, and later that month the Ugandan Government announced that its troops had captured all four main bases in Sudan belonging to the LRA. In late November 2002 the Sudanese authorities agreed to extend permission for Ugandan troops to remain on its territory for as long as Uganda deemed necessary. Meanwhile, the two countries upgraded relations to ambassadorial level.

President Nimeri was one of very few Arab leaders to support President Sadat of Egypt's initiative for peace with Israel in 1978. Sudan's close relations with Egypt were consolidated in 1982, when a 'charter of integration' was signed. The first session of the joint 'Nile Valley Parliament', created by the charter, was convened in 1983 with 60 Sudanese and 60 Egyptian members. After the 1985 coup, the leaders of the two countries reaffirmed links between Khartoum and Cairo, despite the change of government in Sudan. Relations with Egypt deteriorated in 1991, as a result of the Sudanese Government's support for Iraq during the Gulf crisis. Egypt also expressed concern at the perceived growth of Islamic 'fundamentalism' in Sudan. The two countries are involved in a dispute over the Halaib border area, and in early 1992 relations deteriorated sharply following the announcement that Sudan had awarded a Canadian company a concession to explore for petroleum there. Relations deteriorated further, as Egypt repeatedly accused Sudan of supporting illegal Islamic fundamentalist groups in Egypt, while Sudan alleged that Egypt was supporting the SPLA. In August the Sudanese Government sought international arbitration on the Halaib issue, claiming that Egypt had been settling families in the area in an effort to bring it under Egyptian control. A series of bilateral meetings held during the second half of 1992 failed to resolve the issue, and in January 1993 Sudan complained to the UN Security Council that Egyptian troops had infringed Sudan's territorial integrity. In March Egypt announced the construction of a new road link to Halaib. Sudan retaliated by appropriating the Khartoum campus of Cairo University. In June Sudan announced that it was closing two Egyptian consulates in Sudan and two of its own consulates in Egypt. A meeting between Lt-Gen. al-Bashir and President Mubarak of Egypt, during a summit session of the OAU at the end of June appeared, however, to ease tensions between the two countries, and was followed by a meeting of their respective Ministers of Foreign Affairs at the end of July. In May 1994 Sudan accused Egypt of establishing military posts on Sudanese territory, and at the end of the month the Sudanese Ministry of Foreign Affairs announced that Sudan wished to refer its dispute with Egypt to the International Court of Justice (ICJ) in The Hague, Netherlands, for arbitration. In January 1995 Egypt rejected a request by Sudan to refer the dispute over the Halaib border area to a meeting of the OAU's council of Ministers of Foreign Affairs in Addis Ababa. On 26 June relations suffered a further, serious setback after the attempted assassination of President Mubarak of Egypt on his arrival in Addis Ababa to attend the annual conference of the OAU. The Egyptian Government immediately accused Sudan of complicity in the attack, and the OAU made the same allegation in September. In January 1996 the UN Security Council condemned Sudan's role in the attempted assassination and adopted a resolution (No. 1044) seeking the extradition of three individuals implicated in the attack. Relations between Sudan and Egypt appeared to improve in 1997; in December talks were held between President al-Bashir and senior Egyptian officials, and in January 1998 it was agreed that a joint chamber of commerce would be established. In May a joint Sudanese-Egyptian technical committee met in Khartoum to finalize details for the return of several institutions in Sudan to Egyptian control. Both sides were agreed that the institutions, such as the appropriated University of Cairo in Khartoum, should be returned, although differences remained over the time period for this operation. The Sudanese Minister for Foreign Trade made a three-day visit to Egypt in April 1998, during which he praised the *rapprochement* between the two countries, although in August the Sudanese Government stated that it found the Egyptian decision to host an NDA conference regrettable. During the conference meetings were held with Egyptian officials including President Mubarak; Egypt had requested the meetings as it feared that the ongoing civil war in the Sudan could affect control of the Nile, its source of water. In October Sudan and Egypt agreed on a plan to hasten the normalization of relations, and a further meeting was held in Cairo in January 1999 to discuss bilateral relations. Following further meetings, in June it was announced that diplomatic relations between the two countries were to be upgraded. Relations improved further in July when it was announced that Sudan had extradited one of the three suspects implicated in the attempted assassination of Mubarak. In December the two countries agreed to normalize their relations and to resolve their dispute over the Halaib issue amicably. In March 2000 it was announced that the University of Cairo in Khartoum was to be reopened, and later that month Egypt appointed an ambassador to Sudan for the first time since the assassination attempt on Mubarak. The two countries also agreed to establish an Egyptian-Sudanese joint committee. In September the Sudanese and Egyptian ministers responsible for foreign affairs held the first session of the Egyptian-Sudanese Commission for 10 years, at which the two countries expressed their commitment to further bilateral economic development.

The USA has been one of the severest critics of the present Sudanese Government, frequently expressing concern about Sudan's links with Iran. Allegations of Sudanese involvement in terrorism resulted in the detention in the USA, in 1993, of five Sudanese residents suspected of plotting to blow up buildings and road tunnels in New York, and to assassinate President Mubarak of Egypt on a visit to the USA; the USA subsequently added Sudan to its list of countries accused of sponsoring terrorism. The release by the Sudanese to the French authorities, in August 1994, of the Venezuelan-born terrorist, Illich Ramirez Sanchez ('Carlos'), was regarded by many observers as an attempt by the Government to improve its international standing. In August 1997 the USA imposed economic sanctions against Sudan, owing to its alleged continued support for terrorism. The USA reiterated its accusations of Sudanese involvement in terrorism following bomb explosions in its embassies in Kenya and Tanzania in August 1998; the bombings were believed to have been orchestrated by Osama bin Laden, a Saudi-born Islamist activist exiled in Afghanistan. In late August the USA launched a missile attack on what it claimed was a chemical weapons factory in Khartoum in which bin Laden was believed to hold a financial interest. Immediately after the attack, however, the Sudanese Government denied these claims and stated that it was, in fact, a private pharmaceuticals plant. Sudan recalled its ambassador to the USA and refused permission for US aircraft to use its airspace; its requests for a UN inquiry into the attack were unanimously refused by the Security Council, despite backing from the League of Arab States (see p. 260) and the Organization of the Islamic Conference (see p. 295). By February 1999 it had become evident that the US intelligence on which the attack had been based was fundamentally flawed and that bin Laden had had links only with the previous owner. In May Sudan requested compensation for the damage caused by the bomb attack, and in July 2000 the proprietor of the factory announced his intention to sue the US Government for damages. Meanwhile, in April 1999 the USA had announced its decision to ease sanctions on the export of food and medicine to Sudan, and at the end of May Sudan fulfilled one of the conditions set by the USA for a review of the sanctions regime by signing a treaty banning chemical weapons. In September the USA appointed a special envoy to Sudan, whose role was to focus international attention on Sudan's human rights record, highlight the consequences of the civil war and strengthen the IGAD-sponsored peace process. Sudan described the appointment as an 'arrogant decision'. The US Secretary of State, Madeleine Albright, visited Sudan during a tour of Africa in October and held meetings with John Garang, during which she urged him to reinvigorate the IGAD-sponsored peace process and discouraged the rival Egyptian-Libyan initiative. In November, however, the USA enacted controversial legislation allowing food aid to be delivered directly to the Sudanese rebels. An improvement in relations was evident in March 2000 following a visit to Sudan by a US diplomat to discuss the possibility of reopening the US embassy in Khartoum. In mid-April the embassy was duly reopened and a chargé d'affaires appointed. However, relations once again deteriorated in December, when Sudan lodged an official complaint with the UN after the US Assistant Secretary of State, Susan Rice, visited rebel-held areas of southern Sudan in November, without the permission of the Sudanese Government. Later in December a US diplomat was declared *persona non grata* by the Sudanese authorities and given 72 hours to leave the country after he held a meeting with members of the NDA. The Sudanese Minister of External Relations alleged that the incident had posed a threat to the security and stability of the country. Following the election of a new US Administration, under the leadership of President George W. Bush, in January 2001, there was some uncertainty regarding the USA's policy towards Sudan. In early May Bush appointed Andrew Natsios, administrator of the US Agency for International Development, as special humanitarian co-ordinator for Sudan, charged with monitoring the delivery of aid supplies and ensuring they reached their intended destinations. In July the Bush administration outlined its three main policy objectives for Sudan: to deal with the humanitarian crisis, to end Sudan's role as a sanctuary for terrorism, and to promote a just peace by bringing the warring parties together. In September Bush appointed a former senator, John Danforth, as his special envoy to Sudan.

Following the September 2001 suicide attacks on New York and Washington, DC, Sudan agreed to assist the USA with its search for terrorist suspects, and by late September the Suda-

nese authorities had arrested some 30 individuals resident in Sudan who were suspected of having links to bin Laden and the al-Qa'ida (Base) organization, which the USA held responsible for the attacks. Nevertheless, US sanctions remained in place, and Sudan continued to be listed by the US Department of State as a sponsor of terrorism. Furthermore, two Sudanese banks (al-Shamal Islamic Bank and Tadamon Islamic bank) were among numerous institutions under US investigation as possible sources of financial support for bin Laden. Sudan expressed criticism of the US-led military strikes on Afghanistan, which commenced in November, and later that month the USA extended sanctions until November 2002. In February 2002 a suspected senior member of al-Qa'ida, who had been indicted for his alleged involvement in the bombing of the US embassies in Kenya and Tanzania and was also believed to have played a significant role in the September attacks on the USA, was arrested in Sudan. In October Bush approved legislation that allowed the USA to impose further sanctions, including the suspension of multilateral loans, on the Sudanese Government, should it fail to negotiate in good faith with the southern rebels or interfere with humanitarian efforts in the south of the country. The USA also froze the financial assets of 12 Sudanese companies, including the National Broadcasting Corporation. Under the Sudan Peace Act, conditions in Sudan would be evaluated every six months, although the law also made provision for the expenditure of US $100m. a year by the USA until 2005 in areas of Sudan not under the Sudanese Government's control.

Sudan's relations with the United Kingdom deteriorated in May 1998, following a statement made by the British Secretary of State for International Development in which she accused Sudan of using food aid as a weapon in Bahr al-Ghazal. The Sudanese Government vehemently denied this and accused the United Kingdom of having a negative attitude towards forthcoming peace negotiations. In August, following British support for the US bombing of Sudan (see above), Sudan announced that it would recall its ambassador to the United Kingdom and asked the British ambassador to leave. Negotiations were held in an attempt to avert this, but the British envoy was withdrawn in September. Relations improved during 1999, and in September the two countries agreed to appoint ambassadors; both appointments were made by the end of April 2000.

Government

In October 1993 the Revolutionary Command Council for National Salvation, which had assumed power after the military coup of 30 June 1989, was dissolved after appointing Lt-Gen. al-Bashir as President and head of a new civilian Government. In April 1998 a new Constitution was endorsed by the National Assembly, and was presented to President al-Bashir. The document was endorsed by 96.7% of voters in a national referendum held in May. Under its terms, executive power is vested in the Council of Ministers, which is appointed by the President, but is responsible to the National Assembly. Legislative power is vested in the National Assembly. The 360-member National Assembly serves a term of four years. Of its 360 members, 270 are directly elected in single seat constituencies, 35 members represent women, 26 represent university graduates and 29 represent trade unions.

In February 1994 Sudan was redivided into 26 states (rather than the nine that had formed the basis of administration since 1991). A governor assumed responsibility for each state, assisted by five—in the case of the southern states six—state ministers.

Defence

In August 2002 the armed forces comprised: army an estimated 112,500, navy an estimated 1,500, air force 3,000. A paramilitary Popular Defence Force included 7,000 active members and 85,000 reserves. Defence expenditure in 2001 was an estimated US $600m. Sudan has a defence agreement with Egypt and has received military aid from the USA. The People's Republic of China, Iran and Iraq all provide a number of military advisers. Military service is compulsory for males aged 18–30 years and lasts for up to 36 months.

Economic Affairs

In 2001, according to estimates by the World Bank, Sudan's gross national income (GNI), measured at average 1999–2001 prices, was US $10,346m., equivalent to $330 per head (or $1,610 on an international purchasing-power parity basis). During 1990–2001, it was estimated, the population increased at an average annual rate of 2.2%, while gross domestic product (GDP) per head increased, in real terms, by an average of 7.5% per year. Overall GDP increased, in real terms, at an average annual rate of 7.5% in 1990–2001; growth in 2001 was 6.0%.

Agriculture (including forestry and fishing) contributed 37.2% of GDP in 2000, and about 60.2% of the labour force were employed in the sector in 2001. The principal cash crop is sesame seed (including oilcake), which accounted for 6.2% of total export earnings in 2001. The principal subsistence crops are sorghum and wheat. The GDP of the agricultural sector increased by an average of 15.3% per year in 1990–98. Agricultural GDP increased by 3.2% in 1999 and by 2.1% in 2000.

Industry (including mining, manufacturing, construction and power) contributed 18.1% of GDP in 2000, and employed 7.9% of the labour force in 1983. In 1990–97 industrial GDP increased at an average annual rate of 4.7%. Industrial GDP increased by an estimated 4.1% in 1998 and by an estimated 8.5% in 1999.

Mining accounted for only 0.1% of employment in 1983 and an estimated 0.9% of GDP in 1999. Sudan has reserves of petroleum (estimated at 250m.–300m. barrels), chromite, gypsum, gold, iron ore and wollastonite. Sudan began to develop its petroleum reserves in the mid-1990s, and production reached about 220,000 barrels per day in 2001, when crude petroleum accounted for 74.7% of total export earnings; production was expected to double in 2001–04. The GDP of the mining sector increased by about 600% in 1995/96, when gold output rose sharply.

Manufacturing contributed 8.8% of GDP in 2000 and 12.1% in 2001. The most important branch of the sector is food-processing, especially sugar-refining, while the textile industry, cement production and petroleum-refining are also significant. Some 4.6% of the labour force were employed in manufacturing in 1983. In 1990–97 manufacturing GDP increased at an average annual rate of 1.0%. Manufacturing GDP increased by 4.7% in 1999 and by 9.8% in 2000.

Energy is derived from hydroelectric power (which contributed 53.1% of total output in 1999) and petroleum (46.9%). Sudan is a net exporter of fuels, with imports of petroleum comprising an estimated 13.0% of the total value of imports in 1999.

Services contributed 44.7% of GDP in 2000, and employed 18.8% of the labour force in 1983. During 1990–97 the GDP of the services sector increased at an average annual rate of 3.0%. In 1998 the GDP of the services sector was estimated to have stagnated; however, it rose by an estimated 5.0% in 1999.

In 2001 Sudan recorded a visible trade surplus of US $303.6m., but there was a deficit of $618.3m. on the current account of the balance of payments. In 2001 the principal sources of imports were Saudi Arabia (accounting for 12.5% of the total), the People's Republic of China, the United Kingdom, the United Arab Emirates and Germany. In that year the principal markets for Sudanese exports were the People's Republic of China (taking 59.0%) and Japan. The principal exports in 2001 were crude petroleum and sesame seed. The principal imports in 1999 were machinery and equipment, foodstuffs, crude materials (mainly petroleum), basic manufactures, transport equipment and chemicals.

In 1999 Sudan recorded an overall budget deficit of 24,178m. Sudanese dinars, equivalent to 1.0% of GDP. At the end of 2000 Sudan's total external debt was US $15,741m., of which $8,647m. was long-term public debt. In that year the cost of debt-servicing was equivalent to 3.2% of the total value of exports of goods and services. In 1992–2000 the average annual rate of inflation was 64.8%. Consumer prices increased by an annual average of 18.1% in 1999 and 7.4% in 2000.

Sudan is a member of the African Development Bank (see p. 128), the Arab Bank for Economic Development in Africa (see p. 261), the Council of Arab Economic Unity (see p. 178) and the Islamic Development Bank (see p. 257). In 1997 Sudan's membership of both the Arab Fund for Economic and Social Development (AFESD, see p. 136) and the Arab Monetary Fund (see p. 138) was suspended. Membership of the AFESD was reportedly restored in April 2000.

Sudan's formidable economic problems can be traced back to the 1970s, when the country's agricultural potential was neglected and the Government began to borrow heavily. The problems have been compounded by the civil conflict in the south, which, in addition to depressing economic activity in the areas where it has been waged, has caused a massive waste of state resources. Relations with the IMF, which had deteriorated over the preceding years, began to improve in 1997, and substantial economic progress was made in that year. An economic programme for 1998–2003 was announced, which aimed to achieve annual GDP growth of 6%, to increase government revenues by introducing a value-added tax, to continue with the policy of restraint in non-priority spending and to implement a number of structural reforms, including a comprehensive reform of the banking system and the privatization of 107 state enterprises (58 of which had been successfully divested by mid-2001). In late September 1999 the IMF announced that it no longer considered Sudan an unco-operative country, and in August 2000 Sudan's voting rights and full membership of the fund were restored. Sudan began exporting petroleum in late 1999 and, as a result, in 2000 recorded a trade surplus for the first time in modern history. Further discoveries of petroleum in 2001 led to a vast increase in export revenues; however, much of these earnings were used by the Government to fund the war against the rebels in the south, which was estimated to cost US $1m. per day, and the country's reliance on that commodity has caused some concern in recent years. In late 2002, in return for the rescheduling of its repayments to the IMF, the Sudanese Government pledged to display more transparency in the management of its petroleum revenues and to reduce its military expenditure drastically. The inflation rate, which had been as high as 132.8% in 1996, had declined to 5% by 2002, and GDP growth of 6.5% was estimated in 2002. However, despite a number of positive macro-economic indications, widespread famine and drought, as well as the significant number of refugees and internally displaced people in the country, continue adversely to affect the Sudanese economy, and foreign investors remain wary of commitment to Sudan in view of the country's ongoing political instability and its poor relations with international agencies.

Education

The Government provides free primary education from the ages of six to 13 years. Secondary education begins at 14 years of age and lasts for up to three years. In 1996 the total enrolment at primary and secondary schools was equivalent to 44% of children in the appropriate age-groups (47% of boys; 40% of girls). In 1999/2000 enrolment at primary schools included 44.7% of children in the relevant age-group (males 48.6%; females 40.8%), while secondary enrolment was equivalent to 28.8% of children in the relevant age-group (males 21.7%; females 36.2%). About 15% of current government expenditure in 1985 was for primary and secondary education. Pupils from secondary schools are accepted at the University of Khartoum, subject to their reaching the necessary standards. There are three universities at Omdurman: Omdurman Islamic University; Omdurman Ahlia University; and Ahfad University for Women. New universities were opened at Juba and Wadi Medani (University of Gezira) in 1977. There is also a University of Science and Technology in Khartoum.

Public Holidays

2003: 1 January (Independence Day), 12 February* (Id al-Adha, Feast of the Sacrifice), 5 March* (Islamic New Year), 6 April (Uprising Day, anniversary of 1985 coup), 28 April (Sham an-Nassim, Coptic Easter Monday), 14 May* (Mouloud, Birth of the Prophet), 30 June (Revolution Day), 26 November* (Id al-Fitr, end of Ramadan), 25 December (Christmas).

2004: 1 January (Independence Day), 2 February* (Id al-Adha, Feast of the Sacrifice), 22 February* (Islamic New Year), 6 April (Uprising Day, anniversary of 1985 coup), 12 April (Sham an-Nassim, Coptic Easter Monday), 2 May* (Mouloud, Birth of the Prophet), 30 June (Revolution Day), 14 November* (Id al-Fitr, end of Ramadan), 25 December (Christmas).

*The dates of Islamic holidays are determined by sightings of the moon, and may be slightly different from those given above.

Weights and Measures

The metric system is gradually replacing traditional weights and measures.

Statistical Survey

Source (unless otherwise stated): Department of Statistics, Ministry of Finance and National Economy, POB 700, Khartoum; tel. (11) 777003.

Area and Population

AREA, POPULATION AND DENSITY

Area (sq km)	2,505,813*
Population (census results)†	
1 February 1983	20,594,197
15 April 1993‡	
Males	12,518,638
Females.	12,422,045
Total	24,940,683
Population (UN estimates at mid-year)§	
1998	29,790,000
1999	30,423,000
2000	31,095,000
Density (per sq km) at mid-2000	12.4

* 967,500 sq miles.
† Excluding adjustments for underenumeration, estimated to have been 6.7% in 1993.
‡ Provisional result.
§ Source: UN, *World Population Prospects: The 2000 Revision*.

PROVINCES

(1983 census, provisional)*

	Area (sq miles)	Population	Density (per sq mile)
Northern	134,736	433,391	3.2
Nile	49,205	649,633	13.2
Kassala	44,109	1,512,335	34.3
Red Sea	84,977	695,874	8.2
Blue Nile	24,009	1,056,313	44.0
Gezira	13,546	2,023,094	149.3
White Nile	16,161	933,136	57.7
Northern Kordofan	85,744	1,805,769	21.1
Southern Kordofan	61,188	1,287,525	21.0
Northern Darfur	133,754	1,327,947	9.9
Southern Darfur	62,801	1,765,752	28.1
Khartoum	10,883	1,802,299	165.6
Eastern Equatoria	46,073	1,047,125	22.7
Western Equatoria. . . .	30,422	359,056	11.8
Bahr al-Ghazal	52,000	1,492,597	28.7
Al-Bohayrat.	25,625	772,913	30.2
Sobat.	45,266	802,354	17.7
Jonglei	47,003	797,251	17.0
Total	967,500	20,564,364	21.3

* In 1991 a federal system of government was inaugurated, whereby Sudan was divided into nine states, which were sub-divided into 66 provinces and 281 local government areas. A constitutional decree, issued in February 1994, redivided the country into 26 states.

PRINCIPAL TOWNS

(population at 1993 census)

Omdurman . . .	1,271,403	Nyala	227,183
Khartoum (capital) .	947,483	El-Gezira	211,362
Khartoum North . .	700,887	Gedaref	191,164
Port Sudan . .	308,195	Kosti	173,599
Kassala . . .	234,622	El-Fasher	141,884
El-Obeid	229,425	Juba	114,980

Source: UN, *Demographic Yearbook*.

Mid-2000 (UN projection, including suburbs): Khartoum 2,731,000 (Source: UN, *World Urbanization Prospects: The 1999 Revision*).

BIRTHS AND DEATHS

(UN estimates, annual averages)

	1985–90	1990–95	1995–2000
Birth rate (per 1,000)	38.9	37.9	36.1
Death rate (per 1,000)	14.6	13.4	12.2

Source: UN, *World Population Prospects: The 2000 Revision*.

Expectation of life (WHO estimates, years at birth): 55.9 (males 54.1; females 57.9) in 2001 (Source: WHO, *World Health Report*).

ECONOMICALLY ACTIVE POPULATION*

(persons aged 10 years and over, 1983 census, provisional)

	Males	Females	Total
Agriculture, hunting, forestry and fishing	2,638,294	1,390,411	4,028,705
Mining and quarrying . . .	5,861	673	6,534
Manufacturing	205,247	61,446	266,693
Electricity, gas and water . .	42,110	1,618	43,728
Construction	130,977	8,305	139,282
Trade, restaurants and hotels . .	268,382	25,720	294,102
Transport, storage and communications	209,776	5,698	215,474
Financing, insurance, real estate and business services	17,414	3,160	20,574
Community, social and personal services	451,193	99,216	550,409
Activities not adequately defined .	142,691	42,030	184,721
Unemployed persons not previously employed	387,615	205,144	592,759
Total	4,499,560	1,843,421	6,342,981

* Excluding nomads, homeless persons and members of institutional households.

Mid-2001 (estimates in '000): Agriculture, etc. 7,554; Total 12,557 (Source: FAO).

Health and Welfare

KEY INDICATORS

Total fertility rate (children per woman, 2001)	4.6
Under-5 mortality rate (per 1,000 live births, 2001) . . .	107
HIV/AIDS (% of persons aged 15–49, 2001)	2.60
Physicians (per 1,000 head, 1996)	0.09
Hospital beds (per 1,000 head, 1990)	1.09
Health expenditure (2000): US $ per head (PPP)	51
Health expenditure (2000): % of GDP	4.7
Health expenditure (2000): public (% of total)	21.2
Access to water (% of persons, 2000)	75
Access to sanitation (% of persons, 2000)	62
Human Development Index (2000): ranking	139
Human Development Index (2000): value	0.499

For sources and definitions, see explanatory note on p. vi.

Agriculture

PRINCIPAL CROPS
('000 metric tons)

	1999	2000	2001
Wheat	172	214	303
Rice (paddy)	11	7	7*
Maize	37	53	53†
Millet	499	499	481
Sorghum (Durra)	2,347	2,488	4,470
Potatoes*	15	15	16
Cassava (Manioc)*	10	10	10
Yams*	132	135	137
Sugar cane	5,321	4,982	5,000*
Dry beans	19	31	25
Dry broad beans	105†	146†	146*
Other pulses	90	91	91
Groundnuts (in shell)	1,047	1,047	947
Sunflower seed	8	8	4
Sesame seed	329	329	262
Melonseed	12	30*	40*
Cottonseed	94	157	148
Tomatoes*	240	242	243
Pumpkins, etc.*	65	67	68
Aubergines (Eggplants)*	110	112	113
Dry onions*	57	58	59
Garlic*	17	17	17
Melons*	26	27	27
Water melons*	140	142	143
Dates*	176	176	177
Oranges*	17	17	18
Lemons and limes*	58	60	61
Grapefruits and pomelos*	65	66	67
Mangoes*	190	192	193
Bananas*	71	72	73

* FAO estimate(s).
† Unofficial figure.
Source: FAO.

LIVESTOCK
('000 head, year ending September)

	1999	2000	2001
Horses*	26	26	26
Asses*	730	740	750
Cattle	35,825	37,093	38,325
Camels	3,031	3,108	3,203
Sheep	44,802	46,095	47,042
Goats	37,346	38,548	39,952
Chickens	36,465	37,000*	37,500*

* FAO estimate(s).

Source: FAO.

LIVESTOCK PRODUCTS
('000 metric tons)

	1999	2000	2001
Beef and veal*	276	296	367
Mutton and lamb*	142	143	144
Goat meat	114	118	118*
Poultry meat*	30	30	31
Other meat*	77	78	80
Cows' milk*	3,072	3,072	3,072
Sheep's milk	461	462	490*
Goats' milk	1,197	1,245	1,250*
Butter and ghee*	16	16	16
Cheese*	148	150	151
Hen eggs*	44	45	46
Wool: greasy*	45	46	46
Wool: scoured*	23	23	24
Cattle hides*	53	55	56
Sheepskins*	22	22	23
Goatskins*	22	23	23

* FAO estimate(s).

Source: FAO.

Forestry

ROUNDWOOD REMOVALS
(FAO estimates, '000 cubic metres)

	1999	2000	2001
Sawlogs, veneer logs and logs for sleepers	123	123	123
Other industrial wood	2,050	2,050	2,050
Fuel wood	16,549	16,680	16,871
Total	18,722	18,853	19,044

Source: FAO.

Gum arabic ('000 metric tons, year ending 30 June): 24 in 1993/94; 27 in 1994/95; 25 in 1995/96 (Source: IMF, *Sudan—Recent Economic Developments* (March 1997)).

Fishing

('000 metric tons, live weight)

	1998	1999	2000
Capture	49.5	49.5	50.0*
Nile tilapia	16.0	16.0	16.0*
Other freshwater fishes	28.0	28.0	28.0*
Marine fishes	5.5	5.5	6.0*
Aquaculture	1.0	1.0	1.0
Total catch	50.5	50.5	50.5*

* FAO estimate.

Source: FAO, *Yearbook of Fishery Statistics*.

Mining

('000 metric tons, unless otherwise stated)

	1999	2000	2001†
Crude petroleum ('000 barrels)	17,120	67,152	77,755
Salt (unrefined)	117.1	120.0†	120.0
Chromite	48.0	28.5	20.5
Gold ore (kilograms)*	5,565	5,770	5,800

* Figures refer to the metal content of ores.
† Estimated figure(s).
Source: US Geological Survey.

Industry

PETROLEUM PRODUCTS
(estimates, '000 metric tons)

	1996	1997	1998
Motor spirit (petrol)	101	103	105
Aviation gasoline	5	5	5
Naphtha	24	24	24
Jet fuels	91	91	92
Kerosene	26	26	27
Gas-diesel (distillate fuel) oils	328	330	331
Residual fuel oils	320	320	322
Liquefied petroleum gas	7	7	7

Source: UN, *Industrial Commodity Statistics Yearbook*.

SELECTED OTHER PRODUCTS

	1998	1999	2000
Flour ('000 metric tons)	310	532	600
Raw sugar ('000 metric tons)	610	664	662
Vegetable oils ('000 metric tons)	120	100	120
Soft drinks (million boxes)	17	18	20
Footwear (million pairs)	46	48	50
Cigarettes (metric tons)	222	225	232
Rubber tyres ('000)	207	173	212
Cement ('000 metric tons)	206	266	161

Sources: IMF, *Sudan—Statistical Annex* (April 1998 and July 2000); Ministry of Industry.

Finance

CURRENCY AND EXCHANGE RATES

Monetary Units

100 piastres = 1 Sudanese dinar

Sterling, Dollar and Euro Equivalents (31 December 2002)

£1 sterling = 421.78 dinars
US $1 = 261.68 dinars
€1 = 274.42 dinars
1,000 Sudanese dinars = £2.371 = $3.821 = €3.644

Average Exchange Rate (Sudanese dinars per US $)

2000   257.12
2001   258.70
2002   263.31

Note: On 1 March 1999 the Sudanese pound (£S) was replaced by the Sudanese dinar, equivalent to £S10. The pound was withdrawn from circulation on 31 July 1999.

CENTRAL GOVERNMENT BUDGET

('000 million Sudanese dinars)

Revenue	1997	1998	1999
Tax revenue	90.9	126.4	153.3
Taxes on income and profits	21.7	31.2	36.1
Personal income tax	2.1	4.1	3.0
Business profit tax	6.2	8.7	22.9
Remittances from expatriate Sudanese	4.0	4.7	5.4
Taxes on goods and services	21.1	25.9	32.8
Excise duties	21.1	21.3	24.7
Sales taxes	—	4.6	8.1
Taxes on international trade and transactions	48.2	69.3	84.4
Import duties	24.3	35.5	53.8
Export tax	3.3	1.2	1.8
Consumption tax	9.9	17.1	18.4
Non-tax revenue*	16.4	30.4	53.4
Fees and charges on public services	6.3	9.5	9.4
Public enterprise profits, interest, rent and dividends	5.5	8.0	14.1
Receipts from sales of public enterprises	0.1	n.a.	n.a.
Total	107.3	156.9	206.7

Expenditure	1997	1998	1999
Current expenditure	109.8	155.3	195.0
Wages and salaries	37.5	57.3	80.4
Goods and services	45.8	31.2	37.9
Defence	n.a.	19.8	24.3
Current transfers	4.7	8.9	12.8
Interest paid	10.1	13.9	20.2
Capital expenditure and net lending	9.3	15.6	32.2
Development expenditure	9.3	15.6	32.2
Foreign expenses	2.6	3.4	6.5
Local expenses	6.7	12.2	25.7
Total	119.1	170.9	227.2

* Excluding price differential on oil, sugar and cement.

Source: IMF, *Sudan—Statistical Appendix* (July 2000).

INTERNATIONAL RESERVES

(US $ million at 31 December)

	2000	2001	2002
Reserve position in IMF	0.01	0.01	0.01
Foreign exchange	247.30	117.83	477.95
Total	247.31	117.85	477.96

Source: IMF, *International Financial Statistics*.

MONEY SUPPLY

(million Sudanese dinars at 31 December)

	2000	2001	2001
Currency outside banks	142,082	153,836	193.582
Demand deposits at deposit money banks	84,128	109,135	147,459
Total money (incl. others)	234,587	271,388	352,264

Source: IMF, *International Financial Statistics*.

COST OF LIVING

(Consumer Price Index; base: 1992 = 100)

	1998	1999	2000
Food, beverages and tobacco	3,930.8	4,670.3	4,883.3
Clothing and footwear	3,615.7	4,010.5	3,985.6
Housing	3,826.8	5,257.2	6,192.9
Household operations	3,677.7	3,899.3	3,706.4
Health care	5,277.9	6,313.5	6,984.7
Transport and communications	7,107.7	8,661.7	9,082.8
Entertainment	2,261.2	3,046.0	4,149.7
Education	5,947.8	7,057.0	8,048.7
All items (incl. others)	4,299.8	5,077.0	5,451.9

Source: Bank of Sudan.

NATIONAL ACCOUNTS

(estimates, '000 million Sudanese dinars at current prices)

Expenditure on the Gross Domestic Product

	1997	1998	1999
Government final consumption expenditure	91.3	88.5	118.3
Private final consumption expenditure	1,465.9	1,882.2	2,172.6
Gross fixed capital formation	210.7	259.1	318.7
Total domestic expenditure	1,767.9	2,229.8	2,609.6
Exports of goods and services	98.4	122.4	205.7
Less Imports of goods and services	255.4	393.9	383.8
GDP in purchasers' values	1,676.9	2,062.1	2,536.3
GDP at constant 1981/82 prices*	1,201.9	1,262.1	1,338.2

* Million Sudanese dinars.

Source: IMF, *Sudan—Statistical Appendix* (July 2000).

Gross Domestic Product by Economic Activity

	1997	1998	1999
Agriculture and forestry	745.7	841.6	1,040.3
Mining and quarrying	4.2	5.5	20.9
Manufacturing and handicrafts	100.7	177.4	217.3
Electricity and water	14.3	16.1	19.0
Construction	73.1	132.5	156.8
Trade, restaurants and hotels	260.5	405.9	492.0
Transport and communications	150.5	116.3	142.3
Other services	266.0	290.8	354.1
GDP at factor cost	1,615.1	1,986.0	2,442.7
Indirect taxes, *less* subsidies	61.9	76.1	93.6
GDP in purchasers' values	1,677.0	2,062.1	2,536.3

Source: IMF, *Sudan—Statistical Appendix* (July 2000).

BALANCE OF PAYMENTS
(US $ million)

	1999	2000	2001
Exports of goods f.o.b.	780.1	1,806.7	1,698.7
Imports of goods f.o.b.	−1,256.0	−1,366.3	−1,395.1
Trade balance	−475.9	440.4	303.6
Exports of services	81.6	27.4	14.6
Imports of services	−274.9	−647.6	−660.3
Balance on goods and services	−669.2	−179.8	−342.1
Other income received	19.1	4.6	17.8
Other income paid	−123.2	−579.6	−571.9
Balance on goods, services and income	−773.3	−754.8	−896.2
Current transfers received	702.2	651.3	730.4
Current transfers paid	−393.7	−453.3	−452.5
Current balance	−464.8	−556.8	−618.3
Capital account (net)	−22.9	−119.3	−93.3
Direct investment from abroad	370.8	392.2	574.0
Portfolio investment assets	—	—	0.7
Other investment assets	−38.4	−53.4	−55.1
Investment liabilities	102.9	92.8	41.6
Net errors and omissions	167.2	368.4	−0.5
Overall balance	114.8	123.9	−150.9

Source: IMF, *International Financial Statistics*.

External Trade

PRINCIPAL COMMODITIES
(US $ million)

Imports c.i.f.	1997	1998	1999
Foodstuffs	237.9	263.7	275.7
Wheat flour	60.8	59.0	51.2
Crude materials	324.1	307.5	237.2
Petroleum	292.7	255.7	183.9
Chemicals	189.9	157.0	113.9
Fertilizers	47.4	10.6	2.2
Basic manufactures	292.6	592.1	236.9
Machinery and equipment	269.7	348.2	358.3
Transport equipment	173.2	192.7	131.8
Trucks	38.0	86.4	45.1
Spare parts for automobiles	65.7	31.1	22.0
Total (incl. others)	1,579.7	1,924.7	1,412.2

Total imports (US $ million): 1,552.7 in 2000; 1,585.5 in 2001.

Exports f.o.b.	1999	2000	2001
Cotton	44.8	53.0	44.4
Sesame seed (incl. oilcake)	127.0	146.9	104.5
Petroleum and petroleum products	275.9	1,350.8	1,376.2
Crude petroleum	n.a.	1,240.7	1,269.2
Livestock	114.3	66.5	1.7
Gold	55.3	46.2	43.7
Total (incl. others)	780.0	1,806.7	1,698.7

Sources: IMF, *Sudan—Statistical Appendix* (July 2000); Bank of Sudan.

PRINCIPAL TRADING PARTNERS
(US $ million)

Imports c.i.f.	2000	2001
China, People's Repub.	101.9	169.0
Egypt	36.9	46.8
France	62.2	51.7
Germany	80.4	108.9
India	77.5	87.7
Italy	134.7	35.9
Japan	50.9	53.4
Jordan	18.6	19.5
Kenya	31.0	31.3
Korea, Repub.	26.9	33.3
Netherlands	19.6	27.8
Saudi Arabia	155.7	197.8
United Arab Emirates	97.0	122.4
United Kingdom	123.0	137.9
USA	32.1	16.0
Total (incl. others)	1,552.7	1,585.5

Exports f.o.b.	2000	2001
China, People's Repub.	797.1	1,002.2
Egypt	41.2	33.7
Germany	27.8	26.0
Italy	54.1	8.4
Japan	215.2	82.6
Korea, Repub.	105.8	67.0
Netherlands	16.5	26.0
Saudi Arabia	92.2	24.2
Syria	17.6	22.7
United Arab Emirates	43.1	31.7
United Kingdom	62.2	56.2
Yemen	14.0	34.5
Total (incl. others)	1,806.7	1,698.7

Source: Bank of Sudan.

Transport

RAILWAY TRAFFIC*

	1991	1992	1993
Freight ton-km (million)	2,030	2,120	2,240
Passenger-km (million)	1,020	1,130	1,183

* Estimates.

Source: UN Economic Commission for Africa, *African Statistical Yearbook*.

2000 (passengers carried): 258,000 (Source: Sudan Railways).

ROAD TRAFFIC*
(motor vehicles in use)

	1994	1995	1996
Passenger cars	257,000	263,000	285,000
Lorries, trucks, etc.	43,120	48,000	53,000

* Estimates.

Source: International Road Federation, *World Road Statistics*.

SHIPPING

Merchant Fleet
(registered at 31 December)

	1999	2000	2001
Number of vessels	19	19	18
Displacement (grt)	43,078	43,078	42,978

Source: Lloyd's Register-Fairplay, *World Fleet Statistics*.

International Sea-borne Freight Traffic
(estimates, '000 metric tons)

	1991	1992	1993
Goods loaded	1,290	1,387	1,543
Goods unloaded	3,800	4,200	4,300

Source: UN Economic Commission for Africa, *African Statistical Yearbook*.

CIVIL AVIATION
(traffic on scheduled services)

	1996	1997	1998
Kilometres flown (million)	13	7	6
Passengers carried ('000)	491	333	499
Passenger-km (million)	650	471	148
Total ton-km (million)	107	66	19

Source: UN, *Statistical Yearbook*.

Tourism

	1997	1998	1999
Tourist arrivals ('000) . . .	30	38	39
Tourism receipts (US $ million) .	4	2	2

2000: Tourist arrivals 50,000.

Source: World Tourism Organization, mainly *Yearbook of Tourism Statistics*.

Communications Media

	1999	2000	2001
Television receivers ('000 in use)	5,000	8,500	n.a.
Telephones ('000 main lines in use)	251.4	368.8	453.0
Facsimile machines (estimated number in use)	25,000	n.a.	n.a.
Mobile cellular telephones ('000 subscribers)	13	23	105
Personal computers ('000 in use) .	85	100	115
Internet users ('000)	5	30	56

Source: International Telecommunication Union.

1996: Daily newspapers 5 (average circulation 737,000 copies) (Source: UNESCO, *Statistical Yearbook*).

1997: Radio receivers ('000 in use) 7,550 (Source: UNESCO, *Statistical Yearbook*).

Education

(1998)

	Institutions	Teachers*	Students
Pre-primary	5,984	8,897	365,723
Primary	11,982	102,987	2,478,309
Secondary	3,512	14,743	1,010,060
Universities etc.	n.a.	2,043	200,538

* Figures refer to 1996/97.

Source: UNESCO Institute for Statistics.

1999/2000: Primary: 11,923 schools; 117,151 teachers; 3,137,494 pupils. Secondary: 1,694 schools; 21,114 teachers; 401,424 pupils (Source: Ministry of Education).

Adult literacy rate (UNESCO estimates): 57.8% (males 69.5%; females 46.3%) in 2000 (Source: UN Development Programme, *Human Development Report*).

Directory

The Constitution

Following the coup of 6 April 1985, the Constitution of April 1973 was abrogated. A transitional Constitution, which entered into force in October 1985, was suspended following the military coup of 30 June 1989. In April 1998 a new Constitution was approved by the National Assembly, and presented to President al-Bashir. At a referendum held in June, the new Constitution was endorsed by 96.7% of voters. This Constitution, which entered into force on 1 July 1998, vests executive power in the Council of Ministers, which is appointed by the President but responsible to the National Assembly. Legislative power is vested in the National Assembly. The Constitution guarantees freedom of thought and religion, and the right to political association, provided that such activity complies with the law.

The Government

HEAD OF STATE

President: Lt-Gen. OMAR HASSAN AHMAD AL-BASHIR (took power as Chairman of the Revolutionary Command Council for National Salvation (RCC) on 30 June 1989; appointed President by the RCC on 16 October 1993; elected President in March 1996; re-elected in December 2000).

First Vice-President: ALI OSMAN MUHAMMAD TAHA.

Vice-President: MOSES MACHAR KACOUL.

Assistant President: MUBARAK AL-FADIL AL-MAHDI.

COUNCIL OF MINISTERS
(April 2003)

Prime Minister: Lt-Gen. OMAR HASSAN AHMAD AL-BASHIR.

Minister of Presidential Affairs: Maj.-Gen. SALAH AHMAD MUHAMMAD SALIH.

Ministers of Cabinet Affairs: Maj.-Gen. AL-HADI ABDALLAH MUHAMMAD AL-AWAD, MARTIN MALWAL AROP, KARAM AD-DIN SABEH ABD AL-MAWLA.

Minister of National Defence: Maj.-Gen. BAKRI HASSAN SALIH.

Minister of External Relations: Dr MUSTAFA OSMAN ISMAIL.

Minister of Internal Affairs: Maj.-Gen. Eng. ABD AR-RAHIM MUHAMMAD HUSSEIN.

Minister of Justice, Prosecutor-General: ALI MUHAMMAD OSMAN YASSIN.

Minister of Information and Communication: AZ-ZAHAWI IBRAHIM MALIK.

Minister of Federal Relations: Dr NAFI ALI NAFI.

Minister of Finance and National Economy: MUHAMMAD AL-HASAN AZ-ZUBAYR.

Minister of External Trade: ABD AL-HAMID MUSA KASHA.

Minister of International Co-operation: YUSUF SULAYMAN TAKANAH.

Minister of National Industry: JALAL YUSUF MUHAMMAD AL-DUQAYR.

Minister of Investment: ASH-SHARIF AHMAD OMAR BADR.

Minister of Agriculture and Forestry: Dr MAJDHUB AL-KHALIFA AHMAD.

Minister of Animal Resources: Dr RIAK GAI.

Minister of Irrigation and Water Resources: Eng. KAMAL ALI MUHAMMAD.

Minister of Energy and Mining: Dr AWAD AHMAD AL-JAZ.

Minister of Transport: AS-SAMMANI ASH-SHEIKH AL-WASEILAH.

Minister of Roads: MUHAMMAD TAHIR EILA.

Minister of Aviation: Eng. JOSEPH MALWAL.

Minister of Culture: ABD AL-BASIT ABD AL-MAJID.

Minister of Tourism and National Heritage: ABD AL-JALIL AL-PASHA MUHAMMAD AHMAD.

Minister of Higher Education: Prof. MUBARAK MUHAMMAD ALI AL-MAJDHUB.

Minister of Education: Dr AHMAD BABIKR NAHHAR.

Minister of Electricity: ALI TAMIM FARTAK.

Minister of Labour and Administrative Reform: Maj.-Gen. (retd) ALISON MANANI MAGAYA.

Minister of Health: Dr AHMAD BILAL OSMAN.

Minister of Humanitarian Affairs: IBRAHIM MAHMUD HAMID.

Minister of Religious Guidance and Endowment: Dr ISSAM AHMAD AL-BASHIR.

Minister of Welfare and Social Development: Samiyah Ahmad Muhammad.

Minister of the Environment and Urban Development Construction: Maj.-Gen. (retd) at-Tijani Adam at-Tahir.

Minister of Parliamentary Affairs: Abd al-Basit Salih Sabdarat.

Minister of Youth and Sports: Hassan Osman Rizziq.

In addition, there was one presidential adviser and six Ministers of State.

MINISTRIES

All ministries are in Khartoum.

Ministry of Agriculture and Forestry: POB 285, al-Gamaa Ave, Khartoum; tel. (11) 780951; e-mail moafcc@sudanmail.net; internet www.sudagric.net.

Ministry of Aviation: Khartoum; tel. (11) 773000.

Ministry of Education: Khartoum; tel. (11) 78900.

Ministry of Energy and Mining: POB 2087, Khartoum; tel. (11) 775595.

Ministry of the Environment and Urban Development Construction: POB 300, Khartoum; tel. (11) 462604.

Ministry of External Relations: POB 873, Khartoum; tel. (11) 773101; e-mail info@sudmer.com; internet www.sudmer.com.

Ministry of External Trade: Khartoum; tel. (11) 772793.

Ministry of Finance and National Economy: POB 700, Khartoum; tel. (11) 770288.

Ministry of Health: POB 303, Khartoum; tel. (11) 773000.

Ministry of Higher Education: Khartoum; tel. (11) 789970.

Ministry of Internal Affairs: POB 2793, Khartoum; tel. (11) 776554.

Ministry of Irrigation and Water Resources: POB 878, Khartoum; tel. (11) 77533.

Ministry of Justice: POB 302, An-Nil Ave, Khartoum; tel. (11) 774842.

Ministry of National Defence: POB 371, Khartoum; tel. (11) 774910.

Ministry of National Industry: POB 2184, Khartoum; tel. (11) 777830.

Ministry of Roads: POB 1130, Khartoum 11111; tel. (11) 779493; fax (11) 780507.

Ministry of Tourism and National Heritage: Khartoum; tel. (11) 771967.

Ministry of Transport: POB 300, Khartoum; tel. (11) 781629.

STATE GOVERNORS
(May 2003)

Al-Buhayrat: John Angol.

Bahr al-Jabal: Maj.-Gen. (retd) James Loro.

Blue Nile: Abdallah Uthman al-Haj.

Eastern Equatoria: Caesar Baya Lolaya.

Gadarif: Abd ar-Rahman al-Khadr.

Gezira: Lt-Gen. (retd) Abd ar-Rahman Sir al-Khatim.

Jonglei: Michael Mario.

Kassala: Lt-Gen. Faruq Hasan Muhammad Nur.

Khartoum: Dr Abd-al-Halim Ismail al-Muta'afi.

Northern: Maj.-Gen. (retd) al-Hadi Bushra.

Northern Bahr al-Ghazal: Kon Dir Dotjok.

Northern Darfur: Osman Muhammad Yusuf.

Northern Kordofan: Ghulam ad-Din Uthman.

Red Sea: Maj.-Gen. (retd) Hatim al-Wasil Ash-Shaykh as-Sammani.

River Nile: (vacant).

Sennar: Dr Yunis ash-Sharif al-Hussain.

Southern Darfur: Maj.-Gen. (retd) Salah Ali al-Ghali.

Southern Kordofan: Somi Zaydan Attiyah.

Upper Nile: Dr Abdallah Nasar.

Wahdah: John Dor Majok.

Warab: Moses Machar.

Western Bahr al-Ghazal: Michael Mil Hussain.

Western Darfur: Staff Maj.-Gen. (retd) Sulayman Abdallah Adam.

Western Equatoria: James Mima Yanyandi.

Western Kordofan: Maj.-Gen. at-Tayib Abd ar-Rahman Mukhtar.

White Nile: Majdhub Yusuf Babikir.

President

PRESIDENT

Election, 13–22 December 2000

Candidate	% of total votes cast
Omar Hassan Ahmad al-Bashir (National Congress)	86.5
Gaafar Muhammad Nimeri (Alliance of the People's Working Forces)	9.6
Malik Hussain	1.6
as-Samawi'it Husayn Osman Mansur (Independent Democrats)	1.0
Mahmoud Ahmad Juna	1.0

Legislature

MAJLIS WATANI
(National Assembly)

Speaker: Ahmad Ibrahim at-Tahir.

Deputy Speakers: Angelo Beda, Abdallah al-Hardello.

Election, 13–22 December 2000

	Seats
National Congress	355
Others	5
Total	**360***

*Of the 360 members, 270 are directly elected in single seat constituencies; 35 members represent women; 26 represent university graduates and 29 represent trade unions.

Political Organizations

National Congress: Khartoum; successor to National Islamic Front and ruling political org. Pres. Lt-Gen. Omar Hassan Ahmad al-Bashir; Sec.-Gen. Prof. Ibrahim Ahmad Umar.

The right to political association, subject to compliance with the law, was guaranteed in the Constitution approved by referendum in June 1998. (All political organizations had been banned following the military coup of 30 June 1989.) The registration of parties began on 6 January 1999, and by 14 February 32 parties had applied to register. The following parties are among the most active:

Alliance of the People's Working Forces: Khartoum; Head Gaafar Muhammad Nimeri; Acting Sec.-Gen. Kamal ad-Din Muhammad Abdullah.

Democratic Unionist Party (DUP): Khartoum; Leader Osman al-Mirghani; participates in National Democratic Alliance (see below).

Free Sudanese National Party (FSNP): Khartoum; Chair. Fr Philip Abbas Ghabbush.

Independent Democrats: Khartoum; Leader as-Samawi'it Husayn Osman Mansur.

Islamic-Christian Solidarity: Khartoum; Founder Hatim Abdullah az-Zaki Husayn.

Islamic Revival Movement: Khartoum; Founder Siddiq al-Haj as-Siddiq.

Islamic Socialist Party: Khartoum; Leader Salah al-Musbah.

Islamic Ummah Party: Khartoum; Chair. Wali ad-Din al-Hadi al-Mahdi.

Justice Party: Khartoum; f. 2002 by fmr members of the National Congress.

Moderate Trend Party: Khartoum; Leader Mahmud Jiha.

Muslim Brotherhood: Khartoum; Islamic fundamentalist; Leader Dr Habir Nur ad-Din.

National Democratic Party: Khartoum; f. 2002 following merger of the Union of Nationalistic Forces, the Communist Party and the National Solidarity Party.

Nile Valley Conference: Khartoum; Founder Lt-Gen. (retd) UMAR ZARUQ.

Popular Masses' Alliance: Khartoum; Founder FAYSAL MUHMAD HUSAYN.

Popular National Congress (PNC): Khartoum; f. 2000; Founder HASSAN AT-TURABI.

Socialist Popular Party: Khartoum; Founder SAYYID KHALIFAH IDRIS HABBANI.

Sudan Green Party: Khartoum; Founder Prof. ZAKARAIA BASHIR IMAM.

Sudanese Central Movement: Khartoum; Founder Dr MUHAMMAD ABU AL-QASIM HAJ HAMAD.

Sudanese Initiative Party: Khartoum; Leader J'AFAR KARAR.

Sudanese National Party (SNP): Khartoum; Leader HASAN AL-MAHI; participates in the National Democratic Alliance (see below).

Umma Party (UP): e-mail hq@umma.org; internet www.umma .org; Mahdist party based on the Koran and Islamic traditions; Chair. Dr UMAR NUR AD-DA'IM; Leader SADIQ AL-MAHDI; withdrew from the National Democratic Alliance (see below) in March 2000.

United Democratic Salvation Front: Khartoum; political wing of the Sudan People's Defence Force; Chair. Dr RIEK MASHAR TENY-DHURGON.

A number of opposition movements are grouped together in the Asmara-based **National Democratic Alliance (NDA)** (Chair. OSMAN AL-MIRGHANI; Sec. Gen. JOSEPH OKELU). These include the **Beja Congress**, the **Legitimate Command (LC)**, the **Sudan Alliance Forces (SAF)** (internet www.safsudan.com; f. 1994; Cmmdr-in-Chief Brig. ABD EL-AZIZ KHALID OSMAN), the **Sudan Federal Democratic Alliance (SFDA)** (f. 1994; advocates a decentralized, federal structure for Sudan; Chair. AHMAD DREIGE), the **Sudan People's Liberation Movement (SPLM)** (Leader Dr MANSUR KHALID) and its mil. wing, the **Sudan People's Liberation Army (SPLA)** (Leader Col JOHN GARANG; Sec.-Gen. JAMES WANI IGGA).

Diplomatic Representation

EMBASSIES IN SUDAN

Algeria: St 31, New Extension, POB 80, Khartoum; tel. (11) 741954; Ambassador SALIH BEN KOBBI.

Bulgaria: St 31, Middle Rd, New Extension, POB 1690, Khartoum; tel. (11) 743414; Ambassador T. F. MITEV.

Canada: Khartoum.

Chad: 21, St 17, New Extension, POB 1514, Khartoum; tel. (11) 742545; Ambassador MBAILAOU BERAL MOÏSE.

China, People's Republic: 93, St 22, POB 1425, Khartoum; tel. (11) 222036; Ambassador ZHANG DONG.

Congo, Democratic Republic: St 13, Block 12CE, New Extension, 23, POB 4195, Khartoum; tel. (11) 742424; Ambassador MGBAMA MPWA.

Egypt: Al-Gamma St, POB 1126, Khartoum; tel. (11) 772836; Ambassador MUHAMMAD ASIM IBRAHIM.

Eritrea: Khartoum.

Ethiopia: Plot No. 4, Block 384 BC, POB 844, Khartoum; Chargé d'affaires a.i. ABDOU LEGESSE.

France: Amarat, St 3, Plot No. 29, Block 10AE, Burri, POB 377, Khartoum; tel. (11) 225608; Ambassador MICHEL RAIMBAUD.

Germany: Baladia St, Block No. 8DE, Plot No. 2, POB 970, Khartoum; tel. (11) 777990; fax (11) 777622; Ambassador Dr WERNER DAUM.

Greece: Sharia al-Gamhouria, Block 5, No. 30, POB 1182, Khartoum; tel. (11) 773155; Ambassador VASSILIS COUZOPOULOS.

Holy See: Kafouri Belgravia, POB 623, Khartoum (Apostolic Nunciature); tel. (11) 330037; fax (11) 330692; e-mail aponunkrt@email .sudanet.net; Apostolic Nuncio Most Rev. MARCO DINO BROGI (Titular Archbishop of Città Ducale).

India: 61 Africa Rd, POB 707, Khartoum; tel. (11) 471202; fax (11) 472266; e-mail indemb@sudanet.net; Chargé d'affaires a.i. Shri A. C. GOGNA.

Iran: House No. 8, Sq. 2, Mogran, Khartoum; tel. (11) 748843; Chargé d'affaires a.i. NIMATALLAH GADIR.

Iraq: Sharia as-Shareef al-Hindi, POB 1969, Khartoum; tel. (11) 271867; fax (11) 271855; Ambassador NADIM AL-WASSIN.

Italy: St 39, POB 793, Khartoum; tel. (11) 745326; e-mail italsd@usa .net; Ambassador Dr MAURIZIO BATTAGLINI.

Japan: 24, Block AE, St 3, New Extension, POB 1649, Khartoum; tel. (11) 777668; fax (11) 451600; Ambassador YOSHINORI IMAGAWA.

Jordan: 25, St 7, New Extension, Khartoum; tel. (11) 743264; Ambassador MOHAMMED JUMA ASANA.

Kenya: POB 8242, Khartoum; tel. (11) 460386; fax (11) 472265; Ambassador EDWARD N. BWISA.

Korea, Republic: House 2, St 1, New Extension, POB 2414, Khartoum; tel. (11) 451136; fax (11) 452822; Ambassador MUN SONG-MO.

Kuwait: Africa Ave, near the Tennis Club, POB 1457, Khartoum; tel. (11) 781525; Chargé d'affaires FAISAL AL-MALIFIE.

Lebanon: Khartoum; Ambassador NASR AJAJ BAZANA.

Libya: 50 Africa Rd, POB 2091, Khartoum; Secretary of People's Bureau GUMMA AL-FAZANI.

Morocco: 32, St 19, New Extension, POB 2042, Khartoum; tel. (11) 743223; Ambassador MOHAMMED KAMLICHI.

Netherlands: St 47, House No. 6, POB 391, Khartoum; tel. (11) 471200; fax 471204; Ambassador A. H. HUITZING.

Nigeria: St 17, Sharia al-Mek Nimr, POB 1538, Khartoum; tel. (11) 779120; Ambassador IBRAHIM KARLI.

Oman: St 1, New Extension, POB 2839, Khartoum; tel. (11) 745791; Ambassador MOSLIM EBIN ZAIDAN AL-BARAMI.

Pakistan: House No. 94, Block 16, ar-Riyadh, POB 1178, Khartoum; tel. (11) 742518; Ambassador DHAFRALLA SHIEK.

Poland: 73 Africa Rd, POB 902, Khartoum; tel. (11) 744248; Chargé d'affaires a.i. WALDEMAR POPIOLEK.

Qatar: St 15, New Extension, POB 223, Khartoum; tel. (11) 742208; Chargé d'affaires a.i. HASSAN AHMED ABDULLAH ABU HINDI.

Romania: Kassala Rd, Plot No. 172–173, Kafouri Area, POB 1494, Khartoum North; tel. (11) 613445; Chargé d'affaires a.i. GHEORGHE GUSTEA.

Russia: B1, A10 St, New Extension, POB 1161, Khartoum; tel. (11) 471042; fax (11) 471239; e-mail rfsudan@hotmail.com; Ambassador VALERII Y. SUKHIN.

Saudi Arabia: St 11, New Extension, Khartoum; tel. (11) 741938; Ambassador SAYED MOHAMMED SIBRI SULIMAN.

Serbia and Montenegro: St 31, 49A, POB 1180, Khartoum 1; tel. (11) 741252; Ambassador VLADIMIR PETKOVSKI.

Somalia: St 23–25, New Extension, POB 1857, Khartoum; tel. (11) 744800; Ambassador Sheikh MUHAMMAD AHMED.

Switzerland: Amarat, St 15, POB 1707, Khartoum; tel. (11) 451010; fax (11) 452804; Chargé d'affaires a.i. GIANBATTISTA MONDADA.

Syria: St 3, New Extension, POB 1139, Khartoum; tel. (11) 744663; Ambassador MOHAMMED AL-MAHAMEED.

Tunisia: Khartoum.

Turkey: 31, St 29, New Extension, POB 771, Khartoum; tel. (11) 451197; fax (11) 472542; e-mail trembkh@email.sudanet.net; Ambassador Dr ALI ENGIN OBA.

Uganda: Khartoum; Ambassador MULL KATENDE.

United Arab Emirates: St 3, New Extension, POB 1225, Khartoum; tel. (11) 744476; Ambassador ABDULLAH MATAR KHAMIS.

United Kingdom: St 10, off Baladia St, POB 801, Khartoum; tel. (11) 777105; fax (11) 776457; e-mail british@sudanmail.net; Ambassador WILLIAM PATEY.

USA: Khartoum; Chargé d'affaires JEFF MILLINGTON.

Yemen: St 11, New Extension, POB 1010, Khartoum; tel. (11) 743918; Ambassador ABD AS-SALAM HUSSEIN.

Judicial System

Until September 1983 the judicial system was divided into two sections, civil and Islamic, the latter dealing only with personal and family matters. In September 1983 President Nimeri replaced all existing laws with Islamic (*Shari'a*) law. Following the coup in April 1985, the *Shari'a* courts were abolished, and it was announced that the previous system of criminal courts was to be revived. In June 1986 the Prime Minister, Sadiq al-Mahdi, reaffirmed that the *Shari'a* law was to be abolished. It was announced in June 1987 that a new legal code, based on a 'Sudanese legal heritage', was to be introduced. In July 1989 the military Government established special courts to investigate violations of emergency laws concerning corruption. It was announced in June 1991 that these courts were to be incorporated in the general court administration. Islamic law was reintroduced in March 1991, but was not applied in the Southern states of Equatoria, Bahr al-Ghazal and Upper Nile.

Chief Justice: HAFEZ ASH-SHEIKH AZ-ZAKI.

Religion

The majority of the northern Sudanese population are Muslims, while in the south the population are principally Christians or animists.

ISLAM

Islam is the state religion. Sudanese Islam has a strong Sufi element, and is estimated to have more than 15m. adherents.

CHRISTIANITY

Sudan Council of Churches: Inter-Church House, St 35, New Extension, POB 469, Khartoum; tel. (11) 742859; f. 1967; 12 mem. churches; Chair. Most Rev. PAOLINO LUKUDU LORO (Roman Catholic Archbishop of Juba); Gen. Sec. Rev. CLEMENT H. JANDA.

Roman Catholic Church

Latin Rite

Sudan comprises two archdioceses and seven dioceses. At the end of 2000 the estimated number of adherents represented about 8.5% of the total population.

Sudan Catholic Bishops' Conference

General Secretariat, POB 6011, Khartoum; tel. (11) 2250759; fax (11) 703518.

f. 1971; Pres. Most Rev. PAOLINO LUKUDU LORO (Archbishop of Juba).

Archbishop of Juba: Most Rev. PAOLINO LUKUDU LORO, Catholic Church, POB 32, Juba, Equatoria State; tel. 20388; fax 20755.

Archbishop of Khartoum: Most Rev. GABRIEL ZUBEIR WAKO, Catholic Church, POB 49, Khartoum; tel. (11) 782174; fax (11) 783518; e-mail rielei@hotmail.com.

Maronite Rite

Maronite Church in Sudan: POB 244, Khartoum; Rev. Fr YOUSEPH NEAMA.

Melkite Rite

Patriarchal Vicariate of Egypt and Sudan: Patriarcat Grec-Melkite Catholique, 16 rue Daher, 11271 Cairo, Egypt; tel. (2) 5905790; Protosyncellus Most Rev. PAUL ANTAKI (Titular Archbishop of Nubia); Vicar in Sudan Fr GEORGE BANNA; POB 766, Khartoum; tel. (11) 776466.

Syrian Rite

Syrian Church in Sudan: Under the jurisdiction of the Patriarch of Antioch; Protosyncellus Rt Rev. JOSEPH HANNOUCHE (Bishop of Cairo).

Orthodox Churches

Coptic Orthodox Church

Metropolitan of Khartoum, Southern Sudan and Uganda: Rt Rev. ANBA DANIAL, POB 4, Khartoum; tel. (11) 770646; fax (11) 785646; e-mail metaous@email-sudan.net.

Bishop of Atbara, Omdurman and Northern Sudan: Rt Rev. ANBA SARABAMON, POB 628, Omdurman; tel. (11) 550423; fax (11) 556973.

Greek Orthodox Church: POB 47, Khartoum; tel. (11) 772973; Metropolitan of Nubia Archbishop DIONYSSIOS HADZIVASSILIOU.

The Ethiopian Orthodox Church is also active.

The Anglican Communion

Anglicans are adherents of the (Episcopal) Church of the Province of the Sudan. The Province, with 24 dioceses and about 1m. adherents, was established in 1976.

Archbishop in Sudan: Most Rev. JOSEPH BIRINGI, POB 110, Juba; tel. (11) 20065.

Other Christian Churches

Evangelical Church: POB 57, Khartoum; c. 1,500 mems; administers schools, literature centre and training centre; Chair Rev. RADI ELIAS.

Presbyterian Church: POB 40, Malakal; autonomous since 1956; 67,000 mems (1985); Gen. Sec. Rev. THOMAS MALUIT.

SIM Sudan: POB 220, Khartoum; tel. (11) 472790; fax (11) 467213; e-mail fwilson@simintl.sim.org; f. 1937; Dir L. DICK.

The Africa Inland Church, the Sudan Interior Church and the Sudanese Church of Christ are also active.

The Press

DAILIES

Press censorship was imposed following the 1989 coup.

Abbar al-Youm: Khartoum; tel. (11) 779396; daily; Editor AHMED AL-BALAL AT-TAYEB.

Al-Anbaa: Khartoum; tel. (11) 466523; f. 1998; Editor-in-Chief NAJIB ADAM QAMAR AD-DIN.

Al-Nasr: Khartoum; tel. (11) 772494; Editor Col YOUNIS MAHMOUD.

Ar-Rai al-Akhar: Khartoum; tel. (11) 777934; daily; Editor MOHI AD-DIN TITTAWI.

Ar-Rai al-Amm: Khartoum; tel. (11) 778182; e-mail info@rayaam.net; internet www.rayaam.net; daily; Editor SALAH MUHAMMAD IBRAHIM.

Khartoum Monitor: Khartoum; Editor ALBINO OKENY.

Sudan Standard: Ministry of Information and Communication, Khartoum; daily; English.

Al-Wan: Khartoum; tel. (11) 775036; e-mail alwaan@cybergates.net; internet www.alwaan.com/alwaan; daily; independent; pro-Govt; Editor HOUSSEN KHOGALI.

PERIODICALS

Al-Guwwat al-Musallaha (The Armed Forces): Khartoum; f. 1969; publs a weekly newspaper and monthly magazine for the armed forces; Editor-in-Chief Maj. MAHMOUD GALANDER; circ. 7,500.

New Horizon: POB 2651, Khartoum; tel. (11) 777913; f. 1976; publ. by the Sudan House for Printing and Publishing; weekly; English; political and economic affairs, development, home and international news; Editor AS-SIR HASSAN FADL; circ. 7,000.

Sudanow: POB 2651, Khartoum; tel. (11) 777913; f. 1976; publ. by the Sudan House for Printing and Publishing; monthly; English; political and economic affairs, arts, social affairs and diversions; Editor-in-Chief AHMED KAMAL ED-DIN; circ. 10,000.

NEWS AGENCIES

Sudan News Agency (SUNA): Sharia al-Gamhouria, POB 1506, Khartoum; tel. (11) 775770; e-mail suna@sudanet.net; internet www.sudanet.net/suna.htm; Dir-Gen. ALI ABD AR-RAHMAN AN-NUMAYRI.

Sudanese Press Agency: Khartoum; f. 1985; owned by journalists.

Foreign Bureaux

Middle East News Agency (MENA) (Egypt): Dalala Bldg, POB 740, Khartoum.

Xinhua (New China) News Agency (People's Republic of China): No. 100, 12 The Sq., Riad Town, POB 2229, Khartoum; tel. (11) 224174; Correspondent SUN XIAOKE.

The Iraqi News Agency and the Agence Arabe Syrienne d'Information (Syria) also have bureaux in Khartoum.

Publishers

Ahmad Abd ar-Rahman at-Tikeine: POB 299, Port Sudan.

Al-Ayyam Press Co Ltd: POB 363, Aboulela Bldg, United Nations Sq., Khartoum; f. 1953; general fiction and non-fiction, arts, poetry, reference, newspapers, magazines; Man. Dir BESHIR MUHAMMAD SAID.

As-Sahafa Publishing and Printing House: POB 1228, Khartoum; f. 1961; newspapers, pamphlets, fiction and govt publs.

As-Salam Co Ltd: POB 944, Khartoum.

Claudios S. Fellas: POB 641, Khartoum.

Khartoum University Press: POB 321, Khartoum; tel. (11) 776653; f. 1964; academic, general and educational in Arabic and English; Man. Dir ALI EL-MAK.

Government Publishing House

El-Asma Printing Press: POB 38, Khartoum.

Broadcasting and Communications

TELECOMMUNICATIONS

A mobile cellular telephone network for Khartoum State was inaugurated in 1997.

Ministry of Information and Communication: Khartoum; regulatory body; Sec.-Gen. Eng. AWAD E. WIDAA.

Posts and Telegraphs Public Corpn: Khartoum; tel. (11) 770000; fax (11) 772888; e-mail sudanpost@maktoob.com; regulatory body; Dir-Gen. AHMAD AT-TIJANI ALALLIM.

Sudan Telecom Co (SUDATEL): 10th Floor, al-Baraka Tower, POB 11155, Khartoum; tel. (11) 773930; fax (11) 451111; e-mail info@sudatel.net; internet www.sudatel.net; service provider for Sudan; Gen. Man. ABD AL-AZIZ OSMAN.

BROADCASTING

Radio

Sudan National Broadcasting Corpn: POB 572, Omdurman; tel. (11) 552100; state-controlled service broadcasting daily in Arabic, English, French and Swahili; Dir-Gen. SALAH AD-DIN AL-FADHIL USUD.

Voice of Sudan: e-mail sudanvoice@umma.arg; active since 1995; run by the National Democratic Alliance; Arabic and English.

Television

An earth satellite station operated on 36 channels at Umm Haraz has much improved Sudan's telecommunications links. A nationwide satellite network is being established with 14 earth stations in the provinces. There are regional stations at Gezira (Central Region) and Atbara (Northern Region).

Sudan Television: POB 1094, Omdurman; tel. (11) 550022; internet www.sudantv.net; f. 1962; state-controlled; 60 hours of programmes per week; Head of Directorate HADID AS-SIRA.

Finance

(cap. = capital; res = reserves; dep. = deposits; m. = million; brs = branches; amounts in Sudanese pounds, unless otherwise indicated)

BANKING

All domestic banks are controlled by the Bank of Sudan. Foreign banks were permitted to resume operations in 1976. In December 1985 the Government banned the establishment of any further banks. It was announced in December 1990 that Sudan's banking system was to be reorganized to accord with Islamic principles. In 2000 there were a total of 25 banks in Sudan. In May 2000 the Bank of Sudan issued new policy guidelines under which Sudan's banks were to merge into six banking groups to improve their financial strength and international competitiveness; the mergers were expected to be fully implemented by the end of 2003.

Central Bank

Bank of Sudan: Gamaa Ave, POB 313, Khartoum; tel. (11) 774419; fax (11) 780273; e-mail sudanbank@sudanmail.net; internet www .bankofsudan.org; f. 1960; bank of issue; cap. 300,000m. S. dinars, res 1,041m., dep. 491,523,736m. (Dec. 1999); Gov. Dr SABIR MUHAMMAD HASSAN; 9 brs.

Commercial Banks

Al-Baraka Bank: Al-Baraka Tower, Al-qasr Ave, POB 3583, Khartoum; tel. (11) 780688; fax (11) 778948; e-mail baraka2000@ sudanmail.net; internet www.albaraka.com; f. 1984; investment and export promotion; cap. and res 445.8m., total assets 63,613.4m. (Dec. 1998); Pres. Sheikh SALIH ABDALLAH KAMIL; Gen. Man. A. RAHMAN AHMED IBRAHIM; 24 brs.

Al-Shamal Islamic Bank: Zubair Basha Rd, POB 10036, 11111 Khartoum; tel. (11) 773111; fax (11) 773585; e-mail shib@sudanet .net; internet www.shamalbank.com; f. 1990; cap. 494.2m., res 704.9m., dep. 11,692m. (Dec. 1999); Chair. ADIL ABDEL JALEEL BATARJI; Gen. Man. MUHAMMAD SHEIKH MUHAMMAD; 15 brs.

Bank of Khartoum Group: 8 Gamhouria Ave, POB 1008, Khartoum; tel. (11) 772880; fax (11) 781120; internet www .bankofkhartoum.com; f. 1913; absorbed National Export/Import Bank and Unity Bank in 1993; cap. and res 334m. S. dinars, total assets 31,604m. (Dec. 1999); Gen. Man. Dr ISMAIL MUHAMMAD GURASHI; 118 brs.

Farmers Commercial Bank: POB 1116, Al-Qasr Ave, Khartoum; tel. (11) 774960; fax (11) 773687; f. 1960 as Sudan Commercial Bank, name changed as above in 1999 following merger with Farmers Bank for Investment and Rural Development; cap. 666.1m. S. dinars, res 328.4m., dep. 6,127.5m. (Dec. 2000); Chair. EL-TAYB ELOBEID BADR; Gen. Man. BADER ELDIEN MAHMOUD ABBAS; 19 brs.

National Bank of Sudan: Kronfli Bldg, Al-Qasr Ave, POB 1183, Khartoum; tel. (11) 778154; fax (11) 779497; f. 1982; cap. 39.2m. (Dec. 1991); Chair. HASSAN IBRAHIM MALIK; 13 brs in Sudan, 2 abroad.

Omdurman National Bank: POB 11522, Al-Qasr Ave, Khartoum; tel. (11) 770400; fax (11) 770392; e-mail omb@sudanmail.net; internet www.omd-bank.com; f. 1993; cap. 500m. S. dinars, res 720.0m., dep. 16,361.9m. (Dec. 1999); Chair. HASSAN YAHYA; 16 brs.

Sudanese French Bank: Al-Qasr Ave, POB 2775, Khartoum; tel. (11) 771730; fax (11) 771740; e-mail sfbankb@sudanet.net; internet www.sfbank.net; f. 1978 as Sudanese Investment Bank; cap. 1,013m., res 21,414m., dep. 148,624m. (Dec. 1998); Chair. Dr ABBAS MUSTAFA OSMAN; Gen. Man. ABDEL RAHMAN ALI BERRI; 17 brs.

Tadamon Islamic Bank: Baladia St, POB 3154, Khartoum; tel. (11) 771505; fax (11) 773840; e-mail tadamon@sudanmail.net; internet www.tadamonbank.com; f. 1981; cap. 5.0m. S. dinars, res 206.5m., total assets 20,882.5m. (Dec. 2000); Gen. Man. SAYED SALAH ALI ABU ALNAJA; 19 brs.

Foreign Banks

Blue Nile Bank Ltd: Zubeir Pasha Ave, POB 984, Khartoum; tel. (11) 784688; fax (11) 782562; e-mail bnbsudan@yahoo.com; internet www.bluenilebank.com; f. 1983; total assets 1,723.1m. (Dec. 1999); jtly controlled by the Govts of Sudan and the Repub. of Korea; Chair. D. H. KIM.

Faisal Islamic Bank (Sudan) (Saudi Arabia): POB 10143, Khartoum; tel. (11) 774027; fax (11) 780193; e-mail gaafarom@sudanmail .net; f. 1977; cap. 975.0m. S. dinars, res 227.4m., dep. 11,596.4m. (Dec. 2000); Chair. Prince MUHAMMAD AL-FAISAL AS-SAUD; 33 brs.

Habib Bank (Pakistan): Baladia St, POB 8246, Khartoum; tel. (11) 781497; fax (11) 781497; f. 1982; cap. and res 13.8m., total assets 27.3m. (Dec. 1987); Gen. Man. BAZ MUHAMMAD KHAN.

Mashreq Bank PSC (United Arab Emirates): Baladia St, POB 371, Khartoum; tel. (11) 772969; fax (11) 772743; internet www .mashreqbank.com; Man. MUHAMMAD KHEDIR AL-ARAKI.

National Bank of Abu Dhabi (United Arab Emirates): Atbara St, POB 2465, Khartoum; tel. (11) 774870; fax (11) 774892; f. 1976; cap. and res 16.9m., total assets 12.5m. (Dec. 1987); Man. GAAFAR OSMAN.

Saudi Sudanese Bank: Baladia St, POB 1773, Khartoum; tel. (11) 776700; fax (11) 780142; f. 1986; Saudi Arabian shareholders have a 60% interest, Sudanese shareholders 40%; cap. and res 3,276.5m., dep. 30,713.4m. (Dec. 1996); Chair. Sheikh MAHFOUZ SALIM BIN MAHFOUZ.

Development Banks

Agricultural Bank of Sudan: POB 1363, Khartoum; tel. (11) 779410; fax (11) 778296; f. 1957; cap. and res 1,027m. S. dinars, total assets 12,357m. S. dinars (Dec. 1999); provides finance for agricultural projects; Pres. AS-SAYED GAFFER MUHAMMAD AL-HASSAN; Gen. Man. AS-SEED AL-KINDI YOUSIF MUHAMMAD OSMAN; 40 brs.

Islamic Co-operative Development Bank (ICDB): POB 62, Khartoum; tel. (11) 780223; fax (11) 777715; f. 1983; cap. and res 4,100m. S. dinars, total assets 53,080m. (Dec. 1999); Chair. ABDUL GALEEL EL-KARORI; 6 brs.

El-Nilein Industrial Development Bank: 1722 United Nations Sq., POB 1722, Khartoum; tel. (11) 780087; fax (11) 780776; e-mail nidbg@sudan.net; internet www.nidb.com; f. 1993 by merger; provides tech. and financial assistance for private-sector industrial projects and acquires shares in industrial enterprises; cap. 997.1m. S dinars, res 237.6m. S. dinars, dep. 17,588.5m. S. dinars (Dec. 1999); Chair. Dr SABIR MUHAMMAD EL-HASSAN; Man. Dir IBRAHIM ADAM HABIB; 41 brs.

NIMA Development and Investment Bank: Hashim Hago Bldg, As-Suk al-Arabi, POB 665, Khartoum; tel. (11) 779496; fax (11) 781854; f. 1982 as National Devt Bank, name changed as above 1998; 90%-owned by NIMA Groupe, 10% private shareholders; finances or co-finances economic and social development projects; cap. 4,000m., res 106m. (Dec. 1998); Dir-Gen. SALIM EL-SAFI HUGIR; 6 brs.

Sudanese Estates Bank: Baladia St, POB 309, Khartoum; tel. (11) 777917; fax (11) 779465; f. 1967; mortgage bank financing private-sector urban housing development; cap. and res 1,700m., total assets 9,500m. (Dec. 1994); Chair. Eng. MUHAMMAD ALI EL-AMIN; 6 brs.

STOCK EXCHANGE

Sudanese Stock Exchange: Al-Baraka Tower, 5th Floor, POB 10835, Khartoum; tel. (11) 776235; fax (11) 776134; f. 1995; Chair. HAMZA MUHAMMAD JENAWI; 27 mems.

INSURANCE

African Insurance Co (Sudan) Ltd: Muhammad Hussein Bldg, Al-Baladiya Ave, POB 149, Khartoum; f. 1977; fire, accident, marine and motor; Gen. Man. AN-NOMAN AS-SANUSI.

Blue Nile Insurance Co (Sudan) Ltd: POB 2215, Khartoum; Gen. Man. MUHAMMAD AL-AMIN MIRGHANI.

Foja International Insurance Co Ltd: POB 879, Khartoum; tel. (11) 784470; fax (11) 783248; fire, accident, marine, motor and animal; Gen. Man. MAMOON IBRAHIM ABD ALLA.

General Insurance Co (Sudan) Ltd: El-Mek Nimr St, POB 1555, Khartoum; tel. (11) 780616; fax (11) 772122; f. 1961; Gen. Man. ELSAMAWL ELSAYED HAFIZ.

Islamic Insurance Co Ltd: Al-Faiha Commercial Bldg, POB 2776, Khartoum; tel. (11) 772656; e-mail islamicins@sudanmail.net; f. 1979; all classes.

Khartoum Insurance Co Ltd: POB 737, Khartoum; tel. (11) 778647; f. 1953; Chair. MUDAWI M. AHMAD; Gen. Man. ABD AL-MENIM AL-HADARI.

Juba Insurance Co Ltd: Horia Ave, POB 10043, Khartoum; tel. (11) 783245; fax 781617; Gen. Man. ABDUL AAL ELDAWI ABDUL AAL.

Middle East Insurance Co Ltd: POB 3070, Khartoum; tel. (11) 772202; fax (11) 779266; f. 1981; fire, marine, motor and general liability; Chair. AHMAD I. MALIK; Gen. Man. MUAWIA MIRGANI ABBASHER.

Sudanese Insurance and Reinsurance Co Ltd: Sharia al-Gamhouria, Nasr Sq., POB 2332, Khartoum; tel. (11) 770812; f. 1967; Gen. Man. IZZ AD-DIN AS-SAID MUHAMMAD.

United Insurance Co (Sudan) Ltd: Makkawi Bldg, Sharia al-Gamhouria, POB 318, Khartoum; tel. (11) 776630; fax (11) 770783; e-mail abdin@unitedinsurance.ws; internet www.unitedinsurance .ws; f. 1968; Dir-Gen. MUHAMMAD ABDEEN BABIKER.

Trade and Industry

GOVERNMENT AGENCIES

Agricultural Research Corpn: POB 126, Wadi Medani; tel. (511) 42226; fax (511) 43213; e-mail arcsudan@sudanet.net; f. 1967; Dir-Gen. Prof. SALIH HUSSEIN SALIH.

Animal Production Public Corpn: POB 624, Khartoum; tel. (11) 778555; Gen. Man. Dr FOUAD RAMADAN HAMID.

General Petroleum Corpn: POB 2986, Khartoum; tel. (11) 771554; f. 1976; Chair. Dr OSMAN ABDULWAHAB; Dir-Gen. Dr ABD ER-RAHMAN OSMAN ABD ER-RAHMAN.

Gum Arabic Co Ltd: POB 857, Khartoum; tel. (11) 461061; fax (11) 471336; e-mail gmanager@gumarab.com; internet www.gumarab .com; f. 1969; Chair. Dr BABIKIR MUHAMMAD TOM; Gen. Man. Dr MUSA MUHAMMAD KARAMA.

Industrial Production Corpn: POB 1034, Khartoum; tel. (11) 771278; f. 1976; Dir-Gen. OSMAN TAMMAM.

Cement and Building Materials Sector Co-ordination Office: POB 2241, Khartoum; tel. (11) 774269; Dir T. M. KHOGALI.

Food Industries Corpn: POB 2341, Khartoum; tel. (11) 775463; Dir MUHAMMAD AL-GHALI SULIMAN.

Leather Industries Corpn: POB 1639, Khartoum; tel. (11) 778187; f. 1986; Man. Dir IBRAHIM SALIH ALI.

Oil Corpn: POB 64, Khartoum North; tel. (11) 332044; Gen. Man. BUKHARI MAHMOUD BUKHARI.

Spinning and Weaving General Co Ltd: POB 765, Khartoum; tel. (11) 774306; f. 1975; Dir MUHAMMAD SALIH MUHAMMAD ABDALLAH.

Sudan Tea Co Ltd: POB 1219, Khartoum; tel. (11) 781261.

Sudanese Mining Corpn: POB 1034, Khartoum; tel. (11) 770840; f. 1975; Dir IBRAHIM MUDAWI BABIKER.

Sugar and Distilling Industry Corpn: POB 511, Khartoum; tel. (11) 778417; Man. MIRGHANI AHMAD BABIKER.

Mechanized Farming Corpn: POB 2482, Khartoum; Man. Dir AWAD AL-KARIM AL-YASS.

National Cotton and Trade Co Ltd: POB 1552, Khartoum; tel. (11) 80040; f. 1970; Chair. ABD EL-ATI A. MEKKI; Man. Dir ABD AR-RAHMAN A. MONIEM; Gen. Man. ZUBAIR MUHAMMAD AL-BASHIR.

Port Sudan Cotton Trade Co Ltd: POB 590, Port Sudan; POB 590, Khartoum; Gen. Man. SAID MUHAMMAD ADAM.

Public Agricultural Production Corpn: POB 538, Khartoum; Chair. and Man. Dir ABDALLAH BAYOUMO; Sec. SAAD AD-DIN MUHAMMAD ALI.

Public Corpn for Building and Construction: POB 2110, Khartoum; tel. (11) 774544; Dir NAIM AD-DIN.

Public Corpn for Irrigation and Excavation: POB 619, Khartoum; tel. (11) 780167; Gen. Sec. OSMAN AN-NUR.

Public Corpn for Oil Products and Pipelines: POB 1704, Khartoum; tel. (11) 778290; Gen. Man. ABD AR-RAHMAN SULIMAN.

Rahad Corpn: POB 2523, Khartoum; tel. (11) 775175; financed by the World Bank, Kuwait and the USA; by 1983 300,000 ha had been irrigated and 70,000 people settled in 15,000 tenancies; Man. Dir HASSAN SAAD ABDALLA.

The State Trading Corpn: POB 211, Khartoum; tel. (11) 778555; Chair. E. R. M. TOM.

Automobile Corpn: POB 221, Khartoum; tel. (11) 778555; importer of vehicles and spare parts; Gen. Man. DAFALLA AHMAD SIDDIQ.

Captrade Engineering and Automobile Services Co Ltd: POB 97, Khartoum; tel. (11) 789265; fax (11) 775544; e-mail cap1@ sudanmail.net; f. 1925; importers and distributors of engineering and automobile equipment; Gen. Man. ESSAM MOHD EL-HASSAN KAMBAL.

Gezira Trade and Services Co: POB 215, Khartoum; tel. (11) 772687; fax (11) 779060; e-mail gtco@sudanmail.net; f. 1980; importer of agricultural machinery, spare parts, electrical and office equipment, foodstuffs, clothes and footwear; exporter of oilseeds, grains, hides and skins and livestock; provides shipping insurance and warehousing services; agents for Lloyds and P and I Club; Chair. NASR ED-DIN M. OMER.

Khartoum Commercial and Shipping Co: POB 221, Khartoum; tel. (11) 778555; f. 1982; import, export and shipping services, insurance and manufacturing; Gen. Man. IDRIS M. SALIH.

Silos and Storage Corpn: POB 1183, Khartoum; stores and handles agricultural products; Gen. Man. AHMAD AT-TAIEB HARHOOF.

Sudan Cotton Co Ltd: POB 1672, Khartoum; tel. (11) 771567; fax (11) 770703; e-mail sccl@sudanet.net; f. 1970; exports raw cotton; Chair. ABBAS ABD AL-BAGI HAMMAD; Dir-Gen. ABDIN MUHAMMAD ALI.

Sudan Gezira Board: POB 884, HQ Barakat Wadi Medani, Gezira Province; tel. 2412; Sales Office, POB 884, Khartoum; tel. (11) 740145; responsible for Sudan's main cotton-producing area; the Gezira scheme is a partnership between the Govt, the tenants and the board. The Govt provides the land and is responsible for irrigation. Tenants pay a land and water charge and receive the work proceeds. The Board provides agricultural services at cost, technical supervision and execution of govt agricultural policies relating to the scheme. Tenants pay a percentage of their proceeds to the Social Development Fund. The total potential cultivable area of the Gezira scheme is c. 850,000 ha and the total area under systematic irrigation is c. 730,000 ha. In addition to cotton, groundnuts, sorghum, wheat, rice, pulses and vegetables are grown for the benefit of tenant farmers; Man. Dir Prof. FATHI MUHAMMAD KHALIFA.

Sudan Oilseeds Co Ltd: Parliament Ave, POB 167, Khartoum; tel. (11) 780120; f. 1974; 58% state-owned; exporter of oilseeds (groundnuts, sesame seeds and castor beans); importer of foodstuffs and other goods; Chair. SADIQ KARAR AT-TAYEB; Gen. Man. KAMAL ABD AL-HALIM.

DEVELOPMENT CORPORATIONS

Sudan Development Corpn (SDC): 21 al-Amarat, POB 710, Khartoum; tel. (11) 472151; fax (11) 472148; f. 1974 to promote and co-finance development projects with special emphasis on projects in the agricultural, agri-business, and industrial sectors; cap. p.u. US $200m. Man. Dir Dr MUHAMMAD KHIER AHMED EL-ZUBIER.

Sudan Rural Development Co Ltd (SRDC): POB 2190, Khartoum; tel. (11) 773855; fax (11) 773235; e-mail srdfc@hotmail; f. 1980; SDC has 27% shareholding; cap. p.u. US $20m. Gen. Man. EL-AWAD ABDALLA H. HIJAZI (designate).

Sudan Rural Development Finance Co (SRDFC): POB 2190, Khartoum; tel. (11) 773855; fax (11) 773235; f. 1980; Gen. Man. OMRAN MUHAMMAD ALI.

CHAMBER OF COMMERCE

Union of Sudanese Chambers of Commerce: POB 81, Khartoum; tel. (11) 772346; fax (11) 780748; e-mail chamber@ sudanchamber.org; internet www.sudanchamber.org; f. 1908; Pres. ELTAYEB AHMED OSMAN; Sec.-Gen. IBRAHIM MUHAMMAD OSMAN.

INDUSTRIAL ASSOCIATION

Sudanese Industries Association: Africa St, POB 2565, Khartoum; tel. (11) 773151; f. 1974; Chair. FATH AR-RAHMAN AL-BASHIR; Exec. Dir A. IZZ AL-ARAB YOUSUF.

UTILITIES

Public Electricity and Water Corpn: POB 1380, Khartoum; tel. (11) 81021; Dir Dr YASIN AL-HAJ ABDIN.

CO-OPERATIVE SOCIETIES

There are about 600 co-operative societies, of which 570 are officially registered.

Central Co-operative Union: POB 2492, Khartoum; tel. (11) 780624; largest co-operative union operating in 15 provinces.

TRADE UNIONS

All trade union activity was banned following the 1989 coup. The following organizations were active prior to that date.

Federations

Sudan Workers Trade Unions Federation (SWTUF): POB 2258, Khartoum; tel. (11) 777463; includes 42 trade unions representing c. 1.75m. public-service and private-sector workers; affiliated to the Int. Confed. of Arab Trade Unions and the Org. of African Trade Union Unity; Pres. MUHAMMAD OSMAN GAMA; Gen. Sec. YOUSUF ABU SHAMA HAMED.

Sudanese Federation of Employees and Professionals Trade Unions: POB 2398, Khartoum; tel. (11) 773818; f. 1975; includes 54 trade unions representing 250,000 mems; Pres. IBRAHIM AWADALLAH; Sec.-Gen. KAMAL AD-DIN MUHAMMAD ABDALLAH.

Transport

RAILWAYS

The total length of railway in operation in 2000 was 5,901 route-km. The main line runs from Wadi Halfa, on the Egyptian border, to al-Obeid, via Khartoum. Lines from Atbara and Sinnar connect with Port Sudan. There are lines from Sinnar to Damazin on the Blue Nile (227 km) and from Aradeiba to Nyala in the south-western province of Darfur (689 km), with a 445-km branch line from Babanousa to Wau in Bahr al-Ghazal province. In 2001 plans were announced for the construction of a rail link between Port Sudan and Moyale, Ethiopia.

Sudan Railways Corpn: POB 65, Atbara; tel. 2000; f. 1875; Gen. Man. OMAR MUHAMMAD NUR.

ROADS

Roads in northern Sudan, other than town roads, are only cleared tracks and often impassable immediately after rain. Motor traffic on roads in the former Upper Nile province is limited to the drier months of January–May. There are several good gravelled roads in Equatoria and Bahr al-Ghazal provinces which are passable all the year, but in these districts some of the minor roads become impassable after rain. Rehabilitation of communications in Southern Sudan is hampered by the continuing hostilities in the area.

Over 48,000 km of tracks are classed as 'motorable'; there were 3,160 km of main roads and 739 km of secondary roads in 1985. A 1,190-km tarmac road linking the capital with Port Sudan was completed during 1980. In 1996, according to World Bank estimates, some 36.3% of Sudan's roads were paved. By 1997 a 270-km road linking Jaili with Atbara had been completed, as part of a scheme to provide an alternative route from Khartoum to the coast.

National Transport Corpn: POB 723, Khartoum; Gen. Man. MOHI AD-DIN HASSAN MUHAMMAD NUR.

Public Corpn for Roads and Bridges: POB 756, Khartoum; tel. (11) 770794; f. 1976; Chair. ABD AR-RAHMAN HABOUD; Dir-Gen. ABDOU MUHAMMAD ABDOU.

INLAND WATERWAYS

The total length of navigable waterways served by passenger and freight services is 4,068 km, of which approximately 1,723 km is open all year. From the Egyptian border to Wadi Halfa and Khartoum navigation is limited by cataracts to short stretches, but the White Nile from Khartoum to Juba is almost always navigable.

River Transport Corpn (RTC): POB 284, Khartoum North; operates 2,500 route-km of steamers on the Nile; Chair. ALI AMIR TAHA.

River Navigation Corpn: Khartoum; f. 1970; jtly owned by Govts of Egypt and Sudan; operates services between Aswan and Wadi Halfa.

SHIPPING

Port Sudan, on the Red Sea, 784 km from Khartoum, and Suakin are the only commercial seaports.

Axis Trading Co Ltd: POB 1574, Khartoum; tel. (11) 775875; f. 1967; Chair. HASSAN A. M. SULIMAN.

Red Sea Shipping Corpn: POB 116, Khartoum; tel. (11) 777688; fax (11) 774220; e-mail redseaco@sudan.net; Gen. Man. OSMAN AMIN.

Sea Ports Corpn: Port Sudan; tel. 2910; f. 1906; Gen. Man. MUHAMMAD TAHIR AILA.

Sudan Shipping Line Ltd: POB 426, Port Sudan; tel. 2655; and POB 1731, Khartoum; tel. (11) 780017; f. 1960; 10 vessels totalling 54,277 dwt operating between the Red Sea and western Mediterranean, northern Europe and United Kingdom; Chair. ISMAIL BAKHEIT; Gen. Man. SALAH AD-DIN OMER AL-AZIZ.

United African Shipping Co: POB 339, Khartoum; tel. (11) 780967; Gen. Man. MUHAMMAD TAHA AL-GINDI.

CIVIL AVIATION

Civil Aviation Authority: Khartoum; tel. (11) 772264; Dir-Gen. Brig. MAHGOUB MUHAMMAD MAHDI.

Air West Express: POB 10217, Khartoum; tel. (11) 452503; fax (11) 451703; f. 1992; passenger and freight services to destinations in Africa; Chair. SAIF M. S. OMER.

Azza Transport: POB 11586, Mak Nimir St, Khartoum; tel. (11) 783761; fax (11) 770408; e-mail sawasawa@sudanet.net; f. 1993; charter and dedicated freight to Africa and the Middle East; Man. Dir Dr GIBRIL I. MOHAMED.

Sudan Airways Co Ltd: POB 253, SDC Bldg Complex, Amarat St 19, Khartoum; tel. (11) 472451; fax (11) 442377; internet www.sudanair.com; f. 1947; internal flights and international services to Africa, the Middle East and Europe; Man. Dir ELFATIH MUHAMMAD ALI.

Sudanese Aeronautical Services (SASCO): POB 8260, El Amarat, Khartoum; tel. (11) 7463362; fax (11) 4433362; fmrly Sasco Air Charter; chartered services; Chair. M. M. NUR.

Trans Arabian Air Transport (TAAT): POB 1461, Africa St, Khartoum; tel. (11) 451568; fax (11) 451544; e-mail ftaats@sudanmail.net; f. 1983; dedicated freight; services to Africa, Europe and Middle East; Man. Dir Capt. EL-FATI ABDIN.

United Arabian Airlines: POB 3687, Office No. 3, Elekhwa Bldg, Atbara St, Khartoum; tel. (11) 773025; fax (11) 784402; e-mail krthq@uaa.com; internet www.uaa.com; f. 1995; charter and dedicated freight services to Africa and the Middle East; Man. Dir M. KORDOFANI.

Tourism

Public Corpn of Tourism and Hotels: POB 7104, Khartoum; tel. (11) 781764; f. 1977; Dir-Gen. Maj.-Gen. EL-KHATIM MUHAMMAD FADL.

SURINAME

Introductory Survey

Location, Climate, Language, Religion, Flag, Capital

The Republic of Suriname lies on the north-east coast of South America. It is bordered by Guyana to the west, by French Guiana to the east, and by Brazil to the south. The climate is sub-tropical, with fairly heavy rainfall and average temperatures of between 21°C (70°F) and 30°C (86°F). Average annual rainfall varies from 3,720 mm (146 ins) in the north to 804 mm (32 ins) in the south. The official language is Dutch (spoken by 37% of the population in 1964). The other main languages are Hindustani (32%) and Javanese (15%). The majority of the people can speak the native language Sranang Tongo, a Creole language known as Negro English or taki-taki, while Chinese, English, French and Spanish are also used. The principal religions are Christianity (professed by about 48% of the population), Hinduism (27%) and Islam (20%). The national flag (proportions 2 by 3) has five horizontal stripes: a broad central band of red (with a five-pointed yellow star in the centre), edged with white, between bands of green. The capital is Paramaribo.

Recent History

Settlers from England landed in Suriname in the 1630s, and the territory was alternately a British and a Dutch colony until it was eventually awarded to the Netherlands by the Treaty of Vienna in 1815. The colony's economy depended on large sugar plantations, for which labour was provided by slaves of African origin. Following the abolition of slavery in 1863, immigration of labourers from India and the then Dutch East Indies was encouraged, and many of them settled permanently in Suriname. This history explains the country's current ethnic diversity: there are small communities of the original Amerindian population (mainly in the interior) and of ethnic Chinese and Europeans; a Creole population, largely of African descent, constitutes about one-third of the population, as do the Asian-descended 'East' Indians (known locally as Hindustanis); the Indonesian-descended 'Javanese' form about 15% of the population, and another Creole group, the 'boschnegers' or Bush Negroes, forms a further 10% (the Bush Negroes are the Dutch-speaking descendants of escaped slaves, long-established in the rainforest as a tribalized society of four clans). Under a Charter signed in December 1954, Suriname (also known as Dutch Guiana) became an equal partner in the Kingdom of the Netherlands, with the Netherlands Antilles and the Netherlands itself, and gained full autonomy in domestic affairs.

The Hindustani-dominated Government, in power since 1969 and led by Dr Jules Sedney, resigned in February 1973. General elections in November were won by an alliance of parties, the Nationale Partij Kambinatie (NPK), which favoured complete independence from the Netherlands, and in December Henck Arron, leader of the Nationale Partij Suriname (NPS—a predominantly Creole party), became Prime Minister. In May 1975 it was agreed that Suriname would become independent on 25 November. Dr Johan Ferrier, hitherto the Governor of Suriname, became the new republic's first President. Some 40,000 Surinamese emigrated to the Netherlands after independence, leaving Suriname with a severely underskilled work-force. Border disputes with French Guiana and Guyana also ensued. The general election of October 1977 resulted in a clear majority for the NPK, and Henck Arron continued as Prime Minister.

The Arron administration was overthrown in February 1980 by a group of soldiers, who formed a military council, the Nationale Militaire Raad (NMR). President Ferrier refused to agree to the retention of supreme power by the NMR, and in March he appointed a civilian administration led by Dr Henk Chin-A-Sen, a former leader of the Partij Nationalistische Republiek. In August the Army Chief of Staff, NMR member Sgt-Maj. (later Lt-Col) Désiré (Desi) Bouterse (subsequently Commander-in-Chief of the armed forces), led a coup. Ferrier was replaced by Chin-A-Sen; the legislature was dissolved, and a state of emergency declared. A Hindustani-inspired counter-coup, led by Sgt-Maj. Wilfred Hawker, failed in March 1981. In September the President announced details of a draft Constitution, which sought to limit the army to a supervisory role in government. The army responded with the formation of the Revolutionary People's Front, a comprehensive political alliance headed by Bouterse and two other members of the NMR, Maj. Roy Horb and Lt (later Commdr) Iwan Graanoogst, together with three leaders of workers' and students' organizations. In February 1982 the NMR, led by Bouterse, seized power from Chin-A-Sen and his civilian Government. The Vice-President of the Supreme Court, L. Fred Ramdat Misier, was appointed interim President. Hawker was executed after attempting a further coup in March. (Chin-A-Sen left for the Netherlands, where, in January 1983, he formed the Movement for the Liberation of Suriname, which aimed to remove Bouterse from power by peaceful means.)

A state of siege was declared, and martial law was imposed in December 1982. In order to prevent the Netherlands from suspending its aid, a 12-member Cabinet of Ministers with a civilian majority was appointed, and a moderate economist, Henry Neyhorst, became Prime Minister, although Bouterse remained effectively in control. Failure to effect promised social and economic changes lost Bouterse the support of left-wing groups and trade unions, which supported the business community in demanding a return to constitutional rule. In October the arrest of Cyriel Daal, the leader of Suriname's principal trade union (De Moederbond), prompted strikes and demonstrations. In order to avert a general strike, Bouterse agreed to arrange for the election of a constituent assembly to draft a new constitution by March 1983 (to be followed by the establishment of an elected government), but he later reneged on this commitment. In December 1982 members of the armed forces burned down several buildings used by the opposition. During the ensuing disturbances, 15 prominent citizens, including Daal, were killed, in what became known as the 'December Murders'. The Government resigned, the Netherlands and the USA halted all aid, and the country was placed under rule by decree; an interim, military-dominated Government was appointed. An attempted coup in January 1983, the sixth since February 1980, resulted in the dismissal of two-thirds of the officers of the armed forces and the death of Maj. Horb. In February 1983 Dr Errol Alibux, a former Minister of Social Affairs, was appointed Prime Minister. He formed a new Cabinet of Ministers, composed of members of two left-wing parties, the Progressieve Arbeiders en Landbouwers Unie (PALU) and the Revolutionaire Volkspartij. The new Government immediately ended the restrictions imposed in December 1982.

In January 1984, after a series of widely-observed strikes in support of demands for the restoration of civilian rule and the organization of free elections, Bouterse dismissed the Cabinet of Ministers. Agreement was reached with the strike organizers, following the withdrawal of proposals to increase taxation rates. An interim Government, with Wim Udenhout, a former adviser to Bouterse, as Prime Minister, was created in February to formulate a timetable for the gradual restoration of constitutional rule. Nominees of the trade unions and business sector were also included in the new Government. Bouterse hoped to consolidate his position by securing a political base through Standvaste (the 25 February Movement), which he had founded in November 1983. In December 1984 plans for a nominated National Assembly (comprising representatives of Standvaste, the trade unions and the business community) were announced. The Netherlands Government, however, refused to consider the changes as a significant move towards democratic rule, deeming them insufficient to merit the resumption of aid. None the less, the National Assembly was inaugurated in January 1985. A new Cabinet of Ministers, based on the previous administration, was formed by Udenhout.

The tripartite administration collapsed in April 1985, after the withdrawal from the Cabinet of Ministers of three of the four trade union nominees. A reconstituted Cabinet, formed in June, contained new members with links to traditional political parties. In November the ban on political parties was revoked, and in the same month, former NPS Prime Minister Arron, together with Jaggernath Lachmon of the Hindustani-based Vooruitstrevende Hervormings Partij (VHP) and Willy Soemita of the Kaum-Tani Persuatan Indonesia (KTPI), accepted an invitation to join the NMR, renamed the Topberaad (Supreme Council). By July 1986 only two military officers remained on the Topberaad. In that month Bouterse appointed a new Cabinet of Ministers, including representatives from industry, business, political parties, trade unions and Standvaste. Pretaap Radhakishun, a business executive and member of the VHP, was appointed Prime Minister. The Cabinet drafted a new Constitution, which was approved by the National Assembly on 31 March 1987 and by a national referendum in September.

From July 1986 anti-Government guerrillas began a series of attacks on military posts on the eastern border of the country. The guerrillas were led by Ronnie Brunswijk (a former presidential bodyguard). Mainly Bush Negroes, they claimed that government resettlement policies threatened the autonomy of their tribal society, as guaranteed by treaties, signed in 1760, with the former Dutch authorities. It was reported that financial support for the guerrillas (known as the Jungle Commando, or Surinamese Liberation Army—SLA) was being provided by Surinamese exiles in the Netherlands, in particular by members of the Movement for the Liberation of Suriname. By November most of the eastern district of Marowijne was under guerrilla control, and the rebels had also occupied the area near Zanderij (later renamed Johan Adolf Pengel) International Airport, south of Paramaribo. Rebel attacks on the mining town of Moengo forced the closure of the country's principal bauxite mines. The town was recaptured by the armed forces in December, but the mines remained closed. At the beginning of December a state of emergency was declared in eastern and southern Suriname, and a curfew was imposed. Reports that some 200 civilians had been massacred by government troops in the search for guerrillas led to protests by the Netherlands and US Governments.

In February 1987 five members of the Cabinet of Ministers, including Radhakishun, resigned. Jules Wijdenbosch, hitherto the Minister of Internal Affairs and a member of Standvaste, was appointed Prime Minister. The entire Cabinet resigned at the end of March 1987, and a new Cabinet, led by Wijdenbosch, was appointed by Bouterse in April.

In 1987, in preparation for the general election that was to be held in November, several political parties resumed their activities. Standvaste was reconstituted, under Wijdenbosch, as the Nationale Democratische Partij (NDP—National Democratic Party). Three major opposition parties, the NPS, the VHP and the KTPI (whose name was changed to the Kerukanan Tulodo Pranatan Ingil in October 1987), announced an electoral alliance, the Front voor Demokratie en Ontwikkeling (FDO—Front for Democracy and Development). The leaders of the FDO declared that the new alliance would strive for the best possible relationship with the armed forces, while Bouterse stated that the army would respect the outcome of the election. Brunswijk's SLA observed a cease-fire for the duration of the voting.

Elections to the 51-seat National Assembly were held on 25 November 1987. The FDO won a decisive victory, obtaining 40 of the 41 seats that it contested; the PALU and the Progressieve Bosneger Partij each won four seats, while the NDP won three. In January 1988 the National Assembly unanimously elected Ramsewak Shankar (a former Minister of Agriculture) as President of the Republic, and Henck Arron was elected Vice-President and thus (in accordance with the new Constitution) Prime Minister, leading the 14-member Cabinet of Ministers, which comprised members of the alliance. In December 1987 Bouterse was appointed leader of a five-member Military Council, established under the new Constitution to 'guarantee a peaceful transition' to democracy. In July 1988 the Netherlands Government agreed to resume aid to Suriname, but under more restrictive conditions than those previously imposed. Aid was to be provided only on a project-by-project basis until the Suriname Government implemented the International Monetary Fund's (IMF) structural-adjustment programme, considered necessary to correct the economic crisis. However, relations remained tense, largely owing to the Dutch administration's mistrust of the intentions of the Surinamese army.

In June 1988 negotiations finally began between the Government and representatives of the SLA, with the Committee of Christian Churches, led by the Roman Catholic Bishop of Paramaribo, acting as mediator. After preliminary discussions in June 1989, and further negotiations in July, representatives of the Government and the SLA, meeting in French Guiana, signed an agreement at Kourou, which was ratified by the National Assembly in August. The main provisions of the Kourou Accord were: a general amnesty for those involved in the recent conflicts; the ending of the state of emergency; the incorporation of

many members of the SLA into a special police unit for the interior of the country; and significant investment in the interior. The armed forces declared their opposition to the Accord, but took no direct action against continuing negotiations. However, at the end of August there was a further outbreak of guerrilla activity, in the west of the country, by an Amerindian group critical of some of the provisions of the Kourou Accord. The group, known as the Tucayana Amazonica, principally opposed the involvement of the SLA in the proposed police force for the interior; it also requested the restoration of the Bureau for Amerindian Affairs. Several of the group's demands were similar to those of the army command, and there were allegations that Tucayana were being armed and encouraged by the military, exploiting the traditional antipathy between the Amerindians and many of the Bush Negroes. In October, however, the Tucayana spokesmen were augmented by elected representatives of the Amerindian communities (the Commission of Eight) and the two groups met representatives of the National Assembly, who stated that the Government was prepared to supplement, but not rescind, the Kourou Accord.

Also in October 1989 Tucayana received the support of another new insurgent group, the Mandela Bush Negro Liberation Movement (BBM), which declared itself to be dissatisfied with the Kourou Accord. The BBM was formed by members of the most westerly (and, hitherto, least involved in the civil war) of the Bush Negro clans, the Matauriërs. In the same month, however, Brunswijk's SLA secured the support of another new insurgent group, the Union for Liberation and Democracy (UBD), which occupied the mining town of Moengo. Apparently composed of radical former members of the SLA, the UBD declared its support for the Accord.

On 22 December 1990 Bouterse resigned as Commander-in-Chief of the armed forces, after President Shankar failed to issue an official protest at the Netherlands' treatment of Bouterse, who was denied access to the country while in transit at Amsterdam's airport. Suspicions that Bouterse's resignation might portend a military coup were realized two days later, when the acting Commander-in-Chief of the armed forces, Graanoogst, seized power from the Government. The coup was immediately condemned by the Dutch Government, which suspended development aid to Suriname. Johan Kraag (honorary chairman of the NPS and a former Minister of Labour) was appointed provisional President on 29 December, and promptly invited Bouterse to resume command of the armed forces, thus substantiating speculation that Kraag was merely acting on behalf of Bouterse. A transitional Government (led by Jules Wijdenbosch, who had been Prime Minister in 1987) was sworn in on 7 January 1991, and it was announced that a general election would take place within 100 days, later extended to 150 days. In March Brunswijk and Bouterse (who had continued negotiations intermittently since 1989) met in the rebel stronghold of Drietabbetje to sign a peace accord. In April four rebel groups, the SLA, Tucayana, the BBM and Angula (or 'Defiance', led by Carlos Maassi), signed a further agreement with the Government, promising to respect the law and not to obstruct the conduct of free elections.

The elections, which were monitored by a delegation from the Organization of American States (OAS, see p. 288), were held on 25 May 1991. The Nieuw Front (NF), an electoral alliance comprising the members of the former FDO and the Surinaamse Partij van de Arbeid, secured 30 seats in the National Assembly, while the NDP won 12. The remaining nine seats were won by a new coalition, Democratisch Alternatief 1991 (DA '91), mainly comprising former members of the FDO critical of the Government's failure to curb the political influence of the military. Despite the fact that it had not secured the two-thirds' majority in the Assembly necessary to elect automatically its presidential candidate, Runaldo R. Venetiaan, the NF refused to consider the possibility of any agreement involving the formation of a coalition government or the cession of ministerial posts or policy commitments to either the NDP or DA '91. When a series of meetings of the National Assembly in July failed to result in any one presidential candidate securing a majority, the Chairman of the Assembly, Jaggernath Lachman, in accordance with provisions incorporated in the Constitution, convened the Vereinigde Volksvergadering (United People's Assembly), a body comprising the members of the National Assembly and representatives of the municipal and district councils, in order to elect a President. On 7 September Venetiaan was elected with an overwhelming 78.9% of the votes. One of Venetiaan's first acts as President was to announce, in October, the reduction of the armed forces by two-thirds and a reduction in the defence budget of 50%. These measures were introduced as part of a government programme of 'socialization' of the armed forces. In addition, amendments to the Constitution, which were approved in March 1992, included measures to curb the political influence of the military, removing all its constitutional duties except those of national defence and the combating of organized subversion, and banning serving members of the security forces from holding representative public office. In April the Military Council, established under the 1987 Constitution, was abolished.

Following renewed peace negotiations in early 1992 between the Government, the SLA and Tucayana, hostilities, which had resurfaced in late 1991, were suspended in May. In August a peace agreement was signed by the Government and the two rebel groups; the BBM also committed itself to the agreement. Under the terms of the agreement, the amnesty law envisaged under the Kourou Accord of 1989, covering all civil conflicts since 1985 and amended to include insurgent groups formed since the ratification of the Kourou Accord, was to be implemented. All weapons were to be surrendered to the Government, under the supervision of the OAS. Following disarmament, members of all the groups would be eligible for recruitment into a special police force for the interior of the country. In addition, the Government gave assurances that the interior would receive priority in its programmes for economic development and social welfare.

In November 1992 Bouterse resigned as Commander-in-Chief of the armed forces, prompting public concern that the move might once again signal a coup. Bouterse's resignation came as the result of a dispute with the Government over its decision to allow the staging of a march to commemorate the 10th anniversary of the December Murders. Venetiaan's appointment of Col (retd) Arthy Gorré as Bouterse's successor resulted in a confrontation between the Government and senior military officers in April 1993. (Gorré had supported the 1980 coup staged by Bouterse, but had resigned from the armed forces in 1987, following a disagreement with the latter.) Graanoogst, who had occupied the position of Commander-in-Chief on an interim basis since Bouterse's resignation, refused to concede the post to Gorré. He was supported by his fellow members of the military high command and by Bouterse, who, despite his resignation, remained effectively in control of the armed forces. Venetiaan subsequently deferred Gorré's appointment until mid-May, when it was endorsed by a majority in the National Assembly, despite veiled threats of a military coup and an attack on the national television station, which had allegedly been instigated by Bouterse in an attempt to intimidate the legislature. All four members of the military high command subsequently acceded to a request by the National Assembly for their resignations. Three of them, including Graanoogst, later accepted posts as advisers to the Government, thus assuaging fears of an escalation of the conflict. Indications that the Netherlands might intervene to assist the Government were also considered influential in averting further military defiance of civilian rule.

At a general election conducted on 23 May 1996 no single party secured a legislative majority, much less the two-thirds' majority necessary to elect its presidential candidate. The NF secured 24 seats, the NDP 16, DA '91 four, Pendawa Lima four and Alliantie the remaining three seats. Venetiaan, having rejected an offer from Bouterse to form a coalition government, began negotiations with the three other parties with representation in the legislature. However, the negotiations failed to produce agreement on a coalition. Neither Venetiaan nor the candidate of the NDP, former Prime Minister Jules Wijdenbosch, were able to command the two-thirds' majority in the National Assembly necessary to secure the presidency, and responsibility for electing the president consequently passed to the Vereinigde Volksvergadering. With only a simple majority required to win, Wijdenbosch obtained 438 votes, against 407 for Venetiaan, and was inaugurated as President on 14 September. The KTPI and a dissident faction of the VHP, the Beweging voor Vernieuwing en Democratie (BVD), subsequently left the NF alliance, joining an NDP-led coalition. However, the support of the KTPI and the BVD was conditional upon Bouterse's exclusion from the new Government. The parties also stipulated that the portfolios of Foreign Affairs, Finance, Defence and Internal Affairs should not be allocated to the NDP. The new coalition Government, appointed in September, comprised members of the NDP, KTPI, BVD and the Hernieuwde Progressieve Partij (HPP).

In August 1997 the Minister of Finance, Motilal Mungra, was dismissed following a public dispute in which Mungra criticized Wijdenbosch for extravagant expenditure, including the purchase of a presidential yacht. Wijdenbosch was forced to negotiate with members of the BVD, of which Mungra was then Chairman, and two other small parties, in order to maintain a majority in the legislature. In September Wijdenbosch conducted a reorganization of the Cabinet to reflect the new balance of support for his Government. In February 1998, following the withdrawal of support for the administration by four members of the National Assembly, Wijdenbosch was again forced to negotiate with members of minor opposition parties in order to maintain a government majority.

In August 1997 the Government recalled its ambassador to the Netherlands for consultations, following the decision by the Netherlands Government to seek an international arrest warrant for Bouterse on charges of illegal drugs-trafficking. Bouterse was reportedly in hiding following the issue of the warrant. Talks aimed at improving relations between the Governments of Suriname and the Netherlands were conducted, at ministerial level, in New York, USA, in April 1998. However, the fact that Bouterse was continuing to serve on the Council of State, as part of the Suriname Government, remained a serious source of dissatisfaction for the Netherlands' delegation, which refused a request from Suriname's chief of police that the warrant for Bouterse's arrest be withdrawn. In July the Government of Trinidad and Tobago rejected an instruction from the Netherlands Government to arrest Bouterse, who was on a private visit to Trinidad, on the grounds that no extradition treaty existed between the two countries. In March 1999 the Dutch authorities began legal proceedings against Bouterse *in absentia*, on charges of corruption and drugs-trafficking. Similar *in absentia* court proceedings were initiated in the Netherlands against the guerrilla leader Ronnie Brunswijk (who was found guilty on charges of drugs-trafficking in April, and sentenced to eight years' imprisonment) and the President of the Central Bank of Suriname, Henk Goedschalk, who was accused of deliberate financial mismanagement. Despite the Suriname Government's refusal to accede to the demands of the Netherlands Government for the apprehension and extradition of Bouterse, in April President Wijdenbosch dismissed Bouterse from the Council of State, claiming that he represented a divisive force in Surinamese politics. In mid-July Bouterse was convicted and sentenced, *in absentia*, to 16 years in prison (later reduced to 11 years) and fined US $2.3m. The Attorney-General of the Netherlands filed further charges (this time for torture resulting in death) against Bouterse in January 2000. The new charges concerned the 1982 December Murders in 1982 and arose because of a complaint filed by relatives of the victims.

Widespread industrial action, in support of demands by the Trade and Manufacturers' Association for the resignation of the Government in favour of a non-political administration, brought chaos to the country for several days in June 1998. (The action followed a strike in May by petroleum workers opposed to the opening of the sector to overseas participation.) Further labour unrest in the agriculture and mining sectors later in the year was prompted by the Government's delay in adjusting the official currency exchange rate to match the prevailing commercial rate, following a severe decline in the value of the Suriname guilder against the US dollar.

Resentment at the Government's management of the economy erupted again in May 1999. As a result of a national strike, which brought the country to a virtual standstill, President Wijdenbosch's entire Cabinet resigned in late May. On 1 June the National Assembly passed a vote of 'no confidence' in the President by 27 votes to 14 (with 10 abstentions). However, the result fell short of the two-thirds' majority needed to force the President from office and Wijdenbosch refused to tender his own resignation. Instead he called for early elections to be held by 25 May 2000 and asked the cabinet members to remain in office. However, in early December the Government resubmitted its resignation after several of its members were implicated in financial and sexual scandals. President Wijdenbosch accepted several ministers' resignations, distributing their portfolios among the remaining ministers. Prior to the election, in an apparent attempt to distance himself from Bouterse, Wijdenbosch left the NDP and formed a new electoral coalition, Democratisch Nationaal Platform 2000 (DNP 2000). Voting proceeded on 25 May, when Venetiaan's NF (an electoral alliance comprising the NPS, the Pertajah Luhur, the Surinaamse Partij van de Arbeid, and the VHP) secured 33 of the 51 seats; the

Millenium Combinatie (an alliance including the NDP) took 10, and DNP 2000 three. Having narrowly failed to secure the two-third's majority to appoint a new President directly, the NF entered into coalition negotiations with the smaller parties. Following the conclusion of these negotiations, on 4 August Venetiaan was elected to the presidency for the second time, winning 37 of the 51 votes cast in the National Assembly. On assuming office on 12 August, the new President pledged to fight corruption, accelerate economic development and reduce debt. In October Venetiaan announced an economic stabilization programme, to be introduced by the end of the year. Emergency measures included increases in the price of fuel, the utilities and basic necessities, and a devaluation of the currency. In the same month the Dutch Government agreed to resume aid to Suriname, which had been suspended since 1998.

On 1 November 2000 the Suriname Court of Justice ruled that Bouterse must stand trial in Suriname in connection with the December Murders. On 8 February 2001 President Venetiaan announced his intention to seek the amendment of an article in the Constitution which banned the extradition of Surinamese citizens to other countries for trial. In May 2001 a key witness in the case against Bouterse, the former activist and founder of the Labour Party, Fred Derby, died. In September, the Dutch High Court ruled that Bouterse could not be prosecuted in the Netherlands under the UN's Convention on Torture, as the legislation had not been ratified in that country until 1989, seven years after the atrocities took place. However, in the following month it upheld Bouterse's 1999 conviction for drugs-trafficking and demanded he be extradited to serve his 11-year prison sentence. On 18 January 2002 the National Assembly voted to begin corruption proceedings against Errol Alibux, a former finance minister in the Wijdenbosch administration. It was claimed that Alibux, who was also a suspect in the December Murders case, had authorized the purchase of a building in Paramaribo for US $900,000, an amount judged to be nearly three times its actual worth.

The arrival of a detachment of Dutch marines in June 2002 prompted speculation that the Dutch Government would attempt to arrest Bouterse; the Netherlands claimed that the troops were merely engaged in a joint military exercise. However, in the same month, the Dutch Government dispatched forensic specialists to assist Surinamese police officers investigating the December Murders. In December a judge presiding over the case ordered the exhumation of the remains of the 15 murder victims. A series of burglaries at the homes of the Minister of Justice and a leading judge in April 2003 were thought to be connected to the investigation; a former police officer was subsequently arrested for questioning.

In September 2002 the Minister of Trade and Industry, Jack Tjong Tjin Joe, died suddenly while attending a Caribbean Community and Common Market (CARICOM) meeting in Trinidad and Tobago. He was replaced in the following month by Michael Jong Tjien Fa.

The illegal trafficking of drugs continued to be a problem in Suriname. The UN's Drug Control Programme estimated that some 22 metric tons of cocaine were transported annually to Europe via Suriname. In March 2002 three Surinamese, three Brazilians and one Colombian were sentenced to up to 14 years' imprisonment for attempting to bring 1,198 kgs of cocaine into the country. The men had been arrested in March 2001 in what had been the largest ever seizure of illegal drugs by the Surinamese police. In October 2002 the Netherlands announced the provision of training and equipment to assist the Surinamese security forces' campaign against drugs-trafficking and funds for the construction of a new police headquarters in Paramaribo. The following February two Dutch nationals were convicted by a Surinamese court for attempting to transport cocaine, obtained in Suriname, to the Netherlands. Police made some 80 arrests on drugs related charges in early 2003 and in April, some 70 kgs of cocaine were confiscated by authorities at the country's international airport.

Suriname has a territorial dispute with Guyana over an estimated 15,000 sq km (6,000 sq miles) of land in the Corentije region, and another with French Guiana over land to the east of the Litani river. In April 1990, with the mediation of the UN High Commissioner for Refugees, France and Suriname agreed terms providing for the repatriation of an estimated 10,000 Surinamese refugees from French Guiana. In October French Guiana was reported to have begun forcible repatriation of Surinamese refugees. In April 1992, under a plan agreed between France, Suriname and the UN, which had been prompted by the ongoing peace negotiations in Suriname (see above), some 6,000 Surinamese refugees were offered voluntary repatriation. The deadline for the French-funded resettlement scheme, originally scheduled for 30 September, was later extended by the French Government to 31 December. In late July the Suriname Government delivered an official protest to the French authorities concerning the alleged compulsory repatriation of refugees. By that time some 2,500 Surinamese refugees had returned to Suriname.

In 1995 Guyana and Suriname reached agreement on the establishment of a joint commission in order to seek a resolution of the countries' territorial dispute. In October 1998, at the inauguration of a new ferry crossing of the Corentijn River, the Presidents of Suriname and Guyana agreed to reactivate the joint commission, which had not convened at all during the previous two years. In June 1998 Guyana granted the Canadian-based company, CGX Energy Inc, a concession to explore for petroleum and gas along the continental margin off Guyana, part of which lay within the disputed maritime area. In May 2000 Suriname formally claimed that Guyana had violated its territorial integrity, and invited Guyana to begin negotiations regarding the maritime boundary. In early June the Suriname Navy forced CGX to remove the drilling platform. In the same month a Joint Technical Committee was established to resolve the dispute; however, both sides remained at an impasse. It was agreed that talks would resume once the new Government took office. In June 2001, following a further meeting, the Ministers of Foreign Affairs of the two countries issued a declaration of their Governments' commitment to peace and co-operation. In the following month President Venetiaan and President Jagdeo of Guyana met at a regional conference and announced that the Guyana–Suriname Bilateral Co-operation Council was to be revived early in 2002. At the subsequent meeting of the Council in January 2002, the members agreed to investigate the possibility of a joint exploration for petroleum in the disputed territory. At the end of the month, during a visit to Suriname, President Jagdeo addressed the National Assembly. However, his speech was boycotted by opposition members, who objected to the joint oil exploration proposal. A feasibility study undertaken by the Co-operation Council was to report its findings by May. The two Governments also agreed to improve co-operation in trade, investments and joint ventures. However, relations again became strained in March 2003 when the Surinamese Government decreed that maps of the country circulated by all diplomatic missions in Paramaribo must include the disputed territory. Guyana lodged a formal protest and sent a naval detachment to patrol the Corentijn River.

In February 2002 a hand grenade was thrown at the house of the Dutch ambassador, Rudolf Treffers. No one was hurt in the incident and police were unable to divine a motive or identify a suspect. Two days later, the newspaper *De West* received an anonymous telephone call threatening to harm the Dutch ambassador if he did not leave the country within five days. In March, however, a series of meetings between representatives of the Dutch and Surinamese Governments indicated greater co-operation between the two countries. The Minister of Foreign Affairs, Marie Levens, and her Dutch counterpart approved the establishment of a Returned Emigration Committee to oversee the voluntary repatriation of Surinamese with Dutch nationality without the loss of social benefits. Plans were also announced to waive temporarily visa requirements for Dutch visitors over 60 years of age in an effort to increase the number of tourists visiting the country.

Government

Under the provisions of the 1987 Constitution, legislative power is held by the National Assembly, with 51 members, elected by universal adult suffrage for a five-year term. The Assembly elects the President and the Vice-President of the Republic. Executive power is vested in the President, who appoints the Cabinet of Ministers, led by the Vice-President, who is also the Prime Minister. The Cabinet is responsible to the National Assembly. A Council of State, comprising civilians and members of the armed forces, advises the President and the Cabinet of Ministers on policy, and has power of veto over legislation approved by the Assembly. Suriname comprises nine administrative districts.

Defence

Suriname's armed forces numbered 1,840 men and women in August 2002. There is an army of 1,400, a navy of 240, and an air force of about 200. The defence budget for 2001 was estimated at US $9.2m.

Economic Affairs

In 2001, according to estimates by the World Bank, Suriname's gross national income (GNI), measured at average 1999–2001 prices, was US $709m., equivalent to $1,690 per head on an international purchasing-power parity basis). During 1990–2001, it was estimated, the population increased at an average annual rate of 0.4%, while gross domestic product (GDP) per head increased, in real terms, by an average of 1.0% per year. Overall GDP increased, in real terms, at an average annual rate of 1.4% in 1990–2001; growth in 2001 was 2.1%.

Agriculture (including hunting, forestry and fishing) contributed an estimated 11.7% of GDP in 2001 and employed an estimated 6.4% of the employed population in 1999. The principal crop is rice, which supplies domestic demand and provided an estimated 3.8% of export earnings in 1998. The other major agricultural export is bananas, which, together with plantains, earned an estimated 1.4% of total export earnings in 1998. In April 2002 the Government closed the state-run banana company, Surland when it accumulated debt of some US $8m. Sugar cane, citrus fruits and bacoven are cultivated for export, while Suriname also produces coconuts, maize and vegetables. Livestock is being developed, as are the extensive timber reserves (more than 80% of Suriname's total land area is covered by forest). Commercial fishing is important (providing an estimated 8.1% of total export revenue in 2000). Agricultural GDP increased by 1.5% per year in 1990–2000; the sector grew by 18.8% in 1999, but declined by 9.6% in 2000.

Industry (including mining, manufacturing, public utilities and construction) contributed an estimated 34.9% of GDP and engaged an estimated 15.1% of the employed labour force in 1999. The principal activity is the bauxite industry, which dominates both the mining and manufacturing sectors. In 1999 one of the principal aluminium refineries, owned by Suralco, was permanently closed, owing to the high production costs and problems with power generation. In the early 2000s there were plans to build an industrial development zone near to Johan Adolf Pengel International Airport at Zanderij. Industrial GDP increased by an annual average of 0.6% in 1990–2000; the sector declined by 5.5% in 1999 and by a further 8.7% in 2000.

Mining and quarrying contributed an estimated 21.1% of GDP in 2001 and engaged an estimated 2.5% of the employed labour force in 1999. The principal product is bauxite (used in the manufacture of aluminium), of which Suriname is one of the world's leading producers (producing 3.7m. metric tons in 2000). In early 2003 the US-based aluminium company Alcoa concluded negotiations with the Government on plans to develop the bauxite sector in Suriname. An accord was reached to allow Alcoa to increase the capacity of its existing bauxite operations in the country. Alcoa was also granted permission for a joint venture with the Australian company BHP for an aluminium melting plant and hydroelectric dam in the Backhuis Mountains. The large-scale exploitation of gold in central-eastern Suriname was postponed in the late 1990s, owing to falling gold prices; gold reserves at the Gross Rosebel mine, situated some 80 km south of Paramaribo, were estimated at 2.4m. ounces. In late 2002 the Canadian gold-mining corporation Cambior began construction on new facilities at Gross Rosebel; extraction was expected to begin in 2004. Reserves of petroleum in Suriname are exploited at a rate of around 12,500 b/d. Some 40% of production is for export, but much is used domestically in the bauxite industry. Unproven reserves are also thought to exist in the Saramacca district. Suriname also has extensive deposits of iron ore and reserves of manganese, copper, nickel, platinum and kaolin. The GDP of the mining sector was estimated to have increased by an average of 10.7% per year in 1994–98, and by 4.7% in 1998 alone.

Manufacturing contributed an estimated 6.3% of GDP in 2001 and engaged an estimated 4.1% of the employed labour force in 1999. Bauxite refining and smelting is the principal industry (alumina and aluminium accounted for an estimated 62.1% of export revenue in 2000), but there are also important food-processing industries and manufacturers of cigarettes, beverages and chemical products. Manufacturing GDP declined by an estimated average of 2.3% per year in 1990–2000; it declined by 11.1% in 1999 and by a further 17.9% in 2000.

Energy is currently derived principally from hydrocarbon fuels, which are mainly imported; in 2000 fuels accounted for 6.7% of total merchandise imports. The country has considerable potential for the development of hydroelectric power; there is a hydroelectric station for the aluminium industry. In 1998 Suriname produced 1,621m. kWh of electricity, derived mostly from hydroelectric power.

The services sector contributed an estimated 53.4% of GDP and engaged an estimated 78.6% of the employed labour force in 1999. In 1999 the large civil service employed close to 50% of the working population. The GDP of the services sector increased by an estimated average of 3.1% per year in 1990–2000; sectoral growth was 7.4% in 1999 and 7.9% in 2000.

In 2001 Suriname recorded a visible trade surplus of US $139.8m., and there was a deficit of $83.6m. on the current account of the balance of payments. The principal source of imports was the USA (providing 36.6% of total imports in 2000); other significant suppliers were the Netherlands (22.9%) and Japan (7.8%). The principal markets for exports in 2000 was Norway (22.7%), the USA (an estimated 20.1% of the total) and the Netherlands (20.1%). The principal imports in 2000 were machinery and transport equipment, basic manufactures, food and live animals and chemical products. The principal exports in 1998 were crude materials (including alumina), and food and live animals.

In 1998 there was an estimated budgetary deficit of Sf 50,800m. (equivalent to 11.1% of GDP). At the end of 1999 the total external public debt stood at an estimated US $248m. The annual rate of inflation averaged 30.0% in 1995–2002. Consumer prices increased by an average of 38.7% in 2001 and by an average of 1.1% in 2002. In the first six months of 1999 some 14.0% of the labour force were unemployed. Official estimates gave a general rate of unemployment of 20% in early 2001.

In February 1995 Suriname was granted full membership of the Caribbean Community and Common Market (CARICOM, see p. 155).

Economic activity is relatively diversified in range, but the dominant sector is the bauxite industry. In June 1993 the Government introduced a free-market rate for the Suriname guilder. In July 1994 the Government abolished the official exchange rate and introduced a new unified exchange rate system, removing all remaining exchange controls. In that year Suriname's economy experienced hyperinflation (average inflation for the year was 368.5%), rapid currency depreciation and an increasing budgetary deficit. In 1995 intervention in the currency market by the Central Bank succeeded in stabilizing the guilder. The Government also achieved a considerable increase in the level of international reserves, while tax revenue increased four-fold, owing largely to improvements in tax administration. Savings made by the elimination of consumer subsidies in that year were, however, offset by the simultaneous granting of a 200% salary increase to public-sector employees. The budget surplus continued to be eroded by the introduction of further public-sector salary increases. During 1998 economic difficulties arising from drought conditions were exacerbated by labour unrest prompted by the rapid depreciation of the informal, parallel exchange rate for the Suriname guilder. (A 45% devaluation of the currency was finally effected by the Central Bank in January 1999.) However, a gap immediately re-emerged between the official and the unofficial rates (the gap had widened to 75% by August 1999), which led the IMF to recommend a further adjustment of the exchange rate. In 1999 the Government introduced plans to reform the financial sector with the eventual aim of establishing Suriname as an 'offshore' financial centre.

On assuming office in September 2000, the new Government discovered that most of the country's gold reserves had been converted into US dollars. With the country nearing bankruptcy, in October the new President, Runaldo Venetiaan, announced a series of emergency measures, aimed at stabilizing the exchange rate and the domestic inflation rate. The official exchange rate was devalued by 89%, subsidies on petroleum products were eliminated, and tariffs on utilities were raised. As a result, the overall deficit increased to just 13% of GDP in 2000 (from 10% in 1999). The annual inflation rate also fell, to 59.3%, and continued to fall in 2001, partly owing to the ending of central bank credit to the Government. Further corrective measures were introduced in January 2001, including tax increases. The IMF welcomed the new Government's attempts to restore fiscal policy and in 2001 identified the reduction of the public-sector salary bill and an acceleration in the privatization process as essential to the macroeconomic stabilization programme. However, an increase in public-sector wages by some 60% in 2002 threatened to negate progress made in 2001 in reducing the fiscal deficit. The IMF again recommended that the Government reduce its expenditure and continue to rationalize the state sector through privatization. It also suggested that diversification away from the mining sector should be pursued to improve prospects of a more stable economy. In August 2002 the Central Bank again devalued the Surinamese guilder, following its sharp depreciation in the first half of the year. Growth in 2003 was expected to be 2.1%.

Education

Primary education is compulsory for children between seven and 12 years of age. Primary education begins at six years of age and lasts for six years. Secondary education comprises a first cycle of four years and a second cycle of three years. All education in government and denominational schools is provided free of charge. In 1997 the total enrolment at primary and secondary schools was equivalent to 79% of the school-age population (76% of males; 82% of females). In that year, primary enrolment included 99.9% of children in the relevant age-group (males 99.9%; females 99.9%). The traditional educational system, inherited from the Dutch, was amended after the 1980 revolution to place greater emphasis on serving the needs of Sur-

iname's population. This included a literacy campaign and programmes of adult education. Higher education is provided by technical and vocational schools and by the University of Suriname at Paramaribo, which has faculties of law, economics, medicine, social sciences and technology. Of total expenditure by the Central Government in 1996, an estimated Sf 3,480.5m (3.2%) was for education.

Public Holidays

2003: 1 January (New Year's Day), March* (Phagwa), 18 April–21 April (Easter), 1 May (Labour Day), 1 July (National Union Day), 25 November (Independence Day), 26 November (Id al-Fitr, end of Ramadan), 25–26 December (Christmas).

2004: 1 January (New Year's Day), March* (Phagwa), 9–12 April (Easter), 1 May (Labour Day), 1 July (National Union Day), 25 November (Independence Day), 14 November (Id al-Fitr, end of Ramadan), 25–26 December (Christmas).

* Exact date dependent upon sightings of the moon.

Weights and Measures

The metric system is in force.

Statistical Survey

Sources (unless otherwise stated): Algemeen Bureau voor de Statistiek, Kromme Elleboogstraat 10, POB 244, Paramaribo; tel. 473927; fax 425004; e-mail statistics@cq-link.sr; Ministry of Trade and Industry: Nieuwe Haven, POB 557, Paramaribo; tel. 475080; fax 477602.

AREA, POPULATION AND DENSITY

Area: 163,265 sq km (63,037 sq miles).

Population: 355,240 (males 175,814; females 179,426) at census of 1 July 1980; 417,000 (UN estimate) at mid-2000 (Source: UN, *World Population Prospects: The 2000 Revision*).

Density (mid-2000): 2.6 per sq km.

Ethnic Groups (1980 census, percentage): Creole 34.70; Hindustani 33.49; Javanese 16.33; Bush Negro 9.55; Amerindian 3.10; Chinese 1.55; European 0.44; Others 0.84.

Administrative Districts (population at 1 January 2000): Paramaribo 224,218; Wanica 73,219; Nickerie 35,577; Coronie 3,092; Saramacca 13,250; Commewijne 22,134; Marowijne 13,351; Para 15,191; Brokopondo 7,662; Sipaliwini 24,824.

Principal Towns (estimated population at 1 July 1996): Paramaribo (capital) 205,000; Lelydorp 15,600; Nieuw Nickerie 11,100. Source: Thomas Brinkoff, *City Population* (internet www.citypopulation.de).

Births and Deaths (2000): Registered live births 9,804 (birth rate 22.5 per 1,000); Registered deaths 3,090 (death rate 7.1 per 1,000).

Expectation of Life (WHO estimates, years at birth): 67.4 (males 64.2; females 70.7) in 2001. Source: WHO, *World Health Report*.

Economically Active Population (labour force sample survey, '000 persons aged between 15 and 66 years, January–June 1999): Agriculture, hunting, forestry and fishing 4,456; Mining and quarrying 1,727; Manufacturing 2,863; Electricity, gas and water 1,000; Construction 4,953; Trade, restaurants and hotels 17,262; Transport, storage and communication 5,817; Financing, insurance, real estate and business services 4,544; Community, social and personal services 27,305; Activities not adequately defined 2,908; *Total employed* 72,834 (males 47,756; females 25,078); Unemployed 11,812 (males 5,361; females 6,451); *Total labour force* 84,646 (males 53,117; females 31,529).

HEALTH AND WELFARE

Key Indicators

Total Fertility Rate (children per woman, 2001): 2.1.

Under-5 Mortality Rate (per 1,000 live births, 2001): 32.

HIV/AIDS (% of persons aged 15–49, 2001): 1.20.

Physicians (per 1,000 head, 1996): 0.25.

Health Expenditure (2000): US $ per head (PPP): 424.

Health Expenditure (2000): % of GDP: 9.8.

Health Expenditure (2000): public (% of total): 56.1.

Access to Water (% of persons, 2000): 95.

Access to Sanitation (% of persons, 2000): 83.

Human Development Index (2000): ranking: 74.

Human Development Index (2000): value: 0.756.

For sources and definitions, see explanatory note on p. vi.

AGRICULTURE, ETC.

Principal Crops ('000 metric tons, 2001): Rice (paddy) 192; Roots and tubers 6; Sugar cane 120*; Coconuts 8; Vegetables 16; Bananas 43; Plantains 12; Oranges 10; Other citrus fruit 3.
* FAO estimate. Source: partly FAO.

Livestock ('000 head, 2001): Cattle 138; Sheep and Goats 15; Pigs 23; Chickens 3,859.

Livestock Products ('000 metric tons, 2001): Beef and veal 2; Pig meat 1; Poultry meat 5; Cows' milk 5; Hen eggs 9. Source: partly FAO.

Forestry ('000 cu metres, 2001): Roundwood removals: Sawlogs, veneer logs and logs for sleepers 150; Other industrial wood 6; Fuel wood 43 (FAO estimate); *Total* 199. Sawnwood production: Total (incl. railway sleepers) 57. Source: FAO.

Fishing (FAO estimates, '000 metric tons, 2000): Capture 16.2 (Marine fishes 9.8); Aquaculture 0.3; Total catch 16.5. Source: FAO, *Yearbook of Fishery Statistics*.

MINING

Production (2000): Crude petroleum ('000 barrels) 4,400*; Bauxite ('000 metric tons) 3,659.
* Source: US Geological Survey.

INDUSTRY

Production ('000 metric tons, 2000): Soft drinks 230 ('000 hectolitres, 1996); Beer 72 ('000 hectolitres, 1996); Alumina 6,638 (1999); Aluminium 29.0 (1999); Raw sugar 10 (FAO unofficial figure); Cement 65 (estimate); Palm oil 0.22; Cigarettes 483 million (1996); Shoes (pairs, 1995 estimate) 98,990; Plywood ('000 cubic metres) 4 (2000); Electricity (million kWh) 1,621 (1998). Sources: mainly UN, *Industrial Commodity Statistics Yearbook*, and FAO.

FINANCE

Currency and Exchange Rates: 100 cents = 1 Suriname gulden (guilder) or florin (Sf). *Sterling, Dollar and Euro Equivalents* (31 December 2002): £1 sterling = 4,053.7 guilders; US $1 = 2,515.0 guilders; €1 = 2,637.5 guilders; 10,000 Suriname guilders = £2.467 = $3.976 = €3.792. *Average Exchange Rate* (Suriname guilders per US $): 1,322.47 in 2000; 2,178.50 in 2001; 2,346.8 in 2002. *Note:* Between 1971 and 1993 the official market rate was US $1 = 1.785 guilders. A new free market rate was introduced in June 1993, and a unified, market-determined rate took effect in July 1994. A mid-point rate of US $1 = 401.0 guilders was in effect between September 1996 and January 1999.

Budget (Sf '000 million, 1998, estimates): *Revenue:* Direct taxation 49.6; Indirect taxation 55.4; Other revenue (incl. bauxite levy) 15; Grants 17.2; Total 137.2. *Expenditure:* Compensation of employees 73.6; Subsidies 21.9; Goods and services 61.6; Interest payments 2.5; Capital 18.4; Net lending 10; Total 188.0. Source: IMF, *Suriname: Selected Issues* (August 1999).

International Reserves (US $ million at 31 December 2002): Gold (national valuation) 6.13; IMF special drawing rights 1.93; Reserve position in IMF 8.33; Foreign exchange 95.90; Total 112.29. Source: IMF, *International Financial Statistics.*

Money Supply (Sf million at 31 December 2001): Currency outside banks 182,476; Demand deposits at deposit money banks 176,415; Total money (incl. others) 395,059. Source: IMF, *International Financial Statistics.*

Cost of Living (Consumer Price Index for Paramaribo area; base: 1995 = 100): 401.2 in 2000; 556.3 in 2001; 562.6 in 2002.

National Income and Product (Sf million at current prices, 1998): Compensation of employees 213,371; operating surplus 109,143; *Domestic factor incomes* 322,514; Consumption of fixed capital 38,697; *GDP at factor cost* 361,210; Indirect taxes 53,644; *Less* subsidies 7,726; *GDP in purchasers' values* 407,128; Net factor income from abroad –244; *Gross national product* 406,884; *Less* consumption of fixed capital 38,697; *National income in market prices* 368,187. Source: UN Economic Commission for Latin America and the Caribbean, *Statistical Yearbook.*

Expenditure on the Gross Domestic Product (Sf million at current prices, 1998): Government final consumption expenditure 76,326; Private final consumption expenditure 291,097; Increase in stocks 21,174; Gross capital formation 73,301; *Total domestic expenditure* 461,898; Exports of goods and services 172,103; *Less* Imports of goods and services 226,873; *GDP in purchasers' values* 407,128. Source: UN Economic Commission for Latin America and the Caribbean, *Statistical Yearbook.*

Gross Domestic Product by Economic Activity (Sf million at current prices, preliminary figures, 2001): Agriculture, hunting and forestry 118,408; Fishing 46,819; Mining and quarrying 298,318; Manufacturing 89,102; Electricity, gas and water 54,273; Construction 51,598; Wholesale and retail trade 158,170; Restaurants and hotels 34,171; Transport, storage and communications 124,630; Financial intermediation 79,014; Real estate, renting and business services 120,218; Public administration 123,529; Education 74,583; Health and social work 12,839; Other community, social and personal services 28,780; Sub-total 1,414,450; *Less* Imputed bank service charge 50,170; *GDP at factor cost* 1,364,280; Taxes on products *less* subsidies 233,067; *GDP in purchasers' values* 1,597,347.

Balance of Payments (US $ million, 2001): Exports of goods f.o.b. 437.0; Imports of goods f.o.b. –297.2; *Trade balance* 139.8; Exports of services 59.4; Imports of services –174.3; *Balance on goods and services* 24.9; Other income received 5.4; Other income paid –113.0; *Balance on goods, services and income* –82.7; Current transfers received 2.1; Current transfers paid –3.0; *Current balance* –83.6; Capital account (net) 1.5; Direct investment (net) –26.8; Other investment assets 40.7; Other investment liabilities 91.0; Net errors and omissions 55.3; *Overall balance* 78.1. Source: IMF, *International Financial Statistics.*

EXTERNAL TRADE

Principal Commodities (US $ million, 2000): *Imports:* Food and live animals 70.4 ; Beverages and tobacco 16.2; Mineral fuels, lubricants, etc. 35.4 (Refined petroleum products 30.4); Chemicals and related products 53.5 (Artificial resins and plastic materials, etc. 19.1); Basic manufactures 92.7; Machinery and transport equipment 190.5 (Machinery specialized for particular industries 19.1, Telecommunications equipment 16.5, Road vehicles 69.3); Miscellaneous manufactured articles 50.1; Total (incl. others) 526.5. *Exports:* Food and live animals 66.1 (Fish, crustaceans and molluscs 41.5); Crude materials (inedible) except fuels 322.7 (Alumina 319.0); Mineral fuels, lubricants, etc. 34.3 (Crude petroleum 22.3); Total (incl. others) 514.0. Source: UN, *International Trade Statistics Yearbook.*

Principal Trading Partners (US $ million, 2000): *Imports:* Barbados 5.2; Belgium 12.8; Brazil 8.8; Canada 9.0; China, People's Republic 11.3; Colombia 5.3; Guyana 9.0; Italy 6.2; Japan 41.0; Netherlands 120.5; Netherlands Antilles 9.2; Panama 13.5; Trinidad and Tobago 90.4; United Kingdom 5.2; USA 139.9; Total (incl. others) 526.5. *Exports:* Canada 40.4; France 47.6; Guyana 10.6; Iceland 5.8; Japan 21.0; Mexico 8.1; Netherlands 72.4; Netherlands Antilles 7.0; Norway 116.9; Trinidad and Tobago 18.4; United Kingdom 30.5; USA 103.5; Total (incl. others) 514.0. Source: UN, *International Trade Statistics Yearbook.*

TRANSPORT

Road Traffic (registered motor vehicles, 2000 estimates): Passenger cars 61,365; Buses and coaches 2,393; Lorries and vans 20,827; Motor cycles and mopeds 30,598.

Shipping: *International Freight Traffic* (estimates, '000 metric tons, 2001): Goods loaded 2,306; Goods unloaded 1,212. *Merchant Fleet* (registered at 31 December 2001): Number of vessels 13; Total displacement 5,221 grt. (Source: Lloyd's Register-Fairplay, *World Fleet Statistics*).

Civil Aviation (traffic on scheduled services, 1998): Kilometres flown (million) 7; Passengers carried ('000) 278; Passenger-km (million) 1,072; Total ton-km (million) 127. Source: UN, *Statistical Yearbook.*

TOURISM

Tourist Arrivals (number of non-resident arrivals at airports, '000): 72 in 1999; 72 in 2000; 68 in 2001 (preliminary figure).

Tourism Receipts (US $ million): 17 in 1997; 45 in 1998; 44 in 1999. Source: World Bank, *World Development Indicators.*

COMMUNICATIONS MEDIA

Radio Receivers (1997): 300,000 in use.

Television Receivers (2000): 110,000 in use.

Telephones (2001): 77,400 main lines in use.

Facsimile Machines (1996): 800 in use.

Mobile Cellular Telephones (2001): 84,100 subscribers.

Internet Users (2001): 14,500.

Daily Newspapers (2001): 3.

Non-daily Newspapers (2000): 10.

Sources: mainly UNESCO, *Statistical Yearbook*; UN, *Statistical Yearbook*; International Telecommunication Union.

EDUCATION

Pre-primary (2001/02): 637 teachers; 15,746 pupils.

Primary (2001/02, incl. special education): 308 schools; 3,159 teachers (excl. special education); 65,611 pupils.

General Secondary (2001/02, incl. teacher-training): 141 schools; 2,056 teachers (1994/95); 39,858 pupils.

University (2001/02): 1 institution; 2,949 students.

Other Higher (2001/02): 3 institutions; 1,456 students (1999/2000).

Adult Literacy Rate (UNESCO projections): 92.2% (males 93.6%; females 90.7%) in 2001.

Directory

The Constitution

The 1987 Constitution was approved by the National Assembly on 31 March and by 93% of voters in a national referendum in September.

THE LEGISLATURE

Legislative power is exercised jointly by the National Assembly and the Government. The National Assembly comprises 51 members, elected for a five-year term by universal adult suffrage. The Assembly elects a President and a Vice-President and has the right of amendment in any proposal of law by the Government. The approval of a majority of at least two-thirds of the number of members of the National Assembly is required for the amendment of the Constitution, the election of the President or the Vice-President, the decision to organize a plebiscite and a People's Congress and for the amendment of electoral law. If it is unable to obtain a two-thirds' majority following two rounds of voting, the Assembly may convene a People's Congress and supplement its numbers with members of local councils. The approval by a simple majority is sufficient in the People's Congress.

THE EXECUTIVE

Executive authority is vested in the President, who is elected for a term of five years as Head of State, Head of Government, Head of the Armed Forces, Chairman of the Council of State, the Cabinet of Ministers and the Security Council.

The Government comprises the President, the Vice-President and the Cabinet of Ministers. The Cabinet of Ministers is appointed by the President from among the members of the National Assembly. The Vice-President is the Prime Minister and leader of the Cabinet, and is responsible to the President.

In the event of war, a state of siege, or exceptional circumstances to be determined by law, a Security Council assumes all government functions.

THE COUNCIL OF STATE

The Council of State comprises the President (its Chairman) and 14 additional members, composed of two representatives of the combined trade unions, one representative of the associations of employers, one representative of the National Army and 10 representatives of the political parties in the National Assembly. Its duties are to advise the President and the legislature and to supervise the correct execution by the Government of the decisions of the National Assembly. The Council may present proposals of law or of general administrative measures to the Government. The Council has the authority to suspend any legislation approved by the National Assembly which, in the opinion of the Council, is in violation of the Constitution. In this event, the President must decide within one month whether or not to ratify the Council's decision.

The Government

President: Runaldo Ronald Venetiaan (assumed office 12 August 2000).

Council of State: Chair. President of the Republic; 14 mems; 10 to represent the political parties in the National Assembly, one for the Armed Forces, two for the trade unions and one for employers.

CABINET OF MINISTERS
(April 2003)

Vice-President: Jules Rattankoemar Ajodhia (VHP).

Minister of Finance: Humphrey Hildenberg (NPS).

Minister of Foreign Affairs: Marie E. Levens (NPS).

Minster of Defence: Ronald Assen (NPS).

Minister of the Interior: Urmila Joella-Sewnundun (VHP).

Minister of Justice and the Police: Siegfried F. Glids (SPA).

Minister of Planning and Development Co-operation: Keremchand Raghoebarsingh (VHP).

Minister of Agriculture, Livestock and Fisheries: Geetapersad Gangaram Panday (VHP).

Minister of Transport, Communications and Tourism: Guno H. G. Castelen (SPA).

Minister of Public Works: Dewanand Balesar (VHP).

Minister of Social Affairs and Housing: Slamet Paul Somohardjo (PL).

Minister of Trade and Industry: Michael Jong Tjien Fa.

Minister of Regional Development: Romeo W. van Russel (NPS).

Minister of Education and Community Development: Walter T. Sandriman (PL).

Minister of Health: Mohamed Rakieb Khudabux (VHP).

Minister of Labour, Technological Development and the Environment: Clifford Marica (SPA).

Minister of Natural Resources and Energy: Franco R. Demon (NPS).

MINISTRIES

Ministry of Agriculture, Livestock and Fisheries: Letitia Vriesdelaan, Paramaribo; tel. 477698; fax 470301.

Ministry of Defence: Kwattaweg 29, Paramaribo; tel. 474244; fax 420055.

Ministry of Education and Community Development: Dr Samuel Kafilludistraat 117–123, Paramaribo; tel. 498383; fax 495083.

Ministry of Finance: Tamarindelaan 3, Paramaribo; tel. 472610; fax 476314.

Ministry of Foreign Affairs: Gravenstraat, POB 25, Paramaribo; tel. 471209; fax 410411.

Ministry of Health: Gravenstraat 64 boven, POB 201, Paramaribo; tel. 474841; fax 410702.

Ministry of the Interior: Wilhelminastraat 3, Paramaribo; tel. 476461; fax 421170.

Ministry of Justice and the Police: Gravenstraat 1, Paramaribo; tel. 473033; fax 412109.

Ministry of Labour, Technological Development and the Environment: Wagenwegstraat 22, POB 911, Paramaribo; tel. 475241; fax 410465; e-mail arbeid@sr.net.

Ministry of Natural Resources and Energy: Dr J. C. de Mirandastraat 11–15, Paramaribo; tel. 473428; fax 472911.

Ministry of Planning and Development Co-operation: Dr S. Redmondstraat 118, Paramaribo; tel. 473628; fax 421056.

Ministry of Public Works: Verlengde Coppenamestraat 167, Paramaribo; tel. 462500; fax 464901.

Ministry of Regional Development: Van Rooseveltkade 2, Paramaribo; tel. 471574; fax 424517.

Ministry of Social Affairs and Housing: Waterkant 30–32, Paramaribo; tel. 472610; fax 476314.

Ministry of Trade and Industry: Nieuwe Haven, POB 9354, Paramaribo; tel. 404776; fax 402602; internet www.sr.net/users/dirhi.

Ministry of Transport, Communications and Tourism: Prins Hendrikstraat 26–28, Paramaribo; tel. 411951; fax 420425.

President and Legislature

PRESIDENT

Election, 4 August 2000

On 4 August 2000 the National Assembly (see below) held an election to the presidency. Runaldo Ronald Venetiaan, of the New Front coalition, won 37 of the 51 votes cast. His main opponent, Rachid Doekhie, the candidate of the National Democratic Party, attracted 10 votes. Having secured the two-thirds' majority necessary to avoid a further round of voting in the Vereinigde Volksvergadering (United People's Assembly—convened to elect the head of state when the National Assembly failed to do so), Venetiaan was thus elected President. He assumed office on 12 August.

NATIONAL ASSEMBLY

Chairman: M. I. Dwalapersad.

General Election, 25 May 2000

Party	Seats
Nieuwe Front (NF)*	33
Millenium Combinatie (MC)†	10
Democratisch Nationaal Platform 2000 (DNP 2000)‡	3
Democratisch Alternatief 1991 (DA '91)§	2
Politieke Vleugel van de FAL (PVF)	2
Progressieve Arbeiders en Landbouwers Unie (PALU)	1
Total	51

* An alliance of the Nationale Partij Suriname (NPS), the Pertajah Luhur (PL), the Surinaamse Partij van de Arbeid (SPA), and the Vooruitstrevende Hervormingspartij (VHP).

† An alliance of the Nationale Democratische Partij (NDP), Kerukanan Tulodo Pranatan Ingigil (KTPI) and Democratisch Alternatief.

‡ The list of DNP 2000 included candidates of the Democratische Partij (DP) and of Democraten Van de 21 (D21).

§ The list of DA '91 included candidates from the Broederschap en Eenheid in de Politiek (BEP).

Political Organizations

Algemene Bevrijdings- en Ontwikkeling Partij (ABOP) (General Liberation and Development Party): Jaguarstraat 15, Paramaribo; f. 1986.

Alternatief Forum (AF) (Alternative Forum): Gladiolenstraat 26–28, Paramaribo; tel. 432342; Chair. WINSTON JESSURUN.

Amazone Partij Suriname (APS) (Suriname Amazon Party): Wilhelminastraat 91, Paramaribo; tel. 452081.

Basispartij voor Vernieuwing en Democratie (BVD) (Base Party for Renewal and Democracy): Tunalaan 7, Paramaribo; tel. 422231; e-mail info@bvdsuriname.org; internet www.bvdsuriname.org; Chair. TJAN GOBARDHAN.

Broederschap en Eenheid in Politiek (BEP): Ariestraat BR 34, S. O. B. Projekt, Paramaribo; tel. 494466; f. 1986; contested the 2000 election in alliance with DA '91; Chair. CAPRINO ALLENDY.

Democratisch Alternatief 1991 (DA '91) (Democratic Alternative 1991): POB 91, Paramaribo; tel. 470276; fax 493121; internet www.da91.sr; f. 1991; contested the 2000 election in alliance with the BEP; social-democratic; Chair. S. RAMKHELAWAN.

Democratisch Nationaal Platform 2000 (DNP) (National Democratic Platform 2000): Gemenlandsweg 83, Paramaribo; f. 2000; alliance including:

Democratische Partij (DP) (Democratic Party): Paramaribo; f. 1992; Leader FRANK PLAYFAIR.

Democraten Van de 21 (D21) (Democrats of the 21st Century): Goudstraat 22, Paramaribo; f. 1986.

Hernieuwde Progressieve Partij (HPP) (Renewed Progressive Party): Tourtonnelaan 51, Paramaribo; tel. 426965; e-mail hpp@cq-link.sr; internet www.cq-link.net/hpp; f. 1986; Chair. HARRY KISOENSINGH.

Millenium Combinatie (MC) (Millennium Alliance): f. 2000; alliance including:

Democratisch Alternatief (Democratic Alternative): Jadnanansinghlaan 5, Paramaribo.

Kerukanan Tulodo Pranatan Ingigil (KTPI) (Party for National Unity and Solidarity): Bonistraat 64, Geyersvlijt, Paramaribo; tel. 456116; f. 1947 as the Kaum-Tani Persuatan Indonesia; largely Indonesian; Leader WILLY SOEMITA.

Nationale Democratische Partij (NDP) (National Democratic Party): Benjaminstraat 17, Paramaribo; tel. 499183; fax 432174; e-mail ndpsur@sr.net; internet www.sr.net/users/ndp.sur; f. 1987 by Standvaste (the 25 February Movement); army-supported; Chair. Lt-Col DÉSIRÉ (DESI) BOUTERSE.

Nationale Hervormingspartij (NHP) (National Reform Party): Waterkant 54, Paramaribo; tel. 471624.

Nationale Partij Voor Leiderschap en Ontwikkeling (NPLO) (National Party for Leaderhip and Development): Tropicaweg 1, Paramaribo; tel. 551252; f. 1986.

Naya Kadam (New Choice): Naarstraat 5, Paramaribo; tel. 482014; fax 481012; e-mail itsvof@sr.net; Chair. INDRA DJWALAPERSAD; Sec. Ing. WALDO RAMDIHAL.

Nieuw Front (NF) (New Front): Paramaribo; f. 1987 as Front voor Demokratie en Ontwikkeling (FDO—Front for Democracy and Development), an alliance comprising:

Nationale Partij Suriname (NPS) (Suriname National Party): Wanicastraat 77, Paramaribo; tel. 477302; fax 475796; e-mail nps@sr.net; internet www.nps.sr; f. 1946; predominantly Creole; Sec. OTMAR ROEL RODGERS.

Pertajah Luhur (PL) (Full Confidence Party): Hoek Gemenlandsweg-Daniel Coutinhostraat, Paramaribo; tel. 401087; fax 420394.

Surinaamse Partij van de Arbeid (SPA) (Suriname Labour Party): Rust en vredestraat 64, Paramaribo; tel. 425912; fax 420394; f. 1987; affiliated with C-47 trade union; social democratic party; joined FDO in early 1991; Leader (vacant).

Verenigde Hervormings Partij (VHP) (United Reform Party): Coppenamestraat 130, Paramaribo; tel. 425912; fax 420394; f. 1949; leading left-wing party; predominantly Indian; Leader (vacant).

Partij voor Demokratie en Ontwikkeling in Eenheid (DOE) (Party for Democracy through Unity and Development): Kamperfoeliestraat 23, Paramaribo; internet www.angelfire.com/nv/DOE; f. 1999.

Pendawa Lima: Bonistraat 115, Geyersvlij, Paramaribo; tel. 551802; f. 1975; predominantly Indonesian; Chair. SALAM SOMOHARDJO.

Politieke Vleugel van de Fal (PVF): Keizerstraat 150, Paramaribo; Chair. JIWAN SITAL.

Progressieve Arbeiders en Landbouwers Unie (PALU) (Progressive Workers' and Farm Labourers' Union): Dr S. Kafiluddistraat 27, Paramaribo; tel. 400115; socialist party; Chair. IWAN KROLIS.

Progressieve Bosneger Partij (PBP): f. 1968; resumed political activities 1987; represents members of the Bush Negro (Boschneger) ethnic group; associated with the Pendawa Lima (see above).

Progressieve Surinaamse Volkspartij (PSV) (Suriname Progressive People's Party): Keizerstraat 122, Paramaribo; tel. 472979; f. 1946; resumed political activities 1987; Christian democratic party; Chair. W. WONG LOI SING.

Insurgent groups are as follows:

Angula: f. 1990; composed mainly of Saramaccaner Bush Negro clan; Leader CARLOS MAASSI.

Mandela Bush Negro Liberation Movement (BBM): Upper Saramacca region; f. 1989 by mems of the Mataurier Bush Negro clan; Leader 'BIKO' (LEENDERT ADAMS).

Suriname Liberation Front: Leader CORNELIS MAISI.

Surinamese Liberation Army (SLA—Jungle Commando): Langetabbetje (Suriname), via St Laurent du Maroni, French Guiana; f. 1986; Bush Negro guerrilla group; Leader RONNIE BRUNSWIJK.

Tucayana Amazonica: Bigi Poika; f. 1989 by Amerindian insurgents objecting to Kourou Accord between Govt and Bush Negroes of the SLA; Leader THOMAS SABAJO (alias 'Commander Thomas'); Chair. of Tucayana Advisory Group (Commission of Eight) ALEX JUBITANA.

Union for Liberation and Democracy (UBD): Moengo; f. 1989 by radical elements of SLA; Bush Negro; Leader KOFI AJONGPONG.

Diplomatic Representation

EMBASSIES IN SURINAME

Brazil: Maratakkastraat 2, POB 925, Paramaribo; tel. 400200; fax 400205; e-mail brasemb@sr.net; Ambassador RICARDO LUIZ VEANA DE CARVALHO.

China, People's Republic: Anton Dragtenweg 154, POB 3042 Paramaribo; tel. 451570; fax 452540; Ambassador HU SHOUQIN.

France: Gravenstraat 5–7 boven, POB 2648, Paramaribo; tel. 476455; fax 471208; e-mail ambafrance.paramaribo@diplomatie.gouv.fr; internet www.amfrance@sr.net; Ambassador OLIVIER MAITLAND PELEN.

Guyana: Gravenstraat 82, POB 785, Paramaribo; tel. 475209; fax 472679; Ambassador KARSHANJEE ARJUN.

India: Rode Kruislaan 10, POB 1329, Paramaribo; tel. 498344; fax 491106; Chargé d'affaires a.i. RAVI THAPAR.

Indonesia: Van Brussellaan 3, POB 157, Paramaribo; tel. 431230; fax 498234; e-mail indonemb@sr.net; Chargé d'affaires a.i. SUPARMIN SUNJOYO.

Japan: Gravenstraat 23–25, POB 2921, Paramaribo; tel. 474860; fax 412208; e-mail eojparbo@sr.net; Chargé d'affaires a.i. AKIRA NAGAI.

Libya (People's Bureau): Dario Saveedralaan 4, Paramaribo; tel. 490717; fax 464923; Chargé d'affaires A. TAHER AFTEES.

Netherlands: Van Roseveltkade 5; tel. 477211; fax 477792; e-mail prm-cdp@minbuza.nl; Ambassador HENDRIK J. W. SOETERS.

USA: Dr Sophie Redmondstraat 129, POB 1821, Paramaribo; tel. 472900; fax 420800; e-mail embuscen@sr.net; Ambassador MARSHA E. BARNES.

Venezuela: Gravenstraat 23–25, POB 3001, Paramaribo; tel. 475401; fax 475602; e-mail vzla@leda.sr.net; Ambassador FRANCISCO DE JESÚS SIMANCAS.

Judicial System

The administration of justice is entrusted to a Court of Justice, the six members of which are nominated for life, and three Cantonal Courts.

President of the Court of Justice: ALFRED VELDEMA.

Attorney-General: C. G. DE RANDAMIE.

Religion

Many religions are represented in Suriname. Christianity, Hinduism and Islam predominate.

CHRISTIANITY

Committee of Christian Churches: Paramaribo; Chair. Rev. JOHN KENT (Praeses of the Moravian Church).

The Roman Catholic Church

For ecclesiastical purposes, Suriname comprises the single diocese of Paramaribo, suffragan to the archdiocese of Port of Spain (Trinidad and Tobago). The Bishop participates in the Antilles Episcopal Conference (currently based in Port of Spain, Trinidad and Tobago). At 31 December 2000 there were an estimated 100,280 adherents in the diocese, representing about 24% of the population.

Bishop of Paramaribo: Rt Rev. ALOYSIUS FERDINANDUS ZICHEM, Bisschopshuis, Gravenstraat 12, POB 1230, Paramaribo; tel. 473306; fax 471602; e-mail azichem@sr.net.

The Anglican Communion

Within the Church in the Province of the West Indies, Suriname forms part of the diocese of Guyana. The Episcopal Church is also represented.

Anglican Church: St Bridget's, Hoogestraat 44, Paramaribo.

Protestant Churches

Evangelisch-Lutherse Kerk in Suriname: Waterkant 102, POB 585, Paramaribo; tel. 425503; fax 481856; e-mail elks@sr.net; Pres. RAYMON LESLIE WIMPEL; 4,000 mems.

Moravian Church in Suriname: Maagdenstraat 50, POB 1811, Paramaribo; tel. 473073; fax 475797; e-mail ebgs@sr.net; f. 1735; Praeses HESDIE ZAMUEL; Gen. Sec. LILIAN TRUIDEMAN; 57,400 mems (1985).

Also represented are the Christian Reformed Church, the Dutch Reformed Church, the Evangelical Methodist Church, Pentecostal Missions, the Seventh-day Adventists and the Wesleyan Methodist Congregation.

HINDUISM

Sanatan Dharm: Koningstraat 31–33, POB 760, Paramaribo; tel. 404190; f. 1930; Pres. Dr R. M. NANNAN PANDAY; Sec. A. GAJADHARSING; over 150,000 mems.

ISLAM

Surinaamse Moeslim Associatie: Kankantriestraat 55–57, Paramaribo; Chair. A. ABDOELBASHIRE.

Surinaamse Islamitische Organisatie (SIO): Watermolenstraat 10, POB 278, Paramaribo; tel. 475220; f. 1978; Pres. Dr I. JAMALUDIN; Sec. K. M. HOESSEIN; 6 brs.

Stichting Islamitische Gemeenten Suriname: Verlengde Mahonielaan 39, Paramaribo; Chair. Dr T. SOWIRONO.

Federatie Islamitische Gemeenten in Suriname: Paramaribo; Chair. K. KAAIMAN.

JUDAISM

The Dutch Jewish Congregation and the Dutch Portuguese-Jewish Congregation are represented in Suriname.

Jewish Community: The Synagogue Neve Shalom, Keizerstraat, POB 1834, Paramaribo; tel. 400236; fax 402380; e-mail rene-fernandes@cq-link.sr; f. 1854; Pres. RENÉ FERNANDES.

OTHER RELIGIONS

Arya Dewaker: Dr S. Kafilludistraat 1, Paramaribo; tel. 400706; members preach the Vedic Dharma; disciples of Maha Rishi Swami Dayanand Sarswati, the founder of the Arya Samaj in India; f. 1929; Chair. Dr R. BANSRADJ; Sec. D. CHEDAMMI.

The Bahá'í faith is also represented.

The Press

DAILIES

De Ware Tijd: Malebatrumstraat 9, POB 1200, Paramaribo; tel. 472840; fax 472840; internet www.dwt.net; f. 1957; morning; Dutch; independent/liberal; Editor-in-Chief NITA RAMCHARAN.

De West: Dr J. C. de Mirandastraat 2–6, POB 176, Paramaribo; tel. 6923338; fax 470322; f. 1909; midday; Dutch; liberal; Editors G. D. C. FINDLAY, L. KETTIE; circ. 15,000–18,000.

PERIODICALS

Advertentieblad van de Republiek Suriname: Gravenstraat 120, POB 56, Paramaribo; tel. 473501; fax 454782; f. 1871; 2 a week; Dutch; government and official information bulletin; Editor E. D. FINDLAY; circ. 1,000.

CLO Bulletin: Gemenelandsweg 95, Paramaribo; f. 1973; irregular; Dutch; labour information published by civil servants' union.

Hervormd Suriname: POB 2542, Paramaribo; tel. 472344; f. 1895; monthly; religious.

Kerkbode: Burenstraat 17–19, POB 219, Paramaribo; tel. 473079; fax 475635; e-mail stadje@sr.net; f. 1906; weekly; religious; circ. 2,000.

Omhoog: Gravenstraat 21, POB 1802, Paramaribo; tel. 425992; fax 426782; e-mail rkomhoog@sr.net; weekly; f. 1952; Dutch; Catholic bulletin; Editor S. MULDER; circ. 5,000.

NEWS AGENCIES

Surinaams Nieuws Agentschap (SNA) (Suriname News Agency): Paramaribo; two daily bulletins in Dutch, one in English; Dir E. G. J. DE MEES.

Foreign Bureau

Inter Press Service (IPS) (Italy): Malebatrumstraat 1–5, POB 5065, Paramaribo; tel. 471818; Correspondent ERIC KARWOFODI.

Publishers

Anton de Kom Universiteit van Suriname: Universiteitscomplex, Leysweg 1, POB 9212, Paramaribo; tel. 465558; fax 462291.

Educatieve Uitgeverij Sorava NV: Latourweg 10, POB 8382, Paramaribo; tel. and fax 480808.

Publishing Services Suriname: Van Idsingastraat 133, Paramaribo; tel. 472746; e-mail pssmoniz@sr.net; fmrly I. Krishnadath.

Ministerie van Onderwijs en Volksontwikkeling (Ministry of Education and Community Development): Dr Samuel Kafilludistraat 117-123, Paramaribo; tel. 498850; fax 495083.

Pkin Fowru Productions: Jupiterstraat 30, Paramaribo; tel. 455792.

Stichting Al Qalam: Lawtonlaan 6, Paramaribo.

Stichting Volksboekwinkel: Keizerstraat 197, POB 3040, Paramaribo; tel. 472469.

Stichting Volkslectuur: Dr S. Redmondstraat 231, Paramaribo; tel. 497935.

Stichting Wetenschappelijke Informatie: Prins Hendrikstraat 38, Paramaribo; tel. 475232; fax 422195; e-mail swin@sr.net; f. 1977.

VACO, NV: Domineestraat 26, POB 1841, Paramaribo; tel. 472545; fax 410563; f. 1952; Dir EDUARD HOGENBOOM.

PUBLISHERS' ASSOCIATION

Publishers' Association Suriname: Domineestraat 32, POB 1841, Paramaribo; tel. 472545; fax 410563.

Broadcasting and Communications

TELECOMMUNICATIONS

Telecommunication Corporation Suriname (Telesur): Heiligenweg 1, POB 1839, Paramaribo; tel. 473944; fax 404800; supervisory body; Dir Ir LEONARD C. JOHANNS.

BROADCASTING

Radio

Ampi's Broadcasting Corporation (ABC): Maystraat 57, Paramaribo; tel. 465092; f. 1975; re-opened in 1993; commercial; Dutch and some local languages; Dir J. KAMPERVEEN.

Kara's Broadcasting Co (KBC): Verlengde Keizerstraat 5–7, POB 3025, Paramaribo; tel. 475032; fax 474946; f. 1985; commercial; Dutch and some local languages; Dir ORLANDO KARAMAT ALI.

Radio Apintie: Verlengde Gemenelandsweg 37, POB 595, Paramaribo; tel. 498855; fax 400684; e-mail apintie@sr.net; f. 1958; commercial; Dutch and some local languages; Gen. Man. CH. VERVUURT.

Radio Boskopou: Roseveltkade 1, Paramaribo; tel. 410300; govt-owned; Sranang Tongo and Dutch; Head Mr VAN VARSEVELD.

Radio Garuda: Goudstraat 14–16, Paramaribo; tel. 422422; Dir T. RADJI.

Radio Nickerie (RANI): Waterloostraat 3, Nieuw Nickerie; tel. 231462; commercial; Hindi and Dutch; Dir DJOTIES LALTA.

Radio Paramaribo: Verlengde Coppenamestraat 34, POB 975, Paramaribo; tel. 499995; fax 493121; f. 1957; commercial; Dutch and some local languages; Dir R. PIERKHAN.

Radio Radhika: Indira Gandhiweg 165, Paramaribo; tel. 482910; re-opened in 1989; Dutch, Hindi; Dir ROSHNI RADHAKISUN.

Radio Sangeet Mala: Indira Gandhiweg 40, Paramaribo; tel. 423902; Dutch, Hindi; Dir RADJEN SOEKHRADJ.

Stichting Radio Omroep Suriname (SRS): Jacques van Eerstraat 20, POB 271, Paramaribo; tel. 498115; fax 498116; f. 1965; commercial; govt-owned; Dutch and some local languages; Dir L. DARTHUIZEN.

Other stations include: Radika Radio, Radio 10, Radio Bersama, Radio Koyeba, Radio Pertjaya, Radio Sjalom, Radio Sun, and SRS.

Television

Algemene Televisie Verzorging (ATV): Adrianusstraat 55, POB 2995, Paramaribo; tel. 404611; fax 402660; e-mail cooman@sr.net; internet www.atv.sr; f. 1985; govt-owned; commercial; Dutch, English, Portuguese, Spanish and some local languages; Man. GUNO COOMAN.

Surinaamse Televisie Stichting (STVS): Cultuurtuinlaan 34, POB 535, Paramaribo; tel. 473100; fax 477216; f. 1965; govt-owned; commercial; local languages, Dutch and English; Dir FRITS J. PENGEL.

Finance

(cap. = capital; res = reserves; dep. = deposits; m. = million; amounts in Suriname guilders unless otherwise stated)

BANKING

Central Bank

Centrale Bank van Suriname: 18–20 Waterkant, POB 1801, Paramaribo; tel. 473741; fax 476444; e-mail cbvsprv@sr.net; f. 1957; cap. and res 34.5m. (Dec. 1987); Pres. ANDRE E. TELTING.

Commercial Banks

ABN AMRO Bank NV: Kerkplein 1, POB 1836, Paramaribo; tel. 471555; fax 411325; f. 1970; Man. J. M. J. HUISMAN; 8 brs.

Finansbank NV: Dr Sophie Redmondstraat 59–61, Paramaribo; tel. 476111; fax 410471.

Handels-Krediet- en Industriebank (Hakrinbank NV): Dr Sophie Redmondstraat 11–13, POB 1813, Paramaribo; tel. 477722; fax 472066; e-mail hakrindp@sr.net; f. 1936; cap. 50.4m., res 4,535.4m., dep. 45,241.6m (Dec. 2001); Pres. J. J. F. TJANG-A-SJIN; Man. Dir F. W. M. THIJM; 76brs.

Landbouwbank NV: FHR Lim A Postraat 34, POB 929, Paramaribo; tel. 475945; fax 411965; e-mail lbbank@sr.net; f. 1972; agricultural bank; cap. 5m., res 4.6m., dep. 76.0m. (Dec. 1987); Chair. R. KAIMAN; Pres. J. G. BUNDEL; 5brs.

RBTT Bank NV: Kerkplein1, Paramaribo.

De Surinaamsche Bank NV: Gravenstraat 26–30, POB 1806, Paramaribo; tel. 471100; fax 411750; internet www.dsbbank.sr; f. 1865; cap. 48.3m., res 2,842.1m., dep. 124,622.0m. (Dec. 1999); Chair. L. C. JOHANNS; Pres. Dr E. J. MÜLLER; 7 brs.

Surinaamse Postspaarbank: Knuffelsgracht 10–14, POB 1879, Paramaribo; tel. 472256; fax 472952; f. 1904; savings and commercial bank; cap. and res 50.3m., dep. 269.7m. (Dec. 1992); Man. RUDI R. LO FO WONG (acting); 2 brs.

Surinaamse Volkscredietbank: Waterkant 104, POB 1804, Paramaribo; tel. 472616; fax 473257; e-mail btlsvcb@sr.net; f. 1949; cap. and res 170.3m. (Dec. 1997); Man. Dir THAKOERDIEN RAMLAKHAN; 3 brs.

Development Bank

Nationale Ontwikkelingsbank van Suriname NV: Coppenamestraat 160–162, POB 677, Paramaribo; tel. 465000; fax 497192; f. 1963; govt-supported development bank; cap. and res 34m. (Dec. 1992); Man. Dir J. TSAI MEU CHONG.

INSURANCE

American Life Insurance Company (ALICO): Paramaribo; Gen. Man. ABDOEL HAFIZKHAN.

Assuria NV: Grote Combeweg 37, POB 1501, Paramaribo; tel. 477955; fax 472390; f. 1961; life and indemnity insurance; Man. Dir Dr S. SMIT.

Assuria Schadeverzekering NV: Gravenstraat 5–7, POB 1030, Paramaribo; tel. 473400; fax 476669; e-mail assuria@sr.net; Dir M. R. CABENDA.

British American Insurance Company: Klipstenenstraat 29, POB 370, Paramaribo; tel. 476523; Man. H. W. SOESMAN.

CLICO Life Insurance Company (SA) Ltd: Klipstenenstraat 29, POB 3026, Paramaribo; tel. 472525; fax 477219; Gen. Man. C. ABDOELHAFIEZKHAN.

Fatum Levensverzekering NV: Noorderkerkstraat 5–7, Paramaribo.

Hennep Verzorgende Vezerkering NV: Dr Sophie Redmondstraat 246, Paramaribo.

The Manufacturers' Life Insurance Company: c/o Assuria NV, Grote Combeweg 37, Paramaribo; tel. 473400; fax 472390; Man. S. SMIT.

Nationale Nederlanden Levensverzekering Maatschappij NV: Noorderkerkstraat 5–7, POB 1845, Paramaribo; tel. 471541; f. 1955; subsidiary: Fatum Schadeverzekering NV; Man. Dir N. W. LALBIHARIE.

Parsasco NV: Gravenstraat 117 boven, Paramaribo; tel. 421212; e-mail parsasco@sr.net; internet www.parsasco.com; Dir L. KHEDOE.

Self Reliance: Herenstraat 22, Paramaribo; tel. 472582; life insurance; Dir N. J. VEIRA.

Suram NV (Suriname American International Insurance Company): Lim A Postraat 7, Paramaribo; tel. 473908; Man. P. J. KAPPEL.

Trade and Industry

DEVELOPMENT ORGANIZATIONS

Centre for Industrial Development and Export Promotion: Rust en Vredestraat 79–81, POB 1275, Paramaribo; tel. 474830; fax 476311; f. 1981; Man. R. A. LETER.

Stichting Planbureau Suriname (National Planning Bureau of Suriname): Dr Sophie Redmondstraat 118, POB 172, Paramaribo; tel. 476241; fax 475001; responsible for financial administration of development programmes and projects; long- and short-term planning; Gen. Sec. A. J. S. HOK A HIN.

CHAMBER OF COMMERCE

Kamer van Koophandel en Fabrieken (Chamber of Commerce and Industry): Dr J. C. de Mirandastraat 10, POB 149, Paramaribo; tel. 473527; fax 474779; e-mail chamber@sr.net; internet www.sr .net/users/chamber; f. 1910; Pres. R. L. A. AMEERALI; Sec. R. RAMDAT; 16,109 mems.

Surinaams–Nederlandse Kamer voor Handel en Industrie (Suriname–Netherlands Chamber of Commerce and Industry): Coppenamestraat 158, Paramaribo; tel. 463201; fax 463241.

INDUSTRIAL AND TRADE ASSOCIATION

Associatie van Surinaamse Fabrikanten (ASFA) (Suriname Manufacturers' Asscn): Jaggernath Lachmonstraat 187, POB 3046,

Paramaribo; tel. 439797; fax 439798; e-mail asfa@sr.net; Sec. E. VEGA; 317 mems.

EMPLOYERS' ASSOCIATION

Vereniging Surinaams Bedrijfsleven (VSB) (Suriname Trade and Industry Association): Prins Hendrikstraat 18, POB 111, Paramaribo; tel. 475286; fax 472287; f. 1950; Chair. M. A. MEYER; 290 mems.

TRADE UNIONS

Council of the Surinamese Federation of Trade Unions (RVS): f. 1987; comprises:

Algemeen Verbond van Vakverenigingen in Suriname 'De Moederbond' (AVVS) (General Confederation of Trade Unions): Verlengde Coppenamestraat 134, POB 2951, Paramaribo; tel. 463501; fax 465116; right-wing; Pres. IMRO GREP; Chair. A. W. KOORNAAR; 15,000 mems.

Centrale 47 (C-47): Wanicastraat 230, Paramaribo; includes bauxite workers; Chair. (vacant); 7,654 mems.

Centrale Landsdienaren Organisatie (CLO) (Central Organization for Civil Service Employees): Gemenelandsweg 93, Paramaribo; Pres. HENDRIK SYLVESTER; 13,000 mems.

Progressieve Werknemers Organisatie (PWO) (Progressive Workers' Organization): Limesgracht 80, POB 406, Paramaribo; f. 1948; covers the commercial, hotel and banking sectors; Chair. RAMON W. CRUDEN; Sec. M. E. MENT; 4,000 mems.

Progressive Trade Union Federation (C-47): Wanicastraat 230, Paramaribo; tel. 494365; fax 401149; Pres. FRED DERBY; Gen. Sec. R NAARENDORP.

Federation of Civil Servants Organization (CLO): Verlengde Gemenelandsweg 74, Paramaribo; tel. 464200; fax 493918; Pres. RONALD HOOGHART; Gen. Sec. FREDDY WATERBERG.

Federation of Farmers and Agrarians (FAL): Keizerstraat 150, Paramaribo; tel. 464200; fax 499839; Pres. JIWAN SITAL.

Transport

RAILWAYS

There are no public railways operating in Suriname.

Paramaribo Government Railway: Paramaribo; single-track narrow-gauge railway from Onverwacht, via Zanderij, to Brownsweg (87 km—54 miles); operational between Onverwacht and Republiek (13 km—8 miles); Dir S. R. C. VITERLOO.

Suriname Bauxite Railway: POB 1893, Paramaribo; fax 475148; 70 km (44 miles), standard gauge, from the Backhuis Mountains to Apoera on the Corentijn River; owing to the abandonment of plans to mine bauxite in the Backhuis mountains, the railway transports timber and crushed stone; Pres. EMRO R. HOLDER.

ROADS

In 2000 Suriname had an estimated 4,492 km (2,750 miles) of roads, of which 1,220 km (758 miles) were main roads. The principal east–west road, 390 km (242 miles) in length, links Albina, on the eastern border, with Nieuw Nickerie, in the west.

SHIPPING

Suriname is served by many shipping companies and has about 1,500 km (930 miles) of navigable rivers and canals. A number of shipping companies conduct regular international services (principally for freight) to and from Paramaribo including EWL, Fyffesgroup, the Alcoa Steamship Co, Marli Marine Lines, Bic Line, Nedlloyd Line, Maersk Lines and Tecmarine Lines (in addition to those listed below). There are also two ferry services linking Suriname with Guyana, across the Corentijn River, and with French Guiana, across the Marowijne River.

Dienst voor de Scheepvaart (Suriname Maritime Authority): Cornelis Jongbawstraat 2, POB 888, Paramaribo; tel. 476769; fax 472940; e-mail dvsmas@sr.net; government authority supervising and controlling shipping in Surinamese waters; Dir of Maritime Affairs E. FITZ-JIM.

Scheepvaart Maatschappij Suriname NV (SMS) (Suriname Shipping Line Ltd): Waterkant 44, POB 1824, Paramaribo; tel. 472447; fax 474814; f. 1936; regular cargo and passenger services in the interior; Chair. F. VAN DER JAGT; Man. Dir M. E. LIEUW A. PAW.

NV VSH Scheepvaartmij United Suriname Shipping Company: Van het Hogerhuysstraat 9–11, POB 1860, Paramaribo; tel. 402558; fax 403515; e-mail united@sr.net; shipping agents and freight carriers; Man. PATRICK HEALY.

Staatsolie Maatschappij Suriname NV: Industrieterrein 21, Flora, POB 4069, Paramaribo; tel. 480333; fax 480811; Chair. H. G. COLERIDGE; Man. Dir Dr S. E. JHARAP.

Suriname Coast Traders NV: Flocislaan 4, Industrieterrein Flora, POB 9216, Paramaribo; tel. 463020; fax 463040; f. 1981.

CIVIL AVIATION

The main airport is Johan Adolf Pengel International Airport (formerly Zanderij International Airport), 45 km from Paramaribo. Domestic flights operate from Zorg-en-Hoop Airport, located in a suburb of Paramaribo. There are 35 airstrips throughout the country.

Surinaamse Luchtvaart Maatschappij NV (SLM) (Suriname Airways): Coppenamestraat 136, POB 2029, Paramaribo; tel. 433273; fax 491213; e-mail c.cairo@slm.firm.sr; internet www.slm .firm.sr; f. 1962; services to Amsterdam (the Netherlands) and to destinations in North America, South America and the Caribbean; Pres. HENK JESSURUN (acting); Vice-Pres. JAN HOLLUM.

Gonini Air Service Ltd: Doekhiweg 1, Zorg-en-Hoop Airport, POB 1614, Paramaribo; tel. 499098; fax 498363; f. 1976; privately-owned; licensed for scheduled and unscheduled national and international services (charters, lease, etc.); Man. Dir GERARD BRUNINGS.

Gum Air NV: Rijweg naar Kwatta 254, Paramaribo; tel. 497670; privately-owned; unscheduled domestic flights; Man. Mr GUMMELS.

Tourism

Efforts were made to promote the previously undeveloped tourism sector in the 1990s. Attractions include the varied cultural activities, a number of historical sites and an unspoiled interior with many varieties of plants, birds and animals. There are 13 nature reserves and one nature park. There were an estimated 68,000 foreign tourist arrivals at the international airport in 2001. In 1999 tourism receipts totalled US $44m.

Suriname Tourism Foundation: Dr J. F. Nassylaan 2, Paramaribo; tel. 410357; e-mail stsur@sr.net; f. 1996; Exec. Dir Dr H. EDWARD ESSED.

SWAZILAND

Introductory Survey

Location, Climate, Language, Religion, Flag, Capital

The Kingdom of Swaziland is a land-locked country in southern Africa, bordered by South Africa to the north, west, south and south-east, and by Mozambique to the east. The average annual temperature is about 16°C (61°F) on the Highveld, and about 22°C (72°F) in the sub-humid Lowveld, while annual rainfall ranges from 1,000 mm (40 ins) to 2,280 mm (90 ins) on the Highveld, and from 500 mm (20 ins) to 890 mm (35 ins) in the Lowveld. English and siSwati are the official languages. About 60% of the population profess Christianity, while most of the remainder adhere to traditional beliefs. The national flag (proportions 2 by 3) is blue, with a yellow-edged horizontal crimson stripe (one-half of the depth) in the centre. On this stripe is a black and white Swazi shield, superimposed on two spears and a staff, all lying horizontally. The capital is Mbabane.

Recent History

Swaziland, which was previously under the joint rule of the United Kingdom and the South African (Transvaal) Republic, became a British protectorate in 1903, and one of the High Commission Territories in 1907, the others being the colony of Basutoland (now the Kingdom of Lesotho) and the protectorate of Bechuanaland (now the Republic of Botswana). The British Act of Parliament that established the Union of South Africa in 1910 also provided for the inclusion in South Africa of the three High Commission Territories, subject to consultation with the local inhabitants.

Swaziland's first Constitution, which was introduced by the British Government, entered into force in January 1964. The Paramount Chief (Ngwenyama—the Lion), King Sobhuza II, subsequently established a traditionalist political party, the Imbokodvo National Movement (INM), which secured all of the seats in the new Legislative Council at elections in June of that year. In 1965, in response to continued pressure from the INM, the British Government established a committee to draft proposed constitutional amendments. A new Constitution, which was promulgated in 1966 and came into effect in April 1967, provided for the introduction of internal self-government pending the attainment of full independence by the end of 1969. Executive power was vested in King Sobhuza as the hereditary monarch and constitutional Head of State. The Legislative Council was dissolved in March 1967, and elections to the new bicameral Parliament took place in April. The INM secured all 24 elective seats in the House of Assembly, although the Ngwane National Liberatory Congress (NNLC) received 20% of the votes cast. In May King Sobhuza formed Swaziland's first Cabinet, appointing the leader of the INM, Prince Makhosini Dlamini, as Prime Minister. On 6 September 1968 Swaziland was granted full independence within the Commonwealth, and a new Constitution (based on the existing Constitution) was adopted.

At elections to the House of Assembly in May 1972, the INM secured 21 seats, while the NNLC won the remaining three elective seats. In April 1973, in accordance with a parliamentary resolution, King Sobhuza repealed the Constitution, imposed a state of emergency under which all political activity was suspended, introduced legislation providing for detention without trial for a period of 60 days, and announced the formation of a national army. A new Constitution, promulgated on 13 October 1978, confirmed the King's control of executive and legislative decisions. The functions of the bicameral parliament, comprising a House of Assembly and a Senate, were confined to debating government proposals and advising the King. The existing 40 traditional local councils (Tinkhundla—singular: Inkhundla) were each to nominate two members to an 80-member electoral college, which was, in turn, to elect 40 deputies to the House of Assembly. Members of the House of Assembly were to select 10 members of the Senate, while the King was to nominate a further 10 members to each chamber. All political parties (including the INM) were prohibited. Legislative elections took place later that year, and the parliament was inaugurated in January 1979. In June 1982 the Swaziland National Council, an advisory body on matters of Swazi tradi-

tion, comprising members of the royal family, was redesignated as the Supreme Council of State (Liqoqo).

King Sobhuza died in August 1982. In accordance with Swazi tradition, the powers of Head of State devolved upon the Queen Mother (Indlovukazi—Great She Elephant) Dzeliwe, who was authorized to act as Regent until King Sobhuza's designated successor, Prince Makhosetive (born in 1968), attained the age of 21. Shortly afterwards Queen Regent Dzeliwe appointed the Liqoqo, which was to advise her in all affairs of State. Competition to secure supreme executive power subsequently emerged between the Prime Minister, Prince Mabandla N. F. Dlamini, and several prominent members, led by Prince Mfanasibili Dlamini, of the Liqoqo. In March 1983 Prince Mabandla was replaced as Prime Minister by a traditionalist, Prince Bhekimpi Dlamini. In August, under the powers of the 'Authorized Person' (an important hereditary post, held by Prince Sozisa Dlamini, the Chairman of the Liqoqo), Queen Regent Dzeliwe was deposed, apparently as a result of her reluctance to dismiss Prince Mabandla. Following an attempt by Queen Regent Dzeliwe to appeal against her deposition, Prince Mfanasibili and his followers obtained an official declaration that the High Court had no jurisdiction in matters concerning Swazi custom and tradition. Widespread opposition to the deposition of Queen Regent Dzeliwe was suppressed, and in September Queen Ntombi, the mother of Prince Makhosetive, was officially invested as Regent. In November elections to the Libandla took place, and a new Cabinet was appointed, in which only Prince Bhekimpi and the Minister of Foreign Affairs, Richard Dlamini, were retained.

In June 1984 Richard Dlamini and the Minister of Finance, Dr Sishayi Nxumalo, were dismissed, as a result of pressure from Prince Mfanasibili and another leading member of the Liqoqo, Dr George Msibi. Nxumalo had recently been investigating allegations that several prominent Swazi politicians, including Prince Mfanasibili, had been involved in the misappropriation of funds owed to the Southern African Customs Union. In September the Government issued a decree granting immunity from prosecution to members of the Liqoqo on matters arising from their official activities. In the same month it was announced that Prince Sozisa, who was alleged to have attempted a coup in June, had been dismissed as Chairman of the Liqoqo. In November Nxumalo was arrested; together with four senior members of the army and security forces, he was subsequently convicted on charges of conspiring to overthrow the Government.

In October 1985, following protests by prominent members of the royal family at the Liqoqo's monopoly of power, Queen Regent Ntombi dismissed Prince Mfanasibili and Msibi. It was subsequently announced that the Liqoqo was to be reconstituted in its former capacity as an advisory body on matters pertaining to traditional law and custom. In December all those convicted of conspiracy in late 1984 were pardoned and released. In January 1986 it was announced that Prince Makhosetive was to be crowned in April, three years earlier than expected, in order to end the competition for power among vying royal factions. In February Prince Mfanasibili and an associate, Majiji Simelane, were arrested on charges of attempting to subvert justice.

Prince Makhosetive was crowned on 25 April 1986, and assumed the title of King Mswati III. In May King Mswati dissolved the Liqoqo, thereby consolidating his power. In the same month Prince Mfanasibili and Simelane were imprisoned, convicted of fabricating evidence to ensure the continued detention of Nxumalo and his fellow detainees. In July King Mswati reorganized the Cabinet, and in October he appointed a former senior member of the security forces, Sotsha Dlamini, as Prime Minister. In May 1987 12 prominent officials, including Prince Bhekimpi and Prince Mfanasibili, were charged with sedition and treason, in connection with the removal from power of Queen Regent Dzeliwe in 1983. The Minister of Natural Resources, Land Utilization and Energy, Mhambi Mnisi, was dismissed in June; he and Msibi subsequently fled to South Africa. In November King Mswati established a special tribunal to preside over all cases involving alleged offences against the

King or the Queen Regent; defendants appearing before the tribunal were not to be granted the right to legal representation or appeal. In March 1988 10 of those accused of involvement in the deposition of Queen Regent Dzeliwe were convicted of treason by the special tribunal, and received custodial sentences; two defendants were acquitted. In July, however, it was reported that the 10 convicted in March had been released (although Prince Mfanasibili was returned to prison to serve the remainder of the sentence issued in 1986).

In November 1987 elections to the legislature took place, one year earlier than scheduled. Later that month King Mswati reappointed Sotsha Dlamini as Prime Minister; only three members of the previous Government were retained in the new Cabinet. In 1988 widespread dissatisfaction with the Tinkhundla-based electoral system emerged. In October a motion in favour of a comprehensive review of the legislative structure, supported by a majority of members of parliament, was rejected by Sotsha Dlamini, on the grounds that it would be contrary to Swazi tradition to challenge an established institution. In March 1989 it was reported that a conspiracy to release Prince Mfanasibili from prison and to overthrow the Government had been suppressed. In April King Mswati announced his continuing support for the existing electoral system. In July he dismissed Sotsha Dlamini for alleged disobedience, replacing him with Obed Dlamini, a former leader of the Swaziland Federation of Trade Unions (SFTU). This appointment was widely regarded as a measure to appease increasing discontent within some sectors of the labour force; nevertheless, unrest continued throughout 1989. In August it was announced that Prince Mfanasibili had been charged with treason in connection with the alleged coup attempt in March: he was later acquitted, but remained in detention.

In early 1990 the People's United Democratic Movement (PUDEMO), which had been established in 1983, distributed tracts questioning the legitimacy of the monarchy in its existing form and demanding constitutional reform. Security forces subsequently arrested a number of suspected members of PUDEMO, who were variously charged with treason, sedition or conspiring to form a political party. All the defendants were acquitted of the principal charges, although five were convicted of illegally attending a political gathering (the sentences of two of the five were annulled on appeal in October 1991). In November King Mswati dismissed the reformist Minister of Justice, Reginald Dhladhla, reportedly on the advice of the Swaziland National Council (which had been reconstituted from the former Liqoqo), prompting public concern that it continued to exert undue influence on government policies. Later in November five members of PUDEMO (who had previously been acquitted of all charges) were arrested under legislation enabling the detention of suspects without trial. In March 1991 the prisoners were released, as a result of international pressure; Prince Mfanasibili was also released. In an attempt to advance its objectives through legal bodies, PUDEMO subsequently established a number of affiliated organizations, including the Human Rights Association of Swaziland (HUMARAS) and the Swaziland Youth Congress (SWAYOCO), but these were not accorded official recognition.

In September and October 1991 a committee, termed Vusela (Greetings), conducted a series of public forums throughout the country to elicit popular opinion on political reforms. Widespread demands for the abolition of the existing electoral system were reported, while there was substantial criticism of the composition of the Vusela committee itself. In subsequent months several peaceful demonstrations, organized by SWAYOCO to demand the establishment of a democratic system of government, were suppressed by security forces. In October King Mswati announced an extensive reorganization of the Cabinet. In February 1992 PUDEMO declared itself a legal opposition party (in contravention of the prohibition on political association), rejected King Mswati's efforts to institute political reform, and demanded a constitutional referendum. Two further opposition movements, the Swaziland United Front (SUF) and the Swaziland National Front (SWANAFRO), subsequently re-emerged. In February King Mswati appointed a second committee (Vusela 2), which was to present recommendations for consideration by the King, based on the conclusions of the first committee. A member of PUDEMO and a number of HUMARAS representatives joined Vusela 2, but resigned later that year, on the grounds that the committee remained in favour of the existing electoral system.

In October 1992 King Mswati approved several proposals submitted by Vusela 2. The House of Assembly (redesignated the National Assembly) was to be expanded to 65 deputies (of whom 55 were to be directly elected by secret ballot from candidates nominated by the Tinkhundla, and 10 appointed by the King), and the Senate to 30 members (10 selected by the National Assembly and 20 appointed by the King); in addition, the legislation providing for detention without trial was to be abrogated, and a new constitution, incorporating the amendments, enshrining an hereditary monarchy and confirming the fundamental rights of the individual and the independence of the judiciary, was to be drafted. However, opposition groups protested at the committee's failure to recommend the immediate restoration of a multi-party political system: the issue was to be postponed until the forthcoming elections, in order to determine the extent of public support. PUDEMO announced its opposition to the electoral reforms, and demanded that the Government organize a national convention to determine the country's constitutional future. King Mswati subsequently dissolved parliament, and announced that he was to rule by decree, with the assistance of the Council of Ministers (as the Cabinet had been restyled), pending the adoption of the new Constitution and the holding of parliamentary elections. Later in October King Mswati announced that elections to the National Assembly would take place in the first half of 1993. At a series of public meetings convened by Vusela 3 (a third committee intended to instruct the population about the forthcoming amendments), doubts were expressed as to the viability of the reformed electoral system; in early 1993, in response to public concern, it was announced that legislation preventing the heads of the Tinkhundla from exerting undue influence in the nomination of candidates had been introduced.

In early 1993, in response to opposition attempts to organize a campaign against the elections, additional security measures were imposed in order to prevent political meetings from taking place. In March more than 50 opposition activists were arrested and charged in connection with the organization of illegal political gatherings. Although those arrested were subsequently released on bail, legal restrictions prevented them from participating in opposition activity, thereby effectively undermining efforts to prevent the elections. None the less, the subsequent low level of voter registration appeared to reflect widespread objections to the reforms.

The first round of elections to the expanded National Assembly, which was contested by 2,094 candidates nominated by the Tinkhundla, took place on 25 September 1993. At the end of September King Mswati repealed the legislation providing for detention without trial. The second round of parliamentary elections, on 11 October, was contested by the three candidates in each Inkhundla who had obtained the highest number of votes in the first poll; the majority of members of the former Council of Ministers (which had been dissolved in late September), including Obed Dlamini, failed to secure seats in the Assembly. Later in October King Mswati nominated a further 10 deputies to the National Assembly, which elected 10 of its members to the Senate; King Mswati subsequently appointed the remaining 20 senators, among them Obed Dlamini and Prince Bhekimpi. In November the former Minister of Works and Construction, Prince Jameson Mbilini Dlamini, considered a traditionalist, was appointed Prime Minister, and a new Council of Ministers (with Nxumalo as Deputy Prime Minister) was formed.

In February 1994, following a report by the US Department of State concerning human rights in Swaziland, which stated that the parliamentary elections had been 'undemocratic', the Government claimed that the majority of the Swazi people were opposed to the establishment of a multi-party political system. It was announced, however, that King Mswati was to appoint a 15-member commission, comprising representatives of organs of State and non-governmental organizations, to draft a new constitution, and a national policy council, which was to prepare a manifesto of the Swazi people. Elections to the Tinkhundla (which had been postponed from March) finally took place, although a high rate of abstention by voters was reported. (The heads of the Tinkhundla had previously been appointed by the King.)

In early 1995 several incendiary attacks, widely attributed to pro-democracy activists, were targeted against official property, culminating in an incident in February in which the parliament building was severely damaged by fire. SWAYOCO (which had previously threatened violence if the Government failed to rescind the ban on political parties) denied initial reports that it was responsible for the attacks. In March the SFTU undertook a two-day general strike (which was widely observed) in support of a set of 27 demands (first presented in January 1994) that included the repeal of the 1973 decree banning all political activity and the introduction of legislation providing for the reinstatement of dismissed employees. The unions subsequently agreed to suspend further strike action after the Government established an independent committee to consider the SFTU's demands. Further planned strike action was abandoned in July, after the National Assembly approved legislation enabling the Government to impose custodial and financial penalties on organizers of industrial action. In August the Senate approved a motion supporting a statement made by King Mswati (during a visit to South Africa) to the effect that the Swazi population was not in favour of a multi-party system.

In January 1996 PUDEMO announced a campaign of protests and civil disobedience, owing to the Government's failure to respond to demands for the installation of a multi-party system and for the adoption of a constitution restricting the monarch to a largely ceremonial role. Strike action took place later in the month, following a failed attempt by the authorities to have the strike declared illegal. Security forces intervened to suppress demonstrations by SFTU members, and violent clashes ensued, in which three people were reported to have been killed. The SFTU refused to enter into negotiations with the Government, stipulating that the 1973 decree and the restrictions on trade unions be revoked prior to discussions. Meanwhile, it was reported that some members of the Government, including Obed Dlamini, also favoured political reform. King Mswati accused the trade unions of attempting to overthrow the monarchy, and threatened to order his traditional warriors to suppress the strike. The SFTU subsequently suspended strike action to allow negotiations to proceed with the Government (which continued to reject the unions' preconditions for discussions). In February 1996 King Mswati announced that the process of drafting a new constitution would be initiated later that year, and that the ban on political activity would also be reviewed. In May King Mswati indicated that a 'People's Parliament', comprising a series of consultative meetings between citizens and government leaders, had been initiated to solicit public opinion regarding constitutional reform. At the same time King Mswati dismissed Prince Mbilini as Prime Minister, and announced that he would appoint his successor in consultation with the Swaziland National Council.

The country was effectively paralysed in mid-1996 by strike action in the public sector, in support of pay demands. The Government declared the strike illegal, under industrial relations legislation enacted earlier in the year. Although the industrial action was abandoned, the Government deducted approximately one-half from teachers' and civil servants' salaries for July and August.

In late July 1996, following an emergency meeting (attended by Nxumalo, as acting Prime Minister, and the Heads of State of Mozambique, Botswana, Zimbabwe and South Africa) to discuss Swaziland's political situation, King Mswati appointed a Constitutional Review Commission, comprising chiefs, political activists and trade unionists, to collate submissions from the Swazi people and subsequently draft proposals for a new constitution. (The Commission received substantial funds from international donors.) At the same time, Dr Barnabas Sibusiso Dlamini, an IMF Executive Director and former Minister of Finance, was appointed Prime Minister. In August PUDEMO expressed its dissatisfaction with the composition of the Constitutional Review Commission under the chairmanship of the King's brother, Prince Mangaliso, and appealed for regional and international assistance in the review process. In response to accusations by the SFTU of police brutality at a PUDEMO rally in September, the Minister of Commerce and Industry defended police action and blamed political parties for ignoring the 1973 decree prohibiting political activity.

In December 1996 the Prime Minister announced that a 'task force', composed of workers, employers and government representatives, had discussed the SFTU's demands made in March 1995, and that the implementation of the recommendations outlined in the resulting report was to be overseen by the Labour Advisory Board. In January 1997, however, the SFTU claimed that there had been no response to its demands for democratic reform, and resolved to begin indefinite strike action from February. Meanwhile, the PUDEMO President, Mario Masuku, declared that Swaziland's leaders were not committed to

change, and withdrew from the Constitutional Review Commission. At the end of January the four main leaders of the SFTU were arrested and subsequently charged with intimidating bus owners into joining the forthcoming strike; it was believed that the arrests had been made at the behest of the Swaziland National Council. The strike, pronounced illegal by the Government, proceeded, and was apparently observed by approximately one-half of the labour force. Some days later PUDEMO reportedly distributed a pamphlet containing threats to attack and assassinate journalists whose coverage of the strike favoured the Government. On the ninth day of industrial action six strikers were seriously injured in violent clashes with the security forces. The SFTU leaders declined the Government's offer to release them on condition that they end the strike; their trial began, but was dismissed in late February, owing to lack of evidence. At the beginning of March the Congress of South African Trade Unions (COSATU), which had asserted its support for the SFTU throughout the strike, initiated a one-day blockade of the Swazi border. The SFTU decided to suspend the strike shortly afterwards, as the Government had agreed to commence negotiations, but resolved to continue industrial action on the first two days of each month until its 27 demands had been met. It was subsequently announced that King Mswati was reviewing the 1973 decree. In April 1997 the SFTU postponed a further blockade indefinitely, in order to allow the Government adequate time to review the situation.

In October 1997 the SFTU called a nation-wide strike in support of its ongoing demands for democratic reform, after talks with the Government failed to produce any agreement, although support for the strike was low. Teachers none the less resolved to continue with separate industrial action in support of pay demands. There was further civil unrest later in October, when a reported 2,000 demonstrators gathered at Matsapha Airport to await the return of the King from a meeting of Commonwealth Heads of Government; armed paramilitary police intervened, firing tear-gas in an attempt to disperse the crowd. The following day the Government banned a further demonstration at the airport, scheduled to coincide with the arrival of Prince Charles, heir to the British throne. Meanwhile, SFTU and other protesters demanded the recall from Swaziland of the British High Commissioner, whom they accused of colluding with the King and interfering in domestic affairs.

By December 1997 three members of the Constitutional Review Commission had resigned, amid reports of increasing public discontent with the Commission's apparent lack of progress and calls for its dissolution. In April 1998 the Council of Ministers was reshuffled, with the notable departure of Nxumalo, who was appointed to chair the new Swaziland Investment Promotion Authority.

In August 1998 King Mswati dissolved the National Assembly, in preparation for elections scheduled for October. Opposition groups urged voters to boycott the polls, in the absence of the immediate legalization of political parties. Some 350 candidates were nominated by the Tinkhundla to contest the 55 elective seats in the Assembly. Voting took place on 16 and 24 October; turn-out was reportedly low. A new Cabinet, again with Sibusiso Dlamini as Prime Minister, was appointed in mid-November, and a new Senate and Swaziland National Council were formed. On the day of the ceremony to swear in the new Cabinet a powerful bomb exploded in the building in which the offices of the Deputy Prime Minister, Arthur Khoza, were located, killing one person and seriously injuring two others. The Prime Minister denied reports that he had received a letter warning him about the bomb. Officials linked the attack to another bomb explosion, in late October, near a bridge outside the capital, shortly after King Mswati's motorcade had crossed the bridge. Police subsequently seized documents purportedly detailing the manufacture of explosive devices from a house occupied by SWAYOCO. The SFTU leader, Jan Sithole, and members of PUDEMO were subsequently questioned in connection with the dynamiting of the bridge.

In January 1999 the Swazi authorities deregistered the country's biggest labour union, the Swaziland Agriculture, Plantation and Allied Workers' Union, citing its failure to submit annual financial reports for inspection. In April the NNLC, PUDEMO and the SFTU united to form the Swaziland Democratic Alliance (SDA). The NNLC leader, Obed Dlamini, was elected Chairman. The formal launch of the SDA was scheduled for 11 April, to coincide with the end of the Southern African Development Community (SADC) labour conference in Mbabane. However, following warnings from the police that the proposed inauguration, which had been rescheduled for 19 April, was illegal and would not be permitted to take place, the executive of the SDA met and cancelled the event. The SADC labour conference was also the focus of pro-democracy demonstrations by some 2,000 workers in Mbabane and by a larger group, comprising mainly public-sector workers, in Manzini. Protests were swiftly suppressed by security forces.

In September 1999, as a result of an article criticizing the King's choice of a new wife, the Sunday editor of *The Times of Swaziland* was arrested and charged with criminal libel. He was released on bail, but had his passport confiscated. New anti-defamation legislation passed in October required the licensing of all journalists and threatened reporters with criminal penalties for publishing inaccurate stories. The *Swazi Observer*, owned by a national trust controlled by the King, was abruptly closed in February 2000, reportedly as a result of government intervention following the newspaper's recent exposés of power struggles between ministers and of politicians' alleged criminal involvement; the newspaper resumed publication in March 2001, although in October its editor was shot dead, apparently in an indiscriminate attack.

Meanwhile, demands for democracy intensified, and in November 1999 a bomb that exploded 5 km from the royal palace was thought to be connected with the device in Khoza's office in 1998, and was blamed on PUDEMO. Political tensions increased in February 2000 when the leader of the Swaziland Progressive Party was arrested for holding a lone demonstration outside the legislature to protest against the ban on party politics. Shortly afterwards police raided the offices of SWAYOCO, reportedly assaulting delegates at the organization's congress meeting, which had been organized without police permission. At least eight delegates received treatment for injuries caused in the raid. Meanwhile, in the same month King Mswati ordered the Constitutional Review Commission to present its findings by the end of 2000.

In October 2000 there was unrest in several areas following an operation by the armed forces to displace some 200 people from their home villages, allegedly in response to the residents' refusal to abandon support for their local chieftains, in favour of Prince Maguga, the King's brother. Pro-democracy campaigners and trade unions met in South Africa in November to support the displaced residents and to initiate a plan of action in support of democratic reforms. A two-day strike was partially observed, and activists subsequently blockaded the country's border with South Africa for two days in late November. Meanwhile, Masuku was arrested and charged with sedition after allegedly demanding the overthrow of King Mswati at a public meeting; he was subsequently released on bail.

A reorganization of the Council of Ministers, in which six portfolios were redistributed, was effected in February 2001. In May the Government closed down *The Guardian* newspaper (established only three months earlier) and *The Nation*, a monthly magazine, following the publication of reports alleging that the King had been poisoned by one of his wives. The courts quickly overturned the bans, but the Government proceeded to ban the publications again later that month; *The Nation* reached an out-of-court settlement to continue operations immediately, and the second ban on *The Guardian* was eventually overturned in September.

In June 2001 the King provoked international criticism by promulgating a decree that, it was claimed, effectively amounted to the declaration of a state of emergency; the legislation ensured that no person or body, including the courts, had the authority to challenge the King, prevented newspapers from challenging publishing bans, allowed the King to appoint judges and traditional chiefs personally, and made ridiculing or impersonating the King a criminal offence. Opposition groups in Swaziland condemned the decree as reinforcing tyrannical rule, and criticized the international community's lack of interest in the country's political situation. The King revoked the decree in July, in response to international diplomatic pressure, notably a threat by the USA to impose economic sanctions. However, at the same time the King issued a new decree that retained certain sections of the original decree, including a provision allowing the detention of Swazi citizens without the option of bail for some offences.

In August 2001 the Constitutional Review Commission submitted its report, which recommended that the King's powers be extended and political parties remain illegal, but stated that the introduction of a bill of rights that was not in conflict with Swazi laws and customs was a possibility. The SFTU and PUDEMO rejected the Commission's proposals. In February 2002 a 15-member committee, appointed by the King, began drafting a new constitution; PUDEMO criticized the Government for allegedly manipulating the Commission's report and selecting members of the drafting committee who were sympathetic to government policy. Meanwhile, in October 2001 Masuku was re-arrested for defying his bail conditions; his trial on charges of sedition, which he denied, began in February 2002, and in August he was acquitted and released after the High Court ruled that the State had failed to prove its case.

The King introduced the Internal Security Bill in June 2002, intended to suppress political dissent. It provided variously for fines and prison sentences for those found guilty of carrying or wearing banners or flags of banned political formations, or of participating in mass strikes or boycotts. Training abroad to commit acts of insurgency in Swaziland would be punishable by up to 20 years' imprisonment. The bill was severely criticized by the SFTU, PUDEMO and various foreign governments, which considered the bill inconsistent with the proposed new constitution and bill of rights; the bill had still to be passed by the National Assembly in April 2003.

In October 2002 the King was the subject of a legal challenge from the mother of a girl chosen to be his 10th wife; the woman alleged that her daughter had been abducted by two of the King's emissaries. However, she withdrew the case in early November, when her daughter stated that she had no objection to becoming a queen. Chief Justice Stanley Sapire was dismissed following the incident, after ignoring a decree issued by the King to abandon the case against him. Further controversy arose over the King's order for a private aircraft costing around US $45m. The National Assembly voted against the purchase of the aircraft in November, after it was revealed that development funds from international donors had been diverted to pay for it, but the vote was overruled by the Cabinet; the National Assembly intended to vote again to prevent the purchase in mid-2003. The European Union had previously suspended financial aid to the country over the issue in September 2002. In April 2003 a cabinet reshuffle was effected; nine portfolios were redistributed, and the Minister of Public Works and Transport, Titus Mlangeni, was dismissed on suspicion of fraud. Elections to the National Assembly were scheduled for September.

Meanwhile, Swaziland has been severely affected by the HIV/AIDS pandemic. The UN estimated that 33.4% of the adult population (aged between 15 and 49 years) was infected with HIV at December 2001, and the Swaziland National AIDS Programme reported that 34.2% of women attending ante-natal clinics were infected with HIV at March 2001. Estimated figures released by the Swazi Government in January 2003 revealed that almost 40% of the adult population was infected with HIV, and the Prime Minister promised that anti-retroviral drugs would be available at state hospitals from February. The Government had previously been criticized for its reluctance to confront the problem directly; proposed measures have included sterilizing or branding those infected with HIV. In an attempt to prevent the spread of the disease, in September 2001 the Government ordered women aged 18 years or younger to remain celibate and avoid shaking hands with men for a period of five years.

During the apartheid era Swaziland pursued a policy of dialogue and co-operation with South Africa. In 1982 the two countries signed a secret non-aggression pact; several members of the African National Congress of South Africa (ANC), which had increasingly used Swaziland as a base for guerrilla attacks into South Africa, were subsequently arrested and expelled from Swaziland. The signing, in March 1984, of the Nkomati accord between South Africa and Mozambique (which banned both countries from harbouring dissidents) led many ANC members to flee from Mozambique to neighbouring Swaziland. Following the murder, in 1984, of the deputy chief of the Swazi security police, the Government initiated a campaign to arrest all ANC fugitives remaining in the country (the ANC denied involvement in the killing). In 1986 leading Swazi politicians expressed opposition to the imposition of economic sanctions against South Africa, owing to the dependence of Swaziland's own economy on that country. Detentions and deportations of ANC members by the Swazi Government continued, while several suspected ANC members were abducted by South African security forces or killed in Swaziland by gunmen who were widely assumed to be South African. Following the legalization of the ANC in 1990, the Swazi Prime Minister, Obed Dlamini, pledged to conduct an inquiry (which, however, he failed to initiate) into state operations against ANC members. Formal diplomatic relations were established in 1993. From the late 1990s prominent South African organizations, including the ANC and COSATU, expressed support for the SFTU's demands for political reform, prompting the Swazi Government to protest of interference in its domestic affairs. In April 1995 the South African Government announced that it had rejected a long-standing claim by Swaziland to a region in the Mpumalanga province (formerly Eastern Transvaal). However, King Mswati declared in a letter to South African President, Thabo Mbeki, in early 2001 that he had not abandoned his intention to reincorporate parts of Mpumalanga and KwaZulu/Natal provinces into Swaziland.

Following the ratification of the October 1992 peace accord in Mozambique (q.v.), an agreement signed by the Governments of Swaziland and Mozambique and the office of the UN High Commissioner for Refugees in August 1993 provided for the repatriation of some 24,000 Mozambican nationals from Swaziland. In December the number of Swazi troops deployed at the border with Mozambique was increased, following clashes between Swazi and Mozambican forces in the region. Mozambique subsequently protested at alleged border incursions by members of the Swazi armed forces. In early 1994 discussions took place between Swazi and Mozambican officials to seek mutually satisfactory arrangements for the joint patrol of the border, and in 1995 it was announced that the Mhlumeni border post, closed since the 1970s, would reopen as the second official transit point between the two countries. In September 1997, during the first visit to Swaziland made by a Mozambican Prime Minister, a bilateral extradition agreement was signed, with the aim of reducing cross-border crime. In December 1999 the Swazi authorities expelled some 500 Mozambican citizens who had been declared illegal immigrants. In the following month a campaign began to encourage Mozambicans living in Swaziland to register for military service there.

Government

The Constitution of 13 October 1978 vests supreme executive and legislative power in the hereditary King, who is the Head of State, and provides for a bicameral legislature, comprising a House of Assembly and a Senate. The functions of the legislature are confined to debating government proposals and advising the King. Executive power is exercised through the Cabinet (later redesignated the Council of Ministers), which is appointed by the King. The Swaziland National Council (Libandla), which comprises members of the royal family and is headed by the King and the constitutional dual monarch, the Queen Mother, provides advice on matters regulated by traditional law and custom.

Following a number of amendments to the electoral system, which were approved by the King in October 1992, the House of Assembly (which was redesignated as the National Assembly) was expanded to 65 deputies (of whom 55 are directly elected from candidates nominated by traditional local councils, known as Tinkhundla, and 10 appointed by the King), and the Senate to 30 members (of whom 20 are appointed by the King and 10 elected by the National Assembly). Elections to the National Assembly are conducted by secret ballot, in two rounds of voting; the second round of the elections is contested by the three candidates from each of the Tinkhundla who secure the highest number of votes in the first poll. Swaziland is divided into 273 regional tribal areas, comprising 55 elected Tinkhundla. In August 2001 a commission that had been appointed by the King in 1996 to prepare proposals for a draft constitution submitted its report; a constitutional committee began drafting a new constitution in February 2002.

Defence

The Umbutfo Swaziland Defence Force, created in 1973, totalled 2,657 regular troops in November 1983. Swaziland also has a paramilitary police force. Military service is compulsory and lasts for two years. Of total current expenditure by the central Government in the financial year 2001/02, E 168m. (6.6%) was allocated to defence.

Economic Affairs

In 2001, according to estimates by the World Bank, Swaziland's gross national income (GNI), measured at average 1999–2001 prices, was US $1,388m., equivalent to $1,300 per head (or $4,690 per head on an international purchasing-power parity basis). During 1990–2001, it was estimated, the population increased at an average annual rate of 3.0%, while gross

domestic product (GDP) per head increased, in real terms, by an average of 0.1% per year. Overall GDP increased, in real terms, at an average annual rate of 3.1% in 1990–2001; growth in 2001 was 1.6%.

Agriculture (including forestry) contributed 14.2% of GDP in 2001. About 32.9% of the labour force were employed in the agricultural sector in mid-2001. The principal cash crops are sugar cane (sugar accounted for 9.3% of domestic export earnings in 2001), cotton, citrus fruits, pineapples and maize. Tobacco and rice are also cultivated. Livestock-rearing is traditionally important. An outbreak of foot-and-mouth disease occurred in November 2000, but was successfully contained by culling approximately 1,600 infected cattle and vaccinating more than 23,000 animals at risk. Poor harvests in 2001 and 2002 necessitated the imports of basic foods in those years, and around one-quarter of the population was dependent on food aid from the UN World Food Programme in early 2003. Commercial forestry (which employs a significant proportion of the population) provides wood for the manufacture of pulp. During 1990–2001, according to the World Bank, agricultural GDP increased by an average of 0.9% per year. Agricultural GDP increased by 5.2% in 2001.

Industry (including mining, manufacturing, construction and power) contributed 45.1% of GDP in 2001. During 1990–2001, according to the World Bank, industrial GDP increased at an average annual rate of 4.0%. Industrial GDP increased by 7.5% in 2001.

Mining contributed 0.3% of GDP in 2001. Swaziland has extensive reserves of coal, much of which is exported. Asbestos is also an important mineral export. In addition, Swaziland has reserves of tin, kaolin, talc, iron ore, pyrophyllite and silica. During 1996–2001, according to the IMF, mining GDP declined by an average of 3.8% per year. Mining GDP declined by 19.9% in 2001, according to the IMF.

Manufacturing contributed 37.1% of GDP in 2001, and is mainly based on the processing of agricultural, livestock and forestry products. Some 26% of the labour force were employed in the manufacturing sector in 1996/97. During 1990–2001, according to the World Bank, manufacturing GDP increased at an average annual rate of 3.4%. Manufacturing GDP increased by 7.9% in 2001.

Swaziland imports most of its energy requirements from South Africa. Of total electrical energy generated and imported in 1999, 77.1% was imported from South Africa. However, the Swazi Government aimed to increase domestic energy output to cover approximately 50% of the country's needs, following the construction of a hydroelectric power station on the Maguga Dam, which began operations in 2002. Mineral fuels and lubricants accounted for an estimated 11.4% of imports in 2001.

The services sector contributed 40.7% of GDP in 2001. According to the World Bank, the GDP of the services sector increased by an average of 3.3% per year in 1990–2001. Services GDP increased by 4.4% in 2000, but decreased by 1.2% in 2001.

In 2000 Swaziland recorded a visible trade deficit of US $72.7m., while there was a deficit of $52.7m. on the current account of the balance of payments. In 1994 the principal source of imports was South Africa (83.3%); other suppliers are the United Kingdom, the Netherlands and Switzerland. South Africa was also the principal market for exports in 1995 (taking an estimated 58.2% of domestic exports); the United Kingdom is also a significant purchaser. The principal exports in 2001 were edible concentrates, sugar, wood pulp and textiles. The principal imports in that year were machinery and transport equipment, basic manufactures, food and live animals, and chemicals and chemical products.

In the financial year ending 31 March 2002 there was an overall budgetary deficit of E 315m. (equivalent to 2.8% of GDP). Swaziland's external debt totalled US $261.6m. at the end of 2000, of which $198.2m. was long-term public debt. In that year the cost of debt-servicing was equivalent to 2.3% of the value of exports of goods and services. In 1990–2001 annual inflation averaged 9.1%; consumer prices increased by an average of 5.9% in 2001. It was estimated that 40% of the labour force were unemployed in 1995.

Swaziland is a member of the Common Market for Eastern and Southern Africa (see p. 162), of the Southern African Development Community (SADC, see p. 311) and of the Southern African Customs Union (SACU), which also includes Botswana, Lesotho, Namibia and South Africa.

Swaziland's economy is vulnerable to fluctuations in international prices for some major exports, including sugar, as well as to the effects of unfavourable weather conditions. In addition, prevailing economic conditions in neighbouring South Africa have a pronounced impact on the Swazi economy: although Swaziland may determine the exchange rate of its currency, the lilangeni, this has remained at par with the South African rand. The decline in value of the rand and, consequently, the lilangeni from the late 1990s had a detrimental effect on Swaziland's economic performance. In 1997 the Government presented the Economic and Social Reform Agenda, prepared in consultation with the IMF and the World Bank, which aimed to accelerate economic growth, reduce the level of unemployment and encourage investment in the private sector. In 1999 the IMF urged further fiscal and other reforms to strengthen Swaziland's public finances, in order to offset the effects of the new revenue-sharing agreement within SACU (the IMF projected that Swaziland's receipts from SACU would decline from 16% of GDP in 2000 to about 14% in 2004), and of free-trade agreements within the SADC and between South Africa and the European Union (EU). Swaziland was granted some €5.6m. by the EU in September 2000 to assist in this process. In 2000 an improvement in the regional economic environment, particularly in South Africa, also helped the domestic economy. In August 1999 the Government established a National Development Strategy to provide a framework for the formulation of short- and medium-term action programmes. Reforms of the tax system were implemented in 2001 (with rates of corporate and personal taxation reduced), while other government priorities included attracting overseas investment, improving the country's infrastructure and preparing for the privatization of state-owned enterprises. However, continuing demands for constitutional reform ensured that long-term prospects for investment in Swaziland remained dependent on a satisfactory political settlement. The Swaziland Tourism Authority was established in 2001, with funding from the EU and the World Bank, in an attempt to expand the sector. In January 2003 the IMF urged fiscal discipline and increased social and humanitarian spending, and attributed low GDP growth to the country's lack of competitiveness in the region.

Education

Education is neither free nor compulsory in Swaziland. Primary education begins at six years of age and lasts for seven years; the Government announced in the 2001 budget that it hoped to provide free primary education in the future. Secondary education begins at 13 years of age and lasts for up to five years, comprising a first cycle of three years and a second of two years. In 1999/2000 92.8% of children in the relevant age-group (boys 92.1%; girls 93.6%) were enrolled at primary schools, while in 1998/99, according to UNESCO estimates, secondary enrolment included 37.3% of children in the appropriate age-group (boys 40.0%; girls 34.6%). Swaziland has a university, with campuses at Luyengo and Kwaluseni, and a number of other institutions of higher education. According to the IMF, of total expenditure by the central Government in the financial year 2001/02, E 607m. (18.4%) was for education.

Public Holidays

2003: 1 January (New Year's Day), 18–21 April (Easter), 19 April (Birthday of King Mswati), 25 April (National Flag Day), 1 May (Workers' Day), 29 May (Ascension Day), 22 July (Birthday of the late King Sobhuza), 6 September (Somhlolo—Independence—Day), 24 October (UN Day), 25–26 December (Christmas and Boxing Day).

2004: 1 January (New Year's Day), 9–12 April (Easter), 19 April (Birthday of King Mswati), 25 April (National Flag Day), 1 May (Workers' Day), 20 May (Ascension Day), 22 July (Birthday of the late King Sobhuza), 6 September (Somhlolo—Independence—Day), 24 October (UN Day), 25–26 December (Christmas and Boxing Day).

The Incwala and Umhlanga Ceremonies are held in December or January, and August or September (respectively), but the exact dates are variable each year.

Statistical Survey

Source (unless otherwise stated): Central Statistical Office, POB 456, Mbabane; internet www.gov.sz/home.asp?pid=75.

AREA AND POPULATION

Area: 17,363 sq km (6,704 sq miles).

Population (excluding absentee workers): 494,534 (males 231,861, females 262,673) at census of 25 August 1976; 681,059 (males 321,579, females 359,480) at census of 25 August 1986; 980,722 at census of 11–12 May 1997.

Density (1997): 56.5 per sq km.

Ethnic Groups (census of August 1986): Swazi 661,646; Other Africans 14,468; European 1,825; Asiatic 228; Other non-Africans 412; Mixed 2,403; Unknown 77; Total 681,059.

Principal Towns (population at census of August 1986): Mbabane (capital) 38,290; Manzini 18,084. *Mid-2001* (UN projection, including suburbs): Mbabane 80,000 (Source: UN, *World Urbanization Prospects: The 2001 Revision*).

Births and Deaths (UN estimates, 1995–2000): Average annual birth rate 35.6 per 1,000; average annual death rate 14.0 per 1,000. Source: UN, *World Population Prospects: The 2000 Revision*.

Expectation of Life (UN estimates, years at birth): 40.2 (males 40.2; females 40.1) in 2001. Source: WHO, *World Health Report*.

Economically Active Population (persons aged 12 years and over, census of August 1986): Agriculture, hunting, forestry and fishing 30,197; Mining and quarrying 5,245; Manufacturing 14,742; Electricity, gas and water 1,315; Construction 7,661; Trade, restaurants and hotels 12,348; Transport, storage and communications 7,526; Financing, insurance, real estate and business services 1,931; Community, social and personal services 32,309; Activities not adequately defined 3,156; Total employed 116,430 (males 79,528, females 36,902); Unemployed 43,925 (males 25,663, females 18,262); Total labour force 160,355 (males 105,191, females 55,164). Source: UN, *Demographic Yearbook. Mid-2001* (estimates in '000): Agriculture, etc. 114; Total labour force 347. Source: FAO.

HEALTH AND WELFARE

Key Indicators

Total Fertility Rate (children per woman, 2001): 4.5.

Under-5 Mortality Rate (per 1,000 live births, 2001): 149.

HIV/AIDS (% of persons aged 15–49, 2001): 33.44.

Physicians (per 1,000 head, 1996): 0.15.

Health Expenditure (2000): US $ per head (PPP): 210.

Health Expenditure (2000): % of GDP: 4.2.

Health Expenditure (2000): public (% of total): 72.1.

Human Development Index (2000): ranking: 125.

Human Development Index (2000): value: 0.577.

For sources and definitions, see explanatory note on p. vi.

AGRICULTURE

Principal Crops (FAO estimates, '000 metric tons, 2001): Maize 85; Potatoes 6; Sweet potatoes 2; Pulses 3; Cottonseed 15; Cotton (lint) 7; Oranges 36; Grapefruit 37; Pineapples 20; Sugar cane 3,885. Source: FAO.

Livestock (FAO estimates, '000 head, year ending September 2001): Horses 1; Asses 15; Cattle 615; Pigs 34; Sheep 32; Goats 445; Chickens 3. Source: FAO.

Livestock Products (FAO estimates, '000 metric tons, 2001): Beef and veal 18; Goat meat 3; Cows' milk 38; Cattle hides 2. Source: FAO.

FORESTRY

Roundwood Removals (estimates, '000 cubic metres, 2001): Sawlogs, veneer logs and logs for sleepers 260; Other industrial wood 70; Fuel wood 560; Total 890.

Sawnwood Production (estimates, '000 cubic metres, 2001): 102 (Source: FAO).

FISHING

Fishing (metric tons, live weight, 2000): Capture (FAO estimate) 70; Aquaculture 69 (Common carp 20*, Mozambique tilapia 25*, Redbreast tilapia 13, North African catfish 6*, Red claw crayfish 5*); Total catch 139.
* FAO estimate. Source: FAO, *Yearbook of Fishery Statistics*.

MINING

Production (estimates, 2001): Coal 380,000 metric tons; Asbestos 12,690 metric tons (2000); Quarrystone 350,000 cubic metres. Source: US Geological Survey; *Mining Annual Review*.

INDUSTRY

1995: Electric energy 425 million kWh. *1998:* Wood pulp 220,000 metric tons; Raw sugar 476,000 metric tons. Source: UN, *Industrial Commodity Statistics Yearbook*.

FINANCE

Currency and Exchange Rates: 100 cents = 1 lilangeni (plural: emalangeni). *Sterling, Dollar and Euro Equivalents* (31 December 2002): £1 sterling = 13.9260 emalangeni; US $1 = 8.6400 emalangeni; €1 = 9.0608 emalangeni; 1,000 emalangeni = £71.81 = $115.74 = €110.37. *Average Exchange Rate* (US $ per lilangeni): 0.14481 in 2000; 0.11774 in 2001; 0.09539 in 2002. Note: The lilangeni is at par with the South African rand.

Budget (provisional, million emalangeni, year ending 31 March 2002): *Revenue:* Taxes on net income and profits 725; Taxes on property 6; Taxes on goods, services and international trade 2,042 (Receipts from Southern African Customs Union 1,504, Sales tax 408); Other taxes 7; Other current revenue 194; Total 2,973, excl. grants received (121). *Expenditure:* Current expenditure 2,537 (Wages and salaries 1,162, Other purchases of goods and services 781, Interest payments 96, Subsidies and other current transfers 497); Capital expenditure 866; Total 3,402, excl. lending minus repayments (7). Source: IMF, *Swaziland—Selected Issues and Statistical Appendix* (November 2002).

International Reserves (US $ million at 31 December 2002): IMF special drawing rights 3.35; Reserve position in IMF 8.91; Foreign exchange 263.59; Total 275.85. Source: IMF, *International Financial Statistics*.

Money Supply (million emalangeni at 31 December 2002): Currency outside banks 155.44; Demand deposits at commercial banks 670.09; Total money (incl. others) 825.53. Source: IMF, *International Financial Statistics*.

Cost of Living (Retail Price Index, excluding rent, for low-income wage-earners' families in Mbabane and Manzini; base: 1995 = 100): 130.8 in 1999; 146.7 in 2000; 155.4 in 2001. Source: IMF, *International Financial Statistics*.

Expenditure on the Gross Domestic Product (million emalangeni at current prices, 2001): Government final consumption expenditure 1,996.2; Private final consumption expenditure 8,425.9; Gross fixed capital formation 1,984.5; *Total domestic expenditure* 12,406.6; Exports of goods and services 7,699.4; *Less* Imports of goods and services 9,135.0; *GDP in purchasers' values* 10,971.0. Source: IMF, *Swaziland—Selected Issues and Statistical Appendix* (November 2002) .

Gross Domestic Product by Economic Activity (million emalangeni in current purchasers' values, 2001): Agriculture and forestry 1,055.1; Mining and quarrying 24.9; Manufacturing 2,757.2; Electricity, gas and water 111.7; Construction 452.0; Trade, restaurants and hotels 689.2; Transport and communications 391.3; Finance, insurance, real estate, etc. 326.2; Government services 1,367.9; Other non-marketable services 82.6; Owner-occupied dwellings 164.9; *Sub-total* 7,422.9; *Less* Imputed bank service charge 163.7; *GDP at factor cost* 7,259.2; Indirect taxes, *less* subsidies 3,711.8; *GDP in purchasers' values* 10,971.0. Source: IMF, *Swaziland—Selected Issues and Statistical Appendix* (November 2002).

Balance of Payments (estimates, US $ million, 2001): Exports of goods f.o.b. 809.3; Imports of goods f.o.b. –882.0; *Trade balance* –72.7; Exports of services 85.0; Imports of services –179.1; *Balance on goods and services* –166.8; Other income received 118.8; Other income paid–84.3; *Balance on goods, services and income* –132.3; Current transfers received 186.1; Current transfers paid –106.5; *Current balance* –52.7; Capital account (net) 0.5; Direct investment abroad 6.1; Direct investment from abroad –20.8; Portfolio investment assets –0.1; Portfolio investment liabilities 0.0; Other investment assets 39.8; Other investment liabilities –30.2; Net errors and omissions 12.1; *Overall balance* –83.3. Source: IMF, *International Financial Statistics*.

EXTERNAL TRADE

Principal Commodities (US $ million): *Imports c.i.f.* (2001): Food and live animals 132; Beverages and tobacco 20; Inedible crude materials 33; Mineral fuels, lubricants 97; Chemicals and chemical products 112; Manufactures classified by material 148; Machinery and transport equipment 197; Miscellaneous manufactured articles 97; Total (incl. others) 849. *Exports f.o.b.* (2001): Sugar 76; Wood pulp 61; Wood and wood products 19; Canned fruits 10; Citrus 10; Edible concentrates 281; Cotton yarn 10; Other textiles 50; Paper products 18; Eucalyptus 18; Total (incl. others) 813. Figures refer to domestic exports, excluding re-exports (6). Source: IMF, *Swaziland—Selected Issues and Statistical Appendix* (November 2002).

Principal Trading Partners ('000 emalangeni): *Imports* (year ending 31 March 1993): France 1,552.2; Netherlands 10,726.9; South Africa 2,428,294.0; Switzerland 7,499.6; United Kingdom 75,117.8; Total (incl. others) 2,587,338.5. *Exports* (excl. re-exports, 1991): South Africa 804,103.7; United Kingdom 56,561.3; Total (incl. others) 1,711,539.0.

TRANSPORT

Railways (traffic estimates, million, 1991): Passenger-km 1,210 (1988); Freight net ton-km 2,910. Source: UN Economic Commission for Africa, *African Statistical Yearbook*.

Total Freight ('000 metric tons, 1993): 4,203.

Road Traffic (estimates, motor vehicles in use, 31 December 1998): Passenger cars 34,064; Buses and coaches 4,089; Lorries and vans 30,941; Motorcycles and scooters 2,588. Source: International Road Federation, *World Road Statistics*.

Civil Aviation (traffic on scheduled services, 1998): Kilometres flown 1 million; Passengers carried 41,000; Passenger-kilometre 43 million; Total ton-kilometre 4 million. Source: UN, *Statistical Yearbook*.

TOURISM

Tourist Arrivals (at hotels): 284,116 in 1998; 289,383 in 1999; 280,870 in 2000. Source: World Tourism Organization, *Yearbook of Tourism Statistics*.

Tourism Receipts (US $ million): 37 in 1998; 35 in 1999. Source: World Tourism Organization.

COMMUNICATIONS MEDIA

Radio Receivers (1997): 155,000 in use.

Television Receivers (2000): 120,000 in use.

Telephones (2001): 32,000 main lines in use.

Mobile Cellular Telephones (2001): 66,000 subscribers.

Internet Users (2001): 14,000.

Facsimile Machines (year ending 31 March 1998): 1,201 in use.

Daily Newspapers (1996): 3.
Sources: UNESCO, *Statistical Yearbook;* UN, *Statistical Yearbook;* International Telecommunication Union.

EDUCATION

Primary (2001): Institutions 541; Teachers 6,594; Students 212,064.

General Secondary (2001): Institutions 182; Teachers 3,647; Students 61,335.

Teacher Training (1993/94): Institutions 3; Teachers 88; Students 924.

Technical and Vocational Training (1993/94): Institutions 2; Teachers 140; Students 2,034 (Source: partly UNESCO Institute for Statistics).

University Education (1996/97): Institution 1; Teachers 257; Students 3,692 (2000).

Adult Literacy Rate (UNESCO estimates): 79.6% (males 80.8%; females 78.6%) in 2000 (Source: UN Development Programme, *Human Development Report*).

Directory

The Constitution

The Constitution of 13 October 1978 vests supreme executive and legislative power in the hereditary King (Ngwenyama—the Lion). Succession is governed by traditional law and custom. In the event of the death of the King, the powers of Head of State are transferred to the constitutional dual monarch, the Queen Mother (Indlovukazi —Great She Elephant), who is authorized to act as Regent until the designated successor attains the age of 21. The Constitution provides for a bicameral legislature, comprising a House of Assembly and a Senate. The functions of the Swaziland National Council (Libandla) are confined to debating government proposals and advising the King. Executive power is exercised through the Cabinet (later redesignated the Council of Ministers), which is appointed by the King. The Libandla, which comprises members of the royal family, and is headed by the King and Queen Mother, advises on matters regulated by traditional law and custom. The Constitution affirms the fundamental rights of the individual.

Following a number of amendments to the electoral system, which were approved by the King in October 1992, the House of Assembly (which was redesignated as the National Assembly) was expanded to 65 deputies (of whom 55 are directly elected from candidates nominated by traditional local councils, known as Tinkhundla, and 10 appointed by the King), and the Senate to 30 members (of whom 20 are appointed by the King and 10 elected by the National Assembly). Elections to the National Assembly are conducted by secret ballot, in two rounds of voting; the second round of the elections is contested by the three candidates from each of the Tinkhundla who secure the highest number of votes in the first poll. In July 1996 the King appointed a commission to prepare proposals for a draft constitution, which would subsequently be submitted for approval by the Swazi people. The commission submitted its report in August 2001, and in February 2002 a committee began drafting a new constitution, based on the commission's recommendations.

The Government

HEAD OF STATE

King: HM King MSWATI III (succeeded to the throne 25 April 1986).

COUNCIL OF MINISTERS
(April 2003)

Prime Minister: Dr BARNABAS SIBUSISO DLAMINI.

Deputy Prime Minister: ARTHUR R. V. KHOZA.

Minister of Justice and Constitutional Development: MAGWAGWA MDLULI.

Minister of Finance: MAJOZI SITHOLE.

Minister of Home Affairs: Prince SOBANDLA DLAMINI.

Minister of Foreign Affairs and Trade: ROY FERNOUKIS.

Minister of Education: MNTONZIMA DLAMINI.

Minister of Agriculture and Co-operatives: STELLA LUKHELE.

Minister of Broadcasting and Information: MAGWAGWA MDLULI.

Minister of Enterprise and Employment: LUFTO DLAMINI.

Minister of Economic Planning and Development: Prince GUDUZA DLAMINI.

Minister of Health and Social Welfare: Chief SIPHO SHOWNGE.

Minister of Public Service and Information: Rev. ABEDNIGO NTSHANGASE.

Minister of Public Works and Transport: JOHN CARMICHAEL.

Minister of Natural Resources and Energy: MAHLABA MAMBA.

Minister of Tourism, the Environment and Communications: PHETSILE DLAMINI.

Minister of Housing and Urban Development: ALBERT SHABANGU.

MINISTRIES

Office of the Prime Minister: Government House, POB 395, Mbabane; tel. 4042251; fax 4043943; e-mail ppcu@realnet.co.sz.

Office of the Deputy Prime Minister: POB 433, Swazi Plaza, Mbabane; tel. 4042723; fax 4044085.

Ministry of Agriculture and Co-operatives: POB 162, Mbabane; tel. 4042731; fax 4044700; e-mail moac-hq@realnet.co.sz.

Ministry of Broadcasting and Information: POB 338, Mbabane; tel. 4043521; e-mail nhlanhla@realnet.co.sz.

Ministry of Economic Planning and Development: POB 602, Mbabane; tel. 4043765; fax 4042157; e-mail ep_cso@realnet.co.sz.

Ministry of Education: POB 39, Mbabane; tel. 4042491; fax 4043880; e-mail amkhonza@realnet.co.sz.

Ministry of Enterprise and Employment: POB 451, Mbabane; tel. 4043201; fax 4044711; e-mail sglabour@realnet.co.sz.

Ministry of Finance: POB 443, Mbabane; tel. 4048148; fax 4043187; e-mail minfin@realnet.co.sz.

Ministry of Foreign Affairs and Trade: POB 518, Mbabane; tel. 4042661; fax 4042669; e-mail minister-tpu@realnet.co.sz.

Ministry of Health and Social Welfare: POB 5, Mbabane; tel. 4042431; fax 4042092; e-mail minhealth@realnet.co.sz.

Ministry of Home Affairs: POB 432, Mbabane; tel. 4042941; fax 4044303.

Ministry of Housing and Urban Development: POB 1832, Mbabane; tel. 4041739; fax 4045290; e-mail minhouse@realnet.co.sz; internet www.housing.gov.sz.

Ministry of Justice and Constitutional Development: POB 924, Mbabane; tel. 4046010; fax 4044796; e-mail legalgpm@realnet.co.sz.

Ministry of Natural Resources and Energy: POB 57, Mbabane; tel. 4046244; fax 4042436; e-mail nergyswa@realnet.co.sz.

Ministry of Public Service and Information: POB 338, Mbabane; tel. 4042761; fax 4042774.

Ministry of Public Works and Transport: POB 58, Mbabane; tel. 4042321; fax 4042364; e-mail minister-moptw@realnet.co.sz.

Ministry of Tourism, the Environment and Communications: POB 2652, Mbabane; tel. 4046556; fax 4045415; e-mail mintour@realnet.co.sz; internet www.mintour.gov.sz.

Legislature

SENATE

There are 30 senators, of whom 20 are appointed by the King and 10 elected by the National Assembly.

President: MUNTU MSAWANE.

NATIONAL ASSEMBLY

There are 65 deputies, of whom 55 are directly elected from candidates nominated by the Tinkhundla and 10 appointed by the King. The latest elections to the National Assembly took place on 16 and 24 October 1998.

Speaker: SIKAKADZA MATSEBULA.

Political Organizations

Party political activity was banned by royal proclamation in April 1973, and formally prohibited under the 1978 Constitution. Since 1991, following indications that the Constitution was to be revised, a number of political associations have re-emerged.

Imbokodvo National Movement (INM): f. 1964 by King Sobhuza II; traditionalist movement, which also advocates policies of development and the elimination of illiteracy; Leader (vacant).

Ngwane National Liberatory Congress (NNLC): Ilanga Centre, Martin St, Manzini; tel. 5053935; f. 1962 by fmr mems of the SPP; advocates democratic freedoms and universal suffrage, and seeks abolition of the Tinkhundla electoral system; Pres. OBED DLAMINI; Sec.-Gen. DUMISA DLAMINI.

People's United Democratic Movement (PUDEMO): POB 4588, Manzini; tel. and fax 5054181; internet www.members.nbci.com/pudemo; f. 1983; seeks constitutional limitation of the powers of the monarchy; affiliated orgs include the Human Rights Asscn of Swaziland and the Swaziland Youth Congress (SWAYOCO—Pres. BONGANI MASUKU; Sec.-Gen. TEMANGCAMANE MASEKO); Pres. MARIO MASUKU; Sec.-Gen. BONG'NKOSI DLAMINI.

Swaziland National Front (SWANAFRO): Mbabane; Pres. ELMOND SHONGWE; Sec.-Gen. GLENROSE DLAMINI.

Swaziland Progressive Party (SPP): POB 6, Mbabane; tel. 2022648; f. 1929; Pres. J. J. NQUKU.

Swaziland United Front (SUF): POB 14, Kwaluseni; f. 1962 by fmr mems of the SPP; Leader MATSAPA SHONGWE.

Diplomatic Representation

EMBASSIES AND HIGH COMMISSIONS IN SWAZILAND

China (Taiwan): Embassy House, Warner St, POB 56, Mbabane; tel. 4042379; fax 4046688; e-mail chineseembassy@africaonline.co.sz; Ambassador GEORGE JIN-GOU CHANG.

Mozambique: Princess Drive, POB 1212, Mbabane; tel. 4043700; fax 4048402; Ambassador AMOUR ZACIARIAS KAPELA.

South Africa: The New Mall, 2nd Floor, Plasmall St, POB 2597, Mbabane; tel. 4044651; fax 4046944; e-mail sahc@africaonline.co.sz; High Commissioner WALTER SEATE.

United Kingdom: Lilunga House, Gilfillan St, Private Bag, Mbabane; tel. 4042582; fax 4042585; e-mail bhc@realnet.co.sz; High Commissioner DAVID READER.

USA: Central Bank Bldg, Warner St, POB 199, Mbabane; tel. 4046442; fax 4045959; e-mail usembswd@realnet.co.sz; internet usembassy.state.gov/posts/wz1/wwwhhome.html; Ambassador JAMES MCGEE.

Judicial System

Swaziland's legal system operates on a dual basis, comprising both traditional Swazi National Courts as well as Constitutional Courts. The latter are based on Roman-Dutch law and comprise a High Court (which is a Superior Court of Record) with subordinate courts in all the administrative districts. The Court of Appeal sits at Mbabane. The Constitutional Courts are headed by a Chief Justice, subordinate to whom are judges and magistrates. There is also an Industrial Court.

There are 17 Swazi National Courts, including two Courts of Appeal and a Higher Court of Appeal, which have limited jurisdiction in civil and criminal cases. Their jurisdiction excludes non-Swazi nationals. The Constitutional Courts have the final ruling in the event of any conflict between the two legal systems.

Chief Justice: (vacant).

Religion

About 60% of the adult Swazi population profess Christianity. Most of the remainder hold traditional beliefs. There is also a small Muslim community.

CHRISTIANITY

Council of Swaziland Churches: Mandlenkosi Ecumenical House, 142 Esser St, Manzini; POB 1095, Manzini; tel. 5053931; fax 5055841; e-mail c.o.c@africaonline.co.sz; f. 1976; 10 mem. churches; Chair. Rev. R. M. DLAMINI; Gen. Sec. MARIA MBELU.

League of African Churches: POB 230, Lobamba; asscn of 48 independent churches; Pres. ISAAC DLAMINI.

Swaziland Conference of Churches: 175 Ngwane St, POB 1157, Manzini; tel. 5055259; fax 5054430; e-mail cmediac@iafrica.sz; f. 1929; Pres. Rev. NICHOLAS NYAWO; Gen. Sec. JOHANNES V. MAZIBUKO.

The Anglican Communion

Swaziland comprises a single diocese within the Church of the Province of Southern Africa. The Metropolitan of the Province is the Archbishop of Cape Town, South Africa.

Bishop of Swaziland: (vacant), Bishop's House, Muir St, Mbabane; tel. 4043624; fax 4046759; e-mail anglicanchurch@iafrica.sz.

The Roman Catholic Church

The Roman Catholic Church was established in Swaziland in 1913. For ecclesiastical purposes, Swaziland comprises the single diocese of Manzini, suffragan to the archdiocese of Pretoria, South Africa. At 31 December 2000 there were an estimated 53,104 adherents in Swaziland, equivalent to about 5.4% of the total population. The Bishop participates in the Southern African Catholic Bishops' Conference (based in Pretoria, South Africa).

Bishop of Manzini: Rt Rev. LOUIS NCAMISO NDLOVU, Bishop's House,

Sandlane St, POB 19, Manzini; tel. 5056900; fax 5056762; e-mail bishop@iafrica.sz.

Other Christian Churches

Church of the Nazarene: POB 1460, Manzini; tel. 5054732; f. 1910; 7,649 adherents (1994).

The Evangelical Lutheran Church in Southern Africa: POB 117, Mbabane; tel. 4046453; f. 1902; Bishop R. SCHIELE; 2,800 adherents in Swaziland (1994).

Lutheran Development Service: POB 388, Mbabane; tel. 4042562; fax 4043870; e-mail lds@realnet.co.sz.

Mennonite Central Committee: POB 329, Mbabane; tel. 4042805; fax 4044732; f. 1971; Co-ordinators JON RUDY, CAROLYN RUDY.

The Methodist Church in Southern Africa: POB 218, Mbabane; tel. 4042658; f. 1880; 2,578 adherents (1992).

United Christian Church of Africa: POB 253, Nhlangano; tel. 2022648; f. 1944; Pres. Rt Rev. JEREMIAH NDZINISA; Founder and Gen. Sec. Dr J. J. NQUKU.

The National Baptist Church, the Christian Apostolic Holy Spirit Church in Zion and the Religious Society of Friends (Quakers) are also active.

BAHÁ'Í FAITH

National Spiritual Assembly: POB 298, Mbabane; tel. 5052689; f. 1960; mems resident in 153 localities.

ISLAM

Ezulwini Islamic Institute: Al Islam Dawah Movement of Swaziland, POB 133, Ezulwini; c. 3,000 adherents (1994).

The Press

The Guardian of Swaziland: POB 4747, Mbabane; tel. 404838; e-mail info@theguardian.co.sz; f. 2001; daily newspaper; publication suspended May 2001, resumed Sept. 2001; Editor THULANI MTHETHWA.

The Nation: Mbabane House, 3rd Floor, Warner St, POB 4547, Mbabane; tel. 4046611; e-mail thenation@realnet.co.sz; f. 1997; monthly; independent news magazine; publication suspended briefly May 2001; Editor BHEKI MAKHUBU.

The Swazi News: Sheffield Rd, POB 156, Mbabane; tel. 4042520; fax 4042438; e-mail theswazinews@swazinews.com; internet www.swazinews.com; f. 1983; weekly; English; owned by *The Times of Swaziland*; Editor KIMBER FRASER; circ. 18,000.

Swazi Observer: Mbabane; state-owned; publication suspended Feb. 2000, resumed March 2001; Man. Editor JABU MABEBULA.

Swaziland Today: POB 395, Mbabane; tel. 4041432; fax 4043493; internet www.swazi.com/government/sgt-nl.html; weekly; government newsletter; Editor (vacant).

Swaziview: Mbabane; tel. 4042716; monthly magazine; general interest; circ. 3,500.

The Times of Swaziland: Sheffield Rd, POB 156, Mbabane; tel. 4042520; fax 4042438; e-mail theeditor@times.co.sz; internet www.times.co.sz; f. 1897; English; Mon.–Fri., also monthly edn; Editor MARTIN DLAMINI; circ. 18,000.

Publishers

Apollo Services (Pty) Ltd: POB 35, Mbabane; tel. 4042711.

GBS Printing and Publishing (Pty) Ltd: POB 1384, Mbabane; tel. 5052779.

Jubilee Printers: POB 1619, Matsaka; tel. 5184557; fax 5184558.

Longman Swaziland (Pty) Ltd: POB 2207, Manzini; tel. 5053891.

Macmillan Boleswa Publishers (Pty) Ltd: POB 1235, Manzini; tel. 5184533; fax 5185247; Man. Dir T. BALL.

Swaziland Printing & Publishing Co Ltd: POB 28, Mbabane; tel. 4042716; fax 4042710; e-mail veares@iafrica.sz.

Whydah Media Publishers Ltd: Mbabane; tel. 4042716; f. 1978.

Broadcasting and Communications

TELECOMMUNICATIONS

MTN Swaziland: Smuts St, POB 5050, Mbabane; tel. 4060000; fax 4046217; e-mail info@mtn.sz; internet www.swazimtn.sz; f. 1998; operates mobile cellular telephone network.

Posts and Telecommunications Corporation: POB 125, Mbabane; tel. 4043131; fax 4044500; e-mail info@swazi.net; internet www.sptc.co.sz; f. 1986; Man. Dir ALFRED S. DLAMINI; Gen. Man. MZWANDILE R. MABUZA.

BROADCASTING

Radio

Swaziland Broadcasting and Information Service: POB 338, Mbabane; tel. 4042763; fax 4042774; e-mail sbisnews@africaonline .co.sz; f. 1966; broadcasts in English and siSwati; Dir STAN MOTSA.

Swaziland Commercial Radio (Pty) Ltd: POB 1586, Alberton 1450, South Africa; tel. (11) 4344333; fax (11) 4344777; e-mail cicade@icon.co.za; privately-owned commercial service; broadcasts to southern Africa in English and Portuguese; music and religious programmes; Man. Dir A. DE ANDRADE.

Trans World Radio: POB 64, Manzini; tel. 5052781; fax 5055333; internet www.icon.co.za/~ttatlow/Welcome.htm; f. 1974; religious broadcasts from five transmitters in 30 languages to southern, central and eastern Africa and to the Far East; Pres. THOMAS J. LOWELL.

Television

Swaziland Television Authority: POB A146, Swazi Plaza, Mbabane; tel. 4043036; fax 4042093; e-mail swazitv.eng@africaonline.co .sz; f. 1978; state-owned; broadcasts seven hours daily in English; colour transmissions; Gen. Man. DAN S. DLAMINI.

Finance

(cap. = capital; res = reserves; dep. = deposits; m. = million; brs = branches; amounts in emalangeni)

BANKING

Central Bank

Central Bank of Swaziland: POB 546, Warner St, Mbabane; tel. 4043221; fax 4048296; e-mail info@centralbank.org.sz; internet www.centralbank.sz/; f. 1974; bank of issue; cap. 21.8m., res 80.1m., dep. 452.2m. (March 2001); Gov. M. G. DLAMINI; Dep. Gov. S. G. MDLULI.

Commercial Banks

First National Bank of Swaziland Ltd: Sales House Bldg, 2nd Floor, POB 261, Mbabane; tel. 4044501; fax 4044735; e-mail kblakeway@fnbswz.co.sz; f. 1988; fmrly Meridien Bank Swaziland Ltd; cap. and res 41.8m., dep. 525.9m. (June 2001); Chair. Dr D. M. J. VON WISSEL; Man. Dir R. A. PAWSON; 7 brs and 1 agency.

Nedbank (Swaziland) Ltd: Swazi Plaza, POB 68, Mbabane; tel. 4043351; fax 4044060; e-mail nedbank@iafrica.sz; f. 1974; fmrly Standard Chartered Bank Swaziland Ltd; 23% state-owned; cap. and res 32.3m., dep. 432.0m., total assets 482.2m. (Dec. 2000); Chair. A. R. B. SHABANGU; Man. Dir DONALD Q. PRETORIUS; 4 brs and 1 agency.

Development Banks

Standard Bank Swaziland Ltd: Standard House, 1st Floor, Swazi Plaza, POB A294, Mbabane; tel. 4046930; fax 4045899; e-mail StandardBankSwaziland@iafricaonline.co.sz; internet www .standardbank.co.sz; f. 1988; fmrly Stanbic Bank Swaziland, present name since 1997; merged with Barclays Bank of Swaziland in Jan. 1998; 10% state-owned; cap. and res 79.9m., total assets 1,121.7m. (Dec. 2000); Chair. R. J. ROSSOUW (acting); Man. Dir W. G. PRICE; 6 brs.

Swaziland Development and Savings Bank: Engungwini House, Gwamile St, POB 336, Mbabane; tel. 4042551; fax 4042550; e-mail swazibank@swazibank.sz; f. 1965; state-owned; taken over by central bank in 1995; under independent management since 2000; cap. and res 134.2m., total assets 557.9m. (Mar. 2001); Chair. NOKUKHANYA GAMEDZE; Man. Dir STANLEY MATSEBULA; 8 brs.

Financial Institution

Swaziland National Provident Fund: POB 1857, Manzini; tel. 5053731; fax 5054377; total assets 290m. (June 1996).

STOCK EXCHANGE

Swaziland Stock Market: Capital Markets Development Unit, Infumbe House, 1st Floor, Warner St, POB 546, Mbabane; tel. 4041829; fax 4049493; e-mail ssx@centralbank.org.sz; internet www .ssx.org.sz; f. 1993; Chair. M. G. DLAMINI; CEO ANDREW McGUIRE.

INSURANCE

Between 1974 and 1999 the state-controlled Swaziland Royal Insurance Corporation (SRIC) operated as the country's sole authorized insurance company, although cover in a number of areas not served by SRIC was available from several specialized insurers. In 1999 the legislature approved legislation terminating the monopoly of the SRIC and providing for its transfer to private-sector ownership.

Insurance Companies

AON Swaziland (Pty) Ltd: POB 222, Mbabane; tel. 4043226; fax 4046412; e-mail theopheiffer/ars/sz/aon@aonemea; f. 1970; Man. Dir THEO W. PHEIFFER.

Associated Insurance Brokers (Pty) Ltd: POB 1216, Manzini M200; tel. 5056543; fax 5053831; e-mail kdukes@iafrica.sz; Man. Dir K. DUKES.

Swaziland Employee Benefit Consultants (Pty) Ltd: POB 3159, Mbabane; tel. 4044776; fax 4046413; e-mail sebc@iafrica.co.sz; specialized medical cover.

Swaziland Royal Insurance Corporation (SRIC): Liluga House, Gilfillan St, POB 917, Mbabane; tel. 4043231; fax 4046415; e-mail sric@sric.sz; internet www.sric.sz; 51% state-owned; sole auth. insurance co 1974–99; Gen. Man. Z. R. MAGAGULA.

Tibiyo Insurance Brokers: Swazi Plaza, POB 1072, Mbabane; tel. 4042010; fax 4045035; Man. Dir D. T. BAKER.

Insurance Association

Insurance Brokers' Association of Swaziland (IBAS): Swazi Plaza, POB A32, Mbabane; tel. 4042929; fax 4045254; e-mail aon_sib@son.co.sz; f. 1983; 4 mems.

Trade and Industry

GOVERNMENT AGENCY

Swaziland Investment Promotion Authority: POB 4194, Mbabane; tel. 4040470; fax 4043374; e-mail info@sipa.org.uk; internet www.sipa.org.sz; f. 1998; Gen. Man. BHEKI DLAMINI.

DEVELOPMENT ORGANIZATIONS

National Industrial Development Corporation of Swaziland (NIDCS): POB 866, Mbabane; tel. 4043391; fax 4045619; f. 1971; state-owned; administered by Swaziland Industrial Development Co; Admin. Dir P. K. THAMM.

Small Enterprise Development Co (SEDCO): POB A186, Swazi Plaza, Mbabane; tel. 4042811; fax 4040723; e-mail sedco@iafrica.sz; internet www.business-swaziland.com/sedco; f. 1970; govt devt agency; supplies workshop space, training and expertise for 120 local entrepreneurs at seven sites throughout the country.

Swaziland Industrial Development Co (SIDC): Dhlan'Ubeka House, 5th Floor, cnr Tin and Walker Sts, POB 866, Mbabane; tel. 4044010; fax 4045619; e-mail info@sidc.co.sz; internet www.sidc.co .sz; f. 1986; 34.9% state-owned; finances private-sector projects and promotes local and foreign investment; cap. E24.1m., total assets E178.4m. (June 1999); Chair. A. R. SHABANGU; Gen. Man. E. T. GINA.

Swaki (Pty) Ltd: Liqhaga Bldg, 4th Floor, Nkoseluhlaza St, POB 1839, Manzini; tel. 5052693; fax 5052001; jtly owned by SIDC and Kirsh Holdings; comprises a number of cos involved in manufacturing, services and the production and distribution of food (especially maize).

Tibiyo Taka Ngwane (Bowels of the Swazi Nation): POB 181, Kwaluseni; tel. 5184306; fax 5184399; e-mail info@tibiyo.com; internet www.tibiyo.com; f. 1968; nat. devt agency, with investment interests in all sectors of the economy; participates in domestic and foreign jt investment ventures; total assets: E 604m. (1999); Man. Dir A. T. DLAMINI; Gen. Man. C. N. MAMBA.

CHAMBERS OF COMMERCE

Sibakho Chamber of Commerce: POB 2016, Manzini; tel. 5057347.

Swaziland Chamber of Commerce and Industry: POB 72, Mbabane; tel. 4044408; fax 4044258; e-mail chamber@iafricaonline .sz; internet www.business-swaziland.com/html/scci.html; Sec. JOHN FRASER.

INDUSTRIAL AND TRADE ASSOCIATIONS

National Agricultural Marketing Board: POB 4261, Manzini; tel. 5055314; fax 5054072; e-mail encabeni@namboard.co.sz; internet www.swazibusiness.com/namboard.

National Maize Corporation: POB 158, Manzini; tel. 5052261; fax 5052265; e-mail nmc@africaonline.co.sz.

Swaziland Citrus Board: Sokhamila Bldg, cnr Johnston/Walker Sts, H100, Mbabane; tel. 4044266; fax 4043548; e-mail citrus@ realnet.co.sz; f. 1969.

Swaziland Commercial Board: POB 509, Mbabane; tel. 4042930; Man. Dir J. M. D. FAKUDZE.

Swaziland Cotton Board: POB 230, Manzini; tel. 5052775; Gen. Man. T. JELE.

Swaziland Dairy Board: Liqhaga Bldg, 3rd Floor, POB 2975, Manzini; tel. 5058262; fax 5058260; e-mail ceo-swazidairy@ africaonline.co.sz; Gen. Man. N. T. GUMEDE.

Swaziland Sugar Association: MTN Office Park, Smuts St, POB 445, Mbabane; tel. 4042646; fax 4045005; e-mail info@ssa.co.sz; internet www.ssa.co.sz; CEO Dr MICHAEL MATSEBULA.

EMPLOYERS' ORGANIZATIONS

Building Contractors' Association of Swaziland: POB 518, Mbabane; tel. 4040071; fax 4044258; e-mail soconswad@realnet.co .uk.

Swaziland Association of Architects, Engineers and Surveyors: Swazi Plaza, POB A387, Mbabane; tel. 4042309; e-mail ribar@africaonline.co.sz.

Swaziland Institute of Personnel and Training Managers: c/o UNISWA, Private Bag, Kwaluseni; tel. 5184011; fax 5185276.

Employers' Federation

Federation of Swaziland Employers: POB 777, Mbabane; tel. 4040768; fax 4046107; e-mail fse@realnet.co.sz; f. 1964; 376 mems; Pres. R. SEAL; Exec. Dir E. HLOPHE.

UTILITIES

Electricity

Swaziland Electricity Board: POB 258, Mbabane; tel. 4042521; fax 4042335; e-mail solly@seb.co.sz; internet www.seb.co.sz; statutory body; f. 1963; Chair. NKOMEMI NTIWANE; Man. Dir BRUCE FARRER.

Water

Swaziland Water Services Corporation: POB 20, Mbabane; tel. 4043161; fax 4045585; e-mail info@swsc.co.sz; internet www.swsc.co .sz; state authority; Chair. E. N. ZWANE; Man. Dir PETER BHEMBE.

CO-OPERATIVE ASSOCIATIONS

Swaziland Central Co-operatives Union: POB 551, Manzini; tel. 5052787; fax 5052964.

There are more than 123 co-operative associations, of which the most important is:

Swaziland Co-operative Rice Co Ltd: handles rice grown in Mbabane and Manzini areas.

TRADE UNIONS

The following trade unions are recognized by the Department of Labour:

The Association of Lecturers and Academic Personnel of the University of Swaziland, the Building and Construction Workers Union of Swaziland, Swaziland Commercial and Allied Workers' Union, Swaziland Conservation Workers' Union, Swaziland Electricity Supply, Maintenance and Allied Workers' Union, Swaziland Engineering, Metal and Allied Workers' Union, Swaziland Hotel, Catering and Allied Workers' Union, Swaziland Manufacturing and Allied Workers' Union, Swaziland Mining, Quarrying and Allied Workers' Union, Swaziland National Association of Civil Servants, Swaziland National Association of Teachers, Swaziland Post and Telecommunications Workers' Union, Swaziland Transport Workers' Union, Swaziland Union of Financial Institutions and Allied Workers, University of Swaziland Workers' Union, Workers Union of Swaziland Security Guards, Workers' Union of Town Councils.

Trade Union Federations

Swaziland Federation of Labour: mems include workers from the banking sector and mems of the Swaziland Manufacturing and Allied Workers' Union.

Swaziland Federation of Trade Unions (SFTU): POB 1158; Manzini; tel. 5056575; internet www.cosatu.org.za/sftu/index.html; f. 1973; prin. trade union org. since mid-1980s; mems from public and private sectors, incl. agricultural workers; 83,000 mems; Pres. RICHARD NXUMALO; Sec.-Gen. JAN SITHOLE.

Staff Associations

Three staff associations exist for employees whose status lies between that of worker and that of management: the Nyoni Yami Irrigation Scheme Staff Association, the Swazican Staff Association and the Swaziland Electricity Board Staff Association.

Transport

Buses are the principal means of transport for many Swazis. Bus services are provided by private operators who are required to obtain annual permits for each route from the Road Transportation Board, which also regulates fares.

RAILWAYS

The rail network, which totalled 297 km in 1998–99, provides a major transport link for imports and exports. Railway lines connect with the dry port at Matsapha, the South African ports of Richards Bay and Durban in the south, the South African town of Komatipoort in the north and the Mozambican port of Maputo in the east. Goods traffic is mainly in wood pulp, sugar, molasses, coal, citrus fruit and canned fruit. In June 1998 the Trans Lebombo rail service was launched to carry passengers from Durban to Maputo via Swaziland. The service was terminated in May 2000, owing to insufficient demand.

Swaziland Railway Board: Swaziland Railway Bldg, cnr Johnston and Walker Sts, POB 475, Mbabane; tel. 4047211; fax 4047210; e-mail swazirailway@iafrica.sz; f. 1962; Chair. B. A. G. FITZPATRICK; CEO G. J. MAHLALELA.

ROADS

In 1998 there were an estimated 3,247 km of roads, including 1,660 km of main roads and 1,587 of secondary roads. About 28.2% of the road network was paved in 1994. The rehabilitation of about 700 km of main and 600 km of district gravel-surfaced roads began in 1985, financed by World Bank and US loans totalling some E18m. In 1991 work commenced on the reconstruction of Swaziland's main road artery, connecting Mbabane to Manzini, via Matsapha, and in 2001 the Government announced the construction of two main roads in the north of the country, financed by Japanese loans.

Ministry of Public Works and Transport: POB 58, Mbabane; tel. 4042321; fax 4042364; e-mail ps-mopwt@realnet.co.sz; Prin. Sec. EVART MADLOPHA; Sr Roads Engineer A. MANANA.

Roads Department: POB 58, Mbabane; tel. 4042321; e-mail mopwt_rd@realnet.co.sz.

SHIPPING

Royal Swazi National Shipping Corporation Ltd: POB 1915, Manzini; tel. 5053788; fax 5053820; f. 1980 to succeed Royal Swaziland Maritime Co; owns no ships, acting only as a freight agent; Gen. Man. M. S. DLAMINI.

CIVIL AVIATION

Swaziland's only airport is at Matsapha, near Manzini, about 40 km from Mbabane. In mid-1997 the Government initiated a three-year programme to upgrade the airport. In March 2002 it was reported that the Government was delaying the construction of an international airport near Mpaka, in eastern Swaziland, owing to a decline in revenue from the tourism sector.

African International Airways (AIA): Suite 108, Development House, Swazi Plaza, POB 569, Mbabane; tel. 4043875; fax 4043876; e-mail ams@global.co.za; f. 1985; operates cargo services; Chair. PATRICK CORBIN; Man. Dir MARTIN LONGMORE.

Airlink Swaziland: POB 939, Matsapha Airport, Manzini; tel. 5186146; fax 5186156; f. 1999; fmrly Royal Swazi National Airways Corpn; joint venture between SA Airlink of South Africa and the Swazi Government; scheduled passenger services to destinations in Africa.

Air Swazi Cargo: Dhlan'Ubeka House, Walker St, POB 2869, Mbabane; tel. 4045575; fax 4045003; charter services for freight to destinations in Africa and Europe; Man. BRIAN PARMENTER.

Tourism

Swaziland's attractions for tourists include game reserves and magnificent mountain scenery. In 1997 322,000 tourist arrivals were registered at hotels; by 2000 the figure had declined to 280,870. Receipts from tourism in 1999 totalled US $35m, down from $40m. in 1997.

Hotel and Tourism Association of Swaziland: POB 462, Mbabane; tel. 4042218.

Ministry of Tourism, the Environment and Communications: POB 2652, Mbabane; tel. 4046556; fax 4045415; e-mail mintour@realnet.co.sz; internet www.mintour.gov.sz; Tourism Officer MUSA MDLELE.

SWEDEN

Introductory Survey

Location, Climate, Language, Religion, Flag, Capital

The Kingdom of Sweden lies in north-western Europe, occupying about two-thirds of the Scandinavian peninsula. It is bordered by Finland to the north-east, and by Norway to the north-west and west. About 15% of Sweden's area lies north of the Arctic Circle. The Baltic Sea and the Gulf of Bothnia are to the east, the Skagerrak and Kattegat channels to the south-west. The country is relatively flat and is characterized by thousands of inland lakes and small coastal islands. There is a mountain range, the Kjolen mountains, in the north-west. Winters are cold and summers mild. In Stockholm the mean summer temperature is 18°C (64°F) and the mean winter temperature −3°C (27°F). The national language is Swedish, but there are Finnish and Lapp (Sámi) minorities (the latter numbering between 17,000 and 20,000), retaining their own languages. A majority of the inhabitants profess Christianity, and about 86% are adherents of the Evangelical Lutheran Church of Sweden. The national flag (proportions 5 by 8) is light blue with a yellow cross, the upright of the cross being to the left of centre. The capital is Stockholm.

Recent History

Sweden has been a constitutional monarchy, traditionally neutral, since the early 19th century. During this time the country has not participated in any war or entered any military alliance. Norway, formerly united with Sweden, became independent in 1905. Sweden adopted parliamentary government in 1917, and universal adult suffrage was introduced in 1921. From 1932 until 1976, except for a short break in 1936, Sweden was governed by the Socialdemokratiska Arbetareparti (SAP—Social Democratic Labour Party), either alone or as the senior partner in coalitions (1936–45 and 1951–57). During those 44 years the country had only three Prime Ministers, all Social Democrats. Since the Second World War, Sweden has become an active member of many international organizations, including the UN (to which it has given military support), the Council of Europe (see p. 181) and, from 1995, the European Union (EU, see p. 199—formerly the European Community, EC).

Olof Palme succeeded Dr Tage Erlander as Prime Minister and leader of the SAP in October 1969. After a general election in September 1970, Palme formed a minority Government. Under a constitutional reform, the Riksdag (Parliament) was reconstituted from January 1971, its two chambers being replaced by a unicameral assembly. King Gustaf VI Adolf, who had reigned since 1950, died in September 1973 and was succeeded by his grandson, Carl XVI Gustaf. A revised Constitution, effective from January 1975, ended the monarch's prerogative to appoint the Prime Minister: the Speaker of the Riksdag was to have this responsibility in future.

At the September 1976 election, dissatisfaction with high rates of taxation, necessary to maintain the advanced social welfare system that Sweden had developed, brought about the defeat of the SAP. Thorbjörn Fälldin, leader of the Centerpartiet (CP—Centre Party), formed a centre-right coalition in October. The wish of the CP to abandon Sweden's nuclear power programme caused serious controversy in June 1978, when an independent commission recommended its continued use as an energy source. This view was endorsed by the Folkpartiet (FP—Liberals) and Moderata Samlingspartiet (MS—Moderates), whose rejection of a proposal by Fälldin to submit the nuclear issue to a national referendum led to the resignation of the Government in October 1978. The FP formed a minority Government, led by Ola Ullsten. Following a general election in September 1979, Fälldin returned as Prime Minister of a coalition comprising members of the CP, MS and FP, with an overall parliamentary majority of only one seat. A referendum on the future of nuclear power was held in March 1980, at which a narrow majority of the electorate approved a limited programme of nuclear reactor development, to be progressively eliminated by 2010 and replaced by alternative energy resources.

During 1980 the Government's economic policies came under attack, mainly because of the rising rate of inflation, and there was severe industrial unrest. The MS, which disagreed with proposed tax reforms, left the coalition in May 1981. At the next general election, held in September 1982, the SAP were returned to power, winning 45.6% of the votes cast (and 166 of the 349 seats in the Riksdag), but gaining an overall majority over the three non-socialist parties. In October Palme formed a minority Government, following an undertaking by the Vänsterpartiet—Kommunisterna (VpK—Communists), which held 20 parliamentary seats, that they would support the SAP. Palme's Government was returned to power in September 1985, with the support of the VpK, despite a financial scandal in 1983 involving the Minister of Justice. The SAP and the VpK together won 50.0% of the votes cast (securing 178 seats in the Riksdag), while the three main non-socialist parties won 48.0% (and the remaining 171 seats). The FP increased its share of seats in the Riksdag from 21 to 51, attracting voters from all of the other main parties. Palme undertook to continue to follow his 'third way' economic policy, seeking to combat inflation and recession while avoiding both excessively high levels of public spending and reductions in social welfare benefits.

In February 1986 Olof Palme was murdered by an unknown assailant in Stockholm. In March the Deputy Prime Minister, Ingvar Carlsson, took office as Prime Minister and was also appointed acting Chairman of the SAP, pending ratification by the National Congress in 1987. Carlsson retained Palme's Cabinet and declared that he would continue the policies of his predecessor. During 1986–87 little progress was made towards discovering Palme's assassin, and considerable controversy surrounded the case, as disputes increased between the police and successive public prosecutors (officially in charge of the investigation). In December 1988 Christer Pettersson, a man with a history of mental illness and violent crime, was arrested, and in June and July 1989 he was tried for the murder of Palme. He was convicted amid some controversy, only to be acquitted on appeal in October. In December 1997 the public prosecutor's office petitioned the Supreme Court to re-examine the case against Pettersson in the light of the discovery of new, allegedly incriminating evidence. In May 1998, however, the Supreme Court ruled that there was insufficient new evidence to conduct a retrial.

Meanwhile, ecological concerns were heightened in 1988 by two disasters, both of which were attributed to the effects of pollutants: an increase in the concentration of algae devastated the marine environment along the west coast, and this was followed by an outbreak of a virus that reduced the seal population of the North and Baltic Seas by up to two-thirds. At the general election in September the environmentalist Miljöpartiet de Gröna (MpG—Green Party) gained parliamentary representation for the first time, but the SAP remained in power with the continued support of the VpK. The conservative MS remained the second largest party in the Riksdag. In February 1990 the VpK (subsequently restyled the Vänsterpartiet—VP—Left Party) and the MpG refused to support the Government's proposed austerity measures, designed to combat rising inflation, a low rate of economic growth and industrial unrest. Carlsson resigned, but, having secured support for a new and more moderate set of proposals, he formed another minority Government.

During 1990 the Swedish economy entered into recession, and in December the Riksdag approved a new austere economic programme, which was designed to reduce inflation and to restore confidence in the economy. The Government was forced to abandon the long-held belief that the commitment to full employment and the defence of the welfare state (supported by high levels of taxation and of public expenditure) should be overriding priorities.

However, the popularity of the SAP continued to decline, and in the general election of September 1991 the party did not win enough seats to form a government, although it remained the largest party in the Riksdag, with 138 seats. The MS increased its representation to 80 seats, while the Kristdemokratiska Samhällspartiet (KdS—Christian Democrats) and a recently formed right-wing party, Ny demokrati (ND—New Democracy), won 26 and 25 seats respectively, at the expense of the FP and the CP; the MpG failed to secure 4% of the total votes cast, and thereby forfeited all its seats. Ingvar Carlsson resigned as Prime Minister, and in early October Carl Bildt, the leader of the MS (the largest non-socialist party in the legislature) was invited to form a government. He formed a coalition comprising members of four non-socialist parties—the MS, the CP, the FP and the KdS. Since these four parties, even in combination, still formed a minority in the Riksdag, they were obliged to rely on the ND for support in adopting legislation. Without delay, the new Government began to accelerate the deregulation of the economy already undertaken by its predecessor. Bildt emphasized his Government's commitment to membership of the EC.

During 1992 the recession continued in Sweden. Although the Government's austerity measures succeeded in reducing inflation, the high level of the budgetary deficit was a cause of concern. In September speculation on the international currency markets caused a rapid outflow of capital, and in November a fresh outflow of capital, following the SAP's refusal to approve reductions in public expenditure, forced the Government to allow the krona to 'float' in relation to other currencies, thereby effectively devaluing it by some 10%. In March 1993 the Government was defeated in the Riksdag when the ND refused to support budgetary proposals, but later in the same month the Government won a parliamentary vote of confidence, when the ND abstained from voting.

At the general election in September 1994 the SAP secured 45.3% of the votes cast, increasing its representation to 161 seats. The VP won 22 seats (compared with 16 in 1991) and the MpG won 18 seats. Although the MS maintained the level of support it gained at the previous election, the other parties in the incumbent coalition Government fared badly. Bildt resigned as Prime Minister, and in October 1994 Ingvar Carlsson formed a minority SAP Government. The results appeared to indicate a trend of increased support for parties opposed to Sweden's joining the EU (formerly EC). Despite opposition to EU membership within the SAP, Carlsson declared that a major objective of his Government would be to secure a mandate for Sweden to join the EU in the forthcoming national referendum (see below). He also emphasized the need for stringent economic measures (introduced from late 1994) to reduce unemployment, stabilize the budgetary deficit and safeguard welfare provisions.

In August 1995 Carlsson announced that he would relinquish, from March 1996, his dual posts as Prime Minister and leader of the SAP, in order to retire from political life. Göran Persson, hitherto Minister of Finance, was in March elected unopposed as Prime Minister and leader of the SAP. Persson immediately initiated a broad cabinet reshuffle, and stated that the new Government's priorities would be to halve the rate of unemployment by the end of the decade and to reduce the budgetary deficit.

In October 1996 Persson urged that the process to enlarge the EU be accelerated in order to strengthen European security. In November an independent study group, which had been commissioned by the Government to consider Sweden's proposed participation in economic and monetary union (EMU), recommended that Sweden should not join EMU until the unemployment rate had been significantly reduced. In February 1997, however, the Central Bank advocated membership of EMU from its inception in 1999 and claimed that the benefits of membership had been underestimated. Nevertheless, in June 1997 the Government announced that Sweden would not be participating in the first wave of EMU, citing a lack of public support for the project. The Government reiterated this stance in October, when it was also announced that Sweden had no intention of participating in the European exchange rate mechanism (ERM).

In August 1997 details of a national programme of enforced sterilization conducted during 1935–75 against some 60,000 individuals assessed to be of inferior intellectual or physical capabilities, reported in the Swedish daily newspaper *Dagens Nyheter*, provoked national outrage and prompted the Government to announce the creation of a comprehensive public inquiry into the country's post-First World War eugenics programme. It was subsequently revealed by the Minister of Health and Social Affairs that minimal compensation had been paid to just 16 victims of the programme during the previous 10 years. In March 1999 the Ministry of Health and Social Affairs announced that compensation amounting to a maximum of 175,000 kronor would be paid to each surviving victim of the programme. In August 2001 the State Sterilization Compensation Board announced that around 2,000 people had sought financial reparation, and that, of those, about 1,500 had received compensa-

tion, the total amount paid out being approximately 256m. kronor.

In March 1991 the Swedish and Danish Governments agreed to construct a 16-km combined bridge and tunnel for road and rail traffic, across the Öresund strait, between Malmö and Copenhagen (to be known as the Öresund Link). The plan aroused opposition in Sweden, on the grounds that the link might hinder the flow of water into the Baltic Sea, as well as increasing pollution by emissions from vehicles. In May 1994 a Swedish marine commission concluded that plans for the link did not provide sufficient guarantees to protect the flow of water into the Baltic. In the following month, however, the Swedish Government approved construction plans, prompting the resignation from the Government of the Minister of the Environment and leader of the CP, Olof Johansson. The link was opened in July 2000.

Prior to Sweden's membership of the EU (see below), trade with EU countries was conducted by means of a free-trade area, the European Economic Area (EEA), created in 1994 under the aegis of the European Free Trade Association (EFTA, see p. 195). Negotiations on admission to the EU began in February 1993, when the Bildt Government declared that the country's tradition of neutrality would not prevent Sweden from participating fully in the common foreign and security policy of the EU. The negotiations were concluded in March 1994. Sweden obtained safeguards for its traditional policy of freedom of official information, and for its strict environmental standards, and won concessions on the maintenance of subsidies for agriculture in remote areas. A national referendum on membership was held on 13 November, producing a 52.2% majority in favour of joining the EU. The Riksdag formally ratified membership in December, and Sweden's accession to the EU took effect from 1 January 1995. (At the same time Sweden withdrew from EFTA.) It was widely held that concern about the possible effects on the domestic economy of remaining outside the EU, together with fears regarding Sweden's ability to influence international affairs, such as the maintenance of effective environmental controls, had been major factors in the outcome of the referendum. Following the vote, the Carlsson Government reiterated that Sweden would retain its non-aligned policy within the EU and therefore remain outside NATO, although it would apply for observer status within the Western European Union (WEU, see p. 318). Although Sweden remained non-aligned, the Swedish Government none the less expressed its opposition to the US-led military action in Iraq in early 2003.

At the general election held in September 1998 the SAP maintained its position as the largest party in the Riksdag, but suffered a substantial reduction in the number of parliamentary seats that it held—131, compared with 161 in the outgoing Riksdag. This was the SAP's worst electoral performance for some 70 years, and the party was only able to remain in government by subsequently securing the support of the VP and the MpG. The MS retained the position of second largest party in the Riksdag, obtaining 82 parliamentary seats. Like the CP and the KD, the MS indicated its unwillingness to support the SAP in government. At about 81%, the participation rate at the election was the lowest for some 50 years. Post-electoral analysis identified the SAP's pursuit of financial regularity at the perceived expense of socialist policies as the probable cause of its poor performance: many voters had transferred their allegiance from the SAP to the VP. It was reported that, in return for its support, the VP would seek to persuade the Government to increase expenditure on social welfare and employment, and would encourage the slower repayment of Sweden's national debt, higher taxes, the complete decommissioning of Sweden's nuclear power stations, and a less stringent programme of privatization. Both the VP and the MpG remained strongly opposed to any future participation by Sweden in EMU. In early October a new Cabinet was announced. At the same time the Government presented its statement of policy, which envisaged a more active role in Europe for Sweden. The Government would also seek to achieve sustainable economic growth in order to increase labour-force participation to a targeted 80% by 2004. This aim was reflected in the reconstitution of the Ministry of Industry as a so-called 'superministry', with additional responsibility for labour, energy, information technology and infrastructure. In April 1999 the Minister of Finance, Erik Åsbrink, resigned following a reported disagreement with the Prime Minister over the content of the forthcoming spring budget; he was replaced by Bosse Ringholme.

Following the announcement of former Prime Minister Carl Bildt's retirement from party politics, in August 1999 Bo Lundgren was elected to succeed him as leader of the MS.

In March 2000 a national congress of the SAP endorsed the adoption of future EMU entry as official party policy, despite a significant degree of opposition from a number of notable party members. Following the 2002 general election Prime Minister Persson announced that a referendum would be held on the adoption of the euro in September 2003.

In late 1999 it was reported that public spending on defence equipment was to be reduced drastically, in line with the Government's strict fiscal consolidation programme. Proposed reform of the national defence system was also likely to result in the loss of some 10,000 military and civilian jobs. Earlier in the year the military high command had indicated that the Government's programme of defence rationalization would lead to an eventual halving of the strength of the armed forces, in terms of both personnel and hardware, prompting speculation that Sweden might be about to reconsider its non-aligned status with regard to regional security. In November 2000 Persson announced proposals to that effect. He asserted that neutrality was no longer relevant after the end of the Cold War, and that it did not cover all aspects of Sweden's security policy, such as disarmament, the non-proliferation of nuclear weapons and stability in Europe. However, Persson ruled out any move to join NATO, saying it was essential for the stability of northern Europe that Sweden remain non-aligned. Also in November 2000 Sweden pledged to contribute 1,500 troops to the new European rapid reaction force, which was intended to be ready to be deployed by 2003.

In September 2000 the Minister of Justice, Laila Freivalds, resigned amid strong criticism of her decision to buy her council-owned apartment; the SAP was opposed to Stockholm City Council's scheme to sell municipal housing. In March 2002 conservative deputies withheld their support for EU anti-terrorism legislation being debated in the Riksdag, stating that they wanted first to examine exactly which Swedish laws would have to be amended as a result of adopting the proposed common EU anti-terror law and common European arrest warrant. In the same month the Government announced that it was to create a new body to respond to terrorist attacks, large-scale natural disasters and epidemics. The new authority was to replace the Central Board for Civil Readiness, and was to assume some of the responsibilities of the Board for Psychological Defence.

In August 2002 a Tunisian-born Swede was arrested at Västeras airport, 100 km (60 miles) west of Stockholm, as he attempted to smuggle a loaded gun aboard a flight bound for London. He was released from custody one month later when the prosecutor's office stated that it had found no evidence that he had intended to hijack the aircraft; he was convicted of possessing an illegal firearm in December and sentenced to four months' imprisonment.

At the general election held on 15 September 2002 the SAP maintained its position as the party with the largest representation in the Riksdag, winning 39.8% of the votes cast and securing 144 of the 349 seats. Following negotiations during which the MpG demanded, but was refused, governmental posts, Persson appointed a minority SAP Government, which had the parliamentary support of the MpG and the VP. In return for their support, the MpG and the VP expected the Government to espouse some of their policies, including, among others, a reduction of 6,000m. kronor in defence expenditure over five years and a moratorium on cod fishing in the Baltic Sea from 1 January 2003, with compensation for the fishing industry.

In November 2003 national security police arrested two current and one former employee of the telecommunications and defence group Ericsson. The three were accused of supplying sensitive information regarding the company's work on radar and missile guidance systems to Russia via the Russian embassy in Stockholm. The Swedish authorities expelled two Russian diplomats in connection with the incident, one of whom was allegedly caught in the act of receiving illicit information from the former Ericsson employee. The Russian Government expressed it's 'bewilderment and regret' at the Swedish decision, and expelled two Swedish diplomats in retaliation. Two other Ericsson employees were suspended on suspicion of having breached the company's security rules. Sweden also expelled two Iraqi diplomats, in March 2003, following a request from the USA; the two were believed to have been involved in the illegal surveillance of Iraqi dissidents in Sweden.

Government

Sweden is a constitutional monarchy. The hereditary monarch is Head of State but has very limited formal prerogatives. Executive power rests with the Cabinet (Regeringen), which is responsible to the legislature (Riksdag). The unicameral Riksdag was introduced in January 1971. It has 349 members, elected by universal adult suffrage for four years (previously three), on the basis of proportional representation. The Prime Minister is nominated by the Speaker of the Riksdag and later confirmed in office by the whole House. The country is divided into 21 counties (Län) and 288 municipal districts (Kommun): both counties and municipalities have popularly elected councils.

Defence

Proposals for a significant reduction in defence spending and resources were announced during 1999 (see Recent History). In August 2002 Sweden maintained total armed forces of 33,900, compared with 53,100 in 1999. Military service for males (aged between 19 and 47) lasts between seven and 15 months in the army and navy, and between eight and 12 months in the air force. Basic training for women is voluntary. The army consisted of 19,100 men, of whom 9,000 were conscripts; the navy 7,100 men, including 2,300 conscripts, and the air force 7,700 men, including 1,900 conscripts. In addition, there were voluntary defence reservists totalling 262,000, compared with 570,000 in 1999. In November 2000 Sweden committed 1,500 troops to the European rapid reaction force, which was intended to be ready for deployment by 2003. In 2002 defence was allocated 46,299m. kronor in the budget.

Economic Affairs

In 2001, according to estimates by the World Bank, Sweden's gross national income (GNI), measured at average 1999–2001 prices, was US $225,894m., equivalent to $25,400 per head (or $24,670 on an international purchasing-power parity basis). During 1990–2001, it was estimated, the population grew at an average annual rate of 0.3%, while gross domestic product (GDP) per head increased, in real terms, by an average of 1.3% per year. Sweden's overall GDP increased, in real terms, by an average of 1.7% per year in 1990–2001. GDP rose by 3.6% in 2000 and by 1.2% in 2001.

Agriculture (including hunting, forestry and fishing) contributed 2.1% of GDP in 2000 (at constant 1995 prices), and employed 2.4% of the working population in that year. The main agricultural products are dairy produce, meat, cereals and potatoes, primarily for domestic consumption. In 2000 forestry products (wood, pulp and paper) accounted for 13.2% of total merchandise exports. Agricultural GDP remained relatively stagnant during 1990–2000; it increased by 0.6% in 1999, but declined by 0.3% in 2000.

Industry (including mining, manufacturing, construction and power) provided 31.2% of GDP in 2000 (at constant 1995 prices), and employed 24.5% of the working population in that year. Industrial GDP increased by an average of 2.7% per year in 1990–2000. Industrial GDP grew by 3.9% in 1999 and by 5.0% in 2000.

Mining contributed 6.8% of GDP in 2000 (at constant 1995 prices), and employed 0.2% of the working population in that year. The principal product is iron ore, but there are also large reserves of uranium (some 15% of the world's total known reserves), copper, lead and zinc. The GDP of the mining and quarrying sector declined, in real terms, by an average of 2.4% per year in 1995–1999; it decreased by 0.5% in 1998, but increased by 1.2% in 1999.

Manufacturing contributed 25.5% of GDP in 2000 (at constant 1995 prices), and employed 18.2% of the working population in that year. In 1995 the most important manufactures (measured by total value of output) were paper and paper products (10.5% of the total), motor vehicles (9.3%), chemicals (7.2%), basic iron and steel (6.8%), television and radio transmitters and other communications apparatus (6.4%), and general purpose machinery (5.4%). Manufacturing GDP increased, in real terms, by an average of 4.1% per year in 1995–99; it rose by 4.6% in 1998 and by 4.2% in 1999.

Energy is derived principally from nuclear power, which provided some 47.2% of electricity generated in 1999, and hydro-electric power, which provided some 46.1% of electricity generated in the same year; Sweden has 12 nuclear reactors. Imports of petroleum and petroleum products accounted for about 7.8% of total imports in 2001. Alternative sources of energy are also being developed, because of strict environmental legislation, the lack of potential for further hydroelectric projects and, primarily, the Riksdag's resolution to phase out nuclear power by 2010.

The services sector contributed 66.7% of GDP in 2000 (at constant 1995 prices), and engaged 72.9% of the employed population in that year. The GDP of the services sector increased, in real terms, at an average annual rate of 1.7% during 1990–2000; it grew by 4.3% in 1999 and by 3.3% in 2000.

In 2001 Sweden recorded a merchandise trade surplus of US $13,832m., and there was a surplus of $6,696m. on the current account of the balance of payments. The European Union (EU, see p. 199) dominates Swedish trade: in 2001 it provided 66.8% of imports and took 54.7% of exports. The European Free Trade Association (EFTA, see p. 195) is also an important trading partner. In 2001 the principal single source of imports was Germany (contributing 17.8% of total imports); other major suppliers were the United Kingdom (8.9%), Denmark (8.5%) and Norway (8.4%). Germany was also the principal market for exports in that year (accounting for 10.6% of total exports); other major purchasers were the USA (10.5%), the United Kingdom (8.9%) and Norway (8.6%). The principal exports in 2001 were machinery and transport equipment (principally road vehicles and telecommunications equipment), basic manufactured goods (mainly paper) and chemicals. The principal imports in 2001 were machinery and transport equipment, and basic and other manufactures.

In 2000 there was a budget surplus of 125,820m. kronor, equivalent to about 5.7% of GDP. At the end of 1999 the central Government's total external debt was 409,440m. kronor. The annual rate of inflation averaged 2.3% in 1990–2001. Consumer prices increased by an average of 1.0% in 2000, by 2.4% in 2001, and by 2.2% in 2002. An estimated 3.6% of the labour force were unemployed in 2001.

Sweden is a member of the Nordic Council (see p. 266) and the Nordic Council of Ministers (see p. 267). In January 1995 Sweden became a full member of the EU and withdrew from EFTA. Sweden joined the Schengen Agreement (see EU) in March 2001.

From the 1930s and 1940s until the beginning of the 1990s the so-called 'Swedish Model' operated in the economy, the dominating principle of which was the maintenance of full employment. During the late 1980s this became increasingly difficult to achieve, owing to a relatively high level of inflation and a low rate of economic growth. In the early 1990s unwieldy inflation and salary bills, created by high rates of taxation and public-sector employment, coupled with generous welfare provisions, prompted a crisis in the finance sector and Sweden's most serious economic recession in some 60 years. However, the Government's swift response, based on inflation targeting and fiscal consolidation, soon restored confidence, reduced inflation and produced a manageable fiscal surplus. Sweden experienced a considerable economic recovery in the late 1990s with robust GDP growth, owing to the expansion of the high-technology sector, which aided an increase in exports, and an improvement in private consumption. In 2001, however, a sharp decline in exports of high-technology products, and a fall in exports in general, led to a slowdown in Sweden's economy. Decreasing tax revenue exacerbated this, although it was hoped that the Government's programme of tax reductions would stimulate private consumption. In 2002 Sweden's GDP growth was constrained by slow international growth coupled with weak investment activity. This was exacerbated by the onset of the US-led military campaign in Iraq in March 2003, which contributed to a continuing erosion of business and consumer confidence. However, as (by mid-April) the conflict appeared to be short-lived, it was expected that both petroleum prices and uncertainty about future economic development would soon recede, and that this would stimulate the stock markets and investment. The effects of the preceding year's weak growth and sluggish demand were expected to limit GDP growth in 2003 to 1.4%. However, there were some signs of recovery, particularly in the manufacturing and export industries. Moreover, private consumption was expected to recover in mid-2003, once economic uncertainty had dissipated. Increased investment was expected to accelerate GDP growth later on in the year, reaching 2.8% in 2004, while employment was expected to remain stable until 2004, when it would increase (albeit lagging somewhat behind GDP growth). The temporarily high prices of petroleum and electricity, which had pushed up inflation during late 2002, were projected to recede in the latter part of 2003; domestic inflationary pressure was set to remain low, and a strong krona was expected to curb any increase in import prices. Inflation, therefore, was expected to be lower than 2% by the end of 2003. The two biggest risks still facing the Swedish economy were a delayed global economic recovery and continued weakness in the stock markets. Uncertainty over Sweden's possible entry into European economic and monetary union (EMU), which had been destabilizing the krona, continued; a referendum on the subject was scheduled for mid-September 2003.

Education

Basic education, which is compulsory, extends for nine years, starting at the age of six or seven years, and is received at the comprehensive school (grundskolan). At the end of this period a pupil may enter the integrated upper secondary school (gymnasieskolan). In accordance with legislation implemented in 1992–95, courses at upper secondary schools last three years, and are organized into 16 nationally defined study programmes, comprising two university entrance programmes and 14 vocational programmes. In 1996 97.8% of pupils continued to upper secondary school following compulsory education. Enrolment at primary schools included 100% of children in the relevant age-group in the 1990s. There are some 64 universities, university colleges, specialized institutions and university colleges of health science in Sweden. Slightly more than 30% of young people in Sweden proceed to higher education within five years of completing their upper secondary schooling. The budget for 2002 allocated 41,183m. kronor (5.8% of total expenditure) to education and university research.

Public Holidays*

2003: 1 January (New Year's Day), 6 January (Epiphany), 17 April (Maundy Thursday)†, 18 April (Good Friday), 21 April (Easter Monday), 1 May (May Day), 29 May (Ascension Day), 9 June (Whit Monday), 26 June (Midsummer Holiday), 31 October (for All Saints' Day), 25 December (Christmas), 26 December (Saint Stephen's Day).

2004: 1 January (New Year's Day), 6 January (Epiphany), 8 April (Maundy Thursday)†, 9 April (Good Friday), 12 April (Easter Monday), 1 May (May Day), 20 May (Ascension Day), 31 May (Whit Monday), 18 June (Midsummer Holiday), 31 October (for All Saints' Day), 25 December (Christmas), 26 December (St Stephen's Day).

*The eve of a holiday is as important or more so than the holiday itself. Most Swedes have the day off, including those working in the civil service, banks, public transport, hospitals, shops and the media. Others have at least a half-day. This applies especially to Midsummer's Eve, All Saints' Day Eve and Christmas Eve. The eve of May Day is sometimes called Valborg Eve or St Walpurgis.

† Afternoon only.

Weights and Measures

The metric system is in force.

Statistical Survey

Sources (unless otherwise stated): Statistics Sweden, Klostergt. 23, 701 89 Örebro; tel. (19) 17-62-00; fax (19) 17-64-44; e-mail infoservice@scb.se; internet www.scb.se; Nordic Statistical Secretariat (Copenhagen), *Yearbook of Nordic Statistics*.

Area and Population

AREA, POPULATION AND DENSITY

Area (sq km)	
Land	410,934
Inland waters.	39,030
Total	449,964*
Population (census results)†	
1 November 1985	8,360,178
1 November 1990	
Males	4,242,351
Females.	4,345,002
Total	8,587,353
Population (official estimates at 31 December)†	
2000	8,882,792
2001	8,909,128
2002	8,940,788
Density (per sq km) at 31 December 2002	19.9

* 173,732 sq miles.
† Population is *de jure*.

COUNTIES

(31 December 2002)

	Land area (sq km)	Population (estimated)*	Density (per sq km)
Stockholms län	6,490.0	1,850,467	285
Uppsala län	6,989.1	298,655	43
Södermanlands län . . .	6,062.4	259,006	43
Östergötlands län . . .	10,562.0	413,438	39
Jönköpings län	10,474.8	327,971	31
Kronobergs län	8,457.9	176,978	21
Kalmar län	11,170.9	234,627	21
Gotlands län	3,140.1	57,381	18
Blekinge län	2,941.3	149,875	51
Skåne län	11,027.1	1,145,090	104
Hallands län	5,454.3	278,551	51
Västra Götalands län . . .	23,941.6	1,508,230	63
Värmlands län	17,586.0	273,419	16
Örebro län.	8,516.7	273,412	32
Västmanlands län . . .	6,301.7	258,912	41
Dalarnus län	28,193.2	276,636	10
Gävleborgs län	18,191.7	277,012	15
Västernorrlands län . . .	21,678.2	244,319	11
Jämtlands län	49,443.4	127,947	3
Västerbottens län . . .	55,401.2	255,230	5
Norrbottens län	98,910.7	253,632	3
Total	410,934.2	8,940,788	22

* According to the administrative sub-divisions of 1 January 2003.

PRINCIPAL TOWNS

(estimated population at 31 December 2002)

Stockholm (capital) .	758,148	Örebro.	125,520
Göteborg			
(Gothenburg) . .	474,921	Norrköping . .	123,303
Malmö.	265,481	Helsingborg . .	119,406
Uppsala . . .	179,673	Jönköping. . .	118,581
Linköping. . . .	135,066	Umeå . . .	106,525
Västerås . . .	128,902		

BIRTHS, MARRIAGES AND DEATHS

	Registered live births		Registered marriages		Registered deaths	
	Number	Rate (per 1,000)	Number	Rate (per 1,000)	Number	Rate (per 1,000)
1995 . .	103,422	11.7	33,642	3.8	93,955	10.6
1996 . .	95,297	10.8	33,484	3.8	94,133	10.6
1997 . .	90,502	10.2	32,313	3.7	93,326	10.6
1998 . .	89,028	10.1	31,598	3.6	93,271	10.5
1999 . .	88,173	9.9	35,628	4.0	94,726	10.7
2000 . .	90,441	10.2	39,895	4.5	93,461	10.5
2001 . .	91,446	10.3	35,778	4.0	93,752	10.5
2002 . .	95,815	10.7	n.a.	n.a.	95,009	10.6

Expectation of life (WHO estimates, years at birth): 80.0 (males 77.7; females 82.3) in 2001 (Source: WHO, *World Health Report*).

IMMIGRATION AND EMIGRATION

	2000	2001	2002
Immigrants	58,659	60,795	64,087
Emigrants.	34,091	32,141	33,009

ECONOMICALLY ACTIVE POPULATION

(Sample surveys, '000 persons aged 16 to 64 years)

	1998	1999	2000
Agriculture, hunting and forestry .	100	101	95
Fishing	2	2	3
Mining and quarrying	9	9	9
Manufacturing	762	757	757
Electricity, gas and water supply .	32	31	30
Construction	220	225	225
Wholesale and retail trade, repair of motor vehicles, motorcycles and personal and household goods	503	512	520
Hotels and restaurants	110	114	116
Transport, storage and communications	271	275	279
Financial intermediation . . .	84	85	87
Real estate, renting and business activities	411	446	498
Public administration and defence, compulsory social security, extra-territorial organizations and bodies	208	208	223
Education	293	315	329
Health and social work	770	776	770
Other community, social and personal service activities, private households with employed persons	200	207	211
Activities not adequately defined	3	3	6
Total employed.	3,979	4,068	4,159
Unemployed	276	241	203
Total labour force	4,255	4,308	4,362
Males	2,233	2,254	2,281
Females	2,023	2,054	2,081

Source: ILO, *Yearbook of Labour Statistics*.

Health and Welfare

KEY INDICATORS

Total fertility rate (children per woman, 2001)	1.4
Under-5 mortality rate (per 1,000 live births, 2001) . . .	3
HIV/AIDS (% of persons aged 15–49, 2001)	0.08
Physicians (per 1,000 head, 1997)	3.11
Hospital beds (per 1,000 head, 1998)	3.8
Health expenditure (2000): US $ per head (PPP)	2,097
Health expenditure (2000): % of GDP	8.4
Health expenditure (2000): public (% of total)	77.3
Access to water (% of persons, 2000)	100
Access to sanitation (% of persons, 2000)	100
Human Development Index (2000): ranking	2
Human Development Index (2000): value	0.941

For sources and definitions, see explanatory note on p. vi.

Agriculture

PRINCIPAL CROPS

('000 metric tons; holdings of more than 2 ha of arable land)

	1999	2000	2001
Wheat	1,659	2,400	2,345
Rye	117	187	180
Barley	1,853	1,634	1,642
Oats	1,055	1,151	964
Potatoes	991	980	925
Rapeseed	162	122	106
Sugar beets	2,753	2,602	2,659

Source: FAO.

LIVESTOCK

('000 head, year ending September; holdings of more than 2 ha of arable land, or with large numbers of livestock)

	1999	2000	2001
Cattle	1,713	1,684	1,652
Sheep	437	431	452
Pigs	2,115	1,918	1,891
Horses	79	89	86*

* FAO estimate.

Source: FAO.

LIVESTOCK PRODUCTS

('000 metric tons)

	1999	2000	2001
Beef and veal	145	150	143
Horse meat	2	2	1
Mutton and lamb	4	4	4
Pig meat	325	277	276
Poultry meat	96	92	98
Cows' milk	3,299	3,297	3,290
Butter	48	50	51*
Cheese	134	132	130
Hen eggs	107	102	111

* Unofficial figure.

Source: FAO.

Forestry

ROUNDWOOD REMOVALS

('000 cubic metres)

	1999	2000	2001
Sawlogs, veneer logs and logs for sleepers	30,300	32,730	32,670
Pulpwood	21,500	23,760	23,340
Fuel wood	5,900	5,900*	5,900*
Other industrial wood	500	500*	500*
Total	58,200	62,890	62,410

* FAO estimate.

Source: FAO.

SAWNWOOD PRODUCTION

('000 cubic metres, incl. railway sleepers)

	1999	2000	2001
Coniferous (softwood) . . .	14,608	15,970	15,600
Broadleaved (hardwood) . . .	250*	206	210
Total	14,858	16,176	15,810

* FAO estimate.

Source: FAO.

Fishing

('000 metric tons, live weight)

	1998	1999	2000
Capture	410.9	351.3	338.5
Atlantic cod	22.5	22.6	23.2
Blue whiting (Poutassou) . .	6.0	15.5	3.4
Sandeels (Sandlances) . . .	8.6	23.2	28.2
Atlantic herring	201.7	157.5	174.1
European sprat	149.7	112.5	91.2
Aquaculture	5.5	6.1	4.8
Total catch	416.4	357.3	343.4

Note: Figures exclude aquatic mammals, recorded by number rather than by weight. The number of harbour porpoises caught was: 14 in 1998; 2 in 1999; 0 in 2000.

Source: FAO, *Yearbook of Fishery Statistics*.

Mining*

(estimates, '000 metric tons, unless otherwise indicated)

	1999	2000	2001
Iron ore	11,506	13,556	12,811
Copper ore	71.2	77.8	74.3
Gold (kilograms)	4,400	3,570	4,986
Silver (metric tons)	284.1	328.7	306.0
Zinc ore	174.4	176.8	156.3
Lead ore	116.3	106.6	86.0

* Figures relate to the metal content of ores.

Source: US Geological Survey.

Industry

SELECTED PRODUCTS
('000 metric tons, unless otherwise indicated)

	1997	1998	1999
Pig-iron	3,072	3,156	3,816
Crude steel	5,117	5,143	5,038
Aluminium	123.4	122.7	96.0
Copper (refined)	128.4	125.0	115.0
Lead (refined)	66.2	64.5	54.4
Mechanical wood pulp	2,959	3,026	3,029
Chemical wood pulp*	7,272	7,287	7,407
Newsprint	2,411	2,478	2,508
Other printing and writing paper*	2,459	2,545	2,617
Other paper and paperboard	4,886	4,856	4,946
Cement	2,272	2,372	2,307
Dwellings completed (number)	13,007	11,459	11,712
Electricity (million kWh)	149,741	158,277	n.a.

2000 ('000 metric tons, unless otherwise stated): Chemical wood pulp 7,979*; Other paper and paperboard 5,407*; Dwellings completed (number) 12,984.

2001 ('000 metric tons): Chemical wood pulp 7,682*; Other paper and paperboard 5,281*.

* Source: FAO.

Source: mainly UN, *Industrial Commodity Statistics Yearbook*.

Finance

CURRENCY AND EXCHANGE RATES

Monetary Units
100 öre = 1 Swedish krona (plural: kronor)

Sterling, Dollar and Euro Equivalents (31 December 2002)
£1 sterling = 14.224 kronor
US $1 = 8.825 kronor
€1 = 9.255 kronor
1,000 Swedish kronor = £70.30 = $113.31 = €108.05

Average Exchange Rate (kronor per US $)
2000   9.1622
2001   10.3291
2002   9.7371

STATE BUDGET
(million kronor)

Revenue	2000	2001	2002*
Tax revenue	672,831	684,603	654,123
Taxes on income, profits and capital gains	127,514	134,874	68,701
Statutory social security fees	225,900	238,766	249,007
Taxes on property	38,266	39,863	39,507
Taxes on goods and services	265,492	271,515	281,933
Municipality and council tax	19,196	20,874	23,705
Other current revenue	45,542	50,813	49,293
Capital revenue	61,517	188	6
Loan repayment	2,461	2,590	2,614
Computed revenue	8,619	8,447	8,632
EU contributions	9,031	8,485	11,049
Total	800,000	755,126	725,717

Expenditure	2000	2001	2002*
Justice	23,317	22,757	24,051
Defence	46,165	44,895	46,299
Health	28,573	29,492	31,443
Social insurance for the sick and disabled	97,937	107,316	112,962
Social insurance for the elderly	33,538	33,839	33,766
Social insurance for families and children	44,596	48,289	49,935
Social insurance for the unemployed	74,291	59,674	59,963
Employment			
Education and university research	31,363	33,259	41,183
Community planning and housing	11,716	10,434	9,346
Communications	25,196	24,341	24,465
Agriculture, forestry and fisheries	9,727	16,627	10,188
General grants to municipalities	97,535	100,639	101,967
Interest on central government debt	90,213	81,260	62,085
Contributions to the European Union	22,295	23,272	18,619
Total (incl. others)	698,068	716,379	715,157

* Forecasts.

INTERNATIONAL RESERVES
(US $ million at 31 December)

	2000	2001	2002
Gold*	272	262	284
IMF special drawing rights	215	197	179
Reserve position in IMF	890	1,039	1,428
Foreign exchange	13,757	12,740	15,520
Total	15,134	14,238	17,411

* Valued at SDR 35 per troy ounce.

Source: IMF, *International Financial Statistics*.

MONEY SUPPLY
(million kronor at 31 December)

	1998	1999	2000
Currency outside banks	74,633	78,641	89,162

Source: IMF, *International Financial Statistics*.

COST OF LIVING
(Consumer Price Index; base: 1980 = 100)

	2000	2001	2002
Food and non-alcoholic beverages	226.0	232.5	240.0
Alcoholic beverages and tobacco	335.3	339.4	342.2
Clothing and footwear	158.8	162.9	164.5
Housing, water, electricity and fuels	292.1	303.6	312.1
Furniture and household goods	220.1	224.8	229.0
Health	630.5	660.1	686.0
Transport	323.8	324.0	328.7
Communication	230.7	230.4	227.8
Recreation and culture	196.2	197.9	197.8
Restaurants and hotels	345.6	356.6	370.7
Miscellaneous goods and services	254.7	264.9	227.4
All items	260.8	267.1	272.9

NATIONAL ACCOUNTS
(million kronor at current prices)

National Income and Product

	1999	2000	2001
Compensation of employees.	1,108,633	1,217,371	1,289,222
Operating surplus	318,371	308,506	263,609
Domestic factor incomes.	1,427,004	1,525,877	1,552,831
Consumption of fixed capital	279,074	302,687	328,781
Gross domestic product (GDP) at factor cost.	1,706,078	1,828,564	1,881,612
Indirect taxes.	348,644	312,273	329,542
Less Subsidies	50,071	42,386	43,958
GDP in purchasers' values.	2,004,651	2,098,451	2,167,196
Factor income received from abroad (net).	−20,543	−17,087	34,645
Gross national product (GNP)	1,984,108	2,081,364	2,132,551
Less Consumption of fixed capital	279,074	302,687	328,781
National income in market prices.	1,705,034	1,778,677	1,803,770
Other current transfers from abroad (net).	−19,038	−18,737	−21,533
National disposable income.	1,685,996	1,759,940	1,782,237

Expenditure on the Gross Domestic Product

	1999	2000	2001
Government final consumption expenditure.	536,139	549,001	577,701
Private final consumption expenditure.	1,004,605	1,060,424	1,079,731
Changes in stocks	3,529	13,667	3,046
Gross fixed capital formation	340,822	363,286	379,110
Total domestic expenditure.	1,885,095	1,986,378	2,039,588
Exports of goods and services	872,396	990,089	1,006,703
Less Imports of goods and services	752,840	878,016	879,095
GDP in purchasers' values.	2,004,651	2,098,451	2,167,196
GDP at constant 1995 prices.	1,913,547	1,982,619	2,006,526

Gross Domestic Product by Economic Activity

	1999	2000	2001
Agriculture, forestry and fishing	33,702	32,881	33,236
Mining and quarrying	4,485	4,667	5,266
Manufacturing	383,214	402,329	395,099
Electricity, gas and water	41,512	37,157	44,580
Construction	77,685	80,683	84,349
Trade, restaurants and hotels	217,366	233,105	239,003
Transport, storage and communications	144,146	152,554	160,013
Financing, insurance, real estate and business services*	450,532	477,234	494,130
Government services.	383,995	391,650	411,577
Education, health and social services	31,727	36,654	41,109
Other community, social and personal services	35,620	38,267	39,779
Other services†	21,393	32,077	33,881
Sub-total.	1,825,377	1,919,258	1,982,022
Statistical discrepancy	1,800	1,652	1,169
Less Imputed bank service charge	42,423	46,661	50,287
GDP at basic prices	1,784,754	1,874,249	1,932,904
Taxes on products	229,391	233,888	244,413
Less Subsidies on products	9,494	9,686	10,121
GDP in purchasers' values.	2,004,651	2,098,451	2,167,196

* Including imputed rents of owner-occupied dwellings.

† Domestic services and non-profit institutions serving households.

BALANCE OF PAYMENTS
(US $ million)

	1999	2000	2001
Exports of goods f.o.b.	87,568	87,431	76,200
Imports of goods f.o.b.	−71,854	−72,216	−62,368
Trade balance	15,714	15,215	13,832
Exports of services	19,904	20,252	21,997
Imports of services	−22,617	−23,440	−23,020
Balance on goods and services	13,001	12,027	12,809
Other income received	19,871	20,074	17,934
Other income paid	−23,291	−22,137	−20,786
Balance on goods, services and income	9,581	9,964	9,957
Current transfers received	2,341	2,602	2,578
Current transfers paid	−5,940	−5,950	−5,839
Current balance	5,982	6,617	6,696
Capital account (net)	−2,143	384	509
Direct investment abroad	−19,554	−39,962	−6,959
Direct investment from abroad.	59,386	22,125	13,085
Portfolio investment assets.	−36,749	−12,772	−23,041
Portfolio investment liabilities	1,882	9,017	10,338
Financial derivatives assets	22,982	31,481	33,678
Financial derivatives liabilities	−22,923	−31,795	−38,894
Other investment assets	−10,333	−16,000	929
Other investment liabilities	3,897	34,609	12,689
Net errors and omissions	−545	−3,534	−10,078
Overall balance	1,881	170	−1,048

Source: IMF, *International Financial Statistics*.

OFFICIAL ASSISTANCE TO DEVELOPING COUNTRIES
(million kronor)

	2000	2001	2002*
Bilateral assistance	12,132	13,171	12,158
Multilateral assistance	5,207	4,764	4,261
Total	17,339	17,936	16,419

* Projected figures.

External Trade

PRINCIPAL COMMODITIES
(distribution by SITC, million kronor)

Imports c.i.f.	1999	2000	2001*
Food and live animals	33,919	35,172	39,913
Crude materials (inedible) except fuels	17,715	22,241	22,513
Mineral fuels, lubricants, etc.	34,443	60,609	57,707
Petroleum, petroleum products, etc.	30,449	54,509	51,138
Chemicals and related products	62,091	64,086	60,676
Basic manufactures	82,253	92,938	95,138
Iron and steel.	19,672	23,153	22,653
Machinery and transport equipment.	251,955	299,495	271,150
Power-generating machinery and equipment	15,781	20,114	20,044
Machinery specialized for particular industries	17,621	18,285	17,660
General industrial machinery, equipment and parts	30,096	32,837	35,204
Office machines and automatic data-processing equipment	29,784	33,079	31,391
Telecommunications and sound equipment	33,775	45,151	37,879
Other electrical machinery, apparatus, etc.	53,355	68,933	54,124
Road vehicles and parts†	58,748	64,822	60,996
Miscellaneous manufactured articles.	78,882	85,877	91,676
Clothing and accessories (excl. footwear)	19,715	21,199	21,997
Other miscellaneous manufactured articles	24,522	25,295	27,799
Total (incl. others)	568,008	666,863	656,180

Exports f.o.b.	1999	2000	2001*
Crude materials (inedible) except fuels	38,780	48,067	45,765
Mineral fuels, lubricants, etc.	16,514	26,732	26,468
Petroleum, petroleum products, etc.	14,694	25,543	23,437
Chemicals and related products	67,499	75,045	86,839
Medical and pharmaceutical preparations	33,399	36,122	43,190
Basic manufactures	142,934	159,595	169,067
Paper, paperboard and manufactures	55,846	62,473	66,895
Iron and steel	31,846	37,526	38,916
Machinery and transport equipment	354,053	399,734	356,131
Power-generating machinery and equipment	27,535	29,259	30,769
Machinery specialized for particular industries	28,798	33,668	33,988
General industrial machinery, equipment and parts	44,019	46,773	50,913
Telecommunications and sound equipment	105,623	126,918	72,659
Other electrical machinery, apparatus, etc.	41,044	48,901	46,804
Road vehicles and parts†	86,745	90,929	94,546
Miscellaneous manufactured articles	61,132	65,432	72,764
Total (incl. others)	700,960	796,550	783,470

* Provisional.
† Data on parts exclude tyres, engines and electrical parts.

PRINCIPAL TRADING PARTNERS
(million kronor)

Imports c.i.f.	1999	2000	2001*
Austria	5,970	6,865	7,544
Belgium	21,901	24,523	24,889
China, People's Repub.	6,294	8,883	11,042
Denmark	41,956	50,382	55,639
Estonia	5,383	8,118	6,366
Finland	31,993	36,939	35,797
France	35,979	39,295	42,670
Germany	102,467	117,364	116,793
Hong Kong	8,098	9,405	7,946
Ireland	9,083	11,810	11,901
Italy	20,126	21,407	22,328
Japan	16,179	19,714	14,778
Netherlands	46,824	50,669	45,829
Norway	42,370	54,977	55,163
Poland	6,215	8,730	10,005
Spain	9,995	9,544	10,322
Switzerland	9,428	8,908	9,338
United Kingdom	59,531	63,666	58,530
USA	33,248	44,726	35,518
Total (incl. others)	568,008	666,863	656,180

Exports f.o.b.	1999	2000	2001*
Australia	8,284	7,807	7,467
Austria	7,546	8,024	7,726
Belgium	30,334	33,684	35,664
Canada	6,785	9,158	8,465
China, People's Repub.	12,907	17,230	15,986
Denmark	42,257	46,348	48,240
Finland	39,363	44,461	44,797
France	37,518	41,657	40,079
Germany	77,467	87,350	83,389
Italy	26,013	30,745	27,877
Japan	16,798	22,305	22,957
Mexico	4,842	9,898	5,736
Netherlands	42,612	39,670	39,454
Norway	54,729	60,146	67,163
Poland	12,682	13,234	12,768
Russia	4,119	5,076	8,582
Spain	24,403	23,100	19,420
Switzerland	10,133	9,303	10,212
Turkey	10,143	9,593	4,071
United Kingdom	67,016	74,847	69,518
USA	64,261	75,349	82,606
Total (incl. others)	700,960	796,550	783,470

* Provisional figures.

Transport

RAILWAYS
(traffic)

	1999	2000	2001
Passenger-kilometres (million)	7,636	8,251	n.a.
Freight ton-kilometres (million)	19,090	20,088	19,547

ROAD TRAFFIC
('000 motor vehicles in use at 31 December)

	1999	2000	2001
Passenger cars	3,890	3,999	4,019
Buses and coaches	15	14	14
Lorries and vans	354	374	396
Motorcycles	150	165	182

SHIPPING

Merchant Fleet
(registered at 31 December)

	1999	2000	2001
Number of vessels	570	565	578
Total displacement ('000 grt)	2,946.9	2,887.0	2,957.9

Source: Lloyd's Register-Fairplay, *World Fleet Statistics*.

International Sea-borne Freight Traffic

	1999	2000	2001
Vessels entered ('000 grt)	190,647	192,629	98,323
Vessels cleared ('000 grt)	190,587	191,179	97,223
Goods loaded ('000 metric tons)	59,775	59,798	57,781
Goods unloaded ('000 metric tons)	70,446	74,204	70,677

CIVIL AVIATION
(traffic on scheduled services)*

	1997	1998	1999
Kilometres flown (million)	132	143	150
Passengers carried ('000)	11,327	11,878	12,933
Passenger-kilometres (million)	9,749	10,249	10,607
Total ton-kilometres (million)	1,191	1,234	1,309

* Including an apportionment (3/7) of the international services of Scandinavian Airlines System (SAS), operated jointly with Denmark and Norway.

Source: UN, *Statistical Yearbook*.

Tourism*

VISITORS BY ORIGIN
('000 nights in all types of tourist accommodation)

	1998	1999	2000
Denmark	798.6	839.1	832.1
Finland	422.5	502.3	464.7
France	205.4	199.7	210.4
Germany	1,877.3	1,757.0	1,798.5
Japan	166.6	136.6	144.7
Netherlands	468.1	472.2	477.8
Norway	1,542.1	1,951.6	1,869.8
United Kingdom	461.6	503.0	554.5
USA	348.8	380.3	395.4
Total (incl. others)	8,029.1	8,600.8	8,650.3

* Since the introduction of the Scandinavian Passport Control Area, there are no figures available for total arrivals in Sweden.

Source: World Tourism Organization, *Yearbook of Tourism Statistics*.

Tourism receipts (US $ million): 4,189 in 1998; 4,116 in 1999; 4,107 (estimate) in 2000 (Source: World Tourism Organization).

Communications Media

	1999	2000	2001
Television receivers ('000 in use)	4,900	5,100	n.a.
Telephones ('000 main lines in use)	5,889	6,057	6,585
Mobile cellular telephones ('000 subscribers)	5,165	6,338	6,867
Personal computers ('000 in use)	4,000	4,500	5,000
Internet users ('000)	3,666	4,048	4,600

Source: International Telecommunication Union.

Radio receivers ('000 in use, 1997): 8,250.

Facsimile machines (estimated '000 in use, 1996): 450.

Daily newspapers (1997): 169; total circulation ('000 copies) 4,232.

Book production (titles, 1996): 13,496.

Source: mainly UN, *Statistical Yearbook* and UNESCO, *Statistical Yearbook*.

Education

(1996/97)

	Institu- tions	Teachers*	Students
Primary: grade 1–6 / Secondary: grade 7–9	4,936	81,800	958,972
Integrated upper secondary schools	641	28,305	310,000
Higher education	64	20,000†	300,381
People's colleges	147	n.a.	200,000
Municipal adult education	400‡	10,462	174,450

* Full-time and part-time teachers and teachers on leave.
† 1994/95.
‡ 1993/94.

Students: Primary and secondary (grades 1–9) 1,059,122 in 2001/02. Integrated upper secondary 311,121 at 15 Oct. 2000; Higher education 330,156 in 2000/01; People's colleges 122,319 in 2001*; Municipal adult education 317,206 in 2000/01.

* Autumn term.

Teachers (full-time and part-time teachers and teachers on leave, 2001/02): Primary and secondary (grades 1–9) 106,028; Integrated upper secondary 32,791; Municipal adult education 8,878. Total teachers: 154,392.

Institutions (2001/02): Primary and secondary (grades 1–9) 5,075.

Directory

The Constitution

The Swedish Constitution is based on four fundamental laws: the Instrument of Government (originally dating from 6 June 1809), the Act of Succession (1810), the Freedom of the Press Act (1949) and the Riksdag Act. Following partial reforms in 1968 and 1969, a new Instrument of Government and a new Riksdag Act were adopted in 1973 and 1974, and the revised Constitution, summarized below, came into force on 1 January 1975.

GOVERNMENT

The Cabinet governs Sweden and is responsible to the Riksdag (Parliament). The Constitution of 1975 formalized the position of the Monarch relative to the Cabinet and the Riksdag, and laid down rules on the selection and resignation of the Cabinet. In 1978 the Riksdag amended the constitutional law of succession to allow the first-born royal child, whether male or female, to be heir to the throne, with effect from 1980.

As Head of State, the Monarch has representative and ceremonial duties only. The Monarch does not participate in the government of the country, which is conducted rather by the Cabinet at meetings not attended by the Monarch. Decisions of government do not require the Monarch's signature, and it is the Speaker of the Riksdag, and not the Monarch, who leads the procedure resulting in the formation of a new Government. Following consultations within the Riksdag, the Speaker nominates a candidate for Prime Minister. If not more than one-half of the total number of members of the Riksdag vote against the proposed candidate, he or she is approved. Failing this approval, the procedure has to be repeated. After four unsuccessful attempts to secure Riksdag approval of a candidate for the premiership, a new election to the Riksdag must be held within three months. A candidate for the premiership approved by the Riksdag nominates the other members of the Government.

The Prime Minister can be dismissed at his or her own request, by the Speaker of the Riksdag, or in the event of a vote of 'no confidence' in the Riksdag. Other ministers can be dismissed at their own request, by the Prime Minister or by a vote of 'no confidence'. If the Prime Minister should resign or die, all of the ministers in the Cabinet must resign. A Cabinet that is due to resign shall, however, remain in power until a new Prime Minister has been appointed.

A demand for a vote of 'no confidence' will be considered only if it is supported by 10% of the members of the Riksdag. A vote of 'no confidence' requires the support of more than one-half of the Riksdag members. If the Riksdag decides upon a vote of 'no confidence', the Cabinet can avoid resigning if it calls for an extra general election within one week. The Riksdag may continue its business, or be summoned to convene, even after a decision has been made to hold new elections. A Riksdag session may, however, be terminated by a special decision of the Cabinet. Existing terms of office do not expire until the new terms of office have begun.

LEGISLATURE

The Riksdag is the prime representative of the Swedish people. It enacts laws, decides the amount and use of taxation and examines the Government's actions. The Riksdag at present contains 349 members, elected for four years.

In accordance with tradition, the work of the Swedish Riksdag is, to a great extent, carried on in a non-partisan atmosphere. This is largely the result of the thorough attention given to all questions by numerous standing committees elected by the Riksdag on a basis of proportional representation. Besides the Utrikesnämnden (Advisory Council on Foreign Affairs) and Special Committees, every Riksdag appoints from within the assembly a Constitution Committee, a

Finance Committee, a Taxation Committee and at least 12 other committees.

The Constitution Committee has to examine the minutes of the Cabinet and deal with or initiate proposals concerning alterations of the fundamental laws and of laws regulating local government.

ELECTORAL SYSTEM

In order that local and national government terms of office should coincide, the Constitution calls for local and general elections to be held on the same day. In both cases the term of office for the elected candidate is four years. Proportional representation was introduced in Sweden between the years 1906 and 1909, universal and equal suffrage by 1921. Under the provisions of legislation passed in 1976, all aliens resident in the country for three years are permitted to vote in local elections. The minimum voting age is 18 years. In allocating the 349 seats in the Riksdag, the seats are divided into two groups. The first group of 310 'constituency seats' is distributed among the constituencies according to the number of eligible voters, and within each constituency among the parties. The remaining 39 seats are distributed as 'adjustment seats'. First, it is calculated how many seats each party would have obtained if the whole country had been treated as a single constituency and if the distribution of seats had taken place according to a modified Lague method. From this figure is subtracted the number of 'constituency seats' received, the result being the number of 'compensatory seats' to be allocated to each party. These seats are filled by candidates nominated in the constituencies. There is a check to the emergence of small parties in that only parties that have received at least 4% of the total votes cast are entitled to a seat. However, any party that receives 12% or more of the votes in any constituency will be allowed to compete for a permanent seat in that constituency.

The Government

HEAD OF STATE

Monarch: King CARL GUSTAF XVI (succeeded to the throne 15 September 1973).

THE CABINET
(April 2003)

Prime Minister: GÖRAN PERSSON.

Deputy Prime Minister and Minister of Policy Co-ordination: PÄR NUDER.

Minister of Justice: THOMAS BODSTRÖM.

Minister (Democracy and Integration Issues), Ministry of Justice: MONA SAHLIN.

Minister of Foreign Affairs: ANNA LINDH.

Minister (Development Co-operation, Migration and Asylum Policy), Ministry of Foreign Affairs: JAN O. KARLSSON.

Minister of Defence: LENI BJÖRKLUND.

Minister of Health and Social Affairs: LARS ENGQVIST.

Minister (Children and Families), Ministry of Health and Social Affairs: BERIT ANDNOR.

Minister (Public Health and Social Services), Ministry of Health and Social Affairs: MORGAN JOHANSSON.

Minister of Finance: BOSSE RINGHOLM.

Minister, Ministry of Finance: LARS-ERIK LÖVDÉN.

Minister (International Economic Affairs and Financial Markets), Ministry of Finance: GUNNAR LUND.

Minister (Local Government and Housing), Ministry of Finance: LARS-ERIK LÖVDÉN.

Minister of Education and Science: THOMAS ÖSTROS.

Minister (Pre-School Education, Youth Affairs and Adult Learning), Ministry of Education and Science: LENA HALLENGREN.

Minister of Agriculture, Food and Fisheries: ANN-CHRISTIN NYKVIST.

Minister of Culture: MARITA ULVSKOG.

Minister of the Environment: LENA SOMMESTAD.

Minister of Industry, Employment and Communications: LEIF PAGROTSKY.

Minister (Communications and Regional Policy), Ministry of Industry, Employment and Communications: ULRICA MESSING.

Minister (Employment), Ministry of Industry, Employment and Communications: HANS KARLSSON.

MINISTRIES

Prime Minister's Office: Rosenbad 4, 103 33 Stockholm; tel. (8) 405-10-00; fax (8) 723-11-71.

Ministry of Agriculture, Food and Fisheries: Fredsgt. 8, 103 33 Stockholm; tel. (8) 405-10-00; fax (8) 20-64-96; e-mail registrator@agriculture.ministry.se; internet jordbruk.regeringen.se.

Ministry of Culture: Drottninggt. 16, 103 33 Stockholm; tel. (8) 405-10-00; fax (8) 21-68-13; e-mail registrator@culture.ministry.se; internet kultur.regeringen.se.

Ministry of Defence: Jakobsgt. 9, 103 33 Stockholm; tel. (8) 405-25-07; fax (8) 723-11-89; e-mail registrator@defence.ministry.se; internet forsvar.regeringen.se.

Ministry of Education and Science: Drottninggt. 16, 103 33 Stockholm; tel. (8) 405-10-00; fax (8) 723-11-92; e-mail registrator@education.ministry.se; internet utbildning.regeringen.se.

Ministry of the Environment: Tegelbacken 2, 103 33 Stockholm; tel. (8) 405-10-00; fax (8) 24-16-29; e-mail registrator@environment.ministry.se; internet miljo.regeringen.se.

Ministry of Finance: Drottninggt. 21, 103 33 Stockholm; tel. (8) 405-10-00; fax (8) 21-73-86; e-mail registrator@finance.ministry.se; internet finans.regeringen.se.

Ministry of Foreign Affairs: Gustav Adolfs torg 1, 103 39 Stockholm; tel. (8) 405-10-00; fax (8) 723-11-76; e-mail registrator@foreign.ministry.se; internet utrikes.regeringen.se.

Ministry of Health and Social Affairs: Fredsgt. 8, 103 33 Stockholm; tel. (8) 405-10-00; fax (8) 723-11-91; e-mail registrator@social.ministry.se; internet social.regeringen.se.

Ministry of Industry, Employment and Communications: Jakobsgt. 26, 103 33 Stockholm; tel. (8) 405-10-00; fax (8) 411-36-16; e-mail registrator@industry.ministry.se; internet naring.regeringen.se.

Ministry of Justice: Rosenbad 4, 103 33 Stockholm; tel. (8) 405-10-00; fax (8) 20-27-34; e-mail registrator@justice.ministry.se; internet justitie.regeringen.se.

Legislature

RIKSDAG

Sveriges Riksdag

100 12 Stockholm; tel. (8) 786-40-00; e-mail riksdagen@riksdagen.se; internet www.riksdagen.se.

Speaker (Talman): BJÖRN VON SYDOW.

General Election, 15 September 2002

	% of votes	Seats
Sveriges Socialdemokratiska Arbetareparti (SAP)	39.8	144
Moderata Samlingspartiet (MS)	15.2	55
Folkpartiet liberalerna (FP)	13.3	48
Kristdemokraterna (Kd)	9.1	33
Vänsterpartiet (VP)	8.3	30
Centerpartiet (Centern) (CP)	6.1	22
Miljöpartiet de Gröna (MpG)	4.6	17
Others	3.0	—
Total	100.0	349

Political Organizations

Centerpartiet (Centern) (CP) (Centre Party): Bergsgt. 7B, POB 22107, 104 22 Stockholm; tel. (8) 617-38-00; fax (8) 652-64-40; e-mail centerpartiet@centerpartiet.se; internet www.centerpartiet.se; f. 1910 as an agrarian party; aims at social, environmental and progressive development and decentralization; Chair. LENNART DALLÉUS; Sec.-Gen. ÅKE PETTERSSON; 140,000 mems.

Folkpartiet liberalerna (FP) (Liberal Party): POB 6508, 113 83 Stockholm; tel. (8) 509-11-600; fax (8) 509-11-660; e-mail info@liberal.se; internet www.folkpartiet.se; f. 1902; advocates market-orientated economy and social welfare system; Chair. LARS LEIJONBORG; Sec.-Gen. JOHAN JAKOBSSON.

Kristdemokraterna (Kd) (Christian Democratic Party): Målargt. 7, POB 3337, 103 67 Stockholm; tel. (8) 723-25-00; fax (8) 723-25-10; e-mail brev.till@kristdemokrat.se; internet www.kristdemokrat.se; f. 1964 as Kristdemokratiska Samhällspartiet (KdS), to promote emphasis on Christian values in political life; Chair. ALF SVENSSON; Sec.-Gen. URBAN SVENSSON; 25,800 mems.

Miljöpartiet de Gröna (MpG) (Green Party): International Secretary, Swedish Parliament, 100 12 Stockholm; tel. (8) 786-57-44; fax (8) 786-53-75; e-mail info@mp.se; internet www.mp.se; f. 1981; Co-Leaders MARIA WETTERSTRAMEL, PETER ERIKSSON; c. 8,000 mems.

Moderata Samlingspartiet (MS) (Moderate Party): POB 1243, 111 82 Stockholm; tel. (8) 676-80-00; fax (8) 21-61-23; e-mail info@ moderat.se; internet www.moderat.se; f. 1904; advocates liberal-conservative market-orientated economy; Chair. BO LUNDGREN; Sec. GUNNAR HÖKMARK; 100,000 mems.

Ny demokrati (ND) (New Democracy): Stockholm; tel. (8) 786-57-00; fax (8) 20-40-77; e-mail srk@anoden.se; internet www .nydemokrati.se; f. 1991; right-wing populist; Chair. ULF ERIKSSON.

Sveriges Socialdemokratiska Arbetareparti (SAP) (Social Democratic Labour Party of Sweden): Sveavägen 68, 105 60 Stockholm; tel. (8) 700-26-00; fax (8) 21-93-31; e-mail info@sap.se; internet www.sap.se; f. 1889; egalitarian; Chair. GÖRAN PERSSON; Sec.-Gen. LARS STJERNKVIST; 152,118 mems (2001).

Vänsterpartiet (VP) (Left Party): Kungsgt. 84, POB 12660, 112 93 Stockholm; tel. (8) 654-08-20; fax (8) 653-23-85; e-mail ann-marie .ogalde@vansterpartiet.se; internet www.vansterpartiet.se; f. 1917 as Left Social Democratic Party of Sweden; affiliated to the Communists International 1919; renamed the Communist Party in 1921; renamed Left Party—Communists in 1967; renamed Left Party in 1990; policies based on the principles of Marxism, feminism and other theories; Chair. ULLA HOFFMANN; Sec. PERNILLA ZETHRAEUS.

Diplomatic Representation

EMBASSIES IN SWEDEN

Albania: Capellavägen 7, 181 32 Lidingö; tel. (8) 731-09-20; fax (8) 767-65-57; Ambassador SHAHIN KADARE.

Algeria: Danderydsgt. 3–5, POB 26027, 100 41 Stockholm; tel. (8) 679-91-30; fax (8) 611-49-57; e-mail algeriets.ambassad@mailbox .swipnet.se; Ambassador FARIDA AÏOUAZE.

Angola: POB 3199, 103 64 Stockholm; Skeppsbron 8, 111 30 Stockholm; tel. (8) 24-28-90; fax (8) 34-31-27; e-mail info@angolaemb.se; internet www.angolaemb.se; Ambassador LEOVIGILDO DA COSTA E SILVA.

Argentina: Grevgt. 5, POB 14039, 104 40 Stockholm; tel. (8) 663-19-65; fax (8) 661-00-09; e-mail cancilleria@argemb.se; Ambassador JUAN CARLOS ROLAND VIGNALID.

Australia: Sergels Torg 12, POB 7003, 103 86 Stockholm; tel. (8) 613-29-00; fax (8) 24-74-14; e-mail reception@austemb.se; internet www.austemb.se; Ambassador RICHARD ROWE.

Austria: Kommendörsgt. 35, 114 58 Stockholm; tel. (8) 665-17-70; fax (8) 662-69-28; e-mail stockholm-ob@bmaa.gv.at; internet www .algonet.se/~austria; Ambassador PETER PRAMBERGER.

Bangladesh: Anderstorpsvägen 12, 171 54 Solna; tel. (8) 730-58-50; fax (8) 730-58-70; Ambassador MONZURUL ALAM.

Belarus: Herserudsvägen 5, 181 34 Lidingö; tel. (8) 731-57-45; fax (8) 731-57-46; e-mail belarusembassy@telia.com; Ambassador ALEG V. YERMALOVICH.

Belgium: Villagt. 13A, POB 26114, 100 41 Stockholm; tel. (8) 53-48-02-00; fax (8) 53-48-02-07; e-mail stockholm@diplobel.org; Ambassador JAN DEBOUTTE.

Bolivia: Södra Kungsvägen 60, 181 32 Lidingö; tel. (8) 731-58-30; fax (8) 767-63-11; Chargé d'affaires ESTHER ASHTON.

Bosnia and Herzegovina: Birger Jarlsgt. 55, POB 7102, 103 87 Stockholm; tel. (8) 24-74-77; fax (8) 24-98-30; Ambassador Dr HASAN DERVIŠBEGOVIĆ.

Botswana: Tyrgt. 11, POB 26024, 100 41 Stockholm; tel. (8) 545-25-800; Ambassador NAOME ELLEN MAJINDA.

Brazil: Odengt. 3, 114 24 Stockholm; tel. (8) 5451-63-00; fax (8) 5451-63-14; Ambassador ELIM SATURNINO FERREIRA DUTRA.

Bulgaria: Karlavägen 29, 114 31 Stockholm; tel. (8) 723-09-38; fax (8) 21-45-03; e-mail bg.embassy@ebox.tninet.se; Ambassador JASMINE NIKOLOVA POPOVA.

Canada: 7th Floor, Tegelbacken 4, POB 16129, 103 23 Stockholm; tel. (8) 453-30-00; fax (8) 24-24-91; Ambassador PHILLIPPE KIRSCH.

Chile: 3rd Floor, Sturegt. 8, 114 35 Stockholm; tel. (8) 679-82-80; fax (8) 679-85-40; e-mail echilese@chileemb.se; Ambassador JORGE PAYRET ZUBIAUR.

China, People's Republic: Lidovägen 8, 115 25 Stockholm; tel. (8) 5793-64-04; fax (8) 5793-64-03; Ambassador WANG GUISHENG.

Colombia: Östermalmsgt. 46, POB 5627, 114 86 Stockholm; tel. (8) 2143-20; fax (8) 21-84-90; e-mail emsuecia@ebox.tninet.se; Ambassador TERESA IVARS.

Congo, Democratic Republic: Herserudsvägen 5A, POB 1171, 181 23 Lidingö; tel. (8) 765-83-80; fax (8) 765-85-91; Ambassador THOMAS NSENGA KANZA.

Croatia: 1st Floor, Birger Jarlsgt. 13, 111 45 Stockholm; tel. (8) 678-42-20; fax (8) 678-83-20; Ambassador BRANKO CARATAN.

Cuba: Sturevägen 9, 182 73 Stockholm; tel. (8) 545-83-277; fax (8) 545-83-270; Ambassador MARIANELA FERRIOL ECHEVARRÍA.

Cyprus: Birger Jarlsgt. 37, POB 7649, 103 94 Stockholm; tel. (8) 24-50-08; fax (8) 24-45-18; e-mail cy.emb@ebox.tninet.se; Ambassador LEONIDAS PANTELIDES.

Czech Republic: Villagt. 21, POB 26156, 100 41 Stockholm; tel. (8) 440-42-10; fax (8) 440-42-11; e-mail stockholm@embassy.mzv.cz; internet www.czech-embassy.aton.cz; Ambassador MARIE CHATARDOVÁ.

Denmark: Jakobs Torg 1, POB 1638, 111 86 Stockholm; tel. (8) 406-75-00; fax (8) 791-72-20; Ambassador BENT HAAKONSEN.

Dominican Republic: Sibyllegt. 13, 4th Floor, POB 5584, 114 85 Stockholm; tel. (8) 667-46-11; fax (8) 667-51-05; e-mail stockholm@ domemb.se; Ambassador ABIGAÍL MEJÍA-RICART.

Ecuador: Engelbrektsgt. 13, POB 26095, 114 32 Stockholm; tel. (8) 679-60-43; fax (8) 611-55-93; e-mail suecia@embajada-ecuador.se; internet www.embajada-ecuador.se; Ambassador DIEGO STACEY MORENO.

Egypt: Strandvägen 35, POB 14230, 104 40 Stockholm; tel. (8) 662-96-03; fax (8) 661-26-64; e-mail egypt.stockholm@swipnet.se; Ambassador Dr MOHAMED EL-DORGHAMY.

Eritrea: 1st Floor, Östermalmsgt. 34, POB 26068, 100 41 Stockholm; tel. (8) 447-71-70; fax (8) 441-71-71; e-mail eritrea@eriemb.se; internet www.eriemb.se; Ambassador ARAYA DESTA.

Estonia: Tyrgt 3, POB 26076, 100 41 Stockholm; tel. (8) 5451-22-80; fax (8) 5451-22-99; e-mail info@estemb.se; internet www.estemb.se; Ambassador TOOMAS TIIVEL.

Ethiopia: Löjtaantsgt. 17, POB 10148, 100 55 Stockholm; tel. (8) 665-60-30; fax (8) 660-81-77; e-mail ethio.embassy@swipnet.se; Ambassador BIRHANU KEBEDE.

Finland: Gärdesgatan 5–11, POB 24285, 104 51 Stockholm; tel. (8) 676-67-00; fax (8) 20-74-97; internet www.finland.se; e-mail info@ finland.se; Ambassador PERTTI TORSTILA.

France: Kommendörsgt. 13, POB 5135, 102 43 Stockholm; tel. (8) 459-53-00; fax (8) 459-53-13; internet www.ambafrance.se; Ambassador PATRICK IMHAUS.

Germany: Skarpögt. 9, POB 27832, 115 93 Stockholm; tel. (8) 670-15-00; fax (8) 670-15-72; internet www.german-embassy.se; Ambassador Dr BERND VON WALDOW.

Greece: Riddargt. 60, POB 24075, 104 51 Stockholm; tel. (8) 545-660-10; fax (8) 660-54-70; e-mail gremb.stockholm@beta.telenordia .se; Ambassador NICOLAOS COUNINIOTIS.

Guatemala: Wittstocksgt. 30, 115 27 Stockholm; tel. (8) 660-52-29; fax (8) 660-42-29; e-mail svecia@guaemb.se; internet www .guatemalaembassy.com; Ambassador MIGUEL ANGEL VELASCO BITZOL.

Honduras: Stjärnvägen 2, 7th Floor, 181 34 Lidingö; tel. (8) 731-50-84; fax (8) 636-99-83; e-mail embahon@telia.com; internet www .hondurasembassy.se; Ambassador IVÁN ROMERO-MARTÍNEZ.

Hungary: Dag Hammarskjölds Väg 10, POB 24125, 104 51 Stockholm; tel. (8) 661-67-62; fax (8) 660-29-59; e-mail secretariat@ huembsto.se; internet www.huembsto.se; Ambassador Dr LÁSZLÓ SZŐKE.

Iceland: Kommendörsgt. 35, 114 58 Stockholm; tel. (8) 442-83-00; fax (8) 660-74-23; e-mail icemb.stock@utn.strj.is; internet www .island.se; Ambassador SVAVAR GESTSSON.

India: Adolf Fredriks Kyrkogt. 12, POB 1340, 111 83 Stockholm; tel. (8) 10-70-08; fax (8) 24-85-05; e-mail information@indembassy.se; internet www.indianembassy.se; Ambassador CHITRA NARAYANAN.

Indonesia: Sysslomansgt. 18/I, 112 41 Stockholm; POB 12520, 102 29 Stockholm; tel. (8) 650-44-70; fax (8) 650-87-50; e-mail kbri@ indonesiskaambassaden.se; Ambassador TJAHJONO.

Iran: Västra Yttringe Gård, Elfviksvägen, POB 6031, 181 06 Lidingö; tel. (8) 765-08-19; fax (8) 765-31-19; Ambassador MAHMOOD BAYAT.

Iraq: Baldersgt. 6A, POB 26031, 100 41 Stockholm; tel. (8) 411-44-43; fax (8) 796-83-66; Chargé d'affaires a.i. QASSIM H. J. AL-ZUHAIRI.

Ireland: Östermalmsgt. 97, POB 10326, 100 55 Stockholm; tel. (8) 661-80-05; fax (8) 660-13-53; e-mail irish.embassy@swipnet.se; Ambassador PATRICK A. MCCABE.

Israel: Torstenssonsgt. 4, POB 14006, 104 40 Stockholm; tel. (8) 663-04-35; fax (8) 662-53-01; e-mail stockholm@israel.org; internet stockholm.mfa.gov.il; Ambassador ZVI MAZEL.

Italy: Oakhill, Djurgården, 115 21 Stockholm; tel. (8) 54-56-71-04; fax (8) 660-05-05; e-mail itemb@itemb.se; internet www.itemb.se; Ambassador GIULIO CESARE VINCI GIGLIUCCI.

Japan: Gärdesgt. 10, 115 27 Stockholm; tel. (8) 663-04-40; fax (8) 661-88-20; Ambassador TOMIO UCHIDA.

Kenya: 2nd Floor, Birger Jarlsgt. 37, POB 7694, 103 95 Stockholm; tel. (8) 21-83-00; fax (8) 20-92-61; Ambassador MICHAEL ARAP SERGON.

Korea, Democratic People's Republic: Norra Kungsvägen 39, 181 31 Lidingö; tel. (8) 767-38-36; fax (8) 767-38-35; Ambassador SON MU SIN.

Korea, Republic: POB 27237, 102 53 Stockholm; tel. (8) 660-03-30; fax (8) 660-28-18; Ambassador KEUM JUNG-HO.

Kuwait: Banérgt. 37, POB 10030, 100 55 Stockholm; tel. (8) 450-99-80; fax (8) 450-99-55; Chargé d'affaires a.i. FAISAL BADER M. AL-SABAH.

Laos: Badstrandsvägen 11, POB 34050, 112 65 Stockholm; tel. (8) 618-20-10; fax (8) 618-20-01; e-mail embassy.laos@stockholm.mail.telia.com; Ambassador PHOU RASPHONE.

Latvia: Odengt. 5, POB 19167, 104 32 Stockholm; tel. (8) 700-63-00; fax (8) 14-01-51; e-mail embassy.sweden@mfa.gov.lv; Ambassador ARTIS BERTULIS.

Lebanon: Kommendörsgt. 35, POB 5360, 102 49 Stockholm; tel. (8) 665-19-65; fax (8) 662-68-24; Ambassador MOUNIR TALHOUK.

Libya (People's Bureau): Valhallavägen 74, POB 10133, 100 55 Stockholm; tel. (8) 14-34-35; fax (8) 10-43-80; Chargé d'affaires a.i. ABDUSALAM B. S. TOUMI.

Lithuania: Grevgt. 5, 114 53 Stockholm; tel. (8) 667-54-55; fax (8) 667-54-56; e-mail litemb@telia.com; internet se.urm.lt; Ambassador PETRAS ZAPOLSKAS.

Macedonia, former Yugoslav republic: Riddargt. 35, POB 10128, 100 55 Stockholm; tel. (8) 661-18-30; fax (8) 661-03-25; e-mail macedonian.embassy@telia.com; Ambassador MARTIN TRENEVSKI.

Malaysia: Karlavägen 37, POB 26053, 100 41 Stockholm; tel. (8) 791-76-90; fax (8) 791-87-60; e-mail mwstholm@algonet.se; Ambassador Dato' SYEED SULTAN SENI PAKIR.

Mexico: Grevgt. 3, 114 53 Stockholm; tel. (8) 663-51-70; fax (8) 663-24-20; e-mail embamex@telia.com; internet www.sre.gob.mx/suecia; Ambassador JORGE CASTRO VALLE KUEHNE.

Morocco: Kungsholmstorg 16, 112 21 Stockholm; tel. (8) 54-55-11-30; fax (8) 54-55-11-39; e-mail sifamastock@stockholm.mail.telia.com; Ambassador FARIDA JAÏDI.

Mozambique: Sturegt. 46, POB 5801, 102 48 Stockholm; tel. (8) 666-03-50; fax (8) 663-67-29; e-mail info@embassymozambique.se; Ambassador Dr EDUARDO KOLOMA.

Namibia: POB 19151, 104 32 Stockholm; tel. (8) 612-77-88; fax (8) 612-66-55; e-mail namibian.embassy@swipnet.se; internet www.embassyofnamibia; Ambassador WILBARD MANIQUE SHIHEPO HELLAO.

Netherlands: Götgt. 16A, POB 15048, 104 65 Stockholm; tel. (8) 55-69-93-00; fax (8) 55-69-33-11; e-mail nlgovsto@swipnet.se; Ambassador R. S. BEKINK.

Nicaragua: 6th Floor, Sandhamnsgt. 40, 115 28 Stockholm; tel. (8) 667-18-57; fax (8) 662-41-60; e-mail embajada.nicaragua@swipnet.se; Ambassador ALVARO MONTENEGRO MALLONA.

Nigeria: Tyrgt. 8, POB 628, 101 32 Stockholm; tel. (8) 24-63-90; fax (8) 24-63-98; e-mail nigerian.embassy@swipnet.se; Ambassador GEORGE O. AJONYE.

Norway: Skarpögt. 4, POB 27829, 115 27 Stockholm; tel. (8) 665-63-40; e-mail info@norgesambassad.se; internet www.norgesambassad.se; fax (8) 782-98-99; Ambassador EIRIK GLENNE.

Pakistan: 14th Floor, Sergels Torg 12, 111 57 Stockholm; tel. (8) 20-33-00; fax (8) 24-92-33; Chargé d'affaires a.i. MUHAMMAD KHALEEL KHAN.

Panama: Östermalmsgt. 59, 114 50 Stockholm; POB 55547, 102 04 Stockholm; tel. (8) 662-89-81; fax (8) 663-04-07; Ambassador EDUARDO SANTOS CARRASQUILLA LOZANO.

Peru: Brunnsgt. 21B, 111 38 Stockholm; tel. (8) 440-87-40; fax (8) 20-55-92; e-mail emba.perusuec@telia.com; internet www.peruvian-embassy.se; Ambassador Dr EDUARDO LLOSA LARRABURE.

Philippines: Skeppsbron 20, POB 2219, 103 15 Stockholm; tel. (8) 23-56-65; fax (8) 14-07-14; e-mail ph@swipnet.se; Ambassador ERLINDA F. BASILIO.

Poland: Karlavägen 35, 114 31 Stockholm; tel. (8) 411-41-32; fax (8) 10-10-69; e-mail info.polen@swipnet.se; internet www.polemb.se; Ambassador RYSZARD MICHAŁ CZARNY.

Portugal: POB 10194, 100 55 Stockholm; tel. (8) 662-60-28; fax (8) 662-53-29; e-mail portugal@chello.se; Ambassador JOÃO PEDRO ZANATTI.

Romania: Östermalmsgt. 36, POB 26043, 100 41 Stockholm; tel. (8) 10-86-03; fax (8) 21-01-42; e-mail info@romanianembassy.se; Ambassador ADRIAN S. CONSTANTINESCU.

Russia: Gjörwellsgt. 31, 112 60 Stockholm; tel. (8) 13-04-41; fax (8) 618-27-03; e-mail rusembsw@algonet.se; internet www.ryssland.se; Ambassador NIKOLAY I. SADCHIKOV.

Saudi Arabia: Sköldungagt. 5, POB 26073, 100 41 Stockholm; tel. (8) 23-88-00; fax (8) 796-99-56; Chargé d'affaires a.i. BADR O. BAKHSH.

Serbia and Montenegro: Valhallavägen 70, POB 26209, 100 41 Stockholm; tel. (8) 21-84-36; fax (8) 21-84-95; e-mail yuemb@telia.com; Chargé d'affaires a.i. DEJAN VASILJEVIĆ.

Slovakia: 3rd Floor, Arsenalsgt. 2, POB 7183, 103 88 Stockholm; tel. (8) 611-90-05; fax (8) 611-90-02; internet www.slovakemb.se; Ambassador TEODORA CHMELOVA.

Slovenia: 1st Floor, Styrmansgt. 4, 114 54 Stockholm; tel. (8) 662-94-36; fax (8) 662-92-74; Ambassador DARJA BAUDA KURET.

South Africa: Linnégt. 76, 115 23 Stockholm; tel. (8) 24-39-50; fax (8) 660-71-36; e-mail saemb.swe@telia.com; internet www.southafricanemb.se; Ambassador SONTO KUDJOE.

Spain: POB 10295, 100 55 Stockholm; tel. (8) 667-94-30; fax (8) 663-79-65; Ambassador CRISTINA BARRIOS ALMAZOR.

Sri Lanka: Strandvägen 39, POB 24055, 104 50 Stockholm; tel. (8) 663-65-23; fax (8) 660-00-89; e-mail sl.emb@stockholm.mail.telia.com; Ambassador SARALA M. FERNANDO.

Sudan: Birger Jarlsgt. 36, 2nd Floor, POB 26142, 100 41 Stockholm; tel. (8) 611-77-80; fax (8) 611-77-82; Ambassador SASWAN ABDEL-MAGIED ABDELRAHEEM.

Switzerland: Birger Jarlsgt. 64, POB 26143, 100 41 Stockholm; tel. (8) 676-79-00; fax (8) 21-15-04; e-mail vertretung@sto.rep.admin.ch; Ambassador SVEN BEAT MEILI.

Syria: Narvavägen 32, 115 22 Stockholm; tel. (8) 660-88-10; fax (8) 660-88-05; Chargé d'affaires a.i. SAMIR AL-KASSIR.

Tanzania: Wallingatan 11, POB 7255, 103 89 Stockholm; tel. (8) 503-206-01; fax (8) 503-206-02; e-mail balozi@tanemb.se; Ambassador JAMES LUTA KATEKA.

Thailand: Floragt. 3, POB 26220, 100 40 Stockholm; tel. (8) 791-73-40; fax (8) 791-73-51; e-mail info@thaiembassy.se; internet www.thaiembassy.se; Ambassador POKSAK NILUBOL.

Tunisia: Narvavägen 32, 115 22 Stockholm; tel. (8) 5458-55-20; fax (8) 662-19-75; e-mail tunamb@swipnet.se; Ambassador LAZHAR BOUOUNY.

Turkey: Dag Hammarskjölds Väg 20, 115 27 Stockholm; tel. (8) 23-08-40; fax (8) 663-55-14; e-mail turkemb@turkemb.se; Ambassador SELIM KUNERALP.

Ukraine: Stjärnvägen 2A, 181 34 Lidingö; tel. (8) 731-76-90; fax (8) 731-56-90; e-mail ukraina.embassy@ukrainaemb.se; internet www.ukrainaemb.se; Ambassador OLEXANDER S. SLIPCHENKO.

United Kingdom: Skarpög. 6–8, POB 27819, 115 93 Stockholm; tel. (8) 671-30-00; fax (8) 671-99-89; internet www.britishembassy.com; Ambassador JOHN GRANT.

USA: Dag Hammarskjölds Väg 31, 115 89 Stockholm; tel. (8) 783-53-00; fax (8) 661-19-64; internet www.usemb.se; Ambassador CHARLES A. HEIMBOLD, Jr.

Uruguay: POB 10114, 100 55 Stockholm; tel. (8) 660-31-96; fax (8) 665-31-66; e-mail urustoc@uruemb.se; Ambassador JULIO MOREIRA.

Venezuela: Engelbrektsgt. 35B, POB 26012, 100 41 Stockholm; tel. (8) 411-09-96; fax (8) 21-31-00; Chargé d'affaires a.i. LEONARDO VILLALBA PALACIOS.

Viet Nam: Örby Slottsväg 26, 125 71 Älvsjö; tel. (8) 5562-10-70; fax (8) 5562-10-80; e-mail jdh642o@tninet.se; internet www.vietnamemb.se; Ambassador NGUYEN VAN NAM.

Zambia: Engelbrektsgt. 7, POB 26013, 100 41 Stockholm; tel. (8) 679-90-40; fax (8) 679-68-50; e-mail info@zambiaembassy.se; internet www.zambiaembassy.se; Ambassador JOSEPHINE S. KAFWEMBE.

Zimbabwe: Herserudsvägen 5A, 7th Floor, POB 3253, 103 65 Stockholm; tel. (8) 765-53-80; fax (8) 21-91-32; e-mail mbuya@stockholm.mail.telia.com; Ambassador M. MUBI.

Judicial System

The judiciary and the executive are separate. Judges are appointed by the Government. A judge can be removed by an authority other than a court, but may, in such an event, request a judicial trial of the decision.

To supervise the courts in administrative matters, there is a central authority, the Domstolsverket, in Jönköping. This authority has no control over the judicial process, in which the court is independent even of the legislature and Government.

There are state officers who exercise control over the judiciary as well as the administrative authorities. The Justitiekansler (Chancellor of Justice or Attorney-General) and the four Justitieombudsmän supervise the courts and the general administration including the armed forces. The Justitiekansler performs his functions on behalf of the Government. The Justitieombudsmän are appointed by and act on behalf of the legislature.

Justitiekansler: HANS REGNER.

SUPREME COURT

The Supreme Court in Stockholm (Högsta domstolen), consisting of 16 members, is the Court of Highest Instance. The Court works in three chambers, each of which is duly constituted of five members. Certain cases are decided by full session of the Court. There are also special divisions with three members (or, in simple cases, one member) which decide whether the Court is to consider a case.

Chairman of the Supreme Court: A. KNUTSSON.

APPELLATE COURTS

The Court of Appeal, the Court of Second Instance, consists of a president, judges of appeal and associate judges of appeal. The work is apportioned between various divisions, each of which has five or six members. In criminal cases the bench consists of three professional judges and two lay assessors; in petty and civil cases there are three professional judges only. There are six Courts of Appeal (hovrätt).

President of the Court of Appeal (Stockholm): JOHAN HIRSCHFELDT.

President of the Court of Appeal (Jönköping): LARS ÅHLÉN.

President of the Court of Appeal (Malmö): B. BROOMÉ.

President of the Court of Appeal (Göteborg): O. LINDH.

President of the Court of Appeal (Sundsvall): H. WINBERG.

President of the Court of Appeal (Umeå): ANNA-KARIN LUNDIN.

DISTRICT COURTS

The District Court acts as a Court of First Instance in both civil and criminal cases. In January 1998 there were 96 District Courts (tingsrätt). In criminal cases the court is composed of a presiding professional judge and three or, in serious cases, five lay assessors; in petty cases the court consists of the professional judge only. In civil cases the court is ordinarily composed of three professional judges; however, preparatory sessions are conducted by one professional judge. In family law cases, the court is composed of a professional judge and three lay assessors. The lay assessors are elected for a period of four years (during which they are on duty for about 10 days a year). They act as members of the bench and should consequently be distinguished from the jurors of other countries. In certain types of case technical experts may sit alongside the judges.

ADMINISTRATIVE COURTS

In each of the 23 administrative districts of the country there is a County Administrative Court (länsrätten). This Court handles appeal cases concerning the assessment of social security and welfare. The bench ordinarily consists of a professional judge and three lay assessors, although in simple cases a professional judge may preside alone.

Appeals against decisions by the County Administrative Courts may be made to Administrative Courts of Appeal (kammarrätter) consisting of a president, judges of appeal and associate judges of appeal. The courts work in divisions, each of which normally has six members. The bench consists of at least three and not more than four judges. In certain cases there are, however, three professional judges and two lay assessors. There are four Administrative Courts of Appeal.

The Supreme Administrative Court of Sweden (Regeringsrätten) in Stockholm, consisting of 14 members, is the Court of Highest Instance in Administrative cases. The composition of the Court is governed by rules very similar to those that apply to the Supreme Court.

Chairman of the Supreme Administrative Court: GUNNAR BJÖRNE.

President of the Administrative Court of Appeal (Stockholm): R. LAURÉN.

President of the Administrative Court of Appeal (Göteborg): ELISABETH PALM.

President of the Administrative Court of Appeal (Sundsvall): B. ORRHEDE.

President of the Administrative Court of Appeal (Jönköping): J. FRANCKE.

SPECIAL COURTS

Special courts exist for certain categories of cases, e.g. fastighetsdomstolar (real estate courts) for cases concerning real estate.

OMBUDSMEN

The post of Justitieombudsman was created in 1800 to supervise the manner in which judges, government officials and other civil servants observe the laws, and to prosecute those who act illegally, misuse their position or neglect their duties. The Ombudsman is allowed access to all documents and information and has the right to be present at the considerations of the courts and other authorities. Government ministers in Sweden are not subject to supervision by the Ombudsman. The term of office is four years.

Ombudsmen: CLAES EKLUNDH, SUSANNE KNÖÖS, JAN PENNLÖV, RUNE LAVIN.

Religion

The Svenska Kyrkan (Church of Sweden) was traditionally constitutionally linked to the State. In 1996, however, a government proposal for a loosening of the ties between the Church and the State from the year 2000 was approved by both the Riksdag and the General Synod of the Church.

CHRISTIANITY

Sveriges Kristna Råd (Christian Council of Sweden): 172 99 Sundbyberg; tel. (8) 453-68-00; fax (8) 453-68-29; e-mail info@skr .org; internet www.skr.org; f. 1993; 26 mem. churches; Gen. Sec. THORD-OVE THORDSON.

Church of Sweden

**Svenska Kyrkan
(Church of Sweden)**

Kyrkans Hus, Sysslomansgt. 4, 751 70 Uppsala; tel. (18) 16-95-00; fax (18) 16-96-40; e-mail info@svenskakyrkan.se; internet www .svenskakyrkan.se.

Of the Evangelical Lutheran faith. About 86.0% of the population are mems; 13 dioceses, 2,544 parishes, 3,870 active clergy (including missionaries in the mission fields); the Archbishop of Uppsala is head of the Church.

Archbishop of Uppsala: Most Rev. KARL GUSTAF HAMMAR, 751 70 Uppsala; tel. (18) 16-95-00; fax (18) 16-96-25.

Evangeliska Fosterlands-Stiftelsen (Swedish Evangelical Mission): Sysslomansgt. 4, 751 70 Uppsala; tel. (18) 16-98-00; fax (18) 16-98-01; e-mail efs@efs.svenskakyrkan.se; internet www.efs.nu; f. 1856; an independent mission organization within the Church of Sweden; 17,994 mems; Chair. RAY RAWALL; Mission Dir ANDERS SJÖBERG.

Other Protestant Churches

Eesti Evangeeliumi Luteri Usu Kirik (Estonian Evangelical Lutheran Church): POB 450 74, 104 30 Stockholm 45; tel. (8) 20-69-78; 14,000 mems; Archbishop UDO PETERSOO; Gen. Sec. IVAR NIPPAK.

Metodistkyrkan i Sverige (United Methodist Church): 172 99 Sundbyberg; tel. (8) 453-69-90; fax (8) 453-69-95; e-mail info@ metodistkyrkan.se; internet www.metodistkyrkan.se; f. 1868; 3,565 mems; Bishop ØYSTEIN OLSEN; Pres. of Conference Board BIMBI OLLBERG.

Sjundedags Adventistsamfundet (Seventh-day Adventists): POB 536, 101 30 Stockholm; tel. (8) 14-03-65; fax (8) 545–29–770; e-mail per.bolling@adventist.se; internet www.adventist.se; f. 1880; 2,900 mems; Pres. BJORN OTTESEN; Sec. PER BOLLING.

Svenska Baptistsamfundet (Baptist Union of Sweden): 3rd Floor, Ekensbergsvägen 128, 172 69 Sundbyberg; tel. (8) 5648-27-00; fax (8) 5648-27-27; e-mail baptist@baptist.se; f. 1848; 270 churches, 18,631 mems (1997); Pres. Rev. SÖREN CARLSVÄRD; Gen. Sec. Rev. SVEN LINDSTRÖM.

Svenska Missionsförbundet (Mission Covenant Church of Sweden): Tegnérgt. 8, POB 6302, 113 81 Stockholm; tel. (8) 15-18-30; fax (8) 674-07-93; e-mail info@smf.se; internet www.smf.se; f. 1878; 67,041 mems; Gen. Sec. and Pres. KRISTER ANDERSSON; Chair. of Board ULF HÅLLMARKER.

The Roman Catholic Church

For ecclesiastical purposes, Sweden comprises the single diocese of Stockholm, directly responsible to the Holy See. At 31 December 2000 there were 95,291 adherents in the country, representing 1.1% of the total population.

Scandinavian Bishops' Conference

Conferentia Episcopalis Scandiae, Trollbärsvägen 16, 426 55 Västra Frölunda; tel. (31) 709-64-87; fax (31) 709-64-88; e-mail nbk .gensekr@swipnet.se; internet www.katolskakyrkan.se/nbk.

f. 1960; new statutes approved 2000; covers Sweden, Norway, Denmark, Finland and Iceland; Pres. Mgr GERHARD SCHWENZER (Bishop of Oslo); Sec.-Gen. ANGELA CORSTEN.

Bishop of Stockholm: Most Rev. ANDERS ARBORELIUS, Götgt. 68, POB 4114, 102 62 Stockholm; tel. (8) 462-66-00; fax (8) 702-05-55; e-mail biskop@katolskakyrkan.se.

Other Denominations

Other Christian Churches include the Pentecostal Movement (with 90,815 mems in 1997), the Orthodox Churches of the Greeks, Romanians, Russians, Serbians and Finnish (together numbering 97,000 mems in 1994), the Swedish Alliance Missionary Society (12,895 mems in 1997), the Jehovah's Witnesses (33,000 mems in 1994), and the Salvation Army (25,531 mems in 1997).

ISLAM

In 1994 there were more than 100,000 Muslims in Sweden.

Islamiska Radet i Sverige (The Islamic Council of Sweden—IRIS): POB 3053, 14503 Norsborg; tel. (8) 531-70795; fax (8) 531-70665; f. 1986.

Förenade Islamiska Församlingar i Sverge (FIFS): Götgt. 103A, 116 62 Stockholm; tel. (8) 642-16-53; fax (8) 642-34-20.

Islamiska Kulturcenterunionen i Sverige (Union of the Islamic Cultural Centres in Sweden—IKUS): POB 3053, 145 03 Norsborg; tel. (8) 5317-07-95; fax (8) 5317-06-65; f. 1984.

Sveriges Muslimska Förbund (SMUF): Stockholms Moske, Kapellgränd 10, 116 25 Stockholm; tel. and fax (8) 643-10-04; e-mail aldebe@arabia.com.

JUDAISM

In 1994 there were between 15,000 and 20,000 Jews living in Sweden. The largest Jewish community is in Stockholm.

Jewish Community in Stockholm: Wahrendorffsgt. 3B, POB 7427, 103 91 Stockholm; tel. (8) 587-858-00; fax (8) 587-858-58; e-mail info@jf-stockholm.org; internet www.jf-stockholm.org; c. 5,000 mems; Chief Rabbi PHILIP SPECTRE.

BAHÁ'Í FAITH

National Spiritual Assembly: Solhagavägen 11, 163 52 Spånga; tel. (8) 21-51-90; fax (8) 21-51-91; e-mail secretariat@bahai.se; internet www.bahai.se.

The Press

Press freedom in Sweden dates from a law of 1766. The 1949 Freedom of the Press Act, a fundamental law embodying the whole of the press legislation in the Constitution, guarantees the Press's right to print and disseminate ideas; protects those supplying information by forbidding editors to disclose sources under any circumstances; authorizes all public documents to be publicly available, official secrets being the only exception; and contains provision for defamation. Press offences are to be referred to common law, and all cases against the Press must be heard by jury.

In 1916 the Press Council was founded by press organizations to monitor ethical matters within the Press. Lacking judicial status, it has powers to rehabilitate persons wronged by the Press who refuse to apply to courts of law. Its judgments are widely published and highly respected.

In 1969 the office of Press Ombudsman was established to supervise adherence to ethical standards. Public complaints shall be directed to the Press Ombudsman, who is also entitled to act on his own initiative. He may dismiss a complaint if unfounded, or if the newspaper agrees to publish a retraction or rectification acceptable to the complainant. When he finds that the grievance is of a more serious nature, he will file a complaint with the Press Council, which will then publish a statement acquitting or criticizing the newspaper. The findings of the Council are published in the newspaper concerned.

The dominating influence of the few major dailies is largely confined to Stockholm, the provinces having a strong Press of their own. The major dailies are: *Expressen, Dagens Nyheter, Aftonbladet,* *Svenska Dagbladet* (all Stockholm), *Göteborgs-Posten* (Göteborg), *Sydsvenska Dagbladet, Arbetet Nyheterna* (Malmö). In 2000 there were an estimated 118 newspapers (appearing at least twice a week) with a combined circulation of 3.9m.

The two principal magazine publishers in Sweden are the Bonnier group (also a large book publisher and the majority shareholder in the newspapers *Dagens Nyheter, Expressen* and *Sydsvenska Dagbladet*) and the Aller company. Four other companies produce most of the remainder of Sweden's magazine circulation. The most popular weekly periodicals include the family magazines *Året Runt, Hemmets Veckotidning, Allers* and *Hemmets Journal*, and the home and household magazine *ICAKuriren. Vi* caters for serious cultural and political discussion and *Bonniers Litterära Magasin* specializes in literary topics. In 1997 there were some 369 weekly newspapers and magazines in Sweden.

PRINCIPAL NEWSPAPERS

Newspapers with a circulation exceeding 15,000 are listed below.

Ängelholm

Nordvästra Skånes Tidningar: 262 83 Ängelholm; tel. (431) 84-000; fax (431) 26-177; f. 1847; daily; Conservative; Editor-in-Chief BENNIE OHLSSON; circ. 42,400 (1996).

Borås

Borås Tidning: 501 85 Borås; tel. (33) 700-07-00; fax (33) 10-14-36; f. 1826; morning; Conservative; Editor JAN ÖJMERTZ; circ. 53,000 (2001).

Eksjö

Smålands-Tidningen: POB 261, 575 23 Eksjö; tel. (381) 13-200; fax (381) 17-145; f. 1899; morning; independent; Editor BENGT WENDLE; circ. 18,700 (1996).

Eskilstuna

Eskilstuna-Kuriren Strengnäs Tidning: POB 120, 631 02 Eskilstuna; tel. (16) 15-60-00; fax (16) 51-63-04; e-mail ek@ekuriren.se; internet www.ekuriren.se; f. 1890; morning; Liberal; Editors PEO WÄRRING, JERKER NORIN; circ. 33,000 (2002).

Falkenberg

Hallands Nyheter: 311 81 Falkenberg; tel. (346) 29-000; fax (346) 29-115; e-mail administration@hn.se; internet www.hn.se; f. 1905; morning; Centre; Editor KRISTIAN ALM; circ. 31,000 (2001).

Falun

Dala-Demokraten: POB 825, 791 29 Falun; tel. (23) 47-500; fax (23) 20-668; f. 1917; morning; Social Democrat; Editor WILLY BERGSTRÖM; circ. 24,400 (1996).

Falu-Kuriren: POB 265, 791 26 Falun; tel. (23) 93-500; fax (23) 12-073; e-mail red@falukuriren.se; internet www.falukuriren.se; f. 1894; morning; Liberal; Editor CHRISTER GRUHS; circ. 29,400 (1996).

Gävle

Arbetarbladet: POB 287, 801 04 Gävle; tel. (26) 15-93-00; fax (26) 12-14-06; f. 1902; morning; Social Democrat; Editor KENNET LUTTI; circ. 29,100 (1996).

Gefle Dagblad: POB 367, 801 05 Gävle; tel. (26) 15-95-00; fax (26) 15-97-00; f. 1895; morning; Liberal; Editor ROBERT ROSÉN; circ. 30,800 (1996).

Göteborg
(Gothenburg)

Göteborgs-Posten: Polhemsplatsen 5, 405 02 Göteborg; tel. (31) 62-40-00; fax (31) 62-45-85; e-mail redaktion@gp.se; internet www .gp.se; f. 1858; morning; Liberal; Editor-in-Chief JONATHAN FALCK; circ. 264,600 (2000).

Halmstad

Hallandsposten: 301 81 Halmstad; tel. (35) 14-75-00; fax (35) 14-76-88; f. 1850; morning; Liberal; Editor SVERKER EMANUELSSON; circ. 32,200 (1996).

Härnösand

Nya Norrland: POB 120, 871 23 Härnösand; tel. (611) 88-800; fax (611) 17-247; f. 1907; morning; Social Democrat; Editor-in-Chief PER ÅHLSTRÖM; circ. 19,400 (1996).

Directory

Hässleholm

Norra Skåne: 281 81 Hässleholm; tel. (451) 74-50-00; fax (451) 74-50-32; e-mail chefred@nsk.se; internet www.nsk.se; f. 1899; morning; Centre; Editor BILLY BENGTSSON; circ. 21,800 (2001).

Helsingborg

Helsingborgs Dagblad: POB 822, 251 08 Helsingborg; tel. (42) 17-50-00; fax (42) 17-50-02; f. 1867; morning; independent; Editor-in-Chief SVEN-ÅKE OLOFSSON; circ. 49,500 (1996).

Hudiksvall

Hudiksvalls Tidning: POB 1201, 824 15 Hudiksvall; tel. (650) 355-00; fax (650) 355-60; e-mail redaktion@ht.se; internet www.ht.se; f. 1909; includes *Hälsinglands Tidning*; morning; Centre; Man. Dir RUBEN JACOBSSON; Editor JÖRGEN BENGTSON; circ. 17,600 (1998).

Jönköping

Jönköpings-Posten/Smålands Allehanda: 551 80 Jönköping; tel. (36) 30-40-50; fax (36) 12-61-11; f. 1865; morning; independent; Editor STIG FREDRIKSSON; circ. 42,900 (1996).

Kalmar

Barometern med Oskarshamns-Tidningen: 391 88 Kalmar; tel. (480) 59-100; fax (480) 59-131; f. 1841; morning; Conservative; Editor GUNILLA ANDREASSON; circ. 47,400 (1999).

Karlskrona

Blekinge Läns Tidning: 371 89 Karlskrona; tel. (455) 77-000; fax (455) 82-170; internet www.blt.se; f. 1869; morning; Liberal; Editor-in-Chief KERSTIN JOHANSSON; circ. 37,000 (2000).

Sydöstra Sveriges Dagblad: Landbrogt. 17, 371 88 Karlskrona; tel. (455) 19-000; fax (455) 82-237; f. 1903; morning; Social Democrat; Editor ANDERS HAGQUIST; circ. 18,000 (1998).

Karlstad

Nya Wermlands-Tidningen: POB 28, 651 02 Karlstad; tel. (54) 19-90-00; fax (54) 19-92-67; f. 1836; morning; Conservative; Editor STAFFAN ANDER; circ. 59,500 (1996).

Värmlands Folkblad: POB 67, 651 03 Karlstad; tel. (54) 17-55-06; fax (54) 15-16-59; f. 1918; morning; Social Democrat; Editor ROLF H. JANSSON; circ. 25,300 (1996).

Kristianstad

Kristianstadsbladet: 291 84 Kristianstad; tel. (44) 18-55-00; fax (44) 21-17-01; e-mail kb@kristianstadsbladet.se; internet www.kristianstadsbladet.se; f. 1856; morning; Liberal; Man. Dir H. INGE GYLLIN; Editor PETER MELIN; circ. 30,800 (2001).

Lidköping

Nya Läns-Tidningen: 531 81 Lidköping; tel. (510) 89-700; fax (510) 89-796; e-mail post@nlt.se; f. 1903; morning; 3 a week; Liberal; Editor LENNART HÖRLING; circ. 26,300.

Linköping

Östgöta Correspondenten: 581 89 Linköping; tel. (13) 28-00-00; fax (13) 28-03-24; e-mail nyhet@corren.se; internet www.corren.se; f. 1838; morning; Liberal; Editor GUNILLA BEJBRO-HÖGFELDT; circ. 66,100 (2002).

Luleå

Norrbottens-Kuriren: 971 81 Luleå; tel. (920) 37-500; fax (920) 67-107; f. 1861; morning; Conservative; Editor (vacant); circ. 30,700 (1996).

Norrländska Socialdemokraten: 971 83 Luleå; tel. (920) 36-000; fax (920) 36-279; f. 1919; morning; Social Democrat; Editor LENNART HÅKANSSON; circ. 39,600 (1996).

Malmö

Arbetet Nyheterna: Malmö; tel. (40) 20-50-00; fax (40) 611-18-68; e-mail centralred@arbetet.se; internet www.arbetet.se; f. 1887; morning; Social Democrat; Editor BO BERNHARDSSON; circ. 54,600 (1998).

Kvällsposten: 205 26 Malmö; tel. (40) 28-16-00; fax (40) 93-92-24; f. 1990; evening; Liberal; Editor LARS KLINT; circ. 62,900.

Skånska Dagbladet: Östergt. 11, POB 165, 201 21 Malmö; tel. (40) 660-55-00; fax (40) 97-47-70; f. 1888; morning; Centre; Editor JAN A. JOHANSSON; circ. 29,400 (1996).

Sydsvenska Dagbladet: 205 05 Malmö; tel. (40) 28-12-00; fax (40) 93-54-75; e-mail sydsvenskan@sydsvenskan.se; internet sydsvenskan.se; f. 1848; morning; Liberal independent; Editors PER T. OHLSSON, HANS MANSON; circ. 138,000 (2001).

Norrköping

Norrköpings Tidningar: 601 83 Norrköping; tel. (11) 20-00-00; fax (11) 20-02-40; e-mail chefred@nt.se; internet www.nt.se; f. 1758; morning; Conservative; Editor KARL-ÅKE BREDENBERG; circ. 49,900 (2000).

Nyköping

Södermanlands Nyheter: 611 79 Nyköping; tel. (155) 76-700; fax (155) 21-83-50; e-mail redaktionen@sn.se; internet www.sn.se; f. 1893; morning; Centre; Editor LARS J. ERIKSSON; circ. 23,900 (1998).

Örebro

Nerikes Allehanda: 701 92 Örebro; tel. (19) 15-50-00; fax (19) 12-03-83; e-mail vd@nerikes.se; internet www.nerikes.se; f. 1843; morning; Liberal; Editor KRISTER LINNER; circ. 68,000 (1999).

Örnsköldsvik

Örnsköldsviks Allehanda: POB 110, 891 23 Örnsköldsvik; tel. (660) 29-50-00; fax (660) 15-064; e-mail lars.nordstrom@allehanda.se; f. 1843; morning; Liberal; Editor LARS NORDSTRÖM; circ. 20,800 (2001).

Östersund

Länstidningen: 831 89 Östersund; tel. (63) 15-55-00; fax (63) 15-55-95; f. 1924; morning; Social Democrat; Editors PETER SWEDENMARK, CHRISTER SJÖSTRÖM; circ. 25,800 (1996).

Östersunds-Posten: POB 720, 831 28 Östersund; tel. (63) 16-16-00; fax (63) 10-58-02; f. 1877; morning; Centre; Editors BOSSE SVENSSON, HÅKAN LARSSON; circ. 27,100 (1996).

Piteå

Piteå-Tidningen: POB 193, 941 24 Piteå; tel. (911) 64-500; fax (911) 64-650; f. 1915; morning; Social Democrat; Editor OLOV CARLSSON; circ. 17,600 (1996).

Skara

Skaraborgs Läns Tidning: POB 214, 532 23 Skara; tel. (511) 13-010; fax (511) 18-815; f. 1884; morning; Liberal; Editor HANS OLOFSSON; circ. 17,100 (1995).

Skellefteå

Norra Västerbotten: POB 58, 931 21 Skellefteå; tel. (910) 57-700; fax (910) 57-875; e-mail redaktionsavderlning@norran.se; internet www.norran.se; f. 1910; morning; 6 days a week; Liberal; Editor OLA THEANDER; circ. 30,500 (2000).

Skövde

Skaraborgs Allehanda: POB 407, 541 28 Skövde; tel. (500) 46-75-75; fax (500) 48-05-82; f. 1884; morning; Conservative; Editor MÅNS JOHNSON; circ. 23,700 (1997).

Södertälje

Länstidningen: 151 82 Södertälje; tel. (8) 550-921-00; fax (8) 550-877-72; e-mail redaktion@lt.se; f. 1861; morning; 6 a week; Centre; Editor TORSTEN CARLSSON; circ. 18,000 (2000).

Stockholm

Aftonbladet: 105 18 Stockholm; tel. (8) 725-20-00; fax (8) 600-01-70; f. 1830; evening; Social Democrat independent; Editor-in-Chief ANDERS GERDIN; Political Editor HELLE KLEIN; circ. 381,200 (1996).

Dagen: 105 36 Stockholm; tel. (8) 619-24-00; fax (8) 619-60-51; e-mail dagen@dagengruppenab.se; f. 1945; morning; 5 a week; Christian independent; Editor DANIEL GRAHN; circ. 18,200 (1997).

Dagens Industri: 113 90 Stockholm; tel. (8) 736-50-00; fax (8) 31-19-06; f. 1976; 6 a week; business news; Editor HASSE OLSSON; circ. 110,200 (1998).

Dagens Nyheter: 105 15 Stockholm; tel. (8) 738-10-00; fax (8) 738-21-80; e-mail info@dn.se; internet www.dn.se; f. 1864; morning; independent; Man. Editor HANS BERGSTRÖM; CEO FREDRIK ÅHERMAN; circ. 369,200 (2000).

Expressen: Gjörwellsgt. 30, 105 16 Stockholm; tel. (8) 738-30-00; fax (8) 738-33-40; e-mail redaktionen@expressen.se; internet www.expressen.se; f. 1945; evening; Liberal; Editor OTTO SJÖBERG; circ. 374,200 (1996).

Svenska Dagbladet: 105 17 Stockholm; tel. (8) 13-50-00; fax (8) 13-56-80; e-mail svd@svd.se; internet www.svd.se; f. 1884; morning;

Conservative; Editor-in-Chief Hannu Olkinvora; circ. 170,000 (2000).

Sundsvall

Sundsvalls Tidning: 851 72 Sundsvall; tel. (60) 19-70-00; fax (60) 15-44-33; e-mail kjell.c@stonline.se; f. 1841; morning; Liberal; Editor Kjell Carnbro; circ. 38,600 (1997).

Trollhättan

Trollhättans Tidning: POB 54, 461 22 Trollhättan; tel. (520) 49-42-00; fax (520) 49-43-19; f. 1906; morning; 5 a week; independent; Editor Torbjörn Håkansson; circ. 17,300 (1996).

Uddevalla

Bohusläningen med Dals Dagblad: 451 83 Uddevalla; tel. (522) 99-000; fax (522) 51-18-88; f. 1878; morning; Liberal; Editor Ulf Johansson; circ. 32,400 (1996).

Umeå

Västerbottens-Kuriren: 901 70 Umeå; tel. (90) 15-10-00; fax (90) 77-00-53; e-mail info@vk.se; internet www.vk.se; f. 1900; morning; Liberal; circ. 41,500 (1998).

Uppsala

Upsala Nya Tidning: POB 36, Danmarksgt. 28, 751 03 Uppsala; tel. (18) 478-00-00; fax (18) 69-25-94; e-mail lars.nilsson@unt.se; internet www.unt.se; f. 1890; morning; Liberal; Editor Jörgen Ullenhag; circ. 62,600 (2001).

Värnamo

Värnamo Nyheter: 331 84 Värnamo; tel. (370) 30-19-56; fax (370) 493-95; e-mail sten.ake.hjerpe@varnamonyheter.se; internet www.varnamonyheter.se; f. 1917; morning; independent; Editor Sten-Åke Hjerpe; circ. 23,000 (2000).

Västerås

Vestmanlands Läns Tidning: POB 3, 721 03 Västerås; tel. (21) 19-90-00; fax (21) 19-90-60; e-mail nyheter@vlt.se; internet www.vlt.se; f. 1831; morning; Liberal; Editor Anders Ahlberg; circ. 47,600 (2000).

Växjö

Smålandsposten: 351 70 Växjö; tel. (470) 77-05-00; fax (470) 209-49; f. 1866; morning; Conservative; Editor Claes-Göran Hegnell; circ. 41,500 (1996).

Ystad

Ystads Allehanda: 271 81 Ystad; tel. (411) 64-500; fax (411) 10-194; f. 1873; morning; Liberal; Editor Staffan Björnberg; circ. 24,100 (1996).

POPULAR PERIODICALS

Allas Veckotidning: Allers Förlag AB, 205 35 Malmö; tel. (40) 38-59-00; fax (40) 38-59-64; e-mail allas@aller.se; f. 1931; weekly; family; Editor-in-Chief Tina Jansson; circ. 138,400.

Allers: 251 85 Helsingborg; tel. (42) 17-35-00; fax (42) 17-35-68; e-mail redaktionen@allers.aller.se; f. 1877; weekly; family; Editor-in-Chief Åsa Tengvall; circ. 247,400.

Allt om Mat: Sveav. 53, 105 44 Stockholm; tel. (8) 736-53-00; fax (8) 34-00-88; e-mail red@aom.bonnier.se; internet www.alltommat.se; f. 1970; 18 a year; food specialities; Editor-in-Chief Jan Holmström; circ. 125,800.

Antik och Auktion: POB 63, 272 01 Simrishamn; tel. (414) 13-770; fax (414) 13-455; f. 1978; monthly; antiques; Editor Christian Wollin; circ. 56,900.

Året Runt: 105 44 Stockholm; tel. (8) 736-52-00; fax (8) 30-49-00; f. 1946; weekly; family; Editor Arne Winerdal; circ. 243,500.

Det Bästa: Reader's Digest AB, POB 25, 164 93 Kista; tel. (8) 752-03-60; fax (8) 703-99-29; f. 1943; monthly; family; Editor-in-Chief Ulla-Stina Östberg; circ. 169,500.

Bilsport: POB 529, 371 23 Karlskrona; tel. (455) 33-53-25; fax (455) 291-75; e-mail bilsport@fabas.se; internet www.bilsport.se; f. 1962; fortnightly; motor-sport, cars; Editor-in-Chief Fredrik Sjöqvist; circ. 60,400.

Damernas Värld: 105 44 Stockholm; tel. (8) 736-52-00; fax (8) 24-46-46; e-mail red@dv.bonnier.se; f. 1940; monthly; women's; Editor Mona Johansson; circ. 87,700.

Elle: St Eriksplan 2, 113 93 Stockholm; tel. (8) 457-80-00; fax (8) 457-80-80; e-mail elle.red@hachette.se; internet www.elle.se; f. 1988; monthly; women's; Editor Hermine Coyet Ohlén; circ. 69,000.

Femina Månadens Magasin: 251 85 Helsingborg; tel. (42) 17-35-00; fax (42) 17-36-82; e-mail femina@aller.se; f. 1981; monthly; women's; Editor Lisbeth Lundahl; circ. 114,000.

Frida: Hammarby Kajväg 14, 120 30 Stockholm; tel. (8) 5874-81-00; fax (8) 5874-81-07; e-mail frida@frida.forlag.se; internet www.frida.se; fortnightly; for teenage girls; Editor-in-Chief Caroline Engvall; circ. 67,000.

Hänt Extra: POB 27704, 115 91 Stockholm; tel. (8) 679-46-00; fax (8) 679-46-77; f. 1986; weekly; family; Editors-in-Chief Jan Bard, Thord Sköldekrans; circ. 113,300.

Hänt i Veckan: POB 27704, 115 91 Stockholm; tel. (8) 679-46-00; fax (8) 679-46-33; f. 1964; weekly; family; Editor-in-Chief Sten Hedman; circ. 132,300.

Hemmets Journal: Hemmets Journal AB, 212 05 Malmö; tel. (40) 38-52-00; fax (40) 29-42-82; f. 1920; weekly; family; Editor-in-Chief Janne Walles; circ. 272,900.

Hemmets Veckotidning: Allers Förlag AB, 205 35 Malmö; tel. (40) 38-59-00; fax (40) 38-59-14; f. 1929; weekly; family; Editor Ulla Cocke; circ. 215,300.

Hus & Hem: ICA Förlaget AB, POB 6630, 113 84 Stockholm; tel. (8) 728-23-00; fax (8) 34-56-37; e-mail led.husohem@publ.ica.se; internet www.husohem.com; 12 a year; for house-owners; circ. 153,000.

ICA Kuriren: POB 6630, 5-11384 Stockholm; tel. (8) 728-23-00; fax (8) 728-23-50; f. 1942; weekly; home and household; Editor (vacant); circ. 364,300.

Kalle Anka & Co: 205 08 Malmö; tel. (40) 693-94-00; fax (40) 693-94-95; e-mail kalle.anka@egmont.se; internet www.ankeborg.egmont.se; f. 1948; weekly; comics; Editor Tord Jönsson; circ. 138,000.

Kvällsstunden: Lantmännens Tryckeriförening, POB 1080, 721 27 Västerås; tel. (21) 19-04-00; fax (21) 18-84-34; weekly; family magazine; Editor Åke Lindberg; circ. 67,900.

Må Bra: POB 27780, 115 93 Stockholm; tel. (8) 679-46-00; fax (8) 667-34-39; f. 1978; monthly; health and nutrition; Editor-in-Chief Inger Ridström; circ. 97,900.

Månads Journalen: 105 44 Stockholm; tel. (8) 736-53-00; fax (8) 32-78-40; f. 1980; monthly; cultural; Editor-in-Chief Eva Birmann; circ. 41,400.

Mitt Livs Novell: Stockholm; tel. (8) 674-63-60; fax (8) 651-01-88; f. 1964; fortnightly; romance; Editor-in-Chief Anki Partridge; circ. 40,000.

OKEJ: POB 12547, 102 29 Stockholm; tel. (8) 692-01-20; fax (8) 650-86-25; e-mail anders.t@okej.se; internet www.okej.se; f. 1980; monthly pop music magazine; Editor Anders Tengner; circ. 44,400.

Premium Motor: POB 6019, 175 06 Järfälla; tel. (8) 761-09-50; fax (8) 761-09-49; motoring; Editor Staffan Swedenborg; circ. 44,615.

Privata Affärer: Sreav. 53, 105 44 Stockholm; tel. (8) 736-56-00; fax (8) 31-25-60; e-mail red@privataaffarer.se; internet www.privataaffarer.se; f. 1978; monthly; personal money management; Editor-in-Chief Hans Bolander; circ. 111,200.

Röster i Radio/TV: POB 27704, 115 91 Stockholm; tel. (8) 679-46-00; fax (8) 679-46-33; f. 1934; weekly; family magazine and programme guide to radio and television; Editor-in-Chief Edgar Antonsson; circ. 140,000.

Sköna Hem: 105 44 Stockholm; tel. (8) 736-53-00; fax (8) 33-74-11; f. 1979 (Sköna Hem), 1956 (Allt i Hemmet), merged 1992; monthly; interior decoration; Editor-in-Chief Lotti Ander; circ. 97,700.

Svensk Damtidning: POB 27710, 115 91 Stockholm; tel. (8) 679-46-00; fax (8) 679-47-50; f. 1980; weekly; women's; Editor-in-Chief Karin Lenmor; circ. 132,400.

Teknikens Värld: POB 70452, 105 44 Stockholm; tel. (8) 736-53-00; fax (8) 736-00-11; f. 1947; fortnightly; motoring; Editor-in-Chief Calle Carlquist; circ. 58,500.

Vår bostad: POB 12651, 112 93 Stockholm; tel. (8) 692-02-00; fax (8) 650-06-41; e-mail var.bostad@varbostad.se; internet www.varbostad.se; f. 1924; 11 a year; house and home; Editor Ulrica Ambjörn; circ. 949,500.

Vecko-Revyn: Kungsgt. 34, 105 44 Stockholm; tel. (8) 736-52-00; fax (8) 24-16-02; f. 1935; weekly; young women's; Editor Åsa Rydgren; circ. 91,100.

Vi Bilägare: POB 23800, 104 35 Stockholm; tel. (8) 736-12-00; fax (8) 736-12-49; e-mail redaktionen@vibilagare.se; internet www.vibilagare.se; f. 1930; fortnightly; auto and travel; Editor Nils-Eric Frendin; circ. 205,200.

Vi Föräldrar: 105 44 Stockholm; tel. (8) 736-53-00; fax (8) 34-00-43; e-mail red@vf.bonnier.se; f. 1968; monthly; parents' magazine; Editor-in-Chief Helena Rönnberg; circ. 58,400.

SPECIALIST PERIODICALS

Aktuellt i POLITIKEN: Sveavägen 68, 105 60 Stockholm; tel. (8) 700-26-00; fax (8) 11-65-42; weekly; social, political and cultural affairs; organ of Social Democratic Labour Party; circ. 55,000.

Allt om Jakt & Vapen: POB 70452, 107 26 Stockholm; tel. (8) 736-37-00; fax (8) 791-89-04; 11 a year; hunting; circ. 41,500.

Arbetsledaren: POB 12069, 102 22 Stockholm; tel. (8) 652-01-20; fax (8) 653-99-68; f. 1908; 10 a year; journal for foremen and supervisors; Editor INGRID ASKEBERG; circ. 87,400.

Barn: 107 88 Stockholm; tel. (8) 698-90-00; fax (8) 698-90-14; e-mail barn@rb.se; 6 a year; children's rights; circ. 125,700.

Båtliv: Martin Edén Reklam AB, Marinbasen, POB 4070, 183 04 Täby; tel. (8) 544-408-70; fax (8) 544-408-79; e-mail martin.eden@marinbasen.com; 5 a year; for boat-owners and boat-club members; circ. 126,300.

Bonniers Litterära Magasin: Sveavägen 56, POB 3159, 103 63 Stockholm; tel. (8) 696-82-42; fax (8) 696-83-63; e-mail blm@blm.nu; internet www.bok.bonnier.se/abforlag/blm; f. 1932; every 2 months; literary and cinema; Editor-in-Chief KRISTOFFER LEANDOER; circ. 5,000.

Byggnadsarbetaren: 106 32 Stockholm; tel. (8) 728-49-00; fax (8) 728-49-80; e-mail kenneth.petterson@byggnadsarbetaren.nu; internet www.byggnadsarbetaren.nu; f. 1949; 18 a year; building; Editor KENNETH PETTERSON; circ. 135,600 (2001).

Dina Pengar: Stockholm; tel. (8) 23-66-20; fax (8) 10-34-75; 9 a year; finance; circ. 83,000.

Du&jobbet: Maria Skolgt. 83, POB 17550, 118 91 Stockholm; tel. (8) 442-46-00; fax (8) 442-46-07; e-mail redaktionen@duochjobbet.com; internet www.duochjobbet.com; monthly; working environment; circ. 105,000.

Handelsnytt: POB 1146, 111 81 Stockholm; tel. (8) 412-68-00; fax (8) 21-43-33; e-mail handelsnytt@handels.se; internet www.handelsnytt.handels.se; f. 1906; 11 a year; organ of the Union of Commercial Employees; circ. 172,200.

Hundsport: POB 11141, 100 61 Stockholm; tel. (8) 642-37-20; fax (8) 641-00-62; monthly; for dog-owners; Editor TORSTEN WIDHOLM; circ. 101,300.

Jaktmarker och Fiskevatten: Västra Torggt. 18, 652 24 Karlstad; tel. (54) 10-03-70; fax (54) 10-09-83; 11 a year; hunting and fishing; circ. 48,100.

Kommunalarbetaren: POB 19034, 104 32 Stockholm; tel. (8) 728-28-00; fax (8) 30-61-42; e-mail kommunalarbetaren@kommunal.se; internet www.kommunalarbetaren.com; 22 a year; organ of the Union of Municipal Workers; circ. 650,000.

Kyrkans Tidning: POB 15412, 104 65 Stockholm; tel. (8) 462-28-00; fax (8) 644-76-71; e-mail redaktionen@kyrkanstidning.com; internet www.kyrkanstidning.com; f. 1982; weekly; organ of Church of Sweden; Man. Dir THOMAS GRAHL; Editor OLAV S. MELIN; circ. 49,800.

LAND-Familjetidningen: Gävlegt. 22, 113 92 Stockholm; tel. (8) 787-51-00; fax (8) 787-55-02; e-mail familjetidningenland@lrfmedia.lrf.se; internet www.tidningenland.com; f. 1971; weekly; organ of the farmers' asscn; circ. 211,400.

LAND-Lantbruksdelen: Gävlegt. 22, 113 92 Stockholm; tel. (8) 787-51-00; fax (8) 787-55-02; e-mail lantbruksdelen@lrfmedia.lrf.se; internet www.lantbruk.com; f. 1971; weekly; organ of the farmers' asscn; house, garden, cooking, hunting, travel; circ. 118,000.

Lärarförbundet: Segelbåtsvägen 15, POB 12239, 102 26 Stockholm; tel. (8) 737-65-00; e-mail sten.svensson@lararforbundet.se; internet www.lararforbundet.se; 22 a year; for teachers; Editor-in-Chief STEN SVENSSON; circ. 213,700.

Lön & Jobb: POB 30102, 104 25 Stockholm; tel. (8) 737-80-00; fax (8) 618-67-22; e-mail lonjobb@htf.se; internet www.lon-jobb.nu; 18 a year; organ of the Union of Commercial Salaried Employees; Editor-in-Chief CARL VON SCHÉELE; circ. 147,300.

Metallarbetaren: POB 342, 101 24 Stockholm; tel. (8) 10-68-30; fax (8) 11-13-02; f. 1888; weekly; organ of Swedish Metal Workers' Union; Editor PER AHLSTRÖM; circ. 415,400.

Motor: POB 23142, 104 35 Stockholm; tel. (8) 690-38-00; fax (8) 690-38-22; monthly; cars and motoring; circ. 141,700.

Motorföraren: Västertorpsvägen 131, 129 44 Stockholm; tel. (8) 555-765-55; fax (8) 555-765-95; internet www.mhf.se; f. 1927; 7 a year; motoring and tourism; Editor SÖREN SEHLBERG; circ. 36,500.

Musiktidningen Musikomanen: POB 6903, 102 39 Stockholm; tel. (8) 31-00-07; e-mail alexander.scarlat@chello.se; f. 1964; 4 a year; classical and modern music; circ. 90,000.

Ny Teknik: Mäster Samuelsgt. 56, 106 12 Stockholm; tel. (8) 796-66-00; fax (8) 613-30-28; internet www.nyteknik.se; f. 1967; weekly; technical publication owned by the two largest engineering societies of Sweden; Editor-in-Chief DAN MAGNEROT; circ. 150,500.

PRO-Pensionären: POB 3274, 103 65 Stockholm; tel. (8) 701-67-00; fax (8) 20-33-58; e-mail info@pro.se; internet www.pro.se; f. 1942; 10 a year; magazine for pensioners; Editor AGNETA BERG-WAHLSTEDT; circ. 293,900.

SEKO-magasinet: Barnhusgt. 10, POB 1102, 111 81 Stockholm; tel. (8) 791-41-00; fax (8) 21-16-94; f. 1955; 11 a year; organ of the National Union of Services and Communications Employees; Editor-in-Chief BJÖRN FORSBERG; circ. 195,400.

SIA-Skogsindustriarbetaren: Olof Palmesgt. 31, POB 1138, 111 81 Stockholm; tel. (8) 701-77-90; fax (8) 411-27-42; e-mail sia@skogstrafacket.org; monthly; forestry; circ. 69,100.

SIF-Tidningen: SIF-huset, Olof Palmesgt. 17, 105 32 Stockholm; tel. (8) 50-89-70-00; fax (8) 50-89-70-12; e-mail bjorn.oijer@sif.se; internet www.siftidn.sif.se; 19 a year; organ of the Union of Clerical and Technical Employees; Editor-in-Chief BJORN OIJER; circ. 331,800.

Skog & Såg: Sag i Syd, POB 394, 551 15 Jönköping; tel. (36) 19-86-20; fax (36) 12-86-10; f. 1966; 4 a year; sawmills and forestry; Editor HENRIK ASPLUND; circ. 77,200.

SKTF-Tidningen: POB 7825, 103 97 Stockholm; tel. (8) 789-63-00; fax (8) 789-64-79; e-mail sktftidningen@sktf.se; internet www.sktftidningen.nu; 20 a year; organ of the Union of Municipal Employees; circ. 182,800.

Sunt Förnuft: 114 95 Stockholm; tel. (8) 613-17-00; fax (8) 21-38-58; 8 a year; tax-payers' magazine; circ. 175,100.

Svensk Bokhandel (Journal of the Swedish Book Trade): Birkagt. 16C, POB 6888, 113 86 Stockholm; tel. (8) 545-417-70; fax (8) 545-417-75; e-mail redaktion@svb.se; internet www.svb.se; publ. by Swedish Publrs' Asscn, for book-sellers, publishers, antiquarians and librarians; Editor UNO PALSTRÖM; circ. 4,700.

Svensk Golf: POB 84, 182 11 Danderyd; tel. (8) 622-15-00; fax (8) 622-69-30; e-mail info@svenskgolf.se; internet www.svenskgolf.se; monthly; golf; circ. 260,000.

Svensk Jakt: Skedhults Säteri, 575 96 Eksjö; tel. (381) 371-80; fax (381) 371-85; e-mail svenskjakt@telia.com; internet www.jagareforbundet.se/svenskjakt; f. 1862; 11 a year; for hunters and dog-breeders; circ. 167,400 (2001).

Sveriges Natur: POB 4625, 116 91 Stockholm; tel. (8) 702-65-00; fax (8) 702-27-02; e-mail sveriges.natur@snf.se; internet www.sveriges.natur.snf.se; f. 1909; 5 a year; organ of Swedish Society for Nature Conservation; circ. 120,000.

Tidningen C: POB 2200, 103 15 Stockholm; tel. (8) 617-38-30; fax (8) 617-38-10; e-mail c.redaktionen@centrepartiet.se; f. 1929; 10 a year; organ of the Centre Party; Editor EVA-KANN LIND; circ. 68,000.

Tidningen Näringsliv: Blasieholmsgt. 4A, 103 30 Stockholm; tel. (8) 762-60-00; fax (8) 762-68-85; 38 a year; organ of the Employers' Confederation; circ. 60,000.

Transportarbetaren: POB 714, 101 33 Stockholm; tel. (8) 723-77-00; fax (8) 723-00-76; 11 a year; organ of the Swedish Transport Workers Union; Editor JAN LINDKVIST; circ. 72,000.

Turist: 101 20 Stockholm; tel. (8) 463-21-00; 6 a year; tourism and travel; Editor MONIKA TROZELL; circ. 215,000.

NEWS AGENCIES

Svenska Nyhetsbyrån (Swedish Conservative Press Agency): POB 16051, 103 21 Stockholm; tel. (8) 14-07-50; fax (8) 10-10-48; e-mail red@snb.se; internet www.snb.se; Pres. KJELL SVENSSON; Editor-in-Chief and Dir PATRIK STRÖMER.

Svensk-Internationella Pressbyrån (SIP) (Swedish-International Press Bureau): POB 24122, 104 57 Stockholm; tel. (8) 615-40-70; fax (8) 615-43-60; e-mail kjell@ins.se; f. 1927; Editor-in-Chief KJELL ERIKSSON.

Tidningarnas Telegrambyrå (Swedish News Agency): Kungsholmstorg 5, 105 12 Stockholm; tel. (8) 692-26-00; fax (8) 651-53-77; e-mail redaktionen@tt.se; internet www.tt.se; f. 1921; co-operative news agency, working in conjunction with Reuters, AFP, the 'Groupe 39' agencies, dpa and other telegraph agencies; Chair. GUNNAR STRÖMBLAD; Gen. Man. and Editor-in-Chief EBBA LINDSÖ.

Foreign Bureaux

Agence France-Presse (AFP): Kungsholmstorg 5, 3D, 105 12 Stockholm; tel. (8) 651-01-60; fax (8) 650-82-28; e-mail christopher.boian@afp.com; internet www.afp.com; Bureau Chief CHRISTOPHER BOIAN.

Agenzia Nazionale Stampa Associata (ANSA) (Italy): Ynglingagt. 23, 113 47 Stockholm; tel. (8) 33-93-10; Man. GIACOMO OREGLIA.

Associated Press (AP) (USA): Sveavägen 17, POB 1726, 111 87 Stockholm; tel. (8) 5451-30-80; fax (8) 21-24-71; internet www.ap .org; Man. PIERRE-YVES GLASS.

Informatsionnoye Telecommunnikatsionnoye Agentstvo Rossii (TASS) (Russia): Karlavägen 12, 113 31 Stockholm; tel. (8) 411-32-40; e-mail stgm.itar-tass@stockholm.mail.telia.com; internet www.itar-tass.com; Man. ANDREI VARLAMOV.

Kyodo Tsushin (Japan): POB 2130, 145 56 Norsborg; tel. (0753) 83-215.

United Press International (UPI) (USA): Stockholm; tel. (8) 663-21-52; fax (8) 663-21-52; Correspondent PÁL BURMAN.

Xinhua (New China) News Agency (People's Republic of China): Krokvägen 5, 181 33 Lidingö; tel. (8) 765-60-83; fax (8) 731-91-54; Man. LINFENG XIE.

PRESS ASSOCIATIONS

Pre Cent (Centre Party's Press Agency): POB 2033, 103 11 Stockholm; tel. (8) 786-48-84; fax (8) 24-30-04; e-mail red@precent.se; f. 1987; Editor-in-Chief JIMMY DOMINIUS; 33 mems.

Svenska Journalistförbundet (Swedish Union of Journalists): POB 1116, 111 81 Stockholm; tel. (8) 613-75-00; fax (8) 21-26-80; e-mail kansliet@sjf.se; internet www.sjf.se; f. 1901; Pres. AGNETA LINDBLOM HULTÉN; 19,000 mems.

Svenska Tidningsutgivareföreningen (Swedish Newspaper Publishers' Asscn): Kungsholmstorg 5, POB 22500, 104 22 Stockholm; tel. (8) 692-46-00; fax (8) 692-46-38; e-mail tidningsutgivarna@tu.se; internet www.tu.se; f. 1898; Man. Dir BARBRO FISCHERSTRÖM; 190 mems.

Svenska Veckopressens Tidningsutgivareförening (VECTU) (Swedish Magazine Publishers' Asscn): Stockholm; tel. (8) 20-15-10; fax (8) 21-35-20; f. 1943; Man. Dir GUNVOR ENGSTRÖM.

Sveriges Vänsterpressförening (The Liberal Press Asscn): 901 70 Umeå; tel. (90) 15-10-00; fax (90) 77-46-47; f. 1905; Pres. OLOF KLEBERG; Sec. MATS OLOFSSON; c. 130 mems.

Publishers

Alfabeta Bokförlag AB: POB 4284, 102 66 Stockholm; tel. (8) 714-36-30; fax (8) 643-24-31; e-mail info@alfamedia.se; internet www .alfamedia.se; fiction, psychology, biography, cinema, art, music, travel guides, children's books; Man. Dir DAG HERNRIED.

Bokförlaget Atlantis AB: Sturegt. 24, 114 36 Stockholm; tel. (8) 545-660-70; fax (8) 545-660-71; e-mail mail@atlantisbok.se; f. 1977; fiction, non-fiction, art; Man. Dir KJELL PETERSON.

Berghs Förlag AB: Observatoriegt. 10, POB 45084, 104 30 Stockholm; tel. (8) 31-65-59; fax (8) 32-77-45; f. 1954; non-fiction for adults and children, picture books and fiction for children, craft books, popular science, 'New Age' literature; Man. Dir CARL HAFSTRÖM.

Bonnier Carlsen Bokförlag AB: POB 1315, 111 83 Stockholm; tel. (8) 453-89-00; fax (8) 453-89-45; picture books, juvenile books, non-fiction, board books, comics; Man. Dir BODIL SJÖÖ.

Bonnierförlagen AB: Sveavägen 56, POB 3159, 103 63 Stockholm; tel. (8) 696-80-00; fax (8) 696-83-59; f. 1837; fiction, non-fiction, encyclopaedias, reference books, quality paperbacks; includes Albert Bonniers Förlag AB, Bonnier Utbildning AB, Bokförlaget Forum AB, AB Wahlström & Widstrand, Autumn Publ., Bonnier Audio, Bonnier Carlsen, Bokförlaget Rebus, Bokförlaget Max Ström; Chair. PER-OLOV ATLE; Man. Dir MARIA CURMAN.

Bokförlaget Bra Böcker: POB 892, 201 80 Malmö; tel. (40) 665-46-00; f. 1965; Man. Dir JOHAN MÖLLER.

Brombergs Bokförlag AB: Industrigt. 4A, POB 12886, 112 98 Stockholm; tel. (8) 562-62-080; fax (8) 562-62-085; e-mail info@ brombergs.se; quality fiction, non-fiction; Man. Dir DOROTEA BROMBERG.

Brutus Östlings Bokförlag Symposion: POB 148, 241 22 Eslöv; tel. (413) 609-90; e-mail order.symposion@swipnet.se.

Carlsson Bokförlag AB: Stora Nygt. 31, 111 27 Stockholm; tel. (8) 411-23-49; fax (8) 796-84-57; art, photography, ethnology, history, politics; Man. Dir TRYGVE CARLSSON.

Bokförlaget DN: POB 703 21, 107 23 Stockholm; e-mail evafallenius@bokforlagetdn.se; internet www.bokforlagetdn.com; publishing division of *Dagens Nyheter* newspaper; Publr and Pres. ALBERT BONNDER.

Eriksson & Lindgren Bokförlag AB: Hantverkargt. 87, POB 12085, 102 23 Stockholm; tel. (8) 652-32-26; fax (8) 652-32-23; e-mail info@eriksson-lindgren.se; internet www.eriksson-lindgren.se; f. 1990; Man. Dir CLAES ERIKSSON.

Bokförlaget T. Fischer & Co.: Norrlandsgt. 15, 111 43 Stockholm; tel. (8) 24-21-60; fax (8) 24-78-25; e-mail bokforlaget@fischer.co.se; internet www.fischerco.se; Man. Dir KIM MODIN.

Forum Publishers: POB 70321, 107 23 Stockholm; tel. (8) 696-84-40; fax (8) 696-83-67; internet www.forum.se; f. 1943; general fiction, non-fiction; Man. Dir KARIN LEIJON.

C. E. Fritzes AB: 106 47 Stockholm; tel. (8) 690-90-90; fax (8) 690-90-70; f. 1837; Man. Dir CHRISTER BUNGE-MEYER.

Gedins Förlag: Tystagt. 10, 115 20 Stockholm; tel. (8) 662-15-51; fax (8) 663-70-73; fiction, non-fiction, poetry, food, psychology, politics; Man. Dir PER I. GEDIN.

AB Carl Gehrmans Musikförlag: POB 6005, 102 31 Stockholm; tel. (8) 610-06-00; fax (8) 610-06-27; e-mail info@sk-gehrmans.se; e-mail order@sk-gehrmans.se; internet www.sk-gehrmans.se; f. 1893; orchestral music; general music publishing as SK-Gehrmans Musikförlag AB; Pres. JOE LINDSTRÖM; Man. Dir KETTIL SKARBY.

ICA-förlaget AB: 721 85 Västerås; tel. (21) 19-40-00; fax (21) 19-42-83; e-mail bok@publ.ica.se; internet www.publ.ica.se; f. 1945; non-fiction, cookery, handicrafts, gardening, natural history, popular psychology, health, domestic animals, sports; Publr GÖRAN SUNEHAG; Man. Dir HANS RINKEBORN.

Informationsförlaget: Sveavägen 61, POB 6884, 113 86 Stockholm; tel. (8) 34-09-15; fax (8) 31-39-03; f. 1979; publishers of books for companies and organizations on demand; trade books in non-fiction, reference, encyclopaedias, gastronomy, illustrated books; Man. Dir ULF HEIMDAHL.

Liber AB: 113 98 Stockholm; tel. (8) 690-90-00; fax (8) 690-94-70; e-mail export@liber.se; internet www.liber.se; general and educational publishing; Man. Dir BIRGITTA JOHANSSON-HEDBERG.

Liber Hermods AB: Baltzarsgatan 4, 205 10 Malmö; tel. (40) 25-86-00; fax (40) 30-38-39; e-mail guuille.bivered@liber.se; f. 1993; Man. Dir LARS HONT.

LTs förlag: Stockholm; tel. (8) 453-87-25; fax (8) 453-87-98; f. 1934; illustrated do-it-yourself books, agricultural textbooks for adult education; Man. Dir ROLF ELLNEBRAND.

Abraham Lundquist AB Musikförlag: POB 93, 182 11 Danderyd; tel. (8) 732-92-35; fax (8) 732-92-38; e-mail info@abrahamlundquist .se; internet www.abrahamlundquist.se; f. 1838; music; Man. Dir (vacant).

Bokförlaget Natur och Kultur: Karlavägen 31, POB 27323, 102 54 Stockholm; tel. (8) 453-86-00; fax (8) 453-87-90; e-mail info@nok .se; internet www.nok.se; f. 1922; textbooks, general literature, fiction; Man. Dir LARS GRAHN.

Norstedts Förlag AB: Tryckerigt. 4, POB 2052, 103 12 Stockholm; tel. (8) 769-87-50; fax (8) 769-87-64; e-mail info@norstedts.se; internet www.norstedts.se; f. 1823; fiction, non-fiction; Man. Dir SVANTE WEYLER.

Bokförlaget Opal AB: Tegelbergsvägen 31, POB 20113, 161 02 Bromma; tel. (8) 28-21-79; fax (8) 29-66-23; e-mail opal@opal.se; internet www.opal.se; f. 1973; Man. Dir BENGT CHRISTELL.

Ordfront Förlag AB: Bellmansgt. 30, POB 17506, 118 91 Stockholm; tel. (8) 462-44-20; fax (8) 462-44-90; fiction, history, politics; Man. Dir JAN-ERIK PETTERSSON.

Prisma Bokförlaget: Tryckerigt. 4, POB 2052, 103 12 Stockholm; tel. (8) 769-89-00; fax (8) 769-89-13; e-mail prisma@prismabok.se; internet www.prismabok.se; f. 1963; Dir VIVECA EKELUND.

Rabén & Sjögren Bokförlag: Tryckerigt. 4, POB 2052, 103 12 Stockholm; tel. (8) 789-30-00; fax (8) 789-30-52; e-mail raben-sjogren@raben.se; internet www.raben.se; f. 1942; general, juvenile; Dir SUZANNE ÖHMAN-SUNDEN.

Bokförlaget Semic: Landsvägen 57, POB 1243, 172 25 Sundbyberg; tel. (8) 799-30-50; fax (8) 799-30-64; e-mail bokforlaget@semic .se; internet www.semic.se; handbooks, calendars, comic magazines, juvenile; Pres. RICKARD EKSTRÖM.

Stenströms Bokförlag AB: Linnégt. 98, POB 24086, 104 50 Stockholm; tel. (8) 663-76-01; fax (8) 663-22-01; f. 1983; Man. Dir BENGT STENSTRÖM.

Streiffert Förlag AB: Skeppargt. 27, POB 5334, 102 47 Stockholm; tel. (8) 661-58-80; fax (8) 783-04-33; e-mail bo@streiffert.se; internet www.streiffert.se; f. 1990; Man. Dir BO STREIFFERT.

Svenska Förlaget liv & ledarskap AB: POB 3313, 103 66 Stockholm; e-mail kundservice@svenskaforlaget.com; internet www .svenskaforlaget.com; non-fiction.

AB Timbro: POB 5234, 102 45 Stockholm; tel. (8) 5878-98-00; fax (8) 5878-98-55; e-mail info@timbro.se; internet www.timbro.se; economics, political science; Man. Dir MATTIAS BENGTSSON.

Verbum Förlag AB: St Paulsgt. 2, POB 15169, 104 65 Stockholm; tel. (8) 743-65-00; fax (8) 641-45-85; e-mail gunnar.goranzon@

verbum.se; internet www.verbum.se; f. 1911; theology, fiction, juvenile, music; Man. Dir GUNNAR GÖRANZON.

AB Wahlström & Widstrand: Sturegt. 32, POB 5587, 114 85 Stockholm; tel. (8) 696-84-80; fax (8) 696-83-80; f. 1884; fiction, nonfiction, biography, history, science, paperbacks; Man. Dir UNN PALM.

B. Wahlströms Bokförlag AB: Warfvingesvägen 30, POB 30022, 104 25 Stockholm; tel. (8) 619-86-00; fax (8) 618-97-61; e-mail bertil.wahlstrom@wahlstroms.se; internet www.wahlstroms.se; fiction, non-fiction, juvenile, paperbacks; Man. Dir BERTIL WAHLSTRÖM.

PUBLISHERS' ASSOCIATIONS

Föreningen Svenska Läromedelsproducenter (Swedish Asscn of Educational Publishers): Drottninggt. 97, 113 60 Stockholm; tel. (8) 736-19-40; fax (8) 736-19-44; e-mail fsl@forlagskansli.se; f. 1973; Dir JERKER FRANKSSON; 25 mems.

Svenska Förläggareföreningen (Swedish Publishers' Asscn): Drottninggt. 97, 113 60 Stockholm; tel. (8) 736-19-40; fax (8) 736-19-44; e-mail svf@forlagskansli.se; internet www.forlagskansli.se; f. 1843; Chair. LARS GRAHN; Dir KRISTINA AHLINDER; 74 mems.

Broadcasting and Communications

TELECOMMUNICATIONS

Regulatory Authority

Post-och Telestyrelsen (PTS): POB 5398, Binger Jarlsgt. 16, 102 49 Stockholm; tel. (8) 678-50-50; fax (8) 678-55-05; e-mail pts@pts.se; internet www.pts.se; Dir-Gen. CURT ANDERSSON (acting).

Major Service Providers

Global One Services AB: POB 1, 171 18 Solna; tel. (8) 5191-31-00; fax (8) 5191-32-00; Dir PETER JERRY SØRENSEN.

Nordiska Tele 8 AB: Hans Michelsensgt. 6B, 201 20 Malmö; tel. (40) 620-00-88; fax (40) 620-00-89; e-mail info@tele8.se; internet www.tele8.se; Dir of Networks PREBEN E. LARSEN.

Tele 1 Europe AB: Stockholm; tel. (8) 700-22-20; fax (8) 700-22-30.

Tele 2 AB: Borgarfjordsgt. 16, POB 62, 164 94 Kista; tel. (85) 626-40-00; fax (85) 626-42-00; Man. ULF JOHANSSON.

Telefon AB LM Ericsson: Telefonvägen 30, 126 25 Stockholm; tel. (8) 719-00-00; fax (8) 18-40-85; e-mail info@ericsson.se; internet www.ericsson.se; mobile and fixed network provider; world's largest customer base in telecommunications field; represented in 140 countries; Chair. MICHAEL TRESCHOW; CEO KURT HELLSTROM.

Telenordia AB: Årstängsvägen 11A, 117 43 Stockholm; tel. (8) 681-7084; fax (8) 681-7096; Dir TONY THUN.

Telia AB: 123 86 Farsta; tel. (87) 13-00-00; fax (87) 13-36-36; e-mail internet-post@telia.se; merger planned with Sonera, Finland; Pres. and CEO ANDERS IGEL.

TERACOM AB: Medborgarplatsen 3, POB 17666, 118 92 Stockholm; tel. (8) 671-20-00; fax (8) 671-20-82; e-mail info@teracom.se; internet www.teracom.se; Dir VALDEMAR PERSSON.

BROADCASTING

Until the end of 1992 public-service radio and television were organized within the state broadcasting corporation, Sveriges Radio AB, a public-service organization financed by licence fees; this operated two national television channels and three national radio channels, together with 24 local radio stations. On 1 January 1993 the state corporation was replaced by three companies, Sveriges Radio AB, Sveriges Television AB, and Sveriges Utbildningsradio AB, responsible for radio, television and educational radio and television respectively. The operations of these companies are regulated by law and by agreements with the Government. From 1 January 1994 the three companies came into the ownership of three foundations.

Radio

Neighbourhood radio stations were introduced in 1979, and by 1997 there were 160 such stations. During 1993–96 the Local Radio Authority licensed some 90 private local radio stations (financed by advertising) in 35 areas of Sweden.

Sveriges Radio AB: Oxenstiernsgt. 20, 105 10 Stockholm; tel. (8) 784-50-00; fax (8) 667-83-36; e-mail anders.held@kom.sr.se; internet www.sr.se; f. 1993; independent company responsible for national radio broadcasting; Man. Dir LISA SÖDERBERG.

Sveriges Utbildningsradio AB: 115 80 Stockholm; tel. (8) 784-40-00; fax (8) 784-41-00; f. 1979; public company responsible for educational broadcasting on radio and television; Man. Dir LARS HANSSON.

IBRA Radio AB: POB 4033, 141 04 Huddinge; tel. (8) 608-96-80; fax (8) 608-96-89; e-mail ibra@ibra.se; internet www.ibra.org; non-commercial private Christian company broadcasting to all continents; Pres. PER-OVE MORBERG; Dir SUNE ELOFSON.

Television

There are two public-service television channels (SVT 1 and SVT 2) and four public-service radio channels, one of which provides regional broadcasts in 25 areas of Sweden. The broadcasts are financed by licence fees. In 1991 the Government awarded the licence for a third terrestrial nation-wide television channel to TV 4 (which is financed by advertising).

The construction of cable networks for the diffusion of satellite TV programmes began in 1984. In early 1997 an estimated 65% of households in Sweden were connected to cable networks and had access to satellite transmissions. Television channels transmitted by satellite and cable, and directed at the Swedish audience, include: TV 3, Kanal 5, TV 6, Z-TV, and the film channels TV 1000, FilmMax, Filmnet Plus and Filmnet Movie.

Kanal 5: 114 99 Stockholm; tel. (8) 674-15-00; fax (8) 612-05-95; commercial satellite channel.

Sveriges Television AB: TH T2, 105 10 Stockholm; tel. (8) 784-00-00; fax (8) 784-15-00; e-mail information@sut.se; f. 1956; independent; 2 public service channels; Man. Dir SAM NILSSON.

Sveriges Utbildningsradio AB: see Radio.

TV 3: Stockholm; tel. (8) 10-33-33; fax (8) 676-08-12; commercial satellite channel.

TV 4: Tegeluddsvägen 3, 115 79 Stockholm; tel. (8) 459-40-00; fax (8) 459-44-44; internet www.tv4.se; commercial terrestrial channel; Man. Dir JAN SCHERMAN.

Finance

BANKING
(cap. = capital; res = reserves; dep. = deposits; m. = million; brs = branches; amounts in kronor unless otherwise stated)

In 2000 there were 48 commercial banks with total assets of 2,872,419m. kronor.

Central Bank

Sveriges Riksbank (Swedish Central Bank): Brunkebergstorg 11, 103 37 Stockholm; tel. (8) 787-00-00; fax (8) 21-05-31; e-mail registratorn@riksbank.se; internet www.riksbank.se; f. 1668; bank of issue; controlled by a board of eight delegates, seven of whom are appointed by the Riksdag and one, the Governor, by other board members; cap. 1,000m., res 96,291m., dep. 5,962m. (Dec. 2001); Chair. SVEN HULTERSTRÖM; Gov. LARS HEIKENSTEN; 10 brs.

Commercial Banks

FöreningsSparbanken AB (Swedbank): Brunkebergstorg 8, 105 34 Stockholm; tel. (8) 58-59-00-00; fax (8) 796-80-92; e-mail info@foreningssparbanken.se; internet www.foreningssparbanken.se; f. 1997 as a result of merger between Föreningsbanken and Sparbanken Sverige; cap. 10,556m., res 15,372m., dep. 402,589m. (Dec. 2000); Chair. GÖRAN COLLERT; Pres. BIRGITTA JOHANSSON-HEDBERG; 650 brs.

Matteus Bank AB: Kungsgt. 28, 107 81 Stockholm; tel. (8) 50-65-80-00; fax (8) 20-39-10; e-mail info@matteus.se; internet www.matteus.se; f. 1874 as Jämtlands Folkbank, present name adopted 2001; cap. 104m., res 421m., dep. 4,593m. (Dec. 2000); Chair. LEIF B. BERGTSSON; Pres. HANS LARTÉN; 8 brs.

Nordea Bank Sweden AB: Hamngt. 10, 105 71 Stockholm; tel. (8) 614-70-00; fax (8) 20-08-46; internet www.nordea.com; f. 1974 as Post- och Kreditbanken, present name adopted Dec. 2001; part of Nordea Group; cap. 1,182m., res 9,069m., dep. 179,262m. (Dec. 2001); Chair. HANS DALBORG; CEO LARS G. NORDSTRÖM; 280 brs.

Östgöta Enskilda Bank: Storgt. 18, POB 93, 590 10 Stockholm; tel. (8) 14-25-21-60; fax (8) 14-25-20-34; internet www.oeb.se; f. 1837; wholly-owned subsidiary of Den Danske Bank; cap. 563.3m., res 236.5m., dep. 12,778.5m. (Dec. 1996); Chair. PETER STRAARUP; Pres. and CEO ULF LUNDAHL; 30 brs.

Postgirot Bank AB: Mäster Samuelsgt. 70, 105 00 Stockholm; tel. (8) 781-10-00; fax (8) 24-35-11; internet www.postgirot.se; f. 1925; cap. 300m., res 1,659m., dep. 66,376m. (Dec. 2000); Pres. PER-ERIK SCOTTHAG; Chair. LENNART GRABE.

Skandinaviska Enskilda Banken AB: Kungsträdgårdsgt. 8, 106 40 Stockholm; tel. (8) 763-80-00; fax (8) 763-83-89; internet www.sebank.se; f. 1972; cap. 7,046m., res 32,195m., dep. 881,611m. (Dec. 2001); Chair. JACOB WALLENBERG; Pres. and Group CEO LARS H. THUNELL; 260 brs.

Svenska Handelsbanken AB: Kungsträdgårdsgt. 2, 106 70 Stockholm; tel. (8) 701-10-00; fax (8) 701-24-37; e-mail info@handelsbanken.se; internet www.handelsbanken.se; f. 1871; cap. 2,859m., res 36,963m., dep. 944,799m. (Dec. 2001); Chair. ARNE MÅRTENSSON; Pres. and CEO LARS O. GRÖNSTEDT; 480 brs.

Banking Organizations

Finansinspektionen (Financial Supervisory Authority): POB 6750, 113 85 Stockholm; tel. (8) 787-80-00; fax (8) 24-13-35; e-mail finansinspektionen@fi.se; internet www.fi.se; f. 1991 by merger of Bankinspektionen (Bank Inspection Board, f. 1907) and Försäkringsinspektionen (Private Insurance Supervisory Service, f. 1904), for the supervision of commercial and savings banks, financial companies, insurance companies, insurance brokers, friendly societies, mortgage institutions, securities firms and unit trusts, the stock exchange and clearing functions, the securities registry centre and the information registry centre; Dir-Gen. INGRID BONDE.

Svenska Bankföreningen (Swedish Bankers' Asscn): Regeringsgt. 38, POB 7603, 103 94 Stockholm; tel. (8) 453-44-00; fax (8) 796-93-95; e-mail registrator@bankforeningen.se; internet www.bankforeningen.se; f. 1880; Pres. LARS O. GRÖNSTEDT; Man. Dir ULLA LUNDQUIST; 37 mems.

STOCK EXCHANGE

Stockholm Stock Exchange Ltd: Källargränd 2, POB 1256, 111 82 Stockholm; tel. (8) 613-88-00; fax (8) 10-81-10; e-mail info@xsse.se; f. 1863; under government charter; automated trading system introduced by 1990; from 1993 a limited company, owned by members and issuers; merged with OM Group in January 1998; formed an alliance with Copenhagen Stock Exchange (Nordic Exchanges, Norex); since 1999 the Oslo and Iceland Stock Exchanges have joined the group; Chair. INGEMAR ELIASSON; Pres. and CEO BENGT RYDÉN.

INSURANCE

See also Finansinspektionen (under Banking Organizations).

Principal Insurance Companies

Folksam: Bohusgt. 14, 106 60 Stockholm; tel. (8) 772-60-00; fax (8) 643-40-26; internet www.folksam.se; f. 1908; all branches of life and non-life insurance; Pres. and CEO TORE ANDERSSON.

Länsförsäkringsbolagens AB: Tegeluddsvägen 11–13, 106 50 Stockholm; tel. (8) 588-400-50; fax (8) 670-48-23; f. 1936; all branches of life and non-life insurance; Pres. and CEO TOMMY PERSSON.

Skandia Group Försäkrings AB: Sveavägen 44, 103 50 Stockholm; tel. (8) 788-10-00; fax (8) 10-31-74; f. 1855; all branches of life insurance; Chair. LARS RAMQVIST; Pres. and CEO OLA RAMSTEDT.

Trygg-Hansa: Flemminggt. 18, 106 26 Stockholm; tel. (8) 693-10-00; fax (8) 650-93-67; f. 1828; all branches of non-life insurance; Pres. and CEO HÅKAN DANIELSSON.

Insurance Associations

Svenska Försäkringsföreningen (Swedish Insurance Society): Klara Norra Kyrkogt. 33, 111 22 Stockholm; tel. (8) 783-98-90; fax (8) 783-98-95; e-mail anders.kleverman@sff.a.se; internet www.sff.a.se; f. 1875 to promote sound development of the Swedish insurance business; Chair. LARS ROSÉN; Sec. ANDERS KLEVERMAN.

Sveriges Försäkringsförbund (Swedish Insurance Federation): Klara Norra Kyrkogt. 33, 11122 Stockholm; tel. (8) 783-98-00; fax (8) 783-98-15; e-mail kansli@forsakringsforbundet.com; internet www.forsakringsforbundet.com; Chair. HÅKAN DANIELSSON; Man. Dir ANNIKA LUNDIUS.

Trade and Industry

GOVERNMENT AGENCIES

Arbetsmarknadsstyrelsen (AMS) (Labour Market Board): 171 99 Solna, Stockholm; tel. (8) 730-60-00; fax (8) 27-83-68; f. 1948; autonomous public agency, responsible for administration of Sweden's labour market; main aims: to provide social means for easing structural change in the economy, to organize labour market by balancing requirements of workers and employers, and to uphold commitment to concept of full employment; board mems appointed by Govt, employers and trades unions; Dir-Gen. BOSSE RINGHOLM.

Exportrådet (Trade Council): Storgt. 19, POB 5513, 114 85 Stockholm; tel. (8) 783-85-00; fax (8) 662-90-93; e-mail infocenter@swedishtrade.se; internet www.swedishtrade.se; f. 1972; Chair. ANDERS NARVINGER; Man. Dir ULF DINKELSPIEL.

CHAMBERS OF COMMERCE

Handelskammaren i Jönköpings Län: Elmiavägen 11, 554 54 Jönköping; tel. (36) 30-14-30; fax (36) 12-95-79; e-mail jncci@jn.wtc.se; f. 1975; Pres. PER RISBERG; Man. Dir GÖRAN KINNANDER; 600 mems.

Mellansvenska Handelskammaren: POB 296, 801 04 Gävle; tel. (26) 66-20-80; fax (26) 66-20-99; e-mail chamber@mhk.cci.se; internet www.mhk.cci.se; f. 1907; Pres. OVE ANONSEN; Man. Dir ANDERS FRANCK; 465 mems.

Mittsveriges Industri- och Handelskammare (Mid Sweden Chamber of Commerce and Industry): Kyrkogt. 26, 852 32 Sundsvall; tel. (60) 17-18-80; fax (60) 61-86-40; e-mail sdl@mid.chamber.cci.se; internet www.mid.chamber.cci.se; f. 1913; Chair. LARS NÄSMAN; Man. Dir STURE LARSSON; 400 mems.

Norrbottens Handelskammare: Storgt. 9, 972 38 Luleå; tel. (920) 122-10; fax (920) 94-857; e-mail lundgren@north.cci.se; internet www.north.cci.se; f. 1904; Chair. INGA-LILL HOLMGREN; Dir STURE LUNDGREN.

Handelskammaren för Örebro och Västmanlands Län: Örebro; tel. (19) 611-22-23; fax (19) 11-77-50; f. 1907; Pres. EGON LINDEROTH; Sec. SVEN SVENSSON.

Östsvenska Handelskammaren: Nya Rådstugugt. 3, 60224 Norrköping; tel. (11) 28-50-30; fax (11) 13-77-19; e-mail info@east.cci.se; internet www.east.cci.se; f. 1908.

Stockholms Handelskammare: V. Trädgårdsgt. 9, POB 16050, 103 21 Stockholm; tel. (8) 555-100-00; fax (8) 566-316-30; e-mail tradeofficer@chamber.se; internet www.chamber.se; f. 1902; Pres. MARGARETA BOSVED; Dir PETER EGARDT.

Sydsvenska Handelskammaren (Chamber of Commerce and Industry of Southern Sweden): Skeppsbron 2, 211 20 Malmö; tel. (40) 73-550; fax (40) 611-86-09; e-mail info@handelskammaren.com; f. 1905; Pres. HANS CAVALLI-BJÖRKMAN; Man. Dir STEPHAN MÜCHLER; 3,050 mems.

Västsvenska Industri- och Handelskammaren: POB 5253, 402 25 Göteborg; tel. (31) 83-59-00; fax (31) 83-59-36; e-mail info@handelskammaren.net; internet www.handelskammaren.net; f. 1661; Man. Dir ANDERS KÄLLSTRÖM; c. 2,000 mems.

Handelskammaren Värmland: Älvgt. 11, 652 25 Karlstad; tel. (54) 22-14-80; fax (54) 22-14-90; e-mail info@wermland.cci.se; internet www.wermland.cci.se; f. 1912; Pres. TORBJÖRN JOGHED; Sec. ULF LJUNGDAHL; c. 600 mems.

INDUSTRIAL AND TRADE ASSOCIATIONS

Svenskt Näringsliv (Confederation of Swedish Enterprise): Storgt. 19, 114 82 Stockholm; tel. (8) 553-430-00; fax (8) 553-430-99; e-mail info@svensktnaringsliv.se; internet www.svensktnaringsliv.se; f. 2001 by a merger of Sveriges Industriförbund (f. 1910) and Svenska Arbetsgivareföreningen (f. 1902); central organization representing Swedish business and industry; Pres. SÖREN GYLL; Vice-Pres BJÖRN ANDERSSON, SIGRUN HJELMQUIST, MICHAEL TRESCHOW; Dir-Gen. GÖRAN TUNHAMMAR; consists of 52 mem. asscns, representing c. 46,000 cos.

Företagarnas Riksorganisation (Federation of Private Enterprises): 106 67 Stockholm; tel. (8) 406-17-00; fax (8) 24-55-26; e-mail info@fr.se; internet www.fr.se; f. 1990; Chair. ARNE JOHANSSON; Man. Dir CARL-JOHAN WESTHOLM; 60,000 mems.

Grafiska Företagens Förbund (Graphic Companies' Federation): Blasieholmsgt. 4A, POB 16383, 103 27 Stockholm; tel. (8) 762-68-00; fax (8) 611-08-28; e-mail info@grafiska.se; internet www.grafiska.se; f. 1993 by merger; Chair. LARS FREDRIKSSON; Man. Dir LARS FREDRIKSON.

Järnverksföreningen (Swedish Steel Companies' Commercial Association): Kungsträdgårdsgt. 10, POB 1721, 111 87 Stockholm; f. 1889; Pres. CURT JOHANSSON; Sec. P. O. BOMAN; 36 mems.

Jernkontoret (Steel Producers' Asscn): Kungsträdgårdsgt. 10, POB 1721, 111 87 Stockholm; tel. (8) 679-17-00; fax (8) 611-20-89; e-mail office@jernkontoret.se; internet www.jernkontoret.se; f. 1747; Man. Dir HÅKAN MURBY.

Kemikontoret (Asscn of Swedish Chemical Industries): Storgt. 19, POB 5501, 114 85 Stockholm; tel. (8) 783-80-00; fax (8) 663-63-23; e-mail kemikontoret@chemind.se; internet www.chemind.se; f. 1917; Pres. MÅNS COLLIN; Man. Dir OWE FREDHOLM; 161 mems.

Skogsindustrierna (Swedish Forest Industries' Federation): POB 16006, 103 21 Stockholm; tel. (8) 762-72-60; fax (8) 762-72-14; internet www.forestindustries.se; Chair. BJÖRN HÄGGLUND; Dir-Gen. KARL-EWERT LIDMAN.

Svensk Handel (Swedish Federation of Trade): 103 29 Stockholm; tel. (8) 762-77-00; fax (8) 762-77-77; Chair. ROLAND FAHLIN; 20,000 mems.

Svensk Industriförening (Swedish Small Industries' Asscn): Torsgt. 2, POB 1133, 111 81 Stockholm; tel. (8) 23-63-00; f. 1941; Man. Dir SVEN LANGENIUS; 1,800 mems.

Svenska Garveriidkareföreningen (Swedish Tanners' Asscn): c/o Elmo Leather AB, 512 81 Svenljunga; tel. (325) 66-14-00; fax (325) 61-10-04; f. 1901; Chair. BJÖRN JOHANSSON; Man. Dir C. LENNARTSON; 4 mems.

Svenska Glasbruksföreningen (Swedish Crystal Manufacturers' Asscn): POB 5501, 114 85 Stockholm; tel. (8) 783-80-00; fax (8) 663-63-23; e-mail gwn@chemind.se; internet www.chemind.se; Chair. GEORG WERGEMAN.

Svenska Sågverks- och Trävaruexportföreningen (Swedish Wood Exporters' Asscn): Villagt. 1, 114 32 Stockholm; tel. (8) 789-28-00; f. 1875; Pres. P. FREDELL; Man. Dir L. STRÄNGH; 350 mems.

Svenska Skofabrikantföreningen (Swedish Shoe Manufacturers' Asscn): c/o Arbesko-Gruppen AB, POB 1642, 701 16 Örebro; tel. (19) 30-66-00; fax (19) 30-66-50; f. 1910.

Sveriges Handelsagenters Förbund (Federation of Swedish Commercial Agents): POB 1137, 111 81 Stockholm; tel. (8) 411-00-22; fax (8) 411-00-23; f. 1914; Chair. BENGT LINDROTH; Man. Dir ANNA WIGARDT DUHS; 630 mems.

TEKOindustrierna (Textile and Clothing Industries' Asscn): Storgt. 5, POB 5510, 114 85 Stockholm; tel. (8) 762-68-80; fax (8) 762-68-87; f. 1907; Chair. IVAN L. LUDVIGSON; Man. Dirs ANDERS SANDGREN, SVEN CELE; 263 mems.

EMPLOYERS' ORGANIZATIONS

ALMEGA: POB 16105, 103 22 Stockholm; tel. (8) 762-69-00; fax (8) 762-69-48; e-mail almega.epost@almega.se; internet www.almega .se; f. 1921; Chair. HÅKAN BRYNGELSON; Dir-Gen. JONAS MILTON; 8,500 mems.

ARBIO (Swedish Federation of Wood and Furniture Industry): Södra Blasieholmshamnen 4A, POB 16006, 103 21 Stockholm; tel. (8) 762-72-00; fax (8) 762-72-14; internet www.traindustrierna.org; Chair. BJÖRN HÄGGLUND; Man. Dir KARL-EWERT LIDMAN; 5,000 mems.

Biltrafikens Arbetsgivareförbund (Road Transport Employers): Blasieholmsgt. 4A, 111 48 Stockholm; tel. (8) 762-60-00; fax (8) 611-46-99; Chair. REINHOLD ÖHMAN; Man. Dir GÖRAN LJUNGSTRÖM; 5,330 mem. cos.

Byggentreprenörerna (Construction Federation): Stockholm; tel. (8) 665-35-00; fax (8) 662-97-00; f. 1919; Pres. TORSTEN ERIKSSON; Man. Dir BERT LILJA; 2,000 mem. cos.

Byggnadsämnesförbundet (Building Material Manufacturers Employers): POB 16347, 103 26 Stockholm; tel. (8) 762-65-07; fax (8) 762-65-12; Chair. HÅKAN FERNVIK; Man. Dir GUNNAR GÖTHBERG; 278 mem. cos.

Elektriska Installatörsorganisationen EIO (The Swedish Electrical Contractors' Association): POB 17537, 118 91 Stockholm; tel. (8) 762-75-00; fax (8) 668-86-17; e-mail info@eio.se; internet www.eio .se; Chair. GÖSTA ALLTHIN; Man. Dir HANS ENSTRÖM; 2,500 mem. cos.

Försäkringsbranschens Arbetsgivareorganisation (Insurance Employers): Klara Norra Kyrkogt. 33, 111 22 Stockholm; tel. (8) 783-98-60; fax (8) 783-98-95; e-mail info@fao.se; internet www.fao.se; Chair. HÅKAN DANIELSSON; Man. Dir ANNIKA LUNDIUS; 110 mem. cos.

Gruvornas Arbetsgivareförbund (Mine Owners): POB 1721, 111 87 Stockholm; tel. (8) 762-67-35; fax (8) 611-62-64; e-mail bengt .huldt@metallgruppen.se; internet www.metallgruppen.se; Pres. LEIF RÖNNBÄCK; Man. Dir BENGT HULDT; 20 mems with 6,188 employees.

Livsmedelsbranschens Arbetsgivareförbund (Food Producers): POB 16105, 103 22 Stockholm; tel. (8) 762-69-00; fax (8) 762-69-48; Chair. SUNE SIGVARDSSON; Man. Dir GUNNAR GÖTHBERG; 385 mem. cos.

Maskinentreprenörerna (Earth Moving Contractors): POB 1609, 111 86 Stockholm; tel. (8) 762-70-65; fax (8) 611-85-41; Chair. ROLF GUNNARSSON; Man. Dir SVEN-OLA NILSSON; 3,703 mem. cos.

Medie- och Informationsarbetsgivarna (Media and Information Employers' Association): POB 16383, 103 27 Stockholm; tel. (8) 762-70-30; fax (8) 611-41-47; e-mail info@mediearbetsgivarna.org; internet www.mediearbetsgivarna.org; Chair. LENNART WIKLUND; Man. Dir CHARLOTT RICHARDSON; 400 mem. cos.

Motorbranschens Arbetsgivareförbund (Motor Trade Employers): Blasieholmsgt. 4A, POB 1621, 111 86 Stockholm; tel. (8) 762-60-00; fax (8) 611-46-99; Chair. GÖRAN GRERUP; Dir GÖRAN LJUNGSTRÖM; 2,138 mem. cos.

Petroleumbranschens Arbetsgivareförbund (Petroleum Industry Employers): Blasieholmsgt. 4A, POB 1621, 111 86 Stockholm; tel. (8) 762-60-00; fax (8) 611-46-99; f. 1936; Chair. HANS VON UTHMANN; Man. Dir GÖRAN LJUNGSTRÖM; 53 mem. cos.

Plåtslageriernas Riksförbund (Platers): Rosenlundsgt. 40, POB 17536, 118 91 Stockholm; tel. (8) 762-75-85; fax (8) 616-00-72; internet www.plr.se; Chair. LARS SJÖBLOM; Man. Dir CLAES FRANKHAMMAR; 808 mem. cos.

Samhallförbundet (Samhall Employers' Association): POB 16105, 103 22 Stockholm; tel. (8) 762-69-00; fax (8) 762-69-48; Chair. HÅKAN ANDERSSON; Man. Dir JOHAN RIMMERFELDT; 3 mem. cos.

Stål- och Metallförbundet (Steel and Metal Industry Employers): POB 1721, 111 87 Stockholm; tel. (8) 762-67-35; fax (8) 611-62-64; e-mail info@metallgruppen.se; internet www.metallgruppen.se; Pres. BENGT-ÅKE BENGTSSON; Man. Dir BENGT HULDT; 202 mems with 43,953 employees.

Sveriges Bageriförbund (Bakery and Confectionery Employers): POB 16141, 103 23 Stockholm; tel. (8) 762-60-00; fax (8) 678-66-64; e-mail kansli@bageri.se; internet www.bageri.se; f. 1900; Chair. MATS ROSÉU; Man. Dir BJÖRN HELLWAU; 570 mems.

Sveriges Hamnar (Ports): POB 1621, 111 86 Stockholm; tel. (8) 762-71-00; fax (8) 611-12-18; e-mail ports@transportgruppen.se; internet www.sweports.com; f. 1908; Vice-Pres. JAN APPELGREN; 44 mem. cos.

Svets Mekaniska Arbetsgivareförbundet (Welding Engineering): POB 1721, 111 87 Stockholm; tel. (8) 762-67-35; fax (8) 611-62-64; e-mail info@metallgruppen.se; internet www.metallgruppen .se; Pres. GUNNAR SKÖLD; Man. Dir BENGT HULDT; 414 mems with 4,629 employees.

Trä- och Möbelindustriförbundet (Swedish Wood Products Industry Employers' Asscn): POB 16006, 103 21 Stockholm; tel. (8) 762-72-00; fax (8) 611-60-25; e-mail info@traindustrin.org; Chair. LARS-ERIK SANDSTRÖM; Man. Dir KARL-EWERT LIDMAN; 700 mem. cos.

VVS-Installatörerna (Heating, Plumbing, Refrigeration and Insulation Employers): Rosenluundsgt. 40, 118 91 Stockholm; tel. (8) 762-75-00; fax (8) 669-41-19; e-mail kjell.jansson@vvsi.se; internet www.vvsi.se; f. 1918; Chair. KARI KALLIO; Man. Dir KJELL JANSSON; 1,321 mems.

VI Sveriges Verkstadsindustrier (Engineering Industries): Storgt. 5, POB 5510, 114 85 Stockholm; tel. (8) 782-08-00; fax (8) 782-09-00; e-mail vi@vi.se; internet www.vi.se; f. 1896; Pres. LENNART NILSSON; Man. Dir ANDERS NARVINGER; 3,000 mem. cos.

UTILITIES

Major Service Providers

Ängelholms Energi AB: Energig. 1, 262 73 Ängelholm; tel. (431) 878-00.

Billeberga Kraft & Energi AB: Industriv. 5, POB 53, 260 21 Billeberga; tel. (418) 45-08-50.

Gullspång: Forsöv. 4, POB 33, 820 10 Arbrå; tel. (278) 277-00.

Helsingborg Energi: V. Sandg. 4, POB 642, 251 06 Helsingborg; tel. (42) 490-32-70; fax (42) 490-32-56.

Hudiksvalls Energiverk AB: Östanbräcksv. 8, POB 1143, 824 13 Hudiksvall; tel. (650) 373-50.

Höganäs Energi AB: Stadshuset, 253 82 Höganäs; tel. (42) 33-71-00.

KREAB Energi AB: Ljungbyg. 22, 260 70 Lyungbyhed; tel. (20) 41-00-10.

Norrlands Energi Försäljning AB: Kyrkog. 12, POB 736, 851 21 Sundsvall; tel. (60) 19-59-00.

NVSH Energi AB: Verkstadsg. 1, POB 505, 267 25 Bjuv; tel. (42) 856-00.

Skövde Elnät: Badhusg. 22, 541 83 Skövde; tel. (500) 46-82-14.

Sollefteå Energi: Sollefteå; tel. (620) 68-20-00; internet www .solleftea.se.

Sydkraft AB: 205 09 Malmö; tel. (42) 255-000; e-mail info@sydkraft .se; internet www.sydkraft.se.

Vattenfall AB: 162 87 Stockholm; tel. (8) 739-50-00; fax (8) 739-51-29; e-mail info@vattenfall.se; internet www.vattenfall.se; f. 1909; became limited liability company in 1992; 100% state-owned; power generation and distribution; some 90 directly or indirectly owned operational subsidiaries; interests in Germany, Poland, South-East Asia and Latin America; Pres. and CEO CARL-ERIK NYQUIST.

Vinninga Elektriska Förening Ek. för.: Vallmov., POB 3052, 531 03 Vinninga; tel. (510) 500-60.

TRADE UNIONS

The three principal trade union bodies are the Swedish Trade Union Confederation (LO), the Confederation of Professional Employees (TCO) and the Confederation of Professional Associations (SACO).

Landsorganisationen i Sverige (LO) (Swedish Trade Union Confederation): Barnhusgt. 18, 105 53 Stockholm; tel. (8) 796-25-00; fax (8) 796-28-00; e-mail info@lo.se; internet www.lo.se; f. 1898; affiliated to ICFTU; Pres. WANJA LUNDBY-WEDIN; 18 affiliated unions with a total membership of 2,016,218 (Dec. 2000).

Affiliated unions:

Byggnads (Building Workers): 106 32 Stockholm; tel. (8) 728-48-00; fax (8) 34-50-51; Chair. OVE BENGTSBERG; 133,102 mems (Dec. 2000).

Fastighetsanställdas Förbund (Building Maintenance Workers): POB 70446, 107 25 Stockholm; tel. (8) 696-11-50; fax (8) 24-46-90; f. 1936; Chair. BARBRO PALMERLUND; 41,943 mems (Dec. 2000).

Grafiska Fackförbundet (Graphic and Media Workers): POB 1101, 111 81 Stockholm; tel. (8) 791-16-00; fax (8) 411-41-01; e-mail gf@gf.se; internet www.gf.se; Pres. MALTE ERIKSSON; 39,140 mems (Dec. 2000).

Handelsanställdas Förbund (Commercial Employees): Upplandsgt. 5, POB 1146, 111 81 Stockholm; tel. (8) 412-68-00; fax (8) 10-00-62; e-mail handels@handels.se; internet www.handels.se; f. 1916; Pres. NINEL JANSSON; 167,703 mems (Dec. 2000).

Hotell- och Restaurang Facket (Hotel and Restaurant Workers): POB 1143, 111 81 Stockholm; tel. (8) 781-02-00; fax (8) 411-71-18; internet www.hrf.net; Chair. JOHN HERRSTRÖM; 61,069 mems (Dec. 2000).

Industrifacket (Industrial Workers' Union): POB 1114, 111 81 Stockholm; tel. (8) 786-85-00; fax (8) 10-59-68; e-mail postbox.fk@industrifacktet.se; internet www.industrifacket.se; f. 1993 by merger of factory workers' and textile, garment and leather workers' unions; Pres. and Gen. Sec. LEIF OHLSSON; 90,300 mems (Dec. 2002).

SEKO—Facket för Service och Kommunikation (Services and Communications Employees): Barnhusgt. 6–10, POB 1105, 111 81 Stockholm; tel. (8) 791-41-00; fax (8) 21-89-53; e-mail seko@seko.se; internet www.seko.se; f. 1970; present name since 1995; Chair. SVEN-OLAF ARBESTÅL; 172,616 mems (Dec. 2000).

Skogs- och Träfacket (Swedish Forest and Wood Trade Union): POB 1152, 111 81 Stockholm; tel. (8) 701-77-00; fax (8) 20-79-04; e-mail postbox.fk@skogstrafacket.org; internet www.skogstrafacket.org; f. 1998 by merger of Svenska Skogs arbetareförbundet and Svenska Träindustriarbetareförbundet; Chair. and Pres. KJELL DAHLSTRÖM; 60,000 mems.

Svenska Elektrikerförbundet (Electricians): POB 1123, 111 81 Stockholm; tel. (8) 402-14-00; fax (8) 412-82-01; Pres. ALF NORBERG; 26,883 mems (Dec. 2000).

Svenska Kommunalarbetareförbundet (Swedish Municipal Workers' Union): POB 19039, 104 32 Stockholm; tel. (8) 728-28-00; fax (8) 31-87-45; e-mail kommunal.forbundet@kommunal.se; internet www.kommunal.se; merged with Svenska Lantarbetareförbundet in Jan. 2002; Pres. YLVA THÖRN; 595,450 mems.

Svenska Livsmedelsarbetareförbundet (Food Workers): POB 1156, 111 81 Stockholm; tel. (8) 769-29-00; fax (8) 796-29-03; Chair. ÅKE SÖDERGREN; Sec. EVERT KAJHAMMAR; 58,281 mems (Dec. 2000).

Svenska Målareförbundet (Painters): POB 1113, 111 81 Stockholm; tel. (8) 5872-74-00; fax (8) 5872-74-99; e-mail post@malareforbundet.a.se; internet www.malareforbundet.a.se; f. 1887; Chair. LARS-ÅKE LUNDIN; 18,062 mems.

Svenska Metallindustriarbetareförbundet (Swedish Metalworkers' Union): Olof Palmesgt. 11, 105 52 Stockholm; tel. (8) 786-80-00; fax (8) 24-86-74; e-mail post.fk@metall.se; internet www.metall.se; f. 1888; Chair. GÖRAN JOHNSSON; 389,769 mems.

Svenska Musikerförbundet (Musicians): POB 49144, 101 29 Stockholm; tel. (8) 5870-60-00; fax (8) 16-80-20; e-mail info@musikerforbundet.se; f. 1994; Pres. (vacant); 3,700 mems (Dec. 2001).

Svenska Pappersindustriarbetareförbundet (Swedish Paperworkers' Union): POB 1127, 111 81 Stockholm; tel. (8) 796-61-00; fax (8) 411-41-79; e-mail info@pappers.se; internet www.pappers.se; Chair. SUNE EKBÅGE; Sec. BENGT HALLBERG; 25,760 mems.

Svenska Transportarbetareförbundet (Transport Workers): POB 714, 101 33 Stockholm; tel. (8) 723-77-00; fax (8) 24-03-91; e-mail transport.fk@transport.se; internet www.transport.se; Chair. PER NINBERG; 71,403 mems (Dec. 2000).

SACO (Confederation of Professional Asscns): POB 2206, Lilla Nygt. 14, 103 15 Stockholm; tel. (8) 613-48-00; fax (8) 24-77-01; e-mail kansli@saco.se; internet www.saco.se; f. 1947; 26 affiliated unions and professional organizations, of which the largest are:

Civilingenjörsförbundet (90,000 mems), Lärarnas riksförbund (74,000 mems) and Jusek (60,000 mems); Chair. ANNA EKSTRÖM; 500,000 mems (Dec. 2001).

Tjänstemännens Centralorganisation (TCO) (Confederation of Professional Employees): Linnégt. 14, 114 94 Stockholm; tel. (8) 782-91-00; fax (8) 663-75-20; e-mail tco@tco.se; f. 1944; affiliated to ICFTU, European Trade Union Confed. and Council of Nordic Trade Unions; Pres. STURE NORDH; 18 affiliated unions with total membership of 1,045,473 (Dec. 2000), of which the following are the largest:

Finansförbundet (Bank Employees): Roselundsgt. 29B, POB 38151, 100 64 Stockholm; tel. (8) 614-03-00; fax (8) 611-38-98; e-mail info@finansforbundet.se; internet www.finansforbundet.se; Chair. LILLEMOR SMEDENVALL; 34,920 mems.

Lärarförbundet (Teachers): Segelbåtsvägen 15, POB 12229, 102 26 Stockholm; tel. (8) 737-65-00; fax (8) 656-94-15; Chair. CHRISTER ROMILSON; 207,895 mems.

Ledarna (Professional and Managerial Staff): St Eriksgt. 26, POB 12069, 102 22 Stockholm; tel. (8) 598-990-00; fax (8) 598-990-10; e-mail ledarna@ledarna.se; Chair. BJÖRN BERGMAN; 77,192 mems.

SIF (Clerical and Technical Employees in Industry): Olof Palmesgt. 17, 105 32 Stockholm; tel. (8) 508-970-00; fax (8) 508-970-19; e-mail postservice@sif.se; internet www.sif.se; f. as Svenska Industritjänstemannaförbundet, present name adopted 2001; Chair. MARI-ANN KRANTZ; 360,000 mems.

Statstjänstemannaförbundet (Civil Servants): Sturegt. 15, POB 5308, 102 47 Stockholm; tel. (8) 790-51-00; fax (8) 24-29-24; e-mail st@stmf.se; internet www.stmf.se; Chair. ANNETTE CARNHEDE; 97,000 mems.

Sveriges Kommunaltjänstemannaförbund (Local Government Officers): Kungsgt. 28A, POB 7825, 103 97 Stockholm; tel. (8) 789-63-00; fax (8) 21-52-44; e-mail sktf@sktf.se; internet www.sktf.se; Chair. INGER EFRAIMSSON; 176,300 mems.

Tjänstemannaförbundet HTF (Commercial Salaried Employees): Franzengt. 5, POB 30102, 104 25 Stockholm; tel. (8) 737-80-00; fax (8) 618-22-45; fmrly Handelstjänstemannaförbundet; Chair. HOLGER ERIKSSON; 145,286 mems.

Vårdförbundet (Swedish Asscn of Health Professionals): Adolf Fredrik Kyrkogt. 11, POB 3260, 103 65 Stockholm; tel. (8) 14-77-00; fax (8) 411-42-29; e-mail mailbox@vardforbundet.se; internet www.vardforbundet.se; fmrly Svenska Hälso- och Sjukvårdens Tjänstemannaförbund; Chair. EVA FERNVALL MARKSTEDT; 112,186 mems.

Transport

RAILWAYS

At 31 December 1998 there were 10,998 km of standard- and narrow-gauge railways, of which 7,614 km of track was electrified. A railway line, linking Stockholm and Arlanda international airport opened in September 1999.

Statens Järnvägar (SJ): 105 50 Stockholm; tel. (8) 762-20-00; fax (8) 411-12-16; e-mail sjinfo@sj.se; internet www.sj.se; f. 1856; state-owned; runs passenger and freight traffic on all state-owned railway track; the company also controls ferry-boats; 3,500 employees; Dir-Gen. DANIEL JOHANNESSON.

BK Tag AB: Brogardsgt., 574 38 Vetlanda; tel. (383) 19-650; fax (383) 14-757; e-mail info@bktag.se; internet www.bktag.se; passenger services on six routes; Gen. Man. T. HULT; 667 km.

Malmö-Limhamns Järnvägs AB: POB 30022, 200 61 Limhamn; tel. (40) 36-15-04; fax (40) 15-86-24; 5 km of 1,435 mm gauge; Dir UWE JÖHNSON; Traffic Man. K. HOLMBERG.

TGOJ AB: 631 92 Eskilstuna; tel. (16) 17-26-00; fax (16) 17-26-01; internet www.tgoj.se; f. 1877; 300 km of 1,435 mm gauge electrified railways; Chair. R. HELLSTADIUS; Pres. CURT BYLUND.

ROADS

At 31 December 2000 there were an estimated 212,402 km of roads, of which 1,499 km were motorways, 13,580 km were main or national roads and 83,094 km of secondary or regional roads. In 2001 a road-rail link between Malmö and Copenhagen (Denmark), across the 16-km Öresund strait, was opened.

SHIPPING

Principal Shipping Companies

Argonaut AB: Stockholm; tel. (8) 614-45-00; fax (8) 611-62-28; f. 1983; Pres. BJORN ERSMAN.

B & N & Nordsjöfrakt AB: POB 32, 471 21 Skärhamn; tel. (304) 67-47-00; fax (304) 67-47-70; e-mail bn@bn.se; Man. Dir FOLKE PATRIKSSON.

Broström Ship Management AB: POB 39, 471 21 Skärhamn; tel. (304) 67-67-00; fax (304) 67-11-10; e-mail shipman@brostrom.se; internet www.brostrom.se; management company, operating specialized tanker services; Man. Dir OLLE NOORD.

Broström Tankers AB: 403 30 Göteborg; tel. (31) 61-60-00; fax (31) 61-60-12; e-mail brotank@brostrom.se; internet www.brostrom.se; f. 1990; specializes in transporting petroleum products, in north-west Europe and world-wide; Man. Dir TORE ANGERVALL.

EffJohn International: Stockholm; tel. (8) 666-34-00; f. 1990 following merger of Effoa Finland Steamship Co. and Johnson Line (Sweden); passenger ferry operations; EffJohn Group covers operations in the Baltic: Silja Line, SeaWind Line, Wasa Ferries, Sally Line, JBT, Svea Management; elsewhere in Europe: Sally Line UK; in USA: Commodore Cruise Line, Crown Cruise Line; Pres. HANS H. CHRISTNER.

Nordström & Thulin AB: Skeppsbron 34–36, POB 1215, 111 82 Stockholm; tel. (8) 613-19-00; fax (8) 21-22-28; f. 1850; Man. Dir ANDERS BERG.

Stena AB: 405 19 Göteborg; tel. (31) 85-80-00; fax (31) 12-06-51; f. 1939; Stena Line ferry service since 1962; in 1990 acquired Sealink (United Kingdom); Man. Dir DAN STEN OLSSON.

Wallenius Lines AB/Wallenius Rederierna AB: Swedenborgsgt. 19, POB 17086, 104 62 Stockholm; tel. (8) 772-05-00; fax (8) 640-68-54; e-mail postmaster@wallenius.se; f. 1934; car and truck carriers; Pres. CHRISTER OLSSON.

Associations

Föreningen Sveriges Sjöfart och Sjöförsvar (Swedish Maritime League): Kastellet, Kastellholmen, 111 49 Stockholm; tel. (8) 611-74-81; fax (8) 611-74-76; e-mail fsss@algonet.se; f. 1983 by merger of Swedish General Shipping Asscn and Swedish Navy League; Pres. CLAES TORNBERG; Gen. Sec. STEN GÖTHBERG; 2,000 mems.

Sveriges Redareförening (Swedish Shipowners' Asscn): Göteborg; tel. (31) 10-75-00; fax (31) 13-01-26; f. 1906; Pres. CHRISTER OLSSON; Man. Dir HÅKAN GEZELIUS; mems 156 shipping companies with 259 ships (1996).

CIVIL AVIATION

The main international airport is at Arlanda, connected by bus service to Stockholm, 42 km away. There are other international airports at Landvetter, 25 km from Göteborg, and at Sturup, 28 km from Malmö. There are regular flights between the main cities in Sweden. Many domestic flights operate from Bromma (Stockholm's city airport). Measures on the deregulation of civil aviation took effect in 1992 and ended the virtual monopoly of domestic services previously held by the Scandinavian Airlines System.

Civil Aviation Administration: Vikboplan 11, 601 79 Norrköping; tel. (11) 19-20-00; e-mail luftfartsverket@lfv.se; internet www.lfv.se; f. 1923; state body; central government authority for matters concerning civil aviation; Dir-Gen. LARS REKKE.

Scandinavian Airlines System (SAS): Head Office: Frösundavik Allé 1, Solna, 195 87 Stockholm; tel. (8) 797-00-00; fax (8) 797-15-15; internet www.sas.se; f. 1946; the national carrier of Denmark, Norway and Sweden. It is a consortium owned two-sevenths by SAS Danmark A/S, two-sevenths by SAS Norge ASA and three-sevenths by SAS Sverige AB. Each parent organization is a limited company owned 50% by Govt and 50% by private shareholders. The SAS group includes the consortium and the subsidiaries in which the consortium has a majority or otherwise controlling interest; the Board consists of two members from each of the parent companies and the chairmanship rotates among the three national chairmen on an annual basis. SAS absorbed Linjeflyg AB (domestic passenger, newspaper and postal services in Sweden) in 1993; strategic alliance with Lufthansa (Germany) formed in 1995; Chair. BO BERGGREN; Pres. and CEO JAN STENBERG.

AB Aerotransport: POB 5571, 103 96 Stockholm; Chair. KRISTER WICKMAN; Pres. OLLE HEDBERG; Chair. Exec. Cttee CURT NICOLIN; Swedish partner of SAS.

Air Operations of Europe: Hammarbacken 4, 191 49 Sollentuna; tel. (8) 92-66-55; fax (8) 35-07-80; f. 1993; charter services; Man. Dir CAMILLA LENHAMME.

Nordic East Airways: POB 79, 190 45 Stockholm; tel. (8) 5949-0600; fax (8) 5936-1444; f. 1991; charter services; Chair. and CEO GUNNAR OHLSSON.

Swedair AB: 195 87 Stockholm; tel. (8) 797-00-00; fax (8) 85-96-38; f. 1975 as result of merger of Svensk Flygtjanst and Crownair; passenger services to destinations within Scandinavia; Pres. BENNY ZAKRISSON.

Swedeways AB: Skogsta 41, 824 92 Hudiksvall; tel. (650) 24-273; fax (650) 24-224; e-mail webmaster@swedeways.se; internet www.swedeways.se; f. 1995; Man. Dir CARL-JOHAN STÅHLE.

Transwede Airways AB: Stockholm-Arlanda; tel. (593) 65-000; fax (593) 61-710; f. 1985; passenger services within Sweden and from Scandinavia to Europe and the Mediterranean; Chair. BO JOHANSSON; Pres. THOMAS ROSENQUIST.

West Air Sweden: Karlstad; tel. (54) 18-00-10; fax (54) 18-44-10; f. 1963; present name since 1993; Pres. OSKAR NILSSON.

Tourism

Sweden offers a variety of landscape, from the mountains of the 'Midnight Sun', north of the Arctic Circle, to the white sandy beaches of the south. There are many lakes, waterfalls and forests, and Stockholm is famed for its beautiful situation and modern architecture. Most tourists come from the other Scandinavian countries and from Germany. In 2000 tourism receipts totalled an estimated US $4,107m.

Next Stop Sweden: Stockholm; Swedish travel and tourism council; Pres. PER-JOHANN ORRBY.

Svenska Turistföreningen (Swedish Touring Club): Stureplan 4c, POB 25, 101 20 Stockholm; tel. (8) 463-21-00; fax (8) 678-19-58; internet www.stf.turist.se; f. 1885; 300,000 mems; owns and operates mountain hotels, tourist stations, about 300 youth hostels and 480 guest ports; Pres. E. EHN; Sec.-Gen. GORAN LINDSTEDT.

Turistdelegationen (Swedish Tourist Authority): POB 860, 101 37 Stockholm; tel. (8) 5451-54-60; fax (8) 5451-54-69; e-mail kansli@tourist.se; internet www.tourist.se; f. 1995; state-owned; co-ordinates government-sponsored promotion of the tourist industry in Sweden, and monitors trends in the sector; Dir DENNIS BEDCROFF (acting).

SWITZERLAND

Introductory Survey

Location, Climate, Language, Religion, Flag, Capital

The Swiss Confederation lies in central Europe, bounded to the north by Germany, to the east by Austria, to the south by Italy and to the west by France. The climate is generally temperate, but varies considerably with altitude and aspect. In Zürich the average temperature ranges from –1°C (30°F) in winter to 16°C (61°F) in summer. There are three official languages—German, French and Italian, spoken by 73.4%, 20.5% and 4.1% of resident Swiss nationals respectively in 1990. Raeto-Romansch, spoken by 0.7% of Swiss nationals in 1990, mainly in parts of the canton of Graubünden (Grisons) in eastern Switzerland, is expected to become the fourth official language. Other languages are spoken by the remaining 1.3% of the population. Including resident aliens, the linguistic proportions in 1990 were: German 63.6%, French 19.2%, Italian 7.6%. Most Swiss citizens profess Christianity: in 1990 47.3% were Protestants and 43.3% Roman Catholics. Of the total resident population in 1990, 40.0% were Protestants and 46.1% Roman Catholics. The Federal flag, which is square, consists of a white upright cross in the centre of a red ground. The capital is Bern (Berne).

Recent History

Switzerland, whose origins date back to 1291, has occupied its present area since its borders were fixed by treaty in 1815. At the same time, it was internationally recognized as a neutral country. Despite the strategic importance of Switzerland, its 'permanent neutrality' has never since been violated. The country has not entered any military alliances, and it avoided participation in both World Wars. Executive authority is exercised on a collegial basis by the Federal Council (cabinet), with a President who serves, for only one year at a time, as 'the first among equals'. Owing to the restricted powers of the Federal Council, initiatives and referendums form the core of the political process. Switzerland is a confederation of 20 cantons and six half-cantons. In 1979 the mainly French-speaking region of Jura seceded from the predominantly German-speaking canton of Bern, becoming the first new canton to be established since 1815.

Despite the fact that Switzerland has long been the head-quarters of many international organizations, the country has not yet joined the UN. However, Switzerland maintains a permanent observer at the UN and has joined the organization's non-political specialized agencies. At a referendum in 1986 some 75.7% of voters rejected full membership of the UN, although the Government had campaigned in its favour. The proportion of the electorate voting in the referendum, at 50.2%, represented a higher than average level of participation in the Swiss system of direct democracy. In January 2000 the Government announced its intention to propose to the cantons and to the Federal Assembly that the country should join the UN by 2003. In March 2000 a petition favouring membership of the UN forced a future referendum on the issue; it was expected to be held in 2002 (as it, indeed, was—see below). Switzerland was a founder member of the European Free Trade Association (EFTA, see p. 195) in 1960 and joined the Council of Europe (see p. 181) in 1963.

Switzerland began to emerge from its traditional isolation in the early 1990s. This was largely due to economic pressures resulting from the world recession and the further integration of the European Community (EC—now European Union—EU, see p. 199). In May 1992 the Government's proposal for Switzerland to join the IMF and the World Bank was approved in a referendum. On the following day, the Federal Council announced that it was to present an application for membership of the EC. During September and October 1992 the Swiss Parliament approved the necessary legislation to comply with an agreement, signed in May 1992, to create a free-trade zone, the European Economic Area (EEA), encompassing both EC and EFTA member states. In a referendum on 6 December, however, the Swiss electorate voted against ratification of the agreement, by 16 cantons to seven. (The EEA was established, without Switzerland, in January 1994.) Despite this set-back, the Government declared its intention to continue to pursue its application for membership of the EC. During 1993 Switzerland con-fined itself to seeking bilateral negotiations with the EC on issues of particular national interest, including transport and involvement in EC research programmes. In February 1994, however, in defiance of a government campaign, 52% of voters in a referendum approved a proposal to ban transit freight by road through Switzerland within 10 years (requiring its transportation by rail), in order to protect the Swiss Alps. In April 1996 the Federal Council approved the Neue Eisenbahn-Alpen-Transversale (NEAT) project to construct two new Alpine tunnels in order to expedite international freight transport by rail; it was announced that this was to be financed mainly by levying a weight and distance toll on heavy goods vehicles crossing Swiss territory. Agreement was reached in December 1996 to phase out Swiss work permits for citizens of EU member states over a period of six years. At the beginning of December 1998 Switzerland and the EU concluded a bilateral trade agreement, having settled a lengthy dispute concerning the level of the tolls to be imposed on road freight traffic through Switzerland. By February 2000 the Government had negotiated seven bilateral free-trade agreements with the EU. The accords included the gradual elimination of immigration controls between Switzerland and the EU over a 12-year period in order to allay popular anxiety regarding the possibility of EU workers depriving the Swiss of employment. While the Government had taken care to ensure that Swiss sovereignty was not affected by the trade agreements, popular resentment at the EU's imposition of sanctions against Austria during 1999 in protest at the presence of the far-right in the Austrian Government prompted Swiss opponents of the EU to submit a petition to the Swiss Government, thereby forcing a referendum on the trade agreements. At the referendum, which was held in May 2000, 67.2% of those who voted approved the agreements. Following the submission of a petition by pro-EU lobbyists, a referendum was held in March 2001 on whether to begin 'fast-track' accession negotiations with the EU; the ballot attracted an unusually high participation rate and the motion was rejected by an unexpectedly large majority, 77% of the voters. The result was believed to have been influenced in part by a letter from the European Commission in February, widely perceived as coercive, which urged the acceleration of negotiations with the EU regarding co-operation against customs fraud and tax evasion. The Government announced that the vote did not represent a rejection of the EU, but rather reflected the desire to move towards membership at a slower pace, and that its plans for eventual membership of the EU remained unchanged.

Since 1959 government posts have been divided between the members of the Social Democratic Party, the Radical Democratic Party, the Christian Democratic People's Party and the Swiss People's Party. This coalition holds more than 80% of the seats in the National Council (the lower house of the Federal Assembly), and all of the seats in the Council of States (the upper house). The ruling coalition dominated the National Council at elections held between 1975 and 1995, although it lost some support to the Green Party of Switzerland, which grew to become the fifth largest party due to mounting public concern over ecological issues. The results of elections to the National Council and the Council of States, held in October 1999, challenged, initially at least, some of the assumptions generally made about the Swiss political process. They were characterized, above all, by the strong performance of the Swiss People's Party, which, in terms of votes gained, became the country's largest party. In the National Council the Swiss People's Party overtook both the Radical Democrats and the Christian Democratic People's Party to become the second largest party after the Social Democrats. Seats in the National Council are allotted in proportion to votes gained. However, the complex, 'cantonal' nature of the electoral system ensured ultimate victory for the Social Democratic Party. In the Council of States, the success of the Swiss People's Party was similarly diluted by the 'cantonal' nature of majority voting procedures; even so, the People's Party obtained a total of seven seats, thereby overtaking the Social Democrats as the third largest party (after the Radical Democrats and the Christian Democrats).

Analysis of the election results revealed that many of the Swiss People's Party's gains had been made at the expense of extreme right-wing groups. Spurred by one of its factions, the 'Association for an Independent and Neutral Switzerland', led by Christian Blocher, nationalist, isolationist policies had been at the fore of the Party's electoral campaign, together with so-called populist proposals to adopt a more hard-line stance towards asylum-seekers and drug offenders, and to reduce taxation. There was speculation that if the party's representation in the Federal Council were not increased to two seats in December 1999, then Blocher would seek to detach the party from the governing coalition. In the event, Blocher's attempt to gain a seat on the Federal Council was defeated without provoking such a defection. Adolf Ogi, the leader of the Bernese section of the Swiss People's Party, which had criticized Blocher's views, was chosen as President of the Swiss Confederation for 2000. In December the Federal Assembly elected the Head of Federal Department of Environment, Transport, Energy and Communications, Moritz Leuenberger of the Social Democratic Party, to replace Ogi as President for 2001. Leuenberger was, in turn, replaced by Head of Federal Department of Finance, Kaspar Villiger of the Radical Democratic Party, as President for 2002. Pascal Couchepin of the Radical Democratic Party was appointed as President for 2003.

The enfranchisement of women in federal elections was approved at a referendum in February 1971. However, the half-cantons of Appenzell Ausserrhoden and Appenzell Innerrhoden introduced female suffrage only in 1989 and 1990, respectively. In October 1984 the Federal Assembly elected Switzerland's first female cabinet minister, Dr Elisabeth Kopp, a leading member of the Radical Democratic Party, who became Head of the Federal Department of Justice and Police. In December 1988 the Assembly elected Dr Kopp, by a large majority, to be Vice-President of the Swiss Confederation for 1989, concurrently with her other duties in the Federal Council. In the same month, however, she announced her resignation from her post as Head of the Federal Department of Justice and Police, following allegations that she had violated regulations concerning official secrecy. In February 1989, following an official investigation of the case, Dr Kopp was replaced as Vice-President; in February 1990, however, she was finally acquitted by the Federal Supreme Court.

In January 1993 the Head of the Federal Department of Foreign Affairs, René Felber, resigned from the Federal Council. Under the terms of the coalition, Felber was to be replaced by another francophone member of the Social Democratic Party. In March the official Social Democratic candidate, Christiane Brunner, a trade union leader, was rejected by other members of the coalition in favour of a male candidate, Francis Matthey, who, however, following pressure from within the party, refused to accept his election. The Social Democratic Party subsequently reconfirmed Brunner's candidacy but presented another female candidate as well, Ruth Dreifuss, also a trade union activist (and a former journalist and government aid worker). Following three rounds of voting, Dreifuss became the second woman to be elected to a ministerial position in Switzerland. In December 1998 the Federal Assembly elected Dreifuss (by then Head of the Federal Department of Home Affairs) as President of the Confederation for 1999. A female Christian Democratic People's Party candidate, Ruth Metzler, was elected Head of the Federal Department of Justice and Police in March 1999. In the following month 59.2% of voters in a national referendum approved a revised draft Constitution that included new provision for the right to undertake strike action by the labour force.

The commission that had investigated the allegations against Dr Kopp during 1989 (see above) subsequently revealed that the office of the Federal Public Prosecutor held about 900,000 secret files on some 200,000 Swiss citizens and foreigners. In March 1990 about 30,000 people demonstrated in Bern in protest at the existence of such files; the demonstration ended in rioting. The Government subsequently announced that it would commission a report on the activities of the security services and introduce new laws regulating state security; it also opened most of the files to public scrutiny. The completed report, which was published in June 1993, found that security service observation had been largely restricted to left-wing groups since 1945 and that security service personnel had at times behaved in an unprofessional manner.

In September 1995 the Swiss Bankers' Association (SBA) announced the introduction of measures that would enable relatives to trace and recover the assets deposited in Swiss bank accounts by victims of the Nazi massacre of Jews in the Second World War. To assist in this process an accord was signed in May 1996 by the SBA and the World Jewish Congress, establishing an independent commission (the Independent Committee of Eminent Persons), chaired by Paul Volcker, former Chairman of the Board of Governors of the US Federal Reserve, which was responsible for auditing all dormant Swiss bank accounts. In September 1996 controversial documents were released from British and US archives, claiming that gold valued at several thousand million dollars, at current prices, had been deposited in Swiss banks during the Second World War. Much of it was suspected to have belonged to Jews killed in the Holocaust. The Swiss Federal Assembly subsequently approved legislation establishing an independent panel to investigate the ownership of these assets, and legislation ordering banks to release all records that might pertain to dealings with the Nazi regime in Germany or its victims. In December 1996 a nine-member international historical commission was appointed.

From mid-1996 the issue of 'Nazi gold' received much coverage in the international press. Jewish organizations threatened to boycott Swiss financial institutions, claiming that insufficient efforts were being made to recover their assets and expressing outrage at what they regarded as antagonistic comments made by Jean-Pascal Delamuraz (President of the Confederation in 1996) and by Carlo Jagmetti (who subsequently resigned as Switzerland's ambassador to the USA). In March 1997 three of Switzerland's most prominent banks, Crédit Suisse, Swiss Bank Corporation and UBS-Union Bank of Switzerland, established a special humanitarian fund for impoverished survivors of the Holocaust, under the administration of the Federal Government; the first payments from the fund were made in November. In early December Swiss banks issued the first payments to claimants of funds from dormant accounts that had been opened prior to and during the Second World War. In March of that year the Swiss administration had announced a plan, subject to ratification by the Federal Assembly and the electorate, to establish a 'Swiss Foundation for Solidarity', a larger-scale fund with a general humanitarian brief, to be financed by a revaluation of a part of the Swiss National Bank's gold reserves. However, the proposals were rejected by the electorate at a referendum held in September 2002.

In late March 1998 senior US public-finance officials, threatening an imminent boycott of Swiss banks and industrial interests, placed the former under increasing pressure to agree to a speedy 'global settlement' of the issue of Holocaust victims' accounts, involving the establishment of a victims' fund and a timetable for payment; soon afterwards (against the wishes of the Swiss Government, which believed the Independent Committee of Eminent Persons, see above, to be making adequate progress in assessing claims) Swiss Bank Corporation and UBS-Union Bank of Switzerland, which subsequently merged to form UBS AG, and Crédit Suisse announced their intention to negotiate such a 'global settlement'. In August UBS and Crédit Suisse agreed to pay US $1,250m. to the World Jewish Congress as compensation for the role of Swiss financial institutions in retaining dormant Jewish assets, handling gold deposited by the Nazis and lending money during the Second World War to German companies that had utilized Jewish slave labour. In return, all threats of boycotts and legal action against Swiss concerns were withdrawn. The settlement was not endorsed by the Swiss Government.

In December 1999 the Independent Committee of Eminent Persons, established in May 1996, reported that its audit of all dormant Swiss bank accounts had shown that some 54,000 of them might have belonged to Jews murdered in the Holocaust (although that number was subsequently reduced to 36,000). The Committee recommended that details of 25,000 of the 54,000 accounts should be publicized in order to alert survivors of the Holocaust or their heirs to their existence; and it criticized some Swiss banks for their insensitivity and for their obstruction of legitimate claims. The Committee did not attempt to value the funds held in the accounts, but stated that the total would probably not exceed the US $1,250m. already promised by UBS and Crédit Suisse to the World Jewish Congress. The report of the Independent Committee of Eminent Persons was followed, almost immediately, by the release of that of the international historical commission appointed in December 1996. The commission concluded that, by closing its border to an estimated 24,500 fugitive Jews from 1942, Switzerland bore partial responsibility for their deaths at the hands of the Nazis.

Following the release of the historical commission's report the Government formally apologized for Switzerland's role in the Second World War. Further details emerged in August 2001, which indicated that several of Switzerland's largest companies, including Nestlé, had ignored reports of Nazi atrocities and pursued business as usual with Germany during the Second World War, thereby contributing to the German war effort. Moreover, it was revealed that, despite Switzerland's neutrality, the Government had issued Germany and Italy credits to buy Swiss-made machinery and weapons. In December a further report indicated that Switzerland had harboured substantial amounts of Nazi funds and assets, and even dissimilated entire German companies, during the Second World War. The report also stated that Switzerland had provided a refuge for several prominent Nazi war criminals following the end of hostilities.

In May 2000 UBS and Crédit Suisse agreed to allow researchers to examine more than 2m. Nazi-era bank accounts in order to verify or reject claims by Holocaust survivors. The proposed settlement of US \$1,250m. to end the threat of litigation by Holocaust survivors against Swiss banks was approved by a judge in the USA in July 2000. The two banks formally agreed the settlement in August; four Swiss insurers added a further \$50m. in response to claims that the insurance policies of Holocaust survivors had not been honoured. Swiss companies that had used forced labour during the Second World War were also required to contribute. In February 2001, in preparation for the beginning of payments, Swiss banks published lists of dormant bank accounts, thought to be linked to the Holocaust, to be claimed by the account holders or their heirs.

During 1986 the Government introduced legislation which aimed to restrict the number of refugees who were to be granted political asylum in Switzerland. However, the new legislation was criticized by socialist, religious and humanitarian groups, and in April 1987 a national referendum on the issue was held. Of the 41.8% of the electorate who voted at the referendum, a substantial majority was in favour of the new restrictions. In a further national referendum, held in December 1988, 67% of voters rejected a proposal by a small extreme right-wing party to reduce by 300,000 the number of foreigners to be allowed to settle in Switzerland by the year 2003. In 1991 attacks on asylum-seekers' hostels (including incidents of arson) increased to 71, compared with a total of 27 in 1990; subsequently, however, recorded attacks on foreigners reportedly declined. In March 1994, in an attempt to control increasing drugs-related crime (following allegations that immigrants trading in illicit drugs were exploiting the asylum laws to avoid extradition), the Government approved legislation restricting the rights of asylum-seekers and immigrants, which included provisions for their arrest and detention without trial for failure to possess the requisite identification documents; further strong measures against foreigners suspected of trafficking in illegal drugs were approved by national referendum in December. Civil rights groups accused the Government of yielding to popular xenophobic sentiment to divert attention from its failure to overcome the drugs problem. In December 1996 a proposal sponsored by the Swiss People's Party to confiscate the earnings of asylum-seekers in Switzerland and to expel automatically all those without sufficient documentation was narrowly rejected in a national referendum. At the end of 1998 there were 44,660 asylum-seekers in Switzerland, representing about 3.2% of the resident foreign population. In early 2000 the Swiss People's Party was reported to be seeking, increasingly, to make the granting of Swiss citizenship subject to the approval of local electorates. In 1999 Swiss citizenship was granted to 20,363 people. In a referendum held in September 2000 63.7% of voters rejected a motion to reduce the number of foreigners allowed to settle in Switzerland from 20% of the total population to 18%.

On 24 November 2002 a national referendum was held on proposals, drawn up by the Swiss People's Party, under which would-be refugees arriving in Switzerland via any country free of political persecution (in practice, all neighbouring countries) would automatically be denied refugee status and sent back across the border. A total of 1,120,967 voters (51.1%) opposed the proposals, while 1,118,213 (49.9%) were in favour of them; the proposals were thus defeated by a majority of just 2,754 votes. In December the authorities in the town of Meilen, near Zurich, attracted fierce criticism when it emerged that they intended to introduce rules barring asylum-seekers from some public areas, such as schools and sports grounds. Such was the level of opprobrium (including comparisons to apartheid), that the town council was compelled to repeal the rules. However, it was expected that the policy would still operate on an unofficial level, with asylum-seekers 'requested rather than compelled' to avoid certain parts of the town.

In November 1989 64.4% of voters in a referendum rejected a proposal to abolish the armed forces by the year 2000. The referendum, which had been instigated by the Group for Switzerland Without an Army (an alliance of socialist, pacifist, youth and ecological organizations), attracted an unusually high level of participation, almost 70% of the electorate. Following the referendum, the Federal Military (Defence) Department established a working party to examine proposals for reforms in the armed forces; consequently, the strength of the armed forces was considerably reduced during the early 1990s. In June 1993 the Federal Assembly approved legislation that sought permission for Swiss forces to be included in future UN peace-keeping operations. However, at a referendum on the issue, which took place in June 1994, 57.3% of voters rejected the proposal. Switzerland did subsequently join NATO's 'Partnership for Peace' (see p. 273) in 1996. Swiss peace-keepers have participated in operations in Bosnia, while Swiss truce verifiers have worked in Kosovo under the Organization for Security and Co-operation in Europe (OSCE, see p. 283). In November 2000 plans were announced to reduce the size of the army from 360,000 soldiers to 120,000 with 80,000 reservists. In the same month a referendum was held on proposals to cut the military budget by one-third; the motion was rejected by 62% of voters. A further proposal to abolish the armed forces, instigated by the Group for Switzerland Without an Army, was rejected by 79% of voters in a referendum held in December 2001; 78% of voters also rejected a replacement civilian force.

Following the accident in April 1986 at the Chornobyl (Chernobyl) nuclear power station, in the former USSR (Ukraine), public concern about nuclear safety became a national issue in Switzerland. In June a large-scale anti-nuclear demonstration took place at Gösgen, the site of the largest of Switzerland's five nuclear power stations, and in the same month the Social Democratic Party initiated a campaign to collect signatures for a referendum on the nuclear issue, and advocated the progressive elimination of the country's existing reactors, and the cancellation of any future nuclear projects. In March 1989 the Federal Assembly, after protracted debate, approved legislation to cancel the projected construction of a sixth nuclear power station, at Kaiseraugst (near Basel), and to provide compensation for the construction consortium. The decision followed increasing public disapproval of the project. In a referendum held in September 1990, a majority of voters rejected proposals to abandon the use of nuclear power, but approved a proposal for a 10-year moratorium on the construction of further nuclear power stations in Switzerland. The Federal Council announced in October 1998 that the five existing nuclear plants would eventually be closed on environmental grounds; it did not, however, propose a timescale for the withdrawal from nuclear energy. During October it was revealed that the operating licence for one of the stations had just been extended to 2012.

In September 2000 the Federal Prosecutor General, Valentin Roschacher, investigated allegations that two Swiss companies had paid bribes to the former Kremlin property manager, Pavel Borodin, to secure contracts to refurbish the Kremlin in Moscow, Russia. Borodin, his daughter and his son-in-law were believed to have transferred the funds into Swiss bank accounts. As the Russian State Prosecutor was reluctant to investigate the case, Roschacher issued an international arrest warrant; Borodin was subsequently arrested in New York, and in April 2001 he agreed to be voluntarily extradited to Switzerland to face trial. This was just the latest in a series of high-profile money-laundering cases in Switzerland which included the 'freezing' of assets and accounts linked to Sani Abacha and Slobodan Milošević, the former leaders of Nigeria and Yugoslavia respectively, and the former head of the Peruvian secret service. Suspect funds found in Swiss banks accounts were linked to missing IMF aid paid to Russia and to the former leader of the Philippines, Ferdinand Marcos. The total value of suspect funds under investigation in Switzerland increased from 333m. Swiss francs in 1999 (representing 160 cases) to 1,543m. Swiss francs (representing 370 cases) in 2000. These cases, which involved some of Switzerland's most prestigious banks and financial institutions, seriously damaged the country's international reputation as a stable and reliable financial centre. Swiss laws denying foreign investigators access to information about bank accounts unless local laws are broken attracted criticism, as did Switzerland's continued (although diminished) use of anonymous bank accounts. Another source of contention was the Swiss reluctance to co-operate with EU measures to combat tax evasion (which is not a crime in Switzerland).

In January 2001 the annual meeting of the World Economic Forum in Davos attracted large numbers of anti-capitalist demonstrators. Similar demonstrations at the previous meeting had led to violent incidents, as had protests at an IMF meeting in Seattle, USA, during December 1999. In light of these events, Switzerland mounted its largest security operation in 30 years to counter the threat of violence. Riots broke out in Zürich when protesters found themselves unable to reach Davos, during which the police made 121 arrests.

In September 2001 the Federal Assembly approved proposals for Switzerland to join the UN. A referendum was called, at which the proposals required not only the support of the majority of voters, but also the approval of at least one-half of the cantons to be passed. Campaigning focused on Switzerland's independence and neutrality, which some feared would be endangered by membership of the UN. At the referendum, which was held on 3 March 2002, 54.6% of voters and 12 cantons supported the proposals, while 45.4% of voters and 11 cantons rejected them; the participation rate was 57.8%. Consequently, Switzerland was formally admitted as a member of the UN during a session of the UN's General Assembly in September 2002.

In early October 2001 the national airline, Swissair, suspended operations, owing to financial problems which had been exacerbated by the sharp decline in demand for passenger aviation services world-wide following the large-scale terrorist attacks of 11 September on the USA. The Government intervened, using public funds to ensure that the company was able to continue operating until the end of the month, at which time it filed for bankruptcy protection. Further financial support was secured from the Government, UBS AG and Crédit Suisse. In March 2002 a new company, entitled Swiss, was formed to assume responsibility for Swissair's remaining operations. By late 2002, however, the company was implementing redundancies, and reducing the number of aircraft and the number of routes operated in an effort to stem its heavy losses.

Government

The Swiss Confederation, composed of 20 cantons and six half-cantons, has a republican federal Constitution. Legislative power is held by the bicameral Federal Assembly: the Council of States, with 46 members representing the cantons (two for each canton and one for each half-canton), elected for three to four years; and the National Council, with 200 members directly elected by universal adult suffrage for four years, on the basis of proportional representation. Executive power is held by the Federal Council, which has seven members elected for four years by a joint session of the Federal Assembly. The Assembly also elects one of the Federal Councillors to be President of the Confederation (Head of State) for one year at a time.

National policy is the prerogative of the Federal Government, but considerable power is vested in the cantons. Under the Constitution, the autonomous cantons hold all powers not specifically delegated to the federal authorities. The Swiss citizen shares three distinct allegiances—communal, cantonal and national. Direct participation is very important in communal government, and all adult Swiss residents may take part in the communal assemblies or referendums, which decide upon local affairs. Each canton has its own written constitution, government and legislative assembly. The referendum, which can be on a communal, cantonal or national scale, further ensures the possibility of direct public participation in decision-making.

At a national referendum, held on 9 February 2003, 934,264 voters (70.3%) cast their ballots in favour of two proposed reforms, whereby voters would be given the automatic right to challenge treaties signed between Switzerland and other countries (although in practice all important agreements are already subject to a referendum), and petitions with the requisite number of signatures could be used to introduce legislation, rather than solely constitutional amendments as was already the case. The rate of participation in the referendum, however, was markedly low, at only 28%.

Defence

National defence is based on compulsory military service. Switzerland maintains no standing army except for a small permanent personnel of commissioned and non-commissioned officers primarily concerned with training. Military service consists of 15 weeks' recruit training, followed by 10 three-week 'refre-

sher' training courses between the ages of 20 and 42 years. Each soldier keeps his equipment in his own home, and receives compulsory marksmanship training between periods of service. In August 2002 the total strength of the armed forces, when mobilized, was about 320,400. The Confederation belongs to no international defence organizations, and the strategy of the army and air force is defensive. In December 1996 Switzerland signed the NATO 'Partnership for Peace' (see p. 273) framework document. It was emphasized, however, that this in no way compromised the country's 'permanent neutrality', and that Switzerland had no intention of joining NATO itself. Defence expenditure for 2002 was budgeted at 4,800m. Swiss francs.

Economic Affairs

In 2001, according to estimates by the World Bank, Switzerland's gross national income (GNI), measured at average 1999–2001 prices, was US $266,503m., equivalent to $36,970 per head (or $31,320 per head on an international purchasing-power parity basis). During 1990–2001, it was estimated, the population grew by an average of 0.7% per year, while gross domestic product (GDP) per head increased, in real terms, by an average of 0.2% per year. Overall GDP increased, in real terms, by an average of 0.9% per year in 1990–2001; growth in 2001 was 1.3%.

Agriculture (including forestry and fishing) contributed an estimated 1.6% of GDP in 1998, and, according to FAO, engaged 4.1% of the employed labour force in 2001. The principal cash crops are sugar beet, potatoes and wheat. Dairy products, notably cheese, are also important. Agricultural production declined at an average annual rate of 0.7% in 1990–99; it fell by 4.7% in 1997, increased by 6.8% in 1998, but then decreased by 5.4% in 1999.

Industry (including mining and quarrying, manufacturing, power and construction) contributed an estimated 30.3% of GDP in 1998, and engaged 26.3% of the employed labour force in the same year. Industrial GDP increased by 5.3% in 1998.

Switzerland is not richly endowed with mineral deposits, and only rock salt and building materials are mined or quarried in significant quantities. In 1998 only 0.2% of the working population were employed in mining and quarrying.

The manufacturing sector, which contributed (with mining) an estimated 21.3% of GDP in 1993, engaged (excluding mining) 17.8% of the employed labour force in 1998. The most important branches are precision engineering (in particular clocks and watches, which provided 7.4% of export revenue in 1998), heavy engineering, machine-building, textiles, chocolate, chemicals and pharmaceuticals. Mining and manufacturing GDP together increased by 0.4% in 1992, but declined by 2.0% in 1993.

Energy is derived principally from petroleum and from hydro-electric and nuclear power. In 1998 Switzerland imported 82% of the energy that it consumed, mainly in the form of petroleum and related products (which accounted for 61.2% of final energy consumption in that year). Imports of energy products comprised 4.6% of the value of total imports in 2000. Switzerland is, however, a net exporter of electricity. In 1999 58.4% of total electricity output was provided by hydroelectric power, while nuclear power (from five reactors with a total generating capacity of 3,077 MW) provided 37.7% of electricity; a mere 1.5% came from natural gas and 0.2% from petroleum

The services sector contributed an estimated 68.1% of GDP in 1998, and engaged 69.1% of the employed labour force in 1998. Switzerland plays an important role as a centre of international finance, and Swiss markets account for a significant share of international financial transactions. The insurance sector is also highly developed, and Swiss companies are represented throughout the world. The reputation of the banking sector abroad was tarnished in the 1990s by revelations concerning the ignoble role played by Swiss banks in respect of funds deposited by Jewish victims of the Nazi Holocaust (see Recent History). The resolution of this issue in 2001 was overshadowed by a series of high-profile money-laundering scandals, which caused yet more damage to the reputation of Swiss banking. Switzerland draws considerable revenue from tourism. In 1998 this was estimated to be equivalent to about 10% of the value of merchandise exports.

In 2001 Switzerland recorded a visible trade surplus of US $1,564m., and there was a surplus of $22,624m. on the current account of the balance of payments. The European Union (EU, see p. 199) accounted for the majority of Switzerland's trade, providing about 80% of the country's import and taking more than 60% of exports. In 2000 the principal source of imports was Germany (providing 29.1% of total imports), which was also the principal market for exports (taking 21.4% of total exports); other major trading partners were France (providing 10.2% of imports and taking 8.8% of exports), Italy (9.3% and 7.7%, respectively) and the USA (7.4% and 12.8%, respectively). The principal exports in 1999 were pharmaceutical and other chemical products, machinery, clocks and watches and precision instruments and metal products. The main imports in that year were machinery, chemical products, motor vehicles and metal products.

Switzerland recorded a budgetary surplus of 1,367m. Swiss francs (equivalent to 0.3% of GDP) in 2001. General government external debt was equivalent to 0.2% of GDP in 1999. The annual rate of inflation averaged 1.9% in 1990–2001; consumer prices increased by 1.6% in 2000 and by 1.0% in 2001. The rate of unemployment averaged 1.9% in 2000. Of all the major European countries, Switzerland has the highest percentage of foreign workers (about 25% of the working population in 2000).

Switzerland is a founder member of the European Free Trade Association (EFTA, see p. 195). In May 1992 Switzerland was admitted to membership of the IMF and the World Bank.

Economic performance surpassed expectations in 2000: an estimated growth rate of about 3.5%, the highest in a decade, had brought output and employment back to levels consistent with productive capacity, with only moderate pressure on wages. In early 2001 Switzerland was enjoying its best economic performance for many years, following the persistently low levels of growth and relatively high unemployment that characterized the 1990s. Judicious macroeconomic policies and a new monetary policy framework provided a sound basis for ensuring future growth and low inflation. Increased competition and deregulation in the telecommunications sector also compensated for the rapid increase in international petroleum prices to maintain low inflation. However, the economic slowdown in the USA led to a decline in exports throughout most of 2001, although they improved somewhat towards the end of the year, and investment levels were also reduced. This led to economic growth decelerating considerably in 2001, to 2.0%. Growth in 2002 was hampered by the economic stagnation in the euro area —particularly in Germany, Switzerland's main trading partner. Consumption, which had been the mainstay of the Swiss economy during 2001, had slackened, leading to weakening demand, and, in turn, a collapse in investment. However, better-than-expected performance in late 2002 allayed fears of a 'double-dip' recession. Instead, most analysts predicted stagnation, or perhaps only a slight drop in GDP growth for 2002 as a whole, with an upturn expected in the second half of 2003 giving an annual growth rate of between 0.5% and 1.0%. (The Swiss economy was not expected to reach its potential growth rate of between 2.0% and 2.5% until 2004.) Repeated interest rate cuts totalling 2.75% since mid-1999 had failed to control the exchange rate, and the continuing strength of the Swiss franc against both the euro and the US dollar hindered exporters and the tourist industry. Despite this, exports were expected to increase during 2003, with domestic consumption following

rather than leading the recovery. However, as the recovery was to be driven by exports, it was therefore dependent upon a broader economic recovery throughout the euro area. Public expenditure was constrained by government efforts to maintain a balanced budget, while private expenditure was curbed by waning consumer confidence, owing mainly to anxieties over job security. Although unemployment was low by European standards, it had been rising since the end of 2001, and was expected to reach some 3.5% in 2003. Unemployment, therefore, was set to remain a significant restriction on Swiss domestic demand for years to come. The long-term challenge, however, remained to accommodate the pressures on expenditure from a rapidly ageing population. As the main pressure on public finances exerted by pensions and health care was unlikely to be felt until after 2010, long-term planning was essential.

Education

Primary and secondary education are controlled by the cantons, with the result that there are 26 different systems in operation. Responsibility for higher education is shared between the cantons and the Federal Government. Education is compulsory for children between the ages of seven and 16 years. The duration of primary education, which commences at the age of six or seven, is nine years. The duration and system of secondary education depends on individual cantonal policy. Some 20% of 17-year-olds continue their studies at a higher secondary school (Gymnasium/Collège), and a leaving certificate (Matura/Maturité) from one of these is a prerequisite for entry to academic higher education. About 70% proceed to vocational training (trade and technical) for a period of three to four years. There are 10 cantonal universities, two Federal Institutes of Technology (of university standing), as well as seven universities of applied sciences. Numerous private schools exist, and many foreign children receive part of their education in Switzerland. In 1999 federal, cantonal and communal expenditure on education amounted to 21,971m. Swiss francs (18.4% of total public expenditure).

Public Holidays

2003: 1–2 January (New Year), 6 January (Epiphany), 18 April (Good Friday), 21 April (Easter Monday), 1 May (Labour Day), 29 May (Ascension Day), 9 June (Whit Monday), 22 June (Lord's Day), 29 June (St Peter and St Paul), 1 August (National Day), 25 December (Christmas), 26 December (St Stephen's Day).

2004: 1–2 January (New Year), 6 January (Epiphany), 9 April (Good Friday), 12 April (Easter Monday), 1 May (Labour Day), 20 May (Ascension Day), 31 May (Whit Monday), 22 June (Lord's Day), 29 June (St Peter and St Paul), 1 August (National Day), 25 December (Christmas), 26 December (St Stephen's Day).

In addition, various cantonal and local holidays are observed.

Weights and Measures

The metric system is in force.

Statistical Survey

Source (unless otherwise stated): Federal Office of Statistics, 3003 Bern, Hallwylstr. 15; tel. 31618660; fax 31617856; internet www.admin.ch/bfs.

Area and Population

AREA, POPULATION AND DENSITY

Area (sq km)	41,284*
Population (census results)	
4 December 1990	
Males	3,390,446
Females.	3,483,241
Total	6,873,687
5 December 2000.	7,288,010
Population (official estimates at 31 December)†	
1999	7,164,444
2000	7,204,055
2001	7,261,210
Density (per sq km) at 31 December 2001	175.9

* 15,940 sq miles.

† Figures refer to resident population.

LANGUAGES

(%)

	1970	1980	1990
German	64.9	65.0	63.6
French	18.1	18.4	19.2
Italian	11.9	9.8	7.6
Raeto-Romansch	0.8	0.8	0.6
Others	4.3	6.0	8.9

CANTONS

Canton	Area (sq km)*	Population (31 December 1999) Total	Per sq km	Capital (with population, Dec. 1991)
Zürich	1,728.9	1,198,569	693.3	Zürich (343,106)
Bern (Berne) . .	5,959.2	943,427	158.3	Bern (134,393)
Luzern (Lucerne)	1,493.5	345,357	231.2	Luzern (59,811)
Uri	1,076.8	35,487	33.0	Altdorf (8,200)
Schwyz. . . .	908.2	128,248	141.2	Schwyz (12,854)
Unterwalden				
Obwalden . .	490.6	32,225	65.7	Sarnen (8,400)
Nidwalden. . .	275.9	37,657	136.5	Stans (6,200)
Glarus . . .	685.0	38,708	56.5	Glarus (5,700)
Zug (Zoug) . .	238.7	97,758	409.5	Zug (21,719)
Fribourg . .	1,670.6	234,307	140.3	Fribourg (34,200)
Solothurn				
(Soleure). .	790.6	243,908	308.5	Solothurn (15,565)
Basel (Bâle)				
Basel-Stadt (town) . . .	37.0	188,458	5,093.5	Basel (172,768)
Basel-Landschaft (country) . .	517.6	258,602	499.6	Liestal (12,612)
Schaffhausen (Schaffhouse) .	298.5	73,552	246.4	Schaffhausen (34,318)
Appenzell				
Ausserrhoden .	242.8	53,737	221.3	Herisau (16,002)
Innerrhoden . .	172.5	14,946	86.6	Appenzell (5,200)
St Gallen (Saint-Gall) . . .	2,025.7	447,609	221.0	St Gallen (74,106)
Graubünden (Grisons) .	7,105.3	186,026	26.2	Chur (30,284)
Aargau (Argovie)	1,403.6	540,639	385.2	Aarau (16,079)
Thurgau (Thurgovie). .	991.0	227,285	229.3	Frauenfeld (16,908)
Ticino (Tessin) .	2,812.3	308,498	109.7	Bellinzona (16,957)
Vaud . . .	3,211.7	616,275	191.9	Lausanne (123,149)
Valais . . .	5,224.5	275,632	52.8	Sion (25,622)
Neuchâtel . .	807.2	165,649	206.3	Neuchâtel (33,158)
Genève (Genf or Geneva). . .	282.3	403,067	1,427.8	Genève (167,697)
Jura . . .	838.5	68,818	82.1	Delémont (11,652)
Total . . .	41,284.2	7,164,444	173.5	—

* Figures exclude lakes larger than 5 sq km (total area 1,289.5 sq km). Also excluded are special territories (total area 7.2 sq km).

PRINCIPAL TOWNS

(estimated population ('000) at 31 December 2000)

Bern (Berne, the capital) . . .	122.5	Biel (Bienne) . .	48.8
Zürich (Zurich) . .	337.9	Thun (Thoune) . .	40.0
Genève (Genf or Geneva). .	175.0	Köniz	37.2
Basel (Bâle) . . .	166.0	La Chaux-de-Fonds .	36.7
Lausanne . . .	114.9	Schaffhausen (Schaffhouse) . .	33.3
Winterthur (Winterthour) .	88.8	Fribourg (Freiburg) .	31.7
St Gallen (Saint-Gall). . . .	69.8	Neuchâtel (Neuenburg) .	31.6
Luzern (Lucerne) .	57.0	Chur (Coire) . . .	31.3

BIRTHS, MARRIAGES AND DEATHS

	Registered live births Number	Rate (per 1,000)	Registered marriages Number	Rate (per 1,000)	Registered deaths Number	Rate (per 1,000)
1993 . .	83,762	12.1	43,257	6.2	62,512	9.0
1994 . .	82,980	11.9	42,411	6.1	61,987	8.9
1995 . .	82,203	11.7	40,820	5.8	63,387	9.0
1996 . .	83,007	11.7	40,649	5.7	62,637	8.9
1997 . .	80,584	11.4	39,102	5.5	62,839	8.9
1998 . .	78,377	11.0	38,683	5.4	62,569	8.8
1999 . .	78,408	11.0	40,646	5.7	62,503	8.7
2000 . .	78,458	10.9	39,758	5.5	62,528	8.7

Expectation of life (WHO estimates, years at birth): 80.2 (males 77.3; females 82.8) in 2001 (Source: WHO, *World Health Report*).

ECONOMICALLY ACTIVE POPULATION*

(annual averages, '000 persons aged 15 years and over)

	1998	1999	2000
Agriculture, hunting and forestry } Fishing . . . . }	181	187	181
Mining and quarrying. . .	5	5	5
Manufacturing	697	684	703
Electricity, gas and water supply	25	25	24
Construction	290	289	303
Wholesale and retail trade; repair of motor vehicles, motorcycles and personal and household goods	644	645	637
Hotels and restaurants . .	243	241	241
Transport, storage and communications	252	253	254
Financial intermediation . . .	200	202	200
Real estate, renting and business activities	366	378	388
Public administration and defence; compulsory social security	149	150	153
Education	224	229	232
Health and social work . .	398	397	395
Other community, social and personal service activities . .	152	153	153
Private households with employed persons . . .	30	34	42
Total employed †.	3,858	3,873	3,910

* This table refers to workers who are employed for at least six hours per week.

† Including foreigners ('000): 973 in 1998; 956 in 1999; 966 in 2000.

Health and Welfare

KEY INDICATORS

Total fertility rate (children per woman, 2001).	1.4
Under-5 mortality rate (per 1,000 live births, 2001) . . .	6
HIV/AIDS (% of persons aged 15–49, 2001).	0.50
Physicians (per 1,000 head, 1998)	3.23
Hospital beds (per 1,000 head, 1998)	18.1
Health expenditure (2000): US $ per head (PPP)	3,229
Health expenditure (2000): % of GDP	10.7
Health expenditure (2000): public (% of total)	55.6
Access to water (% of persons, 2000).	100
Access to sanitation (% of persons, 2000)	100
Human Development Index (2000): ranking	11
Human Development Index (2000): value	0.928

For sources and definitions, see explanatory note on p. vi.

Agriculture

PRINCIPAL CROPS
('000 metric tons)

	1999	2000	2001
Wheat	506	586	515
Rye	19	23	20
Barley	258	283	253
Oats	29	27	20
Potatoes	484	600	526
Vegetables and melons	291	290	262
Sugar beet	1,186	1,408	1,056
Apples	229	375	170
Pears	798	117	90
Plums	9	8	7
Grapes	169	165	152

Source: FAO.

LIVESTOCK
('000 head, year ending September)

	1999	2000	2001
Cattle	1,609	1,588	1,611
Horses*	46	45	45
Pigs	1,452	1,498	1,548
Sheep	424	421	420
Goats	62	63	63
Chickens	7	7	7
Asses*	2	2	2

* FAO estimates.

Source: FAO.

LIVESTOCK PRODUCTS
('000 metric tons)

	1999	2000	2001
Beef and veal	146	128	138
Mutton and lamb	6	6	6
Pig meat	226	225	234
Poultry meat	46	49	50
Cows' milk	3,852	3,871	3,940
Goats' milk	10	17	17
Butter	38	37	37
Cheese	136	158	162
Poultry eggs	38	36	36

Source: FAO.

Forestry

ROUNDWOOD REMOVALS
('000 cubic metres, excluding bark)

	1999	2000	2001
Sawlogs, veneer logs and logs for sleepers	2,806	6,225	3,000
Pulpwood	462	811	500
Fuel wood	980	1,626	1,000
Total	4,248	8,662	4,500

Source: FAO.

SAWNWOOD PRODUCTION
('000 cubic metres, including railway sleepers)

	1999	2000	2001
Coniferous (softwood)	1,300	1,425	1,250
Broadleaved (hardwood)	225	200	150
Total	1,525	1,625	1,400

Source: FAO.

Fishing

(metric tons, live weight)

	1998	1999	2000
Capture	1,809	1,840	1,659
Roach	168	154	136
European perch	422	491	395
Whitefishes	1,134	1,110	1,017
Aquaculture	1,150	1,135	1,100
Rainbow trout	1,115	1,100	1,065
Total catch	2,959	2,975	2,759

Source: FAO, *Yearbook of Fishery Statistics.*

Industry

SELECTED PRODUCTS
('000 metric tons, unless otherwise indicated)

	1997	1998	1999
Cement	3,568	3,600*	3,600*
Cigars (million)	195	172	203
Cigarettes (million)	37,638	34,453	32,139
Aluminium	35.2†	47.2†	30.0‡
Flour (wheat)§	370	388	395
Chocolate and chocolate products	135.1‖	130.9‖	130.6

* Estimate.
† Source: US Geological Survey.
‡ Source: World Metal Statistics, London.
§ Source: International Grain Council, London.
‖ Salts.

Source: UN, *Industrial Commodity Statistics Yearbook.*

Watches ('000 exported): 17,840 in 1984; 25,137 in 1985; 28,075 in 1986.

New dwellings (units completed): 35,961 in 1997; 33,734 in 1998; 33,108 in 1999.

Electric energy (million kWh): 55,120 in 1996; 60,600 in 1997; 60,948 in 1998.

Finance

CURRENCY AND EXCHANGE RATES

Monetary Units
100 Rappen (centimes) = 1 Schweizer Franken (franc suisse) or Swiss franc

Sterling, Dollar and Euro Equivalents (31 December 2002)
£1 sterling = 2.2352 francs
US $1 = 1.3868 francs
€1 = 1.4543 francs
100 Swiss francs = £44.74 = $72.11 = €68.76

Average Exchange Rates (Swiss francs per US $)
2000   1.6888
2001   1.6876
2002   1.5586

BUDGET
(million Swiss francs)*

Revenue†	1997	1998	1999
Taxes	77,358	83,939	85,711
Taxes on income and wealth	53,057	57,461	57,105
Income and wealth tax	38,502	38,970	40,323
Corporation and capital gains tax	8,899	9,301	10,988
Pre-paid tax	2,320	5,388	1,663
Other taxes on income and wealth	3,336	3,802	4,131
Stamp duty	2,513	3,256	3,126
Taxes on consumption	18,446	19,842	22,015
Turnover tax	12,526	13,287	15,060
Customs duty	1,093	1,034	1,099
Other revenue	30,766	34,884	32,044
Total	108,124	118,823	117,755

Expenditure	1997	1998	1999
General administration	7,336	7,577	7,797
Public order and safety	6,505	6,582	6,544
Defence	5,831	5,771	5,402
Foreign relations	2,043	2,043	2,148
Education	21,448	21,675	21,971
Culture and leisure activities . .	3,389	3,637	3,646
Health	14,563	14,752	15,104
Social welfare	24,945	24,819	23,143
Transport and administration . .	12,006	13,586	12,074
Environment	4,574	4,725	4,819
National economy	6,111	6,199	6,709
Finances and taxes	8,559	8,916	10,084
Total	117,310	120,282	119,439

* Incorporates federal, cantonal and communal budgets.

† Not including parish taxes.

INTERNATIONAL RESERVES
(US $ million at 31 December)

	2000	2001	2002
Gold*	21,219	19,664	21,156
IMF special drawing rights . .	162	283	74
Reserve position in IMF . . .	1,256	1,582	1,917
Foreign exchange	30,854	30,134	38,164
Total	53,491	51,663	61,311

* Gold reserves have totalled 2,590.2 metric tons (83,275,000 troy oz) since 1976. The value in dollars is based on the Swiss national valuation, fixed at 4,595.74 francs per kg (142.95 francs per troy oz) between 1971 and 2000. Beginning in 2000, gold is valued at market-related prices.

Source: IMF, *International Financial Statistics*.

MONEY SUPPLY
(million Swiss francs at 31 December)

	2000	2001	2002
Currency outside banks	37,781	42,169	41,940
Demand deposits at deposit money banks	122,249	131,399	149,320
Total money	160,030	173,568	191,260

Source: IMF, *International Financial Statistics*.

COST OF LIVING
(Consumer Price Index; base: May 2000 = 100)

	1998	1999	2000
Foodstuffs	98.1	98.0	99.6
Alcoholic beverages and tobacco	96.6	99.6	100.9
Clothing and footwear	98.6	99.2	99.5
Housing and energy	96.3	97.3	100.8
Health	99.1	99.6	100.0
Transport	95.5	97.3	100.9
Communication	134.8	124.8	102.5
Education	97.5	98.7	100.2
Recreation and culture	100.1	100.6	100.7
Restaurants and hotels	96.9	99.1	99.9
All items	98.0	98.8	100.3

2001: All items 101.3.

NATIONAL ACCOUNTS
(million Swiss francs)

National Income and Product
(at current prices)

	1997	1998	1999*
Compensation of employees . . .	233,533	237,908	243,274
Operating surplus	60,909	63,113	80,573
Domestic factor incomes . . .	294,442	301,021	303,847
Consumption of fixed capital . .	58,753	59,914	62,332
Gross domestic product (GDP) at factor cost	353,195	360,935	366,179
Indirect taxes	26,208	28,557	30,448
Less Subsidies	8,032	9,503	7,059
GDP in purchasers' values . .	371,372	379,989	388,568
Factor income received from abroad	54,700	70,236	75,648
Less Factor income paid abroad .	28,976	42,445	44,381
Gross national product . . .	397,096	407,780	419,835
Less Consumption of fixed capital	58,753	59,914	62,332
National income in market prices	338,343	347,866	357,503

* Provisional figures.

Expenditure on the Gross Domestic Product
(at current prices)

	1998	1999	2000*
Government final consumption expenditure	56,808	56,771	57,680
Private final consumption expenditure	231,309	237,296	244,886
Increase in stocks	3,245	−2,089	403
Gross fixed capital formation . .	76,017	78,836	85,229
Total domestic expenditure . .	367,379	370,814	388,198
Exports of goods and services . .	137,906	148,375	170,149
Less Imports of goods and services	125,297	130,621	153,956
GDP in purchasers' values . .	379,989	388,568	404,392
GDP at constant 1990 prices .	330,167	335,538	345,519

* Provisional figures.

Gross Domestic Product by Economic Activity
(at constant 1990 prices)

	1998	1999
Agriculture, hunting, forestry and fishing . .	6,817	7,474
Mining and quarrying	682	665
Manufacturing	69,103	69,261
Electricity, gas and water	8,255	8,593
Construction	20,568	20,436
Wholsale and retail trade; repair of motor vehicles, motorcycles and personal and household goods	40,845	41,585
Hotels and restaurants	7,678	7,853
Transport, storage and communications . . .	21,358	22,236
Financial intermediation	39,850	40,192
Real estate, renting and business activities*	43,962	44,894
Public administration and defence, compulsory social security	42,491	42,686
Education	3,938	3,892
Health and social work	14,603	14,445
Other community, social and personal service activities	4,666	4,716
Private households with employed persons . .	1,591	1,598
Sub-total	326,404	330,526
Value-added tax on products	9,955	10,152
Import duties	5,881	6,228
Less Imputed bank service charges	12,073	11,368
GDP in purchasers' values	330,167	335,538

* Including imputed rents of owner-occupied dwellings.

BALANCE OF PAYMENTS
(US $ million)

	1999	2000	2001
Exports of goods f.o.b.	91,823	94,842	95,826
Imports of goods f.o.b.	−90,981	−92,738	−94,262
Trade balance	843	2,104	1,564
Exports of services	28,459	28,877	27,726
Imports of services	−15,888	−15,573	−15,269
Balance on goods and services	13,414	15,408	14,020
Other income received	50,111	61,036	49,751
Other income paid	−29,800	−39,882	−37,074
Balance on goods, services and income	33,725	36,362	26,697
Current transfers received	7,638	6,853	9,682
Current transfers paid	−11,752	−9,777	−13,755
Current balance	29,611	33,638	22,624
Capital account (net)	−302	−3,073	189
Direct investment abroad	−33,277	−42,738	−11,052
Direct investment from abroad	12,342	20,010	8,628
Portfolio investment assets	−46,839	−22,309	−42,840
Portfolio investment liabilities	5,894	10,547	1,896
Other investment assets	−80,612	−93,277	23,059
Other investment liabilities	108,416	99,604	−10,382
Net errors and omissions	2,284	−6,407	8,516
Overall balance	−2,484	−4,005	638

Source: IMF, *International Financial Statistics*.

External Trade

Note: Swiss customs territory includes the Principality of Liechtenstein, the German enclave of Büssingen and the Italian commune of Campione, but excludes the free zone of the Samnaun Valley.

PRINCIPAL COMMODITIES
(million Swiss francs)

Imports c.i.f.	1998	1999	2000
Agricultural and forestry products	9,259.2	9,559.9	9,924.9
Mineral fuels	3,362.6	3,513.5	6,289.6
Textile yarn, fabrics, etc	2,468.9	2,363.6	2,425.0
Clothing (excl. footwear)	5,126.0	5,148.0	5,396.3
Paper, paperboard and graphics	4,429.2	4,593.7	5,025.4
Articles of plastic	2,466.4	2,517.8	2,800.7
Chemical elements and unmoulded plastics	5,906.7	6,142.0	6,885.8
Pharmaceutical products	7,493.8	8,779.5	10,371.0
Building materials, ceramics, glass, etc.	2,122.3	2,164.4	2,314.5
Metal products	5,611.8	5,671.5	6,258.7
Machinery (incl. electrical)	24,656.9	26,966.1	31,583.2
Passenger cars	7,029.1	7,793.8	8,088.4
Aircraft	2,383.9	3,583.4	3,134.4
Precision instruments	3,541.5	3,956.8	4,435.6
Home fittings and furnishings	2,844.8	3,054.0	3,206.0
Total (incl. others)	115,846.5	120,057.2	139,402.2

Exports f.o.b.	1998	1999	2000
Agricultural and forestry products	3,806.8	4,014.2	4,428.0
Textile yarn, fabrics etc	2,728.9	2,572.6	2,664.2
Paper, paperboard and graphics	3,010.8	3,205.0	3,495.2
Leather, rubber and plastic products	3,167.6	3,362.1	3,697.8
Chemicals	31,302.2	33,990.8	35,891.7
Chemical elements and unmoulded plastics	5,042.6	5,208.5	5,582.0
Pharmaceutical products	18,395.1	21,107.2	22,075.9
Pigments	2,486.0	2,351.1	1,540.1
Metal products	9,557.4	9,470.6	10,891.9
Machinery (incl. electrical)	31,922.1	32,641.6	37,136.9
Precision instruments	6,186.0	6,798.9	7,973.6
Clocks and watches	8,422.2	9,003.4	10,297.2
Precious metals and gemstones	3,964.9	5,324.3	8,031.1
Total (incl. others)	114,054.5	120,478.0	135,539.7

PRINCIPAL TRADING PARTNERS
(million Swiss francs)*

Imports c.i.f.	1998	1999	2000
Austria	4,579.0	4,690.5	4,944.6
Belgium-Luxembourg	3,921.0	3,426.0	4,144.7
China, People's Republic	1,682.4	1,800.0	2,300.5
France	12,584.8	14,418.8	14,245.9
Germany	35,316.4	37,251.3	40,584.4
Ireland	2,095.8	2,336.6	3,307.9
Italy	11,187.3	11,625.8	12,950.3
Japan	3,082.2	3,437.7	3,925.5
Netherlands	5,803.2	6,077.1	7,893.7
Russia	1,322.1	1,676.1	3,843.5
Spain	1,950.6	2,045.7	2,418.3
Sweden	1,667.2	1,837.7	1,914.6
United Kingdom	7,233.0	6,786.2	8,129.2
USA	7,963.0	7,701.5	10,288.4
Total (incl. others)	115,846.5	120,057.0	139,402.2

Exports f.o.b.	1998	1999	2000
Austria	3,573.9	3,871.1	4,157.7
Belgium-Luxembourg	2,601.2	2,443.1	2,578.8
Brazil	1,228.8	1,076.5	1,262.0
China, People's Republic	809.1	990.0	1,402.7
France	10,875.4	11,093.1	11,955.8
Germany	26,286.5	27,230.6	29,174.1
Hong Kong	2,564.6	2,912.0	3,841.5
Israel	1,010.1	1,391.6	1,439.6
Italy	8,783.3	9,588.1	10,461.1
Japan	4,387.2	4,852.8	5,767.2
Netherlands	3,338.8	3,798.7	4,152.4
Singapore	1,090.6	1,283.4	1,599.5
Spain	3,213.8	3,492.7	3,772.8
Sweden	1,563.9	1,596.8	1,646.9
Turkey	1,332.2	1,062.8	1,412.4
United Kingdom	6,751.2	6,603.7	7,688.6
USA	12,355.2	14,678.1	17,426.6
Total (incl. others)	114,054.5	120,724.5	136,014.9

* Imports by country of production; exports by country of consumption.

Transport

RAILWAY TRAFFIC

	1995	1996	1997
Passenger-kilometres (million)	13,408	13,326	14,104
Freight ton-kilometres (million)	8,686	7,907	8,688

ROAD TRAFFIC
(motor vehicles in use at 30 September)

	1998	1999	2000
Passenger cars	3,383,273	3,467,275	3,545,247
Buses and coaches	15,461	15,943	16,269
Lorries and vans	267,380	273,954	278,518
Motorcycles and mopeds	733,937	744,357	733,781

Source: IRF, *World Road Statistics*.

INLAND WATERWAYS
(freight traffic at port of Basel, '000 metric tons)

	1996	1997	1998
Goods loaded	876.9	837.5	688.4
Goods unloaded	6,283.4	7,002.4	7,420.3

Source: Federal Department of Transport.

SHIPPING

Merchant Fleet
(at 31 December)

	1999	2000	2001
Number of vessels	21	21	24
Displacement ('000 gross registered tons)	439.1	429.3	502.0

Source: Lloyds Register-Fairplay, *World Fleet Statistics*.

CIVIL AVIATION
(traffic on scheduled services)

	1997	1998	1999
Kilometres flown (million) . . .	230	263	295
Passenger carried ('000) . . .	12,482	14,299	16,209
Passenger-kilometres (million) . .	26,314	29,415	33,309
Total ton-kilometres (million) . .	4,462	4,897	5,195

Source: UN, *Statistical Yearbook*.

Tourism

FOREIGN TOURIST ARRIVALS
(at hotels, and similar establishments)

Country of residence	1998	1999	2000
Belgium	212,147	201,620	216,916
France	450,209	448,477	499,301
Germany	2,168,727	2,143,498	2,221,557
Italy	444,498	437,926	448,718
Japan	536,189	538,416	623,291
Netherlands	151,028	138,804	156,349
Spain	274,072	284,570	315,279
United Kingdom	549,424	585,637	652,555
USA	861,137	832,864	990,961
Total (incl. others)	7,185,379	7,153,967	7,821,158

Total arrivals (estimates, '000, all accommodation): 10,900 in 1998; 10,700 in 1999; 11,400 in 2000.

Tourism receipts (US $ million): 7,973 in 1998; 7,739 in 1999; 7,303 in 2000.

Source: World Tourism Organization, mainly *Yearbook of Tourism Statistics*.

Communications Media

	1999	2000	2001
Television receivers ('000 in use)	3,700	3,950	n.a.
Telephones ('000 main lines in use)	5,062	5,185	5,183
Mobile cellular telephones ('000 subscribers)	3,058	4,618	5,226
Personal computers ('000 in use) .	3,300	3,600	n.a.
Internet users ('000)	1,761	2,134	2,917

Source: International Telecommunication Union.

Facsimile machines ('000 in use, 1996): 207.

Radio licences ('000, 1996): 2,805.

Books published (no. of titles, 1997): 12,435.

Daily newspapers (number, 1997): 76.

Education

(Students)

	1998/99	1999/2000	2000/01
Primary	467,451	475,044	473,739
Secondary	421,972	423,805	423,824
Vocational	206,380	211,230	216,905
Higher	154,838	156,115	162,646

Directory

The Constitution

The Constitution (summarized below) was adopted on 29 May 1874. A revised version of the Constitution, which included new provision for the right to undertake strike action by the labour force, was approved by 59.2% of voters at a federal referendum on 18 April 1999.

Switzerland is divided into federated cantons, which have sovereign authority except where the Constitution defines limits to their powers or accords responsibility to the Federal authority. After a referendum in September 1978, the Constitution was amended to allow for the formation of the canton of Jura, increasing the number of cantons to 23 (three of these are sub-divided and they are sometimes collectively referred to as the 26 states).

Principally, the Federal authority is responsible for civil, penal and commercial law, legislation concerning marriage, residence and settlement, export and import duties, defence, postal and telecommunications services, the mint, forestry, hunting and fishing, hydroelectric power, the economy, railways, important roads and bridges, social insurance, and international affairs. Administration is largely in the hands of the cantons, and in the combined management of Federal authorities and cantons. The cantons derive their revenue from direct taxation. The Federal authority draws its revenue from direct and indirect taxation. The profits from Federal enterprises and customs duties are received by the Federal authorities.

COMMUNES

Each of the more than 3,000 communes of Switzerland has local autonomy over such matters as public utilities and roads, and grants primary citizenship. Decisions are made by communal assemblies. The smallest communes have fewer than 20 inhabitants, the largest, Zürich, around 370,000.

CANTONS

The 26 cantons and half-cantons of the Swiss Confederation each have their own constitution and their own method of choosing the members of the cantonal assembly and cantonal government and the States Councillors who represent them at the federal level. Five cantons, Glarus, Appenzell Ausserrhoden and Innerrhoden, Obwalden and Nidwalden, retain the Landsgemeinde, an assembly of all citizens of the canton held annually, as their decision-making authority. Elsewhere, democracy is less direct, the secret ballot and the referendum having replaced the mass assembly.

FEDERAL ASSEMBLY

The Federal Assembly (Bundesversammlung/Assemblée Fédérale) is the supreme governing body of the Confederation. It is composed of two bodies, the National Council (Nationalrat/Conseil National) and the Council of States (Ständerat/Conseil des Etats), which deliberate separately. The 200 members of the National Council are elected directly, by proportional representation, every four years. The minimum age for voting and eligibility for election in the Confederation is 18 years. In 1971 women gained full political rights at federal level and in almost all the cantons (female suffrage had been introduced in all cantons by late 1990). The Council of States represents the cantons, each of which sends two councillors, elected by the people in various ways according to the cantonal constitutions. Legislative and fiscal measures must be accepted by both houses in order to be adopted, and the Federal Assembly supervises the army, the civil service and the application of the law, exercises the right of pardon and elects the Federal Supreme Court, the Federal Insurance Court, the General who commands the army in times of crisis, and the Federal Council.

FEDERAL COUNCIL

Executive authority is vested in the Federal Council, whose members are each in charge of a Federal Department. Each year the Federal Assembly appoints the President and Vice-President of the Confederation from among the Federal Councillors. Generally, the Councillors are chosen from the members of the Federal Assembly for four years after every general election.

REFERENDUMS AND INITIATIVES

Referendums are held on both cantonal and federal levels. In many cantons all legislation has to be accepted by a majority of the voters, and in some cantons major financial matters have to be submitted to the popular vote. In federal affairs the consent of a majority of the voters and of the cantons must be obtained for amendments to the Federal Constitution, for extraconstitutional emergency legislation and for the decision to join collective security organizations or international bodies, but referendums are optional for other legislation. A petition from 50,000 voters is needed to bring about a national referendum, which can accept or reject any legislation that has been passed by Parliament. The initiative gives voters in many cantons the right to propose a constitutional or legislative amendment and to demand a popular vote on it. A petition by 100,000 voters is needed to initiate a vote on an amendment to the Federal Constitution, but as federal laws cannot be proposed by means of an initiative, some constitutional amendments introduced in this manner concern relatively unimportant matters and participation of the voters is, on average, 30% to 45%. The initiative is also used by the political opposition to effect changes in government policy.

The Government

FEDERAL COUNCIL
(April 2003)

President of the Swiss Confederation for 2003 and Head of Federal Department of Home Affairs: PASCAL COUCHEPIN (Radical Democratic Party).

Vice-President and Head of Federal Department of Justice and Police: RUTH METZLER-ARNOLD (Christian Democratic People's Party).

Head of Federal Department of Finance: KASPAR VILLIGER (Radical Democratic Party).

Head of Federal Department of Defence, Civil Protection and Sports: SAMUEL SCHMID (Swiss People's Party).

Head of Federal Department of Economic Affairs: JOSEPH DEISS (Christian Democratic People's Party).

Head of Federal Department of Foreign Affairs: MICHELINE CALMY-REY (Social Democratic Party).

Head of Federal Department of Transport, Energy and Communications: MORITZ LEUENBERGER (Social Democratic Party).

Chancellor of the Swiss Confederation: ANNEMARIE HUBER-HOTZ.

FEDERAL DEPARTMENTS

Federal Chancellery: Bundeshaus West, 3003 Bern; tel. 313222111; fax 313223706; e-mail webmaster@admin.ch; internet www.admin.ch.

Federal Department of Defence, Civil Protection and Sports: Bundeshaus Ost, 3003 Bern; tel. 313241211; fax 313235782; e-mail postmaster@gs-vbs.admin.ch; internet www.vbs.ch.

Federal Department of Economic Affairs: Bundeshaus Ost, 3003 Bern; tel. 313222007; fax 313222194; e-mail info@gs-evd.admin.ch; internet www.evd.admin.ch.

Federal Department of Environment, Transport, Energy and Communications: Bundeshaus Nord, 3003 Bern; tel. 313225511; fax 313119576; e-mail webmaster@gs-uvek.admin.ch; internet www.uvek.admin.ch.

Federal Department of Finance: Bernerhof, Bundesgasse 3, 3003 Bern; tel. 313226033; fax 313233852; e-mail info@gs-efd.admin.ch; internet www.efd.admin.ch.

Federal Department of Foreign Affairs: Bundeshaus West, 3003 Bern; tel. 313222111; fax 313223237; e-mail info@eda.admin.ch; internet www.eda.admin.ch.

Federal Department of Home Affairs: Bundeshaus, Inselgasse, 3003 Bern; tel. 313229111; fax 313227901; e-mail info@gs-edi.admin.ch; internet www.edi.admin.ch.

Federal Department of Justice and Police: Bundeshaus West, Bundesgasse, 3003 Bern; tel. 313222111; fax 313227832; e-mail webmaster@gs-ejpd.admin.ch; internet www.ejpd.ch.

Legislature

BUNDESVERSAMMLUNG/ASSEMBLÉE FÉDÉRALE
(Federal Assembly)

Nationalrat/Conseil National
(National Council)

President: YVES CHRISTEN (2002/03).

General Election, 24 October 1999

	Seats
Social Democratic Party	51
Swiss People's Party	44
Radical Democratic Party	43
Christian Democratic People's Party	35
Green Party	9
Liberal Party	6
Evangelical People's Party	3
Union of Ticino	2
Workers' Party	2
Christian Socialist Party	1
Independent Alliance	1
Socialist Solidarity Group	1
Swiss Democrats	1
Union of Federal Democrats	1
Total	**200**

Ständerat/Conseil des Etats
(Council of States)

President: GIAN-RETO PLATTNER (2002/03).

Elections, 1999 (Members are elected by canton; method and period of election differs from canton to canton)

	Seats
Radical Democratic Party	18
Christian Democratic People's Party	15
Swiss People's Party	7
Social Democratic Party	6
Total	**46**

Political Organizations

Christlichdemokratische Volkspartei der Schweiz—Parti démocrate-chrétien suisse (Christian Democratic People's Party): Klaraweg 6, Postfach 5835, 3001 Bern; tel. 313522364; fax 313522430; e-mail info@cvp.ch; internet www.cvp.ch; f. 1912; advocates a Christian outlook on world affairs, federalism and Christian social reform by means of professional asscns; non-sectarian; Pres. PHILIPP STAEHELIN; Gen. Sec. RETO NAMSE; Leader of Parliamentary Group JEAN-PHILIPPE MAITRE.

Christlichsoziale Partei—Parti chrétien-social (Christian Socialist Party): Widenstr. 26, 6317 Oberwil-Zug; tel. 417116957; fax 417116947; e-mail monikamathers@gmx.ch; Sec. MONIKA MATHERS-SCHREGENBERGER.

Eidgenössisch-Demokratische Union—Union Démocratique Fédérale (Union of Federal Democrats): Postfach 717, 3607 Thun; tel. 332223637; fax 332223744; e-mail info@edu-udf.ch; internet www.edu-udf.ch; Pres. CHRISTIAN WABER.

Evangelische Volkspartei der Schweiz—Parti évangélique suisse (Protestant People's Party): Josefstr. 32, Postfach 7334, 8023 Zürich; tel. 12727100; fax 12721437; e-mail info@evp-pev.ch; internet www.evppev.ch; f. 1919; Pres. RUEDI AESCHBACHER; Sec. DANIEL REUTER.

Frauen macht Politik (Women in Politics): Postfach 9353, 8036 Zürich; tel. 12424418; fax 12424418; f. 1986; Secs BARBARA HUBER, CLAUDIA SCHÄTTI.

Freiheits-Partei der Schweiz—Die Auto-Partei (Automobile Party): Postfach, 4622 Egerkingen; tel. 913890040; fax 913890045; e-mail fps@bluewin.ch; internet www.freiheits-partei.ch; f. 1985 to support motorists' rights; has subsequently campaigned for restricted immigration; Pres. JÜRG SCHERRER.

Freisinnig-Demokratische Partei der Schweiz—Parti radical-démocratique suisse (Radical Democratic Party): Postfach 6136, 3001 Bern; tel. 313203535; fax 313203500; e-mail gs@fdp.ch; internet www.fdp.ch; led the movement that gave rise to the Federative State and the Constitution of 1848; promotes a strong Fed. Govt, while respecting the legitimate rights of the cantons and all the minorities; liberal democratic principles; Pres. FRANZ STEINEGGER; Sec. JOHANNES MATYASSY; Leader of Parliamentary Group CHRISTINE BEERLI.

Grüne Partei der Schweiz—Parti écologiste suisse (Green Party of Switzerland): Waisenhauspl. 21, 3011 Bern; tel. 313126660; fax 313126662; e-mail gruene@gruene.ch; internet www.gruene.ch; f. 1983; Co-Pres RUEDI BAUMANN, PATRICE MUGNY; Gen. Sec. HUBERT ZURKINDEN; Leader of Parliamentary Group CÉCILE BÜHLMANN.

Grünes Bündnis—Alliance verte et sociale (Green Alliance): Postfach 6411, 3001 Bern; tel. 313018209; fax 313028878; Sec. REGULA RYTZ.

Landesring der Unabhängigen—Alliance des Indépendants (Independent Alliance): Bern; tel. 313821636; fax 313823695; internet www.ldu.ch; f. 1936; 4,000 mems; advocates the application of liberal, social and ecological principles; Pres. MONICA WEBER; Sec. RUDOLF HOFER; Leader of Parliamentary Group VERENA GRENDELMEIER.

Lega dei Ticinesi (Union of Ticino): via Monte Boglia 7, CP 2311, 6901 Lugano; tel. 919713033; fax 919727492; Pres. GIULIANO BIGNASCA; Sec. MAURO MALANDRA.

Liberale Partei der Schweiz—Parti libéral suisse (Liberal Party): Postfach 7107, Spitalgasse 32, 3001 Bern; tel. 313116404; fax 313125474; e-mail info@liberal.ch; internet www.liberal.ch; opposes centralizing tendencies; Pres. CLAUDE RUEY; Sec. CHRISTOPHE BERDAT; Leader of Parliamentary Group RÉMY SCHEURER.

Partei der Arbeit der Schweiz—Parti suisse du travail (Workers' Party): 25 rue du Vieux-Billard, CP 232, 1211 Geneva 8; tel. 223222299; fax 223222295; e-mail pst-pda@bluemail.ch; internet www.pst.ch; f. 1944 by Communist Party mems and left-wing Socialists; Pres. CHRISTIANE JAQUET-BERGER.

Progressive Organisationen der Schweiz—Organisations progressistes suisses (Progressive Swiss Orgs): Postfach 1461, Aarauerstr. 7, 4600 Olten; tel. 62266707; f. 1973; left-wing; Secs GEORGES DEGEN, EDUARD HAFNER.

Schweizer Demokraten—Démocrates suisses (Swiss Democrats): Postfach 8116, 3001 Bern; tel. 319742010; fax 319742011; fmrly Nationale Aktion für Volk und Heimat—Action nationale; 6,000 mems; main objectives are preservation of the country's political independence and of individual freedom, protection of the environment, and a population policy restricting the number of immigrants; Pres. RUDOLF KELLER; Gen. Sec. BERNHARD HESS.

Schweizerische Volkspartei—Union démocratique du centre (Swiss People's Party): Brückfeldstr. 18, 3000 Bern 26; tel. 313025858; fax 313017585; e-mail gs@svp.ch; internet www.svp.ch; f. 1971; Pres. UELI MAURER; Gen. Sec. GREGOR A. RUTZ; Leader of Parliamentary Group WALTER FREY.

Sozialdemokratische Partei der Schweiz—Parti socialiste suisse (Social Democratic Party): Spitalgasse 34, 3001 Bern; tel. 313296969; fax 313296970; e-mail secretariat@sp-ps.ch; internet www.spschweiz.ch; f. 1888; bases its policy on democratic socialism and collaborates with all political parties sharing the same principles; 39,000 mems; Pres. CHRISTIANE BRUNNER; Sec.-Gen. R. GAMMA; Leader of Parliamentary Group HILDEGARD FÄSSLER; International Sec. KASPAR SUTTER.

> **Partito Socialista, sezione ticinese PSS** (Socialist Party): Piazza Governo 4, 6500 Bellinzona; tel. 918259462; fax 918259601; e-mail segreteria@ps-ticino.ch; f. 1992; fmrly the Partito Socialista Unitario; Pres. ANNA BISCOSSA.

Diplomatic Representation

EMBASSIES IN SWITZERLAND

Albania: Bern; tel. 313720707; fax 313724188; e-mail emalb@bluewin.ch; Ambassador VLADIMIR THANAFI.

Algeria: Willadingweg 74, 3000 Bern 15; tel. 313526961; fax 313526268; Ambassador ABDELMALEK GUENAIZIA.

Argentina: Jungfraustr. 1, 3005 Bern; tel. 313523565; fax 313520519; Ambassador JORGE ALBERTO VÁSQUEZ.

Austria: Kirchenfeldstr. 77–79, 3005 Bern; tel. 313565252; fax 313515664; e-mail bern-ob@bmaa.gv.at; Ambassador Dr KARL VON DER LILIE.

Belarus: Quartierweg 6, 3074 Muri bei Bern; tel. 319527914; fax 319527916; e-mail swiss@belembassy.org; Ambassador VLADIMIR KOROLEV.

Belgium: Jubiläumstr. 41, 3005 Bern; tel. 313500150; fax 313500165; e-mail bern@diplobel.org; Ambassador PHILIPPE J. BERG.

Bosnia and Herzegovina: Jungfraustr. 1, 3005 Bern; tel. 313511051; fax 313511079; e-mail emb-ch-brn@tiscalinet.ch; Ambassador JUGOSLAV JOVIČIĆ.

Brazil: Monbijoustr. 68, 3007 Bern; POB 30, 3000 Bern 23; tel. 313718515; fax 313710525; e-mail brasbern@iprolink.ch; Ambassador ROBERTO SOARES-DE-OLIVEIRA.

Bulgaria: Bernastr. 2, 3005 Bern; tel. 313511455; fax 313510064; Chargé d'affaires a.i. PETAR VASSILEV.

Cameroon: Brunnadernrain 29, 3006 Bern; tel. 313524737; Ambassador FRANÇOIS-XAVIER NGOUBEYOU.

Canada: Kirchenfeldstr. 88, 3005 Bern; tel. 313573200; fax 313573210; e-mail bern@dfait-maeci.gc.ca; internet www.dfait-maeci.gc.ca/switzerland; Ambassador JEAN-PAUL HUBERT.

Chile: Eigerpl. 5, 12th Floor, 3007 Bern; tel. 313710745; fax 313720025; e-mail echilech3@my-mail.ch; Ambassador ALEJANDRA FAULBAUM MAYORGA.

China, People's Republic: Kalcheggweg 10, 3006 Bern; tel. 313527333; fax 313514573; Ambassador WU CHUANFU.

Colombia: Dufourstr. 47, 3005 Bern; tel. 313511700; fax 313527072; e-mail colombie@iprolink.ch; Ambassador MARÍA HELENA RAMÍREZ FADUL.

Congo, Democratic Republic: Sulgenheimweg 21, 3007 Bern; tel. 313713538; Ambassador NDEZE MATABARO.

Costa Rica: Schwarztorstr. 11, 3007 Bern; tel. 313727887; fax 313727834; e-mail embajada.costa.rica@thenet.ch; Ambassador ISABEL MONTERO DE LA CÁMARA DE MEISSNER.

Côte d'Ivoire: Thormannstr. 51, 3005 Bern; tel. 313508080; fax 313508081; Ambassador LOUIS ESMEL.

Croatia: Thunstr. 45, 3005 Bern; tel. 313520275; fax 313520373; e-mail croatia.embassy.ch@thenet.ch; Ambassador Dr MLADEN ANDRLIC.

Cuba: Gesellschaftsstr. 8, 3012 Bern; tel. 313022111; fax 313029830; Ambassador TERESITA VICENTE SOTOLONGO.

Czech Republic: Muristr. 53, Postfach 170, 3000 Bern 16; tel. 313523645; fax 313527502; e-mail bern@embassy.mzv.cz; internet www.mfa.cz/bern; Ambassador JOSEF KREUTER.

Denmark: Thunstr. 95, 3006 Bern; tel. 313505454; fax 313505464; e-mail embassy@denmark.ch; internet www.denmark.ch; Ambassador BJARNE BLADBJERG.

Ecuador: Ensingerstr. 48, 3000 Bern 16; tel. 313511755; fax 313512771; e-mail edesuiza@bluewin.ch; Ambassador Dr EDWIN JOHNSON-LÓPEZ.

Egypt: 49 ave Blanc, 1202 Geneva; tel. 227316195; fax 227384415; Ambassador NAÉLA GABR.

Finland: Weltpoststr. 4, Postfach 11, 3015 Bern; tel. 313513031; fax 313513001; e-mail sanomat.brn@formin.fi; Ambassador ANTTI HYNNINEN.

France: Schosshaldenstr. 46, 3006 Bern; tel. 313592111; fax 313592191; e-mail ambassade.fr@iprolink.ch; internet www.itu.int/ambassade/france/berne; Ambassador ANDRÉ GADAUD.

Germany: Willadingweg 83, Postfach 250, 3000 Bern 16; tel. 313594111; fax 313594444; Ambassador Dr REINHARD HILGER.

Georgia: rue Richard Wagner 1, 1202 Geneva; tel. 229191010; fax 227339033; e-mail geomission.geneva@bluewin.ch; Ambassador ALEXANDRE CHIKVAIDZE.

Ghana: Belpstr. 11, Postfach, 3001 Bern; tel. 313817852; fax 313814941; e-mail ghanaemb@tcnet.ch; Ambassador (vacant).

Greece: Bern; tel. 313561414; fax 313681272; e-mail thisseas@iprolink.ch; Ambassador ELEFTHERIOS DANELLIS.

Holy See: Thunstr. 60, 3006 Bern (Apostolic Nunciature); tel. 313526040; fax 313525064; e-mail nunziatura-ch@datacomm.ch; Apostolic Nuncio Most Rev. PIER GIACOMO DE NICOLÒ (Titular Archbishop of Martana).

Hungary: Muristr. 31, 3006 Bern; tel. 313528572; fax 313512001; e-mail huembbrn@bluemail.ch; Ambassador Dr PÁL SCHMITT.

India: Kirchenfeldstr. 28, 3006 Bern; tel. 313511110; fax 313511557; e-mail india@spectraweb.ch.

Indonesia: Elfenauweg 51, 3006 Bern; tel. 313520983; fax 313516767; e-mail 113351.1454@compuserve.com; Ambassador TATI SUMIYATI DARSOYO.

Iran: Thunstr. 68, 3006 Bern; tel. 313510801; fax 313515652; e-mail iran-emb@bluewin.ch; Ambassador MAJID TAKHT RAVANCHI.

Ireland: Kirchenfeldstr. 68, 3005 Bern; tel. 313521442; fax 313521455; e-mail irlemb@bluewin.ch; Ambassador JOHN LAWTON.

Israel: Alpenstr. 32, 3006 Bern; tel. 313563500; fax 313563556; e-mail info@amb-israel.ch; internet www.amb-israel.ch; Ambassador YIGAL ANTEBI.

Italy: Elfenstr. 14, 3006 Bern; tel. 313524151; fax 313511026; e-mail ambital.berna@spectraweb.ch; Ambassador ARDUINO FORNARA.

Japan: Engestr. 53, 3012 Bern; tel. 313002222; fax 313002255; e-mail eojs@bluewin.ch; internet www.ch.emb-japan.go.jp; Ambassador YUJI NAKAMURA.

Jordan: Belpstr. 11, 3007 Bern; tel. 313810404; fax 313810405; e-mail jordanie@bluewin.ch; Ambassador MOHAMMAD AMIN SHAHAN-KARI.

Korea, Democratic People's Republic: Pourtalèsstr. 43, 3074 Muri; tel. 319516621; fax 319515704; Ambassador RI CHOL.

Korea, Republic: Kalcheggweg 38, 3006 Bern; tel. 313511081; fax 313512657; Ambassador KWON SOON-TAE.

Lebanon: Thunstr. 10, 3074 Muri-bei-Bern; tel. 319506565; fax 319506566; e-mail ambalibch@hotmail.com; Ambassador SAMIR HOBEICA.

Libya: Tavelweg 2, 3006 Bern; tel. 313513076; fax 313511325; Chargé d'affaires a.i. SALAHEDDIN A. EL-MESALLATI.

Liechtenstein: Willadingweg 65, 3006 Bern; tel. 313576411; fax 313576415; internet www.firstlink.li; Ambassador Prince STEFAN OF LIECHTENSTEIN.

Luxembourg: Kramgasse 45, 3011 Bern; tel. 313114732; fax 313110019; e-mail embassy.luxembourg@bluewin.ch; Ambassador YVES SPAUTZ.

Mexico: Bernastr. 57, 3005 Bern; tel. 313574747; fax 313574749; e-mail embamex1@swissonline.ch; Ambassador JOSÉ LUIS BERNAL RODRIGUEZ.

Moldova: 28 chemin du Petit-Saconnex, 1209 Geneva; tel. 227339103; fax 227339104; e-mail mission.moldova@bluewin.ch; Ambassador DUMITRU CROITOR.

Monaco: Hallwylstr. 34, 3005 Bern; tel. 313562858; fax 313562855; e-mail ambassademonaco@bluewin.ch; Ambassador BERNARD FAU-TRIER.

Morocco: Helvetiastr. 42, 3005 Bern; tel. 313510362; fax 313510364; Ambassador TAHAR NEJJAR.

Netherlands: Kollerweg 11, 3006 Bern; tel. 313508700; fax 313508710; e-mail nlambassade@bluewin.ch; Ambassador ROELOF R. SMIT.

Nigeria: Zieglerstr. 45, 3007 Bern; tel. 313842600; fax 313821602; e-mail odobande@hotmail.com; Ambassador Dr OGBE D. OBANDE.

Norway: Bubenbergplatz 10, 3011 Bern; tel. 313105555; fax 313105550; e-mail emb.bern@mfa.no; Ambassador HELGA HERNES.

Pakistan: Bernastr. 47, 3005 Bern; tel. 313522992; fax 313515440; e-mail parepberne@bluewin.ch; Ambassador TAYYAB SIDDIQUI.

Peru: Thunstr. 36, 3005 Bern; tel. 313518555; fax 313518570; e-mail lepruberna02@bluewin.ch; Ambassador ARTURO MONTOYA STUVA.

Philippines: Kirchenfeldstr. 73–75, 3005 Bern; tel. 313501717; fax 313522602; e-mail berne_pe@bluewin.ch; Ambassador RORA NAV-ARRO-TOLENTINO.

Poland: Elfenstr. 20A, 3000 Bern 16; tel. 313520452; fax 313523416; e-mail polishemb@dial.eunet.ch; internet www.pol-amb.ch; Ambassador Dr JERZY MARGAŃSKI.

Portugal: Bern; tel. 313528329; fax 313514432; e-mail embportbern@span.ch; Ambassador PEDRO ALVES MACHADO.

Romania: Kirchenfeldstr. 78, 3005 Bern; tel. 313523522; fax 313526455; Ambassador RADU BOROIANU.

Russia: Brunnadernrain 37, 3006 Bern; tel. 313520566; fax 313525595; Ambassador DMITRY CHERKASHIN.

Saudi Arabia: Kramburgstr. 12, 3006 Bern; tel. 313521555; fax 313514581; Chargé d'affaires a.i. IBRAHÍM AMMAR.

Serbia and Montenegro: Seminarstr. 5, 3006 Bern; tel. 313526353; fax 313514474; e-mail info@yuamb.ch; internet www.yuamb.ch; Ambassador DRAGOLJUB POPOVIĆ.

Slovakia: Thunstr. 99, 3006 Bern 1; tel. 313563930; fax 313563933; e-mail slovak@spectraweb.ch; Ambassador (vacant).

Slovenia: Schwanengasse 9, 3011 Bern; tel. 313129009; fax 313124414; Ambassador MIHA VRHUNEC.

South Africa: Alpenstr. 29, Postfach, 3000 Bern 6; tel. 313501313; fax 313501310; e-mail political@southafrica.ch; internet www.southafrica.ch; Ambassador PATRICIA NOZIPHO JANUARY-BARDILL.

Spain: Kalcheggweg 24, 3016 Bern; tel. 313505252; fax 313505255; Ambassador (vacant).

Sweden: Bundesgasse 26, 3001 Bern; tel. 313287000; fax 313287001; e-mail svenska@swissonline.ch; Ambassador LARS MAG-NUSON.

Thailand: Kirchstr. 56, 3097 Liebefeld-Bern; tel. 319703030; fax 319703035; e-mail thai.bern@bluewin.ch; Ambassador JULLAPONG NONSRICHAI.

Tunisia: Kirchenfeldstr. 63, 3005 Bern; tel. 313528226; fax 313510445; Chargé d'affaires a.i. MOHAMED SÉLIM HAMMAMI.

Turkey: Lombachweg 33, 3006 Bern; tel. 313597070; fax 313528819; e-mail turkembsbern@smile.ch; internet www.tr-botschaft.ch; Ambassador METIN ÖRNEKOL.

Ukraine: Feldeggweg 5, 3005 Bern; tel. 313522316; fax 313516416; e-mail emb_ch@mfa.gov.ua; Ambassador YEVHEN BERSHEDA.

United Kingdom: Thunstr. 50, 3000 Bern 15; tel. 313597700; fax 313597701; internet www.britain-in-switzerland.ch; Ambassador BASIL EASTWOOD.

USA: Jubiläumsstr. 93, 3005 Bern; tel. 313577011; fax 313577344; internet www.us-embassy.ch; Ambassador MERCER REYNOLDS.

Uruguay: Kramgasse 63, 3011 Bern; tel. 313122226; fax 313112747; e-mail uruguay@dial.eunet.ch; Ambassador LUIS A. CAR-ROSSO.

Venezuela: Schocchaldenstr. 1, Postfach 1005, 3000 Bern 23; tel. 313505757; fax 313505758; e-mail embavenez@span.ch; Chargé d'affaires a.i. MAGDA RUIZ-PINEDA.

Judicial System

Switzerland has possessed a common Civil Code since 1912, but the Penal Code was only unified in 1942. Under the Code capital punishment was abolished by the few cantons that still retained it. The individual cantons continue to elect and maintain their own magistracy, and retain certain variations in procedure. The canton of Zürich, for example, has justices of the peace (Friedensrichter—normally one for each commune), District Courts (Bezirksgerichte), Labour Courts (Arbeitsgerichte), Courts for Tenancy Matters, an Appeal Court (Obergericht) with various specialized benches, a Cassation Court (Kassationsgericht), and, for the more important cases under penal law, a Jury Court (Geschworenengericht). Apart from military courts, there are only two Federal Judicial authorities, the Federal Supreme Court and the Federal Tribunal of Insurance.

FEDERAL SUPREME COURT

Schweizerisches Bundesgericht—Tribunal fédéral: Mon Repos, 1000 Lausanne 14; tel. 213189111; fax 213233700; internet www.bger.admin.ch; composed of 30 judges elected for a six-year term by the Federal Assembly. According to the Constitution any citizen eligible for election to the National Council can theoretically be elected Justice to the Court, but in practice only lawyers are considered for this office nowadays. All three official Swiss languages must be represented in the Court. The President of the Federal Supreme Court is elected by the Federal Assembly for a two-year term, with no possibility of re-election, from among the senior judges of the Court.

The Court is divided into six permanent branches or chambers, each of which has jurisdiction over cases pertaining to a specific subject, namely:

(a) two 'Public', i.e. Constitutional and Administrative Law Divisions, being composed of seven and six judges respectively.

(b) two Civil or Private Law Divisions of six judges each, which serve mainly as Courts of Appeal in civil matters.

(c) the Debt Execution and Bankruptcy Law Chamber of three judges (members of the Second Civil Law Division).

(d) the Criminal Law Division, the so-called Court of Cassation, which is composed of five judges and which hears mainly appeals in criminal law matters.

There are also four non-permanent divisions hearing exclusively cases that involve certain crimes against the Confederation, certain forms of terrorism, and other offences related to treason.

President: MARTIN SCHUBARTH.

Vice-President: HANS PETER WALTER.

FEDERAL TRIBUNAL OF INSURANCE

Eidgenössisches Versicherungsgericht—Tribunal fédéral des assurances
Schweizerhofquai 6, 6004 Luzern; tel. 414193555; fax 414193669. f. 1918; and consists of 11 members. Since 1969 it has been considered as the Court of Social Insurance (Sozialversicherungsabteilung, Cour des assurances sociales, Corte delle assicurazioni sociali) of the Federal Supreme Court.

President: Dr ULRICH MEYER-BLASER.

Vice-President: ALOIS LUSTENBERGER.

Religion

According to the 1990 census, the religious adherence per 1,000 of the population was as follows: Roman Catholic 461, Protestant 400, Old Catholic 2, Jewish 3, Muslim 22, other denominations (or without religion) 112.

CHRISTIANITY

The Roman Catholic Church

For ecclesiastical purposes, Switzerland comprises six dioceses and two territorial abbacies. All of the dioceses and abbacies are directly responsible to the Holy See. At 31 December 2000 there were an estimated 3,162,993 adherents (45.7% of the total population).

Bishops' Conference

Secrétariat de la Conférence des Evêques Suisses, ave du Moléson 21, CP 122, 1706 Fribourg; tel. 263224794; fax 263224993; e-mail sbk-ces@gmx.ch; internet www.kath.ch/sbk-ces-cvs.
f. 1863; Pres. Mgr AMÉDÉE GRAB (Bishop of Chur); Sec.-Gen. Abbé AGNELL RICKENMANN.

Bishop of Basel: Rt Rev. Dr KURT KOCH, Bischöfliches Ordinariat, Baselstr. 58, Postfach 216, 4501 Solothurn; tel. 326255825; fax 326255845; e-mail kanzlei@bistum-basel.ch; internet www .bistum-basel.ch.

Bishop of Chur: Rt Rev. AMÉDÉE GRAB, Bischöfliches Ordinariat, Hof 19, 7002 Chur; tel. 812586000; fax 812586001; e-mail kanzlei@ bistum-chur.ch; internet www.bistum-chur.ch.

Bishop of Lausanne, Geneva and Fribourg: Rt Rev BERNARD GENOUD, 86 rue de Lausanne, CP 271, 1701 Fribourg; tel. 263474850; fax 263474851; e-mail chancellerie@diocese-lgf.ch.

Bishop of Lugano: Rt Rev. GIUSEPPE TORTI, CP 2337, Borghetto 6, 6901 Lugano; tel. 919138989; fax 919138990; e-mail curialugano@ catt.ch; internet www.catt.ch.

Bishop of St Gallen: Rt Rev. IVO FÜRER, Bischöfliches Ordinariat, Klosterhof 6B, Postfach 263, 9001 St Gallen; tel. 712273340; fax 712273341; e-mail kanzlei@bistum-stgallen.ch.

Bishop of Sion: Rt Rev. NORBERT BRUNNER, ave de la Tour 12, CP 2124, 1950 Sion 2; tel. 273291818; fax 273291836; e-mail diocese .sion@vtx.ch.

Old Catholic Church

Christkatholische Kirche der Schweiz (Old Catholic Church of Switzerland): Willadingweg 39, 3006 Bern; tel. 313513530; fax 313529560; e-mail bischof@christkath.ch; f. 1874; 14,000 mems (1996); Pres. URS STOLZ; Bishop Rt Rev. FRITZ RENÉ MÜLLER.

Protestant Churches

Federation of Swiss Protestant Churches (Schweizerischer Evangelischer Kirchenbund, Fédération des Eglises protestantes de Suisse): Sulgenauweg 26, Postfach, 3000 Bern 23; tel. 313702525; fax 313702580; e-mail info@sek-feps.ch; internet www.sek-feps.ch; f. 1920; comprises the 20 reformed cantonal churches of Aargau, Appenzell, Basel-Stadt, Basel-Landschaft, Bern-Jura, Fribourg, Geneva, Glarus, Graubünden, Luzern, Neuchâtel, St Gallen, Schaffhausen, Solothurn, Tessin, Thurgau, Valais, Vaud, Zug, Zürich, the Kirchenverband Zentralschweiz, the Eglise évangélique libre de Genève and the United Methodist Church; the exec. organ is the Council of the Federation (Rat des Schweizerischen Evangelischen Kirchenbundes, Conseil de la Fédération); Pres. Rev. THOMAS WIPF.

JUDAISM

Schweizerischer Israelitischer Gemeindebund—Fédération suisse des communautés israélites: Gotthardstr. 65, Postfach 564, 8027 Zürich; tel. 12015583; fax 12021672; e-mail info@ swissjews.org; internet www.swissjews.org; Pres. Prof. Dr ALFRED DONATH; Gen. Sec. DENNIS L. RHEIN.

BAHÁ'Í FAITH

Nationaler Geistiger Rat der Bahá'í der Schweiz—Assemblée spirituelle nationale des bahá'ís de Suisse: Dufourstr. 13, 3005 Bern; tel. 313521020; fax 313524716; e-mail bahai@bluewin.ch; internet www.bahai.ch; Chair. DIANE ALA'I; Sec. Dr JOHN-PAUL VADER.

The Press

Freedom of the Press in Switzerland is guaranteed by Article 55 of the amended 1874 Constitution, and the only formal restrictions on the press are the legal restraints concerned with abuses of this freedom. A federal law, enacted in 1968, protects the right of journalists to refuse, in administrative procedures, to reveal their sources of information, except in cases where state security is involved.

Switzerland's federal constitutional structure and the coexistence of diverse languages and religions have tended to produce a decentralized press, fragmented into numerous local papers, often with very low circulations. In 1998 there were 60 daily newspapers, but only 12 had a circulation of over 50,000. The majority of newspapers are regional, even such high circulation ones as *Tages Anzeiger Zürich* and *Basler Zeitung* and national dailies such as *Neue Zürcher Zeitung*. About 67% of newspapers are printed in German, 27% in French, 4% in Italian and less than 1% in Raeto-Romansch. The presence of immigrant workers and the Swiss interest in foreign news has led to the import of 100,000 copies of French, German, Italian and Spanish newspapers every day.

PRINCIPAL DAILIES

Arbon

Bodensee Tagblatt: Romanshornerstr. 36, 9320 Arbon; tel. 714476060; fax 714476070; f. 1849; circ. 14,780.

Baden

Aargauer Zeitung: Stadtturmstr. 19, 5400 Baden; tel. 562042424; fax 562042425; f. 1996 by merger of Aargauer Tagblatt and Badener Tagblatt; non-party; Editor-in-Chief FRANZ STRAUB; Publr PETER WANNER; circ. 120,000.

Basel
(Bâle)

Basellandschaftliche Zeitung: Schützengasse 6, 4410 Liestal; tel. 619272600; fax 619212268; Catholic; Publrs Verlag Lüdin AG; circ. 27,654.

Basler Zeitung: Hochbergerstr. 15, 4002 Basel; tel. 616391111; fax 616311959; f. 1977; liberal; Editor H. P. PLATZ; circ. 114,686.

Bellinzona

La Regione Ticino: Via Ghiringhelli 9, 6500 Bellinzona; tel. 918211121; fax 918211122; e-mail info@laregione.ch; internet www .laregione.ch; f. 1992; circ. 32,556.

Bern
(Berne)

Berner Tagwacht: Bern; tel. 313716469; fax 313715738; independent; circ. 5,697.

Berner Zeitung: Nordring/Dammweg 9, 3001 Bern; tel. 313303730; fax 313316087; internet www.bzonline.ch; f. 1844; independent; Chief Editor ANDREAS Z'GRAGGEN; circ. 131,515.

Der Bund: Bubenbergpl. 8, 3001 Bern; tel. 313851111; fax 313851112; e-mail derbund@derbund.ch; internet www.ebund.ch; f. 1850; liberal; Chief Editor HANSPETER SPOERRI; circ. 68,212.

Bienne
(Biel)

Bieler Tagblatt/Seeländer Bote: Längfeldweg 135, 1501 Bienne; tel. 32428333; fax 32428335; independent; Publr W. GASSMAN; circ. 33,281.

Le Journal du Jura: 15 rue M.-Chipot, CP 624, 2501 Bienne; tel. 3219000; fax 3219009; e-mail redactionjj@journaldujura.ch; internet www.journaldujura.ch; f. 1863; independent; Publr W. GASSMANN; circ. 13,131.

Brig

Walliser Bote: Furkastr. 21, 3900 Brig; tel. 279229988; fax 279229989; Catholic; Editor-in-Chief PIUS RIEDER; circ. 27,493.

Buchs

Werdenberger und Obertoggenburger: Bahnhofstr. 14, 9470 Buchs; tel. 817500202; f. 1869; liberal; circ. 10,450.

La Chaux-de-Fonds

L'impartial: 14 rue Neuve, 2300 La Chaux-de-Fonds; tel. 39210210; fax 39210360; f. 1880; independent; circ. 26,951.

Chur
(Coire)

Bündner Tagblatt: Commercialstr. 22, 7007 Chur; tel. 812555000; fax 812555123; e-mail redaktion-bt@suedostschweiz.ch; f. 1852; independent; circ. 13,000.

Bündner Zeitung: Kasernenstr. 1, 7007 Chur; tel. 812555050; fax 812555100; independent; Publr Gasser AG; circ. 56,144.

La Quotidiana: Via Centrala 4, 7130 Ilanz; tel. 819200710; fax 819200715; e-mail redaktion-lq@suedostschweiz.ch; f. 1997; Romansch-language; Publr Südostschweiz Presse AG; Editor-in-Chief MARTIN CABALZAR; circ. 10,154.

Die Südostschweiz: Comercialstr. 22, 7007 Chur; tel. 812255050; fax 812255102; e-mail zentralredaktion@suedostschweiz.ch; internet www.suedostschweiz.ch; independent; Publr Südostschweiz Presse AG; circ. 140,000.

Delémont

Le Quotidien Jurassien: 6 route de Courroux, 2800 Delémont; tel. 324211818; fax 324211890; e-mail lqj@lqj.ch; internet www.lqj.ch; f. 1993; independent; Editor M. VOISARD; circ. 25,120.

Dielsdorf

Zürcher Unterländer: Schulstr. 12, 8157 Dielsdorf; tel. 18548282; fax 18530690; e-mail redaktion@zuonline.ch; internet www.zuonline.ch; circ. 19,696 (Thur. 74,417).

Flawil

Volksfreund/Wiler Zeitung/Gossauer Zeitung: Burgauerstr. 50, 9230 Flawil; independent; circ. 10,473.

Frauenfeld

Thurgauer Zeitung: Promenadenstr. 16, 8501 Frauenfeld; tel. 527235511; fax 527210002; f. 1798; independent; Publrs Huber & Co AG; circ. 31,866.

Fribourg
(Freiburg)

Freiburger Nachrichten: Bahnhofpl. 5, 1701 Fribourg; tel. 263473000; fax 263473019; e-mail fn.verlag@freiburger-nachrichten.ch; internet www.freiburger-nachrichten.ch; Catholic; circ. 16,393.

Geneva

Le Temps: pl. de Cornavin 3, CP 2570, 1211 Geneva 2; tel. 227995858; fax 227995859; e-mail info@letemps.ch; internet www.letemps.ch; f. 1998 by merger of *Journal de Genève* and *Le Nouveau Quotidien*.

Tribune de Genève: CP 5115, 1211 Geneva 11; tel. 223224000; fax 223215972; f. 1879; independent; morning; Editor GUY METTAN; circ. 78,000.

Glarus

Glarner Nachrichten: Zwinglistr. 6, Postfach 366, 8750 Glarus; tel. 556401921; fax 556406440; f. 1875; liberal; Publrs Tschudi & Co AG; circ. 10,976.

Heerbrugg

Der Rheintaler: Heerbrugg; tel. 71722121; fax 71727936; independent; Editor W. WUFFLI; circ. 11,023.

Herisau

Appenzeller Zeitung: Kasernenstr. 64, 9100 Herisau; tel. 713546464; fax 713546465; radical democratic; f. 1828; Publrs Appenzeller Medienhaus Schläpfer AG; circ. 15,293.

Lausanne

Le Matin: 33 ave de la Gare, 1001 Lausanne; tel. 213494949; fax 21494929; e-mail matin-redaction@edicom.ch; internet www.lematin.ch; f. 1862; independent; Editor DANIEL PITTARD; circ. 66,000, Sunday 220,000.

Nouvelle Revue et Journal politique: 15 ave Ruchonnet, 1001 Lausanne; tel. 213400011; fax 213400030; f. 1868; radical democratic; circ. 6,790.

24 heures: 33 ave de la Gare, 1001 Lausanne; tel. 213494444; fax 213494419; f. 1762; independent; circ. 91,096.

Lucerne
(Luzern)

Neue Luzerner Zeitung: Maihofstr. 76, 6002 Lucerne; tel. 414295151; fax 414295181; e-mail redaktion@neue0lz.ch; f. 1996; Editor THOMAS BORNHAUSER; circ. 133,820.

Lugano

Corriere del Ticino: Ai Mulini, 6933 Muzzano; tel. 919603131; fax 919682779; f. 1891; independent; circ. 37,000.

Giornale del Popolo: Via San Gottardo 50, 6900 Lugano; tel. 919232271; fax 919232805; f. 1926; independent; circ. 26,485.

Mels

Der Sarganserländer: Sarganserstr., 8887 Mels; tel. 817233761; fax 817237018; Catholic; circ. 10,272.

Montreux

La Presse: 22 ave des Planches, 1820 Montreux; tel. 219636131; fax 219635734; e-mail redac@lapresse.ch; internet www.lapresse.ch; f. 1867; independent; circ. 24,655.

Neuchâtel
(Neuenburg)

L'Express: CP 2816, 2001 Neuchâtel; tel. 327235300; fax 327235209; e-mail editeur@lexpress.ch; internet www.lexpress.ch; f. 1738; independent; circ. 29,332.

St Gallen
(St-Gall)

Die Ostschweiz: Oberer Graben 8, 9001 St Gallen; tel. 71308580; f. 1873; Catholic; circ. 21,642.

St Galler Tagblatt: Fürstenlandstr. 122, 9001 St Gallen; tel. 712727711; fax 712727476; e-mail zentralredaktion@tagblatt.ch; internet www.tagblatt.ch; f. 1839; liberal; Editor-in-Chief GOTTLIEB F. HÖPLI; circ. 110,000.

Schaffhausen
(Schaffhouse)

Schaffhauser Nachrichten: Vordergasse 58, 8201 Schaffhausen; tel. 526333111; fax 526333401; e-mail redaktion@shn.ch; internet www.shn.ch; f. 1861; liberal; Editor-in-Chief NORBERT NEIMINGER; Publr Dr MAX U. RAPOLD; circ. 26,000.

Sion

Nouvelliste et Feuille d'Avis du Valais: 13 rue de l'Industrie, 1951 Sion; tel. 273297511; fax 273297565; e-mail redaction@nouvelliste.ch; internet www.lenouvelliste.ch; Catholic; Publrs Imprimerie Moderne SA; Editorial Dir HERMAN PELLEGRINI; circ. 42,066.

Stäfa

Zürichsee-Zeitung: Seestr. 86, 8712 Stäfa; tel. 19285555; fax 19285550; e-mail redstaefa@zsz.ch; internet www.zsz.ch; f. 1845; radical democratic; Publr and Editor-in-Chief LUZI BERNET; circ. 53,000.

Thun
(Thoune)

Berner Oberländer: Rampenstr. 1, 3602 Thun; tel. 332251515; fax 332251505; e-mail redaktion-bo@bom.ch; internet www.berneroberlaender.ch; f. 1898; independent; Publrs Berner Oberland Medien AG; circ. 23,358.

Thuner Tagblatt: Rampenstr. 1, 3602 Thun; tel. 332251515; fax 332251505; independent; Dir KONRAD MAURER; Editor-in-Chief RENÉ E. GYGAX; circ. 23,000.

Uster

Anzeiger von Uster: Oberlandstr. 100, 8610 Uster; tel. 19057979; fax 19057980; e-mail inserat@avu.ch; f. 1846; independent; Publr G. MÜLLER; circ. 11,524.

Wetzikon

Zürcher Oberländer: 8620 Wetzikon; tel. 19333333; fax 19323232; e-mail redaktion@zol.ch; internet www.zo-medien.ch; f. 1852; liberal; circ. 37,040.

Winterthur
(Winterthour)

Der Landbote: Postfach 778, 8401 Winterthur; tel. 522669901; fax 522669911; e-mail redaktion@landbote.ch; internet www .winti-guide.ch; f. 1836; independent; morning; Editor-in-Chief Dr RUDOLF GERBER; circ. 48,000.

Yverdon-les-Bains

La Presse Nord Vaudoise: 6 ave Haldimand, 1401 Yverdon-les-Bains; tel. 244248424; fax 244248425; e-mail redac@lapresse-nv.ch; f. 1773; independent; circ. 11,000.

Zofingen

Zofinger Tagblatt: Vordere Hauptgasse 33, 4800 Zofingen; tel. 627459350; fax 627459419; e-mail pehinger@ztonline.ch; f. 1873; liberal; Editor Dr PAUL EHINGER; circ. 17,200.

Zürich

Blick: Dufourstr. 23, 8008 Zürich; tel. 12596262; fax 12622953; independent; Editor FRIDOLIN LUCHSINGER; circ. 335,143.

Neue Zürcher Zeitung: Falkenstr. 11, Postfach, 8021 Zürich; tel. 12581111; fax 12521329; e-mail redaktion@nzz.ch; internet www .nzz.ch; f. 1780; independent-liberal; Chief Editor Dr HUGO BÜTLER; circ. 170,113.

Tages Anzeiger Zürich: Werdstr. 21, 8021 Zürich; tel. 12484411; fax 12484471; e-mail redaktion@tages-anzeiger.ch; internet www .tagesanzeiger.ch; f. 1893; independent; Chief Editor PHILIPP LOEPFE; circ. 250,000.

PERIODICALS AND JOURNALS

Allgemeine Schweizerische Militärzeitschrift: Verlag Huber & Co AG, Postfach, 8501 Frauenfeld; tel. 527235622; fax 527215404; e-mail redaktion@asmz.ch; f. 1834; 11 a year; Editor LOUIS GEISEL; circ. 28,800.

Die Alpen: Monbijoustr. 61, Postfach, 3000 Bern 23; tel. 313701818; fax 313701890; e-mail alpen@sac-cas.ch; internet www.sac-cas.ch; monthly; publ. by Schweizer Alpen-Club; circ. 80,000.

Annabelle création: Baslerstr. 30, 8048 Zürich; tel. 14046333; fax 14046218; e-mail redaktion@an-creation.ch; creative lifestyle and living magazine; f. 1998; monthly; circ. 102,866.

Auto: Wasserwerkgasse 39, 3000 Bern 13; tel. 313283111; fax 313110310; e-mail acszv@acs.ch; internet www.acs.ch; publ. by the Automobile Club of Switzerland; 10 a year; circ. 63,200.

Automobil Revue: Dammweg 9, 3001 Bern; tel. 313303034; fax 313303032; e-mail office@automobilrevue.ch; f. 1906; weekly publ. in German and French *Revue automobile*; Editor MAX NÖTZLI; circ. 67,412.

Baukader Aktuelles Bauen: Schück Söhne, Bahnhofstr. 24, 8803 Rüschlikon; tel. 17247777; fax 17247877; f. 1944; 10 a year; magazine for the construction industry; publ. by Imprimerie Vogt-Schild AG; circ. 10,500.

Beobachter: Förrlibuckstr. 70, 8021 Zürich; tel. 434445111; fax 434445353; e-mail redaktion@beobachter.ch; internet www .beobachter.ch; f. 1927; 2 a month; circ. 335,226.

Bilanz: Förrlibuckstr. 70, Postfach 8021 Zürich; tel. 434445520; fax 434445521; internet www.bilanz.ch; f. 1977; review of business in Switzerland; circ. 57,548.

Courrier neuchâtelois: Colombier; tel. 38411541; fax 38413179; weekly; Editor RENÉ GESSLER; circ. 88,087.

Du: Postfach, 8021 Zürich; tel. 12486030; fax 12486040; f. 1941; monthly art review; Editor MARCO BEIER; circ. 31,915.

Echo Magazine: rue de Meyrin 12, CP 80, 1211 Geneva 7; tel. 229190404; fax 229190419; e-mail saripres@worldcom.ch; f. 1929; weekly; circ. 22,000.

L'Eco dello Sport: Via Industria, 6933 Muzzano; tel. 919603131; fax 91575750; circ. 44,000.

Finanz und Wirtschaft: Hallwylstr. 71, Postfach, 8021 Zürich; tel. 12983535; fax 12983500; e-mail verlag@fuw.ch; internet www .finanzinfo.ch; f. 1928; 2 a week; finance and economics; circ. 50,397.

Gauchebdo: 18 rue Dancet, CP 366, 1211 Geneva 4; tel. 223206335; fax 223200587; e-mail gauchebdo@worldcom.ch; f. 1944; weekly; left-wing; Publr A. BRINGOLF; Editor-in-Chief R. ABADI; circ. 5,000.

Glücks-Post: Dufourstr. 49, 8008 Zürich; tel. 12596912; fax 12596930; e-mail glueckspost@ringier.ch; women's interest; f. 1977; weekly; Editor-in-Chief HELMUT-MARIA GLOGGER; circ. 170,028.

Graphis: Dufourstr. 107, 8008 Zürich; tel. 13838211; fax 13831643; f. 1944; bi-monthly; graphic art and applied arts; publ. by Graphis Press Corpn; Editor B. MARTIN PEDERSEN; circ. 29,000.

Handels Zeitung: Seestr. 37, 8027 Zürich; tel. 12883555; fax 12883575; e-mail redaktion@handelszeitung.ch; f. 1862; financial, commercial and industrial weekly; Publr RALPH BÜCHI; Chief Editor Dr KURT SPECK; circ. 36,597.

L'Hebdo: 3 Pont Bessières, 1005 Lausanne; tel. 213317600; fax 213317601; f. 1981; news magazine; Editor-in-Chief ARIANE DAYER; circ. 55,388.

L'Illustré: Pont Bessières 3, 1005 Lausanne; tel. 213317500; fax 213317501; e-mail illustre@ringier.ch; internet www.ringier.ch; f. 1921; weekly; Chief Editor FREDERICO CAMPOMODO; circ. 97,974.

Journal suisse d'horlogerie et de bijouterie: La Conversion; tel. 217960096; fax 217914084; e-mail info@jsh.ch; internet www.jsh.ch; f. 1876; 6 a year; publ. in English as *Swiss Watch Journal*; circ. 25,000.

M: 33 ave de la Gare, 1001 Lausanne; tel. 23494545; fax 23494110; f. 1998; men's leisure; Dir PHILIPPE SIMON.

Meyer's: Schachenstr. 80, 8645 Jona; tel. 552242525; fax 552242529; internet www.vmag.ch; weekly; Publr SILVIA AESCHBACH; circ. 122,102.

Museum Helveticum: Steinentorstr. 13, 4010 Basel; tel. 612789565; fax 612789566; e-mail verlag@schwabe.ch; internet www.schwabe.ch; f. 1944; quarterly; Swiss journal for classical philology, ancient history and classical archaeology; Editors Prof. M. BILLERBECK, Prof. A. GIOVANNINI, Prof. TH. GELZER; publ. by Schwabe & Co AG.

Music Scene: 5401 Baden; tel. 562032200; fax 562032299; e-mail info@music-scene.ch; internet www.music-scene.ch; f. 1924; young people's fortnightly; circ. 50,000.

Nebelspalter: Missionsstr. 36, 4012 Basel; tel. 718448924; fax 718412155; e-mail nebelspalter@ep-group.ch; internet www .nebelspalter.ch; f. 1875; 10 a year; satirical; Editor HANS SUTER; publ. By Engeli & Partner Verlag; circ. 17,145.

Orella: Zürich; tel. 12981212; fax 12981277; monthly; fashion, handiwork; circ. 55,000.

Politische Rundschau/Revue politique: Postfach 6136, 3001 Bern; tel. 313203535; f. 1921; quarterly; Swiss and foreign politics, economics and culture; critical reviews; publ. by the Free Democratic Party; circ. 1,500.

PRO: Im Morgental 35, 8126 Zumikou; tel. 19182728; f. 1951; monthly; Editor ANNEMARIE FREY.

RMS-Radsport: Glattbrugg; tel. 18100505; fax 18101160; weekly; organ of Schweizerischer Radfahrer-und Motorfahrer Bund; Editor (vacant); circ. 50,000.

Revue économique et sociale: BFSH 1, 1015 Lausanne/Dorigny; tel. 216915347; fax 216923385; e-mail infosees@hec.unil.ch; internet www.hec.unil.ch/associations; f. 1943; quarterly; Editors A. M. GUÉNETTE, W. RAHM; circ. 1,400.

Revue médicale de la suisse romande: Editions Médecine et Hygiène, 2 ave Bellefontaine, 1003 Lausanne; tel. 213417170; fax 213417179; f. 1880; monthly; Editors Dr J. P. BERGER, Prof. A. PECOUD; circ. 5,600.

Revue militaire suisse: 3 ave de Florimont, 1006 Lausanne; tel. 213114817; fax 213919709; e-mail jcrc@vtxnet.ch; f. 1856; 11 a year; Editor-in-Chief Col HERVÉ DE WECK.

Revue suisse de zoologie: Muséum d'Histoire Naturelle, CP 6434, 1211 Geneva 6; tel. 224186300; fax 224186301; e-mail volker .mahnert@mhn.ville-ge.ch; internet www.ville-ge.ch/musinfo/mhng/page.rsz.htm; f. 1893; quarterly; Dir V. MAHNERT.

Schweizer Archiv für Neurologie und Psychiatrie (Archives Suisses de Neurologie et de Psychiatrie): Schwabe Verlag, Steinentorstr. 13, 4010 Basel; tel. 612789565; fax 612789566; internet www.schwabe.ch; f. 1917; 8 a year.

Schweizer Familie: Baslerstr. 30, Postfach, 8021 Zürich; tel. 14046106; fax 14046096; f. 1893; weekly; Editor ANDREAS DURISCH; Man. Dir JOSEF BURCH; circ. 205,529.

Schweizer Illustrierte: Dufourstr. 23, 8008 Zürich; tel. 12596111; fax 12620442; f. 1911; illustrated weekly; circ. 213,433.

Schweizer Monatshefte: Vogelsangstr. 52, 8006 Zürich; tel. 13612606; fax 13637005; e-mail schweizermonatshefte@swissonline .ch; internet www.schweizermonatshefte.ch; f. 1921; political, economic and cultural monthly; Editors ROBERT NEF, SUZANN RENNINGER, JULIANA SCHWAGER; circ. 2,500.

Schweizerisches Handelsamtsblatt (Feuille officielle suisse du commerce): Effingerstr. 1, Postfach 8164, 3001 Bern; tel. 313240992; fax 313240961; e-mail schab@seco.admin.ch; internet www.shab.ch; f. 1883; commercial daily; publ. by Federal Dept of Foreign Trade; circ. 16,200.

Ski: VS/H Medien, 4500 Solothurn; tel. 326247685; fax 326247251; e-mail j.weibel@vsonline.ch; f. 1968; 7 a year; German and French/Italian editions; Editor JOSEPH WEIBEL; circ. 82,000.

Sport: Förrlibuckstr. 10, 8021 Zürich; tel. 14487373; fax 14487673; f. 1920; weekly; Chief Editor PETER ZWICKY; circ. 55,477.

Swiss Engineering (STZ): Chellenstr. 18E, 6318 Walchwil; tel. 417590202; fax 417590200; e-mail mediakom@bluewin.ch; fortnightly; technical journal in German; circ. 18,000.

Swiss Journal of Psychology (Schweizerische Zeitschrift für Psychologie/Revue suisse de psychologie): Unitobler, Muesmattstr. 45, 3000 Bern 9; e-mail margrit.oswald@psy.unibe.ch; f. 1942; quarterly; Editors Prof. Dr MARGRIT E. OSWALD, Prof. Dr FRIEDRICH WILKENING.

Swiss Medical Weekly: EMH Swiss Medical Publrs Ltd, Steinentorstr. 13, 4010 Basel; tel. 614678555; fax 614678556; e-mail red@smw.ch; internet www.smw.ch; f. 1870; fortnightly; Man. Editor Dr N. MARTY; circ. 3,000.

Swiss Review of World Affairs: Folkenstr. 11, Postfach, 8021 Zürich; tel. 12581111; fax 12521329; monthly; publ. by Neue Zürcher Zeitung; circ. 4,400.

TCS-Revue: Alfred-Escher-Str. 38, 8027 Zürich; tel. 12868613; fax 12868637; official organ of the Zürich Touring Club; monthly; Chief Editor RETO CAVEGN; circ. 200,000.

Tele: Dufourstr. 23, 8008 Zürich; tel. 12596111; fax 12598697; e-mail telesekr@ringier.ch; internet www.tele.ch; f. 1967; television, cinema and multimedia; weekly; Editor KLAUS KRIESEL; circ. 229,508.

Touring: Maulbeerstr. 10, 3001 Bern; tel. 313805000; fax 313805006; f. 1935; fortnightly; German, French and Italian editions; Chief Editor STEFAN SENN; circ. 1,306,000.

TV 8: 3 Pont Bessières, 1005 Lausanne; tel. 213317700; fax 213317701; e-mail tv8@ringier.ch; weekly; circ. 52,720.

Vox Romanica: Länggassstr. 49, 3000 Bern 9; f. 1936; annual review of Romance linguistics and medieval literature.

Weltwoche: Förrlibuckstr. 70, 8021 Zürich; tel. 434445111; fax 434445669; e-mail redaktion@weltwoche.ch; internet www.weltwoche.ch; f. 1933; weekly; independent; Editor-in-Chief ROGER KÖPPEL; circ. 92,337.

Werk, Bauen + Wohnen: Talstr. 39, 8001 Zürich; tel. 12181430; fax 12181434; e-mail wbw.zh@bluewin.ch; internet www.werkbauenundwohnen.ch; f. 1913; monthly; architecture and art; circ. 9,000.

Yakari: Olten; tel. 622130088; fax 622931462; children's monthly; circ. 20,000.

NEWS AGENCIES

Schweizerische Depeschenagentur AG (SDA) (Agence Télégraphique Suisse SA (ATS), Swiss News Agency): Länggassstr. 7, 3001 Bern; tel. 313093333; fax 313018538; f. 1894; agency for political and general news; Chief Editor BERNARD REIST.

Foreign Bureaux

Agence France-Presse (AFP): Bureau C-14, Palais des Nations, 1211 Geneva 10; tel. 227321120; fax 227348292; Bureau Chief (vacant).

Agencia EFE (Spain): Bureau 49, Palais des Nations, 1211 Geneva 10; tel. 227336273; fax 227332041; e-mail efe-ginebra@bluewin.ch; Bureau Chief JOAQUÍN RÁBAGO.

Agenzia Nazionale Stampa Associata (ANSA) (Italy): Salle de Presse 1, Palais des Nations, 1211 Geneva 10; tel. 227334872; fax 227345900; e-mail ansa@itu.ch; Bureau Chief FRANCESCO INDRACEOLO.

Allgemeiner Deutscher Nachrichtendienst (ADN) (Germany): Bureau 53, Palais des Nations, 1211 Geneva 10; Correspondent HELMUT SCHULZ.

Associated Press (AP) (USA): Palais des Nations, 1211 Geneva 10; tel. 229194222; fax 227331337; Bureau Chief ALEXANDER HIGGINS.

Deutsche Presse-Agentur (dpa) (Germany): Bureau 84, Palais des Nations, 1211 Geneva 10; tel. 227315117; fax 227332706; Bureau Chief HEINZ-PETER DIETRICH.

Informatsionnoye Telegrafnoye Agentstvo Rossii— Telegrafnoye Agentstvo Suverennykh Stran (ITAR—TASS) (Russia): Palais des Nations, Bureau 72, 1211 Geneva 10; tel. 227343321; fax 227401147; Correspondent KONSTANTIN F. PRIBYTKOV.

Inter Press Service (IPS) (Italy): Bureau C504, Palais des Nations, 1211 Geneva 10; tel. 227346011; fax 227342430; Correspondent CHAKRAVARTHI RAGHAVAN.

Jiji Tsushin (Japan): 54 chemin du Grand Puits, 1217 Meyrin/Geneva; tel. 227341216; fax 227335115; Man. TOKIHIKO KITAHARA.

Kyodo Tsushin (Japan): C521, Salle de Presse 1, Palais des Nations, 1211 Geneva 10; tel. 227343856; fax 227349669; Bureau Chief YASUSHI FUJII.

Reuters (UK): Palais des Nations, Bureau 70, 1211 Geneva 10; tel. 227333831; fax 227348760; Man. Dir ROBERT EVANS.

United Press International (UPI) (USA): Bureau 76, Palais des Nations, 1211 Geneva 10; tel. 227341740; fax 227341042; Bureau Chief MICHAEL HUGGINS.

Xinhua (New China) News Agency (People's Republic of China): Palais des Nations, Bureau 57, 1211 Geneva 10; tel. 229173710; fax 227343505; Correspondent DASHENG LU.

PRESS ASSOCIATIONS

Association Presse Suisse/Verband Schweizer Presse: Baumackerstr. 42, Postfach, 8050 Zürich; tel. 13186464; fax 13186462; e-mail contact@_schweizerpresse.ch; internet www.schweizerpresse.ch; f. 1899; Pres. Dr H. H. CONINX; 180 mems.

Schweizer Verband der Journalistinnen und Journalisten/Fédération suisse des journalistes/Federazione svizzera dei giornalisti: Postfach 518, Grand'Places 14A, 1701 Fribourg; tel. 263471500; fax 263471509; e-mail info@journalisten.ch; internet www.journalisten.ch; Pres ANTOINE GESSLER, ALBERTO COTTI.

Publishers

FRENCH LANGUAGE PUBLISHING HOUSES

Editions l'Age d'Homme SA: 10 rue de Genève, BP B2, 1003 Lausanne 9; tel. 213120095; fax 213208440; e-mail info@agedhomme.com; internet www.agedhomme.com; f. 1966; fiction, biography, music, art, social science, science fiction, literary criticism; Man. Dir VLADIMIR DIMITRIJEVIC.

Editions de l'Aire SA: 15 rue de l'Union, BP 57, 1800 Vevey; tel. 219236836; fax 219236823; f. 1978; literature, history, philosophy, religion; Man. MICHEL MORET.

La Bibliothèque des Arts: 50 ave de Rumine, 1005 Lausanne; tel. 213123667; e-mail bda@bluewin.ch; internet www.bibliotheque-des-arts.com; f. 1952; art, culture; Dir OLIVIER DAULTE.

Delachaux et Niestlé SA: 79 route d'Oron, 1000 Lausanne 21; tel. 216533044; fax 216534095; f. 1861; natural history, psychology, pedagogy; Man. JEAN ARBEILLE.

Librairie Droz SA: 11 rue Massot, BP 389, 1211 Geneva 12; tel. 223466666; fax 223472391; e-mail droz@droz.org; internet www.droz.org; f. 1924; history, medieval literature, French literature, linguistics, social sciences, economics, archaeology; Dir MAX ENGAMMARE.

Edipresse Publications SA: 33 ave de la Gare, 1001 Lausanne; tel. 23494545; fax 23494110; e-mail edipresse@edicom.ch; internet www.edicom.ch; f. 1988; newspapers, magazines; Dir-Gen. PIERRE LAMUNIÈRE.

Edito Georges Naef SA: 33 quai Wilson, CP 54, 1211 Geneva 21; tel. 227380502; fax 227384224; f. 1986; childrens', health and beauty, history, languages and linguistics, psychology, reference books; Pres. GEORGES NAEF.

Editions Eiselé SA: Confrérie 42, CP 128, 1008 Prilly; tel. 21623650; fax 216236359; internet www.eisele.ch; arts, education, popular science, textbooks.

Editions d'En Bas: BP 304, 1000 Lausanne 17; tel. 213233918; fax 213123240; e-mail enbas@bluewin.ch; internet www.enbas.ch; ; literature, politics, memoirs, travel, poetry; Dir JEAN RICHARD.

Françoise Gonin Editions d'Art: 1 chemin du Grand-Praz, 1012 Lausanne; tel. 217285948; fax 217285948; internet www.biogate.com/ogonin; f. 1926; art books.

Editions du Grand-Pont: 2 place Bel-Air, 1003 Lausanne; tel. 213123222; fax 213113222; f. 1971; general, art books and literature; Dir JEAN-PIERRE LAUBSCHER.

Editions du Griffon: 17 Faubourg du Lac, 2000 Neuchâtel; tel. 327252204; f. 1944; science, arts.

Editions Ides et Calendes: Evole 19, 2001 Neuchâtel; tel. 327253861; fax 327255880; e-mail info@idesetcalendes.com; internet www.idesetcalendes.com; f. 1941; art, photography, literature; Dir ALAIN BOURET.

La Joie de Lire SA: 2 bis rue Saint-Léger, 1205 Geneva; tel. 228073399; fax 228073392; e-mail info@lajoiedelire.ch; f. 1987; juvenile.

Editions Labor & Fides SA: 1 rue Beauregard, 1204 Geneva; tel. 223113290; fax 227813051; f. 1924; theological and religious publs; Dir GABRIEL DE MONTMOLLIN.

Loisirs et Pédagogie SA: en Budron B4A, 1052 Le Mont-sur-Lausanne; tel. 216512570; fax 216535751; e-mail infolep@vtx.ch; Dir PHILIPPE BURDEL.

Médecine et Hygiène: 78 ave de la Roseraie, CP 456, 1211 Geneva 4; tel. 227029311; fax 227029355; e-mail abonnements@medhyg.ch; internet www.medhyg.ch; f. 1943; medicine, psychology, general science, university textbooks; Man. Dirs BERTRAND KIEFER, JACQUELINE MONNIER.

Editions Médecine et Hygiène, Départment Livre Georg: 46 chemin de la Mousse, 1225 Chêne-Bourg; tel. 228690029; fax 228690015; e-mail livres@medhyg.ch; Dir H. WEISSENBACH.

Editions Mon Village: 1085 Vulliens; tel. 219031363; f. 1956; Dir (vacant).

Editions Mondo SA: 7 passage St-Antoine, 1800 Vevey; tel. 219241450; fax 219244662; e-mail info@mondo.ch; internet www .mondo.ch; Dir ARSLAN ALAMIR.

Noir sur Blanc SA: Le Mottâ, 1147 Montricher; tel. 218645931; fax 218644026; e-mail noirsurblanc@bluewin.ch; f. 1986; literature.

Editions Novos SA: ave Nestlé 29, 1800 Vevey; tel. 219254252; fax 219254242; f. 1926; Swiss landscape books, calendars; Dir MAURICETTE JUVET.

Olizane: 11 Vieux-Grenadiers, 1205 Geneva; tel. 223285252; fax 223285796; e-mail guides@olizane.ch; internet www.olizane.ch; f. 1981; travel, tourism, orientalism, photography; Dir MATTHIAS HUBER.

Editions Payot Lausanne: Nadir SA, 18 ave de la Gare, CP 529, 1001 Lausanne; tel. 213290264; fax 213290266; f. 1875; technical, textbooks, medicine, law, popular science, art books, tourism, history, music, general non-fiction, academic publs; Dir JACQUES SCHERRER.

Presses Polytechniques et Universitaires Romandes: EPFL, Centre-Midi, 1015 Lausanne-Ecublens; tel. 216932130; fax 216934027; e-mail ppur@epfl.ch; internet www.ppur.org; f. 1980; technical and scientific; Man. Dir OLIVIER BABEL.

Editions Pro Schola: 3 pl. Chauderon, POB 270, 1000 Lausanne 9; tel. 213236655; fax 213236777; e-mail benedict@benedict-schools .com; internet www.benedict-international.com; f. 1928; education, language textbooks, audio-visual material; Dir JEAN BENEDICT.

Editions Randin SA: Lausanne; tel. and fax 213290194; philosophy, psychology, sport.

Editions Scriptar SA: La Conversion; tel. 217960096; fax 217914084; e-mail info@jsh.ch; internet www.jsh.ch; f. 1946; watches and jewellery, gemmology; Dir. F. MUGNIER.

Editions d'Art Albert Skira SA: Geneva; tel. 223495533; fax 223495535; fine arts and literature; Dir JEAN-MICHEL SKIRA.

Slatkine Reprints: 5 rue des Chaudronniers, CP 3625, 1211 Geneva 3; tel. 227762551; fax 227763527; e-mail slatkine@slatkine .com; internet www.slatkine.com; Dir M.-E. SLATKINE.

Tricorne: 14 rue Lissignol, 1201 Geneva; tel. 227388366; fax 227319749; e-mail tricorne@freesurf.ch; internet www.tricorne.org; f. 1976; philosophy, human sciences, art, religion, psychology, mathematics; Dir SERGE KAPLUN.

Editions Universitaires SA: 42 blvd de Pérolles, 1705 Fribourg; tel. 264264311; fax 264264300; e-mail eduni@st-paul.ch; internet www.st-paul.ch/uni-press-fr; Man. Dir ANTON SCHERER.

Institut Universitaire d'Etudes du Développement: 24 rue Rothschild, 1211 Geneva 21; tel. 229065989; fax 229065994; e-mail jean-pierre.gontard@iued.unige.ch; internet www.unige.ch/iued; f. 1961; educational, health and development; Dir JEAN-LUC MAURER.

Editions 24 heures: 33 ave de la Gare, 1001 Lausanne; tel. 213495013; fax 213495029; Dir J.-P. MÉROT.

Editions Vivez Soleil SA: 17 chemin des Deux Communes, 1226 Thônex; tel. 223492092.

Zoé: 11 rue des Moraines, 1227 Carouge-Geneva; tel. 223093606; fax 223093603; Dir MARLYSE PIETRI-BACHMANN.

GERMAN LANGUAGE PUBLISHING HOUSES

Arche Verlag AG, Raabe + Vitali: Niederdorfstr. 90, Am Central, 8001 Zürich; tel. 12522410; fax 12611115; internet www .arche-verlag.com; f. 1944; literature; Dirs ELISABETH RAABE, REGINA VITALI.

Baufachverlag AG: Schöneggstr. 102, Postfach 933, 8953 Dietikon; f. 1970; building and architecture; Dir WILLY KESSLER.

Benteli Verlags AG: Seftigenstr. 310, 3084 Wabern-Bern; tel. 319608484; fax 319617414; e-mail info@benteliverlag.ch; internet www.benteliverlag.ch; f. 1898; fine arts, photography, non-fiction, philology; Dir TILL SCHAAP.

Birkhäuser Verlag AG: Viaduktstr. 40–44, Postfach 133, 4010 Basel; tel. 612050707; fax 612050799; e-mail info@birkhauser.ch; internet www.birkhauser.ch; scientific and technical books, architecture, periodicals; Man. Dir HANS-PETER THÜR.

Cosmos Verlag: Kräyigenweg 3, 3074 Muri-Bern; tel. 319506464; fax 319506460; e-mail info@cosmosverlag.ch; internet www .cosmosverlag.ch; f. 1923; literature, local history, reference, children's, tax management; Dir RETO M. AEBERLI.

Diogenes Verlag AG: Sprecherstr. 8, 8032 Zürich; tel. 12548511; fax 12528407; e-mail info@diogenes.ch; internet www.diogenes.ch; f. 1952; fiction, graphic arts, children's; Publrs DANIEL KEEL, RUDOLF C. BETTSCHART.

Europa Verlag AG: Rämistr. 5, 8001 Zürich; tel. 12611629; fax 12516081; f. 1933; politics, philosophy, history, biography, sociology, fiction; Dir MARLYS MOSER.

Graphis Press Corpn: Dufourstr. 107, 8008 Zürich; tel. 13838211; fax 13831643; f. 1944; *Graphis* international two-monthly magazine for graphic and applied art, specialized books on visual art and graphic design; Dir B. MARTIN PEDERSEN.

Hallwag: Nordring 4, 3001 Bern; tel. 313355555; fax 313314133; internet www.hallwag.ch; f. 1912; maps and guides, road maps, atlases, travel guides; Man. Dir PETER NIEDERHAUSER.

Huber, Hans AG, Buchhandlung und Verlag: Länggassstr. 76, 3000 Bern 9; tel. 313004500; fax 313004590; e-mail verlag@ hanshuber.com; f. 1927; medicine and psychology; Dir Dr G.-J. HOGREFE.

Huber Verlag: Promenadenstr. 16, Postfach 382, 8501 Frauenfeld; tel. 527235791; fax 527214410; e-mail buchversand@huber.ch; internet www.huberbooks.ch; f. 1809; military, agriculture, art, history, philology, textbooks; Gen. Man. HANSRUDOLF FREY.

S. Karger AG: Allschwilerstr. 10, Postfach, 4009 Basel; tel. 613061111; fax 613061234; e-mail karger@karger.ch; internet www .karger.com; f. 1890; in Berlin, 1937 in Basel; international medical journals, books on medicine, chemistry, psychology; Pres. Dr THOMAS KARGER; CEO STEVEN KARGER.

Kümmerly & Frey Ltd: Alpenstr. 58, 3052 Zollikofen-Bern; tel. 319152211; fax 319152220; e-mail info@swissmaps.ch; internet www.swissmaps.ch; f. 1854; maps, geography; Dir ALEXANDER SOLLBERGER.

Peter Lang AG: Hochfeldstr. 32, POB 746, 3000 Bern 15; tel. 313061717; fax 313061727; e-mail customerservice@peterlang.com; internet www.peterlang.net; humanities, social sciences, German language and literature, Romance literatures and languages, linguistics, music, art, theatre, ethnology.

Manesse Verlag: Badergasse 9, 8001 Zürich; tel. 12525551; fax 12625347; f. 1944; world's classics (Manesse Bibliothek der Weltliteratur), poetry, short stories, essays, novels; Dir ANNE MARIE WELLS.

Müller Rüschlikon Verlags AG: Gewerbestr. 10, 6330 Cham; tel. 417403040; fax 417417115; e-mail info@bucheli-verlag.ch; f. 1936; non-fiction; Dir HEINZ JANSEN.

Nagel & Kimche AG, Verlag: Nordstr. 9, Postfach, Zürich; tel. 523666680; fax 523666688; e-mail info@nagel-kimche.ch; internet www.nagel-kimche.ch; f. 1983; belles-lettres, juvenile; Dir Dr DIRK VAIHINGER.

Neptun Verlag AG: Ermatingen; tel. 72642020; fax 72642023; f. 1946; travel books, children's, contemporary history; Dir H. BERCHTOLD-MÜHLEMANN.

Neue Zürcher Zeitung, Buchverlag: Postfach, 8021 Zürich; tel. 12581505; fax 12581399; e-mail buch.verlag@nzz.ch; internet www .nzz-buchverlag.ch; Man. WALTER KÖPFLI.

Verlag Niggli AG: Steinackerstr. 8, Postfach 135, 8583 Sulgen; tel. 716449111; fax 716449190; internet www.niggli.ch; f. 1950; art, architecture, typography; Gen. Man. Dr J. CHRISTOPH BÜRKLE.

Novalis Verlag AG: Postfach 1021, 8200 Schaffhausen; Neukirchen 86A, 24972 Quern-Neukirchen; tel. 4832875482; fax 4832875488; e-mail novalis@spectraweb.ch; f. 1974; the arts, cultural and social sciences, education; Dirs Dr M. FRENSCH, Dr MAX RAPOLD.

Orell Füssli Verlag: Dietzingerstr. 3, Postfach, 8036 Zürich; tel. 14667711; fax 14667412; e-mail info@ofv.ch; internet www.ofv.ch; f. 1519; management, history, law, schoolbooks, trade directories; Gen. Man. MANFRED HIEFNER-HUG.

Ott Verlag und Druck AG: Länggasse 57, Postfach 802, 3600 Thun 7; tel. 332253939; fax 332253933; e-mail info@ott-verlag.ch;

internet www.ott-verlag.ch; f. 1923; general non-fiction, mineralogy, military, sport, management and commerce; Dir ADOLF A. GROSSERT.

Verlag Pro Juventute/Atlantis Kinderbücher: Seehofstr. 15, 8032 Zürich; tel. 12567717; fax 12567778; e-mail verlag@projuventute.ch; internet www.projuventute.ch; social science, children's, families; Man. URS GYSLING.

Reich Verlag AG: Museggstr. 12, 6000 Lucerne 5; tel. 414103721; fax 414103227; internet www.terramagica.de; f. 1974; 'terra magica' illustrated books; Man. ALFONS WÜEST.

Friedrich Reinhardt Verlag: Missionsstr. 36, Postfach 393, 4012 Basel; tel. 612646464; e-mail verlag@reinhardt.ch; internet www.reinhardt.ch; f. 1900; belles-lettres, theology, periodicals; Dir RUDOLF REINHARDT.

Rex-Verlag: St Karliquai 12, 6000 Lucerne 5; tel. 414194719; fax 414194711; e-mail rex-buch@bluewin.ch; internet www.rex-verlag.ch; f. 1931; theology, pedagogics, fiction, juvenile; Dir MARKUS KAPPELER.

Ringier AG: Dufourstr. 23, 8008 Zürich; tel. 12596111; fax 12598635; e-mail buy@ringier.ch; internet www.ringier.ch; f. 1831; newspapers, magazines, books; CEO MICHAEL RINGIER.

Sauerländer Verlage AG: Laurenzenvorstadt 89, 5001 Aarau; tel. 628368626; fax 628268620; f. 1807; juvenile, school books, textbooks, history, chemistry, periodicals (professional, trade, science); Dir KLAUS WILLBERG.

Scherz Verlag AG: Theaterpl. 4–6, 3000 Bern 7; tel. 313277150; f. 1939; general fiction and non-fiction, crime thrillers, history, psychology and philosophy; Dir PETER LOHMANN.

Schulthess Polygraphischer Verlag AG: Zwinglipl. 2, 8022 Zürich; tel. 12519336; fax 12616394; f. 1791; legal, social science, university textbooks; Man. Dir WERNER STOCKER.

Schwabe & Co AG: Steinentorstr. 13, 4010 Basel; tel. 612789565; fax 612789566; e-mail verlag@schwabe.ch; internet www.schwabe.ch; f. 1488; medicine, art, history, philosophy; Dirs R. BIENZ, Dr U. BREITENSTEIN.

Schweizer Spiegel Verlag: Zürich; tel. 14221666; f. 1925; art, philosophy, psychology, poetry, education, general; Dir Dr P. HUGGLER.

Stämpfli Verlag AG: Hallerstr. 7, Postfach 8326, 3001 Bern; tel. 313006311; fax 313006688; e-mail verlag@staempfli.com; internet www.staempfliverlag.com; f. 1799; law, economics, history, art; Man. Dir Dr RUDOLF STÄMPFLI.

Theologischer Verlag Zürich AG: Badenerstr. 69, Postfach 8026 Zürich; tel. 12993355; fax 12993358; e-mail tvz@ref.ch; internet www.tvz.ref.ch; f. 1934; religion, theology; Dir Dr NIKLAUS PETER.

Tobler Verlag AG: Trogenerstr. 80, Postfach 642, 9450 Altstätten; tel. 717556060; fax 717551254; e-mail books@tobler-verlag.ch; internet www.tobler-verlag.ch; f. 1995.

Walter Verlag AG: Zürich; tel. 12521100; fax 12624792; f. 1916; psychology, religion, history of civilization, literature; Pres. Dr T. AURELIO; Man. RAUL NIEMANN.

Wepf & Co AG Verlag: Eisengasse 5, 4001 Basel; tel. 613119576; fax 613119585; e-mail wepf@dial.eunet.ch; internet www.wepf.ch; f. 1755; architecture, engineering, ethnology, geography, geology, mineralogy; Dir H. HERRMANN.

PUBLISHERS' ASSOCIATIONS

Association Suisse des Editeurs de Langue Française: CP 1215, 1001 Lausanne; tel. 217963300; fax 217963311; e-mail aself@centrepatronal.ch; f. 1975; asscn of French-speaking publrs; Pres. FRANCINE BOUCHET; Vice-Pres. OLIVIER BABEL; Sec.-Gen. FRANÇOIS PERRET; 75 mems.

Schweizer Buchhändler- und Verleger-Verband (SBVV): Alderstr. 40, Postfach, 8034 Zürich; tel. 14212800; fax 14212818; e-mail sbvv@swissbooks.ch; internet www.swissbooks.ch; f. 1849; asscn of German-speaking Swiss booksellers and publrs; Central Pres. MEN HAUPT; Dir Dr MARTIN JANN; 700 mem. and affiliated firms.

Broadcasting and Communications

TELECOMMUNICATIONS

Swisscom AG: Alte Tiefenaustr. 6, 3050 Bern; tel. 313421111; fax 313422549; e-mail swisscom@swisscom.com; internet www.swisscom.com; fmrly Swiss Telecom PTT, transfer to private ownership commenced October 1998; Pres. MARKUS RAUH; CEO JENS ALDER.

BROADCASTING

Radio

SRG SSR idée suisse (Schweizerische Radio- und Fernsehgesellschaft—SRG) (Société suisse de radiodiffusion et télévision—SSR) (Società svizzera di radiotelevisione—SSR) (Societad svizra da radio et televisiun—SSR): Giacomettistr. 3, Postfach 26, 3000 Bern 15; tel. 313509111; fax 313509256; e-mail info@srgssrideesuisse.ch; internet www.srgssrideesuisse.ch; Pres. JEAN-BERNARD MÜNCH; Dir-Gen. ARMIN WALPEN; Sec.-Gen. BEAT DURRER.

The Swiss Broadcasting Corporation (SBC) is a private non-profit-making company which fulfils a public duty on the basis of a licence granted to it by the Federal Government. The SBC uses the electrical and radio-electrical installations of Swisscom for public broadcasting of radio and television programmes. Swisscom is responsible for all technical aspects of transmission. Some 75.08% of the receiver licence fee is allocated to the SBC, while Swisscom takes 24.22% and the remainder is distributed among local radio and television stations.

Radio-Télévision suisse romande (RTSR): 40 ave du Temple, 1010 Lausanne; tel. 213181111; fax 216536767; Pres. JEAN-JACQUES DEMARTINES; Sec.-Gen. ESTHER JOUHET.

Radio suisse romande (RSR): 40 ave du Temple, 1010 Lausanne; tel. 213181111; fax 216523719; e-mail webmaster@rsr.ch; internet www.rsr.ch; Dir GÉRARD TSCHOPP; Dir of Programmes ISABELLE BLINGGELI; Dir of Information PATRICK NUSSBAUM.

Radiotelevisione svizzera di lingua italiana (RTSI): CP, 6903 Lugano; tel. 918035111; fax 918035355; e-mail info@rtsi.ch; internet www.rtsi.ch; Dir DINA BALESTRA; Dir of TV RENIGIO RATTI; Dir of Radio JACKY MARTI.

swissinfo/Swiss Radio International: Giacomettistr. 1, 3000 Bern 15; tel. 313509222; fax 313509569; e-mail info@swissinfo.ch; internet www.swissinfo.org; programmes in English, French, German, Italian and Arabic, short-wave and via satellites, Eutelsat HB3 and Worldspace; short-wave transmitters are situated at Sottens; relay stations in Germany and French Guiana; Dir NICOLAS D. LOMBARD.

Television

A complete TV programme service for each linguistic region and regular broadcasts in Romansch are provided on the 1st (VHF) channel. The 2nd and 3rd (UHF) channels are used in each linguistic region for transmitting programmes of the other two linguistic regions. Limited direct advertising (amounting to an estimated 2% of public broadcast time in 1995) is allowed. There are also five private regional television channels.

SRG SSR idée suisse: see Radio.

Radio- und Fernsehgesellschaft der deutschen und der rätoromanischen Schweiz (RDRS): see Radio.

Schweizer Fernsehen DRS (SF DRS): Fernsehstr. 1–4, Postfach, 8052 Zürich; tel. 13056611; fax 13055660; e-mail sfdrs@sfdrs.ch; Dir PETER SCHELLENBERG.

Radio-Télévision suisse romande (RTSR): see Radio.

Télévision suisse romande (TSR): 20 quai Ernest-Ansermet, CP 234, 1211 Geneva 8; tel. 227082020; fax 223204813; e-mail tsr@tsr.ch; internet www.tsr.ch; Dir GILLES MARCHAND.

Radiotelevisione svizzera di lingua italiana (RTSI): see Radio; TV Programme Dir DINO BALESTRA.

Finance

(cap. = capital; dep. = deposits; res = reserves; m. = million; brs = branches; all values are in Swiss francs)

BANKING

Switzerland's banks have a long-standing reputation as a secure repository for foreign capital. The Swiss Banking Law of 1934 declared it a penal offence for a bank to provide information about its clients without their explicit authorization, unless a court had ordered otherwise. When foreign authorities wish to investigate Swiss accounts, criminal charges must have been made in a foreign court and accepted as valid by Switzerland. The system of numbered accounts has also shielded depositors' shares from investigation. However, the abuse of bank secrecy by organized crime led Switzerland and the USA to sign a treaty in May 1973, under which the banking secrecy rules may be lifted in the case of common-law crime (although not for non-criminal tax evasion and anti-trust law infringements). Further amendments to banking secrecy legislation were introduced in 1990 and 1998. From the mid-1990s the presence in Swiss bank accounts of substantial assets belonging to victims of the Nazi 'Holocaust' attracted international scrutiny, and the probity of Swiss banks during and after the Second World War was called into question. In August 2000 Crédit Suisse Group and UBS AG agreed to pay US $1,250m. to international Jewish organizations, in order to protect Swiss banking and industrial interests from lawsuits and financial sanctions relating to their handling of the dormant assets (see History).

In June 1977 the Swiss banks agreed a code of practice which required the introduction of stricter controls over the handling of foreign funds. The opening of numbered accounts was subjected to closer scrutiny and the practice of actively encouraging the flow of foreign money into the country was checked. The agreement was modified in 1982. In 1987, following the withdrawal from the agreement of the Swiss National Bank, the code was adapted by the Swiss Bankers' Association into rules of professional conduct; further modifications to the code were introduced in 1992. In 1978, in view of the steady increase in Swiss banks' international business, the Federal Banking Commission was given greater supervisory powers. Banks were required for the first time to submit consolidated balance sheets to the Commission and new consolidation requirements forced banks to raise capital to between 6% and 8% of total liabilities. The capital requirement is now one of the highest in the world.

During the 1990s significant restructuring of the retail banking sector was envisaged as a response to a long-term profitability problem which was blamed on overcrowding in the sector. By 1997 approximately one-third of all banks in operation in 1990 had disappeared, mostly through merger or acquisition. The most important amalgamations during the 1990s were the take-over of Swiss Volksbank by Crédit Suisse in 1993 and the creation in 1998 of UBS AG by the merger of UBS-Union Bank of Switzerland and Swiss Bank Corporation.

At the end of 1998 there were 3,199 bank branches (including 722 loan offices) in Switzerland, owned by 376 banks. The total assets of all banks operating in Switzerland at the end of 1998 was 2,057,924m. francs.

The 24 canton banks are mostly financed and controlled by the cantons, and their activities are co-ordinated by the Association of Swiss Cantonal Banks. In 1998 they had 744 branches and controlled more than one-third of Switzerland's savings deposits.

Central Bank

Schweizerische Nationalbank/Banque nationale suisse (Swiss National Bank): Börsenstr. 15, Postfach 2800, 8022 Zürich; tel. 16313111; fax 16313911; e-mail snb@snb.ch; internet www.snb .ch; f. 1907; the object of the bank is to regulate the circulation of money, to facilitate payments transactions and to pursue a credit and monetary policy serving the general interest; Dept I (Zürich) is responsible for economic studies, international affairs, statistics, legal matters, personnel and internal auditing; Dept II (Bern) issues notes, manages metal reserves, runs the main accounting section and banking transactions for the Fed. Govt; Dept III (Zürich) handles foreign-exchange business and credits to the commercial banks in addition to giro and clearing functions; cap. 50m., res 66m., dep. 9,536m. (Dec. 2001); Chair. of Governing Bd Dr JEAN-PIERRE ROTH; 1 br.

Canton Banks

There are 24 cantonal banks, of which the following are the largest:

Aargauische Kantonalbank: Bahnhofstr. 58, 5001 Aarau; tel. 648357777; fax 648357925; e-mail direction@akb.ch; internet www .akb.ch; f. 1913; cap. 200m., res 156m., dep. and bonds 11,292m. (Dec. 2001); Pres. Dr WENDOLIN STUTZ; Chief Exec. Dir U. GRÄTZER; 7 brs.

Banca dello Stato del Cantone Ticino: Viale H. Guisan 5, 6501 Bellinzona; tel. 918037111; fax 918261364; e-mail contatto@bsct.ch; internet www.bsct.ch; f. 1915; cap. 100m., res 97m., dep. and bonds 5,474m. (Dec. 2001); Chair. DONATO BARBUSCIA; 3 brs.

Banque Cantonale de Fribourg: Blvd de Pérolles 1, 1701 Fribourg; tel. 263507111; fax 263507709; internet www.bcf.ch; f. 1892; cap. 70m., res 188m., dep. and bonds 7,085m. (Dec. 2001); Chair. CLAUDE SCHORDERET; CEO ALBERT MICHEL; 21 brs.

Banque Cantonale de Genève: quai de l'Ile 17, CP 2251, 1211 Geneva; tel. 223172727; fax 227935960; e-mail info@bcge.ch; internet www.bcge.ch; f. 1994; cap. 360m., res 324m., dep. and bonds 16,102m. (Dec. 2001); Chair. JACQUES PERROT; CEO BLAISE GOETSCHIN; 28 brs.

Banque Cantonale du Jura: 10 rue de la Chaumont, CP 278, 2900 Porrentruy; tel. 324651301; fax 324651495; e-mail bcj@bcju.ch; internet www.bcju.ch; cap. 45m., res 47m., dep. and bonds 1,483m. (Dec 2001); Chair. Dr PAUL-ANDRÉ SANGLARD.

Banque Cantonale du Valais: CP 133, Pl. des Cèdres, 1951 Sion; tel. 273246111; fax 273246666; e-mail info@bcvs.ch; internet www

.bcvs.ch; cap. 150m., res 193m., dep. and bonds 6,317m. (Dec. 2001); Pres., Chair and Gen. Man. JEAN-DANIEL PAPILLOUD.

Banque Cantonale Neuchâteloise: 4 pl. Pury, 2001 Neuchâtel; tel. 327236111; fax 327236236; e-mail bcn@bcn.ch; internet www .bcn.ch; f. 1883; cap. 125m., res 98m., dep. 3,853m. (Dec. 2000); Pres. WILLY SCHAER.

Banque Cantonale Vaudoise: 14 pl. St François, CP 300, 1003 Lausanne; tel. 212121212; fax 212121222; e-mail info@bcv.ch; internet www.bcv.ch; f. 1845; cap. 589m., res 1,195m., dep. and bonds 32,351m. (Dec. 2000); Gen. Man. GILBERT DUCHOUD; 69 brs.

Basellandschaftliche Kantonalbank: Rheinstr. 7, 4410 Liestal; tel. and fax 619259494; e-mail info@blkb.ch; internet www.blkb.ch; f. 1864; cap. 240m., res 911m., dep. and bonds 11,328m. (Dec. 2000); Pres. WERNER DEGEN; CEO PAUL NYFFELER; 18 brs.

Basler Kantonalbank: Spiegelgasse 2, 4002 Basel; tel. 612662121; fax 612618434; e-mail bkb@bkb.ch; internet www.bkb.ch; f. 1899; cap. 293m., res. 945m., dep. and bonds 10,953m. (Dec. 2001); Chair. Dr WILLI GERSTER; CEO WERNER SIGG; 16 brs.

Berner Kantonalbank: Bundesplatz 8, 3001 Bern; tel. 316661111; fax 316666040; e-mail bekb@bekb.ch; internet www.bekb.ch; f. 1834; cap. 445m., res 460m., dep. and bonds 15,393m. (Dec. 2001); Pres. Dr MAX KOPP; CEO PETER W. KAPPELER; 84 brs.

Graubündner Kantonalbank: Poststr. 2, 7002 Chur; tel. 812569111; fax 812526729; e-mail info@gkb.ch; internet www.gkb .ch; f. 1870; cap. 240m., res 254m., dep. and bonds 10,019m. (Dec. 2001); Pres. Dr HANS HATZ.

Luzerner Kantonalbank: Pilatusstr. 12, 6002 Lucerne; tel. 412062222; fax 412062200; e-mail info@lukb.ch; internet www.lukb .ch; f. 1850; cap. 425m., res 859m., dep. and bonds 14,656m. (Dec. 2002); Chair. PETER GALLIKER; 28 brs.

Schwyzer Kantonalbank: Bahnhofstr. 3, 6431 Schwyz; tel. 418194111; fax 418117355; e-mail info@szkb.ch; internet www.szkb .ch; f. 1889 as Kantonalbank Schwyz, current name adopted 1997; cap. 160m., res 142m., dep. and bonds 7,305m. (Dec. 2001); Pres. EUGEN DIETHELM; Man. Dr HANSJÖRG KOLLER; 10 brs.

St Galler Kantonalbank: St Leonhardstr. 25, Postfach 2063, 9001 St Gallen; tel. 712313131; fax 712313232; e-mail info@emb.net.sgkb .ch; internet www.sgkb.ch; f. 1868; cap. 500m., res 497m., dep. and bonds 14,041m. (Dec. 2001); Pres. Dr U. RÜEGSEGGER; 39 brs.

Thurgauer Kantonalbank: Bankpl. 1, 8570 Weinfelden; tel. 716266111; fax 716266920; e-mail info@tkb.ch; internet www.tkb .ch; f. 1871; cap. 400m., res 137m., dep. and bonds 12,419m. (Dec. 2002); Pres. Dr P. LINDT; Man. THEODOR PRINZ; 15 brs.

Urner Kantonalbank: Bahnhofstr. 1, 6460 Altdorf; tel. 418756000; fax 418756313; e-mail info@urkb.ch; internet www.urkb.ch; f. 1915; cap. 30m., res 36m., dep. and bonds 1,425m. (Dec. 2001); Pres. Dr HANSRUEDI STADLER.

Zuger Kantonalbank: Baarerstr. 37, 6301 Zug; tel. 417091111; fax 417091555; e-mail service@zugerkb.ch; internet www.zugerkb.ch; f. 1892; cap. 133m., res 178m., dep. and bonds 5,083m. (Dec. 1999); Chair. and Pres. WALTER WEBER; Gen. Man. T. LUGINBÜHL; 12 brs.

Zürcher Kantonalbank: Bahnhofstr. 9, Postfach 715, 8010 Zürich; tel. 12201111; fax 12111525; e-mail info@zkb.ch; internet www.zkb .ch; f. 1870; cap. 1,925m., res 551m., total assets 77,500m. (Dec. 2000); Chair Dr HERMANN WEIGOLD; 92 brs.

Commercial Banks (Selected List)

Baloise Bank SoBa: Amthauspl. 4, 4502 Solothurn; tel. 326260202; fax 326233692; e-mail info@soba.ch; internet www.soba .ch; f. 1994; cap. 50m., res 203m., dep. 4,861m. (Dec. 2000); Chair. Dr ROLF SCHÄUBLE; Gen. Man. ALOIS MÜLLER.

Banca del Gottardo: viale S. Franscini 8, CP 2811, 6901 Lugano; tel. 918081111; fax 919239487; e-mail info@gottardo.ch; internet www.gottardo.ch; f. 1957; cap. 170m., res 743m., dep. and bonds 10,824m. (Dec. 2001); Chair. C. GENERALI; 6 brs.

Bank Julius Baer & Co AG: Bahnhofstr. 36, 8010 Zürich; tel. 12285111; fax 12112560; f. 1890; cap. 145m., res 448m., dep. 5,955m. (Dec. 1996); Chair. RUDOLF E. BAER.

Bank Leu AG: Bahnhofstr. 32, 8001 Zürich; tel. 12191111; fax 12193797; e-mail info@leu.com; internet www.leu.com; f. 1755; cap. 200m., res 137m., dep. and bonds 7,719m. (Dec. 2001); Chair. OLIVIER STEIMER; Pres. RETO DONATSCH; 4 brs.

Banque Edouard Constant SA: 11 Cours de Rive, 1204 Geneva; tel. 227873111; fax 227353370; internet www.bec.ch; f. 1964 as Banque Scandinave en Suisse, name changed 1997; cap. 90m., res 63m., dep. 722m. (Dec. 2000); Chair. MARC PANCHAUD; CEO JEAN-BERNARD METTRAUX.

BDL (Banco di Lugano): Piazzetta San Carlo 1, 6901 Lugano; tel. 919108111; fax 919232631; e-mail info@banco-di-lugano.ch; internet www.banco-di-lugano.ch; f. 1947; current name adopted 1990; cap. 50m., res 248m., dep. 3,670m. (Dec. 2001); Chair. KARL JANJÖRI.

BNP Paribas (Suisse) SA: 2 pl. de Hollande, 1204 Geneva; tel. 227877111; fax 227878000; internet www.bnpparibas.com; f. 1961 as United Overseas Bank SA, current name adopted 2001; cap. 338m., res 508m., dep 10,728m. (Dec. 2000); Chair. MICHEL FRANÇOIS-PONCET; Pres. and CEO Jean-Philippe DELCROIX; 4 brs.

BSI AG: via Magatti 2, 6900 Lugano; tel. 918093111; fax 918093678; e-mail info@bsi.ch; internet www.bsi.ch; f. 1873; cap. 290m., res 319m., dep. and bonds 7,920m. (Dec. 2000); Chair. Dr HUGO VON DER CRONE; 6 brs.

Coutts Bank (Switzerland) Ltd: Brandschenkestr. 5, 8022 Zürich; tel. 12145111; fax 12145396; internet www.coutts.com; f. 1930; current name adopted 1997; cap. 110m., res 214m., dep. 2,946m. (Dec. 1996); Chair. THE EARL OF HOME; 4 brs.

Crédit Suisse Group: Crédit Suisse: Paradepl. 8, 8001 Zürich, Postfach 100, 8070 Zürich; tel. 13331111; fax 13325555; internet www.credit-suisse.ch; f. 1869; cap. 3,590m., res 28,304m., dep. 751,871m. (Dec. 2001); Group Chair and CEO. LUKAS MÜHLEMANN; 290 brs.

  Crédit Suisse First Boston: Uetlibergstr. 231, 8045 Zürich, Postfach 1, 8070 Zürich; tel. 13335555; fax 13335599; internet www.csfb.ch; f. 1856; corporate and investment banking; cap. 4,400m., res 14,058m., dep. and bonds 559,273m. (Dec. 2000); CEO JOHN J. MACK; 70 brs.

Discount Bank and Trust Co: 3 quai de l'Ile, 1204 Geneva; tel. 227053111; fax 223101703; e-mail s.post@dbtc.ch; internet www .dbtc.ch; f. 1952 as Discount Bank (Overseas), name changed 1985; cap. 80m., res 445m., dep. 5,318m. (Dec. 2000); Chair. O. RECANATI; 5 brs.

HSBC Republic Bank (Suisse) SA: 3 pl. du Lac, CP 3580, 1211 Geneva 3; tel. 227055555; fax 227055151; internet www .hsbcrepublic.com; f. 1988 as Republic National Bank New York (Suisse) SA, present name adopted 2000; cap. 437m., res 486m., dep. 19,206m. (Dec. 2000); Chair. CHARLES-ANDRÉ JUNOD; 6 brs.

Hyposwiss Privatbank AG: Schützengasse 4, 8023 Zürich; tel. 12143111; fax 12115223; e-mail info@hyposwiss.ch; internet www .hyposwiss.ch; f. 1889; cap. 26m., res 59m., dep. 1,138m. (Dec. 2000); Chair. Dr URS RUERGIEGGER; Exec. Pres. THEODOR HORAT.

Migrosbank AG: Seidengasse 12, 8023 Zürich; tel. 12298111; fax 12298715; e-mail migrosbank@migros.ch; internet www .migrosbank.ch; f. 1957; cap. 689m., res 778m., dep. 21,178m. (Dec. 2001); Chair. Dr ANTON SCHERRER; Exec. Vice-Pres. ERICH HORT; 39 brs.

Neue Aargauer Bank: Bahnhofstr. 49, 5001 Aarau; tel. and fax 628388080; f. 1989; wholly owned by Crédit Suisse; cap. 274m., res 205m., dep. 13,610m. (Dec. 2001); Pres. JOSEF BÜRGE; Gen. Man. JOSEF MEIER; 42 brs.

Schweizer Verband der Raiffeisenbanken/Union Suisse des Banques Raiffeisen: Vadianstr. 17, 9001 St Gallen; tel. 712258888; fax 712258887; internet www.raiffeisen.ch; f. 1902; cap. 190m., res 91m., dep. 15,434m. (June 2001); Chair. Dr MARIUS COTTIER.

UBS AG: Bahnhofstr. 45, 8021 Zürich; tel. 12341111; fax 12365111; e-mail info@ubs.com; internet www.ubs.com; f. 1998 by merger of UBS-Union Bank of Switzerland (f. 1912) and Swiss Bank Corpn (f. 1872); cap. 3,589m., res 34,643m., dep. 782,672m. (Dec. 2001); Chair. MARCEL OSPEL; 357 brs.

Union Bancaire Privée: 96–98 rue du Rhône, CP 1320, 1211 Geneva 1; tel. 228192111; fax 228192200; e-mail ubp@ubp.ch; internet www.ubp.ch; f. 1990; cap. 300m., res 1,073m., dep. 13,970m. (Dec. 2002); Chair. EDGAR DE PICCIOTTO; Pres. GUY DE PICCIOTTO.

Valiant Bank: Bundespl. 4, Postfach 5333, 3001 Bern; tel. 313209111; fax 313209112; internet www.valiant.ch; f. 1857 as Spar- und Leihkasse in Bern/Caisse d'Epargne et de Prêts à Berne, present name adopted 2001; cap. 36m., res 139m., dep. 3,285m. (Dec. 1996); Chair. Prof. Dr ROLAND VON BÜREN.

Private Banks

Switzerland's private banking sector is the largest, in terms of assets, in the world. In 1998 there were 16 privately-owned banks in Switzerland, of which the following are among the most important:

Banque Privée Edmond de Rothschild SA: 18 rue de Hesse, 1204 Geneva; tel. 228189111; fax 228189121; internet www .lcf-rothschild.ch; f. 1924; cap. 45m., res 291m., dep. 534m. (Dec. 2000); Chair. Baron BENJAMIN DE ROTHSCHILD; Gen. Man. CLAUDE MESSULAM; 2 brs.

Darier, Hentsch & Cie: 4 rue de Saussure, 1204 Geneva; tel. 227086000; fax 227086945; internet www.darierhentsch.ch; f. 1991 by merger of Darier & Co and Hentsch & Co; Partners PIERRE DARIER,

BÉNÉDICT HENTSCH, BERTRAND DARIER, ERIC DEMOLE, OLIVIER DUPRAZ, BARTHÉLEMY HELG, THIERRY KERN, JACQUES ROSSIER.

Lombard Odier & Cie: 11 rue de la Corraterie, 1211 Geneva 11; tel. 227092111; fax 227092911; e-mail contact@lombardodier.com; internet www.lombardodier.com; f. 1798; Snr Partner THIERRY LOMBARD; CEO Partner BERNARD DROUX; Man. Partners JEAN A. BONNA, PATRICK ODIER, RICHARD DE TSCHARNER, PHILIPPE A. SARASIN, JEAN PASTRÉ, ANNE MARIE DE WECK.

Pictet & Cie Banquiers: 29 blvd Georges-Favon, CP 5130, 1204 Geneva; tel. 223182211; fax 223182222; e-mail mail@pictet.com; internet www.pictet.com; f. 1805; Snr Partner CHARLES HENRI PICTET; Partners IVAN PICTET, CLAUDE DEMOLE, JACQUES DE SAUSSURE, NICOLAS PICTET, PHILIPPE BERTHERAT, JEAN-FRANÇOIS DEMOLE, RENAUD DE PLANTA.

Central Co-operative Credit Institution

Bank Coop: Aeschenpl. 3, 4002 Basel; tel. 612862121; fax 612714595; e-mail netteam@bankcoop.ch; internet www.bankcoop .ch; f. 1927; fmrly Coop Bank/Banque Coop, present name adopted 2001; cap. 338m., res 299m., dep. 8,230m. (Dec. 2001); Chair. WILLI GERSTER; Exec. Pres. HANS RUDOLF MATTER; 37 brs.

Regulatory Authorities

Eidgenössische Bankenkommission (Federal Banking Commission): Sekretariat, Schwanengasse 12, Postfach, 3001 Bern; tel. 313226911; fax 313226926; e-mail info@ebk.admin.ch; internet www.ebk.admin.ch; Dir DANIEL ZUBERBÜHLER.

Swiss Banking Ombudsman: Schweizergasse 21, Postfach 1818, 8021 Zürich; tel. 12131450; fax 12103720; internet www .bankingombudsman.ch; Ombudsman HANSPETER HÄNI.

Bankers' Organizations

Association of Foreign Banks in Switzerland: Löwenstr. 51, Postfach, 8023 Zürich; tel. 12244070; fax 12210029; e-mail info@ foreignbanks.ch; internet www.foreignbanks.ch; Chair. Dr ALFREDO GYSI; CEO Dr MARTIN MAURER.

Association Suisse des Banquiers/Schweizerische Bankiervereinigung (Swiss Bankers' Asscn): Aeschenpl. 7, Postfach 4182, 4002 Basel; tel. 612959393; fax 612725382; e-mail office@sba.ch; internet www.swissbanking.org; f. 1912; 934 mems; Chair. Dr GEORG F. KRAYER; Man. Dir Dr URS P. ROTH.

Verband Schweizerischer Kantonalbanken/Union des Banques Cantonales Suisses (Asscn of Swiss Cantonal Banks): Wallstr. 8, Postfach, 4002 Basel; tel. 612066666; fax 612066667; e-mail vskb@vskb.ch; internet www.kantonalbank.ch; f. 1907; perm. office est. 1971; Chair. Dr KURT AMSLER; Man. CARLO MATI.

STOCK EXCHANGES

Bern Stock Exchange (Berner Börsenverein): Aarbergergasse 36, 3011 Bern; tel. 313114042; fax 313115309; internet www .bernerboerse.ch; f. 1884; 8 mems, 2 assoc. mems; Dir JÜRG NIEDERHÄUSER.

SWX Swiss Exchange: Selnaustr. 30, 8021 Zürich; tel. 12292111; fax 12292233; e-mail swx@swx.com; internet www.swx.com; f. 1873; 51 mems; Pres. Dr R. FRANCIONI; CEO Dr HEINRICH HENCKEL; Man. A. HUNZIKER-EBNETER.

INSURANCE

In 1997 there were 159 insurance companies in Switzerland, of which 131 were Swiss-owned.

Allianz Continentale Allgemeine Versicherungs AG: Seestr. 356, 8038 Zürich; tel. 14889191; fax 14823580; f. 1974; general; Pres. Dr PETER ALTHER.

Allianz Continentale Lebensversicherungs AG: Seestr. 356, 8038 Zürich; tel. 14889191; fax 14823580; f. 1964; life; Pres. Dr PETER ALTHER.

Alpina Versicherungs AG: Seefeldstr. 123, 8034 Zürich; tel. 16283333; fax 16283255; internet www.alpina.ch; f. 1923; Pres. FRITZ GERBER.

Basler Lebens-Versicherungs-Gesellschaft: Aeschengraben 21, Postfach, 4002 Basel; tel. 612858585; fax 612857070; e-mail group .konzern@basler.ch; f. 1864; life, annuity; Chair. Dr ROLF SCHÄUBLE; Vice-Chair. WALTER FREHNER.

Basler Versicherungs-Gesellschaft: Aeschengraben 21, Postfach, 4002 Basel; tel. 612858585; fax 612857070; e-mail group .konzern@basler.ch; f. 1864; all classes, except life insurance; Chair. Dr ROLF SCHÄUBLE; Vice-Chair. WALTER FREHNER.

Berner Allgemeine Holdingggesellschaft: Sulgeneckstr. 19, 3001 Bern; tel. 313845111; fax 313845300; f. 1909; Pres. (vacant).

ELVIA-Life Swiss Life Insurance Co: 2 ave du Bouchet, 1211 Geneva 28; tel. 227344000; f. 1924; life; Pres. Dr Heinz R. Wuffli; Gen. Man. P. Jungo.

GAN Incendie Accidents, Compagnie Française d'Assurances et de Réassurances: 70 ave C.-F. Ramuz, 1009 Pully-Lausanne; Head Office, Paris; tel. 217297121; fax 217288076; f. 1830.

La Genevoise, Compagnie d'Assurances sur la Vie: 16 ave Eugène-Pittard, 1211 Geneva 25; tel. 227042424; fax 227042704; f. 1872; life; Gen. Man. M. C. Meyer.

La Genevoise, Compagnie générale d'Assurances: 16 ave Eugène-Pittard, 1211 Geneva 25; tel. 227042424; fax 227042704; f. 1950; Gen. Man. M. C. Meyer.

Lebensversicherungs-Gesellschaft: Paulstr. 9, 8401 Winterthur; tel. 522611111; fax 522136620; f. 1923; life; Chair. Dr P. Spälti.

Helvetia Patria Holding: Dufourstr. 40, 9001 St Gallen; tel. 714935111; fax 714935100; e-mail investor@helvetiapatria.com; internet www.helvetiapatria.com; f. 1861; life, fire, burglary, accident liability, motor; Chair. Dr Hans-Rudolf Merz; CEO Erich Walser.

Pax, Schweizerische Lebensversicherungs-Gesellschaft: Aeschenpl. 13, 4002 Basel; tel. 612776666; fax 612776565; e-mail info@pax.ch; internet www.pax.ch; f. 1876; life; Pres. Gianfranco Balestra.

Schweizerische Mobiliar: Bundesgasse 35, 3001 Bern; tel. 313896111; fax 313896852; e-mail mobi@mobi.ch; internet www.mobi.ch; f. 1826; accident, sickness, fire and damage by the elements, theft, valuables, damage by water, glass breakage, machines, construction work, interruption of business, epidemics, warranty, guarantee, third-party liability, motor vehicles, travel, transport; Pres. of Exec. Bd Christian Wegmüller.

Swiss Life/Rentenanstalt: General Guisan-Quai 40, 8022 Zürich; tel. 12843311; fax 12842080; e-mail info.com@swisslife.ch; internet www.swisslife.ch; f. 1857; specializes in international employee benefit and pension plans; brs in Belgium, France, Germany and Netherlands; CEO Rolf Doerig.

Swiss Re (Schweizerische Rückversicherungs-Gesellschaft) (Swiss Reinsurance Co): Mythenquai 50/60, 8022 Zürich; tel. 12852121; fax 12852999; internet www.swissre.com; f. 1863; worldwide reinsurance; Chair. Prof. Dr Peter Forstmoser; CEO John Coomber.

Winterthur Schweizerische Versicherungs-Gesellschaft: Gen. Guisan-Str. 40, Postfach 357, 8401 Winterthur; tel. 522611111; fax 522136620; e-mail info@winterthur.com; internet www.winterthur.com; f. 1875; merged with Crédit Suisse Group in 1997; Chair. Manfred Broska.

Zenith Vie, Compagnie d'assurances sur la vie: 6 ave de la Tour Haldimand, 1009 Pully-Lausanne; tel. 217217000; fax 217217120; f. 1987; life; Gen. Man. Gilbert Smadja.

Zürich Financial Services: Mythenquai 2, 8022 Zürich; tel. 12052121; fax 16253555; internet www.zurich.com; f. 1998 by merger of Zürich Versicherungsgesellschaft (f. 1872) and BAT Industries PLC (UK); non-life, life, reinsurance, asset management; Chair. and CEO (vacant).

Zürich Lebensversicherungs-Gesellschaft: Austr. 46, 8036 Zürich; tel. 12052890; fax 12052029; f. 1922; life; CEO Dr Günther Gose.

Insurance Organization

Schweizerischer Versicherungsverband (Swiss Insurance Asscn): C. F. Meyer-Str. 14, 8022 Zürich; tel. 12082828; fax 12082801; e-mail info@svv.ch; f. 1901; Pres. Dr H J. Frei; 80 mems.

Trade and Industry

GOVERNMENT AGENCIES

Osec Business Network Switzerland: Stampfenbachstr. 85, Postfach 492, 8035 Zürich; tel. 13655151; fax 13655221; e-mail info.zurich@osec.ch; internet www.osec.ch; promotes trade; CEO Balz Hösly.

Staatssekretariat für Wirtschaft—SECO/Secrétariat d'Etat à l'économie—SECO/State Secretariat for Economic Affairs: Gurtengasse 3, 3003 Bern; tel. 313230710; fax 313248600; e-mail invest@seco.admin.ch; internet www.standortschweiz.ch; promotes investment in Switzerland.

PRINCIPAL CHAMBERS OF COMMERCE

Aargauische Industrie- und Handelskammer: Entfelderstr. 11, 5001 Aarau; tel. 628371818; fax 628371819; Pres. H. P. Zehnder.

Berner Handelskammer: Gutenbergstr. 1, 3001 Bern; tel. 313821711; fax 313821715; Pres. Walter Leuenberger.

Bündner Handels- und Industrieverein: Poststr. 43, 7002 Chur; tel. 812526306; fax 812520449; Pres. Otto Beck.

Camera di commercio dell'industria e dell'artigianato del Cantone Ticino: Corso Elvezia 16, 6901 Lugano; tel. 919115111; fax 919115112; e-mail cciati@cci.ch; internet www.cciati.ch; f. 1917; Pres. Franco Ambrosetti; Dir Claudio Camponovo; 900 mems.

Chambre fribourgeoise du commerce, de l'industrie et des services: 37 route du Jura, 1706 Fribourg; tel. 263471220; fax 263471239; e-mail cfcis@cci.ch; internet www.cci.ch/fribourg; f. 1917; Pres. Bernard Sottas; Dir André Uebersax.

Chambre de commerce et d'industrie de Genève: 4 blvd du Théâtre, 1211 Geneva 11; tel. 228199111; fax 228199100; f. 1865; Pres. Gottfried Aeschbacher; Dir Patrick Coidan; 1,500 mems.

Chambre de commerce et d'industrie du Jura: 23 rue de l'Avenir, CP 274, 2800 Delémont 1; tel. 324214545; fax 324214540; e-mail ccjura@cci.ch; Pres. M. Gottfried Aeschbacher; Dir Jean-Frédéric Gerber.

Chambre neuchâteloise du commerce et de l'industrie: 4 rue de la Serre, 2001 Neuchâtel; tel. 327257541; fax 327247092; Pres. Yann Richter; Dir Claude Bernoulli.

Chambre valaisanne de commerce et d'industrie: 6 rue Pré-Fleuri, CP 288, 1951 Sion; tel. 273273535; fax 273273536; Pres. Jacques-Roland Coudray; Dir Thomas Gsponer; 492 mems.

Chambre vaudoise du commerce et de l'industrie: 47 ave d'Ouchy, CP 205, 1000 Lausanne 13; tel. 216133535; fax 216133505; e-mail cvci@cvci.ch; internet www.cvci.ch; Pres. Hubert Barde; Dir Jean-Luc Strohm; 2,100 mems.

Glarner Handelskammer: Spielhof 14A, 8750 Glarus; tel. 556401173; fax 556403639; Pres. Dr Alfred Stöckli; Sec. Dr Karl-Jörg Landolt.

Handelskammer beider Basel: Basel; tel. 612706060; fax 612706005; internet www.hkbb.ch; Pres. Thomas Staehelich; 800 mems.

Handelskammer und Arbeitgebervereinigung Winterthur (HAW): Neumarkt 15, 8401 Winterthur; tel. 522137352; Pres. Dr Viktor Beglinger.

Industrie- und Handelskammer St Gallen-Appenzell: Gallusstr. 16, Postfach, 9001 St Gallen; tel. 712231515; fax 712224727; f. 1466; Pres. Max R. Hungerbuhle.

Industrie- und Handelskammer Thurgau: Schmidstr. 9, Postfach, 8570 Weinfelden; tel. 716221919; fax 716226257; e-mail info@ihk-thurgau.ch; internet www.ihk-thurgau.ch; Pres. P. A. Schifferle.

Schweizerische Junge Wirtschaftskammer/Jeune Chambre économique suisse: c/o Unirevisa, Spielhof 14A, 8750 Glarus; tel. 556407252; fax 556407435; Pres. J. F. Antonioli; Sec. F. Dällenbach.

Schweizerische Zentrale für Handelsförderung/Office suisse d'expansion commerciale (OSEC): Stampfenbachstr. 85, 8035 Zürich; and ave de l'Avant-Poste 4, 1001 Lausanne; tel. 13655151; fax 13655221; e-mail info.zurich@osec.ch; tel. 213203231; fax 213207337; f. 1927; Pres. Philippe Lévy; Dir Martin Monsch; 2,000 mems.

Solothurnische Handelskammer: Grabackerstr. 6, 4502 Solothurn; tel. 326262424; fax 326262426; e-mail info@swk.ch; internet www.swk.ch; Pres. Martin Imbach; Dir Dr H. R. Meyer.

Zentralschweizerische Handelskammer: Kapellpl. 2, 6002 Lucerne; tel. 414106865; fax 414105288; e-mail info@hkz.ch; internet www.hkz.ch; f. 1889; Pres. Doris Russi Schurter; Dir Alex Bruckert; 500 mems.

Zürcher Handelskammer: Bleicherweg 5, Postfach 3058, 8022 Zürich; tel. 12174050; fax 12174051; e-mail direktion@zurichcci.ch; internet www.zurichcci.ch; Pres. Andreas W. Keller; CEO Dr Lukas Briner; 1,300 mems.

INDUSTRIAL AND TRADE ASSOCIATIONS

Associazione Industrie Ticinesi: Corso Elvezia 16, 6901 Lugano; tel. 919235041; fax 919234636; Pres. Giancarlo Bordoni.

Basler Volkswirtschaftsbund: Aeschenvorstadt 71, Postfach 4010 Basel; tel. 612059600; fax 612059600; e-mail bvb@bvb.ch; internet www.bvb.ch; Pres. Hans Ulrich Pfister; Dir Dr Géza Teleki; 9,000 mems.

Chocosuisse—Verband Schweizerischer Schokoladefabrikanten: Münzgraben 6, 3000 Bern 7; tel. 313100990; fax 313100999; e-mail info@chocosuisse.ch; internet www.chocosuisse.ch; f. 1901; asscn of chocolate mfrs; Dir Dr F. U. Schmid; 19 mems.

Communauté de l'industrie suisse de la cigarette (CISC): ave de Beauregard 1, CP 212, 1701 Fribourg; tel. 264255050; fax 264255055; e-mail office@cisc.ch; internet www.swiss-cigarette.ch; f. 1933; cigarette mfrs; Pres. EDGAR OEHLER; Sec.-Gen. CHANTAL AEBY.

Economiesuisse (Swiss Business Federation): Hegibachstr. 47, Postfach 1072, 8032 Zürich; tel. 14213535; fax 14213434; e-mail info@economiesuisse.ch; internet www.economiesuisse.ch; f. 1870 as Schweizerischer Handels- und Industrie-Verein, present name adopted 2000; Pres. UELI FORSTER; Exec. Dir Dr RUDOLOF RAMSAUER; 171 mems.

Fédération de l'Industrie Horlogère Suisse (FH): 6 rue d'Argent, 2501 Bienne; tel. 323280828; fax 323280880; e-mail info@fhs.ch; internet www.fhs.ch; f. 1876; watch industry fed. Pres. J. D. PASCHE; 542 mems.

Föderation der Schweizerischen Nahrungsmittel-Industrien: Thunstr. 82, 3000 Bern 16; Münzgraben 6, 3000 Bern 7; and Elfenstrasse 19, 3000 Bern 16; tel. 313562121; fax 313510065; e-mail info@advo-emmenegger.ch; foodstuffs; Secs B. HODLER, G. EMMENEGGER, Dr F. U. SCHMID; 216 mems.

Schweizerische Gesellschaft für Chemische Industrie (SGCI): Nordstr. 15, Postfach 8035 Zürich; tel. 13681711; fax 13681770; e-mail mailbox@sgci.ch; internet www.sgci.ch; f. 1882; chemical and pharmaceutical industry; Pres. Dr R. WEHRLI; Dir Dr B. MOSER; 190 mems.

Schweizerischer Baumeisterverband (SBV): Weinbergstr. 49, Postfach, 8035 Zürich 10; tel. 12588111; fax 12588335; e-mail verband@baumeister.ch; internet www.baumeister.ch; f. 1897; building contractors; Pres. W. MESSMER; 4,300 mems.

Schweizerischer Elektrotechnischer Verein (SEV): Luppmenstr. 1, 8320 Fehraltorf; tel. 19561111; fax 19561122; electronics; Pres. ANDREAS BELLWALD.

Schweizerischer Gewerbeverband (SGV) (Swiss Union of Small and Medium Enterprises): Schwarztorstr. 26, 3007 Bern; tel. 313801414; fax 313801415; e-mail info@sgv-usam.ch; internet www.sgv-usam.ch; f. 1879; Pres. HANS RUDOLF FRÜH; 289 sections.

Schweizerischer Spenglermeister- und Installateur-Verband: Auf der Mauer 11, 8001 Zürich; tel. 12697400; fax 12697499; e-mail info@ssiv.ch; internet www.ssiv.ch; f. 1891; mfrs of metal goods; Pres. P. HOLINGER; 3,500 mems.

Schweizerischer Verband für visuelle Kommunikation (Viscom): Zürich; tel. 12521440; fax 12521743; f. 1869; printing industry; Pres. R. BALSIGER; Dir HANS-ULRICH BIGLER; 1,256 mems.

Schweizerischer Versicherungsverband: (see under Insurance).

Textilverband Schweiz: Beethovenstr. 20, Postfach 4838, 8022 Zürich; tel. 12897979; fax 12897980; e-mail contact@tvs.ch; internet www.swisstextiles.ch; f. 1874; textiles and fashion; Pres. THOMAS ISLER; Dir Dr TH. SCHWEIZER; 230 mems.

Verband der Schweizerischen Gasindustrie: Grütlistr. 44, 8027 Zürich; tel. 12883131; fax 12021834; f. 1920; Pres. J. CAVADINI.

Verband Schweizerischer Kreditbanken und Finanzierungsinstitute: Löwenstr. 55/57, 8023 Zürich; tel. 12126503; asscn of credit banks and finance institutes; Pres. Dr LYDIA SAXER.

Verband der Schweizerischen Waren- und Kaufhäuser: Zürich; tel. 12524040; fax 12524097; retail trade; Pres. Dr K. HUG; Sec. B. REGLI.

Verband Schweizerische Ziegelindustrie: Obstgartenstr. 28, 8035 Zürich; tel. 13619650; fax 13610205; e-mail info@chziegel.ch; internet www.chziegel.ch; f. 1874; heavy clay; Sec.-Gen. Dr W. P. WELLER.

EMPLOYERS' ORGANIZATIONS

Central Organizations

Schweizerischer Arbeitgeberverband (Confed. of Swiss Employers): Hegibachstr. 47, Postfach, 8032 Zürich; tel. 14211717; fax 14211718; e-mail verband@arbeitgeber.ch; internet www.arbeitgeber.ch; f. 1908; Pres. FRITZ BLASER; Vice-Pres. HUBERT BARDE; Dir Dr PETER HASLER; 73 mems.

Schweizerischer Bauernverband (Union Suisse des Paysans, Lega svizzera dei contadini, Swiss Farmers' Union): Laurstr. 10, 5201 Brugg; tel. 564625111; fax 564415348; e-mail info@bauernverband.ch; internet www.bauernverband.ch; f. 1897; Pres. H. J. WALTER; Dir JACQUES BOURGEOIS.

Principal Regional Organizations

Fédération romande des syndicats patronaux: 98 rue de St-Jean, 1211 Geneva; tel. 227153111; fax 227153213; e-mail fsp@fsp.ch; internet www.fsp.ch; Pres. DANIEL DELAY.

Luzerner Industrie-Vereinigung: Postfach 3142, Kapellpl. 2, 6002 Lucerne; tel. 414106889; Pres. Dr HANS-RUEDI IMBACH.

Union des associations patronales genevoises: 98 rue de Saint-Jean, 1211 Geneva 11; tel. 227153215; fax 227380434; e-mail uapg@uapg.ch; union of employers' asscns in Geneva; Pres. NICOLAS BRUNSCHWIG.

Union des industriels valaisans: Martigny 1; tel. 26222867; Pres. JURG HEROLD; Sec. PASCAL COUCHEPIN.

Verband der Arbeitgeber Region Bern (VAB): Kapellenstr. 14, Postfach 6916, 3001 Bern; tel. 313902581; fax 313902582; f. 1919; employers' asscn for the Bern region; Pres. Dr RUDOLF STÄMPFLI.

Vereinigung Zürcherischer Arbeitgeberorganisationen: Selnaustr. 30, 8021 Zürich; tel. 12292827; fax 12292833; e-mail dieter.sigrist@swx.ch; asscn of Zürich employers' orgs; Pres. THOMAS ISLER; Sec. DIETER SIGRIST.

Sectional Organizations

Arbeitgeberverband Schweizerischer Papier-Industrieller: Bergstr. 110, Postfach 134, 8030 Zürich; tel. 12669921; fax 12669949; e-mail zpk@zpk.ch; internet www.zpk.ch; paper mfrs; Pres. B. LUDWIG; Dir M. FRITZ; 11 mems.

Convention Patronale de l'Industrie Horlogère Suisse: 65 ave Léopold-Robert, 2301 La Chaux-de-Fonds; tel. 329145161; fax 329134606; e-mail info@cpih.ch; internet www.cpih.ch; f. 1937; watch mfrs; Pres. J. CAVADINI; Gen. Sec. F. MATILE; 9 mems.

Swissmem (ASM and VSM) (Mechanical and Electrical Engineering Industries): Kirchenweg 4, Postfach, 8032 Zürich; tel. 13844111; fax 13844242; e-mail info@swissmem.ch; internet www.swissmem.ch; f. 1905; Pres. J. N. SCHNEIDER-AMMANN; Dir THOMAS DAUM; 950 mems.

UTILITIES

Electricity

Verband Schweizerischer Elektrizitätsunternehmen: Gerbergasse 5, Postfach 6140, 8023 Zürich; tel. 12265111; fax 22265191; e-mail info@strom.ch; internet www.strom.ch; electricity producers' asscn; f. 1895; Pres. Dr R. STEINER; Dir A. BUCHER.

Gas

Verband der Schweizerischer Gasindustrie: Grütlistr. 44, 8002 Zürich; tel. 12883131; fax 12021834; e-mail vsg@erdgas.ch; internet www.erdgas.ch; gas industry asscn.

TRADE UNIONS

Schweizerischer Gewerkschaftsbund (Swiss Fed. of Trade Unions): Monbijoustr. 61, 3007 Bern; tel. 313770101; fax 313770102; e-mail info@sgb.ch; internet www.sgb.ch; f. 1880; main trade union org. affiliated to ICFTU; Pres. PAUL RECHSTEINER; total affiliated membership 387,000.

The principal affiliated unions are:

Comedia (Media): Postfach 6336, 3001 Bern; tel. 313906611; fax 313906691; e-mail sekretariat@comedia.ch; internet www.comedia.ch; f. 1858; Pres. C. TIREFORT; 17,000 mems.

Communications Union: Oberdorfstr. 32, 3072 Ostermundigen; tel. 319395211; fax 319395262; e-mail zentralsekretariat@gewerkschaftkom.ch; internet www.gewerkschaftkom.ch; f. 1999; Pres. FRITZ MUENGER; Gen. Sec. HANS U. RUCHTI; 39,500 mems.

Gewerkschaft Bau und Industrie (Building and Industry): Postfach, 8021 Zürich; tel. 12951515; fax 12951799; e-mail hba@gbi.artemis.ch; internet www.gbi-sib-sei.ch; f. 1922; Pres. VASCO PEDRINA; 100,000 mems.

Gewerkschaft Industrie, Gewerbe, Dienstleistungen SMUV (Metal Workers and Watchmakers): Weltpoststr. 20, Postfach 272, 3000 Bern 15; tel. 313502111; fax 313502255; e-mail mail@smuv.ch; internet www.smuv.ch; f. 1888; Pres. RENZO AMBROSETTI; 90,941 mems.

Gewerkschaft Verkauf, Handel, Transport, Lebensmittel (Workers in the Commerce, Transport and Food Industries): Birmensdorferstr. 67, 8036 Zürich; tel. 12423576; fax 12429405; e-mail vhtl@limmat.ch; f. 1904; Pres. BEATRICE ALDER; 20,000 mems.

Schweizerischer Eisenbahn- und Verkehrspersonal-Verband (SEV) (Railway Workers): Steinerstr. 35, 3000 Bern 16; tel. 313575757; fax 313575758; e-mail info@sev-online.ch; internet www.sev-online.ch; f. 1919; Pres. ERNST LEUENBERGER (acting); 54,000 mems.

Schweizerischer Verband des Personals öffentlicher Dienste (Public Services): Sonnenbergstr. 83, Postfach, 8030

Zürich; tel. 12665252; fax 12665253; e-mail vpod@vpod-ssp.ch; internet www.vpod-ssp.ch; f. 1905; Pres. ERIC DECARRO; Gen. Sec. DORIS SCHUEPP; 38,000 mems.

Christlichnationaler Gewerkschaftsbund der Schweiz (CNG) (Confed. of Christian Trade Unions): Hopfenweg 21, Postfach 5775, 3001 Bern; tel. 313702111; fax 313702109; e-mail info@cng-csc.ch; internet www.cng-csc.ch; f. 1907; Pres. H. FASEL; Sec THERESE SCHMID; 102,274 mems.

The principal affiliated unions are:

Christlicher Chemie-Textil-Bekleidungs-Papier-Personalverband (Christian Chemical, Textile, Clothing, Paper and Staff Workers): Zürich; Pres. J. ZUMSTEG; Secs J. FISCHER, J. BLEICHER; 6,630 mems.

Christlicher Holz- und Bauarbeiterverband der Schweiz (CHB) (Christian Building and Woodworkers): Zürich; tel. 12415442; f. 1901; Pres. PETER ALLEMANN.

Christliche Gewerkschaft für Industrie, Handel und Gewerbe (CMV/FCOM) (Christian Metalworkers): Lindstr. 39, 8410 Winterthur; tel. 522680404; fax 522680405; e-mail win@syna.ch; internet www.syna.ch; Pres. H. FASEL; 80,000 mems.

Syna, die Gewerkschaft (syndicat interprofessionnel, sindicato interprofessionale): Josefstr. 59, 8031 Zürich; tel. 12797171; fax 12797172; e-mail zuer@syna.ch; internet www.syna.ch; f. 1998 to replace Landesverband freier Schweizer Arbeitnehmer (f. 1919); Pres. MAX HAAS; Sec. Dr ANDREAS HUBLI; 68,000 mems.

Vereinigung schweizerischer Angestelltenverbände (Salaried Employees): Badenerstr. 332, Postfach 1120, 8040 Zürich; tel. 14912581; fax 14010625; f. 1918; Pres. Dr HANS FURER; 124,103 mems.

Transport

RAILWAYS

Schweizerische Bundesbahnen (SBB) (Chemins de fer fédéraux suisses): Hochschulstr. 6, 3000 Bern 65; tel. 512201111; fax 512204265; e-mail railinfo@sbb.ch; internet www.sbb.ch; f. 1901; 2,910 km in 1998 (of which 2,902 km were electrified); Pres. THIERRY LALIVE D'EPINAY; Gen. Man. Dr BENEDIKT WEIBEL.

In 1996 the Neue Eisenbahn-Alpen-Transversale (NEAT) project was inaugurated with the aim of constructing a 57-km Gotthard tunnel and 33-km Lötschberg tunnel, in order to improve Switzerland's rail freight network and relieve environmental damage to the Alps. In 1997 Switzerland's total rail network had a total length of 5,035 km. There are altogether about 56 small private companies controlling private railways in Switzerland, chiefly along short mountain routes, with a total length of around 2,032 km. The following are among the principal private railways:

BLS Loetschbergbahn Ltd: Genfergasse 11, Postfach, 3001 Bern; tel. 313272727; fax 313272910; e-mail info@bls.ch; internet www.bls.ch; f. 1906; 245 km; six routes; boat services on Lakes Thun and Brienz; Man. Dr M. TROMP.

Bodensee–Toggenburg-Bahn (BT): Bahnhofpl. 1A, Postfach 345, 9001 St Gallen; tel. 712282323; fax 712282333; internet www.bt_bahn.ch; f. 1904; Man. W. DIETZ.

Centovalli Railway: CP 146, 6601 Locarno; tel. 917560400; fax 917560499; e-mail fart@centovalli.ch; internet www.centovalli.ch; f. 1909; 19 km; Locarno–Camedo; Dir DIRK MEYER.

Fribourg Railways (Chemins de fer fribourgeois): 3 rue des Pilettes, 1701 Fribourg; tel. 37812161; fax 37223439; f. 1868; 99 km; Man. ANDRÉ GENOUD.

Furka-Oberalp-Bahn: Postfach 256, 3900 Brig; tel. 279228111; fax 279228103; e-mail dir@fo-bahn.ch; internet www.fo-bahn.ch; f. 1915; Brig–Fiesch–Oberwald–Andermatt–Disentis and Andermatt–Göschenen; 101 km; merger with BVZ Zermatt-Bahn scheduled for 2003; Gen.-Dir HANS-RUDOLF MOOSER.

Montreux-Oberland Bernois: CP 1426, 1820 Montreux; tel. 219898181; fax 219898100; e-mail mob@mob.ch; internet www.mob.ch; f. 1899; 75 km; Montreux–Château d'Oex–Gstaad–Zweisimmen–Lenk i/S; Dir R. KUMMROW.

Rhaetian Railway: Bahnhofstr. 25, 7002 Chur; tel. 812549100; fax 812549118; e-mail info@rhaetische-bahn.ch; internet www.rhaetische-bahn.ch; f. 1889; 375 km; the most extensive of the privately-run railways; Dir S. FASCIATI.

ROADS

Swiss Federal Roads Authority (Bundesamt für Strassen/Office fédéral des routes): Worblentalstr. 68, Ittigen, 3003 Bern; tel. 313229411; fax 313232303; e-mail webmaster@astra.admin.ch; internet www.astra.admin.ch; Dir OLIVIER MICHAUD.

In 1998 Switzerland had 71,086 km of roads: 1,613 km of motorways and expressways, 18,276 km of other main roads and 51,197 km of secondary roads. The construction of a national network of approximately 1,857 km of motorways is scheduled for completion by 2010. The 17-km road tunnel through the Saint Gotthard Pass, a European road link of paramount importance, was opened in 1980. Vehicles of more than 39 metric tons are prohibited from traversing Switzerland. A weight and distance toll on heavy goods vehicles crossing Swiss territory was to be introduced in the late 1990s.

INLAND WATERWAYS

The Swiss Rhine and Canal fleet numbered 127 vessels in 1998. Switzerland had 1,214 km of inland waterways in 1997.

SHIPPING

In 2001 Switzerland's registered merchant fleet comprised 24 vessels with an aggregate displacement of 501,975 grt. The principal shipping companies in Switzerland are:

Acomarit Services Maritimes SA: 3 rue du Mont Blanc, CP 1016, 1211 Geneva 1; tel. 227151800; fax 227322801; e-mail jbille@acomarit.com; internet www.acomarit.com; CEO GIORGIO P. SULSER; Man. Dir A. GAVARONE.

Keller Shipping Ltd: Holbeinstr. 68, Postfach 3479, 4002 Basel; tel. 612818686; fax 612818679; Pres. A. R. KELLER.

Mediterranean Shipping Co SA: 40 ave Eugène-Pittard, 1206 Geneva; tel. 227038888; fax 227038787; Dir G. APONTE.

Natural van Dam AG: Westquaistr. 62, 4019 Basel; tel. 616399234; fax 616399250; e-mail silvia.helbeisen@nvd.ch; internet www.nvd.ch; Dir R. CROWE.

Navirom AG: St Alban-Anlage 64, 4052 Basel; tel. 613135816; fax 613135805.

Schweizerische Reederei & Neptun AG: Wiesendamm 4, 4019 Basel; tel. 616393333; fax 616393466; e-mail info@srn.ch; internet www.srn.ch; Dir H. SCHMITT.

Stolt-Nielsen AG: Uferstr. 90, Postfach, 4057 Basel; tel. 616388200; fax 616388211.

Suisse-Atlantique, Société de Navigation Maritime SA: 7 ave Baumettes, CP 48, 1020 Renens 1; tel. 216372201; fax 216372202; e-mail activity@suisse-atlantique.ch; world-wide tramping services; Pres. E. ANDRE; Dir C. DIDAY; mans of:

Helica SA: c/o Suisse-Atlantique, CP 4140, 1002 Lausanne.

Navemar SA: 1 Grand' Places, 1700 Fribourg.

Suisse-Outremer Reederei AG: Zürich; tel. 13634952; fax 13628362; f. 1956; Man. Dir P. PREISIG.

Van Ommeren (Schweiz) AG: Hafenstr. 87–89, Postfach, 4127 Birsfelden.

Vinalmar SA: 7 rue du Mont-Blanc, 1211 Geneve 1; tel. 229060431; fax 227386467.

CIVIL AVIATION

Switzerland's principal airports are situated at Zürich, Geneva and Basel-Mulhouse.

Swiss International Airlines Ltd: Postfach, 4002 Basel; tel. 615820000; fax 615823333; e-mail communications@swiss.com; internet www.swiss.com; f. 1979 as Crossair, took over operations from Swissair and adopted current name in 2002; national carrier operating routes to 59 countries; 20.5% owned by Federal Govt, 12.1% by Cantons; Pres. and CEO ANDRÉ DOSÉ.

Swiss World Airways (SWA): Geneva; f. 1996; operations commenced Sept. 1998, suspended Dec. 1998; regional connections and service to USA.

Tourism

Switzerland's principal attractions are the lakes and lake resorts and the mountains. Walking, mountaineering and winter sports are the chief pastimes. Tourist arrivals totalled 7.8m. in 2000 and receipts from tourism were an estimated 13,000m. Swiss francs in that year.

Switzerland Tourism: Head Office: Tödistr. 7, 8027 Zürich; tel. 12881111; fax 12881205; e-mail postoffice@switzerlandtourism; f. 1917; Dir MARCO HARTMANN; offices in most major cities of the world.

SYRIA

Introductory Survey

Location, Climate, Language, Religion, Flag, Capital

The Syrian Arab Republic lies in western Asia, with Turkey to the north, Iraq to the east and Jordan to the south. Lebanon and Israel are to the south-west. Syria has a coastline on the eastern shore of the Mediterranean Sea. Much of the country is mountainous and semi-desert. The coastal climate is one of hot summers and mild winters. The inland plateau and plains are dry but cold in winter. Average temperatures in Dimashq (Damascus) range from 2°C to 12°C (36°F to 54°F) in January and from 18°C to 37°C (64°F to 99°F) in August. The national language is Arabic, with Kurdish a minority language. More than 80% of the population are Muslims (mostly Sunnis), but there is a substantial Christian minority of various sects. The national flag (proportions 2 by 3) has three equal horizontal stripes, of red, white and black, with two five-pointed green stars in the centre of the white stripe. The capital is Damascus.

Recent History

Syria was formerly part of Turkey's Ottoman Empire. Turkish forces were defeated in the First World War (1914–18) and Syria was occupied in 1920 by France, in accordance with a League of Nations mandate. Syrian nationalists proclaimed an independent republic in September 1941. French powers were transferred in January 1944, and full independence was achieved on 17 April 1946. In December 1949 Syria came under a military dictatorship, led by Brig. Adib Shishekly. He was elected President in July 1953, but was overthrown by another army coup in February 1954.

In February 1958 Syria merged with Egypt to form the United Arab Republic (UAR). In September 1961, following a military coup in Damascus, Syria seceded and formed the independent Syrian Arab Republic. In 1963 Maj.-Gen. Amin al-Hafiz formed a Government in which members of the Arab Socialist Renaissance (Baath) Party were predominant. In February 1966 the army deposed the Government of President al-Hafiz, replacing him with Dr Nur ed-Din al-Atasi. However, in November 1970, after a bloodless coup, the military (moderate) wing of the Baath Party seized power, led by Lt-Gen. Hafiz al-Assad, who was elected President in March 1971. In March 1972 the National Progressive Front (NPF), a grouping of the five main political parties (including the Baath Party), was formed under the leadership of President Assad.

From 1977 frequent assassinations of Alawites (a minority Islamic sect to which Assad belonged) indicated sectarian tension within Syrian society. Assad attributed much of the opposition to the Muslim Brotherhood, a conservative Islamist group. In February 1982 an uprising in Hamah (Hama), led by the outlawed Brotherhood, was brutally suppressed. From November 1983, after Assad suffered a heart attack, rivals to the succession—including Col Rifaat al-Assad, the President's brother—staged shows of military strength. Ostensibly designed to ease Assad's workload following his illness, the appointment of three Vice-Presidents in March 1984 distributed power evenly between the President's potential successors, giving none the ascendancy. The army, Assad's guarantee of continued power, was still controlled by officers loyal to him.

President Assad was re-elected for a third seven-year term of office in February 1985. At a general election held in February 1986 the Baath Party and other members of the NPF (excluding the Communist Party, which contested the poll independently) obtained 151 of the 195 seats in the People's Assembly. The communists won nine seats, and independents 35. In November 1987, following the resignation of Abd ar-Rauf al-Kassem as Prime Minister, Mahmoud az-Zoubi, the Speaker of the Assembly, was appointed premier. At elections to the People's Assembly (now expanded to 250 seats) in May 1990, the Baath Party won 134 seats and other parties 32, while 84 seats were reserved for independent candidates.

Increasing border tension between Syria and Israel was a major influence leading to the Six-Day War of June 1967, when Israel attacked its Arab neighbours in reprisal for the closure of the Strait of Tiran by the UAR (Egypt). Israeli forces made swift territorial gains, including the Golan Heights region of Syria, which remains under Israeli occupation. An uneasy truce lasted until October 1973, when Egyptian and Syrian forces launched simultaneous attacks on Israeli-held territory. On the Syrian front, there was fierce fighting in the Golan Heights until a cease-fire was agreed after 18 days. In May 1974 the US Secretary of State, Henry Kissinger, secured an agreement for the disengagement of forces. Israel's formal annexation of the Golan Heights in December 1981 effectively impeded the prospect of a negotiated Middle East settlement at this time.

Syria disapproved of the second interim Egyptian-Israeli Disengagement Agreement, signed in September 1975, but agreed to acknowledge it as a *fait accompli* in return for Egypt's acceptance of Syria's role in Lebanon. Syria had progressively intervened in the Lebanese civil war during 1976, finally providing the bulk of the 30,000-strong Arab Deterrent Force (ADF). Syria condemned the Egyptian President, Anwar Sadat, for Egypt's peace initiative with Israel in November and December 1977, the Camp David agreements signed by Egypt and Israel in September 1978, and the subsequent peace treaty concluded between them.

The ADF, based in northern Lebanon, was unable to act when Israel invaded southern Lebanon in June 1982 and advanced to Beirut, surrounding fighters of the Palestine Liberation Organization (PLO) and Syrian troops. In August these forces were evacuated under the supervision of a multinational peace-keeping force, and some 50,000 Syrian troops, deployed in the Beka'a valley and northern Lebanon, faced 25,000 Israelis in the south of the country, even though the ADF's mandate had expired. Syria rejected the May 1983 Israel-Lebanon peace agreement, formulated by US Secretary of State George Shultz, refusing to withdraw its forces from Lebanon and continuing to supply the militias of the Lebanese Druze and Shi'ite factions in their fight against the Lebanese Government and the Christian Phalangists. Meanwhile, Syria supported the revolt against Yasser Arafat's leadership of Fatah (the Palestine National Liberation Movement) which began in the Beka'a valley in May 1983. Syrian and rebel PLO forces finally trapped Arafat, the PLO Chairman, in the Lebanese port of Tarabulus (Tripoli) in November. After fierce fighting, Arafat and some 4,000 of his supporters were evacuated, under UN protection, from Tripoli in December.

Although Israel withdrew its forces from Beirut to the Awali river in September 1983, Syrian troops remained entrenched in northern Lebanon. The state of civil war existing in and around Beirut eventually compelled the evacuation of the multinational force during the first three months of 1984. In March President Amin Gemayel of Lebanon capitulated to Syria's influence over Lebanese affairs, and abrogated the May 1983 agreement with Israel. In April 1984 President Assad approved Gemayel's plans for a Lebanese government of national unity, giving equal representation to Muslims and Christians. Inter-factional fighting continued in Beirut, however, and Syria was repeatedly required to intervene. In September Syria arranged a truce to end fighting in Tripoli between the pro-Syrian Arab Democratic Party and the Sunni Tawheed Islami (Islamic Unification Movement). The Lebanese army entered the city in late 1984, under the terms of a Syrian-backed extended security plan, to assert the authority of the Lebanese Government.

Syria approved Lebanese participation in talks with Israel to co-ordinate the departure of the Israeli Defence Force (IDF) from southern Lebanon with that of other security forces, in order to prevent an outbreak of civil violence. The final stage of the Israeli withdrawal was accomplished by early June 1985. Several hundred Israeli troops and advisers remained in Lebanon to assist the Israeli-backed 'South Lebanon Army' (SLA) in policing a narrow buffer zone along the Lebanese side of the international border. Syria removed 10,000–12,000 troops from the Beka'a valley in July, leaving some 25,000 in position.

Heavy fighting occurred in Muslim west Beirut in April 1985, between the Shi'ite Amal militia, allied with the Druze, and the Sunni Murabitoun militia and its Palestinian allies. This preceded renewed attempts by Syria, through its proxy, Amal, to prevent Yasser Arafat from re-establishing a power-base in

tion being undertaken by the Soviet Union, which had for its part indicated its unwillingness to continue to underwrite Syria's efforts to achieve strategic parity with Israel.

There was speculation in late 1991 that President Assad was preparing to introduce a degree of liberalization into Syria's political system. In December it was announced that 2,864 political prisoners were to be released. In March 1992 Assad indicated that new political parties might in future be established. However, he rejected the implementation of foreign democratic frameworks as unsuited to the country's level of economic development. In January 1994 President Assad's presumed successor, his eldest son, Basel, was killed in a road accident. The President's second son, Bashar, was reportedly instructed to assume the role of his late brother in order to avoid a power struggle. In August senior government officials, including the Commander of the Special Forces, were removed from office in an apparent attempt by Assad to consolidate his position and improve Syria's international standing. At elections to the People's Assembly held in that month, the ruling Baath Party and its NPF allies reinforced their dominance of Syrian affairs, winning 167 of the Assembly's 250 seats. In November 1995—the 25th anniversary of President Assad's seizure of power—some 1,200 political prisoners, including members of the banned Muslim Brotherhood, were released under an amnesty, while a number of the Brotherhood's leaders were allowed to return from exile. During 1996 there were reports of several explosions in Damascus, in addition to a number of attacks on Syrian targets in Lebanon. Syria claimed that Israeli agents were responsible for a bomb attack in central Damascus in December (in which 11 people died), although in January 1997 the Syrian-based Islamic Movement for Change claimed responsibility for the attack.

In February 1998 President Assad unexpectedly dismissed his brother, Col Rifaat al-Assad, as Vice-President (a post he had held since 1984, although he had spent much of the intervening period overseas). It was reported in June that some 225 political prisoners had been released, among them leading members of the Muslim Brotherhood, as well as communists and human rights activists. In July President Assad appointed new chiefs of both the Syrian army and the intelligence service, prompting speculation that he was seeking to extend the political influence of his second son, Bashar.

Elections to the People's Assembly were held on 30 November and 1 December 1998, at which the NPF, led by the ruling Baath Party, again won 167 of the 250 seats. In January 1999 the incoming Assembly voted unanimously to nominate President Assad for a fifth term in office. Assad's re-election was confirmed in a national referendum held on 11 February. There was widespread speculation that the President would shortly announce the formation of a new Government, and that possible changes might include the promotion of Bashar to the vice-presidency. The President's son had already been promoted to the rank of army colonel in January, and had reportedly been granted new powers over important domestic matters, furthering speculation that preparations for his succession were being accelerated. In June the Syrian authorities were said to be undertaking an 'unprecedented' campaign, led by Bashar al-Assad, to counter corruption in public office. Several leading officials and businessmen were subsequently incarcerated, and in October, following a nine-month trial, a former director of Syria's intelligence service received a lengthy prison sentence for alleged corruption and embezzlement of public funds. Details emerged in September of large-scale arrests (involving 1,000 people, according to some reports) by security forces in Damascus and Al-Ladhiqiyah (Latakia) against supporters and relatives of Rifaat al-Assad. The arrests were believed to be linked to the succession issue, since the President's brother had of late sought to increase his public profile in Syria. Moreover, in October the security forces closed down a port in Latakia which they claimed had been built illegally by Rifaat. The action provoked several days of violent clashes between Rifaat's supporters and the security forces, in which, according to certain sources, hundreds of people were killed or injured. However, the Government dismissed such reports, and denied claims that the action of the security forces had been politically motivated.

In July 1999 President Assad ordered a general amnesty for prisoners convicted of certain economic crimes, and for those who had deserted the army and evaded military service. The amnesty was to affect hundreds (some reports claimed thousands) of prisoners, including a number of Muslim Brotherhood activists. In February 2000, however, a report by the British-based Amnesty International alleged that in recent months several hundred Syrians (including many Islamists) opposed to a future peace accord with Israel had been arrested. Meanwhile, it was reported that Syria's military intelligence chief, Gen. Ali Duba, had been removed from his post, owing to alleged 'administrative offences', and replaced by his deputy, Maj.-Gen. Hassan Khalil.

President Assad named as Prime Minister Muhammad Mustafa Mero, formerly governor of Halab (Aleppo), in March 2000, having accepted the resignation of Mahmoud az-Zoubi and his administration. A new Cabinet was subsequently inaugurated, with a programme to accelerate social and economic reforms, to strengthen anti-corruption measures, and to resume peace negotiations with Israel. In all, 22 new ministers were appointed (including a number of younger technocrats and supporters of Bashar al-Assad), although the foreign affairs, defence and interior portfolios did not change hands. In mid-May az-Zoubi was expelled from the Baath Party for alleged 'irregularities and abuses' during his period in office. His assets were subsequently seized, and he was expected to stand trial on corruption charges. However, in late May official sources reported that az-Zoubi had committed suicide. (In early June 2002 Mufid Abd al-Karim, a former Minister of Transport in the az-Zoubi Government, was convicted on corruption charges and handed down a 10-year prison sentence.)

President Assad died on 10 June 2000. Shortly after his death the People's Assembly amended the Constitution, lowering the minimum age required of a president from 40 to 34 years, thus enabling Assad's second son, Bashar, to assume the presidency. Bashar al-Assad was also nominated as Commander-in-Chief of the Armed Forces, and his military rank was upgraded to that of Lieutenant-General. Following approval of Bashar's nomination for the presidency by the People's Assembly in late June (the Baath Party having already endorsed his candidacy), a nationwide referendum on the succession was scheduled to be held in July. Meanwhile, the First Vice-President, Abd al-Halim Khaddam, assumed the role of acting President. In mid-June Bashar al-Assad was elected Secretary-General of the Baath Party. Rifaat al-Assad claimed that the assumed succession by Bashar was unconstitutional, and declared that he would challenge his nephew for the presidency. (The Syrian authorities reportedly issued a warrant for Rifaat's arrest should he attempt to enter the country from exile.) At the national referendum, which proceeded on 10 July, Bashar al-Assad (the sole presidential candidate) received the endorsement of a reported 97.29% of voters. In his inaugural address to the People's Assembly on 17 July, President al-Assad emphasized as priorities for his administration economic reform, elimination of official corruption, and the conclusion of a peace treaty with Israel.

In late July 2000 the new President released a significant number of political prisoners, the majority of whom were Muslim Brotherhood activists and communists. Nevertheless, in September a statement by 99 Syrian intellectuals, published in the Lebanese press, demanded substantive reform of Syria's political system: among the intellectuals' demands were increased democracy and freedom of expression, an end to the state of emergency (in force since 1963) and the release of political detainees. In November the army deployed tanks and armoured vehicles in the southern region of As-Suweida, in order to quell three days of violent clashes between members of the Sunni bedouin and Druze communities; 20 people died in the fighting, and some 200 were injured. On the 30th anniversary of his father's seizure of power, commemorated in mid-November, President Bashar al-Assad declared an amnesty for about 600 political detainees (among them Muslim Brotherhood members and other Islamists and communists), as well as a general amnesty for several non-political offences. The decision to free as many as 100 Lebanese prisoners was widely viewed as a gesture of 'goodwill' at a time when influential elements within Lebanon were demanding a lessening of Syrian influence in Lebanese political life.

In January 2001 a group of at least 1,000 intellectuals, among them a prominent businessman and deputy, Riad Seif, urged the Syrian regime to approve political reforms. The intellectuals demanded the suspension of martial law, the holding of free elections, a free press, the release of political prisoners and an end to discrimination against women. Later that month a new 'liberal' political organization, the Movement for Social Peace, was reportedly established under Seif's leadership. The formation of a new nationalist party, the Grouping for Democracy and Unity, was also reported. Also in January some 70 lawyers signed a statement urging a comprehensive review of Syria's judicial system and an end to martial law. The document followed a statement by the Minister of Information, Adnan Omran, that martial law had been 'frozen'; there was, however, no official suspension of the legislation. Meanwhile, following a decision by the Baath Party in November 2000 to permit the other political parties in the NPF to issue their own newspapers, it was announced in early 2001 that the first non-State-controlled newspaper for several decades was to be published by the Communist Party. Syria's first privately owned newspaper for almost 40 years was also issued from February. The launch was announced in that month of the official newspaper of the Syrian Arab Socialist Unionist Party.

However, although the new regime under President al-Assad had shown itself to be more tolerant of criticism than that of his father, reports emerged in February 2001 that the Baath Party was to restrict the activities of civic discussion forums being held by Syrian intellectuals by requiring that groups should henceforth apply for permission several days in advance of convening meetings. Tensions between traditionalists and reformers in Syria increased in early April when the Deputy Prime Minister and Minister of Defence, Maj.-Gen. Mustafa Tlass, accused Syrian intellectuals of being agents of the US Central Intelligence Agency. Later in the month another civil rights document was issued, defining for President al-Assad a list of the principles on which reforms should be based. Also in April a report published by the UN Human Rights Committee expressed concerns regarding violations of human rights in Syria, including unfair trials and the torture of prisoners, the practice of extrajudicial executions and the continued imposition of martial law. During August and September a series of actions by the authorities against influential opposition activists again prompted speculation that the President was less willing to tolerate dissent than had been initially believed. In early August an independent deputy, Mamoun al-Homsi, was detained after starting a hunger strike in protest at official corruption and the Government's failure to end martial law. In early September the leader of the Communist Party, Riad at-Turk, was taken into custody on charges of defamation of the presidency (he had reportedly criticized the system of 'hereditary succession'). A few days later Riad Seif, who had held an 'illegal' discussion forum on political reform, was arrested. The crack-down continued, with about 10 'pro-reform' campaigners being detained by the authorities during the first part of September; human rights organizations condemned the dissidents' arrests. Trial proceedings began at the end of October against al-Homsi and Seif; the other defendants (some of whom had reportedly begun a hunger strike) were to be tried by state security court. In late March 2002 al-Homsi was convicted of 'attempting to change the Constitution by illegal means' and sentenced to a five-year custodial term. Seif also received a five-year gaol sentence in early April, having been convicted of a similar charges. In mid-May, shortly after the commencement of further hearings, Syrian opposition groups urged the authorities to allow open and fair trials: there were conflicting reports as to whether journalists and representatives of the diplomatic community had been permitted to attend at-Turk's trial, although they had been forbidden access to hearings against two other activists. In late June at-Turk was sentenced to two-and-a-half years' imprisonment, although he was freed by President al-Assad in November, reportedly on 'humanitarian grounds'. The convictions against both al-Homsi and Seif had been upheld by an appeals court in July of that year. Meanwhile, in late November 2001 some 120 political prisoners (mostly Islamists or communists) were released under a general amnesty. Moreover, in January 2002 legislation relating to private broadcasting was relaxed.

Three district governors were replaced by presidential decree in February 2001. On 13 December President al-Assad effected an extensive reorganization of the Government. Prime Minister Mero retained his post, as did the Ministers of Defence and Foreign Affairs (the long-serving Minister of Foreign Affairs, Farouk ash-Shara', additionally became the fourth Deputy Prime Minister), although a new Minister of the Interior, Maj.-Gen. Ali Hammoud (former head of the intelligence service), was named. However, several 'pro-reform' ministers were appointed to strategic portfolios relating to the economy, among them Muhammad al-Atrash as Minister of Finance, Ghassan ar-Rifai as Minister of Economy and Foreign Trade (both experienced economists) and Ibrahim Haddad as Minister of Petroleum and Mineral Resources. The planning ministry was abolished. In

late January 2002 Maj.-Gen. Hassan Turkmani replaced Maj.-Gen. Ali Aslan as the new Chief of Staff of the Armed Forces. In mid-February al-Assad reportedly accepted the resignation of the Deputy Prime Minister and Minister of Defence, Maj.-Gen. Mustafa Tlass, effective from July; however, there were further reports in May that Tlass had been ordered by the President to remain in office for a further two years.

Elections to the People's Assembly were held on 2 and 3 March 2003, at which the NPF, led by the ruling Baath Party, again won 167 of the 250 seats, with the remaining 83 going to independents. Electoral turn-out was estimated to be 63.5%. Opposition parties, under an umbrella grouping called the National Democratic Rally, boycotted the election on the grounds that it was undemocratic. On 9 March the newly reconvened legislature elected the Deputy Prime Minister in charge of Public Services, Muhammad Naji al-Otri, as the new Speaker of the People's Assembly. Al-Otri was replaced as Deputy Prime Minister by Muhammad Safi Abu Wdan in late March.

In July 1991, following a meeting with the US Secretary of State, James Baker, President Assad agreed for the first time to participate in direct negotiations with Israel at a regional peace conference, for which the terms of reference would be a comprehensive settlement based on UN Security Council Resolutions 242 (of 1967) and 338 (1973). In August 1991 the Israeli Cabinet formally agreed to attend a peace conference on terms proposed by the USA and the USSR. An initial, 'symbolic' session of the conference was held in Madrid, Spain, in October, and attended by Israeli, Syrian, Egyptian, Lebanese and Palestinian-Jordanian delegations. Syria's principal aim was to recover the Golan Heights, occupied by Israel since 1967; however, it emphasized that it was not prepared to achieve national goals at the expense of a comprehensive Middle East peace settlement. Syria regarded the Declaration of Principles on Palestinian Self-Rule in the Occupied Territories—the basis of a peace settlement signed by Israel and the PLO in September 1993—as deeply flawed. Furthermore, President Assad viewed the secret negotiations between Israel and the PLO that had preceded the Declaration of Principles as having weakened the united Arab position in the peace process, and Syria gave no indication that it would cease to support those Palestinian factions, such as the Damascus-based Popular Front for the Liberation of Palestine—General Command (PFLP—GC), which actively opposed the accord.

President Assad met US President Bill Clinton in Geneva, Switzerland, in January 1994—his first such meeting with a US leader since 1977—in an attempt to give fresh impetus to what was termed the Syrian track of the peace process. In the following month, however, the Arab delegations temporarily withdrew from negotiations in response to the murder, by a right-wing Jewish extremist, of some 50 Muslim worshippers at a mosque in Hebron on the West Bank. In May 1994 the official Syrian daily newspaper, *Ath-Thawra*, described the agreement between Israel and the PLO that provided for a limited Israeli withdrawal from the Occupied Territories as an obstacle to a comprehensive peace settlement. In June Syria reacted warily to the signing by Jordan and Israel of 'sub-agendas' for future bilateral discussions, and continued to adhere to the principle of a united Arab approach to negotiation with Israel. In September Israel published details of a plan for the partial withdrawal of its armed forces from the Golan Heights; Syria rejected the proposals, although President Assad affirmed his willingness to achieve peace with Israel. Clinton visited Damascus in October for talks with Assad (the first visit by a US President to Syria for some 20 years), in a further attempt to facilitate the resumption of dialogue between Syria and Israel. However, it was not until March 1995 that bilateral negotiations finally resumed.

In May 1995 Israel and Syria concluded a 'framework understanding on security arrangements', in order to facilitate the participation in the discussions of the two countries' military Chiefs of Staff. Israel stated publicly that it had proposed a four-year timetable for the withdrawal of its armed forces from the Golan Heights, but that Syria had insisted on one of 18 months. In June the Israeli and Syrian Chiefs of Staff held talks in Washington, DC. However, negotiations became deadlocked once again, and the situation was aggravated by political turmoil in Israel following the assassination of the Prime Minister, Itzhak Rabin, in November. US and Russian diplomatic efforts led to a resumption of negotiations at the Wye Plantation, Maryland, USA, in December and in January 1996, but no progress was made on the issue of security arrangements in the

Golan Heights. Further talks at Wye Plantation in March were interrupted by the withdrawal of the Israeli delegation after a number of suicide bombings in Israel. The acting Israeli Prime Minister, Shimon Peres, indicated that no further discussions would take place until after the Israeli general election in May, owing to Syria's refusal to condemn the violence in Israel and to take firmer action against terrorism generally. Following the election to the Israeli premiership of Likud leader Binyamin Netanyahu, an emergency Arab League summit meeting, held in Cairo in June, urged the new right-wing Government in Israel not to abandon the principle of negotiating 'land-for-peace', and demanded the removal of all Israeli settlements in the Golan Heights and their return to Syria. Although Netanyahu appealed for the reopening of unconditional peace talks with Arab states, he rejected the 'land-for-peace' policies of his Labour predecessor and also insisted that retaining Israeli sovereignty over the Golan Heights must be the basis of any peace settlement with Syria. The redeployment, in September, of Syrian armed forces in Lebanon to positions in the Beka'a valley gave rise to speculation in Israel that Syria, frustrated at the lack of progress in the peace process, might be preparing an attack on Israeli forces. However, Syria stated that the redeployment merely reflected its increased confidence in the Lebanese army.

In the aftermath of Iraq's defeat by the US-led multinational force, Syria was concerned that the USA might permit Israel to undermine, militarily, the implementation in Lebanon of the Ta'if agreement. The possibility of such military action arose from Syria's decision to allow Hezbollah fighters to continue their attacks on northern Israeli settlements, in the belief that only by continued coercion would Israel withdraw from occupied Arab land. The Israeli Government cited these attacks as justification for its refusal to withdraw its forces from southern Lebanon, in compliance with UN Security Council Resolution 425. Syrian troops began to withdraw from Beirut in March 1992, in preparation for their withdrawal (in accordance with the Ta'if agreement) to eastern Lebanon by September. However, Syrian influence on Lebanese internal affairs remained pervasive. The decision of the Lebanese Government to hold elections to the National Assembly in August and September, before the redeployment of Syrian armed forces to eastern Lebanon had taken place, attracted strong criticism both from Lebanese Christian groups and Western governments, who considered that the continued presence of the Syrian forces would prejudice the outcome of the elections. However, the Lebanese Government argued that its army alone was still unable to guarantee the country's security, and that the timetable for elections, as stipulated by the Ta'if agreement, should be observed. Syria, for its part, denied that the continued presence of its forces contravened the accord, since it allowed for them to remain to assist the Lebanese Government until constitutional reforms had been fully implemented.

The start of construction work on the controversial new Jewish settlement at Jabal Abu Ghunaim (Har Homa) in Arab East Jerusalem in March 1997, and subsequent paralysis in Israeli-Palestinian peace talks, further obstructed the Israeli-Syrian peace initiative. Prospects of a resumption in negotiations were further frustrated after the Israeli Knesset approved a preliminary reading of proposed legislation stipulating that the return of land to Syria would require the approval of at least two-thirds of deputies. A US peace mission to the Middle East in September, led by Secretary of State Madeleine Albright, proved largely unsuccessful: although both Syria and Israel expressed their willingness to resume talks, Israel continued to oppose the principle of 'land-for-peace'. Violence erupted in January 1998 after Israeli occupying forces reportedly attempted to seize land cultivated by Arab farmers. In March Syria accused Israel of attempting to sabotage its relationship with Lebanon after the Israeli Prime Minister offered to withdraw from southern Lebanon in exchange for a security arrangement before reaching a formal agreement with Syria regarding the Golan Heights. Both Syria and Lebanon reiterated that any withdrawal must be unconditional, in compliance with UN Security Council Resolution 425. In October Syrian influence in Lebanon was evident in the selection of Gen. Emile Lahoud as the new Lebanese President, and subsequent appointment of a Lebanese Government of national unity.

Syria announced its scepticism that the US-brokered Wye Memorandum, signed in October 1998 by Israel and the Palestinian (National) Authority (PA), would increase the likelihood of a lasting peace in the Middle East; President Assad again

demanded a resumption of 'land-for-peace' negotiations. In November the Syrian-based militant Islamic Jihad (which opposes the peace process) claimed responsibility for a bomb attack in Jerusalem. In February 1999 Syria apparently rejected an Israeli proposal to resume talks, stating its intention to wait until after the forthcoming Israeli general election. Following the defeat, in elections in May, of Binyamin Netanyahu and his Likud party, Israel's new Prime Minister, Ehud Barak (of the Labour-led One Israel coalition), reportedly proposed a five-phase plan to negotiate peace with Syria and to effect an Israeli withdrawal from southern Lebanon. Syria responded with the demand that Barak uphold his pre-election pledge to withdraw from Lebanon within one year of his election and to resume peace talks from their point of deadlock in 1996.

Syria none the less welcomed Barak's election to the Israeli premiership, and many countries involved in the Middle East peace process, including the USA, expressed hope for a prompt resumption of Israeli-Syrian negotiations. However, Syria strongly condemned air-strikes carried out by Israel on central and southern Lebanon in June 1999, apparently instigated by the outgoing Netanyahu administration. At the inauguration of the new Israeli Cabinet in early July, Barak promised to negotiate a bilateral peace with Syria, based on UN Security Council Resolutions 242 and 338, thus apparently signalling to the Assad regime his intention to return most of the occupied Golan Heights to Syria in exchange for peace and normalized relations. In mid-July, prior to a meeting in Washington, DC, between Barak and President Clinton, Syria was reported to have warned dissidents of Damascus-based Palestinian organizations to cease their military operations against Israel, and to have temporarily disrupted the supply of Iranian weapons to Hezbollah guerrillas in southern Lebanon. Moreover, in late July Syria reported a 'cease-fire' with Israel, although mutual disagreements remained, most notably over the point at which previous negotiations had been suspended. At the beginning of September, as Israel and the PA signed the Sharm esh-Sheikh Memorandum (or Wye Two—see the chapter on Israel) in Egypt, US Secretary of State Albright held talks with President Assad in Damascus. However, no suitable formula emerged for renewed Syria-Israel peace talks. At the end of the month Albright angered Israelis when, for the first time, she openly declared US support for Syrian demands for a complete Israeli withdrawal from the Golan Heights.

In early December 1999, reportedly following mediation by Clinton and secret meetings between Israeli and Syrian officials, Israel and Syria agreed to resume negotiations from the point at which they had stalled in 1996. The first round of discussions between the Syrian Minister of Foreign Affairs, Farouk ash-Shara', and the Israeli premier, Ehud Barak, was opened by the US President in mid-December 1999 in Washington, DC. The talks commenced despite an increase in tension in southern Lebanon, and achieved little progress; both sides, however, agreed to resume discussions in the following month, and in late December Syria and Israel were reported to have agreed an informal 'cease-fire' in order to limit the conflict in Lebanon. A second round of talks between ash-Shara' and Barak proceeded on 3–10 January 2000 (with the involvement of Clinton) in Shepherdstown, West Virginia. Syria and Israel had agreed meanwhile on the establishment of four committees to discuss simultaneously the issues of borders, security, normalization of relations, and water sharing. However, the negotiations were inconclusive, and, although the US Government presented a 'draft working document' to both Syrian and Israeli delegations, intended to act as the basis for a framework agreement, in mid-January the peace talks were postponed indefinitely. Syria declared that it required a 'written' commitment from Israel to withdraw from the Golan Heights prior to a resumption of talks, while Israel demanded the personal involvement of President Assad in the negotiating process and that Syria take action to restrain Hezbollah in southern Lebanon. The informal 'cease-fire' there ended in late January following the killing by Hezbollah of a senior SLA commander. In March the Israeli Cabinet voted unanimously to withdraw its forces from Lebanon by July, even in the absence of peace settlement with Syria, while the Knesset voted to change the majority required in the event of an Israeli withdrawal from the Golan from 50% of participating voters to 50% of the registered electorate. Expectations of a breakthrough on the Syrian-Israeli track were raised briefly in late March, when Assad made a rare overseas trip to meet with Clinton in Geneva. However, the talks collapsed after only three hours, as it became clear that the US President was to convey no new Israeli proposal acceptable to Syria regarding its demand for a full and unconditional withdrawal from the Golan Heights. In April the Israeli Government announced that the building of Jewish settlements in the Golan, declared to have been suspended prior to the December 1999 talks, was to resume.

In May 2000 ash-Shara' hosted discussions in Palmyra with his Egyptian and Saudi Arabian counterparts; the meeting was reportedly convened in an effort to co-ordinate a united Arab position towards the USA and Israel prior to the planned Israeli withdrawal from southern Lebanon. Reports following the talks suggested that Saudi Arabia and Egypt had pledged military support to Syria in the event of Israeli aggression. The accelerated withdrawal of Israeli armed forces from southern Lebanon was completed on 24 May 2000, several weeks ahead of the original Israeli deadline. Hopes for a phased redeployment collapsed when the Israeli-backed SLA fled the buffer zone and Hezbollah fighters intensified their campaign against Israeli military targets there. The Israeli withdrawal was confirmed by the UN Security Council in mid-June; meanwhile, Hezbollah effectively gained control over southern Lebanon. The regular Lebanese army deployed in the south (excluding the border area, where responsibility for security remained with UN peace-keeping forces) in early August. Syria, meanwhile, emphasized that its troops would not fill the vacuum created by the departure of Israeli forces. (See the chapters on Israel and Lebanon for further details of the Israeli withdrawal.)

Following the death, in June 2000, of President Assad, and the succession of his second son, Bashar al-Assad, in mid-July, the Israeli-Syrian track of the Middle East peace process remained stalled. Nevertheless, the new Syrian President indicated a desire to resume negotiations in the near future, although he emphasized that Syrian policy regarding an Israeli withdrawal from the Golan Heights remained unchanged. Syria blamed Israel for the failure of attempts to conclude a framework peace agreement at US-brokered talks held between Ehud Barak and Yasser Arafat in July. Relations between Israel and Syria became further strained from late September, when intense fighting broke out between Palestinians and Israeli forces in the West Bank and Gaza. As tensions increased throughout the Middle East, Israel accused Syria of involvement in the abduction of Israeli military personnel by Hezbollah in the disputed Shebaa Farms area of southern Lebanon. (Shebaa Farms has been interpreted by the UN as being part of Syria, and thus subject to resolution as part of a Syrian-Israeli peace settlement.) During an emergency summit meeting of the Arab League held in Cairo in late October Farouk ash-Shara' urged all Arab countries to sever diplomatic ties with Israel, and Syria welcomed the decision of Jordan and Egypt to withdraw their ambassadors from Tel-Aviv in November of that year.

Following the election of Likud leader Ariel Sharon to the Israeli premiership in early February 2001, President al-Assad again reiterated Syria's position that it would only accept a full Israeli withdrawal from the Golan Heights as the basis for a resumption of negotiations. Tensions between the two sides increased in mid-April following an attack by Israeli forces on a Syrian radar station in eastern Lebanon, in which at least one Syrian soldier died; the raid was in response to the killing by Hezbollah of an Israeli soldier in Shebaa Farms. In early December, following talks in Damascus between Egypt's President Mubarak and President al-Assad, Egypt and Syria issued a joint statement condemning Israeli military actions in the West Bank and Gaza, and called on the international community to put pressure on Israel to halt its 'aggression'. In early January 2003 a Syrian soldier was killed during a rare exchange of gunfire between Israeli and Syrian forces in the Golan Heights.

In early May 2000 Bashar al-Assad undertook his first visit to a Western country since taking office: during discussions with senior officials in Spain, the Syrian President was said to have requested greater EU involvement in the Middle East peace process. Meanwhile, in early May 2001 Pope John Paul II, leader of the Roman Catholic Church, undertook an historic four-day pilgrimage to Syria. The Pope's decision to visit the Israeli-occupied Golan Heights provoked considerable controversy.

The inauguration of a new Syrian President and the Israeli withdrawal from southern Lebanon resulted in more vociferous demands within Lebanon for an end to Syrian influence in Lebanese political affairs. In July 2000 leading Maronite Christians in Lebanon requested that President al-Assad release all Lebanese political prisoners being held in Syria. In the following month a coalition of Christian political parties in Lebanon urged voters there to boycott the forthcoming parliamentary elections,

on the grounds that Syria would dictate the outcome of the poll. In August, shortly before the first round of voting, Bashar al-Assad travelled to Beirut for talks with key political figures, implying that he was seeking to take up his late father's role as power-broker in Lebanon. The results of the elections, at which the Syrian-sponsored Government of Selim al-Hoss was resoundingly defeated by former premier Rafik Hariri, and subsequent demands from elements in Lebanon for a reorganization or withdrawal of Syrian forces (see the chapter on Lebanon), served to intensify speculation as to Syria's future role in Lebanese affairs. Nevertheless, some observers noted that Syria had played a less significant role in consultations leading to the formation of a new Lebanese Government, under Hariri, in late October. Syrian officials reacted angrily when the Lebanese Druze leader and traditional ally of Syria, Walid Joumblatt, demanded a 're-evaluation' of Syria's role in Lebanon. In December 46 Lebanese prisoners (many of whom were Christians detained by Syrian troops during the civil war) were released from Syrian detention; hitherto Syria had never confirmed that it was holding Lebanese political prisoners. In mid-June 2001 Syria withdrew some 6,000–10,000 of its armed forces from predominantly Christian districts of east and south Beirut, and from Mount Lebanon; some of the troops were redeployed in the Beka'a valley. However, Syria retained a number of military bases in strategic areas of the Lebanese capital. In early March 2002 President al-Assad became the first Syrian President to visit Beirut since 1947. His discussions with President Lahoud reportedly centred on the forthcoming Arab League conference in Beirut, at which Saudi Arabia's Crown Prince Abdullah was formally to submit his proposals for a Middle East peace settlement (for further details, see the chapter on Lebanon). The two leaders reportedly demanded that any peace deal should include the right of return for Palestinian refugees. There were reports in early April 2002 that Syria had started to redeploy a number of its armed forces from central Lebanon. In mid-February 2003 Syria was reported to have begun the redeployment of some 4,000 troops from northern Lebanon. The new Lebanese Government formed under Hariri in mid-April was widely considered to be the most pro-Syrian administration in Lebanon for more than a decade. According to many analysts, Syria had precipitated the reorganization in order to consolidate its position in Lebanon and the wider Middle East region as its relations with the USA witnessed a sharp deterioration (see below).

The Syrian Government condemned the massive suicide attacks carried out against US citizens in New York and Washington, DC, on 11 September 2001. However, Syria was openly critical of the decision of the US Administration of George W. Bush—as part of its world-wide 'war on terror'—to launch a military campaign against targets in Afghanistan linked to the Taliban regime and to the militant Islamist organization held principally responsible for the attacks, the al-Qa'ida (Base) network of Osama bin Laden. At the end of October the British Prime Minister, Tony Blair, undertook an official visit to Syria, as part of a wider tour of the region aimed at garnering Arab support for the US-led campaign in Afghanistan. Blair asked the Syrian leadership to end its support for militant groups such as Hezbollah and the PFLP, in order to assist efforts to reinvigorate the Middle East peace process. However, President al-Assad condemned the West's bombing of Afghan civilians and stated that organizations engaged in fighting the Israeli occupation were 'legitimate'. In mid-December 2002 President Bashar al-Assad became the first Syrian leader to visit the United Kingdom; during talks with Tony Blair, the Syrian President expressed his opposition to a US-led military campaign to bring about 'regime change' in Iraq, and rejected Blair's demand that he take action to prevent militant Palestinian groups from operating in Syria. President al-Assad was also strongly critical of Western policies regarding the Israeli–Palestinian issue.

Bashar al-Assad visited Italy in late February 2002 for discussions with Italian political leaders concerning the US-led 'war on terror', the growing Israeli–Palestinian violence, and bilateral trade issues. The Syrian President was reported to have requested that EU countries play a greater role in efforts to resolve the conflict in the Palestinian areas, and to have emphasized Syria's opposition to a possible US military offensive against the regime of Saddam Hussain in Iraq. In early April US Secretary of Defense Donald Rumsfeld accused Syria, Iran and Iraq of involvement in terrorism against Israeli civilians. (The perceived implication in terrorist activities of Syria —which the USA lists as a 'state sponsor of terrorism'—was highlighted in mid-October when gunmen from the Damascus-based Popular Front for the Liberation of Palestine assassinated Israel's Minister of Tourism, Rechavam Ze'evi, in Jerusalem, claiming retaliation for the recent killing by Israeli forces of the organization's leader, Abu Ali Moustafa.) Relations between Syria and the USA deteriorated further during late 2002 and early 2003. Several members of the US Administration proposed the imposition of economic sanctions against Syria as punishment for its continued support for radical Islamist organizations such as Islamic Jihad, Hamas and the PFLP. US officials also accused Syria of involvement in the illegal purchase of oil from Iraq. In late November 2002 the Syrian leadership refused US demands that it close the Damascus office of Islamic Jihad, following a renewed campaign by that organization against targets in Israel. As the US-led coalition forces launched a military campaign to oust the regime of Saddam Hussain in mid-March 2003, the USA also increasingly hinted that Syria might be the next target for a US-imposed 'regime change'. Damascus referred to the US-led campaign in Iraq as an 'illegal invasion'. Moreover, Syrians were angered in late March when a bus close to the border with Iraq was hit by a stray US missile, killing five Syrian civilians. Damascus strongly denied claims by the Bush Administration that it was providing military equipment to Iraq during the conflict. Following the removal of Saddam Hussain's regime by the US-led coalition forces in early April, the USA alleged that Syria had assisted leading members of the Iraqi Baath Party to flee the country and that Iraqi weapons of mass destruction might have been transported across the border into Syria. However, in late April President Bush declared that Syria was co-operating with the US-led coalition, having recently sealed its border with Iraq.

In August 1999 a diplomatic crisis developed between Syria and the Palestinian authorities after the Syrian Deputy Prime Minister and Minister of Defence, Maj.-Gen. Mustafa Tlass, publicly accused Yasser Arafat of having 'sold Jerusalem and the Arab nation' in peace agreements concluded with Israel since 1993, and made other personal insults against the Palestinian leader. The PA demanded that Tlass resign, while President Assad was reportedly angered by the minister's remarks. In mid-2000, after Bashar al-Assad's accession to the Syrian presidency, the PA renewed its demand that Syria free all remaining Palestinian prisoners from its gaols; seven Palestinians were released into Lebanese custody in December. Amid Syrian efforts to support the Palestinians in their escalating conflict with the Israelis, and after talks between al-Assad and Arafat during the summit meeting of Arab League states in Jordan in late March 2001, the two leaders declared that they had achieved a reconciliation.

Meanwhile, in October 1998 the Jordanian Government demanded 'immediate answers' from Syria concerning a list of 239 Jordanians allegedly missing in Syria, and a further 190 whom it claimed were imprisoned there. The Syrian authorities agreed to investigate the matter, although they stated that most of those listed were in fact members of Palestinian organizations linked with Jordan, who had violated Syrian laws. In February 1999 President Assad unexpectedly attended the funeral of King Hussein of Jordan, and reportedly held a private meeting with the new monarch. King Abdullah, whose selection as successor to King Hussein had been welcomed by Syria, made his first official visit there in April. During talks with President Assad the two leaders urged a resumption of the peace process and increased bilateral co-operation; it was also agreed that Syria would supply Jordan with water during 1999 (in order to ease Jordan's drought), and that future discussions should be held regarding the Jordanian prisoners. In May four Jordanian detainees were released by the Syrian authorities. In July, amid Jordanian concerns that any peace agreement concluded by Israel and Syria might isolate and undermine the Palestinian cause in future negotiations, King Abdullah made an unscheduled visit to Syria. The joint Syrian-Jordanian Higher Committee met in August in Amman, under the chairmanship of both countries' premiers—the first time in almost a decade that a senior Syrian delegation had visited Jordan's capital. Meanwhile, the Syrian Government stated that many of the Jordanian prisoners held in Syria had been released under a general amnesty granted in July (see above) and that the 'very few' who remained in Syrian jails were non-political detainees. Later in August Syria ended a 10-year ban on the free circulation of Jordanian newspapers and publications in the country. A further 17 Jordanian prisoners were reportedly released from Syrian gaols in March 2000. Following the death of President

Assad in June, King Abdullah visited Damascus in mid-July for talks with Syria's new President, Bashar al-Assad; Syria again agreed to supply Jordan with water during that summer. It was reported in November that Syria had upgraded its diplomatic representation in Jordan to ambassadorial level. In mid-January 2001 Syrian officials reportedly gave assurances to Jordan that all Jordanian political prisoners would soon be released.

After Iraq's defeat by the multinational force in February 1991, Syria became a centre for elements of the Iraqi opposition. However, it remains committed to the territorial integrity of Iraq, fearing that disintegration might encourage minorities within Syria to pursue their own autonomy. In June 1997 three crossing points on the border between Iraq and Syria were reopened to facilitate bilateral trade (Syria closed its border with Iraq in 1980). In September 1998 Iraq, Iran and Syria agreed to establish a joint forum to co-ordinate their foreign policy (particularly towards the USA). In the same month Syria and Iraq reopened commercial centres in one another's capitals, and in April 1999 a series of mutual agreements were signed, as part of the process of normalizing relations. The Syrian Government expressed strong criticism regarding air-strikes carried out by the USA and United Kingdom against Iraq in late 1998, and operations against Iraqi air defence targets in 1999–2002. Syria also opposed the maintenance of UN sanctions against Iraq. Meanwhile, in August 2000 a rail link between Aleppo and the Iraqi capital was reopened after an interval of some 20 years, and in December the Syrian authorities reportedly removed all restrictions on Iraqi citizens travelling to Syria. In November, furthermore, Iraq was reported to have begun transporting crude petroleum to Syria via a pipeline not used since the early 1980s. When the US Secretary of State, Colin Powell, visited Damascus at the end of February 2001, his discussions with the Syrian President apparently centred on the issue of the supply of petroleum from Iraq. President al-Assad was said to have assured Gen. Powell that Syria was not violating the UN sanctions, and to have agreed to place its oil imports from Iraq under UN control. However, in January 2002 British officials publicly accused Syria of sanctions violations. In mid-August 2001 the Syrian Prime Minister, leading a ministerial and commercial delegation, became the most senior Syrian official to visit Iraq for two decades; Mero made a further visit in early December. Syria was particularly concerned (as was Turkey) at the potential ascendance of Iraqi Kurdish groups should the incumbent regime in Baghdad be overthrown, although, visiting these countries in March 2002, the PUK leader, Jalal Talabani, gave assurances that Iraq's Kurdish groups had no intention of establishing their own state. The presence in the Syrian capital at the same time of the Vice-President of Iraq's Revolutionary Command Council, Izzat Ibrahim, prompted speculation that Syria might attempt to mediate between the Iraqi Government and Kurdish groups. The leader of the Iraqi Kurdistan Democratic Party, Masoud Barzani, again visited Damascus in early May. There were also reports in mid-2002 that Syria was involved in mediation efforts between Iraq and Kuwait. Despite its unexpected support for a UN Security Council resolution (No. 1441), approved in early November, which imposed strict terms according to which Iraq must disarm or else face probable military action, Syria expressed its firm opposition to the US-led military campaign against the Iraqi regime which began in mid-March 2003 (see the chapter on Iraq). Syria had been expected to abstain from the UN vote, but Syrian officials asserted that the resolution did not give the USA the right to use force against the Iraqi regime.

Meanwhile, in the context of a long-standing commitment to establish a regional common market under the auspices of the Council of Arab Economic Unity (see p. 178), plans for a quadripartite free-trade zone encompassing Iraq, Egypt, Libya and Syria were advanced following a meeting of the Council held in the Iraqi capital in early June 2001.

Relations between Syria and Turkey became increasingly strained in the 1990s, owing to disagreements over the sharing of water from the Euphrates river. No permanent agreement on this resource has been concluded, and both Syria and Iraq are concerned that new dams in Turkey will reduce their share of water from the Euphrates. Syria's relations with Turkey deteriorated sharply in April 1996 after it was revealed that Turkey and Israel had concluded a military co-operation agreement earlier in the year. In August 1997 Syria condemned the decision by the USA, Israel and Turkey to conduct joint naval manoeuvres, although the three countries claimed that the exercises (carried out in January 1998) were solely for humanitarian purposes. Tension between Syria and Turkey increased considerably in October 1998, when Turkey threatened to invade Syria if its demands for an end to alleged Syrian support for the separatist Kurdistan Workers' Party (Partiya Karkeren Kurdistan—PKK, now Kurdistan Freedom and Democracy Congress—KADEK) were not met. The Turkish authorities also demanded the extradition of the PKK leader, Abdullah Öcalan (who, they claimed, was directing PKK operations from Damascus), and insisted that Syria renounce its historic claim on the Turkish province of Hatay. The Turkish armed forces Chief of General Staff announced that a state of 'undeclared war' existed between Syria and Turkey. The latter's aggressive stance was viewed by Syria as evidence of a Turkish-Israeli military and political alliance, and as a result both Syria and Turkey ordered troops to be deployed along their joint border. Diplomatic efforts to defuse the crisis by Egypt, Iran and the UN, and Syrian assurances that Öcalan was not residing in Syria, allowed a degree of normalization in bilateral relations. In late October, following two days of negotiations in southern Turkey, representatives of the two countries signed an agreement whereby the PKK was to be banned from entering Syrian territory, while the organization's active bases in Syria and Lebanon's Beka'a valley were to be closed. Turkey and Syria also agreed mutual security guarantees, and resolved to invite Lebanon to participate in further discussions regarding the issue of PKK activity. During 1999 Syrian concerns regarding the close nature of Turkish-Israeli relations persisted. However, it was reported in March 2000 that Syrian and Turkish officials were holding discussions in Damascus on a memorandum of principles, intended to establish a new framework for future bilateral relations. In September Syria and Turkey signed a co-operation agreement relating to countering terrorism and organized crime. It was reported in May 2001 that the two countries had agreed to conduct joint military training exercises, and in June 2002 they signed two military co-operation accords. Moreover, reports in February that the Turkish army was to begin the clearance of landmines along its border with Syria were seen as evidence of a steady improvement in bilateral relations.

In November 1998 Syria and Russia signed a military agreement, whereby Russia would assist in the modernization of Syria's defence systems and provide training to military personnel. However, in January 1999 Syria denied Western reports that it was receiving assistance from Russia in the development of chemical weapons. President Assad visited Moscow in July for talks with President Boris Yeltsin and the then Russian premier, Sergei Stepashin. During the discussions Russia reiterated its support for Syria's demand for a complete Israeli withdrawal from the Golan Heights and southern Lebanon, and that Israeli-Syrian peace negotiations be resumed from their point of suspension in 1996. In May 2000 it was reported that a major arms deal had been concluded whereby Russia would supply Syria with defensive weaponry worth some US $2,000m.

In early October 2001 Syria was elected as a non-permanent member of the UN Security Council for 2002–03.

Government

Under the 1973 Constitution (as subsequently amended), legislative power is vested in the unicameral People's Assembly, with 250 members elected by universal adult suffrage. Executive power is vested in the President, elected by direct popular vote for a seven-year term. He governs with the assistance of an appointed Council of Ministers, led by the Prime Minister. Syria has 14 administrative districts (*mohafazat*).

Defence

National service, which normally lasts 30 months, is compulsory for men. In August 2002 the regular armed forces totalled an estimated 319,000 men: an army of an estimated 215,000 (including conscripts), an air defence command of some 60,000, a navy of 4,000 and an air force of 40,000. In addition, Syria had 354,000-strong reserve forces (army 280,000; air force 70,000; navy 4,000). Paramilitary forces included a gendarmerie of 8,000 and a Baath Party Workers' Militia of some 100,000. An estimated 18,000 Syrian troops were deployed in Lebanon in August 2002. Defence expenditure for 2002 was budgeted at £S53,000m.

Economic Affairs

In 2001, according to estimates by the World Bank, Syria's gross national income (GNI), measured at average 1999–2001 prices, was US $16,608m., equivalent to $1,000 per head (or $3,440 per head on an international purchasing-power parity basis).

During 1990–2001, it was estimated, the population increased at an average annual rate of 2.9%, while gross domestic product (GDP) per head increased, in real terms, by an average of 2.6% per year. Overall GDP increased, in real terms, at an average annual rate of 5.5% in 1990–2001; growth was 0.6% in 2000 and, according to official figures, 5.9% in 2001 (although other sources estimated growth of some 2%).

Agriculture (including forestry and fishing) contributed an estimated 23.8% of GDP in 2001, and engaged 28.4% of the employed labour force (excluding foreign workers) in 1999. The principal cash crops are cotton (which accounted for about 4.5% of export earnings in 1999) and fruit and vegetables. Agricultural GDP increased at an average annual rate of 4.9% in 1990–2001; the sector's GDP decreased by some 17.2% in 1999. Syria experienced its third consecutive year of drought in 1999/2000.

Industry (comprising mining, manufacturing, construction and utilities) provided some 29.7% of GDP in 2001, and engaged 27.3% of the employed labour force (excluding foreign workers) in 1999. The GDP of the industrial sector increased by an average of 8.4% per year during 1990–2001; industrial GDP increased by an estimated 3.9% in 1999.

Mining contributed an estimated 6.6% of GDP in 1994, and employed 0.3% of the working population (excluding foreign workers) in 1999. Crude petroleum is the major mineral export, accounting for 62.9% of total export earnings in 1999, and phosphates are also exported. Syria also has reserves of natural gas and iron ore. By 2001 oil production had declined to an estimated average of 530,000 barrels per day (b/d) (from 600,000 b/d in 1995). Production of natural gas increased substantially in the 1990s, reaching an estimated average of 16m. cu m per day in 2000 and being targeted to reach 30m. cu m per day by 2005. In December 2001 Syria and Lebanon signed an agreement under which Syria is to supply gas to northern Lebanon. During 1995–99 the combined GDP of the mining, manufacturing and power sectors increased by an average of 11.7% per year; growth was 6.2% in 1999.

Manufacturing contributed an estimated 26.5% of GDP in 2001, and employed 12.7% of the working population in 1999. In 1998 the principal branches of manufacturing, measured by gross value of output, were food products, beverages and tobacco (26.3%), chemicals, petroleum, coal, rubber and plastic products (24.2%), textiles, clothing, leather products and footwear (18.7%), metal products, machinery, transport equipment and appliances (12.3%) and non-metallic mineral products (9.7%). The GDP of the manufacturing sector increased by an average of 9.2% per year during 1990–2001.

Energy is derived principally from hydroelectric power (providing 41.1% of total electricity production in 1999) and, to a lesser extent, natural gas (35.1%) and petroleum (23.8%). Imports of mineral fuels comprised an estimated 3.7% of the value of total imports in 2000. A major restructuring of the energy sector is scheduled to be completed by 2005.

Services engaged 44.3% of the employed labour force (excluding foreign workers) in 1999, and provided 46.5% of GDP in 2001. The GDP of the service sectors increased at an average rate of 4.8% per year in 1990–2001; the sectors' combined growth was 6.3% in 1999.

In 2000 Syria recorded a visible trade surplus of US $1,423m., and a surplus of $1,062m. on the current account of the balance of payments. In 1999 the principal source of imports (7.0%) was Germany; other important suppliers were France, Italy and Turkey. Italy was the principal market for exports in that year (26.6%); other major purchasers were France, Turkey, Saudi Arabia and Spain. The principal exports in 1999 were crude petroleum, vegetables and fruit, and textiles, while the principal imports were base metals and manufactures, foodstuffs, and machinery.

A budgetary deficit of £S5,534m. was recorded in 1998, equivalent to 0.7% of GDP. At the end of 2000 Syria's total external debt was US $21,657m., of which $15,930m. was long-term public debt. The cost of debt-servicing in that year was equivalent to 4.8% of the total value of exports of goods and services. Annual inflation averaged 5.7% in 1990–2001. Consumer prices decreased by 0.8% in 2000, but increased by 0.4% in 2001. In that year 10.4% of the labour force were unemployed.

Syria is a member of the UN Economic and Social Commission for Western Asia (ESCWA, see p. 35), the Arab Fund for Economic and Social Development (AFESD, see p. 136), the Arab Monetary Fund (see p. 138), the Council of Arab Economic Unity (see p. 178), the Islamic Development Bank (see p. 257) and the

Organization of Arab Petroleum Exporting Countries (OAPEC, see p. 292).

Under the administration of President Hafiz al-Assad, Syria began to implement a programme of market-orientated economic reforms. However, the pace of change was very slow, partly because Syria is not encumbered by a heavy burden of foreign debt and has thus been relatively unsusceptible to pressure from international agencies to accelerate the reform process. By the end of 2000 Investment Law 10 (enacted in 1991) had attracted more than £S334,000m. of new investment. However, excessive bureaucracy and a politically-motivated multiple exchange rate system have deterred many foreign investors. A bolder reform programme, which appears to be a priority of the regime under President Bashar al-Assad, would almost certainly stimulate investment in tourism and agriculture, where the greatest opportunities are perceived to exist. In 1997 the Government settled its debt of US $526.4m. to the World Bank, prompting forecasts of an improvement in Syria's status within the international financial community, and thus of increased investor confidence in the country. In 1998 a number of amendments were made to Law 10 in order to encourage investment, and amendments approved in May 2000 included a provision permitting foreign investors to own or rent land. In April of that year a decree was promulgated enabling foreign banks to establish branches within Syria's free zones. (A further decree issued in January 2003 will allow other services such as hotels and restaurants to operate in the zones.) In December 2000 draft legislation was proposed allowing for the creation of private banks in Syria for the first time since 1963, as well as laws concerning banking privacy, a proposed stock exchange and the flotation of the Syrian pound. In January 2001 the Government approved the formation of joint-stock banks, while foreign-exchange restrictions were partially rescinded; the new banking law received parliamentary approval in March. In December a framework for the establishment of private banks was announced, as was the formation of a regulatory body, the Monetary and Credit Council; the legislation was enacted in March 2002. The decision to allow private banks (with foreign ownership of 49% being permitted) was expected to encourage foreign investment and to stimulate economic growth. In October Syria announced that henceforth it would permit the purchase and exchange of foreign currency in the domestic market for non-commercial purposes. In April 2003 three private banks—two from Lebanon and one from Jordan—were granted licences to establish branches in Syria. Meanwhile, in November 2001 the Government launched a five-year reform programme focusing on administrative reform and job creation; annual economic growth of 3% was forecast for 2002–04. Official sources estimated growth of 3.4% in 2002. The 2003 budget anticipated increased state expenditure, largely in order to pay government and civil service salaries. The Syrian economy was expected to suffer the consequences of the temporary loss of its trade with Iraq, as a result of the US-led military campaign to oust the regime of Saddam Hussain in March–April 2003. Indeed, Syria's economic prospects following the death of President Assad will largely depend on political factors—most notably the conclusion of a comprehensive peace agreement with Israel, and, possibly, further domestic political reform.

Education

Primary education, which begins at six years of age and lasts for six years, is officially compulsory. In 1996/97 primary enrolment included 91% of children in the relevant age-group (males 95%; females 87%). Secondary education, beginning at 12 years of age, lasts for a further six years, comprising two cycles of three years each. In 1996/97 enrolment at secondary schools included 38% of children in the appropriate age-group (males 40%; females 36%). There are agricultural and technical schools for vocational training, and higher education is provided by the universities of Damascus, Aleppo, Tishrin (the October University, in Latakia) and Hims (Homs—the Baath University, formerly the Homs Institute of Petroleum). There were 167,186 students enrolled at the universities in 1994/95. Expenditure on education by all levels of government in 1999 was estimated at £S26,324m. (10.3% of total government expenditure).

Public Holidays

2003: 1 January (New Year's Day), 12 February* (Id al-Adha, Feast of the Sacrifice), 5 March* (Muharram, Islamic New Year), 8 March (Revolution Day), 25–28 April (Greek Orthodox Easter), 14 May* (Mouloud/Yum an-Nabi, Birth of Muhammad), 23 July (Egypt's Revolution Day), 1 September (Union of Syria, Egypt and Libya), 24 September* (Leilat al-Meiraj, Ascension of Muhammad), 6 October (Martyr's Day, anniversary of the beginning of October War), 16 November (National Day), 26 November* (Id al-Fitr, end of Ramadan), 25 December (Christmas Day).

2004: 1 January (New Year's Day), 2 February* (Id al-Adha, Feast of the Sacrifice), 22 February* (Muharram, Islamic New Year), 8 March (Revolution Day), 9–12 April (Greek Orthodox Easter), 2 May* (Mouloud/Yum an-Nabi, Birth of Muhammad), 23 July (Egypt's Revolution Day), 1 September (Union of Syria, Egypt and Libya), 12 September* (Leilat al-Meiraj, Ascension of Muhammad), 6 October (Martyr's Day, anniversary of the beginning of October War), 14 November* (Id al-Fitr, end of Ramadan), 16 November (National Day), 25 December (Christmas Day).

*These holidays are dependent on the Islamic lunar calendar and may vary by one or two days from the dates given.

Weights and Measures

The metric system is in force.

Statistical Survey

Source (unless otherwise stated): Central Bureau of Statistics, rue Abd al-Malek bin Marwah, Malki Quarter, Damascus; tel. (11) 3335830; fax (11) 3322292.

Area and Population

AREA, POPULATION AND DENSITY

Area (sq km)	
Land	184,050
Inland water	1,130
Total	185,180*
Population (census results)†	
8 September 1981	9,052,628
3 September 1994	
Males	7,048,906
Females	6,733,409
Total	13,782,315
Population (official estimates at mid-year)†	
1999	16,110,000
2000	16,320,000
2001	16,720,000
Density (per sq km) at mid-2001	90.8

* 71,498 sq miles.
† Including Palestinian refugees, numbering 193,000 at mid-1977.

PRINCIPAL TOWNS
(population at census of 3 September 1994)

Halab (Aleppo)	1,582,930	Ar-Raqqah (Rakka)	165,195
Dimashq (Damascus, capital)	1,394,322	Al-Qamishli	144,286
Hims (Homs)	540,133	Deir ez-Zor	140,459
Al-Ladhiqiyah (Latakia)	311,784	Al-Hasakah	119,798
Hamah (Hama)	264,348		

Source: Thomas Brinkhoff, *City Population* (internet www.citypopulation.de).

Mid-2000 (UN estimate, incl. suburbs): Aleppo 2,229,000; Homs 811,000.

Mid-2001 (UN estimate, incl. suburbs): Damascus 2,195,000.

Source: UN, *World Urbanization Prospects: The 2001 Revision*.

REGISTERED BIRTHS, MARRIAGES AND DEATHS

	Births	Marriages	Deaths
1992	404,948	106,545	46,308
1993	433,328	114,979	53,854
1994	447,987	115,994	51,003
1995	478,308	—	52,214
1996	500,953	127,963	53,786
1997	496,140	128,146	53,366
1998	505,008	130,835	57,893
1999	503,473	136,157	56,564

Source: UN, *Demographic Yearbook.*

Expectation of life (WHO estimates, years at birth): 70.9 (males 68.7; females 73.2) in 2001 (Source: WHO, *World Health Report*).

ECONOMICALLY ACTIVE POPULATION

(sample survey, persons aged 10 years and over, 1999)*

	Males	Females	Total
Agriculture, hunting, forestry and fishing	799,181	364,491	1,163,672
Mining and quarrying	10,159	709	10,868
Manufacturing	477,477	43,257	520,734
Electricity, gas and water . . .	3,386	—	3,386
Construction	568,909	13,473	582,382
Trade, restaurants and hotels . .	623,085	24,110	647,195
Transport, storage and communications	216,727	7,800	224,527
Financing, insurance, real estate and business services	27,092	6,382	33,474
Community, social and personal services	660,339	248,903	909,242
Total employed.	3,386,355	709,125	4,095,480
Unemployed	268,703	163,075	431,778
Total labour force	3,655,058	872,200	4,527,258

* Figures refer to Syrians only, excluding armed forces.

2001: Total employed 5,275,717 (males 4,237,644; females 1,038,073); unemployed 613,355 (Source: ILO).

Health and Welfare

KEY INDICATORS

Total fertility rate (children per woman, 2001).	3.8
Under-5 mortality rate (per 1,000 live births, 2001) . . .	28
HIV/AIDS (% of persons aged 15–49, 1994).	0.01
Physicians (per 1,000 head, 1997)	109
Hospital beds (per 1,000 head, 1997)	4.0
Health expenditure (2001): US $ per head (PPP)	51
Health expenditure (2001): % of GDP	2.5
Health expenditure (2001): public (% of total)	63.4
Access to water (% of persons, 2000).	80
Access to sanitation (% of persons, 2000)	90
Human Development Index (2000): ranking	108
Human Development Index (2000): value	0.691

For sources and definitions, see explanatory note on p. vi.

Agriculture

PRINCIPAL CROPS

('000 metric tons)

	1999	2000	2001
Wheat	2,691.5	3,105.5	4,744.6
Barley	425.5	211.9	1,955.6
Maize	181.0	190.3	215.8
Potatoes	496.5	484.8	453.4
Sugar beet.	1,330.4	1,175.3	1,215.5
Chick-peas	28.9	64.5	60.1
Lentils	43.5	73.0	77.5†
Almonds	57.7	62.3	49.5
Olives	400.5	866.1	497.0
Cottonseed	926.1	1,081.9	1,009.8
Cabbages	57.1	42.9	43.2
Lettuce.	49.7	46.3	41.2
Tomatoes	610.2	753.2	771.8
Cauliflowers	50.4	29.8	31.6
Pumpkins, squash and gourds . .	100.0	87.4	87.4*
Cucumbers and gherkins . .	93.8	91.3	91.3*
Aubergines (Eggplants) . . .	114.6	123.7	123.7*
Chillies and green peppers . . .	33.4	43.0	44.9
Green onions and shallots . . .	40.9	51.4	51.4*
Dry onions	91.0	71.9	87.0
Oranges	356.6	407.1	464.9
Lemons and limes	82.9	83.5	79.4
Apples	283.7	286.8	263.0
Apricots	62.9	78.9	66.0
Cherries	54.1	56.3	50.8
Peaches and nectarines . . .	41.6	42.0	37.6
Grapes	387.0	409.5	389.0
Watermelons	258.5	201.5	227.9
Cantaloupes and other melons .	44.7	48.2	48.2*
Figs	41.8	44.1	40.0
Cotton (lint)	306.2	345.0	335.0

* FAO estimate.
† Unofficial figure.

Source: FAO.

LIVESTOCK

('000 head, year ending September)

	1999	2000	2001
Horses	26.6	27.1	27.1*
Mules	14.0	12.9	12.9*
Asses	219.0	216.4	216.4*
Cattle	978	984	837
Camels.	13.3	13.4	13.5*
Sheep	13,998	13,505	12,362
Goats	1,046	1,050	979
Chickens	21,009	21,629	21,009

* FAO estimate.

Source: FAO.

LIVESTOCK PRODUCTS

('000 metric tons)

	1999	2000	2001
Beef and veal	46.7	47.1	42.3
Mutton and lamb.	176.7	184.1	168.5
Chicken meat.	104.4	106.6	114.2
Cows' milk	1,143.4	1,156.4	1,032.3
Sheep's milk	445.9	445.6	482.8
Goats' milk	65.9	70.3	61.7
Cheese.	82.2	87.3	91.9
Butter and ghee	14.4	14.5	15.2
Hen eggs	124.0	127.3*	115.0†
Wool: greasy	25.5*	32.0*	23.5†
Wool: scoured	12.8	15.9	14.0
Cattle hides†	7.2	7.3	6.5
Sheepskins†	29.4	30.6	28.2

* Unofficial figure.
† FAO estimate(s).

Source: FAO.

Forestry

ROUNDWOOD REMOVALS
('000 cubic metres, excl. bark)*

	1999	2000	2001
Sawlogs, veneer logs and logs for sleepers	16	16	16
Other industrial wood	19	19	19
Fuel wood	16	16	16
Total	50	50	50

* Assumed unchanged since 1993 (FAO estimates).

Sawnwood production ('000 cubic metres): 9 per year in 1991–2001.

Source: FAO.

Fishing

(metric tons, live weight)

	1998	1999	2000
Capture	7,097	7,938	6,752
Freshwater fishes	4,347	5,338	3,991
Demersal percomorphs	626	530	392
Aquaculture	7,233	6,079	6,797
Common carp	5,786	4,930	3,790
Tilapias	1,372	1,065	2,626
Total catch	14,330	14,017	13,549

Source: FAO, *Yearbook of Fishery Statistics.*

Mining

('000 metric tons, unless otherwise indicated)

	1999	2000	2001*
Crude petroleum	210	200	194
Phosphate rock	2,084	2,166	2,043
Salt (unrefined)	104	106	106
Gypsum	394	333	345

* Estimates.

Source: US Geological Survey.

Industry

SELECTED PRODUCTS
('000 metric tons, unless otherwise indicated)

	1996	1997	1998
Cotton yarn (pure)	43	53	60
Silk and cotton textiles	15	25	25
Woollen fabrics (metric tons)	0.2	2.7	4.9
Plywood ('000 cu metres)	87.6	78.3	79.8
Cement	4,817	4,840	4,607
Glass and pottery products	58	69	57
Soap	18	18	21
Refined sugar	181	176	89
Olive oil	127	77	145
Other vegetable oils and fats	36	53	65
Cottonseed cake	171	192	201
Manufactured tobacco	9	10	10
Electricity (million kWh)	17,278	18,259	19,841
Refrigerators ('000)	155.2	138.2	136.9
Washing machines ('000)	80	71.5	68.5
Television receivers ('000)	123.8	128.2	150.5

1999 ('000 metric tons, unless otherwise indicated): Cotton yarn (pure) 62; Cement 4,781; Refined sugar 158; Olive oil 80; Other vegetable oils and fats 50; Cottonseed cake (estimate) 208; Electricity (million kWh) 21,568.

2000 ('000 metric tons, unless otherwise indicated): Cement 4,830; Olive oil 165; Other vegetable oils and fats 70; Cottonseed cake (estimate) 214; Electricity (million kWh) 23,952.

2001 ('000 metric tons, unless otherwise indicated): Cement 4,840; Olive oil 95; Cottonseed cake 231 .

Sources: mainly Central Bank of Syria, *Quarterly Bulletin*; FAO; UN, *Monthly Bulletin of Statistics*; US Geological Survey.

Finance

CURRENCY AND EXCHANGE RATES

Monetary Units
100 piastres = 1 Syrian pound (£S)

Sterling, Dollar and Euro Equivalents (31 December 2002)
£1 sterling = £S18.092
US $1 = £S11.225
€1 = £S11.772
£S1,000 = £60.74 sterling = $89.09 = €94.90

Exchange Rate: Between April 1976 and December 1987 the official mid-point rate was fixed at US $1 = £S3.925. On 1 January 1988 a new rate of $1 = £S11.225 was introduced. In addition to the official exchange rate, there is a promotion rate (applicable to most travel and tourism transactions) and a flexible rate. For calculating the value of transactions in the balance of payments, the Central Bank of Syria used the following average exchange rates: $1 = £S44.88 in 1997; $1 = £S49.27 in 1998; $1 = £S48.83 in 1999.

BUDGET
(estimates, £S million)

Revenue	1997	1998	1999
Taxes and duties	69,296.0	75,516.0	82,686.0
Services, commutations and revenues from state properties and their public investments	18,574.0	20,054.0	19,409.0
Various revenues	48,108.0	60,385.0	65,500.0
Supply surplus	44,516.0	47,081.0	50,314.0
Exceptional revenues	30,631.0	34,264.0	37,391.0
Total	211,125.0	237,300.0	255,300.0

Expenditure	1997	1998	1999
Community, social and personal services	116,167.5	127,432.7	144,087.7
Agriculture, forestry and fishing .	24,220.4	25,059.0	24,580.5
Mining and quarrying	8,471.1	8,964.9	8,635.2
Manufacturing	14,033.4	17,049.1	16,734.8
Electricity, gas and water . . .	27,004.4	25,168.2	23,538.7
Building and construction . . .	1,216.2	1,225.3	1,117.6
Trade	3,435.6	3,732.3	3,369.7
Transport, communications and storage	11,012.4	17,679.9	20,288.8
Finance, insurance and companies	1,164.0	1,388.6	1,147.0
Total (incl. others)	211,125.0	237,300.0	255,300.0

2000 (projections, £S million): Revenue 263,000; Expenditure 275,400.

2001 (projections, £S million): Revenue 312,798; Expenditure 322,000.

2002 (projections, £S million): Revenue 356,400; Expenditure 356,400.

CENTRAL BANK RESERVES
(US $ million at 31 December)

	1986	1987	1988
Gold*	29	29	29
Foreign exchange	144	223	193
Total	173	252	222

* Valued at $35 per troy ounce.

Source: IMF, *International Financial Statistics*.

Gold: 1989–2001: 29.

MONEY SUPPLY
(£S million at 31 December)

	1999	2000	2001
Currency outside banks . . .	182,184	203,863	229,266
Demand deposits at commercial banks	121,471	151,753	176,845
Total money (incl. others) . .	313,318	368,670	419,916

Source: IMF, *International Financial Statistics*.

COST OF LIVING
(Consumer Price Index for Damascus; base: 1990 = 100)

	1999	2000	2001
Food and beverages	162.3	159.0	159.3
Electricity, gas and other fuels .	268.3	269.2	269.1
Clothing and footwear	252.6	252.3	253.6
Rent	198.2	199.0	200.3
All items (incl. others) . . .	184.3	182.9	183.6

Source: ILO, *Yearbook of Labour Statistics*.

NATIONAL ACCOUNTS
(£S million at current prices)

Expenditure on the Gross Domestic Product

	1998	1999	2000
Government final consumption expenditure	88,521	86,857	98,403
Private final consumption expenditure	542,374	575,866	579,627
Gross capital formation	162,446	153,706	155,757
Total domestic expenditure. .	793,341	816,429	833,787
Exports of goods and services .	241,316	264,704	326,715
Less Imports of goods and services	244,213	262,041	263,868
GDP in purchasers' values . .	790,444	819,092	896,634
GDP at constant 1995 prices .	675,888	662,396	666,567

Source: IMF, *International Financial Statistics*.

Gross Domestic Product by Economic Activity

	1997	1998	1999*
Agriculture, hunting, forestry and fishing	192,162	232,283	196,743
Mining and quarrying. . . . }			
Manufacturing . . . . . }	184,938	179,687	221,416
Electricity, gas and water. . . }			
Construction	28,102	29,470	27,433
Trade, restaurants and hotels .	149,054	152,130	152,866
Transport, storage and communications	86,409	88,876	104,053
Finance, insurance, real estate and business services . . .	29,459	29,971	35,095
Government services	60,056	61,789	64,859
Other community, social and personal services	15,136	15,935	18,498
Non-profit private services . .	253	303	364
GDP in purchasers' values .	745,569	790,444	821,327

* Preliminary figures.

Source: Central Bank of Syria, *Quarterly Bulletin*.

BALANCE OF PAYMENTS
(US $ million)

	1998	1999	2000
Exports of goods f.o.b.	3,142	3,806	5,146
Imports of goods f.o.b.	−3,320	−3,590	−3,723
Trade balance	−178	216	1,423
Exports of services	1,666	1,651	1,700
Imports of services	−1,491	−1,612	−1,667
Balance on goods and services.	−3	255	1,456
Other income received	369	356	345
Other income paid	−839	−899	−1,224
Balance on goods, services and income	−473	−288	577
Current transfers received . . .	533	491	495
Current transfers paid	−2	−2	−10
Current balance	58	201	1,062
Capital account (net)	27	80	63
Direct investment from abroad. .	82	263	270
Other investment assets . . .	1,422	1,332	1,049
Other investment liabilities . .	−1,308	−1,422	−1,711
Net errors and omissions . . .	153	−195	−192
Overall balance	434	259	541

Source: IMF, *International Financial Statistics*.

External Trade

PRINCIPAL COMMODITIES
(£S million)

Imports c.i.f.	1997	1998	1999*
Cotton textiles, other textile goods and silk	4,287.4	4,376.4	4,279
Mineral fuels and oils	1,914.6	1,747.6	1,212
Sugar	1,700.1	1,622.7	1,796
Other foodstuffs	5,268.1	4,880.7	5,945
Machinery and apparatus . .	6,863.8	6,422.8	5,600
Base metals and manufactures .	6,703.5	7,203.7	7,273
Chemicals and pharmaceutical products.	4,320.8	3,756.1	3,738
Transport equipment	3,452.4	3,797.5	3,807
Paper and paper products . . .	1,336.7	1,259.1	1,400
Resins, artificial rubber, etc. . .	3,071.5	2,929.5	2,503
Total (incl. others)	45,210.7	43,725.5	43,010

Exports f.o.b.	1997	1998	1999*
Raw cotton	2,772.6	3,065.3	1,745
Wheat	2,142.0	1,062.8	272
Textiles	3,200.1	2,430.1	2,805
Vegetables and fruit (fresh and prepared)	3,332.2	3,887.3	4,026
Crude petroleum	24,396.4	15,472.7	24,470
Total (incl. others)	43,953.0	32,443.4	38,880

* Figures are rounded.

Source: Central Bank of Syria, *Quarterly Bulletin*.

PRINCIPAL TRADING PARTNERS
(£S million)

Imports c.i.f.	1997	1998	1999*
Belgium	1,546.7	1,547.6	1,227
Bulgaria	454.8	295.0	376
China, People's Republic	1,626.2	1,570.9	1,425
Czechoslovakia (former)	400.8	455.1	300
Egypt	558.2	640.7	492
France	1,797.1	2,393.6	2,465
Germany	3,680.6	3,099.7	3,031
India	667.0	625.8	634
Italy	3,275.7	2,854.7	2,424
Japan	1,666.6	1,744.2	1,756
Netherlands	912.3	1,067.6	938
Romania	1,615.1	903.2	863
Russia	1,127.3	932.1	887
Saudi Arabia	1,286.7	1,021.7	1,124
Spain	756.6	688.4	642
Turkey	2,414.8	2,098.4	2,137
United Kingdom	1,095.4	1,050.2	995
USA	2,926.7	2,085.8	1,963
Total (incl. others)	45,210.7	43,725.0	43,010

Exports f.o.b.	1997	1998	1999*
Egypt	342.2	329*	391
France	8,650.6	5,707.9	8,013
Germany	666.8	581.1	330
Italy	10,783.3	7,031.3	10,337
Jordan	750.7	473.7	439
Kuwait	467.7	591.5	581
Lebanon	3,702.4	2,778.6	1,537
Russia	1,135.4	519.5	498
Saudi Arabia	2,389.0	2,632.7	3,260
Spain	2,450.5	1,605.9	2,670
Turkey	4,409.7	3,348.2	3,599
United Kingdom	646.7	319.6	927
USA	151.6	181*	503
Total (incl. others)	43,953.1	32,442.5	38,880

* Figures are rounded.

Source: Central Bank of Syria, *Quarterly Bulletin*.

Transport

RAILWAYS
(traffic)

	1996	1997	1998
Passenger-km ('000)	453,886	294,126	181,575
Freight ('000 metric tons)	4,655	4,939	4,983

ROAD TRAFFIC
(motor vehicles in use)

	1996	1997	1998
Passenger cars	139,592	138,460	138,900
Buses and coaches	33,970	47,453	40,143
Lorries, trucks, etc.	251,451	262,060	282,664
Motorcycles	88,490	87,361	88,121

SHIPPING

Merchant Fleet
(registered at 31 December)

	1999	2000	2001
Number of vessels	223	219	215
Total displacement ('000 grt)	440.1	465.4	498.2

Source: Lloyd's Register-Fairplay, *World Fleet Statistics*.

International Sea-borne Traffic

	1996	1997	1998
Vessels entered ('000 net reg. tons)	2,901*	2,640	2,622
Cargo unloaded ('000 metric tons)	4,560	4,788	5,112
Cargo loaded ('000 metric tons)	1,788	2,412	2,136

* Excluding Banias.

Source: mainly UN, *Monthly Bulletin of Statistics* and *Statistical Yearbook*.

1999: Vessels entered 2,928.

CIVIL AVIATION
(traffic on scheduled services)

	1997	1998	1999
Kilometres flown (million)	12	13	12
Passengers carried ('000)	694	665	668
Passenger-km (million)	1,235	1,410	1,287
Total ton-km (million)	127	140	134

Source: UN, *Statistical Yearbook*.

Tourism

FOREIGN VISITOR ARRIVALS
(incl. excursionists)*

Country of nationality	1998	1999	2000
Iran	152,866	199,307	221,380
Iraq	36,375	58,136	85,439
Jordan	477,747	513,783	538,493
Kuwait	66,931	65,868	69,075
Lebanon	827,039	868,051	995,235
Saudi Arabia	245,785	273,161	283,653
Turkey	169,912	186,770	182,801
Total	2,463,724	2,681,534	3,014,758

* Figures exclude Syrian nationals resident abroad.

Source: World Tourism Organization, *Yearbook of Tourism Statistics*.

Tourism receipts (US $ million): 1,190 in 1998, 1,360 in 1999; 474 in 2000 (Source: World Bank).

Communications Media

	1999	2000	2001
Television receivers ('000 in use) .	1,070	1,080	n.a.
Telephones ('000 main lines in use)	1,600.4	1,675.2	1,807.6
Mobile cellular telephones ('000 in use) .	4.0	30.0	200.0
Personal computers ('000 in use) .	230	250	270
Internet users ('000)	20	30	60

1992: Book production 598 titles.

1996: Daily newspapers 8 (average circulation 287,000 copies).

1997 ('000 in use): Radio receivers 4,150.

1998 ('000 in use): Facsimile machines 22.

Sources: UNESCO, *Statistical Yearbook*; UN, *Statistical Yearbook*; International Telecommunication Union.

Education

(1996/97)

	Institutions	Teachers	Pupils/Students		
			Males	Females	Total
Pre-primary . . .	1,096	4,427	52,627	45,524	98,151
Primary	10,783	114,689	1,433,385	1,256,820	2,690,205
Secondary: general .	n.a.	52,182	469,032	396,010	865,042
Secondary: vocational . . .	n.a.	12,479	44,895	47,727	92,622
Higher: universities, etc.*	n.a.	4,733	101,819	65,367	167,186
Higher: others* . .	n.a.	n.a.	25,167	23,381	48,548

* Figures refer to 1994/95.

Source: UNESCO, *Statistical Yearbook*.

Pupils/Students (1999/2000): Pre-primary 115,613 (males 61,458; females 54,155); Primary 2,774,922 (males 1,470,800; females 1,304,122); General secondary 955,272 (males 511,702; females 443,570) (Source: Ministry of Education).

Adult literacy rate (UNESCO estimates): 74.4% (males 88.3%; females 60.5%) in 2000 (Source: UNDP, *Human Development Report*).

Directory

The Constitution

A new and permanent Constitution was endorsed by 97.6% of the voters in a national referendum on 12 March 1973. The 157-article Constitution defines Syria as a 'Socialist popular democracy' with a 'pre-planned Socialist economy'. Under the new Constitution, Lt-Gen. Hafiz al-Assad remained President, with the power to appoint and dismiss his Vice-President, Premier and government ministers, and also became Commander-in-Chief of the Armed Forces, Secretary-General of the Baath Socialist Party and President of the National Progressive Front. Legislative power is vested in the People's Assembly, with 250 members elected by universal adult suffrage (83 seats are reserved for independent candidates).

Following the death of President Hafiz al-Assad on 10 June 2000, the Constitution was amended to allow his son, Lt-Gen. Bashar al-Assad, to accede to the presidency. Bashar al-Assad also became Commander-in-Chief of the armed forces, Secretary-General of the Baath Socialist Party and President of the National Progressive Front.

The Government

HEAD OF STATE

President: Lt-Gen. BASHAR AL-ASSAD (assumed office 17 July 2000).

Vice-Presidents: ABD AL-HALIM KHADDAM (First) (responsible for Political and Foreign Affairs), MUHAMMAD ZUHEIR MASHARKAH (Second) (responsible for Internal and Party Affairs).

COUNCIL OF MINISTERS
(April 2003)

Prime Minister: Dr MUHAMMAD MUSTAFA MERO.

Deputy Prime Minister and Minister of Defence: Maj.-Gen. MUSTAFA TLASS.

Deputy Prime Minister in charge of Public Services: MUHAMMAD SAFI ABU WDAN.

Deputy Prime Minister in charge of Economic Affairs: Dr MUHAMMAD AL-HUSSAIN.

Deputy Prime Minister and Minister of Foreign Affairs: FAROUK ASH-SHARA'.

Minister of Information: ADNAN OMRAN.

Minister of the Interior: Maj.-Gen. ALI HAMMOUD.

Minister of Supply and Internal Trade: BASSAM MUHAMMAD ROSTOM.

Minister of Local Government: HILAL AL-ATRASH.

Minister of Education: Dr MAHMOUD AS-SAYED.

Minister of Higher Education: Dr HASSAN RISHA.

Minister of Electricity: MUNIB ASSAD SAIM AD-DAHER.

Minister of Culture: Dr NAJWA QASSAB HASSAN.

Minister of Transport: Eng. MAKRAM OBEID.

Minister of Economy and Foreign Trade: GHASSAN AR-RIFAI.

Minister of Petroleum and Mineral Resources: Dr IBRAHIM HADDAD.

Minister of Industry: Dr ISSAM AZ-ZAIM.

Minister of Finance: Dr MUHAMMAD AL-ATRASH.

Minister of Housing and Utilities: AYMAN WANLI.

Minister of Justice: NABIL AL-KHATIB.

Minister of Agriculture and Agrarian Reform: Dr NOUR ED-DIN MOUNA.

Minister of Irrigation: Eng. RADWAN MARTINI.

Minister of Communications: Dr BASHIR AL-MUNJID.

Minister of Health: Dr MUHAMMAD IYAD ASH-SHATTI.

Minister of Construction: Dr HASSAN IBRAHIM AL-ASWAD.

Minister of Awqaf (Islamic Endowments): MUHAMMAD ABD AR-RA'UF ZIYADAH.

Minister of Labour and Social Affairs: GHADA AL-JABI.

Minister of Tourism: Dr SAADALLAH AGHA AL-QALLA.

Minister of Presidential Affairs: HAYTHAM DUWAIHI.

Minister of State for Emigration Affairs: NASSER QADDOUR.

Minister of State for the Environment: Eng. ADNAN KHAZAM.

Ministers of State: FAISAL JAWISH, ABD AL-KARIM SAYED YOUSUF, ABD AN-NASSER ABD AL-MU'TI DAOUD.

MINISTRIES

Office of the President: Damascus; internet www.assad.org.

Office of the Prime Minister: rue Chahbandar, Damascus; tel. (11) 2226000.

Ministry of Agriculture and Agrarian Reform: rue Jabri, place Hedjaz, Damascus; tel. (11) 2213613; fax (11) 2216627; e-mail agre-min@syriatel.net; internet www.syrianagriculture.org.

Ministry of Awqaf (Islamic Endowments): Rukeneddin, Damascus; tel. (11) 4419079; fax (11) 419969.

Ministry of Communications: nr Majlis ash-Sha'ab, Damascus; tel. (11) 2227033; fax (11) 2246403.

Ministry of Construction: rue Sa'dallah al-Jaberi, Damascus; tel. (11) 2223595.

Ministry of Culture: rue George Haddad, ar-Rawda, Damascus; tel. (11) 3331556; fax (11) 3320804.

Ministry of Defence: place Omayad, Damascus; tel. (11) 7770700.

Ministry of Economy and Foreign Trade: rue Maysaloun, Damascus; tel. (11) 2213514; fax (11) 2225695; e-mail econ-min@net.sy; internet www.syrecon.org.

Ministry of Education: rue Shahbander, al-Masraa, Damascus; tel. (11) 4444703; fax (11) 4420435; internet www.syrianeducation.org.

Ministry of Electricity: BP 4900, rue al-Kouatly, Damascus; tel. (11) 2223086; fax (11) 2223686.

Ministry of Finance: BP 13136, rue Jule Jammal, Damascus; tel. (11) 2239624; fax (11) 2224701; e-mail mof@net.sy.

Ministry of Foreign Affairs: ave Shora, Muhajireen, Damascus; tel. (11) 3331200; fax (11) 3320686.

Ministry of Health: rue Majlis ash-Sha'ab, Damascus; tel. (11) 3311020; fax (11) 3311114; e-mail health-min@net.sy.

Ministry of Higher Education: ave Kasem Amin, ar-Rawda, Damascus; tel. (11) 3330700; fax (11) 3337719.

Ministry of Housing and Utilities: place Yousuf al-Azmeh, as-Salheyeh, Damascus; tel. (11) 2217571; fax (11) 2217570; e-mail mhu@net.sy.

Ministry of Industry: BP 12835, rue Maysaloun, Damascus; tel. (11) 2231834; fax (11) 2231096; e-mail min-industry@syriatel.net; internet www.syr-industry.org.

Ministry of Information: Imm. Dar al-Baath, Autostrade Mezzeh, Damascus; tel. (11) 6622141; fax (11) 6617665; e-mail moi@net.sy; internet www.moi-syria.com.

Ministry of the Interior: rue al-Bahsah, al-Marjeh, Damascus; tel. (11) 2238682; fax (11) 2246921.

Ministry of Irrigation: rue Fardoss; tel. (11) 2212741; fax (11) 3320691.

Ministry of Justice: rue an-Nasr, Damascus; tel. (11) 2214105; fax (11) 2246250.

Ministry of Labour and Social Affairs: place Yousuf al-Azmeh, as-Salheyeh, Damascus; tel. (11) 2210355; fax (11) 2247499.

Ministry of Petroleum and Mineral Resources: BP 40, al-Adawi, Insha'at, Damascus; tel. (11) 4451624; fax (11) 4463942; e-mail mopmr@net.sy; internet www.mopmr-sy.org.

Ministry of Supply and Internal Trade: opposite Majlis ash-Sha'ab, as-Salheyeh, Damascus; tel. (11) 2219044; fax (11) 2219803.

Ministry of Tourism: Barada St, Damascus; tel. (11) 2233183; e-mail min-tourism@mail.sy; internet www.syriatourism.org.

Ministry of Transport: BP 134, rue al-Jalaa, Damascus; tel. (11) 3336801; fax (11) 3323317; internet www.min-trans.net.

Legislature

MAJLIS ASH-SHA'AB
(People's Assembly)

Speaker: MUHAMMAD NAJI AL-OTRI.

Election, 2 and 3 March 2003

Party	Seats
National Progressive Front*	167
Independents	83
Total	250

* The National Progressive Front reportedly comprised seven political parties, including the Baath Party, Communist Party, Arab Socialist Unionist Party, Syrian Arab Socialist Union Party, Arab Socialist Party and Socialist Unionist Democratic Party.

Political Organizations

The National Progressive Front (NPF): headed by President Assad, was formed in March 1972 by the grouping of the following five parties.

Arab Socialist Party: Damascus; a breakaway socialist party; contested the 1994 election to the People's Assembly as two factions; Leader ABD AL-GHANI KANNOUT.

Arab Socialist Unionist Party: Damascus; Leader SAMI SOUFAN; Sec.-Gen. SAFWAN QUDSI.

Baath Arab Socialist Party: National Command, BP 9389, Autostrade Mezzeh, Damascus; tel. (11) 6622142; fax (11) 6622099; e-mail baath-n@net.sy; internet www.albaath.com; Arab nationalist socialist party; f. 1947; result of merger of the Arab Revival (Baath) Movement (f. 1940) and the Arab Socialist Party (f. 1940); brs in most Arab countries; in power since 1963; supports creation of a unified Arab socialist society; Sec.-Gen. Lt-Gen. BASHAR AL-ASSAD; Asst Sec.-Gen. ABDULLAH AL-AHMAR; Regional Asst Sec.-Gen. Dr SULEIMAN QADDAH; more than 800,000 mems in Syria.

Communist Party of Syria: Damascus; tel. (11) 448243; f. 1924; until 1943 part of joint Communist Party of Syria and Lebanon; Sixth Party Congress January 1987; contested the 1994 election to the People's Assembly as two factions; Sec.-Gen. YOUSUF FAISAL; Sec.-Gen. of Political Bureau RIAD AT-TURK.

Syrian Arab Socialist Union Party: Damascus; tel. (11) 239305; Nasserite; Sec.-Gen. SAFWAN KOUDSI.

A sixth party, the **Socialist Unionist Democratic Party,** has contested elections held to the People's Assembly since 1990 as a member of the National Progressive Front. There is also a **Marxist-Leninist Communist Action Party,** which regards itself as independent of all Arab regimes.

An illegal Syrian-based organization, the **Islamic Movement for Change (IMC)** claimed responsibility for a bomb attack in Damascus in December 1996.

Two new political organizations were formed in early 2001: the **Grouping for Democracy and Unity** (nationalist; Sec.-Gen. MUHAMMAD SAWWAN) and the **Movement for Social Peace** (pro-democratic; Leader RIAD SEIF); however, the latter was reportedly disbanded later that year.

Diplomatic Representation

EMBASSIES IN SYRIA

Afghanistan: BP 12217, ave Secretariat, West Villas, Mezzeh, Damascus; tel. (11) 6112910; fax (11) 6133595; Chargé d'affaires Sheikh ABDULLAH MOHSENI.

Algeria: Immeuble Noss, Raouda, Damascus; Ambassador SALEM BOUJOUMAA.

Argentina: BP 116, rue Ziad ben Abi Soufian, Raouda, Damascus; tel. (11) 3334167; fax (11) 3327326; Ambassador HERNÁN ROBERTO PLORUTTI.

Australia: Immeuble Dakkak, 128A rue Farabi, East Villas, Mezzeh, Damascus; tel. (11) 6664317; fax (11) 6621195; Ambassador JIM DALLIMORE.

Austria: BP 5634, Immeuble Mohamed Naim ad-Deker, 1 rue Farabi, East Villas, Mezzeh, Damascus; tel. (11) 6116730; fax (11) 6116734; e-mail damaskus-ob@bmaa.gv.at; Ambassador Dr MICHAEL LINHART.

Belgium: BP 31, Immeuble du Syndicat des Médecins, rue al-Jalaa, Abou Roumaneh, Damascus; tel. (11) 3332821; fax (11) 3330426; Ambassador PHILIPPE HENRI ARCQ.

Brazil: BP 2219, 7 rue Kassem Amin, Damascus; tel. (11) 3335770; fax (11) 3330054; e-mail braemsyr@net.sy; Ambassador GUILHERME FAUSTO DA CUNHA BASTOS.

Bulgaria: 4 rue Chahbandar, Damascus; Ambassador GEORGI YANKOV.

Canada: BP 3394, Damascus; tel. (11) 6116692; fax (11) 6114000; Ambassador F. D. PILLARELLA.

Chile: BP 3561, 45 rue ar-Rachid, Damascus; tel. (11) 3338443; fax (11) 3331563; e-mail echilesy@scs-net.org; Ambassador LUIS LILLO.

China, People's Republic: 83 rue Ata Ayoubi, Damascus; Ambassador SHI YANCHUN.

Cuba: Immeuble Istouani and Charbati, 40 rue ar-Rachid, Damascus; tel. (11) 3339624; fax (11) 3333802; e-mail embacubasy@net.sy; Ambassador ORLANDO LANCÍS SUÁREZ.

Cyprus: BP 9269, 106 Akram al-Ojjeh, Eastern Mezzeh-Fursan, Damascus; tel. (11) 6130812; fax (11) 6130814; e-mail cyembdam@scs-net.org; Ambassador MARIOS IERONYMIDES.

Czech Republic: BP 2249, place Abou al-Ala'a al-Maari, Damascus; tel. (11) 3331383; fax (11) 3338268; e-mail damascus@embassy.mzv.cz; Ambassador Dr JOSEF KOUTSKY.

Denmark: BP 2244, rue Chekib Arslan, Abou Roumaneh, Damascus; tel. (11) 3331008; fax (11) 3337928; e-mail dk-emb@cyberia.net.lb; Ambassador OLE WØHLERS OLSEN.

Egypt: Damascus; tel. (11) 3330756; Ambassador Dr MUHAMMAD AHMAD ISMAIL.

Finland: BP 3893, Immeuble Yacoubian, Hawakir, West Malki, Damascus; tel. (11) 3338809; fax (11) 3734740; Ambassador ANTTI KOISTINEN.

France: BP 769, rue Ata Ayoubi, Damascus; tel. (11) 3327992; fax (11) 3338632; e-mail ambafr@net.sy; internet www.amb-damas.fr; Ambassador JEAN-FRANÇOIS GIRAULT.

Germany: BP 2237, 16 rue Abd al-Mun'im Riyad, al-Malki, Damascus; tel. (11) 3323800; fax (11) 3323812; e-mail germanemb@net .sy; Ambassador EBERGARD SCHUPPIUS.

Greece: BP 30319, Immeuble Pharaon, 11 rue Farabi, Mezzeh, Damascus; tel. (11) 6113035; fax (11) 6114920; e-mail grembdam@ mail.sy; Ambassador VASSILIS PAPAIOANNOU.

Holy See: BP 2271, 1 place Ma'raket Ajnadin, Malki, Damascus (Apostolic Nunciature); tel. (11) 3332601; fax (11) 3327550; e-mail noncesy@mail.sy; Apostolic Nuncio Most Rev. DIEGO CAUSERO (Titular Archbishop of Grado).

Hungary: BP 2607, 102 rue al-Fursan, East Villas, Mezzeh, al-Akram, Damascus; tel. (11) 6110787; fax (11) 6117917; e-mail hungemb@net.sy; Ambassador BALÁZS BOKOR.

India: BP 685, Immeuble Yassin Noueilati, 40/46 ave Adnan al-Malki, Damascus; tel. (11) 3739082; fax (11) 3326231; e-mail indemcom@scs-net.org; Ambassador ARIF S. KHAN.

Indonesia: BP 3530, 10 rue as-Salam 17, Mezzeh Eastern Villa, Damascus; tel. (11) 6119630; fax (11) 6119632; e-mail kbridams@ cyberia.net.lb; internet www.welcome.to/kbri-damascus; Ambassador ZARKOWI SOEJOETI.

Iran: Autostrade Mezzeh, nr ar-Razi Hospital, Damascus; Ambassador Hojatoleslam MUHAMMAD HASSAN AKHTARI.

Italy: 82 ave al-Mansour, Damascus; tel. (11) 3338338; fax (11) 3320325; e-mail italemb@net.sy; internet www.ambitsir.org; Ambassador LAURA MIRACHIAN.

Japan: 15 ave al-Jala'a, Damascus; tel. (11) 339421; Ambassador RYUJI ONODERA.

Jordan: rue Abou Roumaneh, Damascus; tel. (11) 3334642; fax (11) 3336741; Ambassador Dr SHAKER ARABIAT.

Korea, Democratic People's Republic: rue Fares al-Khouri-Jisr Tora, Damascus; Ambassador JONG CHUN GUN.

Kuwait: rue Ibrahim Hanano, Damascus; Ambassador AHMAD ABD AL-AZIZ AL-JASSEM.

Libya: Abou Roumaneh, Damascus; Head of People's Bureau AHMAD ABD AS-SALAM BIN KHAYAL.

Mauritania: ave al-Jala'a, rue Karameh, Damascus; Ambassador MUHAMMAD MAHMOUD OULD WEDDADY.

Morocco: rue Farabi Villas Est, Mezzeh, Damascus; tel. (11) 6110451; Ambassador IDRIFF DHAHAQ.

Netherlands: BP 702, Immeuble Tello, rue al-Jalaa, Abou Roumaneh, Damascus; tel. (11) 3335119; fax (11) 3339369; Ambassador R. VAN SCHREVEN.

Norway: BP 7703, rue Ahmad Shawki; tel. (11) 3322072; fax (11) 3337114; e-mail emb.damas@mfa.no; Ambassador SVEIN SEVJE.

Oman: BP 9635, rue Ghazzawi, West Villas, Mezzeh, Damascus; tel. (11) 6110408; fax (11) 6110944; Ambassador Sheikh HILLAL BIN SALIM AS-SIYABI.

Pakistan: BP 9284, rue al-Farabi, East Villas, Mezzeh, Damascus; tel. (11) 6132694; fax (11) 6132662; Ambassador AFZAL AKBAR KHAN.

Panama: BP 2548, Apt 7, Immeuble az-Zein, rue al-Bizm, Malki, Damascus; tel. (11) 224743; Chargé d'affaires CARLOS A. DE GRACIA.

Poland: BP 501, rue George Haddad, Abou Roumaneh, Damascus; tel. (11) 3333010; fax (11) 3315318; e-mail dampol@cyberia.net.lb; Ambassador JACEK CHODOROWICZ.

Qatar: BP 4188, 20 Immeuble Allawi, place Madfa, Abou Roumaneh, Damascus; tel. (11) 336717; Ambassador FAHD FAHD AL-KHATER.

Romania: BP 4454, 8 rue Ibrahim Hanano, Damascus; tel. (11) 3327570; fax (11) 3327572; e-mail ro.dam@net.sy; Ambassador ION DOBRECI.

Russia: rue d'Alep, Boustan al-Kouzbari, Damascus; Ambassador ALEKSANDR I. ZOTOV.

Saudi Arabia: ave al-Jala'a, Damascus; Ambassador ABDULLAH BIN SALEH AL-FADL.

Serbia and Montenegro: BP 739, ave al-Jala'a, Damascus; tel. (11) 3336222; fax (11) 3333690; Chargé d'affaires JOVAN VUJASINOVIĆ.

Slovakia: BP 33115, place Mezzeh, rue ash-Shafei, East Villas, Damascus; tel. (11) 6132114; fax (11) 6132598; e-mail slovembdk@ net.sy; Ambassador IVAN ZACHAR.

Somalia: ave Ata Ayoubi, Damascus; Ambassador (vacant).

Spain: BP 392, rue ash-Shafi, Mezzeh East, Damascus; fax (11) 6132941; Ambassador MANUEL CACHO.

Sudan: Damascus; tel. (11) 6111036; fax (11) 6112904; e-mail sud-emb@net.sy; Ambassador ABD AL-HAFIZ IBRAHIM.

Sweden: BP 4266, rue Chakib Arslan, Abou Roumaneh, Damascus; tel. (11) 3327261; fax (11) 3327749; e-mail ambassaden.damaskus@ foreign.ministry.se; Ambassador VIOLA FURUBJELKE.

Switzerland: BP 234, 2 rue ash-Shafi, East Villas, Mezzeh, Damascus; tel. (11) 6111972; fax (11) 6111976; e-mail swissemb@net.sy; Ambassador ROBERT MAYOR.

Tunisia: BP 4114, 6 rue ash-Shafi, blvd Fahim, Mezzeh, Damascus; tel. (11) 6132700; fax (11) 6132704; e-mail at.damas@net.sy; Ambassador MUHAMMAD HASSAIRI.

Turkey: BP 3738, 56–58 ave Ziad bin Abou Soufian, Damascus; tel. (11) 3331370; fax (11) 3339243; e-mail sambe@mfa.gov.tr; Ambassador OGUZ CELIKKOL.

Ukraine: Mezzeh, East Villas, 14 rue as-Salam, Damascus; tel. (11) 6113016; fax (11) 6121355; e-mail ukrembassy@mail.sy.

United Arab Emirates: Immeuble Housami, 62 rue Raouda, Damascus; Ambassador SALIM RASHID AL-AQROUBI.

United Kingdom: BP 37, Immeuble Kotob, 11 rue Muhammad Kurd Ali, Malki, Damascus; tel. (11) 3739241; fax (11) 3731600; e-mail british.embassy.damascus@fco.gov.uk; Ambassador HENRY G. HOGGER.

USA: BP 29, 2 rue al-Mansour, Damascus; tel. (11) 33331324; fax (11) 2247938; e-mail acsdamascus@state.gov; internet www .usembassy.state.gov/damascus; Ambassador THEODORE KATTOUF.

Venezuela: BP 2403, Immeuble at-Tabbah, rue Lisaneddin bin al-Khateb, place Rauda, Damascus; tel. (11) 3336863; fax (11) 3333203; e-mail embavenez@net.sy; Ambassador IVAN URBINA ORTIZ.

Viet Nam: Damascus; tel. (11) 333008; Ambassador LE THANH TAM.

Yemen: Abou Roumaneh, Charkassieh, Damascus; Ambassador ABDULLAH HUSSAIN BARAKAT.

Note: Syria and Lebanon have very close relations but do not exchange formal ambassadors.

Judicial System

The Courts of Law in Syria are principally divided into two juridical court systems: Courts of General Jurisdiction and Administrative Courts. Since 1973 the Supreme Constitutional Court has been established as the paramount body of the Syrian judicial structure.

THE SUPREME CONSTITUTIONAL COURT

This is the highest court in Syria. It has specific jurisdiction over: (i) judicial review of the constitutionality of laws and legislative decrees; (ii) investigation of charges relating to the legality of the election of members of the Majlis ash-Sha'ab (People's Assembly); (iii) trial of infractions committed by the President of the Republic in the exercise of his functions; (iv) resolution of positive and negative jurisdictional conflicts and determination of the competent court between the different juridical court systems, as well as other bodies exercising judicial competence. The Supreme Constitutional Court is composed of a Chief Justice and four Justices. They are appointed by decree of the President of the Republic for a renewable period of four years.

Chief Justice of the Supreme Court: NASRAT MOUNLA-HAYDAR, Damascus; tel. (11) 3331902.

COURTS OF GENERAL JURISDICTION

The Courts of General Jurisdiction in Syria are divided into six categories: (i) The Court of Cassation; (ii) The Courts of Appeal; (iii) The Tribunals of First Instance; (iv) The Tribunals of Peace; (v) The Personal Status Courts; (vi) The Courts for Minors. Each of the above categories (except the Personal Status Courts) is divided into Civil, Penal and Criminal Chambers.

(i) The Court of Cassation: This is the highest court of general jurisdiction. Final judgments rendered by Courts of Appeal in penal and civil litigations may be petitioned to the Court of Cassation by the Defendant or the Public Prosecutor in penal and criminal litigations, and by any of the parties in interest in civil litigations, on grounds of defective application or interpretation of the law as stated in the challenged judgment, on grounds of irregularity of form or procedure, or violation of due process, and on grounds of defective reasoning of judgment rendered. The Court of Cassation is composed of a President, seven Vice-Presidents and 31 other Justices (Councillors).

(ii) The Courts of Appeal: Each court has geographical jurisdiction over one governorate (Mouhafazat). Each court is divided into Penal and Civil Chambers. There are Criminal Chambers which try felonies only. The Civil Chambers hear appeals filed against judgments rendered by the Tribunals of First Instance and the Tribunals of Peace. Each Court of Appeal is composed of a President and sufficient numbers of Vice-Presidents (Presidents of Chambers) and Superior Judges (Councillors). There are 54 Courts of Appeal.

(iii) The Tribunals of First Instance: In each governorate there are one or more Tribunals of First Instance, each of which is divided into several Chambers for penal and civil litigations. Each Chamber is composed of one judge. There are 72 Tribunals of First Instance.

(iv) The Tribunals of Peace: In the administrative centre of each governorate, and in each district, there are one or more Tribunals of Peace, which have jurisdiction over minor civil and penal litigations. There are 227 Tribunals of Peace.

(v) Personal Status Courts: These courts deal with marriage, divorce, etc. For Muslims each court consists of one judge, the 'Qadi Shari'i'. For Druzes there is one court consisting of one judge, the 'Qadi Mazhabi'. For non-Muslim communities there are courts for Roman Catholics, Orthodox believers, Protestants and Jews.

(vi) Courts for Minors: The constitution, officers, sessions, jurisdiction and competence of these courts are determined by a special law.

PUBLIC PROSECUTION

Public prosecution is headed by the Attorney-General, assisted by a number of Senior Deputy and Deputy Attorneys-General, and a sufficient number of chief prosecutors, prosecutors and assistant prosecutors. Public prosecution is represented at all levels of the Courts of General Jurisdiction in all criminal and penal litigations and also in certain civil litigations as required by the law. Public prosecution controls and supervises enforcement of penal judgments.

ADMINISTRATIVE COURTS SYSTEM

The Administrative Courts have jurisdiction over litigations involving the state or any of its governmental agencies. The Administrative Courts system is divided into two courts: the Administrative Courts and the Judicial Administrative Courts, of which the paramount body is the High Administrative Court.

MILITARY COURTS

The Military Courts deal with criminal litigations against military personnel of all ranks and penal litigations against officers only. There are two military courts: one in Damascus, the other in Aleppo. Each court is composed of three military judges. There are other military courts, consisting of one judge, in every governorate, which deal with penal litigations against military personnel below the rank of officer. The different military judgments can be petitioned to the Court of Cassation.

Religion

In religion the majority of Syrians follow a form of Islamic Sunni orthodoxy. There are also a considerable number of religious minorities: Shi'a Muslims; Ismaili Muslims; the Ismaili of the Salamiya district, whose spiritual head is the Aga Khan; a large number of Druzes, the Nusairis or Alawites of the Jebel Ansariyeh (a schism of the Shi'ite branch of Islam, to which President Assad belongs, who comprise about 11% of the population) and the Yezidis of the Jebel Sinjar, and a minority of Christians.

The Constitution states only that 'Islam shall be the religion of the head of the state'. The original draft of the 1973 Constitution made no reference to Islam at all, and this clause was inserted only as a compromise after public protest. The Syrian Constitution is thus unique among the constitutions of Arab states (excluding Lebanon) with a clear Muslim majority in not enshrining Islam as the religion of the state itself.

ISLAM

Grand Mufti: AHMAD KUFTARO.

CHRISTIANITY

Orthodox Churches

Greek Orthodox Patriarchate: Patriarch of Antioch and all the Orient, BP 9, Damascus; His Beatitude IGNATIUS HAZIM; has jurisdiction over Syria, Lebanon, Iran and Iraq.

Syrian Orthodox Patriarchate: BP 914, Bab Touma, Damascus; tel. (11) 447036; Syrian Orthodox Patriarch His Holiness IGNATIUS ZAKKA I IWAS (Patriarch of Antioch and All the East); the Syrian Orthodox Church includes one Catholicose (of the East), 30 Metro-

politans and one Bishop, and has an estimated 3m. adherents throughout the world.

The Armenian Apostolic Church is also represented in Syria.

The Roman Catholic Church

Armenian Rite

Patriarchal Exarchate of Syria: Exarchat Patriarcal Arménien Catholique, BP 22281, Bab Touma, Damascus; tel. (11) 5413820; fax (11) 5419431; f. 1985; represents the Patriarch of Cilicia (resident in Beirut, Lebanon); 4,000 adherents (31 December 2002); Exarch Patriarchal Bishop JOSEPH ARNAOUTIAN.

Archdiocese of Aleppo: Archevêché Arménien Catholique, BP 97, rue 33 at-Tilal, Aleppo; tel. (21) 2213946; fax (21) 2235303; e-mail armen.cath@mail.sy; 17,000 adherents (31 December 2000); Archbishop BOUTROS MARAYATI.

Diocese of Kamichlié: Evêché Arménien Catholique, BP 17, Al-Qamishli; tel. (53) 424211; fax (53) 426211; 4,000 adherents (31 December 2000).

Chaldean Rite

Diocese of Aleppo: Evêché Chaldéen Catholique, BP 4643, 1 rue Patriarche Elias IV Mouawwad, Soulémaniyé, Aleppo; tel. (21) 4441660; fax (21) 4600800; 15,000 adherents (31 December 2000); Bishop ANTOINE AUDO.

Latin Rite

Apostolic Vicariate of Aleppo: BP 327, 19 rue Antaki, Aleppo; tel. (21) 2210204; fax (21) 2219031; e-mail vicariatlatin@mail.sy; f. 1644; 10,000 adherents (31 December 2000); Vicar Apostolic GIUSEPPE NAZZARO (Titular Bishop of Forma).

Maronite Rite

Archdiocese of Aleppo: Archevêché Maronite, BP 203, 57 rue Fares-El-Khoury, Aleppo; tel. (21) 2248048; fax (21) 2248048; 4,105 adherents (31 December 2000); Archbishop YOUSSEF ANIS ABI-AAD.

Archdiocese of Damascus: Archevêché Maronite, BP 2179, 6 rue ad-Deir, Bab Touma, Damascus; tel. (11) 5430129; fax (11) 5435105; 8,000 adherents (31 December 2000); Archbishop RAYMOND EID.

Diocese of Latakia: Evêché Maronite, BP 161, rue Hamrat, Tartous; tel. (43) 223433; fax (43) 322939; 28,000 adherents (31 December 2000); Bishop MASSOUD MASSOUD.

Melkite Rite

Melkite-Greek-Catholic Patriarchate: Patriarcat Grec-Melkite Catholique, BP 22249, 12 ave az-Zeitoon, Bab Charki, Damascus; or BP 70071, Antélias, Lebanon; tel. (11) 5433129; fax (11) 5431266 (Damascus); tel. or (4) 413111; fax (4) 418113; e-mail (Lebanon) gcp@pgc-lb.org(Antélias); jurisdiction over 1.5m. Melkites throughout the world (including 215,000 in Syria); Patriarch of Antioch, Alexandria and Jerusalem S. B. GREGOIRE LAHAM III; The Melkite Church includes the patriarchal sees of Damascus, Cairo and Jerusalem and four other archdioceses in Syria; seven archdioceses in Lebanon; one in Jordan; one in Israel; and six Eparchies (in the USA, Brazil, Canada, Australia, Venezuela, Argentina and Mexico).

Archdiocese of Aleppo: Archevêché Grec-Catholique, BP 146, place Farhat, Aleppo; tel. (21) 2213218; fax (21) 2223106; e-mail gr .melkcath@mail.sy; 20,000 adherents (31 December 2000); Archbishop JEAN-CLÉMENT JEANBART.

Archdiocese of Busra and Hauran: Archevêché Grec-Catholique, Khabab, Hauran; tel. (15) 855012; 27,000 adherents (31 December 2000); Archbishop BOULOS NASSIF BORKHOCHE.

Archdiocese of Homs: Archevêché Grec-Catholique, BP 1525, rue El-Bahri, Boustan ad-Diwan, Homs; tel. (31) 482587; fax (31) 464582; e-mail melkiteh@scs-net.org; 48,000 adherents (31 December 2000); Archbishop ABRAHAM NEHMÉ.

Archdiocese of Latakia: Archevêché Grec-Catholique, BP 151, rue al-Moutannabi, Latakia; tel. (41) 460777; fax (41) 467002; 10,000 adherents (31 December 2000); Archbishop NICOLAS SAWAF.

Syrian Rite

Archdiocese of Aleppo: Archevêché Syrien Catholique, 1 rue Ibn ar-Rumi, Azizié, Aleppo; tel. (21) 2241200; fax (21) 2246651; 8,000 adherents (31 December 2000); Archbishop ANTOINE CHAHDA.

Archdiocese of Damascus: Archevêché Syrien Catholique, BP 2129, 157 rue Al-Mustaqeem, Bab Charki, Damascus; tel. and fax (11) 5432312; e-mail ftouma@mail.sy; 6,400 adherents (31 December 2000); Archbishop GREGORIOS ELIAS TABÉ.

Archdiocese of Hassaké-Nisibi: Archevêché Syrien Catholique, BP 6, Hassaké; tel. (52) 320812; fax (52) 316340; 6,320 adherents (31 December 2000); Archbishop JACQUES BEHNAN HINDO.

Archdiocese of Homs: Archevêché Syrien Catholique, BP 368, rue Hamidieh, Homs; tel. (31) 221575; 10,000 adherents (31 December 2000); Archbishop Théophile Georges Kassab.

The Anglican Communion

Within the Episcopal Church in Jerusalem and the Middle East, Syria forms part of the diocese of Jerusalem (see the chapter on Israel).

Protestant

National Evangelical Synod of Syria and Lebanon: BP 70890, Antélias, Lebanon; tel. (04) 525030; fax (04) 411184; e-mail nessl@minero.net; f. 1920; 80,000 adherents (2003); Gen. Sec. Rev. Adeeb Awad.

Union of the Armenian Evangelical Churches in the Near East: BP 110-377, Beirut, Lebanon; tel. 565628; fax 565629; e-mail uaecne@cyberia.net.lb; f. 1846; in Turkey; comprises about 30 Armenian Evangelical Churches in Syria, Lebanon, Egypt, Cyprus, Greece, Iran, Turkey and Australia; 7,500 mems (1995); Pres. Rev. Megrdich Karagoezian; Office Dir Pastor Sebouh Terzian.

The Press

Since the Baath Arab Socialist Party came to power, the structure of the press has been modified according to socialist patterns. Most publications are issued by political, religious or professional associations (such as trade unions), and several are published by government ministries. Anyone wishing to establish a new paper or periodical must apply for a licence.

The major dailies are *Al-Baath* (the organ of the party), *Tishrin* and *Ath-Thawra* in Damascus, *Al-Jamahir al-Arabia* in Aleppo, and *Al-Fida'* in Hama.

PRINCIPAL DAILIES

Al-Baath (Renaissance): BP 9389, Autostrade Mezzeh, Damascus; tel. (11) 6622142; fax (11) 6622099; e-mail baath-n@net.sy; f. 1946; morning; Arabic; organ of the Baath Arab Socialist Party; Gen. Dir and Chief Editor Turki Saqr; circ. 45,000.

Barq ash-Shimal (The Syrian Telegraph): rue Aziziyah, Aleppo; morning; Arabic; Editor Maurice Djandji; circ. 6,400.

Al-Fida' (Redemption): Al-Wihdat Press, Printing and Publishing Organization, BP 2448, Dawar Kafr Soussat, Damascus; tel. (11) 225219; morning; Arabic; political; publishing concession holder Osman Alouini; Editor A. Aulwani; circ. 4,000.

Al-Jamahir al-Arabia (The Arab People): United Association of Journalists, BP 2448, Damascus; tel. (21) 214309; fax (21) 214308; Arabic; political; Chief Editor Mortada Bakach; circ. 10,000.

Al-Oroubat: Al-Wihdat Press, Printing and Publishing Organization, BP 2448, Dawar Kafr Soussat, Damascus; tel. (11) 225219; morning; Arabic; circ. 5,000.

Ash-Shabab (Youth): rue at-Tawil, Aleppo; morning; Arabic; Editor Muhammad Talas; circ. 9,000.

Syria Times: Tishrin Foundation for Press and Publication, BP 5452, Corniche Meedan, Damascus; tel. (11) 2247359; fax (11) 2247049; e-mail syriatimes@teshreen.com; internet www.teshreen.com/syriatimes; English; Editor Fouad Mardoud; circ. 15,000.

Ath-Thawra (Revolution): United Association of Journalists, BP 2448, Damascus; tel. (11) 2210850; fax (11) 2216851; e-mail thawra@net.sy; internet www.thawra.com; morning; Arabic; political; Editor-in-Chief (vacant); circ. 40,000.

Tishrin (October): Tishrin Foundation for Press and Publication, BP 5452, Corniche Meedan, Damascus; tel. (11) 2131100; fax (11) 2231374; e-mail daily@teshreen.com; Arabic; Chief Editor Khalaf al-Jaraad; circ. 50,000.

Al-Wihdat (Unity): Al-Wihdat Press, Printing and Publishing Organization, Latakia; Arabic.

WEEKLIES AND FORTNIGHTLIES

Al-Ajoua' (The Air): Compagnie de l'Aviation Arabe Syrienne, BP 417, Damascus; fortnightly; Arabic; aviation; Editor Ahmad Allouche.

Ad-Doumari (Lamplighter): Damascus; f. 2001; weekly; Arabic; political satire; privately-owned; Publr Ali Farzat.

Al-Esbou ar-Riadi (The Sports Week): Immeuble Tibi, ave Fardoss, Damascus; weekly; Arabic; sports; Asst Dir and Editor Hasran al-Bounni; circ. 14,000.

Al-Fursan (The Cavalry): Damascus; Arabic; political magazine; Editor Rifaat al-Assad.

Homs: Homs; weekly; Arabic; literary; Publisher and Dir Adib Kaba; Editor Philippe Kaba.

Al-Iqtisadiya: f. 2001; weekly; Arabic; economic; privately-owned; Editor Waddah Abd ar-Rabbo.

Jaysh ash-Sha'ab (The People's Army): Ministry of Defence, BP 3320, blvd Palestine, Damascus; f. 1946; fortnightly; Arabic; army magazine; published by the Political Department of the Syrian Army.

Kifah al-Oummal al-Ishtiraki (The Socialist Workers' Struggle): Fédération Générale des Syndicats des Ouvriers, rue Qanawat, Damascus; weekly; Arabic; labour; published by General Federation of Labour Unions; Editor Said al-Hamami.

Al-Masirah (Progress): Damascus; weekly; Arabic; political; published by Federation of Youth Organizations.

Al-Maukef ar-Riadi (Sport Stance): Al-Wihdat Press, Printing and Publishing Organization, BP 2448, Dawar Kafr Soussat, Damascus; tel. (11) 225219; weekly; Arabic; sports; published by Al-Wihdat Press, Printing and Publishing Organization; circ. 50,000.

An-Nas (The People): BP 926, Aleppo; f. 1953; weekly; Arabic; Publisher Victor Kalous.

Nidal al-Fellahin (Peasants' Struggle): Fédération Générale des Laboureurs, BP 9389, Autostrade Mezzeh, Damascus; weekly; Arabic; peasant workers; Editor Mansour Abu al-Hosn; circ. 8,100.

Ar-Riada (Sport): BP 292, near Electricity Institute, Damascus; weekly; Arabic; sports; Dir Noureddine Rial; Publisher and Editor Ourfane Ubari.

As-Sakafat al-Usbouiya (Weekly Culture): BP 2570, Soukak as-Sakr, Damascus; weekly; Arabic; cultural; Publisher, Dir and Editor Madhat Akkache.

Sawt ash-Shaab (Voice of the People): Damascus; f. 1937; but publication suspended in 1939, 1941, 1947 and 1958; relaunched in 2001; fortnightly; Arabic; organ of the Communist Party of Syria.

Tishrin al–Usbouiya (October Weekly): Damascus; e-mail weekly@teshreen.com; weekly.

Al-Wehdawi (Unionist): Damascus; f. 2001; weekly; Arabic; organ of the Arab Socialist Unionist Party.

Al-Yanbu al-Jadid (New Spring): Immeuble Al-Awkaf, Homs; weekly; Arabic; literary; Publisher, Dir and Editor Mamdou al-Kousseir.

OTHER PERIODICALS

Al-Arabieh (The Arab Lady): Syrian Women's Association, BP 3207, Damascus; tel. (11) 3316560; monthly; Editor S. Bakour.

Ad-Dad: rue Tital, Wakf al-Moiriné Bldg, Aleppo; monthly; Arabic; literary; Dir Riad Hallak; Publisher and Editor Abdullah Yarki Hallak.

Ecos: BP 3320, Damascus; monthly; Spanish; general.

Al-Fikr al-Askari (The Military Idea): BP 4259, blvd Palestine, Damascus; f. 1950; 6 a year; Arabic; official military review published by the Political Dept of the Syrian Army; Editor Nakhle Kallas.

Flash: BP 3320, Damascus; monthly; English and French; general.

Al-Ghad (Tomorrow): Association of Red Cross and Crescent, BP 6095, rue Maysat, Damascus; tel. (11) 2242552; fax (11) 7777040; monthly; environmental health; Editor K. Abed-Rabou.

Al-Irshad az-Zirai (Agricultural Information): Ministry of Agriculture and Agrarian Reform, rue Jabri, Damascus; tel. (11) 2213613; fax (11) 2216627; 6 a year; Arabic; agriculture.

Al-Jundi al-Arabi (The Arab Soldier): BP 3320, blvd Palestine, Damascus; monthly; published by the Political Department of the Syrian Army.

Al-Kalima (The Word): Al-Kalima Association, Aleppo; monthly; Arabic; religious; Publisher and Editor Fathalla Sakal.

Al-Kanoun (The Law): Ministry of Justice, rue an-Nasreh, Damascus; tel. (11) 2214105; fax (11) 2246250; monthly; Arabic; juridical.

Al-Maaloumatieh (Information): National Information Centre, BP 11323, Damascus; tel. (11) 2127551; fax (11) 2127648; e-mail nice@net.sy; f. 1994; quarterly; computer magazine; Editor Abd al-Majid ar-Rifai; circ. 10,000.

Al-Ma'arifa (Knowledge): Ministry of Culture, rue ar-Rouda, Damascus; tel. (11) 3336963; f. 1962; monthly; Arabic; literary; Editor Abd al-Karim Nasif; circ. 7,500.

Al-Majalla al-Batriarquia (The Magazine of the Patriarchate): Syrian Orthodox Patriarchate, BP 914, Damascus; tel. (11) 4447036; f. 1962; monthly; Arabic; religious; Editor Samir Abdoh; circ. 15,000.

Al-Majalla at-Tibbiya al-Arabiyya (Arab Medical Magazine): rue al-Jala'a, Damascus; monthly; Arabic; published by Arab Medical Commission; Dir Dr Y. SAKA; Editor Prof. ADNAN TAKRITI.

Majallat Majma' al-Lughat al-Arabiyya bi-Dimashq (Magazine of the Arab Language Academy of Damascus): Arab Academy of Damascus, BP 327, Damascus; tel. (11) 3713145; fax (11) 3733363; e-mail mla@net.sy; f. 1921; quarterly; Arabic; Islamic culture and Arabic literature, Arabic scientific and cultural terminology; Chief Editor Dr SHAKER FAHAM; circ. 1,600.

Al-Mawkif al-Arabi (The Arab Situation): Ittihab al-Kuttab al-Arab, rue Murshid Khatir, Damascus; monthly; Arabic; literary.

Monthly Survey of Arab Economics: BP 2306, Damascus; BP 6068, Beirut; f. 1958; monthly; English and French editions; published by Centre d'Etudes et de Documentation Economiques, Financières et Sociales; Dir Dr CHAFIC AKHRAS.

Al-Mouallem al-Arabi (The Arab Teacher): National Union of Teachers, BP 2842-3034, Damascus; tel. (11) 225219; f. 1948; monthly; Arabic; educational and cultural.

Al-Mouhandis al-Arabi (The Arab Engineer): Order of Syrian Engineers and Architects, BP 2336, Immeuble Dar al-Mouhandisen, place Azme, Damascus; tel. (11) 2214916; fax (11) 2216948; e-mail lbosea@net.sy; f. 1961; 4 a year; Arabic; scientific and cultural; Dir Eng. M. FAYEZ MAHFOUZ; Chief Editor Dr Eng. AHMAD AL-GHAFARI; circ. 50,000.

Al-Munadel (The Militant): c/o BP 11512, Damascus; fax (11) 2126935; f. 1965; monthly; Arabic; magazine of Baath Arab Socialist Party; Dir Dr FAWWAZ SAYYAGH; circ. 100,000.

An-Nashra al-Iktissad (Economic Bulletin): Damascus Chamber of Commerce; tel. (11) 2218339; fax (11) 2225874; e-mail dcc@net.sy; f. 1922; quarterly; finance and investment; Editor GHASSAN KALLA; circ. 3,000.

Risalat al-Kimia (Chemistry Report): BP 669, Immeuble al-Abid, Damascus; monthly; Arabic; scientific; Publisher, Dir and Editor HASSAN AS-SAKA.

Saut al-Forat: Deir ez-Zor; monthly; Arabic; literary; Publisher, Dir and Editor ABD AL-KADER AYACHE.

Ash-Shourta (The Police): Directorate of Public Affairs and Moral Guidance, Damascus; monthly; Arabic; juridical.

As-Sinaa (Industry): Damascus Chamber of Commerce, BP 1305, rue Mou'awiah, Harika, Damacus; tel. (11) 2222205; fax (11) 2245981; monthly; commerce, industry and management; Editor Y. HINDI.

Souriya al-Arabiyya (Arab Syria): Ministry of Information, Immeuble Dar al-Baath, Autostrade Mezzeh, Damascus; tel. (11) 6622141; fax (11) 6617665; monthly; publicity; in four languages.

At-Tamaddon al-Islami (Islamic Civilization Society): Darwichiyah, Damascus; tel. (11) 2215120; fax (11) 2233815; e-mail raweyah@cyberia.net.lb; f. 1932; monthly; Arabic; religious; published by At-Tamaddon al-Islami Association; Pres. of Asscn AHMAD MOUAZ AL-KHATIB.

At-Taqa Wattanmiya (Energy and Expansion): BP 7748, rue al-Moutanabbi, Damascus; tel. (11) 233529; monthly; Arabic; published by the Syrian Petroleum Co.

Al-Yakza (The Awakening): Al-Yakza Association, BP 6677, rue Sisi, Aleppo; f. 1935; monthly; Arabic; literary social review of charitable institution; Dir HUSNI ABD AL-MASSIH; circ. 12,000.

Az-Zira'a (Agriculture): Ministry of Agriculture and Agrarian Reform, rue Jabri, Damascus; tel. (11) 2213613; fax (11) 2244023; f. 1985; monthly; Arabic; agriculture; circ. 12,000.

PRESS AGENCIES

Syrian Arab News Agency (SANA): BP 2661, Baramka, Damascus; tel. (11) 2228239; fax (11) 2220365; e-mail sana@net.sy; internet www.sana-syria.com; f. 1966; supplies bulletins on Syrian news to foreign news agencies; 14 offices abroad; 14 foreign correspondents; Dir-Gen. GHAZI AD-DIB.

Foreign Bureaux

Agencia EFE (Spain): Damascus; Correspondent ZACHARIAS SARME.

Agence France-Presse (AFP): BP 2400, Immeuble Adel Charaj, place du 17 avril, Damascus; tel. (11) 428253; Correspondent JOSEPH GHASI.

Agenzia Nazionale Stampa Associata (ANSA) (Italy): Hotel Méridien, BP 2712, Damascus; tel. (11) 233116; f. 1962; Correspondent ABDULLAH SAADEL.

Allgemeiner Deutscher Nachrichtendienst (ADN) (Germany): Damascus; tel. (11) 332093; Correspondent FRANK HERRMANN.

Associated Press (AP) (USA): c/o Hotel Méridien, BP 2712, Damascus; tel. (11) 233116; internet www.ap.org.

Deutsche Presse-Agentur (dpa) (Germany): c/o Hotel Méridien, BP 2712, Damascus; tel. (11) 332924.

Kuwait News Agency (KUNA) and Reuters (UK) are also represented in Syria.

Publishers

Arab Advertising Organization: BP 2842-3034, 28 rue Moutanabbi, Damascus; tel. (11) 2225219; fax (11) 2220754; e-mail sy-adv@net.sy; internet www.elan-sy.com; f. 1963; exclusive government establishment responsible for advertising; publishes *Directory of Commerce and Industry, Damascus International Fair Guide, Daily Bulletin of Official Tenders*; Dir-Gen. TALEB QADI AMIN.

Damascus University Press: Damascus; tel. (11) 2215100; fax (11) 2236010; f. 1946; arts, geography, education, history, engineering, medicine, law, sociology, social sciences; Dir HUSSEIN OMRAN.

Institut Français d'Etudes arabes de Damas: BP 344, Damascus; tel. (11) 3330214; fax (11) 3327887; e-mail ifead@net.sy; internet www.univ-aix.fr/ifead; f. 1922; sociology, anthropology, Islamic archaeology, history, language, arts, philosophy, poetry, geography, religion; Dir FLORÉAL SANAGUSTIN.

OFA-Business Consulting Center—Documents Service: BP 3550, 67 place Chahbandar, Damascus; tel. (11) 3318237; fax (11) 4426021; e-mail ofa@net.sy; internet www.ofa-holding.com; f. 1964; numerous periodicals, monographs and surveys on political and economic affairs; Dir-Gen. SAMIR A. DARWICH; has two affiliated branches, OFA-Business Consulting Centre (foreign company representation and services) and OFA-Renseignements Commerciaux (Commercial enquiries on firms and persons in Syria).

The Political Administration Press: BP 3320, blvd Palestine, Damascus; publishes *Al-Fikr al-Askari* (6 a year) and *Jaysh ash-Sha'ab* (fortnightly) and *Al-Jundi al-Arabi* (monthly).

Syrian Documentation Papers: BP 2712, Damascus; f. 1968; publishers of *Bibliography of the Middle East* (annual), *General Directory of the Press and Periodicals in the Arab World* (annual), and numerous publications on political, economic, literary and social affairs, as well as legislative texts concerning Syria and the Arab world; Dir-Gen. LOUIS FARÈS.

United Association of Journalists: BP 2448, Damascus; tel. (11) 2210850; fax (11) 2216851; publishes *Al-Jamahir al-Arabia* and *Ath-Thawra* (dailies).

Al-Wihdat Press, Printing and Publishing Organization (Institut al-Ouedha pour l'impression, édition et distribution): BP 2448, Dawar Kafr Soussat, Damascus; tel. (11) 225219; publishes *Al-Ouroubat, Al-Fida'* and *Al-Wihdat* (dailies), *al-Maukef ar-Riadi* (weekly) and other commercial publications; Dir-Gen. FAHD DIYAB.

Broadcasting and Communications

TELECOMMUNICATIONS

Syrian Telecommunications Establishment (STE): BP 11774, Autostrade Mezzeh, Damascus; tel. (11) 6122226; fax (11) 6120000; e-mail ste-gm@syriatel.net; internet www.syriatel.net; f. 1975; Chair. (vacant).

BROADCASTING

Radio

Directorate-General of Radio and Television: place Omayyad, Damascus; tel. (11) 720700; f. 1945; broadcasts in Arabic, French, English, Russian, German, Spanish, Portuguese, Hebrew, Polish, Turkish, Bulgarian; Dir-Gen. KHUDR OMRAN; Dir SAFWAN GHANIM.

Television

Directorate-General of Radio and Television: see Radio; services started in 1960; Dir-Gen. Dr FAYEZ AS-SAYEGH; Dir of Television M. ABD AS-SALAM HIJAB.

Finance

(cap. = capital; res = reserves; dep. = deposits; m.= million;
brs = branches; amounts in £S)

BANKING

Central Bank

Central Bank of Syria: BP 2254, place At-Tajrida al-Mughrabia, Damascus; tel. (11) 2212642; fax (11) 2213076; e-mail mrksyba-bn@ mail.sy; internet www.syrecon.org; f. 1956; cap. 10m., dep. 391,275m., total assets 773356m. (Dec. 2001); Gov. Dr MUHAMMAD BASHAR KABBARA; 11 brs.

Other Banks

Agricultural Co-operative Bank: BP 4325, rue at-Tajehiz, Damascus; tel. (11) 2213461; fax (11) 2241261; f. 1888; cap. 10,000m., res 671m., dep. 12,000m. (Dec. 2001); Chair. and Dir-Gen. YASSER AS-SAMOR; 106 brs.

Commercial Bank of Syria: BP 933, place Yousuf al-Azmeh, Damascus; tel. (11) 2218890; fax (11) 2216975; e-mail cbos@mail.sy; f. 1967; govt-owned bank; cap. and res 8,197m., dep. 309,545m., total assets 743,000m. (Dec. 2001); Chair. MAHMOUD NADIM MISKAL; Dep. Chair. and Gen. Man. TARREK SARRAJ; 53 brs.

Industrial Bank: BP 7578, Immeuble Dar al-Mohandessin, rue Maysaloon, Damascus; tel. (11) 2228200; fax (11) 2228412; f. 1959; nationalized bank providing finance for industry; cap. 100m.; Chair. ABD AL-QADIR OBEIDO; 13 brs.

Popular Credit Bank: BP 2841, 6e étage, Immeuble Dar al-Mohandessin, rue Maysaloon, Damascus; tel. (11) 2227604; fax (11) 2211291; f. 1967; government bank; provides loans to the services sector and is sole authorized issuer of savings certificates; cap. 25m., res 42,765m., dep. 2,313m. (Dec. 1984); Pres. and Gen. Man. MUHAMMAD HASSAN AL-HOUJJEIRI; 50 brs.

Real Estate Bank: BP 2337, place Yousuf al-Azmeh, Damascus; tel. (11) 2218602; fax (11) 2237938; e-mail reb1@net.sy; f. 1966; govt-owned bank; provides loans and grants for housing, schools, hospitals and hotel construction; cap. 1,000m. (Dec. 2001); Chair. and Gen. Man. MUHAMMAD AHMAD MAKHLOUF; 15 brs.

Syrian Lebanese Commercial Bank SAL: BP 118701-1135127, Damascus; fax (11) 2243224; Chair. and Gen. Man. MAHMOUD NADIM MISKAI.

INSURANCE

Syrian General Organization for Insurance (Syrian Insurance Co): BP 2279, 29 rue Ayyar, Damascus; tel. (11) 2218430; fax (11) 2220494; f. 1953; auth. cap. 1,000m. a nationalized company; operates throughout Syria; Chair. and Gen. Man. GHASSAN BAROUDIT; Assistant Gen. Man. and Admin. Dir SULAYMAN AL-HASSAN.

Trade and Industry

STATE ENTERPRISES

Syrian industry is almost entirely controlled and run by the State. There are national organizations responsible to the appropriate ministry for the operation of all sectors of industry, of which the following are examples:

Cotton Marketing Organization: BP 729, rue Bab al-Faraj, Aleppo; tel. (21) 2238486; fax (21) 2218617; f. 1965; governmental authority for purchase of seed cotton, ginning and sales of cotton lint; Pres. and Dir-Gen. Dr AHMAD SOUHAD GEBBARA.

General Company for Phosphate and Mines (GECOPHAM): BP 288, Homs; tel. (31) 420405; fax (31) 412961; e-mail gecopham@ net.sy; f. 1970; production and export of phosphate rock; Gen. Dir Eng. FARHAN AL-HUHSSIN.

General Organization for the Exploitation and Development of the Euphrates Basin (GOEDEB): Rakka; Dir-Gen. Dr Eng. Dr AHMAD SOUHAD GEBBARA.

General Organization for Food Industries (GOFI): BP 105, rue al-Fardous, Damascus; tel. (11) 2457008; fax (11) 2457021; e-mail foodindustry@mail.sy; internet www.syriafoods.com; f. 1975; food-processing and marketing; Chair. and Gen. Dir KHALIL JAWAD.

General Organization for the Textile Industries: BP 620, rue Fardoss, Damascus; tel. (11) 2216200; fax (11) 2216201; f. 1975; control and planning of the textile industry and supervision of textile manufacture; 13 subsidiary cos. Dir-Gen. MOUSTAFA JAWEESH.

Syrian Petroleum Company (SPC): BP 2849, rue al-Moutanabbi, Damascus; tel. (11) 2228298; fax (11) 2225648; f. 1958; state agency;

holds the oil and gas concession for all Syria; exploits the Suweidiya, Karatchouk, Rumelan and Jbeisseh oilfields; also organizes exploring, production and marketing of oil and gas nationally; Dir-Gen. Dr Eng. MUHAMMAD KHADDOUR.

Al-Furat Petroleum Company: BP 7660, Damascus; tel. (11) 6183333; fax (11) 6184444; e-mail afpc@afpc.net.sy; internet www .afpc-sy.com; f. 1985; owned 50% by SPC and 50% by a foreign consortium of Syria Shell Petroleum Development B.V. and Deminex Syria GmbH; exploits oilfields in the Euphrates river area; Chair. HAITHAM GHANEM; Gen. Man. JOHN MALCOLM.

DEVELOPMENT ORGANIZATIONS

State Planning Commission: Parliament Square, Damascus.

Syrian Consulting Bureau for Development and Investment: Damascus; independent; Chair. NABIL SUKKAR.

CHAMBERS OF COMMERCE

Federation of Syrian Chambers of Commerce: BP 5909, rue Mousa Ben Nousair, Damascus; tel. (11) 3337344; fax (11) 3331127; e-mail syr-trade@mail.sy; internet www.fedcommsyr.org; f. 1975; Pres. Dr RATEB ASH-SHALLAH; Gen. Sec. Dr ABD AR-RAHMAN AL-ATTAR.

Aleppo Chamber of Commerce: BP 1261, Aleppo; tel. (21) 2238236; fax (21) 2213493; e-mail alepchmb@mail.sy; internet www .aleppochamber.com; f. 1885; Pres. M. SALEH AL-MALLAH; Sec. MUHAMMAD MANSOUR.

Alkalamoun Chamber of Commerce: BP 2507, rue Bucher A. Mawla, Damascus; fax (11) 778394; Pres. M. SOUFAN.

Damascus Chamber of Commerce: BP 1040, rue Mou'awiah, Damascus; tel. (11) 2211339; fax (11) 2225874; e-mail dcc@net.sy; internet www.dcc-sy.com; f. 1890; Pres. Dr RATEB ASH-SHALLAH; Gen. Dir HISHAM AL-HAMWY; 11,500 mems.

Hama Chamber of Commerce and Industry: BP 147, rue al-Kouatly, Hama; tel. (33) 233304; fax (33) 517701; e-mail ham-coci@ net.sy; f. 1934; Pres. IZZAT AL-HABBAL; Dir ABD AR-RAZZAK AL-HAIT.

Homs Chamber of Commerce and Industry: BP 440, rue Abou al-Of, Homs; tel. (31) 471000; fax (31) 464247; e-mail homschamber@ homschamber.org; internet www.homschamber.org; f. 1928; Pres. Dr Eng. TARIF AKHRAS; Dir M. FARES AL-HUSSAMY.

Latakia Chamber of Commerce: rue al-Hurriyah, Latakia; Pres. JULE NASRI.

CHAMBERS OF INDUSTRY

Aleppo Chamber of Industry: BP 1859, rue al-Moutanabbi, Aleppo; tel. (21) 339812; f. 1935; Pres. MUHAMMAD M. OUBARI; 7,000 mems.

Damascus Chamber of Industry: BP 1305, rue Harika Mou'awiah, Damascus; tel. (11) 2215042; fax (11) 2245981; Pres. Dr YEHYA AL-HINDI; Dir-Gen. Dr ABD AL-HAMID MALAKANI.

EMPLOYERS' ORGANIZATIONS

Fédération Générale à Damas: Damascus; f. 1951; Dir TALAT TAGLUBI.

Fédération de Damas: Damascus; f. 1949.

Fédération des Patrons et Industriels à Lattaquié: Latakia; f. 1953.

Order of Syrian Engineers and Architects: BP 2336, Immeuble Al Mohandessin, place Azmeh, Damascus; tel. (11) 2214916; fax (11) 2216948; e-mail @lbosea@net.sy; Pres. M. FAYEZ MAHFOUZ.

UTILITIES

Electricity

Public Establishment for Electricity Generation and Transmission (PEEGT): BP 3386, rue Nessan 17, Damascus; tel. (11) 2223086; fax (11) 2229062; e-mail peegt@net.sy; internet www .peegt-syria.org; f. 1965; renamed 1994; state-owned; operates eleven power stations through subsidiary companies; Dir-Gen. Dr A. AL-ALI.

TRADE UNIONS

Ittihad Naqabat al-'Ummal al-'Am fi Suriya (General Federation of Labour Unions): BP 2351, rue Qanawat, Damascus; f. 1948; Chair. 'IZZ AD-DIN NASIR; Sec. MAHMOUD FAHURI.

Transport

RAILWAYS

In 1998 the railway system totalled 2,450 km of track.

Syrian Railways: BP 182, Aleppo; tel. (21) 2213900; fax (21) 2228480; e-mail cfs.syria@net.sy; f. 1897; Pres. and Dir-Gen. Eng. MUHAMMAD IYAD GHAZAL.

General Organization of the Hedjaz-Syrian Railway: BP 134, place Hedjaz, Damascus; tel. (11) 2215815; fax (11) 2227106; f. 1908; the Hedjaz Railway has 347 km of track (gauge 1,050 mm) in Syria; services operate between Damascus and Amman, on a branch line of about 24 km from Damascus to Katana, and there is a further line of 64 km from Damascus to Serghaya; Dir-Gen. S. AHMED.

ROADS

Arterial roads run across the country linking the north to the south and the Mediterranean to the eastern frontier. At 31 December 1999 Syria's total road network was 43,381 km, including 31,189 km of highways, main or national roads and 9,191 km of secondary or regional roads. In 1996 work was scheduled to commence on the first stage of a project costing £S1,800m. to improve the road linking Rakka with Deir ez-Zor. In 2001 the Syrian Government awarded a contract for the construction of a 100-km, four-lane highway, connecting the eastern port town of Latakia with Ariba in the northern governorate of Aleppo, at an estimated cost of US $207m. The project was to be financed by loans from the Kuwaiti-based Arab Fund for Economic and Social Development (AFESD) and the Kuwait Fund for Arab Economic Development (KFAED).

General Co for Roads: BP 3143, Aleppo; tel. (21) 555406; f. 1975; Gen. Man. Eng. M. WALID EL-AJLANI.

PIPELINES

The oil pipelines that cross Syrian territory are of great importance to the national economy, representing a considerable source of foreign exchange. In the late 1990s a number of gas pipelines, linking gas fields in the Palmyra area to Aleppo and Lebanon, were under construction.

Syrian Co for Oil Transport (SCOT): BP 13, Banias; tel. (43) 711300; fax (43) 710418; f. 1972; Dir-Gen. MUHAMMAD DOUBA.

SHIPPING

Latakia is the principal port; the other major ports are at Banias and Tartous. A project to expand the capacities of Latakia and Tartous, and to construct new port facilities near Tartous, commenced in 1997.

General Directorate of Syrian Ports: BP 505, Latakia; tel. (41) 473333; fax (41) 475805; Dir-Gen. ALI RAZZOUK.

Syrian General Organization for Maritime Transport: BP 730, 2 rue Argentina, Damascus; tel. (11) 2226350.

Abdulkader, Abu Bakr: Arwad, Latakia; operates a fleet of 5 general cargo vessels.

Delta Marine Transport: rue de Baghdad, Latakia; tel. (41) 222426; fax (41) 222760.

Ismail, A. M., Shipping Agency Ltd: BP 74, rue Marilyas, Tartous; tel. (43) 220543; operates 8 general cargo vessels; Man. Dir MAHMOUD ISMAIL.

Muhieddine Shipping Co: BP 779, rue du Port, Tartous; tel. (43) 220510; fax (43) 317139; operates 7 general cargo ships.

Riamar Shipping Co Ltd: Al Kornish ash-Sharki, BP 284, Immeuble Tarwin, rue du Port, Tartous; tel. (43) 314999; fax (43) 212616; e-mail tarekg@scs-net.org; operates 6 general cargo vessels; Chair. and Man. Dir ABD AL-KADER SABRA.

Samin Shipping Co Ltd: BP 315, rue al-Mina, Tartous; tel. (43) 318835; fax (43) 318834; operates 10 general cargo ships.

Syro-Jordanian Shipping Co: BP 148, rue Port Said, Latakia; tel. (41) 471635; fax (41) 470250; e-mail syjomar@net.sy; f. 1976; operates 2 general cargo ships; transported 70,551 metric tons of goods in 1992; Chair. OSMAN LEBBADY; Tech. Man. M. CHOUMAN.

CIVIL AVIATION

There is an international airport at Damascus, and the upgrading of Aleppo airport, to enable it to handle international traffic, is planned.

Directorate-General of Civil Aviation: BP 6257, place Nejmeh, Damascus; tel. (11) 3331306; fax (11) 2232201.

Syrian Arab Airlines (Syrianair): BP 417, 5th Floor, Social Insurance Bldg, Youssef al-Azmeh Sq., Damascus; tel. (11) 2220700; fax (11) 224923; e-mail syr-air@syriatel.net; f. 1946; refounded 1961 to succeed Syrian Airways, after revocation of merger with Misrair; domestic passenger and cargo services (from Damascus, Aleppo, Latakia and Deir ez-Zor) and routes to Europe, the Middle East, North Africa and the Far East; Chair. SHAFIK DAOUD.

Tourism

Syria's tourist attractions include a pleasant Mediterranean coastline, the mountains, town bazaars and antiquities of Damascus and Palmyra, as well as hundreds of deserted ancient villages in the north-west of the country. In 2000 some 3m. tourists visited Syria, generating estimated revenues of US $474m.

Ministry of Tourism: Barada St, Damascus; tel. (11) 2233183; e-mail min-tourism@mail.sy; internet www.syriatourism.org; f. 1972; Counsellor to the Minister Mrs SAWSAN JOUZY; Dir of Tourism Promotion and Marketing NIDAL MACHFEJ.

Middle East Tourism: BP 201, rue Fardoss, Damascus; tel. (11) 2211876; fax (11) 2246545; f. 1954; Pres. MUHAMMAD DADOUCHE; 7 brs.

Syrian Arab Co for Hotels and Tourism (SACHA): BP 5549, Mezzeh, Damascus; tel. (11) 2223286; fax (11) 2219415; f. 1977; Chair. DIRAR JUMA'A; Gen. Man. ELIAS ABOUTARA.

TAJIKISTAN

Introductory Survey

Location, Climate, Language, Religion, Flag, Capital

The Republic of Tajikistan (formerly the Tajik Soviet Socialist Republic) is situated in the south-east of Central Asia. To the north and west it borders Uzbekistan, to the north-east Kyrgyzstan, to the east the People's Republic of China and to the south Afghanistan. The climate varies considerably according to altitude. The average temperature in January in Khujand (lowland) is –0.9°C (30.4°F); in July the average is 27.4°C (81.3°F). In the southern lowlands the temperature variation is somewhat more extreme. Rainfall is low in the valleys, in the range of 150–250 mm (6–10 ins) per year. In mountain areas winter temperatures can fall below –45°C (–51°F); the average January temperature in Murgab, in the mountains of south-east Gornyi Badakhshan, is –19.6°C (–3.3°F). Levels of rainfall are very low in mountain regions, seldom exceeding 60–80 mm (2–3 ins) per year. The official language is Tajik. The major religion is Islam. Most Tajiks and ethnic Uzbek residents follow the Sunni tradition, but the Pamiris are mostly of the Isma'ili sect. There are also representatives of the Russian Orthodox Church, and a small Jewish community exists. The national flag (proportions 1 by 2) consists of four unequal horizontal stripes from top to bottom of red, white, green and red, with, on the obverse only, a crossed gold hammer and sickle below a gold-bordered red five-pointed star on the top red stripe, set near the hoist. The capital is Dushanbe.

Recent History

In 1918 northern Tajikistan (which had been under the Russian Empire since the 19th century) was conquered by the Bolsheviks, and the territory was incorporated into the Turkestan Autonomous Soviet Socialist Republic (ASSR). However, Dushanbe and the other southern regions of Tajikistan (which were subject to the Emirate of Bukhara) did not come under the control of the Bolsheviks until 1921. Opposition to Soviet rule was led by the *basmachis* (local guerrilla fighters) and foreign interventionists. In 1924 the Tajik ASSR was established as a part of the Uzbek Soviet Socialist Republic (SSR), and in January 1925 the south-east of Tajikistan was designated a Special Pamir Region (later renamed the Gornyi Badakhshan Autonomous Region) within the Tajik ASSR. On 16 October 1929 the Tajik ASSR became a full Union republic of the USSR and was slightly enlarged by the addition of the Khujand okrug (district) from the Uzbek SSR. Soviet rule brought economic and social benefits to Tajikistan, but living standards remained low, and cattle-breeding, the main occupation in the uplands, was severely disrupted by collectivization. During the repressions of the 1930s almost all ethnic Tajiks in the republican Government were replaced by Russians.

During the 1970s increased Islamic influence was reported, as was violence towards non-indigenous nationalities. In 1978 there were reports of an anti-Russian riot, involving some 13,000 people, and after 1979 there were arrests of some activists opposed to Soviet intervention in Afghanistan. As in other Central Asian republics of the USSR, the first manifestation of the policies of Mikhail Gorbachev, who came to power as Soviet leader in 1985, was a campaign against corruption. Rakhmon Nabiyev, who had been First Secretary of the Communist Party of Tajikistan (CPT) since 1982, was replaced in late 1985 by Kakhar Makhkamov, who accused his predecessor of tolerating nepotism and corruption. Makhkamov was also openly critical of the economic situation in the republic, admitting that there were high levels of both unemployment and poverty. Censorship was relaxed, and there was increased debate in the media of perceived injustices—such as alleged discrimination against Tajiks in Uzbekistan, and the legitimacy of the Uzbek–Tajik boundary. Greater freedom of expression allowed discussion of Tajik culture and language, and an increased interest in other Iranian cultures (links with Iran had been limited since the 1979 Iranian Revolution). The pro-Soviet regime in Afghanistan had developed cultural contacts with Tajikistan, and many Tajiks served in Afghanistan as interpreters. Tajik was declared the state language in 1989, and the teaching of the Arabic script (used by Tajiks prior to sovietization) was begun in schools.

In February 1990, following reports that Armenian refugees were to be settled in the capital, Dushanbe, violence broke out at a protest rally, when about 3,000 demonstrators demanding democratic and economic reforms clashed with police. A state of emergency was declared, and some 5,000 troops of the USSR's Ministry of Internal Affairs, in conjunction with 'civilian militia' units, suppressed the demonstrations; 22 people were reported dead and 565 injured. The unrest prompted a more inflexible attitude towards political pluralism by the republic's leadership. Two nascent opposition parties, Rastokhez (Rebirth), which had been involved in the February demonstrations, and the Democratic Party of Tajikistan (DPT), were refused official registration, and the Islamic Renaissance Party (IRP) was denied permission to hold a founding congress. All three groups, however, retained popular support. Opposition politicians were barred from contesting the elections to the republic's Supreme Soviet, held in March; 94% of the deputies elected were members of the CPT.

In an apparent concession to growing Tajik nationalism, none the less, the Supreme Soviet adopted a declaration of sovereignty on 25 August 1990. Although the declaration emphasized the equality of all nationalities living in Tajikistan, the growth in Islamic influence, the rediscovery of the Tajiks' Iranian heritage and language, and the uncertain political situation all contributed to an increase in emigration, mainly by Europeans and educated Tajiks. In November Makhkamov was elected to the new post of executive President of the Republic by the Supreme Soviet; his only opponent was Nabiyev.

The Tajik Government, possibly anxious about increased Turkic dominance in Central Asia, displayed great enthusiasm for a new Union Treaty (effectively preserving the USSR), and (according to official figures) 90.2% of eligible voters in the republic voted for the preservation of the USSR in the all-Union referendum in March 1991. In August, however, before the Treaty could be signed, conservative leaders of the Communist Party of the Soviet Union and the Soviet security forces staged a *coup d'état* in Moscow. Makhkamov did not oppose the coup, and on 31 August, after the attempted coup had collapsed, he resigned as President, following demonstrations (organized by the DPT, the IRP and Rastokhez), which continued throughout much of September. On 9 September, following the declarations of independence by neighbouring Uzbekistan and Kyrgyzstan, the Tajik Supreme Soviet voted to proclaim Tajikistan an independent state, the Republic of Tajikistan. This did not, however, satisfy the demonstrators, who demanded the dissolution of the CPT and new, multi-party elections. Kadriddin Aslonov, the Chairman of the Supreme Soviet and acting President, issued a decree that banned the CPT and nationalized its assets. In response, the communist majority in the Supreme Soviet demanded Aslonov's resignation, declared a state of emergency in the republic and rescinded the prohibition of the CPT. Aslonov resigned, and was replaced by Nabiyev. Nabiyev was, however, quickly obliged to make substantial concessions to the opposition, and in early October the Supreme Soviet rescinded the state of emergency, suspended the CPT and legalized the IRP, which had previously been banned under legislation that prohibited the formation of religious parties. Shortly afterwards he resigned as acting President, in advance of the presidential election.

Seven candidates contested the direct presidential election, which took place on 24 November 1991. Attracting strong support in rural areas, Nabiyev won 57% of the votes cast, compared with 30% for the candidate favoured by the main opposition parties, Davlat Khudonazarov. Nabiyev took office in December. In January 1992 a new Prime Minister, Akbar Mirzoyev, was appointed to head the Government. Meanwhile, in December 1991 Tajikistan had signed the declaration establishing the Commonwealth of Independent States (CIS, see p. 172), the successor body to the USSR.

Anti-Government demonstrations began in Dushanbe in March 1992, initially prompted by Nabiyev's dismissal of Mamadayez Navzhuvanov, a prominent Badakhshani, from the post of Minister of Internal Affairs. Protests against his dismissal were led by the Pamiri group, Lale Badakhshon, which advocated greater autonomy for the Pamiri peoples of the Gornyi Badakhshan Autonomous Region. It was joined by Rastokhez, the IRP and the DPT, particularly after the arrest, in April, of Maksud Ikramov, the Mayor of Dushanbe and an opposition sympathizer, on charges of abusing his authority. Protesters demanding the resignation of Nabiyev and the Government remained encamped in the centre of Dushanbe for nearly two months; in response, the Government organized rival demonstrations, bringing supporters to the capital from the southern region of Kulob (Kulyab) and Leninabad, in the north—the traditional areas of support for the CPT. In late April members of the newly formed national guard loyal to Nabiyev opened fire on the demonstrators, killing at least eight people. In early May the National Security Committee (NSC—formerly the KGB) allegedly distributed weapons to pro-communist supporters, and the ensuing violent clashes escalated into civil war. Fighting in Dushanbe ended after Nabiyev negotiated a truce with opposition leaders and formed a new 'Government of National Reconciliation' (led by Mirzoyev), in which eight of the 24 ministers were members of opposition parties. However, violent clashes erupted in Kulob region between pro-communist Kulyabi forces, who opposed the President's compromise with the opposition, and members of Islamist and democratic groups. In late May the conflict spread from Kulob region into Qurgonteppa (Kurgan-Tyube or Kurgan Teppe) region (the main base of support for the Islamist and democratic groups), where a Kulyabi militia, the Tajik People's Front (TPF), led by Sangak Safarov (who had spent 23 years in prison for various criminal offences), attempted to suppress the local forces of the informal Islamist-democratic coalition. The Kulyabis alleged that their opponents were receiving weapons and assistance from Islamist groups in Afghanistan, and there were reports that Gulbuddin Hekmatyar, the leader of the Afghan *mujahidin* group, Hizb-i Islami, had established training camps in Afghanistan for Tajik fighters. The Islamic-democratic alliance, for its part, claimed that the ex-Soviet (Russian) garrisons were arming the pro-Government militias.

In late August 1992 several members of the DPT and Lale Badakhshon were killed by Kulyabi militia forces in the town of Qurgonteppa. A violent conflict ensued between local members of the opposition and Kulyabis, in which several hundred people were reportedly killed. Meanwhile, in Dushanbe anti-Government demonstrations resumed, and at the end of August demonstrators entered the presidential palace and took 30 officials hostage. On 7 September Nabiyev was seized by opposition forces at Dushanbe airport, and was forced to announce his resignation. Akbarsho Iskandarov, the Chairman of the Supreme Soviet, temporarily assumed the responsibilities of Head of State. Mirzoyev also resigned, and a Leninabad communist, Abdumalik Abdullojonov, was appointed acting Prime Minister of the coalition Government.

Iskandarov's administration, which had the support of all the main Islamist and democratic groups, had little influence outside the capital; much of the south of the country was under the control of Safarov's TPF militia, and some leaders of the Leninabad region (which has a large Uzbek community) threatened to secede from Tajikistan if there was any attempt to introduce an Islamic state. In October 1992 the Islamist-democratic alliance's control of Dushanbe was threatened when forces led by Safarali Kenjayev, a former Chairman of the Supreme Soviet and a supporter of Nabiyev, entered the capital and attempted to seize power. Kenjayev briefly proclaimed himself Head of State, but his troops were forced to retreat by forces loyal to the regime. During the ensuing two months, however, Kenjayev's militias enforced a virtual economic blockade of the capital.

In November 1992, having failed to end the civil war, Iskandarov and the Government resigned. The legislature abolished the office of President, and Imamali Rakhmonov, a collective-farm chairman from Kulob region, was appointed Chairman of the Supreme Soviet, a post now equivalent to Head of State. The Supreme Soviet elected a new Government, in which Abdullojonov retained the post of Prime Minister. However, all members of the opposition parties lost their portfolios, and the majority of the new ministers were Kulyabis or supporters of ex-President Nabiyev. The Supreme Soviet also voted to combine Qurgonteppa and Kulob regions into one administrative region, Khatlon, in an apparent attempt to ensure control of the south of the country by pro-communist forces from Kulob.

In December 1992 forces loyal to the new Government, the TPF and Kulyabi-Hissarite militias, captured Dushanbe, hith-

erto under the control of the Popular Democratic Army (PDA), a newly formed military coalition of Islamist and democratic groups. Hundreds of PDA fighters were reportedly killed during the attack, and there were also reports of atrocities committed by the militias both in the capital and in the south, particularly against people from Garm (a stronghold of the Islamist and democratic groups) and Gornyi Badakhshan. In February 1993 some of the insurgents in Garm attempted to declare an 'autonomous Islamic republic', but the Government had secured control of most of the country by March. The Government estimated that 30,000 people had been killed and some 800,000 people displaced during the civil war; other sources claimed that as many as 100,000 people had died.

In December 1992 and January 1993 some 60,000 Tajiks fled to Afghanistan, after alleged reprisals against supporters of the democratic and Islamist forces, including executions of opposition members, and attacks on people from Garm by the Kulyabi militias. Such reports were denied by the government and Kulyabi military leaders. Among those who fled was the influential *kazi* (supreme judge) of Tajikistan, Akbar Turajonzoda, the highest-ranking Muslim cleric in the country and a senior member of the IRP, who was accused by the new Government of attempting to establish an Islamic state in Tajikistan. In February 1993 he was replaced as spiritual leader of Tajikistan's Muslims by Fatkhullo Sharifzoda, who was given the title of *mufti*.

Although the civil war effectively ended in early 1993, the continued insurgency of Islamist-democratic forces, notably from across the Afghan border (allegedly supported by Afghan *mujahidin*), continued to destabilize the country. With respect to the interior, government forces ended rebel resistance near Garm in March. The communist Government suspended press and broadcasting freedom in January and February. In June the Supreme Court formally proscribed the IRP, Lale Badakhshon, Rastokhez and the DPT, leaving the CPT as the only legal party in the country. Even the new parties established later in the year—the Party of Economic Freedom and the People's Democratic Party of Tajikistan (PDPT)—were founded or sponsored by members of the Government or its associates.

TIn December 1993 Abdullojonov resigned from the premiership; the new Chairman of the Council of Ministers (Prime Minister) was Abdujalil Samadov. From the end of 1993 Rakhmonov, who secured for his own office responsibility for the powerful Ministries of Defence and Internal Affairs, as well as for the NSC (and, in February 1994, operational supervision of the broadcast media), began to show signs of compromise. In March he announced his willingness to negotiate with the Islamist-democratic opposition, and talks began in April in Moscow, under the auspices of the UN and in the presence of representatives from Iran, Pakistan, Russia and the USA. The negotiations resulted in a protocol on the establishment of a joint commission on refugees. However, reconciliation was far from having been achieved: from March border incursions by Tajik guerrillas intensified, resulting in clashes with the CIS troops stationed on the frontier (see below), and there was also renewed insurgency in Gornyi Badakhshan.

In June 1994 a further round of negotiations between representatives of the Government and the opposition took place in the Iranian capital, Tehran, at which both sides announced their support, in principle, for a cease-fire. However, attacks by opposition forces on CIS and Tajik government troops patrolling the border with Afghanistan intensified in July and August, with many casualties reported on both sides. The continuing conflict along the Tajik–Afghan border was interpreted by some observers as being partly a battle for control of drugs-smuggling routes: since securing independence Tajikistan had become a major conduit for illicit drugs (chiefly opium) from Pakistan, Iran and Afghanistan to Russia and western Europe.

In August 1994 the Government did not renew the state of emergency in effect since October 1992, claiming that greater political freedom would be permitted for the presidential election, scheduled to take place in September. In late August, however, the election was postponed, apparently on the insistence of the Russian Minister of Foreign Affairs, to allow time for opposition candidates to be included in the poll. In mid-September representatives of the Government and the Islamist and democratic opposition, meeting in Tehran, agreed to introduce a temporary cease-fire. Nevertheless, in late September rebel forces launched a large-scale offensive in the district of Tavil Dara, which was repelled by government troops. The cease-fire eventually came into effect in late October, but it remained unclear to what extent the various armed groups based in Afghanistan were under the control of the IRP leadership. In December the UN Security Council authorized the deployment of a Mission of Observers in Tajikistan.

When the presidential election eventually took place on 6 November 1994, the only two candidates were Rakhmonov and Abdullojonov, Tajikistan's ambassador to Russia. Some 85% of eligible voters were reported to have participated in the election, which was won by Rakhmonov, with some 58% of the votes cast; Abdullojonov received about 35% of the votes. The result reflected the regional loyalties of the two candidates; Rakhmonov (of the Kulob clan) secured most of his support in the south of the country, and Abdullojonov received a large proportion of the votes in Leninabad and in Gornyi Badakhshan. At the same time as the presidential election a plebiscite was held on a new constitution, which was approved by more than 90% of voters. Despite allegations of widespread electoral malpractice, Rakhmonov was inaugurated as President in mid-November. In December he made several appointments to the Council of Ministers, with Jamshed Karimov being appointed Chairman, and Mahmadsaid Ubaydulloyev being promoted to First Deputy Chairman.

In February 1995 renewed peace talks between government and opposition representatives opened in Almaty, Kazakhstan, but little progress was achieved. The IRP subsequently announced that it would not participate in parliamentary elections, due to take place later that month. The DPT did not participate either, and in late February the newly formed Party of Popular Unity and Accord (PPUA—led by Abdullojonov) announced that it would not contest the elections, after Abdullojonov's candidature had been disallowed by the electoral authorities. The Organization for Security and Co-operation in Europe (OSCE, see p. 283) refused to send observers to the elections, claiming that the electoral law was severely flawed. Despite the opposition boycott, elections to the new Supreme Assembly took place on 26 February 1995. Although 350 candidates were reported to have contested the 181 seats, in some 40% of constituencies there was only one candidate. An estimated 84% of eligible voters participated in the poll. Most of those elected were reported to be state officials loyal to the President, but largely without party affiliation. The CPT was reported to have won some 60 seats, and its ally, the PPT, five seats. Despite the PPUA's boycott, two representatives of the party were said to have been elected to the legislature. A second round of voting was held on 12 March to decide 19 seats that had not been filled in the previous month. However, when the Supreme Assembly convened in April, two seats reportedly remained vacant.

In March 1995 the opposition announced a unilateral extension of the cease-fire for a further 50 days, but later in that month there were further attacks on border posts on the Tajik–Afghan frontier. In early April there was a serious escalation of the conflict in the border zone, and 34 border guards and 170 rebel troops were reported killed during one week of fighting. In response, Russian aircraft were alleged to have bombed the Afghan town of Taloqan (reported to be the rebels' base in Afghanistan), killing some 125 civilians. (Russian official sources denied the attack.) The opposition forces (comprising the IRP and Lale Badakhshon) claimed that they were responding to a large deployment of Tajik government troops and Russian border guards in Gornyi Badakhshan, in violation of the cease-fire agreement. In mid-April talks opened between the Government and opposition groups in Moscow, but the opposition left the negotiations on the first day, dissatisfied with the Russian response to demands for the withdrawal of troops from Gornyi Badakhshan. Nevertheless, the talks were reconvened, and in late April it was agreed to extend the cease-fire. In mid-May Rakhmonov met Sayed Abdullo Nuri, the leader of the IRP, in Kabul, Afghanistan, for three days of talks. The negotiations resulted in an agreement to extend the cease-fire for three months. Subsequent talks between government and opposition delegations took place in late May in Almaty. Despite the agreement reached earlier in the month, the opposition delegation refused to extend the cease-fire, apparently because government representatives had failed to agree to their demands for a limitation on the deployment of troops in Gornyi Badakhshan and for an assembly to be established to consider constitutional amendments. However, the two sides did agree to exchange prisoners. In July Rakhmonov met Nuri and other opposition leaders for further talks in Tehran, and in mid-August it was agreed to extend the cease-fire for an additional six months. During the second half of 1995 conflict continued in

the south of the country and on the border with Afghanistan. In mid-September fighting was reported in Qurgonteppa between two military units, both formerly loyal to the Government, but now reportedly under the control of local political leaders. By late September, when government forces regained control of the town, some 300 people had reportedly died in the conflict, which some observers claimed was linked to disputes over the control of the lucrative cotton trade. Further negotiations between government and opposition representatives, scheduled for September, were eventually convened, under the auspices of the UN, in Ashgabat, Turkmenistan, in late November. After several days of discussions, however, the opposition withdrew from the negotiations, in response to the Government's refusal to accede to its demand for the formation of what was termed a national reconciliation council to govern the country alongside Rakhmonov during a two-year transition period.

In January 1996 Sharifzoda was killed by gunmen. Although the Government accused the IRP of responsibility for the death of the *mufti*, the opposition denied any involvement. At the end of January opposition forces began a major offensive in the Tavil Dara region, and military commanders of government troops initiated rebellions in two towns. The western town of Tursan-Zade was taken by forces under Ibodullo Boitmatov, and Makhmoud Khudoberdiyev took control of Qurgonteppa. The commanders (both ethnic Uzbeks) claimed that the Government was incompetent and corrupt, and demanded changes in its composition, notably the removal of several Kulyabi ministers. In early February Khudoberdiyev's troops approached Dushanbe, but retreated when they encountered government forces. Following negotiations, Rakhmonov agreed to the demands of the two commanders; Karimov was replaced as Chairman by Yakhyo Azimov, hitherto a company director in the Leninabad region. Ubaydulloyev was succeeded as First Deputy Chairman by Yurii Ponosov, formerly Mayor of Dushanbe.

Following further talks with the opposition in Ashgabat, the Government announced an indefinite extension of the cease-fire. Meanwhile, however, fighting intensified in March and April 1996 in the Tavil Dara region, where it was reported that Russian border guards and aircraft were supporting Tajik government troops in attacks on rebel forces; in May, following intense fighting, opposition forces captured the town of Tavil Dara. Talks resumed in Ashgabat in early July. A cease-fire was brokered in the Tavil Dara region, and agreement was reached on the conduct of further peace negotiations and on a gradual exchange of prisoners of war. In late July the formation of a National Revival bloc, a new opposition movement chaired by three former premiers (Abdullojonov, Karimov and Samadov) was announced. They subsequently declared their intention to participate in the peace talks.

Despite the cease-fire agreement, large-scale hostilities resumed in the Tavil Dara region in late July 1996. Opposition forces regained control of the town in mid-August, and government and rebel troops fought for command of the strategic central region of Tajikistan, notably the towns of Komsomolabad and Garm. Negotiations between representatives of the two sides took place in Tehran in October, and in December a UN-sponsored meeting was held between Rakhmonov and Nuri in Khosdeh, northern Afghanistan. A further cease-fire agreement was reached, but was almost immediately violated as fierce fighting continued in the Garm region. However, significant progress was achieved at discussions held in Moscow later in that month, when Rakhmonov and Nuri agreed to form a National Reconciliation Council (NRC), to be headed by a representative of what had come to be known as the United Tajik Opposition (UTO). The NRC was to have extensive executive powers to revise legislation on elections, political parties and the media, to debate constitutional amendments and to monitor the implementation of the peace agreement. A general amnesty was agreed, as were terms for an exchange of prisoners and the repatriation of refugees.

Negotiations were held in Tehran in January 1997 to determine the structure and composition of the NRC. There was broad consensus on most issues, apart from that of the allocation of seats, with the UTO demanding greater representation. Meanwhile, supporters of the National Revival bloc organized rallies in Khujand, protesting against the exclusion of the secular opposition movement from the peace talks. In early February 15 people, including UN representatives, aid workers and Russian journalists, were taken hostage by Bakhram Sadirov, a rebel fighter who had reportedly changed allegiance on several occasions during the civil war. Also kidnapped was the Tajik

President during the legislative elections. In August 2001 the party was banned, after it failed to re-register its members during its period of suspension. Meanwhile, in January eight members of the banned Uzbek fundamentalist group, Hizb-ut-Tahrir al-Islami (Party of Islamic Liberation), were sentenced to up to six years' imprisonment. (According to government sources, more than 100 militants belonging to the Islamist militant group had been arrested in 2000.) In April 2001 several bomb attacks took place, which killed at least four people. In June a former UTO field commander, Rakhmon Sanginov, took hostage seven police-officers; the police-officers were released after the Government agreed to reassess criminal proceedings brought against eight of his supporters. In the same month a former UTO fighter and supporter of the 1997 peace agreement took hostage 15 members of an aid organization and four Tajik security officials, in protest at four arrests made in connection with the murder of Habib Sanginov; the hostages were released some three days later. (The four men accused of Habib Sanginov's murder were sentenced to death in March 2002.) Also in June 2001 Tajik security forces launched an attack against a group of militants, led by Rakhmon Sanginov, near Dushanbe; it was reported that about 36 rebels were killed and 66 were detained. In August Rakhmon Sanginov was killed by security forces, and at the end of the month Tajik officials claimed that only about 10 of his supporters remained at large.

In early September 2001 the Minister of Culture, Press and Information, Abdurakhim Rakhimov, was assassinated; Karomatullo Olimov was appointed as his successor in October. Also in September some 19,000 prisoners were released under an amnesty to commemorate the 10th anniversary of Tajikistan's independence. In November Hizb-i-Vahdat (the Unity Party) was established; before it could be officially registered the organization had to enlist the support of at least 1,000 members over a three-month period. It was reported in December that 10 men had been sentenced to between eight and 25 years' imprisonment on charges of treason, terrorism and sedition, relating to the November 1998 insurrection in Khujand.

In January 2002 a new Ministry of Industry was created, incorporating six State Committees; Zaid Saidov, hitherto Chairman of the State Committee for Industry, was appointed Minister of Industry. At the same time a Ministry of State Revenues and Tax Collection was established, to which Ghulomjon Boboyev was appointed, as its head. In March a public accord agreement, signed in 1996 by pro-Government political parties and non-governmental organizations to express support for the peace process, and renewed in 1999, was extended indefinitely; the accord was signed by a representative of the IRP for the first time.

Drugs-smuggling remained a significant problem in Tajikistan in the early 2000s, involving government officials as well as Islamist militants. Indeed, in early August 2002 the former Deputy Minister of Defence, Col Nikolai Kim, was sentenced to 13 years' imprisonment for taking part in drugs-trafficking and embezzlement while in office in 1998. Organized crime also remained a problem: in October 2002 a senior police official was sentenced to 25 years' imprisonment on charges of murder, fraud and extortion. Meanwhile, in mid-October two men were sentenced to death, and a further six were reported to have received terms of imprisonment of between two and 25 years, after being found guilty of belonging to an armed grouping loyal to the rebel leader Mahmoud Khudoberdiyev. It was reported that by that time almost 75 supporters of Khudoberdiyev had been convicted since 1999.

In December 2002 the Social Democratic Party of Tajikistan, led by Rakhmatullo Zoirov, was registered; the party had lost its original registration shortly after its foundation in 1999. A government reorganization took place in late January 2003, as part of which a new deputy prime minister, Asadullo Ghulomov, was appointed, replacing Fariddun Mukhiddonov. A referendum on a number of controversial constitutional amendments, which would, *inter alia*, enable Rakhmonov to seek re-election upon the expiry of his presidential term of office, was scheduled to be held on 22 June.

In October 1991 Tajikistan signed, with seven other republics of the USSR, a treaty to establish an economic community, and on 21 December was one of the signatories of the Alma-Ata Declaration, by which the CIS was established. After the dissolution of the USSR, Russian troops remained in Tajikistan, officially adopting a neutral stance during the civil war. However, following the communist victory in Dushanbe in December 1992, they openly assisted pro-communist troops in quelling the opposition forces, and the Tajik Government became increasingly dependent on Russia, both militarily and economically. In January 1993 Russia, Kazakhstan, Kyrgyzstan and Uzbekistan committed themselves to the defence of Tajikistan's southern frontiers, thus supporting the Government in the continuing conflict on the Tajik–Afghan border. In practice, mainly Russian troops were responsible for repelling rebel fighters entering Tajikistan, with Russia defending the southern CIS border as if it were its own. In August Russia and the Central Asian states (excluding Turkmenistan, which refused any involvement in the Tajik conflict) signed an agreement establishing a CIS peace-keeping force to police Tajikistan's border with Afghanistan. By December there were 25,000 troops in place: most units were from the Russian army, but there were also soldiers from Uzbekistan, Kazakhstan, Kyrgyzstan and Tajikistan itself.

Despite Russia's involvement in the Tajik civil conflict, it also sought to mediate between the Government and the opposition leadership in exile. During 1994–95 relations between the Russian authorities and the Rakhmonov regime deteriorated, owing to disagreements regarding the approach of the Tajik Government to the peace talks and to differences concerning the terms of a possible monetary union (see below). However, in 1996 and 1997 Russia hosted several rounds of the UN-sponsored negotiations for a political settlement in Tajikistan, which culminated in the signing of the peace agreement in Moscow, in June 1997. In April 1999 Russia and Tajikistan signed an agreement on the establishment of a Russian military base in Tajikistan; in the same month nine major bilateral agreements were signed, including a Treaty of Alliance and Co-operation.

During the civil conflict in Tajikistan, the Uzbek leadership provided military and political support to the Rakhmonov administration. In October 1994 Tajikistan and Uzbekistan signed a Co-operation Agreement envisaging greater bilateral co-ordination, especially in the fields of foreign policy and security. However, the Uzbek Government reportedly criticized the treatment of its ethnic minority in Tajikistan, alleging that many ethnic Uzbeks had been replaced in their posts by Kulyabis. Despite criticism from Uzbekistan's President Karimov at what he regarded as the intransigence of the Tajik Government in negotiations with the opposition, Uzbekistan continued to provide considerable technical and military support for the Tajik administration. Following the signing of the peace agreement in June 1997, the Uzbek leadership expressed renewed concern at the possible Islamicization of Tajikistan. Relations between the two countries deteriorated somewhat in 1998, as the Tajik Government frequently accused Uzbekistan of involvement in rebel uprisings in Tajikistan. (Such allegations were strongly denied by the Uzbeks.) Renewed tensions occurred in August 1999, when northern Tajikistan came under attack by unidentified aircraft, which, according to the Tajik leadership, belonged to Uzbek forces, which were assisting Kyrgyzstan to repel a group of Islamist militants in that country's nearby Osh region. (The Uzbek Government subsequently admitted that its forces might have accidentally bombed the territory.) In October around 1,000 Uzbek anti-Government rebels entered Tajikistan from Kyrgyzstan (where they were escaping the suppression of Islamists by the Uzbek authorities); the presence of the militants further strained Tajik-Uzbek relations. However, following an ultimatum by the Tajik Government and mediation by the UTO, many of the militants left Tajikistan in November. In April 2000, however, Tajikistan was strongly criticized by the Uzbek and Kyrgyz Governments for failing to expel the rebels' leader, who had allegedly established a permanent base in Tajikistan. Armed incursions into those two countries by insurgents commenced in August. By the end of 2000 hostilities had subsided, although occasional violent incidents continued to be reported. In March 2001, in response to a claim by the Kyrgyz Government that Tajikistan harboured some 2,500 international terrorists, the Tajik Government declared there to be no members of any rebel organization on its territory, and invited the Kyrgyz Government to examine its borders. In the mean time, Uzbekistan, which had begun laying landmines along its border with Tajikistan from mid-2000, in an effort to prevent cross-border incursions by Islamist insurgents, officially informed Tajikistan of its actions only in early May 2001. At the end of the month a Tajik border official accused Uzbekistan of violating international law by planting mines along the Tajik–Uzbek border, which had not been delineated in mountainous areas; it was further observed that, thus far, all of the casualties had been Tajik and Uzbek citizens. However, despite these tensions, the increased vulnerability to terrorist attacks experienced by both countries in late 2001 led to an improvement in bilateral relations. President Rakhmonov visited President Karimov in December; it was announced that a crossing between the Penjakent region of Tajikistan and Uzbekistan's Samarkand region was to re-open, and the two leaders also agreed to collaborate to combat terrorism, crime and drugs-trafficking. In February 2002, at a meeting of the Tajik and Uzbek premiers, an agreement on border-crossing procedures was reached. In October a border agreement was signed by Presidents Rakhmonov and Karimov, although four areas in the northern Soghd Oblast remained in dispute.

Tajikistan had begun to develop relations outside the USSR before its dissolution in 1991, notably with Iran, with which the Tajiks have strong ethnic and linguistic ties. However, the effective collapse of central authority in Tajikistan in 1992 severely hindered further development of foreign relations, although several states attempted to influence the progress of the country's civil war. Anti-Islamist groups in Tajikistan asserted that Iran was supplying armaments and other goods to Islamist elements in Tajikistan, but this was denied by the Iranian authorities, which admitted providing only cultural and humanitarian assistance. In July 1995 President Rakhmonov visited Tehran, where a number of agreements on cultural and economic co-operation were signed. Further agreements were signed in late 1996, providing for Iranian investment in Tajikistan's industrial and agricultural sectors, followed by economic, cultural and defence accords in late 1998. UN-sponsored peace negotiations between Tajik government and opposition representatives were held in Tehran in 1996 and 1997. In April 2002 Tajikistan and Iran signed nine protocols on co-operation in economic, political and social affairs.

Relations with Afghanistan were strained by the apparent inability of the Afghan Government to prevent *mujahidin* fighters and consignments of weapons from crossing the frontier into Tajikistan. The Afghan Government denied any involvement in arms-trafficking: it was widely believed that the main source of armaments was the renegade *mujahidin* leader, Hekmatyar. The election of the largely pro-communist Tajik Government in late 1992 further strained bilateral relations, and in April 1993 the Tajik Government protested to the Afghan authorities about alleged incursions across the border by Afghans, apparently to assist the remaining rebel troops. In December the Afghan President, Burhanuddin Rabbani, made an official visit to Tajikistan, which resulted in the signature of a bilateral friendship and co-operation treaty, as well as agreements on economic co-operation and border security. A tripartite agreement was signed, together with the office of the UN High Commissioner for Refugees, on the safety of refugees returning to Tajikistan. In April 1995 Afghanistan protested strongly against alleged Russian attacks on rebel bases within Afghanistan, and continued to deny any official support of rebel Tajik factions within the country. As hostilities continued, in mid-1996 the Tajik Government temporarily closed the border with Afghanistan, in protest at Afghan support for the opposition forces. The widespread victory of Taliban forces in Afghanistan in that year threatened to destabilize the fragile situation in Tajikistan and, as the Taliban increased their territorial gains in northern Afghanistan, there was increasing concern in Tajikistan and neighbouring countries, which feared an influx of large numbers of refugees. In July 1998, while heavy fighting occurred close to Tajikistan's border with Afghanistan, the frontier was reinforced by Russian troops. A renewed military offensive by the Taliban in July 1999 led President Rakhmonov to demand a further reinforcement of Tajikistan's southern boundaries. As fighting escalated in Afghanistan in late September 2000, the Tajik Government closed its border with that country. By the end of November up to 10,000 Afghan refugees were stranded on marshy islands on the River Pyanj at the Tajik–Afghan border. Heavy fighting occurred close to the border; in early December Russian border guards were engaged in an exchange of fire with Afghan forces.

Following the large-scale terrorist attacks on the USA of 11 September 2001, attributed to the Saudi-born Islamist fundamentalist Osama bin Laden and the al-Qa'ida organization, Russian troops along the Tajik–Afghan border were placed on a state of alert, in anticipation of military strikes against Afghanistan by the USA and allied countries. Initial Tajik reactions to the US-led campaign to combat global terrorism were cautious, and at times contradictory. Although Rakhmonov announced his willingness to co-operate with the USA, both Tajikistan and Russia initially dismissed the possibility of Tajik territory being used as a base for any US-led military action; however, US specialists were granted entry to the country to oversee the distribution of humanitarian aid to Afghanistan. The Tajik Government declared its support for the aerial bombardment of Taliban and al-Qa'ida targets in Afghanistan, which commenced on 7 October, and in early November it was confirmed that Tajikistan had permitted US and NATO troops to utilize three of its airbases.

The Tajik Government expressed great concern that an influx of refugees would encourage a resurgence of Islamist militancy and cause grave problems for a population already on the verge of famine. Thus, the Tajik–Afghan border remained closed, although some refugees succeeded in crossing the border illegally. The anti-Taliban United National Islamic Front for the Salvation of Afghanistan's military successes from November 2001, and the subsequent collapse of the Taliban regime (see chapter on Afghanistan), reduced pressure on Tajikistan to allow Afghan refugees to enter the country. The death of the leader of the fundamentalist Islamist Movement of Uzbekistan (IMU), Juma Namangoniy, which was reported in November, was also thought to reduce the threat of a resurgence of Islamist radicalism in Tajikistan; however, an increasing number of reports in mid-2002 claimed that members of the IMU were attempting to cross the Afghan–Tajik border to regroup in eastern Tajikistan. In mid-July, in response to pressure from other Central Asian states, the Tajik authorities deported several hundred alleged members of the IMU to Afghanistan. At the same time a Tajik border guard and three local inhabitants were kidnapped, provoking fears of renewed Islamist militant activities, amid allegations that Namangoniy was still alive. In September the Chairman of the Kyrgyz National Security Service reported that the IMU had been transformed into the Islamist Movement of Central Asia, incorporating the IMU, Islamist militants from Tajikistan and the separatist Russian republic of Chechnya, and Uygur (Uigur) separatists from the Xinjiang Uygur Autonomous Region of the People's Republic of China. Meanwhile, drugs-smuggling from Afghanistan via Tajikistan continued to represent a significant problem, despite efforts by the Afghan Interim Administration to curb the production of drugs. In late December the six neighbouring countries of Afghanistan (the People's Republic of China, Iran, Pakistan, Tajikistan, Turkmenistan and Uzbekistan) signed the Kabul Declaration, committing themselves to friendly and constructive relations and mutual respect for sovereignty and territorial integrity, and undertaking to warn of any action that might pose a threat to regional security.

In the mid-1990s Tajikistan sought to develop relations with other Asian states, in particular with the People's Republic of China. In April 1996 Tajikistan signed (together with Russia, Kazakhstan and Kyrgyzstan) a wide-ranging border agreement with China. This was supplemented by a further border accord, signed in August 1999. In January 2002 Tajikistan signed a further treaty with China, resolving contentious issues regarding the two countries' joint border on the edge of Gornyi Badakhshan, and in mid-May Tajikistan signed a border agreement, conceding 1,000 sq km of disputed territory to China. Meanwhile, in April 1997 an agreement on confidence-building measures in the military sphere was concluded. In July 2000 members of the Shanghai Forum (China, Kazakhstan, Kyrgyzstan, Tajikistan and Russia) agreed, at a summit meeting held in Dushanbe, to establish a joint anti-terrorist centre to combat cross-border incursions by Islamist militants and drugs-traffickers. The alliance, renamed the Shanghai Co-operation Organization (see p. 351) upon the accession of Uzbekistan, signed the Shanghai Convention on Combating Terrorism, Separatism and Extremism in mid-2001. At an emergency meeting in October, the members agreed to establish an anti-terrorism centre.

In March 2000 joint military exercises were conducted in southern Tajikistan by Kazakhstan, Kyrgyzstan, Tajikistan, Uzbekistan and Russia, as part of a joint commitment to combat international terrorism in the region. In May 2001 the signatory countries of the Collective Security Treaty—Armenia, Belarus, Kazakhstan, Kyrgyzstan, Russia and Tajikistan—formed a Rapid Reaction Force to combat Islamist militancy in Central Asia; in January 2002 it was announced that the force was ready to undertake combat missions. In March the Central Asian Economic Community, which Tajikistan joined in March 1998, was superseded by the Central Asian Co-operation Organization. The Organization was to co-ordinate anti-terrorism efforts, as well as to further economic, political and technical co-operation.

In January 2002 it was announced that US restrictions on the transfer of defence equipment to Tajikistan, imposed in 1993, had been lifted, as a result of Tajikistan's close co-operation with the US-led coalition against global terrorism. In February 2002 Tajikistan joined NATO's 'Partnership for Peace' programme of military co-operation.

Government

Under the Constitution of November 1994 (to which a number of amendments were passed in September 1999), Tajikistan has a presidential system of government. The President is Head of State and also heads the executive branch of power. The President appoints a Prime Minister (or Chairman) to head the Government (Council of Ministers). Legislative power is vested in the 63-member lower chamber, the Assembly of Representatives, and the 33-member upper chamber, the National Assembly. For administrative purposes, the country is divided into three regions (oblasts): Soghd (known as Leninabad until 2000), in the north; Khatlon (formerly two regions of Kulob and Kurgan-Tyube), in the south; and the autonomous region of Gornyi Badakhshan. These regions are further subdivided into districts and towns. The city of Dushanbe has a separate status, and is administratively independent of the three regions.

Defence

A Ministry of Defence was established in September 1992; in December it was announced that Tajikistan's national armed forces were to be formed on the basis of the Tajik People's Front and other paramilitary units supporting the Government. In 1998 integration of United Tajik Opposition (UTO) force members into the Tajik armed forces began; by March 2000 4,498 UTO fighters had been integrated into the army or security forces. Military service lasts for 24 months. In August 2002 there was an army of some 6,000. There were also an estimated 1,200 paramilitary border guards attached to the Ministry of Internal Affairs. There were plans to form an Air Force squadron. A number of Tajik conscripts were serving as border guards with the Russian armed forces. The budget for 2002 allocated an estimated US $14.8m. to defence. Tajikistan became a member of NATO's Partnership for Peace (see p. 273) programme of military co-operation in February 2002.

Economic Affairs

In 2001, according to estimates by the World Bank, Tajikistan's gross national income (GNI), measured at average 1999–2001 prices, was US $1,051m., equivalent to $170 per head (or $1,150 per head on an international purchasing-power parity basis). During 1990–2001, it was estimated, the population increased by an annual average of 1.5%, while gross domestic product (GDP) per head decreased by an annual average of 9.3%, in real terms. Overall GDP decreased, in real terms, by an average of 8.0% per year; however, GDP increased by 8.3% in 2000 and by 5.0% in 2001.

Despite the fact that only 7% of Tajikistan's land is arable (the remainder being largely mountainous), the Tajik economy has traditionally been predominantly agricultural: agriculture and forestry contributed 26.7% of GDP in 2001, and provided 66.0% of employment. The principal crop is grain, followed in importance by cotton, vegetables and fruit. Approximately 95% of the country's arable land is irrigated. Agricultural production was severely disrupted by the civil war in 1992–93. In 1996 proposals were announced to transfer collective and state farms to private ownership. However, although in mid-1998 legislation was passed on the establishment of a centre to aid farm privatization, agricultural reform has proceeded slowly. The IMF estimated that 51% of Tajikistan's arable land was privately owned at the end of 2001. During 1990–2000 agricultural GDP decreased, in real terms, by an average of 4.8% annually. However, real agricultural GDP increased by 3.8% in 2000 and by 12.4% in 2001.

Industry (comprising manufacturing, mining, utilities and construction) contributed 22.6% of GDP in 2001, and provided 9.2% of employment. There is little heavy industry, except for mineral extraction, aluminium production and power generation. Light industry concentrates on food-processing, textiles and carpet-making. Industrial GDP declined, in real terms, by an annual average of 13.5% in 1990–2000. Sectoral GDP decreased by 4.3% in 1999, but increased by 13.4% in 2000.

Tajikistan has considerable mineral deposits, including gold, antimony, silver, aluminium, iron, lead, mercury and tin. Alu-

minium production increased by 30.4% in 2000 compared with the previous year, owing to regular energy and raw mineral supplies, which were hitherto impeded by military operations in and around Tajikistan. There are deposits of coal as well as reserves of petroleum and natural gas. Mineral extraction is hampered by the mountainous terrain.

According to the World Bank, the manufacturing sector contributed 22.6% of GDP in 2000. The GDP of the manufacturing sector declined, in real terms, by an annual average of 10.2% in 1990–2000. However, real manufacturing GDP increased by 4.9% in 1999 and by 10.2% in 2000.

Although imports of fuel and energy comprised 29.5% of the value of merchandise imports in 2001 (mainly supplied by Turkmenistan, Uzbekistan, Kazakhstan and Russia), Tajikistan is believed to have sufficient unexploited reserves of petroleum and natural gas to meet its requirements. The mountain river system is widely used for hydroelectric power generation, and Tajikistan is one of the largest producers of hydroelectric power world-wide. Electric energy production amounted to some 15,797m. kWh in 1999, of which 15,300m. kWh (97%) was provided by hydroelectric power.

The services sector contributed 50.8% of GDP in 2001, and provided 24.8% of employment. The GDP of the services sector declined, in real terms, by an annual average of 0.5% in 1990–2000; however, real services GDP increased by 22.0% in 1999 and by 5.1% in 2000.

In 2001, according to IMF figures, Tajikistan recorded a visible trade deficit of US $121m., while there was a deficit of $74m. on the current account of the balance of payments. In 2001 the principal source of imports was Uzbekistan (accounting for 21.9% of the total); other important suppliers were Russia, Kazakhstan, Ukraine and Turkmenistan. The major market for exports in that year was Russia (accounting for 16.1% of the total). Uzbekistan was also a significant purchaser. The principal exports in 2001 were alumina (accounting for some 60.9% of the total value of exports), electricity and cotton fibre. The principal imports in 2001 were alumina, electricity, petroleum products, and grain and flour.

In 2001 there was an overall budgetary surplus of 11.3m. somoni (equivalent to some 0.4% of GDP). Tajikistan's total external debt was US $1,170.0m. at the end of 2000, of which $625.6m. was long-term public debt. The cost of debt-servicing in that year was equivalent to 10.9% of the value of exports of goods and services. The average annual rate of inflation was 303.4% in 1990–2000. The annual rate of inflation reached 2,195% in 1993, but had declined significantly by 1996, to some 40.5%. According to IMF figures, the rate of inflation was 26.7% in 1999 and 23.4% in 2000. The official unemployment rate was 2.4% in 2001; however, according to unofficial estimates the rate of unemployment was as high as 30%.

In 1992 Tajikistan joined the Economic Co-operation Organization (ECO, see p. 192) and the European Bank for Reconstruction and Development (EBRD, see p. 193); it became a member of the IMF and the World Bank in 1993. Tajikistan has sought to promote closer economic integration among the member states of the Commonwealth of Independent States (CIS, see p. 172). In April 1998 Tajikistan was admitted to the CIS Customs Union (already comprising Russia, Kazakhstan, Kyrgyzstan and Belarus). In October 2000 a treaty was signed, establishing the Eurasian Economic Community (EAEC) to supersede the Customs Union. In November 1996 Tajikistan joined the Islamic Development Bank (see p. 257) and it became a member of the Asian Development Bank (ADB, see p. 143) in February 1998. In July 2001 Tajikistan was granted observer status at the World Trade Organization (WTO, see p. 323).

Already the poorest of the republics of the former USSR, during the early 1990s the Tajik economy was very seriously affected by the widespread disruption to the former Soviet trading system, caused by the collapse of the USSR, and by the civil war that broke out in 1992 (see Recent History). In May 1995 Tajikistan introduced the Tajik rouble, and in September the Government announced an ambitious five-year programme of economic reform. Following the conclusion of the peace agreement in June 1997, a number of international financial organizations allocated credit to Tajikistan to facilitate the structural reform process, and to assist in rebuilding the country's infrastructure. However, the financial crisis in Russia in mid-1998 had a strongly adverse effect on the Tajik economy, as did the sharp decline in world cotton prices. The introduction of a new currency, the somoni, at the end of October 2000 was expected to strengthen Tajikistan's monetary and banking system, and the country's economic performance improved significantly in 2000–01, despite the effects of drought. Economic growth, however, had failed to reduce poverty (affecting almost 80% of the population in 2001, according to the ADB) or increase employment; an estimated 200,000 people left Tajikistan in 2001 to seek work abroad. In early 2002 it became evident that the IMF had released funding in 2000–01 on the basis of incorrect information, supplied by the Tajik Government, relating to the country's level of external debt. However, the IMF continued to support the Government's economic programme, and in December it approved a new, three-year loan under its Poverty Reduction and Growth Facility. Meanwhile, in August the European Commission announced that it was to resume its programme of assistance to Tajikistan, following a four-year suspension. Although strong economic growth was sustained in 2002, there was a high level of external debt and the deficit on the current account of the balance of payments remained significant, partly owing to low global prices for aluminium and cotton. Moreover, there was little foreign investment, and substantial further reform was required to promote private-sector development.

Education

Education is controlled by the Ministry of Education and is fully funded by the State at all levels. Education is officially compulsory for nine years, to be undertaken between seven and 17 years of age. Primary education begins at seven years of age and lasts for four years. Secondary education, beginning at the age of 11, lasts for up to seven years, comprising a first cycle of five years and a second of two years. In 1996 the total enrolment at primary schools was equivalent to 95% of the relevant age-group (males 96%; females 94%). The total enrolment in secondary education in that year was equivalent to 78% of the relevant age-group (males 83%; females 74%). Since independence, greater emphasis has been placed in the curriculum on Tajik language and literature, including classical Persian literature. In 2000/01 84,400 students were enrolled at 31 institutes of higher education. In 2001 expenditure on education by all levels of government was 64.0m. somoni (18.9% of total government expenditure).

Public Holidays

2003: 1 January (New Year's Day), 12 February* (Id-al-Adha—Feast of the Sacrifice), 8 March (International Women's Day), 20–22 March (Navrus), 1 May (International Labour Day), 9 May (Victory Day), 9 September (Independence Day), 6 November (Constitution Day), 26 November* (Id-al-Fitr, end of Ramadan).

2004: 1 January (New Year's Day), 2 February* (Id-al-Adha—Feast of the Sacrifice), 8 March (International Women's Day), 20–22 March (Navrus), 1 May (International Labour Day), 9 May (Victory Day), 9 September (Independence Day), 6 November (Constitution Day), 14 November* (Id-al-Fitr, end of Ramadan).

*These holidays are dependent on the Islamic lunar calendar and may vary by one or two days from the dates given.

Weights and Measures

The metric system is in force.

Statistical Survey

Source (unless otherwise indicated): State Committee for Statistics, 734025 Dushanbe, Bokhtar 17; tel. (372) 27-63-31; fax (372) 21-43-75; e-mail stat@tajikistan.com.

Area and Population

AREA, POPULATION AND DENSITY

Area (sq km)	143,100*
Population (census results)†	
12 January 1989	5,092,603
20 January 2000	
Males	3,069,100
Females.	3,058,393
Total	6,127,493
Population (official estimates at 31 December)	
1999	6,126,747
2000	6,249,985
Density (per sq km) at 31 December 2000	43.7

*55,251 sq miles.

† Figures refer to *de jure* population. The *de facto* total at the 1989 census was 5,108,576.

POPULATION BY ETHNIC GROUP

(2000 census)

	%
Tajik	80.0
Uzbek.	15.3
Russian	1.1
Tatar	0.3
Others	3.3
Total	100.0

PRINCIPAL TOWNS

(population at 1 January 2002)

Dushanbe (capital) .	575,900	Kanibadam . . .	45,100
Khujand			
(Khodzhent)* . .	147,400	Kofarnihon‡ . . .	45,100
Kulob		Tursunzade	
(Kulyab) . .	79,500	(Tursunzoda) . .	38,100
Qurgonteppa			
(Kurgan-Tyube) .	61,200	Isfara	37,300
Istravshan† . . .	51,700	Panjakent	
		(Pendzhikent) . .	33,200

* Known as Leninabad between 1936 and 1992.

† Also known as Urateppa (Ura-Tyube).

‡ Formerly Ordzhonikidzeabad.

BIRTHS, MARRIAGES AND DEATHS

	Registered live births		Registered marriages		Registered deaths	
	Number	Rate (per 1,000)	Number	Rate (per 1,000)	Number	Rate (per 1,000)
1994 . .	191,596	34.2	38,820	6.8	39,943	7.1
1995 . .	193,182	34.1	32,078	5.7	34,274	6.0
1996 . .	172,341	30.0	28,019	4.8	31,610	5.5
1997 . .	178,127	30.6	27,250	4.7	27,888	4.8
1998 . .	185,733	31.3	22,276	3.8	29,261	4.9
1999 . .	180,888	29.8	22,536	3.9	25,384	4.2
2000 . .	167,246	27.0	26,257	4.2	29,387	4.7
2001 . .	171,623	27.2	28,827	4.6	32,015	5.1

Expectation of life (WHO estimates, years at birth): 63.3 (males 59.9; females 66.9) in 2001 (Source: WHO, *World Health Report*).

ECONOMICALLY ACTIVE POPULATION
(annual averages, '000 persons)

	1999	2000	2001
Activities of the material sphere .	1,420	1,416	1,452
Agriculture*	1,118	1,135	1,167
Industry†	133	121	131
Construction	44	36	31
Trade and catering‡	70	72	72
Transport and communications	44	42	43
Activities of the non-material			
sphere	313	326	316
Housing and municipal services	24	27	29
Health care, social security,			
physical culture and sports	75	82	72
Education, culture and arts .	179	179	178
Science, research and			
development	5	5	5
Government and finance . .	31	34	23
Total employed	1,737	1,745	1,769
Unemployed	54	49	43
Total labour force	1,791	1,794	1,812

* Including forestry.

† Comprising manufacturing (except printing and publishing), mining and quarrying, electricity, gas, water, logging and fishing.

‡ Including material and technical supply.

Health and Welfare

KEY INDICATORS

Total fertility rate (children per woman, 2001).	3.1
Under-5 mortality rate (per 1,000 live births, 2001) . . .	72
HIV/AIDS (% of persons aged 15–49, 2001).	<0.10
Physicians (per 1,000 head, 1998)	2.01
Hospital beds (per 1,000 head, 1994)	8.8
Health expenditure (2000): US $ per head (PPP) . . .	29
Health expenditure (2000): % of GDP	2.5
Health expenditure (2000): public (% of total)	80.8
Human Development Index (2000): ranking	112
Human Development Index (2000): value	0.667

For sources and definitions, see explanatory note on p. vi.

Agriculture

PRINCIPAL CROPS
('000 metric tons)

	1999	2000	2001
Wheat	365	406	388
Rice (paddy)	47	82	40
Barley	25	19	16
Maize	36	38	42
Potatoes	240	303	318
Cottonseed	313	335	453
Cabbages	16	18	23
Tomatoes	133	129	127
Dry onions	153	110	129
Carrots	52	48	69
Other vegetables	31	49	51
Watermelons*	84	95	97
Grapes	54	110	111
Other fruits and berries . . .	78	170	152
Cotton (lint)	98†	93†	96‡
Tobacco (leaves)	7	7	4

* Including melons, pumpkins and squash.

† Unofficial figure.

‡ FAO estimate.

Sources: State Committee for Statistics, Dushanbe; and FAO.

LIVESTOCK
('000 head at 1 January)

	1999	2000	2001
Horses	72	72	71
Asses*	32	30	32
Cattle	1,037	1,062	1,091
Camels*	43	43	42
Sheep	1,472	1,478	1,490
Goats	706	744	779
Poultry	771	1,061	1,320

* FAO estimates.

Sources: State Committee for Statistics, Dushanbe; and FAO.

LIVESTOCK PRODUCTS
('000 metric tons)

	1999	2000	2001
Beef and veal	15.0	14.8	14.8
Mutton, lamb and goat meat . .	13.2	13.0	12.8
Poultry meat	0.1	0.1	0.4
Cows' milk	302	310	316
Goats' milk	22.0*	24.5*	25.0†
Cheese	6.2	6.6	6.7
Wool: greasy	2.1	2.1	2.2
Sheepskins (fresh)	1.7	2.1	2.0

* Unofficial figure.

† FAO estimate.

Sources: State Committee for Statistics, Dushanbe; and FAO.

Fishing

(aquaculture only, metric tons, live weight)

	1998	1999	2000
Silver carp	81	58	55
Common carp	0	8	10
Grass carp	0	8	21
Total catch (incl. others) . . .	81	74	86

Source: FAO, *Yearbook of Fishery Statistics*.

Mining

(metric tons, unless otherwise indicated)

	1998	1999	2000
Hard coal	18,500	19,100	22,200
Crude petroleum	19,400	18,700	18,400
Natural gas (million cu m) . . .	32.4	36.1	40.0
Lead concentrate*†	800	800	800‡
Antimony ore*†	1,500	1,800	2,000‡
Mercury*†	35	35	40‡
Silver*	5	5†	5‡
Gold (kilograms)*	3,000	2,700†	2,700‡
Gypsum (crude)†	31,700	35,000	35,000‡

* Figures refer to the metal content of ores and concentrates.

† Estimated production.

‡ Provisional figure.

Sources: US Geological Survey and State Committee for Statistics, Dushanbe.

2001: Hard coal 24,200 metric tons; Crude petroleum 16,100 metric tons; Natural gas 81.6 million cu m.

Industry

SELECTED PRODUCTS

('000 metric tons, unless otherwise indicated)

	1999	2000	2001
Cottonseed oil (refined)	22	23	16.3
Wheat flour	341	307	312
Ethyl alcohol ('000 hectolitres) . .	28	23	27
Wine ('000 hectolitres)	51	39	45
Beer ('000 hectolitres)	7	4	8
Soft drinks ('000 hectolitres) . .	19	49	118
Cigarettes (million)	209	667	1,155
Wool yarn (pure and mixed) . .	0.8	0.5	0.6
Cotton yarn (pure and mixed) . .	14.7	15.0	14.9
Woven cotton fabrics (million sq			
metres)	11.5	10.9	13.0
Woven silk fabrics ('000 sq metres)	386	253	247
Knotted wool carpets and rugs ('000			
sq metres)	1,045	341	509
Footwear, excl. rubber ('000 pairs).	72	110	94
Caustic soda (Sodium hydroxide) .	0.7	3.7	3.0
Nitrogenous fertilizers*	4.6	11.1	3.4
Clay building bricks (million) . .	33	30	26
Cement	33.2	54.8	68.9
Aluminium (unwrought): primary	229.1	269.2	289.1
Electric energy (million kWh) . .	15,797	14,247	14,336

* Production in terms of nitrogen.

Finance

CURRENCY AND EXCHANGE RATES

Monetary Units

100 diram = 1 somoni

Sterling, Dollar and Euro Equivalents (31 December 2002)

£1 sterling = 4.835 somoni

US $1 = 3.000 somoni

€1 = 3.146 somoni

100 somoni = £20.68 = $33.33 = €31.79

Average Exchange Rate (somoni per US $)

2000   2.0763

2001   2.3722

2002   2.7641

Note: The Tajik rouble was introduced in May 1995, replacing the Russian (formerly Soviet) rouble at the rate of 1 Tajik rouble = 100 Russian roubles. A new currency, the somoni (equivalent to 1,000 Tajik roubles), was introduced in October 2000. Some figures in this Survey are still in terms of Tajik roubles.

BUDGET

('000 somoni)*

Revenue†	1999	2000	2001
Tax revenue	158,244	205,409	313,491
Individual income tax. . . .	14,412	22,255	32,842
Enterprise profits tax	17,158	11,008	14,300
Excise taxes	8,002	9,010	15,521
Tax on vehicles	610	890	1,225
Value-added tax	30,561	44,466	86,041
Customs revenue	17,873	27,351	51,566
Taxes on aluminium and cotton .	47,408	58,934	62,797
Land tax	7,250	7,876	9,537
Prospection tax	1,134	1,930	3,251
State duties and local taxes . .	13,836	21,690	36,411
Non-tax revenue	10,059	13,393	28,825
Total	168,303	218,803	342,316

Expenditure	1999	2000‡	2001‡
General public services	20,417	49,957	66,743
Law enforcement	22,060	21,993	13,821
Defence	18,723	21,496	29,577
Social services	49,905	69,286	106,586
Education	28,363	40,851	63,967
Health	13,893	16,600	24,595
Social security	2,500	2,442	2,706
Cash compensation payments . .	1,579	4,996	9,476
Housing	15,557	17,183	n.a.
Recreational, cultural and other			
services	6,586	−30	n.a.
Economic services	47,518	37,220	58,815
Agriculture, forestry, fishing and			
hunting	8,347	8,574	n.a.
Transport and communications	20,950	18,138	n.a.
Science	1,508	—	—
Interest payments	7,939	6,518	13,821
Other purposes	30,730	16,549	39,580
Total	200,379	228,015	338,418
Current	154,082	178,814	262,342
Capital	46,204	47,802	73,624
Lending minus repayments. . .	93	1,399	2,452

* Figures refer to the consolidated operations of the State Budget, comprising the budgets of the central (republican) Government and local authorities, and the Social Security Fund.

† Excluding grants received ('000 somoni): 3,582 in 1999; 1,688 in 2000. Also excluded are the proceeds of privatization ('000 somoni): 10,805 in 1999; 17,478 in 2000; 7,413 in 2001.

‡ Owing to changes in classification, figures are not strictly comparable with those for earlier years.

Source: IMF, *Republic of Tajikistan: Statistical Appendix* (December 2002).

MONEY SUPPLY

('000 somoni at 31 December)

	2000	2001	2002
Currency outside banks	86,773	103,631	135,768
Demand deposits	15,709	23,792	36,329
Total money (incl. others) . .	102,715	128,830	173,192

Source: IMF, *International Financial Statistics*.

COST OF LIVING

(Consumer price index for December; base: previous December = 100)

	1998	1999	2000
Food	99.1	129.7	166.4
Other goods	119.2	136.5	144.2
Services	132.0	147.7	133.9
All items	102.7	130.1	160.6

Source: partly IMF, *Republic of Tajikistan: Statistical Appendix* (January 2003).

Annual averages (base: 1990 = 0.1): All items 73,107 in 1998; 92,114 in 1999; 114,222 in 2000 (Source: ILO, *Yearbook of Labour Statistics*).

NATIONAL ACCOUNTS

('000 somoni at current prices)

Expenditure on the Gross Domestic Product

	1998	1999	2000
Government final consumption			
expenditure.	79,966	116,520	153,170
Private final consumption			
expenditure.	706,371	967,799	1,322,416
Increase in stocks	20,504	9,534	39,914
Gross fixed capital formation . .	137,639	223,621	169,309
Total domestic expenditure	944,480	1,317,473	1,684,809
Exports of goods and services . .	509,560	852,128	1,537,684
Less Imports of goods and services	589,259	821,332	1,353,462
Sub-total	864,781	1,348,269	1,869,031
Statistical discrepancy* . . .	160,430	−3,316	−62,264
GDP in purchasers' values . .	1,025,211	1,344,953	1,806,767

* Referring to the difference between the sum of the expenditure components and official estimates of GDP, compiled from the production approach.

TAJIKISTAN

Gross Domestic Product by Economic Activity

	1998	1999	2000
Agriculture	257,191	341,332	487,828
Forestry	173	146	132
Industry*	206,067	291,550	431,661
Construction	39,538	72,948	61,059
Transport and communications	42,643	99,029	88,270
Trade and catering†	231,845	270,002	334,169
Other activities of the material sphere	10,245	4,838	5,784
Finance and insurance	7,872	14,111	20,445
Housing and public utilities	54,594	39,968	74,765
General administration and defence	23,821	32,492	55,845
Education, culture and art	41,443	51,496	70,732
Health care, social security and sports	29,061	17,666	18,261
Other marketable non-material services	3,690	11,543	6,351
Private non-profit institutions	2,510	4,491	6,452
Sub-total	950,691	1,251,611	1,661,752
Less Imputed bank service charge	3,298	4,632	4,666
GDP at factor cost	947,394	1,246,979	1,657,086
Indirect taxes	79,011	106,012	154,174
Less Subsidies	1,193	8,038	4,494
GDP in purchasers' values	1,025,211	1,344,953	1,806,767

* Comprising manufacturing (except printing and publishing), mining and quarrying, electricity, gas, water, logging and fishing.
† Including material and technical supply.

BALANCE OF PAYMENTS
(US $ million)

	1998	1999	2000
Exports of goods f.o.b.	586	666	789
Imports of goods c.i.f.	−731	−693	−836
Trade balance	−145	−27	−46
Other services (net)	18	11	5
Balance on goods and services	−127	−16	−42
Other income (net)	−38	−55	−57
Balance on goods, services and income	−165	−71	−99
Current transfers (net)	57	35	37
Current balance	−108	−36	−62
Capital transfers (net)	0	0	5
Direct investment (net)	24	21	22
Other public-sector capital (net)	28	5	11
Other capital (net). Net errors and omissions	16	−17	3
Overall balance	−40	−26	−22

Source: IMF, *Republic of Tajikistan: Statistical Appendix* (May 2001) and Staff Report (July 2001).

External Trade

PRINCIPAL COMMODITIES
(US $ million)

Imports c.i.f.	1999	2000	2001
Alumina	81	198	184
Natural gas	36	35	27
Petroleum products	54	48	78
Electricity	179	119	98
Grain and flour	46	45	38
Total (incl. others)	663	675	688

Exports f.o.b.	1999	2000	2001
Aluminium	309	433	397
Cotton fibre	82	84	62
Electricity	175	92	79
Total (incl. others)	689	784	652

PRINCIPAL TRADING PARTNERS
(US $ million)

Imports c.i.f.	1999	2000	2001
Azerbaijan	15.6	63.1	n.a.
Iran	10.4	7.6	10.0
Kazakhstan	78.8	82.4	89.1
Romania	3.3	41.0	n.a.
Russia	92.4	105.1	129.4
Switzerland	25.1	0.6	n.a.
Turkmenistan	15.2	29.3	62.3
Ukraine	37.7	84.3	63.6
United Kingdom	70.5	86.9	n.a.
Uzbekistan	264.4	185.6	150.7
Total (incl. others)	663.1	675.0	687.5

Exports f.o.b.	1999	2000	2001
Belgium	7.0	5.1	n.a.
Iran	13.5	12.5	n.a.
Italy	4.9	21.4	5.7
Korea, Republic	7.4	10.9	7.0
Moldova	—	14.3	n.a.
Netherlands	222.3	178.2	n.a.
Russia	115.1	258.8	104.7
Switzerland	75.1	72.2	n.a.
Turkey	1.0	58.4	n.a.
Uzbekistan	181.0	97.8	87.2
Total (incl. others)	688.7	784.3	651.6

Source: partly Asian Development Bank, *Key Indicators of Developing Asian and Pacific Countries*.

Transport

RAILWAYS
(traffic)

	1999	2000	2001
Passenger-km (million)	61	73	32
Freight ton-km (million)	1,282	1,326	1,248

CIVIL AVIATION
(estimated traffic on scheduled services)

	1997	1998	1999
Kilometres flown (million)	7	5	4
Passengers carried ('000)	594	217	156
Passenger-km (million)	1,825	322	229
Freight ton-km (million)	166	32	23

Source: UN, *Statistical Yearbook*.

Communications Media

	1998	1999	2000
Television receivers ('000 in use) .	1,900	2,000	2,000
Telephones ('000 main lines in use)	221.3	212.5	218.5
Facsimile machines (number in use)	2,000	2,100	n.a.
Mobile cellular telephones ('000 subscribers).	0.4	0.6	1.2
Internet users ('000)	—	2.0	3.0

Books published: 132 titles and 997,000 copies in 1996.

Daily newspapers (estimates): 2 titles and 120,000 copies (average circulation) in 1996.

Non-daily newspapers: 73 titles and 153,000 copies (average circulation) in 1996.

Other periodicals: 11 titles and 130,000 copies (average circulation) in 1996.

Radio receivers ('000 in use): 850 in 1997.

2001: Telephones ('000 main lines in use) 223.0; Mobile cellular telephones ('000 subscribers) 1.6.

Sources: UNESCO, *Statistical Yearbook*; International Telecommunication Union.

Education

(2001/02, unless otherwise indicated)

	Institutions	Teachers	Students
Pre-primary	501	6,615*	57,812
Primary.	660	100,200	33,000
Secondary:			
general	2,861		1,487,600
specialist	128		39,400
vocational	55	n.a.	29,842†
Higher (incl. universities)	31	6,100	84,400

* 1996/97.
† 1994/95.

Source: partly UNESCO, *Statistical Yearbook*.

Adult literacy rate (UNESCO estimates): 99.2% (males 99.6%; females 98.8%) in 2000 (Source: UN Development Programme, *Human Development Report*).

Directory

The Constitution

Tajikistan's Constitution entered into force on 6 November 1994, when it was approved by a majority of voters in a nation-wide plebiscite. It replaced the previous Soviet-style Constitution, adopted in 1978. The following is a summary of its main provisions:

PRINCIPLES OF THE CONSTITUTIONAL SYSTEM

The Republic of Tajikistan is a sovereign, democratic, law-governed, secular and unitary state. The state language is Tajik, but Russian is accorded the status of a language of communication between nationalities.

Recognition, observance and protection of human and civil rights and freedoms is the obligation of the State. The people of Tajikistan are the expression of sovereignty and the sole source of power of the State, which they express through their elected representatives.

Tajikistan consists of Gornyi Badakhshan Autonomous Region, regions, towns, districts, settlements and villages. The territory of the State is indivisible and inviolable. Agitation and actions aimed at disunity of the State are prohibited.

No ideology, including religious ideology, may be granted the status of a state ideology. Religious organizations are separate from the State and may not interfere in state affairs.

The Constitution of Tajikistan has supreme legal authority and its norms have direct application. Laws and other legal acts which run counter to the Constitution have no legal validity. The State, its bodies and officials are bound to observe the provisions of the Constitution.

Tajikistan will implement a peaceful policy, respecting the sovereignty and independence of other states of the world and will determine foreign relations on the basis of international norms. Agitation for war is prohibited.

The economy of Tajikistan is based on various forms of ownership. The State guarantees freedom of economic activity, entrepreneurship, equality of rights and the protection of all forms of ownership, including private ownership. Land and natural resources are under state ownership.

FUNDAMENTAL DUTIES OF INDIVIDUALS AND CITIZENS

The freedoms and rights of individuals are protected by the Constitution, the laws of the republic and international documents to which Tajikistan is a signatory. The State guarantees the rights and freedoms of every person, regardless of nationality, race, sex, language, religious beliefs, political persuasion, social status, knowledge and property. Men and women have the same rights. Every person has the right to life. No one may be subjected to torture, punishment or inhuman treatment. No one may be arrested, kept in custody or exiled without a legal basis, and no one is adjudged guilty of a crime except by the sentence of a court in accordance with the law. Every person has the right freely to choose their place of residence, to leave the republic and return to it. Every person has the right to profess any religion individually or with others, or not to profess any, and to take part in religious ceremonies. Every citizen has the right to take part in political life and state administration; to elect and be elected from the age of 18; to join and leave political parties, trade unions and other associations; to take part in meetings, rallies or demonstrations. Every person is guaranteed freedom of speech. State censorship is prohibited.

Every person has the right: to ownership and inheritance; to work; to housing; to health care, provided free of charge by the State; to social security in old age, or in the event of sickness or disability. Every person has the right to education. Basic general education is compulsory.

A state of emergency is declared as a temporary measure to ensure the security of citizens and of the State in the instance of a direct threat to the freedom of citizens, the State's independence, its territorial integrity, or natural disasters. The period of a state of emergency is up to three months; it can be prolonged by the President of the Republic.

THE SUPREME ASSEMBLY

The Supreme Assembly is the highest representative and legislative body of the republic. Its 181 members are elected for a five-year term. Any citizen over the age of 25 may be elected to the Supreme Assembly.

The powers of the Supreme Assembly include: enactment and amendment of laws, and their annulment; interpretation of the Constitution and laws; determination of the basic direction of domestic and foreign policy; ratification of presidential decrees on the appointment and dismissal of the Chairman of the National Bank, the Chairman and members of the Constitutional Court, the Supreme Court and the Supreme Economic Court; ratification of the state budget; determining and altering the structure of administrative territorial units; ratification and annulment of international treaties; ratification of presidential decrees on a state of war and a state of emergency.

Laws are adopted by a majority of the deputies of the Supreme Assembly. If the President does not agree with the law, he may return it to the Supreme Assembly. If the Supreme Assembly once again approves the law, with at least a two-thirds majority, the President must sign it.

THE PRESIDENT OF THE REPUBLIC

The President of the Republic is the Head of State and the head of the executive. The President is elected by the citizens of Tajikistan on the basis of universal, direct and equal suffrage for a five-year term. Any citizen who knows the state language and has lived on the territory of Tajikistan for the preceding 10 years may be nominated to the post of President of the Republic. A person may not be nominated to the office of President for more than two consecutive terms.

The President has the authority: to represent Tajikistan inside the country and in international relations; to establish or abolish ministries with the approval of the Supreme Assembly; to appoint or dismiss the Chairman (Prime Minister) and other members of the Council of Ministers and to propose them for approval to the Supreme Assembly; to appoint and dismiss chairmen of regions, towns and districts, and propose new appointments for approval to the relevant assemblies of people's deputies; to appoint and dismiss members of the Constitutional Court, the Supreme Court and the Supreme Economic Court (with the approval of the Supreme Assembly); to appoint and dismiss judges of lower courts; to sign laws; to lead the implementation of foreign policy and sign international treaties; to appoint diplomatic representatives abroad; to be Commander-in-Chief of the armed forces of Tajikistan; to declare a state of war or a state of emergency (with the approval of the Supreme Assembly).

In the event of the President's death, resignation, removal from office or inability to perform his duties, the duties of the President will be carried out by the Chairman of the Supreme Assembly until further presidential elections can be held. New elections must be held within three months of these circumstances. The President may be removed from office in the case of his committing a crime, by the decision of at least two-thirds of deputies of the Supreme Assembly, taking into account the decisions of the Constitutional Court.

THE COUNCIL OF MINISTERS

The Council of Ministers consists of the Chairman (Prime Minister), the First Deputy Chairman, Deputy Chairmen, Ministers and Chairmen of State Committees. The Council of Ministers is responsible for implementation of laws and decrees of the Supreme Assembly and decrees and orders of the President. The Council of Ministers leaves office when a new President is elected.

LOCAL GOVERNMENT

The local representative authority in regions, towns and districts is the assembly of people's deputies. Assemblies are elected for a five-year term. Local executive government is the responsibility of the President's representative: the chairman of the assembly of people's deputies, who is proposed by the President and approved by the relevant assembly. The Supreme Assembly may dissolve local representative bodies, if their actions do not conform to the Constitution and the law.

THE GORNYI BADAKHSHAN AUTONOMOUS REGION

The Gornyi Badakhshan Autonomous Region is an integral and indivisible part of Tajikistan, the territory of which cannot be changed without the consent of the regional assembly of people's deputies.

JUDICIARY

The judiciary is independent and protects the rights and freedoms of the individual, the interests of the State, organizations and institutions, and legality and justice. Judicial power is implemented by the Constitutional Court, the Supreme Court, the Supreme Economic Court, the Military Court, the Court of Gornyi Badakhshan Autonomous Region, and courts of regions, the city of Dushanbe, towns and districts. The term of judges is five years. The creation of emergency courts is not permitted.

Judges are independent and are subordinate only to the Constitution and the law. Interference in their activity is not permitted.

THE OFFICE OF THE PROCURATOR-GENERAL

The Procurator-General and procurators subordinate to him ensure the control and observance of laws within the framework of their authority in the territory of Tajikistan. The Procurator-General is responsible to the Supreme Assembly and the President, and is elected for a five-year term.

PROCEDURES FOR INTRODUCING AMENDMENTS TO THE CONSTITUTION

Amendments and addenda to the Constitution are made by means of a referendum. A referendum takes place with the support of at least two-thirds of the people's deputies. The President, or at least one-third of the people's deputies, may submit amendments and addenda to the Constitution. The form of public administration, the territorial integrity and the democratic, law-governed and secular nature of the State are irrevocable.

Note: In September 1999 Parliament enacted a number of constitutional amendments, including: the creation of a bicameral legislature, the extension of the President's term of office to seven years, and the legalization of religious-based political parties.

The Government

HEAD OF STATE

President of the Republic of Tajikistan: IMAMALI SHARIPOVICH RAKHMONOV (elected by popular vote on 6 November 1994; re-elected on 6 November 1999).

COUNCIL OF MINISTERS
(April 2003)

Chairman (Prime Minister) and Minister of Construction: AKIL AKILOV.

First Deputy Chairman: Haji AKBAR TURAJONZODA.

Deputy Chairmen: NIGINA SHARIPOVA, Maj.-Gen. SAIDAMIR ZUKHUROV, KOZIDAVLAT KOIMDODOV, ZOKIR VAZIROV, ASADULLO GHULOMOV.

Minister of Agriculture: TURSUN RAKHMATOV.

Minister of Communications: SAIDMAHMAD ZUBAIDOV.

Minister of Culture, Press and Information: KAROMATULLO OLIMOV.

Minister of Defence: Maj.-Gen. SHERALI KHAYRULLOYEV.

Minister of the Economy and Foreign Economic Relations: KHAKIM SOLIYEV.

Minister of Education: SAFARALI RAJABOV.

Minister of Emergency Situations and Civil Defence: Maj.-Gen. MIRZO ZIYOYEV.

Minister of Energy: ABDULLO YOROV.

Minister of Environmental Protection: USMONKUL SHOKIROV.

Minister of Finance: SAFARALI NAJMIDDINOV.

Minister of Foreign Affairs: TALBAK NAZAROV.

Minister of Grain Products: BEKMUROD UROKOV.

Minister of Health: NUSRATULLO FAIZULLOYEV.

Minister of Industry: ZAID SAIDOV.

Minister of Internal Affairs: KHOMIDDIN SHARIPOV.

Minister of Justice: KHALIFABOBO KHAMIDOV.

Minister of Labour, Employment and Social Welfare: MAHMADSHO ILOLOV.

Minister of Land Improvement and Water Economy: ABDUKAKHIR NAZIROV.

Minister of Security: KHAYRIDDIN ABDURAKHIMOV.

Minister of State Revenues and Tax Collection: GHULOMJON BOBOYEV.

Minister of Transport and Roads: ABDUJALOL SALIMOV.

Chairmen of State Committees

Chairman of State Committee for Construction and Architecture: ISMAT ESHMIRZOYEV.

Chairman for State Committee on Land Resources and Reclamation: DAVLATSHO GULMAKHMADOV.

Chairman of State Committee for Oil and Gas: SALAMSHO MUKHABBATOV.

Chairman of State Committee for Religious Affairs: SAID AKHMEDOV.

Chairman of State Committee for State Property: SHERALI GULOV.

Chairman of State Committee for Statistics: KHOLMAMED AZIMOV.

Chairman of State Committee for Television and Radio: UBAYDULLO RAJABOV.

Deputy Chairman of State Committee for State Border Protection: Maj.-Gen. SAFAR SAYFULLOYEV.

MINISTRIES

Office of the President: 734023 Dushanbe, pr. Rudaki 80; tel. (372) 21-04-18; fax (372) 21-18-37.

Secretariat of the Prime Minister: 734023 Dushanbe, pr. Rudaki 80; tel. (372) 21-18-71; fax (372) 21-51-10.

Ministry of Agriculture: 734025 Dushanbe, pr. Rudaki 44; tel. (372) 22-31-46; fax (372) 21-57-94.

Ministry of Communications: 734025 Dushanbe, pr. Rudaki 57; tel. (372) 21-22-84; fax (372) 21-29-53; e-mail mincom@mincom.netrt .org; internet www.netrt.org/mincomtj/.

Ministry of Construction: Dushanbe, Kirova 36; tel. (372) 22-61-43; fax (372) 27-86-17.

Ministry of Culture, Press and Information: 734025 Dushanbe, N. Karabayeva 17; tel. (372) 21-03-05; fax (372) 21-36-30.

Ministry of Defence: 734025 Dushanbe, kuchai Bokhtar 59; tel. (372) 23-19-89; fax (372) 23-19-37.

Ministry of the Economy and Foreign Economic Relations: 734002 Dushanbe, pr. Rudaki 42; tel. (372) 23-29-44; fax (372) 21-04-04.

Ministry of Education: 734025 Dushanbe, Chekhova 13A; tel. (372) 21-46-05; fax (372) 21-70-41.

Ministry of Emergency Situations and Civil Defence: 734025 Dushanbe, kuchai Bokhtar 59; tel. (372) 21-12-42; fax (372) 21-13-31.

Ministry of Energy: Dushanbe.

Ministry of Environmental Protection: 734025 Dushanbe, kuchai Bokhtar 12; tel. (372) 21-30-39; fax (372) 21-18-39.

Ministry of Finance: 734025 Dushanbe, kuchai Akademikov Radjabovii 3; tel. (372) 21-14-17; fax (372) 21-33-29.

Ministry of Foreign Affairs: 734051 Dushanbe, pr. Rudaki 42; tel. (372) 21-18-08; fax (372) 21-02-59; e-mail dushanbe@mfaumo.td.silk.org.

Ministry of Grain Products: 734025 Dushanbe, pr. Rudaki 42; tel. (372) 27-61-31; fax (372) 27-95-71.

Ministry of Health: 734025 Dushanbe, Shevchenko 69; tel. (372) 21-18-35; fax (372) 21-48-71.

Ministry of Industry: Dushanbe.

Ministry of Internal Affairs: 734025 Dushanbe, Dzerzhinskogo 29; tel. (372) 21-30-53; fax (372) 21-26-05.

Ministry of Justice: 734025 Dushanbe, pr. Rudaki 25; tel. (372) 21-44-05; fax (372) 21-80-66.

Ministry of Labour, Employment and Social Welfare: 734028 Dushanbe, kuchai Alishepa Navoi 52; tel. (372) 35-18-37; fax (372) 36-24-15.

Ministry of Land Improvement and Water Economy: 734001 Dushanbe, pr. Rudaki 78; tel. (372) 21-20-31.

Ministry of Security: 734025 Dushanbe, Gorkogo 8; tel. (372) 23-29-12; fax (372) 21-15-65.

Ministry of State Revenues and Tax Collection: Dushanbe.

Ministry of Transport and Roads: 734042 Dushanbe, kuchai Aini 14; tel. (372) 21-17-13; fax (372) 21-20-03.

Principal State Committees

State Committee for Construction and Architecture: 734025 Dushanbe, Mazayeva 1911; tel. and fax (372) 23-18-82.

State Committee for Land Resources and Reclamation: Dushanbe.

State Committee for Oil and Gas: Dushanbe.

State Committee for Religious Affairs: Dushanbe.

State Committee for State Border Protection: Dushanbe.

State Committee for State Property: Dushanbe, pr. Rudaki 25; tel. (372) 21-86-59; e-mail privatization@tajikistan.com; internet privatization.tajikistan.com.

State Committee for Statistics: 734025 Dushanbe, Bokhtar 17; tel. (372) 27-63-31; fax (372) 21-43-75; e-mail stat@tojikiston.com.

State Committee for Television and Radio: Dushanbe, kuchai Chapayeva 31; tel. (372) 27-65-69.

President and Legislature

PRESIDENT

A presidential election took place on 6 November 1999. There were two candidates, Davlat Usmon and Imamali Rakhmonov. According to official sources, Rakhmonov obtained an estimated 97% of the votes cast, while Davlat Usmon received about 2%. Rakhmonov was inaugurated as President on 16 November.

PARLIAMENT

Constitutional amendments approved by a referendum in September 1999 provided for the establishment of a 96-member bicameral legislative body, comprising a 63-member lower chamber, the Majlisi Namoyandagon (Assembly of Representatives), and a 33-member upper chamber, the Majlisi Milliy (National Assembly).

MAJLISI NAMOYANDAGON

The 63 members of the lower chamber are elected for a five-year term: 22 are elected by proportional representation and 41 in single-mandate constituencies. At the first elections to the Assembly of Representatives, held on 27 February 2000, only 49 of the 63 seats were filled. Invalid results were declared in three constituencies, while in 11 no party achieved the requisite 50% of the vote. This necessitated a second round of voting on 12 March 2000, at which the 11 seats were filled. Two further seats were filled in April and December, respectively; however, one seat remained vacant.

President: SAIDULLO KHAIRULLAYEV.

MAJLISI MILLIY

The 33 members of the upper chamber are indirectly elected for five years: of these, 25 are selected by local deputies, while the remaining eight are appointed by the President. Elections to the National Assembly were held for the first time on 23 March 2000.

President: MAKHMADSAID UBAYDULLAYEV.

Political Organizations

Adolatkoh (Justice): Kanibadam, Mira 44; tel. (3467) 2-58-38; f. 1996; campaigns for the establishment of social justice; banned in Aug. 2001; Leader ABDURAKHMON KARIMOV; c. 7,200 mems.

Communist Party of Tajikistan (CPT): Dushanbe; f. 1924; sole registered party until 1991; Chair. SHODI SHABDOLOV; c. 70,000 mems (2001)*.

Hizb-i-Vahdat (Unity): Dushanbe; f. 2001.

Justice and Progress of Tajikistan: Khujand; f. 1996; moderate opposition party; Chair. KARIM ABDULOV.

Party of Popular Unity and Accord (PPUA): Dushanbe; f. 1994; represents interests of northern Tajikistan; Leader ABDUMALIK ABDULLOJONOV.

People's Democratic Party of Tajikistan (PDPT): Dushanbe, pr. Rudaki 107; tel. (372) 21-63-21; fax (372) 24-34-79; f. 1993; campaigns for a united, democratic, secular and law-based state; joined by the Lale Badakhshon Movement in 2000; Chair. IMAMALI RAKHMONOV; c. 90,000 mems*.

Social Democratic Party of Tajikistan (SDPT): Dushanbe; f. 1999; Chair. RAKHMATULLO ZOIROV*.

Socialist Party of Tajikistan: Dushanbe, Gafurova 30; f. 1996; campaigns for a socialist, law-based state; Chair. KURBON VOSSE (acting); c. 24,000 mems*.

Taraqqiyot Party (Development Party): Dushanbe; f. 2001; Chair. SULTON KUVVATOV; 3,000 mems (2001).

The following parties were formally banned by the Supreme Court in June 1993. The DPT was relegalized in 1996. However, one faction of the DPT (led by Jumaboy Niyazov) continued to oppose any accommodation with the Government. The legalization of opposition parties and their media was a term of the peace agreement concluded in June 1997. It was not, however, granted by the President until August 1999. In March and December of that year the further re-registration of parties was carried out.

Democratic Party of Tajikistan (DPT): Dushanbe, Yakkachinora 42; f. 1990; permitted to reregister 1996 and 1999; secular nationalist and pro-Western; Chair. MUKHAMMADRUZI ISKANDAROV; c. 16,000 mems (1996)*.

Islamic Rebirth Party of Tajikistan (IRP): Dushanbe, Tolstaya 5; tel. (372) 27-25-30; fax (372) 27-53-93; leadership formerly based in Tehran, Iran; registered in 1991 as the Islamic Renaissance Party of Tajikistan; br. of what was the Soviet IRP; renamed in 1999; formerly a moderate Islamist party; Chair. SAYED ABDULLO NURI; c. 50,000 mems*.

Rastokhez (Rebirth): f. 1990; nationalist-religious party favoured by intellectuals; Chair. TAKHIR ABDUZHABBOROV*.

During 1992–97 the supporters of the IRP and other opposition parties maintained guerrilla warfare against the regime, often with the support of the Afghan *mujahidin*. Most paramilitary groups were members of the IRP-led **United Tajik Opposition** (UTO, Leader Sayed Abdullo Nuri; Dep. Leader Muhammadsharif Himmafzoda). In 1997, however, following the conclusion of the peace agreement between the Government and the UTO, a National Reconciliation Council (NRC) was formed, comprising 26 members drawn equally from the UTO and the Government to debate executive and constitutional changes. Nevertheless, some opposition elements continued to perpetrate dissident attacks, in an attempt to disrupt the peace process. Following legislative elections, held in

February and March 2000, at the end of March the NRC was dissolved.

*Denotes parties re-registered from December 1999.

Diplomatic Representation

EMBASSIES IN TAJIKISTAN

Afghanistan: Dushanbe, Pushkina 34; tel. (372) 21-60-72; fax (372) 51-00-96; Ambassador MUHAMMAD DAUD PANSHERI.

Bangladesh: Dushanbe; Ambassador ABDUS SALEM.

China, People's Republic: 734002 Dushanbe, Parvina 143; tel. (372) 24-41-83; fax 51-00-24; e-mail chinaembassy@tajnet.com; internet www.chinaembassy-tj.org; Ambassador WU HONGBIN.

Germany: Dushanbe, Warsobskaja 16; tel. (372) 21-21-89; fax (372) 21-22-45; e-mail deutschebotschaftduschanbe@tajnet.com; Ambassador WOLFGANG NEUEN.

Holy See: 734006 Dushanbe, pr. Titova 21/10; tel. (372) 23-42-69; e-mail avila@romecc.td.silk.glas.apc.org; Apostolic Nuncio Most Rev. JÓZEF WESOŁOWSKI (Titular Archbishop of Slebte).

India: Dushanbe, Bukhoro 45; tel. (372) 21-23-50; fax (372) 21-24-61; e-mail eoi@netrt.org; Ambassador BONDAL JAISHANKER (designate).

Iran: Dushanbe, Tehran 18; tel. (372) 21-12-32; Ambassador NASER SARMADI-PARSA.

Kazakhstan: Dushanbe; tel. (372) 27-18-38; fax (372) 21-89-40; e-mail dipmiskz@tajik.net; Ambassador AMANZHOLA ZHANKULIYEV.

Korea, Democratic People's Republic: Dushanbe; Ambassador LI CHER HVAN.

Korea, Republic: Dushanbe; Ambassador KIM SUNG-HWAN.

Kyrgyzstan: Dushanbe, Abu Ali ibn Sina 46; tel. and fax (372) 21-18-31; fax (372) 21-03-66; Ambassador ERIK ASANALIYEV.

Pakistan: 734000 Dushanbe, pr. Rudaki 37A; tel. (372) 21-19-65; fax (372) 21-17-29; e-mail parepdushanbe@tajnet.com; Ambassador KHALID AMIRKHAN.

Russia: Dushanbe, ul. A. A. Sino 29/31; tel. (372) 21-10-05; fax (372) 21-10-85; e-mail rambtadjik@rambler.ru; internet www.rusembassy.tajnet.ru; Ambassador MAKSIM PESHKOV.

Turkey: 734019 Dushanbe, pr. Rudaki 15; tel. (372) 21-00-36; fax (372) 51-00-12; e-mail turkdusa@tajnet.com; Ambassador A. FERIT ÜLKER.

Turkmenistan: 734000 Dushanbe, pr. Rudaki 105/1; tel. (372) 21-04-61.

United Kingdom: Dushanbe; Ambassador MICHAEL FORBES SMITH.

USA: 734003 Dushanbe, Pavlova 10; tel. (372) 21-03-50; fax (372) 21-03-62; e-mail reception@amemb.tajik.net; Ambassador FRANKLIN P. HUDDLE.

Uzbekistan: Dushanbe; Ambassador BAKHTIYOR URDASHEV.

Judicial System

Chairman of the Supreme Court: UBAIDULLO DAVLATOV.

Procurator-General: AMIRQUL AZIMOV.

Religion

ISLAM

The majority of Tajiks are adherents of Islam and are mainly Sunnis (Hanafi school). Some of the Pamiri peoples, however, are Isma'ilis (followers of the Aga Khan), a Shi'ite sect. Under the Soviet regime the Muslims of Tajikistan were subject to the Muslim Board of Central Asia and a muftiate, both of which were based in Tashkent, Uzbekistan. The senior Muslim cleric in Tajikistan was the *kazi* (supreme judge). In 1992 the incumbent *kazi* fled to Afghanistan, and in 1993 the Government established an independent muftiate.

Chief Mufti: AMONULLO NEMATZODA, Dushanbe.

CHRISTIANITY

Most of the minority Christian population is Slav, the main denomination being the Russian Orthodox Church. There are some Protestant and other groups, notably a Baptist Church in Dushanbe.

Roman Catholic Church

The Church is represented in Tajikistan by a Mission, established in September 1997. There were an estimated 245 adherents at 31 December 2000.

Superior: Rev. CARLOS AVILA, 734006 Dushanbe, pr. Titova 21/10; tel. (372) 27-68-21; e-mail carlosavila@tajnet.com.

The Press

In 2000 there were four national newspapers. In 1996 two daily newspapers and 73 non-daily newspapers were published in Tajikistan. There were also 11 periodicals published in that year.

PRINCIPAL NEWSPAPERS

Adabiyet va sanat (Literature and Art): 734001 Dushanbe, Ismail Somoni 8; tel. (372) 24-57-39; f. 1959; weekly; organ of Union of Writers of Tajikistan and Ministry of Culture, Press and Information; in Tajik; Editor GULNAZAR KELDI; circ. 4,000.

Biznes i Politika (Business and Politics): 734018 Dushanbe, pr. S. Sherozi 16; tel. (372) 33-43-96; f. 1991; weekly; in Russian; Editor-in-Chief V. KRASOTIN; circ. 30,000.

Djavononi Tochikiston (Tajikistan Youth): 734018 Dushanbe, pr. S. Sherozi 16; tel. (372) 22-60-07; f. 1930; weekly; organ of the Union of Youth of Tajikistan; in Tajik; Editor DAVLAT NAZRIYEV; circ. 3,000.

Golos Tajikistana (Voice of Tajikistan): 734018 Dushanbe, pr. S. Sherozi 16; tel. (372) 33-76-27; f. 1992; weekly; organ of the Communist Party of Tajikistan; in Russian; Editor G. SHCHERBATOV; circ. 2,300.

Jumhuriyat (Republic): 734018 Dushanbe, pr. S. Sherozi 16; tel. (372) 33-08-11; f. 1925; organ of the President; 3 a week; in Tajik; Editor-in-Chief SARDABIR MUKHABBATSHOYEV; circ. 8,000.

Khabar: 734018 Dushanbe, pr. S. Sherozi 16; tel. (372) 22-33-13; Editorial Dir ZAINIDDIN NASPEDDINOV.

Khalk ovozi (People's Voice): 734018 Dushanbe, pr. S. Sherozi 16; tel. (372) 33-05-04; f. 1929; organ of the President; 3 a week; in Uzbek; Editor I. MUKHSINOV; circ. 8,600.

Kurer Tajikistana (Tajikistan Courier): 734018 Dushanbe, pr. S. Sherozi 16; tel. (372) 33-08-15; e-mail ttemirov@td.silk.org; weekly; independent; Editor KH. YUSIPOV; circ. 40,000.

Najot: Dushanbe Toktogulya 55; tel. (372) 31-47-38; organ of the Islamic Rebirth Party of Tajikistan; weekly.

Narodnaya Gazeta (People's Newspaper): 734018 Dushanbe, pr. S. Sherozi 16; tel. (372) 33-08-30; f. 1929; fmrly *Kommunist Tajikistana*(Tajik Communist); organ of the President; 3 a week; in Russian; Editor NIKOLAI NIKOLAIYEVICH; circ. 7,000.

Nidoi ranchbar (Call of the Workers): 734018 Dushanbe, pr. S. Sherozi 16; tel. (372) 33-38-50; f. 1992; weekly; organ of the Communist Party of Tajikistan; in Tajik; Editor-in-Chief KH. YOROV; circ. 6,000.

Omuzgor (Teacher): Dushanbe, kuchai Aini 45; tel. (372) 27-25-49; f. 1932; weekly; organ of the Ministry of Education; in Tajik; Editor-in-Chief S. SAIFULLOYEV; circ. 3,000.

Posukh (Answer): 734018 Dushanbe, N. Karabayeva 17; tel. (372) 33-35-60; f. 1994; organ of the Ministry of Culture, Press and Information and the Union of Journalists; weekly; in Tajik; Editor-in-Chief A. KURBANOV; circ. 3,000.

Sadoi mardum (The Voice of the People): 734018 Dushanbe, pr. S. Sherozi 16; tel. (372) 22-42-47; f. 1991; 3 a week; organ of the legislature; in Tajik; Editor MURADULLO SHERALIYEV; circ. 8,000.

Tojikiston ovozi (Voice of Tajikistan): 734018 Dushanbe, pr. S. Sherozi 16; tel. (372) 33-06-08; f. 1992; organ of the Central Committee of the Communist Party of Tajikistan; weekly; in Tajik and Russian; Editors SULAYMAN ERMATOV, INOM MUSOYEV; circ. 24,700.

Vechernii Dushanbe (Dunshanbe Evening Newspaper): 734018 Dushanbe, pr. S. Sherozi 16; tel. (372) 33-55-59; fax (372) 33-30-25; e-mail vecherka@vd.td; f. 1968; weekly; social and political; in Russian; closed down by the Government in 2001; Editor-in-Chief S. LAGUTOV.

PRINCIPAL PERIODICALS

Monthly, unless otherwise indicated.

Adab: 734025 Dushanbe, ul. Chekhova 13; tel. (372) 23-49-36; organ of the Ministry of Education; in Tajik; Editor SH. SHOKIRZODA; circ. (annual) 24,000.

Bunyod-i Adab (Culture Fund): f. 1996 to foster cultural links among the country's Persian-speaking peoples; weekly; Editor ASKAR KHAKIM.

Djashma (Spring): 734018 Dushanbe, pr. S. Sherozi 16; tel. (372) 33-08-48; f. 1986; journal of the Ministry of Culture, Press and Information; for children; Editor KAMOL NASRULLO; circ. (annual) 10,000.

Farkhang (Culture): 734003 Dushanbe, pr. Rudaki 124; tel. (372) 24-02-39; f. 1991; journal of the Culture Fund and Ministry of Culture, Press and Information; in Tajik; Editor-in-Chief J. AKOBIR; circ. 15,000.

Firuza: 734018 Dushanbe, pr. S. Sherozi 16; tel. (372) 33-89-10; f. 1932; organ of the Ministry of Culture, Press and Information; social and literary journal for women; Editor ZULFIYA ATOI; circ. (annual) 29,400.

Ilm va khayot (Science and Life): 734025 Dushanbe, pr. Rudaki 34; tel. (372) 27-48-61; f. 1989; organ of the Academy of Sciences; popular science; Editor T. BOIBOBO; circ. (annual) 12,000.

Istikbol: 734018 Dushanbe, pr. S. Sherozi 16; tel. (372) 33-14-52; f. 1952; organ of the Ministry of Culture, Press and Information; in Tajik; Editor K. KENJAYEVA; circ. (annual) 7,200.

Marifat: 734024 Dushanbe, kuchai Aini 45; tel. (372) 23-42-84; organ of the Ministry of Education; in Tajik; Editor O. BOZOROV; circ. (annual) 40,000.

Pamir: 734001 Dushanbe, Ismail Somoni 8; tel. (372) 24-56-56; f. 1949; journal of the Union of Writers of Tajikistan; fiction; in Russian; Editor-in-Chief BORIS PSHENICHNYI.

Sadoi shark (Voice of the East): 734001 Dushanbe, Ismail Somoni 8; tel. (372) 24-56-79; f. 1927; journal of the Union of Writers of Tajikistan; fiction; in Tajik; Editor URUN KUKHZOD; circ. 1,600.

Tochikiston (Tajikistan): 734018 Dushanbe, pr. S. Sherozi 16; tel. (372) 33-89-89; f. 1938; social and political; in Tajik; Editor-in-Chief D. ASHUROV; circ. (annual) 9,000.

Zdravookhraneniye Tajikistana (Tajikistan Public Health): 734026 Dushanbe, Ismail Somoni 59; tel. (372) 36-16-37; f. 1933; 6 a year; journal of the Ministry of Health; medical research; in Russian; Editor-in-Chief AZAM T. PULATOV; circ. (annual) 10,500.

NEWS AGENCIES

Asia-Plus: 734002 Dushanbe, Bokhtar 35/1, 8th floor; tel. (372) 21-78-63; fax (372) 51-01-36; e-mail info@asiaplus.tajik.net; internet www.asiaplus.tajnet.com; independent information and consulting agency; Dir UMED BABAKHANOV; Man. DALER NURKHANOV.

Khovar (East): 734025 Dushanbe, pr. Rudaki 37; tel. (372) 21-33-13; f. 1991 to replace TajikTA (Tajik Telegraph Agency); govt information agency; Dir NABI KARIMOV.

Mizon: Dushanbe; independent information agency.

Varorud: Khujand; independent information agency.

Foreign Bureau

Rossiiskoye Informatsionnoye Agentstvo—Novosti (RIA—Novosti) (Russia): 734025 Dushanbe, Putovskogo 73/2; tel. (372) 23-49-06.

PRESS ASSOCIATION

National Association of Independent Mass Media: Dushanbe; e-mail nansmit@tojikiston.com; f. 1999.

Publishers

Adib (Literary Publishing House): Dushanbe, pr. Rudaki 37; tel. (372) 23-27-37; f. 1987; literary fiction; Dir K. MIRZOYEV.

Irfon (Light of Knowledge Publishing House): 731018 Dushanbe, N. Karabayeva 17; tel. (372) 33-39-06; f. 1926; politics, social sciences, economics, agriculture, medicine and technology; Dir J. SHARIFOV; Editor-in-Chief A. OLIMOV.

Maorif (Education Publishing House): Dushanbe, kuchai Aini 126; tel. (372) 25-10-50; educational, academic; Dir A. GHAFUROV.

Sarredaksiyai Ilmii Entsiklopediyai Millii Tajik (Tajik Scientific Encyclopaedia Publishing House): Dushanbe, kuchai Aini 126; tel. (372) 25-18-41; f. 1969; Editor-in-Chief A. QURBONOV.

Broadcasting and Communications

TELECOMMUNICATIONS

Joint Venture 'TajikTel': 734000 Dushanbe, pr. Rudaki 57; tel. (372) 21-01-45; fax (372) 51-01-25; e-mail office@tajiktel.tajik.net; mobile cellular telephone co; Dir-Gen. ZVI SHWA.

JSC Tajiktelecom: 734025 Dushanbe; tel. (372) 23-44-44; fax (372) 21-04-04; e-mail tajiktelekom@netrt.org; f. 1996; national telecommunications operator; Dir-Gen. FARKHOD S. SHUKUROV.

BROADCASTING

In February 1994 President Rakhmonov placed the State TV-Radio Broadcasting Co of Tajikistan under the direct operational supervision of the Chairman of the legislature. Transmissions of a rebel opposition group, calling itself Voice of Free Tajikistan, began in 1993. In 1996 a new, Iranian-funded television station, Samaniyan, began broadcasting a selection of Iranian and local programmes. In December 2001 there were some 20 independent television stations.

Radio

State TV-Radio Broadcasting Co of Tajikistan: 734025 Dushanbe, kuchai Chapayev 31; tel. (372) 27-75-27; fax (372) 21-34-95; e-mail soro@ctvrtj.td.silk.org; Chair. MIRBOBO MIRRAKHIMOV; Dep. Chair. G. MAKHMUDOV.

Asia-Plus Radio: Dushanbe; country's first independent radio station; broadcasts 14 hours per day in Russian and Tajik; Man. Dir DALER NURKHONOV.

Tajik Radio: 734025 Dushanbe, kuchai Chapayev 31; tel. (372) 27-65-69; broadcasts in Russian, Tajik and Uzbek.

Tiroz: 735700 Khujand, Mikroraion 27; tel. (342) 25–66–89; e-mail trrktiroz@sugdien.com; internet www.tiroz.sugdien.com; Dir KHURSHED ULMASOV.

Television

State TV-Radio Broadcasting Co of Tajikistan: see Radio.

Tajik Television (TTV): 734013 Dushanbe, kuchai Behzod 7; tel. (372) 22-43-57.

Internews Tajikistan: 434001 Dushanbe, pr. Rudaki 92, 4th floor, apt 23; tel. (372) 24-54-83; fax (372) 21-43-12; e-mail bahodoor@internews.tj; internet www.internews.tj; f. 1982; non-governmental organization to promote free and independent media; includes the Asia-Plus agency; Man. Dir BAHODOOR KOSIMOV.

Poitakht: 734013 Dushanbe, Azizbekova 20; tel. (372) 23-26-29; independent; Dir RAKHMON OSTONOV.

Samaniyan: Dushanbe, pr. S. Sherozi 16; tel. (372) 21-65-91; f. 1996; Iranian-funded; Dir GULOMALI KURBONOV.

Finance

(cap. = capital; res = reserves; dep. = deposits; brs = branches; m. = million; amounts in Tajik roubles, unless otherwise stated)

BANKING

Central Bank

National Bank of the Republic of Tajikistan: 734025 Dushanbe, pr. Rudaki 23/2; tel. (372) 21-26-28; fax (372) 51-00-68; e-mail root@natbank.tajnet.com; f. 1991; cap. 1,594m. Russian old roubles, res 1,025m. Russian old roubles, dep. 1,334,659m. Russian old roubles (Dec. 1993); Chair. MURODALI ALIMARDONOV; First Dep. Chair. SHARIF RAKHIMOV.

Other Banks

According to the IMF, the number of commercial banks declined from 28 in 1997 to 14 in 2002, owing to consolidation.

Joint-Stock Commercial Agroindustrial Investment Bank (Agroinvestbank): 734018 Dushanbe, pr. S. Sherozi 21; tel. (372) 21-03-85; fax (372) 21-12-06; e-mail invest@agrobank.td.silk.org; f. 1991; fmrly Agroprombank; cap. 198,411m., res 22,993m., dep. 3,218m. (Jan. 1998); Chair. MAKSUDJON SALYAMOVICH KADIROV; 64 brs.

Orienbank: 734001 Dushanbe, pr. Rudaki 95/1; tel. (372) 21-06-57; fax (372) 21-18-77; e-mail ved@orien.tojikiston.com; f. 1922 as republican office of Industrial Bank; cap. 1.2m. somoni, res 3.2m. somoni, dep. 21.8m. somoni (Dec. 2001); commercial bank; Chair. KURBONOV SAMIKHON; Chair. of Bd MALIKOV SHERMALIK; 28 brs.

Sberbank (Savings Bank): Dushanbe; f. 1991; fmrly br. of USSR Sberbank; licensed by presidential decree and not subject to the same controls as the commercial and trading banks; 58 brs, 480 sub-brs.

Somonbank: 734025 Dushanbe, proyezd 1, Tursunzoda 3; tel. and fax (372) 21-78-13.

Tajbank: 734064 Dushanbe, Ismail Somoni 59/1; tel. (372) 27-46-54.

Tajprombank: 734025 Dushanbe, Kh. Dekhlavi 4; tel. (372) 21-26-42; fax (372) 21-25-85.

Tajikvneshekonombank (Bank for Foreign Economic Affairs of the Republic of Tajikistan—also known as Tojiksodirotbonk): 734012 Dushanbe, Dekhlavi 4; tel. (372) 21-47-38; fax (372) 21-59-52; e-mail shamatsob@tojikiston.com; fmrly br. of USSR Vneshekonombank; underwent restructuring in 1999; Chair. I. L. LALBEKOV; 6 brs.

COMMODITY EXCHANGES

Tajik Republican Commodity Exchange (NAVRUZ): 374001 Dushanbe, Orjonikidze 37; tel. (372) 23-48-74; fax (372) 27-03-91; f. 1991; Chair. SULEYMAN CHULEBAYEV.

Vostok-Mercury Torgovyi Dom: Dushanbe; tel. and fax (372) 24-60-61; f. 1991; trades in a wide range of goods.

INSURANCE

Tajikgosstrakh: Dushanbe, Akademikov Rajabovykh 3; tel. (372) 27-58-49; state-owned; Dir-Gen. MANSUR OCHILDEV.

Trade and Industry

GOVERNMENT AGENCY

Drug Control Agency: Dushanbe; f. 1999; documents and curbs regional drugs-trafficking; receives financial and technical assistance from the UN Office for Drug Control and Crime Prevention; Dir RUSTAM NAZAROV.

CHAMBER OF COMMERCE

Chamber of Commerce and Industry: 734012 Dushanbe, Mazayeva 21; tel. (372) 27-95-19; Chair. KAMOL SUFIYEV.

INDUSTRIAL ASSOCIATION

Tajikvneshtorg Industrial Association: 734035 Dushanbe, POB 48, pr. Rudaki 25; tel. (372) 23-29-03; fax (372) 22-81-20; f. 1988; co-ordinates trade with foreign countries in a wide range of goods; Pres. ABDURAKHMON MUKHTASHOV.

EMPLOYERS' ORGANIZATION

National Association of Small and Medium-Sized Businesses of Tajikistan: Dushanbe, Bofanda 9; tel. (372) 27-79-78; fax (372) 21-17-26; f. 1993 with govt support; independent org. Chair. MATLJUBA ULJABAEVA.

UTILITIES

Electricity

Barqi Tojik (Tajik Electricity): Dushanbe, kuchai Ismoili Somoni 64; tel. (372) 35-87-66; Chair. NURMUHAMMADOV; First Dep. Chair. ALEKSEI SILANTAYEV.

Pamir Energy Co (PamirEnergy): Khorog; f. 2002; jt venture between Governments of Tajikistan and Switzerland, the Aga Khan Fund for Economic Development, International Finance Corpn and the International Development Association to provide electricity to Gornyi Badakhshan.

Gas

Dushanbe Gas Co: supplies gas to Dushanbe region.

TRADE UNIONS

Federation of Trade Unions: Dushanbe, pr. Rudaki 20; tel. (372) 23-35-16; Chair. MURODALI SALIKHOV.

Transport

RAILWAYS

There are few railways in Tajikistan. In 1999 the total length of the rail network was 482 km. Lines link the major centres of the country with the railway network of Uzbekistan, connecting Khujand (Khodzhent) to the Fergana valley lines, and the cotton-growing centre of Qurgonteppa (Kurgan-Tyube) to Termez. A new line, between the town of Isfara, in Soghd region, and Khavast, in Uzbekistan, was opened in 1995 and in 1997 a passenger route between Dushanbe and Volgograd, Russia, was inaugurated. The first section of a new line, between Qurgonteppa and Kulob (Kulyab) in the south-west of the country, was inaugurated in 1998. In October 2002 a new route from Kulob to Astrakhan, Russia, was opened. The predominantly mountainous terrain makes the construction of a more extensive network unlikely.

Tajik Railways: 734012 Dushanbe, Nazarshoyeva 35; tel. (372) 21-83-34; fax (372) 21-60-59; f. 1994; comprises part of the former Soviet Railways' Central Asian network; Pres. AMONULLO KHUKUMOV.

ROADS

In mid-2002 Tajikistan's road network totalled an estimated 30,000 km (13,747 km highways and 8,965 km local roads). The principal highway of Tajikistan is the road that links the northern city of Khujand, across the Anzob Pass (3,372 m), with the capital, Dushanbe, and carries on to the border town of Khorog (Gornyi Badakhshan), before wending through the Pamir Mountains, north, to the Kyrgyz city of Osh, across the Akbaytal Pass (4,655 m). This arterial route exhibits problems common to much of the country's land transport: winter weather is likely to cause the road to be closed by snow for up to eight months of the year. In early 2000 Tajikistan and the Asian Development Bank (ADB) signed a memorandum of understanding for the rehabilitation of the road linking Dushanbe to the south-western cities of Qurgonteppa and Kulob. In the same year a road linking eastern Tajikistan with the People's Republic of China was completed, giving Tajikistan access to the Karakorum highway, which connects China and Pakistan.

CIVIL AVIATION

The main international airport is at Dushanbe, although there is also a major airport at Khujand. The country is linked to cities in Russia and other former Soviet republics, and also to a growing number of destinations in Europe and Asia. The reconstruction of Khujand airport was completed by a joint Tajik-Indian company in late 2000.

Tajikistan Airlines (TZK): 734006 Dushanbe, Dushanbe Airport, Titova 31/2; tel. (372) 21-21-45; fax (372) 51-00-41; e-mail tt_gart@tajnet.com; f. 1990; formerly known as Tajik Air; state-owned; operates flights to Russia, India, Pakistan, Iran, Turkey, Kazakhstan, Kyrgyzstan, Germany, the United Arab Emirates and Uzbekistan; commenced weekly flights to Afghanistan in March 2002; Gen. Dir MIRZO ALIMOV; Gen. Man. F. ISHANKULOV.

Tourism

There was little tourism in Tajikistan even before the outbreak of civil war. There is some spectacular mountain scenery, hitherto mainly visited by climbers, and, particularly in the Fergana valley, in the north of the country, there are sites of historical interest, notably the city of Khujand.

Tajikistan Republican Council of Tourism and Excursions: 734018 Dushanbe, S. Sherozi 11; tel. (372) 33-27-70; fax (372) 33-44-20.

'Sayoh' State Enterprise: 734025 Dushanbe, Pushkinskaya 14; tel. (372) 23-14-01; fax (372) 21-90-72; e-mail sayoh@netrt.org; internet www.sayoh.tojikiston.com; Chair. GAFAROV KASIM.

TANZANIA

Introductory Survey

Location, Climate, Language, Religion, Flag, Capital

The United Republic of Tanzania consists of Tanganyika, on the African mainland, and the nearby islands of Zanzibar and Pemba. Tanganyika lies on the east coast of Africa, bordered by Uganda and Kenya to the north, by Rwanda, Burundi and the Democratic Republic of the Congo (formerly Zaire) to the west, and by Zambia, Malawi and Mozambique to the south. Zanzibar and Pemba are in the Indian Ocean, about 40 km (25 miles) off the coast of Tanganyika, north of Dar es Salaam. The climate varies with altitude, ranging from tropical in Zanzibar and on the coast and plains to semi-temperate in the highlands. The official languages are Swahili and English, and there are numerous tribal languages. There are Muslim, Christian and Hindu communities. Many Africans follow traditional beliefs. The national flag (proportions 2 by 3) comprises two triangles, one of green (with its base at the hoist and its apex in the upper fly) and the other of blue (with its base in the fly and its apex at the lower hoist), separated by a broad, yellow-edged black diagonal stripe, from the lower hoist to the upper fly. The administrative functions of the capital are being transferred from Dar es Salaam to Dodoma.

Recent History

Tanzania was formed in 1964 by a merger of the two independent states of Tanganyika and Zanzibar (see below).

Tanganyika became a German colony in 1884, and was later incorporated into German East Africa, which also included present-day Rwanda and Burundi. In 1918, at the end of the First World War, the German forces in the area surrendered, and Tanganyika was placed under a League of Nations mandate, with the United Kingdom as the administering power. In 1946 Tanganyika became a UN Trust Territory, still under British rule. Tanganyika's first general election was held in September 1958 and February 1959. A new Council of Ministers, including African members, was formed in July 1959. At the next election, in September 1960, the Tanganyika African National Union (TANU) won 70 of the 71 seats in the National Assembly. The party's leader, Dr Julius Nyerere, became Chief Minister. Internal self-government was achieved in May 1961, when Nyerere became Prime Minister. Tanganyika became independent, within the Commonwealth, on 9 December 1961, but Nyerere resigned as Prime Minister in January 1962, in order to devote himself to the direction of TANU. He was succeeded as premier by Rashidi Kawawa. On 9 December 1962, following elections in November, Tanganyika became a republic, with Nyerere as the country's first President. Kawawa became Vice-President. Zanzibar (including the island of Pemba), a British protectorate since 1890, became an independent sultanate in December 1963. Following an armed uprising by the Afro-Shirazi Party in January 1964, the Sultan was deposed and a republic proclaimed. The new Government signed an Act of Union with Tanganyika in April 1964, thus creating the United Republic. The union was named Tanzania in October 1964, and a new Constitution was introduced in July 1965, which provided for a one-party state (although, until 1977, TANU and the Afro-Shirazi Party remained the respective official parties of mainland Tanzania and Zanzibar, and co-operated in affairs of state). Nyerere was elected President of the United Republic in September 1965, and was subsequently re-elected in 1970, 1975 and 1980.

Despite its incorporation in Tanzania, Zanzibar retained a separate administration, which ruthlessly suppressed all opposition. In April 1972 Sheikh Abeid Karume, Chairman of the ruling Revolutionary Council of Zanzibar and First Vice-President of the United Republic, was assassinated. His successor, Aboud Jumbe, extended the powers of the Afro-Shirazi Party. A separate Constitution for Zanzibar was adopted in October 1979, providing for a popularly elected President and a House of Representatives elected by delegates of the ruling party. The first elections to the 40-member Zanzibar House of Representatives were held in January 1980. In June of that year a coup plot against Jumbe was thwarted; Jumbe won an overwhelming majority at Zanzibar's first presidential election, held in

October. However, mounting dissatisfaction among Zanzibaris concerning the union with Tanganyika culminated in the resignation, in January 1984, of Jumbe and three of his ministers. In April Ali Hassan Mwinyi, a former Zanzibari Minister of Natural Resources and Tourism, was elected unopposed as President of Zanzibar, winning 87.5% of the votes cast. A new Constitution for Zanzibar came into force in January 1985, providing for the House of Representatives to be directly elected by universal adult suffrage.

In February 1977 TANU and the Afro-Shirazi Party were amalgamated to form Chama Cha Mapinduzi (CCM), the Revolutionary Party of Tanzania. In April the National Assembly approved a permanent Constitution for Tanzania; this provided for the election to the National Assembly of representatives from Zanzibar, in addition to those from the Tanzanian mainland. At a general election in October 1980 about one-half of the elected members of the Assembly, including several ministers, failed to retain their seats; this was interpreted as a protest by voters against commodity shortages and inefficient bureaucracy. In January 1983 several civilians and soldiers were arrested and charged with plotting a coup: in December 1985 nine of the accused were found guilty and sentenced to life imprisonment. (All those convicted eventually received a presidential pardon in October 1995.) Major changes to the Constitution were approved by the National Assembly in October 1984, limiting the President's powers and increasing those of the National Assembly.

President Nyerere retired in November 1985, and was succeeded by Ali Hassan Mwinyi (President of Zanzibar and Vice-President of Tanzania since April 1984), who, as the sole candidate, had won 96% of the votes cast at a presidential election in October. Elections to the National Assembly were held on the same day. Mwinyi appointed Joseph Warioba (previously Minister of Justice) as Prime Minister and First Vice-President. At presidential and legislative elections in Zanzibar, also held in October, Idris Abdul Wakil (formerly Speaker of the Zanzibar House of Representatives) was elected President of Zanzibar to replace Mwinyi; although the sole candidate, he received only 61% of the votes. Nyerere remained Chairman of the CCM.

In July 1986 Mwinyi declared an offensive against corruption and mismanagement within the CCM: in the following months several regional party officials and directors of parastatal bodies were dismissed or demoted, and in some cases expelled from the party. By late 1987 a division was apparent between 'conservative' socialists, who supported the CCM's traditional socialist ideology (as favoured by Nyerere), and 'pragmatists', who advocated a more liberal approach to government (as favoured by Mwinyi). It was thought that Nyerere's decision to accept renomination as Chairman of the CCM at this time reflected his desire to counter reformist influence in government: in October he was re-elected Chairman of the CCM. Nyerere resigned in August 1990, and Mwinyi was appointed Chairman of the CCM. In cabinet reshuffles in December 1997 and March 1990 Mwinyi dismissed several 'conservative' socialist ministers who had opposed his policies of economic liberalization.

In early 1988 tension began to increase in Zanzibar, reflecting underlying rivalries between the inhabitants of the main island and those of the smaller island of Pemba, between Zanzibar's African and Arab populations, and between supporters and opponents of unity with Tanganyika. In January Wakil suspended the islands' Government, the Supreme Revolutionary Council, and assumed control of the armed forces from the office of his main rival, Chief Minister Seif Sharrif Hamad, following earlier claims by Wakil that a group of dissidents, including members of the Council, had been plotting the overthrow of his administration. When Wakil appointed a new Council later in that month, Hamad was among the five ministers dismissed. Dr Omar Ali Juma was appointed as the new Chief Minister. In May Hamad and six other officials were expelled from the CCM for allegedly opposing the party's aims and endangering Tanzanian unity.

In October 1990 concurrent parliamentary and presidential elections were held in Zanzibar. Wakil did not stand for re-election; the sole presidential candidate, Dr Salmin Amour, was elected as Wakil's successor by 97.7% of the votes cast. Amour subsequently reappointed Juma as Chief Minister of Zanzibar. At the end of October national parliamentary and presidential elections took place. Mwinyi, the sole candidate in the presidential election, was re-elected for a second term, taking 95.5% of the votes cast. In November Mwinyi replaced Warioba as Prime Minister with John Malecela, previously the Tanzanian High Commissioner to the United Kingdom.

In December 1991 a presidential commission published recommendations for the establishment of a multi-party political system. In February 1992 proposed constitutional amendments to this effect were ratified by a special congress of the CCM, which stipulated that, in order to protect national unity, all new political organizations should command support in both Zanzibar and mainland Tanzania, and should be free of tribal, religious and racial bias. In May the Constitutions of both the United Republic and Zanzibar were amended to enshrine a multi-party system. Several political organizations were officially registered from mid-1992. In December Zanzibar unilaterally joined the Organization of the Islamic Conference (OIC, see p. 295), thereby precipitating controversy regarding the future of the Tanzanian union. An *ad hoc* parliamentary commission concluded in February 1993 that Zanzibar's membership of the OIC contravened the Constitution of the United Republic. Zanzibar withdrew from the organization in August.

During 1993 opposition leaders were detained and charged with sedition on a number of occasions. Violent clashes occurred during April between Islamic fundamentalists and the security forces; some 40 Islamists were arrested and charged with holding illegal demonstrations, and Sheikh Yahya Hussein, the leader of the Balukta Islamic movement, was charged with plotting against the Government. Balukta was outlawed later in the month, although charges against Hussein and several other defendants were subsequently withdrawn. During October some 30,000 opposition supporters organized a demonstration in Zanzibar to demand the right to hold authorized meetings.

In November 1994 some members of the international donor community reportedly threatened to withdraw aid to Tanzania unless the Government acted to eradicate alleged irregular activities by the Ministry of Finance. In December Mwinyi reorganized the Cabinet. Malecela was replaced as Prime Minister and First Vice-President by Cleopa Msuya, hitherto the Minister of Industry and Trade and previously Prime Minister during 1980–83; Lt-Col Jakaya Kikwete, hitherto Minister of Energy, Minerals and Water, was appointed Minister of Finance. In February 1995 Augustine Mrema, the Minister of Home Affairs, was dismissed, having criticized government policy. Mrema subsequently became Chairman of the opposition National Convention for Reconstruction and Reform (NCCR—Mageuzi).

In October 1995 multi-party legislative elections were held for the first time, concurrently with presidential elections, both in Zanzibar and throughout the Tanzanian union. At elections on 22 October the CCM secured 26 of the 50 elective seats in the Zanzibari House of Representatives, while the Civic United Front (CUF, campaigning for increased Zanzibari autonomy) took 24 seats. Amour was re-elected President of the islands by 50.2% of the votes cast, only narrowly defeating Seif Sharrif Hamad (the former Zanzibari Chief Minister), who represented the CUF. Amour appointed a new ruling council, with Dr Mohamed Gharib Bilali, formerly a government official, as Chief Minister. The CUF contested the election results, accusing the Zanzibari authorities of electoral malpractice and refusing to recognize the legitimacy of the new Amour administration, while party delegates initially declined to take up their seats in the House of Representatives. The Tanzanian national elections, on 29 October, were disrupted by a combination of apparent organizational chaos and further allegations by opposition parties of electoral fraud. Administrative inefficiency led to the cancellation of the election results in seven constituencies in Dar es Salaam; these polls were repeated in mid-November. The opposition parties, alleging that the CCM was manipulating the voting process, refused to rerun, withdrew their candidates from the presidential election, and unsuccessfully petitioned the High Court to declare all results null and void. The Government proceeded to publish the results, whereby the CCM won 186 of the 232 elective seats in the National Assembly, the CUF 24, NCCR—Mageuzi 16, and Chama Cha Democrasia na Maendeleo (Chadema) and the United Democratic Party three seats each. Benjamin Mkapa, hitherto Minister of Science, Technology and Higher Education, was deemed to have been elected President, winning 61.8% of the votes cast. Mrema, his closest rival, took 27.8% of the votes. President Mkapa was inaugurated in late November; Omar Ali Juma (hitherto Chief Minister of Zanzibar) was appointed Vice-President. Shortly afterwards Mkapa announced a new Cabinet, with Frederick Sumaye (formerly Minister of Agriculture) as Prime Minister. Many long-serving ministers were not reappointed.

In his election campaign Mkapa had promised a crusade against corruption in high public office, and in January 1996 he appointed a special presidential commission (chaired by former Prime Minister Joseph Warioba). At a special congress of the CCM in June, Mkapa was elected party Chairman. Also in June the allegedly corrupt Dar es Salaam city council was disbanded. In September a parliamentary select committee investigating bribery allegations against the Minister of Finance, Simon Mbilinyi, published a report recommending that he be made accountable for having illegally granted tax exemptions. Mbilinyi subsequently resigned. Meanwhile, in October Mrema unexpectedly won a parliamentary by-election for NCCR—Mageuzi in a Dar es Salaam constituency; although his campaign had focused on financial impropriety in government, Mrema had recently been accused of having presented false evidence to the parliamentary select committee on corruption in order to undermine the Government's credibility. In December the Warioba Commission issued a report asserting that corruption was widespread in the public sector.

In May 1997 a faction of NCCR—Mageuzi attempted to remove Mrema from the party chairmanship, reportedly after he ordered an investigation into the disappearance of substantial party funds. In June the High Court banned a NCCR—Mageuzi special congress from taking place, apparently in order to prevent violent confrontation between the opposing factions. Following allegations that opposition members were frequently being harassed by the security forces, reports emerged in August that some opposition groupings had formed their own militias.

In February 1996 the Zanzibari Government banned demonstrations by the CUF in southern Pemba; allegations persisted that numerous human rights abuses were being perpetrated by the authorities against supporters of the CUF. During 1996 external donors began to suspend aid disbursements to Zanzibar in view of the continuing political deadlock between the CUF and the islands' administration. There were signs of a *rapprochement* in January 1997, when representatives of the mainland branch of the CUF reportedly agreed to accept the legitimacy of the Amour Government. During December 1997 and early January 1998, however, 17 members of the CUF, including some delegates to the House of Representatives, were arrested on suspicion of conspiring to overthrow the Amour Government. From January CUF members refused to attend sessions of the House of Representatives in protest; consequently, in February all CUF deputies were officially suspended from the House for 10 days as a punitive measure. During January the Secretary-General of the Commonwealth, Chief Emeka Anyaoku, visited Zanzibar and presented proposals for a peaceful solution to the dispute, including a cessation of confrontational statements, the removal of restrictions on party political activity and a return to the House of Representatives by CUF delegates. Both the CUF and the Zanzibari section of the CCM contained elements that were strongly opposed to negotiating a compromise. Chief Anyaoku subsequently appointed a special envoy, Dr Moses Anafu, to continue mediation efforts, and in early May the UN Secretary-General, Kofi Annan, declared the full support of his organization for the Commonwealth's initiative. During that month a member of a CUF delegation that had been negotiating with Dr Anafu was arrested on suspicion of treason. Treason charges against the 18 CUF members who had been detained in 1997 and 1998 were finally presented in February 1999. The Zanzibari CCM came under considerable pressure from senior mainland CCM officials to reach an agreement with the CUF, while that party's leadership eventually resigned itself to accepting Amour's tenure of the presidency until the end of his term of office in 2000; a mutual accord was finally concluded in June 1999. In January 2000 45 deputies of the mainland CCM were reported to have petitioned the Zanzibari President to withdraw the charges against the 18 CUF members being tried for treason. By that time the court proceedings had already been adjourned several times, and two days prior to the deputies' appeal the Zanzibari Attorney-General had been dismissed after he had ordered the arrest of two more leading members of the CUF. Nevertheless, in February President Amour declared that the trial would not be abandoned. (The charges were dropped in November by Amani Abeid Karume following his election as President of Zanzibar—see below.) Later in February the National Executive Committee of the CCM rejected a proposal to amend the Zanzibari Constitution in order to allow President Amour to serve a third term of office.

In August 1998 a car bomb exploded outside the US Embassy in Dar es Salaam (concurrently with a similar attack at the US mission in Nairobi, Kenya); 11 people were killed in Dar es Salaam and some 75 were injured. The attacks were believed to have been co-ordinated by international Islamic fundamentalist terrorists led by a Saudi-born dissident, Osama bin Laden, and the USA retaliated by launching air-strikes against targets in Afghanistan and Sudan. In the aftermath of the bomb attacks, Tanzanian investigators and US federal agents made extensive nation-wide inquiries. Four men were convicted of involvement in the bombings by a court in New York, USA, in May 2001 and were later sentenced to life imprisonment.

A committee was appointed by the Government in July 1998 to assess public opinion on constitutional reform. In September Mkapa reorganized the Cabinet, following the nullification of the election to the National Assembly, in 1995, of two ministers and the resignation, in August, of the Minister of State in the President's Office, Hassy Kitine, who was alleged to have used state funds to finance medical treatment abroad for his wife. In April 1999 Mrema and his faction of NCCR—Mageuzi defected to the Tanzania Labour Party (TLP). Mrema initially assumed the chairmanship of the TLP, but in May he was banned by the High Court from holding any official post in that party. There was speculation that the death, in October, of former President Nyerere might give rise to increased pressure for a restructuring of the United Republic of Tanzania. This was, to some extent, reinforced by the release, in December, of the report of the committee charged with assessing public opinion on constitutional reform. While it found that some 96.25% of Zanzibaris and 84.97% of mainland Tanzanians favoured a 'two-tier' government for the United Republic, the committee itself recommended the establishment of a 'three-tier' system. In so doing it was adjudged by President Mkapa to have exceeded its mandate. In February 2000 the National Assembly approved draft legislation to amend the Constitution in accordance with citizens' recommendations as reported by the committee. Among these recommendations was one that the President should henceforth be elected by a majority vote. Opposition deputies declared that they would prevent the enactment of the proposed legislation, if necessary by resorting to legal action.

At a presidential election held on 29 October 2000 Benjamin Mkapa was re-elected as President, securing 71.7% of votes cast; Ibrahim Lipumba won 16.3% of the votes cast, Augustine Mrema 7.8% and John Cheyo 4.2%. The participation rate was 84%. The CUF, Chadema and the UDP had initially planned to field joint candidates, but in July a judge ruled that the Constitution forbade the presidential running-mate from being drawn from a different party to the presidential candidate. In the following month the CUF and Chadema agreed to form a five-year alliance and field joint candidates for the presidential elections in both the United Republic of Tanzania and in Zanzibar. It was agreed that if either candidate (both from the CUF) won, the respective prime minister would be drawn from Chadema. Candidates from the TPP and NCCR—Mageuzi failed to secure the minimum 200 referees and thus were not allowed to stand for election. At legislative elections, held at the same time, the CCM secured 244 seats in the National Assembly. The largest opposition group to obtain representation was the CUF, with 15 seats; the three other opposition parties (Chadema, the TLP and the UDP) won four, three and two seats, respectively. The polls were declared by international observers to have been freely and fairly conducted. In November Mkapa appointed a new Cabinet, reappointing Frederick Sumaye as Prime Minister.

In marked contrast, presidential and legislative elections were also held in Zanzibar and Pemba on 29 October 2000, amid widespread accusations of electoral fraud. Voting in 16 of the islands' 50 constituencies was annulled owing to a lack of ballot papers and voter registration lists. The Zanzibar Electoral Commission (ZEC) announced that new polls would be held in the 16 constituencies (all areas where the CUF enjoyed strong support), and that counting for the presidential elections for both Zanzibar and the United Republic would be delayed until the new results were received. Opposition parties and Commonwealth electoral observers called for a full rerun of the elections, but this was rejected by the ZEC. The CUF subsequently called for a boycott of the partial rerun of the election. Following a week of confusion and violent clashes between the police and opposition supporters, the repeated polls were held on 5 November. Accusations of electoral fraud persisted, and the participation rate was reported to be low. Following the poll, the CCM claimed that it had won 67% of the votes cast (thereby winning 34 seats in the House of Representatives). The CUF refused to recognize the results of the ballot. Despite the concerns of the opposition parties and international observers, the ZEC proclaimed Amani Abeid Karume of the CCM as President of Zanzibar. The CUF refused to recognize Karume as President and demanded that a repeat election be held within four months. During Karume's subsequent appointment of a new Government, popular unrest and a series of bomb attacks occurred throughout the islands. In January 2001 police in Zanzibar and Pemba recovered 112 explosive devices and arrested 59 people in connection with the bomb attacks. In September John Tendwa, the Registrar of Political Parties, announced that he would investigate the results of the elections to ascertain whether electoral rules had been adhered to properly, and that he would consider whether a change of electoral legislation was necessary. He was expected to issue his report in July 2002.

Meanwhile, throughout late 2000 and January 2001 there were, often violent, opposition demonstrations calling for new elections. On 27 and 28 January clashes between the police and opposition supporters left an estimated 37 people dead (including one police-officer and five other members of the security forces) and 100 people injured; more than 400 protesters were arrested and imprisoned. Police used tear gas and live ammunition to disperse the crowds, and troops were deployed to restore order in Pemba. (On the mainland 100 people were arrested in Dar es Salaam.) Police were reportedly refusing to allow local hospitals to treat the wounded, with many fleeing by boat to seek treatment in Kenya, and about 100 people were believed to have drowned when two boats carrying refugees sank. By February the number of Zanzibari refugees in Kenya had reached 636, although the Government claimed that a large number of these were not legitimate political refugees, but CUF activists trying to discredit the Government. (Many of the refugees remained in Kenya at April 2002, despite the Government's assurances that they would face no reprisals on their return to Zanzibar.)

In February 2001 two prominent CUF leaders, including the Deputy Secretary-General, were arrested and charged with the murder of a police-officer during the January demonstrations; the human rights organization Amnesty International criticized the charges as politically motivated. One of Karume's first acts as President had been to drop treason charges that the two, along with 16 other CUF members, had been facing since 1997 (see above). The Tanzania Court of Appeal had subsequently ruled that treason was not possible in Zanzibar because the isles were not a sovereign state. In November 2001 the 18 CUF members brought legal actions against the National Chief of Police, the Zanzibari Police Commissioner and the Zanzibari Attorney-General. The 18 were seeking damages for income lost and fees incurred during their three-year imprisonment, as well as for losing the chance to contend the 2000 elections.

In April 2001 an estimated 60,000 supporters of 12 opposition parties gathered peacefully in Dar es Salaam to demand that the Government hold fresh elections in Zanzibar, draft a new Constitution for the United Republic and establish independent electoral commissions. A similar, peaceful demonstration in Zanzibar later that month was attended by an estimated 60,000–85,000 protesters. President Karume, however, continued to reject the opposition's demands. In May 11 members of the Zanzibar House of Representatives and five members of the National Assembly were dismissed from their respective legislatures for having boycotted three successive sittings—their actions were part of the CUF's ongoing refusal to recognize the 2000 election results. The Attorney-General rejected subsequent demands from the CUF for their reinstatement, and by-elections were to be held in 2003.

At the beginning of July 2001 a week of official mourning was announced to mark the death of Vice-President Omar Ali Juma; his successor, Dr Ali Mohamed Sheni, was sworn in later that month.

In August 2001 a Muslim group (denounced by the National Muslim Council of Tanzania) marched on the High Court in Dar es Salaam to protest against the imprisonment of one of its members for defaming Christianity. The group was dispersed after violent clashes with the police, and the prisoner was later freed. The unrest continued with a bomb attack on the CCM headquarters, which was believed to have been carried out by the same group, and culminated in more violent clashes between the police and armed Muslims, who were threatening to invade the central police station in an attempt to free some 40 people being detained in its cells. The police arrested 170 people, 41 of whom later stood trial, and were released on bail in September.

Idi Simba, the Minister for Industry and Commerce, resigned in November 2001, following allegations that he had fradulently issued licences to sugar importers. He was replaced by Dr Juma Ngasongwa.

Meanwhile, in June 2001 it emerged that, following the violence of the 2000 elections, the CCM and the CUF had been holding a series of secret negotiations intended to resolve the political impasse in Zanzibar. The negotiations concluded with the signing of a *muafaka* (peace accord) between the two parties in Zanzibar in October 2001. Shortly afterwards the State withdrew all 109 legal cases related to the January demonstrations, including the murder charges against the two CUF leaders. In December, however, the CUF threatened to withdraw from the accord, after the House of Representatives amended draft legislation on the establishment of a presidential commission to oversee its implementation, without consulting the party. Talks subsequently took place between the CCM and the CUF, and in January 2002 they resolved to continue with the implementation process; it was agreed that if any amendments to the accord were necessary, the Zanzibari Government would seek the consent of both parties. The joint presidential monitoring commission was subsequently appointed by Karume. At the same time President Mkapa appointed a commission to investigate the killings of CUF protesters at the demonstrations of January 2001. In November 2002 the commission reported that 31 of the people killed during violent disturbances in Zanzibar on 27 and 28 January 2001 had been shot dead by the police. The commission stated that the police were poorly equipped and under-trained, but that inflammatory articles in the press were also partly responsible for the events. The commission suggested that future political disputes be settled by a council of elders, religious leaders, academics and retired public servants, and urged the CCM and the CUF to sign a joint declaration apologizing for the damage caused. The commission also recommended that the Government compensate those injured during the clashes.

In accordance with the CCM-CUF accord signed in October 2001, amendments to the Zanzibari Constitution were approved by the House of Representatives in April 2002. The amendments provided for the restructuring of the electoral commission to include opposition representatives (duly appointed in October 2002), the creation of a permanent voters register and the removal of legislation requiring a person to live in a particular area for five consecutive years in order to qualify as a voter. Also included were the introduction of the right to appeal against High Court decisions and the appointment of a separate director of public prosecutions for Zanzibar.

In June 2002 the Democratic Party (DP) was officially registered. In August its leader, Rev. Christopher Mtikila, was arrested after claiming that President Mkapa was not a Tanzanian national (which, if true, would debar him from the presidency), but a Mozambican; he was later charged with sedition.

President Mkapa was re-elected Chairman of the CCM at the party's general convention, which was held in October 2002. Following the success of the opposition National Rainbow Coalition in presidential and legislative elections in Kenya in December, 11 Tanzanian opposition parties (including Chademn, NCCR—Mageuzi and the CUF) agreed in principle to field a joint candidate to contest the 2005 presidential election; the proposal remained subject to approval by the parties' members.

Tanzania's relations with Uganda and Kenya were strained throughout the 1970s, particularly after the dissolution of the East African Community (EAC) in 1977. Uganda briefly annexed the Kagera salient from Tanzania in November 1978. In early 1979 Tanzanian troops supported the Uganda National Liberation Front in the overthrow of President Idi Amin Dada. In June 2000 Tanzania called on Uganda to pay 98,500m. shillings to cover the cost of the operation. President Mkapa later stated that the amount was to be regarded as a military debt and not, as some claimed, as compensation for those killed

during the war. The Tanzania–Kenya border, closed since 1977, was reopened in November 1983, following an agreement on the distribution of the EAC's assets and liabilities. In the following month Tanzania and Kenya agreed to establish full diplomatic relations. The two countries reached agreement on a trade treaty and on the establishment of a joint co-operation commission in 1986. Tanzania pledged its support for the Government of Yoweri Museveni, which took power in Uganda in January of that year, and in November Tanzania began to send military instructors to Uganda to organize the training of Ugandan government troops. In November 1991 the Presidents of Tanzania, Kenya and Uganda met in Nairobi, Kenya, and declared their commitment to developing mutual co-operation. In November 1994, meeting in Arusha, the three leaders established a commission for co-operation; in March 1996 they met again in Nairobi to inaugurate formally the Secretariat of the Permanent Tripartite Commission for East African Co-operation, which aimed to revive the EAC. A treaty for the re-establishment of the EAC (see p. 339), providing for the creation of a free trade area (with the eventual introduction of a single currency), for the development of infrastructure, tourism and agriculture within the Community, and for the establishment of a regional legislative assembly and court, was formally ratified by the Tanzanian, Kenyan and Ugandan Heads of State in November 1999. The new East African Council of Ministers held its first meeting in Tanzania in January 2001.

In August 1993, following a protracted mediation effort by the Mwinyi Government, a peace agreement was signed in Arusha by the Rwandan authorities and the rebel Front patriotique rwandais. In April 1994, however, following the assassination of the Rwandan President, Juvénal Habyarimana, hundreds of thousands of Rwandans fled to Tanzania to escape the atrocities being perpetrated in their homeland: in one 24-hour period in late April some 250,000 refugees were reported to have crossed the Rwanda–Tanzania border. In May the Tanzanian authorities appealed for international emergency aid to assist in the care of the refugees, many of whom were sheltering in makeshift camps in the border region. In March 1995 Tanzania banned the admission of further refugees from both Rwanda and Burundi (where violent unrest had erupted in late 1994); some 800,000 Rwandan and Burundian refugees were reportedly sheltering in Tanzania in September 1995. The International Criminal Tribunal for Rwanda, authorized by the UN to charge and try Rwandan nationals accused of direct involvement in the genocide perpetrated in that country during 1994, was inaugurated in June 1995 in Arusha. After the Tutsi-led military coup, which took place in Burundi in July 1996 (following the failure of peace talks mediated by former President Nyerere), the Mkapa administration imposed economic sanctions against the new regime of President Pierre Buyoya, in co-operation with other regional governments. Relations between Tanzania and Burundi remained strained, owing both to the presence of Burundian rebels in northern Tanzania, which the Buyoya regime accused the Mkapa administration of supporting, and to the increasing numbers of Burundians seeking refuge in Tanzania throughout 1996 and 1997. Talks between the Buyoya Government and opposition politicians, once again mediated by Nyerere, were convened in Arusha, Tanzania, in 1998 and early 1999. The regional economic sanctions that were imposed against Burundi in 1996 were suspended in January 1999. In July 2002, following a meeting between President Mkapa and the Burundian Vice-President, Domitien Ndayizeye, the two countries stated that they were to normalize their relations. Peace negotiations between the Burundian transitional Government and rebel groups took place in Dar es Salaam in August and October of that year.

In December 1996 some of the Rwandan refugees remaining in Tanzania were repatriated, following the threat of forcible repatriation by the Tanzanian Government; however, 200,000 refugees, unwilling to return to Rwanda, reportedly fled their camps. In March 1997 the Tanzanian Government appealed for further international assistance in coping with the remaining refugees (an estimated 200,000 Burundians and 250,000 Zaireans). In June 1997 it was agreed to repatriate some 100,000 refugees to the Democratic Republic of the Congo (DRC—formerly Zaire). At the end of December the office of the UN High Commissioner for Refugees (UNHCR) estimated that some 74,300 refugees from the DRC remained in Tanzania, while the number of Burundian refugees was believed to have increased to 459,400; the total refugee population was estimated at 570,400.

In July 1999 the Government rejected allegations by a human rights organization, the US-based Human Rights Watch, that it had confined in camps in the west of the country refugees who had, in some cases, been living in Tanzania for as long as 20 years. In December it was reported that UNHCR was providing protection and assistance to a total 415,000 refugees. In February 2000 the Government announced that nine refugee camps in the Kigoma region of west Tanzania had become saturated. Instability in Burundi and the DRC had recently led to further heavy influxes of refugees from those countries. At that time the number of officially registered refugees in west Tanzania reportedly totalled 468,000, but it was claimed that an additional 200,000 unregistered refugees were also present in the region. Burundians accounted for 70% of all refugees, and refugees from the DRC for 29%. The remainder had originated in Rwanda. In August 2000 a peace accord was signed in Arusha between the Burundian Government and various rebel groups; however, the main rebel groups refused to sign the agreement. Although the agreement neither stopped the fighting in Burundi, nor allowed the refugees to return home, it nevertheless resulted in a serious decline in the level of aid donations (for example, the UNHCR allocation for refugee camps in Tanzania was reduced by 55%). At the end of 2000 UNHCR estimated that the number of officially registered refugees in Tanzania totalled 509,223, of whom 72% were from Burundi, 22% from the DRC and 5% from Rwanda; the remainder had originated in Somalia. In May 2001 UNHCR and the Governments of Tanzania and Burundi signed an agreement to establish a tripartite commission for the voluntary repatriation of Burundian refugees in Tanzania, of whom there were an estimated 800,000 at that time. Although some 26,000 refugees were repatriated to Burundi during the first nine months of 2002, with hostilities in Burundi continuing, about 512,000 remained in Tanzania at September.

Government

Under the provisions of the 1977 Constitution, with subsequent amendments, legislative power is held by the unicameral National Assembly, whose members serve for a term of five years. There is constitutional provision for both directly elected members (chosen by universal suffrage) and nominated members (including five members elected by and from the Zanzibar House of Representatives). The number of directly elected members exceeds the number of nominated members. The Electoral Commission may review and, if necessary, increase the number of constituencies before every general election. Executive power lies with the President, elected by popular vote for five years. The President must be at least 40 years of age and his mandate is limited to a maximum of two five-year terms. The President appoints a Vice-President, to assist him in carrying out his functions, and presides over the Cabinet, which is composed of a Prime Minister and other ministers who are appointed from among the members of the National Assembly.

Zanzibar has its own administration for internal affairs, and the amended Zanzibar Constitution, which came into force in January 1985, provides for the President, elected by universal adult suffrage, to hold office for a maximum of two five-year terms, and for the House of Representatives, of 45–55 members, to be directly elected by universal adult suffrage. The President of Zanzibar appoints the Chief Minister, and the two co-operate in choosing the other members of the Supreme Revolutionary Council, which has a maximum of 20 members.

In May 1992 the United Republic's Constitution was amended to legalize a multi-party political system.

Defence

In August 2002 the total active armed forces numbered an estimated 27,000, of whom about 23,000 were in the army, 1,000 in the navy and 3,000 in the air force. There are also paramilitary forces including a 1,400-strong Police Field Force and an 80,000-strong reservist Citizens' Militia. The estimated defence budget was 140,000m. shillings in 2002.

Economic Affairs

In 2001, according to estimates by the World Bank, mainland Tanzania's gross national income (GNI), measured at average 1999–2001 prices, was US $9,198m., equivalent to $270 per head (or $540 per head on an international purchasing-power parity basis). During 1990–2001, it was estimated, the population of the country as a whole increased at an average annual rate of 2.8%, while gross domestic product (GDP) per head increased, in real terms, by an average of 0.3% per year. Overall GDP increased, in real terms, at an average annual rate of 3.1% in 1990–2001; growth was 4.6% in 2001.

Agriculture (including hunting, forestry and fishing) contributed 44.6% of GDP in 2001, and employed some 80.0% of the labour force in that year. The principal cash crops are coffee (which provided an estimated 14.2% of export revenues in 1999), cashew nuts (18.3%), cotton (5.2%) and cloves (Zanzibar's most important export, cultivated on the island of Pemba). Other cash crops include tobacco, tea, sisal, pyrethrum, coconuts, sugar and cardamom. Exports of cut flowers (grown in the vicinity of Kilimanjaro Airport and freighted to Europe) commenced in the mid-1990s. Seaweed production is an important activity in Zanzibar. Farmers have been encouraged to produce essential food crops, most importantly cassava and maize. The rearing of cattle is also significant. A large proportion of agricultural output is produced by subsistence farmers. Tanzania's agricultural GDP increased at an average annual rate of 3.2% during 1990–2001, according to the World Bank; agricultural GDP increased by 3.8% in 2001.

Industry (including mining, manufacturing, construction and power) contributed 16.4% of GDP in 2001, and employed an estimated 4.5% of the working population in 1980. During 1990–2001 industrial GDP increased by an average of 3.6% per year, according to the World Bank; growth in 2001 was 8.9%.

Mining provided only 1.5% of GDP in 2000. Gold, diamonds, other gemstones (including rubies and sapphires), salt, phosphates, coal, gypsum, tin, kaolin, limestone and graphite are mined, and it is planned to exploit reserves of natural gas. Other mineral deposits include nickel, silver, cobalt, copper, soda ash, iron ore and uranium, and exploration for petroleum is in progress. According to the IMF, the GDP of the mining sector increased by an average of 12.9% per year in 1990–99; it grew by 9.1% in 1999.

Manufacturing contributed 7.5% of GDP in 2001. The most important manufacturing activities are food-processing, textile production, cigarette production and brewing. Pulp and paper, fertilizers, cement, clothing, footwear, tyres, batteries, pharmaceuticals, paint, bricks and tiles and electrical goods are also produced, while other activities include oil-refining, metalworking, vehicle assembly and engineering. Tanzania's manufacturing GDP increased at an average annual rate of 2.8% in 1990–2001, according to the World Bank; it grew by 5.3% in 2001.

Energy is derived principally from hydroelectric power, which supplied 96.5% of Tanzania's electricity in 1999 (the remainder was supplied by petroleum). Imports of petroleum and petroleum products accounted for about 5.8% of imports in 1999.

The services sector contributed 39.0% of GDP in 2001, and employed an estimated 9.9% of the labour force in 1980. Tourism is an important potential growth sector: tourism receipts were approximately US $739m. in 2000. According to the World Bank, the GDP of the services sector increased by an average of 3.1% per year in 1990–2001. Growth in the sector was 4.3% in 2001.

In 2000 Tanzania recorded a visible trade deficit of US $674.1m., and there was a deficit of $480.3m. on the current account of the balance of payments. In 1999 the principal sources of imports were Japan (10.9%), South Africa, the United Kingdom and the USA, while the main markets for exports were India (20.6%), the United Kingdom, Japan and Germany. The principal exports in 1999 were coffee beans, minerals, tobacco and manufactured products. The principal imports were consumer goods, machinery, intermediate goods and transport equipment.

In the financial year ending 30 June 2001 there was a budgetary deficit of 87,860m. shillings, equivalent to 1.1% of GDP. In the year ending 30 June 2002 the budgetary deficit was 38,195m. shillings. At the end of 2000 Tanzania's external debt totalled US $7,445m., of which $6,325m. was long-term public debt. In that year the cost of debt-servicing was equivalent to 16.2% of the value of exports of goods and services. The annual rate of inflation averaged 18.4% in 1990–2001; consumer prices increased by 5.1% in 2001.

Tanzania is a member of the African Development Bank (see p. 128) and of the Southern African Development Community (see p. 311). Tanzania is a founder member (with Kenya and Uganda) of the restored East African Community (EAC, see p. 339).

In terms of GNI per head, Tanzania is one of the world's poorest countries. Perhaps the greatest of all the country's economic problems is the very high level of its external debt. In

September 1999 Tanzania was admitted to the World Bank's Heavily Indebted Poor Countries initiative, thereby qualifying for concessionary debt relief. By that time the Government had achieved greater control over public expenditure and a reduction in inflation. In November of that year the Heads of State of Tanzania, Kenya and Uganda ratified a treaty re-establishing the EAC. The treaty envisaged the creation of a customs union, to be followed, eventually, by monetary and political union. In March 2000 the IMF approved a three-year loan equivalent to some US $181.5m. for Tanzania, under its Poverty Reduction and Growth Facility, and in November 2001 the country was granted enhanced debt relief, effectively halving its external debt. However, there was concern about Tanzania's continued dependence on foreign aid. Moreover, studies indicated that poverty had not diminished over the last decade, and that the proportion of malnourished people had grown, while AIDS was still rife throughout much of the country. The agricultural sector had generally failed to fulfil its potential (despite good growth in 2001), and, while much of this could be attributed to the sharp decline in commodity prices (especially for coffee), critics maintained that the Government had not done enough to address the sector that could most improve the lives of ordinary Tanzanians. The tourism sector also suffered severe set-backs in 2001, following post-election violence in Zanzibar (see Recent History) and the suicide attacks on the USA on 11 September. Tanzania has achieved considerable success with its privatization programme, and in January 2002 it was announced that some 326 of a total of 369 parastatals had been transferred to the private sector. However, a number of enterprises in sensitive sectors, such as utilities and transport, remained to be divested. Notably, the decision to place the Tanzania Electric Supply Co under South African management from May 2002, ahead of its privatization, provoked a series of demonstrations by employees who feared job losses. GDP growth was estimated at 6.0% in 2002, with growth exceeding 5.0% in almost all sectors of the economy. At the end of the year inflation had declined to 4.4%, owing to a significant deceleration in the rise of food prices; non-food inflation, however, increased markedly. Unemployment was expected to increase in 2003, with 9,100 job losses announced in the Tanzania Railways Corporation alone.

Education

Education at primary level is officially compulsory and is provided free of charge. In secondary schools a government-stipulated fee is paid: from January 1995 this was 8,000 shillings per year for day pupils at state-owned schools and 50,000–60,000 shillings per year for day pupils at private schools. Villages and districts are encouraged to construct their own schools with government assistance. Almost all primary schools are government-owned. Primary education begins at seven years of age and lasts for seven years. Secondary education, beginning at the age of 14, lasts for a further six years, comprising a first cycle of four years and a second of two years. Enrolment at primary schools in 1999/2000 included 46.7% of children in the relevant age-group (males 45.8%; females 47.6%). Secondary enrolment in that year included only 4.8% of children in the appropriate age-group (males 4.9%; females 4.6%), according to UNESCO estimates. In November 2001 it was announced that approximately 7m. children were to be enrolled in primary schools, under the Government's five year plan to reintroduce universal primary education by 2005. There is a university at Dar es Salaam. Tanzania also has an agricultural university at Morogoro, and a number of vocational training centres and technical colleges. Education was allocated 23% of total recurrent budgetary expenditure by the central Government in 1994.

Public Holidays

2003: 1 January (New Year's Day), 12 January (Zanzibar Revolution Day), 5 February (Chama Cha Mapinduzi Day), 12 February* (Id El Haji, Feast of the Sacrifice), 5 March* (Muharram, New Year), 18–21 April (Easter), 26 April (Union Day), 1 May (International Labour Day), 14 May* (Maulid, Birth of the Prophet), 7 July (Saba Saba, Industry's Day), 8 August (Peasants' Day), 26 August (Sultan's Birthday)†, 29 October (Naming Day), 26 November* (Id El Fitr, end of Ramadan), 9 December (Independence Day), 25–26 December (Christmas).

2004: 1 January (New Year's Day), 12 January (Zanzibar Revolution Day), 2 February* (Id El Haji, Feast of the Sacrifice), 5 February (Chama Cha Mapinduzi Day), 22 February* (Muharram, New Year), 9–12 April (Easter), 26 April (Union Day), 1 May (International Labour Day), 2 May* (Maulid, Birth of the Prophet), 7 July (Saba Saba, Industry's Day), 8 August (Peasants' Day), 26 August (Sultan's Birthday)†, 29 October (Naming Day), 14 November* (Id El Fitr, end of Ramadan), 9 December (Independence Day), 25–26 December (Christmas).

* These holidays are dependent on the Islamic lunar calendar and may vary by one or two days from the dates given.

† Zanzibar only.

Weights and Measures

The metric system is in force.

Statistical Survey

Source (unless otherwise stated): Economic and Research Policy Dept, Bank of Tanzania, POB 2939, Dar es Salaam; tel. (22) 2110946; fax (22) 2113325; e-mail info@hq.bot-tz.org; internet www.bot-tz.org.

Area and Population

AREA, POPULATION AND DENSITY

Area (sq km)	945,087*
Population (census results)	
28 August 1988	23,126,310
25 August 2002	
Males	16,910,321
Females	17,658,911
Total	34,569,232
Population (UN estimates at mid-year)†	
1999	34,285,000
2000	35,119,000
2001	35,965,000
Density (per sq km) at mid-2001	38.1

* 364,900 sq miles. Of this total, Tanzania mainland is 942,626 sq km (363,950 sq miles), and Zanzibar 2,461 sq km (950 sq miles).

† Source: UN *World Population Prospects: The 2000 Revision.*

ETHNIC GROUPS
(private households, census of 26 August 1967)

African	11,481,595	Others	839
Asian	75,015	Not stated . . .	159,042
Arabs	29,775	**Total**	11,763,150
European	16,884		

REGIONS
(at census of 25 August 2002)

Arusha	1,292,973	Mwanza	2,942,148
Dar es Salaam	2,497,940	Pwani	889,154
Dodoma	1,698,996	North Pemba*	186,013
Iringa	1,495,333	North Unguja*	136,953
Kagera	2,033,888	Rukwa	1,141,743
Kigoma	1,679,109	Ruvuma	1,117,166
Kilimanjaro	1,381,149	Shinyanga	2,805,580
Lindi	791,306	Singida	1,090,758
Manyara†	603,691	South Pemba*	176,153
Mara	1,368,602	South Unguja*	94,504
Mbeya	2,070,046	Urban West*	391,002
Morogoro	1,759,809	Tabora	1,717,908
Mtwara	1,128,523	Tanga	1,642,015

* Part of the autonomous territory of Zanzibar.
† Before the 2002 census Manyara was inlcuded in the region of Arusha.

PRINCIPAL TOWNS
(estimated population at mid-1988)

Dar es Salaam	1,360,850	Mbeya	152,844
Mwanza	223,013	Arusha	134,708
Dodoma	203,833	Morogoro	117,760
Tanga	187,455	Shinyanga	100,724
Zanzibar	157,634		

Source: UN, *Demographic Yearbook.*

BIRTHS AND DEATHS
(UN estimates, annual averages)

	1990–95	1995–2000	2000–2005
Birth rate (per 1,000)	42.6	40.4	37.9
Death rate (per 1,000)	12.8	13.3	13.1

Source: UN, *World Population Prospects: The 2000 Revision.*

Expectation of life (WHO estimates, years at birth): 46.5 (males 45.8; females 47.2) in 2001 (Source: WHO, *World Health Report*).

ECONOMICALLY ACTIVE POPULATION
(1967 census)

	Males	Females	Total
Agriculture, forestry, hunting and fishing	2,549,688	2,666,805	5,216,493
Mining and quarrying	4,918	99	5,017
Manufacturing	85,659	13,205	98,864
Construction	32,755	318	33,073
Electricity, gas, water and sanitary services	5,704	158	5,862
Commerce	71,088	7,716	78,804
Transport, storage and communications	46,121	711	46,832
Other services	169,693	38,803	208,496
Other activities (not adequately defined)	35,574	18,081	53,655
Total labour force	3,001,200	2,745,896	5,747,096

1978 census: Total labour force 7,845,105 (males 3,809,135; females 4,035,970) aged 5 years and over.

Mid-1990 (ILO estimates, '000 persons): Agriculture etc. 11,291 (males 5,239, females 6,052); Industry 654 (males 534, females 120); Services 1,431 (males 957, females 474); Total 13,376 (males 6,730, females 6,646) (Source: ILO).

Mid-2001 (estimates in '000): Agriculture, etc. 14,845; Total labour force 18,556 (Source: FAO).

Health and Welfare

KEY INDICATORS

Total fertility rate (children per woman, 2001)	5.2
Under-5 mortality rate (per 1,000 live births, 2001)	165
HIV/AIDS (% of persons aged 15–49, 2001)	7.83
Hospital beds (per 1,000 head, 1992)	0.89
Health expenditure (2000): US $ per head (PPP)	27
Health expenditure (2000): % of GDP	5.9
Health expenditure (2000): public (% of total)	47
Human Development Index (2000): ranking	151
Human Development Index (2000): value	0.440

For sources and definitions, see explanatory note on p. vi.

Agriculture

PRINCIPAL CROPS
('000 metric tons)

	1999	2000	2001
Wheat	82	90*	90
Rice (paddy)	506	508	514
Maize	2,452	2,551	2,616
Millet	194	153	170
Sorghum	561	664	736
Potatoes†	255	270	270
Sweet potatoes	597	798	453
Cassava (Manioc)	7,182	5,758	5,650†
Yams†	10	10	10
Sugar cane	1,269	1,355	1,500
Dry beans†	255	260	260
Dry peas†	27	28	28
Chick-peas†	23	24	24
Other pulses†	26	27	27
Groundnuts (in shell)†	74	75	75
Sunflower seed	28*	28*	28†
Sesame seed*	40	42	39
Coconuts†	350	370	370
Oil palm fruit†	62	64	64
Tomatoes	139	140†	140†
Onions (dry)†	55	56	56
Other vegetables†	935	940	940
Citrus fruits†	38	39	39
Mangoes†	189	190	190
Pineapples†	75	76	76
Bananas	150	141	156
Plantains	601	562	624
Other fruit†	199	200	200
Cashew nuts	107	121	122
Coffee (green)	47	48	58
Tea (made)	25	24	26
Tobacco (leaves)	38	37†	24
Sisal	24	21	21
Cotton (lint)	35	41	81

* Unofficial figure(s).
† FAO estimate(s).

Source: FAO.

LIVESTOCK
('000 head, year ending September)

	1999	2000	2001
Asses*	179	180	180
Cattle*	15,000	17,000	17,000
Pigs	446†	450*	450*
Sheep	3,489	3,400*	3,400*
Goats	11,643	11,640*	11,643*
Chickens	28	28	30*
Ducks	1	1*	1*

* FAO estimate(s).
† Unofficial figure.

Source: FAO.

LIVESTOCK PRODUCTS

(FAO estimates, '000 metric tons)

	1999	2000	2001
Beef and veal	215	225	225
Mutton and lamb	11	10	10
Goat meat	29	29	29
Pig meat	12	13	13
Poultry meat	41	41	41
Cows' milk	687*	715*	715
Goats' milk	95	96	96
Butter	5	5	5
Hen eggs	56	61	61
Other poultry eggs	2	2	2
Honey	26	26	26
Cattle hides	42	44	44
Sheepskins	3	3	3
Goatskins	6	6	6

* Unofficial figure.

Source: FAO.

Forestry

ROUNDWOOD REMOVALS

('000 cubic metres, excluding bark)

	1999	2000	2001
Sawlogs, veneer logs and logs for sleepers*	170	170	170
Pulpwood†	153	153	153
Other industrial wood*	1,844	1,844	1,844
Fuel wood*	20,737	20,787	20,951
Total	22,904	22,954	23,118

* FAO estimates.

† Annual output assumed to be unchanged since 1987.

Source: FAO.

SAWNWOOD PRODUCTION

(FAO estimates, '000 cubic metres, including railway sleepers)

	1999	2000	2001
Coniferous (softwood)	13	13	13
Broadleaved (hardwood)	11	11	11
Total	24	24	24

Source: FAO.

Fishing

('000 metric tons, live weight)

	1998	1999	2000
Capture	348.0	310.0	332.8
Tilapias	24.0	38.0	40.0
Mouthbrooding cichlids	10.5	8.0	9.0
Nile perch	150.0	100.0	90.0
Other freshwater fishes	58.7	67.5	96.7
Dagaas	46.8	42.0	40.0
Sardinellas	4.5	14.0	15.0
Aquaculture*	0.3	0.3	0.2
Total catch	348.3	310.3	333.0

Note: Figures exclude aquatic plants ('000 metric tons): 7.0 (capture 4.0, aquaculture 3.0*) in 1998; 7.0 (capture 0.0, aquaculture 7.0) in 1999; 12.0 (capture 5.0, aquaculture 7.0) in 2000. Also excluded are crocodiles, recorded by number rather than by weight. The number of Nile crocodiles caught was: 777 in 1998; 827 in 1999; 1,302 in 2000.

* FAO estimate(s).

Source: FAO, *Yearbook of Fishery Statistics*.

Mining

('000 metric tons, unless otherwise indicated)

	1998	1999	2000
Gold (refined, kilograms)	427	4,767	15,060
Salt	75	35	70
Gypsum and anhydrite	59	40	60

Source: US Geological Survey.

Industry

SELECTED PRODUCTS

('000 metric tons, unless otherwise indicated)

	1998	1999	2000
Wheat flour	87.7	144.7	162.6
Sugar (refined)	93.0	110.0	135.3
Cigarettes (million)	3.9	3.4	3.7
Beer (million litres)	170.7	167.4	183.0
Textiles (million sq metres)	45.5	49.8	73.6
Cement	778.0	833.0	833.0
Rolled steel	9.5	9.0	11.2
Iron sheets	14.9	23.0	25.0
Aluminium	0.2	0.2	0.1
Petroleum products	312.0	287.0	117.0
Sisal ropes	4.3	3.3	3.9
Paints (million litres)	4.9	12.9	7.1

Source: Bank of Tanzania.

Finance

CURRENCY AND EXCHANGE RATES

Monetary Units

100 cents = 1 Tanzanian shilling

Sterling, Dollar and Euro Equivalents (31 December 2002)

£1 sterling = 1,528.0 Tanzanian shillings
US $1 = 984.5 Tanzanian shillings
€1 = 977.4 Tanzanian shillings
10,000 Tanzanian shillings = £6.544 = $10.157 = €10.232

Average Exchange Rate (Tanzanian shillings per US $)

2000   800.41
2001   876.41
2002   966.58

BUDGET

(million shillings, year ending 30 June)*

Revenue†	1997/98	1998/99	1999/2000
Tax revenue	566,122.1	616,284.1	685,107.4
Taxes on imports	183,002.8	171,993.2	178,000.7
Sales taxes and excises on local goods	138,179.3	208,040.4	222,341.1
Income taxes	149,787.4	162,894.1	209,713.6
Other taxes	95,152.6	73,356.4	75,052.0
Non-tax revenue	52,960.5	73,041.2	92,537.3
Total	619,082.6	689,325.3	777,644.7

Expenditure‡	1997/98	1998/99	1999/2000
Recurrent expenditure	669,592.4	791,208.3	808,865.4
Current payments	442,569.7	589,354.5	680,687.0
Debt service (incl. redemption)	227,022.7	201,853.8	128,178.4
Development expenditure‡	186,585.0	136,523.9	359,913.4
Total	856,177.4	927,732.2	1,168,778.8

* Figures refer to the Tanzania Government, excluding the revenue and expenditure of the separate Zanzibar Government.

† Excluding grants received (million shillings): 119,358.3 in 1997/98; 169,945.6 in 1998/99; 280,306.7 in 1999/2000.

‡ Including lending minus repayments.

Source: Bank of Tanzania.

INTERNATIONAL RESERVES
(US $ million at 31 December)

	2000	2001	2002
IMF special drawing rights	0.1	0.5	0.1
Reserve position in IMF	13.0	12.5	13.6
Foreign exchange	961.1	1,143.6	1,512.2
Total	974.2	1,156.6	1,525.9

Source: IMF, *International Financial Statistics*.

MONEY SUPPLY
(million shillings at 31 December)

	2000	2001	2002
Currency outside banks	392,404	411,639	495,450
Demand deposits at commercial banks	302,602	354,381	463,340
Total money	695,006	766,020	958,790

Source: IMF, *International Financial Statistics*.

COST OF LIVING
(Consumer Price Index for Tanzania mainland; base: 1990 = 100)

	1998	1999	2000
Food (incl. beverages)	562.3	611.7	653.3
Fuel, light and water	666.2	731.5	782.1
Clothing (incl. footwear)	376.7	416.7	427.4
Rent	686.1	719.9	760.6
All items (incl. others)	531.9	573.6	607.8

2001: Food 693.1; All items 638.8.

Source: ILO.

NATIONAL ACCOUNTS
(Tanzania mainland, million shillings at current prices)

National Income and Product
(provisional)

	1992	1993	1994
Compensation of employees	88,230	119,119	148,194
Operating surplus	906,923	1,132,774	1,462,193
Domestic factor incomes	995,153	1,251,894	1,610,387
Consumption of fixed capital	35,802	36,697	49,542
Gross domestic product (GDP) at factor cost	1,030,955	1,288,591	1,659,929
Indirect taxes	109,442	183,389	260,039
Less Subsidies	9,801	67,611	97,398
GDP in purchasers' values	1,130,596	1,404,369	1,822,570
Factor income received from abroad	2,563	7,934	8,648
Less Factor income paid abroad	72,969	67,842	78,173
Gross national product (GNP)	1,060,190	1,344,460	1,753,045
Less Consumption of fixed capital	35,802	36,697	49,542
National income in market prices	1,024,387	1,307,763	1,703,504
Other current transfers from abroad (net)	282,813	291,673	308,518
National disposable income	1,307,200	1,599,436	2,084,022

Expenditure on the Gross Domestic Product*

	1998	1999	2000
Government final consumption expenditure	433,790	451,140	473,690
Private final consumption expenditure	4,909,250	5,667,440	6,069,580
Increase in stocks	9,910	10,310	14,370
Gross fixed capital formation	892,700	989,340	1,266,680
Total domestic expenditure*	6,245,650	7,118,230	7,824,320
Exports of goods and services	748,970	885,940	1,060,530
Less Imports of goods and services	1,565,330	1,703,760	1,675,880
Sub-total	5,429,300	6,300,410	7,208,970
Statistical discrepancy	142,340	140,880	16,720
GDP in purchasers' values	5,571,640	6,441,290	7,225,690
GDP at constant 1992 prices	1,636,960	1,694,740	1,781,260

* Figures are rounded to the nearest 10 million shillings.

Source: IMF, *International Financial Statistics*.

Gross Domestic Product by Economic Activity
(at factor cost)

	1998	1999	2000
Agriculture, hunting, forestry and fishing	2,295,413	2,694,373	3,003,903
Mining and quarrying	74,386	85,792	99,519
Manufacturing	382,901	434,544	499,726
Electricity, gas and water	81,751	101,301	112,753
Construction	255,330	305,859	343,354
Trade, restaurants and hotels	635,305	740,181	823,025
Transport, storage and communications	250,081	294,180	328,259
Public administration	424,278	495,377	516,865
Financial and business services	312,847	345,071	377,996
Other services	553,928	625,777	709,617
Sub-total	5,266,220	6,122,455	6,815,017
Less Imputed bank service charge	140,909	144,756	151,359
Total	5,125,311	5,977,699	6,663,658

Source: Bank of Tanzania.

BALANCE OF PAYMENTS
(US $ million)

	1998	1999	2000
Exports of goods f.o.b.	589.5	542.9	665.7
Imports of goods f.o.b.	−1,365.3	−1,368.3	−1,339.8
Trade balance	−775.9	−825.4	−674.1
Exports of services	555.0	624.4	614.6
Imports of services	−988.1	−762.3	−670.3
Balance on goods and services	−1,209.0	−963.3	−729.8
Other income received	35.1	54.8	59.5
Other income paid	−173.7	−127.6	−139.0
Balance on goods, services and income	−1,347.7	−1,036.0	−809.3
Current transfers received	426.6	413.4	406.0
Current transfers paid	−35.5	−123.3	−77.0
Current balance	−956.5	−745.9	−480.3
Capital account (net)	422.9	322.5	331.7
Direct investment from abroad	172.3	183.4	193.5
Other investment assets	−50.7	14.8	10.2
Other investment liabilities	−44.0	−117.5	−327.5
Net errors and omissions	−53.5	269.3	137.7
Overall balance	−509.4	−73.4	−134.8

Source: IMF, *International Financial Statistics*.

External Trade

PRINCIPAL COMMODITIES
(US $ million)

Imports c.i.f.	1997	1998	1999
Capital goods	513.6	764.4	770.2
Transport equipment	233.1	241.0	297.0
Building and construction	35.1	132.2	132.0
Machinery	225.4	391.2	341.1
Intermediate goods	382.9	268.1	308.0
Petroleum and petroleum products	173.0	102.4	95.1
Crude petroleum	104.9	102.4	95.1
Petroleum products	68.2	0.0	0.0
Consumer goods	373.1	537.6	552.4
Food and foodstuffs	97.0	226.7	176.4
Total	1,269.5	1,570.1	1,630.6

Exports f.o.b.	1997	1998	1999
Coffee	119.3	108.7	76.6
Cotton	130.4	47.6	28.3
Tea	31.8	30.4	24.4
Tobacco	53.6	55.4	43.4
Cashew nuts	91.1	107.3	98.9
Minerals	51.1	26.4	71.6
Total (incl. others)	752.6	588.5	541.0

Source: IMF, *Tanzania—Statistical Annex* (September 2000).

PRINCIPAL TRADING PARTNERS
(million shillings)

Imports c.i.f.	1997	1998	1999
Argentina	1,798.4	4,338.4	14,256.2
Australia	1,177.2	18,966.6	60,646.6
Belgium	15,632.2	16,236.8	17,166.0
Brazil	5,258.3	9,685.7	12,936.4
Canada	7,651.9	11,080.2	19,853.0
China, People's Repub.	37,671.0	32,401.2	43,213.3
Denmark	5,281.6	17,828.7	17,865.7
France	12,449.2	10,513.2	15,993.3
Germany	30,368.5	51,601.1	46,524.0
India	47,443.7	59,659.7	70,444.1
Iran	38,938.0	43,556.5	59,734.3
Italy	23,730.2	45,348.5	36,418.0
Japan	45,322.9	87,044.5	132,711.7
Kenya	58,558.4	70,319.2	70,799.0
Malaysia	10,510.4	23,346.9	17,865.9
Netherlands	17,246.4	62,065.2	27,425.0
Pakistan	6,387.6	11,827.3	11,660.7
Singapore	23,716.2	8,546.5	7,266.9
South Africa	58,757.8	86,885.6	127,231.3
Sweden	11,183.6	19,466.5	13,299.4
Switzerland	18,209.9	11,917.0	10,918.3
Thailand	11,821.9	16,016.1	13,345.6
United Arab Emirates	57,200.3	39,704.7	38,006.4
United Kingdom	75,342.0	81,558.9	95,553.6
USA	32,215.4	54,046.5	73,963.0
Zambia	15,303.8	11,324.2	5,408.4
Total (incl. others)	808,167.9	1,403,096.9	1,219,957.4

Exports	1997	1998	1999
Belgium	5,019.1	17,353.5	12,527.6
China, People's Repub.	10,595.9	1,320.1	90.6
France	8,769.1	1,885.7	1,672.9
Germany	41,518.3	32,560.0	26,178.0
Hong Kong	11,153.6	3,321.4	5,828.0
India	40,710.6	76,272.7	84,022.3
Indonesia	11,711.3	3,922.9	6,737.9
Ireland	1,115.4	13,304.2	10,716.9
Italy	7,499.9	4,374.3	4,797.2
Japan	36,729.9	30,276.2	32,702.9
Kenya	7,807.5	17,306.9	15,630.9
Netherlands	24,537.9	30,035.6	23,234.5
Pakistan	7,067.9	6,147.6	5,662.3
Portugal	9,207.8	7,988.8	4,678.3
St Helena	0.6	3,556.7	6,546.0
Singapore	8,922.9	7,267.6	18,399.4
South Africa	4,852.0	4,190.1	4,771.0
Spain	7,807.5	3,703.6	2,548.8
Switzerland	3,596.1	7,463.0	1,802.0
Taiwan	12,672.8	4,617.5	2,210.7
Thailand	8,624.1	5,086.1	2,870.0
Uganda	7,096.0	4,336.8	3,467.2
United Arab Emirates	3,031.0	4,546.4	4,969.7
United Kingdom	22,864.8	39,679.4	69,113.2
USA	13,076.7	8,519.9	13,372.8
Zambia	6,134.5	2,442.0	2,119.5
Total (incl. others)	459,549.0	391,804.4	407,118.1

Source: Bank of Tanzania.

Transport

RAILWAYS
(estimated traffic)

	1989	1990	1991
Passenger-km (million)	3,630	3,690	3,740
Freight ton-km (million)	1,420	1,470	1,490

Source: UN Economic Commission for Africa, *African Statistical Yearbook*.

ROAD TRAFFIC
(estimates, '000 motor vehicles in use)

	1994	1995	1996
Passenger cars	28.0	26.0	23.8
Buses and coaches	78.0	81.0	86.0
Lorries and vans	27.2	27.7	29.7
Road tractors	6.7	6.7	6.6

Source: IRF, *World Road Statistics*.

SHIPPING

Merchant fleet
(registered at 31 December)

	1999	2000	2001
Number of vessels	56	59	57
Displacement ('000 grt)	36.2	38.0	37.6

Source: Lloyd's Register-Fairplay, *World Fleet Statistics*.

International sea-borne freight traffic
(estimates '000 metric tons)

	1988	1989	1990
Goods loaded	1,208	1,197	1,249
Goods unloaded	3,140	3,077	2,721

Source: Government Printer, *Economic Survey 1990*.

CIVIL AVIATION
(traffic on scheduled services)

	1997	1998	1999
Kilometres flown (million)	4	5	3
Passengers carried ('000)	218	220	190
Passenger-km (million)	231	236	176
Total ton-km (million)	26	25	18

Source: UN, *Statistical Yearbook*.

Tourism

FOREIGN VISITOR ARRIVALS
(by country of origin)

	1998	1999	2000
Burundi	21,777	28,329	22,651
France	16,523	21,493	17,186
Germany	21,734	28,272	22,606
India	18,118	23,567	18,844
Kenya	81,717	106,297	84,993
Malawi	11,086	14,421	11,531
South Africa	14,400	18,732	14,977
Sweden	15,430	20,071	16,049
Uganda	20,224	26,307	21,035
United Kingdom	33,180	43,161	34,511
USA	31,786	41,348	33,060
Total (incl. others)	482,331	627,417	501,669

Source: World Tourism Organization, *Yearbook of Tourism Statistics*.

Tourism receipts (US $ million): 570 in 1998; 733 in 1999; 739 in 2000 (Source: World Bank).

Communications Media

	1999	2000	2001
Television receivers ('000 in use) .	690	700	n.a.
Telephones ('000 main lines in use)	149.6	173.6	148.5
Mobile cellular telephones ('000 subscribers).	51.0	180.2	427.0
Personal computers ('000 in use)	80	100	120
Internet users ('000)	25	115	300

Source: International Telecommunication Union.

Radio receivers ('000 in use, estimate, 1997): 8,800 (Source: UNESCO, *Statistical Yearbook*).

Daily newspapers (1996): 3; average circulation ('000 copies, estimate) 120 (Source: UNESCO, *Statistical Yearbook*).

Education

(1998)

	Teachers	Pupils/Students		
		Males	Females	Total
Primary	106,329	2,033,281	2,009,287	4,042,568
General secondary .	11,691	121,429	105,474	226,903
Tertiary	2,064	14,897	3,970	18,867

Institutions: 11,339 primary schools in 1998.

Adult literacy rate (UNESCO estimates): 75.1% (males 83.9%; females 66.5%) in 2000 (Source: UN Development Programme, *Human Development Report*).

Source: UNESCO Institute for Statistics.

Directory

The Constitution

The United Republic of Tanzania was established on 26 April 1964, when Tanganyika and Zanzibar, hitherto separate independent countries, merged. An interim Constitution of 1965 was replaced, on 25 April 1977, by a permanent Constitution for the United Republic. In October 1979 the Revolutionary Council of Zanzibar adopted a separate Constitution, governing Zanzibar's internal administration, with provisions for a popularly elected President and a legislative House of Representatives elected by delegates of the then ruling party. A new Constitution for Zanzibar, which came into force in January 1985, provided for direct elections to the Zanzibar House of Representatives. The provisions below relate to the 1977 Constitution of the United Republic, as subsequently amended.

GOVERNMENT

Legislative power is exercised by the Parliament of the United Republic, which is vested by the Constitution with complete sovereign power, and of which the present National Assembly is the legislative house. The Assembly also enacts all legislation concerning the mainland. Internal matters in Zanzibar are the exclusive jurisdiction of the Zanzibar executive, the Supreme Revolutionary Council of Zanzibar, and the Zanzibar legislature, the House of Representatives.

National Assembly

The National Assembly comprises both directly elected members (chosen by universal adult suffrage) and nominated members (including five members elected from the Zanzibar House of Representatives). The number of directly elected members exceeds the number of nominated members. The Electoral Commission may review and, if necessary, increase the number of electoral constituencies before every general election. The National Assembly has a term of five years.

President

The President is the Head of State, Head of the Government and Commander-in-Chief of the Armed Forces. The President has no power to legislate without recourse to Parliament. The assent of the President is required before any bill passed by the National Assembly becomes law. Should the President withhold his assent and the bill be repassed by the National Assembly by a two-thirds' majority, the President is required by law to give his assent within 21 days unless, before that time, he has dissolved the National Assembly, in which case he must stand for re-election.

The President appoints a Vice-President to assist him in carrying out his functions. The President presides over the Cabinet, which comprises a Prime Minister and other ministers who are appointed from among the members of the National Assembly.

JUDICIARY

The independence of the judges is secured by provisions which prevent their removal, except on account of misbehaviour or incapacity when they may be dismissed at the discretion of the President. The Constitution also makes provision for a Permanent Commission of Enquiry, which has wide powers to investigate any abuses of authority.

CONSTITUTIONAL AMENDMENTS

The Constitution can be amended by an act of the Parliament of the United Republic, when the proposed amendment is supported by the votes of not fewer than two-thirds of all the members of the Assembly.

The Government

HEAD OF STATE

President: BENJAMIN WILLIAM MKAPA (took office 23 November 1995; re-elected 29 October 2000).

Vice-President: Dr ALI MOHAMMED SHENI.

CABINET
(April 2003)

President and Commander-in-Chief of the Armed Forces: BENJAMIN WILLIAM MKAPA.

Vice-President: Dr ALI MOHAMMED SHENI.

Prime Minister: FREDERICK SUMAYE.

Ministers of State in the President's Office: ABDALLA KIGODA, WILSON MASILINGI, MARY NAGU, Brig.-Gen. HASSAN NGWILIZI.

Ministers of State in the Vice-President's Office: ARCADO NTAGAZWA, DANIEL YONA.

Ministers of State in the Prime Minister's Office: WILLIAM LUKUVI, OMAR RAMADHANI MAPURI.

Minister of Foreign Affairs and International Co-operation: Lt-Col JAKAYA MRISHO KIKWETE.

Minister of Home Affairs: MOHAMMED SEIF KHATIB.

Minister of Finance: BASIL MRAMBA.

Minister of Industry and Commerce: Dr JUMA NGASONGWA.

Minister of Communications and Transport: Prof. MARK MWANDOSYA.

Minister of Food and Agriculture: CHARLES KEENJA.

Minister of Health: ANNA ABDALLAH.

Minister of Education: JOSEPH MUNGAI.

Minister of Energy and Mineral Resources: EDGAR MAOKOLA MAJOGO.

Minister of Water and Livestock Development: EDWARD LOWASSA.

Minister of Natural Resources and Tourism: ZAKHIA MEGHJI.

Minister of Lands and Human Settlement: GIDEON CHEYO.

Minister of Science, Technology and Higher Education: Dr PIUS NG'WANDU.

Minister of Works: JOHN MAGUFULI.

Minister of Labour, Youth Development and Sports: Prof. JUMA KAPUYA.

Minister of Community Development, Women's Affairs and Children: Dr ASHA ROSE MIGIRO.

Minister of Justice and Constitutional Affairs: HARITH BAKARI MWAPACHU.

Minister of Defence: Prof. PHILEMON SARUNGI.

Minister of Co-operatives and Marketing: GEORGE KAHAMA.

MINISTRIES

All ministries in Dar es Salaam are to be transferred to Dodoma by 2005.

Office of the President: State House, POB 9120, Dar es Salaam; tel. (22) 2116898; fax (22) 2113425.

Office of the Vice-President: State House, POB 9120, Dar es Salaam; tel. (22) 2116919; fax (22) 2110614.

Office of the Prime Minister: POB 980, Dodoma; tel. (61) 20511.

Ministry of Community Development, Women's Affairs and Children: Dar es Salaam.

Ministry of Co-operatives and Marketing: Dar es Salaam.

Ministry of Defence: POB 9544, Dar es Salaam; tel. (22) 228291.

Ministry of Education: POB 9121, Dar es Salaam; tel. (22) 227211.

Ministry of Energy and Mineral Resources: POB 2000, Dar es Salaam; tel. (22) 2110414; fax (22) 2116719.

Ministry of Finance: POB 9111, Dar es Salaam; tel. (22) 2111174; fax (22) 238573.

Ministry of Food and Agriculture: POB 9192, Dar es Salaam; tel. (22) 2112323.

Ministry of Foreign Affairs and International Co-operation: POB 9000, Dar es Salaam; tel. (22) 2111906.

Ministry of Health: POB 9083, Dar es Salaam; tel. (22) 220261.

Ministry of Home Affairs: POB 9223, Dar es Salaam; tel. (22) 2112034.

Ministry of Industry and Commerce: POB 9503, Dar es Salaam; tel. (22) 227251.

Ministry of Justice and Constitutional Affairs: Dar es Salaam.

Ministry of Labour, Youth Development and Sports: POB 2483, Dar es Salaam; tel. (22) 220781.

Ministry of Lands and Human Settlement: POB 9372, Dar es Salaam; tel. (22) 227271.

Ministry of Natural Resources and Tourism: Dar es Salaam.

Ministry of Science, Technology and Higher Education: Dar es Salaam.

Ministry of Water and Livestock Development: POB 9153, Dar es Salaam; tel. (22) 2117153; fax (22) 2118075.

Ministry of Works, Communications and Transport: POB 9423, Dar es Salaam; tel. (22) 223235.

SUPREME REVOLUTIONARY COUNCIL OF ZANZIBAR
(April 2003)

President and Chairman: AMANI ABEID KARUME.

Chief Minister: SHAMSI VUAI NAHODHA.

Minister of State in the President's Office: SULELMAN OTHMAN NYANGA.

Minister of Constitution and Good Governance: Dr ALI MOHAMED SHENI.

Minister of Regional Administration and Government Forces: ALI ABDALLAH ALI.

Minister of State in the Chief Minister's Office: SALUM JUMA OTHMAN.

Minister for Transport and Communications: ZUBEIR ALI MAULID.

Minister for Commerce, Industry, Markets and Tourism: MOHAMED ABOUD MOHAMED.

Minister for Agriculture, Natural Resources, Environment and Co-operatives: MUSSA AME SIRIMA.

Minister for Youth, Employment, Women's Development and Children: SAMLA SULUHU.

Minister for Education, Culture and Sports: HAROUN SULELMAN.

Minister for Health and Social Welfare: MWINYI HAJI MAKAME.

Minister for Water, Works, Energy and Lands: BURHAN SAADAT HAJI.

Minister without Portfolio: KHAMIS SALUM ALI.

President and Legislature

PRESIDENT

Election, 29 October 2000

Candidate	Votes	%
Benjamin William Mkapa	5,863,201	71.7
Prof. Ibrahim Haruna Lipumba	1,329,077	16.3
Augustine Lyatonga Mrema	637,115	7.8
John Momose Cheyo	342,891	4.2
Total	8,172,284	100.0

NATIONAL ASSEMBLY

Speaker: PIUS MSEKWA.

Election, 29 October 2000

Party	Seats*
CCM	244
CUF	15
Chadema	4
TLP	3
UDP	2
Total	268

*In addition to the 231 elective seats, 10 seats are reserved for presidential nominees and 27 seats for women (included in the figures above), five to members of the Zanzibar House of Representatives and one to the Attorney-General.

ZANZIBAR PRESIDENT

Election, 29 October 2000

Candidate	Votes	%
Amani Abeid Karume	248,000	67
Seif Sharif Hamad	122,000	33
Total	370,000	100

ZANZIBAR HOUSE OF REPRESENTATIVES

Speaker: PANDU AMIR KIFICHO.

Election, 29 October 2000

Party	Seats*
CCM	34
CUF	16
Total	50

*In addition to the 50 elective seats, five seats are reserved for regional commissioners, 10 for presidential nominees, and 10 for women.

Political Organizations

Bismillah Party: Pemba; seeks a referendum on the terms of the 1964 union of Zanzibar with mainland Tanzania.

Chama Cha Demokrasia Makini (MAKINI): Dar es Salaam; officially regd 2001.

Chama Cha Demokrasia na Maendeleo (Chadema—Party for Democracy and Progress): Plot No. 922/7, Block 186005, Kisutu St, POB 5330, Dar es Salaam; supports democracy and social development; Chair. EDWIN I. M. MTEI; Sec.-Gen. BOB NYANGA MAKANI.

Chama Cha Haki na Usitawi (Chausta—Party for Justice and Development): Dar es Salaam; f. 1998; officially registered in 2001; Chair. JAMES MAPALALA.

Chama Cha Mapinduzi (CCM) (Revolutionary Party of Tanzania): Kuu St, POB 50, Dodoma; tel. (61) 2282; f. 1977 by merger of the mainland-based Tanganyika African National Union (TANU) with the Afro-Shirazi Party, which operated on Zanzibar and Pemba; sole legal party 1977–92; socialist orientation; Chair. BENJAMIN WILLIAM MKAPA; Vice-Chair. Dr SALMIN AMOUR; Sec.-Gen. PHILIP MANGULA.

Civic United Front (CUF): Mtendeni St, Urban District, POB 3637, Zanzibar; tel. (54) 237446; fax (54) 237445; e-mail headquarters@cuftz.org; internet www.cuftz.org; f. 1992 by merger of Zanzibar opposition party Kamahuru and the mainland-based Chama Cha Wananchi; commands substantial support in Zanzibar and Pemba, for which it demands increased autonomy; Sec.-Gen. SEIF SHARIFF HAMAD.

Democratic Party (DP): Dar es Salaam; Leader Rev. CHRISTOPHER MTIKILA.

Movement for Democratic Alternative (MDA): Zanzibar; seeks to review the terms of the 1964 union of Zanzibar with mainland Tanzania; supports democratic institutions and opposes detention without trial and press censorship.

National Convention for Construction and Reform (NCCR—Mageuzi): Plot No. 48, Mchikichi St, Kariakoo Area, POB 5316, Dar es Salaam; f. 1992; Chair. Dr KASSIM MAGUTU; Sec.-Gen. MABERE MARANDO.

National League for Democracy (NLD): Sinza D/73, POB 352, Dar es Salaam; Chair. EMMANUEL J. E. MAKAIDI; Sec.-Gen. MICHAEL E. A. MHINA.

National Reconstruction Alliance (NRA): House No. 4, Mvita St, Jangwani Ward, POB 16542, Dar es Salaam; Chair. ULOTU ABUBAKAR ULOTU; Sec.-Gen. SALIM R. MATINGA.

Popular National Party (PONA): Plot 104, Songea St, Ilala, POB 21561, Dar es Salaam; Chair. WILFREM R. MWAKITWANGE; Sec.-Gen. NICOLAUS MCHAINA.

Tanzania Democratic Alliance Party (TADEA): Block 3, Plot No. 37, Buguruni Malapa, POB 63133, Dar es Salaam; Pres. FLORA M. KAMOONA; Sec.-Gen. JOHN D. LIFA-CHIPAKA.

Tanzania Labour Party (TLP): Dar es Salaam; Chair. LEO LWE-KAMWA.

Tanzania People's Party (TPP): Mbezi Juu, Kawe, POB 60847, Dar es Salaam; removed from register of political parties 2002; Chair. ALEC H. CHE-MPONDA; Sec.-Gen. GRAVEL LIMO.

United Democratic Party (UDP): Leader JOHN MOMOSE CHEYO.

United People's Democratic Party (UPDP): Al Aziza Restaurant, Kokoni and Narrow Sts, POB 3903, Zanzibar; Chair. KHALFANI ALI ABDULLAH; Sec.-Gen. AHMED M. RASHID.

Union for Multi-Party Democracy of Tanzania (UMD): 77 Tosheka St, Magomeni Mapiga, POB 41093, Dar es Salaam; Chair. ABDALLAH FUNDIKIRA.

Diplomatic Representation

EMBASSIES AND HIGH COMMISSIONS IN TANZANIA

Albania: 93 Msese Rd, POB 1034, Kinondoni, Dar es Salaam; Ambassador MEHDI SHAQIRI.

Algeria: 34 Upanga Rd, POB 2963, Dar es Salaam; Ambassador (vacant).

Angola: Plot 78, Lugalo Rd, Upanga, POB 20793, Dar es Salaam; tel. (22) 2117674; fax (22) 2132349; Ambassador BRITO SOZINHO.

Belgium: NIC Investment House, 7th Floor, Samora Machel Ave, POB 9210, Dar es Salaam; tel. (22) 2112688; fax (22) 2117621; Ambassador BEATRIX VAN HEMELDONCK.

Brazil: IPS Bldg, 9th Floor, POB 9654, Dar es Salaam; tel. (22) 221780; Ambassador JOSÉ FERREIRA LOPES.

Burundi: Plot 10007, Lugalo Rd, POB 2752, Upanga, Dar es Salaam; tel. (22) 238608; Ambassador (vacant).

Canada: 38 Mirambo St, POB 1022, Dar es Salaam; tel. (22) 2112831; fax (22) 2116897; e-mail dslam@dfait-maeci.gc.ca; High Commissioner JANET L. GRAHAM.

China, People's Republic: 2 Kajificheni Close at Toure Drive, POB 1649, Dar es Salaam; tel. (22) 2667212; Ambassador XIE YOUKUN.

Congo, Democratic Republic: 438 Malik Rd, POB 975, Upanga, Dar es Salaam; tel. (22) 2150282; fax (22) 2153341; e-mail drcemba@intafrica.com; Chargé d'affaires a.i. NSINGI ZI LUBAKI.

Cuba: Plot 313, Lugalo Rd, POB 9282, Upanga, Dar es Salaam; Ambassador A. ROLANDO GALLARDO FERNÁNDEZ.

Denmark: Ghana Ave, POB 9171, Dar es Salaam; tel. (22) 2113887; fax (22) 2116433; Ambassador PETER LYSHOLT HANSEN.

Egypt: 24 Garden Ave, POB 1668, Dar es Salaam; tel. (22) 2117622; Ambassador BAHER M. EL-SADEK.

Finland: Mirambo St and Garden Ave, POB 2455, Dar es Salaam; tel. (22) 2119170; fax (22) 2119173; e-mail finemb@twiga.com; Ambassador RITRA SOLKKONEN.

France: Ali Hassan Mwinyi Rd, POB 2349, Dar es Salaam; tel. (22) 2666021; fax (22) 2668435; e-mail ambfrance@africaonline.co.tz; Ambassador JACQUES MIGOZZI.

Germany: NIC Investment House, Samora Ave, POB 9541, Dar es Salaam; tel. (22) 2117409; fax (22) 2112944; e-mail german.emb .dar@raha.com; Ambassador Dr ENNO BARKER.

Guinea: 35 Haile Selassie Rd, POB 2969, Oyster Bay, Dar es Salaam; tel. (22) 268626; Ambassador M. BANGOURA.

Holy See: Oyster Bay, Haile Selassie Rd, POB 480, Dar es Salaam (Apostolic Nunciature); tel. (22) 2666422; fax (22) 2668059; e-mail nunzio@cats-net.com; Apostolic Nuncio Most Rev. LUIGI PEZZUTO (Titular Archbishop of Turris in Proconsulari).

Hungary: Plot 294, Chake Chake Rd, POB 672, Dar es Salaam; tel. (22) 2668573; fax (22) 2667214; Ambassador JÁNOS ZEGNAL.

India: POB 2684, Dar es Salaam; tel. (22) 246341; fax (22) 246747; High Commissioner OM PRAKASH GUPTA.

Indonesia: 299 Ali Hassan Mwinyi Rd, POB 572, Dar es Salaam; tel. (22) 246024; fax (5) 46350; Ambassador R. CHARIS.

Iraq: Dar es Salaam; tel. (22) 225728; Ambassador FAWZ ALI AL-BANDER.

Ireland: Plot 1131, Msasani Rd, Msasani Peninsular, POB 9612, Dar es Salaam; tel. (22) 2602355; fax (22) 2602362; e-mail iremb@raha.com; Chargé d'affaires RONAN CORVIN.

Italy: Plot 316, Lugalo Rd, POB 2106, Dar es Salaam; tel. (22) 2115935; fax (22) 2115938; e-mail italdipl@raha.com; Ambassador MARCELLO GRICCIOLI.

Japan: 1018 Upanga Rd, POB 2577, Dar es Salaam; tel. (22) 246356; fax (22) 246360; Ambassador MITSURU EGUCHI.

Kenya: NIC Investment House, Samora Machel Ave, POB 5231, Dar es Salaam; tel. (22) 2112955; fax (22) 2113098; High Commissioner NJNUNA NGUNJIRI.

Korea, Democratic People's Republic: Plot 460B, United Nations Rd, POB 2690, Dar es Salaam; Ambassador RO MIN SU.

Libya: Dar es Salaam; Secretary of People's Bureau BASHIR ABDA AL-DA'IM BASHIR.

Madagascar: Magoret St, POB 5254, Dar es Salaam; tel. (22) 241761; Chargé d'affaires a.i. RAHDRAY DESIRÉ.

Malawi: IPS Bldg, POB 23168, Dar es Salaam; tel. (22) 237260; High Commissioner L. B. MALUNGA.

Mozambique: 25 Garden Ave, POB 9370, Dar es Salaam; tel. and fax (22) 2116502; High Commissioner PEDRO DAVANE.

Netherlands: New ATC Town Terminal Bldg, cnr Ohio St and Garden Ave, POB 9534, Dar es Salaam; tel. (22) 2118566; fax (22) 2112828; e-mail nlgovdar@intafrica.com; Ambassador B. S. M. BERENDSEN.

Nigeria: 83 Haile Selassie Rd, POB 9214, Oyster Bay, Dar es Salaam; tel. (22) 2666000; fax (22) 2668947; e-mail nhc-dsm@raha .com; High Commissioner AHMED M. USMAN.

Norway: 160 Mirambo St, POB 2646, Dar es Salaam; tel. (22) 2113366; fax (22) 2116564; Ambassador SIGRID ROMUNDSET.

Pakistan: 149 Malik Rd, Upanga, POB 2925, Dar es Salaam; tel. (22) 2117630; fax (22) 2113205; High Commissioner (vacant).

Poland: 63 Alykhan Rd, POB 2188, Dar es Salaam; tel. (22) 115271; fax (22) 2115812; Chargé d'affaires EUGENIUSZ RZEWUSKI.

Romania: POB 590, Dar es Salaam; Chargé d'affaires a.i. IOAN BUNEA.

Russia: Plot No. 73, Kenyatta Dr., POB 1905, Dar es Salaam; tel. (22) 2666005; fax (22) 2666818; e-mail embrussia@intafrica.com; Ambassador DOKU G. ZAVGAYEV.

Rwanda: Plot 32, Upanga Rd, POB 2918, Dar es Salaam; tel. and fax (22) 2133382; e-mail ambarwa.dsm@raha.com; Ambassador ZEPHYR MUTANGUHA.

Serbia and Montenegro: Plot 35/36, Upanga Rd, POB 2838, Dar es Salaam; tel. (22) 2115891; fax (22) 2115893; Ambassador (vacant).

South Africa: Plot 1338/1339, Mwanya Rd, Msaski, POB 10723, Dar es Salaam; tel. (22) 2600484; fax (22) 2600618; High Commissioner T. LUJABE RANKOE.

Spain: 99B Kinondoni Rd, POB 842, Dar es Salaam; tel. (22) 2666936; fax (22) 2666938; e-mail embesptz@mail.mae.es; Ambassador JOSÉ MARÍA CASTROVIEJO Y BOLIBAR.

Sudan: 'Albaraka', 64 Ali Hassan Mwinyi Rd, POB 2266, Dar es Salaam; tel. (22) 2117641; fax (22) 2115811; Ambassador CHARLES DE WOL.

Sweden: Mirambo St and Garden Ave, POB 9274, Dar es Salaam; tel. (22) 2111235; internet www.swedemb-dar.com; Ambassador STEN RYLANDER.

Switzerland: POB 2454, Dar es Salaam; tel. (22) 2666008; fax (22) 2666736; Ambassador THOMAS FÜGLISTER.

Syria: POB 2442, Dar es Salaam; tel. (22) 2117655; Chargé d'affaires M. B. IMADI.

United Kingdom: Social Security House, Samora Machel Ave, POB 9200, Dar es Salaam; tel. (22) 2117659; fax (22) 2112952; e-mail bhc.dar@dar.mail.fco.gov.uk; High Commissioner RICHARD CLARK.

USA: 140 Msese Rd, Kinondoni, POB 9123, Dar es Salaam; tel. (22) 2666010; fax (22) 2666701; e-mail usembassy-dar2@cats-net.com; Ambassador Rev. CHARLES STITH.

Viet Nam: 9 Ocean Rd, Dar es Salaam; Ambassador TRAN MY.

Yemen: 353 United Nations Rd, POB 349, Dar es Salaam; tel. (22) 221722; fax (22) 266791; Chargé d'affaires MOHAMED ABDULLA ALMAS.

Zambia: 5–6 Ohio St/City Drive Junction, POB 2525, Dar es Salaam; tel. (22) 2118481; High Commissioner JOHN KASHONKA CHITAFU.

Zimbabwe: NIC Life Bldg, 6th Floor, POB 20762, Dar es Salaam; tel. (22) 2116789; fax (22) 2112913; High Commissioner J. M. SHAVA.

Judicial System

Permanent Commission of Enquiry: POB 2643, Dar es Salaam; tel. (22) 2113690; fax (22) 2111533; Chair. and Official Ombudsman Prof. JOSEPH F. MBWILIZA; Sec. A. P. GUVETTE.

Court of Appeal
Consists of the Chief Justice and four Judges of Appeal.

Chief Justice of Tanzania: BARNABAS SAMATTA.

Chief Justice of Zanzibar: HAMID MAHMOUD HAMID.

High Court: headquarters at Dar es Salaam, but regular sessions held in all Regions; consists of a Jaji Kiongozi and 29 Judges.

District Courts: situated in each district and presided over by either a Resident Magistrate or District Magistrate; limited jurisdiction, with a right of appeal to the High Court.

Primary Courts: established in every district and presided over by Primary Court Magistrates; limited jurisdiction, with a right of appeal to the District Courts and then to the High Court.

Attorney-General: ANDREW CHENGE.

Director of Public Prosecutions: KULWA MASSABA.

People's Courts were established in Zanzibar in 1970. Magistrates are elected by the people and have two assistants each. Under the Zanzibar Constitution, which came into force in January 1985, defence lawyers and the right of appeal, abolished in 1970, were reintroduced.

Religion

ISLAM
Islam is the religion of about 98% of the population in Zanzibar and of about one-third of the mainland population. A large proportion of the Asian community is Isma'ili. In March 2002 it was announced that a *Mufti* was to be appointed in Zanzibar, with the power to impose fines or prison sentences on Muslims contravening his directives.

Ismalia Provincial Church: POB 460, Dar es Salaam.

National Muslim Council of Tanzania: POB 21422, Dar es Salaam; tel. (22) 234934; f. 1969; supervises Islamic affairs on the mainland only; Chair. Sheikh HEMED BIN JUMA BIN HEMED; Exec. Sec. Alhaj MUHAMMAD MTULIA.

Supreme Muslim Council: Zanzibar; f. 1991; supervises Islamic affairs in Zanzibar.

Wakf and Trust Commission: POB 4092, Zanzibar; tel. (54) 30853; f. 1980; Islamic affairs; Exec. Sec. YUSUF ABDULRAHMAN MUHAMMAD.

CHRISTIANITY
In 1993 it was estimated that about one-half of the mainland population professed Christianity.

Jumuiya ya Kikristo Tanzania (Christian Council of Tanzania): Church House, POB 1454, Dodoma; tel. (61) 321204; fax (61) 324445; f. 1934; Chair. Rt Rev. JOHN ACLAND RAMADHANI (Bishop of the Anglican Church); Gen. Sec. Dr WILSON LWEGANWA MTEBE.

The Anglican Communion
Anglicans are adherents of the Church of the Province of Tanzania, comprising 16 dioceses.

Archbishop of the Province of Tanzania and Bishop of

Ruaha: Most Rev. DONALD LEO MTETEMELA, POB 1028, Iringa; fax (26) 2702479; e-mail ruaha@maf.or.tz.

Provincial Secretary: Dr R. MWITA AKIRI (acting), POB 899, Dodoma; tel. (26) 2321437; fax (26) 2324265; e-mail cpt@maf.org.

Greek Orthodox

Archbishop of East Africa: NICADEMUS OF IRINOUPOULIS (resident in Nairobi, Kenya); jurisdiction covers Kenya, Uganda and Tanzania.

Lutheran

Evangelical Lutheran Church in Tanzania: POB 3033, Arusha; tel. (57) 8855; fax (57) 8858; 1.5m. mems; Presiding Bishop Rt Rev. Dr SAMSON MUSHEMBA (acting); Exec. Sec. AMANI MWENEGOHA.

The Roman Catholic Church
Tanzania comprises five archdioceses and 24 dioceses. There were an estimated 9,470,310 adherents at 31 December 2000, equivalent to about 24.6% of the total population.

Tanzania Episcopal Conference
Catholic Secretariat, Mandela Rd, POB 2133, Dar es Salaam; tel. (22) 2851075; fax (22) 2851133; e-mail tec@cats-net.com; internet www.rc.net/tanzania/tec.

f. 1980; Pres. Mgr SEVERINE NIWEMUGIZI (Bishop of Rulenge).

Archbishop of Arusha: Most Rev. JOSAPHAT LOUIS LEBULU, Archbishop's House, POB 3044, Arusha; tel. (27) 2544361; fax (27) 2548004; e-mail archbishoplebulu@habari.co.tz.

Archbishop of Dar es Salaam: Cardinal POLYCARP PENGO, Archbishop's House, POB 167, Dar es Salaam; tel. (22) 2113223; fax (22) 2125751; e-mail nyumba@cats-net.com.

Archbishop of Mwanza: Most Rev. ANTHONY MAYALA, Archbishop's House, POB 1421, Mwanza; tel. and fax (68) 501029; e-mail archdiocese-mwanza@africaonline.co.tz.

Archbishop of Songea: Most Rev. NORBERT WENDELIN MTEGA, Archbishop's House, POB 152, Songea; tel. (65) 602004; fax (65) 602593; e-mail songea-archdiocese@cats-net.com.

Archbishop of Tabora: Most Rev. MARIO EPIFANIO ABDALLAH MGULUNDE, Archbishop's House, Private Bag, PO Tabora; tel. (62) 2329; fax (62) 4536.

Other Christian Churches

Baptist Mission of Tanzania: POB 9414, Dar es Salaam; tel. (22) 2170130; fax (22) 2170127; f. 1956; Admin. FRANK PEVEY.

Christian Missions in Many Lands (Tanzania): German Branch, POB 34, Tunduru, Ruvuma Region; f. 1957; Gen. Sec. KARLGERHARD WARTH.

Moravian Church: POB 377, Mbeya; 113,656 mems; Gen. Sec. Rev. SHADRACK MWAKASEGE.

Pentecostal Church: POB 34, Kahama.

Presbyterian Church: POB 2510, Dar es Salaam; tel. (22) 229075.

BAHÁ'Í FAITH

National Spiritual Assembly: POB 585, Dar es Salaam; tel. and fax (22) 2152766; e-mail bahaitz@africaonline.tz; mems resident in 2,301 localities.

OTHER RELIGIONS
Many people follow traditional beliefs. There are also some Hindu communities.

The Press

NEWSPAPERS

Daily

The African: Sinza Rd, POB 4793, Dar es Salaam; e-mail dimba@africaonline.co.tz; Editor-in-Chief JOHN KULEKANA.

Alasiri: POB 31042, Dar es Salaam; Swahili; Editor LUCAS MNUBI.

Daily News: POB 9033, Dar es Salaam; tel. (22) 2110165; fax (22) 2112881; f. 1972; govt-owned; Man. Editor SETHI KAMUHANDA; circ. 50,000.

The Democrat: Dar es Salaam; independent; Editor IDRISS LUGULU; circ. 15,000.

The Guardian: POB 31042, Dar es Salaam; tel. (22) 275250; fax (22) 273583; e-mail guardian@ipp.co.tz; internet www.ippmedia

.com; f. 1994; English and Swahili; Man Dir Vumi Urasa; Man. Editor Pascal Shija.

Kipanga: POB 199, Zanzibar; Swahili; publ. by Information and Broadcasting Services.

Majira: POB 71439, Dar es Salaam; tel. (22) 238901; fax (22) 231104; independent; Swahili; Editor Theophil Makunga; circ. 15,000.

Nipashe: POB 31042, Dar es Salaam; Swahili; Editor Hamisi Mzee.

Uhuru: POB 9221, Dar es Salaam; tel. (22) 2182224; fax (22) 2185065; e-mail uhuru@intafrica.com; f. 1961; official publ. of CCM; Swahili; Man. Editor Saidi Nguba; circ. 100,000.

Weekly

Business Times: POB 71439, Dar es Salaam; tel. (22) 238901; fax (22) 231104; e-mail majira@bcsmedia.com; internet www.bcstimes .com; independent; English; Editor Alli Mwambola; circ. 15,000.

The Express: Bakwata Bldg, 2nd Floor, POB 20588, Dar es Salaam; tel. (22) 2180058; fax (22) 2182659; e-mail express@raha.com; internet www.theexpress.com; independent; English; Editor Fayuz Bhojani; circ. 20,000.

Gazette of the United Republic: POB 9142, Dar es Salaam; tel. (22) 231817; official announcements; Editor H. Haji; circ. 6,000.

Government Gazette: POB 261, Zanzibar; f. 1964; official announcements.

Kasheshe: POB 31042, Dar es Salaam; Swahili; Editor Venance Mlay.

Mfanyakazi (The Worker): POB 15359, Dar es Salaam; tel. (22) 226111; Swahili; trade union publ. Editor Ndugu Mtawa; circ. 100,000.

The Family Mirror: Faru/Nyamwezi St, Karikoo Area, POB 6804, Dar es Salaam; tel. (22) 181331; Editor Zephaniah Musendo.

Mzalendo: POB 9221, Dar es Salaam; tel. (22) 2182224; fax (22) 2185065; e-mail uhuru@intafrica.com; f. 1972; publ. by CCM; Swahili; Man. Editor Saidi Ngaba; circ. 115,000.

Leta Raha: POB 31042, Dar es Salaam; Swahili; Editor Edmond Msangi.

Nipashe Jumapili: POB 31042, Dar es Salaam; Swahili.

Sunday News: POB 9033, Dar es Salaam; tel. (22) 2116072; fax (22) 2112881; f. 1954; govt-owned; Man. Editor Sethi Kamuchanda; circ. 50,000.

Sunday Observer: POB 31042, Dar es Salaam; e-mail guardian@ ipp.co.tz; Man. Dir Vumi Urasa; Man. Editor Peter Msungu.

Taifa Letu: POB 31042, Dar es Salaam; Swahili.

PERIODICALS

The African Review: POB 35042, Dar es Salaam; tel. (22) 243500; 2 a year; journal of African politics, development and international affairs; publ. by the Dept of Political Science, Univ. of Dar es Salaam; Chief Editor Dr C. Gasarasi; circ. 1,000.

Eastern African Law Review: POB 35093, Dar es Salaam; tel. (22) 243254; f. 1967; 2 a year; Chief Editor N. N. N. Nditi; circ. 1,000.

Elimu Haina Mwisho: POB 1986, Mwanza; monthly; circ. 45,000.

Habari za Washirika: POB 2567, Dar es Salaam; tel. (22) 223346; monthly; publ. by Co-operative Union of Tanzania; Editor H. V. N. Chibulunje; circ. 40,000.

Jenga: POB 2669, Dar es Salaam; tel. (22) 2112893; fax (22) 2113618; journal of the National Development Corpn; circ. 2,000.

Kiongozi (The Leader): POB 9400, Dar es Salaam; tel. (22) 229505; f. 1950; fortnightly; Swahili; Roman Catholic; Editor Robert Mfugale; circ. 33,500.

Kweupe: POB 222, Zanzibar; weekly; Swahili; publ. by Information and Broadcasting Services.

Mlezi (The Educator): POB 41, Peramiho; tel. 30; f. 1970; every 2 months; Editor Fr Dominic Weis; circ. 8,000.

Mwenge (Firebrand): POB 1, Peramiho; tel. 30; f. 1937; monthly; Editor John P. Mbonde; circ. 10,000.

Nchi Yetu (Our Country): POB 9142, Dar es Salaam; tel. (22) 2110200; f. 1964; govt publ. monthly; Swahili; circ. 50,000.

Nuru: POB 1893, Zanzibar; tel. (54) 23253; fax (54) 33457; f. 1992; bi-monthly; official publ. of Zanzibar Govt; circ. 8,000.

Safina: POB 21422, Dar es Salaam; tel. (22) 234934; publ. by National Muslim Council of Tanzania; Editor Yassin Sadik; circ. 10,000.

Sikiliza: POB 635, Morogoro; tel. (56) 3338; fax (56) 4374; quarterly; Seventh-day Adventist; Editor Mel H. M. Matinyi; circ. 100,000.

Taamuli: POB 899, Dar es Salaam; tel. (22) 243500; 2 a year; journal of political science; publ. by the Dept of Political Science, Univ. of Dar es Salaam; circ. 1,000.

Tantravel: POB 2485, Dar es Salaam; tel. (22) 2111244; fax (22) 2116420; e-mail safari@ud.co.tz; internet www.tanzaniaweb.com/ home2/htm; quarterly; publ. by Tanzania Tourist Board; Editor Steve Foreman.

Tanzania Education Journal: POB 9121, Dar es Salaam; tel. (22) 227211; f. 1984; 3 a year; publ. by Institute of Education, Ministry of Education; circ. 8,000.

Tanzania Trade Currents: POB 5402, Dar es Salaam; tel. (22) 2851706; fax (22) 851700; e-mail betis@intafrica.com; bimonthly; publ. by Board of External Trade; circ. 2,000.

Uhuru na Amani: POB 3033, Arusha; tel. (57) 8855; fax (57) 8858; quarterly; Swahili; publ. by Evangelical Lutheran Church in Tanzania; Editor Elizabeth Lobulu; circ. 15,000.

Ukulima wa Kisasa (Modern Farming): Farmers' Education and Publicity Unit, POB 2308, Dar es Salaam; tel. (22) 2116496; fax (22) 2122923; e-mail fepu@twiga.com; f. 1955; bi-monthly; Swahili; publ. by Ministry of Food and Agriculture; Editor H. Mlaki; circ. 15,000.

Ushirika Wetu: POB 2567, Dar es Salaam; tel. (22) 2184081; e-mail ushirika@covision2000.com; monthly; publ. by Tanzania Federation of Co-operatives; Editor Simon J. Keraryo; circ. 40,000.

Wela: POB 180, Dodoma; Swahili.

NEWS AGENCIES

Press Services Tanzania (PST) Ltd: POB 31042, Dar es Salaam; tel. and fax (22) 2119195.

Foreign Bureaux

Inter Press Service (IPS) (Italy): 304 Nkomo Rd, POB 4755, Dar es Salaam; tel. (22) 229311; Chief Correspondent Paul Chintowa.

Newslink Africa (UK): POB 5165, Dar es Salaam; Correspondent Nizar Fazal.

Rossiyskoye Informatsionnoye Agentstvo—Novosti (RIA—Novosti) (Russia): POB 2271, Dar es Salaam; tel. (22) 223897; Dir Anatolii Tkachenko.

Xinhua (New China) News Agency: 72 Upanga Rd, POB 2682, Dar es Salaam; tel. (22) 223967; Correspondent Huai Chengbo.

Reuters (UK) is also represented in Tanzania.

Publishers

Central Tanganyika Press: POB 15, Dodoma; tel. (61) 22140; fax (61) 324565; f. 1954; religious; Man. Rev. James Lifa Chipaka.

DUP (1996) Ltd: POB 7028, Dar es Salaam; tel. and fax (22) 2410137; e-mail director@dup.udsm.ac.tz; f. 1979; educational, academic and cultural texts in Swahili and English; Dir Dr N. G. Mwitta.

Eastern Africa Publications Ltd: POB 1002 Arusha; tel. (57) 3176; f. 1979; general and school textbooks; Gen. Man. Abdullah Saiwaad.

Inland Publishers: POB 125, Mwanza; tel. (68) 40064; general non-fiction, religion, in Kiswahili and English; Dir Rev. S. M. Magesa.

Oxford University Press: Maktaba Rd, POB 5299, Dar es Salaam; tel. (22) 229209; f. 1969; literature, literary criticism, essays, poetry; Man. Salim Shaaban Salim.

Tanzania Publishing House: 47 Samora Machel Ave, POB 2138, Dar es Salaam; tel. (22) 232164; f. 1966; educational and general books in Swahili and English; Gen. Man. Primus Isidor Karugendo.

Government Publishing House

Government Printer: POB 9124, Dar es Salaam; tel. (22) 220291; Dir Jonas Oforo.

Broadcasting and Communications

TELECOMMUNICATIONS

Tanzania Communications Commission: POB 474, Dar es Salaam; tel. (22) 2118947; fax (22) 2116664; e-mail moa@tcc.go.tz; internet www.tcc.go.tz; f. 1993; licenses postal and telecommunications service operators; manages radio spectrum; acts as ombudsman.

Tanzania Telecommunications Co Ltd (TTCL): POB 9070, Dar es Salaam; tel. (22) 2110055; fax (22) 2113232; e-mail ttcl@ttcl.co.tz; 35% sold to consortium of Detecon (Germany) and Mobile Systems International (Netherlands) in Feb. 2001; Man. Dir ASMATH N. MPATWA.

Tri-Telecommunication Tanzania Ltd, MIC Ltd, Vodacom and Zanzibar Telecom Ltd also provide telecommunications services.

BROADCASTING

Radio

Radio Kwizera: N'Gara.

Radio One: POB 4374, Dar es Salaam; tel. (22) 275914; e-mail ipptech@ipp.co.tz; internet www.ippmedia.com.

Radio Tanzania Dar es Salaam (RTD): POB 9191, Dar es Salaam; tel. (22) 2860760; fax (22) 2865577; f. 1951; state-owned; domestic services in Swahili; external services in English; Dir ABDUL NGARAWA.

Radio Tumaini (Hope): 1 Bridge St, POB 167, Dar es Salaam; tel. (22) 2117307; fax (22) 2112594; e-mail tumaini@africaonline.co.tz; broadcasts in Swahili within Dar es Salaam; operated by the Roman Catholic Church; broadcasts on religious, social and economic issues; Dir Fr JEAN-FRANÇOIS GALTIER.

Sauti Ya Tanzania Zanzibar (The Voice of Tanzania Zanzibar): POB 1178, Zanzibar; tel. (54) 31088; fax (54) 31985; f. 1951; state-owned; broadcasts in Swahili on three wavelengths; Dir SULEIMAN JUMA.

Television

Dar Television (DTV): POB 21122, Dar es Salaam; tel. (22) 2116341; fax (22) 2113112; e-mail franco.dtv@raha.com; Man. Dir FRANCO TRAMONTANO.

Independent Television (ITV): Dar es Salaam.

Television Zanzibar: POB 314, Zanzibar; tel. (54) 32816; f. 1973; Dir JAMA SIMBA.

Finance

(cap. = capital; res = reserves; dep. = deposits; m. = million; brs = branches; amounts in Tanzanian shillings, unless otherwise indicated)

BANKING

Central Bank

Bank of Tanzania (Benki Kuu Ya Tanzania): 10 Mirambo St, POB 2939, Dar es Salaam; tel. (22) 2110946; fax (22) 2113325; e-mail info@hq.bot-tz.org; internet www.bot.tz.org; f. 1966; bank of issue; cap. 10,000m., res 61,824m., dep. 200,507m. (June 2000); Gov. and Chair. Dr DAUDI T. S. BALLALI; Dep. Gov. M. H. MBAYE; 4 brs.

Principal Banks

CRDB (1996) Ltd: Azikiwe St, POB 268, Dar es Salaam; tel. (22) 2117442; fax (22) 2119146; e-mail crdb@raha.com; internet www.crdb.com; f. as Co-operative and Rural Development Bank in 1984, transferred to private ownership and current name adopted 1996; 30% owned by DANIDA Investment; provides commercial banking services and loans for rural development; cap. and res 13,803m., dep. 160,991m. (Dec. 2000); Chair JERRY SOLOMON; Man. Dir C. S. KIMEI.

Eurafrican Bank Tanzania Ltd: NDC Development House, cnr Kivukoni Front and Ohio St, POB 3054, Dar es Salaam; tel. (22) 2111229; fax (22) 2113740; f. 1994; 76.6% owned by Belgolaise/Fortis Bank Group; other shareholders: FMO-Netherlands Development Co. (10%), Tanzania Development Finance (9.4%), Inernational Finance Corpn (1.3%), PROPARCO (0.6%), others (2.1%); cap. 6,500m. (Dec. 2000); Chair. FULGENCE M. KAZAURA; Man. Dir STEFAAN MATTHEEUWS.

EXIM Bank (Tanzania) Ltd: 9 Samora Ave, POB 1431, Dar es Salaam; tel. (22) 2113091; fax (22) 2119737; e-mail eximbank.tz@cats.net.com; Chair. Y. MANEK; Man. Dir S. M. J. MWAMBENJA.

National Microfinance Bank Ltd (NMB): POB 9213, Dar es Salaam; tel. (22) 2118785; fax (22) 2110077; e-mail nmb.ltd@raha.com; f. 1997 following disbandment of The National Bank of Commerce; state-owned; transfer to private-sector ownership pending; Chair. IBRAHIM M. KADUMA; Man. Dir JAMES A. N. KARASHANI.

NBC Ltd: NBC House, Sokoine Drive, POB 1863, Dar es Salaam; tel. (22) 2112082; fax (22) 2112887; e-mail nbcltd@nbctz.com; f. 1997 following disbandment of National Bank of Commerce; 55% owned by ABSA Group Ltd (South Africa), 30% by Govt and 15% by International Finance Corpn; cap. and res US $29.5m., dep. US $320m. (Dec. 2001); Chair. CHARLES M. NYIRABU; Man. Dir GERALD JORDAN; 33 brs.

People's Bank of Zanzibar Ltd (PBZ): POB 1173, Forodhani, Zanzibar; tel. (54) 31118; fax (54) 31121; f. 1966; controlled by Zanzibar Govt; cap. 16m. (June 1991); Chair. MOHAMED ABOUD; Gen. Man. N. S. NASSOR; 1 br.

Stanbic Bank Tanzania Ltd: Sukari House, cnr Ohio St and Sokoine Drive, POB 72647, Dar es Salaam; tel. (22) 2112195; fax (22) 2113742; e-mail tanzaniainfo@stanbic.com; internet www.stanbic.co.tz; f. 1993; wholly owned by Standard Africa Holdings PLC; cap. and res 12,985m., dep. 65,928m. (Dec. 1998); Chair R. E. NORVAL; Man. Dir I. J. MITCHELL.

Standard Chartered Bank Tanzania Ltd: POB 9011, Dar es Salaam; tel. (22) 2117350; fax (22) 2113770; f. 1992; wholly owned by Standard Chartered Holdings (Africa) BV, Netherlands; cap. 1,000m., dep. 139,381m., total assets 197,540m. (Dec. 2000); Man. Dir C. LOW.

Tanzania Development Finance Co Ltd (TDFL): TDFL Bldg, Plot 1008, cnr Upanga Rd/Ohio St, POB 2478, Dar es Salaam; tel. (22) 2116417; fax (22) 2116418; e-mail mail@tdfl.co.tz; f. 1962; owned by Govt (32%), govt agencies of the Netherlands and Germany (5% and 26% respectively), the Commonwealth Development Corpn (26%) and the European Investment Bank (11%); cap. and res 1,284m. (Dec. 1996); Chair. H. K. SENKORO; CEO J. MCGUFFOG.

Tanzania Investment Bank (TIB): cnr Zanaki St and Samora Machel Ave, POB 9373, Dar es Salaam; tel. (22) 2111708; fax (22) 2113438; e-mail tib-tz@intafrica.com; f. 1970; provides finance, tech. assistance and consultancy, fund administration and loan guarantee for economic devt; 99% govt-owned; total assets 129,707m. (Dec. 2002); Chair. F. M. KAZAURA; Man. Dir WILLIAM A. MLAKI.

Tanzania Postal Bank (TPB): Samora Ave, POB 9300, Dar es Salaam; tel. (22) 2115258; fax (22) 2114815; e-mail md@postalbank.co.tz; internet www.postalbank.co.tz; f. 1991; cap. 1,041m., res 1,899m. (Dec. 2000), dep. 43,611m. (Dec. 2001); Man. Dir and CEO ALPHONCE R. KIHWELE; 4 brs and 113 agencies.

Ulc (Tanzania) Ltd: 1st Floor, Sukari House, cnr Ohio St and Sokoine Drive, POB 31, Dar es Salaam; tel. (22) 2111990; fax (22) 2112402; e-mail info@ulc.co.tz; internet www.ulc.co.tz; cap. 2,204 (Dec. 1999); Chair Dr JONAS KIPOKOLA; CEO JAMES MACHARIA.

STOCK EXCHANGE

Dar es Salaam Stock Exchange: Twigga Bldg, 4th floor, Samora Ave, POB 70081, Dar es Salaam; tel. (22) 2133659; fax (22) 2122421; e-mail des@cats-net.com; internet www.darstock.com; f. 1998; Chair. ERNEST MASSAWE; Chief Exec. Dr HAMIS KIBOLA.

INSURANCE

Jubilee Insurance Co of Tanzania Ltd (JICT): Dar es Salaam; 40% owned by Jubilee Insurance Kenya, 24% by local investors, 15% by the IFC, 15% by the Aga Khan Fund for Economic Devt, 6% by others; cap. US $2m.

National Insurance Corporation of Tanzania Ltd (NIC): POB 9264, Dar es Salaam; tel. (22) 2113823; fax (22) 2113403; f. 1963; state-owned; all classes of insurance; Chair. Prof. J. L. KANYWANYI; Man. Dir OCTAVIAN W. TEMU; 30 brs.

Trade and Industry

GOVERNMENT AGENCIES

Board of External Trade (BET): POB 5402, Dar es Salaam; tel. (22) 2851706; fax (22) 2851700; e-mail betis@intafrica.com; f. 1978; trade and export information and promotion, market research, marketing advisory and consultancy services; Dir-Gen. MBARUK K. MWANDORO.

Board of Internal Trade (BIT): POB 883, Dar es Salaam; tel. (22) 228301; f. 1967 as State Trading Corpn, reorg. 1973; state-owned; supervises seven national and 21 regional trading cos; distribution of general merchandise, agricultural and industrial machinery, pharmaceuticals, foodstuffs and textiles; shipping and other transport services; Dir-Gen. J. E. MAKOYE.

Parastatal Sector Reform Commission (PSRC): Sukari House, POB 9252, Dar es Salaam; tel. (22) 2115482; fax (22) 2113065; e-mail masalla@raha.com.

Tanzania Investment Centre (TIC): POB 938, Dar es Salaam; tel. (22) 2116328; fax (22) 2118253; e-mail information@tic.co.tz; internet www.tic.co.tz; f. 1997; promotes and facilitates investment in Tanzania; Exec. Dir SAMUEL SITTA.

CHAMBERS OF COMMERCE

Dar es Salaam Chamber of Commerce: Kelvin House, Samora Machel Ave, POB 41, Dar es Salaam; tel. (22) 221893; Exec. Officer I. K. MKWAWA.

Tanzania Chamber of Commerce, Industry and Agriculture: POB 9713, Dar es Salaam; tel. and fax (22) 2119437; e-mail tccia .info@cats-net.com; internet www.tccia.co.tz; f. 1988; Pres. E. MUSIBA.

Zanzibar Chamber of Commerce: POB 1407, Zanzibar; tel. (54) 233083; fax (54) 233349.

DEVELOPMENT CORPORATIONS

Capital Development Authority: POB 1, Dodoma; tel. (61) 324053; f. 1973 to develop the new capital city of Dodoma; govt-controlled.

Economic Development Commission: POB 9242, Dar es Salaam; tel. (22) 2112681; f. 1962 to plan national economic development; state-controlled.

National Development Corporation: POB 2669, Dar es Salaam; tel. (22) 2112893; fax (22) 2113618; f. 1965; state-owned; cap. Ts. 21.4m. promotes progress and expansion in production and investment.

Small Industries Development Organization (SIDO): POB 2476, Dar es Salaam; tel. (22) 2151945; fax (22) 2152070; e-mail sido-dg@africaonline.co.tz; internet www.sido.co.tz; f. 1973; promotes and assists development of small-scale enterprises in public, co-operative and private sectors, aims to increase the involvement of women in small businesses; Chair. E. M. K. MSELLA; Dir-Gen. E. B. TOROKA.

Sugar Development Corporation: Dar es Salaam; tel. (22) 2112969; fax (22) 230598; Gen. Man. GEORGE G. MBATI.

Tanzania Petroleum Development Corporation (TPDC): POB 2774, Dar es Salaam; tel. (22) 2181407; fax (22) 2180047; f. 1969; state-owned; oversees petroleum exploration and undertakes autonomous exploration, imports crude petroleum and distributes refined products; Man. Dir YONA S. M. KILLAGANE.

There is also a development corporation for textiles.

INDUSTRIAL AND TRADE ASSOCIATONS

Cashewnut Board of Tanzania: POB 533, Mtwara; tel. (59) 333445; fax (59) 333536; govt-owned; regulates the marketing, processing and export of cashews; Chair. GALUS ABEID; Gen. Man. Dr ALI F. MANDALI.

Confederation of Tanzania Industries (CTI): POB 71783, Dar es Salaam; tel. (22) 2123802; fax (22) 2115414; e-mail cti@raha.com; Dir JUMA MWAPACHU.

National Coconut Development Programme: POB 6226, Dar es Salaam; tel. (22) 2700552; fax (22) 275549; e-mail arim@arim .africaonline.co.tz; f. 1979 to revive coconut industry; processing and marketing via research and devt in disease and pest control, agronomy and farming systems, breeding and post-harvest technology; based at Mikocheni Agricultural Research Inst. Dir Dr ALOIS K. KULLAYA.

Tanganyika Coffee Growers' Association Ltd: POB 102, Moshi.

Tanzania Association of Floriculture (TAFA): POB 11123, Arusha; tel. (57) 4432; fax (57) 4214; e-mail aru.cut@kabari.co.tz; Sec. MATTHIAS OLE KISSAMBU.

Tanzania Coffee Board (TCB): POB 732, Moshi; tel. (55) 52324; fax (55) 53033; e-mail coffee@eoltz.com; internet www.newafrica .com; Man. Dir LESLIE OMARI.

Tanzania Cotton Lint and Seed Board: Pamba House, Garden Ave, POB 9161, Dar es Salaam; tel. (22) 2112555; fax (22) 2112894; e-mail tclb@raha.com; f. 1984; regulates the marketing and export of cotton lint; Gen. Man. ALI N. NGONGOLO.

Tanzania Exporters' Association: Plot No. 139, Sembeti Rd, POB 1175, Dar es Salaam; tel. (22) 2781035; fax (22) 2112752; e-mail smutabuz@hotmail.com.

Tanzania Pyrethrum Board: POB 149, Iringa; f. 1960; Chair. Brig. LUHANGA; CEO P. B. G. HANGAYA.

Tanzania Sisal Authority: POB 277, Tanga; tel. (53) 44401; fax (53) 42759; Chair. W. H. SHELLUKINDO; Man. Dir S. SHAMTE.

Tanzania Tobacco Board: POB 227, Mazimbu Rd, Morogoro; tel. (56) 4517; fax (56) 4401; Chair. S. GALINOMA; CEO HAMISI HASANI LIANA.

Tanzania Wood Industry Corporation: POB 9160, Dar es Salaam; Gen. Man. E. M. MNZAVA.

Tea Association of Tanzania: POB 2177, Dar es Salaam; tel. (22) 2122033; e-mail trit@twiga.com; f. 1989; Chair. Dr NORMAN C. KELLY; Exec. Dir DAVID E. A. MGWASSA.

Tea Board of Tanzania: POB 2663, Dar es Salaam; tel. and fax (22) 2114400; Chair. A. MDEE; Exec. Dir H. S. MIJINGA.

Zanzibar State Trading Corporation: POB 26, Zanzibar; tel. (54) 30272; fax (54) 31550; govt-controlled since 1964; sole exporter of cloves, clove stem oil, chillies, copra, copra cake, lime oil and lime juice; Gen. Man. ABDULRAHMAN RASHID.

UTILITIES

Electricity

Tanzania Electric Supply Co Ltd (TANESCO): POB 9024, Dar es Salaam; tel. (22) 2112891; fax (22) 2113836; e-mail mdtan@ intafrica.com; state-owned; placed under private management in May 2002; privatization planned for 2005, following restructuring; Chair. NDEWIRWA KITOMARI; Man. Dir BARUANY LUHANGA.

Gas

Enertan Corpn Ltd: POB 3746, Dar es Salaam.

Songas Ltd: POB 6342, Dar es Salaam; tel. (22) 2117313; fax (22) 2113614; internet www.songas.com; f. 1998; Gen. Man. JIM MCCARDLE.

Water

Dar es Salaam Water and Sanitation Authority: POB 1573, Dar es Salaam; e-mail dawasapiu@raha.com; privatization pending.

National Urban Water Authority: POB 5340, Dar es Salaam; tel. (22) 2667505.

CO-OPERATIVES

There are some 1,670 primary marketing societies under the aegis of about 20 regional co-operative unions. The Co-operative Union of Tanzania is the national organization to which all unions belong.

Co-operative Union of Tanzania Ltd (Washirika): POB 2567, Dar es Salaam; tel. (22) 223346; f. 1962; Sec.-Gen. D. HOLELA; 700,000 mems.

Department of Co-operative Societies: POB 1287, Zanzibar; tel. (54) 30747; f. 1952; promotes formation and development of co-operative societies in Zanzibar.

Principal Societies

Bukoba Co-operative Union Ltd: POB 5, Bukoba; 74 affiliated societies; 75,000 mems.

Kilimanjaro Native Co-operative Union 1984 Ltd: POB 3032, Moshi; tel. (27) 2752785; fax (27) 2754204; e-mail knacu@ africaonline.co.tz; f. 1984; 88 regd co-operative societies.

Nyanza Co-operative Union Ltd: POB 9, Mwanza.

TRADE UNIONS

Union of Tanzania Workers (Juwata): POB 15359, Dar es Salaam; tel. (22) 226111; f. 1978; Sec.-Gen. JOSEPH C. RWEGASIRA; Dep. Secs-Gen. C. MANYANDA (mainland Tanzania), I. M. ISSA (Zanzibar); 500,000 mems (1991).

  Agricultural Workers: Sec. G. P. NYINDO.

  Central and Local Government and Medical Workers: Sec. R. UTUKULU.

  Commerce and Construction: Sec. P. O. OLUM.

  Communications and Transport Workers: Sec. M. E. KALUWA.

  Domestic, Hotels and General Workers: Sec. E. KAZOKA.

  Industrial and Mines Workers: Sec. J. V. MWAMBUMA.

  Railway Workers: Sec. C. SAMMANG' OMBE.

  Teachers: Sec. W. MWENURA.

Principal Unaffiliated Unions

Organization of Tanzanian Trade Unions (OTTU): Dar es Salaam; Sec.-Gen. BRUNO MPANGAL.

Workers' Department of Chama Cha Mapinduzi: POB 389, Vikokotoni, Zanzibar; f. 1965.

Transport

RAILWAYS

Tanzania Railways Corporation (TRC): POB 468, Dar es Salaam; tel. and fax (22) 2110599; e-mail ccm_shamte@trctz.com; f. 1977 after dissolution of East African Railways; privatization pending; operates 2,600 km of lines within Tanzania; Chair. J. K. CHANDE; Dir-Gen. LINFORD MBOMA.

Tanzania-Zambia Railway Authority (Tazara): POB 2834, Dar es Salaam; tel. (22) 2860340; fax (22) 2865338; e-mail acistz@twiga.com; jtly owned and administered by the Tanzanian and Zambian Govts; operates a 1,860-km railway link between Dar es Salaam and New Kapiri Mposhi, Zambia, of which 969 km are within Tanzania; plans to privatize the line, which has incurred heavy losses in recent years, were under consideration in 1999; Chair. SALIM MSOMA; Man. Dir K. MKANDAWIRE; Regional Man. (Tanzania) A. F. S. NALITOLELA.

ROADS

In 1996 Tanzania had an estimated 88,200 km of classified roads, of which 10,400 km were primary roads and 17,900 km were secondary roads. A 1,930-km main road links Zambia and Tanzania, and there is a road link with Rwanda. A 10-year Integrated Roads Programme, funded by international donors and co-ordinated by the World Bank, commenced in 1991: its aim was to upgrade 70% of Tanzania's trunk roads and to construct 2,828 km of roads and 205 bridges, at an estimated cost of US $650m.

The island of Zanzibar has 619 km of roads, of which 442 km are bituminized, and Pemba has 363 km, of which 130 km are bituminized.

INLAND WATERWAYS

Steamers connect with Kenya, Uganda, the Democratic Republic of the Congo, Burundi, Zambia and Malawi. A joint shipping company was formed with Burundi in 1976 to operate services on Lake Tanganyika. A rail ferry service operates on Lake Victoria between Mwanza and Port Bell.

SHIPPING

Tanzania's major harbours are at Dar es Salaam (eight deep-water berths for general cargo, three berths for container ships, eight anchorages, lighter wharf, one oil jetty for small oil tankers up to 36,000 gross tons, offshore mooring for oil supertankers up to 100,000 tons, one 30,000-ton automated grain terminal) and Mtwara (two deep-water berths). There are also ports at Tanga (seven anchorages and lighterage quay), Bagamoyo, Zanzibar and Pemba. A programme to extend and deepen the harbour entrance at Dar es Salaam commenced in 1997.

Tanzania Harbours Authority (THA): POB 9184, Dar es Salaam; tel. (22) 2110371; fax (22) 232066; internet www.bandari.com; privatization pending; Exec. Chair. J. K. CHANDE; Gen. Man. A. S. M. JANGUO; 3 brs.

Chinese-Tanzanian Joint Shipping Co: POB 696, Dar es Salaam; tel. (22) 2113389; fax (22) 25011380; f. 1967; services to People's Republic of China, South East Asia, Eastern and Southern Africa, Red Sea and Mediterranean ports.

National Shipping Agencies Co Ltd (NASACO): POB 9082, Dar es Salaam; f. 1973; state-owned shipping co; reorg. into five operating divisions and removal of monopoly on dealings with foreign shipping cos pending in 1999; Man. Dir D. R. M. LWIMBO.

Tanzania Central Freight Bureau (TCFB): POB 3093, Dar es Salaam; tel. (22) 2114174; fax (22) 2116697; e-mail tcfb@cats-net.com.

Tanzania Coastal Shipping Line Ltd: POB 9461, Dar es Salaam; tel. (22) 237034; fax (22) 2116436; regular services to Tanzanian coastal ports; occasional special services to Zanzibar and Pemba; also tramp charter services to Kenya, Mozambique, the Persian (Arabian) Gulf, Indian Ocean islands and the Middle East; Gen. Man. RICHARD D. NZOWA.

CIVIL AVIATION

There are 53 airports and landing strips. The major international airport is at Dar es Salaam, 13 km from the city centre, and there are also international airports at Kilimanjaro and Zanzibar.

Tanzania Civil Aviation Authority (TCAA): IPS Bldg, cnr Samora Machel Ave and Azikiwe St, POB 2819, Dar es Salaam; tel. (22) 2115079; fax (22) 2118905; e-mail civil-aviation@twiga.com; internet www.aviationauthority.org; f. 1999; govt agency; replaces Directorate of Civil Aviation (f. 1977); ensures aviation safety and security; Dir-Gen. MARGARET T. MUNYAGI.

Air Tanzania Corporation: ATC House, Ohio St/Garden Ave, POB 543, Dar es Salaam; tel. (22) 2110245; fax (22) 2113114; f. 1977; operates an 18-point domestic network and international services to Africa, the Middle East and Europe; Chair. ABBAS SYKES; CEO JOSEPH S. MARANDUS; Dir-Gen. MELKIZEDECK SANARE.

Air Zanzibar: POB 1784, Zanzibar; tel. (54) 32512; fax (54) 33098; f. 1990; operates scheduled and charter services between Zanzibar and destinations in Tanzania, Kenya and Uganda.

New ACS Ltd: Peugeot House, 36 Upanga Rd, POB 21236, Dar es Salaam; fax (22) 237017; operates domestic and regional services; Dir MOHSIN RAHEMTULLAH.

Precisionair: POB 70770, Dar es Salaam; tel. (22) 2113036; e-mail information@precisionairtz.com; operates domestic and regional services.

Tanzanair: Royal Palm Hotel, POB 364, Dar es Salaam; tel. (22) 2113151; fax (22) 2112946; e-mail tanzanair@raha.com; operates domestic charter services.

Tourism

Tanzania has set aside about one-quarter of its land area for 12 national parks, 17 game reserves, 50 controlled game areas and a conservation area. Other attractions for tourists include beaches and coral reefs along the Indian Ocean coast, and the island of Zanzibar (which received 86,495 tourists in 1997 and is expanding and upgrading its tourism facilities). Visitor arrivals reached a record 627,417 in 1999, but declined to 501,669 in 2000, when revenue from tourism was estimated to total US $739m.

Tanzania Tourist Board: IPS Bldg, cnr Azikiwe St and Samora Machel Ave, POB 2485, Dar es Salaam; tel. (22) 2111244; fax (22) 2116420; e-mail safari@ud.co.tz; internet www.tanzania-web.com/home2.htm; state-owned; supervises the development and promotion of tourism; Man. Dir PETER J. MWENGUO.

Tanzania Wildlife Corporation: POB 1144, Arusha; tel. (57) 8830; fax (57) 8239; e-mail tawico@marie.gn.apc.org; organizes safaris; also exports and deals in live animals, birds and game-skin products; Gen. Man. DAVID S. BABU.

Zanzibar Tourist Corporation: POB 216, Zanzibar; tel. (54) 238630; fax (54) 233430; e-mail ztc@zanzinet.com; f. 1985; operates tours and hotel services; Gen. Man. ALPHONCE KATEMA.

THAILAND

Introductory Survey

Location, Climate, Language, Religion, Flag, Capital

The Kingdom of Thailand lies in South-East Asia. It is bordered to the west and north by Myanmar (Burma), to the north-east by Laos and to the south-east by Cambodia. Thailand extends southward, along the isthmus of Kra, to the Malay Peninsula, where it borders Malaysia. The isthmus, shared with Myanmar, gives Thailand a short coastline on the Indian Ocean, and the country also has a long Pacific coastline on the Gulf of Thailand. The climate is tropical and humid, with an average annual temperature of 29°C (85°F). There are three main seasons: hot, rainy and cool. Temperatures in Bangkok are generally between 20°C (68°F) and 35°C (95°F). The national language is Thai. There are small minorities of Chinese, Malays and indigenous hill peoples. The predominant religion is Buddhism, mainly of the Hinayana (Theravada) form. About 4% of the population, predominantly Malays, are Muslims, and there is also a Christian minority, mainly in Bangkok and the north. The national flag (proportions 2 by 3) has five horizontal stripes, of red, white, blue, white and red, the central blue stripe being twice as wide as each of the others. The capital is Bangkok.

Recent History

Formerly known as Siam, Thailand took its present name in 1939. Under the leadership of Marshal Phibul Songkhram, Thailand entered the Second World War as an ally of Japan. Phibul was deposed in 1944, but returned to power in 1947 after a military coup. However, his influence declined during the 1950s, and in 1957 he was overthrown in a bloodless coup, led by Field Marshal Sarit Thanarat. Elections took place, but in 1958 martial law was declared and all political parties were dissolved. Sarit died in 1963 and was succeeded as Prime Minister by Gen. (later Field Marshal) Thanom Kittikachorn, who had served as Deputy Prime Minister since 1959. Thanom continued the combination of military authoritarianism and economic development instituted by his predecessor. A Constitution was introduced in 1968, and elections to a National Assembly took place in 1969, but in November 1971, following an increase in communist insurgency and internal political unrest, Thanom annulled the Constitution, dissolved the National Assembly and imposed martial law.

During 1972 there were frequent student demonstrations against the military regime, and in October 1973 the Government was forced to resign, after the army refused to use force to disperse student protesters, and King Bhumibol withdrew his support from the administration. An interim Government was formed under Dr Sanya Dharmasakti, the President of the Privy Council. In October 1974 a new Constitution, legalizing political parties, was promulgated, and in January 1975 elections were held to the new House of Representatives. A coalition Government was formed in February by Seni Pramoj, the leader of the Democratic Party (DP), but it was defeated by a vote of 'no confidence' in the following month.

A new right-wing coalition Government, headed by the leader of the Social Action Party (SAP), Kukrit Pramoj (brother of Seni), was unable to maintain its unity, and Kukrit resigned in January 1976. After further general elections in April, a four-party coalition Government was formed, with Seni as Prime Minister. However, following violent student demonstrations in October during which the security forces killed perhaps hundreds of demonstrators, the Seni Government was dissolved, and a right-wing military junta, the National Administrative Reform Council (NARC), seized power. Martial law was declared, the 1974 Constitution was annulled, political parties were banned and strict press censorship was imposed. A new Constitution was promulgated, and a new Cabinet was announced, with Thanin Kraivixien, a Supreme Court judge, as Prime Minister.

Under the Thanin Government there was considerable repression of students and political activists. In October 1977 the Government was overthrown in a bloodless coup by a Revolutionary Council (later known as the National Policy Council—NPC) of military leaders, most of whom had been members of the NARC which had brought Thanin to power. The 1976

Constitution was abrogated, and the Secretary-General of the NPC (who was also the Supreme Commander of the Armed Forces), Gen. Kriangsak Chomanan, became Prime Minister. Many detainees were released, censorship was partially relaxed and the King nominated a National Assembly on the advice of the NPC. In December 1978 the National Assembly approved a new Constitution, and elections to a new House of Representatives were held in April 1979. Members of the Senate, however, were all nominated by the Prime Minister, and were almost all military officers. Kriangsak remained Prime Minister and formed a new Council of Ministers, after which the NPC was dissolved. However, Kriangsak resigned in March 1980, and was replaced by Gen. Prem Tinsulanonda, the Commander-in-Chief of the Army and the Minister of Defence. A new coalition Government, composed largely of centre-right politicians acceptable to the armed forces, was formed.

Although Prem's administration initially appeared to lack authority, it survived an abortive coup attempt in April 1981. In December of that year Prem effected a ministerial reshuffle, reincorporating members of the SAP (who had been excluded from the Government in March), in order to repulse a challenge from the new National Democracy Party (NDP), established by the former Prime Minister, Kriangsak. In April 1983 elections took place to the new House of Representatives. No single party won an overall majority, and a coalition Government was formed by the SAP, Prachakorn Thai, the DP and the NDP. Chart Thai, despite being the party with the largest number of seats, formed the opposition, and Prem was again appointed Prime Minister.

In September 1985 a group of military officers, dissatisfied with the decline of the role of the armed forces in politics, staged a coup attempt in Bangkok. Troops loyal to the Government quickly suppressed the revolt, but at least five people were killed and about 60 were injured during the fighting. The leader of the revolt, Col Manoon Roopkachorn (who had also led the coup attempt in 1981), fled the country, but 40 others, including Kriangsak, were put on trial in October, accused of inciting sedition and rebellion. Gen. Arthit Kamlang-ek, the Supreme Commander of the Armed Forces and Commander-in-Chief of the Army (who was believed to have been sympathetic to the aims of the coup leaders), was replaced in his posts by Gen. Chavalit Yongchaiyudh, hitherto the army Chief of Staff.

In September 1985 and January 1986 there were extensive changes in the Government, including the replacement of all members of the SAP, following the resignation of Kukrit as the party's leader, and the introduction of members of the Progress Party into the coalition. In May 1986, following a parliamentary defeat for the Government over proposed vehicle taxation, the House of Representatives was dissolved, 11 months before the expiry of its term. A general election for an enlarged legislature was held in July, when the DP won 100 of the 347 seats (compared with 56 of the 324 seats at the previous election). A coalition Government was formed, including members of the DP, Chart Thai, the SAP, Rassadorn and seven 'independent' ministers not belonging to the House of Representatives. Prem remained as Prime Minister.

In November 1987 a crisis arose concerning proposed legislation on copyright, which would have made illegal the previously uncontrolled counterfeiting of foreign manufactures and intellectual property. In April 1988 dissident members of the DP voted to reject the copyright legislation, and 16 ministers belonging to the DP resigned, on the grounds that they had failed to maintain party unity. As a result, Prem asked the King to dissolve the House of Representatives, and new elections were held in July (two years before the expiry of the legislature's mandate). Internal disputes weakened support for the DP at the elections (25 dissidents had resigned in May), and Chart Thai gained the largest number of seats (87). Gen. Chatichai Choonhavan, the leader of Chart Thai, was appointed Prime Minister in early August, after Prem declined an invitation to remain in the post. A new Council of Ministers was formed, comprising members of six parties (Chart Thai, the DP, the SAP, Rassadorn, the United Democratic Party and the Muan Chon party).

Chatichai introduced reforms to encourage private enterprise and greater foreign investment, and also assumed an active role in foreign affairs. In an abrupt change of Thai policy, he sought to improve relations with Laos, Cambodia and Viet Nam. In April 1989 Ruam Thai, the Community Action Party, the Prachachon Party and the Progressive Party merged to form an opposition grouping called Ekkaparb (Solidarity). Nine members of the Prachachon Party subsequently defected to Chart Thai, giving the ruling coalition control of 229 of the 357 seats in the House of Representatives.

Popular support for Chatichai declined towards the end of 1989. The Government's response to damage caused by a typhoon in November was widely perceived as inadequate and compounded allegations that Chatichai was preoccupied with foreign affairs to the detriment of domestic issues. In early 1990 the Government's public image was further damaged by corruption scandals and labour unrest. In March 1990 Chavalit resigned as acting Supreme Commander of the Armed Forces; he also resigned as Commander-in-Chief of the Army, in which post he was succeeded by Gen. Suchinda Kraprayoon, hitherto his deputy.

In July 1990, despite growing criticism of the administration, the House of Representatives overwhelmingly rejected a motion of 'no confidence' in the Government (sponsored by the opposition on the grounds of incompetence and corruption). In August, however, Chatichai reorganized the Council of Ministers, incorporating Puangchon Chao Thai (the party of the former Commander-in-Chief, Gen. Arthit Kamlang-ek) in the ruling coalition, and reducing the influence of the SAP, following the implication of many of its members in allegations of corruption.

In November 1990, in a further reorganization of the Government, Chatichai demoted the leader of the Muan Chon party, Chalerm Yubamrung, an outspoken critic of the armed forces, from his position as Minister to the Prime Minister's Office. The leadership of the armed forces had demanded Chalerm's dismissal, threatening unspecified intervention if government changes did not take place. In early December Chatichai resigned as Prime Minister; he was reappointed on the next day and subsequently formed a coalition Government comprising Chart Thai, Rassadorn, Puangchon Chao Thai and former opposition parties Prachakorn Thai and Ekkaparb. The DP, the SAP and the Muan Chon party were not included in the coalition, the composition of which provided Chatichai with reduced support (227 of the 357 seats) in the House of Representatives.

On 23 February 1991 Chatichai's Government was ousted in a bloodless military coup. Gen. Sunthorn Kongsompong, the Supreme Commander of the Armed Forces, assumed administrative power as the Chairman of the newly created National Peace-keeping Council (NPC). The NPC was actually dominated by the effective head of the armed forces in Thailand, Gen. Suchinda Kraprayoon, who was appointed joint Deputy Chairman of the NPC together with the Commanders-in-Chief of the Air Force and Navy and the Director-General of the Police. The coup leaders cited government corruption and abuse of power to justify their action; however, the coup was also widely believed to have been organized in response to the recent erosion of military influence under Chatichai.

Under the NPC, the Constitution was abrogated, the House of Representatives, the Senate and the Council of Ministers were dissolved, and martial law was imposed. The NPC won unprecedented royal approval, and in early March 1991 an interim Constitution, approved by the King, was published. Anand Panyarachun, a business executive and former diplomat, was appointed acting Prime Minister pending fresh elections. Anand appointed a predominantly civilian 35-member interim Cabinet, comprised mainly of respected technocrats and former ministers, and including only eight members of the armed forces. Chatichai and Arthit, who had been arrested at the time of the coup, were released after two weeks. The NPC appointed a 292-member National Legislative Assembly, which included 149 serving or former military personnel, as well as many civilians known to have connections with the armed forces.

In May 1991 martial law was repealed in most areas, and political activity was permitted to resume. The New Aspiration Party (NAP—formed in October 1990 by Gen. Chavalit) gathered support as the traditional parties were in disarray, largely owing to investigations of corruption by the newly created Assets Examination Committee. In June 1991 a new party, Samakkhi Tham, was created to compete with the NAP. It was sponsored by the Commander-in-Chief of the Air Force, Air Chief Marshal Kaset Rojananin, and led by Narong Wongwan, a former leader of Ekkaparb. In August Suchinda assumed, in addition to the post of Commander-in-Chief of the Army, the role of Supreme Commander of the Armed Forces, replacing Sunthorn, who remained Chairman of the NPC.

In November 1991 the Constitution Scrutiny Committee, which had been effectively nominated by the NPC, presented a draft Constitution to the National Legislative Assembly. Following public criticism of the draft (including a demonstration by 50,000 protesters in Bangkok), the document was amended to reduce the number of nominated senators from 360 (equal to the number of elected members of the House of Representatives) to 270, and to abolish provisions that allowed the Senate the right to participate in the selection of the Prime Minister. Opposition parties, including the NAP and Palang Dharma (led by the popular and influential Governor of Bangkok, Maj.-Gen. Chamlong Srimuang), continued to oppose the draft, claiming that it perpetuated the power of the NPC. Despite public criticism, the National Legislative Assembly approved the new Constitution in early December, but campaigners continued to express concern over certain provisional clauses (which were to remain in effect for four years), under which the NPC was to appoint the Prime Minister and the Senate, and regarding the Senate's right to vote jointly with the elected House on motions of 'no confidence', thus enabling the Senate to dismiss a government with the support of only 46 elected representatives.

The general election took place on 22 March 1992, when 2,185 candidates, representing 15 parties, contested the 360 seats; 59.2% of the electorate voted. Despite the establishment by Anand of an independent organization, Poll Watch, to monitor the elections, the practice of 'vote-buying' persisted in the poorer northern and north-eastern regions. Samakkhi Tham and Chart Thai secured the largest number of seats, 79 and 74 respectively. The NAP gained 72 seats and Palang Dharma won 41 seats, 32 of which were in Bangkok. On the day of the election the NPC appointed the 270 members of the Senate, 154 of whom were officers of the armed forces or police.

In late March 1992 it was announced that Narong Wongwan would lead a coalition government comprising his own party (Samakkhi Tham), Chart Thai, Prachakorn Thai, the SAP and Rassadorn, which together controlled 195 seats in the House of Representatives. US allegations of Narong's involvement in illicit drugs-trafficking, however, caused the nomination to be rescinded. In early April 1992 Suchinda was named as Prime Minister, despite his assurances before the election that he would not accept the post. He was replaced as Supreme Commander of the Armed Forces by Kaset and as Commander-in-Chief of the Army by his brother-in-law, Gen. Issarapong Noonpakdi, hitherto his deputy. Suchinda's accession to the premiership prompted an immediate popular protest by more than 50,000 demonstrators against the appointment of an unelected Prime Minister. Later in April Suchinda appointed eight other unelected members to a new Cabinet, retaining several technocrats from Anand's interim Government. The 49-member Council of Ministers also included three ministers who had been found guilty of 'possessing unusual wealth' by the Assets Examination Committee. Thus Suchinda's standing was damaged both by his failure to honour his pledge not to become Prime Minister and by the inclusion in the Government of the very politicians that the armed forces had overthrown on the grounds of corruption.

In early May 1992 Chamlong announced, at a rally attended by 100,000 demonstrators, that he would fast until death unless Suchinda resigned. The demonstrations continued uninterrupted for one week until the government parties agreed to amend the Constitution to prevent an unelected Prime Minister (including the incumbent Suchinda, who would have to resign) from taking office, and to limit the power of the unelected Senate. Chamlong abandoned his hunger strike, and temporarily suspended the demonstration. However, violent anti-Government demonstrations erupted in Bangkok when it appeared that the Government might renege on its commitments. The Government declared a state of emergency in Bangkok and neighbouring provinces, introducing a curfew and banning any large gatherings. Chamlong was arrested and more than 3,000 people were detained by security forces in a brutal attempt to suppress the riots, which continued for several days.

Following unprecedented intervention by King Bhumibol, Suchinda ordered the release of Chamlong, announced a general amnesty for those involved in the protests and pledged to introduce amendments to the Constitution. On 24 May 1992 Suchinda resigned, after failing to retain the support of the five coalition parties, which agreed to introduce a constitutional amendment preventing Suchinda's continued tenure of office as Prime Minister. On 10 June the National Assembly approved constitutional amendments, whereby the Prime Minister was required to be a member of the House of Representatives, the authority of the Senate was restricted and the President of the House of Representatives was to be the President of the National Assembly. On the same day the King, contrary to expectations, named Anand as Prime Minister. Anand appointed a politically neutral, unelected Cabinet, which included many of the figures from his previous administrations, and dissolved the National Assembly in preparation for a general election.

At the end of June 1992 the four parties that had opposed the military Government (the DP, the NAP, Palang Dharma and Ekkaparb) formed an alliance, the National Democratic Front (NDF), to contest the forthcoming elections. In July, in an effort to dissociate himself from the traditional coalition parties that had supported the Suchinda regime, Chatichai declined the leadership of Chart Thai and formed a new party, Chart Pattana, which quickly gained widespread support.

During June and July 1992 Anand introduced measures to curb the political power of the armed forces, reduce military control of state enterprises, and remove the authority of the armed forces to intervene in situations of social unrest. In early August, as part of a limited reorganization of the armed forces, Kaset and Issarapong were dismissed from their positions at the head of the armed forces and demoted to inactive posts. A more extensive military reshuffle took place in September. The new Commander-in-Chief of the Army, Gen. Wimol Wongwanit, pledged that the army would not interfere in politics during his period of command.

The general election took place on 13 September 1992, when 12 parties contested the 360 seats in the House of Representatives; 62.1% of the electorate voted. Poll Watch reported that 'vote-buying' and violence persisted, especially in the north-eastern region. The DP won the largest number of seats (79), while Chart Thai and Chart Pattana secured 77 and 60 seats respectively. The DP was able to form a coalition, with the NAP, Palang Dharma and Ekkaparb, which commanded 185 of the 360 seats. Despite its participation in the previous administration, the SAP (with 22 seats) was also subsequently invited to join the Government. On 23 September Chuan Leekpai, the leader of the DP, was formally approved as Prime Minister. Chuan declared his intention to eradicate corrupt practices, to decentralize government, to enhance rural development and to reduce the powers of the Senate.

Although Chuan's integrity as Prime Minister remained unquestioned, widespread dissatisfaction with his style of leadership began to emerge in early 1993. The SAP was openly critical of Chuan's alleged indecisiveness and slow progress in the implementation of national policy. The coalition was also adversely affected by the association of certain members of the Government with companies linked to major share price manipulation in 1992. In June 1993 Chuan's administration was threatened by two motions of 'no confidence' in the Cabinet, introduced by Chart Pattana and Chart Thai. The rejection of the motions by a considerable margin, however, consolidated the Government's position. In early September the SAP announced that it was to merge with four opposition parties, including Chart Pattana, under the leadership of Chatichai, while remaining in the ruling coalition. This appeared to be an attempt to secure the premiership for Chatichai, as the new SAP would command more seats than any other member of the coalition. However, four days after the merger plans were announced, the SAP was expelled from the Government. It was replaced by the Seritham Party, which was considered a more suitable coalition partner than the SAP as its policies were closer to those of the Government.

In September 1994 Chamlong resumed the leadership of Palang Dharma in party elections, and subsequently persuaded the party executive committee to approve the replacement of all 11 of the party's cabinet members. Chamlong's nominations for inclusion in the Cabinet included Thaksin Shinawatra, a prominent business executive, and Vichit Surapongchai, a banking executive, as Minister of Foreign Affairs and Minister of Transport and Communications respectively. Prasong and his supporters expressed opposition to the selection of non-elected candidates and also objected to Chamlong's authoritarian style of leadership. The appointments were, however, confirmed in a cabinet reorganization in October, when Chamlong was named a Deputy Prime Minister.

In December 1994 the NAP withdrew from the ruling coalition over a constitutional amendment providing for the future election of local government representatives, including village headmen. The NAP voted against the Government to protect the vested interests of incumbent local administrators who would control many votes at the next election. In order to secure a parliamentary majority Chuan was subsequently obliged to include Chatichai's Chart Pattana in the governing coalition, although this severely compromised the Government's claims to represent honesty and reform. A cabinet reorganization was implemented to replace NAP members and include members of Chart Pattana.

In January 1995 Chuan finally obtained the approval of the National Assembly for a series of amendments to the Constitution to expand the country's democratic base. Attempts in the previous year had been obstructed by the opposition with the support of the majority of senators (who were mostly appointees of the 1991 coup leaders). The reforms adopted in 1995 included a reduction in the size of the appointed Senate to two-thirds of that of the elective House of Representatives, the lowering of the eligible voting age from 20 years to 18, equality for women, the establishment of an administrative court, the introduction of parliamentary ombudsmen and the prohibition of senators and members of the Government from holding monopolistic concessions with government or state bodies. This last amendment necessitated the resignation of Thaksin as Minister of Foreign Affairs, owing to his extensive business interests.

In May 1995 the opposition tabled a motion of 'no confidence' in the Government, in connection with a land reform scandal, which had prompted the resignation of the Minister of Agriculture and Co-operatives in December 1994. During a government investigation allegations that the land reform programme had been used to benefit wealthy landowners were substantiated. In April 1995, in what was regarded by the opposition as an inadequate response, land titles were removed from seven deed-holders and a senior official was dismissed from the land reform department. Following an announcement by Chamlong that Palang Dharma would not support the coalition in the 'no confidence' vote, Chuan dissolved the House of Representatives on 19 May and scheduled a general election for early July.

At elections to an enlarged House of Representatives, which took place on 2 July 1995, 12 political parties contested 391 seats; 62.0% of eligible voters participated in the election. Chart Thai won the largest number of seats (92), followed by the DP (86) and the NAP (57). Support for these parties was based on provincial patronage politics and allegations of vote-buying were widespread. Chart Thai failed to secure a single seat in Bangkok, where the electorate was widely regarded as more politically sophisticated. The leader of Chart Thai, Banharn Silapa-Archa (who was among those accused of 'possessing unusual wealth' by the military junta in 1991) formed a coalition Government comprising Chart Thai, the NAP, Palang Dharma, the SAP, Prachakorn Thai, Muan Chon and later Nam Thai (a business-orientated party formed in 1994 by Amnuay Viravan, a former minister). Thaksin (who had relinquished majority control of his company) had been elected to the leadership of Palang Dharma in May, following the resignation of Chamlong. Banharn appointed all the leaders of the coalition parties (except for the Muan Chon party) as Deputy Prime Ministers. Banharn assumed responsibility for the interior portfolio pending the findings of a commission established to investigate US allegations of drugs-trafficking by two leaders of powerful factions within Chart Thai who demanded control of the ministry. The composition of Banharn's Cabinet was widely criticized, owing to the lack of technocrats and the predominance, despite pre-election assurances, of professional politicians (who were often subject to allegations of corruption and vote-buying). There was also dissatisfaction at the appointment of the inexperienced Surakiart Sathirathai, a lawyer, as Minister of Finance while the country was undergoing a process of financial liberalization. The administration was subjected to severe criticism by the national media, which accused the regime of corruption and nepotism.

In early 1996 the stability of the ruling coalition was jeopardized by an armed forces' plan to launch a US $1,000m. satellite system with both commercial and military applications. Thaksin opposed the unnecessary expenditure, which would contribute to the large current account deficit, while Chavalit, the Minister of Defence, who wished to maintain his popularity with the armed forces, threatened to withdraw the NAP from the coalition if the project were cancelled. Chavalit had already consolidated his position with the armed forces in September by appointing a close associate, Gen. Pramon Phalasin, as Commander-in-Chief of the Army, contrary to the recommendations for promotions of the outgoing Commander-in-Chief, which were traditionally observed.

In March 1996 Banharn announced the composition of the new Senate, the first to be appointed by a democratically elected Prime Minister. In contrast to the previous Senate, only 39 active military officers were named as senators; other appointees included academics and business executives.

In May 1996 10 government ministers, including the Prime Minister, survived motions of 'no confidence', despite opposition revelations of financial irregularities at the Bangkok Bank of Commerce, including loans extended without collateral to members of the Thai Cabinet, notably the Deputy Minister of the Interior, Suchart Tancharoen, and the Deputy Minister of Finance, Newin Chidchob, both members of Chart Thai. Palang Dharma refused to support Suchart in the debate, probably in an attempt to dissociate itself from government corruption prior to the gubernatorial elections in Bangkok. In order to pre-empt the withdrawal of Palang Dharma from the ruling coalition, five members of Chart Thai, including Suchart and Newin, resigned from their government positions. Palang Dharma subsequently agreed to remain in the coalition but announced the resignation of all five of its ministers from the Cabinet. In the ensuing cabinet reorganization at the end of May Surakiart, who had failed to take action to prevent huge losses at the Bangkok Bank of Commerce, was replaced by a former official in the Ministry of Finance, Bodi Chunnananda, Amnuay was appointed Minister of Foreign Affairs and the Palang Dharma ministers all agreed to return to their positions in the Cabinet.

In the gubernatorial election in Bangkok which took place in June 1996, Bhichit Rattakul, an environmental activist who contested the election as an independent, secured 48.4% of the votes cast, defeating Chamlong (32.6%) and the incumbent, Krisda Arunvongse Na Ayutthya (15.5%). Krisda, who had won the governorship as a Palang Dharma representative, was supported by Prachakorn Thai following Palang Dharma's decision to support Chamlong's candidacy. Palang Dharma, which relied on its popularity in Bangkok to secure its national political position, was severely weakened by the defeat. Chamlong subsequently announced that he was retiring from politics.

In July 1996 Vijit Supinit resigned from his position as Governor of the Bank of Thailand following a series of financial scandals, most notably the near collapse of the Bangkok Bank of Commerce and the arrest of several of the latter's officials on suspicion of fraud and embezzlement. The Central Bank's regulatory capability was thus brought into question. In August the Government suffered a set-back following the withdrawal of the Palang Dharma from the ruling coalition. This defection, which was the apparent result of a cabinet dispute over alleged bribery in the awarding of bank licences, reduced the Government's legislative majority by 23 seats. In September Banharn was able to secure the support of his coalition partners in a scheduled motion of 'no confidence' in his administration only by undertaking to resign from the premiership to make way for another candidate. However, the inability of the coalition partners to agree on the appointment of a new Prime Minister led to the dissolution of the House of Representatives on 27 September.

In the general election, which was held on 17 November 1996 and was marred by violence and alleged extensive ballot-rigging, the NAP won 125 of the 393 seats, while the DP secured 123 seats. The majority of NAP seats were gained through provincial patronage politics, while the more politically-aware electorate of Bangkok returned the DP to 29 of the city's 37 seats. Chavalit, the leader of the NAP, was appointed to the office of Prime Minister, heading a coalition that incorporated Chart Pattana, the SAP, Prachakorn Thai, Muan Chon and the Seritham Party. The ruling coalition thus held 221 seats in the House of Representatives. Chatichai was appointed as the Chairman of the Prime Minister's special advisory group on economic and foreign affairs, and the majority of the other influential cabinet posts were assigned to other members of Chart Pattana and the NAP. Thaksin resigned as leader of Palang Dharma following the party's failure to win more than one seat in the House of Representatives.

As evidence of Chavalit's avowed intention to revive the economy, he allocated the finance portfolio and the deputy premiership with responsibility for economic affairs to Amnuay,

a respected technocrat. However, Chavalit subsequently failed to give Amnuay the necessary support to overcome the obstacles imposed by other coalition members anxious to prevent the implementation of austere fiscal policies. In June Amnuay resigned and was replaced by the little-known Thanong Bidaya, the President of the Thai Military Bank. The Government's indecisive handling of the economy contributed to a financial crisis in mid-1997, following a series of sustained assaults on the Thai baht by currency speculators, which led to the baht's effective devaluation in early July. At the end of July the Governor of the Central Bank, Rerngchai Marakanonda, also resigned, citing political interference. The deterioration in the state of the economy in 1997 was reflected in an increase in popular protests. The most significant of these was an encampment of about 15,000 representatives of the Assembly of the Poor (a non-governmental organization campaigning for the improvement of conditions for impoverished farmers and landless agricultural labourers) outside the Prime Minister's office in January. The protesters dispersed in May, following the establishment of a fund to compensate villagers for relocation and destruction caused by government infrastructure projects. The Government introduced measures in June to constrain media attacks on the authorities and to limit mass protests.

In August 1997 Chavalit and Thanong had an audience with the King to discuss the economic crisis. Later that month Chavalit implemented a cabinet reorganization in an attempt to regain public confidence. On the advice of former Prime Minister Prem, the former Minister of Finance, Virabongsa Ramangkura, an outspoken critic of the Government's handling of the economic crisis, was appointed Deputy Prime Minister with responsibility for economic affairs, while Thaksin joined the Cabinet as Deputy Prime Minister with responsibility for regional development and trade. Despite the announcement of strict austerity measures and the intervention of the IMF, the economic situation continued to deteriorate.

In January 1997 an assembly of 99 members was elected by the legislature to draft a new constitution following the unanimous approval of a constitution amendment bill by the National Assembly in September 1996. Uthai Pimchaichon, a former Minister of Commerce and advocate of the eradication of the influence of money in politics, was appointed as Chairman of the Constitution Drafting Assembly. The draft Constitution included provisions for: a directly elected Senate; the replacement in the House of Representatives of 393 deputies from multi-member constituencies by 400 deputies from single-member constituencies and 100 deputies elected by proportional representation; the resignation of cabinet ministers from the legislature; the establishment of a minimum educational requirement for members of the National Assembly; the formation of an Election Commission to supervise elections (in place of the Ministry of the Interior); the centralization of vote-counting; compulsory voting; and the guarantee of press freedom. Although the draft gained the support of opposition parties and the media, there was considerable opposition to the new charter from within the ruling administration. Chavalit himself reneged on his pledge to support the overwhelmingly popular draft, but then finally gave it his endorsement following the application of pressure by both business representatives and the armed forces.

Chavalit ensured his survival of a 'no confidence' motion tabled by the opposition by scheduling the censure debate prior to the vote on the draft Constitution. If defeated Chavalit could thus dissolve the National Assembly rather than resign, delaying the vote on the draft Constitution and forcing fresh elections under the existing Constitution. In the event the Government won the 'no confidence' vote and the draft Constitution was approved on 27 September 1997, with 578 votes in favour, 16 opposed, 17 abstentions and 40 absences. Chavalit was then prohibited by law from dissolving the National Assembly and was allowed 240 days to complete enabling legislation for the new Constitution, prior to a general election (although the King subsequently urged the accelerated completion of the necessary reforms). The new Constitution was promulgated on 11 October.

In October 1997 Thanong resigned as Minister of Finance, citing obstruction of his attempts to implement the extensive reforms required to resolve the economic crisis. His resignation was precipitated by the Government's reversal of an increase in fuel tax that had formed part of a programme of reforms initiated by Thanong earlier in the month. Popular demonstrations demanding the resignation of Chavalit took place in the capital in October. A cabinet reorganization was announced at the end of October, in conjunction with a statement declaring that the Government would set a date for a general election before the end of the year. The new appointments, however, which included that of the Executive Vice-President of Bangkok Bank and a former minister, Khosit Panpiamrat, as the Minister of Finance, failed to restore public or investor confidence in the Government, and the Thai currency continued to depreciate. At the beginning of November Chavalit's announcement that he would resign from the premiership on 6 November, following the adoption of important electoral and financial legislation by the National Assembly, caused a slight recovery of the Thai baht. Both Prem and Chatichai rejected approaches by members of the ruling coalition to prevent its collapse by assuming the leadership. Finally, on 9 November Chuan, who maintained his reputation for integrity, assumed the premiership, following the formation of a coalition comprising Chuan's DP, Chart Thai, the SAP, Ekkaparb, the Seritham Party, Palang Dharma and the Thai Party (as well as 12 of the 18 members of Prachakorn Thai) commanding the support of 210 of the 393 seats in the House of Representatives.

The transfer of power to Chuan, under the terms of the new Constitution, without the intervention of the armed forces or resort to a non-elected leader, received widespread approval and represented significant democratic progress in Thailand. The new Cabinet included the appointment of Tarrin Nimmanhae-minda as Minister of Finance (a post he had occupied in Chuan's previous administration) and the allocation of the commerce portfolio to the former Deputy Prime Minister, Supachai Pan-ichpakdi. However, the baht continued to depreciate, causing intermittent social unrest. In March, however, a vote of 'no confidence' in Chuan's Government was defeated by 208 votes to 177, and the Government retained popular support in the country. This was demonstrated at the elections to the Bangkok city council, which took place on 26 April, when the DP won 22 of the 60 seats, followed by the non-political supporters of the incumbent Governor, Bhichit Rattakul, styled Worker Ants, who secured 20 seats.

In May 1998 the Governor of the Central Bank, Chaiyawat Wibulsawadi, announced his resignation, shortly before the publication of an independent report into the alleged misman-agement of the economy preceding the devaluation of the baht in July 1997 and the onset of the subsequent financial crisis. The report attributed much blame for the country's difficulties to the economic strategy followed by Chaiyawat, his predecessor Rerngchai Marakanonda, the former Prime Minister, Chavalit, and the former Minister of Finance, Amnuay Viravan. Chaiyawat was replaced by Chatu Mongol Sonakul, a former permanent secretary of finance. Also in May new electoral legislation was approved, enabling polls to be held six months later. However, despite pressure from the opposition, Chuan stated that elections would not be held until specific economic reforms had been put in place. At the same time there were fears that, under the new legislation, the 12 members of the ruling coalition who had defected from Prachakorn Thai to help form the Government in November 1997 might lose their legal status as legislators. (The 12 were formally expelled from Prachakorn Thai in October 1998 but continued to form part of the coalition Government.) In July a new political party, Thai Rak Thai, was established by the former Deputy Prime Minister, Thaksin Shinawatra.

By August 1998 Thailand's economy appeared to have stabi-lized, and Chuan received rare public praise from Queen Sirikit. However, the Government was beset by allegations of corrup-tion. These resulted in the resignation in mid-September of the Minister of Public Health, Rakkait Sukthana, over alleged cor-ruption in the purchase of medicine for state hospitals, and in early October of the Deputy Minister of Agriculture, Virat Rattanaset, as the consequence of an alleged misuse of Ministry of Agriculture funds. Gen. Surayud Chulanont was appointed as the new Commander-in-Chief of the Army, replacing Gen. Chettah Thanajaro. On 5 October Chuan announced a reorgan-ization of his Government, bringing the Chart Pattana party into the ruling coalition and thereby increasing to 257 the number of seats held by the coalition in the House of Repre-sentatives. In a reorganization of the Cabinet effected on the same day, five new ministers were appointed to the Cabinet, including the Secretary-General of Chart Pattana, Suwat Lipta-panlop, who was assigned the industry portfolio; however, many of the most influential portfolios were retained by the DP. In late 1998 and early 1999 the Government came under renewed pressure from the opposition. In December 1998 the opposition

filed a motion to remove Chuan and Tarrin from office, on the grounds that they had allegedly acted in breach of the Con-stitution by submitting four Letters of Intent to the IMF without first securing the approval of the House of Representatives; the motion was unsuccessful. In January 1999 the opposition filed a censure motion against three DP ministers (the Deputy Prime Minister and Minister of the Interior, Maj.-Gen. Sanan Kajorn-prasart, the Minister of Transport and Communications, Suthep Thaungsuban, and Tarrin), who were accused by the opposition of corruption, nepotism, incompetence and dishonesty. All three ministers survived the vote on the motion held in late January.

A series of minor bombings of government buildings, which occurred in December 1998 and January 1999, and included an attack on the DP headquarters in mid-January, were believed by a number of observers to be politically motivated. The Gov-ernment reportedly attributed blame for the bombings to a group of unidentified opposition sympathizers. In early April Chuan became subject to criticism following the revelation that in the previous year he had countersigned the honorary appoint-ment of Field Marshal Thanom Kittikachorn (the former dic-tator accused of being responsible for the killing by troops of large numbers of mainly student protesters in Bangkok in 1973) as a Royal Guards officer. Chuan refused to apologize for author-izing the appointment, which had also been approved by the King; however, Thanom subsequently resigned from the posi-tion.

In July 1999 the SAP withdrew from the governing coalition, reportedly as a result of intense disputes within the party concerning the allocation of cabinet positions, prompting a reor-ganization of the Cabinet. By August, however, public approval of the Government appeared to be in decline, and the coalition faced increasing demands from the opposition that the House of Representatives be dissolved and that elections be called. The recently established opposition party, Thai Rak Thai, led by Thaksin Shinawatra, intensified its recruitment campaign from mid-1999 onwards; a public debate on the alleged use of finan-cial inducements by Thai Rak Thai to recruit members of other parties was initiated by members of the DP in an attempt to prevent support for the DP being lost to Thai Rak Thai. In November Chavalit pledged his willingness to support Thai Rak Thai in the forthcoming general election in the event of his own NAP performing poorly at the polls.

In August 1999 a report on the state-owned Krung Thai Bank which exposed the bank's dubious loan policies and other irreg-ularities, and revealed that 84% (rather than 59%, as the bank itself claimed) of the bank's loans were failing to be serviced, was disclosed to the Senate and the press. The report led to criticism of the Government and also resulted in direct allegations of corruption being made against Tarrin, whose brother, Sirin Nimmanhaeminda, had been the President of Krung Thai Bank until his resignation in January. Although the Government was reported in October to have exonerated a number of senior Krung Thai executives, including Sirin, of allegations of ineffi-ciency and dishonesty, the controversy surrounding the bank continued and constituted the main focus of a joint no-con-fidence motion filed by three main opposition parties against the Government in December, in which the ruling coalition was accused of mismanagement of the economy and of condoning corruption. The Government survived the censure debate, win-ning 229 votes against the opposition's 125. However, the debate exposed divisions within the governing coalition (particularly between the DP and Chart Thai), and also proved particularly damaging to Tarrin and to the Deputy Prime Minister and Minister of the Interior, Maj.-Gen. (retd) Sanan Kajornprasart.

The DP fared badly in provincial elections held in February 2000, possibly owing to discontent among the rural population with the Government's refusal to subsidize crop prices. In late January, however, the opposition NAP had also suffered a serious reverse when as many as 40 of its members of the House of Representatives, led by the former NAP Secretary-General, Sano Thianthong, boycotted a gathering intended to reaffirm their allegiance to the party in the approach to the anticipated elections. Sano, who had been forcibly removed from the party leadership in March 1999, was subsequently reported to have claimed that the dissident legislators were engaged in negotia-tions with representatives of Thai Rak Thai regarding a possible merger between the two groups. (Public support for Thai Rak Thai had increased throughout the second half of 1999, and continued to grow in early 2000.) Allegations of corruption against the ruling coalition re-emerged in 2000. In March Sanan was accused by the National Anti-Corruption Committee

(NACC) of having falsified his assets declaration statement (recently required of all cabinet ministers) in order to conceal the source of funds in his personal bank account. Although he denied the NACC's allegations, Sanan swiftly resigned from his ministerial positions and from his membership of the legislature, pending a ruling on the NACC's report by Thailand's Constitutional Court. (Sanan did, however, retain his position as Secretary-General of the DP.) Although Sanan's prompt removal from the Government was expected to aid the DP's survival of the scandal, the credibility of the party was damaged by the revelations; the ruling coalition was also regarded as having been markedly weakened by the loss of such an influential minister. A reorganization of the Cabinet was effected on 11 April; Banyat Bantadtan was appointed to replace Sanan as Deputy Prime Minister and Minister of the Interior. In August Sanan was convicted of corruption by the Constitutional Court.

On 4 March 2000, in the first significant test of the country's new reformist Constitution, elections to the new 200-member Senate were contested by more than 1,500 candidates. The level of voter participation in the polls was reported at 70%, with voting being compulsory for the first time. Although an increased focus on the suitability of the candidates themselves was reported, the widespread practice of vote-buying persisted, and on 21 March the Election Commission (EC), empowered by the Constitution to declare results invalid at its discretion, disqualified 78 of the 200 winning candidates (including the wives of two cabinet ministers) on the grounds of either vote-buying or fraudulent conduct. The EC subsequently announced that a second round of polling would be held in the 78 affected constituencies on 29 April, in which all but two of the disqualified contestants would be permitted to stand again. However, there were further allegations of electoral fraud following the second round of voting, with 34 of the previously disqualified candidates being accused of various electoral violations. The EC responded by declaring that a second rerun of the polls would be held in at least nine of the affected constituencies, rejecting appeals for the dismissal of the allegations of fraud in the interest of political continuity. (While the final results of the elections remained in dispute, none of the declared winners were able to assume their seats as they lacked the necessary quorum, resulting in a backlog of legislation and obliging the outgoing Senate to remain in office in a interim capacity.) Although in May it was reported that 22 senatorial candidates had been cleared of allegations of fraud by the EC owing to lack of evidence, a third round of polling was scheduled to be held in June in a number of constituencies. The EC also announced that a number of prominent individuals were likely to be prosecuted for their involvement in electoral misconduct. While the insistence of the EC on the holding of a further round of polls led to fears that the recent constitutional reforms might result in the paralysis of the legislature, the disclosures of electoral fraud were welcomed by many as demonstrating the Government's commitment to the elimination of political corruption. Further allegations of electoral fraud necessitated a fourth and fifth round of polling in June and July respectively. Despite the resignation of almost 100 NAP deputies from the House of Representatives in June and July in support of an early dissolution of the House, Chuan reiterated his intention to dissolve the House in October. The SAP also withdrew from the House of Representatives in July in a similar attempt to gain an early dissolution. On 1 August Thailand's first-ever democratically elected Senate was formally inaugurated.

In November 2000 it was announced that elections to the House of Representatives would be held in January 2001. In December 2000 the NACC recommended that Thaksin Shinawatra, the leader of the opposition Thai Rak Thai, should be indicted for having violated the Constitution by concealing financial assets and seeking to avoid the payment of taxes. One notable feature of Thai Rak Thai's electoral campaign was its targeting of rural votes by pledging grants of 1m. baht for each of Thailand's 70,000 villages and offering a debt-relief scheme for farmers. At the legislative elections held on 6 January 2001 Thai Rak Thai won 248 of the 500 seats in the House of Representatives, thereby almost gaining an unprecedented absolute majority. However, the elections were marred by widespread allegations of malpractice; indeed, many domestic and international observers declared that, despite the vigilance of the EC, they had been the most corrupt ever held in Thailand. In late January repolling was held in more than 60 constituencies where the EC had found evidence of fraudulent practice. In February a new cabinet nominated by Thaksin Shinawatra was

formally approved by the King. All but five of the appointees were members of Thai Rak Thai, with which the Seritham Party had merged since the election, thus affording Thai Rak Thai an absolute majority in the House of Representatives. With the support of its coalition partners, the NAP and Chart Thai, the incoming Thai Rak Thai administration controlled 339 of the 500 seats in the House.

In March 2001 a Thai Airways airliner, which the Prime Minister was about to board, was destroyed in an explosion. Despite the Prime Minister's claim that this had been an assassination attempt, investigators were subsequently unable to find any conclusive evidence to confirm that the explosion had been caused by a bomb. In April the Constitutional Court formally commenced hearing charges of corruption brought against the Prime Minister, as recommended by the NACC in December 2000. In the same month two bombs exploded in southern Thailand, killing a child and injuring 42 people. The involvement of a militant Islamist separatist organization, the Pattani United Liberation Organization (PULO), was suspected.

In May 2001 Prime Minister Thaksin dismissed the Governor of the central bank, Chatu Mongol Sonakul, following a dispute over monetary policy. Pridiyathorn Davakula was appointed as his replacement. The incident raised questions about the extent of governmental interference in the bank's affairs. In June Thaksin Shinawatra appeared in court for the first time to contest the accusations of corruption that had been made against him. In the same month there was a bomb attack on the Vietnamese embassy. It was believed to have been perpetrated by members of the Free Vietnam Movement. Three men from the USA were arrested shortly afterwards in connection with the incident.

On 30 June 2001 by-elections were held in seven constituencies to fill seats in the House of Representatives vacated by members disqualified for breaches of campaign rules after the January elections. However, the polls were again marred by allegations of corruption. In July King Bhumibol appointed the former Deputy Interior Permanent Secretary, Palakorn Suwannarat, and the former Minister of Education, Kasem Watanachai, to the Privy Council. Watanchai had resigned from his post in the previous month; he was succeeded by Suwit Khunkitti in September of that year.

The Prime Minister was acquitted of the charges against him regarding concealment of his assets in August 2001. The judges ruled by a narrow eight-to-seven majority in his favour, following the conclusion of the hearing one month previously. His exoneration was welcomed by his many supporters, who had conducted a popular campaign which was thought to have exerted some influence over the court's verdict. The court issued a lengthy exposition of its decision intended to rebut concerns that its judges had been placed under pressure to deliver a favourable verdict. In September the Prime Minister dismissed the president of Thai Airways International and brought about the resignation of the entire board of directors. His actions were prompted by a series of recent bomb threats against the airline and by disputes between its management and the Deputy Minister of Transport and Communications, Pracha Maleenanont.

In October 2001 the Government introduced a plan to provide low-cost health care for the nation's poorest people, thus implementing one of the Prime Minister's election pledges. Doubts remained over the quality of the service provided. Later in the same month the limits to the Government's reform efforts were highlighted when army Sub-Lt Duangchalerm Yoobamrung, son of Chalerm Yoobamrung, an influential NAP member of the House of Representatives, allegedly murdered a police officer during a fight in a night-club. Duangchalerm subsequently fled to Cambodia. As a result of his son's actions and subsequent popular criticism of the Government for its ineffectual attempts to bring him to justice, Chalerm was forced to resign from the deputy leadership of the NAP, although he retained an influential position within the Government. Duangchalerm's trial was scheduled *in absentia* for January 2002, at which point the Government requested that the Cambodian authorities extradite the fugitive to face trial. In May 2002 Duangchalerm finally surrendered himself to the Thai embassy in Malaysia, having entered the country illegally, and agreed to return home, where he entered a plea of not guilty to the charges against him. A court hearing took place in July 2002 and Duangchalerm remained in prison, awaiting trial, in early 2003.

In November 2001 a panel of judges acting for the Public Prosecutor recommended that the former Governor of the Central Bank, Rerngchai Marakanonda, face a civil lawsuit for the part that he had played in precipitating the 1997 financial crisis. The hearing began in February 2002. Rerngchai later filed a countersuit in which he alleged that the people who had accused him were attempting to damage his reputation. In December King Bhumibol made a speech to mark his birthday in which he publicly criticized the Prime Minister, commenting that his Government's 'double standards' were effectively leading Thailand towards 'catastrophe'. His criticism was thought to be linked to his reported disapproval of the business relationship that existed between the Prime Minister and the King's son, Crown Prince Vajiralongkorn.

Prime Minister Thaksin's apparent sensitivity to criticism was reflected in his Government's increasingly repressive policies towards the media. In January 2002 an edition of the *Far Eastern Economic Review*, a Hong Kong-based publication, was banned for its inclusion of an article that suggested that tensions existed in the relationship between King Bhumibol and the Prime Minister. In February 2002 the reporters responsible for the article were summoned by the Thai immigration authorities as it was alleged that they posed a threat to national security. Their visas were subsequently revoked but reinstated in March. Meanwhile, it was reported that the Ministry of Defence had ordered the Nation Media Group to cease its provision of news programmes to a Bangkok radio station. The ban followed the broadcast of an interview with a senior opposition figure which was deemed to have been critical of the Prime Minister. The armed forces, which controlled all Thai radio frequencies, claimed that the decision had been taken for commercial reasons. The Prime Minister rebuffed allegations that his Government was attempting to impose restraints upon media freedom by commenting that the media were permitted to report freely but that any criticism should be constructive.

In January 2002 the NAP voted to merge with its coalition partner, Thai Rak Thai. However, the move was opposed by several NAP politicians, and deputy leader Chingchai Mongkoltham stated that he would pursue legal action in an attempt to maintain the party's independence. Despite this opposition, the party was legally dissolved in March. In the same month the Government was further strengthened when Chart Pattana joined the ruling coalition; a minor cabinet reorganization took place shortly afterwards in which Suwat Liptapanlop, Secretary-General of Chart Pattana, was allocated a ministerial position. Meanwhile, by-elections were held in 14 constituencies where the January 2001 general election results had been invalidated owing to substantiated allegations of electoral fraud and corruption. Thai Rak Thai lost five seats as a result, but retained its commanding majority in the National Assembly. Shortly afterwards six policemen died after gunmen attacked three security outposts—two in Pattani province and one in Yala province. The attacks were suspected to have been carried out by one of the militant Islamist separatist organizations known to exist in the area. Two bombs later exploded in Yala province, coinciding with a tour of the region by the Minister of the Interior. Further outbreaks of violence against the Thai police occurred in the area throughout the month. A Thai military official attributed the attacks to the Guragan Mujahideen Islam Pattani, a group thought to be linked to the international terrorist network al-Qa'ida. In April the Constitutional Court formally granted the NAP's request that it be permitted to merge with Thai Rak Thai.

In May 2002 the Government succeeded in defeating no-confidence motions that had been brought against 15 of its ministers, including nine members of the Cabinet, by the opposition. It was also reported that the National Counter-Corruption Commission (NCCC) had begun an investigation into impeachment petitions that had been filed against the nine cabinet ministers. It was expected, however, that the ministers concerned would evade censure. In October Prime Minister Thaksin implemented an extensive cabinet reorganization. Chavalit Yongchaiyudh was replaced as Minister of Defence by Thammarak Issarangkun Na Ayutthaya, while former Minister of Transport Wan Muhamad Nor Matha became Minister of the Interior. Purachai Piemsomboon was allocated the justice portfolio and Suwit Khunkitti was replaced as Minister of Education by Pongpol Adireksarn. Six ministers were also appointed to take responsibility for new ministries that had been created as part of the Government's ongoing bureaucratic reforms. Later in the month a bomb exploded in the province of Yala, while in the neighbouring province of Songkhla five schools were subjected to arson attacks.

In February 2003 a further redistribution of cabinet portfolios took place. The Minister of Finance, Somkid Jatusripitak, and the Minister of Justice, Purachai Piemsomboon, were both appointed Deputy Prime Ministers; Somkid was replaced by his deputy, Suchart Jaovisidha, while Purachai was succeeded by former Minister of Energy Pongthep Thepkanjana. Deputy Prime Minister Prommin Lertsuridej was awarded the energy portfolio. Meanwhile, the Government announced the commencement of an intensive anti-drugs campaign intended to eliminate Thailand's drug problem within three months. As the campaign continued, the huge number of suspected drug dealers being killed prompted criticism from both local and international human rights groups, which claimed that the Thai authorities were operating an illegal 'shoot to kill' policy and effectively condoning extra-judicial violence. The office of the UN High Commissioner for Human Rights (OHCHR, see p. 39) subsequently requested that it be permitted to send a representative to the country to investigate the killings, but its demand was rejected by the Government. In March Thaksin acknowledged that mistakes had been made during the campaign, which had resulted in an estimated 1,128 deaths in the previous month, but denied that the police had been responsible for any extra-judicial killings.

Thailand is a member of the Association of South East Asian Nations (ASEAN, see p. 146) and generally maintains good relations with the other member states. Its former dependence on the USA has been greatly reduced by the increasing importance of regional trade and diplomatic relations. In the late 1980s Prime Minister Chatichai adopted a new business-orientated policy towards Cambodia, Laos, Viet Nam and Myanmar, encouraging investment in their developing economies; a policy successfully pursued by subsequent premiers. In April 1995, following lengthy discussions with Viet Nam, Cambodia and Laos, the four countries established the Mekong River Commission (see p. 341) to promote the joint development of the Mekong's resources. Relations with the People's Republic of China also improved as Thailand became one of China's most significant trading partners. In October 1993 Thailand was accepted as a full member of the Non-aligned Movement (see p. 350).

In January 1993, despite its previous reluctance to do so, Thailand officially closed its border with Cambodia to trade with areas controlled by the communist Cambodian insurgent group, the Party of Democratic Kampuchea (known as the Khmers Rouges), in compliance with UN sanctions against the movement. Nevertheless, violations of the embargo (mainly exports of logs and gems from Cambodia through Thailand) were widely reported during 1993. Accusations by representatives of the Cambodian Government that Thai complicity with the Khmers Rouges was undermining Cambodian attempts to end the insurgency were substantiated by reports from UN peace-keeping troops that members of the Thai armed forces were providing transport, medical care and other support for the Khmers Rouges. Official Thai government policy was to support the elected Government of Cambodia, but the armed forces controlled the border and were unwilling to jeopardize their lucrative business relations with the Khmers Rouges.

In January 1994 Chuan Leekpai made an official visit to Cambodia (the first such visit by a Thai premier) to improve bilateral relations, which had been adversely affected by the continuing allegations. Following this visit more strenuous efforts were made to control illicit border trade and to prevent members of the armed forces from co-operating with the Khmers Rouges. However, clashes between Thai and Cambodian troops continued as a result of incursions into Thai territory by Cambodian government forces in pursuit of the Khmers Rouges. In September 1995 Thailand and Cambodia signed an agreement to establish a border co-ordination committee. At its first meeting in November three border checkpoints, which had been closed in April, were reopened. In the latter half of 1997 intense fighting in Cambodia between forces loyal to the First Prime Minister, Hun Sen, and those of the former Second Prime Minister, Prince Norodom Ranariddh, led to further incursions, across Thailand's eastern border with Cambodia, and resulted in an influx of refugees to Thailand. In May 1998 Hun Sen visited Bangkok to hold discussions with Prime Minister Chuan. In January 1997, meanwhile, the Thai Government adopted a potentially controversial resolution unilaterally to extend Thailand's maritime jurisdiction over waters that were also claimed by Cambodia and Viet Nam. The Thai Government, however, insisted that its decision was legal under international practice.

In January 2003 Thai–Cambodian relations were severely strained when the Thai embassy and several Thai businesses situated in the Cambodian capital, Phnom-Penh, were attacked by Cambodian demonstrators. Those who perpetuated the attacks were protesting against remarks, allegedly made by a Thai actress, claiming that the temples at Angkor Wat in Cambodia in fact belonged to Thailand. In response to the rioting, Prime Minister Thaksin downgraded diplomatic relations with Cambodia and announced plans to evacuate all Thai citizens from the country and to expel illegal Cambodian immigrants living in Thailand; the joint border was subsequently closed. The Cambodian Government issued a formal apology for the incident and promised compensation for those who had been affected by the violence. The Thai Government permitted a limited reopening of the border for commercial reasons in February. In early March Cambodia's Prime Minister, Hun Sen, ordered the border to be closed again, owing to alleged security concerns and in protest at the economic inequality between the two countries. However, later in that month the border was fully reopened and, in April, diplomatic relations were upgraded.

Following a military coup in Burma (now Myanmar) in September 1988, thousands of Burmese students fled to Thailand to avoid government repression. A prominent human rights group, Amnesty International, subsequently accused the Thai Government of coercing the students to return (resulting in their arrest and, in some cases, execution). In 1990 Myanma soldiers achieved unprecedented success in attacks on the strongholds of ethnic minorities on the Thai–Myanma border, since they were able to launch offensives from inside Thailand. The attacks resulted in a new influx of Myanma students and members of rebel ethnic groups seeking refuge in Thailand. The Thai Government refused to recognize those fleeing from Myanmar as refugees or to offer them aid. This refusal was motivated by its wish not to jeopardize the preferential treatment that it received from the Myanmar Government, which had recently granted many licences to Thai businesses for the exploitation of Myanmar's natural resources.

In 1992 Myanma forces intensified their attacks on rebel bases near the Thai border. In March the Myanma Government warned Thai armed forces to withdraw from nearby border areas, but later in the month Thai troops clashed with Myanma forces which had entered Thailand to attack a nearby rebel base. In early December King Bhumibol appealed for a peaceful agreement to end the tension caused by the continued occupation by Myanma forces of Hill 491 in Chumphan province. In accordance with a bilateral agreement signed shortly afterwards, Myanma troops were withdrawn from the hill by late December. In February 1993 the two countries resolved to demarcate their common border. In April 1994 Thailand invited Myanmar to attend the annual ASEAN meeting of ministers responsible for foreign affairs in Bangkok. In early 1995, however, relations with Myanmar were strained by the persistent border incursions into Thailand by forces of the Myanma Government during their offensive to capture the headquarters of the rebel Karen (Kayin) National Union (KNU) and subsequent attacks on disarmed Kayin refugees held in Thai camps along the border. In August Myanmar closed its land border with Thailand in protest at the alleged killing of a substantial number of Myanma seamen by Thai fishermen. A visit by Prime Minister Chavalit to Yangon, the capital of Myanmar, in September failed to resolve the situation and further discussions were held in November. In October 1996 the Thai Government approved the opening of three border checkpoints.

In late 1996 and early 1997 attacks allegedly carried out by breakaway Kayin rebels on Kayin refugee camps in Thailand resulted in a number of minor clashes between the Thai army and the rebels. In December 1997 the Thai and Myanma Governments agreed jointly to establish a panel to determine the legitimacy of an estimated 98,000 Kayin refugees sheltered along Thailand's border with Myanmar. In the same month, relief agencies operating along the border accused the Thai military authorities of using oppressive tactics to encourage the refugees to return to Myanmar, although the Thai military had earlier denied reports of its involvement in the forced repatriation of Kayin refugees. In March 1998 the Thai Government announced plans for the forced repatriation of several hundred thousand Myanma immigrants working illegally in Thailand, in response to the economic crisis afflicting the country. In the same month one of the largest Kayin refugee camps along the Thai–Myanma border was destroyed in a cross-border attack by the pro-Government grouping, the Democratic Karen (Kayin)

Buddhist Organization. In March 1999 the Myanma Prime Minister, Senior Gen. Than Shwe, made an official visit to Thailand.

Relations between Thailand and Myanmar were placed under some strain in late 1999 when a group of armed Myanma student activists seized control of the Myanma embassy in Bangkok in early October, taking 89 people hostage and demanding the release of all political prisoners in Myanmar and the opening of a dialogue between the military Government and the opposition. All the hostages were released by the gunmen within 24 hours, in exchange for the Thai Government's provision of helicopter transport to give the hostage-takers safe passage to the Thai–Myanma border. The Thai Government's release of the hostage-takers angered the ruling military junta in Myanmar, prompting the country to close its border with Thailand. In November, in a further indication of a deterioration in relations between the two countries, Thai forces expelled thousands of illegal Myanma migrant workers from the town of Mai Sot on the Thai–Myanma border, despite threats made by Myanma government troops to shoot the returnees. Although the border was reopened to commerce in late November, relations between the two countries remained fraught.

In January 2000 10 armed Myanma rebels took control of a hospital in Ratchaburi, Thailand, holding hundreds of people hostage. The hostage-takers, reported by some sources to be linked to the Kayin insurgent group, God's Army (a small breakaway faction of the KNU—the main KNU denied any connection with the gunmen), issued several demands, including that the shelling of their base on the Thai–Myanma border by the Thai military be halted, that co-operation between Thai and Myanma government forces against the Kayins should cease, and that their people be allowed to seek refuge in Thailand. However, in contrast to its peaceful handling of the siege of the Myanma embassy in Bangkok in October 1999, the response of the Thai Government to this second hostage crisis (which raised doubts about Thailand's national security and provoked further criticism from both the Thai political opposition and the general population of the Thai Government's relative tolerance of Myanma dissident activity in Thailand) was severe: government forces stormed the hospital, killing all 10 of the hostage-takers and releasing all of the hostages unharmed. This uncompromising resolution of the incident was praised by the military Government in Myanmar, and was regarded by many observers as the signal of a broader campaign by the Thai authorities against dissident activity by ethnic Myanma opposition groups operating in Thailand.

In February 2001 a border incident erupted between Thailand and Myanmar after Myanma forces pursued rebels belonging to the Shan State Army (SSA) into the northern Thai province of Chiang Rai, prompting reprisals by Thai troops. Despite the agreement of a cease-fire, Thailand sealed its border with Myanmar, and the situation was aggravated by Myanmar's assertion that Thailand was assisting the SSA. In April officials belonging to a non-governmental organization in Thailand claimed that the number of refugees of Myanma origin in Thailand had been underestimated and that, as of early April, they totalled almost 131,000. In May the Minister of Foreign Affairs, Surakiart Sathirathai, visited Myanmar in an effort to resolve the ongoing border tensions, but with little success. In the same month the United Wa State Army (UWSA), a Myanma ethnic militia, captured Hua Lone Hill near Chiang Mai; Thai troops recaptured the hill following a four-day battle in which at least 20 members of the UWSA were killed. The Government later lodged a formal protest with the Myanma Government after its forces allegedly bombed a Thai outpost situated near the hill. The Myanma Government responded by accusing the Thai armed forces of having launched air strikes into its territory. The problems were exacerbated when an article appeared in a Myanma newspaper that the Thai authorities claimed was insulting to the monarchy. In June 2001, after repeatedly denying reports that he intended to visit Myanmar, Thaksin Shinawatra became the first Thai Prime Minister to visit Yangon since 1997. While the subsequent discussions succeeded in defusing the immediate tensions, the two sides failed to come to any firm agreement as to how they would overcome the problems affecting bilateral relations. In July the Minister of Defence, Chavalit Yongchaiyudh, also visited Myanmar, and the two countries agreed to work together to expedite the repatriation of refugees on the common border. In September Gen. Khin Nyunt of Myanmar visited Thailand on a trip considered by many to constitute a starting point for a new era of improved relations. In January 2002 a joint Thai-Myanma commission met for the first time since 1999 to discuss plans to establish a task force which would aid in the repatriation of illegal Myanma immigrants. Further talks were held in February, intended to facilitate bilateral co-operation in controlling the cross-border narcotics trade.

In March 2002 Thai-Myanma relations were placed under severe strain when Thai soldiers clashed with members of the UWSA in Chiang Mai. Following the incident, in which one Thai soldier and 12 UWSA guerrillas were killed, the Thai Government lodged a formal protest with Myanmar's ruling military junta. In April a bomb exploded on the so-called 'Friendship Bridge' linking the two countries, resulting in the deaths of at least seven people. Later in the same month the Vice-Chairman of Myanmar's ruling State Peace and Development Council (SPDC) visited Thailand to hold talks with the Government concerning drug-smuggling and the continued border tensions. However, in May fighting broke out along the joint border between Myanma government troops, together with their UWSA allies, and the SSA; the SPDC subsequently accused the Thai Government of supporting the SSA, following which it closed the shared border, owing to the deterioration of bilateral relations. In June masked gunmen dressed in a similar manner to members of the KNU opened fire on a Thai school bus travelling near the border, killing three children. The KNU denied responsibility for the attack and Prime Minister Thaksin declared that he did not believe the group to have been responsible. Meanwhile, following the commencement of a Myanma military campaign on the border, intended to reclaim outposts and camps in the country's Shan State, Thai troops fired across the frontier when two Thai soldiers were allegedly injured by Myanma shells. The Government denied that it supported Myanma insurgent ethnic militias but admitted that it had allowed refugees from Myanmar to cross into Thailand. Shortly afterwards Thaksin claimed that bilateral relations had deteriorated to a new low point and that only an apology from Myanmar would improve the situation. In August the Minister of Foreign Affairs stated that the two countries had agreed to hold talks in an effort to resolve the ongoing bilateral tensions; the joint border finally reopened in October. Relations continued to improve in early 2003 and, in February, Thaksin paid a visit to Myanmar, during which the possibility of bilateral co-operation to address the problems posed by the cross-border narcotics trade and illegal immigration were discussed.

Relations with Malaysia were adversely affected in November 1995 by the killing of two Thai fishermen by a Malaysian patrol vessel. In December an understanding was reached on the issue and it was agreed to establish a joint committee to resolve a long-standing dispute over fishing rights. Relations were also strained in early 1996 by Thai opposition to the Malaysian construction of a wall along the countries' common border. In late 1996 and early 1997 Thailand co-operated with Malaysia to prevent illegal Bangladeshi workers from entering Malaysia. Relations between the two countries continued to improve during 1998: by April, Prime Minister Chuan and his Malaysian counterpart, Mahathir Mohamad, had met five times in as many months to discuss bilateral issues. In January the Malaysian authorities arrested, and transferred to the Thai authorities, three alleged Muslim separatist leaders wanted in Thailand in connection with terrorist activities in the southern provinces of the country. In February 1997 Malaysia and Thailand established the Kolok river as the border demarcation between the two countries. In April 2001 responsibility for two bomb attacks in southern Thailand was attributed by the Government to a newly established separatist organization, Bersatu, which, the Government claimed, was seeking to establish a Muslim state in southern Thailand. The two countries agreed to co-operate to find those responsible. In the same month Prime Minister Thaksin paid an official visit to Malaysia during which the two countries discussed border demarcation issues and agreed that the planned construction of a gas pipeline between Thailand and Malaysia would proceed as originally intended. Relations remained cordial and, in December 2002, the cabinets of the two countries held an historical joint meeting, during which trade and security issues were discussed.

In November 1996 the Government approved a proposal for the establishment of a Joint Thai-Lao Border Committee. In December 1997 it was announced by the office of the UN High Commissioner for Refugees that the review of the status of the last remaining group of Laotian refugees at the Ban Napho refugee camp in the Nakhan Phanom province of Thailand was scheduled to be completed by January 1998, after which the refugees were to be either allowed to settle in a third country or repatriated. In September 1999 282 Laotian refugees who had been residing at the camp were compulsorily repatriated by Thai officials and the UN High Commissioner for Refugees after having been refused refugee status; a further 291 Laotian refugees were repatriated in December. In March 1999 the Laotian Prime Minister, Gen. Sisavat Keobounphan, made an official visit to Thailand. In August 2000 a border dispute arose between Thailand and Laos apparently attempted to assert sovereignty over all islands in the Mekong river, as it claimed was its right under the Siam-Franco treaty of 1926. The occupation by Laotian armed forces of the Mano I and Mano II islands took place during the demarcation of the river boundary (due to be completed by the end of 2000) between the two countries. In March 2002 a Thai court convicted 28 people, including 17 Laotian nationals, of charges relating to the dispute. Despite the existence of a bilateral extradition treaty, concluded in 2001, it was thought unlikely that Thailand would comply with a Lao Government request to extradite its citizens to Laos.

In February 1998 it was reported that, owing to the country's ongoing economic crisis, Thailand was to reduce financial aid to neighbouring countries, including Cambodia, Laos, Myanmar and Viet Nam. In October the Vietnamese President, Tran Duc Luong, paid an official visit to Thailand, the first visit to the country by a Vietnamese head of state since the establishment of diplomatic relations more than 20 years previously. At the 31st annual ASEAN ministerial meeting in July, Thailand's Minister of Foreign Affairs, Surin Pitsuwan, proposed the modification of ASEAN's long-standing policy of non-interference in the internal affairs of member countries in favour of a policy of 'flexible engagement'; however, the proposal met with a generally negative response from most other ASEAN members.

In 1999 Thailand contributed 1,500 troops to the multi-national peace-keeping force in the UN-administered territory of East Timor (now Timor-Leste), following the territory's vote for independence from Indonesia in a referendum held in August. The country also maintained a cordial bilateral relationship with Indonesia, affirmed when the Thai Prime Minister visited Jakarta in February 2002.

In December 2001 the Prime Minister paid an official visit to the USA. During his stay he held talks with US President George W. Bush and assured him that Thailand would remain a strong ally in the US-led war on terrorism in the aftermath of the September terrorist attacks (see the chapter on the USA). In response, the US President praised the Thai Government for its consistent support throughout the campaign.

Following the terrorist attack on the Indonesian island of Bali in October 2002 (see the chapter on Indonesia), the Thai Government increased security in the country owing to speculation that Thailand, and in particular the tourist resort of Phuket, might be the target of further regional terrorist activity. Evidence was discovered suggesting that southern Thailand had been one of the locations used by those responsible for planning the Bali attack. Meanwhile, several foreign governments issued advisories warning against unnecessary travel to the country. However, the Thai Government expressed its concern that such warnings were unnecessary and called for them to be rescinded.

Government

In December 1991 a new Constitution was promulgated, which provided for a National Assembly (comprising an elected House of Representatives and an appointed Senate) and a Cabinet headed by a Prime Minister. In June 1992 the National Assembly approved a constitutional amendment requiring the Prime Minister to be a member of the House of Representatives. In January 1995 the National Assembly approved a constitutional charter, which provided for a number of amendments; these included lowering the voting age from 20 to 18 years and reducing the membership of the Senate to two-thirds of that of the House of Representatives.

A new draft Constitution was promulgated on 11 October 1997 (see Constitution, below): enabling legislation for the new Constitution was completed within 240 days.

Defence

In August 2002 the Thai armed forces had an estimated total strength of 306,000: 190,000 in the army, 68,000 in the navy and an estimated 48,000 in the air force. Military service is compulsory for two years between the ages of 21 and 30. Paramilitary forces, including a volunteer irregular force, numbered 113,000. The defence budget was 78,600m. baht for 2002/03.

Economic Affairs

In 2001, according to estimates by the World Bank, Thailand's gross national income (GNI), measured at average 1999–2001 prices, was US $120,871m., equivalent to $1,970 per head (or $6,550 per head on an international purchasing-power parity basis). During 1990–2001, it was estimated, the population increased at an annual average rate of 0.9%, while gross domestic product (GDP) per head increased, in real terms, by an average of 3.3% per year. Overall GDP increased, in real terms, at an average annual rate of 4.2% in 1990–2001. According to official figures, GDP increased by 1.8% in 2001 and by 5.2% in 2002.

Agriculture (including forestry, hunting and fishing) contributed an estimated 8.6% of GDP in 2001. In that year 42.2% of the employed labour force were engaged in the sector. Thailand's staple crop and principal agricultural export commodity is rice (Thailand was the world's largest exporter of rice in 1996). Rice exports accounted for 2.4% of the total value of exports in 2001. Other major crops include sugar cane, cassava (tapioca), maize, natural rubber, pineapples, bananas and coconuts. Timber was formerly a major source of export revenue, but a ban on uncontrolled logging was imposed in 1989, following severe flooding as a result of deforestation; a reafforestation programme, initiated in the late 1980s, recommenced during 1993. Fisheries products and livestock (mainly cattle, buffaloes, pigs and poultry) are also important. Thailand is one of the world's largest exporters of farmed shrimp. During 1990–2001, according to the Asian Development Bank (ADB), agricultural GDP increased by an estimated annual average of 1.4%; the GDP of the sector increased by 4.9% in 2000, but declined by 10.1% in 2001.

Industry (including mining, manufacturing, construction and power) provided an estimated 42.1% of GDP in 2001. In that year 24.6% of the employed labour force were engaged in industrial activities. During 1990–2001, according to the ADB, industrial GDP increased at an annual average rate of 5.7%; the GDP of the sector increased by an estimated 5.2% in 2000 and by 4.4% in 2001.

Mining and quarrying contributed an estimated 2.5% of GDP in 2001: the sector engaged only 1.5% of the employed labour force in that year. Gemstones, notably diamonds, are the principal mineral export, accounting for 2.6% of the total value of exports in 2001. Natural gas and, to a lesser extent, petroleum are also exploited, and production of these fuels increased substantially from the late 1990s onwards. Tin, lignite, gypsum, tungsten, lead, antimony, manganese, gold, zinc, iron and fluorite are also mined. In 2001 licences had reportedly been granted to permit the exploitation of a large deposit of potash at Somboon; it is eventually expected to yield up to 2m. metric tons per year, making it the world's second largest potash mine. In late 2001 a new gold mine was opened in Pichit province, the first to have been opened since the country ceased gold production in 1996. During 1990–2001, according to the ADB, the GDP of the mining sector increased at an average annual rate of 6.9%. Mining GDP increased by an estimated 5.5% in 2000 and by an estimated 0.5% in 2001.

Manufacturing provided an estimated 33.5% of GDP in 2001. In that year 17.7% of the employed labour force were engaged in the sector. In 1999 manufacturing's contribution to export earnings was 80%. Textiles and garments and electronics and electrical goods (particularly semiconductors) constitute Thailand's principal branches of manufacturing. Other manufacturing activities include the production of cigarettes, chemicals, cement and beer, sugar and petroleum refining, motor vehicle production, rubber production and the production of iron and steel. During 1990–2001, according to the ADB, manufacturing GDP increased by an estimated annual average of 6.7%; the GDP of the sector increased by an estimated 6.0% in 2000 and by an estimated 5.0% in 2001.

Energy is derived principally from hydrocarbons. At the end of 2001 there were estimated proven gas reserves of some 360,000m. cu m, enough to sustain production at that year's level for less than 20 years. Estimated proven petroleum reserves were some 500m. barrels, enough to sustain production at 2001 levels for less than 10 years. In 2001 7.1m. metric tons of petroleum were produced and 16.3m. metric tons of natural gas. In 2001 petroleum accounted for 53.6% of total fuel consumption, natural gas for 30.2%, coal for 14.0% and hydroelectricity for 2.2%. Lignite is also exploited. Solar and wind energy account for about 1% of electric power. Thailand

remains, however, heavily dependent on imported petroleum and electricity. In 2000 approximately 86% of its petroleum requirements were met by imports. In February 1996 licences were awarded by the state-owned Electricity Generating Authority of Thailand to two companies to provide an additional generating capacity of 1,380 MW by 2000 under the Independent Power Producers programme, Asia's largest scheme for private-sector electricity supply. A further 2,000 MW were to be produced by independent producers by 2002 and an additional 4,000 MW by 2006. In 2001 imports of mineral fuels comprised 11.5% of the value of merchandise imports.

Services (including transport and communications, commerce, banking and finance, public administration and other services) contributed an estimated 49.3% of GDP in 2001; 34.5% of the employed labour force were engaged in the services sector in that year. In 2002 tourism was one of the principal sources of foreign exchange; 10,872,976 tourists visited Thailand in that year. Receipts from tourism totalled some US $7,119m. in 2000. It was feared that Thailand's tourism sector would be affected by the repercussions of the terrorist attack on the tourist resort of Bali, Indonesia, in October 2002. In the aftermath of the attack several foreign governments advised their citizens to avoid unnecessary travel to Thailand, owing to speculation that the country was vulnerable to the terrorist threat. During 1990–2001, according to the ADB, the GDP of the services sector expanded by an estimated annual average of 3.6%; the GDP of the sector increased by 4.0% in 2000 and by 2.3% in 2001.

In 2001 Thailand recorded a visible trade surplus of US $8,582m.; in the same year there was a surplus of $6,221m. on the current account of the balance of payments. In 2001 the principal source of imports (22.4%) was Japan; other major suppliers in that year were the USA, the People's Republic of China and Malaysia. The principal market for exports in 2001 was the USA (20.3%); other important purchasers were Japan, Singapore and Hong Kong. The principal imports in 2000 were machinery and transport equipment (particularly electrical and industrial machinery and parts, and road vehicles and parts), basic manufactures, petroleum and petroleum products and chemical products. The principal exports were machinery and transport equipment, food and live animals (particularly fish, crustaceans and molluscs), basic manufactures, chemicals and related products and clothing and accessories.

In 2002 there was a budgetary deficit of 80,615m. baht. Thailand's external debt totalled US $79,675m. at the end of 2000, of which $29,418m. was long-term public debt. In that year the cost of debt-servicing was equivalent to 16.3% of the value of exports of goods and services. The annual rate of inflation averaged 4.3% in 1990–2001. Consumer prices increased by 1.7% in 2001 and by 0.6% in 2002. In 2001 3.3% of the labour force were unemployed.

Thailand is a member of the Asian Development Bank (ADB, see p. 143), the Association of South East Asian Nations (ASEAN, see p. 146), the Colombo Plan (see p. 339) and the Asia-Pacific Economic Co-operation (APEC, see p. 139). In January 1993 the establishment of the ASEAN Free Trade Area (AFTA) commenced; the reduction of tariffs to between 0% and 5% was originally to be implemented by 2008 but this was subsequently brought forward to 2002. The target date for zero tariffs was advanced from 2015 to 2010 in November 1999. AFTA was formally established on 1 January 2002.

Thailand's emergence from the regional economic crisis precipitated, in 1997, by the collapse of the Thai baht, was mainly export-driven. In 2001 the deceleration of the global economy, in particular the economies of the USA and Japan, exacerbated by the September terrorist attacks on the USA, significantly slowed this recovery, as GDP increased by only 1.8%. In August 2001 fears that the Government was resorting to a protectionist economic policy were partially realized when legislation was approved restricting the limit on foreign ownership of Thai telecommunications companies to 25% from a previous limit of 49%. Some observers feared that such measures would damage investor confidence at a time when greater foreign direct investment was needed in order to exploit Thailand's highly competitive operating costs in such sectors as food-processing and plastics. In an attempt to reduce the country's substantial public debt (which was equivalent to almost 60% of GDP) and restore investor confidence, the Government implemented a programme of privatization, partially listing the state-owned Petroleum Authority of Thailand on the stock exchange in November 2001, in the first of a planned series of 18 sales. However, by late 2002 the indefinite postponement of several planned listings prompted speculation as to the extent of the Government's commitment to its reform programme. In December 2001 Prime Minister Thaksin Shinawatra rebuffed accusations that his Government was averse to encouraging foreign investment when his Cabinet approved a 'package' of tax incentives for foreign companies establishing bases in the country. However, the measures were criticized for their failure to address more long-term problems. In 2002 GDP rose by 5.2%, owing largely to increased domestic demand, stimulated by high levels of government spending. In January 2003, in a further attempt to encourage foreign investment, the Government announced its intention to repay earlier than the scheduled date of May 2005 an outstanding loan of US $4,800m. awarded by the IMF and other international donors in the aftermath of the 1997 economic crisis. Also in January 2003 a five-year 80,000m.-baht plan was introduced to build 1m. low-income homes. The initiative was intended to encourage growth in the construction industry and thus sustain domestic demand. From March 2003 it was feared that the US-led campaign to effect regime change in Iraq would adversely affect the performance of the Thai economy, owing to an increase in global petroleum prices and a possible slowdown in the US economy, Thailand's largest export market. The threat of regional terrorist activity also continued to deter foreign investment, while high levels of government spending contributed to an increasing budget deficit. The Central Bank forecast growth of 3.5%–4.5% in 2003.

Education

Education is officially compulsory for six years, to be undertaken between the ages of six and 11 years. In 1995 the Government announced that it would extend the period of compulsory education to nine years, beginning in 1996. Primary education begins at six years of age and lasts for six years. In 1996 total enrolment in primary education was equivalent to 87% of children in the relevant age-group. Secondary education, beginning at 12 years

of age, also lasts for six years, divided into two equal cycles. In 1996 total secondary enrolment was equivalent to 56% of children in the relevant age-group. In the same year the total enrolment at primary and secondary schools was equivalent to 71% of all school-age children. There were 20 state universities (12 of which were in Bangkok) and 26 private universities and colleges in 1995. In the same year enrolment at tertiary level was equivalent to 22% of the relevant age-group. Budgetary expenditure on education by the central Government was 222,989.8m. baht (21.8% of total spending) in the financial year ending 30 September 2002.

Public Holidays

2003: 1 January (New Year's Day), 16 February (Makhabuja*), 6 April (Chakri Day), 13–15 April (Songkran Festival), 1 May (Labour Day), 5 May (Coronation Day), 15 May (Visakhabuja*), May (Royal Ploughing Ceremony Day*), 1 July (Half Year Bank Holiday), July (Asalhabuja*), 14 July (beginning of Buddhist Lent*), 12 August (Queen's Birthday), 23 October (Chulalongkorn Day), 5 December (King's Birthday), 10 December (Constitution Day), 31 December (New Year's Eve).

2004: 1 January (New Year's Day), February (Makhabuja*), 6 April (Chakri Day), 13–15 April (Songkran Festival), 1 May (Labour Day), 5 May (Coronation Day), May (Royal Ploughing Ceremony Day*), May (Visakhabuja*), 1 July (Half Year Bank Holiday), July (Asalhabuja*), July (beginning of Buddhist Lent*), 12 August (Queen's Birthday), 23 October (Chulalongkorn Day), 5 December (King's Birthday), 10 December (Constitution Day), 31 December (New Year's Eve).

*Regulated by the Buddhist lunar calendar.

Weights and Measures

The metric system is in force, but a number of traditional measures are also used.

Statistical Survey

Source (unless otherwise stated): National Statistical Office, Thanon Larn Luang, Bangkok 10100; tel. (2) 281-8606; fax (2) 281-3815; internet www.nso.go.th.

Area and Population

AREA, POPULATION AND DENSITY

Area (sq km)	513,115*
Population (census results)†	
1 April 1990	54,548,530
1 April 2000	
Males	29,844,870
Females.	30,762,077
Total	60,606,947
Population (official estimates at mid-year)	
2001	62,914,000
Density (per sq km) at mid-2001	122.6

* 198,115 sq miles.

† Excluding adjustment for underenumeration.

REGIONS

(2000 census)

	Area (sq km)	Population	Density (per sq km)
Bangkok	1,565	6,320,174	4,038.4
Central Region (excl. Bangkok) .	102,335	14,101,530	137.8
Northern Region	169,645	11,367,826	67.0
Northeastern Region . . .	168,855	20,759,899	122.9
Southern Region	70,715	8,057,518	113.9
Total	513,115	60,606,947	118.1

PRINCIPAL TOWNS

(population at 2000 census)

Bangkok Metropolis*	6,320,174	Pak Kret . . .	141,788
Samut Prakan .	378,694	Si Racha . . .	141,334
Nanthaburi . .	291,307	Khon Kaen . .	141,034
Udon Thani . .	220,493	Nakhon Pathom . .	120,657
Nakhon Ratchasima	204,391	Nakhon Si	
		Thammarat . .	118,764
Hat Yai . . .	185,557	Thanya Buri . .	113,818
Chon Buri. . .	182,641	Surat Thani . .	111,276
Chiang Mai . .	167,776	Rayong . . .	106,585
Phra Padaeng .	166,828	Ubon Ratchathani .	106,552
Lampang . . .	147,812	Khlong Luang . .	103,282

* Formerly Bangkok and Thonburi.

Mid-2001 (UN estimate, including suburbs): Bangkok 7,527,000 (Source: UN, *World Urbanization Prospects: The 2001 Revision*).

BIRTHS, MARRIAGES AND DEATHS*

	Registered live births		Registered marriages		Registered deaths	
	Number	Rate (per 1,000)	Number	Rate (per 1,000)	Number	Rate (per 1,000)
1993 . .	957,832	16.5	484,569	8.4	285,731	4.9
1994 . .	960,248	16.4	n.a.	n.a.	305,526	5.2
1995 . .	963,678	16.2	470,751	7.9	324,842	5.5
1996 . .	944,118	15.7	436,831	7.3	342,645	5.7
1997 . .	897,604	14.8	396,928	6.5	303,918	5.0
1998 . .	897,495	14.7	324,262	5.3	317,793	5.2
1999 . .	754,685	12.3	348,803	5.7	362,607	5.9
2000 . .	773,009	12.4	339,443	5.4	365,741	5.9

* Registration is incomplete. According to UN estimates, the average annual rates in 1990–95 were: Births 19.9 per 1,000; Deaths 5.7 per 1,000; and in 1995–2000: Births 19.6 per 1,000; Deaths 6.1 per 1,000 (Source: UN, *World Population Prospects: The 2000 Revision*).

Source: mainly Ministry of Public Health, Ministry of the Interior, Thailand.

Expectation of life (WHO estimates, years at birth): 68.9 (males 65.7; females 72.2) in 2001 (Source: WHO, *World Health Report*).

ECONOMICALLY ACTIVE POPULATION*
(million persons aged 15 years and over)

	1999	2000	2001
Agriculture, hunting, forestry and fishing	13.88	13.89	13.59
Mining and quarrying	0.64	0.45	0.47
Manufacturing	4.60	4.99	5.68
Electricity, gas, water and sanitary services	0.16	0.17	0.17
Construction	1.40	1.50	1.58
Trade, financing, insurance and real estate	4.76	4.89	4.49
Transport, storage and communications	1.01	0.97	1.02
Other services (incl. restaurants and hotels)	4.79	4.83	5.60
Total employed	30.66	31.29	32.17
Unemployed	2.06	1.93	1.75
Total labour force	32.72	33.22	33.92

* Excluding the armed forces.

Source: IMF, *Thailand: Selected Issues and Statistical Appendix* (September 2002).

Health and Welfare

KEY INDICATORS

Total fertility rate (children per woman, 2001)	2.0
Under-5 mortality rate (per 1,000 live births, 2001) . . .	28
HIV/AIDS (% of persons aged 15–49, 2001)	1.79
Physicians (per 1,000 head, 1995)	0.24
Hospital beds (per 1,000 head, 1995)	1.99
Health expenditure (2000): US $ per head (PPP)	237
Health expenditure (2000): % of GDP	3.7
Health expenditure (2000): public (% of total)	57.4
Access to water (% of persons, 2000)	80
Access to sanitation (% of persons, 2000)	96
Human Development Index (2000): ranking	70
Human Development Index (2000): value	0.762

For sources and definitions, see explanatory note on p. vi.

Agriculture

PRINCIPAL CROPS
('000 metric tons)

	1999	2000	2001
Rice (paddy)	24,172	25,608	26,954
Maize	4,286	4,397	4,470
Sorghum	142	148	145
Sweet potatoes	100	91	91†
Cassava (Manioc, Tapioca) .	16,507	19,064	18,270
Dry beans	249	233	240
Soybeans (Soya beans) . .	319	324	294
Groundnuts (in shell) . .	138	135	129
Coconuts	1,381	1,400	1,400†
Oil palm fruit	3,512	3,256	3,880
Kapok fruit	132*	138*	138†
Cabbages†	200	205	205
Tomatoes	219	236	236†
Pumpkins, squash, gourds† . .	210	210	210
Cucumbers and gherkins† . .	210	210	210
Dry onions	316	270	270†
Garlic	126	128	124
Other vegetables† . . .	1,217	1,244	1,244
Watermelons†	400	400	400
Sugar cane	53,494	59,436	60,042
Bananas†	1,720	1,750	1,750
Oranges†	320	325	325
Tangerines, mandarins, clementines, satsumas† . .	640	650	650
Mangoes	1,462	1,633	1,633†
Pineapples	2,372	2,287	1,979
Papayas†	119	119	119
Other fruits†	1,109	1,110	1,110
Tobacco (leaves)	79	74	74†
Natural rubber	2,199	2,346*	2,357*

* Unofficial figure.
† FAO estimate(s).

Source: FAO.

LIVESTOCK
('000 head, year ending September)

	1999	2000	2001
Horses	7	9	9*
Cattle	5,677	4,602	4,640
Buffaloes	1,912	1,900*	2,000*
Pigs	6,370	6,558	6,689
Sheep	39	37	43*
Goats	133	144	132*
Chickens*	230,000	232,000	190,000
Ducks	22,330	27,884	23,000*
Geese	226	233	500*

* FAO estimate(s).

Source: FAO.

LIVESTOCK PRODUCTS
('000 metric tons)

	1999	2000	2001
Beef and veal†	188	174	180
Buffalo meat†	60	51	52
Pig meat†	451	462	475
Chicken meat*	1,087	1,117	1,260
Duck meat	102	103*	105*
Cows' milk	465	495	530*
Hen eggs	496	515	530†
Other poultry eggs† . . .	280	293	293
Cattle hides (fresh)† . . .	44	44	44
Buffalo hides (fresh)† . .	7	6	6

* Unofficial figure(s).
† FAO estimate(s).

Source: FAO.

Forestry

ROUNDWOOD REMOVALS
('000 cubic metres, excl. bark)

	1999	2000	2001
Sawlogs, veneer logs and logs for sleepers	50	158	210
Other industrial wood*	2,848*	4,576	5,053
Fuel wood*	20,548	20,553	20,396
Total	23,446	25,287	25,659

* FAO estimates.

Source: FAO.

SAWNWOOD PRODUCTION
('000 cubic metres, incl. railway sleepers)

	1999	2000	2001
Coniferous (softwood)	41	17	18
Broadleaved (hardwood). . . .	137	203	215
Total	178	220	233

Source: FAO.

Fishing

('000 metric tons, live weight)

	1998	1999	2000
Capture	2,927.5	2,928.8	2,923.6
Sardinellas	185.9	187.0	187.8
Anchovies, etc.	157.2	160.5	158.8
Indian mackerels	151.0	152.2	152.6
Aquaculture	594.6	691.8	707.0
Giant tiger prawn	247.5	271.0	294.7
Total catch	3,522.1	3,620.6	3,630.6

Source: FAO, *Yearbook of Fishery Statistics*.

Mining

(production in metric tons, rounded, unless otherwise indicated)

	1999	2000	2001
Tin concentrates*	3,400	2,363	2,383
Tungsten concentrates*	54	54	92
Lead ore*	23,783	24,760	800
Zinc ore*	185,752	159,093	139,050
Antimony ore*	130	178	40
Iron ore*	122,633	100	50
Gypsum ('000 metric tons) . . .	5,005	5,830	6,191
Barite	76,092	56,180	23,559
Dolomite	485,393	625,127	871,308
Feldspar	626,415	542,991	710,543
Gemstones ('000 carats). . . .	1,267	928	1,071
Lignite ('000 metric tons) . . .	18,266	17,714	19,617
Fluorspar†	13,005	4,745	3,020
Manganese ore†	721	225	45
Crude petroleum (million barrels) .	12.4	21.1	22.6
Natural gas (million cu m) . . .	19,307	20,134	19,638

* Figures refer to the gross weight of ores and concentrates.
† Metallurgical grade.

Source: US Geological Survey.

Industry

SELECTED PRODUCTS
('000 metric tons, unless otherwise indicated)

	1999	2000	2001
Synthetic fibre*	696	735	727
Raw sugar.	5,630	6,447	4,865
Cement	25,354	25,499	27,913
Galvanized iron sheets	299	369	434
Pulp	854	917	n.a.
Petroleum products (million litres)	41,414	41,060	n.a.
Beer (million litres)	1,042	1,165	1,238
Integrated circuits (million pieces)	5,182	7,070	n.a.
Tin metal	17	17	n.a.

* Source: Asian Development Bank, *Key Indicators of Developing Asian and Pacific Countries*.

Sources: IMF, *Thailand: Statistical Appendix* (August 2001); and Bank of Thailand, Bangkok.

Finance

CURRENCY AND EXCHANGE RATES

Monetary Units
100 satangs = 1 baht

Sterling, Dollar and Euro Equivalents (31 December 2002)
£1 sterling = 69.55 baht
US $1 = 43.15 baht
€1 = 45.25 baht
1,000 baht = £14.38 = $23.17 = €22.10

Average Exchange Rate (baht per US $)
2000   40.112
2001   44.432
2002   42.960

Note: Figures refer to the average mid-point rate of exchange available from commercial banks. In July 1997 the Bank of Thailand began operating a managed 'float' of the baht. In addition, a two-tier market was introduced, creating separate exchange rates for purchasers of baht in domestic markets and those who buy the currency overseas.

BUDGET
(million baht, year ending 30 September)

Revenue	1999/2000	2000/01	2001/02
Tax revenue	723,611.1	783,809.3	815,920.6
Direct taxes	245,800.0	237,600.0	259,360.0
Personal income tax . . .	105,000.0	101,830.0	102,000.0
Corporate income tax . . .	135,000.0	125,770.0	145,360.0
Indirect taxes	477,810.9	546,209.3	556,560.6
Value-added tax.	n.a.	226,450.0	235,790.0
Specific business tax . . .	n.a.	22,440.0	16,200.0
Tax on petroleum and petroleum products . . .	64,750.0	67,000.0	67,200.0
Excise taxes	8,215.8	17,695.0	17,258.0
Consumption tax	86,973.2	99,524.0	97,376.0
Taxes on international trade .	72,234.0	98,625.0	104,100.0
Non-tax revenue	99,286.1	87,330.8	87,629.4
State enterprises	56,072.0	47,510.0	40,908.5
Other	28,288.4	23,960.8	35,731.1
Total	822,897.2	871,140.0	903,550.0

Expenditure	1999/2000	2000/01	2001/02
General governmental services . .	175,488.8	178,642.7	186,161.1
General public services . . .	42,672.2	44,338.2	52,275.2
Defence	76,421.5	76,445.7	77,207.4
Public order and safety . . .	56,395.1	57,858.8	56,678.5
Community and social services . .	374,840.7	382,398.2	425,846.8
Education	220,620.8	221,591.5	222,989.8
Health	63,501.2	65,041.2	72,769.7
Social security and welfare . .	46,101.1	51,562.1	70,781.0
Housing and community amenities.	37,165.5	37,494.1	52,984.2
Economic affairs and services . .	190,176.7	205,094.5	238,763.1
Agriculture, forestry, fishing and hunting	67,728.0	73,860.4	75,497.5
Transportation and communication	86,354.2	76,851.2	64,176.7
Others	29,041.3	46,932.4	91,628.0
Miscellaneous and unclassified items	119,493.8	143,864.6	172,229.0
Total	860,000	910,000	1,023,000.0
Current expenditure. . . .	635,585.1	679,286.5	773,714.1
Capital expenditure	217,097.6	218,578.2	223,617.0
Principal repayment	7,317.3	12,135.3	25,668.9

Source: Bureau of the Budget, Office of the Prime Minister.

INTERNATIONAL RESERVES
(US $ million at 31 December)

	2000	2001	2002
Gold*	645	686	869
IMF special drawing rights . . .	83	5	4
Foreign exchange.	31,933	32,350	38,042
Total	32,661	33,041	38,915

* Revalued annually on the basis of the London market price.

Source: IMF, *International Financial Statistics.*

MONEY SUPPLY
('000 million baht at 31 December)

	2000	2001	2002
Currency outside banks . . .	406.8	440.9	496.0
Demand deposits at deposit money banks	114.0	134.4	157.8
Total money (incl. others) . .	684.3	650.6	674.9

Source: IMF, *International Financial Statistics.*

COST OF LIVING
(Consumer Price Index; base: 1990 = 100)

	1999	2000	2001
Food (incl. beverages) . . .	166.9	165.1	166.2
Fuel and light	152.7	164.6	177.4
Clothing (incl. footwear). . .	152.8	154.3	155.9
Rent	126.3	126.1	125.8
All items (incl. others) . . .	153.2	155.6	158.1

Source: ILO, *Yearbook of Labour Statistics.*

2002 (base: 1995 = 100): All items 125.8 (Source: IMF, *International Financial Statistics*).

NATIONAL ACCOUNTS
(million baht at current prices)

National Income and Product

	1998	1999	2000*
Compensation of employees. . .	1,440,186	1,450,914	1,542,959
Operating surplus	2,030,906	2,005,769	2,149,228
Domestic factor incomes. . .	3,471,092	3,456,683	3,692,187
Consumption of fixed capital . .	679,148	703,867	728,287
Gross domestic product (GDP) at factor cost	4,150,240	4,160,550	4,420,474
Indirect taxes, *less* subsidies . .	476,207	471,582	484,251
GDP in purchasers' values . .	4,626,447	4,632,132	4,904,725
Net factor income from abroad . .	−160,044	−126,436	−76,874

— *continued*	1998	1999	2000*
Gross national product . . .	4,466,403	4,505,696	4,827,851
Less Consumption of fixed capital	679,148	703,867	728,287
National income in market prices	3,787,255	3,801,829	4,099,564

* Provisional figures.

Source: National Economic and Social Development Board.

Expenditure on the Gross Domestic Product

	1999	2000*	2001*
Government final consumption expenditure.	533,507	560,767	593,202
Private final consumption expenditure.	2,591,129	2,751,901	2,903,664
Increase in stocks	−16,693	31,853	35,175
Gross fixed capital formation . .	966,343	1,082,651	1,188,965
Statistical discrepancy . . .	−25,114	50,148	69,657
Total domestic expenditure. .	4,049,172	4,477,320	4,788,663
Exports of goods and services . .	2,703,308	3,289,675	3,379,634
Less Imports of goods and services	2,120,348	2,862,270	3,070,655
GDP in purchasers' values . .	4,632,132	4,904,725	5,099,642

* Provisional figures.

Sources: National Economic and Social Development Board and Asian Development Bank, *Key Indicators of Developing Asian and Pacific Countries.*

Gross Domestic Product by Economic Activity

	1999	2000*	2001*
Agriculture, forestry and fishing.	497,149	504,513	436,160
Mining and quarrying	87,352	116,798	125,869
Manufacturing	1,446,554	1,570,842	1,706,695
Construction	166,332	150,333	148,996
Electricity and water	130,378	146,155	167,850
Transport and communications .	376,777	396,667	410,701
Wholesale and retail trade, restaurants and hotels . . .	743,185	784,478	875,850
Banking, insurance and real estate services	164,109	157,306	319,623
Ownership of dwellings . . .	123,101	125,008	
Public administration and defence	204,102	212,515	229,425
Other services	693,093	740,110	678,473
GDP in purchasers' values . .	4,632,132	4,904,725	5,099,642

* Provisional figures.

Sources: National Economic and Social Development Board and Asian Development Bank, *Key Indicators of Developing Asian and Pacific Countries.*

BALANCE OF PAYMENTS
(US $ million)

	1999	2000	2001
Exports of goods f.o.b.	56,775	67,894	63,202
Imports of goods f.o.b.	−42,762	−56,193	−54,620
Trade balance	14,013	11,701	8,582
Exports of services	14,635	13,868	13,024
Imports of services	−13,583	−15,460	−14,619
Balance on goods and services	15,066	10,109	6,987
Other income received	3,092	4,235	3,833
Other income paid	−6,083	−5,616	−5,200
Balance on goods, services and income	12,075	8,727	5,621
Current transfers received . . .	806	952	990
Current transfers paid . . .	−452	−366	−389
Current balance	12,428	9,313	6,221
Direct investment abroad . . .	−346	23	−162
Direct investment from abroad. .	6,213	3,366	3,820
Portfolio investment assets . . .	−2	−160	−287
Portfolio investment liabilities . .	77	−546	−932
Other investment assets . . .	−1,755	−2,203	250
Other investment liabilities . . .	−15,261	−10,914	−6,597
Net errors and omissions . . .	33	−685	161
Overall balance	1,388	−1,806	2,475

Source: IMF, *International Financial Statistics.*

External Trade

PRINCIPAL COMMODITIES
(distribution by SITC, US $ million)

Imports c.i.f.	1998	1999	2000
Food and live animals	1,993.3	2,019.4	2,068.1
Crude materials (inedible)			
except fuels	1,812.2	2,047.3	2,556.6
Mineral fuels, lubricants, etc.	3,479.5	4,879.3	7,606.7
Petroleum and petroleum products	3,428.9	4,775.5	7,371.8
Crude petroleum	2,905.4	3,897.1	6,108.5
Chemicals and related			
products	4,680.7	5,448.1	6,539.4
Organic chemicals	1,309.1	1,391.2	1,777.4
Basic manufactures	7,932.1	9,816.9	10,484.2
Iron and steel	1,944.4	2,728.7	2,809.0
Other metal manufactures	2,098.6	2,509.4	2,006.0
Machinery and transport			
equipment	18,489.5	21,675.9	27,392.6
Power-generating machinery and equipment	1,389.7	1,035.3	1,236.6
Machinery specialized for particular industries	1,126.2	1,219.7	1,872.0
Office machines and automatic data-processing equipment	2,165.8	2,567.7	3,821.1
Parts and accessories for office machines, etc.	1,846.5	2,138.1	3,125.3
Telecommunications and sound equipment	960.4	1,256.3	1,868.3
Other electrical machinery, apparatus, etc.	8,751.4	9,739.4	12,986.8
Switchgear, etc., and parts	1,623.0	1,522.9	1,835.0
Thermionic valves, tubes, etc.	4,910.4	5,928.1	8,365.8
Road vehicles and parts*	519.4	1,304.7	1,976.6
Other transport equipment	749.5	2,108.6	409.3
Aircraft, associated equipment and parts	605.9	1,809.4	330.5
Miscellaneous manufactured			
articles	2,757.8	3,011.1	3,548.4
Total (incl. others)	42,370.1	50,309.1	61,450.6

* Excluding tyres, engines and electrical parts.

Exports f.o.b.	1998	1999	2000
Food and live animals	9,460.1	9,687.7	9,662.1
Fish, crustaceans and molluscs	4,023.9	4,095.7	4,335.8
Fresh, chilled, frozen, salted or dried crustaceans and molluscs	1,754.8	1,648.3	1,865.0
Prepared or preserved fish, crustaceans and molluscs	1,875.8	2,016.0	2,057.9
Cereals and cereal preparations	2,309.5	2,165.9	1,860.3
Milled rice	2,050.1	1,906.9	1,590.3
Crude materials (inedible)			
except fuels	2,117.7	2,104.5	2,790.7
Chemicals and related			
products	2,391.2	2,942.4	4,039.4
Basic manufactures	6,396.9	6,917.5	8,157.8
Textile yarn, fabrics, etc.	1,786.2	1,833.1	1,976.5
Machinery and transport			
equipment	21,869.5	24,490.8	30,016.1
General industrial machinery, equipment and parts	1,504.3	1,747.5	2,066.5
Office machines and automatic data-processing equipment	8,042.2	8,211.8	8,790.4
Automatic data-processing machines and units	1,810.7	1,935.3	1,999.2
Parts and accessories for office machines, etc.	5,917.8	6,033.0	6,522.0
Telecommunications and sound equipment	3,091.3	2,997.1	4,014.4
Other electrical machinery, apparatus, etc.	6,694.3	8,153.5	10,891.5
Thermionic valves, tubes, etc.	3,169.2	4,031.1	5,876.3
Miscellaneous manufactured			
articles	8,947.8	9,075.9	9,954.7
Clothing and accessories (excl. footwear)	3,576.0	3,495.9	3,790.1
Total (incl. others)	53,583.5	58,423.1	68,786.7

Source: UN, *International Trade Statistics Yearbook*.

PRINCIPAL TRADING PARTNERS
(US $ million)

Imports c.i.f.	1999	2000	2001
Australia	977	1,160	1,380
China, People's Repub.	2,495	3,377	3,711
Germany	1,589	1,947	2,562
Japan	12,256	15,315	13,881
Korea, Repub.	1,770	2,165	2,121
Malaysia	2,512	3,344	3,078
Oman	1,060	958	1,264
Singapore	2,980	3,416	2,854
United Arab Emirates	872	1,766	1,529
USA	6,443	7,291	7,198
Total (incl. others)	50,350	61,923	62,057

Exports f.o.b.	1999	2000	2001
Australia	1,315	1,615	1,358
China, People's Repub.	1,861	2,806	2,863
Germany	1,459	1,640	1,568
Hong Kong	2,979	3,474	3,298
Japan	8,259	10,164	9,964
Malaysia	2,124	2,813	2,722
Netherlands	2,197	2,245	2,028
Singapore	5,073	5,997	5,287
United Kingdom	2,090	2,357	2,328
USA	12,667	14,706	13,246
Total (incl. others)	58,495	68,961	65,112

Source: Asian Development Bank, *Key Indicators of Developing Asian and Pacific Countries*.

Transport

RAILWAYS
('000)

	1991	1992	1993
Passenger journeys	86,906	87,769	87,183
Passenger-km.	12,819,567	14,135,915	14,717,667
Freight (ton-km)	3,365,431	3,074,786	3,059,043
Freight carried (metric tons)	7,990	7,600	7,498

Source: The State Railway of Thailand.

1994: Passenger-km ('000) 13,814,000; Freight (ton-km, '000) 3,072,000.

1995: Passenger-km ('000) 12,975,000; Freight (ton-km, '000) 3,242,000.

1996: Passenger-km ('000) 12,205,000; Freight (ton-km, '000) 3,286,000.

1997: Passenger-km ('000) 11,804,000; Freight (ton-km, '000) 3,410,000.

1998: Passenger-km ('000) 10,947,000; Freight (ton-km, '000) 2,874,000.

1999: Passenger-km ('000) 9,894,000; Freight (ton-km, '000) 2,929,000.

2000: Passenger-km ('000) 10,040,000; Freight (ton-km, '000) 3,347,000.

Source (1994–2000): UN, *Statistical Yearbook*.

ROAD TRAFFIC
('000 motor vehicles in use at 31 December)

	1999	2000	2001
Passenger cars	2,124	2,111	2,281
Buses and trucks	731	775	804
Vans and pick-ups	3,098	3,209	3,341
Motorcycles	13,245	13,817	15,236

Source: Ministry of Transport and Communications.

SHIPPING

Merchant Fleet
(registered at 31 December)

	1999	2000	2001
Number of vessels	551	561	568
Total displacement ('000 grt)	1,956.1	1,944.5	1,771.4

Source: Lloyd's Register-Fairplay, *World Fleet Statistics*.

International Sea-borne Freight Traffic
(Ports of Bangkok and Laem Chabang)

	2000	2001	2002
Goods loaded ('000 metric tons)	12,153	12,744	14,803
Goods unloaded ('000 metric tons)	20,055	21,912	24,755
Vessels entered	6,145	6,625	7,000

Source: Port Authority of Thailand.

CIVIL AVIATION

	1988	1989	1990
Kilometres flown	85,003,000	93,871,689	101,589,000
Passengers carried: number	6,282,438	7,394,199	8,272,516
Passengers carried: passenger-km ('000)	16,742,348	18,876,972	19,869,143
Freight carried: tons	157,964	165,502	199,399
Freight carried: ton-km ('000)	589,064	626,497	799,267
Mail carried: tons	7,636	8,893	9,287
Mail carried: ton-km ('000)	33,576	39,104	39,070

Source: Airport Authority of Thailand and the Department of Aviation.

Kilometres flown ('000): 153,000 in 1997; 158,000 in 1998; 163,000 in 1999 (Source: UN, *Statistical Yearbook*).

Passengers carried ('000): 14,236 in 1997; 15,015 in 1998; 15,950 in 1999 (Source: UN, *Statistical Yearbook*).

Passenger-km (million): 30,827 in 1997; 34,340 in 1998; 38,345 in 1999 (Source: UN, *Statistical Yearbook*).

Total ton-km (million): 4,460 in 1997; 4,682 in 1998; 5,184 in 1999 (Source: UN, *Statistical Yearbook*).

Tourism

FOREIGN TOURIST ARRIVALS

Country of origin	2000	2001	2002
Australia	326,003	366,468	358,616
China, People's Republic	704,463	695,372	763,708
France	240,568	238,550	254,610
Germany	387,904	407,353	412,968
Hong Kong	495,153	531,300	533,798
India	203,221	206,541	253,475
Japan	1,206,549	1,179,202	1,233,239
Korea, Republic	448,207	553,441	717,361
Malaysia	1,055,933	1,161,490	1,297,619
Singapore	659,539	669,166	687,982
Sweden	210,504	224,268	222,154
Taiwan	711,702	728,953	678,511
United Kingdom	480,303	522,117	574,007
USA	485,701	494,920	519,668
Total (incl. others)	9,578,826	10,132,509	10,872,976

Receipts from tourism (million baht): 220,754 in 1997; 242,177 in 1998; 269,882 in 1999.

Source: Tourism Authority of Thailand.

2000: Receipts from tourism (US $ million) 7,119 (Source: World Tourism Organization).

Communications Media

	1999	2000	2001
Television receivers ('000 in use)	16,700	17,200	n.a.
Telephones ('000 main lines in use)	5,215.6	5,591.1	5,973.5
Mobile cellular telephones ('000 subscribers)	2,339.4	3,056.0	7,550.0
Personal computers ('000 in use)	1,382.4	1,471.0	1,700.0
Internet users ('000)	950	2,300	3,536

Source: International Telecommunication Union.

Radio receivers ('000 in use): 13,959 in 1997.

Facsimile machines ('000 in use): 150 in 1997.

Book production (titles, excluding pamphlets): 8,142 in 1996.

Daily newspapers: 35 (with average circulation of 2,766,000 copies) in 1994; 35 (with average circulation of 2,700,000* copies) in 1995; 30 (with average circulation of 3,808,000 copies) in 1996.

Non-daily newspapers: 280 in 1995; 320 in 1996.
* Provisional.

Sources: UNESCO, *Statistical Yearbook*; UN, *Statistical Yearbook*.

Education

(2002)

	Institutions	Teachers	Students
Office of the Permanent Secretary	—	1,720	—
Religious Affairs Department	16,006	—	1,258,201
Non-Formal Education Department	998	2,777	2,364,879
Physical Education Department	27	1,673	24,902
Fine Arts Department	16	1,146	10,416
General Education Department	2,668	125,797	2,590,392
Vocational Education Department	413	17,679	592,406
Rajamangala Institute of Technology	55	4,718	92,179
Office of the National Primary Education Commission	30,476	344,581	6,633,809
Office of the Private Education Commission	7,258	854	2,049,150
Office of Rajabhat Institutes Council	41	7,522	275,737
Mahachulalongkornrajavidyalaya University	25	—	9,292
Mahamakut Buddhist University	8	—	5,765
Mahidol Withayanuson School	1	—	877
Total (incl. others)	57,991	508,467	15,872,418

Source: Office of the Permanent Secretary, Ministry of Education.

Adult literacy rate (UNESCO estimates): 95.5% (males 97.1%; females 93.9%) in 2000 (Source: UN Development Programme, *Human Development Report*).

Directory

The Constitution

On 27 September 1997 the National Assembly approved a new Constitution, which was endorsed by the King and promulgated on 11 October. The main provisions are summarized below.

GENERAL PROVISIONS

Sovereignty resides in the people. The King as Head of State exercises power through the National Assembly, the Council of Ministers (Cabinet) and the Courts in accordance with the provisions of the Constitution. The human dignity, rights and liberty of the people shall be protected. The people, irrespective of their origin, sex or religion, shall enjoy equal protection under the Constitution. The Constitution is the supreme law of the State.

THE KING

The King is a Buddhist and upholder of religions. He holds the position of Head of the Thai Armed Forces. He selects and appoints qualified persons to be the President of the Privy Council and not more than 18 Privy Councillors to constitute the Privy Council. The Privy Council has a duty to render such advice to the King on all matters pertaining to His functions as He may consult. Whenever the King is absent from the Kingdom or unable to perform His functions, He will appoint a Regent. For the purposes of maintaining national or public safety or national economic security, or averting public calamity, the King may issue an Emergency Decree which shall have the force of an Act.

RIGHTS, LIBERTIES AND DUTIES OF THE THAI PEOPLE

All persons are equal before the law and shall enjoy equal protection under the law. Men and women shall enjoy equal rights. Unjust discrimination against a person on the grounds of origin, race, language, sex, age, physical or health condition, personal status, economic or social standing, religious belief, education or constitutionally political view, shall not be permitted. A person shall enjoy full liberty to profess a religion, a religious sect or creed, and observe religious precepts or exercise a form of worship in accordance with his or her belief, provided that it is not contrary to his or her civic duty, public order or good morals. A person shall enjoy the liberty to express his or her opinion, make speeches, write, print, publicize, and make expression by other means. A person shall enjoy an equal right to receive the fundamental education for the duration of not less than 12 years which shall be provided by the State without charge. A person shall enjoy the liberty to assemble peacefully and without arms, to unite and form an association, a union, league, cooperative, farmer group, private organization or any other group, and to unite and form a political party. A person shall enjoy an equal right to receive standard public health service, and the indigent shall have the right to receive free medical treatment from public health centres of the State. Every person shall have a duty to exercise his or her right to vote at an election. Failure to vote will result in the withdrawal of the right to vote as provided by law.

THE NATIONAL ASSEMBLY

The National Assembly consists of the House of Representatives and the Senate. The President of the House of Representatives is President of the National Assembly. The President of the Senate is Vice-President of the National Assembly. A bill approved by the National Assembly is presented by the Prime Minister to the King to be signed within 20 days from the date of receipt, and shall come into force upon its publication in the Government Gazette. If the King refuses his assent, the National Assembly must re-deliberate such bill. If the National Assembly resolves to reaffirm the bill with a two-thirds' majority, the Prime Minister shall present such bill to the King for signature once again. If the King does not sign and return the bill within 30 days, the Prime Minister shall cause the bill to be promulgated as an Act in the Government Gazette as if the King had signed it.

The House of Representatives consists of 500 members, 100 of whom are from the election on a party-list basis and 400 of whom are from the election on a constituency basis. Election is by direct suffrage and secret ballot. The list of any political party receiving votes of less than 5% of the total number of votes throughout the country shall be regarded as one for which no person listed therein is elected and such votes shall not be reckoned in the determination of the proportional number of the members of the House of Representatives. A person seeking election to the House of Representatives must be of Thai nationality by birth, be not less than 25 years of age, have graduated with not lower than a Bachelor's degree or its equivalent, except for the case of having been a member of the House of Representatives or a Senator before, and be a member of any and only one political party, for a consecutive period of not less than 90 days, up to the date of applying for candidacy in an election. The term of the House of Representatives is four years from the election day. The King has the prerogative power to dissolve the House of Representatives for a new election of members of the House. Members of the House may not renounce their party affiliation without resigning their seats.

The Senate consists of 200 members, elected by direct suffrage and secret ballot. A person seeking election to the Senate must be of Thai nationality by birth, of not less than 40 years of age, and have graduated with not lower than a Bachelor's degree or its equivalent. The term of the Senate is six years as from the election day.

When it is necessary for the interests of the State, the King may convoke an extraordinary session of the National Assembly.

The Election Commission consists of a Chairman and four other Commissioners appointed, by the King with the advice of the Senate, from persons of apparent political impartiality and integrity. Election Commissioners shall hold office for a term of seven years.

The National Human Rights Commission consists of a President and 10 other members appointed, by the King with the advice of the Senate, from persons having apparent knowledge and experiences in the protection of rights and liberties of the people. The term of office of members of the National Human Rights Commission is six years. The National Human Rights Commission has the duty to examine and report the commission or omission of acts which violate human rights or which do not comply with obligations under international treaties to which Thailand is a party.

THE COUNCIL OF MINISTERS

The King appoints the Prime Minister and not more than 35 other Ministers to constitute the Council of Ministers (Cabinet) having the duties to carry out the administration of state affairs. The Prime Minister must be appointed from members of the House of Representatives and must receive the approval of more than half the total number of members of the House. No Prime Minister or Ministers shall be members of the House of Representatives or Senators simultaneously. A Minister must be of Thai nationality by birth, of not less than 35 years of age and be a graduate with not lower than a Bachelor's degree or its equivalent.

The State shall establish the National Economic and Social Council to be charged with the duty to give advice and recommendations to the Council of Ministers on economic and social problems. A national economic and social development plan and other plans as provided by law shall obtain opinions of the National Economic and Social Council before they can be adopted and published.

LOCAL GOVERNMENT

Any locality which meets the conditions of self-government shall have the right to be formed as a local administrative organization as provided by law. A local administrative organization shall have a local assembly and a local administrative committee or local administrators. Members of a local assembly shall be elected by direct suffrage and secret ballot. A local administrative committee or local administrators shall be directly elected by the people or by the approval of a local assembly. Members of a local assembly, local administrative committee or local administrators shall hold office for a period of four years. A member of a local administrative committee or local administrator shall not be a government official holding a permanent position or receiving a salary, or an official or an employee of a state agency, state enterprise or local administration.

AMENDMENT OF THE CONSTITUTION

A motion for amendment must be proposed either by the Council of Ministers or by not less than one-fifth of the total number of members of the House of Representatives or the National Assembly as a whole. A motion for amendment must be proposed in the form of a draft Constitution Amendment and the National Assembly shall consider it in three readings. Promulgation must be approved by the votes of more than half of the total number of members of both Houses.

The Government

HEAD OF STATE

King: HM King BHUMIBOL ADULYADEJ (King Rama IX); succeeded to the throne June 1946).

PRIVY COUNCIL

Gen. (retd) PREM TINSULANONDA (President), Dr SANYA DHARMASAKTI, M. L. CHIRAYU NAVAWONGS, Dr CHAOVANA NASYLVANTA, THANIN KRAI-VIXIEN, Rear-Adm. M. L. USNI PRAMOJ, Air Vice-Marshal KAMTHON SINDHAVANANDA, Air Chief Marshal SIDDHI SAVETSILA, CHULANOPE SNID-VONGS, M. R. ADULKIT KITIYAKARA, Gen. PICHITR KULLAVANIJAYA, AMPOL SENANARONG, CHAMRAS KEMACHARU, M. L. THAWISAN LADAWAN, M. R. THEP DEVAKULA, SAKDA MOKKAMAKKUL, PALAKORN SUWANNARAT, KASEM WATANACHAI.

CABINET
(April 2003)

A coalition of the Thai Rak Thai, Chart Thai and Chart Pattana.

Prime Minister: THAKSIN SHINAWATRA.

Deputy Prime Ministers: Gen. CHAVALIT YONGCHAIYUDH, KORN DAB-BARANSI, SUWIT KHUNKITTI, CHATURON CHAISAENG, WISSANU KREA-NGAM, PURACHAI PIEMSOMBOON, SOMKID JATUSRIPITAK.

Minister of Defence: THAMMARAK ISSARANGKUN NA AYUTTHAYA.

Minister of Labour and Social Welfare: SUWAT LIPTAPANLOP.

Minister of Finance: SUCHART JAOVISIDHA.

Minister of Culture: URAIWAN TIENGTHONG.

Minister of Education and of University Affairs: PONGPOL ADIR-EKSARN.

Minister of Foreign Affairs: SURAKIART SATHIRATHAI.

Minister of the Interior: WAN MUHAMAD NOR MATHA.

Minister of Justice: PONGTHEP THEPKANJANA.

Minister of Natural Resources and Environment: PRAPAT PAN-YACHARTRAK.

Minister of Energy: PROMMIN LERTSURIDEJ.

Minister of Agriculture and Co-operatives: SORA-AT KLINPRATUM.

Minister of Tourism and Sports: SONTHAYA KHUNPLUEM.

Minister of Transport: SURIYA JUNGRUNGRUANGKIT.

Minister of Commerce: ADISAI PHOTHARAMIK.

Minister of Public Health: SUDARAT KEYURAPHUN.

Minister of Industry: SOMSAK THEPSUTHIN.

Minister of Information and Communications Technology: SURAPONG SUEBWONGLEE.

Minister of Science and Technology: PINIT JARUSOMBAT.

Minister of Social Development and Human Security: ANURAK JUREEMAT.

MINISTRIES

Office of the Prime Minister: Government House, Thanon Nakhon Pathom, Bangkok 10300; tel. (2) 280-3526; fax (2) 282-8792; internet www.pmoffice.go.th.

Ministry of Agriculture and Co-operatives: Thanon Ratcha-damnoen Nok, Bangkok 10200; tel. (2) 281-5955; fax (2) 282-1425; internet www.moac.go.th.

Ministry of Commerce: Thanon Sanamchai, Pranakorn, Bangkok 10200; tel. (2) 282-6171; fax (2) 280-0775; internet www.moc.go.th.

Ministry of Culture: Bangkok; internet www.culture.go.th.

Ministry of Defence: Thanon Sanamchai, Bangkok 10200; tel. (2) 222-1121; fax (2) 226-3117; internet www.mod.go.th.

Ministry of Education: Wang Chankasem, Thanon Ratcha-damnoen Nok, Bangkok 10300; tel. (2) 281-9809; fax (2) 281-8218; e-mail website@emisc.moe.go.th; internet www.moe.go.th.

Ministry of Energy: Bangkok; internet www.energy.go.th.

Ministry of Finance: Thanon Rama VI, Samsennai, Phaya Thai, Rajatevi, Bangkok 10400; tel. (2) 273-9021; e-mail foc@vayu.mof.go.th; internet www.mof.go.th.

Ministry of Foreign Affairs: Thanon Sri Ayudhya, Bangkok 10400; tel. (2) 643-5000; fax (2) 225-6155; e-mail thaiinfo@mfa.go.th; internet www.mfa.go.th.

Ministry of Industry: 75/6 Thanon Rama VI, Ratchathewi, Bangkok 10400; tel. (2) 202-3000; fax (2) 202-3048; internet www.industry.go.th.

Ministry of Information and Communications Technology: Bangkok 10500; tel. (2) 238-5422; fax (2) 238-5423; internet www.ict.go.th.

Ministry of the Interior: Thanon Atsadang, Bangkok 10200; tel. (2) 222-1141; fax (2) 223-8851; internet www.moi.go.th.

Ministry of Justice: Thanon Ratchadaphisek, Chatuchak, Bangkok 10900; tel. (2) 502-8051; fax (2) 502-8059; internet www.moj.go.th.

Ministry of Labour and Social Welfare: Thanon Mitmaitri, Din-daeng, Huay Kwang, Bangkok 10400; tel. (2) 245-4782; fax (2) 246-1520; internet www.molsw.go.th.

Ministry of Natural Resources and Environment: Bangkok; e-mail monre@environnet.in.th; internet www.monre.go.th.

Ministry of Public Health: Thanon Tiwanon, Amphoe Muang, Nonthaburi 11000; tel. (2) 591-8495; fax (2) 591-8492; internet www.moph.go.th.

Ministry of Science and Technology: Thanon Phra Ram VI, Ratchathewi, Bangkok 10400; tel. (2) 246-0064; fax (2) 247-1449; internet www.moste.go.th.

Ministry of Social Development and Human Security: Bangkok; e-mail society@m-society.go.th; internet www.social.go.th.

Ministry of Tourism and Sports: Bangkok 10330; tel. (2) 214-0120; fax (2) 216-7390; internet www.mts.go.th.

Ministry of Transport: 38 Thanon Ratchadamnoen Nok, Khet Pom Prab Sattruphai, Bangkok 10100; tel. (2) 283-3044; fax (2) 280-1714; internet www.motc.go.th.

Ministry of University Affairs: 328 Thanon Sri Ayudhya, Bangkok 10400; tel. (2) 246-0025; fax (2) 245-8636; internet www.inter.mua.go.th.

Legislature

RATHA SAPHA
(National Assembly)

Woothi Sapha
(Senate)

A constitutional amendment was enacted in January 1995, limiting the membership of the Senate to two-thirds of that of the House of Representatives.

On 22 March 1996 the Prime Minister appointed a new Senate, comprising 260 members, only 39 of whom were active members of the armed forces. (Under the new Constitution promulgated in October 1997, the Senate was to comprise 200 directly elected members.) Elections to the new 200-member Senate were held on 4 March 2000; however, owing to the repeated incidence of electoral fraud, a second round of voting took place in April and a third round was held in a number of constituencies in June, by which time only 197 members had been elected to the new Senate, which had yet to take office pending the election of its three remaining members. A fourth round of polling was held in June/July, which resulted in the election of a further two members to the Senate. At a fifth round of voting held later that month the final member was elected to the Senate. The 200-member Senate was subsequently sworn in on 1 August 2000.

President of the Senate: Maj.-Gen. MANOONKRIT ROOBKAJORN.

Sapha Poothaen Rassadorn
(House of Representatives)

Speaker of the House of Representatives and President of the National Assembly: UTHAI PHIMCHAICHON.

General Election, 6 January 2001*

Party	Seats
Thai Rak Thai	248
Democrat Party	128
Chart Thai	41
New Aspiration Party	36
Chart Pattana	29
Seritham Party	14
Social Action Party	1
Independents	3
Total	**500**

*The new Constitution of 1997 provided for an increase in the number of deputies in the House of Representatives from 393 to 500. Of those who gained seats in January 2001, 400 contested the election in single-member constituencies and 100 through a party-list system.

Political Organizations

Chart Pattana (National Development): c/o House of Representatives, Bangkok; tel. (2) 668–9111; e-mail contact@chartpattana.or .th; internet www.chartpattana.or.th; f. 1992; Leader KORN DABBAR-ANSI; Sec.-Gen. SUWAT LIPTAPANLOP.

Chart Thai (Thai Nation): 1 Thanon Pichai, Dusit, Bangkok 10300; tel. (2) 243-8070; fax (2) 243-8074; e-mail chartthai@chartthai.or.th; internet www.chartthai.or.th; f. 1981; right-wing; founded political reform policy; includes mems of fmr United Thai People's Party and fmr Samakkhi Tham (f. 1991); Leader BANHARN SILAPA-ARCHA.

Democrat Party (DP) (Prachatipat): 67 Thanon Setsiri, Samsen Nai, Phyathai, 10400 Bangkok; tel. (2) 270-0036; fax (2) 279-6086; e-mail admin@democrat.or.th; internet www.democrat.or.th; f. 1946; liberal; Leader CHUAN LEEKPAI; Sec.-Gen. Maj.-Gen. SANAN KAJORNPRASART.

Ekkaparb (Solidarity): 670/104 Soi Thepnimit, Thanon Jaransanitwong, Bangpaid, Bangkok 10700; tel. (2) 424-0291; fax (2) 424-8630; f. 1989; opposition merger by the Community Action Party, the Prachachon Party, the Progressive Party and Ruam Thai; Leader CHAIYOS SASOMSAP; Sec.-Gen. NEWIN CHIDCHOB.

Muan Chon (Mass Party): 630/182 Thanon Prapinklao, Bangkok 10700; tel. and fax (2) 424-0851; f. 1985; dissolved after defection of leader Capt. Chalerm Yoobamrung to New Aspiration Party (NAP); re-formed in 2002 following merger of NAP with Thai Rak Thai; Leader Gen. VORAVIT PIBOONSILP; Sec.-Gen. KAROON RAKSASUK.

Nam Thai (Leadership of Thailand): c/o House of Representatives, Bangkok; f. 1994; business-orientated; Leader AMNUAY VIRAVAN.

Palang Dharma (PD) (Righteous Force): 445/15 Ramkhamhaeng, 39 Bangkapi, Bangkok 10310; tel. (2) 718-5626; fax (2) 718-5634; internet www.pdp.or.th; f. 1988; Leader CHAIWAT SINSUWONG; Sec.-Gen. RAVEE MASCHAMADOL.

Prachakorn Thai (Thai Citizens Party): 1213/323 Thanon Srivara, Bangkapi, Bangkok 10310; tel. (2) 559-0008; fax (2) 559-0016; f. 1981; right-wing; monarchist; Leader SAMAK SUNDARAVEJ; Sec.-Gen. YINGPAN MANSIKARN.

Seritham Party (Justice Freedom Party): c/o House of Representatives, Bangkok; f. 1992; merged with Thai Rak Thai in June 2001; Leader PRACHUAB CHAIYASARN.

Social Action Party (SAP) (Kij Sangkhom): 126 Soi Ongkarak Samsen, 28 Thanon Nakhon Chaisi, Dusit, Bangkok 10300; tel. (2) 243-0100; fax (2) 243-3224; f. 1981; conservative; Leader MONTREE PONGPANIT; Sec.-Gen. SUWIT KHUNKITTI.

Thai Party: 193 Thanon Amnauy Songkram, Dusit, Bangkok; tel. and fax (2) 669-4367; f. 1997; Leader THANABORDIN SANGSATHAPORN; Gen. Sec. Rear Adm. THAVEEP NAKSOOK.

Thai Freedom Party: c/o House of Representatives, Bangkok; f. Aug. 2002; Leader NIT SORASIT.

Thai Rak Thai (Thais Love Thais): c/o House of Representatives, Bangkok; tel. (2) 668-2000; fax (2) 668-6000; e-mail public@thairakthai.or.th; internet www.thairakthai.or.th; f. 1998; Leader THAKSIN SHINAWATRA.

Groupings in armed conflict with the Government include:

National Revolutionary Front: Yala; Muslim secessionists.

Pattani United Liberation Organization (PULO): e-mail p_u_l_@hotmail.com; internet www.pulo.org; advocates secession of the five southern provinces (Satun, Narathiwat, Yala, Pattani and Songkhla); Leader SIAMA-IL TAHNAM.

Diplomatic Representation

EMBASSIES IN THAILAND

Argentina: 16th Floor, Suite 1601, Glas Haus Bldg, 1 Soi Sukhumvit 25, Klongtoey, Bangkok 10110; tel. (2) 259-0401; fax (2) 259-0402; e-mail embtail@mozart.inet.co.th; Ambassador CARLOS FAUSTINO GARCÍA.

Australia: 37 Thanon Sathorn Tai, Bangkok 10120; tel. (2) 287-2680; fax (2) 287-2029; e-mail austembassy.bangkok@dfat.gov.au; internet www.austembassy.or.th; Ambassador MILES KUPA.

Austria: 14 Soi Nandha, off Thanon Sathorn Tai, Soi 1, Bangkok 10120; tel. (2) 287-3970; fax (2) 287-3925; e-mail bangkok-ob@bmaa .gv.at; Ambassador Dr HERBERT TRAXL.

Bangladesh: 727 Thanon Thonglor Sukhumvit, Soi 55, Bangkok 10110; tel. (2) 392-9437; fax (2) 391-8070; e-mail bdoot@samart.co .th; Ambassador HEMAYETUDDIN.

Belgium: 17th Floor, Sathorn City Tower, 175 Thanon Sathorn Tai, Tungmahamek, Sathorn, Bangkok 10120; tel. (2) 679-5454; fax (2) 679-5467; e-mail bangkok@diplobel.org; Ambassador PIERRE VAESEN.

Bhutan: 375/1 Soi Ratchadanivej, Thanon Pracha-Uthit, Huay Kwang, Bangkok 10320; tel. (2) 274-4740; fax (2) 274-4743; e-mail bht_emb_bkk@yahoo.com; Ambassador CHENKYAB DORJI.

Brazil: 34F Lumpini Tower, 1168/101 Thanon Rama IV, Sathorn, Bangkok 10120; tel. (2) 679-8567; fax (2) 679-8569; e-mail EMBRASbkk@mozart.inet.co.th; Ambassador MARCO ANTÔNIO DINIZ BRANDÃO.

Brunei: 132 Sukhumvit, Soi 23, Thanon Sukhumvit, Bangkok 10110; tel. (2) 204-1476; fax (2) 204-1486; Ambassador Dato' Paduka Haji MOHD YUNOS BIN Haji MOHD HUSSEIN.

Bulgaria: 64/4 Soi Charoenmitr, Sukhumvit 63, Wattana, Bangkok 10110; tel. (2) 391-6180; fax (2) 391-6182; e-mail bulgemth@asianet .co.th; Ambassador ROUMEN IVANOV SABEV.

Cambodia: 185 Thanon Ratchadamri, Lumpini, Bangkok 10330; tel. (2) 254-6630; fax (2) 253-9859; e-mail recanbot@loxinfo.co.tlt; Chargé d'affaires a.i. CHOEUNG BUN THENG.

Canada: Abdulrahim Bldg, 15th Floor, 990 Thanon Rama IV, Bangrak, Bangkok 10500; tel. (2) 2636-0540; fax (2) 2636-0565; e-mail bngkk@dfait-maeci.gc.ca; internet www.bangkok.gc.ca; Ambassador Dr ANDREW MCALISTER.

Chile: 10th Floor, Charan Tower, 19 Thanon Sukhumvit, Soi 43, Wattana, Bangkok 10110; tel. (2) 260-3870; fax (2) 260-4328; e-mail embajada@chile-thai.com; internet www.chile-thai.com; Ambassador LUIS PINOCHET SEPÚLVEDA.

China, People's Republic: 57 Thanon Ratchadaphisek, Bangkok 10310; tel. (2) 245-7043; internet www.chinaembassy.or.th; Ambassador YAN TINGAI.

Czech Republic: 71/6 Soi Ruamrudi 2, Thanon Ploenchit, Bangkok 10330; tel. (2) 255-3027; fax (2) 253-7637; e-mail bangkok@embassy .mzv.cz; internet www.mfa.cz/bangkok; Ambassador Dr JIŘÍ SITLER.

Denmark: 10 Soi Attakarn Prasit, Thanon Sathorn Tai, Bangkok 10120; tel. (2) 213-2021; fax (2) 213-1752; e-mail bkkamb@um.dk; internet www.denmark-embassy.or.th; Ambassador ULRIK HELWEG-LARSEN.

Egypt: 6 Las Colinas Bldg, 42nd Floor, Sukhumvit 21, Wattana, Bangkok 10110; tel. (2) 661–7184; fax (2) 262–0235; e-mail egyptemb@loxinfo.co.th; Ambassador TAMER ABDEL-AZIZ ABDALLA KHALIL.

Finland: Amarin Tower, 16th Floor, 500 Thanon Ploenchit, Bangkok 10330; tel. (2) 256-9306; fax (2) 256-9310; e-mail Sanomat .BAN@formin.fi; Ambassador HEIKKI TUUANEN.

France: 35 Soi Rong Phasi Kao, Thanon Charoenkrung, Bangkok 10500; tel. (2) 266-8250; fax (2) 236-7973; e-mail press@ ambafrance-th.org; internet www.ambafrance-th.org/; Ambassador LAURENT AUBLIN.

Germany: 9 Thanon Sathorn Tai, Bangkok 10120; tel. (2) 287-9000; fax (2) 287-1776; e-mail rk@german-embassy.or.th; internet www .german-embassy.or.th; Ambassador ANDREAS VON STECHOW.

Greece: Thai Wah Tower II, 30th Floor, 21/159 Thanon Sathorn Tai, Bangkok 10120; tel. (2) 679-1462; fax (2) 679-1463; e-mail bagremb@ksc.th.com; Ambassador NICHOLAS ZAFIROPOLOUS.

Holy See: 217/1 Thanon Sathorn Tai, POB 12–178, Bangkok 10120 (Apostolic Nunciature); tel. (2) 212-5853; fax (2) 212-0932; e-mail vatemb@mozart.inet.co.th; Apostolic Nuncio Most Rev. ADRIANO BERNARDINI (Titular Archbishop of Faleri).

Hungary: Oak Tower, 20th Floor, President Park Condominium, 95 Sukhumvit Soi 24, Prakhanong, Bangkok 10110; tel. (2) 661-1150; fax (2) 661-1153; e-mail huembbgk@mozart.inet.co.th; Ambassador SANDOR JOLSVAI.

India: 46 Soi Prasarnmitr, 23 Thanon Sukhumvit, Bangkok 10110; tel. (2) 258-0300; fax (2) 258-4627; e-mail indiaemb@mozart.inet.co .th; internet www.indiaemb.or.th; Ambassador L. K. PONAPPA.

Indonesia: 600–602 Thanon Phetchburi, Phyathai, Bangkok 10400; tel. (2) 252-3135; fax (2) 255-1267; Ambassador Air Chief Marshall (retd) SUTRIA TUBAGUS.

Iran: 602 Thanon Sukhumvit, between Soi 22–24, Bangkok 10110; tel. (2) 259-0611; fax (2) 259-9111; e-mail emb@mozart.inet.co.th; Ambassador RASOUL ESLAMI.

Iraq: 47 Thanon Pradipat, Samsen Nai, Phya Thai, Bangkok 10400; tel. (2) 278-5355; fax (2) 271-4218; e-mail iraqyia-bkk@hotmail.com; Ambassador NASSER HUSSAIN A. SWAILEM.

Israel: Ocean Tower II, 25th Floor, 75 Sukhumvit, Soi 19, Thanon Asoke, Bangkok 10110; tel. (2) 204-9200; fax (2) 204-9255; e-mail bangkok@israel.org; Ambassador GERSHON ZOHAR.

Italy: 399 Thanon Nang Linchee, Thungmahamek, Yannawa, Bangkok 10120; tel. (2) 285-4090; fax (2) 285-4793; e-mail ambitbkk@loxinfo.co.th; internet www.ambasciatabangkok.org; Ambassador STEFANO STARACE JANFOLLA.

Japan: 1674 Thanon Phetchburi Tadmai, Bangkok 10320; tel. (2) 252-6151; fax (2) 253-4153; internet embjp-th.org; Ambassador ATSUSHI TOKINOYA.

Kazakhstan: Suite 3E1–3E2, 3rd Floor, 139 Rimco House, Sukhumvit 63, Klongton Nua, Wattana, Bangkok 10110; tel. (2) 714-9890; fax (2) 714-7588; e-mail kzdipmis@asianet.co.th; Ambassador RASHIT RAKHIMBEKOV.

Korea, Democratic People's Republic: 14 Mooban Suanlaemthong 2, Thanon Pattanakarn, Suan Luang, Bangkok 10250; tel. (2) 319-2686; fax (2) 318-6333; Ambassador JO IN CHOL.

Korea, Republic: 23 Thanon Thiam-Ruammit, Huay Kwang, Bangkok 10320; tel. (2) 247-7537; fax (2) 247-7535; e-mail korea_emb_th@yahoo.co.kr; Ambassador CHOI HYUCK.

Kuwait: 100/44 Sathorn Nakhon Tower, 24th Floor, Thanon Sathorn Nua, Bangrak, Bangkok 10500; tel. (2) 636-6600; fax (2) 636-7363; e-mail hamood@mozart.inet.co.th; Ambassador KHALED MOHAMMAD AHMAD AL-SHAIBANI.

Laos: 520/502/1–3 Soi Sahakarnpramoon, Thanon Pracha Uthit, Wangthonglang, Bangkok 10310; tel. (2) 539-6667; fax (2) 539-3827; e-mail sabaidee@bkklaoembassy.com; internet www.bkklaoembassy.com; Ambassador HIEM PHOMMACHANH.

Malaysia: 35 Thanon Sathorn, Tungmahamek, Sathorn, Bangkok 10120; tel. (2) 679-2190; fax (2) 679-2208; e-mail mwbngkok@samart.co.th; Ambassador Dato' SYED NORULZAMAN SYED KAMARULZAMAN.

Mexico: 20/60–62 Thai Wah Tower I, 20th Floor, Thanon Sathorn Tai, Bangkok 10120; tel. (2) 285-0995; fax (2) 285-0667; e-mail mexthai@loxinfo.co.th; internet www.sre.gob.mx/tailandia; Ambassador JAVIER RAMON BRITO MONCADA.

Mongolia: 251 Soi Rojana, Thanon Sukhumvit 21, Klongtoey Nua, Wattana, Bangkok 10110; tel. (2) 640–8017–8; fax (2) 258–3849; e-mail mongemb@loxinfo.co.th; Ambassador LUVSANDORJ DAWAGIV.

Morocco: One Pacific Place, 19th Floor, 140 Thanon Sukhumvit, between Soi 4–6, Bangkok 10110; tel. (2) 653-2444; fax (2) 653-2449; e-mail sifambkk@samart.co.th; Ambassador SAMIR ARROUR.

Myanmar: 132 Thanon Sathorn Nua, Bangkok 10500; tel. (2) 233-2237; fax (2) 236-6898; e-mail mebkk@asianet.co.th; Ambassador U MYO MYINT.

Nepal: 189 Soi 71, Thanon Sukhumvit, Bangkok 10110; tel. (2) 390-2280; fax (2) 381-2406; e-mail nepembkk@asiaaccess.net.th; internet www.royalnepaleseembassy.org; Ambassador JANAK BAHADUR SINGH.

Netherlands: 106 Thanon Witthayu, Bangkok 10330; tel. (2) 254-7701; fax (2) 254-5579; e-mail ban@minbuza.nl; internet www.netherlandsembassy.in.th; Ambassador G. J. H. C. KRAMER.

New Zealand: M Thai Tower, 14th Floor, All Season's Place, 87 Thanon Witthayu, Lumpini, Bangkok 10330; tel. (2) 254-2530; fax (2) 253-9045; e-mail nzembbkk@loxinfo.co.th; Ambassador PETER RIDER.

Nigeria: 100 Sukhumvit, Soi 38, Prakhanong, Klongtoey, Bangkok 10110; tel. (2) 391-5197; fax (2) 391-8819; e-mail nigeriabkk@hotmail.com; internet www.embnigeriabkk.com; Ambassador Prince ADEMOLA O. ADERELE.

Norway: UBC II Bldg, 18th Floor, 591 Thanon Sukhumvit, Soi 33, Bangkok 10110; tel. (2) 261-0230; fax (2) 262-0218; e-mail emb.bangkok@mfa.no; internet www.emb-norway.or.th/; Ambassador RAGNE BIRTE LUND.

Oman: 82 Saeng Thong Thani Tower, 32nd Floor, Thanon Sathorn Nua, Bangkok 10500; tel. (2) 235-4222; fax (2) 639-9390; e-mail oman_embassy@pacific.net.th; Ambassador MOHAMMED YOUSUF DAWOOD SHALWANI.

Pakistan: 31 Soi Nana Nua, Thanon Sukhumvit, Bangkok 10110; tel. (2) 253-0288; fax (2) 253-0290; e-mail parepbkk@ji-net.com; Ambassador Maj.-Gen. (retd) MUHAMMAD HASAN AQAEL.

Panama: 14 Sarasin Bldg, 7th Floor, 14 Thanon Surasak, Bangrak, Bangkok 10500; tel. (2) 237-9008; fax (2) 237-9009; e-mail ptybkk@ksc.th.com; Ambassador XIOMARA JUDITH DE ARROCHA.

Peru: Glas Haus Bldg, 16th Floor, 1 Soi Sukhumvit 25, Khet Wattana, Bangkok 10110; tel. (2) 260-6243; fax (2) 260-6244; e-mail peru@peruthai.or.th; internet www.peruthai.or.th; Ambassador (vacant).

Philippines: 760 Thanon Sukhumvit, cnr Soi 30/1, Klongtan, Klongtoey, Bangkok 10110; tel. (2) 259-0139; fax (2) 259-2809; e-mail inquiry@philembassy-bangkok.net; internet www.philembassy-bangkok.net; Ambassador SONIA C. BRADY.

Poland: Sriyukon Bldg, 84 Sukhumvit, Soi 5, Bangkok 10110; tel. (2) 251-8891; fax (2) 251-8895; Ambassador JERZY SURDYKOWSKI.

Portugal: 26 Bush Lane, Thanon Charoenkrung, Bangkok 10500; tel. (2) 234-2123; fax (2) 238-4275; e-mail portemb@loxinfo.co.th; Ambassador JOÃO LIMA PIMENTEL.

Romania: 20/1 Soi Rajakhru, Phaholyothin Soi 5, Thanon Phaholyothin, Phayathai, Bangkok 10400; tel. (2) 617-1551; fax (2) 617-1113; e-mail romembkk@ksc.th.com; Ambassador CRISTIAN TEODORESCU.

Russia: 78 Thanon Sap, Bangrak, Bangkok 10500; tel. (2) 234-9824; fax (2) 237-8488; e-mail rosposol@cscoms.com; internet www.thailand.mid.ru; Ambassador YEVGENY OSTROVENKO.

Saudi Arabia: Sathorn Thani Bldg, 10th Floor, 82 Thanon Sathorn Nua, Bangkok 10500; tel. (2) 639-2999; fax (2) 639-2950; Chargé d'affaires HANI ABDULLAH MOMINAH.

Singapore: Rajanakarn Bldg, 9th and 18th Floors, 183 Thanon Sathorn Tai, Bangkok 10120; tel. (2) 286-2111; fax (2) 287-2578; e-mail singemb@pacific.net.th; internet www.mfa.gov.sg/bangkok; Ambassador CHAN HENG WING.

Slovakia: Thai Wah Tower II, 22nd Floor, 21/144 Thanon Sathorn Tai, Bangkok 10120; tel. (2) 677-3445; fax (2) 677-3447; e-mail slovakemb@actions.net; Ambassador MARIÁN TOMÁŠIK.

South Africa: The Park Place, 6th Floor, 231 Soi Sarasin, Lumpini, Bangkok 10330; tel. (2) 253-8473; fax (2) 253-8477; e-mail saembbkk@loxinfo.co.th; Ambassador BUYISIWE MAUREEN PHETO.

Spain: Diethelm Towers, 7th Floor, 93/1 Thanon Witthayu, Bangkok 10330; tel. (2) 252-6112; fax (2) 255-2388; e-mail embesp@bkk3.loxinfo.co.th; internet www.embesp.or.th; Ambassador JOSÉ EUGENIO SALARICH FERNÁNDEZ DE VALDERRAMA.

Sri Lanka: Ocean Tower II, 13th Floor, 75/6–7 Sukhumvit, Soi 19, Bangkok 10110; tel. (2) 261-1934; fax (2) 261-1936; e-mail slemb@ksc.th.com; Ambassador H. M. G. S. PALIHAKKARA.

Sweden: First Pacific Place, 20th Floor, 140 Thanon Sukhumvit, Bangkok 10110; tel. (2) 263-7200; fax (2) 263-7260; e-mail ambassaden.bangkok@foreign.ministry.se; internet www.swedenabroad.com/bangkok; Ambassador JAN NORDLANDER.

Switzerland: 35 Thanon Witthayu, Bangkok 10330; tel. (2) 253-0156; fax (2) 255-4481; e-mail vertretung@ban.rep.admin.ch; internet www.eda.admin.ch/bangkok_emb/e/home.html; Ambassador HANS-PETER ERISMANN.

Turkey: 61/1 Soi Chatsan, Thanon Suthisarn, Huaykwang, Bangkok 10310; tel. (2) 274-7262; fax (2) 274-7261; e-mail tcturkbe@mail.cscoms.com; Ambassador MUMIN ALANAT.

United Arab Emirates: 82 Seng Thong Thani Bldg, 25th Floor, Thanon Sathorn Nua, Bangkok 10500; tel. (2) 639-9820; fax (2) 639-9818; Ambassador SALIM ISSA ALI AL-KATTAM AL-ZAABI.

United Kingdom: 1031 Thanon Witthayu, Pathumwan, Bangkok 10330; tel. (2) 305-8333; fax (2) 255-8619; e-mail info.bangkok@fco.gov.uk; internet www.britishemb.or.th; Ambassador LLOYD BARNABY SMITH.

USA: 95 Thanon Witthayu, Bangkok 10330; tel. (2) 205-4000; fax (2) 254-2990; internet www.usa.or.th/; Ambassador DARRYL N. JOHNSON.

Viet Nam: 83/1 Thanon Witthayu, Lumpini, Pathumwan, Bangkok 10330; tel. (2) 251-3551; fax (2) 251-7203; e-mail vnembassy@bkk.a-net.net.th; Ambassador NGUYEN QUOC KHANH.

Judicial System

SUPREME COURT

Sarn Dika

Thanon Ratchadamnoen Nai, Bangkok 10200.

The final court of appeal in all civil, bankruptcy, labour, juvenile and criminal cases. Its quorum consists of three judges. However, the Court occasionally sits in plenary session to determine cases of exceptional importance or where there are reasons for reconsideration or overruling of its own precedents. The quorum, in such cases, is one-half of the total number of judges in the Supreme Court.

President (Chief Justice): SANTI THAKRAL.

Vice-President: UDOM FRUNGFOONG.

COURT OF APPEALS

Sarn Uthorn

Thanon Ratchadaphisek, Chatuchak, Bangkok 10900.

Appellate jurisdiction in all civil, bankruptcy, juvenile and criminal matters; appeals from all the Courts of First Instance throughout the country, except the Central Labour Court, come to this Court. Two judges form a quorum.

Chief Justice: KAIT CHATANIBAND.

Deputy Chief Justices: PORNCHAI SMATTAVET, CHATISAK THAMMA-SAKDI, SOMPOB CHOTIKAVANICH, SOMPHOL SATTAYA-APHITARN.

COURTS OF FIRST INSTANCE

Civil Court
(Sarn Pang)
Thanon Ratchadaphisek, Chatuchak, Bangkok 10900.
Court of first instance in civil and bankruptcy cases in Bangkok. Two judges form a quorum.

Chief Justice: PENG PENG-NITI.

Criminal Court
(Sarn Aya)
Thanon Ratchadaphisek, Bangkok 10900.
Court of first instance in criminal cases in Bangkok. Two judges form a quorum.

Chief Justice: PRADIT EKMANEE.

Central Juvenile and Family Court
(Sarn Yaowachon Lae Krobkrow Klang)
Thanon Rachini, Bangkok 10200; fax (2) 224-1546.
Original jurisdiction over juvenile delinquency and matters affecting children and young persons. Two judges and two associate judges (one of whom must be a woman) form a quorum.

Chief Justice: JIRA BOONPOJANASUNTHON.

Central Labour Court
(Sarn Rang Ngan Klang)
404 Thanon Phra Ram IV, Bangkok 10500.
Jurisdiction in labour cases throughout the country.

Chief Justice: CHAVALIT PRAY-POO.

Central Tax Court
(Sarn Phasi-Arkorn Klang)
Thanon Ratchadaphisek, Chatuchak, Bangkok 10900.
Jurisdiction over tax cases throughout the country.

Chief Justice: SANTI TAKRAL.

Provincial Courts (Sarn Changwat): Exercise unlimited original jurisdiction in all civil and criminal matters, including bankruptcy, within their own district, which is generally the province itself. Two judges form a quorum. At each of the five Provincial Courts in the south of Thailand (i.e. Pattani, Yala, Betong, Satun and Narathiwat) where the majority of the population are Muslims, there are two Dato Yutithum or Kadis (Muslim judges). A Kadi sits with two trial judges in order to administer *Shari'a* (Islamic) laws and usages in civil cases involving family and inheritance where all parties concerned are Muslims. Questions on Islamic laws and usages which are interpreted by a Kadi are final.

Thon Buri Civil Court (Sarn Pang Thon Buri): Civil jurisdiction over nine districts of metropolitan Bangkok.

Thon Buri Criminal Court (Sarn Aya Thon Buri): Criminal jurisdiction over nine districts of metropolitan Bangkok.

South Bangkok Civil Court (Sarn Pang Krungthep Tai): Civil jurisdiction over southern districts of Bangkok.

South Bangkok Criminal Court (Sarn Aya Krungthep Tai): Criminal jurisdiction over southern districts of Bangkok.

Magistrates' Courts (Sarn Kwaeng): Adjudicate in minor cases with minimum formality and expense. Judges sit singly.

Religion

Buddhism is the predominant religion, professed by more than 95% of Thailand's total population. About 4% of the population are Muslims, being ethnic Malays, mainly in the south. Most of the immigrant Chinese are Confucians. The Christians number about 305,000, of whom about 75% are Roman Catholic, mainly in Bangkok and northern Thailand. Brahmins, Hindus and Sikhs number about 85,000.

BUDDHISM

Sangha Supreme Council
The Religious Affairs Dept, Thanon Ratchadamnoen Nok, Bangkok 10300; tel. (2) 281-6080; fax (2) 281-5415.
Governing body of Thailand's 350,000 monks, novices and nuns.

Supreme Patriarch of Thailand: SOMDEJ PHRA YANSANGWARA.

The Buddhist Association of Thailand: 41 Thanon Phra Aditya, Bangkok 10200; tel. (2) 281-9563; f. 1934; under royal patronage; 4,183 mems; Pres. PRAPASANA AUYCHAI.

CHRISTIANITY

The Roman Catholic Church
For ecclesiastical purposes, Thailand comprises two archdioceses and eight dioceses. At 31 December 2000 there were an estimated 273,147 adherents in the country, representing about 0.4% of the population.

Catholic Bishops' Conference of Thailand: 122/6–7 Soi Naak-suwan, Thanon Nonsi, Yannawa, Bangkok 10120; tel. (2) 681-5361; fax (2) 681-5370; e-mail cbct@ksc.th.com; f. 1969; Pres. Cardinal MICHAEL MICHAI KITBUNCHU (Archbishop of Bangkok).

Catholic Association of Thailand
57 Soi Burapa, Bangrak, Bangkok 10500; tel. (2) 233-2976.

Archbishop of Bangkok: Cardinal MICHAEL MICHAI KITBUNCHU, Assumption Cathedral, 40 Thanon Charoenkrung, Bangrak, Bangkok 10500; tel. (2) 237-1031; fax (2) 237-1033; e-mail arcdibkk@loxinfo.co.th.

Archbishop of Tharé and Nonseng: Most Rev. LAWRENCE KHAI SAEN-PHON-ON, Archbishop's House, POB 6, Sakon Nakhon 47000; tel. (42) 711718; fax (42) 712023.

The Anglican Communion
Thailand is within the jurisdiction of the Anglican Bishop of Singapore (q.v.).

Other Christian Churches
Baptist Church Foundation (Foreign Mission Board): 90 Soi 2, Thanon Sukhumvit, Bangkok 10110; tel. (2) 252-7078; Mission Admin. TOM WILLIAMS (POB 832, Bangkok 10501).

Church of Christ in Thailand: CCT Bldg, 13th Floor, 109 Thanon Surawong, Bangkok 10500; tel. (2) 236-2900; fax (2) 238-3520; e-mail cctecume@loxinfo.co.th; f. 1934; 129,935 communicants; Moderator Rev. Dr BOONRATNA BOAYEN; Gen. Sec. Rev. Dr SINT KIMHACHANDRA.

ISLAM
Office of the Chularajmontri: 100 Soi Prom Pak, Thanon Sukhumvit, Bangkok 10110; Sheikh Al-Islam (Chularajmontri) Haji SAWASDI SUMALAYASAK.

BAHÁ'Í FAITH
National Spiritual Assembly: 77/1 Soi Lang Suan 4, Thanon Ploenchit, Lumpini Patumwan, Bangkok 10330; tel. (2) 252-5355; fax (2) 254-4199; mems resident in 76 provinces.

The Press

DAILIES

Thai Language
Baan Muang: 1 Soi Pluem-Manee, Thanon Vibhavadi Rangsit, Bangkok 10900; tel. (2) 513-3101; fax (2) 513-3106; Editor MANA PRAEBHAND; circ. 200,000.

Daily News: 1/4 Thanon Vibhavadi Rangsit, Laksi, Bangkok 10210; tel. (2) 561-1456; fax (2) 940-9875; internet www.dailynews.co.th; f. 1964; Editor PRACHA HETRAKUL; circ. 800,000.

Dao Siam: 60 Mansion 4, Thanon Rajdamnern, Bangkok 10200; tel. (2) 222-6001; fax (2) 222-6885; f. 1974; Editor SANTI ÜNTRAKARN; circ. 120,000.

Khao Panich (Daily Trade News): 22/27 Thanon Ratchadaphisek, Bangkok 10900; tel. (2) 511-5066; Editor SAMRUANE SUMPHANDHARAK; circ. 30,000.

Khao Sod (Fresh News): Bangkok; Editor-in-Chief KIATICHAI PONG-PANICH; circ. 350,000.

Krungthep Turakij Daily: Nation Multimedia Group Public Co Ltd, 44 Moo 10, Thanon Bangna-Trad, Bangna, Prakanong, Bangkok 10260; tel. (2) 317-0042; fax (2) 317-1489; e-mail ktwebmaster@bangkokbiznews.com; internet www .bangkokbiznews.com; f. 1987; Publr and Group Editor SUTHICHAI YOON; Editor ADISAK LIMPRUNGPATANAKIT; circ. 75,882.

Matichon: 12 Thanon Thedsaban Naruban, Prachanivate 1, Cha-tuchak, Bangkok 10900; tel. (2) 589-0020; fax (2) 589-9112; e-mail matisale@matichon.co.th; internet www.matichon.co.th; f. 1977; Man. Editor PRASONG LERTRATANAVISUTH; circ. 180,000.

Naew Na (Frontline): 96 Moo 7, Thanon Vibhavadi Rangsit, Bangkok; tel. (2) 521-4647; fax (2) 552-3800; Editor WANCHAI WONG-MEECHAI; circ. 200,000.

Siam Daily: 192/8–9 Soi Vorapong, Thanon Visuthikasat, Bangkok; tel. (2) 281-7422; Editor NARONG CHARUSOPHON.

Siam Post: Bangkok; internet www.siampost.co.th; Man. Dir PAISAL SRICHARATCHANYA.

Siam Rath (Siam Nation): 12 Mansion 6, Thanon Rajdamnern, Bangkok 10200; tel. (2) 224-1952; fax (2) 224-1982; f. 1950; Editor ASSIRI THAMMACHOT; circ. 120,000.

Sue Tuakij: Bangkok; f. 1995; evening; business news.

Thai: 423–425 Thanon Chao Khamrop, Bangkok; tel. (2) 223-3175; Editor VICHIEN MANA-NATHEETHORATHAM.

Thai Rath: 1 Thanon Vibhavadi Rangsit, Bangkok 10900; tel. (2) 272-1030; fax (2) 272-1324; internet www.thairath.co.th; f. 1948; Editor PITHOON SUNTHORN; circ. 800,000.

English Language

Asia Times: 102/1 Thanon Phra Arthit, 5th Floor, Pranakorn, Bangkok 10200; tel. (2) 288-4160; fax (2) 288-4161; internet www .atimes.com; f. 1995; regional; business news; Editor PANSAK VINYARATN; Deputy Editor UWE VON PARPART.

Bangkok Post: Bangkok Post Bldg, 136 Soi Na Ranong, Klongtoey, Bangkok 10110; tel. (2) 240-3700; fax (2) 240-3666; e-mail editor@ bangkokpost.co.th; internet www.bangkokpost.net; f. 1946; morning; Editor VEERA PRATEEPCHAIKUL; circ. 49,378 (Dec. 1999).

Business Day: Olympia Thai Tower, 22nd Floor, 444 Thanon Ratchadaphisek, Huay Kwang, Bangkok 10310; tel. (2) 512-3579; fax (2) 512-3565; e-mail info@bday.net; internet www.bday.net; f. 1994; business news; Man. Editor CHATCHAI YENBAMROONG.

The Nation: 44 Moo 10, Thanon Bangna Trad, km 4.5 Bangna, Phra Khanong, Bangkok 10260; tel. (2) 317-0420; fax (2) 317-2071; e-mail info@nationgroup.com; internet www.nationmultimedia.com; f. 1971; morning; Publr and Group Editor SUTHICHAI YOON; Editor PANA JANVIROJ; circ. 55,000.

Thailand Times: 88 Thanon Boromrajachonnee, Taling Chan, Bangkok; tel. (2) 434-0330; Editor WUTHIPONG LAKKHAM.

Chinese Language

Kia Hua Tong Huan: 108 Thanon Suapa, Bangkok; tel. (2) 221-4182; f. 1959; Editor SURADECH KORNKITTICHAI; circ. 80,000.

New Chinese Daily News: 1022–1030 Thanon Charoenkrung, Talad-Noi, Bangkok; tel. (2) 234-0684; fax 234-0684; Editor PUSADEE KEETAWORANART; circ. 72,000.

Sing Sian Yit Pao Daily News: 267 Thanon Charoenkrung, Bangkok 10100; tel. (2) 222-6601; fax (2) 225-4663; e-mail singpau@ loxinfo.co.th; f. 1950; Man. Dir NETRA RUTHAIYANONT; Editor TAWEE YODPETCH; circ. 70,000.

Tong Hua Daily News: 877/879 Thanon Charoenkrung, Talad-Noi, Bangkok 10100; tel. (2) 236-9172; fax (2) 238-5286; Editor CHART PAYONITHIKARN; circ. 85,000.

WEEKLIES

Thai Language

Bangkok Weekly: 533–539 Thanon Sri Ayuthaya, Bangkok 10400; tel. (2) 245-2546; fax (2) 247-3410; Editor VICHIT ROJANAPRABHA.

Mathichon Weekly Review: 12 Thanon Thedsaban Naruban, Prachanivate 1, Chatuchak, Bangkok 10900; tel. (2) 589-0020; fax (2) 589-9112; Editor RUANGCHAI SABNIRAND; circ. 150,000.

Satri Sarn: 83/35 Arkarntrithosthep 2, Thanon Prachathipatai, Bangkok 10300; tel. (2) 281-9136; f. 1948; women's magazine; Editor NILAWAN PINTONG.

Siam Rath Weekly Review: 12 Mansion 6, Thanon Rajdamnern, Bangkok 10200; Editor PRACHUAB THONGURAI.

Skul Thai: 58 Soi 36, Thanon Sukhumvit, Bangkok 10110; tel. (2) 258-5861; fax (2) 258-9130; Editor SANTI SONGSEMSAWAS.

Wattachak: 88 Thanon Boromrajachonnee, Talingchan, Bangkok 10170; tel. (2) 434-0330; fax (2) 435-0900; e-mail rattanasingha@ wattachak.com; internet www.wattachak.com; Editor PRAPHAN BOO-NYAKIAT; circ. 80,000.

English Language

Bangkok Post Weekly Review: U-Chuliang Bldg, 3rd Floor, 968 Thanon Phra Ram Si, Bangkok 10500; tel. (2) 233-8030; fax (2) 238-5430; f. 1989; Editor ANUSSORN THAVISIN; circ. 10,782.

Business Times: Thai Bldg, 1400 Thanon Phra Ram IV, Bangkok 10110.

FORTNIGHTLIES

Thai Language

Darathai: 9-9/1 Soi Sri Ak-Sorn, Thanon Chuapleung, Tungma-hamek, Sathorn, Bangkok 10120; tel. (2) 249-1576; fax (2) 249-1575; f. 1954; television and entertainment; Editor USA BUKKAVESA; circ 80,000.

Dichan: 1400 Thai Bldg, Thanon Phra Ram Si, Bangkok; tel. (2) 249-0351; fax (2) 249-9455; Editor KHUNYING TIPYAVADI PRAMOJ NA AYUDHYA.

Lalana: 44 Moo 10, Thanon Bangna-Trad, Bangna, Bangkok 10260; tel. (2) 317-1400; fax (2) 317-1409; f. 1972; Editor NANTAWAN YOON; circ. 65,000.

Praew: 7/9–18 Thanon Arun-Amarin, Bangkoknoi, Bangkok 10700; tel. (2) 434-0286; fax (2) 433-8792; e-mail praew@amarin.co.th; internet www.amarin.com; f. 1979; women and fashion; Editorial Dir SUPAWADEE KOMARADAT; Editor NUANCHAN SUPANIMIT; circ. 150,000.

MONTHLIES

Bangkok 30: 98/5–6 Thanon Phra Arthit, Bangkok 10200; tel. (2) 282-5467; fax (2) 280-1302; f. 1986; Thai; business; Publr SONCHAI LIMTHONGKUL; Editor BOONSIRI NAMBOONSRI; circ. 65,000.

Chao Krung: 12 Mansion 6, Thanon Rajdamnern, Bangkok 10200; Thai; Editor NOPPHORN BUNYARIT.

The Dharmachaksu (Dharma-vision): Foundation of Mahamakut Rajavidyalai, 241 Thanon Phra Sumeru, Bangkok 10200; tel. (2) 629-1417; fax (2) 629-4015; e-mail books@mahamakuta.inet.co.th; internet www.mahamakuta.inet.co.th; f. 1894; Thai; Buddhism and related subjects; Editor WASIN INDASARA; circ. 5,000.

Grand Prix: 4/299 Moo 5, Soi Ladplakhao 66, Thanon Ladplakhao, Bangkhan, Bangkok 10220; tel. (2) 971-6450; fax (2) 971-6469; e-mail grandprix@grandprixgroup.com; internet www .grandprixgroup.com/gpi/maggrandprix/grandprix.asp; Editor VEERA JUNKAJIT; circ. 80,000.

The Investor: Pansak Bldg, 4th Floor, 138/1 Thanon Petchburi, Bangkok 10400; tel. (2) 282-8166; f. 1968; English language; busi-ness, industry, finance and economics; Editor TOS PATUMSEN; circ. 6,000.

Kasikorn: Dept of Agriculture, Catuchak, Bangkok 10900; tel. (2) 561-4677; fax (2) 579-5369; f. 1928; Thai; agriculture and agricul-tural research; Editor-in-Chief ORANAN LEKAGUL; Editor PANNEE WICHACHOO.

Look: 1/54 Thanon Sukhumvit 30, Pra Khanong, Bangkok 10110; tel. (2) 258-1265; Editor KANOKWAN MILINDAVANIJ.

Look East: 52/38 Soi Saladaeng 2, Silom Condominium, 12th Floor, Thanon Silom, Bangkok 10500; tel. (2) 235-6185; fax (2) 236-6764; f. 1969; English; Editor ASHA SEHGAL; circ. 30,000.

Motorcycle Magazine: 4/299 Moo 5, Soi Ladplakhao 66, Thanon Ladplakhao, Bangkhan, Bangkok 10220; tel. (2) 971-6450; fax (2) 971-6469; e-mail motorcycle@grandprixgroup.com; internet www .grandprixgroup.com/gpi/magmotor/motorcycle.asp; monthly; Publr PRACHIN EAMLAMNOW; circ. 70,000.

Saen Sanuk: 50 Soi Saeng Chan, Thanon Sukhumvit 42, Bangkok 10110; tel. (2) 392-0052; fax (2) 391-1486; English; travel and tourist attractions in Thailand; Editor SOMTAWIN KONGSAWATKIAT; circ. 85,000.

Satawa Liang: 689 Thanon Wang Burapa, Bangkok; Thai; Editor THAMRONGSAK SRICHAND.

Villa Wina Magazine: Chalerm Ketr Theatre Bldg, 3rd Floor, Bangkok; Thai; Editor BHONGSAKDI PIAMLAP.

NEWS AGENCIES

Foreign Bureaux

Agence France-Presse (AFP): 18th Floor, Alma Link Bldg, 25 Soi Chidlom, Thanon Ploenchit, Lumpini Patumwan, Bangkok 10330;

tel. (2) 650-3230; fax (2) 650-3234; e-mail afpbgk@samart.co.th; Bureau Chief PHILIPPE AGRET.

Associated Press (AP) (USA): Charn Issara Tower, 14th Floor, 942/51 Thanon Phra Ram IV, POB 775, Bangkok; tel. (2) 234-5553; Bureau Chief DENIS D. GRAY.

Jiji Tsushin (Jiji Press) (Japan): Boonmitr Bldg, 8th Floor, 138 Thanon Silom, Bangkok; tel. (2) 236-8793; fax (2) 236-6800; Bureau Chief JUNICHI ISHIKAWA.

Kyodo News Service (Japan): U Chuliang Bldg, 2nd Floor, 968 Thanon Phra Ram IV, Bangkok 10500; tel. (2) 236-6822; Bureau Chief YOSHISUKE YASUO.

Reuters (UK): Maneeya Centre Bldg, 518/5 Thanon Ploenchit, 10330 Bangkok; tel. (2) 637-5500; Man. (Myanmar, Thailand and Indo-China) GRAHAM D. SPENCER.

United Press International (UPI) (USA): U Chuliang Bldg, 968 Thanon Phra Ram IV, Bangkok; tel. (2) 238-5244; Bureau Chief JOHN B. HAIL.

Viet Nam News Agency (VNA): 3/81 Soi Chokchai Ruamit, Bangkok; Bureau Chief NGUYEN VU QUANG.

Xinhua (New China) News Agency (People's Republic of China): Room 407, Capital Mansion, 1371 Thanon Phaholyothin, Saphan Kwai, Bangkok 10400; tel. and fax (2) 271-1413; Chief Correspondent YU ZUNCHENG.

PRESS ASSOCIATIONS

Confederation of Thai Journalists: 55 Mansion 8, Thanon Ratchadamnoen Klang, Bangkok 10200; tel. (2) 629-0022; fax (2) 280-0337; internet www.ctj.in.th; Pres. SMARN SUDTO; Sec.-Gen. SUWAT THONGTHANAKUL.

Press Association of Thailand: 299 Thanon Ratchasima, Dusit, Bangkok 10300; tel. (2) 241-2064; e-mail webmaster@thaipressasso .com; internet www.thaipressasso.com; f. 1941; Pres. PREECHA SAMAK-KIDHAM.

There are also regional press organizations and journalists' organizations.

Publishers

Advance Media: 1400 Rama IV Shopping Centre, Klongtoey, Bangkok 10110; tel. (2) 249-0358; Man. PRASERTSAK SIVASAHONG.

Bhannakij Trading: 34 Thanon Nakornsawan, Bangkok 10100; tel. (2) 282-5520; fax (2) 282-0076; Thai fiction, school textbooks; Man. SOMSAK TECHAKASHEM.

Chalermnit Press: 108 Thanon Sukhumvit, Soi 53, Bangkok 10110; tel. (2) 662-6264; fax (2) 662-6265; e-mail chalermnit@ hotmail.com; internet www.chalermnit.com; f. 1937; dictionaries, history, literature, guides to Thai language, works on Thailand and South-East Asia; Man. Dir Dr PARICHART (JUMSAI) SUKSONGKROH.

Dhamabuja: 5/1–2 Thanon Asadang, Bangkok; religious; Man. VIROCHANA SIRI-ATH.

Graphic Art Publishing: 105/19–2 Thanon Naret, Bangkok 10500; tel. (2) 233-0302; f. 1972; textbooks, science fiction, photography; CEO Mrs ANGKANA SAJJARAKTRAKUL.

Prae Pittaya Ltd: POB 914, 716–718 Wangburabha, Bangkok; tel. (2) 221-4283; general Thai books; Man. CHIT PRAEPANICH.

Praphansarn: Siam Sq., Soi 2, Thanon Phra Ram I, Bangkok; tel. (2) 251-2342; e-mail editor@praphansarn.com; internet www .praphansarn.com; Thai pocket books; Man. Dir SUPHOL TAECHATADA.

Ruamsarn (1977): 864 Wangburabha, Thanon Panurangsri, Bangkok 10200; tel. (2) 221-6483; fax (2) 222-2036; f. 1951; fiction and history; Man. PITI TAWEWATANASARN.

Ruang Silpa: 663 Thanon Samsen Nai, Bangkok; Thai pocket books; Propr DHAMNOON RUANG SILPA.

Sermvitr Barnakarn: 222 Werng Nakorn Kasem, Bangkok 10100; general Thai books; Man. PRAVIT SAMMAVONG.

Silkworm Books: 104/5 Thanon Chiang Mai-Hot, M.7, T. Suthep, Muang, Chiang Mai 50200; tel. (53) 271-889; fax (53) 275-178; e-mail silkworm@loxinfo.co.th; internet www.silkwormbooks.info; f. 1991; South-East Asian studies.

Suksapan Panit (Business Organization of Teachers' Institute): 128/1 Thanon Ratchasima, Bangkok 10300; tel. (2) 811-845; e-mail ssp@suksapan.or.th; internet www.suksapan.or.th; f. 1950; general, textbooks, children's, pocket books; Pres. PANOM KAW KAMNERD.

Suriyabarn Publishers: 14 Thanon Pramuan, Bangkok 10500; tel. (2) 234-7991; f. 1953; religion, literature, Thai culture; Man. Dir PRASIT SAETANG.

Thai Watana Panit: 599 Thanon Maitrijit, Bangkok 10100; tel. (2) 221-0111; children's, school textbooks; Man. Dir VIRA T. SUWAN.

Watana Panit Printing and Publishing Co Ltd: 31/1–2 Soi Siripat, Thanon Mahachai, Samranrat, Pranakorn, Bangkok 10120; tel. (2) 222-1016; fax (2) 225-6556; school textbooks; Man. ROENGCHAI CHONGPIPATANASOOK.

White Lotus Co Ltd: 11/2 Soi 58, Thanon Sukhumvit, POB 1141, Bangkok 10250; tel. (2) 332-4915; fax (2) 311-4575; e-mail ande@ loxinfo.co.th; internet www.thailine.com/lotus; f. 1992; regional interests; Chief Exec. D. ANDE.

PUBLISHERS' ASSOCIATION

Publishers' and Booksellers' Association of Thailand: 947/158–159 Moo 12, Thanon Bang Na-Trad, Bang Na, Bangkok 10260; tel. (2) 744-0863; fax (2) 744-0873; e-mail pubat@usa.net; internet www.pubat.or.th; Pres. M. L. MANICH JUMSAI; Gen. Sec. PLEARNPIT PRAEPANIT.

Broadcasting and Communications

TELECOMMUNICATIONS

Post and Telegraph Department: Thanon Phaholyothin, Payathai, Bangkok 10400; tel. (2) 271-0151; fax (2) 271-3511; e-mail webadmin@ptd.go.th; internet www.ptd.go.th; Dir-Gen. SETHAPORN CUSRIPITUCK.

Advanced Info Service Public Co Ltd: 414 Thanon Phaholyothin, Shinawatra Tower I, Phayathai, Bangkok 10400; tel. (2) 299-5000; fax (2) 299-5719; e-mail callcenter@ais900.com; internet www .ais900.com; mobile telephone network operator; Chair. PAIBOON LIMPAPHAYOM.

Communications Authority of Thailand (CAT): 99 Thanon Changwattana, Laksi, Bangkok 10002; tel. (2) 506-3299; fax (2) 573-6507; e-mail prcat@cat.or.th; internet www.cat.or.th; state-owned; telephone operator; *de facto* regulator; scheduled for partial transfer to the private sector; Chair. SRISOOK CHANDRANGSU; Pres. and CEO DHIRAPHONG SUDDHINOND.

Samart Corpn Public Co Ltd: Moo 4, Software Park Bldg, 38th Floor, 99 Thanon Chaengwattana, Klong Gluar, Pak-kred, Nonthaburi 11120; tel. (2) 502-6000; fax (2) 502-6043; e-mail nikhila@ samartcorp.com; internet www.samartcorp.com; telecommunications installation and distribution; cap. and res 700m., sales 4,692m. (1996); Chair. PICHAI VASANASONG; Exec. Chair. CHAROENRATH VILAI-LUCK.

Telecomasia Corpn Public Co Ltd: Telecom Tower, 18 Thanon Ratchadaphisek, Huay Kwang, Bangkok 10320; tel. (2) 643-1111; fax (2) 643-9669; e-mail iroffice@asianet.co.th; internet www .telecomasia.co.th; telecommunications services; Chair. DHANIN CHEARAVANONT; Pres. and CEO SUPACHAI CHEARAVANONT.

Telephone Organization of Thailand (TOT): 89/2 Moo 3, Thanon Chaengwattana, Thungsonghong, Laksi, Bangkok 10210; tel. (2) 505-1000; internet www.tot.co.th; state-owned; telephone operator; *de facto* regulator; scheduled for partial transfer to the private sector; Pres. SUTHAM MALILA.

Thai Telephone and Telecommunication Public Co Ltd (TT&T): Muang Thai Phatra Complex Tower 1, 24th Floor, 252/30 Thanon Ratchadaphisek, Huay Kwang, Bangkok; tel. (2) 693-2100; fax (2) 693-2126; internet www.ttt.co.th; distributors of telecommunications equipment and services; Chair. DHONGCHAI LAMSAM; Pres. and CEO Dr PISIT LEEAHTAM.

Total Access Communications Public Co Ltd: Chai Bldg, 19th Floor, 333/3 Moo 4, Thanon Vibhavadi Rangsit, Ladyao Chatuchak, Bangkok 10900; tel. (2) 202-8000; fax (2) 202-8102; internet www .dtac.co.th; mobile telephone network operator; 71.6% owned by United Communication Industry Public Co Ltd; Chair. and Man. Dir BOONCHAI BENCHARONGKUL.

United Communication Industry Public Co Ltd: 499 Moo 3, Benchachinda Bldg, Thanon Vibhavadi Rangsit, Chatuchak, Bangkok 10900; tel. (2) 953-1111; fax (2) 953-0248; e-mail hr@ucom .co.th; internet www.ucom.co.th; telecommunications service provider; Chair. SRIBHUMI SUKHANETR; Pres. and Chief Exec. BOONCHAI BENCHARONGKUL.

BROADCASTING

Regulatory Authority

Radio and Television Executive Committee (RTEC): Programme, Administration and Law Section, Division of RTEC Works, Government Public Relations Department, Thanon Ratchadamnoen Klang, Phra Nakhon Region, Bangkok 10200; constituted under the

Broadcasting and TV Rule 1975, the committee consists of 17 representatives from 14 government agencies and controls the administrative, legal, technical and programming aspects of broadcasting in Thailand.

Radio

Radio Thailand (RTH): National Broadcasting Services of Thailand, Government Public Relations Dept, Soi Aree Sampan, Thanon Phra Ram VI, Khet Phayathai, Bangkok 10400; tel. (2) 618-2323; fax (2) 618-2340; internet www.prd.go.th/mcic/radio.htm; f. 1930; govt-controlled; educational, entertainment, cultural and news programmes; operates 109 stations throughout Thailand; Dir of Radio Thailand SOMPHONG VISUTTIPAT.

> **Home Service:** 12 stations in Bangkok and 97 affiliated stations in 50 provinces; operates three programmes; Dir CHAIVICHIT ATISAB.

> **External Services:** f. 1928; in Thai, English, French, Vietnamese, Khmer, Japanese, Burmese, Lao, Malay, Chinese (Mandarin), German and Bahasa Indonesia; Dir AMPORN SAMOSORN.

Ministry of Education Broadcasting Service: Centre for Innovation and Technology, Ministry of Education, Bangkok; tel. (2) 246-0026; f. 1954; morning programmes for schools (Mon.–Fri.); afternoon and evening programmes for general public (daily); Dir of Centre PISAN SIWAYABRAHM.

Pituksuntirad Radio Stations: stations at Bangkok, Nakorn Rachasima, Chiangmai, Pitsanuloke and Songkla; programmes in Thai; Dir-Gen. PAITOON WAIJANYA.

Radio Saranrom: Thanon Ratchadamnoen, POB 2-131, Bangkok 10200; tel. (2) 224-4904; fax (2) 226-1825; f. 1968 as Voice of Free Asia; name changed as above in 1998; operated by the Ministry of Foreign Affairs; broadcasts in Thai; Dir of Broadcasting PAIBOON KUSKUL.

Television

Radio and Television Executive Committee (RTEC): see Radio.

Bangkok Broadcasting & TV Co Ltd (Channel 7): 998/1 Soi Sirimitr, Phaholyothin, Talad Mawchid, POB 456, Bangkok 10900; tel. (2) 278-1255; fax (2) 270-1976; e-mail prdept@ch7.com; internet www.ch7.com; commercial.

Bangkok Entertainment Co Ltd (Channel 3): 1126/1 Thanon Petchburi Tadmai, Bangkok 10400; tel. (2) 204-3333; fax (2) 204-1384; internet www.tv3.co.th; Programme Dir PRAVIT MALEENONT.

Independent Television (ITV): 19 SCB Park Plaza, East Tower 3, Thanon Rachadapisek, Bangkok; tel. (2) 937-8080; e-mail webmaster@itv.co.th; internet www.itv.co.th; f. 1996; owned by a consortium including Nation Publishing Co, Siam Commercial Bank Public Co Ltd and Daily News media group.

The Mass Communication Organization of Thailand (Channel 9): 222 Thanon Asoke-Dindaeng, Bangkok 10300; tel. (2) 245-1844; fax (2) 245-1855; e-mail webmaster@mcot.or.th; internet www.mcot.or.th; f. 1952 as Thai Television Co Ltd; colour service; Dir-Gen. (vacant).

The Royal Thai Army Television HSA-TV (Channel 5): Thanon Phaholyothin, Sanam Pao, Bangkok 10400; tel. (2) 278-1470; fax (2) 279-0430; internet www.tv5.co.th; f. 1958; operates channels nationwide; Dir-Gen. Maj. Gen. VIJIT JUNAPART.

Television of Thailand (Channel 11): Public Relations Dept, Fortune Town Bldg, 26th Floor, Thanon Ratchadaphisek, Huay Kwang, Bangkok 10310; tel. and fax (2) 248-1601; internet www.prd.go.th/prdnew/thai/tv11; operates 16 colour stations; Dir-Gen. (vacant).

Thai Sky TV: 21 Vibhavadi Rangsit, Bangkok; tel. (2) 273-8977; pay-television; owned by Wattachak Co.

TV Pool of Thailand: c/o Royal Thai Army HSA-TV, Thanon Phaholyothin, Sanam Pao, Bangkok 10400; tel. (2) 271-0060; fax (2) 279-0430; established with the co-operation of all stations to present coverage of special events; Chair. Maj.-Gen. SOONTHORN SOPHONSIRI.

Finance

(cap. = capital; p.u. = paid up; res = reserves; dep. = deposits; m. = million; brs = branches; amounts in baht)

BANKING

Central Bank

Bank of Thailand: POB 154, 273 Thanon Samsen, Bangkhunprom, Bangkok 10200; tel. (2) 283-5353; fax (2) 280-0449; e-mail webmaster@bot.or.th; internet www.bot.or.th; f. 1942; bank of issue; cap. 20m., res 75,502m., dep. 748,072m. (Dec. 2000); Gov. PRIDIYA-THORN DAVAKULA; Asst Gov. BANDID NIJATHAWORN; 4 brs.

Commercial Banks

Bangkok Bank Public Co Ltd: 333 Thanon Silom, Bangkok 10500; tel. (2) 231-4333; fax (2) 236-8281; internet www.bbl.co.th; f. 1944; cap. 14,668m., res 145,928m., dep. 1,083,352m. (Dec. 2000); 49% foreign-owned; Chair. CHATRI SOPHONPANICH; Pres. CHARTSIRI SOPHONPANICH; 548 brs.

Bank of Asia Public Co Ltd: 191 Thanon Sathorn Tai, Khet Sathorn, Bangkok 10120; tel. (2) 287-2211; fax (2) 287-2973; e-mail webmaster@boa.co.th; internet www.bankasia4u.com; f. 1939; cap. 50,954m., res 8,560m., dep. 142,462m. (June 2002); 78.85%-owned by ABN-AMRO Bank N.V. Pres. and CEO CHULAKORN SINGHAKOWIN; 129 brs.

Bank of Ayudhya Public Co Ltd: 1222 Thanon Rama III, Bangkok 10120; tel. (2) 296-2000; fax (2) 683-1304; e-mail prs007@bay.co.th; internet www.bay.co.th; f. 1945; cap. 18,503m., res 35,965m., dep. 365,390m. (Dec. 2000); Chair. KRIT RATANARAK; Pres. JAMLONG ATIKUL; 424 brs.

Bankthai Public Co Ltd: 44 Thanon Sathorn, Silom, Bangrak, Bangkok 10500; tel. (2) 638-8000; fax (2) 633-9026; e-mail bankthai_pr2@hotmail.com; internet www.bankthai.co.th; f. 1998; cap. 70,631m., dep. 186,606m. (Aug. 2002); Chair. PRAMON SUTIVONG; Pres. PHIRASILP SUBHAPHOLSIRI; 80 brs.

DBS Thai Danu Bank Public Co Ltd: 393 Thanon Silom, Bangkok 10500; tel. (2) 230-5000; fax (2) 236-7939; internet www.dbs.co.th; f. 1949; cap. 17,001m., res 20,116m., dep. 72,407m. (Dec. 2000); fmrly Thai Danu Bank Public Co Ltd, 51.8% share purchased by DBS Bank (Singapore) in 1999; Chair. PAKORN THAVISIN; Pres. and CEO PORNSANONG TUCHINDA; 96 brs.

Krung Thai Bank Public Co Ltd (State Commercial Bank of Thailand): 35 Thanon Sukhumvit, Klongtoey, Bangkok 10110, POB 44 BMC, Bangkok 10000; tel. (2) 255-2222; fax (2) 255-9391; e-mail ptsirana@ktb.co.th; internet www.ktb.co.th; f. 1966; cap. 219,850m., res 34,747m., dep. 854,011m. (Dec. 1999); taken under the control of the central bank in 1998, pending transfer to private sector; merged with First Bangkok City Bank Public Co Ltd in 1999; Chair. SUPHA-CHAI PHISITVANICH; Pres. VIROJ NUALKHAIR; 617 local brs, 8 overseas brs.

Siam City Bank Public Co Ltd: POB 488, 1101 Thanon Petchburi Tadmai, Bangkok 10400; tel. (2) 208-5000; fax (2) 253-1240; e-mail webmaster@siamcity.co.th; internet www.siamcity.co.th; f. 1941; cap. 31,421m., res –4,613m., dep. 248,035m. (Dec. 2000); taken under the control of the central bank in Feb. 1998; merged with Bangkok Metropolitan Bank Public Co Ltd in April 2002; Pres. SOMPOL KIATPHAIBOOL; 211 brs.

Siam Commercial Bank Public Co Ltd: 9 Thanon Ratchadaphisek, Lardyao, Chatuchak, Bangkok 10900; tel. (2) 544-1111; fax (2) 937-7754; e-mail ccs@telecom.scb.co.th; internet www.scb.co.th; f. 1906; cap. 60,175m., res 22,808m., dep. 593,107m. (Dec. 2000); Chair. Dr CHIRAYU ISARANGKUN NA AYUTHAYA; Pres. and CEO JADA WATTANSIRITHAM; 477 brs.

Standard Chartered Nakornthon Bank Public Co Ltd: 90 Thanon Sathorn Nua, POB 2731, Bangkok 10500; tel. (2) 233-2111; fax (2) 236-1968; e-mail suteel@samart.co.th; internet www.ntb.co.th; f. 1933 as Wang Lee Bank Ltd, renamed 1985; cap. 7,003m., res 114m., dep. 55,220m. (Dec. 1999); taken under the control of the central bank in July 1999, 75% share sold to Standard Chartered Bank (United Kingdom); name changed as above in September 1999; CEO and Pres. VISHNU MOHAN; 67 brs.

Thai Farmers Bank Public Co Ltd: 1 Thai Farmers Lane, Thanon Ratburana, Bangkok 10140; tel. (2) 470-1122; fax (2) 470-1144; internet www.tfb.co.th; f. 1945; cap. 27,072m., dep. 664,846m. (Dec. 2001); 48.98% foreign-owned; Chair. BANYONG LAMSAM; Pres. BANTHOON LAMSAM; 529 brs.

Thai Military Bank Public Co Ltd: 3000 Thanon Phahon Yothin, Bangkok 10900; tel. (2) 299-1111; fax (2) 273-7121; e-mail tmbir@tmb.co.th; internet www.tmb.co.th; f. 1957; cap. 36,102m., res 10,906m., dep. 268,588m. (Dec. 2000); Pres. and CEO SIRI GARN-JAROENDEE; (acting); 367 brs.

Thanachart Bank Public Co Ltd: 1st, 2nd, 14th and 15th Floors, Thonson Bldg, 900 Thanon Phoenchit, Lumpini, Patumwan, Bangkok 10330; tel. (2) 655–9000; fax (2) 655–9001; e-mail nfs_rb@nfs.co.th; internet www.thanachart.com; f. 2002; Man. Dir SUVAR-NAPHA SUVARNAPRATHIP.

UOB Radanasin Bank Public Co Ltd: 690 Thanon Sukhumvit, Bangkok 10110; tel. (2) 260-0090; fax (2) 260-5310; internet www.uob-radanasin.co.th; f. 1998 as the result of the merger of Laem Thong Bank Ltd with Radanasin Bank; name changed as above Nov. 1999; cap. 19,795m., res –7,618m., dep. 40,870m. (Dec. 1998); Chair. WEE CHO YAW; CEO SAMUEL POON HON THANG; 68 brs.

Foreign Banks

ABN AMRO Bank N.V. (Netherlands): Bangkok City Tower, 1st–4th Floors, 179/3 Thanon Sathorn Tai, Bangkok 10120; tel. (2) 679-5900; fax (2) 679-5901; cap. p.u. 2,003m., dep. 903m. (March 1996); Country Man. Burno Schrieke.

Bank of America, NA (USA): Bank of America Centre, 2/2 Thanon Witthayu, Bangkok 10330; tel. (2) 251-6333; fax (2) 253-1905; f. 1949; cap. p.u. 2,000m. (May 1998); Man. Dir and Country Man. Frederick Chin.

Bank of China (People's Republic of China): Bangkok City Tower, 179 Thanon Sathorn Tai, Bangkok 10120; tel. (2) 268-1010; fax (2) 268-1020.

Bank of Nova Scotia (Canada): Ground Floor, Ploenchit Tower, 898 Thanon Ploenchit, Bangkok 10330; tel. (2) 263–0303; fax (2) 263–0150; e-mail bbangkok@scotiabank.com.

Bank of Tokyo-Mitsubishi Ltd (Japan): Harindhorn Tower, 54 Thanon Sathorn Nua, Bangrak, Bangkok 10500; tel. (2) 266-3011; fax (2) 266-3055; cap. p.u. 3,100m., dep. 17,213m. (March 1996); Dir and Gen. Man. Hiroshi Motomura.

Bharat Overseas Bank Ltd (India): 221 Thanon Rajawongse, Sumpphanthawongse, Bangkok 10100; tel. (2) 224-5412; fax (2) 224-5405; f. 1974; cap. p.u. 225m., dep. 1,254m. (March 1996); Man. K. S. Ganapathy.

BNP Paribas (France): 29th Floor, Abdulrahim Place, 990 Thanon Rama IV, Silom, Bangrak, Bangkok 10500; tel. (2) 636–1900.

Citibank, NA (USA): Sangtongtanee Bldg, 82 Thanon Sathorn Nua, Bangrak, Bangkok 10500; tel. (2) 232-2000; fax (2) 639-2564; internet www.citibank.com/thailand; cap. p.u. 3,849m., dep. 9,483m. (Feb. 1996); Man. David L. Hendrix.

Crédit Agricole Indosuez (France): CA Indosuez House, 152 Thanon Witthayu, POB 303, Bangkok 10330; tel. (2) 651-4590; fax (2) 651-4586; cap. p.u. 1,400m., dep. 2,241m. (April 1996); Man. Dr Jean-François Cahet.

Deutsche Bank AG (Germany): 208 Thanon Witthayu, Bangkok 10330; tel. (2) 651-5000; fax (2) 651-5151; cap. p.u. 1,200m., dep. 3,703m. (March 1996); Man. Gerhard Heigl.

Hongkong and Shanghai Banking Corpn (HSBC) (Hong Kong): HSBC Bldg, 968 Thanon Rama IV, Silom, Bangkok 10500; tel. (2) 614-4000; fax (2) 632-4818; cap. p.u. 2,000m., dep. 8,328m. (March 1996); Man. R. J. O. Cromwell.

International Commercial Bank of China (Taiwan): 36/12 P. S. Tower Asoke, 21 Thanon Sukhumvit, Phrakhanong, Bangkok 10110; tel. (2) 259-2000; fax (2) 259-1330; cap. p.u. 500m., dep. 1,334m. (Feb. 1996); Gen. Man. Chia-Nan Wang.

JP Morgan Chase Bank (USA): Bubhajit Bldg, 2nd Floor, 20 Thanon Sathorn Nua, Silom Bangrak, Bangkok 10500; tel. (2) 234-5992; fax (2) 234-8386; Man. Dir Raymond C. C. Chang.

Mizuho Corporate Bank Ltd (Japan): 18th Floor, Tisco Tower, 48 Thanon Sathorn Nua, Silom, Bangrak, Bangkok 10500; tel. (2) 638–0200–5; fax (2) 638–0218.

Oversea-Chinese Banking Corpn Ltd (Singapore): Charn Issara Tower, 2nd Floor, 942/80 Thanon Rama IV, Suriwongse, Bangkok 10500; tel. (2) 236-6730; fax (2) 237-7390; cap. p.u. 651m., dep. 455m. (Feb. 1996); Gen. Man. New Jing Yan.

RHB Bank Bhd (Malaysia): Liberty Sq. Bldg, 10th Floor, 287 Thanon Silom, Bangrak, Bangkok 10500; tel. (2) 631-2010; fax (2) 631-2018; Man. Leh Thiam Guan.

Standard Chartered Bank (UK): Sathorn Nakorn Tower, 100 Thanon Sathon Nua, Silom, Bangrak, Bangkok 10500; tel. (2) 724–4000; fax (2) 636-0536; internet www.stanchart.com/th/; cap. p.u. 1,200m., dep. 5,585m. (March 1996); Man. Bruce Darrington.

Sumitomo Mitsui Banking Corpn (Japan): Boon-Mitr Bldg, 138 Thanon Silom, Bangkok 10500; tel. (2) 353-8000; fax (2) 353-8100; cap. p.u. 3,200m., dep. 8,343m. (Feb. 1996); Gen. Rep. Yoshihiro Yoshimura.

Development Banks

Bank for Agriculture and Agricultural Co-operatives (BAAC): 469 Thanon Nakorn Sawan, Dusit, Bangkok 10300; tel. (2) 280-0180; fax (2) 280-0442; e-mail train@baac.or.th; internet www .baac.or.th; f. 1966 to provide credit for agriculture; cap. 22,761m., dep. 180,563m. (Dec. 2000); Exec. Chair. Varathep Ratanakorn; Pres. Pittayapol Nattaradol; 491 brs.

Export-Import Bank of Thailand (EXIM THAILAND): EXIM Bldg, 1193 Thanon Phaholyothin, Phayathai, Bangkok 10400; tel. (2) 271-3700; fax (2) 271-3204; e-mail info@exim.go.th; internet www .exim.go.th; f. 1993; provides financial services to Thai exporters and Thai investors investing abroad; cap. 6,500m. (Dec. 2001); Chair. Dr Somchai Richupan; Pres. (vacant); 7 brs.

Government Housing Bank: 63 Thanon Phra Ram IX, Huay Kwang, Bangkok 10310; tel. (2) 246-0303; fax (2) 246-1789; e-mail ghb_pr@housing.ghb.co.th; internet www.ghb.co.th; f. 1953 to provide housing finance; cap. 9,483m., assets 152,973m., dep. 80,251m. (Dec. 1995); Chair. Dr Somchai Richupan; Pres. Sidhijai Tanphiphat; 120 brs.

Small and Medium Enterprise Development Bank of Thailand: 9th Floor, Siripinyo Bldg, 475 Thanon Sri Ayudhaya, Rajtavee, Bangkok 10400; tel. (2) 201–3700; fax (2) 201–3723–34; e-mail sme@smebank.co.th; internet www.smebank.co.th; f. 2002; fmrly Small Industrial Finance Co.

Savings Bank

Government Savings Bank: 470 Thanon Phaholyothin, Phayathai, Bangkok 10400; tel. (2) 299-8000; fax (2) 299-8490; e-mail vicheal@gsb.or.th; internet www.gsb.or.th; f. 1913; cap. 0.1m., res 4,647m., dep. 377,773m. (Dec. 1999); Chair. Suphachai Phisitvanich; Dir-Gen. Paiboon Wattanasiritham; 566 brs.

Bankers' Association

Thai Bankers' Association: Lake Rachada Office Complex, 4th Floor, 195/8–10 Thanon Ratchadaphisek, Klongtoey, Bangkok 10110; tel. (2) 264-0883; fax (2) 264-0888; e-mail atmpool@tba.or.th; internet www.tba.or.th; Chair. Chatri Sophonpanich.

STOCK EXCHANGE

Stock Exchange of Thailand (SET): The Stock Exchange of Thailand Bldg, 62 Thanon Ratchadaphisek, Klongtoey, Bangkok 10110; tel. (2) 229-2000; fax (2) 654-5649; e-mail clientsupport@set .or.th; internet www.set.or.th; f. 1975; 27 mems; Pres. Kittirat Na Ranong; Chair. Chavalit Thanachanan.

Securities and Exchange Commission: Diethelm Towers B, 10th/13th–16th Floors, 93/1 Thanon Witthayu, Lumpini, Patumwan, Bangkok 10330; tel. (2) 252-3223; fax (2) 256-7711; e-mail info@sec.or.th; internet www.sec.or.th; f. 1992; supervises new share issues and trading in existing shares; Chair. Minister of Finance (vacant); Sec.-Gen. Prasorn Trairvosakul.

INSURANCE

In March 1997 the Government granted licences to 12 life assurance companies and 16 general insurance companies, bringing the total number of life insurance companies to 25 and non-life insurance companies to 83.

Selected Domestic Insurance Companies

American International Assurance Co Ltd: American International Tower, 181 Thanon Surawongse, Bangkok 10500; tel. (2) 634-8888; fax (2) 236-6452; internet www.aia.co.th; f. 1983; ordinary and group life, group and personal accident, credit life; Exec. Vice-Pres. and Gen. Man. Dhadol Bunnag.

Ayudhya Insurance Public Co Ltd: Ploenchit Tower, 7th Floor, Thanon Ploenchit, Pathumwan, Bangkok 10330; tel. (2) 263-0335; fax (2) 263-0589; internet www.ayud.co.th; non-life; Chair. Krit Ratanarak.

Bangkok Insurance Public Co Ltd: Bangkok Insurance Bldg, 25 Thanon Sathorn Tai, Bangkok 10120; tel. (2) 285-8888; fax (2) 677-3777; e-mail corp.comm@bki.co.th; internet www.bki.co.th; f. 1947; non-life; Chair. and Pres. Chai Sophonpanich.

Bangkok Union Insurance Public Co Ltd: 175–177 Thanon Surawongse, Bangkok 10500; tel. (2) 233-6920; fax (2) 237-1856; f. 1929; non-life; Chair. Manu Liewpairot.

China Insurance Co (Siam) Ltd: 36/68–69, 20th Floor, PS Tower, Thanon Asoke, Sukhumvit 21, Bangkok 10110; tel. (2) 259-3718; fax (2) 259-1402; f. 1948; non-life; Chair. James C. Cheng; Man. Dir Fang Rong-Cheng.

Indara Insurance Public Co Ltd: 364/29 Thanon Si Ayutthaya, Ratchthewi, Bangkok 10400; tel. (2) 247-9261; fax (2) 247-9260; e-mail webmaster@indara.co.th; internet www.indara.co.th; f. 1949; non-life; Chair. Pratip Wongnirund; Man. Dir Sophon Dejthevaporn.

International Assurance Co Ltd: 488/7–9 Thanon Henri Dunant, Patumwan, Bangkok 10330; tel. (2) 658-1919; fax (2) 285-8679; f. 1952; non-life, fire, marine, general; Chair. Pichai Kulavanich; Man. Dir Somchai Mahasantipiya.

Mittare Insurance Co Ltd: 295 Thanon Si Phraya, Bangrak, Bangkok 10500; tel. (2) 237-4646; fax (2) 236-1376; internet www .mittare.com; f. 1947; life, fire, marine, health, personal accident, automobile and general; fmrly Thai Prasit Insurance Co Ltd; Chair. Surachan Chansrichawla; Man. Dir Sukhathep Chansrichawla.

Ocean Life Insurance Co Ltd: 170/74–83 Ocean Tower I Bldg, Thanon Rachadapisek, Klongtoey, Bangkok 10110; tel. (2) 261-2300;

fax (2) 261-3344; e-mail info@oiclife.com; internet www.oiclife.com; f. 1949; life; Chair. and Man. Dir KIRATI ASSAKUL.

Paiboon Insurance Co Ltd: Thai Life Insurance Bldg, 19th–20th Floors, 123 Thanon Ratchadapisek, Bangkok 10310; tel. (2) 246-9635; fax (2) 246-9660; f. 1927; non-life; Chair. ANUTHRA ASSAWANONDA; Pres. VANICH CHAIYAWAN.

Prudential TS Life Assurance Public Co Ltd: Sengthong Thani Tower, 30th–32nd Floors, 82 Thanon Sathorn Nua, Bangkok 10500; tel. (2) 639-9500; fax (2) 639-9699; e-mail customer.service.ptsl@ibm.net; internet www.prudential.co.th; f. 1983; Chair. Prof. BUNCHANA ATTHAKOR; Vice-Chair. DAN R. BARDIN.

Siam Commercial New York Life Insurance Public Co Ltd: 4th Floor, SCB Bldg 1, 1060 Thanon Petchburi, SCB Chidlom, Ratchathewi, Bangkok 10400; tel. (2) 655-3000; fax (2) 256-1517; e-mail don@scnyl.com; internet www.scnyl.com; f. 1976; life; Pres. and CEO C. DONALD CARDEN.

Southeast Insurance (2000) Co Ltd (Arkanay Prakan Pai Co Ltd): Southeast Insurance Bldg, 315G, 1–3 Thanon Silom, Bangrak, Bangkok 10500; tel. (2) 631-1331; f. 1946; life and non-life; Chair. CHAYUT CHIRALERSPONG; Gen. Man. NATDANAI INDRASUKHSRI.

Syn Mun Kong Insurance Public Co Ltd: 279 Thanon Srinakarin, Bangkapi, Bangkok 10240; tel. (2) 379-3140; fax (2) 731-6590; e-mail info@smk.co.th; internet www.smk.co.th; f. 1951; fire, marine, automobile and personal accident; Chair. THANAVIT DUSADEESURAPOJ; Man. Dir RUENGDEJ DUSADEESURAPOJ.

Thai Commercial Insurance Public Co Ltd: TISCO Tower Bldg, 12th Floor, 48/21 Thanon Sathorn Nua, Bangrak, Bangkok 10500; tel. (2) 236-5987; fax (2) 236-5990; f. 1940; automobile, fire, marine and casualty; Chair. SUKIT WANGLEE, SUCHIN WANGLEE; Man. Dir SURAJIT WANGLEE.

Thai Health Insurance Co Ltd: 123 Thanon Ratchadaphisek, Ding-Daeng, Bangkok 10320; tel. (2) 246-9680; fax (2) 246-9806; f. 1979; Chair. APIRAK THAIPATANAKUL; Man. Dir PRANEET VIRAKUL.

Thai Insurance Public Co Ltd: 34/3 Soi Lang Suan, Thanon Ploenchit, Lumpini, Pathumwan, Bangkok 10330; tel. (2) 652-2880; fax (2) 652-2870; e-mail tic@thaiins.com; internet www.thaiins.com; f. 1938; non-life; Chair. KAVI ANSVANANDA.

Thai Life Insurance Co Ltd: 123 Thanon Ratchadaphisek, Din-Daeng, Bangkok 10320; tel. (2) 247-0247; fax (2) 246-9945; e-mail prcenter@thailife.com; internet www.thailife.com; f. 1942; life; Chair. and CEO VANICH CHAIYAWAN; Pres. APIRAK THAIPATANAGUL.

Viriyah Insurance Co Ltd: Viriya Panich Bldg, 1242 Thanon Krung Kasem, Pomprapsattrupuy, Bangkok 10100; tel. (2) 223-0851; fax (2) 224-9876; e-mail info@viriyah.co.th; internet www.viriyah.co.th; Man. Dir SUVAPORN THONGTHEW.

Wilson Insurance Co Ltd: 18th Bangkok Insurance/YWCA Bldg, 25 Thanon Sathorn Tai, Thungmahamek, Sathorn, Bangkok 10120; tel. (2) 677-3999; fax (2) 677-3978–9; e-mail wilson@wilsonins.co.th; f. 1951; fire, marine, motor car, general; Chair. CHOTE SOPHONPANICH; Pres. NOPADOL SANTIPAKORN.

Associations

General Insurance Association: 223 Soi Ruamrudee, Thanon Witthayu, Bangkok 10330; tel. (2) 256-6032–8; fax (2) 256-6039–40; e-mail general@thaigia.com; internet www.thaigia.com; Exec. Dir CHALAW FUANGAROMYA.

Thai Life Assurance Association: 36/1 Soi Sapanku, Thanon Rama IV, Thungmahamek, Sathorn, Bangkok 10120; tel. (2) 287-4596; fax (2) 679-7100; e-mail tlaa@tlaa.org; internet www.tlaa.org; Pres. SUTTI RAJITRANGSON.

Trade and Industry

GOVERNMENT AGENCIES

Board of Investment (BOI): 555 Thanon Vipavadee Rangsit, Chatuchak, Bangkok 10900; tel. (2) 537-8111; fax (2) 537-8177; e-mail head@boi.go.th; internet www.boi.go.th; f. 1958 to publicize investment potential and encourage economically and socially beneficial investments and also to provide investment information; Chair. THAKSIN SHINAWATRA; Sec.-Gen. SOMPHONG WANAPHA.

Board of Trade of Thailand: 150/2 Thanon Rajbopit, Bangkok 10200; tel. (2) 221-1827; fax (2) 225-3995; e-mail bot@tcc.or.th; internet www.tcc.or.th/bot/index2.htm; f. 1955; mems: chambers of commerce, trade asscns, state enterprises and co-operative societies (large and medium-sized companies have associate membership); Chair. AIVA TAULANANDA.

Central Sugar Marketing Centre: Bangkok; f. 1981; responsible for domestic marketing and price stabilization.

Financial Sector Restructuring Authority (FSRA): 130–132 Tower 3, Thanon Witthayu, Patumwan, Bangkok 10330; tel. (2) 263-2620; fax (2) 650-9872; e-mail webmaster@fra.or.th; internet www.fra.or.th; f. 1997 to oversee the restructuring of Thailand's financial system; Chair. KAMOL JUNTIMA; Sec. Gen. MONTRI CHENVIDAYAKAM.

Forest Industry Organization: 76 Thanon Ratchadamnoen Nok, Bangkok 10200; tel. (2) 282-3243; fax (2) 282-5197; e-mail info@fio.or.th; internet www.fio.or.th; f. 1947; oversees all aspects of forestry and wood industries; Man. Col M. R. ADULDEJ CHAKRABANDHU.

Office of the Cane and Sugar Board: Ministry of Industry, Thanon Phra Ram Hok, Bangkok 10400; tel. (2) 202-3291; fax (2) 202-3293; e-mail wimonlak@narai.oie.go.th.

Rubber Estate Organization: Nabon Station, Nakhon Si Thammarat Province 80220; tel. (75) 411554; internet www.reothai.com; Man. Dir SOMPHOL ISARATHANACHAI.

DEVELOPMENT ORGANIZATIONS

Industrial Finance Corpn of Thailand (IFCT): 1770 Thanon Petchburi Tadmai, Bangkok 10320; tel. (2) 253-7111; fax (2) 253-9677; e-mail info@ifct.co.th; internet www.ifct.co.th; f. 1959 to assist in the establishment, expansion or modernization of industrial enterprises in the private sector; organizes pooling of funds and capital market development; makes medium- and long-term loans, complementary working capital loans, investment advisory services, underwriting shares and securities and guaranteeing loans; Chair. Dr ARAN THAMMANO; Pres. ANOTHAI TECHAMONTRIKUL.

National Economic and Social Development Board: 962 Thanon Krung Kasem, Bangkok 10100; tel. (2) 282-8454; fax (2) 628-2871; e-mail mis@nesdb.go.th; internet www.nesdb.go.th; economic and social planning agency; Sec.-Gen. CHAKRAMON PHASUKAVANICH.

Royal Developments Projects Board: Office of the Prime Minister, Bangkok; internet www.rdpb.go.th; Sec.-Gen. Dr SUMET TANTIVEJKUL.

Small Industries Finance Office (SIFO): 24 Mansion 5, Thanon Ratchadamnoen, Bangkok 10200; tel. (2) 224-1919; f. 1964 to provide finance for small-scale industries; Chair. PISAL KONGSAMRAN; Man. VICHIEN OPASWATTANA.

CHAMBER OF COMMERCE

Thai Chamber of Commerce: 150 Thanon Rajbopit, Bangkok 10200; tel. (2) 622-1880; fax (2) 225-3372; e-mail tcc@tcc.or.th; internet www.tcc.or.th; f. 1946; 2,000 mems, 10 assoc. mems (1998); Chair Dr. AJVA TAULANANDA; Pres. VICHIEN TEJAPHAIBOON.

INDUSTRIAL AND TRADE ASSOCIATIONS

Bangkok Rice Millers' Association: 14/3 Thanon Sathorn Tai, Bangkok 10120; tel. (2) 286-8298.

The Federation of Thai Industries: Queen Sirikit National Convention Center, Zone C, 4th Floor, 60 Thanon Ratchadaphisek Tadmai, Klongtoey, Bangkok 10110; tel. (2) 229-4255; fax (2) 229-4941; e-mail fa-dept@off.fti.or.th; internet www.fti.or.th; f. 1987; fmrly The Association of Thai Industries; 4,800 mems; Chair. TAWEE BUTSUNTORN.

Mining Industry Council of Thailand: Soi 222/2, Thai Chamber of Commerce University, Thanon Vibhavadi Rangsit, Dindaeng, Bangkok 10400; tel. (2) 275-7684–6; fax (2) 692–3321; e-mail miningthai@miningthai.org; internet www.miningthai.org; f. 1983; intermediary between govt organizations and private mining enterprises; Chair. YONGYOTH PETCHSUWAN; Sec.-Gen. PUNYA ADULYAPICHIT.

Rice Exporters' Association of Thailand: 37 Soi Ngamdupli, Thanon Phra Ram IV, Bangkok 10120; tel. (2) 287-2674; fax (2) 287-2678; e-mail reat@ksc.th.com; Chair. SMARN OPHASWONGSE.

Rice Mill Association of Thailand: 81–81/1 Trok Rongnamkheng, 24 Thanon Charoenkrung, Talat Noi, Sampanthawong, Bangkok 10100; tel. (2) 235-7863; fax (2) 234-7286; Pres. NIPHON WONGTRAGARN.

Sawmills Association: 101 Thanon Amnuaysongkhram, Dusit, Bangkok 10300; tel. (2) 243-4754; fax (2) 243-8629; e-mail smassoc@mail.cscoms.com; Pres. VITOON PONGPASIT.

Thai Diamond Manufacturers Association: Bangkok; tel. (2) 390-0341; 11-mem. board; Pres. CHIRAKITTI TANGKATHAC.

Thai Food Processors' Association: Tower 1, Ocean Bldg, 9th Floor, 170/21–22 Thanon Rajchadapisaktadmai, Klongtoey, Bangkok 10110; tel. (2) 261-2995; fax (2) 261-2996-7; e-mail thaifood@thaifood.org; internet www.thaifood.org.

Thai Jute Mill Association: Sivadol Bldg, 10th Floor, Rm 10, 1 Thanon Convent, Silom, Bangrak, Bangkok 10500; tel. (2) 234-1438; fax (2) 234-1439.

Thai Lac Association: 66 Soi Chalermkhetr 1, Thanon Yukul, Pomprab, Bangkok 10100; tel. (2) 233-8331.

Thai Maize and Produce Traders' Association: Sathorn Thani II Bldg, 11th Floor, 92/26–27 Thanon Sathorn Nua, Bangrak, Bangkok 10500; tel. (2) 234-4387; fax (2) 236-8413.

Thai Pharmaceutical Manufacturers Association: 188/107 Thanon Charansanitwongs, Banchanglaw, Bangkoknoi, Bangkok 10700; tel. (2) 863-5106; fax (2) 863-5108; e-mail tpma@asiaaccess .net.th; f. 1969; Pres. CHERNPORN TENGAMNUAY.

Thai Rubber Traders' Association: 57 Thanon Rongmuang 5, Pathumwan, Bangkok 10500; tel. (2) 214-3420; f. 1951; Pres. SANG UDOMJARUMANCE.

Thai Silk Association: Textile Industry Division, Soi Trimitr, Thanon Rama IV, Klongtoey, Bangkok 10110; tel. (2) 712-4328; fax (2) 391-2896; e-mail thsilkas@thaitextile.org; internet www .thaitextile.org/tsa; f. 1962; Pres. MONTIGAN LOVICHIT.

Thai Sugar Producers' Association: 8th Floor, Thai Ruam Toon Bldg, 794 Thanon Krung Kasem, Pomprap, Bangkok 10100; tel. (2) 282-0990; fax (2) 281-0342.

Thai Sugar Manufacturing Association: 20th Floor, Gypsum Metropolitan Tower, 539/2 Thanon Sri Ayudhya, Rajdhareé, Bangkok 10400; tel. (2) 642-5248; fax (2) 642-5251; e-mail tsma2000@cscoms.com.

Thai Tapioca Trade Association: Sathorn Thani II Bldg, 20th Floor, 92/58 Thanon Sathorn Nua, Silom, Bangkok 10500; tel. (2) 234-4724; fax (2) 236-6084; e-mail ttta@loxinfo.co.th; internet www .ttta-tapioca.org; Pres. SEREE DENWORALAK.

Thai Textile Manufacturing Association: 454–460 Thanon Sukhumvit, Klongton, Klongtoey, Bangkok 10110; tel. (2) 258-2023; fax (2) 260-1525; e-mail ttma@thaitextile.org; internet www .thaitextile.org/ttma.

Thai Timber Exporters' Association: Ratchada Trade Centre, 4th Floor, 410/73–76 Thanon Ratchadaphisek, Bangkok 10310; tel. (2) 278-3229; fax (2) 259-0481.

Timber Merchants' Association: 4 Thanon Yen-Arkad, Thung-Mahamek, Yannawa, Bangkok 10120; tel. (2) 249-5565.

Union Textile Merchants' Association: 562 ESPREME Bldg, 4th Floor, Soi Watgunmatuyalarm, Thanon Rajchawong, Samphantha-wong, Bangkok 10100; tel. (2) 622-6711; fax (2) 622-6714; e-mail utma@thaitextile.org; internet www.thaitextile.org/utma; Chair. SURAPHOL TIYAVACHRAPONG.

UTILITIES

Electricity

Cogeneration Public Co Ltd: Grand Amarin Tower, 29th Floor, 1550 Thanon Petchburi Tadmai, Rachtavee, Bangkok 10320; tel. (2) 207-0970; fax (2) 207-0910; generation and supply of cogeneration power; cap. and res 5,634m., sales 3,424m. (1996/97); Chair. PIERRE CHARLES E. SWARTENBROEK; Pres. CHANCHAI JIVACATE.

Electricity Generating Authority of Thailand (EGAT): 53 Thanon Charan Sanit Wong, Bang Kruai, Nothaburi, Bangkok 11130; tel. (2) 436-4800; fax (2) 436-4879; internet www.egat.or.th; f. 1969; scheduled for transfer to the private sector; Gov. VITAYA KOTCHARUG.

Electricity Generating Public Co Ltd (EGCO): EGCO Bldg, 222 Moo 5, Thanon Vibhavadi Rangsit, Tungsonghong, Laksi, Bangkok 10210; tel. (2) 955-0955; fax (2) 955-0956; e-mail electric@egco.com; internet www.egco.com; a subsidiary of the Electricity Generating Authority of Thailand (EGAT); 59% transferred to the private sector in 1994–96; 14.9%-owned by China Light and Power Co (Hong Kong); Pres. SITTHIPORN RATANOPAS.

The Metropolitan Electricity Authority: 30 Soi Chidlom Ploen-chit, Lumpini, Pathumwan, Bangkok 10330; tel. (2) 254-9550; fax (2) 253-1424; internet www.mea.or.th; one of the two main power distribution agencies in Thailand; Gov. YONGYUTH SRICHAROEN.

The Provincial Electricity Authority: 200 Thanon Ngam Wongwan, Chatuchak, Bangkok 10900; tel. (2) 589-0100; fax (2) 589-4850; e-mail vibulya@pca.or.th; f. 1960; one of the two main power distribution agencies in Thailand.

Water

Metropolitan Waterworks Authority: 18/137 Thanon Pracha-chuen, Don Muang, Bangkok 10210; tel. (2) 504-0123; fax (2) 503-9493; e-mail mwa1125@water.mwa.or.th; internet www.mwa.or.th; f. 1967; state-owned; provides water supply systems in Bangkok; Gov. CHUANPIT DHAMASIRI.

Provincial Waterworks Authority: 72 Thanon Chaengwattana, Don Muang, Bangkok 10210; tel. (2) 551-1020; fax (2) 552-1547; e-mail pwait2000@yahoo.com; internet www.pwa.thaigov.net; f. 1979; provides water supply systems except in Bangkok Metropolis; Gov. THANYA HARNPOL; Dep. Gov. WANCHAI GHOOPRASERT.

CO-OPERATIVES

In 1992 there were 4m. members of co-operatives, including 1.6m. in agriculture.

TRADE UNIONS

Under the Labour Relations Act (1975), a minimum of 10 employees are required in order to form a union; by August 1997 there were an estimated 1,028 such unions.

Confederation of Thai Labour (CTL): 25/20 Thanon Sukhumvit, Viphavill Village, Tambol Paknam, Amphur Muang, Samutprakarn, Bangkok 10270; tel. (2) 756-5346; fax (2) 323-1074; represents 44 labour unions; Pres. AMPORN BANDASAK.

Labour Congress of Thailand (LCT): 420/393–394 Thippavan Village 1, Thanon Teparak, Samrong-Nua, Muang, Samutprakarn, Bangkok 10270; tel. and fax (2) 384-6789; e-mail lct_org@hotmail .com; f. 1978; represents 224 labour unions, four labour federations and approx. 140,000 mems; Pres. PRATNENG SAENGSANK; Gen. Sec. SAMAM THOMYA.

National Congress of Private Employees of Thailand (NPET): 142/6 Thanon Phrathoonam Phrakanong, Phrakanong, Klongtoey, Bangkok 10110; tel. and fax (2) 392-9955; represents 31 labour unions; Pres. BANJONG PORNPATTANANIKOM.

National Congress of Thai Labour (NCTL): 1614/876 Samut-prakarn Community Housing Project, Sukhumvit Highway Km 30, Tai Baan, Muang, Samutprakarn, Bangkok 10280; tel. (2) 389-5134; fax (2) 385-8975; represents 171 unions; Pres. PANAS THAILUAN.

National Free Labour Union Congress (NFLUC): 277 Moo 3, Thanon Ratburana, Bangkok 10140; tel. (2) 427-6506; fax (2) 428-4543; represents 51 labour unions; Pres. ANUSSAKDI BOONYAPRANAI.

National Labour Congress (NLC): 586/248–250 Moo 2, Mooban City Village, Thanon Sukhumvit, Bang Phu Mai, Mueng, Samut-prakarn, Bangkok 10280; tel. and fax (2) 709-9426; represents 41 labour unions; Pres. CHIN THAPPHLI.

Thai Trade Union Congress (TTUC): 420/393–394 Thippavan Village 1, Thanon Teparak, Tambol Samrong-nua, Amphur Muang, Samutprakarn, Bangkok 10270; tel. and fax (2) 384-0438; f. 1983; represents 172 unions; Pres. PANIT CHAROENPHAO.

Thailand Council of Industrial Labour (TCIL): 99 Moo 4, Thanon Sukhaphibarn 2, Khannayao, Bungkum, Bangkok; tel. (2) 517-0022; fax (2) 517-0628; represents 23 labour unions; Pres. TAVEE DEEYING.

Transport

RAILWAYS

Thailand has a railway network of 4,041 km, connecting Bangkok with Chiang Mai, Nong Khai, Ubon Rathathani, Nam Tok and towns on the isthmus.

State Railway of Thailand: 1 Thanon Rong Muang, Rong Muang, Pathumwan, Bangkok 10330; tel. (2) 220-4567; fax (2) 225-3801; e-mail info@srt.or.th; internet www.srt.or.th; f. 1897; 4,041 km of track in 2002; responsible for licensing a 4,044-km passenger and freight rail system, above ground; Chair. PRINYA JINDAPRASERT; Gov. CHITSANTI DHANASOBHON.

Bangkok Mass Transit System Corpn Ltd: Alma Link Bldg, 9th Floor, 25 Soi Chidlom, Thanon Ploenchit, Lumpini, Bangkok 10330; fax (2) 255-8651; responsible for the construction and management of the Skytrain, a two-line, 23.5-km elevated rail system, under the supervision of the Bangkok Metropolitan Area, the initial stage of which was opened in December 1999; Chair. KASAME CHATIKAVANIJ; Exec. Vice-Pres. DAVID RACE.

Mass Rapid Transit Authority of Thailand: 175 Thanon Rama IX, Huay Kwang, Bangkok 10320; tel. (2) 246-5733; fax (2) 246-3687; e-mail pr@mrta.or.th; internet www.mrta.or.th; in September 1995 it was announced that 21 km of the planned rail network for Bangkok would be underground; the subway system was scheduled to open in 2004; Gov. THEERAPONG ATTAIJARUSIT.

ROADS

The total length of the road network was an estimated 53,436 km in 2001. A network of toll roads has been introduced in Bangkok in an attempt to alleviate the city's severe congestion problems.

Bangkok Mass Transit Authority (BMTA): 131 Thanon Thiam Ruammit, Huay Kwang, Bangkok 10310; tel. (2) 246-0973; fax (2) 247-2189; e-mail cnai.bmta@motc.go.th; internet www.bmta.motc

.go.th; controls Bangkok's urban transport system; Chair. WANCHAI SARAIHUHIHAT; Dir and Sec. PHIRAPHONG ISARABHAKDI.

Department of Highways: Thanon Sri Ayudhaya, Ratchathevi, Bangkok 10400; tel. (2) 246-1122; e-mail prosdoh@motc.go.th; internet www.doh.motc.go.th; Dir-Gen. TERDSAK SEDTHAMANOP.

Department of Land Transport: 1032 Thanon Phaholyothin, Chatuchak, Bangkok 10900; tel. (2) 272-5671; fax (2) 272-5680; e-mail admin@dlt.motc.go.th; internet www.dlt.motc.go.th; Dir-Gen. PREECHA ORPRASIRTH.

Express Transportation Organization of Thailand (ETO): 485/1 Thanon Sri Ayudhaya, Ratchathevi, Bangkok 10400; tel. (2) 245-3231; internet www.eto.motc.go.th; f. 1947; Pres. KOVIT THANYAR-ATTAKUL.

SHIPPING

There is an extensive network of canals, providing transport for bulk goods. The port of Bangkok is an important shipping junction for South-East Asia, and consists of 37 berths for conventional and container vessels.

Harbour Department: 1278 Thanon Yotha, Talardnoi, Samphan-thawong, Bangkok 10100; tel. (2) 266-3972; fax (2) 233-7167; e-mail webmaster@hd.motc.go.th; internet www.hd.motc.go.th; Dir-Gen. WIT WORAKUPT.

Office of the Maritime Promotion Commission: 19 Thanon Phra Atit, Bangkok 10200; tel. (2) 281-9367; e-mail motc@motc.go .th; internet www.ompc.moto.go.th; f. 1979; Sec.-Gen. SOMSAK PIENSA-KOOL.

Port Authority of Thailand: 444 Thanon Tarua, Klongtoey, Bangkok 10110; tel. (2) 269-3000; fax (2) 249-0885; e-mail patodga@ loxinfo.co.th; internet www.pat.or.th; 18 berths at Bangkok Port, 12 berths at Laem Chabang Port; Chair. WANCHAI SARATHULTHAT; Dir-Gen. MANA PATRAM.

Principal Shipping Companies

Jutha Maritime Public Co Ltd: Mano Tower, 2nd Floor, 153 Soi 39, Thanon Sukhumvit, Bangkok 10110; tel. (2) 260-0050; fax (2) 259-9825; e-mail jutha@loxinfo.co.th; services between Thailand, Malaysia, Korea, Japan and Viet Nam; Chair. Rear-Adm. CHANO PHENJATI; Man. Dir CHANET PHENJATI.

Precious Shipping Public Co Ltd: Cathay House, 7th Floor, 8/30 Thanon Sathorn Nua, Khet Bangrak, Bangkok 10500; tel. (2) 237-8700; fax (2) 633-8460; e-mail psl@preciousshipping.com; internet www.preciousshipping.com; Chair. Adm. AMNARD CHANDANAMATTHA; Man. Dir HASHIM KHALID MOINUDDIN.

Regional Container Lines Public Co Ltd: Panjathani Tower, 30th Floor, 127/35 Thanon Ratchadaphisek, Chongnonsee Yan-nawa, Bangkok 10120; tel. (2) 296-1088; fax (2) 296-1098; e-mail rclbkk@rclgroup.com; Chair. KUA PHEK LONG; Pres. SUMATE TANTHU-WANIT.

Siam United Services Public Co Ltd: 30 Thanon Ratburana, Bangprakok, Ratburana, Bangkok 10140; tel. (2) 428-0029; fax (2) 427-6270; f. 1977; Chair. and Man. Dir MONGKHOL SIMAROJ.

Thai International Maritime Enterprises Ltd: Sarasin Bldg, 5th Floor, 14 Thanon Surasak, Bangkok 10500; tel. (2) 236-8835; services from Bangkok to Japan; Chair. and Man. Dir SUN SUNDI-SAMRIT.

Thai Maritime Navigation Co Ltd: Manorom Bldg, 15th Floor, 51 Thanon Phra Ram IV, Klongtoey, Bangkok 10110; tel. (2) 249-0100; fax (2) 249-0108; internet www.tmn.co.th; services from Bangkok to Japan, the USA, Europe and ASEAN countries; Chair. VORASUGDI VORAPAMORN; Vice-Chair. ORMSIN CHIVAPRUCK.

Thai Mercantile Marine Ltd: 599/1 Thanon Chua Phloeng, Klong-toey, Bangkok 10110; tel. (2) 240-2582; fax (2) 249-5656; e-mail tmmbkk@asiaaccess.net.th; f. 1967; services between Japan and Thailand; Chair. SUTHAM TANPHAIBUL; Man. Dir TANAN TANPHAIBUL.

Thai Petroleum Transports Co Ltd: 355 Thanon Sunthornkosa, POB 2172, Klongtoey, Bangkok 10110; tel. (2) 249-0255; Chair. C. CHOWKWANYUN; Man. Capt. B. HAM.

Thoresen Thai Agencies Public Co Ltd: 26/26–27 Orakarn Bldg, 8th Floor, 26–27 Soi Chidlom, Thanon Ploenchit, Kwang Lumpinee, Khet Pathumwan, Bangkok 10330; tel. (2) 254-8437; fax (2) 253-9497; e-mail tta@thoresen.th.com; transports bulk cargo around Asia and the Middle East; Chair. M. R. CHANDRAM S. CHANDRATAT; Man. Dir ARNE TEIGEN.

Unithai Group: 11th Floor, 25 Alma Link Bldg, Soi Chidlom, Thanon Ploenchit, Pathumwan, Bangkok 10330; tel. (2) 254-8400; fax (2) 253-3093; e-mail gerrit.d@unithai.com; internet www.unithai

.com; regular containerized/break-bulk services to Europe, Africa and Far East; also bulk shipping/chartering; Chair. SIVAVONG CHANG-KASIRI; CEO GERRIT J. DE NYS.

CIVIL AVIATION

Bangkok, Chiang Mai, Chiang Rai, Hat Yai, Phuket and Surat Thani airports are of international standard. U-Tapao is an alternative airport. In May 1991 plans were approved to build a new airport at Nong Ngu Hao, south-east of Bangkok, at an estimated cost of US $1,200m. Construction began in 1995, and the project was scheduled for completion in 2000. In January 1997, however, it was announced that, due to the Government's financial problems, the Nong Ngu Hao project was to be suspended; priority was, instead, to be given to the existing airport at Don Muang in Bangkok, which was to be expanded to handle 45m. passengers annually by 2007, compared with 25m. in 1997. In December 2001 construction of the passenger terminal complex of Bangkok's second airport, Suvarnab-humi International Airport, commenced. The project was scheduled for completion in 2005.

Airports Authority of Thailand: Bangkok International Airport, 171 Thanon Vibhavadi Rangsit, Don Muang, Bangkok 10210; tel. (2) 535-1111; fax (2) 535-5559; e-mail aatpr@airportthai.or.th; internet www.airportthai.or.th; f. 1998; Man. Dir Air Chief Marshal TERDSAK SUJJARUK.

Department of Aviation: 71 Soi Ngarmduplee, Thanon Phra Ram IV, Tung Mahamek, Sathorn District, Bangkok 10120; tel. (2) 287-0320; fax (2) 286-1295; e-mail tiva@aviation.go.th; internet www .aviation.go.th; f. 1963; Dir-Gen. SUPOTE KUMPEERA.

Air Andaman: 87 Nailert Bldg, 4th Floor, Unit 402A, Thanon Sukhumvit, Bangkok; tel. (2) 2514905; fax (2) 6552378; internet www.airandaman.com; f. 2000; regional, scheduled passenger and charter services; Pres. ATICHART ATHAKRAVISUNTHORN.

Bangkok Airways: 60 Queen Sirikit Nat. Convention Centre, Thanon Ratchadaphisek Tadmai, Klongtoey, Bangkok 10110; tel. (2) 229-3434; fax (2) 229-3450; e-mail reservation@bangkokair.co.th; internet www.bangkokair.com; f. 1968 as Sahakol Air, name changed as above in 1989; privately owned; scheduled and charter passenger services to regional and domestic destinations; Pres. and CEO Dr PRASERT PRASARTTONG-OSOTH.

Kampuchea Airlines (OX): 138/70 Jewellery Centre, 17th Floor, Thanon Nares, Bangrak, Bangkok 10500; tel. (2) 267-3210; fax (2) 267-3216; e-mail bondmx@yahoo.com; f. 1997; owned by Cambodian govt (51%) and Orient Thai Airlines (49%); regional passenger flights from Phnom-Penh to Hong Kong and Bangkok; CEO UDOM TANTIPRASONGCHAI.

PB Air: 101 Thanon Samsen, Bangkok 10300; tel. (2) 669-2066; fax (2) 669-2092; internet www.pbair.com; f. 1990; scheduled domestic passenger services; Chair. PIYA BHIROM BHAKDI.

Phuket Airlines: 1168/71, 25th Floor, Lumpini Tower Bldg, Thungmahamek, Bangkok; tel. (67) 982-3840; internet www .phuketairlines.com; f. 1999; domestic passenger services linking Ranong to Bangkok, Had Yai and Phuket.

Thai Airways International Public Co Ltd (THAI): 89 Thanon Vibhavadi Rangsit, Bangkok 10900; tel. (2) 513-0121; fax (2) 513-0203; e-mail public.info@thaiairways.co.th; internet www.thaiair .com; f. 1960; 93% govt-owned; shares listed in July 1991, began trading in July 1992; merged with Thai Airways Co in 1988; scheduled for partial privatization in late 2000; domestic services from Bangkok to 20 cities; international services to over 50 destinations in Australasia, Europe, North America and Asia; Chair. THANONG BHIDAYA; Pres. KANOK ABHIRADEE.

Tourism

Thailand is a popular tourist destination, noted for its temples, palaces, beaches and islands. In 2002 tourist arrivals totalled 10.87m. Revenue from tourism totalled 269,882m. baht in 1999 and, according to the World Tourism Organization, was an estimated US $7,119m. in 2000.

Tourism Authority of Thailand (TAT): Head Office: 1600 Thanon New Phetburi, Makkasan, Rachathewi, Bangkok 10400; tel. (2) 250–5500; fax (2) 250–5511; e-mail center@tat.or.th; internet www.tat.or.th; f. 1960; Chair. ADISAI BODHACAMIK; Gov. PRADECH PHAYAKVICHIEN.

Tourist Association of Northern Thailand: 51/20 Thanon Mahidol (Northern Tour), Chiang Mai 50100; tel. (53) 276-848; fax (53) 272-394; Pres. AURAWAN NIMANANDA.

TIMOR-LESTE

(EAST TIMOR)

Introductory Survey

Location, Climate, Language, Religion, Flag, Capital

The Democratic Republic of Timor-Leste, which is styled Timor Loro Sa'e (Timor of the rising sun) in the principal indigenous language, Tetum, occupies the eastern half of the island of Timor, which lies off the north coast of Western Australia. The western half of the island is Indonesian territory and constitutes part of the East Nusa Tenggara Province. In addition to the eastern half of Timor island, the territory also includes an enclave around Oecusse (Oekussi) Ambeno on the north-west coast of the island, and the islands of Ataúro (Pulo Cambing) and Jaco (Pulo Jako). Timor's climate is dominated by intense monsoon rain, succeeded by a pronounced dry season. The north coast of the island has a brief rainy season from December to February; the south coast a double rainy season from December to June, with a respite in March. The mountainous spine of the island has heavy rains that feed torrential floods. Tetum and Portuguese are the official languages. More than 30 languages are in use in Timor-Leste. The predominant religion is Christianity; 86% of the population were adherents of Roman Catholicism in 1997. Islam and animism are also practised. A national flag was officially adopted on 20 May 2002. The flag (proportions 1 by 2) displays a black triangle at the hoist (approximately one-third of the length of the flag) overlapping a yellow triangle (approximately one-half of the length of the flag) on a red background. The black triangle bears a five-pointed white star with one point aimed at the upper hoist corner. The capital is Dili.

Recent History

The Portuguese began trading in Timor in about 1520, principally for sandalwood, and they later established settlements and several ports on the island. They were forced to move to the north and east of the island by the Dutch, who had arrived in the early part of the 18th century and had established themselves at Kupana in the south-west. The division of the island between Portugal and the Netherlands was formalized in a treaty of 1859, although the boundaries were modified slightly in 1904. Portuguese Timor and Macau were administered as a single entity until 1896, when Portuguese Timor became a separate province. The eastern half remained a Portuguese overseas province when the Dutch recognized the western area as part of Indonesia in 1949.

The military coup in Portugal in April 1974 was followed by increased political activity in Portuguese Timor. In August 1975 the União Democrática Timorense (UDT, Timorese Democratic Union) demanded independence for Timor. The UDT allied with two other parties, the Associação Popular Democrática de Timor (APODETI) and Kota, against the alleged threat of a Communist regime being established by the Frente Revolucionária do Timor Leste Independente (Fretilin, Revolutionary Front for an Independent East Timor), and fighting broke out. The UDT forces were supported by the Indonesians. Gains on both sides were uneven, with Fretilin in control of Dili in mid-September. In the same month the Portuguese administration abandoned the capital and moved to the offshore island of Ataúro. A Portuguese attempt to arrange peace talks was rejected in October. The Indonesians intervened directly and by the beginning of December Indonesian troops controlled the capital. Portuguese-Indonesian peace talks in Rome in November were unsuccessful, and diplomatic relations were suspended after Indonesian military involvement. Two meetings of the UN Security Council voted for immediate withdrawal of Indonesian troops. Fretilin's unilateral declaration of independence in November was recognized in December by the People's Republic of China. In December the enclave of Oecusse (Oekussi) Ambeno in West Timor was declared part of Indonesian territory. In May 1976 the People's Representative Council of East Timor voted for integration with Indonesia. The UN did not recognize the composition of the Council as being representative, however, and by mid-1976 the Portuguese had not formally ceded the right to govern, although they had no remaining presence in the territory.

In July 1976 East Timor was declared the 27th province of Indonesia. Human rights organizations claimed that as many as 200,000 people, from a total population of 650,000, might have been killed by the Indonesian armed forces during the annexation. In February 1983 the UN Commission on Human Rights adopted a resolution affirming East Timor's right to independence and self-determination. In September, following a five-month cease-fire (during which government representatives negotiated with Fretilin), the armed forces launched a major new offensive. During 1984 conditions in East Timor deteriorated, with widespread hunger, disease and repression among civilians, and continuing battles between rebels and Indonesian troops. The rebels suffered a serious set-back in August 1985, when the Australian Government recognized Indonesia's incorporation of East Timor. In November 1988 Gen. Suharto, the President of Indonesia, visited East Timor, prior to announcing that travel restrictions (in force since the annexation in 1976) were to be withdrawn. The territory was opened to visitors in December. In October 1989 the Pope visited East Timor, as part of a tour of Indonesia, and made a plea to the Government to halt violations of human rights. In November 1990 the Government rejected proposals by the military commander of Fretilin, José Alexandre (Xanana) Gusmão, for unconditional peace negotiations aimed at ending the armed struggle in East Timor.

In 1991 tension in East Timor increased prior to a proposed visit by a Portuguese parliamentary delegation. Some Timorese alleged that the armed forces had initiated a campaign of intimidation to discourage demonstrations during the Portuguese visit. The mission, which was to have taken place in November, was postponed, owing to Indonesia's objection to the inclusion of an Australian journalist who was a prominent critic of Indonesia's policies in East Timor. In November the armed forces fired on a peaceful demonstration (believed to have been originally organized to coincide with the Portuguese visit) at the funeral of a separatist sympathizer in Dili. The Indonesian Armed Forces (ABRI), which admitted killing 20 civilians, claimed that the attack had been provoked by armed Fretilin activists. Independent observers and human rights groups refuted this and estimated the number of deaths at between 100 and 180. There were also subsequent allegations of the summary execution of as many as 100 witnesses. Under intense international pressure, Suharto established a National Investigation Commission. The impartiality of the Commission was challenged, however, on the grounds that it excluded non-governmental organizations, and Fretilin announced that it would boycott the investigation. Despite this, the Commission's findings received cautious foreign approbation, as they were mildly critical of ABRI and stated that 50 people had died, and 90 disappeared, in the massacre. The senior military officers in East Timor were replaced, and 14 members of the armed forces were tried by a military tribunal. The most severe penalty received by any of the soldiers involved was 18 months' imprisonment; this contrasted starkly with the sentences of convicted demonstrators, which ranged from five years' to life imprisonment.

In July 1992 Indonesia and Portugal agreed to resume discussions on East Timor under the auspices of the UN Secretary-General (although without a representative from Fretilin, which had indicated in May that it was prepared to take part in the negotiations). In August the UN General Assembly adopted its first resolution condemning Indonesia's violations of fundamental human rights in East Timor. In September the appointment of Abílio Soares as Governor of East Timor provoked widespread criticism in the province; although Soares was a native of East Timor, he was a leading advocate of the Indonesian occupation. In October the US Congress suspended defence training aid to Indonesia, in protest at the killing of separatist demonstrators in November 1991. In October 1992, prior to the anniversary of the massacre, Amnesty International reported that hundreds of suspected supporters of independence had been arrested and tortured to prevent a commemorative demonstration.

In November 1992 Xanana Gusmão was arrested. He was subsequently taken to Jakarta, where he was to be tried in February 1993 on charges of subversion and illegal possession of firearms. Xanana Gusmão's detention provoked international concern, and his replacement as leader of Fretilin, António Gomes da Costa (Mau Huno—who was himself arrested in April), claimed that his predecessor had been tortured. Two weeks after his capture, Xanana Gusmão publicly recanted his opposition to Indonesian rule in East Timor and advised Fretilin members to surrender. It transpired, however, that he was only co-operating with the authorities in order to gain the opportunity to speak publicly at a later date. During his trial, he was prevented from reading a prepared statement; the document was, however, illicitly conveyed to the press and was widely disseminated. In May Xanana Gusmão was found guilty of rebellion, conspiracy, attempting to establish a separate state and illegal possession of weapons, and was condemned to life imprisonment. The sentence was commuted to 20 years by Suharto in August. During the same month it was announced that all government combat forces were to be withdrawn from East Timor, leaving only troops involved in development projects. In September, however, the new acting leader of Fretilin, Konis Santana, declared that, contrary to announcements, the Indonesians were renewing their forces in East Timor and that killings and atrocities continued.

In December 1993 Xanana Gusmão managed to convey letters to the Portuguese Government and the International Commission of Jurists demanding an annulment of his trial, owing to the lack of impartiality of his defence lawyer. The Government subsequently banned Xanana Gusmão from receiving visitors. Also in December the first reconciliation talks took place in the United Kingdom between an Indonesian government official and a former leader of Timorese exiles opposed to Indonesia's occupation of East Timor. In January 1994 Indonesia announced to the UN Secretary-General's envoy that it would facilitate access to East Timor by human rights and UN organizations. In May, however, a privately-organized human rights conference being held in the Philippines, entitled the Asia-Pacific Conference on East Timor, provoked diplomatic tension with the Indonesian Government, which had attempted to force the abandonment of the conference. The outcome of the conference was the establishment of an Asia-Pacific coalition on East Timor, which consisted mainly of non-governmental organizations active in the region.

In July 1994 the Indonesian authorities suppressed a demonstration in Dili, following weeks of increasing tension in the capital; at least three people were reportedly killed during the protest. In August it was reported that the armed forces had held talks with Xanana Gusmão, included in which was the discussion of the possibility of holding a referendum under the auspices of the UN to determine the future status of the disputed territory. A second round of reconciliation talks between Indonesian officials and East Timorese exiles was held between late September and early October in the United Kingdom, and was attended by a UN envoy, although the main East Timorese opposition groups opposed the discussions, on the grounds that the participating East Timorese exiles were mostly in favour of Indonesian rule. The Indonesian Minister of Foreign Affairs, Ali Alatas, also held discussions in October in New York, in the USA, with José Ramos Horta, the Secretary for International Relations of Fretilin, the first such talks to be officially recognized. At the beginning of November President Suharto agreed to hold talks with exiled East Timorese dissidents. The Government's increasingly conciliatory position on East Timor was, however, reported largely to be a superficial attempt to improve the country's human rights image prior to the holding of the Asia-Pacific Economic Co-operation (APEC, see p. 139) summit meeting in Bogor, 60 km south of Jakarta, in mid-November.

In January 1995 Alatas, the Portuguese Minister of Foreign Affairs and the UN Secretary-General met in Geneva, Switzerland, for the fifth round of talks on East Timor. Agreement was reached to convene a meeting between separatist and pro-integrationist Timorese activists under the auspices of the UN, called the All-Inclusive Intra-East Timorese Dialogue (AETD). The AETD, which was held in June 1995, March 1996 and October 1997, failed to achieve any conclusive progress. The sixth and seventh rounds of talks between the Portuguese and

Indonesian ministers responsible for foreign affairs took place in July 1995 and January 1996, again with little progress.

In September 1995 the worst rioting that year took place in protest against Indonesian Muslim immigrants, following an Indonesian prison official's alleged insult to Roman Catholicism. Mosques and Muslim businesses were burned, and some Muslims were forced to flee the island. Further riots erupted in October, in which rival groups of separatists and integrationists clashed on the streets. The Roman Catholic Apostolic Administrator in Dili, the Rt Rev. Carlos Filipe Ximenes Belo, persuaded the rioters to return home following an agreement with ABRI; however, the agreement was subsequently broken by the armed forces, who arrested more than 250 alleged rioters.

From September 1995 East Timorese activists began forcing entry into foreign embassies in Jakarta and appealing for political asylum. They were granted asylum by the Portuguese, who were still officially recognized by the UN as the administrative power in East Timor. The Indonesian Government permitted the asylum-seekers to leave, but denied that there was any persecution in East Timor. The culmination of the successful campaign was the storming in December of the Dutch and Russian embassies by 58 and 47 activists respectively. The demonstrators, some of whom were non-Timorese and belonged to a radical group called the People's Democratic Union, demanded unsuccessfully a meeting with the UN High Commissioner for Human Rights, José Ayala Lasso, who was visiting Indonesia and who, following a brief visit to East Timor, confirmed the occurrence of severe violations of human rights in the province.

In February 1996 President Suharto and the Portuguese Prime Minister met in Bangkok, Thailand (the first meeting on East Timor by heads of government). During the negotiations Portugal offered to re-establish diplomatic links in return for the release of Xanana Gusmão and the guarantee of human rights in East Timor. International awareness of East Timor was heightened in October, when Belo and José Ramos Horta were jointly awarded the Nobel Prize for Peace. The Indonesian Government, displeased with the Nobel committee's choice, declared that there would be no change in its policy on East Timor. Four days after the announcement of the award, Suharto visited East Timor for the first time in eight years.

Following the announcement of the Nobel Peace Prize, Bishop Belo repeated demands that the Government conduct a referendum on the issue of autonomy for East Timor. In November 1996 he became involved in a controversy regarding an interview that he had given to a German periodical, *Der Spiegel*, which quoted several controversial remarks, allegedly made by Belo, about the treatment of the East Timorese people by the Indonesian Government and ABRI. Belo denied having made the remarks, but was requested to appear before a parliamentary commission in Jakarta to explain the matter. This controversy, and the temporary confiscation of Belo's passport by the Indonesian authorities (which threatened to prevent Belo's visit to Norway to receive the Nobel award), prompted five days of demonstrations in his support in Dili. The rallies were reportedly the largest since 1975, but were conducted peacefully.

The award of the Nobel Peace Prize to José Ramos Horta proved even more controversial. The Governor of East Timor accused Ramos Horta of ordering the torture and killing of East Timorese people. Ramos Horta himself declared that the award should have been made to Xanana Gusmão and invited the Indonesian Government to enter into serious negotiations on the future of East Timor. Ramos Horta was banned from visiting the Philippines for the duration of an APEC summit meeting which took place there in late 1996; this ban was subsequently extended.

In November 1996 the Indonesian Government withdrew permission for foreign journalists to visit East Timor, where they had planned to attend a press conference conducted by Belo. In December Ramos Horta and Belo attended the Nobel Prize ceremony in Oslo, Norway. Riots in Dili (following a gathering of Belo's supporters to welcome him upon his return) resulted in the death of a member of ABRI; it was reported later in the month that at least one East Timorese citizen had been killed by the Indonesian authorities in a raid to capture those believed to be responsible for the soldier's death. (It was, however, generally recognized by non-governmental organizations working in East Timor that the Indonesian authorities had become more lenient about allowing demonstrations in 1996.)

Following an increase in clashes between resistance forces and ABRI prior to the general election, in June 1997 a military commander of Fretilin, David Alex, was apprehended by the Indonesian armed forces. His subsequent death in custody was highly controversial; resistance groups rejected the official explanation that he had been fatally injured in a clash with security forces and claimed that he had been tortured to death. Guerrilla activity subsequently intensified and in September at least seven Indonesian soldiers were killed in a clash with resistance forces. Further fighting took place in November and December.

In July 1997 the President of South Africa, Nelson Mandela, met Xanana Gusmão, with the approval of Suharto. Mandela subsequently announced that he had written to Suharto to request the prisoner's release. In September Mandela continued his attempts to mediate in the Timorese conflict by holding talks with Bishop Belo; despite international optimism, however, Mandela's initiative ultimately proved fruitless.

In November 1997 the Australia-East Timor Association released a report cataloguing human rights abuses perpetrated by members of the Indonesian armed forces against Timorese women; abuses cited in the report included enforced prostitution, rape and compulsory sterilization programmes. Also in November shots were fired when Indonesian troops stormed the campus of the University of East Timor in Dili, following a vigil held by students to commemorate the massacre in Dili in 1991. According to reports, at least one student was killed in the incident, a number of others were injured and many were arrested. Belo accused the Indonesian security forces of having used 'excessive force', and this was confirmed by a report made by the Indonesian National Commission on Human Rights in early December. Also in December the Commission demanded the abolition of the country's anti-subversion legislation. In the same month two Timorese were sentenced to death under the legislation for their part in an ambush of election security officials earlier in the year, prompting threats of increased guerrilla activities by separatist forces, and a further four were sentenced to 12 years' imprisonment for taking part in armed resistance operations. Meanwhile, Abílio Soares, who had been re-elected as Governor of East Timor in September, ordered the arrest of the leaders of the recently formed Movement for the Reconciliation and Unity of the People of East Timor (MRUPT), which he declared to be a proscribed movement.

In January 1998 Ramos Horta attempted to exploit the Government's economic difficulties by urging Suharto to agree to a cease-fire and to co-operate with the UN in creating protection zones to ensure the safety of disarmed resistance fighters; the Government, however, failed to respond to his requests. In the same month it was announced that a Timorese resistance congress that was due to be held in Portugal in March was to be replaced by a national convention to ensure the participation of the UDT. The convention, held in April, unanimously approved the 'Magna Carta' of East Timor, a charter intended to provide the basis for the constitution of future self-determination within the territory, and ratified plans for the establishment of the National Council of Timorese Resistance (CNRT), a body intended to give the Timorese resistance movement a single national structure and to bring together representatives of the defunct National Council of Maubere Resistance (CNRM), Fretilin and the UDT. Xanana Gusmão was appointed President of the new CNRT, and Ramos Horta was named as Vice-President. In March 1998, meanwhile, Konis Santana, the acting military leader of Fretilin, died following an accident; Taur Matan Ruak was appointed as his successor.

The accession of B. J. Habibie to the Indonesian presidency in May 1998 raised hopes that independence for East Timor might be granted in the near future. However, while President Habibie publicly suggested that the territory might be given a new 'special' status within Indonesia and that troops might be withdrawn, there was no initial indication that the Government was contemplating independence for the territory. While a number of prominent political prisoners were released soon after Habibie replaced Suharto as President, Xanana Gusmão's 20-year sentence was reduced by a mere four months. Following the killing of an East Timorese youth by Indonesian soldiers in June, the Government renewed efforts to demonstrate its conciliatory position and, in late July, effected a much-publicized withdrawal of a limited number of troops from the territory. However, opposition groups subsequently claimed that fresh troops were being sent by the Indonesian Government to replace those leaving (a claim denied by Indonesian military leaders).

In August 1998 it was announced that Indonesia and Portugal had agreed to hold discussions on the possibility of 'wide-ranging' autonomy for East Timor, and in early November the UN was reported to be opening discussions with the two countries regarding a UN plan for extensive autonomy for the territory. Following an outbreak of severe violence in the Alas region of East Timor later that month, in which 82 people were reported to have been killed, Portugal suspended its involvement in the talks; however, in January 1999 it was announced that the talks were to resume. During his visit to East Timor in December 1998, UN special envoy Jamsheed Marker held talks with both Xanana Gusmão and Belo; in the same month, Xanana Gusmão reportedly advocated that the Timorese people should consider the UN's proposal for autonomy, but only as a transitional stage prior to the holding of a referendum (the possibility of which, in December, was still ruled out by the Indonesian Government).

In January 1999 the Australian Government announced a significant change in its policy on East Timor, stating that it intended actively to promote 'self-determination' in the territory (although the precise intended meaning of 'self-determination' remained unclear). Later the same month, total independence for East Timor in the near future emerged as an apparent possibility when, in its boldest move to date to appease the East Timorese and the international community, the Indonesian Government suggested that a vote might be held in the national legislature, the Majelis Permusyawaratan Rakyat (MPR, People's Consultative Assembly), following the election to the House of Representatives (part of the MPR) scheduled for June, on the issue of Indonesia's granting independence to the territory. As a result of a request from the UN Secretary-General, Kofi Annan, the Government also announced that it was to allow Xanana Gusmão to serve the remainder of his 20-year prison sentence under house arrest in Jakarta. Following the Government's announcement regarding the possibility of independence for East Timor, a number of outbreaks of violence, attributed to supporters of the territory's integration with Indonesia, were reported to have occurred.

On 27 January 1999 the Indonesian Government unexpectedly announced that, if the East Timorese voted to reject Indonesia's proposals for autonomy, it would consider granting independence to the province. Although the Indonesian Government was initially opposed to a referendum on the issue of independence for East Timor, it signed an agreement with Portugal on 5 May, giving its assent to a process of 'popular consultation' taking the form of a UN-supervised poll to determine the future status of East Timor. The United Nations Mission in East Timor (UNAMET) was established by the UN Security Council in June to organize the poll in which the East Timorese could opt for a form of political autonomy or for independence. The 'popular consultation' was initially scheduled to be held on 8 August, and all East Timorese, including those living in exile, were to be allowed to participate in the ballot.

Following the announcement of the scheduled referendum, violence in the territory escalated. Anti-independence militia groups based within East Timor initiated a campaign of violence and intimidation in advance of the poll, which included summary killings, kidnappings, harassment and the forced recruitment of young East Timorese. The Indonesian military itself was discovered to be not only supporting but also recruiting, training and organizing many of the militias. Violence continued to escalate throughout the territory during April and May 1999. In one incident in April anti-independence militia members massacred 57 people in a churchyard in the town of Liquiça (Likisia); further massacres were reported to have occurred in other areas, including Dili. Also in April Xanana Gusmão (who in February had been moved from Cipinang prison in Jakarta to serve the remainder of his 20-year sentence under effective house arrest in the capital) responded to the increasing violence from anti-independence militias by reversing his previous position and urging guerrillas in Fretilin's military wing, the Forças Armadas Libertação Nacional de Timor Leste (Falintil), to resume their struggle. Although rival pro-independence and integrationist factions signed a peace accord in June supporting a cease-fire and disarmament in advance of the scheduled referendum, the violence continued unabated.

The escalating violence in the territory, together with logistical difficulties, led the UN to postpone the referendum to 21 August 1999 and then to 30 August. Although intimidation and violence by the militias continued, the referendum proceeded on 30 August. About 98.5% of those eligible to vote participated in the poll, which resulted in an overwhelming rejection, by 78.5%

of voters, of the Indonesian Government's proposals for autonomy and in the endorsement of independence for East Timor. The announcement of the result of the referendum, however, precipitated a rapid descent into anarchy. Pro-Jakarta militias embarked upon a campaign of murder and destruction in which hundreds of civilians were killed; as many as 500,000 (according to the UN) were forced to flee their homes, and many buildings were destroyed in arson attacks. While many of those who were displaced from their homes sought refuge in the hills, about one-half were estimated by the UN to have left the territory (a large number having entered West Timor), some involuntarily. In one incident during the campaign of extreme violence that followed the announcement of the result of the referendum, anti-independence militia members stormed the residence of Bishop Belo, evicting at gunpoint some 6,000 refugees who had sought shelter in the compound; the home of the bishop was burned down and dozens of East Timorese were reported to have been killed in the attack. Bishop Belo was evacuated to Australia, while Xanana Gusmão (who was released from house arrest in Jakarta by the Indonesian Government on 7 September) took refuge in the British embassy in Jakarta. Thousands of civilians besieged the UN compound in Dili, the premises of other international agencies, churches and police stations, seeking protection from the indiscriminate attacks of the militias. On 7 September martial law was declared in the territory, and a curfew was imposed. The violence continued unabated, however, and in mid-September, following international condemnation of the situation and intense diplomatic pressure, the Indonesian Government reversed its earlier opposition to a proposal by the Australian Government and agreed to permit the deployment of a multinational peace-keeping force. As the massacre of civilians continued, thousands of refugees were airlifted to safety in northern Australia, along with the remaining employees of the UN (many local staff members of UNAMET were among the victims of the violence); shortly after the UN withdrew its staff, anti-independence militia members set fire to the UN compound in Dili. Meanwhile, aid agencies warned that as many as 300,000 East Timorese people would starve if humanitarian assistance were not urgently provided.

The first contingent of several thousand UN peace-keeping troops, forming the International Force for East Timor (Interfet), was deployed in the territory on 20 September 1999. Led by Australia, which committed 4,500 troops, the force gradually restored order. Other substantial contributions to the operation were made by the Philippines and Thailand, each of which provided 1,000 soldiers. A week later the Indonesian armed forces formally relinquished responsibility for security to the multi-national force. At the end of October, after 24 years as an occupying force, the last Indonesian soldiers left East Timor. In late September Indonesia and Portugal reiterated their agreement for the transfer of authority in East Timor to the UN. On 19 October the result of the referendum was ratified by the MPR, thus permitting East Timor's accession to independence to proceed. Shortly thereafter, on 25 October, the UN Security Council established the United Nations Transitional Administration in East Timor (UNTAET—now UNMISET) as an integrated peace-keeping operation fully responsible for the administration of East Timor during its transition to independence. UNTAET, with an initial mandate until 31 January 2001, was to exercise all judicial and executive authority in East Timor, to undertake the establishment and training of a new police force, and to assume responsibility for the co-ordination and provision of humanitarian assistance and emergency rehabilitation; the transfer of command of military operations in the territory from Interfet to the UNTAET peace-keeping force was completed on 23 February 2000. Meanwhile, the UN also began a large-scale emergency humanitarian relief effort; however, many displaced and homeless East Timorese remained without access to adequate food supplies, shelter and basic health-care facilities.

Following reports that in mid-October 1999 Indonesian troops and militias had entered the isolated East Timorese enclave of Oecusse (situated within West Timor) and allegedly massacred around 50 people, Interfet troops were deployed in Oecusse; most of the enclave's population of 57,000 were believed to have been removed to refugee camps in West Timor, and by early November only 10,000 of its citizens had been accounted for. Following his popularly-acclaimed return to Dili in October, Xanana Gusmão met with the UNTAET Transitional Administrator, Sérgio Vieira de Mello, in November, and reportedly communicated the concerns of local East Timorese organiza-

tions that they were being marginalized by UNTAET officials. In late November he visited Jakarta in order to establish relations with the Indonesian Government, and in early December he visited Australia, where he met with representatives of the Australian Government to discuss the Timor Gap Treaty. (The Treaty, which had been concluded between Australia and Indonesia in 1991, provided a framework for petroleum and gas exploration in the maritime zone between Australia and East Timor and for the division of any resulting royalties between Australia and Indonesia. Indonesia ceased to be party to the original Treaty when it relinquished control of East Timor in October 1999, however, and the transitional administration in East Timor subsequently expressed a desire to renegotiate the terms of the Treaty, which the UN considered to have no legal standing, as Indonesian sovereignty over East Timor had never been recognized by the international body. In February 2000 a memorandum of understanding—MOU—relating to the Treaty was signed by the Australian Government and East Timor's UN administrators, temporarily maintaining the arrangement for the division of royalties—although between Australia and East Timor rather than Australia and Indonesia—and East Timor received its first payment of royalties from Australia under the MOU in October 2000. In the same month, however, the formal renegotiation of the Treaty began, with East Timor requesting the redrawing of the boundaries covered by the Treaty and a larger share of petroleum and gas royalties. Following independence in May 2002 both countries formally signed the Treaty. However, owing to prolonged negotiations over the division of royalties, Australia did not ratify the agreement until March 2003.)

On 1 December 1999 José Ramos Horta returned to East Timor after 24 years of exile. Ramos Horta, who commanded much popular support, urged the East Timorese people to show forgiveness towards their former oppressors and called for reconciliation between Indonesia and East Timor. On 11 December Vieira de Mello convened the first meeting of the National Consultative Council (NCC) in Dili; the 15-member Council, comprising members of the CNRT and other East Timorese political representatives as well as UNTAET officials, was established in late 1999 to advise UNTAET.

A number of mass graves containing the bodies of suspected victims of the violence perpetrated by the anti-independence militias both before and after the holding of the referendum in August 1999 were discovered in East Timor (including two in the Oecusse enclave) in late 1999 and early 2000. In December 1999 Sonia Picado Sotela, the Chair of the International Commission of Inquiry in East Timor, confirmed that the team of UN investigators had discovered evidence of 'systematic killing'.

In January 2000 a panel appointed by the Indonesian Government to investigate human rights abuses in East Timor delivered its report to the Indonesian Attorney-General. The panel reportedly named 24 individuals whom it recommended should be prosecuted for their alleged involvement in violations of human rights in the territory. One of those named was the former Minister of Defence and Security and Commander-in-Chief of the Indonesian armed forces, Gen. Wiranto, who had since been appointed Co-ordinating Minister for Politics and Security in the Indonesian Government; also named were a number of senior military officers, as well as leaders of the pro-Jakarta militias responsible for the extreme violence perpetrated during the period following the referendum. However, pro-independence leaders in East Timor strongly criticized the report as inadequate. In the same month the International Commission of Inquiry in East Timor recommended that the UN establish an independent international body to investigate allegations of human rights violations in East Timor, and an international tribunal to deal with the cases of those accused by the investigators. In February the recently-appointed President of Indonesia, Abdurrahman Wahid, visited East Timor and publicly apologized for the atrocities committed by the Indonesian armed forces during the Republic's occupation of the territory. Wahid reaffirmed the commitment of the Indonesian Government to the prosecution of any individuals implicated in the violation of human rights in East Timor. In the same month Wahid suspended Gen. Wiranto from the Indonesian Government. (Wiranto subsequently resigned in May.) The UN Secretary-General, Kofi Annan, made an official visit to East Timor in mid-February, during which he pledged that investigations into violations of human rights in the territory would be carried out.

In April 2000 UNTAET signed an agreement with the Indonesian Government regarding the extradition to East Timor of

Indonesian citizens facing charges relating to the violence of 1999, and in July 2000 a team from the Indonesian Attorney-General's Office visited East Timor to investigate a limited number of cases of human rights violations. However, relations between East Timor and Indonesia remained tense, and the introduction in August 2000 (in the closing stages of the annual session of the country's principal legislative body, the MPR) of an amendment to Indonesia's Constitution providing for the exclusion of military personnel from retroactive prosecution prompted fears among many international observers that the possibility of the prosecution of members of the Indonesian military believed responsible for recent human rights abuses in East Timor would be placed in serious jeopardy (despite the suggestions of senior Indonesian legislators that the amendment would probably not apply to crimes such as genocide, war crimes and terrorism). In September the Indonesian Attorney General's Office named 19 people whom it suspected of involvement in the violence of 1999. Whilst human rights groups in both East Timor and Indonesia welcomed the publication of the list, which included the names of several former high-ranking members of the Indonesian armed forces, there was widespread disappointment that Gen. Wiranto was not among those named.

In June 2000 an agreement was reached between UNTAET and East Timorese leaders on the formation of a new transitional coalition Government, in which the two sides were to share political responsibility. The Cabinet of the new transitional Government, which was formally appointed in July, initially included four East Timorese cabinet ministers: João Carrascalão, President of the UDT and a Vice-President of the CNRT, who was allocated responsibility for infrastructure; Mari Alkatiri, Secretary-General of Fretilin, who was appointed Minister for Economic Affairs; Father Filomeno Jacob, who was appointed to oversee social affairs; and Ana Pessôa, who was placed in charge of internal administration. The new Cabinet also included four international representatives: Jean-Christian Cady, the UNTAET Deputy Special Representative of the Secretary-General for Governance and Public Administration, was allocated responsibility for the police and emergency services, while the three remaining non-East Timorese cabinet members were to be responsible for the judicial affairs, finance and political affairs portfolios. Mariano Lopes da Cruz, an East Timorese national, was appointed as Inspector-General. It was reported that Xanana Gusmão, whilst holding no formal position in the new Government, was to be consulted on an informal basis by Sérgio Vieira de Mello (who was to retain ultimate control over the approval of any draft legislation proposed to the Cabinet) with respect to all political decisions. In October the Cabinet was expanded to nine members, with the appointment of José Ramos Horta as Minister of Foreign Affairs.

In mid-July 2000 UNTAET approved the establishment of a 'National Council' to advise the new Cabinet. The East Timorese National Council, the membership of which was expanded from 33 to 36 in October, consisted of a selection of East Timorese representatives from the political, religious and private sectors. The new National Council was inaugurated on 23 October and replaced the 15-member NCC. In the same month Xanana Gusmão was elected to lead the National Council.

In August 2000, meanwhile, Xanana Gusmão retired as the Military Commander of Falintil, in order to concentrate on his political role in the process of guiding East Timor towards full independence. Xanana Gusmão relinquished control of the guerrilla army to his deputy, Taur Matan Ruak. Initially, Falintil faced an uncertain future, and the refusal of the UN to allow the active involvement of the unit in attempts to combat incursions by Indonesian paramilitaries into East Timor led Xanana Gusmão to voice indirect criticism of the international organization in his resignation speech. In February 2001, however, a new East Timorese Defence Force (ETDF) was established, consisting of an initial 650 recruits drawn exclusively from the ranks of Falintil, which was itself to be dissolved. The former Military Commander of the guerrilla army, Taur Matan Ruak, was promoted to the rank of Brigadier-General and appointed to command the new force. Meanwhile, a fund was established to finance the support and retraining of an estimated 1,000 Falintil veterans who were to be demobilized. Training of the new Defence Force was to be conducted by Portugal and Australia; its role was described as that of 'policing', with the defence of the territory remaining the responsibility of UNTAET peace-keeping troops.

In December 2000 four of the five East Timorese members of the transitional Cabinet threatened to resign, reportedly in

protest at their treatment by the UN. The ministers, who allegedly claimed that they were merely 'puppet ministers' in the new coalition Government, demanded further clarification of the legal status of the Cabinet and of their authority as individual cabinet ministers, and called for the establishment of a more clearly defined relationship between UNTAET and the Cabinet. Further complaints about UNTAET's treatment of East Timorese officials were voiced at a donors' conference for East Timor held in the same month, and press reports suggested the existence of a level of public resentment of the UN's presence in East Timor. However, in January 2001 Ramos Horta warned that any attempt to scale down the UN's presence in East Timor would destabilize the territory's progression towards independence. In late January 2001 the UN Security Council extended UNTAET's mandate (which had initially been scheduled to expire on 31 January 2001) until 31 January 2002. It was acknowledged, however, that modifications of the mandate might be necessary to take into account developments in East Timor's progression towards full independence and, in January 2002, the mandate was extended until 20 May 2002, the date set for independence. From August 2000, meanwhile, in a move that allowed for greater formal East Timorese influence in the governing of the territory during the period preceding the territory's accession to full independence, a process commenced whereby the transitional Government began to be redefined as the East Timorese Transitional Administration (ETTA). Consisting of both UNTAET and East Timorese staff, ETTA was composed of the transitional Cabinet, the National Council and the judiciary. Final authority over ETTA rested with the Special Representative of the UN Secretary-General and Transitional Administrator, Sérgio Vieira de Mello.

In February 2001 legislation providing for an election to an 88-seat Constituent Assembly, to be conducted on 30 August, was approved. The single chamber was to comprise 75 deputies elected on a national basis, using proportional representation, and one elected delegate from each of East Timor's 13 districts, chosen on a 'first-past-the-post' basis. The members of the Constituent Assembly were to be responsible for the preparation and adoption of a constitution, which would require the endorsement of at least 60 members. Meanwhile, a National Constitutional Commission, comprising representatives of various groups, was to be established in order to facilitate consultation with the people of East Timor.

In March 2001 Xanana Gusmão tendered his resignation as Speaker of the National Council, having become disaffected by the stagnation of the political process. At the same time he announced that he would not stand for President in the forthcoming elections for the post, despite commanding an overwhelming level of public support for his candidacy. In April UNTAET announced that José Ramos Horta would serve as Gusmão's replacement on the National Council, prompting his resignation as the Minister for Foreign Affairs (the two posts could not be held simultaneously). However, in the 9 April election for the post of Speaker, Manuel Carrascalão emerged victorious, defeating Ramos Horta, and criticized UNTAET for supporting his rival. Two weeks later José Ramos Horta resigned from the National Council and resumed his position in the transitional Cabinet. In June the CNRT announced its dissolution, reportedly in order to enable the groups of which it was comprised to evolve into fully independent political parties, and, in August, Xanana Gusmão finally yielded to immense popular pressure and international encouragement and announced his intention to stand for the presidency in 2002.

On 30 August 2001 91.3% of the eligible populace turned out to vote in the country's first free parliamentary election. Fretilin secured 55 of the 88 seats available in the Constituent Assembly, commanding 57% of the votes cast. In second place, with seven seats, was the Partido Democrático (PD). The Partido Social Democrata (PSD) and the Associação Social-Democrata Timorense (ASDT) won six seats each. In September Sérgio Vieira de Mello swore in the members of the Constituent Assembly, and five days later the second transitional Government was appointed. Mari Alkatiri of Fretilin was appointed leader of the Cabinet and retained the economy portfolio. José Ramos Horta continued as Minister for Foreign Affairs. Of 20 available government positions, nine were allocated to Fretilin, two to the PD and the remaining nine to independents and various experts. In October the Constituent Assembly appointed a committee to oversee the drafting of the Constitution, taking into account the views of over 36,000 East Timorese summarized in reports presented by 13 Constitutional Commissions. In

November 2001 the Assembly approved the structure of the draft Constitution.

In December 2000 UNTAET issued its first indictments for crimes committed against humanity in connection with the violence that had surrounded the referendum in 1999, charging 11 people (including an officer of the Indonesian special forces) with the murder of nine civilians in September 1999. In January 2001 an East Timor court sentenced a former pro-Jakarta militia member to 12 years' imprisonment for the murder of a village chief in September 1999, marking the first successful prosecution related to the violence of 1999. In September 2001 the UN filed 'extermination' charges against nine militiamen and two Indonesian soldiers accused of murdering 65 people two years previously. In October, in the first civil case of its kind, a US federal court awarded six East Timorese a total of US $66m. in damages after Indonesian Gen. Johny Lumintang was found to bear responsibility for human rights abuses. In December 2001 a UN tribunal took the first step in bringing those responsible for the atrocities committed in 1999 to justice. Of the 11 individuals indicted in December 2000, 10 were convicted of crimes against humanity and sentenced to prison terms of up to 33 years. However, the Jakarta authorities resisted the extradition of the indicted Indonesian Special Forces Officer to face trial.

In February 2000, meanwhile, the Australian Government announced that all 470 East Timorese refugees remaining in Australia were expected to be returned to East Timor by the end of the month. Also in February, however, the UN expressed its concern that very few of the estimated 90,000 East Timorese refugees remaining in camps across the border in West Timor were returning to East Timor; it had earlier been reported that pro-Jakarta militias had been intimidating the refugees in West Timor and preventing them from returning home. In September the UN temporarily suspended its relief work among East Timorese refugees in West Timor, following the murder by pro-Jakarta militias of three UN aid workers in the territory earlier in the month. The murders prompted international criticism of the Indonesian Government for its failure to control the militia groups operating in West Timor. In November Ramos Horta alleged that estimates of the number of East Timorese refugees residing in West Timor (reported by some sources to be as high as 130,000) were being deliberately exaggerated by the Indonesian Government, and estimated the actual number of refugees to be no higher than 60,000–70,000. In December 2000 and January 2001, in an attempt to dispel the fears of refugees remaining in West Timor about the security situation in East Timor, UNTAET arranged for a number of groups of refugees to visit their homeland. The visits resulted in a number of refugees opting to return permanently to East Timor.

In June 2001 refugees from East Timor participated in a process of registration through which they were permitted to decide whether or not they wished to return to the newly independent state. Of the 113,791 refugees who took part, 98% wished to remain in Indonesia. However, it was thought that intimidation by pro-Indonesia militias might have influenced the result and that the survey did not necessarily reflect the participants' long-term intentions. In the same month the six men accused of the murder of the three UN aid workers in September 2000 were found guilty of violence against people and property rather than murder and given light sentences. The UN criticized the verdicts and pressed for a review.

Following the formal declaration of the election results, the families of former East Timorese militiamen began returning to their homeland in mid-September 2001. In October the Indonesian authorities announced the imminent halting of aid to an estimated 80,000 East Timorese who remained in refugee camps in West Timor and in November Xanana Gusmão visited West Timor in an effort to promote reconciliation and encourage thousands of the remaining refugees to return home.

In October 2001 the newly elected Constituent Assembly requested that the UN formally grant East Timor independence on 20 May 2002. Xanana Gusmão reluctantly lent his support to the request, although he commented that the choice of date was too politically partisan as it commemorated the 28th anniversary of the founding of the country's first political party. However, the UN Security Council endorsed the Assembly's request, and agreed to maintain a peace-keeping presence in the region for between six months and two years after the granting of independence.

On 22 March 2002 the Constituent Assembly finally promulgated East Timor's first Constitution, which was to become effective upon independence on 20 May of that year. The document provided for the adoption of Tetum and Portuguese as the country's official languages.

On 14 April 2002 East Timor held its first presidential election, which resulted in an overwhelming victory for Xanana Gusmão, who secured almost 83% of the votes cast. The only other candidate was Francisco Xavier do Amaral. Later in the same month Madalena Brites Boavida was sworn in as Minister of Finance and Planning in the second transitional Government, following the resignation of Fernando Borges.

On 20 May 2002 East Timor celebrated its formal accession to independence, upon which it became known officially as the Democratic Republic of Timor-Leste. The tenure of the UN interim administration was officially terminated and UNTAET was replaced by a smaller mission, the UN Mission of Support in East Timor (UNMISET), which was to remain in the country for two years to support administrative development and to assist in the maintenance of law and order, whilst downsizing its military presence as rapidly as possible. Xanana Gusmão was officially inaugurated as President and swore in the country's first Government. Parliament then held its inaugural session, during which it elected to become a signatory to the UN Declaration of Human Rights and to apply for membership of the UN. Prime Minister Alkatiri stressed that the new Government would give priority to spending on health and education. The President of Indonesia, Megawati Sukarnoputri, attended the independence day celebrations, despite criticism from several members of the Indonesian legislature. On the following day Sérgio Vieira de Mello left the country; he was succeeded by Kamalesh Sharma, the head of UNMISET.

In July 2002 President Gusmão visited Indonesia on his first official trip abroad since assuming the presidency. In September Timor-Leste became the 191st member of the UN. In the same month the Indonesian Government announced that the remaining refugee camps in West Timor would be closed at the end of 2002 and, in November, Gusmão visited the province in an effort to encourage the estimated 30,000 refugees who remained there to return to their homeland. In the following month Bishop Belo announced that he was leaving his position in Dili for health reasons. In the same month the Government declared a state of alert in the country following an outbreak of rioting in Dili during which two people were killed. The protests had begun when a police officer allegedly shot at a student participating in a peaceful demonstration outside the police headquarters in the city. During the rioting two houses owned by Prime Minister Alkatiri were burnt down. The violence was the worst to have been experienced in the country since independence. In January 2003 further violence occurred when a group of armed men attacked villages near the town of Atsabe in the Ermera district, resulting in the deaths of five people. In the following month a bus travelling to Dili was attacked by a group of men with guns; two people subsequently died. It was feared that the violence reflected the possible establishment of several militias and insurgent groups intending to undermine the stability of the new nation.

In March 2003 Prime Minister Alkatiri announced the appointment of Ana Pessôa to the newly created post of Deputy Prime Minister. The justice portfolio, formerly held by Pessôa, was allocated to her deputy, Domingos Sarmento. In addition, Virgílio Guterres was appointed to the new post of Secretary of State for Telecommunications. In the following month, owing to the apparent increase of violence in Timor-Leste in the preceding months, the UN Security Council announced that UNMISET would no longer follow its original downsizing plan (under which the phased withdrawal of UN troops from the country would have commenced in July 2003) and would instead implement an alternative two-phase plan. Under the new strategy, UNMISET would retain primary responsibility for national security until December 2003, maintaining its peace-keeping force at its existing level, before preparing to hand over full responsibility for national defence to Falintil-ETDF (see Defence) on 20 May 2004, as planned.

From mid-2002, at a specially created court in Jakarta, the trials took place of 18 officers, government officials and militiamen believed to have participated in the violence that had surrounded the referendum for independence in 1999. In August 2002 Abílio Soares, the former governor of East Timor, was found guilty of two charges of 'gross rights violations'; he was sentenced to a three-year prison term. The sentence was widely criticized for its apparent leniency. In the same month the former chief of police in East Timor, Timbul Silaen, was acquitted of charges of failing to control his subordinates. Five other Indonesian police and army officers were also acquitted shortly afterwards, prompting widespread criticism of the verdicts from human rights organizations. In November former Indonesian militia leader Eurico Guterres was sentenced to 10 years in prison, having been convicted of crimes against humanity. In the following month the former military chief of Dili, Lt-Col Soedjarwo, was sentenced to a five-year prison term for his role in the violence. In March 2003 the court sentenced Brig.-Gen. Noer Moeis, a former army chief in East Timor, to five years in prison for crimes against humanity; he was the highest ranking officer to have been convicted of charges relating to the violence. By early April, however, 11 of those tried had been acquitted and the five convicted remained at liberty pending appeals.

In early 2003 prosecutors in Timor-Leste began to issue indictments for crimes against humanity against several military officials in relation to the violence surrounding the referendum in 1999, including the former chief of the Indonesian armed forces, Gen. Wiranto, who faced prosecution for the first time. Wiranto denied the charges against him. The Indonesian Government, however, stated that it would refuse to permit the extradition of those charged to face trial. In April 2003 a court in Timor-Leste sentenced José Cardosa Fereira, an East Timorese militia leader, to a 12-year prison term following his conviction for crimes against humanity.

Government

On 25 October 1999 the UN Security Council established the UN Transitional Administration in East Timor (UNTAET) as an integrated, multi-dimensional peace-keeping operation responsible for the administration of East Timor during its transition to independence. Under the terms of UN Security Council Resolution 1272 of 25 October 1999, UNTAET was empowered to exercise all legislative and executive authority in East Timor, including the administration of justice. Under the guidance of UNTAET, an 88-member Constituent Assembly, which was responsible for drafting a new constitution for East Timor, was elected in August 2001. A total of 75 deputies were elected nationally by proportional representation, the remaining members being elected by each of East Timor's 13 districts. On 22 March 2002 the Constituent Assembly promulgated East Timor's first Constitution and, on 14 April, the territory held its first presidential election. The President serves a five-year term. Upon the territory's accession to independence on 20 May, the Constituent Assembly transformed itself into the National Parliament and the Government, which was largely composed of the same Cabinet members who had constituted the pre-independence Council of Ministers, was formally inaugurated by the President. UNTAET formally relinquished its responsibility for the administration of the country and was succeeded by the UN Mission for Support in East Timor (UNMISET), which was to remain in the country, in a supporting role, for two years.

Defence

Within the framework of its mandate, the UN Transitional Administration in East Timor (UNTAET) was required to provide security and to maintain law and order throughout East Timor. (The authorized maximum strength of UNTAET was 8,950 troops, 200 military observers and 1,640 civilian police.) In early February 2001 a new East Timorese Defence Force (Falintil-ETDF) was established; the force was initially to fulfil a 'policing' role, with the defence of the territory remaining the responsibility of UNTAET troops. The first 650 recruits for the new Defence Force, which was ultimately to consist of 1,500 regulars and 1,500 reservists, were drawn from the ranks of the former guerrilla army, Falintil. The new force was trained by Portugal and Australia, and the first troops from Falintil-ETDF were deployed into the peace-keeping structure in early August 2001. In December Timor-Leste's navy was founded with the acquisition of two armed patrol boats from Portugal. The UN Mission of Support in East Timor (UNMISET), which replaced UNTAET in May 2002, had an authorized maximum strength of up to 5,000 troops, including 120 military observers, 1,250 police officers and 100 civilian experts. Provision was also made for 455 international civilian staff, 100 experts for a Civilian Support Group, 977 locally recruited staff and 241 UN Volunteers. In February 2003 UNMISET comprised 3,761 troops, 108 military observers and 682 civilian police, supported by 432 international and 995 local civilians. The peace-keeping force was to be replaced, through a two-year process of phased withdrawal, by Falintil-ETDF. In July 2002 the first battalion of Falintil-ETDF

assumed responsibility from UNMISET's peace-keeping force for the district of Lautem. In August Falintil-ETDF comprised 636 army personnel.

Economic Affairs

In 2001, according to estimates by the World Bank, Timor-Leste's gross national income (GNI), measured at average 1999–2001 prices, was US $403.1m., equivalent to $520 per head. During 1990–2001, it was estimated, the population increased at an average annual rate of 0.2%, while gross domestic product (GDP) per head, in real terms, remained constant during 1996–2001. Overall GDP decreased, in real terms, at an average annual rate of 2.1% during 1996–2001. GDP decreased by an estimated 35.4% in 1999, but increased by an estimated 15.4% in 2000 and by 18.3% in 2001. In 2002 GDP was estimated to be $369m., equivalent to $431 per head.

The economy of Timor-Leste is based principally on the agricultural sector, which normally employs more than 90% of the Timorese population. In 1999 the agricultural sector contributed an estimated 21.3% of GDP. This contribution increased to an estimated 26% in 2000. The only significant export commodity is coffee, which was expected to remain the country's most important source of income until 2004 (when revenues were expected to be generated primarily from petroleum and gas production in the Timor Sea—see below). It was thought that reforms in Timor-Leste's coffee industry could result in a threefold increase in coffee production levels. However, the sector remained extremely susceptible to climatic conditions, which were primarily responsible for significant fluctuations in annual output. There are small plantations of coconut, cloves and cinnamon. Subsistence crops include rice and maize. Livestock raised includes cattle and water buffalo. The forestry sector possesses potential. By 2000 UNTAET had announced that a comprehensive survey of Timor-Leste's forestry resources was to be conducted, and work had commenced on a sandalwood replanting project. In addition to ocean fishing, there is also some small-scale aquaculture. Agricultural GDP increased at an average annual rate of 2.7%, in real terms, in 1994–96. Following annual increases of 7.1% and 0.2% in 1997 and 1998 respectively, the GDP of the sector decreased by an estimated 48.4% in 1999, as a consequence of the widespread destruction and violence that followed the referendum on independence held in that year. However, in 2001 favourable climatic conditions and the implementation of efforts to increase crop production contributed to an ongoing agricultural recovery. The recovery continued throughout 2002, owing in part to the greater availability of seed and to the ongoing restoration of farming equipment in the country. However, it was feared that a drought later in the year might adversely affect agricultural production.

There is a small industrial sector, which is mainly concerned with the production of textiles, the bottling of water and the processing of coffee. In 1999 the manufacturing sector provided an estimated 3.5% of GDP. The GDP of the manufacturing sector increased at an average annual rate of 15%, in real terms, in 1994–96. Following an annual increase of 11.7% in 1997, however, the GDP of the sector decreased by 4.2% in 1998 and by an estimated 37.4% in 1999.

The mining sector contributed an estimated 1.4% of GDP in 1999. Mineral resources include high-grade marble and offshore petroleum and gas. The GDP of the mining sector increased at an average annual rate of 11%, in real terms, in 1994–96. However, following an increase of 22.2% in 1997, the GDP of the sector decreased by 8.6% in 1998 and by an estimated further 13.8% in 1999.

The construction sector contributed an estimated 23.2% of GDP in 1999 and an estimated 14% in 2000. The GDP of the sector increased at an average annual rate of 12.1%, in real terms, in 1994–96. However, following an increase of 2.1% in 1997, the sector's GDP decreased by 9.1% in 1998 and by an estimated 9.0% in 1999.

The power sector (including electricity, gas and water) provided an estimated 0.7% of GDP in 1999. Timor-Leste's generating capacity amounted to some 40 MW prior to the civil conflict in 1999, of which about 50% was contained in two power stations at Dili. However, the territory's power facilities suffered extensive damage in the civil conflict, and in 2003 supplies of electricity remained intermittent. In October 2002 the Government elected to transfer control of the national power authority, Electricidade de Timor-Leste (EDTL), to external management, owing to a continuing deterioration in the financial position of the authority. The rehabilitation of the power sector was ongoing in 2003, although the physical rehabilitation of the rural power sector was largely complete by April of that year. Approximately one-half of budgetary capital expenditure in that year was allocated to the introduction of a pre-paid electricity meter system in Timor-Leste. The GDP of the power sector increased at an average annual rate of 19.1%, in real terms, in 1994–96. The sector's GDP increased by 4.8% in 1997 and by 4.2% in 1998, but decreased by an estimated 49.9% in 1999.

The services sector (including trade, transport and communications, finance, public administration and other services) contributed an estimated 49.8% of GDP in 1999. The GDP of all branches of the services sector recorded a sharp contraction in 1999. In 2000 public administration contributed an estimated 33% of GDP, trade and hospitality services 8%, and transport and communications 7%.

In 1999 Timor-Leste recorded a visible trade deficit of an estimated US $36m. This increased to an estimated $84m. in 2000 and was predicted to rise to $131m. in 2001. In early 2001 substantial official aid continued to dominate the country's trade flows. Although this aid contributed towards the rehabilitation and reconstruction of the economy, it also resulted in a marked deterioration in the territory's trade and current-account deficits. Exports declined following the violence of 1999, and export earnings in 2000, including those from coffee (Timor-Leste's principal export commodity), were projected to be significantly below the pre-conflict average.

Following independence on 20 May 2002, Timor-Leste became a member of the Asian Development Bank (ADB, see p. 143) and of the Comunidade dos Países de Língua Portuguesa (Community of Portuguese-Speaking Countries, see p. 349). The country also holds observer status in the Association of South East Asian Nations (ASEAN, see p. 146). It attended the third Summit of the African, Caribbean and Pacific group of states (ACP), held in Fiji in July 2002, as an observer.

A US $65m. budget for 2001/02 was approved at the Fourth Donors' Meeting in Canberra in June 2001. A $20m. shortfall was to be financed through donor contributions. The fiscal deficit for the year was budgeted at $137m.; 40% of current and proposed spending was allocated to the health and education sectors, with a further 25% directed towards agriculture and infrastructure. At the Sixth Donors' Meeting, held in Dili in May 2002, a $77.7m. budget for 2002/03 was approved. Owing to funding shortfalls, the budget was revised downwards prior to its submittal to the National Parliament in December of that year; expenditure was reduced by $3.5m. Donors pledged $29.3m. in budgetary support for the year. Consumer prices increased by 80% in 1998 and by an estimated 140% in 1999. However, inflation was only an estimated 3% in 2000. In late 2000 the rate of unemployment in East Timor was estimated at around 80%. In January 2000 a regulation was passed by the UNTAET Transitional Administrator establishing the US dollar as the official currency of East Timor; however, as a result of the scarcity of low-denomination dollar notes, the absence of coins and a lack of familiarity with the new currency amongst the East Timorese, the use of the US dollar by 2001 was not as widespread as had been anticipated. By the end of 2002, however, the process of dollarization had been largely completed.

In December 1999 the Joint Assessment Mission of the World Bank reported that both the public and private sectors of the East Timorese economy had suffered almost total collapse as a consequence of the recent violence in the territory, with real GDP having declined by an estimated 35.4% in 1999. At a meeting in Tokyo in December 1999 international donors pledged US $523m. to the humanitarian aid programme for East Timor. Following the meeting a multi-donor Trust Fund for East Timor (TFET) was established; the fund was administered by the World Bank and the ADB and provided grants for economic reconstruction and development in the territory. Significant economic progress was made in 2000, with real GDP growing at an estimated average annual rate of 15.4% in that year. In October 2000 East Timor received its first payment of royalties from Australia for petroleum and gas mined in the Timor Gap, under the Timor Gap Treaty originally concluded between Australia and Indonesia in 1991. (Since the signing of the original Treaty in 1991, sizeable natural gas fields had been discovered in and around the Timor Gap zone, and petroleum reserves in the region were estimated by some sources to total a potential 500m. barrels, valued at more than $17,000m. in early 2001. Although East Timor had agreed temporarily to maintain the arrangement covering the sharing of petroleum and gas royalties with Australia after Indonesia ceased to be party to the original Treaty in 1999, the transitional administration in East Timor ultimately considered the Treaty to be invalid and sought to secure a larger share of the royalties.) In July 2001 East Timorese and Australian officials initialled the Timor Sea Arrangement. This awarded East Timor 90% of petroleum and gas production in the region covered by the original Timor Gap Treaty. The Arrangement was signed by both parties at independence in May 2002 and, in December, the National Parliament of Timor-Leste ratified the arrangement, although the Australian Government did not do so until March 2003, owing to prolonged disputes over the distribution of revenues from one of the fields covered by the Treaty. The revenues that the Arrangement would provide were expected to constitute the new nation's primary source of income from 2004 onwards. Real GDP increased by an estimated 18.3% in 2001, growth being led by agriculture, commerce, basic services and reconstruction of public and residential buildings. The rebuilding of Dili Port and the transfer of its management to the East Timorese Government in November 2001 promised to provide a valuable means of promoting foreign trade, investment and tourism. In 2001 donors pledged $153m. in aid for East Timor, excluding the contributions made by UNTAET.

Following independence on 20 May 2002 Timor-Leste's first National Development Plan (NDP), drafted following a nation-wide process of popular consultation in the preceding months, came into operation. The Plan's principal objectives, over a 20-year period, were the reduction of poverty and the promotion of economic growth in Timor-Leste. It proposed the implementation of a phased programme of economic development, under which priority would be given in the short term to the creation of a legislative framework, the enlargement of institutional capacity and further infrastructural growth, following which it was hoped that more sustainable development could be achieved. However, the decreasing international presence in the country after independence, a result of the conclusion of the UN's interim administration period, contributed significantly to an economic slowdown, particularly evident in the construction and services sectors, the expansion of which had hitherto driven growth. A delay in the resolution of many new country agreements for bilateral donor projects resulted in levels of investment that were lower than had initially been expected. A rapid increase in levels of private sector investment was considered integral to future economic expansion. By late 2002 preparations had been made to introduce key economic legislation into the National Parliament that would enable the development of a legal framework to regulate business activity in the new nation. The banking sector remained primarily localized in nature, although the level of deposits within the developing banking system continued to rise, and the country remained dependent on external grants to finance the majority of its public sector spending. In the immediate post-independence period external aid continued to be of absolutely vital importance to the Timorese economy, and the IMF cautioned that sound economic management would be critical to the preservation of macroeconomic stability, along with the provision of reasonable assurances to donors and other parties that the resources made available to Timor-Leste were being used effectively and accounted for properly. GDP was projected to contract by 1.2% in 2002 and by a further 2.3% in 2003.

Education

Prior to the civil conflict in 1999 there were 167,000 primary students, 32,000 junior secondary students and 19,000 senior secondary students. Primary school enrolment included 70% of those in the relevant age-group and secondary enrolment about 39%. Some 4,000 students were engaged in further education at the university and the polytechnic in Dili, while in addition several thousand East Timorese were following courses at Indonesian universities. It was estimated that, as a result of the civil conflict in 1999, 75%–80% of primary and secondary schools were either partially or completely destroyed. A total of 240,000 students registered for the 2000/01 academic year, however, a much higher number than anticipated. Literacy rates were reported to have reached only 41% by 1998, with lower rates recorded for women than for men. In January 2001, however, the reopening of the university improved the country's tertiary education facilities, enabling the enrolment of 4,500 students on degree courses and 3,000 on bridging programmes. By July 2001 373 schools had been rehabilitated to a basic operational level. The draft budget for 2000/01 allocated US $12m. to the education sector.

Public Holidays

2003: 1 January (New Year's Day), 18 April (Good Friday), 1 May (Labour Day), 20 May (Independence Day), 15 August (Assumption), 30 August (Constitution Day), 20 September (Liberation Day), 1 November (All Saints' Day), 12 November (Santa Cruz Day), 8 December (Immaculate Conception), 25 December (Christmas Day).

2004: 1 January (New Year's Day), 9 April (Good Friday), 1 May (Labour Day), 20 May (Independence Day), 15 August (Assumption), 30 August (Constitution Day), 20 September (Liberation Day), 1 November (All Saints' Day), 12 November (Santa Cruz Day), 8 December (Immaculate Conception), 25 December (Christmas Day).

Statistical Survey

Sources (unless otherwise stated): Indonesian Central Bureau of Statistics, Jalan Dr Sutomo 8, Jakarta 10710, Indonesia; tel. (21) 363360; fax (21) 3857046; internet www.bps.go.id; IMF, *East Timor: Establishing the Foundations of Sound Macroeconomic Management*.

AREA AND POPULATION

Area: 14,609 sq km (5,641 sq miles).

Population: 555,350 at census of 31 October 1980; 747,750 (males 386,939, females 360,811) at census of 31 October 1990; 1998: 884,000; 2001 (UN registration): 737,811.

Density (2001): 50.5 per sq km.

Principal Towns (population in 2000): Dili (capital) 48,200; Dare 17,100; Baucau 14,200; Maliana 12,300; Ermera 12,000. Source: Stefan Helders, *World Gazetteer* (internet www.world-gazetteer.com).

Births and Deaths (UN estimates, annual averages): Birth rate per 1,000: 1985–90: 43.3; 1990–95: 36.8; 1995–2000: 29.4; Death rate per 1,000: 1985–90: 20.4; 1990–95: 17.5. 1995–2000: 14.8. Source: UN, *World Population Prospects: The 2000 Revision*.

Expectation of Life (UN estimates, years at birth, 1995–2000): 47.5 (males 46.7; females 48.4). Source: UN, *World Population Prospects: The 2000 Revision*.

Economically Active Population (survey, persons aged 10 years and over, August 1993): Total employed 336,490; Unemployed 5,397; Total labour force 341,887.

AGRICULTURE, ETC.

Principal Crops ('000 metric tons, 1996): Rice (paddy) 46; Maize 101; Cassava (Manioc) 66; Sweet potatoes 16; Soybeans 1; Potatoes 6; Cabbages 3; Mustard greens 2; Avocados 1; Mangoes 5; Oranges 1; Papayas 1; Pineapples 2; Bananas 4.

Livestock ('000 head, 1996): Cattle 137; Sheep 32; Goats 187; Pigs 378; Horses 32; Buffaloes 69; Chickens 1,021; Ducks 28.

Fishing (metric tons): Total catch 2,459 in 1994; 2,462 in 1995.

FINANCE

Currency and Exchange Rate: United States currency is used: 100 cents = 1 US dollar ($). *Sterling and Euro Equivalents* (31 December 2002): £1 sterling = US $1.6118; €1 = US $1.0487; US $100 = £62.04 = €95.34.

Budget (US $ million, year ending 30 June 2002): *Revenue*: Domestic revenue 20.5 (Direct taxes 5.4; Indirect taxes 12.7; Non-tax revenue 2.4); Timor Sea revenue 10.8 (Tax revenues 6.5; Royalties and interest 4.3); Total 31.3. *Expenditure:* Recurrent expenditure 41.5 (Salaries and wages 18.9; Goods and services 22.6); Capital expenditure 11.6; Total 53.1. Source: IMF, *Interim Donors' Meeting —IMF Staff Statement* (December 2002).

Money Supply (estimate, '000 million rupiah, 31 December 1998): Currency in circulation 58.

Cost of Living (Consumer Price Index for Dili; base: year ending March 1989 = 100): 146.4 in 1994; 158.6 in 1995; 169.3 in 1996.

Gross National Product (US $ million at current prices): 326 in 2000; 402 in 2001; 391 in 2002. Source: IMF, *Interim Donors' Meeting—IMF Staff Statement* (December 2002).

Gross Domestic Product (US $ million at current prices): 321 (income from oil 5) in 2000; 389 (income from oil 13) in 2001; 369 (income from oil 22) in 2002. Source: IMF, *Interim Donors' Meeting —IMF Staff Statement* (December 2002.

Balance of Payments (estimates, US $ million, 1999): Exports of goods 46; Imports of goods –82; *Trade balance* –36; Services and other income (net) –12; *Balance on goods, services and income* –48; Current transfers 49; *Current balance* 1; Capital transfers 3; Other capital flows (net) –3; Net errors and omissions –1; *Overall balance* 0.

EXTERNAL TRADE

Principal Commodities (US $ million, 1998): *Imports*: Rice 13; Other foodstuffs 22; Petroleum products 14; Construction materials 20; Total (incl. others) 135. *Exports*: Products of agriculture, forestry and fishing 51 (Food crops 8, Other crops 28, Livestock 12); Products of manufacturing 3; Total (incl. others) 55.

Principal Trading Partner (US $ million, 1998): *Imports*: Indonesia 135. *Exports*: Indonesia 53.

TOURISM

Tourist Arrivals ('000 foreign visitors, excl. Indonesians, at hotels): 0.8 in 1996; 1.0 in 1997; 0.3 in 1998. Figures exclude arrivals at non-classified hotels: 204 in 1996; 245 in 1997; 41 in 1998.

Directory

The Constitution

The Constitution of the Democratic Republic of East Timor was promulgated by the Constituent Assembly on 22 March 2002 and became effective on 20 May 2002, when the nation formalized its independence. (From this date the country elected to be known by its official name, the Democratic Republic of Timor-Leste.) The main provisions of the Constitution are summarized below:

FUNDAMENTAL PRINCIPLES

The Democratic Republic of East Timor is a democratic, sovereign, independent and unitary state. Its territory comprises the historically defined eastern part of Timor island, the enclave of Oecussi, the island of Ataúro and the islet of Jaco. Oecussi Ambeno and Ataúro shall receive special administrative and economic treatment.

The fundamental objectives of the State include the following: to safeguard national sovereignty; to guarantee fundamental rights and freedoms; to defend political democracy; to promote the building of a society based on social justice; and to guarantee the effective equality of opportunities between women and men.

Sovereignty is vested in the people. The people shall exercise the political power through universal, free, equal, direct, secret and periodic suffrage and through other forms stated in the Constitution.

In matters of international relations, the Democratic Republic of East Timor shall establish relations of friendship and co-operation with all other peoples. It shall maintain privileged ties with countries whose official language is Portuguese.

The State shall recognize and respect the different religious denominations, which are free in their organization. Tetum and Portuguese shall be the official languages.

FUNDAMENTAL RIGHTS, DUTIES, LIBERTIES AND GUARANTEES

All citizens are equal before the law and no one shall be discriminated against on grounds of colour, race, marital status, gender, ethnic origin, language, social or economic status, political or ideological convictions, religion, education and physical or mental condition. Women and men shall have the same rights and duties in family, political, economic, social and cultural life. Rights, freedoms and safeguards are upheld by the State and include the following: the right to life; to personal freedom, security and integrity; to habeas corpus; to the inviolability of the home and of correspondence; to freedom of expression and conscience; to freedom of movement, assembly and association; and to participate in political life. Freedom of the press is guaranteed.

Rights and duties of citizens include the following: the right and the duty to work; the right to vote (at over 17 years of age); the right to petition; the right and duty to contribute towards the defence of sovereignty; the freedom to form trade unions and the right to strike; consumer rights; the right to private property; the duty to pay taxes; the right to health and medical care; the right to education and culture.

ORGANIZATION OF THE POLITICAL POWER

Political power lies with the people. The organs of sovereignty shall be the President of the Republic, the National Parliament, the Government and the Courts. They shall observe the principle of separation and interdependence of powers. There shall be free, direct, secret, personal and regular universal suffrage. No one shall hold political office for life.

PRESIDENT OF THE REPUBLIC

The President of the Republic is the Head of State and the Supreme Commander of the Defence Force. The President symbolizes and guarantees national independence and unity and the effective functioning of democratic institutions. The President of the Republic shall be elected by universal, free, direct, secret and personal suffrage. The candidate who receives more than half of the valid votes shall be elected President. Candidates shall be original citizens of the Democratic Republic of East Timor, at least 35 years of age, in possession of his/her full faculties and have been proposed by a minimum of 5,000 voters. The President shall hold office for five years. The President may not be re-elected for a third consecutive term of office.

The duties of the President include the following: to preside over the Supreme Council of Defence and Security and the Council of State; to set dates for elections; to convene extraordinary sessions of the National Parliament; to dissolve the National Parliament; to promulgate laws; to exercise the functions of the Supreme Commander of the Defence Force; to veto laws; to appoint and dismiss the Prime Minister and other Government members; to apply to the Supreme Court of Justice; to submit relevant issues of national interest to a referendum; to declare a State of Emergency following the authorization of the National Parliament; to appoint and dismiss diplomatic representatives; to accredit foreign diplomatic representatives; to declare war and make peace with the prior approval of the National Parliament.

COUNCIL OF STATE

The Council of State is the political advisory body of the President of the Republic. It is presided over by the President of the Republic and comprises former Presidents of the Republic who were not removed from office, the Speaker of the National Parliament, the Prime Minister, five citizens elected by the National Parliament and five citizens nominated by the President of the Republic.

NATIONAL PARLIAMENT

The National Parliament represents all Timorese citizens, and shall have a minimum of 52 and a maximum of 65 members, elected by universal, free, direct, equal, secret and personal suffrage for a term of five years. The duties of the National Parliament include the following: to enact legislation; to confer legislative authority on the Government; to approve plans and the Budget and monitor their execution; to ratify international treaties and conventions; to approve revisions of the Constitution; to propose to the President of the Republic that issues of national interest be submitted to a referendum. The legislative term shall comprise five legislative sessions, and each legislative session shall have the duration of one year.

GOVERNMENT

The Government is the supreme organ of public administration and is responsible for the formulation and execution of general policy. It shall comprise the Prime Minister, the Ministers and the Secretaries of State, and may include one or more Deputy Prime Ministers and Deputy Ministers. The Council of Ministers shall comprise the Prime Minister, the Deputy Prime Ministers, if any, and the Ministers. It shall be convened and presided over by the Prime Minister. The Prime Minister shall be appointed by the President of the Republic. Other members of the Government shall be appointed by the President at the proposal of the Prime Minister. The Government shall be responsible to the President and the National Parlia-

ment. The Government's programme shall be submitted to the National Parliament for consideration within 30 days of the appointment of the Government.

JUDICIARY

The Courts are independent organs of sovereignty with competence to administer justice. There shall be the Supreme Court of Justice and other courts of law, the High Administrative, Tax and Audit Court, other administrative courts of first instance and military courts. There may also be maritime courts and courts of arbitration.

It is the duty of the Public Prosecutors to represent the State. The Office of the Prosecutor-General shall be the highest authority in public prosecution and shall be presided over by the Prosecutor-General, who is appointed and dismissed by the President of the Republic. The Prosecutor-General shall serve for a term of six years.

ECONOMIC AND FINANCIAL ORGANIZATION

The economic organization of East Timor shall be based on the co-existence of the public, private, co-operative and social sectors of ownership, and on the combination of community forms with free initiative and business management. The State shall promote national investment. The State Budget shall be prepared by the Government and approved by the National Parliament. Its execution shall be monitored by the High Administrative, Tax and Audit Court and by the National Parliament.

NATIONAL DEFENCE AND SECURITY

The East Timor defence force—Falintil-ETDF—is composed exclusively of national citizens and shall be responsible for the provision of military defence to the Democratic Republic of East Timor. There shall be a single system of organization for the whole national territory. Falintil-ETDF shall act as a guarantor of national independence, territorial integrity and the freedom and security of the population against any external threat or aggression. The police shall guarantee the internal security of the citizens.

The Superior Council for Defence and Security is the consultative organ of the President of the Republic on matters relating to defence and security. It shall be presided over by the President of the Republic and shall include a higher number of civilian than military entities.

GUARANTEE AND REVISION OF THE CONSTITUTION

Declaration of unconstitutionality may be requested by: the President of the Republic; the Speaker of the National Parliament; the Prosecutor-General; the Prime Minister; one-fifth of the Members of the National Parliament; the Ombudsman.

Changes to the Constitution shall be approved by a majority of two-thirds of Members of Parliament and the President shall not refuse to promulgate a revision statute.

FINAL AND TRANSITIONAL PROVISIONS

Confirmation, accession and ratification of bilateral and multilateral conventions, treaties, agreements or alliances that took place before the Constitution entered into force shall be decided by the respective bodies concerned; the Democratic Republic of East Timor shall not be bound by any treaty, agreement or alliance not thus ratified. Any acts or contracts concerning natural resources entered into prior to the entry into force of the Constitution and not subsequently confirmed by the competent bodies shall not be recognized.

Indonesian and English shall be working languages, together with the official languages, for as long as is deemed necessary.

Acts committed between 25 April 1974 and 31 December 1999 that can be considered to be crimes of humanity, of genocide or of war shall be liable to criminal proceedings within the national or international courts.

The Government

Until 20 May 2002 all legislative and executive authority in East Timor was exercised by the UN Transitional Administration in East Timor (UNTAET). Under its guidance the Constituent Assembly promulgated a new Constitution on 22 March 2002 and the people of East Timor elected their first President on 14 April. Having satisfied both these preconditions East Timor was formally granted independence on 20 May, at which time the Constituent Assembly transformed itself into East Timor's first Parliament and the Government was formally inaugurated by the President. The Government was largely composed of the same Cabinet members who had constituted the pre-independence Council of Ministers.

Upon independence UNTAET was succeeded by the UN Mission of Support in East Timor (UNMISET, see p. 67), which was to remain in the country for an initial period of one year. UNMISET's mandate comprised the following elements: to provide support to core administrative structures critical to the political stability and viability of the new country; to assist in interim law enforcement and public security; to aid in the development of a new law enforcement agency —the East Timor Police Force (ETPF); and to contribute to the maintenance of internal and external security. Downsizing of the mission was to take place as rapidly as possible and it was intended that, over a period of two years, all operational responsibilities would be fully devolved to the East Timorese authorities.

HEAD OF STATE

President: José Alexandre (Xanana) Gusmão (took office 20 May 2002).

CABINET
(April 2003)

Prime Minister and Minister for Development and the Environment: Mari bin Amude Alkatiri.

Deputy Prime Minister: Ana Maria Pessôa Pereira da Silva Pinto.

Senior Minister for Foreign Affairs and Co-operation: José Ramos Horta.

Minister for Justice: Domingos Sarmento.

Minister for Planning and Finance: Madalena Brites Boavida.

Minister for Internal Administration: Rogério Tiago Lobato.

Minister for Health: Rui Maria de Araújo.

Minister for Transport, Communications and Public Works: Ovídio de Jesus Amaral.

Minister for Education, Culture, Youth and Sport: Armindo Maia.

Minister for Agriculture, Fisheries and Forestry: Estanislau Aleixo da Silva.

Secretary of State for Defence: Felix de Jesús Rodrigues.

Secretary of State for Labour and Solidarity: Arsênio Paixão Bano.

Secretary of State for Commerce and Industry: Arlindo Rangel.

Secretary of State for Tourism, Environment and Investment: José Texeira.

Secretary of State for the Council of Ministers: Gregorio José da Conceição Ferreira de Sousa.

Secretary of State for Parliamentary Affairs: Antoninho Bianco.

Secretary of State for Electricity and Water: Egídio de Jesús.

Secretary of State for Telecommunications: Virgílio da Silva Guterres.

There are, in addition, seven Vice-Ministers.

MINISTRIES

Office of the President: Palácio das Cinzas, Kaikoli, Dili; tel. (390) 3339011; e-mail presidente-tl@easttimor.minihub.org.

Office of the Prime Minister: Dili; e-mail opm@gov.east-timor .org.

Ministry of Agriculture, Forestry and Fisheries: Dili; e-mail agriculture@gov.east-timor.org.

Ministry of Economic Affairs and Planning: Dili; e-mail economic.affairs@gov.east-timor.org.

Ministry of Education, Culture, Youth and Sport: Dili; e-mail education@gov.east-timor.org.

Ministry of Planning and Finance: Dili; e-mail finance@gov .east-timor.org.

Ministry of Foreign Affairs and Co-operation: Edif. GPA 1, Ground Floor, Dili; tel. (390) 3339608; internet www.mfac.gov.tp.

Ministry of Health: Palácio das Repartições, Edif. 3, Unit 4, POB 374, Dili; tel. (390) 322467; fax (390) 325189; e-mail health@gov .east-timor.org.

Ministry of Internal Administration: Dili; e-mail internal .admin@gov.east-timor.org.

Ministry of Justice: Dili; e-mail justice@gov.east-timor.org.

Ministry of Transport, Communications and Public Works: Dili; e-mail transport@gov.east-timor.org.

President and Legislature

PRESIDENT
Presidential Election, 14 April 2002

Candidate	Votes	%
José Alexandre Gusmão	301,634	82.69
Francisco Xavier do Amaral	63,146	17.31
Total	**364,780**	**100.0**

NATIONAL PARLIAMENT

A single-chamber Constituent Assembly was elected by popular vote on 30 August 2001. Its 88 members included 75 deputies elected under a national system of proportional representation and one representative from each of Timor-Leste's 13 districts, elected under a 'first-past-the-post' system. Upon independence on 20 May 2002 the Constituent Assembly became the National Parliament; it held its inaugural session upon the same day.

Speaker: Francisco Guterres.

General Election, 30 August 2001

	Seats
Frente Revolucionária do Timor Leste Independente (Fretilin)	55
Partido Democrático (PD)	7
Associação Social-Democrata Timorense (ASDT) . .	6
Partido Social Democrata (PSD)	6
Klibur Oan Timor Asuwain (KOTA)	2
Partido Democrata Cristão (PDC)	2
Partido Nacionalista Timorense (PNT)	2
Partido do Povo de Timor (PPT)	2
União Democrática Timorense (UDT)	2
Partido Democrata Cristão de Timor (UDC/PDC) . .	1
Partido Liberal (PL)	1
Partido Socialista de Timor (PST)	1
Independent	1
Total	**88**

Political Organizations

Associação Popular Democrática de Timor Pro Referendo (Apodeti Pro Referendo) (Pro Referendum Popular Democratic Association of Timor): c/o Frederico Almeida Santos Costa, CNRT Office, Balide, Dili; tel. (390) 324994; f. 1974 as Apodeti; adopted present name in August 2000; fmrly supported autonomous integration with Indonesia; Pres. Frederico Almeida Santos Costa.

Associação Social-Democrata Timorense (ASDT) (Timor Social Democratic Association): Av. Direitos Humanos Lecidere, Dili; tel. (0408) 983331; f. 2001; Pres. Francisco Xavier do Amaral.

Barisan Rakyat Timor Timur (BRTT) (East Timor People's Front): fmrly supported autonomous integration with Indonesia; Pres. Francisco Lopes da Cruz.

Conselho Popular pela Defesa da República Democrática de Timor Leste (CPD-RDTL) (Popular Council for the Defence of the Democratic Republic of East Timor): opp. the Church, Balide, Dili; tel. (0409) 481462; f. 1999; promotes adoption of 1975 Constitution of Democratic Republic of East Timor; Spokesperson Cristiano da Costa.

Frente Revolucionária do Timor Leste Independente (Fretilin) (Revolutionary Front for an Independent East Timor): Rua dos Mártires da Pátria, Dili; tel. (390) 321409; internet www.geocities .com/SoHo/Study/4141/; f. 1974 to seek full independence for East Timor; entered into alliance with the UDT in 1986; Pres. Francisco Guterres; Sec. for International Relations José Ramos Horta.

Klibur Oan Timor Asuwain (KOTA) (Association of Timorese Heroes): Rua dos Mártires da Pátria, Fatuhada, Dili; tel. (390) 324661; e-mail clementinoamaral@hotmail.com; f. 1974 as pro-integration party; currently supports independence with Timorese traditions; Pres. Clementino dos Reis Amaral (acting).

Movement for the Reconciliation and Unity of the People of East Timor (MRUPT): f. 1997; Chair. Manuel Viegas Carrascalão.

Partai Liberal (PL) (Liberal Party): Talbessi Sentral, Dili; tel. (0408) 786448; Pres. Armando José Dourado da Silva.

Partido Democrata Cristão (PDC) (Christian Democrat Party): Former Escola Cartilha, Rua Quintal Kiik, Bairo Economico, Dili;

tel. (390) 324683; e-mail arlindom@octa4.net.au; f. 2000; Pres. ANTÓNIO XIMENES.

Partido Democrático (PD) (Democratic Party): 1 Rua Democracia, Pantai Kelapa, Dili; tel. (0419) 608421; e-mail flazama@hotmail.com; Pres. FERNANDO DE ARAÚJO.

Partido Democratik Maubere (PDM) (Maubere Democratic Party): Blk B II, 16 Surikmas Lama Kraik, Fatumeta, Dili; tel. (0407) 184508; e-mail pdm_party@hotmail.com; f. 2000; Pres. PAOLO PINTO.

Partido Nacionalista Timorense (PNT) (Nationalist Party of Timor): Dili; tel. (390) 323518; Pres. Dr ABÍLIO ARAÚJO (acting).

Partido do Povo de Timor (PPT) (Timorese People's Party): Dili; tel. (0409) 568325; f. 2000; pro-integration; supported candidacy of Xanana Gusmão for presidency of East Timor; Pres. Dr JACOB XAVIER.

Partido Republika National Timor Leste (PARENTIL) (National Republic Party of East Timor): Perumnar Bairopite Bob Madey Ran, Fahan Jalam, Ailobu Laran RTK; tel. (0419) 361393; Pres. FLAVIANO PEREIRA LOPEZ.

Partido Social Democrata Timor Lorosae (PSD) (Social Democrat Party of East Timor): Apartado 312, Correios de Dili, Dili; tel. (0418) 357027; e-mail psdtimor@hotmail.com; f. 2000; Pres. MÁRIO VIEGAS CARRASCALÃO.

Partido Socialista de Timor (PST) (Socialist Party of Timor): Rua Colegio das Madras, Balide, Dili; tel. (0407) 560246; e-mail kaynaga@hotmail.com; Marxist-Leninist Fretilin splinter group; Pres. AVELINO DA SILVA.

Partido Trabalhista Timorense (PTT) (Timor Labour Party): 2B Rua Travessa de Befonte, 2 Bairro Formosa, Dili; tel. (390) 322807; f. 1974; Pres. PAULO FREITAS DA SILVA.

União Democrática Timorense (UDT) (Timorese Democratic Union): Palapagoa Rua da India, Dili; tel. (409) 881453; e-mail uchimov2001@yahoo.com; internet www.unitel.net/udttimor; f. 1974; allied itself with Fretilin in 1986; Pres. JOÃO CARRASCALÃO; Sec.-Gen. DOMINGOS OLIVEIRA.

União Democrata-Cristão de Timor (UDC/PDC) (Christian Democratic Union of Timor): 62 Rua Americo Thomaz, Mandarin, Dili; tel. (390) 325042; f. 1998; Pres. VINCENTE DA SILVA GUTERRES.

Diplomatic Representation

EMBASSIES IN TIMOR-LESTE

Australia: Av. dos Mártires da Pátria, Dili; tel. (390) 322111; fax (390) 323615; Ambassador PAUL FOLEY.

Brazil: Rua Governador Serpa Rosa, POB 157, Farol, Dili; tel. (390) 324203; fax (390) 324620; e-mail esctimor@yahoo.com.br; Ambassador Dr KYWAL DE OLIVEIRA.

China, People's Republic: Av. Governador Serpa Rosa, Farol, Dili; tel. (438) 881918; fax (390) 325166; e-mail chinaemb_tp@mfa.gov.cn; Ambassador GUANFU SHAO.

Indonesia: Kompleks Pertamina, Pantai Kelapa, Correios Timor Leste, Dili; tel. (390) 312333; fax (390) 312332; e-mail kukridil@hotmail.com; Chargé d'affaires KRISTIO WAHYONO.

Japan: Av. de Portugal, Pantai Kelapa Dili, POB 175, Dili; tel. (390) 323131; fax (390) 323130; e-mail japrepet@yahoo.co.jp; Ambassador YUTAKA IIMURA.

Korea, Republic: Dili; e-mail koreadili@hotmail.com; Ambassador LIM BYONG-HYO.

Malaysia: Av. Almirante Americo Thomas, rue de Thomas, Mandarin, Dili; tel. (390) 311141; fax (390) 321805; e-mail mwdili@bigpond.com; Chargé d'affaires a.i. MOHAMED RAMEEZ YAHAYA.

Portugal: Av. Presidente Nicolau Lobato, Dili; tel. (390) 312155; fax (390) 312526; e-mail embaixada.dili@portugal.minihub.org; Ambassador RUI QUARTIM DOS SANTOS.

Thailand: Central Maritime Hotel, Dili.

United Kingdom: Pantai Kelapa, Av. do Portugal, Dili; tel. (408) 010991; e-mail dili.fco@gtnet.gov.uk; Ambassador HAMISH ST CLAIR DANIEL.

USA: Av. do Portugal, Dili; tel. (390) 313205; fax (390) 313206; Ambassador GROVER JOSEPH REES.

Judicial System

Until independence was granted on 20 May 2002 all legislative and executive authority with respect to the administration of the judiciary in East Timor was vested in UNTAET. During the transitional period of administration a two-tier court structure was established, consisting of District Courts and a Court of Appeal. The Constitution, promulgated in March, specified that Timor-Leste should have three categories of courts: the Supreme Court of Justice and other law courts; the High Administrative, Tax and Audit Court and other administrative courts of first instance; and military courts. The judiciary would be regulated by the Superior Council of the Judiciary, the function of which would be to oversee the judicial sector and, in particular, to control the appointment, promotion, discipline and dismissal of judges. The effectiveness of the newly established judicial system was severely impaired by Timor-Leste's lack of human and material resources. In July there were only 22 judges in Timor-Leste, none of whom possessed more than two years of legal experience.

Office of the Prosecutor-General: Dili; Prosecutor-General LONGUINHOS MONTEIRO; Dep. Prosecutor-General AMANDIO BENEVIDES.

Religion

In 1998 it was estimated that about 86.3% of the total population were Roman Catholic.

CHRISTIANITY

The Roman Catholic Church

Timor-Leste comprises the dioceses of Dili and Baucau, directly responsible to the Holy See. In December 2000 the country had an estimated 750,047 Roman Catholics.

Bishop of Baucau: (vacant), Largo da Catedral, Baucau 88810; tel. (399) 21209; fax (399) 21380.

Bishop of Dili: (vacant); Apostolic Administrator: Rt Rev. Basílio do Nascimento Martins (Titular Bishop of Septimuncia); Av. Direitos Humanos, Bidau Lecidere, CP 4, Dili 88010; tel. (390) 321177.

Protestant Church

Igreja Protestante iha Timor Lorosa'e: Jl. Raya Comoro, POB 1186, Dili 88110; tel. and fax (390) 323128; f. 1988 as Gereja Kristen Timor Timur (GKTT); adopted present name 2000; Moderator Rev. FRANCISCO DE VASCONCELOS; 30,000 mems.

The Press

The office and printing plant of the largest newspaper in East Timor under Indonesian rule, *Suara Timor Timur* (Voice of East Timor, circulation of 8,000), were destroyed prior to the referendum on independence in August 1999. The Constitution promulgated in March 2002 guarantees freedom of the press in Timor-Leste.

Lalenok (Mirror): Rua Gov. Celestino da Silva, Farol, Dili; tel. (390) 321607; e-mail lalenok@hotmail.com; f. 2000; publ. by Kamelin Media Group; Tetum; 3 a week; Dir Gen. and Chief Editor VIRGÍLIO DA SILVA GUTERRES; Editor JOSÉ MARIA POMPELA; circ. 300.

Lian Maubere: Dili; f. 1999; weekly.

Suara Timor Lorosae: Dili; e-mail stl_redaksi@yahoo.com; internet www.suaratimorlorosae.com; daily.

The Official Gazette of East Timor: Dili; f. 1999 by UNTAET; forum for publication of all govt regulations and directives, acts of organs or institutions of East Timor and other acts of public interest requiring general notification; published in English, Portuguese and Tetum, with translations in Bahasa Indonesia available on request.

Tais Timor: Dili; f. 2000; fmrly published by the Office of Communication and Public Information (OCPI) of the UN; Tetum, English, Portuguese and Bahasa Indonesia; every fortnight; distributed free of charge; circ. 75,000.

Talit@kum: Dili; f. 2000; news magazine; publ. by Kdadlak Media Group; Bahasa Indonesia; monthly; Chief Editor HUGO FERNANDEZ.

Timor Post: Rua D. Aleixo Corte Real No. 6, Dili; f. 2000; managed by editors and staff of the former *Suara Timor Timur*; Bahasa Indonesia, Tetum, Portuguese and English; daily; Chief Editor ADERITO HUGO DA COSTA.

PRESS ASSOCIATION

Timor Lorosae Journalists Association (TLJA): Jalan Kaikoli, Dili; tel. (390) 324047; fax (408) 327505; e-mail timorjournal@eudoramail.com; f. 1999; Co-ordinator OTELIO OTE; Pres. VIRGÍLIO DA SILVA GUTERRES.

Broadcasting and Communications

TELECOMMUNICATIONS

Prior to the civil conflict in 1999, East Timor's telephone lines totalled about 12,000. Telecommunications transmission towers were reported to have suffered significant damage in the civil conflict. Indonesia withdrew its telecommunication services in September. A cellular telephone network service was subsequently provided by an Australian company, Telstra. In July 2002 the Government granted a consortium led by Portugal Telecom a 15-year concession permitting it to establish and operate Timor-Leste's telecommunications systems. Under the terms of the concession the consortium agreed to provide every district in Timor-Leste with telecommunications services at the most inexpensive tariffs viable within 15 months. At the expiry of the concession in 2017 the telecommunications system was to be transferred to government control. In February 2003 Timor-Leste Telecom assumed control of the country's telephone network from Telstra.

Timor-Leste Telecom (TT): Dili; f. 2003; jt venture mainly operated by Portugal Telecom; provides telecommunications services in Timor-Leste.

BROADCASTING

Following independence UNMISET transferred control of public television and radio in Timor-Leste to the new Government. Legislation was passed in mid-2002 requesting the establishment of a Public Broadcasting Service controlled by an independent board of directors. In the interim MARIANO LOPES was appointed to serve as head of television and radio.

Radio

In May 2002 Radio UNTAET, launched by the UN, became Radio Timor-Leste, which broadcasts in four languages to an estimated 90% of Timor-Leste's population. The Roman Catholic Church also operates a radio station, Radio Kamanak, while a third populist station, Voz Esperança, broadcasts in Dili. A fourth radio station, Radio Falintil FM, also operates in Dili. In 2000 the US radio station, Voice of America, began broadcasting to Timor-Leste seven days a week in English, Portuguese and Bahasa Indonesia.

Television

TV Timor-Leste (TVTL): Dili; f. 2000 as Televisaun Timor Lorosa'e by UNTAET; adopted present name in May 2002; broadcasts in Tetum and Portuguese.

Finance

In January 2000 a Central Fiscal Authority was established by the UNTAET Transitional Administrator. This later became the country's Ministry of Finance. On 24 January the National Consultative Council formally adopted the US dollar as Timor-Leste's transitional currency; the process of dollarization had been largely completed by early 2003.

BANKING

Timor-Leste's banking system collapsed as a result of the violent unrest that afflicted the territory in 1999. In late 1999 Portugal's main overseas bank, Banco Nacional Ultramarino, opened a branch in Dili. In January 2001 the Australia and New Zealand Banking Group also opened a branch in the capital. In February the East Timor Central Payments Office was officially opened. This was succeeded in November 2001 by the Banking and Payments Authority, which was intended to function as a precursor to a central bank.

Banking and Payments Authority (BPA): Av. Bispo Medeiros, POB 59, Dili; tel. (390) 313718; fax (390) 313716; e-mail bancocentraltimor@yahoo.com; inaugurated Nov. 2001; regulates and supervises Timor-Leste's financial system, formulates and implements payments system policies, provides banking services to Timor-Leste's administration and foreign official institutions, manages fiscal reserves; fmrly Central Payments Office; Gen. Man. LUÍS QUINTANEIRO; Dep. Gen. Mans ABRAAO VASCONSELOS, SAM ROBINSON.

Foreign Banks

Australia and New Zealand Banking Group Ltd (ANZ) (Australia): POB 264, Unit 2, 17–19 Rua José Maria Marques, Dili; tel. (390) 324800; fax (390) 324822; e-mail anzeasttimor@anz.com; internet www.anz.com/TimorLeste; retail and commercial banking services; Gen. Man. CHRIS DURMAN; Chief Operating Officer RICHARD HARE.

Banco Nacional Ultramarino (Portugal): 11–12 Rua Presidente Nicolau Lobato, Dili; tel. (390) 323385; fax (390) 323678; e-mail timor@bnu.com.mo; internet www.bnu.pt; Dir-Gen. Dr CORREIA PINTO.

Trade and Industry

UTILITIES

Timor-Leste's total generating capacity amounted to some 40 MW. As a result of the civil conflict in 1999, some 13–23 power stations were reported to require repairs ranging from moderate maintenance to almost complete rehabilitation. The rehabilitation of the power sector was ongoing in 2003, with funding largely provided by foreign donors. The physical rehabilitation of the rural power sector was expected to have been completed by April of that year.

Electricidade de Timor-Leste (EDTL): Dili; govt dept; responsible for power generation, distribution and financial management of power sector in Timor-Leste; transferred to external management in 2002.

Transport

ROADS

The road network in Timor-Leste is poorly designed and has suffered from long-term neglect. In December 1999 the World Bank reported that some 57% of the country's 1,414 km of paved roads were in poor or damaged condition. Many gravel roads are rough and potholed and are inaccessible to most vehicles. Some repair and maintenance work on the road network was being carried out in 2003, using funding supplied by external donors.

SHIPPING

Timor-Leste's maritime infrastructure includes ports at Dili, Carabela and Com, smaller wharves at Oecusse (Oekussi) and Liquiça (Likisia), and slip-landing structures in Oecusse, Batugade and Suai. In November 2001, following its reconstruction, the management of the port at Dili was transferred to the Government. The port was expected to be a significant source of revenue.

CIVIL AVIATION

Timor-Leste has two international airports and eight grass runways. At mid-2000 operators of international flights to East Timor included Qantas Airways and Air North of Australia. In June 2001 Dili Express Pte was the first Timor-based company to begin international flights, with a service to Singapore.

TOGO

Introductory Survey

Location, Climate, Language, Religion, Flag, Capital

The Togolese Republic lies in West Africa, forming a narrow strip stretching north from a coastline of about 50 km (30 miles) on the Gulf of Guinea. It is bordered by Ghana to the west, by Benin to the east, and by Burkina Faso to the north. The climate in the coastal area is hot and humid, with an average annual temperature of 27°C (81°F), rainfall in this zone averages 875 mm (34.4 ins) per year, and is heaviest during May–October. Precipitation in the central region is heaviest in May–June and in October, and in the north, where the average annual temperature is 30°C (86°F), there is a rainy season from July–September. The official languages are French, Kabiye and Ewe. About one-half of the population follows animist beliefs, while about 35% are Christians and 15% Muslims. The national flag (approximate proportions 3 by 5) has five equal horizontal stripes, alternately green and yellow, with a square red canton, containing a five-pointed white star, in the upper hoist. The capital is Lomé.

Recent History

Togoland, of which modern Togo was formerly a part, became a German colony in 1894. Shortly after the outbreak of the First World War, the colony was occupied by French and British forces. After the war, a League of Nations mandate divided Togoland into two administrative zones, with France controlling the larger eastern section, while the United Kingdom governed the west. The partition of Togoland split the homeland of the Ewe people, who inhabit the southern part of the territory, and this has been a continuing source of friction. After the Second World War, French and British Togoland became UN Trust Territories. In May 1956 a UN-supervised plebiscite in British Togoland produced, despite Ewe opposition, majority support for a merger with the neighbouring territory of the Gold Coast, then a British colony, in an independent state. The region accordingly became part of Ghana in the following year. In October 1956, in another plebiscite, French Togoland voted to become an autonomous republic within the French Community. The new Togolese Republic had internal self-government until becoming fully independent on 27 April 1960.

Prior to independence Togo's foremost political parties were the Comité de l'unité togolaise (usually known as the Unité togolaise—UT), led by Sylvanus Olympio, and the Parti togolais du progrès (PTP), led by Nicolas Grunitzky, Olympio's brother-in-law. In 1956 Grunitzky became Prime Minister in the first autonomous Government, but in April 1958 a UN-supervised election was won by the UT. Olympio became Prime Minister and led Togo to independence.

At elections in April 1961 Olympio became Togo's first President, while the UT was elected (unopposed) to all 51 seats in the Assemblée nationale. At the same time a referendum approved a new Constitution. On 13 January 1963 the UT regime was overthrown by a military revolt, in which Olympio was killed. Grunitzky subsequently assumed the presidency on a provisional basis. A referendum in May approved another Constitution, confirmed Grunitzky as President and elected a new legislature from a single list of candidates, giving equal representation to the four main political parties.

President Grunitzky was deposed by a bloodless military coup on 13 January 1967. The Constitution was abrogated, and the Assemblée nationale was dissolved. The coup was led by Lt-Col (later Gen.) Etienne (Gnassingbé) Eyadéma, the Army Chief of Staff, who assumed the office of President in April. Political parties were banned, and the President ruled by decree. Eyadéma, a member of the Kabiye ethnic group, had taken a prominent part in the 1963 rising and was reputedly Olympio's assassin. In November 1969 a new ruling party, the Rassemblement du peuple togolais (RPT), was founded, led by Eyadéma. Comprehensive government changes in January 1977 left Eyadéma as the sole representative of the armed forces in the Council of Ministers.

In Togo's first elections for 16 years, held on 30 December 1979, Eyadéma (the sole candidate) was confirmed as President of the Republic for a seven-year term. At the same time a new Constitution was overwhelmingly endorsed, while the list of 67 candidates for a single-party Assemblée nationale was approved by 96% of votes cast. On 13 January 1980 Eyadéma proclaimed the 'Third Republic'. At the legislative elections of March 1985 a choice of RPT candidates was permitted, although the RPT remained the sole legal political party. However, in May the Constitution was amended to allow deputies to be elected without first being proposed by the party.

In December 1986 President Eyadéma was re-elected, unopposed, for a further seven-year term. In the same month 13 people were sentenced to death for complicity in an attempted *coup d'état* staged in September 1985 (the exiled opposition leader, Gilchrist Olympio, son of the former President, was sentenced *in absentia*), although most of the death sentences were subsequently commuted.

In March 1990 230 candidates, all loyal to the RPT, contested the Assemblée nationale's 77 seats. In October a commission was established to draft a new constitution, to be submitted to a national referendum in December 1991. In December 1990 the constitutional commission presented a draft document, which envisaged the existence of a Prime Minister, a Constitutional Council and a plurality of political parties. Meanwhile, several recently formed, unofficial opposition movements formed a co-ordinating organization, the Front des associations pour le renouveau (FAR), led by Yawovi Agboyivo, to campaign for the immediate introduction of a multi-party political system. Eyadéma subsequently agreed to implement a general amnesty for political dissidents and to permit the legalization of political organizations.

Following instances of violent unrest in April 1991, Eyadéma, fearing a civil conflict between the Kabiye and Ewe ethnic groups (the Government and armed forces were composed overwhelmingly of members of the first group, while opposition groups for the most part represented the Ewe people), announced that a new constitution would be introduced within one year, and that legislative elections, in the context of a multi-party political system, would be organized. At the end of the month it was announced that the FAR was to be disbanded. Agboyibo subsequently formed his own party, the Comité d'action pour le renouveau (CAR), and in early May 10 parties, including the CAR, announced the formation of a Front de l'opposition démocratique (FOD, later renamed the Coalition de l'opposition démocratique—COD), to co-ordinate the activities of opposition groups in preparation for the proposed national meeting.

In May 1991 representatives of the Government and the FOD disputed the status of the forthcoming meeting: the former designated it a 'national forum of dialogue', while the latter insisted that it should be a 'sovereign national conference' (akin to those that had recently been held in other countries of the region, notably in Benin, and which had been instrumental in the introduction of democratic institutions). Following the organization of a general strike by the FOD, the Government agreed, in June, that a 'national conference' would be held, with the power to choose a transitional Prime Minister and to establish a transitional legislative body, prior to legislative and presidential elections. The conference opened in July, attended by some 1,000 delegates, representing the organs of state, political parties, and religious and professional groups, although the armed forces boycotted the conference. Gilchrist Olympio returned from exile to participate. When the conference adopted resolutions suspending the Constitution, dissolving the Assemblée nationale and giving the conference sovereign power, government representatives withdrew. Subsequently the conference resolved to 'freeze' the assets of the RPT, to transfer most of the powers of the President to a Prime Minister, and to prevent Eyadéma from contesting future elections. In defiance of a decree issued by Eyadéma temporarily suspending proceedings, the conference elected a Prime Minister, Joseph Kokou Koffigoh (a senior lawyer and prominent human rights activist, announced the dissolution of the RPT and the formation of a transitional legislature, the Haut Conseil de la République (HCR). Eyadéma capitulated, signing a decree that proclaimed

Koffigoh as transitional Prime Minister. In September Koffigoh formed a transitional Government, most of whose members had not previously held office: he himself assumed the defence portfolio.

In October 1991 members of the armed forces seized control of the national broadcasting station, demanding that full executive powers be restored to Eyadéma. They returned to barracks on Eyadéma's orders. Later in October a new commission was established to draft a constitution, and Koffigoh confirmed that a constitutional referendum and elections would be held in 1992. In November 1991, following the adoption of legislation by the HCR confirming the dissolution of the RPT, troops seized the broadcasting headquarters and surrounded the Prime Minister's residence, demanding that Eyadéma nominate a new government and that the HCR be abolished. At least 20 people were killed in the fighting that ensued. In December troops captured Koffigoh during an attack on his residence, killing several of his guards. Koffigoh agreed to form a new government. At the end of December the reconvened HCR restored legal status to the RPT and announced the formation of a transitional 'Government of National Union', which comprised many of the members of the previous transitional administration, but also two close associates of Eyadéma, including Aboudou Assouma, the new minister with responsibility for the armed forces.

In January 1992 an electoral schedule was announced, envisaging the holding of a referendum on a new constitution and of local, legislative and presidential elections by June of that year. In March the Government approved the newly drafted Constitution, and an electoral census commenced. In May the attempted assassination of Gilchrist Olympio, who was regarded as a potential presidential candidate, and the murder of another prominent member of the opposition, Dr Marc Attidépé, provoked renewed unrest. In late May the Council of Ministers abandoned the electoral timetable. In June Koffigoh dismissed Assouma, prompting the resignation of another minister, and precipitating a wider ministerial reorganization in July. Also in July the HCR adopted the draft Constitution and an electoral code, and the constitutional referendum was scheduled for late August, although it was subsequently postponed. Meanwhile, a report published by the International Federation of Human Rights concluded that members of the armed forces had been responsible for the attempted murder of Olympio, implicating Eyadéma's son (a military officer) of involvement. Later in July Tavio Ayao Amorin, a member of the HCR and leader of the radical Parti pan-africain socialiste, was shot and fatally wounded. In response, the recently formed Collectif de l'opposition démocratique (COD-2), an alliance of some 25 political organizations and trade unions, called a general strike, which was widely observed. In August agreement was reached on opposition access to the state-controlled media, and on the extension until 31 December of the transition period (which was subsequently approved by the HCR). In late August the HCR restored to Eyadéma the power to preside over the Council of Ministers, and to represent Togo abroad; furthermore, his agreement would henceforth be necessary in the appointment of members of the Government. Moreover, the draft Constitution was amended so that members of the armed forces would no longer be obliged to resign their commissions before seeking election to public office.

The transitional Government was dissolved on 1 September 1992. In late September a new transitional Government, under Koffigoh's premiership, was appointed; representatives of 10 parties were included, although the most influential ministries were allocated to members of the RPT. On 27 September the new Constitution was approved in a referendum by 98.11% of the votes cast. At the end of the month, however, it was announced that the local, legislative and presidential elections were to be further postponed. In October eight opposition parties announced the formation of a 'Patriotic Front', to be led by the leader of the Union togolaise pour la démocratie (UTD), Edem Kodjo, and Agboyibo of the CAR. In November Koffigoh dismissed two ministers (both adherents of the RPT) for their conduct during an attack on the HCR by members of the armed forces in October, but Eyadéma overruled this decision. In the same month a general strike was organized by the COD-2 and independent trade unions in support of their demands, which included the expedited holding of elections, the neutrality of the armed forces and the bringing to justice of those responsible for the attacks on the HCR. The strike was widely observed, except in the north of Togo (where support for Eyadéma was strongest),

and continued until mid-1993, causing considerable economic disruption.

In January 1993 Eyadéma dissolved the Government, reappointing Koffigoh as Prime Minister, and stated that he would appoint a new government of national unity to organize elections. His action provoked protests by the opposition parties, who claimed that, according to the Constitution, the HCR should appoint a Prime Minister since the transition period had now expired. In the same month two ministers representing the French and German Governments visited Togo to offer mediation in the political crisis. During their visit at least 20 people were killed when police opened fire on anti-Government protesters. Thousands of Togolese subsequently fled from Lomé, many seeking refuge in Benin or Ghana. In February discussions organized by the French and German Governments in France, and attended by representatives of Eyadéma, the RPT, Koffigoh, the HCR and the COD-2, failed when the presidential delegation withdrew after one day. In that month the French, German and US Governments suspended their programmes of aid to Togo. A new 'Crisis Government', in which supporters of Eyadéma retained the principal posts, was formed in February. In March COD-2 member parties, meeting in Benin, stated that they now regarded Koffigoh as an obstacle to democratization, and nominated a 'parallel' Prime Minister, Jean-Lucien Savi de Tové (of the Parti des démocrates pour l'unité). In late March more than 20 people were killed in an armed attack on the military camp in Lomé where Eyadéma had his residence. The Government declared that Gilchrist Olympio, with assistance from Ghana, had instigated the attack, although both parties denied these accusations.

In April 1993 a new electoral schedule was announced. As subsequently modified, it envisaged elections to the presidency and the legislature in July and August, respectively. The RPT designated Eyadéma as its presidential candidate. In May the COD-2 declared that it would boycott the elections, alleging that they would not be fairly conducted, and that opposition politicians had no guarantee of their safety. In June and July, however, discussions took place in Burkina Faso, between the Togolese Government and the COD-2, and in July they signed an agreement establishing 25 August as the date for the presidential election (with a second round to be held on 8 September, should no candidate gain an absolute majority in the first round). The agreement stipulated that the Togolese armed forces should be confined to barracks during the election period, and that international military observers should be present to confirm this, while international civilian observers should also be present for the election. An independent, nine-member National Electoral Commission (NEC) was to be established, to include three members nominated by the opposition parties. Gilchrist Olympio, who remained outside Togo, denounced the agreement, stating that the Government would retain too much control over the election, and that Togolese refugees abroad should be allowed to return home in safety before the poll. (By now the number of Togolese refugees in neighbouring countries —mostly in Ghana and Benin—was estimated at between 200,000 and 350,000.)

Later in July 1993 the COD-2 nominated Kodjo, of the UTD, as its presidential candidate; however, in the same month two other candidates—Agboyibo of the CAR and Abou Djobo Boukari of Démocratie sociale togolaise—were nominated by parties affiliated to the COD-2. Gilchrist Olympio also announced his nomination as the presidential candidate of the Union des forces de changement (UFC), but in August the Supreme Court rejected his candidacy, on the grounds that he had not produced the requisite Togolese medical certificates. After intervention by the international monitoring committee, Olympio was invited to undergo a medical examination in Togo, but stated that he would not return until security conditions permitted the return of all other Togolese exiles. The Prime Minister, Koffigoh (who had formed his own political party, the Coordination nationale des forces nouvelles—CFN, in June) expressed support for Eyadéma's re-election. In August Boukari, Kodjo and Agboyibo announced their withdrawal from the election, expressing dissatisfaction with electoral preparations. Teams of US and German observers withdrew shortly before the election took place; French observers remained, but concluded that the poll was not satisfactorily conducted. Three candidates contested the presidency: Eyadéma and two little-known candidates. Eyadéma was reported to have obtained 96.49% of the votes cast.

In early January 1994 an armed attack on Eyadéma's official residence was attributed by the Government to forces organized by Olympio, with Ghanaian support. A total of 67 people were officially reported to have died in the violence. The human rights organization Amnesty International claimed that at least 48 deaths took the form of summary executions by the armed forces.

In the legislative elections, finally held, after several postponements, on 6 and 20 February 1994, 347 candidates contested 81 seats. Despite the murder of an elected CAR representative after the first round, and violent incidents at polling stations during the second round, international observers expressed themselves satisfied with the conduct of the elections. The opposition won a narrow victory in the polls, with the CAR winning 36 seats and the UTD seven; the RPT obtained 35 seats and two other smaller pro-Eyadéma parties won three. During March Eyadéma consulted the main opposition parties on the formation of a new government. In late March the CAR and the UTD reached an agreement on the terms of their alliance and jointly proposed the candidacy of Agboyibo for Prime Minister. In March and April the Supreme Court declared the results of the legislative elections invalid in three constituencies (in which the CAR had won two seats and the UTD one) and ordered by-elections. In protest, the CAR and the UTD staged a boycott of the new Assemblée nationale. In April Eyadéma nominated Kodjo (of the UTD) as Prime Minister, an appointment that Kodjo accepted, in spite of an agreement between the UTD and the CAR that their candidate for the premiership should be a member of the CAR. The CAR subsequently declared that it would not participate in an administration formed by Kodjo. Kodjo took office on 25 April; his Government, formed in late May, comprised eight members of the RPT and other pro-Eyadéma parties, three members of the UTD, and eight independents. Shortly beforehand the CAR had announced (in response to the postponement of the parliamentary by-elections) that it was to end its boycott of the Assemblée nationale.

In November 1994 the CAR again suspended its participation in the Assemblée nationale, and indicated that it would return only when agreement had been reached with the Government on the conduct of the by-elections, which were consequently postponed. In early 1995 the Government and the major opposition parties reached an agreement providing for the Government and the legislative opposition to have equal representation on national, district and local electoral commissions. In August the CAR officially resumed participation in the legislature, following the approval of legislation concerning the independence of the judiciary. In April 1996 a deputy of the CAR resigned from the party. In May the CAR withdrew from the by-elections, following the rejection by the Government of its demands that the elections be conducted in the presence of an international monitoring committee. In the same month a UTD deputy was dismissed from the party.

At the by-elections, conducted on 4 and 18 August 1996 in the presence of 22 international observers, the RPT won control of all three constituencies. Consequently, the RPT and its allies were able to command a majority in the legislature, thus precipitating the resignation of the Kodjo administration. On 20 August Eyadéma appointed Kwassi Klutse, hitherto Minister of Planning and Territorial Development, as Prime Minister, and the new Council of Ministers, appointed in late August, comprised almost exclusively supporters of Eyadéma.

In October 1996 a further CAR deputy resigned from the party, to join the RPT. In November the Union pour la justice et la démocratie, which held two seats in the legislature, announced that it was officially to merge with the RPT, thus giving the RPT an overall majority, with 41 seats. A new Constitutional Court was inaugurated in February 1997; the legislative vote that, in December 1996, had approved the creation of the Court, had been boycotted by the CAR and the UTD as a result of the rejection of a proposal of the CAR that the Court be empowered to rule on disputes arising from legislative and presidential elections.

In September 1997 a new electoral code was approved, providing for an NEC comprising nine members, chaired by the President of the Court of Appeal and including four members appointed by the opposition. The CAR, however, boycotted the legislative session in protest at the Government's refusal to reveal the findings of a report by a mission of the European Union (EU, see p. 199) on the country's electoral process. Later that month the CAR, the UFC and the Parti pour la démocratie et le renouveau (PDR) organized a demonstration in the capital in protest at the new electoral law and condemned as fraudulent

the Government's preparations for the forthcoming presidential election.

During campaigning for the presidential election, scheduled for 21 June 1998, Eyadéma permitted rival candidates to make brief campaign speeches on state television. Shortly before the election, however, the Government refused to permit the presence of 500 national observers trained by the EU. The election proceeded amid accusations of electoral malpractice, and on the following day counting of votes was halted without explanation, reportedly when the early returns showed Eyadéma to be in second place. Four members of the NEC resigned the same day, alleging intimidation. The Minister of the Interior and Security, Gen. Seyi Memene, announced that he assumed responsibility for the ballot count, and that Eyadéma had been re-elected President with 52.13% of the valid votes cast. Gilchrist Olympio, who had contested the election from exile in Ghana, was officially stated to have won 34.12%. Following the announcement of the result, violent protests erupted throughout Lomé. The USA condemned the conduct of the election, and called on the Government to respect its own laws and electoral code, while the EU decided not to recognize the result, which was, none the less, confirmed by the Togolese Constitutional Court.

In September 1998 Klutse announced his new Council of Ministers. Despite Eyadéma's stated intention to form a government of national unity, no opposition figures were willing to be included. Few new appointments were made, although former Prime Minister Koffigoh was appointed as Minister of State, responsible for Foreign Affairs and Co-operation. In November the Government survived a vote of censure tabled by the CAR and the UTD. In the same month Olympio urged Eyadéma to resign, offering to concede defeat at the June presidential elections, and not to stand in future elections, if he did so.

In January 1999 the Government announced that the first round of legislative elections would be held on 7 March. In February the opposition parties appealed for discussions with the Government prior to the elections, on the grounds that the issue of the disputed presidential election should be settled first. The Government agreed to postpone voting until later in March, but rejected the opposition's proposal that the Constitution be amended in order to allow the extension of the mandate of the incumbent Assemblée nationale; the eight main opposition parties therefore announced a boycott of the elections.

Elections to the Assemblée nationale took place on 21 March 1999, contested by the RPT and by two small parties loyal to Eyadéma, Koffigoh's CFN and the Parti écologiste pan-africain, as well as by 12 independent candidates. The 50 international observers present noted that the elections had taken place in an atmosphere of calm. The Constitutional Court ruled that the RPT had won 77 seats, and that independent candidates had taken two seats. By-elections were to take place in two constituencies in which voting had been invalidated. (Both of these seats were subsequently won by the RPT.) The Court estimated turn-out at 66%, although the opposition stated that it was little more than 10%. Despite international criticism, Eyadéma rejected demands for fresh elections, declaring that the opposition had been afforded ample opportunity to participate. In April Klutse tendered his Government's resignation; in May Eugene Koffi Adogboli, a former UN official, was appointed Prime Minister. Adogboli subsequently nominated a Council of Ministers dominated by long-standing supporters of Eyadéma.

In May 1999 Amnesty International published a report detailing numerous abuses of human rights committed by Togolese security forces, alleging that hundreds of political opponents of Eyadéma had been killed following the 1998 presidential election. The Government reacted angrily to the report, threatening to institute legal proceedings against Amnesty International. In July a Beninois human rights organization reported that, following the 1998 presidential election in Togo, corpses had been discovered on the beaches of Benin. The Beninois Government, however, stated that it had received no such information. In late July 1999 Eyadéma urged the UN and the Organization of African Unity (now the African Union, see p. 130) to assist in the establishment of an international commission of inquiry into the allegations; such a commission was established in June 2000.

Discussions began in Lomé in July 1999 between four international facilitators, representing France, Germany, the EU and La Francophonie (see p. 349). Both the Government and opposition rejected a demand made by Gilchrist Olympio that the UFC meet government representatives separately in order to resolve the issue of the disputed presidential election; Olympio therefore withdrew from discussions and returned to Ghana, although the UFC continued to be represented in the discussions. Eyadéma's announcement, reportedly advocated by French President Jacques Chirac, that he would not stand for re-election in 2003 and that new legislative elections would be held, was widely credited with breaking the deadlock in negotiations, and, after the opposition had agreed to accept Eyadéma's victory in the presidential election, an accord was signed on 29 July 1999 by all the parties involved in negotiations, including the UFC. The accord made provision for the creation of an independent electoral body and for the creation of a code of conduct to regulate political activity.

The first meeting took place in early August 1999 of the 24-member Comité paritaire de suivi (CPS) responsible for the implementation of the accord, composed of an equal number of opposition and pro-Eyadéma representatives, and also including intermediaries from the EU. Harry Octavianus Olympio, the cousin of Gilchrist Olympio and the Minister for the Promotion of Democracy and the Rule of Law, was appointed to head the CPS. Despite the reservations of the UFC, a compromise agreement on announcing election results was reached in late September, and in December agreement was reached on a revised electoral code, providing for the establishment of an independent electoral commission. In April 2000 Eyadéma obliged the Assemblée nationale to accept the new electoral code, and announced that no obstacle remained to the creation of an independent electoral commission. Three parties, including the UFC and the CAR, which had withdrawn from discussions in January, following the initial refusal of the legislature to accept the new arrangements, therefore returned to negotiations. The EU expressed its satisfaction at the adoption of the electoral code, and subsequently offered to provide financial support for the elections, which were scheduled to be held later in 2000.

In January 2000 the Government amended legislation regulating the press, introducing terms of imprisonment and substantial fines for those found guilty of violating the press code, as well as the seizure and destruction of the offending publication, and the possible suspension of the publication's future activities. The new regulations were widely condemned as detrimental to the freedom of the press, and several leading journalists were arrested on various charges during the first half of 2000, while other senior journalists subsequently went into hiding in order, they claimed, to evade arrest.

In April 2000 the CPS began discussions regarding the appointment of an independent electoral commission. The 20 members of the new electoral commission were finally named in June, and following the withdrawal of the UFC candidate for the presidency of the Commission électorale nationale indépendante (CENI), Arthème Ahoomey-Zounou of the Convergence patriotique panafricaine (CPP—formed in 1999 by the amalgamation of the UTD and three smaller parties, and headed by Edem Kodjo) was elected to this position in late July. Meanwhile, in May Harry Octavianus Olympio announced that he had survived an attempt on his life. However, in June Olympio was dismissed from the Government, after evidence was discovered, which apparently indicated that he had himself engineered the alleged assassination attempt; his former portfolios were subsequently assimilated into that of justice.

In August 2000 three activists of the UFC, who had been arrested in February for violence and disturbing public order, were given 12-month prison sentences. In that month Adogboli was overwhelmingly defeated in a legislative vote of 'no confidence'; he therefore presented his resignation and that of his Government to Eyadéma. In late August Eyadéma appointed Agbéyomè Kodjo, hitherto the President of the Assemblée nationale, and regarded as a close ally of the President, as Prime Minister. A government reshuffle was effected in early October.

In December 2000 Eyadéma requested that the CENI publish a new electoral calendar. In January 2001 the four international facilitators of inter-Togolese dialogue expressed disappointment at the continued failure of the commission to establish a date for the repeatedly postponed legislative elections. Shortly afterwards the CENI announced that the legislative elections would now be held in two rounds, on 14 and 28 October 2001. The CENI also announced that the disputed electoral registers from the 1998 presidential election would be used in the forthcoming polls.

In February 2001 the Minister of the Interior, Security and Decentralization, Gen. Sizing Akawilou Walla, accused Amnesty International of having received US $500,000m. from Gilchrist Olympio prior to the publication of its 1999 report,

which had accused the Togolese Government of committing human rights abuses. Walla claimed that the Government possessed letters from Gilchrist Olympio to the Secretary-General of Amnesty International that confirmed these allegations, although these claims were rejected by the UFC. Later in February the report of the joint UN-OAU commission was published. The report concluded that 'systematic violations of human rights' had occurred in Togo in 1998 and stated that allegations of extra-judicial executions, particularly of opposition party activists, could not be disproven. Although the commission had been unable to establish the quantity of corpses found in the sea or on beaches following the election, it stated that individuals linked to the security forces appeared to be responsible for such killings, and recommended that the authorities punish those responsible, and that a special rapporteur be appointed to monitor human rights in Togo. However, both the Government and the President of the Assemblée nationale, Ouattara Fambaré Natchaba, dismissed the report's conclusions, emphasizing that the commission had been unable to substantiate some of its findings. At the end of the month security forces used tear gas to disperse a demonstration in Lomé, which had been organized by the CAR to protest at the findings of the UN-OAU report; the rally, which was attended by 100 people, according to government figures, or by more than 5,000, according to the CAR, had been declared unlawful several days earlier. In late March Prime Minister Agbéyomè Kodjo appeared before the office of the UN High Commissioner for Human Rights to deny the findings of the report.

Concern regarding the freedom of the Togolese press was again expressed internationally in May 2001, when Lucien Messan, the editor of the pro-opposition weekly newspaper *Le Combat du Peuple*, was arrested on charges of fraud, for which he was subsequently sentenced to 18 months' imprisonment. Observers noted that the offence with which Messan had been charged was of a technical nature and that the arrest occurred prior to the publication of an article that allegedly documented government involvement in the attempted assassination of Harry Octavianus Olympio. (All copies of the relevant edition of the publication were seized.) In late June Harry Octavianus Olympio was himself sentenced to 18 months' imprisonment, having been convicted of the illegal possession and manufacture of explosives. In early August Agboyibo, the leader of the CAR, was jailed for six months and fined 100,000 Francs CFA, having been convicted of libelling Prime Minister Agbéyomè Kodjo. Several opposition groups withdrew from the CPS in protest at Agboyibo's detention, and two protest marches in support of his release were prohibited by the authorities.

In late August 2001 Prime Minister Kodjo announced that the legislative elections would be further postponed until 2002, and declared his support for a proposed constitutional change that would allow Eyadéma to contest a further term of office as President. (A report issued in September by the four international facilitators of inter-Togolese dialogue confirmed the need for further preparations prior to the holding of elections.) In late October Eyadéma issued presidential decrees pardoning and permitting the release from prison of Harry Octavianus Olympio and Lucien Messan. In late November Eyadéma implied that he would be prepared to offer a pardon to Agboyibo, should he request one. Agboyibo, however, launched an appeal against his conviction. Although the appeals court found in favour of Agboyibo in mid-January 2002, he was immediately rearrested on charges of conspiring to commit violence during the 1998 presidential election campaign; Agboyibo was finally released from prison in mid-March 2002, on the orders of Eyadéma, who stated that the release was intended to facilitate national reconciliation; the charges against Agboyibo of conspiring to commit violence were also withdrawn.

In February 2002, following several unresolved disputes within the CENI, the Assemblée nationale approved amendments to electoral legislation and to the remit of the CENI; henceforth all candidates for legislative elections were required to have been continuously resident in Togo for six months prior to elections, with presidential candidates to have been resident for a continuous 12 months. The CENI was also to be reduced in size from 20 to 10 members, and decisions were henceforth to be taken by a two-thirds' majority, instead of the four-fifths' majority required hitherto; these amendments led to a further postponement of the elections, which had been scheduled to take place in March. The UFC opposed the amendments, which effectively prevented its leader, Gilchrist Olympio, who remained resident in Ghana, from seeking election. The measures also attracted international disapproval, notably prompting the EU to suspend aid intended to finance the legislative elections. In mid-February five opposition parties, including the CAR, the CPP and the UFC, issued a joint communiqué accusing the Government of having broken the conditions of the accord signed in July 1999, and in early March they rejected an invitation by Kodjo to nominate representatives to the CENI. The Government consequently announced that no date for the legislative elections could be announced until a complete electoral commission had been formed. In late March 10 opposition parties, which had not been party to the accord signed in 1999 and were therefore excluded from the CPS, announced the formation of a Coordination des partis de l'opposition constructive, headed by Harry Octavianus Olympio, who was also now the leader of the Rassemblement pour le soutien de la démocratie et du développement (RSDD).

In mid-May 2002 a committee of seven judges (the Comité de sept magistrats—C-7), charged with monitoring the electoral process at the proposed legislative elections, was appointed, in accordance with a provision of the revised electoral code that permitted the appointment of such a committee in the event that the CENI could not be formed by consensus. Several opposition parties, including the CAR, the CPP and the UFC condemned this decision, and announced their intention to boycott any elections organized by the C-7. None the less, in early June Cornelius Aidam, a senior figure in the CPP, urged supporters of the opposition to participate in the elections, apparently in an attempt to prevent Eyadéma from introducing legislation that would permit him to stand for a further term of office. Meanwhile, at the end of May the EU announced that it would not renew funding for the three facilitators it supported (representing France, Germany and the EU), in view of the continued lack of progress towards democracy in Togo.

At the end of June 2002 Eyadéma dismissed Kodjo as Prime Minister, following a dispute within the RPT between party factions loyal to the President and those close to a reformist deputy, Dahuku Pere. Eyadéma appointed Koffi Sama, the Secretary-General of the RPT and hitherto Minister of National Education and Research, as Prime Minister, and a new Government, which included several principal members of the former administration, was appointed in early July. Kodjo subsequently issued a statement criticizing the 'monarchic, despotic' regime of Eyadéma, and (in contrast to his former stated position) called for measures to ensure that Eyadéma would be unable to amend the Constitution to stand for a further term of office; it was subsequently reported that the former premier had received death threats from a relation of the President. Moreover, the state prosecutor filed a suit against Kodjo on charges of disseminating false information and demeaning the honour of the President, in response to statements issued by Kodjo, alleging corruption and human rights abuses by representatives of the Government; Kodjo subsequently left Togo, taking up residence in France. In early August Kodjo and Pere were both expelled from the RPT, and in mid-September an international arrest warrant, on charges of fraud, was issued against Kodjo. However, in late October Kodjo's bank accounts in France were 'unfrozen', after a judicial inquiry failed to establish that the accounts had been used fraudulently.

Meanwhile, in early August 2002 four parties, including the CAR, announced the formation of an opposition alliance, the Front uni de l'opposition (Le Front), headed by Agboyibo. In late August renewed concern about the freedom of the press in Togo arose, following the approval by the Council of Ministers of a draft text of modifications to the press code; notably, journalists convicted of insulting the President could be sentenced to five years' imprisonment under the new proposed legislation. The approval of the text followed the arrest, in June, of a newspaper editor on charges of defamation and printing false information, in connection with the death threats allegedly issued against Kodjo, and the arrest, in August, of the editor and director of the *Nouvel Echo* (see p. 4084), Julien Ayih and Alphonse Nevame Klu, respectively, who had published reports claiming that Eyadéma had a personal fortune of up to US \$5,000m., which were denied by the President. The leader of the Parti des travailleurs, Claude Ameganvi, was also detained on charges related to these reports; Ameganvi and Ayih were each sentenced to four months' imprisonment in mid-September, and Klu, who had gone into hiding, was sentenced *in absentia* to six months' imprisonment. Also in mid-September, the authorities announced that the legislative elections were to be held on 27 October. In late September the Secretary-General of the UFC,

Jean-Pierre Fabre, was arrested, following a ban on public meetings by the party imposed by the Minister of the Interior, Security and Decentralization, who stated that the UFC's meetings frequently resulted in violence and disruption to public order.

In mid-October 2002 Eyadéma issued two decrees, in accordance with which the Assemblée nationale was dissolved, although deputies were to retain their responsibilities and powers until the holding of the forthcoming legislative elections. These measures, which were approved by an overwhelming majority in the outgoing Assemblée nationale, provoked controversy, as the Constitution required 30 days to elapse between the dissolution of the legislature and the holding of elections; however, the Government described the measures as a means to ensure stability in the event of any further delays in the organization of the polls. In late October nine opposition parties that had declined to participate in the elections announced the formation of a new alliance, the Coalition des forces démocrates (CFD); members of the grouping included the CAR, the CPP and the UFC, in addition to a faction of 'renovators' within the RPT. The elections proceeded as scheduled, without the participation of the principal opposition parties, on 27 October. The 81 seats of the Assemblée nationale were contested by 126 candidates, comprising 118 candidates nominated by 15 parties and eight independent candidates, although the RPT was the sole party to contest every seat. According to the official results, published at the end of October, the RPT won 72 seats (of which 46 had been secured unopposed) and the RSDD three, while three other parties won a total of five seats, and one independent candidate was elected. The C-7, which now comprised six judges (following the resignation of one member of the committee on the day before the elections), estimated electoral turn-out at 67.43%, although the CFD claimed that no more than 10% of the electorate had voted.

Eyadéma re-appointed Sama as Prime Minister in mid-November 2002; a new Government, comprising 21 ministers, was formed in early December. Gen. Walla was replaced as Minister of the Interior, Security and Decentralization by Maj. Akila Esso Boco, and the former chief administrator of the port of Lomé, Katari Foli Bazi, was appointed as Keeper of the Seals, Minister of Justice responsible for the Promotion of Democracy and the Rule of Law. Roland Yao Kpotsra, a former ambassador to Belgium, was appointed as Minister of Foreign Affairs and Cooperation. All ministers were members of the RPT, with the exception of Harry Octavianus Olympio, who was appointed Minister responsible for Relations with Parliament.

At the end of December 2002 the Assemblée nationale approved several constitutional amendments regarding the eligibility of presidential candidates. The restriction that had limited the President to serving two terms of office was to be removed, and the age of eligibility was to be reduced from 45 to 35 years. (It was widely believed that these measures were intended to permit Eyadéma to serve a further term of office, and also to permit the possible presidential candidacy of Eyadéma's son.) Candidates were henceforth to be required to hold solely Togolese citizenship, although those holding dual or multiple nationalities were to be permitted to renounce them, prior to seeking election. Although these measures were adopted unanimously by the 80 members of the legislature present at the vote, they were vociferously denounced by the extra-parliamentary opposition; in particular, the UFC announced its intention of commencing a campaign of civil disobedience in response to the amendments. In late February 2003 the UFC announced its withdrawal from the CFD, after other parties within the grouping agreed to appoint representatives to the CENI prior to the holding of a presidential election later in the year. In mid-March Gilchrist Olympio announced that he intended to contest the presidential election as the candidate of the UFC, although it appeared that his candidacy would not meet residency requirements. Also in mid-March, a prominent leader of the UFC in northern Togo, Marc Palanga, was arrested on charges of illicitly importing military equipment to Togo. In mid-April the Government announced that the presidential election was to be held on 1 June. In late April Eyadéma confirmed that he was to seek re-election. In early May the CENI rejected the candidacy of Olympio, who had recently returned to Togo. By mid-May six opposition candidates (including four representatives of the constituent parties of the CFD) had emerged. Emmanuel Bob Akitani, the First Vice-President of the UFC, was announced as his party's candidate, following Olympio's debarment.

Relations with neighbouring Ghana have frequently become strained, as the common border with Togo has periodically been closed in an effort to combat smuggling and to curb political activity by exiles on both sides. In March 1993 and January 1994 the Togolese Government accused Ghana of supporting armed attacks on Eyadéma's residence, reflecting earlier accusations of Ghanaian involvement in unrest in Togo in early 1991. Full diplomatic relations between the two countries, suspended since 1982, were formally resumed in November 1994, and various joint commissions were subsequently reactivated. The newly elected President of Ghana, John Kufuor, visited Togo to mark the celebrations for Liberation Day on 13 January 2001; this visit provoked controversy internationally, within Ghana, and among the Togolese opposition. The Togolese authorities emphasized that the annual holiday commemorated the bloodless coup of 13 January 1967, and not the military uprising that occurred on the same day in 1963.

From mid-1998 President Eyadéma mediated in the conflict in Guinea-Bissau. Togolese troops were sent to the country as peace-keepers, and a peace conference was held in Lomé in February 1999. In June, after the failure of the peace agreement, the Togolese contingent withdrew from Guinea-Bissau. Eyadéma also hosted talks on the conflict in Sierra Leone in the first half of 1999. A peace agreement between the warring rebel factions and the Sierra Leonean Government was concluded in Lomé in July, in the presence of Eyadéma and other regional leaders. From late 2002 Eyadéma also played a leading role in mediation in the conflict in Côte d'Ivoire, under the auspices of the Economic Community of West African States.

Government

Under the terms of the Constitution that was approved in a national referendum on 27 September 1993, and subsequently modified, executive power is vested in the President of the Republic, who is directly elected, by universal adult suffrage, for a period of five years. The legislature is the unicameral Assemblée nationale, whose 81 members are also elected, by universal suffrage, for a five-year period. All elections take place in the context of a multi-party political system. The Prime Minister is appointed by the President from among the majority in the legislature, and the Prime Minister, in consultation with the President, nominates other ministers. For administrative purposes, the country is divided into five regions. It is further divided into 30 prefectures and sub-prefectures.

Defence

In August 2002 Togo's armed forces officially numbered about 9,450 (army 9,000, air force 250, naval force 200). Paramilitary forces comprised a 750-strong gendarmerie. Military service is by selective conscription and lasts for two years. Togo receives assistance with training and equipment from France. The defence budget was estimated at 24,000m. francs CFA in 2002.

Economic Affairs

In 2001, according to estimates by the World Bank, Togo's gross national income (GNI), measured at average 1999–2001 prices, was US $1,279m., equivalent to $270 per head (or $1,420 on an international purchasing-power parity basis). During 1990–2001, it was estimated, the population increased at an average annual rate of 2.7%, while gross domestic product (GDP) per head declined by an average of 1.4% per year. Overall GDP increased, in real terms, at an average annual rate of 1.3% in 1990–2001. Real GDP declined by 1.9% in 2000, but increased by 2.7% in 2001.

Agriculture (including forestry and fishing) contributed 38.6% of GDP in 2001, when 59.1% of the working population were employed in the sector. The principal cash crops are cotton (which contributed 22.0% of earnings from merchandise exports in 2000), coffee and cocoa. Togo has generally been self-sufficient in basic foodstuffs: the principal subsistence crops are cassava, yams, maize, millet and sorghum. Imports of livestock products and fish are necessary to satisfy domestic needs. During 1990–2001, according to the World Bank, agricultural GDP increased at an average annual rate of 3.1%; agricultural GDP declined by 4.5% in 2000, but increased by 5.6% in 2001.

Industry (including mining, manufacturing, construction and power) contributed 21.1% of GDP in 2001, and employed 10.1% of the working population in 1990. During 1990–2001, according to the World Bank, industrial GDP increased by an average of 2.0% per year; industrial GDP increased by 7.3% in 2000 and by 0.9% in 2001.

Only 0.3% of the labour force were employed in the mining sector in 1981; in 1999, however, extractive activities contributed 5.1% of GDP. Togo has the world's richest reserves of first-grade calcium phosphates. Concerns regarding the high cadmium content of Togolese phosphate rock have prompted interest in the development of lower-grade carbon phosphates, which have a less significant cadmium content; exports of crude fertilizers and unground crude minerals provided 25.1% of earnings from merchandise exports in 2000. Limestone and marble are also exploited. There are, in addition, smaller deposits of iron ore, gold, diamonds, zinc, rutile and platinum. In 1998 marine exploration revealed petroleum and gas deposits within Togo's territorial waters. In October 2002 the Togolese Government, the Hunt Oil Co of the USA and Petronas Carigali of Malaysia signed a joint-venture oil-production agreement, providing for the first offshore drilling in Togolese territorial waters. The GDP of the mining sector was estimated to have declined at an average annual rate of 3.2% in 1991–95.

Manufacturing contributed 9.7% of GDP in 2001. About 6.6% of the labour force were employed in the sector in 1990. Major companies are engaged notably in agro-industrial activities, the processing of phosphates, steel-rolling and in the production of cement. An industrial 'free zone' was inaugurated in Lomé in 1990, with the aim of attracting investment by local and foreign interests by offering certain (notably fiscal) advantages in return for guarantees regarding export levels and employment; a second 'free zone' has since opened, and provision has been made for 'free zone' terms to apply to certain businesses operating outside the regions. According to the World Bank, manufacturing GDP increased by an average of 2.8% per year in 1990–2001; manufacturing GDP increased by 12.5% in 2000 and by 4.9% in 2001.

Togo's dependence on imports of electrical energy from Ghana was reduced following the completion, in 1988, of a 65-MW hydroelectric installation (constructed in co-operation with Benin) at Nangbeto, on the Mono river. None the less, in 1999 some 96.9% of electricity produced in Togo was generated from petroleum. In 2000 fuel imports constituted 18.8% of all merchandise imports by value, less than one-half of the proportion recorded in the previous year. It was planned to connect the electricity grids of Togo and Benin, and to construct further power stations in both countries. A pipeline to supply natural gas from Nigeria to Togo (and also to Benin and Ghana) was expected to come on stream by 2005.

The services sector contributed 40.3% of GDP in 2001, and engaged 24.4% of the employed labour force in 1990. Lomé has been of considerable importance as an entrepôt for the foreign trade of land-locked countries of the region. However, political instability in the early 1990s resulted in the diversion of a large part of this activity to neighbouring Benin and undermined the tourism industry (previously an important source of foreign exchange). According to the World Bank, the GDP of the services sector declined by an average of 0.9% per year in 1990–2001; services GDP declined by 4.3% in 2000, but increased by 0.8% in 2001.

In 2000 Togo recorded a visible trade deficit of US $122.8m., while there was a deficit of $139.6m. on the current account of the balance of payments. In 2000 the principal source of imports was France (23.3%); other major suppliers were Côte d'Ivoire and the Netherlands. The principal market for exports in that year was Ghana (which took 16.6% of Togo's exports in that year); other significant purchasers were Benin, the Philippines, South Africa and Iran. The principal exports in 2000 were crude fertilizers and unground crude minerals, cotton, cement and coffee. The principal imports in that year were refined petroleum products, road vehicles, iron and steel, cement, woven cotton fabrics, and cereals and cereal preparations.

Togo's overall budget deficit for 2000 was 43,000m. francs CFA (equivalent to 4.6% of GDP). Togo's total external debt was US $1,435m. at the end of 2000, of which $1,232m. was long-term public debt. In that year the cost of debt-servicing was equivalent to 6.1% of the value of exports of goods and services. Annual inflation averaged 2.6% in 1990–93. Following the devaluation of the CFA franc in January 1994, inflation in that year averaged 39.2%. Consumer prices increased by an annual average of 3.2% in 1995–2002, according to the IMF. Consumer prices increased by 3.4% in 2001 and by 3.0% in 2002, according to the Banque centrale des états de l'Afrique centrale.

Togo is a member of the Economic Community of West African States (see p. 187), of the West African organs of the Franc Zone (see p. 238), of the International Cocoa Organization (see p. 336), of the International Coffee Organization (see p. 336) and of the Conseil de l'Entente (see p. 339). Togo was admitted to the Islamic Development Bank (see p. 257) in 1998.

Following the devaluation of the CFA franc in early 1994, the IMF approved a series of credits in support of Togo's 1994–97 economic adjustment programme. During this period Togo recorded a decline in inflation, a decrease in its external debt and budget deficit, and an increase in GDP per head. In 1998 a decline in agricultural production and energy shortages contributed to a decline in real GDP of 2.1%. During the late 1990s and early 2000s the Togolese economy was adversely affected by a number of economic and political factors: a decline in the output of phosphates (by an average of 22.1% per year in 1998–2001), historically one of Togo's major source of export earnings, persistently low international prices for another of Togo's principal exports, cotton, and high international prices for a principal import, petroleum, had a negative impact on the trade balance. Moreover, foreign assistance to Togo has been limited in the aftermath of the disputed presidential election of 1998, and as a result of delays in the implementation of an accord signed in July 1999 (see Recent History), providing for fresh legislative and presidential elections. Togo received no multilateral or bilateral aid in 1999 and 2000, compared with the annual average of 29,200m. francs CFA that it received in 1994–98. The refusal of the European Union (EU), previously a major source of support, to maintain financial assistance to the country has been particularly significant. Tourism has also suffered as a result of the political instability that has prevailed since the early 1990s; only 69,458 international arrivals were recorded in 1998, compared with 121,346 in 1988. Although the Government of Agbéyomè Kodjo, formed in late 2000, announced a number of economic reform measures, which were intended to strengthen public finances and to restructure public enterprises further, only limited aspects of the programme were implemented before Kodjo's dismissal in June 2002, and attempts to restore normal relations with Togo's principal international donors remained dependent on the holding of credible and transparent democratic elections. The eventual holding of the repeatedly delayed legislative elections in October 2002 appeared unlikely to lead to a restoration of international aid, as both the EU and the USA declared themselves dissatisfied with the conduct of the polls. The return to growth in 2001 was largely attributable to a recovery in the agricultural sector. In late 2001 the World Bank announced that it would finance the construction of a new facility at Lomé's port, to be completed by 2004, which, it was hoped, would establish the port as a principal regional centre of container trade, while the port has also been a beneficiary of entrepôt trade displaced from Côte d'Ivoire as a result of the civil conflict in that country from late 2002. However, to a large extent, Togo's long-term economic prospects remained dependent on the encouragement of inward investment, which was unlikely to be achieved without a restoration of political stability.

Education

Primary education, which begins at six years of age and lasts for six years, is (in theory) compulsory. Secondary education, beginning at the age of 12, lasts for a further seven years, comprising a first cycle of four years and a second of three years. In 1999/2000 enrolment at primary schools included 91.4% of children in the relevant age-group (100.0% of boys; 82.0% of girls). In the same year secondary enrolment was equivalent to only 36.2% of the appropriate age-group (boys 50.2%; girls 22.2%), according to UNESCO estimates. Proficiency in the two national languages, Ewe and Kabiye, is compulsory. Mission schools are important, educating almost one-half of all pupils. The Université du Bénin at Lomé (which was renamed the Université du Lomé in early 2001) had about 11,000 students in the mid-1990s, and scholarships to French universities are available. Current expenditure on education was an estimated 23,800m. francs CFA in 1995 (16.2% of total expenditure by the central Government), and a further 3,700m. francs CFA was allocated to scholarships and training (2.5% of total expenditure).

Public Holidays

2003: 1 January (New Year's Day), 13 January (Liberation Day, anniversary of the 1967 coup), 24 January (Day of Victory, anniversary of the failed attack at Sarakawa), 12 February* (Tabaski, Feast of the Sacrifice), 21 April (Easter Monday), 24 April (Day of Victory), 27 April (Independence Day), 1 May (Labour Day), 29 May (Ascension Day), 9 June (Whit Monday), 15 August (Assumption), 24 September (anniversary of the failed attack on Lomé), 1 November (All Saints' Day), 26 November* (Id al-Fitr, end of Ramadan), 25 December (Christmas).

2004: 1 January (New Year's Day), 13 January (Liberation Day, anniversary of the 1967 coup), 24 January (Day of Victory, anniversary of the failed attack at Sarakawa), 2 February* (Tabaski, Feast of the Sacrifice), 12 April (Easter Monday), 24 April (Day of Victory), 27 April (Independence Day), 1 May (Labour Day), 20 May (Ascension Day), 31 May (Whit Monday), 15 August (Assumption), 24 September (anniversary of the failed attack on Lomé), 1 November (All Saints' Day), 14 November* (Id al-Fitr, end of Ramadan), 25 December (Christmas).

*These holidays are dependent on the Islamic lunar calendar and may vary by one or two days from the dates given.

Weights and Measures

The metric system is in force.

Statistical Survey

Source (except where otherwise indicated): Direction de la Statistique, BP 118, Lomé; tel. 221-22-87.

Area and Population

AREA, POPULATION AND DENSITY

Area (sq km)	56,785*
Population (census results)	
1 March–30 April 1970	1,997,109
22 November 1981	2,703,250
Population (UN estimates at mid-year)†	
1998	4,242,000
1999	4,388,000
2000	4,527,000
Density (per sq km) at mid-2000	79.7

* 21,925 sq miles.
† Source: UN, *World Population Prospects: The 2000 Revision.*

ETHNIC GROUPS (percentage of total, 1995): Kabré 23.7; Ewe 21.9; Kabiyé 12.9; Watchi 10.1; Guin 6.0; Tem 6.0; Mobamba 4.9; Gourmantché 3.9; Lamba 3.2; Ncam 2.4; Fon 1.2; Adja 0.9; Others 2.9 (Source: La Francophonie).

PRINCIPAL TOWNS
(official estimates in 1997)

Lomé (capital, incl.			
suburbs) . . .	700,000	Kpalimé	30,000
Sokodé	51,000	Kara	30,000

Mid-2001 (UN estimate, incl. suburbs): Lomé 732,000 (Source: UN, *World Urbanization Prospects: The 2001 Revision*).

BIRTHS AND DEATHS
(UN estimates, annual averages)

	1985–90	1990–95	1995–2000
Birth rate (per 1,000)	43.9	42.3	40.5
Death rate (per 1,000)	14.3	14.1	13.9

Source: UN, *World Population Prospects: The 2000 Revision.*

Expectation of life (WHO estimates, years at birth): 51.7 (males 50.3; females 53.1) in 2001 (Source: WHO, *World Health Report*).

ECONOMICALLY ACTIVE POPULATION
(census of 22 November 1981)

	Males	Females	Total
Agriculture, hunting, forestry and fishing	324,870	254,491	579,361
Mining and quarrying	2,781	91	2,872
Manufacturing	29,307	25,065	54,372
Electricity, gas and water	2,107	96	2,203
Construction	20,847	301	21,148
Trade, restaurants and hotels	17,427	87,415	104,842
Transport, storage and communications	20,337	529	20,866
Financing, insurance, real estate and business services	1,650	413	2,063
Community, social and personal services	50,750	12,859	63,609
Activities not adequately defined	14,607	6,346	20,953
Total employed	484,683	387,606	872,289
Unemployed	21,666	7,588	29,254
Total labour force	506,349	395,194	901,543

Mid-2001 (estimates in '000): Agriculture, etc. 1,166; Total labour force 1,972 (Source: FAO).

Health and Welfare

KEY INDICATORS

Total fertility rate (children per woman, 2001)	5.5
Under-5 mortality rate (per 1,000 live births, 2001)	141
HIV/AIDS (% of persons aged 15–49, 2001)	6.00
Physicians (per 1,000 head, 1995)	0.08
Hospital beds (per 1,000 head, 1990)	1.51
Health expenditure (2000): US $ per head (PPP)	36
Health expenditure (2000): % of GDP	2.8
Health expenditure (2000): public (% of total)	54.3
Access to water (% of persons, 2000)	54
Access to sanitation (% of persons, 2000)	34
Human Development Index (2000): ranking	141
Human Development Index (2000): value	0.493

For sources and definitions, see explanatory note on p. vi.

Agriculture

PRINCIPAL CROPS
('000 metric tons)

	1999	2000	2001
Rice (paddy)	81.1	62.3	63.7
Maize	493.6	482.1	463.9
Millet	39.3	37.4	41.2
Sorghum	141.7	151.4	141.7
Cassava (Manioc)	694.0	700.7	651.5
Taro (Coco Yam)	32.1	22.3	15.5
Yams	665.6	563.3v	549.1
Dry beans	45.4	41.8	41.3
Groundnuts (in shell)	35.4	26.0	33.0
Coconuts*	14	14	14
Oil palm fruit*	115	115	115
Cottonseed*	60	50	85
Vegetables*	130.7	130.7	130.7
Bananas*	16.1	16.1	16.1
Oranges*	12.1	12.1	12.1
Other fruit*	20.5	20.5	20.5
Cotton (lint)	50.2	58.1†	60.0*
Coffee (green)	17.0	15.2	17.0*
Cocoa beans	7.0	6.6	8.0†

* FAO estimate(s).
† Unofficial figure.

Source: FAO.

LIVESTOCK
('000 head, year ending September)

	1999	2000	2001*
Cattle	275	277	277
Sheep	1,415	1,570	1,600
Pigs	284	289	289
Goats	1,357	1,425	1,425
Horses*	2	2	2
Asses*	3	3	3
Poultry	8,262	8,500*	8,500

* FAO estimate(s).
Source: FAO.

LIVESTOCK PRODUCTS
(FAO estimates, '000 metric tons)

	1999	2000	2001
Beef and veal	5.2	5.2	5.2
Mutton and lamb	3.1	3.5	3.5
Goat meat	3.4	3.6	3.6
Pig meat	4.4	4.5	4.5
Poultry meat	10.0	10.4	10.4
Game meat	4	4	4
Cows' milk	8.8	9.0	9.0
Hen eggs	6.3	6.3	6.3

Source: FAO.

Forestry

ROUNDWOOD REMOVALS
('000 cubic metres, excluding bark)

	1998	1999	2000
Sawlogs, veneer logs and logs for sleepers	55	67	62
Other industrial wood	232	247	244
Fuel wood*	5,364	5,431	5,499
Total	5,651	5,745	5,805

* FAO estimates.
Source: FAO.

Fishing

('000 metric tons, live weight)

	1998	1999	2000
Capture	16.7	22.9	22.3
Tilapias	3.5	3.5	3.5
Freshwater siluroids	0.5	0.5	0.5
Other freshwater fishes	1.0	1.0	1.0
Bigeye grunt	0.0	0.5	0.7
Pandoras	0.6	1.3	0.2
Round sardinella	1.0	1.9	1.9
Madeiran sardinella	0.4	0.6	0.6
European anchovy	6.3	6.7	7.2
Flyingfishes	0.6	0.2	0.1
Jack and horse mackerels	0.1	0.8	0.4
Aquaculture	0.0	0.2	0.1
Total catch	16.7	23.1	22.4

Source: FAO, *Yearbook of Fishery Statistics*.

Mining

('000 metric tons)

	1999	2000	2001
Calcium phosphates (gross weight)	1,714.5	1,370.1	1,066.6

Source: Banque centrale des états de l'Afrique de l'ouest.

Industry

SELECTED PRODUCTS
('000 metric tons, unless otherwise indicated)

	1997	1998	1999
Palm oil*	7	7	7
Cement†	421	565	560
Electric energy (million kWh) . .	412.7	413.0	462.1

* FAO estimates.

† Data from US Geological Survey.

2000 (FAO estimate, '000 metric tons): Palm oil 7.

2001 (FAO estimate, '000 metric tons): Palm oil 7.

Sources: mainly UN, *Industrial Commodity Statistics Yearbook*, and Banque centrale des états de l'Afrique de l'ouest.

Finance

CURRENCY AND EXCHANGE RATES

Monetary Units
100 centimes = 1 franc de la Communauté financière africaine (CFA)

Sterling, Dollar and Euro Equivalents (31 December 2002)
£1 sterling = 1,008.17 francs CFA
US $1 = 625.50 francs CFA
€1 = 655.96 francs CFA
10,000 francs CFA = £9.919 = $15.987 = €15.245

Average Exchange Rate (francs CFA per US $)
2000   711.98
2001   733.04
2002   696.99

Note: An exchange rate of 1 French franc = 50 francs CFA, established in 1948, remained in force until January 1994, when the CFA franc was devalued by 50%, with the exchange rate adjusted to 1 French franc = 100 francs CFA. This relationship to French currency remained in effect with the introduction of the euro on 1 January 1999. From that date, accordingly, a fixed exchange rate of €1 = 655.957 francs CFA has been in operation.

BUDGET
(million francs CFA)

Revenue*	1997	1998	1999
Tax revenue	115,700	115,000	112,700
Direct tax revenue.	34,400	29,600	n.a.
Indirect tax revenue . . .	81,300	85,400	n.a.
Taxes on goods and services	48,400	52,200	n.a.
Taxes on international trade	29,700	29,400	n.a.
Import duties	28,000	27,800	n.a.
Other current revenue . . .	12,800	11,800	12,900
Total	128,500	126,800	125,600

Expenditure†	1997	1998	1999
Current expenditure. . . .	139,800	153,600	144,700
Salaries and wages . . .	57,000	58,700	58,800
External debt repayments . .	17,600	18,000	18,800
Investment expenditure. . . .	17,600	34,200	29,000
Total	157,400	187,800	173,700

* Excluding grants received (million francs CFA): 11,900 in 1997; 13,700 in 1998; 14,800 in 1999.

† Excluding lending minus repayments (million francs CFA): 0 in 1997; 500 in 1998; 500 in 1999.

Source: Banque centrale des états de l'Afrique de l'ouest.

INTERNATIONAL RESERVES
(excl. gold, US $ million at 31 December)

	1999	2000	2001
IMF special drawing rights. . .	0.2	—	0.2
Reserve position in IMF. . . .	0.3	0.4	0.4
Foreign exchange.	121.5	151.9	125.8
Total	125.6	152.3	126.4

* Valued at market-related prices.

2002 (US $ million at 31 December): IMF special drawing rights 0.3; Reserve position in IMF 0.4.

Source: IMF, *International Financial Statistics*.

MONEY SUPPLY
(million francs CFA at 31 December)

	1999	2000	2001
Currency outside banks	79,481	95,694	85,669
Demand deposits at deposit money banks	61,056	78,376	73,005
Total money (incl. others). . .	144,774	176,890	161,550

Source: IMF, *International Financial Statistics*.

COST OF LIVING
(Consumer price index for Lomé; base: 1996 = 100)

	2000	2001	2002
Food, beverages and tobacco . .	100.0	105.2	109.3
Clothing	104.1	102.4	103.0
Housing, water, electricity and gas	104.0	105.0	107.8
All items (incl. others)	108.8	112.5	115.9

Source: Banque centrale des états de l'Afrique de l'ouest.

NATIONAL ACCOUNTS

Expenditure on the Gross Domestic Product
('000 million francs CFA at current prices)

	1998	1999	2000
Government final consumption expenditure.	103.0	95.4	89.3
Private final consumption expenditure.	726.4	752.2	820.0
Increase in stocks	−0.6	4.6	5.5
Gross fixed capital formation . .	128.3	123.0	142.9
Total domestic expenditure. .	957.1	975.2	1,057.7
Exports of goods and services . .	292.7	269.8	280.5
Less Imports of goods and services	414.4	374.1	408.3
GDP in purchasers' values . .	835.4	870.9	929.9

Source: IMF, *International Financial Statistics*.

Gross Domestic Product by Economic Activity
(million francs CFA at current prices)

	1997	1998	1999
Agriculture, hunting, forestry and fishing	369,600	325,700	366,300
Mining and quarrying	48,200	51,600	44,900
Manufacturing	73,600	78,600	80,600
Electricity, gas and water . . .	29,300	27,400	32,300
Construction	25,000	26,700	27,800
Trade, restaurants and hotels . .	155,800	151,400	150,700
Transport, storage and communications	47,900	47,300	47,500
Other marketable services* . . .	65,900	63,700	66,100
Non-marketable services . . .	60,100	61,700	60,900
GDP in purchasers' values . .	875,400	834,100	877,100

* After deduction of imputed bank service charges.

Source: Banque centrale des états de l'Afrique de l'ouest.

BALANCE OF PAYMENTS
(US $ million)

	1998	1999	2000
Exports of goods f.o.b.	420.3	391.5	361.8
Imports of goods f.o.b.	−553.5	−489.4	−484.6
Trade balance	−133.2	−98.0	−122.8
Exports of services	76.0	68.4	61.8
Imports of services	−149.2	−130.6	−117.5
Balance on goods and services	−206.4	−160.1	−178.5
Other income received	44.4	40.2	32.9
Other income paid	−67.7	−78.6	−62.0
Balance on goods, services and			
income	−229.7	−198.5	−207.6
Current transfers received . . .	101.8	73.6	73.3
Current transfers paid	−12.2	−2.2	−5.4
Current balance	−140.1	−127.1	−139.6
Capital account (net)	6.1	6.9	8.7
Direct investment abroad . . .	−10.6	−2.9	−0.4
Direct investment from abroad	30.2	42.6	41.9
Portfolio investment assets . . .	−5.2	−1.3	0.8
Portfolio investment liabilities . .	11.4	8.6	6.1
Financial derivatives assets .	−0.1	—	−0.1
Financial derivatives liabilities .	−0.2	−0.3	—
Other investment assets . . .	16.2	13.0	8.8
Other investment liabilities . .	72.3	95.8	105.7
Net errors and omissions . . .	2.7	−3.7	5.0
Overall balance	−17.2	31.6	36.8

Source: IMF, *International Financial Statistics*.

External Trade

PRINCIPAL COMMODITIES
(US $ million)

Imports c.i.f.	1998	1999	2000
Food and live animals . . .	64.9	56.0	46.2
Fish, crustaceans and molluscs and			
preparations thereof . . .	17.9	13.1	11.8
Fish, fresh, chilled or frozen . .	16.3	12.3	11.3
Cereals and cereal preparations .	24.8	23.5	17.3
Mineral fuels, lubricants, etc.	222.0	265.6	61.0
Petroleum products, refined . .	219.9	264.1	60.4
Animal and vegetable oils, fats			
and waxes	5.2	41.0	4.1
Fixed vegetable oils and fats . .	4.8	40.5	3.9
Palm oil	1.2	36.8	2.9
Chemicals and related			
products	49.3	48.5	34.0
Medicinal and pharmaceutical			
products.	14.0	12.6	10.3
Basic manufactures . . .	132.8	114.8	83.6
Textile yarn, fabrics, made-up			
articles and related products. .	33.1	28.4	21.5
Cotton fabrics, woven* . .	23.6	20.2	18.1
Other woven fabrics, 85% plus			
of cotton, bleached, etc.,			
finished	20.5	18.7	17.7
Non-metallic mineral			
manufactures	38.2	32.1	24.4
Cement	32.6	25.5	20.5
Iron and steel.	25.8	28.8	21.8
Machinery and transport			
equipment.	145.9	73.9	60.1
Power-generating machinery and			
equipment	35.2	3.6	1.4
Rotating electric plant and parts			
thereof	25.2	2.7	1.1
Electric motors, generators			
(not direct current);			
generating sets	22.3	2.3	0.5
Generating sets with			
internal combustion piston			
engines	22.0	0.9	0.2
General industrial machinery and			
equipment and parts thereof. .	22.1	14.7	8.0
Telecommunications, sound			
recording and reproducing			
equipment	22.1	6.4	7.0
Telecommunication equipment,			
parts and accessories . . .	19.0	4.7	6.3
Road vehicles	30.6	21.9	26.2
Passenger motor vehicles (excl.			
buses).	18.0	13.3	15.6
Miscellaneous manufactured			
articles.	32.8	35.4	17.6
Total (incl. others)	686.9	668.2	323.6

Exports f.o.b.	1998	1999	2000
Food and live animals . . .	55.6	58.0	30.2
Coffee, tea, cocoa, spices, and			
manufactures thereof . . .	25.7	34.7	16.7
Coffee, green, roasted; coffee			
substitutes containing coffee .	16.5	25.5	11.5
Coffee, not roasted; coffee			
husks and skins	15.9	25.4	11.4
Cocoa	16.8	8.2	9.3
Crude materials, inedible,			
except fuels	223.3	165.9	96.9
Textile fibres and their waste† .	100.4	95.8	42.1
Cotton	96.4	87.2	42.1
Raw cotton, excl. linters, not			
carded or combed . . .	67.4	54.6	23.9
Cotton, carded or combined .	27.7	32.5	18.0
Crude fertilizers and crude			
minerals (unground) . . .	115.7	65.0	48.2
Mineral fuels, lubricants, etc. .	10.6	13.3	1.2
Petroleum, petroleum products and			
related materials	10.1	12.6	1.2
Petroleum products, refined . .	9.0	12.2	1.2
Basic manufactures	44.8	65.1	45.1
Non-metallic mineral			
manufactures, etc..	27.3	43.7	29.3
Cement	27.0	31.6	29.1
Glazed ceramic sets, flags and			
paving, hearth and wall tiles .	0.0	11.7	0.0
Iron and steel	2.8	4.8	6.9
Machinery and transport			
equipment	16.8	17.6	7.4
Total (incl. others)	393.4	360.3	191.7

* Excluding narrow or special fabrics.
† Excluding wool tops and wastes in yarn.

Source: UN, *International Trade Statistics Yearbook*.

PRINCIPAL TRADING PARTNERS
(US $ million)

Imports c.i.f.	1998	1999	2000
Belgium	15.3*	27.9	16.1
Benin	4.9	40.1	1.9
Canada	15.0	15.9	9.1
China, People's Repub. . . .	7.4	10.0	9.3
Côte d'Ivoire	63.5	77.4	38.0
Denmark	2.7	3.0	3.8
France (incl. Monaco) . . .	191.8	117.1	75.5
Germany	27.2	21.3	14.0
Ghana	13.4	11.3	8.0
Hong Kong	9.4	9.2	5.5
India	9.1	4.4	4.5
Italy	37.4	27.6	7.9
Japan	26.4v	24.8	10.4
Korea, Republic	7.4	10.9	2.5
Mauritania	13.7	10.3	9.9
Netherlands	43.7	27.1	20.8
Nigeria	17.5	13.3	5.0
Romania	11.8	4.3	0.1
Russia	6.6	9.1	9.3
SACU†	12.1	28.7	n.a.
Senegal	6.5	10.4	3.8
Spain	29.2	10.6	5.3
Thailand	9.9	7.8	2.8
United Kingdom	22.4	25.0	11.7
USA	14.9	9.4	5.0
Total (incl. others)	686.9	668.2	323.6

Exports f.o.b.	1998	1999	2000
Belgium	6.8*	12.1	2.9
Benin	44.7	59.8	18.9
Brazil	12.4	17.4	6.0
Burkina Faso	5.9	7.9	2.8
Canada	46.4	18.4	—
Côte d'Ivoire	2.3	6.7	0.8
France (incl. Monaco) . . .	12.4	9.0	8.5
Gabon	4.1	2.4	1.3
Germany	1.5	4.9	2.1
Ghana	33.6	39.3	31.8
Greece	0.7	4.7	3.4
India	4.3	6.8	9.0
Indonesia	13.7	7.5	5.7
Iran	1.7	—	10.1
Italy	5.1	6.5	5.2
Malaysia	8.9	5.5	0.9
Morocco	1.9	3.8	n.a.
Netherlands	8.2	8.1	4.9
Nigeria	6.0	14.7	8.3
Philippines	38.3	17.3	12.0
Poland	3.8	7.4	5.4
SACU†	16.1	13.9	10.8‡
Spain	0.7	0.4	4.0
Switzerland-Liechtenstein . .	24.3	22.5	1.6
Thailand	4.3	4.2	1.4
Total (incl. others)	393.4	360.3	191.7

* Including trade with Luxembourg.
† Southern African Customs Union, comprising Botswana, Lesotho, Namibia, South Africa and Swaziland.
‡ Trade with South Africa only.

Source: UN, *International Trade Statistics Yearbook*.

Transport

RAILWAYS
(traffic)

	1997	1998	1999
Passengers carried ('000) . . .	152.0	35.0	4.4
Freight carried ('000 metric tons) .	250	759	1,090
Passenger-km (million) . . .	12.7	3.4	0.4
Freight ton-km (million) . . .	28.8	70.6	92.4

Source: Société Nationale de Chemin de Fer du Togo, Lomé.

ROAD TRAFFIC
(motor vehicles registered at 31 December)

	1994	1995	1996*
Passenger cars	67,936	74,662	79,200
Buses and coaches	529	547	580
Goods vehicles	31,457	32,514	33,660
Tractors (road)	1,466	1,544	1,620
Motorcycles and scooters . . .	39,019	52,902	59,000

* Estimates.

Source: IRF, *World Road Statistics*.

SHIPPING

Merchant Fleet
(registered at 31 December)

	1999	2000	2001
Number of vessels	13	1	1
Total displacement (grt) . . .	47,035	4,212	4,212

Source: Lloyd's Register-Fairplay, *World Fleet Statistics*.

International Sea-borne Freight Traffic
('000 metric tons)

Port Lomé	1997	1998	1999
Goods loaded	432.4	794.6	1,021.4
Goods unloaded	1,913.9	1,912.9	1,812.4

Source: Port Autonome de Lomé.

CIVIL AVIATION
(traffic on scheduled services)*

	1997	1998	1999
Kilometres flown (million) . . .	3	3	3
Passengers carried ('000) . . .	86	91	84
Passenger-km (million)	242	258	235
Total ton-km (million)	38	38	36

* Including an apportionment of the traffic of Air Afrique.

Source: UN, *Statistical Yearbook*.

Tourism

FOREIGN TOURIST ARRIVALS*

	1996	1997	1998
International arrivals	58,049	92,081	69,461
National arrivals	23,252	22,594	24,754
Receipts from tourism (million francs CFA).	5,601	7,442	5,612

1999: International arrivals 69,818*; receipts (US $ million) 6.

2000: International arrivals 59,541*.

* Arrivals at hotels and similar establishments.

Sources: Direction des Etudes et de la Planification, Ministère du Tourisme et des Loisirs; World Tourism Organization.

Communications Media

	1999	2000	2001
Television receivers ('000 in use) .	100	150	n.a.
Telephones ('000 main lines in use)	38.2	42.8	48.1
Mobile cellular telephones ('000 subscribers).	17	50	95
Personal computers ('000 in use) .	100	100	230
Internet users ('000).	15	50	50

Radio receivers ('000 in use): 940 in 1997.

Facsimile machines ('000 in use): 17 in 1997.

Daily newspapers: 1 (average circulation 15,000 copies) in 1996.

Sources: International Telecommunication Union; UNESCO, *Statistical Yearbook; UN, Statistical Yearbook*.

Education
(1998)

	Institu- tions	Teachers	Pupils/Students		
			Males	Females	Total
Pre-primary . .	319	566	5,640	5,601	11,241
Primary . . .	4,701	23,107	542,992	410,894	953,886
Secondary:					
general . .	n.a.}	6,595{	153,942	62,542	216,484
vocational . .	n.a.}		11,623	3,841	15,464
Tertiary . . .	n.a.	384	12,413	2,615	15,028

Source: UNESCO Institute for Statistics.

Adult literacy rate (UNESCO estimates): 57.1% (males 72.4%; females 42.5%) in 2000 (Source: UN Development Programme, *Human Development Report*).

Directory

The Constitution

The Constitution that was approved in a national referendum on 27 September 1992, and subsequently amended, defines the rights, freedoms and obligations of Togolese citizens, and defines the separation of powers among the executive, legislative and judicial organs of state.

Executive power is vested in the President of the Republic, who is elected, by direct universal adult suffrage, with a five-year mandate. The legislature, the Assemblée nationale, is similarly elected for a period of five years, its 81 members being directly elected by universal suffrage. The President of the Republic appoints a Prime Minister who is able to command a majority in the legislature, and the Prime Minister, in consultation with the President, appoints other government ministers. A Constitutional Court is designated as the highest court of jurisdiction in constitutional matters.

Constitutional amendments, approved by the Assemblée nationale in late December 2002, removed the previous restriction limiting the President to serving two terms of office; reduced the minimum age for presidential candidates from 45 to 35 years; and required presidential candidates holding dual or multiple citizenships to renounce their non-Togolese nationality or nationalities.

The Government

HEAD OF STATE

President: Gen. GNASSINGBÉ EYADÉMA (assumed power 13 January 1967; proclaimed President 14 April 1967; elected 30 December 1979; re-elected 21 December 1986, 25 August 1993 and 21 June 1998).

COUNCIL OF MINISTERS
(April 2003)

President: Gen. GNASSINGBÉ EYADÉMA.

Prime Minister, Head of the Government: KOFFI SAMA.

Minister of Defence and Former Combatants: Gen. ASSANI TIDJANI.

Minister of Equipment, Mines, Energy, Posts and Telecommunications: TCHAMDJA ANDJO.

Minister of Technical Education and Professional Training: EDO KODJO MAURILLE AGBOGBLI.

Minister of Foreign Affairs and Co-operation: YAO ROLAND KPOTSRA.

Minister of Tourism, Crafts and Leisure: TANKPADJA LALLÉ.

Minister of the Civil Service, Labour and Employment: BIOSSEY KOKOU TOZOUN.

Minister of Trade, Industry, Transport and Development of the Free Zone: DAMA DRAMANI.

Minister of National Education and Research: CHARLES KONDI AGBA.

Minister of Agriculture, Stockbreeding and Fisheries: KOMIKPINE BAMENANTE.

Minister of Culture, Youth and Sports: KOMI KLASSOU.

Minister of the Environment and Forest Resources: RODOLPHE OSSEYI.

Minister of Health, Social Affairs, the Promotion of Women and the Protection of Childhood: SUZANNE AHO.

Minister of Communication and Civic Training: PITANG TCHALLA.

Minister of the Interior, Security and Decentralization: Maj. AKILA ESSO BOCO.

Keeper of the Seals, Minister of Justice responsible for the Promotion of Democracy and the Rule of Law: KATARI FOLI-BAZI.

Minister of the Economy, Finance and Privatization: AYAOVI DEMBA TIGNONKPA.

Minister responsible for Relations with Parliament: HARRY OCTAVIANUS OLYMPIO.

Minister of Town Planning and Housing: DOVI KAVÉGUÉ.

Minister-delegate to the Prime Minister's Office, responsible for the Private Sector: ANGÈLE AGUIGAH.

Secretary of State to the Minister of the Economy, Finance and Privatization, responsible for the Budget: M'BA LEKEZIM.

MINISTRIES

Office of the President: Palais Présidentiel, ave de la Marina, Lomé; tel. 221-27-01; fax 221-18-97; e-mail presidence@republicoftogo.com; internet www.republicoftogo.com.

Office of the Prime Minister: Palais de la Primature, Lomé; tel. 221-29-52; fax 221-20-19; e-mail info@republicoftogo.com.

Ministry of Agriculture, Stockbreeding and Fisheries: ave de Sarakawa, BP 341, Lomé; tel. 221-02-48; fax 221-10-62.

Ministry of the Civil Service, Labour and Employment: angle ave de la Marina et rue Kpalimé, Lomé; tel. 221-26-53.

Ministry of Communication and Civic Training: Lomé; e-mail info@republicoftogo.com.

Ministry of Culture, Youth and Sports: BP 3193, Lomé; tel. 221-23-52.

Ministry of Defence and Former Combatants: Lomé; tel. 221-28-91.

Ministry of the Economy, Finance and Privatization: CASEF, ave Sarakawa, BP 387, Lomé; tel. 221-35-54; fax 221-09-05; e-mail eco@republicoftogo.com.

Ministry of the Environment and Forest Resources: Lomé; tel. 221-56-58; fax 221-68-12.

Ministry of Equipment, Mines, Energy, Posts and Telecommunications: ave de Sarakawa, Lomé; tel. 223-14-00; fax 221-68-12; e-mail eco@republicoftogo.com.

Ministry of Foreign Affairs and Co-operation: place du Monument aux Morts, Lomé; tel. 221-36-01; fax 221-39-79; e-mail diplo@republicoftogo.com.

Ministry of Health, Social Affairs, the Promotion of Women and the Protection of Childhood: rue Branly, Lomé; tel. 221-29-83.

Ministry of the Interior, Security and Decentralization: rue Albert Sarraut, Lomé; tel. 221-23-19; fax 221-36-30; e-mail info@republicoftogo.com.

Ministry of Justice: ave de la Marina, rue Colonel de Roux, Lomé; tel. 221-26-53; fax 222-29-06.

Ministry of National Education and Research: rue Colonel de Roux, BP 12175, Lomé; tel. 222-09-83; fax 222-07-83.

Ministry of Relations with Parliament: Lomé.

Ministry of Technical Education and Professional Training: Lomé.

Ministry of Tourism, Crafts and Leisure: rue du Lac Togo, BP 1289, Lomé; tel. 221-43-13; fax 221-89-27.

Ministry of Town Planning and Housing: Lomé.

Ministry of Trade, Industry, Transport and Development of the Free Zone: 1 ave de Sarakawa, face au Monument aux Morts, BP 383, Lomé; tel. 221-05-52; fax 221-05-72; e-mail eco@republicoftogo.com.

President and Legislature

PRESIDENT

Presidential Election, 21 June 1998

Candidate	Votes	% of votes
Gen. Gnassingbé Eyadéma	813,313	52.13
Gilchrist Olympio	532,328	34.12
Yawovi Agboyibo	149,308	9.57
Zarifou Ayeva	47,117	3.02
Others	18,197	1.17
Total	**1,560,263**	**100.00**

ASSEMBLÉE NATIONALE

Assemblée nationale: Palais des Congrès, BP 327, Lomé; tel. 221-23-61; fax 222-11-88; e-mail assemblee.nationale@syfed.tg.refer.org.

President: OUATTARA FAMBARÉ NATCHABA.

General Election, 27 October 2002

Party	Seats
Rassemblement du peuple togolais (RPT)	72
Rassemblement pour le soutien de la démocratie et du développement (RSDD)	3
Union pour la démocratie et le progrès social (UDPS)	2
Juvento—Mouvement de la jeunesse togolaise	2
Mouvement des croyants pour l'égalité et la paix (MOCEP)	1
Independents	1
Total	**81**

Political Organizations

In mid-1993 there were 63 registered political parties. Of those active in early 2003, the following were among the most influential:

Alliance togolaise pour la démocratie (ATD): Lomé; Leader ADANI IFÉ ATAKPAMEVI.

Convergence patriotique panafricaine (CPP): BP 12703, Lomé; f. 1999 by merger of the Parti d'action pour la démocratie (PAD), the Parti des démocrates pour l'unité (PDU), the Union pour la démocratie et la solidarité (UDS) and the Union togolaise pour la démocratie (UTD); did not participate in legislative elections in 2002; Pres. EDEM KODJO; First Vice-Pres. JEAN-LUCIEN SAVI DE TOVÉ.

Coordination nationale des forces nouvelles (CFN): Lomé; f. 1993; centrist; Pres. Me JOSEPH KOKOU KOFFIGOH.

Front uni de l'opposition (Le Front): Lomé; f. 2002; constituent parties did not contest legislative elections in 2002; opposes Govt of Pres. Eyadéma; Co-ordinator Me YAWOVI AGBOYIBO.

Alliance des démocrates pour le développement intégrale (ADDI): Lomé; Leader NAGBANDJA KAMPATIBE.

Comité d'action pour le renouveau (CAR): 58 ave du 24 janvier, BP06, Lomé; tel. 222-05-66; fax 221-62-54; e-mail yagboyibo@bibway.com; moderately conservative; Leader Me YAWOVI AGBOYIBO; Sec.-Gen. DODJI APEVON; 251,349 mems (Dec. 1999).

Convention démocratique des peuples africains—Branche togolaise (CDPA—BT): 2 rue des Cheminots, BP 13963, Lomé; tel. 221-71-75; fax 226-46-55; e-mail cdpa-bt@cdpa-bt.org; internet www.cdpa-bt.com; f. 1991; socialist; First Sec. Prof. EMMANUEL Y. GU-KONU.

Union pour la démocratie et la solidarité—Togo (UDS—Togo): 276 blvd Circulaire, BP 8580, Lomé; tel. 222-55-64; fax 221-81-95; e-mail uds-togo@wanadoo.fr; Leader ANTOINE FOLLY.

Juvento—Mouvement de la jeunesse togolaise: Lomé; f. 2001; nationalist youth movement; supports Pres. Eyadéma; Leaders MONSILIA DJATO, ABALO FIRMIN.

Mouvement des croyants pour l'égalité et la paix (MOCEP): Lomé; Leader ALMEIDA MAWUTOÈ.

Parti pour la démocratie et le renouveau (PDR): 30 rue de l'Entente, BP 1270, Lomé; tel. 221-10-02; e-mail contactpdr@yahoo.fr; internet www.pdr-togo.org; f. 1991; social-democratic; did not participate in legislative elections in 2002; Pres. of Exec. Bd ZARIFOU AYÉVA; First Vice-Pres. ISSA AFFO; Sec.-Gen. HENRI KOLANI.

Parti démocratique togolais (PDT): Lomé; Leader M'BA KABASSÉMA.

Parti des travailleurs (PT): 49 ave de Calais, BP 13974, Nyekonapoe, Lomé; tel. 913-65-54; socialist; Co-ordinating Sec. CLAUDE AMEGANVI.

Rassemblement du peuple togolais (RPT): place de l'Indépendance, BP 1208, Lomé; tel. 221-20-18; e-mail rpttogo@yahoo.fr; internet www.rpt-13togo.com; f. 1969; sole legal party 1969–91; Pres. Gen. GNASSINGBÉ EYADÉMA; Sec.-Gen. KOFFI SAMA.

Rassemblement pour le soutien de la démocratie et du développement (RSDD): Lomé; Leader HARRY OCTAVIANUS OLYMPIO.

Union des forces de changement (UFC): 59 rue Koudadzé, Lom-Nava, BP 62168 Lomé; tel. and fax 221-33-32; e-mail contact@ufctogo.com; internet www.ufctogo.com; f. 1992; social-democratic; Pres. GILCHRIST OLYMPIO; First Vice-Pres. EMMANUEL BOB AKITANI; Sec.-Gen. JEAN-PIERRE FABRE.

Union des libéraux indépendants (ULI): f. 1993 to succeed Union des démocrates pour le renouveau; Leader KWAMI MENSAN JACQUES AMOUZOU.

Union pour la démocratie et le progrès social (UDPS): Lomé.

Note: In October 2002 nine opposition parties, which were boycotting the legislative elections held in that month, announced the formation of a new alliance, with the intention of ensuring the retirement from public life of Pres. Eyadéma. The **Coalition des forces démocrates (CFD)** included the four constituent parties of the Front uni de l'opposition, the CPP, the PDR and the UFC, in addition to a 'renovationist' faction of the RPT. The UFC withdrew from the alliance in February 2002.

Diplomatic Representation

EMBASSIES IN TOGO

China, People's Republic: 131 rue de l'Entente, BP 2690, Lomé; tel. 221-31-59; fax 221-40-75; Ambassador ZHANG SHIXIAN.

Congo, Democratic Republic: Lomé; tel. 221-51-55; Ambassador LOKOKA IKUKELE BOMOLO.

Egypt: 143 rue de l'OCAM, BP 8, Lomé; tel. 221-24-43; fax 221-10-22; Ambassador ZEKRI RAMZY ABDEL-SHAHID.

France: 51 rue du Golfe, BP 337, Lomé; tel. 221-25-71; fax 221-87-60; e-mail ambafrance-lome@tg.refer.org; internet www.ambafrance-tg.org; Ambassador JEAN-FRANÇOIS VALETTE.

Gabon: Lomé; tel. 222-18-93; fax 222-18-92; Ambassador (vacant).

Germany: blvd de la République, BP 1175, Lomé; tel. 221-23-38; fax 222-18-88; e-mail amballtogo@cafe.tg; Ambassador Dr DIETER PAPENFUSS.

Ghana: 8 rue Paulin Eklou, Tokoin-Ouest, BP 92, Lomé; tel. 221-31-94; fax 221-77-36; Ambassador DAVID ANAGLATE.

Guinea: Lomé; tel. 221-74-98; fax 221-81-16.

Libya: blvd du 13 janvier, BP 4872, Lomé; tel. 221-40-63; Chargé d'affaires a.i. AHMED M. ABDULKAFI.

Nigeria: 311 blvd du 13 janvier, BP 1189, Lomé; tel. and fax 221-59-76; Ambassador Chief BAYO YUSEF.

USA: angle rue Kouenou et rue 15 Beniglato, BP 852, Lomé; tel. 221-29-94; fax 221-79-52; e-mail RobertsonJJ2@state.gov; internet togo.usembassy.gov; Ambassador GREGORY W. ENGLE (designate).

Judicial System

Justice is administered by the Constitutional Court, the Supreme Court, two Appeal Courts and the Tribunaux de première instance, which hear civil, commercial and criminal cases. There is a labour tribunal and a tribunal for children's rights. In addition, there are two exceptional courts, the Cour de sûreté de l'Etat, which judges crimes against internal and external state security, and the Tribunal spécial chargé de la répression des détournements de deniers publics, which deals with cases of misuse of public funds.

Constitutional Court: 32 ave Augustino de Souza, Lomé; tel. 221-72-98; fax 221-39-74; f. 1997; seven mems; Pres. ATSU KOFFI AMEGA.

Supreme Court: BP 906, Lomé; tel. 221-22-58; f. 1961; consists of three chambers (judicial, administrative and auditing); Chair. FESSOU LAWSON; Attorney-General KOUAMI AMADOS-DJOKO.

State Attorney: ATARA NDAKENA.

Religion

It is estimated that about 50% of the population follow traditional animist beliefs, some 35% are Christians and 15% are Muslims.

CHRISTIANITY

The Roman Catholic Church

Togo comprises one archdiocese and six dioceses. At 31 December 2000 there were an estimated 1,258,935 adherents in the country, representing about 23.4% of the total population.

Bishops' Conference

Conférence Episcopale du Togo, 561 rue Aniko Palako, BP 348, Lomé; tel. 221-82-00; fax 222-48-08.

Statutes approved 1979; Pres. Most Rev. PHILIPPE FANOKO KOSSI KPODZRO (Archbishop of Lomé).

Archbishop of Lomé: Most Rev. PHILIPPE FANOKO KOSSI KPODZRO, Archevêché, 561 rue Aniko Palako, BP 348, Lomé; tel. 221-82-00; fax 222-48-08; e-mail archlome@lome.ocicnet.net.

Protestant Churches

There are about 250 mission centres, with a personnel of some 250, affiliated to European and US societies and administered by a Conseil Synodal, presided over by a moderator.

Directorate of Protestant Churches: 1 rue Maréchal Foch, BP 378, Lomé; Moderator Pastor AWUME (acting).

Eglise Evangélique Presbytérienne du Togo: 1 rue Tokmake, BP 2, Lomé; tel. 221-46-69; fax 222-23-63; Moderator Pastor YAWO FATSÈME AMIOU.

BAHÁ'Í FAITH

Assemblée spirituelle nationale: BP 1659, Lomé; tel. 221-21-99; e-mail asnbaha@laposte.tg.

The Press

DAILY

Togo-Presse: BP 891, Lomé; tel. 221-37-18; fax 222-14-89; f. 1961; official govt publ. French, Kabiye and Ewe; political, economic and cultural; circ. 8,000.

PERIODICALS

L'Aurore: Lomé; tel. 222-65-41; fax 222-65-89; e-mail aurore37@caramail.com; weekly; independent; Editor-in-Chief ANKOU SALVADOR; circ. 2,500.

Carrefour: 596 rue Ablogame, BP 6125, Lomé; tel. 944-45-43; e-mail carrefour1@caramail.com; f. 1991; pro-opposition; weekly; Dir HOLONOU HOUKPATI; circ. 3,000 (2000).

Cité Magazine: 50 ave Pas de Souza, BP 6275, Lomé; tel. and fax 222-67-40; e-mail citemag@cafe.tg; internet www.cafe.tg/citemag; monthly; Editor-in-Chief GAËTAN K. GNATCHIKO.

Le Citoyen: Lomé; tel. 221-73-44; independent.

La Colombe: Lomé; f. 2001; weekly.

Le Combat du Peuple: 62 rue Blagogee, BP 4682, Lomé; tel. 904-53-83; fax 222-65-89; e-mail combat@webmails.com; f. 1994; pro-opposition weekly; Editor LUCIEN DJOSSOU MESSAN; circ. 3,500 (2000).

Le Courrier du Golfe: Rue de l'OCAM, angle rue Sotomarcy, BP 660, Lomé; tel. 221-67-92.

Crocodile: 299 rue Kuévidjin, no 27 Bé-Château, BP 60087, Lomé; tel. 221-38-21; fax 226-13-70; e-mail crocodile@caramail.com; f. 1993; pro-opposition; weekly; Dir VIGNO KOFFI HOUNKANLY; Editor FRANCIS-PEDRO AMAZUN; circ. 3,500 (2000).

Le Débat: BP 8737, Lomé; tel. 222-42-84; f. 1991; 2 a month; Dir PROSPER ETEH.

La Dépêche: BP 20039, Lomé; tel. and fax 221-09-32; e-mail ladepeche@hotmail.com; f. 1993; 2 a week; Editor ESSO-WE APPOLINAIRE MÈWÈNAMÈSSÈ; circ. 3,000.

Echos d'Afrique: BP 13963, Lomé; e-mail cdpa-bt@cdpa-bt.org; internet www.cdpa-bt.com; weekly; published by the CDPA—BT; Editor RIGOBERT BASSADOU.

L'Etoile du matin: S/C Maison du journalisme, Casier no 50, Lomé; e-mail wielfridsewa18@hotmail.com; f. 2000; weekly; Dir WIELFRID SÉWA TCHOUKOULI.

Etudes Togolaises: Institut National de la Recherche Scientifique, BP 2240, Lomé; tel. 221-57-39; f. 1965; quarterly; scientific review, mainly anthropology.

L'Evénement: 44–50 rue Douka, Kotokoucondji, BP 1800, Lomé; tel. 222-65-89; f. 1999; independent; weekly; Dir MENSAH KOUDJODJI; circ. 3,000 (2000).

L'Eveil du Peuple: Lomé; weekly; re-established in 2002, having ceased publication in 1999.

L'Exilé: Maison du journalisme, Casier no 28, Lomé; e-mail jexil@hotmail.com; f. 2000; weekly; independent; Editor HIPPOLYTE AGBOH.

Game su/Tev Fema: 125 ave de la Nouvelle Marche, BP 1247, Lomé; tel. 221-28-44; f. 1997; monthly; Ewe and Kabiye; govt publ. for the newly literate; circ. 3,000.

Hébdo-forum: 60 rue Tamakloe, BP 3681, Lomé; weekly.

Journal Officiel de la République du Togo (JORT): BP 891, Lomé; tel. 221-37-18; fax 222-14-89; government acts, laws, decrees and decisions.

Kpakpa Désenchanté: BP 8917, Lomé; tel. 221-37-39; weekly; independent; satirical.

Kyrielle: BP 81213, Lomé; e-mail noel@journaliste.org; f. 1999; monthly; culture, sport; Dir CREDO TETTEH; circ. 3,000 (2000).

Libre Togovi: BP 81190, Lomé; tel. 904-43-36; e-mail libretogovi@mail.com; 2 a week; pro-democracy, opposed to Govt of Pres. Eyadéma; distributed by the Comité presse et communication de la concertation nationale de la société civile.

La Matinée: Tokoin Nkafu, rue Kpoguédé, BP 30368, Lomé; tel. 226-69-02; f. 1999; monthly; Dir KASSÉRÉ PIERRE SABI.

Le Miroir du Peuple: 48 rue Defale, BP 81231, Lomé; tel. 946-60-24; e-mail nouveau90@hotmail.com; f. 1998; fmrly *Le Nouveau Combat*; weekly; independent; Dir ELIAS EDOH HOUNKANLY; circ. 1,000 (2000).

Motion d'Information: Lomé; f. 1997; weekly; pro-opposition.

Nouvel Echo: BP 3681, Lomé; tel. 947-72-40; f. 1997; pro-opposition; weekly; Dir ALPHONSE NEVAME KLU; Editor JULIEN AYIH.

Nouvel Eclat: S/C BP 20312, Lomé; tel. 945-55-42; e-mail nouvel.eclat@caramail.com; f. 2000; weekly; supports Pres. Eyadéma; Dir CHARLES PASSOU; circ. 2,500 (2000).

Nouvel Horizon: Maison du journalisme, Casier no 38, BP 81213, Lomé; tel. 222-09-55; f. 2000; weekly; Dir DONNAS A. AMOZOUGAN; circ. 3,000 (2000).

La Nouvelle République: BP 20378, Lomé; tel. 945-55-43; e-mail nouvelle.republique@caramail.com; f. 1999; supports Pres. Eyadéma; Dir WILFRIED SÉWA TCHOUKOULI; circ. 2,500 (2000).

La Parole: Lomé; tel. 221-55-90.

Politicos: BP 20312, Lomé; tel. 945-32-66; fax 226-13-70; e-mail politicos@hotmail.com; f. 1993; weekly; sympathetic to Pres. Eyadéma; Editor ELVIS A. KAO; circ. 1,500 (2000).

Le Regard: BP 81213, Lomé; tel. 222-65-89; fax 226-13-70; e-mail leregard@webmails.com; f. 1996; weekly; pro-opposition; supports promotion of human rights; Editor ABASS MIKAÏLA SAIBOU; circ. 3,000 (2000).

Le Reporter des Temps Nouveaux: Maison du journalisme, Casier no 22, BP 1800, Lomé; tel. 945-40-45; fax 226-18-22; e-mail le_reporter@hotmail.com; f. 1998; weekly; independent; political criticism and analysis; Man. Editor ROMAIN ATTISO KOUDJODJI; circ. 3,000 (2000).

Le Scorpion—Akéklé: S/C Maison du journalisme, BP 81213, Lomé; tel. 944-43-80; fax 226-13-70; e-mail lescorpion@webmails.com; f. 1998; opposition weekly; Dir DIDIER AGBLETO; circ. 3,500 (2000).

Le Secteur Privé: angle ave de la Présidence, BP 360, Lomé; tel. 221-70-65; fax 221-47-30; monthly; publ. by Chambre de Commerce et d'Industrie du Togo.

Le Soleil: BP 12785, Lomé; tel. 944-41-97; e-mail joel12@dromadaire.com; f. 1999; weekly; supports Pres. Eyadéma; Dir ARISTO GABA; circ. 2,000 (2000).

Témoin de la Nation: Maison du journalisme, Casier no 48, BP 434, Lomé; tel. 221-24-92; f. 2000; weekly; Dir ELIAS EBOH.

Tingo Tingo: 44–50 rue Douka, Kotokoucondji, BP 80419, Lomé; tel. 222-17-53; e-mail jtingo-tingo@yahoo.fr; f. 1996; weekly; independent; Editor AUGUSTIN ASIONBO; circ. 3,500 (2000).

Togo-Images: BP 4869, Lomé; tel. 221-56-80; f. 1962; monthly series of wall posters depicting recent political, economic and cultural events in Togo; publ. by govt information service; Dir AKOBI BEDOU; circ. 5,000.

Togo-Presse: BP 891, Lomé; tel. 221-53-95; fax 22-37-66; f. 1962; publ by Govt in French, Ewe and Kabre; political, economic and cultural affairs; Dir WIYAO DADJA POUWI; circ. 5,000 (2000).

La Tribune du Peuple: Lomé; weekly; pro-opposition; Dir KODJO AFATSAO SILIADIN.

PRESS ASSOCIATION

Union des Journalistes Indépendants du Togo: BP 81213, Lomé; tel. 226-13-00; fax 226-13-70; e-mail maison-du-journalisme@ids.tg; also operates Maison de Presse; Sec.-Gen. GABRIEL AYITÉ BAGLO.

NEWS AGENCY

Agence Togolaise de Presse (ATOP): 35 rue des Media, BP 2327, Lomé; tel. 221-25-07; f. 1975; Dir SESHIE SEYENA BIAVA.

Publishers

Centre Togolais de Communication Evangélique—Editions Haho (CTCE—Editions Haho): 1 rue de Commerce, BP 378, Lomé; tel. 221-45-82; fax 221-29-67; e-mail ctcte@cafe.tg; f. 1983; general literature, popular science, poetry, school textbooks, Christian interest; Dir KODJO MAWULI ETSÉ.

Editions Akpagnon: BP 3531, Lomé; tel. and fax 222-02-44; e-mail yedogbe.akpagnon@laposte.tg; f. 1978; general literature and non-fiction; Man. Dir YVES-EMMANUEL DOGBÉ.

Editions de la Rose Bleue: BP 12452, Lomé; tel. 222-93-39; fax 222-96-69; e-mail dorkenoo_ephrem@yahoo.fr; general literature, poetry; Dir EPHREM SETH DORKENOO.

Les Nouvelles Editions Africaines du Togo (NEA-TOGO): 239 blvd du 13 janvier, BP 4862, Lomé; tel. and fax 222-10-19; e-mail neatogo@yahoo.fr; general fiction, non-fiction and textbooks; Dir-Gen. KOKOU A. KALIPE; Editorial Dir TCHOTCHO CHRISTIANE EKUE.

Les Presses de l'Université du Lomé: BP 1515, Lomé; tel. 225-48-44; fax 225-87-84.

Société National des Editions du Togo (EDITOGO): BP 891, Lomé; tel. 221-61-06; f. 1961; govt-owned; general and educational; Pres. BIOSSEY KOKOU TOZOUN; Man. Dir WIYAO DADJA POUWI.

Broadcasting and Communications

TELECOMMUNICATIONS

Télécel Togo: Cité Maman N'Danida, route de Kpalimé, BP 14511, Lomé; tel. 225-82-50; fax 225-82-51; e-mail telecel@telecel.tg; internet www.telecel.tg; operates mobile cellular telecommunications network in Lomé and six other towns.

Togo Télécom: ave N. Grunitzky, BP 333, Lomé; tel. 221-44-01; fax 221-03-73; e-mail contact@togotel.net.tg; internet www.togotel.net.tg; also operates mobile cellular telecommunications network in major cities as TOGOCEL; Dir-Gen. KOSSIVI PAUL AYIKOE.

BROADCASTING

Radio

Legislation providing for the liberalization of radio broadcasting was ratified in November 1990. However, no definitive licences for radio stations had been issued by mid-2002, when 11 private stations were, nevertheless, in operation.

Radiodiffusion du Togo (Internationale)—Radio Lomé: BP 434, Lomé; tel. 221-24-93; fax 221-36-73; e-mail radiolome@yahoo.fr; f. 1953; state-controlled; radio programmes in French, English and vernacular languages; Dir AMÉVI DABLA.

Radiodiffusion du Togo (Nationale): BP 21, Kara; tel. 660-60-60; f. 1974 as Radiodiffusion Kara (Togo); state-controlled; radio programmes in French and vernacular languages; Dir M'BA KPENOUGOU.

Radio Avenir: BP 20183, 76 blvd de la Kara, Doumassessé, Lomé; tel. 221-20-88; fax 221-03-01; f. 1998; broadcasts in French, English, Ewe and Kotokoli; Dir KPÉLE-KOFFI AHOOMEY-ZUNU.

Radio Carré Jeunes: BP 2550, Adidogomé, Lomé; tel. 225-77-44; e-mail carrejeunes@yahoo.fr; f. 1999; community radio stn; popular education, cultural information; broadcasts in French, Ewe, Kabyè and other local languages; Dir FOLY ALODÉ GLIDJITO AMAGLI.

Radio Evangile Jésus Vous Aime (JVA): Bretelle de Klimamé, BP 2313, Lomé; tel. 225-06-63; e-mail brucejosyl@hotmail.com; f. 1995; Christian; education and development; broadcasts in French, English and nine local languages; Dir Pastor SYLVESTRE KWABLAN BRUCE.

Radio Galaxy: BP 20822, 253 rue 48, Doumassessé, Lomé; tel. and fax 221-63-18; e-mail radiogalaxy@yahoo.fr; f. 1996; broadcasts in French, English, Ewe and Kabyè; Dir PAUL S. TCHASSOUA.

Radio Kanal FM: rue Kuyoua, Tokoin Protestant, BP 61554, Lomé; tel. 221-33-74; fax 226-13-70; e-mail kanalfm@cafe.tg; f. 1997; broadcasts in French and Mina; independent; Dir MODESTE MESSAVUSSUA-KUE.

Radio Maria Togo: BP 30162, 155 de la rue 158, Hédzranawoé, Lomé; tel. 226-11-31; fax 226-35-00; e-mail rmariatg@ids.tg; f. 1997; Roman Catholic; broadcasts in French, English and six local languages; Dir R. P. GUSTAVE SANVEE.

Radio Metropolys: 157 rue Missahoé, Tokoin Hôpital, derrière Pharmacie Ave Marie, Lomé; tel. 222-86-81; e-mail metropolys.lome@voila.fr; internet site.voila.fr/metropolys; f. 2000; secular and apolitical broadcasts in French only; Dir NOÉLIE ASSOGBAVI.

Radio Nana FM: BP 6035, Immeuble du Grand Marché du Lomé, Lomé; tel. 221-02-63; e-mail petdog2@yahoo.fr; f. 1999; broadcasts in French and Mina; community stn; political, economic and cultural information; Dir PETER DOGBE.

Radio Nostalgie: 378 ave de la Victoire, quartier Tokoin-Hôpital, BP 13836, Lomé; tel. 222-25-41; f. 1995; broadcasts in French, Ewe and Mina; Dir RACHEL YWASSA-BABA.

Radio Tropik FM: BP 2276, quartier Wuiti, Lomé; tel. 226-11-11; e-mail tropikfm@nomade.fr; f. 1995; broadcasts in French, Kabyè and Tem; Dir Blaise Yao Amedodji.

Radio Zion: BP 13853, Adidogomé, Lomé; tel. 225-64-99; f. 1999; religious; broadcasts in French, Ewe and Kabyè; Dir Luc Adjaho.

Television

Télévision Togolaise: BP 3286, Lomé; tel. 221-53-57; fax 221-57-86; e-mail televisiontogolaise@yahoo.fr; internet www.tvt.tg; f. 1973; state-controlled; three stations; programmes in French and vernacular languages; Dir Pitang Tchalla.

Broadcasting Association

Organisation Togolaise des Radios et Télévisions Indépendantes (ORTI): BP 81302, Lomé; tel. 221-33-74; e-mail kawokou@syfed.tg.refer.org; Pres. Raymond Awokou Koukou.

Finance

(cap. = capital; res = reserves; dep. = deposits; m. = million; br. = branch; amounts in francs CFA)

BANKING

Central Bank

Banque Centrale des Etats de l'Afrique de l'Ouest (BCEAO): ave de Sarakawa, BP 120, Lomé; HQ in Dakar, Senegal; tel. 221-53-83; fax 221-76-02; f. 1962; bank of issue for the mem. states of the Union économique et monétaire ouest-africaine (UEMOA, comprising Benin, Burkina Faso, Côte d'Ivoire, Guinea-Bissau, Mali, Niger, Senegal and Togo); cap. and res 850,500m., total assets 5,157,700m. (Dec. 2001); Gov. Charles Konan Banny; Dir in Togo Ayéwanou Agetoho Gbeasor; br. at Kara.

Commercial Banks

Banque Togolaise pour le Commerce et l'Industrie (BTCI): 169 blvd du 13 janvier, BP 363, Lomé; tel. 221-46-41; fax 221-32-65; e-mail btci@btci.tg; internet www.btci.tg; f. 1974; 24.8% owned by Société Financière pour les Pays d'Outre-mer, 23.8% by BNP Paribas (France); cap. 1,700m., dep. 40,170m., total assets 51,228m. (Dec. 2000); Pres. Abdoul Hamid Segoun Tidjani-Dourodjaye; Man. Dir Yao Patrice Kanekatoua; 8 brs.

Banque Internationale pour l'Afrique au Togo (BIA—Togo): 13 rue de Commerce, BP 346, Lomé; tel. 221-32-86; fax 221-10-19; e-mail bia-togo@cafe.tg; f. 1965; fmrly Meridien BIAO—Togo; 33% owned by Banque Belgolaise (Belgium); cap. 5,000m., dep. 20,890m., total assets 46,751m. (Dec. 2000); Pres. Victor Alipui; Dir-Gen. Jean-Paul Le Calm; 7 brs.

Ecobank Togo: 20 rue de Commerce, BP 3302, Lomé; tel. 221-72-14; fax 221-42-37; e-mail ecobanktg@ecobank.com; internet www.ecobank.com; f. 1988; 80.8% owned by Ecobank Transnational Inc (operating under the auspices of the Economic Community of West African States), 14.0% by Togolese private investors; cap. 2,000.0m., res 1,932.4m., dep. 53,718.0m. (Dec. 2001); Chair. Ogamo Bagnah; Man. Dir Gabriel Lopes; 2 brs.

Société Interafricaine de Banque (SIAB): 14 rue de Commerce, BP 4874, Lomé; tel. 221-28-30; fax 221-58-29; f. 1975; fmrly Banque Arabe Libyenne-Togolaise du Commerce Extérieur; 50% state-owned, 50% owned by Libyan Arab Foreign Bank; cap. and res 1,114m., total assets 2,579m. (Dec. 1999); Dir-Gen. Khalifa Achour Ettluaa.

Union Togolaise de Banques (UTB): blvd Circulaire, BP 359, Lomé; tel. 221-64-11; fax 221-22-06; f. 1964; 63% state-owned; transfer to majority private ownership pending in 2003; cap. and res −8,768m., total assets 44,915m. (Dec. 1999); Chair. Elom K. Dadzie; Dir-Gen. Alexis Lamseh Looky; 11 brs.

Development Banks

Banque Ouest-Africaine de Développement (BOAD): 68 ave de la Libération, BP 1172, Lomé; tel. 221-42-44; fax 221-72-69; e-mail boadsiege@boad.org; internet www.boad.org; f. 1973; promotes West African economic development and integration; total assets 550,193m. (Dec. 1998); Pres. Dr Yayi Boni; Dir O. Nanga.

Banque Togolaise de Développement (BTD): BP 65, Lomé; tel. 221-36-41; fax 221-44-56; e-mail togo-devbank@bibway.com; f. 1966; 43% state-owned, 20% owned by BCEAO, 13% by BOAD; transfer to majority private ownership pending in 2003; cap. and res 5,847m., dep. 12,782m. (Dec. 2001); Pres. Esso Kandja; Dir-Gen. Zakari Darou-Salim; 8 brs.

Société Nationale d'Investissement: 11 ave du 24 janvier, BP 2682, Lomé; tel. 221-62-21; fax 221-62-25; e-mail sni@ids.tg; f. 1971; fmrly Société Nationale d'Investissement et Fonds Annexes; 33% state-owned; cap. 3,963m., total assets 18,243m. (Dec. 1999); Pres. Palouki Massina; Dir-Gen. Richard K. Attipoe.

Savings Bank

Caisse d'Epargne du Togo (CET): 23 ave de la Nouvelle Marché, Lomé; tel. 221-20-60; fax 221-85-83; e-mail cet@ids.tg; internet www.cet.tg; state-owned; privatization pending in 2003; cap. 120.0m., res 5.0m., dep. 19,833.9m. (Dec. 2002); Dir-Gen. Mindi Lamboni.

Credit Institution

Société Togolaise de Crédit Auto (STOCA): 3 rue du Mono, BP 899, Lomé; tel. 221-37-59; fax 221-08-28; e-mail stoca@ids.tg; f. 1962; 93.3% owned by SAFCA; cap. and res 176m., total assets 1,827m. (Dec. 1999); Pres. Diack Diawar; Dir-Gen. Eric Leclère.

Bankers' Association

Association Professionnelle des Banques et Etablissements Financiers du Togo: Lomé; tel. 221-24-84; fax 221-85-83.

STOCK EXCHANGE

Bourse Régionale des Valeurs Mobilières (BRVM): BP 3263, Lomé; tel. 221-23-05; fax 221-23-41; e-mail natcholi@brvm.org; internet www.brvm.org; f. 1998; national branch of BRVM (regional stock exchange based in Abidjan, Côte d'Ivoire, serving the member states of UEMOA); Man. in Togo Nathalie Bitho Atcholi.

INSURANCE

Colina Togo: 10 rue du Commerce, BP 1349, Lomé; tel. 221-79-91; fax 221-73-58; e-mail c-togo@colina-sa.com; internet www.colina-sa.com; affiliated to Colina SA (Côte d'Ivoire); Dir-Gen. Marcus Laban.

Compagnie Commune de Réassurance des Etats Membres de la CICA (CICA—RE): ave du 24 janvier, BP 12410, Lomé; tel. 221-62-69; fax 221-49-64; e-mail cicare@cafe.tg; f. 1981; reinsurance co operating in 12 west and central African states; cap. 1,500m. Chair. Léon-Paul N'Goulakia; Gen. Man. Digbeu Kipre.

Groupement Togolais d'Assurances (GTA): route d'Atakpamé, BP 3298, Lomé; tel. 225-60-75; fax 225-26-78; f. 1974; 62.9% state-owned; all classes of insurance and reinsurance; Pres. Minister of the Economy, Finance and Privatization; Man. Dir Kossi Nambea.

Sicar Gras Savoye Togo: 14 ave de la Nouvelle Marché, BP 2932, Lomé; tel. 221-35-38; fax 221-82-11; Dir Alexandre Wilson.

UAT: Immeuble BICI, 169 blvd du 13 Janvier, BP 495, Lomé; tel. 221-10-34; fax 221-87-24.

Trade and Industry

ECONOMIC AND SOCIAL COUNCIL

Conseil Economique et Social: Lomé; tel. 221-53-01; f. 1967; advisory body of 25 mems, comprising five trade unionists, five reps of industry and commerce, five reps of agriculture, five economists and sociologists, and five technologists; Pres. Koffi Gbodzidi Djondo.

GOVERNMENT AGENCIES

Direction Générale des Mines et de la Géologie: BP 356, Lomé; tel. 221-30-01; fax 221-31-93; organization and administration of mining in Togo; Dir-Gen. Ankoume P. Aregba.

EPZ Promotion Board: BP 3250, Lomé; tel. 221-13-74; fax 221-52-31; promotes the Export Processing Zone at Lomé internationally.

Société d'Administration des Zones Franches (SAZOF): BP 2748, Lomé; tel. 221-07-44; fax 221-43-05; administers and promotes free zones; Dir Gen. Yazaz Egbaré.

Société Nationale de Commerce (SONACOM): 29 blvd Circulaire, BP 3009, Lomé; tel. 221-31-18; f. 1972; cap. 2,000m. francs CFA; importer of staple foods; Dir-Gen. Jean Ladoux.

Société Nationale d'Investissement et Fonds Annexes (SNI & FA): 11 ave du 24 Janvier, BP 2682, Lomé; tel. 221-62-21; fax 221-62-25; e-mail martialg@cafe.tg; f. 1971; state-owned investment co. cap. 2,600m. francs CFA (Dec. 2000); Pres. Palouki Massina; Dir-Gen. Kuaku Richard Attipoe.

DEVELOPMENT ORGANIZATIONS

Agricultural development is under the supervision of five regional development authorities, the Sociétés régionales d'aménagement et de développement.

Agence Française de Développement (AFD): 9 ave de Sarakawa, BP 33, Lomé; tel. 221-04-98; fax 221-79-32; e-mail afdlom@laposte.tg; internet www.afd.fr; fmrly Caisse Française de Développement; Dir in Togo YVES TERRACOL.

Association Française des Volontaires du Progrès (AFVP): BP 1511, Lomé; tel. 221-09-45; fax 221-85-04; e-mail afvp@togo-imet.com; internet www.afvp.org; f. 1965; Nat. Del. PATRICK ROBERT.

Association Villages Entreprises: BP 23, Kpalimé; tel. and fax 441-00-62; e-mail averafp@hotmail.com; Dir KOMI AFELETE JULIEN NYUIADZI.

Office de Développement et d'Exploitation des Forêts (ODEF): 15 rue des Conseillers Municipaux, BP 334, Lomé; tel. 221-71-28; fax 221-34-91; f. 1971; develops and manages forest resources; Man. Dir KOFFI AGOGNO.

Recherche, Appui et Formation aux Initiatives d'Autodéveloppement (RAFIA): BP 43, Dapaong; tel. 770-80-89; fax 770-82-37; f. 1992; Dir NOIGUE TAMBILA LENNE.

Service de Coopération et d'Action Culturelle: BP 91, Lomé; tel. 221-21-26; fax 221-21-28; e-mail scac-lome@tg.refer.org; administers bilateral aid from the French Ministry of Foreign Affairs; Dir HENRI-LUC THIBAULT.

Société d'Appui a la Filière Café-Cacao-Coton (SAFICC): Lomé; f. 1992; development of coffee, cocoa and cotton production.

CHAMBER OF COMMERCE

Chambre de Commerce et d'Industrie du Togo (CCIT): ave de la Présidence, angle ave Georges Pompidou, BP 360, Lomé; tel. 221-70-65; fax 221-47-30; e-mail ccit@rdd.tg; f. 1921; Pres. ALEXIS LAMSEH LOOKY; Sec.-Gen. YAZAS EGBARÈ TCHOHOU.

EMPLOYERS' ORGANIZATIONS

Conseil National du Patronat: 55 ave N. Grunitzky, BP 12429, Lomé; tel. and fax 221-08-30; f. 1989; Pres. A. J. KOUDOYOR.

Groupement Interprofessionnel des Entreprises du Togo (GITO): BP 345, Lomé; Pres. CLARENCE OLYMPIO.

Syndicat des Commerçants Importateurs et Exportateurs du Togo (SCIMPEXTO): BP 1166, Lomé; tel. 222-59-86; Pres. C. SITTERLIN.

Syndicat des Entrepreneurs de Travaux Publics, Bâtiments et Mines du Togo: BP 12429, Lomé; tel. 221-19-06; fax 221-08-30; Pres. JOSÈPHE NAKU.

UTILITIES

Electricity

Communauté Electrique du Bénin: ave de la Kozah, BP 1368, Lomé; tel. 221-61-32; fax 221-37-64; e-mail dg@cebnet.org; f. 1968 as a jt venture between Togo and Benin to exploit the energy resources in the two countries; Chair. CODJO DÉLAVA; Man. KOUAGOU CYR MPO.

Togo Electricité: 426 ave du Golfe, BP 42, Lomé; tel. 221-27-43; fax 221-64-98; e-mail m.ducommun@ids.tg; f. 2000 to replace Compagnie Energie Electrique du Togo; production, transportation and distribution of electricity; managed by consortium led by Hydro-Quebec (Canada) and Elyo (France); Man. Dir MARC DUCOMMUN-RICOUX.

Gas

Société Togolaise de Gaz SA (Togogaz): BP 1082, Lomé; tel. 221-44-31; fax 221-55-30; 71% privatization pending; Dir-Gen. JOËL POMPA.

Water

Régie Nationale des Eaux du Togo (RNET): 53 ave de la Libération, BP 1301, Lomé; tel. 221-34-81; fax 221-46-13; e-mail rnetdg@togo-imet.com; f. 1964; cap. 252m. francs CFA; state-owned; production and distribution of drinking water; Chair. ANATO AGBOZOUHOUE; Man. Dir Y. BADJO.

TRADE UNIONS

Collectif des Syndicats Indépendants (CSI): Lomé; f. 1992 as co-ordinating org. for three trade union confederations.

Confédération Nationale des Travailleurs du Togo (CNTT): Bourse du Travail, BP 163, 160 blvd du 13 Janvier, Lomé; tel. 222-02-55; fax 221-48-33; f. 1973; Sec.-Gen. DOUEVI TCHIVIAKOU.

Confédération Syndicale des Travailleurs du Togo (CSTT): 14 rue Van Lare, BP 3058, Lomé; tel. 222-11-17; fax 222-44-41; e-mail cstt-tg@cstt-togo.org; f. 1949, dissolved 1972, re-established 1991; comprises 36 unions and 7 professional federations (Agro-Alimentation, Education, General Employees, Industry, Public Services,

Transport, Woodwork and Construction); Sec.-Gen. BELIKI ADRIEN AKOUETE; 50,000 mems.

Union Nationale des Syndicats Indépendants du Togo (UNSIT): Tokoin-Wuiti, BP 30082, Lomé; tel. 221-32-88; fax 221-95-66; e-mail unsit@netcom.tg; f. 1991; Sec.-Gen. NORBERT GBIKPI-BENISSAN; 17 affiliated unions.

Transport

RAILWAYS

Société Nationale des Chemins de Fer du Togo (SNCT): BP 340, Lomé; tel. 221-43-01; fax 221-22-19; f. 1900; owned by West African Cement (Wacem) since Jan. 2002; total length 355 km, incl. lines running inland from Lomé to Atakpamé and Blitta (280 km); a coastal line, running through Lomé and Aného, which links with the Benin railway system, was closed to passenger traffic in 1987 (a service from Lomé to Palimé—119 km—has also been suspended); passengers carried (1999): 4,400 (compared with 628,200 in 1990), freight handled (1999): 1,090,000 metric tons; Gen. Man. ROY GEMMELL.

ROADS

In 1996 there were an estimated 7,520 km of roads, of which 2,376 km were paved. The rehabilitation of the 675-km axis road that links the port of Lomé with Burkina Faso, and thus provides an important transport corridor for land-locked West African countries, was considered essential to Togo's economic competitiveness; in 1997 the World Bank provided a credit of US $50m. for the rehabilitation of a severely deteriorated 105-km section of the road between Atakpamé and Blitta. In 1998 Kuwait awarded Togo a loan of 6,000m. CFA francs to improve the Notse-Atakpamé highway. Other principal roads run from Lomé to the borders of Ghana, Nigeria and Benin.

Africa Route International (ARI—La Gazelle): km 9, route d'Atakpamé, BP 4730, Lomé; tel. 225-27-32; f. 1991 to succeed Société Nationale de Transports Routiers; Pres. and Man. Dir BAWA S. MANKOUBI.

SHIPPING

The major port, at Lomé, generally handles a substantial volume of transit trade for the land-locked countries of Mali, Niger and Burkina Faso, although political unrest in Togo, in the early 1990s, resulted in the diversion of much of this trade to neighbouring Benin. In 1995 the Banque ouest-africaine de développement approved a loan of 5,000m. francs CFA to help finance the rehabilitation of the infrastructure at Lomé port. The project aimed to re-establish Lomé as one of the principal transit ports on the west coast of Africa, and further upgrading of the port's facilities, including the computerization of port operations and the construction of a new container terminal, was implemented in the late 1990s, with private-sector funding. By 1999 freight traffic had recovered to 2.8m. metric tons, compared with only 1.1m. tons in 1993. There is another port at Kpémé for the export of phosphates.

Port Autonome de Lomé: BP 1225, Lomé; tel. 227-47-42; fax 227-26-27; e-mail togoport@togoport.tg; internet www.togoport.tg; f. 1968; transferred to private management in Jan. 2002; Pres. KOUAMI AGBOGBOLI IHOU; Man. Dir AWA BELEYI; 1,746 employees (2001).

Conseil National des Chargeurs Togolais: BP 2991, Lomé; tel. 223-71-00; fax 227-08-37; e-mail cnct@cnct.tg; internet www.cnct.tg; Man. Dir MAGUÉNANI KOMOU.

Ecomarine International (Togo): Immeuble Ecomarine, Zone Portuaire, BP 6014, Lomé; tel. 227-48-04; fax 227-48-06; e-mail kegbeto@ecomarineint.com; f. 2001 to develop container-handling facility at Lomé Port, to be operational by 2004; operates maritime transport between Togo, Senegal and Angola; Chief Exec. KOFI I. J. EGBETO.

Société Ouest-Africaine d'Entreprises Maritimes Togo (SOAEM—Togo): Zone Industrielle Portuaire, BP 3285, Lomé; tel. 221-07-20; fax 221-34-17; f. 1959; forwarding agents, warehousing, sea and road freight transport; Pres. JEAN FABRY; Man. Dir JOHN M. AQUEREBURU.

Société Togolaise de Navigation Maritime (SOTONAM): place des Quatre Etoiles, rond-point du Port, BP 4086, Lomé; tel. 221-51-73; fax 227-69-38; state-owned; privatization pending; Man. PAKOUM KPEMA.

SOCOPAO—Togo: 18 rue du Commerce, BP 821, Lomé; tel. 221-55-88; fax 221-73-17; f. 1959; freight transport, shipping agents; Pres. GUY MIRABAUD; Man. Dir HENRI CHAULIER.

TOGO

Directory

SORINCO—Marine: 110 rue de l'OCAM, BP 2806, Lomé; tel. 221-56-94; freight transport, forwarding agents, warehousing, etc. Man. AHMED EDGAR COLLINGWOOD WILLIAMS.

Togolaise d'Armements et d'Agence de Lignes SA (TAAL): 21 blvd du Mono, BP 9089, Lomé; tel. 222-02-43; fax 221-06-09; f. 1992; shipping agents, haulage management, crewing agency, forwarding agents; Pres. and Man. Dir LAURENT GBATI TAKASSI-KIKPA.

CIVIL AVIATION

There are international airports at Tokoin, near Lomé, and at Niamtougou. In addition, there are smaller airfields at Sokodé, Sansanné-Mango, Dapaong and Atakpamé.

Air Togo—Compagnie Aerienne Togolaise: Aéroport International de Lomé-Tokoin, BP 20393, Lomé; tel. 226-22-11; fax 226-22-30; e-mail airtogo@airtogo.net; internet www.airtogo.net; f. 1963; cap. 5m. francs CFA; scheduled internal services; Man. Dir AMADOU ISAAC ADE.

Peace Air Togo (PAT): Lomé; tel. and fax 222-71-40; internal services and services to Burkina Faso, Côte d'Ivoire and Ghana; Man. Dir PELSSEY NORMAN.

Société aéroportuaire de Lomé (SALT): Aéroport de Lomé-Tokoin, BP 10112, Lomé; tel. 226-71-21; fax 226-88-95; e-mail salt@cafe.tg; Dir-Gen. Dr AKRIMA KOGOE.

Transtel Togo: Lomé; f. 2001; flights between Togo and France and Belgium; Gen. Man. M. MOROU.

Tourism

Togo's tourist industry declined precipitously in the wake of the political instability of the early 1990s; occupancy rates in the capital's hotels dropped from 33% in 1990 to 10% in 1993. The tourist industry did, however, recover in the late 1990s. Some 69,818 foreign tourist arrivals were reported in 1999, although numbers declined to 59,541 in 2000. In 1998 hotel receipts from tourism totalled 5,612m. CFA francs. In 1998 occupancy rates were estimated at 20%. In that year there were 2,258 hotel rooms and 4,289 hotel beds available.

Office National Togolais du Tourisme (ONTT): BP 1289, Lomé; tel. 221-43-13; fax 221-89-27; Dir FOLEY DAHLEN (acting).

TONGA

Introductory Survey

Location, Climate, Language, Religion, Flag, Capital

The Kingdom of Tonga comprises 170 islands in the south-western Pacific Ocean, about 650 km (400 miles) east of Fiji. The Tonga (or Friendly) Islands are divided into three main groups: Vava'u, Ha'apai and Tongatapu. Only 36 of the islands are permanently inhabited. The climate is mild (16°–21°C or 61°–71°F) for most of the year, though usually hotter (27°C–81°F) in December and January. The languages are Tongan, which is a Polynesian language, and English. Tongans are predominantly Christians of the Wesleyan faith, although there are some Roman Catholics and Anglicans. The national flag (proportions 1 by 2) is red, with a rectangular white canton, containing a red cross, in the upper hoist. The capital is Nuku'-alofa, on Tonga-tapu Island.

Recent History

The foundations of the constitutional monarchy were laid in the 19th century. The kingdom was neutral until 1900, when it became a British Protected State. The treaty establishing the Protectorate was revised in 1958 and 1967, giving Tonga increasing control over its affairs. Prince Tupouto'a Tungi, who had been Prime Minister since 1949, succeeded to the throne as King Taufa'ahau Tupou IV in December 1965 and appointed his brother, Prince Fatafehi Tu'ipelehake, to be Prime Minister. Tonga achieved full independence, within the Commonwealth, on 4 June 1970.

Elections to the Legislative Assembly held in May 1981 resulted unexpectedly in the new Assembly becoming dominated by traditionalist conservatives. In March 1982 the Minister of Finance, Mahe Tupouniua, resigned at the King's request after refusing to grant him extrabudgetary travel funds. Further elections to the Legislative Assembly took place in May 1984. In September 1985 the King declared his support for the French Government's programme of testing nuclear weapons in the South Pacific, on the grounds that it was in the broader interests of the Western alliance. However, he upheld his former statement of opposition to the tests in French Polynesia.

Elections were held in February 1987 to the nine commoner seats in the Legislative Assembly; among the six newcomers to the legislature were reported to be some of the Government's harshest critics. In July 1988 the Supreme Court awarded $T26,500 in damages to 'Akilisi Pohiva, the editor of a local independent journal and an elected member of the Legislative Assembly, after the Government had been found guilty of unfairly dismissing him from his job in the Ministry of Education in 1985, because he had reported on controversial issues. The court ruling intensified opposition demands for the abolition of perceived feudal aspects within Tongan society.

In September 1989 the commoner members of the Legislative Assembly boycotted the Assembly, leaving it without a quorum, in protest at the absence of the Minister of Finance when they had wanted to question him about the proceeds of the Government's sale of Tongan passports to foreign nationals, a process which had begun in 1983 as a means of acquiring revenue. Upon resuming their seats in the Assembly later in the month, the commoners introduced a motion demanding the reform of the Assembly to make it more accountable to the people. The motion proposed the creation of a more balanced legislature by increasing elected representation from nine to 15 seats and reducing noble representation to three seats (the Cabinet's 12 members also sit in the Assembly). In March 1990 a group of Tongan conservatives submitted an electoral petition, alleging bribery and corruption against Pohiva, the leader of the pro-reform commoners, and his colleagues, who had been re-elected by substantial majorities in the February general election. (In July 1988 the King had indicated his opposition to majority rule, claiming that the monarchical Government reacted more quickly to the needs of the people than the Government of a parliamentary democracy.)

In October 1990 Pohiva initiated a court case against the Government, claiming that its controversial sale of passports to foreign citizens was unconstitutional and illegal. The passports were sold mainly in Hong Kong, for as much as US $30,000 each,

allowing the purchasers, in theory, to avoid travel restrictions imposed on Chinese passport-holders. In February 1991, however, a constitutional amendment to legalize the naturalization of the new passport-holders was adopted by an emergency session of the Legislative Assembly, and the case was therefore dismissed. In March a large demonstration was held in protest at the Government's actions, and a petition urging the King to invalidate the 426 passports in question, and to dismiss the Minister of Police (who was responsible for their sale), was presented by prominent commoners and church leaders. In the following month the Government admitted that the former President of the Philippines, Ferdinand Marcos, and his family had been given Tongan passports as gifts, after his fall from power in 1986. The events that ensued from the sale of passports were widely viewed as indicative of the growing support for reform and for greater accountability in the government of the country. By 1996, however, most of the 6,600 passports sold under the scheme had expired.

In August 1991 the Prime Minister, Prince Fatafehi Tu'ipelehake, retired from office, owing to ill health (the Prince died in April 1999), and was succeeded by the King's cousin, Baron Vaea of Houma, who had previously held the position of Minister of Labour, Commerce and Industries.

Plans by campaigners for democratic reform to establish a formal political organization were realized in November 1992, when the Pro-Democracy Movement was founded. The group, led by Fr Seluini 'Akau'ola (a Roman Catholic priest), organized a constitutional convention in the same month, at which options for the introduction of democratic reform were discussed. The Government, however, refused to recognize or to participate in the convention, prohibiting any publicity of the event and denying visas to invited speakers from abroad. Nevertheless, the pro-democracy reformists appeared to be enjoying increased public support, and, at elections in February 1993, won six of the nine elective seats in the Legislative Assembly. However, Pohiva's position was undermined when, in December 1993 and February 1994, he lost two defamation cases in the Supreme Court, following the publication of allegations of fraudulent practice in his journal, Kele'a. In August 1994 Tonga's first political party was formed when the Pro-Democracy Movement launched its People's Party, under the chairmanship of a local businessman, Huliki Watab.

In May 1995 the Minister of Finance, Cecil Cocker, resigned from the Cabinet following allegations that he had sexually harassed three women while attending a regional conference in Auckland. Cocker received an official reprimand for his conduct from New Zealand's acting Prime Minister, Don McKinnon.

Elections took place on 24 January 1996, at which pro-democracy candidates retained six seats in the Legislative Assembly. In March three journalists, including the editor of The Times of Tonga, were arrested and imprisoned in connection with an article in the newspaper that criticized the newly-appointed Minister of Police, Fire Services and Prisons, Clive Edwards, for unfavourable remarks that he had made regarding the People's Party. All three were subsequently released, but were found guilty in April under a law against angering a civil servant.

In July 1996 the Legislative Assembly voted to resume the sale of Tongan passports to Hong Kong Chinese, despite the controversy caused by a similar scheme in the early 1990s. As many as 7,000 citizenships were to be made available for between $T10,000 and $T20,000, granting purchasers all the rights of Tongan nationality, except ownership of land.

In September 1996 a motion to impeach the Minister of Justice and Attorney-General, Tevita Topou, was proposed in the Legislative Assembly. The motion alleged that Topou had continued to receive his daily parliamentary allowance during an unauthorized absence from the Assembly. Moreover, the publication of details of the impeachment motion, which had been reported to The Times of Tonga by Pohiva, before it had been submitted to the Legislative Assembly, resulted in the imprisonment of Pohiva and of the newspaper's editor, Kalafi Moala, and deputy editor, Filakalafi Akau'ola, for contempt of parliament. The three were subsequently released, although in

October Moala was found guilty on a further charge of contempt. In the same month the King closed the Assembly (which had been expected to sit until mid-November) until further notice. He denied that he had taken this decision in order to prevent further impeachment proceedings against Topou. Furthermore, in February 1997 the Speaker of the Legislative Assembly was found guilty of contempt of court for criticizing the Chief Justice's decision to release the three journalists imprisoned in September of the previous year. The Government rejected accusations made in early 1997 by journalists in Tonga and media organizations throughout the region that it was attempting to force the closure of *The Times of Tonga*, despite forbidding Moala (who was resident in New Zealand) to enter Tonga without written permission from the Government, banning all government-funded advertising in the publication and forbidding all government employees to give interviews to its journalists.

Parliament reopened in late May 1997. In June Akau'ola was arrested once again and charged with sedition for publishing a letter in *The Times of Tonga* that questioned government policy. However, in the same month the Government suffered a significant reverse when the Court of Appeal ruled that the imprisonment of Pohiva and the two journalists in late 1996 had been unlawful. In August the Prime Minister of New Zealand, Jim Bolger, paid an official visit to Tonga. Following the visit, Pohiva, who had unsuccessfully sought a meeting with Bolger, criticized New Zealand's relationship with Tonga, claiming that financial assistance from the country hindered democratic reform.

In September 1997, following a formal apology from Topou, the Legislative Assembly voted to abandon impeachment proceedings against him. In October Pohiva announced that he was helping to prepare a proposed draft Constitution for presentation to the Legislative Assembly; the document's principal recommendation was to be the direct election of all 30 members of the Assembly.

In March 1998 Fakafanua, a former Minister of Lands, Survey and Natural Resources, was arrested and remanded on bail in connection with charges of fraud, extortion and accepting bribes. He was released by the Supreme Court later in the month after he accused the police of unlawful imprisonment. One police-officer was convicted of this charge in April, while five other men, including Edwards, were acquitted.

In mid-September 1998 the King closed the Legislative Assembly in response to a petition, signed by more than 1,000 people, which sought the removal from office of the Speaker, Eseta Fusitu'a. A parliamentary committee was forced to conduct an inquiry into the activities of Fusitu'a, who was accused of misappropriating public funds and of abusing his position. Pohiva and other pro-democracy activists commended the king for his decisive action in response to the petition. Legislation presented to the legislature later that month, which proposed that in future the Legislative Assembly should appoint cabinet ministers (a responsibility hitherto reserved for the King), was seen as further evidence of the increasing influence of the pro-democracy lobby in the political life of the country.

At the general election held on 11 March 1999 five members of the reformist Human Rights and Democracy Movement (formerly People's Party) were returned to the Legislative Assembly, compared with six at the previous election. In April Veikune was appointed as Speaker and Chairman of the Legislative Assembly, replacing Eseta Fusitu'a, who had lost his seat at the general election. In late 1999 the former Minister for Lands, Survey and Natural Resources, Fakafanua, appeared in court on charges of forgery and bribery.

On 3 January 2000 the King appointed Prince 'Ulukalala-Lavaka-Ata as Prime Minister, replacing Baron Vaea who had in 1995 announced his desire to retire. It had been expected that Crown Prince Tupouto'a would take up the position, but his support for constitutional reform in Tonga (notably the abolition of life-time terms for the Prime Minister and Ministers) contrasted with the King's more conservative approach. In March of that year a report published by the US State Department claimed that Tonga's system of Government, whereby the Legislative Assembly is not directly elected, was in breach of UN and Commonwealth human rights guide-lines. The report was welcomed by 'Akilisi Pohiva, the leader of the Tonga Human Rights and Democracy Movement, who reiterated the party's demands for greater democracy, set out in a draft constitution completed in late 1999.

In November 2000 the Human Rights and Democracy Movement condemned the Government's decision to co-operate with an Australian biotechnology company wishing to carry out research into the genetic causes of a range of diseases. Tonga's extended family structures and the genetic isolation of its ethnically homogenous Polynesian population were cited as providing a rare opportunity for research. In return for its co-operation in the project, Tonga was to receive a share of the royalties from the sale of any drugs developed.

In January 2001 the Prime Minister announced a reallocation of cabinet positions in which he assumed responsibility for the newly created telecommunications portfolio. In the same month claims which appeared in a newspaper report that members of the pro-democracy movement had been involved in a plot to assist a prison break-out, to seize weapons from the army and to assassinate a cabinet minister were vehemently denied by representatives of the group. A spokesperson for the movement stated that the allegations were merely the latest in a series of claims aimed at discrediting the organization. Meanwhile, ongoing concerns for the freedom of the media in Tonga were renewed following the arrest of the deputy editor of *The Times of Tonga* on charges of criminal libel.

In February 2001 the Human Rights and Democracy Movement launched a public petition to amend Tonga's Nationality Act to allow Tongans who had taken up citizenship in other countries to retain Tongan citizenship. Their stated objective in undertaking the petition was to acknowledge Tonga's dependence on remittances from Tongans living overseas.

In September 2000, meanwhile, protests took place in Nuku'alofa, prompted by concerns that Chinese immigrant businesses, encouraged by the Government to establish themselves in Tonga, were creating unfavourable economic conditions for Tongan businesses. The Human Rights and Democracy Movement appealed to the Government to cease issuing work permits to foreign (predominantly Chinese) business people and to end the sale of Tongan passports, which had raised an estimated US $30m. during the 1980s. In order to protect this money from his ministers, whom he feared would squander it on unsuitable public works projects should it enter Tonga, the King requested that the funds be placed in the Tonga Trust Fund, held in a cheque account at the San Francisco, CA, branch of the Bank of America. In June 1999 Jesse Bogdonoff, a Bank of America employee, successfully sought royal approval to invest the money in a company in Nevada called Millennium Asset Management, where Bogdonoff was named as the Fund's Advising Officer. Bogdonoff later claimed that he had made a profit of about $11m., which so impressed the King that he appointed Bogdonoff as Court Jester. The balance of the Fund and the interest it had accrued (altogether some $40m.) was due to be returned to Tonga on 6 June 2001; instead the money appeared to have vanished, along with Millennium Asset Management, which had ceased to exist. In September Princess Pilolevu, acting as Regent in the absence of the King and the Crown Prince, dismissed Kinikinilau Tutoatasi Fakafanua, currently Minister of Education but who at the time of the incident had been Minister of Finance, along with the Deputy Prime Minister and Minister of Justice, Tevita Tupou, both of whom were trustees of the fund. She appointed the Minister of Police, Fire Services and Prisons, Clive Edwards, as Acting Deputy Prime Minister. Parliament created a committee to investigate the crime and tabled a motion to impeach Fakafanua and Tupou. There were no apparent reprisals, or legal action, against Bogdonoff, who claimed that he had been deliberately misled as to the value of the funds. In October the Acting Deputy Prime Minister denied that the Privy Council had directed the transfers from the Fund or that any ministers were implicated. He stressed that at least $2.1m. of the fund, invested in Tongan banks, was duly accounted for. In June 2002, however, the Government admitted that about $26m. had been lost as a result of Bogdanoff's actions and that legal proceedings had been initiated in the USA. It was announced in February 2003 that the case would be heard in December of that year; also in February the Legislative Assembly began impeachment proceedings against the ministers implicated in the matter.

In January 2002 Pohiva published allegations that the King held a secret offshore bank account containing US $350m., some of which was believed to be the proceeds of gold recovered from an 18th century shipwreck. He claimed to possess a letter written to the King from within the palace referring to the account. The Government dismissed the letter as a forgery. Nevertheless, Pohiva was briefly held in custody in February, whilst police searched the offices of the Tonga Human Rights and Democracy Movement and confiscated the hard drives of its computers in an attempt to find the source material of the allegations. Later that month New Zealand's Minister for Foreign Affairs and Trade condemned Tonga as being endemically corrupt, implying that New Zealand's annual $NZ6m. profited the élite rather than the Tongan people as a whole. In February the King admitted that he did possess an overseas account, with the Bank of Hawaii, but it contained the profits of vanilla sales from his own plantation. Nevertheless, Pohiva was formally charged with the use and publication of a forged document. In May 2002 he was acquitted of charges of sedition.

A general election was held on 6–7 March 2002, at which 52 candidates competed for the nine commoners' seats in the Legislative Assembly. The Tonga Human Rights and Democracy Movement won seven seats.

In late July 2002 it was reported that Pohiva, Moala and Akau'ola were seeking damages from the Tongan Government for wrongful imprisonment, following their incarceration in 1996 on charges of contempt of parliament.

Concerns for the freedom of the media re-emerged in February 2003 when the Government declared *The Times of Tonga*, the twice-weekly newspaper printed in New Zealand, to be a 'prohibited import', describing it as a foreign publication with a political agenda. The ban was challenged, and in April Tonga's Chief Justice ruled that it was both illegal and unconstitutional. However, within hours of the ruling the Government ordered a new ban under different legislation.

A friendship treaty that Tonga signed with the USA in July 1988 provided for the safe transit within Tongan waters of US ships capable of carrying nuclear weapons. Tonga was virtually alone in the region in failing to condemn the French Government for its decision to resume nuclear-weapons tests in the South Pacific in mid-1995. However, in May 1996 it was announced that Tonga was finally to accede to the South Pacific Nuclear-Free Zone Treaty (see p. 306).

In September 1990 Tongasat, a Tongan telecommunications company founded earlier that year by Tongan citizens jointly with a US entrepreneur, laid claim to the last 16 satellite positions remaining in the earth's orbit that were suitable for trans-Pacific communications. Despite the protests of leading member nations of Intelsat (the international consortium responsible for most of the world's satellite services), the International Telecommunication Union (see p. 104), was obliged to approve the claim, and Tongasat was subsequently granted six positions. A dispute with Indonesia, concerning that country's use of satellite positions reserved by Tonga in 1990, was resolved by the signing of an agreement in December 1993. In May of the following year the two countries established diplomatic relations at ambassadorial level.

In November 1998 Tonga announced that it had decided to terminate its diplomatic links with Taiwan and to establish relations with the People's Republic of China.

In January 2002, in the Red Sea, Israeli commandos seized a ship that was allegedly transporting weapons to Palestinians. The ship was flying a Tongan 'flag of convenience' and had been registered in the Kingdom, although its ownership was uncertain. 'Akilisi Pohiva criticized Tonga's policy of international ship registration, which generated income through sales of flags of convenience. (The issue of international shipping registration had never been debated in Parliament.) Following the seizure, the registration system was closed in June. However, in September another Tongan-registered ship was seized off the coast of Italy and its crew arrested on suspicion of plotting an al-Qa'ida-sponsored terrorist attack in Europe. Furthermore, it was reported in early October that the Greek businessman in charge of the Tongan International Registry of Ships, Pelopidas Papadopoulos, had absconded with the proceeds of the operation owed to the Tongan Government, totalling some US $0.3m.

Government

Tonga is a hereditary monarchy. The King is Head of State and Head of Government. He appoints, and presides over, the Privy Council which acts as the national Cabinet. Apart from the King, the Council includes 10 ministers, appointed for life and led by the Prime Minister, and the Governors of Ha'apai and Vava'u. The unicameral Legislative Assembly comprises the King and 30 members: the Privy Council, nine hereditary nobles (chosen by their peers) and nine representatives elected by all adult Tongan citizens. Elected members hold office for three years. There are no official political parties, although an oppo-

sition group was founded in late 1992 to campaign for democratic reform.

Defence

Tonga has its own defence force, consisting of both regular and reserve units. Projected government expenditure on defence in the financial year 1999/2000 was $T3.3m. (5.0% of total budgetary expenditure); in the same year estimated expenditure on law and order was $T4.6m. (6.9% of total current expenditure).

Economic Affairs

In 2001, according to estimates by the World Bank, Tonga's gross national income (GNI), measured at average 1999–2001 prices, was US $154m., equivalent to $1,530 per head. During 1990–2001, it was estimated, the population increased at an average annual rate of 0.5%, while gross domestic product (GDP) per head increased, in real terms, by an average of 2.4% per year. Overall GDP increased, in real terms, at an average annual rate of 2.8 % in 1990–2001; growth in 2001 was 3.1%.

Agriculture (including forestry and fishing) contributed 27.2% of GDP in 2000/01, and engaged 33.8% of the employed labour force in 1996. According to the Asian Development Bank (ADB), agricultural GDP increased at an average annual rate of 0.8% in 1996–2001, rising by 10.8% in 2000 and by 1.3% in 2001. The principal cash crops are coconuts, vanilla and squash, which normally form the major part of Tonga's exports. In 2000/01 exports of squash provided almost half of total export earnings (some 45%). Vanilla acquired comparable significance, accounting for 13.4% in 1995/96; however, production subsequently declined and accounted for only 3.3% of total export earnings in 2000/01. Yams, taro, sweet potatoes, watermelons, tomatoes, cassava, lemons and limes, oranges, groundnuts and breadfruit are also cultivated as food crops, while the islanders keep pigs, goats, poultry and cattle. Food imports accounted for some 32% of total import costs in 2000/01. The fishing industry is relatively undeveloped. However, in early 2001 the Australian Government agreed to fund a four-year fishing project in the islands, which was to include the provision of equipment to small-scale fishermen, improved marketing opportunities and the development of commercial long-line fishing for tuna. The fishing sector contributed some 30% of total export earnings in 2000/01.

Industry (including mining, manufacturing, construction and power) provided 13.5% of GDP in 2000/01 and engaged 26.4% of the employed labour force in 1996. Compared with the previous year, industrial GDP was estimated by the ADB to have increased by 12.4% in 1999, by 3.0% in 2000 and by 5.4% in 2001. Manufacturing contributed 5.2% of GDP in 2000/01, and (with mining) employed 22.8% of the labour force in 1996. Food products and beverages accounted for 56.8% of total manufactured goods produced in 1999/2000. The food and textile sectors of manufacturing registered the largest increases in 1999/2000, raising the value of their production by 14.6% and 56.8% respectively. Other industrial activities are the production of concrete blocks, small excavators, furniture, handicrafts, leather goods, sports equipment (including small boats), brewing and coconut oil. There is also a factory for processing sandalwood. In early 2003 permission was granted for a Chinese businessman to establish a cigarette factory in the islands.

In an attempt to reduce fuel imports, a 2-MW wave-energy power plant was constructed in the early 1990s, and would, it was hoped, supply one-third of the islands' total electricity requirements when in full operation. Fuel and chemical imports accounted for 25.5% of total import costs in 2000/01. A project to provide all the outer islands with solar power by 2000 was begun in 1996.

Service industries contributed 59.3% of GDP in 2000/01 and engaged 39.5% of the employed labour force in 1996. According to the ADB, the GDP of the services sector expanded by 5.6% in 2000 and by an estimated 3.2% in 2001. Tourism makes a significant contribution to the economy. Tourism receipts, however, declined from 16.5m. pa'anga in 1999/2000 to 12.7m. pa'anga in 2000/01. The trade, restaurants and hotels sector contributed 13.7% of GDP in 2000/01 and engaged 8.5% of the employed labour force in 1996. Visitor arrivals totalled 33,868 in 1999/2000, when cruise-ship passengers accounted for a further 5,151 visitors. Total arrivals declined to 33,722 in 2000/01

In 2000/01 Tonga recorded a visible trade deficit of US $56m., and a deficit of US $14m. on the current account of the balance of payments. In 2001 the principal sources of imports were New Zealand (32.5%) and Fiji (21.9%), while Japan and the USA were the principal markets for exports (purchasing 42.2% and 40.1%

respectively). Other major trading partners are Australia and Fiji. The principal exports in that year were foodstuffs. The principal imports were foodstuffs, machinery and transport equipment, basic manufactures and mineral fuels.

In the financial year ending 30 June 2002 there was an estimated budgetary deficit of 1.4m. pa'anga. Tonga's total external debt was US $62.3m. in 1999/2000. In that year the cost of debt-servicing was equivalent to 12.1% of the total revenue from exports of goods and services. Official development assistance totalled US $18.8m. in 2000, of which US $14.8m. was bilateral aid. In 2002/03 official development assistance from Australia totalled $A11.4m. and from New Zealand $NZ5.6m. According to ADB figures, the annual rate of inflation averaged 3.8% in 1990–2001. Consumer prices increased by an average of 6.3% in 2001. Some 13.3% of the labour force were unemployed in 1996.

Tonga is a member of the Pacific Community (see p. 304), the Pacific Islands Forum (see p. 306), the Asian Development Bank (ADB, see p. 143), the UN Economic and Social Commission for Asia and the Pacific (ESCAP, see p. 28) and is a signatory of the Lomé Conventions and the successor Cotonou Agreement with the European Union (EU, see p. 199).

During much of the 1990s Tonga's economic development was adversely affected by inclement weather, inflationary pressures, a high level of unemployment, large-scale emigration and over-reliance on the agricultural sector. Diversifying sources of income and establishing an efficient source of energy, to enable a reduction in fuel imports, remained important issues for Tonga in the 1990s. In late 1993 the King announced the conclusion of a joint-venture agreement between Tonga and the State Government of Sarawak in Malaysia. The agreement provided for the settlement of Tongan workers on farms in the state, jointly owned by the Tongan and Sarawak Governments, where various crops would be produced for export. Similar agreements were concluded with the Government of Papua New Guinea in 1994 and with American Samoa and Hawaii in 1999 providing for use of leased land for commercial crop cultivation. Following the decline in earnings from squash exports, various proposals for diversifying agricultural production were considered in the late 1990s, including the cultivation of tea, papaya and aloe vera, as well as the establishment of gas and petroleum refineries, the construction of new hotels to encourage growth in the tourist industry and the expansion of passenger and freight air services (with the purchase of 10 Russian aircraft and the development of new flight routes to Asia in an attempt to secure new markets for Tonga's exports). Proposals have also been mooted for a regional free-trade agreement and export promotion on a regional basis. In 1999 Tonga signed a bilateral trade agreement with the People's Republic of China, and a trade delegation from that country visited the islands in the following year. It was thought that China was considering using Tonga as a base for the production of export goods (including garments and agricultural products) for the Australian and New Zealand markets. In August 2001, as a result of Tonga's action against the problem of international 'money-laundering', the country was removed from a list of unco-operative tax havens, drawn up by the Paris-based Financial Action Task Force (FATF, see p. 343). The repercussions of the terrorist attacks on the USA in September 2001 not only depressed Tonga's tourism industry in the short term but were also expected to reduce overseas remittances to the islands, as many emigrant workers were employed in the airline industry in the USA. It was reported in early 2002 that the Tongan Government had reached an agreement with a US company to develop the island of 'Eua as a rocket-launching site for the purposes of 'space tourism'. The first launch was expected to take place in 2005. Meanwhile, the sharp rise in the Government's unbudgeted expenditure continued to cause concern in early 2002. The ADB projected a GDP growth rate of 2.9% for 2002 and of 2.6% for 2003.

Education

Free state education is compulsory for children between five and 14 years of age, while the Government and other Commonwealth countries offer scholarship schemes enabling students to go abroad for higher education. In 1999 there were 117 primary schools, with a total of 16,206 pupils, and there was a total of 13,987 pupils in 39 secondary schools. There were also four technical and vocational colleges in 1999, with a total of 467 students, and one teacher-training college, with 288 students. In 1990 there were 230 Tongans studying overseas. Some degree courses are offered at the university division of 'Atenisi Institute. Recurrent government expenditure on education in 1999/2000 was an estimated $T10.9m. (equivalent to 16.5% of total recurrent budgetary expenditure).

Public Holidays

2003: 1 January (New Year's Day), 18–21 April (Easter), 25 April (ANZAC Day), 4 May (HRH the Crown Prince's Birthday), 4 June (Independence Day), 4 July (HM the King's Birthday), 4 November (Constitution Day), 4 December (Tupou I Day), 25–26 December (Christmas Day and Boxing Day).

2004: 1 January (New Year's Day), 9–12 April (Easter), 25 April (ANZAC Day), 4 May (HRH the Crown Prince's Birthday), 4 June (Independence Day), 4 July (HM the King's Birthday), 4 November (Constitution Day), 4 December (Tupou I Day), 25–26 December (Christmas Day and Boxing Day).

Weights and Measures

In 1980 Tonga adopted the metric system of weights and measures in place of the imperial system.

Statistical Survey

Source (unless otherwise indicated): Tonga Government Department of Statistics, POB 149, Nuku'alofa; tel. 23300; fax 24303; e-mail statdept@tongatapu.net.to.

AREA AND POPULATION

Area: 748 sq km (289 sq miles).

Population: 94,649 at census of 28 November 1986; 97,784 (males 49,615, females 48,169) at census of 30 November 1996; 100,672 (official estimate) at mid-2001. *By group* (1996 census, provisional): Tongatapu 66,577; Vava'u 15,779; Ha'apai 8,148; 'Eua 4,924; Niuas 2,018.

Density (2001): 134.6 per sq km.

Principal Towns (population in '000, 1986): Nuku'alofa (capital) 21.3; Mu'a 4.1; Neiafu 3.9. Source: Stefan Helders, *World Gazetteer* (internet www.world-gazetteer.com).

Births, Marriages and Deaths (1998): Registered live births 2,737 (birth rate 27.0 per 1,000 at 1996 census); Registered marriages 736 (marriage rate 7.7 per 1,000); Registered deaths 498 (death rate 6.5 per 1,000 at 1996 census).

Expectation of Life (WHO estimates, years at birth): 69.4 (males 68.1; females 70.8) in 2001. Source: WHO, *World Health Report*.

Economically Active Population (persons aged 15 years and over, 1996): Agriculture, forestry and fishing 9,953; Mining and quarrying 43; Manufacturing 6,710; Electricity, gas and water 504; Construction 500; Trade, restaurants and hotels 2,506; Transport, storage and communications 1,209; Financing, insurance, real estate and business services 657; Public administration and defence 3,701; Education 1,721; Health and social work 510; Other community, social and personal services 1,320; Extra-territorial organizations 72; Total employed 29,406 (males 18,402, females 11,004); Total unemployed 4,502 (males 3,293, females 1,209); Total labour force 33,908 (males 21,695; females 12,213). The totals shown may differ from the sum of the component parts.

AGRICULTURE, ETC.

Principal Crops (metric tons, 2000): Sweet potatoes 8,000; Cassava 9,070; Taro 3,720; Yams 5,040; Copra 4,109*; Coconuts 57,685†; Pumpkins, squash and gourds 17,000*; Bananas 710; Plantains 2,961; Oranges 690; Lemons and limes 2,500*; Other fruits 3,000*.
* Unofficial figure.
† FAO estimate. Source: FAO.

Livestock (FAO estimates, '000 head, year ending September 2001): Pigs 81; Horses 11; Cattle 11; Goats 13; Chickens 300. Source: FAO.

Livestock Products (FAO estimates, metric tons, 2001): Pig meat 1,496; Other meat 684; Hen eggs 28; Honey 12; Cattle hides 40; Cow's milk 370. Source: FAO.

Forestry (Roundwood removals, '000 cu m, excluding bark): 4 in 1998; 2 in 1999; 2 in 2000; 2 in 2001. Source: FAO.

Fishing (metric tons, live weight, 2000): Total catch 3,531 (Albacore 822, Marine crustaceans 175). Source: FAO, *Yearbook of Fishery Statistics*.

INDUSTRY

Production (1999): Electric energy 29.5 million kWh.

FINANCE

Currency and Exchange Rates: 100 seniti (cents) = 1 pa'anga (Tongan dollar or $T). *Sterling, US Dollar and Euro Equivalents* (31 December 2002): £1 sterling = $T3.592; US $1 = $T2.228; €1 = $T2.337; $T100 = £27.84 = US $44.87 = €42.79. *Average Exchange Rate* (pa'anga per US $): 1.7585 in 2000; 2.1236 in 2001; 2.1952 in 2002.

Budget (estimates, million pa'anga, year ending 30 June 2002): *Revenue:* Taxation 74.5 (Taxes on international transactions 48.5); Other current revenue 18.7; Total 93.2 (excl. grants received from abroad 2.0). *Expenditure:* Current expenditure 80.6; Capital expenditure 10.2; Total 91.8 (excl. lending minus repayments 0.6). Source: IMF, *Tonga: Statistical Appendix* (February 2003).

International Reserves (US $ million at 31 December 2002): IMF special drawing rights 0.26; Reserve position in the IMF 2.33; Foreign exchange 25.11; Total 27.70. Source: IMF, *International Financial Statistics*.

Money Supply ('000 pa'anga at 31 December 2001): Currency outside banks 11,355; Demand deposits at deposit money banks 30,389; Total money 41,744. Source: IMF, *International Financial Statistics*.

Cost of Living (Consumer Price Index, excl. rent; base: 1995 = 100): 113.9 in 1999; 120.6 in 2000; 130.7 in 2001. Source: IMF, *International Financial Statistics*.

Gross Domestic Product (million pa'anga at current prices, year ending 30 June): 260.6 in 1999/2000; 270.3 (preliminary) in 2000/01; 296.5 (estimate) in 2001/02. Source: IMF, *Tonga: Statistical Appendix* (February 2003).

Gross Domestic Product by Economic Activity (preliminary figures, million pa'anga at current prices, year ending 30 June 2001): Agriculture, forestry and fishing 65.0; Mining and quarrying 0.9; Manufacturing 12.3; Electricity, gas and water 4.5; Construction 14.5; Trade, restaurants and hotels 32.8; Transport, storage and communications 18.7; Finance and real estate 23.8; Government services 42.7; Entertainment and private services 13.5; Ownership of dwellings 9.9; *Sub-total* 238.6; *Less:* Imputed bank service charge 12.6; *GDP at factor cost* 226.0; Indirect taxes, *less* subsidies 44.3; *GDP in purchasers' values* 270.3. Source: IMF, *Tonga: Statistical Appendix* (February 2003).

Balance of Payments (US $ million, year ending 30 June 2001): Exports of goods f.o.b. 7; Imports of goods f.o.b. –63; *Trade balance* –56; Exports of services and income 18; Imports of services and income –28; *Balance on goods, services and income* –66; Current transfers (net) 52; *Current balance* –14; Direct investment 4; Portfolio investment 0; Other long-term capital 9; Other short-term capital 2; Net errors and omissions 1; *Overall balance* 2 (Source: Asian Development Bank, *Key Indicators of Developing Asian and Pacific Countries*). *2001* (US $ million): Trade balance –49; Current balance –12 (Source: Asian Development Bank, *Asian Development Outlook 2002*).

EXTERNAL TRADE

Principal Commodities (US $ million, year ending 30 June 2001): *Imports:* Food and live animals, beverages and tobacco 22.2; Crude materials (inedible) except fuels 5.2; Fuels, minerals and chemicals 17.6; Basic manufactures 7.7; Machinery and transport equipment 7.7; Miscellaneous manufactured articles 8.4; Total (incl. others) 68.9. *Exports:* Squash 2.7; Root crops 1.0; Vanilla 0.2; Fish 1.8; Manufactured goods 0.4; Total 6.0. Source: IMF, *Tonga: Statistical Appendix* (February 2003).

Principal Trading Partners (US $ million, 2001): *Imports:* Australia 7.8; China, People's Repub. 2.0; Fiji 16.5; France 2.0; Indonesia 1.1; Japan 3.5; New Zealand 24.5; Thailand 6.3; United Kingdom 2.0; USA 5.8; Total (incl. others) 75.3. *Exports:* Australia 0.4; Fiji 0.3; Japan 8.1; New Zealand 1.1; United Kingdom 0.3; USA 7.7; Total (incl. others) 19.2. Source: Asian Development Bank, *Key Indicators of Developing Asian and Pacific Countries*.

TRANSPORT

Road Traffic (registered vehicles in use, 1998): Passenger cars 6,419; Buses and coaches 171; Lorries and vans 9,018.

Shipping (international traffic, '000 metric tons, 1998): Goods loaded 13.8; Goods unloaded 80.4. 1991: Vessels entered ('000 net registered tons) 1,950 (Source: UN, *Statistical Yearbook*). *Merchant Fleet* (registered at 31 December 2001): Vessels 165; Total displacement ('000 grt) 337.6 (Source: Lloyd's Register-Fairplay, *World Fleet Statistics*).

Civil Aviation (traffic on scheduled services, 1999): Passengers carried 91,000; Passenger-km 19 million; Total ton-km 2 million. Source: UN, *Statistical Yearbook*.

TOURISM

Foreign Tourist Arrivals: 27,709 (excl. cruise-ship passengers 5,737) in 1998/99; 33,868 (excl. cruise-ship passengers 5,151) in 1999/2000; 33,722 (excl. cruise-ship passengers 4,976) in 2000/01.

Tourist Arrivals by Country (2000/01): Australia 5,453; New Zealand 10,674; Pacific islands 2,797; USA 7,053; Total (incl. others) 33,722.

Tourism Receipts (million pa'anga): 11.6 in 1998/99; 16.5 in 1999/2000; 12.7 in 2000/01.
Source: IMF, *Tonga: Statistical Appendix* (February 2003).

COMMUNICATIONS MEDIA

Radio Receivers (1997): 61,000 in use.

Television Receivers (1997): 2,000 in use.

Telephones ('000 main lines, 2000): 9.7 in use.

Mobile Cellular Telephones (1999): 140 subscribers.

Internet Users (1999): 1,000.

Facsimile Machines (1996): 250 in use.

Daily Newspapers (1996): 1; estimated circulation 7,000.

Non-daily Newspapers (2001): 2; estimated circulation 13,000.
Sources: UNESCO, *Statistical Yearbook*; UN, *Statistical Yearbook*; Audit Bureau of Circulations, Australia; and International Telecommunication Union.

EDUCATION

Primary (1999): 117 schools; 745 teachers; 16,206 pupils.

General Secondary (1999): 39 schools; 961 teachers; 13,987 pupils.

Technical and Vocational (1999): 4 colleges; 45 teachers (1990); 467 students.

Teacher-training (1999): 1 college; 22 teachers (1994); 288 students.

Universities, etc. (1985): 17 teachers; 85 students.

Other Higher Education (1985): 36 teachers (1980); 620 students.

In 1990 230 students were studying overseas on government scholarships.

Directory

The Constitution

The Constitution of Tonga is based on that granted in 1875 by King George Tupou I. It provides for a government consisting of the Sovereign; a Privy Council, which is appointed by the Sovereign and consists of the Sovereign and the Cabinet; the Cabinet, which consists of a Prime Minister, a Deputy Prime Minister, eight other ministers and the Governors of Ha'apai and Vava'u; a Legislative Assembly and a Judiciary. Limited law-making power is vested in the Privy Council and any legislation passed by the Executive is subject to review by the Legislative Assembly. The unicameral Legislative Assembly comprises the King, the Cabinet, nine hereditary nobles (chosen by their peers) and nine representatives elected by all adult Tongan citizens. Elected members hold office for three years.

The Government

The Sovereign: HM King TAUFA'AHAU TUPOU IV (succeeded to the throne 15 December 1965).

CABINET
(April 2003)

Prime Minister and Minister of Foreign Affairs, Defence, Agriculture, Forestry and Fisheries and Civil Aviation, responsible for Telecommunications: HRH Prince 'ULUKALALA-LAVAKA-ATA.

Deputy Prime Minister and Minister of Works responsible for Disaster Relief, Environment and Marine Affairs and Ports: CECIL COCKER.

Minister of Finance: SIOSIUA 'UTOIKAMANU.

Minister of Education: PAULA SUNIA BLOOMFIELD.

Minister of Labour, Commerce, Industries and Tourism: Dr MASASO PAUNGA.

Minister of Police, Fire Services and Prisons: CLIVE EDWARDS.

Minister of Lands, Survey and Natural Resources: FIELAKEPA.

Minister of Health: Dr VILIAMI TA'U TANGI.

Attorney-General and Minister of Justice: FRANKIE SUE DEL PAPA.

Governor of Ha'apai: MALUPO.

Governor of Vava'u: S. M. TUITA.

GOVERNMENT MINISTRIES AND OFFICES

Office of the Prime Minister: POB 62, Taufa'ahau Rd, Kolofo'ou, Nuku'alofa; tel. 24644; fax 23888; e-mail fttuita@pmo.gov.to; internet www.pmo.gov.to.

Palace Office: Salote Rd, Kolofo'ou, Nuku'alofa; tel. 21000; fax 24102.

Ministry of Agriculture and Fisheries: Administration Office, Vuna Rd, Kolofo'ou, Nuku'alofa; tel. 23038; fax 23039; e-mail maf-holo@candw.to.

Ministry of Civil Aviation: POB 845, Salote Rd, Nuku'alofa; tel. 24144; fax 24145; e-mail info@mca.gov.to; internet www.mca.gov.to.

Ministry of Education: POB 61, Vuna Rd, Kolofo'ou, Nuku'alofa; tel. 23511; fax 23596; e-mail moe@kalianet.to.

Ministry of Finance: Treasury Building, POB 87, Vuna Rd, Kolofo'ou, Nuku'alofa; tel. 23066; fax 21010; e-mail minfin@candw.to.

Ministry of Foreign Affairs: National Reserve Bank Building, Salote Rd, Kolofo'ou, Nuku'alofa; tel. 23600; fax 23360; e-mail secfo@candw.to.

Ministry of Health: POB 59, Taufa'ahau Rd, Tofoa, Nuku'alofa; tel. 23200; fax 24921.

Ministry of Justice: POB 130, Railway Rd, Kolofo'ou, Nuku'alofa; tel. 21055; fax 23098.

Ministry of Labour, Commerce and Industries: POB 110, Salote Rd, Fasi-moe-afi, Nuku'alofa; tel. 23688; fax 23880; e-mail tongatrade@candw.to.

Ministry of Lands, Survey and Natural Resources: POB 5, Vuna Rd, Kolofo'ou, Nuku'alofa; tel. 23611; fax 23216.

Ministry of Marine and Ports: Fakafanua Centre, Vuna Rd, Ma'ufanga, Nuku'alofa; tel. 22555; fax 26234.

Ministry of Police, Fire Services and Prisons: Mauikisikisi Rd, Longolongo, Nuku'alofa; tel. 23233; fax 23226.

Ministry of Telecommunications: Nuku'alofa.

Ministry of Works and Disaster Relief Activities: 'Alaivahamama'o Rd, Vaololoa, Nuku'alofa; tel. 23100; fax 23102; e-mail mowtonga@kalianet.to.

Department of Civil Aviation: Salote Rd, Fasi-moe-afi; tel. 24144; fax 24145.

Legislative Assembly

The Legislative Assembly consists of the Speaker, the members of the Cabinet, nine nobles chosen by the 33 Nobles of Tonga, and nine representatives elected by all Tongans over 21 years of age. There are elections every three years, and the Assembly is required to meet at least once every year. The most recent election was held on 6–7 March 2002, when seven of the nine elected representatives were members of the reformist Tonga Human Rights and Democracy Movement.

Speaker and Chairman of the Legislative Assembly: TU'IVAKANO.

Political Organizations

Kotoa Movement: f. 2001; campaigns in support of monarchy.

Human Rights and Democracy Movement in Tonga (HRDMT): POB 843, Nuku'alofa; tel. 25501; fax 26330; e-mail demo@kalianet.to; f. 1992 as Tonga Pro-Democracy Movement; campaigns for democratic reform and increased parliamentary representation for the Tongan people; Chair. Rev. SIMOTE VEA; Sec. 'AKILISI POHIVA.

Diplomatic Representation

EMBASSY AND HIGH COMMISSIONS IN TONGA

Australia: Salote Rd, Nuku'alofa; tel. 23244; fax 23243; High Commissioner COLIN HILL (designate).

China, People's Republic: Nuku'alofa; Ambassador GAO SHANHAI.

New Zealand: cnr Taufa'ahau and Salote Rds, POB 830, Nuku'alofa; tel. 23122; fax 23487; e-mail nzhcnuk@kalianet.to; High Commissioner WARWICK A. HAWKER.

United Kingdom: Vuna Rd, POB 56, Nuku'alofa; tel. 24285; fax 24109; e-mail britcomt@kalianet.to; High Commissioner PAUL NESSLING.

Judicial System

There are eight Magistrates' Courts, the Land Court, the Supreme Court and the Court of Appeal.

Appeal from the Magistrates' Courts is to the Supreme Court, and from the Supreme Court and Land Court to the Court of Appeal (except in certain matters relating to hereditary estates, where appeal lies to the Privy Council). The Chief Justice and Puisne Judge are resident in Tonga and are judges of the Supreme Court and Land Court. The Court of Appeal is presided over by the Chief Justice and consists of three judges from other Commonwealth countries. In the Supreme Court the accused in criminal cases, and either party in civil suits, may elect trial by jury. In the Land Court the judge sits with a Tongan assessor. Proceedings in the Magistrates' Courts are in Tongan, and in the Supreme Court and Court of Appeal in Tongan and English.

Supreme Court
POB 11, Nuku'alofa; tel. 23599; fax 24771.

Chief Justice: GORDON WARD.

Puisne Judge: TONY FORD.

Chief Registrar: MANAKOVI PAHULU.

Religion

The Tongans are almost all Christians, and about 36% of the population belong to Methodist (Wesleyan) communities. There are also significant numbers of Roman Catholics (15%) and Latter-day Saints (Mormons—15%). Anglicans (1%) and Seventh-day Adventists (5%) are also represented. Fourteen churches are represented in total.

CHRISTIANITY

Kosilio 'ae Ngaahi Siasi 'i Tonga (Tonga National Council of Churches): POB 1205, Nuku'alofa; tel. 23291; fax 27506; e-mail tncc@kalianet.to; f. 1973; four mem. churches (Free Wesleyan, Roman Catholic, Anglican and Free Constitutional Church of Tonga); Chair. Archdeacon TUINIUA FINAU; Gen. Sec. Rev. SIMOTE M. VEA.

The Anglican Communion

Tonga lies within the diocese of Polynesia, part of the Church of the Province of New Zealand. The Bishop of Polynesia is resident in Fiji.

Archdeacon of Tonga and Samoa: The Ven. SAM KOY, The Vicarage, POB 31, Nuku'alofa; tel. 22136.

The Roman Catholic Church

The diocese of Tonga, directly responsible to the Holy See, comprises Tonga and the New Zealand dependency of Niue. At 31 December 2000 there were an estimated 15,339 adherents in the diocese. The Bishop participates in the Catholic Bishops' Conference of the Pacific, based in Fiji.

Bishop of Tonga: Dr SOANE LILO FOLIAKI, Toutai-mana Catholic Centre, POB 1, Nuku'alofa; tel. 23822; fax 23854; e-mail cathbish@kalianet.to.

Other Churches

Church of Jesus Christ of Latter-day Saints (Mormon): Mission Centre, POB 58, Nuku'alofa; tel. 26007; fax 23763; 40,000 mems; Pres. DOUGLAS W. BANKS.

Church of Tonga: Nuku'alofa; f. 1928; a branch of Methodism; 6,912 mems; Pres. Rev. FINAU KATOANGA.

Free Constitutional Church of Tonga: POB 23, Nuku'alofa; tel. 23966; fax 24458; f. 1885; 15,941 mems (1996); Pres. Rev. SEMISI FONUA; brs in Australia, New Zealand and USA.

Free Wesleyan Church of Tonga (Koe Siasi Uesiliana Tau'ataina 'o Tonga): POB 57, Nuku'alofa; tel. 23432; fax 24020; e-mail fwc@candw.to; f. 1826; 36,500 mems; Pres. Rev. Dr 'ALIFALETI MONE.

Tokaikolo Christian Fellowship: Nuku'alofa; f. 1978 as breakaway group from Free Wesleyan Church; 5,000 mems.

BAHÁ'Í FAITH

National Spiritual Assembly: POB 133, Nuku'alofa; tel. 21568; fax 23120; e-mail patco@kalianet.to; mems resident in 156 localities.

The Press

Eva, Your Guide to Tonga: POB 958, Nuku'alofa; tel. 25779; fax 24749; e-mail vapress@kalianet.to; internet www.matangitonga.to; f. 1989; 4 a year; Editor PESI FONUA; circ. 4,500.

Ko e Kele'a (Conch Shell): POB 1567, Nuku'alofa; tel. 25501; fax 26330; f. 1986; monthly; activist-oriented publication, economic and political; Editor SIOSINA PO'OI POHIVA; circ. 3,500.

Lali: Nuku'alofa; f. 1994; monthly; English; national business magazine; Publr KALAFI MOALA.

Lao and Hia: POB 2808, Nuku'alofa; tel. 14105; weekly; Tongan; legal newspaper; Editor SIONE HAFOKA.

Matangi Tonga: POB 958, Nuku'alofa; tel. 25779; fax 24749; e-mail vapress@kalianet.to; internet www.matangitonga.to; f. 1986; 4 a year; national news magazine; Editor PESI FONUA; circ. 2,000.

'Ofa ki Tonga: c/o Tokaikolo Fellowship, POB 2055, Nuku'alofa; tel. 24190; monthly; newspaper of Tokaikolo Christian Fellowship; Editor Rev. LIUFAU VAILEA SAULALA.

Taumu'a Lelei: POB 1, Nuku'alofa; tel. 27161; fax 23854; e-mail tmlcath@kalianet.to; f. 1931; monthly; Roman Catholic; Editor Dr SOANE LILO FOLIAKI.

The Times of Tonga/Koe Taimi'o Tonga: POB 880, Hala Velingatoni, Kolomotu'a; tel. 23177; fax 23292; e-mail times@kalianet.to; internet www.tongatimes.com; f. 1989; twice-weekly; English edition covers Pacific and world news, Tongan edition concentrates on

local news; Editor KALAFI MOALA; Deputy Editor MATENI TAPUELUELU; circ. 8,000.

Tohi Fanongonongo: POB 57, Nuku'alofa; tel. 26533; fax 24020; e-mail fwctf@kalianet.to; monthly; Wesleyan; Editor Rev. TEVITA PAUKAMEA TIUETI.

Tonga Chronicle/Kalonikali Tonga: POB 197, Nuku'alofa; tel. 23302; fax 23336; e-mail chroni@kalianet.to; internet www .netstorage.com/kami/tonga/news; f. 1964; govt-sponsored; weekly; Editor PAUA MANU'ATA; circ. 6,000 (Tongan), 1,200 (English).

Publisher

Vava'u Press Ltd: POB 958, Nuku'alofa; tel. 25779; fax 24749; e-mail vapress@kalianet.to; internet www.matangitonga.to; f. 1980; books and magazines; Pres. PESI FONUA.

Broadcasting and Communications

TELECOMMUNICATIONS

Tonga Communications Corporation: Private Bag 4, Nuku'alofa; tel. 26700; fax 26701; internet www.tcc.to; responsible for domestic and international telecommunications services; Gen. Man. JON E. MORRIS.

Tongasat—Friendly Islands Satellite Communications Ltd: POB 2921, Nuku'alofa; tel. 24160; fax 23322; e-mail kite@tongasat .com; 80% Tongan-owned; private co but co-operates with Govt in management and leasing of orbital satellite positions; Chair. Princess PILOLEVU TUITA; Man. Dir SIONE KITE; Sec. WILLIAM CLIVE EDWARDS.

BROADCASTING

Radio

Tonga Broadcasting Commission: POB 36, Tungi Rd, Fasi-moe-afi, Nuku'alofa; tel. 23555; fax 24417; independent statutory board; commercially operated; manages two stations, A3Z Radio Tonga 1 and Radio Tonga 2, with programmes in Tongan and English; Gen. Man. TAVAKE FUSIMALOHI.

93FM: Pacific Partners Trust, POB 478, Nuku'alofa; tel. 23076; fax 24970; broadcasts in English, Tongan, German, Mandarin and Hindi.

A3V The Millennium Radio 2000: POB 838, Nuku'alofa; tel. 25891; fax 24195; e-mail a3v@tongatapu.net.to; broadcasts on FM; musical programmes; Gen. Man. SAM VEA.

Tonga News Association: Nuku'alofa; Pres. PESI FONUA.

Television

The introduction of a television service has been mooted since 1984. Oceania Broadcasting Inc started relaying US television programmes in 1991. The Tonga Broadcasting Commission was expected to launch the country's first television service in July 2000.

Oceania Broadcasting Network: POB 91, Nuku'alofa; tel. 23314; fax 23658.

Finance

(cap. = capital; res = reserves; dep. = deposits; m. = million; amounts in Tongan dollars)

BANKING

Australia and New Zealand Banking Group Ltd: Cnr of Salote and Railway Rds, POB 910, Nuku'alofa; tel. 24944; fax 23870; internet www.candw.to/banks.

Bank of Tonga: POB 924, Nuku'alofa; tel. 23933; fax 23634; e-mail bot-gm@kalianet.to; f. 1974; owned by Govt of Tonga (40%) and Westpac Banking Corpn (60%); cap. 3.0m., res 12.2m., dep. 65.2m. (Sept. 2001); Chair. ALAN WALTER; Gen. Man. BRIAN HARRIS; 4 brs.

MBf Bank Ltd: POB 3118, Nuku'alofa; tel. 24600; fax 24662; e-mail mbfbank@kalianet.to; 93.35% owned by MBf Asia Capital Corpn Holdings Ltd, 4.75% owned by Crown Prince Tupouto'a, 0.95% owned by Tonga Investments Ltd, 0.95% owned by Tonga Co-operative Federation Society.

National Reserve Bank of Tonga: POB 25, Post Office, Nuku'alofa; tel. 24057; fax 24201; e-mail nrbt@kalianet.to; f. 1989 to assume central bank functions of Bank of Tonga; issues currency; manages exchange rates and international reserves; cap. 1.0m., res

0.2m., dep. 41.9m. (June 2000); Gov. Siosiua 'Utoikamanu; Chair. Prince 'Ulukalala-Lavaka-Ata.

Tonga Development Bank: Fatafehi Rd, POB 126, Nuku'alofa; tel. 23333; fax 23775; e-mail tdevbank@tdb.to; f. 1977 to provide credit for developmental purposes, mainly in agriculture, fishery, tourism and housing; cap. 10.5m., res 1.502m. (Dec. 2001); Man. Dir 'Otenifi Afu'alo Matoto; 5 brs.

Westpac Banking Corporation: c/o Bank of Tonga, Railway Rd, Nuku'alofala; tel. 23933; fax 23781.

Trade and Industry

DEVELOPMENT ORGANIZATIONS

Tonga Investments Ltd: POB 27, Nuku'alofa; tel. 24388; fax 24313; f. 1992 to replace Commodities Board; govt-owned; manages five subsidiary companies; Chair. Baron Vaea of Houma; Man. Dir Anthony Wayne Madden.

Tonga Association of Small Businesses: Nuku'alofa; f. 1990 to cater for the needs of small businesses; Chair. Simi Silapelu.

CHAMBER OF COMMERCE

Tonga Chamber of Commerce and Industries: Tungi Arcade, POB 1704, Nuku'alofa; tel. 25168; fax 26039; e-mail chamber@kalianet.to; Pres. Aisake Eke.

TRADE ASSOCIATION

Tonga Kava Council: Nuku'alofa; to promote the development of the industry both locally and abroad; Chair. Toiimoana Takataka.

UTILITIES

Tonga Electric Power Board: POB 47, Taufa'ahau Rd, Kolofo'ou, Nuku'alofa; tel. 23311; fax 23632; provides electricity via diesel motor generation.

Tonga Water Board: POB 92, Taufa'ahau Rd, Kolofo'ou, Nuku'alofa; tel. 23298; fax 23518; operates four urban water systems, serving about 25% of the population; Man. Saimone P. Helu.

CO-OPERATIVES

In April 1990 there were 78 registered co-operative societies, including the first co-operative registered under the Agricultural Organization Act.

Tonga Co-operative Federation Society: Tungi Arcade, Nuku'alofa.

TRADE UNIONS

Association of Tongatapu Squash Pumpkin Growers: Nuku'alofa; f. 1998.

Tonga Nurses' Association and Friendly Islands Teachers' Association (TNA/FITA): POB 150, Nuku'alofa; tel. 23200; fax 24291; Pres. Finau Tutone; Gen. Sec. 'Ana Fotu Kavaefiafi.

Transport

ROADS

Total road length was estimated at 680 km in 1996, of which some 27% were all-weather paved roads. Most of the network comprises fair-weather-only dirt or coral roads.

SHIPPING

The chief ports are Nuku'alofa, on Tongatapu, and Neiafu, on Vava'u, with two smaller ports at Pangai and Niuatoputapu.

Shipping Corporation of Polynesia Ltd: Vuna Rd, POB 453, Nuku'alofa; tel. 23853; fax 22334; e-mail shipcorp@kalianet.to; regular inter-islands passenger and cargo services; Chair. Prince 'Ulukalala-Lavaka-Ata; Gen. Man. Capt. Volker Pahl.

Uata Shipping Lines: 'Uliti Uata, POB 100, Nuku'alofa; tel. 23855; fax 23860.

Warner Pacific Line: POB 93, Nuku'alofa; tel. 21088; services to Samoa, American Samoa, Australia and New Zealand; Man. Dir Ma'ake Faka'osifolau.

CIVIL AVIATION

Tonga is served by Fua'amotu International Airport, 22 km from Nuku'alofa, and airstrips at Vava'u, Ha'apai, Niuatoputapu, Niuafo'ou and 'Eua.

Royal Tongan Airlines: Private Bag 9, Royco Building, Fatafehi Rd, Nuku'alofa; tel. 23414; fax 24056; e-mail rta_per@kalianet.to; internet www.candw.to/rta; f. 1985 as Friendly Islands Airways Ltd; govt-owned; operates international service to Auckland (New Zealand), Nadi (Fiji), Niue, Honolulu (Hawaii), Samoa and Sydney (Australia) and internal services to Fua'amotu, Ha'apai, Vava'u, 'Eua, Niuatoputapu and Niuafo'ou; Chair. Prince 'Ulukalala-Lavaka-Ata; Gen. Man. Logan Appu.

Tourism

Tonga's attractions include scenic beauty and a mild climate. There were 33,868 visitors to the islands in 1999/2000 (an increase of more than 20% compared with the previous year). In addition 5,151 cruise-ship passengers visited the islands in 1999/2000. In that year tourism earned $T16.5m. In 1999/2000 the majority of tourists were from New Zealand, the USA and Australia.

Tonga Tourist Association: POB 74, Nuku'alofa; tel. 23344; fax 23833; e-mail royale@kalianet.to; Pres. Joseph Ramanlal.

Tonga Visitors' Bureau: Vuna Rd, POB 37, Nuku'alofa; tel. 25334; fax 23507; e-mail tvb@kalianet.to; internet www.tongaholiday.com; f. 1978; Dir Semisi P. Taumoepeau.

TRINIDAD AND TOBAGO

Introductory Survey

Location, Climate, Language, Religion, Flag, Capital

The Republic of Trinidad and Tobago consists of Trinidad, the southernmost of the Caribbean islands, and Tobago, which is 32 km (20 miles) to the north-east. Trinidad, which accounts for 94% of the total area, lies just off the north coast of Venezuela, on the South American mainland, while the country's nearest neighbour to the north is Grenada. The climate is tropical, with a dry season from January to May. Rainfall averages 1,561 mm (61.5 ins) per year. Annual average daytime temperatures range between 32°C (90°F) and 21°C (70°F). The official and main language is English, but French, Spanish, Hindi and Chinese are also spoken. In 1990 some 40.3% of the population were Christians, mainly Roman Catholics (29.4%) and Anglicans (10.9%), while 23.8% were Hindus and 5.8% Muslims. The national flag (proportions 3 by 5) is deep red, divided by a white-edged black diagonal stripe from upper hoist to lower fly. The capital is Port of Spain, on the island of Trinidad.

Recent History

Trinidad was first colonized by the Spanish in 1532, but was ceded to the British in 1802. Africans were transported to the island to work as slaves, but slavery was abolished in 1834. Shortage of labour led to the arrival of large numbers of Indian and Chinese immigrants, as indentured labourers, during the second half of the 19th century. In 1888 the island of Tobago, which had finally been ceded to the British in 1814, was joined with Trinidad as one political and administrative unit, and the territory remained a British colony until its independence on 31 August 1962.

Modern politics emerged in the 1930s with the formation of a trade union movement. The first political party, the People's National Movement (PNM), was founded in 1956 by Dr Eric Williams. It campaigned successfully at the elections to the Legislative Council in September 1956, and Williams became the colony's first Chief Minister in October. In 1958 the territory became a member of the newly-established Federation of the West Indies, and in the following year achieved full internal self-government, with Williams as Premier. The Federation collapsed in 1961, however, following the secession of Jamaica and, subsequently, Trinidad and Tobago. After independence, in 1962, Williams was restyled Prime Minister, and the Governor became Governor-General. In 1967 Trinidad and Tobago became the first member of the Commonwealth (see p. 164) to join the Organization of American States (OAS, see p. 288).

In April 1970 the Government declared a state of emergency, following violent demonstrations, lasting several weeks, by supporters of 'Black Power', protesting against foreign influence in the country's economy and demanding solutions to the problem of unemployment, which was particularly severe among Trinidadians of African descent. On the day that the emergency was proclaimed, part of the Trinidad and Tobago Regiment (the country's army) mutinied. The mutiny collapsed after only three days, and some officers and soldiers who participated were subsequently imprisoned. At a general election in May 1971, the PNM won all 36 seats in the House of Representatives.

A new Constitution came into effect on 1 August 1976, whereby Trinidad and Tobago became a republic, within the Commonwealth. The first parliamentary elections of the republic were held in September, when the PNM won 24 of the 36 seats in the House of Representatives. The United Labour Front (ULF), a newly-formed party led by trade unionists, won 10 seats, while the Democratic Action Congress (DAC) won the two Tobago seats. The former Governor-General, Ellis Clarke, was sworn in as the country's first President in December 1976. A parliamentary resolution in 1977 to grant Tobago self-rule resulted, after long resistance from the Government, in the formation in 1980 of a Tobago House of Assembly, giving the island limited autonomy. Tobago was granted full internal self-government in January 1987.

Williams died in March 1981, having consistently refused to nominate a successor. The President selected George Chambers, a deputy leader of the PNM and Minister of Agriculture, to assume the leadership on an interim basis. He was formally adopted as party leader in May and confirmed as Prime Minister. The PNM increased its majority in the House of Representatives by two seats in a general election in November. The ULF, the DAC and the Tapia House Movement, campaigning jointly as the Trinidad and Tobago National Alliance, succeeded in retaining only 10 seats. The newly-formed Organization for National Reconstruction (ONR), led by a former PNM minister, Karl Hudson-Phillips, secured 22.3% of the total vote but no seats.

Co-operation between the four opposition parties increased, and, at local elections in August 1983, they combined to oppose the PNM. This new coalition, called the 'Accommodation', won 66 of the 120 council seats being contested. The PNM won the remaining 54, thus suffering its first electoral defeat since its foundation in 1956. In August 1984 the National Alliance and the ONR established a common front, to be known as the National Alliance for Reconstruction (NAR). At elections to the Tobago House of Assembly in November 1984, the DAC achieved a convincing victory, reducing the PNM's representation from four seats to one. In September 1985 Arthur Napoleon Raymond (A. N. R.) Robinson, leader of the DAC and a former Deputy Prime Minister in the PNM Government, was elected leader of the NAR. In February 1986 the four parties merged to form one opposition party, still known as the NAR.

The stringent economic policies of the PNM Government undermined its public support and provoked labour unrest over wage restraint, notably in a bitter strike at Trinidad's petroleum refineries during May 1984. The next general election, held in December 1986, resulted in a decisive victory for the NAR, which won 33 of the 36 seats in the House of Representatives. Robinson was appointed Prime Minister. Chambers was among those members of the PNM who lost their seats, and in January 1987 Patrick Manning, the former Minister of Energy, was appointed leader of the parliamentary opposition. In March Noor Mohammed Hassanali, formerly a senior judge, took office as President, following the retirement of Ellis Clarke.

Although the NAR increased its majority of borough and county council seats at local elections held in Trinidad in September, the party experienced internal difficulties during 1987 and 1988. In June 1987 former members of the Tapia House Movement announced that they were to leave the NAR, and in November the Minister of Public Works and Settlements, formerly a member of the ULF, was dismissed from the Cabinet. In February 1988 more than 100 NAR members met to discuss the leadership of the alliance and the direction of its policies. Two cabinet ministers (including Basdeo Panday, the Minister of External Affairs) and one junior minister were subsequently dismissed from the Government. All three were former members of the ULF, which derived most of its support from the 'East' Indian community. Despite their accusations of racism against the NAR leadership, they were expelled from the party in October. In April 1989 Panday and the other dissidents announced the formation of a left-wing opposition party, the United National Congress (UNC). In July 1990 Panday was elected leader of the UNC at the party's first national assembly. In September President Hassanali confirmed Panday as the leader of the parliamentary opposition, replacing Manning. The UNC, with six seats in the House of Representatives, replaced the PNM, with only three seats, as the principal opposition party.

In July 1990 members of the Jamaat al Muslimeen, a small Muslim group led by Yasin Abu Bakr, attempted to seize power. The rebels destroyed the capital's police headquarters and took control of the parliament building and the state television station. Some 45 people were taken hostage, among them Robinson and several cabinet ministers. The rebels demanded Robinson's resignation, elections within 90 days and an amnesty for those taking part in the attempted coup. On 28 July a state of emergency was declared and a curfew was imposed: police preoccupation with the political crisis had resulted in widespread looting in the capital. On 31 July the Prime Minister, who had sustained gunshot wounds, was released from captivity by the rebels. On 1 August the attempted coup, in which some 30 people were killed and another 500 injured, ended after the rebels surrendered unconditionally. An amnesty pardoning them, signed by the President of the Senate, Joseph Emmanuel Carter, in his capacity as acting Head of State, was proclaimed invalid, on the grounds that it had been signed under duress. In mid-August Bakr and his followers were charged with treason, a capital offence.

In November 1991 the imprisoned Jamaat al Muslimeen rebels won an appeal to the Judicial Committee of the Privy Council in the United Kingdom (the final court of appeal for Trinidad and Tobago), which ruled that the validity of the presidential pardon issued during the attempted coup in July 1990 should be determined before the rebels were brought to trial, and that an application for their release should be heard by the High Court of Trinidad and Tobago immediately. On 30 June 1992 the High Court ruled that the pardon was valid, and ordered the immediate release of the 114 defendants. The Government announced that it would pursue all legal means of appeal against the decision, which it deemed to be of great constitutional significance. In March 1993 delays in the payment of compensation to the rebels, for what the High Court ruled was their wrongful imprisonment, led Bakr to threaten 'action' against the Government. In October the Court of Appeal ruled to uphold the decision of the High Court. In October 1994 the Privy Council ruled to overturn the decisions of the High Court and the Court of Appeal, declaring the pardon invalid. As a result, the Jamaat al Muslimeen would be unable to claim compensation for wrongful imprisonment. However, it was also ruled that to rearrest the rebels and try them for offences committed during the insurrection would constitute an abuse of the legal process. However, the Jamaat al Muslimeen was subsequently awarded some TT \$2.1m. in compensation for the destruction of its buildings following the coup attempt.

General elections, held on 16 December 1991, resulted in a decisive victory for the PNM, which secured 45.1% of the votes and won 21 seats in the House of Representatives. The implementation of unpopular austerity measures was widely acknowledged as the main cause of the defeat of the NAR, which lost all but two of its legislative seats. As a result of his party's defeat, Robinson resigned as leader. A notable feature of the elections was the re-emergence of ethnic voting, with the vast majority of the votes divided between the Afro-Trinidadian-orientated PNM and the largely Indo-Trinidadian UNC, which secured 13 seats in the House of Representatives. On 17 December Patrick Manning was sworn in as Prime Minister. A promise made by the PNM in its election manifesto to settle a public-sector claim for salaries and allowances withheld during the austerity programme of the outgoing NAR Government was honoured in the budget submitted to Parliament in January 1992. However, the Government's continued failure to effect a settlement led to escalating industrial unrest. In February 1993 several thousand public-sector employees joined protests against the delay in payments and at the Government's plans to restructure inefficient state enterprises, involving some 2,600 redundancies. In early 1994 a government offer of a settlement of the public-sector claim was rejected by the majority of employees. In mid-1995 the Government introduced a new plan to settle the claim, involving the issue of bonds with tax credits, which was accepted by the Trinidad and Tobago Unified Teachers' Association. However, industrial action resumed in September, when some 25,000 public-sector employees observed a 24-hour strike in support of demands for a more favourable settlement. In March 1996, following a further 48-hour stoppage, agreement was finally reached on a settlement involving the issue, over a period of four years, of bonds worth TT \$1,000m. Meanwhile, industrial unrest persisted in opposition to continuing government plans for the rationalization and privatization of unproductive public utilities.

At elections to the Tobago House of Assembly, held on 7 December 1992, the NAR retained control, securing 11 seats, with the remaining elective seat won by the PNM. In July 1993 the Government and the Tobago House of Assembly agreed to begin discussions concerning the upgrading of Tobago's constitutional status. Measures subsequently submitted for consideration by the legislature included the establishment of an executive council on Tobago and the appointment of an independent senator to represent the island.

Appeals for the restoration of capital punishment, prompted by growing public concern at the increasing rate of murder and violent crime in Trinidad and Tobago, gained considerable impetus in August 1993 following the murder of the country's

Prison Commissioner. Warrants issued shortly afterwards for the execution of two convicted murderers were suspended following protests by human rights organization Amnesty International. In July 1994 Trinidad and Tobago conducted its first execution since 1979. However, the convicted murderer, Glen Ashby, was hanged only minutes before a facsimile transmission from the Privy Council in the United Kingdom was sent to the Court of Appeal in Trinidad granting a stay of execution. Reportedly, an undertaking had been given by the Attorney-General, Keith Sobion, that the execution would not be conducted until all applications for a stay had been exhausted. In July 1994 the Privy Council issued a conservatory order whereby, in the case of two men due to be heard by the Trinidad Court of Appeal, should their execution be ordered, it could not be conducted until the case had been heard by the Privy Council itself. This decision provoked protest from the Chief Justice of Trinidad and Tobago, who accused the Privy Council of pre-empting the Court of Appeal's exercise of its jurisdiction. Subsequently, the Government announced its intention to introduce legislation establishing the Court of Appeal as the final appeal court for criminal cases, pending regional agreement on a Caribbean appeal court. In March 1995 an international jurists' inquiry into the Ashby case reported that the execution of Ashby was illegal and that sufficient evidence existed to cite Sobion for contempt of court. However, the report was non-binding, and no action was taken.

In July 1995 the Speaker of the House of Representatives, Occah Seapaul, was accused by the Government of bringing her office into disrepute; an unsuccessful attempt by Seapaul to sue a former business partner, Victor Jattan, had led the court to question the veracity of Seapaul's testimony. Seapaul refused to accede to demands for her resignation, and rejected as unconstitutional the proposal, by the Attorney-General, to conduct a confidence motion on the matter. Lacking the necessary two-thirds' majority in the legislature to unseat Seapaul, the Government introduced draft legislation to amend the Constitution in order to allow the removal of the Speaker by means of a simple majority. The proposal was approved by the Senate, but debate of the bill was obstructed in the House of Representatives by Seapaul, who adjourned the session and ordered the suspension of the leader of the House, Ken Valley, for six months, on a charge of contempt. (Valley subsequently secured a High Court order reinstating him.) In August acting President Joseph Emmanuel Carter declared a limited state of emergency in the capital, thus empowering the Government to place Seapaul under house arrest and facilitating the prompt approval in the House of Representatives of the constitutional amendment. In protest at the Government's action, Seapaul's brother, Ralph Maraj, resigned as the Minister of Public Utilities. Maraj subsequently relinquished his seat in the legislature and his membership of the PNM, later joining the UNC. The state of emergency was ended after four days, and Seapaul was released from detention, having agreed to vacate her position pending a High Court ruling on constitutional motions filed by her against the Government.

In October 1995, with the Government's legislative majority reduced to three, Manning called an early general election for 6 November. At the election the PNM and the UNC each secured 17 seats, while the NAR won the remaining two. Following discussions between the leader of the UNC, Basdeo Panday, and Robinson, who had resumed the leadership of the NAR in October, a coalition Government was established, with Panday as Prime Minister. The Cabinet included Robinson as Minister Extraordinaire and Adviser to the Cabinet, with special responsibility for Tobago. It was widely understood that the NAR's support for the UNC in forming the Government had been dependent on undertakings concerning the prompt upgrading of Tobago's constitutional status.

The results of local elections in June 1996 reflected a decline in support for the PNM. At elections to the Tobago House of Assembly, held on 9 December, the NAR secured 10 of the 12 elective seats; the PNM obtained one seat, and the remaining seat was won by an independent candidate.

On 14 February 1997 Robinson was elected President to replace Noor Mohammed Hassanali on his retirement from the position in March. However, the appointment (by an electoral college comprising the members of the Senate and the House of Representatives) was, for the first time, contested: traditionally, all parties support the nominee of the Government for the Presidency, which is a ceremonial position only. On this occasion the PNM, which objected to the Government's nomination of Robinson (owing to his status as an active politician with party affiliation), presented its own candidate, a High Court Judge, Anthony Lucky. Lucky received 18 votes, compared with the 46 votes obtained by Robinson, who was inaugurated on 19 March.

Following the appointment of Robinson as President, a by-election was scheduled for May 1997 to elect a replacement to occupy the seat vacated by him in the House of Representatives. A dispute within the NAR concerning the selection of a candidate to contest the seat resulted, in April, in the resignation from the party of its only remaining member of the House of Representatives and sole cabinet member, the Minister of Sport and Youth Affairs, Pamela Nicholson, who declared herself independent. The by-election was won by the candidate of the NAR, Morgan Job, who was named Minister of Tobago Affairs. In July the interim leader of the NAR, Nizam Mohammed, was formally elected party leader.

In March 1998 militia of the Jamaat al Muslimeen prevented employees of the Ministry of Works and Transport from establishing a barrier around land inhabited by the Jamaat al Muslimeen, in order to halt further expansion of settlements. Bakr denounced the Government for attempting to provoke a violent reaction from the militants. A fence was eventually constructed after Government employees resumed their task, under the protection of the police force. In December 1999 the Jamaat al Muslimeen repeated their warning that they would not permit building work to take place adjacent to their headquarters.

In early January 2000 Hanraj Sumairsingh, a member of the UNC, was found murdered. It was subsequently reported that Sumairsingh had written to the Prime Minister several times regarding threats by the Minister of Local Government, Dhanraj Singh, following Sumairsingh's revelation of alleged corruption in the unemployment relief programme administered by Singh's ministry. Although Panday denied having received any letters, a copy of one was later produced by a PNM member. In a separate incident, a petrol bomb was thrown at the house of Patricia Mehijas, a member of a regional development corporation, which had also recently reported corruption in the unemployment scheme. A full investigation was initiated and in October Singh was dismissed from his government post and replaced by the junior works minister, Carlos John. On 19 February 2001 Singh was charged with the murder of Sumairsingh and, in the following month, remanded in custody. In late June, however, he was moved to a psychiatric hospital on the orders of Panday, after it was discovered that he was suffering from depression.

In mid-January 2000 two government-appointed Tobagan senators were dismissed from their posts, following their earlier failure to support a government-sponsored bill. President Robinson refused, however, to revoke their appointments, stating that their dismissal would damage relations between the two islands. Robinson's refusal to follow the Prime Minister's advice created a constitutional *impasse*, and in late January Robinson publicly announced that Panday had ceased to attend their weekly discussions of current affairs. Robinson also sought an apology from Panday following what he termed a defamatory attack on his person, and continued to emphasize his disquiet at the state of relations between the Government and the Tobago House of Assembly. Following mediation by the Archbishop of Port of Spain, Robinson announced that, having brought the state of relations between the two islands to the public's attention, he would agree to revoke the senators' appointments.

In April 2000 Hochoy Charles, the Chief Secretary of the Tobagan House of Assembly, met Prime Minister Panday in order to discuss the deterioration in the relationship between the two islands. Charles had previously announced his intention to create a 'Tobago assembly of villages' in order to counterbalance what he termed the central Government's lack of interest in Tobago. Charles had also criticized the Government for failing to intervene in a dispute over public access to beaches on Tobago. In May a draft agreement was reached on the creation of a seven-member 'task force', which was to consider the constitutional and legal position of Tobago and to attempt to resolve the problems affecting its governance. In the same month Anthony Smart was formally elected leader of the NAR. Smith had been serving as acting leader since the NAR's dismissal of Nizam Mohammed as leader in October 1999.

In October 1997 it was announced that the Government had approved a proposal by the Attorney-General to expedite executions of persons convicted of murder, whereby the Government would allow only 18 months for completion of a hearing before the UN Human Rights Committee (UNHRC) and the Inter-American Commission on Human Rights (IACHR), in the event

of the Privy Council rejecting an appeal. The Government hoped, by imposing a time limit on the UNHRC and the IACHR, to complete the appeals process within the five years allowed by the Privy Council as the maximum length of time between sentencing and execution. In April 1998 the Government refused to grant leave for the hearing of appeals against the death penalty made by nine men convicted of murder (the so-called 'Chadee gang'). The nine subsequently appealed to the UNHRC. In late May 1998 the Government announced that it was withdrawing from the UNHRC and the IACHR, as neither body had been able to guarantee to hear appeals within the 18 months requested by the Government. Many Caribbean states expressed their support for Trinidad and Tobago, although the opposition PNM criticized the withdrawals as damaging the islands' international reputation, while the Roman Catholic Church and Amnesty International also criticized the move on humanitarian grounds. In June 1998 the IACHR ordered Trinidad and Tobago not to execute five people whose cases it had been due to review; however, the authorities announced that the IACHR no longer had any jurisdiction over the cases, and that the executions would be carried out.

In October 1998, in what was considered a landmark case, the Privy Council rejected the appeals of two convicted murderers, who had claimed that their constitutional rights had been infringed by the conditions in which they had been imprisoned. In January 1999, in a further landmark judgment, the Privy Council ruled that, even though Trinidad and Tobago had withdrawn from the IACHR, two convicted killers could not be executed while their appeals were being considered by the Commission, since the appeals had been made prior to the withdrawal. In April the Privy Council ordered the release of three prisoners who had spent almost four years awaiting execution.

In May 1999 the Privy Council rejected an appeal for clemency made by the nine members of the Chadee gang, who had claimed that they were being held in cruel and degrading conditions. The men had been granted stays of execution by the Chief Justice of Trinidad and Tobago in December 1998. Later in May 1999 the Privy Council granted a further stay of execution on the grounds that the Court of Appeal in Trinidad and Tobago had been hurried into a decision by the Government. The stay was granted in order to allow the Privy Council time to consider the legality of hanging as a means of administering the death penalty. At the end of May the Privy Council ruled that Trinidad and Tobago could legally proceed with the nine executions, which, despite international protests, were carried out in early June. A further execution was carried out in late July.

In April 2000 the Government announced that it was to withdraw from the first optional protocol to the International Covenant on Civil and Political Rights, following a judgment from the UNHRC that Trinidad and Tobago could not continue to adhere to the resolution while differing on the subject of the death sentence. The announcement attracted widespread international condemnation, and was variously described as weakening the protection of human rights on the islands and as an attempt by the Government to withdraw from international scrutiny. The Government, however, stated that the withdrawal was intended purely to prevent condemned murders from addressing lengthy appeals to the UNHRC. The Government also announced the introduction of a constitutional amendment, which would allow executions to proceed before the IACHR and the UNHRC had ruled on the cases. The amendment was reportedly intended to ensure that murderers did not escape the death sentence on the grounds that more than five years had elapsed since their sentencing. However, Amnesty International denounced these claims, noting that the Privy Council had ruled that in the event of international bodies taking an excessive time to process appeals, the delay would not count towards the five-year limit. On 14 February 2001, at a CARICOM summit in Barbados, the leaders of 11 Caribbean states signed an agreement to establish the Caribbean Court of Justice. The Court would replace the Privy Council as the final court of appeal, and was to be based in Trinidad and Tobago. The Court would be established upon ratification by three states, at the annual summit in July; the Government of Trinidad and Tobago had already stated that it would ratify the agreement. However, the Court was unlikely to be fully established before 2003.

In early June 2000, following the suspension of the Opposition Chief Whip for 'objectionable' behaviour, opposition members withdrew from the House of Representatives in protest. In August legislation was approved to give the courts jurisdiction to seize the profits from drugs-trafficking and other serious crimes. The legislation introduced regulations demanding greater legal and administrative transparency, in efforts to combat money-laundering, and imposed heavy fines on individuals and institutions in breach of the regulations.

At the general election of 11 December 2000, the UNC secured 19 of the 36 seats in the House of Representatives, while the PNM won 16 seats and the NAR secured one. On 20 December, following a delay owing to a recount of votes, Panday was inaugurated as Prime Minister for the second time. The PNM subsequently challenged the legality of the victory of two UNC candidates, Winston Peters and Bill Chaitan, claiming that they had made false declarations on their nomination forms by failing to disclose their dual nationality. The High Court rejected attempts by Peters and Chaitan to obstruct the electoral petitions brought against them in March 2001, prompting the Attorney-General, Ramesh Maharaj, to accuse the judiciary of bias. The two ministers began proceedings to appeal against the decision. In late August, after the Appeal Court had confirmed the High Court's ruling, the two ministers declared their intention to take the matter to the Privy Council. At elections to the Tobago House of Assembly, held on 29 January 2001, the PNM secured eight of the 12 elective seats, ending the traditional domination of the House by the NAR, which obtained the remaining four seats.

In January 2001 Panday announced his Cabinet and his nominations to the Senate. However, President Robinson refused to approve the senate nominations of seven UNC members, declaring them to be unconstitutional, as they had been defeated as candidates in the election. The Jamaat al Muslimeen threatened to hold widespread demonstrations should the seven nominations be approved. Nevertheless, on 14 February the President reluctantly approved all of Panday's nominations (as he was constitutionally obliged to do), though he urged the Prime Minister not to appoint any of the seven controversial senators to the Cabinet. The previous day, following rumours of a planned coup attempt by opposition members, Panday announced that he would assume the national security portfolio. (In April the acting Commissioner of Police revealed that evidence of a plot had been discovered, and further evidence of a conspiracy to overthrow the Government was discovered in June.) In March Panday announced that, owing to health problems, he was to relinquish the public administration and Tobago affairs portfolios in order to reduce his workload.

In May 2001 several PNM members withdrew from Parliament in protest at the suspension of their colleague, Keith Rowley, for alleged 'objectionable behaviour' and disrespect towards the Speaker. Rowley was reinstated after Manning agreed to withdraw a motion of censure against Panday. In early June the Jamaat al Muslimeen leader, Yasin Abu Bakr, claimed that his group had discovered a conspiracy by the state to murder him. At elections for the deputy leadership of the UNC in June, party members rejected Panday's preferred candidates, Carlos John and Kamla Persad-Bissessar, the Minister of Education, in favour of Ramesh Maharaj.

The Government was beset by allegations of corruption in mid-2001. In July a report in the *Sunday Express* newspaper claimed that government ministers, including the former Minister of Energy, Finabar Gangar, had received payments in exchange for supporting various tenders for contracts with the state-owned oil company, Petrotrin. The allegations were based on an earlier report by a British forensic firm, against which Gangar issued a writ in December. Furthermore, in mid-July a report by the Auditor-General on the North West Regional Health Authority (NWRHA) claimed to have discovered irregularities in the health authority's accounts and accused three of its executives of corruption. The Minister of Finance, Gerald Yetming, suspended the executives and authorized a police investigation. The revelations provoked intense debate in Parliament, with Panday incurring criticism both from the opposition and from within his Government. In July, during a heated debate in which the Prime Minister was accused of protecting those implicated in the scandal, Panday apparently walked out of the chamber. A government spokesman later claimed that Panday had left the debate early to keep an important appointment. On the same day, the Minister of Communications and Information Technology, Ralph Maraj, threatened to resign if Panday did not act to curb corruption. Panday responded by divesting Maraj of responsibility for the National Broadcasting Network and Freedom of Information Act. Panday's party rival, Attorney-General Ramesh Maharaj, also was relinquished of

some of his responsibilities. Relations between the Attorney-General and the Prime Minister continued to deteriorate throughout September. Maharaj, with Maraj and two other cabinet members, Minister of Food Production and Marine Resources, Trevor Sudama, and Minister of Housing and Settlements, Sadiq Baksh, formed a faction within the UNC. This faction, which was known as Team Unity, subsequently gained control of the party's national executive. Despite attempts by Team Unity to prevent UNC constituent elections from taking place on 9 September, supporters of Panday were victorious in 30 of the 34 constituencies.

On 1 October 2001 it was confirmed that Maharaj and Sudama had been dismissed from their government posts for their continued criticism of the Prime Minister. Maraj subsequently also resigned from his position. The Government's legislative majority was effectively lost when the three ministers subsequently formed a coalition with the PNM and the NAR and obstructed attempts by Panday to approve the budget. Amid increasing pressure from the opposition for his resignation and threats of a vote of 'no confidence' in his Government, on 10 October Panday asked President Robinson to dissolve Parliament. Parliament was duly suspended and on 19 October it was announced that elections were to be held on 10 December.

The opposition parties indicated in mid-October 2001 that their alliance with the three dissident UNC ministers would not extend to the election, however. Maharaj and his allies subsequently challenged Panday for control of the UNC and petitioned the Elections and Boundaries Commission (EBC) for an injunction to prevent Panday from issuing the party's list of electoral candidates under the UNC name. The action was rejected by the EBC in early November, and a further appeal by Team Unity was similarly unsuccessful. In addition, at a special assembly of the UNC, members loyal to Panday voted to ban Maharaj, Maraj and Sudama from party activities. The dissidents claimed the vote was not sanctioned by the party constitution and registered their own list of Team Unity candidates for the elections. If re-elected, Panday pledged to establish a commission to investigate corruption in the public and private sectors, while Manning's electoral campaign included promises to reduce taxes, create jobs and instigate housing programmes.

Meanwhile, in September 2001 a report published by the independent Personnel Management Services into the allegations of corruption at the NWRHA recommended the dismissal of four senior executives. In mid-November, Dr Tim Gopiesingh, the former Chairman of the NWRHA, admitted to charges of fraud and was taken into police custody. Several days earlier, two senior managers of the health authority appeared in court charged with embezzling TT $1.6m. In late November the Director of Public Prosecutions (DPP) announced that police were investigating the case of a cheque for US $50,000 issued to Panday by Gopiesingh in his capacity as leader of UNC's North-west Liaison Office, at the time of the 2000 elections. Panday maintained that the cheque was paid into a constituency bank account, but this was disputed by a UNC treasurer. Also in November, the DPP authorized police to investigate allegations that the Minister of Energy and Energy Industries, Lindsay Gillette, had exploited his position to gain a valuable mobile cellular phone contract for his family's company in 2000. In December Panday and other government ministers were implicated in alleged instances of misconduct relating to contracts given to the US-owned power company Inncogen Ltd, to supply electricity to four new factories in Trinidad, which had failed to be built.

Preliminary results of the elections of 10 December 2001 indicated that the UNC and the PNM had secured an equal number (18) of seats in the House of Representatives and that no other parties had gained legislative representation (Team Unity secured only 2.5% of the valid votes cast). Following a recount of votes in two marginal constituencies, in mid-December the EBC announced that the UNC had secured 49.7% of votes cast, while the PNM had won 46.3%. Team Unity attracted only 2.5% of the ballot. On 15 December the two party leaders announced they had reached an agreement on political collaboration in government, though not a coalition arrangement, that would allow the President to appoint the Prime Minister and Speaker in the House of Representatives and to reform the electoral process. It was reported that while the UNC had favoured the formation of a Government of National Unity, the PNM remained committed to the appointment of their leader as Prime Minister. The PNM had also demanded a complete revision of the electoral register. However, following the appointment of Manning as Prime Minister on 24 December and PNM nominee Max Richards as Speaker of the House of Representatives, the UNC withdrew from the post-election agreement. The following day, Manning announced the provisional composition of his Cabinet. The appointment of his wife, Hazel Manning, as Minister of Education provoked accusations of nepotism and there was further controversy over the inclusion of Knowlson Gift as Minister of Foreign Affairs, since he had been forced to resign from this position in a former administration following allegations of misconduct.

Panday's refusal to be sworn in as leader of the opposition and to agree to elect a Speaker in the House of Representatives (Richards had withdrawn from the position after his impartiality was questioned) prevented the convening of the new Parliament in early January 2002. Panday announced the UNC's intention to prevent Parliament from sitting for the next six months, thereby forcing Manning to call new elections, according to the provisions of the Constitution. Following concern expressed by the business community at the effect of the political impasse on the country's economy, at the end of January Manning and Panday met for discussions. However, neither these meetings, nor negotiations mediated by leaders of the Caribbean Community and Common Market (CARICOM, see p. 155) in February, provided a solution to the dispute. Later in February Manning agreed to put the UNC's proposals for an executive comprising equal numbers of PNM and UNC representatives to the PNM party council. The UNC accused the Prime Minister of deliberately delaying the process and warned of civil unrest if a date for fresh elections was not set. The following month controversy also arose over Robinson's continued occupation of the position of President. His tenure expired on 18 March, but as the legislature had not been convened, Robinson obtained Manning's permission to remain in office.

The first session of the new House of Representatives was reconvened on 5 April 2002; however, owing to the failure of the two parties to elect a Speaker, Manning was forced to adjourn proceedings. He promised to call a further session before the end of 2002. While Panday repeated his demands that elections be held within the next few months, there was increasing speculation that the PNM would seek to persuade members of the UNC to defect in order to gain a legislative majority and thus end the political impasse.

Meanwhile, in mid-March 2002, Panday's former finance minister, Brian Kuei Tung, and several senior government officials and prominent businessmen were arrested on charges of fraud and misbehaviour in public office with regard to the recent construction of a new terminal at Piarco Airport. Manning ordered a Commission of Inquiry into the project. Panday himself was also questioned by the authorities regarding his failure to declare a large deposit made to his wife's bank account in the United Kingdom. In late March doctors in public hospitals went on strike for three days in protest at the delay of several months in the payment of their salaries. Doctors staged a further strike in late April, to demand better pay and working conditions. In May Ralph Maraj was appointed to a position in the Ministry of Public Administration and Information, a move which Panday took to be further evidence that Maraj had conspired with other dissidents to remove the party from power.

The conflict between the UNC and PNM continued throughout mid-2002. In June the opposition demanded the resignation of the Minister of Labour and Small and Micro-Enterprise Development, Lawrence Achong, and a ministerial colleague, following their mistaken announcement that the troubled Hindu Credit Union was the subject of an investigation. In July two more UNC members of parliament were accused of criminal activity by the Commission of Inquiry into the airport project. The former works minister Carlos John was accused of ignoring tender procedures during his time in office and in the same month US $246,000-worth of cocaine and two missiles were apparently found at the home of the former housing minister Sadiq Baksh. President Robinson, meanwhile, declared his intention to sue Panday for slander following the latter's assertion that the President's choice of Manning as Prime Minister was racially motivated.

A report by the Commission of Inquiry into the Electoral and Boundaries Commission (ECB) in early June documented countless flaws in its practices and recommended that all its members should resign. However, its members failed to relinquish their posts, despite Manning's pledge to implement the reforms recommended by the report. Mounting concern, especially among

business leaders and the regional community, at the lack of progress in resolving the political impasse forced Manning in late July to announce that if Parliament failed to elect a Speaker by 31 October, further elections would be held.

Manning made a final attempt to convene Parliament on 28 August 2002; however, the members again failed to elect a Speaker, some UNC representatives resorting deliberately to voting against their own candidate. The following day Manning dissolved Parliament and announced that elections would take place on 7 October. The decision was welcomed by trade-union and business leaders, who attributed the fall in foreign investment in the first half of 2002 to the uncertain political situation. On 20 September Panday was officially charged with fraud in connection with the bank account held by his wife in London. The PNM sought to make political gain from this and from the allegations made by the Commissions of Inquiry against the various UNC members by focusing on corruption in its electoral campaign. The opposition responded by criticizing the Government for its failure to combat a recent rise in crime, in particular an increase in the abduction (and, in some cases, murder) of members of the business community; Manning claimed that the violence was gang-related. Earlier in the month, a new political party, the Citizens' Alliance, was formed. It was led by a former PNM finance minister, Wendell Mottley, and aimed to prevent another tied election.

In elections held on 7 October 2002 the PNM won 50.7% of votes cast and 20 seats in the House of Representatives, while the UNC secured 46.6% of votes and 16 seats. Voter turn-out was estimated at 69.6%. Manning again acceded to the office of Prime Minister, stating his intention to seek solutions to issues which divided the nation's political and racial communities. He appointed a new Cabinet, which included most of the members of the previous administration in their former positions. One of the new Government's first acts was the proposal of legislation aimed at preventing abduction and acts of terrorism, as well as a planned increase in penalties for acts of corruption committed by holders of public office. Manning, in his capacity as Minister of Finance, also presented a generous budget that included a 12% increase in expenditure on education and health, as well as a rise in public-sector salaries.

Following the party's electoral defeat, Panday resigned as leader of the UNC in October 2002. Party members failed to agree on a new leader and attempts to persuade Panday's rival and leader of Team Unity, Ralph Maharaj, to return to the party caused a bitter dispute. Panday subsequently agreed to remain in office until a new leader could be elected.

Despite the new administration's attempts to restore order, the crime rate continued to concern community and business groups in late 2002 and early 2003. Following a warning to travellers issued by the British Office of Foreign and Commonwealth Affairs, in January 2003 it was announced that a delegation of ministers would travel to the United Kingdom and the USA to reassure the Governments there that the country was safe. In the same month Panday caused controversy by accusing Manning of associating with the Jamaat al-Muslimeen group, which, he claimed, had links with the al-Qa'ida (Base) organization, a network of fundamentalist Islamist militants, thought to be responsible for terrorist attacks. Later in January two newspaper reporters claimed that they had been taken to a chemical weapons laboratory owned by an radical Islamist group which had threatened to attack US and British visitors to the country. The claims prompted further warnings from the US and British Governments and led to the cancellation of trips to the islands by some cruise-ship operators.

The Government's preferred candidate, Maxwell Richards, was elected President on 14 February 2003. In early April the UNC proposed a motion of 'no confidence' in the President of the Senate, Linda Baboolal, whom the party accused of exploiting her office to restrict criticism of government policies.

In July 1991 Trinidad and Tobago ratified with Venezuela a joint declaration on maritime boundaries, under which Trinidad and Tobago's maritime boundary was to be extended from 200 nautical miles (370 km) to 350 nautical miles (648 km). Relations with Venezuela deteriorated in late 1996 and early 1997 owing to a series of incidents involving Trinidadian fishing vessels. In May 1997 a two-year fishing agreement was completed for approval by both Governments. However, tensions were revived later in the month after 15 Trinidadian fishermen were arrested by Venezuelan coast-guards. In June Trinidad and Tobago's Minister of Foreign Affairs accused Venezuela of violating his country's sovereignty, and the Trinidadian Government referred the issue to the OAS. In response, Venezuela briefly withdrew its ambassador from the country. A revised two-year treaty was endorsed in December, permitting an unlimited number of vessels from each country into a shared fishing area. A joint fisheries commission was also re-established. In October 1998 it was agreed that the two countries would negotiate treaties on free trade and on co-operation against drugs-trafficking. Treaties on extradition, mutual legal assistance and prisoner exchange were also planned. In July 2000 talks were held to find a solution to the maritime border dispute between Trinidad and Barbados. Despite further talks being held over the next two years, little progress was made. In December 2001 the Minister of Foreign Affairs and Enterprise Development, Mervyn Assam, asserted that the Barbadian Government had been in possession of a draft fisheries agreement since June of that year. However, Barbados maintained that no such document had been received. In June 2001, following a visit to Trinidad by the Prime Minister of Grenada a joint commission was established by the two Governments to promote bilateral co-operation and begin the process of boundary delimitation.

Government

Legislative power is vested in the bicameral Parliament, consisting of the Senate, with 31 members, and the House of Representatives, with 36 members. Representatives are elected for a five-year term by universal adult suffrage. The President is a constitutional Head of State, chosen by an electoral college of members of both the Senate and the House of Representatives. Members of the Senate are nominated by the President in consultation with, and on the advice of, the Prime Minister and the Leader of the Opposition. The Cabinet has effective control of the Government and is responsible to Parliament. Tobago Island was granted its own House of Assembly in 1980 and given full internal self-government in January 1987. The Tobago House of Assembly has 15 members, of whom 12 are elected. The remaining three are selected by the majority party.

Defence

In August 2002 the defence forces consisted of an army estimated at 2,000 men, and a coastguard of 700, with 12 patrol craft. Included in the coastguard is an air force of 50. The defence budget for 2002 was an estimated TT $420m.

Economic Affairs

In 2001, according to estimates by the World Bank, Trinidad and Tobago's gross national income (GNI), measured at average 1999–2001 prices, was US $7,249m., equivalent to US $5,540 per head (or US $9,080 on an international purchasing-power parity basis). During 1990–2001, it was estimated, the population increased at an average annual rate of 0.7%, while gross domestic product (GDP) per head increased, in real terms, by an average of 2.8% per year. Overall GDP increased, in real terms, at an average annual rate of 3.5% in 1990–2001; growth in 2001 was 5.0%.

Agriculture (including forestry, hunting and fishing) contributed an estimated 1.6% of GDP in 2000 and employed an estimated 7.8% of the working population in 2001. The principal cash crops are sugar cane, coffee, cocoa and citrus fruits. The fishing sector is small-scale, but is an important local source of food. In 2001 the Government allocated TT $5m. to create an Agriculture Disaster Relief Fund, designed to alleviate the effects of natural disasters upon the agricultural sector. During 1990–2000, according to the World Bank, agricultural GDP increased by an average of 1.2% per year. Agricultural GDP expanded by 4.8% in 1999 and by 0.8% in 2000.

Industry (including mining and quarrying, manufacturing, construction and power) provided an estimated 43.2% of GDP in 2000 and employed an estimated 28.9% of the working population in 2001. In 1999 there were eight ammonia plants, one urea plant, and four methanol plants in Trinidad. During 1990–2000, according to the World Bank, industrial GDP increased at an average annual rate of 3.3%. Industrial GDP increased by 8.7% in 1999 and by 5.3% in 2000.

The mining and refining industry provided an estimated 25.7% of GDP in 2000. Some 3.2% of the working population were employed in the mining sector in 2001. The petroleum industry is the principal sector of Trinidad and Tobago's economy. In 1990 it accounted for 47% of government revenue, although by 1997 the proportion had been reduced to an estimated 22.8%, owing to declines in production and international prices. According to the IMF, the GDP of the petroleum sector increased at an annual average rate of 3.7% between 1996–2000; the

sector grew by 8.1% in 1999 and by 3.3% in 2000. Trinidad has the world's largest deposits of natural asphalt, and substantial reserves of natural gas. Cement, limestone and sulphur are also mined.

Manufacturing contributed an estimated 7.7% of GDP in 2000, and employed 10.3% of the working population in 2001. In 1998 the principal branches (measured by value of output) were petroleum-refining, fertilizers, iron and steel, food products, paper and paperboard, and cement, lime and plaster. During 1990–2000, according to the World Bank, manufacturing GDP increased at an average annual rate of 6.2%. Manufacturing GDP increased by 12.4% in 1999 and by 8.0% in 2000.

Energy is derived principally from natural gas and petroleum. Locally-extracted natural gas generates most of Trinidad and Tobago's electricity supply, and is also used as fuel for the country's two petroleum refineries and several manufacturing plants. In 1999 18 international companies were involved in petroleum and gas exploration in Trinidad and Tobago's offshore areas. In 2001 it was predicted that natural gas would soon overtake oil as the country's principal foreign-exchange earner. Imports of fuel products comprised only 0.4% of the value of merchandise imports in 1995, but the proportion increased to an estimated 32.3% in 2001.

The services sector contributed an estimated 55.2% of GDP in 2000 and employed some 63.3% of the working population in 2001. Tourism is a major source of foreign exchange, and in 2000 398,559 foreign tourists visited the islands. However, the majority of visitors are private or business visitors, and only a minority stay in hotels. In October 2000 Air Caribbean, the smaller of Trinidad and Tobago's national airlines, was put into receivership. The Government subsequently initiated an investigation into its failure. According to the World Bank, the GDP of the services sector increased at an average annual rate of 2.8% in 1990–2000. Sectoral GDP increased by 2.2% in 1999 and by 4.6% in 2000. Earnings from the tourist sector grew by an estimated 22.4% in 1997 and by an estimated 42.1% in 1998.

In 2001, according to Central Bank figures, Trinidad and Tobago recorded an estimated visible trade surplus of US $7,84m., and there was a surplus of US $666m. on the current account of the balance of payments. In 1999 the principal source of imports was the USA (39.8%); other major suppliers were Latin America and Canada. The USA was also the principal market for exports (38.9%) in that year; other important purchasers were Jamaica, Barbados and Latin America. The principal exports in 2000 were mineral fuels and lubricants (64.8%); chemicals and basic manufactures were also significant exports. The principal imports were fuels, foodstuffs and construction materials. In 2000 Trinidad and Tobago retained its position as the leading exporter to the Caribbean region, providing petroleum products and manufactured goods.

In 2001/02 there was a projected budgetary deficit of TT $83.3m. At the end of 2000 Trinidad and Tobago's total external debt was US $2,467m., of which US $1,606m. was long-term public debt. In that year the cost of debt-servicing was equivalent to 10.3% of the value of exports of goods and services. The annual rate of inflation averaged 5.5% in 1990–2001. Consumer prices increased by an estimated average of 3.5% in 2000 and by 5.6% in 2001. Some 10.9% of the labour force were unemployed in 2001.

Trinidad and Tobago is a member of CARICOM (see p. 155), the Inter-American Development Bank (IDB, see p. 239), the Latin American Economic System (SELA, see p. 340), and the Association of Caribbean States (ACS, see p. 338).

By 1995 the policy of offering incentives for foreign investment in petroleum exploration had succeeded in reversing the decline in production, and in early 1996 the first significant discovery of petroleum deposits for many years lent further impetus to explorative activity, while the discovery in the late 1990s of several significant deposits of natural gas led to the development of a major liquefied natural gas (LNG) plant at Point Fortin. In 1999 Atlantic LNG, a consortium of Spanish- and British-owned energy companies, announced that operations at the plant were to be expanded, and that production was to triple by 2003, although by 2003 construction had not begun, owing to legal problems. In 2001, however, further expansion proposals were announced, which, when complete, would make Trinidad and Tobago one of the world's leading suppliers of LNG. In June 2000 construction began on the world's first gas-to-liquid fuel conversion plant, at the Point Lisas industrial estate. The US $300m. plant was to be completed by 2003. In September BP Energy Company of Trinidad and Tobago (formerly BP Amoco) announced the discovery of the country's largest ever natural gas deposit. Substantial foreign investment in the country has allowed increased industrialization, and many new factories have opened or are planned; the majority to process hydrocarbons and ammonia. Despite the growth of the industrial and tourist sectors in recent years, the economy remains greatly dependent on the export of hydrocarbons, and the Government was obliged to revise its budgetary estimates for 1998/99 when the international price for petroleum declined dramatically in early 1998. Increased production and a recovery in the price of petroleum in 1999 contributed to GDP growth of 6.0% in that year. Although moves had been made to liberalize the telecommunications sector, in 2003 it was still a monopoly, controlled by Telecommunication Services of Trinidad and Tobago (TSTT) Ltd, 51% of which was owned by the Government and 49% by a British company, Cable & Wireless. In June 2000 the Government was accused of lacking transparency in the liberalization process of the telecommunications sector. There was controversy in the bidding process for cellular licences, following the removal of the Caribbean Communications Network from the bidding shortlist, and the successful bid of Open Telecom Ltd, owned by the family of government minister Lindsay Gillette. The Director of Public Prosecutions ordered an investigation into allegations of misconduct by Gillette in November 2001 (see Recent History, above). It was also believed that the licences should not be awarded until appropriate legislation for the telecommunications sector was in place. Following the elections of December 2001, the Government's failure to convene Parliament and pass a budget caused problems for both public and private sectors in 2002. In January the state sugar company, Caroni, warned that it would be forced to close in March unless legislation was passed allocating the company more funds. Following the elections of October 2002, the new Government announced that some 10,000 of Caroni's employees would be made redundant and that private-sector investment would be sought for the non-sugar-producing part of its operations. In April 2003 the Government approved the release US $80.1m. of funds to help restore the company's finances. Business leaders blamed the political situation for low levels of foreign investment in 2002. Furthermore, concerns about rising crime rates threatened the tourist industry; in August 2002 the country's airline, BWIA International Airways, announced that the company would be reorganized owing to falling profits, and in 2003 the British cruise-ship operator P&O cancelled services to Trinidad and Tobago following fears over the safety of British visitors. The 2003 budget included the highest ever public expenditure, which the Government envisaged would be funded by rapid expansion in the energy sector. In August 2002 it was announced that a new oil refinery would be constructed which, when it began production in 2005, would more than double the country's current output. In the same month, the second train at the Point Fortin LNG plant began production and a third train was scheduled to begin operation in mid-2003. At consultations regarding plans for a fourth train in October, however, Prime Minister Manning warned that any future expansion would be conditional on the Government receiving favourable returns. In March 2003 construction began on an oil extraction plant in the Greater Angostura field; output was expected by begin in 2004. The Central Bank estimated that the economy grew by 2.7% in 2002.

Education

Primary and secondary education is provided free of charge. Attendance at school is officially compulsory for children between five and 12 years of age. Primary education begins at the age of five and lasts for seven years. Secondary education, beginning at 12 years of age, lasts for up to five years, comprising a first cycle of three years and a second of two years. Entrance to secondary schools is determined by the Common Entrance Examination. Many schools are administered jointly by the State and religious bodies. In 1997 enrolment at primary schools included 99.9% of children in the relevant age-group (males 99.9%; females 99.9%), while enrolment at secondary schools was equivalent to 71.5% of children in the relevant age-group (males 70.8%; females 72.2%). In 2000 the Government announced an education reform programme to improve access to, and levels of, education. A school-to-work apprenticeship programme was also to be established.

The Trinidad campus of the University of the West Indies (UWI), at St Augustine, offers undergraduate and postgraduate programmes. The UWI Institute of Business offers postgraduate courses, and develops programmes for local companies. Other institutions of higher education are the Eric Williams Medical Sciences complex, the Polytechnic Institute and the East Caribbean Farm Institute. The country has one teacher training college and three government-controlled technical institutes and vocational centres, including the Trinidad and Tobago Hotel School. In the late 1990s the Government established the Trinidad and Tobago Institute of Technology, and the College of Science, Technology and Applied Arts of Trinidad and Tobago. Distance learning was also being expanded. Expenditure on education by the central Government in 2000 was TT $2,111.0m.

Public Holidays

2003: 1 January (New Year's Day), 3–4 March (Carnival), 30 March (Spiritual Baptist Shouters' Liberation Day), 18–21 April (Easter), 30 May (Indian Arrival Day), 19 June (Corpus Christi), 1 August (Emancipation Day), 1 September (for Independence Day), 25 October† (Divali), 26 November* (Id al-Fitr, end of Ramadan), 25–26 December (Christmas).

2004: 1 January (New Year's Day), 23–24 February (Carnival), 9–12 April (Easter), 30 March (Spiritual Baptist Shouters' Liberation Day), 30 May (Indian Arrival Day), 10 June (Corpus Christi), 21 June (Labour Day), 2 August (Emancipation Day), 31 August (Independence Day), 4 November† (Divali), 12 November* (Id al-Fitr, end of Ramadan), 25–26 December (Christmas).

*These holidays are dependent on the Islamic lunar calendar and may vary by one or two days from the dates given.

†Dependent on lunar sightings.

Weights and Measures

The metric system is replacing the imperial system of weights and measures.

Statistical Survey

Source (unless otherwise stated): Central Statistical Office, 35-41 Queen St, POB 98, Port of Spain; tel. 623-7069.

Area and Population

AREA, POPULATION AND DENSITY

Area (sq km)	5,128*
Population (census results)	
12 May 1980	1,079,791
2 May 1990	
Males	606,388
Females	607,345
Total	1,213,733
Population (official estimates at September)	
2000	1,294,000
2001	1,296,000
Density (per sq km) at September 2001	252.7

* 1,980 sq miles. Of the total area, Trinidad is 4,828 sq km (1,864 sq miles) and Tobago 300 sq km (116 sq miles).

POPULATION BY ETHNIC GROUP
(1990 census*)

	Males	Females	Total	%
African	223,561	221,883	445,444	39.59
Chinese	2,317	1,997	4,314	0.38
'East' Indian . . .	226,967	226,102	453,069	40.27
Lebanese	493	441	934	0.08
Mixed	100,842	106,716	207,558	18.45
White	3,483	3,771	7,254	0.64
Other	886	838	1,724	0.15
Unknown	2,385	2,446	4,831	0.43
Total	560,934	564,194	1,125,128	100.00

* Excludes some institutional population and members of unenumerated households, totalling 44,444.

PRINCIPAL TOWNS
(population at mid-1991)

Port of Spain (capital). . .	54,000		Arima (borough) . .	29,483
San Fernando . .	30,115			

2001 (UN estimate, incl. suburbs): Port of Spain 54,000 (Source: UN, *World Urbanization Prospects: The 2001 Revision*).

BIRTHS AND DEATHS
(official estimates, annual averages)

	1996	1997	1998
Birth rate (per 1,000)	14.2	14.3	13.9
Death rate (per 1,000)	7.4	7.1	7.2

Expectation of life (WHO estimates, years at birth): 69.9 (males 67.3; females 72.6) in 2001 (Source: WHO, *World Health Report*).

EMPLOYMENT
('000 persons aged 15 years and over)

	1999	2000	2001
Agriculture, forestry, hunting and fishing	39.7	36.3	40.3
Mining and quarrying	15.6	16.5	16.6
Manufacturing	53.0	54.9	52.7
Electricity, gas and water . . .	6.2	6.9	7.5
Construction	60.8	62.8	71.2
Wholesale and retail trade, restaurants and hotels . . .	88.8	95.2	89.9
Transport, storage and communication.	35.7	39.2	38.9
Finance, insurance, real estate and business services . . .	37.6	39.2	41.0
Community, social and personal services	151.5	151.4	154.6
Activities not adequately defined	0.4	0.5	1.5
Total employed	489.4	502.9	514.2
Males	310.1	316.7	326.2
Females.	179.3	186.2	188.0
Unemployed	74.0	69.3	62.7
Total labour force	563.4	572.2	576.9

Source: ILO.

Health and Welfare

KEY INDICATORS

Total fertility rate (children per woman, 2001)	1.4
Under-5 mortality rate (per 1,000 live births, 2001) . . .	20
HIV/AIDS (% of persons, aged 15–49, 2001)	2.5
Physicians (per 1,000 head, 1994)	0.79
Hospital beds (per 1,000 head, 1996)	5.11
Health expenditure (2000): US $ per head (PPP) . . .	468
Health expenditure (2000): % of GDP	5.2
Health expenditure (2000): public (% of total)	50.7
Access to water (% of persons, 2000).	86
Access to sanitation (% of persons, 2000)	88
Human Development Index (2000): ranking	50
Human Development Index (2000): value	0.805

For sources and definitions, see explanatory note on p. vi.

Agriculture

PRINCIPAL CROPS
('000 metric tons)

	1999	2000*	2001
Rice (paddy)*	10.0	13.0	16.0
Maize*	5.0	5.3	5.4
Taro (Coco yam)*	3.5	3.6	3.7
Sugar cane	1,255.9	1,373.0	1,500.0*
Pigeon peas	2.6	2.8*	2.8*
Coconuts*	23.0	23.0	23.5
Cabbages	1.5	1.7*	1.7*
Tomatoes	2.7	2.8	2.9
Pumpkins, squash and gourds . .	2.1*	6.5*	7.6
Cucumbers and gherkins . . .	2.5	2.5	2.8
Aubergines	1.3	1.8*	2.0*
Other fresh vegetables*	4.7	5.0	5.2
Bananas*	6.0	6.1	6.2
Plantains*	3.9	4.0	4.2
Oranges*	20.5	12.0	15.0
Grapefruit and pomelo* . . .	7.9	8.1	8.2
Watermelons*	2.8	2.8	2.9
Pineapples*	3.4	3.5	3.5
Other fruit*	34.7	40.4	47.2
Coffee (green)	0.3	0.6	0.8†
Cocoa beans	1.2	1.5	1.6

* FAO estimate(s).
† Unofficial estimate.

Source: FAO.

LIVESTOCK
(FAO estimates, '000 head, year ending September)

	1999	2000	2001
Horses	1.0	1.0	1.0
Mules	1.7	1.7	1.7
Asses	2.0	2.0	2.0
Cattle	35.0	35.5	36.0
Buffaloes	5.4	5.5	5.5
Pigs	41.0	41.0	42.0
Sheep	12.0	12.0	12.5
Goats	59.0	59.0	60.0

Poultry (million): 15.3 in 1999; 15.5 in 2000; 16.0 in 2001.

Source: FAO.

LIVESTOCK PRODUCTS
('000 metric tons)

	1999	2000	2001
Beef and veal	1.0	1.0*	1.0*
Pig meat	1.9	2.0*	2.0*
Poultry meat*	26.5	26.5	26.5
Cows' milk	10.2	10.4*	10.5*
Hen eggs	3.2*	3.4†	3.4†

* FAO estimate(s).
† Unofficial estimate.

Source: FAO.

Forestry

ROUNDWOOD REMOVALS
('000 cubic metres, excl. bark)

	1999	2000	2001
Sawlogs, veneer logs and logs for sleepers	34.0	72.0	56.0
Fuel wood*	36.8	36.5	36.1
Total	70.8	108.5	92.1

* FAO estimates.

Source: FAO.

SAWNWOOD PRODUCTION
('000 cubic metres, incl. railway sleepers)

	1999	2000	2001
Coniferous (softwood)	8	5	—
Broadleaved (hardwood) . . .	10	27	41
Total	18	32	41

Source: FAO.

Fishing

('000 metric tons, live weight)

	1998	1999	2000
Capture	9.0	8.7	9.7
Demersal percomorphs . . .	2.0	1.9	1.8
Clupeoids	0.6	0.9	—
King mackerel	0.7	0.4	0.4
Serra Spanish mackerel . .	2.1	1.3	1.7
Tuna-like fishes	3.0	3.0	3.0
Sharks, rays, skates, etc. . .	0.6	0.7	0.8
Other marine fishes . . .	1.4	1.9	2.0
Penaeus shrimps	0.6	0.7	0.6
Aquaculture*	0.0	0.0	0.0
Total catch	9.0	8.7	9.7

* FAO estimates.

Source: FAO, *Yearbook of Fishery Statistics*.

Mining

('000 barrels, unless otherwise indicated)

	1998	1999	2000
Crude petroleum	44,759	45,662	43,593
Natural gas liquids	5,254	5,753	6,932
Natural gas (million cu m) . .	10,294	13,240	15,483

Source: US Geological Survey.

Industry

SELECTED PRODUCTS
('000 metric tons, unless otherwise indicated)

	1998	1999	2000
Raw sugar†	65	69	120*
Rum ('000 proof gallons) . . .	5,425*	n.a.	n.a.
Beer and stout ('000 hectolitres) .	391*	n.a.	n.a.
Cigarettes (metric tons) . . .	1,282*	n.a.	n.a.
Nitrogenous fertilizers . . .	3,247	n.a.	n.a.
Jet fuels and kerosene ('000 barrels)‡	5,501	5,480	5,927
Motor spirit—petrol ('000 barrels)‡	10,672	8,889	11,652
Gas-diesel (distillate fuel) oil ('000 barrels)‡	11,103	13,048	12,659
Residual fuel oils ('000 barrels)‡	20,088	20,689	21,807
Lubricating oils ('000 barrels)‡	379	192	−51
Cement‡	690	688	743
Wire rods	650*	n.a.	n.a.
Electric energy (million kWh) . .	5,194*	n.a.	n.a.

2001: Raw sugar 180*†.
* Provisional figure.
† Source: FAO.
‡ Source: IMF, *Trinidad and Tobago: Statistical Appendix* (July 2001).

Finance

CURRENCY AND EXCHANGE RATES

Monetary Units
100 cents = 1 Trinidad and Tobago dollar (TT $)

Sterling, US Dollar and Euro Equivalents (31 December 2002)
£1 sterling = TT $10.130
US $1 = TT $6.285
€1 = TT $6.591
TT $1,000 = £98.714= US $159.106 = €151.718

Average Exchange Rate (TT $ per US $)
2000   6.2998
2001   6.2332
2002   6.2342

BUDGET
(TT $ million)*

Revenue	1998	1998/99	1999/2000
Oil sector	661	1,092	3,206
Corporation tax	173	480	2,441
Withholding tax	450	520	575
Other	38	93	191
Non-oil sector	9,012	8,907	8,926
Taxes on income	3,389	3,442	3,610
Taxes on property	60	62	64
Taxes on goods and services . .	3,426	3,207	3,128
Taxes on international trade.	781	776	782
Other taxes	98	93	93
Non-tax revenue	1,259	1,327	1,221
Capital revenue and grants. . .	29	265	11
Total	9,702	10,264	12,144

Expenditure	1998	1998/99	1999/2000
Current expenditure.	9,540	10,008	10,860
Wages and salaries†	3,522	3,665	3,141
Other goods and services . .	960	1,095	1,236
Interest payments	1,916	1,986	2,520
Domestic	1,207	1,272	1,681
External	710	714	839
Transfers and subsidies . . .	3,143	3,262	3,962
Households	1,122	1,193	1,344
Public sector bodies. . . .	1,151	1,129	1,334
Local governments . .	707	724	724
Statutory authorities. . .	80	71	71
State enterprises . . .	222	186	186
Public utilities . . .	143	148	148
Non-profit organizations . .	434	471	471
Abroad	67	69	69
Other	368	368	368
Capital expenditure and net lending	860	518	1,208
Capital formation	1,078	742	1,448
Net lending.	−219	−224	−241
Total	10,400	10,526	12,068

* The central Government switched to a 1 October–30 September fiscal
  year in 1998.
† Includes contributions to the National Insurance Board.

Source: IMF, *Trinidad and Tobago: Statistical Appendix* (July 2001).

INTERNATIONAL RESERVES
(US $ million at 31 December)

	1999	2000	2001
Gold*	17.4	16.4	16.8
IMF special drawing rights . .	—	0.1	0.2
Foreign exchange	945.4	1,386.2	1,876.0
Total	962.9	1,402.7	1,893.0

* National valuation of gold reserves.

Source: IMF, *International Financial Statistics*.

MONEY SUPPLY
(TT $ million at 31 December)

	1999	2000	2001
Currency outside banks . . .	1,292.4	1,271.0	1,373.5
Demand deposits at commercial banks	3,182.0	3,722.4	4,829.4
Total money (incl. others) . .	5,306.8	5,658.0	6,766.6

Source: IMF, *International Financial Statistics*.

COST OF LIVING
(Consumer Price Index; base: 1990 = 100)

	1999	2000	2001
Food (incl. beverages and tobacco)	285.2	308.8	351.9
Rent	111.7	115.0	116.2
Clothing (incl. footwear) . . .	92.2	90.6	89.5
Electricity and gas	—	114.8	115.1
All items (incl. others)	164.1	169.9	179.4

Source: ILO.

NATIONAL ACCOUNTS
(TT $ million at current prices)

Expenditure on the Gross Domestic Product

	1997	1998	1999
Government final consumption expenditure	5,578.8	6,280.9	6,637.4
Private final consumption expenditure	18,853.4	23,027.4	25,480.3
Gross fixed capital formation* . .	13,215.0	10,745.6	9,030.5
Total domestic expenditure. . .	37,647.2	40,053.9	41,148.2
Exports of goods and services . .	19,305.6	18,452.5	19,017.5
Less Imports of goods and services	20,440.6	20,469.7	19,131.7
GDP in purchasers' values . .	36,512.2	38,036.7	41,034.0
GDP at constant 1985 prices .	18,507.0	19,326.7	20,659.3

* Including increase in stocks.

Source: UN, Economic Commission for Latin America and the Caribbean,
Statistical Yearbook.

Gross Domestic Product by Economic Activity

	1997	1998	1999
Agriculture, hunting, forestry and fishing	618.8	567.5	629.8
Mining and quarrying	4,811.1	3,769.8	4,367.7
Manufacturing	5,699.1	5,584.7	6,320.1
Electricity, gas and water . . .	587.0	820.1	848.7
Construction	3,674.3	4,156.6	4,701.9
Wholesale and retail trade, restaurants and hotels . . .	7,192.8	8,026.0	8,764.3
Transport, storage and communications	3,294.0	3,391.3	3,758.6
Finance, insurance, real estate and business services	5,193.9	5,622.2	5,706.1
Community, social and personal services	5,190.9	5,583.6	6,032.2
Sub-total	36,261.9	37,521.8	41,129.4
Less Imputed bank service charges	1,373.7	1,645.5	1,844.4
Value-added tax	1,624.0	2,160.4	1,749.0
GDP in purchaser's values . .	36,512.2	38,036.7	41,034.0

Source: UN Economic Commission for Latin America and the Caribbean,
Statistical Yearbook.

GDP in purchasers' values (TT $ million at current prices): 50,871.5 in
2000; 55,815.1 in 2001 (Source: Central Bank of Trinidad and Tobago).

BALANCE OF PAYMENTS
(US $ million)

	1996	1997	1998
Exports of goods f.o.b.	2,354.1	2,448.0	2,258.0
Imports of goods f.o.b.	−1,971.6	−2,976.6	−2,998.9
Trade balance	382.4	−528.6	−740.8
Exports of services	461.2	546.5	671.7
Imports of services	−217.5	−254.1	−255.4
Balance on goods and services	626.2	−236.2	−324.5
Other income received	39.1	63.8	64.0
Other income paid	−553.1	−445.0	−405.3
Balance on goods, services and income	112.2	−617.4	−665.8
Current transfers received	34.2	37.0	58.4
Current transfers paid	−41.3	−33.2	−36.2
Current balance	105.1	−613.6	−643.5
Direct investment from abroad	355.4	999.3	729.8
Portfolio investment assets	—	—	−0.4
Other investment assets	3.0	32.6	1.0
Other investment liabilities	−315.4	−334.7	−258.8
Net errors and omissions	90.0	110.0	252.2
Overall balance	238.1	193.6	80.2

Source: IMF, *International Financial Statistics*.

External Trade

PRINCIPAL COMMODITIES
(US $ million)

Imports c.i.f.	1998	1999	2000*
Consumer goods	460	502	548
Foodstuffs	189	192	212
Raw materials and intermediate goods	1,198	1,332	1,982
Fuels	300	554	935
Construction materials	123	123	205
Capital goods	1,246	885	986
Transport equipment	191	154	191
Oil-refining and mining machinery	88	43	51
Total †	3,008	2,752	3,557

Exports f.o.b.	1998	1999	2000*
Fuels	1,008	1,524	2,736
Crude petroleum	253	367	557
National gas liquids	63	237	517
Refined petroleum products	692	920	1,661
Chemicals	496	529	735
Anhydrous ammonia	248	293	360
Urea	50	48	60
Methanol	148	144	267
Manufactures	352	328	360
Steel products	206	164	169
Food and live animals	145	144	149
Sugar	32	34	37
Beverages and tobacco	89	78	78
Total (incl. others)‡	2,264	2,816	4,220

* Estimates.
† Including imports for processing: 104 in 1998; 33 in 1999; 40 in 2000.
‡ Including re-exports: 89 in 1998; 123 in 1999; 75 in 2000.

Source: IMF, *Trinidad and Tobago: Statistical Appendix* (July 2001).

PRINCIPAL TRADING PARTNERS
(US $ million)

Imports c.i.f.	1997	1998	1999
Barbados	16	24	38
Canada	80	105	134
France	18	56	47
Germany	136	89	68
Guyana	13	11	12
Jamaica	17	18	18
Japan	107	145	140
Latin America	497	572	605
United Kingdom	148	148	128
USA	1,564	1,340	1,095
Total (incl. others)	3,036	3,008	2,752

Exports f.o.b.	1997	1998	1999
Barbados	94	127	151
Canada	23	26	42
Guyana	109	84	76
Jamaica	210	237	246
Latin America	261	251	131
USA	999	825	1,096
Total (incl. others)	2,544	2,264	2,816

Source: IMF, *Trinidad and Tobago: Statistical Appendix* (July 2001).

Transport

ROAD TRAFFIC
(motor vehicles in use)

	1994	1995	1996
Passenger cars	122,000	122,000	122,000
Lorries and vans	24,000	24,000	24,000

Source: IRF, *World Road Statistics*.

Total number of registered vehicles: 215,895 in 1995; 226,380 in 1996; 237,299 in 1997.

SHIPPING

Merchant Fleet
(registered at 31 December)

	1999	2000	2001
Number of vessels	59	61	67
Total displacement ('000 grt)	30.7	21.6	26.6

Source: Lloyd's Register-Fairplay, *World Fleet Statistics*.

International Sea-borne Freight Traffic
(estimates, '000 metric tons)

	1988	1989	1990
Goods loaded	7,736	7,992	9,622
Goods unloaded	4,076	4,091	10,961

Source: UN, *Monthly Bulletin of Statistics*.

1998: Port of Spain handled 3.3m. metric tons of cargo.

CIVIL AVIATION
(traffic on scheduled services)

	1997	1998	1999
Kilometres flown (million)	18	21	24
Passengers carried ('000)	807	880	1,046
Passenger-km (million)	2,392	2,567	2,715
Total ton-km (million)	239	315	309

Source: UN, *Statistical Yearbook*.

Tourism

FOREIGN TOURIST ARRIVALS

Country of origin	1998	1999	2000
Barbados	22,706	28,694	31,126
Canada	39,827	43,459	47,382
Germany	10,736	10,306	11,266
Grenada	12,216	14,050	15,492
Guyana	17,583	21,607	23,686
Jamaica	4,954	4,828	6,255
Saint Lucia	5,986	6,740	7,374
Saint Vincent and Grenadines	8,220	8,000	8,265
United Kingdom	46,324	49,480	55,048
USA	114,416	118,390	132,578
Venezuela	10,022	10,182	11,450
Total (incl. others)	334,037	358,220	398,559

Receipts from tourism (US $ million): 73 in 1997; 201 in 1998; 210 in 1999.

Source: World Tourism Organization, *Yearbook of Tourism Statistics*.

Communications Media

	1999	2000	2001
Television receivers ('000 in use) .	435	440	n.a.
Telephones ('000 main lines in use)	278.9	299.1	311.8
Mobile cellular telephones ('000 subscribers).	38.7	133.2	225.4
Personal computers ('000 in use) .	70	80	90
Internet users ('000)	75	100	120

Radio receivers (1997, '000 in use): 680*.

Facsimile machines (1998, number in use): 5,024*.

Daily newspapers: 4 in 1997 (estimated average circulation 156,000 in 1996)†.

Non-daily newspapers: 5 in 1997 (estimated average circulation 150,000 in 1996)†.

* Source: UN, *Statistical Yearbook*.
† Source: UNESCO, *Statistical Yearbook*.

Source (unless otherwise stated): International Telecommunication Union.

Education

(1996/97, unless otherwise indicated)

	Institu-tions	Tea-chers	Students		
			Males	Females	Total
Pre-primary* † . .	50	126	727	691	1,418
Primary*	476	7,311	92,015	89,015	181,030
Secondary: general .	} 101 {		5,070	51,096	53,253	104,349
Secondary: vocational† . . .			n.a.	575	113	688
University and equivalent . . .	3§	421§	2,727	3,280	6,007

* Government-maintained and government-aided schools only.
† 1992/93.
‡ 1993/94.
§ 1995/96.

Source: mainly UNESCO, *Statistical Yearbook*.

Adult literacy rate (UNESCO estimates): 93.8% (males 95.5%; females 92.1%) in 2000 (Source: UN Development Programme, *Human Development Report*).

Directory

The Constitution

Trinidad and Tobago became a republic, within the Commonwealth, under a new Constitution on 1 August 1976. The Constitution provides for a President and a bicameral Parliament comprising a Senate and a House of Representatives. The President is elected by an Electoral College of members of both the Senate and the House of Representatives. The Senate consists of 31 members appointed by the President: 16 on the advice of the Prime Minister, six on the advice of the Leader of the Opposition and nine at the President's own discretion from among outstanding persons from economic, social or community organizations. The House of Representatives consists of 36 members who are elected by universal adult suffrage. The duration of a Parliament is five years. The Cabinet, presided over by the Prime Minister, is responsible for the general direction and control of the Government. It is collectively responsible to Parliament.

The Government

HEAD OF STATE

President: Prof. GEORGE MAXWELL RICHARDS (took office 17 March 2003).

THE CABINET
(April 2003)

Prime Minister, Minister of Finance and Minister of Tobago Affairs: PATRICK MANNING.

Attorney-General: GLENDA MOREAN PHILLIP.

Minister of Legal Affairs: CAMILLE ROBINSON-REGIS.

Minister of Science, Technology and Tertiary Education: DANNY MONTANO.

Minister of Community Development and Gender Affairs: JOAN YUILLE-WILLIAMS.

Minister of Education: HAZEL ANNE MARIE MANNING.

Minister of Energy and Energy Industries: ERIC WILLIAMS.

Minister of Public Utilties and the Environment: RENNIE DUMAS.

Minister of Agriculture, Land and Marine Resources: JOHN RAHAEL.

Minister of Foreign Affairs: KNOWLSON GIFT.

Minister of Health: COLM IMBERT.

Minister of Housing: MARTIN JOSEPH.

Minister of Culture and Tourism: PENELOPE BECKLES.

Minister of Local Government: JARRETTE NARINE.

Minister of Planning and Development: KEITH ROWLEY.

Minister of Labour and Small and Micro Enterprise Development: LAWRENCE ACHONG.

Minister of Works and Transport: FRANKLYN KHAN.

Minister of Public Administration and Information: LENNY SAITH.

Minister of Social Development: MUSTAPHA ABDUL-HAMID.

Minister of Sports and Youth Affairs: ROGER BOYNES.

Minister of Trade, Industry and Consumer Affairs: KENNETH VALLEY.

Minister of National Security: HOWARD CHIN LEE.

MINISTRIES

Office of the President: President's House, Circular Rd, St Ann's, Port of Spain; tel. 624-1261; fax 625-7950; e-mail presoftt@carib-link.net.

Office of the Prime Minister: Whitehall, Maraval Rd, Port of Spain; tel. 622-1625; fax 622-0055; e-mail opm@trinidad.net; internet www.opm.gov.tt.

Office of the Attorney-General: Cabildo Chambers, 23–27 St Vincent St, Port of Spain; tel. 623-7010; fax 625-0470; e-mail attorneygeneral@tstt.net.tt.

Ministry of Agriculture, Land and Marine Resources: St Clair Circle, St Clair, Port of Spain; tel. 622-1221; fax 622-8202; e-mail apdmalmr@trinidad.net.

Ministry of Community Development and Gender Affairs: Algico Bldg, Jerningham Ave, Belmont; tel. 625-3012; fax 625-3278; e-mail minscdps@tstt.net.tt.

Ministry of Education: 18 Alexandra St, St Clair, Port of Spain; tel. 622-2181; fax 622-7818.

Ministry of Energy and Energy Industries: Level 9, Riverside Plaza, cnr Besson and Piccadilly Sts, Port of Spain; tel. 623-6708; fax 623-2726; e-mail admin@energy.gov.tt; internet www.meei.gov.tt.

Ministry of Finance: Eric Williams Finance Bldg, Independence Sq., Port of Spain; tel. 627-9700; fax 627-6108.

Ministry of Foreign Affairs: Knowsley Bldg, 1 Queen's Park West, Port of Spain; tel. 623-4116; fax 624-4220; e-mail permanentsecretary@foreign.gov.tt; internet www.tradeind.gov.tt.

Ministry of Health: IDC Bldg, 10–12 Independence Sq., Port of Spain; tel. 627-0012; fax 623-9528; e-mail scdda@carib-link.net.

Ministry of Housing: 44–46 South Quay, Port of Spain; tel. 624-5058; fax 625-2793; e-mail mohas@tstt.tt.

Ministry of Culture and Tourism: ANSA Finance Bldg, Independence Sq., Port of Spain; tel. 624-1403; fax 625-0437.

Ministry of Planning and Development: Level 14, Eric Williams Finance Bldg, Eric Williams Plaza, Independence Sq., Port of Spain; tel. 627-9700; fax 623-8123.

Ministry of Labour and Small and Micro Enterprise: Level 11, Riverside Plaza, Cnr Besson and Piccadilly Sts, Port of Spain; tel. 623-4451; fax 624-4091; e-mail minlab@trinidad.net.

Ministry of Legal Affairs: Registration House, Huggins Bldg, South Quay, Port of Spain; tel. 623-7163; fax 625-9805.

Ministry of Local Government: Kent House, Long Circular Rd, Maraval; tel. 622-1667; fax 622-4783; e-mail molg1@carib-link.net; internet www.molg.bizland.com.

Ministry of National Security: Temple Court, 31–33 Abercromby St, Port of Spain; tel. 623-2441; fax 627-8044; e-mail mns@tstt.net.tt.

Ministry of Public Administration and Information: 45A-C St Vincent St, Port of Spain; tel. 623-8578; fax 623-6027.

Ministry of Public Utilities and the Environment: Sacred Heart Bldg, 16 18 Sackville St, Port of Spain; tel. 625-6083; fax 625-7003; e-mail environment@tstt.net.tt.

Ministry of Science, Technology and Tertiary Education: Cnr Agra and Patna Sts, St James; tel. 628-9925.

Ministry of Social Development: Autorama Bldg, El Socorro Rd, San Juan; tel. 675-6728; fax 638-1364.

Ministry of Tobago Affairs: 10 St Vincent St, Port of Spain; tel. 624-1403; fax 625-0437.

Ministry of Trade, Industry and Consumer Affairs: Level 15, Riverside Plaza, Cnr Besson and Picadilly St, Port of Spain; tel. 623-2931; fax 627-8488.

Ministry of Works and Transport: Cnr Richmond and London Sts, Port of Spain; tel. 625-1225; fax 627-9886.

Legislature

PARLIAMENT

Senate

President: Dr LINDA BABOOLAL.

House of Representatives

Speaker: BARENDRA SINANAN.

Election, 7 October 2002

Party	% of votes	Seats
People's National Movement	50.7	20
United National Congress	46.6	16
National Alliance for Reconstruction	1.1	—
Citizens' Alliance	1.0	—
Total (incl. others)	100.0	36

TOBAGO HOUSE OF ASSEMBLY

The House is elected for a four-year term of office and consists of 12 elected members and three members selected by the majority party.

Chief Secretary: ORVILLE LONDON.

Election, 29 January 2001

Party	Seats
People's National Movement	8
National Alliance for Reconstruction	4
Total	12

Political Organizations

Citizens' Alliance: Port of Spain; formed to contest the October 2002 elections; Leader WENDELL MOTTLEY.

Lavantille Out-Reach for Vertical Enrichment: L. P. 50, Juman Dr., Morvant; tel. 625-7840; f. 2000; Leader LENNOX SMITH; Gen. Sec. VAUGHN CATON.

The Mercy Society: L. P. 216, Mount Zion, Luango Village, Maracas; tel. 628-1753.

National Alliance for Reconstruction (NAR): 37 Victoria Sq., Port of Spain; tel. 627-6163; f. 1983 as a coalition of moderate opposition parties; reorganized as a single party in 1986; Leader (vacant); Chair. ABDOOL WAHAB.

National Democratic Organization (NDO): L. P. 2, Freedom St, Enterprise, Chaguanas; tel. 750 9063; e-mail ndotrini@yahoo.dom; f. 2000; Leader ENOCH JOHN; Sec. RICHARD JOODEEN.

People's Empowerment Party (PEP): Miggins Chamber, Young St, Scarborough; tel. 639-3175; by independent mems of the Tobago House of Assembly; Leader DEBORAH MOORE-MIGGINS; Gen. Sec. RICHARD ALFRED.

People's National Movement (PNM): 1 Tranquillity St, Port of Spain; tel. 625-1533; e-mail pnm@carib-link.net; internet www.pnm.org.tt; f. 1956; moderate nationalist party; Leader PATRICK MANNING; Chair. Dr LINDA BABOOLAL; Gen. Sec. MARTIN JOSEPH.

United National Congress (UNC): Rienzi Complex, 78–81 Southern Main Rd, Couva; tel. 636-8145; e-mail unc@tstt.net.tt; internet www.unc.org.tt; f. 1989; social-democratic; Leader BASDEO PANDAY; Deputy Leader RAMESH LAWRENCE MAHARAJ; Chair. WADE MARK; Gen. Sec. FAZAL KARIM.

Diplomatic Representation

EMBASSIES AND HIGH COMMISSIONS IN TRINIDAD AND TOBAGO

Argentina: TATIL Bldg, 4th Floor, 11 Maraval Rd, POB 162; Port of Spain; tel. 628-7557; fax 628-7544; e-mail embargen-pos@carib-link.net; Ambassador JULIO ALBERTO MILLER.

Brazil: 18 Sweet Briar Rd, St Clair, POB 382, Port of Spain; tel. 622-5779; fax 622-4323; e-mail brastt@wow.net; Ambassador JOSÉ MARCUS VINÍCIUS DE SOUSA.

Canada: Maple House, 3-3A Sweet Briar Rd, St Clair, POB 1246, Port of Spain; tel. 622-6232; fax 628-1830; e-mail chcpspan@opus.co.tt; High Commissioner SIMON WADE.

China, People's Republic: 39 Alexandra St, St Clair, Port of Spain; tel. 622-6976; fax 622-7613; e-mail tian@wow.net; Ambassador XU YA'NAN.

Cuba: Furness Bldg, 2nd Floor, 90 Independence Sq., Port of Spain; tel. 627-1306; fax 627-3515; e-mail cuba_tt@cablenet.tt; Ambassador FÉLIX RAÚL ROJAS CRUZ.

Dominican Republic: Suite 8, 1 Dere St, Queen's Park West, Port of Spain; tel. 624-7930; fax 623-7779; Ambassador JORGE LUIS PÉREZ ALVARADO.

France: TATIL Bldg, 6th Floor, 11 Maraval Rd, Port of Spain; tel. 622-7447; fax 628-2632; e-mail francett@wow.net; internet www.ambafrance-tt.org; Ambassador ALAIN GIRMA.

Germany: 7–9 Marli St, Newtown, POB 828, Port of Spain; tel. 628-1630; fax 628-5278; e-mail germanemb@carib-link.net; internet www.germanemb-portofspain.de; Ambassador ULRICH NITZSCHKE.

Holy See: 11 Mary St, St Clair, POB 854, Port of Spain; tel. 622-5009; fax 628-5457; e-mail apnun@trinidad.net; Apostolic Pro-Nuncio Most Rev. EMIL PAUL TSCHERRIG (Titular Archbishop of Tiddi).

India: 6 Victoria Ave, POB 530, Port of Spain; tel. 627-7480; fax 627-6985; High Commissioner SHRI VIRENDRA GUPTA.

Jamaica: 2 Newbold St, St Clair, Port of Spain; tel. 622-4995; fax 628-9043; e-mail jhctnt@tstt.net.tt; High Commissioner LORNE McDONNOUGH.

Japan: 5 Hayes St, St Clair, Port of Spain; tel. 628-5991; fax 622-0858; e-mail jpemb@wow.net; Ambassador YOSHIO YAMAGISHI.

Mexico: 4th Floor, Algico Bldg, 91–93 St Vincent St, Port of Spain; tel. 627-7047; fax 627-1028; e-mail embamex@carib-link.net; Ambassador ROSALBA OJEDA.

Netherlands: Life of Barbados Bldg, 3rd Floor, 69–71 Edward St, POB 870, Port of Spain; tel. 625-1210; fax 625-1704; e-mail info@holland.tt; internet www.holland.tt; Ambassador MAARTEN M. VAN DER GAAG.

Nigeria: 3 Maxwell-Phillip St, St Clair, Port of Spain; tel. 622-4002; fax 622-7162; High Commissioner NNE FURO KURUBO.

Panama: Suite 6, 1A Dere St, Port of Spain; tel. 623-3435; fax 623-3440; e-mail embapatt@wow.net; Ambassador VASCO DEL MAR HUERTA.

Suriname: TATIL Bldg, 5th Floor, Maraval Rd, Port of Spain; tel. 628-0704; fax 628-0086; e-mail ambsurpde@opus.co.tt; Chargé d'affaires a.i. EDWARD R. HALFHUID.

United Kingdom: 19 St Clair Circle, St Clair, POB 778, Port of Spain; tel. 622-2748; fax 622-4555; e-mail ppabhc@opus.co.tt; High Commissioner PETER HARBORNE.

USA: 15 Queen's Park West, POB 752, Port of Spain; tel. 622-6371; fax 625-5462; e-mail usispos@trinidad.net; internet usembassy.state.gov/trinidad; Ambassador Dr ROY AUSTIN.

Venezuela: 16 Victoria Ave, POB 1300, Port of Spain; tel. 627-9821; fax 624-2508; e-mail embaveneztt@carib-link.net; Ambassador HECTOR AZOCAR.

Judicial System

The Chief Justice, who has overall responsibility for the administration of justice in Trinidad and Tobago, is appointed by the President after consultation with the Prime Minister and the Leader of the Opposition. The President appoints and promotes judges on the advice of the Judicial and Legal Service Commission. The Judicial and Legal Service Commission, which comprises the Chief Justice as chairman, the chairman of the Public Service Commission, two former judges and a senior member of the bar, appoints all judicial and legal officers. The Judiciary comprises the higher judiciary (the Supreme Court) and the lower judiciary (the Magistracy).

Chief Justice: MICHAEL DE LA BASTIDE.

Supreme Court of Judicature: Knox St, Port of Spain; tel. 623-2417; fax 627-5477; e-mail ttlaw@wow.net; internet www.ttlawcourts.org; the Supreme Court consists of the High Court of Justice and the Court of Appeal. The Supreme Court is housed in four locations: Port of Spain, San Fernando, Chaguaramas and Tobago. There are 20 Supreme Court Puisne Judges who sit in criminal, civil, and matrimonial divisions; Registrar EVELYN PETERSEN.

Court of Appeal: The Court of Appeal hears appeals against decisions of the Magistracy and the High Court. Further appeals are directed to the Judicial Committee of the Privy Council of the United Kingdom, sometimes as of right and sometimes with leave of the Court. The Court of Appeal consists of the Chief Justice, who is President, and six other Justices of Appeal.

The Magistracy and High Court of Justice

The Magistracy and the High Court exercise original jurisdiction in civil and criminal matters. The High Court hears indictable criminal matters, family matters where the parties are married, and civil matters involving sums over the petty civil court limit. High Court judges are referred to as either Judges of the High Court or Puisne Judges. The Masters of the High Court, of which there are three, have the jurisdiction of judges in civil chamber courts. The Magistracy (in its petty civil division) deals with civil matters involving sums of less than TT $15,000. It exercises summary jurisdiction in criminal matters and hears preliminary inquiries in indictable matters. The Magistracy, which is divided into 13 districts, consists of a Chief Magistrate, a Deputy Chief Magistrate, 13 Senior Magistrates and 29 Magistrates.

Chief Magistrate: SHERMAN MCNICHOLLS, Magistrate's Court, St Vincent St, Port of Spain; tel. 625-2781.

Director of Public Prosecutions: MARK MOHAMMED.

Attorney-General: GLENDA MOREAN PHILLIP.

Religion

In 1990 it was estimated that 29.4% of the population were members of the Roman Catholic Church, 23.8% Hindus, 10.9% Anglicans, 5.8% Muslims and 3.4% Presbyterians.

CHRISTIANITY

Caribbean Conference of Churches: POB 876, Port of Spain; tel. 628-2028; fax 628-2031; e-mail caconftt@Trinidad.net.

Christian Council of Trinidad and Tobago: Hayes Court, 21 Maraval Rd, Port of Spain; tel. 637-9329; f. 1967; church unity organization formed by the Roman Catholic, Anglican, Presbyterian, Methodist, African Methodist, Spiritual Baptist and Moravian Churches, the Church of Scotland and the Salvation Army, with the Ethiopian Orthodox Church and the Baptist Union as observers; Pres. The Rt Rev. CALVIN BESS (Anglican Archbishop of Trinidad and Tobago); Sec. GRACE STEELE.

The Anglican Communion

Anglicans are adherents of the Church in the Province of the West Indies, comprising eight dioceses. The Archbishop of the West Indies is the Bishop of Nassau and the Bahamas.

Bishop of Trinidad and Tobago: The Rt Rev. RAWLE E. DOUGLIN, Hayes Court, 21 Maraval Rd, Port of Spain; tel. 622-7387; fax 628-1319; e-mail red@trinidad.net.

Protestant Churches

Presbyterian Church in Trinidad and Tobago: POB 92, Paradise Hill, San Fernando; tel. and fax 652-4829; e-mail pctt@tstt.net.tt; f. 1868; Moderator Rt Rev. ALLISON KEN NOBBEE; 45,000 mems.

Baptist Union of Trinidad and Tobago: 104 High St, Princes Town; tel. 655-2291; f. 1816; Pres. Rev. ALBERT EARL-ELLIS; Gen. Sec. Rev. ANSLEM WARRICK.

The Roman Catholic Church

For ecclesiastical purposes, Trinidad and Tobago comprises the single archdiocese of Port of Spain. At 31 December 2000 there were some 383,302 adherents in the country, representing about 29.6% of the total population.

Antilles Episcopal Conference: 9A Gray St, Port of Spain; tel. 622-2932; fax 622-8255; e-mail aec@carib-link.net; internet www.catholiccaribbean.org; f. 1975; 21 mems from the Caribbean and Central American regions; Pres. Most Rev. EDGERTON ROLAND CLARKE (Archbishop of Kingston (Jamaica)); Gen. Sec. Rev. GERARD E. FARFAN.

Archbishop of Port of Spain: 27 Maraval Rd, Port of Spain; tel. 622-1103; fax 622-1165; e-mail abishop@carib-link.net; EDWARD J. GILBERT.

HINDUISM

Hindu immigrants from India first arrived in Trinidad and Tobago in 1845. The vast majority of migrants, who were generally from Uttar Pradesh, were Vishnavite Hindus, who belonged to sects such as the Ramanandi, the Kabir and the Sieunaraini. The majority of Hindus, estimated in 1990 at 23.8% of the total population, currently subscribe to the doctrine of Sanathan Dharma, which evolved from Ramanandi teaching.

Arya Pratinidhi Sabha of Trinidad Inc (Arya Samaj): Seereeram Memorial Vedic School, Old Southern Main Rd, Montrose Village, Chaguanas; tel. 663-1721; e-mail sadananramnarine@hotmail.com; Pres. SADANAN RAMNARINE.

Pandits' Parishad (Council of Pandits): Maha Sabha Headquarters, Eastern Main Rd, St Augustine; tel. 645-3240; works towards the co-ordination of temple activities and the standardization of ritual procedure; affiliated to the Maha Sabha; 200 mems.

Sanathan Dharma Maha Sabha of Trinidad and Tobago Inc: Maha Sabha Headquarters, Eastern Main Rd, St Augustine; tel. 645-3240; e-mail mahasabha@ttemail.com; internet www.websitetech.com/mahasabha; f. 1952; Hindu pressure group and public organization; organizes the provision of Hindu education; Pres. Dr D. OMAH MAHARAJH; Sec. Gen. SATNARAYAN MAHARAJ.

The Press

DAILIES

Newsday: 19–21 Chacon St, Port of Spain; tel. 623-4949; fax 625-8362; f. 1993; CEO and Editor-in-Chief THERESE MILLS; circ. 2,200,000.

Trinidad Guardian: 22 St Vincent St, POB 122, Port of Spain; tel. 623-8870; e-mail letters@ttol.co.tt; internet www.guardian.co.tt; f. 1917; morning; independent; Editor-in-Chief LENNOX GRANT; circ. 52,617.

Trinidad and Tobago Express: 35 Independence Sq., Port of Spain; tel. 623-1711; fax 627-1451; e-mail express@trinidadexpress.com; internet www.trinidadexpress.com; f. 1967; morning; CEO KEN GORDON; Editor KEITH SMITH; circ. 55,000.

PERIODICALS

Blast: 5–6 Hingoo Lane, El Socorro, San Juan; tel. 674-4414; weekly; Editor ZAID MOHAMMED; circ. 22,000.

The Boca: Crews Inn Marina and Boatyard, Village Sq., Chaguaramas; tel. 634-2055; fax 634-2056; e-mail boaters@trinidad.net; internet www.boatersenterprise.com/boca; monthly; magazine of the sailing and boating community.

The Bomb: Southern Main Rd, Curepe; tel. 645-2744; weekly.

Caribbean Beat: 6 Prospect Ave, Maraval, Port of Spain; tel. 622-3821; fax 628-0639; e-mail mep@wow.net; internet www.caribbeanbeat.com; 6 a year; distributed by BWIA International Airways Ltd; Editor JEREMY TAYLOR.

Catholic News: 31 Independence Sq., Port of Spain; tel. 623-6093; fax 623-9468; e-mail cathnews@trinidad.net; internet www.trinidad.net/catholicnews; f. 1892; weekly; Editor Fr MICHEL DE VERTEUIL; circ. 15,600.

Naturalist: Port of Spain; tel. 622-3428; f. 1975; 9 a year; natural heritage and conservation in the Caribbean; Publr/Editor-in-Chief STEPHEN MOHAMMED; circ. 25,000.

Quarterly Economic Bulletin: 35–41 Queen St, POB 98, Port of Spain; tel. 623-7069; fax 625-3802; f. 1950; issued by the Central Statistical Office.

Showtime: Cnr 9th St and 9th Ave, Barataria; tel. 674-1692; fax 674-3228; circ. 30,000.

Sunday Express: 35 Independence Sq., Port of Spain; tel. 623-1711; fax 627-1451; e-mail express@trinidadexpress.com; internet www.trinidadexpress.com; f. 1967; Editor EARL BEST; circ. 51,405.

Sunday Guardian: 22 St Vincent St, POB 122, Port of Spain; tel. 623-8870; fax 625-7211; e-mail esunday@ttol.co.tt; internet www .guardian.co.tt; f. 1917; independent; morning; Editor-in-Chief LENNOX GRANT; circ. 48,324.

Sunday Punch: Cnr 9th St and 9th Ave, Barataria; tel. 674-1692; fax 674-3228; weekly; Editor ANTHONY ALEXIS; circ. 40,000.

Tobago News: Milford Rd, Scarborough; tel. 639-5565; f. 1985; weekly; Editor COMPTON DELPH.

Trinidad and Tobago Exporter: 6 Prospect Ave, Maraval, Port of Spain; tel. 622-3821; fax 628-0639; e-mail mep@wow.net; internet www.readcaribbean.com; f. 1996; quarterly; promotes exports from Trinidad and Tobago and the Caribbean; Man. Dir JEREMY TAYLOR.

Trinidad and Tobago Gazette: 2–4 Victoria Ave, Port of Spain; tel. 625-4139; weekly; official government paper; circ. 3,300.

Trinidad and Tobago Mirror: Cnr 9th St and 9th Ave, Barataria; tel. 674-1692; fax 674-3228; 2 a week; Editors KEN ALI, KEITH SHEPHERD; circ. 35,000.

Tropical Agriculture: Faculty of Agriculture and Natural Sciences, University of the West Indies, St Augustine; tel. and fax 645-3640; e-mail tropicalagri@fans.uwi.tt; f. 1924; journal of the School of Agriculture (fmrly Imperial College of Tropical Agriculture); quarterly; Editor-in-Chief Prof. FRANK A. GUMBS.

Weekend Heat: Southern Main Rd, Curepe; tel. 645-2744; weekly; Editor STAN MORA.

NEWS AGENCY

Caribbean Media Corporation (CMC) (Barbados): 92 Queen St, Port of Spain; tel. 627-2262; f. by merger of Caribbean News Agency and Caribbean Broadcasting Union.

Publishers

Caribbean Book Distributors (1996) Ltd: 10 Boundary Rd, San Juan, POB 462, Port of Spain; tel. 674-4720; fax 674-0497; publish and distribute school textbooks and general books; Man. GERRY BABOOLAL.

Caribbean Children's Press: 1A Lazare St, St James; tel. 628-4248; fax 628-4248; e-mail caripres@tstt.net.tt; internet www .trinidadinternet.com/ccp; f. 1987; educational publishers for primary schools.

Caribbean Educational Publishers: 49 High St, San Fernando; tel. 657-1012; fax 657-5620.

Charran Educational Publishers: 53 Eastern Main Rd, Port of Spain; tel. 663-1884.

Lexicon Trinidad Ltd: 53 Boundary Rd, San Juan; tel. 675-3395.

Media and Editorial Projects Ltd: 6 Prospect Ave, Maraval, Port of Spain; tel. 622-3821; fax 628-0639; e-mail mep@wow.net; internet www.readcaribbean.com; f. 1991; magazine and book publishing; Man. Dir JEREMY TAYLOR.

Trinidad Publishing Co Ltd: 22–24 St Vincent St, Port of Spain; tel. 623-8870; fax 625-7211; e-mail guardian@ttol.co.tt; internet www.guardian.co.tt; f. 1917; Gen. Man. and CEO GRENFELL KISSOON.

University of the West Indies: St Augustine; tel. 662-2002; fax 663-9684; e-mail campreg@centre.uwi.tt; f. 1960; academic books and periodicals; Principal Pro-Vice Chancellor BHOENDRADATT TEWARIE.

Broadcasting and Communications

TELECOMMUNICATIONS

Telecommunication Services of Trinidad and Tobago (TSTT) Ltd: 1 Edward St, POB 3, Port of Spain; tel. 625-4431; fax 627-0856; e-mail tsttceo@tstt.net.tt; internet www.tstt.co.tt; 51% state-owned, 49% by Cable & Wireless (United Kingdom); 51% privatization pending; CEO SAMUEL A. MARTIN.

TSTT Cellnet: 114 Frederick St, Port of Spain; fax 625-5807; internet www.tstt.co.tt/cellservices.html; f. 1991; mobile cellular telephone operator.

Caribbean Communications Network (CCN): 10 Nook Ave, Port of Spain; tel. 624-5735; Chair. KEN GORDON.

Open Telecom Ltd: 88 Edward St, Port of Spain; tel. 627-6559.

BROADCASTING

Radio

Central Radio 90.5: 1 Morequito Ave, Port of Spain; tel. 662-4309.

Hott 93 FM: Cumulus Broadcasting Inc, 3A Queens Park West, Port of Spain; tel. 623-4688; fax 624-3234; e-mail studio@gemradio.com.

Love 94 88–90 and Power 102 FM: 88–90 Abercromby St, Port of Spain; tel. 627-6937.

MW & C Radio 97: Long Circular Rd, St James; tel. 622-9797.

National Broadcasting Network Ltd (FM 100, Yes 98.9 FM, Swar Milan 91.1, Radio 610): 11A Maraval Rd, Port of Spain; tel. 662-4141; fax 622-0344; e-mail bdesilva@nbn.co.tt; f. 1957; AM and FM transmitters at Chaguanas, Cumberland Hill, Hospedales and French Fort, Tobago; govt-owned; CEO INGRID ISAAC; Programme Man. BRENDA DE SILVA; est. regular audience 105,000.

Trinidad Broadcasting Co Ltd (Radio Trinidad, Radio Nine Five): Broadcasting House, 11B Maraval Rd, POB 716, Port of Spain; tel. 622 1151; fax 622 2380; commercial.

Trinidad Broadcasting Radio Network (Rhythm Radio, Caribbean Tempo and Sangeet 106.1 FM): 22 St Vincent St, Port of Spain; tel. 623-9202; fax 622-2380; internet www.ttol.co.tt/caribbeantempo; f. 1947; commercial; three programmes; Man. Dir GRENFELL KISSOON.

Trinidad and Tobago Radio Network: 35 Independence Sq., Port of Spain; tel. 624-7078.

Television

CCN TV6: 35 Express House, Independence Sq., Port of Spain; tel. 627-8806; fax 627-2721; e-mail jlumyoung@trinidadexpress.com; f. 1991; owned by Caribbean Communications Network (CCN); CEO CRAIG REYNALD; Gen. Man. RASHIDAN BOLAI.

National Broadcasting Network Ltd: 11A Maraval Rd, POB 665, Port of Spain; tel. 622-4141; fax 622-0344; f. 1962; state-owned commercial station; CEO JOHN BARSOTTI.

Finance

(cap. = capital; dep. = deposits; res = reserves; m. = million; brs = branches; amounts in TT $ unless otherwise stated)

BANKING

Central Bank

Central Bank of Trinidad and Tobago: Eric Williams Plaza, Independence Sq., POB 1250, Port of Spain; tel. 625-4835; fax 627-4696; e-mail info@central-bank.org.tt; internet www.central-bank .org.tt; f. 1964; cap. 100.0m., res 93.8m., dep. 8,603m. (Sept. 2002); Gov. EWART S. WILLIAMS.

Commercial Banks

Citibank (Trinidad and Tobago) Ltd: 12 Queen's Park East, POB 1249, Port of Spain; tel. 625-1046; fax 624-8131; internet www .citicorp.com; f. 1983; fmrly The United Bank of Trinidad and Tobago Ltd; name changed as above 1989; owned by Citicorp Merchant Bank Ltd; cap. 30.0m., res 14.7m., dep. 455.5m. (Dec. 1996); Chair. IAN E. DASENT; Man. Dir STEVE BIDESHI; 2 brs.

First Citizens Bank Ltd: 62 Independence Sq., Port of Spain; tel. 625-2893; fax 623-3393; e-mail itc@firstcitizenstt.com; internet www .firstcitizenstt.com; f. 1993; as merger of National Commercial Bank of Trinidad and Tobago Ltd, Trinidad Co-operative Bank Ltd and Workers' Bank of Trinidad and Tobago; state-owned; cap. 340.0m., res 559.8m., dep. 2,402.9m. (Sept. 2000); CEO LARRY HOWAI; 22 brs.

RBTT Ltd: Royal Court, 19–21 Park St, POB 287, Port of Spain; tel. 623-1322; fax 625-3764; e-mail royalinfo@rbtt.co.tt; internet www .rbtt.com; f. 1972 as Royal Bank of Trinidad and Tobago to take over local branches of Royal Bank of Canada, present name adopted April 2002; cap. 404.0m., res 152.9m., dep. 5,632.7m. (March 2001); Chair. PETER J. JULY; Man. Dir TERRENCE A. J. MARTINS; 21 brs.

Republic Bank Ltd: 9–17 Park St, POB 1153, Port of Spain; tel. 623-1056; fax 624-1323; e-mail email@republictt.com; internet www .republictt.com; f. 1837 as Colonial Bank; 1972 Barclays Bank; 1981 name changed as above; 1997 merged with Bank of Commerce Trinidad and Tobago Ltd; cap. 77.9m., res 235.1m., dep. 1,570.5m. (Sept. 2001); Chair. FRANK A. BARSOTTI; Man. Dir RONALD HARFORD; 47 brs.

Scotiabank Trinidad and Tobago Ltd: Cnr of Park and Richmond Sts, POB 621, Port of Spain; tel. 625-3566; fax 627-5278; e-mail scotiamain@carib.link.net; internet www.scotiabankttt.com; cap. 117.6m., res 544.4m., dep. 4,420m. (Oct. 2001); Chair. B. R. BIRMINGHAM; Man. Dir R. P. YOUNG; 23 brs.

Development Banks

Agricultural Development Bank of Trinidad and Tobago: 87 Henry St, POB 154, Port of Spain; tel. 623-6261; fax 624-3087; e-mail adp.o.s@tstt.net.tt; f. 1968; provides long-, medium- and short-term loans to farmers and the agri-business sector; Chair. HUBERT ALLEYNE; CEO JACQUELINE RAWLINS.

Development Finance Ltd (DFL): 10 Cipriani Blvd, POB 187, Port of Spain; tel. 623-4665; fax 624-3563; e-mail dfinbank@dflpos .com; internet www.dflpos.com; provides short- and long-term finance, and equity financing for projects in manufacturing, agro-processing, tourism, industrial and commercial enterprises; total assets US $84.2m. (Dec. 1998); Man. Dir GERARD M. PEMBERTON.

Credit Unions

Co-operative Credit Union League of Trinidad and Tobago Ltd: 32–34 Maraval Rd, St Clair; tel. 622-3100; fax 622-4800; e-mail culeague@tstt.net.tt.

Hindu Credit Union Co-operative Society Ltd: Chaguanas; tel. 671-3718.

INSURANCE

American Life and General Insurance Co (Trinidad and Tobago) Ltd: ALGICO Plaza, 91–93 St Vincent St, POB 943, Port of Spain; tel. 625-4425; fax 623-6218; e-mail algico@wow.net.

Bankers Insurance Co of Trinidad and Tobago Ltd: 177 Tragarete Rd, Port of Spain; tel. 622-4613; fax 628-6808.

Barbados Mutual Life Assurance Society: The Mutual Centre, 16 Queen's Park West, POB 356, Port of Spain; tel. 628-1636; Gen. Man. HUGH MAZELY.

Capital Insurance Ltd: 38–42 Cipero St, San Fernando; tel. 657-8077; fax 652-7306; f. 1958; motor and fire insurance; total assets TT $65m. 10 brs and 9 agencies.

Caribbean Home Insurance Co Ltd: 63 Park St, Port of Spain; tel. 625-4461; fax 625-5985; e-mail insure@caribbeanhome.com; f. 1973; cap. 100m. general and group life; Chair. DAVID N. COLLENS; Man. Dir FRANKLIN DE MOBRIGA.

Colonial Life Insurance Co (Trinidad) Ltd: Colonial Life Bldg, 29 St Vincent St, POB 443, Port of Spain; tel. 623-1421; fax 627-3821; e-mail info@clico.com; internet www.clico.com; f. 1936; Chair. LAWRENCE A. DUPREY; Man. Dir A. CLAUDE MUSAIB-ALI.

CUNA Caribbean Insurance Services Ltd: 2 Rust St, St Clair, Port of Spain; tel. 628-2862; fax 628-0841; e-mail cunaweb@trinidad .net; internet www.cunacaribbean.com; f. 1991; marine aviation and transport; motor vehicle, personal accident, property; Gen. Man. ERIC PHILLIP; 3 brs.

Furness Anchorage General Insurance Ltd: 11–13 Milling Ave, Sea Lots, POB 283, Port of Spain; tel. 623-0868; fax 625-1243; e-mail furness@wow.net; internet www.furnessgroup.com; f. 1979; general; Man. Dir IGNATIUS S. FERREIRA.

Great Northern Insurance Co Ltd: 29A Edward St, Port of Spain; tel. 625-1116.

GTM Fire Insurance Co Ltd: 95–97 Queen St, Port of Spain; tel. 623-1525.

Guardian Life of the Caribbean: 80 Independence Sq., Port of Spain; tel. 625-5433.

Gulf Insurance Ltd: 1 Gray St, St Clair, Port of Spain; tel. 622-5878; fax 628-0272; e-mail gulf@wow.net; f. 1974; general.

Maritime Financial Group: Maritime Centre, 10th Ave, Barataria; tel. 674-0130; f. 1978; property and casualty; CEO RICHARD ESPINET.

Motor and General Insurance Co Ltd: 1–3 Havelock St, St Clair, Port of Spain; tel. 622-2637; fax 622-5345.

NEMWIL: NEMWIL House, 12 Abercromby St, Port of Spain; tel. 623-4741; fax 623-4320; e-mail info@nemwil.com; internet www .nemwil.com; f. 1960; general insurer; Chair. HENRY PETER GANTEAUME; CEO and Man. Dir GERRARD LEE-INNIS; 3 brs.

New India Assurance Co (T & T) Ltd: 22 St Vincent St, Port of Spain; tel. 623-1326; fax 625-0670; e-mail newindia@wow.net.

Presidential Insurance Co Ltd: 54 Richmond St, Port of Spain; tel. 625-4788.

Royal Caribbean Insurance Ltd: 109 St Vincent St, Port of Spain; tel. 625-9980; fax 623-7895; e-mail rci@trinidad.net; f. 1977.

Trinidad and Tobago Export Credit Insurance Co Ltd: 14-17 Victoria Park Suites, 5th Floor, Victoria Sq., Port of Spain; tel. and fax 624-0028; CEO ROGER MIKE.

Trinidad and Tobago Insurance Ltd (TATIL): 11 Maraval Rd, POB 1004, Port of Spain; tel. 622-5351; fax 628-0035; Chair. JOHN JARDIM; Man. Dir GERRY BROOKS.

INSURANCE ORGANIZATIONS

Association of Trinidad and Tobago Insurance Companies: 28 Sackville St, Port of Spain; tel. 624-2817; fax 625-5132; e-mail jsc-attic@trinidad.net; internet attic.org.tt.

National Insurance Board: Cipriani Place, 2A Cipriani Blvd, POB 1195, Port of Spain; tel. 625-2171; fax 624-0276; f. 1971; statutory corporation; Chair. EDWARD BAYLEY; Exec. Dir TREVOR J. ROMANO.

STOCK EXCHANGE

Trinidad and Tobago Stock Exchange Ltd: 1st Floor, 1 Ajax St, Port of Spain; tel. 625-5107; fax 623-0089; e-mail ttstockx@tstt.net .tt; internet www.stockex.co.tt; f. 1981; 28 companies listed (2002); electronic depository system came into operation in 1999; Chair. RONALD HUGGINS; Gen. Man. HUGH EDWARDS.

Trade and Industry

GOVERNMENT AGENCIES

Caribbean Food Corporation (CFC): Port of Spain; tel. 622-5211; fax 622-4430; e-mail cfc@trinidad.net; f. 1976; promotion of agricultural development; Man. Dir E. C. CLYDE PARRIS.

Caroni (1975) Ltd: Brechin Castle, Couva; tel. 636-2311; fax 636-1259; sugar-cane plantations and mills; producers of rum and other sugar by-products; Chair. Dr JOE RAMKISSOON; Gen. Man. J. R. WOTHERSPOON.

Cocoa and Coffee Industry Board: 27 Frederick St, POB 1, Port of Spain; tel. 625-0289; fax 627-4172; e-mail ccib@carib-link.net; f. 1962; marketing of coffee and cocoa beans, regulation of cocoa and coffee industry; Man. KENT VILLAFANA.

Export-Import Bank of Trinidad and Tobago Ltd (EXIM-BANK): 30 Queens Park West, Port of Spain; tel. 628-2762; fax 622-3545; e-mail eximbank@wow.net; CEO ROGER L. L. MIKE; Gen. Man. JOSEPHINE IBLE.

Trinidad and Tobago Forest Products Ltd (TANTEAK): Connector Rd, Carlsen Field, Chaguanas; tel. 665-0078; fax 665-6645; f. 1975; harvesting, processing and marketing of state plantation-grown teak and pine; privatization pending; Chair. RUSKIN PUNCH; Man. Dir CLARENCE BACCHUS.

DEVELOPMENT ORGANIZATIONS

National Energy Corporation of Trinidad and Tobago Ltd: PLIPDECO House, Orinoco Dr., POB 191, Point Lisas, Couva; tel. 636-4662; fax 679-2384; e-mail infocent@carib-link.net; f. 1979; Chair. KENNETH BIRCHWOOD.

National Housing Authority: 44–46 South Quay, POB 555, Port of Spain; tel. 627-1703; fax 625-3963; f. 1962; Chair. BRIAN GEORGE; Exec. Dir Dr KEITH BAILEY.

Point Lisas Industrial Port Development Corporation Ltd (PLIPDECO): PLIPDECO House, Orinoco Dr., POB 191, Point Lisas, Couva; tel. 636-2201; fax 636-4008; e-mail plipdeco@plipdeco .com; internet www.plipdeco.com; f. 1966; privatized in the late 1990s; deep-water port handling general cargo, liquid and dry bulk, to serve adjacent industrial estate, which now includes iron and steel complex, methanol, ammonia, urea and related downstream industries; Chair. NIRMAL RAMPERSAD; CEO NEIL ROLINGSON.

Tourism and Industrial Development Company of Trinidad and Tobago (TIDCO): 10–14 Philipps St, POB 222, Port of Spain; tel. 623-6022; fax 624-3848; e-mail invest-info@tidco.co.tt; internet www.tidco.co.tt; Pres. (vacant).

CHAMBERS OF COMMERCE

South Trinidad Chamber of Industry and Commerce: Suite 311, Cross Crossing Shopping Centre, Lady Hailes Ave, San Fernando; tel. 652-5613; e-mail secretariat@southchamber.com; internet www.southchamber.com; f. 1956; Pres. BRIAN SAMLALSINGH.

Trinidad and Tobago Chamber of Industry and Commerce (Inc): Chamber Bldg, Columbus Circle, Westmoorings, POB 499, Port of Spain; tel. 627-6966; fax 637-7425; f. 1891; Pres. MICHAEL ARNEAUD; CEO DAVID MARTIN; Gen. Man. CARMENA BAIRD; 299 mems.

INDUSTRIAL AND TRADE ASSOCIATIONS

Agricultural Society of Trinidad and Tobago: 2A Alexandra St, Port of Spain; tel. 628-2486.

Coconut Growers' Association (CGA) Ltd: Eastern Main Rd, Laventille, POB 229, Port of Spain; tel. 623-5207; fax 623-2359; e-mail cgaltd@tstt.net.tt; f. 1936; 354 mems; Chair. PHILLIP AGOSTINI.

Co-operative Citrus Growers' Association of Trinidad and Tobago Ltd: Eastern Main Rd, POB 174, Laventille, Port of Spain; tel. 623-2255; fax 623-2487; e-mail ccga@wow.net; f. 1932; 437 mems; Pres. AINSLEY NICHOLS; Sec. N. WEEKES.

Pan Trinbago: Victoria Park Suites, 14–17 Park St, Port of Spain; tel. 623-4486; fax 625-6715; e-mail admin@pantrinbago.co.tt; f. 1971; official body for Trinidad and Tobago steelbands; Pres. PATRICK LOUIS ARNOLD; Sec. RICHARD FORTEAN.

Shipping Association of Trinidad and Tobago: 15 Scott Bushe St, Port of Spain; tel. 623-8070; e-mail satt@wow.net; f. 1938; Pres. NOEL JENVEY; Exec. Sec. S. JULUMSINGH.

Sugar Association of the Caribbean: Brechin Castle, Couva; tel. 636-2449; fax 636-2847; f. 1942; promotes and protects sugar industry in the Caribbean; 6 mem. associations; Chair. KARL JAMES; Sec. A. MOHAMMED.

Trinidad and Tobago Contractors' Association: 8 Stanmore Ave, Port of Spain; tel. 625-0196; fax 625-0247; internet www.ttca.com; f. 1968; represents contractors and manufacturers and suppliers to the sector.

Trinidad and Tobago Manufacturers' Association: 8 Stanmore Ave, St Clair, POB 971, Port of Spain; tel. 623-1029; fax 623-1031; e-mail ttmagm@opus.co.tt; internet www.ttma.com; f. 1956; 260 mems; Pres. AMJAD ALI.

EMPLOYERS' ORGANIZATION

Employers' Consultative Association of Trinidad and Tobago (ECA): 43 Dundonald St, POB 911, Port of Spain; tel. 625-4723; fax 625-4891; e-mail eca@wow.net; internet www.wow.net/community/eca; f. 1959; CEO GERARD PINARD; 156 mems.

STATE HYDROCARBONS COMPANIES

National Gas Co of Trinidad and Tobago Ltd: Goodrich Bay Rd, Point Lisas, POB 1127, Port of Spain; tel. 636-4662; fax 679-2384; e-mail infocent@carib-link.net; f. 1975; purchases, sells, compresses, transmits and distributes natural gas to consumers; Pres. FRANK LOOK KIN.

Petroleum Company of Trinidad and Tobago Ltd (Petrotrin): Petrotrin Administration Bldg, Cnr Queen's Park West and Cipriani Blvd, Port of Spain; tel. 625-5240; fax 624-4661; e-mail petroprd@petrotrin.com; internet www.petrotrin.com; f. 1993 following merger between Trinidad and Tobago Oil Company Ltd (Trintoc) and Trinidad and Tobago Petroleum Company Ltd (Trintopec); petroleum and gas exploration and production; operates refineries and a manufacturing complex, producing a variety of petroleum and petrochemical products; Chair. (vacant); Pres. RODNEY JAGAI; Vice-Pres ALEEM HOSEIN, WAYNE BERTRAND, SOLOMON SINANAN.

> **Petroleum Company of Trinidad and Tobago Ltd (Trinmar SBU):** Administration Bldg, Point Fortin; tel. 648-2127; fax 648-2519; internet www.trinmar.com; f. 1962; owned by Petrotrin; marine petroleum and natural gas co; Vice Pres. ALEEM HOSEIN; 705 employees.

UTILITIES

Regulatory Authority

Regulated Industries Commission: 90 Independence Sq., Port of Spain; tel. 627-0821; fax 624-2027; e-mail ttric@wow.net.

Electricity

Inncogen Ltd: 10 Marine Villas, Columbus Blvd, West Moorings by the Sea; tel. 632-7339; fax 632-7341; Chair. ROBERT PALEDINE.

Power Generation Co of Trinidad and Tobago (PowerGen): 6A Queen's Park West, Port of Spain; tel. 624-0383; fax 625-3759; Gen. Man. LARRY PORTER.

Trinidad and Tobago Electricity Commission (TTEC): 63 Frederick St, POB 121, Port of Spain; tel. 623-2611; fax 623-3759; e-mail ttecisd@trinidad.net; state-owned electricity transmission and distribution company; 51% owned by Power Generation Company of Trinidad and Tobago, 49% owned by Southern Electric Int./Amoco; Chair. DEVANAND RAMLAL; Gen. Man. DENIS SINGH (acting).

Gas

National Gas Co of Trinidad and Tobago Ltd: see State Hydrocarbons Companies.

Water

Water and Sewerage Authority (WASA): Farm Rd, St Joseph; tel. 662-9272; fax 652-1253.

TRADE UNIONS

National Trade Union Centre (NATUC): c/o NUGFW Complex, 145–147 Henry St, Port of Spain; tel. 623-4591; fax 625-7756; f. June 1991 as umbrella organization unifying entire trade-union movement, including former Trinidad and Tobago Labour Congress and Council of Progressive Trade Unions; Pres. ERROL K. McLEOD; Gen. Sec. SELWYN JOHN.

Principal Affiliates

Airline Superintendent's Association: c/o Data Centre Bldg, B. W. I. A., Piarco; tel. 664-3401; fax 664-3303; Pres. JEFFERSON JOSEPH; Gen. Sec. THEO OLIVER.

All-Trinidad Sugar and General Workers' Trade Union (ATSGWTU): Rienzi Complex, Exchange Village, Southern Main Rd, Couva; tel. 636-2354; fax 636-3372; e-mail atsgwtu@opus.co.tt; f. 1937; Pres. BOYSIE MOORE JONES; Gen. Sec. RUDRANATH INDARSINGH; 8,500 mems.

Amalgamated Workers' Union: 16 New St, Port of Spain; tel. 627-6717; fax 627-8993; f. 1953; Pres.-Gen. CYRIL LOPEZ; Sec. FLAVIUS NURSE; c. 7,000 mems.

Association of Technical, Administrative and Supervisory Staff: c/o Caroni (1975) Ltd, Brechin Castle, Couva.

Aviation, Communication and Allied Workers' Union: 315 McConie St, Dinsley Village, Tacarigua; tel. 669-1762; f. 1982; Pres. PAUL HARRISON; Gen. Sec. MARTIN ELIGON.

Bank and General Workers' Union: 27 Borde St, Woodbrook, Port of Spain; tel. 627-3931; fax 627-0278; e-mail bgwu@cariblink.net; f. 1974; Pres. VINCENT CABRERA; Gen. Sec. CHRISTOPHER JACKSON-SMITH.

Communication, Transport and General Workers' Trade Union: Golden Grove Rd, Piarco; tel. 669-1593; Pres. Gen. MARTIN PACHECO; Gen. Sec. ALSTON WILSON.

Communication Workers' Union: 146 Henry St, Port of Spain; tel. 623-5588; f. 1953; Pres. LAWRENCE BROWN; Gen. Sec. LYLE TOWNSEND; c. 2,100 mems.

Contractors' and General Workers' Trade Union: 37 Rushworth St, San Fernando; tel. 657-8072; fax 657-6834; Pres. OWEN HINDS; Gen. Sec. AINSLEY MATTHEWS.

Customs and Excise Extra Guard Association: Nicholas Court, Abercromby St, Port of Spain; tel. 625-3311-9; Pres. ALEXANDER BABB; Gen. Sec. NATHAN HERBERT.

National Farmers' and Workers' Union: 25 Coffee St, San Fernando; Pres. Gen. RAFFIQUE SHAH; Gen. Sec. DOOLIN RANKISSOON.

National General Workers' Union: c/o 143 Charlotte St, Port of Spain; tel. 623-0694; Pres. JIMMY SINGH; Gen. Sec. CHRISTOPHER ABRAHAM.

National Union of Government and Federated Workers: 145–147 Henry St, Port of Spain; tel. 623-4591; fax 625-7756; f. 1937; Pres. Gen. ROBERT GUISEPPI; Gen. Sec. JACQUELINE JACK; c. 20,000 mems.

Oilfield Workers' Trade Union: Paramount Bldg, 99A Circular Rd, San Fernando; tel. 652-2701; fax 652-7170; e-mail owtu@cariblink.net; f. 1937; Pres. ERROL McLEOD; Gen. Sec. DOODNATH MAHARAJ; 10,000 mems.

Public Services Association: 89–91 Abercromby St, POB 353, Port of Spain; tel. 623-7987; fax 627-2980; f. 1938; Pres. JENNIFER BAPTISTE; c. 15,000 mems.

Seamen and Waterfront Workers' Trade Union: 1D Wrightson Rd, Port of Spain; tel. 625-1351; fax 625 1182; f. 1937; Pres.-Gen. FRANCIS MUNGROO; Sec.-Gen. ROSS ALEXANDER; c. 3,000 mems.

Steel Workers' Union of Trinidad and Tobago: 115 Southern Main Rd, California; tel. 679-4666; e-mail swutt@tstt.net.tt; Pres. GRAFTON WOODLEY; Gen. Sec. WAYNE ROBERTS.

Transport and Industrial Workers' Union of Trinidad and Tobago: 114 Eastern Main St, Laventille, Port of Spain; tel. 623-4943; fax 623-2361; f. 1962; Pres. ALDWYN BREWSTER; Gen Sec. DESMOND O. BISHOP; *c.* 5,000 mems.

Trinidad and Tobago Postmen's Union: c/o General Post Office, Wrightson Rd, POB 692, Port of Spain; Pres. KENNETH SOOKOO; Gen. Sec. EVERALD SAMUEL.

Trinidad and Tobago Unified Teachers' Association: Cnr Fowler and Southern Main Rd, Curepe; tel. 645-2134; fax 662-1813; Pres. TREVOR OLIVER; Gen. Sec. PETER WILSON.

Union of Commercial and Industrial Workers: 130–132 Henry St, Port of Spain; tel. 623-8381; f. 1951; Asst Sec. M. WILSON; *c.* 1,500 mems.

Transport

RAILWAYS

The railway service was discontinued in 1968.

ROADS

In 1999 there were 7,900 km (4,910 miles) of roads in Trinidad and Tobago.

Public Transport Service Corporation: Railway Bldgs, South Quay, POB 391, Port of Spain; tel. 623-2341; fax 625-6502; f. 1965 to operate national bus services; Chair. (vacant); Gen. Man. EDISON ISAAC; operates a fleet of buses.

SHIPPING

The chief ports are Port of Spain, Pointe-à-Pierre and Point Lisas in Trinidad and Scarborough in Tobago. Port of Spain handles 85% of all container traffic, and all international cruise arrivals. In 1998 Port of Spain handled 3.3m. metric tons of cargo. Port of Spain and Scarborough each have a deep-water wharf. Port of Spain possesses a dedicated container terminal, with two large overhead cranes. Plans were in place in 2002 for an expansion of operations, through the purchase of an additional crane, the computerization of operations, and the deepening of the harbour (from 9.75m to 12m).

Caribbean Drydock Ltd: Port Chaguaramas, Western Main Rd, Chaguaramas; tel. 634-4127; fax 625-1215; e-mail caridoc@trinidad.org; internet www.caridoc.org; ship repair, marine transport, barge and boat construction.

Point Lisas Industrial Port Development Corporation Ltd (PLIPDECO): see Development Organizations.

Port Authority of Trinidad and Tobago: Dock Rd, POB 549, Port of Spain; tel. 623-2901; fax 627-2666; e-mail patt@wow.net; internet www.patnt.com; f. 1962; Chair. TAWARI TOTA-MAHARAJ; Gen. Man. COLIN LUCAS.

Shipping Association of Trinidad and Tobago: 1st Level, Cruise Ship Complex, Wrightson Rd, Port of Spain; tel. 623-3352; fax 623-8570; Pres. RAWLE BADDALOO; Exec. Sec. S. JULUMSINGH.

CIVIL AVIATION

Piarco International Airport is situated 25.7 km (16 miles) southeast of Port of Spain and is used by numerous airlines. The airport was expanded and a new terminal was constructed in 2001. Piarco remains the principal air transportation facility in Trinidad and Tobago. However, following extensive aerodrome development at Crown Point Airport (located 13 km from Scarborough) in 1992 the airport was opened to jet aircraft. It is now officially named Crown Point International Airport. A further re-development of the airport was to begin in 2002. There is a domestic service between Trinidad and Tobago.

Airports Authority of Trinidad and Tobago (AATT): Airport Administration Centre, Piarco International Airport; tel. 669-8047; fax 669-2319; e-mail airport@tstt.net.tt; internet www.airporttnt.com; administers Piarco and Crown Point International Airports; Chair. TYRONE GOPEE.

BWIA International Airways Ltd (Trinidad and Tobago): Administration Bldg, Golden Grove Rd, Piarco International Airport, POB 604, Port of Spain; tel. 669-3000; fax 669-1865; e-mail mail@bwee.com; internet www.bwee.com; f. 1980 by merger of BWIA International (f. 1940) and Trinidad and Tobago Air Services (f. 1974); 51% owned by consortium headed by Acker Group (USA), 33.5% state-owned; operates scheduled passenger and cargo services linking destinations in the Caribbean region, South America, North America and Europe; began service between Trinidad and Tobago, the Tobago Express, in March 2001; Chair. LAWRENCE DUPREY; Pres. and CEO CONRAD ALEONG.

Tourism

The climate and coastline attract visitors to Trinidad and Tobago. The latter island is generally believed to be the more beautiful and is less developed. The annual pre-Lenten carnival is a major attraction. In 2000 there were an estimated 398,559 foreign visitors, excluding cruise-ship passengers, and tourist receipts were estimated at US $210m. In the same year there were an estimated 82,859 cruise-ship passenger arrivals. In 2000 there were 4,532 hotel rooms in Trinidad and Tobago. The Government announced plans to increase first-class hotel room accommodation by 8,000 in 2001, marketing the islands as a sophisticated cultural destination. There were additional tourism developments in Chaguaramas and Toco Bay.

Tourism and Industrial Development Company of Trinidad and Tobago (TIDCO): see Development Organizations.

Trinidad and Tobago Hotel and Tourism Association (TTHTA): Unit 'B', 36 Scott Bushe St, POB 243, Port of Spain; tel. 627-4515; fax 627-4516; e-mail hotelassoc@wow.net; internet www.tnthotels.com; Pres. SHAZAM ALI; Exec. Dir GREER ASSAM.

> **Tobago Chapter:** Goddard's Bldg, Auchenskeoch, Carnbee; tel. and fax 639-9543; e-mail tthtatob@tstt.net.tt; Vice-Pres. RENE SEEPERSADSINGH.

TUNISIA

Introductory Survey

Location, Climate, Language, Religion, Flag, Capital

The Republic of Tunisia lies in North Africa, bordered by Algeria to the west and by Libya to the south-east. To the north and east, Tunisia has a coastline on the Mediterranean Sea. The climate is temperate on the coast, with winter rain, but hot and dry inland. Temperatures in Tunis are generally between 6°C (43°F) and 33°C (91°F). The country's highest recorded temperature is 55°C. Average annual rainfall is up to 1,500 mm in the north, but less than 200 mm in the southern desert. The official language is Arabic, and there is a small Berber Tamazight-speaking minority. French is widely used as a second language. Islam is the state religion, and almost all of the inhabitants are Muslims. There are small minorities of Christians and Jews. The national flag (proportions 2 by 3) is red, with a white disc, containing a red crescent moon and a five-pointed red star, in the centre. The capital is Tunis.

Recent History

Tunisia formally became a French protectorate in 1883. In the 1930s a campaign for independence from French rule began, led by the Néo-Destour (New Constitution) Party, founded in 1934 by Habib Bourguiba and a section of active former members of the Destour movement. Tunisia was granted internal self-government by France in September 1955 and full independence on 20 March 1956. Five days later elections were held for a Constitutional Assembly, which met in April and appointed Bourguiba as Prime Minister in a Government dominated by members of the Néo-Destour Party. In July 1957 a republic was established, with Bourguiba as Head of State, and a new Constitution was promulgated in June 1959. At elections held in November Bourguiba was elected unopposed to the new office of President, and the Néo-Destour Party won all 90 seats in the new National Assembly.

By 1964 the Néo-Destour Party had become the only legal political organization and in November of that year it was renamed the Parti socialiste destourien (PSD). A moderate socialist economic programme was introduced, which began with the expropriation of foreign-owned lands. However, attempts to introduce agricultural collectivization in 1964–69, under the direction of Ahmad Ben Salah, Minister of Finance and Planning, were abandoned in September 1969 because of resistance from the rural population. Ben Salah was dismissed, arrested and subsequently sentenced to 10 years' hard labour. He escaped in 1973 and fled to Europe, from where he organized the radical Mouvement de l'unité populaire (MUP). In 1970 Hédi Nouira, hitherto governor of the Tunisian Central Bank, was appointed Prime Minister. He began to reverse Ben Salah's socialist economic policies, with the introduction of liberal economic reforms in the sectors of industry and agriculture.

Liberalization of the economy was not accompanied by political reform, and the extensive powers of Nouira and Bourguiba were increasingly challenged by younger PSD members in the early 1970s. However, at the 1974 PSD Congress, Bourguiba was elected President-for-Life of the PSD and Nouira was confirmed as Secretary-General. In March 1975, after approving the necessary amendments to the Constitution, the National Assembly elected Bourguiba President-for-Life of Tunisia. Political differences emerged concerning economic policy, and the previously loyal trade union movement, the Union Générale des Travailleurs Tunisiens (UGTT), led by Habib Achour, began to assert its independence from the PSD. In January 1978, for the first time since independence, a 24-hour general strike took place, organized by the UGTT. In violent clashes between troops and strikers, at least 50 people were killed and many trade union leaders, including Achour, were arrested. Subsequently Achour was sentenced to 10 years' hard labour and a new Secretary-General of the UGTT, Tijani Abid, declared the willingness of trade unions to co-operate with the Government.

In April 1980 Nouira resigned, owing to ill health, and was succeeded as Prime Minister and Secretary-General of the PSD by Muhammad Mzali. Under Mzali, signs of greater political tolerance became apparent. The one-party system ended in mid-1981, when the Parti communiste tunisien (PCT), which had been proscribed in 1963, was granted legal status. The Government announced that any political group that gained more than 5% of the votes cast in the forthcoming legislative elections would also be officially recognized. Many of the UGTT leaders imprisoned after the 1978 disturbances were pardoned, and Achour was reappointed Secretary-General of the UGTT. At elections to the National Assembly in November 1981 the PSD and the UGTT formed an electoral alliance, the Front national, which received 94.6% of the total votes cast and won all 126 seats in the new Assembly.

In July 1986 Mzali was replaced as Prime Minister by Rachid Sfar (hitherto Minister of Finance), and was dismissed as Secretary-General of the PSD. Mzali subsequently fled to Algeria, and was sentenced in absentia to terms of imprisonment and hard labour for defamatory comments against Tunisian leaders and mismanagement of public funds. Elections to the National Assembly, in November, were boycotted by the opposition parties, with the result that the PSD, opposed only by 15 independent candidates, won all 125 seats.

During late 1987 President Bourguiba's behaviour became increasingly erratic. In October he revoked several of his recent appointments of leading state officials, and dismissed Sfar from the premiership. Zine al-Abidine Ben Ali was appointed Prime Minister and Secretary-General of the PSD; he retained the interior portfolio, which he had held since 1986. In early November 1987 a disagreement between Bourguiba and Ben Ali was reported, apparently concerning the recent trial of 90 Islamists accused of plotting against the Government. On 7 November 1987 seven doctors declared that President Bourguiba was unfit to govern, owing to senility and ill health. In accordance with the Constitution, Ben Ali was sworn in as President. Hedi Baccouche (previously Minister of Social Affairs) was appointed Prime Minister, and a new Council of Ministers was formed, which excluded several close associates of Bourguiba. Ben Ali announced plans to reform the Constitution and to permit greater political freedom. In the same month the Government permitted the publication of previously suspended opposition newspapers, and by early 1988 some 3,000 political and non-political detainees had been released. In February the PSD was renamed the Rassemblement constitutionnel démocratique (RCD), in order to reflect the new administration's commitment to democratic reform.

In April 1988 legislation was enacted by the National Assembly to institute a multi-party political system, and in July the Assembly approved a series of proposals to reform the Constitution. The office of President-for-Life was abolished, and the President was, henceforth, to be elected by universal suffrage every five years and limited to two consecutive terms of office. In the same month there was a significant reorganization of the Government, notably affecting ministers who had served under Bourguiba. In September two further opposition parties, the left-wing Rassemblement socialiste progressiste and the liberal Parti social pour le progrès (renamed the Parti social libéral—PSL—in October 1993) were legalized. In November the Government claimed that there were no longer any political prisoners in Tunisia, a total of 8,000 people having been released during the first year of Ben Ali's regime.

Ben Ali was nominated as the sole candidate (supported by all the officially-recognized parties) for the presidential election of 2 April 1989, and was duly elected President, receiving 99.3% of the votes cast. In legislative elections, the RCD won all 141 seats in the National Assembly, with some 80% of the votes cast. The fundamentalist Hizb an-Nahdah or the Parti de la renaissance (whose candidates contested the election as independents, since the party was not officially recognized), won some 13% of the votes cast, but failed to win any seats under an electoral system that favoured the ruling party. A general amnesty declared by President Ben Ali later that month restored political and civil rights to 5,416 people who had been condemned by the previous regime. In September Ben Ali dismissed Prime Minister Baccouche, following a disagreement concerning the Government's economic policy, and appointed Hamed Karoui, the former Minister of Justice, in his place.

In May 1990 the National Assembly approved a reformed electoral code, introducing a system of partial proportional representation for forthcoming municipal elections. The winning party was to receive 50% of the seats, while the remainder were to be distributed among all the parties, according to the number of votes received by each one. However, the six legal opposition parties boycotted the elections, held in June, arguing that they were neither free nor fair. Consequently, the RCD won control of all but one of the 245 municipal councils.

Ben Ali stated in December 1991 that changes to the electoral system, to be formulated in consultation with opposition parties, would be implemented during 1992, with the aim of ensuring greater representation at the national level for parties other than the RCD. In December 1992 Ben Ali announced a revision of the electoral code, to include the introduction of partial proportional representation at legislative elections scheduled for March 1994. Additional revisions of the press laws were also envisaged. However, this apparent willingness to co-operate with the legalized opposition was accompanied by further repression of the Islamist movement, with increased censorship of publications sympathetic to their cause, and the harassment of suspected activists. In February 1992 two an-Nahdah leaders, who were alleged to have been implicated in attempts to overthrow the Government, were sentenced to eight years' imprisonment for membership of an illegal organization.

In March 1992 the human rights organization Amnesty International published a report which detailed the arrests of some 8,000 suspected an-Nahdah members over an 18-month period, and cited 200 cases of the torture and ill-treatment of detainees. It also claimed that at least seven Islamists had died while in custody. The Government initially denied the allegations, but later conceded that some violations of human rights had occurred. In mid-March it was announced that human rights 'units' were to be established within the Ministries of Foreign Affairs, Justice and the Interior, although new restrictions were imposed on the activities of unofficial, quasi-political groups such as the Ligue tunisienne des droits de l'homme (LTDH). In the same month an amnesty was granted to more than 1,000 detainees. In July and August 1992 the trials were held in Tunis of 171 alleged members of an-Nahdah, and of 108 alleged members of the organization's military wing, who were all accused of conspiring to overthrow the Government; 46 of the defendants were sentenced to life imprisonment, 16, including Rached Ghanouchi, the leader of an-Nahdah, *in absentia*. (In 1993 Ghanouchi was granted political asylum in the United Kingdom.) Prison sentences of between one and 24 years were imposed on the remainder. In October appeals on behalf of 265 of those convicted were rejected, and another 20 an-Nahdah sympathizers were reportedly arrested and quantities of weapons and explosives seized in police raids. During 1993–94 Amnesty International issued reports detailing widespread abuses of human rights in Tunisia, including the victimization of female relatives of an-Nahdah members.

There were indications in 1993 of a revival of political activity, and in April a new political organization, the Mouvement de la rénovation (MR), held its first Congress. In November Ben Ali announced that presidential and legislative elections were to take place in March 1994. His candidacy for the presidency was supported not only by the RCD, but also by most of the legal opposition parties. In January 1994 the National Assembly adopted reforms to the electoral code: thenceforth 19 of the 163 seats in the enlarged Assembly were to be allocated to opposition parties in proportion to their overall national vote. In March, prior to the elections, the Government imposed restrictions on the reporting and distribution of the international press. At the presidential election, which took place concurrently with the legislative elections on 20 March 1994, Ben Ali was re-elected President, receiving 99.9% of the votes cast. The RCD received 97.7% of the total votes cast in the legislative elections, securing all 144 seats that were contested under a simple majority system. Of the 19 seats reserved for opposition candidates, the Mouvement des démocrates socialistes (MDS) secured 10, the MR four, the Union démocratique unioniste (UDU) three and the Parti de l'unité populaire (PUP) two. The rate of voter participation was officially estimated at 95.5%.

In October 1995 Muhammad Mouada, the MDS Secretary-General, was arrested and accused of having received money from an unnamed foreign country. Mouada was detained the day after he had, in an open letter to the President, criticized the lack of political freedom in Tunisia; however, government officials denied any connection between the letter and Mouada's arrest. In late October the Tunisian authorities prevented Khemais Chamari, an MDS member of the National Assembly, from travelling to Malta to attend an international conference on human rights. In the following month Chamari's parliamentary immunity was withdrawn, in order to allow judicial charges (relating to Mouada's trial) to be brought against him. Meanwhile, in an apparently conciliatory gesture towards the opposition, Ben Ali pardoned the leader of the Parti des ouvriers communistes tunisiens (POCT), Hamma Hammani, who had been imprisoned in April 1994, and his associate Muhammad Kilani, the former editor of the POCT journal. (Nevertheless, Hammani apparently remained the object of official harassment and in March 1996 his passport was confiscated.) In February 1996 Mouada was sentenced to two years' imprisonment for 'illegal detention of currency'. Although a court of appeal subsequently reduced his term by one year, at the end of the month Mouada was sentenced to 11 years' imprisonment for maintaining links with and receiving money from Libya. In July Chamari was sentenced to five years' imprisonment for breaching security proceedings relating to Mouada's trial. Human rights organizations protested at the severity of the sentence and appealed to the Tunisian authorities to release all political detainees. In December Mouada and Chamari were released conditionally on humanitarian grounds. Najib Hosni, an outspoken human rights lawyer (arrested in mid-1994 and sentenced in January 1996 to eight years' imprisonment for fraud) was also released in December, following a presidential pardon. However, in December 2000 Hosni was convicted of the 'unauthorized practice of his profession', after having defended several Islamist activists, and received a shorter prison sentence. In May 2001 Hosni was again granted a presidential pardon and released from detention.

In June 1996 President Ben Ali reorganized the Government and appointed Abd al-Aziz Ben Dhia as Secretary-General of the RCD. Wide-ranging ministerial changes were effected in January 1997, and Ben Ali again reorganized the Council of Ministers in October—notably appointing Said Ben Mustapha as Minister of Foreign Affairs and Ali Chaouch as Minister of the Interior. In December 1996 Ben Ali announced plans to amend the electoral law, which, *inter alia*, would lower the minimum eligible age of candidates for the National Assembly (from 25 to 23 years) and increase the representation of legal opposition parties in the Assembly and in municipal councils. Political parties would not be permitted to be based on religion, language, race or region, nor to have foreign links. The scope of referendums was also to be widened. In December 1997 the Council of Ministers reached consensus on draft legislation to amend the electoral law.

In July 1997 several international human rights groups strongly criticized the Tunisian authorities for an alleged campaign of intimidation which effectively prevented Tunisian human rights activists from attending a meeting of the European Parliament. In May an-Nahdah announced the death in detention of Sheikh Mabrouk Zren, one of its founder members, while serving a seven-year sentence. In August Ridha Khemeri, an Islamist activist, died in prison after a hunger strike to protest at his illegal imprisonment. Khemeri had been reincarcerated on the day of his release from a seven-and-a-half-year prison sentence. In February 1998 Khémais Ksila, the Vice-President of the LTDH, who had been arrested in September 1997 after announcing his intention to begin a hunger strike, was given a combined sentence of three years' imprisonment for offending public order, spreading rumours and inciting others to break the law.

In January 1999 draft legislation was presented to the National Assembly to introduce extraordinary provisions to the Constitution in order to allow pluralism in the presidential election scheduled to be held that year. The amendments, which were approved in March, allowed for the leaders of all political parties to contest the presidency provided that they had held their current leadership position for at least five consecutive years, and that their party was represented by one or more deputies in the legislature. (Hitherto opposition parties had been unable to present candidates, owing to the requirement that they be supported by at least 30 deputies in the Assembly.) Despite the new provisions, only two leaders of opposition parties were eligible to contest the presidency, namely Abderrahmane Tlili (UDU) and Muhammad Belhadj Amor (PUP). Ben Ali had himself been re-elected Chairman of the RCD at a party congress in July 1998, when he had been formally nominated as the party's presidential candidate.

The first contested presidential election since independence was held on 24 October 1999. As expected, Ben Ali comprehensively defeated his two rivals, securing 99.45% of the vote. Voter participation was officially estimated at 91.4%. At elections to the National Assembly, which were held concurrently, the RCD won all of the 148 seats contested under a simple majority system. Of the 34 seats reserved for opposition candidates, 13 were won by the MDS, the UDU and the PUP both took seven seats, the MR won five, and the PSL two. Some 91.5% of the electorate voted, according to official sources. In November Ben Ali pardoned some 600 prisoners and reduced or annulled the sentences of more than 3,100. Later that month the President effected a major government reorganization; Hamed Karoui was replaced as Prime Minister by Muhammad Ghannouchi (previously Minister of International Co-operation and Foreign Investment) and Abdallah Kallel succeeded Ali Chaouch as Minister of the Interior.

In April 2000 Taoufik Ben Brik, a Tunisian journalist, commenced a hunger strike after the Tunisian authorities responded to his critical writings by seizing his passport and accusing him of defaming public institutions. After four weeks of fasting Ben Brik was admitted to hospital and he temporarily suspended his hunger strike. However, he resumed the protest following the arrest of his brother, Jalal, who was subsequently sentenced to three months' imprisonment for attacking a policeman. In May Taoufik Ben Brik was allowed to travel to France for medical treatment. and, following the release of his brother from prison, he ended his hunger strike later that month.

At municipal elections held in May 2000 the RCD won more than 94% of the 4,128 seats being contested, and maintained control over all local councils. Representatives of the legal opposition parties and independent candidates, standing in 80 of the 257 constituencies, took 243 seats, compared with only six (out of 4,090) in 1995. However, many analysts had forecast a more successful result for the opposition parties, following changes to electoral regulations approved in 1997.

In June 2000 the President of the Conseil national pour les libertés en Tunisie (CNLT), Moncef Marzouki, visited London, United Kingdom, where he declared that a national democratic conference was to be held later in the year. Marzouki reportedly held talks with the leader of an-Nahdah, Rached Ghanouchi, and proposed future co-operation between secular and Islamist factions of the Tunisian opposition. In September it was reported that the Secretary-General of the UGTT, Ismail Sahbani, had resigned his post; he was replaced in an acting capacity by Abdessalem Djerad. At the same time the LTDH issued a statement alleging that, since May, three people had died while in detention as a result of police violence or negligence. In June 2001 Sahbani was sentenced to a total of 13 years' imprisonment after he was found guilty of two separate cases of embezzlement and forgery.

In early November 2000 President Ben Ali announced a number of initiatives aimed at furthering the democratization process and promoting human rights in Tunisia. The measures included: state compensation for detainees held in police custody without reasonable grounds; the transfer of responsibility for the prison system from the Ministry of the Interior to the Ministry of Justice; new legislation to improve conditions in prisons and to reduce censorship of the press; and an increase, by 50%, in government subsidies allocated for other political parties and their publications. In late November 14 alleged members of an illegal Islamist organization were sentenced to prison terms of between two and 17 years. In December Marzouki received a one-year prison sentence, having been convicted of belonging to an illegal group and of disseminating false information. Marzouki's defence lawyers claimed that his trial had not been conducted fairly, although they announced that no appeal would be launched against the verdict. However, the prosecution announced that it would appeal against the leniency of the sentence. In September the court of appeal announced the suspension of Marzouki's one-year sentence, although his civil rights were not restored. Marzouki, who had been prevented from travelling abroad on several occasions during 2001, finally had the ban on him lifted on leaving Tunisia in early December, and he departed for France later that month.

Meanwhile, at the fifth congress of the LTDH, held in October 2000, a new executive board was elected, with Mokhtar Trifi, an outspoken critic of the Ben Ali regime, as President. Four former members of the board subsequently filed a suit against the new leadership, claiming that, owing to procedural irregularities, it was invalid, and in late November a court imposed a moratorium on the activities of the LTDH. The Tunisian Government denied having ordered the ruling, but was strongly criticized by international and local human rights groups for its perceived role in the affair. Trial proceedings against the LTDH began at the end of January 2001, and in mid-February a judgment was issued that the results of the October congress should be invalidated. In March Trifi was charged with dissemination of false information and violation of the recent court ruling; however, in mid-June the court of appeal ruled that the LTDH could resume its activities and ordered it to hold another congress within a year.

President Ben Ali effected a significant reorganization of the Government in late January 2001. Muhammad Ghannouchi remained as Prime Minister, but several portfolios were reallocated. The most notable change in the enlarged Government (which included 19 new ministers) was the promotion of the former Government Secretary-General, Abdallah Kaabi, to become Minister of the Interior. In late February Slaheddine Maâoui replaced Afif Hindaoui as Minister-delegate to the Prime Minister in charge of Human Rights, Communications and Relations with the National Assembly. There was a further minor reorganization of the Council of Ministers in October.

In March 2001 more than 250 human rights activists in Tunisia produced a petition that demanded wide-ranging democratic reforms in the country prior to the presidential and legislative elections scheduled for 2004. Also in March 2001 some 100 moderate figures in civil society signed a separate petition accusing Ben Ali of corruption and nepotism and denouncing his plans to amend the Constitution so as to permit him to seek a fourth term in office. In April an-Nahdah released a joint communiqué with Mouada's faction of the MDS, proposing the formation of an opposition coalition to unite Islamists and liberals against the Ben Ali regime. Later that month the President instructed the Ministry of the Interior to investigate all alleged abuses by the security forces against Tunisian citizens and to ensure that those found guilty were punished. In a newspaper interview in mid-May he expressed his commitment to accelerating the pace of democratic change and reaffirmed that those responsible for human rights abuses would be brought to justice. Ben Ali also made a series of conciliatory gestures, including the release of a number of political prisoners. Meanwhile, in late April the National Assembly approved revisions to the press code under which the offence of 'defamation of public order' was abolished. The amendments also removed the threat of prison sentences for certain violations of the code. The changes were, however, condemned as inadequate by the Association des journalistes tunisiens.

During 2001–02 Tunisian courts took stern action against several high-profile individuals who had come into conflict with the Ben Ali regime. In late June 2001 Sihem Ben Sedrine, a spokesperson for the CNLT, was arrested and imprisoned by the authorities after she revealed details of a corruption scandal allegedly involving a close relative of President Ben Ali. Ben Sedrine was subsequently charged with spreading false information. In protest at her detention, some 20 members of Reporters sans frontiers temporarily occupied the offices of the Tunisian tourism office in Paris to demand her release and in mid-August she was released. In early July Mokhtar Yahyaoui, a senior Tunisian judge, had, in an open letter addressed to the President, condemned the absence of independence among the country's judiciary and claimed that judges were forced to deliver verdicts 'dictated in advance' and which were not in accordance with the law. Yahyaoui was subsequently suspended from duty and deprived of his salary, and in late December Yahyaoui (who had in the mean time been temporarily reinstated) was dismissed after being found guilty of attacking the honour of the magistrature and defaming the judiciary. In early February 2002 Hamma Hammani and two other members of the proscribed POCT, Abdeljabar Maduri and Samir Taamallah, appeared in court after surrendering to the authorities following four years in hiding, in order to appeal against the nine-year prison terms imposed upon them *in absentia* in July 1999 for belonging to an illegal organization. However, their arrival at court provoked clashes between demonstrators and security forces. and the defendants were forcibly removed from the court by police on two separate occasions. The presiding judge swiftly announced that he had upheld the prison terms initially imposed on the three men and also sentenced Maduri, who failed to reappear before the court after allegedly being injured during the skirmishes, to a further two years' imprisonment for contempt of court. Later that month Hammani commenced a hunger strike to protest at the conditions under which he was being detained, and the three men lodged an appeal against their sentences. In early April Hammani's sentence was reduced to 38 months, while Maduri's and Taamallah's terms were revised to 21 months. In September Hammani was conditionally released on health grounds just days after the appeal against his sentence was rejected. Taamallah was also freed owing to ill health.

Meanwhile, in late September 2001 the central committee of the ruling RCD announced that it would formally propose changes to the country's Constitution in order to enable Ben Ali to seek a fourth presidential term. In April 2002 members of the National Assembly overwhelmingly approved a constitutional reform bill, and at a referendum held on 26 May, according to official figures, the constitutional changes were approved by 99.5% of voters; the rate of voter participation was officially recorded at 95.6%. The amendments raised the age limit for presidential candidates from 70 to 75 years, and removed the limit on the number of terms that could be served by a President. Provision was also made for the creation of a second legislative chamber, for the establishment of a two-round presidential election system, and for a number of measures that would improve civil liberties and public freedoms.

In early April 2002 a tanker lorry exploded outside a synagogue on the island of Djerba. More than 20 people were killed in the incident, most of them German tourists, and a similar number suffered injuries. The Tunisian authorities initially claimed that the explosion had been an accident, but a spokesman for the Israeli Ministry of Foreign Affairs insisted that it was an anti-Semitic 'terrorist' attack. The Tunisian authorities subsequently confirmed that the explosion had been a 'premeditated criminal act'. A number of Arabic newspapers immediately carried claims that the al-Qa'ida (Base) organization of Osama bin Laden—the principal suspect in the September 2001 attacks on New York and Washington, DC—was responsible, and in late June 2002 the Qatar-based satellite television station Al-Jazeera broadcast a statement by a spokesman for al-Qa'ida, asserting that the attack had been perpetrated in the name of al-Qa'ida, in protest against Israel's recent military offensive against Palestinian-controlled areas of the West Bank.

Later in April 2002, apparently in response to the Djerba attack, Abdallah Kaabi was replaced as Minister of the Interior by Hédi M'henni, hitherto Minister of Social Affairs. A new director-general of national security was also appointed. In May 13 senior military officers, including the army chief of staff, were killed when the helicopter in which they were travelling crashed to the west of Tunis.

In September 2002 President Ben Ali implemented a major reorganization of the Council of Ministers. In an attempt to improve efficiency in government operations, a number of ministries were merged or abolished, although most strategic posts remained unaltered. In early November eight people were arrested in Lyon, France, in connection with the Djerba explosion. Among those detained was the brother of the man suspected of having driven the lorry, and later that month he was one of three people to be questioned further in Paris by a senior French judge as part of ongoing anti-terrorism investigations. The other five suspects were released without charge. In early March 2003 five people were arrested in Spain in connection with the incident, and another person was detained in France shortly afterwards; in the following month police in Saudi Arabia arrested a German citizen who had been briefly detained by the authorities in that country following the explosion. However, by late April no charges had been brought against any of those detained.

Relations with the other countries of the Maghreb improved considerably in the 1980s. A meeting between President Bourguiba and President Ben Djedid Chadli of Algeria in March 1983 led to the drafting of the Maghreb Fraternity and Co-operation Treaty, which envisaged the eventual creation of a Greater Maghreb Union, and was signed by Mauritania in December. In January 1988 Tunisia and Algeria held further discussions on the establishment of a greater Arab Maghreb, and in April border restrictions between Tunisia and Libya were removed. In February 1989, at a meeting of North African Heads of State in Morocco, a treaty was concluded that proclaimed the Union of the Arab Maghreb (Union du Maghreb arabe—UMA, see p. 342), comprising Algeria, Libya, Mauritania, Morocco and Tunisia. The treaty envisaged the establishment of a council of heads of

state; regular meetings of ministers responsible for foreign affairs; and, eventually, the free movement of goods, people, services and capital throughout the countries of the region.

In 1982 President Bourguiba permitted the Palestine Liberation Organization (PLO) to establish its headquarters near Tunis. In October 1985 Israeli aircraft attacked the PLO headquarters, causing the deaths of some 72 people, including 12 Tunisians. US support for the right of Israel to retaliate (the attack was a reprisal for the murder of three Israeli citizens in Cyprus) severely strained relations between Tunisia and the USA. In April 1988 Abu Jihad, the military commander of the PLO, was assassinated at his home in Tunis. The Tunisian Government blamed Israel for the murder, and complained to the UN Security Council. The PLO transferred its offices to Gaza in mid-1994, following the signing of the PLO-Israeli Cairo Agreement on implementing Palestinian self-rule in the Gaza Strip and in Jericho.

In January 1988 the Tunisian Government announced that diplomatic relations with Egypt, which had been severed in 1979, would be resumed. In March 1990 Ben Ali made the first visit to Cairo by a Tunisian President since 1965, and signed several agreements on bilateral co-operation. In September 1990 a majority of members of the League of Arab States (the Arab League, see p. 260) resolved to move the League's headquarters from Tunis (where it had been established 'temporarily' in 1979) to its original site in Cairo: the Tunisian Government protested at the decision.

In January 1993 Tunisia assumed the annual presidency of the UMA. The Government made clear its determination to reactivate the process of Maghreb union, as well as dialogue with the European Community (now European Union—EU, see p. 199). In April 1994 the UMA ratified 11 agreements designed to improve co-operation and trade within the Maghreb. However, tensions between the UMA's member states subsequently undermined the activities of the Union. In March 1999 Ben Ali made his first official visit to Morocco, during which he pledged to strengthen relations with that country, and to revive the UMA. A summit meeting of ministers responsible for foreign affairs of the five UMA member states was arranged, and proceeded in the Algerian capital in mid-March 2001. However, the meeting, which was to have made preparations for the first summit meeting of UMA Heads of State since 1995, quickly broke down following disagreements between Moroccan and Algerian representatives.

Relations with Algeria improved appreciably after the second round of Algerian elections, at which the fundamentalist Front islamique du salut (FIS) had been expected to secure victory, was suspended in January 1992, and Tunisia welcomed the appointment of Muhammad Boudiaf as Chairman of the High Council of State, as well as the suppression of the FIS. During a visit to Tunis in February 1993, Boudiaf's successor, Ali Kafi, exchanged letters with Ben Ali to ratify the official demarcation of the 1,000-km border between Tunisia and Algeria, which had been the subject of dispute since Algerian independence. Ben Ali and Kafi also pledged to co-operate in countering the threat of terrorism in the region. In early 1995 six Tunisian border guards were killed in an attack perpetrated by Algerian Islamists in protest at the Tunisian authorities' alleged support for the Algerian security forces. Another serious incident occurred at the joint border in May 2000, when Tunisian security forces responded to an attack by Algerian Islamists; three of the Islamists were killed and two Tunisian soldiers wounded. The attack followed the signing of a bilateral customs agreement aimed at ending cross-border smuggling, considered by the Algerian Government to facilitate the activities of Islamist groups in Algeria. A number of bilateral agreements were signed during a visit to Algeria by Ben Ali in February 2002; most notably, the two countries pledged to formalize delineation of their maritime border.

In October 1994 Tunisia and Israel signalled the beginning of the normalization of bilateral relations with the announcement of plans to establish interests offices in the Belgian embassies in Tunis and Tel-Aviv. The offices opened in April and May 1996, respectively. Relations between the two countries were strained in early 1997, following Tunisia's criticism of Israel's alleged failure to implement agreements concluded with the PLO; although the two countries' respective interests offices remained open, Tunisia suspended the process of normalizing relations with Israel. The Tunisian Government installed a liaison office in the Gaza Strip in April 1995; a second office was planned for Jericho. In February 2000 a senior-level delegation from Tunisia visited Israel, where it was agreed, *inter alia*, that the two countries would establish a joint committee for advancing trade and tourism. However, in October, in response to the escalating Israeli–Palestinian crisis, Tunisia announced that it had severed all diplomatic ties with Israel. As violence continued to escalate in the Palestinian territories in early 2002, the Tunisian authorities again denounced Israeli aggression and urged international organizations to take firm action to end the crisis.

In June 1993 President Ben Ali, addressing the European Parliament in Strasbourg, advocated the establishment of a Euro-Maghreb Development Bank, which, by stimulating economic growth in North Africa, would alleviate illegal immigration into Europe. In July 1995 Tunisia concluded an association agreement with the EU, designed to foster closer commercial and political co-operation between the two. In October the new French President, Jacques Chirac, made an official visit to Tunisia. Chirac and Ben Ali agreed that henceforth they would meet annually, in order to consolidate bilateral relations. Although the two leaders failed to meet as scheduled in late 1996, Ben Ali made an official visit to France in October 1997, during which he countered criticisms regarding his country's record on human rights by claiming that there were currently no political prisoners in Tunisia. Several Tunisian deputies demanded a suspension of the association agreement in June 2000, after EU member states (particularly France) criticized the Tunisian authorities' failure to protect human rights in view of the Ben Brik affair (see above). Relations between France and Tunisia deteriorated further during 2001 when the French Government again criticized the growing use of violence against human rights activists and voiced its concern at gaol sentences imposed upon prominent opposition figures (see above). In May the Tunisian authorities cancelled part of a planned visit to Tunisia by the French Minister-delegate in charge of Co-operation and Francophone Affairs, Charles Josselin, who had been scheduled to meet several prominent human rights activists. Josselin subsequently postponed his visit, which had also been expected to renew dialogue between the two countries, until later that month. Following the arrest of the CNLT spokesperson Sihem Ben Sedrine in late June (see above), Josselin wrote to the Tunisian Minister-delegate to the Prime Minister in charge of Human Rights, Communications and Relations with the National Assembly, Slaheddine Maâoui, informing him that Ben Sedrine's detention had aroused strong emotions in France. Despite a brief visit to Tunisia by President Chirac in December, bilateral relations remained strained.

Government

Under the 1959 Constitution, legislative power is held by the unicameral National Assembly, with 182 members who are elected by universal adult suffrage for a five-year term. (Of the 182 members, 148 are elected under a simple majority system, while 34 seats are reserved for the opposition, allotted according to the proportion of votes received nationally by each party.) In 1988 a multi-party system was officially permitted by law. Executive power is held by the President, elected for five years by popular vote at the same time as the Assembly. The President, who is Head of State and Head of Government, appoints a Council of Ministers, led by a Prime Minister, which is responsible to him. Constitutional amendments relating to the presidency and legislature were approved at a national referendum in May 2002 (see Recent History). For local administration the country is divided into 18 governorates.

Defence

In August 2002 total armed forces numbered an estimated 35,000 (including 23,400 conscripts), consisting of an army of 27,000, a navy of about 4,500 and an air force of 3,500. Paramilitary forces included a 12,000-strong national guard. From 2003 women were required to complete military service. Officer-training is undertaken in the USA and France as well as in Tunisia. The defence budget for 2000 totalled TD 461m.

Economic Affairs

In 2001, according to estimates by the World Bank, Tunisia's gross national income (GNI), measured at average 1999–2001 prices, was US $20,051m., equivalent to $2,070 per head (or $6,450 per head on an international purchasing-power parity basis). During 1990–2001, it was estimated, the population increased at an average annual rate of 1.6%, while gross domestic product (GDP) per head increased, in real terms, by an average of 3.2%. Overall GDP increased, in real terms, at an

average annual rate of 4.8% per year in 1990–2001; it grew by 4.7% in 2000 and by 5.4% in 2001.

Agriculture (including forestry and fishing) contributed an estimated 13.0% of GDP in 2001 and employed an estimated 24.3% of the working population in that year. The principal cereal crops are wheat and barley. However, Tunisia imports large quantities of cereals, dairy produce, meat and sugar. The country's main agricultural export is olive oil; olives, citrus fruit and dates are also grown for export. During 1990–2001 agricultural GDP increased at an average annual rate of 2.9%. Agricultural GDP declined by 1.0% in 2000, but rose by 1.5% in 2001.

Industry (including mining, manufacturing, construction and power) contributed an estimated 32.2% of GDP in 2001, and engaged 34.4% of the employed labour force in 1994. During 1990–2001 industrial GDP increased by an average of 4.7% per year. Industrial GDP increased 5.2% in 2000 and by the same figure in 2001.

Mining (excluding hydrocarbons) contributed an estimated 0.9% of GDP in 2001. In 1994 mining (with gas, electricity and water) employed 1.6% of the working population. In 1999 the principal mineral export was petroleum (which accounted for 6.6% of total export earnings). At 1 January 2002 Tunisia's proven published oil reserves were estimated at 300m. barrels, sufficient to maintain production (at 2001 levels) for a further 12 years. Iron, zinc, lead, aluminium fluoride, fluorspar and sea salt are also mined. In addition, Tunisia possesses large reserves of natural gas. The GDP of the mining sector increased by 5.0% in 2000 and by 1.5% in 2001.

Manufacturing contributed an estimated 20.7% of GDP in 2001, and employed 19.6% of the working population in 1994. Manufacturing is based on the processing of the country's principal agricultural and mineral products. Other important sectors include textiles, construction materials, machinery, chemicals, and paper and wood. In 1990–2001 manufacturing GDP increased at an average annual rate of 5.4%. Manufacturing GDP increased by 6.2% in 2000 and 4.8% in 2001.

Energy is derived principally from gas (which contributed 85.5% of total electricity output in 1999) and petroleum (13.5%), although Tunisia also has several hydroelectric plants. Imports of mineral fuels and lubricants comprised 6.7% of the value of total imports in 1999. In the late 1990s a project was under way to link the Tunisian electricity grid to that of Libya.

The services sector accounted for an estimated 54.8% of GDP in 2001 and employed 42.3% of the working population in 1994. Tourism represents an important source of revenue; receipts from tourism in 2001 totalled 2,343m. dinars. In 2001 there were 5.4m. tourist arrivals, an increase of 6.5%% compared with 2000. The GDP of the services sector increased by an average of 5.3% per year in 1990–2001. Growth in the sector's GDP was recorded at 5.9% in 2000 and at 6.4% in 2001.

In 2001 Tunisia recorded a visible trade deficit of US $2,391m., and a deficit of $863m. on the current account of the balance of payments. In 2002 the principal sources of imports were France (accounting for 25.6% of the total), Italy (19.5%) and Germany (8.9%). The principal market for Tunisian exports in that year were also France (taking 31.3%), Italy (21.6%) and Germany (11.5%). The member states of the European Union (EU, see p. 199) accounted for 80.5% of Tunisia's exports and 71.4% of its imports in 1999. Tunisia's principal exports in 1999 were clothing and accessories, petroleum and petroleum products, machinery and transport equipment, phosphates and fertilizers, and food and live animals. The principal imports were machinery and transport equipment, textiles, food and live animals, road vehicles and parts, and petroleum and petroleum products.

In 1999 there was an estimated budgetary deficit of TD 646.2m. (equivalent to 2.6% of GDP). At the end of 2000 Tunisia's total external debt was US $10,610m., of which $8,869m. was long-term public debt. In that year the cost of debt-servicing was equivalent to 20.2% of the value of exports of goods and services. The average annual rate of inflation was 4.1% in 1990–2002; the annual rate of inflation averaged 1.9% in 2001 and 2.8% in 2002. An estimated 15% of the labour force were unemployed in 2001.

Tunisia is a member of the Arab Fund for Economic and Social Development (AFESD, see p. 136), the Arab Monetary Fund (see p. 138) and the Union of the Arab Maghreb (Union du Maghreb arabe—UMA, see p. 342).

In 1986 Tunisia adopted a structural adjustment programme, under the auspices of the IMF, and initiated measures to liberalize the economy and restructure the financial sector and public enterprises. These reforms stimulated economic activity and reduced inflation and the country's external debt. The dinar became fully convertible on international currency markets in 1993. In 1995 Tunisia secured an association agreement with the EU (formalized in March 1998) that provided for a 12-year transitional period during which the Tunisian economy would be more closely integrated with those of EU member states. The agreement was expected to afford Tunisia greater access to EU funds and promote investment, albeit at the expense of exposing the agricultural and industrial sectors to increased competition from abroad. The divestiture of a large number state-owned enterprises from the late 1990s significantly reduced government debt levels; however, the privatization programme slowed during 2002, with just three of a possible 26 companies given over to private control. The 10th development plan (for 2002–06) aimed to increase international trade and accelerate structural reforms in order to create a more competitive economy. Furthermore, President Ben Ali introduced a 15-point 'Programme for the Future', which aimed to further eradicate poverty and combat unemployment. Tunisia's tourism industry, which provides an estimated 7% of total GDP and employs some 300,000 people, was adversely affected by the recession in global travel following the suicide attacks against the USA in September 2001, with revenue from that sector falling by 14% in 2002, compared with the previous year. Nevertheless, the Government is proceeding with an ambitious programme to develop the sector, which aims to double the number of visitors to the country to 10m. by 2010. GDP expanded by 5.0% in 2002, and the anticipated recovery of the tourism and agricultural sectors, combined with an increase in the value of exports, was expected to result in GDP growth of some 5.5% in 2003.

Education

Education is compulsory in Tunisia for a period of nine years between the ages of six and 16. Primary education begins at six years of age and normally lasts for six years. Secondary educa-tion begins at the age of 12 and lasts for seven years, comprising a first cycle of three years and a second cycle of four years. In 1996 the total enrolment at primary and secondary schools, which are mostly state-run, was equivalent to 89% of the school-age population (91% of boys; 87% of girls). In that year an estimated 98% of children in the primary age-group (99% of boys; 96% of girls) were enrolled at primary schools; enrolment at secondary schools included 66% of children in the relevant age-group (67% of boys; 65% of girls). Arabic is the first language of instruction in primary and secondary schools, but French is also used. The University of Tunis was divided in 1988 to form separate institutions, one for the arts, the other for the sciences, and two new universities were opened in 1986, at Monastir and Sfax. In 2001/02 a total of 225,102 students were enrolled at higher educational establishments in Tunisia. Proposed administrative budget expenditure on education was TD 1,395m. dinars (17.7% of total government spending) in 1999.

Public Holidays

2003: 1 January (New Year's Day), 12 February* (Aid el-Kebir, Feast of the Sacrifice), 20 March (Independence Day), 21 March (Youth Day), 9 April (Martyrs' Day), 1 May (Labour Day), 25 July (Republic Day), 13 August (Women's Day), 15 October (Evacuation of Bizerta), 7 November (accession of President Ben Ali), 26 November* (Aid es-Seghir, end of Ramadan).

2004: 1 January (New Year's Day), 2 February* (Aid el-Kebir, Feast of the Sacrifice), 20 March (Independence Day), 21 March (Youth Day), 9 April (Martyrs' Day), 1 May (Labour Day), 25 July (Republic Day), 13 August (Women's Day), 15 October (Evacuation of Bizerta), 7 November (accession of President Ben Ali), 14 November* (Aid es-Seghir, end of Ramadan).

*These holidays are dependent on the Islamic lunar calendar and may differ by one or two days from the dates given.

Weights and Measures

The metric system is in force.

Statistical Survey

Source (unless otherwise stated): Institut National de la Statistique, Ministère du Développement Economique, 70 rue ach-Cham, 1002 Tunis; tel. (1) 891-002; fax (1) 792-559; e-mail ins@e-mail.ati.tn; internet www.ins.nat.tn.

Area and Population

AREA, POPULATION AND DENSITY

Area (sq km)		
Land	. . . .	154,530
Inland waters	. . . .	9,080
Total	. . . .	163,610*
Population (census results)		
30 March 1984	. . . .	6,966,173
20 April 1994		
Males	. . . .	4,447,341
Females	. . . .	4,338,023
Total	. . . .	8,785,364
Population (official estimates at mid-year)		
2000	. . . .	9,563,500
2001	. . . .	9,673,600
2002	. . . .	9,779,800
Density (per sq km) at mid-2002	. . . .	59.8

* 63,170 sq miles.

GOVERNORATES

(population at 1 July 2002)

	Area (sq km)	Population	Density (per sq km)
Tunis	346	933,700	2,698.6
Ariana	498	382,600	768.3
Ben Arous	761	467,200	613.9
Manouba	1,060	327,000	308.5
Nabeul	2,788	649,900	233.1
Zaghouan	2,768	157,300	56.8
Bizerte	3,685	527,600	143.2
Béja	3,558	320,200	90.0
Jendouba	3,102	430,100	138.6
Le Kef	4,965	281,900	56.8
Siliana	4,631	258,100	55.7
Kairouan	6,712	571,000	85.1
Kasserine	8,066	424,800	52.7
Sidi Bouzid	6,994	404,100	57.8
Sousse	2,621	510,000	194.6
Monastir	1,019	429,100	421.1
Mahdia	2,966	376,400	126.9
Sfax	7,545	832,50	110.3
Gafsa	8,990	333,400	37.1
Tozeur	4,719	98,500	20.9
Kébili	22,084	144,200	6.5
Gabés	7,175	337,700	47.1
Médenine	8,588	432,000	50.3
Tataouine	38,889	150,500	3.9
Total	163,610	9,779,800	59.8

PRINCIPAL TOWNS
(population at 1994 census)

Tunis (capital) . .	674,100	Kairouan (Qairawan)	102,600
Sfax (Safaqis). .	230,900	Gabés	98,900
Ariana. . . .	152,700	Bizerta (Bizerte). .	98,900
Ettadhamen . .	149,200	Bardo	72,700
Sousse. . . .	125,000	Gafsa	71,100

Mid-2001 (UN estimate, incl. suburbs): Tunis 1,927,000 (Source: UN, *World Urbanization Prospects: The 2001 Revision*).

BIRTHS, MARRIAGES AND DEATHS*

	Registered live births		Registered marriages		Registered deaths	
	Number	Rate (per 1,000)	Number	Rate (per 1,000)	Number	Rate (per 1,000)
1990 . .	205,345	25.4	55,612	6.8	45,700	5.6
1991 . .	207,455	25.2	59,010	7.1	46,500	5.6
1992 . .	211,649	25.2	64,700	7.6	46,300	5.5
1993 . .	207,786	24.1	54,120	6.3	49,400	5.7
1994 . .	200,223	22.7	52,431	5.9	50,300	5.7
1995 . .	186,416	20.8	53,726	6.0	52,000	5.8
1996 . .	178,801	19.7	56,349	6.2	40,817	5.5
1997 . .	173,757	18.9	57,861	6.3	42,426	5.6

Birth rate (per 1,000): 16.9 in 1999; 17.1 in 2000; 16.9 in 2001.

Death rate (per 1,000): 5.7 in 1999; 5.6 in 2000; 5.5 in 2001.

* Birth registration is reported to be 100% complete. Death registration is estimated to be about 73% complete. UN estimates for average annual death rates are: 8.5 per 1,000 in 1980–85, 7.3 per 1,000 in 1985–90, 6.4 per 1,000 in 1990–95. UN estimates for average annual birth rates are: 33.7 per 1,000 in 1980–85, 30.9 per 1,000 in 1985–90, 24.1 per 1,000 in 1990–95.

Expectation of life (WHO, estimates, years at birth): 71.1 (males 69.0; females 73.5) in 2001 (Source: WHO, *World Health Report*).

EMPLOYMENT
('000 persons aged 15 years and over at 20 April 1994)

	Males	Females	Total
Agriculture, forestry and fishing .	393.7	107.3	501.0
Manufacturing	244.7	211.0	455.7
Electricity, gas and water* . . .	34.4	2.4	36.8
Construction	302.6	3.2	305.8
Trade, restaurants and hotels† . .	277.8	37.8	315.6
Community, social and personal services‡	503.9	163.2	667.1
Activities not adequately defined .	28.6	10.0	38.6
Total employed	1,785.7	534.9	2,320.6

* Including mining and quarrying.
† Including financing, insurance, real estate and business services.
‡ Including transport, storage and communications.

Mid-2001 (estimates in '000): Agriculture, etc. 949; Total labour force 3,913 (Source: FAO).

Health and Welfare

KEY INDICATORS

Total fertility rate (children per woman, 2001)	2.2
Under-5 mortality rate (per 1,000 live births, 2001) . . .	27
HIV/AIDS (% of persons aged 15–49, 1994).	0.04
Physicians (per 1,000 head, 1997)	0.70
Hospital beds (per 1,000 head, 1997)	1.7
Health expenditure (2000): US $ per head (PPP) . . .	472
Health expenditure (2000): % of GDP	7.0
Health expenditure (2000): public (% of total)	78.2
Human Development Index (2000): ranking	97
Human Development Index (2000): value	0.722

For sources and definitions, see explanatory note on p. vi.

Agriculture

PRINCIPAL CROPS
('000 metric tons)

	1999	2000	2001
Wheat	1,390	824	1,120
Barley	420	240	233
Other cereals	26	24	29
Potatoes	320	290	330
Sugar beet.	89	21	30
Broad beans (dry)	45	29	46
Peas (dry)	3†	3	4
Chick-peas	9	8	7
Almonds	58	62	30
Olives	1,125	1,125	550
Sunflower seed†	10	10	10
Tomatoes	930	812	750
Cabbages	12	12	12†
Artichokes.	19	17	—
Lettuce.	14	14	14†
Spinach	12	13	12†
Chillies and green peppers . . .	185	190	214
Dry onions	127	133	120*
Pumpkins, etc.	36	37	37†
Cucumbers and gherkins . . .	28	29	28†
Green peas	20	21	21†
Green broad beans	25	22	22†
Carrots	46	47	47†
Watermelons	350	360	380
Grapes	132	141	125
Dates	119	105	113
Apples	97	108	108†
Pears	50	54	55
Peaches and nectarines . . .	70	73	75
Plums	15	15	15†
Oranges	105	115	110
Tangerines, mandarins, clementines and satsumas . .	38	38	41
Lemons and limes	17	18	23
Grapefruit and pomelos . . .	50	50†	66
Apricots	31	32	26

* Unofficial figure(s).
† FAO estimate(s).

Source: FAO.

LIVESTOCK
('000 head, year ending September)

	1999	2000	2001
Horses*	56	56	56
Mules*	81	81	81
Asses*	230	230	230
Cattle	750*	767	759
Camels*	231	231	231
Sheep	6,800*	6,926	6,861
Goats	1,350*	1,448	1,450
Chickens*	38,000	43,000	43,000
Turkeys*	2,800	2,900	2,900

* FAO estimate(s).

Source: FAO.

LIVESTOCK PRODUCTS
('000 metric tons)

	1999	2000	2001
Beef and veal	58	60	62
Mutton and lamb	53	54	56
Poultry meat	101	107	108
Cows' milk	817	908	940
Sheep's milk*	17	17	17
Goats' milk*	12	12	12
Hen eggs*	75	78	78
Wool: greasy*	9	9	9
Wool: scoured*	6	6	6
Cattle hides*	5	5	6
Sheepskins*	8	8	8

* FAO estimates.

Source: FAO.

Forestry

ROUNDWOOD REMOVALS
(FAO estimates, '000 cu m, excl. bark)

	1999	2000	2001
Sawlogs, veneer logs and logs for sleepers	21	21	21
Pulpwood	75	75	75
Other industrial wood	118	118	118
Fuel wood	2,080	2,094	2,105
Total	2,294	2,308	2,319

Source: FAO, *Yearbook of Forest Products*.

SAWNWOOD PRODUCTION
(FAO estimates, '000 cu m, incl. sleepers)

	1999	2000	2001
Coniferous (softwood)	7	7	7
Broadleaved (hardwood)	14	14	14
Total	20	20	20

Source: FAO, *Yearbook of Forest Products*.

Fishing

('000 metric tons, live weight)

	1998	1999	2000
Capture	88.1	92.1	95.6
Common pandora	3.0	3.1	3.1
Sargo breams	2.1	3.0	3.1
Bogue	2.5	3.9	3.1
Jack and horse mackerels	3.9	5.6	4.9
Sardinellas	6.3	7.5	11.8
European pilchard	8.9	13.4	15.0
Chub mackerel	3.2	3.5	2.2
Caramote prawn	3.8	4.7	6.2
Common cuttlefish	4.9	6.6	6.0
Common octopus	3.1	2.3	2.1
Aquaculture	1.8	1.1	1.6
Total catch (incl. others)	89.9	93.2	97.1

Source: FAO, *Yearbook of Fishery Statistics*.

Mining

('000 metric tons, unless otherwise indicated)

	1999	2000	2001*
Crude petroleum ('000 barrels)	30,960	28,207	26,300
Natural gas (million cu m)	1,819	1,985	2,254
Iron ore: gross weight	219	182	204
Iron ore: metal content	119	98	109†
Lead concentrates (metric tons)‡	6,589	6,602	6,820†
Zinc concentrates (metric tons)‡	49,066	41,247	40,000†
Phosphate rock§	8,006	8,339	8,144
Barite (Barytes) (metric tons)	530	3,702	4,000
Salt (marine)	447	620	654
Gypsum (crude)†	110	125	125

* Preliminary figures.

† Estimated production.

‡ Figures refer to metal content of concentrates.

§ Figures refer to gross weight. The estimated phosphoric acid content (in '000 metric tons) was: 2,400 in 1999; 2,500 in 2000; 2,440 in 2001.

Source: US Geological Survey.

Industry

SELECTED PRODUCTS
('000 metric tons, unless otherwise indicated)

	1997	1998	1999
Superphosphates	349	362	384
Phosphoric acid	604	629	905
Cement	4,378	4,588	4,864
Electric power (million kWh)	8,389	8,958	n.a.
Beer ('000 hl)	780	813	911.9
Cigarettes (million units)	7,735	9,813	11,066
Wine ('000 hl)	372	352	469
Olive oil	96	200	180
Flour	697	708	721.3
Refined sugar	75	101	123.5
Crude steel	195	171	231
Quicklime	471	483	475
Motor gasoline	362	294*	n.a.
Kerosene	119	127*	n.a.
Diesel oil	571	560*	n.a.
Residual fuel oil	646	635*	n.a.

* Estimate.

Source: partly UN, *Industrial Commodity Statistics, Yearbook*.

2000 ('000 metric tons, unless otherwise indicated): Cement 5,647.3; Beer ('000 hl) 1,065.7; Wine ('000 hl) 413.3; Olive oil 225; Flour 745.5; Refined sugar 103.2.

2001 ('000 metric tons, unless otherwise indicated): Cement 5,720.4; Beer ('000 hl) 1,087.2; Wine ('000 hl) 336.0; Olive oil 115; Flour 755.6; Refined sugar 102.2.

Finance

CURRENCY AND EXCHANGE RATES

Monetary Units
1,000 millimes = 1 Tunisian dinar (TD)

Sterling, Dollar and Euro Equivalents (31 December 2002)
£1 sterling = 2.150
US $1 = 1.334 dinars
€1 = 1.399 dinars
100 Tunisian dinars = £46.51 = $74.96 = €71.48

Average Exchange Rate (dinars per US $)
2000   1.3707
2001   1.4387
2002   1.4217

BUDGET
(million dinars)*

Revenue†	1997	1998	1999
Taxation	5,224	5,884	6,427
Taxes on income, profits, etc.	1,113	1,294	1,387
Social security contributions	993	1,114	1,220
Taxes on payroll or work-force	78	69	79
Taxes on property	78	83	98
Domestic taxes on goods and services	2,112	2,438	2,733
Value-added tax	1,170	1,443	1,625
Excises	722	775	858
Taxes on international trade	736	751	731
Import duties	717	742	723
Export duties	11	9	9
Other current revenue	702	691	750
Capital revenue	7	5	6
Total	5,933	6,579	7,183

Expenditure‡	1997	1998	1999
General public services	474	549	659
Defence	379	411	424
Public order and safety	548	584	624
Education	1,192	1,263	1,395
Health	437	465	491
Social security and welfare . .	1,030	1,170	1,327
Housing and infrastructure . .	237	264	287
Recreational, cultural and religious affairs and services	166	182	207
Economic affairs and services . .	1,029	1,092	1,151
Agriculture, forestry and fishing	394	418	474
Transport and telecommunications . . .	110	111	184
Other purposes	1,126	1,135	1,302
Total	6,618	7,115	7,866
Current	5,283	5,644	6,153
Capital	1,335	1,471	1,713

* Figures refer to the consolidated accounts of the central Government, including administrative agencies and social security funds. The data exclude the operations of economic and social agencies with their own budgets.

† Excluding grants from abroad (million dinars): 66 in 1997; 89 in 1998; 83 in 1999. Also excluded are receipts from privatization (million dinars): 3 in 1997; 418 in 1998; 1 in 1999.

‡ Excluding net lending (million dinars): 186 in 1997; 108 in 1998.

Source: IMF, *Tunisia: Statistical Appendix* (February 2001).

State Budget (million dinars): *Revenue:* 6,872.5 in 2000; 7,105.4 (estimate) in 2001; 7,561.0 (projection) in 2002. *Expenditure:* 7,524.2 in 2000; 8,025.5 (estimate) in 2001; 8,261.0 (projection) in 2002.

CENTRAL BANK RESERVES
(US $ million at 31 December)

	1999	2000	2001
Gold*	3.5	3.2	3.0
IMF special drawing rights . .	26.5	3.9	1.7
Reserve position in IMF . . .	27.7	26.3	25.3
Foreign exchange	2,207.3	1,780.9	1,962.2
Total	2,265.0	1,814.2	1,992.2

* National valuation.

Source: IMF, *International Financial Statistics*.

MONEY SUPPLY
(million dinars at 31 December)

	1999	2000	2001
Currency outside banks . . .	1,994	2,229	2,376
Demand deposits at commercial banks	3,435	3,779	4,169
Total money (incl. others) . .	5,794	6,369	6,926

Source: IMF, *International Financial Statistics*.

COST OF LIVING
(Consumer Price Index; base: 1990 = 100)

	2000	2001	2002
Food	156.7	159.4	165.3
Housing	144.5	148.5	151.6
Clothing	164.7	167.5	170.0
Transport	150.0	153.4	157.7
All items (incl. others) . . .	155.2	158.2	162.6

NATIONAL ACCOUNTS
(million dinars at current prices)

Expenditure on the Gross Domestic Product

	2000*	2001†	2002†
Government final consumption expenditure.	4,165.0	4,548.7	4,941.7
Private final consumption expenditure.	16,181.4	17,424.4	18,825.3
Increase in stocks	289.6	392.4	464.7
Gross fixed capital formation . .	7,020.3	7,625.0	8,260.0
Total domestic expenditure. .	27,656.3	29,990.5	32,491.7
Exports of goods and services . .	11,868.4	13,360.3	14,290.4
Less Imports of goods and services	12,839.3	14,471.9	15,514.3
GDP in purchasers' values . .	26,685.4	28,878.9	31,267.8
GDP at constant 1990 prices	17,181.2	18,070.7	18,964.2

* Provisional figures.
† Projections.

Source: IMF, *International Financial Statistics*.

Gross Domestic Product by Economic Activity

	1999	2000*	2001*
Agriculture and fishing . . .	3,210.4	3,297.5	3,347.0
Mining (excluding hydrocarbons) .	209.7	234.4	220.1
Manufacturing (excluding hydrocarbons)	4,469.6	4,847.5	5,325.6
Hydrocarbons, electricity and water	1,161.9	1,287.5	1,351.9
Construction and public works .	1,121.0	1,252.4	1,391.2
Transport and telecommunications	1,906.0	2,138.3	2,390.7
Trade, finance, etc.	5,139.9	5,610.0	6,071.4
Hotels and restaurants . . .	1,540.1	1,632.4	1,713.0
Non-market services.	3,335.0	3,593.4	3,913.5
Sub-total	22,094.4†	23,893.7†	25,724.4
Less Imputed bank service charges	722.2	793.9	862.6
GDP at factor cost. . . .	21,372.2	23,099.8	24,861.8
Indirect taxes, *less* subsidies . .	3,299.3	3,585.5	3,931.3
GDP in purchasers' values . .	24,671.6	26,685.3	28,793.1

* Provisional figures.
† Including adjustment.

BALANCE OF PAYMENTS
(US $ million)

	1999	2000	2001
Exports of goods f.o.b.	5,873	5,840	6,006
Imports of goods f.o.b.	−8,014	−8,092	−8,997
Trade balance	−2,141	−2,252	−2,391
Exports of services	2,920	2,767	2,912
Imports of services	−1,234	−1,218	−1,425
Balance on goods and services.	−455	−705	−904
Other income received . . .	89	94	95
Other income paid	−978	−1,036	−1,036
Balance on goods, services and income.	−1,344	−1,647	−1,845
Current transfers received . .	920	825	958
Current transfers paid . . .	−18	—	24
Current balance	−442	−821	−863
Capital account (net)	59	3	53
Direct investment abroad . .	−3	−1	−1
Direct investment from abroad. .	350	752	457
Portfolio investment liabilities . .	10	−20	−15
Other investment assets . . .	−228	−624	−416
Other investment liabilities . .	954	540	1,099
Net errors and omissions . . .	38	−33	−27
Overall balance	738	−205	288

Source: IMF, *International Financial Statistics*.

External Trade

PRINCIPAL COMMODITIES
(distribution by SITC, US $ million)

Imports c.i.f.	1997	1998	1999
Food and live animals . . .	672.8	646.4	506.1
Cereals and cereal preparations .	324.1	303.4	240.2
Crude materials (inedible) except fuels	400.7	374.8	351.1
Mineral fuels, lubricants, etc. .	634.9	436.7	559.2
Petroleum, petroleum products, etc.	512.3	359.6	443.4
Refined petroleum products . .	361.6	261.4	286.2
Chemicals and related products	663.8	710.8	673.6
Basic manufactures	2,152.9	2,474.0	2,296.5
Textile yarn, fabrics, etc. . .	1,245.3	1,440.9	1,330.8
Woven cotton fabrics* . . .	575.5	666.5	605.8
Bleached and mercerized fabrics*.	539.3	634.6	574.1
Woven fabrics of man-made fibres*	339.2	410.4	379.0
Iron and steel.	258.2	318.3	270.5
Machinery and transport equipment.	2,349.2	2,554.9	2,848.5
Machinery specialized for particular industries . . .	368.3	458.3	456.5
General industrial machinery, equipment and parts . .	388.4	443.6	406.6
Electrical machinery, apparatus, etc.	598.5	693.3	633.3
Road vehicles and parts† . .	526.4	527.2	612.3
Passenger motor cars (excl. buses).	284.2	254.2	323.2
Other transport equipment† . .	165.2	122.5	445.5
Aircraft and associated equipment	3.5	90.4	252.6
Miscellaneous manufactured articles.	879.5	932.2	908.3
Clothing and accessories (excl. footwear)	492.5	517.4	476.2
Total (incl. others)	7,947.0	8,347.3	8,336.9

* Excluding narrow or special fabrics.

† Excluding tyres, engines and electrical parts.

Exports f.o.b.	1997	1998	1999
Food and live animals . . .	253.0	277.5	250.4
Mineral fuels, lubricants, etc. .	504.6	369.3	414.6
Petroleum, petroleum products, etc.	503.8	369.1	414.6
Crude petroleum oils, etc. .	376.2	282.1	380.9
Animal and vegetable oils, fats and waxes.	268.1	199.6	341.5
Fixed vegetable oils and fats . .	267.9	199.4	341.3
Olive oil.	263.7	188.8	321.0
Chemicals and related products	694.5	723.1	673.1
Inorganic chemicals	334.0	331.7	312.7
Inorganic chemical elements, oxides and halogen salts .	256.1	246.6	230.7
Manufactured fertilizers . .	279.7	303.7	288.6
Basic manufactures . . .	517.5	568.1	582.6
Machinery and transport equipment.	602.3	738.2	723.7
Electrical machinery, apparatus, etc.	475.8	601.4	585.7
Equipment for distributing electricity.	215.3	257.8	252.0
Miscellaneous manufactured articles.	2,527.9	2,708.2	2,639.7
Clothing and accessories (excl. footwear)	2,298.6	2,474.2	2,375.0
Total (incl. others)	5,559.4	5,737.9	5,788.0

Source: UN, *International Trade Statistics Yearbook.*

PRINCIPAL TRADING PARTNERS
(million dinars)*

Imports c.i.f.	2000	2001	2002
Algeria.	119.9	119.1	128.1
Belgium	402.5	478.6	419.7
China, People's Republic . .	138.2	187.8	198.1
France	3,088.1	3,544.7	3,456.9
Germany	1,126.3	1,322.6	1205.5
Italy	2,243.4	2,620.3	2,632.5
Japan	239.3	254.6	225.1
Libya	437.7	466.0	408.1
Netherlands	244.7	251.2	244.9
Spain	468.4	624.1	669.0
Sweden	161.9	223.9	211.3
Switzerland	109.2	150.0	187.6
United Kingdom	283.6	343.1	319.6
USA	540.8	562.1	427.2
Total (incl. others) . .	11,738.0	13,697.3	13,512.3

Exports f.o.b.	2000	2001	2002
Algeria.	84.3	109.0	121.5
Belgium	406.1	464.2	414.2
France	2,145.7	2,751.3	3,023.2
Germany	1,001.8	1,114.0	1109.8
India	149.1	118.3	114.8
Italy	1,842.2	2,207.0	2,079.1
Libya	288.9	357.5	447.3
Netherlands	280.7	233.9	210.5
Spain	434.4	460.4	460.9
United Kingdom	175.7	226.3	241.6
Total (incl. others) . .	8,004.8	9,503.7	9,646.2

* Imports by country of production; exports by country of last destination.

Transport

RAILWAYS
(traffic)

	1999	2000	2001
Passengers carried ('000) . .	34,410.0	35,581.6	36,819.0
Passenger-kilometres (million) .	1,196.0	1,258.1	1,283.5
Freight carried ('000 metric tons) .	12,551.0	12,370.9	12,294.1
Freight net ton-kilometres (million)	2,373.9	2,283.1	2,286.1

ROAD TRAFFIC
(estimates, motor vehicles in use at 31 December)

	1997	1998	1999
Passenger cars	415,200	445,600	482,700
Commercial vehicles	217,100	233,000	250,300

Source: UN, *Statistical Yearbook.*

SHIPPING

Merchant Fleet
(vessels registered at 31 December)

	1999	2000	2001
Number of vessels	79	78	77
Total displacement ('000 grt) . .	199.5	208.3	202.7

Source: Lloyd's Register-Fairplay, *World Fleet Statistics.*

International Sea-borne Freight Traffic
('000 metric tons)

	1999	2000	2001
Goods loaded*	6,783	6,367	6,777
Goods unloaded	13,154	14,424	14,971

* Excluding Algerian crude petroleum loaded at La Skhirra.

CIVIL AVIATION
(traffic on scheduled services)

	1996	1997	1998
Kilometres flown (million) . . .	18	24	27
Passengers carried ('000) . . .	1,371	1,779	1,888
Passenger-km (million)	2,118	2,479	2,683
Total ton-km (million)	212	249	266

Source: UN, *Statistical Yearbook*.

Tourism

FOREIGN TOURIST ARRIVALS BY NATIONALITY
('000)

	1999	2000	2001
Algeria.	616.4	611.6	623.1
Austria.	138.3	110.2	114.8
Belgium	132.4	139.8	150.7
France	893.7	997.9	1,047.4
Germany	1,036.3	1,011.3	934.7
Italy	354.6	393.9	398.3
Libya	603.1	685.2	1,016.6
Switzerland	110.2	118.4	114.2
United Kingdom	261.9	299.4	314.7
Total (incl. others)	4,813.7	5,057.2	5,387.3

Receipts from tourism (million dinars): 1,950 in 1999; 2,095.1 in 2000; 2,343.0 in 2001.

Communications Media

	1999	2000	2001
Television receivers ('000 in use) .	1,800	1,900	n.a.
Telephones ('000 main lines in use)	850.4	n.a.	15,056.2
Mobile cellular telephones ('000 subscribers).	55.3	n.a.	389.2
Personal computers ('000 in use) .	145	219	230
Internet users ('000)	30	100	400

Radio receivers ('000 in use): 2,060 in 1997.

Facsimile machines (number in use): 31,000 in 1997.

Daily newspapers: 8 (average circulation 280,000) in 1996.

Non-daily newspapers: 25 (estimated average circulation 900,000) in 1996.

Sources: UNESCO, *Statistical Yearbook*; UN, *Statistical Yearbook*; and International Telecommunication Union.

Education

	1999/2000	2000/01	2001/02
Institutions:			
primary	4,497	5,406	4,518
secondary	1,301	1,323	1,356
higher	101	114	128
Teachers:			
primary	60,912	60,706	60,556
secondary	52,432	55,155	57,821
Pupils:			
primary	1,413,795	1,373,904	1,325,707
secondary	965,607	1,015,996	1,074,391
higher	180,044	207,388	225,102

Adult literacy rate (UNESCO estimates): 71.0% (males 81.4%; females 60.6%) in 2000 (Source: UNDP, *Human Development Report*).

Directory

The Constitution

A new Constitution for the Republic of Tunisia was promulgated on 1 June 1959 and amended on 12 July 1988; further amendments were approved by referendum on 26 May 2002. Its main provisions are summarized below:

NATIONAL ASSEMBLY

Legislative power is exercised by the National Assembly, which is elected (at the same time as the President) every five years by direct universal suffrage. Every citizen who has had Tunisian nationality for at least five years and who has attained 20 years of age has the right to vote. The National Assembly shall hold two sessions every year, each session lasting not more than three months. Additional meetings may be held at the demand of the President or of a majority of the deputies.

Note: The constitutional amendments approved in May 2002 envisaged the establishment of a second legislative chamber, the Chamber of Councillors.

HEAD OF STATE

The President of the Republic is both Head of State and Head of the Executive. He must be not less than 40 years of age and not more than 75 (not more than 70, prior to the May 2002 amendments). The President is elected by universal suffrage for a five-year term. The amendments approved in May 2002 removed restrictions on the renewal of the presidential mandate (previously, this was renewable twice consecutively). The President is also the Commander-in-Chief of the army and makes both civil and military appointments. The Government may be censured by the National Assembly, in which case the President may dismiss the Assembly and hold fresh elections. If censured by the new Assembly thus elected, the Government must resign. Should the presidency fall vacant for any reason before the end of a President's term of office, the President of the National Assembly shall take charge of affairs of the state for a period of 45 to 60 days. At the end of this period, a presidential election shall be organized. The President of the National Assembly shall not be eligible as a presidential candidate.

COUNCIL OF STATE

Comprises two judicial bodies: an administrative body dealing with legal disputes between individuals and state or public bodies, and an audit office to verify the accounts of the state and submit reports.

ECONOMIC AND SOCIAL COUNCIL

Deals with economic and social planning and studies projects submitted by the National Assembly. Members are grouped in seven categories representing various sections of the community.

The Government

HEAD OF STATE

President: ZINE AL-ABIDINE BEN ALI (took office on 7 November 1987; re-elected 2 April 1989, 20 March 1994 and 24 October 1999).

COUNCIL OF MINISTERS
(April 2003)

Prime Minister: MUHAMMAD GHANNOUCHI.

Minister of State, Special Adviser to the President: ABD AL-AZIZ BEN DHIA.

Minister of Foreign Affairs: HABIB BEN YAHIA.

Minister of the Interior and Local Development: HÉDI M'HENNI.

Minister of National Defence: DALI JAZI.

Minister of Justice and Human Rights: BÉCHIR TEKKARI.

Minister of Religious Affairs: JEALLOUL JERIBI.

Minister Director of the Presidential Office: Ahmad Iyadhi Ouederni.

Minister of Women's, Family and Children's Affairs: Naziha Ben Yedder.

Minister of Social Affairs and Solidarity: Chedli Neffati.

Minister of Education and Training: Moncer Rouissi.

Minister of Higher Education, Scientific Research and Technology: Sadok Chaâbane.

Minister of Culture, Youth and Leisure: Abdelbaki Hermassi.

Minister of Public Health: Habib M'Barek.

Minister of Sport: Abderrahim Zouari.

Minister of Employment: Chadli Laroussi.

Minister of Finance: Taoufik Baccar.

Minister of Agriculture, the Environment and Water Resources: Habib Haddadi.

Minister of Communication Technologies and Transport: Sadok Rabah.

Minister of Tourism, Trade and Handicrafts: Mondher Zenaidi.

Minister of Equipment, Housing and Territorial Development: Slaheddine Belaïd.

Minister of Development and International Co-operation: Muhammad Nouri Jouini.

Minister of State Domains and Property Affairs: Ridha Grira.

Minister of Industry and Energy: Moncef Ben Abdallah.

Government Secretary-General in charge of Relations with the Chamber of Deputies and the Chamber of Councillors: Muhammad Rachid Kechich.

There are, in addition, 19 Secretaries of State.

MINISTRIES

Ministry of Agriculture, Environment and Water Resources: Centre Urbain Nord, Anana, 2000 Tunis; tel. (71) 704–000; fax (71) 704-430; e-mail boc@mineat.gov.tn.

Ministry of Children and Youth: ave Muhammad Ali Akid, Cité Nationale Sportive, al-Menzah, 1004 Tunis; tel. (71) 841-433; fax (71) 789-047; e-mail mje@ministeres.tn.

Ministry of Communications: 3 bis rue d'Angleterre, 1000 Tunis; tel. (71) 359-000; fax (71) 352-353; e-mail mcom@ministeres.tn.

Ministry of Culture: 8 rue du 2 Mars 1934, la Kasbah, 1006 Tunis; tel. (71) 562-661; fax (71) 574-580; e-mail mcu@ministeres.tn.

Ministry of Economic Development: Place de la monnaie, 1000 Tunis; tel. (71) 351-515; fax (71) 787-234; e-mail mde@ministeres.tn.

Ministry of Education: ave Bab Benat, 1030 Tunis; tel. (71) 263-336; fax (71) 569-230; e-mail med@ministeres.tn.

Ministry of the Environment and Land Planning: Centre Urbain Nord, 2080 Ariana, Tunis; tel. (71) 704-000; fax (71) 702-431; e-mail meat@ministeres.tn.

Ministry of Equipment and Housing: 10 blvd Habib Chita, Cité Jardin, 1002 Tunis; tel. (71) 842-244; fax (71) 780-397; e-mail meh@ministeres.tn.

Ministry of Family and Women's Affairs: 2 rue d'Alger, 1000 Tunis; tel. (71) 332-781; fax (71) 349-900; e-mail maff@email.ati.tn.

Ministry of Finance: place du Gouvernement, 1008 Tunis; tel. (71) 571-888; fax (71) 963-959; e-mail mfi@ministeres.tn.

Ministry of Foreign Affairs: place du Gouvernement, la Kasbah, 1006 Tunis; tel. (71) 660-088; e-mail mae@ministeres.tn.

Ministry of Higher Education: ave Ouled Haffouz, 1030 Tunis; tel. (71) 786-300; fax (71) 786-711; e-mail mes@ministeres.tn.

Ministry of Industry: 37 ave Kheireddine Pacha, 1002 Tunis; tel. (71) 289-368; fax (71) 892-350; e-mail mind@ministeres.tn.

Ministry of the Interior: ave Habib Bourguiba, 1000 Tunis; tel. (71) 333-000; fax (71) 340-888; e-mail mint@ministeres.tn.

Ministry of International Co-operation and Foreign Investment: 98 ave Muhammad V, 1002 Tunis; tel. (71) 798-522; fax (71) 799-069; e-mail mciie@ministeres.tn.

Ministry of Justice: 31 ave Bab Benat, 1006 Tunis; tel. (71) 560-502; fax (71) 586-106; e-mail mju@ministeres.tn.

Ministry of National Defence: blvd Bab Menara, 1030 Tunis; tel. (71) 560-240; fax (71) 561-804; e-mail mdn@ministeres.tn.

Ministry of Professional Training and Employment: 10 ave Ouled Haffouz, 1005 Tunis; tel. (71) 790-838; fax (71) 794-615; e-mail mfpe@ministeres.tn.

Ministry of Public Health: Bab Saâdoun, 1006 Tunis; tel. (71) 560-545; fax (71) 567-100; e-mail msp@ministeres.tn.

Ministry of Religious Affairs: 176 ave Bab Benat, 1009 Tunis; tel. (71) 570-147; fax (71) 570-283; e-mail mar@ministeres.tn.

Ministry of Social Affairs: 25 ave Bab Benat, 1006 Tunis; tel. (71) 567-502; fax (71) 568-722; e-mail mas@ministeres.tn.

Ministry of State Domains: 19 ave de Paris, 1000 Tunis; tel. (71) 341-644; fax (71) 342-410; e-mail mdeaf@ministeres.tn.

Ministry of Tourism, Leisure and Handicrafts: 1 ave Muhammad V, 1001 Tunis; tel. (71) 341-077; fax (71) 332-070; e-mail info@tourismtunisia.com; internet www.tourismtunisia.com.

Ministry of Trade: 37 ave Kheireddine Pacha, 1002 Tunis; tel. (71) 892-313; fax (71) 792-420; e-mail mcmr@ministeres.tn.

Ministry of Transport: rue 8006 Montplaislir par l'ave Muhammad V, Tunis; tel. (71) 781-824; fax (71) 790-149; e-mail mtr@ministeres.tn.

President and Legislature

PRESIDENT

Presidential Election, 24 October 1999

Candidate	Votes	% of votes
Zine al-Abidine Ben Ali	3,269,067	99.45
Muhammad Belhadj Amor	10,492	0.32
Abderrahmane Tlili	7,662	0.23
Total*	3,287,221	100.00

* Excluding 8,779 invalid votes.

ASSEMBLÉE NATIONALE

President: Fouad Mebazaa.

Election, 24 October 1999

Party	Votes	%	Seats
Rassemblement constitutionnel démocratique	2,831,030	91.59	148
Mouvement des démocrates socialistes	98,550	3.19	13
Union démocratique unioniste	52,612	1.70	7
Parti de l'unité populaire	52,054	1.68	7
Mouvement de la rénovation	32,220	1.04	5
Parti social libéral	15,024	0.49	2
Rassemblement socialiste progressiste	5,835	0.19	0
Independents	3,737	0.12	0
Total*	3,091,062	100.00	182†

* Excluding 9,036 spoilt ballot papers.
† Under the terms of an amendment to the electoral code adopted by the National Assembly in 1998, 34 of the 182 seats in the National Assembly were reserved for candidates of opposition parties. These were allotted according to the proportion of votes received nationally by each party.

Political Organizations

Ettajdid (Renewal): Tunis; f. 1993; legal.

Congrès pour la République: Tunis; f. 2001; Leader Moncef Marzouki.

Forum démocratique pour le travail et les libertés (FDTL): Tunis; f. 2002; Leader Dr Mustapha Ben Jafaar.

Mouvement des démocrates socialistes (MDS): Tunis; in favour of a pluralist political system; participated in 1981 election and was officially recognized in Nov. 1983; Political Bureau of 11 mems, National Council of 60 mems, normally elected by the party Congress; Sec.-Gen. Ismail Boulahya.

Mouvement de la rénovation (MR): 6 rue Metouia, 1000 Tunis; tel. (71) 256-400; fax (71) 240-981; f. 1993; Sec.-Gen. Muhammad Harmel.

Mouvement de l'unité populaire (MUP): Tunis; supports radical reform; split into two factions, one led by Ahmad Ben Salah living in exile until 1988; the other became the Parti de l'unité populaire (see below); Co-ordinator Brahim Hayder.

Parti Democratique Progressiste (PDP): Tunis; f. 1983 as Rassemblement socialiste progressiste, officially recognized in Sept. 1988; changed name as above in 2001; leftist; Sec.-Gen. Nejib Chebbi.

Parti de la renaissance—Hizb an-Nahdah: Tunis; formerly Mouvement de la tendance islamique (banned in 1981); Leader RACHED GHANOUCHI; Sec.-Gen. Sheikh ABD AL-FATHA MOUROU.

Parti des ouvriers communistes tunisiens (POCT): Tunis; illegal; Leader HAMMA HAMMANI.

Parti social libéral (PSL): 38 rue Gandhi, 1001 Tunis; tel. and fax (71) 341-093; f. 1988; officially recognized in Sept. 1988 as the Parti social pour le progrès; adopted present name in 1993; liberal; Pres. MOUNIR BEJI; Vice-Pres. HOSNI LAHMAR.

Parti de l'unité populaire (PUP): 7 rue d'Autriche, 1002 Tunis; tel. (71) 289-678; fax (71) 796-031; split from MUP (see above); officially recognized in Nov. 1983; Leader MUHAMMAD BOUCHIHA.

Rassemblement constitutionnel démocratique (RCD): blvd 9 avril 1938, Tunis; e-mail info@rcd.tn; internet www.rcd.tn; f. 1934 as the Néo-Destour Party, following a split in the Destour (Constitution) Party; renamed Parti socialiste destourien in 1964; adopted present name in Feb. 1988; moderate left-wing republican party, which achieved Tunisian independence; Political Bureau of nine mems, and a Cen. Cttee of 200, elected by the party Congress; Chair. ZINE AL-ABIDINE BEN ALI; Vice-Chair. HAMED KAROUI; Sec.-Gen. ALI CHAOUCH.

Rassemblement national arabe: Tunis; banned in 1981; Leader BASHIR ASSAD.

Union démocratique unioniste (UDU): Tunis; officially recognized in Nov. 1988; supports Arab unity; Sec.-Gen. ABDERRAHMANE TLILI.

Diplomatic Representation

EMBASSIES IN TUNISIA

Algeria: 18 rue de Niger, 1002 Tunis; tel. (71) 783-166; fax (71) 788-804; Ambassador SMAÏL ALLAOUA.

Argentina: 10 rue al-Hassan et Houssaine, al-Menzah IV, 1002 Tunis; tel. (71) 231-222; fax (71) 750-058; e-mail fetune@mrecic.gov.ar; Ambassador HÉCTOR TEJERINA.

Austria: 16 rue ibn Hamdiss, BP 23, al-Menzah, 1004 Tunis; tel. (71) 751-091; fax (71) 767-824; e-mail autriche@ambassade_autriche.intl.tn; Ambassador Dr MAXIMILIAN PAMMER.

Bahrain: 72 rue Mouaouia ibn Soufiane, al-Menzah VI, Tunis; tel. (71) 750-865; Ambassador JASSIM BUALLAY.

Belgium: 47 rue du 1er juin, BP 24, 1002 Tunis; tel. (71) 781-655; fax (71) 792-797; Ambassador DANIEL LEROY.

Brazil: 37 ave d'Afrique, BP 64, al-Menzah V, 1004 Tunis; tel. (71) 232-538; fax (71) 750-367; Ambassador LUIZ JORGE RANGEL DE CASTRO.

Bulgaria: 5 rue Ryhane, Cité Mahragène, 1082 Tunis; tel. (71) 798-962; fax (71) 791-667; Ambassador TCHAVDAR TCHERVENKOV.

Canada: 3 rue du Sénégal, place d'Afrique, BP 31, Belvédère, 1002 Tunis; tel. (71) 796-577; fax (71) 792-371; Ambassador JACQUES SIMARD.

China, People's Republic: 41 ave Jugurtha, Mutuelleville, Tunis; tel. (71) 282-090; Ambassador ZHU BANGZAO.

Congo, Democratic Republic: 11 rue Tertullien, Notre Dame, Tunis; tel. (71) 281-833; Ambassador MBOLADINGA KATAKO.

Côte d'Ivoire: 7 rue Fatma al-Fahria, BP 21, Belvédère, 1002 Tunis; tel. (71) 796-601; fax (71) 798-852; Ambassador KOUASSI GUSTAVE OUFFOUÉ.

Cuba: 20 ave du Golfe Arabe, al-Menzah VIII, 1004 Tunis; tel. (71) 712-844; fax (71) 714-198; Ambassador JORGE MANFUGAS-LAVIGNE.

Czech Republic: 98 rue de Palestine, BP 53, Belvédère, 1002 Tunis; tel. (71) 780-456; fax (71) 793-228.

Denmark: 5 rue de Mauritanie, BP 254, Belvédère, 1002 Tunis; tel. (71) 792-600; fax (71) 790-797; e-mail dannebrog@planet.tn; Ambassador HERLUF HANSEN.

Djibouti: Tunis; Ambassador ALI ABDOU MUHAMMAD.

Egypt: ave Muhammad V, Quartier Montplaisir, rue 8007, Tunis; tel. (71) 792-233; fax (71) 794-389; Ambassador MAHDI FATHALLA.

France: 1 place de l'Indépendance, 1000 Tunis; tel. (71) 358-111; fax (71) 358-198; e-mail courrier@ambafrance-tn.org; Ambassador YVES AUBIN DE LA MESSUZIÈRE.

Germany: 1 rue al-Hamra, Mutuelleville, BP 35, 1002 Tunis-Mutuelleville; tel. (71) 786-455; fax (71) 788-242; Ambassador Dr CHRISTOPH DERIX.

Greece: 6 rue Saint Fulgence, Notre Dame, 1082 Tunis; tel. (71) 288-411; fax (71) 789-518; e-mail amb.grec@planet.tn; Ambassador PETROS AVIERINOS.

Hungary: 12 rue Achtart, Nord Hilton, Tunis; tel. (71) 780-544; fax (71) 781-264; e-mail huembtun@planet.tn; Ambassador Dr GYÖRGY SZATHMÀRY.

India: 4 place Didon, Notre Dame, Tunis; tel. (71) 787-819; fax (71) 783-394; e-mail india_emb@emb_india.intl.tn; Ambassador RAM MOHAN.

Indonesia: BP 63, al-Menzah, 1004 Tunis; tel. (71) 860-377; fax (71) 861-758; e-mail ss.alink@kbritun.intl.tn; Ambassador IS ISNAEDI.

Iran: 10 rue de Docteur Burnet, Belvédère, 1002 Tunis; tel. (71) 792-578; Ambassador JAHAN BAKHSH MOZAFARI.

Iraq: ave Tahar B. Achour, route X2 m 10, Mutuelleville, Tunis; tel. (71) 890-633; Ambassador Dr ISAM SHARIF.

Italy: 37 rue Gamal Abd an-Nasser, 1000 Tunis; tel. (71) 321-811; fax (71) 324-155; e-mail seg.ambit@email.ati.tn; Ambassador ARMANDO SANGUINI.

Japan: 9 rue Apollo XI, Cité Mahrajène, BP 163,1082 Tunis; tel. (71) 791-251937; fax (71) 786-625; Ambassador NORITAKE NAI.

Jordan: 87 ave Jugurtha, Mutuelleville, Tunis; tel. (71) 288-401; Ambassador NABIH AN-NIMR.

Korea, Republic: 16 rue Caracalla, Notre Dame, BP 297, 1082 Tunis; tel. (71) 799-905; fax (71) 791-923; Ambassador CHOE IN-SOP.

Kuwait: 40 route Ariane, al-Menzah, Tunis; tel. (71) 236-811; Ambassador MEJREN AHMAD AL-HAMAD.

Libya: 48 bis rue du 1er juin, Tunis; tel. (71) 236-666; Ambassador ABD AL-ATTI OBEIDI.

Mauritania: 17 rue Fatma Ennechi, BP 62, al-Menzah, Tunis; tel. (71) 234-935; Ambassador MOHAMED LAMINE OULD YAHYA.

Morocco: 39 ave du 1er juin, Tunis; tel. (71) 782-775; fax (71) 787-103; Ambassador ABD AL-KADER BENSLIMANE.

Netherlands: 6–8 rue Meycen, Belvédère, BP 47, 1082 Tunis; tel. (71) 797-724; fax (71) 785-557; Ambassador Baron BENTINCK VAN SCHOONHETEN.

Norway: 20 rue de la Kahéna, BP 9, 1082 Tunis; tel. (71) 802-158; fax (71) 801-944; e-mail noramb@planet.tn; Ambassador SVEN OSTRAT OWE.

Pakistan: 7 rue Ali ibn Abi Talib, BP 42, al-Menzah VI, 1004 Tunis; tel. (71) 234-366; fax (71) 752-477; Ambassador Vice-Adm. (rtd) SHAMOON ALAM KHAN.

Poland: 5 Impasse No. 1, rue de Cordoue, El Manar I, Tunis; tel. (71) 873-837; fax (71) 872-987; e-mail polamba.tunis@email.ati.tn; Ambassador RAFAL KARPINSKI.

Portugal: 2 rue Sufétula, Belvédère, 1002 Tunis; tel. (71) 893-981; fax (71) 791-189; Ambassador MANUEL MOREIRA DE ANDRADE.

Qatar: 2 Nahj al-Hakim Bourni, Belvédère, Tunis; tel. (71) 285-600; Chargé d'affaires MAJID AL-ALI.

Romania: 18 ave d'Afrique, al-Menzah V, 1004 Tunis; tel. (71) 766-926; fax (71) 767-695; e-mail amb.roumanie@planet.tn; Chargé d'affaires a.i. NICOLAE IORDACHE.

Russia: 4 rue Bergamotes, BP 48, 2092 el Manar I, Tunis; tel. (71) 882-446; fax (71) 882-478; e-mail russie@emb_rus.intl.tn; Ambassador VENYAMIN V. POPOV.

Saudi Arabia: 16 rue d'Autriche, Belvédère, Tunis; tel. (71) 281-295; Ambassador Sheikh ABBAS FAIK GHAZZAOUI.

Senegal: 122 ave de la Liberté, Tunis; tel. (71) 282-544; Ambassador IBRA DEGUENE KA.

Serbia and Montenegro: 4 rue de Libéria, 1002 Tunis; tel. (71) 783-057; fax (71) 796-482; e-mail yuamb.1@gnet.tn; Ambassador MOMCILO BOJOVIĆ.

Somalia: 6 rue Hadramout, Mutuelleville, Tunis; tel. (71) 289-505; Ambassador AHMAD ABDALLAH MUHAMMAD.

South Africa: 7 rue Achtart, Nord Hilton, 1082 Tunis; tel. (71) 800-311; fax (71) 796-742; e-mail sa@emb-safrica.intl.tn; internet www.southafrica.itnl.tn; Ambassador AUBREY MASIZA J. MFABE.

Spain: 22-24 ave Dr Ernest Conseil, Cité Jardin, 1002 Tunis; tel. (71) 782-217; fax (71) 786-267; Ambassador SENEN FLORENSA PALAU.

Sudan: 30 ave d'Afrique, Tunis; tel. (71) 238-544; fax (71) 750-884.

Sweden: Les Berges du Lac, Lot 12-01-03, Tunis; tel. (71) 860-580; fax (71) 860-810; e-mail ambsuedetunis@planet.tn; Ambassador STAFFAN ÅBERG.

Switzerland: Immeuble Stramica, BP 501, Les Berges du Lac, 1025 Tunis; tel. (71) 962-997; fax (71) 965-796; e-mail swissembtun@email.ati.tn; Ambassador PETER VON GRAFFENRIED.

Syria: 119 Azzouz Ribai-Almanar 3, Tunis; tel. (71) 888-188; Ambassador Dr SAMI GLAIEL.

Turkey: Lot 4, ave heidi Karray, Centre Urban Nord, 1082 Tunis; tel. (71) 750-668; fax (71) 767-045; e-mail tunus.be@planet.tn; Ambassador H. SELAH KORUTÜRK.

Ukraine: 30 rue du docteur Burnet, Mutuelleville, 1002 Tunis; tel. (71) 849-861; fax (71) 840-866.

United Arab Emirates: 15 rue du 1er juin, Mutuelleville, Tunis; tel. (71) 783-522; Ambassador HAMAD SALEM AL-MAQAMI.

United Kingdom: 5 place de la Victoire, 1000 Tunis; tel. (71) 341-444; fax (71) 354-877; e-mail british.emb@planet.tn; internet www.british-emb.intl.tn; Ambassador ROBIN KEALY.

USA: 144 ave de la Liberté, 1002 Tunis; tel. (71) 782-566; fax (71) 789-719; internet usembassy.state.gov/tunis; Ambassador RUST DEMING.

Venezuela: 30 rue de Niger, 1002 Tunis; tel. (71) 285-075; Ambassador JOSÉ ANTONIO QUIJADA SÁNCHEZ.

Yemen: rue Mouaouia ibn Soufiane, al-Menzah VI, Tunis; tel. (71) 237-933; Ambassador RASHID MUHAMMAD THABIT.

Judicial System

The **Cour de Cassation** in Tunis has three civil and one criminal sections. There are three **Cours d'Appel** at Tunis, Sousse and Sfax, and 13 **Cours de Première Instance,** each having three chambers, except the **Cour de Première Instance** at Tunis which has eight chambers. **Justices Cantonales** exist in 51 areas.

Religion

The Constitution of 1956 recognizes Islam as the state religion, with the introduction of certain reforms, such as the abolition of polygamy. An estimated 99% of the population are Muslims. Minority religions include Judaism (an estimated 2,000 adherents in 1993) and Christianity. The Christian population comprises Roman Catholics, Greek Orthodox and French and English Protestants.

ISLAM

Grand Mufti of Tunisia: Sheikh MUHAMMAD HABIR BELKHODJA.

CHRISTIANITY

Reformed Church of Tunisia: 36 rue Charles de Gaulle, 1000 Tunis; tel. (71) 327-886; e-mail williambrown@bigfoot.com; internet members.truepath.com/ertunis; f. 1880; c.100 mems; Pastor WILLIAM BROWN.

Roman Catholic Church: 4 rue d'Alger, 1000 Tunis; tel. (71) 335-831; fax (71) 335-832; e-mail eveche.tunisie@gnet.tn; f. 1964; Bishop of Tunis Most Rev. FOUAD TWAL; 22,000 adherents (2000).

The Press

DAILIES

Ach-Chourouk (Sunrise): 10 rue ach-Cham, Tunis; tel. (71) 834-000; fax (71) 830-337; Dir SLAHEDDINE AL-AMRI; circ. 70,000.

El-Horria: 8 rue de Rome, Tunis; tel. (71) 352-255; Arabic; organ of the RCD; Dir MUHAMMAD HEDI TRIKI; circ. 50,000.

La Presse de Tunisie: 6 rue Ali Bach-Hamba, Tunis; tel. (71) 341-066; fax (71) 349-720; e-mail contact@lapresse.tn; internet www.lapresse.tn; f. 1936; French; Dir MONCEF GOUJA; circ. 40,000.

Le Quotidien: 25 rue Jean Jaures, 1000 Tunis; f. 2001; French; Dir SLAHEDDINE AL-AMRI; circ. 30,000.

Le Renouveau: 8 rue de Rome, 1000 Tunis; tel. (71) 352-255; fax (71) 351-927; internet www.tunisieinfo.com/LeRenouveau/; f. 1988; organ of the RCD; French; Dir ZOHRA BEN ROMDHANE; Editor ZINE AMARA.

As-Sabah (The Morning): blvd du 7 novembre, BP 441, al-Menzah, 1004 Tunis; tel. (71) 717-222; fax (71) 718-420; e-mail info@assabah.com.tn; internet www.tunisie.com/Assabah; f. 1951; Arabic; Dir HABIB CHEIKHROUHOU; circ. 50,000.

As-Sahafa: 6 rue Ali Bach-Hamba, Tunis; tel. (71) 341-066; fax (71) 349-720; internet www.sahafa.com; f. 1936; Arabic; Dir MONCEF GUUJA.

Le Temps: 4 rue Ali Bach-Hamba, Tunis; tel. (71) 340-222; f. 1975; French; Dir HABIB CHEIKHROUHOU; circ. 42,000.

PERIODICALS

Afrique Economie: 16 rue de Rome, BP 61, 1015 Tunis; tel. (71) 347-441; fax (71) 353-172; e-mail iea@planet.tn; f. 1970; monthly; Dir MUHAMMAD ZERZERI.

Al-Akhbar (The News): 1 passage d'al-Houdaybiyah, Tunis; tel. (71) 344-100; f. 1984; weekly; general; Dir MUHAMMAD BEN YOUSUF; circ. 75,000.

Les Annonces: 6 rue de Sparte, BP 1343, Tunis; tel. (71) 350-177; fax (71) 347-184; f. 1978; 2 a week; French/Arabic; Dir MUHAMMAD NEJIB AZOUZ; circ. 170,000.

Al-Anouar at-Tounissia (Tunisian Lights): 10 rue ach-Cham, 1002 Tunis; tel. (71) 331-000; fax (71) 340-600; SLAHEDDINE AL-AMRI; circ. 165,000.

L'Avenir: 26 rue Gamal Abd an-Nasser, BP 1200, Tunis; tel. (71) 258-941; f. 1980; weekly; organ of Mouvement des démocrates socialistes (MDS).

Al-Bayan (The Manifesto): 87 ave Jughurta, Belvédère, 1002 Tunis; tel. (71) 791-098; fax (71) 796-400; f. 1977; weekly; general; Dir HÉDI DJILANI; circ. 120,000.

Al-Biladi (My Country): 15 rue 2 mars 1934, Tunis; f. 1974; Arabic; political and general weekly for Tunisian workers abroad; Dir HÉDI AL-GHALI; circ. 90,000.

Bulletin Mensuel de Statistiques: Institut National de la Statistique, 70 rue Ech-cham, BP 265, 1080 Tunis; tel. (71) 891-002; fax (71) 792-559; e-mail ins@email.ati.tn; internet www.ins.nat.tn; monthly.

Conjoncture: 37 ave Kheireddine Pacha, 1002 Tunis; tel. (71) 784-223; fax (71) 782-742; f. 1974; monthly; economic and financial surveys; Dir HOSNI TOUMI; circ. 5,000.

Démocratie: Tunis; f. 1978; monthly; French; organ of the MDS; Dir HASSIB BEN AMMAR; circ. 5,000.

Dialogue: 15 rue 2 mars 1934, Tunis; tel. (71) 264899; f. 1974; weekly; French; cultural and political organ of the RCD; Dir NACEUR BECHEKH; circ. 30,000.

Etudiant Tunisien: Tunis; f. 1953; French and Arabic; Chief Editor FAOUZI AOUAM.

Al-Fajr (Dawn): Tunis; f. 1990; weekly; Arabic; publ. of the Hizb an-Nahdah movement; Dir HAMADI JEBALI (imprisoned Jan. 1991).

Al-Falah: rue Alain Savary, al-Khadra, 1003 Tunis; tel. (71) 800-800; fax (71) 797-292; weekly; agricultural; Dir ABD AL-BAKI BACHA; Editor GHARBI HAMOUDA; circ. 7,000.

Al-Fikr (Thought): Tunis; f. 1955; monthly; Arabic; cultural review.

L'Hebdo Touristique: rue 8601, 40, Zone Industrielle, La Charguia 2, 2035 Tunis; tel. (71) 786-866; fax (71) 794-891; f. 1971; weekly; French; tourism; Dir TIJANI HADDAD; circ. 5,000.

IBLA: Institut des Belles Lettres Arabes, 12 rue Jemaâ el-Haoua, 1008 Tunis; tel. (71) 560-133; fax (71) 572-683; e-mail ibla@gnet.tn; 2 a year; French; social and cultural review on Maghreb and Muslim-Arab affairs; Dirs J. FONTAINE; and; D. BOND; circ. 800.

Al-Idhaa wa Talvaza (Radio and Television): 71 ave de la Liberté, Tunis; tel. (71) 287-300; fax (71) 781-058; f. 1956; fortnightly; Arabic language broadcasting magazine; Dir Gen. ABD AL-HAFIDH HERGUEM; Editor WAHID BRAHAM; circ. 10,000.

Irfane (Children): 6 rue Muhammad Ali, 1000 Tunis; tel. (71) 256-877; fax (71) 351-521; f. 1965; monthly; Arabic; Dir-Gen. RIDHA EL OUADI; circ. 100,000.

Jeunesse Magazine: 6 rue Muhammad Ali, 1000 Tunis; tel. (71) 256-877; fax (71) 351-521; f. 1980; monthly; Arabic; Dir-Gen. RIDHA EL OUADI; circ. 30,000.

Journal Officiel de la République Tunisienne: ave Farhat Hached, 2040 Radès; tel. (71) 299-914; fax (71) 297-234; f. 1860; the official gazette; French and Arabic editions published twice weekly by the Imprimerie Officielle (The State Press); Pres. and Dir-Gen. ROMDHANE BEN MIMOUN; circ. 20,000.

Al-Maoukif: Tunis; weekly; organ of the Rassemblement socialiste progressiste; Dir AHMAD NEJIB CHABI.

Al-Maraa (The Woman): 56 blvd Bab Benat, 1006 Tunis; tel. (71) 567-845; fax (71) 567-131; e-mail unft@email.a.t.i.tn; f. 1961; monthly; Arabic/French; political, economic and social affairs; issued by the Union Nationale de la Femme Tunisienne; Pres. CHEDLIA BOUKHCHINA; circ. 10,000.

Le Mensuel: Tunis; f. 1984; monthly; economic, social and cultural affairs.

Al-Moussawar: 10 rue ach-Cham, Tunis; tel. (71) 289-000; fax (71) 289-357; weekly; circ. 75,000.

Outrouhat: Tunis; monthly; scientific; Dir LOTFI BEN AISSA.

Ar-Rai (Opinion): Tunis; f. 1977 by MDS; weekly; opposition newspaper; Dir HASSIB BEN AMAR; circ. 20,000.

Réalités: 85 rue de Palestine, Belvédère, BP 227, 1002 Tunis; tel. (71) 788-313; fax (71) 893-489; f. 1979; weekly; French/Arabic; Dir TAÏEB ZAHAR; circ. 25,000.

At-Tariq al-Jadid (New Road): 6 rue Metouia, Tunis; tel. (71) 256-400; fax (71) 350-748; e-mail sof@realites.com.tn; internet www .tunisieinfo.com/realites; f. 1981; organ of the Mouvement de la rénovation; Editor MUHAMMAD HARMEL.

Tounes al-Khadra: rue Alain Savary, 1003 Tunis; tel. (71) 800-800; fax (71) 798-598; f. 1976; monthly; agricultural, scientific and technical; Dir ABD AL-BAKI BACHA; Editor GHARBI HAMOUDA; circ. 5,000.

Tunis Hebdo: 1 passage d'al-Houdaybiyah, Tunis; tel. (71) 344-100; fax (71) 355-079; internet www.tunishebdo.com.tn; f. 1973; weekly; French; general and sport; Dir M'HAMEÓ BEN YOUSUF; circ. 35,000.

Tunisia News: rue 8601, 40, Zone Industrielle, La Charguia 1, 2035 Tunis; tel. (71) 786-866; fax (71) 794-891; e-mail haddad.tijani@ planet.tn; f. 1993; weekly; English; Dir TIJANI HADDAD; circ. 5,000.

NEWS AGENCIES

Tunis Afrique Presse (TAP): 7 ave Slimane Ben Slimane, 2092 al-Manar, Tunis; tel. (71) 889-000; fax (71) 883-500; f. 1961; Arab, French and English; offices in Algiers, Rabat, Paris and New York; daily news services; Chair. and Gen. Man. BRAHIM FRIDHI.

Foreign Bureaux

Agence France-Presse (AFP): 45 ave Habib Bourguiba, Tunis; tel. (71) 337-896; fax (71) 352-414; e-mail pvro.afp@gnet.tn; Chief PATRICK VAN ROEKEGHEM.

Agencia EFE (Spain): 126 rue de Yougoslavie, 1000 Tunis; tel. (71) 321-497; fax (71) 325-976; e-mail manostos@gnet.tn; Chief MANUEL OSTOS LÓPEZ.

Agenzia Nazionale Stampa Associata (ANSA) (Italy): Tunis; Chief MANUELA FONTANA.

Informatsionnoye Telegrafnoye Agentstvo Rossii—Telegrafnoye Agentstvo Suverennykh Stran (ITAR—TASS) (Russia): Tunis; Chief VIKTOR LEBEDEV.

Inter Press Service (IPS) (Italy): 80 ave Tahar Ben Ammar, al-Menzah IX, 1013 Tunis; tel. (71) 880-182; fax (71) 880-848; f. 1976; Chief ABD AL-MAJID BEJAR.

Kuwait News Agency (KUNA): Tunis; tel. (71) 717-624; fax (71) 718-062.

Reuters (United Kingdom): 3 rue Ibn Rachiq, BP 369, Belvédère, 1002 Tunis; tel. (71) 787-711; fax (71) 787-454; Senior Correspondent ABD AL-AZIZ BARROUHI.

Rossiiskoye Informatsionnoye Agentstvo—Novosti (RIA—Novosti) (Russia): 102 ave de la Liberté, Tunis; tel. (71) 283-781; Chief NICOLAS SOLOGUBOVSKII.

Saudi Press Agency (SPA): Tunis.

Xinhua (New China) News Agency (People's Republic of China): 6 rue Smyrne, Notre Dame, Tunis; tel. (71) 281-308; Dir XIE BINYU.

Publishers

Addar al-Arabia Lil Kitab: 4 ave Mohieddine El Klibi, al-Manar, BP 32, al-Manar 2, 2092 Tunis; tel. (71) 888-255; fax (71) 888-365; f. 1975; general literature, children's books, non-fiction; Dir-Gen. REBAH DEKHILI.

Agence de Promotion de l'Industrie (API): 63 rue de Syrie, Belvédère, 1002 Tunis; tel. (71) 792-144; fax (71) 782-482; e-mail api@api.com.tn; internet www.tunisieindustrie.nat.tn; f. 1987 by merger; responsible for the implementation of the Government's policies relative to the promotion of the industrial sector; provides a support structure for companies and promoters; 23 regional offices; Gen. Man. KHELIL LAGIMI.

Bouslama Editions: 15 ave de France, 1000 Tunis; tel. (71) 243-745; fax (71) 381-100; f. 1960; history, children's books; Man. Dir ALI BOUSLAMA.

Ceres Productions: rue Lac Victoria, Immeuble Lac des Cygnes, 2035 Les Berges du Lac; tel. (71) 960-980; fax (71) 960-977; e-mail nbic.ceres@planet.tn; f. 1964; art books, literature, novels; Pres. MUHAMMAD BEN SMAIL.

Dar al-Amal: 8 rue de Rome, Tunis; tel. (71) 352-255; f. 1976; economics, sociology, politics; Dir-Gen. MAHMOUD MEFTAH.

Dar al-Kitab: 5 ave Bourguiba, 4000 Sousse; tel. (73) 25097; f. 1950; literature, children's books, legal studies, foreign books; Pres. TAIEB KACEM; Dir FAYÇAL KACEM.

Dar as-Sabah: Centre Interurbain, BP 441, al-Menzah, 1004 Tunis; tel. (71) 717-222; fax (71) 718-366; f. 1951; 200 mems; publishes daily and weekly papers which circulate throughout Tunisia, North Africa, France, Belgium, Luxembourg and Germany; Dir-Gen. MONCEF CHEIKHROUHOU.

Institut National de la Statistique: 70 rue Ech-Cham, BP 265, 1080 Tunis; tel. (71) 891-002; fax (71) 792-559; e-mail ins@email.ati .tn; internet www.ins.nat.tn; publishes a variety of annuals, periodicals and papers concerned with the economic policy and devt of Tunisia.

Librairie al-Manar: 60 ave Bab Djedid, Case Postale 179, 1008 Tunis; tel. (71) 253-224; fax (71) 336-565; e-mail librairie.almanar@ planet.tn; f. 1938; general, educational, Islam; Man. Dir HABIB M'HAMDI.

Maison Tunisienne d'Edition: Tunis; f. 1966; all kinds of books, magazines, etc. Dir ABDELAZIZ ACHOURI.

En-Najah—Editions Hedi Ben Abdelgheni: 11 ave de France, 1000 Tunis; tel. (71) 334-246; fax (71) 336-471; Arab and French books, Koranic texts.

Société d'Arts Graphiques, d'Edition et de Presse: 15 rue 2 mars 1934, La Kasbah, Tunis; tel. (71) 264-988; fax (71) 569-736; f. 1974; prints and publishes daily papers, magazines, books, etc. Chair. and Man. Dir HASSEN FERJANI.

Sud Editions: 79 rue de Palestine, 1002 Tunis; tel. (71) 785-179; fax (71) 792-905; f. 1976; Arab literature, art and art history; Man. Dir M. MASMOUDI.

Government Publishing House

Imprimerie Officielle de la République Tunisienne: ave Farhat Hached, 2040 Radès; tel. (71) 434-211; fax (71) 434-234; f. 1860; Man. Dir ROMDHANE BEN MIMOUN.

Broadcasting and Communications

TELECOMMUNICATIONS

Société Tunisienne d'Entreprises des Télécommunications (SOTETEL): rue des Entrepreneurs, Zone Industrielle, la Charguia 2, 1080 Tunis; tel. (71) 703-345; internet www.sototel.com.tn; transferred to private ownership in 1998.

Orascom Telecom Tunisia: Tunis; Chair. FETHI HOUDI; CEO JEAN-PIERRE ROELAND.

Tunisie Télécom: 41 rue Asdrubal, 1002 Tunis; tel. (71) 801-717; fax (71) 800-777; internet www.tunisietelecom.tn; CEO KHÉDIJA GHARIANI; Gen. Man. AHMED MAHJOUB.

BROADCASTING

Radio

Etablissement de la Radiodiffusion-Télévision Tunisienne (ERTT): 71 ave de la Liberté, 1002 Tunis; tel. (71) 847-300; fax (71) 781-058; e-mail presidence@ertt.net.tn; internet www.radiotunis .com; govt service; broadcasts in Arabic, French, Italian, Spanish and English; stations at Gafsa, El-Kef, Monastir, Sfax, Tataouine and Tunis (three); Pres. RAOUF BASTI.

Television

Etablissement de la Radiodiffusion-Télévision Tunisienne: see Radio.

Office National de la Télédiffusion (ONT): 13 rue de Bizerte, 1006 Tunis; tel. (71) 794-609.

Television was introduced in northern and central Tunisia in January 1966, and by 1972 transmission covered the country. A relay station to link up with European transmissions was built at al-Haouaria in 1967, and a second channel was introduced in 1983.

Finance

(cap. = capital; dep. = deposits; res = reserves; m. = million; brs = branches; amounts in dinars unless otherwise stated)

BANKING

Central Bank

Banque Centrale de Tunisie (BCT): 25 rue Hédi Nouira, BP 369, 1080 Tunis; tel. (71) 340-588; fax (71) 354-214; e-mail bct@bct.gov.tn; internet www.bct.gov.tn; f. 1958; cap. 6.0m., dep. 2,099.8m., res

20.2m., total assets 4,666.8m., (Dec. 1999); Gov. Muhammad Daouas; 10 brs.

Commercial Banks

AMEN Bank: ave Muhammad V, 1002 Tunis; tel. (71) 835-500; fax (71) 834-770; e-mail amen.bank@amenbank.com.tn; internet www .amenbank.com.tn; f. 1967 as Crédit Foncier et Commercial de Tunisie; changed name as above in 1995; cap. and res 85.3m., total assets 1,348.5m. (Dec. 1998); Chair. and Pres. Rachid Ben Yedder; Gen. Man. Ahmed El Karm; 73 brs.

Arab Banking Corpn Tunisie: ABC Building, rue du Lac d'Annecy, Les Berges du Lac, 1053 Tunis; tel. (71) 861-861; fax (71) 860-921; e-mail abc.tunis@arabbanking.com; internet www .arabbanking.com; f. 2000; cap. 18m. CEO Ezzedine Saidane; 3 brs.

Arab Tunisian Bank: 9 rue Hédi Nouira, POB 520, 1001 Tunis; tel. (71) 351-155; fax (71) 349-278; e-mail atbbank@atb.com.tn; internet www.atb.com.tn; f. 1982; cap. 35m., res 46.2m., dep. 810.5m. (Dec. 2000); Dir-Gen. Hammouda Belkhodja; 30 brs.

Banque de l'Habitat: 21 ave Kheireddine Pacha, BP 242, 1002 Tunis; tel. (71) 785-277; fax (71) 784-417; e-mail banquehabitat@bh .fin.tn; f. 1984; 57.4% govt-owned; cap. and res 79.3m., total assets 1,590.7m. (Dec. 1998); Chair. Tahar Bourkhis; 49 brs.

Banque Internationale Arabe de Tunisie (BIAT): 70–72 ave Habib Bourguiba, BP 520, 1080 Tunis; tel. (71) 340-733; fax (71) 340-680; e-mail abderrazak.lahiani@biat.com.tn; internet www.biat.com .tn; f. 1976; cap. 100.0m., res 99.6m., dep. 1,994.8m. (Dec. 2000); Pres. Mokhtar Fakhfakh; 92 brs.

Banque Nationale Agricole: rue Hédi Nouira, 1001 Tunis; tel. (71) 831-000; fax (71) 835-551; f. 1989 by merger of the Banque Nationale du Développement Agricole and the Banque Nationale de Tunisie; cap. 100.0m., res 226.5m., dep. 2,453.3m. (Dec. 2000); Chair. Muhammad Ferid Ben Tanfous; Gen. Man. Fadhel Ben Othman; 140 brs.

Banque du Sud: 95 ave de la Liberté, 1002 Tunis; tel. (71) 849-400; fax (71) 782-663; e-mail courier@banksud.com.tn; internet www .banksud.com.tn; f. 1968; cap. 100.0m., res 42.6m., dep. 969.1m. (1999); Pres. Laroussi Bayoudh; 86 brs.

Banque de Tunisie SA: 2 rue de Turquie, BP 289, 1001 Tunis; tel. (71) 332-188; fax (71) 347-756; e-mail finance@bt.com.tn; f. 1884; cap. 40.0m., res 60.6m., dep. 944.7m. (Dec. 2001); Chair. and Man. Dir Faouzi Bel Kahia; 5 brs and 77 agencies.

Citibank N.A.: 55 ave Jugurtha, BP 72, Belvédère, 1001 Tunis; tel. (71) 790-066; fax (71) 785-556; f. 1989; cap. 10m., total assets 387m. (Dec. 1998); Gen. Man. Nayera N. Amin; 2 brs.

Société Tunisienne de Banque (STB): rue Hédi Nouira, BP 638, 1001 Tunis; tel. (71) 340-477; fax (71) 348-400; internet www.stb .com.tn; f. 1957; 50% govt-owned; merged with Banque Nationale de Développement Touristique and Banque de Développement Econo-mique de Tunisie in 2000; cap. 124.3m., res 228.6m., dep. 2,281.0m. (Dec. 2000); Chair. and Gen. Man. Ali Debaya; 113 brs.

Union Bancaire pour le Commerce et l'Industrie: 139 ave de la Liberté, Belvédère, 1002 Tunis; tel. (71) 340-635; fax (71) 328-823; e-mail dg@ubci.com.tn; internet www.ubci.com.tn; f. 1961; cap. 35.0m., res 82.9m., dep. 875.4. (Dec. 2000); affiliated to Banque Nationale de Paris Intercontinentale; Pres. and Gen. Man. Slah Eddine Bougerra; 39 brs.

Union Internationale de Banques SA: 65 ave Habib Bourguiba, BP 109, 1000 Tunis; tel. (71) 347-000; fax (71) 353-090; e-mail nessafiuib@planet.tn; f. 1963 as a merging of Tunisian interests by the Société Tunisienne de Banque with Crédit Lyonnais (France) and other foreign banks, including Banca Commerciale Italiana; cap. and res 97.5m., total assets 1,323.1m. (Dec. 1998); scheduled for privatization in 2002; Pres. and Gen. Man. Brahim Saâda; 94 brs.

Merchant Banks

Banque d'Affaires de Tunisie (BAT): Les Berges du Lac, 1001 Tunis; tel. (71) 860-080; fax (71) 861-081; f. 1997; cap. 3m. Gen. Man. Arnaud Dinashin.

International Maghreb Merchant Bank (IM Bank): Immeuble Maghrebia, Bloc B, 2035 Tunis; tel. (71) 860-816; fax (71) 860-057; f. 1995; auth. cap. 3m., total assets 3.1m. (Dec. 1995); Pres. Moncef Cheikh-Rouhou; CEO Kacem Bousnina.

Development Banks

Banque Arabe Tuniso-Libyenne pour le Développement et le Commerce Extérieur: 25 ave Kheireddine Pacha, BP 102, Belvé-dère, 1002 Tunis; tel. (71) 781-500; fax (71) 782-818; f. 1983; pro-motes trade and devt projects between Tunisia and Libya, and provides funds for investment in poorer areas; cap. 100.0m., res 17.6m., dep. 38.7m. (Dec. 1999); Chair. Said M'rabet.

Banque de Coopération du Maghreb Arabe: ave Muhammad V, BP 46, Belvédère, 1002 Tunis; tel. (71) 780-311; fax (71) 781-056; f. 1981; began operations 1982; finances jt devt projects between Tunisia and Algeria; cap. and res US $53.7m., total assets $77.8m. (Dec. 1998); Chair. Abdelkarim Lakehal; Gen. Man. Chafik Ben Hamza.

Banque de Tunisie et des Emirats d'Investissement: 5 bis Blvd Muhammad Badra, 1002 Tunis; tel. (71) 783-600; fax (71) 783-756; scheduled to merge with Union Internationale de Banques.

Banque Tunisienne de Solidarité: 56 ave Muhammad V, 1002 Tunis; tel. (71) 849-400; fax (71) 847-352; e-mail BTS@e-mail.ati.tn; f. 1997; provides long-term finance for small-scale projects; cap. 30m. Pres. Anouar Belarbi.

Banque Tuniso-Koweïtienne de Développement: 10 bis ave Muhammad V, BP 49, 1001 Tunis; tel. (71) 340-000; fax (71) 343-106; e-mail ask@btkd-bank.com; internet www.btkd-bank.com; f. 1981; provides long-term finance for devt projects; cap. 100m., res 74.9m. (Dec. 2000); Dir-Gen. Anouar Belarbi.

Société Tuniso-Séoudienne d'Investissement et de Dével-oppement (STUSID): 32 rue Hédi Karray, BP 20, 1002 Tunis; tel. (71) 718-233; fax (71) 719-515; e-mail stusid@gnet.tn; f. 1981; pro-vides long-term finance for devt projects; cap. and res 173.8m., total assets 237.3m. (Dec. 1998); Chair. Dr Mahsoun Bahjet Jalal; Pres. Abdelghaffar Ezzeddine.

'Offshore' Banks

Alubaf International Bank: BP 51, rue Montplaisir, Belvédère, 1002 Tunis; tel. (71) 783-500; fax (71) 793-905; e-mail alub.tn@gnet .tn; f. 1985; cap. US $25.0m., res 5,618m., dep. 49,210m. (Dec. 2000); Pres. Muhammad Abduljawad; Gen. Man. Farag Ali Gamra.

Arab Banking Corpn Tunis: ABC Bulding, rue du Lac d'Annecy, Les Berges du Lac, 1053 Tunis; tel. (71) 861-861; fax (71) 860-921; e-mail abc.tunis@arabbanking.com; internet www.arabbanking .com; f. 1993; cap. US $6m., res 5,645m. Gen. Man. Ezzedine Saidane.

Beit Ettamwil Saudi Tounsi (BEST): 88 ave Hédi Chaker, 1002 Tunis; tel. (71) 790-000; fax (71) 780-235; f. 1983; cap. US $50m., total assets $156.0m. (Dec. 1996); Pres. Dr Salah Jemil Malaika.

North Africa International Bank: BP 485, 1080 Tunis; tel. (71) 950-800; fax (71) 950-840; f. 1984; cap. US $30.0m., res $12.0m. (2001); Pres., Chair. and Gen. Man. Saddiq M. Hijjaji.

Tunis International Bank: 18 ave des Etats-Unis d'Amérique, BP 81, 1002 Tunis; tel. (71) 782-411; fax (71) 782-479; e-mail tib1-tib@ planet.tn; f. 1982; cap. US $25.0m., res 9.6m., dep. 185.3m. (Dec. 2000); Chair. Zouhair Khouri; 3 brs.

STOCK EXCHANGE

Bourse de Tunis: Centre Babel, Bloc E, Zone Montplaisir, 1002 Tunis; tel. (71) 799-414; fax (71) 789-189; e-mail hamdi.bannour@ bvmt.com.tn; internet www.bvmt.com.tn; Chair. Ahmed Haddouej.

INSURANCE

Caisse Tunisienne d'Assurances Mutuelles Agricoles: 6 ave Habib Thameur, 1069 Tunis; tel. (71) 340-933; fax (71) 332-276; f. 1912; Pres. Moktar Bellagha; Dir-Gen. Mezri Jelizi.

Cie d'Assurances Tous Risques et de Réassurance (ASTREE): 45 ave Kheireddine Pacha, BP 780, 1002 Tunis; tel. (71) 792-211; fax (71) 794-723; f. 1950; cap. 4m. dinars; Pres. and Dir-Gen. Muhammad Hachicha.

Cie Tunisienne pour l'Assurance du Commerce Extérieur (COTUNACE): ave Muhammad V/Montplaisir I, rue 8006, 1002 Tunis; tel. (71) 783-000; fax (71) 782-539; e-mail cotunace2@email .ati.tn; internet www.cotunace.com.tn; f. 1984; cap. 5m. dinars; 65 mem. cos; Pres. and Dir-Gen. Moncef Zouari.

Lloyd Tunisien: 7 ave de Carthage, 1000 Tunis; tel. (71) 340-911; fax (71) 340-909; f. 1945; fire, accident, liability, marine, life; cap. 1m. dinars; Chair. and Man. Dir Abd al-Karim Merdassi.

Société Tunisienne d'Assurance et de Réassurance (STAR): ave de Paris, Tunis; tel. (71) 340-866; fax (71) 340-835; f. 1958.

Tunis-Ré (Société Tunisienne de Réassurance): ave Muhammad V, Montplaisir 1, POB 133, 1082 Tunis; tel. (71) 844-011; fax (71) 787-573; e-mail tunis.re@email.ati.tn; f. 1981; various kinds of reinsur-ance; cap. 24.4m. dinars; Chair. and Gen. Man. Muhammad el-Fateh Maherzi.

Trade and Industry

GOVERNMENT AGENCIES

Centre de Promotion des Exportations (CEPEX): 28 rue Ghandi, 1001 Tunis; tel. (71) 350-344; fax (71) 353-683; e-mail cepexedpuc@attmail.com; f. 1973; state export promotion org. Pres. and Dir-Gen. HAMDANE BEN OTHMAN.

Foreign Investment Promotion Agency (FIPA): Centre Urbain Nord, 1004 Tunis; tel. (71) 7032-140; fax (71) 702-600; e-mail fipa.tunisia@mci.gov.tn; internet www.investintunisia.com; f. 1995; Dir-Gen. ABDESSALEM MANSOUR.

Office du Commerce de Tunisie (OCT): 1 rue de Syrie, 1060 Tunis; tel. (71) 682-901; Dir-Gen. MUHAMMAD AMOR.

CHAMBERS OF COMMERCE AND INDUSTRY

Chambre de Commerce et d'Industrie de Tunis: 1 rue des Entrepreneurs, 1000 Tunis; tel. (71) 350-300; fax (71) 354-744; e-mail ccitunis@planet.tn; f. 1885; 25 mems; Pres. JILANI BENM'BAREK.

Chambre de Commerce et d'Industrie du Centre: rue Chadli Khaznadar, 4000 Sousse; tel. (73) 225-044; fax (73) 224-227; f. 1895; 25 mems; Pres. KABOUDI MONCEF; Dir FATEN BASLY.

Chambre de Commerce et d'Industrie du Nord-Est: Tom Bereaux Bizerte Center, Angle rues 1er Mai, Med Ali, 7000 Bizerte; tel. (72) 431-044; fax (72) 431-922; f. 1903; 5 mems; Pres. KAMEL BELKAHIA; Dir MOUFIDA CHAKROUN.

Chambre de Commerce et d'Industrie de Sfax: 10 rue Tahar Sfar, BP 794, 3018 Sfax; tel. (74) 296-120; fax (74) 296-121; e-mail ccis@ccis.org.tn; internet www.ccis.org.tn; f. 1895; 35,000 mems; Dir IKRAM MAKNI.

INDUSTRIAL AND TRADE ASSOCIATIONS

Agence de Promotion de l'Industrie (API): 63 rue de Syrie, 1002 Tunis; tel. (71) 792-144; fax (71) 782-482; e-mail api@api.com.tn; internet www.tunisieindustrie.nat.tn; f. 1987 by merger; co-ordinates industrial policy, undertakes feasibility studies, organizes industrial training and establishes industrial zones; overseas offices in Belgium, France, Germany, Italy, the United Kingdom, Sweden and the USA; Pres. and Dir-Gen. KHELIL LAGIMI.

Centre Technique du Textile (CETTEX): ave des Industries, Zone Industrielle, Bir El Kassaa, 2013 Ben Arous, BP 279, Tunis; tel. (71) 381-133; fax (71) 382-558; e-mail cettex@textiletunisia.com.tn; responsible for the textile industry; Dir MONJI JLAIEL.

Cie des Phosphates de Gafsa (CPG): Cité Bayech, Gafsa; tel. (76) 22022; f. 1897; production and marketing of phosphates; Pres. MUHAMMAD AL-FADHEL KHELIL.

Entreprise Tunisienne d'Activités Pétrolières (ETAP): 27 ave Kheireddine Pacha, BP 367, 1002 Tunis; tel. (71) 782-288; fax (71) 784-092; responsible for exploration and investment in hydrocarbons.

Office des Céréales: Ministry of Agriculture, 30 rue Alain Savary, 1002 Tunis; tel. (71) 790-351; fax (71) 789-573; f. 1962; responsible for the cereals industry; Chair. and Dir-Gen. A. SADDEM.

Office National des Mines: 24 rue 8601, BP 215, 1080 Tunis; tel. (71) 787-366; fax (71) 794-016; f. 1963; mining of iron ores; research and study of mineral wealth; Chair. and CEO MOHAMMED FADHEL ZERELLI.

Office National des Pêches (ONP): Le Port, La Goulette, Tunis; tel. (71) 275-093; marine and fishing authority; Dir-Gen. L. HALAB.

Office des Terres Domaniales (OTD): 30 rue Alain Savary, 1002 Tunis; tel. (71) 800-322; fax (71) 795-026; e-mail otd@email.ati.tn; f. 1961; responsible for agricultural production and the management of state-owned lands; Dir BECHIR BEN SMAIL.

UTILITIES

Electricity and Gas

Société Tunisienne de l'Electricité et du Gaz (STEG): 38 rue Kemal Atatürk, BP 190, 1080 Tunis; tel. (71) 341-311; fax (71) 349-981; e-mail dpsc@steg.com.tn; f. 1962; responsible for generation and distribution of electricity and for production of natural gas; Pres. and Gen. Man. MUHAMMAD MONCEF BOUSSEN; 35 brs.

Water

Société Nationale d'Exploitation et de Distribution des Eaux (SONEDE): Ave Slimane ben Sliman el-Manar 2,Tunis; tel. (71) 887-000; fax (71) 881-000; e-mail commuson@gnet.tn; f. 1968; Pres. and Dir. Gen. MABROUK ABDELLAZIZ.

TRADE AND OTHER UNIONS

Union Générale des Etudiants de Tunisie (UGET): 11 rue d'Espagne, Tunis; f. 1953; 600 mems; Pres. MEKKI FITOURI.

Union Générale Tunisienne du Travail (UGTT): 9 rue de Grèce, Tunis; e-mail ugtt.relaintl@planet.tn; f. 1946 by Farhat Hached; affiliated to ICFTU; mems 360,000 in 23 affiliated unions; 18-member exec. bureau; Sec.-Gen. ABDESSALEM DJERAD.

Union Nationale des Agriculteurs (UNA): 6 ave Habib Thameur, 1000 Tunis; tel. (71) 246-920; fax (71) 349-843; f. 1955; Pres. BACHA ABD AL-BAKI.

Union Nationale de la Femme Tunisienne (UNFT): 56 blvd Bab Benat, Tunis; tel. (71) 561-845; fax (71) 567-131; e-mail unft@email.ati.tn; f. 1956; 100,000 mems; promotes the rights of women; 27 regional delegations; Pres. CHEDLIA BOUKHCHINA; Vice-Pres. FAIZA AZOUZ.

Union Tunisienne de l'Industrie, du Commerce et de l'Artisanat (UTICAL): 103 ave de la Liberté, Belvédère, 1002 Tunis; tel. (71) 780-366; fax (71) 782-143; f. 1946; mems: 15 national federations and 170 syndical chambers at national levels; Pres. HEDI JILANI.

Transport

RAILWAYS

In 1999 the total length of railways was 2,168 km. A total of 36.819m. passengers travelled by rail in Tunisia in 2001.

Société du Métro Léger de Tunis (SMLT): 60–62 ave Jean-Jaurès, BP 4, 1002 Tunis; tel. (71) 348-555; fax (71) 338-100; f. 1981; operates light railway system in and around Tunis (total length 53 km); Pres. and Dir-Gen. CHEDLY HAJRI.

Société Nationale des Chemins de Fer Tunisiens (SNCFT): Bâtiment La Gare Tunis Ville, Place Barcelona, 1001 Tunis; tel. (71) 333-343; fax (71) 344-045; f. 1956; state org. controlling all Tunisian railways; Pres. and Dir-Gen. ABD AL-AZIZ CHAÂBEN.

ROADS

In 1996 there were an estimated 23,100 km of roads. Of these, 6,240 km were main roads and 7,900 km secondary roads.

Société Nationale des Transports (SNT): 1 ave Habib Bourguiba, BP 660, 1025 Tunis; tel. (71) 259-422; fax (71) 342-727; internet www.snt-smlt.com.tn; f. 1963; operates 199 local bus routes with 1,033 buses; Chair. and Man. Dir CHEDLY HAJRI; Gen. Man. MONCEF CHENITI.

Société Nationale de Transport Interurbain (SNTRI): ave Muhammad V, BP 40, Belvédère, 1002 Tunis; tel. (71) 784-433; fax (71) 786-605; e-mail drn@sntri.com.tn; f. 1981; Dir-Gen. SASSI YAHIA.

There are 12 **Sociétés Régionales des Transports,** responsible for road transport, operating in different regions in Tunisia.

SHIPPING

Tunisia has seven major ports: Tunis-La Goulette, Radès, Bizerta, Sousse, Sfax, Gabès and Zarzis. There is a special petroleum port at La Skhirra.

Office de la Marine Marchande et des Ports: Bâtiment Administratif, Port de la Goulette, 2060 La Goulette; tel. (71) 735-300; fax (71) 735-812; maritime port administration; Pres. and Dir-Gen. ALI LABIEDH.

ie Générale Maritime: Résidence Alain Savary, Bloc D7, Apt 74, 1003 Tunis; tel. and fax (71) 860-430; e-mail logwan.girgen@gnet.tn; Chair. ELIAS MAHERZI.

Cie Méditerranéenne de Navigation: Tunis; tel. (71) 331-544; fax (71) 332-124.

Cie Tunisienne de Navigation SA (CTN): 5 ave Dag Hammarskjoeld, BP 40, 1001 Tunis; tel. (71) 341-777; fax (71) 350-976; f. 1959; state-owned; brs at Bizerta, Gabès, La Skhirra, La Goulette, Radès, Sfax and Sousse; Chair. M. YONSAA.

Gabès Marine Tankers: Immeuble SETCAR, route de Sousse, km 13, 2034 Tunis; tel. (71) 445-644; fax (71) 454-650; Chair. FÉRID ABBES.

Gas Marine: Immeuble SETCAR, route de Sousse, km 13, 2034 Ez-Zahra; tel. (71) 454-644; fax (71) 454-650; Chair. HAMMADI ABBES.

Hannibal Marine Tankers: 10 rue 8161, Cité Olympique, 1003 Tunis; tel. (71) 807-032; fax (71) 773-805; Gen. Man. AMEUR MAHJOUB.

Société Tunisienne de Navigation Maritime (PETRONAV): Immeuble Saâdi, BP 85, 2080 Ariana; tel. (71) 861-125; fax (71) 861-780; Chair. HICHEM KHATTECH.

SONOTRAK: 179 ave Muhammad Hédi Khefacha, Gare Maritime de Kerkenna, 3000 Sfax; tel. (74) 498-216; fax (74) 497-496; e-mail jabeur.m@planet.tn; Chair. Taoufi Jrad.

Tunisian Shipping Agency: Zone Industrielle, Radès 2040, BP 166, Tunis; tel. (71) 448-379; fax (71) 448-410; e-mail tsa.rades@planet.tn; Chair. Muhammad Ben Sedrine.

CIVIL AVIATION

There are international airports at Tunis-Carthage, Sfax, Djerba, Monastir, Tabarka, Gafsa and Tozeur. In January 2000 it was announced that a new airport was to be built at Enfidha, 100 km south of Tunis. The new airport was to be operational by mid-2004.

Office de l'Aviation Civile et des Aéroports: BP 137, Aéroport International de Tunis-Carthage, 1080 Tunis; tel. (71) 754-000; fax (71) 755-133; e-mail hayet.amri@laposte.net; internet www.oaca.nat .tn; f. 1972; air traffic control and airport administration; Pres. and Dir-Gen. Abderrahmen Tlili.

Nouvelair Tunisie: Zone Touristique Dkhila, 5065 Monastir; tel. (73) 520-600; fax (73) 520-666; e-mail info@nouvelair.com.tn; internet www.nouvelair.com; f. 1989 as Air Liberté Tunisie; name changed as above in 1996; Tunisian charter co; flights from Tunis, Djerba and Monastir airports to Scandinavia and other European countries; Chair. Aziz Milad; Gen. Man. Sami Zitouni.

Tuninter: BP 1080, Immeuble Securas ZI Charguia 11, 1080 Tunis; tel. (71) 701-717; fax (71) 712-193; e-mail tuninter@mail.gnet.tn; f. 1992; Tunisian charter co; Man. Dir Abd al-Karim Ouertani.

TunisAir (Société Tunisienne de l'Air): blvd du 7 novembre 1987, 2035 Tunis; tel. (71) 700-100; fax (71) 700-897; internet www .tunisair.com.tn; f. 1948; 45.2% govt-owned; 20% of assets privatized in 1995; flights to Africa, Europe and the Middle East; Pres. and Dir-Gen. Rafaa Dekhil.

Tunisavia (Société de Transports, Services et Travaux Aériens): Immeuble Saadi Spric, Tour CD, 1082 al-Menzah, Tunis; tel. (71) 717-600; fax (71) 718-100; e-mail tunisaviasiege@planet.tn; internet www.tunisavia.com.tn; f. 1974; helicopter and charter operator; Pres. Aziz Milad; Dir-Gen. Slaheddine Kastalli.

Tourism

The main tourist attractions are the magnificent sandy beaches, Moorish architecture and remains of the Roman Empire. Tunisia contains the site of the ancient Phoenician city of Carthage. Tourism, a principal source of foreign exchange, has expanded rapidly, following extensive government investment in hotels, improved roads and other facilities. The number of hotel beds increased from 71,529 in 1980 to 188,600 in 1999. Foreign tourist arrivals totalled 5.4m. in 2001 (compared with 4.7m. in 1998). Receipts from tourism in 2001 totalled 2,343m. dinars.

Office National du Tourisme Tunisien: 1 ave Muhammad V, 1001 Tunis; tel. (71) 341-077; fax (71) 350-997; e-mail info@tourismtunisia.com; internet www.tourismtunisia.com; f. 1958; Dir-Gen. Fakhreddine Messai.

TURKEY

Introductory Survey

Location, Climate, Language, Religion, Flag, Capital

The Republic of Turkey lies partly in south-eastern Europe and partly in western Asia. The European and Asian portions of the country (known, respectively, as Thrace and Anatolia) are separated by the Sea of Marmara, linking the Black Sea and the Aegean Sea. Turkey has an extensive coastline: on the Black Sea, to the north; on the Mediterranean Sea, to the south; and on the Aegean Sea, to the west. Most of Turkey lies in Asia, the vast Anatolian peninsula being bordered to the east by Armenia, Georgia, the Nakhichevan Autonomous Republic (part of Azerbaijan) and Iran, and to the south by Iraq and Syria. The smaller European part of the country is bordered to the west by Greece and Bulgaria. In the Asian interior the climate is one of great extremes, with hot dry summers and cold, snowy winters on the plateau. Temperatures in Ankara are generally between –4°C (25°F) and 30°C (86°F). On the Mediterranean coast it is more equable, with mild winters and warm summers. The principal language is Turkish, spoken by 90% of the population. About 7% speak Kurdish, mainly in the south-east. In 1928 the Arabic characters of the written Turkish language were superseded by Western-style script. Islam is the religion of 99% of the population. The national flag (proportions 2 by 3) is red, with a white crescent and a five-pointed white star to the left of centre. The capital is Ankara.

Recent History

Turkey was formerly a monarchy, ruled by a Sultan, with his capital in Constantinople (now İstanbul). At its zenith, the Turkish Empire, under the Osmanlı (Ottoman) dynasty, extended from the Persian (Arabian) Gulf to Morocco, including most Arab regions and south-eastern Europe. Following the dissolution of the Ottoman Empire after the First World War, political control of Turkey itself passed to the nationalist movement led by Mustafa Kemal, a distinguished army officer. On 23 April 1920, in defiance of the Sultan, a newly-elected assembly established a provisional Government, led by Kemal, in Ankara, then a minor provincial town. Kemal's forces waged war against the Greek army in 1920–22, forcing the Greeks to evacuate Smyrna (İzmir) and eastern Thrace (the European portion of Turkey). The new regime abolished the sultanate in November 1922 and declared Turkey a republic, with Ankara as its capital and Kemal as its first President, on 29 October 1923. The Ottoman caliphate (the former monarch's position as Islamic religious leader) was abolished in March 1924.

Kemal remained President of Turkey, with extensive dictatorial powers, until his death in 1938. He vigorously pursued a radical programme of far-reaching reform and modernization, including the secularization of the state (in 1928), the abolition of Islamic courts and religious instruction in schools, the emancipation of women (enfranchised in 1934), the banning of polygamy, the development of industry, the introduction of a Latin alphabet, the adoption of the Gregorian (in place of the Islamic) calendar, and the encouragement of European culture and technology. Another westernizing reform was the introduction of surnames in 1934: Kemal assumed the name Atatürk ('Father of the Turks'). His autocratic regime attempted, with considerable success, to replace the country's Islamic traditions by the principles of republicanism, nationalism, populism and state control.

Following Atatürk's death, his Cumhuriyet Halk Partisi (CHP —Republican People's Party), the only authorized political grouping, remained in power under his close associate, İsmet İnönü, who had been Prime Minister in 1923–24 and from 1925 to 1937. İnönü was President from 1938 to 1950, and maintained Turkey's neutrality during most of the Second World War (Turkey declared war on Germany in February 1945). After the war İnönü introduced some liberalization of the regime. The one-party system was ended in 1946, when opposition leaders, including Celâl Bayar and Adnan Menderes, registered the Demokratik Parti (DP—Democratic Party). Numerous other parties were subsequently formed. The DP won Turkey's first free election, in 1950, and ruled for the next decade. Bayar became President, with Menderes as Prime Minister.

In May 1960 the Government was overthrown by a military coup, led by Gen. Cemal Gürsel, who assumed the presidency, claiming that the DP regime had betrayed Atatürk's principle of secularism. A series of coalition governments, mostly led by İnönü, held office from November 1961 until October 1965, when an election was won by the conservative Adalet Partisi (Justice Party), led by Süleyman Demirel, which appealed to supporters of the former DP. The Demirel Government remained in power until March 1971, when escalating student and labour unrest caused the armed forces to demand its resignation. 'Guided democracy', under military supervision, continued until October 1973, with a succession of right-wing 'non-party' administrations, martial law and the rigorous suppression of all left-wing activities.

The return to civilian rule began in April 1973, when the Turkish Grand National Assembly (TGNA—the legislative body established in 1961) chose Adm. Fahri Korutürk as President, in preference to a candidate supported by the armed forces. Military participation in government was ended by an election in October 1973. No single party received sufficient support to form a government, and negotiations on the creation of a coalition continued until January 1974, when Bülent Ecevit, leader of the CHP (which had become a left-of-centre party), took office as Prime Minister, having negotiated a coalition with the Milli Selamet Partisi (MSP—National Salvation Party), a pro-Islamic right-wing group. Deteriorating relations with Greece were exacerbated by the Greek-backed coup in Cyprus (q.v.) in July 1974, when Turkey responded by dispatching troops, and occupying the northern part of the island, to protect the Turkish Cypriot population. Despite the failure of the coup, Turkish forces kept control of northern Cyprus, and the island remained effectively partitioned.

A long period of political instability was fostered by a succession of unsuccessful coalitions, headed by either Ecevit or Demirel, and prompted an escalation in political violence, mainly involving clashes between left-wing and right-wing groups. On 12 September 1980, as the violence neared the scale of a civil war, the armed forces, led by Gen. Kenan Evren, Chief of the General Staff, seized power in a bloodless coup; a five-member National Security Council (NSC) was formed, which appointed a mainly civilian Cabinet. Martial law was declared throughout the country. In December the NSC published a decree endowing the military regime with unlimited powers. During 1981–83 a campaign to eradicate all possible sources of political violence was undertaken. In April 1981 former politicians were banned from future political activity, and in October all political parties were disbanded.

The new Government succeeded in reducing the level of political violence in Turkey and in restoring law and order. However, that this had been achieved at the expense of respect for human rights caused concern among Western governments: Turkey was banned from the Parliamentary Assembly of the Council of Europe (see p. 181), aid from the European Community (EC, now European Union—EU, see p. 199) was suspended, and fellow members of NATO urged Turkey to return to democratic rule as soon as possible. In October 1981 a Consultative Assembly was established to draft a new constitution, which was approved by referendum in November 1982; objections were widely expressed that the President was to be accorded excessive powers while judicial powers and the rights of trade unions and the press were to be curtailed. An appended 'temporary article' installed Evren as President for a seven-year term.

In May 1983 the NSC revoked the ban on political organizations, permitting the formation of parties, subject to strict rules, in preparation for the first election to be held under the new Constitution. All the former political parties remained proscribed, and 723 former members of the TGNA and leading party officials were banned from political activity for up to 10 years. Followers of the former political parties regrouped under new names and with new leaders. Of the 15 new parties, however, only three were allowed to take part in the election: the Milliyetçi Demokrasi Partisi (MDP—Nationalist Democracy

Party) and the Halkçı Partisi (HP—Populist Party), both of which had the tacit support of the NSC, and the conservative Anavatan Partisi (ANAP—Motherland Party), led by Turgut Özal, the former Deputy Prime Minister for Economic Affairs. In the November general election ANAP won 211 of the 400 seats in the unicameral legislature. Accordingly, Özal was appointed Prime Minister in December. Although this result suggested a decisive rejection of military rule, martial law was still in operation in almost one-half of the provinces a year after the election.

In November 1985 the HP and the Sosyal Demokrasi Partisi (Social Democratic Party), respectively the main opposition parties within and outside the National Assembly, merged to form the Sosyal Demokrat Halkçı Parti (SHP—Social Democratic Populist Party). However, the left-wing opposition was split as a result of the immediate formation of the Demokratik Sol Parti (DSP—Democratic Left Party), which drew support from the former CHP. The MDP voted to disband in May 1986.

At a national referendum in September 1987 a narrow majority approved the repeal of the ban on participation in political affairs imposed on more than 200 politicians in 1981. This enabled Ecevit to assume the leadership of the DSP, while Demirel was elected as leader of the Doğru Yol Partisi (DYP— True Path Party). In a general election conducted in November 1987 ANAP obtained 292 of the 450 seats in the enlarged TGNA, while the SHP won 99 seats and the DYP 59.

Özal succeeded Evren as President in November 1989, having secured the support of the simple majority required in a third round of voting by the TGNA at the end of October. Yıldırım Akbulut, the Speaker of the TGNA and a former Minister of the Interior, was subsequently appointed Prime Minister. At an ANAP party congress convened in June 1991 Akbulut was defeated by former Minister of Foreign Affairs Mesut Yılmaz in a contest for the party leadership. Akbulut subsequently resigned as Prime Minister, and, in accordance with the Constitution, President Özal invited Yılmaz, the leader of ANAP's liberal faction, to head a new administration.

In a general election held on 20 October 1991 the DYP, under the leadership of Demirel, received an estimated 27.3% of the votes cast, narrowly defeating ANAP (with 23.9%) and the SHP (with 20.6%). Demirel formed a coalition administration with the SHP (who with the DYP accounted for 266 of the 450 newly elected deputies in the TGNA), with Erdal İnönü, the SHP party leader, as deputy premier. The coalition set out a programme for political and economic reform, and international observers were impressed by Demirel's apparent commitment to human rights. The implementation of amendments designed to discourage torture were, however, impeded by a lack of consensus within the Government, and the problems were exacerbated during 1992 by a succession of political defections from the SHP, which by September had reduced the representation of the coalition parties in the TGNA to 229. Although the DYP and the SHP performed well at municipal elections in early June, the reactivation of the CHP in September (following a relaxation of guide-lines for the formation of political parties) threatened to undermine left-wing support for the Government.

At a special ANAP party conference in December 1992, concern was expressed that right-wing extremism had become the dominant force behind the party leadership, prompting the emergence of a dissident, more conservative faction of the party. Subsequently some 70 deputies announced their intention to leave ANAP in order to form a new party headed by President Özal. In April 1993, however, Özal died of heart failure. In May Süleyman Demirel was elected to the presidency, with a simple majority in a third round of voting by the TGNA. Minister of State Tansu Çiller was elected to the DYP party leadership in early June and promptly assumed the premiership. Çiller (Turkey's first female Prime Minister) formed a new Cabinet, retaining the 12 SHP members of the previous Government but replacing 17 former DYP ministers—notably several Demirel loyalists. The Prime Minister's personal support was consolidated in December when five DYP ministers were replaced.

The new administration was strained by a sharp escalation of violence on the part of the outlawed Partiya Karkeren Kurdistan (PKK—Kurdistan Workers' Party). Plans to extend cultural and educational rights to the Kurds were abandoned following strong opposition from Demirel, right-wing members of the DYP and military leaders, who, in October, effectively resisted a proposal to discuss the establishment of local autonomy for the Kurdish population in the south-east of the country.

In early 1994 Çiller's political standing was damaged by a devaluation of the Turkish lira following a loss of confidence in the currency on the part of international credit agencies. The DYP performed unexpectedly well in municipal elections in March, however, obtaining 24% of the national vote; Çiller was thus able to pursue her programme of economic austerity, although in July the Constitutional Court halted Çiller's accelerated privatization plans for state-owned enterprises—a key aspect of her economic programme. In October an attempt to introduce new legislation on privatization revealed serious political differences within the coalition Government. Proposals for the democratization of the Constitution also provoked disagreements concerning the extent to which should be enshrined freedoms of expression and movement. Some SHP members threatened to withhold support for the privatization bill until assurances were made that the reform measures would be implemented. In late November the TGNA approved legislation enabling the sale of some 100 state enterprises; thousands of workers subsequently participated in a demonstration in Ankara, organized by trade unions, to protest against the new law.

In February 1995 a special conference of the SHP voted to merge with the CHP (under the latter's name). The merger increased the Government's parliamentary majority but forced a renegotiation of the conditions of the coalition. Agreement was reached by Çiller and Hikmet Çetin, the CHP leader, in March, and an extensive reorganization of the Government was undertaken in order to accommodate the party. Çetin became Deputy Prime Minister and Minister of State; İnönü assumed the foreign affairs portfolio.

In June 1995 the DYP obtained 39% of votes cast in municipal elections, a result depicted by Çiller as a vindication of her personal standing as leader and of her Government's policies, in particular the pursuit of closer relations with the EU. However, efforts by Çiller to extend democratic rights within the Constitution encountered considerable opposition, both from conservative elements within her own party and from the fundamentalist Islamist Refah Partisi (RP—Welfare Party). Certain constitutional reforms, including the removal of restrictions on political associations and trade unions, the lowering of the age of eligibility to vote from 21 to 18 years, and the expansion of the TGNA by 100 parliamentary seats to 550, were finally approved at the end of July. Çiller, however, failed to obtain sufficient support for the amendment of the 'anti-terrorism' legislation, which was expected to be crucial in securing the European Parliament's ratification of the EU-Turkish customs union (see below).

Deniz Baykal was elected leader of the CHP in September 1995. All CHP ministers subsequently resigned their cabinet positions, and ensuing negotiations with Çiller for a new coalition agreement failed as it became apparent that the political differences between the two leaders were insurmountable. Later in September Demirel was forced to accept the Prime Minister's resignation, but Çiller was immediately invited to form a new government. An attempt by Çiller to form a coalition with ANAP was unsuccessful, and in October a minority DYP administration failed to secure a parliamentary vote of confidence. A significant obstacle to a new DYP-CHP agreement was removed when Çiller conceded the necessity of holding an early general election; in addition, an agreement was reached to resolve a damaging public-sector wage dispute. A DYP-CHP Government, headed by Çiller with Baykal as Deputy Prime Minister and Minister of Foreign Affairs, took office in early November.

At the general election, in December 1995, the RP, which had campaigned to strengthen political and economic relations with other Islamic countries, to withdraw from NATO and the EU customs union, and to increase state involvement in the economy, secured the largest number of parliamentary seats (158), with 21.4% of the votes cast. The DYP won 135 seats with 19.2% of the votes, while ANAP took 132, with 19.7% of the votes. Since no party had an absolute majority, the two other parties securing parliamentary representation, the DSP and the CHP, were expected to have considerable political leverage in the new parliament. (Under the new electoral arrangements, eight other parties secured no seats in the legislature, having failed to reach the minimum requirement of 10% of support.) Although during the election campaign the DYP and ANAP leaders had both declared their opposition to participating in a coalition administration with the RP, in January 1996 President Demirel invited RP leader Necmettin Erbakan to attempt to form a government. Despite Erbakan's declared willingness to negotiate an agreement with any of the four main parties, as well as to compromise on the RP's main policies, no coalition partner could be found. Subsequent efforts by Çiller to form a government through an agreement with ANAP also failed, and in early February Demirel invited Mesut Yılmaz, of ANAP, to establish a new administration. Following protracted negotiations, Yılmaz and Çiller reached a coalition agreement, which was signed and approved by Demirel in March; Çiller conceded the first turn at leading the Government to Yılmaz, under a rotating premiership arrangement. The new Government secured a parliamentary vote of confidence by 257 votes to 207. Almost immediately, however, the Government was strained by tensions between the two leaders, and allegations of corruption against Çiller. In April and May 1996 ANAP deputies failed to support Çiller following votes in the TGNA to establish commissions to investigate her alleged illegal involvement in the sale of the TEDAŞ state electricity company and of a Turkish car manufacturer. Members of the DYP accused Yılmaz of further undermining Çiller's position, by passing information to the media detailing evidence of the misappropriation of secret security funds under her premiership, in order to force her resignation before her scheduled assumption of the office of Prime Minister in 1997. Meanwhile, opposition parties questioned the credibility of the Government after the Constitutional Court annulled the March 1996 vote of confidence. At the end of May Çiller announced the withdrawal of her party's support for the Government and publicly called for Yılmaz's resignation. Political tensions were heightened in that month by an assassination attempt on President Demirel.

In early June 1996 the RP renewed its demands for a general election after it won 34% of the votes cast in municipal elections. At the same time the RP secured the DYP's support for a censure motion against the Government to be considered in the TGNA. This was withdrawn when Yılmaz announced the resignation of his Government, following the official publication of the Constitutional Court's ruling. Necmettin Erbakan was subsequently invited to form a government, and at the end of June the RP concluded an agreement with the DYP; Erbakan was to lead the new coalition administration, with Çiller assuming the deputy premiership and foreign affairs portfolio. The leaders asserted that the objective of the new Government was to secure political and economic stability, and they guaranteed that Turkey would adhere to its existing international and strategic agreements. Eight DYP deputies in the TGNA resigned from the party in protest at the coalition with the RP, and a further 15 DYP deputies failed to endorse the new administration in a parliamentary vote of confidence conducted in July. The Government, however, secured a narrow majority (winning by 278 votes to 265). The new Government was immediately confronted by local demonstrations and mounting international concern regarding several hundred left-wing prisoners who had initiated a hunger strike in May, in protest at their treatment and conditions of confinement. At the end of July, following the deaths of 12 protesters and widespread unrest within many prisons, the Government concluded an agreement with the prisoners to end their action in return for guarantees that included the transfer of 102 activists from a high-security prison in Anatolya and greater access to medical care.

The contradictions inherent in the new RP-DYP administration became evident in many aspects of government policy. In foreign affairs, the Government attempted to reassure its Western allies of its continued support. At the end of July 1996 the mandate for the use of Turkish airbases by allied forces engaged in 'Operation Provide Comfort' (see below) was extended, and in August a new military co-operation agreement was signed with Israel, expanding on an accord concluded in February. In addition, there was evidence of the military's asserting its authority by dismissing 13 officers in August on disciplinary charges relating to Islamist practices (50 officers had been dismissed on similar grounds in December 1995). At the same time, however, Prime Minister Erbakan embarked on a tour of Asian and Middle Eastern Muslim countries in order to strengthen bilateral relations and co-operation. In August Turkey and Iran finalized an economic agreement, shortly after legislation had been ratified in the USA that threatened punitive measures against countries undertaking investments in Iran. A visit by Erbakan to Libya in October became politically damaging when the Libyan leader, Col Muammar al-Qaddafi, expressed opposition to Turkey's relations with NATO and the EU and, moreover, advocated the establishment of a Kurdish homeland. Turkey's ambassador to Libya was temporarily

recalled. However, censure motions brought against Erbakan's administration by three opposition parties were defeated in a single vote in the TGNA.

In January 1997 the TGNA cleared Çiller of the last of the corruption charges that had been filed against her. In the same month a new party was established to absorb dissident DYP deputies. The leader of this Demokrat Türkiye Partisi (DTP—Democratic Turkey Party) was Hüsamettin Cindoruk, who had been expelled from the DYP in October 1995.

In November 1996, meanwhile, the Government was confronted by allegations of state involvement in criminal activities following a traffic accident at Susurluk, in the north-west, in which a senior police-officer and a wanted criminal were killed; a DYP deputy travelling in the same car was injured. The resignation a few days later of the Minister of the Interior, Mehmet Agar, was said to be unconnected to the incident. Details subsequently emerged of the activities of the alleged mafia member, Abdullah Catli, which included drugs-trafficking as well as intelligence work for the state (which some commentators suspected included the assassination of left-wing activists during the 1980s), while there was evidence that Agar had held meetings with members of organized criminal groups and had secured Catli a gun licence. In December 1996 İstanbul's Director of Security and five other senior officers were suspended during investigation proceedings into the death, in July, of a casino owner, in which Catli was a leading suspect. In January 1997 a report on the Susurluk incident by the Prime Minister's office recommended that judicial inquiries be initiated into the conduct of some 35 people, including Agar and the former İstanbul security director. A popular protest against corruption in government and aimed at ensuring full judicial consideration of the Susurluk case was initiated the following month, when nightly demonstrations emphasized the increasing tension between secularists and Islamists.

There were civil disturbances in early February 1997 following an Islamist rally in the Sincan district of Ankara, at which Iran's ambassador to Turkey criticized Turkey's relations with Israel and its NATO allies and advocated the introduction of *Shari'a* law. The RP district mayor, who had organized the rally, was suspended. A few days later military tanks were driven through Sincan, generating concern at the prospect of extreme military intervention in the country's administration. At the same time pressure from the military and DYP members of the Government forced the RP to withdraw proposals to extend Muslim education and to allow religious garments to be worn by public workers. In late February the Government defeated a censure motion in the TGNA, tabled by the DSP and CHP in protest at the Government's alleged undermining of the secular state. At a meeting of the NSC held at the end of February, the military leadership presented a list of 18 measures that would ensure the secular state traditions, including greater supervision of Islamic financial and media operations, the removal of Islamists from public administration and closure of all unauthorized Islamic groupings; the military warned of punitive action if the proposals were not implemented. Political tension was defused when Erbakan, who had initially criticized the NSC for attempting to impose laws on the Government, signed a memorandum endorsing the NSC measures and declared that the leaders of all the main political parties were unanimous in their view that the Constitution must be upheld. The Council of Ministers agreed in March to implement the NSC proposals, but concern subsequently arose that the failure of the Government to act on the measures would result in the collapse of the administration—owing to increasing pressure from the military on the DYP to withdraw from the coalition arrangement, as well as pressure from extreme elements within the governing parties. Two dissident DYP government ministers resigned in protest at Erbakan's leadership, and demanded an early election on the grounds that their party leader, Çiller, had failed to restrain the Islamist tendencies of the RP. At a meeting of the NSC held in late April the political crisis was again temporarily resolved when Erbakan agreed to pursue the military's demands, including restrictions on Islamic education. At the end of April 122 members of an Islamist sect were sentenced to up to four years' imprisonment for forming an illegal group and contravening a ban on Islamic dress, and in May Erbakan approved the dismissal of 161 army officers for allegedly demonstrating Islamist sympathies. Although the Government defeated an opposition attempt in that month to pursue a censure motion in the TGNA, the political situation remained critical, and charges from the military, opposition parties and dissident members of the DYP that the Government was undermining the modern secular tradition were reinforced when the country's chief prosecutor initiated legal proceedings to ban the RP (on the grounds that the party had violated the Constitution). By June the coalition had lost its majority in the TGNA as a result of defections principally from the DYP. Erbakan announced that he would seek an early election, but the military continued to exert pressure on the Government, and the Prime Minister finally resigned in mid-June. President Demirel asked the ANAP leader, Mesut Yılmaz, to form a new administration, and a coalition with the DSP and the DTP was inaugurated at the beginning of July; the coalition controlled only a minority of seats in the TGNA, and was dependent on the support of the CHP. The tripartite Government pledged to improve law and order, implement previously proposed changes to the education system, and vigorously pursue EU membership. Defections from the DYP continued through July, and by the end of the month its representation in the TGNA had been reduced from 135 to 93.

In August 1997 the TGNA approved legislation extending compulsory education from five to eight years. This was intended to raise the entry age to Islamic schools from 11 to 14, thus reducing attendance at such schools and lessening Islamic influence. The RP organized popular demonstrations in protest against the legislation (which constituted a principal demand of the military) during July and August and following the implementation of the measures in September. In August a further 73 members of the armed forces were expelled owing to suspected affiliation to Islamist organizations. Further public demonstrations were prompted by the military's insistence on the strict enforcement of the ban on wearing Islamic dress in public buildings, notably educational establishments. The largest of these demonstrations was attended by 10,000 people in İstanbul at the end of February 1998. In early March the University of İstanbul temporarily annulled the ban and the Government stated that the ban would not be strictly enforced. In mid-March the Government survived its third censure motion, which was presented against the Minister for Education for his handling of the issue of Islamic dress. A few days later 20 members of a proscribed Islamic organization were arrested for inciting the demonstrations. At the end of the month the NSC criticized the Government for advocating a relaxation of the enforcement of anti-Islamic legislation; the Government subsequently proposed further measures to curb Islamist radicalism, and the universities announced their decision to enforce the dress code.

Meanwhile, Çiller's participation in the coalition with the RP and her opposition to a possible ban on the party had caused offence to the secular establishment, causing a deterioration in the previously good relations between Çiller and the armed forces. In March 1998 the Court of Appeals ruled that Çiller could not be prosecuted in connection with a particular allegation that she had misused government funds during her premiership owing to the threat to national security interests. However, (although previous similar attempts had failed) in April her loss of support in the TGNA led to a vote in favour of the commencement of an investigation into alleged irregularities in Çiller's accumulation of wealth between 1991 and 1996. In October 1997 Çiller's husband, Ozer Çiller, had been charged with forgery.

In January 1998 the Constitutional Court ordered the dissolution of the RP on the grounds that it was responsible for undermining the secular regime, and banned seven of its members, including Erbakan, from holding political office for five years. The ban attracted widespread international criticism and human rights organizations condemned the decision. The ruling took effect in February; many former RP deputies joined the Fazilet Partisi (FP—Virtue Party), which had been established in December 1997. By March 1998 the FP's representation in the TGNA had risen to 140 seats, making it the largest parliamentary party (ANAP controlled 139 seats). In April the mayor of İstanbul, Recep Tayyip Erdoğan, who was expected to assume the leadership of the FP, was sentenced to 10 months' imprisonment for inciting hatred. He was released pending an appeal. His conviction and the investigation of hundreds of civil servants, teachers and government officials for their alleged support of Islamist organizations were widely criticized.

The stability of Yılmaz's minority Government was threatened by the demands of the CHP for an early general election. The CHP demonstrated its power in April 1998 by voting with the opposition in favour of an investigation into allegations of corruption against the Prime Minister. Following an agreement signed by Yılmaz and CHP leader Deniz Baykal, the Prime

Minister announced in June 1998 that he was to resign at the end of the year; he was to be succeeded by an interim government which would call early elections for April 1999.

In May 1998 it was announced that former Minister of the Interior, Mehmet Agar, was to be tried for his involvement in the Susurluk incident. In that month Çiller's husband was found guilty of misleading a parliamentary commission; his sentence, of five months' imprisonment, was later commuted to a fine. In August 12 former RP politicians, including Erbakan and FP leader Recai Kutan, were charged with illegally diverting funds from the party prior to its dissolution. An investigation into Çiller's assets was begun in September. Further investigations were launched in that month into Çiller and the former Minister of Finance for financial irregularities, and the immunity of the former TGNA Speaker was revoked, to allow an investigation, at his request, into his conduct following corruption allegations.

In September 1998 the Court of Appeal upheld the prison sentence on the mayor of İstanbul. Public demonstrations were held in protest at the sentence. As a result of his conviction Erdoğan was deprived of his position of mayor; he also resigned from the FP. In December new charges were filed against him for insulting the judiciary in a speech following his sentencing in September. In November the TGNA approved an investigation into the Minister of Public Works and Housing, Yaşar Topçu, on charges that he misused his office in the tender for the İzmit Bay Project. In that month corruption charges against Çiller were dismissed by a parliamentary commission, owing to insufficient evidence, while Erbakan was acquitted on charges of slandering the judiciary, and Minister of State Güneş Taner was removed from office following a parliamentary censure motion arising from corruption allegations. In December Ozer Çiller was acquitted on charges of falsifying documents.

In November 1998 the Government resigned, after the TGNA approved a motion of 'no confidence' submitted by the CHP in response to accusations of corruption against Yılmaz. In December Bülent Ecevit of the DSP was invited to form a government. He abandoned the task after three weeks of negotiations, primarily with the DYP, failed to reach an agreement. Yalim Erez, the Minister of Trade and Industry, was subsequently offered the premiership. In early January 1999, however, the DYP indicated that it would support Ecevit. Erez relinquished his mandate, and in mid-January Ecevit named his Government, formed of DSP and independent deputies, which would govern until the elections in April; the administration subsequently secured a vote of confidence in the TGNA. Also in January a motion was filed for the dissolution of the pro-Kurdish nationalist Halkın Demokrasi Partisi (HADEP—People's Democracy Party), owing to its alleged links with the Kurdish separatist PKK (see below); in March, however, the Constitutional Court ruled that HADEP was to be allowed to contest the elections.

In February 1999 the trial began of 79 alleged Islamists, including Erbakan. Hasan Celal Güzel, the leader of the Yeniden Doğuş Partisi (YDP—Rebirth Party), was sentenced to one year's imprisonment in February for inciting hatred in a speech at a meeting in Kayseri province; he received a further one-year sentence in May for insulting the President, and was imprisoned for five months from December for incitement to vengeance and hostility. In February the Minister of Finance and Customs resigned in order to stand for election as mayor of İstanbul. In February the High Election Council ruled that former RP deputies would not be allowed to take part in the forthcoming elections as independent candidates.

Despite pressure to postpone the elections, voting proceeded as scheduled on 18 April 1999. No party won an outright majority in the TGNA; the DSP won 136 of the 550 seats, and subsequently formed a coalition with the Milliyetçi Hareket Partisi (MHP—Nationalist Movement Party), which had won 129 seats, and ANAP, which had won 86 seats. The remaining seats in the TGNA were won by the FP (111), and the DYP (85), with three seats won by independent candidates. HADEP performed strongly in the south-east, but failed to secure the 10% of the national vote necessary for a seat in the TGNA. The CHP leader, Deniz Baykal, resigned following the poor performance of his party. The new Government, led by Bülent Ecevit, won a parliamentary vote of confidence on 9 June. In May the Chief Prosecutor instituted a court case against the FP, with the aim of dissolving the party.

In late August 1999 an earthquake measuring 7.8 on the Richter scale stuck near İzmit in north-west Turkey. Some 17,100 people died, a further 44,000 were injured and at least

350,000 were left homeless. Both the Government and the armed forces were criticized for the lack of co-ordination and the slowness of the response to the crisis. A second earthquake, measuring 7.2 on the Richter scale, struck the same region in November, resulting in a further 800 deaths. In that month Turkey enacted legislation to allow men to pay to shorten their military service in order to raise funds for reconstruction after the earthquake; some 73,500 applied to take part.

In August 1999 several articles of a political parties act relating to the closure of parties were approved: no party would be permitted to reform, even under a different name, party officials would be prohibited from active politics for five years and would be forbidden from standing as candidates for the party, although they would be permitted to stand as independent candidates. In September the FP submitted its preliminary defence against the motion to ban it. In October 1999 the assets of Erbakan and nine other former RP officials were 'frozen' as part of the continuing trial of a case brought by the Treasury demanding the repayment of aid given to the RP in 1997 as well as the repayment of allegedly unregistered party funds. In March 2000 Erbakan was sentenced to one year in prison and a lifetime ban from politics for provoking animosity and hatred in a speech made in 1994; his conviction was upheld by an appeals court in July, and in September he was issued with an arrest warrant. In December 1999, meanwhile, 300 people were detained following protests over the ban on wearing headscarves in universities and in that month the Court of Appeals ruled that the prerogative to wear Islamic headscarves was not a democratic right.

Internal power struggles within the FP became increasingly evident in 1999 and 2000, with growing instability, a loss of voters and alleged domination of the party by Erbakan (who had been banned from politics after the closure of the RP). In July 1999, following the appointment of a new secretary-general, a number of members, including the deputy leader, resigned in protest at these appointments which they claimed had been made without their knowledge and in March 2000 Abdullah Gül announced his intention to challenge Kutan for the leadership of the party. However, Gül was narrowly defeated (by 633 to 521) in a vote in May. In February the party was again threatened with closure following its accusations that the army had links with Hezbollah, a fundamentalist guerrilla organization (see below).

In January 2000, following a lack of agreement within the TGNA on a suitable presidential candidate (Demirel's term of office was to end in May), Ecevit announced plans for a constitutional amendment that would allow Demirel to renew his term. Despite the agreement of the governing coalition for the proposal, a vote in the TGNA failed to achieve the necessary level of support for the amendment to be carried. In April the parties of the governing coalition agreed to nominate the chairman of the Constitutional Court, Ahmet Necdet Sezer, as their joint candidate for the presidency; he was elected in a third round of voting by 330 votes out of 533.

In June 2000 the TGNA rejected a recommendation to indict former Prime Minister Mesut Yılmaz on corruption charges related to the sale of state-owned land. The rejection came after Yılmaz suggested that ANAP could be forced to withdraw its support from the governing coalition, which could in turn have led to the collapse of the Government. In July a minor reshuffle saw Yılmaz appointed Minister of State and replace Cumhur Ersümer, the Minister of Energy and Natural Resources, as Deputy Prime Minister. His remit was to include EU affairs. Yılmaz's inclusion in Government was welcomed by the FP.

Ecevit spoke out in June 2000 in favour of abolishing capital punishment, emphasizing this as a prerequisite for Turkey if it was to be fully integrated with the EU; he also stated that the extradition of offenders to Turkey would be facilitated by the abolition. The issue was one which was said to divide the ruling coalition. In August 2000 the State Security Court issued an arrest warrant for a popular religious leader, Fethullah Gülen, charging him with attempting to undermine the secular system. However, following a televised appearance by Ecevit in which he expressed his regret at the court's decision, the arrest warrant was dismissed by a higher court, which claimed that the case against Gülen was too weak. In that same month the military claimed that thousands of civil servants were trying to destroy the secular system and urged the TGNA to enact measures enabling their removal. The Government had already attempted to change laws by cabinet decree which would authorize the dismissal of civil servants suspected of supporting radical Is-

lamist or Kurdish groups, but Sezer twice vetoed the measures, insisting that the proposals had to be introduced by parliamentary legislation.

At HADEP's national conference in November 2000 Murat Bozlak was elected unopposed as leader, replacing Ahmet Turan Demir. Deniz Baykal was re-elected leader of the CHP in the same month. In December the case was brought before the Constitutional Court seeking the closure of the FP on the grounds of its being a focus for fundamentalist activities and an illegally established successor to RP.

Under the relative stability of the Ecevit Government the Turkish economy appeared to be making significant improvements throughout most of 2000, with the implementation of a stability programme, structural reform and increased regulation of the financial system considered imperative by the Government and international investors. A privatization programme was also under way, albeit at a slower rate than initially intended, and progress was made towards eliminating double-digit inflation. In November the Government was also preparing legal reform, which would grant bank mergers immunity from taxation in an attempt to encourage consolidation in the overcrowded banking sector. In that same month, however, a severe banking crisis was provoked by an investigation by the Banking and Supervision Agency into 10 failed banks. The investigation exposed the vulnerability of the banking sector and the lack of confidence of foreign investors in the Turkish economy as a result of a widening current-account deficit and delays to the structural reform programme. The crisis was exacerbated by massive capital outflow resulting in sharp declines in share prices and rapid inflation increases. In early December overnight interest rates reached a high point of 1,700%. The IMF agreed to an emergency loan US $7,500m., aimed at averting a further crisis (subject to a number of conditions, such as the privatization of Turkey's state telecommunications company), in addition to $2,900m. already available under a stand-by arrangement. The World Bank also pledged $5,000m. in support of the Government's undertaking to strengthen the financial sector and accelerate privatizations. In mid-February 2001 a second economic crisis was precipitated following a dispute between the President and Prime Minister: Sezer had accused Ecevit of not responding adequately to allegations of government corruption. Opposition parties and the business community had demanded the dismissal of deputy premier Hüsamettin Özkan, Minister of Energy, Cumhur Ersümer, and the Minister of Public Works, Koray Aydın, and for there to be a parliamentary investigation into the affairs of Ersümer and Aydın. The precarious balance of power within the governing coalition was, however, thought to have dissuaded Ecevit from undertaking any action against the alleged corruption. On 21 February Turkey, with the support of the IMF, abandoned its exchange-rate controls and allowed the lira to float, while empowering the central bank to pursue a rigorous monetary policy to control inflation; the immediate result was a sharp decline in value against the US dollar and a huge rise in interest rates (to as high as 7,500%, falling back to 500%, from 60% before the crisis).

Following the crisis, in March 2001 Ecevit replaced the Minister of Finance, Recep Onal, with Kemal Derviş, a senior economist at the World Bank, in a clear attempt to salvage Turkey's economic reforms and restore confidence in the financial markets. He also replaced the governor of the central bank, Gazi Erçel, with Süreyya Serdegeçti. Following Derviş's appointment, the head of the Banking and Supervision Agency resigned. Derviş outlined a structural reform package to bring the Turkish economy out of crisis. It included the restructuring of three state-owned banks under one supervisory board. Derviş reached a framework agreement with the IMF, combining plans for restructuring the banking sector and fiscal and monetary discipline aimed at reducing high interest rates and restoring investor confidence. In response to the reform package the IMF and the World Bank pledged additional financing.

In November 2000, meanwhile, the World Commission on Dams found that the planned Ilisu dam project on the Tigris river was in breach of seven key principles for dam building, including gaining public acceptance and sustaining rivers and livelihoods. (In September a Swedish construction firm had withdrawn from the project, in what was interpreted by many observers as an attempt to preserve its environmental reputation.) Construction of the dam was likely to displace in excess of 25,000 Kurdish people in south-east Turkey and submerge sites of archaeological and historical interest. In July 2001 a British government report reiterated such concerns, and in November 2001 and February 2002 Italian and British construction firms and a major Swiss Bank respectively withdrew from the project, placing its future in doubt.

The political implications of the financial crisis continued to be felt throughout April 2001 as anti-Government demonstrations involving tens of thousands of people degenerated into riots in Ankara and İzmir; police used water cannon and tear gas to disperse the crowds. However, Ecevit rejected calls for his government to resign. Later in the month it was announced that 15 officials and business executives were to be tried on conspiracy and bribery charges following a high-profile investigation into corruption in the state energy sector. The testimonies of the indicted men resulted in the resignation of the Minister of Energy and Natural Resources, Cumhur Ersümer, who was succeeded by Zeki Cakan of the ANAP in early May.

In May 2001 the TGNA approved legislation designed to meet conditions demanded by the IMF before the latter was to release US $10,000m. in financial aid. A major condition was the privatization of Turkey's telecommunications sector, which was widely opposed by TGNA members. At the end of the month the Minister of State for Privatization, Yuksel Yalova, resigned owing to disagreements within the Government over the liberalization of the tobacco industry—a key demand of the IMF. Prime Minister Ecevit attempted to replace Yalova with the Minister of the Interior, Sadettin Tantan, but the latter refused the transfer and resigned from his cabinet and ANAP posts in early June following disagreements with Mesut Yılmaz. Tantan had been widely respected for his anti-corruption measures, and his departure from the Government was regarded as a set-back to such reforms. He was succeeded as Minister of the Interior by Rüştü Kazim Yücelen, hitherto State Minister in charge of human rights. In late July the Minister of Communications, Enis Öksüz, resigned owing to his opposition to the planned IMF-imposed reforms in the communications sector. In early August the IMF released a further $1,500m. instalment of emergency funding. In early September the Minister of Public Works and Housing, Koray Aydin, resigned from his government post and from the TGNA after corruption charges were brought against him in respect of his alleged receipt of money from contracts relating to reconstruction in the aftermath of the 1999 earthquake damage.

In late June 2001 the Constitutional Court banned the FP on the grounds that it was essentially a continuation of the banned Islamist RP and was thus regarded as seeking to undermine the secular system. The Court expelled two FP members from the TGNA; however, it refrained from ordering the mass expulsions of the 100 remaining FP members from the legislature, who were allowed to remain in place as independents or join two planned successor parties. The ban was nevertheless opposed by most TGNA members, who were reportedly concerned that it would lead to more political instability and drive the Islamists underground. In July 2001 the European Court of Human Rights (ECHR) upheld the Government's 1998 decision to ban the RP. In July 2001 former FP leader Recai Kutan established a new Islamist party, Saadet Partisi (SP—Felicity Party), incorporating about one half of the former members of the FP (mainly from the conservative wing); the new party pledged to defend religious rights without challenging the secular State. It was believed that, as with the FP, Necmettin Erbakan was the main force in the party. In mid-August the remaining members of the FP joined the new reformist Islamist AK Partisi (Justice and Development Party), established by the former mayor of İstanbul, Recep Tayyip Erdoğan and FP member Abdullah Gül as an alternative to the SP. Erdoğan came under investigation within days for comments he reportedly made in 1994 that allegedly insulted the Turkish State. The split in the former FP seemed to coincide with a broader political realignment: Murat Karayalcin of the defunct SHP and Erdal İnönü of the CHP announced their intention to form a new centre-left party, while former Minister of the Interior Sadettin Tantan announced that he would form a new conservative party. Growing opposition to Mesut Yılmaz also provoked speculation of a likely split in ANAP.

Meanwhile, in late June 2001 President Sezer vetoed legislation designed to curb internet content to which there was access in Turkey on the grounds that it was undemocratic; many politicians held fears that the internet would be used to spread Kurdish separatism or pro-Islamist sentiment, thereby undermining the secular state.

In early October 2001 the TGNA overwhelmingly approved a number of constitutional amendments designed to facilitate Turkey's admission to the EU. The changes largely pertained to political freedoms and civil liberties, including minority rights (notably regarding the use of the Kurdish language); however, amendments to articles concerning the death penalty refrained from abolishing capital punishment outright. Significantly, the number of civilians on the powerful NSC would rise from five to nine, thereby lessening the power of the military (which would retain five members). Improved rights for women were approved in late November.

In January 2002 the Constitutional Court imposed restrictions on the political activities of AK Partisi leader Erdoğan, owing to his earlier allegedly seditious activities. The Court banned him from contesting the elections to the TGNA, and ordered his party to remove him from its leadership within six months. Meanwhile, attempts by Murat Karayalcin to establish a new centre-left party with various elements from the former CHP (see above) apparently foundered in February as they failed to agree on a leader or platform. At the same time, there were reports that former Constitutional Court Chief Justice Yekta Gungor Ozden, former Court of Cassation Chief Prosecutor Vural Savas, and retired generals Cevik Bir and Osman Ozbek, were planning to form a new 'Kemalist' party dedicated to the secular cause. The plans were interpreted as reflecting a broader realignment of political forces between secularists and Islamists in place of the traditional left–right divide. In early March it appeared that Necmettin Erbakan's political career was at an end, after Ankara's Higher Criminal Court sentenced him to two years and four months in prison for embezzling party funds.

In early February 2002 the TGNA approved additional laws on freedom of thought and expression by means of a 'mini-reform' programme designed to satisfy EU standards. In subsequent weeks the ruling coalition experienced increasing disagreement over the possible execution of PKK leader Abdullah Öcalan, and on broadcasting and education in the Kurdish language, with the MHP taking an uncompromising stance on these issues in opposition to ANAP. The discord prompted rumours of a possible general election, which intensified towards mid-2002 as it became apparent that the Prime Minister was in poor health. In late June, none the less, Ecevit, who was reportedly under pressure from members of his own party to resign, discounted the possibility of an early election, considering that this would undermine the economic recovery programme.

In July 2002, however, Ecevit was finally forced to call early elections to the TGNA for November after several of his ministers and numerous DSP party legislators resigned, thereby denying the ruling coalition a majority in the TGNA. The MHP had earlier that month publicly called for an early election. Notable resignations included those of Deputy Prime Minister and Minister of State Hüsamettin Özkan, Minister of Foreign Affairs İsmail Cem and Minister of Culture İstemihan Talay. Cem formed a new party, the Yeni Türkiye Partisi (YTP—New Turkey Party), with 62 defectors from the DSP, whose representation in the TGNA had fallen from 128 seats to 65 seats. Ecevit appointed DSP member Şükrü Sina Gürel as Deputy Prime Minister and Minister of State, and concurrently Minister of Foreign Affairs. In early August the Minister of Finance, Kemal Derviş, also resigned, having offered to resign in July, but remaining in office at President Sezer's request. Derviş initially indicated that he would join the YTP, but subsequently agreed to co-operate with the CHP. The Minister of Labour and Social Security also resigned in August, underscoring the disintegration of Ecevit's Government.

Meanwhile, at the end of August 2002 the notably pro-EU and strongly secularist commander of the army's ground forces, Gen. Hilmi Özkök, was appointed to the powerful position of Chief of the General Staff for a four-year term.

In late September 2002 the AK Partisi, which was leading in opinion polls, received a set-back when Turkey's highest election board confirmed the Constitutional Court's decision to ban Erdoğan from holding public office. Although he had publicly professed secular and pro-European views, Erdoğan retained the distrust of the secularist military and judiciary, and in October the chief prosecutor sought to obtain an outright ban on the AK Partisi—although this was not implemented. Attempts by several political parties to delay the election also failed.

The elections to the TGNA, held on 3 November 2002, significantly transformed the Turkish political landscape. The AK

Partisi won 34.3% of the votes cast, securing 363 seats in the TGNA. Only one other party—the CHP—achieved the 10% of the vote required for representation in the TGNA, winning 19.4% of the votes cast and securing 178 seats. The DSP, which had won the majority of seats in the April 1999 election, won just 1.2% of the votes cast, while its coalition partners, the MHP and ANAP, won 8.3% and 5.1% of the vote, respectively. The new Genç Partisi (Youth Party), founded in 2002 by the millionaire businessman, Cem Uzan, won 7.3% of the votes cast. Voter turnout was 79.0%. Following the election President Sezer appointed AK Partisi deputy leader Abdullah Gül as Prime Minister, since Erdoğan was no longer eligible for the position. None the less, Erdoğan acted as *de facto* Prime Minister, exerting a strong influence on the new Government and making a number of foreign official visits. The new Council of Ministers largely consisted of technocrats from the AK Partisi with limited experience of government. Three Deputy Prime Ministers—Abdullatif Şener, Mehmet Ali Şahin and Ertuğrul Yalçınbayır—were appointed, while Ali Babacan became Minister of State for the Economy and Kemal Unakıtan acquired the financial portfolio. Yaşar Yakış was appointed Minister of Foreign Affairs and Mehmet Vecdi Gönül, Minister of National Defence. Owing to the fact that AK Partisi's representation in the TGNA was only four seats short of the two-thirds' majority needed to amend the Constitution, and the party could rely on the support of several independents, in early December constitutional reforms were introduced that would allow Erdoğan to become Prime Minister. Initially vetoed by Sezer, these changes were subsequently re-endorsed by the TGNA, forcing the President to accept them.

In January 2003 Erdoğan was re-elected leader of the AK Partisi and immediately announced plans to stand in a by-election for the TGNA, membership of which would allow him to become Prime Minister. In February the electoral commission endorsed his candidacy, and Erdoğan was elected to the TGNA on 9 March. Two days later President Sezer appointed Erdoğan as Prime Minister, after Abdullah Gül agreed to step down from the post, as expected. Erdoğan appointed a new Council of Ministers, with Gül as Minister of State and concurrently Minister of Foreign Affairs, but retained most ministers from the incumbent Government. Immediately after assuming office Erdoğan was faced with the need to resolve the political stand-off concerning the TGNA's refusal to allow the USA to deploy 62,000 troops in the country in preparation for its war against Saddam Hussain's regime in Iraq. Erdoğan was expected to implement a second vote in the TGNA, at the request of the USA, but eventually refrained from doing so (see below).

Although Turkey was readmitted to the Parliamentary Assembly of the Council of Europe in May 1984, the Assembly continued to advocate the establishment of full democracy and political freedom in the country. In July 1987 all martial law decrees were repealed when martial law was replaced with a state of emergency in several provinces. The Government's signing, in January 1988, of UN and Council of Europe agreements denouncing torture, however, met with a cynical response from both the domestic and international media. Turkey's human rights record has since continued to be a focus of international scrutiny, and recent initiatives to amend articles of the Constitution pertaining to guarantees of basic rights and freedoms have been linked to the country's application for EU membership.

In July 1999 the ECHR found Turkey guilty of 13 counts of violating rights of free speech and ordered it to pay some 110,000m. lira in damages. In August a proposed amnesty law was approved by the TGNA; it was intended to ease the extreme overcrowding in Turkish prisons, with the release of some 26,500 prisoners (of a total prison population of 69,000) and the reduction in sentence for a further 32,000. Although the bill was initially intended to encourage Kurdish rebels to surrender, it was subsequently altered so that prisoners serving sentences for terrorism would not benefit from the law. However, the bill received widespread criticism and was vetoed by President Demirel in early September. Unrest broke out in that month in prisons across the country as a result of the poor conditions and overcrowding; 10 prisoners were killed and a number of guards were taken hostage. The Minister of Justice later announced that a special force was to be established to ensure prison security. In September some 100 people were arrested in İstanbul while trying to issue a press release on the prison incidents. Prison unrest continued, and in February 2000 a protocol was signed providing for the education of prison inmates. During April and May a number of prison officials were dismissed for improper conduct and contacts with prisoners.

In December 1999 the ECHR found Turkey guilty of breaking the European Convention on Human Rights by its closure of the pro-Kurdish Demokrasi Partisi (DEP—Democracy Party, see below) and ordered it to pay compensation of 70,000 French francs. It was also announced that a human rights consultation committee was to be established to provide information and to act on any complaints received.

A report published by the Turkish Human Rights Foundation in June 2000 asserted that as many as 1m. people had been victims of torture over the preceding decade. The report criticized the fact that perpetrators of torture were not subjected to due investigation. The Government admitted in a separate report in December to the Council of Europe that a trade unionist who died in police custody in March 1999 may have been tortured.

In November 2000 hundreds of political prisoners throughout Turkey—mainly members of left-wing organizations—embarked on a hunger strike, in protest against plans to transfer them to high security prisons where they would to be held in so-called 'F-type' cells. The prisoners feared that their isolation in these cells would make them more vulnerable to abuse by prison staff. (The hunger strike was later joined by a small number of the prisoners' relatives.) Following attempts to force-feed the prisoners, in violation of international medical ethics, a stand-off ensued between the prisoners and the authorities. In December Turkish security forces raided some 20 prisons in an attempt to end the hunger strikes. The three-day action resulted in the deaths of 30 prisoners and two soldiers. After the authorities regained control of the prisons over 1,000 prisoners were transferred to the 'F-type' cells. There were widespread allegations, supported by human rights organizations Human Rights Watch and Amnesty International, that many prisoners had been subjected to beatings and torture both before and after their transfer to these cells, where many prisoners resumed their hunger strike. Also in December the TGNA approved legislation to grant amnesty to as many as 35,000 prisoners by reducing gaol sentences by 10 years. The bill was, however, rejected by President Sezer on the grounds that it was divisive and would not serve the cause of justice. In March 2001 the hunger strike claimed its first victim, and by the end of April, the number of deaths had reached 20, with some 30 more seriously ill. The Government refused to open negotiations with the prisoners, although the Minister of Justice announced an initiative to improve prison inspections. Meanwhile, Human Rights Watch claimed that the new prison accommodation was below international standards. In May EU officials warned that failure to resolve the issue could jeopardize Turkey's candidacy for the EU. During the remainder of 2001 many of the strikers were released or hospitalized; of these, some subsequently ended their strike. In November police stormed the houses of some of the released strikers in an attempt forcibly to end the strikes; four protesters reportedly died of self-immolation during the police operation. By January 2003 a total of 104 people had died as a result of the ongoing hunger strikes, but there had hitherto been no compromise on the issue of prison accommodation.

Meanwhile, during 2001 the TGNA introduced new legislation, including constitutional amendments, designed to improve the country's human rights and civil liberties in preparation for eventual EU accession (see above). In March the Government had announced a new programme aimed at facilitating EU membership that entailed, *inter alia*, the eventual abolition of the death penalty and ending restrictions on freedom of expression, as well as improving the rights of minorities, but EU officials criticized the programme for its lack of specifics. Despite such plans, the TGNA approved a four-month extension of the state of emergency in the predominantly Kurdish south-east of the country, and in May the Turkish Radio and Television Supreme Council ordered the closure of 89 radio and television stations for broadcasting separatist and disruptive programmes. In October 2001 the TGNA approved wide-ranging constitutional amendments embracing improvements in civil liberties and human rights; further liberalizing reforms were approved in February 2002 (see above). Meanwhile, in November women were granted new rights, including equal status to men in several key areas. In February 2002 the Government rescinded a law that allowed schoolgirls to be forced to undergo 'virginity tests'—a practice long criticized by human rights organizations and women's groups.

In June 2002 the Government proposed additional reforms that abolished the death penalty and removed a ban on broadcasting and education in the Kurdish language. In early August the TGNA formally abolished the death penalty in peacetime; in September, however, Turkey's reputation on human rights issues suffered a set-back when Amnesty International released a report alleging the widespread use of torture by police, citing testimony from more than 60 individuals during the first half of 2002. In mid-October a court in İstanbul sentenced 10 police officers to prison terms ranging from five to 10 years for beating, torturing and sexually abusing 15 teenage suspects in 1995. The case had received considerable publicity both in Turkey and abroad, and the police officers had been acquitted on two previous occasions, resulting in strong condemnation by human rights groups. The officers launched an appeal against their verdict, but in early April 2003 the Court of Appeals upheld the sentences.

Following his appointment as Prime Minister in March 2003 Erdoğan immediately pledged to bring about major improvements in Turkey's human rights record and to eliminate the use of torture. Further objectives outlined by the new administration included the implementation of outstanding rulings by the ECHR, the removal of restrictions on freedom of expression and conscience, the permitting of non-Muslim religious foundations to own real estate and the creation of a new legislative committee to bring Turkey's human rights into line with EU standards.

The Government's position on the Kurdish situation remained a major element of its human rights policy. In September 2001 hundreds of Kurds were reportedly arrested to prevent their attending a mass rally in Ankara. In January 2002 the Government acted against a campaign to allow the Kurdish language to be taught in schools and universities by arresting hundreds of activists. In February an İstanbul court acquitted a publisher, Fatih Tas, for disseminating 'separatist' articles, written by US academic and linguist Noam Chomsky, which criticized US support for Turkish military operations aimed at suppressing Kurdish nationalism. Chomsky himself attended the trial in support of Tas. In March an internationally acclaimed film focusing on the relationship between Turks and Kurds was withdrawn from cinemas and banned in Turkey on the grounds that it portrayed the police in a negative light and promoted Kurdish nationalism. At the same time the Government postponed the trial of an expatriate Kurdish novelist, who had been charged with violating the ban on the Kurdish language. In late March clashes between security forces and Kurds at a HADEP-organized Kurdish new year celebration in Mersin resulted in the death of two policemen and one demonstrator. The decision by the AK Partisi Government in November 2002 to permit a maximum of 30 minutes per day of Kurdish language programmes on state television and a maximum of 45 minutes on state radio was greeted with disappointment by Kurdish groups, who had long sought unlimited broadcasting of Kurdish programmes on commercial and local radio and television stations.

In mid-March 2003 a ruling by Turkey's Constitutional Court banned HADEP from political activity on the grounds that it had been aiding the PKK—a charge which the party denied. Some 46 members of the party were also subjected to a five-year ban.

A significant increase in outbreaks of urban terrorism in early 1990, coupled with a perceived increase in the influence of fundamentalist thought, led to widespread fears of a return to the extremist violence of the late 1970s. The increase in terrorist attacks by Islamist and left-wing groups, especially the Dev-Sol (Revolutionary Left), was exacerbated by the Government's stance in the Gulf crisis of 1990–91 (see below), and both factions unleashed a series of attacks against Western targets in Turkey, including US civilians, diplomatic missions and offices of several national airlines and banks in İstanbul and Ankara. The leader of Dev-Sol, Dursun Karatas, was detained in France in September 1994, and diplomatic efforts began to ensure his extradition. Two weeks later a former Minister of Justice, Mehmet Topaç, was shot dead by Dev-Sol members in Ankara. In August 1995 several bombs exploded in İstanbul (killing two civilians and injuring some 40 others), at least one of which was reported to have been placed by a previously unknown Islamist group. In January 1996 a left-wing faction of Dev-Sol, Devrimci Halk Kurtuluş Partisi—Cephesi (DHKP—C, the Revolutionary People's Liberation Party—Front), claimed responsibility for the murder of two leading Turkish business executives in İstanbul. At the end of the year it was reported that Dev-Sol had been subsumed by the DHKP—C. The IBDA—C (Islamic Great Eastern Raiders—Front) also claimed responsibility for a number of terrorist attacks in late 1999 and early 2000.

In January 2000 the Government launched a major operation against the fundamentalist guerrilla group Hezbollah (apparently sponsored by fundamentalist elements in Iran but unrelated to the Lebanese group of the same name). An armed confrontation between police and Hezbollah members resulted in the death of its leader, Hüseyin Velioğlu, and the capture of two of his closest associates; information provided by these associates led to the discovery of the bodies of nine men, believed to have been abducted by the group in İstanbul. In early 2000 the operation succeeded in detaining some 690 suspected Hezbollah members and the bodies of more than 50 people, believed to have been victims of the group, were discovered. At that time the Government denied that it had tolerated the activities of Hezbollah, owing to its anti-PKK activities, and the office of the Chief of the General Staff strongly denied allegations of links between Hezbollah and the army. In February Çiller denied that the state had supplied weapons to Hezbollah during her time as Prime Minister and in March two regional FP staff were arrested on suspicion of membership of Hezbollah; the FP said it would expel them if found guilty. In October 2000 Turkish security forces captured Mehmet Sudan, Velioğlu's successor, and the Ministry of the Interior reported that since January some 1,600 people with ties to Hezbollah had been arrested.

In December 2000 two police-officers were killed and a further three were injured following an attack on a police bus in İstanbul. In January 2001 a suicide bomb attack on a police building killed two people. The DHKP—C claimed responsibility for the attack. The DHKP—C was also accused by the authorities of supporting the prisoners' hunger strikes (see above). In April 2001 Sahil Izzet Erdis, the leader of the outlawed IBDA—C, was sentenced to death on charges of seeking to overthrow the secular state. In early September 2001 a suicide bomber, believed to be acting on behalf of the DHKP—C, killed two policemen and a foreign tourist in central İstanbul. In May 2002 the EU designated the DHKP—C as a terrorist organization.

In 1984 the outlawed PKK, seeking the creation of a Kurdish national homeland in Turkey, launched a violent guerrilla campaign against the Turkish authorities in the south-eastern provinces. The Government responded by arresting suspected Kurdish leaders, sending in more security forces, establishing local militia groups, and imposing martial law (and later states of emergency) in the troubled provinces. Violence continued to escalate, however, and in April and May 1990 clashes between rebel Kurds, security forces and civilians resulted in the deaths of 140 people. The conflict entered a new phase when in August and October 1991, and March 1992 (in retaliation for continuing cross-border attacks on Turkish troops), government fighter planes conducted numerous sorties into northern Iraq in order to attack suspected PKK bases there. In the course of these raids many civilians and refugees (including Iraqi Kurds) were reportedly killed, prompting international observers and relief workers publicly to call into question the integrity of the exercises. The Iraqi Government lodged formal complaints with the UN, denouncing Turkish violations of Iraq's territorial integrity.

Violence in the south-eastern provinces, resulting from ethnic tension, persisted throughout 1992 and 1993, despite the stated commitment of the Demirel administration to foster new initiatives for improved relations with ethnic minorities. In late 1992 Turkish air and ground forces (in excess of 20,000 troops), conducted further attacks upon PKK bases inside northern Iraq, hoping to take advantage of losses inflicted on the Kurdish rebels by an offensive in October initiated by Iraqi Kurdish *peshmerga* forces, aimed at forcing the PKK from Iraq. Hopes that a negotiated resolution to the conflict might be achieved, following the unilateral declaration of a cease-fire by the PKK in March 1993, were frustrated by renewed fighting in May and an intensification of the conflict in June. The bombing of several coastal resorts and of tourist attractions in central İstanbul confirmed the PKK's intention to disrupt the country's economy and to attract international attention to the conflict. PKK activists and supporters also conducted protests and attacked Turkish property throughout Europe.

In November 1993 a 10,000-strong élite anti-terrorist force was created to counter the PKK fighters, in addition to the estimated 150,000–200,000 troops already positioned in the area of conflict. In early 1994 the security forces mounted a heavy offensive against the separatists, and again conducted air attacks on suspected PKK strongholds in south-eastern Turkey and in northern Iraq. Reports that an estimated 6,000 Kurds were forcibly displaced into northern Iraq as a result of the destruction of their villages by security forces were denied by the Minister of Foreign Affairs. Further air offensives against Kurdish targets in northern Iraq were undertaken in August, while clashes between the PKK and security forces were reported in south-eastern Turkey. In late September security forces initiated an operation in the eastern Munzur mountains to destroy PKK stores and supply routes. In November a Kurdish proposal for a cease-fire, accompanied by international mediation, to achieve a peaceful settlement to the conflict was rejected by the Government, which emphasized the success of its anti-terrorist campaign.

On 20 March 1995 a massive offensive, involving 35,000 air and ground force troops, was initiated against PKK targets in northern Iraq. Turkish forces advanced some 40 km across the border, prompting protests from Iraq, as well as concern on the part of the USA and the EU that the military intervention should not be consolidated into a permanent occupation force. The Turkish Government insisted that the offensive was designed to destroy PKK base camps and to force the separatists from northern Iraq (where, it claimed, the PKK had taken advantage of a power vacuum in the region to become securely established). The UN assisted in the evacuation of several thousand Kurds from the northern Iraqi town of Zakho, amid reports of intimidation by the occupying Turkish troops. Under increasing international pressure, Turkey undertook a complete withdrawal of its troops by May. Official figures stated that 555 Kurdish separatists and 58 Turkish soldiers were killed as a result of the operation. Earlier, in April, the PKK had obtained permission to convene in the Netherlands, in an attempt to establish a Kurdish parliament-in-exile. Turkey temporarily recalled its ambassador to the Netherlands in protest. Fighting was again resumed in the south-east of the country in June, and in July a further week-long offensive was conducted against Kurdish bases in northern Iraq. In December the PKK leader, Abdullah Öcalan, announced a unilateral cease-fire on the part of his organization. By March 1996, having received no assurances of a cease-fire from the Turkish authorities, Öcalan advised tourists against visiting the country, warning of possible renewed attacks against major tourist sites. During April an estimated 400 PKK members were killed in the renewed military operation. In the following months PKK activists were frequently pursued into northern Iraq by Turkish ground and air forces, provoking protests from the Iraqi Government, and fighting in the south-eastern provinces escalated. At the end of June five soldiers were killed in a suicide bomb attack in Tunceli, eastern Turkey. A further two suicide attacks, reportedly by PKK members, were perpetrated in October killing 10 people. In response Turkish security forces conducted air raids against PKK targets in northern Iraq in November and December. An estimated 2,800 PKK activists were killed during 1996 as a result of the conflict, in addition to 532 members of the security forces and 145 civilians. A cross-border operation involving 5,000 Turkish troops at the start of 1997 resulted in the deaths of some 200 separatists in five days. In March Öcalan called for a process of political dialogue to reach a settlement of the conflict.

In May 1997 Turkey again launched a massive military offensive against the PKK in northern Iraq, involving the mobilization of 50,000 troops. Turkey claimed the incursion was in response to an appeal by the Iraqi-based Kurdistan Democratic Party (KDP), which co-operated with the Turkish attack. The operation elicited rigorous condemnation from Iraq, Iran and Syria, but the response from members of NATO was muted. Turkish military officials claimed that the attack, which continued through June, had achieved its objectives of destroying several PKK bases in northern Iraq and estimated that more than 3,000 PKK troops had been killed. A further offensive, launched in September, was speculated to be part of a Turkish plan to establish a security zone in northern Iraq to prevent cross-border attacks by the PKK. This assumption was apparently confirmed by the lifting of the state of emergency in three of the nine south-eastern provinces at the beginning of October.

Despite PKK threats to extend the separatist struggle throughout Turkey, if the Turkish Government refused to seek a political solution to the conflict, further Turkish troops entered northern Iraq in February 1998. Further operations against the PKK took place in April, including the capture of a former PKK commander, Semdin Sakik. Sakik had surrendered to the DPK in March, following a disagreement with Öcalan, which fuelled

speculation concerning internal dissent within the movement. The Government undertook heavy offensive action in northern Iraq in late May and early June. At the end of August the PKK declared a unilateral cease-fire; this was, however, rejected by the Government.

Relations with Syria, which had already deteriorated in July 1998 (owing to Syria's repeated claim to the Hatay region of Turkey), worsened in early October after Turkey threatened the use of force if Syria did not expel Öcalan and close down terrorist training camps both in Syria and the Beka'a valley in Lebanon. It was reported that 10,000 Turkish troops had been deployed near the border; the Turkish ambassador to Syria was also recalled. Egypt and, later, Iran both attempted to mediate in the dispute, and following a meeting of Turkish and Syrian officials in late October an agreement was signed under which Syria would not allow the PKK to operate on its territory; Öcalan was thus forced to leave the country, and he arrived in Italy in November. Turkey had already temporarily recalled its ambassador to Italy in October after a meeting of the Kurdish parliament-in-exile was hosted there. Relations deteriorated further when Italy refused to extradite Öcalan to Turkey and Öcalan applied for asylum. Demonstrations were held in Turkey against Italy, and Italian goods were boycotted; Turkey also threatened to end diplomatic relations with Italy if Öcalan's asylum request was granted. PKK attacks in the south-east were reported during November, and government operations against the PKK continued. In January 1999 Öcalan was reported to have left Italy after his asylum application was turned down. His whereabouts were unclear, until, in February, Öcalan was captured at the Greek embassy in Kenya and returned to Turkey. Widespread Kurdish protests were held throughout Europe.

At the end of February 1999 Öcalan was formally charged, in the absence of defence counsel, and the first hearing was set for late March. PKK violence in protest at the trial continued in that month, and there were also threats of violence against tourists in Turkey. A series of bomb attacks in İstanbul were later attributed to a new Kurdish group, the Nationalist Kurdish Revenge Teams (MKIT). In early March Turkey conveyed information to the ECHR regarding Öcalan's trial; at that time it was reported that he had appointed two lawyers. In April a further operation was launched against the PKK, involving the deployment of some 15,000 Turkish troops in northern Iraq. Semdin Sakik, the former PKK commander who had been captured in March 1998, was sentenced to death in May 1999; his sentence was upheld by the Supreme Court in October. In late June Öcalan was convicted on treason charges and sentenced to death; violent demonstrations were held in protest at his sentence. A third PKK leader, Cevat Soysal, was arrested in Moldova in July.

In early August 1999 the PKK agreed to a cease-fire, and at that time Öcalan announced that the PKK was prepared to surrender its arms in exchange for Kurdish rights; PKK fighters withdrew from Turkey at the end of the month. However, the Chief of Staff of the Army said that the PKK must also abandon arms entirely in order for Turkey to reassess the situation. Following a statement issued by Öcalan in September in which he urged PKK rebels to show their commitment to the end of hostilities by surrendering to Turkish forces, two eight-member PKK delegations travelled to Ankara where they were arrested and detained by the authorities.

In September 1999 the Kurdish parliament-in-exile convened in Brussels where it voted to dissolve and to join the Kurdistan National Congress. Following the cease-fire, the number of armed confrontations in the south-east had declined substantially and in October the Government reduced the number of check-points in the region. In November Öcalan's death sentence was upheld on appeal and the chief prosecutor rejected his application for a final appeal; his lawyers referred the case to the ECHR. A second trial against Öcalan, together with 101 other defendants, began in Ankara in December for a series of offences including extortion and murder allegedly carried out in the 1970s; the trial was adjourned until February 2000. In January 2000 the parties of the governing coalition announced that they had agreed to delay Öcalan's execution until a ruling had been given by the ECHR.

In February 2000 the PKK announced formally the end to its war against Turkey and said it would campaign for Kurdish rights within a framework of peace and democracy. In February three HADEP mayors were arrested and charged with aiding the PKK; they were released on bail following protests both from within Turkey and internationally, including from the EU. Relations with the EU further deteriorated in February when Turkey denied EU politicians permission to visit Öcalan in prison. At that time 18 people, including the HADEP leader, Ahmet Turan Demir, were sentenced to almost four years' imprisonment for organizing demonstrations in support of Öcalan. Despite the PKK's cease-fire declaration, Turkish troops continued to push into Kurdish strongholds throughout the year. Some 16 members of the PKK were reportedly killed in late May in renewed fighting in south-eastern Turkey. In September at least 38 civilians were reported killed following sorties by Turkish fighter planes into northern Iraq targeting suspected PKK bases and in January 2001 Turkish troops pushed 160 km into Kurdish northern Iraq. Some 2,500 PKK rebels were believed to be based along the Iran–Iraq border at this time. In late March thousands of Turkish troops again advanced into northern Iraq in an attempt to suppress PKK activities.

In June 2000 there were a number of reports of increased tension within the PKK leadership, with some members, including, according to some sources, Öcalan's brother, Osman, no longer acknowledging Abdullah Öcalan as leader of the organization. In September Selahattin Celik, a founder member of the PKK, formed a breakaway group styling itself 'the Initiative' to continue the PKK's armed struggle. However, Celik, who was based in Germany, lacked the resources and manpower to wage a guerrilla war. The hearing of the appeal against Öcalan's death sentence began at the ECHR in November 2000. Öcalan's appeal was based on the grounds that he had not received a fair trial in Turkey under the terms of the European Convention on Human Rights.

In April 2002 the PKK formally announced a change of name to the Congress for Freedom and Democracy in Kurdistan (KADEK), under the leadership of Öcalan, and asserted its wish to campaign peacefully for Kurdish rights. Although the movement had abandoned its initiative for an independent Kurdish state, the announcement was greeted with scepticism on the part of the Turkish Government. In May the EU designated the PKK a terrorist organization, and moved to freeze the group's assets. However, KADEK was not included in the EU's list of terrorist organizations, and it was believed that its agenda had been designed to win support from the EU.

In June 2002 the ECHR awarded compensation to 13 Kurdish former members of the TGNA who had been imprisoned by the Government in 1994 for supporting the PKK. The ECHR accused the authorities of violating the right to free elections by expelling the legislators from the TGNA. At the end of November, in a sign that the Government had acknowledged the final defeat of the PKK, the state of emergency that prevailed in the two remaining south-eastern provinces of Diyarbakır and Sirnak was finally lifted.

In early October 2002, meanwhile, the State Security Court officially commuted Öcalan's death sentence to life imprisonment (albeit with no possibility of parole), in accordance with the abolition of the death penalty in peacetime by the TGNA in August. The court's decision was controversial, since Öcalan was widely despised by the Turkish public for his armed insurrections during the 1980s and 1990s. In March 2003 the ECHR issued a non-binding ruling that Öcalan had not received a fair trial, and criticized Turkey for violating some of Öcalan's rights, although also rejecting accusations by Öcalan's lawyers of inhumane treatment and illegal detention. Turkey immediately appealed against the ECHR, fearing renewed pressure from the EU to hold a retrial if the ruling was upheld. Despite its success in defeating Kurdish separatism, the Government continued to fear the possible emergence of a Kurdish state in northern Iraq after the USA's successful war against Iraqi President Saddam Hussein's regime in March–April 2003 (see below).

Turkey has been a member of NATO since 1952, and is widely considered to have fulfilled a crucial role in NATO defence strategy in south-eastern Europe. During the 1990s Turkey's importance to its key ally, the USA, increased as its strategic location allowed it to co-operate with the USA in regional security issues. The Turkish Government responded positively to requests from the USA for logistical aid, following the forcible annexation of Kuwait by Iraq in August 1990, and complied with UN proposals for economic sanctions against Iraq by closing its border to all non-essential trade and, later, to traffic. In September Turkey and the USA extended an agreement to allow the USA access to more than 25 military establishments, in return for military and economic aid, that had been initially signed in 1980, and renewed in 1987. In mid-January 1991 a resolution to extend the war powers of the Government and effectively endorse the unrestricted use of Turkish air bases by coalition forces was agreed by the TGNA. On the following day US aircraft embarked upon bombing missions into north-east Iraq from NATO bases inside south-east Turkey. In February and March the US Government announced substantial increases in military and economic aid to Turkey. In April an estimated 600,000 Kurds attempted to flee northern Iraq into Turkey. Following a massive international relief effort and the subsequent repatriation of the majority of refugees, the Turkish Government agreed to the deployment in south-east Turkey of a 3,000-strong multi-national 'rapid reaction force', which would respond to any further acts of aggression by Iraq against the Kurds in the newly-created 'safe havens'. While all ground forces were withdrawn in October, the Turkish Government agreed to the continued use of its air bases by a small allied air-strike force to conduct patrols of northern Iraq under the mandate of 'Operation Provide Comfort'. The mandate was granted six-month extensions, despite increasing unease on the part of the Turkish authorities that the Kurdish enclave was providing a refuge for PKK separatists. Difficulties in Turkey's relations with the USA arose in 1994, following a decision by the US Congress to withhold a portion of military and economic aid in order to encourage greater respect for human rights in the Turkish Government's treatment of Kurdish separatists. In early 1996 human rights organizations revealed that weapons supplied by NATO countries were being used in military offensives against Kurdish separatists.

In March 1996 the Turkish Government assured parliament that the mandate for the use of Turkish bases for allied aircraft engaged in 'Operation Provide Comfort' would be terminated following the approval of a final three-month extension. At the end of July, however, the new RP Prime Minister, Necmettin Erbakan, in spite of his earlier election pledge to conclude the arrangement, secured a final extension of the operation's mandate until the end of the year. In September the Turkish Government refused permission for the use of its air bases for a US military operation against Iraqi forces that had violated the Kurdish area in northern Iraq. Turkey amassed an estimated additional 20,000 troops along the border and revealed proposals to establish a temporary security zone in the region in order to stem any influx of refugees from Iraq and to prevent the PKK from exploiting the situation. The Government also undertook to relocate the military co-ordination centre of 'Operation Provide Comfort' from Zakho in northern Iraq to Silopi in south-eastern Turkey. ('Operation Provide Comfort' was superseded by the more limited aerial surveillance operation 'Northern Watch' in January 1997.) In October 1996 the Turkish Government was actively involved in negotiations between the conflicting Kurdish factions in northern Iraq to secure a peace agreement, not least in an attempt to end the power vacuum in that region which threatened Turkey's security. A second round of talks, following the conclusion of a preliminary agreement at the end of October, was initiated in November. During 1996 Turkey pursued diplomatic efforts to secure the reopening of the petroleum pipeline from Kirkuk in northern Iraq to Yumurtalik in Turkey, which had been closed since August 1990 as a result of UN-imposed economic sanctions. The pipeline was finally reactivated in December, in accordance with a UN agreement permitting the export of US $2,000m. of petroleum by Iraq over a six-month period, in order to fund the purchase of essential medical and other humanitarian supplies. As relations between Iraq and the UN deteriorated towards the end of 1997 and in early 1998, Turkey announced that it opposed the use of its Incirlik air base for potential US-led strikes against Iraq and urged a peaceful solution to the crisis. Relations deteriorated further in late 1998, and Turkey again urged a diplomatic solution. Although Turkey was informed of the air-strikes against Iraq in December, in January 1999 it announced that Turkish air bases would not be used in any new operation against Iraq. The Iraqi Deputy Prime Minister, Tareq Aziz, visited Turkey in February and held talks with Turkish officials in which relations with the UN were discussed, along with other bilateral issues.

Following the terrorist attacks on the USA in September 2001, Turkey emerged as a crucial ally in the former's 'war against terror', immediately pledging its co-operation. In October the TGNA agreed in principle to send troops to Afghanistan and allow foreign forces to be stationed in Turkey, and in December US Secretary of State Colin Powell visited Turkey to discuss security and bilateral trade issues. (It was believed that in return for assisting in the US-led campaign, Turkey would gain financial assistance from the USA and persuade the USA to pressure the EU into accepting Turkey's membership.) Meanwhile, hundreds of Turkish commandos were deployed in Uzbekistan in preparation for possible combat in Afghanistan, and 90 of these entered northern Afghanistan to train the opposition United National Islamic Front for the Salvation of Afghanistan (the United Front—UF, or 'Northern Alliance'). Turkey had for some years had contacts with the UF's Gen. Abdulrashid Dostam, having given him asylum in the late 1990s. Turkey assumed command of the International Security Assistance Force (ISAF) in Afghanistan in June 2002, raising its troop presence in that country to 1,000. (Turkish command of the ISAF ended in February 2003, whereupon control of the force passed to Germany and the Netherlands.)

Throughout 2002 Turkish leaders became increasingly concerned about the possibility that the USA would open a 'second front' in its 'war against terror', to overthrow the regime of Saddam Hussain. In particular the Government feared a breakup of the Iraqi state and the creation of a Kurdish state in northern Iraq that could be used to foster Kurdish nationalism in its own territory, and the possible mass exodus of Iraqi Kurds into Turkey. There were also concerns about the disruption to Turkish-Iraqi trade and economic co-operation that any US-led attack would bring. (It was estimated that the Gulf War of 1991 and subsequent sanctions had cost the Turkish economy some US $30,000m.–$40,000m.) Ecevit's illness and the subsequent preparations for elections to the TGNA in November meant that no agreements between Turkey and the USA were reached over the latter's planned invasion of Iraq. Relations between the two countries were further complicated by the victory of the AK Partisi in the elections, and overwhelming public opposition to war against Iraq. By January 2003 a number of senior US officials had visited Turkey to persuade the Government to accept the deployment of 62,000 US troops in the south-east of the country, and the use of the region as a staging post for a 'northern front' in the planned conflict. Following lengthy negotiations the US Government offered a financial package of US $6,000m. in direct grants and an additional $20,000m. in loans and trade concessions in compensation for any economic losses incurred during the war, but Turkish officials considered this figure too low, instead seeking $10,000m. in grants, $15,000m. in credits and loans, and $7,000m. in forgiveness of military debts, as well as written guarantees of US aid. President Sezer in late February warned that US forces could only be deployed in Turkey if the USA obtained a second UN resolution from the UN Security Council authorising the use of force against Iraq.

On 1 March 2003 the TGNA rejected a motion allowing the USA to deploy troops in Turkey. (Although 264 members of the TGNA had voted in favour of the deployment, with 250 against, the motion was four votes short of a majority of deputies in attendance.) As many as 50 AK Partisi legislators voted against the Government, underscoring the level of opposition to US plans for a military campaign to oust the Iraqi regime. On 20 March the TGNA voted only to allow the use of Turkish airspace for the conflict, but endorsed the deployment of Turkish troops in Iraq if considered necessary. The US-led coalition forces initiated attacks against the Iraqi regime on 20 March, and shortly thereafter abandoned attempts to negotiate the use of Turkish bases. The aid package was withdrawn following the TGNA vote, but in early April the USA offered a new, reduced package totalling a maximum of US $8,500m. (including loans) in order to repair bilateral relations. The US Secretary of State, Colin Powell, visited Ankara at that time and secured Turkish permission for humanitarian aid and US logistical supplies to be delivered to US and coalition troops in Iraq via Turkish territory.

Meanwhile, during the US-led military campaign against Iraq, Turkey massed tens of thousands of its troops on its border with Iraq in preparation for deployment in the north of that country, both to prevent the emergence of a Kurdish state and to block an influx of refugees into Turkey. Following the collapse of the regime of Saddam Hussain in mid-April 2003, tensions between Turkey and the USA again momentarily increased, with the latter warning Ankara to withdraw any forces which had crossed the border into Iraq. In place of these, Turkey sent a number of military observers into the northern Iraqi city of Kirkuk, which had been captured by US-backed Iraqi Kurdish forces.

Although Turkey and Greece are both members of NATO, long-standing disputes over sovereignty in the Aegean Sea and concerning Cyprus have strained relations between the two countries, and tension was exacerbated when Turkey granted recognition to the 'Turkish Republic of Northern Cyprus' ('TRNC'), proclaimed in November 1983 (see chapter on Cyprus). In April 1988 the Greek Prime Minister, Andreas Papandreou, officially accepted Turkey's status as an associate of the EC by signing the Protocol of Adaptation (consequent on Greece's accession to the EC) to the EC-Turkey Association Agreement, which the Greek Government had hitherto refused to do, and in June Turgut Özal became the first Turkish Prime Minister to visit Greece for 36 years. In February 1990 relations deteriorated again, following violent clashes between Christians and the Muslim minority in western Thrace, in Greece. Throughout the early 1990s Turkey and Greece maintained strong support for their respective communities in Cyprus during the ongoing, but frequently interrupted, negotiations to resolve the issue.

The issue of the demarcation of territorial waters in the Aegean re-emerged as a source of tension with Greece in 1994. Turkey insisted that it would retaliate against any expansion of territorial waters in the region, as provided for under the terms of the UN Convention on the Law of the Sea (UNCLOS, see p. 000), which entered into force in November. Military exercises in the region were undertaken, by both Turkish and Greek naval vessels, and resumed in June 1995 following ratification of UNCLOS by the Greek Parliament. Relations between the two countries, which remained strained during 1995 over the issue of the treatment of the Muslim minority in western Thrace, deteriorated sharply in early 1996 owing to a series of incidents in the Aegean in which both countries claimed sovereignty of Imia (Kardak), a small, uninhabited island. Turkey's claim was based on a concession granted by Italy prior to the 1947 settlement that awarded the main Dodecanese islands to Greece. The dispute was exploited by nationalist media in both countries, however, the threat of military action was averted in February 1996 when the two sides agreed to a petition of the US Government to withdraw naval vessels from the region and to pursue efforts to conclude a diplomatic solution. Differences remained on the means of achieving a settlement, with Greece proposing to take the dispute to international arbitration, an option endorsed by the EU Council of Ministers, and Turkey advocating bilateral negotiations. Throughout 1996 relations between the two countries remained strained as a result of several minor confrontations between Greek and Turkish patrol vessels in the Aegean, persistent Greek allegations of violations of its airspace by Turkish aircraft and Turkish concern at the treatment of the ethnic population in western Thrace. From mid-1996 an escalation in intercommunal tension in Cyprus emphasized divisions between the two countries. Turkey remained committed in its support for the 'TRNC' authorities and resolved to respond with military action to the proposed deployment of an anti-aircraft missile system in the Greek Cypriot territory. A joint defence doctrine was agreed by the Turkish and 'TRNC' authorities in January 1997, and in March a co-operation accord, providing for some US $250m. in economic assistance to the 'TRNC', was ratified by the two sides.

In April 1997, following Greece's continued refusal to conduct bilateral discussions with Turkey over sovereignty rights in the Aegean, Turkey rejected proposals to refer the dispute over Imia (Kardak) to the International Court of Justice (ICJ). At the end of April the Greek and Turkish ministers responsible for foreign affairs held bilateral talks in Malta under EU auspices, during which it was agreed that each country would establish a committee of experts to help resolve bilateral disputes. The two committees were to be separate and independent and were to communicate through the EU. In July, at a NATO summit in Madrid, Spain, direct talks took place between Demirel and the Greek Prime Minister, Konstantinos Simitis (the first such meeting for three years). An agreement, known as the Madrid agreement, was signed in which both sides pledged to respect the other's sovereign rights and to renounce violence, and the threat of violence, in their dealings with each other. Later in July, following earlier statements from Turkey expressing the hope that Greece would revoke its veto on EU aid, Greece stated that the veto would not be removed unless Turkey agreed to international arbitration over the disputed islet of Imia (Kardak).

In July 1997 Turkey announced the formation of a joint committee to implement partial integration between Turkey and the 'TRNC', in response to the EU's agreement to commence accession talks with Cyprus. Turkey also declared in September that should the EU continue to conduct membership talks with the Greek Cypriot Government, then it would seek further integration with the 'TRNC'. Shortly afterwards Turkey banned all Greek Cypriot ships from entering Turkish ports. Following the involvement of Greece in Greek Cypriot military exercises in October, in November Turkish forces engaged in military manoeuvres in the 'TRNC'. However, Yılmaz and Simitis held a cordial meeting later in November and agreed to explore confidence-building measures. Throughout 1997 and early 1998 relations were strained by accusations of violations of airspace and territorial waters, made by both Greece and Turkey. The most serious incident occurred in October when Greece accused Turkey of harassing a plane carrying the Greek Minister of Defence. In January 1998 Turkey declared that a Greek plan to extend its territorial waters from six to 12 miles under UNCLOS was unacceptable, as were plans to open several Aegean islets for settlement. Turkey also protested to the UN that the proposed opening of an airbase at Paphos in southern Cyprus would destabilize the military situation on the island. In April Greece again vetoed the release of aid promised to Turkey under the Turkish-EU customs union.

Relations deteriorated in 1998 as a result of a purchase agreement between the Greek-Cypriot Government and Russia for anti-aircraft missiles. Turkey maintained that their deployment would be a threat to its territory and in July announced that it planned to deploy missiles in the 'TRNC' if the missiles deal proceeded. In December, however, the Greek Cypriot Government announced that it would not be deploying the missiles in Cyprus and that they would be deployed on Crete, Greece. In January 1999 Turkey refused to pay compensation which had been awarded by the ECHR to a Greek Cypriot woman for land lost as a result of the Turkish occupation of northern Cyprus.

Relations with Greece deteriorated in early 1999 following repeated Turkish accusations of Greek support for the PKK; Greece denied the accusations, although Öcalan was later captured at the Greek embassy in Kenya. In March Turkey alleged that Greece had unilaterally suspended 'confidence-building' talks on the dispute in the Aegean, and denied a claim that Turkish aircraft had violated Greek airspace. At the end of August relations between the two countries improved markedly, following the Greek response to the earthquake that occurred in north-west Turkey at the end of that month. Greek rescue teams were among the first to arrive in Turkey, and Greece agreed to lift its veto on EU development loans and aid to Turkey; Turkey reciprocated the gesture by sending a rescue team to Greece following a smaller-scale earthquake in Athens in September. A joint business council announced it was to resume its activities in September and in that month the Turkish and Greek ministers responsible for foreign affairs met in Brussels, Belgium, where they emphasized the positive atmosphere between the two countries. Train services linking Greece and Turkey were introduced in November. In January 2000 the Greek Minister of Foreign Affairs made the first official visit to Turkey by a Greek foreign minister in 38 years, during which it was agreed that direct talks would be held to reduce military tensions in the Aegean. In February the Turkish Minister of Foreign Affairs made an equally historic visit, becoming the first Turkish foreign minister to visit Greece in 40 years. In October 2000, however, relations with Greece were strained once again, when Greece withdrew from a joint NATO military exercise in the Aegean, after it accused Turkey of preventing Greek aircraft from flying over the disputed islands of Limnos and Ikaria. This followed a joint NATO military exercise with Greek and Turkish troops on a Greek beach in June, which had been considered to be a mark of considerable progress in Greek–Turkish relations. Relations with Greece were further strained in February 2001 when the Greek parliament decreed a 'Genocide Day' to commemorate the Turkish assault on the Greek community in eastern Turkey by Atatürk's forces in 1922. However, in April 2001 both Turkey and Greece announced major reductions in their weapons-procurement programmes, and in May Greece announced measures to improve the rights of its ethnic Turks (mainly in Thrace). In June the two countries discussed the possibility of allowing Turkish nationals to visit Greek islands in the Aegean for day trips without the need for visas, and the Minister of Foreign Affairs, İsmail Cem, received his Greek counterpart, Georgios Papandreou, to discuss friendship-building measures such as the de-mining of their mutual border and co-hosting the 2008 European Football Championship. In November Turkey and Greece signed an agreement that allowed Greece to repatriate illegal Turkish immigrants.

None the less, Cyprus continued to overshadow bilateral relations, and in May 2001 Cem warned that there would be 'no limits' to Turkey's response were Cyprus to be admitted to EU membership before a political settlement had been reached; in early November Ecevit warned that Turkey could annex the 'TRNC' if this were to occur. In February 2002 the Turkish and Greek foreign ministers recommenced talks, following the resumption of negotiations between the Greek and Turkish Cypriot sides on the island.

In mid-March 2002 Turkey and Greece discussed ongoing disputes over the Aegean Sea, including the control of the continental shelves and the resources beneath them. Later in the month the two Governments signed an agreement to build a 285-km natural gas pipeline from Ankara to Komotini, Greece, thereby allowing Iranian gas to flow to the EU via the existing Tabriz (Iran)–Ankara pipeline. In late April the Turkish and Greek foreign ministers announced that they would send a joint mission to the Middle East to support efforts to end the Israeli–Palestinian violence. In September 2002 a series of meetings took place between Turkish and Greek officials and government ministers, and in October Greece offered its support for the scheduling of EU accession negotiations with Turkey.

Following the elections to the TGNA in November 2002, Recep Tayyip Erdoğan stated that a final peace agreement over Cyprus would accelerate Turkey's chances of joining the EU. Erdoğan, whose political priority was Turkey's membership of the EU, was increasingly at odds with Turkish Cypriot President Rauf Denktaş's unyielding stance on reaching a political solution. In January 2003 Erdoğan publicly criticized Denktaş and stated that he was in favour of a new policy for Cyprus, with a view to achieving a solution by 28 February 2003—a date set by the UN —in order to allow the 'TRNC' to join the EU in 2004 at the same time as the Greek part of the island. During late 2002 and early 2003 the Turkish- and Greek-Cypriot leaders had made significant progress towards reaching a final agreement, which would permit the entire island to accede to the EU in May 2004. However, the subsequent collapse of the peace plan in March 2003 (see chapter on Cyprus) meant that only the Greek part of Cyprus would accede to the EU in the following year, thereby threatening Turkey's improving relations with Greece and jeopardizing Turkey's EU accession bid.

Following the 1980 military coup, the EC-Turkish Association Council (which had been established in 1963) was suspended, together with all community aid to the country. Turkey was readmitted to associate membership of the EC in September 1986, but failed to gain access to the suspended EC aid or to extend the rights of the large number of Turkish workers in Europe. In April 1987 Turkey made a formal application to become a full member of the EC. In December 1989 the application was effectively rejected, at least until 1993, by the Commission of the European Communities. The Commission cited factors including Turkey's unsatisfactory human rights record, high rate of inflation, dependence upon the rural population and inadequate social security provisions as falling short of EC expectations. During informal discussions in 1993 representatives of the EC reiterated their concern at abuses of human rights in Turkey and the lack of progress in the political negotiations regarding Cyprus; however, they recognized the strategic importance of Turkey's role as a stable regional influence. The Turkish Government began to implement measures to construct a customs union with the EU, which was to become effective on 1 January 1995. Human rights issues remained the main obstacle to securing an agreement, and in December 1994 the customs union was postponed on these grounds. An attempt to conclude the agreement in January 1995 was unsuccessful, owing to opposition from the Greek Government. (The negotiations were complicated by Greek demands concerning EU relations with Cyprus.) In February Greece withdrew its veto on the customs union, having received assurance on the accession of Cyprus to the EU, and the agreement was signed in March; however, it was to be subject to ratification by the European Parliament. The Turkish Government subsequently pursued efforts to introduce new democratization legislation and to secure the support of European leaders for the customs union by extending guarantees on human rights and treatment of its Kurdish population. The final terms of the arrangement were agreed at a meeting of the EU-Turkish Association Council in October, and were approved by the European Parliament in December. The EU was expected to provide a total of ECU

1,800m. over a five-year period, in order to assist the implementation of the new trade regime and to alleviate any initial hardships resulting from the agreement. The customs union came into effect on 1 January 1996. Its implementation was, however, delayed owing to Greek opposition to the release of ECU 375m. in aid, claiming that Turkish action in the Aegean was a violation of the agreement. In July Greece withdrew its opposition to Turkey's participation in an EU-Mediterranean assistance programme, although the block on funds from the customs union remained in effect. Throughout 1996 the Turkish Government criticized the EU for its failure to adhere to the terms of the economic agreement. In January 1997 Turkey warned that it would disrupt any expansion of NATO if the EU refused to consider the Turkish membership application. Previously, Turkey had prevented the use of NATO facilities by members of Western European Union owing to Greek opposition to Turkey's full participation in the regional defence grouping. In late January the foreign affairs ministers of five EU countries assured Çiller that there were no obstacles, in principle, to Turkey's membership of the EU.

Relations with the EU were tense in 1997 as the next group of EU applicants was selected. In December, following EU announcements that Turkey would not be invited to join the EU, but that it would be invited to a newly-created EU Conference, which was to include both EU and non-EU states, Turkey stated that it would not attend such a conference and that it would also cease negotiations on Cyprus, human rights and the Aegean disputes. It further threatened to boycott EU goods and to withdraw its application to the EU if it was not included in a list of candidates by June. On 20 December Turkey announced a six-month freeze in relations with the EU. The EU later announced it was withholding all aid to Turkey for 1998, owing to the situation in the south-east of the country and its human rights problems. Turkey officially declined its invitation to the EU Conference in March 1998 and in May Turkey declined to attend a scheduled meeting of the EU-Turkish Association Council. Relations with France deteriorated in May when the French National Assembly adopted a motion recognizing the Turkish 'genocide' against the Armenians between 1915 and 1923; a number of bilateral military and commercial contracts were suspended as a result. Relations with France temporarily improved in February 2000, following a decision by the French Senate not to place the draft law recognizing the Armenian 'genocide' (approved by the National Assembly in 1998) on its agenda for discussion.

In October 1999 an EU report declared Turkey to be a suitable candidate to join that body, although at that time Turkey said that it would not accept any extraordinary conditions attached to such a candidacy, particularly with relation to Öcalan and the Kurdish problem. A number of EU members declared their support for Turkey in late 1999, including Greece and Italy; Turkish relations with both countries had improved in that year. In December Turkey was invited to attend the EU summit in Helsinki and to accept formal status as a candidate for membership. Turkey initially objected, owing to attached conditions concerning Cyprus and the Aegean dispute with Greece, but following a visit to Turkey by Javier Solana, the Secretary General of the Council of the European Union, Turkey accepted. It announced at that time that it would seek an end to its territorial disputes with Greece by 2004, the deadline set by the EU for a review.

In August 2000 Turkey signed the International Covenant of Civil and Political Rights and the International Covenant on Economic, Social and Cultural Rights. This was described as a positive step by the EU in its progress to accession report on Turkey in November 2000, although it pointed out that Turkey had not yet acceded to a number of other major human rights instruments, such as the abolition of the death penalty and the Convention on the Elimination of All Forms of Racial Discrimination. The report concluded that Turkey did not yet meet the Copenhagen criteria (which state that a country must have achieved 'stability of institutions guaranteeing democracy, the rule of law, human rights and respect for and protection of minorities'), thus making accession negotiations impossible, and described the overall human rights record in Turkey as worrying. It also stated that although Turkey had the basic features of a democratic system, it was slow to implement institutional reforms. Accession was also conditional on a satisfactory settlement of the Cyprus problem. This condition led to the Turkish withdrawal from the UN-sponsored proximity talks in protest. Prime Minister Ecevit accused the EU of 'deception' over Tur-

key's membership application, stating that the EU had reneged on a promise not to link Turkey's application to a resolution of the Cyprus problem and disputes with Greece over territorial rights in the Aegean Sea. A rewording of the Cyprus condition was later approved by Turkey, although tensions between Ankara and Brussels remained following the EU decision to defer negotiations on Turkish membership to 2010. Further tension was caused by Turkey's obstruction of an EU-NATO agreement enabling the EU's planned Rapid Reaction Force to use NATO assets, despite Turkey's offer to contribute up to 6,000 troops to the Rapid Reaction Force.

In February 2001 the NSC sought to make compromises on disagreements over Turkey's action plan for achieving EU membership. The NSC decided that further efforts would be made to 'remove obstacles' to Kurdish-language broadcasting and education, and increase the number of civilians on the NSC.

In 2000 and 2001 the issue of the Armenian 'genocide' question also continued to provoke tension between Turkey and the international community. In April 2000 Turkey complained to Israel after the Israeli education minister stated that he believed school pupils should be taught of the 'genocide' of the Armenians; the minister was speaking at a meeting to mark the 85th anniversary of the massacre. In October the Turkish parliament threatened not to renew the USA's mandate to use a Turkish airbase if the US Congress backed a draft resolution which referred to the killing of the 1.5m. Armenians by Turkey in 1915 as 'genocide'. Following intervention by President Bill Clinton the House of Representatives agreed to withdraw the resolution. The European Parliament adopted a resolution in mid-November which formally accused Turkey of genocide against Armenians in 1915 (at the same time it also called on Turkey to pull its forces out of the 'TRNC'). Turkey reacted angrily, with the FP proposing a legislative investigation 'with the aim of removing wrong and biased opinions'. Relations with France were, however, more seriously damaged in January 2001, after the French National Assembly unanimously voted to recognize the 1915 massacre of the Armenians under the Ottoman Empire as 'genocide', against the wishes of the Government. In November 2000 the French Senate had already voted to recognize the massacre as genocide; none the less, the French Government attempted to reassure Turkey that relations between the two countries remained intact. Following the National Assembly vote, however, Ecevit stated that the French action would damage relations between the two countries and recalled Turkey's ambassador to France immediately after the vote for consultations. In late January 2001 Turkey cancelled a surveillance satellite contract with a French firm. Another French company was barred from tendering for a major defence contract and the minister for health threatened to ban French medical imports. Turkey also removed a French telecommunications group from the list of bidders for the privatization of the state-owned telecommunications company. The Government further announced plans to erect a 'genocide' monument to the 1.5m. Algerians killed in the 1954–62 war of independence against the French. In that same month Turkey also reacted angrily at the presence of Armenians at Holocaust memorial ceremonies in the United Kingdom.

Relations between Turkey and the EU received a set-back in early May 2001 when the ECHR ruled that Turkey had grossly violated the human rights of thousands of Greek Cypriots during its invasion, and subsequent occupation of northern Cyprus since 1974. The court highlighted the failure of the Turkish Government to investigate the fate of missing Greek Cypriots, and their forcible eviction from the north and the subsequent confiscation of their property.

In late May 2001 Turkey nominally agreed to grant the EU's Rapid Reaction Force access to NATO assets for future operations. Although Turkey would be consulted on such matters, it would not have the same participation rights or veto powers as the existing 15 EU members. However, Turkish officials remained dissatisfied at the arrangements, having lobbied strongly for a greater influence in EU security planning—some 13 of the 16 potential EU crisis scenarios were in Turkey's geographical vicinity. Turkey also feared that an upsurge of violence in Cyprus would necessitate the deployment of the Rapid Reaction Force on the island, placing the EU directly against itself, and had unsuccessfully sought guarantees against such an eventuality. In early December Turkey finally reached agreement with the EU regarding the Rapid Reaction Force after months of British diplomacy.

In August 2001 meanwhile, the ECHR ruled that the Government's decision to ban the Islamist FP did not violate human rights laws. In October the TGNA passed constitutional amendments designed to facilitate EU membership but stopped short of abolishing the death penalty, a crucial EU demand. The issue of capital punishment placed the EU at odds with the ultra-nationalist MHP in the ruling coalition, which had pledged to exact the death penalty imposed on PKK leader Abdullah Öcalan.

In late January 2002 the French Minister of Defence, Alain Richard, visited Turkey in an attempt to improve bilateral relations following the diplomatic crisis over the Armenian 'genocide' in 2001. In mid-February Turkey hosted a meeting of EU ministers and ministers from the Organization of the Islamic Conference (OIC) in İstanbul in an effort to promote dialogue between the West and the Muslim world in the aftermath of the US-led war in Afghanistan.

In August 2002 the EU welcomed the TGNA's vote to abolish the death penalty in peacetime, as part of a broader package of reforms, and, similarly, reacted positively to the commutation of Öcalan's death sentence to life imprisonment in October of that year (see above).

The new AK Partisi Government elected in November 2002 pledged to accelerate efforts to join the EU. However, in that month Valéry Giscard d'Estaing, the Chairman of the Convention on the Future of Europe, made controversial remarks when he publicly stated that Turkey should never be allowed to join the EU, and that its accession would mean the 'end of the European Union'. Senior EU officials distanced themselves from the remarks, which were also dismissed by Erdoğan. At the EU summit in Copenhagen, Denmark, in December 2002, EU leaders agreed to delay negotiations on Turkish membership until after December 2004, and to resume discussions then only if Turkey had fulfilled all the entry obligations. Several EU members, notably France and Germany, remained less enthusiastic about Turkish membership, citing its poor human rights record, which Turkey again pledged to improve. The delays angered the Turkish Government, and Erdoğan warned that continuing delays to negotiations and attempts to exclude Turkey from the EU could lead to a 'Muslim' backlash against the organization. Turkey was further angered in February 2003 by France, Germany, and Belgium's initial obstruction of NATO plans to deploy defensive equipment to Turkey as a precaution against possible retaliation from Iraq in the run-up to the US-led military campaign against the regime of President Saddam Hussein.

A further complication to Turkish ambitions for EU membership emerged with the failure of the Cyprus peace plan in March 2003. The accession to the EU of the Greek part of the island in 2004 would mean that Turkey did not recognize one of the organization's constituent members—a situation that the EU was unwilling to countenance. Furthermore, a precondition for Turkey's EU membership was the successful resolution of territorial disputes with all members of the union.

In March 2003 the EU criticized the Turkish Constitutional Court's decision to ban HADEP, stating that the ban contradicted the process of political reform. Also in that month the Turkish State Security Court acquitted nine German and six Turkish nationals who had been accused of forming a 'secret alliance' aimed at undermining the Turkish state. The case had strained relations between Turkey and Germany in preceding months.

Following the formal dissolution of the USSR in December 1991, the Turkish Government sought to further its political, economic and cultural influence in the Caucasus and Central Asia, in particular with Azerbaijan, Kazakhstan, Kyrgyzstan, Turkmenistan, and Uzbekistan, all of which share ethno-linguistic ties with Turkey. Following the outbreak of war between Armenia and Azerbaijan in 1991, Turkey blockaded Armenia and provided support to its 'Turkic' ally, Azerbaijan. In April 1992 Prime Minister Demirel undertook an official visit to several former Soviet republics, pledging aid of more than US $1,000m. in the form of credits for the purchase of Turkish goods and contracts. At the same time programmes broadcast by the Turkish national television company began to be relayed, by satellite, to the region. In June leaders of 11 nations, including Turkey, Greece, Albania and six former Soviet republics, established the Organization of the Black Sea Economic Co-operation (see p. 293), and expressed their commitment to promoting greater co-operation with regard to transport, energy, information, communications and ecology. In October 1994 a meeting of the Heads of State of Turkey, Azerbaijan, Turkmenistan, Uzbekistan, Kazakhstan and Kyrgyzstan took place in İstanbul, in an effort to develop and improve relations among the 'Turkic' republics. Summit meetings have subsequently been convened each year. In the late 1990s, Turkey sought to encourage Western firms to build a new petroleum pipeline from Baku, Azerbaijan, to the Turkish port of Ceyhan, thereby allowing the transportation of petroleum from the Caspian Sea to the Mediterranean, via Azerbaijan and Georgia. Such a scheme would also increase Turkey's importance to the EU by making it the centre of the Transport Corridor Europe–Caucasus–Asia (TRACECA) project. Despite the cost of the pipeline, construction began in June 2002. In October 2000 President Sezer signed military co-operation pacts with Kyrgyzstan and Uzbekistan, allowing Turkey to train and equip their armed forces. In mid-2001 work began on a new natural gas pipeline from Dzhubga, Russia, to Samsun, Turkey, beneath the Black Sea, which would increase Turkey's dependency on Russian natural gas.

In late 1995 a long-standing dispute with Syria and Iraq concerning the water supply from the Euphrates and Tigris rivers re-emerged as a major source of tension in Turkey's external relations. (Hostilities with Syria had already intensified during the year over that country's apparent support for the PKK, with the Turkish Government accusing Syria of supplying armaments to the separatist organization.) In December Syria issued a formal protest at the construction of a new hydroelectric dam on the Euphrates river (as part of the extensive southern Anatolia project—GAP) arguing that it would adversely affect the supply of water flowing into Syria. Further protests by Syria and Iraq that Turkey was storing their share of water from the two rivers and restricting flow, in contravention of previous agreements, resulted in a ruling, in March 1996, by the Council of the Arab League that the waters of the rivers should be shared equally between the three countries. In September 1997, President Demirel appealed for talks with Syria and Iraq on the use of the waters of the Euphrates. In August 1998, however, the Government refused to revive water talks with Syria and Iraq, citing issues that had first to be improved between the countries, primarily that of terrorism. Relations between Syria and Turkey improved during 1999 and in October officials from the two countries reportedly agreed to open a new border crossing. However, in January 2000 Turkey appealed to the USA not to remove Syria from its list of nations accused of sponsoring terrorism, until such time as all PKK bases had been removed from Syria, and in that month Turkey ruled out any concessions on the water issue in order to aid talks between Israel and Syria. In March Turkey and Syria announced a new framework for bilateral relations and discussed the basic principles which would apply to them, although in that month Turkey warned against the use of a map, prepared by Syria for use at a trade fair, which showed the Turkish region of Hatay as Syrian territory. A major improvement in relations materialized in early 2002 when Turkey signed an agreement with Syria allowing for joint military exercises. In early 2003 Turkey and Syria agreed to co-operate in bringing about a peaceful solution to the crisis over Iraq's alleged weapons of mass destruction and the US pursuit of regime change in Iraq.

In early 1996 Turkey signed a new military and intelligence co-operation agreement with Israel, which permitted the use of Turkish airbases and airspace for military training purposes. The pact stemmed from common concerns about Iran, Iraq, and Syria, and received support from the USA, a strong ally of both Turkey and Israel. The Arab League denounced the agreement as 'an act of aggression'. Business deals quickly followed, especially those concerning the supply of Turkish water to Israel. However, the gradual improvement in Turkey's relations with its Arab neighbours from 2000 made the pact with Israel less significant, and, in response to the increasing violence between Israelis and Palestinians in the West Bank and Gaza, Prime Minister Ecevit in April 2002 accused Israel of 'genocide' against the Palestinians. He appeared to be responding to increasing public sympathy in Turkey to the Palestinian cause. None the less, in August 2002 Turkey signed an agreement with Israel according to which it would sell the latter 50m. cu m of water every year for the next 20 years. The election of the AK Partisi Government in November 2002 initially raised Israeli fears of a deterioration in bilateral relations, although by mid-2003 this had failed to materialize.

In April 1996 the Turkish and Iranian authorities ordered the expulsion of diplomatic personnel following accusations of Iranian involvement in Islamic terrorist attacks committed in

Turkey in the early 1990s. In August relations with Iran were strengthened by the conclusion of an agreement providing for the construction of a 320-km pipeline between the two countries and the export of substantial supplies of natural gas from Iran by 1999 (later revised to 1998). In December 1996 the Presidents of Turkey and Iran agreed to pursue greater economic and security co-operation. A trade agreement was concluded granting each other the status of most favoured nation. In February 1997 the Iranian ambassador to Turkey provoked a diplomatic crisis by advocating the introduction of Islamic law in Turkey. Criticism of the actions of the Turkish military by an Iranian consul-general later in that month resulted in both men being asked to leave the country. Iran responded by expelling two Turkish diplomats. However, both countries immediately undertook diplomatic initiatives to restore relations, and in March it was agreed that all bilateral agreements were to be pursued. Following negotiations, it was announced at the end of September that full diplomatic relations were to be resumed.

In October 1998 Iran and Turkey established a committee to demarcate their joint border; they later signed a memorandum to increase customs co-operation at their main border crossing. In February 1999, during discussions on bilateral relations the two countries agreed to implement measures aimed at more effective co-operation on border security. In that month the border crossing with Iran was closed for security reasons owing to PKK activity in the area in protest at Öcalan's arrest. In June a meeting of the Turkish-Iranian border committee was held for the first time since 1994; a number of issues were discussed and it was agreed that the committee should meet every year. In July, however, the Turkish chargé d'affaires was twice summoned to the Iranian Ministry of Foreign Affairs following the alleged bombing of an Iranian border region by Turkey in which five people died, although Turkey claimed that its air force had bombed Kurdish targets in Iraq not Iran. In August a meeting of the Turkish-Iranian security commission ended with the signing of a memorandum of understanding in which the two countries agreed to combat illegal organizations within their respective territories. In October Turkey announced it would contribute to compensation for the Iranian bomb damage; a Turkish report into the incident concluded that Turkey had bombed Iraq not Iran, although some people with Iranian citizenship, living in northern Iraq, might have been affected. In October Iran's President Muhammad Khatami welcomed the improvement in ties with Turkey although in that month Iran expressed concern about Turkey's co-operation with Israel. In December Turkey protested to Iran following the death of a soldier in a clash on the border. In January 2000 the Iranian and Turkish ministers responsible for foreign affairs held talks in Ankara and signed a memorandum of understanding to promote co-operation between the two countries. During 2001 both countries sought to improve co-operation in combating drugs-trafficking and organized crime. However, rising tensions between Azerbaijan and Iran over claims to the Caspian Sea, Turkey's strong support for Azerbaijan, its continuing alliance with Israel, and competition for influence in the Caucasus and Central Asia, threatened to bring occasional tensions to the relationship. In early 2003 both Turkey and Iran were seeking to increase their influence in Iraq during the build-up of US military forces in the region, and after the subsequent collapse of the regime of Saddam Hussain, Turkey sought to develop ties with Iraq's ethnic Turkoman minority, with Iran favouring the majority Shi'a population of Iraq.

In January 1997 the Ministers of Foreign Affairs of eight Islamic developing countries—Bangladesh, Egypt, Indonesia, Iran, Malaysia, Nigeria, Pakistan and Turkey—convened in İstanbul to formulate a joint position and conclude agreement on the organizational structures of a new Developing Eight (D-8, see p. 339). A summit meeting of D-8 heads of state was held in June, in order formally to inaugurate the organization.

Government

Under the Constitution approved by referendum in November 1982, legislative power is vested in the unicameral Turkish Grand National Assembly (TGNA), with 400 deputies, who are elected by universal adult suffrage for a five-year term. Executive power is vested in the President, to be elected by the TGNA for a seven-year term and empowered to appoint a Prime Minister and senior members of the judiciary, the Central Bank and broadcasting organizations; to dissolve the TGNA; and to declare a state of emergency entailing rule by decree. An amendment adopted in June 1987 increased the number of deputies in the TGNA from 400 to 450. Further amendments adopted by the

TGNA in July 1995 increased the number of deputies to 550 and reduced the minimum age of suffrage from 21 to 18 years.

For administrative purposes, Turkey comprises 67 provinces and 2,074 municipalities.

Defence

Turkey joined the North Atlantic Treaty Organization (NATO) in 1952. Military service in the army lasts for 18 months. The total strength of the active armed forces at 1 August 2002 was 514,850 (including 391,000 conscripts), comprising an army of 402,000, a navy of 52,750 and an air force of 60,100. There was a gendarmerie numbering 150,000 and a coast guard of 2,200. Reserve forces totalled 378,700 in the armed forces and 50,000 in the gendarmerie. Defence expenditure for 2002 was budgeted at TL 9,700,000,000m.

Economic Affairs

In 2001, according to estimates by the World Bank, Turkey's gross national income (GNI), measured at average 1999–2001 prices, was US \$168,335m., equivalent to \$2,540 per head (or \$6,640 per head on an international purchasing-power parity basis). During 1990–2001, it was estimated, the population increased at an annual average rate of 1.5%, while gross domestic product (GDP) per head increased, in real terms, by an average annual rate of 1.1%. Overall GDP increased, in real terms, by an annual average of 2.6% in 1990–2001. GDP decreased by 6.1% in 1999, but showed an increase of 6.3% in 2000 before declining again, by 9.4%, in 2001.

Agriculture (including forestry and fishing) contributed 12.6% to GDP in 2001 and employed 45.8% of the economically active population in 1999. The country is self-sufficient in most basic foodstuffs. The principal agricultural exports are cotton, tobacco, wheat, fruit and nuts. Other important crops are barley, sunflower and other oilseeds, maize, sugar beet, potatoes, tea and olives. The raising of sheep, goats, cattle and poultry is also an important branch of the economy. During 1990–2001 agricultural GDP increased by an annual average of 0.6%.

Industry (including mining, manufacturing, construction and power) contributed 29.6% to GDP in 2001 and engaged 20.5% of the employed population in 1999. During 1990–2001 industrial GDP increased by an annual average of 2.8%.

Mining contributed 1.1% to GDP in 2001 and engaged 0.6% of the employed population in 1999. Chromium, copper and borax are the major mineral exports. Coal, petroleum, natural gas, bauxite, iron ore, manganese and sulphur are also mined. In the late 1990s the country's first gold mine, near Bergama on the Aegean coast, was being developed. During 1990–2001 manufacturing GDP increased by an annual average of 0.8%.

Manufacturing contributed 19.7% to GDP in 2001 and employed 14.1% of the employed population in 1999. The most important branches, measured by gross value of output, are textiles, food-processing, petroleum refineries, iron and steel, and industrial chemicals. In 1997 the textiles and clothing sector accounted for 39.5% of total export revenues. During 1990–2001 manufacturing GDP increased by an annual average of 3.4%.

Energy is derived principally from thermal power plants. In 1999 31.8% of energy was derived from coal, with 31.2% from natural gas, 29.8% from hydroelectric power, and a further 6.9% from petroleum. The energy sector contributed 3.8% to GDP in 2001 and employed 0.4% of the employed population in 1999. Total domestic output of crude petroleum and natural gas accounts for roughly 12% of the country's hydrocarbon requirements. Imports of crude petroleum comprised 13.9% of the value of total imports in 2000. In the long term, a major development project for south-east Anatolia, scheduled for completion in 2010, aims to increase Turkey's energy production by 70% and to irrigate 1.6m. ha of uncultivable or inadequately irrigated land, by constructing dams and hydroelectric plants on the Tigris and Euphrates rivers and their tributaries. In June 2000 the TGNA approved the construction of an petroleum pipeline between Baku, Azerbaijan, and the Turkish terminal at Ceyhan. The pipeline was also to cross Georgian territory and was expected to raise substantial future revenues for the Government. In mid-2001 construction began on a new 'blue stream' natural gas pipeline running between Russia and Turkey under the Black Sea. During 1990–99 the GDP of the energy sector grew by an annual average of 0.6%.

The services sector contributed 57.8% of GDP in 2001, and engaged 33.7% of the employed labour force in 1999. Tourism is one of Turkey's fastest growing sources of revenue. In 2000 revenues from around 10.4m. visitors to the country totalled

US $7,636m., compared with $5,203m. from 7.5m. tourists in the previous year. Tourism rose sharply in 2001, with around 11.6m. visitors, generating $8,090m. in revenue, as a result of the sharp decline in the value of the lira following its devaluation in February 2001. Remittances from Turkish workers abroad also make an important contribution to the economy, amounting to $2,835m. in 2001. During 1990–2001 the GDP of the services sector increased by an annual average of 2.5%.

In 2001 Turkey recorded a visible trade deficit of US $4,537m., and a surplus of $3,396m. on the current account of the balance of payments. In 2001 the principal source of imports (13.2%) was Germany, which was also the principal market for exports (18.1%). Other major trading partners in that year were the USA, Italy, France, Japan, the United Kingdom and Russia. The UN restrictions on trade with Iraq reversed Turkey's previously strong trading relations with that country. Exports in 2001 were dominated by clothing and textiles, vegetables and fruit and road vehicles and related components. In that year the principal imports were machinery, crude petroleum, iron and steel, transport vehicles and chemical products.

In 2002 there was a provisional budgetary deficit of TL 26,913,000,000m. (equivalent to some 11.5% of GDP). Turkey's external debt at the end of 2000 was US $116,209m., of which $55,293m. was long-term public debt. In that year the cost of debt-servicing was equivalent to 36.1% of the value of exports of goods and services. The annual rate of inflation averaged 80.5% in 1994–99. It stood at 39.0% in 2000, but increased to an estimated 68.5% in 2001. In 2002 unemployment was estimated at 10.8% of the labour force, and was forecast to increase to 11.2% in 2003.

Turkey is a member of numerous international and regional organizations, including the Developing Eight (D-8, see p. 339), the Economic Co-operation Organization (ECO, see p. 192), and the Organization of the Black Sea Economic Co-operation (see p. 293). Turkey was accepted as a candidate for membership of the European Union (EU, see p. 199) in December 1999.

Turkey's economy has been afflicted by persistently high rates of inflation, an expanding public-sector deficit, ongoing political instability and a poor rate of tax collection. In November 1999 Turkey concluded a three-year loan agreement with the IMF, under which Turkey aimed to achieve a lasting reduction in inflation through the implementation of strict fiscal and monetary policies, and of structural reforms. The privatization programme, which had been suspended in 1998, resumed in early 2000 and envisaged the divestment of 74 state enterprises, including banking and telecommunications concerns. However, the country experienced a severe financial crisis in November 2000 and a further crisis in February 2001 (see Recent History), which resulted in soaring interest rates and an effective devaluation of the lira as the Government was obliged to allow the currency to float. As part of a recovery programme announced in March, the Turkish Government reasserted its commitment to the privatization programme (which had hitherto proceeded only slowly) as a precondition for the extension of funds from the IMF and the World Bank. Radical restructuring of the banking sector was also envisaged. In May 2001 the legislature approved proposals to sell a 45% stake in the national telecommunications company, Türk Telekom, to a strategic foreign investor. By that month pledged IMF support for the Government's economic reform programme had reached US $19,000m.—including loans to the value of US $8,000m. approved in mid-May. The sale of the national airline was also identified as a priority, and it was planned to end the state monopoly in production of sugar, alcohol and tobacco. There were major concerns, however, about the social effects of these reforms, which had resulted in unemployment increasing from 6.6% in 2000 to 10.8% in 2001. In July the IMF warned Turkey that it would withhold loans until stipulated reforms were implemented. After the Government agreed to appoint professionals rather than political appointees to the board of Türk Telekom as part of the privatization

process, and seized five troubled banks, the IMF released $3,200m. in loans. Meanwhile, the banking sector was subject to foreign takeovers, partnerships, or mergers, as part of a broader consolidation process, securing the release of further IMF funding later that year. The reforms often proved particularly unpopular in the agricultural sector, which depended on state subsidies, and feared greater foreign competition. Meanwhile, there was recognition that Turkey's strategic importance to the USA would ensure that IMF funding was maintained. In February 2002 the IMF approved an extra $12,000m. to Turkey, raising Turkey's debt to the organization to $31,000m.: the World Bank had estimated that Turkey's foreign debt stood at 58% of GDP at the beginning of 2001, and this figure increased to 78% by the end of that year. As a result of the financial crisis, GDP declined by 9.4% in 2001, although the Government estimated growth, at 4.2%, in 2002. The AK Partisi Government, elected in November of that year, pledged to meet the IMF's conditions for receiving the last US $6,100m. of loans allocated for 2002; by the end of the year, inflation had been reduced to below 35%. Analysts hoped that the party's overwhelming majority in the TGNA would allow it to increase the pace of privatization where previous coalition governments had faced internal opposition. However, a major economic consideration for the economy in early 2003 was the impact of the US-led war against the regime of Saddam Hussain in Iraq. The Government surprised observers by rejecting a $26,000m. package of direct grants and loans in return for basing US troops in the south-east of the country (see above). The loss of the US package resulted in the lira and the stock market reaching record lows in late March. None the less, a modest recovery was expected in 2003, with growth forecast at 3.5%.

Education

Legislation took effect in September 1997 to increase the duration of compulsory primary education from five to eight years, for children between six and 14 years of age. All state education up to University or Higher Institute levels is co-educational and provided free of charge. The number of primary schools reached 45,112 in 1998, compared with 12,511 in 1950, and about 9.6m. children were receiving primary education. Secondary education, which lasts for at least three years, may be undertaken in general high schools, open high schools or vocational and technical high schools. In 1996 the total enrolment at primary and secondary schools was equivalent to 79% of the school-age population (boys 86%; girls 71%). A state examination must be passed by high school students wishing to proceed to a university or to an Institute of Higher Education. In 1998 there were 1,222 higher education institutes, attended by almost 1.5m. students. In 1997 expenditure on education by the central Government was about TL 967,811,000m. (11.2% of total spending).

Public Holidays

2003: 1 January (New Year's Day), 12–15 February* (Kurban Bayram—Feast of the Sacrifice), 23 April (National Sovereignty and Children's Day), 19 May (Commemoration of Atatürk and Youth and Sports Day), 30 August (Victory Day), 29 October (Republic Day), 26–27 November* (Şeker Bayram—End of Ramadan).

2004: 1 January (New Year's Day), 2–5 February* (Kurban Bayram—Feast of the Sacrifice), 23 April (National Sovereignty and Children's Day), 19 May (Commemoration of Atatürk and Youth and Sports Day), 30 August (Victory Day), 29 October (Republic Day), 14–16 November* (Şeker Bayram—End of Ramadan).

*These holidays are dependent on the Islamic lunar calendar and may vary by one or two days from the dates given.

Weights and Measures

The metric system is in force.

Statistical Survey

Source (unless otherwise stated): Türkiye İş Bankası AŞ, Economic Research and Planning Dept, İstiklal Cad. 300, Beyoğlu, İstanbul; tel. (212) 2927764; fax (212) 2498298; internet www.isbank.com.tr.

Area and Population

AREA, POPULATION AND DENSITY

Area (sq km)	779,452*
Population (census results)	
21 October 1990	
Males	28,607,047
Females.	27,865,988
Total	56,473,035†
30 November 1997	62,865,574
22 October 2000	67,803,927
Population (official estimates at mid-year)‡	
1999	65,819,000
2000	66,835,000
2001	67,829,000
Density (per sq km) at mid-2001.	87.0

* 300,948 sq miles. The total comprises Anatolia (Turkey in Asia or Asia Minor), with an area of 755,688 sq km (291,773 sq miles), and Thrace (Turkey in Europe), with an area of 23,764 sq km (9,175 sq miles).
† Comprising 50,497,586 in Anatolia and 5,975,449 in Thrace.
‡ Source: State Institute of Statistics.

PRINCIPAL TOWNS
(population at census of 22 October 2000, within municipal boundaries)

İstanbul . . .	8,803,468	Samsun	363,180
Ankara (capital) .	3,203,362	Erzurum . . .	361,235
İzmir (Smyrna) .	2,232,265	Kahramanmaraş. .	326,198
Bursa . . .	1,194,687	Van	284,464
Adana	1,130,710	Sakarya . . .	283,752
Gaziantep. . .	853,513	Denizli. . . .	275,480
Konya . . .	742,690	Elâziğ . . .	266,495
Antalya . . .	603,190	Gebze . . .	253,487
Diyarbakır . .	545,983	Sivas	251,776
Mersin (İçel) . .	537,842	Batman . . .	246,678
Kayseri . . .	536,392	Tarsus. . . .	216,382
Eskişehir . . .	482,793	Balıkesir . . .	215,436
Şanlıurfa . . .	385,588	Trabzon . . .	214,949
Malatya . . .	381,081	Manisa	214,345

Source: Thomas Brinkhoff, *City Population* (www.citypopulation.de).

Mid-2001 (UN estimate, '000 incl. suburbs): Ankara 3,208.

Source: UN, *World Urbanization Prospects: The 2001 Revision*.

BIRTHS, MARRIAGES AND DEATHS

	Registered live births		Registered marriages		Registered deaths	
	Number	Rate (per 1,000)	Number	Rate (per 1,000)	Number	Rate (per 1,000)
1994 . .	1,383,000	22.8	462,415	7.7	401,000	6.6
1995 . .	1,381,000	22.4	463,105	7.6	405,000	6.6
1996 . .	1,379,000	22.0	486,734	7.9	408,000	6.5
1997 . .	1,340,000	21.5	518,856	8.3	395,000	6.3
1998 . .	1,339,000	21.1	485,112	7.6	402,000	6.3
1999 . .	1,405,000	21.8	n.a.	n.a.	438,000	6.8
2000 . .	1,504,000	22.3	n.a.	n.a.	439,000	6.5
2001 . .	1,507,000	22.0	n.a.	n.a.	463,000	6.7

Sources: UN, *Demographic Yearbook* and *Population and Vital Statistics Report*; State Institute of Statistics.

Expectation of life (WHO estimates, years at birth): 69.0 (males 67.0; females 71.2) in 2001 (Source: WHO, *World Health Report*).

ECONOMICALLY ACTIVE POPULATION*
(sample surveys, '000 persons aged 12 years and over, October)

	1997	1998	1999
Agriculture, hunting, forestry and fishing . . .	8,219	9,534	10,096
Mining and quarrying	176	171	134
Manufacturing	3,602	3,300	3,117
Electricity, gas and water . . .	111	106	78
Construction	1,323	1,335	1,192
Trade, restaurants and hotels . .	2,916	2,901	2,944
Transport, storage and communications	926	953	863
Financing, insurance, real estate and business services . . .	516	516	520
Community, social and personal services	3,024	3,142	3,107
Total employed. . . .	20,815	21,958	22,049
Males	15,364	15,587	15,167
Females.	5,450	6,371	6,882
Unemployed	1,545	1,547	1,730
Total labour force	22,360	23,505	23,779

* Excluding armed forces.

Source: ILO.

WORKERS ABROAD
('000)

	1997	1998*	1999
Australia	21	17	13
Austria.	51	48	55
Belgium	38	27	27
CIS	40	25	25
France	73	96	79
Germany	740	731	741
Libya	6	6	3
Netherlands	65	56	48
Saudi Arabia	120	115	115
Switzerland	34	34	33
Total (incl. others) . . .	1,264	1,219	1,206

* Figures at October.

WORKERS' REMITTANCES FROM ABROAD
(US $ million)

	1999	2000	2001
Total	4,576	4,603	2,835

Source: Secretariat of the State Planning Organization.

Health and Welfare

KEY INDICATORS

Total fertility rate (children per woman, 2001)	2.4
Under-5 mortality rate (per 1,000 live births, 2001) . . .	43
HIV/AIDS (% of persons aged 15–49, 2001).	<0.1
Physicians (per 1,000 head, 2001)	1.21
Hospital beds (per 1,000 head, 1999)	2.6
Health expenditure (2000): US $ per head (PPP)	323
Health expenditure (2000): % of GDP	5.0
Health expenditure (2000): public (% of total)	71.1
Access to water (% of persons, 2000).	83
Access to sanitation (% of persons, 2000)	91
Human Development Index (2000): ranking	85
Human Development Index (2000): value	0.742

For sources and definitions, see explanatory note on p. vi.

Agriculture

PRINCIPAL CROPS
('000 metric tons)

	1999	2000	2001
Wheat	18,009	21,009	19,007
Rice (paddy)	340	350	360
Rye	233	260	220
Barley	7,700	8,000	7,500
Maize	2,297	2,300	2,200
Oats	290	314	265
Dry beans	237	230	225
Chick peas	560	548	535
Lentils	380	353	520
Vetch	134	138	130
Broad beans (dry)	39	37	35
Potatoes	6,000	5,370	5,200
Onions (dry)	2,500	2,200	2,150
Garlic (dry)	109	102	103
Tomatoes	8,956	8,890	8,425
Cabbages (incl. black)	717	725	710
Carrots	239	235	230
Melons and watermelons*	5,725	5,805	5,795
Aubergines (Eggplants)	976	924	945
Apples	2,500	2,400	2,450
Grapes	3,400	3,600	3,250
Pears	360	380	360
Hazel-nuts (Filberts)	530	470	625
Figs (dried)	275	240	235
Walnuts	120	116	116
Pistachios (in shell)	40	75	30
Almonds	43	47	42
Chestnuts	53	50	47
Oranges	1,100	1,070	1,250
Lemons and limes	520	460	510
Tangerines, mandarins, etc.	500	560	580
Peaches and nectarines	400	430	460
Plums	195	195	200
Apricots (incl. wild)	378	579	517
Cherries (incl. sour)	375	336	370
Cotton (lint)	791	791	n.a.
Tobacco (leaves)	243	200	145
Sugar beet	17,102	18,821	12,633
Sesame seed	28	24	23
Sunflower seed	950	800	650
Olives	581	1,800	600
Olive oil	54	180	n.a.
Tea (made)	199	139	143

* FAO estimates.

Source: FAO.

LIVESTOCK
('000 head, year ending September)

	1999	2000	2001
Horses	330	309	271
Mules	133	125	99
Asses	603	555	489
Cattle	11,031	11,054	10,761
Buffaloes	176	165	146
Camels	1	1	1
Pigs	5	3	3
Sheep	29,435	30,256	28,492
Goats	8,057	7,774	7,201
Chickens	236,997	239,748	258,168
Ducks	1,339	1,295	1,104
Geese	1,771	1,671	1,497
Turkeys	3,805	3,763	3,682

Source: FAO.

LIVESTOCK PRODUCTS
('000 metric tons)

	1999	2000	2001
Beef and veal	350	355	332
Buffalo meat	5.2	4.0	2.3
Mutton and lamb	313*	321†	303†
Goat meat	55*	53†	48†
Horse meat†	2.1	2.0	2.0
Poultry meat	614.8	660.9	631.4
Cows' milk	8,966	8,732	8,489
Buffalo milk	75.0	67.3	63.3
Sheep milk	805	774	723
Goats' milk	236	228†	228†
Butter and ghee	119	119	115
Cheese	130.4	130.1	127.1
Hen eggs*	705	675	529
Honey	67	61	60
Wool (greasy)	45.7	46.6†	46.6†
Cattle and buffalo hides	34.7	36.2	31.6
Sheepskins†	55.4	56.8	53.8
Goatskins†	7.0	6.8	6.2

* FAO estimate(s).
† Unofficial figure(s).

Source: FAO.

Forestry

ROUNDWOOD REMOVALS
('000 cubic metres, excl. bark)

	1999	2000	2001
Sawlogs, veneer logs and logs for sleepers	4,933	5,178	4,978
Pulpwood	1,610	3,369	3,259
Other industrial wood	3,522	1,882	1,739
Fuel wood	7,550	6,358	6,186
Total	17,615	16,787	16,162

Source: FAO.

SAWNWOOD PRODUCTION
('000 cubic metres, incl. railway sleepers)

	1999	2000	2001
Coniferous (softwood)	2,280	3,033	2,391
Broadleaved (hardwood)	2,020	2,710	2,645
Total	4,300	5,743	5,036

Source: FAO.

Fishing

('000 metric tons, live weight)

	1998	1999	2000
Capture	487.2	575.1	503.3
Common carp	20.0	17.8	14.1
Blue whiting	27.2	17.0	18.2
Whiting	13.2	14.1	18.0
Mullets	45.4	46.8	43.4
European pilchard	23.6	22.0	16.5
European anchovy	228.0	350.0	280.0
Atlantic bonito	24.0	17.9	12.0
Aquaculture	56.7	63.0	79.0
Trout	34.6	38.6	44.5
Seabasses	8.7	12.0	17.9
Total catch	543.9	638.1	582.4

Note: Figures exclude aquatic plants and aquatic mammals.

Source: FAO, *Yearbook of Fishery Statistics*.

Mining

('000 metric tons)

	1999	2000	2001
Crude petroleum	2,939	2,748	2,551
Lignite	64,897	59,686	56,542
Coal	2,738	3,330	3,639
Copper (blister)	43	30	25

Source: Secretariat of the State Planning Organization.

Industry

SELECTED PRODUCTS

('000 metric tons, unless otherwise indicated)

	1999	2000	2001
Paper*	1,349	1,566	n.a.
Cotton yarn	126	n.a.	n.a.
Woollen yarn	8	n.a.	n.a.
Cotton fabrics (million metres)	177	n.a.	n.a.
Woollen fabrics (million metres)	28	n.a.	n.a.
Raki (million litres)	79 }	759	764
Beer (million litres)	669 }		
Cigarettes	119	123	126
Crude steel	14,309	14,325	n.a.
Pig-iron	315	n.a.	n.a.
Cement	34,216	36,237	30,125
Sugar (raw)*	2,921	2,162	2,755
Commercial fertilizers†	3,216	n.a.	n.a.
Electrolytic copper‡	43	n.a.	n.a.
Polyethylene	217	225	207
Polyvinyl chloride compositions§	191	177	147
Coke‖¶	2,144	2,811	2,090
Motor spirit (petrol)	3,412	2,758	3,027
Kerosene ('000 barrels)¶	730	638*	n.a.
Fuel oils	6,584	6,532	7,250
Tractors (number)	24,864	35,908	15,054
Domestic refrigerators ('000)	2,102	2,355	2,237
Domestic washing machines ('000)	1,227	1,391	1,022
Vacuum cleaners ('000)	1,067	1,173	591
Television receivers ('000)	6,940	8,789	8,025
Passenger motor cars ('000)	222	306	227
Buses and minibuses ('000)	32	47	12
Electricity (million kWh)	116,441	124,922	123,001

* Data from FAO.

† Excluding potassic fertilizers.

‡ Private sector only.

§ Including precipitated calcium carbonate.

‖ Including semi-coke.

¶ Data from US Geological Survey.

Source (unless otherwise indicated): mainly Secretariat of the State Planning Organization.

Finance

CURRENCY AND EXCHANGE RATES

Monetary Units

100 kuruş = 1 Turkish lira (TL) or pound

Sterling, Dollar and Euro Equivalents (31 December 2002)

£1 sterling = 2,649,314 liras

US $1 = 1,643,699 liras

€1 = 1,723,747 liras

10,000,000 Turkish liras = £3.775 = $6.084 = €5.801

Average Exchange Rate (liras per US $)

2000   625,219

2001   1,225,588

2002   1,507,226

CONSOLIDATED BUDGET

(TL '000 million)

Revenue	2000	2001	2002*
General budget	33,040,903	51,143,596	70,918,000
Taxation	26,503,698	39,767,892	57,911,000
Taxes on income	10,503,316	15,647,113	19,027,000
Income tax	6,212,977	11,578,894	15,401,000
Corporate tax	2,356,787	3,675,662	3,595,000
Interest tax	1,640,655	382,208	31,000
Taxes on goods and services	11,363,785	18,135,668	28,625,000
Domestic value-added tax	4,487,808	7,289,376	10,608,000
Petroleum consumption tax	3,268,774	5,658,565	10,509,000
Banking and Institutions Transactions tax	858,154	1,511,194	1,588,000
Stamp tax	704,478	834,256	1,345,000
Taxes on foreign trade	4,289,401	5,551,053	9,560,000
Value-added on imports	3,891,746	5,149,317	8,892,000
Non-tax revenue	3,486,493	7,398,155	7,007,000
Property	1,548,821	4,490,549	2,845,000
Special revenue and funds	3,050,712	3,977,549	6,000,000
Funds	2,206,054	2,933,055	5,000,000
Annexed budget revenues	399,240	668,946	300,000
Total	**33,440,143**	**51,812,542**	**71,218,000**

Expenditure	2000	2001	2002*
Personnel	9,978,784	15,203,977	21,891,000
Wages	1,708,554	2,538,942	3,200,000
Other current expenditure	3,635,153	5,164,362	7,783,230
Ministry of National Defence	2,326,906	3,220,858	5,350,000
Investment expenditure	2,475,116	4,139,803	5,735,940
Transfers	30,615,975	55,870,862	62,720,830
Interest payments	20,439,862	41,064,609	42,795,000
Domestic debt interest	18,791,862	37,949,301	36,900,000
Foreign debt interest	1,648,000	3,570,308	5,895,000
Tax rebates	1,632,049	2,918,178	3,400,000
VAT rebates on exports	770,983	1,691,353	2,000,000
Social security payments	3,321,098	5,112,000	7,930,000
Payments to retirement fund	1,775,000	2,625,000	400,000
Payments to institution for the self-employed	1,050,685	1,437,000	1,740,000
Agricultural subsidies	358,501	1,032,578	2,125,000
Fund appropriation	1,995,073	1,480,501	300,000
Total	**46,705,028**	**80,379,004**	**98,131,000**

* Rounded projections.

Source: General Directorate of Public Accounts, Ministry of Finance.

INTERNATIONAL RESERVES

(US $ million at 31 December)

	2000	2001	2002
Gold*	1,009	1,008	1,008
IMF special drawing rights	29	4	31
Reserve position in IMF	147	142	153
Foreign exchange	22,313	18,733	26,884
Total	**23,491**	**19,887**	**28,076**

* National valuation.

Source: IMF, *International Financial Statistics*.

MONEY SUPPLY

(TL '000 million at 31 December*)

	1999	2000	2001
Currency outside banks	1,887,150	3,196,940	4,462,900
Demand deposits at deposit money banks	2,802,400	4,187,400	6,338,700
Total money (incl. others)	4,709,800	7,406,900	10,839,600

* Figures are rounded.

Source: IMF, *International Financial Statistics*.

COST OF LIVING
(Consumer Price Index for urban areas at December; base: 1994 = 100)

	1998	1999	2000
Food	1,410.3	2,186.3	2,907.3
Clothing	1,517.1	2,195.9	2,981.5
Household expenditures	1,154.4	1,813.8	n.a.
Medical and personal care	1,575.9	2,696.8	4,071.5
Transport	1,477.8	2,865.1	3,658.1
Cultural and recreational expenditures	1,392.2	2,206.5	3,014.5
Dwelling expenditures*	1,570.9	2,973.2	4,350.4
All items	1,455.4	2,456.6	3,415.5

* Rent is assumed to be fixed.

December 2001 (base: December 2000 = 100): All items 168.5.

NATIONAL ACCOUNTS

Expenditure on the Gross Domestic Product
(TL '000,000 million at current prices)

	1999	2000	2001
Government final consumption expenditure	11,748	17,539	25,405
Private final consumption expenditure	55,928	88,978	128,513
Increase in stocks	1,149	2,685	−2,475
Gross fixed capital formation	16,931	27,848	32,409
Total domestic expenditure	85,756	137,050	183,852
Exports of goods and services	17,972	29,959	60,151
Less Imports of goods and services	20,801	39,285	55,862
Sub-total	82,926	127,724	188,141
Statistical discrepancy	−5,510	−2,442	−9,729
GDP in purchasers' values	77,416	125,282	178,412
GDP at constant 1987 prices	111	119	110

Source: IMF, *International Financial Statistics*.

Gross Domestic Product by Economic Activity
(TL '000 million, at current prices)

	1999	2000	2001
Agriculture, forestry and fishing	11,851,055	17,540,631	23,427,659
Mining and quarrying	883,737	1,422,903	2,128,387
Manufacturing	14,839,451	23,888,136	36,730,882
Electricity, gas and water	2,250,677	3,716,743	7,015,153
Construction	4,362,039	6,483,106	9,202,185
Wholesale and retail trade	14,750,945	24,906,513	37,867,860
Transport, storage and communications	10,868,376	17,645,564	28,462,322
Financial institutions	4,228,349	4,698,024	6,639,387
Ownership of dwellings	3,465,420	5,772,955	8,491,506
Other private services	2,830,826	4,430,360	6,704,663
Government services	8,781,478	12,633,650	18,781,015
Private non-profit institutions	272,486	477,141	918,063
Sub-total	79,384,839	123,615,726	186,369,082
Import duties	2,314,575	5,065,425	6,573,910
Less Imputed bank service charges	4,284,141	4,097,693	11,534,431
GDP in purchasers' values *	77,415,272	124,583,458	181,408,563

* Based on unrounded data.

BALANCE OF PAYMENTS
(US $ million)

	1999	2000	2001
Exports of goods f.o.b.	28,842	30,721	34,379
Imports of goods f.o.b.	−39,326	−53,131	−38,916
Trade balance	−10,484	−22,410	−4,537
Exports of services	16,881	20,429	16,059
Imports of services	−9,395	−9,061	−6,929
Balance on goods and services	−2,998	−11,042	4,593
Other income received	2,350	2,836	2,753
Other income paid	−5,887	−6,838	−7,753
Balance on goods, services and income	−6,535	−15,044	−407
Current transfers received	5,295	5,317	3,861
Current transfers paid	−120	−92	−58
Current balance	−1,360	−9,819	3,396
Direct investment abroad	−645	−870	−497
Direct investment from abroad	783	982	3,266
Portfolio investment assets	−759	−594	−788
Portfolio investment liabilities	4,188	1,615	−3,727
Other investment assets	−2,198	−1,913	−156
Other investment liabilities	3,716	9,389	−12,296
Net errors and omissions	1,629	−2,725	−2,086
Overall balance	5,354	−3,934	−12,888

Source: IMF, *International Financial Statistics*.

External Trade

PRINCIPAL COMMODITIES
(distribution by SITC, US $ million, excl. military goods)

Imports c.i.f.	1999	2000	2001
Crude materials (inedible) except fuels	2,521.8	3,304.1	2,434.7
Mineral fuels, lubricants, etc.	5,375.3	9,529.3	8,288.6
Petroleum, petroleum products, etc.	3,482.2	5,642.7	4,665.0
Gas (natural and manufactured)	1,466.8	3,078.7	3,119.3
Chemicals and related products	6,303.8	7,414.7	6,242.4
Organic chemicals	1,361.3	1,760.1	1,397.6
Medicinal and pharmaceutical products	1,159.3	1,344.8	1,345.3
Plastics in primary forms	1,259.4	1,561.9	1,200.4
Basic manufactures	6,539.4	8,465.1	6,634.8
Textile yarn, fabrics, etc.	1,906.9	2,135.8	1,920.7
Iron and steel	1,564.8	2,422.2	1,795.6
Machinery and transport equipment	15,378.5	20,508.6	12,826.7
Power-generating machinery and equipment	1,200.2	1,428.5	1,956.9
Machinery specialized for particular industries	1,819.0	2,340.1	1,638.3
General industrial machinery, equipment and parts	1,990.0	2,182.6	1,809.1
Office machines and automatic data processing machines	1,206.9	1,594.7	781.1
Telecommunications and sound equipment	2,348.6	3,009.8	1,206.1
Road vehicles and parts*	3,003.4	5,432.2	1,814.1
Miscellaneous manufactured articles	2,749.4	3,381.2	2,695.7
Total (incl. others)	40,687.3	54,502.9	40,474.8

Exports f.o.b.	1999	2000	2001
Food and live animals . . .	3,190.3	2,890.7	3,277.4
Vegetables and fruit	2,132.7	1,816.9	2,127.8
Chemicals and related products	1,120.6	1,242.9	1,343.1
Basic manufactures . . .	6,071.9	6,585.4	7,475.2
Textile yarn, fabrics, etc. . .	3,477.8	3,705.7	3,936.2
Non-metallic mineral manufactures	856.8	1,015.3	1,091.5
Iron and steel	1,737.3	1,864.5	2,447.5
Machinery and transport equipment	5,036.8	5,740.5	7,132.2
Telecommunications and sound equipment	753.0	944.5	987.2
Electrical machinery, apparatus, etc. (excl. telecommunications and sound equipment) . .	1,017.7	1,163.0	1,422.7
Road vehicles and parts* . . .	1,438.3	1,520.5	2,295.8
Miscellaneous manufactured articles	7,640.4	7,928.4	8,128.2
Clothing and accessories (excl. footwear)	6,516.0	6,586.0	6,655.5
Total (incl. others)	26,587.2	27,774.9	31,128.9

* Including air-cushion vehicles.

Source: Secretariat of the State Planning Organization.

PRINCIPAL TRADING PARTNERS
(US $ million, excl. military goods)

Imports c.i.f. (excl. grants)	1999	2000	2001
Austria	508	n.a.	n.a.
Belgium-Luxembourg . . .	1,133	1,661	890
China, People's Republic . . .	895	n.a.	n.a.
France	3,127	3,532	2,284
Germany	5,880	7,198	5,334
Iran	636	n.a.	n.a.
Italy	3,192	4,333	3,480
Japan	1,393	1,621	1,307
Korea, Republic	871	n.a.	n.a.
Libya	502	n.a.	n.a.
Netherlands	1,315	1,585	1,042
Russia	2,374	3,887	3,476
Saudi Arabia	579	961	771
Spain	1,262	1,678	1,062
Sweden	1,444	1,440	544
Switzerland	749	891	683
Ukraine	774	982	758
United Kingdom	2,190	2,748	1,800
USA	3,080	3,911	3,253
Total (incl. others)	40,687	54,503	40,507

Exports f.o.b.	1999	2000	2001
Algeria	408	384	421
Austria	312	n.a.	n.a.
Belgium-Luxembourg . . .	624	647	681
Egypt	467	376	421
France	1,570	1,657	1,893
Germany	5,475	5,180	5,362
Italy	1,683	1,789	2,333
Netherlands	932	874	890
Russia	763	644	923
Saudi Arabia	367	387	492
Spain	763	714	945
Switzerland	268	n.a.	n.a.
United Arab Emirates . . .	391	n.a.	n.a.
United Kingdom	1,830	2,037	2,173
USA	2,437	3,135	3,121
Total (incl. others)	26,587	27,775	31,186

Source: Secretariat of the State Planning Organization.

Transport

RAILWAYS
(traffic)

	1998	1999	2000
Passenger-km (million) . . .	6,160	6,147	5,813
Freight ton-km (million) . . .	8,377	8,265	9,731

Source: UN, *Statistical Yearbook*.

ROAD TRAFFIC
(motor vehicles at end of February)

	2000	2001	2002
Passenger cars	4,422,180	4,534,803	4,539,944
Minibuses	235,885	239,381	239,525
Buses and coaches	118,454	119,306	119,357
Small trucks	794,459	833,175	836,438
Trucks	394,283	396,493	396,668
Motorcycles and mopeds . .	1,011,284	1,031,221	1,032,079
Special purpose vehicles . . .	55,677	57,490	57,766

Source: State Institute of Statistics.

SHIPPING

Merchant Fleet
(registered at 31 December)

	1999	2000	2001
Number of vessels	1,152	1,153	1,146
Total displacement ('000 grt) . .	6,324.6	5,832.7	5,896.7

Source: Lloyd's Register-Fairplay, *World Fleet Statistics*.

International Sea-borne Freight Traffic
('000 metric tons)

	1998	1999	2000*
Goods loaded†	24,756	37,332	25,476
Goods unloaded	78,168	58,080	77,916

* Estimates.
† Excluding livestock and timber.

Source: UN, *Monthly Bulletin of Statistics*.

CIVIL AVIATION
(Turkish Airlines)

	1995	1996	1997*
Number of passengers ('000) . .	8,599	9,281	10,405
Freight handled (metric tons)† . .	90,846	91,688	109,242

* Figures are provisional.
† Cargo and mail.

Tourism

TOURISTS BY COUNTRY OF ORIGIN*

Country	1999	2000	2001
Bulgaria	259,075	381,545	540,437
France	270,280	449,727	523,777
Germany	1,388,787	2,277,505	2,881,550
Greece	146,871	218,092	189,028
Iran	351,937	380,819	327,067
Italy	79,029	218,768	315,134
Romania	483,184	265,128	180,941
Russian Federation	n.a.	677,152	757,121
Syria	102,444	122,417	109,723
United Kingdom	814,889	915,286	845,932
USA	395,006	515,284	428,989
Yugoslavia (former)	213,776	128,383	125,818
Total (incl. others)	7,487,285	10,428,153	11,619,909

* Including same-day tourists.

Sources: State Institute of Statistics; World Tourism Organization, *Yearbook of Tourism Statistics*.

Tourism receipts (million US $): 5,203 in 1999; 7,636 in 2000; 8,090* in 2001 (Source: Secretariat of the State Planning Organization).

* Provisional.

Communications Media

	1999	2000	2001
Television receivers ('000 in use)	n.a.	29,500	n.a.
Telephones ('000 main lines in use)	18,054.0	18,395.2	18,900.9
Mobile cellular telephones ('000 subscribers)	8,121.5	16,133.4	20,000
Personal computers ('000 in use)	2,200	2,500	2,700
Internet users ('000)	1,500	2,000	2,500

Source: International Telecommunication Union.

Radio receivers ('000 in use): 11,300 in 1997.

Facsimile machines (number in use): 108,014 in 1997.

Book production (titles): 6,546 in 1996.

Daily newspapers (number): 57 in 1996; (Circulation, '000) 5,600 in 1996.

Non-daily newspapers (number): 1,468 in 1996.

Sources: UNESCO, *Statistical Yearbook*; and UN, *Statistical Yearbook*.

Education

(1998)

	Institutions	Teachers	Total students
Pre-primary	6,868	10,979	204,000
Primary	45,112	317,795	9,625,400
Secondary:			
general	2,598	71,344	1,282,600
vocational and teacher training	3,367	74,559	998,000
Higher	1,222	60,129	1,465,000

Source: UN, *Statistical Yearbook for Asia and the Pacific*.

Adult literacy rate (UNESCO estimates): 85.1% (males 93.5%; females 76.5%) in 2000 (Source: UN Development Programme, *Human Development Report*).

Directory

The Constitution

In October 1981 the National Security Council (NSC), which took power in September 1980, announced the formation of a Consultative Assembly to draft a new constitution, replacing that of 1961. The Assembly consisted of 40 members appointed directly by the NSC and 120 members chosen by the NSC from candidates put forward by the governors of the 67 provinces; all former politicians were excluded. The draft Constitution was approved by the Assembly in September 1982 and by a national referendum in November. Its main provisions are summarized below:

Legislative power is vested in the unicameral Grand National Assembly, with 400 deputies, who are elected by universal adult suffrage for a five-year term. Executive power is vested in the President, who is elected by the Grand National Assembly for a seven-year term and is empowered to appoint a Prime Minister and senior members of the judiciary, the Central Bank and broadcasting organizations; to dissolve the Grand National Assembly; and to declare a state of emergency entailing rule by decree. Strict controls on the powers of trades unions, the press and political parties were also included. An appended 'temporary article' automatically installed the incumbent President of the NSC as Head of State for a seven-year term, assisted by a Presidential Council comprising members of the NSC.

An amendment adopted in June 1987 increased the number of deputies in the Grand National Assembly from 400 to 450. The number was increased to 550 in a further amendment adopted in July 1995.

The Government

HEAD OF STATE

President: AHMET NECDET SEZER (took office 16 May 2000).

COUNCIL OF MINISTERS
(April 2003)

All ministers were members of the Adalet ve Kalkınma (AK) Partisi.

Prime Minister: RECEP TAYYIP ERDOĞAN.

Minister of State and Minister of Foreign Affairs: ABDULLAH GÜL.

Deputy Prime Minister and Minister of State: ABDULLATIF ŞENER.

Deputy Prime Minister and Minister of State: MEHMET ALI ŞAHIN.

Ministers of State: BEŞIR ATALAY, ALI BABACAN, MEHMET AYDIN.

Minister of Justice: CEMIL ÇIÇEK.

Minister of National Defence: MEHMET VECDI GÖNÜL.

Minister of Intenal Affairs: ABDÜLKADIR AKSU.

Minister of Finance: KEMAL UNAKITAN.

Minister of National Education: HÜSEYIN ÇELIK.

Minister of State: ZEKI ERGEZEN.

Minister of Health: RECEP AKDAD.

TURKEY

Directory

Minister of Transport and Communications: Binali Yıldırım.

Minister of Agriculture and Rural Affairs: Sami Güçlü.

Minister of Labour and Social Security: Murat Başeskioğlu.

Minister of Trade and Industry: Ali Coşkun.

Minister of Energy and Natural Resources: Hilmi Güler.

Minister of Culture: Erkan Mumcu.

Minister of Tourism: Güldal Akşit.

Minister of Forestry: Osman Pepe.

Minister of the Environment: Kürşat Tüzmen.

MINISTRIES

President's Office: Cumhurbaşkanlığı Köşkü, Çankaya, Ankara; tel. (312) 4685030; fax (312) 4271330; e-mail cankaya@tccb.gov.tr; internet www.cankaya.gov.tr.

Prime Minister's Office: Başbakanlık, Bakanlıklar, Ankara; tel. (312) 4189056; fax (312) 4180476; e-mail info@basbakanlik.gov.tr; internet www.basbakanlik.gov.tr.

Deputy Prime Minister's Office: Başbakan yard. ve Devlet Bakanı, Bakanlıklar, Ankara; tel. (312) 4191621; fax (312) 4191547.

Ministry of Agriculture and Rural Affairs: Tarım ve Köyişleri Bakanlığı, Şehit Adem Yavuz Sok. 10, 06140 Kızılay, Ankara; tel. (312) 4191677; fax (312) 4177168; e-mail admin@tarim.gov.tr; internet www.tarim.gov.tr.

Ministry of Culture: Kültür Bakanlığı, Atatürk Bul. 29, 06050 Opera, Ankara; tel. (312) 3090850; fax (312) 3126473; e-mail kultur@kultur.gov.tr; internet www.kultur.gov.tr.

Ministry of Energy and Natural Resources: Enerji ve Tabii Kaynaklar Bakanlığı, İnönü Bul. 27, Ankara; tel. (312) 2126915; fax (312) 2864769; e-mail webmaster@enerji.gov.tr; internet www.enerji.gov.tr.

Ministry of the Environment: Gevre Bakanlığı, Eskişehir Yolu 8, 06530 Ankara; tel. (312) 2879965; fax (312) 2852742.

Ministry of Finance: Maliye Bakanlığı, Dikmen Cad., Ankara; tel. (312) 4250018; fax (312) 4250058; e-mail bshalk@maliye.gov.tr; internet www.maliye.gov.tr.

Ministry of Foreign Affairs: Dişişleri Bakanlığı, Yeni Hizmet Binası, 06520 Balgat, Ankara; tel. (312) 2873556; fax (312) 2873869; internet www.mfa.gov.tr.

Ministry of Forestry: Orman Bakanlığı, Atatürk Bul., Bakanlıklar, Ankara; tel. (312) 4176000.

Ministry of Health: Sağlık Bakanlığı, Yenişehir, Ankara; tel. (312) 4312486; fax (312) 4339885; e-mail adres@saglik.gov.tr; internet www.saglik.gov.tr.

Ministry of the Interior: İçişleri Bakanlığı, Bakanlıklar, Ankara; tel. (312) 4181368; fax (312) 4181795.

Ministry of Justice: Adalet Bakanlığı, 06440 Bakanlıklar, Ankara; tel. (312) 4196050; fax (312) 4173954.

Ministry of Labour and Social Security: Çalışma ve Sosyal Güvenlik Bakanlığı, İnönü Bul. 42, 06100 Emek, Ankara; tel. (312) 4170727; fax (312) 4179765; internet www.calisma.gov.tr.

Ministry of National Defence: Milli Savunma Bakanlığı, 06100 Ankara; tel. (312) 4254596; fax (312) 4184737; e-mail meb@meb.gov.tr; internet www.msb.gov.tr.

Ministry of National Education: Milli Eğitim Bakanlığı, Atatürk Bul., Bakanlıklar, Ankara; tel. (312) 4191410; fax (312) 4177027; internet www.meb.gov.tr.

Ministry of Public Works and Housing: Bayındırlık ve İskan Bakanlığı, Vekaletler Cad. 1, 06100 Ankara; tel. (312) 4255711; fax (312) 4180406.

Ministry of Tourism: Turizm Bakanlığı, İsmet İnönü Bul. 5, 06100 Bahçelievler, Ankara; tel. (312) 2128300; fax (312) 2128391; internet www.turizm.gov.tr.

Ministry of Trade and Industry: Sanayi ve Ticaret Bakanlığı, Eskişehir yolu üzeri 7 km Ankara; tel. (312) 2860365; internet www.sanayi.gov.tr.

Ministry of Transport and Communications: Ulaştırma Bakanlığı, Sok. 5, Emek, Ankara; tel. (312) 2124416; fax (312) 2124930; internet www.ubak.gov.tr.

Legislature

BÜYÜK MİLLET MECLİSİ
(Grand National Assembly)

Speaker: Bülent Arınç.

General Election, 3 November 2002

Party	% of votes	Seats
AK Partisi	34.28	363
Cumhuriyet Halk Partisi (CHP)	19.40	178
Doğru Yol Partisi (DYP)	9.55	0
Milliyetçi Hareket Partisi (MHP)	8.34	0
Genç Partisi (GP)	7.25	0
Demokratik Halk Partisi (DHP)*	6.23	0
Anavatan Partisi (ANAP)	5.13	0
Saadet Partisi (SP)	2.48	0
Demokratik Sol Parti (DSP)	1.22	0
Yeni Türkiye Partisi (YTP)	1.15	0
Büyük Birlik Partisi (BBP)	1.02	0
Independents	0.99	9
Others	2.96	0
Total	100.00	550

*Alliance based on Halkın Demokrasi Partisi (HADEP).

Political Organizations

Political parties were banned from 1980–83. Legislation enacted in March 1986 stipulated that a party must have organizations in at least 45 provinces, and in two-thirds of the districts in each of these provinces, in order to take part in an election. A political party is recognized by the Government as a legitimate parliamentary group only if it has at least 20 deputies in the Grand National Assembly.

In mid-1992, following the adoption of more lenient guidelines for the formation of political parties (proposed by the Demirel Administration), several new parties were established, and the left-wing CHP, dissolved in 1981, was reactivated.

Following the November 2002 legislative elections, only two parties—the AK Partisi and the CHP—were represented in the Grand National Assembly.

Adalet ve Kalkınma (AK) Partisi (Justice and Development Party): internet www.akparti.org.tr; f. 2001; Islamist-orientated; Leader Recep Tayyip Erdoğan.

Anavatan Partisi (ANAP) (Motherland Party): 13 Cad. 3, Balgat, Ankara; tel. (312) 2865000; fax (312) 2865019; e-mail anavatan@anap.org.tr; internet www.anap.org.tr; f. 1983; supports free-market economic system, moderate nationalist and conservative policies, rational social justice system, integration with the EU, and closer ties with the Islamic world; Chair. Mesut Yilmaz; Sec.-Gen. Yaşar Okuyan.

Büyük Birlik Partisi (BBP) (Great Unity Party): Tuna Cad. 28, Yenişehir, Ankara; tel. (312) 4340923; fax (312) 4355818; e-mail bbp@bbp.org.tr; internet www.bbp.org.tr; f. 1993; Chair. Muhsin Yazicioğlu.

Cumhuriyet Halk Partisi (CHP) (Republican People's Party): Çevre Sok. 38, Ankara; tel. and fax (312) 4685969; e-mail chpbim@chp.org.tr; internet www.chp.org.tr; f. 1923 by Kemal Atatürk, dissolved in 1981 and reactivated in 1992; merged with Sosyal Demokrat Halkçı Parti (Social Democratic Populist Party) in February 1995; left-wing; Leader Deniz Baykal; Sec.-Gen. Tarhan Erdem.

Değişen Türkiye Partisi (DEPAR) (Changing Turkey Party): Aşağlı Öveçler 6, Cad. 78, Sok. 15/2, Dikmen, Ankara; tel. (312) 4794875; fax (312) 4795964; e-mail webmaster@depar.org; internet www.depar.org; f. 1998; Chair. Gökhan Çapoğlu.

Demokrasi ve Barış Partisi (DBP) (Democracy and Peace Party): Menekşe 1, Sok. 10-A/7, Kızılay, Ankara; tel. (312) 4173587; f. 1996; pro-Kurdish; Leader Refik Karakoç.

Demokrat Türkiye Partisi (DTP) (Democratic Turkey Party): Mesnevi Sok 27, Ankara; tel. (312) 4420151; fax (312) 4421263; e-mail sevginazlioglu@dtp.org.tr; internet www.dtp.org.tr; Leader İsmet Sezgin.

Demokratik Sol Partisi (DSP) (Democratic Left Party): Fevzi Çakmak Cad. 17, Ankara; tel. (312) 2124950; fax (312) 2213474; e-mail akguvercinist@dsp.org.tr; internet www.dsp.org.tr; f. 1985; centre-left; drawing support from members of the fmr Republican People's Party; Chair. Bülent Ecevit; Sec.-Gen. Zeki Sezer.

Doğru Yol Partisi (DYP) (True Path Party): Selanik Cad. 40, Kızılay, Ankara; tel. (312) 4191818; fax (312) 4176090; internet www.dyp.org.tr; f. 1983; centre-right; replaced the Justice Party (f. 1961 and banned in 1981); Chair. TANSU ÇILLER; Sec.-Gen. NURHAN TEKINEL.

Emeğin Partisi (EMEP) (Labour Party): Ulufeci Sok Fındıkoba Ishani 2/2, Kocamustafapaşa, İstanbul; tel. (212) 5884332; fax (212) 5884341; e-mail info@emep.org; internet www.emep.org; Pres. LEVENT TÜZEL.

Genç Partisi (GP) (Youth Party): internet www.gp.org.tr; f. 2002; populist, nationalist; Leader CEM UZAN.

Halkın Demokrasi Partisi (HADEP) (People's Democracy Party): 2 Cadde, 32 Sok 37, Ankara; tel. (312) 2852200; fax (312) 2852297; e-mail hadepgm@yahoo.com; internet www.hadep.org.tr; f. 1994; pro-Kurdish nationalist party; Chair. MURAT BOZLAK.

İşçi Partisi (IP) (Workers' Party): Mithatpaşa Cad. 10/8, Sıhhıye, Ankara; tel. (312) 4352999; fax (312) 4343386; e-mail ip@ip.org.tr; internet www.ip.org.tr; f. 1992; Chair. DOĞU PERINÇEK.

Liberal Demokratik Parti (LDP) (Liberal Democratic Party): Gazi Mustafa Kemal Bul., 108/18 Maltepe, 06570 Ankara; tel. (312) 2323374; fax (312) 4687597; e-mail info@ldp.org.tr; internet www.ldp.org.tr; f. 1994; Chair. BESIM TIBUK.

Millet Partisi (MP) (Nation Party): İstanbul Cad., Rüzgarlı Gayret Sok. 2, Ankara; tel. (312) 3127626; fax (312) 3127651; internet www.mp.org.tr; f. 1992; Chair. AYKUT EDIBALI.

Milliyetçi Hareket Partisi (MHP) (Nationalist Movement Party): Karanfil Sokak 69, 06640 Bakanlıklar, Ankara; tel. (312) 4195956; fax (312) 2311424; e-mail mhp@mhp.org.tr; internet www.mhp.org.tr; f. 1983; fmrly the Democratic and Conservative Party; Leader DEVLET BAHÇELI; Sec.-Gen. FARUK BAL.

Özgürlük ve Dayanisma Partisi (ODP) (Freedom and Solidarity Party): Necatibey Cad. 23/11, Ankara; e-mail ozgurluk@odp.org.tr; internet www.odp.org.tr; f. 1996; Leader UFUK URAZ.

Saadet Partisi (SP) (Felicity Party): f. 2001; replaced conservative wing of Islamic fundamentalist and free-market advocating Fazilet Partisi (Virtue Party), which was banned in June 2001; Leader RECAI KUTAN.

Türkiye Komünist Partisi (TKP) (Communist Party of Turkey): Osmanağa Mahallesi Nüzhet Efendi Sok 38, Kadıköy, İstanbul; tel. (216) 4185351; fax (216) 3461137; e-mail tkp@tkp.org.tr; internet www.tkp.org.tr; f. 1981 as the Party of Socialist Power, name changed as above in 2001; Gen. Sec. KEMAL OKUYAN.

Yeniden Doğuş Partisi (YDP) (Rebirth Party): Sağlık Sok 3, Sıhhıye, Ankara; tel. (312) 4356565; fax (312) 4356564; f. 1992; Chair. HASAN CELAL GÜZEL.

Yeni Parti (YP) (New Party): Rabat Sok 27, Gaziosmanpaşa, Ankara; tel. (312) 4469254; fax (312) 4469579; f. 1993; Leader YUSUF BOZKURT ÖZAL.

Yeni Turkiye Partisi (YTP) (New Turkey Party): f. 2002; comprised of former DSP politicians; Leader İSMAIL CEM.

The following proscribed organizations were engaged in an armed struggle against the Government:

KADEK (Congress for Freedom and Democracy in Kurdistan): internet www.pkk.org; f. 1978 as the Partiya Karkeren Kurdistan (PKK) (Kurdistan Workers' Party); 57-member directorate; launched struggle for an independent Kurdistan in 1984; ceased activities in 2000; assumed present name in April 2002; Chair. ABDULLAH ÖCALAN.

Devrimici Halk Kurtuluş—Cephesi (DHKP—C) (Revolutionary People's Liberation Party—Front): e-mail dhkc@ozgurluk.org; internet www.ozgurluk.org/dhkc; left wing faction of Dev-Sol; subsumed parent organization in 1996.

Diplomatic Representation

EMBASSIES IN TURKEY

Afghanistan: Cinnah Cad. 88, 06551 Çankaya, Ankara; tel. (312) 4381121; fax (312) 4387745; Ambassador Dr ABD as-SALAM AUSEM.

Albania: Ebuziya Tevfik Sok 17, Çankaya, Ankara; tel. (312) 4416103; fax (312) 4416104; Ambassador SAIMAR BALA.

Algeria: Şehit Ersan Cad. 42, 06680 Çankaya, Ankara; tel. (312) 4687719; fax (312) 4687619; Ambassador RABAH HADID.

Argentina: Uğar Mumcu Cad. 60/3, 06700 Gaziosmanpaşa, Ankara; tel. (312) 4462062; fax (312) 4462063; Ambassador JOSÉ PEDRO PICO.

Australia: Nenehatun Cad. 83, 06680 Gaziosmanpaşa, Ankara; tel. (312) 4461180; fax (312) 4461188; e-mail ausemank@ibm.net; internet www.embaustralia.org.tr; Ambassador JONATHAN PHILP.

Austria: Atatürk Bul. 189, Kavaklıdere, Ankara; tel. (312) 4190431; fax (312) 4189454; e-mail austroambtr@superonline.com; Ambassador Dr MARIUS CALLIGARIS.

Azerbaijan: Cemal Nadir Sok 20, Çelikler Apt, Çankaya, Ankara; tel. (312) 4412620; fax (312) 4412600; Ambassador MEHMET NEHROZODLU ALIEV.

Bangladesh: Cinnah Cad. 78/7–10, Çankaya, Ankara; tel. (312) 4392750; fax (312) 4392408; Ambassador MAHBOOB ALAM.

Belarus: Han Sok 13/1–2, Gaziosmanpaşa, Ankara; tel. (312) 4463042; fax (312) 4460150; Ambassador MIKALAY LEPESHKO.

Belgium: Mahatma Gandhi Cad. 55, Gaziosmanpaşa, Ankara; tel. (312) 4468247; fax (312) 4468251; e-mail ankara@diplobel.org; Ambassador ALEXIS BROUHNS.

Bosnia and Herzegovina: Turan Emeksiz So. 3/9, Park Evleri B Blok, Gaziosmanpaşa, Ankara; tel. (312) 4273602; fax (312) 4273604; e-mail bh_emb@ttnet.net.tr; Ambassador NERKEZ ARIF-HODŽIĆ.

Brazil: Reşit Galip Cad., İlkadım Sok 1, Ankara; tel. (312) 4481840; fax (312) 4481838; Ambassador LUIZ ANTÔNIO JARDIM GAGLIARDI.

Bulgaria: Atatürk Bul. 124, 06680 Kavaklıdere, Ankara; tel. (312) 4671948; fax (312) 4672574; Ambassador VIKTOR VALKOV.

Canada: Nenehatun Cad. 75, 06700 Gaziosmanpaşa, Ankara; tel. (312) 4599200; fax (312) 4599361; e-mail ankra@dfait-maeci.gc.ca; Ambassador MICHAEL LEIR.

Chile: Reşit Galip Cad., İrfanli Sok 14/1-3, 06700 Gaziosmanpaşa, Ankara; tel. (312) 4473418; fax (312) 4474725; e-mail echiletr@ttnet.net.tr; Ambassador PEDRO BARROS.

China, People's Republic: Gölgeli Sok 34, 06700 Gaziosmanpaşa, Ankara; tel. (312) 4360628; fax (312) 4464248; Ambassador YAO KUANGYI.

Croatia: Kelebek Sok 15/A, Gaziosmanpaşa, Ankara; tel. (312) 4469460; fax (312) 4366212; Ambassador Dr I. TOMIĆ.

Cuba: Komşu Sok 7/2, 06690 Çankaya, Ankara; tel. (312) 4394110; fax (312) 4414007; Ambassador JORGE CASTRO BENÍTEZ.

Czech Republic: Uğur Mumcu Cad. 100/3, 06700 Gaziosmanpaşa, Ankara; tel. (312) 4461244; fax (312) 4461245; e-mail ankara@embassy.mzv.cz; Ambassador JOZEF BRAUN.

Denmark: Kırlangıç Sok 42, 06700 Gaziosmanpaşa, Ankara; tel. (312) 4667760; fax (312) 4684559; e-mail danemb@ada.net.tr; internet www.danimarka.org.tr; Ambassador CHRISTIAN HOPPE.

Egypt: Atatürk Bul. 126, 06680 Kavaklıdere, Ankara; tel. (312) 4261026; fax (312) 4270099; Ambassador MAHDI FATHALLAH.

Finland: Kader Sok 44, 06700 Gaziosmanpaşa, Ankara; tel. (312) 4261930; fax (312) 4680072; Ambassador BJÖRN EKBLOM.

France: Paris Cad. 70, 06540 Kavaklıdere, Ankara; tel. (312) 4681154; fax (312) 4679434; e-mail ambafr@ada.net.tr; Ambassador BERNARD GARCIA.

Georgia: Abdullah Cevdat Sok 15, Çankaya; Ankara; tel. (312) 4426508; fax (312) 4421507; Ambassador TARIEL LEBANIDZE.

Germany: Atatürk Bul. 114, 06680 Kavaklıdere, Ankara; tel. (312) 4555100; fax (312) 4266959; e-mail infomail@germanembassyank.com; internet www.germanembassyank.com; Ambassador Dr RUDOLF SCHMIDT.

Greece: Ziya ül-Rahman Cad. 9–11, 06610 Gaziosmanpaşa, Ankara; tel. (312) 4368860; fax (312) 4463191; Ambassador YANNIS KORANDIS.

Holy See: Birlik Mah. 3, Cad. 37, PK 33, 06552 Çankaya, Ankara (Apostolic Nunciature); tel. (312) 4953514; fax (312) 4953540; e-mail vatican@tr.net; Apostolic Nuncio Most Rev. EDMOND FARHAT (Titular Archbishop of Byblus).

Hungary: Sancak Mah. 1, Kahite Cad. 30, Yıldız, Çankaya, Ankara; tel. (312) 4422273; fax (312) 4415049; e-mail huembtur@isnet.net.tr; Ambassador Dr ZSOLT G. SZALAY.

India: Cinnah Cad. 77/A, 06680 Çankaya, Ankara; tel. (312) 4382195; fax (312) 4403429; Ambassador ALOKE SEN.

Indonesia: Abdullah Cevdet Sok 10, 06552 Çankaya, Ankara; tel. (312) 4382190; fax (312) 4382193; Ambassador SOEMARSO H. SUEBROTO.

Iran: Tahran Cad. 10, Kavaklıdere, Ankara; tel. (312) 4682820; fax (312) 4682823; Ambassador SAYED MUHAMMAD HUSEIN LAVASANI.

Iraq: Turan Emeksiz Sok 11, 06700 Gaziosmanpaşa, Ankara; tel. (312) 4687421; fax (312) 4684832; Ambassador FAROK A. YAHYA.

Ireland: Uğur Mumcu Cad 88, MNG Binası B Blok Kat 3, Gaziosmanpaşa 06700 Ankara; tel. (312) 4466172; fax (312) 4468061; e-mail ireland@superonline.com; Ambassador SÉAN WHELAN.

Israel: Mahatma Gandhi Cad. 85, Gaziosmanpaşa, Ankara; tel. (312) 4463605; fax (312) 4261533; e-mail israel@marketweb.net.tr; Ambassador URI BAR-NER.

Italy: Atatürk Bul. 118, Kavaklıdere, Ankara; tel. (312) 4265460; fax (312) 4265800; e-mail itaamb@superonline.com; internet www .itaamb.org.tr; Ambassador Dr VITTORIO CLAUDIO SORDO.

Japan: Reşit Galip Cad 81, Gaziosmanpaşa, Ankara; tel. (312) 4460500; fax (312) 4372504; Ambassador ATSUKO TOYAMA.

Jordan: Dede Korkut Sok 18, 06690 Çankaya, Ankara; tel. (312) 4402054; fax (312) 4404327; Ambassador Dr MOUSA SULAYMAN BRAIZAT.

Kazakhstan: Ebuziya Tevfik Sok 6, Çankaya, Ankara; tel. (312) 4412301; fax (312) 4412303; e-mail kazank@ada.net.tr; Ambassador KANAT B. SAUDABAYEV.

Korea, Republic: Cinnah Cad., Alaçam Sok 5, 06690 Çankaya, Ankara; tel. (312) 4684822; fax (312) 4682279; Ambassador BYUNG WOO YU.

Kuwait: Reşit Galip Cad. Kelebek Sok 110, Gaziosmanpaşa, Ankara; tel. (312) 4450576; fax (312) 4466839; Ambassador ABDULLAH AL-MURAD.

Kyrgyzstan: Çayhane Sok 24, GOP, Ankara 11; tel. (312) 4468408; fax (312) 4468413; e-mail kirgiz-o@tr.net; Ambassador AMANBEK KARYPKULOV.

Lebanon: Kızkulesi Sok 44, Gaziosmanpaşa, Ankara; tel. (312) 4467486; fax (312) 4461023; Ambassador JAFFER MUAVI.

Libya: Cinnah Cad. 60, 06690 Çankaya, Ankara; tel. (312) 4381110; fax (312) 4403862; e-mail ashaabiankara@hotmail.com; Ambassador MOHAMED A. MANGUSH.

Lithuania: Mahatma Gandhi Cad 17/8–9, Gaziosmanpaşa, Ankara; tel. (312) 4470766; fax (312) 4470663; e-mail lrambasd@ada.net.tr.

Macedonia, former Yugoslav republic: Filistin Sok 30/2, Gaziosmanpaşa, Ankara; tel. (312) 4469204; fax (312) 4469206; Ambassador TRAJAN PETROVSKI.

Malaysia: Mahatma Gandhi 58, 06700 Gaziosmanpaşa, Ankara; tel. (312) 4463547; fax (312) 4464130; Ambassador ABDUL JALIL HARON.

Mexico: Kırkpınar Sok 18/6, 06540 Çankaya, Ankara; tel. (312) 4423033; fax (312) 4420221; e-mail mexico@embamextur.com; Ambassador RAÚL CARDOSO.

Moldova: Kaptanpaşa Sok 49, Ankara; tel. (312) 4465527; fax (312) 4465816; Ambassador ION BOTNARU.

Mongolia: Koza Sok 109, Gaziosmanpaşa, Ankara; tel. (312) 4467977; fax (312) 4467791.

Morocco: Reşit Galip Cad., Rabat Sok 11, Gaziosmanpaşa, Ankara; tel. (312) 4376020; fax (312) 4471405; Ambassador BABANA EL-ALAOUI.

Netherlands: Uğur Mumcu Cad. 16, 06700 Gaziosmanpaşa, Ankara; tel. (312) 4460470; fax (312) 4463358; e-mail nlgovank@ domi.net.tr; internet www.dutchembassy.org.tr; Ambassador I. H. GOSSES.

New Zealand: PK 162, İran Cad. 13/4, 06700 Kavaklıdere, Ankara; tel. (312) 4679054; fax (312) 4679013; e-mail newzealand@ superonline.com; Ambassador JAN HENDERSON.

Norway: Kelebek Sok 18, 06700 Gaziosmanpaşa, Ankara; tel. (312) 4478690; fax (312) 4478694; e-mail emb.ankara@mfa.no; Ambassador FINN K. FOSTERVOLL.

Oman: Mahatma Gandhi Cad. 63, 06700 Gaziosmanpaşa, Ankara; tel. (312) 4470630; fax (312) 4470632; Ambassador MUHAMMAD AL-VAHIBI.

Pakistan: İran Cad. 37, 06700 Gaziosmanpaşa, Ankara; tel. (312) 4271410; fax (312) 4671023; e-mail parepank@marketweb.net.tr; Ambassador QAZI HUMAYUN.

Philippines: Mahatma Gandi Cad. 56, Gaziosmanpaşa, Ankara; tel. (312) 4465831; fax (312) 4465733; e-mail jochar@surf.net.tr; Ambassador JOSE LINO B. GUERRERO.

Poland: Atatürk Bul. 241, 06650 Kavaklıdere, Ankara; tel. (312) 4675619; fax (312) 4678963; e-mail polamb@ada.net.tr; internet www.polonya.org.tr; Chargé d'affaires a.i. GRZEGORZ MICHALSKI.

Portugal: Kuleli Sok 26, 06700 Gaziosmanpaşa, Ankara; tel. (312) 4461890; fax (312) 4461892; e-mail embport@domi.com.tr; Ambassador ANTÓNIO MONTEIRO PORTUGAL.

Qatar: Karaca Sok 19, 06610 Gaziosmanpaşa, Ankara; tel. (312) 4411364; fax (312) 4411544; Ambassador Dr HASSAN ALI HUSSEIN EN-NIMAH.

Romania: Bükreş Sok 4, 06680 Çankaya, Ankara; tel. (312) 4271243; fax (312) 4271530; e-mail romania@attglobal.net; Ambassador GEORGE CIAMBA.

Russia: Karyağdı Sok 5, 06692 Çankaya, Ankara; tel. (312) 4392122; fax (312) 4383952; Ambassador ALEKSANDR LEBEDEV.

Saudi Arabia: Turan Emeksiz Sok 6, Gaziosmanpaşa, Ankara; tel. (312) 4685540; fax (312) 4274886; Ambassador NAJI MUFTI.

Serbia and Montenegro: Paris Cad. 47, 06450 Kavaklıdere, Ankara; tel. (312) 4260236; fax (312) 4278345; e-mail yugoslav@tr .net; Ambassador ZORAN S. POPOVIĆ.

Slovakia: Atatürk Bul. 245, 06692 Kavaklıdere, Ankara; tel. (312) 4675075; fax (312) 4682689; e-mail slovakya@optima.net.tr; Ambassador JAN LISUCH.

Slovenia: Küpe Sok 1/3, Gaziosmanpaşa, Ankara; tel. (312) 4056007; fax (312) 4466887; Ambassador ANDREJ GRASSELLI.

South Africa: Filistin Cad. 27, Gaziosmanpaşa, Ankara; tel. (312) 4464056; fax (312) 4466434; e-mail saemb@ada.net.tr; internet www .southafrica.org.tr; Ambassador THOMAS WHEELER.

Spain: Abdullah Cevdat Sok 8, 06680 Çankaya, Ankara; tel. (312) 4380392; fax (312) 4395170; Ambassador JESÚS ATIENZA.

Sudan: Koza Sok 51, Gaziasmanpaşa, Ankara; tel. (312) 4413885; fax (312) 4413886; e-mail sudani@superonline.com.tr; Ambassador Dr BAHA'ALDIN HANAFI.

Sweden: Katip Çelebi Sok 7, 06692 Kavaklıdere, Ankara; tel. (312) 4664558; fax (312) 4685020; Ambassador HENRIK LILJEGREN.

Switzerland: Atatürk Bul. 247, 06692 Kavaklıdere, Ankara; tel. (312) 4675555; fax (312) 4671199; e-mail 100634.3643@compuserve .com; Ambassador ANDRÉ FAIVET.

Syria: Sedat Simavi Sok 40, 06680 Çankaya, Ankara; tel. (312) 4409657; fax (312) 4385609; Chargé d'affaires a.i. MAMDOUH HAIDAR.

Tajikistan: Mahatma Gandhi Cad. 36, Gaziosmanpaşa, Ankara; tel. (312) 4461602; fax (312) 4463621; Chargé d'affaires a.i. ROUSTAM DODCNOV.

Thailand: Çankaya Cad. Kader Sok 45/3, 06700 Gaziosmanpaşa, Ankara; tel. (312) 4673059; fax (312) 4277284; e-mail thaiank@mbex .marketweb.net.tr; Ambassador KAROON RUECHUYOTHIN.

Tunisia: Kuleli Sok 12, 06700 Gaziosmanpaşa, Ankara; tel. (312) 4377812; fax (312) 4377100; e-mail atunisa@superonline.com; Ambassador MOHAMED LESSIR.

'Turkish Republic of Northern Cyprus': Rabat Sok 20, 06700 Gaziosmanpaşa, Ankara; tel. (312) 4462920; fax (312) 4465238; Ambassador NAZIF BORMAN.

Turkmenistan: Koza Sok 28, Çankaya, Ankara; tel. (312) 4417122; fax (312) 4417125; Ambassador NUR MUHAMMAD HANAMOV.

Ukraine: Sancak Mahallesi, Sok 206, 8470, 17 Yıldyz, Çankaya, Ankara; tel. (312) 4415499; fax (312) 4406815; e-mail ukremb_tr@ kablonet.com.tr; internet web.ttnet.net.tr/ukremb; Ambassador Dr IHOR DOLHOV.

United Arab Emirates: Reşit Galip Cad. Şairler Sok. 28, Gaziosmanpaşa, Ankara; tel. (312) 4476861; fax (312) 4475545; Ambassador SALEM RASHED SALEM AL-AGROOBI.

United Kingdom: Şehit Ersan Cad. 46/A, Çankaya, Ankara; tel. (312) 4553344; fax (312) 4553351; e-mail britembank@celik.net.tr; internet www.britishembassy.org.tr; Ambassador Sir DAVID LOGAN.

USA: Atatürk Bul. 110, 06540 Kavaklıdere, Ankara; tel. (312) 4686110; fax (312) 4670019; internet www.usis-ankara.org.tr; Ambassador W. ROBERT PEARSON.

Uzbekistan: Willy Brand Sok. 13, Çankaya, Ankara; tel. (312) 4413871; fax (312) 4427058; e-mail uzbekembassy@superonline .com; Ambassador ABDULAKHAT JALILOV.

Venezuela: Cinnah Cad. 78/2, Çankaya, Ankara; tel. (312) 4387135; fax (312) 4406619; e-mail venezemb@dominet.in.com.tr; Ambassador RAMÓN DELGADO.

Yemen: Fethiye Sok 2, 06700 Gaziosmanpaşa, Ankara; tel. (312) 4462637; fax (312) 4461778; Ambassador MUHAMMAD ABDULLAH AL-GAIFI.

Judicial System

Until the foundation of the Turkish Republic, a large part of the Turkish civil law—the laws affecting the family, inheritance, property, obligations, etc.—was based on the Koran, and the holy law was administered by special religious (*Shari'a*) courts. The legal reform of 1926 was not only a process of secularization, but also a radical change of the legal system. The Swiss Civil Code and the Code of Obligation, the Italian Penal Code and the Neuchâtel (Cantonal) Code of Civil Procedure were adopted and modified to fit Turkish customs and traditions.

According to current Turkish law, the power of the judiciary is exercised by judicial (criminal), military and administrative courts.

These courts render their verdicts in the first instance, while superior courts examine the verdict for subsequent rulings.

SUPERIOR COURTS

Constitutional Court: Consists of 11 regular and four substitute members, appointed by the President. Reviews the constitutionality of laws, at the request of the President of the Republic, parliamentary groups of the governing party or of the main opposition party, or of one-fifth of the members of the National Assembly, and sits as a high council empowered to try senior members of state. The rulings of the Constitutional Court are final. Decisions of the Court are published immediately in the Official Gazette, and shall be binding on the legislative executive, and judicial organs of the state. Chair. MUSTAFA BUMIN.

Court of Appeals: The court of the last instance for reviewing the decisions and verdicts rendered by judicial courts. It has original and final jurisdiction in specific cases defined by law. Members are elected by the Supreme Council of Judges and Prosecutors. Chair. SAMI SELCUK.

Council of State: An administrative court of the first and last instance in matters not referred by law to other administrative courts, and an administrative court of the last instance in general. Hears and settles administrative disputes and expresses opinions on draft laws submitted by the Council of Ministers. Three-quarters of the members are appointed by the Supreme Council of Judges and Public Prosecutors, the remaining quarter is selected by the President of the Republic.

Military Court of Appeals: A court of the last instance to review decisions and verdicts rendered by military courts, and a court of first and last instance with jurisdiction over certain military persons, stipulated by law, with responsibility for the specific trials of these persons. Members are selected by the President of the Republic from nominations made by the Military Court of Appeals.

Supreme Military Administrative Court: A military court for the judicial control of administrative acts concerning military personnel. Members are selected by the President of the Republic from nominations made by the Court.

Court of Jurisdictional Disputes: Settles disputes among judicial, administrative and military courts arising from disagreements on jurisdictional matters and verdicts.

The Court of Accounts: A court charged with the auditing of all accounts of revenue, expenditure and government property, which renders rulings related to transactions and accounts of authorized bodies on behalf of the National Assembly.

Supreme Council of Judges and Public Prosecutors: The President of the Council shall be the Minister of Justice, and the Under-Secretary to the Minister of Justice shall serve as an *ex-officio* member of the Council. Three regular and three substitute members from the Court of Appeals, together with two regular and two substitute members of the Council of State, shall be appointed to the Supreme Council by the President of the Republic for a four-year term. Decides all personnel matters relating to judges and public prosecutors.

Public Prosecutor: The law shall make provision for the tenure of public prosecutors and attorneys of the Council of State and their functions. The Chief Prosecutor of the Republic, the Chief Attorney of the Council of State and the Chief Prosecutor of the Military Court of Appeals are subject to the provisions applicable to judges of higher courts.

Military Trial: Military trials are conducted by military and disciplinary courts. These courts are entitled to try the military offences of military personnel and those offences committed against military personnel or in military areas, or offences connected with military service and duties. Military courts may try non-military persons only for military offences prescribed by special laws.

Religion

ISLAM

More than 99% of the Turkish people are Muslims. However, Turkey is a secular state. Although Islam was stated to be the official religion in the Constitution of 1924, an amendment in 1928 removed this privilege. After 1950 subsequent governments have tried to re-establish links between religion and state affairs, but secularity was protected by the revolution of 1960, the 1980 military takeover and the 1982 Constitution.

Diyanet İşleri Reisi: Head of Religious Affairs in Turkey Prof. MUSTAFA SAIT YAZICIOĞLU.

CHRISTIANITY

The town of Antioch (now Antakya) was one of the earliest strongholds of Christianity, and by the the 4th century had become a patriarchal see. Formerly in Syria, the town was incorporated in Turkey in 1939. Constantinople (now İstanbul) was also a patriarchal see, and by the 6th century the Patriarch of Constantinople was recognized as the Ecumenical Patriarch in the East. Gradual estrangement from Rome developed, leading to the final breach between the Catholic West and the Orthodox East, usually assigned to the year 1054.

In 1986 it was estimated that there were about 100,000 Christians in Turkey.

The Orthodox Churches

Armenian Patriarchate: Ermeni Patrikliği, 34480 Kumkapı, İstanbul; tel. (212) 5170970; fax (212) 5164833; e-mail arm.pat.ist@amicus.com; f. 1461; 65,000 adherents (1999); Patriarch MESROB II.

Bulgarian Orthodox Church: Bulgar Ortodoks Kilisesi, Halâskâr Gazi Cad. 319, Şişli, İstanbul; Rev. Archimandrite GANCO ÇOBANOF.

Greek Orthodox Church: The Ecumenical Patriarchate (Rum Ortodoks Patrikhanesi), Sadrazam Ali Paşa Cad. No. 35, TR-34220 Fener-İstanbul; tel. (212) 5319671; fax (212) 5349037; e-mail www.elpidof@attglobal.net; internet www.patriarchate.org; Archbishop of Constantinople (New Rome) and Ecumenical Patriarch BARTHOLOMEOS I.

The Roman Catholic Church

At 31 December 2001 there were an estimated 28,000 adherents in the country.

Bishops' Conference: Conferenza Episcopale di Turchia, Satırcı Sok 2, Harbiye, 34373 İstanbul; tel. (212) 2190089; fax (212) 2411543; f. 1987; Pres. Mgr FRANCESCHINI RUGGERO (Vicar Apostolic of Anatolia).

Armenian Rite

Patriarchate of Cilicia: f. 1742; Patriarch NERSES BEDROS TARMOUNI XIX (resident in Beirut, Lebanon).

Archbishopric of İstanbul: Sakızağacı Cad. 31, PK 183, 80072 Beyoğlu, İstanbul; tel. (212) 2441258; fax (212) 2432364; f. 1830; Archbishop HOVHANNES TCHOLAKIAN.

Byzantine Rite

Apostolic Exarchate of İstanbul: Hamalbaşı Cad. 44, PK 259, 80070 Beyoğlu, İstanbul; tel. (212) 2497104; fax (212) 2411543; f. 1861; Vicar Delegate LOUIS PELÂTRE (Titular Bishop of Sasima).

Bulgarian Catholic Church: Bulgar Katolik Kilisesi, Eski Parmakkapı Sok. 15, Galata, İstanbul.

Chaldean Rite

Archbishopric of Diyarbakır: Hamalbaşı Cad. 48, 80070 Beyoğlu, İstanbul; tel. (212) 2440351; fax (212) 2932064; Archbishop PAUL KARATAS.

Latin Rite

Metropolitan See of İzmir: Church of St Polycarp, Necatibey Bul. 2, PK 267, 35212 İzmir; tel. (232) 4840531; fax (232) 4845358; e-mail padrestefano@hotmail.com; Archbishop of İzmir GIUSEPPE GERMANO BERNARDINI.

Apostolic Vicariate of Anatolia: Uray Cad. 85, PK 35, 33001 Mersin; tel. (324) 2320578; fax (324) 2320595; e-mail curiaves@future.net.tr; e-mail vic.ap@softhome.com; f. 1990; Vicar Apostolic RUGGERO FRANCESCHINI (Titular Bishop of Sicilibba).

Apostolic Vicariate of İstanbul: Ölçek Sok 83, 80230 Harbiye, İstanbul; tel. (212) 2480775; fax (212) 2411543; f. 1742; Vicar Apostolic LOUIS PELÂTRE (Titular Bishop of Sasima).

Maronite Rite

The Maronite Patriarch of Antioch, Cardinal Nasrallah Pierre Sfeir, is resident in Lebanon.

Melkite Rite

The Greek Melkite Patriarch of Antioch, Gregoire III Laham, is resident in Damascus, Syria.

Syrian Rite

The Syrian Catholic Patriarch of Antioch, Ignace Pierre VIII Abdel Ahad, is resident in Beirut, Lebanon.

Patriarchal Vicariate of Turkey: Sarayarkası Sok 15, PK 84, 80090 Ayazpaşa, İstanbul; tel. (212) 2432521; fax (212) 2490261; Vicar Patriarchal Rev. YUSUF SAĞ.

The Anglican Communion

Within the Church of England, Turkey forms part of the diocese of Gibraltar in Europe. The Bishop is resident in England.

Archdeacon of the Aegean: Canon JEREMY PEAKE (resident in Vienna, Austria).

JUDAISM

In 1996 it was estimated that there were about 25,000 Jews in Turkey.

Jewish Community of Turkey: Türkiye Hahambaşılığı, Yemenici Sok 23, Beyoğlu, 80050 Tünel, İstanbul; tel. (212) 2938794; fax (212) 2441980; e-mail jcommnty@atlas.net.tr; Chief Rabbi ISAK HALEVA.

The Press

Almost all İstanbul papers are also printed in Ankara and İzmir on the same day, and some in Adana. Among the most serious and influential papers are the dailies *Milliyet* and *Cumhuriyet*. The weekly *Gırgır* is noted for its political satire. The most popular dailies are the İstanbul papers *Sabah, Hürriyet, Milliyet* and *Zaman; Yeni Asır*, published in İzmir, is the best-selling quality daily of the Aegean region. There are numerous provincial newspapers with limited circulation.

PRINCIPAL DAILIES

Adana

Yeni Adana: Abidinpaşa Cad. 56, Adana; tel. (322) 3599006; fax (322) 3593655; e-mail yeniadana@ttnet.net.tr; f. 1918; political; Propr ÇETIN REMZI YÜREĞIR; Chief Editor YALÇIN REMZI YÜREĞIR; circ. 2,000.

Ankara

Ankara Ticaret: Rüzgârlı Sok O. V. Han 2/6, Ankara; tel. (312) 4182832; f. 1954; commercial; Man. Editor NURAY TÜZMEN; Chief Editor MUAMMER SOLMAZ; circ. 1,351.

Belde: Rüzgarlı Gayret Sok 7/1, Ulus, Ankara; tel. (312) 3106820; f. 1968; Propr İLHAN İŞBILEN; circ. 3,399.

Tasvir: Ulus Meydanı, Ulus İş Hanı, Kat 4, Ankara; tel. (312) 4111241; f. 1960; conservative; Editor ENDER YOKDAR; circ. 3,055.

Turkish Daily News: Hülya Sok 45, 06700 GOP, Ankara; tel. (312) 4475647; fax (312) 4468374; e-mail tdn-f@tr.net; internet www.turkishdailynews.com; f. 1961; English language; Publisher İLHAN ÇEVIK; Editor-in-Chief İLNUR ÇEVIK; circ. 54,500.

Türkiye Ticaret Sicili: Karanfil Sok 56, Bakanlıklar, Ankara; f. 1957; commercial; Editor YALÇIN KAYA AYDOS.

Vakit: Konya Yolu 8 km, 68 Balgat, Ankara; tel. (312) 2877906; f. 1978; Man. Editor NALI ALAN; circ. 3,384.

Yeni Tanin: Ankara; f. 1964; political; Propr BURHANETTIN GÖGEN; Man. Editor AHMET TEKEŞ; circ. 3,123.

Yirmidört Saat: Gazeteciler Cemiyeti Çevre Sok 35, Çankaya, Ankara; tel. (312) 1682384; f. 1978; Propr BEYHAN CENKÇI.

Eskişehir

Istikbal: Köprübaşı Değirmen Cad. 19/4, Eskişehir; tel. (222) 2318975; fax (222) 2345888; f. 1950; morning; Editor VEDAT ALP.

Gaziantep

Olay (Event): Gaziantep; Man. EROL MARAS.

İstanbul

Akşam: Davutpaşa Cad. 34, Zeytinburnu, İstanbul; tel. (212) 4493000; fax (212) 4819561; internet www.aksam.com.tr.

Apoyevmatini: İstiklâl Cad., Suriye Pasajı 348, Beyoğlu, İstanbul; tel. (212) 2437635; f. 1925; Greek language; Publr Dr Y. A. ADAŞOĞLU; Editor İSTEFAN PAPADOPOULOS; circ. 1,200.

Bugün: Medya Plaza Basın Ekspres Yolu, 34540 Güneşli, İstanbul; tel. (212) 5504850; fax (212) 5023340; f. 1989; Propr ÖNAY BILGIN; circ. 184,884.

Cumhuriyet (Republic): Türkocağı Cad. 39, 34334 Cağaloğlu, İstanbul; tel. (212) 5120505; fax (212) 5138595; internet www.cumhuriyet.com.tr; f. 1924; morning; liberal; Man. Editor HIKMET ÇETINKAYA; circ. 75,000.

Dünya (World): Yil Mahallesi 100, 34440 Bağcilar, İstanbul; tel. (212) 6290808; fax (212) 6200313; internet www.dunya.com; f. 1952; morning; economic; Editor-in-Chief NEZIH DEMIRKENT; circ. 50,000.

Fotomaç: Medya Plaza Basın Ekspres Yolu, 34540 Güneşli, İstanbul; tel. (212) 5504900; fax (212) 5028217; f. 1991; Chief Officer İBRAHIM SETEN; circ. 250,000.

Günaydın-Tan: Alayköşkü, Cad. Eryilmaz Sok 13, Cağaloğlu, İstanbul; tel. (212) 5120050; fax (212) 5260823; f. 1968; Editor-in-Chief SECKIN TURESAY.

Hürriyet: Babiali Cad. 15–17, Guneslikoy, 34540 Bakırköy, İstanbul; tel. (212) 5550050; fax (212) 5156705; internet www.hurriyet.com.tr; f. 1948; morning; independent political; Propr AYDIN DOĞAN; Chief Editor ERTUĞRUL ÖZKÖK; circ. 542,797.

Meydan (Nationalism): Yüzyıl Mahallesi, Mahmutbey Viyadüğü Altı, İkitelli, 34410 Cağaloğlu, İstanbul; tel. (212) 5056111; fax (212) 5056436; f. 1990; Propr REFIK ARAS; Ed. UFUK GULDEMIR.

Milli Gazete: Çayhane Sok 1, 34040 Topkapı, İstanbul; tel. (212) 5674775; fax (212) 5674024; f. 1973; pro-Islamic; right-wing; Editor-in-Chief EKREM KIZILTAŞ; circ. 51,000.

Milliyet: Doğan Medya Center, Bağcilar, 34554 İstanbul; tel. (212) 5056111; fax (212) 5056233; internet www.milliyet.com.tr; f. 1950; morning; political; Publr AYDIN DOĞAN; Editor-in-Chief DERYA SAZAK; circ. 630,000.

Nor Marmara: İstiklâl Cad., Solakzade Sok 5, PK 507, İstanbul; tel. (212) 2444736; f. 1940; Armenian language; Propr and Editor-in-Chief ROBER HADDELER; Gen. Man. ARI HADDELER; circ. 2,200.

Sabah (Morning): Medya Plaza, Basın Ekspres Yolu, Günesli, İstanbul; tel. (212) 5504810; fax (212) 5028143; internet www.sabah.com.tr; Propr DINÇ BILGIN; Editor ZAFER MUTLU; circ. 550,000.

Tercüman: Sercekale Sok 4, 34370 Topkapı, İstanbul; tel. (212) 5017505; fax (212) 5446562; f. 1961; right-wing; Propr SEDAT COLAK; Chief Editor NAZIF OKUMUS; circ. 32,869.

Türkiye (Turkey): Çatalçeşme Sok 17, 34410 Cağaloğlu, İstanbul; tel. (212) 5139900; fax (212) 5209362; e-mail bulend@ihlas.net.tr; internet www.turkiyegazetesi.com; f. 1970; Editor-in-Chief KENAN AKIN; circ. 450,000.

Yeni Nesil (New Generation): Sanayi Cad., Selvi Sok 5, Yenibosna, Bakırköy, İstanbul; tel. (212) 5846261; fax (212) 5567289; f. 1970 as *Yeni Asya*; political; Editor-in-Chief UMIT SIMSEK.

Yeni Şafak: Yenidoğan Mah., Şenay Sokak 2, Kat 1, Bayrampaşa, İstanbul; tel. (212) 6122390; fax (212) 6121944; internet www.yenisafak.com.tr.

Yeniyüzyıl: Medya Plaza Basın Ekspres Yolu, 34540 Güneşli, İstanbul; tel. (212) 5028877; fax (212) 5028295; Editor KEREM ÇALISKAN.

Zaman (Time): Çobançeşme, Kalendar Sok 21, 34530 Yenibosna, İstanbul; tel. (212) 6393450; fax (212) 6522423; e-mail okurhatti@zaman.com.tr; internet www.zaman.com.tr; f. 1962; morning; political, independent; Man. Editor ADEM KALAC; circ. 210,000.

İzmir

Rapor: Gazi Osman Paşa Bul. 5, İzmir; tel. (232) 4254400; f. 1949; Owner DINÇ BILGIN; Man. Editor TANJU ATEŞER; circ. 9,000.

Ticaret Gazetesi: 1571 Sok 16, 35110 Çınarlı, 35110 İzmir; tel. (232) 4619642; fax (232) 4619646; e-mail ticinfo@unimedya.net.tr; internet www.ticaretgazetesi.com; f. 1942; commercial news; Editor-in-Chief AHMET SUKÜTI TÜKEL; Man. Editor CEMAL M. TÜKEL; circ. 5,009.

Yeni Asır (New Century): Yeni Asır Plaza, Ankara Cad. 3, İzmir; tel. (232) 4615000; fax (232) 4610757; e-mail yeniasir@yeniasir.com.tr; internet www.yeniasir.com.tr; f. 1895; political; Man. Editor AYDIN BILGIN; Editorial Dir HAMDI TÜRKMEN; circ. 60,000.

Konya

Yeni Konya: Mevlâna Cad. 4, Konya; tel. (332) 2112594; f. 1945; political; Man. Editor M. NACI GÜCÜYENER; Chief Editor ADIL GÜCÜYENER; monthly circ. 1,657.

Yeni Meram: Babu Aksaray Mah. Piroğlu Sok 4, Konya; tel. (332) 3512699; fax (332) 3507565; e-mail yenimeram@yenimeram.com; internet www.yenimeram.com; f. 1949; political; Propr M. YALÇIN BAHÇIVAN; Chief Editor TUFAN BAHÇIVAN; monthly circ. 44,000.

WEEKLIES

Ankara

EBA Briefing: Bestekar Sok 59/3, Kavaklıdere, Ankara; tel. (312) 4685376; fax (312) 4684114; f. 1975; publ. by Ekonomik Basın Ajansı (Economic Press Agency); political and economic survey; Publrs YAVUZ TOLUN, MELEK TOLUN.

Ekonomi ve Politika: Kavaklıdere, Ankara; f. 1966; economic and political; Publisher ZIYA TANSU.

Türkiye İktisat Gazetesi: Karanfil Sok 56, 06582 Bakanlıklar, Ankara; tel. (312) 4184321; fax (312) 4183268; f. 1953; commercial; Chief Editor MEHMET SAĞLAM; circ. 11,500.

Turkish Economic Gazette: Atatürk Bul. 149, Bakanlıklar, Ankara; tel. (312) 4177700; publ. by UCCET.

Turkish Probe: Hülya Sok. 45, 06700 GOP, Ankara; tel. (312) 4475647; fax (312) 4468374; English language; Publr A. İLHAN ÇEVİK; Editor-in-Chief İLNUR ÇEVİK; circ. 2,500.

Antalya

Pulse: PK 7, Kemer, Antalya; tel. and fax (242) 8180105; e-mail uras@ada.net.tr; internet www.turkpulse.com; politics and business; English; published online; Publr VEDAT URAS.

İstanbul

Aktüel: Medya Plaza Basın Ekspres Yolu, 34540 Güneşli, İstanbul; tel. (212) 5504870; e-mail aktuel@birnumara.com.tr; internet aktuel .birnumara.com.tr; f. 1991; Gen. Man. GÜLAY GÖKTÜRK; Man. Editor ALEV ER.

Bayrak: Çatalçeşme Sok 50/5, 34410 Cağaloğlu, İstanbul; tel. (212) 5275575; fax (212) 5268363; f. 1970; political; Editor MEHMET GÜNGÖR; circ. 10,000.

Doğan Kardeş: Türbedar Sok 22, Cağaloğlu, İstanbul; f. 1945; illustrated children's magazine; Editor ŞEVKET RADO; circ. 40,000.

Elegans: Valikonağı Cad. Y.K.V. Binası K:5 D:3 Nişantaşı 80220 İstanbul; tel. (212) 2336506; fax (212) 2412738; e-mail editor@ yumak.com.tr; internet www.elegans.com.tr; f. 1985; social, economic, and global issues; Editor-in-Chief MURAT BEKDIK.

Ekonomik Panaroma: Büyükdere Cad. Ali Kaya Sok 8, 80720 Levent, İstanbul; tel. (212) 2696680; f. 1988; Gen. Man. AYDIN DEMİRER.

Ekonomist: Hürgüç Gazetecilik AŞ Hurriyet Tesisleri, Kireçocaği Mevkii, Evren Mah., Güneşli Köy, İstanbul; tel. (212) 5500050; f. 1991; Gen. Man. ADIL ÖZKOL.

Gırgır: Alayköşkü Cad., Çağaloğlu, İstanbul; tel. (212) 2285000; satirical; Propr and Editor OĞUZ ARAL; circ. 500,000.

İstanbul Ticaret: İstanbul Chamber of Commerce, Ragip Gümüşpala Cad. 84, 34378, Eminönü, İstanbul; tel. (212) 5114150; fax (212) 5131565; f. 1958; commercial news; Publr MEHMET YILDIRIM.

Nokta: Gelisim Yayinlari, Büyükdere Cad., Ali Kaya Sok 8, 80720 Levent, İstanbul; tel. (212) 2782930; fax (212) 2794378; Editor ARDA USKAN; circ. 60,000.

Tempo: Hürgüç Gazetecilik AŞ Hürriyet Tesisleri, Güneşli, İstanbul; tel. (212) 5500081; f. 1987; Dir SEDAT SIMAVI; Gen. Man. MEHMET Y. YILMAZ.

Türk Dünyası Araştırmalar Dergisi: Hürgüç Gazetecilik AŞ Hürriyet Tesisleri, Güneşli, İstanbul; tel. (212) 5500081; Dir SEDAT SIMAVI; Gen. Man. MEHMET Y. YILMAZ.

PERIODICALS

Ankara

Azerbaycan Türk Kültür Dergisi: Vakıf İş Hanı 324, Anafartalar, Ankara; f. 1949; literary and cultural periodical of Azerbaijani Turks; Editor Dr AHMET YAŞAT.

Bayrak Dergisi: Bestckar Sok 44/5, Kavaklıdere, Ankara; f. 1964; Publr and Editor HAMI KARTAY.

Bilim ve Teknik: Bilim ve Teknik Dergisi Tübitak, Atatürk Bul. 221, Kavaklıdere, 06100 Ankara; tel. (312) 4270625; fax (312) 4276677; e-mail bteknik@tubitak.gov.tr; internet www.biltek .tubitak.gov.tr; f. 1967; monthly; science; Propr NAMIK KEMAL PAK; Man. Editor RAŞIT GÜRDILEK.

Devlet Opera ve Balesi Genel Müdürlügü: Ankara; tel. (312) 3241476; fax (312) 3107248; f. 1949; state opera and ballet; Gen. Dir. RENGIM GOKMEN.

Devlet Tiyatrosu: Devlet Tiyatrosu Um. Md., Ankara; f. 1952; art, theatre.

Eğitim ve Bilim: Kızılırmak Sok 8, Kocatepe, Ankara; tel. (312) 4174202; fax (312) 4175365; e-mail tedgmrk@superonline.com; 4313488; f. 1928; quarterly; education and science; publ. by the Turkish Educational Asscn (TED); Editors Dr GÜLTEKIN ÖZDEMIR, MARGARET SÖNMEZ; circ. 500.

Elektrik Mühendisliği Mecmuası: Gülden Sok. 2/A Güvenevler, Kavaklıdere, Ankara; f. 1954; publ. by the Chamber of Turkish Electrical Engineers; Pres. SEFA GÖMDENIZ.

Karınca: Türk Kooperatifçilik Kurumu, Mithatpaşa Cad. 38/A, 06420 Kızılay, Ankara; tel. (312) 4316125; fax (312) 4340646; f. 1934;

monthly review publ. by the Turkish Co-operative Asscn; Editor Prof. Dr CELÂL ER; circ. 5,000.

Maden Tetkik Arama Genel Müdürlüğü: İnönü Bul., Ankara; f. 1935; 2 a year; publ. by Mineral Research and Exploration Institute of Turkey; English Edition *Bulletin of Mineral Research and Exploration* (2 a year).

Mimarlık (Architecture): Konur Sok 4, Kızılay, Ankara; tel. (312) 4173727; fax (312) 4180361; e-mail mimarlarodasi@superonline .com; internet www.mimarlarodasi.org.tr; f. 1963; every 2 months; publ. by the Chamber of Architects of Turkey; Editor KADRI ATABAŞ; circ. 12,500.

Mühendis ve Makina: Sümer 2 Sok 36/1-A, 06640 Demirtepe, Ankara; tel. (312) 2313159; fax (312) 2313165; f. 1957; engineering; monthly; Publr Chamber of Mechanical Engineers; Propr MEHMET SOĞANCI; Editor YÜKSEL KÖKEN; circ. 30,000.

Teknik ve Uygulama: Konur Sok 4/4, 06442 Kızılay, Ankara; tel. (312) 4182374; f. 1986; engineering; every 2 months; publ. by the Chamber of Mechanical Engineers; Propr İSMET RIZA ÇEBI; Editor UĞUR DOĞAN; circ. 3,000.

Türk Arkeoloji ve Etnoğrafya Dergisi (General Directorate of Monuments and Museums): Kültür Bakanlığı, Anıtlar ve Müzeler Genel Müdürlüğü-II. Meclis Binası Ulus, Ankara; tel. (312) 3105363; fax (312) 3111417; archaeological.

Türk Dili: Türk Dil Kurumu, Atatürk Bul. 217, 06680 Kavaklıdere, Ankara; tel. (312) 4286100; fax (312) 4285288; e-mail tdili@tdk.gov .tr; internet www.tdk.gov.tr; f. 1951; monthly; Turkish literature and language; Editor Prof. Dr ŞÜKRÜ HALUK AKALIN.

Turkey—Economic News Digest: Karanfil Sok 56, Ankara; f. 1960; Editor-in-Chief BEHZAT TANIR; Man. Editor SADIK BALKAN.

Turkish Review: Atatürk Bul. 203, 06688 Kavaklıdere, Ankara; tel. (312) 4671180; fax (312) 4682100; f. 1985; 4 a year; cultural, social and economic; English; publ. by the Directorate General of Press and Information; Chief Officers MURAT ERSAVCI, OSMAN ÜNTÜRK, NAZAN ER, MINE CANPOLAT.

Türkiye Bankacılık: PK 121, Ankara; f. 1955; commercial; Publisher MUSTAFA ATALAY.

Türkiye Bibliyografyası: Milli Kütüphane Başkanlığı, 06490 Bahçelievler, Ankara; tel. (312) 2126200; fax (312) 2230451; e-mail katalog@mkutup.gov.tr; internet www.mkutup.gov.tr; f. 1928; monthly; Turkish national bibliography; publ. by the Turkish National Library, Cataloguing and Classification Dept; Dir AHMET ÇELENKOĞLU.

Türkiye Makaleler Bibliyografyası (Bibliography of Articles in Turkish Periodicals): Milli Kütüphane Başkanlığı, 06490 Bahçelievler, Ankara; tel. (312) 2126200; fax (312) 2230451; e-mail bibliografya@mkutup.gov.tr; internet www.mkutup.gov.tr; f. 1952; monthly; Turkish articles, bibliography; publ. by the Turkish National Library, Bibliography Preparation Dept; Dir DENIZ AYGÜNEŞ.

İstanbul

Arkeoloji ve Sanat Dergesi (Archaeology and Art Magazine): Hayriye Cad. 3/5 Çorlu Apt., Beyoğlu 80060, İstanbul; tel. (212) 2456838; fax (212) 2456877; e-mail info@arkeolojisanat.com; internet arkeolojisanat.com; f. 1978; bimonthly; publ. by Archaeology and Art Publications; Publr and Editor NEZIH BAŞGELEN; English-Language Submissions Editor BRIAN JOHNSON.

Bankacılar: Nışpetiye Cad. Akmerkez, B3 Blok. Kat 13–14, 80630 Etiler, İstanbul; tel. (212) 2820973; fax (212) 2820946; publ. by Banks' Asscn of Turkey; quarterly.

İstanbul Ticaret Odası Mecmuası: Gümüşpala Cad. 84, 34378 Eminönü, İstanbul; tel. (212) 5114150; fax (212) 5131565; f. 1884; quarterly; journal of the İstanbul Chamber of Commerce (ICOC); English; Editor-in-Chief CENGIZ ERSUN.

Musiki Mecmuası (Music Magazine): Sem'i Bey Sok 19/3, Yıldızbakkal, Kadıköy 81130, İstanbul; tel. (216) 3306299; e-mail etemungor@hotmail.com; f. 1948; monthly; music and musicology; Editor ETEM RUHI ÜNGÖR.

Nûr (the Light): Nuruosmaniye Cad., Sorkun Han 28/2, 34410, Cağaloğlu, İstanbul; tel. (212) 5277607; fax (212) 5208231; e-mail sozler@ihlas.net.tr; internet www.sozler.com.tr; f. 1986; religion; Publr MEHMET NURI GÜLEÇ; Editor CEMAL UŞAK; circ. 10,000.

Pirelli Mecmuası: Büyükdere Cad. 117, Gayrettepe, İstanbul; tel. (212) 2663200; fax (212) 2520718; e-mail bilyay@ibm.net; f. 1964; monthly; Publr Türk-Pirelli Lâstikleri AS; Editor UĞUR CANAL; circ. 24,500.

Présence (Aylık Dergi): Ölçek Sok 82, 80230 Harbiye, İstanbul; tel. and fax (212) 2408801; f. 1986; 10 a year; publ. by the Apostolic Vicariate of İstanbul; Gen. Man. FUAT ÇÖLLÜ.

Ruh ve Madde Dergisi (Spirit and Matter): Ruh ve Madde Publications and Health Services Co., PK 9, 80072 Beyoğlu, İstanbul; tel. (212) 2431814; fax (212) 2520718; e-mail bilyay@bilyay.org.tr; internet www.ruhvemadde.com; f. 1959; organ of the Foundation for Spreading the Knowledge to Unify Humanity; Editor HALUK HACALOGLU.

Sevgi Dünyası (World of Respect): Aydede Cad. 4/5, 80090 Taksim, İstanbul; tel. (212) 2504242; f. 1963; monthly; social, psychological and spiritual; Publr and Editor Dr REFET KAYSERILIOĞLU.

Turkey: Ihlas Holding Merkez Binası, Ekim Cad. 29, 34520 Yenibosna, İstanbul; tel. (212) 4542530; fax (212) 4542555; e-mail img@img.com.tr; internet www.img.com.tr; f. 1982; monthly; English language, economics; Editor MEHMET SOZTUTAN; circ. 43,000.

Türkiye Turing ve Otomobil Kurumu Belleteni: Oto Sanayi Sitesi Yanı 4, Levent, İstanbul; tel. (212) 2828140; f. 1930; quarterly; publ. by the Touring and Automobile Club of Turkey; Publr Prof. NEJAT ÖLCAY; Editor ÇELIK GÜLERSOY.

Varlık: Ayberk Ap. Piyerloti Cad. 7–9, Çemberlitaş, 34400 İstanbul; tel. (212) 5226924; fax (212) 5162004; e-mail varlik@varlik.com.tr; internet www.varlik.com.tr; f. 1933; monthly; literary; Editors FILIZ NAYIR DENIZTEKIN, ENVER ERCAN; circ. 4,000.

İzmir

İzmir Ticaret Odası Dergisi: Atatürk Cad. 126, 35210 İzmir; tel. (232) 4417777; fax (232) 4837853; f. 1927; every 2 months; publ. by Chamber of Commerce of İzmir; Sec.-Gen. Prof. Dr İLTER AKAT; Man. ÜMIT ALEMDAROĞLU.

NEWS AGENCIES

Anadolu Ajansı: Mustafa Kemal Bul. 128/C, Tandogan, Ankara; tel. (312) 2317000; fax (312) 2312174; e-mail disyayin@anadoluajansi.com.tr; internet www.anadoluajansi.com.tr; f. 1920; Chair. ALI AYDIN DUNDAR; Gen. Dir BEHIÇ EKŞI.

ANKA Ajansı: Büklüm Sok 20–22, Kavaklıdere, Ankara; tel. (312) 4172500; fax (312) 4180254; e-mail anka@ankaajansi.com.tr; Dir-Gen. MÜŞERREF HEKIMOĞLU.

Bagımsiz Basın Ajansı (BBA): Saglam Fikir Sok 11, Esentepe, İstanbul; tel. (212) 2122936; fax (212) 2122940; e-mail bba@bba.tv; internet www.bba.tv; f. 1971; provides camera crewing, editing and satellite services in Turkey, the Balkans, the Middle East and the former Soviet republics to broadcasters worldwide.

EBA Ekonomik Basın Ajansı (Economic Press Agency): Bestekar Sok 59/3, Kavakıdere, 06680 Ankara; tel. (312) 4685376; fax (312) 4684114; e-mail ebainfo@superonline.com; internet www.ebanews.com; f. 1969; private economic news service; Propr MELEK TOLUN; Editor YAVUZ TOLUN.

Hürriyet Haber Ajansı: Hürriyet Medya Towers, Güneşli, 34544 İstanbul; tel. (212) 6770365; fax (212) 6770372; e-mail ucebeci@hurriyet.com.tr; f. 1963; Dir-Gen. UĞUR ÇEBECI.

İKA Haber Ajansı (Economic and Commercial News Agency): Atatürk Bul. 199/A-45, Kavaklıdere, Ankara; tel. (312) 1267327; f. 1954; Dir ZIYA TANSU.

Milha News Agency: Doğan Medya Center, Bağcılar, 34554 İstanbul; tel. (212) 5056111; fax (212) 5056233.

Ulusal Basın Ajansı (UBA): Meşrutiyet Cad. 5/10, Ankara; Man. Editor OĞUZ SEREN.

Foreign Bureaux

Agence France-Presse (AFP): And Sok 8/13, Çankaya, Ankara; tel. (312) 4689680; fax (312) 4689683; e-mail afpank@ada.net.tr; Correspondent FLORENCE BIEDERMANN.

Agenzia Nazionale Stampa Associata (ANSA) (Italy): Sedat Simavı Sok 30/5, Ankara; tel. (312) 4406084; fax (312) 4405029; Correspondent ROMANO DAMIANI.

Associated Press (AP) (USA): Tunus Cad. 87/3, Kavaklıdere, Ankara; tel. (312) 4282709; Correspondent EMEL ANIL.

Bulgarska Telegrafna Agentsia (BTA) (Bulgaria): Hatır Sok. 25/6, Gaziosmanpaşa, Ankara; tel. (312) 4273899; Correspondent LUBOMIR GABROVSKI.

Deutsche Presse-Agentur (dpa) (Germany): Yesil Yalı Sok, Liman Apt 6/6 Yesilköy, İstanbul; tel. (212) 5738607; Correspondent BAHADETTIN GÜNGÖR.

Informatsionnoye Telegrafnoye Agentstvo Rossii—Telegrafnoye Agentstvo Suverennykh Stran (ITAR—TASS) (Russia): Romşu Sok 7/7, Ankara; tel. (312) 4405781; fax (312) 4391955; e-mail tassankara@superonline.com; Correspondent ANDREI PALARIA.

Reuters: Emirhan Cad. 145/A, Dikilitaş Beşiktaş, 80700 İstanbul; tel. (212) 2750875; fax (212) 2116794; e-mail turkey.marketing@reuters.com; internet www.reuters.com/turkey; Gen. Man. SAMEEH EL-DIN.

United Press International (UPI) (USA): Cağaloğlu, İstanbul; tel. (212) 2285238; Correspondent ISMET IMSET.

Xinhua (New China) News Agency (People's Republic of China): Horasan Sok 16/4, Gaziosmanpaşa, Ankara; tel. (312) 4361456; fax (312) 4465229; Correspondent WANG QIANG.

Zhongguo Xinwen She (China News Agency) (People's Republic of China): Nenehatun Cad. 88-2, Ata Apartmanı, Gaziosmanpaşa, Ankara; tel. (312) 4362261; Correspondent CHANG CHILIANG.

AFP also has representatives in İstanbul and İzmir; AP is also represented in İstanbul.

JOURNALISTS' ASSOCIATION

Gazeteciler Cemiyeti: Cağaloğlu, İstanbul; tel. (212) 5138300; fax (212) 5268046; f. 1946; Pres. NECMI TANYOLAÇ; Sec. RIDVAN YELE.

Publishers

Altın Kitaplar Yayınevi Anonim ŞTİ: Celal Ferdi Gökçay Sok, Nebioğlu Han, Kat. 1, Cağaloğlu, İstanbul; tel. (212) 5268012; fax (212) 5268011; e-mail info@altinkitaplar.com.tr; internet www.altinkitaplar.com; f. 1959; fiction, non-fiction, biography, children's books, encyclopaedias, dictionaries; Publrs FETHI UL, TURHAN BOZKURT; Chief Editor MÜRSIT UL.

Arkadas Co Ltd: Mithatpaşa Cad. 28C, 06441 Yenisehir, Ankara; tel. (312) 4344624; fax (312) 4356057; e-mail arkadas@arkadas.tr; internet www.arkadas.com.tr; f. 1979; fiction, educational and reference books; Dir of Publs MELTEM ÖZDEMIR.

Arkeoloji ve Sanat Yayınları (Archaeology and Art Publications): Hayriye Cad. 3/4 Çorlu Apt., Beyoğlu, 80060 İstanbul; tel. (212) 2456838; fax (212) 2456877; e-mail info@arkeolojisanat.com; internet www.arkeolojisanat.com; f. 1978; classical, Byzantine and Turkish studies, art and archaeology, numismatics and ethnography books; Publr NEZIH BASGELEN; Senior Editor BRIAN JOHNSON.

Bilgi Yayınevi: Meşrutiyet Cad. 46/A, Yenişehir, 06420 Ankara; tel. (312) 4318122; fax (312) 4317758; e-mail info@bilgiyayinevi.com.tr; internet www.bilgiyayinevi.com.tr.

IKI NOKTA (Research Press & Publications Industry & Trade Ltd): Moda Cad. 180/10, Kadıköy, 81300 İstanbul; tel. (216) 3490141; fax (216) 3376756; e-mail info@ikinokta.com; internet www.ikinokta.com; humanities; Pres. YÜCEL YAMAN.

Iletisim Yayınları: Klodfarer Cd Iletisim Han 7/2, Cağaloğlu, 34400 İstanbul; tel. (212) 5162263; fax (212) 5161258; e-mail iletisim@iletisim.com.tr; internet www.iletisim.com.tr; f. 1984; fiction, non-fiction, encyclopaedias, reference; Gen. Man. NIHAT TUNA.

Inkilap Kitabevi: Ankara Cad. 99, Sirkeci, İstanbul; tel. (212) 5140610; fax (212) 5140612; e-mail posta@inkilap.com; internet www.inkilap.com; f. 1935; general reference and fiction; Man. Dir A. FIKRI; Dir of Foreign Rights S. DIKER.

Kabalci Yayınevi: Himaye-i Etfal Sok 8-B, 34410 Cağaloğlu, İstanbul; tel. (212) 5268685; fax (212) 5136305; e-mail info@kabalci.com.tr; internet www.kabalci.com.tr; art, history, literature, social sciences; Pres. SABRI KABALCI.

Kök Yayıncılık: Konur Sok. 8/6, 06550 Kızılay, Ankara; tel. (312) 4172868; fax (312) 4315013; f. 1987; childcare, education, health; Editor OSMAN CAN.

Metis Yayınları: Ipek Sok. 9, 80060 Beyoğlu, İstanbul; tel. (212) 2454509; fax (212) 2454519; e-mail metis@turk.net; internet www.metisbooks.com; f. 1982; fiction, literature, non-fiction, social sciences; Dir SEMIH SÖKMEN.

Nurdan Yayınları Sanayi ve Ticaret Ltd Sti: Prof. Kâzim Ismail Gürkan Cad. 13, Kati 1, 34410 Cağaloğlu, İstanbul; tel. (212) 5225504; fax (212) 5125186; e-mail info@nurdan.com.tr; internet www.nurdan.com.tr; f. 1980; children's and educational; Dir NURDAN TÜZÜNER.

Parantez Yayınları AŞ: Istikal Cad. 212 Alt Kat 8, Beyoğlu, İstanbul; tel. and fax (212) 2528567; e-mail parantez@yahoo.com; internet www.planet.com.tr/bilisim/parantez; f. 1991; Publr METIN ZEYNIOĞLU.

Payel Yayınevi: Cağaloğlu Yokusu Evren han Kat 3/51, 34400 Cağaloğlu, İstanbul; tel. (212) 5284409; fax (212) 5118233; f. 1966; science, history, literature; Editor AHMET ÖZTÜRK.

Remzi Kitabevi AŞ: Selvili Mescit Sok 3, 34440 Cağaloğlu, İstanbul; tel. (212) 5139424; fax (212) 5229055; e-mail post@remzi.com.tr; internet www.remzi.com.tr; f. 1927; general and educational; Dirs EROL ERDURAN, ÖMER ERDURAN, AHMET ERDURAN.

Saray Medikal Yayın Tıc Ltd Sti: 168 Sok. 5/1, Bornova, İzmir; tel. (232) 3394969; fax (232) 3733700; e-mail eozkarahan@novell.cs .eng.dev.edu.tr; f. 1993; medicine, social sciences.

Seçkin Yayınevi: Saglik Sok. 19B, 06410 Sihhiye, Ankara; tel. (312) 4353030; fax (312) 4352472; e-mail yayin@seckin.com.tr; internet www.seckin.com.tr; f. 1959; accounting, computer science, economics, law.

Türk Dil Kurumu (Turkish Language Institute): Atatürk Bul. 217, 06680 Kavaklıdere, Ankara; tel. (312) 4268124; fax (312) 4285288; e-mail bilgi@tdk.gov.tr; internet tdk.gov.tr; f. 1932; non-fiction, research, language; Pres. Prof. Dr ŞÜKRÜ HALUK AKALIN.

Varlık Yayınları: Ayberk Ap. Piyerloti Cad. 7–9, Çemberlitaş, 34400 İstanbul; tel. (212) 5129528; fax (212) 5162004; e-mail varlik@ varlik.com.tr; internet www.varlik.com.tr; f. 1946; fiction and non-fiction books; Dirs FİLİZ NAYIR DENİZTEKİN, OSMAN DENİZTEKİN.

Government Publishing House

Ministry of Culture: Directorate of Publications, Necatibey Cad. 55, 06440 Kızılay, Ankara; tel. (312) 2315450; fax (312) 2315036; e-mail yayimlar@kutuphanelergm.gov.tr; internet www.kultur.gov .tr; f. 1973; Dir ALİ OSMAN GÜZEL.

PUBLISHERS' ASSOCIATION

Türkiye Yayıncılar Birliği Derneği (The Publishers' Association of Turkey): Kazım Ismail Gürkan Cad. 12, Ortaklar Han Kat 3/17, Cağaloğlu, İstanbul; tel. (212) 5125602; fax (212) 5117794; e-mail info@turkyaybir.com.tr; internet www.turkyaybir.org.tr; f. 1985; Pres. ÇETIN TÜZÜNER; Sec. METIN CELAL ZEYNİOĞLU; 230 mems.

Broadcasting and Communications

TELECOMMUNICATIONS

General Directorate of Communications: 90 Str. no. 5, 06338 Ankara; tel. (312) 2128088; fax (312) 2121775; regulatory authority; Dir-Gen. HAYRETTIN SOYTAS.

Türk Telekomünikayson AŞ: Ankara; internet www.telekom.gov .tr; 51% privatized in 2001, further sale pending in late 2002; provides telecoms services throughout Turkey; Dir-Gen. İBRAHIM HAKKI ALPTÜRK.

Turkcell: Ankara; internet www.turkcell.com.tr; subsidiary of Turk Telekomunikayson AŞ; provides mobile cellular services.

BROADCASTING

Regulatory Authority

Türkiye Radyo ve Televizyon Üst Kurulu (Turkish Radio and Television Supreme Council): Bilkent Plaza B2 Blok, Bilkent, 06530 Ankara; tel. (312) 2662013; fax (312) 2661964; e-mail rtuk2@ttnet .net.tr; responsible for assignment of channels, frequencies and bands, controls transmitting facilities of radio stations and TV networks, draws up regulations on related matters, monitors broadcasting and issues warnings in case of violation of the Broadcasting law; Chair SEDAT NURI KAYIS.

Radio

Türkiye Radyo ve Televizyon Kurumu (TRT) (Turkish Radio and Television Corpn): Oran Sitesi, B Blok Kat 9, 06450 Oran, Ankara; tel. (312) 4901797; fax (312) 4905936; internet www.trt.net .tr; f. 1964; controls Turkish radio and television services incl. four national radio channels; Dir-Gen. YÜCEL YENER; Head of Radio ÇETIN TEZCAN.

Voice of Turkey: PK 333, 06443 Yenişehir, Ankara; tel. (312) 4909800; fax (312) 4909845; e-mail englishservice@tsr.gov.tr; internet www.tsr.gov.tr; foreign service of the TRT; Man. Dir DANYAL GÜRDAL.

There are also more than 50 local radio stations, an educational radio service for schools and a station run by the Turkish State Meteorological Service. The US forces have their own radio and television service.

Television

Türkiye Radyo ve Televizyon Kurumu (TRT): (Turkish Radio and Television Corpn): Oran Sitesi Turan Günes Bul. A Block Kat 6, 06450 Oran, Ankara; e-mail nilgun.artun@trt.net.tr; internet www .trt.net.tr; five national channels in 2000 and two satellite channels broadcasting to Europe; Head of Television NILGÜN ARTUN; Dir Ankara TV GÜRKAN ELÇI.

In addition there are also 11 other TV stations, including cable networks. These are; ATV (www.atv.com.tr), Cine 5 (www.cine5 .com.tr), Kanal D (www.kanald.com.tr), Kanal 6 (www.kanal6.com .tr), Kral TV (www.kraltv.com.tr), No1 TV (www.levi.com.tr/no1tv), NTV Online (www.ntv.co.tr), Show TV (www.showtv.net), Star (www.star.com.tr), TGRT (www.tgrt.com.tr), and NTVMSNBC (www.ntvmsnbc.com).

Finance

(cap. = capital; res = reserves; dep. = deposits; m. = million; brs = branches; amounts in Turkish liras unless otherwise stated)

The Central Bank of the Republic of Turkey was originally founded in 1930, and constituted in its present form in 1970. The Central Bank is the bank of issue and is also responsible for the execution of monetary and credit policies, the regulation of the foreign and domestic value of the Turkish lira jointly with the government, and the supervision of the credit system. In 1987 a decree was issued to bring the governorship of the Central Bank under direct government control.

Several banks were created by special laws to fulfil specialized services for particular industries. Etibank operates primarily in the extractive industries and electric power industries; the Ziraat Bankası makes loans for agriculture; the Emlâk Bankası participates in construction and in industrial undertakings.

The largest of the private sector Turkish banks is the Türkiye İş Bankası, which operates 854 branches.

There are several credit institutions in Turkey, including the Sınai Kalınma Bankası (Industrial Development Bank), which was founded in 1950, with the assistance of the World Bank, to encourage private investment in industry by acting as underwriter in the issue of share capital.

There are numerous co-operative organizations, including agricultural co-operatives in rural areas. There are also a number of savings institutions.

In 1990 the Turkish Government announced plans to establish a structure for offshore banking. A decree issued in October 1990 exempted foreign banks, operating in six designated free zones, from local banking obligations.

In June 1999 an independent supervisory body, the Regulatory and Supervisory Board for Banking, was established by law to monitor the financial sector. The treasury, the Ministry of Finance, the Central Bank, the state planning organization, the Capital Markets Board and the Banks' Association of Turkey were each to nominate one member to the Board for a six-year term. The Board was operational from mid-2000. Other legislation passed in June 1999 incorporated core principles of the Basle Committee on Banking Supervision relating to risk-based capital requirements, loan administration procedures, auditing practices and credit risk issues.

BANKING

Regulatory Authority

Bancacılık Düzenleme ve Denetleme Kurumu (BDDK) (Banking Regulation and Supervisory Agency): Atatürk Bulvaı 191, 06680 Kavaklidere, Ankara; tel. (312) 4556500; fax (312) 4240877; e-mail bilgi@bddk.org.tr; internet www.bddk.org.tr; Chair. ENGIN AKCAKOCA.

Central Bank

Türkiye Cumhuriyet Merkez Bankası AŞ (Central Bank of the Republic of Turkey): Head Office, İstiklal Cad. 10, 06100 Ulus, Ankara; tel. (312) 3103646; fax (312) 3107434; e-mail info@tcmb.gov .tr; internet www.tcmb.gov.tr; f. 1931; bank of issue; cap. 25,000.0m., res 2,390,298,019m., dep. 22,572,549,565m. (Dec. 2000); Gov., Pres. and Chair. SUREYYA SERDEGEÇTI; 21 brs.

State Banks

Türkiye Cumhuriyeti Ziraat Bankası (Agricultural Bank of the Turkish Republic): Bankalar Cad. 42, 06107 Ulus, Ankara; tel. (312) 3122957; fax (312) 3101135; e-mail zbmail@ziraatbank.com.tr; internet www.ziraatbank.com.tr; f. 1863; absorbed Türkiye Emlâk Bankası AŞ (Real Estate Bank of Turkey) in July 2001; cap. 261,305,000m., res 179,789,000m., dep. 14,587,301,000m. (Dec. 2000); Chair. and Pres. SAFA OCAK; Gen. Man. Dr NIYAZI ERDOĞAN; 1,177 brs.

Türkiye Halk Bankası AŞ: Esikişehir Yolu, 2 Cad. 63, Söğütözü, 06520 Ankara; tel. (312) 2892000; fax (312) 2892378; e-mail dciner@ halkbank.com.tr; internet www.halkbank.com.tr; f. 1938; absorbed Turkiye Öğretmenler Bankası TAŞ in May 1992; cap. 315,901,000m., dep. 8,894,332,000m. (Dec. 2000); Chair. A. VURAL AKIŞIK; Gen. Man. EMEL ÇABUKOĞLU; 804 brs.

Türkiye İhracat Kredi Bankası AŞ (Türk Eximbank) (Export Credit Bank of Turkey): Milli Müdafa Cad. 20, 06100 Bakanlıklar, Ankara; tel. (312) 4171300; fax (312) 4257896; e-mail ankara@eximbank.gov.tr; internet www.eximbank.gov.tr; f. 1987; fmrly Devlet Yatırım Bankası AŞ (f. 1964); cap. 529,513,000m., res 71,658,000m., total assets 4,445,213,000m. (Dec. 2001); extends credit to exporters, insures and guarantees export transactions; Chair., CEO and Gen. Man. H. AHMET KILIÇOĞLU; 2 brs.

Türkiye Vakıflar Bankası TAO (Foundation Bank of Turkey): Atatürk Bul. 207, 06683 Kavaklıdere, Ankara; tel. (312) 4557575; fax (312) 4684541; e-mail international@vakifbank.com.tr; internet www.vakifbank.com.tr; f. 1954; cap. 319,666,000m., res 959,290,000m., dep. 7,140,585,900m. (Dec. 2001); Chair. and Gen. Man. İRFAN ERCIYAS; 301 brs.

Principal Commercial Banks

Akbank TAŞ: Sabancı Center, 4 Levent, 80745 İstanbul; tel. (212) 2699822; fax (212) 2818188; internet www.akbank.com.tr; f. 1948; cap. 500,000,000m., res 57,486,000m., dep. 4,375,895m. (Dec. 2000); Chair. EROL SABANCI; CEO and Gen. Man. ZAFER KURTUL; 606 brs.

Alternatifbank AŞ: Cumhuriyet Cad. 22–24, Elmadağ, 80200 İstanbul; tel. (212) 3156500; fax (212) 2331500; e-mail sakir.somek@abank.com.tr; internet www.abank.com.tr; cap. 160,000,000m., dep. 873,832,000m. (Sept. 2002); Chair. TUNCAY ÖZILHAN; CEO MURAT ARIG; 22 brs.

Bank Ekspres AŞ: Istınye Yokuşu, 80860 Istınye, İstanbul; tel. (212) 2852525; fax (212) 2854646; e-mail bilgi@bankekspres.com.tr; internet www.bankekspres.com.tr; f. 1992; taken into govt control in Oct. 1998; cap 30,000,000m. (Dec. 1998), dep. 164,287,000m., total assets 221,932,000m. (Sept. 1998); Chair MUHSIN YENER GÜRMEN; Pres. and CEO DOGAN TUNALI; 26 brs.

Denizbank AŞ: Büyükdere Cad 110, Esentepe, 80496 İstanbul; tel. (212) 3550800; fax (212) 2747993; e-mail info@denizbank.com; internet www.denizbank.com; f. 1997; cap. 42,960,000m., res 7,137,078m., dep. 347,310,992m. (Dec. 2000); Pres. and CEO HAKAN ATEŞ; Chair. Dr VEYSI SEVIG.

Eskişehir Bankası TAŞ (Esbank): Meşrutiyet Cad. 141, 80050 Tepebaşı, İstanbul; tel. (212) 2517270; fax (212) 2432396; e-mail webmaster@esbank.com.tr; internet www.esbank.com.tr; f. 1927; taken into govt control in Dec. 1999; cap. 45,000,000m., res 8,878,806m., dep. 443,897,966m. (Dec. 1998); Chair. MESUT EREZ; Gen. Man. CANKUT LAC; 84 brs.

Etibank AŞ: Emirhan Cad. 145, Atakule B Blok, 80700 Dikilitaş, Beşiktaş, İstanbul; tel. (212) 2368585; fax (212) 2584360; e-mail mail@etibank.com.tr; internet www.etibank.com.tr; f. 1935; privatized 1998; absorbed Esbank and Interbank AS in July 2001; cap. US $70m., dep. $830m. (March 1999); Chair. DINC BILGIN; Gen. Man. ZEKI ÜNAL; 151 brs.

Finansbank AŞ: Büyükdere Cad. 129, 80300 Mecidiyeköy, İstanbul; tel. (212) 2167070; fax (212) 2161217; internet www.finansbank.com; f. 1987; sold to Banque National de Paris in mid-2001; cap. 304,759,480m., res −105,275,721m., dep. 914,927,701m. (Dec. 2000); Man. Dir Dr ÖMER ARAS; 73 brs.

İktisat Bankası TAŞ: Büyükdere Cad. 165, 80504 Esentepe, İstanbul; tel. (212) 2747111; fax (212) 2747028; internet www.iktisatbank.com.tr; f. 1927; cap. 30,000,000m. res 419,355,000m., dep. 264,679,000m. (Dec. 1999); Chair. TEVFIK ALTINOK; Pres. DOĞAN TUNALI; 28 brs.

Kentbank AŞ: Süzer Plaza Askerocagi Cad 15, Elmadag, Şişli, 80200 İstanbul; tel. (212) 3343434; e-mail ugurg@kentbank.com.tr; internet www.kentbank.com.tr; f. 1992; cap. 68,901,000m., res −26,302m., dep 412,420,000m. (Dec. 1999); Gen. Man. and CEO VEYSEL BILEN; 74 brs.

Koçbank AS: Barbaros Bulvari, Morbasan Sokak, Koza İş Merkezi-C Blok Balmumu, İstanbul; tel. (212) 2747777; fax (212) 2672987; e-mail fim@kocbank.com.tr; internet www.kocbank.com.tr; f. 1986; cap. 283,135,000m., res −42,704,000m., dep. 2,151,501,000m. (Dec. 2000); Chair. BURHAN KARAÇAM; Gen. Man. HALIL EGÜR; brs 112.

Körfezbank: Maçka Cad. Bronz Sok, Maçka Palas, 80210 Teşuikiye, İstanbul; tel. (212) 2191111; fax (212) 2194112; e-mail cemb@korfezbank.com.tr; internet www.korfezbank.com.tr; f. 1988; cap. 324,866,000m., res −172,451,000m., dep. 689,110,000m. (Dec. 2000); Pres. and CEO HÜSNÜ AKHAN; 9 brs.

Oyak Bank AŞ: Büyükdere Cad., Ali Kaya Sok. 4, Polat Plaza A Blok, 80620 Levent, İstanbul; tel. (212) 3252929; fax (212) 2808716; e-mail gm@oyakbank.com.tr; internet www.oyakbank.com.tr; f. 1990; cap. 62,749,000m., res −5,461,586m., dep. 213,717,968m. (Dec. 2000); Chair. ALI CANER ONER; Gen. Man. A. MEHMET ÖZDENIZ; 177 brs.

Pamukbank TAŞ: Büyükdere Cad. 82, 34387 Gayrettepe, İstanbul; tel. (212) 2752424; fax (212) 2758606; internet www.pamukbank.com.tr; f. 1955; cap. 170,000,000m., res 649,967,000m., dep.

3,137,439,000m. (Dec. 2000); taken into govt control in June 2002; Chair. HASAN ULUKANLI; Pres. and CEO AHMET TUREL AYAYDIN; 196 brs.

Şekerbank TAŞ: Atatürk Bul. 171, 06680 Kavaklıdere, 06680 Ankara; tel. (312) 4179120; fax (312) 4178233; e-mail seker1@sekerbank.com.tr; internet www.sekerbank.com.tr; f. 1953; cap. 30,000,000m., res 654,893,000m., dep. 70,237,000m. (Dec. 2000); Chair. KAMIL ÖZDEMIR; Gen. Man. HASAN BASRI GÖKTAN; 182 brs.

Sümerbank AŞ: Büyükdere Cad. 106, Esentepe, 80280 İstanbul; tel. (212) 3364000; fax (212) 3364989; e-mail corrbanking@sumerbank.com.tr; internet www.sumerbank.com.tr; f. 1933; taken into govt control in Dec. 1999, absorbed Türkiye Tütüncüler Bankasi Yaşarbank AŞ in Jan. 2001 and Ulusal Bank TAS in Apr. 2001; sale pending in mid-2001; cap. 17,500,000., res 7,577,173m., dep. 244,406,954m. (Dec. 1998); Chair. and Gen. Man. ATILLA TAŞDEMIR; 87 brs.

Tekstilbank AŞ: Abide-i Hürriyet Cad. Geçit Sok 10, 80270 Şişli, İstanbul; tel. (212) 2241313; fax (212) 2241334; internet www.tekstilbank.com.tr; f. 1986; cap. 40,000,000m., res 22,714,000m., dep. 404,945,000m. (Dec. 2000); Chair. MUSTAFA ŞENDAĞ; CEO PULAT AKÇIN; Gen. Man. GIM GÜZELAYDINLI; 23 brs.

Toprakbank AŞ: Büyükdere Cad. 23, 80220 Şişli, İstanbul; tel. (212) 2332211; fax (212) 2255800; e-mail toprakbank@toprakbank.com.tr; internet www.toprakbank.com.tr; f. 1992; cap. 131,080,000m., res −22,754,000; dep. 736,270,000m. (Dec. 2000); Chair. and Gen. Man. CEMALETTIN HASDEMIR; 165 brs.

Türk Dış Ticaret Bankası AŞ (Turkish Foreign Trade Bank): Yıldız Posta Cad. 54, 80280 Gayrettepe, İstanbul; tel. (212) 2744280; fax (212) 2725278; internet www.disbank.com.tr; f. 1964; cap. 100,000,000m., res 186,490,395m., dep. 976,159,686m. (Dec. 2000); Chair. M. Ç. HACALOĞLU; Gen. Man. FAIK AÇIKALIN; 105 brs.

Türk Ekonomi Bankası AŞ: Meclisi Mebusan Cad. 35, 80040 Fındıklı, İstanbul; tel. (212) 2512121; fax (212) 2496568; internet www.teb.com.tr; f. 1927; fmrly Kocaeli Bankası TAŞ; cap. 69,602,000m., res 32,983,000m., dep. 662,304,000m. (Dec. 2000); Chair. YAVUZ CANEVI; Man. Dir Dr AKIN AKBAYGIL; 10 brs.

Türk Ticaret Bankası AŞ (Turkbank): Yıldız Posta Cad. 2, 80280 Gayrettepe, İstanbul; tel. (212) 2885900; fax (212) 2886113; internet www.turkbank.com.tr; f. 1913; cap. 109,249,236m., res −104,228,585m., dep. 520,482,945m. (Dec. 1999); Chair. ERDAL ARSLAN (acting); Gen. Man. ISMET TUĞUL (acting); 258 brs.

Türkiye Garanti Bankası AŞ (Garantibank): Büyükdere Cad. 63, 80670 Maslak, İstanbul; tel. (212) 3353240; fax (212) 3353535; e-mail mutlus@garanti.com.tr; internet www.garantibank.com; f. 1946; merged with Osmanli Bankasi AŞ (f. 1863) in Dec. 2001; cap. 807,313,000m., dep. 7,394,925,000m., total assets 9,791,928,000m. (Dec. 1999); Chair. FERIT FAIK ŞAHENK; Pres., CEO, and Gen. Man. ERGUN ÖZEN; 283 brs.

Türkiye İmar Bankası TAŞ: Büyükdere Cad. Doğuş Han. 42-46, 80290 Mecidiyeköy, İstanbul; tel. (212) 2670607; fax (212) 2665514; internet www.imarbankasi.com.tr; f. 1928; cap. 140,000,000m., res 5,603,107m., dep. 1,306,751,463m. (Dec. 2001); Chair. KEMAL UZAN; Gen. Man. HILMI BAŞARAN; 171 brs.

Türkiye İş Bankası AŞ (İşbank): İş Kuleleri, Büyükdere Cad., 80620 Levent, İstanbul; tel. (212) 3160000; fax (212) 3160900; e-mail halkla.iliskiler@isbank.com.tr; internet www.isbank.com.tr; f. 1924; cap. US $44m., res US $226m., dep. US $7,029m. (Dec. 2000); Chair. Dr AHMET KIRMAN; CEO and Gen. Man. ERSIN OZINCE; 854 brs.

Yapı ve Kredi Bankası AŞ: Yapı Kredi Plaza, Blok D, Büyükdere Cad., 80620 Levent, İstanbul; tel. (212) 3397000; fax (212) 2781289; e-mail yi@ykb.com; internet www.ykb.com.tr; f. 1944; cap. 1,000,507,000m., res 611,629,000m., dep. 5,823,567,000m. (Dec. 2000); Chair. RONA YIRCALI; CEO NACI SIĞIN; 414 brs.

Development and Investment Banks

Park Yatırım Bankası AŞ: Büyükdere Cad., Meşeli Sok 9, Kat 4, 80620 Levent, İstanbul; tel. (212) 2814820; fax (212) 2780445; e-mail webmaster@parkmaster.com.tr; internet www.parkbank.com.tr; f. 1992; cap. 2,000,000m., res 374,264m., dep. 3,885,680m. (Dec. 1998); Chair. HASAN KARAMEHMET; Gen. Man. RIZA SUAT GÖKDEL.

Sınai Yatırım Bankası AŞ (Industrial Investment Bank): Büyükdere Cad. 129, Esentepe, 80300 İstanbul; tel. (212) 2131600; fax (212) 2131303; e-mail form@syb.com.tr; internet www.syb.com.tr; f. 1963; cap. 22,500,000m., res 30,166,236m., dep. 15,123,746m. (Dec. 2000); Chair. CAHIT KOCAÖMER; Pres. and Gen. Man. HALIL EROĞLU.

Türkiye Kalkınma Bankası AS (Development Bank of Turkey): İzmir Cad. 35, Kızılay, 06440 Ankara; tel. (312) 4171220; fax (312) 4183967; e-mail tkb@tkb.com.tr; internet www.tkb.com.tr; f. 1975; cap. 75,000,000m., res 37,275,314m. (Dec. 2000); Pres. and Gen. Man. TACI BAYHAN; 6 brs.

Türkiye Sınai Kalkınma Bankası AŞ (Industrial Development Bank of Turkey): Meclisi Mebusan Cad. 161, Findikli, 80040 İstanbul; tel. (212) 3345050; fax (212) 2432975; e-mail ergund@tskb .com.tr; internet www.tskb.com.tr; f. 1950; cap. 28,000,000m., res 9,215,000m. (Dec. 2000), total assets 525,824,000m. (Dec. 2001); Chair. İSMET CAHIT KOCAÖMER; Pres. and Gen. Man. HALIL EROĞLU; 2 brs.

Foreign Banks

ABN AMRO NV (Netherlands): İnönü Cad. 13/17, Taksim, Gümüş-suyu, 80090 İstanbul; tel. (212) 2938802; fax (212) 2492008; f. 1921; Gen. Man. ALBERT MEIJER; 1 br.

Arap Türk Bankası AŞ (Arab Turkish Bank): Vali Konağı Cad. 10, PK 380, 80223 Nişantaşı, İstanbul; tel. (212) 2250500; fax (212) 2250526; e-mail webmaster@arabturkbank.com; internet www .arabturkbank.com.tr; f. 1977; cap. 62,846,515m., res 3,991,596m., dep. 66,497,837m. (Dec 2000); 54% owned Arabbanks; Chair. A. AYKUT DEMIRAY; Gen. Man. MUHAMMAD NAJIB H. EL-JAMAL; 3 brs.

Banca di Roma (Italy): Büyükdere Cad. Üç Yol Mevlik, Noramin Is Merkezi Kat 5, Maslak, 80670 İstanbul; tel. (212) 2859310; fax (212) 2769425; f. 1911; cap. 26,777m., res 5,868m. (Dec. 1992); Gen. Man. VALERIO BERT; 2 brs.

Bank Mellat (Iran): Büyükdere Cad. Binbirçiçek Sok 1, PK 67, 80620 Levent, İstanbul; tel. (212) 2798015; fax (212) 2846214; e-mail mellat@mellatbank.com; f. 1982; cap. and res US $2.1m., dep. US $18.4m. (Dec. 2001); Chair. MOSTAFA BEHESHTI ROUY; 3 brs.

BNP-Ak-Dresdner Bank AŞ: 1 Levent Plaza, Büyükdere Cad. 173, A Blok Kat. 8, Levent, İstanbul; tel. (212) 3395700; fax (212) 3395705; e-mail fininst@bnp-ak-dresdner.com.tr; internet www .bnp-ak-dresdner.com.tr; f. 1985; cap. 24,000,000m., res 35,493,472m., dep. 388,258,656m. (Dec. 2000); Pres. and Chair. AKIN KOZANOĞLU; Gen. Man. Dr ROLF SUTTER.

Chase Manhattan Bank (USA): Kat 11, Atakule A Blok, Emirhan Cad. 145, Beşiktaş, 80700 İstanbul; tel. (212) 2279700; fax (212) 2279729; f. 1984; Gen. Man. I ANTIKA; 1 br.

Citibank NA (USA): Büyükdere Cad. 100, Maya Akar Centre, 24th Floor, 80280 Esentepe, İstanbul; tel. (212) 2887700; fax (212) 2887760; e-mail dardo.sabarots@citicorp.com; internet www.citicorp .com; f. 1981; Gen. Man. SEBASTIAN PARADES; 3 brs.

Credit Agricole Indosuez Türk Bank AŞ (France): Büyükdere Cad. Plaza C Blok K Yapi Kredi Plaza, Levent, 80620 İstanbul; tel. (212) 2797070; fax (212) 2826301; e-mail indosuez@turk.net; f. 1990; cap. 11,265,000m., res 2,900,000m. (Dec. 2001); Pres. HENRI GUIL-LEMIN; Gen. Man. GILLES SERRA.

Cyprus Turkish Co-operative Central Bank Ltd ('TRNC'): PO Box Mersin 10; tel. (392) 2273398; fax (392) 2276787; internet www .koopbank.com; f. 1959; cap. and res 4,344,363m., dep. 117,722,019m. (Dec. 2000); Chair. AHMET ALPER; Gen. Man. Dr TUNCER ARIFOĞLU; 12 brs.

Habib Bank Ltd (Pakistan): Abide-i Hürriyet Cad. 12, PK 8, 80222 Şişli, İstanbul; tel. (212) 2460235; fax (212) 2340807; e-mail habibbank@fornet.net.tr; f. 1983; cap. 50,000m., res 2,125m., dep. 158,207m. (Dec. 1998); Gen. Man. A. B. TÜRKAY; 1 br.

HSBC Bank AŞ: Büyükdere Cad. 2, Levent, 80620 İstanbul; tel. (212) 2751900; fax (212) 2826020; internet www.hsbc.com.tr; f. 1990 as Midland Bank AŞ, name changed as above in 1999; acquired Demirbank TAŞ (f. 1953) in 2001; Chair. KEITH R. WHITSON; CEO PIRAYE Y. ANTIKA.

Kuwait Turkish Evkaf Finance House: Büyükdere Cad. 129, 34394 Esentepe, İstanbul; tel. (212) 3541111; fax (212) 3541212; e-mail kuveytturk@kuveytturk.com.tr; internet www.kuveytturk .com.tr; f. 1988; cap. 95,310,000m., res 12,407,111m., dep. 600,812,373m. (Dec. 2002); Chair. MUHAMMED S. AL OMAR; Gen. Man. UFUK UYAN; brs 36.

Société Générale SA (France): Akmerkez E-3, Nispetiye Cad., Blok Kat. 9, Eitler, 80600 İstanbul; tel. (212) 2821942; fax (212) 2821848; f. 1990; Gen. Man. ERIC FAIVRE; 1 br.

Turkish Bank AŞ ('TRNC'): Valikonağı Cad. 7, 80200 Nişantaşı, İstanbul; tel. (212) 2250330; fax (212) 2250353; e-mail dmm@ turkishbank.com; internet www.turkishbank.com; f. 1982; cap. 3,327,000m., res 812,448m., dep. 79,884,401m. (Dec. 2000); Chair. HAMIT B. BELLI; 13 brs.

Westdeutsche Landesbank Girozentrale (Germany): Ebulula Mardin Cad., Maya Park Towers, 80630 İstanbul; tel. (212) 3392500; fax (212) 3522258; f. 1990; Gen. Man. JOHN CHRISTOPHER DUTHIE; 2 brs.

Banking Organization

Banks' Association of Turkey: Nıspetıye Cad. Akmerkez B3 Blok. Kat 13–14, 80630 Etiler, İstanbul; tel. (212) 2820973; fax (212) 2820946; e-mail gensek@tbb.org.tr; internet www.tbb.org.tr; f. 1958; Chair. OSMAN TUNABOYLU (acting); Sec.-Gen. Dr EKREM KESKIN.

STOCK EXCHANGE

İstanbul Menkul Kıymetler Borsası (İMKB): Resitpaşa Mah., Tuncay Artun Cad., 34467 Emirgan, İstanbul; tel. (212) 2982100; fax (212) 2982500; e-mail dis@imkb.gov.tr; internet www.ise.org; f. 1866; revived in 1986 after being dormant for about 60 years; 119 mems of stock market, 146 mems of bond and bills market; Chair. and CEO OSMAN BIRSEN; Senior Vice-Chair ARIL SEREN.

INSURANCE

Anadolu Sigorta TAŞ (Anadolu Insurance Co): Rıhtım Cad. 57, 80030 Karaköy, İstanbul; tel. (212) 2516540; fax (212) 2432690; internet www.anadolusigorta.com.tr; f. 1925; Chair. BURHAN KAR-AGÖZ; Gen. Man. AHMET YAVUZ.

Ankara Sigorta TAŞ (Ankara Insurance Co): Bankalar Cad. 80, 80020 Karaköy, İstanbul; tel. (212) 2521010; fax (212) 2524744; f. 1936; Chair. and Gen. Man. Dr SEBAHATTIN BEYAZ.

Destek Reasürans TAŞ: Abdi İpekçi Cad. 75, 80200 Maçka, İstanbul; tel. (212) 2312832; fax (212) 2415704; f. 1945; reinsurance; Pres. ONUR ÖKTEN; Gen. Man. İBRAHIM YAYCIOĞLU.

Doğan Sigorta AŞ: Serdarı Ekrem Sok 48, 80020 Kuledibi, İstanbul; tel. (212) 2516374; fax (212) 2516379; f. 1942; fire, marine, accident; Chair. T. GÜNGÖR URAS.

Güven Sigorta TAŞ: Bankalar Cad. 81, 80000 Karaköy, İstanbul; tel. (212) 2547900; fax (212) 2551360; e-mail bilgeog@guvensigorta .com; internet www.guvensigorta.com.tr; f. 1924; all branches of insurance; Chair. and Gen. Man. HAYATI CETIN.

Hür Sigorta AŞ: Büyükdere Cad., Hür Han 15/A, 80260 Şişli, İstanbul; tel. (212) 2322010; fax (212) 2463673; Chair. BÜLENT SEMILER; Gen. Man. GÜNER YALÇINER.

İMTAŞ İttihadı Milli Sigorta TAŞ: Büyükdere Cad. 116, 80300 Zincirlikuyu, İstanbul; tel. (212) 2747000; fax (212) 2720837; f. 1918; Chair. Prof. Dr ASAF SAVAŞ AKAT; Gen. Man. MUSTAFA AKAN.

İstanbul Reasürans AŞ: Güneş Plaza, Büyükdere Caddesi No. 110 Kat 9, 80280 Esentepe-Şişli/İstanbul; tel. (212) 3556891; fax (212) 2173723; f. 1979; Chair. HASAN ALTANER; Gen. Man. GÜLGÜN ÜNLÜOĞLU.

Koç Allianz Sigorta AŞ: Bağlarbaşı, Kısıklı Cad. 11, 81180 Altu-nizade, İstanbul; tel. (212) 3101250; fax (212) 3101349; e-mail kocallianz@kocallianz.com.tr; f. 1923; Chair. M. RAHMI KOÇ; Gen. Man. GÜNEL BAŞER.

Milli Reasürans TAŞ: Teşvikiye Cad. 43–57, 34368 Teşvikiye, İstanbul; tel. (212) 2314730; fax (212) 2308608; e-mail info@millire .com.tr; internet www.millire.com.tr; f. 1929; premium income 257,433,972m., total assets 250,959,762m. (Dec. 2001); Chair. Prof. Dr AHMET KIRMAN; Dir and Gen. Man. CAHIT NOMER.

Şeker Sigorta AŞ: Meclisi Mebusan Cad. 87, Şeker Sigorta Hanı, PK 519, 80040 Fındıklı, İstanbul; tel. (212) 2514035; fax (212) 2491046; e-mail info@sekersigorta.com.tr; internet www .sekersigorta.com.tr; f. 1954; Chair. HASAN BASRI GÖKTAN; Gen. Man. KÂMIL YIĞIT.

Tam Sigorta AŞ: Meclisi Mebusan Cad. 27/1, Setüstü, Kabataş, İstanbul; tel. (212) 2934064; fax (212) 2517181; f. 1964; all types of insurance except life; Chair. REHA BAVBEK; Gen. Man. MEHMET NEZIR UCA.

Türkiye Genel Sigorta AŞ: Meclisi Mebusan Cad. 91, 80040 Salıpazarı, İstanbul; tel. (212) 2520010; fax (212) 2499651; f. 1948; Chair. MEHMET E. KARAMEHMET; Gen. Man. HULUSI TAŞKIRAN.

Yapi Kredi Sigorta AŞ: Yapi Kredi Plaza, Blok A, Büyükdere Cad., 34330 Levent, İstanbul; tel. (212) 3360606; fax (212) 3360808; e-mail yksigorta@yksigorta.com.tr; internet www.yksigorta.com.tr; f. 1944; Chair. HALUK CILLOV; Gen. Man. ERHAN DUMANLI.

Trade and Industry

GOVERNMENT AGENCY

Özelleştirme İdaresi Başkanlığı (Privatization Administration): Hüseyin Rahmi Gürpınar Sok. 2, Çankaya, 06680 Ankara; tel. (312) 4411500; fax (312) 4403271; e-mail info@oib.gov.tr; internet www .oib.gov.tr; co-ordinates privatization programme; Pres. UGUR BAYAR.

DEVELOPMENT ORGANIZATIONS

Turkish Atomic Energy Authority: Prime Minister's Office, 06530 Ankara; tel. (312) 2876536; fax (312) 2871224; e-mail mehmet .tomak@taek.gov.tr; internet www.taek.gov.tr; f. 1956; controls the development of peaceful uses of atomic energy; 11 mems; Pres. Prof. Dr MEHMET TOMAK; Vice-Pres. Dr ERDENER BIROL.

Turkish Electricity Authority (TEAS) (Nuclear Power Plants Department): İnönü Bul. 27, 06440 Ankara; tel. (312) 2229855; fax (312) 2127853; state enterprise to supervise the construction and operation of nuclear power plants; attached to the Ministry of Energy and Natural Resources; Head of Dept NEVZAT ŞAHIN.

CHAMBERS OF COMMERCE AND INDUSTRY

Union of Chambers of Commerce, Industry, Maritime Commerce and Commodity Exchanges of Turkey (UCCET): 149 Atatürk Bul. 149, Bakanlıklar, Ankara; tel. (312) 4184325; fax (312) 4254854; e-mail info@info.tobb.org.tr; f. 1952; represents 335 chambers and commodity exchanges; Pres. FUAT MIRE; Sec.-Gen. ŞEFIK TOKAT.

Ankara Chamber of Commerce: Ato Sarayi Eskişehir Yolu Söğütözü Mahallesi Cad. 5, Ankara; tel. (312) 2857950; fax (312) 2863446; internet www.atonet.org.

Ankara Chamber of Industry: Atatürk Bul. 193/4-5, Kavaklıdere, Ankara; tel. (312) 4171200; fax (312) 4175205; e-mail aso@aso.org.tr; internet www.aso.org.

İstanbul Chamber of Commerce (ICOC): Reşadiye Cad. 84,34378 Eminönü, İstanbul; tel. (212) 5114150; fax (212) 5131565; internet www.ito.org.tr; f. 1882; more than 230,000 mems; Chair. MEHMET YILDIRIM.

İstanbul Chamber of Industry: Meşrutiyet Cad. 118, Tepebaşi, İstanbul; tel. (212) 2522900; fax (212) 2934398; e-mail mkabasahal@iso.org.tr.

İzmir Chamber of Commerce: Atatürk Cad. 126, 35210 İzmir; tel. (232) 4417777; fax (232) 4837853; e-mail info@izto.org.tr; internet www.izto.org.tr; f. 1885; Pres. EKREM DEMIRTAŞ; Sec.-Gen. Prof. Dr İLTER AKAT.

EMPLOYERS' ASSOCIATIONS

Türk Sanayicileri ve İşadamları Derneği (TÜSİAD) (Turkish Industrialists' and Businessmen's Association): Meşrutiyet Cad. 74, 80050 Tepebaşı, İstanbul; tel. (212) 2495448; fax (212) 2491350; e-mail webmaster@tusiad.org; internet www.tusiad.org; f. 1971; 451 mems; Pres. TUNCAY ÖZILHAN; Chair. ERKUT YÜCAOĞLU; Sec.-Gen. Dr HALUK R. TÜKEL.

Türkiye İşveren Sendikaları Konfederasyonu (TİSK) (Turkish Confederation of Employers' Associations): Meşrutiyet Cad. 1/4-5, 06650 Kızılay, Ankara; tel. (312) 4183217; fax (312) 4184473; e-mail gensec@tisk.org.tr; internet www.tisk.org.tr; f. 1962; represents (on national level) 20 employers' associations with 8,000 affiliated member employers or companies; official representative in labour relations; Pres. REFIK BAYDUR; Sec.-Gen. BÜLENT PIRLER.

UTILITIES

Electricity

Türkiye Elektrik Üretim-İletim AŞ (TEAŞ-Turkish Electricity Authority): Inönü Bul. 27, 06440 Ankara; tel. (312) 2229855; fax (312) 2127853; attached to Ministry of Energy and Natural Resources.

TRADE UNIONS

Confederations

DİSK (Türkiye Devrimci İşçi Sendikaları Konfederasyonu) (Confederation of Progressive Trade Unions of Turkey): Cad. Abide-I Hürriyet 117, Kat. 5-6-7, Şişli, İstanbul; tel. (212) 2910005; fax (212) 2342075; e-mail disk-f@tr.net.tr; internet www.disk.org.tr; f. 1967; member of ICFTU, ETUC and TUAC; 26 affiliated unions; Pres. SÜLEYMAN ÇELEBI; Sec.-Gen. MURAT TOKMAK.

Türk-İş (Türkiye İşçi Sendikaları Konfederasyonu Genel Başkanlığı) (Confederation of Turkish Trade Unions): Bayındır Sok 10, Yenişehir, Ankara; tel. (312) 4333125; fax (312) 4336809; e-mail turkis@turkis.org.tr; f. 1952; member of ICFTU, ETUC, ICFTU-APRO and OECD/TUAC; 32 national unions and federations with 1.7m. mems; Pres. BAYRAM MERAL; Gen. Sec. HÜSEYIN KARAKOÇ.

Principal DİSK Trade Unions

Bank-Sen (Türkiye Devrimci Banka ve Sigorta İşçileri Sendikası): Nakiye Elgun Sok 117, Şişli, İstanbul; tel. (212) 2321000; fax (212) 2311911; Pres. VEYSEL KALAY; 15,000 mems.

Basın-İş (Türkiye Basın İşçileri Sendikası) (Press Workers' Union): İstanbul; f. 1964; Pres. YILMAZ ÖZDEMIR; Gen. Sec. DERVIŞ BOYOĞLU; 5,000 mems.

Birlesik Metal-İs (Birlesik Metal İşçileri Sendikası): Tünel Yolu Cad. 2, 81110 Bostancı, Kadıköy, İstanbul; tel. (216) 3622091; fax (216) 3736502; e-mail info@birlesikmetal.com; Gen. Sec. MUZAFFER ŞAHIN; 58,800 mems.

Demiryol-İş (Türkiye Demiryolu İşçileri Sendikası) (Railway Workers): Necatibey Cad., Sezenler Sok 5, 06430 Yenişehir, Ankara; tel. (312) 2318029; fax (312) 2318032; internet www.sendikaonline .com; f. 1952; Pres. ERGÜN ATALAY; Gen. Sec. HÜSEYIN DEMIR; 25,000 mems.

Deri-İş (Türkiye Deri İşçileri Sendikası) (Leather Industry): Ahmet Kutsi Tecer Cad. 12/6, Merter, İstanbul; tel. (212) 5048083; fax (212) 5061079; f. 1948; Pres. NUSRETTIN YILMAZ; Gen. Sec. ALI SEL; 11,000 mems.

Dev. Sağlık-İş (Türkiye Devrimci Sağlık İşçileri Sendikası) (Health Employees): İstanbul; f. 1961; Pres. DOĞAN HALIS; Gen. Sec. SABRI TANYERI; 15,000 mems.

Genel-İş (Türkiye Genel Hizmet İşçileri Sendikası) (Municipal Workers): Çankırı Cad. 28, Kat 5-9, Ulus, Ankara; tel. (312) 3091547; fax (312) 3091046; f. 1983; Pres. ISMAIL HAKKI ÖNAL; Gen. Sec. ATILA ÖNGEL; 50,000 mems.

Gıda-İş (Türkiye Gıda Sanayii İşçileri Sendikası): Ahmet Kutsi Tecer Cad. 12/3, 34010 Merter, İstanbul; tel. (212) 5751540; fax (212) 5753099; Pres. MEHMET MUHLACI; Gen. Sec. YURDAKUL GÖZDE; 31,000 mems.

Koop-İş (Türkiye Kooperatif ve Büro İşçileri Sendikası) (Co-operative and Office Workers): İzmir Cad. Fevzi Çakmak Sok 15/11–12, Yenişehir, Ankara; tel. (312) 4300855; f. 1964; Pres. AHMET BALAMAN; Gen. Sec. AHMET GÜVEN; 29,000 mems.

Limter-İş (Liman, Tersane Gemi Yapım Onarım İşçileri Sendikası) (Harbour, Shipyard, Ship Building and Repairs): İcmeler Tren İstasyonu Yanı 12/1, Tuzla, İstanbul; tel. (216) 3955271; f. 1947; Pres. EMIR BABAKUŞ; Gen. Sec. ASKER ŞIT; 7,000 mems.

Nakliyat-İş (Nakliye İşçileri Sendikası) (Transportation Workers): Guraba Hüseyin Ağa Mah. Kakmacı Sok 10, Daire 11 Vatan Cad. Tranvay, Durağı Karşısı, Aksaray, İstanbul; tel. (212) 5332069; Pres. ŞEMSI ERCAN; Gen. Sec. NEDIM FIRAT.

OLEYİS (Otel, Lokanta, Eğlence Yerleri İşçileri Sendikası) (Hotel, Restaurant and Places of Entertainment Workers' Union): Necatibey Cad. 96/1-3, Kızılay, Ankara; tel. (312) 2311845; fax (312) 2311846; e-mail oleyis@oleyis.org.tr; internet www.oleyis.org.tr; f. 1947; Pres. ENVER ÖKTEM; Gen. Sec. ETHEM KAYNAR OLGUNER; 4,000 mems.

Petkim-İş (Türkiye Petrol, Kimya ve Lastik Sanayii İşçileri Sendikası): İzmir Cad., Fevzi Çakmak Sok. 7/13, Ankara; tel. (312) 2300861; fax (312) 2299429; Pres. MUSTAFA KARADAYI; 18,000 mems.

Sosyal-İş (Türkiye Sosyal Sigortalar, Eğitim, Büro, Ticaret Kooperatif Banka ve Güzel Sanatlar İşçileri Sendikası) (Banking, Insurance and Trading): Necatibey Cad. Sezenler Sok. Lozan Apt. 2/14, Yenişehir, Ankara; tel. (312) 2318178; fax (312) 2294638; Pres. ÖZCAN KESGEÇ; Gen. Sec. H. BEDRI DOĞANAY; 31,000 mems.

Tekstil İşçileri Sendikası: Ahmet Kutsi Tecer Cad. 12/1, Merter, İstanbul; tel. (212) 6429742; fax (212) 5044887; Pres. RIDVAN BUDAK; 45,000 mems.

Tümka-İş (Türkiye Tüm Kağıt Selüloz Sanayii İşçileri Sendikası): Gündoğdu Sok 19/3, Merter, İstanbul; tel. (212) 5750843; Pres. SABRI KAPLAN; 3,000 mems.

Other Principal Trade Unions

Denizciler (Türkiye Denizciler Sendikası) (Seamen): Rıhtım Cad., Denizciler Sok. 7, Tophane, İstanbul; tel. (212) 2929081; fax (212) 2933938; e-mail selimataergin@hotmail.com; f. 1959; Pres. TURHAN UZUN; Gen. Sec. ÇEMIL YENIAY; 4,272 mems.

Fındık-İş (Fiskobirlik İşçileri Sendikası) (Hazel-nut producers): Giresun; Pres. AKÇIN KOÇ; Gen. Sec. ERSAIT ŞEN.

Hava-İş (Türkiye Sivil Havacılık Sendikası) (Civil Aviation): İncirli Cad., Volkan Apt., 68/1 Bakırköy, İstanbul; tel. (212) 6601495; fax (212) 5719051; e-mail havais@mail.turk.net; Pres. ATILAY AYÇIN; Gen. Sec. MUSTAFA YAĞCI; 7,000 mems.

Liman-İş (Türkiye Liman ve Kara Tahmil İşçileri Sendikası) (Longshoremen): Necatibey Cad., Sezenler Sok 4, Kat. 5, Sıhhıye, Ankara; tel. (312) 2317418; fax (312) 2302484; e-mail liman-is@tr-net.net.tr; f. 1963; Pres. RAIF KILIÇ; Gen. Sec. ERDING ÇAKIR; 5,000 mems.

Şeker-İş (Türkiye Şeker Sanayii İşçileri Sendikası) (Sugar Industry): Karanfil Sok 59, Bakanlıklar, Ankara; tel. (312) 4184273; fax (312) 4259258; f. 1952; Pres. ÖMER ÇELIK; Gen. Sec. FETHI TEKIN; 35,000 mems.

Tarım-İş (Türkiye Orman, Topraksu, Tarım ve Tarım Sanayii İşçileri Sendikası) (Forestry, Agriculture and Agricultural Industry Workers): Bankacı Sok 10, 06700 Kocatepe, Ankara; tel. (312) 4190456; fax (312) 4193113; e-mail tarim-is@tr.net; f. 1961; Pres. BEDRETTIN KAYKAÇ; Gen. Sec. İ. SABRI KESKIN; 40,500 mems.

Tekgıda-İş (Türkiye Tütün, Müskirat Gıda ve Yardımcı İşçileri Sendikası) (Tobacco, Drink, Food and Allied Workers' Union of Turkey): 4 Levent Konaklar Sok, İstanbul; tel. (212) 2644996; fax (212) 2789534; e-mail bilgi@tekgida.org.tr; internet www.tekgida .org.tr; f. 1952; Pres. HÜSEYIN KARAKOÇ; Gen. Sec. MUSTAFA TÜRKEL; 176,000 mems.

Teksif (Türkiye Tekstil, Örme ve Giyim Sanayii İşçileri Sendikası) (Textile, Knitting and Clothing): Ziya Gökalp Cad. Aydoğmuş Sok 1, Kurtuluş, Ankara; tel. (312) 4312170; fax (312) 4357826; f. 1951; Pres. ZEKI POLAT; 80,000 mems.

Tez-Koop-İş (Türkiye, Ticaret, Kooperatif, Eğitim, Büro ve Güzel Sanatlar İşçileri Sendikası) (Commercial and Clerical Employees): Üç Yıldız Cad. 29, Subayevleri, Ayınlıkevler, 06130 Ankara; tel. (312) 3183979; fax (312) 3183988; f. 1962; Pres. SADIK ÖZBEN; Gen. Sec. H. FARAK ÜSTÜN; 30,000 mems.

Türk Harb-İş (Türkiye Harb Sanayii ve Yardımcı İşkolları İşçileri Sendikası) (Defence Industry and Allied Workers): İnkılap Sok 20, Kızılay, Ankara; tel. (312) 4175097; fax (312) 4171364; f. 1956; Pres. İZZET CETIN; Gen. Sec. NURI AYCICER; 35,000 mems.

Türk-Metal (Türkiye Metal, Çelik, Mühimmat, Makina ve Metalden Mamul, Eşya ve Oto, Montaj ve Yardımcı İşçileri Sendikası) (Auto, Metal and Allied Workers): Kızılırmak Mah., Adalararası Sok. 3, Eskişehir Yolu 1 km, 06560 Söğütözü, Ankara; tel. (312) 2844010; fax (312) 2844018; e-mail bilgiislem@turkmetal .org.tr; f. 1963; Pres. MUSTAFA ÖZBEK; 247,000 mems.

Yol-İş (Türkiye Yol, Yapı ve İnşaat İşçileri Sendikası) (Road, Construction and Building Workers' Unions): Sümer 1 Sok 18, Kızıloy, Ankara; tel. (312) 2324687; fax (312) 2324810; f. 1963; Pres. BAYRAM MERAL; Gen. Sec. TEVFIK ÖZÇELIK; 170,000 mems.

Transport

RAILWAYS

The total length of the railways operated within the national frontiers is 10,922 km (2000), of which 8,671 km are main lines, 2,122 km are electrified, and 2,505 km are signalled. A new direct rail link between Ankara and İstanbul, cutting the distance from 577 km to 416 km, was to be completed by 2000. There are direct rail links with Bulgaria to Iran and Syria. A new line connecting Turkey with Georgia was to be completed by 2000. İstanbul operates an 18-km light railway system, and opened its first metro line in September 2000. Both systems are being expanded. Ankara and İzmir both operate metro railways.

Türkiye Cumhuriyeti Devlet Demiryolları İşletmesi Genel Müdürlüğü (TCDD) (Turkish Republic State Railways): Talatpaşa Bul., 06330 Gar, Ankara; tel. (312) 3090515; fax (312) 3123215; e-mail tcddapk@superonline.com; internet tcdd.gov.tr; f. 1924; operates all railways and connecting ports (see below) of the State Railway Administration, which acquired the status of a state economic enterprise in 1953, and a state economic establishment in 1984; 479 main-line diesel locomotives, 78 main-line electric locomotives, 1,031 passenger coaches and 16,624 freight wagons; Chair. of Board and Gen. Dir VEDAT BILGIN.

ROADS

At 1 January 2000 1,746 km of motorways were open to traffic and nearly 511 km of motorways were under construction; the total length of the highway network was 62,672 km and the total length of village roads was 319,218 km. In 1999 there were 59,894 km of roads in the maintenance programme.

Bayındırlık ve İskan Bakanlığı, Karayolları Genel Müdürlüğü (KGM) (General Directorate of Highways): Yücetepe, 06100 Ankara; tel. (312) 4252343; fax (312) 4186996; e-mail info@kgm.gov .tr; internet www.kgm.gov.tr; f. 1950; Dir-Gen. DINÇER YIĞIT.

SHIPPING

At the end of 2001 Turkey's merchant fleet comprised 1,146 vessels and had an aggregate displacement of 5,896,708m. grt.

General-purpose public ports are operated by two state economic enterprises. The ports of Bandırma, Derince, Haydarpaşa (İstanbul), İskenderun, İzmir, Mersin and Samsun, all of which are connected to the railway network, are operated by Turkish State Railways (TCDD) (see above), while the smaller ports of Antalya, Giresun, Hopa, Tekirdağ and Trabzon are operated by the Turkish Maritime Organization (TDI).

Turkish Maritime Organization (TDI): Genel Müdürlüğü, Karaköy, İstanbul; tel. (212) 2515000; fax (212) 2495391.

Port of Bandırma: TCDD Liman İşletme Müdürlüğü, Bandırma; tel. (266) 2234966; fax (266) 2236011; Port Man. OKKES DEMIREL; Harbour Master RUSEN OKAN.

Port of Derince: TCDD Liman İşletme Müdürlüğü, Derince; Port Man. ALI ARIF AYTAÇ; Harbour Master HAYDAR DOĞAN.

Port of Haydarpaşa (İstanbul): TCDD Liman İşletme Müdürlüğü Haydarpaşa, İstanbul; tel. (212) 3379988; fax (212) 3451705; Port Man. NEDIM OZCAN; Harbour Master İSMAIL SAFAER.

Port of İskenderun: TCDD Liman İşletme Müdürlüğü, İskenderun; tel. (326) 6140047; fax (326) 6132424; Port Man. HILMI SÖNMEZ; Harbour Master İSHAK ÖZDEMIR.

Port of İzmir: TCDD Liman İşletme Müdürlüğü, İzmir; tel. (232) 4632252; fax (232) 4632248; Port Man. GÜNGÖR ERKAYA; Harbour Master MEHMET ONGEL.

Port of Mersin: TCDD Liman İşletme Müdürlüğü, Mersin; tel. (324) 2330687; fax (324) 2311350; Port Man. FAHRI SAYILI; Harbour Master RACI TARHUSOĞLU.

Port of Samsun: TCDD Liman İşletme Müdürlüğü, Samsun; tel. (362) 4357616; fax (362) 4317849; Port Man. SAFFET YAMAK; Harbour Master Capt. ARIF H. UZUNOĞLU.

Private Companies

Deniz Nakliyatı TAŞ (Turkish Cargo Lines): Meclisı Mebusan Cad. 151, 80040 Fındıklı, İstanbul; tel. (212) 2522600; fax (212) 2512696; f. 1955; privatization pending 1997; regular liner services between Turkey and Mediterranean, Adriatic, Red Sea, US Atlantic, and Indian and Far East ports; Gen. Man. NEVZAT BILICAN; 17 general cargo ships, 4 roll-on, roll-off, 8 bulk/ore carriers.

İstanbul Deniz Otobusleri Sanayi ve Ticaret AŞ: POB 81110, Bostanci, İstanbul; tel. (216) 3628013; fax (216) 3620443; ferry company; Chair. MUSTAFA ACIKALIN; Man. Dir BINALI YILDIRIM; 23 vessels.

Kiran Shipping Group of Companies: Fahrettin Kerim Gorkay Cad. 22, Denizcilar İş Merkezi B Blok Kat 2, 81190 Altunizade, İstanbul; tel. (216) 3916150; fax (216) 3916168; Chair. TURGUT KIRAN; Man. Dir TAMER KIRAN; 16 vessels.

Ozsay Seatransportation Co Inc: Iskele Sok Ozsay Bldg 44 Kat 3, 81320 Kadikoy, İstanbul; tel. (216) 3451827; fax (216) 3469532; Pres. IHSAN KALKAVAN; Man. Dir OZNUR CALIS; 10 vessels.

Pinat Gida Sanayi ve Ticaret AŞ: Pak Ismerkezi Prof. Dr Bulent Tarcan Sok 5/3, 80290 Gayrettepe, İstanbul; tel. (212) 2747533; fax (212) 2750317; e-mail pinat@pinat.com.tr; Pres. ENGIN PAK; Man. Dir ALPAY CITAK; 7 vessels.

T.D.I Sehir Hatlan İşletmesi: Mayis Han, Bahcekapi 27, 34420 Sirkeci, İstanbul; tel. (212) 5264020; fax (212) 2495391; 14 vessels.

Türkiye Denizcilik İşletmeleri Denizyolları İşletmesi Müdürlüğü (TDI): Meclisı Mebusan Cad. 18, 80040 Salıpazarı, İstanbul; tel. (212) 2521700; fax (212) 2515767; internet www.tdi.com.tr; ferry company; Chair. ERKAN ARIKAN; Man. Dir KADIR KURTOĞLU; 5 vessels.

Vakif Deniz Finansal Kiralama AŞ: Rihtim Cad. 201 Tahir Han kat 6, PK 853, 80040 Karaköy, İstanbul; 15 vessels.

Yardimci Shipping Group of Companies: Aydintepe Mah. Tersaneler Cad. 50 Sok 7, 81700 Tuzla, İstanbul; tel. (216) 4938000; fax (216) 4928080; e-mail moliva@turk.net; Chair. KEMAL YARDIMCI; Man. Dir HUSEYIN YARDIMCI; 11 vessels.

Shipping Associations

SS Gemi Armatörleri Motorlu Taşıyıcılar Kooperatifi (Turkish Shipowners' Asscn): Meclisı Mebusan Cad., Dursun Han, Kat. 7, No 89, Salıpazarı İstanbul; tel. (212) 2510945; fax (212) 2492786; f. 1960; Pres. GÜNDÜZ KAPTANOĞLU; Man. Dir A. GÖKSU; 699 vessels; 5,509,112 dwt (1993).

Türk Armatörler Birliği (Turkish Shipowners' Union): Meclisı Mebusan Cad. Dursun Han, Kat. 7 No. 89, Salıpazarı, İstanbul; tel. (212) 2453022; fax (212) 2492786; f. 1972; 460 mems; Pres. ŞADAN KALKAVAN; Co-ordinator HAKAN ÜNSALER; 8,780,436 dwt (1997).

Vapur Donatanları ve Acenteleri Derneği (Turkish Shipowners' and Shipping Agents' Asscn): Mumhane Cad. Emek İş Hanı Kat. 3 No. 31, Karaköy, İstanbul; tel. (212) 2443294; fax (212) 2432865; e-mail vapurd@vda.org.tr; internet www.vda.org.tr; f. 1902; world-wide agency service; Pres. Capt. M. LEBLEBICIOĞLU; Man. Dir C. KAPLAN.

CIVIL AVIATION

There are airports for scheduled international and internal flights at Atatürk (İstanbul), Esenboğa (Ankara), Adnan Menderes (İzmir and Trabzon), while international charter flights are handled by Adana,

Dalaman and Antalya. Fifteen other airports handle internal flights only.

Alfa Hava Yolları AŞ (Alfa Airlines Inc.): Fatih Cad. 21, Günesli, 34540 İstanbul; tel. (212) 6303348; fax (212) 6575869; e-mail hkeser@airalfa.com.tr; internet www.airalfa.com.tr; f. 1992; charter services to Europe; Man. Dir. NECMETTIN METINER.

Eurosun Airlines (ESN): Fener Mah, Bul. Ozgurluk, Melda 2/7, Antalya 07134; tel. (242) 3235060; fax (242) 3241252; f. 1999 as Air Rose, assumed present name in June 2000; charter flights to European destinations; Man. Dir. MESUT SENER.

İstanbul Hava Yolları AŞ (Istanbul Airlines): Firuzköy Yolu, Bağlar İçi Mevzii 26, 34850 Avcılar, İstanbul; tel. (212) 5092100; fax (212) 5938742; internet www.istanbulairlines.com.tr; f. 1985; charter services from major Turkish cities to European destinations; Gen. Man. SAFI ERGIN.

Onur Air Taşımacılık AŞ: Senlik Mahallesi, Gatal Sok. 3, 34810 Florya, İstanbul; tel. (212) 6632300; fax (212) 6632319; internet www.onurair.de; f. 1992; regional and domestic passenger and cargo charter services; Chair. CANKUT BAGANA.

Pegasus Hava Taşımacılığı AŞ: İstasyon Cad. 24, Kat. 1, 34800 Yeşilyurt, İstanbul; tel. (212) 6632934; fax (212) 5739627; internet www.pgtair.com; f. 1989; charter services; Chair. S. ALTUN; Gen. Man. L. J. LOWTH.

Sky Airlines: Jalan Cad., Suite 41, Baranaklar-Anatalya 07100; tel. (242) 3237576; fax (242) 3237567; f. 2000; regional passenger charter flights; CEO TALHA GORGULU.

Sonmez Hava Yolları: 9 km Yakova Yolu, PK 189, Bursa; tel. (224) 2610440; fax (224) 2465445; f. 1984; scheduled flights and dedicated freight; Chair. ALI OSMAN SÖNMEZ.

SunExpress: Fener Mahallesi Sinanoghu Cad., Oktay Airport, PK 28, 07100 Antalya; tel. (242) 3234047; fax (242) 3234057; e-mail sunexpress@condor.de; internet www.sunexpress.de; f. 1990; charter and scheduled passenger and freight; serves European destinations; Man. Dir PAUL SCHWAIGER.

Top Air: Atatürk Havalimani, E-Kapısı, Polis Okulu Arkası, 34640 Sefaköy, İstanbul; tel. (212) 5416040; fax (212) 5985060; e-mail info@topair.com.tr; internet www.topair.com.tr; f. 1990; charter and scheduled flights for tour operators.

Türk Hava Yolları AO (THY) (Turkish Airlines Inc.): Genel Müdürlük Binas, Atatürk Hava Limanı, 34830 Yeşilköy, İstanbul; tel. (212) 6636300; fax (212) 6634744; e-mail turkishairlines@thy .com; internet www.turkishairlines.com; f. 1933; majority state-owned, but earmarked 51% privatization in 2001; extensive internal network and scheduled and charter flights to destinations in the Middle East, Africa, the Far East, Central Asia, the USA and Europe; Pres. and CEO YUSUF BOLAYIRLI.

Tourism

Visitors to Turkey are attracted by the climate, fine beaches and ancient monuments. Tourism is being stimulated by the Government, and the industry is expanding rapidly. In 2001 provisional receipts from tourism were a record US $8,090m., compared with $7,636m. in 2000, while the number of tourists increased from 7.5m. in 1999 to 10.4m. in 2000 and 11.6m. in 2001.

Ministry of Tourism: İsmet İnönü Bul. 5, Bahçelievler, Ankara; tel. (312) 2128300; fax (312) 2128391; e-mail tbtgmos@tr-net.net.tr; internet www.tourism.gov.tr; f. 1963; Dir-Gen. of Establishments YENAL ÜNSEL; Dir-Gen. of Information MUSTAFA SYAHHAN; Dir-Gen. of Investments HALUK AKAR.

TURKMENISTAN

Introductory Survey

Location, Climate, Language, Religion, Flag, Capital

The Republic of Turkmenistan (or Turkmenia), formerly the Turkmen Soviet Socialist Republic, is situated in the south-west of Central Asia. It is bordered to the north by Uzbekistan, to the north-west by Kazakhstan, to the west by the Caspian Sea, to the south by Iran and to the south-east by Afghanistan. The climate is severely continental, with extremely hot summers and cold winters. The average temperature in January is –4°C (25°F), but winter temperatures can fall as low as –33°C (–27°F). In summer temperatures often reach 50°C (122°F) in the south-east Kara-Kum desert; the average temperature in July is 28°C (82°F). Precipitation is slight throughout much of the country: average annual rainfall ranges from only 80 mm (3.1 ins) in the north-west to about 300 mm (11.8 ins) in mountainous regions. In 1990 Turkmen was declared the official language of the republic. Turkmen is a member of the Southern Turkic group; in 1929 the traditional Arabic script was replaced by a Latin script, which was, in turn, replaced by the Cyrillic script in 1940. In 1993 it was announced that the republic would gradually change to a Latin-based Turkish script, which was formally adopted in January 2000. Most of the population are Sunni Muslims. Islam in Turkmenistan has traditionally featured elements of Sufi mysticism and shamanism, and pilgrimages to local religious sites are reported to be common. The national flag (proportions 2 by 3) consists of three unequal vertical stripes (proportions 4–6–23), of green, maroon and green; the maroon stripe bears a vertical design of five different carpet patterns above an orange wreath of olive branches, while the green stripe nearest the fly has in its upper dexter corner five white five-pointed stars framed by a narrow white crescent moon. The capital is Ashgabat (Ashkhabad).

Recent History

In 1877 Russia began a campaign against the Turkmen, which culminated in the battle of Gök Tepe, in 1881, at which some 20,000 Turkmen are estimated to have been killed. In 1895 the Russian conquest was confirmed by agreement with the British; the international boundary thus established divided some Turkmen under Russian rule from others in the British sphere of influence. In 1917 the Bolsheviks attempted to take power in the region, but there was little support from among the local population. An anti-Bolshevik Russian Provisional Government of Transcaspia was formed, and a Turkmen Congress was also established. Soviet forces were sent to Ashgabat (Ashkhabad), and a Turkestan Autonomous Soviet Socialist Republic, which included Transcaspia, was declared on 30 April 1918. In July, however, nationalists, aided by British forces, overthrew the Bolshevik Government and established an independent Government in Ashgabat, protected by a British garrison. After the British withdrew, however, the Government was soon overthrown, and by 1920 the Red Army, led by Gen. Frunze, was in control of Ashgabat. As part of the National Delimitation of Central Asia, the Turkmen Soviet Socialist Republic (SSR) was established on 27 October 1924. In May 1925 it became a constituent republic of the Union of Soviet Socialist Republics (USSR, established in December 1922). Political power in the republic became the preserve of the Communist Party of Turkmenistan (CPT).

The Soviet agricultural collectivization programme, which was begun in 1929 and entailed the forcible settlement of traditionally nomadic people in collective farms, provoked further military resistance; guerrilla warfare against Soviet power continued until 1936. In 1928 a campaign against the practice of religion in Turkmenistan was launched: almost all Islamic institutions were closed, including schools, courts and mosques. In the early 1930s there was a campaign among the Turkmen intelligentsia for greater political autonomy for Turkmenistan. As a result, many Turkmen intellectuals were imprisoned or executed. The scope of the purges widened in the late 1930s to include government and CPT officials, notably the Chairman of the republic's Supreme Soviet (legislature), Nederbai Aitakov, who was executed in c. 1937.

After the early 1930s there was little development in the industrial sector. Agriculture was encouraged and irrigation extended, although with little regard for the possible ecological effects. Irrigation projects such as the Kara-Kum Canal, the largest such scheme in the USSR, enabled rapid development of cotton-growing, especially after 1945. However, the ecological consequences for the Aral Sea, to the north of the republic, were catastrophic.

The immigration of Russians into the urban areas of Turkmenistan, from the 1920s, gradually diminished the proportion of Turkmen in leading posts in the republic. In 1958 the First Secretary (leader) of the CPT, Babayev, proposed that Turkmen should occupy more leading positions. He was dismissed, together with many of his colleagues in government.

The major issues in Turkmenistan in the late 1980s were economic, environmental and cultural. Turkmenistan's position as a provider of raw materials (mainly natural gas and cotton) to more developed republics in the European parts of the USSR provoked strong criticism of the relationship between Turkmenistan and the all-Union authorities. The environmental and health hazards connected with over-intensive agriculture, notably the cultivation of cotton, were also widely discussed in the republican media. These issues, combined with those of language and history, provoked dissatisfaction with the relationship with the USSR. However, the geographical remoteness of the republic and its poor level of communications with other parts of the USSR inhibited its involvement in the political changes occurring in other Soviet republics. Moreover, the lack of any history as a unified nation, together with the continuing tribal divisions, did not engender any mass movement for national autonomy, as occurred elsewhere.

In the absence of any significant democratic movement, the CPT dominated the republic's elections to the all-Union Congress of People's Deputies in Moscow in early 1989. In September of that year, however, Turkmen intellectuals met to form Agzybirlik, a 'popular front' organization concerned with the status of the Turkmen language, indigenous arts, environmental matters and economic issues. In the following month it was officially registered, albeit with some reluctance on the part of the authorities and, after support for the movement increased, it was banned in January 1990. Nevertheless, Agzybirlik's founding congress took place in the following month. As a result of the official animosity towards the nascent democratic movement, only the CPT and its approved organizations were permitted to participate in elections to the republican Supreme Soviet on 7 January, at which CPT members won the majority of the 175 seats. When the new Supreme Soviet convened, Saparmyrat Niyazov, the First Secretary of the CPT since 1985, was elected Chairman of the Supreme Soviet, the highest government office in the republic.

Despite the continuing dominance of the CPT, some concessions were made to popular pressure. In May 1990 Turkmen officially became the state language, replacing Russian; Turkmenistan was the last of the Soviet republics to introduce such legislation. On 22 August the Turkmen Supreme Soviet adopted a declaration of sovereignty, which proclaimed the republic to be a zone free of nuclear and chemical weapons, and asserted the right of the republic to determine its own political and social system and to secede from the USSR. On 27 October Niyazov was elected, by direct ballot, to the new post of executive President of Turkmenistan. He was unopposed in the election and received a reported 98.3% of the votes cast.

In late 1990 and early 1991 Turkmenistan participated in negotiations towards a new Union Treaty, which would redefine the status of the republics within the structure of the USSR. The underdeveloped state of the Turkmen economy, and the republic's dependence on the central Government for subsidies, ensured that the republic's leadership was one of the most enthusiastic proponents of the preservation of the USSR. At the all-Union referendum on the status of the USSR, in March 1991, 95.7% of eligible voters in Turkmenistan approved the preservation of the USSR as a 'renewed federation', the highest proportion of any Soviet republic.

President Niyazov made no public announcements either opposing or supporting the attempted coup in Moscow of August 1991. However, opposition groups, including Agzybirlik, publicly opposed the coup, which led to the arrest of several of their leaders. Following the failure of the coup attempt, Niyazov remained in power and announced that the CPT would be retained as the ruling party, unlike in other republics, where the Communist parties had been suspended or dissolved; however, in December the CPT changed its name to the Democratic Party of Turkmenistan (DPT), with Niyazov as its Chairman. On 18 October Turkmenistan was among the signatories of the treaty establishing an economic community of eight republics. This was followed on 26 October by a national referendum at which, according to the official results, 94.1% of the electorate voted for independence. On the following day the Turkmen Supreme Soviet adopted a law on independence, declaring 27 October to be Independence Day. The name of the republic was changed from the Turkmen SSR to the Republic of Turkmenistan, and a new state emblem, flag and national anthem were adopted. In November the Turkmen leadership agreed to draft proposals for a new political union, the Union of Sovereign States. However, when this plan was superseded by the Commonwealth of Independent States (CIS, see p. 172), initially proposed by the three Slav republics, Turkmenistan indicated its wish to participate. On 21 December it became a signatory, with 10 other republics, of the Alma-Ata (Almaty) Declaration, by which the CIS was formally established; this decision was subsequently ratified by the Turkmen Supreme Soviet.

In the first half of 1992 Turkmenistan's state structures remained unchanged, with the DPT dominant both in the Council of Ministers and the Supreme Soviet—effectively the same position that the CPT had held during the Soviet period. However, ultimate power resided with Niyazov, in his capacity as President of the Republic and leader of the DPT. Although Niyazov reportedly continued to enjoy widespread popular support, there was some criticism of his increasingly authoritarian style of leadership, which involved the rigid control of the media, the restriction of opposition activity, and the promotion of a presidential 'personality cult'. It was reportedly the last ambition that prompted the resignation, in August, of the Minister of Foreign Affairs, Abdy Kuliyev.

The new Constitution, adopted on 18 May 1992, further enhanced presidential authority, making Niyazov Head of Government (Prime Minister), as well as Head of State, and giving him certain legislative prerogatives. He was also to act concurrently as the Supreme Commander of the Armed Forces. In June Niyazov was re-elected, unopposed, to the presidency, receiving a purported 99.5% of the votes cast in a direct ballot.

Certain other significant structural changes were introduced under the new Constitution. The Supreme Soviet was to be replaced as Turkmenistan's legislature by a 50-member Majlis (Assembly); however, until the expiry of its five-year term, the Supreme Soviet elected in 1990 (although renamed the Majlis), was to be retained as the republican legislature. A People's Council (Khalk Maslakhaty) was established as the 'supreme representative body of popular power'. The Council was to act only in a supervisory capacity, and it would not diminish the authority of the President or the Majlis; however, it was to debate and decide important political and economic issues, and would also be empowered to demand changes to the Constitution as well as to vote to express 'no confidence' in the President, if it found his actions to be at variance with the law. The Council was to comprise the 50 deputies of the Majlis in addition to 50 elected and 10 appointed representatives from the electoral districts of Turkmenistan (the former were directly elected in November–December 1992); it was also to include other prominent figures of Turkmen society, including the members of the Government and the Chairman of the Supreme Court, and was to be headed by the President. At its first session, in mid-December, the Council awarded Niyazov the rank of General, further enhancing his authority.

Following the adoption of the new Constitution, there were fears that the rights of Turkmenistan's ethnic minorities (the largest two groups of which, Russians and Uzbeks, represented 10% and 9%, respectively, of the total population in the early 1990s) were in jeopardy, as the document stipulated that only ethnic Turkmen would be eligible for employment in state enterprises. Moreover, the Russian language was no longer to be used as the means of inter-ethnic communication (the status that it had held since 1990, when Turkmen replaced Russian as the official language). Nevertheless, Turkmenistan did not experience inter-ethnic violence or religious conflict, such as occurred in some other former republics of the USSR. Although the population is predominantly Muslim, Turkmenistan's Constitution guaranteed state secularism, a principle that was strongly emphasized by President Niyazov.

The presidential 'personality cult' was further strengthened during 1993, with numerous institutions, streets and public buildings being named after Niyazov—the Caspian Sea port of Krasnovodsk was renamed Turkmenbashy ('Head of the Turkmen', a recently introduced mode of address for Niyazov). The construction also continued of a number of extravagantly furbished palaces for Niyazov. In November senior members of the DPT proposed that the presidential election scheduled for 1997 be cancelled. In the following month the Majlis voted to extend Niyazov's term of office until 2002, on the grounds that the republic's political and economic stability depended on the realization of Niyazov's '10 Years of Prosperity' programme of gradual reforms. The extension of Niyazov's presidency was endorsed by a reported 99.99% of the electorate in a referendum held on 15 January 1994.

Elections to the new, 50-member Majlis were held in December 1994, officially with the participation of 99.8% of the registered electorate. It was reported that 49 of the 50 deputies had been elected unopposed. The Majlis convened for the first time in late December; the overwhelming majority of the deputies were believed to be members of the DPT.

Despite the result of the referendum of January 1994, elements of opposition to Niyazov were believed to be active in Turkmenistan. Anti-Niyazov activists were also based in exile, in other republics of the CIS, in particular Russia, where Abdy Kuliyev led one branch of the opposition—the so-called Turkmenistan Fund. In November two leading members of the Turkmen opposition-in-exile were arrested in Moscow by Russian security forces (allegedly acting at the behest of Niyazov). The Turkmen Government accused them of planning to assassinate Niyazov, and it urged the Russian authorities to extradite the suspects to Turkmenistan. However, following vocal protests by Russian human rights groups, the two men were released in December. In June 1995 the Turkmen Supreme Court sentenced two further opposition leaders to respective terms of 12 and 15 years' imprisonment in a labour colony, having found them guilty of involvement in the same alleged plot to overthrow Niyazov. In July a protest rally took place in Ashgabat (reportedly the first to be held in Turkmenistan since independence in 1991), at which as many as 1,000 demonstrators criticized Niyazov's leadership and the continuing economic hardships. In January 1996 27 people were tried and imprisoned in connection with the demonstration, although some 20 of these were released shortly afterwards under an amnesty.

In August 1995, in what was interpreted as a response to the previous month's unrest, Niyazov dismissed 10 of Turkmenistan's 50 local administrative leaders. At a meeting of the People's Council in October, the President announced his dismissal of a number of senior members of the Council of Ministers, having drawn attention to 'serious shortcomings' in their discharge of office. In an apparent attempt to deflect international criticism of Turkmenistan's treatment of political opponents of the regime, Niyazov indicated in December that an institute for human rights would be established. In the same month the People's Council conferred upon Niyazov his second 'hero of Turkmenistan' award (the country's highest honour). The Institute for Democracy and Human Rights was inaugurated in Ashgabat in October 1996, with Niyazov as its director.

In 1996 and 1997 Niyazov exercised his powers as Head of Government by effecting widespread dismissals of government officials, as well as local administrative leaders and members of the judiciary. In February 1998 the President revealed that he planned to amend the Constitution after the legislative elections of December 1999, devolving certain presidential powers to the Majlis and relinquishing the post of Prime Minister (a post that he retained, however, in 2003). In April 1998 elections to the People's Council were held, with the reported participation of 99.5% of the electorate.

Turkmenistan continued to attract the censure of a number of international human rights organizations during the late 1990s. There was also criticism of the undiminished 'personality cult' of Niyazov. In April 1998 a delegation of the Organization for Security and Co-operation in Europe (OSCE, see p. 283) appealed to Niyazov to release eight political prisoners who had been detained since the Ashgabat demonstration of July 1995.

Niyazov agreed to their release, following which he made his first official visit to the USA where, it was reported, President Bill Clinton discussed with him the question of human rights in Turkmenistan, as well as the need for political and economic reforms. In an unexpected development, the most prominent of the Turkmen opposition leaders-in-exile, Abdy Kuliyev, returned to Turkmenistan in April 1998; he was arrested upon arrival, on charges of sedition and 'economic crimes'. Following Russian intervention, however, he was released.

Niyazov's systematic purging of government and other officials continued in May 1998. An attempted military rebellion that occurred in western Turkmenistan in September was followed by the dismissal of the Minister of Defence, and the comprehensive reorganization of senior personnel of the armed forces and border troops. In the same month a number of regional governors were purged from office, while in October Niyazov criticized the National Television and Radio Company for its 'failure to contribute to the revival of the nation's spiritual wealth', also dismissing the organization's chairman. In the wake of public disorder outside an Ashgabat bank in December, wide-ranging dismissals of municipal police and security officials were effected, as well as personnel changes within the Ministry of the Economy and Finance.

The promotion of the presidential 'personality cult' appeared to intensify during 1998: in October Niyazov was honoured with his third 'hero of Turkmenistan' award, while in December a giant ceremonial arch, surmounted by a revolving gold-plated statue of the President, was inaugurated in central Ashgabat. In the same month Niyazov was unanimously re-elected Chairman of the DPT. In what was interpreted as an effort to counter growing international accusations of dictatorial methods, the President declared, in December, that the elections to the Majlis scheduled for late 1999 would be contested on a multi-party basis, and that the establishment of new political parties would be permitted in advance of the poll. In early 1999, in a further attempt to prove his commitment to human rights, the President declared a moratorium on the death penalty; this was followed by an amnesty for several thousand prisoners. (In December the Khalk Maslakhaty voted to abolish the death penalty; Turkmenistan thus became the first Central Asian republic to proscribe capital punishment.) In April Niyazov reiterated his pledge that, following the legislative elections, greater powers would be divested to the Majlis, and also to the People's Council.

Elections to the Majlis were conducted on 12 December 1999. According to official reports, some 99% of the registered electorate participated in the poll. In the event, the DPT was the only party represented and, despite the assertion of President Niyazov that the elections had been conducted in accordance with the Constitution, the OSCE declined an invitation to monitor the poll, claiming that there was minimal evidence of a genuinely democratic process. Previous undertakings of the President to establish political pluralism prior to the elections appeared to have been abandoned. In late December the new Majlis approved an amendment to the Constitution whereby Niyazov's presidential term was extended indefinitely. Niyazov had made repeated claims that the success of democratic and economic reform would be dependent on the continuity of successive 10-year plans. Following the Majlis' endorsement of the amendment, Niyazov announced that the creation of opposition political parties would not be contemplated before 2010, when, he explained, the 'political conscience' of the Turkmen people would be fully formed. These developments further aroused the concerns of the international community, and there was considerable outrage when, in March 2000, the leader of the unofficial popular opposition front, Agzybirlik, Nurberdy Nurmamedov, was sentenced to five years' imprisonment on charges of hooliganism and intent to murder, after he protested that the December 1999 amendment to the Constitution was undemocratic.

On 1 January 2000 Turkmenistan formally adopted the Latin script. In early 2000 Niyazov enacted a law that detailed the first phase of extensive reforms to administrative, economic and social structures. The reform programme was to be considered by the Majlis, which had been granted new legislative and regulatory powers following the December 1999 elections. In January 2000 the Majlis announced the creation of four permanent parliamentary committees to examine: legislation; science, education and culture; economy and social policy; and international and interparliamentary relations.

Meanwhile, Niyazov continued to be uncompromising in his management of the Council of Ministers. In January 2000 Niyazov dismissed a number of prominent government officials for alleged professional shortcomings, including the Deputy Prime Minister and Minister of the Economy and Finance and the Deputy Prime Minister and Minister of Energy and Industry. In June Babayev was dismissed as Deputy Prime Minister and Minister of Agriculture and Water Economy.

In June 2000 the President approved the founding of a joint Council for the Supervision of Foreigners, which gave Turkmenistan's security services the power to monitor the movements of foreigners arriving or temporarily residing in the country. At the same time, President Niyazov instructed Turkmen citizens and government organizations to close any bank accounts held abroad, in order to curtail the flow of capital outside Turkmenistan. In July Niyazov issued an order declaring that, henceforth, knowledge of the Turkmen language would be a mandatory requirement for all government officials; heads of state organizations, ministries and higher-education institutions were given 30 days to learn the language or lose their positions. Furthermore, all candidates for leadership posts were to have their genealogies over the previous three generations verified. At the end of July the President dismissed Boris Shikhmuradov, the Minister of Foreign Affairs; he was replaced by Batyr Berdiyev. All officials were, henceforth, to be appointed for a six-month probation period.

In mid-February 2001 President Niyazov announced that he would retire from office by 2010, but implemented stringent criteria for potential presidential candidates. In the mean time Niyazov continued a process of nation-building in an attempt to develop a strong national identity. In April 2001 the President closed the opera and ballet theatre, which he denounced as 'alien' to Turkmen culture; it was replaced with a national music and drama theatre instructed to produce the works of contemporary Turkmen authors. In October Niyazov published the multi-volume *Rukhnama*, or national code of spiritual conduct. In the same month the Khalk Maslakhaty voted to confer President Niyazov with his fourth 'hero of Turkmenistan' award.

In July 2001 Batyr Berdiyev was dismissed as Minister of Foreign Affairs, accused of professional shortcomings; he was replaced by Rashid Merepov. In late October former Minister of Foreign Affairs Boris Shikhmuradov was dismissed from his post of ambassador to the People's Republic of China. He fled to exile in Moscow from where, in early November, he issued a statement condemning President Niyazov's rule. At the same time it was reported that a warrant for Shikhmuradov's arrest had been issued by the Prosecutor-General, along with a request for his extradition from Russia. Shikhmuradov had been accused of misappropriating state property, charges which he denied. Turkmen officials claimed that his actions were an attempt to avoid prosecution; however, it was widely speculated that Shikhmuradov intended to replace Niyazov by means of a *coup d'état*, possibly with foreign support. In January 2002 he established the Turkmenistan Popular Democratic Movement, with the aim of deposing Niyazov. In early February Nurmukhammed Khanamov resigned as ambassador to Turkey in order to join the opposition movement. In mid-February a former Deputy Prime Minister, Khudayberdy Orazov, announced his support for the opposition-in-exile. Consequently, the Turkmen authorities issued a request for the extradition of Khanamov and accused Orazov of embezzling state funds. By May a former Deputy Prime Minister, Aleksandr Dodonov, the ambassador to the United Arab Emirates, and a senior diplomat from the Turkmen embassy in the USA had also joined the opposition democratic movement. Niyazov reacted to these developments by dismissing a number of senior officials from the defence, intelligence and security services (including the Minister of Defence) in March, whom he accused of plotting to overthrow him. In addition, the State Border Service was placed under the direct control of the President. In mid-April a rare public demonstration took place, by some 300 citizens protesting against the treatment of citizens by officers of the Committee for National Security. In May the Turkmen authorities, believing Shikhmuradov to have fled to the USA, requested his extradition from that country, without success.

Meanwhile, in December 2001 President Niyazov signed a resolution abolishing the requirement that citizens intending to cross the country's border be in possession of an exit visa, with effect from January 2002. However, the movement of citizens with access to state secrets, residents under investigation or with existing criminal convictions, those being sued in a civil court, and citizens who had been called up for compulsory military service, were to be subject to temporary legal restrictions.

A major reorganization of the interior ministry, announced in May 2002, saw the appointment of a new Minister of Internal Affairs, the permanent dismissal of 9,000 staff and the transfer of the fire department and traffic police to the jurisdiction of the Ministry of Defence. In the same month Deputy Prime Minister Seitbay Gandimov was dismissed as Chairman of the Central Bank, following allegations of links to Orazov; he was replaced by Imamdurdy Gandimov, and the Minister of the Economy and Finance was elevated to Deputy Prime Minister. A further cabinet reshuffle followed in August, with the replacement of the Minister of Agriculture and the Minister for the Textile Industry. In the same month Niyazov issued a decree renaming the calendar months after Turkmen national heroes. Government changes in September included the appointment of three new ministers and the creation of a Ministry of National Security, to replace the Committee for National Security; Batyr Busakov, erstwhile Deputy Minister of Internal Affairs, was granted the portfolio. In late September Imamgurdy Gandimov was dismissed, accused of gross negligence, following the theft of US \$41.5m. from the Central Bank. In the same month Niyazov announced the creation of so-called 'labour armies', comprising 20,000 men under the age of 35. The armies were to be drafted to work without remuneration on public projects; the term of service was to be two years, irrespective of previous army service. In mid-November, in a major cabinet reshuffle, Gurbansoltan Handurdiyeva was appointed Deputy Prime Minister. Also in November Ovezgeldy Atayev was elected Chairman of the Majlis.

On 25 November 2002 it was widely reported that an assassination attempt had been made against the presidential motorcade, as it travelled through Ashgabat. An emergency cabinet meeting was held, and Niyazov publicly accused former officials Shikhmuradov and Khanamov, among others, of an attempted coup. An official announcement the following day reported the arrest of 16 suspects. However, Amnesty International and other human rights organizations reported hundreds of detentions in subsequent days; in mid-December the Uzbek embassy was searched, in violation of the UN's Vienna Convention on Diplomatic Relations. Shikhmuradov's arrest was reported on 26 December; following a televised confession, a one-day trial at the Supreme Court on 30 December found Shikhmuradov, Orazov and Khanamov guilty of the attempt on Niyazov's life. Shikhmuradov was sentenced to 25 years' imprisonment (subsequently increased to a life sentence by the Majlis). Another former minister, Sapar Yklymov, was given the same sentence *in absentia*; Yklymov was one of more than 50 people sentenced for involvement in the attack. Opposition leader Murad Esenov, in exile in Sweden, claimed that the assassination attempt had been staged as a pretext for the arrest of Shikhmuradov and other members of the opposition, while the OSCE, concerned at the circumstances surrounding Shikhmuradov's trial and confession, sent a fact-finding mission to Ashgabat. In late December the Uzbek ambassador to Turkmenistan was expelled from the country, having been accused of harbouring Shikhmuradov immediately after the attack (see below).

Meanwhile, in November 2002 the failure of the cotton harvest, which achieved only 24% of the predicted yield, led to the dismissal of four regional governors and the Minister of Agriculture, Poran Berdiyev; the latter was later reported to have been found dead at his home. In early January 2003 the International Crisis Group, based in Brussels, Belgium, warned of persistent human rights abuses in Turkmenistan and claimed that the country had become a transit route for drugs-trafficking and a refuge to members of the deposed Taliban regime fleeing neighbouring Afghanistan. Decrees issued by Niyazov in February reinstated the requirement for exit visas and specified that only students wishing to study abroad who had been nominated by the Ministry of Education would be able to exchange Turkmen currency, the manat, for convertible currencies. In response to the events of November 2002, media access was severely limited in the country, with the closure of all internet cafés and non-official websites; this followed a ban on the import of foreign periodicals in late 2002. During April 2003 the UN Human Rights Commission denounced Turkmenistan's obstruction of political opposition. Meanwhile, a rate of participation of 89.3% was declared for elections on 6 April to the Khalk Maslakhaty and to 5,535 local councils. The OSCE, which

had accused the Turkmen authorities of widespread human rights abuses in a report issued in March, questioned the legitimacy of the electoral process.

One of the fundamental principles of Turkmenistan's foreign policy is that of 'permanent neutrality', a concept that is enshrined in the country's Constitution. The republic's neutral status was recognized by the UN General Assembly in December 1995, two months after Turkmenistan became the first of the former Soviet republics to join the Non-aligned Movement (see p. 350). The policy of neutrality has led Turkmenistan to adopt a somewhat equivocal attitude towards its membership of the CIS. President Niyazov has consistently voiced his opposition to any centralized structures within the Commonwealth, preferring to regard it as a 'consultative body'. Moreover, the republic has refused to sign a number of CIS agreements on closer political, military and economic integration.

None the less, Turkmenistan's most important political ally and economic partner remains Russia, the leading CIS state. In December 1993 Turkmenistan became the first of the former Soviet republics to sign an agreement on dual citizenship with Russia—an accord which, it was hoped, would further strengthen Turkmen-Russian relations, while also helping to stem the exodus of ethnic Russians from the republic.

However, a persistent cause of friction between the two countries concerned Turkmenistan's natural gas exports, which were dependent on the use of the former Soviet pipeline system, under Russian control. In 1993 Turkmenistan's access via this system to European markets was effectively curbed by Russia's decision to direct Turkmen gas exports to Ukraine and the Transcaucasian republics of the former USSR. However, as a result of the recipient countries' failure or delay in paying for their gas imports, Turkmenistan suspended all deliveries in 1993–95, which in turn had a severely detrimental impact on the Turkmen economy. Gas exports to Ukraine and Transcaucasia were resumed in 1996. However, in March 1997 Niyazov announced the dissolution of the Turkmen-Russian company, Turkmenrosgaz—which held a monopoly on the sale and export of Turkmen gas—owing to the company's reported extreme indebtedness. In response, the Russian Government denied Turkmenistan access to the regional pipeline system. Despite Ukraine's commencement of payment of its outstanding debt to Turkmenistan, delivery was hampered by Russia's refusal to lower its transport tariffs to the level demanded by Turkmenistan. However, in December 1998 Turkmenistan reached an agreement with Russia regarding the transport of natural gas, and deliveries to Ukraine were resumed in January 1999, only to be suspended again in May, owing to further payment problems. In May 2000 the Turkmen authorities agreed to deliver to Russia an additional 10,000m. cu m of natural gas for the next three to four years until the level of imports reached 50,000m.–60,000m. cu m per year. At the beginning of 2001, however, Turkmenistan halted its deliveries to Russia, owing to the failure of the two sides to agree on a mutually acceptable price; agreement was finally reached in February with Itera, an affiliate of the Russian gas monopoly, Gazprom. The agreement was renewed in December. At the same time, Turkmenistan signed an agreement with Itera and a Russian energy company, Zarubezhneft, for the development of Turkmenistan's onshore and offshore hydrocarbons deposits. In November 2000 Turkmenistan resumed natural gas deliveries to Ukraine after receiving payment from that country. In May 2001 Turkmenistan agreed to supply Ukraine with 250,000m. cu m of natural gas in 2002–06.

Of the remaining CIS member states, Turkmenistan has concentrated on developing closer relations with the neighbouring Central Asian republics of Kazakhstan, Kyrgyzstan, Tajikistan and Uzbekistan. However, unlike Kazakhstan, Kyrgyzstan and Uzbekistan, Turkmenistan remained neutral regarding the civil war in Tajikistan (q.v.), and it did not contribute troops to the joint CIS peace-keeping forces in the region. None the less, Ashgabat did become one of the venues for the Tajik peace negotiations. In September 2000 Turkmenistan and Uzbekistan signed a treaty demarcating their 1,867 km border. Under President Niyazov's orders, a 1,700 km fence was installed along the border in 2001. However, increased control of the border led to local tensions. By January 2002 both the Turkmen and Uzbek authorities had introduced fees for citizens wishing to cross the border. In early 2002 there were reports of shooting incidents involving people who had attempted to cross the border illegally, and protests by residents of border zones against the closure of some border posts.

Relations with Uzbekistan deteriorated sharply in December 2002, following the alleged coup attempt of 25 November (see above). In mid-December the Uzbek embassy in Ashgabat was searched for evidence, and Uzbekistan's ambassador to Turkmenistan was subsequently declared *persona non grata*, on the grounds that he supported the alleged instigator of the coup, Boris Shikhmuradov. The Uzbek authorities reacted with hostility; open confrontation quickly led to the deployment of troops from both countries along the border and an increase in border security. The construction of an additional border station was ordered and a number crossings were closed. It was reported in early 2003 that Niyazov was forcibly relocating Uzbek residents of Turkmenistan away from the border area.

The legal status of the Caspian Sea, and the ownership of the extensive deposits of petroleum and natural gas beneath it, was a source of controversy in the mid-1990s between Turkmenistan and the other littoral states (Azerbaijan, Russia, Kazakhstan and Iran). Although the Sea had been divided into national economic zones during the Soviet period, after 1992 there were demands by some states for a new demarcation. At a special conference on the Sea's status, held in Ashgabat in November 1996, the ministers of foreign affairs of all five countries agreed that a new convention on the Caspian Sea should be formulated, and a working group was established for this purpose. Nevertheless, in early 1997 Turkmenistan and Azerbaijan were engaged in a dispute over the status of two Caspian oilfields (the Azeri and Chirag fields—known as the Khazar and Kaverochkin fields to the Turkmen), which were being developed by Azerbaijan and a consortium of international companies. The situation deteriorated in July 1997, when Azerbaijan announced its intention to develop, in conjunction with a consortium of Russian companies, a third oilfield—known as Kyapaz to the Azeris and as Serdar to the Turkmen—ownership of which was claimed by both countries. Despite the subsequent Russian withdrawal from the project, Azerbaijan refused to abandon its claim to the field. Apparently in response, in September Turkmenistan launched its first international tender for petroleum and gas exploration in the Caspian Sea, and announced that it expected to receive compensation from Azerbaijan for developing the Azeri and Chirag fields. The commercial exploitation of the latter field began in November. In October 2000 Kazakhstan signed an agreement with Russia on the definition of the legal status of the Caspian Sea; the two Governments urged the remaining littoral states (Azerbaijan, Iran and Turkmenistan) to hold a summit meeting to discuss the issue. The meeting was postponed twice in 2001, because it was clear that a final agreement would not be reached. Although negotiations finally took place in April 2002, in Ashgabat, they ended inconclusively; talks between Turkmenistan and Iran recommenced in March 2003. In July 2001 Turkmenistan and Kazakhstan signed a treaty on the demarcation of their shared border.

Iran plays the most important role in Turkmenistan's foreign relations outside the CIS. In 1992 a number of agreements on closer political, economic and cultural integration were signed, including an accord to construct a railway line between Iran and Turkmenistan. The line, which linked the Turkmen city of Tejen with the northern Iranian city of Mashad, was opened in May 1996, thus affording Turkmenistan access both to the Persian (Arabian) Gulf and to İstanbul, Turkey. Turkmenistan and Iran also signed an agreement on constructing a 140-km-long gas pipeline between the Korpeje natural gas deposit in south-western Turkmenistan and the city of Kord Kuy in northern Iran. The pipeline—which was to be the first segment on a route, which, it was envisaged, would eventually transport Turkmen gas via Iran to Turkey and thence to western Europe—was completed in mid-1997. The inauguration of the pipeline in December opened the first alternative export route for Turkmenistan's natural gas (see above), and thus promised greater economic independence for the republic from Russia. In April 2000 Iran reduced its gas exports from Turkmenistan by one-half, reportedly in response to Turkmenistan's improved relations with Russia; in November, however, an agreement to increase supplies was reached. In February 2001, partly owing to Turkmenistan's support in negotiations over the status of the Caspian Sea (see above), Iran agreed to increase its gas imports from Turkmenistan by more than twofold in 2001, to 6,000m. cu m. In April 2002 Turkmenistan and Iran signed agreements on trade, economic integration, and co-operation in the fields of science and technology.

Plans were also under investigation for other alternative gas export pipelines, including one to Turkey, via Azerbaijan and Georgia, which would involve the construction of an underwater trans-Caspian pipeline. In November 1999, at a summit meeting of the OSCE in İstanbul, the Presidents of Turkmenistan, Turkey, Azerbaijan and Georgia met and signed a preliminary agreement to construct the pipeline, which was expected to cost some US $3,000m. and allow Turkmen exports of up to 30,000m. cu m of natural gas per year. However, the trans-Caspian project encountered difficulties in 2000, when negotiations over the division of the pipeline's anticipated throughput resulted in serious disagreement between Turkmenistan and Azerbaijan. In October 2001 the USA reiterated its support for the project and advised Turkmenistan to reassess its objections to Azerbaijan's demand to export its own gas through the pipeline, and to allow private investors to support the project. In 1998 the proposed construction of a 1,460-km gas pipeline from Turkmenistan to central Pakistan via Afghanistan, led by the US company Unocal, was suspended indefinitely, owing to conflict in Afghanistan and the lack of an internationally recognized government there. However, following the collapse of the Taliban regime in Afghanistan in late 2001, Turkmenistan attempted to resurrect interest in the project. In late April 2002 President Niyazov requested UN support for the construction of the pipeline. The Afghan Interim Administration supported the proposal; at the end of May the leaders of Turkmenistan, Afghanistan and Pakistan signed a memorandum of understanding on a feasibility study for the project. In December 2002 a deal was signed for the construction of the pipeline, at a preliminary cost of US $2,000m.–$3,200m.

President Niyazov confirmed his country's neutral stance by developing equal relations with the Taliban and their opposition, the United National Islamic Front for the Salvation of Afghanistan, commonly known as the United Front, in the late 1990s. Turkmenistan was central in organizing peace negotiations between the Taliban and United Front in both July 1999 and December 2000. Niyazov maintained the country's neutrality following the large-scale suicide attacks on the USA in September 2001, which were attributed to the Saudi-born leader of the Islamist militant al-Qa'ida (Base) organization, Osama bin Laden. However, Niyazov expressed general support for attempts to form an international coalition to combat global terrorism, although he declared that its formation should be co-ordinated by the UN, rather than the USA. None the less, the President gave his consent to the use of Turkmenistan's ground and air transport 'corridors' for the delivery of humanitarian aid to Afghanistan during airstrikes against al-Qa'ida and its Taliban hosts; Niyazov refused US troops access to Turkmenistan's military bases, however, reaffirming the country's policy of non-interference. It was widely speculated that Niyazov would seek support for the pipeline project via Afghanistan to Pakistan (see above) in return for his co-operation.

During a visit to Turkmenistan in July 2000, the Chinese President, Jiang Zemin, resumed discussion of the proposed construction of an 8,000-km gas pipeline from Turkmenistan to the People's Republic of China and Japan, under consideration since 1997. In mid-September the leaders of Turkmenistan and China signed a joint declaration on energy co-operation.

Turkmenistan enjoys close relations with Turkey (which has been regarded as competing with Iran for political and economic influence in the region), not least owing to the Turkmen's ethnic and linguistic ties with the Turks. Turkmenistan is a member, with both Turkey and Iran (among others), of the Economic Co-operation Organization (ECO, see p. 192). In April 2001 at a meeting of leaders of the Turkic-speaking countries, the Presidents of Azerbaijan, Kazakhstan, Kyrgyzstan, Turkey and Turkmenistan, and the Chairman of Uzbekistan's Oly Majlis (Supreme Assembly) signed an agreement on regional co-operation to combat terrorism and drugs-trafficking, the revival of the old 'Silk Road' trade route between China and Europe, and the protection of the environment.

Government

Under the terms of the 1992 Constitution, the President of the Republic is directly elected, by universal adult suffrage, for five years, although in December 1993 the legislature voted to extend President Niyazov's mandate—due to expire in 1997— until 2002 (this was endorsed in a national referendum in January 1994). In December 1998 the Khalk Maslakhaty endorsed an amendment to the Constitution whereby Niyazov's mandate was extended indefinitely. In February 2001, however, Niyazov announced he was to retire by 2010. The President is both Head of State and Head of Government (Prime Minister in the Council of Ministers), holding executive power in conjunction with the Council of Ministers (which is appointed by the President), and is concurrently Supreme Commander of the Armed Forces. The supreme legislative body is the Majlis (Assembly), whose 50 members are directly elected for a term of five years. The deputies of the Majlis also sit on the Khalk Maslakhaty (People's Council), a supervisory organ which is described as the 'supreme representative body of popular power' and which also includes 65 directly elected and 10 appointed representatives from all districts of Turkmenistan, the members of the Council of Ministers and other prominent figures, and is headed by the President of the Republic. For administrative purposes, Turkmenistan is divided into five velayats (regions), which are subdivided into 50 etraps (districts).

Defence

In mid-1992 Turkmenistan began the establishment of national armed forces, based upon the former Soviet military units still stationed in the republic; under an agreement with Russia, these forces were initially under joint Turkmen and Russian command. In August 2002 the national army numbered 14,500. There is a small air force (of 3,000), and the Government also intended to establish a navy/coastguard; since 1993 Turkmenistan has co-operated with Russia and Kazakhstan in the operation of the Caspian Sea Flotilla, another former Soviet force, based, under Russian command, at Astrakhan, Russia. In May 1994 Turkmenistan became the first Central Asian republic of the former USSR to join NATO's 'Partnership for Peace' programme (see p. 273). The defence budget for 2001 allocated US $163m.

Economic Affairs

In 2001, according to estimates by the World Bank, Turkmenistan's gross national income (GNI), measured at average 1999–2001 prices, was US $5,236m., equivalent to $950 per head (or $4,580 per head on an international purchasing-power parity basis). During 1990–2001, it was estimated, the population increased at an average annual rate of 3.4%, while gross domestic product (GDP) per head decreased, in real terms, by an average of 4.1% per year. Overall GDP decreased, in real terms, at an average annual rate of 0.8% per year in 1990–2001. However, real GDP increased by 17.6% in 2000 and by 20.5% in 2001.

Agriculture contributed an estimated 25.8% of GDP in 2000. In 1998 the sector employed 48.5% of the working population, according to provisional figures. Although the Kara-Kum desert covers some 80% of the country's territory, widespread irrigation has enabled rapid agricultural development; in recent years, however, over-intensive cultivation of the principal crop, cotton, together with massive irrigation projects, have led to serious ecological damage. In 1996 cotton contributed an estimated 11.5% of GDP, although the Government planned to reduce cotton production in favour of food production by 2010. Other important crops include grain, vegetables and fruit (in particular grapes and melons), although the country remains heavily dependent on imports of foodstuffs. Livestock husbandry (including the production of astrakhan and karakul wools) plays a central role in the sector. Silkworm breeding is also practised. According to the World Bank, agricultural production declined, in real terms, by an annual average of 2.6% in 1990–2000. However, real agricultural GDP increased by 26.0% in 1999 and by 17.0% in 2000. Agricultural production was affected by drought in 2000, but recovered in 2001 owing to favourable climatic conditions.

Industry (including mining, manufacturing, construction and power) contributed an estimated 47.6% of GDP in 2000. In 1998 18.2% of the working population were employed in the sector. Industrial activity is chiefly associated with the extraction and processing of the country's mineral resources (predominantly natural gas and petroleum), energy generation and cotton-processing. In 1995 fuels accounted for 47.4% of the value of total industrial production, while a further 14.4% was provided by textiles. During 1990–2000, according to the World Bank, industrial GDP decreased, in real terms, at an average annual rate of 1.6%. However, real industrial GDP increased by 15.5% in 1999 and by 24.5% in 2000.

Turkmenistan is richly endowed with mineral resources, in particular natural gas and petroleum (recoverable reserves of which were estimated to be some 2,860,000m. cu m and 100m. metric tons, respectively, at the end of 2000). In February and May 2000 major discoveries of petroleum and natural gas

reserves were announced. In that year, according to the European Bank for Reconstruction and Development (EBRD, see p. 193), Turkmenistan produced 7.1m. tons of petroleum and approximately 38,000m. cu m of gas. Petroleum is refined at three refineries, at Turkmenbashy (Krasnovodsk), Seidi and Türkmenatat (Charjou). In 2001 work began on upgrading the refinery at Turkmenbashy at an estimated cost of US $1,000m. Annual production was expected to increase to 6m. metric tons as a result. An associated petrochemicals complex was under development and was expected to become fully operational in late 2002. The refinery at Seidi was also undergoing modernization and construction of a smaller refinery near Atamurat, Lebap province, was in progress in 2002. In addition, Turkmenistan has large deposits of iodine, bromine, sodium sulphate, clay, gypsum and different types of salt.

The manufacturing sector contributed 37.8% of GDP in 2000. The sector is largely associated with the processing of the country's mineral extracts and cotton products. Textile manufacturing increased considerably in the 1990s; in 2000 it was the second fastest-growing industry in Turkmenistan. According to official statistics production in the manufacturing sector increased by 11% in that year.

In 1993 Turkmenistan had an installed electricity capacity of 2,640 MW, all of which was thermally fired by the country's two major thermal power stations (which were fuelled by domestically-produced natural gas). In 1995 an estimated 9,800m. kWh of electricity was produced in Turkmenistan; of electricity produced in 1994, some 20% was reported to have been exported, while a proportion of the remainder was distributed free of charge to domestic users. (Some charges for domestic electricity use were introduced in 1996; however, the 2003 budget provided for free distribution.)

The services sector provided 26.7% of GDP in 2000 and some 33.2% of total employment in 1998. Trade and catering services form the major part of the sector, providing some 6% of employment in 1998. According to the World Bank, services GDP declined, in real terms, at an average annual rate of 3.6% in 1990–2000. However, real services GDP increased by 10.0% in 1999 and by 9.1% in 2000.

According to the EBRD, in 2000 Turkmenistan recorded a visible trade surplus of an estimated US $550m., and there was a deficit of $60m. on the current account of the balance of payments. According to the ADB there was an estimated visible trade surplus of $535m. in 2001. In 2001 the principal source of imports (accounting for 14.2% of the total) was Turkey; other major suppliers were the USA (13.9%) and Ukraine (12.6%). The principal market for exports (17.7%) was Iran; other major purchasers were Turkey (15.1%) and Ukraine (12.1%). In 2000 the principal exports were mineral fuels and lubricants (accounting for some 81.0% of the value of total exports), followed by crude materials (10.3%) and basic manufactures (4.3%). The principal imports were machinery and transport equipment (43.8% of total imports), basic manufactures (21.4%) and chemicals (8.9%).

In 2001 Turkmenistan recorded a budget surplus of 268,000 Turkmen manats. At the end of 1999 Turkmenistan's total external debt was US $2,015m., of which $1,678m. was long-term public debt. In that year the cost of debt-servicing was equivalent to 31.1% of the value of exports of goods and services. Consumer prices increased by an annual average of 1,150% in 1993 and by 1,748% in 1994, but the inflation rate declined to 1,005% in 1995, to 992% in 1996 and to an estimated 84% in 1997. Average prices rose by only 16.8% in 1998 and by 24.2% in 1999. The inflation rate declined again in 2000 to an annual average of 7.4%. In 1995 some 50,000 people were believed to be unemployed (about 3% of the labour force); however, unofficial sources estimated the rate to be considerably higher.

Turkmenistan became a member of the IMF and the World Bank in 1992. It also joined the EBRD as a 'Country of Operations' and, with five other former Soviet republics, the Economic Co-operation Organization (ECO, see p. 192). In 1994 Turkmenistan became a member of the Islamic Development Bank (IDB, see p. 257), and it joined the Asian Development Bank (ADB, see p. 143) in September 2000.

The disruptions in inter-republican trade that followed the dissolution of the USSR in December 1991 adversely affected Turkmenistan's industrial sector, which was heavily reliant on imported finished and intermediate goods. Moreover, the failure, or delay, of many of Turkmenistan's CIS trading partners to pay for imports of natural gas (the mainstay of the republic's economy) resulted in huge arrears, and Turkmenistan was forced to suspend deliveries in 1993–95, in 1997–98 and in 1999, with adverse consequences for the economy as a whole. The opening of a new gas pipeline to Iran in late 1997 was regarded as of major importance in the revival of the economically crucial gas sector, and by 2001 the economy was benefiting from the fuller capacity utilization of the pipeline. After two years of disrupted gas supplies to Russia and Ukraine, in late 2000 gas deliveries to Ukraine resumed. The economy was further assisted by agreements to export gas to Russia. The rate of inflation decreased significantly and GDP registered strong growth in 2000–01, largely owing to the export of natural gas, petroleum and cotton. Natural gas production increased by 9% in 2001 compared with the previous year, petroleum output rose by 12% and cotton yields increased by 10%. None the less, there were concerns that Turkmenistan's economy would become over-dependent on the hydrocarbons sector. Moreover, an inefficient tax system and a poorly-regulated banking sector, largely under state control, continued to present significant obstacles to economic stability, and estimates of the private sector's contribution to GDP varied between 20% and 30%, reflecting the continuing high levels of state control of the economy, as well as the slow pace of structural reform and market liberalization. Turkmenistan's failure to prioritize the process of democratization also resulted in financial penalties; in April 2000 the EBRD announced the suspension of public-sector loans to Turkmenistan. In October the Government initiated a project to build a 4,000 sq km artificial lake in the Kara-Kum desert, to enable the development of 10,000 ha of land and to fulfil water requirements for a period of 50 years. The official estimate for GDP growth in 2002 was about 21%, although some international financial institutions questioned Turkmenistan's exceptional rates of growth. In December 2002 a budget of 52,532,997m. manats was passed for the following year, with projected expenditure allowing for the provision of free natural gas, electricity and water supplies.

Education

There were few educational establishments in pre-revolutionary Turkmenistan, but a state-funded education system was introduced under Soviet rule. Most school education is conducted in Turkmen (76.9% of all pupils at general day-schools in 1988), but there are also schools using Russian (16.0%), Uzbek (6.1%) and Kazakh (1.0%). President Niyazov has pledged to eradicate teaching in languages other than Turkmen. Primary education begins at seven years of age and lasts for four years. Secondary education, beginning at 11, lasts for seven years. In 1990 the total enrolment at higher schools was equivalent to 21.7% of the relevant age-group. In the early 1990s some 30% of school-children in Turkmenistan reportedly studied in shifts, owing to inadequate staffing and facilities. There are 14 institutes of higher education and some 90 technical colleges. The 1999 budget allocated 26.9% of total expenditure (1,048,700m. manats) to education.

Public Holidays

2003: 1 January (New Year's Day), 12 January (Memorial Day), 11–13 February* (Kurban Bairam, Id al-Adha or Feast of the Sacrifice), 19 February (National Flag Day; President Niyazov's Birthday), 8 March (International Women's Day), 21 March (Novrus Bairam, Turkmen New Year), 8–9 May (Victory Day), 18 May (Revival and Unity Day), 6 October (Remembrance Day), 27–28 October (Independence Day), 26 November* (Oraza Bairam, Id al-Fitr or end of Ramadan), 12 December (Turkmenistan Neutrality Day).

2004: 1 January (New Year's Day), 12 January (Memorial Day), 19 February (National Flag Day; President Niyazov's Birthday), 1–3 February* (Kurban Bairam, Id al-Adha or Feast of the Sacrifice), 8 March (International Women's Day), 21 March (Novrus Bairam, Turkmen New Year), 8–9 May (Victory Day), 18 May (Revival and Unity Day), 6 October (Remembrance Day), 27–28 October (Independence Day), 12 December* (Turkmenistan Neutrality Day), 14 December (Oraza Bairam, Id al Fitr or end of Ramadan).

*These holidays are dependent on the Islamic calendar and may vary by one or two days from the dates given.

Weights and Measures

The metric system is in force.

Statistical Survey

Principal sources (unless otherwise stated): IMF, *Turkmenistan, Economic Review, Turkmenistan—Recent Economic Developments* (December 1999); World Bank, *Statistical Handbook: States of the Former USSR*.

Area and Population

AREA, POPULATION AND DENSITY

Area (sq km)	488,100*
Population (census results)	
12 January 1989	3,533,925
10 January 1995	
Males	2,225,331
Females	2,257,920
Total	4,483,251
Population (UN estimates at mid-year)†	
1999	4,636,000
2000	4,737,000
2001	4,835,000
Density (per sq km) at mid-2001	9.9

* 188,456 sq miles.

† Source: UN, *World Population Prospects: The 2000 Revision*.

Population (official estimates): 5,369,400 at 1 January 2001; 5,725,200 at 1 July 2002.

POPULATION BY ETHNIC GROUP
(official estimates at 1 January 1993)

	Number	%
Turkmen	3,118,000	73.3
Russian	419,000	9.8
Uzbek	382,000	9.0
Kazakh	87,000	2.0
Tatar	39,000	0.9
Ukrainian	34,000	0.8
Azeri	34,000	0.8
Armenian	32,000	0.8
Belarusian	9,000	0.2
Others	100,000	2.4
Total	4,254,000	100.0

PRINCIPAL TOWNS
(estimated population at 1 January 1999)

Ashgabat (capital)	605,000	Türkmenbashi		
Türkmenabat* . .	203,000	(Turkmenbashy)‡ .		70,000
Dashkhovuz		Bayramaly (Bayram-		
(Tashauz) . .	165,000	Ali)		60,000
Mari (Mary) . .	123,000	Tejen (Tedzhen) . .		54,000
Balkanabat† . .	119,000	Serdar§		51,000

* Formerly Charjew (Chardzhou).

‡ Formerly Krasnovodsk.

† Formerly Nebit-Dag.

§ Formerly Gyzylarbat (Kizyl-Arvat).

1 July 2002 (official estimates): Ashgabat 743,000.

BIRTHS, MARRIAGES AND DEATHS

	Registered live births		Registered marriages		Registered deaths	
	Number	Rate (per 1,000)	Number	Rate (per 1,000)	Number	Rate (per 1,000)
1987 . .	126,787	37.2	31,484	9.2	26,802	7.9
1988 . .	125,887	36.0	33,008	9.4	27,317	7.8
1989 . .	124,992	34.9	34,890	9.8	27,609	7.7

Registered deaths: 25,755 (death rate 7.0 per 1,000) in 1990; 27,403 (7.3 per 1,000) in 1991; 27,509 (6.8 per 1,000) in 1992; 31,171 (7.2 per 1,000) in 1993; 32,067 (7.3 per 1,000) in 1994.

1998 (provisional): Live births 98,461 (birth rate 20.3 per 1,000); Marriages 26,361 (marriage rate 5.4 per 1,000); Deaths 29,628 (death rate 6.1 per 1,000).

Source: UN, *Demographic Yearbook*.

Expectation of life (WHO estimates, years at birth): 62.5 (males 58.9; females 66.5) in 2001 (Source: WHO, *World Health Report*).

EMPLOYMENT
('000 persons at 31 December)

	1996	1997	1998*
Agriculture	769.8	778.8	890.5
Forestry	2.5	2.9	1.9
Industry†	172.0	188.1	226.8
Construction	136.2	122.8	108.2
Trade and catering . . .	91.8	101.2	115.8
Transport and communications	77.7	77.9	90.7
Information-computing services	1.3	1.0	1.2
Housing and municipal services	50.2	46.8	48.3
Health care and social security .	97.4	100.4	89.2
Education, culture and arts. . .	183.8	185.9	190.5
Science, research and development	9.2	6.9	5.2
General administration . . .	24.7	25.3	28.8
Finance and insurance . . .	8.7	9.6	12.6
Other activities	41.5	28.3	29.0
Total	1,666.8	1,675.9	1,838.7

* Provisional.

† Comprising manufacturing (except printing and publishing), mining and quarrying, electricity, gas, water, logging and fishing.

Total employed ('000 persons at 31 December): 1,872 in 1999; 1,950 (estimate) in 2000 (Source: Asian Development Bank, *Key Indicators of Developing Asian and Pacific Countries*).

Health and Welfare

KEY INDICATORS

Total fertility rate (children per woman, 2001).	3.3
Under-5 mortality rate (per 1,000 live births, 2001) . . .	99
HIV/AIDS (% of persons aged 15–49, 2001).	<0.10
Physicians (per 1,000 head, 1998)	2.61
Hospital beds (per 1,000 head, 1998)	11.15
Health expenditure (2000): US $ per head (PPP) . . .	286
Health expenditure (2000): % of GDP	5.4
Health expenditure (2000): public (% of total)	84.9
Human Development Index (2000): ranking	87
Human Development Index (2000): value	0.741

For sources and definitions, see explanatory note on p. vi.

Agriculture

PRINCIPAL CROPS
('000 metric tons)

	1999	2000	2001
Wheat	1,506	1,150*	1,760*
Rice (paddy)	33.3	27.3	39.1*
Barley	19.5	22*	23*
Potatoes	28.1	29†	30†
Cottonseed	1,300	1,030	1,100
Cabbages	29.3	35†	32†
Tomatoes	139.0	145†	155†
Dry onions	48.7	53†	49†
Carrots	28.9	32†	36†
Other vegetables†	32.5	31.6	31.7
Watermelons‡	244*	240†	235†
Grapes	145.0	140†	135†
Apples	20.0	19†	18†
Other fruits and berries† . .	29.6	27	26
Cotton (lint)	234.3	232.6	187.0*

* Unofficial figure.

† FAO estimate(s).

‡ Including melons, pumpkins and squash.

Source: FAO.

LIVESTOCK
(FAO estimates, '000 head at 1 January)

	1999	2000	2001
Horses	16	16	17
Asses	25	24	25
Camels.	41	40	42
Cattle	880	850	860
Pigs	48	46	45
Sheep	5,650	5,600	6,000
Goats	375	368	375
Chickens	4,000	4,300	4,800
Turkeys	250	250	200

Source: FAO.

LIVESTOCK PRODUCTS
('000 metric tons)

	1999	2000	2001
Beef and veal	63.0	65.0*	67.0*
Mutton and lamb. . . .	60.0†	58.5*	57.0*
Goat meat	3.3†	3.2*	3.0*
Poultry meat	4.6	4.9*	5.0*
Other meat*	2.6	2.7	2.6
Cows' milk	875.4	820.0*	830.0*
Cheese*	1.6	1.5	1.6
Butter*	1.3	1.1	0.8
Hen eggs	15.9†	13.0*	15.0*
Honey	9.9	8.0*	8.0*
Raw silk (incl. waste) . . .	5.0*	4.7†	5.0*
Wool: greasy	21.9	20.0*	21.0*
Wool: scoured	13.1	12.0*	12.6*
Cattle hides (fresh)* . . .	6.7	6.8	7.0
Sheepskins (fresh)* . . .	8.0	7.8	7.6

* FAO estimate(s).

† Unofficial figure.

Source: FAO.

Fishing

(metric tons, live weight)

	1998	1999	2000
Capture	7,010	9,058	12,228
Azov sea sprat	6,324	8,370	11,540
Aquaculture	559	549	547
Silver carp	445	422	427
Total catch	7,569	9,607	12,775

Source: FAO, *Yearbook of Fishery Statistics*.

Mining

('000 metric tons, unless otherwise indicated)

	1998	1999	2000*
Crude petroleum	6,500†	7,800†	7,350
Natural gas (million cu metres)	14,000†	22,800†	47,000
Bentonite†	50	50	50
Salt (unrefined)	215†	215†	215
Gypsum (crude)†	100	100	100

* Preliminary figures.
† Estimated production.

Source: US Geological Survey.

Industry

SELECTED PRODUCTS
('000 metric tons, unless otherwise indicated)

	1996	1997	1998
Vegetable oil	36	22	33
Wheat flour	329	303	339
Ethyl alcohol ('000 hectolitres) . .	2	2	1
Woven cotton fabrics (million sq metres)	18	14	15
Woven silk fabrics (million sq metres)	4,468	4,479	4,529
Woven woollen fabrics (million sq metres)	2.8	3.2	2.5
Blankets	15	19	24
Knotted wool carpets and rugs ('000 sq metres)	417	326	315
Footwear, excl. rubber ('000 pairs)	1,546	1,108	561
Nitric acid (100%)	121	109	145
Ammonia (nitrogen content) . .	85	74	93
Nitrogenous fertilizers (a)*† . .	50	49	62
Phosphate fertilizers (b)*† . .	13	5	6
Soap	1.7	0.4	0.7
Motor spirit (petrol)	677	766	693‡
Gas-diesel (distillate fuel) oil . .	1,253	1,520	1,575‡
Residual fuel oils	1,301	1,600	2,214‡
Clay building bricks (million) . .	371	278	245
Quicklime	21	28	16
Cement	438	601	750
Electric energy (million kWh) . .	10,100‡	9,498	9,416‡

* Production in terms of (a) nitrogen or (b) phosphoric acid.
† Official figures.
‡ Provisional or estimated figure.

Source: mainly UN, *Industrial Commodity Statistics Yearbook*.

1999 ('000 metric tons, unless otherwise indicated): Wheat flour 437; Phosphate fertilizers 5; Gas-diesel (distillate fuel) oil 1,349; Cement 780; Electric energy (million kWh) 8,860.

2000 (million kWh): Electric energy 9,850.

Source: mainly Asian Development Bank, *Key Indicators of Developing Asian and Pacific Countries*.

Finance

CURRENCY AND EXCHANGE RATES
Monetary Units
100 tenge = 1 Turkmen manat

Sterling, Dollar and Euro Equivalents (31 December 2002)
£1 sterling = 8,381.4 manats
US $1 = 5,200.0 manats
€1 = 5,453.2 manats
10,000 Turkmen manats = £1.193 = $1.923 = €1.834

Note: The Turkmen manat was introduced on 1 November 1993, replacing the Russian (formerly Soviet) rouble at a rate of 1 manat = 500 roubles. Following the introduction of the Turkmen manat, a multiple exchange rate system was established. The foregoing information refers to the official rate of exchange. This rate was maintained at US $1 = 4,165 manats between May 1997 and April 1998. It was adjusted to $1 = 5,200 manats in April 1998. In addition to the official rate, there was a commercial bank rate of exchange until this market was closed in December 1998. There is also a 'parallel' market rate, which averaged $1 = 6,493 manats in 1998 and reached $1 = 14,200 manats at mid-1999.

BUDGET
('000 million manats)

Revenue*	1997	1998	1999†
State budget	2,067.3	1,867.5	2,382.3
Personal income tax	108.3	157.4	224.9
Profit tax	579.6	412.0	422.0
Value-added tax	797.9	714.9	946.3
Natural resources tax . . .	231.2	43.1	201.1
Excise tax	92.4	221.3	377.8
Other receipts*	257.9	318.8	210.1
Pension and Social Security Fund	471.0	711.0	832.5
Medical Insurance Fund . . .	32.7	8.2	0.0
Repayments on rescheduled gas debt	246.6	474.1	478.3
Total	**2,817.6**	**3,060.8**	**3,693.1**

Expenditure	1997	1998	1999‡
National economy	843.9	461.1	623.3
Agriculture	632.5	331.4	223.2
Transport and communications	121.1	63.4	190.0
Other	90.3	66.3	210.1
Socio-cultural services† . . .	975.7	1,850.0	1,907.9
Education	435.3	919.2	1,048.7
Health	443.1	493.8	550.6
Communal services . . .	9.1	337.9	188.6
Culture, recreation and other	88.2	99.1	120.0
Defence§	440.2	435.8	582.0
Pension and Social Security Fund	387.8	511.5	605.9
Interest payments	72.1	11.1	18.0
Public administration and other purposes	94.3	153.4	157.2
Total	**2,814.0**	**3,422.8**	**3,894.3**

* Including grants received and road fund revenues.
† Approved budget.
‡ Excluding expenditure of the Pension and Social Security Fund.
§ Variable coverage, owing to changes in classification.

MONEY SUPPLY
(million manats at 31 December)

	1995	1996	1997
Currency in circulation . . .	56,629	270,248	408,000
Demand deposits at banks . .	48,475	408,000	401,000

Currency in circulation ('000 million manats at 31 December): 1,040.2 in 1998; 1,009.4 in 1999; 1,517.0 in 2000 (Source: Asian Development Bank, *Key Indicators of Developing Asian and Pacific Countries*).

COST OF LIVING
(Consumer Price Index; base: previous year = 100)

	1995	1996	1997
All items	1,105.3	1,092.4	183.7

NATIONAL ACCOUNTS

Gross Domestic Product by Economic Activity
(million manats, at current prices)

	1998	1999	2000
Agriculture	3,521,700	4,981,900	5,903,300
Industry*	3,850,500	6,304,600	8,644,500
Construction	1,828,300	2,449,300	2,244,000
Trade and catering	505,000	815,300	1,008,100
Transport and communications .	1,093,500	1,341,200	1,043,700
Other activities	3,195,700	4,163,600	4,051,000
Total	**13,994,700**	**20,055,900**	**22,894,600**

* Comprising manufacturing, mining and quarrying, electricity, gas, water, logging and fishing.

2001: Total GDP 31,000,000 million manats.

Source: Asian Development Bank, *Key Indicators of Developing Asian and Pacific Countries*.

BALANCE OF PAYMENTS
(US $ million)

	1996	1997	1998
Exports of goods f.o.b.	1,692.0	774.0	614.1
Imports of goods f.o.b.	−1,388.3	−1,005.0	−1,137.1
Trade balance	303.7	−230.9	−523.0
Services (net)	−323.4	−402.5	−471.0
Balance on goods and services	−19.7	−633.5	−994.0
Other income (net)	16.7	84.8	32.6
Balance on goods, services and income	−3.0	−548.7	−961.4
Current transfers (net)	4.8	−31.2	26.9
Current account	1.8	−579.9	−934.5
Direct investment	108.1	102.4	64.1
Trade credit (net)	60.8	−266.5	56.5
Other (net)	−211.6	1,035.9	749.7
Net errors and omissions	46.4	−71.4	33.9
Overall balance	5.4	220.6	−30.3

External Trade

PRINCIPAL COMMODITIES
(US $ million)

Imports c.i.f.	1998	1999	2000
Food and live animals	75.2	170.5	180.4
Beverages and tobacco	7.5	96.5	25.2
Mineral fuels, lubricants, etc.	46.5	60.0	21.3
Chemicals	103.4	150.0	159.0
Basic manufactures	215.2	286.5	382.4
Machinery and transport equipment	439.9	483.8	782.5
Miscellaneous manufactured articles	53.3	116.1	111.1
Total (incl. others)	1,007.5	1,478.0	1,785.0

Exports f.o.b.	1998	1999	2000
Crude materials (inedible) except fuels	154.8	233.1	257.1
Mineral fuels, lubricants, etc.	347.5	761.3	2,029.7
Basic manufactures	70.1	101.3	107.0
Miscellaneous manufactured articles	9.5	16.2	32.8
Total (incl. others)	593.9	1,187.0	2,506.0

Source: Asian Development Bank, *Key Indicators of Developing Asian and Pacific Countries.*

PRINCIPAL TRADING PARTNERS
(US $ million)

Imports c.i.f.	1999	2000	2001
France	85.4	75.7	50.2
Germany	71.0	52.6	123.0
Iran	66.2	90.9	98.1
Japan	64.1	144.4	36.8
Russia	167.3	254.5	153.4
Turkey	260.1	253.3	278.6
Ukraine	182.0	214.3	246.6
United Arab Emirates	123.7	146.6	158.2
USA	66.3	62.8	273.4
Uzbekistan	49.8	35.3	35.3
Total (incl. others)	1,478.3	1,787.8	1,960.9

Exports f.o.b.	1999	2000	2001
Afghanistan	40.9	38.0	42.0
Azerbaijan	48.2	37.1	37.1
Germany	119.0	404.8	148.9
Iran	163.0	242.0	241.0
Russia	43.5	1,029.3	35.5
Switzerland	66.3	91.9	94.7
Tajikistan	11.9	29.1	46.3
Turkey	128.3	186.0	205.3
Ukraine	321.8	164.9	164.9
United Kingdom	40.8	54.1	13.3
Total (incl. others)	1,187.1	2,505.2	1,362.5

Source: Asian Development Bank, *Key Indicators of Developing Asian and Pacific Countries.*

Transport

RAILWAYS
(traffic)

	1996	1997*	1999
Passenger journeys (million)	7.8	6.4	3.1
Passenger-km (million)	2,104	958	701
Freight transported (million metric tons)	15.9	18.5	17.2
Freight ton-km (million)	6,779	7,445	7,337

* Data for 1998 not available.

Source: *Railway Directory.*

SHIPPING

Merchant Fleet
(registered at 31 December)

	1999	2000	2001
Number of vessels	40	40	41
Total displacement ('000 grt)	43.6	41.8	45.7

Source: Lloyd's Register-Fairplay, *World Fleet Statistics.*

CIVIL AVIATION
(estimated traffic on scheduled services)

	1997	1998	1999
Kilometres flown (million)	15	11	9
Passengers carried ('000)	523	890	220
Passenger-kilometres (million)	1,093	832	640
Total ton-kilometres (million)	101	79	74

Source: UN, *Statistical Yearbook.*

Tourism

FOREIGN VISITOR ARRIVALS
(incl. excursionists)

Country of nationality	1995	1996	1997
Afghanistan	11,803	18,301	n.a.
Azerbaijan	n.a.	10,642	114
Iran	82,925	82,386	171,071
Kazakhstan	n.a.	9,466	4,971
Kyrgyzstan	n.a.	15,798	22,066
Pakistan	7,000	5,837	3,075
Russia	n.a.	3,916	6,979
Tajikistan	n.a.	10,623	11,310
Turkey	46,414	52,230	62,915
Uzbekistan	n.a.	45,259	31,784
Total (incl. others)	232,832	281,988	332,425

Source: World Tourism Organization, *Yearbook of Tourism Statistics.*

Tourism receipts (US $ million): 66 in 1996; 74 in 1997; 192 in 1998 (Source: World Bank).

Communications Media

	1998	1999	2000
Television receivers ('000 in use) .	865	870	875
Telephones ('000 main lines in use)	354.0	358.9	364
Mobile cellular telephones ('000 subscribers).	3.0	4.0	9.5
Personal computers ('000 in use) .	n.a.	2.0	n.a.
Internet users ('000)	n.a.	2	6

1994: Book production (including pamphlets): 450 titles (5,493,000 copies).

1997: Radio receivers in use 1,225,000.

2001: Telephones ('000 main lines in use): 387.6; Internet users 8,000.

Sources: International Telecommunication Union; UNESCO, *Statistical Yearbook*.

Education

(1984/85)

	Institutions	Students
Secondary schools	1,900	800,000
Secondary specialized schools	35	36,900
Higher schools (incl. universities). . . .	9	38,900

1990/91: 76,000 students at higher schools (Source: UNESCO, *Statistical Yearbook*).

Adult literacy rate (UNESCO estimates): 97.7% (males 98.8%; females 96.6%) at 1989 census (Source: UNESCO, *Statistical Yearbook*).

Directory

The Constitution

A new Constitution was adopted on 18 May 1992. The Constitution was organized into eight sections (detailing: fundamentals of the constitutional system; fundamental human and civil rights, freedoms and duties; the system of state governmental bodies; local self-government; the electoral system and provisions for referendum; judicial authority; the office of the prosecutor-general and final provisions), and included the following among its main provisions:

The President of the Republic is directly elected by universal adult suffrage for a five-year term. A President may hold office for a maximum of two terms. The President is not only Head of State, but also head of Government (Prime Minister in the Council of Ministers) and Supreme Commander of the Armed Forces. The President must ratify all parliamentary legislation and in certain circumstances may legislate by decree. The President appoints the Council of Ministers and chairs sessions of the Khalk Maslakhaty (People's Council).

Supreme legislative power resides with the 50-member Majlis, a unicameral parliament which is directly elected for a five-year term. Sovereignty, however, is vested in the people of Turkmenistan, and the supreme representative body of popular power is the Khalk Maslakhaty. This is described as a supervisory organ with no legislative or executive functions, but it is authorized to perform certain duties normally reserved for a legislature or constituent assembly. Not only does it debate and approve measures pertaining to the political and economic situation in the country, but it examines possible changes to the Constitution and may vote to express 'no confidence' in the President of the Republic, on grounds of unconstitutionality. The Khalk Maslakhaty is comprised of all the deputies of the Majlis, a further 50 directly elected and 10 appointed representatives from all districts of the country, the members of the Council of Ministers, the respective Chairmen of the Supreme Court and the Supreme Economic Court, the Prosecutor-General and the heads of local councils.

The Constitution, which defines Turkmenistan as a democratic state, also guarantees the independence of the judiciary and the basic human rights of the individual. The age of majority is 18 years (parliamentary deputies must be aged at least 21). Ethnic minorities are granted equality under the law, although Turkmen is the only official language. A central tenet of Turkmenistan's foreign policy is that of 'permanent neutrality'.

Note: On 15 January 1994 a referendum confirmed President Saparmyrat Niyazov's exemption from the need to be re-elected in 1997. An amendment to the Constitution, approved by the Khalk Maslakhaty in December 1999, extended the term of Niyazov's presidency indefinitely. In February 2001, following Niyazov's announcement that he would retire by 2010, the Khalk Maslakhaty endorsed a resolution to hold open presidential elections in 2008–10, following his retirement.

The Government

HEAD OF STATE

President of the Republic: Gen. SAPARMYRAT A. NIYAZOV (directly elected 27 October 1990; re-elected 21 June 1992—a constitutional amendment of 28 December 1999 extended his term of office indefinitely, although in February 2001 Niyazov announced that he would retire no later than 2010).

COUNCIL OF MINISTERS
(April 2003)

Prime Minister: Gen. SAPARMYRAT A. NIYAZOV.

Deputy Prime Minister and Minister of Construction and Construction Materials: MUKHAMMETNAZAR KHUDAYGULYYEV.

Deputy Prime Minister and Minister of Foreign Affairs: RASHID MEREDOV.

Deputy Prime Minister and Minister of Health and the Pharmaceutical Industry: GURBANGULY BERDYMUKHAMMETOV.

Deputy Prime Minister and Minister of the Textile Industry: DORTKULI AYDOGYEV.

Deputy Prime Ministers: YOLLY GURBANMYRADOV, GURBANSOLTAN HANDURDIYEVA.

Minister of Agriculture: BEGENC ATAMRADOV.

Minister of Culture: ORAZGELDY AYDOGDIYEV.

Minister of Defence: REJEPBAY ARAZOV.

Minister of the Economy and Finance: YAZGULY KAKALYEV.

Minister of Education: MAMEDDURDY SARYKHANOV.

Minister of Energy and Industry: ATAMYRAT BERDIYEV.

Minister of Environmental Protection: MATKARIM RAJAPOV.

Minister of Trade and Foreign Economic Relations: CHARYMAMMED GAYIBOV.

Minister of Internal Affairs: ASHYR ATAYEV.

Minister of Justice: GURBAN KASIMOV.

Minister of National Security: Gen. BATYR BUSAKOV.

Minister of Petroleum, Natural Gas and Mineral Resources: TACHBERDY TAGIYEV.

Minister of Social Security: ORAZMURAT BEGMURADOV.

Minister of Water Resources: GURBANGELDI VELMYRADOV.

Minister of Communications: RESULBERDI KHOZHAGURBANOV.

State Minister: GULYA GARAJAYEVA.

Chairmen of State Committees

Chairman of the State Committee for the Border Service: Gen. SAPARMYRAT A. NIYAZOV.

Chairman of the State Committee for Fisheries: HUDAJBERDY YAZOVICH YAKATOV.

Chairman of the State Committee for Hydrometeorology: SUKHANBERDY BAIRAMOV.

Chairman of the State Committee for Land Use and Land Reform: (vacant).

Chairman of the State Committee for Tourism and Sport: (vacant).

MINISTRIES

Office of the President and the Council of Ministers: 744000 Ashgabat, ul. Karl Marxa 24, Presidential Palace; tel. (12) 35-45-34; fax (12) 35-43-88.

Ministry of Agriculture: 744000 Ashgabat, ul. Azadi 63; tel. (12) 35-66-91; fax (12) 35-01-18; e-mail minselhoz@online.tm.

Ministry of Communications: 744000 Ashgabat, ul. Bitarap Turkmenistan 40; tel. (12) 35-21-52; fax (12) 35-05-95; e-mail mincom@telecom.tm; internet www.mct.gov.tm.

Ministry of Construction and Construction Materials: 744000 Ashgabat, ul. Steklozavodskoy 1; tel. (12) 47-40-87; fax (12) 47-50-69.

Ministry of Culture: 744000 Ashgabat, ul. Pushkina 14; tel. (12) 35-30-61; fax (12) 35-35-60.

Ministry of Defence: 744000 Ashgabat, ul. Galkynysh 4; tel. (12) 35-22-59.

Ministry of the Economy and Finance: 744000 Ashgabat, ul. Nurberdy Pomma 4; tel. (12) 51-05-63; fax (12) 51-18-23.

Ministry of Education: 744000 Ashgabat, ul. Bitarap Turkmenistan 2; tel. (12) 35-58-03; fax (12) 39-88-11.

Ministry of Energy and Industry: 744000 Ashgabat, ul. Nurberdy Pomma 6; tel. (12) 35-38-70; fax (12) 39-06-82; e-mail kuwwat@online.tm.

Ministry of Environmental Protection: 744000 Ashgabat, ul. Azadi 28; tel. (12) 39-65-12; fax (12) 51-13-97.

Ministry of Foreign Affairs: Ashgabat, pr. Magtymguly 83; tel. (12) 26-62-11; fax (12) 25-35-83.

Ministry of Health and the Pharmaceutical Industry: 744000 Ashgabat, pr. Magtymguly 95; tel. (12) 35-60-47; fax (12) 35-50-32.

Ministry of Internal Affairs: Ashgabat, pr. Magtymguly 85; tel. (12) 25-13-28.

Ministry of Justice: Ashgabat.

Ministry for National Security: Ashgabat.

Ministry of Petroleum, Natural Gas and Mineral Resources: 744000 Ashgabat, ul. Bitarap Turkmenistan 28; tel. (12) 39-38-27; fax (12) 39-38-21; e-mail ministryoilgas@online.tm.

Ministry of Social Security: 744007 Ashgabat, ul. Mollanepes 3; tel. (12) 25-30-03.

Ministry of Trade and Foreign Economic Relations: 744000 Ashgabat, ul. Bitarap Turkmenistan 1; tel. (12) 35-10-47; fax (12) 35-73-24; e-mail mtfer@online.tm.

Ministry of Water Resources: 744000 Ashgabat, ul. Seidi 1; tel. (12) 39-06-15; fax (12) 39-85-39.

All the principal state committees are also based in Ashgabat.

KHALK MASLAKHATY
(People's Council)

Under the Constitution of May 1992, the Khalk Maslakhaty is established as the supreme representative body in the country. Formally, it is neither a legislative nor an executive body, although its decisions supersede those of both parliament and presidency. The People's Council is composed of all the Majlis deputies, 65 directly elected representatives and 10 appointed representatives from all districts (etraps) of Turkmenistan, the members of the Council of Ministers, the Chairman of the Supreme Court, the Chairman of the Supreme Economic Court, the Prosecutor-General and the prefects (hakims) of the five regions (velayats). It is headed by the President of the Republic. Elections for the 50 district representatives were held in November and December 1992; the Council convened for the first time later in December. Fresh elections were held in April 1998 and on 6 April 2003.

Legislature

MAJLIS
(Assembly)

Under the Constitution of May 1992, the highest legislative body in Turkmenistan is the 50-member Majlis, directly elected for a term of five years. Until the expiry of its term, the former legislature, the Supreme Soviet, acted as the Majlis. Elections to the Majlis were held on 12 December 1999, officially with the participation of 98.9% of the registered electorate. All contestants were believed to be members of the ruling party, the Democratic Party of Turkmenistan. The new Majlis convened for the first time in late December. Following the December 1999 elections, the new Majlis was granted greater legislative and regulatory powers by the President. The deputies of the Majlis also form part of the Khalk Maslakhaty (see above).

Chairman: OVEZGELDY ATAYEV.

Political Organizations

Agzybirlik: Ashgabat; f. 1989; popular front organization; denied official registration except from Oct. 1991 to Jan. 1992; Leader NURBERDY NURMAMEDOV (imprisoned February–December 2000).

Democratic Party of Turkmenistan: 744014 Ashgabat 14, ul. Bitarap Turkmenistan 28; tel. (12) 25-12-12; name changed from Communist Party of Turkmenistan in 1991; Chair. Gen. SAPARMYRAT A. NIYAZOV; 116,000 mems (1991).

National Revival Movement of Turkmenistan (Galkynysh): Ashgabat; Chair. Gen. SAPARMYRAT A. NIYAZOV.

Peasants' Justice Party: Ashgabat; f. 1993 by deputies of the agrarian faction in parliament; still awaited official registration in 2002.

Turkmenistan is effectively a one-party state, with the Democratic Party of Turkmenistan (led by the President of the Republic) dominant in all areas of government. There are, however, several unregistered opposition groups, such as the Islamic Renaissance Party, which had been an all-Union Muslim party in the former USSR, and Agzybirlik. In early 1994 President Niyazov indicated that the Peasants' Justice Party would be permitted registration (although this had apparently not happened by the early 2000s). A Social Democratic Party was reportedly established in Ashgabat in August 1996, upon the merger of several small unofficial groups.

Other opposition elements are based in other republics of the CIS, in particular Russia. A leading opposition figure in exile is the former Minister of Foreign Affairs, Abdy Kuliyev, whose Turkmenistan Fund is based in Moscow. In January 1996 several of the Turkmenistan Fund's leaders left to form the Movement for Democratic Reform (based in Sweden). The Vatan (Motherland) movement (also based in Sweden) comprises Turkmen and other Central Asian oppositionists. In January 2002 the former Minister of Foreign Affairs, Boris Shikhmuradov, established the opposition People's Democratic Movement of Turkmenistan; however, he was imprisoned in December.

Diplomatic Representation

EMBASSIES IN TURKMENISTAN

Afghanistan: 744000 Ashgabat, ul. Bitarap Turkmenistan 14; tel. (12) 39-58-20; fax (12) 39-58-23; Ambassador SHAH MARDANKUL.

Armenia: 744000 Ashgabat, ul. Bitarap Turkmenistan 14; tel. (12) 35-44-18; fax (12) 39-55-38; e-mail eat@online.tm; Ambassador ARAM GRIGORYAN.

Azerbaijan: Ashgabat.

China, People's Republic: 744036 Ashgabat, Berzengi District, Hotel 'Kuwwat'; tel. (12) 51-81-31; fax (12) 51-88-78; e-mail chemb@cat.glasnet; Ambassador GAO YUSHENG.

France: 744000 Ashgabat, Four Points Ak Altin Hotel, Office Bldg, pr. Magtymguly 141/1; tel. (12) 36-35-50; fax (12) 36-35-46; e-mail alain.couanon@diplomatie.fr; Ambassador ALAIN COUANON.

Georgia: 744000 Ashgabat, ul. Azady 139A; tel. (12) 34-48-38; fax (12) 34-32-48; e-mail georgia@online.tm; Ambassador PETER CHKHEIDZE.

Germany: 744000 Ashgabat, Hotel Sheraton 'Four Points Ak Altin', pr. Magtymguly; tel. (12) 36-35-15; fax (12) 36-35-22; e-mail grembtkm@online.tm; Ambassador HANS GÜNTHER MATTERN.

India: 744000 Ashgabat, ul. Nogina 11, Rm 103, Hotel 'Nogina'; tel. (12) 34-46-31; fax (12) 46-90-30; e-mail ambtm@online.tm; Ambassador GEORGE JOSEPH.

Iran: 744000 Ashgabat, Tegeranskaya 3; tel. (12) 35-02-37; fax (12) 35-05-65; e-mail isroiref@online.tm; Ambassador SAYED IBRAHIM DERAZGISOU.

Kazakhstan: Ashgabat, ul. Bitarap Turkmenistan 14, 3rd Floor; tel. (12) 39-55-48; fax (12) 39-59-32; e-mail turemb@online.tm; Ambassador AMANGELDY JUMABAYEV.

Korea, Democratic People's Republic: Ashgabat; Ambassador SON SONG PHIL.

Kyrgyzstan: Ashgabat, ul. Bitarap Turkmenistan 14; tel. (12) 39-20-64; fax (12) 35-55-06; e-mail embassy@meerim.ashgabat.su; Ambassador MARKIL IBRAYEVICH IBRAYEV.

Libya: Ashgabat, ul. Shota Rustaveli 15; tel. (12) 35-49-17; fax (12) 39-05-69; Chargé d'affaires a.i. OMAR ELHADI SHIN-SHIN.

Pakistan: Ashgabat, ul. Kemine 92; tel. (12) 35-00-97; fax (12) 39-76-40; e-mail parepashgabat@online.tm; Ambassador BABAR MALIK.

Romania: Ashgabat, ul. Miati Kusaeva 107; tel. (12) 34-67-15; fax (12) 34-76-20; e-mail ambromas@online.tm; Ambassador ION POROJAN.

Russia: 744004 Ashgabat, Saparmyrat Turkmenbashy shayoly 11; tel. (12) 35-39-57; fax (12) 39-84-66; Ambassador (vacant).

Saudi Arabia: Ashgabat, 1 Younes Amra Area (2/1), Internal Imperial Centre for Business; tel. (12) 45-49-63; fax (12) 45-49-70; e-mail tmemb@mofa.gov.sa.

Tajikistan: 744000 Ashgabat; ul. Bitarap Turkmenistan 14; tel. (12) 35-56-96; fax (12) 39-31-74; e-mail embtd@online.tm; Ambassador MARDONY TAJIDDIN NURIDDIN.

Thailand: Ashgabat; Ambassador KARUN RUCHUYOTIN.

Turkey: 744007 Ashgabat, ul. Shevchenka 9; tel. (12) 35-14-61; fax (12) 39-19-14; e-mail askabat.be@mfa.gov.tr; Ambassador MEHMET BAHATTIN GÜRSÖZ.

Ukraine: 744001 Ashgabat, ul. Azadi 49; tel. (12) 39-13-73; fax (12) 39-10-28; e-mail ukremb@online.tm; Ambassador VADIM CHUPRUN.

United Arab Emirates: Ashgabat; Ambassador HASSAN ABDULLAH AL-AZZAB AL-ZARUUNA.

United Kingdom: 744001 Ashgabat, Four Points Ak Altin Hotel, 3rd Floor Office Bldg; tel. (12) 36-34-62; fax (12) 36-34-65; e-mail beasb@online.tm; internet www.britishembassytm.org.uk; Ambassador PAUL BRUMMELL.

USA: 744000 Ashgabat, ul. Pushkina 9; tel. (12) 35-00-45; fax (12) 39-26-14; e-mail irc-ashgabat@iatp.edu.tm; internet www.usemb-ashgabat.rpo.at; Ambassador TRACEY ANN JACOBSON (designate).

Uzbekistan: Ashgabat; tel. (12) 34-24-34; fax (12) 34-23-37; e-mail emuzbek@online.tm.

Judicial System

Chairman of the Supreme Court: YAGSHIGELDY ESENOV.

Vice-Chairman of the Supreme Court: REJEPNIYAZ CHERKEZOV.

Prosecutor-General: GURBANBIBI ATAJANOVA.

Religion

The majority of the population are adherents of Islam. In June 1991 the Turkmen Supreme Soviet adopted a Law on Freedom of Conscience and Religious Organizations. This law and subsequent amendments have been criticized abroad for the stipulation that religious organizations must have 500 members (of 18 years of age or more) to achieve formal recognition from the Ministry of Justice. In April 1994 a council (Gengesh) for religious affairs was established, within the office of the President; it was chaired by the Kazi of Turkmenistan and his deputy was the head of the Orthodox Church in Turkmenistan.

ISLAM

Turkmen are traditionally Sunni Muslims, but with elements of Sufism. Islam, the religion of the Turkmen for many centuries, was severely persecuted by the Soviet regime from the late 1920s. Until July 1989 Ashgabat was the only Central Asian capital without a functioning mosque. The Muslims of Turkmenistan are officially under the jurisdiction of the Muslim Board of Central Asia, based in Tashkent, Uzbekistan, but, in practice, the Government permits little external influence in religious affairs. The Board is represented in Turkmenistan by a *kazi*, who is responsible for appointing Muslim clerics in all rural areas.

Kazi of Turkmenistan: KAKAGELDY VEPAYEV.

CHRISTIANITY

Roman Catholic Church

The Church is represented in Turkmenistan by a Mission, established in September 1997. There were an estimated 500 adherents at 31 December 2000.

Superior: Fr ANDRZEJ MADEJ, 744000 Ashgabat, ul. Gorogly 20A, POB 98; tel. (12) 39-11-40; fax (12) 35-36-83; e-mail aszomi@online.tm.

The Press

All publications listed below are in Turkmen, except where otherwise stated.

PRINCIPAL NEWSPAPERS

Adalat: 744000 Ashgabat, ul. Steklozavodskoy 4; tel. (12) 47-84-53; weekly; Editor-in-Chief KHUDAYBERDY GYRBANDURDIYEV; circ. 42,575.

Ashgabat: 744004 Ashgabat, ul. Galkynysh 20; tel. (12) 35-16-38; f. 1960; 3 a week; journal of the Union of Writers of Turkmenistan; popular; in Russian and Turkmen; Editor-in-Chief ORAZNAZAR HESHDEKOV; circ. 20,577.

Edebiyat ve sungat (Literature and Art): 744604 Ashgabat, ul. Galkynysh 20; tel. (12) 35-30-34; f. 1958; weekly; Editor ANNAMYRAT POLADOV; circ. 1,500.

Esger: 744004 Ashgabat, Atamurat Niyazov shayoly 29; tel. (12) 35-68-09; f. 1993; weekly; organ of the Council of Ministers; Editor-in-Chief GUVANCH MAMMETGELDIYEV (acting); circ. 23,769.

Galkynysh: Ashgabat 744604, ul. Galkynysh 20; tel. (12) 46-68-53; weekly; Editor-in-Chief KHUDAYBERDY DIVANGULIYEV; circ. 24,465.

Habarlar: 744004 Ashgabat, ul. Galkynysh 20; tel. (12) 46-84-70; weekly; in Russian and Turkmen; business; Editor-in-Chief R. BALABAN; circ. 5,500.

Khalk sesi (Voice of the People): 744000 Ashgabat, Saparmyrat Turkmenbashy shayoly 13; tel. (12) 25-39-98; f. 1991; weekly; organ of the Federation of Trade Unions of Turkmenistan; Editor P. ALLAGULOV.

Mugallymlar gazeti (Teachers' Newspaper): 744004 Ashgabat, ul. Galkynysh 20; tel. (12) 39-59-25; f. 1952; 3 a week; organ of the Ministry of Education; Editor DORTKULI BALAKAYEV; circ. 52,771.

Neitralnyi Turkmenistan (Neutral Turkmenistan): 744004 Ashgabat, ul. Galkynysh 20; tel. and fax (12) 46-84-75; e-mail nt@online.tm; internet www.tmpress.gov.tm; f. 1924; 6 a week; organ of the Majlis and the Council of Ministers; in Russian; Editor-in-Chief GOZEL NURALYEVA; circ. 23,000.

Nesil (Generation): 744604 Ashgabat, ul. Galkynysh 20; tel. (12) 39-17-64; f. 1922; 3 a week; for young people; Editor GULMURAD MURADOV; circ. 15,386.

Novosti Turkmenistana (Turkmenistan News): 744000 Ashgabat, ul. Bitarap Turkmenistan 24a; tel. (12) 39-12-21; fax (12) 51-02-34; f. 1994; weekly; in Russian, English and Turkmen; organ of the Turkmen Dowlet Khabarlar Gullugy news agency; circ. 500.

Turkmen demiryolchusy (Turkmen Railwayman): 744007 Ashgabat, Saparmyrat Turkmenbashy shayoly 7; tel. (12) 29-17-81; f. 1936; weekly; organ of the Turkmenistan State Railways; Editor BAIRAM SEKHEDOV.

Turkmenistan: 744004 Ashgabat, ul. Galkynysh 20; tel. (12) 39-14-55; f. 1920; 6 a week; organ of the Council of Ministers and the Majlis; Editor KAKABAY ILYASOV; circ. 22,500.

Syyasy sokhbetdesh (Political Symposium): 744604 Ashgabat, ul. Galkynysh 20; tel. (12) 25-10-84; f. 1992; weekly; organ of the Democratic Party of Turkmenistan; Editor AKBIBI YUSUPOVA; circ. 14,500.

Vatan (Motherland): 744604 Ashgabat, ul. Galkynysh 20; tel. (12) 35-43-10; f. 1925; 3 a week; Editor-in-Chief AMANMUHAMMAD REPOV; circ. 23,672.

PRINCIPAL PERIODICALS

Monthly, unless otherwise indicated.

Diller duniesi (World of Languages): 744014 Ashgabat, ul. O. Kuliyeva 22; tel. (12) 29-15-41; f. 1972; 6 a year; publ. by the Ministry of Education; in Russian and Turkmen.

Diyar: 744004 Ashgabat, ul. Galkynysh 20; tel. (12) 35-53-97; f. 1992; socio-political and literary magazine; publ. by the President of the Republic and the Council of Ministers; Editor-in-Chief ORAZGELDY AYDOGDIYEV; circ. 3,000.

Finansovye vesti (Financial News): 744004 Ashgabat, ul. Galkynysh 20; tel. (12) 29-42-76; f. 1994; in Russian, English and Turkmen; publ. by the Ministry of the Economy and Finance.

Garagum (Kara-Kum): 744005 Ashgabat, ul. Galkynysh 20; tel. (12) 46-86-26; f. 1928; cultural; Editor SAPAR OREYEV; circ. 2,000.

Gunesh: 744000 Ashgabat, ul. Garaja Burunova 8; tel. (12) 51-17-83; for children; Editor-in-Chief SHDURDY CHARYGYLLIYEV; circ. 7,415.

Gurbansoltan Edzhe: 744604 Ashgabat, ul. Galkynysh 20; tel. (12) 25-20-64; f. 1931 as Ovadan (Beautiful) for women; Editor A. B. SEITKULIYEVA.

Izvestiya Akademii Nauk Turkmenistana (Academy of Sciences of Turkmenistan News): 744000 Ashgabat, ul. Azadi 59; f. 1946; 6 a year; in Russian and Turkmen.

Khalypa (Tutor): 744014 Ashgabat, ul. O. Kuliyeva 22; tel. (12) 25-36-31; f. 1931; 6 a year; publ. by the Ministry of Education.

Politicheskii sobesednik (Political Symposium): 744604 Ashgabat, ul. Galkynysh 20; tel. (12) 25-10-84; f. 1937; in Russian; publ. by the Democratic Party of Turkmenistan; circ. 2,300.

Saglyk (Health): 744000 Ashgabat, ul. Kerbabayeva 39/57; tel. (12) 39-16-21; f. 1990; 6 a year; publ. by the Ministry of Health and the Pharmaceutical Industry; Editor-in-Chief BAYRAM TYACHMAMEDOV; circ. 13,828.

Turkmen dili khem edebiyati (Turkmen Language and Literature): Ashgabat; tel. (12) 41-88-03; f. 1991; 6 a year; publ. by the Ministry of Education.

Turkmen dunyasi: 744004 Ashgabat, ul. Azadi 20; tel. (12) 47-81-18; organ of the Humanitarian Association of World Turkmen; Editor-in-Chief ANNABERDY AGABAYEV; circ. 11,956.

Turkmenistanyn oba khozhalygy (Agriculture of Turkmenistan): 744000 Ashgabat, ul. Azadi 63; tel. (12) 35-19-38; f. 1929; Editor BYASHIM TALLYKOV; circ. 3,500.

Turkmen medeniyeti (Turkmen Culture): 744007 Ashgabat, ul. O. Kuliyeva 21; tel. (12) 25-37-22; f. 1993; 2 a year; publ. by the Ministry of Culture; Editor GELDYMYRAT NURMUKHAMMEDOV.

Turkmen sesi (Voice of the Turkmen): 744007 Ashgabat, ul. Azadi 20; tel. (12) 47-81-67; f. 1991; organ of the humanitarian asscn 'Turkmeny Mira'; Editor A. AGABAYEV.

Vedomosti Majlisa Turkmenistana (Bulletin of the Majlis of Turkmenistan): 744000 Ashgabat, ul. Bitarap Turkmenistan 17; f. 1960; 4 a year; in Russian and Turkmen.

Vozrozhdeniye: 744604 Ashgabat, ul. Galkynysh 20; tel. (12) 35-10-84; in Russian; political; Editor-in-Chief H. DIVANGULYEV; circ. 1,500.

NEWS AGENCY

Turkmen Dowlet Khabarlar Gullugy (Turkmen State News Service): 744000 Ashgabat, ul. Bitarap Turkmenistan 24A; tel. (12) 39-12-21; fax (12) 51-02-34; e-mail tpress@online.tm; f. 1967; Dir JEREN TAIMOVA.

Publishers

Magaryf Publishing House: Ashgabat; Dir N. ATAYEV.

Turkmenistan State Publishing Service: 744000 Ashgabat, ul. Galkynysh 20; tel. (12) 46-90-13; f. 1965; politics, science and fiction; Dir A. M. JANMURADOV; Editor-in-Chief A. ALLANAZAROV.

Ylym Publishing House: 744000 Ashgabat, ul. Azadi 59; tel. (12) 29-04-84; f. 1952; desert development, science; Dir N. I. FAIZULAYEVA.

Broadcasting and Communications

TELECOMMUNICATIONS

Turkmentelekom: 744000 Ashgabat, ul. Asudalyk 36; tel. (12) 51-12-77; fax (12) 51-02-40; e-mail admin@telecom.tm; internet www .telecom.tm; f. 1993; Dir-Gen. REJEPMURAD M. ATAYEV.

BROADCASTING

National Television and Radio Co of Turkmenistan (Turkmenistanin Milli Teleradiokompaniyasi): 744000 Ashgabat, ul. Navoi 5; tel. (12) 35-15-15; fax (12) 36-48-21; Chair. (vacant).

Radio

Turkmen Radio: 744000 Ashgabat, pr. Magtymguly 89; tel. (12) 25-15-15; fax (12) 25-14-21; broadcasts local programmes and relays from Russia in Turkmen and Russian.

Television

Turkmen Television: see Radio.

Finance

(cap. = capital; res = reserves; dep. = deposits; m. = million; brs = branches; amounts in Turkmen manats)

BANKING

Long-standing lack of confidence in the banking sector, together with a regional financial crisis, prompted a restructuring of the sector, in December 1998, by presidential decree. Government ownership of banks was increased, while restrictions on lending by the Central Bank were intensified and the merger of smaller banks was encouraged. By late 2002 there were 12 commercial banks.

Central Bank

Central Bank of Turkmenistan: 744000 Ashgabat, ul. Bitarap Turkmenistan 22; tel. (12) 51-06-73; fax (12) 51-08-12; e-mail cbtmode@cat.glasnet.ru; f. 1991; central monetary authority, issuing bank and supervisory authority; Chair. of Bd SHAKERSOLTAN MUKHAMMEDOVA (acting); 5 brs.

Other Banks

Daykhanbank: 744000 Ashgabat, ul. Galkynysh 62; tel. (12) 41-98-73; fax (12) 39-15-42; e-mail daybank@online.tm; f. 1989 as independent bank, Agrombank, reorganized 1999; specializes in agricultural sector; Chair. of Bd NURBERDY BAYRAMOV; 70 brs.

Garagum Bank: 744000 Ashgabat, ul. Kulieyeva 3; tel. (12) 35-22-01; fax (12) 35-38-54; f. 1993 as International Bank for Reconstruction, Development and Support of Entrepreneurship, name changed 2000; Chair. BEKMAMED SOLTANMEMEDOV.

Garashsyslyk Bank: Ashgabat, ul. Schevchenko 30A; tel. (12) 39-01-24; fax (12) 39-78-92; e-mail garash@cbtm.net; f. 1999 following merger of Gas Bank and Ashgabat Bank; Chair. CHARYGELDY BAYGELDIYEV.

President Bank: 744000 Ashgabat, ul. Neitralnaya 22; tel. (12) 35-79-43; fax (12) 51-08-12; e-mail presidentbank@cbtm.net; f. 2000; cap. US $60m. Exec. Dir (vacant).

Savings Bank of Turkmenistan (Sberbank): 744000 Ashgabat, pr. Magtymguly 86; tel. (12) 35-46-71; fax (12) 35-40-04; f. 1923, reorganized 1989; wholly state-owned; cap. 726m., res 125m., dep. 7,304m. (1997); Chair. BEGENCH BAYMUKHAMEDOV; 120 brs.

Senagatbank: 744017 Ashgabat, ul. Turkmenbashy 42; tel. (12) 51-03-05; fax (12) 35-06-93; e-mail senagat@online.tm; Chair. GELDYMURAD CHAPAYEV.

State Bank for Foreign Economic Affairs of Turkmenistan (Turkmenvnesheconombank): 744000 Ashgabat, ul. Asudalyk 22; tel. (12) 35-02-52; fax (12) 39-79-82; e-mail tveb@online.tm; f. 1992 as independent bank, from Soviet Vneshekonombank; wholly state-owned; cap. 100,705m., res 54,181m., dep. 1,487,087m. (Jan. 2001); Chair. GUVANCH B. GEOKLENOV; 5 brs.

State Commercial Bank 'Turkmenistan' (Turkmenbank): 744000 Ashgabat, ul. Bitarap Turkmenistan 10A; tel. (12) 51-07-21; fax (12) 39-67-35; e-mail turkmenbank@ctbm.net; f. 1992; Chair. ATAMYRAT REJEPOV.

Turkmenbashy Bank: 744000 Ashgabat, ul. Annadurdiyeva 54; tel. (12) 51-24-50; fax (12) 51-11-11; e-mail mail@investbank.org; internet www.turkmenbashi.net; f. 1992 as Investbank, renamed in 2000; Chair. AMANMURAT PAJAYEV; 23 brs.

Foreign and Joint-Venture Banks

Bank Saderat Iran: Ashgabat, pr. Magtymguly 181; tel. (12) 34-67-67; fax (12) 34-20-70; Man. ALI AMOLI.

Kreditbank: 744000 Ashgabat, pr. Magtymguly 73; tel. (12) 35-02-22; fax (12) 35-03-09; e-mail kreditbank@online.tm; f. 1995; fmrly Rossiiskii Kredit; jt venture with Russia; Chair. BATYR BAYRIYEV.

National Bank of Pakistan: 744000 Ashgabat, ul Bitarap Turkmenistan 7, Hotel 'Emperyal Grand Turkmen'; tel. (12) 35-35-16; fax (12) 35-04-65; e-mail nbptm@online.tm; Gen. Man. SHAKHZAD JAKHANGIR KOKAR.

Turkmen Turkish Commercial Bank: 744014 Ashgabat, pr. Magtymguly 111/2, POB 15; tel. (12) 51-14-07; fax (12) 51-11-23; e-mail ttcb@online.tm; f. 1993, with 50% Turkish ownership; cap. 28,570m., res –18,474m., dep. 36,911m. (Dec. 2000).

COMMODITY EXCHANGE

State Commodity and Raw Materials Exchange of Turkmenistan: 744000 Ashgabat, pr. Magtymguly 111; tel. (12) 35-43-21; fax (12) 51-03-04; e-mail exchange@cbtm.net; internet www .exchangetm.com; f. 1994; Chair. CHARY GAIBOV.

Trade and Industry

GOVERNMENT AGENCIES

National Institute of State Statistics and Information on Turkmenistan (Turkmenmillihasabat): 744000 Ashgabat, pr. Magtymguly 72; tel. (12) 39-42-65; fax (12) 35-43-79; e-mail office@ natstat.gov.tm; f. 1997; Dir JUMADURDY BAIRAMOV.

State Agency for Foreign Investment (SAFI): 744000 Ashgabat, ul. Azadi 53; tel. (12) 35-03-18; fax (12) 35-04-13; f. 1996; monitors and regulates all foreign investment in Turkmenistan.

DEVELOPMENT ORGANIZATION

Small and Medium Enterprise Development Agency (SMEDA): 744000 Ashgabat, ul. Sokolovskogo 8; tel. (12) 34-42-59; fax (12) 34-51-49; e-mail smeda@online.tm; internet www.icctm.org/ Smeda; jt venture between Turkmen Govt and EU; Dir SERDAR BABAYEV.

CHAMBER OF COMMERCE

Chamber of Commerce of Turkmenistan: 744000 Ashgabat, ul. B. Karrieva 17; tel. (12) 35-64-03; fax (12) 35-13-52; e-mail mission@ online.tm; f. 1959; Chair. ARSLAN F. NEPESOV; Dep. Chair. AGAMAMED SAKHATOV.

UTILITIES

Electricity

Kuvvat: Ashgabat; e-mail kuvvat@online.tm; state electrical power generation co and agency; Chair. DAVYDOV YUSUP.

STATE HYDROCARBONS COMPANIES

Turkmengaz: 744000 Ashgabat, ul. Mollanepec 1; tel. (12) 35-59-59; fax (12) 39–26–00; e-mail tmgas@online.tm; f. 1996; govt agency responsible for natural gas operations, inc. development of system of extraction, processing of gas and gas concentrate and gas transportation; Chair. GUYCHNAZAR TACHNAZAROV.

Turkmengeologiya: 744000 Ashgabat, ul. Myati Kosayev 7/32; tel. (12) 35-13-46; fax (12) 35-50-15; govt agency responsible for natural gas and petroleum exploration; Chair. ORAZMUKHAMMET ATAGELDYEV.

Turkmenneft: 745100 Balkanabat, pr. Magtymguly 49; tel. (00243) 2-19-45; govt agency responsible for petroleum operations and production; Pres. SAPARMAMMET VALIYEV; Gen. Dir KHAKIM IMAMOV.

Turkmenneftegaz: 744000 Ashgabat, ul Bitarap Turkmenistan 28; tel. (12) 35-58-94; fax (12) 35-27-28; e-mail tngaz@online.tm; f. 1996; govt trade corpn for petroleum and natural gas marketing; includes Chelekenmorneftegaz (CMNG); Chair. ILYAS CHARIYEV.

> **Turkmenbashy Oil Refinery:** 745000 Balkan, Turkmenbashy, POB 5; tel. (00222) 7-45-45; fax (00222) 7-45-44; production and refining of petroleum; Dir V. I. GUBANOV.

Turkmenneftegazstroy: 744000 Ashgabat, ul. Mollanepec 5; tel. (12) 35-58-65; fax (12) 51-08-54; govt agency for construction projects in the hydrocarbons sector; Chair. REJEPTURDY ATAYEV.

TRADE UNIONS

Association of Trade Unions of Turkmenistan: 744000 Ashgabat, Saparmyrat Turkmenbashy shayoly 13; tel. (12) 35-62-08; fax (12) 35-21-30; national centre; Chair. ENEBAY G. ATAEVA.

Committee of Trade Unions of Dashkhovuz Velayat: 746311 Niyazovsk, Saparmyrat Turkmenbashy shayoly 8; Dir SH. IGAMOV.

Union of Trade Unions of Akhal Velayat: Gyaver etrap, Annau; tel. 41-39-19; Dir A. TAGANOV.

Transport

RAILWAYS

The main rail line in the country runs from Turkmenbashy (Krasnovodsk), on the Caspian Sea, in the west, via Ashgabat and Mary, to Türkmenabat (Charjew) in the east. From Türkmenabat one line runs further east, to the other Central Asian countries of the former USSR, while another runs north-west, via Uzbekistan and Kazakhstan, to join the rail network of the Russian Federation. In 1998 the total length of rail track in use in Turkmenistan was 2,313 km. A 203-km rail link from Türkmenabat to Atamarut was opened in 1999. In 1996 a rail link was established with Iran (on the route Tejen–Serakhs–Mashhad), thus providing the possibility of rail travel and transportation between Turkmenistan and İstanbul, Turkey, as well as giving access to the Persian (Arabian) Gulf.

Turkmenistan State Railways: 744000 Ashgabat, Saparmyrat Turkmenbashy shayoly 7; tel. (12) 35-55-45; fax (12) 51-06-32; f. 1992 following the dissolution of the former Soviet Railways (SZhD) organization; 19,200 employees (1998); Chair. BATYR SARJAYEV.

ROADS

In 1999 there was an estimated total of 24,000 km of roads, of which some 19,500 km were hard-surfaced. In 2000 construction began on a 600-km road linking Ashgabat and Dashoguz.

Turkmenavtoyollary: 744000 Ashgabat, ul. Bitarap Turkmenistan 316; tel. (12) 34-84-16; fax (12) 34-52-77; joint-venture co between the state and AML; construction of highway connecting Ashgabat and Kaakha; Chair. BAYMUKHAMMET KELOV.

SHIPPING

Shipping services link Turkmenbashy (Krasnovodsk) with Baku, Azerbaijan, Makhachkala, Russia, and the major Iranian ports on the Caspian Sea. The Amu-Dar'ya river is an important inland waterway. From 2000 Turkmenbashy port was undergoing an extensive process of modernization.

Shipowning Companies

Neftec Ltd: Turkmenbashy; tel. (2) 765-81; fax (2) 766-89.

Turkmen Maritime Steamship Company: Turkmenbashy, ul. Shagadama 8; tel. (2) 767-34.

Turkmen Shipping Co: Turkmenbashy, ul. Shagadama 8; tel. (2) 972-67; fax (2) 767-85.

Turkmennefteflot: Turkmenbashy, Pochtovyi Yashchik 6; tel. (2) 762-62.

CIVIL AVIATION

Turkmenistan's international airport is at Ashgabat. A new terminal building was completed in late 1994, thus expanding the airport's capacity. A second phase of redevelopment (involving the construction of a new runway and the installation of modern airport systems) was completed in 1998. In 2000 an additional runway was opened at the airport.

National Civil Aviation Authority of Turkmenistan: 744008 Ashgabat Airport; tel. (12) 35-10-52; fax (12) 35-44-02; f. 1992; Chief Exec. ILYAE BERDIEV.

Turkmenistan Airlines: 744000 Ashgabat, pr. Magtymguly 80; tel. (12) 35-10-52; fax (12) 35-44-02; e-mail info@ turkmenistanairline.com; internet www.t5turkmenistan.com; f. 1992; domestic and international scheduled and charter passenger flights, incl. services within Europe, Central and South-East Asia, and the Middle East; operates under three divisions: Akhal Air Co, Khazar Air and Lebap Air Co; Gen. Dir ALEKSEI P. BONDAREV.

Tourism

Although the tourism sector in Turkmenistan remains relatively undeveloped, owing, in part, to the vast expanse of the Kara-Kum desert (some 80% of the country's total area), the Government has made efforts to improve the standard of visitor accommodation (there are a number of new luxury hotels in Ashgabat) and to improve the capacity and efficiency of the capital's international airport (see Civil Aviation). The scenic Kopet Dagh mountains, the Caspian Sea coast, the archaeological sites and mountain caves of Kugitang and the hot subterranean mineral lake at Kov-Ata are among the country's natural attractions, while the ancient cities of Merv (Mary) and Nisa—former capitals of the Seljuk and Parthian empires, respectively—are of considerable historical interest. In addition, Kunya-Urgench is an important site of Muslim pilgrimage. In 1997, according to the World Tourism Organization, there were 332,425 visitors from abroad, compared with 232,832 foreign tourists in 1995.

State Committee for Tourism and Sport: 744000 Ashgabat, ul. Pushkina 17; tel. (12) 35-47-77; fax (12) 39-67-40; e-mail travel@ online.tm; internet www.tourism-sport.gov.tm; f. 2000; Chair. (vacant).

National Institute of Tourism and Sport: 744001 Ashgabat, ul. Atamyrat Niyazov 15A, Hero of Turkmenistan; tel. (12) 36-25-40; fax (12) 36-24-49; f. 1981; Rector ASHIR MOMMADOV.

TUVALU

Introductory Survey

Location, Climate, Language, Religion, Flag, Capital

Tuvalu is a scattered group of nine small atolls (five of which enclose sizeable lagoons), extending about 560 km (350 miles) from north to south, in the western Pacific Ocean. Its nearest neighbours are Fiji to the south, Kiribati to the north and Solomon Islands to the west. The climate is warm and pleasant, with a mean annual temperature of 30°C (86°F), and there is very little seasonal variation. The average annual rainfall is about 3,500 mm (140 ins), the wettest months being November to February. The inhabitants speak Tuvaluan and English. Almost all of them profess Christianity, and about 98% are Protestants. The national flag (proportions 1 by 2) is light blue with the United Kingdom flag as a rectangular canton in the upper hoist, occupying one-quarter of the area, and nine five-pointed yellow stars (arranged to symbolize a map of the archipelago) in the fly. The flag was reintroduced in February 1997 to replace a design, adopted in October 1995, omitting the British union flag. The capital is on Funafuti Atoll.

Recent History

Tuvalu was formerly known as the Ellice (or Lagoon) Islands. Between about 1850 and 1875 many of the islanders were captured by slave-traders and this, together with European diseases, reduced the population from about 20,000 to 3,000. In 1877 the United Kingdom established the Western Pacific High Commission (WPHC), with its headquarters in Fiji, and the Ellice Islands and other groups were placed under its jurisdiction. In 1892 a British protectorate was declared over the Ellice Islands, and the group was linked administratively with the Gilbert Islands to the north. In 1916 the United Kingdom annexed the protectorate, which was renamed the Gilbert and Ellice Islands Colony (GEIC). During the Japanese occupation of the Gilbert Islands in 1942–43, the administration of the GEIC was temporarily moved to Funafuti in the Ellice Islands. (For more details of the history of the GEIC, see the chapter on Kiribati.)

A series of advisory and legislative bodies prepared the GEIC for self-government. In May 1974 the last of these, the Legislative Council, was replaced by the House of Assembly, with 28 elected members (including eight Ellice Islanders) and three official members. A Chief Minister was elected by the House and chose between four and six other ministers, one of whom had to be from the Ellice Islands.

In January 1972 the appointment of a separate GEIC Governor, who assumed most of the functions previously exercised by the High Commissioner for the Western Pacific, increased the long-standing anxiety of the Ellice Islanders over their minority position as Polynesians in the colony, dominated by the Micronesians of the Gilbert Islands. In a referendum held in the Ellice Islands in August and September 1974, more than 90% of the voters favoured separate status for the group, and in October 1975 the Ellice Islands, under the old native name of Tuvalu ('eight standing together', which referred to the eight populated atolls), became a separate British dependency. The Deputy Governor of the GEIC took office as Her Majesty's Commissioner for Tuvalu. The eight Ellice representatives in the GEIC House of Assembly became the first elected members of the new Tuvalu House of Assembly. They elected one of their number, Toaripi Lauti, to be Chief Minister. Tuvalu was completely separated from the GEIC administration in January 1976. The remainder of the GEIC was renamed the Gilbert Islands and achieved independence, as Kiribati, in July 1979.

Tuvalu's first separate elections took place in August 1977, when the number of elective seats in the House of Assembly was increased to 12. An independence Constitution was finalized at a conference in London in February 1978. After five months of internal self-government, Tuvalu became independent on 1 October 1978, with Lauti as the first Prime Minister. The pre-independence House of Assembly was redesignated Parliament. In September 2000 Tuvalu was formally admitted to the UN.

In 1983 the USA formally renounced its claim, dating from 1856, to the four southernmost atolls. Following elections to Parliament in September 1981, Lauti was replaced as Prime Minister by Dr Tomasi (later Sir Tomasi) Puapua. Puapua was re-elected Prime Minister following subsequent elections in September 1985.

In February 1986 a nation-wide poll was conducted to establish public opinion as to whether Tuvalu should remain an independent constitutional monarchy, with the British monarch at its head, or become a republic. Only on one atoll did the community appear to be in favour of the adoption of republican status. In March Tupua (later Sir Tupua) Leupena, a former Speaker of Parliament, was appointed Governor-General, replacing Sir Penitala Teo, who had occupied the post since independence in 1978.

At a general election in September 1989 supporters of Puapua were reported to have been defeated in the election, and an opponent, Bikenibeu Paeniu (who had been appointed Minister for Community Services within the previous year), was elected Prime Minister. In October 1990 Toaripi Lauti succeeded Sir Tupua Leupena as Governor-General.

Legislation approved by Parliament in mid-1991, which sought to prohibit all new religions from the islands and to establish the Church of Tuvalu as the State Church, caused considerable controversy and extensive debate. A survey showed the population to be almost equally divided over the matter, although Paeniu firmly opposed the motion, describing it as incompatible with basic human rights.

In August 1991 the Government announced that it was to prepare a compensation claim against the United Kingdom for the allegedly poor condition of Tuvalu's economy and infrastructure at the time of the country's achievement of independence in 1979. Moreover, Tuvalu was to seek additional compensation for damage caused during the Second World War when the United Kingdom gave permission for the USA to build airstrips on the islands (some 40% of Funafuti is uninhabitable because of large pits created by US troops during the construction of an airstrip on the atoll). Relations with the United Kingdom deteriorated further in late 1992, when the British Government harshly criticized the financial policy of Paeniu's Government. Paeniu defended his Government's policies, and stated that continued delays in the approval of aid projects from the United Kingdom meant that Tuvalu would not be seeking further development funds from the British Government.

At a general election held in September 1993, three of the 12 incumbent members of Parliament lost their seats. At elections to the premiership held in the same month, however, Paeniu and Puapua received six votes each. When a second vote produced a similar result, the Governor-General dissolved Parliament, in accordance with the Constitution. Paeniu and his Cabinet remained in office until the holding of a further general election in November. At elections to the premiership in the following month Kamuta Latasi defeated Paeniu by seven votes to five. Puapua, who had agreed not to challenge Paeniu in the contest in favour of supporting Latasi, was elected Speaker of Parliament. In June 1994 Latasi removed the Governor-General, Toomu Malaefono Sione, from office, some seven months after he had been appointed to the position, and replaced him with Tulaga (later Sir Tulaga) Manuella. Latasi alleged that Paeniu's appointment of Sione had been politically motivated.

In December 1994, in what was widely regarded as a significant rejection of its political links with the United Kingdom, the Tuvaluan Parliament voted to remove the British union flag from the Tuvalu national flag. A new design was selected and the new flag was inaugurated in October 1995. Speculation that the British monarch would be removed as Head of State intensified during 1995, following the appointment of a committee to review the Constitution. The three-member committee was to examine the procedure surrounding the appointment and removal of the Governor-General, and, particularly, to consider the adoption of a republican system of government.

In late 1996 the Deputy Prime Minister, Otinielu Tausi, and the parliamentary Speaker, Dr Tomasi Puapua, both announced their decision to withdraw their support for Latasi's Government, thereby increasing the number of opposition members in Parliament from five to seven. This reversal appeared to be in response to increasing dissatisfaction among the population with Latasi. This had been perceived firstly with his unpopular initiative to replace the country's national flag, and was exacerbated by revelations that the leasing of Tuvalu's telephone code to a foreign company had resulted in the use of the islands' telephone system for personal services considered indecent by the majority of islanders. (It was announced by the Government in October 2000 that the lease was to cease by the end of the year.) Opponents of the Prime Minister submitted a parliamentary motion of 'no confidence' in his Government in December, which was approved by seven votes to five. Paeniu subsequently defeated Latasi, by a similar margin, to become Prime Minister, and a new Cabinet was appointed. The new premier acted promptly to restore the country's original flag, by proposing a parliamentary motion in February 1997, which was approved by seven votes to five.

A total of 35 candidates contested a general election on 26 March 1998. The period prior to the election had been characterized by a series of bitter disputes between Paeniu and Latasi, in which both had made serious accusations of sexual and financial misconduct against the other. Five members of the previous Parliament were returned to office, although Latasi unexpectedly failed to secure re-election. Paeniu was subsequently re-elected Prime Minister by 10 votes to two. In June the new Government announced a series of development plans and proposals for constitutional reform, including the introduction of a code of conduct for political leaders and the creation of an ombudsman's office. Paeniu stated that his administration intended to consult widely with the population before any changes were implemented. Also in 1998 Puapua was appointed Governor-General, replacing Manuella.

On 13 April 1999 Paeniu lost a parliamentary vote of confidence and was forced to resign. Later in the month Ionatana Ionatana, hitherto the minister for Health, Education, Culture, Women and Community Affairs, was elected by Parliament as the new Prime Minister. On his appointment Ionatana immediately effected a reshuffle of the Cabinet.

Potentially the most significant new source of revenue for many years was established in September 1998 when the Government signed an agreement to lease the country's national internet suffix '.tv' to a Canadian information company. The company, which defeated several other business interests to secure the deal, was expected to market the internet address to international television companies. Although that arrangement subsequently failed, it was announced in February 2000 that a US $50m. deal on the sale of the '.tv' suffix had been concluded with a US company. The sale was expected to generate some US $10m. annually in revenue. The funds generated from the sale enabled Tuvalu officially to join the UN, and participate in the 55th annual UN General Assembly Meeting, held in September 2000.

In March 2000 18 schoolgirls and their supervisor were killed in a fire in a school dormitory on Vaitupu atoll. A government inquiry was established into the disaster, which was reportedly the worst in independent Tuvalu's history.

In early December 2000 Prime Minister Ionatana Ionatana died unexpectedly. The Deputy Prime Minister, Lagitupu Tuilimu was immediately appointed as interim Prime Minister, pending the election of a replacement. In late February 2001 Parliament elected as Prime Minister the Minister for Internal Affairs and Rural and Urban Development, Faimalaga Luka; he assumed responsibility for the additional portfolios of foreign affairs, finance and economic planning, and trade and commerce, and immediately named a new cabinet.

A vote of 'no confidence' was upheld against Luka in December 2001 while he was in New Zealand for a medical examination. Koloa Talake, a former Minister for Finance, was elected Prime Minister in the same month, winning eight of the 15 votes cast. He appointed an entirely new Cabinet. The next general election was scheduled for 25 July 2002.

Talake announced in March 2002 that lawyers were preparing evidence for legal action against the United Kingdom, seeking compensation for the alleged inequality of the division of assets between Tuvalu and Kiribati when the two nations had achieved independence in the late 1970s. Following general elections held on 25 July 2002, Saufatu Sopoanga, a former Minister for Finance, defeated Amasone Kilei, the opposition candidate, by eight votes to seven to become the new Prime Minister. Sopoanga subsequently announced his intention to hold a referendum on the adoption of a republican system of Government in Tuvalu.

In 1989 a UN report on the 'greenhouse effect' (the heating of the earth's atmosphere) listed Tuvalu as one of the island groups which would completely disappear beneath the sea in the 21st century, unless drastic action were taken. At the UN World Climate Conference, held in Geneva in November 1990, Paeniu appealed for urgent action by developed nations to combat the environmental changes caused by the 'greenhouse effect', which were believed to include a 10-fold increase in cyclone frequency (from two in 1940 to 21 in 1990), an increase in salinity in ground water and a considerable decrease in the average annual rainfall. The Government remained critical, however, of the inertia with which it considered certain countries had reacted to its appeal for assistance and reiterated the Tuvaluan people's fears of physical and cultural extinction. The subsequent Prime Minister, Kamuta Latasi, was similarly critical of the industrial world's apparent disregard for the plight of small island nations vulnerable to the effects of climate change, particularly when Tuvalu was struck by tidal waves in 1994 (believed to be the first experienced by the islands). Attempts during the mid-1990s to secure approval for resettlement plans for Tuvaluans to other countries, including Australia and New Zealand, were largely unsuccessful. The Government of Tuvalu was strongly critical of Australia's refusal to reduce its emission of pollutant gases (known to contribute to the 'greenhouse effect') at the Conference of the Parties to the Framework Convention on Climate Change (see UN Environment Programme, see p. 49) in Kyoto, Japan, in late 1997. In July 2001, however, Australia adopted the Kyoto Protocol, which urged industrial nations to reduce carbon-dioxide emissions by 5.2% from 1990 levels by 2012. In March 2001 Tuvalu, Kiribati and the Maldives announced their decision to take legal action against the USA for its refusal to sign the Kyoto Protocol. In August Tuvalu was one of six states at the Pacific Islands Forum to demand a meeting with US President George W. Bush to try to enlist his support for the Kyoto Protocol. (The USA produced nearly one-third of the industrialized countries' carbon-dioxide emissions, and was the only nation in the world not to have adopted the Protocol.)

The installation of a new sea-level monitoring station began in December 2001 as part of the South Pacific Sea Level and Climate Monitoring Project administered by the Australian aid agency, Ausaid. In January 2002 it was reported that the Government had engaged a US law firm to prosecute the USA and other nations for failing to meet their commitments to the United Nations Framework Convention on Climate Change (UNFCC). In September 2002 at the World Summit for Sustainable Development held in Johannesburg, South Africa, government delegates attempted to persuade representatives of other Pacific islands to join their campaign against the USA and Australia.

Government

Tuvalu is a constitutional monarchy. Executive authority is vested in the British sovereign, as Head of State, and is exercisable by her representative, the Governor-General, who is appointed on the recommendation of the Prime Minister and acts, in almost all cases, on the advice of the Cabinet. Legislative power is vested in the unicameral Parliament, with 12 members elected by universal adult suffrage for four years (subject to dissolution). The Cabinet is led by the Prime Minister, who is elected by and from the members of Parliament. On the Prime Minister's recommendation, other ministers are appointed by the Governor-General. The Cabinet is responsible to Parliament. Each of the inhabited atolls has its own elected Island Council, which is responsible for local government.

Economic Affairs

In 1999 the UN calculated Tuvalu's gross domestic product (GDP) at current prices to be US $16m., equivalent to US $1,556 per head. According to provisional estimates by the Asian Development Bank (ADB), in 2000 GDP totalled $A23.4m., equivalent to $A2,236 per head. During 1990–2000, it was estimated, the population increased at an average annual rate of 1.5%, while GDP per head increased, in real terms, by an average of 4.9% per year. Overall GDP increased, in real terms, at an average annual rate of 4.9% in 1990–2000. Compared with the previous year, GDP rose by an estimated 4.0% in 2001.

Agriculture (including fishing) is, with the exception of copra production, of a basic subsistence nature. The sector contributed some 16.8% of GDP in 1998. According to ADB figures, the GDP of the agricultural sector declined at an average annual rate of 1.8% in 1990–98. Compared with the previous year, agricultural GDP increased by 5.8% in 1997 and by 0.7% in 1998. Some 60%

of Tuvaluans are engaged in subsistence farming. Coconuts (the source of copra) are the only cash crop; exports of copra were worth $A6,000 in 1997. Pulaka, taro, papayas, the screw-pine (*Pandanus*) and bananas are cultivated as food crops and honey is produced. Livestock comprises pigs, poultry and goats. Fish and other sea products are staple constituents of the islanders' diet. The sale of fishing licences to foreign fleets is an important source of income, which was equivalent to an estimated 40% of total government revenue in 1998, and earned US $6.1m. in 2001.

Industry (including mining, manufacturing, construction and utilities) accounted for 24.3% of GDP in 1998. In 1990–98, according to ADB figures, industrial GDP expanded at an average annual rate of 14.0%. Compared with the previous year, the sector's GDP increased by 4.0% in 1997 and by 21.5% in 1998. Manufacturing is confined to the small-scale production of coconut-based products, soap and handicrafts. The manufacturing sector contributed some 4.2% of GDP in 1998.

Energy is derived principally from a power plant (fuelled by petroleum) and, on the outer islands, solar power. In 1989 mineral fuels accounted for almost 13% of total import costs.

The Government is an important employer (engaging almost one-half of the labour force) and consequently the services sector makes a relatively large contribution to Tuvalu's economy (providing some 58.9% of GDP in 1998). In 1990–98, according to ADB figures, the GDP of the services sector increased at an average annual rate of 5.1%. Compared with the previous year, the sector's GDP expanded by 2.7% in 1997 and by 16.0% in 1998. The islands' remote situation and lack of amenities have hindered the development of a tourist industry. Tourist arrivals totalled only 1,504 in 2000. An important source of revenue, however, has been provided by remittances from Tuvaluans working abroad. In the early 1990s some 1,200 Tuvaluans were working overseas, principally in the phosphate industry on Nauru, although many of these workers returned to Tuvalu during the late 1990s, as Nauruan phosphate reserves became exhausted. Remittances from Tuvaluan seafarers were estimated at US $2.6m. in 2001. In the same year receipts from the leasing of the islands' internet domain address reached US $1.6m., while revenue from telecommunication licence fees totalled US $0.31m.

In 2001 Tuvalu recorded a visible trade deficit of US $13.09m. The principal sources of imports in that year were Fiji (65.5%) and Australia (17.8%). The principal market for exports was Sweden, which purchased 35.0% of the total. In 1997 copra was the only domestic export of any significance. The principal imports in 1989 were foodstuffs (29.3% of the total), basic manufactures, machinery and transport equipment and mineral fuels. In 2001 total export earnings were equivalent to only 7.3% of the value of imports.

The 2002 budget allowed for operating expenditure of as much as US $11.6m. and for special development spending of $2.5m., while capital expenditure of $5.6m. was envisaged. An overall budgetary surplus of $6.4m. was projected, equivalent to 47% of GDP (compared with a surplus equivalent to 20% in 2001). In 1987 the Tuvalu Trust Fund was established, with assistance from New Zealand, Australia and the United Kingdom, to generate funding, through overseas investment, for development projects. In September 2001 its market value totalled $A32.6m. During the late 1990s the Fund contributed some $A7m. towards total annual expenditure. Official development assistance in 2000totalled US $4.0m., of which US $3.8m. was bilateral aid. In 2002/03 New Zealand provided bilateral assistance worth $NZ2.05m. Aid from Australia totalled $A3.3m. in 1999/2000. The annual rate of inflation averaged 3.2% in 1990–99. The average rate was 1.0% in 1999, 5.3% in 2000 and 1.8% in 2001.

Tuvalu is a member of the Pacific Community, see p. 304, the Pacific Islands Forum (see p. 306) and the UN Economic and Social Commission for Asia and the Pacific (ESCAP, see p. 28).

In May 1993 the country was admitted to the Asian Development Bank (ADB, see p. 143).

According to UN criteria, Tuvalu is one of the world's least developed nations. Its economic development has been adversely affected by inclement weather (as illustrated by Cyclone Kelo, which devastated the islands of Niulakita and Nukulaelae in mid-1997) and inadequate infrastructure. Tuvalu's vulnerability to fluctuations in the price of copra on the international market and the country's dependence on imports have resulted in a persistent visible trade deficit; it has also remained reliant on foreign assistance for its development budget. Owing to a high rate of population growth and a drift from the outer islands to the capital, there is a serious problem of overcrowding on Funafuti. In August 1999 a US $4m. loan was secured to establish an outer islands development fund. It was expected that responsibility for development in the outer islands would be transferred from the Government to local communities. The Island Development Programme aimed not only to decentralize administration but also to raise the standards of local public services and to encourage the development of small businesses. The capital assets of the Falekaupule Trust Fund, which was charged with promoting sustainable increases in funding for the development of the outer islands, reached US $8.2m. in 2001. In February 2000, meanwhile, the sale of the '.tv' internet suffix (see Recent History) substantially increased the islands' income. Government revenues in that year were almost twice the projected budgeted amount. Proceeds from the sale were used to develop the country's infrastructure and were channelled largely into improving roads and the education system, also allowing the Government to investigate the possibility of buying land in Fiji, should the resettlement of Tuvalu's population become necessary. In an attempt to ensure the continuity of flights to Tuvalu, the Government committed itself to the purchase of majority shares in Air Fiji in March 2002, using a loan from the National Bank of Tuvalu. The ADB envisaged a GDP growth rate of 3.0% in 2002, with a similar rate being anticipated in 2003.

Education

Education is provided by the Government, and is compulsory between the ages of six and 15 years. In 1994 there were 12 primary schools, with a total of 1,811 pupils and 91 teachers in 1999. There was one secondary school in 2000, with 31 teachers and 345 pupils in 1990. The only tertiary institution is a Maritime Training School at Amatuku on Funafuti. Further training or vocational courses are available in Fiji and Kiribati. The University of the South Pacific (based in Fiji) has an extension centre on Funafuti. A programme of major reforms in the education system in Tuvalu, begun in the early 1990s, resulted in the lengthening of primary schooling (from six to eight years) and a compulsory two years of secondary education, as well as the introduction of vocational, technical and commerce-related courses at the Maritime Training School. Adult literacy was estimated at 98% at the 1991 census. Total government expenditure on education in 1998 amounted to $A277,813, equivalent to 40.3% of total budgetary expenditure.

Public Holidays

2003: 1 January (New Year's Day), 13 March (Commonwealth Day), 29 March–1 April (Easter), 8 June (Queen's Official Birthday), 4 August (National Children's Day), 1–2 October (Tuvalu Day, anniversary of independence), 14 November (Prince of Wales's Birthday), 25 December (Christmas Day), 26 December (Boxing Day).

2004: 1 January (New Year's Day), 13 March (Commonwealth Day), 9–12 April (Easter), 8 June (Queen's Official Birthday), 4 August (National Children's Day), 1–2 October (Tuvalu Day, anniversary of independence), 14 November (Prince of Wales's Birthday), 25 December (Christmas Day), 26 December (Boxing Day).

Statistical Survey

AREA AND POPULATION

Land Area: 26 sq km (10 sq miles).

Population: 8,229 (males 3,902; females 4,327) at mini-census of June 1985; 9,043 (males 4,376; females 4,667) at census of 17 November 1991; 10,450 (official estimate) at mid-2000; 10,660 at 1 July 2001 (Source: Asian Development Bank, *Key Indicators of Developing Asian and Pacific Countries*). *By atoll* (1996): Funafuti 3,836; Vaitupu 1,205; Niutao 749; Nanumea 818; Nukufetau 756; Nanumaga 644; Nui 608; Nukulaelae 370; Niulakita 75.

Density (2001): 410.0 per sq km.

Principal Town (population at mid-2000): Vaiaku (capital) 4,590.

Births and Deaths (1999): Birth rate 20.3 per 1,000; Death rate 7.6 per 1,000. Source: UN, *Statistical Yearbook for Asia and the Pacific*.

Expectation of Life (WHO estimates, years at birth): 63.5 (males 61.9; females 65.4) in 2001. Source: WHO, *World Health Report*.

Economically Active Population: In 1979 there were 936 people in paid employment, 50% of them in government service. In 1979 114 Tuvaluans were employed by the Nauru Phosphate Co, with a smaller number employed in Kiribati and about 255 on foreign ships. At the 1991 census the total economically active population (aged 15 years and over) stood at 2,383 (males 1,605, females 778).

AGRICULTURE, ETC.

Principal Crops (FAO estimates, metric tons, 2001): Coconuts 1,000; Fruit (excl. melons) 650. Source: FAO.

Livestock (FAO estimate, '000 head, 2001): Pigs 13. Source: FAO.

Livestock Products (FAO estimates, metric tons, 2001): Poultry meat 30, Pig meat 70, Hen eggs 12; Honey 1. Source: FAO.

Fishing (FAO estimates, metric tons, live weight, 2000): Total catch 400 (Skipjack tuna 260, Yellowfin tuna 15). Source: FAO, *Yearbook of Fishery Statistics*.

FINANCE

Currency and Exchange Rates: Australian and Tuvaluan currencies are both in use. Australian currency: 100 cents = 1 Australian dollar ($A). *Sterling, US Dollar and Euro Equivalents* (31 December 2002): £1 sterling = $A2.8467; US $1 = $A1.7661; €1 = $A1.8522; $A100 = £35.13 = US $56.62 = €53.99. *Average Exchange Rate* (US $ per Australian dollar): 0.5823 in 2000; 0.5176 in 2001; 0.5439 in 2002.

Budget (provisional, $A '000, 2001): Revenue 33,519; Expenditure 24,091. Source: Asian Development Bank, *Key Indicators of Developing Asian and Pacific Countries*.

Development Budget (provisional capital expenditure, $A '000, 1991): Australia 1,300; New Zealand 1,500; United Kingdom 1,500; Taiwan 2,340; European Development Fund 900; Japan 500; UNDP 900; France 250; USA 200; Total (incl. others) 10,077. *2000:* Total development expenditure $A30m.

Cost of Living (Consumer Price Index for Funafuti; base: November 1983 = 100): 161.5 in 1997; 162.5 in 1998; 173.8 in 1999. Source: Asian Development Bank, *Key Indicators of Developing Asian and Pacific Countries*.

Gross Domestic Product by Economic Activity ($A '000 at current prices, 1998): Agriculture 3,484; Mining 638; Manufacturing 881; Electricity, gas and water 574; Construction 2,952; Trade, restaurants and hotels 2,972; Transport storage and communications 1,380; Finance and real estate 2,376; Community, social and personal services 4,806; *Sub-total (incl. others)* 20,769; Indirect taxes, *less* subsidies 1,275; *GDP in purchasers' values* 22,045. Source: Asian Development Bank, *Key Indicators of Developing Asian and Pacific Countries*.

Balance of Payments ($A '000, 1996): Exports of goods f.o.b. 361; Imports of goods f.o.b. –10,740; *Trade balance* –10,379; Exports of services and other income 10,502; Imports of services and other income –8,758; *Balance on goods, services and income* 8,635; Unrequited transfers (net) 9,082; *Current balance* 447; Capital account (net) 2,088; Net errors and omissions –55; *Overall balance* 2,480. Source: Asian Development Bank, *Key Indicators of Developing Asian and Pacific Countries*.

EXTERNAL TRADE

Principal Commodities ($A '000, 1989): *Imports*: Food and live animals 1,514.6; Beverages and tobacco 201.6; Crude materials, inedible, except fuels 239.6; Mineral fuels, lubricants, etc. 660.7; Chemicals 369.1; Basic manufactures 1,001.3; Machinery and transport equipment 631.9; Miscellaneous manufactured articles 455.2; Total (incl. others) 5,170.3. *Exports*: (1990) Copra 29.0; Handicrafts 2.0; Stamps 147.0; Total 178.0; (1997) Copra 6.0.

Principal Trading Partners (US $ million, 2001): *Imports*: Australia 2.51; Fiji 9.25; Japan 0.24; New Zealand 1.09; United Kingdom 0.23; Total (incl. others) 14.12. *Exports*: Belgium 0.01; Fiji 0.11; Poland 0.02; Total (incl. others) 1.03 (Source: Asian Development Bank, *Key Indicators of Developing Asian and Pacific Countries*).

TRANSPORT

Shipping: *Merchant Fleet* (vessels registered, '000 grt at 31 December): 43 in 1999; 59 in 2000; 36 in 2001. Source: Lloyd's Register-Fairplay, *World Fleet Statistics*.

TOURISM

Tourist Arrivals: 1,029 in 1997; 1,077 in 1998; 1,504 in 2000.

Tourist Arrivals by Country of Residence (1998): Australia 163; Germany 35; Japan 71; New Zealand 104; United Kingdom 42; USA 101; Total (incl. others) 1,077 (Source: World Tourism Organization, *Yearbook of Tourism Statistics*, and South Pacific Tourism Organization).

COMMUNICATIONS MEDIA

Non-daily Newspapers (1996): 1; estimated circulation 300*.

Telephones (main lines, 2000): 660 in use†.

Radio Receivers (1997): 4,000 in use*.

Telefax Stations (1993): 10 in use‡.
* Source: UNESCO, *Statistical Yearbook*.
† Source: International Telecommunication Union.
‡ Source: UN, *Statistical Yearbook*.

EDUCATION

Primary (1998): 9 government schools, 3 church schools (1994); 91 teachers; 1,811 pupils.

General Secondary (1990): 1 government school (2000); 31 teachers; 345 pupils. In 1988 there were 13 kindergartens, three private primary schools, eight community training centres (mainly for the use of primary school leavers) and one maritime school for the training of 25 merchant seamen per year. Education reforms, begun in 1991, resulted in the closure of the largely unsuccessful community training centres and the expansion of the maritime school to offer vocational, technical and commerce-related courses.

Directory

The Constitution

A new Constitution came into effect at independence on 1 October 1978. Its main provisions are as follows:

The Constitution states that Tuvalu is a democratic sovereign state and that the Constitution is the Supreme Law. It guarantees protection of all fundamental rights and freedoms and provides for the determination of citizenship.

The British sovereign is represented by the Governor-General, who must be a citizen of Tuvalu and is appointed on the recommendation of the Prime Minister. The Prime Minister is elected by Parliament, and up to four other ministers are appointed by the Governor-General from among the members of Parliament, after consultation with the Prime Minister. The Cabinet, which is directly responsible to Parliament, consists of the Prime Minister and the other ministers, whose functions are to advise the Governor-General upon the government of Tuvalu. The Attorney-General is the principal legal adviser to the Government. Parliament is composed of 12 members directly elected by universal adult suffrage for four years, subject to dissolution, and is presided over by the Speaker (who is elected by the members). The Constitution also provides for the operation of a Judiciary (see Judicial System) and for an independent Public Service. Under a revised Constitution that took effect on 1 October 1986, the Governor-General no longer has the authority to reject the advice of the Government.

The Government

Head of State: HM Queen ELIZABETH II.

Governor-General: Sir TOMASI PUAPUA (took office June 1998).

CABINET
(April 2003)

Prime Minister, Minister for Foreign Affairs and Labour: SAUFATU SOPOANGA.

Deputy Prime Minister, Minister Works, Communications and Transport: MAATIA TOAFA.

Minister for Education, Sports and Culture, and Health: ALESANA KLIES SELUKA.

Minister for Finance and Economic Planning and and Industries: BIKENIBEU PAENIU.

Minister for Home Affairs and Rural Development: OTINIELU T TAUSI.

Minister for Natural Resources, Energy, the Environment and Tourism: SAMUELU P TEO.

MINISTRIES

The majority of ministries are situated on Vaiaku, Funafuti; the remainder are on Vaitupu.

Ministry of Tourism, Trade and Industries: see under Tourism.

Ministry of Works, Communications and Energy: PMB, Vaiaku, Funafuti; tel. 20055; fax 20772.

Legislature

PARLIAMENT

Parliament has 12 members who hold office for a term of up to four years. A general election was held on 25 July 2002. There are no political parties.

Speaker: SALOA TAUIA.

Diplomatic Representation

There are no embassies or high commissions in Tuvalu. The British High Commissioner in Fiji is also accredited as High Commissioner to Tuvalu. Other Ambassadors or High Commissioners accredited to Tuvalu include the Australian, New Zealand, US, French and Japanese Ambassadors in Fiji.

Judicial System

The Supreme Law is embodied in the Constitution. The High Court is the superior court of record, presided over by the Chief Justice, and has jurisdiction to consider appeals from judgments of the Magistrates' Courts and the Island Courts. Appeals from the High Court lie with the Court of Appeal in Fiji or, in the ultimate case, with the Judicial Committee of the Privy Council in the United Kingdom.

There are eight Island Courts with limited jurisdiction in criminal and civil cases.

Chief Justice: Sir GAVEN DONNE (non-resident).

Attorney-General: TELETI TEO.

Religion

CHRISTIANITY

Te Ekalesia Kelisiano Tuvalu (The Christian Church of Tuvalu): POB 2, Funafuti; tel. 20755; fax 20651; f. 1861; autonomous since 1968; derived from the Congregationalist foundation of the London Missionary Society; some 98% of the population are adherents; Pres. Rev. ETI KINE; Gen. Sec. Rev. FILOIMEA TELIFO.

Roman Catholic Church: Catholic Centre, POB 58, Funafuti; tel. and fax 20527; e-mail cathcent@tuvalu.tv; 109 adherents (31 December 1999); Superior Fr CAMILLE DESROSIERS.

Other churches with adherents in Tuvalu include the Church of Jesus Christ of Latter-day Saints (Mormons), the Jehovah's Witnesses, the New Apostolic Church and the Seventh-day Adventists.

BAHÁ'Í FAITH

National Spiritual Assembly: POB 48, Funafuti; tel. 20860; mems resident in 8 localities.

The Press

Tuvalu Echoes: Broadcasting and Information Office, Vaiaku, Funafuti; tel. 20731; fax 20732; f. 1984; fortnightly; English; Editor VAIATOA UALE; circ. 250.

Te Lama: Ekalesia Kelisiano Tuvalu, POB 2, Funafuti; tel. 20755; fax 20651; quarterly; religious; Pres. Rev. ETI KINE; Editor Rev. KITIONA TAUSI; circ. 1,000.

Broadcasting and Communications

TELECOMMUNICATIONS

Telecom Tuvalu: Vaiaku, Funafuti; tel. 20010; fax 20002.

BROADCASTING

Tuvalu Media Corporation: PMB, Vaiaku, Funafuti; tel. 20731; fax 20732; govt-owned; Chief Broadcasting and Information Officer PUSINELLI LAAFAI.

Radio

Radio Tuvalu: Broadcasting and Information Office, PMB, Vaiaku, Funafuti; tel. 20138; fax 20732; f. 1975; daily broadcasts in Tuvaluan and English, 43 hours per week; Programme Dir FALAHEA HALETI.

Finance

BANKS

Development Bank of Tuvalu: PMB 9, Vaiaku, Funafuti; tel. 20199; fax 20850; f. 1993 to replace the Business Development Advisory Bureau.

National Bank of Tuvalu: POB 13, Vaiaku, Funafuti; tel. 20803; fax 20802; e-mail nbt@tuvalu.tv; f. 1980; commercial bank; govt-owned; ('000 A$) cap. 471.0, res 1,479.0, dep. 24,808.9 (Dec. 1999); Chair. AFELE PITA; Gen. Man. IONATANA PEIA; brs on all atolls.

Trade and Industry

GOVERNMENT AGENCY

National Fishing Corporation of Tuvalu (NAFICOT): POB 93, Funafuti; tel. 20724; fax 20800; fishing vessel operators; seafood processing and marketing; agents for diesel engine spare parts, fishing supplies and marine electronics; Gen. Man. SEMU SOPOANGA TAAFAKI.

CHAMBER OF COMMERCE

Tuvalu Chamber of Commerce: POB 27, Vaiaku, Funafuti; tel. 20917; fax 20646; e-mail tpasefika@hotmail.com; Chair. MATANILE IOSEFA; Sec. TEO PASEFIKA.

UTILITIES

Electricity

Tuvalu Electricity Corporation (TEC): POB 32, Funafuti; tel. 20350; fax 20351; e-mail thomas@tuvalu.tv.

CO-OPERATIVE

Tuvalu Co-operative Society Ltd: POB 11, Funafuti; tel. 20747; fax 20748; f. 1979 by amalgamation of the eight island socs; controls retail trade in the islands; Gen. Man. MONISE LAAFAI; Registrar SIMETI LOPATI.

Tuvalu Coconut Traders Co-operative: Contact TAAI KATALAKE.

TRADE UNION

Tuvalu Overseas Seamen's Union (TOSU): POB 99, Funafuti; tel. 20609; fax 20610; e-mail tosu@tuvalu.tv; Gen. Sec. TOMMY ALEFAIO.

Transport

ROADS

Funafuti has some impacted-coral roads; elsewhere, tracks exist.

SHIPPING

There is a deep-water lagoon at the point of entry, Funafuti, and ships are able to enter the lagoon at Nukufetau. Irregular shipping services connect Tuvalu with Fiji and elsewhere. The Government operates an inter-island vessel.

CIVIL AVIATION

In 1992 a new runway was constructed with EU aid to replace the grass landing strip on Funafuti. Air Marshall Islands operates three-weekly service between Funafuti, Nadi (Fiji) and Majuro (Marshall Islands). In June 1995 Tuvalu, Kiribati, the Marshall Islands and Nauru agreed to begin discussions on the establishment of a joint regional airline. The Government of Tuvalu planned to purchase a majority shareholding in Air Fiji in 2002.

Tourism

In 1994 there was one hotel, with 17 rooms, on Funafuti. There were an estimated 1,077 tourist arrivals in 1998. In that year 15.1% of tourists came from Australia, 9.4% from the USA, 9.7% from New Zealand, 6.6% from Japan, 3.9% from the United Kingdom and 3.3% from Germany. Tourist arrivals totalled 1,504 in 2000.

Ministry of Tourism, Trade and Commerce: PMB, Vaiaku, Funafuti; tel. 20184; fax 20829.

Tuvalu Tourism Office: PMB, Funafuti; tel. 20184; fax 20829.

UGANDA

Introductory Survey

Location, Climate, Language, Religion, Flag, Capital

The Republic of Uganda is a land-locked equatorial country in East Africa, bordered by Sudan to the north, the Democratic Republic of the Congo to the west, Kenya to the east and Rwanda, Tanzania and Lake Victoria to the south. The climate is tropical, with temperatures, moderated by the altitude of the country, varying between 15°C and 30°C. The official language is English and there are many local languages, the most important of which is Luganda. More than 60% of the population follow Christian beliefs, while about 5% are Muslims. The national flag (proportions 2 by 3) has six horizontal stripes: black, gold, red, black, gold and red. In the centre is a white disc containing a crested crane. The capital is Kampala.

Recent History

Formerly a British protectorate, Uganda became an independent member of the Commonwealth on 9 October 1962. The Government was led by Dr Milton Obote, leader of the Uganda People's Congress (UPC) from 1960 and Prime Minister from April 1962. At independence the country comprised four regions, including the kingdom of Buganda, which had federal status. Exactly one year after independence Uganda became a republic, with Mutesa II, Kabaka (King) of Buganda, as first President. In February 1966 Obote led a successful coup against the Kabaka, and in April he became executive President. In September 1967 a new Constitution was introduced, establishing a unitary republic, and Buganda was brought under the control of the central Government. After an assassination attempt on President Obote in December 1969 all opposition parties were banned.

Obote was overthrown in January 1971 by the army, led by Maj.-Gen. (later Field Marshal) Idi Amin Dada, who assumed full executive powers and suspended political activity. The National Assembly was dissolved in February, when Amin declared himself Head of State, took over legislative powers and suspended parts of the 1967 Constitution. Obote fled to Tanzania. In August 1972 Amin, proclaiming an 'economic war' to free Uganda from foreign domination, undertook a mass expulsion of non-citizen Asians (who comprised the majority of the resident Asian population), thereby incurring widespread international condemnation.

Amin's regime was characterized by the ruthless elimination of suspected opponents, mass flights of refugees to neighbouring countries and periodic purges of the army (which, in turn, perpetrated numerous atrocities). In February 1977 the Anglican Archbishop of Uganda and two government ministers were murdered, arousing further world-wide indignation. Relations within the East African Community (EAC), comprising Uganda, Kenya and Tanzania, deteriorated during the 1970s. In February 1976 Amin claimed that large areas of western Kenya were historically part of Uganda, and in November 1978 Uganda annexed the Kagera salient from Tanzania. In early 1979 an invasion force comprising Tanzanian troops and the Uganda National Liberation Army (UNLA), formed by Ugandan exiles, gained control of the southern region of Uganda. Amin's forces capitulated, and in April a Tanzanian assault force entered Kampala. The remaining pro-Amin troops were defeated in June. Amin fled initially to Libya, and in 1980 took up permanent residence in Saudi Arabia.

A provisional Government, the National Executive Council (NEC), was established in April 1979 from the ranks of the Uganda National Liberation Front (UNLF, a coalition of 18 previously exiled groups), with Dr Yusuf Lule, a former vice-chancellor of Makerere University, as President. When Lule attempted to reshuffle the NEC in June, opposition from within the UNLF forced his resignation. Lule was succeeded by Godfrey Binaisa (a former Attorney-General), who was, in turn, overthrown by the Military Commission of the UNLF in May 1980, after he had decided to allow only UNLF members to stand in parliamentary elections and attempted to reorganize the leadership of the UNLA. The elections, in December, were contested by four parties and won by the UPC, with Obote, who remained its leader, becoming President for the second time. The defeated parties complained of gross electoral malpractice by UPC supporters.

The Obote Government was subject to constant attack from guerrilla groups operating inside the country. Hundreds of Obote's opponents were detained, including Democratic Party (DP) members of the National Assembly, and several newspapers were banned. Following the withdrawal of Tanzanian troops in June 1981, there were reports from the West Nile Region of further atrocities by Ugandan soldiers. In January 1982 the Uganda Popular Front was formed to co-ordinate, from abroad, the activities of the main opposition groups in exile: the Uganda Freedom Movement (UFM), the Uganda National Rescue Front and the National Resistance Movement (NRM, led by Lule and his former Minister of Defence, Yoweri Museveni). The NRM had a military wing, the National Resistance Army (NRA), led by Museveni. Lule died in 1985, whereupon Museveni became sole leader of the NRM and NRA. From 1982 thousands of Ugandans were reported to have fled to Sudan, Rwanda and Zaire, to escape fighting between guerrilla forces and UNLA troops. In March 1983, during a campaign by the UNLA to repel an NRA offensive, attacks on refugee camps resulted in the deaths of hundreds of civilians, and more than 100,000 people were displaced. The NRA denied involvement in the massacres.

In July 1985 Obote was overthrown in a military coup, led by Brig. (later Lt-Gen.) Basilio Okello. (The deposed President was subsequently granted political asylum by Zambia.) A Military Council, headed by Lt-Gen. (later Gen.) Tito Okello, the Commander-in-Chief of the army, was established to govern the country, pending elections to be held one year later. In subsequent months groups that had been in opposition to Obote, with the exception of the NRA and the NRM (see below), reached agreement with the new administration, and accepted positions on the Military Council. An amnesty was declared for exiles who had supported Amin. The UNLA allegedly continued to perpetrate atrocities under the Okello regime.

In August 1985 the NRA, led by Museveni, entered into negotiations with the Government (under the auspices of President Daniel arap Moi of Kenya), while conducting a simultaneous military campaign to overthrow Okello. During the following two months the NRA gained control of large areas of the country. In December the NRA and the Government signed a peace agreement; the terms of the accord were never implemented, however, and on 26 January 1986 the NRA took control of Kampala by force and dissolved the Military Council. Okello fled to Sudan, and then to Tanzania. On 29 January Museveni was sworn in as President, and in February he announced the formation of a new Cabinet, comprising mainly members of the NRA and NRM, but also representatives of other political groups including the DP, the UPC, the UFM, the Federal Democratic Movement (FEDEMO), and three members of the previous administration. A National Resistance Council (NRC) was formed to act in place of a legislature for an indefinite period. All party political activity was banned in March, although political organizations were not proscribed. At a summit meeting in March the Heads of State of all the countries adjoining Uganda pledged their support for Museveni.

Initial attempts to integrate defeated rebel forces into the NRA were only partially successful, and guerrilla groups remained active in northern Uganda. An association of opposition groups, the Uganda People's Democratic Movement (UPDM), was formed in May 1986. In October 26 people were arrested and charged with treason, among them Andrew Kayiira, the Minister of Energy and leader of the UFM, and David Lwanga, the Minister of Environment Protection and leader of the FEDEMO. Although treason charges against eight of the accused, including Lwanga and Kayiira, were retracted in February 1987, the murder of Kayiira in March caused the UFM to withdraw its support from the Government. Three of the accused were sentenced to death in March 1988.

In June 1987 the NRC offered an amnesty to rebels (except those accused of murder or rape). In August, however, the UPDM joined with a faction of the FEDEMO and another opposition group, the United National Front, to form an alliance seeking Museveni's overthrow. The most widespread source of disruption during 1987 was a rebellion that had arisen in northern and eastern Uganda in late 1986 by the cultish 'Holy Spirit' movement; between December 1986 and November 1987 some 5,000 ill-equipped 'Holy Spirit' fighters were reportedly killed in clashes with the NRA. By December 1987 the rebellion had been suppressed, and its leader had escaped to Kenya. Surviving members of the movement, however, regrouped as the Lord's Resistance Army (LRA—see below). In early 1988 the NRC extended the period of its amnesty to guerrilla groups: by mid-April it was reported that almost 30,000 rebels had surrendered. Many of these were integrated into the NRA. In October 24 people were arrested and charged with plotting against the Government.

In February 1989 the first national election since 1980 was held. The NRC, hitherto composed solely of presidential nominees, was expanded from 98 to 278 members, to include 210 elected representatives. While 20 ministerial posts were reserved for nominated members of the NRC, 50 were allocated to elected members. Also in February Museveni appointed a constitutional commission to assess public opinion on Uganda's political future and to draft a new constitution.

In October 1989 (despite opposition from the DP) the NRC approved draft legislation to prolong the Government's term of office by five years from January 1990 (when its mandate had been due to expire): the NRM justified seeking to extend its rule by claiming that it required further time in which to prepare a new constitution, organize elections, eliminate guerrilla activity, improve the judiciary, police force and civil service and rehabilitate the country's infrastructure. In November 1989 Museveni replaced the Minister of State for Defence and members of the NRA command, reportedly as a measure to combat corruption and indiscipline in the armed forces. It was announced in January 1990 that several army officers and civilians had been charged with plotting to overthrow the Government. In March the NRM extended the national ban on party political activity (imposed in March 1986) for a further five years. In the following month the Minister of Culture, Youth and Sports, Brig. Moses Ali, was removed from his post and charged with plotting terrorist activities. (Ali was subsequently acquitted of this charge, but in January 1991 was found guilty of illegally possessing ammunition.) In July 1990 the leader of the UPDM, Eric Otema Allimadi, signed a peace accord with the Government; nevertheless, some members of the rebel organization reportedly did not take advantage of the Government's continuing amnesty. In April 1991 Daniel Omara Atubo, the Minister of State for Foreign Affairs and Regional Co-operation, was arrested, together with two other members of the NRC, and charged with plotting to overthrow the Museveni administration; 15 other people (including further members of the NRC) were subsequently arrested on the same charge. During April the NRA initiated a campaign to combat continuing rebel activity in the north and east: by July it was reported that at least 1,500 guerrillas had been killed and more than 1,000 arrested. In May Museveni formally invited all former resident Asians expelled at the time of the Amin regime to return, pledging the restitution of expropriated property. In October 1992 the Government undertook a three-year programme to reduce the size of the NRA by about one-half, in response to pressure from the international donor community to reduce the exorbitant military budget.

At the end of December 1992 the Constitutional Commission presented its draft Constitution to the Government. The draft was published in March 1993, and in the following month the NRC passed legislation authorizing the establishment of a Constituent Assembly (see below). In July 1993 the NRC adopted a constitutional amendment revoking the abolition of traditional rulers, as provided for under the 1967 Constitution. Restored traditional rulers would, however, have only ceremonial significance.

In January 1994 the Ugandan National Democratic Alliance and the Ugandan Federal Army agreed to suspend their armed struggle, under the provisions of a government amnesty, and in March the surrender of senior members of the Ruwenzunuru Kingdom Freedom Movement in the south-west signified the end of a conflict dating from independence. During January the Government took part in negotiations with the LRA. However, following the collapse of the discussions the LRA intensified guerrilla activities in northern Uganda. During 1994–99 large numbers of security forces were deployed in the region, repre-

senting a considerable burden on national resources; they failed, however, to suppress the rebellion (see below).

At elections to the 288-member Constituent Assembly, which took place on 28 March 1994, more than 1,500 candidates contested the 214 elective seats. Although the elections were officially conducted on a non-party basis, NRM members were believed to have secured the majority of votes in the centre, west and south-west of the country, whereas UPC and DP members, who advocated an immediate return to multi-party politics, secured the most seats in the north and east. The Constituent Assembly, which also comprised nominated representatives of the armed forces, political parties, trade unions, and youth and disabled organizations, debated and amended the draft Constitution, finally enacting it in September 1995. The Constitution, under whose terms a national referendum on the future introduction of a multi-party political system took place in 2000 (see below), was promulgated in October 1995.

A presidential election took place on 9 May 1996, at which Museveni was returned to office, winning 74.2% of the votes cast. The election was pronounced free and fair by international observers. Museveni's main rival, Paul Ssemogerere (the Chairman of the DP, who had resigned as Second Deputy Prime Minister and Minister of Public Service in June 1995), took 23.7% of the votes. As the unofficial representative of an electoral alliance between the DP and the UPC, Ssemogerere was widely perceived to be associated with the UPC's exiled leader, Dr Milton Obote. Legislative elections took place in June 1996. The total membership of the NRC, redesignated the Parliament under the new Constitution, was reduced from 278 to 276, comprising 214 elected and 62 nominated representatives. Also in June elections were held for new local councils (to replace the resistance committees). In July Museveni appointed an enlarged Government.

From the mid-1990s the Museveni administration was greatly preoccupied with combating insurrections perpetrated by three main rebel groups in northern and western Uganda. In the north the LRA (reportedly backed by Sudan) was becoming increasingly disruptive. During 1993–98 the LRA was alleged to have killed as many as 10,000 people, while some 220,000 sought refuge in protected camps; economic activity in the region was devastated. The LRA's use of abducted children as soldiers (reportedly some 10,000 by early 1999) attracted widespread international condemnation. The Government strongly resisted pressure to resume negotiations with the LRA, prompting some speculation that Museveni (a Southerner) might be prepared to profit from the disablement of opposition strongholds in the northern region. In May 1999, however, the Government appeared to modify its policy towards the LRA by offering it an amnesty and promising its leader, Joseph Kony, a cabinet post in the event of his being democratically elected. In the west, meanwhile, the Uganda People's Defence Forces (UPDF, as the NRA had become) fought intermittently with two rebel groups: the Allied Democratic Front (ADF), mainly comprising Ugandan Islamic fundamentalist rebels, exiled Rwandan Hutu militiamen and former soldiers from Zaire (which became the Democratic Republic of the Congo—DRC—in May 1997), and the West Nile Bank Front (WNBF). Although WNBF activities subsided in mid-1997, following the killing of several hundred of its members by Sudanese rebels, the ADF mounted a persistent terror campaign from mid-1997 against western Ugandan targets, threatening tourism to the region and disrupting economic activity. In May 1999 Roman Catholic leaders in the Ruwenzori region offered to mediate between the Ugandan Government and the ADF, which was believed to bear the main responsibility for a series of bomb attacks on civilian targets in Kampala from 1998. In August, confronted by escalating security problems on various fronts, the Government was reported to have recalled for military service some 10,000 demobilized troops, and in September the command structure of the UPDF was reorganized. In October the High Court dismissed charges of treason against some 340 alleged members of the now defunct WNBF who had been detained for more than two years. In November the UPDF launched a new offensive against the ADF in the Ruwenzori region. In December the Parliament adopted legislation (the so-called Amnesty Bill) that extended (not without conditions, in some cases) an amnesty to all rebels in opposition to President Museveni. The ADF's response was apparently to intensify its struggle. In January 2000 the Chief of Staff of the army publicly questioned the likelihood of the Amnesty Bill's persuading the ADF to cease hostilities. In February President Museveni was reported to be personally co-ordinating military operations against the ADF in western Uganda, and to have renewed his appeal to the rebels to avail themselves of the new amnesty legislation.

In July 1999 legislation was enacted providing for the proposed referendum on a multi-party political system to take place in 2000 as planned. However, most political parties announced that they would boycott the referendum on the grounds that it would be manipulated by the NRM for its own objectives. In October a US-based human rights organization, Human Rights Watch, criticized Uganda's political system and claimed that the country was moving away from democracy. Ugandan political leaders had criticized the readiness of some Western donors (in particular those that formed the Referendum 2000 Group in December 1999) to support the referendum process, claiming that by so doing they were legitimizing the prevailing suspension of active political opposition. In February 2000 Uganda's Multi-Party National Referendum Committee appealed for a postponement of the referendum on the grounds that the Electoral Commission had not made funds available to some advocates of a return to political pluralism. In the same month the Referendum 2000 Group expressed concern at the Government's failure to implement measures on which it had made conditional its support of the referendum process. At the referendum, which proceeded on 29 June, 90.7% of participants voted in favour of retaining the existing 'no-party' political system.

A presidential election was held on 12 March 2001. The election had been scheduled for 7 March, but was delayed to allow the Electoral Commission time to check and amend the electoral register after it was found to contain about 2.5m. more voters than there were citizens eligible to vote. At the election, which had a participation rate of 70%, Museveni was re-elected President, winning 69.3% of the votes cast. His main challenger, Kiiza Besigye, won 27.8%, while Aggrey Awori and Mohamed Kibirige Mayanja won 1.4% and 1.0% respectively. There were some allegations of electoral malpractice and intimidation of opposition politicians, with up to 15% of the votes compromised by serious irregularities; however, international observers held that this did not affect the overall result, and that the Ugandan people had been able to express their democratic will. Besigye, who had served with Museveni during the civil war as his personal physician, represented the first real challenge to Museveni's authority. He commanded considerable support within the army and was perceived as similar enough to Museveni to allay public fears of change and a mistrust of politicians, yet different enough for his promises of reform to appear convincing. His criticism of the UPDF's continuing involvement in the civil war in the DRC was also very popular.

Legislative elections were held on 26 June 2001, at which 50 parliamentarians, including 10 ministers, failed to secure re-election. The rate of voter participation was reported as being low. The total number of seats in Parliament was increased to 292 (comprising 214 elected and 78 nominated representatives), of which the NRM reportedly secured more than 70%. Earlier in June government representatives and local leaders had held talks with the LRA in Gulu, northern Uganda. In July Museveni appointed a new Cabinet, which included the 10 ministers who had failed to retain their parliamentary seats in June. Notably, Amama Mbabazi was appointed as Minister of Defence, a portfolio hitherto held by Museveni. Besigye fled to the USA in August, claiming to have feared for his personal security in Uganda, and subsequently held talks with senior US officials. Local elections were held on 4 January 2002. In January 2003 some 200,000 members of the Baganda tribe were reported to have demonstrated in Kampala for a new federal constitution and semi-autonomous status for the region of Buganda.

In late May 2003 Museveni effected a cabinet reshuffle, notably appointing Prof. Gilbert Bukenya as Vice-President, following the resignation of the incumbent, Dr Specioza Kazibwe, and dismissing a number of ministers who had recently expressed opposition to a proposal to revoke the current two-term limit on the presidential mandate.

During 1987 Uganda's relations with neighbouring Kenya deteriorated, with the Museveni Government accusing the regime of President Daniel arap Moi of sheltering and supporting Ugandan rebels. In March the Kenyan authorities expelled hundreds of Ugandans. When, in October, Uganda stationed troops at the two countries' common border, Kenya threatened to retaliate with force against any attempts by Ugandan military personnel to cross the frontier in pursuit of rebels. In December there were clashes between Kenyan and Ugandan security forces, and the border was temporarily closed.

In late December, following the intervention of the Organization of African Unity (now the African Union, see p. 130), discussions between the Heads of State of the two countries led to a resumption of normal traffic across the border. However, several incursions into Kenya by Ugandan troops were subsequently reported. In November 1994 the Presidents of Uganda, Kenya and Tanzania met in Arusha, Tanzania, and established a permanent commission for co-operation between the three countries. During early 1995 Kenya protested strongly to the UN following the granting of refugee status in Uganda to an alleged Kenyan guerrilla leader; the Ugandan Government subsequently claimed to have deported the dissident to an unspecified third country. In March 1996 Museveni, Moi and President Benjamin Mkapa of Tanzania, meeting in Nairobi, Kenya, formally inaugurated the Secretariat of the Permanent Tripartite Commission for East African Co-operation, which aimed to revive the EAC (see p. 339). A treaty for the re-establishment of the EAC, providing for the creation of a free trade area (with the eventual introduction of a single currency), for the development of infrastructure, tourism and agriculture within the Community and for the establishment of a regional legislature and court was ratified by the three Heads of State in November 1999. In January 2003 it was reported that Kenyan tribesmen had crossed the border into Nakapiripirit province and attacked local herdsmen, resulting in the deaths of more than 50 people.

During 1988 tension arose along Uganda's border with Zaire (now the DRC—see above), owing to a number of attacks by Zairean troops on NRA units; further border clashes occurred in 1992. In November 1996 Ugandan rebels were reportedly operating from within Zaire with the support of Zairean troops. In late 1996 and early 1997 the Ugandan authorities repeatedly denied allegations that Ugandan forces were occupying territory in eastern Zaire; however, it was widely reported that the Museveni Government supplied armaments and tactical support to Laurent-Désiré Kabila's Alliance des forces démocratiques pour la libération du Congo-Zaïre, which took power in Zaire in May 1997. The Museveni administration, however, subsequently withdrew its support from the new regime in the DRC, as President Kabila made no attempt to sever the ongoing supply of armaments to Ugandan guerrilla groups operating in the DRC–Uganda border region. In August 1998 the Museveni administration, in co-operation with the Rwandan Government, deployed troops in the eastern part of the DRC, avowedly to protect Ugandan and Rwandan security interests; the two Governments formed a joint military command in November 1998. The Kabila regime accused Uganda and Rwanda of creating, with DRC rebels, a Tutsi-dominated alliance with expansionist ambitions; it was also alleged that the DRC's two eastern neighbours were illegally exploiting mineral interests in the area occupied by their forces. In April 1999 Museveni and Kabila were reported to have met in Sirte, Libya, (without their Rwandan counterpart) and to have signed a cease-fire agreement, which entailed the withdrawal of all Ugandan troops and their replacement by an African peace-keeping force. In July, however, the Sirte agreement gave way to another, comprehensive cease-fire agreement, the Lusaka accord, concluded in Lusaka, Zambia, by the Heads of State of all the countries engaged militarily in the civil war in the DRC, including those of Angola, Namibia and Zimbabwe, who had supported the DRC Government. Under the terms of the Lusaka accord, the cease-fire was to be monitored by a joint military commission, while a UN peace-keeping force was to be deployed on the withdrawal from the DRC of all foreign troops. However, the implementation of the Lusaka accord did not proceed smoothly. In May tensions had arisen between Uganda and Rwanda when the DRC rebel group that they had been jointly supporting divided into two factions, backed, respectively, by the Ugandan and Rwandan Governments. In mid-August these tensions escalated into hostilities between Ugandan and Rwandan armed forces around the city of Kisangani, in the DRC. In November President Museveni and President Bizimungu of Rwanda met in Uganda and reaffirmed their commitment to the Lusaka accord. In May 2000 the DRC Government signed an agreement in which it consented to the deployment of 500 UN military observers and 5,000 support troops, the Mission des nations unies en République démocratique du Congo (MONUC, see p. 66), to monitor the by-now frequently violated cease-fire that had been inaugurated by the Lusaka accord. Almost immediately afterwards, however, hostilities erupted again between Ugandan and Rwandan troops in Kisangani. In mid-May Uganda and Rwanda withdrew their troops in Kisangani to positions some 100 km from the city, to prepare the way for its eventual cession to the control of MONUC. In September Uganda claimed to have withdrawn all its troops from zones declared as demilitarized under the Lusaka accord. In December Uganda, along with the other parties in the conflict, met in Harare, Zimbabwe, to sign an agreement under which all forces would withdraw 15 km from positions of military engagement by January 2001, to allow UN peace-keepers to ensure that the cease-fire called for in the Lusaka accord was being observed. In January 2001 President Kabila was assassinated by one of his bodyguards; he was succeeded by his son, Joseph Kabila, who immediately engaged in international efforts to end the conflict. In mid-March the groups involved in the conflict, under the aegis of the UN Security Council, commenced the military disengagement of their forces. However, factions subsequently refused to proceed with the withdrawal from military positions until MONUC guaranteed security in the region. Following the publication of a UN report, in April, alleging that Burundi, Rwanda and Uganda were illegally exploiting the DRC's mineral reserves, Museveni announced that Uganda would withdraw its remaining troops from the DRC and pull out of the UN-sponsored Lusaka accord. In late 2001 Rwandan troops occupied positions in the eastern DRC that had been vacated by the UPDF in June of that year, prompting fears that clashes would again erupt between Rwanda and Ugandan forces. Furthermore, each side accused the other of supporting rebel groups. In October it was reported that a new rebel group, known as the People's Redemption Army, had been formed in the Rwanda-controlled part of the DRC by dissident UPDF officers who had defected earlier in the year. However, following negotiations between Museveni and Kagame (now the President of Rwanda), which were held in London, United Kingdom, in November, both sides exchanged delegations of inspectors to verify that the dissidents based in their respective countries were not receiving government support, and relations began to stabilize once more. Despite the redeployment of Ugandan troops in the north-east of the DRC in January 2002, to prevent escalating fighting between the rebel factions from reaching the border with Uganda, negotiations between Uganda and Rwanda continued, with British mediation, and in April 2002 the two countries signed a peace agreement in Kigali. In September a peace accord was signed by Uganda and the DRC in Luanda, Angola, providing for the normalization of relations between the two countries and the complete withdrawal of Ugandan troops from the DRC. Uganda subsequently began the withdrawal of its troops, although the UN permitted some of them to remain near the north-eastern town of Bunia to assist with maintaining security. In March 2003 skirmishes between Ugandan forces and a local rebel group were reported near Bunia, as was the redeployment of Rwandan troops on the border with the DRC, prompting the Ugandan Government to dispatch reinforcements to the region. The Governments of Uganda and the DRC and local rebel groups subsequently signed a cease-fire agreement, although later that month the Rwandan Government threatened to resume military engagement in eastern DRC if the UN failed to secure the withdrawal of all Ugandan troops. In response to the continuing violence around Bunia, which was in contravention of the peace agreement, the UN Security Council issued a resolution calling for increased numbers of military and humanitarian observers to be stationed in the DRC under the MONUC mandate, and the immediate withdrawal of Ugandan troops. On the same day it was reported that the Rwandan legislature had approved the redeployment of troops in eastern DRC. Most Ugandan troops were reported to have withdrawn from the DRC by early May.

From the late 1980s Sudanese troops reportedly made repeated incursions into Ugandan territory in pursuit of Sudanese rebels. In early 1992 nearly 80,000 Sudanese refugees fled to Uganda, followed by a further 50,000 in August 1993. Relations between the two countries deteriorated seriously in 1994, when each Government accused the other of harbouring and supporting their respective outlawed guerrilla groups; in April 1995 Uganda severed diplomatic relations with Sudan. In October 1995 intense fighting between Sudanese rebels and government forces resulted in the displacement of several thousand Ugandans residing in the border region. In November the Ugandan Government dispatched troops to protect the area. Subsequent allegations by the Sudanese authorities that Ugandan forces were massing on the two countries' common border in order to invade southern Sudan were strongly denied by the Museveni regime. In the following month, however, Museveni threatened to launch military assaults into Sudan in retaliation for the

Sudanese Government's alleged continuing support for the LRA. Sudanese troops shelled the border area for three consecutive days in April 1996, provoking strong protest from the Ugandan Government. In September 1996 Sudan and Uganda resumed diplomatic relations, and in the following month a preliminary accord was signed in the Iranian capital, Tehran. Relations between the two countries did not, however, improve: in September 1996 and in February 1997 it was alleged that Sudanese aircraft had once again attacked northern Uganda, and in April, despite a continuing dialogue mediated by Iran and Libya, the Sudanese authorities claimed that their forces had killed several hundred Ugandan soldiers who had been assisting Sudanese rebels from within Sudanese territory. At the end of August President Nelson Mandela of South Africa mediated a meeting between the Ugandan and Sudanese leaderships, the outcome of which was described as 'positive'. In December, however, the Museveni administration banned a number of Sudanese non-governmental organizations which were accused of providing assistance to Ugandan rebel groups. In February 1998 Uganda deployed troops along the Uganda–Sudan border, with the aim of preventing LRA rebels from taking captives over the frontier into Sudan. In September Uganda denied allegations by the Sudanese Government that it had made incursions into Sudanese territory and that it had shelled border villages and refugee camps. In December, in Kenya, the Presidents of Uganda and Sudan unexpectedly signed an accord that set out a comprehensive resolution of all of the two countries' differences. The so-called Nairobi Agreement, which had been mediated by former US President Jimmy Carter, committed Uganda and Sudan to the renunciation of force as a means of settling disputes; to the disarmament and disbandment of terrorist groups and the cessation of support for rebel groups; to the repatriation of prisoners of war; and to the restoration of full diplomatic relations by the end of February 2000. Joint committees were to be established to oversee the implementation of the Agreement from January 2000. In June negotiations to uphold the peace process were held in the USA. Further meetings were held in Kampala in September, during which Uganda and Sudan agreed to disarm the LRA, which had been active throughout 2000, and to relocate it at least 1,000 km deeper within Sudanese territory. It was also agreed that the Governments of Uganda, Sudan, Libya and Egypt, in collaboration with the Carter Center, Canada, the UN Children's Fund and the office of the UN High Commissioner for Refugees (UNHCR), would set up a body to find and repatriate all children abducted from Sudan by rebel groups. Rebel attacks continued in northern Uganda, however, and in January 2001 President Museveni threatened to send troops to pursue rebel groups into Sudanese territory. In February there were reports of incursions by Sudanese military aircraft into Ugandan airspace. In the same month Museveni deployed troops in northern Uganda, reportedly to defend against possible LRA attacks during the presidential election. In mid-May the Sudanese President, Omar al-Bashir, attended Museveni's presidential inauguration in Kampala. Following a Libyan diplomatic initiative in that month, Sudan and Uganda agreed to restore diplomatic relations. In August the Ugandan embassy reopened in the Sudanese capital, Khartoum, and a chargé d'affaires was appointed; relations were upgraded to an ambassadorial level in April 2002. In August 2001 al-Bashir announced that his Government would no longer provide support for the LRA, and in December bank accounts used by the LRA in London, United Kingdom, were frozen. Negotiations between Sudan and Uganda continued successfully throughout early 2002, with both countries remaining committed to implementing the Nairobi Agreement. In March it was announced that Sudan was to allow the UPDF to deploy forces within its borders in order to pursue operations against the LRA, and later that month the Ugandan Government announced that its troops had captured all four main bases in Sudan belonging to the LRA. In November the Sudanese authorities agreed to extend permission for Ugandan troops to remain on its territory for as long as Uganda deemed necessary.

During the late 1980s an estimated 250,000 Rwandan refugees were sheltering in Uganda. Relations with Rwanda deteriorated in October 1990, following the infiltration of northern Rwanda by an invasion force of some 4,000 Rwandan rebels who had been based in Uganda; their leader, Maj.-Gen. Fred Rwigyema (who was killed by the Rwandan armed forces), was a deputy commander of the NRA and a former Ugandan Deputy Minister of Defence. In November President Museveni dismissed all non-Ugandan members of the NRA. In February 1991 a conference was held on the Rwandan security situation; an amnesty was agreed for all Rwandans who were exiled abroad, and the rebels were urged to observe a cease-fire. Nevertheless, the allegedly Uganda-based Rwandan rebels continued to operate in northern Rwanda during 1991–93. In January 1992 it was reported that 64,000 Ugandans residing near the two countries' common border had been displaced, owing to cross-border shelling by Rwandan troops. In August 1993 the UN Observer Mission Uganda-Rwanda (subsequently disbanded) stationed troops on the Ugandan side of this border to verify that no military assistance reached Rwandan rebels. In May 1994 the Ugandan authorities appealed for emergency assistance, claiming that the corpses of thousands of victims of massacres taking place in Rwanda were contaminating the water supply of districts abutting Lake Victoria. The victory in Rwanda of the Front patriotique rwandais (FPR) in mid-1994 brought about a significant change in bilateral relations; Maj.-Gen. Paul Kagame, Rwandan Vice-President and Minister of National Defence, had previously served in the Ugandan NRA, as had other members of the FPR administration. In August 1995 Museveni made an official visit to Rwanda, and both countries made commitments to enhance economic and social co-operation. In August 1998 Uganda and Rwanda jointly deployed troops in the DRC (see above). The Ugandan Government has strenuously denied allegations that a Uganda-Rwanda military alliance has been formed with the ultimate aim of extending Tutsi rule as far as Burundi and the DRC. Relations between the two countries worsened again during their involvement in the hostilities in the DRC; there were frequent reports of fighting, especially around the town of Kisangani. However, this tension eased when both armies withdrew from Kisangani during May 2000 (see above), and in July Museveni and Kagame met to discuss relations between their respective countries. In January 2001 at least 15,000 Rwandan refugees, most of them Hutu, entered Uganda following an order in Tanzania to expel all non-citizens. A further 7,000 Rwandan refugees had entered Uganda through Tanzania by July. Tension between Rwanda and Uganda increased in March 2003, when the Rwandan Government approved the redeployment of troops in eastern DRC (see above), in response to the continuing presence of Ugandan troops in the north-east of that country.

At the end of 2001, according to UNHCR, there were a total of 199,736 refugees in Uganda, including 176,766 from Sudan (compared with 212,156 at the beginning of the year), 14,288 from Rwanda and 7,613 from the DRC.

Government

Following the January 1986 coup, power was vested in a broad-based interim Government, headed by an executive President. A National Resistance Council (NRC) was formed to legislate by decree. In addition, resistance committees were formed at local and district level. Political activity was suspended, although political parties were not banned. National elections were held in February 1989. Representatives were elected directly to local-level resistance committees; these elected representatives to district-level resistance committees, and these, in turn, elected representatives to the NRC. The NRC was expanded from 98 members, all nominated by the President, to 278 members, of whom 68 were nominated by the President and 210 were elected. In October 1989 the NRC approved legislation prolonging the Government's term of office by five years from January 1990, when its mandate had been due to expire. A new Constitution was enacted by an elected Constituent Assembly in September 1995 and came into force in the following month. The first direct presidential election was held in May 1996, and national legislative elections took place in the following month to a 276-member Parliament, as the NRC became—comprising 214 directly elected and 62 nominated members. Voting also took place in June for local councils (which replaced the resistance committees). Further local elections were held in November 1997 and January 2002. Under the terms of the new Constitution, a national referendum on the future introduction of a multi-party political system took place in June 2000, at which voters overwhelmingly endorsed the retention of the existing 'no-party' system. Following legislative elections in June 2001, the number of seats in Parliament stood at 292, comprising 214 directly elected representatives and 78 nominated members.

Defence

In August 2002 the Uganda People's Defence Forces was estimated to number 50,000–60,000 men, including paramilitary forces (a border defence unit of about 600 men, a police air wing

of about 800 men, about 400 marines and local defence units of about 15,000 men). Defence was allocated an estimated 250,000m. shillings by the central Government in 2002.

Economic Affairs

In 2001, according to estimates by the World Bank, Uganda's gross national income (GNI), measured at average 1999–2001 prices, was US $6,286m., equivalent to $280 per head (or $1,250 per head on an international purchasing-power parity basis). During 1990–2001, it was estimated, the population increased at an average annual rate of 3.1%, while gross domestic product (GDP) per head increased, in real terms, by an average of 3.2% per year. Overall GDP increased, in real terms, at an average annual rate of 6.4% in 1990–2001; growth was 4.6% in 2001.

Agriculture (including hunting, forestry and fishing) contributed 42.4% of GDP in 2001, and the sector employed an estimated 79.6% of the labour force in that year. The principal cash crops are coffee (which provided about 57.0% of export earnings in 1999), tea, cotton and maize. Tobacco, sugar cane and cocoa are also cultivated, and the production of cut flowers is an important activity. The main subsistence crops are plantains, cassava, sweet potatoes, millet, sorghum, maize, beans, groundnuts and rice. In addition, livestock (chiefly cattle, goats, sheep and poultry) are reared, and freshwater fishing is an important rural activity. Agricultural GDP increased by an average of 3.8% per year in 1990–2001, according to the World Bank; it increased by 4.9% in 2001.

Industry (including mining, manufacturing, construction and power) contributed 19.2% of GDP in 2001, and employed 6.3% of the working population in 1994. Industrial GDP increased at an average annual rate of 10.7% in 1990–2001, according to the World Bank; it increased by 5.4% in 2001.

Mining has made a negligible contribution to GDP since the 1970s (0.7% in 2000/01). The Government aims to encourage renewed investment in the sector. Output of copper, formerly an important export, virtually ceased during the late 1970s. However, the state-owned Kilembe copper mine in western Uganda is expected to be transferred to private ownership and reopened. The production of cobalt from stockpiled copper pyrites commenced in 1999. Uganda is believed to possess the world's second largest deposit of gold, which began to be exploited again in the mid-1990s. Apatite and limestone are also mined. There are, in addition, reserves of iron ore, magnetite, tin, tungsten, beryllium, bismuth, asbestos, graphite, phosphate and tantalite. Mining GDP increased by 8.9% in the financial year to June 1999.

Manufacturing contributed 8.9% of GDP in 2001. The most important manufacturing activities are the processing of agricultural commodities, brewing, vehicle assembly and the production of textiles, cement, soap, fertilizers, paper products, metal products, shoes, paints, matches and batteries. Manufacturing GDP increased by an average of 11.3% per year in 1990–2001, according to the World Bank; it increased by 2.4% in 2001.

Energy is derived principally from hydroelectric power. In 1998 Uganda generated only about two-thirds of national energy requirements. However, plans are under way to expand hydroelectric production. Imports of fuel accounted for 17.5% of the value of Uganda's merchandise imports in 2000.

The services sector contributed 38.5% of GDP in 2001, and engaged an estimated 9.7% of the employed labour force in 1980. Trade is the most important aspect of the sector. Services GDP increased by an average of 7.4% per year in 1990–2001, according to the World Bank. GDP in the sector increased by 5.0% in 2001.

In 2001 Uganda recorded a visible trade deficit of US $575.0m., and there was a deficit of $802.4m. on the current account of the balance of payments. In 1999 the principal sources of imports were Kenya (23.8%), the United Kingdom, Japan and India, while the United Kingdom (18.0%), the Southern African Customs Union, Kenya and Singapore were the main markets for exports in that year. The principal export in 1999 was coffee; the main imports in that year were petroleum products, road vehicles, medicinal and pharmaceutical products, and cereals and cereal preparations.

In the financial year ending 30 June 2002 Uganda's central government budgetary deficit was 587,600m. shillings, equivalent to 5.7% of GDP. Uganda's external debt totalled US $3,409m. at the end of 2000, of which $2,997m. was long-term public debt. In that year the cost of debt-servicing was equivalent to 23.7% of the value of exports of goods and services.

The annual average rate of inflation was 11.0% in 1990–2001; consumer prices increased by an average of 1.9% in 2001.

Uganda is a member of the Common Market for Eastern and Southern Africa (see p. 162), the African Development Bank (see p. 128) and the East African Community (see p. 339).

Uganda has an open, deregulated economy, with conditions favourable to investment. Inflation has remained low since the late 1990s, the foreign exchange regime has been liberalized since the mid-1990s and privatization is well advanced. As such, Uganda has enjoyed good relations with international donors. In February 1995 international creditor Governments agreed to cancel some two-thirds of Uganda's bilateral government-guaranteed debt. During 1998–2000 Uganda received approximately US $1,500m. from international aid and debt-relief packages, including the IMF's Heavily Indebted Poor Countries initiative. It was estimated that these funds would reduce Uganda's annual debt-servicing obligations by about 65%–75%. In March 2000 donor countries granted Uganda $2,000m.–$3,000m. in support of its economic development programme, commending the country for having focused its economic policies on the reduction of poverty and for its commitment to reduce defence spending to 2% of GDP. Certain weaknesses have, however, tended to be overlooked. For instance, a large part of Uganda's GDP growth is needed each year just to keep pace with the rapid increase in population (more than 3.0% per year). By 2003 there were two main challenges for Uganda's economy. Firstly, growth, which was still largely dependent on agricultural exports, needed to be sustained at a sufficient level to enable the reduction of poverty. Secondly, Uganda had to reduce its reliance on foreign aid, which in 2003 financed around one-half of the country's expenditure. In 2002/03 revenue from aid and private capital offset a widening current-account deficit. The flexibility of a floating currency also enabled Uganda to move towards a more diversified economic base and lessened the adverse effects of low export prices for coffee and cotton and high prices for petroleum imports. (The value of Uganda's exports increased in early 2003, owing to a recovery in coffee prices.) However, the IMF was concerned that Uganda was not reaching its target growth rate of 7% per year, and that this could jeopardize the country's poverty reduction plan. The IMF concluded that Uganda required more private investment and better use of its funds to stay on course with its economic programme, and urged Uganda to reduce its reliance on foreign aid.

Education

Education is not compulsory. Most schools are supported by the Government, although a small proportion are sponsored by missions. Traditionally all schools have charged fees. In 1997, however, the Government introduced an initiative known as Universal Primary Education (UPE), whereby free primary education was to be phased in for up to four children per family. Primary education begins at six years of age and lasts for seven years. Secondary education, beginning at the age of 13, lasts for a further six years, comprising a first cycle of four years and a second of two years. In 1995 the number of pupils attending government-aided primary and secondary schools was equivalent to 48% of children in the relevant age-group (males 53%; females 43%). In 1999 there were 6,591,429 pupils enrolled at primary schools, and 427,492 pupils attending general secondary schools. According to the IMF, enrolment in primary education had risen to 94% of the relevant age-group in 1999. In addition to Makerere University in Kampala there is a university of science and technology at Mbarara, and a small Islamic university is located at Mbale. Education expenditure in the financial year ending 30 June 1997 accounted for 24.9% of government current expenditure.

Public Holidays

2003: 1 January (New Year's Day), 26 January (Liberation Day), 12 February* (Id al-Adha, Feast of the Sacrifice), 8 March (International Women's Day), 18–21 April (Easter), 1 May (Labour Day), 3 June (Martyrs' Day), 9 June (National Heroes' Day), 9 October (Independence Day), 26 November* (Id al-Fitr, end of Ramadan), 25 December (Christmas), 26 December (Boxing Day).

2004: 1 January (New Year's Day), 26 January (Liberation Day), 2 February* (Id al-Adha, Feast of the Sacrifice), 8 March (International Women's Day), 9–12 April (Easter), 1 May (Labour Day), 3 June (Martyrs' Day), 9 June (National Heroes' Day), 9 October (Independence Day), 14 November* (Id al-Fitr, end of Ramadan), 25 December (Christmas), 26 December (Boxing Day).

*These holidays are dependent on the Islamic lunar calendar and the exact dates may vary by one or two days from those given.

Weights and Measures

The metric system is in force.

Statistical Survey

Sources (unless otherwise stated): Uganda Bureau of Statistics, POB 13, Entebbe; tel. (41) 320165; fax (41) 320147; e-mail ubos@infocom.co.ug; internet www.ubos.org; Statistics Department, Ministry of Finance, Planning and Economic Development, POB 8147, Kampala.

Area and Population

AREA, POPULATION AND DENSITY

Area (sq km)	
Land	197,058
Inland water	44,081
Total	241,139*
Population (census results)	
18 January 1980	12,636,179
12 January 1991	
Males	8,185,747
Females.	8,485,958
Total	16,671,705
Population (official estimates at mid-year)	
1999	21,620,000
2000	22,210,000
2001	22,788,000
Density (per sq km) at mid-2001	94.5

* 93,104 sq miles. Source: Lands and Surveys Department.

DISTRICTS
(population at 1991 census)

District	Population	District	Population
Apac	454,504	Kumi	236,694
Arua	637,941	Lira	500,965
Bundibugyo . . .	116,566	Luwero	449,691
Bushenyi	579,137	Masaka	838,736
Gulu	338,427	Masindi	260,796
Hoima	197,851	Mbale	710,980
Iganga	945,783	Mbarara	798,774
Jinja	289,476	Moroto	174,417
Kabale	417,218	Moyo	175,645
Kabarole	746,800	Mpigi	913,867
Kalangala	16,371	Mubende	500,976
Kampala	774,241	Mukono	824,604
Kamuli	485,214	Nebbi	316,866
Kapchorwa . . .	116,702	Ntungamo . . .	289,222
Kasese	343,601	Pallisa	357,656
Kibaale	220,261	Rakai	383,501
Kiboga	141,607	Rukungiri . . .	390,780
Kisoro	186,681	Soroti	430,390
Kitgum	357,184	Tororo	585,574
Kotido	196,006		

PRINCIPAL TOWNS
(population at census of 18 August 1969)

Kampala (capital) .	330,700	Mbale	23,544
Jinja and Njeru .	52,509	Entebbe	21,096
Bugembe planning			
area	46,884	Gulu	18,170

1980 (provisional census results): Kampala 458,423; Jinja 45,060; Masaka 29,123; Mbale 28,039; Mbarara 23,155; Gulu 14,958.

Mid-2001 (UN projection, including suburbs): Kampala 1,274,000 (Source: UN, *World Urbanization Prospects: The 2001 Revision*).

BIRTHS AND DEATHS
(UN estimates, annual averages)

	1985–90	1990–95	1995–2000
Birth rate (per 1,000) . . .	50.5	50.5	50.4
Death rate (per 1,000) . . .	19.7	21.3	20.3

Source: UN, *World Population Prospects: The 2000 Revision*.

Expectation of life (WHO estimates, years at birth): 46.4 (males 45.8; females 47.2) in 2001 (Source: WHO, *World Health Report*).

ECONOMICALLY ACTIVE POPULATION
(ILO estimates, '000 persons at mid-1990)

	Males	Females	Total
Agriculture, etc.	3,729	3,697	7,425
Industry	340	77	417
Manufacturing	143	73	216
Services	536	408	944
Total labour force	4,605	4,181	8,786

Source: ILO.

Mid-2001 (estimates in '000): Agriculture, etc. 9,326; Total labour force 11,714 (Source: FAO).

Health and Welfare

KEY INDICATORS

Total fertility rate (children per woman, 2001)	7.1
Under-5 mortality rate (per 1,000 live births, 2001) . . .	124
HIV/AIDS (% of persons aged 15–49, 2001)	5.00
Hospital beds (per 1,000 head, 1991)	0.92
Health expenditure (2000): US $ per head (PPP)	36
Health expenditure (2000): % of GDP	3.9
Health expenditure (2000): public (% of total)	38
Access to water (% of persons, 2000)	80
Access to sanitation (% of persons, 2000)	75
Human Development Index (2000): ranking	150
Human Development Index (2000): value	0.444

For sources and definitions, see explanatory note on p. vi.

Agriculture

PRINCIPAL CROPS
('000 metric tons)

	1999	2000	2001
Wheat	11	12	14
Rice (paddy)	95	109	114
Maize	1,053	1,096	1,174
Millet	606	534	584
Sorghum	413	361	423
Potatoes	449	478	508
Sweet potatoes	2,354	2,398	2,515
Cassava (Manioc)	4,875	4,966	5,265
Dry beans	401	420	511
Other pulses	160*	n.a.	n.a.
Soybeans	101	120	144
Groundnuts (in shell) . . .	137	139	146
Sesame seed	93	97	102
Seed cotton	66†	67*	67*
Vegetables and melons . . .	527	546	556
Sugar cane*	1,600	1,550	1,500
Bananas	895	943	973
Plantains	8,949	9,533	9,533*
Other fruit*	50	51	51
Coffee (green)	252	143	197
Tea (made)	25	29	33
Tobacco (leaves)	21	23	23
Cotton (lint)	14	21	13

* FAO estimate(s).
† Unofficial figure.

Source: FAO.

LIVESTOCK
('000 head, year ending September)

	1999	2000	2001*
Asses*	18	18	18
Cattle	5,820	5,966	5,900
Sheep	1,044	1,050*	1,100
Goats	6,180	6,200*	6,200
Pigs	1,520	1,550*	1,550
Chickens	24,622	25,000*	25,500

* FAO estimate(s).

Source: FAO.

LIVESTOCK PRODUCTS
(FAO estimates, '000 metric tons)

	1999	2000	2001
Beef and veal	96	97	97
Mutton and lamb	5	5	5
Goat meat	24	24	24
Pig meat	75	78	78
Poultry meat	40	41	41
Other meat	18	18	18
Cows' milk	509	511	511
Poultry eggs	18	20	20
Cattle hides	13	14	14

Source: FAO.

Forestry

ROUNDWOOD REMOVALS
('000 cubic metres, excl. bark)

	1999	2000*	2001*
Sawlogs, veneer logs and logs for			
sleepers	1,055	1,055	1,055
Other industrial wood* . . .	2,120	2,120	2,120
Fuel wood*	33,726	34,090	34,611
Total	36,901	37,265	37,786

* FAO estimates.

Source: FAO.

SAWNWOOD PRODUCTION
('000 cubic metres, incl. railway sleepers)

	1999	2000*	2001*
Coniferous (softwood) . . .	67	67	67
Broadleaved (hardwood). . .	197	197	197
Total	264	264	264

* FAO estimates.

Source: FAO.

Fishing

('000 metric tons, live weight)

	1998	1999	2000
Capture	220.6	226.1	355.8
Cyprinids	15.7	17.6	152.3
Tilapias	78.5	84.5	97.4
African lungfishes .	7.6	9.2	5.8
Characins	11.7	13.2	7.2
Naked catfishes . . .	5.2	8.6	4.4
Nile perch	98.8	69.2	83.9
Aquaculture	0.4*	0.4	0.2
Total catch	221.0	226.5	356.0

* FAO estimate.

Note: Figures exclude aquatic mammals, recorded by number rather than by weight. The number of Nile crocodiles caught was: 508 in 2000.

Source: FAO, *Yearbook of Fishery Statistics*.

Mining

('000 metric tons, unless otherwise indicated)

	1999	2000	2001
Iron ore (gross weight)	3.2	4.6	1.2
Tantalum and niobium (columbium) concentrates (kilograms)	—	2,712	11,092
Cobalt (metric tons)	77	411	634
Gold (kilograms)	5	56	0
Limestone	121.5	253.0	229.8
Salt (unrefined)*	5	5	5

* Estimated production.

Source: US Geological Survey.

Industry

SELECTED PRODUCTS
('000 metric tons, unless otherwise indicated)

	1998	1999	2000
Beer (million litres)	108.8	106.4	126.1
Soft drinks (million litres) . . .	68.7	80.8	72.6
Cigarettes (million)	1,846	1,602	1,344
Sugar	102.7	126.9	222.9
Soap	72.8	83.8	75.2
Cement	321.3	347.3	367.5
Paint (metric tons)	2,466	2,450	2,792
Edible oil and fat ('000 litres) .	28.3	40.5	42.8
Animal feed	17.2	17.2	31.7
Footwear ('000 pairs) . . .	1,471	1,725	1,696
Wheat flour	18.0	14.5	12.2
Electricity (million kWh) . .	1,233.6	1,341.7	1,638.9

Source: Bank of Uganda.

Finance

CURRENCY AND EXCHANGE RATES

Monetary Units
100 cents = 1 new Uganda shilling

Sterling, Dollar and Euro Equivalents (31 December 2002)
£1 sterling = 2,986.0 new Uganda shillings
US $1 = 1,852.6 new Uganda shillings
€1 = 1,942.8 new Uganda shillings
10,000 new Uganda shillings = £3.349 = $5.398 = €5.147

Average Exchange Rate (new Uganda shillings per US $)
2000   1,644.5
2001   1,755.7
2002   1,797.6

Note: Between December 1985 and May 1987 the official exchange rate was fixed at US $1 = 1,400 shillings. In May 1987 a new shilling, equivalent to 100 of the former units, was introduced. At the same time, the currency was devalued by 76.7%, with the exchange rate set at $1 = 60 new shillings. Further adjustments were implemented in subsequent years. Foreign exchange controls were mostly abolished in 1993.

BUDGET
(million new shillings, year ending 30 June)

Revenue	1998/99	1999/2000	2000/01
Revenue*	951,273	1,010,260	1,085,400
Grants	406,936	600,640	883,880
Total	1,358,210	1,610,900	1,969,280

Expenditure	1998/99	1999/2000	2000/01
Recurrent expenditure	863,786	957,360	1,143,520
Wages and salaries . . .	341,163	373,890	436,600
Interest payments	68,841	75,520	126,700
Development expenditure . . .	635,067	903,060	1,001,380
External expenditure . . .	490,400	640,140	663,380
Domestic expenditure . . .	144,667	262,920	338,000
Net lending and investment . .	2,319	9,860	−25,810
Total	1,501,173	1,870,280	2,119,090

* Tax revenue excludes tax refunds and government payments.

Source: Bank of Uganda, *Annual Report 2000/2001*.

INTERNATIONAL RESERVES
(US $ million at 31 December)

	2000	2001	2002
IMF special drawing rights . . .	3.5	1.9	3.0
Foreign exchange	804.5	981.5	931.1
Total	808.0	983.4	934.0

Source: IMF, *International Financial Statistics*.

MONEY SUPPLY
(million new shillings at 31 December)

	2000	2001	2002
Currency outside banks	362,248	393,433	466,610
Demand deposits at commercial banks	443,244	515,363	632,830
Total money	805,492	908,796	1,099,440

Source: IMF, *International Financial Statistics*.

COST OF LIVING
(Consumer Price Index for all urban households; base: 1990 = 100)

	1998	1999	2000
Food	293.9	314.1	317.2
Clothing	164.8	175.8	181.3
Rent, fuel and light	327.2	330.4	338.3
All items (incl. others) . . .	283.4	299.7	309.7

Source: ILO.

2001: Food 306.4; All items 315.5 (Source: UN, *Monthly Bulletin of Statistics*).

NATIONAL ACCOUNTS
(million new shillings at current prices, year ending 30 June)

Expenditure on the Gross Domestic Product

	1993/94	1994/95	1995/96
Government final consumption expenditure.	453,929	504,008	594,881
Private final consumption expenditure.	3,730,985	4,447,233	5,154,110
Increase in stocks	2,091	44,692	49,431
Gross fixed capital formation	641,311	819,893	1,062,422
Total domestic expenditure.	4,828,316	5,815,826	6,761,982
Exports of goods and services	384,788	631,227	734,365
Less Imports of goods and services	850,477	1,105,522	1,363,759
GDP in purchasers' values*.	4,366,721	5,273,248	6,077,035
GDP at constant 1991 prices	2,572,413	2,868,209	3,150,019

* Including statistical discrepancy (million shillings): 4,094 in 1993/94; −68,282 in 1994/95; −55,554 in 1995/96.

Gross Domestic Product by Economic Activity
(at factor cost)

	1998/99	1999/2000	2000/01
Agriculture, hunting, forestry and fishing	3,183,450	3,478,605	3,673,126
Mining and quarrying	50,279	56,083	63,566
Manufacturing	697,466	737,684	799,777
Electricity, gas and water	109,450	119,254	128,730
Construction	582,945	669,493	786,881
Trade, restaurants and hotels	1,096,033	1,191,829	1,299,629
Transport, storage and communications	374,043	447,681	541,119
General government services	319,572	351,965	406,816
Education	308,976	342,827	381,129
Health	91,471	98,916	107,176
Other services	879,041	952,353	1,067,979
GDP at factor cost*	7,693,118	8,446,690	9,255,928

* Based on unrounded data.

Source: Bank of Uganda, *Annual Report 2000/2001.*

BALANCE OF PAYMENTS
(US $ million)

	1999	2000	2001
Exports of goods f.o.b.	483.5	449.9	451.6
Imports of goods f.o.b.	−989.1	−949.7	−1,026.6
Trade balance	−505.6	−499.8	−575.0
Exports of services	196.0	213.2	221.0
Imports of services	−419.2	−458.8	−523.2
Balance on goods and services	−728.8	−745.4	−877.2
Other income received	35.1	53.1	37.3
Other income paid	−162.5	−165.5	−177.6
Balance on goods, services and income	−856.2	−857.8	−1,017.5
Current transfers received	329.7	340.0	583.0
Current transfers paid	−184.2	−307.3	−367.9
Current balance	−710.7	−824.4	−802.4
Direct investment from abroad.	140.2	160.7	144.7
Investment assets	−8.2	−0.9	−15.0
Other investment liabilities	121.3	160.7	370.0
Net errors and omissions	2.0	40.6	63.8
Overall balance	−455.4	−464.3	−238.9

Source: IMF, *International Financial Statistics.*

External Trade

PRINCIPAL COMMODITIES
(distribution by SITC, US $ million)

Imports c.i.f.	1996	1998*	1999
Food and live animals	77.6	125.5	90.2
Cereals and cereal preparations	48.7	71.9	57.6
Sugar, sugar preparations and honey	10.9	35.6	21.1
Crude materials (inedible) except fuels	44.0	44.2	37.2
Mineral fuels, lubricants, etc.	107.5	115.0	125.3
Petroleum products, refined	104.4	111.5	121.5
Animal and vegetable oils, fats and waxes.	54.9	63.5	50.1
Fixed vegetable fats and oils	30.4	39.5	26.8
Chemicals and related products	114.6	136.2	146.0
Medicinal and pharmaceutical products.	47.4	53.4	73.6
Medicaments (incl. veterinary medicaments)	37.4	44.4	65.3
Medicaments (excl. antibiotics)	24.8	32.2	53.3
Basic manufactures	201.6	201.9	186.6
Non-metallic mineral manufactures	43.9	44.0	38.5
Lime, cement and fabricated construction materials	29.3	27.8	25.4
Iron and steel.	47.7	46.8	43.0
Machinery and transport equipment.	269.7	322.7	277.6
Machinery specialized for particular industries	33.3	35.7	31.7
General industrial machinery, equipment and parts	30.4	37.2	26.6
Electrical machinery, apparatus, etc.	55.7	80.6	74.0
Road vehicles (incl. air-cushion vehicles) and parts (excl. tyres, engines and electrical parts)	122.1	121.2	95.6
Passenger motor vehicles (excl. buses).	34.0	21.4	28.8
Motor vehicles for the transport of goods or materials	46.0	41.6	33.2
Miscellaneous manufactured articles.	81.4	93.5	100.1
Total (incl. others)	952.8	1,105.5	1,015.2

Exports f.o.b.	1996	1998*	1999
Food and live animals	495.9	406.2	346.2
Fish, fresh, chilled or frozen	43.9	64.2	23.8
Coffee, tea, cocoa, spices and manufactures	399.9	318.1	311.6
Coffee, green, roasted, coffee substitutes containing coffee	396.8	287.1	288.0
Coffee, not roasted, coffee husks and skins	396.5	266.5	267.2
Coffee, roasted	—	11.9	20.8
Tea	1.1	28.2	21.4
Crude materials (inedible) except fuels	77.3	30.1	88.7
Textile fibres (not wool tops) and their wastes (not in yarn)	52.2	3.8	30.9
Cotton	45.0	3.0	20.3
Cotton waste, not carded or combed	3.1	1.1	17.4
Cotton, carded or combed	26.5	—	—
Fish waste	0.7	3.8	40.7
Animal and vegetable oils, fats and waxes	23.2	5.4	2.5
Fixed vegetable oils and fats	22.5	5.2	2.4
Palm oil	21.7	4.8	1.5
Chemicals and related products	46.7	8.5	3.1
Inorganic chemicals	42.0	5.4	0.1
Colloidal precious metals; amalgams, salts, etc., of precious metals	40.6	4.9	—
Basic manufactures	27.8	7.2	3.8
Gold, non-monetary (excl. gold ores and concentrates)	24.5	7.5	33.5
Gold, non-monetary, unwrought or semi-manufactured	24.5	6.1	13.0
Goldsmiths', silversmiths' and jewellers' sweepings, residues, lemels, waste, etc.	—	1.4	20.5
Total (incl. others)	714.7	509.9	505.7

* Figures for 1997 are unavailable.

Source: UN, *International Trade Statistical Yearbook*.

PRINCIPAL TRADING PARTNERS
(US $ million)

Imports c.i.f.	1996	1998*	1999
Belgium-Luxembourg	20.0	26.3	20.1†
China, People's Repub.	13.2	15.2	22.5
France (incl. Monaco)	24.3	21.7	19.5
Germany	35.0	28.9	28.4
Hong Kong	24.6	22.4	22.8
India	52.0	66.5	65.4
Italy	34.5	45.4	21.8
Japan	75.3	68.7	82.2
Kenya	250.4	265.6	241.9
Malaysia	24.0	13.6	21.2
Netherlands	12.7	14.7	20.1
Pakistan	6.7	10.9	18.3
SACU‡	27.5	75.3	57.0
Singapore	36.2	56.0	18.4
Tanzania	11.7	23.3	11.1
United Arab Emirates	49.7	57.2	55.4
United Kingdom	120.2	132.0	103.1
USA	24.7	34.3	57.0
Total (incl. others)	952.8	1,105.5	1,015.2

Exports f.o.b.	1996	1998*	1999
Australia	12.2	3.6	11.2
Bahrain	3.3	—	6.8
Belgium-Luxembourg	23.1	8.3	n.a.
Congo, Democratic Repub.	40.3	4.4	3.7
Congo, Repub.	—	7.3	9.1
Egypt	2.3	1.2	7.8
Ethiopia	0.2	3.8	15.1
France (incl. Monaco)	12.1	23.9	14.6
Germany	19.0	22.8	17.5
Hong Kong	2.1	5.9	4.1
Hungary	—	4.4	6.9
Italy	0.3	7.1	8.2
Japan	2.1	4.4	19.1
Kenya	52.1	48.8	32.1
Netherlands	21.1	52.8	18.6
Norway	0.3	4.5	8.7
Pakistan	1.6	6.4	0.8
Poland	—	4.4	14.3
Russian Federation	—	9.8	—
Rwanda	51.4	21.4	16.8
SACU‡	1.4	14.4	33.1
Singapore	25.5	22.9	24.8
Spain	8.6	21.4	15.1
Sudan	19.7	18.7	16.5
Switzerland (incl. Liechtenstein)	205.4	47.7	24.3
Tanzania	6.4	8.6	5.9
United Kingdom	175.4	57.7	91.0
USA	2.0	26.5	8.9
Total (incl. others)	714.7	509.9	505.7

* Figures for 1997 are unavailable.

† Excluding Luxembourg.

‡ Southern African Customs Union, comprising Botswana, Lesotho, Namibia, South Africa and Swaziland.

Source: UN, *International Trade Statistics Yearbook*.

Transport

RAILWAYS
(traffic)

	1994	1995	1996
Passenger-km (million)	35	30	28
Freight ton-km (million)	208	236	187

ROAD TRAFFIC
(vehicles in use)

	1998	1999	2000
Passenger cars	46,930	48,392	49,016
Buses and coaches	15,829	16,042	16,323
Lorries and vans	48,650	54,166	55,683
Motorcycles	61,044	63,769	64,305

Source: Bank of Uganda, *Annual Report 2000/2001*.

CIVIL AVIATION
(traffic on scheduled services)

	1997	1998	1999
Kilometers flown (million)	2	2	5
Passengers carried ('000)	100	100	179
Passenger-km (million)	110	110	356
Total ton-km (million)	11	11	54

Source: UN, *Statistical Yearbook*.

Tourism

FOREIGN TOURIST ARRIVALS

Country of residence	1998	1999	2000
Congo, Democratic Repub. . . .	4,006	7,552	7,957
India	7,107	6,206	4,841
Kenya	65,501	68,167	60,900
Norway	8,554	8,642	6,717
Rwanda	10,584	7,293	36,041
Tanzania	22,318	20,780	14,375
United Kingdom	17,603	15,744	13,954
USA	11,263	9,802	9,593
Total (incl. others)	192,012	186,937	191,276

Source: World Tourism Organization, *Yearbook of Tourism Statistics*.

Tourism receipts (US $ million): 78 in 1997; 144 in 1998; 149 in 1999 (Source: World Tourism Organization).

Communications Media

	1999	2000	2001
Television receivers ('000 in use)	600	610	n.a.
Telephones ('000 main lines in use)	57.2	61.7	63.7
Mobile cellular telephones ('000 subscribers)*	56.4	188.6	322.7
Personal computers ('000 in use)	55	60	70
Internet users ('000)	25	40	60

Source: International Telecommunication Union.

Radio receivers ('000 in use, 1997): 2,600.

Facsimile machines (number in use, 1996): 3,000 (estimate)*.

Book production (titles, excl. pamphlets and govt publications, 1996): 288.

Daily newspapers (1996): titles 2; average circulation ('000 copies) 40.

* Year ending 30 June.

Sources: mainly UNESCO, *Statistical Yearbook*; UN, *Statistical Yearbook*.

Education

(1999)

	Teachers	Students
Primary	109,733	6,591,429
Secondary: general	22,599	427,492
Secondary: vocational*‡	1,138	17,772
Secondary: primary teacher training colleges‡	956	20,728
Higher: university	1,134	14,279
Higher: other†‡	1,344	23,994

* Technical schools and institutes.
† Includes secondary teacher training colleges.
‡ 1998 data.

Adult literacy rate (UNESCO estimates): 67.1% (males 77.5%; females 56.8%) in 2000 (Source: UN Development Programme, *Human Development Report*).

Directory

The Constitution

Following the military coup in July 1985, the 1967 Constitution was suspended, and all legislative and executive powers were vested in a Military Council, whose Chairman was Head of State. In January 1986 a further military coup established an executive Presidency, assisted by a Cabinet of Ministers and a legislative National Resistance Council (NRC). In September 1995 a Constituent Assembly (comprising 214 elected and 74 nominated members) enacted a draft Constitution. The new Constitution was promulgated on 8 October 1995. Under its terms, a national referendum on the introduction of a multi-party political system was to take place in 2000. The referendum produced an overwhelming vote in favour of retaining the existing 'no-party' system. A direct presidential election took place in May 1996, followed in June of that year by legislative elections to the Parliament. This body, comprising 214 elected members and 62 nominated members, replaced the NRC. At the general election of June 2001 the number of nominated members was increased to 78.

The Government

HEAD OF STATE

President: Lt-Gen. YOWERI KAGUTA MUSEVENI (took office 29 January 1986; elected 9 May 1996, re-elected 12 March 2001).

THE CABINET
(May 2003)

President and Commander-in-Chief: Lt-Gen. YOWERI KAGUTA MUSEVENI.

Vice-President: Prof. GILBERT BALIBASEKA BUKENYA.

Prime Minister: Prof. APOLO NSIBAMBI.

First Deputy Prime Minister and Minister of Disaster Preparedness and Refugees: Lt-Gen. MOSES ALI.

Second Deputy Prime Minister and Minister of Foreign Affairs: JAMES WAMBOGO WAPAKHABULO.

Third Deputy Prime Minister and Minister of Public Service: HENRY MUGANWA KAJURA.

Minister in Charge of the Presidency: KIRUNDA KIVENJINJA.

Minister of Agriculture, Animal Industry and Fisheries: WILBERFORCE KISAMBA MUGERWA.

Minister of Defence: AMAMA MBABAZI.

Minister of Internal Affairs: RUHAKANA RUGUNDA.

Minister of Education and Sports: EDWARD KIDDU MAKUBUYA.

Minister of Energy and Mineral Development: SYDA NAMIREMBE BBUMBA.

Minister of Finance, Planning and Economic Development: GERALD SSENDAWULA.

Minister of Gender, Labour and Social Services: ZOE BAKOKO BAKORU.

Minister of Health: JIM KATUGUGU MUHWEZI.

Minister of Justice and Constitutional Affairs: JANET BALUNZI MUKWAYA.

Minister of Local Government: Prof. TARSIS KABWEGYERE.

Minister of Tourism, Trade and Industry: Prof. EDWARD RUGUMAYO.

Minister of Water, Lands and Environment: Col KAHINDA OTAFIRE.

Minister of Works, Transport, Housing and Communications: JOHN NASASIRA.

Minister without Portfolio and National Political Commissar: Dr CRISPUS W. C. B. KIYONGA.

Minister in the Office of the Prime Minister: Prof. MONDO GEORGE KAGONYERA.

Attorney-General: FRANCIS AYUME.

In addition to the Cabinet Ministers, there are 44 Ministers of State.

MINISTRIES

Office of the President: Parliament Bldg, POB 7168, Kampala; tel. (41) 258441; fax (41) 256143; e-mail info@gouexecutive.net; internet www.gouexecutive.net.

Office of the Prime Minister: POB 341, Kampala; tel. (41) 259518; fax (41) 242341.

Ministry of Agriculture, Animal Industry and Fisheries: POB 102, Entebbe; tel. (42) 20752; fax (42) 21042; internet www.agriculture.go.ug.

Ministry of Defence: Bombo, POB 7069, Kampala; tel. (41) 270331; fax (41) 245911.

Ministry of Education and Sports: Embassy House and Development Bldg, Plot 9/11, Parliament Ave, POB 7063, Kampala; tel. (41) 234451; fax (41) 230437; internet www.education.go.ug.

Ministry of Energy and Mineral Development: Amber House, Kampala Rd, Kampala.

Ministry of Finance, Planning and Economic Development: Appollo Kaggwa Rd, Plot 2/4, POB 8147, Kampala; tel. (41) 234700; fax (41) 230163; e-mail efmp@imul.com; internet www.finance.go.ug.

Ministry of Foreign Affairs: Embassy House, POB 7048, Kampala; tel. (41) 258251; fax (41) 258722; e-mail info@mofa.go.ug; internet www.mofa.go.ug.

Ministry of Gender, Labour and Social Development: Udyam House, Jinja Rd, POB 7168, Kampala; tel. (41) 258334.

Ministry of Health: POB 7272, Kampala; tel. (41) 340884; fax (41) 340887; e-mail info@health.go.ug; internet www.health.go.ug.

Ministry of Internal Affairs: Jinja Rd, POB 7191, Kampala; tel. (41) 231103; fax (41) 231188; e-mail psmia@infocom.co.ug.

Ministry of Justice and Constitutional Affairs: Parliament Bldg, POB 7183, Kampala; tel. (41) 230538; fax (41) 254829; e-mail mojca@africaonline.co.ug; internet www.justice.go.ug.

Ministry of Local Government: Uganda House, 8/10 Kampala Rd, POB 7037, Kampala; tel. (41) 256533; fax (41) 258127; e-mail decsec@imul.com; internet www.ugandamolg.org.

Ministry of Public Service: 12 Nakasero Hill Rd, POB 7003, Kampala; tel. (41) 250570; fax (41) 255363; e-mail info@publicservice.go.ug; internet www.publicservice.go.ug.

Ministry of Tourism, Trade and Industry: 6/8 Parliament Ave, POB 7103, Kampala; tel. (41) 232971; fax (41) 242188; e-mail ps@mintrade.org.

Ministry of Water, Lands and Environment: POB 7096, Kampala; tel. (41) 342931; e-mail mwle@mwle.go.ug; internet www.mwle.go.ug.

Ministry of Works, Transport, Housing and Communications: POB 10, Entebbe; tel. (42) 320101; fax (42) 320135; e-mail mowh@infocom.co.ug; internet www.miniworks.go.ug.

President and Legislature

PRESIDENT

Election, 12 March 2001

Candidate		Votes	%
Lt-Gen. Yoweri Kaguta Museveni	. .	5,123,360	69.3
Kiiza Besigye		2,055,795	27.8
Aggrey Awori		103,915	1.4
Mohamed Kibirige Mayanja		73,790	1.0
Francis Bwengye		22,751	0.3
Karuhanga Chapaa		10,080	0.1
Total		**7,389,691**	**100.0**

PARLIAMENT

Speaker: EDWARD SSEKANDI.

Deputy Speaker: REBECCA KADAGA.

The National Resistance Movement, which took office in January 1986, established a National Resistance Council (NRC), initially comprising 80 nominated members, to act as a legislative body. National elections were held on 11–28 February 1989, at which 210 members of an expanded NRC were elected by members of district-level Resistance Committees (themselves elected by local-level Resistance Committees, who were directly elected by universal adult suffrage). The remaining 68 seats in the NRC were reserved for candidates nominated by the President (to include 34 women and representatives of youth organizations and trades unions). Political parties were not allowed to participate in the election campaign. In October 1989 the NRC approved legislation extending the Government's term of office by five years from January 1990, when its mandate was to expire. The Constituent Assembly (see Constitution) extended further the NRM's term of office in November 1994. Under the terms of the Constitution that was promulgated in October 1995, the NRC was restyled as the Ugandan Parliament. Legislative elections to the Parliament took place in June 1996 (again officially on a 'no-party' basis). The total membership of the Parliament was reduced from 278 to 276, comprising 214 elected and 62 nominated representatives. A national referendum on the future introduction of a multi-party political system was staged in June 2000, at which 90.7% of participants voted in favour of retaining the 'no-party' political system. A general election was held on 26 June 2001, following which the number of seats in Parliament stood at 292, comprising 214 directly elected representatives, 53 nominated female representatives, 10 nominated representatives from the UPDF, five nominated representatives for workers, five for people with disabilities and five for young people.

Political Organizations

Political parties were ordered to suspend active operations, although not formally banned, in March 1986. At a referendum on the future restoration of a plural political system, which took place on 29 June 2000, the retention of the existing 'no-party' system was overwhelmingly endorsed by voters.

Bazzukulu ba Buganda (Grandchildren of Buganda): Bagandan separatist movement.

Buganda Youth Movement: f. 1994; seeks autonomy for Buganda; Leader STANLEY KATO.

Conservative Party (CP): f. 1979; Leader JEHOASH MAYANJA-NKANGI.

Democratic Party (DP): City House, Plot 2/3 William St, POB 7098, Kampala; tel. and fax (41) 252536; e-mail info@dpuganda.org; internet www.dpuganda.org; f. 1954; main support in southern Uganda; seeks a multi-party political system; Pres. Dr PAUL KAWANGA SSEMOGERERE; Vice-Pres. ZACHARY OLUM.

Federal Democratic Movement (FEDEMO): Kampala.

Forum for Multi-Party Democracy: Kampala; Gen. Sec. JESSE MASHATTE.

Movement for New Democracy in Uganda: based in Zambia; f. 1994 to campaign for multi-party political system; Leader DAN OKELLO-OGWANG.

National Resistance Movement (NRM): f. to oppose the UPC Govt 1980–85; also opposed the mil. Govt in power from July 1985 to Jan. 1986; its fmr. mil. wing, the National Resistance Army (NRA), led by Lt-Gen. Yoweri Kaguta Museveni, took power in Jan. 1986; Chair. Dr SAMSON KISEKKA.

Nationalist Liberal Party: Kampala; f. 1984 by a breakaway faction of the DP; Leader TIBERIO OKENY.

Uganda Democratic Alliance: opposes the NRM Govt; Leader APOLO KIRONDE.

Uganda Democratic Freedom Front: Leader Maj. HERBERT ITONGA.

Uganda Freedom Movement (UFM): Kampala; mainly Baganda support; withdrew from NRM coalition Govt in April 1987; Sec.-Gen. (vacant).

Uganda Independence Revolutionary Movement: f. 1989; opposes the NRM Govt; Chair. Maj. OKELLO KOLO.

Uganda Islamic Revolutionary Party (UIRP): Kampala; f. 1993; Chair. IDRIS MUWONGE.

Uganda National Unity Movement: opposes the NRM Govt; Chair. Alhaji SULEIMAN SSALONGO.

Uganda Patriotic Movement: Kampala; f. 1980; Sec.-Gen. JABERI SSALI.

Uganda People's Congress (UPC): POB 1951, Kampala; internet www.members.home.net/upc; f. 1960; socialist-based philosophy; mainly northern support; ruling party 1962–71 and 1980–85, sole legal political party 1969–71; Pres. Dr APOLO MILTON OBOTE (in exile in Zambia); Nat. Leader Dr JAMES RWANYARARE.

Ugandan People's Democratic Movement (UPDM): seeks democratic reforms; support mainly from north and east of the country; includes mems of fmr govt armed forces; signed a peace accord with the Govt in 1990; Chair. ERIC OTEMA ALLIMADI; Sec.-Gen. EMMANUEL OTENG.

Uganda Progressive Union (UPU): Kampala; Chair. ALFRED BANYA.

The following organizations are in armed conflict with the Government:

Alliance of Democratic Forces (ADF): active since 1996 in southeastern Uganda; combines Ugandan Islamic fundamentalist rebels, exiled Rwandan Hutus and guerrillas from the Democratic Republic of the Congo; Pres. Sheikh JAMIL MUKULU.

Lord's Resistance Army (LRA): f. 1987; claims to be conducting a Christian fundamentalist 'holy war' against the Govt; forces est. to number up to 6,000, operating mainly from bases in Sudan; Leader JOSEPH KONY; a breakaway faction (LRA—Democratic) is led by RONALD OTIM KOMAKECH.

Uganda National Rescue Front Part Two (UNRF II): based in Juba, Sudan; Leader ALI BAMUZE.

Uganda People's Freedom Movement (UPFM): based in Tororo and Kenya; f. 1994 by mems of the fmr Uganda People's Army; Leader PETER OTAI.

West Nile Bank Front (WNBF): operates in northern Uganda.

Diplomatic Representation

EMBASSIES AND HIGH COMMISSIONS IN UGANDA

Algeria: POB 4025, Kampala; tel. (41) 232918; fax (41) 341015; e-mail ambalka@imul.com; Ambassador MOHAMED EL AMINE DERRAGUI.

Austria: POB 7457, Kampala; tel. (41) 235103; fax (41) 235160; Chargé d'affaires ANTON MAIR.

Belgium: POB 7043, Kampala; tel. (41) 345969; fax (41) 347212; e-mail kampala@diplobel.org; Ambassador (vacant).

Burundi: POB 4379, Kampala; tel. (41) 221697; Ambassador GEORGES NTZEZIMANA.

China, People's Republic: POB 4106, Kampala; tel. (41) 236895; fax (41) 235087; e-mail chinaemb@infocom.co.ug; Ambassador LI QIANGMIN.

Congo, Democratic Republic: POB 4972, Kampala; tel. (41) 233777; Chargé d'affaires a.i. BWANAMAZURI KAMONGU.

Cuba: POB 9226, Kampala; tel. (41) 233742; fax (41) 233320; e-mail ecuba@africaonline.co.ug; Chargé d'affaires a.i. ANGEL NICHOLAS.

Denmark: Plot 3, Lumumba Ave, POB 11234, Kampala; tel. (41) 256783; fax (41) 256687; e-mail kmtamb@kmtamb.um.dk; internet www.imul.com/danemb; Ambassador FLEMMING BJØRK PEDERSEN.

Egypt: POB 4280, Kampala; tel. (41) 254525; fax (41) 232103; Ambassador SAMIR ABDALLAH.

Ethiopia: POB 7745, Kampala; tel. (41) 348340; fax (41) 341885; e-mail ethiokam@starcom.co.ug; Ambassador CHAM UGALA URIAT.

France: POB 7212, Kampala; tel. (41) 242120; fax (41) 241252; e-mail amba.kampala@diplomatie.gouv.fr; Ambassador RENÉ ROUDAUT.

Germany: 15 Philip Rd, POB 7016, Kampala; tel. (41) 256767; fax (41) 343136; Ambassador HANS-JOACHIM HELDT.

Holy See: POB 7177, Kampala (Apostolic Nunciature); tel. (41) 505619; fax (41) 221774; e-mail nuntius@imul.com; Apostolic Nuncio Most Rev. CHRISTOPHE PIERRE (Titular Archbishop of Gunela).

India: Plot 11, Kyodondo Rd, Nakaseru, POB 7040, Kampala; tel. (41) 257368; fax (41) 254943; e-mail hc@hicomindkampala.org; High Commissioner B. S. PRAKASH.

Ireland: POB 7791, Kampala; tel. (41) 344348; fax (41) 344353; e-mail irishaid@starcom.co.ug; Chargé d'affaires a.i. BRENDAN ROGERS.

Italy: 10 Lourdel Rd, Nakasero, POB 4646, Kampala; tel. (41) 341786; fax (41) 349526; e-mail ambkamp@imul.com; internet www.imul.com/embitaly; Ambassador Dr LUIGI NAPOLITANO.

Kenya: POB 5220, Kampala; tel. (41) 258235; fax (41) 258239; e-mail kenhicom@africaonline.co.ug; High Commissioner (vacant).

Korea, Democratic People's Republic: POB 3717, Kampala; tel. (41) 233667; Ambassador RI KWANG ROK.

Libya: POB 6079, Kampala; tel. (41) 344924; fax (41) 344969; Sec. of People's Bureau (vacant).

Netherlands: Rwenzori Courts, 4th floor, Plot 2, Nakasero Rd, POB 7728, Kampala; tel. (41) 346000; fax (41) 231861; e-mail kam@minbuza.nl; Ambassador MATTHIEU PETERS.

Nigeria: 33 Nakasero Rd, POB 4338, Kampala; tel. (41) 233691; fax (41) 232543; e-mail nighicom-sgu@africaonline.co.ug; High Commissioner MAMMAN DAURA.

Norway: 8a John Babiiha Ave, Kololo, Kampala; tel. (41) 343621; fax (41) 343936; e-mail emb-kampala@mfa.no; internet ud69.mogul.no; Ambassador TORE GJØS.

Pakistan: POB 7022, Kampala; tel. and fax (41) 231142.

Russia: 28 Malcolm X Ave, POB 7022, Kampala; tel. (41) 345698; fax (41) 345798; e-mail ruscon@imul.com; Ambassador ALEKSANDR A. SADOVNIKOV.

Rwanda: POB 2468, Kampala; tel. (41) 244045; fax (41) 258547; Ambassador SAGAHUTU MURASHI ISAIE.

South Africa: POB 22667, Kampala; tel. (41) 343543; fax (41) 348216; e-mail sahc@infocom.co.ug; High Commissioner (vacant).

Sudan: Kampala; tel. (41) 243518.

Sweden: POB 22669, Kampala; tel. (41) 340970; fax (41) 340979; e-mail ambassaden.kampala@sida.se; Ambassador HANS ANDERSSON.

Tanzania: POB 5750, Kampala; tel. (41) 257357; fax (41) 342890; High Commissioner JOSHUA OPANGA.

United Kingdom: 10–12 Parliament Ave, POB 7070, Kampala; tel. (41) 257054; fax (41) 257304; e-mail bhcinfo@starcom.co.ug; internet www.britain.or.ug; High Commissioner TOM R. V. PHILLIPS.

USA: POB 7007, Kampala; tel. (41) 259791; fax (41) 341768; Ambassador MARTIN BRENNAN.

Judicial System

Courts of Judicature: POB 7085, Kampala; tel. (41) 233420; e-mail hclib@imul.com; internet www.judiciature.go.ug.

The Supreme Court
Kabaka Anjagala Rd, Mengo.

Hears appeals from the Court of Appeal. Also acts as a constitutional court.

Chief Justice: BENJAMIN ODOKI.

Deputy Chief Justice: L. E. M. MUKASA-KIKONYOGO.

The Court of Appeal: 5 Parliament Ave, Kampala; hears appeals from the High Court; the Court of Appeal consists of the Deputy Chief Justice and no fewer than seven Justices of Appeal, the number thereof being prescribed by Parliament.

The High Court
POB 7085, Kampala; tel. (41) 233422.

Has full criminal and civil jurisdiction and also serves as a Constitutional Court. The High Court consists of the Principal Judge and 27 Puisne Judges.

Principal Judge: H. J. NTABGOBA.

Magistrates' Courts: These are established under the Magistrates' Courts Act of 1970 and exercise limited jurisdiction in criminal and civil matters. The country is divided into magisterial areas, presided over by a Chief Magistrate. Under the Chief Magistrate there are two categories of Magistrates. The Magistrates preside alone over their courts. Appeals from the first category of Magistrates' Court lie directly to the High Court, while appeals from the second categories of Magistrates' Court lie to the Chief Magistrate's Court, and from there to the High Court. There are 27 Chief Magistrates' Courts, 52 Magistrates' Grade I Courts and 428 Magistrates' Grade II Courts.

Religion

It is estimated that more than 60% of the population profess Christianity. About 5% of the population are Muslims.

CHRISTIANITY

The Anglican Communion
Anglicans are adherents of the Church of the Province of Uganda, comprising 29 dioceses. There are about 8m. adherents.

Archbishop of Uganda and Bishop of Kampala: Most Rev. LIVINGSTONE MPALANYI-NKOYOYO, POB 14123, Kampala; tel. (41) 270218; fax (41) 251925; e-mail couab@uol.co.ug.

Greek Orthodox Church

Archbishop of East Africa: NICADEMUS OF IRINOUPOULIS (resident in Nairobi, Kenya); jurisdiction covers Kenya, Tanzania and Uganda.

The Roman Catholic Church

Uganda comprises four archdioceses and 15 dioceses. At 31 December 2000 there were an estimated 10,057,388 adherents (an estimated 44.9% of the total population).

Uganda Episcopal Conference

Uganda Catholic Secretariat, POB 2886, Kampala; tel. (41) 268175; fax (41) 268713.

f. 1974; Pres. Mgr PAUL L. KALANDA (Bishop of Fort Portal).

Archbishop of Gula: Most Rev. JOHN BAPTISTE ODAMA, Archbishop's House, POB 200, Gula; tel. (471) 32026.

Archbishop of Kampala: Cardinal EMMANUEL WAMALA, Archbishop's House, POB 14125, Mengo, Kampala; tel. (41) 270183; fax (41) 345441.

Archbishop of Mbarare: Most Rev. PAUL BAKYENGA, Archbishop's Office, Nyamitanga, POB 184, Mbarare; tel. (485) 20052; fax (485) 21249.

Archbishop of Tororo: Most Rev. JAMES ODONGO, Archbishop's House, POB 933, Mbale; tel. (45) 33269; fax (45) 33754.

ISLAM

The Uganda Muslim Supreme Council: POB 3247, Kampala; Mufti of Uganda IBRAHIM SAID LUWEMBA; Chief Kadi and Pres. of Council HUSAYN RAJAB KAKOOZA.

BAHÁ'Í FAITH

National Spiritual Assembly: POB 2662, Kampala; tel. (41) 540511; fax (41) 530147; e-mail bahai@spacenetuganda.com; mems resident in 2,721 localities.

The Press

DAILY AND OTHER NEWSPAPERS

The Citizen: Kampala; official publ. of the Democratic Party; English; Editor JOHN KYEYUNE.

The Crusader: Kampala Rd, Kampala; publ. suspended April 1999; Editor GEORGE LUGALAMBI.

The Economy: POB 6787, Kampala; weekly; English; Editor ROLAND KAKOOZA.

Financial Times: Plot 17/19, Station Rd, POB 31399, Kampala; tel. (41) 245798; bi-weekly; English; Editor G. A. ONEGI OBEL.

Focus: POB 268, Kampala; tel. (41) 235086; fax (41) 242796; f. 1983; publ. by Islamic Information Service and Material Centre; 4 a week; English; Editor HAJJI KATENDE; circ. 12,000.

Guide: POB 5350, Kampala; tel. (41) 233486; fax (41) 268045; f. 1989; weekly; English; Editor-in-Chief A. A. KALIISA; circ. 30,000.

The Monitor: POB 12141, Kampala; tel. (41) 231541; fax (41) 251352; e-mail info@monitor.co.ug; internet www.monitor.co.ug; f. 1992; daily; English; Editor-in-Chief WAFULA OGUTTU; Editor CHARLES ONYANGO-OBBO; circ. 25,000 (Mon.–Sat.), 30,000 (Sun.).

Mulengera: POB 6787, Kampala; weekly; Luganda; Editor ROLAND KAKOOZA.

Munnansi News Bulletin: POB 7098, Kampala; f. 1980; weekly; English; owned by the Democratic Party; Editor ANTHONY SGEKWEYAMA.

Munno: POB 4027, Kampala; f. 1911; daily; Luganda; publ. by the Roman Catholic Church; Editor ANTHONY SSEKWEYAMA; circ. 7,000.

New Vision: POB 9815, Kampala; tel. (41) 235846; fax (41) 235221; e-mail wpike@newvision.co.ug; internet www.newvision.co.ug; f. 1986; official govt newspaper; daily; English; Editor WILLIAM PIKE; circ. 34,000 (Mon.–Sat.), 42,000 (Sun.).

Bukedde: daily; Luganda; Editor MAURICE SSEKWAUNGU; circ. 16,000.

Etop: weekly; vernacular; Editor KENNETH OLUKA; circ. 5,000.

Ormuri: tel. (485) 21265; e-mail visionmb@infocom.co.ug; weekly; vernacular; Editor JOSSY MUHANGI; circ. 11,000.

Rupiny: weekly; vernacular; Editor CHRIS BANYA; circ. 5,000.

Ngabo: POB 9362, Kampala; tel. (41) 42637; f. 1979; daily; Luganda; Editor MAURICE SEKAWUNGU; circ. 7,000.

The Star: POB 9362, Kampala; tel. (41) 42637; f. 1980; revived 1984; daily; English; Editor SAMUEL KATWERE; circ. 5,000.

Taifa Uganda Empya: POB 1986, Kampala; tel. (41) 254652; f. 1953; daily; Luganda; Editor A. SEMBOGA; circ. 24,000.

Weekly Topic: POB 1725, Kampala; tel. (41) 233834; weekly; English; Editor JOHN WASSWA; circ. 13,000.

PERIODICALS

Eastern Africa Journal of Rural Development: Dept of Agriculture, Makerere University, POB 7062, Kampala; 2 a year; circ. 800.

The Exposure: POB 3179, Kampala; tel. (41) 267203; fax (41) 259549; monthly; politics.

Leadership: POB 2522, Kampala; tel. (41) 221358; fax (41) 221576; f. 1956; 6 a year; English; Roman Catholic; circ. 7,400.

Mkombozi: c/o Ministry of Defence, Republic House, POB 3798, Kampala; tel. (41) 270331; f. 1982; military affairs; Editor A. OPOLOTT.

Musizi: POB 4027, Mengo, Kampala; f. 1955; monthly; Luganda; Roman Catholic; Editor F. GITTA; circ. 30,000.

Pearl of Africa: POB 7142, Kampala; monthly; govt publ.

Uganda Confidential: POB 5576, Kampala; tel. (41) 250273; fax (41) 255288; e-mail ucl@swiftuganda.com; internet www .swiftuganda.com/~confidential; f. 1990; monthly; Editor TEDDY SSEZI-CHEEYE.

NEWS AGENCIES

Uganda News Agency (UNA): POB 7142, Kampala; tel. (41) 232734; fax (41) 342259; Dir CRISPUS MUNDUA (acting).

Foreign Bureaux

Inter Press Service (IPS) (Italy): Plot 4, 3rd St, Industrial Area, POB 16514, Wandegeya, Kampala; tel. (41) 235846; fax (41) 235211; Correspondent DAVID MUSOKE.

Newslink Africa (United Kingdom): POB 6032, Kampala.

Rossiiskoye Informatsionnoye Agentstvo—Novosti (RIA—Novosti) (Russia): POB 4412, Kampala; tel. (41) 232383; Correspondent Dr OLEG TETERIN.

Xinhua (New China) News Agency (People's Republic of China): Plot 27, Prince Charles Drive, Kampala; tel. (41) 347109; fax (41) 254951; Chief Correspondent WANG SHANGZHI.

Publishers

Centenary Publishing House Ltd: POB 6246, Kampala; tel. (41) 241599; fax (41) 250427; f. 1977; religious (Anglican); Man. Dir Rev. SAM KAKIZA.

Fountain Publishers Ltd: POB 488, Kampala; tel. (41) 259163; fax (41) 251160; e-mail fountain@starcom.co.ug; internet www .fountainpublishers.co.ug; f. 1989; general, school textbooks, children's books, academic; Man. Dir JAMES TUMUSIIME.

Longman Uganda Ltd: POB 3409, Kampala; tel. (41) 42940; f. 1965; Man. Dir M. K. L. MUTYABA.

Uganda Printing and Publishing Corporation: POB 33, Entebbe; tel. (42) 20639; fax (42) 20530; f. 1993; Man. Dir P. A. BAKER.

Broadcasting and Communications

TELECOMMUNICATIONS

CelTel Ltd: POB 6771, Kampala; tel. (41) 230110; fax (41) 230106; e-mail celmail@imul.com; Man. Dir A. K. SSEMMANDA.

MTN Uganda Ltd: POB 24624, Kampala; fax (41) 078212250; internet www.mtn.co.ug; f. 1998.

Uganda Communications Commission: Kampala; f. 1998; regulatory body.

Uganda Telecom Ltd (UTL): POB 7171, Kampala; tel. (41) 258855; fax (41) 345907; f. 1998; state-owned; privatization pending.

BROADCASTING

Radio

91.3 Capital FM: POB 7638, Kampala; tel. (41) 235092; fax (41) 344556; e-mail capital@imul.com; f. 1993; independent music station broadcasting from Kampala, Mbarara and Mbale; Chief Officers WILLIAM PIKE, PATRICK QUARCOO.

Central Broadcasting Service (CBS): POB 12760, Kampala; tel. (41) 272993; fax (41) 340031; e-mail cbs@imul.com; f. 1996; independent station broadcasting in local languages and English to most of Uganda.

Radio One: POB 4589, Kampala.

Radio Uganda: POB 7142, Kampala; tel. (41) 257256; fax (41) 256888; f. 1954; state-controlled; broadcasts in 24 languages, including English, Swahili and Ugandan vernacular languages; Commr for Broadcasting JACK TURYAMWIJUKA.

Sanyu Radio: Katto Plaza, Nkrumah Rd, Kampala; f. 1993; independent station broadcasting to Kampala and its environs.

Voice of Toro: POB 2203, Kampala.

Television

Sanyu Television: Naguru; f. 1994; independent station broadcasting to Kampala and its environs.

Uganda Television (UTV): POB 7142, Kampala; tel. (41) 254461; f. 1962; state-controlled commercial service; programmes mainly in English, also in Swahili and Luganda; transmits over a radius of 320 km from Kampala; five relay stations are in operation, others are under construction; Controller of Programmes FAUSTIN MISANVU.

Finance

(cap. = capital; res = reserves; dep. = deposits; m. = million; brs = branches; amounts in new Uganda shillings unless otherwise indicated)

BANKING

Central Bank

Bank of Uganda: 37–43 Kampala Rd, POB 7120, Kampala; tel. (41) 258441; fax (41) 255983; e-mail info@bou.or.ug; internet www.bou.or.ug; f. 1966; bank of issue; cap. 20,000m., res 186,036m., dep. 1,753,966m. (June 2000); Gov. EMMANUEL TUMUSIIME-MUTEBILE; Dep. Gov. Dr LOUIS AUSTIN KASEKENDE.

State Banks

Uganda Commercial Bank Ltd (UCBL): Plot 12, Kampala Rd, POB 973, Kampala; tel. (41) 234710; fax (41) 259012; e-mail ucb@starcom.co.ug; f. 1965; 51% state-owned; operations placed under the control of Bank of Uganda April 1999; cap. 1,500m., res 5,705m., dep. 246,531m. (Sept. 1999); Chair. I. K. KABANDA; Dirs CHRIS KASSAMI, Dr RUTARO-MUTORO, Dr GERMINA SEMOGERERE; 67 brs.

Uganda Development Bank: UDB Towers, 22 Hannington Rd, POB 7210, Kampala; tel. (41) 230446; fax (41) 258571; e-mail udb@afsat.com; f. 1972; state-owned; reorg. 2001; privatization pending; cap. 11m. (Dec. 1993); Chair. JOHN R. DOWNER.

Commercial Banks

Allied Bank International (Uganda) Ltd: 24 Jinja Rd, POB 2750, Kampala; tel. (41) 236535; fax (41) 230439; e-mail allied@starcom.co.ug; reorg. in 1996; 59.7% owned by Banque Belgolaise SA, 23.4% by Netherlands govt agency; cap. 2,264m., res 391m., dep 18,596m. (Dec. 2000); Man. Dir J. J. LAING; 3 brs.

Crane Bank Ltd: 38 Kampala Rd, POB 22572, Kampala; tel. (41) 231337; fax (41) 231578; e-mail cranebnk@cranebanklimited.com; internet www.cranebanklimited.com; 33.33% owned by M/S Anglo Universal Holdings Ltd, 16.67% by M/S Meera Investments Ltd, remainder owned by private investors; cap. 5,000m., dep. 69,446m. (March 2001); Chair. SAMSON MUWANGUZI; Man. Dir A. M. RAO.

DFCU Bank Ltd: Impala House, 13 Kimathi Ave, POB 70, Kampala; tel. (41) 231784; fax (41) 231687; e-mail dfcubank@dfcugroup.com; f. 1984 as Gold Trust Bank Ltd, current name adopted 2000; cap. and res 8,500m., dep. 29,801m. (Dec. 2001); Chair. Dr WILLIAM KALEMA; Man. Dir JOHN TAYLOR.

International Credit Bank Ltd: Katto Plaza, Plot 11/13, Nkrumah Rd, POB 22212, Kampala; tel. (41) 342291; fax (41) 230408; f. 1977; cap. and res 2,060m., dep. 9,794m. (June 1996); Chair. THOMAS I. KATTO; Gen. Man. S. BALARAMAN.

Nile Bank Ltd: Spear House, Plot 22, Jinja Rd, POB 2834, Kampala; tel. (41) 346904; fax (41) 257779; e-mail nilebkug@imul.com; f. 1988; 15.88% owned by East African Development Bank, remainder owned by private investors; cap. and res 3,150m., dep. 18,237m. (Dec. 1999); Chair. MARY GUMISIRIZA (acting); Man. Dir ANTON BENTLEY; 3 brs.

Orient Bank Ltd: Orient Plaza, Plot 6/6A, Kampala Rd, POB 3072, Kampala; tel. (41) 236012; fax (41) 236066; e-mail mail@orient-bank.com; internet www.orient-bank.com; f. 1993; cap. 5,000m., dep. 47,461m. (June 2002); Chair. KETAN MORJARIA; Man. Dir SAMWIRI H. K. NJIIKI; 6 brs.

Development Banks

Development Finance Co of Uganda Ltd: Rwenzori House, Lumumba Rd, POB 2767, Kampala; tel. (41) 231215; fax (41) 259435; e-mail dfcu@dfc-ug.com; owned by Commonwealth Devt Corpn, Uganda Devt Corpn, Int. Finance Corpn and DEG (25% each); cap. and res 6,953m. (Dec. 1995); Chair. WILLIAM KALEMA; CEO JOHN S. TAYLOR.

East African Development Bank (EADB): East African Development Bank Bldg, 4 Nile Ave, POB 7128, Kampala; tel. (41) 230021; fax (41) 259763; e-mail dg@eadb.com; internet www.eadb.com; f. 1967; provides financial and tech. assistance to promote industrial development within Uganda, Kenya and Tanzania, whose Govts each hold 25.46% of the equity, the remaining 23.62% being shared by FMO Netherlands, Deutsche Investitions- und Entwicklungs-GmbH, the African Development Bank and others; regional offices in Nairobi and Dar es Salaam; cap. SDR 37.5m., res SDR 2.8m. (Dec. 2000); Dir (Uganda) E. TUMUSIIME-MUTEBILE.

Foreign Banks

Bank of Baroda (Uganda) Ltd (India): 18 Kampala Rd, POB 7197, Kampala; tel. (41) 233680; fax (41) 230781; e-mail bob12@calva.com; f. 1969; wholly owned by Bank of Baroda (India); cap. 2,000m., res 1,127m., dep. 73,016m. (Dec. 2000); Chair. Dr A. K. KHANDELWAL; Man. Dir P. L. KAGALWALA; 7 brs.

Barclays Bank of Uganda Ltd (United Kingdom): 16 Kampala Rd, POB 2971, Kampala; tel. (41) 232594; fax (41) 259467; e-mail barclays-uganda@barclays.com; internet www.barclays.com/uganda.htm; f. 1969; wholly owned by Barclays Bank PLC (UK); cap. 2,000m., res 9,533m., dep. 125,887m. (Dec. 2000); Chair. and Man. Dir FRANK GRIFFITHS; 4 brs.

Stanbic Bank Uganda Ltd (United Kingdom): 45 Kampala Rd, POB 72647, Kampala; tel. (41) 231151; fax (41) 231116; e-mail ugandainfo@stanbic.com; internet www.stanbic.co.ug; f. 1906 as National Bank of India Uganda, adopted present name 1993; wholly owned by Stanbic Africa Holdings Ltd (UK); cap. 4,000m., res 8,842m., dep. 197,962m. (Dec. 2000); Chair. R. E. NORVAL; Man. Dir A. C. KLEINSCHMIDT; 2 brs.

Standard Chartered Bank Uganda Ltd (United Kingdom): 5 Speke Rd, POB 7111, Kampala; tel. (41) 258211; fax (41) 231473; e-mail sbc.uganda@ug.standardchartered.com; internet www.standardchartered.com/ug; f. 1969; wholly owned by Standard Chartered Bank Africa PLC; cap. 2,000m., res 14,986m., dep. 231,847m. (Dec. 1999); Chair. A. E. H. GROAG; CEO W. MATSAIRA.

Tropical Africa Bank Ltd (Libya): Plot 27, Kampala Rd, POB 9485, Kampala; tel. (41) 241408; fax (41) 232296; e-mail tabu10@calva.com; f. 1972; 50% govt-owned, 50% owned by Libyan Arab Foreign Bank; cap. 7,000m. (Jan. 2000); Chair. EMMANUEL TUMUSIIME-MUTEBILE; Gen. Man. KAMEL M. EL KHALLAS.

STOCK EXCHANGE

Kampala Stock Exchange: East African Development Bank Bldg, 4 Nile Ave, POB 24565, Kampala; tel. (41) 342788; fax (41) 343803; e-mail cma@starcom.co.ug; f. 1997; Chair. LEO KIBIRANGO; Chief Exec. JAPHETH KATTO.

INSURANCE

East Africa General Insurance Co Ltd: Plot 14, Kampala Rd, POB 1392, Kampala; tel. and fax (41) 343234; life, fire, motor, marine and accident; Gen. Man. E. MULONDO.

National Insurance Corporation: Plot 3, Pilkington Rd, POB 7134, Kampala; tel. (41) 258001; fax (41) 259925; f. 1964; general and life; Man. Dir S. SEBUUFU.

Pan World Insurance Co Ltd: POB 7658, Kampala; tel. (41) 341618; fax (41) 341593; e-mail pwico@imul.com; Gen. Man. GORDON SENTIBA.

Uganda American Insurance Co Ltd: POB 7077, Kampala; tel. and fax (41) 533781; f. 1970; Man. Dir STAN MENSAH.

Uganda Co-operative Insurance Ltd: Plot 10, Bombo Rd, POB 6176, Kampala; tel. (41) 241836; fax (41) 258231; f. 1982; general; Chair. EPHRAIM KAKURU; Gen. Man. D. S. MASWERE.

Trade and Industry

GOVERNMENT AGENCIES

Capital Markets Authority: East African Development Bank Bldg, 4 Nile Ave, POB 24565, Kampala; tel. (41) 342788; fax (41) 342803; e-mail cma@starcom.co.ug; f. 1996 to develop, promote and regulate capital markets sector; CEO JAPHETH KATTO.

Enterprise Development Unit (EPD): Kampala; oversees privatization programme; Exec. Dir LEONARD MUGANWA.

Export and Import Licensing Division: POB 7000, Kampala; tel. (41) 258795; f. 1987; advises importers and exporters and issues import and export licences; Prin. Commercial Officer JOHN MUHWEZI.

Uganda Advisory Board of Trade: POB 6877, Kampala; tel. (41) 33311; f. 1974; issues trade licences and service for exporters.

Uganda Export Promotion Board: POB 5045, Kampala; tel. (41) 230233; fax (41) 259779; e-mail uepc@starcom.co.ug; internet www .ugandaexportsonline.com; f. 1983; provides market intelligence, organizes training, trade exhbns, etc. Exec. Dir FLORENCE KATE.

Uganda Investment Authority: Investment Centre, Plot 28, Kampala Rd, POB 7418, Kampala; tel. (41) 251562; fax (41) 342903; e-mail uia@starcom.co.ug; internet www.ugandainvest.com; f. 1991; promotes foreign and local investment, assists investors, provides business information, issues investment licences; Exec. Dir YOB YOBE OKELLO.

DEVELOPMENT ORGANIZATIONS

Agriculture and Livestock Development Fund: f. 1976; provides loans to farmers.

National Housing and Construction Corporation: Crested Towers, POB 659, Kampala; tel. (41) 257461; fax (41) 258708; e-mail nhcc@imul.com; internet www.nhcc.ug.com; f. 1964; govt agent for building works; also develops residential housing; Chair. Dr COLIN SENTONGO; Gen. Man. M. S. KASEKENDE.

Uganda Industrial Development Corporation Ltd (ULDC): 9–11 Parliament Ave, POB 7042, Kampala; f. 1952; Chair. SAM RUTEGA.

CHAMBER OF COMMERCE

Uganda National Chamber of Commerce and Industry: Plot 17/19, Jinja Rd, POB 3809, Kampala; tel. (41) 258792; fax (41) 258793; e-mail uma@starcom.co.ug; Chair. Pres. BONEY KATATUMBA.

INDUSTRIAL AND TRADE ASSOCIATIONS

CMB Ltd (Coffee Marketing Board): POB 7154, Kampala; tel. (41) 254051; fax (41) 230790; state-owned; privatization pending; purchases and exports coffee; Chair. Dr DDUMBA SSENTAMU; Man. Dir SAM KIGGUNDU.

Cotton Development Organization: POB 7018, Kampala; tel. (41) 232968; fax (41) 232975; Man. Dir JOLLY SABUNE.

Produce Marketing Board: POB 3705, Kampala; tel. (41) 236238; Gen. Man. ESTHER KAMPAMPARA.

Uganda Coffee Development Authority: Coffee House, Plot 35, Jinja Rd, POB 7267, Kampala; tel. (41) 256940; fax (41) 256994; e-mail ucdajc@ugandacoffee.org; internet www.ugandacoffee.org; f. 1991; enforces quality control and promotes coffee exports, maintains statistical data, advises Govt on local and world prices and trains processors and quality controllers; Man. Dir HENRY NGA-BIRANO.

Uganda Importers', Exporters' and Traders' Association: Kampala.

Uganda Manufacturers' Association (UMA): POB 6966, Kampala; tel. (41) 221034; fax (41) 220285; e-mail uma@starcom.co.ug; internet www.uganda.co.ug/uma.htm; promotes mfrs' interests; Chair. JAMES MULWANA.

Uganda Tea Authority: POB 4161, Kampala; tel. (41) 231003; state-owned; controls and co-ordinates activities of the tea industry; Gen. Man. MIRIA MARGARITA MUGABI.

EMPLOYERS' ORGANIZATION

Federation of Uganda Employers: POB 3820, Kampala; tel. (41) 220201; fax (41) 221257; e-mail fue@infocom.co.ug; Chair. ALOYSIUS K. SSEMMANDA; Exec. Dir ROSEMARY N. SSENABULYA.

UTILITIES

Electricity

Uganda Electricity Board: POB 7059, Kampala; tel. (41) 254071; fax (41) 235119; e-mail okumu@infocom.co.ug; f. 1948; privatization pending; Chair. J. E. N. KAGULE-MAGAMBO; 36 brs.

Water

National Water & Sewerage Corpn: Plot 39, Jinja Rd, POB 7053, Kampala; tel. (41) 256596; fax (41) 346532; e-mail nwscmd@infocom .co.ug; internet www.nwsc.co.ug; f. 1972; privatization pending; Man. Dir WILLIAM TSIMWA MUHAIRWE; 12 brs.

CO-OPERATIVES

In 2000 there were 6,313 co-operative societies, grouped in 34 unions. There is at least one co-operative union in each administrative district.

Uganda Co-operative Alliance: Kampala; co-ordinating body for co-operative unions, of which the following are among the most important:

Bugisu Co-operative Union Ltd: Palisa Rd, Private Bag, Mbale; tel. (45) 33027; f. 1954; processors and exporters of Bugisu arabica coffee; 226 mem. socs; Gen. Man. WOMUTU.

East Mengo Growers' Co-operative Union Ltd: POB 7092, Kampala; tel. (41) 270383; fax (41) 243502; f. 1968; processors and exporters of coffee and cotton; 280 mem. socs; Chair. FRANCIS MUKAMA; Man. JOSEPH SSEMOGERERE.

Kakumiro Growers' Co-operative Union: POB 511, Kakumiro; processing of coffee and cotton; Sec. and Man. TIBIHWA-RUKEERA.

Kimeeme Livestock Co-operative Society: Mwanga II Rd, POB 6670, Kampala; f. 1984; farming and marketing of livestock; Chair. SAMUSI LUKIMA.

Lango Co-operative Union: POB 59, Lira; tel. (473) 79; f. 1956; ginning and exporting of conventional and organic cotton produce; Gen. Man. PATRICK ORYANG.

Masaka Co-operative Union Ltd: POB 284, Masaka; tel. (481) 20260; f. 1951; coffee, dairy farming, food processing, carpentry; 245 primary co-operative socs; Chair. J. M. KASOZI; Gen. Man. EDWARD C. SSERUUMA.

Mubende District Co-operative Union: coffee growers.

Nyakatonzi Growers Co-operative Union: Fort Portal Rd, POB 32, Kasese; tel. (483) 4370; fax (483) 44135; f. 1957; processors and exporters of coffee and cotton; Gen. Man. ADAM BWAMBALE.

South Bukedi Co-operative Union: 6 Busia Rd, POB 101, Tororo; tel. (45) 44327; f. 1952; ginning and export of cotton lint; Gen. Man. MICHAEL O. OGUNDY.

South-west Nile Co-operative Union: POB 33, Pakwach, Nebbi; f. 1958; ginning and export of cotton; Gen. Man. PHILIP UPAKRWOTH.

Uganda Co-operative Savings and Credit Society: 62 Parliament Ave, POB 9452, Kampala; tel. (41) 257410; f. 1973; Chair PATRICK KAYONGO.

Uganda Co-operative Transport Union: 41 Bombo Rd, POB 5486, Kampala; tel. (41) 567571; f. 1971; general transport, imports of motor vehicles, vehicle repair and maintenance; Gen. Man. STEPHEN TASHOBYA.

Wamala Growers' Co-operative Union Ltd: POB 99, Mityana; tel. (46) 2036; f. 1968; coffee and cotton growers, real estate agents, cattle ranchers, printers, mfrs of edible oils, bricks, tiles and clay products; 250 mem. socs; Gen. Man. HERBERT KIZITO.

West Mengo Growers' Co-operative Union Ltd: POB 7039, Kampala; tel. (41) 567511; f. 1948; cotton growing and buying, coffee buying and processing, maize milling; 250 mem. socs; Chair. H. E. KATABALWA MIIRO.

West Nile Tobacco Co-operative Union: Wandi, POB 71, Arua; f. 1965; growing, curing and marketing of tobacco; Gen. Man. ANDAMAH BABWA.

TRADE UNION

National Organization of Trade Unions (NOTU): POB 2150, Kampala; tel. (41) 256295; f. 1973; Chair. E. KATURAMU; Sec.-Gen. MATHIAS MUKASA.

Transport

RAILWAYS

In 1992 there were 1,241 km of 1000-mm-gauge track in operation. A programme to rehabilitate the railway network is under way.

Uganda Railways Corporation: Nasser Rd, POB 7150, Kampala; tel. (41) 254961; fax (41) 344405; f. 1977 following the dissolution of East African Railways; Man. Dir D. C. MURUNGI.

ROADS

In 1985 there was a total road network of 28,332 km, including 7,782 km of main roads and 18,508 km of secondary roads. About 22% of roads were paved. By early 1997 about 60% of main roads (by then totalling some 10,000 km) had been rehabilitated, and it was planned to invest some US $1,500m. in a further 10-year rehabilitation project.

INLAND WATERWAYS

A rail wagon ferry service connecting Jinja with the Tanzanian port of Tanga, via Mwanza, was inaugurated in 1983, thus reducing Uganda's dependence on the Kenyan port of Mombasa. In 1986 the Uganda and Kenya Railways Corporations began the joint operation of Lake Victoria Marine Services, to ferry goods between the two countries via Lake Victoria.

CIVIL AVIATION

The international airport is at Entebbe, on Lake Victoria, some 40 km from Kampala. There are also several small airfields.

Civil Aviation Authority (CAA): Passenger Terminal Bldg, 2nd floor, Entebbe International Airport, POB 5536, Kampala; tel. (41) 20516; fax (41) 321401; e-mail aviation@caa.co.ug; internet www.caa.co.ug; Man. Dir AMBROSE AKANDONDA.

Principal Airlines

Air Alexander: Entebbe International Airport; f. 1999; operates cargo and passenger services between Entebbe and Kisangani (Democratic Republic of the Congo).

Dairo Air Cargo Services: 24 Jinja Rd, POB 5480, Kampala; tel. (41) 257731.

Eagle Air Ltd: Entebbe International Airport, POB 7392, Kampala; tel. (41) 344292; fax (41) 344501; e-mail eagle@swiftuganda.com; internet www.eagleuganda.com; f. 1994; domestic services, charter flights to neighbouring countries; Man. Dir Capt. ANTHONY RUBOMBORA.

East African Airlines: Airways House, 6 Colville St, POB 5740, Kampala; tel. (41) 232990; fax (41) 257279; f. 2002; services to Africa and the Middle East; CEO BENEDICT MUTYABA.

Inter Air: Nile Ave, POB 22658, Kampala; tel. (41) 255508.

Tourism

Uganda's principal attractions for tourists are the forests, lakes, mountains and wildlife and an equable climate. A programme to revive the tourist industry by building or improving hotels and creating new national parks began in the late 1980s. There were 191,276 tourist arrivals in 2000 (compared with 12,786 in 1983). Revenue from the sector in 1999 was estimated at US $149m. Unrest in western Uganda during the late 1990s had a negative impact on tourism.

Ministry of Tourism: Parliament Ave, POB 4241, Kampala; tel. (41) 232971; fax (41) 242188; provides some tourist information.

Uganda Tourist Board: Kimatti Ave, POB 7211, Kampala; tel. (41) 342196; fax (41) 342188; e-mail utb@starcom.co.ug; internet www.visituganda.com; Chair. PETER KAMYA; Gen. Man. IGNATIUS NAKISHERO.

UKRAINE

Introductory Survey

Location, Climate, Language, Religion, Flag, Capital

The Republic of Ukraine is situated in east-central Europe. It is bordered by Poland, Slovakia, Hungary, Romania and Moldova to the west, by Belarus to the north and by Russia to the north-east and east. To the south lie the Black Sea and the Sea of Azov. The climate is temperate, especially in the south. The north and north-west share many of the continental climatic features of Poland or Belarus, but the Black Sea coast is noted for its mild winters. Droughts are not infrequent in southern areas. Average temperatures in Kiev range from –6.1°C (21°F) in January to 20.4°C (69°F) in July, and average annual rainfall is 615 mm (24 ins). The official state language is Ukrainian, although Russian is widely spoken, particularly in the south and the east. Most of the population are adherents of Orthodox Christianity (which has three separate jurisdictions in Ukraine) and there are many adherents to the Roman Catholic Church (mostly 'Greek' Catholics, followers of the Eastern rites), particularly in western regions. There are also a number of Protestant churches, and small communities of Jews and Muslims. The national flag (proportions 2 by 3) has two equal horizontal stripes, of pale blue over yellow. The capital is Kiev (Kyiv).

Recent History

The original East Slavic state, Kievan Rus, founded in the late 10th century, was based in what is now Ukraine ('the Borderlands'), and is claimed as the precursor of Russia, Belarus and Ukraine. Following the fall of the Rus principalities, in the 13th and 14th centuries, during the Mongol invasions, the Ukrainians (sometimes known as Little Russians or Ruthenians) developed distinctively from the other Eastern Slavs, mainly under Polish and Lithuanian rulers. Ukrainians first entered the Russian Empire in 1654, when a Cossack state east of the Dnipro (Dniepr) river sought Russian protection from Polish invasion. In 1667 Ukraine was divided: the regions east of the Dnipro became part of Russia, while Western Ukraine was annexed by Poland. Russia gained more Ukrainian lands as a result of subsequent partitions of Poland (1793 and 1795) and, in the south, from the Ottoman Empire; the western regions were acquired by Austria.

When the Russian Empire collapsed, in 1917, Ukrainian nationalists set up a central Rada (council or soviet) in Kiev and demanded autonomy from the Provisional Government in Petrograd (St Petersburg). After the Bolshevik coup, in November, the Rada proclaimed a Ukrainian People's Republic. Although they initially recognized the new republic, in December the Bolsheviks established a rival Government in Kharkiv (Kharkov), and by February 1918 much of Ukraine was occupied by Soviet forces. In March, however, the Bolsheviks were forced to cede Ukraine to Germany, under the terms of the Treaty of Brest-Litovsk. Ukraine was the battleground for much of the fighting in the Civil War over the next two years, but in December 1920 a Ukrainian Soviet Socialist Republic (SSR) was established.

The Treaty of Rīga, which formally ended the Soviet–Polish War in 1921, assigned territories in western Ukraine to Poland, Czechoslovakia and Romania. Eastern and central lands formed the Ukrainian SSR, one of the founding members of the Union of Soviet Socialist Republics (USSR), in December 1922. The 1920s were a period of national development for Ukrainians: in particular, the use of the Ukrainian language was encouraged and literacy improved. However, the collectivization of agriculture from 1929 had severe consequences for the republic; between 5m. and 20m. Ukrainians were estimated to have died in a famine in 1933, which resulted from collectivization. In the 1930s advocates of the wider use of the Ukrainian language, or of greater autonomy for the republic, were arrested, and by the late 1930s almost the entire Ukrainian cultural and political élite had been imprisoned, killed or exiled. Ukraine also suffered greatly during the Second World War, which resulted in an estimated 6m. deaths in the republic, and great material losses.

Soviet victory in the war, and the annexing of territories from Czechoslovakia, Poland and Romania resulted in the uniting of the western and eastern areas of Ukraine, and the republic gained representation, nominally separate from that of the USSR, at the UN. In 1954 Crimea (formerly part of the Russian Federation), the Tatar inhabitants of which had been deported *en masse* to Soviet Central Asia in 1944, was transferred to Ukrainian control.

During the 1960s there was an increase in covert opposition to the regime, manifested in the production of independent publications, known as *samvydav* (*samizdat*—self-publishing). In 1972, however, there was widespread repression of dissidents and a purge of the membership of the ruling Communist Party of Ukraine (CPU). In 1973 Petro Shelest, First Secretary (leader) of the CPU, who had been accused of tolerating dissent in the republic, was replaced by Vladimir Shcherbitsky, a loyal ally of the Soviet leader, Leonid Brezhnev.

The accession of the reformist Mikhail Gorbachev to the Soviet leadership, in 1985, had little initial effect in Ukraine, largely owing to the authoritarianism of the Shcherbitsky administration. On 26 April 1986 a serious explosion occurred at the Chornobyl (Chernobyl) nuclear power station, in northern Ukraine. Only after unusually high levels of radiation were reported in other European countries did Soviet officials admit that large amounts of radioactivity had leaked into the atmosphere. A 50-km (30-mile) exclusion zone was created around Chornobyl (including large areas within neighbouring Belarus), from which 135,000 people were evacuated. Thirty-one people were killed in the initial explosion, but in 1996 it was reported that an estimated 2,500 deaths in Ukraine may have been caused by the accident, while a further 3.2m. people had been affected by the disaster, as a result of increased numbers of cancers and other related illnesses.

Official secrecy surrounding the Chornobyl accident led to greater public support for opposition movements in Ukraine, particularly the environmental group Green World. In 1988, moreover, the liberal nationalist Ukrainian People's Movement for Restructuring (Rukh) was founded by a group of prominent writers and intellectuals. Despite official opposition, Rukh's manifesto was published in 1989, and local branches were established throughout the republic. Furthermore, economic problems contributed to a growing militancy among mining communities in the Donbass region (around Donetsk, in eastern Ukraine), producing 11 strikes in the first three months of 1989. The revival of hitherto 'underground' religious groups from 1988 also assumed a national character in Ukraine. Notably, the Ukrainian (Byzantine rite) Catholic Church was legalized in December 1989, when Gorbachev met Pope John Paul II.

Shcherbitsky was dismissed in September 1989, and Volodymyr Ivashko was elected in his place. In local and republican elections, held on 4 March 1990, candidates supported by the Democratic Bloc, a coalition led by Rukh (which had been registered in February), won 108 of the 450 seats in the Verkhovna Rada (Supreme Soviet—republican legislature). Independents supported by the Bloc won about 60 seats, giving the opposition parties some 170 votes, although an estimated 280 supported the CPU leadership. The Bloc was particularly successful in western Ukraine, but performed poorly in the Russian-speaking communities of eastern and southern Ukraine.

In June 1990 Ivashko was elected Chairman of the Verkhovna Rada (the highest state post in the republic). In response to protests by deputies of the Democratic Bloc, he resigned later in the month as First Secretary of the CPU. On 16 July the Verkhovna Rada adopted a declaration of sovereignty, proclaiming the supremacy of republican authority within the Ukrainian SSR. Also in July Ivashko was appointed as the Deputy General Secretary of the Communist Party of the Soviet Union, precipitating his resignation as Chairman of the Verkhovna Rada. The new Chairman of the Verkhovna Rada was Leonid Kravchuk, hitherto Second Secretary of the CPU.

In October 1990 Vitaliy Masol resigned as Chairman of the Council of Ministers (Prime Minister); he was succeeded by Vitold Fokin, who was regarded as a supporter of moderate reforms. The Government participated in negotiations on a new union treaty and signed the protocol to a draft treaty in March

1991. The Government also agreed to conduct the all-Union referendum on the future of the USSR (see chapter on the Russian Federation), but appended a further question to the referendum, asking if Ukraine's 1990 declaration of sovereignty should form the basis for participation in a renewed federation. Of the electorate, 84% participated in the referendum, 70% of whom approved Gorbachev's proposal to preserve the USSR as a 'renewed federation'. However, Ukraine's own question received greater support (80%), and an additional question in certain regions of Western Ukraine, which asked voters if they supported a fully independent Ukraine, gained the support of 90% of those voting.

Following the attempted *coup d'état* in Moscow on 19 August 1991, led by the conservative communist State Committee for the State of Emergency, the Verkhovna Rada, on 24 August, adopted a declaration of independence, pending confirmation by a referendum on 1 December, when direct presidential elections were also scheduled. The CPU was banned at the end of August.

Despite his background in the CPU, Kravchuk's support for Ukrainian independence ensured his election as President of the Republic on 1 December 1991, with 62% of the votes cast. His closest rival, Vyacheslav Chornovil, a member of Rukh and a former dissident who had been imprisoned by the authorities under Brezhnev and Shcherbitsky, received 23%. In the referendum, held concurrently with the presidential election, some 90% of the electorate voted in favour of independence (84% of the electorate participated), which thereby took effect. Outwith Crimea, where 54% voted in favour of Ukrainian independence, more than 80% of the electorate voted for independence in every administrative region of Ukraine. In early December an independent Ukrainian armed forces was established, on the basis of those Soviet troops operative on Ukrainian territory at that time. In January 1992 a new interim currency coupon, which retained the Ukrainian name of the Soviet currency, the karbovanets, was introduced, and the Government formally adopted new national symbols early that year.

In June 1992 the Government narrowly avoided defeat in a vote of 'no confidence' in the Verkhovna Rada, in particular as the result of its economic policies; this criticism intensified as inflation increased sharply following the withdrawal of subsidies from foodstuffs in July. The Government resigned in September, having been conclusively defeated in a second vote of 'no confidence'. In October Leonid Kuchma, hitherto director-general of the Pivdenne/Yuzhnoye missiles factory in Dnipropetrovsk, and who had been first elected as a deputy in 1990, was appointed Prime Minister. The new Government consisted largely of moderate reformers.

In November 1992 the Verkhovna Rada granted Kuchma special powers to rule by decree for a period of six months. He proposed an extensive programme of economic reform, including privatization and severe reductions in government expenditure; in that month Ukraine withdrew from the so-called rouble zone. These measures were strongly opposed by left-wing groups, including the Socialist Party of Ukraine (SPU), which had been formed from elements of the CPU and which, in association with other left-wing groups, began a campaign to rescind the ban on the CPU. In January 1993 Viktor Yushchenko, a leading exponent of market reforms, was appointed Governor of the National Bank of Ukraine (NBU). In March Ihor Yukhnovskiy, the First Deputy Prime Minister and a leading reformer, resigned, apparently in protest at Kravchuk's perceived failure to combat corruption. In May, following the refusal of the legislature to renew the special powers granted to Kuchma in November 1992, the Prime Minister offered to resign, although the legislature rejected Kuchma's resignation after President Kravchuk had requested special constitutional powers to enable him to head the Government. As Ukraine began to experience hyperinflation, more than 2m. miners and factory workers, mainly in the Donbass region, joined a strike, in June 1993, to protest at the declining standard of living, demanding a referendum of confidence in the President and in the Verkhovna Rada; a plebiscite was subsequently scheduled for September.

Viktor Pynzenyk's resignation as Deputy Prime Minister, in August 1993, was regarded as marking the departure from the Government of the last serious advocate of economic reform. In September Kuchma again tendered his resignation, which was accepted by the legislature; Yukhym Zvyahilsky, hitherto First Deputy Prime Minister and a former Mayor of Donetsk and coal-mine director (in which capacity he had been a prominent leader of the protests earlier in the year), was appointed as Prime Minister, in an acting capacity, although after several days

President Kravchuk assumed direct control of the Government. The proposed referendum on confidence in the President and legislature was cancelled and early elections to the Verkhovna Rada were scheduled.

The elections to the new, 450-member Verkhovna Rada were held on 27 March 1994, with two subsequent rounds of voting in April, in constituencies where candidates had failed to secure 50% of the votes cast. The CPU (which had been permitted to contest the elections in advance of its subsequent re-legalization, pending the outcome of parliamentary discussion) won 86 seats, more than any other group, and, in alliance with the SPU and the Peasants' Party of Ukraine (PPU), formed the largest bloc in the Verkhovna Rada, although independent candidates were more numerous, with 170 seats. Rukh won 20 seats, and other moderate nationalist parties received 13. A notable political division between eastern Ukraine (where left-wing parties obtained greater support) and the west of the country (where moderate nationalist parties won the greatest share of the votes) was evident in the election results. Further rounds of voting, held in late 1994 to fill the 112 vacant seats, failed to elect candidates in more than 50 seats, which thus remained empty. In May Oleksandr Moroz, the leader of the SPU, was elected Chairman of the Verkhovna Rada, which in June elected Vitaliy Masol, premier of the Ukrainian SSR in 1987–90, as Prime Minister. Zvyahilsky, meanwhile, fled to Israel, seemingly in order to escape investigation into charges of corruption issued against him: he subsequently returned to Ukraine, having been granted immunity from prosecution.

A presidential election, held on 26 June 1994, proved inconclusive, as none of the seven candidates secured the minimum 50% of the votes necessary for election. Kravchuk received the greatest share of votes cast, with 37.7%, followed by Kuchma, with 31.3%. In a second round of voting, held on 10 July, Kuchma was elected President, securing 52.1% of the votes, while Kravchuk obtained 45.1%. The election result evidenced a continuing polarity in voting patterns between the east, where voters largely supported Kuchma, and the west, where Kravchuk secured a majority of votes cast.

In October 1994 Pynzenyk was reappointed to the Cabinet of Ministers, as First Deputy Prime Minister, responsible for Economic Reform. In March 1995 Masol resigned as Prime Minister; he was replaced, in an acting capacity, by Yevhen Marchuk, hitherto Deputy Prime Minister and Chairman of the State Security Service. As the economic crisis continued (although the rate of inflation had decreased considerably since 1993), President Kuchma sought greater executive powers, although the legislature consistently rejected any extension of presidential authority. In June 1995 the President and the Verkhovna Rada signed a Constitutional Agreement, announcing the cancellation of a referendum of confidence in the President and the legislature, previously announced by Kuchma, but granting the President additional powers, including the right to appoint leading officials, at national, regional and local levels, without the approval of the Verkhovna Rada, and to issue decrees with the force of legislation. These provisions were to remain in effect until the adoption of a new Constitution. Exceptionally, the President was to retain the prerogative to legislate economic reform by decree until the expiry of his term, in 1999.

In July 1995 a major government reshuffle was initiated, in which several reformist ministers were demoted, and more conservative politicians, known as 'red directors', including several regarded as close allies of Kuchma, were appointed. In particular, the First Deputy Prime Minister, Pavlo Lazarenko, and the Deputy Prime Minister, responsible for Industrial Policy, Anatoliy Kinakh, were regarded as hostile to further economic reform. In November the Verkhovna Rada voted to suspend the privatization of petroleum and gas enterprises, and blocked other economic legislation. Meanwhile, a Constitutional Commission completed work on a draft Constitution, which proposed an increase in the powers of the President, in March 1996; this text was rejected by the Verkhovna Rada. In May Kuchma dismissed Marchuk as premier, appointing Lazarenko in his place. As the legislature continued to oppose aspects of the draft, Kuchma threatened to call a referendum if it had not been approved by 25 June. Following lengthy discussions, the new Constitution was adopted on 28 June. It confirmed the extensive new powers of appointment granted to the President in the interim Constitutional Agreement, including the right to nominate the Prime Minister, and, *inter alia*, guaranteed the right to private ownership.

In July 1996 the Cabinet of Ministers resigned; Lazarenko retained the premiership in the new Government. As unrest in the coal-mining industry continued, the Government commenced a structural reorganization of the sector, and in mid-July an agreement to end a strike, which had been pursued intermittently since February, was reached with the trade unions. The attempted assassination of Lazarenko, shortly after the signing of the agreement, was linked by some observers to his role in resolving the dispute. In September Kinakh stepped down from his position as Deputy Prime Minister, becoming the President's special adviser on industrial policy. The long-awaited introduction of a new currency, the hryvnya, in September, was regarded as a significant indication that the serious economic difficulties that had affected Ukraine for several years were beginning to relent. In October Kinakh was selected as Chairman of an influential grouping of business leaders, the Ukrainian Union of Industrialists and Entrepreneurs.

In December 1996 Kuchma issued two decrees specifying the future composition of the Cabinet and stipulating that, henceforth, the Ministries of Internal Affairs, Foreign Affairs, Defence and Information were to be directly subordinated to the President. The newly reorganized Ministry of Information had already been granted extensive powers to co-ordinate the state-owned media. In April 1997 Pynzenyk tendered his resignation, citing the legislature's continued opposition to reform, although in May his successor, Serhiy Tyhypko, gained the legislature's approval for proposed agricultural reforms. In June Kuchma dismissed Lazarenko and appointed Vasyl Durdynets as acting Prime Minister until mid-July, when Valeriy Pustovoytenko, latterly Minister without Portfolio, was narrowly approved by the legislature as the new Prime Minister. In a subsequent governmental reorganization several ministries were transformed into state committees, which were to be directly answerable to the President.

In September 1997 the legislature approved a new electoral law, which provided for 225 seats in the 450-member Verkhovna Rada to be allocated by proportional representation on the basis of party lists, subject to their receiving a minimum of 4% of the total votes, and for the remaining 225 to be elected from single-seat constituencies. However, Kuchma's refusal to approve the law unless certain amendments were made led to the legislature's rejection, in October, of the Government's 1998 budget proposals. Following negotiations between Kuchma and the Chairman of the legislature, Moroz, the electoral law was approved with the required amendments; the 1998 budget was adopted in December 1997. In that month Kuchma revoked deputies' immunity from prosecution, after the Verkhovna Rada had refused to confirm the President's nominee to the position of Procurator-General. Meanwhile, it was announced that Lazarenko (who had been appointed Chairman of the Hromada—Community—party) was to be prosecuted on charges of embezzlement. In October the formation of a new, centrist party, headed by Pustovoytenko, the People's Democratic Party of Ukraine (PDPU), was announced.

A total of 30 parties and electoral blocs contested the elections to the Verkhovna Rada held on 29 March 1998, in which 70.8% of the electorate participated. The result of the elections demonstrated widespread support for left-wing parties, including the CPU, which obtained a total of 123 seats, becoming the largest party in the legislature. Eight parties exceeded the 4% threshold required to secure representation on the basis of party lists and some 136 independent deputies were elected. Several serious violations of the electoral law were reported by independent observers, in particular regarding the imposition of restrictions on the opposition media in the period prior to the elections. In order to comply with a Constitutional Court ruling that ministers could not simultaneously sit in the Verkhovna Rada, several ministers resigned from the Government following their election to the legislature. Repeated attempts by the new legislature to elect a chairman were unsuccessful, and in June Kuchma declared that economic-reform legislation would be introduced by presidential decree. In July, after 19 attempts, Oleksandr Tkachenko, the leader of the PPU, was elected as Chairman of the legislature.

Lazarenko was arrested in early December 1998 as he attempted to enter Switzerland, and charged with money-'laundering'. After his release on bail he returned to Ukraine later that month and denied the charges in a speech to the legislature. However, in February 1999 the Verkhovna Rada endorsed a resolution allowing for Lazarenko to be charged, and shortly afterwards he was detained in the USA.

In January 1999 the Verkhovna Rada approved a law on the presidential elections, to be held in October–November, stipulating that candidates must be supported by 1m. signatures from Ukrainians eligible to vote. In early 1999 Rukh split into two factions: Chornovil formed the Ukrainian People's Movement-Rukh (UPM-R), while the former Minister of Foreign Affairs, Hennadiy Udovenko, continued to head the People's Movement of Ukraine—Rukh (PMU-R). (In March Yuriy Kostenko assumed leadership of the UPM-R, after Chornovil's death in a motoring collision.) A government reorganization took place in March, as part of which the Ministry of Information was, notably, dissolved. During 1999 a number of ministers were dismissed, resulting in a high turnover of government members. In early August Kinakh was appointed as First Deputy Prime Minister, responsible for Economic Policy.

As campaigning for the presidential elections got under way, in mid-1999 Kuchma (who had declared his candidacy earlier in the year) was accused of irregularities including the illegal use of state funds to finance his campaign. In October, in a co-ordinated attempt to inhibit the chances of Kuchma gaining re-election, four left-wing nominees for the presidential elections—Marchuk, Tkachenko, Moroz and Volodymyr Oliynyk—announced their intention to unite around the candidacy of Marchuk. However, Moroz subsequently decided not to withdraw his candidacy, and Tkachenko declared his support for the candidate of the CPU, Petro Symonenko. The rate of participation in the first round of voting, on 31 October, was 70%. Kuchma won the largest proportion of the votes cast for any candidate, with 36.5%; his opponent in the second round, to be held on 14 November, was Symonenko, with 22.2%. Moroz was the third-placed candidate, with 11.3%. In early November Kuchma undertook a number of measures that were regarded as being intended to ensure his re-election in the second round. Notably, the governors of three oblasts (regions), in which the popular vote had supported Symonenko or Moroz, were dismissed. Shortly afterwards Kuchma appointed Marchuk as Chairman of the National Security and Defence Council. In the following days Nataliya Vitrenko (a first-round candidate, and leader of the Progressive Socialist Party of Ukraine) and Moroz announced their support for Symonenko. In the second ballot, on 14 November, Kuchma retained the presidency, with some 57.7% of the votes; Symonenko received 37.8%. Notably, the regional division in voting patterns evident in earlier presidential and parliamentary elections was not repeated. International observers stated that the election campaign and voting in the second round had been flawed, but that the overall result, none the less, adequately represented the will of the people. Kuchma was inaugurated on 30 November and, in accordance with the Constitution, the Government was immediately dismissed, pending the nomination of a new Prime Minister.

Having rejected a proposal to re-appoint Pustovoytenko as premier, the Verkhovna Rada endorsed the nomination of Viktor Yushchenko in mid-December 1999. The appointment to the premiership of Yushchenko was widely welcomed, in particular by centre-right factions and internationally, as he had gained a reputation as a competent and trustworthy economic reformer during his tenure as Governor of the NBU. In the new Cabinet of Ministers the number of ministries was again reduced. The appointment to the premiership of a prominent proponent of increased economic liberalization precipitated discontent within left-wing factions in the legislature. In January 2000 some 240 deputies, mainly members of centre-right and reformist parties, in addition to a number of independent deputies, announced the formation of a parliamentary majority, led by former president Kravchuk, and sought to remove Tkachenko from the chairmanship of the legislature, and to dismiss his deputy, Adam Martynyuk. In the face of left-wing opposition, in mid-January the majority faction held a separate session in a nearby exhibition centre and voted unanimously to remove Tkachenko and Martynyuk from office. The opposition continued to meet in the Verkhovna Rada building, although the faction was insufficient to constitute the quorum of 226 deputies specified by the Constitution. In February the majority faction elected Ivan Plyushch of the PDPU, who had previously held the post in 1994, as speaker. The left-wing 'rump' denied the majority access to the parliamentary building for several days, until several deputies of the centre-right grouping forced their way into the building, and subsequently won control of the legislature.

Meanwhile, deputies from all factions criticized a decree issued by Kuchma in mid-January 2000, scheduling a referendum on proposed constitutional change for 16 April; more than 3m. signatures had been collected in favour of this proposal, which appeared to be intended to strengthen the constitutional position of the President at the expense of that of the legislature. Of the six questions initially intended to feature in the referendum, two—on the dissolution of the Verkhovna Rada should deputies fail to form a majority government, and on the possibility of adopting a national constitution by means of a referendum—were excluded from the plebiscite by the Constitutional Court in late March. The four remaining questions—on the dissolution of the Verkhovna Rada should deputies fail to approve the state budget within three months of its submission, the reduction of the number of deputies from 450 to 300, the establishment of a bicameral legislature and the placing of limitations on the immunity enjoyed by deputies—were all approved by a majority of the 81% of the electorate that participated in the referendum. There was, however, no indication as to when or whether the proposals (which remained in abeyance in early 2003) would be implemented, heightening suspicions that the referendum had served primarily as a device to increase the President's authority over the legislature.

In January 2000 Lazarenko, who remained in custody in the USA, despite Swiss and Ukrainian attempts to extradite him, alleged that associates of Kuchma had benefited from the illegal diversion of IMF funds. The Government vigorously denied the claims, but the IMF decided to investigate the matter. In February the Fund also opened an inquiry into allegations that in 1997 and 1998 Ukraine exaggerated the extent of its foreign-exchange reserves in order to fulfil the criteria for assistance. In March 2000 the IMF confirmed that the NBU had indeed provided incorrect data on the size of its reserves, but was unable to prove that Ukrainian officials had been involved in embezzlement or abuse of power. In June Serhiy Tulub resigned as Minister of Fuel and Energy; later that month the Minister of the Economy, Tyhypko, the leader of the Working Ukraine party, won a seat in a legislative by-election, thereby excluding him from the Council of Ministers. Also in June Lazarenko was convicted *in absentia* of money-'laundering' by a court in Switzerland, and given an 18-month suspended prison sentence. Serhiy Yermilov was appointed as Minister of Fuel and Energy in July, and in August Kuchma appointed Vasyl Rohoviy, hitherto first deputy head of the presidential administration, as Minister of the Economy, a position that he had held in 1998–99. In July 2000 the Deputy Prime Minister, responsible for Energy Issues, Yuliya Tymoshenko, a prominent instigator of reforms in the energy sector and the leader of the Batkivshchyna—Fatherland party, faced charges of corruption, as a result of investigations into her former ally, Lazarenko, in the USA.

In September 2000 the State Security Service announced that it had successfully thwarted a coup attempt; President Kuchma conducted a reshuffle of military intelligence chiefs at the Ministry of Defence shortly afterwards. Also in September, the pro-Government majority alliance in the Verkhovna Rada elected the head of the parliamentary faction of the PDPU, Oleksandr Karpov, as its leader, in place of Kravchuk. In late September Kuchma dismissed the Minister of Foreign Affairs, Boris Tarasyuk, and appointed Anatoliy Zlenko in his place.

In early November 2000 a decapitated corpse, believed to be that of an investigative journalist, Heorhiy Honhadze, missing since mid-September, was discovered by police, near Kiev. Honhadze, who had edited an internet news site, *Ukrainska Pravda* (Ukrainian Truth), which had investigated incidents of high-level political corruption, had been a vocal critic of Kuchma; he had also made allegations of harassment by state officials. In late November Moroz released tape recordings in which Kuchma, the head of the presidential administration, Volodymyr Lytvyn, and the Minister of Internal Affairs, Yuriy Kravchenko, were alleged to discuss possible means of killing Honhadze. Over subsequent months several hours of audio recordings were released, precipitating a serious political crisis. Kuchma dismissed Moroz's demands for his resignation and, in early December, made a national address in which he claimed the scandal to be a carefully planned campaign to undermine Ukraine's international reputation. Controversy surrounded the authenticity of the recordings, which a former presidential security adviser, Maj. Mykola Melnychenko, claimed to have made over a period of several months, prior to fleeing Ukraine. (Melnychenko was granted exile in the USA in April 2001.) In late December 2000 demonstrations urging the resignation of Kuchma began in a number of cities, and continued throughout

early 2001 with support from a wide range of political parties, with the notable exception of the CPU.

In January 2001 Kuchma dismissed Tymoshenko, as an investigation into her alleged involvement in tax evasion and the smuggling of Russian gas proceeded; her duties were assumed by Oleh Dubyna, who Kuchma appointed as Deputy Prime Minister, responsible for Industrial Policy. In February further audio recordings were made public, in which President Kuchma was alleged to have ordered electoral fraud in the presidential election of 1999 and the bribery of senior energy officials. After initially denying the authenticity of the recordings, Kuchma admitted that the recordings were of his voice, but stated that they had been edited in an attempt to incriminate him. Demonstrations in Kiev, to demand a 'Ukraine without Kuchma' continued for several weeks, in which Tymoshenko, leading a loose coalition of opposition movements, the National Salvation Forum (NSF), was one of the most prominent leaders. In February, in an apparent concession to the demands of the protestors, Kuchma dismissed the head of the national security service, Gen. Leonid Derkach, and the head of the presidential bodyguard. In mid-February Tymoshenko was arrested on charges of tax evasion. Meanwhile, President Kuchma, parliamentary Chairman Plyushch and Prime Minister Yushchenko issued a statement, urging an end to the protests.

In late February 2001 the Prosecutor-General's office formally identified the body discovered in November as that of Honhadze, and opened a murder inquiry. In early March a demonstration by up to 18,000 anti-Kuchma protesters in Kiev, degenerated into violent clashes and was dispersed by police with tear-gas. In mid-March Kuchma ordered government officials to resign or publicly disassociate themselves from the protests. Although Yushchenko denounced the actions of the demonstrators, his position was regarded as being particularly vulnerable, as a result of his increasing unpopularity with both members of the Verkhovna Rada and with so-called 'oligarchs' (politically influential businessmen); this was despite the economic growth achieved during his premiership—in 2000 Ukraine's GDP had increased for the first time since independence. In late March, in a further apparent conciliatory gesture towards the opposition, Kuchma dismissed Minister of Internal Affairs Yuriy Kravchenko, replacing him with Yuriy Smirnov. At the end of the month Tymoshenko was released from prison, and all charges against her were dismissed. However, four days later Tymoshenko was re-arrested, while receiving medical treatment. In early April the Supreme Court suspended Tymoshenko's arrest, although the charges against her remained a subject of investigation; meanwhile, Tymoshenko was prohibited from leaving Ukraine.

In late April 2001 the Verkhovna Rada approved a motion of 'no confidence' in the Prime Minister and his Cabinet of Ministers. Yushchenko submitted his resignation, but was asked by Kuchma to remain in office until a new government had been formed. In mid-May Smirnov attributed Honhadze's death to a criminal attack, with no political motives, and announced that the investigation into his death would be closed. In late May Kinakh was appointed as Prime Minister; this appointment was widely regarded as an indication that the measures towards economic reform associated with Yushchenko were unlikely to be continued. In the new Government appointed in May–June, notable appointments included the promotion of Dubyna to the post of First Deputy Prime Minister, and of Rohoviy to Deputy Prime Minister, responsible for Economic Policy. At the end of July Kuchma dismissed the judge who had ordered Tymoshenko's release from custody. In mid-September several of the charges against Tymoshenko were dropped, although she was not permitted to travel outside Kiev.

In the latter half of 2001 a number of electoral blocs were formed in preparation for the forthcoming legislative elections. In late September Tymoshenko issued an appeal for other opposition groupings to join the NSF (of which she had been elected as leader in July), but rejected the suggestion that the NSF unite with the Our Ukraine bloc of centrist and nationalist parties, headed by Yushchenko; her supporters subsequently become known as the Yuliya Tymoshenko Bloc (YuTB). Meanwhile, the leader of the SPU, Moroz, appealed for the construction of another opposition grouping, but stated that he regarded Yushchenko as insufficiently independent of the presidential administration to lead such a group. In late September the Parliamentary Assembly of the Council of Europe (PACE, see p. 181) announced that a commission would be established to investigate the death of Honhadze. Meanwhile, supporters of

Kuchma formed the For a United Ukraine (FUU) bloc, headed by Lytvyn, which incorporated five parties, including several generally regarded as sympathetic to the interests of the 'oligarchs': among the members of the FUU were the PDPU, Kinakh's Party of Industrialists and Entrepreneurs of Ukraine, the Party of the Regions (PR), led by Volodymyr Semynozhenko, and Tyhypko's Working Ukraine.

In mid-October 2001 the Minister of Defence, Col-Gen. Oleksandr Kuzmuk resigned, following an incident in which a passenger aircraft flying from Tel-Aviv, Israel, to Novosibirsk, Russia, was accidentally shot down during Ukrainian military exercises over the Black Sea, killing all 78 people on board; Kuzmuk was replaced, initially in acting capacity, by Gen. Volodymyr Shkidchenko. (A similar incident, in which a missile hit an apartment block near Kiev in 2000, had resulted in 20 deaths.) In mid-November 2001 Kuchma dismissed Stanislav Stashevskyi as Minister of Fuel and Energy; Vitaliy Haiduk, who had been deputy fuel minister in Yushchenko's Government in 2000–01, was appointed in his place. In the following month Ihor Yushko was appointed to replace Ihor Mityukov as Minister of Finance.

In early February 2002 Ukrainian prosecutors charged Lazarenko, *in absentia*, with having ordered the murders of two parliamentary deputies in 1996 and 1998; in March 2002 the Prosecutor-General was reported to have rejected a motion approved by the Verkhovna Rada for the initiation of a legal investigation into Kuchma's alleged role in the case. In March the Government's director of arms exports, Valeriy Malev, was killed in an automobile collision. It subsequently emerged that several days before Malev's death Kuchma had been informed of the discovery of audio recordings made by Melnychenko, in which Kuchma and Malev were allegedly heard to discuss the illegal sale of air-defence equipment to Iraq, in violation of UN sanctions.

In the legislative election, held on 31 March 2002, Our Ukraine, which by this time comprised 10 moderate and nationalist parties, including two factions of Rukh (a third had been formed in late 2001), obtained both the largest share of the vote (23.57%) and the largest number of seats to be won by any party, receiving 112 (of which 70 were allocated on the basis of party-list voting); FUU received the second largest number of seats (101, including 35 from party lists), but only 11.78% of the votes cast. The CPU obtained 19.99% of the votes cast, but received only 66 seats (59 from party lists), compared with the 123 it had obtained in 1998. The Social-Democratic Party of Ukraine—United (SDPU—U) received 24 seats (19 from party lists) and 6.28% of the votes cast, the SPU 23 seats (20 from party lists) and 6.87% of the votes and the YuTB 22 seats—all of which were from party lists, and 7.26% of the votes. Four other parties obtained representation in single-mandate constituency seats, and 93 independent candidates were elected. An electoral bloc 'For Yushchenko' which, however, had no association with the former Prime Minister, failed to achieve legislative representation. Opposition spokesmen alleged that incidents of electoral fraud had been perpetrated, and a report by observers from the Organization for Security and Co-operation in Europe (OSCE, see p. 283) indicated 'important flaws' in the organization of the election. Additionally, on the eve of the polls, in what appeared to be a political assassination, a candidate of the pro-Kuchma SDPU—U was shot dead in the Ivano-Frankivsk region. In the subsequent formation of parliamentary factions, supporters of Kuchma were able to establish a larger grouping than those of Yushchenko, with the 'United Ukraine' faction (led by FUU) comprising 165 deputies, compared with the 120 deputies of the Our Ukraine faction. As neither grouping was sufficiently large to constitute a parliamentary majority in its own right, it appeared likely that the ability of the new Verkhovna Rada to pass legislation would be restricted, and attempts to form a coherent majority in the legislature continued throughout 2002. After the elections Viktor Medvedchuk, a former Deputy Chairman of the Verkhovna Rada and the Chairman of the SDPU—U, was appointed to head the presidential administration, following the election of the incumbent, Lytvyn, as Chairman of the Verkhovna Rada.

In late May 2002 Kuchma announced that, henceforth, first deputy ministers and deputy ministers were to be replaced by state secretaries, appointed by the President for a tenure of five years, concurrently with the presidential term of office, and not subject to removal during government re-organizations. It appeared likely that this restructuring would permit greater continuity in the work of ministries, while also representing an enhancement of the powers of the executive; a state secretary was, additionally, to be appointed to the Council of Ministers. In late July some 76 civilians were killed when a Ukrainian military plane crashed into a crowd of spectators at an airshow near Lviv, prompting renewed concern at standards of safety and discipline within the military; following a declaration by the Prosecutor-General, Svyatoslav Pyskun, that criminal negligence by pilots and military officials had played a part in the accident, the Chief of the General Staff and the Chief of the Military Air Force resigned, and were replaced by new appointees in August. However, Shkidchenko's offer to resign as Minister of Defence was declined.

As attempts to form a working majority in the Verkhovna Rada continued, in August 2002 Kuchma announced that a Constitutional Commission was to be formed to look into the possibility of introducing constitutional reforms, with the intention of surmounting the executive–parliamentary tensions that had characterized much of Ukrainian politics since independence; in particular, Kuchma expressed support for the introduction of a bicameral parliament and for a wider usage of proportional representation in the election of deputies. In early October supporters of Kuchma finally announced the formation of a majority grouping in the Verkhovna Rada, following the defection of several, hitherto, opposition deputies. However, the faction lost its majority after only one week, when five deputies left the group. In mid-October a senior judge in Kiev, Yuriy Vasylenko, opened a criminal investigation into Kuchma, who was charged with violating 11 articles of the criminal code, including charges of corruption, abuse of power and the sale of military radar equipment to Iraq. In late October the Supreme Court rejected an appeal by Pyskun declaring the case illegal. However, in early November, an ally of Kuchma, Vasyl Malyarenko, was elected as Chairman of the Supreme Court, replacing Vitaliy Boyko, and in late December the court ruled that the investigation into Kuchma had, indeed, been opened illegally.

In mid-November 2002 Kuchma dismissed Kinakh as Prime Minister; he was replaced, on 16 November, by Viktor Yanukovych, latterly Governor of Donetsk Oblast; a new Government, in which several principal positions remained unchanged, was appointed later in the month. In early December a pro-presidential majority was finally established in the Verkhovna Rada. Later in the month, amid violent scuffles, the legislature voted, at the second attempt, to dismiss Volodymyr Stelmakh as Governor of the NBU, and to approve Tyhypko as his replacement; this appointment had been rejected by the legislature in late November. Tyhypko's appointment to the post necessitated his resignation as a parliamentary deputy. Kuchma's position also appeared to be strengthened following the signing of an agreement, in early December, by the President, Yanukovych and Lytvyn on power-sharing between their respective domains, and by the removal, following a vote in the Verkhovna Rada later in the month, of opponents of Kuchma (principally deputies of Our Ukraine) from the leadership of parliamentary committees.

In late January 2003 the UPM-R renamed itself the Ukrainian People's Party, after proposals to re-unite the party, led by Kostenko, with the PMU-R, led by Udovenko, in a renewed Rukh movement had been abandoned; both parties, however, remained members of Our Ukraine. (In mid-May the former Minister of Foreign Affairs, Borys Tarasyuk, was elected to lead the PMU-R) In late February Yushchenko issued a public statement, addressed to Kuchma, Yanukovych and Lytvyn, urging an end to what was described as 'political terror', including physical assaults reportedly committed against several political activists and the unsolved murders of several journalists. Meanwhile, the office of the Prosecutor-General, the Ministry of Internal Affairs and the State Security Service commenced an investigation into the distribution by post, in early 2003, of at least 900,000 leaflets bearing Yushchenko's name and the representation of his signature, which had apparently been intended to discredit both Yushchenko and Tymoshenko; Yushchenko expressed dissatisfaction at the progress of the investigation, and in early March the distribution of all political leaflets by means of the state postal system was prohibited. Later in the month anti-Kuchma demonstrations were held in several major cities; attendance at a rally in Kiev, at which Yushchenko, Tymoshenko and Symonenko issued addresses, was estimated at up to 15,000, according to police figures, or up to 150,000, according to the organizers of the rally.

Meanwhile, in mid-February 2003 the Verkhovna Rada rejected draft legislation on constitutional reform, presented by deputies of the SDP—U and SDU, providing for the election of all 450 deputies on the basis of party lists and proportional representation, within the existing 225 constituencies; the draft, which was supported by deputies of Our Ukraine, the CPU and the YuTB, in addition to allies of the Government, was again rejected by the Verkhovna Rada in mid-April. However, in early March Kuchma submitted a draft on constitutional reform to the legislature: the draft envisaged that the Verkhovna Rada be replaced with a 300-seat State Assembly elected under a party-list system, and an 81-member House of Regions; moreover, the parliament was to be granted the power to dismiss the Prime Minister, and the President the power to dissolve parliament. Also in early March the Verkhovna Rada ordered Pyskun to investigate whether his predecessor as Prosecutor-General, Mykhaylo Potebenko, had abused his position by seeking the closure of the investigation into the Honhadze case. In early April Kuchma appointed Ivan Tkalenko, a former deputy of the PR, to a new ministerial post, the Minister of Relations with the Verkhovna Rada. In late March Leonid Kozachenko, a Deputy Prime Minister in the Kinakh Government, and a leading proponent of agricultural reform, was arrested, on charges of tax evasion and abuse of office. In mid-April the Verkhovna Rada, including, notably, the YuTB and SPU factions, and 55 deputies of Our Ukraine, approved the 'Programme of Activity' of the Cabinet of Ministers, outlining its priorities for economic development: in accordance with the Constitution the Verkhovna Rada was thereby forbidden to seek a vote of censure against the Cabinet for the period of one year. Also in mid-April, the Constitutional Court ruled that, in certain circumstances, deputies could be held accountable for administrative offences without prior approval from the Verkhovna Rada. In late April the two highest-ranking members of the Government were elected to senior positions in the PR: Yanukovych was elected as party Chairman and the First Deputy Prime Minister and Minister of Finance, Mykola Azarov, became the Chairman of the party's Political Council.

Despite the political differences between the Ukrainian-speaking western regions and the Russian-speaking eastern regions that were evident in parliamentary and presidential elections during the 1990s, only in the Crimean peninsula did any significant movement for re-unification with Russia emerge. The situation was further complicated by the status of the Crimean Tatars, who had been forcibly deported to Uzbekistan and elsewhere in Soviet Central Asia in 1944, and who began to return to their homeland from late 1989. In a referendum held in January 1991, residents of Crimea (which then had the status of an ordinary oblast) voted to restore it to the status of a nominally autonomous republic. The decision, although it had no legal basis in law, was ratified by the Verkhovna Rada. In June Crimean Tatars established 'parallel' institutions to those of the state, without any constitutional or legal status. The Kurultay was a popular assembly that was intended to convene once a year, the Mejlis was a national assembly that was to meet throughout the year, and a number of local assemblies were also established. Following Russia's decision, in January 1992, to re-examine the status of the transfer of Crimea from the Russian Federation to Ukraine in 1954, the Verkhovna Rada declared that this contravened a number of treaties, including one on the formation of the Commonwealth of Independent States (see p. 172). In February 1992 the Crimean Supreme Council, the regional legislature, voted to transform the region into the Republic of Crimea, and in May declared Crimea an independent state, adopting a new Constitution. However, following threats from the Verkhovna Rada to impose an economic blockade and direct rule on Crimea, the independence declaration was rescinded. In June the Ukrainian Government confirmed Crimea's status as an autonomous republic within Ukraine, which was otherwise to remain a unitary state. Meanwhile, relations between the local leadership and Crimean Tatars, some 250,000 of whom had returned to their homeland by late 1992, deteriorated steadily, primarily as a result of disputes over the ownership of land and property, and the right to gain Ukrainian citizenship. In October a Tatar encampment was dispersed on the orders of the Crimean Government, and in response some 6,000 Tatars stormed the Crimean parliament building.

With the election of Yurii Meshkov (an ethnic Russian and the leader of the Republican Party of Crimea) as President of Crimea in January 1994, it appeared likely that the region would renew moves towards sovereignty, as well as establish closer links with Russia. In response, the Verkhovna Rada approved constitutional amendments, according to which the Ukrainian President could nullify any measures taken by the Crimean authorities that he deemed to be illegal. In March a referendum was held in Crimea, simultaneously with the Ukrainian legislative elections; 70% of those voting in the referendum supported broader autonomous powers for Crimea. In May, following a vote by the Crimean parliament to restore the suspended Crimean Constitution of May 1992, the Ukrainian Government ordered the Crimean legislature to rescind its decision within 10 days; the crisis appeared to have been defused by June 1994, when delegations from the Ukrainian and Crimean parliaments met in Simferopol, the Crimean capital, where it was agreed that Crimea would continue to be subject to Ukrainian law. In September the Crimean legislature voted to restrict the Crimean President's executive authority, in response to which Meshkov suspended parliament, although the Crimean parliament was reconvened later in the month. Meanwhile, the Verkhovna Rada approved a constitutional amendment, permitting it to nullify any legislation adopted by the Crimean parliament that contravened the Ukrainian Constitution. In March 1995 the Ukrainian legislature voted to abolish both the Crimean Constitution of May 1992 and the Crimean presidency. In April 1995 Kuchma imposed direct rule on Crimea, and the Verkhovna Rada debated draft legislation to dissolve the Crimean parliament. A subsequent proposal by the Crimean parliament, that a referendum be held on the 1992 Constitution, was declared illegal by Kuchma, leading to its rescission, and to an agreement to prepare a new constitution.

Results of local elections in Crimea in June and July 1995 showed a marked decrease in support for pro-Russia parties, although in July the Crimean parliament elected a new Chairman, Yevhen Suprunyuk, who was reputed to be more conciliatory towards the Ukrainian Government. In October the Crimean legislature approved a new Constitution. Before its final adoption by the Verkhovna Rada in December 1996, the Constitution underwent several amendments; notably, Ukrainian was recognized as the state language, although Russian was to be the language of all official correspondence of the autonomous republic.

In October 1996 Suprunyuk resigned, and was replaced by Vasyl Kiselev, who pledged efforts to achieve a more united legislature. In January 1997 the Crimean legislature approved a motion of 'no confidence' in the regional Government, led by Arkadii Demydenko. In February, contrary to national law, which stipulates that the appointment of the Crimean Prime Minister is the prerogative of the Ukrainian President, the Crimean parliament arrogated to itself the power to appoint the regional Government. Additionally, Kiselev was dismissed by the legislature and replaced by Anatolii Gritsenko. In April the Crimean parliament appointed Anatolii Franchuk as the new Crimean premier, in place of Demydenko. Kuchma suspended this resolution, declaring it to be a violation of the Ukrainian Constitution but, following the approval of a further motion of 'no confidence' in Demydenko, in June Kuchma consented to his dismissal. A new Council of Ministers headed by Franchuk was subsequently approved by the Crimean legislature.

In October 1997 Kuchma exercised his veto over items of legislation approved by the Crimean Supreme Council—the adoption of Russian as the peninsula's official language of business communication, and the realignment of Crimea's time zone with that of Moscow—that were regarded as an assertion of the primacy of Crimea's links with Russia. Further conflict arose between the national Government and the Crimean legislature in February 1998, following the approval of legislation by the Verkhovna Rada, whereby all Ukrainian citizens were to be eligible to contest the seats in the Crimean legislature—hitherto, only citizens resident in Crimea had been eligible. In addition, the new legislation stated that elections to the Crimean parliament were to be held simultaneously with the elections to the Verkhovna Rada in March and not in September, as previously decided by the Crimean Supreme Council.

Elections to the Crimean legislature in March 1998 brought the issue of the status of the Crimean Tatars to the fore, when demonstrations were staged by Tatars appealing for the right to vote. The OSCE estimated that about one-half of the 165,000 Tatars resident in Crimea did not have Ukrainian citizenship and were, therefore, ineligible to vote. Leonid Grach, the leader of the CPU in Crimea, was elected Chairman of the new Crimean Supreme Council. In May a new Council of Ministers was appointed, with Sergei Kunitsyn as Chairman. In January 1999 a new Crimean Constitution came into effect, which granted the Crimean authorities the right to manage its own property and to pass a budget. Although citizenship had recently been granted to a number of Crimean Tatars, representatives of the group held a demonstration in May in Simferopol, demanding constitutional changes to ensure better representation and rights for Crimean Tatars and for the Crimean Tatar language to be recognized as a state language, and subsequent protests culminated in a 20,000-strong demonstration in Simferopol in May 2000.

A political impasse developed from the second half of 2000, apparently as a result of political rivalry between Kunitsyn and Grach, and as a result of alleged corruption within the Crimean Government; in September five ministers and two deputy prime ministers, all of whom were members of the CPU, resigned from the cabinet. Kunitsyn nominated new ministers in their place in December. In mid-July 2001 the Supreme Council dismissed Kunitsyn from the premiership for the third time, appointing Deputy Chairman Lentun Bezaziyev as acting premier. Although Kuchma had refused to recognize the previous two dismissals, in late July Kuchma accepted Kunitsyn's dismissal, and expressed support for the new premier elected by the Crimean Supreme Council, Valerii Gorbatov of the Working Ukraine party. A new Crimean Government was appointed in mid-September, although 11 of the 30 ministerial posts remained vacant in late November.

As campaigning for the concurrent elections to the Verkhovna Rada and the Crimean Supreme Council, to be held on 31 March 2002, commenced, controversy was provoked at the end of February by the invalidation of Grach's candidacy for a seat in the Supreme Council, on technical grounds. Some 30 candidates opposed to Grach were also disqualified. Following the rejection of Grach's appeal by the Crimean Court of Appeal, the case was referred to the national Supreme Court, but was not heard until after the elections, in April. Meanwhile, despite his disqualification, Grach's name appeared on ballot papers, and he was re-elected to the Supreme Council in defiance of the decision of the Crimean Court of Appeal. The elections to the Crimean Supreme Council demonstrated a sizeable shift in support away from the communists, towards centrists, whose grouping, known as the Kunitsyn Team, after its leader, won 39 of the 100 seats in the Council; a pro-communist electoral alliance known as the Grach bloc received 28 seats; three other parties obtained representation, and 29 independent candidates were elected. In late April the national Supreme Court approved Grach's appeal, thereby serving to legitimize his status as a deputy of the Crimean legislature. However, Grach was unsuccessful in his campaign for re-election as speaker of the legislature, being resoundingly defeated by a former deputy speaker, Boris Deich, at the opening session in late April. The new parliament also voted for the dismissal of Gorbatov and the re-appointment of Kunitsyn as Prime Minister, and reformists loyal to Kunitsyn were successful in establishing a majority in the legislature, with 67 of the 100 deputies. None the less, in the concurrent elections to the Verkhovna Rada, the CPU remained the most popular party on the peninsula. Notably, for the first time, Crimean Tatar deputies were elected to the Verkhovna Rada, within the Our Ukraine bloc. Russian nationalists only successfully captured votes in the Crimean city of Sevastopol.

Following the collapse of the USSR in 1991, the Ukrainian leadership was notably reluctant to sign any union agreement with the other former Soviet republics that might compromise its declaration of independence. It was this reluctance to enter into a renewed political union that led to the establishment of the CIS by President Kravchuk, and the leaders of the Russian Federation and Belarus, on 8 December. Although relations with Russia, as Ukraine's major trading partner and a country with close ethnic, historic, cultural and familial links with Ukraine, remained generally good following independence, tensions existed between those who sought to renew closer relations with Russia and countries of 'Eurasia', and those who sought to emphasize Ukraine's independence and 'European' status. Initially there were considerable difficulties over the details of the agreements, particularly in relation to the armed forces. Ukraine agreed to a unified command for the strategic forces of the former USSR, but began to establish its own conventional armed forces. In January 1994 a trilateral agreement on the denuclearization of Ukraine was signed by Ukraine, Russia and the USA, and in November the Verkhovna Rada voted to ratify the Treaty on the Non-Proliferation of Nuclear Weapons (see p. 82). In December Kuchma formally signed the Treaty, and the Strategic Arms' Reduction Treaty (START) I entered into force.

The transfer to Russia of Ukraine's nuclear weapons was completed by June 1996.

Ukraine refused to sign the CIS charter on closer political and economic co-operation, agreed by seven other CIS members in January 1993, regarding it as a threat to Ukraine's independent status. Although President Kuchma was regarded as being more sympathetic to Russian interests than Kravchuk had been, Ukraine consistently refused to participate in organizations that it perceived as being unduly dominated by Russia. However, in 1995 Ukraine became an associate member of the CIS Air Defence Agreement. In 1996 Ukraine rejected membership of a Customs Union, established by Belarus, Russia, Kazakhstan and Kyrgyzstan (which, in 2000, following the accession of Tajikistan, was renamed the Eurasian Economic Community). In 1997 Ukraine initiated the establishment of the GUAM (Georgia-Ukraine-Azerbaijan-Moldova) grouping, in an attempt to establish a counter-balance to Russia's dominant status in the CIS. In 2001 a permanent office of the grouping was opened in Yalta, Crimea. In September 1998 Kuchma rejected Russia's suggestion that Ukraine should join the Union of Russia and Belarus. In January 2003 Kuchma was elected as Chairman of the CIS, becoming the first non-Russian to hold that post.

The principal controversy between Ukraine and Russia concerned ownership of the former Soviet Black Sea Fleet, based in Sevastopol, Crimea. An initial agreement between the two countries to divide the fleet was abrogated. Although both countries agreed in July 1992 to exercise joint control over the fleet for a transitional period of three years, subsequent negotiations between Kravchuk and Russian President Boris Yeltsin made no progress, and in April 1995 the Russian parliament imposed a moratorium on plans to divide the fleet. Nevertheless, in June Presidents Yeltsin and Kuchma agreed to the equal division of the fleet, with separate Ukrainian and Russian bases. The main Russian base was to be at Sevastopol, although the exact legal status of the city was left unresolved. Negotiations continued, and by October 1996 it was reported that agreement had been reached on most issues, except that of ownership of the infrastructure in Sevastopol. The Russian legislature's decision, apparently in defiance of Ukrainian territorial integrity, in December, to accord Sevastopol the status of a Russian city threatened further to hinder the progress of the negotiations. None the less, Yeltsin and Kuchma signed an agreement on 31 May 1997, in accordance with which the Russian fleet was to lease three bays in Sevastopol for 20 years, while the Ukrainian fleet was to use the remaining bays. Upon expiry, the treaty could be renewed for five years, should both parties agree, but would then be subject to renegotiation. A bilateral Treaty of Friendship, Co-operation and Partnership was also signed, in which, significantly, Russia for the first time recognized the sovereignty of Ukraine. Russia finally ratified the treaty in February 1999, and further agreements were signed between Russia and Ukraine on compensation for the former Black Sea Fleet, in June, and on payment for the operations and services of jointly-used facilities, in March 2000.

Relations with Russia were also affected by questions of bilateral trade, and in particular by the failure of Ukraine to settle its debts for energy deliveries made by Russia, and by Ukraine's unauthorized 'siphoning' of petroleum and gas belonging to Russia. However, in December 2000 Russia agreed to defer Ukraine's gas debt repayments for 10 years. In February 2001, in a meeting that was regarded as expressing support for the beleaguered Ukrainian President, the Russian President, Vladimir Putin, met Kuchma in Dnipropetrovsk, and the two countries agreed, *inter alia*, to reconnect their countries' power grids and to create a joint aerospace consortium. In January 2003 a treaty delineating the land boundary (which remained largely unmarked and unregulated) between Russia and Ukraine was signed by Kuchma and Putin, although discussions on the status of the Sea of Azov, which lies between the two countries, was to continue.

Ukraine has sought to counterbalance its close relations with Russia by a policy of engagement with Western nations and organizations, as part of what was termed a 'multi-vector' foreign policy. In 1994 Ukraine joined NATO's 'Partnership for Peace' programme (see p. 273); although it was emphasized that Ukraine had no intention of applying for NATO membership, a 'Charter on a Distinctive Relationship' was signed with the Organization in 1997, envisaging enhanced co-operation between NATO and Ukraine. However, in April 1999, in protest at NATO airstrikes against Yugoslavia (now Serbia and Montenegro), the Verkhovna Rada voted for Ukraine to leave the

'Partnership for Peace' programme. When the conflict ended Ukraine rejoined the programme, and in July sent troops to form part of the peace-keeping force in the province of Kosovo and Metohija (Kosovo) in Serbia.

Following pressure from the USA, in 1998 Ukraine cancelled an agreement to supply turbines to Bushehr nuclear power station in Iran. The USA, in return, pledged to allocate additional investment to the development of Ukraine's energy sector. In March 2000 the USA, one of the major aid donors to Ukraine in the mid-1990s, became concerned about allegations that Ukraine had misused IMF funds, and demanded a full audit of the central bank before any more assistance would be forthcoming. Prime Minister Yushchenko visited Washington, DC, the USA, in May and held talks with President Bill Clinton on bilateral relations and international financial aid to Ukraine. During a visit to Ukraine in June, President Clinton pledged aid towards the closure of the Chornobyl reactor, which was closed in December. Relations with the USA deteriorated somewhat during 2002, following allegations that Ukraine, with the complicity of President Kuchma, had transferred military equipment to Iraq. In October a joint British-US inquiry failed to determine the veracity of the allegations, which the Ukrainian Government continued to deny. However, in March 2003, following the commencement of US-led military action in Iraq, Ukraine agreed to a request by the USA to dispatch an antinuclear, anti-biological and anti-chemical warfare unit, comprising 448 troops to Kuwait, which were to be used in the event that Iraq should use any such weapons. The Verkhovna Rada approved this measure in mid-March, although it also approved a motion condemning the US-led action in Iraq.

In June 1995 Ukraine signed a trade agreement with the European Union (EU, see p. 199), and the Ukrainian leadership has expressed an intention to pursue full membership of the EU. Ukraine was formally admitted to the Council of Europe (see p. 181) in November 1995. However, the failure to abolish capital punishment (which is prohibited by the conditions of membership of the organization) before March 2000 was a source of tension, as was the slow pace of political and economic reform. Allegations that President Kuchma was implicated in the murder of investigative journalist Heorhiy Honhadze in late 2000 led to demands by PACE for Ukraine's expulsion from the Council.

In December 2000 Ukraine announced that it would be contributing 800 troops to the UN peace-keeping mission in Sierra Leone (see chapter on that country), and in early 2001 Ukraine provided military assistance to the Government of the former Yugoslav republic of Macedonia, in order to quell a rebellion by ethnic Albanians.

Government

Executive power is vested in the President and the Prime Minister, while legislative power is the prerogative of the 450-member Verkhovna Rada. The President is elected by direct, popular vote for a mandate of five years. The President appoints the Prime Minister and the members of the Cabinet of Ministers. Ukraine is a unitary state, divided for administrative purposes into 24 oblasts (regions), one Autonomous Republic (Crimea), and two metropolitan areas (Kiev—Kyiv and Sevastopol). The Constitution guarantees local self-government to regions, cities, settlements and villages.

Defence

In December 1991 the Verkhovna Rada adopted legislation, which established independent Ukrainian armed forces. In August 2002 there were an estimated 302,300 active personnel in the Ukrainian armed forces (excluding the Black Sea Fleet), including 150,700 ground forces, 49,100 in the air force and air defence forces (which were expected to merge by the mid-2000s), and an estimated 13,500 in the navy. There were also paramilitary forces, comprising some 45,000 in the Border Guard, 44,000 serving under the Ministry of Internal Affairs, 14,000 serving in the Coast Guard, and some 9,500 serving in civil defence troops answerable to the Ministry for Emergency Situations and Protection of the Population from the Consequences of the Chornobyl Catastrophe. There were, additionally, some 1m. reserves. Military service is compulsory for males over 18 years of age, for a period of 18 months in the ground forces and air forces, and two years in the navy. The 2002 budget allocated an estimated 3,400m. hryvnyas to defence. In 1998 proposals to end conscription by 2015 were announced as part of a programme of military reforms.

Economic Affairs

In 2001, according to the World Bank, Ukraine's gross national income (GNI), measured at average 1999–2001 prices, was US $35,185m., equivalent to $720 per head (or $4,150 per head on an international purchasing-power parity basis). During 1990–2001 gross domestic product (GDP) per head declined, in real terms, at an average rate of 6.1% per year. Over the same period, the population decreased by an annual average of 0.5%. Ukraine's GDP declined, in real terms, by an average of 6.6% annually during 1990–2001. However, GDP increased by 5.8% in 2000, and by 9.1% in 2001.

Agriculture (including forestry and fishing) contributed 16.6% of GDP in 2001, according to estimates by the World Bank, and it provided 14.0% of employment in that year, according to FAO. Ukraine has large areas of extremely fertile land, forming part of the 'black earth' belt, and the country is self-sufficient in almost all aspects of agricultural production. The principal crops are grain, sugar beet, potatoes and other vegetables. A programme to transfer state collective farms to private ownership was initiated in 1991. In January 1997 only 14% of land was managed by private farms, although in that year private farms contributed some 46% of total agricultural output. During 1990–2001, according to the World Bank, agricultural GDP declined by an annual average of 4.5%, in real terms. However, agricultural GDP increased by 5.9% in 2000, and by 10.0% in 2001.

Industry (including mining, manufacturing, construction and power) contributed an estimated 39.0% of GDP in 2001, according to the World Bank, and it provided 24.5% of employment in 2000, when utilities are excluded. Heavy industry dominates the sector, particularly metalworking, mechanical engineering, chemicals, and machinery products. The mining and metallurgical sector accounted for 27.2% of Ukraine's industrial output in 1997. Defence-related industrial activity, traditionally important, was being converted to non-military production, and by 1997 some 80% of defence-industry factories had been transformed. According to the World Bank, industrial GDP decreased by an average of 8.2% annually, in real terms, in 1990–2001. However, real industrial GDP increased by 10.9% in 2000, and by 8.6% in 2001.

In 2000 3.4% of the work-force were engaged in mining and quarrying. Ukraine has large deposits of coal (mainly in the huge Donbass coal basin) and high-grade iron ore, and there are also significant reserves of manganese, titanium, graphite, natural gas and petroleum. Production of coal declined significantly in the early 1990s (by some 53% in 1989–95), and in 1996 the Government implemented a major reorganization of the coal-mining industry, including the closure of several loss-making mines.

The manufacturing sector contributed 35.0% of GDP in 2001, according to the World Bank, and the sector provided 16.1% of employment. During 1990–95 production of iron and steel declined by some 60%. During 1990–2001 manufacturing GDP decreased by an annual average of 7.5%, in real terms. However, the GDP of the sector increased by 12.8% in 2000, and by 13.0% in 2001.

Ukraine is highly dependent on imports of energy products (importing 90% of its petroleum requirements and 80% of its natural gas needs in 1997). Russia and Turkmenistan are the principal suppliers. Imports of mineral fuels comprised an estimated 44.0% of the value of total imports in 1999. Ukraine has five nuclear power stations. However, following the accident at the Chornobyl station in 1986, the viability of the country's nuclear power programme was called into question. Financial assistance was to be provided by the mid-2000s for the construction of two further nuclear reactors to meet the country's energy requirements. In 1999 nuclear power accounted for 41.9% of Ukraine's electricity production; coal accounted for 29.5%, and natural gas for 17.3%.

The services sector contributed an estimated 44.4% of GDP in 2001, according to the World Bank, and employed 47.9% of the labour force in 2000. During 1990–2001 the GDP of the sector decreased by an average of 6.8% annually, in real terms. The real GDP of the sector increased by 4.6% in 2000, but declined dramatically, by 54.1%, in 2001.

In 2001 Ukraine recorded a trade surplus of US $198m., while there was a surplus of $1,402m. on the current account of the balance of payments. In 2000 the principal markets for exports were Russia (24.1%), Turkey, the USA and the People's Republic of China. The principal source of imports in 2000 was Russia (providing 41.6% of all imports), followed by Germany (8.1%). The principal imports in 2000 were mineral fuels and lubricants (which accounted for 43.7% of the total), machinery and transport equipment, basic manufactures and chemical products. The principal exports in that year were basic manufactures (some 50.6% of the total, comprising principally iron and steel), machinery and transport equipment, and chemical products.

In 2000 there was a budgetary deficit of 1,060.9m. hryvnyas, equivalent to 0.8% of GDP. In 2001 a budgetary deficit of 1,800.4m. hryvnyas was recorded. Ukraine's total external debt was US $12,166m. at the end of 2000, of which $9,646m. was long-term public debt. In that year the cost of debt-servicing was equivalent to 18.6% of the value of exports of goods and services. In 1992–2001 the average annual inflation rate was 176.0%. The average rate of inflation reached 4,735% in 1993, but declined thereafter, to reach just 13.2% in 1997. Consumer prices increased by 22.7% in 1999 and by 28.2% in 2000. In 2000 some 1,155,200 people were officially registered as unemployed (some 6.0% of the labour force), although at the end of 1998 the World Bank estimated the unemployment rate to be 11.3%, more than twice the officially recorded level.

Ukraine became a member of the IMF and the World Bank in 1992. It also joined the European Bank for Reconstruction and Development (EBRD, see p. 193) as a 'Country of Operations'. In June 1994 Ukraine signed an agreement of partnership and co-operation with the European Union (EU, see p. 199), which was ratified in 1998. An interim trade accord was signed with the EU in June 1995. Ukraine is a member of the Organization of the Black Sea Economic Co-operation (see p. 293), and is seeking membership of the World Trade Organization (see p. 323).

Ukraine faced severe economic problems following the dissolution of the USSR, and all sectors of the economy experienced sharp declines in production (by 2001 GDP was equivalent to just 44% of the level recorded in 1991). A reform programme was agreed with the IMF in 1994, and by 1996 a significant reduction in the rate of inflation contributed to the stabilization of the economy, and the annual rate of GDP declined more slowly during the second half of the 1990s. (It should be noted, however, that published figures take into account neither the significance of the unofficial sector, nor Soviet-era over-production; thus the decline in recorded output was in fact less precipitous than might appear to be the case.) A second stage of economic reform, inaugurated in 1996, was only inconsistently implemented, and Ukraine was adversely affected by the financial crisis in Russia, its principal trading partner, in mid-1998; none the less, some 60,000 enterprises were transferred to private ownership in 1991–98, while the number of people employed by medium and large enterprises owned by the central Government declined from 13m. in 1992 to 5m. in 1997. Ukraine's inability to pay for deliveries of fuel supplies, on which it is highly dependent, caused difficulties throughout the 1990s and early 2000s, with frequent losses of power. The privatization of six regional energy companies in 2001 represented progress towards implementing deeper reform in the sector; in October of that year Russia rescheduled Ukraine's gas-debt repayments over a period of 12 years. Despite Ukraine's geographical proximity to western Europe, and a generally well-educated and urbanized population, foreign investment remained relatively low, partly because of a lack of clear fiscal regulation, and partly owing to perceptions of widespread corruption. Moreover, in January 2003 economic sanctions against Ukraine were imposed by Canada and the USA, because of concerns, highlighted by the Financial Action Task Force on Money Laundering (FATF), that flaws in Ukraine's financial regulatory system made it permissive to money-'laundering'. It was also reported in that month that the USA was to reduce financial assistance to the Ukrainian Government (which had been one of the principal recipients of US overseas aid in the mid-1990s), because of its perceived failure to co-operate adequately with an investigation into the alleged illegal transfer of Ukrainian military equipment to Iraq; although by that time some US $55m. of assistance of Ukraine had been suspended, the US administration announced that future support would be directed towards civil society organizations. However, the economy showed significant signs of improvement from 2000, when GDP registered positive growth for the first time since the dissolution of the USSR, although GDP per head remains significantly lower than in Russia. In December 2000 the IMF resumed lending to Ukraine, which had been suspended while an investigation into the alleged misuse of funds was undertaken. Following substantial growth in 2001, GDP increased by 4.1% in 2002, according to provisional figures.

Education

After Ukrainian was decreed the state language, in 1990, policies were adopted to ensure that all pupils were granted the opportunity of tuition in Ukrainian. In 2001 there was also tuition in Russian, as well as in Romanian, Hungarian, Moldovan, Crimean Tatar and Polish. In the early 1990s there were significant changes to the curriculum, with a greater emphasis on Ukrainian history and literature. Some religious and private educational institutions were established in the early 1990s. Education is officially compulsory between seven and 15 years of age. Primary education begins at seven years of age and lasts for four years. Secondary education, beginning at 11, lasts for a maximum of seven years, comprising a first cycle of five years and a second of two years. In 1993 total enrolment at primary and secondary schools was equivalent to 90% of the school-age population (88% of males; 92% of females). Primary enrolment in that year was equivalent to 87% of children in the relevant age-group, while the comparable ratio for secondary enrolment was 91%. In 2001/02 there were 2,109,300 students enrolled in higher education. Combined enrolment at the primary, secondary and tertiary levels was some 78% in 1998. In 2001, according to preliminary figures, government expenditure on education totalled 9,449m. hryvnyas (12.8% of the total budgetary expenditure).

Public Holidays

2003: 1 January (New Year), 7 January (Orthodox Christmas), 8 March (International Women's Day), 28 April (Orthodox Easter Monday), 1–2 May (Labour Day), 9 May (Victory Day), 28 June (Constitution Day), 24 August (Independence Day).

2004: 1 January (New Year), 7 January (Orthodox Christmas), 8 March (International Women's Day), 12 April (Orthodox Easter Monday), 1–2 May (Labour Day), 9 May (Victory Day), 28 June (Constitution Day), 24 August (Independence Day).

Weights and Measures

The metric system is in force.

Statistical Survey

Principal sources (unless otherwise stated): State Committee of Statistics of Ukraine, 01023 Kiev, vul. Sh. Rustaveli 3; tel. (44) 226-20-21; fax (44) 235-37-39; e-mail info@ukrstat.gov.ua; internet www.ukrstat.gov.ua; IMF, *Ukraine: Statistical Appendix* (February 2001).

Area and Population

AREA, POPULATION AND DENSITY

Area (sq km)	603,700*
Population (census results)	
12 January 1989	51,706,742
5 December 2001†	
Males	22,441,000
Females.	26,016,000
Total	48,457,000
Population (official estimates at 31 December)	
2002	48,003,500
Density (per sq km) at 31 December 2002	79.5

* 233,090 sq miles.
† Rounded figures.

POPULATION BY ETHNIC GROUP
(permanent inhabitants, census of 5 December 2001)

	'000	%
Ukrainian	37,541.7	78.13
Russian . . .	8,334.1	17.34
Belarusian . . .	275.8	0.57
Moldovan . . .	258.6	0.54
Crimean Tatar . .	248.2	0.52
Bulgarian. . .	204.6	0.43
Hungarian . .	156.6	0.33
Romanian. . .	151.0	0.31
Polish . . .	144.1	0.30
Jewish. . .	103.6	0.22
Armenian. .	99.9	0.21
Greek . . .	91.5	0.19
Tatar . . .	73.3	0.15
Roma (Gypsy) . .	47.6	0.10
Others. . .	321.7	0.67
Total . . .	48,052.3	100.00

ADMINISTRATIVE DIVISIONS

	Area ('000 sq km)	Population ('000 at 31 Dec. 2002)*	Density (per sq km)
Regions†			
Cherkasy (Cherkassy)	20.9	1,386.6	66.3
Chernihiv (Chernigov) . . .	31.9	1,225.2	38.4
Chernivtsi (Chernovtsy) . .	8.1	918.5	113.4
Dnipropetrovsk (Dnepropetrovsk) . .	31.9	3,532.8	110.7
Donetsk	26.5	4,774.4	180.2
Ivano-Frankivsk (Ivano-Frankovsk) . .	13.9	1,403.7	101.0
Kharkiv (Kharkov) . . .	31.4	2,887.9	92.0
Kherson	28.5	1,161.4	40.8
Khmelnytskiy (Khmelnitskii) . .	20.6	1,414.9	68.7
Kirovohrad (Kirovograd) . .	24.6	1,115.7	45.4
Kyiv (Kiev)	28.1	1,808.3	64.4
Luhansk (Lugansk). . . .	26.7	2,507.3	93.9
Lviv (Lvov)	21.8	2,611.0	119.8
Mykolayiv (Nikolayev) . .	24.6	1,251.5	50.9
Odesa (Odessa) . . .	33.3	2,448.2	73.5
Poltava . . .	28.8	1,609.4	55.9
Rivne (Rovno) . . .	20.1	1,168.3	58.1
Sumy . . .	23.8	1,279.9	53.8
Ternopil (Ternopol) . . .	13.8	1,134.2	82.2
Transcarpathia . . .	12.8	1,253.9	98.3
Vinnytsia (Vinnitsa) . .	26.5	1,753.9	66.9
Volyn . . .	20.2	1,054.7	52.5
Zaporizhzhia (Zaporozhe) . . .	27.2	1,909.3	70.8
Zhytomyr (Zhitomir)	29.9	1,373.9	46.5

—continued	Area ('000 sq km)	Population ('000 at 31 Dec. 2002)*	Density (per sq km)
Cities			
Kyiv (Kiev)	0.8	2,621.7	3,277.1
Sevastopol . . .	0.9	378.5	420.6
Autonomous Republic			
Crimea	26.1	2,018.4	77.8
Total	603.7	48,003.5	79.5

* Official estimates.
† With the exception of Crimea and Transcarpathia, the names of regions are given in Ukrainian, with alternative Russian versions in brackets where applicable.

PRINCIPAL TOWNS*
(population at census of 5 December 2001, rounded)

Kyiv (Kiev, capital) .	2,611,000	Cherkasy	
Kharkiv (Kharkov) .	1,470,000	(Cherkassy) . .	295,000
Dnipropetrovsk		Sumy . . .	293,000
(Dnepropetrovsk) .	1,065,000	Horlivka (Gorlovka) .	292,000
Odesa (Odessa) . .	1,029,000	Zhytomyr (Zhitomir).	284,000
Donetsk . . .	1,016,000	Dniprodzerzhinsk	
Zaporizhzhia		(Dneprodzerzhinsk)	256,000
(Zaporozhe). .	815,000	Khmelnytskiy	
Lviv (Lvov) . .	733,000	(Khmelnitskii) . .	254,000
Kryvyi Rih (Krivoi		Kirovohrad	
Rog) . . .	669,000	(Kirovograd) . .	254,000
Mykolayiv		Rivne (Rovno) . .	249,000
(Nikolayev). . .	514,000	Chernivtsi	
Mariupol† . . .	492,000	(Chernovtsy) . .	241,000
Luhansk (Lugansk)‡	463,000	Kremenchuk	
Makiyivka		(Kremenchug) . .	234,000
(Makayevka) . .	390,000	Ternopil (Ternopol) .	228,000
Vinnytsia (Vinnitsa).	357,000	Ivano-Frankivsk	
Simferopol . . .	344,000	(Ivano-Frankovsk).	218,000
Sevastopol . . .	342,000	Lutsk . . .	209,000
Kherson . . .	328,000	Bila Tserkva (Belaya	
Poltava . . .	318,000	Tserkov) . . .	200,000
Chernihiv			
(Chernigov). . .	305,000		

* The names of towns are given in Ukrainian, with alternative Russian versions in brackets where applicable.
† Known as Zhdanov from 1948 to 1989.
‡ Known as Voroshylovhrad (Voroshilovgrad) from 1935 to 1958 and from 1970 to 1989.

BIRTHS, MARRIAGES AND DEATHS*

	Registered live births		Registered marriages		Registered deaths	
	Number	Rate (per 1,000)	Number	Rate (per 1,000)	Number	Rate (per 1,000)
1995 . .	492,861	9.6	431,731	8.4	792,587	15.5
1996 . .	467,211	9.1	307,543	6.0	776,717	15.2
1997 . .	442,581	8.8	345,013	6.8	754,152	15.0
1998 . .	419,238	8.4	310,504	6.2	719,955	14.3
1999 . .	389,208	7.8	344,888	6.9	739,170	14.8
2000 . .	385,126	7.8	274,523	5.5	758,082	15.3
2001 . .	376,479	7.8	309,602	6.4	745,953	15.4
2002 . .	390,687	8.1	317,228	6.6	754,911	15.7

* Rates for 1995–2000 are based on unrevised population estimates.

Expectation of Life (WHO estimates, years at birth): 67.7 (males 62.2; females 73.3) in 2001 (Source: WHO, *World Health Report*).

EMPLOYMENT
(annual averages, '000 employees)

	1998	1999	2000
Agriculture, hunting, forestry and fishing	5,060	4,961	4,977
Mining and quarrying	687	639	618
Manufacturing	3,540	3,319	2,914
Construction	1,097	974	895
Trade, restaurants and hotels	1,514	1,604	1,406
Transport, storage and communications	1,400	1,329	1,228
Finance, insurance, real estate and business services	213	197	196
Total employed (incl. others)	19,415	18,790	18,063

Registered unemployed (annual averages, '000 persons): 1,003.2 in 1998; 1,174.5 in 1999; 1,155.2 in 2000.

Economically active population (sample surveys, '000 persons aged 15 years and over, October each year): 22,747.0 (males 11,733.7, females 11,013.3) in 1999; 23,127.4 (males 11,896.6, females 11,230.8) in 2000; 22,755.0 (males 11,678.5, females 11,076.5) in 2001. Figures include unemployed ('000): 2,698.8 in 1999; 2,707.6 in 2000, 2.516.9 in 2001.

Source: ILO.

Health and Welfare

KEY INDICATORS

Total fertility rate (children per woman, 2001)	1.1
Under-5 mortality rate (per 1,000 live births, 2001)	20
HIV/AIDS (% of persons aged 15–49, 2001)	0.99
Physicians (per 1,000 head, 1998)	2.99
Hospital beds (per 1,000 head, 1995)	11.83
Health expenditure (2000): US $ per head (PPP)	152
Health expenditure (2000): % of GDP	4.1
Health expenditure (2000): public (% of total)	70.1
Human Development Index (2000): ranking	80
Human Development Index (2000): value	0.748

For sources and definitions, see explanatory note on p. vi.

Agriculture

PRINCIPAL CROPS
('000 metric tons)

	1999	2000	2001
Wheat	13,585.3	10,197.0	21,348.0
Barley	6,424.6	6,871.9	10,186.0
Maize	1,736.9	3,848.1	3,641.0
Rye	918.9	968.3	1,822.0
Oats	760.4	881.4	1,116.0
Millet	196.0	426.1	266.0
Buckwheat	222.1	480.6	380.0*
Potatoes	12,723	19,838	17,344
Sugar beet	14,064.0	13,198.8	15,575.0
Dry peas	498	499	619
Sunflower seed	2,794.0	3,457.4	2,251.0
Rapeseed	147.9	132.0	135.0
Cabbages	931.7	1,104.6	1,234.0
Tomatoes	1,325.0	1,126.5	1,053.0
Pumpkins, squash and gourds	783.0	891.1	901.0
Cucumbers and gherkins	641.1	709.0	467.0
Chillies and green peppers	108.5	108.9	120.0
Dry onions	437.8	563.0	547.0
Garlic	89.1	127.0	127.0
Carrots	384.7	496.5	463.0†
Other vegetables†	146.3	321.7	344.5
Apples	296.8	648.2	475.0
Pears	101.7	155.7	102.0
Apricots	57.2	102.1	44.0
Plums	83.4	123.0	138.0
Grapes	306.3	513.8	336.0
Watermelons	425.0	325.3	354.0
Other fruits and berries	250.3*	421.2*	469.5†

* Unofficial figure.
† FAO estimate(s).

Source: FAO.

LIVESTOCK
('000 head at 1 January)

	1999	2000	2001
Horses	721	698	701
Cattle	11,722	10,627	9,424
Pigs	10,083	10,073	7,652
Sheep	1,198	1,060	963
Goats	828	825	912
Chickens	105,000	118,000	130,000

Source: FAO.

LIVESTOCK PRODUCTS
('000 metric tons)

	1999	2000	2001
Beef and veal	791.2	754.3	646.0
Mutton and lamb	15.0	9.2	8.0
Pig meat	656.3	675.9	591.0
Poultry meat	204.2	193.2	239.0
Other meat	29.1	30.2	33.0
Cows' milk	13,140	12,436	13,169
Sheep's milk	18	17	9
Goats' milk	204	257	257
Cheese	64.0	80.3	110.6
Butter	108.3	135.4	151.6
Poultry eggs	502.0	505.3	553.8
Hen eggs	491.5	496.6	546.4
Honey	55.5	52.4	60.0
Cattle hides (fresh)*	120.5	118.5	111.6

* FAO estimates.

Source: FAO.

Forestry

ROUNDWOOD REMOVALS
('000 cubic metres, excl. bark)

	1998	1999	2000
Sawlogs, veneer logs and logs for sleepers*	3,290	3,379	3,379
Other industrial wood*	953	775	775
Fuel wood	1,810*	1,766*	4,058†
Total	8,453	7,920	9,859

* FAO estimate(s).
† Unofficial figure.
Source: FAO.

Fishing

('000 metric tons, live weight)

	1998	1999	2000
Capture	462.3	407.9	392.7
Blue grenadier	16.1	15.1	19.3
Sardinellas	161.8	74.7	38.1
European pilchard (sardine)	12.8	49.1	40.9
European sprat	30.3	29.2	32.7
European anchovy	3.9	5.5	16.4
Cape horse mackerel	18.3	4.6	13.8
Greenback horse mackerel	9.3	15.3	12.2
Chub mackerel	73.0	42.3	45.0
Aquaculture	28.3	33.8	31.0
Common carp	18.0	20.0	20.0
Total catch	490.6	441.7	423.7

Source: FAO, *Yearbook of Fishery Statistics*.

Mining

('000 metric tons, unless otherwise indicated)

	1998	1999	2000
Hard (incl. coking) coal	74,358	80,640	79,923
Brown coal (incl. lignite)	1,409	1,184	1,067
Crude petroleum	3,894.8	3,797.9	3,692.9
Natural gas (million cu m)	17,967	18,092	17,847
Iron ore: gross weight	50,758	47,769	55,883
Iron ore: metal content*	28,000	26,200	30,600
Manganese ore*†	755	675	930
Ilmenite concentrate	507.4	536.5	576.7
Rutile concentrate	50.0*	49.0*	58.6
Zirconium concentrates*	65	69	75
Uranium concentrate (metric tons)†	500*	500*	600
Bentonite*	300	300	300
Kaolin	201.7	221.5	225.0*
Potash salts (crude)*‡	35	35	30
Native sulphur*	97	80	80
Salt (unrefined)	2,500*	2,185	2,287
Graphite (metric tons)	5,104	7,461	7,431
Peat*	1,000	1,000	1,000

* Estimated production.

† Figures refer to the metal content of ores and concentrates.

‡ Figures refer to potassium oxide content.

Source: US Geological Survey.

Industry

SELECTED PRODUCTS

('000 metric tons, unless otherwise indicated)

	1997	1998	1999
Margarine	78	90	108
Flour	3,986	3,608	3,036
Raw sugar*	2,034	1,984	1,858
Ethyl alcohol ('000 hectolitres)	2,461	1,576	1,360
Wine ('000 hectolitres)	990	771	856
Beer ('000 hectolitres)	6,125	6,842	8,407
Cigarettes (million)	54,488	59,275	54,105
Wool yarn: pure and mixed	4.5	3.2	3.0
Cotton yarn: pure and mixed	6.4	10.6	5.4
Flax yarn	6.5	2.9	1.7
Woven cotton fabrics (million sq metres)	28	57	27
Woven woollen fabrics (million sq metres)	8.2	5.8	3.8
Linen fabrics (million sq metres)	19.7	9.9	5.5
Footwear, excl. rubber ('000 pairs)	10,580	11,389	11,875
Hydrochloric acid	107.6	81.7	47.7
Sulphuric acid	1,438	1,354	1,393
Nitric acid	17	11	11
Phosphoric acid	230.6	220.3	169.5
Caustic soda (Sodium hydroxide)	156	127	99
Soda ash (Sodium carbonate)	368	390	456
Nitrogenous fertilizers (a)†	2,022	1,675	2,060
Phosphatic fertilizers (b)†	305	240	238
Potassic fertilizers (c)†	49	21	21
Rubber tyres ('000)‡	6,940	7,941	7,477
Rubber footwear ('000 pairs)	3,060	2,390	2,207
Clay building bricks (million)	1,606	1,579	1,629
Quicklime	3,535	3,358	3,385
Cement	5,101	5,591	5,828
Pig-iron	21,060	21,239	23,315
Crude steel: for castings	343	342	480
Crude steel: ingots	25,629	24,447	27,393
Tractors (number)§	4,645	3,248	4,984
Household refrigerators ('000)	382	390	409
Household washing machines ('000)	147	138	127
Radio receivers ('000)	25	10	27
Television receivers ('000)	50	93	81
Passenger motor cars ('000)	2	26	10
Buses and motor coaches (number)	1,771	2,454	2,032
Lorries (number)	3,386	4,768	7,769
Motorcycles, scooters, etc. ('000)	1	—	1
Bicycles ('000)‖	28	13	31
Electric energy (million kWh)	181,986	172,822¶	172,000

* Production from home-grown sugar beet.

† Production of fertilizers is in terms of (a) nitrogen; (b) phosphoric acid; or (c) potassium oxide.

‡ Tyres for road motor vehicles.

§ Tractors of 10 horse-power and over, excluding industrial tractors and road tractors for tractor-trailer combinations.

‖ Excluding children's bicycles.

¶ Estimate.

Source: mainly UN, *Industrial Commodity Statistics Yearbook*.

Raw sugar (production from home-grown sugar beet, '000 metric tons): 1,780 in 2000; 1,947 in 2001.

Footwear, excl. rubber ('000 pairs): 13,500 in 2000; 14,600 in 2001.

Cement ('000 metric tons): 5,300 in 2000; 5,800 in 2001.

Household refrigerators ('000): 451 in 2000; 509 in 2001.

Passenger motor cars ('000): 32 in 2000; 35 in 2001.

Electric energy (million kWh): 171,000 in 2000; 173,000 in 2001.

Finance

CURRENCY AND EXCHANGE RATES

Monetary Units
100 kopiykas = 1 hryvnya

Sterling, Dollar and Euro Equivalents (31 December 2002)
£1 sterling = 8.5948 hryvnyas
US $1 = 5.3324 hryvnyas
€1 = 5.5921 hryvnyas
100 hryvnyas = £11.63 = $18.75 = €17.88

Average Exchange Rate (hryvnyas per US $)
2000   5.4402
2001   5.3722
2002   5.3266

Note: Following the dissolution of the USSR in December 1991, Russia and several other former Soviet republics retained the rouble (known as the karbovanets—KRB in Ukraine) as their monetary unit. In November 1992 this currency ceased to be legal tender in Ukraine, and was replaced (initially at par) by a currency coupon, also known as the karbovanets, or kupon, for a transitional period. Following the introduction of the transitional currency, Ukraine operated a system of multiple exchange rates, but in October 1994 the official and auction rates were merged. The unified exchange rate at 31 December 1995 was $1 = 179,400 KRB. On 2 September 1996 Ukraine introduced a new currency, the hryvnya, at a rate of 100,000 KRB per hryvnya (1.750 hryvnyas per US $).

GENERAL BUDGET
(million hryvnyas)*

Revenue†	1999	2000	2001
Current revenue	30,431.1	45,549.2	54,225.5
Taxation	28,712.0	38,281.3	44,265.8
Taxes on income, profits and capital gains	3,364.0	5,802.3	6,313.8
Social security contributions	11,765.3	14,300.8	19,637.7
Taxes on payroll	835.3	868.9	20.7
Domestic taxes on goods and services	11,395.2	15,362.1	15,871.6
General sales tax, turnover tax and value-added tax	9,786.1	11,396.4	10,743.0
Excises	1,203.3	2,089.1	2,383.2
Taxes on international trade and transactions	1,262.7	1,947.0	2,422.0
Import duties	1,236.6	1,555.1	1,938.0
Other current revenue	1,719.1	7,267.9	9,959.7
Income from property	799.1	1,222.0	3,468.1
Adminstration fees, charges and non-industrial sales	263.2	4,728.9	4,962.7
Capital revenue	427.3	42.1	343.8
Total (incl. others)	30,858.4	45,591.3	54,569.3

Expenditure‡	1999	2000	2001
General public services	1,654.3	4,084.4	4,327.8
Defence	1,766.9	2,578.8	3,446.8
Public order and safety	1,428.1	2,492.5	3,615.2
Education	1,248.9	2,749.3	3,651.0
Health	388.2	758.4	1,140.4
Social security and welfare	16,983.6	21,311.2	25,466.9
Economic affairs and services	3,730.5	4,051.2	4,813.2
Interest payments	3,010.2	4,303.4	3,925.0
Total (incl. others)	33,900.2	48,074.0	58,973.6

* Figures refer to the consolidated accounts of central government, excluding the operations of social security and pension funds (excepting figures for 2000, which include the operations of the Social Security Fund) and those of local government.
† Excluding grants received (million hryvnyas): 314.0 in 1999; 1,470.3 in 2000; 2,784.6 in 2001.
‡ Excluding net lending (million hryvnyas): 19.2 in 1999; 48.5 in 2000; 180.7 in 2001.

Source: IMF, *Government Finance Statistics Yearbook*.

INTERNATIONAL RESERVES
(US $ million at 31 December)

	2000	2001	2002
Gold*	123.7	134.1	175.4
IMF special drawing rights	249.1	251.1	28.3
Foreign exchange	1,103.6	2,704.3	4,212.8
Total	1,476.4	3,089.5	4,416.5

* National valuation.
Source: IMF, *International Financial Statistics*.

MONEY SUPPLY
(million hryvnyas at 31 December)

	2000	2001	2002
Currency outside banks	12,799.0	19,464.8	26,433.8
Demand deposits at banks	8,013.5	10,301.5	13,806.8
Total money (incl. others)	20,825.3	29,795.6	40,451.1

Source: IMF, *International Financial Statistics*.

COST OF LIVING
(Index of consumer prices; base: 1992 = 100)

	1998	1999	2000
Food (incl. tobacco)	446,690.4	570,891.4	767,854.9
All items	527,662.7	647,356.0	829,930.5

Source: ILO.

NATIONAL ACCOUNTS
(million hryvnyas at current prices)

Expenditure on the Gross Domestic Product

	1998	1999	2000
Final consumption expenditure	83,569	100,481	128,901
Household	58,323	71,310	92,406
Non-profit institutions serving households	3,126	3,305	3,909
General government	22,120	25,866	32,586
Gross capital formation	21,357	22,746	33,531
Gross fixed capital formation	20,096	25,131	33,427
Changes in inventories	1,128	−2,519	−42
Acquisitions, *less* disposals, of valuables	133	134	146
Total domestic expenditure	104,926	126,034	162,432
Exports of goods and services	42,974	70,884	106,200
Less Imports of goods and services	45,307	63,669	98,562
GDP in purchasers' values	102,593	130,442	170,070

Source: UN, *National Accounts Statistics*.

Gross domestic product (million hryvnyas at current prices): 130,442 (revised) in 1999; 170,070 in 2000; 201,927 (provisional) in 2001.

Gross Domestic Product by Economic Activity

	1998	1999	2000
Agriculture	12,400	15,500	24,600
Manufacturing*	27,600	37,700	47,700
Construction	4,900	5,400	6,100
Trade and catering	7,600	9,300	15,200
Transport, storage and communications	12,600	15400	19,800
Public adminstration and defence; compulsory social security	4,700	5,200	6,800
Education; health and social work; other community, social and personal services	13,200	14,900	17,500
Sub-total (incl. others)	88,000	109,600	146,000
Less Financial intermediation services, indirectly measured	1,000	1,200	1,700
Gross value added in basic prices	87,000	108,400	144,300
Taxes on products	17,300	24,100	27,300
Less Subsidies on products	1,700	2,100	1,500
GDP in market prices	102,600	130,400	170,100

* Including mining and quarrying, manufacturing (except printing and publishing), electricity, gas and water.
Source: UN, *National Accounts Statistics*.

BALANCE OF PAYMENTS
(US $ million)

	1999	2000	2001
Exports of goods f.o.b.	13,189	15,722	17,091
Imports of goods f.o.b.	−12,945	−14,943	−16,893
Trade balance	244	779	198
Exports of services	3,869	3,800	3,995
Imports of services	−2,292	−3,004	−3,580
Balance on goods and services	1,821	1,575	613
Other income received	98	143	167
Other income paid	−967	−1,085	−834
Balance on goods, services and income	952	633	−54
Current transfers received	754	967	1,516
Current transfers paid	−48	−119	−60
Current balance	1,658	1,481	1,402
Capital account (net)	−10	−8	3
Direct investment abroad	−7	−1	−23
Direct investment from abroad	496	595	792
Portfolio investment assets	−11	−4	1
Portfolio investment liabilities	−75	−197	−867
Other investment assets	−2,264	−449	−1,015
Other investment liabilities	982	−696	921
Net errors and omissions	−953	−148	−221
Overall balance	−184	573	993

Sources: IMF, *International Financial Statistics*.

External Trade

PRINCIPAL COMMODITIES
(distribution by SITC, US $ million)

Imports f.o.b.	1998	1999	2000
Food and live animals	593.8	595.3	624.0
Crude materials (inedible) except fuels	669.6	628.5	824.0
Metalliferous ores and metal scrap	229.1	227.6	421.0
Mineral fuels, lubricants, etc.	5,940.7	5,213.6	5,998.0
Chemicals and related products	1,338.3	1,093.7	1,304.0
Artificial resins and plastic materials, celluose esters etc	354.5	315.6	416.0
Basic manufactures	1,851.8	1,345.7	1,752.0
Machinery and transport equipment	3,172.1	2,078.7	2,445.0
Road vehicles	752.7	423.3	430.0
Miscellaneous manufactured articles	511.2	409.4	409.0
Total (incl. others)	14,675.6	11,846.1	13,719.0

Exports f.o.b.	1998	1999	2000
Food and live animals	918.0	1,073.8	815.0
Cereals and cereal preparations	378.1	551.7	159.0
Crude materials (inedible) except fuels	903.9	620.9	805.0
Metalliferous ores and metal scrap	502.4	355.5	465.0
Mineral fuels, lubricants, etc.	520.7	701.0	808.0
Chemicals and related products	1,350.8	1,134.6	1,626.0
Inorganic chemicals	508.2	443.2	630.0
Basic manufactures	6,107.1	5,574.0	7,383.0
Iron and steel	4,204.4	3,888.8	5,031.0
Non-ferrous metals	325.2	408.4	540.0
Machinery and transport equipment	1,721.7	1,331.4	1,797.0
Miscellaneous manufactured articles	569.6	523.1	633.0
Total (incl. others)	12,637.4	11,581.6	14,579.6

Source: UN, *International Trade Statistics Yearbook*.

PRINCIPAL TRADING PARTNERS
(US $ million)

Imports f.o.b.	1998	1999	2000
Austria	193.8	133.4	185.1
Belarus	352.9	343.5	601.9
Czech Republic	208.8	131.4	162.9
France (incl. Monaco)	300.2	236.9	237.4
Germany	1,263.6	942.9	1,134.4
Hungary	193.9	123.6	165.4
Italy	409.5	277.0	346.6
Kazakhstan	345.7	164.9	412.8
Korea, Republic	196.4	79.4	109.9
Lithuania	239.9	82.5	135.4
Netherlands	161.5	133.6	146.6
Poland	486.2	258.5	312.5
Russia	7,064.3	5,592.2	5,824.9
Slovakia	170.4	131.6	124.4
Sweden	148.9	114.5	150.4
Switzerland-Liechtenstein	122.7	93.1	217.7
Turkey	135.7	142.7	159.9
Turkmenistan	1.3	481.0	946.2
United Kingdom	204.7	143.6	202.8
USA	590.3	401.7	360.5
Uzbekistan	29.7	87.3	178.0
Total (incl. others)	15,478.1	11,846.1	14,010.8

Exports f.o.b.	1998	1999	2000
Algeria	108.1	184.5	235.8
Austria	135.2	139.8	163.6
Belarus	548.0	345.7	272.1
Bulgaria	205.4	294.5	382.5
China, People's Republic	737.4	730.4	628.9
Czech Republic	171.5	141.4	188.9
Egypt	186.9	171.3	221.0
Germany	638.7	560.1	741.4
Hungary	263.1	278.2	327.3
India	137.6	173.8	168.3
Israel	134.1	153.8	105.9
Italy	553.9	463.6	644.2
Moldova	180.4	122.8	176.3
Pakistan	194.6	182.4	30.2
Poland	313.1	301.4	417.9
Romania	160.9	75.6	164.6
Russia	2,905.5	2,396.4	3,515.6
Slovakia	245.2	199.2	230.9
Spain	131.3	105.8	162.9
Syria	204.1	122.5	160.4
Turkey	696.3	673.4	868.5
Turkmenistan	121.1	102.1	148.5
USA	502.3	435.9	727.4
Uzbekistan	139.5	77.6	114.1
Total (incl. others)	12,637.4	11,581.6	14,579.6

Source: UN, *International Trade Statistics Yearbook*.

Transport

RAILWAYS
(traffic)

	1997	1998	1999
Passenger-kilometres (million)	54,540	49,938	47,600
Freight ton-kilometres (million)	160,433	158,693	156,336

Source: UN, *Statistical Yearbook*.

ROAD TRAFFIC
('000 motor vehicles in use)

	1998	1999	2000
Passenger cars	4,877.8	5,210.8	5,250.1

Source: International Road Federation, *World Road Statistics*.

SHIPPING

Merchant Fleet
(registered at 31 December)

	1999	2000	2001
Number of vessels	936	894	838
Total displacement ('000 grt) . .	1,775.2	1,546.3	1,407.7

Source: Lloyd's Register-Fairplay, *World Fleet Statistics*.

International Sea-borne Freight Traffic
('000 metric tons)

	1997	1998	1999
Goods loaded	55,236	64,656	77,004
Goods unloaded	5,760	7,044	7,116

Source: UN, *Monthly Bulletin of Statistics*.

CIVIL AVIATION
(traffic on scheduled services)

	1997	1998	1999
Kilometres flown (million) . .	36	37	31
Passengers carried ('000) . .	1,190	1,064	891
Passenger-kilometres (million) . .	1,853	1,720	1,312
Total ton-kilometres (million) . .	186	188	138

Source: UN, *Statistical Yearbook*.

Tourism

FOREIGN TOURIST ARRIVALS
('000)

Country of residence	1998	1999	2000
Belarus	1,238.9	548.4	530.9
Czech Republic	75.6	59.9	39.9
Germany	62.5	59.3	62.4
Hungary	440.9	506.4	480.3
Moldova	1,292.8	1,051.7	1,199.1
Poland	256.0	184.7	182.2
Russian Federation	2,116.8	1,222.4	1,332.8
Slovakia	149.0	84.5	57.7
USA	46.0	54.0	52.9
Total (incl. others)	6,207.6	4,232.4	4,405.7

Tourist receipts (US $ million): 270 in 1997; 315 in 1998; 327 in 1999; 394 in 2000; 573 in 2001.

Sources: World Tourism Organization, *Yearbook of Tourism Statistics*; and National Bank of Ukraine.

Communications Media

	1999	2000	2001
Television receivers ('000 in use) .	22,000	23,000	n.a.
Telephones ('000 main lines in use)	10,074.0	10,417.2	10,669.6
Facsimile machines (number in use)	47,700	42,161	n.a.
Mobile cellular telephones ('000 subscribers).	216.6	818.5	2,224.6
Personal computers ('000 in use)	800	890	920
Internet users ('000)	200	300	600

Radio receivers ('000 in use): 45,050 in 1997.

Book production (incl. pamphlets, 1996): Titles 6,460; Copies ('000) 50,905.

Daily newspapers (1996): Number 44; Average circulation ('000) 2,780.

Periodicals (1996): Titles 2,162; Average circulation ('000) 19,934.

Sources: UNESCO, *Statistical Yearbook*; International Telecommunication Union.

Education

(2001/02)

	Institutions	Teachers	Students
Pre-primary	15,400	107,700	968,000
Primary . . . . }	22,200	568,000	6,601,000
General secondary . . . . . }			
Specialized secondary: teacher training*	38	n.a.	21,300
Specialized secondary: vocational	965	n.a.	512,300
Higher†	983	121,300*	2,109,300

* 1993/94.
† Including evening and correspondence courses.

Adult literacy rate (UNESCO estimates): 99.6% (males 99.7%; females 99.5%) in 2000 (Source: UN Development Programme, *Human Development Report*).

Directory

Constitution

The Constitution of the Republic of Ukraine, summarized below, was adopted at the Fifth Session of the Verkhovna Rada on 28 June 1996. It replaced the Soviet-era Constitution (Fundamental Law), originally approved on 12 April 1978, but amended several times after Ukraine gained independence in 1991, and entered into force the day of its adoption.

FUNDAMENTAL PRINCIPLES

The Republic of Ukraine is a sovereign and independent, unitary and law-based state, in which power is exercised directly by the people through the bodies of state power and local self-government. The life, honour, dignity and health of the individual are recognized as the highest social value. The Constitution is the highest legal authority; the power of the State is divided between the legislative, the executive and the judicial branches. The state language is Ukrainian. The use and protection of Russian and other languages of national minorities, and the development of minorities' ethnic and cultural traditions is guaranteed. The State ensures protection of all forms of ownership rights and management, as well as the social orientation of the economy. The state symbols of Ukraine, its flag, coat of arms and anthem, are established.

THE RIGHTS, FREEDOMS AND DUTIES OF CITIZENS

The rights and freedoms of individuals are declared to be unalienable and inviolable regardless of race, sex, political or religious affiliation, wealth, social origin or other characteristics. Fundamental rights, such as the freedoms of speech and association and the right to private property, are guaranteed. Citizens have the right to engage in political activity and to own private property. All individuals are entitled to work and to join professional unions to protect their employment rights. The Constitution commits the State to the provision of health care, housing, social security and education. All citizens have the right to legal assistance. Obligations of the citizenry include military service and taxes. The age of enfranchisement for Ukrainian citizens is 18 years. Elections to organs of state authority are declared to be free and conducted on the basis of universal, equal and direct suffrage by secret ballot.

THE VERKHOVNA RADA

The Verkhovna Rada is the sole organ of legislative authority in Ukraine. It consists of 450 members, elected for a four-year term. Only Ukrainian citizens aged over 21 years, who have resided in Ukraine for the five previous years and have not been convicted for a criminal offence, are eligible for election to parliament. The Verkhovna Rada is a permanently acting body, which elects its own Chairman and Deputy Chairmen.

The most important functions of the legislature include: the enactment of laws; the approval of the state budget and other state programmes; the scheduling of presidential elections; the removal (impeachment) of the President; consenting to the President's appointment of the Prime Minister; the declaration of war or conclusion of peace; the foreign deployment of troops; and consenting to international treaty obligations within the time-limit prescribed by law. Within 15 days of a law passed by the Verkhovna Rada being received by the President, the President shall officially promulgate it or return it for repeat consideration by parliament. If, during such consideration, the legislature re-adopts the law by a two-thirds' majority, the President is obliged to sign it and officially promulgate it within 10 days. The President of Ukraine may terminate the authority of the Verkhovna Rada if, within 30 days of a single, regular session a plenary session cannot be convened, except within the last six months of the President's term of office.

Some of the Verkhovna Rada's financial responsibilities, such as the oversight of fiscal resources by the Accounting Chamber on its behalf, are specified in the Constitution. The monetary unit of Ukraine is the hryvnya and providing for the stability of the currency is the primary function of the central state bank, the National Bank of Ukraine.

THE PRESIDENT OF THE REPUBLIC

The President of the Republic of Ukraine is the Head of State, and is guarantor of state sovereignty and the territorial integrity of Ukraine. The President is directly elected for a period of five years. A presidential candidate must be aged over 35 years and a resident of the country for the 10 years prior to the election. The President may hold office for no more than two consecutive terms.

The President's main responsibilities include: the scheduling of elections and of referendums on constitutional amendments, the conclusion of international treaties; and the promulgation of laws. The President is responsible for appointing a Prime Minister, with the consent of the Verkhovna Rada, and for dismissing the Prime Minister and deciding the issue of his resignation. The President appoints members of the Cabinet of Ministers on the recommendation of the Prime Minister.

The President is the Supreme Commander of the Armed Forces of the Republic of Ukraine and chairs the National Security and Defence Council. The President may be removed from office by the Verkhovna Rada by impeachment, for reasons of state treason or another crime. The decision to remove the President must be approved by at least a three-quarters' majority in the Verkhovna Rada. In the event of the termination of the authority of the President, the Prime Minister executes the duties of the President until the election and entry into office of a new President.

THE CABINET OF MINISTERS

The principal organ of executive government is the Cabinet of Ministers, which is responsible before the President and accountable to the Verkhovna Rada. The Cabinet supervises the implementation of state policy and the state budget and the maintenance of law and order. The Cabinet of Ministers is headed by the Prime Minister, appointed by the President with the approval of more than one-half of the parliamentary deputies. The duties of the Prime Minister include the submission of proposals to the President on the creation, reorganization and liquidation of ministries and other central bodies of executive authority. The members of the Cabinet, which also include a First Deputy Prime Minister and three Deputy Prime Ministers, are appointed by the President upon the recommendation of the Prime Minister. The Cabinet of Ministers must resign when a new President is elected, or in the event of the adoption of a vote of 'no confidence' by the Verkhovna Rada.

JUDICIAL POWER

Justice in Ukraine is administered by the Constitutional Court and by courts of general jurisdiction. The Supreme Court of Ukraine is the highest judicial organ of general jurisdiction. Judges hold their position permanently, except for justices of the Constitutional Court and first judicial appointments, which are made by the President for a five-year term. Other judges, with the exception of justices of the Constitutional Court, are elected by the Verkhovna Rada. Judges must be at least 25 years of age, have a higher legal education and at least three years' work experience in the field of law, and have resided in Ukraine for no fewer than 10 years. The Procuracy of Ukraine is headed by the General Procurator, who is appointed with the consent of parliament and dismissed by the President. The term of office of the General Procurator is five years.

A Superior Justice Council, responsible for the submission of proposals regarding the appointment or dismissal of judges, functions in Ukraine. The Council consists of 20 members. The Chairman of the Supreme Court of Ukraine, the Minister of Justice, and the General Procurator are *ex-officio* members of the Superior Justice Council.

LOCAL SELF-GOVERNMENT

The administrative and territorial division of Ukraine consists of the Autonomous Republic of Crimea, 24 provinces (oblasts), the cities of Kiev and Sevastopol (which possess special status), districts (raions), cities, settlements and villages. Local self-government is the right of territorial communities. The principal organs of territorial communities are the district and provincial councils, which, with their chairmen, are directly elected for a term of four years. The chairmen of district and provincial councils are elected by the relevant council and head their executive structure. Provincial and district councils monitor the implementation of programmes of socioeconomic and cultural development of the relevant provinces and districts, and adopt and monitor the implementation of district and provincial budgets, which are derived from the state budget.

THE AUTONOMOUS REPUBLIC OF CRIMEA

The Autonomous Republic of Crimea is an inseparable, integral part of Ukraine. It has its own Constitution, which is adopted by the Supreme Council of the Autonomous Republic of Crimea (the representative organ of Crimea) and approved by the Verkhovna Rada. Legislation adopted by the Autonomous Republic's Supreme Council and the decisions of its Council of Ministers must not contravene the Constitution and laws of Ukraine. The Chairman of the Council of Ministers is appointed and dismissed by the Supreme Council of the Autonomous Republic of Crimea with the consent of the President of Ukraine. Justice in Crimea is administered by courts belonging to the single court system of Ukraine. An Office of the Representative of the President of Ukraine functions in Crimea.

The jurisdiction of the Autonomous Republic of Crimea includes: organizing and conducting local referendums; implementing the republican budget on the basis of the state policy of Ukraine; ensuring the function and development of the state and national languages and cultures; participating in the development and fulfilment of programmes for the return of deported peoples.

THE CONSTITUTIONAL COURT

The Constitutional Court consists of 18 justices, six of whom are appointed by the President, six by the Verkhovna Rada and six by the assembly of judges of Ukraine. Candidates must be citizens of Ukraine, who are at least 40 years of age and have resided in Ukraine for the previous 20 years. Justices of the Constitutional Court serve a term of nine years, with no right to reappointment. A Chairman is elected by a secret ballot of the members for a single three-year term.

The Constitutional Court provides binding interpretations of the Constitution. It rules on the constitutionality of: parliamentary legislation; acts of the President and the Cabinet of Ministers; the official interpretation of the Constitution of Ukraine; international agreements; and the impeachment of the President of Ukraine.

CONSTITUTIONAL AMENDMENTS AND THE ADOPTION OF A NEW CONSTITUTION

A draft law on amending the Constitution may be presented to the Verkhovna Rada by the President or at least one-third of the constitutional composition of the parliament. A draft law on amending the Constitution, which has been given preliminary approval by a majority of the constitutional composition of the Verkhovna Rada, is considered adopted if it receives the support of at least a two-thirds' parliamentary majority. In the case of its approval it is confirmed by a nation-wide referendum designated by the President.

Note: In April 2000 participants in a national referendum approved a number of constitutional amendments permitting: the dissolution of the Verkhovna Rada, should it fail to approve the state budget within a three-month period; the reduction of the number of deputies from 450 to 300; the limitation of deputies' immunity from prosecution; and the introduction of a bicameral legislature.

The Government

HEAD OF STATE

President: Leonid D. Kuchma (elected 10 July 1994, re-elected 14 November 1999, re-inaugurated 30 November 1999).

CABINET OF MINISTERS
(April 2003)

Prime Minister: Viktor F. Yanukovych.

First Deputy Prime Minister, Minister of Finance: Mykola Ya. Azarov.

Deputy Prime Minister: Vitaliy A. Haiduk.

Deputy Prime Minister, responsible for the Agro-industrial Complex: IVAN H. KYRYLENKO.

Deputy Prime Minister, responsible for Humanitarian Issues: DMYTRO V. TABACHNYK.

Minister of Agricultural Policy: SERHIY M. RYZHUK.

Minister of Internal Affairs: Col-Gen. YURIY O. SMIRNOV.

Minister of the Economy and Progress Towards European Integration: VALERIY I. KHOROSHKOVSKYI.

Minister of Transport: HEORHIY M. KIRPA.

Minister of Defence: Gen. VOLODYMYR P. SHKIDCHENKO.

Minister of Ecology and Natural Resources: VASYL YA. SHEV-CHUK.

Minister of Foreign Affairs: ANATOLIY M. ZLENKO.

Minister for Emergency Situations and Protection of the Population from the Consequences of the Chornobyl Catastrophe: HRYHORIY V. REVA.

Minister of Relations with the Verkhovna Rada: IVAN I. TKA-LENKO.

Minister of Art and Culture: YURIY P. BOHUTSKYI.

Minister of Education and Science: VASYL H. KREMEN.

Minister of Health Care: ANDRIY V. PIDAYEV.

Minister of Fuel and Energy: SERHIY F. YERMILOV.

Minister of Labour and Social Policy: MYKHAILO M. PAPIYEV.

Minister of Industrial Policy: ANATOLIY K. MYALYTSYA.

Minister of Justice: OLEKSANDR V. LAVRYNOVYCH.

State Secretary to the Cabinet of Ministers: VOLODYMYR H. YATSUBA.

MINISTRIES

Office of the President: 01220 Kiev, vul. Bankova 11; tel. (44) 291-53-33; fax (44) 293-61-61; e-mail president@adm.gov.ua; internet www.president.gov.ua.

Cabinet of Ministers: 01008 Kiev, vul. M. Hrushevskoho 12/2; tel. (44) 293-21-71; fax (44) 293-20-93; e-mail web@kmu.gov.ua; internet www.kmu.gov.ua.

Ministry of Agricultural Policy: 01001 Kiev, vul. Khreshchatyk 24; tel. (44) 226-34-66; fax (44) 229-87-56; e-mail ministr@minapk .kiev.ua; internet www.minagro.gov.ua.

Ministry of Art and Culture: 01030 Kiev, vul. Ivana Franka 19; tel. (44) 226-26-45; fax (44) 225-32-57; e-mail info@mincult.gov.ua; internet www.mincult.gov.ua.

Ministry of Defence: 03168 Kiev, Povitroflotskyi pr. 6; tel. (44) 226-26-56; fax (44) 226-20-15; e-mail pressmou@pressmou.kiev.ua; internet www.mil.gov.ua.

Ministry of Ecology and Natural Resources: 01601 Kiev, vul. Khreshchatyk 5; tel. (44) 228-06-44; fax (44) 229-83-83; e-mail menr@menr.gov.ua; internet www.menr.gov.ua.

Ministry of the Economy and Progress Towards European Integration: 01008 Kiev, vul. M. Hrushevskoho 12/2; tel. (44) 293-93-94; fax (44) 226-31-81; e-mail meconomy@me.gov.ua; internet www.me.gov.ua.

Ministry of Education and Science: 01135 Kiev, pr. Peremohy 10; tel. (44) 226-26-61; fax (44) 274-10-49; e-mail vgk@ministry .edu-ua.net; internet www.mon.gov.ua.

Ministry for Emergency Situations and Protection of the Population from the Consequences of the Chornobyl Catastrophe: 01030 Kiev, vul. O. Honchara 55; tel. (44) 247-30-50; e-mail main@mns.gov.ua; internet www.mns.gov.ua.

Ministry of Finance: 01008 Kiev, vul. M. Hrushevskoho 12/2; tel. (44) 293-74-66; fax (44) 293-21-78; e-mail infomf@minfin.gov.ua.

Ministry of Foreign Affairs: 01018 Kiev, pl. Mykhailivska 1; tel. (44) 21-28-33; fax (44) 226-31-69; internet www.mfa.gov.ua.

Ministry of Fuel and Energy: 01601 Kiev, vul. Khreshchatik 30; tel. (44) 221-43-64; fax (44) 462-05-61; e-mail kanc@mintop.energy .gov.ua; internet mpe.energy.gov.ua.

Ministry of Health Care: 01021 Kiev, vul. M. Hrushevskoho 7; tel. (44) 253-24-39; fax (44) 253-69-75; internet www.moz.gov.ua.

Ministry of Industrial Policy: 03035 Kiev, vul. Surikova 3; tel. (44) 245-47-78; fax (44) 246-32-14.

Ministry of Internal Affairs: 01024 Kiev, vul. Akademika Boho-moltsya 10; tel. (44) 291-18-30; fax (44) 291-16-52; e-mail mail@ centrmia.gov.ua; internet www.centrmia.gov.ua.

Ministry of Justice: 01001 Kiev, vul. Horodetskoho 13; tel. and fax (44) 228-37-23; e-mail themis@minjust.gov.ua; internet www .minjust.gov.ua.

Ministry of Labour and Social Policy: 01023 Kiev, vul. Espla-nadna 8/10; tel. (44) 220-90-97; fax (44) 220-90-64; e-mail public@ subs-mspp.kiev.ua; internet www.minpraci.gov.ua.

Ministry of Relations with the Verkhovna Rada: 01008 Kiev, vul. M. Hrushevskoho 12/2.

Ministry of Transport: 03680 Kiev, vul. Shchorsa 7/9; tel. (44) 446-30-30; e-mail info@mintrans.gov.ua; internet www.mintrans.kiev .ua.

State Committees

State Committee for Archives: 03110 Kiev, vul. Solomyanska 24; tel. (44) 277-36-55; fax (44) 277-34-44; e-mail mail@archives.gov.ua; internet www.archives.gov.ua; Chair. Prof. HENNADIY V. BORYAK.

State Committee for Border Control: 01034 Kiev, vul. Volody-myrska 26; tel. (44) 212-87-77; fax (44) 212-39-80; e-mail dkk@pvu .gov.ua; internet www.pvu.gov.ua; Chair. MYKOLA M. LYTVYN.

State Committee for Communication and Information: 01001 Kiev, vul. Khreshchatyk 22; tel. (44) 228-15-00; fax (44) 212-30-74; e-mail l.bychenok@stc.gov.ua; internet www.stc.gov.ua; Chair. MYKOLA V. HONCHAR.

State Committee for Construction and Architecture: 03150 Kiev, vul. Dymytrova 24; tel. (44) 226-22-08; fax (44) 227-23-35; e-mail untp@build.gov.ua; internet www.build.gov.ua; Chair. VALERIY I. CHEREP.

State Committee for Energy Conservation: 04112 Kiev, vul. Honty 1; tel. (44) 456-81-83; fax (44) 456-80-23; e-mail cenef@elan-ua .net; internet www.cenef.kiev.ua; Chair. YURIY I. SHULGA.

State Committee for Exercise and Sports: 01023 Kiev, vul. Esplanadna 42; tel. (44) 220-03-66; fax (44) 220-12-94; e-mail komitet@sport.kiev.ua; internet www.sport.gov.ua; Chair. MARIYA M. BULATOVA.

State Committee for Family and Youth Affairs: 01025 Kiev, vul. Desyatynna 14; tel. (44) 229-11-24; fax (44) 228-55-40; e-mail dovzhenko@dksm.gov.ua; Chair. VALENTYNA DOVZHENKO.

State Committee for Forestry: 01023 Kiev, vul. Sh. Rustaveli 9A; tel. (44) 226-32-53; fax (44) 228-77-94; e-mail dklg@nbi.com.ua; internet www.dklg.kiev.ua; Chair. MYKOLA V. KOLISNYCHENKO.

State Committee for Housing: 03150 Kiev, vul. Dymytrova 24; tel. (44) 244-39-82; fax (44) 227-23-35; e-mail iass@ndiasb.kiev.ua; internet www.djkg.gov.ua; Chair. HRIHORIY M. SEMCHUK.

State Committee for Information Policy, Television and Radio Broadcasting: 01001 Kiev, vul. Prorizna 2; tel. (44) 228-87-69; fax (44) 229-41-48; e-mail admin@scriptrb.gov.ua; internet www .sciptrb.gov.ua; Chair. IVAN S. CHYZH.

State Committee for Land Resources: 01601 Kiev, Muzeinyi provulok 12; tel. (44) 226-21-70; fax (44) 226-21-54; e-mail myland@ iatp.kiev.ua; internet myland.org.ua/uk/(main)/790; Chair. ANATOLIY S. DANYLENKO.

State Committee for Nationalities and Migration: 01034 Kiev, vul. Volodymyrska 9; tel. (44) 228-17-18; fax (44) 226-23-39; e-mail ksenia@minjust.gov.ua; Chair. HENNADIY H. MOSKAL.

State Committee for Nuclear Regulation: 01011 Kiev, vul. Arsenalna 9/11; tel. (44) 254-33-47; fax (44) 254-33-11; e-mail pr@hq .snrc .gov.ua; internet www.snrcu.gov.ua; Chair. VADYM V. HRYSH-CHENKO.

State Committee for Regulatory Policy and the Development of Enterprise: 04053 Kiev, vul. Sichovykh Striltsiv 73; tel. (44) 246-84-49; fax (44) 246-86-39; internet www.dkrp.gov.ua; Chair. (vacant).

State Committee for Religions: 01601 Kiev, vul. Prorizna 15/5; tel. (44) 229-37-16; fax (44) 229-36-43; e-mail dkrelig@iptelecom.net .ua; Chair. VIKTOR D. BONDARENKO.

State Committee for Statistics: 01023 Kiev, vul. Sh. Rustaveli 3; tel. (44) 226-20-21; fax (44) 235-37-39; e-mail info@ukrstat.gov.ua; internet www.ukrstat.gov.ua; Chair. OLEKSANDR H. OSAULENKO.

State Committee for Technical Regulation and Consumption Policy: 01150 Kiev, vul. Horkoho 174; tel. 226-29-71; fax 226-29-70; e-mail dstu1@dstu.gov.ua; internet www.dss u.gov.ua; Chair. LEONID S. SHKOLNYK.

State Committee for Veterans: 04053 Kiev, vul. Lvivska 8/18/1803; tel. (44) 212-51-30; fax (44) 212-02-30; e-mail kiev_veteran@ukrpost.com.ua; internet www.dkusv.cjb.net; Chair. SERHIY V. CHERVONOPYSKYI.

State Committee for Water Resources: 01601 Kiev, vul. Vasyl-kivska 8; tel. (44) 226-26-07; fax (44) 225-31-92; e-mail webmaster@

scwm.gov.ua; internet www.scwm.gov.ua; Chair. Viktor M. Khoryev.

State Customs Committee: 04119 Kiev, vul. Degtyarivska 11н; tel. (44) 274-82-83; internet www.customs.gov.ua; Chair. Mykola M. Kalenskiy.

President and Legislature

PRESIDENT

Presidential Election, First Ballot, 31 October 1999

Candidates	Votes	%
Leonid D. Kuchma	9,598,672	36.49
Petro M. Symonenko	5,849,077	22.24
Oleksandr O. Moroz	2,969,896	11.29
Nataliya M. Vitrenko	2,886,972	10.97
Yevhen K. Marchuk	2,138,356	8.13
Yuriy I. Kostenko	570,623	2.17
Hennadiy Y. Udovenko	319,778	1.22
Others	456,021	1.73
Against all candidates	477,019	1.81
Total*	26,305,163	100.00

* Including invalid votes, totalling 1,038,749.

Second Ballot, 14 November 1999

Candidate	Votes	%
Leonid D. Kuchma	15,870,722	57.70
Petro M. Symonenko	10,665,420	38.77
Against all candidates	970,181	3.52
Total*	27,506,323	100.00

* Excluding invalid votes, totalling 706,161.

VERKHOVNA RADA
(Supreme Council)

Verkhovna Rada

01008 Kiev, vul. M. Hrushevskoho 5; tel. (44) 226-22-92; fax (44) 293-06-53; e-mail vfsev@rada.gov.ua; internet www.rada.gov.ua.

Chairman: Volodymyr M. Lytvyn.

First Deputy Chairman: Hennadiy A. Vasylyev.

Deputy Chairman: Oleksandr O. Zinchenko.

General Election, 31 March 2002

Parties and blocs	Federal party lists		Total seats*
	% of votes	Seats	
Our Ukraine	23.57	70	112
For A United Ukraine	11.78	35	101
Communist Party of Ukraine	19.99	59	66
Social-Democratic Party of Ukraine (United)	6.28	19	24
Socialist Party of Ukraine	6.87	20	23
Yuliya Tymoshenko Bloc	7.26	22	22
Democratic Party of Ukraine—Democratic Union	0.88	—	4
Unity	1.09	—	3
Ukrainian Maritime Party	0.11	—	1
Party of National Economic Development of Ukraine	—	—	1
Nataliya Vitrenko bloc	3.23	—	—
Women for the Future	2.11	—	—
Team of the Winter Crop Generation	2.03	—	—
Communist Party of Ukraine (Renewed)	1.40	—	—
Green Party of Ukraine	1.31	—	—
Yabluko	1.16	—	—
Others†	4.77	—	—
Independents	—	—	93
Against all lists	2.45	—	—
Total	100.00‡	225	450

* Including seats filled by voting in single-member constituencies, totalling 225.
† There were 19 other groups.
‡ Including spoilt ballot papers (3.71% of the total). The total number of votes cast was 25,909,407.

Political Organizations

Until 1990 the only legal political party in Ukraine was the Communist Party of Ukraine (CPU), an integral part of the Communist Party of the Soviet Union. In 1988, however, a Ukrainian People's Movement for Restructuring (known as Rukh) was established to support greater democratization and freedom of speech, and several other political organizations were also founded. In 1990, after the CPU's constitutional monopoly was abolished, many new political parties were established. Rukh, which had been the main coalition of forces opposed to the CPU in 1988–91, became a political party (as the People's Movement of Ukraine) in 1993. President Leonid Kuchma, who was elected to that position in 1994, and re-elected in 1999, has been associated with a number of so-called 'parties of power', including the Inter-regional Bloc for Reform movement (which was registered as a political party in 1994) and the Party of Industrialists and Entrepreneurs of Ukraine (founded in 2001), which contested the parliamentary elections in 2002 as part of the For a United Ukraine bloc. In December 2001 there were 127 political parties officially registered in Ukraine; the following were among the most important at early 2003.

Batkivshchyna (Fatherland): 01133 Kiev, vul. L. Ukrainky 26/916; tel. (44) 294-42-21; e-mail info@byti.org.ua; internet www.tymoshenko.com.ua; f. 1999 by members of Hromada—Community Party; democratic, seeks to combine patriotism,a liberal approach towards economics and provision of social protection for citizens; contested 2002 parliamentary elections as Yuliya Tymoshenko Bloc; Chair. Yuliya V. Tymoshenko; 203,000 mems (2002).

Christian Democratic Party of Ukraine (Khrystyyansko-Demokratychna Partiya Ukrainy): 01004 Kiev, vul. Baseyna 1/2a; tel. (44) 235-39-96; fax (44) 234-19-49; e-mail info@cdpu.org.ua; internet cdpu.org.ua; centrist democratic party; Chair. Vitaliy S. Zhuravskiy; 42,000 mems.

Communist Party of Ukraine (CPU) (Komunistychna Partiya Ukrainy): 04070 Kiev, vul. Borysohlibska 7; tel. (44) 416-54-87; fax (44) 416-31-37; internet www.kppu.kiev.ua; banned 1991–93; advocates state control of economy and confederation with Russia; Sec. of Cen. Cttee Petro M. Symonenko.

Communist Party of Ukraine (Renewed) (CPU—R) (Komunistychna Partiya Ukrainy—Onovlena): 02098 Kiev, pr. Tychyny 10/35; tel. (44) 554-28-34; f. 2000 by faction of CPU; Leader Mykhaylo M. Savenko.

Democratic Party of Ukraine—Democratic Union (Demokratychna Partiya Ukrainy—Demokratychnyi Soyuz): 04010 Kiev, vul. Chapayeva 4/4; tel. (44) 235-39-40; e-mail rada@demunion.kiev.ua; internet www.demunion.kiev.ua; Pres. Volodomyr P. Horbulin.

For a United Ukraine (FUU) (Za Yedinu Ukrainu): 04070 Kiev, vul. Florivska 1; tel. (44) 238-65-16; e-mail info@zaedu.org.ua; internet www.zaedu.org.ua; electoral bloc formed 2001 to contest 2002 parliamentary elections; supports Govt of President Kuchma; Chair. Volodymyr M. Lytvyn.

Agrarian Party of Ukraine (Agrarna Partiya Ukrainy): 01034 Kiev, vul. Reitarska 6a; tel. (44) 464-01-86; fax (44) 464-05-91; e-mail webmaster@partiya.net.ua; internet www.apu.org.ua; f. 1996; advocates revival of the Ukrainian countryside; Chair. Mykhaylo V. Hladiy.

People's Democratic Party (PDP) (Narodno-Demokratychna Partiya—NDP): 03150 Kiev, vul. Antonovicha 107; tel. (44) 252-84-18; fax (44) 252-87-26; e-mail zagal@s ndp.kiev.ua; internet ndp.org.ua; f. 1996; centrist; Leader Valeriy P. Pustovoytenko; 242,792 mems (2002).

Party of Industrialists and Entrepreneurs of Ukraine (Partiya promyslovtsiv i pidpryyemtsiv Ukrainy): 01023 Kiev, vul. Baseyna 30/46; tel. (44) 234-37-07; fax (44) 235-82-58; e-mail pppu@ukr.net; internet pppu.com.ua; f. 2001 by faction of PDPU; Chair. Anatoliy K. Kinakh.

Party of the Regions (PR) (Partiya Regioniv): 04053 Kiev, vul. Kudryavska 3/5; tel. (44) 212-55-70; fax (44) 212-55-83; e-mail PressCenter@partyofregions.org.ua; internet www.partyofregions.org.ua; f. 1997 as Party of Regional Rebirth of Ukraine; present name adopted 2001; Chair. Viktor F. Yanukovych; 460,000 mems (Dec. 2001).

Working Ukraine (Trudova Ukraina): 01021 Kiev, vul. Shovkovychna 4; tel. (44) 229-89-03; e-mail inform@tu.privat-online.net; internet www.trud.org.ua; f. 2000; Pres. Serhiy L. Tyhypko; Chair. of Political Committee Andriy Derkach; 20,000 mems (2002).

Green Party of Ukraine (Partiya Zelenykh Ukrainy): 01023 Kiev, vul. Sh. Rustaveli 38; tel. (44) 220-50-80; fax (44) 220-66-94; e-mail office@greenparty.org.ua; internet www.greenparty.org.ua; f. 1990 as political wing of environmental organization, Green World (f. 1987); Pres. Vitaliy M. Kononov.

Hromada (Community): 01133 Kiev, Laboratornyi provylok 1; tel. and fax (44) 252-88-57; e-mail office@hromada.kiev.ua; internet www.hromada.kiev.ua; f. 1994; social democratic; Leader PAVLO I. LAZARENKO.

Our Ukraine (Nasha Ukraina): Kiev; e-mail forum@ua.org.ua; internet www.razom.org.ua; electoral bloc f. 2001 to contest 2002 parliamentary elections; broadly nationalist and supportive of greater economic liberalization; Chair. VIKTOR A. YUSHCHENKO; affiliated parties include.

> **Congress of Ukrainian Nationalists** (Kongres Ukrainskykh Natsionalistiv): 01034 Kiev, vul. Yaroslaviv 9/4; tel. (44) 224-70-20; e-mail mkun@ukr.net; f. 1992; Chair. (vacant).

> **People's Movement of Ukraine-Rukh (PMU-R)** (Narodnyi Rukh Ukrainy): 01034 Kiev, vul. O. Honchara 33; tel. (44) 246-47-67; e-mail nruorg@ukrtel.com; internet www.nru.org.ua; f. 1989 as popular movement (Ukrainian People's Movement for Restructuring); registered as political party in 1993; national democratic party; Chair. BORIS I. TARASYUK.

> **Reforms and Order Party** (Reformy i poryadok): 01021 Kiev, vul. Instytutska 28; tel. (44) 201-41-16; fax (44) 201-41-17; e-mail webmaster@reformy.org; internet www.reformy.org; f. 1997; supports economic reform and greater integration of Ukraine with central and western European organizations; Chair. VIKTOR M. PYNZENYK.

> **Ukrainian People's Party (UPP)** (Ukrainska Narodna Partiya): 01004 Kiev, vul. Pushkinska 28A; tel. (44) 224-59-17; fax (44) 224-10-30; e-mail org@rukh-unr.org; internet www.rukh-unr.org; f. 1999 as breakaway faction of People's Movement of Ukraine-Rukh by former leader Vyacheslav Chornovil; fmrly Ukrainian People's Movement-Rukh; present name adopted 2003; Chair. YURIY I. KOSTENKO.

Party of National Economic Development of Ukraine (Partiya Natsionalno-Ekonoichnoho Ukrainy): 01001 Kiev, vul. Sofiyivska 7; tel. (44) 226-21-63; fax (44) 226-21-08; f. 1996; Leader PAVLO V. MATVIYENKO.

Progressive Socialist Party of Ukraine (Prohresyvna Sotsialistychna Partiya Ukrainy): 01032 Kiev, vul. Kominterna 15; tel. (44) 291-74-60; e-mail pspu@aport2000.ru; internet www.vitrenko.org; f. 1996 by members of the Socialist Party of Ukraine; contested parliamentary elections in 2002 as Nataliya Vitrenko bloc; favours extension of Belarus-Russia Union to incorporate Ukraine; opposed to Ukraine seeking membership of NATO; Chair. NATALIYA M. VITRENKO.

Russian Movement of Ukraine (Russkoye Dvizheniye Ukrainy): 79008 Lviv, vul. Smolskoho 2/7; tel. and fax (322) 75-80-59; e-mail rdu@rdu.org.ua; internet www.rdu.org.ua; f. 1999; seeks by moderate means to re-establish a political union of Belarus, Russia and Ukraine, and to restore the status of Russian as an official language of Ukraine, alongside Ukrainian; Chair. ALEKSANDR G. SVISTUNOV; affiliated parties include.

> **Union** (Soyuz): 95017 Crimea, Simferopol, vul. Krupskoyi 5/9; tel. (652) 24-17-55; fax (652) 24-18-94; f. 1997; Chair. VLADIMIR KLYCHNIKOV.

Social-Democratic Party of Ukraine (United) (SDPU—U) (Sotsial-Demokratychna Partiya Ukrainy—Obyednana): 01030 Kiev, vul. Ivano-Franko 18; tel. (44) 536-15-71; fax (44) 536-15-78; e-mail sdpuo@org.ukr.net; internet www.sdpuo.org.ua; f. 1995, by merger of the Social Democratic Party, the Ukrainian Party of Justice and the Party of Human Rights; advocates economic and political reform; social democratic; Chair. VIKTOR V. MEDVEDCHUK; 370,000 mems (2002).

Socialist Party of Ukraine (SPU) (Sotsialistychna Partiya Ukrainy): 01054 Kiev, vul. Vorovskoho 45; tel. (44) 216-88-82; fax (44) 244-51-66; e-mail press@socinfo.kiev.ua; internet www.socinfo .kiev.ua; f. 1991; formed as partial successor to CPU; advocates democratic socialism; Leader OLEKSANDR O. MOROZ; c. 69,000 mems.

Team of the Winter Crop Generation (Komanda Ozymoho Pokolinnya): Kiev; tel. (44) 254-08-07; e-mail info@zbirna.org.ua; internet zbirna.org.ua; f. 1997; supports economic reform, constitutional democracy and private property; advocates closer links with western Europe; Leader VALERIY I. KHOROSHKOVSKIY.

Ukrainian Maritime Party (Ukrainska Morska Partiya): 65000 Odesa, vul. Kanatna 42; represents the interests of sailors; Leader SERHIY V. KIVALOV.

Unity (Yednist): 03039 Kiev, vul. Yaroslaviv val 21; tel. (44) 227-55-27; internet www.yednist.org.ua; f. 2000; contested the 2002 parliamentary elections in alliance with Young Ukraine, Social Democratic Union and the Party of Justice–Union of Veterans, Invalids, survivors of the Chernobyl catastrophe and the Soviet–Afghan War; Chair. OLEKSANDR O. OMELCHENKO.

Women for the Future (Zhinky za maibutne): 04080 Kiev, vul. Turivska 13; tel. (44) 229-51-08; internet www.woman.org.ua; f. 2001; supports Govt of President Kuchma; Chair. VALENTYNA I. DOVZHENKO.

Yabluko (Apple): 01010 Kiev, vul. Moskovska 37/2/1/45; tel. (44) 254-52-88; fax (44) 293-56-71; e-mail yabluko@yabluko.org.ua; internet www.yabluko.org.ua; supports the protection of private property; Chair. MYKHAYLO BRODSKYI.

CRIMEAN POLITICAL ORGANIZATIONS

Like its Ukrainian counterpart, the Communist Party of Crimea was banned in August 1991. In September 1993, however, a new organization of that name was registered. Several other political groups emerged in 1993–94. The 'Russia' bloc consisted of various pro-Russian parties, including the Republican Party of Crimea, the former leader of which, YURII MESHKOV, won the Crimean presidential elections in January 1994. Several parties promoting business interests were formed, including the Party for the Economic Rebirth of Crimea, and Working Ukraine, which was founded in 2000. The dominant political party among the Crimean Tatars was the Organization of the Crimean Tatar Movement (OCTM—f. 1991), which advocates the restoration of Tatar statehood in the Crimea. The OCTM also organized a Crimean Tatar representative body, the Majlis, led by MUSTAFA DZHEMLYEV. The National Movement of the Crimean Tatars is a more moderate organization, committed to co-operation with the existing political structures in the Crimea, and in March 2002 seven Crimean Tatars were elected to the Crimean Supreme Council, compared with just one in 1998. The National Party (Milli Firka—National Party) is a radical nationalist group. In the elections to the Verkhovna Rada held concurrently with elections to the Crimean Supreme Council in March 2002, the CPU were the most popular party, receiving 33.9% of the votes cast, one of the highest proportions in any region in Ukraine, while the Social-Democratic Party of Ukraine (United) also received a markedly higher proportion of the votes cast (12.5%) than was the case nationwide. Although the Our Ukraine bloc only received 9.8% of the votes cast in Crimea, it was believed to have gained particular support among Crimean Tatars, partially because of the inclusion of MUSTAFA DZHEMLYEV and another leader of the Majlis, REFAT CHUBAROV, on the party's list.

Diplomatic Representation

EMBASSIES IN UKRAINE

Afghanistan: 03037 Kiev, pr. Chervonozoryanyi 42; tel. (44) 245-81-04; e-mail afghanem@afghanem.kiev.ua; Chargé d'affaires a.i. MUKHAYEDDIN MASUD.

Algeria: 01001 Kiev, vul. B. Khmelnytskoho 64; tel. (44) 216-70-79; fax (44) 216-70-08; e-mail ambkv@ksv.net.ua; Ambassador CHERIF SHIKHI.

Armenia: 01901 Kiev, vul. Volodymyrska 45; tel. (44) 224-90-05; fax (44) 224-05-00; e-mail armenia@desp.kiev.ua; Ambassador HRACH H. SILVANYAN.

Austria: 01901 Kiev, vul. Ivana Franka 33; tel. (44) 244-39-43; fax (44) 230-23-52; e-mail kiew-ob@bmaa.gv.at; Ambassador KLAUS FABJAN.

Azerbaijan: 04050 Kiev, vul. Hlubochytska 24; tel. (44) 461-91-99; fax (44) 461-93-44; e-mail embass@faust.kiev.ua; Ambassador TALYAT MUSEIB OLGY ALIYEV.

Belarus: 01010 Kiev, vul. Sichnevoho Povstannya 6; tel. (44) 290-02-01; fax (44) 290-34-13; e-mail ukraine@belembassy.org; Ambassador VALENTYN V. VELICHKO.

Belgium: 01030 Kiev, vul. Leontovicha 4; tel. (44) 238-26-00; fax (44) 238-26-01; e-mail ambbkiev@gu.net; Ambassador PIERRE CLEMENT DUBUISSON.

Brazil: 01010 Kiev, bulv. L. Ukrainky 21/17; tel. (44) 290-63-01; fax (44) 290-95-68; e-mail kivbrem@public.ua.net; Ambassador ELDER MARTINS DE MORAES.

Bulgaria: 01023 Kiev, vul. Hospitalna 1; tel. (44) 235-52-96; fax (44) 224-99-29; e-mail embbul@carrier.kiev.ua; Ambassador ALEKSANDR DYMYTROV.

Canada: 01901 Kiev, vul. Yaroslaviv Val 31; tel. (44) 464-11-44; fax (44) 464-11-33; e-mail kyiv@dfait-maeci.gc.ca; internet www.kyiv.gc .ca; Ambassador ANDREW N. ROBINSON.

China, People's Republic: 01901 Kiev, vul. M. Hrushevskoho 32; tel. and fax (44) 253-10-49; fax (44) 253-15-24; e-mail cxjl@ukrpack .net; Ambassador LI GOUBANG.

Croatia: 01091 Kiev, vul. Sichovykh Striltsiv 51/50; tel. (44) 216-58-62; fax (44) 224-69-43; e-mail croemb@carrier.kiev.ua; Ambassador Dr MARIO MIKOLIĆ.

Cuba: 01901 Kiev, prov. Byekhtyerevskyi 5; tel. (44) 216-57-43; fax (44) 216-19-07; e-mail embacuba@naverex.kiev.ua; Ambassador JOSÉ DIONISIO PERAZA CHAPEAU.

Czech Republic: 01901 Kiev, vul. Yaroslaviv Val 34A; tel. (44) 212-04-31; fax (44) 229-74-69; e-mail kiev@embassy.mzv.cz; Ambassador Dr KAREL ŠTINDL.

Egypt: 01901 Kiev, vul. Observatorna 19; tel. (44) 212-13-27; fax (44) 216-94-28; e-mail boustan@egypt-emb.kiev.ua; Ambassador MONA ALY KHASHABA.

Estonia: 01901 Kiev, vul. Volodymyrska 61/11; tel. (44) 235-85-82; fax (44) 234-14-03; e-mail embassy@estemb.kiev.ua; internet www.estemb.kiev.ua; Ambassador PAUL LETTENS.

Finland: 01901 Kiev, vul. Striletska 14; tel. (44) 228-70-49; fax (44) 228-20-32; e-mail sanomat.kio@formin.fi; Ambassador LAURA REINILÄ.

France: 01034 Kiev, vul. Reitarska 39; tel. (44) 228-87-28; fax (44) 229-08-70; e-mail scfr@carrier.kiev.ua; internet www.ambafrance.kiev.ua; Ambassador PHILIPPE DE SUREMAIN.

Georgia: 04119 Kiev, vul. Melnikova 83D; tel. (44) 451-43-53; fax (44) 451-43-56; e-mail embassy@geo.kiev.ua; Ambassador GRIGOL SH. KATAMADZE.

Germany: 0901 Kiev, vul. B. Khmelnytskoho 25; tel. (44) 247-68-00; fax (44) 247-68-18; e-mail wi@german-embassy.kiev.ua; internet www.deutsche-botschaft.kiev.ua; Ambassador DIETMAR GERHARD STÜDEMANN.

Greece: 01901 Kiev, vul. Sofiyisvka 19; tel. (44) 299-57-30; fax (44) 229-13-38; e-mail greece@inec.kiev.ua; Ambassador DIMITRIS KONTOUMAS.

Holy See: 01901 Kiev, vul. Turhenyevska 40; tel. (44) 246-95-57; fax (44) 246-95-53; e-mail nunziatura@public.ua.net; Apostolic Nuncio Most Rev. NIKOLA ETEROVIĆ (Titular Archbishop of Sisak).

Hungary: 01034 Kiev, vul. Reitarska 33; tel. (44) 238-63-81; fax (44) 212-20-90; e-mail po.box@hunemb.com.ua; Chargé d'affaires a.i. SÁNDOR ALMÁSI.

India: 01901 Kiev, vul. Teryokhina 4; tel. (44) 468-66-61; fax (44) 468-66-19; e-mail com@indianembassy.org.ua; internet www.indianembassy.org.ua; Ambassador SHEHKHOLEN KIPGEN.

Indonesia: 01054 Kiev, vul. Nahorna 27B; tel. (44) 205-54-46; fax (44) 205-54-40; e-mail kbri@indo.ru.kiev.ua; internet www.kbri.kiev.ua; Ambassador REMY ROMAULI SIAHAAN.

Iran: 01901 Kiev, vul. Kruhlouniversytetska 12; tel. (44) 229-44-63; fax (44) 229-32-55; Ambassador AHMAD SADEGH-BONAB.

Iraq: 03150 Kiev, vul. A. Barbyusa 49; tel. (44) 268-64-42; fax (44) 269-46-49.

Israel: 01901 Kiev, bulv. L. Ukrainky 34; tel. (44) 295-69-36; fax (44) 294-97-48; e-mail embisr@carrier.kiev.ua; Ambassador ANNA AZARI.

Italy: 01901 Kiev, vul. Yaroslaviv val 32B; tel. (44) 230-31-00; fax (44) 230-31-03; e-mail ambital.kiev@utel.net.ua; internet www.ambital.kiev.ua; Ambassador JOLANDA BRUNETTI.

Japan: 01901 Kiev, Muzeiniy prov. 4; tel. (44) 490-55-00; fax (44) 490-55-02; e-mail jpembua@sovamua.com; internet www.embjapan.com.ua; Ambassador KISHCHINO AMAE.

Kazakhstan: 04050 Kiev, vul. Melnykova 26; tel. and fax (44) 213-11-98; e-mail admin@kazemb.kiev.ua; Ambassador RAVIL T. CHERDABAYEV.

Korea, Republic: 01034 Kiev, vul. Volodymyrska 43; tel. (44) 246-37-59; fax (44) 246-37-57; e-mail korea@koremb.kiev.ua; Ambassador CHUNG SHIN.

Kuwait: 04053 Kiev, vul. Kudryavska 13–19; tel. (44) 238-27-32; fax (44) 238-63-94; Ambassador KHALED MUTLAK ZAED AL-DUWAILAH.

Kyrgyzstan: 4053 Kiev, vul. Sichovykh Striltsiv 51/50; tel. (44) 219-13-97; fax (44) 246-88-89; Ambassador ESENGUL K. OMURALIYEV.

Latvia: 01901 Kiev, vul. Sichnevoho Povstannya 6B; tel. (44) 490-70-30; fax (44) 490-70-35; e-mail cha@latemb.kiev.ua; Ambassador ANDRIS VILCĀNS.

Libya: 04050 Kiev, vul. Ovrutska 6; tel. (44) 238-60-70; fax (44) 238-60-68; Chargé d'affaires a.i. MOHAMED AL-BUAISHI.

Lithuania: 01901 Kiev, vul. Buslivska 21; tel. (44) 254-09-20; fax (44) 254-09-28; e-mail embassy@ltembua.org; Ambassador VIKTORAS BAUBLYS.

Macedonia, former Yugoslav Republic: 01024 Kiev, vul. Borychiv Tik 28; tel. (44) 238-66-16; fax (44) 238-66-17; e-mail embmac@carrier.kiev.ua; Ambassador VLADO BLAZHEVSKI.

Moldova: 01010 Kiev, vul. Sichnevoho Povstannya 6; tel. (44) 290-77-21; fax (44) 290-77-22; Ambassador NICOLAE CERNOMAZ.

Netherlands: 01901 Kiev, pl. Kontraktova 7; tel. (44) 490-82-00; fax (44) 490-82-09; e-mail nlambkie@ukrpack.net; Ambassador M. P. FRANK.

Nigeria: 03067 Kiev, bulv. I. Lepse 4, 'Silver-Centre'; tel. (44) 201-44-59; fax (44) 201-44-63; Ambassador ALFRED NANNA.

Norway: 01901 Kiev, vul. Striletska 15; tel. (44) 234-00-66; fax (44) 234-06-55; e-mail emb.kiev@mfa.no; Ambassador IOSTEIN BERNHARDSEN.

Pakistan: 01015 Kiev, pr. Panfilovtsiv 7; tel. and fax (44) 290-25-77; e-mail parepkiev@mail.kar.net; Ambassador Vice-Adm. (retd) SHAMOON ALAM KHAN.

Poland: 01034 Kiev, vul. Yaroslaviv Val 12; tel. (44) 230-07-03; fax (44) 464-13-36; e-mail ambasada@polska.com.ua; Ambassador MAREK ZIOŁKOWSKI.

Portugal: 01901 Kiev, vul. V. Vasylkivska 9/2/12; tel. (44) 227-24-42; fax (44) 230-26-25; e-mail embport@ukrpack.net; Ambassador PEDRO MANUEL SARMENTO DE VASCOUCELOS E CASTRO.

Romania: 01030 Kiev, vul. M. Kotsyubynskoho 8; tel. (44) 224-52-61; fax (44) 235-20-25; e-mail romania@iptelecom.net.ua; Ambassador ALEXANDRU CORNEA.

Russia: 03049 Kiev, Povitroflotskyi pr. 27; tel. (44) 244-09-63; fax (44) 246-34-69; e-mail embrus@public.icyb.kiev.ua; Ambassador VIKTOR S. CHERNOMYRDIN.

Serbia and Montenegro: 04070 Kiev, vul. Voloska 4; tel. (44) 416-60-60; fax (44) 416-60-47; e-mail ambayu@svitonline.com; Ambassador (vacant).

Slovakia: 01901 Kiev, vul. Yaroslaviv Val 34; tel. (44) 229-79-29; fax (44) 212-32-71; e-mail slovak@i.kiev.ua; Ambassador VASIL GRIVNA.

South Africa: 01004 Kiev, vul. V. Vasylkivska 9/2, POB 7; tel. (44) 227-71-72; fax (44) 220-72-06; e-mail saemb@utel.net.ua; Ambassador DELAREY VAN TONDER.

Spain: 01901 Kiev, vul. Dekhtyarivska 38–44; tel. (44) 213-04-81; fax (44) 213-00-31; e-mail embespua@mail.mae.es; Ambassador LUIS GÓMEZ DE ARANDA Y VILLÉN.

Sweden: 01901 Kiev, vul. Ivana Franka 34/33; tel. (44) 462-05-80; fax (44) 462-05-81; e-mail ambassaden.kiev@foreign.ministry.se; internet www.sweemb.kiev.ua; Ambassador ÅKE PETERSON.

Switzerland: 01901 Kiev, vul. I. Fedorova 12/2/111; tel. (44) 220-54-73; fax (44) 246-65-13; e-mail vertretung@kie.rep.admin.ch; Ambassador JEAN-FRANÇOIS KAMMER.

Turkey: 01901 Kiev, vul. Arsenalna 18; tel. (44) 294-99-64; fax (44) 295-64-23; e-mail kiev.be@mfa.gov.tr; Ambassador ALI BILGE CANKOREL.

Turkmenistan: 01901 Kiev, vul. Pushkinska 6; tel. (44) 229-34-49; fax (44) 229-30-34; e-mail ambturkm@ukrpack.net; Ambassador AMANGELDY O. BAYRAMOV.

United Kingdom: 01025 Kiev, vul. Desyatynna 9; tel. (44) 462-00-11; fax (44) 462-00-13; e-mail ukembinf@sovam.com; internet www.britemb-ukraine.net; Ambassador ROBERT BRINKLEY.

USA: 01901 Kiev, vul. Yu. Kotsyubynskoho 10; tel. (44) 490-40-00; fax (44) 244-73-50; e-mail press@usinfo.usemb.kiev.ua; internet www.usemb.kiev.ua; Ambassador CARLOS E. PASCUAL.

Uzbekistan: 01901 Kiev, vul. Volodymyrska 16; tel. (44) 228-12-46; fax 229-55-09; Ambassador SHAMANSUR SH. SHAHALILOV.

Viet Nam: 01011 Kiev, vul. Lyeskova 5; tel. and fax (44) 295-28-37; fax (44) 294–80–87; Ambassador DOAN DUC.

Judicial System

Constitutional Court: 01033 Kiev, vul. Zhylianska 14; tel. (44) 220-93-98; fax (44) 227-20-01; internet www.ccu.gov.ua; f. 1996; Chair. MYKOLA F. SELIVAN; Permanent Rep. of the President at the Constitutional Court VLADYSLAV NOSOV.

Supreme Court: 01024 Kiev, vul. P. Orlyka 4; tel. (44) 226-23-04; e-mail interdep@scourt.gov.ua; internet www.scourt.gov.ua; Chair. VASYL MALYARENKO.

Supreme Arbitration Court: 01011 Kiev, vul. Kopylenka 6; tel. (44) 536-05-00; fax (44) 536-18-18; e-mail kantselariya@vasu.arbitr.gov.ua; internet www.arbitr.gov.ua; f. 1991; Chief Justice DMYTRO M. PRYTYKA.

Prosecutor-General: 01061 Kiev, vul. Riznytska 13/15; tel. (44) 226-20-27; fax (44) 290-26-03; Prosecutor-General SVYATOSLAV PYSKUN; Deputy Prosecutor-General OLEKSIY BAHANETS.

Religion

CHRISTIANITY

The Eastern Orthodox Church

Eastern Orthodoxy is the principal religious affiliation in Ukraine. Until 1990 all Orthodox churches were part of the Ukrainian Exarchate of the Russian Orthodox Church (Moscow Patriarchate). In that year the Russian Orthodox Church in Ukraine was renamed the Ukrainian Orthodox Church (UOC), partly to counter the growing influence of the previously prohibited Ukrainian Autocephalous Orthodox Church (UAOC). In the early 1990s there was considerable tension between the UOC and the UAOC over the issue of church property seized in 1930. A new ecclesiastical organization was formed in June 1992, when Filaret (Denisenko), the disgraced former Metropolitan of Kiev, united with a faction of the UAOC to form the Kievan Patriarchate. The UOC (Kievan Patriarchate) elected a Patriarch, Volodymyr (Romaniuk), in October. Following Volodymyr's death in July 1995, Filaret was elected as Patriarch, prompting some senior clergy to leave the church and join the UAOC, although in the early 2000s the UOC (Kievan Patriarchate) remained the largest church organization in Ukraine.

Ukrainian Autocephalous Orthodox Church: 01001 Kiev, vul. Tryokhsvyatytelska 8A; e-mail info@uapc.org.ua; internet uapc.org.ua; f. 1921, forcibly incorporated into the Russian Orthodox Church in 1930; continued to operate clandestinely; formally revived in 1990; 1,015 parishes in 2001; Patriarch of Kiev and All Ukraine DMYTRO (YAREMA).

Ukrainian Orthodox Church (Moscow Patriarchate): 01015 Kiev, vul. I. Mazepy 25/49; tel. (44) 290-15-08; internet www.orthodox.org.ua; exarchate of the Russian Orthodox Church (Moscow Patriarchate); 9,049 parishes in 2001; Metropolitan of Kiev VLADIMIR (SABODAN).

Ukrainian Orthodox Church (Kievan Patriarchate): 01034 Kiev, vul. Pushkinska 36; tel. (44) 224-10-96; internet www.kievpatr.org.ua; f. 1992 by factions of Ukrainian Orthodox Church and Ukrainian Autocephalous Orthodox Church; 2,781 parishes in 2001; 'Patriarch of Kiev and all Rus-Ukraine' FILARET (DENISENKO).

Old Believers (The Old Ritualists): 49017 Dnipropetrovsk, pr. K. Marksa 60/8; tel. (562) 52-17-75; internet www.staroobryad.narod.ru; f. 1652 by separation from the Moscow Patriarchate; 55 parishes in Ukraine in 2001; Leader MARIYA BUZOVSKAYA; Bishop of Kiev and all Ukraine, Savvatiye.

The Roman Catholic Church

Most Roman Catholics in Ukraine are adherents of the Byzantine Rites, the so-called 'Greek' Catholic Church, which is based principally in Western Ukraine and Transcarpathia. In 2001 there were 3,317 parishes of the Byzantine rites in Ukraine, 807 Roman Catholic parishes of the Latin Rite and 15 parishes of the Armenian rite. Ukraine comprises three archdioceses (including one each for Catholics of the Latin, Byzantine and Armenian rites), 14 dioceses (of which one is directly responsible to the Holy See) and one Apostolic Administration. At 31 December 2000 there were an estimated 4,244,183 adherents. Adherents of Latin-Rite Catholicism in Ukraine are predominantly ethnic Poles.

Bishops' Conference (Conferenza Episcopale Ucraina): 79008 Lviv, pl. Katedralna 1; tel. (322) 79-70-92; e-mail www.rkc.lviv.ua; f. 1992; Pres. Cardinal MARIAN JAWORSKI (Archbishop of Lviv).

Byzantine Ukrainian Rite

Archbishop-Major of Lviv: Cardinal LUBOMYR HUSAR, 79000 Lviv, pl. Sviatoho Yura 5; tel. (322) 97-12-56; fax (322) 72-00-07; e-mail lv.archeparchy@ugkc.lviv.ua; internet www.ugcc.org.ua; head of Ukrainian Greek Catholic Church; established in 1596 by the Union of Brest, which permitted Orthodox clergymen to retain the Eastern rite, but transferred their allegiance to the Pope in 1946, at the self-styled Synod of Lvov (Lviv Sobor), the Catholics of the Byzantine rite were forcibly integrated into the Russian Orthodox Church (Moscow Patriarchate), but continued to function in an 'underground' capacity; re-legalized in 1989.

Latin Rite

Metropolitan Archbishop of Lviv: Cardinal MARIAN JAWORSKI, 79008 Lviv, pl. Katedralna 1; tel. (322) 76-94-15; fax (322) 96-61-14; e-mail k@rkc.lviv.ua; internet www.rkc.lviv.ua.

Armenian Rite

Archbishop of Lviv: (vacant).

Protestant Churches

There were 6,578 protestant communities registered in Ukraine in 2001. These comprised both those churches that had been repressed and forced to operate clandestinely during the period of Soviet rule, the largest of which were the All-Ukrainian Union of United Evangelical Christians-Baptists, and the All-Ukrainian Union of Christians of the Evangelical Faith—Pentecostalists ('Pyatydesyatnykiv'), and a number of confessions introduced to Ukraine during the 1990s by missionaries, primarily from Europe and North America.

All-Ukrainian Union of Christians of the Evangelical Faith—Pentecostalists ('Pyatydesyatnykiv'): 01033 Kiev, vul. Karyerna 44; 1,196 parishes in 2001.

All-Ukrainian Union of United Churches of Evangelical Christians-Baptists: 01004 Kiev, vul. L. Tolstoho 3A; tel. (44) 224-04-05; fax (44) 227-74-80; 2,000 parishes, 125,950 adherents in 2001; affiliated to the Euro-Asiatic Federation of the Union of Evangelical Christians-Baptists; Pres. HRIHORIY I. KOMENDANT.

Ukrainian Lutheran Church: 01004 Kiev, vul. V. Vasylkivska 14/15; tel. (44) 235-77-21; fax (44) 234-08-00; e-mail vhorpynchuk@yahoo.com0; internet www.ukrlc.org; 30 parishes in 2001; Head of Church Bishop VYACHESLAV HORPYNCHUK.

ISLAM

In 2001 there were 391 Islamic communities officially registered in Ukraine, of which 293 were located in the Autonomous Republic of Crimea, and an estimated 2m. adherents in total. The return of Crimean Tatars to Crimea from Central Asia, to where they were exiled at Stalin's behest during the Second World War, has had a significant impact upon the growth of Islamic communities in the republic since the early 1990s. An Islamic University was established in Donetsk in 1998.

Independent Federation of Muslim Social Organizations of Ukraine (Arraid): 04119 Kiev, vul. Dekhtyarivska 25A; tel. (44) 490-99-00; fax (44) 490-99-22; e-mail office@arraid.org; internet www.arraid.org; f. 1997; brs in Dnipropetrovsk, Donetsk, Kharkiv, Luhansk, Lviv, Odesa, Simferopol, Vinnytsya and Zaporizhzhya; publishes periodical 'Arraid' (*Forward*) in Arabic and Russian and educational material in Russian, Tatar and Ukrainian; undertakes charitable and eductional work; Chair. FAROUK ASHOUR.

Spiritual Direction of Muslims in Ukraine: Kiev; f. 1993; Mufti Sheikh TAMIN AHMED MUHAMED MUTAH.

Mufti of Crimea: ADZHE NURALI ABLAIYEV, 95000 Crimea, Simferopol, Kebir Çami Mosque.

JUDAISM

In the mid-1990s there were an estimated 500,000 Jews in Ukraine, despite high levels of emigration from the 1970s. From 1989 there was a considerable revival in the activities of Jewish communities. In 2001 there were 221 Jewish communities in Ukraine, compared with 12 synagogues in 1989. The majority of Jews in Ukraine live in Kiev, Dnipropetrovsk, Kharkiv and Odesa.

All-Ukrainian Jewish Congress: 01023 Kiev, vul. Mechnykova 14/1; tel. (44) 235-71-20; fax (44) 235-10-67; e-mail vek@i.kiev.ua; internet www.jewish.kiev.ua; f. 1997; Chief Rabbi of Kiev and All-Ukraine YAAKOV DOV BLEICH; Chair. VADYM RABYNOVYCH.

The Press

In 1992 there were 1,695 officially registered newspaper titles published in Ukraine and in 1996 there were an estimated 44 daily newspapers and 2,162 periodicals. In addition to newspapers published in Ukraine, several newspapers and magazines published in the Russian Federation (see p. 3468) have a large circulation in Ukraine.

The publications listed below are in Ukrainian, except where otherwise stated.

PRINCIPAL NEWSPAPERS

Demokratychna Ukraina (Democratic Ukraine): 03047 Kiev, pr. Peremohy 50; tel. (44) 441-83-33; f. 1918; fmrly *Radyanska Ukraina* (Soviet Ukraine); 3 a week; independent; Editor OLEKSANDR POBIGAI; circ. 10,000 (2001).

Den (The Day): 04212 Kiev, vul Marshala Tymoshenka 2L; tel. (44) 414-40-66; fax (44) 414-49-20; e-mail master@day.kiev.ua; internet www.day.kiev.ua; f. 1998; in Ukrainian and Russian; 5 a week; publ. by the Presa Ukrainy (Press of Ukraine) Publishing House; Editor-in-Chief LARYSA IVSHYNA; circ.62,500 (2001).

Fakty i Kommentarii (Facts and Commentaries): 04116 Kiev, vul. Vandy Vasylevskoy 27–29; tel. (44) 244-57-81; fax (44) 216-85-80; e-mail info@facts.kiev.ua; internet www.facts.kiev.ua; daily; politics, economics, sport, law, culture; in Russian; daily.

Holos Ukrainy/Golos Ukrainy (Voice of Ukraine): 03047 Kiev, vul. Nesterova 4; tel. (44) 441-88-11; fax (44) 224-72-54; e-mail mail@

golos.com.ua; f. 1991; organ of the Verkhovna Rada; in Ukrainian and Russian; 5 a week; Editor SERHIY M. PRAVDENKO; circ. 150,000 (2002).

Kievskiye Vedomosti (Kiev Gazette): 04086 Kiev, vul. Olzhycha 29; tel. (44) 238-28-07; internet www.kv.com.ua; f. 1992; in Russian; national daily; Dir-Gen. VLADIMIR P. DERIKIT; Editor-in-Chief NIKOLAI V. ZAKREVSKII; circ. 138,300 (2002); also weekly edition (Fridays), in Ukrainian, *Kyivski Vidomosti*.

Kyiv Post: 01133 Kiev, vul. L. Ukrainky 34/401; tel. (44) 573-83-53; fax (44) 254-31-13; e-mail editor@kppublications.com; internet www .kpnews.com; f. 1995; weekly; in English; Publisher JED SUNDEN; Exec. Editor GREG BLOOM; circ. 25,000 (2002).

Literaturna Ukraina (Literary Ukraine): 01061 Kiev, bulv. L. Ukrainky 20; tel. (44) 296-36-39; f. 1927; weekly; organ of Union of Writers of Ukraine; Editor VASYL PLUSHCH; circ. 15,000 (1999).

Molod Ukrainy (The Youth of Ukraine): 03047 Kiev, pr. Peremohy 50; tel. (44) 441-83-83; fax (44) 225-31-52; e-mail my@molod.kiev.ua; f. 1994; 3 a week; Editor-in-Chief V. I. BODENCHUK; circ. 37,893 (2001).

News from Ukraine: Kiev; tel. and fax (44) 244-58-45; f. 1964; weekly; publ. by the joint-stock co News from Ukraine; in English; readership in 70 countries; Editor VOLODYMYR KANASH; circ. 20,000.

Pravda Ukrainy (The Truth of Ukraine): 03047 Kiev, pr. Peremohy 50; tel. (44) 441-85-34; f. 1938; deregistered Jan. 1998, re-registered Jan. 1999; 5 a week; in Russian; Editor-in-Chief OLHA PRONINA; circ. 40,000.

Robitnycha Hazeta/Rabochaya Gazeta (Workers' Gazette): 03047 Kiev, pr. Peremohy 50; tel. (44) 441-83-33; fax (44) 446-68-85; f. 1957; 5 a week; publ. by the Cabinet of Ministers and Interregional Association of Manufacturers; editions in Russian and Ukrainian; Editor-in-Chief IVAN G. LITVIN; circ. 113,666 (2001).

Silski Visti (Rural News): 03047 Kiev, pr. Peremohy 50; tel. (44) 441-86-32; fax (44) 446-93-71; e-mail silvis@visti.com; internet www .silskivisti.kiev.ua; f. 1920; 3 a week; Editor I. V. SPODARENKO; circ. 572,262 (2002).

Ukraina Moloda (Ukraine The Young): 03047 Kiev, pr. Peremohy 50; tel. and fax (44) 454-83-92; e-mail post@umoloda.kiev.ua; 5 a week; independent; opposed to Govt of President Kuchma; Editor MYKHAYLO DOROSHENKO; circ. 103,171 (2002).

Ukrainska Pravda (Ukrainian Truth): Kiev; e-mail pravda@ svitonline.com; internet www2.pravda.com.ua; online only, in English, Russian and Ukrainian; Editor-in-Chief OLENA PRYTULA.

Ukrainske Slovo (The Ukrainian Word): 01010 Kiev, vul. Sichnevoho Povstannya 6; tel. (44) 290-17-30; fax (44) 290-70-59; e-mail info@ukrslovo.kiev.ua; internet www.ukrslovo.kiev.ua; f. 1933; weekly; nationalist; Editor-in-Chief BOHDAN CHERVAK.

Uryadoviy Kuryer (Official Courier): 01008 Kiev, vul. Sadova 1; tel. (44) 253-12-95; fax (44) 253-39-50; e-mail letter@ukcc.com.ua; internet www.ukcc.com.ua; f. 1990; 5 a week; organ of the Cabinet of Ministers; Editor-in-Chief MYKHAYLO M. SOROKA; circ. 125,000 (2002).

Vechirniy Kiev (Evening Kiev): 04136 Kiev, vul. Marshala Hrechka 13; tel. (44) 434-61-09; fax (44) 443-96-09; e-mail office@ vecherniykyiv.com; internet www.vecherniykyiv.com; f. 1906; 5 a week; Editor-in-Chief VITALIY KARPENKO; circ. 80,000 (2001).

Vladi i Polityka/Vlast i Politika (Power and Politics): 01042 Kiev, vul. P. Lumumby 4v/200; tel. (44) 201-01-28; fax (44) 201-01-29; e-mail vip@vipnews.com.ua; internet www.vipnews.com.ua; f. 2001; weekly; in Ukrainian and Russian; Dir-Gen. ANDRIY V. NAKONECHNYI; Editor-in-Chief YURIY L. UZDEMYR; circ. 22,000 (2002).

Za Vilnu Ukrainu (For a Free Ukraine): 79000 Lviv, vul. Voronoho 3; tel. (322) 97-92-49; fax (322) 72-95-27; e-mail zwuky@mail.lviv.ua; f. 1990; 5 a week; independent; Editor-in-Chief MYKHAYLO SIRKIV; circ. 30,058 (2001).

PRINCIPAL PERIODICALS

Avto-Tsentr (Auto-Centre): Kiev-47, POB 2; tel. and fax (44) 441-85-91; e-mail gazeta@avtocentr.kiev.ua; internet www.autocentre .ua; f. 1997; weekly; motoring; in Russian; Editor-in-Chief SERGEI TARNAVSKII; circ. 140,000.

Barvinok (Periwinkle): 04119 Kiev, vul. Dekhtyarivska 38–44; tel. (44) 213-99-13; fax (44) 211-04-36; e-mail barvinok@kievweb.com .ua; f. 1928; fortnightly; illustrated popular fiction for school-age children; in Ukrainian and Russian; Editor VASYL VORONOVYCH; circ. 40,000.

Berezil: 61002 Kharkiv, vul. Chernyshevskoho 59; tel. (572) 43-41-84; fax (572) 47-61-62; f. 1956; fmrly *Prapor*; monthly; journal of Union of Writers of Ukraine; fiction and socio-political articles; Editor-in-Chief VOLODYMYR NAUMENKO; circ. 5,000.

Delovaya Stolitsya (Capital City Business): 01135 Kiev, vul. Pavlovska 29; tel. (44) 461-91-32; fax (44) 461-91-40; e-mail dsnews@ dsnews.com.ua; internet www.dsnews.com.ua; f. 2001; weekly; in Russian; Editor-in-Chief INNA KOVTUN; circ. 35,900 (2002).

Dnipro (The Dnieper): 04119 Kiev, vul. Dekhtyarivska 38–44; tel. (44) 446-11-42; f. 1927; 2 a month; novels, short stories, essays, poetry; social and political topics; Editor MYKOLA LUKIV.

Donbas/Donbass: 83055 Donetsk, vul. Artema 80A; tel. (622) 93-82-26; f. 1923; monthly; journal of Union of Writers of Ukraine; fiction; in Ukrainian and Russian; circ. 20,000 (1991).

Dzerkalo Tyzhnya/Zerkalo Nedyeli (Weekly Mirror): 03680 Kiev, vul. Shchorsa 18; tel. (44) 261-82-08; e-mail postmaster@ mirror.kiev.ua; internet www.zn.kiev.ua; weekly; politics, economics, the arts; Ukrainian and Russian editions.

Dzvin (Bell): 79005 Lviv, vul. Kn. Romana 6; tel. (322) 72-36-20; f. 1940; monthly; journal of Union of Writers of Ukraine; fiction; Editor ROMAN FEDORIV; circ. 152,500.

Interesna Hazeta (Interesting Magazine): 03047 Kiev, pr. Peremohy 50; tel. (44) 441-82-59; e-mail postmail@avkpress.kiev.ua; 2 a month; general; circ. 700,000.

Kiev: 01025 Kiev, vul. Desyatinna 11; tel. (44) 229-02-80; f. 1983; monthly; journal of the Union of Writers of Ukraine and the Kiev Writers' Organization; fiction; Editor-in-Chief PETRO M. PEREBYJNIS.

Kompanyon (Companion): 01103 Kiev, vul. Kykbydze 39; tel. and fax (44) 267-64-07; e-mail komp@maximum.com.ua; internet www .companion.com.ua; f. 1996; weekly; in Russian; economics, politics, business; Editor-in-Chief V. ZUBANYUK; circ. 25,000 (2002).

Malyatko (Child): 04119 Kiev, vul. Dekhtyarivska 38–44; tel. and fax (44) 213-98-91; f. 1960; monthly; illustrated; for pre-school children; Editor-in-Chief ANATOLIY GRIGORUK; circ. 25,800 (2002).

Nataly: 02156 Kiev, vul. Kyoto 25; tel. (44) 519-34-33; fax (44) 518-77-90; internet www.nataly.com.ua; monthly; women's interest; Editor-in-Chief ZHANNA LAVROVA; circ. 679,115 (2002).

Natsionalna Bezpeka i Oborona (National Security and Defence): 01034 Kiev, vul. Volodymyrska 46; tel. (44) 201-11-98; fax (44) 201-11-99; e-mail info@uceps.com.ua; internet www.uceps.com .ua/eng/work/work_journal.shtml; f. 2000; publ. by Oleksandr Razumkov Ukrainian Centre for Political and Economic Research; monthly; politics, economics, international relations; in Ukrainian and English; Pres. ANATOLIY HRYTSENKO.

Obrazotvorche Mistetstvo (Fine Arts): 04655 Kiev, vul. Sichovykh Striltsiv 1–5; tel. (44) 212-02-86; fax (44) 212-14-54; e-mail spilka@nbi.com.ua; f. 1933; 4 a year; publ. by the Artists' Union of Ukraine; fine arts; Editor-in-Chief MYKOLA MARYCHEVSKIY; circ. 1,500.

Perets (Pepper): 03047 Kiev, pr. Peremohy 50; tel. (44) 441-82-14; fax (44) 441-89-11; f. 1927; fortnightly; publ. by the Presa Ukrainy Publishing House; satirical; Editor YURIY PROKOPENKO; circ. 19,300.

Politychna Dumka/Politicheskaya Mysl (Political Thought): 01030 Kiev, vul. Leontovycha 5; tel. and fax (44) 235-02-29; e-mail politdumka@bigmir.net; internet www.politdumka.kiev.ua; f. 1993; current affairs and political analysis; Ukrainian, Russian and English editions; Editor-in-Chief VOLODYMYR POLOKHALO.

Polityka i Chas/Politics and the Times: 02160 Kiev, pr. Vozyednanya 15–17; tel. and fax (44) 550-31-44; e-mail times@uct.kiev.ua; f. 1992 to replace *Pid praporam Lenina* (Under the Banner of Lenin); monthly; organ of the Ministry of Foreign Affairs; domestic affairs and foreign relations of Ukraine, domestic economic matters; in Ukrainian (monthly) and English (quarterly); Editor-in-Chief LEONID BAIDAK; circ. 1,500.

Ukraina (Ukraine): 03047 Kiev, pr. Peremohy 50; tel. and fax (44) 446-63-16; internet uamedia.visti.net/ukraine/; f. 1941; monthly; social and political life in Ukraine; illustrated; Editor-in-Chief YURIY PERESUNKO; circ. 70,000.

Ukraina Business (Ukraine Business): 01004 Kiev, vul. Pushkinska 20/24; tel. and fax (44) 224-25-55; e-mail malva@ukrbus.kiev .ua; f. 1990; weekly; Editor-in-Chief YURIY VASYLCHUK; circ. 22,000 (2001).

Ukrainskiy Teatr (Ukrainian Theatre): Kiev; tel. (44) 228-24-74; f. 1936; 6 a year; publ. by the Mistetstvo (Fine Art) Publishing House; journal of the Ministry of Art and Culture, and the Union of Theatrical Workers of Ukraine; Editor-in-Chief YURIY BOHDASHEVSKIY; circ. 4,100.

Visti z Ukrainy (News from Ukraine): 01034 Kiev, vul. Zolotovoritska 6; tel. (44) 228-56-42; fax (44) 228-04-28; f. 1960; weekly; aimed at Ukrainian diaspora; Editor VALERIY STETSENKO; circ. 50,000.

Vitchyzna (Fatherland): 01021 Kiev, vul. M. Hrushevskoho 34; tel. (44) 253-28-51; f. 1933; 6 a year; Ukrainian prose and poetry; Editor OLEKSANDR HLUSHKO; circ. 50,100.

Vsesvit (The Whole World): 01021 Kiev, vul. M. Hrushevskoho 34/1; tel. (44) 293-13-18; fax (44) 253-28-88; e-mail myk@vsesvit-review .kiev.ua; f. 1925; monthly; publ. by the Vsesvit Publishing House; foreign fiction, critical works and reviews of foreign literature and art; Editor-in-Chief OLEH MYKYTENKO; circ. 3,000.

Yeva (Eve): 04050 Kiev, vul. Melnykova 12A/8; tel. (44) 568-59-53; e-mail centre@yanko.com.ua; internet www.evamag.kiev.ua; f. 1998; six a year; fashion, design; Editor-in-Chief IRYNA B. DANY-LEVSKA; circ. 10,000 (2002).

Zhinka (Woman): 03047 Kiev, pr. Peremohy 50; tel. and fax (44) 446-90-34; e-mail zhinka@cki.ipri.kiev.ua; f. 1920; monthly; publ. by Presa Ukrainy Publishing House; social and political subjects; fiction; for women; Editor LIDIYA MAZUR; circ. 250,000.

NEWS AGENCIES

Interfax-Ukraina (Interfax-Ukraine): 01034 Kiev, vul. Reitarska 8/5a; tel. (44) 464-04-65; fax (44) 464-05-69; internet www.interfax .kiev.ua; f. 1992.

Respublika Ukrainian Independent Information Agency (UNIAR): 02005 Kiev, vul. Mechnykova 14/1; tel. (44) 246-46-34; e-mail naboka@uniar.kiev.ua; internet www.uniar.com.ua; independent press agency; Dir S. NABOKA.

Ukrainian Independent Information and News Agency (UNIAN): 01001 Kiev, vul. Khreshchatyk 4; tel. (44) 229-33-53; fax (44) 461-91-11; e-mail info@unian.net; internet www.unian.net; press agency and monitoring service; publishes weekly bulletins concerning finance, technology, business, construction; photographic agency; selected services are provided in Ukrainian, Russian and English; Gen. Man. MYKHAYLO I. BATIH; Editor-in-Chief OLEKSANDR KHARCHENKO.

Ukrainski Novyni Informatsyonnoye Ahentstvo (Ukrainian News Information Agency): 01033 Kiev, vul. Volodymyrska 61/11/41; tel. (44) 494-31-60; fax (44) 494-31-67; e-mail office@ ukranews.com; internet www.ukranews.com; f. 1993; economic and political news; in Ukrainian, Russian and English.

UkrInform–Ukrainian National Information Agency: 01001 Kiev, vul. B. Khmelnytskoho 8/16B; tel. (44) 229-22-42; fax (44) 229-81-52; e-mail chiefadm@ukrinform.com; internet www.dinau.com; f. 1918; until 1990 Ukrainian branch of TASS (State Information Agency of the Soviet Union).

Foreign Bureaux

Agenzia Nazionale Stampa Associata (ANSA) (Italy): Kiev, vul. Chitadelna 5–9/45; tel. and fax (44) 290-21-38; internet www.ansa.it; Correspondent ALESSANDRO PARONE.

Česká tisková kancelář (ČTK) (Czech Republic): 01042 Kiev, vul. I. Kudri 41/22/49; tel. and fax (44) 295-91-61; internet www.ctk.cz.

Deutsche Presse-Agentur (dpa) (Germany): 01001 Kiev, vul. Khreshchatyk 29/32; tel. (44) 225-57-60; internet www.dpa.de.

Magyar Távirati Iroda (MTI) (Hungary): 01030 Kiev, vul. Ivana Franka 24A /8; tel. and fax (44) 235-62-04; e-mail mti@gu.kiev.ua; internet www.mti.ua; Correspondent KATALIN BENKONE OZE.

Reuters Ltd (United Kingdom): 01001 Kiev, vul. B. Khmelnytskoho 8–16/112; tel. (44) 244-91-50; fax (44) 244-91-53; e-mail kiev .newsroom@reuters.com; internet www.reuters.com; Chief Correspondent T. RODDAM.

RIA—Novosti (Russian Information Agency—News) (Russia): 03150 Kiev, vul. V. Vasylivska 134/49; tel. and fax (44) 434-48-45.

Publishers

In 1996 there were 6,460 book titles (including pamphlets and brochures) published in Ukraine (total circulation 50.9m.).

Budivelnik (Builder): 04053 Kiev, vul. Observatorna 25; tel. (44) 212-10-90; f. 1947; books on building and architecture; in Ukrainian and Russian; Dir S. N. BALATSKII.

Carpaty (The Carpathians): 88000 Transcarpathian obl., Uzhhorod, Radyanska pl. 3; tel. (312) 23-25-13; fiction and criticism; in Ukrainian and Russian; Dir V. I. DANKANICH.

Dnipro (The Dnieper): 01061 Kiev, vul. Volodymyrska 42; tel. (44) 224-31-82; f. 1919; fiction, poetry and critical works; in Ukrainian and Russian; Dir TARAS I. SERGIYCHUK.

Donbas/Donbass: 83002 Donetsk, vul. B. Khmelnytskoho 102; tel. (622) 93-25-84; fiction and criticism; in Ukrainian and Russian; Dir B. F. KRAVCHENKO.

Folio: Kharkiv; tel. and fax (572) 47-61-25; e-mail foliosp@kharkov .ukrpack.net; internet folio.com.ua; f. 1992; classic and contempo-

rary fiction in Russian, Ukrainian and French; Gen. Man. ALEKSANDR V. KRASOVITSKII.

Kamenyar (Stonecrusher): 79000 Lviv, vul. Pidvalna 3; tel. (322) 72-19-49; fax (322) 72-79-22; fiction and criticism; in Ukrainian; Dir DMYTRO I. SAPIGA.

Konsum: 61057 Kharkiv, POB 9123; tel. (572) 17-01-19; fax (572) 23–76–75; e-mail book@konsum.kharkov.ua; internet konsum .kharkov.ua; politics, economics, human rights, legal and medical books.

Lybid (Swan): 01001 Kiev, vul. Pushkinska 32; tel. (44) 228-10-93; fax (44) 229-11-71; e-mail info@lybid.org.ua; internet www.lybid.org .ua; f. 1835; University of Kiev press; Dir OLENA A. BOIKO.

Mayak (Beacon): 65001 Odesa, vul. Zhukovskoho 14; tel. (482) 22-35-95; fiction and criticism; in Ukrainian and Russian; Dir D. A. BUKHANENKO.

Medytsyna Svitu (Medicines of the World): 79017 Lviv, vul. Rodyny Krushelnytskykh 14; tel. and fax (322) 75-51-12; e-mail msvitu@mail.lviv.ua; internet www.msvitu.lviv.ua; f. 1997; medical journals and books, books pertaining to history, art and religion; Dirs VOLODYMYR PAVLIUK, ZENON MATCHAK.

Mistetstvo (Fine Art): 01034 Kiev, vul. Zolotovoritska 11; tel. (44) 225-53-92; fax (44) 229-05-64; f. 1932; fine art criticism, theatre and screen art, tourism, Ukrainian culture; in Ukrainian, Russian, English, French and German; Dir VALENTIN M. KUZMENKO.

Molod (Youth): 04119 Kiev, vul. Dekhtyarivska 38–44; tel. (44) 213-11-60; fax (44) 213-11-92; in Ukrainian; Dir O. I. POLONSKA.

Muzichna Ukraina (Music of Ukraine): 01034 Kiev, vul. Pushkinska 32; tel. (44) 225-63-56; fax (44) 224-63-00; f. 1966; books on music; in Ukrainian; Dir N. P. LINNIK; Editor-in-Chief B. R. VERESHCHAGIN.

Naukova Dumka (Scientific Thought): 01601 Kiev, vul. Tereshchenkivska 3; tel. (44) 234-40-68; fax (44) 234-70-60; e-mail ndumka@i.kiev.ua; f. 1922; scientific books and periodicals in all branches of science; research monographs; Ukrainian literature; dictionaries and reference books; in Ukrainian, Russian and English; Dir I. R. ALEKSEYENKO.

Osvita (Education): 04053 Kiev, vul. Y. Kotsyubynski 5; tel. and fax (44) 216-54-44; e-mail osvita@kv.ukrtel.net; f. 1920; educational books for schools of all levels; Dir-Gen. IRAYIDA PODOLYUK.

Prapor (Flag): 61002 Kharkiv, vul. Chubarya 11; tel. (572) 47-72-52; fax (572) 43-07-21; fmrly named *Berezil*; general; in Ukrainian and Russian; Dir V. S. LEBETS.

Prosvita (Enlightenment): 01032 Kiev, bulv. Shevchenka 46; tel. (44) 224-15-86; fax (44) 224-95-23; e-mail office@prosvita.kiev.ua; internet www.prosvita.kiev.ua; f. 1990; textbooks for all levels from education from pre-school to higher education.

Rodovid: 01015 Kiev, vul. I. Mazepy 29; tel. (44) 254-32-37; fax (44) 290-29-31; e-mail rodovid@carrier.kiev.ua; internet www.rodovid .net; history, ethnography, poetry, cultural history.

Sich (Camp): 49070 Dnipropetrovsk, pr. K. Marksa 60; tel. (562) 45-22-01; fax (562) 45-44-04; f. 1964; fiction, juvenile, socio-political, criticism; in Ukrainian, English, German, French and Russian; Dir V. A. SIROTA; Editor-in-Chief V. V. LEVCHENKO.

Tavria: 95000 Crimea, Simferopol, vul. Gorkogo 5; tel. (652) 27-45-66; fax (652) 27-65-74; fiction, criticism, folklore and geography; in Ukrainian, Russian and Crimean Tatar; Dir Y. IVANICHENKO.

Tekhnika (Technologyi): 01034 Kiev, vul. Pushkinska 28/9; tel. (44) 228-22-43; f. 1930; industry and transport books, popular science, posters and booklets; in Ukrainian and Russian; Dir M. G. PISARENKO.

Tsentr Yevropy (The Centre of Europe): 79000 Lviv, vul. Kostyushko 18/317; tel. (322) 72-35-66; fax (322) 72-76-71; e-mail centrevr@is.lviv.ua; internet www.centrevtr@is.lviv.ua; f. 1994; books related to the history and culture of Halychyna; Dir SERHIY E. FRUKHT.

Ukraina: 01054 Kiev, vul. Hoholivska 7H; tel. (44) 216-36-02; fax (44) 216-97-35; e-mail ua@alfacom.net; internet www.ua.alfacom .net; f. 1922; humanities, science, reference and literary works; Dir MYKOLA V. STETYUHA; Editor-in-Chief OLEKSANDR P. KOSYUK.

Ukrainska Ensyklopedia (Ukrainian Encyclopedia): 01030 Kiev, vul. B. Khmelnytskoho 51; tel. (44) 224-80-85; encyclopedias, dictionaries and reference books; Dir A. V. KUDRITSKIY.

Ukrainskiy Pysmennyk (Ukrainian Writer): 01054 Kiev, vul. O. Honshara 52; tel. (44) 216-25-92; f. 1933; publishing house of the Union of Writers of Ukraine; fiction; in Ukrainian; Dir V. P. SKOMAROVSKIY.

Urozhai (Harvest): 03035 Kiev, vul. Uritskoho 45; tel. (44) 220-16-26; f. 1925; books and journals about agriculture; Dir V. G. PRIKHODKO.

Veselka (Rainbow): 04050 Kiev, vul. Melnikova 63; tel. (44) 213-95-01; fax (44) 213-33-59; e-mail veskiev@iptelecom.net.ua; f. 1934; books for pre-school and school age children; in Ukrainian and foreign languages; Dir YAREMA HOYAN.

Vyscha Shkola (High School): 01054 Kiev, vul. Hoholivska 7; tel. and fax (44) 216-33-05; f. 1968; educational, scientific, reference, etc. Dir V. P. KHOVKHUN; Editor-in-Chief V. V. PIVEN.

Zdorovya (Health): 01054 Kiev, vul. O. Honshara 65; tel. (44) 216-89-08; books on medicine, physical fitness and sport; in Ukrainian; Dir A. P. RODZIYEVSKIY.

Znannya (Knowledge): 01034 Kiev, vul. Striletska 28; tel. (44) 234-80-43; fax (44) 234-23-36; e-mail znannia@society.kiev.ua; internet www.znannia.com.ua; f. 1948; general non-fiction; Dir VOLODOMYR KARASOV.

Broadcasting and Communications

TELECOMMUNICATIONS

Regulatory Authorities

RRT: 04112 Kiev, vul. Dorohozhytska 10; tel. (44) 226-22-60; fax (44) 440-87-22; e-mail vvu@concernbrn.kiev.ua; f. 1970; leases satellite communications channels for radio and television broadcasting and telecommunications; Pres. VOLODYMYR ISHCHUK.

State Committee for Communication and Information: see section on The Government.

Major Service Providers

Golden Telecom GSM: 01021 Kiev, vul. Mechnikova 14/1; tel. (44) 247-56-65; internet www.goldentele.com; mobile cellular telephone services; Gen. Man. YURIY BEZBORODIV.

Ukrainian Mobile Communications (UMC): 01010 Kiev, vul. Moskovska 21; tel. (44) 311-95-59; fax (44) 314-22-48; e-mail slavik@umc.com.ua; internet www.umc.com.ua; f. 1991; 51% owned by Ukrtelecom; Deutsche Telekom AG (Germany), TDC Tele Danmark (Denmark) and Royal KPN NV (Netherlands) each own 16.3% of shares; operates mobile cellular telephone network; Gen. Man. MARTIN DIRKS; 1,110,000 subscribers (March 2002).

UkrTelecom: 01030 Kiev, bulv. Shevchenka 18; tel. (44) 226-25-41; fax (44) 229-25-06; e-mail ukrtelecom@ukrtel.net; internet www.ukrtel.net; f. 1993; national fixed telecommunications network operator; provides national and international telecommunications services; Gen. Man. P. NETUDYTHATA.

BROADCASTING

Regulatory Authorities

National Council for Television and Radio Broadcasting (Natsionalna Rada Ukrainy z pytan Telebachennya i Radiomovlennya): 01025 Kiev, vul. Desyatynna 14; tel. (44) 228-74-11; fax (44) 228-75-75; e-mail tvr@i.com.ua; internet www.nradatvr.kiev.ua; f. 1994; monitoring and supervisory functions; issues broadcasting licences; Chair. BORYS KHOLOD.

State Committee for Information Policy, Television and Radio Broadcasting: see section on The Government.

Radio

Ukrainian State Television and Radio Co (Derzhavna Teleradiomovna Kompaniya Ukrainy): 01001 Kiev, vul. Khreshchatyk 26; Chair. ZYNOVIY V. KULYK.

Hromadske—Community Radio: Kiev, vul. Volodymyrska 61/11/50; tel. (44) 494-40-14; e-mail roman@radio.org.ua; internet www.radio.org.ua; information, news and discussion programmes; Pres. (vacant).

National Radio Co Ukraine-Ukrainian Radio (Natsionalna Radiokompaniya Ukrainy-Ukrainske Radio): 01001 Kiev, vul. Khreshchatyk 26; tel. (44) 229-12-85; fax (44) 299-11-70; e-mail vsru@nrcu.gov.ua.

Radio Ukraine International: 01001 Kiev, vul. Khreshchatyk 26; tel. (44) 229-45-86; e-mail vsru@nrcu.gov.ua; broadcasts in English, German, Romanian and Ukrainian; Chief Editor VIKTOR I. NABRUSKO.

There were, in addition, several independent radio stations broadcasting to the major cities of Ukraine.

Television

Ukrainian State Television and Radio Co (Derzhavna Teleradiomovna Kompaniya Ukrainy): see Radio (above); Chair. of Television OLEKSANDR M. SAVENKO.

1+1: 01023 Kiev, vul. Mechnikova 14/1; tel. (44) 246-46-00; fax (44) 246-45-18; e-mail contact@1plus1.tv; internet www.1plus1.tv; f. 1995; independent; broadcasts for 15 hours daily to 95% of Ukrainian population; Dir-Gen. OLEKSANDR YU. RODNYANSKY.

Inter: 01601 Kiev, vul. Dmitriyevska 30; tel. and fax (44) 490-67-65; e-mail pr@inter.ua; internet www.inter.kiev.ua; f. 1996.

Novy Kanal (New Channel): 04107 Kiev, vul. Nahorna 24/1; tel. (44) 238-80-28; fax (44) 238-80-20; e-mail post@novy.tv; internet www.novy.tv; f. 1998; broadcasts in Ukrainian and Russian; Chair. OLEKSANDR M. TKACHENKO.

Pershyi Natsionalnyi (First National): 04119 Kiev, vul. Melnykova 42; tel. (44) 241-39-09; fax (44) 246-88-48; e-mail office@firstnational.kiev.ua; internet www.fn.com.ua; state-owned.

STB: Kiev; e-mail y@stb.ua; internet stb.ua; Dirs VLAD STAROVOYTOV, KYRYL BYSTRYAKOV.

Finance

(cap. = capital; res = reserves; dep. = deposits; brs = branches; m. = million; amounts in hryvnyas, unless otherwise indicated)

BANKING

Reform of the banking sector was initiated in 1996, when responsibility for the issuing of licences was transferred to the Committee on Banking Supervision. A division of the National Bank of Ukraine was established to identify those banks in need of restructuring.

In May 1998 there were 217 commercial banks and seven foreign banks in Ukraine. Most of the commercial banks were single-branch banks, operating solely within the region in which they were registered.

Central Bank

National Bank of Ukraine: 01008 Kiev, vul. Institutska 9; tel. (44) 293-69-21; fax (44) 253-26-02; e-mail smm@bank.gov.ua; internet www.bank.gov.ua; f. 1991; cap. 5m., res 1,251m., dep. 5,780m. (Dec. 2000); Gov. SERHIY L. TYHYPKO; First Vice-Gov. ANATOLIY V. SHAPOVALOV.

Other State Banks

Republican Bank of Crimea: 95000 Crimea, Simferopol, ul. Gorkogo; tel. (652) 51-09-46; e-mail webmaster@rbc.crimea.ua.

UkrExImBank JSC—State Export-Import Bank of Ukraine: 03150 Kiev, vul. Horkoho 127; tel. (44) 226-27-45; fax (44) 247-80-82; e-mail bank@eximb.com; internet www.eximb.com; f. 1992; fmrly br. of USSR Vneshekonombank; deals with foreign firms, joint ventures and import-export associations; cap. US $76.6m., res $16.0m., dep. $470.8m. (July 2002); Chair. of Bd OLEKSANDR N. SOROKIN; 28 brs.

Commercial Banks

AVAL Bank—JS Postal-Pension Bank Aval: 01011 Kiev, vul. Leskova 9; tel. (44) 490-88-01; fax (44) 490-87-55; e-mail office@head.aval.kiev.ua; internet www.avalbank.com; f. 1992; 92.9% privately-owned; cap. US $63.8m., dep. $869.7m., total assets $952.8m. (Dec. 2001); Pres. FEDIR SHPIG; Chair. of Bd OLEKSANDR DERKACH; 977 brs.

Bank Pekao (Ukraine) Ltd: 43016 Volyn obl., Lutsk, vul. Halytskoho 14; tel. (332) 77-62-10; fax (332) 72-03-57; e-mail pekao@pekao.com.ua; internet www.pekao.com.ua; f. 1997; present name adopted 2000; cap. 22.5m., res 1.7m., dep. 8.7m. (Dec. 1999); Pres. DARIUSZ KLIMONT.

Crédit Lyonnais Bank Ukraine (CLBU): 01034 Kiev, vul. Volodymyrska 23A; tel. (44) 490-14-01; fax (44) 490-14-02; e-mail general@clu.kiev.ua; internet www.creditlyonnais.kiev.ua; f. 1993; cap. 29.6m., res 2.1m., dep. 207.9m. (Dec. 2001); Chair. and Dir-Gen. JACQUES MOUNIER.

Crimea-Bank: 95000 Crimea, Simferopol, vul. Krylova 37; tel. (652) 27-04-76; fax (652) 27-04-56.

EnergoBank: 01001 Kiev, vul. Luteranska 9/9; tel. (44) 221-49-68; fax (44) 229-50-64; e-mail bank@enbank.kiev.ua; internet www.enbank.kiev.ua; f. 1991; cap. 13.5m., res 6.2m., dep. 147.8m. (Dec. 2000); Pres. YEVHEN M. PATRUSHEV.

Fiatbank: 29000 Khmelnytsky, vul. Proskurovska 19; tel. (382) 26-47-18; fax (382) 226-91-18; Gen. Dir VALERIY BEZVERKHNIY.

Finance and Credit Banking Corpn: 04050 Kiev, vul. Sichovykh Striltsiv 60; tel. (44) 490-68-70; fax (44) 238-24-65; e-mail common@fc.kiev.ua; internet www.fc.kiev.ua; f. 1990; present name adopted 1995; cap. US $13.3m., res $3.3m., dep. $63.7m. (Aug. 2002); Chair. of Bd VADYM PUSHAREV; 11 brs.

First Ukrainian International Bank/Pershyi Ukrainskyi Mizhnarodnyi Bank: 83000 Donetsk, vul. Universitetska 2A; tel. (623)

32-45-03; fax (623) 32-47-00; e-mail info@fuib.com; internet www
.fuib.com; f. 1991; 26.4% owned by AzovStal Iron and Steel Works,
20% by Fortis Bank (Netherlands); cap. US \$12.4m., res \$52.7m.,
dep. \$144.0m. (Dec. 2001); Chair of Bd. N. P. VINOGRADOV.

Inko Joint-Stock Bank: 01021 Kiev, vul. Mechnikova 18; tel. (44)
294-92-19; fax (44) 293-87-90.

Khreshchatyk Open Joint-Stock Bank: 01001 Kiev, vul.
Khreshchatyk 8A; tel. and fax (44) 464-12-28; e-mail bank@xbank
.com.ua; internet www.xcitibank.com.ua; f. 1993 as Zgoda Commercial Bank; 53.3% owned by Central Financial Dept of Kiev City State
Administration; present name adopted 2001; cap. 59.9m., res 4.5m.,
dep. 187.0m. (Dec. 2001); Chair. of Bd DMYTRO M. HRYDZHUK.

Kredyt Bank (Ukraina)—Credit Bank (Ukraine): 79026 Lviv,
vul. Sakharova 78; tel. (322) 97-23-20; fax (322) 97-02-33; e-mail
office@wucb.lviv.net; internet www.kredytbank.com.ua; f. 1990;
fmrly West Ukrainian Commercial Bank—Zakhidno-Ukrainskyi
Komertsiinyi Bank; present name adopted 2001; 67% owned by
Kredyt Bank SA (Poland); cap. 75.1m., res 3.2m., dep. 511.8m.
(Dec. 2001); Pres. STEPAN I. KUBIV.

Kredytprombank: 01014 Kiev, 38 bulv. Druzhby Naradiv; tel. and
fax (44) 244-43-65; e-mail kpb@kreditprombank.com; internet www
.kreditprombank.com; f. 1997, as Inkombank-Ukraina; present
name adopted 1999; 43.6% owned by Homerton Trading Ltd (Ireland); dep. 314.5m., total assets 434.9m. (Dec. 2000); Chair. of Bd
VALERIY HILKO; Chief Exec. NIKOLAI P. ROZHKO.

Legbank: 01033 Kiev, vul. Zhilyanska 27; tel. (44) 227-95-20; fax
(44) 227-95-19; e-mail legbank@legbank.kiev.ua; internet www
.legbank.kiev.ua.

Lesbank: 88000 Uzhhorod, vul. Voloshina 52; tel. (312) 23-31-01;
fax (312) 23-25-04; Pres. and Chair. VASYLIY D. SIVULYA.

Megabank-East Ukrainian Power Bank 'Megabank': 61002
Kharkiv, vul. Artema 30; tel. (572) 14-33-63; fax (572) 47-20-79;
e-mail mega@megabank.net; internet www.megabank.net; f. 1990
as Dobrodiy; present name adopted 1996; cap. US \$14.5m., dep.
\$32.2m. (Dec. 2000); Pres. OLEKSIY LOHVINENKO.

Nadra Bank: 04053 Kiev, vul. Sichovykh Striltsiv 15; tel. (44) 238-
84-00; fax (44) 246-48-40; e-mail pr@nadrabank.kiev.ua; internet
www.nadra.com.ua; f. 1993; cap. 221.1m., res 128.3m. (Jan. 2003);
Pres. I. GILENKO; 152 brs.

JSCB Perkombank—Personal Computer Bank: 04070 Kiev,
vul. P. Sahaidachniy 17; tel. (44) 255-86-23; fax (44) 255-86-54;
e-mail bank@percombank.kiev.ua; f. 1990; cap. 20.1m., res 9.3m.,
dep. 63.4m. (Jan. 2002); Chair. of Bd SERHIY P. BELY; 2 brs.

Pravex–Bank: 01021 Kiev, uzviz Klovskiy 9/2; tel. (44) 294-81-80;
fax (44) 294-81-03; e-mail bank@pravex.com; internet www.pravex
.com; f. 1992; cap. and res US \$24.0m., dep. \$39.5m. (Dec. 1999);
Chair. of Council LEONID CHERNOVETSKIY; Chair. of Bd ANATOLIY KIL-
CHEVSKIY.

Premierbank: 49000 Dnipropetrovsk, vul. Lenina 10; tel. (562) 37-
34-37; fax (56) 770-02-71; e-mail post@premierbank.dp.ua; internet
www.premierbank.dp.ua; f. 1994; present name adopted 1999; cap.
30.0m., res 12.4m., dep. 172.6m. (Dec. 2001); Pres. VOLODYMYR M.
HAVRYLOV; Chair. of Bd OLEKSANDR O. BEZZUB; 5 brs.

PrivatBank: 49094 Dnipropetrovsk, nab. Peremohy 50; tel. (562)
39-05-11; fax (56) 778-54-74; e-mail privatbank@pbank.dp.ua;
internet www.privbank.com.ua; cap. 186.0m., res 184.2m., dep.
4,240.5m (Dec. 2001); Chair. of Bd A. DOUBILET.

Prominvestbank (Industrial-Investment Bank): 01001 Kiev, provulok Shevchenka 12; tel. (44) 201-51-20; fax (44) 229-14-56; e-mail
alf@pib.com.ua; internet www.pib.com.ua; f. 1922 as Stroibank,
name changed 1992; 90% privately owned; cap. 774.0m., res
302.4m., dep. 2,993.0m. (Jan. 2002); Chair. VOLODYMYR P. MAT-
VYENKO; 600 brs.

Raiffeisenbank Ukraine: 01054 Kiev, vul. Vorovskoho 40; tel. (44)
490-05-00; fax (44) 490-05-01; internet www.raiffeisenbank.com.ua;
f. 1998; cap. 44.1m., res 54.7m., dep. 6.7m. (Dec. 2000); Chair. of Bd
IHOR FRANTSKEVYCH.

Real Bank: 61001 Kharkiv, vul. Lenina 60A; tel. (572) 33-27-14; fax
(572) 33-31-06; e-mail bank@real.kharkov.ua; internet www.real
.kharkov.ua; cap. 15.8m., res 2.4m., dep. 102.7m. (April 1999);
Chair. YURIY SHRAMKO.

Rostok Bank: 03067 Kiev, bulv. I. Lepse 4; tel. (44) 484-50-35; fax
(44) 488-74-21; e-mail rostok_bank@svitonline.com; internet www
.rostok-bank.kiev.ua; f. 1994; cap. US \$3.4m., res \$0.8m., dep.
\$2.6m. (Dec. 2002); Pres. IHOR MASOL; Chair. ANATOLIY KOSMIN; 3 brs.

Tavrika Bank: 99028 Crimea, Sevastopol, ul. Relina 1; tel. (692)
45-42-01; fax (692) 45-42-02; e-mail bank@ukr.net; internet www
.tavrika.com; f. 1991; cap. 41.4m., res 7.0m., dep. 69.6m. (Dec. 2002);
Chair. of Bd. SERGEI A. BOGATYREV; 6 brs.

Transbank: 03150 Kiev, vul. Fizkultury 9; tel. (44) 227-27-83; fax
(44) 220-45-88; e-mail common@transbank.kiev.ua; internet www
.transbank.kiev.ua; f. 1991; cap. 25.0m., res 3.8m., dep. 35.7m.
(Dec. 2002); Pres. ANTON Y. TRETYAKOV; Chair. of Bd VALENTINA V.
LASHKEVICH; 3 brs.

**Ukrainian Bank for Trade Co-operation (Bank Torhovoho
Spivrobitnytstva):** 61003 Kharkiv, vul. Klochkivska 3; tel. (572)
23-58-68; fax (572) 12-18-52; e-mail bank@ubtc.kharkov.ua; internet
www.ubtc.kharkov.ua; f. 1992; cap. 5.0m., res 0.2m., dep. 3.0m.
(Jan. 2001); Pres. ZAKHAR BRUK.

Ukrainian Credit Bank: 03056 Kiev, pr. Peremohy 37; tel. (44)
236-96-31; fax (44) 230-23-86; e-mail roleg@viaduk.net; internet
www.ucb.com.ua; f. 1992; cap. 28.2m., res 29.4m., dep. 501.2m.
(Dec. 2002); Pres. VALENTIN A. ZHURSKIY; 1 br.

Ukrainian Innovation Bank—Ukrinbank: 04053 Kiev, Vozne-
senskiy uzviz 10A; tel. (44) 247-20-02; fax (44) 247-21-18; e-mail
ukrinbank@ukrinbank.com; internet www.ukrinbank.com; f. 1989;
long-term investment credits; commercial and foreign exchange
transactions; cap. 40m., res 24m., dep. 293m. (Aug. 2002); Chair.
SERHIY MESCHERYAK; 27 brs.

UkrGazPromBank: 02098 Kiev, Dniprovska nab. 13; tel. (44) 553-
65-45; fax (44) 553-29-39; e-mail ukrgazprombank@ugpb.com;
internet www.ugpb.com; f. 1996; cap. 18.2m., res 0.0m., dep. 8.8m.
(Dec. 2000); Pres. VOLODYMYR MAKIYINKO; Chair. LEONID STOVBCHATY.

UkrSibbank: 61005 Kharkiv, pr. Moskovskyi 60; tel. (572) 21-92-
12; fax (572) 28-26-20; e-mail bank@ukrsib.kharkov.com; internet
www.ukrsibbank.com; f. 1990; present name adopted 1992; cap.
90.0m., res 57.9m., dep. 892.0m. (Dec. 2001); Pres. OLEKSANDR YARO-
SLAVSKIY; 20 brs; 10 sub-brs.

UkrSotsBank—Joint-Stock Bank for Social Development:
03150 Kiev, vul. Kovpak 29; tel. (44) 269-08-36; fax (44) 269-13-07;
e-mail info@ukrsotsbank.com; internet www.usb.com.ua; f. 1990;
cap. 48.6m., res 179.4m., dep. 1,367.1m. (Dec. 2000); Pres. VALERIY
HOROSHKOVSKIY; Chair. of Bd BORYS TYMONKYN.

Ukrspetsimpexbank: 01034 Kiev, vul. Yaroslaviv val 36A; tel. (44)
464-00-00; fax (44) 464-00-22; f. 1993 as Ascold Bank, name changed
to Banker's House Ukraine 1994, changed as above 1999; cap. 8.3m.,
res 2.0m, dep. 32.0m. (April 1999); Chair. ROSTISLAV SCHILLER.

VA Bank-Vseukrainsky Aktsionerny Bank (All-Ukrainian
Share Bank): 04119 Kiev, vul. Zoolohichna 5; tel. (44) 490-06-09; fax
(44) 216-00-33; e-mail bank@vabank.com.ua; internet www.vabank
.com.ua; f. 1992; cap. 91.0m., res 25.1m., dep. 201.6m. (Dec. 2002);
Pres. SERHIY MAKSIMOV; Chair. YURIY BLASHCHUK; 7 brs.

Vidrodzhennia (Rebirth—Kiev Joint Stock Commercial Bank
Vidrodzhennia): Kiev; tel. (44) 224-50-12; fax (44) 225-30-42; Gen.
Dir ANATOLIY SKOPENKO; 27 brs.

Savings Bank

State Oschadny Bank of Ukraine JSC (Oschadbank): 01023
Kiev, vul. Hospitalna 12H; tel. (44) 247-85-69; fax (44) 247-85-68;
internet www.oschadnybank.com; f. 1922; cap. 100m., res 117m.,
dep. 1,705m. (April 2001); Pres. VIKTOR GRYBKOV.

Banking Association

Association of Ukrainian Banks: Kiev; tel. (44) 516-87-75; fax
(44) 516-87-76; e-mail aub@carrier.kiev.ua; fmrly Commercial Bank
Asscn; unites 116 of Ukraine's 155 commercial banks; Pres. OLEK-
SANDR SUHONYAKO.

COMMODITY EXCHANGES

Crimea Universal Exchange: 95050 Crimea, Simferopol, vul.
L. Chaikinoy 1/421; tel. (652) 22-04-32; fax (652) 22-12-73; f. 1923 as
Simferopol Commodity Exchange; present name adopted 1991; Pres.
NATALIYA S. SYUMAK.

Donetsk Commodity Exchange: 83086 Donetsk, vul. Persho-
travnevska 12; tel. (62) 338-10-93; fax (62) 335-92-91; e-mail
oltradex@pub.dn.ua; f. 1991; Gen. Man. PETRO O. VYSHNEVSKYI.

Kharkiv Commodity Exchange: 61003 Kharkiv, vul. Universy-
tetska 5; tel. (572) 12-33-21; fax (572) 12-74-95; e-mail ss@htb
.kharkov.ua; f. 1993; Pres. IHOR V. ZOTOV.

Kiev Universal Exchange: 01103 Kiev, Zaliznychne shose 57; tel.
(44) 295-11-29; fax (44) 295-44-36; e-mail nva@iptelecom.net.ua;
internet www.kue.kiev.ua; f. 1990; Pres. NIKOLAY DETOCHKA.

Odesa Commodity Exchange: 65114 Odesa, vul. Lyustdorfska
doroha 140A; tel. (482) 61-89-92; fax (482) 47-72-84; e-mail yuri@oce
.odessa.ua; originally; f. 1796, re-established 1990; Gen. Man.
MYKOLA O. NIKOLISHEN.

Transcarpathian Regional Commodity Exchange: 78200
Ivano-Frankivsk obl., Kolomiya, vul. Vahylevycha 1, POB 210; tel.
and fax (343) 32-19-61; f. 1996; Gen. Man. IVAN P. VATUTIN.

Transdnipro Commodity Exchange: 49094 Dnipropetrovsk, vul. Nab. Peremohi 32; tel. (562) 46-31-59; fax (562) 46-45-53; e-mail oleg@pce.dp.ua; internet www.pce.dp.ua; originally; f. 1908 as Katerinoslav Commodity Exchange; re-established with present name in 1991; brs in Dniprodzerzhynsk, Kryvyi Rih, Marhanets, Pavlohrad and Synelnykove; Gen. Man. VADYM F. KAMEKO.

Ukrainian Universal Commodity Exchange: 03680 Kiev, pr. Akadmika Hlushkova 1, pavillion 6; tel. (44) 261-67-43; fax (44) 251-95-40; e-mail birga@uutb.kiev.ua; internet www.uutb.com.ua; f. 1991; Pres. OLEKSANDR M. BORKOVSKYI.

Zaporizhzhya Commodity Exchange 'Hileya': 69037 Zaporizhzhya, vul. 40 rokiv Radyanskoyi Ukrainy 41; tel. (612) 33-32-73; fax (612) 34-76-62; originally; f. 1991; re-established 1996; Gen. Man. ANTON A. KHULAKHSIZ.

INSURANCE

State Insurance Companies

Crimean Insurance Co: 99011 Crimea, Sevastopol, vul. Butakov 4; tel. (692) 55-30-28; e-mail ksk@stel.sebastopol.ua.

DASK UkrinMedStrakh: 01601 Kiev, vul. O. Honshara 65; tel. (44) 216-30-21; fax (44) 216-96-92; e-mail ukrmed@ukrpack.com; f. 1999; provides compulsory medical insurance to foreigners and stateless persons temporarily resident in Ukraine.

National Joint-Stock Insurance Co (ORANTA): 01021 Kiev, vul. M. Hrushevskoho 34/1; tel. (44) 293-62-31; fax (44) 253-06-59; e-mail oranta@oranta.ua; internet www.oranta.ua; f. 1921; insurance, reinsurance; Chair. of Bd OLEKSANDR ZAVADA.

Commercial Insurance Companies
A selection of companies is given below.

AIG Ukraine: 01004 Kiev, vul. Shovkovychna 42–44; tel. (44) 490-65-50; fax (44) 490-65-48; e-mail reception@aig.com.ua; internet www.aig.com.ua; affiliated to American International Group (USA); f. 2000; Gen. Man. IHOR KOVALENKO.

AKB Garant Ukrainian-Swiss Joint Stock Insurance Co: 03062 Kiev, pr. Peremohy 67; tel. (44) 459-52-01; e-mail akb@garant.kiev.ua; internet www.garant.kiev.ua; f. 1994; general insurance services; Gen. Man. OLEKSANDR I. DYACHENKO.

Alcona Insurance Co: 03150 Kiev, vul V. Vasylivska 102; tel. (44) 247-44-77; e-mail alcona@alcona.kiev.ua; internet www.insurance.kiev.ua/alcona; f. 1992; insurance and reinsurance.

ASKA Insurance Co: 03186 Kiev, vul. Antonova 5; tel. (44) 241-11-67; e-mail office@aska.com.ua; internet www.aska.com.ua; life and non-life insurance; Chair. HALINA N. TRETYAKOVA; Gen. Man. A. SOSYS.

DASK Insurance Co: 49000 Dnipropetrovsk, vul. K. Libkhnekhta 4D; tel. (562) 32-09-75; fax (562) 32-09-81; e-mail dask@dask.dp.ua; internet www.dask.com.ua; f. 1993; affiliated to DASK Insurance Group; Dir GALINA MAZURETS.

DISCO Insurance Co: 49000 Dnipropetrovsk, vul. K. Lybknekhta 4D; tel. (562) 32-09-78; fax (562) 32-09-81; e-mail disco@disco.dp.ua; internet www.disco.com.ua; f. 1992; affilated to Dask Insurance Group.

ECCO Insurance Co: 01034 Kiev, vul. Prorizna 4/23; tel. (44) 228-10-82; e-mail insurance@ecco-alpha.kiev.ua; internet www.ecco-insurance.at; f. 1991; affiliated to ECCO (Austria); life and non-life insurance.

EnergoPolis Insurance Co: 03049 Kiev, vul. Bohdanivska 10; tel. (44) 244-02-36; fax (44) 244-05-94; e-mail office@enpolis.viaduk.net; internet www.energopolis.com.ua; Pres. and Gen. Man. VASYL MAKHNO.

Galinstrakh Insurance Co: 79012 Lviv, vul. Ak. Sakharova 34; tel. (322) 75-70-30; fax (322) 97-10-40; e-mail gis@is.lviv.ua; internet www.gis.com.ua; f. 1991; general insurance services; Chair. of Bd VOLODYMYR ROMANYSHYN.

INPRO Insurance Co: 03110 Kiev, vul. I. Klymenka 23/219; tel. (44) 227-72-39; fax (44) 240-20-28; e-mail mb@dnister.kiev.ua; internet www.inpro.kiev.ua; f. 1992; life and non-life insurance.

InterPolis Insurance Co: 01025 Kiev, vul. Volodymyrska 69; tel. (44) 227-70-96; fax (44) 220-74-45; e-mail inpolis@gu.kiev.ua; internet www.users.gu.net/inpolis; f. 1993.

Kiev Insurance Co: 04053 Kiev, vul. Yu. Kotsubynskoho 20; tel. (44) 461-92-41; fax (44) 461-92-43; e-mail info@kic.kiev.ua; internet www.kic.kiev.ua; f. 1998.

Ostra Insurance Co: 65026 Odesa, vul. Pushkinska 13; tel. (482) 23-38-87; e-mail main@ostra.com.ua; internet www.ostra.com.ua; non-life insurance; Chair. KHYRACH MAHDYEV.

Ostra-Kiev Insurance Co: 01011 Kiev, vul. Kutuzova 4A; tel. (44) 490-27-44; fax (44) 490-27-48; e-mail office@ostra-kiev.com.ua;

internet www.ostra-kiev.com.ua; f. 1994; re-insurance, medical, travel, property and cargo insurance; Chair. of Bd IHOR N. HORDYENKO.

QBE Ukraina Insurance: 02098 Kiev, Dniprovska nab. 13; tel. (44) 559-82-96; fax (44) 559-28-92; e-mail insurance@qbe-ukraine.com; internet www.qbe-ukraine.com; affiliate of QBE Insurance (New Zealand); f. 1998.

Skide Insurance Co: 04050 Kiev, vul. Hlybochytska 72; tel. (44) 417-40-04; fax (44) 228-40-33; e-mail skide@iptelecom.net.ua; f. 1991; Pres. VOLODYMYR BESARAB.

Skide-West Insurance Co: 04053 Kiev, vul. Sichovykh Striltsiv 40; tel. (44) 238-62-38; e-mail mail@skide-west.kiev.ua; internet www.skide-west.com.ua; f. 1993; Pres. ANDRIY PERETYAZHKO.

Sun Life Ukraine: 01032 Kiev, vul. Starovokzalna 17; tel. (44) 235-20-02; fax (44) 235-89-17; e-mail office@sunlife.com.ua; internet www.sunlife.com.ua; f. 1993; life insurance; Pres. ROSTYSLAV B. TALSKYI.

UkrGazPromPolis Insurance Co: 01034 Kiev, vul. O. Honshara 41; tel. (44) 235-25-00; e-mail office@ugpp.com.ua; internet www.ugpp.com.ua; f. 1996; jointly owned by UkrGazProm, UkrGazPromBank and KievTransGaz; Pres. KONSTANTYN O. YEFYMENKO.

Insurance Association

League of Insurance Organizations of Ukraine: 02002 Kiev, vul. M. Raskovoyi 11/523; tel. and fax (44) 516-82-30; e-mail liga@uainsur.com; internet www.uainsur.com; f. 1992; non-profit association to protect the interests of the members and other participants of the insurance services market; Pres. ALEKSANDR FILONYUK.

Trade and Industry

GOVERNMENT AGENCY

State Property Fund: 01133 Kiev, vul. Kutuzova 18/9; tel. (44) 295-12-74; fax (44) 296-69-84; e-mail marketing@spfu.kiev.ua; internet www.spfu.gov.ua; Chair. MYKHAYLO V. CHECHETOV.

NATIONAL CHAMBER OF COMMERCE

Ukrainian Chamber of Commerce and Industry: 01601 Kiev, vul. V. Zhytomyrska 33; tel. (44) 212-28-40; fax (44) 212-33-53; e-mail ucci@ucci.org.ua; internet www.ucci.org.ua; f. 1972; Chair. SERHIY SKRYPCHECNKO; 28 brs.

REGIONAL CHAMBERS OF COMMERCE
Chambers of Commerce are located in every administrative region of Ukraine, including the following.

Chamber of Commerce of Crimea: 95013 Crimea, Simferopol, ul. Sevastopolskaya 45; tel. (652) 49-97-31; fax (652) 44-58-13; e-mail cci@cci.crimea.ua; internet www.cci.crimea.ua; 1974; sub-brs in Armyansk, Dzhankoi; Feodosiya, Kerch, Yalta and Yevpatoriya; Pres. NEONILA M. GRACHEVA.

Dnipropetrovsk Chamber of Commerce: 49044 Dnipropetrovsk, vul. Shevchenka 4; tel. (562) 36-22-58; fax (562) 36-22-59; e-mail miv@dcci.dp.ua; internet www.dcci.dp.ua; brs at Kryvyi Rih and Dniprodzerzhynsk; Pres. VYTALIY H. ZHMURENKO.

Donetsk Chamber of Commerce: 83000 Donetsk, pr. Dzherzhynskoho 12; tel. (622) 92-80-60; fax (622) 92-80-48; e-mail dcci@dttp.donetsk.ua; internet www.cci.donbass.com; brs at Artemovsk, Horlivka, Kramatorsk and Mariupol; Gov. OLHA H. PSHONKA.

Kharkhiv Chamber of Commerce: 61012 Kharkiv, vul. Katsarksa 3A; tel. (572) 14-96-90; fax (572) 14-96-82; e-mail info@kcci.kharkov.ua; internet www.kcci.kharkov.ua; Pres. VIKTOR I. LOBODA.

Kiev Chamber of Commerce: 01601 Kyiv-54, vul. B. Khmelnytskoho 55; tel. (44) 246-83-01; fax (44) 246-99-66; e-mail info@kiev-chamber.org.ua; internet www.kiev-chamber.org.ua; Pres. MYKOLA V. ZASULSKIY.

Lviv Chamber of Commerce: 79011 Lviv, Stryiskiy park 14; tel. (322) 76-46-11; fax (322) 76-79-72; e-mail lcci@cscd.lviv.ua; internet www.lviv.net/tpp; Pres. OLEH M. KHUSTOCHKA.

Odesa Chamber of Commerce: 65011 Odesa, vul. Bazarna 47; tel. (482) 28-66-10; fax (482) 22-48-22; e-mail orcci@orcci.odessa.ua; internet www.orcci.odessa.ua; brs at Illichivsk, Izmayil and Reni; Pres. SERHIY V. LOKAREV.

Sevastopol Chamber of Commerce: 99011 Crimea, Sevastopol, ul. B. Morskaya 34; tel. (692) 54-35-36; fax (692) 54-06-44; e-mail root@stpp.stel.sebastopol.ua; Pres. LYUDMILA I. VISHNYA.

Transcarpathian (Zakarpatska) Chamber of Commerce: 88015 Transcarpathian obl., Uzhhorod, vul. Hrushevskoho 62; tel.

(312) 26-22-14; fax (312) 21-64-77; e-mail tpp@karpaty.uzhgorod.ua; br. at Mukachevo; Pres. Otto O. Kobchar.

Zaporizhzhya Chamber of Commerce: 69000 Zaporizhzhya, bulv. Tsentralnyi 4; tel. (612) 39-04-16; fax (612) 33-11-72; e-mail cci@cci.zp.ua; internet www.cci.zp.ua; brs at Berdyansk and Melitopol; Pres. Volodomyr I. Shamylov.

EMPLOYERS' ORGANIZATION

Congress of Business Circles of Ukraine: 01061 Kiev, vul. Prorizna 15; tel. (44) 228-64-81; fax (44) 229-52-84; Pres. Valeriy G. Babich.

UTILITIES

Regulatory Bodies

National Electricity Regulatory Commission of Ukraine: 03057 Kiev, vul. Smolenska 19; tel. (44) 241-90-01; fax (44) 241-90-47; e-mail box@nerc.gov.ua; f. 1994; promotion of competition and protection of consumer interests; Chair. Oleksandr Hrydassov.

State Committee for Nuclear Regulation: see section on The Government.

Electricity

EnergoAtom: 71500 Zaporizhzhya obl., Energodar; tel. (44) 294-48-89; e-mail pr@nae.atom.gov.ua; internet www.energoatom.com.ua; f. 1996; responsible for scientific and technical policy within the nuclear-power industry; manages all five nuclear-power producing installations in Ukraine; Pres. Yuriy Hedashkovskyi.

There are 27 electricity distribution companies in Ukraine, including Dniproenergo (serves Dnipropetrovsk), Kievenergo (serves Kiev) and Zaporizhoblenergo (serves the Zaporizhzhya province). These companies were previously grouped in the Unified Energy Systems of Ukraine. Thirteen regional distribution companies were privatized in 1998–2001; a further 12 companies were scheduled to be transferred to majority private ownership during 2002.

Kievenergo: 01001 Kiev, 1 pl. Ivana Franka 5; tel. (44) 201-03-37; fax (44) 201-03-38; e-mail pubrel@me-press.kiev.ua; internet www.kievenergo.com.ua; power generation and distribution; Chair. Ivan Plachkov.

Zakhidenergo (West Energy): 79011 Lviv, vul. Sventitskoho 2; tel. (322) 79-89-41; fax (322) 78-90-59; e-mail z_vtv@rdc.west.energy.gov.ua; f. 1995; power generation; Pres. and Gen. Dir Volodymyr Pavlyuk.

Gas

Naftogaz Ukrainy JSC (Oil and Gas of Ukraine): 01001 Kiev, vul. B. Khmelnytskoho 6в; tel. (44) 461-25-37; fax (44) 220-15-26; e-mail ngu@naftogaz.net; internet www.naftogaz.com; f. 1998; production, processing and storage of gas and petroleum; gas- and condensate-processing; Chair. of Bd Yuriy A. Boyko.

TRADE UNION FEDERATIONS

Confederation of Free Trade Unions of Ukraine (CFTUU): Kiev; independent; Chair. Mykhaylo Volynets.

Federation of Trade Unions of Ukraine (FTUU): 01012 Kiev, maydan Nezalezhnosti 2; tel. (44) 228-87-88; fax (44) 229-80-57; e-mail belova@uprotel.net.ua; f. 1990; fmrly Ukrainian branch of General Confederation of Trade Unions of the USSR; affiliation of 40 trade union brs; Chair. Oleksandr M. Stoyan.

Transport

RAILWAYS

In 2001 there were 22,218 km of railway track in use, of which more than 9,000 km were electrified. Lines link most towns and cities in the republic. Kiev is connected by rail to all the other republics of the former USSR, and there are direct lines to Vienna (Austria), Warsaw (Poland), Budapest (Hungary), Bucharest (Romania), Bratislava (Slovakia) and Berlin (Germany).

State Railway Transport Administration—Ukrzaliznytsia: 03680 Kiev, vul. Tverska 5; tel. (44) 223-00-10; fax (44) 258-80-11; e-mail ci@uz.gov.ua; internet www.uz.gov.ua; Dir-Gen. Minister of Transport; Dir, International Dept Ihor B. Matviyiv.

Ukrreftrans: 03049 Kiev, vul. Furmanova 1/7; tel. (44) 245-47-22; e-mail sekretar@interntrans.com.ua; internet www.intertrans.com.ua; state-owned freight transportation service.

City Underground Railways

Dnipropetrovsk Metro: 49000 Dnipropetrovsk, vul. Kurchatova 8; tel. (562) 42-37-68; e-mail master@gorod.dp.ua; internet gorod.dp.ua/metro; f. 1995; one line with six stations; total length 8 km; total planned network of 74 km.

Kharkiv Metro: 61012 Kharkiv, vul. Engelsa 29; tel. (572) 12-59-83; fax (572) 23-21-41; e-mail metro@tender.kharkov.com; internet www.metro.kharkov.ua; f. 1975; three lines with 26 stations, total length 34 km; Gen. Man. Leonid A. Isayev.

Kiev Metro: 03055 Kiev, pr. Peremohy 35; tel. (44) 238-44-21; fax (44) 229-18-57; e-mail nto@metro.kiev.ua; internet www.metro.kiev.ua; f. 1960; three lines with 40 stations; Dir Mykola M. Shavlovskiy.

ROADS

At 31 December 2001 there were 169,630 km of roads, of which 96.7% were paved. In December 2000 there were 13,081 km of main or national roads, and 156,410 km of secondary or regional roads. A major new road-building programme was announced in March 1998, under which 3,375 km of roads were to be constructed by 2005.

INLAND WATERWAYS

The length of navigable inland waterways in Ukraine declined notably during the 1990s, from 4,405 km in 1990 to 2,281 km in 2001. The Dnipro (Dniepr—Dnieper) river, which links Kiev, Cherkasy, Dnipropetrovsk and Zaporizhzhya with the Black Sea, is the most important route for river freight.

SHIPPING

The main ports are Yalta and Yevpatoriya in Crimea, and Odesa. In addition to long-distance international shipping lines, there are services to the Russian ports of Novorossiisk and Sochi, and Batumi and Sukhumi in Georgia. Although many passenger routes on the Black Sea ceased to operate in the 1990s, there are frequent passenger services from Odesa to Haifa (Israel) and İstanbul (Turkey). In 2001 Ukraine's merchant fleet (838 vessels) had a total displacement of 1.4m. grt.

Port Authority

Port of Odesa Authority: 65026 Odesa, pl. Mytna 1; tel. (48) 729-35-55; fax (48) 729-36-27; e-mail bev@port.odessa.ua; internet www.port.odessa.ua; cargo handling and storage; Gen. Man. Oleksandr S. Soborov.

Shipping Companies

Azov Shipping Co: 87510 Donetsk obl., Mariupol, pr. Admirala Lunina 89; tel. (629) 31-15-00; fax (629) 31-12-25; e-mail admin@c2smtp.azsco.anet.donetsk.ua; f. 1871; Pres. Serhiy V. Prusikov.

State Black Sea Shipping Co: 65026 Odesa, vul. Lanzheronovska 1; tel. (482) 25-21-60; fax (482) 60-57-33; Pres. Boris Scherbak.

Ukrainian Danube Shipping Co: 68600 Odesa obl., Izmayil, vul. Chervonaflotska 28; tel. (4841) 2-55-50; fax (4841) 2-53-55; e-mail udp_t@udp.izmail.uptel.net; f. 1944; cargo and passenger services; Pres. Petr S. Suvorov.

Ukrainian Shipping Co (UkrShip): 65014 Odesa, vul. Marazlyevska 8; tel. (482) 34-73-50; fax (487) 77-07-00; e-mail admin@ukrship.odessa.ua; f. 1996; Pres. A. Savitskiy.

Ukrrechflot Joint-Stock Shipping Co: 04071 Kiev, Nizhny val. 51; tel. (44) 416-88-79; fax (44) 417-86-82; Pres. Nikolay A. Slavov.

Yugreftransflot JSC: 99014 Crimea, Sevastopol, ul. Rybakov 5; tel. (692) 41-25-79; fax (692) 42-39-39; Chair. Volodymyr Andreyev.

CIVIL AVIATION

Ukraine has air links with cities throughout the former USSR and with major European, North American, Asian and African cities. The principal international airport is at Boryspil (Kiev).

AeroSvit Airlines: 01032 Kiev, bulv. Shevchenko 58а; tel. (44) 246-50-70; fax (44) 246-50-46; e-mail av@aswt.kiev.ua; internet www.aerosvit.com; f. 1994; operates scheduled and charter passenger services to domestic and international destinations; Chief Exec. and Dir-Gen. Hrihoriy Hurtovoy.

Air Urga: 25005 Kirovohrad, vul. Dobrovolskoho 1а; tel. (522) 35-11-25; fax (522) 35-11-52; e-mail office@urga.com.ua; internet www.urga.com.ua; f. 1993; regional and international passenger and cargo flights; Dir-Gen. Leonid Shmayevich.

Khors Air Company: 01133 Kiev, vul. L. Ukrainki 34; tel. (44) 294-64-69; fax (44) 573-86-72; e-mail info@khors.com.ua; internet www.khors.com.ua; f. 1990; operates international, regional and domestic cargo and passenger services; Gen. Dir Serhiy Shamenko.

Ukraine International Airlines JSC (Mizhnarodni Avialinyi Ukraini): 01135 Kiev, pr. Peremohy 14; tel. (44) 461-56-56; fax (44)

216-79-94; e-mail uia@ps.kiev.ua; internet www
.ukraine-international.com; f. 1992; 61% state-owned, 22.5% owned
jointly by SAir (Switzerland) and Austrian Airlines (Austria); operates services to domestic and European destinations; Pres. VITALIY
M. POTEMSKIY.

Tourism

The Black Sea coast of Ukraine has several popular resorts,
including Odesa and Yalta. The Crimean peninsula is a popular
tourist centre in both summer and winter, owing to its temperate
climate. Kiev, Lviv and Odesa have important historical attractions
and there are many archaeological monuments on the Black Sea
coast, including the remains of ancient Greek and Ottoman settlements. However, the tourist industry is little developed outside
Kiev, Lviv and the Black Sea resorts, with few hotels or other
facilities. There were 4.4m. foreign tourist arrivals in Ukraine in
2000, and receipts from tourism totalled US $573m. in 2001, com-
pared with $394m. in the previous year.

Ministry of Resorts and Tourism of Crimea: 95005 Crimea,
Sevastopol, pr. Kirova 13; tel. (652) 54-46-68; e-mail ministry@
tourism.crimea.ua; internet www.tourism.crimea.ua.

State Tourism Adminstration of Ukraine: 01034 Kiev, vul.
Yaroslaviv val 36; tel. (44) 212-42-15; e-mail info@tourism.gov.ua;
internet www.tourism.gov.ua; f. 1999; Chair. VALERIY I. TSYBUKH.

THE UNITED ARAB EMIRATES

Introductory Survey

Location, Climate, Language, Religion, Flag, Capital

The United Arab Emirates (UAE) lies in the east of the Arabian peninsula. It is bordered by Saudi Arabia to the west and south, and by Oman to the east. In the north the UAE has a short frontier with Qatar and a coastline of about 650 km on the southern shore of the Persian (Arabian) Gulf, separated by a detached portion of Omani territory from a small section of coast on the western shore of the Gulf of Oman. The climate is exceptionally hot in summer, with average maximum temperatures exceeding 40°C, and humidity is very high. Winter is mild, with temperatures ranging from 17°C to 20°C. Average annual rainfall is very low: between 100 mm and 200 mm. The official language is Arabic, spoken by almost all of the native population. Arabs are, however, outnumbered by non-Arab immigrants, mainly from India, Pakistan, Bangladesh and Iran. According to official estimates, UAE nationals represented about 25% of the total population in 1994. Most of the inhabitants are Muslims, mainly of the Sunni sect. The national flag (proportions 1 by 2) has three equal horizontal stripes, of green, white and black, with a vertical red stripe at the hoist. The capital is Abu Dhabi.

Recent History

Prior to independence, the UAE was Trucial Oman, also known as the Trucial States, and the component sheikhdoms of the territory were under British protection. Although, from 1892, the United Kingdom assumed responsibility for the sheikhdoms' defence and external relations, they were otherwise autonomous and followed the traditional form of Arab monarchy, with each ruler having virtually absolute power over his subjects.

In 1952 the Trucial Council, comprising the rulers of the seven sheikhdoms, was established in order to encourage the adoption of common policies in administrative matters, possibly leading to a federation of the states. Petroleum, the basis of the area's modern prosperity, was first discovered in 1958, when deposits were located beneath the coastal waters of Abu Dhabi, the largest of the sheikhdoms. Onshore petroleum was found in Abu Dhabi in 1960. Commercial exploitation of petroleum began there in 1962, providing the state with greatly increased revenue. However, Sheikh Shakhbut bin Sultan an-Nahyan, the Ruler of Abu Dhabi since 1928, failed to use the income from petroleum royalties to develop his domain. As a result, the ruling family deposed him in August 1966 and installed his younger brother, Sheikh Zayed bin Sultan. Under the rule of Sheikh Zayed, Abu Dhabi was transformed, with considerable income from the petroleum industry allocated for public works and the provision of welfare services. In 1966 petroleum was discovered in neighbouring Dubai (the second largest of the Trucial States), which also underwent a rapid development.

In January 1968 the United Kingdom announced its intention to withdraw British military forces from the area by 1971. In March 1968 the Trucial States joined nearby Bahrain and Qatar (which were also under British protection) in what was named the Federation of Arab Emirates. It was intended that the Federation should become fully independent, but the interests of Bahrain and Qatar proved to be incompatible with those of the smaller sheikhdoms, and both seceded from the Federation in August 1971 to become separate independent states. In July six of the Trucial States (Abu Dhabi, Dubai, Sharjah, Umm al-Qaiwain, Ajman and Fujairah) had agreed on a federal Constitution for achieving independence as the United Arab Emirates (UAE). The United Kingdom accordingly terminated its special treaty relationship with the States, and the UAE became independent on 2 December 1971. The remaining sheikhdom, Ras al-Khaimah, joined the UAE in February 1972. At independence Sheikh Zayed of Abu Dhabi took office as the first President of the UAE. Sheikh Rashid bin Said al-Maktoum, the Ruler of Dubai since 1958, became Vice-President, while his eldest son, Sheikh Maktoum bin Rashid al-Maktoum (Crown Prince of Dubai), became Prime Minister in the Federal Council of Ministers. A 40-member consultative assembly, the Federal National Council, was also inaugurated.

In January 1972 the Ruler of Sharjah, Sheikh Khalid bin Muhammad al-Qasimi, was killed by rebels under the leadership of his cousin, Sheikh Saqr bin Sultan, who had been deposed as the sheikhdom's Ruler in June 1965. However, the rebels were defeated, and Sheikh Khalid was succeeded by his brother, Sheikh Sultan bin Muhammad al-Qasimi.

In August 1976 Sheikh Zayed, disappointed with progress towards centralization, reportedly announced that he was not prepared to accept another five-year term as President. In November, however, the highest federal authority, the Supreme Council of Rulers (comprising the Rulers of the seven emirates), re-elected him unanimously, following agreements granting the Federal Government greater control over defence, intelligence services, immigration, public security and border control.

Owing to a dispute over a senior appointment in February 1978, the forces of Dubai and Ras al-Khaimah refused to accept orders from the Federal Defence Force. Although Ras al-Khaimah later reintegrated with the Federal Defence Force, Dubai's armed forces effectively remained a separate entity. In March 1979 a 10-point memorandum from the National Council, containing proposals for increased unity, was rejected by Dubai, which, together with Ras al-Khaimah, boycotted a meeting of the Supreme Council. In April Sheikh Maktoum resigned as Prime Minister; he was replaced by his father, Sheikh Rashid, who formed a new Council of Ministers in July, while retaining the post of Vice-President. Although Sheikh Rashid's health was deteriorating, both he and Sheikh Zayed were re-elected to their posts by the Supreme Council in November 1981. Meanwhile, Sheikh Ahmad bin Rashid al-Mu'alla, the Ruler of Umm al-Qaiwain (the smallest of the emirates) since 1929, died in February 1981, and was succeeded by his son, Rashid. Sheikh Rashid bin Humaid an-Nuaimi, the Ruler of Ajman since 1928, died in September 1981, and was succeeded by his son, Humaid.

In October 1986 the provisional federal Constitution was renewed for a further five years, and Sheikh Zayed and Sheikh Rashid were unanimously re-elected to the posts of President, and Vice-President and Prime Minister, respectively.

There was an attempted coup in Sharjah in June 1987, when Sheikh Abd al-Aziz, a brother of Sheikh Sultan, announced (in his brother's absence) the abdication of the Ruler, on the grounds that he had mismanaged the economy. The Supreme Council of Rulers intervened to endorse Sheikh Sultan's claim to be the legitimate Ruler of Sharjah, effectively restoring him to power. Sheikh Abd al-Aziz was given the title of Crown Prince and was granted a seat on the Supreme Council. In February 1990, however, Sheikh Sultan removed his brother from the post of Crown Prince and revoked his right to succeed him as Ruler. In July Sheikh Sultan appointed Sheikh Ahmad bin Muhammad al-Qasimi, the head of Sharjah's petroleum and mineral affairs office, as Deputy Ruler of Sharjah, although he was not given the title of Crown Prince.

In October 1990, upon the death of his father, Sheikh Maktoum acceded to the positions of Ruler of Dubai and Vice-President and Prime Minister of the UAE. In October 1991 the Supreme Council confirmed Sheikh Zayed and Sheikh Maktoum as, respectively, President, and Vice-President and Prime Minister, each for a further five-year term. The Constitution was also renewed for a further period of five years.

In January 1995 the Ruler of Dubai, Sheikh Maktoum bin Rashid al-Maktoum, issued a decree naming Sheikh Muhammad bin Rashid al-Maktoum as Crown Prince, and Sheikh Hamdan bin Rashid al-Maktoum as Deputy Ruler of Dubai. In June 1996 legislation designed to make the provisional Constitution permanent was endorsed by the Federal National Council, following its approval by the Supreme Council of Rulers. At the same time Abu Dhabi was formally designated capital of the UAE. Sheikh Zayed was subsequently re-elected to the presidency.

In July 1991 the UAE became involved in a major international financial scandal, when regulatory authorities in seven countries abruptly closed down the operations of the Bank of Credit and Commerce International (BCCI), in which the Abu Dhabi ruling family and agencies had held a controlling interest

(77%) since April 1990. The termination of the bank's activities followed the disclosure of systematic, large-scale fraud by BCCI authorities prior to April 1990. By the end of July 1991 BCCI's activities had been suspended in all 69 countries in which it had operated. At the conclusion of fraud trials in May 1994 all but one of the defendants were sentenced to terms of imprisonment ranging from three to 14 years. (In June 1995 a court of appeal overturned the guilty verdicts of two of those imprisoned.) In March 1998, as new legislation was being prepared to strengthen the role of the Central Bank and to enforce stricter regulation of the financial sector, the Government intervened in the affairs of Dubai Islamic Bank which was reportedly experiencing financial difficulties. In 1999 an expatriate business executive defaulted on loans and bank credits totalling an estimated $866m.; subsequent investigations into his business revealed fraudulent activity. The Central Bank called an emergency meeting to discuss the recovery of the monies owed, and UAE banks were later criticized by the police for their lack of vigilance in potential fraud cases.

In April 2001 Dubai's Director-General of Ports and Customs, Dr Obeid Saqer bin Busit, was sentenced to 27 years' imprisonment, having been convicted on two charges of corruption arising from abuse of his position; bin Busit was the highest ranking civil servant ever to have been tried for corruption in the UAE. Six other defendants (three UAE nationals and three Pakistani expatriates) were also convicted—among them the head of Dubai's Hamriya port, who was found guilty of four charges and given a 31-year prison sentence. The arrests had been ordered personally by Dubai's Crown Prince in February, following a two-year investigation, and it was subsequently reported that the federal Minister of Justice and Islamic Affairs and Awqaf (Religious Endowments) had proposed the establishment of an anti-corruption commission and the institution of more stringent legislation to counter corruption. There were, however, subsequent reports that those convicted of the customs fraud had been pardoned.

Meanwhile, in January 2001 the Minister of Information and Culture was reported to have urged a review of criminal legislation, in force since 1980, prohibiting journalists from reporting on contentious matters relating to legislation or criticizing public institutions.

In December 2001 the Supreme Council re-elected Sheikh Zayed as President and Sheikh Maktoum (the Prime Minister) as Vice-President for a further five-year term.

Industrial safety concerns emerged during 2002 after 27 workers were killed when the Dubai dry docks flooded in March and an unknown number of construction workers were killed and injured when the roof of a new power plant under construction at the Jebel Ali industrial centre near Dubai city collapsed in August.

In February 2003 Said Muhammad Said al-Ghandi was appointed as Speaker of the Federal National Council after a secret ballot.

The UAE was a founder member of the Co-operation Council for the Arab States of the Gulf (the Gulf Co-operation Council—GCC, see p. 175) in May 1981. The GCC aims to achieve greater political and economic integration between Gulf countries, and in December 2001 the UAE joined with other member states in agreeing to establish a Supreme Joint Defence Council and to formulate a joint strategy on terrorism. A new GCC combined defence force was to be established by 2004 under joint GCC command.

Conflict arose between the UAE and Iran in 1992 concerning the sovereignty of Abu Musa, an island situated between the states in the Persian (Arabian) Gulf. The island had been administered since 1991 under a joint agreement between Iran and Sharjah, in accordance with which an Iranian garrison was stationed on the island. In that year Iran had also seized the smaller neighbouring islands of Greater and Lesser Tunb. In April 1992 the Iranian garrison on Abu Musa was said to have seized civilian installations on the island. There were further allegations that Iranian officials were attempting to force expatriate workers employed by the UAE to leave the island, preventing the entry of other expatriates, and increasing the number of Iranian nationals there. In Syrian-sponsored indirect contacts later in the year the Iranian Government was reported to be prepared to negotiate over the administration of Abu Musa alone, and in April 1993 all those who had been expelled from or refused entry to Abu Musa in 1992 were reportedly permitted to return. In October 1993 Sheikh Zayed announced the introduction of a federal law standardizing the limits of the UAE's

territorial waters to 12 nautical miles (22.2 km) off shore, in response to a similar announcement by the Iranian authorities. Despite the purported commitment of both Governments to enter into direct negotiations during the following year, by late 1994 no significant progress had been made towards resolving the conflict, and in December the UAE announced its intention to refer the dispute to the International Court of Justice in The Hague, Netherlands. In February 1995 it was alleged that Iran had deployed air defence systems on the islands. In November officials from the UAE and Iran, meeting in Qatar, failed to reach agreement on establishing an agenda for ministerial-level negotiations. In March 1996 bilateral relations deteriorated further when Iran opened an airport on Abu Musa; in the following month Iran established a power station on Greater Tunb. In February 1999 the UAE protested at the construction by Iran of municipal facilities on Abu Musa and at recent Iranian military exercises near the disputed islands. Iran subsequently complained to the UN that, in disputing the location of its military exercises, the UAE was interfering in Iranian internal affairs. During 1999 the UAE was increasingly critical of the *rapprochement* between Saudi Arabia and Iran, claiming that it was at the expense of Saudi relations with the UAE. (The UAE also boycotted a meeting of GCC oil ministers in March 1999, in protest at the decision by Saudi Arabia to begin petroleum production in disputed land prior to an agreement being reached on the ownership of the land.) In November a tripartite committee, established by the GCC and comprising representatives of Oman, Qatar and Saudi Arabia, announced that it would continue efforts to facilitate a settlement. At the end of the month Sheikh Zayed boycotted a meeting of GCC leaders in Saudi Arabia, in protest at the lack of attention given to the dispute with Iran by the other GCC members at a time when they were increasingly moving towards improved relations with Iran. In December the UAE renewed its request for Iran to enter into direct negotiations or to agree to international arbitration over the islands. In March 2000, following a statement by Iran that it would be prepared to negotiate over the islands, the UAE asserted that it would refer it to the GCC tripartite committee. By mid-2002 no progress had been reached concerning a resolution of the territorial dispute.

In response to Iraq's occupation of Kuwait in August 1990, the UAE (which supported the US-led multinational effort against Iraq) announced that foreign armed forces opposing the Iraqi invasion would be provided with military facilities in the Emirates. By the mid-1990s, however, the UAE was among those states questioning the justification for the continued maintenance of international sanctions (imposed in 1990) against Iraq, in view of the resultant humanitarian consequences for the Iraqi population. In June 1998 the UAE reiterated its support for an end to the economic blockade against Iraq, and in August it was announced that the UAE was to restore diplomatic ties with Iraq. The UAE reopened its embassy in the Iraqi capital in April 2000. However, the Ruler of Fujairah was criticized in Iraq following a speech, at the UN Millennium Summit in New York in September, in which he called on Iraq to apply all pertinent UN resolutions, particularly those related to the issue of prisoners of war. Although Iraq's Minister of Trade visited Abu Dhabi in December, where he was received by Sheikh Zayed, the UAE lent its support to a declaration of the GCC annual summit meeting that urged Iraq to conform with UN Security Council Resolutions: it was generally considered that the Emirates had been compelled to endorse the declaration in return for emphasis of GCC support for the UAE in its territorial dispute with Iran. Addressing the Arab Inter-Parliamentary Union in February 2001, Sheikh Zayed none the less urged Arab states to work jointly towards an end to the sanctions regime in force against Iraq. In November the UAE and Iraq signed a free trade agreement, which was ratified by Sheikh Zayed in early May 2002.

The UAE severed diplomatic relations with the Taliban regime in Afghanistan in late September 2001, in response to the suicide attacks against New York and Washington, DC, on 11 September. Hitherto, the UAE had been one of only three states to maintain ties with the Taliban (the UAE's relations with the Taliban were at chargé d'affaires level), although an air link between Dubai and Kabul had been suspended in compliance with UN sanctions imposed against Afghanistan in late 2000. The Saudi-born Osama bin Laden, whose al-Qa'ida (Base) organization was based in Afghanistan, was now the USA's principal suspect in having orchestrated the September 2001 suicide attacks. After diplomatic relations were severed, the

UAE's Minister of Foreign Affairs stated that the Emirates had sought to persuade the Taliban to hand over bin Laden so that he might stand trial in an international court. In common with other GCC members, the UAE pledged support for the US Administration in its efforts to bring to justice the perpetrators of terrorism, swiftly extraditing a suspected militant Islamist wanted for questioning in France. None the less, the UAE emphasized that the success of the US-led 'coalition against terror' must be linked to a resumption of the Arab–Israeli peace process, and expressed concerns that military action should not target any Arab state. The UAE's banking sector came under international scrutiny after US investigators claimed to have evidence of transactions between banks in the UAE and USA linking bin Laden with the terrorist attacks. At the end of September the Emirates' Central Bank ordered that the assets in the UAE of 27 individuals and organizations accused by the USA of involvement in terrorism be 'frozen'; in early November the Central Bank reportedly ordered a 'freeze' on the assets of a further 62 entities. Following the swift defeat of the Taliban regime in the US-led military offensive which began in early October, and the inauguration of a new Afghan interim administration in late December 2001, in early February 2002 the Afghan embassy in the UAE was reopened; the opening of the Emirates' embassy in Kabul was announced in mid-March. In November the Central Bank tightened regulations on an informal money-transfer system known as 'hawala', after the practice was criticized by western law enforcement agencies as an important element in the financing of terrorism. In December UAE authorities announced that they had arrested Abdul Rahim Nashiri, al-Qa'ida's alleged chief in the Gulf, and had handed him over to the US military.

At the summit meeting of the Council of the League of Arab States (the Arab League, see p. 260) convened in Beirut, Lebanon, in late March 2002, the Minister of State for Foreign Affairs, Sheikh Hamdan bin Zaid an-Nahyan, declared the UAE to be opposed to any future US-led campaign to oust the regime of Saddam Hussein in Iraq as a potential second phase in the USA's declared 'war against terror'. The UAE continued to urge a diplomatic solution to the crisis, and promoted a plan for the Iraqi leader to go into exile in order to prevent a war to oust his regime; however, in March 2003 the UAE disregarded calls by some members of the Arab League to refuse to provide facilities for military action in Iraq. At the commencement of the conflict later in the same month some 3,000 US air force personnel and 72 combat aircraft were stationed in the UAE.

Government

The highest federal authority is the Supreme Council of Rulers, comprising the hereditary rulers of the seven emirates, each of whom is virtually an absolute monarch in his own domain. Decisions of the Supreme Council require the approval of at least five members, including the rulers of both Abu Dhabi and Dubai. From its seven members, the Supreme Council elects a President and a Vice-President. The President appoints the Prime Minister and the Federal Council of Ministers, responsible to the Supreme Council, to hold executive authority. The legislature is the Federal National Council, a consultative assembly (comprising 40 members appointed for two years by the emirates) which considers laws proposed by the Council of Ministers. There are no political parties.

Defence

In August 2002 the armed forces totalled an estimated 41,500 men (of whom some 30% were thought to be expatriates): an army of 35,000, an air force of 4,000 and a navy of around 2,500. The Union Defence Force and the armed forces of Abu Dhabi, Dubai, Ras al-Khaimah and Sharjah were formally merged in 1976, although Dubai still maintains a degree of independence (as to a lesser extent do other emirates). Military service is voluntary. The defence budget for 2002 was estimated at AED 6,000m.

Economic Affairs

In 1998, according to estimates by the World Bank, the UAE's gross national income (GNI), measured at average 1996–98 prices, was US $49,205m., equivalent to US $18,060 per head (or $19,410 on an international purchasing-power parity basis). During 1990–2001, it was estimated, the population increased by an average annual rate of 4.4%, while gross domestic product (GDP) per head decreased, in real terms, by an average of 2.8% per year during 1990–98. Overall GDP increased, in real terms,

by an average annual rate of 2.9% in 1990–2000; growth in 2000 was an estimated 6.0%.

Agriculture (including livestock and fishing) contributed an estimated 3.4% of GDP in 2001, and engaged 7.9% of the employed population in 2000. The principal crops are tomatoes, dates, melons and cabbages. The UAE imports some 70% of food requirements, but is self-sufficient in salad vegetables, eggs and poultry. Some agricultural products are exported, on a small scale. Livestock-rearing and fishing are also important. During 1997–2001 agricultural GDP increased at an average annual rate of 9.2%. Agricultural production increased by an average of 9.6% per year in 1990–2000.

Industry (including mining, manufacturing, construction and power) contributed an estimated 51.2% of GDP in 2001, and engaged 33.4% of the working population in 2000. During 1997–2001 industrial GDP increased by an average of 2.4% per year.

Mining and quarrying contributed an estimated 29.1% of GDP in 2001, and employed 2.3% of the working population in 2000. Petroleum production is the most important industry in the UAE, with exports of crude petroleum and related products providing an estimated 41.3% of total export revenues in 2001. At the end of 2001 the UAE's proven recoverable reserves of petroleum were 97,800m. barrels, representing 9.3% of world reserves. Production levels in 2001 averaged 2.4m. barrels per day (b/d). From 1 February 2003 the UAE's production quota within the Organization of the Petroleum Exporting Countries (OPEC, see p. 298) was 2.1m. b/d. The UAE has large natural gas reserves, estimated at 6,010,000m. cu m at the end of 2001 (3.9% of world reserves). Most petroleum and natural gas reserves are concentrated in Abu Dhabi. Dubai is the second largest producer of petroleum in the UAE. Marble and sand are also quarried.

The major heavy industries in the UAE are related to hydrocarbons, and activities are concentrated in the Jebel Ali Free Zone (in Dubai) and the Jebel Dhanna-Ruwais industrial zone in Abu Dhabi. The most important products are liquefied petroleum gas, distillate fuel oils and jet fuels. There are two petroleum refineries in Abu Dhabi, and the emirate has 'downstream' interests abroad. Manufacturing contributed an estimated 13.5% of GDP in 2001, and employed 11.0% of the working population in 2000. The most important sectors are aluminium, steel and chemicals. During 1997–2001 manufacturing GDP increased at an average annual rate of 7.6%.

Electric energy is generated largely by thermal power stations, utilizing the UAE's own petroleum and natural gas resources. Each of the emirates is responsible for its own energy production. In 1994 the total installed capacity of UAE power stations was 5,000 MW. A further 2,500 MW was expected to be installed by 2000 to meet rising demand.

The services sector contributed an estimated 45.4% of GDP in 2001, and engaged 58.7% of the working population in 2000. The establishment of the Jebel Ali Free Zone in 1985 enhanced Dubai's reputation as a well-equipped entrepôt for regional trade, and significant growth in both re-exports and tourism has been recorded in recent years. During 1997–2001 the GDP of the services sector increased by an average of 6.9% per year.

In 2001, according to preliminary estimates, the UAE recorded a visible trade surplus of AED 56,300m., and there was a surplus of AED 39,700m. on the current account of the balance of payments. In 1999 the principal source of imports (9.9%) was the USA. Other important suppliers in that year were Japan, the United Kingdom, India, Germany, France and the People's Republic of China. In 1998 the principal market for exports was Japan (29.5%). Other important markets in that year were the Republic of Korea, India, Oman and Singapore. All of Sharjah's exports of crude petroleum are taken by the USA. According to IMF estimates, in 2001 the principal source of imports and the principal market for exports was Japan, with 10.2% and 36.4%, respectively. The principal exports in 2001, excluding hydrocarbons, base metals and articles of base metal, textiles and textile articles and chemical products. The principal imports in 2001 were machinery and electrical equipment, vehicles and other transport equipment and textiles and textile articles.

A federal budgetary deficit of AED 2,169m. was forecast for 2002. The federal budget reflects only about one-half of the country's total public expenditure, as the individual emirates also have their own budgets for municipal expenditure and local projects. Abu Dhabi is the major contributor to the federal budget. Annual inflation averaged 2.1% in 1995–2001. Consumer prices rose by an average of 1.4% in 2000 and an estimated 2.2% in 2001. Some 2.3% of the labour force were recorded as unemployed in 2000. About 80% of the work-force are estimated to be non-UAE nationals.

In addition to its membership of OPEC (see p. 298) and the Co-operation Council for the Arab States of the Gulf (GCC, see p. 175), the UAE and also belongs to the Organization of Arab Petroleum Exporting Countries (OAPEC, see p. 292) and the Arab Fund for Economic and Social Development (AFESD, see p. 136). The UAE, and Abu Dhabi in particular, is a major aid donor. Abu Dhabi disburses loans through the Abu Dhabi Fund for Development (ADFD). GCC member states established a unified regional customs tariff in January 2003 and agreed to create a single market and currency no later than January 2010.

Abu Dhabi and Dubai, the principal petroleum producers, dominate the economy of the UAE, while the northern emirates remain relatively undeveloped; there is little co-ordination in the economic affairs of the emirates. The UAE is less dependent than other petroleum-producing countries on the hydrocarbons sector (crude oil accounted for some 28.8% of GDP in 2001), and Dubai is of particular importance as an entrepôt for regional trade. Following a period of reduced international petroleum prices, by late 1999 oil prices had increased dramatically, leading to an economic recovery. Despite the anticipated decline in Government revenue in 1999, no spending cuts were enforced, with the emirates focusing instead on ways to maximize revenues; Abu Dhabi continued with its privatization programme, divesting the electricity and water sector along with telecommunications; Dubai encouraged self-reliance and greater profitability among its state enterprises; and the northern emirates continued to expand non-oil-sector activities. Social welfare reforms instituted in 1999 included the establishment of a General Authority for Pensions and Social Security. Following a sharp decline in values on the informal stock exchange in mid-1998, an official stock exchange was inaugurated in Dubai in March 2000; a second exchange was scheduled to open in Abu Dhabi. The sustained recovery in international petroleum prices was the principal factor contributing to a 23.4% increase in the value of the UAE's exports and re-exports in 2000, compared with a 4.1% increase in spending on imports; the value of non-hydrocarbons exports increased by 3.4%. In view of continuing high oil prices, overall growth in excess of 5% was forecast for 2001, although this assessment was thrown into doubt as the world economy suffered a downturn in the aftermath of the terrorist attacks on the USA in September. The build-up towards the US-led military campaign to oust the regime of Saddam Hussein in Iraq pushed oil prices even higher, leading to forecasts of strong export performance in 2002 and 2003. The UAE was concerned that its tourism sector, which had enjoyed particularly strong growth in Dubai during the 1990s, would be severely affected. However, since the UAE has tended to base revenue forecasts on oil prices somewhat lower than prevailing world rates, there was speculation that budget revenues would exceed projections in 2002. The education, health, social security and utilities sectors were to receive substantial investment under that year's federal budget, which anticipated a deficit of AED 2,169m.

Education

Primary education is compulsory, beginning at six years of age and lasting for six years. Secondary education, starting at the age of 12, also lasts for six years, comprising two equal cycles of three years. As a proportion of all school-age children, the total enrolment at primary and secondary schools was equivalent to 85% in 1996 (males 85%; females 85%), compared with only 61% in 1970. Secondary enrolment included 71% of children in the relevant age-group in 1996 (males 68%; females 74%). Most of the teachers are from other Arab countries. In September 1988 four higher colleges of technology (two for male and two for female students) opened, admitting a total of 425 students, all of whom were citizens of the UAE; by 1992/93 the four colleges enrolled 1,150 students, all of whom were UAE citizens. In 1996/97 16,213 students were enrolled at the University at Al-Ain in Abu Dhabi, or at equivalent institutions abroad. Many other students currently receive higher education abroad. Federal government expenditure in 1995 allocated AED 2,699m. to education (15.1% of total expenditure by the central Government).

Public Holidays

2003: 1 January (New Year's Day), 12 February* (Id al-Adha, Feast of the Sacrifice), 5 March* (Muharram, Islamic New Year), 14 May* (Mouloud, Birth of Muhammad), 6 August† (Accession of the Ruler of Abu Dhabi), 24 September* (Leilat al-Meiraj, Ascension of Muhammad), 27 October* (first day of Ramadan), 26 November* (Id al-Fitr, end of Ramadan), 2 December (National Day), 25 December (Christmas Day).

2004: 1 January (New Year's Day), 2 February* (Id al-Adha, Feast of the Sacrifice), 22 February* (Muharram, Islamic New Year), 2 May* (Mouloud, Birth of Muhammad), 6 August† (Accession of the Ruler of Abu Dhabi), 12 September* (Leilat al-Meiraj, Ascension of Muhammad), 15 October* (first day of Ramadan), 14 November* (Id al-Fitr, end of Ramadan), 2 December (National Day), 25 December (Christmas Day).

*These holidays are dependent on the Islamic lunar calendar and may vary slightly from the dates given.

†Applies only in Abu Dhabi.

Weights and Measures

The imperial, metric and local systems are all in use.

Statistical Survey

Area and Population

AREA, POPULATION AND DENSITY

Area (sq km)	77,700*
Population (census results)	
December 1985	1,622,464
17 December 1995 (provisional)	
Males	1,579,743
Females.	797,710
Total	2,377,453
Population (official estimates at mid-year)	
1999	3,033,000
2000	3,247,000
2001†	3,488,000
Density (per sq km) at mid-2001	44.9

* 30,000 sq miles.

† Preliminary.

POPULATION BY EMIRATE
(preliminary figures, mid-2001)

	Area (sq km)	Population*	Density (per sq km)
Abu Dhabi	67,350	1,362,000	20.2
Dubai	3,900	1,029,000	263.8
Sharjah	2,600	562,000	216.2
Ajman	250	196,000	784.0
Ras al-Khaimah . . .	1,700	181,000	106.5
Fujairah.	1,150	106,000	92.2
Umm al-Qaiwain . . .	750	52,000	69.3
Total	77,700	3,247,000	41.8

* Source: IMF, *UAE—Selected Issues and Statistical Appendix* (March 2003).

PRINCIPAL TOWNS
(population at December 1995 census)

Dubai	669,181	Ajman	114,395
Abu Dhabi (capital) .	398,695	Ras al-Khaimah . .	77,550
Sharjah	320,095	Fujairah . . .	33,176
Al-Ain	225,970		

Source: Thomas Brinkhoff, *City Population* (internet www.citypopulation.de).

Mid-2000 (UN estimate, incl. suburbs): Dubai 886,000 (Source: UN, *World Urbanization Prospects: The 2001 Revision*).

Mid-2001 (UN estimate, incl. suburbs): Abu Dhabi 471,000 (Source: UN, *World Urbanization Prospects: The 2001 Revision*).

BIRTHS AND DEATHS
(UN estimates, annual averages)

	1985–90	1990–95	1995–2000
Birth rate (per 1,000)	27.0	19.6	16.0
Death rate (per 1,000)	3.9	3.7	3.6

Source: UN, *World Population Prospects: The 2000 Revision*.

1995: 4,779 registered deaths (death rate 2.1 per 1,000) (Source: UN, *Population and Vital Statistics Report*).

1996: 47,050 registered live births (birth rate 19.3 per 1,000) (Source: UN, *Population and Vital Statistics Report*).

Expectation of life (WHO estimates, years at birth): 71.7 (males 70.7; females 74.7) in 2001 (Source: WHO, *World Health Report*).

ECONOMICALLY ACTIVE POPULATION
('000 persons)

	1995*	2000
Agriculture, hunting and forestry	96.8	129.6
Fishing	8.1	10.8
Mining and quarrying	30.3	40.8
Manufacturing	143.6	195.0
Electricity, gas and water supply	13.1	17.5
Construction	253.8	340.1
Wholesale and retail trade; repair of motor vehicles, motorcycles and personal and household goods	183.1	246.6
Hotels and restaurants	45.8	61.9
Transport, storage and communications . . .	93.8	126.2
Financial intermediation	16.7	22.8
Real estate, renting and business activities	33.5	45.3
Public administration and defence; compulsory social security	175.1	235.4
Education.	49.2	69.5
Health and social work	23.6	33.3
Other community, social and personal service activities	40.0	53.8
Private households with employed persons . .	103.2	147.4
Extra-territorial organizations and bodies . .	1.2	1.7
Not classifiable by economic activity	0.9	1.2
Total employed	1,311.8	1,779.0
Unemployed	24.1	41.0
Total labour force.	1,335.9	1,820.0
Males	1,180.1	1,587.7
Females	155.8	232.3

* Census figures.

Source: ILO, *Yearbook of Labour Statistics*.

Health and Welfare

KEY INDICATORS

Total fertility rate (children per woman, 2001) . . .	3.0
Under-5 mortality rate (per 1,000 live births, 2001) . . .	9
HIV/AIDS (% of persons aged 15–49, 1994).	0.18
Physicians (per 1,000 head, 1997)	1.81
Hospital beds (per 1,000 head, 1996)	2.64
Health expenditure (2000): US $ per head (PPP)	767
Health expenditure (2000): % of GDP	3.2
Health expenditure (2000): public (% of total)	77.7
Access to water (% of persons, 2000).	–
Access to sanitation (% of persons, 2000)	–
Human Development Index (2000): ranking	46
Human Development Index (2000): value	0.812

For sources and definitions, see explanatory note on p. vi.

Agriculture

PRINCIPAL CROPS
('000 metric tons)

	1999	2000	2001
Potatoes	5.3	15.6	11.5
Cabbages	53.7	294.3	294.3*
Spinach	148.7	619.8	619.8*
Tomatoes	1,157.4	946.4	331.1
Cauliflower	19.6	22.8	12.5
Pumpkins, squash and gourds	42.6	40.2	40.2*
Cucumbers and gherkins	16.9	36.8	36.8*
Aubergines (Eggplants)	25.9	140.9	140.9*
Chillies and green peppers	6.6	17.8	4.3
Green onions and shallots	20.2	83.1	83.1*
Lemons and limes	18.5	17.2	16.2
Watermelons	12.2	13.3	5.6
Cantaloupes and other melons	100.9	165.3	165.3*
Mangoes	9.7	9.6	9.1
Dates	536.0	757.6	757.6*

* FAO estimate.

Source: FAO.

LIVESTOCK
('000 head, year ending September)

	1999	2000	2001*
Cattle	91	96	96
Camels	207	220	220
Sheep	467	495	500
Goats	1,207	1,279	1,279
Chickens*	13,680	16,800	16,900

* FAO estimates.

Source: FAO.

LIVESTOCK PRODUCTS
('000 metric tons)

	1999	2000	2001*
Beef and veal*	7.6	8.5	8.8
Camel meat*	12.3	13.1	13.1
Mutton and lamb*	18.2	16.0	14.4
Goat meat*	7.9	8.4	8.4
Poultry meat*	29.4	36.3	36.3
Cows' milk*	8.7	9.8	9.8
Camels' milk	31.5	33.3	33.3
Sheep's milk	9.3	9.8	9.8
Goats' milk	27.9	29.6	29.6
Hen eggs	13.0	14.6†	14.8

* FAO estimates.
† Unofficial figure.

Source: FAO.

Fishing

('000 metric tons, live weight)

	1998	1999	2000
Capture	114.7	117.6	105.5
Groupers	7.3	7.4	24.0
Snappers and jobfishes	3.7	3.8	1.7
Grunts and sweetlips	1.9	2.0	4.2
Emperors (Scavengers)	12.3	12.6	19.6
King soldier bream	2.8	2.9	3.6
Indian oil sardine	4.1	4.1	—
Sardinellas	9.2	9.5	6.1
Stolephorus anchovies	10.3	10.6	2.7
Narrow-barred Spanish mackerel	7.1	7.3	6.6
Longtail tuna	3.7	3.7	—
Jacks and crevalles	7.4	7.6	3.1
Carangids	6.8	7.0	3.1
Indian mackerel	4.7	4.8	4.8
Aquaculture	0.0	0.0	0.0
Total catch	114.7	117.6	105.5

Source: FAO, *Yearbook of Fishery Statistics*.

Mining*

	1999	2000	2001
Crude petroleum (million barrels)	756	815	790
Natural gas (million cu metres)†	38,500	39,800	41,300

* Estimates.
† On a dry basis.

Source: US Geological Survey.

Industry

SELECTED PRODUCTS
('000 metric tons, unless otherwise indicated)

	1996	1997	1998*
Jet fuels	2,474	2,980	2,550
Motor spirit (petrol)	1,468	1,507	1,539
Naphthas	983	1,250	1,536
Kerosene	144	174	148
Gas-diesel (distillate fuel) oil	3,210	3,309	3,258
Residual fuel oils	2,269	2,113	1,845
Liquefied petroleum gas:			
from natural gas plants	6,147	6,1492	7,509
from petroleum refineries	258	272	272
Electric energy (million kWh)*	26,5727	28,464	31,392

* Provisional or estimated figure(s).

Source: UN, *Industrial Commodity Statistics Yearbook*.

Finance

CURRENCY AND EXCHANGE RATES

Monetary Units
    100 fils = 1 UAE dirham (AED)

Sterling, Dollar and Euro Equivalents (31 December 2002)
    £1 sterling = 5.9193 dirhams
    US $1 = 3.6725 dirhams
    €1 = 3.8514 dirhams
    100 UAE dirhams = £16.89 = $27.23 = €25.96

Exchange Rate: The Central Bank's official rate was set at US $1 = 3.671 dirhams in November 1980. This remained in force until December 1997, when the rate was adjusted to $1 = 3.6725 dirhams.

FEDERAL BUDGET
(million UAE dirhams)

Revenue	1999	2000	2001*
Emirate contributions	13,382	13,312	13,403
Abu Dhabi	12,182	12,112	12,203
Dubai	1,200	1,200	1,200
Other receipts	6,886	6,965	7,422
Enterprise profits	2,351	2,827	2,350
Electricity and water . . .	508	0	0
Other fees and charges . .	4,027	4,138	5,072
Total	20,268	20,277	20,825

Expenditure	1999	2000	2001*
Current expenditure.	19,067	19,680	20,135
Interior and defence†	8,953	8,688	8,796
Education and health	4,771	5,079	5,243
Other ministries	1,986	2,179	2,230
Subsidies and transfers . .	3,357	3,734	3,867
Foreign grants	47	148	260
Development expenditure . .	823	5187	418
Loans and equity.	268	356	205
Total	20,205	20,702	21,018

* Preliminary.

† Partly financed by grants from Abu Dhabi.

Source: IMF, *UAE—Selected Issues and Statistical Appendix* (March 2003).

INTERNATIONAL RESERVES
(US $ million at 31 December)

	2000	2001	2002
Gold*	90.7	90.7	90.7
IMF special drawing rights . .	4.0	2.2	1.5
Reserve position in IMF . .	214.7	225.9	320.6
Foreign exchange†	13,303.9	13,918.2	14,897.2
Total	13,613.3	14,237.0	15,310.0

* Valued at US $228 per troy ounce.

† Figures exclude the Central Bank's foreign assets and accrued interest attributable to the governments of individual emirates.

Source: IMF, *International Financial Statistics.*

MONEY SUPPLY
(million UAE dirhams at 31 December)

	2000	2001	2002
Currency outside banks . . .	10,017	10,537	11,938
Demand deposits at commercial banks	24,050	28,927	35,116
Total money	34,067	39,464	47,054

Source: IMF, *International Financial Statistics.*

COST OF LIVING
(Consumer Price Index; base: 1995 = 100)

	1999	2000	2001*
Food, beverages and tobacco . .	112.8	113.4	113.6
Clothing and footwear	113.5	114.2	114.6
Housing (incl. rent)	96.2	96.1	98.1
Furniture, etc.	112.0	116.4	116.7
Medical care and health services .	125.7	132.5	137.0
Transport and communications .	126.2	130.3	133.0
Recreation and education . . .	114.6	115.2	125.0
All items (incl. others)	109.23	110.7	113.1

* Preliminary.

Source: IMF, *UAE—Selected Issues and Statistical Appendix* (March 2003).

NATIONAL ACCOUNTS
(million UAE dirhams at current prices)

National Income and Product

	1988	1989	1990
Compensation of employees . .	25,226	26,769	27,996
Operating surplus	49,193	60,848	81,633
Domestic factor incomes . .	74,419	87,617	109,629
Consumption of fixed capital . .	14,382	15,127	16,078
Gross domestic product (GDP) at factor cost	88,801	102,744	125,707
Indirect taxes, *less* subsidies . .	−1,695	−1,768	−1,699
GDP in purchasers' values . .	87,106	100,976	124,008
Factor income from abroad . . .	9,940	10,600	10,900
Less Factor income paid abroad .	9,690	10,178	12,200
Gross national income . . .	87,356	101,398	122,708
Less Consumption of fixed capital .	14,382	15,127	16,078
National income in market prices	72,974	86,271	106,630
Other current transfers from abroad (net)	−1,040	−744	−11,000
National disposable income. .	71,934	85,527	95,630

Source: UN, *National Accounts Statistics.*

Expenditure on the Gross Domestic Product

	1999	2000	2001*
Government final consumption expenditure	36,117	39,885	42,131
Private final consumption expenditure	100,365	112,674	118,632
Increase in stocks	2,500	2,680	2,792
Gross fixed capital formation . .	53,916	57,398	59,823
Total domestic expenditure . .	192,898	212,637	223,378
Exports of goods and services . .	141,710	190,070	185,466
Less Imports of goods and services	131,910	143,460	152,280
GDP in purchasers' values . .	202,698	258,991	256,564

* Preliminary.

Source: IMF, *UAE—Selected Issues and Statistical Appendix* (March 2003).

Gross Domestic Product by Economic Activity

	1999	2000	2001*
Agriculture and fishing	7,551	9,047	8,862
Mining and quarrying	50,450	87,372	75,589
Crude oil	49,794	86,690	74,892
Manufacturing	26,539	34,762	35,087
Electricity and water	4,416	4,615	4,890
Construction	16,621	16,857	17,446
Wholesale and retail trade . . .	21,535	22,268	22,838
Restaurants and hotels	4,720	5,026	5,700
Transport, storage and communications	15,247	17,247	19,381
Financial institutions and insurance	13,663	14,862	16,903
Real estate and business services .	18,384	19,068	19,662
Government services	22,458	25,561	27,504
Other community, social and personal services	5,071	5,465	6,007
Sub-total	206,656	262,150	259,869
Less Imputed bank service charge	4,858	4,171	4,566
Total	201,797	257,979	255,303

* Preliminary.

Source: IMF, *UAE—Selected Issues and Statistical Appendix* (March 2003).

BALANCE OF PAYMENTS
(million UAE dirhams)*

	1999	2000	2001†
Exports of goods f.o.b.	134,100	182,100	176,900
Imports of goods c.i.f.	−102,500	−113,100	−120,600
Trade balance	31,600	69,000	56,300
Services and other income (net)	4,900	12,700	−1,100
Balance on goods, services and income	36,500	81,700	55,200
Current transfers (net)	−14,400	−14,600	−15,500
Current balance	22,100	67,100	39,700
Short-term private capital	6,100	−13,300	−11,000
Other capital	9,500	−13,700	2,800
Net errors and omissions	−324,100	−29,700	−29,700
Overall balance	5,600	10,400	1,800

* Figures are rounded to the nearest 100 million dirhams.
† Preliminary.

Source: IMF, *UAE—Selected Issues and Statistical Appendix* (March 2003).

External Trade

PRINCIPAL COMMODITIES (million UAE dirhams)

Imports c.i.f.*	1999	2000	2001†
Live animals and animal products.	2,834	2,900	3,314
Vegetable products	4,815	5,135	5,831
Prepared foodstuffs, beverages, spirits and tobacco.	2,578	2,540	3,387
Chemical products, etc.	5,750	5,998	6,914
Plastics, rubber and articles thereof	3,668	3,760	4,810
Textiles and textile articles.	10,914	10,642	15,322
Pearls, precious or semi-precious stones, precious metals, etc.	2,925	3,499	2,481
Base metals and articles of base metal	8,263	8,587	9,267
Machinery and electrical equipment	22,845	24,871	26,067
Vehicles and other transport equipment	13,609	15,880	15,464
Miscellaneous manufactured articles	2,944	3,007	3,302
Total (incl. others)	91,711	98,119	110,454

Exports f.o.b.‡	1999	2000	2001†
Live animals and animal products.	122	102	201
Prepared foodstuffs, beverages, spirits and tobacco.	309	343	365
Mineral products.	297	349	335
Chemical products, etc.	297	293	422
Textiles and textile articles.	942	1,005	1,160
Stone, plaster, cement, ceramic and glassware	175	162	217
Pearls, precious stones and precious metals	237	276	224
Base metals and articles of base metal	2,656	3,052	2,997
Machinery and electrical equipment	163	246	95
Vehicles and other transport equipment	158	135	286
Total (incl. others)§	5,934	6,561	7,012

* Imports of the Emirates of Abu Dhabi, Dubai and Sharjah only.
† Preliminary.
‡ Excluding hydrocarbons.
§ Excluding free zone exports.

Source: IMF, *UAE—Selected Issues and Statistical Appendix.*

PRINCIPAL TRADING PARTNERS
(US $ million)

Imports	1997	1998	1999
Australia	452.1	425.0	58.9
Belgium-Luxembourg	264.7	321.0	—
China, People's Republic	1,894.2	1,718.0	1,604.3
France (incl. Monaco)	848.0	1,062.0	1,697.6
Germany	1,557.8	1,849.0	1,845.3
Hong Kong	1,739.2	202.0	200.4
India	1,333.2	1,339.0	1,983.8
Indonesia	640.2	610.0	551.3
Iran	343.0	325.0	300.4
Italy (incl. San Marino and Vatican).	1,195.3	1,350.0	1,522.8
Japan	2,298.9	2,606.0	2,451.0
Korea, Republic	1,177.7	1,180.0	1,168.3
Malaysia	350.9	329.0	368.2
Netherlands	386.4	453.0	531.8
Pakistan	260.7	264.0	297.9
Saudi Arabia	0.0	843.0	904.3
Singapore	207.9	309.0	340.8
Spain	257.6	297.0	264.2
Sweden	180.5	340.0	243.5
Switzerland-Liechtenstein	248.3	372.0	398.3
Thailand	451.0	469.0	484.0
Turkey.	207.4	224.0	281.0
United Kingdom	1,986.5	1,872.0	2,094.7
USA	2,773.4	2,493.0	2,570.6
Total (incl. others)	24,562.6	24,728.0	25,911.3

Exports*	1991†	1992†
Bahrain	34.7	43.3
Congo, Republic	17.7	0.0
France (incl. Monaco)	22.9	20.3
Germany	45.6	54.2
India	12.4	22.1
Japan	244.3	148.7
Korea, Republic	35.3	42.4
Kuwait	20.0	36.5
Netherlands	9.2	35.5
Oman	70.5	72.9
Pakistan	15.2	14.9
Saudi Arabia.	19.1	35.0
Thailand	22.0	19.2
United Kingdom.	28.0	89.9
USA	26.1	45.7
Yemen.	20.2	35.5
Total (incl. others)	754.4	899.3

* Excluding crude petroleum.
† Excluding re-exports.

1998: Bahrain 86.0; France (incl. Monaco) 106.6; Germany 186.6; India 1,637.6; Iran 500.8; Japan 7,582.6; Kenya 283.4; Korea, Republic 1,930.9; Kuwait 168.7; Netherlands 81.2; Oman 1,302.2; Pakistan 529.4; Saudi Arabia 447.2; Singapore 956.9; Thailand 657.3; United Kingdom 841.8; USA 644.0; Yemen 177.4; Total (incl. others) 25,662.0.

Source: UN, *International Trade Statistics Yearbook.*

Transport

ROAD TRAFFIC
('000 motor vehicles in use)

	1994	1995	1996
Passenger cars	332.5	321.6	346.3
Commercial vehicles.	87.2	84.2	89.3

Source: UN, *Statistical Yearbook.*

SHIPPING

Merchant Fleet
(registered at 31 December)

	1999	2000	2001
Number of vessels	322	350	341
Total displacement ('000 grt)	786.5	978.8	746.4

Source: Lloyd's Register of Shipping, *World Fleet Statistics.*

International Sea-borne Shipping
(estimated freight traffic, '000 metric tons)

	1988	1989	1990
Goods loaded	63,380	72,896	88,153
Crude petroleum	54,159	63,387	78,927
Other cargo.	9,221	9,509	9,226
Goods unloaded	8,973	8,960	9,595

Source: UN, *Monthly Bulletin of Statistics*.

CIVIL AVIATION
(traffic on scheduled services)*

	1997	1998	1999
Kilometres flown (million) . . .	85	94	106
Passengers carried ('000) . . .	4,720	5,264	5,848
Passenger-km (million)	13,519	15,633	18,154
Total ton-km (million) . . .	2,107	2,403	2,950

* Figures include an apportionment (one-quarter) of the traffic of Gulf Air, a multinational airline with its headquarters in Bahrain.

Source: UN, *Statistical Yearbook*.

Tourism

ARRIVALS BY NATIONALITY

Country	1998	1999	2000
Egypt	77,876	85,259	94,058
France	52,136	65,755	60,955
Germany	100,958	147,736	171,519
India	175,237	216,219	235,493
Iran	127,571	137,678	154,861
Pakistan	97,827	115,441	136,061
Russia	331,026	232,081	228,785
United Kingdom	229,631	293,025	337,865
USA	75,805	94,502	100,547
Total (incl. others)*	2,990,539	3,392,614	3,906,545

* Total includes domestic tourists.

Dubai tourism receipts (US $ million): 562 in 1998; 607 in 1999.

Source: partly World Tourism Organization, *Yearbook of Tourism Statistics*.

Communications Media

	1999	2000	2001
Television receivers ('000 in use) .	740	760	n.a.
Telephones ('000 main lines in use)	975.2	1,020.1	1,052.9
Mobile cellular telephones ('000 subscribers).	832.3	1,428.1	1,909.3
Personal computers ('000 in use)	300	400	n.a.
Internet users ('000)	400	735	900

1996: Daily newspapers 7 (combined circulation 384,000 copies).

1997 ('000 in use): Radio receivers 820; Facsimile machines 50.

Sources: UNESCO, *Statistical Yearbook*; UN, *Statistical Yearbook*; International Telecommunication Union.

Education

(1996/97, unless otherwise indicated)

	Teachers	Pupils/Students		
		Males	Females	Total
Pre-primary	3,110	28,920	26,704	55,624
Primary.	16,148	134,817	124,692	259,509
Secondary:				
general	9,832*	88,644	90,195	178,839
vocational	249	n.a.	n.a.	1,925
University	728†	4,519	11,694	16,213
Other higher†	354	627	1,110	1,737

* Figure refers to 1995/96.
† Figure(s) refer to 1991/92.

Source: UNESCO, *Statistical Yearbook*.

Adult literacy rate (UNESCO estimates): 76.3% (males 75.0%; females 79.3%) in 2000 (Source: UNDP, *Human Development Report*).

Directory

The Constitution

A provisional Constitution for the UAE took effect in December 1971. This laid the foundation for the federal structure of the Union of the seven emirates, previously known as the Trucial States.

The highest federal authority is the Supreme Council of Rulers, which comprises the rulers of the seven emirates. It elects the President and Vice-President from among its members. The President appoints a Prime Minister and a Council of Ministers. Proposals submitted to the Council require the approval of at least five of the Rulers, including those of Abu Dhabi and Dubai. The legislature is the Federal National Council, a consultative assembly comprising 40 members appointed by the emirates for a two-year term.

In July 1975 a committee was appointed to draft a permanent federal constitution, but the National Council decided in 1976 to extend the provisional document for five years. The provisional Constitution was extended for another five years in December 1981, and for further periods of five years in 1986 and 1991. In November 1976, however, the Supreme Council amended Article 142 of the provisional Constitution so that the authority to levy armed forces was placed exclusively under the control of the federal Government. Legislation designed to make the provisional Constitution permanent was endorsed by the Federal National Council in June 1996, after it had been approved by the Supreme Council of Rulers.

The Government

HEAD OF STATE

President: Sheikh ZAYED BIN SULTAN AN-NAHYAN (Ruler of Abu Dhabi, took office as President of the UAE on 2 December 1971; re-elected 1976, 1981, 1991, 1996 and 2 December 2001).

Vice-President: Sheikh MAKTOUM BIN RASHID AL-MAKTOUM (Ruler of Dubai).

SUPREME COUNCIL OF RULERS
(with each Ruler's date of accession)

Ruler of Abu Dhabi: Sheikh ZAYED BIN SULTAN AN-NAHYAN (1966).

Ruler of Dubai: Sheikh MAKTOUM BIN RASHID AL-MAKTOUM (1990).

Ruler of Sharjah: Sheikh SULTAN BIN MUHAMMAD AL-QASIMI (1972).

Ruler of Ras al-Khaimah: Sheikh SAQR BIN MUHAMMAD AL-QASIMI (1948).

Ruler of Umm al-Qaiwain: Sheikh RASHID BIN AHMAD AL-MU'ALLA (1981).

Ruler of Ajman: Sheikh HUMAID BIN RASHID AN-NUAIMI (1981).

Ruler of Fujairah: Sheikh HAMAD BIN MUHAMMAD ASH-SHARQI (1974).

COUNCIL OF MINISTERS
(April 2003)

Prime Minister: Sheikh MAKTOUM BIN RASHID AL-MAKTOUM.

Deputy Prime Minister: Sheikh SULTAN BIN ZAYED AN-NAHYAN.

Minister of the Interior: Lt-Gen. Dr MUHAMMAD SAID AL-BADI.

Minister of Foreign Affairs: RASHID ABDULLAH AN-NUAIMI.

Minister of Finance and Industry: Sheikh HAMDAN BIN RASHID AL-MAKTOUM.

Minister of Defence: Sheikh MUHAMMAD BIN RASHID AL-MAKTOUM.

Minister of Economy and Commerce: Sheikh FAHIM BIN SULTAN AL-QASIMI.

Minister of Information and Culture: Sheikh ABDULLAH BIN ZAYED AN-NAHYAN.

Minister of Communications: AHMAD BIN HUMAID AT-TAYER.

Minister of Public Works and Housing: RAKKAD BIN SALEM AR-RAKKAD.

Minister of Higher Education and Scientific Research: Sheikh NAHYAN BIN MUBARAK AN-NAHYAN.

Minister of Health: HAMAD ABD AR-RAHMAN AL-MADFA.

Minister of Electricity and Water: HUMAID BIN NASSER AL-OWAIS.

Minister of Labour and Social Affairs: MATEER HUMAID AT-TAYER.

Minister of Planning: Sheikh HUMAID BIN AHMAD AL-MU'ALLA.

Minister of Petroleum and Mineral Resources: OBEID BIN SAIF AN-NASIRI.

Minister of Agriculture and Fisheries: SAID MUHAMMAD AR-RAGABANI.

Minister of Education and Youth: ALI ABD AL-AZIZ ASH-SHARHAN.

Minister of Justice, Islamic Affairs and Awqaf (Religious Endowments): MUHAMMAD NAKHIRA ADH-DHAHERI.

Minister of State for Cabinet Affairs: SAID KHALFAN AL-GHAITH.

Minister of State for Finance and Industry: MUHAMMAD KHALFAN BIN KHARBASH.

Minister of State for Foreign Affairs: Sheikh HAMDAN BIN ZAYED AN-NAHYAN.

Minister of State for Affairs of the Supreme Council: Sheikh MAJEED BIN SAID AN-NUAIMI.

Director-General of the President's Office: Sheikh MANSOUR BIN ZAYED AN-NAHYAN.

FEDERAL MINISTRIES

Office of the Prime Minister: POB 12848, Dubai; tel. (4) 3534550; fax (4) 3530111.

Office of the Deputy Prime Minister: POB 831, Abu Dhabi; tel. (2) 4451000; fax (2) 4450066.

Ministry of Agriculture and Fisheries: POB 213, Abu Dhabi; tel. (2) 6662781; fax (2) 6654787; e-mail maf@uae.gov.ae; internet www.uae.gov.ae/maf.

Ministry of Communications: POB 900, Abu Dhabi; tel. (2) 6651900; fax (2) 6651691.

Ministry of Defence: POB 46616, Abu Dhabi; tel. (4) 4461300; fax (4) 4463286.

Ministry of Economy and Commerce: POB 901, Abu Dhabi; tel. (2) 6265000; fax (2) 6215339; e-mail moec@uae.gov.ae; internet www.uae.gov.ae/moec.

Ministry of Education and Youth: POB 295, Abu Dhabi; tel. (2) 6213800; fax (2) 6313778; internet www.education.gov.ae.

Ministry of Electricity and Water: POB 629, Abu Dhabi; tel. (2) 6274222; fax (2) 6269738; e-mail moew@uae.gov.ae; internet www.uae.gov.ae/moew.

Ministry of Finance and Industry: POB 433, Abu Dhabi; tel. (2) 6726000; fax (2) 6768414; e-mail mofi@uae.gov.ae; internet www.uae.gov.ae/mofi.

Ministry of Foreign Affairs: POB 1, Abu Dhabi; tel. (2) 6652200; fax (2) 6668015; e-mail mofa@uae.gov.ae.

Ministry of Health: POB 848, Abu Dhabi; tel. (2) 6330000; fax (2) 6726000; e-mail moh@uae.gov.ae; internet www.uae.gov.ae/moh.

Ministry of Higher Education and Scientific Research: POB 45253, Abu Dhabi; tel. (2) 6428000; fax (2) 6427262; e-mail mohe@uae.gov.ae; internet www.uae.gov.ae/mohe.

Ministry of Information and Culture: POB 17, Abu Dhabi; tel. (2) 4453000; fax (2) 4452504; e-mail mic@uae.gov.ae.

Ministry of the Interior: POB 398, Abu Dhabi; tel. (2) 4414666; fax (2) 4414938.

Ministry of Justice and Islamic Affairs and Awqaf (Religious Endowments): POB 260, Abu Dhabi; tel. (2) 6814000; fax (2) 6810680; e-mail moia@uae.gov.ae; internet www.uae.gov.ae/moia.

Ministry of Labour and Social Affairs: POB 809, Abu Dhabi; tel. (2) 6671700; fax (2) 6665889; e-mail molsa@uae.gov.ae.

Ministry of Petroleum and Mineral Resources: POB 59, Abu Dhabi; tel. (2) 6651810; fax (2) 6664573; e-mail mopmr@uae.gov.ae.

Ministry of Planning: POB 904, Abu Dhabi; tel. (2) 6271100; fax (2) 6269942; e-mail mop@uae.gov.ae; internet www.uae.gov.ae/mop.

Ministry of Public Works and Housing: POB 878, Abu Dhabi; tel. (2) 6651778; fax (2) 6665598; e-mail mpwh@uae.gov.ae.

Ministry of State for Affairs of the Supreme Council: POB 545, Abu Dhabi; tel. (2) 6323900; fax (2) 6344225.

Ministry of State for Cabinet Affairs: POB 899, Abu Dhabi; tel. (2) 6811106; fax (2) 6812968; e-mail moca@uae.gov.ae; internet www.uae.gov.ae/moca.

Ministry of State for Finance and Industrial Affairs: POB 433, Abu Dhabi; tel. (2) 771133; fax (2) 793255.

Ministry of State for Foreign Affairs: POB 1, Abu Dhabi; tel. (2) 6660888; fax (2) 6652883.

Legislature

FEDERAL NATIONAL COUNCIL

Formed under the provisional Constitution, the Council is composed of 40 members from the various emirates (eight each from Abu Dhabi and Dubai, six each from Sharjah and Ras al-Khaimah, and four each from Ajman, Fujairah and Umm al-Qaiwain). Each emirate appoints its own representatives separately. The Council studies laws proposed by the Council of Ministers and can reject them or suggest amendments.

Speaker: SAID MUHAMMAD SAID AL-GHANDI.

Diplomatic Representation

EMBASSIES IN THE UNITED ARAB EMIRATES

Afghanistan: Abu Dhabi; POB 5687, Abu Dhabi; tel. (2) 661244; fax (2) 655310; reopened February 2002.

Algeria: POB 3070, Abu Dhabi; tel. (2) 448943; fax (2) 447068; Ambassador MUHAMMAD MELLOUH.

Argentina: POB 3325, Abu Dhabi; tel. (2) 4436838; fax (2) 4431392; e-mail embar@emirates.net.ae; Ambassador MARIO QUADRI CASTILLO.

Bahrain: POB 3367, Abu Dhabi; tel. (2) 6657500; fax (2) 6674141; Ambassador Sheikh AHMAD BIN KHALIFA AL-KHALIFA.

Bangladesh: POB 2504, Abu Dhabi; tel. (2) 4465100; fax (2) 4464733; e-mail banglaad@emirates.net.ae; Ambassador MIRZA SHAMSUZZAMAN.

Belgium: POB 3686, Abu Dhabi; tel. (2) 319449; fax (2) 319353; Ambassador HENRY O. LOBERT.

Belize: POB 43432, Abu Dhabi; tel. (2) 333554; fax (2) 330429; Ambassador ELHAM S. FREIHA.

Bosnia and Herzegovina: POB 43362, Abu Dhabi; tel. (2) 6444164; fax (2) 6443619; Chargé d'affaires a.i. SALKO ČANIĆ.

Brazil: POB 3027, Abu Dhabi; tel. (2) 665352; fax (2) 654559; Ambassador JOSÉ FERREIRA LOPES.

Brunei: POB 5836, Abu Dhabi; tel. (2) 4491100; fax (2) 4491567; e-mail kbdauh98@emirates.net.ae; Ambassador Dato MALAI HAJI AHMAD BIN SYED HAJI MASHOR.

Canada: POB 6970, Abu Dhabi; tel. (2) 4456969; fax (2) 4458787; internet www.dfait-maeci.gc.ca/world/embassies/abudhabi; e-mail abdbi@dfait-maeci.gc.ca; Ambassador DAVID HUTTON.

China, People's Republic: POB 2741, Abu Dhabi; tel. (2) 434276; fax (2) 435440; Ambassador ZHANG ZHIJUN.

Czech Republic: POB 27009, Abu Dhabi; tel. (2) 782800; fax (2) 795716; Chargé d'affaires JOSEF KOUTSKY.

Egypt: POB 4026, Abu Dhabi; tel. (2) 445566; fax (2) 449878; Ambassador BAHAA ELDIN MOSTAFA REDA.

Eritrea: POB 2597, Abu Dhabi; tel. (2) 331838; fax (2) 346451; Ambassador MUHAMMAD OMAR MAHMOUD.

Finland: POB 3634, Abu Dhabi; tel. (2) 6328927; fax (2) 6325063; e-mail finemb@emirates.net.ae; internet www.finabu.com; Ambassador RISTO REKOLA.

France: POB 4014, Abu Dhabi; tel. (2) 4435100; fax (2) 4434158; e-mail ambafr@emirates.net.ae; internet www.ambafrance.org.ae; Ambassador FRANÇOIS GOUYETTE.

Germany: POB 2591, Abu Dhabi; tel. (2) 4435630; fax (2) 4455712; e-mail germemb@emirates.net.ae; internet www.germemb.org.ae; Ambassador Dr ALEXANDER MÜHLEN.

Greece: POB 5483, Abu Dhabi; tel. (2) 6654847; fax (2) 6656008; e-mail grembauh@emirates.net.ae; Ambassador GEORGE ZOIS.

Hungary: POB 44450, Abu Dhabi; tel. (2) 6660107; fax (2) 6667877; e-mail hungexad@emirates.net.ae; Chargé d'affaires a.i. IVAN P. NOVAK.

India: POB 4090, Abu Dhabi; tel. (2) 6664800; fax (2) 6651518; e-mail indiauae@emirates.net.ae; internet www.indiaembassyuae.org; Ambassador K. C. SINGH.

Indonesia: POB 7256, Abu Dhabi; tel. (2) 454448; fax (2) 455453; Ambassador ABDULLAH FUAD RACHMAN.

Iran: POB 4080, Abu Dhabi; tel. (2) 447618; fax (2) 448714; e-mail iranemb@emirates.net.ae; internet www.iranembassy.org.ae; Ambassador KAMAL SADEQI.

Italy: POB 46752, Abu Dhabi; tel. (2) 4435622; fax (2) 4434337; e-mail ambitcom@emirates.net.ae; internet www.italian-embassy.org.ae; Ambassador DOMENICO PEDATA.

Japan: POB 2430, Abu Dhabi; tel. (2) 4435969; fax (2) 4434219; Ambassador TOSHIO MOCHIZUKI.

Jordan: POB 4024, Abu Dhabi; tel. (2) 4447100; fax (2) 4449157; Ambassador EID KAMEL AR-RODAN.

Kenya: POB 3854, Abu Dhabi; tel. (2) 666300; fax (2) 652827; Ambassador MUDE DAE MUDE.

Korea, Republic: POB 3270, Abu Dhabi; tel. (2) 4435337; fax (2) 4435348; e-mail keauhlee@emirates.net.ae; Ambassador SUN-YONG KANG.

Kuwait: POB 926, Abu Dhabi; tel. (2) 446888; fax (2) 444990; Ambassador IBRAHIM AL-MANSOUR.

Kyrgyzstan: Abu Dhabi.

Lebanon: POB 4023, Abu Dhabi; tel. (2) 4492100; fax (2) 4493500; e-mail libanamb@emirates.net.ae; Ambassador HASSAN BERRO.

Libya: POB 5739, Abu Dhabi; tel. (2) 450030; fax (2) 450033; Chargé d'affaires ABDUL HAMID ALI SHAIKHY.

Malaysia: POB 3887, Abu Dhabi; tel. (2) 4482775; fax (2) 4482779; e-mail mwadhabi@emirates.net.ae; Ambassador Dato' Syed HUSSEIN AL-HABSHEE.

Mauritania: POB 2714, Abu Dhabi; tel. (2) 462724; fax (2) 465772; Ambassador TELMIDI OULD MUHAMMAD AMMAR.

Morocco: POB 4066, Abu Dhabi; tel. (2) 433963; fax (2) 433917; Ambassador ABDELLAH AZMANI.

Netherlands: POB 46560, Abu Dhabi; tel. (2) 6321920; fax (2) 6313158; e-mail nlgovabu@emirates.net.ae; Ambassador JOSEPH P. M. WOLFSWINKEL.

Norway: POB 47270, Abu Dhabi; tel. (2) 6211221; fax (2) 6213313; e-mail emb.abudhabi@mfa.no; Ambassador ULF CHRISTIANSEN.

Oman: POB 2517, Abu Dhabi; tel. (2) 463333; fax (2) 464633; Ambassador SULTAN AL-BUSAIDI.

Pakistan: POB 846, Abu Dhabi; tel. (2) 447800; fax (2) 447172; Chargé d'affaires ABDUL RAZZAK SOOMRO.

Philippines: Abu Dhabi; tel. (2) 345665; fax (2) 313559; Ambassador JOSEPH GERARD B. ANGELES.

Poland: POB 2334, Abu Dhabi; tel. (2) 4465200; fax (2) 4462967; e-mail polcon99@emirates.net.ae; internet www.plembassy.gov.ae; Chargé d'affaires MIROSLAW ADAMCZYK.

Qatar: 26th St, Al-Minaseer, POB 3503, Abu Dhabi; tel. (2) 435900; fax (2) 434800; Ambassador ABDULLAH M. AL-UTHMAN.

Romania: 9 Sudan St, Sector 2/35, POB 70416, Abu Dhabi; tel. (2) 6666346; fax (2) 6651598; e-mail romaniae@emirates.net.ae; Ambassador IOAN EMIL VASILIU.

Russia: POB 8211, Abu Dhabi; tel. (2) 721797; fax (2) 788731; Ambassador OLEG DERKOVSKII.

Saudi Arabia: POB 4057, Abu Dhabi; tel. (2) 445700; fax (2) 448491; Ambassador SALEH MUHAMMAD AL-GHUFAILI.

Slovakia: POB 3382, Abu Dhabi; tel. (2) 6321674; fax (2) 6315839; e-mail slovemb@emirates.net.ae; Ambassador PETER ZSOLDOS.

Somalia: POB 4155, Abu Dhabi; tel. (2) 669700; fax (2) 651580; Ambassador HUSSEIN MUHAMMAD BULLALEH.

South Africa: Madinat Zayed, an-Najdah St, 8th St, Villa 12A, POB 29446, Abu Dhabi; tel. (2) 6337565; fax (2) 6333909; e-mail saemb@emirates.net.ae; internet www.southafrica.co.ae; Ambassador DIK-GANG MOOPELOP.

Spain: POB 46474, Abu Dhabi; tel. (2) 213544; fax (2) 342978; Ambassador MANUEL POMBO.

Sri Lanka: POB 46534, Abu Dhabi; tel. (2) 6426666; fax (2) 6428289; e-mail lankemba@emirates.net.ae; Ambassador J. B. NAKKAWITA.

Sudan: POB 4027, Abu Dhabi; tel. (2) 666788; fax (2) 654231; Chargé d'affaires MOHIEDDIN SLAIM AHMED.

Switzerland: POB 46116, Abu Dhabi; tel. (2) 6274636; fax (2) 6269627; e-mail swiemadh@emirates.net.ae; Ambassador FRANÇOIS BARRAS.

Syria: POB 4011, Abu Dhabi; tel. (2) 4448768; fax (2) 4449387; Ambassador H. E. AHMAD HALLAK.

Thailand: POB 47466, Abu Dhabi; tel. (2) 6421772; fax (2) 6421773; e-mail thaiauh@emirates.net.ae; Ambassador SNANCHART DEVAHASTIN.

Tunisia: POB 4166, Abu Dhabi; tel. (2) 6811331; fax (2) 6812707; e-mail ambtunad@emirates.net.ae; Ambassador MUSTAPHA TLILI.

Turkey: POB 3204, Abu Dhabi; tel. (2) 6655466; fax (2) 6662691; e-mail tcabudbe@emirates.net.ae; Ambassador ERCAN ÖZER.

Ukraine: POB 45714, Abu Dhabi; tel. (2) 327586; fax (2) 327506; e-mail emb_ae@mfa.gov.ua; Ambassador Dr OLEH SEMENETS.

United Kingdom: POB 248, Abu Dhabi; tel. (2) 6326600; fax (2) 6345968; e-mail britembc@emirates.net.ae; internet www.britain-uae.org; Ambassador RICHARD MAKEPEACE.

USA: POB 4009, Abu Dhabi; tel. (2) 4436691; fax (2) 4435441; e-mail paoabud@exchange.usia.gov; internet www.usembabu.gov.ae; Ambassador MARCELLE M. WAHBA.

Yemen: POB 2095, Abu Dhabi; tel. (2) 448454; fax (2) 447978; Ambassador Dr ABDULLAH HUSSAIN BARAKAT.

Judicial System

The 95th article of the Constitution of 1971 provided for the establishment of the Union Supreme Court and Union Primary Tribunals as the judicial organs of State.

The Union has exclusive legislative and executive jurisdiction over all matters that are concerned with the strengthening of the federation, such as foreign affairs, defence and Union armed forces, security, finance, communications, traffic control, education, currency, measures, standards and weights, matters relating to nationality and emigration, Union information, etc.

President Sheikh Zayed signed the law establishing the new federal courts on 9 June 1978. The new law effectively transferred local judicial authorities into the jurisdiction of the federal system.

Primary tribunals in Abu Dhabi, Sharjah, Ajman and Fujairah are now primary federal tribunals, and primary tribunals in other towns in those emirates have become circuits of the primary federal tribunals.

The primary federal tribunal may sit in any of the capitals of the four emirates and have jurisdiction on all administrative disputes between the Union and individuals, whether the Union is plaintiff or defendant. Civil disputes between Union and individuals will be heard by primary federal tribunals in the defendant's place of normal residence.

The law requires that all judges take a constitutional oath before the Minister of Justice and that the courts apply the rules of *Shari'a* (Islamic religious law) and that no judgment contradicts the *Shari'a*. All employees of the old judiciaries will be transferred to the federal authority without loss of salary or seniority.

In February 1994 President Sheikh Zayed ordered that an extensive range of crimes, including murder, theft and adultery, be tried in *Shari'a* courts rather than in civil courts.

Chief Shari'a Justice: AHMAD ABD AL-AZIZ AL-MUBARAK.

Religion

ISLAM

Most of the inhabitants are Muslims of the Sunni sect. About 16% of the Muslims are Shi'ites.

CHRISTIANITY

Roman Catholic Church

Apostolic Vicariate of Arabia: POB 54, Abu Dhabi; tel. (2) 4461895; fax (2) 4465177; e-mail apvicar@emirates.net.ae; responsible for a territory covering most of the Arabian peninsula (including Saudi Arabia, the UAE, Oman, Qatar, Bahrain and Yemen), containing an estimated 1,300,000 Catholics (31 December 2001); Vicar Apostolic Fr GIOVANNI BERNARDO GREMOLI (Titular Bishop of Masuccaba).

The Anglican Communion

Within the Episcopal Church in Jerusalem and the Middle East, the UAE forms part of the diocese of Cyprus and the Gulf. The Anglican congregations in the UAE are entirely expatriate. The Bishop in Cyprus and the Gulf resides in Cyprus, while the Archdeacon in the Gulf is resident in Qatar.

Chaplain, St Andrew's Church: Rev. CLIVE WINDEBANK, St Andrew's Church, POB 262, Abu Dhabi; tel. (2) 4461631; fax (2) 4465869; e-mail standrew@emirates.net.ae.

The Press

The Ministry of Information and Culture has placed a moratorium on new titles.

Abu Dhabi

Abu Dhabi Magazine: POB 662, Abu Dhabi; tel. (2) 214000; fax (2) 348954; f. 1969; Arabic, some articles in English; monthly; Editor ZUHAIR AL-QADI; circ. 18,000.

Adh-Dhafra: POB 4288, Abu Dhabi; tel. (2) 328103; Arabic; weekly; independent; publ. by Dar al-Wahdah.

Emirates News: POB 791, Abu Dhabi; tel. (2) 451446; fax (2) 453662; e-mail emrtnews@emirates.net.ae; f. 1975; English; daily; publ. by Al-Ittihad Press, Publishing and Distribution Corpn; Chair. Sheikh ABDULLAH BIN ZAYED AN-NAHYAN; Man. Editor PETER HELLYER; circ. 21,150.

Al-Fajr (The Dawn): POB 505, Abu Dhabi; tel. (2) 478300; fax (2) 474326; Arabic; daily; Man. Editor OBEID AL-MAZROUI; circ. 28,000.

Hiya (She): POB 2488, Abu Dhabi; tel. (2) 474121; Arabic; weekly for women; publ. by Dar al-Wahdah.

Al-Ittihad (Unity): POB 791, Abu Dhabi; tel. (2) 452206; fax (2) 455126; f. 1972; Arabic; daily and weekly; publ. by Al-Ittihad Press, Publishing and Distribution Corpn; Man. Editor OBEID SULTAN; circ. 58,000 daily, 60,000 weekly.

Majed: POB 791, Abu Dhabi; tel. (2) 4451804; fax (2) 4451455; e-mail majid-magazine@emi.co.ae; internet www.emi.co.ae; Arabic; f. 1979; weekly; children's magazine; Man. Editor AHMAD OMAR; circ. 145,300.

Ar-Riyada wa-Shabab (Sport and Youth): POB 2710, Dubai; tel. (4) 444400; fax (4) 445973; Arabic; weekly; general interest.

UAE and Abu Dhabi Official Gazette: POB 899, Abu Dhabi; tel. (2) 660604; Arabic; daily; official reports and papers.

UAE Press Service Daily News: POB 2035, Abu Dhabi; tel. (2) 44292; f. 1973; English; daily; Editor RASHID AL-MAZROUI.

Al-Wahdah (Unity): POB 2488, Abu Dhabi; tel. (2) 478400; fax (2) 478937; f. 1973; daily; independent; Man. Editor RASHID AWEIDHA; Gen. Man. KHALIFA AL-MASHWI; circ. 20,000.

Zahrat al-Khaleej (Splendour of the Gulf): POB 791, Abu Dhabi; tel. (2) 461600; fax (2) 451653; f. 1979; Arabic; weekly; publ. by Al-Ittihad Press, Publishing and Distribution Corpn; women's magazine; circ. 10,000.

Dubai

Akhbar Dubai (Dubai News): Department of Information, Dubai Municipality, POB 1420, Dubai; f. 1965; Arabic; weekly.

Al-Bayan (The Official Report): POB 2710, Dubai; tel. (4) 688222; fax (4) 688222; f. 1980; owned by Dubai authorities; Arabic; daily; Editor-in-Chief Sheikh HASHER MAKTOUM; circ. 82,575.

Emirates Woman: POB 2331, Dubai; tel. (4) 2824060; fax (4) 2827593; e-mail annabel@motivate.co.ae; f. 1979; Motivate Publishing; English; monthly; fashion, health and beauty; Editor ANNABEL KANTARIA; circ. 18,690.

Gulf News: POB 6519, Dubai; tel. (4) 447100; fax (4) 441627; e-mail editorial@gulf-news.co.ae; internet www.gulf-news.co.ae; f. 1978; An-Nisr Publishing; English; daily; two weekly supplements, *Junior News* (Wednesday), *Gulf Weekly* (Thursday); Editor-in-Chief OBAID HUMAID AT-TAYER; Editor FRANCIS MATTHEW; circ. 86,900.

Al-Jundi (The Soldier): POB 2838, Dubai; tel. (4) 3433033; fax (4) 3433343; e-mail mod5@emirates.net.ae; f. 1973; Arabic; monthly; military and cultural; Editor Brig. KHAMIS BIN HASHER; circ. 4,000–7,000.

Khaleej Times: POB 11243, Dubai; tel. (4) 4382400; fax (4) 4390519; e-mail ktimes@emirates.net.ae; internet www.khaleejtimes.com; f. 1978; a Galadari enterprise; English; daily; free weekly supplement, *Weekend* (Friday); Man. Dir QASSIM MUHAMMAD YOUSUF; Editor S. NIHAL SINGH; circ. 70,000.

Trade and Industry: POB 1457, Dubai; tel. (4) 280000; fax (4) 2028597; e-mail dcciinfo@dcci.org; internet www.dcci.org; f. 1975; Arabic and English; monthly; publ. by Dubai Chamber of Commerce and Industry; circ. 26,000.

What's On: POB 2331, Dubai; tel. (4) 2824060; fax (4) 2824436; e-mail editor-wo@motivate.co.ae; f. 1979; Motivate Publishing; English; monthly; Exec. Editor IAN FAIRSERVICE; circ. 17,905.

Ras al-Khaimah

Akhbar Ras al-Khaimah (Ras al-Khaimah News): POB 87, Ras al-Khaimah; Arabic; monthly; local news.

Al-Ghorfa: POB 87, Ras al-Khaimah; tel. (7) 333511; fax (7) 330233; f. 1970; Arabic and English; free monthly; publ. by Ras al-Khaimah Chamber of Commerce; Editor ZAKI H. SAQR.

Ras al-Khaimah Magazine: POB 200, Ras al-Khaimah; Arabic; monthly; commerce and trade; Chief Editor AHMAD AT-TADMORI.

Sharjah

Al-Azman al-Arabia (Times of Arabia): POB 5823, Sharjah; tel. (6) 356034.

The Gulf Today: POB 30, Sharjah; tel. (6) 5591919; fax (6) 5532737; e-mail tgtmkt@alkhaleej.co.ae; f. 1995; English; daily; circ. 38,000.

Al-Khaleej (The Gulf): POB 30, Sharjah; tel. (6) 625304; fax (6) 598547; f. 1970; Arabic; daily; political, independent; Editor GHASSAN TAHBOUB; circ. 82,750.

Sawt al-Khaleej (Voice of the Gulf): Sharjah; tel. (6) 358003.

Ash-Sharooq (Sunrise): POB 30, Sharjah; tel. (6) 598777; fax (6) 599336; f. 1970; Arabic; weekly; general interest; Editor YOUSUF AL-HASSAN.

At-Tijarah (Commerce): Sharjah Chamber of Commerce and Industry, POB 580, Sharjah; tel. (6) 5116600; fax (6) 5681119; e-mail scci@emirates.net.ae; internet www.sharjah.gov.ae; f. 1970; Arabic/English; monthly magazine; circ. 50,000; annual trade directory; circ. 100,000.

UAE Digest: Sharjah; tel. (6) 354633; fax (6) 354627; English; monthly; publ. by Universal Publishing; commerce and finance; Man. Dir FARAJ YASSINE; circ. 10,000.

NEWS AGENCIES

Emirates News Agency (WAM): POB 3790, Abu Dhabi; tel. (2) 454545; fax (2) 454694; f. 1977; operated by the Ministry of Information and Culture; Dir IBRAHIM AL-ABED.

UAE Press Service: POB 2035, Abu Dhabi; tel. (2) 820424.

Foreign Bureaux

Agenzia Nazionale Stampa Associata (ANSA) (Italy): POB 44106, Abu Dhabi; tel. (2) 454545.

Kuwait News Agency (KUNA): Apartment 907, 9th Floor, Building No. 728, Zayed I St, Khalidiya, Abu Dhabi; tel. (2) 666994; fax (2) 666935.

Reuters (UK): POB 7872, Abu Dhabi; tel. (2) 328000; fax (2) 333380; Man. JEREMY HARRIS.

Publishers

Al-Ittihad Press, Publishing and Distribution Corpn: POB 791, New Airport Rd, Abu Dhabi; tel. (2) 455555; fax (2) 451653; Chair. KHALFAN BIN MUHAMMAD AR-ROUMI.

All Prints: POB 857, Abu Dhabi; tel. (2) 338235; publishing and distribution; Partners BUSHRA KHAYAT, TAHSEEN S. KHAYAT.

Motivate Publishing: POB 2331, Dubai; tel. (4) 824060; fax (4) 824436; e-mail motivate@emirates.net.ae; f. 1979; books and magazines; Dirs OBAID HUMAID AT-TAYER, IAN FAIRSERVICE.

Broadcasting and Communications

TELECOMMUNICATIONS

Ministry of Communications: see Ministries, above; regulatory authority.

Emirates Telecommunications Corpn (Etisalat): POB 3838, Abu Dhabi; tel. (2) 283333; fax (2) 725456; internet www.etisalat.co .ae; provides telecommunications services throughout the UAE; privatization pending in 1998.

Radio

Abu Dhabi Radio: Abu Dhabi; tel. (2) 451111; fax (2) 451155; f. 1968; broadcasts in Arabic over a wide area; also broadcasts in French, Bengali, Filipino and Urdu; Dir-Gen. ABD AL-WAHAB AR-RADWAN.

Capital Radio: POB 63, Abu Dhabi; tel. (2) 451000; fax (2) 451155; English-language FM music and news station, operated by the Ministry of Information and Culture; Station Manager AIDA HAMZA.

Dubai Radio and Colour Television: POB 1695, Dubai; tel. (4) 370255; fax (4) 374111; broadcasts domestic Arabic and European programmes; Chair. Sheikh HASHER MAKTOUM; Dir-Gen. ABD AL-GHAFOOR SAID IBRAHIM.

Ras al-Khaimah Broadcasting Station: POB 141, Ras al-Khaimah; tel. (7) 851151; fax (7) 353441; two transmitters broadcast in Arabic and Urdu; Dir Sheikh ABD AL-AZIZ BIN HUMAID.

Sharjah Broadcasting Station: POB 155, Sharjah; broadcasts in Arabic and French.

Umm al-Qaiwain Broadcasting Station: POB 444, Umm al-Qaiwain; tel. (6) 7666044; fax (6) 7666055; e-mail uaqfm@emirates .net.ae; f. 1978; broadcasts music and news in Arabic, Malayalam, Sinhala and Urdu; Gen. Man. ALI JASSEM.

UAE Radio and Television—Dubai: POB 1695, Dubai; tel. (4) 3369999; fax (4) 3374111; e-mail dubairtv@emirates.net.ae; internet www.ecssr.ac.ae/05uae.6television.html; broadcasts in Arabic and English to the USA, India and Pakistan, the Far East, Australia and New Zealand, Europe and North and East Africa; Chair. Sheikh HASHEM MAKTOUM; Dir-Gen. AHMED SAEED AL-GAOUD; Controller of Radio HASSAN AHMAD.

Television

Dubai Radio and Colour Television: (see Radio).

UAE Radio and Television-Dubai: see Radio; Controller of Programmes NASIB BITAR.

UAE TV—Abu Dhabi: POB 637, Abu Dhabi; tel. (2) 452000; fax (2) 451470; internet www.ecssr.ac.ae/05uae.6television.html; f. 1968; broadcasts programmes incorporating information, entertainment, religion, culture, news and politics; Dir-Gen. ALI OBAID.

UAE Television—Sharjah: POB 111, Sharjah; tel. (6) 361111; fax (6) 541755; f. 1989; broadcasts in Arabic and Urdu in the northern emirates; Executive Dir MUHAMMAD DIAB AL-MUSA.

Finance

(cap. = capital; dep. = deposits; res = reserves; m. = million; brs = branches; amounts in dirhams, unless otherwise indicated)

BANKING

Central Bank

Central Bank of the United Arab Emirates: POB 854, Abu Dhabi; tel. (2) 6652220; fax (2) 66652504; e-mail uaccbadm@ emirates.net.ae; internet www.uaecb.gov.ae; f. 1973; acts as issuing authority for local currency; superseded UAE Currency Board December 1980; auth. cap. 300m. total assets 50,136m. (Dec. 2000); Chair. MUHAMMAD EID AL-MURAIKHI; Gov. SULTAN NASSER AS-SUWAIDI; 6 brs.

Principal Banks

Abu Dhabi Commercial Bank (ADCB): POB 939, Abu Dhabi; tel. (2) 6962222; fax (2) 6776499; internet www.adcbuae.com; f. 1985 by merger; 65% govt-owned, 35% owned by private investors; cap. 1,250.0m., res 2,858.3m., dep. 20,858.3m. (Dec. 2001); Chair. FADHEL SAEED AD-DARMAKI; CEO and Man. Dir KHALIFA MUHAMMAD HASSAN; 32 brs.

Abu Dhabi Islamic Bank: POB 313, Najda St, Abu Dhabi; tel. (2) 6343000; fax (2) 6342222; e-mail adib@adib.co.ae; internet www .e-adib.com; f. 1997; cap. 1,000.0m., res 127.8m., dep. 4,687.1m. (Dec.

2001); Chair. OBAID SAIF AN-NASSERI; CEO ABD AR-RAHMAN ABD AL-MALIK.

Arab Bank for Investment and Foreign Trade (ARBIFT): POB 46733, ARBIFT Bldg, Hamdan St, Tourist Club Area, Abu Dhabi; tel. (2) 6721900; fax (2) 6777550; e-mail arbiftho@emirates.net.ae; internet www.arbift.com; f. 1976; jointly owned by the UAE Govt, the Libyan Arab Foreign Bank and the Banque Extérieure d'Algérie; cap. 570.0m., res 659.3m., dep. 4,463.1m. (Dec. 2001); Chair. Dr ABD AL-HAFID ZLITNI; Gen. Man. IBRAHIM M. LOOTAH; 2 brs in Abu Dhabi, 1 in Dubai, 1 in al-Ain.

Arab Emirates Investment Bank PJSC: POB 5503, Dubai; tel. (4) 2222191; fax (4) 274351; e-mail aeibank@emirates.net.ae; cap. 40.9m., res 8.9m., dep. 143.5m. (Dec. 1999); Chair. KHALID MUHAMMAD SAEED AL-MULLA; Gen.-Man. SAJJAD AHMAD.

Bank of Sharjah Ltd: POB 1394, Sharjah; tel. (6) 5694411; fax (6) 5694422; e-mail bankshj@emirates.net.ae; internet www .bank-of-sharjah.com; f. 1973; cap. 240m., res 138.8m., dep. 1,503.1m. (Dec. 2001); Chair. AHMAD AN-NOMAN; Gen. Man. VAROUJ NERGUIZIAN; brs in Abu Dhabi and Dubai.

Commercial Bank of Dubai PSC: POB 2668, Deira, Dubai; tel. (4) 3523355; fax (4) 3520444; e-mail cbd-ho@cbd.co.ae; internet www .cbd.co.ae; f. 1969; cap. 450.9m., res 909.1m., dep. 5,909.5m. (Dec. 2001); Chair. AHMAD HUMAID AT-TAYER; Gen. Man. OMAR ABD AR-RAHIM LEYAS; 15 brs.

Commercial Bank International PLC: POB 4449, Dubai; tel. (4) 2275265; fax (4) 2279038; e-mail cbiho@emirates.net.ae; internet www.cbiuae.com; f. 1991; cap. 230.2m., res 96.6m., dep. 2,015.2m. (Dec. 2001); Chair. and Man. Dir SALEH AHMAD ASH-SHALL.

Dubai Bank: Dubai; f. 2002; cap. 300.0m.

Dubai Islamic Bank PLC: POB 1080, Dubai; tel. (4) 2953000; fax (4) 2954000; internet www.alislami.com; f. 1975; cap. 1,000.0m., res 235.0m., dep. 13,337.9 (Dec. 2001); Chair. Dr MUHAMMAD KHALIFAN BIN KHARBASH; 9 brs.

Emirates Bank International PJSC: POB 2923, Dubai; tel. (4) 2256256; fax (4) 2268005; e-mail pnd@emiratesbank.com; internet www.emiratesbank.com; f. 1977 by merger; 77% owned by Govt of Dubai; cap. 918.4m., res 3,095.0m., dep. 13,482.5m. (Dec. 2001); Chair. AHMAD HUMAID AT-TAYER; Man. Dir and CEO ANIS AL-JALLAF; 25 brs in UAE.

First Gulf Bank: POB 3662, Sheikh Zayed St, Abu Dhabi; tel. (2) 6394000; fax (2) 6217721; e-mail fgbabd@emirates.net.ae; f. 1979; cap. 360m., res 135.9m., dep. 1,798.3m. (Dec. 2000); Chair. Sheikh TAHNOON BIN ZAYED AN-NAHYAN; Man. Dir AHMED SAIF AN-NASRI; 5 brs.

Investbank PSC: Al-Borj Ave, POB 1885, Sharjah; tel. (6) 5695550; fax (6) 5694442; e-mail sharjah@invest-bank.com; internet www .invest-bank.com; f. 1975; cap. 300m., res 158.7m., dep. 2,018.3m. (Dec. 2001); Chair. Dr ABDULLAH OMRAN TARYAM; 5 brs.

MashreqBank PSC: POB 1250, Deira, Dubai; tel. (4) 2229131; fax (4) 2226061; internet www.mashreqbank.com; f. 1967 as Bank of Oman; adopted present name 1993; cap. 715.9m., res 837.6m., dep. 18,777.8m. (Dec. 2001); Chair. ABDULLAH AHMAD AL-GHURAIR; Man. Dir and CEO ABD AL-AZIZ AL-GHURAIR; 30 brs.

Middle East Bank PJSC: POB 5547, Deira, Dubai; tel. (4) 2256256; fax (4) 2255322; e-mail pnd@emiratesbank.com; internet www.emiratesbank.com/meb; f. 1976; subsid. (99.8%-owned) of EBI; cap. 500.0m., res 161.5m., dep. 1,718.3m. (Dec. 2001); Vice-Chair. FARDAN BIN ALI AL-FARDAN; 12 brs.

National Bank of Abu Dhabi (NBAD): POB 4, Abu Dhabi; tel. (2) 6666800; fax (2) 6655329; internet www.nbad.co.ae; f. 1968; owned jointly by Abu Dhabi Investment Authority and UAE citizens; cap. 941.6m., res 2,545.6m., dep. 27,729.6m. (Dec. 2001); Chair. Sheikh MUHAMMAD BIN HABROUSH AS-SUWAIDI; CEO MICHAEL H. TOMALIN; 56 brs in UAE.

National Bank of Dubai PJSC: POB 777, Dubai; tel. (4) 2222111; fax (4) 2283000; e-mail contactus@nbd.co.ae; internet www.nbd.co .ae; f. 1963; cap. 864.5m., res 3,609.3m., dep. 27,595.0m. (Dec. 2001); Chair. Dr KHALIFA MUHAMMAD AHMAD SULAYMAN; Gen. Man. R. DOUGLAS DOWIE; 32 brs.

National Bank of Fujairah: POB 887, Fujairah; tel. (9) 2224513; fax (9) 2224516; e-mail fujairah@emirates.net.ae; internet www.nbf .co.ae; f. 1982; owned jointly by Govt of Fujairah (36.78%), Govt of Dubai (9.78%), and UAE citizens and cos (51.25%); cap. 330.0m., res 145.0m., dep. 2,034.6m. (Dec. 2001); Chair. Sheikh SALEH BIN MUHAMMAD ASH-SHARQI; Gen. Man. MICHAEL H. WILLIAMS; 5 brs.

National Bank of Ras al-Khaimah PSC: POB 5300, Ras al-Khaimah; tel. (7) 2281127; fax (7) 2283238; e-mail nbrakho@ emirates.net.ae; f. 1976; cap. 250.0m., res 228.6m., dep. 1,853.7m. (Dec. 2001); Chair. Sheikh KHALID BIN SAQR AL-QASIMI; Gen. Man. J. G. HONEYBILL; 13 brs.

National Bank of Sharjah: POB 4, Al-Borj Ave, Sharjah; tel. (6) 5681000; fax (6) 5680101; e-mail nbsmail@emirates.net.ae; f. 1976; commercial bank; cap. 349.8m., res 267.8m., dep. 1,303.9m. (Dec. 2001); Chair. Sheikh SULTAN BIN MUHAMMAD BIN SULTAN AL-QASSIMI; Gen. Man. SAID MUHAMMAD; 9 brs.

National Bank of Umm al-Qaiwain PSC: POB 800, Umm al-Qaiwain; tel. (6) 7655225; fax (6) 7655440; e-mail edpnbuaq@emirates.net.ae; Chair. Sheikh SA'UD BIN RASHID AL-MU'ALLA; Man. Dir and CEO Sheikh NASSER BIN RASHID AL-MU'ALLA; 10 brs.

Union National Bank: POB 3865, Abu Dhabi; tel. (2) 6741600; fax (2) 6786080; e-mail feedback@unb.co.ae; internet www.unb.co.ae; f. 1983; fmrly Bank of Credit and Commerce (Emirates); cap. 747.4m., res 556.5m., dep. 11,641.3m. (Dec. 2001); Chair. Sheikh NAHYAN BIN MUBARAK AL-NAHYAN; CEO MUHAMMAD NASR ABDEEN; 12 brs in Abu Dhabi, 7 brs in Dubai, 2 each in Sharjah and al-Ain, and one each in Ras al-Khaimah, Ajman and Fujairah.

United Arab Bank: POB 25022, Sharjah; tel. (6) 5733900; fax (6) 5733907; e-mail uarbae@emirates.net.ae; f. 1975; affiliated to Société Générale, France; cap. 227.3m., res 130.6m., dep. 1,286.0m. (Dec. 2000); Chair. Sheikh FAISAL BIN SULTAN AL-QASSIMI; Gen. Man. BERTRAND GIRAUD; 9 brs.

Development Banks

Emirates Industrial Bank: POB 2722, Abu Dhabi; tel. (2) 339700; fax (2) 319191; f. 1982; offers low-cost loans to enterprises with at least 51% local ownership; 51% state-owned; cap. 200m. Chair. MUHAMMAD KHALFAN KHIRBASH; Gen. Man. MUHAMMAD ABD AL-BAKI MUHAMMAD.

United Arab Emirates Development Bank: Abu Dhabi; tel. (2) 344986; f. 1974; participates in development of real estate, agriculture, fishery, livestock and light industries; cap. 500m. Gen. Man. MUHAMMAD SALEM AL-MELEHY.

Foreign Banks

ABN AMRO Bank NV (Netherlands): Istiqlal St, POB 22401, Abu Dhabi; POB 2567, Deira, Dubai; POB 1971, Sharjah; tel. (2) 6335400; fax (2) 6330182; tel. (4) 3512200; fax (4) 3511555; tel. (6) 5093101; fax (6) 5360099; internet www.abnamro-uae.com; f. 1974; cap. 223m., total assets 3,677m. (1999); Man. (Abu Dhabi) BRICE ROPION.

Al-Ahli Bank of Kuwait KSC: POB 1719, Deira, Dubai; tel. (4) 2681118; fax (4) 2684445; e-mail abkdub@emirates.net.ae; Chair. MURAD YOUSUF BEHBEHANI.

Arab-African International Bank (Egypt): POB 1049, Dubai; POB 928, Abu Dhabi; tel. (4) 2223131; fax (4) 2222257; e-mail aaibdxb@emirates.net.ae; internet www.aaibank.com; tel. (2) 6323400; fax (2) 6216009; e-mail aaib@emirates.net.ae; f. 1970; f. 1976; Chair. Dr FAHD AR-RASHID; Gen. Man. (Dubai) MUHAMMAD FARAMAOUI.

Arab Bank PLC (Jordan): POB 875, Abu Dhabi; POB 11364, Dubai; POB 130, Sharjah; POB 4972, Ras al-Khaimah; POB 300, Fujairah; POB 17, Ajman; tel. (2) 334111; fax (2) 336433; tel. (4) 228845; fax (4) 285974; tel. (6) 353994; fax (6) 357182; tel. (7) 228473; fax (7) 222837; tel. (9) 222050; fax (9) 568249; tel. (6) 422431; fax (6) 426871; f. 1970; Man. NAIM KHUSHASHI; 8 local brs.

Bank of Baroda (India): POB 3162, Dubai; tel. (2) 538093; fax (2) 536962; e-mail barbaead@emirates.net.ae; f. 1974; Chair. K. KANNAN; CEO PAR KASH SINGH; also brs in Abu Dhabi, al-Ain, Deira (Dubai), Sharjah and Ras al-Khaimah.

Bank Melli Iran: Regional Office and Main Branch, POB 1894, Dubai; tel. (4) 221462; fax (4) 269157; e-mail bmirodxb@emirates.net.ae; f. 1969; Regional Dir AZIZ AZIMI NOBAR; brs in Dubai, Abu Dhabi, al-Ain, Sharjah, Fujairah and Ras al-Khaimah.

Bank Saderat Iran: POB 700, Abu Dhabi; POB 4182, Dubai; tel. (2) 225155; fax (2) 225062; tel. (4) 221161; fax (4) 215961; also Sharjah, Ajman, Fujairah and al-Ain; Man. ALI VERDI.

Banque Banorabe (France): POB 4370, Dubai; POB 5803, Sharjah; tel. (4) 2284655; fax (4) 2236260; tel. (6) 5736100; fax (6) 5736080; e-mail banorabe@emirates.net.ae; f. 1974; fmrly Banque de l'Orient Arabe et d'Outre Mer; Chair. and Gen. Man. Dr NAAMAN AZHARI; UAE Regional Man. BASSEM M. AL-ARISS.

Banque du Caire (Egypt): POB 533, Abu Dhabi; POB 1502, Dubai; POB 254, Sharjah; POB 618, Ras al-Khaimah; tel. (2) 224900; fax (2) 225081; tel. (4) 715175; fax (4) 713013; tel. (6) 5739222; fax (6) 5739292; tel. (7) 333245; fax (7) 334202; Gulf Regional Man. FOUAD ABD AL-KHALEK TAHOON.

Banque Libanaise pour le Commerce SA (France): POB 4207, Dubai; POB 854, Sharjah; POB 3771, Abu Dhabi; POB 771, Ras al-Khaimah; tel. (4) 222291; fax (4) 279861; e-mail blcad@emirates.net.ae; tel. (6) 724561; fax (6) 727843; e-mail blcdxbrm@emirates.net

.ae; tel. (2) 270909; fax (2) 268851; UAE Regional Man. ELIE N. SALIBA.

Barclays Bank PLC (UK): POB 2734, Abu Dhabi; POB 1891, Zabeel, Dubai; tel. (2) 275313; fax (2) 268060; tel. (4) 351555; fax (4) 366700; Corporate Dir of Gulf JONATHAN PINE.

BNP Paribas (France): POB 2742, Abu Dhabi; POB 7233, Dubai; tel. (2) 6267800; fax (2) 6268638; tel. (4) 2225200; fax (4) 2225849; Gen. Man. (Abu Dhabi) LUC FICHTER; Gen. Man. (Dubai) MICHEL DUBOIS.

Citibank NA (USA): POB 749, Dubai; POB 346, Sharjah; POB 999, Abu Dhabi; POB 294, Ras al-Khaimah; POB 1430, al-Ain; tel. (4) 522100; fax (4) 524942; tel. (6) 354511; tel. (2) 742484; fax (2) 334524; f. 1963; Gen. Man. AHM BIN BREK.

Credit Agricole Indosuez Gulf (France): POB 9256, Dubai; POB 46786, Abu Dhabi; tel. (4) 3314211; fax (4) 3313201; tel. (2) 6267500; fax (2) 6275581; f. 1975; f. 1981; Regional Man. FRANÇOIS RIVIER.

El Nilein Industrial Development Bank (Sudan): POB 6013, Abu Dhabi; tel. (2) 326453; Man. ABDULLAH MAHMOUD AWAD.

Habib Bank AG Zurich (Switzerland): POB 2681, Abu Dhabi; POB 1166, Sharjah; POB 3306, Dubai; tel. (2) 322838; fax (2) 351822; f. 1974; Joint Pres. H. M. HABIB; Vice-Pres. HATIM HUSAIN; 8 brs throughout UAE.

Habib Bank Ltd (Pakistan): POB 888, Dubai; POB 897, Abu Dhabi; tel. (4) 268171; fax (4) 260198; tel. (2) 325665; fax (2) 333620; f. 1967; f. 1975; Sr Vice-Pres. JAVED AKHTAR CHATTHA; 6 other brs in UAE.

HSBC Bank Middle East (United Kingdom): POB 66, Dubai; tel. (4) 3535000; fax (4) 35315641; e-mail hsbcuae@emirates.net.ae; internet www.banking.middleeast.hsbc.com; f. 1946; total assets US $7,832m. (1999); Dep. Chair. ANDREW DIXON; CEO MUKHTAR HUSSAIN; 8 brs throughout UAE.

IntesaBCI SpA: POB 3839, Abu Dhabi; tel. (2) 274224; fax (2) 273709; Dep, Chief Man. DANIÈLE PANIN.

Janata Bank (Bangladesh): POB 2630, Abu Dhabi; POB 3342, Dubai; tel. (2) 344542; fax (2) 348749; tel. (4) 281442; fax (4) 246023; Chair. MUHAMMAD ALI; Man. Dir M. A. HASHEM; brs in al-Ain, Dubai and Sharjah.

Lloyds TSB Bank PLC (UK): POB 3766, Dubai; tel. (4) 3422000; fax (4) 3422660; e-mail ltsbbank@emirates.net.ae; f. 1977; Area Man. RICHARD STOCKDALE.

National Bank of Bahrain BSC: POB 46080, Abu Dhabi; tel. (2) 335288; fax (2) 333783; Sr Man. FAROUK KHALAF.

National Bank of Oman SAOG: POB 3822, Abu Dhabi; tel. (2) 348111; fax (2) 321043; Man. O. R. QUADRI.

Rafidain Bank (Iraq): POB 2727, Abu Dhabi; tel. (2) 335882; fax (2) 326996; Gen. Man. ZANAIB TALEB.

Standard Chartered Bank (UK): POB 240, Abu Dhabi; POB 999, Dubai; POB 5, Sharjah; POB 1240, al-Ain; tel. (2) 330077; fax (2) 341511; tel. (4) 520455; fax (4) 526679; tel. (6) 357788; fax (6) 543604; tel. (3) 641253; fax (3) 654824; Gen. Man. COLIN AVERY.

United Bank Ltd (Pakistan): POB 1367, Dubai; POB 237, Abu Dhabi; tel. (4) 3552020; fax (4) 3514525; e-mail ubldra@emirates.net.ae; tel. (2) 6391507; fax (2) 6315052; e-mail ublman@emirates.net.ae; f. 1959; Gen. Man. SHAUKAT MIR; 8 brs in UAE.

Bankers' Association

United Arab Emirates Bankers' Association: POB 44307, Abu Dhabi; tel. (2) 6272541; fax (2) 6274155; e-mail ebauae@emirates.net.ae; internet www.eba_ae.com; f. 1983.

STOCK EXCHANGE

Dubai Financial Market (DFM): World Trade Centre, POB 9700, Dubai; tel. (4) 3055555; fax (4) 3314924; e-mail ekazim@dfm.co.ae; internet www.dfm.co.ae; f. 2000; 12 listed cos; market capitalization AED 35,866m. (Nov. 2002); Dir-Gen. ESSA ABDUL FATTAH KAZIM.

A second trading floor, the Abu Dhabi Stock Exchange (ADSE), is also planned.

INSURANCE

Abu Dhabi National Insurance Co (Adnic): POB 839, Abu Dhabi; tel. (2) 6264000; fax (2) 6268600; e-mail adnic@emirates.net.ae; internet www.adnic-uae.com; f. 1972; subscribed 25% by the Govt of Abu Dhabi and 75% by UAE nationals; all classes of insurance; Chair. and Gen. Man. KHALAF A. AL-OTAIBA.

Al-Ahlia Insurance Co: POB 128, Ras al-Khaimah; tel. (7) 221479; f. 1977; Chair. Sheikh OMAR BIN ABDULLAH AL-QASSIMI; 3 brs.

Al-Ain Ahlia Insurance Co: POB 3077, Abu Dhabi; tel. (2) 4459900; fax (2) 4456685; e-mail alainins@emirates.net.ae; internet www.alainsurance.com; f. 1975; Chair. MUHAMMAD BIN J. R. AL-

BADIE ADH-DHAHIRI; Gen. Man. M. MAZHAR HAMADEH; brs in Dubai, Sharjah, Tarif, Ghouifat and al-Ain.

Dubai Insurance Co PSC: POB 3027, Dubai; tel. (4) 2693030; fax (4) 2693727; e-mail dubins@emirates.net.ae; f. 1970; Chair. MAJID AL-FUTTAIM.

Sharjah Insurance Co: POB 792, Sharjah; tel. (6) 5686690; fax (6) 5686545; e-mail sirco@emirates.net.ae; internet www .sharjahinsurance.co.ae; f. 1970; Gen. Man. MUHAMMAD FAWZI NAJI.

Union Insurance Co: Head Office: POB 460, Umm al-Qaiwain; POB 4623, Dubai; POB 3196, Abu Dhabi; tel. (6) 666223; Gen. Man. L. F. DOKOV.

Trade and Industry

DEVELOPMENT ORGANIZATIONS

Abu Dhabi Development Finance Corpn: POB 814, Abu Dhabi; tel. (2) 6441000; fax (2) 6440800; e-mail opadfdmn@emirates.net.ae; purpose is to provide finance to the private sector; Chair. Sheikh KHALIFA BIN ZAYED AN-NAHYAN; Dir-Gen. SAEED KHALFAN MATAR AR-ROMAITHI.

Abu Dhabi Fund for Development (ADFD): POB 814, as-Salam St, Abu Dhabi; tel. (2) 6441000; fax (2) 6440800; e-mail opadfdmn@ emirates.net.ae; f. 1971; purpose is to offer economic aid to other Arab states and other developing countries in support of their development; cap. AED 4,000m. Dir-Gen. SAEED KHALFAN MATTAR AR-ROMAITHI.

Abu Dhabi Investment Authority (ADIA): POB 3600, Abu Dhabi; tel. (2) 213100; f. 1976; responsible for co-ordinating Abu Dhabi's investment policy; Chair. Sheikh KHALIFA BIN ZAYED AN-NAHYAN; Pres. Sheikh MUHAMMAD HABROUSH AS-SUWAIDI; 1 br. overseas.

Abu Dhabi Investment Company (ADIC): POB 46309, Abu Dhabi; tel. (2) 658100; fax (2) 650575; e-mail adic@emirates.net.ae; internet www.adic.co.ae; f. 1977; investment and merchant banking activities in the UAE and abroad; 98% owned by ADIA and 2% by National Bank of Abu Dhabi; total assets AED 5,947m. (1997); Chair. HAREB MASOOD AD-DARMAKI; Gen. Man. HUMAID DARWISH AL-KATBI.

Abu Dhabi Planning Department: POB 12, Abu Dhabi; tel. (2) 727200; fax (2) 727749; f. 1974; supervises Abu Dhabi's Development Programme; Chair. MUSALLAM SAEED ABDULLAH AL-QUBAISI; Under-Sec. AHMED M. HILAL AL-MAZRUI.

General Industry Corpn (GIC): POB 4499, Abu Dhabi; tel. (2) 6214900; fax (2) 6325034; e-mail info@gic.co; internet www.gic.co.ae; f. 1979; responsible for the promotion of non-petroleum-related industry; Chair. Sheikh HAMAD BIN TAHNOON AN-NAHYAN; Deputy Dir-Gen. SUHAIL MUHAMMAD AL-AMERI.

International Petroleum Investment Co (IPIC): POB 7528, Abu Dhabi; tel. (2) 336200; fax (2) 216045; f. 1984; cap. US $200m. state-owned venture to develop overseas investments in energy and energy-related projects; Chair. JOUAN SALEM ADH-DHAHIRI; Man. Dir KHALIFA MUHAMMAD ASH-SHAMSI.

Sharjah Economic Development Corpn (SHEDCO): Sharjah; tel. (6) 371212; industrial investment co; jt venture between Sharjah authorities and private sector; auth. cap. AED 1,000m. Gen. Man. J. T. PICKLES.

CHAMBERS OF COMMERCE

Federation of UAE Chambers of Commerce and Industry: POB 3014, Abu Dhabi; POB 8886, Dubai; tel. (2) 6214144; fax (2) 6339210; e-mail fcciauh@emirates.net.ae; tel. (4) 2212977; fax (4) 2235498; e-mail fccidxb@emirates.net.ae; internet www.fcci-uae .com; f. 1976; 7 mbr chambers; Pres. SAEED SAIF BIN JABER AL-SUWAIDI; Sec.-Gen. ABDULLAH SULTAN ABDULLAH.

Abu Dhabi Chamber of Commerce and Industry: POB 662, Abu Dhabi; tel. (2) 6214000; fax (2) 6215867; e-mail services@adcci.gov .ae; internet www.adcci-uae.com; f. 1969; 45,000 mems; Pres. SAID SEIF BIN JABER AS-SUWAIDI; Dir-Gen. MUHAMMAD OMAR ABDULLAH.

Ajman Chamber of Commerce and Industry: POB 662, Ajman; tel. (6) 422177; fax (6) 427591; e-mail ajmchmbr@emirates.net.ae; internet www.ajcci.co.ae; f. 1977; Pres. HAMAD MUHAMMAD ABU SHIHAB; Dir-Gen. MUHAMMAD BIN ABDULLAH AL-HUMRANI.

Dubai Chamber of Commerce and Industry: POB 1457, Dubai; tel. (4) 280000; fax (4) 211646; e-mail dcci@dcci.gov.ae; internet www .dcci.org; f. 1965; 40,000 mems; Pres. HASSAN BIN ASH-SHEIKH; Dir-Gen. ABD AR-RAHMAN GHANEM AL-MUTAIWEE.

Fujairah Chamber of Commerce, Industry and Agriculture: POB 738, Fujairah; tel. (9) 222400; fax (9) 221464; e-mail fujccia@

emirates.net.ae; Pres. SAID ALI KHAMAS; Dir-Gen. SHAHEEN ALI SHA-HEEN.

Ras al-Khaimah Chamber of Commerce, Industry and Agriculture: POB 87, Ras al-Khaimah; tel. (7) 333511; fax (7) 330233; e-mail rakchmbr@emirates.net.ae; f. 1967; 800 mems; Pres. ALI ABDULLAH MUSSABEH; Dir-Gen. ALI MUHAMMAD ALI AL-HARANKI.

Sharjah Chamber of Commerce and Industry: POB 580, Sharjah; tel. (6) 5116600; fax (6) 5681119; e-mail scci@sharjah.gov .ae; internet www.sharjah.gov.ae; f. 1970; 25,000 mems; Chair. AHMAD MUHAMMAD AL-MIDFA'A; Dir-Gen. SAID OBEID AL-JARWAN.

Umm al-Qaiwain Chamber of Commerce and Industry: POB 436, Umm al-Qaiwain; tel. (6) 656915; fax (6) 657056; Pres. ABDULLAH RASHID AL-KHARJI; Man. Dir SHAKIR AZ-ZAYANI.

STATE HYDROCARBONS COMPANIES

Abu Dhabi

Supreme Petroleum Council: POB 898, Abu Dhabi; tel. (2) 602000; fax (2) 6023389; f. 1988; assumed authority and responsibility for the administration and supervision of all petroleum affairs in Abu Dhabi; Chair. Sheikh KHALIFA BIN ZAYED AN-NAHYAN; Sec.-Gen. YOUSUF BIN OMEIR BIN YOUSUF.

Abu Dhabi National Oil Co (ADNOC): POB 898, Abu Dhabi; tel. (2) 6020000; fax (2) 6023389; e-mail adnoc@adnoc.com; internet www.adnoc.com; f. 1971; cap. AED 7,500m. state company; deals in all phases of oil industry; owns two refineries: one on Umm an-Nar island and one at Ruwais; Habshan Gas Treatment Plant (scheduled for partial privatization); gas pipeline distribution network; a salt and chlorine plant; holds 60% participation in operations of ADMA-OPCO and ADCO, and 88% of ZADCO; has 100% control of Abu Dhabi National Oil Company for Oil Distribution (ADNOC-FOD), Abu Dhabi National Tanker Co (ADNATCO), National Drilling Co (NDC) and interests in numerous other companies, both in the UAE and overseas; ADNOC is operated by Supreme Petroleum Council, Chair. SHEIKH KHALIFA BIN ZAYED AN-NAHYAN; Gen. Man. YOUSUF BIN OMEIR BIN YOUSUF.

Subsidiaries include:

Abu Dhabi Co for Onshore Oil Operations (ADCO): POB 270, Abu Dhabi; tel. (2) 6040000; fax (2) 669785; shareholders are ADNOC (60%), British Petroleum, Shell and Total (9.5% each), Exxon and Mobil (4.75% each) and Partex (2%); oil exploration, production and export operations from onshore oilfields; average production (1990): 1.2m. b/d; Chair. YOUSUF BIN OMEIR BIN YOUSUF; Gen. Man. KEVIN DUNNE.

Abu Dhabi Drilling Chemicals and Products Ltd (ADDCAP): POB 46121, Abu Dhabi; tel. (2) 6029000; fax (2) 6029010; e-mail addcap@emirates.net.ae; f. 1975; production of drilling chemicals and provision of marine services; wholly-owned subsidiary of ADNOC; Chair. YOUSUF BIN OMEIR BIN YOUSUF; Gen. Man. MAHFOUD A. DARBOUL ASH-SHEHHI.

Abu Dhabi Gas Co (ATHEER): POB 345, Abu Dhabi; tel. (2) 6020000; fax (2) 6027150; processing and distribution of natural gas.

Abu Dhabi Gas Industries Co (GASCO): POB 665, Abu Dhabi; tel. (2) 6041111; fax (2) 6047414; started production in 1981; recovers condensate and LPG from Asab, Bab and Bu Hasa fields for delivery to Ruwais natural gas liquids fractionation plant; capacity of 22,000 tons per day; ADNOC has a 68% share; Total, Shell Gas and Partex have a minority interest; Chair. SAHAIL AL-MAZROUI; Gen. Man. PHILIPPE HILAIREAUD.

Abu Dhabi Gas Liquefaction Co (ADGAS): POB 3500, Abu Dhabi; tel. (2) 6061111; fax (2) 6065456; f. 1973; owned by ADNOC, 51%; British Petroleum (BP), 16%; Total, 8%; Mitsui and Co, 22%; Mitsui Liquefied Gas Co, 3%; operates LGSC and the LNG plant on Das Island which uses natural gas produced in association with oil from offshore fields and has a design capacity of approx. 2.3m. tons of LNG per year and 1.29m. tons of LPG per year; the liquefied gas is sold to the Tokyo Electric Power Co, Japan; Chair. A. N. AS-SUWEIDI; Gen. Man. P. J. CARR.

Abu Dhabi Marine Operating Co (ADMA-OPCO): POB 303, Abu Dhabi; tel. (2) 6060000; fax (2) 6065062; operates a concession 60% owned by ADNOC, 40% by Abu Dhabi Marine Areas Ltd; f. 1977 as an operator for the concession; production (1984): 67,884,769 barrels (8,955,721 metric tons); Chair. YOUSUF BIN OMEIR BIN YOUSUF; Gen. Man. HENRY BACCONNIER.

Abu Dhabi Oil Refining Co (TAKREER): POB 3593, Abu Dhabi; tel. (2) 6027000; fax (2) 6065062; refining of crude oil; production of chlorine and related chemicals.

ADNOC Distribution: POB 4188, Abu Dhabi; tel. (2) 771300; fax (2) 722322; e-mail adnoc-fod@adnoc-fod.co.ae; internet www .adnoc-fod.co.ae; 100% owned by ADNOC; distributes petroleum products in UAE and worldwide; Chair. Yousuf bin Omeir bin Yousuf; Gen. Man. Jamal Jaber adh-Dhareef.

National Drilling Co (NDC): POB 4017, Abu Dhabi; tel. (2) 316600; fax (2) 317045; e-mail ndcisc@emirates.net.ae; drilling operations; Chair. Abdullah Nasser as-Suwaidi; Gen. Man. Najeeb Hassan az-Zaabi.

National Petroleum Construction Co (NPCC): POB 2058, Abu Dhabi; tel. (2) 5549000; fax (2) 5549111; e-mail npccnet@emirates .net.ae; f. 1973; 'turnkey' construction and maintenance of offshore facilities for the petroleum and gas industries; cap. AED 100m. Chair. Muhammad Butti K. al-Qubaisi; Gen. Man. Aqeel A. Madhi.

Ajman

Ajman National Oil Co (AJNOC): POB 410, Ajman; tel. (6) 421218; f. 1983; 50% govt-owned, 50% held by Canadian and private Arab interests.

Dubai

DUGAS (Dubai Natural Gas Co Ltd): POB 4311, Dubai (Location: Jebel Ali); tel. (4) 846000; fax (4) 846118; wholly owned by Dubai authorities; Dep. Chair. and Dir Sultan Ahmed bin Sulayem.

Dubai Petroleum Co (DPC): POB 2222, Dubai; tel. (4) 846000; fax (4) 846118; holds offshore concession which began production in 1969; wholly owned by Dubai authorities; Pres. S. L. Cornelius.

Emirates General Petroleum Corpn (Emarat): POB 9400, Dubai; tel. (4) 444444; fax (4) 444292; f. 1981; wholly owned by Ministry of Finance and Industry; distribution of petroleum; Gen. Man. Ahmad Muhammad al-Kamda.

Emirates National Oil Co (ENOC): POB 6442, Enoc House, 4th Floor, al-Qutaeyat Road, Dubai; tel. (4) 3374400; fax (4) 3031221; e-mail webmaster@enoc.co.ae; f. 1993; responsible for management of Dubai-owned cos in petroleum-marketing sector; Chief Exec. Hussain M. Sultan.

Emirates Petroleum Products Co Pvt. Ltd: POB 5589, Dubai; tel. (4) 372131; fax (4) 3031605; f. 1980; jt venture between Govt of Dubai and Caltex Alkhaleej Marketing; sales of petroleum products, bunkering fuel and bitumen; Chair. Sheikh Hamdan bin Rashid al-Maktoum.

Sedco-Houston Oil Group: POB 702, Dubai; tel. (4) 224141; holds onshore concession of over 400,000 ha as well as the offshore concession formerly held by Texas Pacific Oil; Pres. Carl F. Thorne.

Sharjah

In 1999 a Supreme Petroleum Council was established in Sharjah. Chaired by Ahmad bin Sultan al-Qasimi, it was to assume the responsibilities of the Petroleum and Mineral Affairs Department.

Petroleum and Mineral Affairs Department: POB 188, Sharjah; tel. (6) 541888; Dir Ismail A. Wahid.

Sharjah Liquefied Petroleum Gas Co (SHALCO): POB 787, Sharjah; tel. (6) 5286333; fax (6) 5286111; e-mail shalco@emirates .net.ae; f. 1984; gas processing; 60% owned by Sharjah authorities, 25% Sharjah BP Amoco-Oil Co, 7.5% each Itochu Corpn and Tokyo Boeki of Japan; Gen. Man. Saleh Ali.

Umm al-Qaiwain

Petroleum and Mineral Affairs Department: POB 9, Umm al-Qaiwain; tel. (6) 666034; Chair. Sheikh Sultan bin Ahmad al-Mu'alla.

UTILITIES

Abu Dhabi

A decree issued in late February 1998 restructured the Abu Dhabi utilities sector in preparation for its privatization.

Abu Dhabi Water and Electricity Authority (ADWEA): POB 6120, Abu Dhabi; tel. (2) 6943333; fax (2) 6943491; internet www .adwea.gov.ae; f. 1999 to oversee the privatization of the water and electricity sectors; Chair. Sheikh Diab Zayed an-Nahyan.

Abu Dhabi Distribution Co: POB 219, Abu Dhabi; tel. (2) 642300; fax (2) 6426033; e-mail customerservice@addc.co.ae; internet www.adwea.gov.ae/addc; f. 1999; distribution of water and electricity.

Abu Dhabi Transmission and Dispatch Co: POB 173, Abu Dhabi; tel. (2) 6414000; fax 92) 6426333; internet www.adwea.gov .ae/transco; f. 1999.

Abu Dhabi Water and Electricity Co (ADWEC): POB 51111, Abu Dhabi; tel. (2) 6943333; fax (2) 6425773; internet www.adwea .gov.ae/adwec; f. 1999.

Al-Ain Distribution Co: POB 1065, al-Ain; tel. (3) 7636000; fax (3) 7632025; e-mail aadc@aadc.cc; internet www.adwea.gov.ae/ aadc; f. 1999; distribution of water and electricity.

Bayounah Power Co.: POB 3477, Abu Dhabi; tel. (2) 731100; fax (2) 730403; internet www.adwea.gov.ae/bpc; f. 1999.

Al-Mirfa Power Co: POB 32277, Abu Dhabi; tel. (2) 8833044; fax (2) 8833011; e-mail mirfa@emirates.net.ae; internet www.adwea .gov.ae/ampc; f. 1999 to control Mirfa and Madinat Zayed plants; capacity 300 MW electricity per day, 16m. gallons water per day; Chair. Abdullah al-Ahbabi; Gen. Man. Philip Graham Tilson.

Al-Taweelah Power Co: POB 32255, Abu Dhabi; tel. (2) 5627000; fax (2) 5627055; internet www.adwea.gov.ae/atpc; f. 1999.

Emirates CMS Power Co: POB 47688, Abu Dhabi; tel. (2) 5067100; fax (2) 5067157; e-mail zgdesouza@cmsenergy.com; internet www.adwea.gov.ae/ecpc; f. 1999; owns and operated the Al-Taweelah plant; Man. Dir Brian S. Jackson.

Umm an-Nar Power Co: POB 33488, Abu Dhabi; tel. (2) 5582700; fax (2) 5582405; internet www.adwea.gov.ae/uanpc; f. 1999.

Dubai

Dubai Electricity and Water Authority (DEWA): POB 564, Dubai; tel. (4) 3244444; fax (4) 3248111; e-mail dewa@dewa.gov.ae; internet www.dewa.gov.ae.

Northern Emirates (Ajman, Fujairah, Ras al-Khaimah and Umm al-Qaiwain)

Ministry of Electricity and Water: see Ministries, above.

Sharjah

Sharjah Electricity and Water Authority (SEWA): Sharjah; tel. (2) 5288888; fax (2) 5288000; internet www.sewa.gov.ae.

Transport

ROADS

Roads are rapidly being developed in the United Arab Emirates, and Abu Dhabi and Dubai are linked by a good road which is dual carriageway for most of its length. This road forms part of a west coast route from Shaam, at the UAE border with the northern enclave of Oman, through Dubai and Abu Dhabi to Tarif. An east coast route links Dibba with Muscat. Other roads include the Abu Dhabi–al-Ain highway and roads linking Sharjah and Ras al-Khaimah, and Sharjah and Dhaid. An underwater tunnel links Dubai Town and Deira by dual carriageway and pedestrian subway. In 1998 there was a total road network of roads of 1,088 km, of which 253 km were motorways and 139 km were main roads.

SHIPPING

Dubai has been the main commercial centre in the Gulf for many years. Abu Dhabi has also become an important port since the opening of the first section of its artificial harbour, Port Zayed. There are smaller ports in Sharjah, Fujairah, Ras al-Khaimah and Umm al-Qaiwain. Dubai possesses two docks capable of handling 500,000-ton tankers, seven repair berths and a third dock able to accommodate 1,000,000-ton tankers. The Dubai port of Mina Jebel Ali has the largest man-made harbour in the world.

Abu Dhabi

Abu Dhabi Seaport Authority: POB 422, Port Zayed, Abu Dhabi; tel. (2) 6730600; fax (2) 6731023; e-mail Mrktdept@emirates.net.ae; internet www.portzayed.gov.ae; f. 1972; administers Port Zayed; facilities at the port include 21 deep-water berths and five container gantry cranes of 40 metric tons capacity; cold storage 20,500 metric tons; in 2000 Port Zayed handled 315,810 20-ft equivalent units (TEUs); Chair. Sheikh Said bin Zayed an-Nahyan; Dir Mubarak Muhammad al-Buainain.

Abu Dhabi National Tanker Co (ADNATCO): POB 2977, Abu Dhabi; tel. (2) 277733; fax (2) 272940; subsidiary company of ADNOC, operating owned and chartered tankships, and transporting crude petroleum, refined products and sulphur; Chair. Nasser Ahmad as-Suwaidi; Gen. Man. Bader M. as-Suwaidi.

Abu Dhabi Petroleum Ports Operating Co (ADPPOC): POB 61, Abu Dhabi; tel. (2) 333500; fax (2) 333567; e-mail adppoc@emirates .net.ae; f. 1979; manages Jebel Dhanna, Ruwais, Das Island, Umm an-Nar and Zirku Island SPM terminal, Mubarraz; cap. AED 50m. 60% owned by ADNOC, 40% by LAMNALCO Kuwait; Chair. Yousuf bin Omeir bin Yousuf; Gen. Man. Khalifa M. al-Gobaisi.

National Marine Services Co (NMS): POB 7202, Abu Dhabi; tel. (2) 339800; fax (2) 211239; operate, charter and lease specialized offshore support vessels; cap. AED 25m. owned 60% by ADNOC and

40% by Jackson Marine Corpn USA; Chair. SOHAIL FARES AL-MAZRUI; Gen. Man. Capt. HASSAN A. SHAREEF.

Dubai

Dubai Ports Authority (DPA): POB 17000, Dubai; tel. (4) 8815000; fax (4) 8816093; e-mail mktg@dpa.co.ae; internet www.dpa .co.ae; storage areas and facilities for loading and discharge of vessels; supervises ports of Jebel Ali and Mina Rashid; handled 3m. TEUs in 2000; Chair. SULTAN AHMAD BIN SULAYEM; Man. Dir JAMAL MAJID BIN THANIAH.

Dubai Drydocks: POB 8988, Dubai; tel. (4) 3450626; fax (4) 3450116; e-mail drydocks@drydocks.gov.ae; internet www.drydocks .gov.ae; f. 1983; state-owned; dry-docking and repairs, floating dock, tank cleaning, construction of vessels and floating docks, conversions, galvanizing plant, dredging, etc. Chief Exec. KEITH BURGESS.

Sea Bridge Shipping: POB 8458, Dubai; tel. (4) 379858; fax (4) 372600; cargo ships; Chair. S. RAMAKRISHNAN; Man. Dir L. B. CULAS.

Vela International Marine: POB 26373, City Towers 2, Sheikh Zayed Road, Dubai; tel. (4) 312800; fax (4) 315675; operates tankships; Chair. DHAIFALLAH F. ALUTAIBI; Man. Dir ADEL M. AD-DULAIJIN.

Fujairah

Fujairah Port: POB 787, Fujairah; tel. (9) 228800; fax (9) 228811; f. 1982; offers facilities for handling full container, general cargo and 'roll on, roll off' traffic; handled 565,723 TEUs in 1999; Chair. Sheikh SALEH BIN MUHAMMAD ASH-SHARQI; Harbour Master TAMER MASOUD.

Ras al-Khaimah

Mina Saqr Port Authority: POB 5130, Ras al-Khaimah; tel. (7) 668444; fax (7) 668533; Port operators handling bulk cargoes, containers, general cargo and 'roll on, roll off' traffic; govt owned; Chair. Sheikh MUHAMMAD BIN SAQR AL-QASIMI; Man. DAVID ALLAN.

Sharjah

Sharjah Ports and Customs Department: POB 510, Sharjah; tel. (6) 281666; fax (6) 281425; the authority administers Port Khalid and Port Khor Fakkan and offers specialized facilities for container and 'roll on roll off' traffic, reefer cargo and project and general cargo; in 1999 Port Khalid handled 90,972 TEUs of containerized shipping, and Port Khor Fakkan 989,028 TEUs; Chair. (Ports and Customs) Sheikh SAUD BIN KHALID AL-QASIMI; Dir-Gen. ABD AL-AZIZ SULAIMAN AS-SARKAL.

Fal Shipping Co Ltd: POB 6600, Sharjah; tel. (6) 286666; fax (6) 280861; operates tankships; Chair. ABDULLA JUMA AS-SARI; Gen. Man. MUHAMMAD OSMAN FADUL.

Umm al-Qaiwain

Ahmed bin Rashid Port and Free Zone Authority: POB 279, Umm al-Qaiwain; tel. (6) 7655882; fax 7651552; e-mail abrpaftz@ emirates.net.ae.

CIVIL AVIATION

There are six international airports at Abu Dhabi, al-Ain (Abu Dhabi), Dubai, Fujairah and Ras al-Khaimah, and a smaller one at Sharjah, which forms part of Sharjah port, linking air, sea and overland transportation services. In 1995 a total of 11.6m. pas-

sengers used the six UAE airports, 3.3m. of them passing through Abu Dhabi airports; and in 1996 a record 8.5m. passengers used Dubai airport.

Civil Aviation Department: POB 20, Abu Dhabi; tel. (2) 757500; responsible for all aspects of civil aviation; Chair. HAMDAN BIN MUBARAK AN-NAHYAN.

Abu Dhabi Aviation: POB 2723, Abu Dhabi; tel. (2) 449100; fax (2) 449081; f. 1976; domestic charter flights; Chair. HAMDAN BIN MUBARAK AN-NAHYAN; Gen. Man. MUHAMMAD IBRAHIM AL-MAZROUI.

> **Emirates Air Service:** POB 2723, Abu Dhabi; tel. (2) 757021; fax (2) 449100; f. 1976 as Abu Dhabi Air Services; overhaul, engine and avionics servicing, component repairs and complete refurbishment.

Emirates Airline: POB 686, Dubai; tel. (4) 2951111; fax (4) 2955817; e-mail corpcom@emiratesairline.com; internet www .emiratesairline.com; f. 1985; services to 52 destinations world-wide; owned by the Dubai Govt; in 2000/01 the airline carried 5.7m. passengers and 335,194 tons of freight; Chair. Sheikh AHMAD BIN SAID AL-MAKTOUM; Group Man. Dir. MAURICE FLANAGAN.

Falcon Express Cargo Airlines: Dubai International Airport, POB 93722, Dubai; tel. (4) 2826886; fax (4) 2823125; e-mail feca@ emirates.net.ae; f. 1995; dedicated courier freight.

Gulf Air Co: POB 5015, Sharjah; tel. (6) 356356; fax (6) 354354; internet www.gulfairco.com; f. 1950; jointly owned by Govts of Bahrain, Oman and Abu Dhabi since 1974; flights world-wide; Pres. and Chief Exec. SALIM BIN ALI BIN NASSER.

Tourism

Tourism is an established industry in Sharjah, and plans are being implemented to foster tourism in other emirates, notably in Abu Dhabi and Dubai. In 1994 foreign visitors to the UAE totalled more than 1.9m., compared with 616,000 in 1990. In 1999 some 2.5m. tourists visited Dubai.

Department of Tourism and Commerce Marketing: POB 594, Dubai; tel. (4) 2230000; fax (4) 2230022; e-mail info@dubaitourism .co.ae; internet www.dubaitourism.com.ae.

Dubai Information Department: POB 1420, Dubai; Dir OMAR DEESI.

Fujairah Tourism Bureau: POB 829, Fujairah; tel. (9) 231554; fax (9) 231006; e-mail fujtourb@emirates.net.ae; internet www .fujairah-tourism.com; f. 1995; Chair. Sheikh SAEED ASH-SHARQI; Dir WAHID BIN YOUSSEF.

National Corporation for Tourism and Hotels (NCTH): Abu Dhabi; 20% owned by Government of Abu Dhabi.

Ras al-Khaimah Information and Tourism Department: POB 141, Ras al-Khaimah; tel. (7) 751151; Chair. Sheikh ABD AL-AZIZ BIN HUMAID AL-QASIMI.

Sharjah Commerce and Tourism Development Authority: POB 26661, 11th Floor, Crescent Tower, Buheirah Corniche, Sharjah; tel. (6) 5562777; fax (6) 5563000; e-mail sctda@ sharjahcommerce-tourism.gov.ae; internet www.sharjah-welcome .com; f. 1980; Dir. MUHAMMAD SAIF AL-HAJRI.

THE UNITED KINGDOM

GREAT BRITAIN

Introductory Survey

Location, Climate, Language, Religion, Flag, Capital

The United Kingdom of Great Britain and Northern Ireland lies in north-western Europe, occupying the major portion of the British Isles. The country's only land boundary is with the Republic of Ireland. Northern Ireland is a constitutionally distinct part of the United Kingdom (see the subsequent chapter). Great Britain, consisting of one large island and a number of smaller ones, comprises England, Scotland to the north and Wales to the west. It is separated from the coast of western Europe by the English Channel to the south and by the North Sea to the east. The northern and western shores are washed by the Atlantic Ocean. Ireland lies to the west across the Irish Sea. The climate is generally temperate but variable. The average temperature is about 15°C (59°F) in summer and about 5°C (41°F) in winter. Average annual rainfall is 900–1,000 mm (35–40 ins). The language is English, but Welsh is spoken by about one-fifth of the Welsh population. The Church of England is the established church in England. Other large Christian denominations are Roman Catholicism, Methodism, the United Reformed Church and the Baptists. The national flag (proportions 1 by 2), known as the Union Jack, is a superimposition of the red cross of Saint George of England, the white saltire of Saint Andrew of Scotland and the red saltire of Ireland, all on a blue background. The capital is London.

Recent History

At the end of the Second World War the United Kingdom still ruled a vast overseas empire, and successive British Governments, in response both to nationalist aspirations and world pressure, gradually granted independence to the colonies; almost all of these became members of the Commonwealth (see p. 164). Britain's dominance diminished over the Commonwealth, which became a free association of states, and by the end of the 1970s the country looked exclusively to the NATO (see p. 271) and to the European Community (EC—now restructured as the European Union—EU, see p. 199) for its future security.

In 1951 a Conservative Government was formed by Winston Churchill, the wartime Prime Minister. The Conservatives remained in power for 13 years, led successively by Churchill, Sir Anthony Eden (1955–57), Harold Macmillan (1957–63) and Sir Alec Douglas-Home (1963–64). The election of 1964 gave a small parliamentary majority to the Labour Party, led by Harold Wilson. The Labour Party was re-elected in 1966, but in 1970 a Conservative Government, under Edward Heath, was returned.

After the general election of February 1974 Wilson formed a minority Government; at a further election in October the Labour Party achieved a small majority in the House of Commons. Wilson resigned as Prime Minister in April 1976, and was succeeded by James Callaghan. His Labour Government immediately encountered a serious monetary crisis and, following a series of by-election defeats, became a minority Government again. In March 1977 the Government formed a pact with the Liberal Party, which held 13 parliamentary seats; the pact ended in May 1978.

In the general election of May 1979 the Conservative Party won a parliamentary majority. A Government was formed under Margaret Thatcher, who became the United Kingdom's first female Prime Minister. Thatcherite policy, which emphasized non-intervention in industry and the encouragement of private enterprise, while aiming to reduce public expenditure in central and local government, proved controversial, owing to the austerity of certain economic measures and an accompanying increase in unemployment. New employment legislation restricted the power of the trade unions.

Michael Foot was elected Leader of the Labour Party in November 1980. The increasing prominence of extreme left-wing members caused serious rifts in the Labour Party, and in March 1981 four former ministers from the right wing of the party formed the Social Democratic Party (SDP). The SDP rapidly gained support, including that of other Labour Members of Parliament (MPs), and a political alliance was formed with the Liberals in 1981.

In April 1982 Argentine forces invaded the British dependency of the Falkland Islands (q.v.). The successful military campaign to recover the islands in June significantly increased the Government's popularity, despite rising unemployment and strict monetary control of the economy. In the general election of June 1983 the Conservative Party won a decisive victory, increasing its majority in the House of Commons to 146 seats. The Labour Party suffered a significant reduction in its parliamentary representation and Neil Kinnock subsequently replaced Foot as the Labour Leader.

At a general election in June 1987 the Conservative Party won an overall majority of 102 seats in the House of Commons. In September the SDP-Liberal Alliance (support for which had declined at the election) agreed to merge as the Social and Liberal Democrats (SLD—later known as the Liberal Democrats). The party was formally established in March 1988 and in July Paddy Ashdown (of the former Liberal Party) was elected sole leader of the SLD.

In April 1990 a new local tax, the community charge (or 'poll tax'), payable at a uniform rate within each local authority by every resident over 18 years of age, came into force in England and Wales to replace the existing system of domestic rates (charges on property collected by local authorities). The introduction of the community charge—in conjunction with an economic recession (and accompanying high levels of inflation and interest rates), and the unpopularity of changes to the education system and of proposed reforms to the National Health Service (NHS)—contributed to considerable national dissatisfaction with the Thatcher administration. There were also divisions within the Government, chiefly concerning its policy on integration with the EC. In November 1990 Sir Geoffrey Howe resigned as the Lord President of the Council, Leader of the House of Commons and Deputy Prime Minister, in protest against Thatcher's hostility towards economic and political union within the EC. Michael Heseltine (who had abruptly resigned as Secretary of State for Defence in 1986, owing to policy differences with the Prime Minister) announced that he would challenge Thatcher for the leadership of the Conservative Party. In the first ballot of the leadership election (conducted among Conservative MPs) Thatcher narrowly failed to achieve an outright victory and she subsequently withdrew her candidacy. The contest was finally won by John Major, Chancellor of the Exchequer since October 1989. Major was officially appointed Prime Minister at the end of November 1990. In the ensuing cabinet reshuffle Norman Lamont, hitherto Chief Secretary to the Treasury, was appointed Chancellor of the Exchequer; Heseltine was awarded the environment portfolio, with the task of reforming the community charge. (Legislation to replace the charge with a new local 'council tax', to be based on property values, took effect in April 1993.)

Prior to the general election of 9 April 1992 opinion polls indicated that the Labour Party had sufficient popular support to secure its first election victory since 1974. However, the Conservative Party was re-elected with an overall, but substantially reduced, majority in the House of Commons. The Conservative Party obtained 336 (of 651) seats and 41.9% of the votes cast, the Labour Party 271 seats and 34.4% of the votes, and the Liberal Democrats 21 seats and 17.9% of the votes.

As the economic recession continued, the Government's economic policies were criticized not only by political opponents, but also increasingly by industrial and business leaders. Serious divisions in the Conservative Party over the provisions of the Treaty on European Union (the 'Maastricht Treaty') were exacerbated by the United Kingdom's departure from the exchange rate mechanism of the European Monetary System (see p. 225) in September 1992, owing to the weakness of the pound sterling. The Labour Party, which largely favoured the Treaty, objected to the Government's refusal to adopt the Social Policy Agreement (which provided for the protection of workers' rights). In November Labour and 26 dissident Conservative MPs voted against a motion to proceed with draft legislation approving the Maastricht Treaty. However, the Government, supported on this occasion by the Liberal Democrats, won by a margin of three votes. The Treaty was endorsed by the House of Lords, the non-elected upper chamber, in July 1993, in spite of fierce opposition by some Conservatives; Labour peers abstained. In a crucial vote to ratify the Treaty, by adopting a motion on its so-called 'social chapter', conducted in the House of Commons later in July, 'rebel' Conservatives joined the Opposition to defeat the motion. The Prime Minister introduced a confidence motion the following day, and speculation that Major would call a general election in the event of a defeat for the Government was sufficient to ensure the support of the dissident MPs.

Following the Labour Party's fourth successive general election defeat, in April 1992, Kinnock announced his resignation as Leader of the party. In July John Smith was elected to replace him. Prior to his sudden death, in May 1994, Smith notably undertook the reform of the relationship between the Labour Party and the trade unions, effectively reducing the unions' bloc influence over policy formulation and the election of party chiefs and parliamentary candidates. In July Anthony (Tony) Blair, Labour's parliamentary spokesman on home affairs, was elected Leader by the party's electoral college. John Prescott became Deputy Leader. A 'modernization' of the party was pledged, in an attempt to increase its electoral appeal. Blair's initiative to abandon Labour's socialist commitment to the common ownership of the means of production provoked a much-publicized reassessment of party ideology, and became a test of support for the new leadership. In April 1995, despite strong resistance by two large trade unions and left-wing party delegates, a special party conference endorsed a draft text to replace the relevant clause of the party's constitution.

In November 1994 parliamentary consideration of legislation to increase the United Kingdom's contribution to EU finances emphasized the persistence of divisions within the Conservative Party with regard to the EU. Following disclosures that the Government was presenting the bill as a vote of confidence in the administration, the legislation was approved in the House of Commons by 330 votes to 303. In a by-election in December the Government's parliamentary majority was further reduced (following the loss of a seat to the Liberal Democrats in June) after the Conservatives lost the seat to the Labour Party candidate, who took 68.8% of the votes cast. In a parliamentary vote in March 1995, however, the Government achieved a narrow margin of support for its policy on Europe. Later that month a more secure victory was achieved in a vote on reform of the EU's Common Agricultural Policy (CAP), as a result, in particular, of regaining the support of the Ulster Unionist Party (UUP), which had earlier opposed the Government in protest at developments in the Northern Ireland peace process

At local elections held in Scotland in April 1995 the Conservative party obtained only 11% of the votes cast. The Labour Party, which had disclosed proposals for devolution in the event of its forming a government, won 47% of the votes, and the Scottish National Party (SNP) 27%. By May the Government's majority in the House of Commons had been reduced to 10 members. In June Major abruptly announced his resignation as Leader of the Conservative Party, asserting that persistent speculation of a possible challenge to his leadership, was undermining both his authority as Prime Minister and that of the Government. The Secretary of State for Wales, John Redwood, resigned from the Cabinet in order to challenge Major as party leader. In the ballot for the leadership, held in July, Major obtained 218 of the 329 votes of the parliamentary party (compared with Redwood's 89). In a subsequent extensive reorganization of the Government Major appointed Heseltine (who had held the Cabinet post of President of the Board of Trade since 1992) to a new position of First Secretary of State and Deputy Prime Minister. The Government was, none the less, further

unsettled by the loss of another seat at a by-election later in July 1995, and by the defection of three Conservative MPs in late 1995 and early 1996. In April 1996 the Government's majority in the House of Commons declined to a single seat, following the defeat of its candidate in a by-election with a substantial loss of votes to the Labour Party.

In March 1996 the imposition by the EU of a comprehensive trade ban on British beef products, in response to a major public health alert (see below), reinforced the position of those Conservative MPs demanding a limitation in the country's convergence with the EU. In April Major committed a future Conservative administration to conducting a popular referendum on the country's participation in a European single currency. The Prime Minister also stipulated that the Government would approach a new parliamentary term maintaining all policy options on future participation in European economic and monetary union (EMU) until the final terms of entry and the prevailing economic conditions could be determined. In June more than 70 Conservative MPs declared their support for a wider referendum on EU membership, demonstrating the increasingly organized strength of the so-called 'Euro-sceptic' faction of the party.

In December 1996 the Government officially lost its majority in the House of Commons when the Labour Party won a by-election for a previously Conservative-held seat. In February 1997 the Labour Party attempted to force a government defeat, in order to prompt a general election, by introducing a parliamentary censure motion against the Minister of Agriculture, Fisheries and Food, Douglas Hogg, for his administration of the bovine spongiform encephalopathy (BSE) crisis (see below). However, the Ulster Unionists upheld the Government's position by abstaining. By March the Conservatives' parliamentary minority had deepened, following a further Labour by-election victory and the defection of a 'Euro-sceptic' MP.

In March 1997 John Major announced that a general election was to be conducted on 1 May. The Conservative Party had been weakened by an investigation by the Parliamentary Commissioner for Standards, into improper conduct by several of its MPs, and also by disunity over the issue of future participation in a European single currency. The Labour Party, which maintained a constant strong lead in opinion polls, appealed to voters on the possibilities presented by a change of government, and emphasized the political reforms undertaken by the party (now frequently referred to as 'New Labour'), under Blair's leadership. In the event, the Labour Party secured an overwhelming victory, winning 418 of the 659 parliamentary seats, with 44.3% of the votes cast in Britain. The Conservative Party won only 165 seats with 31.5% of the vote. Moreover, for the first time in its history, the Conservative Party failed to win any parliamentary representation in Scotland or Wales. The Liberal Democrats increased their number of seats to 46, although with a slightly reduced share of the votes (17.2%, compared with 17.9% in 1992). Major immediately announced his resignation as leader of the Conservative Party: William Hague, hitherto Secretary of State for Wales, was elected to the post (and thus Leader of the Opposition) by Conservative MPs in June.

The new Labour Government incorporated the key figures of Blair's front-bench administration in Opposition. Gordon Brown was named as Chancellor of the Exchequer, Robin Cook became the new Secretary of State for Foreign and Commonwealth Affairs, while John Prescott, appointed Deputy Prime Minister, assumed additional responsibility for the environment, transport and the regions. Peter Mandelson, one of Blair's closest advisers and regarded as highly influential in the organization of Labour's election campaign, was appointed Minister without portfolio, with responsibility for co-ordinating government policy (a non-Cabinet post). The new administration announced a series of radical policy proposals and government reforms, including an employment initiative, aimed initially at long-term unemployed 18–24 year olds, which was to be financed by a single taxation levy on the profits of privatized industries. Brown announced changes to the management and regulation of the economy and the financial sector (including a transfer of operational responsibility for monetary policy to the Bank of England), while Cook defined the Government's broad approach to foreign affairs, with greater emphasis on the country's role in international organizations and the incorporation of human rights concerns into foreign policy and trade decisions. A new Department for International Development was established, to assume the functions of the former Overseas Development Administration (previously under the authority of the Foreign and Commonwealth Office) at cabinet level. The Government's parliamentary programme included additional legislation for improved standards in education, the adoption of a national minimum wage, and constitutional reform.

In July 1997 the Blair Government formally published its proposals for the establishment of devolved legislative authorities in Scotland and Wales. The most significant constitutional development was proposed for Scotland, where a new elected parliament was envisaged as having powers to legislate on all domestic matters, including education, health, local government, law and order, and the possible mandate to vary taxes set by the United Kingdom Government. An executive level of government was to be headed by a First Minister. The 129 Members of the Scottish Parliament (MSPs) were to be elected every four years by a combined system of direct voting, on the basis of Westminster parliamentary constituencies, and a form of proportional representation, whereby additional members would be elected from a party list on the basis of the larger constituencies used for elections to the European Parliament. The Welsh Assembly, like the Scottish body, was envisaged as assuming control of the annual block grant for the region from central government, and as undertaking responsibility for issues covered by the Welsh Office. The 60-member Assembly was to be elected under the same system as in Scotland. In a referendum on the issue held in Scotland in September, 74.3% of voters supported a new Parliament, while 63.5% approved its having tax-raising powers. The results, although representing only an estimated 44.7% and 38.1% of eligible voters, respectively, were considered by the Labour Government as being an endorsement of its proposals for constitutional change. The outcome of the referendum in Wales, held one week later, was less conclusive, with only 50.3% of voters (or some 25% of the eligible electorate) in support of the Assembly. None the less, the Government declared its intention of implementing the majority decision. Legislation providing for the establishment of the authorities on 1 January 2000, with elections to be held in May 1999, was presented to Parliament in December 1997. The political settlement on the future governance of Northern Ireland (q.v.), concluded in April, provided for new constitutional arrangements regarding the status of Northern Ireland within the United Kingdom and for the establishment of a British-Ireland Council comprising representatives of the British and Irish Governments, members of the proposed Assemblies in Scotland, Wales and Northern Ireland, and representatives of the Isle of Man and the Channel Islands.

In July 1998 Blair implemented a major reorganization of the Government, dismissing four members of the Cabinet, in a move widely interpreted as strengthening support for the Prime Minister and curbing the influence of Brown. Among the new appointments was that of Peter Mandelson as President of the Board of Trade and Secretary of State for Trade and Industry. In that month the Government's declared commitment to restoring probity in public life was undermined following allegations in the national press that former Labour Party advisers working as professional lobbyists were using party contacts to secure preferential access to ministers and advisers and to obtain confidential information of commercial value. While the Government denied any impropriety on the part of ministers or their current advisers, a new code of conduct was issued by the Cabinet Office later that month, establishing strict regulations for government contact with lobbyists.

In December 1998 the Government suffered a serious crisis when Mandelson and the Paymaster General, Geoffrey Robinson, resigned following allegations of financial impropriety. The allegations centred on the revelation that, in 1996, Mandelson had received from Robinson a substantial loan on preferential terms in order to purchase a house. Since his appointment as Paymaster General in May 1997, Robinson had come under several investigations for alleged irregularities in his business affairs, and, in September 1998, the Department of Trade and Industry, of which Mandelson was Secretary of State, had begun one such investigation. Mandelson later contended that he had excluded himself from the process and that no conflict of interest had arisen; however, he had failed to disclose the existence of the loan to the permanent secretary of the Department.

In October 1998 the leader of the Government in the House of Lords, Baroness Jay of Paddington, announced that legislation was to be introduced to remove the voting rights of hereditary peers, and that a Royal Commission was to be appointed to consider options for a definitive reform of the second chamber. Opposition from within the House of Lords was appeased in

December when a compromise agreement was reached under which 92 hereditary peers were to retain their seats in an interim second chamber pending the definitive reform. (In return, opposition peers undertook to ensure the passage of European parliamentary elections legislation, which had hitherto been repeatedly blocked in the House of Lords). Draft legislation for the abolition of hereditary peers and the establishment of an interim chamber was published in January 1999. Despite renewed opposition from within the House of Lords, including an unsuccessful challenge to the constitutional legality of the proposed reform, in October the upper chamber approved the House of Lords Bill, and in November it received royal assent. In the same month an election was conducted to elect 75 of the 92 hereditary peers who would sit in the new interim chamber. Candidates for these seats were elected by their fellow hereditary peers. A further 15 office-holders had been elected by the whole house in the previous month, while the two remaining seats were reserved for the incumbents of the offices of Lord Great Chamberlain and Earl Marshal. In January 2000 the Royal Commission, headed by Lord Wakeham, published its proposals for the definitive reform of the upper house. Its principal recommendations were that the new chamber should comprise some 550 members, the majority of whom would be chosen by an independent commission, while a 'significant minority' (between 65 and 195) would be elected by regional proportional representation. In response Baroness Jay announced that time was needed to study the report but that there were no immediate plans to establish the joint committee of the House of Lords and Commons, which, as envisaged in the Government's original proposals, would consider the report prior to the formulation of definitive legislation.

At elections to the new legislative authorities in Scotland and Wales, held in early May 1999, the Labour Party, while securing the greatest number of seats, failed to gain an overall majority in either assembly. In Scotland the Labour Party obtained 56 of the total 129 seats, while the SNP won 35 seats, the Conservative Party 18 seats, and the Liberal Democrats 17 seats; the remaining three seats were won by independent candidates. The Labour Party and the Liberal Democrats subsequently formed a coalition administration comprising nine Labour and two Liberal Democrat members, headed by Donald Dewar as First Minister. In Wales the Labour Party secured 28 of the total 60 seats, while Plaid Cymru obtained 17 seats, the Conservative Party nine seats and the Liberal Democrats six seats. Despite the Labour Party's lack of an overall majority, in mid-May the Welsh First Minister, Alun Michael, rejected plans for a formal coalition, opting instead to form a minority administration. Simultaneous local council elections held in England were notable for their low participation rate, which, at about 29%, was the lowest on record. The results were expected to prompt the Government to expedite plans for a far-reaching reform of local government.

The transfer of powers to both the Scottish and the Welsh Assemblies took place on 1 July 1999. In August the Liberal Democrats elected Charles Kennedy to succeed Paddy Ashdown as leader of the party. In October Blair conducted a further government reorganization, particularly notable for the return to the Cabinet of Peter Mandelson, who replaced Marjorie (Mo) Mowlam as Secretary of State for Northern Ireland. In February 2000 Rhodri Morgan succeeded Alun Michael as Welsh First Minister. Michael had resigned shortly before the Welsh National Assembly adopted a vote of no confidence in his leadership. The development was regarded as a serious reverse for Blair, who had supported Michael against Morgan in controversial Welsh Labour leadership elections in February 1999.

During 2000 there was considerable political upheaval in both Wales and Scotland. In July Alex Salmond unexpectedly announced his resignation as the leader of the SNP precipitating a leadership contest at which John Swinney defeated his sole rival, Alex Neil, by securing 67% of the votes cast. Following the death in October of the First Minister, Dewar, the Labour Party in Scotland narrowly elected Henry McLeish to succeed him as their leader. Later that month McLeish, hitherto Minister for Enterprise and Lifelong Learning, was also elected to succeed Dewar as First Minister. Meanwhile, in Wales the leader of Plaid Cymru, Dafydd Wigley, resigned in May owing to ill health; he was replaced by Ieuan Wyn Jones in August. In October the ruling Labour Party entered into a coalition agreement with the Liberal Democrats, who obtained two portfolios, including that of Deputy First Minister, in the reorganized nine-member Welsh Cabinet. The coalition was to remain in force until the elections to the Welsh Assembly in 2003.

In early September 2000 the Labour administration suffered its most serious domestic crisis since coming to power when protesters (primarily road hauliers and farmers) angered by rising fuel prices, staged a nation-wide blockade of the country's major petroleum refineries and distribution depots, exhausting supplies at more than 90% of British retail fuel outlets. In mid-September Blair, who had rejected the protesters' demands for concessions, predicted a swift end to the crisis after invoking 'contingency powers' under the 1976 Energy Act in an attempt to force the oil companies to break the blockade and deliver supplies; however, to Blair's embarrassment the blockades remained in place. The following day troops were placed on stand-by in an attempt to pressurize the protesters into ending their blockade and Blair warned of the genuine possibility of the loss of life if supplies to hospitals were not immediately restored. Faced with the prospect of losing popular support the protesters finally called off the blockades (though they pledged to resume action if fuel prices had not been reduced within 60 days) and deliveries of fuel recommenced. Three major petroleum companies concurrently announced further price rises, which were fiercely condemned by both the Government and protesters and as a result subsequently reversed. As fuel distribution gradually returned to normal, Blair announced that legislation would be introduced to place a statutory duty on petroleum companies to maintain fuel supplies. The crisis resulted in a temporary loss of popular support for the Labour Government. In November the Government announced concessions aimed at road hauliers and motorists, notably a small reduction in the price of petroleum and the freezing of duty on fuel until at least April 2002.

In late January 2001 the Government suffered a further reverse when Mandelson resigned as Secretary of State for Northern Ireland after his initial denial of any direct involvement in an enquiry to the Home Office in June 1998 regarding the application for British citizenship of an Indian business executive, Srichand Hinduja, appeared to be false. Mandelson insisted that he had not acted improperly, maintaining that he could not recall making the enquiry, but acknowledged that he had failed to disclose the whole truth about his role in the application and had been responsible for 'wrong information' given out by the Government. Blair immediately launched an inquiry into the incident, to be headed by Sir Anthony Hammond, and which would also investigate the conduct of a minister of state, Keith Vaz, who had also made representations on behalf of Hinduja and his brother, Gopichand, to the Home Office. In the ensuing cabinet reorganization Dr John Reid, hitherto Secretary of State for Scotland, was appointed to succeed Mandelson, thus becoming the first Roman Catholic to hold the Northern Ireland portfolio. In March 2001 Hammond's report exonerated Mandelson of any wrongdoing and affirmed that Mandelson's initial belief that he had not personally contacted the Home Office had been honestly held.

On 20 February 2001 incidences of foot-and-mouth disease (FMD–a non-fatal yet highly contagious virus carried by cloven-hoofed animals) were discovered at an abattoir in south-east England. The following day, in response to the outbreak, the European Commission imposed a temporary ban on the export of live animals, meat and dairy products from the United Kingdom and on 23 February the Government outlawed the movement of all British livestock. Furthermore, legislation was invoked empowering local authorities to prohibit the use of footpaths and public rights of way in areas affected by the outbreak and vast areas of the countryside were closed to the public. Despite these measures FMD spread at a rapid rate and cases were confirmed in various locations throughout the United Kingdom. By the end of February some 30,000 animals had been consigned to slaughter and in mid-March plans were announced for an emergency preventative cull of all sheep, pigs and goats residing within a 3-km radius of infected farms. In that month the announcement that in many areas long delays were occurring between the diagnosis, slaughter and disposal of infected animals provoked opposition criticism of the Government's handling of the crisis. Belated government proposals to vaccinate cattle against FMD were abandoned in mid-April, owing to a lack of support for the policy from farmers. It had been widely anticipated (though not officially confirmed) that a general election would be conducted concurrently with local elections scheduled for 3 May. The Government initially insisted that local elections (and thus perhaps the general election) would proceed as intended on that date. However, the continuing rise

in the number of cases of FMD, mounting pressure from agricultural interest groups and popular opposition to the timing of the polls, led to a government announcement on 2 April that emergency legislation would be introduced to provide for a five-week postponement of the local elections (the first time such legislation had been required during peacetime). By late April new outbreaks of FMD were declining rapidly in number and it appeared that the situation had been brought under control. The Government announced the relaxation of its slaughter policy (giving veterinary surgeons discretion regarding the slaughter of healthy animals within a 3-km radius of an infection), and restrictions on the movement of animals in the south-west of the country (one of the areas most affected by the outbreak) were partially lifted.

In early May 2001 Blair announced that a general election (as well as the postponed local elections) would be conducted on 7 June, although new incidences of FMD continued to be discovered. It was estimated that the resultant loss of revenue from the tourism and agricultural sectors would amount to several million pounds and the Government attracted criticism for its failure adequately to compensate the tourism sector for losses incurred as a result of restrictions on access to the countryside. In August the Government announced the establishment of three separate independent inquiries into the outbreak of FMD, which would examine the Government's handling of the crisis, investigate ways of preventing future epidemics of FMD, and review the future of farming and food in the United Kingdom; however, the Government rejected opposition calls for a full public inquiry into the crisis. The last case of FMD was identified in late September and in mid-January 2002 the Government announced that the United Kingdom was free of FMD. Nevertheless, the Blair administration was heavily criticized by the National Farmer's Union, which accused the Government of presiding over a catalogue of failures and inadequacies in its handling of the crisis, and demanded the introduction of stricter controls on the import of foodstuffs. In early February the European Commission agreed to lift the remaining restrictions on the import and export of British meat, animal products and livestock. According to official figures released by the Department of the Environment, Food and Rural Affairs the 2,030 confirmed cases of FMD in the United Kingdom resulted in the slaughter of 4,077,000 animals for disease control, with a further 2,573,000 slaughtered for welfare reasons. According to a report published by the National Audit Office in June 2002, the total cost of the crisis amounted to more than £3,000m., £1,100m. of which was allocated to the compensation of farmers. The report also confirmed that the losses to the British economy resulting from the FMD crisis totalled some £5,000m. In July the inquiry into the Government's handling of the crisis was published and was highly critical of the Government's response to the outbreak, stating that FMD spread far wider than it should have as a result of inadequate contingency plans and the Government's sluggish response.

At the general election held on 7 June 2001 the Labour Party won a further comprehensive victory, securing 413 of the 659 parliamentary seats with 40.7% of the votes cast. The Conservative Party won 166 seats with 31.7% of the votes cast, while the Liberal Democrats increased their parliamentary representation to 53 seats, with 18.3% of the votes cast. The election was, however, marred by a low rate of voter participation, 59.4% (the lowest since 1918). Following his party's poor performance, Hague announced his intention to resign the leadership of the Conservative Party; in September Iain Duncan Smith, hitherto the Conservative Party's parliamentary spokesman on defence, was elected to replace Hague as Leader of the Conservative Party and thus of the opposition. Meanwhile, Blair effected a major reorganization of the Cabinet and created several new ministries. Most notably Jack Straw, hitherto Secretary of State for the Home Department, replaced Cook as Secretary of State for Foreign and Commonwealth Affairs and David Blunkett, formerly Secretary of State for Education, assumed Straw's vacated portfolio. The Ministry of Agriculture, Fisheries and Food, which had been heavily criticized for its handling of the FMD outbreak, was replaced by the Department for Environment, Food and Rural Affairs and a new Department for Work and Pensions was created. Furthermore, Blair removed the responsibility for transport, environment and the regions from the Deputy Prime Minister, John Prescott, appointing Stephen Byers, previously Secretary of State for Trade and Industry, as head of the newly formed Department for Transport, Local Government and the Regions (DTLR).

In early July 2001 the Deputy First Minister of the Welsh Assembly and Minister for Economic Development, Michael German, temporarily vacated his post after police announced that they had commenced an investigation into fraudulent activities at the Welsh Joint Education Committee's European unit, of which German was formerly in charge. Jenny Randerson, the Minister for Culture, Sport and the Welsh Language, became acting Deputy First Minister. In June 2002 German was cleared of any impropriety and reassumed the position of Deputy First Minister. Later that month Morgan effected a minor cabinet reshuffle. In late October 2001 it was revealed that the Scottish First Minister, Henry McLeish, was under police investigation for financial improprieties relating to the sub-letting of his Westminster constituency office and his apparent failure to declare the revenue received therefrom. In April the PCS had begun investigations into the matter (McLeish continued to assist the inquiry despite the fact that he had resigned his British parliamentary seat prior to the general election in June) and earlier in October he had agreed to repay the sum of £9,000. However, in early November McLeish resigned after he admitted his failure to declare rental income of more than £36,000 paid by five tenants of his constituency office over a 14-year period. Nevertheless, he maintained that he had not profited personally from the rental and had not been aware of the total sum of money involved. Later that month Jack McConnell of the Labour Party, hitherto Minister for Education, was elected First Minister defeating his nearest rival John Swinney, the leader of SNP, by 70 votes to 34. McConnell immediately effected a major reorganization of the Scottish Cabinet, dismissing five ministers, including the Minister for Finance. In early May 2002 Wendy Alexander resigned from her post as Scotland's Minister of Enterprise, Transport and Lifelong Learning. McConnell subsequently announced further changes to the Scottish Executive.

In early November 2001 the Government revealed its proposals for the reform of the House of Lords. Under the plans the number of members of the upper house would be reduced from over 700 to 600, 120 of whom would be to be directly elected. A total of 332 members would be nominated by the political parties represented in the House of Commons (the exact number nominated by each party would depend on their percentage of the vote at the most recent legislative elections), while a further 120 'People's Peers', unaffiliated to any political party, were to be appointed by an independent commission. The number of Church of England bishops entitled to sit in the House of Lords would be reduced from 26 to 16, although at least 12 Law Lords would be granted seats in the new chamber. Furthermore, at least 30% of the 600 seats would be reserved for women. The remaining 92 hereditary peers would lose their right to sit, and although the new House of Lords would retain its right to delay laws (for a three-month period) its power to veto legislation passed in the House of Commons would be removed. It was envisaged that the reforms would take place over a 10-year transitional period. However, the proposals were criticized by Conservative and Liberal Democrat MPs, as well as by several senior figures within the Labour Party, who demanded that a larger number of members of the new upper house be elected, and at a debate in the House of Commons in January 2002 some 100 Labour MPs voiced their opposition to the proposals. The President of the Council and Leader of the House of Commons, Robin Cook, who was charged with overseeing the reform process, insisted that there would be no compromise on the removal of the 92 hereditary peers, but did indicate his willingness to consider plans to increase the number of elected members. The public consultation process on the proposals ended in late January and Cook announced that there would be an extended period of reflection and predicted that the definitive reform of the House of Lords would be achieved during the next session of Parliament, due to commence in November. In mid-May, however, the Government effectively abandoned the recommendations produced in November 2001 and announced plans to establish a new joint committee of MPs and peers, which would be charged with formulating new proposals regarding the role and composition of the House of Lords. In December 2002 the committee presented seven options for the future proportion of elected members in the House of Lords, ranging from a wholly elected chamber to a wholly appointed house. However, in early February all seven options were rejected by MPs voting in the House of Commons and it was conceded that there would be little progress on the issue prior to the next general election.

In mid-December 2001 a Labour MP announced his defection to the Liberal Democrats in protest at the Government's continued failure to bring about improvements in public services. Furthermore, Blair also encountered criticism for allegedly neglecting domestic issues and increasingly concentrating on foreign policy, most notably the war in Afghanistan (see below). Also in December emergency anti-terrorism legislation was introduced in response to the events of 11 September in the USA (see below), which, most notably, provided Blunkett with the power to detain suspected international terrorists without trial if their deportation was not deemed possible. However, in July 2002 the legislation was deemed unlawful and in breach of the European Convention on Human Rights by the Special Immigration Appeals Committee. In October the British Court of Appeal ruled against the July decision. Since December 2001 12 people had been arrested and detained under the new legislation and it was expected that they would appeal against the latest judgment declaring their detention legal.

In late May 2002 Byers, who had been under increasing pressure regarding his decision to place Railtrack (the operating company responsible for rail infrastructure in the United Kingdom) in administration (see below), and who had faced allegations that he had deliberately misled Parliament, resigned as Secretary of State for Transport, Local Government and the Regions. The resignation precipitated a major reorganization of several government departments. Most notably, the DTLR was abolished and a new Department for Transport, to be headed by Alistair Darling, hitherto Secretary of State for Work and Pensions, was created. Most of the other responsibilities of the former DTLR were transferred to the Office of the Deputy Prime Minister.

In mid-October 2002 members of the Fire Brigades Union (FBU) voted overwhelmingly in favour of industrial action, following the breakdown of negotiations between local government employers and the FBU. An independent review of the fire service by Sir George Bain, a former chairman of the Low Pay Commission, had recommended an 11% pay increase, linked to the modernization of working practices; however, the FBU demanded a 40% pay increase and opposed the modernization plans. In mid-November firefighters commenced a 48-hour strike, the first of a threatened 32 days of strike action. Emergency services were covered by the armed forces. An offer of a 16% two-year increase, again linked to reforms, failed to prevent a second strike of eight days' duration, later that month. In December both sides agreed to negotiations with the Advisory, Conciliation and Arbitration Service; the talks proved unsuccessful and further strikes of 24 and 48 hours were held on 21 and 28 January 2003, respectively. The dispute continued, although planned strikes in February and March were postponed. In mid-March FBU members had defied the union's executive and rejected a revised pay offer worth 16% over three years, prompting Prescott to announce his intention to introduce legislation which would allow him to impose an agreement on pay and conditions upon the FBU members. In April local government employers were ordered to commence plans to modernize the fire service despite the fact that no pay agreement had been reached.

Meanwhile, in late October 2002 the Secretary of State for Education and Skills, Estelle Morris, resigned following a series of educational crises. In the ensuing cabinet reshuffle, Charles Clarke, hitherto Minister without Portfolio and Party Chair., assumed Morris's vacated position. Clarke was replaced by Dr John Reid and Paul Murphy, previously Secretary of State for Wales, was appointed as Reid's successor as Secretary of State for Northern Ireland.

In early January 2003 six men of North African origin were arrested, following a raid by anti-terrorist police and agents from the defence intelligence unit, MI5, on a flat in London, in which traces of the deadly poison ricin were discovered. Additional arrests were made country-wide as part of an ongoing investigation and in mid-January a police officer was fatally stabbed during an anti-terrorist raid in Manchester. Those arrested were alleged to have links with the al-Qa'ida (Base) organization of the Islamist fundamentalist Osama bin Laden, which was believed to have been responsible for the September 2001 suicide attacks on the USA, and in February three men appeared in court charged with conspiring to produce a chemical weapon. Later in January security forces arrested seven people after arms were discovered during a raid on a London mosque. Two suspects were detained on charges of involvement in terrorism-related offences. In early April Blunkett announced the withdrawal of British citizenship from the mosque's imam, Sheikh Abu Hamza, under new legislation which allowed British nationality to be removed from people with dual citizenship who were believed to have acted against the vital interests of the country. Hamza subsequently appealed against the decision. Meanwhile, the United Kingdom was placed on high alert in mid-February as troops and armoured vehicles were temporarily stationed at London's Heathrow airport, following intelligence reports of the possibility of a terrorist attack involving the use of surface-to-air missiles to bring down aircraft.

In mid-March 2003 Clare Short announced that she would resign as Secretary of State for International Development if Blair approved British participation in the US-led campaign to oust the regime of Saddam Hussain in Iraq (see below) without the support of a UN resolution. Following the collapse of diplomatic efforts to secure a second UN resolution authorizing military action in Iraq and the announcement that British troops would be deployed as part of the US-led coalition to remove Hussain, Cook announced his resignation as Leader of the House of Commons, citing his unwillingness to accept collective responsibility for the decision to commit the United Kingdom to military action in Iraq without international agreement or domestic support. Two ministers of state and a number of ministerial aides also resigned in protest at Blair's decision. However, Short stated that she intended to remain in her post; her decision attracted criticism from across the political spectrum. Blair suffered another major reverse after 139 Labour MPs voted in favour of a motion stating that there was no moral justification for an attack in Iraq, although another motion endorsing the Prime Minister's strategy was approved by a total of 412 votes to 149. In early April Blair appointed Reid to replace Cook. Ian McCartney, hitherto Secretary of State for Work and Pensions, succeeded Reid as Minister without Portfolio and Party Chair. Short resigned as Secretary of State for International Development in mid-May as rumours abounded that Blair was preparing to remove her from the Cabinet; she accused Blair of reneging on assurances he had made to her concerning the need for a UN mandate to establish a legitimate Iraqi Government. Short was succeeded by Baroness Amos, who became Britain's first black female Cabinet minister.

At elections to the Scottish and Welsh legislative authorities held on 1 May 2003 the Labour Party again won the largest number of seats in both assemblies. In Wales Labour secured 30 of the 60 available seats, thus narrowly failing to achieve an overall majority. Plaid Cymru won 12 seats, the Conservatives 11, and the Liberal Democrats six; the remaining seat was taken by an independent candidate. Morgan subsequently unveiled a nine-member, all-Labour Cabinet. In Scotland the Labour Party obtained 50 of the total 129 seats, while the SNP took 27, the Conservatives 18, the Liberal Democrats 17, the Scottish Green Party seven, and the Scottish Socialist Party six; the remaining four seats were won by independent candidates. Following negotiations between the Labour Party and the Liberal Democrats, the two parties agreed to continue their coalition and in mid-May McConnell announced a new 11-member administration comprising eight Labour and three Liberal Democrat ministers.

In the 1980s and early 1990s the Irish Republican Army (IRA) continued its campaign of violence and mounted frequent attacks against targets on the British mainland. In July 1993 a security cordon was formed around the City of London, which permitted police to stop and search vehicles at road-blocks at access routes. Responsibility for countering the IRA's campaign was transferred from the police force to MI5. In late 1993 and early 1994 police made several large seizures of explosives, which the Government claimed to be evidence of improving anti-terrorist surveillance. During this period frequent discoveries of IRA devices and bomb alerts caused much disruption, especially to public transport services. In August 1994 the IRA declared a complete cessation of violence, as part of the process to achieve a political settlement in Northern Ireland. Following the cease-fire, security measures were relaxed, although Prevention of Terrorism legislation was renewed for a further year in March 1995. In December certain provisions of the Prevention of Terrorism Act (PTA), enabling the Government to exclude suspected IRA activists from Britain, were ruled to be in breach of the Treaty of Rome by the European Court of Justice.

In February 1996 the IRA's cessation of hostilities was abruptly terminated with a large bomb explosion near the City of London, which killed two people and caused extensive structural damage. Security measures in the capital were again intensified, although considerable disruption was caused by the discovery of a further device and several bomb alerts. Later in February a man killed in a second explosion in London was found to be an IRA activist, and in subsequent investigations the security forces uncovered details of a revived bombing campaign on the mainland. In April new legislation was approved by parliament to extend police powers under the PTA (despite criticism by civil liberties groups), in order to counter the renewed terrorist threat. In June, following the opening of political negotiations (excluding the IRA's political grouping, Sinn Féin) in Northern Ireland, an IRA bomb caused extensive damage to the centre of Manchester. In July and September raids undertaken by the security forces against suspected IRA bases in southern England resulted in the seizure of significant amounts of explosives and equipment, and were reported by the police to have averted planned attacks on infrastructural and political targets. In January 1997 the security restrictions encircling the City of London were extended. In the weeks prior to the May general election the IRA undertook a co-ordinated programme of disruption. However, in July the IRA once again announced a cessation of hostilities, and anti-terrorist measures in mainland Britain were promptly reduced. In October the Government revoked the last exclusion orders still in place under the PTA, and announced its intention to begin consideration of replacement legislation following its renewal in March 1998. Between June 2000 and August 2001 there were seven attacks on mainland Britain by an Irish dissident republican group, the Real IRA, who were opposed to the peace settlement agreed in April 1998 (the Good Friday Agreement); prompting the intensification of mainland security measures. (For Northern Ireland, see the subsequent chapter.)

In May 1997 the newly elected Labour Government announced proposals to incorporate the provisions of the European Convention on Human Rights into domestic legislation and to extend the jurisdiction of United Kingdom courts to cover the rights guaranteed in the Convention. The Human Rights Act received Royal Assent in November 1998 and came into force in October 2000.

In October 1999, following the United Kingdom's worst rail disaster for more than 10 years—a collision between two trains near London's Paddington station that resulted in 31 fatalities —the Government established an official inquiry, under senior Scottish judge Lord Cullen, to investigate the circumstances of the accident. The inquiry was to operate jointly with an ongoing inquiry into an earlier major rail disaster at Southall, London, in 1997, which resulted in seven fatalities. In addition, the Government announced that a separate inquiry, under the chairmanship of the President of the Royal Academy of Engineering, Sir David Davies, would examine existing rail safety systems and assess the merits of alternative systems. In December 1999 the Government announced a 10-year programme for upgrading the United Kingdom's transport system involving expenditure of at least £80,000m. by the public and private sectors combined. In February 2000 the Government was widely criticized following the announcement that responsibility for rail safety was to be vested in a new subsidiary of Railtrack rather than in a wholly independent body as envisaged in the wake of the Paddington disaster. However, the subsidiary was to have its own board and chief executive whose pay would not be linked to Railtrack's commercial performance. Later that month the inquiry into the Southall accident published its report, which concluded that a major cause of the crash had been confused and inadequate safety rules in the various privatized rail companies.

In mid-October 2000 the derailing of a high-speed train at Hatfield (north of London), which resulted in the death of four passengers, deepened public concern about safety standards on British railways. An investigation into the incident established that a cracked rail in a section of the track had been the cause of the accident. Railtrack admitted that that particular stretch of track had been in 'appalling' condition and that trains should not have been permitted to travel at full speed along it. An emergency programme of repairs to sub-standard sections of railway lines was subsequently implemented in some 300 locations along with wide-scale speed restrictions resulting in major disruptions to rail services throughout late 2000 and early 2001. In late February 2001 a further major railway disaster occurred, when a motor vehicle veered from an adjacent motorway onto a railway line where it was struck by an express train, which was derailed and collided with an oncoming freight train. The incident came just days after speed restrictions had been lifted on that particular stretch of track and resulted in the death of 10 passengers. Although no blame was attached to the rail industry for the accident it resulted in a further loss of confidence in the safety of rail services in the United Kingdom. In June Cullen issued a report on the Paddington rail crash in which he accused Railtrack of having 'lamentably failed' to act on a number of occasions over complaints that the signal through which the train incorrectly travelled was not clearly visible. He also severely criticized the inadequate safety and training procedures of Thames Trains (the company responsible for operating services on that part of the rail network) and produced 89 recommendations, which he insisted be introduced and adhered to within two years. Cullen issued a second report in September in which, most notably, he called for the establishment of two new bodies to monitor industry safety standards and to investigate rail accidents. Furthermore he also recommended the installation of the sophisticated automatic train protection (ATP) safety system on all stretches of the United Kingdom rail network by 2010.

The British rail network suffered a further major setback in October 2001 when the Secretary of State for Transport, Local Government and the Regions, Stephen Byers, controversially placed the heavily-indebted Railtrack into administration and announced plans to replace it with a 'not-for-profit' company to be formed by train operators, freight companies, passenger groups and trade unions. Shortly before announcing the decision, Byers had refused Railtrack's request for substantial further government funding and informed the company's Chairman, John Robinson, that a £150m. tranche of a £1,500m. emergency credit, agreed by the Government in April, would not be released. The following day Railtrack's Chief Executive, Steve Marshall, denounced the Government's treatment of the company and its shareholders as 'shoddy and unacceptable' and announced his resignation (although he was to remain in his post for up to six months while the company was in administration). Nevertheless, Byers insisted that he was not prepared to use public money to reimburse shareholders in the failed company. Railtrack's directors subsequently announced that they were investigating the possibility of suing the Government to recover losses on behalf of their shareholders. The Government endured further criticism from investors and shareholders when Marshall revealed that Byers had threatened to introduce legislation preventing Railtrack from being granted any extra capital, even if approval for the funding had been agreed by the Rail Regulator. Robinson, meanwhile, stated that he had offered to relinquish control over Railtrack and its entire equity to the Government in return for a government guarantee to subsidize the company for three years. In mid-December John Armitt replaced Marshall as Chief Executive of Railtrack and Robinson also resigned as Chairman of the company. Meanwhile, in November the DTLR confirmed that some £3,500m., a much larger figure than had previously been officially quoted, would be required to fund Railtrack for the duration of its period in administration. However, in January 2002 Railtrack's administrators, Ernst and Young, announced that the amount required would far exceed the Government's initial estimates. In early February it was revealed that the Government would not be able to meet the 2010 deadline for the installation of the ATP system recommended in the Cullen report, and that it was not likely to be in operation until 2015.

During early 2002 Byers came under increasing pressure from financial institutions in the City of London to compensate Railtrack shareholders and a series of one-day strikes by railway workers in the south-west of the country intensified the crisis on the British rail network. In late March a £500m. bid for Railtrack was tabled by Network Rail, a company that had been formed by Byers in October 2001 and had no shareholders, and thus pledged to reinvest any operating surplus in the rail infrastructure. Network Rail's offer included a government grant worth £300m., although, Byers stressed that this sum would only be payable to the company if it succeeded in swiftly removing the rail system from the control of the administrators. Network Rail's chairman subsequently declared his optimism that Railtrack could be released from administration as early as the end of July 2002. Shortly after the Network Rail offer was received Railtrack announced that it would no longer seek to proceed with legal action to recover losses for shareholders (as they would be receiving a return on their investment if Network Rail's bid was successful). Byers' handling of the affair was nevertheless severely criticized by both Labour and opposition MPs, who accused him of reneging on his earlier pledge not to use public money to compensate Railtrack shareholders. Byers,

however, maintained that the £300m. was not extra money but, in fact, capital that represented the value of an early exit from administration. Public confidence in the British rail network was further undermined by a rail crash at Potters Bar (just 10 km south of the site of the Hatfield disaster) in early May in which seven people were killed and some 70 people were injured; later that month Byers announced his resignation (see above). In early October Railtrack was released from administration and Network Rail assumed the responsibility for running the United Kingdom's railway infrastructure.

The United Kingdom became a full member of the EC in January 1973. A referendum in 1975 endorsed British membership by a large majority. The first direct election of British representatives to the European Parliament took place in June 1979. During the 1980s the Thatcher Government demanded controls on spending by the EC, and particularly reform of the CAP, and expressed scepticism regarding proposals for greater European economic unity, on the grounds that this was likely to entail a loss of national sovereignty. In October 1990, however, the United Kingdom joined the ERM. Following Major's assumption of the British premiership, relations with individual members of the EC (particularly Germany) improved, and the Government adopted a more pragmatic approach towards European developments. Nevertheless, the British Government agreed to the terms of the Treaty on European Union only after several months of negotiations had produced substantial concessions for the United Kingdom. In particular, the United Kingdom's participation in the final stage of EMU (including the adoption of a single EC currency by 2000) was made optional. Following the implementation of the Maastricht Treaty in November 1993, proposals to extend membership of the EU (as the EC became) to other European countries provoked concern on the part of the British Government over voting rights for larger countries within the EU's Council of Ministers; however, a compromise agreement effectively permitting new members to join the EU was concluded in March 1994. In December, despite objections on the part of the United Kingdom, EU ministers approved a new fisheries agreement, which permitted controlled access for Spanish trawlers to an area of water around Ireland. The accord was deeply unpopular among British fishing communities, who advocated a withdrawal from the Common Fisheries Policy (CFP).

British relations with the EU were adversely affected by concerns over the safety of beef from British cattle. In March 1996 a report by a government health advisory committee recognized a possible link between BSE, evident in cattle herds in all parts of the country, and a new strain of Creutzfeldt-Jakob disease (CJD), a degenerative disease affecting humans. The findings of the report provoked a serious crisis of consumer confidence within the United Kingdom and abroad, and several countries announced a ban on all imports of beef and related products from the United Kingdom. At the end of March comprehensive restrictions on the export from the United Kingdom of all live cattle, beef and derivatives were imposed by the European Commission. EU ministers of agriculture undertook to support the British Government in compensating farmers for any necessary slaughter of cattle herds, on condition that adequate measures were adopted to eradicate BSE. In February 1997 the European Parliament adopted the report of a special committee charged with consideration of the BSE affair, which was highly critical of the response to the crisis of the British Government, which had adopted a policy on 'non-co-operation' with the work of the EU in an attempt to force the removal of the trade restrictions.

The election, in May 1997, of the Labour Government generated expectations of a significant improvement of relations between the United Kingdom and the EU. The Blair administration immediately announced its intention to withdraw the country's option not to participate in the 'social chapter' of the Maastricht Treaty, and to promote completion of the internal economic market and enlargement of the EU. However, the Government's opposition to greater EU authority over national borders and immigration controls, and its demands for reform of the CAP, remained as potential obstacles to a successful conclusion of the negotiations to review the implementation of the Maastricht Treaty. In June 1997 EU Heads of Government signed the Treaty of Amsterdam, amending the Maastricht Treaty. The new agreement incorporated the social chapter, given the Labour Government's willingness to subscribe to the protocol, although it was not expected to be enforced in the United Kingdom until the new Treaty had been ratified by all members. The United Kingdom, together with Ireland, secured an exemption from obligations with regard to immigration, asylum and visa policies; however, Blair negotiated an option to participate in certain co-operative aspects of the border arrangements.

In July 1997 the European Commission criticized the Government for failing to prevent illegal exports of beef. The Minister of Agriculture, Fisheries and Food, Jack Cunningham, agreed to tighten measures to act against meat-processing plants and suppliers who were breaching the EU ban. The Government's efforts to restore confidence in British beef products included pursuing the selective slaughter of cattle, agreed under the previous administration, developing the certified herd scheme (initially proposed by the Major Government) to allow for the export of beef from herds where computerized records could prove there had been no cases of BSE for at least eight years, and promoting a date-based scheme to export meat from animals born since August 1996 (when the last stocks of contaminated animal feed had been destroyed). In late 1997 the Government further angered farmers when it unilaterally imposed a ban on the sale of beef still on the bone, on the basis of scientific evidence that it carried a small risk of BSE infection. (This ban was lifted in December 1999.) In March 1998 EU agriculture ministers endorsed the application of the certified herds scheme, which, in June, provided for the first export sales of beef from approved farms in Northern Ireland. Also in March a public inquiry was established in the United Kingdom to review the emergence and identification of BSE and the new variant of CJD over the 10 years prior to March 1996. Sir Nicholas Phillips, a judge of the Court of Appeal, was appointed to lead the inquiry. In October 2000 the long-delayed report of the Phillips inquiry into the BSE crisis was finally published. In the 16-volume report Lord Phillips attributed the BSE crisis to intensive farming and the practice of feeding cattle and sheep remains to cows, yet stated that neither the BSE epidemic nor the infection of consumers could have been prevented because, owing to the long incubation period of the disease, it had taken hold before the first cattle were identified as suffering from the disease. Furthermore, he exonerated the previous Conservative administration of accusations that it had lied to the public and concealed the threat posed by the epidemic. The report did, however, maintain that the then Government had been preoccupied with preventing an alarmist overreaction and had failed to inform the public of the risk to human health from BSE, which it mistakenly believed was remote. The report was also critical of the Ministry of Agriculture, Fisheries and Food and 25 individuals (including two former Conservative Ministers of Agriculture) for their handling of the crisis.

In July 1999 the European Commission formally ended the ban on British beef exports, with effect from 1 August, subject to the provision that all beef was de-boned and came from animals the pedigree of which could be traced. However, despite the Commission's ruling, France announced that it would maintain its embargo on British beef pending a report by its own food safety agency on the advisability of ending restrictions. Similarly, Germany also delayed ending the ban pending a decision by its parliament. In October, following the recommendation by the French food safety agency that its Government maintain the ban, France presented new evidence to the European Commission and demanded that a new scientific study be conducted. However, the results of the study, conducted that month by an EU scientific steering committee, concluded that there was no justification for the continuing French ban. In November, in the light of continued French intransigence, the European Commission announced its intention to initiate legal proceedings to secure French compliance. In late November it was envisaged that an understanding reached between the British and French Governments, involving a minor revision of the conditions under which British beef would be exported, would facilitate an ending of the French ban. However, in early December, following the French food safety agency's inability to reach a decision on the advisability of the new proposal, the French Government announced its decision to maintain its embargo. In January 2000 the European Commission formally began legal proceedings against France at the European Court of Justice (ECJ) in Luxembourg. However, the legal process was complicated by a French counter-claim already submitted to the court asserting that the European Commission had breached EU law by failing to protect public health when it rejected the French submission that it was unsafe to end the ban on British beef. Later that month the European Commission announced that it would not

seek an interim judgment to force France to lift its ban pending a ruling by the ECJ, which, it was envisaged, could take up to two years. Legal action was also initiated by the Commission against Germany, which continued to uphold its ban. In September 2001 the ECJ issued a preliminary ruling, which stated that the French ban on British beef was illegal; that initial ruling was upheld at a subsequent ECJ hearing in December. In March 2002 the European Commission issued France with a letter of formal notice identifying France's failure to end the embargo on British beef and to which the French Government was expected to respond within 30 days. However, the French Minister of Agriculture and Fisheries insisted that the ban would remain in place at least until after the legislative elections in that country, scheduled to be held in June. In October the French Government removed the ban on British beef. Later that month relations between France and the United Kingdom were again strained following disagreements between Blair and the French President, Jacques Chirac, over EU agricultural policy reform. Chirac subsequently postponed an British–French summit scheduled for December, although in November it was announced that the summit would take place in February 2003. Bilateral relations deteriorated further after France invited the President of Zimbabwe, Robert Mugabe, to attend a summit of African leaders in Paris. Sanctions prohibiting Mugabe and other Zimbabwean political leaders from travelling to EU countries had been imposed in February 2002 in response to Zimbabwe's prevention of the deployment of an EU observation mission which was to monitor elections in that country. Relations between the United Kingdom and France were also strained by their differing views on the necessity of military action in Iraq (see below).

At the end of October 1997 the Chancellor of the Exchequer, Gordon Brown, attempted to clarify the Government's stance on the European single currency, following a period of intense speculation. He identified five key principles for participation in EMU, relating to its impact on the British economy and employment, and insisted that membership would have to be preceded by a sustained period of economic stability. In December 1997 Blair objected to a decision of other EU leaders to establish a new economic policy group comprising representatives of countries adopting the single currency from 1 January 1999. None the less, the Government emphasized its commitment to the successful introduction of the euro (as the currency was designated). In May 1999 Blair expressed his intention to end what he termed Britain's 'ambivalence' towards the EU and to make the country a 'leading partner' in the bloc. Earlier in the year he had predicted that the relevant conditions for participation in EMU would be in place shortly after the next general election. Following the Labour party's re-election in June 2001, speculation mounted that a referendum on the United Kingdom's participation in the single currency would be held by late 2002. However, in November 2001 Brown played down the prospect of such a referendum and insisted that the assessment of the five key principles would not take place until 2003. Nevertheless, later that month in a speech to the European Research Institute Blair insisted that the country was 'inextricably linked' to Europe, and speculation again increased that a referendum would be held in late 2002.

Following Iraq's forcible annexation of Kuwait in August 1990, the British Government promptly supported the efforts of the USA in defending Saudi Arabia from potential Iraqi aggression and deployed some 42,000 personnel in the subsequent engagement in hostilities against Iraq, under the auspices of the UN. British troops also participated in subsequent humanitarian efforts to protect the Kurdish population within Iraq from persecution by the Iraqi armed forces. In January 1993 British fighter aircraft participated in US-led attacks on military targets in Iraq, launched in response to renewed Iraqi incursions into Kuwait and obstruction of a UN investigation into a suspected Iraqi nuclear weapons programme. In September 1996 the British Government awarded political and logistical support to a series of air-strikes by the USA against targets in Iraq. In December 1998, following Iraq's refusal to co-operate with weapons inspections by the UN Special Commission (see p. 14), the USA and the United Kingdom conducted a further series of air-strikes in an effort to 'degrade' Iraq's military capabilities. Further airborne attacks were conducted in early 1999 and mid-2000 in response to alleged violations by Iraq of the UN air exclusion zone. In February 2001 the United Kingdom and the USA were again involved in the bombardment of a number of targets in Iraq, in response to a reportedly increased threat to aircraft from those countries in the preceding weeks. The action was, however, condemned by several Western and Arab countries. Further air-strikes against targets in southern Iraq were carried out in by British and US military aircraft in August. In March 2002 Blair faced opposition from within the Labour Party as speculation mounted about the possibility of further military action in Iraq. Blair indicated in July that he had 'tremendous concerns' about any possible military strikes on Iraq and subsequently announced his support for the UN Security Council's proposal that UN weapons inspectors be re-admitted to Iraq. He did, however, stress in late August that the British Government was determined to deal with the threat posed by Iraq's posession of weapons of mass destruction. In early September in response to mounting public opposition to possible military action in Iraq, Blair insisted that no decision on such moves had yet been taken but stated that he would publish a dossier outlining the 'real and unique threat' posed by the regime of the Iraqi President, Saddam Hussain, by the end of the month. Following a meeting with US President George W. Bush, Blair announced that the United Kingdom and the USA would attempt to secure a new UN Security Council resolution that would approve military action in Iraq, should that country fail to comply with UN weapons inspectors; days later the Prime Minister also approved the emergency recall of Parliament in order to discuss the crisis. Both British and US officials greeted with scepticism Iraq's declaration, made on 16 September, of its willingness to readmit weapons inspectors 'without conditions'; however, the People's Republic of China, France and Russia cautiously welcomed the move. In late September the British Government published the dossier outlining its case against the Iraqi regime and the perceived threat posed by that country's 'illicit weapons programmes' to the security of both the West and the Middle East. However, it appeared that the United Kingdom and the USA were becoming increasingly isolated in their attempts to secure approval for the use of military force against Iraq. On 8 November, after a compromise had been reached between the five permanent members, the UN Security Council unanimously adopted Resolution 1441, which demanded, *inter alia*, that Iraq permit weapons inspectors from the UN Monitoring, Verification and Inspection Commission (UNMOVIC, see p. 14) and the International Atomic Energy Agency (IAEA, see p. 80) unrestricted access to sites suspected of holding illegal weapons and required the Iraqi leadership to make a full declaration of its chemical, biological, nuclear and ballistic weapons, as well as related materials used in civilian industries, within 30 days. The resolution warned that this represented a 'final opportunity' for the Iraqi authorities to comply with its disarmament obligations under previous UN resolutions, affirming that Iraq would face 'serious consequences' in the event of non-compliance with the UN inspectors or of any 'false statements and omissions' in its weapons declaration. Later in November the Liberal Democrat's parliamentary motion proposing that no military action should be taken against Iraq without a fresh mandate from the UN and a vote in the House of Commons was defeated by 452 votes to 85; 32 Labour MPs voted in favour of the motion.

In mid-December 2002 the British Secretary of State for Foreign and Commonwealth Affairs, Jack Straw, stated that Hussain's claims that he had destroyed all weapons of mass destruction were an 'obvious falsehood'. The USA also stated that Iraq was in 'material breach' of UN Resolution 1441 since it had failed to give a complete account of its weapons capabilities, citing in particular Iraq's failure to account for stocks of biological weapons such as anthrax. During January 2003 Blair, while asserting that conflict was not inevitable if Iraq complied with the UN's disarmament terms and insisting that UNMOVIC and the IAEA be granted sufficient time in order to complete their inspections, ordered large numbers of troops to the Persian (Arabian) Gulf region to join the increasing number of US forces already in position there. However, it also became apparent that month that disagreements over policy on Iraq within the Government, the Labour Party and Parliament as a whole were increasing, particularly following Blair's refusal in mid-January to guarantee that British troops would not be involved in a military campaign in Iraq should there be no UN resolution approving such action. On 27 January, 60 days after the resumption of UN weapons inspections in Iraq (as stipulated under Resolution 1441), the head of UNMOVIC, Hans Blix, and the Director-General of the IAEA, Muhammad el-Baradei, briefed the UN Security Council on the progress of inspections. El-Baradei stated that IAEA inspectors had found no evidence

that Iraq had restarted its nuclear weapons programme, but requested more time for the organization to complete its research. Blix, for his part, claimed that there was no evidence that Iraq had destroyed known stocks of illegal chemical and long-range ballistic weapons, and announced that he was sceptical about Baghdad's willingness to disarm. Following the briefing Straw, declared Iraq to be in 'material breach' of Resolution 1441.

In late January 2003, as the likelihood of a US-led military response to the crisis increased, the United Kingdom was one of eight European countries to sign a joint statement expressing support for the USA's stance on Iraq. The following month increasing British popular opposition to military action against Iraq precipitated nation-wide 'anti-war' demonstrations, including a march in London attended by some 1m. people. Blair continued with his efforts to secure a second UN Security Council resolution authorizing a US-led campaign in Iraq should inspectors from UNMOVIC continue to report Baghdad's non-compliance; however, on 26 February he suffered a damaging reverse when 122 Labour MPs supported an all-party motion in the House of Commons stating that the case for military action against Iraq was 'as yet unproven'. Earlier in February the USA had presented to the Security Council what it claimed to be overwhelming evidence of Iraq's possession of weapons of mass destruction, its attempts to conceal such weapons from the UN inspectorate and its links with international terrorism, including the al-Qa'ida network. Despite signs of progress being reported by Blix in mid-February in his report to the UN Security Council, on 24 February the United Kingdom, the USA and Spain presented a draft resolution to the Security Council effectively authorizing a US-led military campaign against Hussain's regime, in response to Iraq's failure to disarm peacefully. The resolution stated that a deadline of 17 March would be set, by which time Iraq should prove that it was disarming; however, no specific mention was made of consequent military action in the event of the deadline not being met by Baghdad, apparently in an effort by the US-led coalition to persuade France, Russia and China not to exercise their right of veto. Officials from France, Russia and Germany responded to the draft resolution by presenting an alternative proposal involving an extended timetable of weapons inspections in order to avert a war. On 7 March Straw submitted an amended draft resolution to the Security Council which concluded that Iraq would have 'failed to take the final opportunity to disarm unless on or before 17 March the Council concludes that Iraq has demonstrated full, unconditional, immediate and active co-operation with its disarmament obligations under resolution 1441'. On 12 March Blair proposed six new conditions that Iraq must meet in order to prove that it was serious about disarmament: this was seen as an attempt at a compromise that might encourage wavering countries in the Security Council to support an amended resolution. The British proposals came a day after President Bush had rejected a suggested 45-day postponement of any decision to go to war by six countries that had the power to influence the Security Council vote, although Blair also indicated that British forces would participate in the anticipated US-led campaign in Iraq without the passing of a second UN resolution.

On 16 March 2003 Blair attended a summit meeting in the Azores, Portugal, along with President Bush and the Spanish Prime Minister, José María Aznar López. The following day the United Kingdom, the USA and Spain withdrew their resolution from the UN, stating that they reserved the right to take their own action to ensure Iraqi disarmament. Later that day Bush issued an ultimatum giving Saddam Hussain and his two sons 48 hours to leave Baghdad or face military action. Shortly after the expiry of Bush's 48-hour deadline, on 19 March US and British armed forces launched a 'broad and concerted campaign' (code-named 'Operation Iraqi Freedom') to oust the regime of Saddam Hussain. US-led coalition forces crossed into Iraq from Kuwait and began a steady advance towards the capital. At the same time a campaign of massive air-strikes was launched against the key symbols of the Iraqi regime in and around Baghdad, including selected military bases, communications sites, government buildings and broadcasting headquarters. The US and British forces adopted a simultaneous campaign of issuing leaflets and broadcasting radio messages, in an effort to persuade Iraqi citizens to abandon their support for the incumbent regime: their declared intention was that Operation Iraqi Freedom would precipitate the disintegration of the regime 'from within'. British troops were principally engaged in securing towns in southern Iraq, including Iraq's second city of Basra, after the US-led coalition had seized control of the key southern port of Umm Qasr and the Al-Faw Peninsular. During the campaign Blair frequently stressed his desire that the UN should play a central role in the future of Iraq. Baghdad was captured by US forces on 9 April and the Iraqi regime appeared to have collapsed. Although the whereabouts of Saddam Hussain and his sons was unknown, a number of senior Iraqi officials had been captured by late April. According to the British Ministry of Defence, at late April there had been 32 British military fatalities resulting from the conflict. Sporadic fighting was ongoing in parts of Iraq in late April, despite the arrival, earlier in the month, of US Gen. (retd) Jay Garner, as Civil Administrator, with the intention of overseeing the peaceful transition to civilian rule by Iraqi nationals. Garner claimed that appointments to a new Government would begin in May. At the end of April it was announced that at least one-third of the 45,000 British troops deployed in the Gulf region during the conflict would be withdrawn by mid-May.

In November 1992 the United Kingdom began dispatching troops to the former Yugoslav republic of Bosnia and Herzegovina, as part of the UN peace-keeping efforts. The British Government subsequently participated in diplomatic efforts to achieve a peace settlement in Bosnia and Herzegovina. Following the conclusion of the Dayton peace agreement by all parties to the Yugoslav conflict in November 1995 British troops have continued to serve in the region under NATO-led operations to secure implementation of the accord.

In early 1999 the United Kingdom was one of the principal participants in a NATO air offensive against the Federal Republic of Yugoslavia (now Serbia and Montenegro). The campaign, which began in March, was intended to end the atrocities committed by Serb forces against ethnic Albanians in the Serbian province of Kosovo (see the chapter on Serbia and Montenegro). Although NATO did not have a direct mandate from the UN Security Council for the offensive, it insisted that earlier UN resolutions provided ample justification for the use of force on humanitarian grounds. However, although NATO's stated targets were to be exclusively military, the campaign was widely criticized for the number of civilian casualties caused by NATO errors. It was also widely held that NATO was failing in its stated aim of averting a humanitarian disaster in Kosovo, because the air offensive had prompted Serbia to intensify its attacks on Kosovars, provoking a severe refugee crisis with hundreds of thousands of Kosovars attempting to escape the province. In view of the refugee crisis, in late March Blair announced the establishment of a cross-departmental group to respond to the problem, and pledged £10m. in aid. Following a visit to Kosovar refugee encampments in the former Yugoslav republic of Macedonia (FYRM) in May, Blair promised to increase aid to £40m. and announced that the United Kingdom would receive 1,000 refugees a week. The Government had earlier been criticized by its NATO partners for its reluctance to accept the refugees. As the military campaign developed Blair was perceived as the most determined of NATO's leaders in his effort to force the Yugoslav President, Slobodan Milošević, to accept the alliance's terms for a cessation of hostilities. In early June Milošević conceded to these demands, and by the end of that month Serb forces had withdrawn from Kosovo. British troops formed part of the peace implementation force which entered the province to enforce the peace process. In early August 2000 two British police officers who were training local police forces in Kosovo were arrested along with two Canadian citizens by Yugoslav security forces who claimed they had evidence that the men were preparing acts of terrorism against Yugoslavia. Despite growing international pressure for their release, the four men, who had initially been denied access to diplomats and were reportedly subjected to torture, appeared in a Yugoslav court later that month and were charged with attempting to plan terrorist actions, the intent to establish an armed group and the possession of explosives. However, in early October all four men were released from detention after the British ambassador to Yugoslavia appealed to the Yugoslav prosecutor to make a gesture of goodwill. In November diplomatic relations between the two countries were restored.

In late August 2001 some 2,000 British troops were deployed in the FYRM as part of a multinational 3,500-strong NATO mission (Operation Essential Harvest) mandated to disarm members of the ethnic Albanian National Liberation Army and destroy their weapons during a 30-day period. The large proportion of British troops involved in the operation provoked criticism from opposition parties and the death of a British member of the mission later that month (caused by a missile attack on a NATO vehicle by Macedonian nationals) led to increased popular opposition in the United Kingdom to the British forces' presence in the FYRM. Nevertheless, following the successful completion of Operation Essential Harvest some 3,900 British troops remained stationed in the Balkans as part of NATO's Kosovo Force. In July 2002 it was announced that the majority of the remaining 2,000 British troops in Kosovo would be withdrawn by the end of August.

In May 2000 the United Kingdom dispatched troops to the former British colony of Sierra Leone, ostensibly to help evacuate British and other European and Commonwealth citizens following a considerable deterioration in the security situation in that country (see chapter on Sierra Leone). Having reneged on commitments made in a peace accord with the Sierra Leonean Government in July 1999, rebel troops of the Revolutionary United Front had taken hostage some 300 peacekeepers belonging to the UN mission charged with enforcing the peace process, and were advancing on the country's capital, Freetown. The British Government, which had been instrumental in brokering the fragile peace accord, rejected pleas from the Government of Sierra Leone to commit troops to the UN peacekeeping force, but, under considerable pressure from the UN, affirmed that it would remain in the country for at least one month while reinforcements to the UN force arrived. Fears that British troops would be drawn into the conflict were rejected by the British Government, which ruled out the possibility of involvement in combative action. Although it was initially announced that all British troops would be withdrawn from Sierra Leone by mid-June 2000, in early June the long-term stationing of some 300 British military personnel in Sierra Leone (primarily to train that country's armed forces and occupy key security and judicial posts) was approved by the British Government. Furthermore, the Government agreed to provide the Sierra Leonean army with an estimated 10,000 rifles. In late August 11 British troops were abducted by a rebel militia group, the West Side Boys (WSB). Five of the hostages were released on 30 August, however, negotiations to secure the release of the remaining six failed and in early September Blair ordered the intervention of a 150-strong team of paratroopers to forcibly liberate the captives. In a swift attack all six hostages were successfully freed unharmed, however, one British serviceman and 25 WSB members were killed during the rescue mission. An inquiry into the incident conducted later that month severely criticized the officer in charge of the captured group (concluding that he made a 'grave mistake' in leading his troops into rebel-held territory) and confirmed that he would face disciplinary action. Despite cross-party calls for a complete withdrawal of British troops from Sierra Leone, Cook affirmed that the incident did not adversely affect Britain's long-term commitment to the country and in mid-October more British troops arrived in Sierra Leone. In September 2001 it was announced that the number of British troops in Sierra Leone would be lowered from some 600 to 360.

The terrorist attacks on New York and Washington, DC, on 11 September 2001, for which the USA held the al-Qa'ida (Base) organization of Osama bin Laden responsible and during which 78 British citizens were killed, were denounced by Blair as an attack on the democratic world. The Prime Minister pledged that the United Kingdom would stand 'shoulder to shoulder' with the USA in its quest to bring the perpetrators of the attacks to justice and offered to provide military and diplomatic assistance to the US Government. Blair, who by late October had held talks with more than 50 foreign heads of government, played a significant role in strengthening the international coalition against terrorism and obtaining support for military action against the Islamist Taliban regime in Afghanistan, which was suspected of harbouring senior al-Qa'ida figures, including bin Laden.

On 4 October 2001 the British Government released documents detailing evidence of al-Qa'ida's responsibility for the attacks on the USA, and three days later US and British armed forces commenced the aerial bombardment of suspected al-Qa'ida camps and strategic Taliban positions in Afghanistan. Blair, however, stressed that military strikes were part of a wider, lengthy campaign against terrorism involving diplomatic, economic and political action. In mid-October British military leaders agreed the deployment of up to 1,000 ground troops in Afghanistan and the following month the Secretary of State for Defence, Geoffrey Hoon, confirmed that British troops were involved in ground operations in Afghanistan. In mid-

November 100 British soldiers, belonging to the Special Boat Service unit, seized control of Bagram airbase outside the Afghanistan capital, Kabul, and the number of British troops on 48-hour stand-by was raised from 4,000 to 6,000. The first British casualties were reported in late November after four soldiers were injured during exchanges of fire with Taliban forces. Despite this Blair announced that it was unlikely that the deployment of a large number of British soldiers would occur and by the end of November only 400 of 6,000 troops remained on high alert.

In mid-December 2001 it was announced that the United Kingdom had agreed to lead the multi-national International Security Assistance Force (ISAF), which was granted a six-month mandate by the UN to provide security in Kabul and its environs. ISAF was expected to comprise as many as 5,000 troops from 17 countries, some 2,000 of whom would be from the United Kingdom. The first British peacekeeping troops arrived in Afghanistan later in December. In March 2002 a separate force of 1,700 British combat troops was deployed in Afghanistan to assist US special forces with their pursuit of the remaining Taliban and al-Qa'ida fighters, and later that month Hoon stated that British troops would not be withdrawn from Afghanistan until the threat of al-Qa'ida and the Taliban had been completely removed. In early June Turkey assumed control of ISAF and the number of British troops in the force was reduced to 400.

In November 1991 the United Kingdom and the USA demanded that Libya extradite for trial, either in the United Kingdom or the USA, two suspected intelligence agents who were alleged to be responsible for an explosion that destroyed a US passenger aircraft over Lockerbie, Scotland, in 1988. The United Kingdom subsequently supported the imposition, by the UN, of economic and political sanctions against Libya. In view of Libya's continued refusal to allow the suspects to be tried in Scotland, in August 1998 the United Kingdom and the USA conceded to a Libyan proposal that the suspects be tried on neutral territory in the Netherlands. The proposed trial, which received the endorsement of the UN Security Council, would be heard under Scottish law by a panel of Scottish judges in the presence of international observers. In March 1999, following mediation by the South African President, Nelson Mandela, Libya finally agreed to the extradition of the suspects, who arrived for trial at Camp Zeist, a former US air base near The Hague, in early April. The UN sanctions against Libya were subsequently suspended. The trial of Abd al-Baset Ali Muhammad al-Megrahi and Al-Amin Khalifa Fhimah commenced in May 2000. At the end of January 2001 the judges announced that they had unanimously found Megrahi guilty of the murder of 270 people and sentenced him to life imprisonment, with the recommendation that he serve a minimum of 20 years. Fhimah was, however, acquitted, owing to lack of evidence of his involvement in the bombing, and freed to return to Libya. Despite mounting pressure from Arab League states, the British Foreign Secretary, Robin Cook, maintained that sanctions against Libya would not be permanently revoked until Libya accepted responsibility for the bombing and paid 'substantial' compensation. Demands for further investigation into the bombing were rejected by senior Scottish legal officials, who stated that there was insufficient evidence to justify any further proceedings against those alleged to have abetted Megrahi, although it was apparent that he had not acted alone. Shortly afterwards lawyers for Megrahi formally lodged an appeal against the conviction. The appeal hearing, before five Scottish judges, began at Camp Zeist in late January 2002. Megrahi's lawyers based their case on what they termed new 'strong circumstantial evidence', which raised the possibility that the bomb had been placed on the aircraft in the United Kingdom, and not in Malta as the trial judges had concluded. In mid-March the appeal was unanimously rejected, and Megrahi was transferred to a prison in Scotland to begin his sentence. Also that month Libya appointed an ambassador to the United Kingdom for the first time in 17 years. In early August a minister of the British Foreign and Commonwealth Office visited Libya for talks with Qaddafi, representing the first visit by a British government minister to Libya for some 20 years. After the meeting it was reported that Libya had given strong indications that it was ready to accept responsibility for the Lockerbie bombing, while the Libyan Secretary for Foreign Affairs declared that Libya was ready 'in principle' to take steps to compensate the relatives of victims. Qaddafi had also expressed his willingness to co-operate with the international community on issues such as weapons of mass destruction and the 'war against terror'.

In February 1990 diplomatic relations (severed in 1982) were restored between the United Kingdom and Argentina. While both countries continued to indicate that their respective claims to sovereignty over the Falkland Islands were not negotiable, political dialogue was able to proceed under a mutual arrangement to circumvent the issue of sovereignty. In September 1995 the two sides concluded an accord to allow for the exploration for offshore petroleum and gas deposits in the disputed waters around the Islands. A joint commission was to be established to supervise licensing and revenue-sharing. (The first licences were awarded in October 1996.) In October 1995 Major met with the Argentine President, Carlos Menem (the first meeting at this level since the 1982 war) at the UN headquarters in New York, USA. In October 1998 Menem made an official visit to the United Kingdom, the first by an Argentinian President in almost 40 years. In June 2000 relatives of the 323 Argentinians who were killed when a British submarine sank an Argentinian battleship during the Falklands conflict in 1982 announced their intention to take their claim for compensation from the British Government to the European Court of Human Rights. However, the claim was judged inadmissible the following month owing to the amount of time that had elapsed between the incident and the claim being lodged. In July 2001 Blair became the first serving British Prime Minister to visit Argentina.

The long-standing dispute with Spain over the sovereignty of Gibraltar has frequently strained relations between the two countries (see the chapters on Spain and Gibraltar). Dialogue between the United Kingdom and Spain over the future of Gibraltar resumed in July 2001 for the first time since 1998, and further discussions were held in Luxembourg in October 2001, although Gibraltar's Chief Minister, Peter Caruana, refused to attend either meeting. In November the British Government announced it would be willing to consider joint sovereignty of the territory with Spain. This statement angered Caruana, who again boycotted talks between the British and Spanish Foreign Ministers, held in Barcelona, Spain, later that month at which the British and Spanish Government concluded that they would reach an agreement on the future of the territory by mid-2002. In January Caruana agreed to attend discussions scheduled for the following month, on the condition that Gibraltar was granted equal status at the meeting and that Britain and Spain guaranteed that any proposal regarding British-Spanish joint sovereignty of the territory would be withdrawn if rejected at a referendum. Caruana's conditions were not met and he was again absent from talks held in early February. In March some 25,000 people protested in Gibraltar against the proposed power-sharing arrangement, nevertheless, both the Spanish and British Governments reiterated their determination to proceed with plans for a joint sovereignty agreement. However, in April, just days before talks on the future of Gibraltar were scheduled to recommence, the Spanish Prime Minister stated that Spain would never cede its claim to sovereignty over the territory. In response to this announcement, Caruana insisted that if the British Government entered an agreement with Spain granting concessions over sovereignty, the Gibraltar Government would organize its own referendum, thus making it even more difficult for the British and Spanish Governments to secure popular approval for their proposals. In early May Jack Straw, the Secretary of State for Foreign and Commonwealth Affairs, visited Gibraltar and stated that he would not enter into an agreement with Spain that was not in the best interests of the citizens of Gibraltar. Following talks with his Spanish counterpart, José María Aznar López, later that month Blair admitted that the process faced 'real difficulties'. In July Straw confirmed that the United Kingdom was willing to share sovereignty of the territory with Spain, subject to approval by the residents of Gibraltar at a referendum, provoking angry protests in Gibraltar, and later in July Caruana announced that Gibraltar would conduct its own referendum on the sovereignty issue by the end of October. The British Government had also agreed to allow Spain access to the military base on Gibraltar, by allowing NATO members to use it. Both the Spanish and the British Governments condemned Caruana's decision to hold a referendum and stated that it would lack any validity. The Gibraltar referendum held on 7 November, which explicitly asked if Gibraltarians approved 'of the principle that Britain and Spain should share sovereignty over Gibraltar' resulted in an overwhelming rejection of the Spanish and British proposals. Of the electorate, 99.0% voted against shared sovereignty; the rate of voter participation was recorded at 87.9%. Nevertheless, the British and Spanish Governments insisted that talks between the two countries aimed at resolving the issue would continue.

Government

The United Kingdom is a constitutional monarchy. The Sovereign is the Head of State and the monarchy is hereditary. Parliament consists of the House of Commons and the House of Lords. The 659 members of the Commons are elected for a maximum of five years by direct suffrage by all citizens of 18 years and over, using single-member constituencies. The House of Lords is composed of hereditary Peers of the Realm and Life Peers and Peeresses created by the Sovereign for outstanding public service. Legislation may be initiated in either House but it usually originates in the Commons. Each bill has three readings in the Commons and it is then passed to the House of Lords who may return it to the Commons with amendments or suggestions. The House of Lords may delay, but cannot prevent, any bill from becoming law once it has been passed by the Commons. Executive power is held by the Cabinet, headed by the Prime Minister. The Cabinet is responsible to the House of Commons.

In 1999 devolved legislative authorities were established in Scotland and Wales. In Scotland a new elected parliament, based in Edinburgh, was established with powers to legislate on all domestic matters (incl. education, health, local government and law and order) and with a mandate to vary taxes set by the Government of the United Kingdom by 3%. The Assembly has 129 members, elected every four years by a combined system of direct voting, on the basis of Westminster parliamentary constituencies, and a form of proportional representation, whereby additional members are elected from a party list on the basis of the larger constituencies used for elections to the European Parliament. The Welsh Assembly, located in Cardiff, undertook responsibility for issues covered by the Welsh Office of the Government of the United Kingdom. The 60-member Assembly was elected under the same system as in Scotland. Elections to the two Assemblies took place simultaneously in May 1999 and the transfer of powers took place on 1 July.

Legislation providing for the abolition of all but 92 hereditary peers and the establishment of an interim second chamber pending a definitive reform of the House of Lords was passed in November 1999.

Defence

The United Kingdom is a member of the North Atlantic Treaty Organization (NATO, see p. 271) and maintains a regular army. The total strength of the armed forces at 1 August 2002, including women's services (17,350) and those enlisted outside Britain (3,780), was 210,450 (army 114,800, navy 42,350, air force 53,300). In November 2000 the United Kingdom pledged to contribute 12,500 troops to a European Union rapid reaction force, which was to be ready to be deployed by 2003. There is no compulsory military service. The United Kingdom possesses its own nuclear weapons. Government defence expenditure for 2001 totalled £27,692m.

Economic Affairs

In 2001, according to estimates by the World Bank, the United Kingdom's gross national income (GNI), measured at average 1999–2001 prices, was US $1,451,442m., equivalent to $24,230 per head (or $24,460 per head on an international purchasing-power parity basis). During 1990–2001, it was estimated, the population increased at an average annual rate of 0.4%, while gross domestic product (GDP) per head increased, in real terms, by an average of 1.8% per year. Overall GDP increased, in real terms, at an average annual rate of 2.2% per year in 1990–2001; it increased by 3.0% in 2000 and by 2.2% in 2001.

Agriculture (including hunting, forestry and fishing) contributed 1.0% of GDP in 2001, and engaged 1.4% of the employed labour force in 2002. The principal crops include wheat, sugar beet, potatoes and barley. Livestock-rearing (particularly poultry and cattle) and animal products are important, as is fishing. In 2001 the agricultural sector was adversely affected by the outbreak of foot-and-mouth disease, which resulted in the slaughter of more than 6.5m. animals. The GDP of the agricultural sector decreased, in real terms, by 0.2% during 1993–2001; it declined by 3.2% in 2000 and by 11.6% in 2001, largely owing to the adverse effects of the foot-and-mouth crisis (see above).

Industry (including mining, manufacturing, construction and power) contributed 26.5% of GDP in 2001, and in 2002 engaged 20.2% of the employed labour force. Excluding the construction sector (which increased by 3.6% in 2001), industrial GDP increased, in real terms, at an average annual rate of 1.3% during 1993–2001; it increased by 1.6% in 2000, but declined by 2.1% in 2001.

Mining (including petroleum and gas extraction) contributed 2.8% of GDP in 2001 and engaged 0.8% of the employed labour force in 1990. Crude petroleum, natural gas, coal and limestone are the principal minerals produced. The GDP of the mining sector increased, in real terms, at an average annual rate of 2.4% during 1993–2001, but declined by 1.2% in 2000 and by 5.0% in 2001.

Manufacturing provided 16.8% of GDP in 2001 and engaged 13.1% of the employed labour force in 2002. Measured by the value of output, the principal branches of manufacturing in 1997 were transport equipment (accounting for 12.5% of the total), food products (11.8%), machinery (10.8%), chemical products (10.0%) and metals and metal products (7.6%). In real terms, the GDP of the manufacturing sector increased at an average annual rate of 1.1% during 1993–2001; manufacturing GDP increased by 2.0% in 2000, but declined by 2.3% in 2001.

Energy is derived principally from natural gas, petroleum and coal, although natural gas is increasingly favoured in preference to coal. Of the United Kingdom's total consumption of energy in 2000, 40.8% was derived from natural gas, 32.3% from petroleum, 16.3% from coal and 9.2% from primary electricity (including nuclear power, hydroelectric power and imports). In mid-2001 33 nuclear power reactors were operating in the United Kingdom. In 2001 mineral fuels accounted for about 4.8% of the value of total merchandise imports.

Services accounted for 72.6% of GDP in 2001. In 2002 the sector engaged 78.4% of the employed labour force. The United Kingdom is an important international centre for business and financial services. Financial intermediation and other business services (including renting and real estate) contributed 28.0% of GDP in 2001. Receipts from tourism totalled £12,805m. in 2000. However, the tourism industry suffered badly in 2001 as a result of the foot-and-mouth crisis and the events of 11 September, and tourism receipts declined by almost 12% to £11,306m. Transport and communications are also important, and the sector contributed 7.7% of GDP in 2001. In real terms, the GDP of the services sector increased at an average annual rate of 3.8% during 1993–2001, and by 3.3% in 2001.

In 2000 the United Kingdom recorded a visible trade deficit of £33,534m., and there was a deficit of £20,453m. on the current account of the balance of payments. In 2001 the principal source of imports (13.2%) was the USA, which was also the principal market for exports (15.4%) in that year. Other major trading partners include Germany, France, the Netherlands, Belgium-Luxembourg and Ireland. The principal imports in 2001 were mechanical and electrical machinery and road vehicles. The principal exports were also mechanical and electrical machinery and road vehicles.

In 2001 there was a budgetary surplus of £7,490m. (equivalent to 0.9% of GDP). At 1997 external government debt was £60,213m. The annual rate of inflation averaged 2.9% in 1990–2001; it declined to 1.8% in 2001 and to 1.7% in 2002. The rate of unemployment, according to OECD figures, averaged 5.0% of the labour force in 2001 and 5.1% in 2002.

The United Kingdom is a member of the European Union (EU —, see p. 199). It is also a member of the Organisation for Economic Co-operation and Development (OECD, see p. 277).

In the early 1990s the British economy experienced a recession; however, by 1994 the economy had recovered and strong GDP growth was recorded during the late 1990s. In May 1997 the newly-elected Labour Government confirmed its commitment to restricting the inflation rate to 2.5%, and granted the Bank of England (BoE) operational independence for monetary policy to achieve the target, within the framework of long-term economic stability. The Government also adhered to controls on public expenditure implemented under the previous administration, which, in conjunction with increased tax revenue, contributed to a reduction in the Public Sector Borrowing Requirement. The budget for 2000 marked a transition from nearly three years of restraint to substantial real increases in public spending, made possible by the continuing expansion of the economy, and in July that year the Government announced a 'comprehensive spending review' for the period 2001–04 which pledged a £43,000m. increase in public expenditure on health, education, transport and law and order. Further increases in expenditure on public services were announced in July 2002 with total funds allocated to those sectors scheduled to rise to £511,000m. in the financial year 2005–06. During the early 2000s the global economic slowdown, partly caused by the effects of the terrorist attacks on the USA in September 2001 (see Recent History), prompted the BoE to introduce a series of interest rate reductions and in February 2003 the interest rate was cut to just 3.75%—the lowest level since 1964. Although the number of Britons in employment continued to rise, reaching its highest level since 1979 in late 2002, the Government encountered a number of economic reverses in late 2002 and early 2003. The Chancellor of the Exchequer, Gordon Brown, announced large increases in the amount of money the Treasury would have to borrow—predicted to reach £24,000m. in 2003—in order to fulfil public service expenditure pledges, and both the European Commission and the IMF expressed concern at the optimism of Brown's GDP growth predictions for 2003. Furthermore, by early 2003 the rate of inflation had remained above the 2.5% desired upper limit for three consecutive months and there were increasing fears of the development of a 'two-speed' economy, as the divide between the service and manufacturing sectors failed significantly to contract. The United Kingdom's trade deficit had also risen to unprecedented levels after the value of exports declined during 2002, and GDP growth in that year was officially recorded at just 1.6%.

Education

Education takes place in five stages: nursery (now part of the 'foundation' stage in England), primary, secondary, further and higher, and is compulsory for all children between the ages of five (four in Northern Ireland) and 16. The non-compulsory fourth stage, further education, covers non-advanced education, which can be taken at both further (including tertiary) education colleges, higher education institutions and increasingly in secondary schools. For most full-time students, the fifth stage, higher education, which is study beyond Advanced Level (A Level) and their equivalent, takes place in higher education institutions.

Educational establishments in the United Kingdom are administered and financed in several ways. Most schools are controlled by local education authorities (LEAs), which are part of the structure of local government, but some are 'assisted', receiving grants direct from central government sources and being controlled by governing bodies, which have a substantial degree of autonomy. Alongside the state system, there are independent schools, which do not receive grants from public funds but are financed by fees and endowments; many of these schools are administered by charitable trusts and church organizations.

Until March 2001, further education courses in further education sector colleges in England and in Wales were largely funded through grants from the respective Further Education Funding Councils (FEFC). In April 2001, however, the Learning and Skills Council (LSC) assumed the responsibility for funding the further education sector in England, and the National Council for Education and Training for Wales (part of Education and Learning Wales—ELWa) did so for Wales. The LSC in England is also responsible for funding provision for further education and some non-prescribed higher education in further education sector colleges; it also funds some further education provided by LEA maintained and other institutions referred to as 'external institutions'. In Wales ELWa funds further education provision made by further education institutions via a third party or sponsored arrangements. The Scottish FEFC funds further education colleges in Scotland, while the Department for Employment and Learning funds further education colleges in Northern Ireland.

Government finance for publicly funded higher education institutions (to help meet the costs of teaching, research and related activities) is distributed by the Higher Education Funding Councils (HEFC) in England and Scotland, the Higher Education Council—ELWa in Wales, and the Department of Employment and Learning in Northern Ireland. In addition, some designated higher education (mainly Higher National Diplomas/Higher National Certificates and Certificates of Higher Education) is also funded by these sources. The further education sources mentioned above fund the remainder.

Student loans are the main form of support for assistance with living costs for higher education students. The maximum loan in 2002/03 for full-time students living away from home was £3,905 (£4,815 for those studying in London). The amount of loan depends on where a student lives or studies, the length of the academic year, the course of study and the year of the course.

The amount of loan paid also depends on the student's and their family's income. Loans are repaid on the basis of income after the student has left their course. Most students who began full-time undergraduate courses at publicly-funded higher academic institutions in or after 1998/99, or their parents or spouse, have to contribute towards the tuition fees for each year of the course. The level of the contribution is means-tested, although those on lower family incomes get free tuition and the maximum contribution for those on higher incomes is currently about £1,000. Since the 2000/01 academic year, eligible full-time Scottish-domiciled or EU students who are studying in Scotland no longer pay tuition fees. Other additional forms of student support include, dependant's allowances, young and mature student bursaries, hardship funds, disabled students' allowance and care leavers' grants.

Responsibility for education is substantially devolved: the Secretary of State for Education and Skills is responsible, in principle, for all sectors of education in England (the individual LEAs have substantial autonomy over the education system in their area), while the Secretary of State for Wales is responsible for all non-university education in Wales and, since April 1993, for the college of the University of Wales. The Secretaries of State for Scotland and Northern Ireland have full educational responsibilities. Assessment of the quality of schools is undertaken in England by an inspectorate, the Office for Standards in Education, in Wales by Her Majesty's Chief Inspectorate For Education and Training in Wales, in Scotland by Her Majesty's Inspectorate of Education and in Northern Ireland by the Education and Training Inspectorate.

In recent years there has been a major expansion of pre-school education. Many children under the age of five attend state nursery schools or nursery schools attached to primary schools. Others may attend playgroups in the voluntary sector or privately run nurseries. In England and Wales many primary schools also operate an early admission policy where they admit children under the age of five into 'reception classes'. The primary stage covers three age ranges: nursery (under five), infant (five to seven or eight) and junior (up to 11 or 12) but in Scotland and Northern Ireland there is generally no distinction between infant and junior schools. Most public sector primary schools take both boys and girls in mixed classes. It is usual to transfer straight to secondary school at age 11 (in England, Wales and Northern Ireland) or 12 (in Scotland), but in England some children make the transition via middle schools catering for various age ranges between eight and 14. Depending on their individual age ranges middle schools are classified as either primary or secondary.

Secondary education generally begins at the age of 11, although in England many areas have 'middle schools', as mentioned above. In most areas, the state-maintained system of comprehensive schools prevails. Pupils are admitted to such schools without reference to ability. Some localities, however, retain a system of grammar and secondary modern schools, to which admission is determined through a test of ability. The Specialist Schools Programme in England enables secondary schools to develop strength in a particular subject area, often in partnership with an employer with an interest in that same area, while still delivering a broad and balanced education through the National Curriculum, as referred to below. Any maintained secondary school in England may apply to be designated as a specialist school in one of eight specialist areas: language, sports, arts (performing, visual or media), business and enterprise, technology, engineering, science, and mathematics and computing. Schools can also combine two specialisms. Special schools (day or boarding) are provided by LEAs for certain children with special educational needs, although the vast majority are educated in ordinary schools. All children attending special schools are offered a curriculum designed to overcome their learning difficulties and to enable them to become self-reliant.

In 1989 the Government implemented legislation introduced under the Education Reform Act (1988), which provided for a national curriculum and national testing of pupils aged seven, 11 and 14 years in state schools in England and Wales (Key Stages 1, 2 and 3, respectively). All state schools in England, Wales and Northern Ireland must conform to the national curricula, which set out which subjects pupils should study, what they should be taught and what standards they should achieve. In Scotland the curriculum in state schools is not prescribed by statute; however, the Secretary of State for Scotland issues national advice and guidance to schools and Scottish

Local Authorities. The Qualifications and Curriculum Authority is the statutory body that advises the Government on all matters concerned with the curriculum and all aspects of school examinations and assessment in state schools in England. It is also responsible for vocational qualifications. Similar arrangements operate for Wales, Scotland and Northern Ireland. Examinations for the single-system General Certificate of Secondary Education (GCSE) may be taken (usually at the age of 16) in as many subjects as a candidate wishes. The General Certificate of Education Advanced Level (A Level) is generally taken at the age of 18, in a few selected subjects, and serves as a qualification for entrance to higher education. An additional examination, the Advanced Supplementary (AS) Level, was introduced in 1987. The first examinations were held in 1989; the AS Level is intended to broaden the studies of pupils pursuing A Level courses. In 1999/2000 National Qualifications (NQ) were introduced in Scotland. NQs include Standard Grades, Intermediate 1 and 2 and Higher Grades. Pupils study for the Scottish Certificate of Education (SCE)/NQ Standard Grade, approximately equivalent to GCSE, in their third and fourth years of secondary schooling (roughly ages 14 and 15). Each subject has several elements, some of which are internally assessed in school, and an award is only made (on a scale of one to seven) if the whole course has been completed and examined. The Higher Grade requires one further year of study and for the more able candidates the range of subjects taken may be as wide as at Standard Grade with as many as five or six subjects spanning both arts and science. Three or more Highers are regarded as being approximately the equivalent of two or more A Levels.

Since 1986 the National Council for Vocational Qualifications (NCVQ) has established a framework of National Vocational Qualifications (NVQs) in England, Wales and Northern Ireland. The framework is based on five defined levels of achievement, ranging from Level 1, broadly equating to foundation skills in semi-skilled occupations, to Level 5, equating to professional/senior management occupations. The competence-based system has also been extended in Scotland through a system of Scottish Vocational Qualifications (SVQs) along similar lines to the NVQs. General National Vocational Qualifications (GNVQs), along with General Scottish Vocational Qualifications (GSVQs) have also been introduced. GNVQs, which are normally studied in school or college, aim to incorporate skills required by employers and are designed to develop the skills and understanding needed in vocational areas such as business, engineering or health and social care, in order to provide an introduction into both further education and employment. GSVQs are awarded on the basis of a modular framework of National Certificate Units, which give candidates practical and knowledge-based vocational skills and are taken in secondary schools and colleges.

Further and higher education may be pursued through vocational or academic courses, on a full-time, part-time or 'sandwich' basis. The decision to admit students is made by each institution according to its own entrance requirements. The term 'further education' may be used in a general sense to cover all non-advanced courses taken after the period of compulsory education, but more commonly it excludes those staying on at secondary school and those in higher education, i.e. courses in universities and colleges leading to qualifications above A Level, SCE Higher Grade, GNVQ/NVQ level three, and their equivalents. Since 1 April 1993 sixth form colleges have been included in the further education sector.

Higher education is defined as courses that are of a standard that is higher than A Level, the SCE Higher Grade of the SCE, GNVQ/NVQ Level 3 or the Edexcel (formerly BTEC) or SQA National Certificate/Diploma. The first degree course normally lasts three or four years and leads to a Bachelor of Arts or Sciences (BA or BSc) degree. One-year postgraduate and four-year undergraduate initial teacher training courses are provided at colleges and university departments of education. There are also some two-year Bachelor of Education (BEd) courses available in the subjects for which there is a shortage of teachers. Entrants to these courses may be admitted with an Edexcel higher national award, Higher National Diploma (HND) level qualification or an advanced City and Guilds certificate and some relevant experience. Some two-year 'conversion' Postgraduate Certificate of Education courses are also available for intending secondary school teachers who wish to change subject to teach a 'shortage' subject and whose initial degree is related to the intended teaching subject. In addition to the minimum requirements listed above, entrants to initial teacher training must have reached GCSE standard in mathematics and English.

Under the provisions of the Further and Higher Education Act (1992), polytechnics and equivalent institutions were granted the same status as universities and were to be permitted to adopt the title 'university'. Polytechnics were henceforth empowered to award their own degrees, a function previously performed by the Council for National Academic Awards. Universities and polytechnics, previously funded separately, were to be financed by a single HEFC for England, the Scottish Higher Education Funding Council or the Welsh Funding Council (Higher Education Division). In 2001/02 there were 89 publicly-funded universities (47 'traditional' universities and 42 former polytechnics and colleges accorded 'university' status—including the London and Manchester Business Schools), 63 other higher education institutions as well as the Open University and the privately-funded University of Buckingham, offering courses of higher education in the United Kingdom. The Open University, which is funded directly by the Department for Education and Skills, provides degree and other courses through a combination of printed texts, correspondence tuition, television broadcasts, audio/visual cassettes and, for some courses, short residential schools. No formal qualifications are required for entry to its courses.

Total Managed Expenditure on education during the 2000–01 financial year totalled £44,108m, and represented 4.6% of GDP.

Public Holidays

2003: 1 January (New Year's Day), 2 January* (Scotland only), 18 April* (Good Friday), 21 April† (Easter Monday), 5 May* (Early May Holiday), 26 May (Spring Holiday), 4 August* (Summer Bank Holiday, Scotland only), 25 August† (Late Summer Bank Holiday), 25 December (Christmas Day), 26 December* (Boxing Day).

2004: 1 January (New Year's Day), 2 January* (Scotland only), 9 April* (Good Friday), 12 April† (Easter Monday), 3 May* (Early May Holiday), 7 June (Spring Holiday), 2 August* (Summer Bank Holiday, Scotland only), 30 August† (Late Summer Bank Holiday), 25 December (Christmas Day), 26 December* (Boxing Day).

* Bank Holidays but not national holidays in Scotland.

† Excluding Scotland.

Weights and Measures

The metric system of weights and measures is now the primary system in force, although the imperial system is still used in limited areas.

Weight
1 pound (lb) = 16 ounces (oz) = 453.59 grams.
14 pounds = 1 stone = 6.35 kilograms.
112 pounds = 1 hundredweight (cwt) = 50.8 kilograms.
20 hundredweights = 1 ton = 1,016 kilograms.

Length
1 yard (yd) = 3 feet (ft) = 36 inches (ins) = 0.9144 metre.
1,760 yards = 1 mile = 1.609 kilometres.

Capacity
1 gallon = 4 quarts = 8 pints = 4.546 litres.

Statistical Survey

Statistics refer to the United Kingdom unless otherwise indicated

Area and Population

AREA, POPULATION AND DENSITY

Area (sq km)	242,910*
Population usually resident (census results)	
21 April 1991	56,466,700
29 April 2001	
Males	28,581,233
Females	30,207,961
Total	58,789,194
Population (official estimates at mid-year)	
1999	58,481,100
2000	58,643,200
2001	58,836,700
Density (per sq km) at mid-2001	242.2

* 93,788 sq miles.

Source: Office for National Statistics.

DISTRIBUTION OF POPULATION

(estimates, at mid–2001)

	Area (sq km)	Population	Density (per sq km)
Great Britain	229,334	57,148,700	249.2
England	130,422	49,181,300	377.1
Wales	20,779	2,903,200	139.7
Scotland	78,133	5,064,200	64.8
Northern Ireland	13,576	1,689,300	124.4
Total	242,910	58,836,700	242.2

Source: Office for National Statistics.

ADMINISTRATIVE AREAS

(Great Britain only; population estimates at mid-2001, '000)

England

Greater London . .	7,188.0	Lincolnshire . . .	647.6
Metropolitan		Norfolk	797.9
Counties:		North Yorkshire . .	570.1
Greater Manchester .	2,482.8	Northamptonshire . .	630.4
Merseyside . . .	1,361.7	Northumberland . .	307.4
South Yorkshire . .	1,226.5	Nottinghamshire . .	748.8
Tyne and Wear . .	1,076.3	Oxfordshire . . .	605.9
West Midlands . .	2,554.4	Shropshire . . .	283.3
West Yorkshire . .	2,080.2	Somerset	498.7
Unitary Authorities:		Staffordshire . . .	807.1
Bath and North-east		Suffolk	669.4
Somerset . . .	169.2	Surrey	1,059.5
Blackburn with		Warwickshire . . .	506.2
Darwen	137.6	West Sussex . . .	754.3
Blackpool	142.3	Wiltshire	433.5
Bournemouth . . .	163.6	Worcestershire . .	542.2
Bracknell Forest . .	109.6		
Brighton and Hove .	248.1	**Wales**	
Bristol	380.8	*Unitary Authorities:* .	
Darlington . . .	97.9	Blaenau Gwent . .	70.0
Derby	221.7	Bridgend	128.7
East Riding of		Caerphilly	169.6
Yorkshire . . .	314.8	Cardiff	305.2
Halton	118.2	Carmarthenshire . .	173.7
Hartlepool	88.7	Ceredigion	75.3
Herefordshire . .	174.9	Conwy	109.8
Isle of Wight . . .	132.9	Denbighshire . . .	93.1
Kingston upon Hull .	243.4	Flintshire	148.6
Leicester	279.8	Gwynedd	116.8
Luton	184.3	Isle of Anglesea . .	66.7
Medway	249.7	Merthyr Tydfil . .	56.0
Middlesbrough . .	134.8	Monmouthshire . .	85.0
Milton Keynes . .	207.6	Neath Port Talbot .	134.4
North Lincolnshire .	153.0	Newport	137.0
North Somerset . .	188.8	Nottingham	267.0
North-east		Peterborough . . .	156.5
Lincolnshire . .	158.0	Plymouth	241.0
		Poole	138.4

Portsmouth . . .	186.9	Rhondda, Cynon,	
Reading	143.2	Taff	231.9
Redcar and		Swansea	223.2
Cleveland . . .	139.2	Torfaen	90.9
Rutland	34.6	The Vale of	
Slough	119.1	Glamorgan . . .	119.3
South		Wrexham	128.5
Gloucestershire .	246.0		
Southampton . . .	217.6		
Southend	160.49	**Scotland**	
Stockton-on-Tees . .	178.6	*Unitary Authorities:* .	
Stoke-on-Trent . .	240.4	Aberdeen City . .	211.9
Swindon	180.2	Aberdeenshire . .	226.9
Telford and Wrekin .	158.5	Angus	108.4
Thurrock	143.2	Argyll and Bute . .	91.3
Torbay	130.0	Clackmannanshire .	48.1
Warrington . . .	191.2	Dumfries and	
West Berkshire . .	144.5	Galloway . . .	147.8
Windsor and		Dundee City . . .	145.4
Maidenhead . .	133.5	East Ayrshire . .	120.3
Wokingham . . .	150.4	East Dunbartonshire	108.3
York	181.3	East Lothian . . .	90.2
Non-Metropolitan		East Renfrewshire .	89.4
Counties:		Edinburgh, City of .	449.0
Bedfordshire . . .	382.1	Eilean Siar . . .	26.5
Buckinghamshire . .	479.1	Falkirk	145.3
Cambridgeshire . .	553.6	Fife	349.8
Cheshire	674.2	Glasgow City . . .	578.7
Cornwall/Isles of		Highland	208.9
Scilly	502.1	Inverclyde	84.2
Cumbria	487.8	Midlothian	81.0
Derbyshire . . .	734.9	Moray	87.0
Devon	705.6	North Ayrshire . .	135.8
Dorset	391.5	North Lanarkshire .	321.2
Durham	493.7	Orkney Islands . .	19.2
East Sussex . . .	493.1	Perth and Kinross .	135.0
Essex	1,312.7	Renfrewshire . . .	172.9
Gloucestershire . .	565.0	Scottish Borders . .	107.0
Hampshire . . .	1,240.8	Shetland Islands . .	22.0
Hertfordshire . . .	1,034.9	South Ayrshire . .	112.2
Kent	1,331.1	South Lanarkshire .	302.3
Lancashire . . .	1,135.8	Stirling	86.2
Leicestershire . .	610.3	West	
Pembrokeshire . .	113.0	Dunbartonshire .	93.3
Powys	126.4	West Lothian . . .	159.0

Sources: Office for National Statistics; General Register Office for Scotland.

PRINCIPAL LOCALITIES*
(population estimates at mid-2001, '000)

Greater London			Nottingham . . .	267.0
(capital). . .	7,188.0		Belfast.	277.2
Birmingham . . .	976.4		Bolton	261.3
Leeds	715.5		Newcastle upon Tyne	259.6
Glasgow City . . .	578.7		Walsall	253.3
Sheffield	513.1		Medway	249.7
Bradford	467.9		Rotherham . . .	248.4
Liverpool	439.2		Brighton and Hove .	248.1
Edinburgh . . .	449.0		South	
Manchester . . .	392.9		Gloucestershire .	246.0
Kirklees	388.9		Kingston upon Hull .	243.4
Bristol	380.8		Plymouth	241.0
Fife	349.8		Stoke-on-Trent . .	240.4
North Lanarkshire .	321.2		Wolverhampton . .	236.4
Wakefield	315.4		Rhondda, Cynon,	
East Riding of			Taff	231.9
Yorkshire . . .	314.8		Aberdeenshire . .	226.9
Wirral	312.2		Swansea	223.2
Cardiff	305.2		Derby	221.7
Dudley	305.1		Barnsley	218.1
South Lanarkshire .	302.3		Southampton . . .	217.6
Wigan	301.5		Oldham	217.5
Coventry	300.7		Salford	215.9
Doncaster	286.9		Tameside	213.1
Stockport	284.6		Trafford	210.2
Sefton	282.9		Aberdeen City . .	211.3
Sandwell	282.8		Highland	208.9
Sunderland . . .	280.8		Milton Keynes . .	207.6
Leicester	279.8		Rochdale	205.2

* Local authority areas with populations greater than 200,000.

Sources: Office for National Statistics; General Register Offices for Scotland and Northern Ireland.

BIRTHS, MARRIAGES AND DEATHS*

	Registered live births		Registered marriages		Registered deaths	
	Number	Rate (per 1,000)	Number	Rate (per 1,000)	Number	Rate (per 1,000)
1994 . .	750,480	13.0	331,232	5.7	626,222	10.8
1995 . .	731,882	12.6	322,251	5.6	641,712	11.1
1996 . .	733,163	12.6	317,514	5.5	638,879	11.0
1997 . .	726,622	12.5	310,218	5.3	632,517	10.9
1998 . .	716,888	12.3	304,797	5.2	627,592	10.8
1999 . .	699,976	12.0	310,083	5.3	629,476	10.8
2000 . .	697,029	11.6	305,912	5.2	610,579	10.4
2001 . .	669,123	11.4	286,133	4.9	604,393	10.3

* In England and Wales, figures for births are tabulated by year of occurrence, while figures for Scotland and Northern Ireland are tabulated by year of registration. Births to non-resident mothers in Northern Ireland are excluded from the figures for the United Kingdom.

Sources: Office for National Statistics; General Register Office for Scotland; Northern Ireland Statistics and Research Agency.

Expectation of life (WHO estimates, years at birth): 77.5 (males 75.1; females 79.9) in 2001 (Source: WHO, *World Health Report*).

IMMIGRATION AND EMIGRATION*

Immigrants
('000)

Nationality and country†	1999	2000	2001
Commonwealth citizens . . .	215	218	229
EU‡	32	35	28
Commonwealth countries. . .	149	152	164
Australia	40	35	50
Canada	6	8	6
New Zealand.	17	19	16
South Africa	28	20	18
Other African countries . .	17	19	22
Bangladesh, India, Sri Lanka .	17	23	23
Pakistan	8	11	13
Caribbean§	4	2	3
Other foreign countries . .	34	31	37
USA	12	9	11
Foreign citizens	139	146	144
EU‡	58	55	55
Commonwealth countries. . .	2	5	6
Other foreign countries‖ . . .	79	86	83
USA	17	15	12
Total	354	364	372

Emigrants
('000)

Nationality and country†	1999	2000	2001
Commonwealth citizens . . .	153	184	178
EU‡	39	41	43
Commonwealth countries. . .	83	96	94
Australia	42	46	46
Canada	6	7	9
New Zealand.	10	16	14
South Africa	6	7	7
Other African countries . .	2	6	4
Bangladesh, India, Sri Lanka .	2	3	5
Pakistan	0	2	2
Caribbean§	2	2	2
Other foreign countries . .	31	47	42
USA	17	21	17
Foreign citizens	92	93	73
EU‡	41	42	35
Commonwealth countries. . .	5	3	4
Other foreign countries‖ . . .	46	48	35
USA	15	11	8
Total	245	278	251

* Figures are derived from a small sample of passengers and refer to long-term migration only, excluding all movements between the UK and the Republic of Ireland and short-term visitors who are granted extensions of stay in the UK or abroad. Long-term migrants are defined as persons who have resided (or intend to reside) for one year or more in the UK and intend to reside (or have resided) outside the UK for one year or more.

† Figures refer to the country of immigrants' last permanent residence or emigrants' intended future residence.

‡ Figures for all years show the EU as it was constituted on 1 January 1995.

§ Including Guyana and Belize.

‖ Including Hong Kong.

Source: International Passenger Survey, Office for National Statistics.

WORKFORCE JOBS BY INDUSTRY
('000)

	2000	2001	2002
Agriculture, hunting, forestry and fishing	509	461	422
Energy and water	210	218	217
Manufacturing	4,228	4,054	3,880
Construction	1,858	1,860	1,869
Distribution, hotels and restaurants	6,696	6,795	6,856
Transport, storage and communications	1,741	1,814	1,804
Banking, finance, insurance, etc.	5,488	5,709	5,679
Public administration, education and health	6,803	6,868	6,988
Other services	1,740	1,737	1,806
Total	29,273	29,515	29,519
Males	15,601	15,679	15,681
Females	13,672	13,836	13,838

Source: Office for National Statistics.

Health and Welfare

KEY INDICATORS

Total fertility rate (children per woman, 2001)	1.6
Under-5 mortality rate (per 1,000 live births, 2001)	7
HIV/AIDS (% of persons aged 15–49, 2001)	0.10
Physicians (per 1,000 head, 1993)	1.64
Hospital beds (per 1,000 head, 1999)	4.1
Health expenditure (2000): US $ per head (PPP)	1,774
Health expenditure (2000): % of GDP	7.3
Health expenditure (2000): public (% of total)	81.0
Access to water (% of persons, 2000)	100
Access to sanitation (% of persons, 2000)	100
Human Development Index (2000): ranking	13
Human Development Index (2000): value	0.928

For sources and definitions, see explanatory note on p. vi.

Agriculture

PRINCIPAL CROPS
('000 metric tons)

	1998	1999	2000
Wheat	15,450	14,870	16,700
Barley	6,620	6,580	6,490
Oats	585	540	640
Rye	55	43	44
Potatoes	6,417	7,100	n.a.
Sugar beet	10,002	10,584	9,335
Rapeseed	1,566	1,737	1,129
Beetroot	66	61	72
Carrots	626	702	455
Turnips and swedes	121	126	106
Parsnips	99	95	77
Dry onions	376	406	379
Leeks	55	46	40
Brussels sprouts	71	79	63
Cabbages, savoys, etc.	286	268	251
Cauliflowers	192	168	152
Beans, broad, runner and French	43	36	35
Green peas	159	150	181
Celery	35	40	36
Lettuce	152	156	138
Tomatoes	109	117	113
Cucumbers	84	84	80
Apples	184	246	201
Pears	26	23	27
Soft fruit	61	66	61

Source: Office for National Statistics, *Annual Abstract of Statistics*.

LIVESTOCK ON AGRICULTURAL HOLDINGS
('000 head at June)

	1999	2000	2001
Cattle	11,423	11,135	10,602
Sheep and lambs	44,656	42,264	36,716
Pigs	7,284	6,482	5,845
Chickens*	140,300	157,100	167,500
Ducks and geese†	3,600	3,600	4,100
Turkeys‡	9,900	9,500	9,500

* FAO figures.
† FAO estimates.
‡ Unofficial figures.

Source: mainly the Office for National Statistics, *Annual Abstract of Statistics*.

LIVESTOCK PRODUCTS
('000 metric tons, unless otherwise indicated)

	1999	2000	2001
Beef and veal[1]	677	708	653
Mutton and lamb[1]	361	359	258
Pork[1]	829	731	611
Poultry meat*	1,525	1,513	1,564
Offal	272	269	249
Butter	141	132	126
Cheese (incl. farmhouse)	368	340	395
Condensed milk[3]	177	162	161
Milk powder[4]	204	188	154
Cream[5]	275	270	263
Hen eggs*	586	597	629
Wool: greasy	66	63	50
Wool: scoured	47	46	34†

Cattle hides (FAO estimates, '000 metric tons): 65 in 1998; 64 in 1999; 68 in 2000.
* FAO figures.
† Unofficial figure.
[1] Production of home-killed meat, including meat subsequently canned.
[2] Sold for food.
[3] Including skim concentrate and condensed milk used in the manufacture of chocolate crumb.
[4] Including skimmed milk; excluding buttermilk and whey powder.
[5] Fresh and sterilized (including farm) cream.

Source: mainly the Office for National Statistics, *Annual Abstract of Statistics*.

Forestry

ROUNDWOOD REMOVALS
('000 cubic metres, excl. bark)

	1998	1999	2000
Sawlogs, veneer logs and logs for sleepers	3,981	4,271	4,253
Pulpwood	2,597	2,518	2,560
Other industrial wood	449	459	404
Fuel wood	233	234	234
Total	7,260	7,482	7,451

Source: FAO.

SAWNWOOD PRODUCTION
('000 cubic metres, incl. railway sleepers)

	1998	1999	2000
Coniferous (softwood)	2,253	2,416	2,389
Broadleaved (hardwood)	129	121	103
Total	2,382	2,537	2,492

Source: FAO.

Fishing

LANDINGS BY BRITISH VESSELS
(Great Britain, '000 metric tons, excluding freshwater fish and seaweeds)

	1999	2000	2001
Marine ('wet') fish	389.8	337.6	332.1
Atlantic cod	46.8	37.0	28.1
Haddock	71.3	50.3	42.3
European plaice	9.5	8.6	7.7
Monks or anglers.	15.5	14.7	15.1
Whiting	25.4	23.3	15.1
Atlantic herring*	45.3	39.5	43.8
Atlantic mackerel*	41.3	54.6	63.9
Crustaceans, molluscs, etc. . .	116.7	127.0	136.2
Cockles	14.2	20.3	19.0
Crabs	23.0	25.7	25.0
Nephrops (Norway lobster) . .	31.1	28.3	28.4
Scallops	19.1	19.7	19.5
Total	506.5	464.7	458.3

* Figures include transhipments (caught by British vessels but not landed at British ports).

Source: Office for National Statistics, *Annual Abstract of Statistics*.

Mining and Quarrying

('000 metric tons, unless otherwise indicated)

	1999	2000	2001
Hard coal (incl. slurries) . . .	37,077	31,198	31,513
Natural gas and petroleum:			
Methane—colliery[1]	41	42	35
Methane—North Sea[1]	99,024	108,169	105,753
Crude petroleum	128,286	117,882	108,387
Condensates and others[2] . .	8,839	8,362	8,293
Iron ore[3]	1*	1	1
China clay (sales)[4]	2,304	2,376	2,204
Ball clay (sales)	931	1,069	999
Fireclay[5]	545	595	459
Fuller's earth (sales)[6] . . .	75	66	52
Common clay and shale[5] . . .	11,355	10,838	10,426
Slate[7]	361	479	551
Limestone	86,933	84,348	88,238
Dolomite	13,698	13,069	14,314
Chalk[5]	9,667	9,213	8,205
Sandstone[8]	15,485	14,900	19,967
Common sand and gravel[9] . .	100,953	101,621	101,397
Igneous rock	53,155	54,133	51,501
Gypsum*	1,800	1,500	1,700
Rock salt*	1,500	1,700	1,900
Salt from brine	1,200	1,200	1,200
Salt in brine[10]	3,000*	3,000	3,000
Fluorspar*	40	36	50
Barytes	59	54	66*
Talc	6	5	5
Sulphur[11]	136	n.a.	n.a.
Potash[12]	825	966	882

[1] Approximate oil equivalent: converted from original data at 397 therms = 1 metric ton.

[2] Includes ethane, propane and butane, in addition to condensates (pentane and hydrocarbons).

[3] Figures refer to gross weight. The estimated iron content is 55%.

[4] Dry weight.

[5] Excluding production in Northern Ireland.

[6] Estimates based on data from producing companies.

[7] Including waste used for constructional fill and powder and granules used in industry.

[8] Including grit and conglomerate.

[9] Including marine-dredged sand and gravel for both home consumption and export.

[10] Used for purposes other than salt-making.

[11] Sulphur recovered from oil refineries.

[12] Marketable product (kc1).

* Estimate(s).

Source: British Geological Survey.

Industry

SELECTED PRODUCTS
('000 metric tons, unless otherwise indicated)

	1998	1999	2000
Wheat flour	4,582	5,668	5,617
Refined sugar[1]	1,557	n.a.	n.a.
Margarine and other table spreads	448	421	388
Crude seed and nut oil[2] . . .	915	832	820
Beer ('000 hectolitres)	56,652	57,854	55,279
Cigarettes ('000 million). . . .	67.8	28.2	49.3
Woven cotton fabrics (million metres)	74	n.a.	n.a.
Woven fabrics of man-made fibres (million metres)[3]	171.8	n.a.	n.a.
Newsprint	1,046	1,071	1,100
Other printing and writing paper	1,742	1,745	1,747
Other paper and paperboard . .	3,689	3,760	3,758
Synthetic rubber*	252.2	282.8	285.7
Rubber tyres—for cars, lorries, etc. ('000)*†	32,660	n.a.	n.a.
Butane and propane[4]	1,978	2,002	1,957
Petroleum naphtha[4]	2,335	2,465	3,145
Motor spirit (petrol)[4]	27,392	25,587	23,929
Aviation turbine fuel[4] . . .	7,942	7,352	6,620
Burning oil[4]	3,471	3,603	3,141
Diesel fuel and gas oil[4] . . .	27,859	26,226	28,879
Fuel oil[4]	11,066	10,289	10,302
Lubricating oils[4]	1,134	920	717
Petroleum bitumen (asphalt)[4] .	2,190	1,667	1,468
Cement	12,409	12,697	12,452
Pig-iron[5]	12,746	12,139	10,890
Crude steel (usable)	17,315	16,284	15,155
Aluminium—unwrought . .	533.2	555.0	542.8
Refined copper—unwrought . .	53.8	50.3	n.a.
Refined lead—unwrought[6] . .	349.7	349.7	n.a.
Zinc—unwrought: primary . .	99.6	132.8	n.a.
Passenger motor cars ('000). . .	1,748.3	1,786.6	1,641.5
Road goods vehicles ('000) . .	227.4	185.9	172.4
Electric energy (million kWh) . .	362,720	368,364	374,900

[1] Production from home-grown sugar beet only.

[2] Including maize oil.

[3] Including mixtures of man-made fibres and cotton.

[4] Refinery production only (excluding supplies from other sources).

[5] Including blast-furnace ferro-alloys.

[6] Excluding hard lead.

* Figure(s) from UN, *Monthly Bulletin of Statistics*.

† Source: International Rubber Study Group.

Source: mainly Office for National Statistics, *Annual Abstract of Statistics*.

Finance

CURRENCY AND EXCHANGE RATES

Monetary Units
100 pence (pennies) = 1 pound sterling (£)

Dollar and Euro Equivalents (31 December 2002)
US $1 = 62.04 pence
€1 = 65.06 pence
£100 = $161.18 = €153.70

Average Exchange Rate (US $ per pound sterling)
2000	1.5161
2001	1.4400
2002	1.5013

BUDGET
(general government transactions, £ million)*

Revenue	1999	2000	2001
Tax revenue	327,050	351,173	366,181
Taxes on income and wealth	129,483	140,153	147,504
Income tax	95,289	103,762	109,011
Corporation tax	33,722	34,851	36,967
Taxes on production and imports	124,411	131,150	134,772
Value-added tax	58,313	60,713	64,506
Other taxes on products	48,442	51,956	50,318
Tobacco duties	7,693	7,666	7,638
Excise on hydrocarbon oils	22,391	23,041	22,046
Non-domestic rates	15,508	16,526	17,725
Council Tax	12,699	13,845	14,976
National Insurance contributions	55,008	60,430	63,413
Gross operating surplus	7,707	7,929	8,200
Interest and dividends from private sector and abroad	4,150	5,155	4,895
Interest and dividends (net) from public sector	7,562	6,767	7,069
Rent	528	1,283	1,859
Other current transfers	259	280	153
Total	347,256	372,587	388,357

Expenditure	1999	2000	2001
General public services	17,611	18,516	19,385
Defence	25,199	28,453	27,692
Public order and safety	18,059	18,103	19,288
Education	41,338	42,666	46,700
Health	51,356	55,093	61,465
Social protection	138,758	145,678	159,202
Housing and community amenities	4,537	4,233	4,857
Recreational, cultural and religious affairs	4,730	5,072	5,257
Economic affairs	19,586	23,231	25,726
Environmental protection	4,475	4,456	5,080
Interest and dividends paid to private sector and abroad	25,908	26,062	23,522
Sub-total	351,557	371,645	398,174
Adjustments:			
Social contributions (incl. imputed)	−10,656	−11,342	−12,709
Insurance claims and attributed income	−443	−488	−476
International co-operation (receipts from European Union)	−3,176	−2,084	−4,561
Net ac. of f.a.	705	3,339	3,538
Others†	1,181	−1,347	−3,099
Total	339,098	359,723	380,867

* Consolidated accounts, covering current and capital transactions, of the central Government (all funds and accounts, including the National Insurance Funds) and local authorities. Figures have been adjusted to the official national definitions, whereby some receipts are treated as deductions from expenditure.

† Including revisions to expenditure by sector.

Source: Office for National Statistics, mainly *United Kingdom National Accounts*.

OFFICIAL RESERVES
(US $ million at 31 December)*

	1998	1999	2000
Gold	5,078	5,965	4,273
IMF special drawing rights	444	512	327
Convertible currencies†	25,664	30,087	38,087
Reserve position in IMF	4,157	5,270	4,298
Total	35,343	41,824	48,179

* Reserves are revalued at 31 March each year.

† Including European currency units (ECUs) acquired from swaps with the European Monetary Institute (now the European Central Bank).

Source: Bank of England.

CURRENCY IN CIRCULATION
(£ million)

	1999	2000	2001
Annual averages:			
Bank of England notes*	24,443	26,418	28,184
Scottish bank notes	1,858	1,988	2,164
Northern Ireland bank notes	889	986	1,114
Total bank notes	27,190	29,392	31,462
Estimated coin*	2,686	2,837	3,008
Total outstanding	29,875	32,230	34,470
of which:			
In public circulation†	24,292	26,647	28,484
At 31 December:			
Currency in public circulation†	28,229	30,227	32,460

* Average of Wednesdays. Includes amounts held by Scottish and Northern Irish banks as backing for their own note issues.

† Outside of monetary financial institutions.

Source: Bank of England.

COST OF LIVING
(General Index of Retail Prices, annual averages; base: January 1987 = 100)

	2000	2001	2002
Food	143.4	148.1	149.2
Catering	203.6	211.8	219.6
Alcoholic drink	187.4	191.3	195.7
Tobacco	270.4	285.1	293.7
Housing	214.4	221.1	226.9
Fuel and light	123.9	124.9	128.8
Household goods	140.2	141.4	142.3
Household services	157.1	158.9	166.1
Clothing and footwear	112.3	107.5	102.4
Personal goods and services	185.5	191.5	194.9
Motoring expenditure	181.3	180.3	178.9
Fares and other travel costs	184.6	190.5	195.9
Leisure goods	112.1	109.8	106.6
Leisure services	207.9	220.3	238.5
All items	170.3	173.3	176.2

Source: Office for National Statistics.

NATIONAL ACCOUNTS
(£ million at current prices)

National Income and Product

	1999	2000	2001
Compensation of employees	492,724	524,890	556,371
Operating surplus	187,275	189,385	187,423
Domestic factor incomes	679,999	714,275	743,794
Consumption of fixed capital	99,502	106,099	111,275
Gross domestic product (GDP) at factor cost	779,501	820,374	855,069
Indirect taxes	130,292	137,484	140,447
Less Subsidies	7,334	7,443	7,884
Statistical discrepancy	—	—	382
GDP in purchasers' values	902,459	950,415	988,014
Factor income from abroad	101,134	135,529	140,178
Less Factor income paid abroad	100,852	129,997	134,422
Gross national product	902,741	955,947	993,770
Less Consumption of fixed capital	99,502	106,099	111,275
National income in market prices	803,239	849,848	882,495
Other current transfers from abroad	10,439	9,749	13,946
Less Other current transfers paid abroad	14,874	16,005	17,699
National disposable income	798,804	843,592	878,742

Source: Office for National Statistics, *United Kingdom National Accounts*.

UNITED KINGDOM (GREAT BRITAIN)

Statistical Survey

Expenditure on the Gross Domestic Product

	1999	2000	2001
Government final consumption expenditure	166,614	177,801	220,663
Private final consumption expenditure	591,631	626,584	655,265
Increase in stocks	5,829	5,590	1,078
Gross fixed capital formation	153,501	158,918	162,244
Total domestic expenditure	917,575	968,893	1,039,250
Exports of goods and services	236,609	265,135	268,451
Less Imports of goods and services	252,187	283,623	290,912
Statistical discrepancy	—	—	499
GDP in purchasers' values	902,459	950,415	988,014
GDP at constant 1995 prices	804,713	829,517	845,552

Source: Office for National Statistics, *United Kingdom National Accounts*.

Gross Domestic Product by Economic Activity

	1999	2000	2001
Agriculture, hunting, forestry and fishing	9,478	8,801	8,241
Mining and quarrying	17,402	25,308	25,665
Manufacturing	152,402	153,671	153,132
Electricity, gas and water supply	15,968	15,731	15,713
Construction	41,516	44,047	47,327
Wholesale and retail trade; repair of motor vehicles, motorcycles and personal and household goods	99,144	102,333	106,766
Hotels and restaurants	26,098	28,296	29,359
Transport, storage and communication	65,096	68,842	70,252
Financial intermediation	43,190	45,784	46,034
Real estate, renting and business activities*	178,319	193,963	209,837
Public administration and defence	39,372	40,848	42,096
Education	45,417	49,162	52,659
Health and social work	52,783	56,496	61,410
Other community, social and personal services	40,209	42,731	45,101
Sub-total	826,394	876,014	913,594
Less Imputed bank service charge	30,121	37,949	39,367
GDP at basic prices	796,273	838,065	874,227
Taxes on products	112,636	119,003	120,499
Less Subsidies on products	6,450	6,653	6,712
GDP in purchasers' values	902,459	950,415	988,014

* Including imputed rents of owner-occupied dwellings.

Source: Office for National Statistics, *United Kingdom National Accounts*.

BALANCE OF PAYMENTS
(£ million)

	1999	2000	2001
Exports of goods f.o.b.	166,166	187,936	191,644
Imports of goods f.o.b.	−193,538	−218,262	−225,178
Trade balance	−27,372	−30,326	−33,534
Exports of services	70,443	77,199	76,807
Imports of services	−58,649	−65,361	−65,734
Balance on goods and services	−15,578	−18,488	−22,461
Other income received	100,825	135,237	139,880
Other income paid	−98,289	−125,925	−130,718
Balance on goods, service and income	−13,042	−9,176	−13,299
Current transfers received	14,006	12,273	16,183
Current transfers paid	−20,693	−22,305	−23,337
Current balance	−19,729	−19,208	−20,453
Capital account (net)	943	1,823	1,499
Direct investment abroad	−125,028	−168,554	−23,710
Direct investment from abroad	55,189	79,101	43,775
Portfolio investment abroad	−20,642	−67,327	−93,284
Portfolio investment from abroad	115,417	166,410	44,182
Financial derivatives (net)	2,685	1,553	8,432
Other investment abroad	−57,569	−265,945	−176,573
Other investment from abroad	49,044	272,670	213,386
Net errors and omissions	−949	3,392	−337
Overall balance	−639	3,915	−3,083

Source: Office for National Statistics, *United Kingdom Balance of Payments*.

GROSS PUBLIC EXPENDITURE ON OVERSEAS AID
(£ million, year ending 31 March)

	1999/2000	2000/01	2001/02
DFID* bilateral programmes	1,323.9	1,414.8	1,506.2
Financial aid	176.2	185.5	256.0
Technical co-operation	513.5	573.0	656.9
Aid and trade provision	37.8	27.6	23.1
Programme aid	140.4	251.6	248.5
Emergency aid	226.2	179.8	165.5
Food aid	6.5	12.8	9.9
DFID debt relief	23.1	21.2	18.3
Official advances to CDC†	38.7	—	—
Other bilateral programmes	369.8	343.3	447.9
CDC investment	269.1	194.2	132.4
Other‡	100.7	149.1	315.5
Total bilateral aid§	1,655.0	1,758.1	1,954.2
DFID multilateral programmes	1,179.8	1,298.4	1,314.6
European Community	739.3	708.5	723.5
World Bank Group	170.6	277.1	243.9
International Monetary Fund	17.0	—	10.0
Global Environmental Assistance‖	16.9	21.0	25.2
Regional development banks	67.2	54.8	76.7
Commonwealth	7.4	6.9	7.6
UN agencies	151.6	219.2	213.5
International research organizations	9.7	10.7	14.2
Other multilateral programmes	45.0	47.2	52.8
EC/EU	18.5	19.5	27.1
Global Environmental Assistance‖	0.2	0.1	0.1
UN agencies	25.4	26.6	24.6
Commonwealth	0.7	0.7	0.7
International research organizations	0.2	0.2	0.2
Total multilateral aid	1,224.8	1,345.6	1,367.4
Administrative costs	105.6	122.7	120.0
Total gross expenditure on aid	2,985.6	3,226.3	3,441.6

* Department for International Development; assumed the responsibilities of the Overseas Development Administration in May 1997.
† Commonwealth Development Corporation.
‡ Mainly non-DFID debt relief.
§ Excluding official advances to CDC.
‖ Comprising 100%, in 1999/2000, 2000/01 and 2001/02, of the United Kingdom's contribution to the Global Environment Facility and 100% of contributions to the Montreal Protocol; defined as official development assistance since 1994.

Source: Department for International Development, *Statistics on International Development*.

External Trade

(Note: Figures include the Isle of Man and the Channel Islands)

PRINCIPAL COMMODITIES
(£ million)

Imports c.i.f.	1999	2000	2001
Food and live animals	13,292	13,268	14,429
Mineral fuels, lubricants, etc.	5,427	10,016	10,799
Petroleum, petroleum products, etc.	4,674	9,048	9,529
Chemicals and related products	18,619	20,633	23,050
Basic manufactures*	26,930	29,231	30,525
Machinery and transport equipment	88,502	99,622	98,865
Mechanical machinery and equipment	17,319	17,863	18,885
Electrical machinery, apparatus, etc.	40,727	50,840	44,363
Road vehicles and parts†	24,009	23,115	26,333
Other transport equipment	6,447	7,804	9,284
Miscellaneous manufactured articles	29,043	32,802	35,528
Clothing and footwear	9,530	10,494	11,458
Scientific and photographic apparatus	6,174	7,272	7,696
Total (incl. others)	193,538	218,262	225,295

* Sorted industrial diamonds, usually classified with natural abrasives (under 'crude materials'), are included with 'basic manufactures'.
† Excluding tyres, engines and electrical parts.

Source: Office for National Statistics, *Annual Abstract of Statistics*.

Exports f.o.b.	1999	2000	2001
Food and live animals	5,924	5,829	5,545
Mineral fuels, lubricants, etc.	9,929	17,057	16,518
Petroleum, petroleum products, etc.	9,123	15,584	14,934
Chemicals and related products	23,071	24,992	28,095
Organic chemicals	5,489	5,716	6,140
Medicinal products	6,279	7,219	9,429
Basic manufactures*	20,302	22,673	22,890
Machinery and transport equipment	78,872	87,821	88,487
Mechanical machinery and equipment	21,885	22,145	24,704
Electrical machinery, apparatus, etc.	36,009	42,685	42,541
Road vehicles and parts†	15,079	15,602	14,090
Other transport equipment	5,899	7,389	7,152
Miscellaneous manufactured articles	20,265	21,197	22,373
Scientific and photographic apparatus	6,738	7,331	7,948
Total (incl. others)	166,166	187,936	191,754

* Sorted industrial diamonds, usually classified with natural abrasives (under 'crude materials'), are included with 'basic manufactures'.
† Excluding tyres, engines and electrical parts.

Source: Office for National Statistics, *Annual Abstract of Statistics*.

PRINCIPAL TRADING PARTNERS
(£ million)

Imports c.i.f.	1999	2000	2001
Australia	1,338	1,543	1,790
Austria	1,452	1,398	1,881
Belgium-Luxembourg	10,475	11,411	12,860
Canada	3,014	4,007	3,703
China, People's Republic	3,384	4,824	5,786
Denmark	2,227	2,364	2,685
Finland	2,361	2,757	2,975
France	18,167	18,274	19,390
Germany	26,486	27,800	28,688
Hong Kong	4,911	5,915	5,799
India	1,423	1,650	1,829
Ireland	8,492	9,538	9,454
Italy	9,332	9,467	9,883
Japan	9,119	10,212	9,138
Korea, Republic	2,784	3,414	2,771
Malaysia	1,955	2,287	1,954
Netherlands	13,414	15,169	15,121
Norway	3,544	5,562	5,601
Philippines	983	1,155	1,163
Portugal	1,817	1,720	1,592
Russia	1,307	1,472	2,034
Singapore	2,349	2,392	2,085
South Africa	1,569	2,553	2,866
Spain (excl. Canary Is)	5,894	6,010	6,911
Sweden	4,606	4,921	4,692
Switzerland	5,308	5,484	4,606
Taiwan	2,625	3,559	2,808
Thailand	1,291	1,601	1,621
Turkey	1,205	1,448	1,692
USA	24,355	28,404	29,662
Total (incl. others)	193,538	218,262	225,295

Exports f.o.b.	1999	2000	2001
Australia	2,163	2,699	2,344
Austria	1,168	1,148	1,244
Belgium-Luxembourg	9,241	10,321	10,055
Canada	2,546	3,488	3,239
China, People's Republic	1,212	1,469	1,735
Denmark	2,055	2,315	2,304
Finland	1,353	1,470	1,633
France	16,908	18,575	19,537
Germany	20,465	22,790	24,009
Greece	1,148	1,234	1,127
Hong Kong	2,312	2,673	2,717
India	1,451	2,058	1,797
Ireland	10,784	12,374	14,061
Israel	1,295	1,516	1,376
Italy	7,832	8,428	8,533
Japan	3,305	3,671	3,743
Korea, Republic	948	1,350	1,284
Netherlands	13,634	15,163	14,807
Norway	2,052	2,017	1,862
Poland	1,179	1,304	1,310
Portugal	1,712	1,660	1,600
Saudi Arabia	1,485	1,557	1,523
Singapore	1,599	1,624	1,613
South Africa	1,281	1,413	1,558
Spain (excl. Canary Is)	7,526	8,302	8,490
Sweden	4,034	4,210	4,014
Switzerland	2,732	3,062	3,578
Turkey	1,210	1,799	1,179
USA	24,238	29,276	29,561
Total (incl. others)	166,166	187,936	191,754

Source: Office for National Statistics, *Annual Abstract of Statistics*.

Transport

RAILWAYS
(Great Britain)

	1999/2000	2000/01	2001/02
National railways:			
Passenger journeys (million) . .	931	957	960
Passenger-kilometres (million) .	38,454	39,218	39,104
Freight traffic (million metric tons)	91.9	95.4	94.4
Freight metric ton-kilometres (million)	18,400	n.a.	n.a.
London Transport:			
Passenger journeys (million) . .	927	970	953
Passenger-kilometres (million) .	7,171	7,470	7,451

Source: Department of the Environment, Transport and the Regions.

ROAD TRAFFIC
('000 licensed vehicles in Great Britain at 31 December)

	1999	2000	2001
Private motor cars*	22,785	23,196	23,899
Motorcycles, scooters and mopeds	760	825	882
Light goods vehicles† . . .	2,427	2,469	2,544
Heavy goods vehicles . . .	415	418	422
Public passenger vehicles‡ . . .	84	86	89

* Including vans used privately; from 1 July 1995 included taxis and private hire cars.

† Goods vehicles less than 3,500 kg in weight.

‡ From 1 July 1995 included only public transportation vehicles with more than eight seats.

Source: Department of the Environment, Transport and the Regions.

SHIPPING

Merchant Fleet
(registered at 31 December)

	1999	2000	2001
Number of vessels	1,391	1,448	1,462
Total displacement ('000 grt) . .	4,331.0	5,532.0	6,029.1

Source: Lloyd's Register-Fairplay, *World Fleet Statistics.*

International Sea-borne Freight Traffic
('000 metric tons)

	1992	1993	1994*
Goods imported	176,599	175,062	177,607
Goods exported†	134,660	151,142	174,203

* Provisional.

† Including re-exports.

Source: the former Department of Transport.

CIVIL AVIATION
(United Kingdom airlines)

	1999	2000	2001
All scheduled services:			
Aircraft stage flights (number) .	835,031	878,582	921,556
Aircraft-kilometres flown (million)	946.9	1,016.3	1,048.6
Passengers carried (million) . .	65.4	70.3	69.7
Passenger-kilometres flown (million)	160,336.4	170,469.0	158,650.7
Total cargo carried (metric tons)	860,291	897,184	742,705
Total metric ton-kilometres (million)	20,595.6	21,846.1	19,908.2
Freight metric ton-kilometres (million)	4,924.9	5,159.9	4,548.3
Mail metric ton-kilometres (million)	153.0	179.2	101.9

— continued	1999	2000	2001
Domestic scheduled services:			
Aircraft stage flights (number) .	354,864	353,525	365,881
Aircraft-kilometres flown (million)	119.6	121.4	128.2
Passengers carried (million) . .	17.1	18.0	18.2
Passenger-kilometres flown (million)	7,183.9	7,541.8	7,644.5
Total cargo carried (metric tons)	25,964	24,644	19,498
Total metric ton-kilometres (million)	619.9	649.7	656.1
Freight metric ton-kilometres (million)	6.0	5.8	4.1
Mail metric ton-kilometres (million)	4.0	3.7	3.5
International scheduled services:			
Aircraft stage flights (number) .	480,167	525,057	555,675
Aircraft-kilometres flown (million)	827.3	894.9	920.5
Passengers carried (million) . .	48.2	52.2	51.5
Passenger-kilometres flown (million)	153,152.5	162,927.2	151,005.5
Total cargo carried (metric tons)	834,300	872,540	723,206
Total metric ton-kilometres (million)	19,976.0	18,940.7	19,252.1
Freight metric ton-kilometres (million)	4,919.0	5,154.1	4,544.3
Mail metric ton-kilometres (million)	149.0	175.5	98.3

Source: Civil Aviation Authority.

Tourism

FOREIGN VISITORS BY REGION OF ORIGIN
('000)

	1999	2000	2001
EU	14,584	14,020	12,865
Other Europe	2,232	2,066	1,992
North America	4,559	4,869	4,228
Other countries	3,979	4,253	3,751
Total	25,394	25,209	22,835
Total expenditure (£ million) . .	12,498	12,805	11,306

Source: International Passenger Survey, Office for National Statistics, *Travel Trends.*

VISITS BY COUNTRY OF PERMANENT RESIDENCE
('000)

	1999	2000	2001
Austria	242	227	191
Belgium-Luxembourg . . .	1,130	1,048	971
France	3,223	3,087	2,852
Germany	2,794	2,758	2,309
Ireland	2,075	2,087	2,039
Italy	1,076	949	857
Netherlands	1,617	1,440	1,411
Scandinavia and Finland . .	1,730	1,632	1,424
Spain	829	849	856
Switzerland	616	579	514
Other Europe	1,484	1,430	1,431
USA	3,939	4,097	3,580
Canada	660	772	4,228
Japan	495	557	366
Australia/New Zealand	921	951	845
South Africa	300	304	319
Latin America	300	317	259
Middle East	607	614	580
Other countries	1,356	1,510	1,384
Total	25,394	25,209	22,835

Source: International Passenger Survey, Office for National Statistics, *Travel Trends.*

Communications Media

	1999	2000	2001
Television receivers ('000)	38,800	39,000	n.a.
Telephones ('000 main lines in use)	34,197	35,177	34,710
Mobile cellular telephones ('000 subscribers).	27,185	43,452	47,026
Personal computers ('000 in use) .	18,000	20,190	22,000
Internet users ('000) .	12,500	15,400	24,000

1996: Book production (titles) 107,263; Daily newspapers 99 (average circulation 19,332,000); Facsimile machines (number in use) 1,992,000.

1997: Radio receivers ('000 in use) 84,500.

Sources: UNESCO, *Statistical Yearbook*; UN, *Statistical Yearbook* and International Telecommunication Union.

Education

ENGLAND AND WALES

	1999/2000	2000/01[1]	2001/02
Number of schools (at January)	27,964	27,774	27,634
Teachers ('000, at January):[2]			
Maintained primary schools[3]. .	196.4	198.3	200.3
Maintained secondary schools[3] .	197.9	201.7	205.9
Other schools	77.0	78.7	77.3
Total	471.4	478.7	483.5
Full-time pupils ('000, at January):			
Nursery schools[4]	8.9	8.9	9.2
Maintained primary schools[3].	4,386.7	4,360.4	4,325.2
Maintained secondary schools[3] .	3,389.7	3,442.2	3,476.1
All Special schools.	97.9	96.9	96.0
Pupil referral units[5]	8.8	9.7	10.4
Independent schools[6]	558.9	566.3	574.9
Total	8,450.9	8,484.5	8,491.8
Part-time pupils ('000, at January)	407.3	401.9	387.9
Further education establishments	452	427	420
Students in further education ('000):[7,8]			
Full-time students.	977.3	1,023.9	1,050.3
Part-time students	2,684.2	3,532.3	3,953.9

[1] Includes revised figures.
[2] Qualified teachers only. Full-time teachers and the full time equivalent of part-time teachers.
[3] Including middle schools deemed either primary or secondary.
[4] Including Direct Grant nursery schools.
[5] Excluding pupils registered elsewhere.
[6] Including City Technology Colleges.
[7] Whole year counts. Figures for 2000/01 are provisional estimates.
[8] Further education institution figures for England from 2000/01 include external institutions and specialist designated colleges and are not directly comparable with previous years.

Sources: Department for Education and Skills; National Assembly for Wales; Scottish Executive; Northern Ireland Department of Education; Northern Ireland Department for Employment and Learning; Higher Education Statistics Authority.

SCOTLAND[1]

	1999/2000	2000/01	2001/02
Education authority and grant-aided:			
Schools:			
Nursery	2,213	2,586	2,597
Primary	2,293	2,278	2,271
Secondary	389	389	387
Special	195	195	197
Total	5,090	5,448	5,452
Teachers:			
Nursery	1,566	n.a.	1,811
Primary	22,643	22,429	22,289
Secondary	24,446	24,525	24,552
Special	1,967	1,974	2,029
Total	50,622	48,928	50,681
Pupils:			
Nursery[2]	88,799	98,837	98,769
Primary	431,414	425,221	420,523
Secondary	315,356	317,704	316,368
Special	8,311	8,318	8,183
Total	843,880	850,080	843,843
Further education day colleges:			
Establishments	47	47	46
Full-time academic staff[3]	4,938	4,997	4,997
Full-time students	68,017	72,641	72,630
Higher education institutions:			
Establishments	19	19	20
Full-time academic staff[4]	9,279	9,147	9,105
Full-time students	132,153	134,296	142,751

[1] Response rates to data collections vary. In 2000/01, a new data collection, the Census of Children's Daycare and Pre-school Education Centres, replaced the former Census of Pre-school Education Centres and the Survey of Daycare Services for Children. This change may have resulted in some inconsistencies between figures shown here for prior to 2000/01 (taken from the Pre-school Census only) and those for 2000/01 (taken from the new Daycare and Pre-school Census).
[2] Nursery figures refer to centres registered to provide pre-school education. Nursery teacher figures only include qualified teachers. Nursery information comes from surveys carried out on an individual centre basis. Any children attending more than one centre will be counted by each centre and will appear more than once in the total figures.
[3] The figures quoted are for full-time teaching staff.
[4] The figures quoted are for full-time teaching and teaching and research staff.

Source: Scottish Office Education and Industry Department.

HIGHER EDUCATION INSTITUTIONS
('000 United Kingdom—academic years)*

	1999/2000	2000/01†	2001/02
Number of universities .	88	90	89
Number of other higher education institutes	58	58	63
Full-time teaching and research staff	113.8	116.4	n.a.
Students taking higher education courses:			
Full-time students .	1,259.7	1,276.3	1,311.8
Part-time students	764.4	791.0	928.9

* Generally annual 'snapshots' at November/December each year; including Open University students.
† Includes revised figures.

Sources: Department for Education and Skills; National Assembly for Wales; Scottish Executive; Northern Ireland Department of Education; Northern Ireland Department for Employment and Learning; Higher Education Statistics Agency.

Directory

The Constitution

The United Kingdom is a constitutional monarchy. In the ninth century, when England was first united under a Saxon King, the monarchy was the only central power and the Constitution did not exist. Today, the Sovereign acts on the advice of her Ministers which she cannot, constitutionally, ignore; power, which has been at various times and in varying degrees in the hands of kings, feudal barons, ministers, councils and parliaments, or of particular groups or sections of society, is vested in the people as a whole, and the Sovereign is an essential part of the machinery of government which has gradually been devised to give expression to the popular will.

Both the powers of the Government and the functions of the Sovereign are determined by the Constitution, by the body of fundamental principles on which the State is governed and the methods, institutions and procedures which give them effect. But the United Kingdom has no written Constitution: there is no document, no one law or statute, to which reference can be made. The Constitution is an accumulation of convention, precedent and tradition which, although continually changing as the times change, is at any one moment binding and exact.

Some of the principles and many of the practices are secured by Statute, some are avowed by Declaration or Manifesto and many are incorporated in the Common Law. Magna Carta, in 1215, began the process by which the law of the land acquired a status of its own, independent of King and Parliament; the Bill of Rights of 1689 ended the long era of rivalry between Crown and Parliament and began the story of their co-operation; and the Reform Bill of 1832 dramatically broadened the basis of representative government and prepared the way for further changes. The Constitution is, above all, based on usage. It has been modified to match changing customs and to meet successive situations. Any one Parliament could, if it chose, revise or repeal every law and disown every convention that has constitutional significance. It could destroy the whole fabric of political and social existence, including its own; because, according to the Constitution, Parliament, which represents the people, is supreme. The work of one Parliament is not binding on its successors, except in so far as changes must be made by constitutional means. Parliament cannot disobey the law, but it can change it.

It would be impossible to enumerate the principles which are extant in the British Constitution. In constitutional as in legal practice, the way has been to admit the general principle in quite practical terms related to specific practical problems: the Habeas Corpus Act, for example, which establishes the principle of no imprisonment without trial, makes no mention of the principle itself but lays down in most concrete terms the punishments that shall be inflicted on a judge, or other law officer, if he fails to issue the Writ (commanding the prisoner to be brought before the court) when applied for. The principles of the Constitution and constitutional practice are in fact inherent in the Common Law on the one hand and in the structure, functions and procedures of the various instruments of government on the other: of the Crown, of Parliament, of the Privy Council, of the Government and the Cabinet and of the government departments.

THE SOVEREIGN

The monarchy is hereditary, descending to the sons of the Sovereign in order of seniority or, if there are no sons, to the daughters.

The constitutional position of the Queen as head of the State, quite apart from her position as head of the Commonwealth, demands that she keep herself informed on all aspects of the life of her subjects, that she maintain absolute impartiality and that she should personally visit the different parts of her realm as often as it is possible for her to do so, but she has also quite specific functions, all exercised on ministerial advice: she summons, prorogues and dissolves Parliament; she must give Royal Assent to a Bill which has passed through both Houses of Parliament, before it becomes law; she is head of the judiciary (although the judiciary is now quite independent of the executive); she appoints all important state officials, including judges, officers of the forces and representatives abroad, and she confers honours and awards. Her formal consent is necessary before a Minister can take up office or a Cabinet be formed; and before a treaty may be concluded, war declared or peace made. These are some of the more essential functions. However, the Queen also has many residuary responsibilities, such as the guardianship of infants and persons of unsound mind, the creation of corporations, granting of printing rights for the Bible and Prayer Book and for state documents; and her signature and consent are necessary to many important state papers. Constitutional government cannot in fact be carried on without the Sovereign, so much so that provision has been made by Act of Parliament for the appointment of a Regent should the Sovereign be incapacitated or under age and for Counsellors of State to act in the temporary absence of the Queen.

PARLIAMENT*

The Queen in Parliament—the House of Commons and the House of Lords—is the supreme legislative authority in the United Kingdom. Under the Parliament Act of 1911 the maximum life of one Parliament was fixed at five years: if, that is, Parliament has not meanwhile been dissolved for any other reason, such as the fall of the Government, then a general election is at the end of five years necessary by law. During its lifetime, the power of Parliament is theoretically absolute; it can make or unmake any law. In practice, of course, it must take account of the electorate. Parliament is prorogued at intervals during its life, which therefore consists of a number of sessions; by present custom, a session has normally 160 sitting days and is divided into five periods: from November (when the session is opened) until Christmas (about 30 days), from January till Easter (50), from Easter till Whitsun (30), from Whitsun until the end of July (40) and 10 days in October.

The House of Commons has 659 members, each elected for one geographical constituency. The Speaker, who is elected by the members immediately a new parliament meets, presides. Members of Parliament may be elected either at a general election or at a by-election (held in the event of the death, resignation or expulsion of the sitting member) and in either case hold their seats during the life of the existing parliament. All British subjects who are more than 18 years of age (and subjects of any Commonwealth country and of the Republic of Ireland who are resident in the United Kingdom) have the vote unless legally barred (e.g. for insanity). Anyone who has the vote may stand as a candidate for election except clergymen of the Church of England, the established Churches of Scotland and Northern Ireland and the Roman Catholic Church, and certain officers of the Crown; civil servants must resign from the service if they wish to stand as a Member of Parliament.

There are over 600 peers who have the right to a seat in the House of Lords, including Princes of the Blood Royal (who, by tradition, take no part in the proceedings); hereditary peers of England and of the United Kingdom (peerages created since the Act of Union of England and Scotland of 1707 are all peerages of the United Kingdom); several Lords of Appeal in Ordinary (appointed for life to carry out the judicial duties of the House); Scottish peers; created life peers and life peeresses; and the two archbishops and the 24 senior bishops of the Church of England. All except the spiritual, judicial and life peerages are hereditary. The Lord Chancellor is the Speaker of the House. The 1963 Peerage Act made three main amendments to the Constitution: (1) An hereditary peerage may be disclaimed by the holder for the duration of his lifetime. The peerage can be reclaimed at his death by his heir, but he himself cannot reclaim it. (2) All Scottish peers, instead of only 16 representatives, and (3) peeresses in their own right, may take their seats in the House of Lords.

Members of Parliament whose views coincide form parties which agree in each case to support the policies put forward by their chosen leaders, and to present a common front on all important issues both in Parliament and to the electorate. This system evolved during the 17th and 18th centuries and is now essential to the working of the British Constitution. Under the party system, the Queen sends for the leader of the party which wins the majority of seats (although not necessarily of votes) at a general election and asks him or her to form a government. The party with the second largest number of seats forms the Opposition, which has quite specific functions. Members of other minority parties and independents may support the Government or Opposition as they choose. Each party has its own Whips, officials whose duty it is to arrange, (in consultation with the Whips of other parties), matters of procedure and organization; to ensure that members attend debates; and to muster for their party its maximum voting strength. In addition, each party has its own national and local organizations outside Parliament.

Parliamentary procedure, like the Constitution itself, is determined by rules, customs, forms and practices which have accumulated over many centuries. The Speaker is responsible for their application, and generally for controlling the course of business and debates in the house.

It is the duty of Parliament to make the laws which govern the life of the community, to appropriate the necessary funds for the various services of state and to criticize and control the Government. Parliament is also consulted before the ratification of certain international treaties and agreements.

Legislation may (with some exceptions) be initiated in either House and on either side of the House. In practice, most Public Bills are introduced into the House of Commons by the Government in power (the chief exceptions are Private Members' Bills) as the result of Cabinet decisions. Each Bill which is passed by the Commons at its third reading is sent to the House of Lords, who either accept it or return it to the Commons with suggested amendments. The Lords cannot in any instance prevent Bills passed by the Commons from becoming law: over Money Bills or Bills affecting the duration of Parliament they have no power at all, and by the Parliament Act of 1949 any other Bill passed by the Commons in two successive sessions may be presented for Royal Assent without the consent of the Lords, provided one year has elapsed between the date of the second reading in the Commons and the date of its final passing. In practice, the House of Lords is extremely unlikely to delay matters thus far, and its main function is to scrutinize the work of the Commons, to caution and suggest. Bills of a non-controversial kind are sometimes introduced initially in the House of Lords.

* In 1999 devolved legislative authorities were established in Scotland and Wales. In Scotland a new elected parliament, based in Edinburgh, was established with powers to legislate on all domestic matters (incl. education, health, local government and law and order) and with a mandate to vary taxes set by the Government of the United Kingdom by 3%. The Assembly has 129 members, elected every four years by a combined system of direct voting, on the basis of Westminster parliamentary constituencies, and a form of proportional representation, whereby additional members are elected from a party list on the basis of the larger constituencies used for elections to the European Parliament. The Welsh Assembly, located in Cardiff, undertook responsibility for issues covered by the Welsh Office of the Government of the United Kingdom. The 60-member Assembly was elected under the same system as in Scotland. Elections to the two Assemblies took place simultaneously in May 1999 and the transfer of powers took place on 1 July.

THE PRIVY COUNCIL

The power of the Privy Council has declined with the development of the Cabinet and its main function today is to give effect to decisions made elsewhere. There are at present over 300 Privy Counsellors, including Cabinet Ministers (who are automatically created Privy Counsellors), and people who have reached eminence in some branch of public affairs. Meetings are presided over by the Queen, and the responsible minister is the Lord President of the Council, an office which, since 1600, has always been held by a member of the party in power, who is usually also a leading member of the Cabinet. The Privy Council is responsible for making Orders in Council, of which there are two kinds: those made in virtue of the Royal prerogative, e.g. the ratification of treaties, and those which are authorized by Act of Parliament and are, in fact, a form of delegated legislation. It has also various advisory functions which cover such subjects as scientific, industrial, medical and agricultural research. An important organ of the Privy Council is the Judicial Committee.

HER MAJESTY'S GOVERNMENT

The Government is headed by the Prime Minister, who is also the leader of the party which holds the majority in the House of Commons. It includes ministers who are in charge of government departments and those who hold traditional offices which involve no special departmental duties; the Chancellor of the Exchequer and the Lord Chancellor, who are specially responsible for financial and economic, and legal affairs respectively; the law officers of the Crown (the Attorney-General and Solicitor-General, the Lord Advocate for Scotland and the Solicitor-General for Scotland); the Ministers of State, who are usually appointed to assist Ministers in charge of departments; and Parliamentary Secretaries and Under-Secretaries.

The cabinet system developed during the 18th century from the informal meetings of Privy Counsellors who were also ministers, and who formed a committee of manageable size which could take decisions far more quickly and simply than larger bodies. The Cabinet today has between 15–25 members at the discretion of the Prime Minister—its main duty is to formulate policy for submission to Parliament.

The doctrine of ministerial responsibility has also evolved gradually, but was generally accepted by the middle of the last century. Each Minister must take full responsibility, particularly in Parliament, for the work of his own department; if his department fails over any important matter, he will be expected to resign. Ministers also assume collective responsibility for the work of the Government and for any advice which it may offer to the Crown.

Legislation providing for the abolition of all but 92 hereditary peers and the establishment of an interim second chamber, pending a definitive reform of the House of Lords, was passed in November 1999.

The Government
HEAD OF STATE

Sovereign: Her Majesty Queen ELIZABETH II (Elizabeth Alexandra Mary), succeeded to the throne 6 February 1952.

THE MINISTRY
(May 2003)
The Cabinet

Prime Minister, First Lord of the Treasury and Minister for the Civil Service: ANTHONY (TONY) BLAIR.

Deputy Prime Minister and First Secretary of State: JOHN PRESCOTT.

Chancellor of the Exchequer: GORDON BROWN.

President of the Council and Leader of the House of Commons: Dr JOHN REID.

Lord Chancellor: Lord IRVINE OF LAIRG.

Secretary of State for Foreign and Commonwealth Affairs: JOHN (JACK) STRAW.

Secretary of State for the Home Department: DAVID BLUNKETT.

Secretary of State for the Environment, Food and Rural Affairs: MARGARET BECKETT.

Secretary of State for International Development: Baroness AMOS.

Secretary of State for Transport: ALISTAIR DARLING.

Secretary of State for Health: ALAN MILBURN.

Minister without Portfolio and Party Chair: IAN McCARTNEY.

Secretary of State for Northern Ireland: PAUL MURPHY.

Secretary of State for Defence: GEOFFREY HOON.

Secretary of State for Work and Pensions: ANDREW SMITH.

Secretary of State for Scotland: HELEN LIDDELL.

Lord Privy Seal and Leader of the House of Lords: Lord WILLIAMS OF MOSTYN.

Secretary of State for Trade and Industry: PATRICIA HEWITT.

Secretary of State for Culture, Media and Sport: TESSA JOWELL.

Parliamentary Secretary to the Treasury: HILARY ARMSTRONG.

Seretary of State for Education and Skills: CHARLES CLARKE.

Chief Secretary to the Treasury: PAUL BOATENG.

Secretary of State for Wales: PETER HAIN.

Also attending Cabinet

Captain of the Gentlemen at Arms: Lord GROCOTT.

Law Officers

Attorney-General: Lord GOLDSMITH.

Lord Advocate: COLIN BOYD.

Solicitor-General: HARRIET HARMAN.

Advocate-General for Scotland: Dr LYNDA CLARK.

Ministers not in the Cabinet

Minister for the Cabinet Office and Chancellor of the Duchy of Lancaster: Lord MACDONALD OF TRADESTON.

Minister of State, Cabinet Office: DOUGLAS ALEXANDER.

Paymaster General: DAWN PRIMAROLO.

Financial Secretary to the Treasury: RUTH KELLY.

Economic Secretary to the Treasury: JOHN HEALEY.

Minister of State for Trade, Foreign and Commonwealth Office and Department of Trade and Industry: Baroness SYMONS OF VERNHAM DEAN.

Minister of State for Europe, Foreign and Commonwealth Office: DENNIS McSHANE.

Minister of State for Police and Crime Reduction, Home Department: (vacant).

Minister of State for the Criminal Justice System, Home Department: Lord FALCONER OF THOROTON.

Minister of State for Citizenship and Immigration, Home Department: BEVERLEY HUGHES.

Minister of State for the Environment, Department for Environment, Food and Rural Affairs: MICHAEL MEACHER.

Minister of State for Rural Affairs, Department for Environment, Food and Rural Affairs: ALUN MICHAEL.

Minister of State for Work, Department for Work and Pensions (with right to attend Cabinet): NICHOLAS (NICK) BROWN.

Minister of State for Pensions, Department for Work and Pensions: (vacant).

Minister of State for Transport, Department for Transport: JOHN SPELLAR.

Minister of State for Local Government and the Regions, Office of the Deputy Prime Minister: NICOLLS (NICK) RAYNSFORD.

Minister of State for Housing and Planning, Office of the Deputy Prime Minister: Lord ROOKER.

Minister of State for Social Exclusion and Deputy Minister for Women, Office of the Deputy Prime Minister: BARBARA ROCHE.

Ministers of State for Health, Department for Health: JOHN HUTTON, JACQUELINE (JACQUI) SMITH.

Minister of State, Northern Ireland Office: JANE KENNEDY.

Minister of State, Ministry of Defence: ADAM INGRAM.

Minister of State for E-Commerce, Department of Trade and Industry: STEPHEN TIMMS.

Minister of State for Industry and Energy, Department of Trade and Industry: BRIAN WILSON.

Minister of State for Employment, Manufacturing and the Regions, Department of Trade and Industry: ALAN JOHNSON.

Minister of State for Schools, Department for Education and Skills: DAVID MILIBAND.

Minister of State for Universities and Lifelong Learning, Department for Education and Skills: MARGARET HODGE.

Minister of State for Sport, Department for Culture, Media and Sport: RICHARD CABORN.

Minister of State for Arts, Department for Culture, Media and Sport: Baroness BLACKSTONE.

Minister of State, Department for International Development: HILARY BENN.

MINISTRIES

Prime Minister's Office: 10 Downing St, London, SW1A 2AA; tel. (20) 7270-3000; internet www.number-10.gov.uk.

Office of the Deputy Prime Minister: Dover House, Whitehall, London, SW1A 2AU; tel. (20) 7276-0400; internet www.odpm.gov.uk.

Cabinet Office and the Office of the Chancellor of the Duchy of Lancaster (Office of Public Service): 70 Whitehall, London SW1A 2AS; tel. (20) 7276-1250; fax (20) 7276-1257; internet www.cabinet-office.gov.uk.

Department for Culture, Media and Sport: 2–4 Cockspur St, London SW1Y 5DH; tel. (20) 7211-6200; fax (20) 7211-6032; e-mail enquiries@culture.gov.uk; internet www.culture.gov.uk.

Ministry of Defence: Main Bldg, Whitehall, London, SW1A 2HB; tel. (20) 7218-9000; e-mail webmaster@dgics.mod.uk; internet www.mod.uk.

Department for Education and Skills: Sanctuary Bldgs, Great Smith St, London, SW1P 3BT; tel. (870) 001-2345; fax (20) 7925-6000; e-mail info@dfes.gsi.gov.uk; internet www.dfes.gov.uk.

Department of the Environment, Food and Rural Affairs (DEFRA): Nobel House, 17 Smith Street, London, SW1P 3JR; tel. (20) 7238-6000; fax (20) 7238-6591; internet www.defra.gov.uk.

Foreign and Commonwealth Office: Whitehall, London, SW1A 2AH; tel. (20) 7270-3000; internet www.fco.gov.uk.

Department of Health: Richmond House, 79 Whitehall, London, SW1A 2NS; tel. (20) 7210-4850; fax (20) 7210-5523; e-mail dhmail@doh.gsi.gov.uk; internet www.doh.gov.uk.

Home Office: 50 Queen Anne's Gate, London, SW1H 9AT; tel. (20) 7273-4000; fax (20) 7273-2065; e-mail public.enquiries@homeoffice.gsi.gov.uk; internet www.homeoffice.gov.uk.

Department for International Development: 1 Palace St, London, SW1E 5HE; tel. and fax (20) 7023-0000; e-mail enquiry@dfid.gov.uk; internet www.dfid.gov.uk.

Lord Chancellor's Department: Selborne House, 54–60 Victoria St, London, SW1E 6QW; tel. (20) 7210-8500; e-mail general.enquiries@lcdhq.gsi.gov.uk; internet www.lcd.gov.uk.

Northern Ireland Office: 11 Millbank, London, SW1P 4PN; tel. (20) 7210-3000; fax (20) 7210-0249; e-mail press.nio@nics.gov.uk; internet www.nio.gov.uk.

Scotland Office: Dover House, Whitehall, London, SW1A 2AU; tel. (20) 7270-6754; fax (20) 7270-6812; e-mail scottish.secretary@scotland.gsi.gov.uk; internet www.scottishsecretary.gov.uk.

Department of Trade and Industry: 1 Victoria St, London, SW1H 0ET; tel. (20) 7215-5000; fax (20) 7222-0612; e-mail enquiries@dti.gsi.gov.uk; internet www.dti.gov.uk.

Department for Transport: Great Minster House, 76 Marsham St, London, SW1P 4DR; tel. (20) 7944-83000; internet www.dft.gov.uk.

HM Treasury: Treasury Chambers, Parliament St, London, SW1P 3AG; tel. (20) 7270-5000; fax (20) 7270-5653; e-mail public.enquiries@hm-treasury.gov.uk; internet www.hm-treasury.gov.uk.

Wales Office: Gwydyr House, Whitehall, London, SW1A 2ER; tel. (20) 7270-0549; fax (20) 7270-0568; e-mail wales.office@wales.gsi.gov.uk; internet www.walesoffice.gov.uk.

Department for Work and Pensions: Richmond House, 79 Whitehall, London, SW1A 2NS; tel. (20) 7238-0800; internet www.dwp.gov.uk.

Legislature

PARLIAMENT

House of Commons

Speaker: MICHAEL MARTIN.

Chairman of Ways and Means: SIR ALAN HASELHURST.

Leader of the House: Dr JOHN REID.

General Election, 7 June 2001

	Votes	%	Seats
Labour Party	10,740,168	40.7	413*
Conservative Party . . .	8,355,267	31.7	166
Liberal Democrats . . .	4,815,249	18.3	52
Scottish National Party . .	464,314	1.8	5
Ulster Unionist Party . . .	216,839	0.8	6
Plaid Cymru (Welsh National Party)	195,892	0.7	4
Democratic Unionist Party .	181,999	0.7	5
Sinn Féin	175,933	0.7	4
Social Democratic and Labour Party	169,874	0.6	3
Others	1,049,657	4.0	1
Total	26,365,192	100.0	659

*Including the Speaker.

House of Lords
(April 2003)

Lord High Chancellor: Lord IRVINE OF LAIRG.

Lord Chairman of Committees: Lord TORDOFF.

Leader of the House: Lord WILLIAMS OF MOSTYN.

	Seats
Archbishops and Bishops	26
Life Peers under the Appelate Jurisdiction Act 1876 . . .	27
Life Peers under the Life Peerages Act 1958	547
Peers under the House of Lords Act 1999	91
Total	691

The Legislative Authorities and Executive Bodies of Scotland and Wales

In 1999 devolved legislative authorities were established for Scotland and Wales. An executive level of government, headed by a First Minister, was also established for each country. The Scottish Assembly assumed powers to legislate on all domestic matters, including education, health, local government and law and order. It also had a mandate to vary taxes set by the United Kingdom Government by 3%. The Welsh Assembly (Cynulliad Cenedlaethol Cymru) assumed responsibility for issues covered by the Welsh Office of the United Kingdom Government. Both Assemblies were elected, for a term of four years, by a combined system of direct voting, on the basis of Westminster parliamentary constituencies, and a form of proportional representation, whereby additional members were elected from a party list on the basis of the larger constituencies used for election to the European Parliament. The transfer of powers to both the Scottish and the Welsh authorities took place on 1 July.

SCOTLAND

Legislature

Scottish Parliament

Presiding Officer: GEORGE REID.

Election, 1 May 2003

	Total votes	%	Seats
Labour Party	1,225,464	33.1	50
Scottish National Party	855,381	23.1	27
Conservative Party	615,208	16.6	18
Liberal Democrats	520,157	14.1	17
Green Party	132,138	3.6	7
Scottish Socialist Party	244,139	6.6	6
Others	108,895	3.1	4
Total	**3,701,382**	**100.0**	**129**

Cabinet
(May 2003)

First Minister: JACK McCONNELL.

Deputy First Minister and Minister for Enterprise and Lifelong Learning: JIM WALLACE.

Minister for Justice: CATHY JAMIESON.

Minister for Education and Young People: PETER PEACOCK.

Minister for Health and Community Care: MALCOLM CHISHOLM.

Minister for Environment and Rural Development: ROSS FINNIE.

Minister for Finance and Public Services: ANDY KERR.

Minister for Communities: MARGARET CURRAN.

Minister for Parliamentary Business: PATRICIA FERGUSON.

Minister for Tourism, Culture and Sport: FRANK McAVEETY.

Minister for Transport: NICOL.

Lord Advocate: COLIN BOYD.

Solicitor General: EILISH ANGIOLINI.

WALES

Legislature

Welsh Assembly

Presiding Officer: Lord DAFYDD ELIS-THOMAS.

Election, 1 May 2003

	Total votes	%	Seats
Labour Party	647,073	41.0	30
Plaid Cymru	347,838	22.0	12
Conservative	336,657	21.3	11
Liberal Democrats	228,263	14.4	6
Others	19,757	1.3	1
Total	**1,579,588**	**100.0**	**60**

Cabinet
(May 2003)

First Minister: RHODRI MORGAN.

Minister for Finance, Local Government and Public Services: SUE ESSEX.

Minister for Assembly Business: KAREN SINCLAIR.

Minister for Social Justice and Regeneration: EDWINA HART.

Minister for Health and Social Care: JANE HUTT.

Minister for Economic Development: ANDREW DAVIES.

Minister for Education and Lifelong Learning: JANE DAVIDSON.

Minister for the Environment, Planning and Countryside: CARWYN JONES.

Minister for Culture, the Welsh Language and Sports: ALAN PUGH.

Political Organizations

British National Party: POB 287, Waltham Cross, Hertfordshire, EN8 8ZU; tel. (870) 757-6267; e-mail bnp@bnp.to; internet www.bnp .net; f. 1982 as a breakaway faction from the National Front; National Chair. NICK GRIFFIN.

Communist Party of Britain: Unit F11, Cape House, 787 Commercial Road, London, E14 7HG; tel. (20) 7517-9722; fax (20) 7517-9733; e-mail office@communist-party.org.uk; internet www .communist-party.org.uk; f. 1920; re-established 1988; militant Marxist-Leninist; Gen.-Sec. ROBERT GRIFFITHS.

Conservative and Unionist Party: 32 Smith Sq., London, SW1P 3HH; tel. (20) 7222-9000; fax (20) 7222-1135; internet www .conservatives.com; f. 1870 as Conservative Central Office; aims to uphold the Crown and the Constitution; to build a sound economy based on freedom and enterprise; to encourage personal responsibility and a wider spread of ownership of property; to look after those most in need; to ensure respect for law and order; to improve educational standards and widen parents' choice; to strengthen Britain's defences, maintain its interests and increase its influence abroad, not least through commitment to the European Union; member of the International Democrat Union and the European Democrat Union; in the European Parliament part of the European People's Party-European Democrat Group; 330,000 mems (adherent on a local, rather than national, basis); Leader IAIN DUNCAN SMITH; Chair. THERESA MAY.

Co-operative Party: 77 Weston St, London, SE1 3SD; tel. (20) 7357-0230; fax (20) 7407-4476; e-mail p.hunt@co-op-party.org.uk; internet www.co-op-party.org.uk; f. 1917; part of the Co-operative Union Ltd, but has its own Annual Conference and National Executive Committee. Under an Agreement with the Labour Party it is recognized as the political party representing the co-operative movement, and fields candidates, jointly with the Labour Party, who are Labour and Co-operative candidates at local, UK and European parliamentary elections; promotes the principles of the co-operative movement; seeks to extend co-operative enterprise and cares for the interests of the consumer; individual mems in 269 brs; 47 societies arc affiliated; Chair. G. THOMAS; Sec. PETER HUNT.

Green Party: 1a Waterlow Rd, London, N19 5NJ; tel. (20) 7272-4474; fax (20) 7272-6653; e-mail office@greenparty.org.uk; internet www.greenparty.org.uk; f. 1973 as the Ecology Party; present name adopted in 1985; campaigns for the protection of the environment and the promotion of social justice; approx. 5,500 mems; Exec. Chair. ANDREW CORNWELL; Principal Speakers DARREN JOHNSON, MARGARET WRIGHT.

Labour Party: 16 Old Queen St, London, SW1H 9HP; tel. (8705) 900200; fax (20) 7802-1234; e-mail join@labour.org.uk; internet www.labour.org.uk; f. 1900; a democratic socialist party affiliated to the Socialist International and the Party of European Socialists; aims to achieve a dynamic economy, serving the public interest, with a strong private sector and high quality public services; a just society, with full equality of opportunity; an open democracy, guaranteeing fundamental human rights and governmental accountability; and a healthy environment. The Labour Party is committed to co-operating with European institutions, the UN, the Commonwealth and other international bodies to secure peace, freedom, democracy, economic security and environmental protection for all; also committed to pursuing these aims with trade unions, co-operative societies, voluntary organizations, consumer groups and other representative bodies. The party has been a member of the Socialist Group in the European Parliament since 1973; supports European economic and political union; 311,000 individual mems (2001), total individual and affiliated membership 3,965,000 (1995). Leader ANTHONY (TONY) BLAIR; Chair. IAN McCARTNEY; Gen. Sec. DAVID TRIESMAN.

Liberal Democrats: 4 Cowley St, London, SW1P 3NB; tel. (20) 7222-7999; fax (20) 7799-2170; e-mail libdems@cix.co.uk; internet www.libdems.org.uk; f. 1988 following the merger of the Liberal Party (f. 1877) and the Social Democratic Party (f. 1981, disbanded 1990); c. 100,500 mems; Leader CHARLES KENNEDY; Pres. Lord (NAVNIT) DHOLAKIA.

Plaid Cymru—The Party of Wales: Ty Gwynfor, 18 Park Grove, Cardiff, CF10 3BN; tel. (29) 2064-6000; fax (29) 2064-6001; e-mail post@plaidcymru.org; internet www.plaidcymru.org; f. 1925; promotes Welsh interests and seeks national status for Wales; formed a parliamentary alliance with the SNP in April 1986; 10,000 mems; Leader (vacant); Chair. ELIN JONES; Gen. Sec. DAFYDD TRISTAN.

Scottish National Party (SNP): 107 McDonald Rd, Edinburgh, EH7 4NW; tel. (131) 525-8900; fax (131) 525-8901; e-mail snp.hq@ snp.org; internet www.snp.org; f. 1934; advocates independence for Scotland as a member of the EU and Scottish control of national resources; National Convener (Leader) JOHN SWINNEY; Pres. WINIFRED EWING; Nat. Sec. STEWART HOSIE.

Socialist Labour Party: 9 Victoria Rd, Barnsley, South Yorkshire, S70 2BB; tel. and fax (1226) 770957; e-mail info@ socialist-labour-party.org.uk; internet www.socialist-labour-party .org.uk; supports renationalization of industry, constitutional reform, withdrawal from the European Union; Founder ARTHUR SCARGILL.

Socialist Workers' Party (SWP): POB 82, London, E3 3LH; tel. (20) 7538-5821; fax (20) 7538-4672; e-mail enquiries@swp.org.uk; internet www.swp.org.uk; f. 1950; advocates workers' control through revolution, not reform; c. 9,000 mems; Chair. DUNCAN HALLAS.

UK Independence Party: Bridgeman House, 54 Broadwick St, London, W1F 7AH; tel. (20) 7434-4559; fax (20) 7439-4659; e-mail mail@ukip.org; internet www.ukip.org; f. 1993; advocates withdrawal from the EU; 16,000 mems; Leader JEFFREY TITFORD; Chair. MICHAEL NATTRASS.

Diplomatic Representation

EMBASSIES AND HIGH COMMISSIONS IN THE UNITED KINGDOM

Afghanistan: 31 Prince's Gate, London, SW7 1QQ; tel. (20) 7589-8891; fax (20) 7584-4801; e-mail afghanembassy@btinternet.com; Chargé d'affaires AHMAD WALI MASOUD.

Albania: 2nd Floor, 24 Buckingham Gate, London, SW1E 6LB; tel. (20) 7828-8897; fax (20) 7828-8869; Ambassador KASTRIOT ROBO.

Algeria: 54 Holland Park, London, W11 3RS; tel. (20) 7221-7800; fax (20) 7221-0448; Ambassador AHMAD ATTAF.

Angola: 22 Dorset St, London, W1U 6QY; tel. (20) 7299-9850; fax (20) 7486-9397; e-mail embassy@angola.org.uk; internet www .angola.org.uk; Ambassador ANTÓNIO DA COSTA FERNANDES.

Antigua and Barbuda: 15 Thayer St, London, W1U 3JT; tel. (20) 7486-7073; fax (20) 7486-9970; e-mail ronald@antiguahc.sonnet.co .uk; internet www.antigua-barbuda.com; High Commr Sir RONALD MICHAEL SANDERS.

Argentina: 65 Brook St, London, W1Y 1YE; tel. (20) 7318-1300; fax (20) 7318-1301; internet www.argentine-embassy-uk.org; Ambassador VICENTE E. BERASATEGUI.

Armenia: 25A Cheniston Gdns, London, W8 6TG; tel. (20) 7938-5435; fax (20) 7938-2595; e-mail armembuk@dircon.co.uk; Ambassador Dr VAHRAM ABADJIAN.

Australia: Australia House, Strand, London, WC2B 4LA; tel. (20) 7379-4334; fax (20) 7240-5333; internet www.australia.org.uk; High Commr MICHAEL L'ESTRANGE.

Austria: 18 Belgrave Mews West, London, SW1X 8HU; tel. (20) 7235-3731; fax (20) 7344-0292; e-mail embassy@austria.org.uk; internet www.austria.org.uk; Ambassador Dr ALEXANDER CHRISTIANI.

Azerbaijan: 4 Kensington Court, London, W8 5DL; tel. (20) 7938-3412; fax (20) 7937-1783; e-mail sefir@btinternet.com; internet www .president.az; Ambassador RAFAEL IBRAHIMOV.

Bahamas: 10 Chesterfield St, London, W1J 5JL; tel. (20) 7408-4488; fax (20) 7499-9937; e-mail information@bahamashclondon.net; High Commr BASIL G. O' BRIEN.

Bahrain: 30 Belgrave Sq., London, SW1X 8QB; tel. (20) 7201-9170; fax (20) 7201-9189; Ambassador SHAIKH KHALID BIN AHMAD AL-KALIFA.

Bangladesh: 28 Queen's Gate, London, SW7 5JA; tel. (20) 7584-0081; fax (20) 7581-7477; e-mail bdesh.lon@dial.pipex.com; internet www.bangladeshhighcommission.co.uk; High Commr SHEIKH RAZZAK ALI.

Barbados: 1 Great Russell St, London, WC1B 3ND; tel. (20) 7631-4975; fax (20) 7323-6872; e-mail london@foreign.gov.bb; High Commr PETER SIMMONS.

Belarus: 6 Kensington Court, London, W8 5DL; tel. (20) 7937-3288; fax (20) 7361-0005; e-mail belarus@belemb.freeserve.co.uk; internet www.belemb.freeserve.co.uk; Ambassador Dr ALYAKSEI MAZHUKHOU.

Belgium: 103 Eaton Sq., London, SW1W 9AB; tel. (20) 7470-3700; fax (20) 7259-6213; e-mail info@belgium-embassy.co.uk; internet www.belgium-embassy.co.uk; Ambassador Baron THIERRY DE GRUBEN.

Belize: 22 Harcourt House, 19 Cavendish Sq., London, W1E 0PL; tel. (20) 7499-9728; fax (20) 7491-4139; e-mail bzhc-lon@btconnect .com; internet www.belize.gov.bz; High Commr ALEXIS ROSADO.

Bolivia: 106 Eaton Sq., London, SW1W 9AD; tel. (20) 7235-4248; fax (20) 7235-1286; e-mail info@embassyofbolivia.co.uk; internet www .embassyofbolivia.co.uk; Chargé d'affaires a.i. ROBERTO CALZADILLA SARMIENTO.

Bosnia and Herzegovina: 5–7 Lexham Gardens, London, W8 5JJ; tel. (20) 7373-0867; fax (20) 7373-0871; e-mail bosnia@bhembassy .london.ision.co.uk; Ambassador ELVIRA BEGOVIĆ.

Botswana: 6 Stratford Pl., London, W1C 1AY; tel. (20) 7499-0031; fax (20) 7495-8595; High Commr ROY BLACKBEARD.

Brazil: 32 Green St, London, W1Y 4AT; tel. (20) 7499-0877; fax (20) 7493-5105; e-mail infolondres@infolondres.org.uk; internet www .brazil.org.uk; Ambassador JOSÉ MAURICIO BUSTANI.

Brunei: 19–20 Belgrave Sq., London, SW1X 8PG; tel. (20) 7581-0521; fax (20) 7235-9717; e-mail bruhighcomlondon@hotmail.com; High Commr PENGIRAN HAJI YUNUS.

Bulgaria: 186–188 Queen's Gate, London, SW7 5HL; tel. (20) 7584-9400; fax (20) 7584-4948; e-mail bgembassy@yahoo.com; internet www.bulgarianembassy.org.uk; Ambassador VALENTIN DOBREV.

Cameroon: 84 Holland Park, London, W11 3SB; tel. (20) 7727-0771; fax (20) 7792-9353; High Commr SAMUEL LIBOCK MBEI.

Canada: 38 Grosvenor St, London, W1K 4AA; tel. (20) 7258-6600; fax (20) 7258-6506; e-mail ldn@dfait-maeci.gc.ca; internet www .dfait-maeci.gc.ca/london; High Commr MEL CAPPE.

Chile: 12 Devonshire St, London, W1G 7DS; tel. (20) 7580-6392; fax (20) 7436-5204; e-mail embachile@embachile.co.uk; internet www .echileuk.demon.co.uk; Ambassador MARIANO FERNÁNDEZ.

China, People's Republic: 49–51 Portland Pl., London, W1B 1JL; tel. (20) 7299-4049; internet www.chinese-embassy.org.uk; Ambassador ZHA PEIXIN.

Colombia: Flat 3A, 3 Hans Cres., London, SW1X 0LN; tel. (20) 7589-9177; fax (20) 7581-1829; e-mail mail@colombianembassy.co.uk; internet www.colombianembassy.co.uk; Ambassador Dr ALFONSO LOPEZ-CABALLERO.

Congo, Democratic Republic: 38 Holne Chase, London, N2 0QQ; tel. and fax (20) 8458-0254; Chargé d'affaires HENRY N'SWANA.

Costa Rica: Flat 1, 14 Lancaster Gate, London, W2 3LH; tel. (20) 7706-8844; fax (20) 7706-8655; e-mail info@embcrlon.demon.co.uk; internet www.embcrlon.demon.co.uk; Ambassador RODOLFO GUTIÉRREZ.

Côte d'Ivoire: 2 Upper Belgrave St, London, SW1X 8BJ; tel. (20) 7235-6991; fax (20) 7259-5320; Ambassador YOUSSOUFU BAMBA.

Croatia: 21 Conway St, London, W1T 6BN; tel. (20) 7387-2022; fax (20) 7387-0310; Ambassador JOŠKO PARO.

Cuba: 167 High Holborn, London, WC1V 6PA; tel. (20) 7240-2488; fax (20) 7836-2602; e-mail embacuba.lnd@virgin.net; Ambassador JOSÉ FERNANDEZ DE COSSÍO.

Cyprus: 93 Park St, London, W1K 7ET; tel. (20) 7499-8272; fax (20) 7491-0691; e-mail cyphclondon@dial.pipex.com; internet www .cyprus.gov.cy; High Commr MYRNA Y. KLEOPAS.

Czech Republic: 26 Kensington Palace Gdns, London, W8 4QY; tel. (20) 7243-1115; fax (20) 7727-9654; e-mail london@embassy.mzv.cz; internet www.czech.org.uk; Ambassador ŠTEFAN FÜLE.

Denmark: 55 Sloane St, London, SW1X 9SR; tel. (20) 7333-0200; fax (20) 7333-0270; e-mail lonamb@um.dk; internet www.denmark .org.uk; Ambassador TOM RISDAHL JENSEN.

Dominica: 1 Collingham Gdns, London, SW5 0HW; tel. (20) 7370-5194; fax (20) 7373-8743; e-mail highcommission@dominica.co.uk; internet www.dominica.co.uk; High Commr BRIAN RICHARD BELLEVUE (acting).

Dominican Republic: 139 Inverness Terrace, London, W2 6JF; tel. (20) 7727-6285; fax (20) 7727-3693; internet www.serex.gov.do; Ambassador RAFAEL LUDOVINO FERNÁNDEZ.

Ecuador: Flat 3B, 3 Hans Cres, Knightsbridge, London, SW1X 0LS; tel. (20) 7584-1367; fax (20) 7823-9701; e-mail embajada@ecuador .freeserve.co.uk; Ambassador (vacant).

Egypt: 26 South St, London, W1K 1DW; tel. (20) 7499-3304; fax (20) 7491-1542; e-mail etembuk@hotmail.com; internet www .egypt-embassy.org.uk; Ambassador ADEL EL-GAZZAR.

El Salvador: Mayfair House, 39 Great Portland St, London, W1W 7JZ; tel. (20) 7436-8282; fax (20) 7436-8181; e-mail evilanova@rree .gob.sv; Ambassador EDUARDO VILANOVA-MOLINA.

Eritrea: 96 White Lion St, London N1 9PF; tel. (20) 7713-0096; fax (20) 7713-0161; Ambassador GHIRMAI GHEBREMARIAM.

Estonia: 16 Hyde Park Gate, London, SW7 5DG; tel. (20) 7589-3428; fax (20) 7589-3430; e-mail embassy.london@estonia.gov.uk; internet www.estonia.gov.uk; Ambassador KAJA TAEL.

Ethiopia: 17 Prince's Gate, London, SW7 1PZ; tel. (20) 7589-7212; fax (20) 7584-7054; e-mail info@ethioembassy.org.uk; internet www.ethioembassy.org.uk; Ambassador FISSEHA ADUGNA.

Fiji: 34 Hyde Park Gate, London, SW7 5DN; tel. (20) 7584-3661; fax (20) 7584-2838; e-mail fijirepuk@compuserve.com; High Commr EMITAI LAUSIKI BOLADUADUA.

Finland: 38 Chesham Pl., London, SW1X 8HW; tel. (20) 7838-6200; fax (20) 7235-3680; internet www.finemb.org.uk; Ambassador PERTTI SALOLAINEN.

France: 58 Knightsbridge, London, SW1X 7JT; tel. (20) 7073-1000; fax (20) 7073-1053; e-mail press.londres-amba@diplomatie.fr; internet www.ambafrance-uk.org; Ambassador GERARD ERRERA.

Gabon: 27 Elvaston Pl., London, SW7 5NL; tel. (20) 7823-9986; fax (20) 7584-0047; Chargé d'affaires CARLOS VICTOR BOUNGOU.

Gambia: 57 Kensington Court, London, W8 5DG; tel. (20) 7937-6316; fax (20) 7937-9095; e-mail gambia@gamhighcom.fsnet.co.uk; High Commr GIBRIL SEMAN JOOF.

Georgia: 4 Russell Gardens, London, W14 8EZ; tel. (20) 7603-7799; fax (20) 7603-6682; e-mail geoemb@dircon.co.uk; internet www.embassyofgeorgia.org.uk; Ambassador TEIMURAZ MAMATSASHVILI.

Germany: 23 Belgrave Sq., London, SW1X 8PZ; tel. (20) 7824-1300; fax (20) 7824-1435; e-mail mail@german-embassy.org.uk; internet www.german-embassy.org.uk; Ambassador THOMAS MUTUSSEK.

Ghana: 13 Belgrave Sq., London, SW1X 8PN; tel. (20) 7235-4142; fax (20) 7245-9552; e-mail enquiries@ghana-com.co.uk; internet www.ghana-com.co.uk; High Commr ISAAC OSEI.

Greece: 1A Holland Park, London, W11 3TP; tel. (20) 7229-3850; fax (20) 7229-7221; e-mail political@greekembassy.org.uk; internet www.greekembassy.org.uk; Ambassador ALEXANDROS SANDIS.

Grenada: 5 Chandos St, London, W1G 9DG; tel. (20) 7631-4277; fax (20) 7631-4274; e-mail grenada@high-commission.freeserve.co.uk; High Commr RUTH ROUSE.

Guatemala: 13 Fawcett St, London, SW10 9HN; tel. (20) 7351-3042; fax (20) 7376-5708; e-mail embaguatelondon@btinternet.com; internet www.travel-guatemala.org.gt; Ambassador GLADYS MARITHZA RUIZ SANCHEZ DE VIELMAN.

Guyana: 3 Palace Court, Bayswater Rd, London, W2 4LP; tel. (20) 7229-7684; fax (20) 7727-9809; e-mail ghc.l@ic24.net; High Commr LALESHWAR K. N. SINGH.

Holy See: 54 Parkside, London, SW19 5NE (Apostolic Nunciature); tel. (20) 8946-1410; fax (20) 8947-2494; e-mail nuntius@globalnet.co.uk; Apostolic Nuncio Most Rev. PABLO PUENTE (Titular Archbishop of Macri).

Honduras: 115 Gloucester Pl., London, W1H 3PJ; tel. (20) 7486-4880; fax (20) 7486-4550; e-mail honduras@lineone.net; Ambassador HERNÁN ANTONIO BERMÚDEZ-AGUILAR.

Hungary: 35 Eaton Pl., London, SW1X 8BY; tel. (20) 7235-5218; fax (20) 7823-1348; e-mail office@huemblon.org.uk; internet www.huemblon.org.uk; Ambassador BÉLA SZOMBATI.

Iceland: 2A Hans St, London, SW1X 0JE; tel. (20) 7259-3999; fax (20) 7245-9649; e-mail icemb.london@utn.stjr.is; internet www.iceland.org.uk; Ambassador SVERRIR HAUKUR GUNNLAUGSSON.

India: India House, Aldwych, London, WC2B 4NA; tel. (20) 7836-8484; fax (20) 7836-4331; internet www.hcilondon.org; High Commr SHRI RANENDRA SEN.

Indonesia: 38 Grosvenor Sq., London, W1X 9AD; tel. (20) 7499-7661; fax (20) 7491-4993; e-mail kbri@indolondon.freeserve.co.uk; internet www.indonesianembassy.org.uk; Chargé d'affaires NICHOLAS TANDI DAMMEN.

Iran: 16 Prince's Gate, London, SW7 1PT; tel. (20) 7225-3000; fax (20) 7589-4440; e-mail info@iran-embassy.org.uk; internet www.iran-embassy.org.uk; Ambassador MORTEZA SARMADI.

Iraq: see Jordan.

Ireland: 17 Grosvenor Pl., London, SW1X 7HR; tel. (20) 7235-2171; fax (20) 7245-2851; Ambassador DÁITHÍ O'CEALLAIGH.

Israel: 2 Palace Green, Kensington, London, W8 4QB; tel. (20) 7957-9500; fax (20) 7957-9555; e-mail info@israel-embassy.org.uk; internet www.israel-embassy.org.uk/london/; Ambassador ZVI SHTAUBER.

Italy: 14 Three Kings Yard, Davies St, London, W1K 4EH; tel. (20) 7312-2200; fax (20) 7312-2230; e-mail emblondon@embitaly.org.uk; internet www.embitaly.org.uk; Ambassador LUIGI AMADUZZI.

Jamaica: 1–2 Prince Consort Rd, London, SW7 2BZ; tel. (20) 7823-9911; fax (20) 7589-5154; e-mail jamhigh@jhcuk.com; internet www.jhcuk.com; High Commr MAXINE ROBERTS.

Japan: 101–104 Piccadilly, London, W1J 7JT; tel. (20) 7465-6500; fax (20) 7491-9348; e-mail info@embjapan.org.uk; internet www.embjapan.org.uk; Ambassador MASAKI ORITA.

Jordan: 6 Upper Phillimore Gdns, London, W8 7HA; Iraqi Interests Section: 21 Queen's Gate, London, SW7 5JG; tel. (20) 7937-3685; fax (20) 7937-8795; e-mail info@jordanembassyuk.org; internet www.jordanembassyuk.org; tel. (20) 7584-7141; fax (20) 7584-7716; Ambassador TIMOOR DAGHISTANI; Head of Section MUDHAFFAR AMIN.

Kazakhstan: 33 Thurloe Sq., London, SW7 2SD; tel. (20) 7581-4646; fax (20) 7584-8481; e-mail london@kazakhstan-embassy.org; internet www.kazakhstan-embassy.org.uk; Ambassador ERLAN IDRISSOV.

Kenya: 45 Portland Pl., London, W1N 4AS; tel. (20) 7636-2371; fax (20) 7323-6717; e-mail kcomm45@aol.com; internet www.kenyahighcommission.com; High Commr NANCY C. KIRUI.

Korea, Democratic People's Republic: 73 Gunnersbury Ave, London, W5 4LP; tel. (20) 8992–4965; fax (20) 8992–2053; Ambassador RI SI HONG (acting).

Korea, Republic: 60 Buckingham Gate, London, SW1E 6AJ; tel. (20) 7227-5500; fax (20) 7227-5503; internet www.mofat.go.kr/uk.htm; Ambassador KIM IL-SOO.

Kuwait: 2 Albert Gate, London, SW1X 7JU; tel. (20) 7590-3400; fax (20) 7823-1712; e-mail kuwait@dircon.co.uk; internet www.kuwaitinfo.org.uk; Ambassador KHALID AL-DUWAISAN.

Kyrgyzstan: Ascot House, 119 Crawford St, London W1U 6BJ; tel. (20) 7935-1462; fax (20) 7935-7449; e-mail embassy@kyrgyz-embassy.org.uk; internet www.kyrgyz-embassy.org.uk; Ambassador (vacant).

Latvia: 45 Nottingham Pl., London, W1U 5LY; tel. (20) 7312-0040; fax (20) 7312-0042; e-mail embassy@embassyoflatvia.co.uk; Chargé d'affaires JĀNIS DRIPE.

Lebanon: 15–21 Palace Gardens Mews, London, W8 4QN; tel. (20) 7229-7265; fax (20) 7243-1699; e-mail emb.leb@btinternet.com; Ambassador JIHAD MORTADA.

Lesotho: 7 Chesham Pl., London, SW1 8HN; tel. (20) 7235-5686; fax (20) 7235-5023; e-mail lhc@lesotholondon.org.uk; internet www.lesotholondon.org.uk; High Commr LEBOHANG RAMOHLANKA.

Liberia: 2 Pembridge Pl., London W2 4XB; tel. (20) 7221-1036; fax (20) 7727-2914; Chargé d'affaires JEFF GONGOER DOWANA Sr.

Libya: 61–62 Ennismore Gardens, London, SW7 1NH; tel. (20) 7589-6109; fax (20) 7589-6087; Ambassador MUHAMMAD A. A. QUASIM.

Lithuania: 84 Gloucester Pl., London, W1U 6AU; tel. (20) 7486-6401; fax (20) 7486-6403; e-mail chancery@lithuanianembassy.co.uk; internet www.lithuanianembassy.co.ukt; Ambassador AURIMAS TAURANTAS.

Luxembourg: 27 Wilton Cres., London, SW1X 8SD; tel. (20) 7235-6961; fax (20) 7235-9734; Ambassador JEAN-LOUIS WOLZFELD.

Macedonia, former Yugoslav republic: 10 Harcourt House, 19A Cavendish Sq., London, W1M 9AD; tel. (20) 7499-5152; fax (20) 7499-2864; e-mail mkuk@btinternet.com; Ambassador STEVO CRVENKOVSKI.

Malawi: 33 Grosvenor St, London, W1K 4QT; tel. (20) 7491-4172; fax (20) 7491-9916; e-mail kwacha@malawihighcomm.prestel.co.uk; High Commr BRIGHT McBIN MSAKA.

Malaysia: 45/46 Belgrave Sq., London, SW1X 8QT; tel. (20) 7235-8033; fax (20) 7235-5161; e-mail mwlondon@btinternet.com; High Commr Dato' SALIM HASHIM.

Maldives: 22 Nottingham Pl., London, W1U 5NJ; tel. (20) 7224-2135; fax (20) 7224-2157; e-mail maldives.high.commission@virgin.net; High Commr ADAM HASSAN (acting).

Malta: 36–38 Piccadilly, London, W1V 0PQ; tel. (20) 7292-4800; fax (20) 7734-1831; High Commr Dr GEORGE BONELLO DU PUIS.

Mauritania: 8 Carlos Pl., London, W1K 3AS; tel. (20) 7478-9323; fax (20) 7478-9339; Ambassador Dr DIAGANA YOUSSOUF.

Mauritius: 32–33 Elvaston Pl., London, SW7 5NW; tel. (20) 7581-0294; fax (20) 7823-8437; e-mail londonmhc@btinternet.com; High Commr MOHUNLALL GOBURDHUN.

Mexico: 42 Hertford St, London, W1J 7JR; tel. (20) 7499-8586; fax (20) 7495-4035; e-mail mexuk@easynet.co.uk; internet www.mexicanembassy.co.uk; Ambassador ALMA ROSA MORENO-RAZO.

Mongolia: 7 Kensington Court, London, W8 5DL; tel. (20) 7937-0150; fax (20) 7937-1117; e-mail office@embassyofmongolia.co.uk; internet www.embassyofmongolia.co.uk; Ambassador DAVAASAMBUU DALRAIN.

Morocco: 49 Queen's Gate Gdns, London, SW7 5NE; tel. (20) 7581-5001; fax (20) 7225-3862; e-mail mail@sifamaldn.org; Ambassador MUHAMMAD BELMAHI.

Mozambique: 21 Fitzroy Sq., London, W1P 5HJ; tel. (20) 7383-3800; fax (20) 7383-3801; e-mail mozalon@compuserve.com; High Commr ANTONIO GUMENDE.

Myanmar: 19A Charles St, Berkeley Sq., London, W1J 5DX; tel. (20) 7499-8841; fax (20) 7629-4169; e-mail memblondon@aol.com; Ambassador Dr KYAW WIN.

Namibia: 6 Chandos St, London, W1G 9LU; tel. (20) 7636-6244; fax (20) 7637-5694; e-mail namibia-highcomm@btconnect.com; High Commr MONICA NDILIAWIKE NASHANDI.

Nepal: 12A Kensington Palace Gdns, London, W8 4QU; tel. (20) 7229-1594; fax (20) 7792-9861; e-mail info@nepalembassy.org.uk; internet www.nepembassy.org.uk; Ambassador (vacant).

Netherlands: 38 Hyde Park Gate, London, SW7 5DP; tel. (20) 7590-3200; fax (20) 7581-0053; e-mail london@netherlands-embassy.org.uk; internet www.netherlands-embassy.org.uk; Ambassador Count JAN M. V. A. DE MARCHANT ET D'ANSEMBOURGH.

New Zealand: New Zealand House, 80 Haymarket, London, SW1Y 4TQ; tel. (20) 7930-8422; fax (20) 7839-4580; e-mail email@newzealandhc.org.uk; internet www.nzembassy.com/uk; High Commr RUSSELL MARSHALL.

Nicaragua: Suite 31, Vicarage House, 58–60 Kensington Church St, London, W8 4DB; tel. (20) 7938-2373; fax (20) 7937-0952; e-mail emb.ofnicaragua@virgin.net; Ambassador JUAN B. SACASA.

Nigeria: Nigeria House, 9 Northumberland Ave, London, WC2N 5BX; tel. (20) 7839-1244; fax (20) 7839-8746; e-mail chancery@nigeriahighcommissionuk.com; internet www.nigeriahighcommissionuk.com; High Commr Dr CHRISTOPHER KOLADE.

Norway: 25 Belgrave Sq., London, SW1X 8QD; tel. (20) 7591-5500; fax (20) 7245-6993; e-mail emb.london@mfa.no; internet www.norway.org.uk; Ambassador TARALD O. BRAUTASET.

Oman: 167 Queen's Gate, London, SW7 5HE; tel. (20) 7225-0001; fax (20) 7589-2505; Ambassador HUSSAIN ALI ABDULLATIF.

Pakistan: 35 Lowndes Sq., London, SW1X 9JN; tel. (20) 7664-9200; fax (20) 7664-9224; e-mail pareplondon@supanet.com; internet www.pakmission-uk.gov.pk; High Commr ABDUL KADER JAFFER.

Panama: 40 Hertford St, London, W1J 7SH; tel. (20) 7493-4646; fax (20) 7493-4333; e-mail emb.pan@lineone.net; Ambassador ARIADNE SINGARES ROBINSON.

Papua New Guinea: 3rd Floor, 14 Waterloo Pl., London, SW1R 4AR; tel. (20) 7930-0922; fax (20) 7930-0828; e-mail kduldn@compuserve.com; High Commr JEAN L. KEKEDO.

Paraguay: 3rd Floor, 344 Kensington High St, London, W14 8NS; tel. (20) 7610-4180; fax (20) 7371-4279; e-mail embapar@londresdy.freeserve.co.uk; Ambassador RAÚL DOS SANTOS.

Peru: 52 Sloane St, London, SW1X 9SP; tel. (20) 7235-1917; fax (20) 7235-4463; e-mail postmaster@peruembassy-uk.com; internet www.peruembassy-uk.com; Ambassador ARMANDO LECAROS-DE COSSIO.

Philippines: 9A Palace Green, London, W8 4QE; tel. (20) 7937-1600; fax (20) 7937-2925; e-mail embassy@philemb.co.uk; internet www.philemb.co.uk; Ambassador CESAR B. BAUTISTA.

Poland: 47 Portland Pl., London, W1B 1JH; tel. (20) 7580-4324; fax (20) 7323-4018; e-mail polishembassy@polishembassy.org.uk; internet www.polishembassy.org.uk; Ambassador Dr STANISŁAW KOMOROWSKI.

Portugal: 11 Belgrave Sq., London, SW1X 8PP; tel. (20) 7235-5331; fax (20) 7245-1287; e-mail london@portembassy.co.uk; internet www.portembassy.gla.ac.uk; Ambassador JOSÉ GREGÓRIO FARIA.

Qatar: 1 South Audley St, London, W1K 1NB; tel. (20) 7493-2200; fax (20) 7493-2661; e-mail qatar.embassy.london@btclick.com; Ambassador NASSER BIN HAMAD AL-KHALIFA.

Romania: Arundel House, 4 Palace Green, London, W8 4QD; tel. (20) 7937-9666; fax (20) 7937-8069; e-mail press@roemb.co.uk; internet www.roemb.co.uk; Ambassador DAN GHIBERNEA.

Russia: 13 Kensington Palace Gdns, London, W8 4QX; tel. (20) 7229-3628; fax (20) 7727-8625; e-mail office@rusemblon.org; internet www.great-britain.mid.ru; Ambassador GRIGORII KARASIN.

Rwanda: 58/59 Trafalgar Sq., London, WC2N 5DW; tel. (20) 7930-2570; fax (20) 7930-2572; e-mail ambrwanda@compuserve.com; Ambassador ROSEMARY MUSEMINALI.

Saint Christopher and Nevis: 2nd Floor, 10 Kensington Court, London, W8 5DL; tel. (20) 7460-6500; fax (20) 7460-6505; e-mail sknhighcomm@aol.com; High Commr JAMES E. WILLIAMS.

Saint Lucia: 10 Kensington Court, London, W8 5DL; tel. (20) 7937-9522; fax (20) 7937-8704; e-mail hclsu@btconnect.com; High Commr EMMANUEL H. COTTER.

Saint Vincent and the Grenadines: 10 Kensington Court, London, W8 5DL; tel. (20) 7565-2874; fax (20) 7937-6040; e-mail svghighcom@clara.co.uk; High Commr CENIO E. LEWIS.

Saudi Arabia: 30 Charles St, London, W1J 5DZ; tel. (20) 7917-3000; fax (20) 7917-3330; internet www.saudiembassy.org.uk; Ambassador Prince TURKI AL-FAISAL.

Senegal: 39 Marloes Rd, London, W8 6LA; tel. (20) 7937-7237; fax (20) 7938-2546; Ambassador EL HADJ AMADOU NIANG.

Serbia and Montenegro: 28 Belgrave Sq., London, SW1X 8QB; tel. (20) 7235-9049; fax (20) 7235-7092; e-mail londre@jugisek.demon.co.uk; internet www.yugoslavembassy.org.uk; Ambassador Dr VLADETA JANKOVIC.

Seychelles: Eros House, 2nd Floor, 111 Baker St, London, W1U 6RR; tel. (20) 7224-1660; fax (20) 7487-5756; e-mail seyhclon@aol.com; High Commr BERTRAND RASSOOL.

Sierra Leone: Oxford Circus House, 245 Oxford St, London, W1D 2LX; tel. (20) 7287-9884; fax (20) 7734-3822; e-mail info@slhc-uk.org.uk; internet www.slhc-uk.org.uk; High Commr SULAIMAN TEJAN-JALLOH.

Singapore: 9 Wilton Cres., London, SW1X 8SP; tel. (20) 7235-8315; fax (20) 7245-6583; e-mail info@singaporehc.org.uk; internet www.gov.sg/mfa/London; High Commr MICHAEL TEO ENG CHENG.

Slovakia: 25 Kensington Palace Gdns, London, W8 4QY; tel. (20) 7313-6470; fax (20) 7313-6481; e-mail mail@slovakembassy.co.uk; internet www.slovakembassy.co.uk; Ambassador FRANTIŠEK DLHO-POLČEK.

Slovenia: 10 Little Cottage St, London, SW1P 3SH; tel. (20) 7222-5400; fax (20) 7222-5277; e-mail vlo@mzz-dkp.gov.si; internet www.embassy-slovenia.org.uk; Ambassador Dr MARJAN SENJUR.

South Africa: South Africa House, Trafalgar Sq., London, WC2N 5DP; tel. (20) 7451-7299; fax (20) 7451-7284; e-mail general@southafricahouse.com; internet www.southafricahouse.com; High Commr LINDIWE MABUZA.

Spain: 39 Chesham Pl., London, SW1X 8SB; tel. (20) 7235-5555; fax (20) 7259-5392; Ambassador: Marqués de TAMARÓN.

Sri Lanka: 13 Hyde Park Gdns, London, W2 2LU; tel. (20) 7262-1841; fax (20) 7262-7970; e-mail mail@slhc.globalnet.co.uk; internet www.slhc.london.org; High Commr FAISZ MUSTAPHA.

Sudan: 3 Cleveland Row, St James's, London, SW1A 1DD; tel. (20) 7839-8080; fax (20) 7839-7560; e-mail admin@sudanebassy.co.uk; internet www.sudanembassy.co.uk; Ambassador HASAN ABDIN.

Swaziland: 20 Buckingham Gate, London, SW1E 6LB; tel. (20) 7630-6611; fax (20) 7630-6564; e-mail swaziland@swaziland.btinternet.com; High Commr Rev. PERCY SIPHO MNGOMEZULU.

Sweden: 11 Montagu Pl., London, W1H 2AL; tel. (20) 7917-6400; fax (20) 7724-4174; e-mail embassy@swednet.org.uk; internet www.swedish-embassy.org.uk; Ambassador Dr MATS BERGQUIST.

Switzerland: 16–18 Montagu Pl., London, W1H 2BQ; tel. (20) 7616-6000; fax (20) 7724-7001; e-mail swissembassy@lon.rep.admin.ch; internet www.swissembassy.org.uk; Ambassador BRUNO SPINNER.

Syria: 8 Belgrave Sq., London, SW1X 8PH; tel. (20) 7245-9012; fax (20) 7235-4621; e-mail embassy500@netscapeonline.co.uk; Ambassador MOUFAIC NASSAR.

Tanzania: 43 Hertford St, London, W1Y 8DB; tel. (20) 7499-8951; fax (20) 7491-9321; e-mail tanzarep@tanzania-online.gov.uk; internet www.tanzania-online.gov.uk; High Commr HASSAN OMAR GUMBO KIBELLOH.

Thailand: 29–30 Queen's Gate, London, SW7 5JB; tel. (20) 7589-2944; fax (20) 7823-9695; e-mail thaiduto@btinternet.com; internet www.thaiinuk.com/th_emuk.html; Ambassador (vacant).

Tonga: 36 Molyneux St, London, W1H 5BQ; tel. (20) 7724-5828; fax (20) 7723-9074; e-mail fetu@btinternet.com; High Commr Col FETU'UTOLU TUPOU.

Trinidad and Tobago: 42 Belgrave Sq., London, SW1X 8NT; tel. (20) 7245-9351; fax (20) 7823-1065; e-mail tthc.info@virgin.net; High Commr SANDRA MCINTYRE-TROTMAN; (acting).

Tunisia: 29 Prince's Gate, London, SW7 1QG; tel. (20) 7584-8117; fax (20) 7225-2884; Ambassador KHEMAIES JHINAOUI.

Turkey: 43 Belgrave Sq., London, SW1X 8PA; tel. (20) 7393-0202; fax (20) 7393-0066; e-mail info@turkishembassy-london.com; internet www.turkishembassy-london.com; Ambassador AKIN ALP-TUNA.

Turkmenistan: 2nd Floor South, St George's House, 14–17 Wells St, London, W1P 3FP; tel. (20) 7255-1071; fax (20) 7323-9184; Ambassador (vacant).

Uganda: Uganda House, 58/59 Trafalgar Sq., London, WC2N 5DX; tel. (20) 7839-5783; fax (20) 7839-8925; High Commr Prof. GEORGE KIRYA.

Ukraine: 60 Holland Park, London, W11 3SJ; tel. (20) 7727-6312; internet www.ukrainianembassy.org.uk; Ambassador IHOR MITIUKOV.

United Arab Emirates: 30 Princes Gate, London, SW7 1PT; tel. (20) 7581-1281; fax (20) 7581-9616; e-mail embinfo@cocoon.co.uk; Ambassador EASA SALEH AL-GURG.

USA: 24–32 Grosvenor Sq., London, W1A 1AE; tel. (20) 7499-9000; fax (20) 7629-9124; internet www.usembassy.org.uk; Ambassador WILLIAM FARISH.

Uruguay: 2nd Floor, 140 Brompton Rd, London, SW3 1HY; tel. (20) 7589-8835; fax (20) 7581-9585; e-mail emb@urubri.demon.co.uk; Ambassador MIGUEL JORGE BERTHET.

Uzbekistan: 41 Holland Park, London, W11 2RP; tel. (20) 7229-7679; fax (20) 7229-7029; e-mail info@uzbekistanembassy.uk.net; internet www.uzbekistanembassy.uk.net; Ambassador ALISHER FAIZULLUEV.

Venezuela: 1 Cromwell Rd, London, SW7 2HW; tel. (20) 7584-4206; fax (20) 7589-8887; e-mail venezlon@venezlon.demon.co.uk; internet www.venezlon.demon.co.uk; Ambassador ALFREDO TORO-HARDY.

Viet Nam: 12–14 Victoria Rd, London, W8 5RD; tel. (20) 7937-1912; fax (20) 7937-6108; e-mail embassy@vietnamembassy.org.uk; internet www.vietnamembassy.org.uk; Ambassador VUONG THUA PHONG.

Yemen: 57 Cromwell Rd, London, SW7 2ED; tel. (20) 7584-6607; fax (20) 7589-3350; internet users.pgen.net/embassy/yemen.htm; Ambassador Dr MUTAHAR ADBULLAH AL-SAEEDE.

Zambia: 2 Palace Gate, London, W8 5NG; tel. (20) 7589-6655; fax (20) 7581-1353; High Commr SILUMELUME K. MUBUKWANU.

Zimbabwe: Zimbabwe House, 429 Strand, London, WC2R 0QE; tel. (20) 7836-7755; fax (20) 7379-1167; e-mail zimlondon@callnetuk.com; internet www.zimbabwelink.com; High Commr SIMBARASHE SIMBANENDUKU MUMBENGEGWI.

Judicial System

There are, historically, three sources of the law as administered in the law courts today: Statute Law, which is written law and consists mainly of Acts of Parliament, Common Law, which originated in ancient usage and has not been formally enacted, and Equity, which was the system evolved by the Lord Chancellor's court (Court of Chancery) to mitigate the strictness of some of the common law rules. The law of the European Community has now been added to these.

Scottish common and statute law differ in some respects from that current in the rest of the United Kingdom, owing to Scotland's retention of her own legal system under the Act of Union with England of 1707.

Three factors help to ensure a fair trial: the independence of judges, who, in the case of High Court Judges, are outside the control of the executive and can be removed from office only after an address from Parliament to the Sovereign (Circuit Judges can be removed by the Lord Chancellor); the participation of private citizens in all important criminal and some civil cases, in the form of a summoned jury of 12 persons, who judge, if necessary by a majority, the facts of a case, questions of law being decided by the judge; and the system of appeals to a higher court, including the Criminal and Civil Divisions of the Court of Appeal, and, thereafter, the House of Lords.

The Courts and Legal Services Act 1990 provided for radical change in the legal profession, including legislation permitting solicitors to appear in higher courts, and extensive reform of the civil courts, whereby the civil cases formerly heard in the High Court, could be transferred to the county courts.

MAGISTRATES' COURTS OR PETTY SESSIONS

The criminal courts of lowest jurisdiction are presided over by Justices of the Peace, who are unpaid lay people appointed by the Lord Chancellor. They have power to try all non-indictable offences, and some of the less serious indictable offences, if the defendant agrees. The trial of nearly all criminal offences begins in the magistrates' court. Approximately 95% of all criminal offences are dealt with solely by magistrates' courts. In the vast majority of committals for trial in the Crown Court magistrates are not required to consider evidence.

In London and in certain other large towns there are a small number of professional salaried magistrates, known as metropolitan stipendiary magistrates in London and as stipendiary magistrates in the provinces, who sit alone, whereas lay justices normally sit in threes when acting judicially.

Youth Courts, composed of specially trained justices selected by the justices of each petty sessional division (in London, by the Lord Chancellor), have power to try most charges against children under 18 years. The general public is excluded and there are restrictions on newspaper reports of the proceedings.

Magistrates also have power to grant, renew, transfer or remove or order the forfeiture of licences for the sale of alcoholic drinks, and to control the structural design of premises where alcohol is sold for consumption on the premises. They also control the licensing of betting shops, and grant bookmakers' permits.

COUNTY COURTS

A high proportion of civil actions are tried in these courts, which are presided over by a circuit judge, or, in some cases, a district judge, sitting alone. From 1 July 1991 county courts were granted unlimited jurisdiction.

THE CROWN COURT

The Crown Court came into being on 1 January 1972, under the Courts Act 1971, replacing Quarter Sessions and Assizes, to deal with serious criminal cases where trial by jury is required. The Crown Court sits at various centres throughout England and Wales. Court centres have been administratively divided into three tiers. The most serious offences are tried at first and second tier centres presided over by High Court Judges, Circuit Judges or Recorders. Circuit Judges or Recorders preside over third tier centres, where the less serious offences are tried. The Crown Court for the City of London is the Central Criminal Court (the Old Bailey).

HIGH COURT OF JUSTICE

Certain civil cases are heard in the three divisions of this court—Chancery, Queen's Bench and Family. The Chancery Division deals with litigation about property, patents, family trusts, companies, dissolution of partnerships and disputed estates. The Queen's Bench Division hears cases involving damage to property, personal injuries, etc. and also includes the Commercial and Admiralty Courts. The Family Division hears contested or complex divorce and separation cases and matters relating to children such as adoption, wardship or guardianship of minors.

Chancery Division

President: Lord IRVINE OF LAIRG (Lord High Chancellor).

Judges: Sir ROBERT ANDREW MORRITT (Vice-Chancellor), Sir FRANCIS MURSELL FERRIS, Sir JOHN EDMUND FREDERIC LINDSAY, Sir EDWARD CHRISTOPHER EVANS-LOMBE, Sir ROBERT (ROBIN) RAPHAEL HAYIM JACOB, Sir WILLIAM ANTHONY BLACKBURNE, Sir GAVIN ANTHONY LIGHTMAN, Sir PERCY FARQUHARSON COLIN RIMER, Sir HUGH IAN LANG LADDIE, Sir TIMOTHY ANTHONY WIGRAM LLOYD, Sir DAVID EDMUND NEUBERGER, Sir ANDREW EDWARD WILSON PARK, Sir NICHOLAS RICHARD PUMFREY, Sir MICHAEL CHRISTOPHER CAMPBELL HART, Sir LAWRENCE ANTHONY COLLINS, Sir NICHOLAS JOHN PATTEN, Sir TERRENCE MICHAEL ELKAN BARNET ETHERTON, Sir PETER WINSTON SMITH.

Queen's Bench Division

Lord Chief Justice of England: Lord WOOLF (President).

Judges: Sir STUART NEIL McKINNON, Sir DOUGLAS DUNLOP BROWN, Sir MICHAEL MORLAND, Sir ROGER JOHN BUCKLEY, Sir ANTHONY BRIAN HIDDEN, Sir JOHN MICHAEL WRIGHT, Sir PETER JOHN CRESSWELL, Sir CHRISTOPHER JOHN HOLLAND, Sir RICHARD HERBERT CURTIS, Sir ANTHONY DAVID COLMAN, Sir JOHN THAYNE FORBES, Sir MICHAEL ALEXANDER GEDDES SACHS, Sir STEPHEN GEORGE MITCHELL, Sir RODGER BELL, Sir MICHAEL GUY VICAT HARRISON, Sir WILLIAM MARCUS GAGE, Sir THOMAS RICHARD ATKIN MORISON, Sir ANDREW DAVID COLLINS, Sir MAURICE RALPH KAY, Sir ANTHONY HOOPER, Sir ALEXANDER NEIL LOGIE BUTTERFIELD, Sir GEORGE MICHAEL NEWMAN, Sir DAVID ANTHONY POOLE, Sir MARTIN JAMES MOORE-BICK, Sir GORDON JULIAN HUGH LANGLEY, Sir RODGER JOHN LAUGHARNE THOMAS, Sir ROBERT FRANKLYN NELSON, Sir ROGER GRENFELL TOULSON (also Chairman of the Law Commission), Sir MICHAEL JOHN ASTILL, Sir ALAN GEORGE MOSES, Sir DAVID EADY, Sir JEREMY MIRTH SULLIVAN, Sir DAVID HERBERT PENRY-DAVEY, Sir STEPHEN PRICE RICHARDS, Sir DAVID WILLIAM STEEL, Sir CHARLES ANTHONY ST JOHN GRAY, Sir NICOLAS DUŠAN BRATZA (Judge of the European Court of Human Rights), Sir MICHAEL JOHN BURTON, Sir RUPERT MATTHEW JACKSON, Dame HEATHER CAROL HALLETT, Sir PATRICK ELIAS, Sir RICHARD JOHN PEARSON AIKENS, Sir STEPHEN ROBERT SILBER, Sir JOHN BERNARD GOLDRING, Sir PETER FRANCIS CRANE, Sir GEOFFREY DOUGLAS GRIGSON, Sir RICHARD JOHN HEDLEY GIBBS, Sir RICHARD HENRY QUIXANO HENRIQUES, Sir STEPHEN MILES TOMLINSON, Dame ANNE JUDITH RAFFERTY, Sir ANDREW CHARLES SMITH, Sir STANLEY JEFFREY BURNTON, Sir PATRICK JAMES HUNT, Sir CHRISTOPHER JOHN PITCHFORD, Sir BRIAN HENRY LEVESON, Sir DUNCAN BRIAN WALTER OUSELEY, Sir RICHARD GEORGE BRAMWELL McCOMBE, Sir RAYMOND EVAN JACK, Sir ROBERT

MICHAEL OWEN, Sir COLIN CRICHTON MACKAY, Sir JOHN EDWARD MITTING, Sir DAVID RODERICK EVANS, Sir NIGEL ANTHONY LAMERT DAVIS, Sir PETER HENRY GROSS, Sir BRIAN RICHARD KEITH, Sir JEREMY LIONEL COOKE, Sir RICHARD ALAN FIELD, Sir CHRISTOPHER JOHN PITCHERS, Sir COLMAN MAURICE TREACY, Sir PEREGRINE CHARLES HUGO SIMON, Sir ROGER JOHN ROYCE, Dame LAURA MARY COX, Sir ADRIAN BRUCE FULFORD.

Family Division

President: Dame ANN ELIZABETH BUTLER-SLOSS.

Judges: Sir ROBERT LIONEL JOHNSON, Dame JOYANNE WINIFRED BRACE-WELL, Sir JAN PETER SINGER, Sir NICHOLAS ALLAN ROY WILSON, Sir NICHOLAS PETER RATHBONE WALL, Sir ANDREW TRISTAM HAMMETT KIRKWOOD, Sir HUGH PETER DERWYN BENNETT, Sir EDWARD JAMES HOLMAN, Dame MARY CLAIRE HOGG, Sir CHRISTOPHER JOHN SUMNER, Sir ANTHONY PHILIP GILSON HUGHES, Sir ARTHUR WILLIAM HESSIN CHARLES, Sir DAVID RODERICK LESSITER BODEY, Dame JILL MARGARET BLACK, Sir JAMES LAWRENCE MUNBY, Sir PAUL JAMES COLERIDGE, Sir MARK HEDLEY.

COURT OF APPEAL

An appeal lies in civil cases to this court from County Courts and the High Court of Justice and in criminal cases from the Crown Courts. The Master of the Rolls is the effective head of the court.

Ex-Officio Judges

Lord High Chancellor: Lord IRVINE OF LAIRG (President).

Lord Chief Justice of England: Lord WOOLF.

Master of the Rolls: Lord PHILLIPS OF WORTH MATRAVERS.

President of the Family Division: Dame ELIZABETH BUTLER-SLOSS.

Vice-Chancellor: Sir (ROBERT) ANDREW MORRITT.

Lords Justices of Appeal: Sir PAUL JOSEPH MORROW KENNEDY, Sir SIMON DENIS BROWN, Sir CHRISTOPHER DUDLEY RODGER ROSE, Sir PETER LESLIE GIBSON, Sir ROBIN ERNEST AULD, Sir MALCOLM THOMAS PILL, Sir WILLIAM ALDOUS, Sir ALAN HYLTON WARD, Sir KONRAD HERMANN THEODOR SCHIEMANN, Sir MATHEW ALEXANDER THORPE, Sir MARK HOWARD POTTER, Sir HENRY BROOKE, Sir IGOR JUDGE (Senior Presiding Judge), Sir GEORGE MARK WALLER, Sir JOHN FRANK MUMMERY, Sir CHARLES BARRIE KNIGHT MANTELL, Sir JOHN MURRAY CHADWICK, Sir RICHARD JOSEPH BUXTON, Sir ANTHONY TRISTAM KENNETH MAY, Sir SIMON LANE TUCKEY, Sir ANTHONY PETER CLARKE, Sir JOHN GRANT McKENZIE LAWS, Sir STEPHEN JOHN SEDLEY, Sir JONATHAN HUGH MANCE, Dame BRENDA MARJORIE HALE, Sir DAVID NICHOLAS RAMSEY LATHAM, Sir JOHN WILLIAM KAY, Sir BERNARD ANTHONY RIX, Sir JONATHAN FREDERIC PARKER, Dame MARY HOWARTH ARDEN, Sir DAVID WOLFE KEENE, Sir JOHN ANTHONY DYSON, Sir ANDREW CENTLIVRES LONGMORE, Sir ROBERT JOHN ANDERSON CARNWATH, Sir THOMAS SCOTT GILLESPIE BAKER, Dame JANET HILARY SMITH.

HOUSE OF LORDS

In civil and criminal cases this is the final court of appeal.

Lord High Chancellor: Lord IRVINE OF LAIRG.

Lords of Appeal in Ordinary: Lord BINGHAM OF CORNHILL, Lord NICHOLLS OF BIRKENHEAD, Lord STEYN, Lord HOFFMANN, Lord HOPE OF CRAIGHEAD, Lord HUTTON OF BRESAGH, Lord SAVILLE OF NEWDIGATE, Lord HOBHOUSE OF WOODBOROUGH, Lord MILLETT, Lord SCOTT OF FOSCOTE, Lord RODGER OF EARLSFERRY, Lord WALKER OF GESTINGTHORPE.

JUDICIAL COMMITTEE OF THE PRIVY COUNCIL

Final court of appeal for appeals from certain Commonwealth territories; also exercises domestic jurisdiction in ecclesiastical matters and appeals from disciplinary tribunals of certain professions.

Scottish Judicial System

CRIMINAL COURTS

Minor offences are dealt with in District courts.

Sheriff Court

Most criminal actions, including all but the most serious offences, are tried in this court. Each of the six sheriffdoms of Scotland has a Sheriff Principal and a number of Sheriffs, who hear the cases.

High Court of Justiciary

This is the supreme criminal court in Scotland: all the most serious cases are taken there. Appeal may be made to it from the Sheriff Court and from the District courts; there is, however, no further appeal to the House of Lords.

The 32 judges of this court are known as Lords Commissioners of Justiciary and are headed by the Lord Justice General and the Lord Justice Clerk. Apart from their criminal jurisdiction in this court, these judges are also judges of the Court of Session (see below) in civil cases. The Lord Justice General is also the President of the Court of Session.

CIVIL COURTS

Sheriff Court

This court hears civil as well as criminal cases, and in civil cases its jurisdiction is practically unlimited. It has concurrent jurisdiction with the Court of Session in divorce actions. Appeal may be made to the Court of Session or the Sheriff Principal.

Court of Session

This is the supreme civil court in Scotland. It has an Inner House and an Outer House.

The Inner House has two divisions of equal standing, each consisting of four judges (the quorum is three although due to pressure of business an extra division of three judges frequently sits) under the presidency of the Lord President and the Lord Justice Clerk respectively; it is mainly an appeal court, whence further appeal may be made to the House of Lords.

First Division

Lord Justice General and President of the Court of Session: Lord CULLEN.

Judges: Lady COSGROVE, Lord PENROSE, Lord MARNOCH, Lord HAMILTON.

Second Division

Lord Justice Clerk: Lord GILL.

Judges: Lord KIRKWOOD, Lord MACFAYDEN, Lord MACLEAN, Lord OSBORNE.

The Outer House deals with the major civil cases and divorce actions. The judges are those of the High Court of Justiciary, sitting in a civil capacity as judges of the Court of Session.

Judges: Lord ABERNETHY, Lord JOHNSTON, Lord DAWSON, Lord NIMMO SMITH, Lord PHILIP, Lord KINGARTH, Lord BONOMY, Lord EASSIE, Lord REED, Lord WHEATLEY, Lady PATON, Lord CARLOWAY, Lord CLARKE, Lord HARDIE, Lord MACKAY OF DRUMADOON, Lord McEWAN, Lord MENZIES, Lord DRUMMOND YOUNG, Lord EMSLIE, Lady SMITH, Lord BRODIE, Lord BRACADALE.

Religion

CHRISTIANITY

Churches Together in Britain and Ireland: Inter-Church House, 35–41 Lower Marsh, London SE1 7SA; tel. (20) 7523-2121; fax (20) 7928-0010; e-mail info@ctbi.org.uk; internet www.ctbi.org.uk; f. 1990 as successor to the British Council of Churches; co-ordinates the activities of its 32 member churches and liaises with ecumenical bodies in Britain and Ireland. Its work divisions include Church Life, Church and Society and International Affairs, Spirituality, Racial Justice and Inter-faith Relations. It provides a forum for joint decision-making and enables the churches to take action together; Gen. Sec. Dr DAVID GOODBOURN.

Action of Churches Together in Scotland (ACTS): Scottish Churches' House, Dunblane, Perthshire, FK15 0AJ; tel. (1786) 823588; fax (1786) 825844; e-mail acts.ecum@dial.pipex.com; internet www.acts-scotland.org; aims to encourage and express unity of Christian Churches in Scotland; Convener Sr. MAIRE GALLAGHER; Gen. Sec. Rev. KEVIN FRANZ.

The Irish Council of Churches: Inter-Church Centre, 48 Elmwood Ave, Belfast, BT9 6AZ; tel. (28) 9066-4160; fax (28) 9038-2750; e-mail icpep@email.com; internet www.irishchurches.org; 12 mem. bodies; Pres. Rev. ROBERT HERRON; Gen. Sec. Dr DAVID STEVENS.

Churches Together in England (CTE): 27 Tavistock Sq., London, WC1H 9HH; tel. (20) 7529-8141; fax (20) 7529-8134; e-mail <name>@cte.org.uk; internet www.churches-together.org.uk; 22 mem. bodies; Pres Most Rev. and Rt Hon. Dr ROWAN WILLIAMS, Rev. ANTHONY BURNHAM, Rev. ESME BESWICK, H.E. Cardinal CORMAC MURPHY-O'CONNOR; Gen. Sec. Rev. BILL SNELSON.

Churches Together in Wales (CYTÛN): 11 St Helen's Rd, Swansea, SA1 4AL; tel. (1792) 460876; fax (1792) 469391; e-mail gensec@cytun.org.uk; internet www.cytun.org.uk; fmrly the Council of Churches for Wales; 11 mem. bodies; Pres. Rt Rev. D. HUW JONES, EURWEN RICHARDS, Rev. DANIEL MULLINS, JOHN SOUTHERN, Rev ADRIAN WILLIAMS; Gen. Sec. Rev. GETHIN ABRAHAM-WILLIAMS.

The Anglican Communion

The Church of England

The Church of England is the Established Church, and as such acknowledges the authority of Parliament in matters in which secular authority is competent to exercise control. Queen Elizabeth I was declared 'supreme Governor on Earth' of the Church of England, and the Sovereign is consecrated to this office at coronation In England, there are two Provinces, Canterbury and York. The former contains 30, the latter 14, dioceses. Each Province has its ancient Convocations, the Upper and Lower House. By the Enabling Act the Constitution of the National Assembly of the Church of England ('Church Assembly') received statutory recognition in 1920, with power, subject to the control and authority of Parliament, of initiating legislation on all matters concerning the Church of England. Measures passed by the Assembly and approved by Parliament were submitted for the Royal Assent, having the force of Acts of Parliament.

In 1970, by the Synodical Government Measure (1969), the Church Assembly was reconstituted as the General Synod and was also given authority to exercise most of the functions of the Convocations. The House of Bishops consists of members of the Upper House of the Convocations (53 persons). The House of Clergy consists of the Lower Houses (a maximum of 259 persons). The House of Laity consists almost entirely of representatives of the dioceses elected by the deanery synods (a maximum of 258 persons).

In 2000 there were 1,377,000 people on the Church's electoral rolls.

The Archbishops and the 24 senior Bishops sit in the House of Lords.

Archbishop of Canterbury, Primate of All England and Metropolitan: Most Rev. and Rt Hon. ROWAN WILLIAMS, Lambeth Palace, London, SE1 7JU; tel. (20) 7898-1200; fax (20) 7261-9836; internet www.archbishopofcanterbury.org.

Archbishop of York, Primate of England and Metropolitan: Most Rev. and Rt Hon. Dr DAVID M. HOPE, Bishopthorpe Palace, Bishopthorpe, York, YO23 2GE; tel. (1904) 707021; fax (1904) 709204; e-mail office@bishopthorpe.u-net.com; internet www.bishopthorpepalace.co.uk.

General Synod of the Church of England: Church House, Great Smith St, London, SW1P 3NZ; tel. (20) 7898-1000; fax (20) 7898-1369; e-mail synod@c-of-e.org.uk; internet www.cofe.anglican.org; Sec.-Gen. WILLIAM FITTALL.

The Church in Wales

39 Cathedral Rd, Cardiff, CF11 9XF; tel. (29) 2023-1638; fax (29) 2038-7835; e-mail information@rb.churchinwales.org.uk; internet www.churchinwales.org.uk.

the Province of Wales was created as a result of the Welsh Church Act of 1914, which took effect on 31 March 1920 and separated the four Welsh Dioceses from the Province of Canterbury. It is divided into six Dioceses served by 650 stipendiary clerics. The number of Easter communicants is approximately 90,000. The Church in Wales has an administrative governing body which is a legislative assembly composed of bishops, clergy and laity, and a representative body incorporated by Royal Charter, which holds and manages the property and central funds of the Church. Provincial Sec. JOHN SHIRLEY.

Archbishop of Wales: Right Rev. BARRY MORGAN, Bishopstow, Stow Hill, Newport, NP20 4EA; tel. (1633) 263510; fax (1633) 259946; e-mail archbishop@churchinwales.org.uk; internet wales.anglican.org.

The Scottish Episcopal Church

21 Grosvenor Cres., Edinburgh, EH12 5EE; tel. (131) 225-6357; fax (131) 346-7247; e-mail office@scotland.anglican.org; internet www.scotland.anglican.org.

Formerly the Established Church of Scotland, was disestablished and disendowed in 1689; is in full communion with all branches of the Anglican Communion; seven dioceses: Aberdeen and Orkney, Argyll and The Isles, Brechin, Edinburgh, Glasgow and Galloway, Moray, Ross and Caithness, and St Andrews, Dunkeld and Dunblane. There is a Bishop in each diocese; one of them is elected by the other Bishops as The Primus; Churches, mission stations, etc. 310, clergy 402, communicants 29,810; Sec.-Gen. to the General Synod JOHN STUART.

The Primus: Most Rev. BRUCE CAMERON (Bishop of Aberdeen and Orkney), The Diocesan Office, 39 King's Cres., Aberdeen, AB24 3HP; tel. (1224) 636653; fax (1224) 636186; e-mail office@aberdeen .anglican.org.

The Roman Catholic Church

For ecclesiastical purposes Great Britain comprises seven archdioceses and 23 dioceses. There is also an apostolic exarchate for the Ukrainian Rite. At 31 December 2000 there were an estimated 4,175,738 adherents in England and Wales, of whom about 15,000 were of the Ukrainian Rite, and an estimated 694,076 adherents in Scotland.

Latin Rite

Bishops' Conference of England and Wales

39 Eccleston Sq., London, SW1V 1BX; tel. (20) 7630-8220; fax (20) 7901-4821; e-mail secretariat@cbcew.org.uk; internet catholic-ew .org.uk.

President H.E. Cardinal CORMAC MURPHY-O'CONNOR (Archbishop of Westminster).

Archbishop of Westminster: H.E. Cardinal CORMAC MURPHY-O'CONNOR, Archbishop's House, Westminster, London, SW1P 1QJ; tel. (20) 7798-9033; fax (20) 7798-9077; e-mail archbishop@rcdow .org.uk; internet www.rcdow.org.uk/archbishop.

Archbishop of Birmingham: Most Rev. VINCENT NICHOLS, Archbishop's House, 8 Shadwell St, Queensway, Birmingham, B4 6EY; tel. (121) 236-9090; fax (121) 212-0171; e-mail archbishop@ rc-birmingham.org; internet www.birminghamdiocese.org.uk.

Archbishop of Liverpool: Most Rev. PATRICK ALTHAM KELLY, Archbishop's House, Lowood, Carnatic Road, Mossley Hill, Liverpool, L18 8BY; tel. (151) 724-6398; fax (151) 724-6405; e-mail archbishop .liverpool@rcaolp.co.uk; internet www.archdiocese-of-liverpool.co .uk.

Archbishop of Southwark: Most Rev. MICHAEL GEORGE BOWEN, Archbishop's House, 150 St George's Rd, Southwark, London, SE1 6HX; tel. (20) 7928-2495; fax (20) 7928-7833; internet www .rcsouthwark.co.uk.

Archbishop of Cardiff: Most Rev. PETER SMITH, Archbishop's House, 41–43 Cathedral Rd, Cardiff, South Glamorgan, CF11 9HD; tel. (29) 2022-0411; fax (29) 2034-5950; e-mail arch@rcacd.org.

Bishops' Conference of Scotland

64 Aitken St, Airdrie, ML6 6LT; tel. (1236) 764061; fax (1236) 762489; e-mail gensec@bpsconfscot.com; internet www.scmo.org.uk.

President Most Rev. KEITH MICHAEL PATRICK O'BRIEN.

Archbishop of St Andrews and Edinburgh: Most Rev. KEITH MICHAEL PATRICK O'BRIEN, 113 White House Loan, Edinburgh, EH9 1BD; tel. (131) 452-8244; fax (131) 452-9153; e-mail archkp@lineone .net; internet www.archbishopedin.free-online.co.uk.

Archbishop of Glasgow: Most Rev. MARIO JOSEPH CONTI, Curial Offices, 196 Clyde St, Glasgow, G1 4JY; tel. (141) 226-5898; fax (141) 225-2600; e-mail curia@rcag.org.uk; internet www.rcag.org.uk.

Ukrainian Rite

Apostolic Exarch: Rt. Rev. MICHAEL KUCHMIAK, Bishop's House, 22 Binney St, London, W1K 5BQ; tel. (20) 7629-1073; fax (20) 7355-3314.

Protestant Churches

Free Churches' Group, Churches Together in England: 27 Tavistock Sq., London, WC1H 9HH; tel. (20) 7529-8141; fax (20) 7529-8134; e-mail freechurch@cte.org.uk; internet www .churches-together.org.uk; central body for the co-ordination of the work of the Free Churches throughout England and Wales; Moderator Rev. ANTHONY BURNHAM (1999–2003), Rev. DAVID COFFEY (from March 2003); Sec. Rev. GEOFFREY H. ROPER.

Baptist Union of Great Britain: Baptist House, POB 44, 129 Broadway, Didcot, Oxfordshire, OX11 8RT; tel. (1235) 517700; fax (1235) 517715; e-mail info@baptist.org.uk; internet www.baptist.org .uk; f. 1813; the Baptist form of church government is congregational; baptism by immersion of believers is practised. The Churches are grouped in associations; mems (2001) 141,515; Pres. (2003/2004) Rev. JOHN C. RACKLEY; Gen. Sec. Rev. DAVID R. COFFEY.

The Church of Scotland: 121 George St, Edinburgh, EH2 4YN; tel. (131) 225-5722; fax (131) 220-3113; internet www .churchofscotland.org.uk; The National Church of Scotland was reformed in 1560, and became Presbyterian in doctrine and constitution. In 1921 'The Church of Scotland Act' was passed, by which the articles declaring the full spiritual freedom of the Church are recognized as lawful. In 1925 'The Church of Scotland (Property and Endowments) Act' became law, and made over to the Church of Scotland places of worship, manses and endowments in absolute property, vesting the future control of them in Trustees. The union of the Church of Scotland and the United Free Church was effected in 1929; Moderator of the General Assembly Rt Rev. Dr FINLAY MACDONALD; Lord High Commr to the 2002 General Assembly Viscount YOUNGER OF LECKIE; 600,000 mems.

Elim Pentecostal Church: PO Box 38, Cheltenham, Glos, GL50 3HN; tel. (1242) 519904; fax (1242) 222279; e-mail info@elimhq.org.uk; internet www.elim.org.uk; f. 1915; c. 580 churches and 60,000 adherents in Great Britain; Gen. Superintendent Rev. J. J. GLASS.

The Free Church of Scotland: The Mound, Edinburgh, EH1 2LS; tel. (131) 226-5286; fax (131) 220-0597; e-mail offices@freechurchofscotland.org.uk; internet www.freechurch.org; f. 1843; 130 congregations; Principal Clerk of Assembly Rev. JAMES MACIVER.

Lutheran Church in Great Britain: Lutheran Church House, 9 Alma Rd, Headingley, Leeds LS6 2AH; tel. (113) 275-9042; fax (113) 275-9042; e-mail info@lutheransinleeds.freeserve.co.uk; internet www.lutheran.org.uk; Bishop Rt Rev. WALTER JAGUCKI.

The Methodist Church: Methodist Church House, 25 Marylebone Rd, London, NW1 5JR; tel. (20) 7486-5502; fax (20) 7467-5228; e-mail pressoffice@methodistchurch.org.uk; internet www.methodist.org.uk; f. 1739 by Rev. John Wesley, a priest of the Church of England; the governing body of the Church is the Annual Conference, which consists of ministers and lay representatives. The Church throughout Great Britain is divided into 33 Districts, and these hold their Synod Meetings in the autumn and the spring. The Districts are divided into Circuits, which hold regular Circuit Meetings, made up of representatives from the churches within the Circuit. There are also local Church Councils; 327,724 mems (2001); Pres. of the Methodist Conference (2002/2003) Rev. IAN T. WHITE; Sec. of the Methodist Conference Rev. NIGEL T. COLLINSON.

Moravian Church: 5 Muswell Hill, London, N10 3TJ; tel. (20) 8883-3409; fax (20) 8365-3371; e-mail RevdNewman@aol.com; internet www.moravian.org.uk; f. 1457; Sec. Provincial Board Rev. D. J. NEWMAN.

Presbyterian Church of Wales: 53 Richmond Rd, Cardiff, CF24 3WJ; tel. (29) 2049-4913; fax (29) 2046-4293; e-mail ebcpcw@aol.com; internet www.ebcpcw.org.uk; f. 1811; 832 churches, 88 full-time ministers, 38,805 mems (2002); Moderator of General Assembly Rev. DAFFYD HOWER; Gen. Sec. Rev. IFAN RH ROBERTS.

The Religious Society of Friends (Quakers) in Britain: Friends House, 173 Euston Rd, London, NW1 2BJ; tel. (20) 7663-1000; fax (20) 7663-1001; e-mail qcomms@quaker.org.uk; internet www.quaker.org.uk; by George Fox, about the middle of the 17th century; the Quakers have 16,500 mems and 14,000 'attenders' in Great Britain; Recording Clerk (Sec.) ELSA DICKS.

Salvation Army: 101 Newington Causeway, London, SE1 6BN; tel. (20) 7367-4500; fax (20) 7367-4728; e-mail thq@salvationarmy.org.uk; internet www.salvationarmy.org.uk; f. 1865; International Leader Gen. JOHN LARSSON.

Union of Welsh Independents: 11 Heol Sant Helen, Swansea, SA1 4AL; tel. (1792) 652542; fax (1792) 650647; e-mail tyjp@tyjp.co.uk; internet www.annibynwyr.com; Pres. Rev. GERAINT TUDOR; Gen. Sec. Rev. DEWI MYRDDIN HUGHES.

The United Free Church of Scotland: 11 Newton Pl, Glasgow, G3 7PR; tel. (141) 332-3435; fax (141) 333-1973; e-mail office@ufcos.org.uk; internet www.ufcos.org.uk; f. 1900; 68 congregations, 45 ministers and pastors, 4,950 mems; Moderator of the General Assembly Rev. COLIN C. BROWN, Rev. DONALD MACKENZIE (from June 2003); Gen. Sec. Rev. JOHN O. FULTON.

United Reformed Church: United Reformed Church House, 86 Tavistock Pl., London, WC1H 9RT; tel. (20) 7916-2020; fax (20) 7916-2021; e-mail urc@urc.org.uk; internet www.urc.org.uk; f. 1972 by union of the Congregational Church in England and Wales and the Presbyterian Church of England; joined by the Churches of Christ 1981 and by the Scottish Congregational Church 2000; approx. 1,725 churches and 90,000 mems; Moderator Rev. JOHN WALLER; Gen. Sec. Rev. Dr DAVID CORNICK.

Orthodox Churches

Council of the Oriental Orthodox Churches: 34 Chertsey Rd, Church Sq., Shepperton, Middx, TW17 9LF; tel. and fax (20) 8368-8447; Sec. Deacon AZIZ M. A. NOUR.

Armenian Apostolic Church: The Armenian Vicarage, St Sarkis Church, Iverna Gdns, London, W8 6TP; tel. (20) 7937-0152; fax (20) 7937-9049; Bishop NATHAN HOUHANMISSIAN.

Greek Orthodox Church (Archdiocese of Thyateira and Great Britain of the Oecumenical Patriarchate): Thyateira House, 5 Craven Hill, London, W2 3EN; tel. (20) 7723-4787; fax (20) 7224-9301; f. 1922; Archbishop of Thyateira and Great Britain GREGORIOS; Chancellor Bishop ATHANASIOS OF TROPAEOU.

Russian Orthodox Patriarchal Church in Great Britain: Cathedral of the Assumption and All Saints, Ennismore Gdns, London, SW7 1NH; tel. (20) 7584-0096; fax (20) 7584-9864; e-mail webdeacon@sourozh.org; internet www.sourozh.org; Archbishop ANTHONY OF SOUROZH.

Serbian Orthodox Church: 131 Cob Lane, Bournville, Birmingham, B30 1QE; tel. (121) 458-5273; fax (121) 458-4986; Very Rev. MILENKO ZEBIC.

Other Christian Churches

The First Church of Christ, Scientist: Christian Science Committee on Publication, 9 Elysium Gate, 126 New Kings Rd, London, SW6 4LZ; tel. (20) 7384-8600; fax (20) 7371-9204; e-mail londoncs@compub.org; internet www.spirituality.com; f. 1879; The Mother Church, The First Church of Christ, Scientist, in Boston, Mass (USA); approx. 150 churches in Great Britain; District Man. for Great Britain and Ireland TONY LOBL.

The Church of Jesus Christ of Latter-day Saints (Mormon): Press Office, 751 Warwick Rd, Solihull, West Midlands, B91 3DQ; tel. (121) 712-1202; fax (121) 712-1126; e-mail mclavertymw@ldschurch.org; f. 1830; c. 181,000 mems (1998); Area Pres. HAROLD G. HILLAM.

The General Assembly of Unitarian and Free Christian Churches: Essex Hall, 1-6 Essex St, London, WC2R 3HY; tel. (20) 7240-2384; fax (20) 7240-3089; e-mail ga@unitarian.org.uk; internet www.unitarian.org.uk; f. 1928; Gen. Sec. JEFFREY J. TEAGLE.

Jehovah's Witnesses: Watch Tower House, The Ridgeway, London, NW7 1RN; tel. (20) 8906-2211; fax (20) 8906-3938; e-mail pr@wtbts.org.uk; internet www.watchtower.org; f. 1900; there were an estimated 130,000 Jehovah's Witnesses in the UK in 2000.

Seventh-day Adventist Church Headquarters: Stanborough Park, Watford, Herts, WD25 9JZ; tel. (1923) 672251; fax (1923) 893212; e-mail jsurridge@adventist.org.uk; internet www.adventist.org.uk; Communication Dir JOHN C. SURRIDGE.

The Spiritualists' National Union: Redwoods, Stansted Hall, Stansted Mountfitchet, Essex, CM24 8UD; tel. (1279) 816363; fax (1279) 812034; e-mail snu@snu.org.uk; internet www.snu.org.uk; f. 1891; (and incorporated 1901) for the advancement of Spiritualism as a religion and a religious philosophy, it is a trust corporation officially recognized as the central and national body representing the Spiritualists of Great Britain; conducts the Arthur Findlay College of Psychic Science; 400 Spiritualist churches, societies and 20,000 individual mems; Pres. D. P. GASCOYNE; 40 Newmarket, Otley, LS21 3AE; Gen. Sec. CHARLES S. COULSTON.

ISLAM

The Muslim community in the United Kingdom, which is estimated to number 1.5m., consists mainly of people from the Indian subcontinent and their British-born descendants. The chief concentrations of Muslims are in London, the Midlands, South Wales, Lancashire and Yorkshire. There are more than 900 mosques in the United Kingdom; the oldest is the Shah Jehan Mosque in Woking, Surrey.

London Central Mosque Trust and Islamic Cultural Centre: 146 Park Rd, London, NW8 7RG; tel. (20) 7724-3363; fax (20) 7724-0493; e-mail islamic200@aol.com; internet www.islamicculturalcentre.co.uk; Dir-Gen. Dr AHMAD AL-DUBAYAN.

SIKHISM

There are an estimated 400,000 Sikhs in the United Kingdom, who originally came from the Punjab region of the Indian sub-continent as well as from East Africa, although many are now British-born. Each gurdwara (temple) is independent, and there is no central national body.

Sikh Missionary Society, UK: 8–10 Featherstone Rd, Southall, Middx, UB2 5AA; tel. (20) 8574-1902; fax (20) 8574-1912; internet www.sikh-ms.demon.co.uk; promotes Sikhism and acts as a resource centre for information and literature; Hon. Gen. Sec. MOHINDER SINGH CHAHAL.

HINDUISM

There are an estimated 350,000 Hindus in the United Kingdom, with their own origins in India, East Africa and Sri Lanka, although many are now British by birth. Hindus in the United Kingdom are concentrated in London, the Midlands and Yorkshire. By mid-1996 there were some 120 Hindu temples in the country, the largest being the Swaminarayan Hindu Mission in Neasden, north-west London.

JUDAISM

The Jewish community in the United Kingdom is estimated to number 300,000. There are about 350 synagogues in the United Kingdom.

Chief Rabbi of the United Hebrew Congregations of the Commonwealth: Rabbi Prof. JONATHAN SACKS, Office of the Chief Rabbi, Alder House, 735 High Rd, London, N12 0US; tel. (20) 8343-6301; fax (20) 8343-6310; e-mail info@chiefrabbi.org; internet www.chiefrabbi.org.

Court of the Chief Rabbi (Beth Din): 735 High Rd, North Finchley, London, N12 0US; tel. (20) 8343-6270; fax (20) 8343-6257; e-mail info@bethdin.org.uk; Registrar D. FREI.

There is no comprehensive organization of synagogues covering the country as a whole. In London and the South-East there are the following major synagogue organizations:

Council of Reform and Liberal Rabbis: c/o Rabbi Danny Rich, 25 Westmont Rd, Hinchley Wood, Surrey, KT10 9BE; tel. (20) 8398-4252; e-mail rabdrich@aol.com; f. 1968; its Chairs are the Chair of the Rabbinic Conference of the Union, the Chair. of the Union of Liberal and Progressive Synagogues and the Chair. of the Assembly of Reform Rabbis who represent and speak for Progressive Jewry, which does not recognize the authority of the Chief Rabbi of the United Hebrew Congregations; about 60 rabbis serving about 70 congregations in Great Britain and Ireland; Chair. Rabbi DANNY RICH.

Federation of Synagogues: 65 Watford Way, London, NW4 3AQ; tel. (20) 8202-2263; fax (20) 8203-0610; internet www.kfkosher.org; f. 1887; 30 constituent and affiliated synagogues with a total membership of about 12,000 families; Chief Exec. G. D. COLEMAN.

Spanish and Portuguese Jews' Congregation: 2 Ashworth Rd, London, W9 1JY; tel. (20) 7289-2573; fax (20) 7289-2709; e-mail howard@sandpsyn.demon.co.uk; f. 1657; Pres. of the Bd of Elders CESARE SACEROSTI; Chief Exec. HOWARD MILLER.

Union of Liberal and Progressive Synagogues: The Montagu Centre, 21 Maple St, London, W1T 4BE; tel. (20) 7580-1663; fax (20) 7436-4184; e-mail montagu@ulps.org; internet www.ulps.org; f. 1902; 9,300 mems, 31 affiliated synagogues, 3 assoc. communities; Administrative Dir MICHAEL A. BURMAN.

Union of Orthodox Hebrew Congregations: 140 Stamford Hill, London, N16 6QT; tel. (20) 8802-6226; fax (20) 8809-7902; f. 1926; over 6,000 mems; Exec. Dir Rabbi A. KLEIN.

United Synagogue: Adler House, 735 High Rd, London, N12 0YS; tel. (20) 8343-8989; fax (20) 8343-6262; e-mail infogeneral@unitedsynagogue.org.uk; internet www.unitedsynagogue.org.uk; f. 1870 by Act of Parliament; Pres. PETER SHELDON.

West London Synagogue of British Jews: 33 Seymour Pl., London, W1H 5AU; tel. (20) 7723-4404; fax (20) 7224-8258; e-mail admin@wls.org.uk; internet www.wls.org.uk; f. 1840; c. 2,500 mems; Senior Rabbi MARK L. WINER; Exec. Dir MAURICE ROSS.

BUDDHISM

The Buddhist community in the United Kingdom numbers about 25,000.

The Buddhist Society: 58 Eccleston Sq., London, SW1V 1PH; tel. (20) 7834-5858; fax (20) 7976-5238; e-mail info@thebuddhistsociety .org.uk; internet www.thebuddhistsociety.org.uk; f. 1924; Gen. Sec. PAUL SETO.

BAHÁ'Í FAITH

National Spiritual Assembly of the Bahá'ís of the United Kingdom: 27 Rutland Gate, London, SW7 1PD; tel. (20) 7584-2566; fax (20) 7584-9402; e-mail nsa@bahai.org.uk; internet www.bahai .org.uk; f. 1923; Sec.-Gen. BARNABAS LEITH; Chair. SHIRIN TAHZIB.

The Press

The United Kingdom has some of the highest circulation figures in the world for individual newspapers (*Daily Mirror* 2.0m., *The Sun* 3.5m., *News of the World* 3.8m.). In 2000 there were more than 1,300 regional and local daily and weekly newspapers in the United Kingdom and in 2001 the total weekly circulation of all newspapers was 159m.

There is no law which specifies the operations of the press but several items of legislation bear directly on press activities. Although exact reporting of legal proceedings appearing at the time of trial is protected from later charges of defamation, the freedom to report cases is subject to certain restrictions as defined in the Judicial Proceedings Act of 1926, in the Children's and Young Persons' Act of 1933 and in the Criminal Justice Act 1967. The strict laws of contempt of court and of libel somewhat limit the scope of the press. Journalists are subject to the former if they publish material liable to interfere with a matter which is *sub judice* but this law is qualified by the Administration of Justice Act of 1960 which declares an editor not guilty of contempt if, after taking reasonable care, he remained ignorant of the fact that proceedings were pending. The Scottish law of contempt is more severe than the English. Libel cases can involve the awarding of punitive damages against the press. The Defamation Act of 1952 lessened the possible repercussions of unin-

tentional libel and made provision for the claim of fair comment by the defence.

The Official Secrets Act of 1911 prohibits the publication of secret information where this is judged not to be in the national interest. The Secretary of State for the Home Department is empowered to require a person with information about a violation of the Act to disclose his source. Journalists have no exemption here. The publication of morally objectionable and harmful material is treated in the Children's and Young Persons' (Harmful Publications) Act of 1955 and in the Obscene Publications Act.

In recent years legislative measures have been taken to limit the excessive development of concentrations of newspaper ownership and the extent of the control by newspaper owners over other mass media such as the television. The Television Act of 1964 provided for intervention by the Postmaster-General or the Independent Broadcasting Authority where investments by newspaper owners in television companies are judged liable to lead to abuses. The Monopolies and Mergers Act of 1965 requires the written consent of the Department of Trade and Industry for the transfer of daily or weekly papers with an aggregate average of over 500,000 copies per day of publication. The Department's decision is based on the conclusions of the Monopolies Commission to which, with exception of cases of papers judged to be uneconomical and of papers with an average daily circulation of no more than 25,000 copies, all cases are referred for investigation.

The Press Complaints Commission, which replaced the Press Council in 1991, has an independent chairman and 16 members, drawn from the lay public and the press. It deals with complaints from the public and upholds a 18-point Code of Practice.

Among the most influential newspapers may be included: *The Times, The Guardian, The Independent, Daily Telegraph* and *Financial Times* (daily), *The Observer, The Independent on Sunday, The Sunday Times* and *Sunday Telegraph* (Sunday newspapers). Prominent among the popular press are: *Daily Mail, Daily Mirror, The Express* and *The Sun* (daily), *Sunday Mirror, News of the World* and *The People* (Sunday newspapers).

No important newspaper is directly owned by a political party. The great rate of news consumption has fostered the growth of large national groups or chains of papers controlled by a single organization or individual. The largest of these chains are as follows:

Daily Mail and General Trust PLC: Northcliffe House, 2 Derry St, London, W8 5TT; tel. (20) 7938-6000; fax (20) 7938-6747; e-mail webmaster@dmgt.co.uk; internet www.dmgt.co.uk; controls through Associated Newspapers one national daily *Daily Mail*, one national Sunday *The Mail on Sunday*, one London daily *Evening Standard*; through the Northcliffe Newspapers Group Ltd controls 20 daily titles, 27 weekly titles and 50 free newspapers; Group Chair. Viscount ROTHERMERE; Group CEO CHARLES SINCLAIR.

Guardian Media Group PLC: 164 Deansgate, Manchester, M60 2RD; tel. (161) 832-7200; fax (161) 831-7308; internet www.gmgplc .co.uk; subsidiary publishing cos include Guardian Newspapers Ltd (controls *The Guardian, The Observer*) and Manchester Evening News Ltd; Chair. PAUL MYNERS; CEO BOB PHILLIS.

Independent Newspapers UK: 1 Canada Sq., Canary Wharf, London, E14 5DL; tel. (20) 7293-2000; fax (20) 7293-2435; internet www.independentnewsmedia.com; UK subsidiary of Ireland's Independent News & Media PLC; publishes one national daily, *The Independent*, and one national Sunday paper, *The Independent on Sunday*; Chair. TONY O'REILLY; Man. Dir TERRY GROTE.

News International PLC: 1 Virginia St, Wapping, London, E98 1XY; tel. (20) 7782-6000; UK subsidiary of USA's News Corporation; subsidiary cos: News Group Newspapers Ltd (controls *The Sun* and *News of the World*), Times Newspapers Ltd (controls *The Times* and *The Sunday Times*); Exec. Chair. LESLIE HINTON.

Trinity Mirror PLC: 1 Canada Sq., Canary Wharf, London, E14 5AP; tel. (20) 7293-3000; fax (20) 7293-3280; internet www.trinity .plc.uk; f. 1999; by merger of Mirror Group Newspapers Ltd and Trinity International Holdings; controls a total of over 250 newspapers, including one national daily paper *Daily Mirror*, two national Sunday papers *The People, Sunday Mirror* and two Scottish national papers *Daily Record* and *Sunday Mail* and numerous regional and local papers; Chair. Sir VICTOR BLANK; Chief Executive SYLVIA (SLY) BAILEY.

United Business Media PLC: Ludgate House, 245 Blackfriars Rd, London, SE1 9UY; tel. (20) 7921-5000; internet www .unitedbusinessmedia.com; f. 1996; by merger of United Newspapers and MAI group; international media and information group; three core business divisions—professional media, market research, news distribution; Chair. GEOFF UNWIN; CEO Lord HOLLICK.

PRINCIPAL NATIONAL DAILIES

Daily Mail: Northcliffe House, 2 Derry St, Kensington, London, W8 5TT; tel. (20) 7938-6000; fax (20) 7937-4463; internet www.dailymail .co.uk; f. 1896; inc. *News Chronicle* 1960 and *Daily Sketch* 1971;

Propr Associated Newspaper Holdings; Editor-in-Chief PAUL DACRE; circ. 2,427,032.

Daily Mirror: 1 Canada Sq., Canary Wharf, London, E14 5AP; tel. (20) 7293-3000; fax (20) 7293-3280; e-mail mailbox@mirror.co.uk; internet www.mirror.co.uk; f. 1903; Propr Trinity Mirror PLC; Editor PIERS MORGAN; circ. 1,997,846.

Daily Star: Ludgate House, 245 Blackfriars Rd, London, SE1 9UX; tel. (20) 7928-8000; fax (20) 7633-0244; e-mail dailystarnewsdesk@dailystar.co.uk; internet www.dailystar.co.uk; f. 1978; Propr Express Newspapers PLC; Editor PETER HILL; circ. 850,043.

Daily Telegraph: 1 Canada Sq., Canary Wharf, London, E14 5DT; tel. (20) 7538-5000; fax (20) 7513-2506; e-mail dtletters@telegraph.co.uk; internet www.telegraph.co.uk; *Daily Telegraph*, f. 1855, *Morning Post*, f. 1772; amalgamated 1937; Propr Hollinger International Inc. Chair. CONRAD BLACK; Editor CHARLES MOORE; circ. 926,500.

The Express: Ludgate House, 245 Blackfriars Rd, London, SE1 9UX; tel. (20) 7928-8000; fax (20) 7633-0244; e-mail expressletters@express.co.uk; internet www.express.co.uk; f. 1900; Propr Northern and Shell Group; Editor CHRIS WILLIAMS; circ. 932,560.

Financial Times: Number One Southwark Bridge, London, SE1 9HL; tel. (20) 7873-3000; fax (20) 7873-3076; internet www.ft.com; f. 1880; Propr Pearson PLC; Chair. DAVID BELL; Editor ANDREW GOWERS; circ. 472,969.

The Guardian: 119 Farringdon Rd, London, EC1R 3ER; and 164 Deansgate, Manchester, M3 3GG; tel. (20) 7278-2332; fax (20) 7837-2114; e-mail newmedia@guardian.co.uk; internet www.guardian.co.uk; tel. (161) 832-7200; fax (161) 832-5351; f. 1821; Propr Guardian Newspapers Ltd; Editor ALAN RUSBRIDGER; circ. 412,341.

The Independent: Independent House, 191 Marsh Wall, London, E14 9RS; tel. (20) 7005-2000; fax (20) 7005-2056; e-mail customerservices@independent.co.uk; internet www.independent.co.uk; f. 1986; Editor SIMON KELNER; circ. 223,867.

Racing Post: 1 Canada Sq., Canary Wharf, London, E14 5AP; tel. (20) 7293-3000; fax (20) 7293-2630; e-mail editor@racingpost.co.uk; internet www.racingpost.co.uk; f. 1986; covers national and international horse racing, greyhound racing, general sport and betting; Editor CHRIS SMITH; circ. 70,684.

The Sport: 19 Gt Ancoats St, Manchester, M60 4BT; tel. (161) 236-4466; fax (161) 236-4535; internet www.dailysport.net; f. 1988; Propr Sport Newspapers Ltd; Editor DAVID BEEVERS.

The Sun: 1 Virginia St, Wapping, London, E1 9XR; tel. (20) 7782-4000; fax (20) 7782-4108; e-mail news@the-sun.co.uk; internet www.thesun.co.uk; f. 1921 as *Daily Herald*, present name since 1964; Propr News International PLC; Editor REBEKAH WADE; circ. 3,521,348.

The Times: 1 Pennington St, Wapping, London, E98 1XY; tel. (20) 7782-5000; fax (20) 7782-5988; internet www.thetimes.co.uk; f. 1785; Propr News International PLC; Editor ROBERT THOMSON; circ. 655,484.

LONDON DAILIES

Evening Standard: Northcliffe House, 2 Derry St, Kensington, London, W8 5TT; tel. (20) 7938-6000; fax (20) 7937-2648; internet www.thisislondon.co.uk; f. 1827; merged with *Evening News* 1980; Monday–Friday; evening paper; Propr Associated Newspaper Holdings PLC; Editor VERONICA WADLEY; circ. 402,223.

Metro: Harmsworth Quays Printing, Surrey Quays Rd, Rotherhithe, London, SE16 7ND; tel. (20) 7651-5200; fax (20) 7651-5342; e-mail editorial@londonmetro.co.uk; internet www.metro.co.uk; f. 1999; Monday–Friday; morning; also distributed in Scotland, Manchester, Newcastle, Birmingham, South Yorkshire and Leeds; Propr Associated Newspaper Holdings PLC; Editor KENNY CAMPBELL; circ. 408,403 (London); 485,557 (total UK).

PRINCIPAL PROVINCIAL DAILIES

Aberdeen

Evening Express: Aberdeen Journals Ltd, POB 43, Lang Stracht, Mastrick, Aberdeen, AB15 6DF; tel. (1224) 690222; fax (1224) 699575; e-mail ee.news@ajl.co.uk; internet www.thisisnorthscotland.co.uk; f. 1879; Editor DONALD MARTIN; circ. 62,764.

Press and Journal: POB 43, Lang Stracht, Mastrick, Aberdeen, AB15 6DF; tel. (1224) 690222; fax (1224) 663575; e-mail pj.editor@ajl.co.uk; internet www.thisisnorthscotland.co.uk; f. 1747; morning; Propr Northcliffe Newspapers Ltd; Editor DEREK TUCKER; circ. 96,235.

Birmingham

Birmingham Post: 28 Colmore Circus, Queensway, Birmingham, B4 6AX; tel. (121) 236-3366; fax (121) 625-1105; internet www.icbirmingham.co.uk; f. 1857; acquired by Mirror Group Newspapers Ltd in 1997; morning; independent; Editor N. HASTILOW; circ. 17,836.

The Evening Mail: 28 Colmore Circus, Queensway, Birmingham, B4 6AX; tel. (121) 234-5678; fax (121) 233-0271; e-mail eveningmail@mrn.co.uk; internet www.icbirmingham.co.uk; f. 1870; acquired by Mirror Group Newspapers Ltd in 1997; evening; independent; Editor ROGER BORRELL; circ. 121,159.

Bradford

Telegraph & Argus: Newsquest (Bradford) Ltd, Hall Ings, Bradford, BD1 1JR; tel. (1274) 729511; fax (1274) 723634; e-mail newsdesk@bradford.newsquest.co.uk; internet www.thisisbradford.co.uk; f. 1868; evening; Editor PERRY AUSTIN-CLARKE; circ. 50,142.

Brighton

The Argus: Newsquest (Sussex) Ltd, Argus House, Crowhurst Rd, Hollingbury, Brighton, BN1 8AR; tel. (1273) 544544; fax (1273) 566114; e-mail simonb@argus-btn.co.uk; internet www.thisisbrightonandhove.co.uk; f. 1880; Man. Dir HOWARD SCOTT; Editor SIMON BRADSHAW; circ. 46,627.

Bristol

Evening Post: Temple Way, Old Market, Bristol, BS99 7HD; tel. (117) 934-3000; fax (117) 934-3575; e-mail epnews@bepp.co.uk; internet www.thisisbristol.com; f. 1932; inc. the *Evening World*; Propr Northcliffe Newspapers; independent; Editor MIKE LOWE; circ. 66,610.

Western Daily Press: Temple Way, Bristol, BS99 7HD; tel. (117) 934-3000; fax (117) 934-3574; e-mail wdnews@bepp.co.uk; internet www.westpress.co.uk; f. 1858; inc. *Bristol Times and Mirror*; Propr Bristol Evening Post and Press Ltd; morning; independent; Man. Dir PAUL KEARNEY; Editor TERRY MANNERS; circ. 51,181.

Cardiff

South Wales Echo: Havelock St, Cardiff, CF1 1XR; tel. (29) 2058-3622; fax (29) 2058-3411; e-mail rfletcher@wme.co.uk; internet www.icwales.co.uk; f. 1884; Propr Trinity Mirror PLC; evening; independent; Editor ALASTAIR MILBURN; circ. 67,504.

The Western Mail: Havelock St, Cardiff, CF1 1XR; tel. (29) 2058-3583; fax (29) 2058-3652; e-mail readers@wme.co.uk; internet www.icwales.co.uk; f. 1869; independent; Man. Dir MARK HAYSOM; Editor NEIL FOWLER; circ. 50,306.

Coventry

Coventry Evening Telegraph: Corporation St, Coventry, CV1 1FP; tel. (24) 7663-3633; fax (24) 7655-0869; e-mail covnews@innotts.co.uk; internet www.iccoventry.co.uk; f. 1891 as *Midland Daily Telegraph*; Propr. Trinity Mirror PLC; independent; Man. Dir GERALDINE AITKEN; Editor ALAN KIRBY; circ. (Mon-Sat) 69,695.

Darlington

Northern Echo: Newsquest (North East) Ltd, POB 14, Priestgate, Darlington, Co Durham, DL1 1NF; tel. (1325) 381313; fax (1325) 380539; e-mail echo@nne.co.uk; internet www.thisisthenortheast.co.uk; f. 1869; morning; independent; Editor PETER BARRON; circ. 61,053.

Derby

Derby Evening Telegraph: Derby Daily Telegraph Ltd, Northcliffe House, Meadow Rd, Derby, DE1 2DW; tel. (1332) 291111; fax (1332) 253027; e-mail newsdesk@derbytelegraph.co.uk; internet www.thisisderbyshire.co.uk; f. 1932; inc. *Derby Daily Telegraph*, f. 1879, *Derby Daily Express*, f. 1884; Editor MICHAEL NORTON; circ. 53,876.

Dundee

Courier and Advertiser: 80 Kingsway East, Dundee, DD4 8SL; tel. (1382) 223131; fax (1382) 454590; e-mail courier@dcthompson.co.uk; internet www.thecourier.co.uk; f. 1810; morning; Editor ADRIAN ARTHUR; circ. 87,764.

Edinburgh

Edinburgh Evening News: Barclay House, 108 Holyrood Rd, Edinburgh, EH8 8AS; tel. (131) 620-8620; fax (131) 620-8696; e-mail istewart@edinburghnews.com; internet www.edinburghnews.com; f. 1873; Propr European Press Holdings; Editor IAN STEWART; circ. 70,205.

The Scotsman: Barclay House, 108 Holyrood Rd, Edinburgh, EH8 8AS; tel. (131) 620-8620; fax (131) 620-8615; e-mail enquiries@ scotsman.com; internet www.scotsman.com; f. 1817; morning; Propr Press Holdings Ltd; Editor IAIN MARTIN; circ. 81,421.

Glasgow

Daily Record: 1 Central Quay, Glasgow, G3 8DA; tel. (141) 309-3000; fax (141) 309-3340; internet www.dailyrecord.co.uk; morning; independent; f. 1895; Propr Trinity Mirror PLC; Editor-in-Chief PETER COX; circ. 517,248.

The Express: Park House, Park Circus Pl., Glasgow, G3 6AF; tel. (141) 332-9600; fax (141) 332-5448; morning; regional edition of The Express; Propr Northern and Shell Group; Editor JOHN MURRAY; circ. 155,000.

Glasgow Evening Times: 200 Renfield St, Glasgow, G2 3PR; tel. (141) 302-7000; fax (141) 302-6600; e-mail times@eveningtimes.co .uk; internet www.eveningtimes.co.uk; f. 1876; independent; Propr Scottish Media Group; Editor CHARLES MCGHEE; circ. 102,231.

The Herald: 200 Renfield St, Glasgow, G2 3PR; tel. (141) 302-7000; fax (141) 333-1147; e-mail news@theherald.co.uk; internet www .theherald.co.uk; f. 1783; morning; independent; Propr SMG; Editor MARK DOUGLAS-HOME; circ. 92,615.

Grimsby

Grimsby Telegraph: 80 Cleethorpe Rd, Grimsby, DN31 3EH; tel. (1472) 360360; fax (1472) 372257; e-mail newsdesk@ grimsbytelegraph.co.uk; internet www.thisisgrimsby.co.uk; f. 1898; evening; Editor MICHELLE LALOR; circ. 41,546.

Ipswich

East Anglian Daily Times: Press House, 30 Lower Brook St, Ipswich, IP4 1AN; tel. (1473) 230023; e-mail eadt.newsdesk@eadt.co .uk; internet www.eadt.co.uk; morning; Editor TERRY HUNT; circ. 42,773.

Kingston upon Hull

Hull Daily Mail: POB 34, Blundell's Corner, Beverley Rd, Kingston upon Hull, HU3 1XS; tel. (1482) 327111; fax (1482) 584353; e-mail news@hulldailymail.co.uk; internet www.thisishull.co.uk; f. 1885; evening; Editor JOHN MEEHAN; circ. 77,199.

Leeds

Yorkshire Evening Post: Wellington St, Leeds, LS1 1RF; tel. (113) 243-2701; fax (113) 238-8536; e-mail epad@ypn.co.uk; internet www .thisisleeds.co.uk; f. 1890; independent; Publr Regional Independent Media; Editor NEIL HODGKINSON; circ. 89,931.

Yorkshire Post: Wellington St, Leeds, LS1 1RF; tel. (113) 2432701; fax (113) 244-3430; e-mail yp.newsdesk@ypn.co.uk; internet www .ypn.co.uk; f. 1754; morning; Conservative; Publr Yorkshire Post Newspapers Ltd; Editor RACHEL CAMPEY; circ. 67,651.

Leicester

Leicester Mercury: St George St, Leicester, LE1 9FQ; tel. (116) 251-2512; fax (116) 253-0645; e-mail nickcarter@leicestermercury.co .uk; internet www.thisisleicestershire.co.uk; f. 1874; evening; Editor NICK CARTER; circ. 98,599.

Liverpool

Daily Post: Liverpool Daily Post and Echo Ltd, POB 48, Old Hall St, Liverpool, L69 3EB; tel. (151) 227-2000; fax (151) 236-4682; e-mail newsdesk@dailypost.co.uk; internet www.icliverpool.co.uk; f. 1855; inc. *Liverpool Mercury*, f. 1811; morning; independent; Propr Trinity Mirror PLC; Editor JANE WOLSTENHOLME; circ. 64,366.

Liverpool Echo: Liverpool Daily Post and Echo Ltd, POB 48, Old Hall St, Liverpool, L69 3EB; tel. (151) 227-2000; fax (151) 236-4682; e-mail letters@liverpoolecho.co.uk; internet www.icliverpool.co.uk; f. 1879; evening; independent; Propr Trinity Mirror PLC; Editor MARK DICKINSON; circ. 146,656.

Manchester

Manchester Evening News: 164 Deansgate, Manchester, M60 2RD; tel. (161) 832-7200; fax (161) 834-3814; e-mail newsdesk@ men-news.co.uk; internet www.manchesteronline.co.uk; f. 1868; independent; Editor PAUL HORROCKS; circ. 164,237.

Middlesbrough

Evening Gazette: Borough Rd, Middlesbrough, Cleveland, TS1 3AZ; tel. (1642) 245401; fax (1642) 210565; e-mail editor@ eveninggazette.co.uk; internet www.icteeside.co.uk; f. 1869; Propr Trinity Mirror PLC; Man. Dir NEIL BENSON; Editor PAUL ROBERTSON; circ. 60,993.

Newcastle upon Tyne

Evening Chronicle: Groat Market, Newcastle upon Tyne, NE1 1ED; tel. (191) 232-7500; fax (191) 230-4144; e-mail chron@ cjchronicle.demon.co.uk; internet www.icnewcastle.co.uk; f. 1885; Propr Trinity Mirror PLC; Editor PAUL ROBERTSON; circ. 99,389.

The Journal: Groat Market, Newcastle upon Tyne, NE1 1ED; tel. (191) 232-7500; fax (191) 230-4144; e-mail jnl.newsdesk@ncjmedia .co.uk; internet www.icnewcastle.co.uk; f. 1832; morning; Propr Trinity Mirror PLC; Editor GERARD HENDERSON; circ. 47,146.

Norwich

Eastern Daily Press: Prospect House, Rouen Rd, Norwich, NR1 1RE; tel. (1603) 628311; fax (1603) 612930; e-mail edp@archant.co .uk; internet www.edp24.co.uk; f. 1870; independent; Propr Archant Regional Ltd; Editor PETER FRANZEN; circ. 74,832.

Nottingham

Nottingham Evening Post: Castle Wharf House, Nottingham, NG1 7EU; tel. (115) 948-2000; fax (115) 964-4032; e-mail nep .editorial@dial.pipex.com; internet www.thisisnottingham.co.uk; f. 1878; Editor GRAHAM GLEN; circ. 80,633.

Plymouth

Western Morning News: 17 Brest Rd, Derriford Business Park, Plymouth, PL6 5AA; tel. (1752) 765500; fax (1752) 765535; internet www.westernmorningnews.co.uk; f. 1860; Editor BARRIE WILLIAMS; circ. 57,923; companion evening paper, *Evening Herald*; Editor ALAN QUALTROUGH; circ. 48,766.

Portsmouth

The News: The News Centre, Hilsea, Portsmouth, PO2 9SX; tel. (23) 9266-4488; fax (23) 9267-3363; e-mail newsdesk@thenews.co .uk; internet www.thenews.co.uk; f. 1877; evening; Editor MIKE GILSON; circ. 67,133.

Preston

Lancashire Evening Post: Oliver's Pl., Eastway, Fulwood, Preston, PR2 9ZA; tel. (1772) 254841; fax (1772) 880173; e-mail lep .newsdesk@rim.co.uk; internet www.prestononline.co.uk; f. 1886; Editor SIMON REYNOLDS; circ. 45,516.

Sheffield

The Star: York St, Sheffield, S1 1PU; tel. (114) 276-7676; fax (114) 272-5978; e-mail peter.charlton@sheffieldnewspapers.co.uk; internet www.thisissheffield.net; f. 1887; evening; independent; Propr Johnston Press; Editor PETER CHARLTON; circ. (Mon.–Fri.) 76,421.

Southampton

Southern Daily Echo: Newspaper House, Test Lane, Redbridge, Southampton, SO16 9JX; tel. (23) 8042-4424; fax (23) 8042-4770; e-mail newsdesk@southern-echo.co.uk; internet www .thisishampshire.co.uk; f. 1888; Propr Southern Newspapers; Editor IAN MURRAY; circ. 51,657.

Stoke-on-Trent

The Sentinel: Staffordshire Sentinel Newspapers Ltd, Sentinel House, Etruria, Stoke-on-Trent, ST1 5SS; tel. (1782) 602525; fax (1782) 602616; e-mail editor@thesentinel.co.uk; internet www .thisisstaffordshire.co.uk; f. 1873; Editor SEAN DOOLEY; circ. 81,498.

Sunderland

Sunderland Echo: Echo House, Pennywell, Sunderland, Tyne and Wear, SR4 9ER; tel. (191) 501-5800; fax (191) 534-3807; e-mail echo .news@northeast-press.co.uk; internet www.sunderlandtoday.co.uk; f. 1873; evening; Editor ROB LAWSON; circ. 52,345.

Swansea

South Wales Evening Post: South-West Wales Publs Ltd, Adelaide St, Swansea, SA1 1QT; tel. (1792) 510000; fax (1792) 514197; internet www.thisissouthwales.co.uk; f. 1930; Editor GEORGE EDWARDS; circ. 60,248.

Telford

Shropshire Star: Ketley, Telford, Shropshire, TF1 4HU; tel. (1952) 242424; fax (1952) 254605; internet www.shropshirestar.com; f. 1964; evening; Propr Shropshire Newspapers Ltd; Editor SARAH-JANE SMITH; circ. 87,684.

Wolverhampton

Express and Star: 51–53 Queen St, Wolverhampton, West Midlands, WV1 1ES; tel. (1902) 313131; fax (1902) 710106; e-mail queries@expressandstar.co.uk; internet www.westmidlands.com; f. 1874; evening; Propr The Midland News Association Ltd; Editor W. WILSON; circ. 172,476.

York

York Evening Press: POB 29, 76–86 Walmgate, York, YO1 9YN; tel. (1904) 653051; fax (1904) 612853; e-mail newsdesk@ycp.co.uk; internet www.thisisyork.co.uk; Editor LIZ PAGE; circ. 42,674.

PRINCIPAL WEEKLY NEWSPAPERS

Asian Times: Ethnic Media Group, 65 Whitechapel Rd, London, E1 1DU; tel. (20) 7650-2000; fax (20) 7650-2001; internet www.ethnicmedia.co.uk; Man. Editor MUJIB ISLAM.

The Business: 292 Vauxhall Bridge Rd, London, SW1V 1DE; tel. (20) 7961-0000; fax (20) 7961-0101; f. 1996; relaunched in 1998; Propr European Press Holdings; Editor ANDREW NEIL; circ. 81,405.

Daily Star Sunday: Ludgate House, 245 Blackfriars Rd, London, SE1 9UX; tel. (20) 7928-8000; fax (20) 7633-0244; e-mail dailystarnewsdesk@dailystar.co.uk; internet www.dailystar.co.uk; f. 1978; Propr Express Newspapers PLC; Editor HUGH WITTOW; circ. 437,766.

Express on Sunday: Ludgate House, 245 Blackfriars Rd., London, SE1 9UX; tel. (20) 7928-8000; fax (20) 7620-1656; f. 1918; inc. *Sunday Despatch* 1961; independent; Propr Northern and Shell Group; Editor-in-Chief MARTIN TOWNSEND; circ. 924,047.

The Independent on Sunday: Independent House, 191 Marsh Wall, London, E14 9RS; tel. (20) 7005-2000; fax (20) 7005-2627; internet www.independent.co.uk; f. 1990; Propr Independent Newspapers UK; Editor TRISTAN DAVIES; circ. 222,238.

The Mail on Sunday: Northcliffe House, 2 Derry St, London, W8 5TS; tel. (20) 7938-6000; fax (20) 7937-1004; f. 1982; Propr Associated Newspaper Holdings; Editor PETER WRIGHT; circ. 2,339,222.

News of the World: 1 Virginia St, Wapping, London, E1 9XR; tel. (20) 7782-1000; fax (20) 7583-9504; e-mail newsdesk@news-of-the-world.co.uk; f. 1843; Propr News International PLC; independent; Sunday; Editor ANDY COULSON; circ. 3,849,189.

The Observer: 119 Farringdon Rd, London, EC1R 3ER; tel. (20) 7278-2332; fax (20) 7713-4250; e-mail newmedia@guardian.co.uk; internet www.observer.co.uk; f. 1791; acquisition by Guardian Newspapers Ltd approved in May 1993; independent; Sunday; Editor ROGER ALTON; circ. 455,387.

Scotland on Sunday: Barclay House, 108 Holyrood Rd, Edinburgh, EH8 8AS; tel. (131) 620-8620; fax (131) 620-8491; e-mail letters_sos@scotlandonsunday.com; internet www.scotlandonsunday.com; f. 1988; Propr Scotish Publications Ltd; Editor JOHN MCLELLAN; circ. 84,449.

Sunday Herald: 200 Renfield St, Glasgow, G2 3PR; tel. (141) 302-7800; e-mail editor@sundayherald.com; internet www.sundayherald.com; f. 1999; Propr Scottish Media Group; Editor ANDREW JASPAN; circ. 56,874.

Sunday Mail: 40 Anderston Quay, Glasgow, G3 8DA; tel. (141) 248-7000; fax (141) 242-3587; internet www.record-mail.co.uk/rm/; Propr Mirror Group Newspapers Ltd; Editor ALLAN RENNIE; circ. 621,956.

Sunday Mercury: 28 Colmore Circus, Queensway, Birmingham, B4 6AX; tel. (121) 236-3366; fax (121) 234-5877; e-mail Sundaymercury@mrn.co.uk; internet www.icbirmingham.co.uk; Propr Trinity Mirror PLC; f. 1918; Editor DAVID BROOKES; circ. 95,661.

Sunday Mirror: 1 Canada Sq., Canary Wharf, London, E14 5AP; tel. (20) 7293-3000; fax (20) 7822-3280; internet www.sundaymirror.co.uk; f. 1915; Propr Trinity Mirror PLC; independent; Editor TINA WEAVER; circ. 1,603,578.

Sunday People: 1 Canada Sq., Canary Wharf, London, E14 5AP; tel. (20) 7293-3000; fax (20) 7293-3280; internet www.thepeople.co.uk; f. 1881; Propr Trinity Mirror PLC; Editor NEIL WALLIS; circ. 1,107,0481,341,825.

The Sunday Post: 2 Albert Square, Dundee, DD1 9QJ; Glasgow Office: 144 Port Dundas Rd; tel. (1382) 223131; fax (1382) 201064; e-mail mail@sundaypost.com; internet www.sundaypost.com; tel. (141) 332-9933; fax (141) 331-1595; f. 1919; Editor DAVID POLLINGTON; circ. 596,160.

Sunday Sport: 19 Gt Ancoats St, Manchester, M60 4BT; tel. (161) 236-4466; fax (161) 236-4535; f. 1986; Editor MARK HARRIS; circ. 189,879.

Sunday Sun: Thomson House, Groat Market, Newcastle upon Tyne, NE1 1ED; tel. (191) 232-7500; fax (191) 230-0238; e-mail scoop.sundaysun@ncjmedia.co.uk; internet www.sundaysun.co.uk; f. 1919; Propr Trinity Mirror PLC; independent; north-east England; Editor PETER MONTELLIER; circ. 97,624.

Sunday Telegraph: 1 Canada Sq., Canary Wharf, London, E14 5DT; tel. (20) 7538-5000; fax (20) 7538-6242; e-mail stletters@telegraph.co.uk; internet www.telegraph.co.uk; f. 1961; Propr Hollinger International Inc. Chair. CONRAD BLACK; Editor DOMINIC LAWSON; circ. 716,362.

The Sunday Times: 1 Pennington St, Wapping, London, E98 1ST; tel. (20) 7782-5000; fax (20) 7782-5658; internet www.sunday-times.co.uk; f. 1822; Propr News International PLC; Editor JOHN WITHEROW; circ. 1,382,778.

Wales on Sunday: Havelock St, Cardiff, CF1 1XR; tel. (29) 2058-3583; internet www.icwales.co.uk; f. 1991; Editor ALAN EDMUNDS; circ. 58,198.

SELECTED PERIODICALS

Arts and Literature

Apollo Magazine: 1 Castle Lane, London, SW1E 6DR; tel. (20) 7233-8906; fax (20) 7233-7159; e-mail advertising@apollomag.com; internet www.apollomagazine.com; f. 1925; monthly; fine and decorative art; Publr PAUL JOSEFOWITZ; Editor DAVID EKSERDJIAN.

Architects' Journal: EMAP Construct, 151 Rosebery Ave, London, EC1R 4GB; tel. (20) 7505-6700; fax (20) 7505-6701; e-mail isabel.allen@construct.emap.com; internet www.ajplus.co.uk; f. 1895; Wednesday; Editor ISABEL ALLEN; circ. 16,921.

Architectural Review: EMAP Construct, 151 Rosebery Ave, London, EC1R 4GB; tel. (20) 7505-6725; fax (20) 7505-6701; e-mail peter.davey@ebc.emap.com; internet www.arplus.com; f. 1896; monthly; Editor PETER DAVEY; circ. 23,925.

The Artist: Caxton House, 63–65 High St, Tenterden, Kent, TN30 6BD; tel. (1580) 763673; fax (1580) 765411; e-mail sally@tapc.co.uk; internet www.theartistmagazine.co.uk; f. 1931; monthly; Editor SALLY BULGIN.

Art Review: Art Review Ltd, Hereford House, 23–24 Smithfield St, London, EC1A 9LF; tel. (20) 7236-4880; fax (20) 7236-4881; e-mail info@art-review.co.uk; internet www.art-review.co.uk; f. 1949; monthly; Editor MEREDITH ETHERINGTON-SMITH; circ. 13,500.

BBC Music Magazine: BBC Worldwide Ltd, Rm A1004, Woodlands, 80 Wood Lane, London, W12 0TT; tel. (20) 8433-3283; fax (20) 8433-3292; e-mail music.magazine@bbc.co.uk; internet www.bbcmusicmagazine.com; f. 1992; monthly; classical music; Editor HELEN WALLACE; circ. 78,707.

Books Magazine: 39 Store St, London, WC1E 7DB; tel. (20) 7692-2900; fax (20) 7419-2111; e-mail lizthomson@publishingnews.co.uk; f. 1955; quarterly; literature and books of general interest; Editor LIZ THOMSON.

The Bookseller: Endeavour House, 189 Shaftesbury Ave, London, WC2H 8TJ; tel. (20) 7420-6006; fax (20) 7420-6103; e-mail letters.to.editor@bookseller.co.uk; internet www.thebookseller.com; f. 1858; incorporates *Bent's Literary Advertiser* (f. 1802); Friday; Propr VNU Entertainment Media UK Ltd; Publ. Dir SARAH PERCIVAL; Editor NICHOLAS CLEE; circ. 10,700.

The Burlington Magazine: 14–16 Dukes Rd, London, WC1H 9SZ; tel. (20) 7388-1228; fax (20) 7388-1230; e-mail burlington@burlington.org.uk; internet www.burlington.org.uk; f. 1903; monthly; all forms of art, ancient and modern; Editor ANDREW HOPKINS.

Classical Music: 241 Shaftesbury Avenue, London, WC2H 8TF; tel. (20) 7333-1720; fax (20) 7333-1769; e-mail classical.music@rhinegold.co.uk; internet www.rhinegold.co.uk; f. 1976; Editor KEITH CLARKE; circ. 18,000.

Dancing Times: Clerkenwell House, 45–47 Clerkenwell Green, London, EC1R 0EB; tel. (20) 7250-3006; fax (20) 7253-6679; e-mail dt@dancing-times.co.uk; internet www.dancing-times.co.uk; f. 1910; monthly; ballet and modern dance; Editor MARY CLARKE; circ. 12,000.

Empire: 7th Floor, Endeavour House, Shaftesbury Ave, WC2H 8JG; tel. (20) 7437-9011; fax (20) 7859-8613; e-mail empire@emap.com; internet www.empireonline.co.uk; monthly; film and video; Editor EMMA COCHRANE; circ. 160,305.

Film Review: Visual Imagination Ltd, 9 Blades Court, Deodar Rd, London, SW15 2NU; tel. (20) 8875-1520; fax (20) 8875-1588; e-mail filmreview@visimag.com; internet www.visimag.com/filmreview; f. 1954; monthly; international cinema and video; Editor NEIL CORRY.

Folklore: The Folklore Society, c/o The Warburg Institute, Woburn Sq., London, WC1H 0AB; tel. (20) 7862-8564; e-mail folklore-society@talk21.com; internet www.folklore-society.com; f. 1878; 3 a year; Hon. Sec. Dr JULIETTE WOOD.

Gramophone: 38–42 Hampton Rd, Teddington, Middlesex, TW11 0JE; tel. (20) 8267-5050; fax (20) 8267-5844; e-mail gramophone@ haynet.com; internet www.gramophone.co.uk; f. 1923; monthly; Publr NICOLE LEVESCONTE; Editor JAMES JOLLY; circ. 50,125.

Granta: 2/3 Hanover Yard, Noel Rd, London, N1 8BE; tel. (20) 7704-9776; fax (20) 7704-0474; e-mail editorial@granta.com; internet www.granta.com; quarterly; Editor IAN JACK; circ. 80,000.

Index on Censorship: Writers and Scholars International Ltd, 33 Islington High St, London, N1 9LH; tel. (20) 7278-2313; fax (20) 7278-1878; e-mail contact@indexoncensorship.org; internet www .indexoncensorship.org; f. 1972; four a year; concerned with freedom of expression throughout the world; Editor URSULA OWEN; circ. 12,000.

Jazz Journal International: Jazz Journal Ltd, 3 & 3A Forest Rd, Loughton, Essex IG10 1DR; tel. (20) 8532-0456; fax (20) 8532-0440; f. 1948; monthly; Editor EDDIE COOK; circ. 8,000.

Language Learning Journal: Association for Language Learning, 150 Railway Terrace, Rugby, CV21 3HN; tel. (1788) 546443; fax (1788) 544149; e-mail langlearn@all-languages.org.uk; internet www.all-languages.org.uk; f. 1990; 2 a year; Editors NORBERT PACHLER, DOUGLAS ALLFORD; circ. 5,000.

mixmag: EMAP Metro Publications Ltd, 2nd Floor, Mappin House, 4 Winsley St, London, W1N 7AR; tel. (20) 7436-1515; fax (20) 7312-8977; e-mail mixmag@emap.com; internet www.mixmag.net; f. 1983; monthly; dance music and club culture; Editor TOM WHITNELL; circ. 100,277.

Mojo: Mappin House, 4 Winsley St, London, W1W 8HF; tel. (20) 7436-1515; fax (20) 7312-8296; e-mail mojo@emap.com; internet www.mojo4music.com; f. 1993; monthly; popular music; Editor PAT GILBERT; circ. 96,837.

NME: IPC Media Ltd, 25th Floor, King's Reach Tower, Stamford St, London, SE1 9LS; tel. (20) 7261-5000; e-mail connor_mcnicholas@ ipcmedia.com; internet www.nme.com; f. 1952; Wednesday; popular music; Editor CONNOR MCNICHOLAS; circ. 70,456.

Opera: 36 Black Lion Lane, London, W6 9BE; tel. (20) 8563-8893; fax (20) 8563-8635; e-mail editor@operamag.clara.co.uk; internet www.opera.co.uk; f. 1950; monthly; Editor JOHN ALLISON.

Poetry Review: 22 Betterton St, London, WC2H 9BX; tel. (20) 7420-9880; fax (20) 7240-4818; e-mail poetryreview@poetrysoc.com; internet www.poetrysoc.com; f. 1909; quarterly; Editors ROBERT POTTS, DAVID HERD; circ. 5,000.

Q Magazine: EMAP Metro Publications, Mappin House, 5th Floor, 4 Winsley St, London, W1W 8HF; tel. (20) 7436-1515; fax (20) 7312-8247; e-mail q@emap.com; internet www.q4music.com; f. 1986; monthly; music, general features; Editor PAUL REES; circ. 200,636.

Sight and Sound: British Film Institute, 21 Stephen St, London, W1T 1LN; tel. (20) 7255-1444; fax (20) 7436-2327; e-mail s&s@bfi .org.uk; internet www.bfi.org.uk/sightandsound; f. 1932; monthly; international film review; Editor NICK JAMES; circ. 23,429.

Smash Hits: Mappin House, 4 Winsley St, London, W1W 8HF; tel. (20) 7436-1515; fax (20) 7636-5792; e-mail letters@smashhits.net; internet www.smashhits.net; f. 1978; fortnightly; popular music; Editor LISA SMOSARSKI; circ. 190,177.

The Stage: Stage House, 47 Bermondsey St, London, SE1 3XT; tel. (20) 7403-1818; fax (20) 7403-1418; e-mail info@thestage.co.uk; internet www.thestage.co.uk; f. 1880; Thursday; theatre, light entertainment, television, opera, dance; Editor BRIAN ATTWOOD; circ. 41,859.

The Times Literary Supplement: Admiral House, 66–68 East Smithfield, London, E1W 1BX; tel. (20) 7782-3000; fax (20) 7782-3100; e-mail letters@the-tls.co.uk; internet www.the-tls.co.uk; f. 1902; Friday; weekly journal of literary criticism; Editor PETER STOTHARD; circ. 34,007.

Top of the Pops: Room A1136, Woodlands, 80 Wood Lane London, W12 0TT; e-mail totp.magazine@bbc.co.uk; internet www.beeb.com/ totp; monthly; popular music; Editor CORINNA SHAFFER; circ. 281,417.

Current Affairs and History

Antiquity: New Hall, Cambridge, CB3 0DF; tel. (1223) 762298; fax (1223) 357075; e-mail catm20@cam.ac.uk; internet www.intarch.ac .uk/antiquity; f. 1927; quarterly; archaeological; Editor SIMON STODDART.

The Big Issue: 1–5 Wandsworth Rd, London, SW8 2LN; tel. (20) 7526-3200; fax (20) 7526-3201; e-mail press@bigissue.com; internet www.bigissue.com; also offices based in Cardiff, Glasgow, Manchester, the Midlands and Bristol producing regional weekly editions; f. 1991; weekly; current affairs, social issues; Editor MATT FORD; total circ. 253,645.

Classical Quarterly: Journals Marketing, Oxford University Press, Great Clarendon St, Oxford, OX2 6DP; tel. (1865) 556767; fax (1865) 267835; e-mail chris.collard@1.thum.ox.ac.uk; internet www3.oup.co.uk/clquaj; f. 1906; 2 a year; language, literature, history and philosophy; Editors Prof. R. MALTBY, Prof. C. COLLARD.

Contemporary Review: POB 1242, Oxford OX1 4FJ; tel. and fax (1865) 201529; e-mail editorial@contemporaryreview.co.uk; internet www.contemporaryreview.co.uk; f. 1866; monthly; publ by Contemporary Review Co Ltd; politics, international affairs, social subjects, the arts; Editor Dr RICHARD MULLEN.

English Historical Review: Oxford University Press, Gt Clarendon St, Oxford, OX2 6DP; tel. (1865) 556767; fax (1865) 267485; e-mail ehr@oup.co.uk; internet www3.oup.co.uk/enghis; f. 1886; 5 a year; learned articles and book reviews; Editors JEAN DUNBABIN, G. W. BERNARD.

The Historian: The Historical Association, 59A Kennington Park Rd, London, SE11 4JH; tel. (20) 7735-3901; fax (20) 7582-4989; e-mail enquiry@history.org.uk; internet www.history.org.uk; f. 1912; 4 a year; Editor Prof. MURIEL CHAMBERLAIN; circ. 8,000.

History Today: 20 Old Compton St, London, W1D 4TW; tel. (20) 7534-8000; fax (20) 7534-8008; e-mail p.furtado@historytoday.com; internet www.historytoday.com; f. 1951; monthly; illustrated general historical magazine; Editor PETER FURTADO; circ. 29,496.

Illustrated London News: 20 Upper Ground, London, SE1 9PF; tel. (20) 7805-5555; fax (20) 7805-5911; e-mail iln@ilng.co.uk; internet www.ilng.co.uk; 2 a year; Editor ALISON BOOTH; circ. 40,000.

International Affairs: Royal Institute of International Affairs, Chatham House, 10 St James's Sq., London, SW1Y 4LE; tel. (20) 7957-5700; fax (20) 7957-5710; e-mail csoper@riia.org; internet www .riia.org; f. 1922; quarterly; publ. by Blackwell Publishers Ltd; original articles, and reviews of publications on international affairs; Editor CAROLINE SOPER; circ. 6,000.

Journal of Contemporary History: 4 Devonshire St, London, W1W 5BH; tel. (20) 7580-4330; fax (20) 7436-6428; e-mail aileen .kent@sagepub.co.uk; f. 1966; quarterly; publ. by Sage Publications Ltd; Editors WALTER LAQUEUR, RICHARD J. EVANS, STANLEY PAYNE.

London Gazette: The Stationery Office Ltd, POB 7923, London, SE1 5ZH; tel. (20) 7394-4580; fax (20) 7394-4581; internet www .london-gazette.co.uk; f. 1665; 5 a week; the oldest existing world newspaper; government journal of official, legal and public notices.

New Left Review: 6 Meard St, London, W1F 0EG; tel. (20) 7734-8830; fax (20) 7439-3869; e-mail mail@newleftreview.org; internet www.newleftreview.org; f. 1960; 6 a year; international politics, economics and culture; Editor PERRY ANDERSON.

New Statesman: Victoria Station House, 7th Floor, 191 Victoria St, London, SW1E 5NE; tel. (20) 7828-1232; fax (20) 7828-1881; e-mail info@newstatesman.com; internet www.newstatesman.com; f. 1913; weekly; current affairs, politics and the arts; Editor PETER WILBY; circ. 22,806.

People in Power: Cambridge International Reference on Current Affairs Ltd (CIRCA), 13–17 Sturton St, Cambridge, CB1 2SN; tel. (1223) 568017; fax (1223) 354643; e-mail pip@circa-uk.demon.co.uk; internet www.circaworld.com; f. 1987; bi-monthly; current worldwide government listings; Editor ROGER EAST.

The Political Quarterly: Blackwell Publishers Ltd, 108 Cowley Rd, Oxford, OX4 1JF; tel. (1865) 791100; fax (1865) 791347; internet www.blackwellpublishers.co.uk; f. 1930; 5 a year; Editors ANDREW GAMBLE, ANTHONY WRIGHT.

Prospect: 2 Bloomsbury Pl., London, WC1A 2QA; tel. (20) 7255-1344; fax (20) 7255-1279; e-mail editorial@prospect-magazine.co.uk; internet www.prospect-magazine.co.uk; f. 1995; 12 a year; political and cultural; Editor DAVID GOODHART; circ. 18,165.

Race & Class: The Institute of Race Relations, 2–6 Leeke St, London, WC1X 9HS; tel. (20) 7837-0041; fax (20) 7278-0623; e-mail info@irr.org.uk; internet www.irr.org.uk; f. 1959; quarterly; journal for black and Third World liberation; Editors A. SIVANANDAN, HAZEL WATERS.

The Spectator: 56 Doughty St, London, WC1N 2LL; tel. (20) 7405-1706; fax (20) 7242-0603; e-mail editor@spectator.co.uk; internet www.spectator.co.uk; f. 1828; Thursday; independent political and literary review; Editor BORIS JOHNSON; circ. 61,617.

Tribune: 9 Arkwright Rd, London, NW3 6AN; tel. (20) 7433-6410; fax (20) 7433-6419; internet www.tribuneuk.co.uk; f. 1937; Friday; Labour's independent weekly; politics, current affairs, arts; Editor MARK SEDDON.

Economics and Business

Accountancy Age: 32–34 Broadwick St, London, W1A 2HG; tel. (20) 7316-9236; fax (20) 7316-9250; e-mail news@accountancyage .com; internet www.accountancyage.co.uk; f. 1969; weekly; Man. Dir TONY LOYNES; Editor DAMIAN WILD; circ. 69,419.

The Banker: Maple House, 149 Tottenham Court Rd, London, W1T 7LB; tel. (20) 7896-2525; fax (20) 7896-2586; e-mail stephen .timewell@ft.com; internet www.thebanker.com; f. 1926; monthly; monetary and economic policy, international and domestic banking and finance, banking technology, country surveys; Editor STEPHEN TIMEWELL; circ. 32,000.

Campaign: Haymarket Marketing Publications Ltd, 174 Hammersmith Rd, London, W6 7JP; tel. (20) 8267-4656; fax (20) 8267-4915; e-mail campaign@haynet.com; internet www.campaignlive.com; f. 1968; advertising, marketing and media; Thursday; Editor CAROLINE MARSHALL; circ. 14,987.

Crops: Reed Farmers Publishing, Quadrant House, The Quadrant, Sutton, Surrey, SM2 5AS; tel. (20) 8652-4080; fax (20) 8652-8928; e-mail crops@rbi.co.uk; internet www.fwi.co.uk; f. 1984; fortnightly; Editor DEBBIE BEATON; circ. 29,000.

Economic Journal: Blackwell Publrs, 9600 Garsington Rd, Oxford, OX4 2QD; tel. (1865) 791100; fax (1865) 791347; e-mail jnlinfo@blackwellpublishers.co.uk; internet www.blackwellpub .com; f. 1891; eight a year; Editors CHRISTOPHER BLISS, DAVID DE MEZA, STEVE MACHIN, GERARD VAN DEN BERG; Co-ordinating Editor MIKE MICKENS.

The Economist: 25 St James's St, London, SW1A 1HG; tel. (20) 7830-7000; fax (20) 7839-2968; e-mail inquiries@economist.com; internet www.economist.com; f. 1843; 50% owned by Pearson PLC, 50% by individual shareholders; Friday; Publr DAVID HANGER; Editor-in-Chief BILL EMMOTT; circ. (world-wide) 870,080.

Euromoney: Nestor House, Playhouse Yard, London, EC4V 5EX; tel. (20) 7779-8888; fax (20) 7779-8653; e-mail hotline@ euromoneyplc.com; internet www.euromoney.com; f. 1969; monthly; Editor PETER LEE; circ. 28,102.

Farmers Weekly: Reed Business Information, Quadrant House, The Quadrant, Sutton, Surrey, SM2 5AS; tel. (20) 8652-4911; fax (20) 8652-4005; e-mail farmers.weekly@rbi.co.uk; internet www.fwi .co.uk; f. 1934; Friday; Editor STEPHEN HOWE; circ. 89,000.

Investors Chronicle: FT Finance, Maple House, 149 Tottenham Court Rd, London, W1TP 7LB; tel. (20) 7896-2525; fax (20) 7896-2054; e-mail 100617.1135@compuserve.com; internet www .investorschronicle.co.uk; f. as *Money Market Review* 1860; amalgamated with *Investors Chronicle* 1914; amalgamated with the *Stock Exchange Gazette* 1967; Friday; independent financial and economic review; Editor MATTHEW VINCENT; circ. 51,121.

Management Today: 174 Hammersmith Rd, London, W6 7JP; tel. (20) 8267-4610; fax (20) 8267-4966; e-mail management.today@ haynet.com; internet www.clickmt.com; f. 1966; monthly; Editor-in-Chief RUFUS OLINS; Editor MATTHEW GWYTHER; circ. 102,117.

Education

Higher Education Quarterly: Blackwell Publishers Ltd, 108 Cowley Rd, Oxford, OX4 1JF; tel. (1865) 244083; fax (1865) 381381; e-mail jnlinfo@blackwellpublishers.co.uk; internet www .blackwellpublishers.co.uk; f. 1946; quarterly; Editors OLIVER FULTON, GARETH PARRY, MALCOLM TIGHT, PETER WRIGHT.

The Teacher: Hamilton House, Mabledon Pl., London, WC1H 9BD; tel. (20) 7380-4708; fax (20) 7383-7230; e-mail teacher@nut.org.uk; f. 1872; magazine of the NUT; news, comments and articles on all aspects of education; eight times a year; Editor MITCH HOWARD; circ. 280,000.

The Times Educational Supplement: Admiral House, 66–68 East Smithfield, London, E1W 1BX; tel. (20) 7782-3000; fax (20) 7782-3200; e-mail editor@tes.co.uk; internet www.tes.co.uk; f. 1910; Friday; Editor BOB DOE; circ. 116,947.

The Times Higher Education Supplement: Admiral House, 66–68 East Smithfield, London, E1W 1BX; tel. (20) 7782-3000; fax (20) 7782-3300; e-mail editor@thes.co.uk; internet www.thesis.co.uk; f. 1971; Friday; Editor JOHN O'LEARY; circ. 25,648.

Home, Fashion and General

Arena: Exmouth House, Pine St, London, EC1R 0JL; tel. (20) 7689-9999; fax (20) 7689-0902; e-mail editorial@arenamag.co.uk; monthly; men's interest; Editor ANTHONY NOGUERA; circ. 38,182.

B: 17–18 Berners St, London W1T 3LN; tel. (20) 7664-6470; fax (20) 7070-3401; e-mail letters@bmagazine.co.uk; internet www.hf-uk .com; f. 1997; monthly; fashion, beauty, lifestyle, travel; Editor GINA JOHNSON; circ. 193,807.

Bella: H. Bauer Publishing Ltd, 1st Floor, 24–28 Oval Rd, London, NW1 7DT; tel. (20) 7241-8000; fax (20) 7241-8056; e-mail bella@ natmags.co.uk; internet www.natmags.co.uk; f. 1987; weekly; fashion, beauty, health, cookery, handicrafts; Editor-in-Chief JACKIE HIGHE; circ. 468,937.

Best: National Magazine Company, 72 Broadwick St, London, W1F 9EP; tel. (20) 7439-5000; fax (20) 7312-4176; e-mail best@natmags .co.uk; internet www.natmags.co.uk; f. 1987; weekly; women's interest; Editor LOUISE COURT; circ. 430,433.

Chat: IPC Connect Ltd, King's Reach Tower, Stamford St, London, SE1 9LS; tel. (20) 7261-6565; fax (20) 7261-6534; e-mail paul_merrill@ipcmedia.com; internet www.ipcmedia.com; weekly; women's interest; Editor PAUL MERRILL; circ. 510,000.

Company: National Magazine House, 72 Broadwick St, London, W1F 9EP; tel. (20) 7439-5000; fax (20) 7439-5117; e-mail company .mail@natmags.co.uk; internet www.company.co.uk; monthly; Editor SAM BAKER; circ. 261,117.

Cosmopolitan: National Magazine House, 72 Broadwick St, London, W1V 2BP; tel. (20) 7439-5000; fax (20) 7439-5016; e-mail contact@cosmopolitan.co.uk; internet www.cosmopolitan.co.uk; f. 1972; monthly; women's interest; Editor-in-Chief LORRAINE CANDY; circ. 463,010.

Elle: EMAP Elan, Endeavour House, 189 Shaftesbury Ave, London, WC2H 8JG; tel. (20) 7437-9011; fax (20) 7208-3599; e-mail danielle .hine@emap.com; internet www.ellemagazine.co.uk; f. 1985; monthly; women's interest; Editor SARAH BAILEY; circ. 210,861.

Esquire: National Magazine House, 72 Broadwick St, London, W1F 9EP; tel. (20) 7439-5000; fax (20) 7439-5675; e-mail contact@esquire .co.uk; internet www.esquire.co.uk; f. 1991; monthly; men's interest; Editor SIMON TIFFIN; circ. 62,007.

The Face: Exmouth House, 3rd Floor, Block A, Pine St, London, EC1R 0JL; tel. (20) 7689-9999; fax (20) 7689-0300; e-mail editorial@ theface.co.uk; f. 1980; monthly; Editor NEIL STEVENSON; circ. 55,329.

FHM: EMAP élan Network Ltd, The Network Building, 97 Tottenham Court Rd, London, W1T 4TP; tel. (20) 7504-6000; fax (20) 7504-6300; e-mail dan.elk@fhm.com; internet www.fhm.com; f. 1987; monthly; men's interest; Editor DAVID DAVIES; circ. 570,719.

Glamour: 6–8 Old Bond St, London, WIS 4PH; tel. (20) 7499-9080; fax (20) 7491-2551; e-mail letters@glamourmagazine.co.uk; internet www.glamour.com; f. 2001; monthly; women's interest; Editor JO ELVIN; circ. 520,000.

Good Housekeeping: National Magazine House, 72 Broadwick St, London, W1F 9EP; tel. (20) 7439-5000; fax (20) 7439-5591; e-mail contact@goodhousekeeping.co.uk; internet www.goodhousekeeping .co.uk; f. 1922; monthly; Editor-in-Chief LINDSAY NICHOLSON; circ. 405,140.

GQ: The Condé Nast Publications Ltd, Vogue House, Hanover Sq., London, W1S 1JU; tel. (20) 7499-9080; fax (20) 7495-1679; internet www.gq-magazine.co.uk; f. 1988; monthly; Editor DYLAN JONES; circ. 125,885.

Harpers & Queen: National Magazine House, 72 Broadwick St, London, W1F 9EP; tel. (20) 7439-5000; fax (20) 7439-5506; e-mail lucy@harpersandqueen.co.uk; internet www.harpersandqueen.co .uk; f. 1929; Prprs National Magazine Co Ltd; monthly; international fashion, beauty, general features; Editor LUCY YEOMANS; circ. 88,521.

Heat: Endeavour House, 189 Shaftesbury Ave, London, WC2H 8JG; tel. (20) 7436-1515; fax (20) 7859-8570; e-mail heat@emap.com; internet www.heatmagazine.co.uk; f. 1999; Tuesdays; celebrity news, TV, radio, films; Editor MARK FRITH; circ. 450,000.

Hello!: Hello! Ltd, Wellington House, 69–71 Upper Ground, London, SE1 9PQ; tel. (20) 7667-8700; fax (20) 7667-8716; e-mail amanda .synott@hellomagazine.com; internet www.hellomagazine.com; Propr. HOLA S.A. (Spain); weekly; Publr SALLY CARTWRIGHT; Editor MARIA TRKULJA; circ. 517,883.

Homes and Gardens: King's Reach Tower, Stamford St, London, SE1 9LS; tel. (20) 7261-5000; fax (20) 7261-6247; f. 1919; monthly; Editor ISOBEL MCKENZIE-PRICE; circ. 148,106.

House & Garden: The Condé Nast Publications Ltd, Vogue House, Hanover Sq., London, W1R 0AD; tel. (20) 7499-9080; fax (20) 7629-2907; internet www.houseandgarden.co.uk; f. 1920; monthly; Editor SUSAN CREWE; circ. 150,593.

Ideal Home: IPC Media Ltd, King's Reach Tower, Stamford St, London, SE1 9LS; tel. (20) 7261-6474; fax (20) 7261-6697; e-mail ideal_home@ipcmedia.com; f. 1920; 11 a year; Editor JANE PARBURY; circ. 244,870.

InStyle: 12th Floor, King's Reach Tower, Stamford St, London, SE1 9LS; tel. (20) 7261-4747; fax (20) 7261-6664; f. 2001; monthly; fashion, beauty; Editor LOUISE CHUM.

The Lady: 39–40 Bedford St, London, WC2E 9ER; tel. (20) 7379-4717; fax (20) 7836-4620; e-mail editors@lady.co.uk; internet www .lady.co.uk; f. 1885; Tuesday; Editor ARLINE USDEN; circ. 41,242.

Loaded: IPC Media Ltd, King's Reach Tower, Stamford St, London, SE1 9LS; tel. (20) 7261-5562; fax (20) 7261-5557; e-mail tammy_butt@ipc.co.uk; internet www.uploaded.com; f. 1994;

monthly; music, fashion, contemporary lifestyles; Editor KEITH KEN-DRICK; circ. 308,711.

Marie Claire: IPC Media Ltd, 2 Hatfields, London, SE1 9PG; tel. (20) 7261-5240; fax (20) 7261-5277; e-mail marieclaire@ipcmedia.com; internet www.marieclaire.co.uk; f. 1988; monthly; women's interest; Man. Editor MARIE O'RIORDAN; circ. 382,094.

Maxim: 30 Cleveland St, London, W1P 5FF; tel. (20) 7907-6410; fax (20) 7907-6000; e-mail editorial@maxim-magazine.co.uk; internet www.maximonline.co.uk; f. 1995; monthly; health, fitness, fashion, finance; Editor TOM LOXLEY; circ. 276,640.

My Weekly: D. C. Thomson & Co Ltd, 80 Kingsway East, Dundee, DD4 8SL; tel. (1382) 223131; fax (1382) 452491; e-mail myweekly@dcthompson.co.uk; f. 1910; Friday; women's interest; Editor HARRISON G. WATSON; circ. 305,407.

New Woman: EMAP Elan, Endeavour House, 189 Shaftesbury Ave, London, WC2H 8JG; tel. (20) 7437-9011; fax (20) 7208-3585; e-mail lizzi.hosking@emap.com; internet www.newwomanonline.co.uk; monthly; women's interest; Editor SARA CREMER; circ. 305,088.

Now: King's Reach Tower, Stamford St, London SE1 9LS; tel. (870) 4445000; fax (20) 7261-6789; internet www.ipc.co.uk; weekly; celebrity news, TV, radio, films; Editor JANE ENNIS; circ. 552,744.

OK!: Ludgate House, 245 Blackfriars Rd, London SE1 9UX; tel. (20) 7928-8000; fax (20) 7579-4607; weekly; Editor NICK McCARTHY; circ. 486,858.

The People's Friend: D. C. Thomson & Co Ltd, 80 Kingsway East, Dundee, DD4 8SL; tel. (1382) 223131; fax (1382) 452491; e-mail peoplesfriend@dcthompson.co.uk; f. 1869; Wednesday; women's fiction, home, crafts, general; Editor MARGARET McCOY; circ. 412,570.

Prima: 72 Broadwick St, London, W1F 9EP; tel. (20) 7439–5000; fax (20) 7312-4100; e-mail prima@natmags.co.uk; internet www.primamagazine.co.uk; f. 1986; English edition; monthly; seeks to cover over 100 topics of women's interest in every issue; Editor MARIE FAHEY; circ. 380,040.

Private Eye: 6 Carlisle St, London, W1D 3BN; tel. (20) 7437-4017; fax (20) 7437-0705; e-mail strobes@private-eye.co.uk; internet www.private.eye.co.uk; f. 1961; fortnightly; satirical; Editor IAN HISLOP; circ. 188,081.

Reader's Digest: Reader's Digest Association Ltd, (British Edition) 11 Westferry Circus, Canary Wharf, London, E14 4HE; tel. (20) 7715-8000; fax (20) 7715-8181; e-mail theeditor@readersdigest.co.uk; internet www.readersdigest.co.uk; f. 1938; monthly; Editor KATHERINE WALKER; circ. 1,005,006.

The Scots Magazine: D. C. Thomson & Co. Ltd, 2 Albert Sq., Dundee, DD1 9QJ; tel. (1382) 223131; fax (1382) 322214; e-mail mail@scotsmagazine.com; internet www.scotsmagazine.com; f. 1739; monthly; Scottish interest; circ. 53,071.

She: 72 Broadwick St, London, W1V 2BP; tel. (20) 7439-5000; fax (20) 7312-3981; e-mail contact@she.co.uk; internet www.she.co.uk; f. 1955; monthly; Editor EVE CAMERON; circ. 176,183.

Take a Break: Bauer Publishing Ltd, 24–28 Oval Rd, London, NW1 9LL; tel. (20) 7241-0000; fax (20) 7241-8052; e-mail janelenny@tabreak.demon.co.uk; Thursday; Editor JOHN DALE; circ. 1,148,634.

Tatler: The Condé Nast Publications Ltd, Vogue House, Hanover Sq., London, W1S 1JV; tel. (20) 7499-9080; fax (20) 7409-0451; internet www.tatler.co.uk; f. 1709; monthly; Editor GEORDIE GREIG; circ. 82,026.

Vanity Fair: The Condé Nast Publications Ltd, Vogue House, Hanover Sq., London, W1R 0AD; tel. (20) 7499-9080; fax (20) 7499-4415; internet www.vanityfair.co.uk; monthly; Editor HENRY PORTER; circ. 89,177.

Viz: IFG Ltd, 9 Dallington St, London, EC1V 0BQ; tel. (20) 7687-7000; fax (20) 7687-7099; e-mail viz@viz.co.uk; internet www.viz.co.uk; f. 1979; ten a year; Publr BRUCE SANDELL; Editor SIMON DONALD; circ. 178,745.

Vogue: The Condé Nast Publications Ltd, Vogue House, Hanover Sq., London, W1S 1JU; tel. (20) 7499-9080; fax (20) 7408-0559; internet www.vogue.co.uk; f. 1916; monthly; Editor ALEXANDRA SHULMAN; circ. 195,167.

The Voice: Blue Star House, 234–244 Stockwell Rd, London, SW9 9SP; tel. (20) 7737-7377; fax (20) 7274-8994; e-mail newsdesk@the-voice.co.uk; internet www.voice-online.co.uk; f. 1982; Monday; black interest; Editor MIKE BEST; circ. 42,508.

Woman: IPC Media Ltd, King's Reach Tower, Stamford St, London, SE1 9LS; tel. (20) 7261-5000; fax (20) 7261-5997; e-mail woman@ipc.co.uk; internet www.beme.com; f. 1937; Tuesday; Editor CAROLE RUSSELL; circ. 631,451.

Woman and Home: IPC Media Ltd, King's Reach Tower, Stamford St, London, SE1 9LS; tel. (20) 7261-5000; fax (20) 7261-7346; e-mail woman&home@ipcmedia.com; f. 1926; monthly; Editor SARAH KILBY; circ. 253,008.

Woman's Own: IPC Media Ltd, King's Reach Tower, Stamford St, London, SE1 9LS; tel. (20) 7261-5500; fax (20) 7261-5346; f. 1932; Tuesday; Editor-in-Chief ELSA McALONAN; circ. 518,495.

Woman's Weekly: IPC Media Ltd, King's Reach Tower, Stamford St, London, SE1 9LS; tel. (20) 7261-5000; f. 1911; Tuesday; Editor GILLY SINCLAIR; circ. 504,531.

Law

Law Quarterly Review: The Hatchery, Hall Bank Lane, Mytholmroyd, West Yorks, HX7 5HQ; tel. (1422) 888000; fax (1422) 888002; e-mail sarah.kennedy@sweetandmaxwell.co.uk; internet www.sweetandmaxwell.co.uk; f. 1885; quarterly; Editor SARAH KENNEDY.

Law Society's Gazette: 6th Floor, Newspaper House, 8–16 Great New St, London, EC4A 3BN; tel. (20) 7320-5820; fax (20) 7831-0869; e-mail gazette-editorial@lawsociety.org.uk; internet www.lawgazette.co.uk; f. 1903; weekly; Editor JONATHAN AMES; circ. 99,705.

The Lawyer: 50 Poland St, London, W1V 4AX; tel. (20) 7970-4614; fax (20) 7970-4640; e-mail fiona.callister@thelawyer.co.uk; internet www.thelawyer.co.uk; weekly; Editor CATRIN GRIFFITHS; circ. 30,756.

Leisure Interests and Sport

Autocar Magazine: Haymarket Publishing Ltd, 60 Waldegrave Rd, Teddington, Middx, TW11 8LG; tel. (20) 8267-5630; fax (20) 8267-5759; e-mail autocar@haynet.com; f. 1895; Wednesday; Editor STEVE FOWLER; circ. 70,073.

Autosport: Haymarket Magazines Ltd, Somerset House, Somerset Rd, Teddington, Middx, TW11 8RV; tel. (20) 8267-5998; fax (20) 8267-5922; e-mail autosport@aol.com; internet www.autosport.com; f. 1950; Thursday; covers all aspects of motor sport; Editor-in-Chief LAWRENCE FOSTER; circ. 65,000.

Car: Angel House, 338–346 Goswell Rd, London, EC1V 7QP; tel. (20) 7477-7399; fax (20) 7477-7279; e-mail car@emap.com; f. 1962; monthly; Editor GREG FOUNTAIN; circ. 108,253.

Country Life: IPC Media Ltd, 20th Floor, King's Reach Tower, Stamford St, London, SE1 9LS; tel. (20) 7261-7058; fax (20) 7261-5139; e-mail sally_smith@ipcmedia.com; internet www.countrylife.co.uk; f. 1897; Thursday; Editor CLIVE ASLET; circ. 43,491.

The Countryman: Stable Courtyard, Broughton Hall, Skipton, N. Yorkshire, BD23 3AZ; tel. (1756) 701381; fax (1756) 701326; e-mail burford@countrymanmagazine.co.uk; f. 1927; monthly; independent; Editor DAVID HORAN; circ. 29,676.

The Cricketer International: Third Street, Langton Green, Tunbridge Wells, TN3 9ST; tel. (1892) 862551; fax (1892) 863755; e-mail editorial@cricketer.co.uk; internet www.cricketer.com; f. 1921; monthly; Editor PETER PERCHARD; circ. 26,604.

FourFourTwo: Somerset House, Somerset Rd, Teddington, TW11 8RT; tel. (20) 8267-5848; fax (20) 8267-5354; e-mail 442@haynet.com; internet www.fourfourtwo.com; f. 1994; monthly; football; Editor MAT SNOW; circ. 67,246.

BBC Gardeners' World Magazine: BBC Worldwide Ltd, 80 Wood Lane, London, W12 0TT; tel. (20) 8433-3959; fax (20) 8433-3986; e-mail adam.pasco@bbc.co.uk; f. 1991; monthly; Editor ADAM PASCO; circ. 350,064.

Golf Monthly: King's Reach Tower, Stamford St, London, SE1 9LS; tel. (20) 7261-7237; fax (20) 7261-7240; e-mail golfmonthly@ipcmedia.com; internet www.ipcmedia.com; monthly; Editor JANE CARTER; circ. 74,397.

BBC Good Food: BBC Worldwide Ltd, 80 Wood Lane, London, W12 0TT; tel. (20) 8433-2000; fax (20) 8433-3931; e-mail goodfoodrs@galleon.co.uk; f. 1989; monthly; Editor ORLANDO MURRIN; circ. 322,614.

Hi-Fi News: Focus House, Dingwall Ave, Croydon, Surrey, CR9 2TA; tel. (20) 8774-0846; fax (20) 8774-0940; e-mail hi-finews@ipcmedia.co.uk; internet www.hifinews.com; f. 1956; monthly; all aspects of high quality sound reproduction, record reviews; Editor STEVE HARRIS; circ. 18,415.

Men's Health: Rodale Press, 7/10 Chandos St, London, W1M 0AD; tel. (20) 7291-6000; fax (20) 7291-6053; e-mail simon.geller@rodale.co.uk; internet www.menshealth.co.uk; f. 1995; monthly; lifestyle, health, general features; Editor SIMON GELLER; circ. 215,517.

Practical Photography: Bretton Ct, Bretton, Peterborough, PE3 8DZ; tel. (1733) 264666; fax (1733) 465246; e-mail practical.photography@emap.com; monthly; Editor WILLIAM CHEUNG; circ. 64,123.

Radio Times: BBC Worldwide Ltd, Woodlands, 80 Wood Lane, London, W12 0TT; tel. (870) 608-4455; fax (20) 8433-3923; e-mail radio.times@bbc.co.uk; internet www.radiotimes.com; f. 1923; weekly; programme guide to television and radio broadcasts; Editor GILL HUDSON; circ. 1,200,615.

Rugby World: Room 2318, King's Reach Tower, Stamford St, London, SE1 9LS; tel. (20) 7261-6830; fax (20) 7261-5419; e-mail paul_morgan@ipcmedia.com; internet www.rugbyworld.com; monthly; Editor PAUL MORGAN; circ. 36,926.

Time Out: Time Out Magazine Ltd, Universal House, 251 Tottenham Court Rd, London, W1P 0AB; tel. (20) 7813-3000; fax (20) 7813-6001; e-mail net@timeout.co.uk; internet www.timeout.co.uk; f. 1968; Wednesday; listings and reviews of events in London; Editor LAURA LEE DAVIES; circ. 84,486.

TVTimes: IPC Media Ltd, 10th Floor, King's Reach Tower, Stamford St, London, SE1 9LS; tel. (20) 7261-7000; fax (20) 7261-7777; e-mail tvtimes_letters@ipcmedia.com; f. 1955; features and listings of all television broadcasts; Editor MIKE HOLLINGSWORTH; circ. 689,137.

What Car?: Haymarket Motoring Publications Ltd, 60 Waldegrave Rd, Teddington, Middx, TW11 8LG; tel. (20) 8267-5688; fax (20) 8267-5750; e-mail whatcar@haynet.com; internet www.whatcar.co.uk; f. 1973; Editor ROB AHERNE; circ. 144,087.

What's On TV: IPC Media Ltd, King's Reach Tower, Stamford St, London, SE1 9LS; tel. (20) 7261-7769; fax (20) 7261-7739; e-mail wotv-postbag@ipcmedia.com; f. 1991; weekly; television programme guide and features; Editor COLIN TOUGH; circ. 1,652,138.

Zest: 72 Broadwick St, London, W1F 9EP; tel. (20) 7312-3050; fax (20) 7312-3750; e-mail contact@zest.co.uk; internet www.zest.co.uk; health, beauty, fitness and nutrition; Editor ALISON PYLKKANEN; circ. 118,042.

Medicine, Science and Technology

Biochemical Journal: Portland Press Ltd, 59 Portland Pl., London, W1B 1QW; tel. (20) 7637-5873; fax (20) 7323-1136; e-mail editorial@portlandpress.com; internet www.biochemj.org; f. 1906; 2 a month; publ. by Portland Press on behalf of the Biochemical Society; Chair. Editorial Board PETER J. PARKER; Publisher P. J. STARLEY.

British Journal of Psychiatry: 17 Belgrave Sq., London, SW1X 8PG; tel. (20) 7235-2351; fax (20) 7259-6507; e-mail publications@rcpsych.ac.uk; internet www.rcpsych.ac.uk; monthly; original articles, reviews and correspondence; publ. by the Royal College of Psychiatrists; Editor GREG WILKINSON; circ. 13,245.

British Journal of Psychology: St Andrew's House, 48 Princess Rd East, Leicester, LE1 7DR; tel. (116) 254-9568; fax (116) 247-0787; e-mail journals@bps.org.uk; internet www.bps.org.uk; f. 1904; quarterly; publ. by the British Psychological Society; Editor Prof. GEOFFREY UNDERWOOD; circ. 3,000.

British Journal of Sociology: London School of Economics, Houghton St, London, WC2A 2AE; tel. (20) 7955-7283; fax (20) 7955-6311; e-mail bjs@lse.ac.uk; internet www.lse.ac.uk/serials/bjs/Homepage.htm; f. 1950; quarterly; Editor BRIDGET HUTTER.

British Medical Journal: British Medical Assen House, Tavistock Sq., London, WC1H 9JR; tel. (20) 7387-4499; fax (20) 7383-6418; e-mail bmj@bmj.com; internet www.bmj.com; f. 1840; Saturday; 10 overseas editions; Editor Prof. RICHARD SMITH; circ. 115,000.

Computer Weekly: Reed Business Information, Quadrant House, The Quadrant, Sutton, Surrey, SM2 5AS; tel. (20) 8652-8642; fax (20) 8652-8979; e-mail cwnews@rbi.co.uk; internet www.computerweekly.com; f. 1966; Thursday; Editor KARL SCHNEIDER; circ. 133,000.

Computing: VNU Business Publications BV, VNU House, 32–34 Broadwick St, London, W1A 2HG; tel. (20) 7316-9000; fax (20) 7316-9160; e-mail computing@vnu.co.uk; internet www.computing.co.uk; f. 1973; Thursday; Editor COLIN BARKER; circ. 135,000.

The Ecologist: Unit 18, Chelsea Wharf, 15 Lots Rd, London, SW10 0QJ; tel. (20) 7351-3578; fax (20) 7351-3617; e-mail belinda@theecologist.org; internet www.theecologist.org; f. 1970; ten per year; all aspects of ecology, the environment, etc.; Editor ZAC GOLDSMITH; circ. 25,000.

Flight International: Reed Business Information, Quadrant House, The Quadrant, Sutton, Surrey, SM2 5AS; tel. (20) 8652-3842; fax (20) 8652-3840; e-mail flight.international@rbi.co.uk; internet www.flightinternational.com; f. 1909; Tuesday; Editor MURDO MORRISON; circ. 53,552.

The Geographical Magazine: Campion Interactive Publishing Ltd, Unit 11, Pall Mall Deposit, 124–128 Barlby Rd, London, W10 6BL; tel. (20) 8960-6400; fax (20) 8960-6004; e-mail magazine@geographical.co.uk; internet www.geographical.co.uk; f. 1935; monthly; Editor CAROLYN FRY; circ. 23,708.

Lancet: 32 Jamestown Rd, London, NW1 7BY; tel. (20) 7424-4910; fax (20) 7424-4911; e-mail editorial@lancet.com; internet www.lancet.com; f. 1823; Saturday; medical; Editor Dr RICHARD HORTON; circ. 40,000 world-wide.

Nature: Macmillan Magazines Ltd, Porters South, 4 Crinan St, London, N1 9XW; tel. (20) 7833-4000; fax (20) 7843-4596; e-mail nature@nature.com; internet www.nature.com/nature; f. 1869; Thursday; scientific; Editor Dr PHILIP CAMPBELL; circ. 55,000.

New Scientist: Reed Business Information, 151 Wardour St, London, W1F 8WE; tel. (20) 7331-2701; fax (20) 7331-2777; e-mail news@newscientist.com; internet www.newscientist.com; f. 1956; Thursday; science and technology; Editor JEREMY WEBB; circ. 136,505.

Nursing Times: EMAP Healthcare Ltd, Greater London House, Hampstead Rd, London, NW1 7EJ; tel. (20) 7874-0500; fax (20) 7874-0505; e-mail nt@emap.com; internet www.nursingtimes.net; f. 1905; Thursday; professional nursing journal; Editor TRICIA REID; circ. 58,785.

The Practitioner: CMPi Ltd, City Reach, 5 Greenwich View Place, Millharbour, London, E149NN; tel. (20) 7861-6478; fax (20) 7861-6544; e-mail gatkin@cmpinformation.com; f. 1868; 12 per year; medical journal for General Practitioners; Editor GAVIN ATKIN; circ. 40,567.

Religion and Philosophy

Catholic Herald: Herald House, Lambs Passage, Bunhill Row, London, EC1Y 8TQ; tel. (20) 7588-3101; fax (20) 7256-9728; e-mail editorial@catholicherald.co.uk; internet www.catholicherald.co.uk; f. 1888; Catholic weekly newspaper; Friday; Editor Dr WILLIAM ODDIE; circ. 30,000.

Christian Herald: Garcia Estate, Canterbury Rd, Worthing, W. Sussex, BN14 1EH; tel. (1903) 821082; fax (1903) 821081; e-mail editor@christianherald.org.uk; internet www.christianherald.org.uk; f. 1996; Saturday; Editorial Dir RUSS BRAVO; circ. 15,000.

Church Times: 33 Upper St, London, N1 0PN; tel. (20) 7359-4570; fax (20) 7226-3073; e-mail editor@churchtimes.co.uk; internet www.churchtimes.co.uk; f. 1863; Church of England and world-wide Anglican news; Friday; Editor PAUL HANDLEY; circ. 35,701.

Jewish Chronicle: Jewish Chronicle Newspaper Ltd, 25 Furnival St, London, EC4A 1JT; tel. (20) 7415-1500; fax (20) 7405-9040; e-mail jconline@thejc.com; internet www.thejc.com; f. 1841; Friday; Editor EDWARD J. TEMKO; circ. 40,106.

Methodist Recorder: 122 Golden Lane, London, EC1Y 0TL; tel. (20) 7251-8414; fax (20) 7608-3490; e-mail editorial@methodistrecorder.co.uk; internet www.methodistrecorder.co.uk; f. 1861; Thursday; Editor MOIRA SLEIGHT; circ. 21,379.

New Blackfriars: Blackfriars, Oxford, OX1 3LY; tel. (1865) 278401; fax (1865) 278403; f. 1920; monthly; religious and cultural; Editor Rev. FERGUS KERR.

Philosophy: Royal Institute of Philosophy, 14 Gordon Sq., London, WC1H 0AR; tel. (20) 7387-4130; e-mail j.garvey@royalinstitutephilosophy.org; internet www.royalinstitutephilosophy.org; f. 1925; quarterly; Editor ANTHONY O'HEAR.

The Universe: 1st Floor, St James's Bldgs, Oxford St, Manchester, M1 6FP; tel. (161) 236-8856; fax (161) 236-8530; e-mail newsdesk@the-universe.net; internet www.the-universe.net; f. 1860; Sunday; illustrated Catholic newspaper and review; publ. by Gabriel Communications Ltd; Editor JOE KELLY; circ. 55,922.

Woman Alive: Christian Media Centre Ltd, Garcia Estate, Canterbury Rd, Worthing, West Sussex, BN13 1EH; tel. (1903) 821082; fax (1903) 821081; e-mail womanalive@christianmedia.org.uk; internet www.womanalive.co.uk; f. 1982; monthly; Editor ELIZABETH TRUNDLE; circ. 10,000.

PRESS ORGANIZATION

The Press Complaints Commission: 1 Salisbury Sq., London, EC4Y 8JB; tel. (20) 7353-1248; fax (20) 7353-8355; e-mail pcc@pcc.org.uk; internet www.pcc.org.uk; f. 1991 to replace the Press Council, following the report of the Committee on Privacy and Related Matters; an independent organization established by the newspaper and magazine industry through the Press Standards Board of Finance to deal with complaints from the public about the contents and conduct of newspapers and magazines; the Commission has an independent chairman and 16 members, drawn from the lay public (who are in the majority) and the press. It upholds a 16-point Code of Practice, agreed by a committee of editors representing the newspaper and magazine industry. It aims to ensure that the British press maintains the highest professional standards, having regard to generally established press freedoms; Chair. Sir CHRISTOPHER MEYER; Dir GUY BLACK.

NEWS AGENCIES

Associated Press Ltd: Associated Press House, 12 Norwich St, London, EC4A 1BP; tel. (20) 7353-1515; fax (20) 7353-8118; f. 1931; British subsidiary of Associated Press of USA; delivers a world-wide foreign news and photographic service to Commonwealth and foreign papers; Chair. LOUIS D. BOCCARDI; Bureau Chief BARRY RENFREW.

Press Association Ltd: 292 Vauxhall Bridge Rd, London, SW1V 1AE; tel. (20) 7963-7000; fax (20) 7963-7192; e-mail info@pa.press .net; internet www.pa.press.net; f. 1868; national news agency of the United Kingdom and the Republic of Ireland; Chair. Sir HARRY ROCHE; CEO and Editor-in-Chief PAUL POTTS; Editor JONATHAN GRUN.

Reuters Group PLC: 85 Fleet St, London, EC4P 4AJ; tel. (20) 7250-1122; fax (20) 7324-5400; e-mail editor@reuters.com; internet www.reuters.co.uk; f. 1851; world-wide news and information service to media and business clients in 57,900 organizations and media clients in 157 countries; Chair. Sir CHRISTOPHER HOGG; CEO TOM GLOCER.

United Press International (UPI): Prince Consort House, 27–29 Albert Embankment, London, SE1 7TJ; tel. (20) 7820-4180; internet www.upi.com; supplies world-wide news and news-picture coverage in English and Arabic to newspapers, radio and television stations throughout the world; Editor-in-Chief HOSSEIN HINDAWI; Man. Dir TOBY ALDRICH.

Principal Foreign Bureaux

Agence France-Presse (AFP): 78 Fleet St, London, EC4Y 1NB; tel. (20) 7353-7461; fax (20) 7353-8359; e-mail london.bureau@afp .com; internet www.afp.com; Bureau Chief HERVÉ GUILBAUD.

Agencia EFE (Spain): 6th Floor, 299 Oxford St, London, W1C 2DZ; tel. (20) 7493-7313; fax (20) 7493-7314; e-mail efelondon@btclick .com; internet www.efe.es; Bureau Chief FERNANDO PAJARES GIMÉNEZ.

Agenzia Nazionale Stampa Associata (ANSA) (Italy): Essex House, 12–13 Essex St, London, WC2R 3AA; tel. (20) 7240-5514; fax (20) 7240-5518; Bureau Chief FRANCESCO BIANCHINI.

Australian Associated Press Ltd (AAP): 12 Norwich St, London, EC4A 1QJ; tel. (20) 7353-0153; fax (20) 7583-3563; e-mail aaplondon@hotmail.com; Chief Correspondent MARIA HAWTHORNE.

Canadian Press: Associated Press House, 12 Norwich St, London, EC4A 1QE; tel. (20) 7353-6355; fax (20) 7583-4238; Bureau Chief KEVIN WARD.

Česká tisková kancelář (ČTK) (Czech Republic): 12 Elliott Sq., London, NW3 3SU; tel. (20) 7483-1958; fax (20) 7586-6377; e-mail jiri.chrast@btinternet.com; Chief Correspondent JIŘÍ CHRÁST.

Cyprus News Agency: 23 Chase Way, London, N14 5EB; tel. and fax (20) 8368-1946; internet www.cyna.org.cy/corr.htm; Chief Correspondent KYRIACOS TSIOUPRAS.

Deutsche Presse-Agentur (dpa) (Germany): 30 Old Queen St, London, SW1H 9HP; tel. (20) 7233-2888; fax (20) 7233-3534; Bureau Chief DIETER EBELING.

Dow Jones Newswires (USA): 5th Floor, 10 Fleet Pl. Limeburner Lane, London, EC4M 7QN; tel. (20) 7842-9300; fax (20) 7842-9361; internet www.djnewswires.com; Senior Ed. GABRIELLA STERN.

Informatsionnoye Telegrafnoye Agentstvo Rossii— Telegrafnoye Agentstvo Suverennykh Stran (ITAR—TASS) (Russia): Suite 12–20, Second Floor, Morley House, 314–320 Regent St, London, W1R 5AB; tel. (20) 7580-5543; fax (20) 7580-5547; internet www.itar-tass.com; Bureau Chief IGOR E. BORISENKO.

Jiji Press (Japan): International Press Centre, 76 Shoe Lane, London, EC4A 3JB; tel. (20) 7936-2847; fax (20) 7583-8353; e-mail jijildn2@ma.kew.net; Bureau Chief J. ANUMA.

Kyodo News (Japan): 2nd Floor, 34 Threadneedle St, London, EC2R 8AY; tel. (20) 7330-8000; fax (20) 7330-8012; e-mail london@ kyodonews.jp; internet www.kyodo.co.jp; Bureau Chief KEN HAYASHI.

Maghreb Arabe Presse (Moroccan News Agency): 35 Westminster Bridge Rd, London, SE1 7JB; tel. (20) 7401-8146; fax (20) 7401-8148; e-mail maplon@aol.com; Bureau Chief ALI BAHAIJOUB.

Press Trust of India (PTI): Third Floor, Radnor House, 93–97 Regent St, London, W1B 4ET; tel. (20) 7494-0602; fax (20) 7494-0603; e-mail ptilondon@aol.com; Chief of Bureau H. S. RAO.

Rossiiskoye Informatsionnoye Agentstvo—Novosti (RIA— Novosti) (Russia): 3 Rosary Gardens, London, SW7 4NW; tel. (20) 7370-3002; fax (20) 7244-7875; e-mail ria@novosti.co.uk; internet www.rian.ru; Bureau Chief SERGEI BORISOV; Correspondent SERGEI KUDASOV.

Saudi Press Agency (SPA): 18 Cavendish Sq., London, W1G 0AQ; tel. (20) 7495-0418.

Xinhua (New China) News Agency (People's Republic of China): 8 Swiss Terrace, Belsize Rd, Swiss Cottage, London, NW6 4RR; tel. (20) 7586-8271; fax (20) 7722-8512; Chief Correspondent LI ZHIGAO.

INSTITUTIONS

Chartered Institute of Journalists: 2 Dock Offices, Surrey Quays Rd, London, SE16 2XU; tel. (20) 7252-1187; fax (20) 7232-2302; e-mail memberservices@ioj.co.uk; internet www.ioj.co.uk; f. 1884; Pres. ANDREW SMITH; Gen. Sec CHRIS UNDERWOOD.

Newspaper Press Fund: Dickens House, 35 Wathen Rd, Dorking, Surrey, RH4 1JY; tel. (1306) 887511; fax (1306) 888212; f. 1864; charity for journalists and their dependants; Pres. Lord ROTHERMERE; Sec. D. J. ILOTT; 5,500 mems.

Newspaper Publishers' Association: 34 Southwark Bridge Rd, London, SE1 9EU; tel. (20) 7207-2200; fax (20) 7928-2067; f. 1906; comprises 8 national newspaper groups and 22 titles; Chair. TERRY GROTE; Dir STEPHEN ORAM.

Newspaper Society: Bloomsbury House, 74–77 Great Russell St, London, WC1B 3DA; tel. (20) 7636-7014; fax (20) 7631-5119; e-mail ns@newspapersoc.org.uk; internet www.newspapersoc.org.uk; f. 1836; represents the regional and local press; Pres. TIM BOWDLER; Dir DAVID NEWELL.

Periodical Publishers' Association Ltd: Queen's House, 28 Kingsway, London, WC2B 6JR; tel. (20) 7404-4166; fax (20) 7404-4167; e-mail info1@ppa.co.uk; internet www.ppa.co.uk; f. 1913; trade association for the UK magazine industry; Chair. DEREK CARTER; Chief Exec. IAN LOCKS; more than 300 mems.

Association of Publishing Agencies: Queen's House, Lincoln's Inn Fields, London, WC2A 3LJ; tel. (20) 7404-4166; fax (20) 7404-4167; e-mail info@apa.co.uk; internet www.apa.co.uk; f. 1993; trade association for the customer publishing industry; Chair. GRAHAM WEAVER.

UK Association of Online Publishers: Queen's House, 28 Kingsway, London, WC2B 6JR; tel. (20) 7404-4166; fax (20) 7404-4167; e-mail alex.daley@ukaop.org.uk; internet www.ukaop.org .uk; f. 2002; represents the interests of online content providers.

Scottish Daily Newspaper Society: 48 Palmerston Pl., Edinburgh, EH12 5DE; tel. (131) 220-4353; fax (131) 220-4344; e-mail info@sdns.org.uk; f. 1915; Dir JAMES B. RAEBURN.

Scottish Newspaper Publishers' Association: 48 Palmerston Pl., Edinburgh, EH12 5DE; tel. (131) 220-4353; fax (131) 220-4344; e-mail info@snpa.org.uk; internet www.snpa.org.uk; Dir JAMES B. RAEBURN.

See also under Employers' Organizations and Trade Unions.

Principal Publishers

Publishing firms in the United Kingdom are mainly located in London and many are members of large publishing groups, notably Reed Elsevier, Random Century, the Pearson Group and the Thomson Corporation. Fiction remains the largest category. The United Kingdom publishes more new titles every year than any other European country. In 2000 some 116,415 new titles were issued.

Academic Press Ltd: 32 Jamestown Rd, London, NW1 7BY; tel. (20) 7424-4200; fax (20) 7424-2293; internet www .harcourt-international.com; f. 1958; academic, medical, technical and scientific; a Harcourt Science and Technology Co; Man. Dir JAN WELTEROP.

Asean Academic Press Ltd: POB 13945, London E5 0XY; fax (20) 8533-5856; e-mail aapub@attglobal.net; internet www .aseanacademicpress.com; educational, technical, professional and scientific books on Asia.

Ashgate Publishing Ltd: Gower House, Croft Rd, Aldershot, Hants, GU11 3HR; tel. (1252) 331551; fax (1252) 317446; e-mail info@ashgatepub.co.uk; internet www.ashgate.com; f. 1967; social sciences and humanities, business and public sector management books; imprints: Ashgate, Dartmouth, Gower, Lund Humphries, Variorum; Chair. N. FARROW.

Bartholomew: HarperCollins Cartographic, Westerhill Rd, Bishopbriggs, Glasgow, G64 2QT; tel. (141) 772-3200; fax (141) 3063130; e-mail bartholomew@harpercollins.co.uk; internet www .bartholomewmaps.com; f. 1826; bought by News International PLC 1985; the cartographic division of HarperCollins; maps, atlases and guide books; Man. Dir THOMAS WEBSTER; Cartographic Dir SHEENA BARCLAY.

B. T. Batsford Ltd: 64 Brewery Rd, London, N7 9NT; tel. (20) 7697-3000; e-mail info@chrysalisbooks.co.uk; internet www.chrsalisbooks .co.uk; f. 1843; part of Chrysalis Books PLC; crafts, design, architecture, art techniques, fashion, film, chess, bridge, gardening, English heritage, historic Scotland; Chief Exec. MARK LEAVER.

BBC Worldwide Ltd: Woodlands, 80 Wood Lane, London, W12 0YY; tel. (20) 8433-2000; fax (20) 8749-0358; e-mail bbcworldwide@bbc.co.uk; internet www.bbcworldwide.com; Man. Dir PETER TEAGUE.

Berlitz Publishing Co Ltd: Lincoln House, 296–302 High Holborn, London, W1V 7JH; tel. (20) 7611-9640; fax (20) 7611-9656; e-mail publishing@berlitz.co.uk; internet www.berlitz.com; f. 1970; travel, languages, reference, leisure, children's books; Man. Dir ROGER KIRKPATRICK.

A. & C. Black (Publishers) Ltd: 37 Soho Sq., London, W1V 3QZ; tel. (20) 7758-0200; fax (20) 7758-0222; e-mail enquiries@acblack.com; internet www.acblack.com; f. 1807; inc. Adlard Coles Nautical, Christopher Helm, Herbert Press, Pica Press, T & AD Poyser, Thomas Reed; acquired by Bloomsbury Publishing PLC in 2001; children's and educational books, music, arts and crafts, drama, reference, sport, theatre, travel, sailing, ornithology; Chair. NIGEL NEWTON; Man. Dir JILL COLEMAN.

Blackwell Publishers: 108 Cowley Rd, Oxford, OX4 1JF; tel. (1865) 791100; fax (1865) 791347; e-mail general@blackwellpublishers.co.uk; internet www.blackwellpublishers.co.uk; f. 1921; academic, professional, business and finance books and journals; allied cos Polity Press, NCC Blackwell, Marston Book Services Ltd, Shakespeare Head Press; Chair. NIGEL BLACKWELL; Man. Dir RENÉ OLIVIERI.

Blackwell Science Ltd: Osney Mead, Oxford, OX2 0EL; tel. (1865) 206206; fax (1865) 721205; internet www.blackwell-science.co.uk; f. 1939; medical, scientific, veterinary, technical, agricultural, botanical, ecological, geological, allied health; Chair. NIGEL BLACKWELL; Man. Dir ROBERT CAMPBELL.

Bloomsbury Publishing PLC: 38 Soho Sq., London, W1D 3HB; tel. (20) 7494-2111; fax (20) 7434-0151; internet www.bloomsbury.com; f. 1986; fiction, non-fiction, children's, music and reference; Chair. and CEO NIGEL NEWTON; Publishing Dir LIZ CALDER.

Boosey and Hawkes Music Publishers Ltd: 295 Regent St, London, W1R 8JH; tel. (20) 7580-2060; fax (20) 7291-7109; internet www.boosey.com; music, textbooks; Man. Dir. J. MINCH.

Bowker: East Grinstead House, Winsor Court, East Grinstead, West Sussex, RH19 1XA; tel. (1342) 336149; fax (1342) 336192; e-mail customer.services@bowker.co.uk; internet www.bowker.co.uk; business information, general reference and bibliographies; Man. Dir JACKI HEPPARD.

Marion Boyars Publishers Ltd: 24 Lacy Rd, London, SW15 1NL; tel. (20) 8788-9522; fax (20) 8789-8122; e-mail marion.boyars@talk21.com; internet www.marionboyars.co.uk; fiction, plays, cinema, music, translations, literary criticism, sociology; Man. Dir CATHERYN KILGARRIFF.

Butterworth-Heinemann: Linacre House, Jordan Hill, Oxford, OX2 8DP; tel. (1865) 310366; fax (1865) 310898; e-mail bhmarketing@repp.co.uk; internet www.bh.com; a division of Reed Education and Professional Publishing Ltd; imprints: Butterworth Architecture, Butterworth Medical, Butterworth Scientific, Digital Press, Focal Press, Made Simple, Heinemann Professional Publishing; Chair. JOHN PHILBIN; Man. Dir PHILIP SHAW.

Butterworths Tolley: Halsbury House, 35 Chancery Lane, London, WC2A 1EL; tel. (20) 7400-2500; fax (20) 7400-2842; internet www.butterworths.co.uk; f. 1818; a division of Reed Elsevier UK Ltd; law, tax, accountancy, banking books and journals; Man. Dir STEPHEN STOUT.

Calder Publications Ltd: 51 The Cut, London, SE1 8LF; tel. (20) 7633-0599; fax (20) 7928-5930; e-mail info@calderpubublications.com; internet www.calderpublications.com; f. 1950; fiction, plays, music, opera, European classics, translations, general books, social science, politics, Calderbooks, Journal of Beckett Studies, English National Opera guides, Frank: International Literary Journal; Man. Dir JOHN CALDER.

Cambridge University Press: The Edinburgh Bldg, Shaftesbury Rd, Cambridge, CB2 2RU; tel. (1223) 312393; fax (1223) 315052; e-mail information@cambridge.org; internet www.cambridge.org; f. 1534; academic and scientific monographs and textbooks, educational, English language teaching materials, microsoftware, bibles, prayer books and academic journals; Chief Exec. STEPHEN R. R. BOURNE.

Jonathan Cape Ltd: Random House, 20 Vauxhall Bridge Rd, London, SW1V 2SA; tel. (20) 7840-8400; fax (20) 7233-6117; e-mail enquiries@randomhouse.co.uk; internet www.randomhouse.co.uk; f. 1921; imprint of The Random House Group Ltd; general, biography, travel, belles-lettres, fiction, history, poetry; subsidiary imprint: The Bodley Head (biography, current affairs, humour); Publishing Dir DAN FRANKLIN.

Carlton Books: 20 Mortimer St, London W1T 3JW; tel. (20) 7612-0400; fax (20) 7612-0401; e-mail sales@carltonbooks.co.uk; internet www.carltonbooks.co.uk; f. 1992; Propr Carlton Communications PLC; Chief Exec. JONATHAN GOODMAN.

Frank Cass & Co Ltd: Crown House, 47 Chase Side, Southgate, London, N14 5BP; tel. (20) 8920-2100; fax (20) 8447-8548; e-mail info@frankcass.com; internet www.frankcass.com; f. 1957; politics, international relations, military studies, development studies, Jewish studies, Irish studies, economics, European and colonial history, economic and social history, business, sociology, slavery, African, Middle Eastern; reprints, original studies, journals; Chair. FRANK CASS; Man. Dir STEWART CASS.

Century: Random House, 20 Vauxhall Bridge Rd, London, SW1V 2SA; tel. (20) 7840-8400; fax (20) 7233-6127; e-mail enquiries@randomhouse.co.uk; internet www.randomhouse.co.uk; f. 1987; imprint of Random House Group Ltd; general, biography, travel, current affairs, fiction, memoirs, music, philosophy; Man. Dir RICHARD CABLE.

Chatto and Windus, Ltd: 20 Vauxhall Bridge Rd, London, SW1V 2SA; tel. (20) 7840-8400; fax (20) 7233-6117; internet www.randomhouse.co.uk; imprint of The Random House Group Ltd (see below); general, academic, biography, memoirs, politics, history, literary criticism, current affairs, cultural studies and fiction; imprint: Hogarth Press; Dir ALISON SAMUEL.

Chrysalis Books PLC: 64 Brewery Rd, London, N7 9NT; tel. (20) 7697-3000; fax (20) 7697-3001; e-mail info@chrysalisbooks.co.uk; internet www.chrysalisbooks.co.uk; f. 1989; Chief Exec. JOHN NEEDLEMAN.

Church House Publishing: Church House, Great Smith St, London, SW1P 3NZ; tel. (20) 7898-1451; fax (20) 7898-1449; e-mail publishing@c-of-e.org.uk; internet www.chpublishing.co.uk; Publ. Man. ALAN MITCHELL.

Churchill Livingstone: Robert Stevenson House, 1–3 Baxter's Place, Leith Walk, Edinburgh, EH1 3AF; tel. (131) 556-2424; fax (131) 558-1278; e-mail andrewstevenson@compuserve.com; f. 1863; imprint of Harcourt Brace and Co Ltd; medical science, dental, nursing books, allied health, medical and biomedical periodicals; Div. Man. Dir ANDREW STEVENSON.

James Clarke and Co Ltd: POB 60, Cambridge, CB1 2NT; tel. (1223) 350865; fax (1223) 366951; e-mail publishing@jamesclarke.co.uk; internet www.jamesclarke.co.uk; f. 1859; religious, reference and academic; imprints: Acorn Editions, Patrick Hardy Books; Man. Dir ADRIAN BRINK.

CMP Information Data and Information Services Division: Riverbank House, Angel Lane, Tonbridge, Kent, TN9 1SE; tel. (1732) 377591; fax (1732) 367301; internet www.cmpdata.co.uk; reference and buyers' guides; Group Publishing Dir SARA CREECH.

Conran Octopus: 2–4 Heron Quays, London, E14 4JP; tel. (20) 7531-8628; fax (20) 7531-8627; e-mail info-co@conran-octopus.co.uk; internet www.conran-octopus.co.uk; illustrated reference books; imprint of Octopus Publishing Group; Publishing Dir LORRAINE DICKIE.

Constable and Robinson Ltd: 3 The Lanchesters, 162 Fulham Palace Rd, London, W6 9ER; tel. (20) 8741-3663; fax (20) 8748-7562; e-mail enquiries@constablerobinson.com; internet www.constablerobinson.com; all branches of literature; Man. Dir NICHOLAS ROBINSON.

James Currey Publishers: 73 Botley Rd, Oxford, OX2 0BS; tel. (1865) 244111; fax (1865) 246454; e-mail editorial@jamescurrey.co.uk; internet www.jamescurrey.co.uk; African and Caribbean; Chair. JAMES CURREY; Man. Dir DOUGLAS H. JOHNSON.

Darton, Longman and Todd Ltd: 1 Spencer Court, 140–142 Wandsworth High St, London, SW18 4JJ; tel. (20) 8875-0155; fax (20) 8875-0133; e-mail tradesales@darton-longman-todd.co.uk; f. 1959; theology, spirituality, religious biography and history, Bibles; Sales and Marketing Dir A. MORDUE.

David & Charles Ltd: Brunel House, Forde Close, Newton Abbot, Devon, TQ12 4PU; tel. (1626) 323200; fax (1626) 323319; e-mail postmaster@davidandcharles.co.uk; internet www.davidandcharles.co.uk; f. 1960; general, trade and reference; Man. Dir BUDGE WALLIS (acting).

André Deutsch Ltd: 20 Mortimer St, London, W1T 3JW; tel. (20) 7612-0400; fax (20) 7612-0401; f. 1950; fiction, belles-lettres, biography, memoirs, cookery, poetry, humour, art, politics, history, travel, sport; imprint of Carlton Books.

Dorling Kindersley PLC: 9 Henrietta St, London, WC2E 8PS; tel. (20) 7836-5411; fax (20) 7836-7570; internet www.dk.com/uk; f. 1974; acquired by Pearson PLC in 2000; illustrated reference books; Chief Exec. ANTHONY FORBES WATSON; Man. Dir ANDREW WELHAM.

Gerald Duckworth and Co Ltd: 61 Frith St, London, W1D 3JL; tel. (20) 7434-4242; fax (20) 7434-4420; e-mail info@

Directory

duckworth-publishers.co.uk; internet www.ducknet.co.uk; f. 1898; fiction, academic; Chair. STEPHEN HILL; CEO GILLIAN HALKINS.

Edinburgh University Press: 22 George Sq., Edinburgh, EH8 9LF; tel. (131) 650-4218; fax (131) 662-0053; e-mail timothy.wright@eup.ed.ac.uk; internet www.eup.ed.ac.uk; learned books and journals; Chair. TIM RIX.

Edward Elgar Publishing Ltd: Glensanda House, Montpellier Parade, Cheltenham, GL50 1UA; tel. (1242) 226934; fax (1242) 262111; e-mail info@e-elgar.co.uk; internet www.e-elgar.co.uk; f. 1986; economics and other social sciences; Chair. ALEX RYAN; Man. Dir E. ELGAR.

Element Books: Old School House, The Courtyard, Bell St, Shaftesbury, Dorset, SP7 8BP; internet www.elementbooks.co.uk; f. 1978; imprint of HarperCollins Publishers; alternative health, personal development, philosophy, psychology, world religions, divination; Chair. MICHAEL MANN; Man. Dir BELINDA BUDGE.

Elsevier Science Ltd: The Boulevard, Langford Lane, Kidlington, Oxon, OX5 1GB; tel. (1865) 843000; fax (1865) 843010; e-mail g.mcgurran@elsevier.co.uk; internet www.elsevier.nl; Propr Reed Elsevier PLC; scientific, academic, engineering, architectural and technical books and journals; Man. Dir GAVIN HOWE.

Encyclopaedia Britannica UK Ltd: 2nd Floor, Unity Wharf, Mill St, London, SE1 2BH; tel. (20) 7500-7800; fax (20) 7500-7878; e-mail enquiries@britannica.co.uk; internet www.britannica.co.uk; f. 1768; publs *Encyclopaedia Britannica, Britannica Book of the Year, Great Books of the Western World, Children's Britannica, Britannica CD*; Man. Dir LEAH MANSOOR.

Euromonitor plc: 60–61 Britton St, London, EC1M 5UX; tel. (20) 7251-8024; fax (20) 7608-3149; e-mail info@euromonitor.com; internet www.euromonitor.com; f. 1972; business and commercial reference; Chair. R. N. SENIOR; Man. Dir T. J. FENWICK.

Europa Publications Ltd: 11 New Fetter Lane, London, EC4P 4EE; tel. (20) 7583-9855; fax (20) 7842-2391; e-mail edit.europa@tandf.co.uk; internet www.europapublications.com; f. 1926; international reference books, social and economic history and international affairs; division of Taylor and Francis Group plc; Chief Exec. DAVID SMITH; Editorial Dir PAUL KELLY.

Evans Brothers Ltd: 2A Portman Mansions, Chiltern St, London, W1M 1LE; tel. (20) 7487-0920; fax (20) 7487-0921; e-mail sales@evansbrothers.co.uk; internet www.evansbooks.co.uk; f. 1906; educational, children's, general and overseas books; Man. Dir S. T. PAWLEY; Publr SU SWALLOW.

Everyman Publishers: Gloucester Mansions, 140A Shaftesbury Ave, London, WC2H 8HD; tel. (20) 7539-7600; fax (20) 7379-4060; e-mail books@everyman.uk.com; internet www.everyman.uk.com; incorporates The Everyman's Library, David Campbell Publishers, Everyman Chess; Publr DAVID CAMPBELL.

Faber and Faber Ltd: 3 Queen Sq., London, WC1N 3AU; tel. (20) 7465-0045; fax (20) 7465-0034; internet www.faber.co.uk; f. 1929; biography, autobiography, children's, film, drama, popular science, economics, fiction, history, music, poetry; Man. Dir STEPHEN PAGE.

The Folio Society Ltd: 44 Eagle St, London, WC1R 4FS; tel. (20) 7400-4222; fax (20) 7400-4242; internet www.foliosoc.co.uk; f. 1947; fine illustrated editions of fiction, history, biographies, drama and poetry; Man. Dir NICK RICE.

Footprint Handbooks Ltd: 6 Riverside Court, Lower Bristol Rd, Bath, BA2 3DZ; tel. (1225) 469141; fax (1225) 469461; e-mail discover@footprintbooks.com; internet www.footprintbooks.com; Dirs JAMES DAWSON, PATRICK DAWSON.

W. Foulsham & Co Ltd: The Publishing House, Cippenham, Slough, Berks, SL1 5AP; tel. (1753) 526769; fax (1753) 535003; e-mail reception@foulsham.com; internet www.foulsham.com; f. 1819; finance, reference; Man. Dir BARRY BELASCO.

Fourth Estate: 77–85 Fulham Palace Rd, London, W6 8JB; tel. (20) 8741-4414; fax (20) 8307-4466; e-mail general@4thestate.co.uk; internet www.fourthestate.com; f. 1984; general reference, current affairs; literary and commercial fiction; cookery; division of Harper-Collins Publishers; Man. Dir CHRISTOPHER POTTER.

Samuel French Ltd: 52 Fitzroy St, London, W1T 5JR; tel. (20) 7387-9373; fax (20) 7387-2161; e-mail theatre@samuelfrench-london.co.uk; internet www.samuelfrench-london.co.uk; f. 1830; drama; Chair. CHARLES VAN NOSTRAND; Man. Dir VIVIEN GOODWIN.

Robert Gibson and Sons, Glasgow, Ltd: 2A Christie St, Paisley, Renfrewshire, PA1 1NB; tel. (141) 848-1609; fax (141) 889-6315; e-mail hoddergibson@hodder.co.uk; internet hodderheadline.co.uk; f. 1883; educational and textbooks; Man. Dir JOHN MITCHELL.

Ginn and Co: Linacre House, Jordan Hill, Oxford OX2 8DP; tel. (1865) 310533; fax (1865) 393433; e-mail services@ginn.co.uk; internet www.ginn.co.uk; f. 1924; imprint of Harcourt Education UK Ltd; educational; Chair. JOHN PHILBIN; Man. Dir PAUL SHUTER.

Victor Gollancz Ltd: Orion House, 5 Upper St Martin's Lane, London, WC2H 9EA; tel. (20) 7420-5555; fax (20) 7240-7261; f. 1928; imprint of Orion Publishing Group Ltd; science fiction and fantasy; Dirs SIMON SPANTON, JO FLETCHER.

Granta Books: 2/3 Hanover Yard, Noel Rd, London, N1 8BE; tel. (20) 7704-9776; fax (20) 7354-3469; e-mail glynch@granta.com; internet www.granta.com; fiction, political non-fiction; Publrs GAIL LYNCH, GEORGE MILLER, IAN JACK.

Gresham Books Ltd: 46 Victoria Rd, Summertown, Oxford OX2 7QD; tel. (1865) 513582; fax (1865) 512718; e-mail greshambks@btinternet.com; internet www.gresham-books.co.uk; f. 1978; hymn books, school histories, music folders; Chief Exec. P. A. LEWIS.

Guinness World Records Ltd: 338 Euston Rd, London, NW1 3BD; tel. (20) 7891-4567; fax (20) 7891-4501; e-mail info@guinnessrecords.com; internet www.guinnessworldrecords.com; f. 1954; acquired by Gullane Entertainment in 2001; music and general interest; CEO STEPHEN NELSON; Man. Dir CHRISTOPHER IRWIN.

Robert Hale Ltd: Clerkenwell House, 45–47 Clerkenwell Green, London, EC1R 0HT; tel. (20) 7251-2661; fax (20) 7490-4958; e-mail enquire@halebooks.com; internet www.halebooks.com; f. 1936; memoirs, biography, travel, sport, fiction, belles-lettres, general non-fiction; Man. Dir JOHN HALE.

Hamlyn Octopus: 2–4 Heron Quays, London, E14 4JP; tel. (20) 7531-8400; fax (20) 7531-8650; e-mail info-ho@hamlyn.co.uk; internet www.hamlyn.co.uk; imprint of Octopus Publishing Group; cookery, DIY, gardening, sports, history, animals; Man. Dir ALISON GOFF.

Harcourt Publishers Ltd: Harcourt Pl., 32 Jamestown Rd, London, NW1 7BY; tel. (20) 7424-4200; fax (20) 7482-2293; internet www.harcourt-international.com; academic, scientific and medical; Man. Dir PETER H. LENGEMANN.

Harlequin Mills and Boon Ltd: Eton House, 18–24 Paradise Rd, Richmond, Surrey, TW9 1SR; tel. (20) 8288-2800; fax (20) 8288-2899; internet www.millsandboon.co.uk; f. 1908; romantic fiction; Man. Dir A. LOW.

HarperCollins Publishers Ltd: 77–85 Fulham Palace Rd, London, W6 8JB; tel. (20) 8741-7070; fax (20) 8307-4440; e-mail contact@harpercollins.co.uk; internet www.harpercollins.co.uk; William Collins; f. 1819; bought by News International 1989; fiction and non-fiction of all classes, including biographies, history, travel, nature, sport, art, children's, classics, atlases, reference, religion; imprints: Armada, Bartholomew, Collins, Collins Bibles, Collins Cartographic, Collins Classics, Collins Crime, Collins English Dictionaries, Collins Liturgical, Flamingo, Fontana, HarperCollins, HarperCollins Audio, HarperCollins Paperbacks, HarperCollins Science Fiction and Fantasy, Jets, Lions, Marshall Pickering, Nicholson, Thorsons, Times Books, Tolkien, Tracks, Young Lions; CEO VICTORIA BARNSLEY.

The Harvill Press: The Random House Group Ltd, 20 Vauxhall Bridge Rd, London, SW1V 2SA; tel. (20) 7840-8400; fax (20) 7840-8664; e-mail enquiries@randomhouse.co.uk/harvill; internet www.randomhouse.co.uk/harvill; fiction, non-fiction, illustrated books; Publr CHRISTOPHER MACLEHOSE.

Haynes Publishing: Sparkford, Yeovil, Somerset, BA22 7JJ; tel. (1963) 440635; fax (1963) 440001; e-mail sales@haynes-manual.co.uk; internet www.haynes.co.uk; f. 1960; transport, manuals etc. Chair. J. H. HAYNES; Man. Dir K. C. FULLMAN.

Headline Book Publishing Ltd: 338 Euston Rd, London, NW1 3BH; tel. (20) 7873-6000; fax (20) 7873-6124; e-mail headline.books@headline.co.uk; internet www.headline.co.uk; division of Hodder Headline Ltd; fiction, autobiography, biography, food and wine, gardening, popular science, sport and TV tie-ins; Chief Exec. TIM HELY HUTCHINSON; Man. Dir MARTIN NEILD.

William Heinemann Ltd: Random House, 20 Vauxhall Bridge Rd, London, SW1V 2SA; tel. (20) 7840-8400; fax (20) 7233-6127; internet www.randomhouse.co.uk; arts, biography, fiction, history, science, travel; Publishing Dirs RAVI MIRCHANDANI, KIRSTY FOWKES.

Heinemann Educational: Halley Court, Jordan Hill, Oxford, OX2 8EJ; tel. (1865) 311366; fax (1865) 310043; e-mail uk.schools@repp.co.uk; internet www.heinemann.co.uk; imprint of Reed Educational and Professional Publishing; educational textbooks for UK and abroad; Man. Dir BOB OSBORNE.

Hodder Arnold: 338 Euston Rd, London, NW1 3BH; tel. (20) 7873-6000; fax (20) 7873-6325; e-mail feedback.arnold@hodder.co.uk; internet www.arnoldpublishers.com; f. 1890; imprint of Hodder Headline (see below); humanities, medical, nursing, health sciences, statistics; journals cover scientific, technical, engineering; Man. Dir PHILIP WALTERS.

Hodder Headline: 338 Euston Rd, London, NW1 3BH; tel. (20) 7873-6000; fax (20) 7873-6124; internet www.madaboutbooks.com; f. 1993; bought by WH Smith PLC 1999; imprints: Edward Arnold,

Headline Book Publishing Ltd, Hodder and Stoughton Ltd; Group Chief Exec. TIM HELY HUTCHINSON.

Hodder and Stoughton: 338 Euston Rd, London, NW1 3BH; tel. (20) 7873-6000; fax (20) 7873-6024; f. 1868; imprints: Coronet, Flame, LIR, Mobius, New English Library, Sceptre; general, biography, travel, religion, juvenile, fiction, current affairs, educational, academic and medical paperbacks; Man. Dir JAMIE HODDER-WILLIAMS.

IOP Publishing Ltd: Dirac House, Temple Back, Bristol, BS1 6BE; tel. (117) 929-7481; fax (117) 929-4318; e-mail info@iop.org; internet www.iop.org; f. 1874; scientific and technical publishers; Man. Dir J. R. COWHIG.

Jane's Information Group: 163 Brighton Rd, Coulsdon, Surrey, CR5 2YH; tel. (20) 8700-3700; fax (20) 8763-1006; e-mail info@janes.co.uk; internet www.janes.com; military, aviation, transport and security analysis; CEO ALFRED ROLINGTON.

Jordan Publishing Ltd: 21 St Thomas St, Bristol, BS1 6JS; tel. (117) 923-0600; fax (117) 923-0063; e-mail rhudson@jordanpublishing.co.uk; internet www.jordanpublishing.co.uk; f. 1863; practical law books covering family law, litigation, company, property and private client law; Man. Dir RICHARD HUDSON.

Michael Joseph Ltd: 80 Strand, London, WC2R 0RL; tel. (20) 7010-3000; fax (20) 7010-6060; internet www.penguin.co.uk; f. 1936; general, fiction; division of Penguin; Publishing Dir LOUISE MOORE.

Richard Joseph Publishers Ltd: POB 15, Torrington, Ex38 8ZJ; tel. (1805) 625750; fax (1805) 625376; e-mail rjoe01@aol.com; internet www.sheppardsdirectories.co.uk; reference and directories; Man. Dir RICHARD JOSEPH.

Kenyon-Deane: 10 Station Rd, Industrial Estate, Malvern, Worcs., WR13 6RN; tel. and fax (1684) 540154; e-mail simonsmith@cressrelles4drama.fsbusiness.co.uk; f. 1971; incorporates Kenyon House Press, H. F. W. Deane Ltd; plays and drama textbooks, specialists in all-women plays and plays for young people; Man. Dir LESLIE SMITH.

Kingfisher Publications PLC: New Penderel House, 283–288 High Holborn, London, WC1V 7HZ; tel. (20) 7903-9999; fax (20) 7242-5009; e-mail sales@kingfisherpub.com; internet www.kingfisherpub.com; children's books; imprints: Kingfisher; Man. Dir JOHN RICHARDS.

Kogan Page Ltd: 120 Pentonville Rd, London, N1 9JN; tel. (20) 7278-0433; fax (20) 7837-6348; e-mail kpinfo@kogan-page.co.uk; internet www.kogan-page.co.uk; f. 1967; business, education, management, accountancy, textbooks, transport, careers, personal development, training, journals; Man. Dir PHILIP KOGAN.

Lawrence and Wishart Ltd: 99A Wallis Rd, London, E9 5LN; tel. (20) 8533-2506; fax (20) 8533-7369; e-mail lw@l-w-bks.demon.co.uk; internet www.l-w-bks.co.uk; f. 1936; politics, history, feminism, race, economics, Marxist theory, cultural studies; Man. Dir SALLY DAVISON.

Letts Educational: The Chiswick Centre, 414 Chiswick High Rd, London, W4 5TF; tel. (20) 8996-3333; fax (20) 8742-8390; e-mail mail@lettsed.co.uk; internet www.letts-education.com; children's, educational, textbooks; Man. Dir STEPHEN BAKER.

Liverpool University Press: 4 Cambridge St, Liverpool, L69 7ZU; tel. (151) 794-2233; fax (151) 794-2235; e-mail J.M.Smith@liverpool.ac.uk; internet www.liverpool-unipress.co.uk; f. 1899; European and American literature, education, social, political, economic and ancient history, geography, planning and environmental science, hispanic studies, archaeology, population studies, veterinary science, architecture, art, art history, cultural studies, science fiction criticism series; Publr ROBIN BLOXSIDGE.

Lonely Planet Publications: 10A Spring Place, London, NW5 3BH; tel. (20) 7428-4800; fax (20) 7428-4828; e-mail go@lonelyplanet.co.uk; internet www.lonelyplanet.com; cookery, travel, languages, photography; Publr KATHARINE LECK.

Lund Humphries: Gower House, Croft Rd, Aldershot, Hants GU11 3HR; tel. (1252) 331551; fax (1252) 344405; e-mail info@ashgatepub.co.uk; internet www.lundhumphries.com; f. 1969; arts, graphic arts, design, architecture, photography, scholarly, Arabic language; Dir NIGEL FARROW.

Lutterworth Press: POB 60, Cambridge, CB1 2NT; tel. (1223) 350865; fax (1223) 366951; e-mail sales@lutterworth.com; internet www.lutterworth.com; f. 1799; subsidiary of James Clarke & Co Ltd; the arts, crafts, biography, educational, environmental, history, theology, travel, sport, juvenile fiction and non-fiction; Man. Dir ADRIAN BRINK.

McGraw-Hill Education: McGraw-Hill House, Shoppenhangers Rd, Maidenhead, Berks., SL6 2QL; tel. (1628) 502500; fax (1628) 770224; internet www.mcgraw-hill.co.uk; technical, scientific, computer studies, professional reference, general and medical books; Man. Dir SIMON ALLEN.

Macmillan Publishers Ltd: 20 New Wharf Rd, London, N1 9RR; tel. (20) 7014-6000; fax (20) 7014-6001; e-mail books@macmillan.co.uk; internet www.macmillan.co.uk; fiction and non-fiction, general reference; imprints: Picador, Pan Paperbacks, Sidgwick & Jackson, Macmillan; Chief Exec. RICHARD CHARKIN.

Macmillan Education Ltd: Between Towns Rd, Oxford, OX4 3PP; tel. (1865) 405700; fax (1865) 405701; e-mail info@macmillan.com; internet www.macmillaneducation.com; a division of Macmillan Publishers Ltd; English Language Teaching and educational books; Chair. CHRISTOPHER PATERSON; Man. Dir CHRIS HARRISON.

Manchester University Press: Oxford Rd, Manchester, M13 9NR; tel. (161) 275-2310; fax (161) 274-3346; e-mail mup@man.ac.uk; internet www.manchesteruniversitypress.co.uk; f. 1904; all branches of higher education, arts, science and social sciences; Chief Exec. DAVID ROGERS.

Methuen Publishing Ltd: 215 Vauxhall Bridge Rd, London, SW1V 1EJ; tel. (20) 7798-1600; fax (20) 7828-2098; e-mail name@methuen.co.uk; internet www.methuen.co.uk; f. 1889; literature, fiction, non-fiction, biography, sport, theatre, drama, humour, music; Man. Dir PETER TUMMONS; Publishing Dir MAX EILENBERG.

Mitchell Beazley: 2–4 Heron Quays, London, E14 4JP; tel. (20) 7531-8400; fax (20) 7537-0773; e-mail info-mb@mitchell-beazley.co.uk; internet www.mitchell-beazley.com; f. 1969; imprint of Octopus Publishing Group Ltd; Miller's antiques, arts and design, interiors and style, gardening, reference, wine and food; Publr JANE ASPDEN.

John Murray Publishers Ltd: 50 Albemarle St, London, W1S 4BD; tel. (20) 7493-4361; fax (20) 7499-1792; e-mail johnmurray@dial.pipex.com; f. 1768; acquired by Hodder Headline in 2002; art, architecture, biography, autobiography, history, travel, crafts, decorative arts; secondary, higher and self-teaching educational books; Chair. JOHN R. MURRAY.

Nelson Thornes Ltd: Delta Pl., 27 Bath Rd, Cheltenham, GL53 7TH; tel. (1242) 267100; fax (1242) 267311; e-mail mail@nelsonthornes.com; internet www.nelsonthornes.com; educational; Man. Dir OLIVER GADSBY.

New English Library Ltd: 338 Euston Rd, London, NW1 3BH; tel. (20) 7873-6000; fax (20) 7873-6124; f. 1957; imprint of Hodder and Stoughton Ltd; publishers of NEL, NEL Hardcovers; Publr CAROLYN MAYS.

James Nisbet and Co Ltd: Pirton Ct, Priors Hill, Pirton, Hitchin, Herts., SG5 3QA; tel. and fax (1462) 713444; f. 1810; business management, educational; Chair. E. M. MACKENZIE-WOOD.

Novello and Co Ltd: 8/9 Frith St, London, W1D 3JB; tel. (20) 7434-0066; fax (20) 7287-6329; e-mail promotion@musicsales.co.uk; internet www.chester-novello.com; music; Man. Dir JAMES RUSHTON.

Octopus Publishing: 2–4 Heron Quays, London, E14 4JP; tel. (20) 7531-8400; fax (20) 7531-8650; internet www.octopus-publishing.co.uk; imprints: Brimax, Bounty, Cassell Illustrated, Conran Octopus, Hamlyn, Mitchell Beazley, Philip's; Chief Exec. DEREK FREEMAN.

Open University Press: Celtic Court 22 Ballmoor, Buckingham, MK18 1XW; tel. (1280) 823388; fax (1280) 823233; e-mail enquiries@openup.co.uk; internet www.openup.co.uk; academic, politics, medical, sociology; Man. Dir JOHN SKELTON.

Orion Publishing Group: Orion House, 5 Upper St Martin's Lane, London, WC2H 9EA; tel. (20) 7240-3444; fax (20) 7240-4822; f. 1991; imprints: Everyman, Orion, Phoenix, Gollancz, Cassell, Millenium, Chapmans, Weidenfeld and Nicolson; Chief Exec. ANTHONY CHEETHAM.

Peter Owen Ltd: 73 Kenway Rd, London, SW5 0RE; tel. (20) 7373-5628; fax (20) 7373-6760; e-mail admin@peter.owen.com; internet www.peterowen.com; f. 1951; general publishers of fiction, autobiography, biography, translations, etc. publishers of books in the UNESCO series of Representative Works; Man. Dir PETER OWEN; Editorial Dir ANTONIA OWEN.

Oxford University Press: Gt Clarendon St, Oxford, OX2 6DP; tel. (1865) 556767; fax (1865) 556646; e-mail enquiry@oup.co.uk; internet www.oup.co.uk; f. c.1478; Bibles, prayer books, *Oxford English Dictionary* the *Dictionary of National Biography* and many other dictionaries and books of reference, learned and general works from the humanities to the sciences, educational, electronic, music and children's books and audio-visual and English language teaching material; Sec. to the Delegates of the Press and Chief Exec. HENRY REECE.

Palgrave Macmillan Ltd: Houndmills, Basingstoke, Hants., RG21 6XS; tel. (1256) 329242; fax (1256) 479476; internet www.palgrave.com; academic, professional, textbooks and journals; Man. Dir D. J. G. KNIGHT.

Pavilion Books Ltd: Chrysalis Books, 64 Brewery Rd, London, N7 9NT; tel. (20) 7697-3000; fax (20) 7697-3001; e-mail info@pavilionbooks.co.uk; internet www.chrysalisbooks.co.uk; general; acquired by Chrysalis Group PLC in 2001; Publr VIVIEN JAMES.

Pearson Education Ltd: Edinburgh Gate, Harlow, Essex, CM20 2JE; tel. (1279) 623623; fax (1279) 431059; internet www .pearsoned-ema.com; Propr Pearson PLC; educational; Chief Exec. NIGEL PORTWOOD.

Pearson Professional Ltd: 3 Burlington Gdns, London, W1S 3EP; tel. (20) 7411-2000; fax (20) 7411-2390; f. 1994 by amalgamation of business and professional publishing divisions of Financial Times Group and Longman Group; Chief Exec. MARJORIE SCARDINO.

Penguin Books Ltd: 80 The Strand, London WC2R 0RL; tel. (20) 7010-3000; fax (20) 7416-3099; e-mail editor@penguin.co.uk; internet www.penguin.co.uk; f. 1936; holding co Pearson PLC; paperback imprints: Penguin and Puffin; reprints and original works of fiction and non-fiction including travel, biography, science and social studies, reference books, handbooks, plays, poetry, classics and children's books; hardback imprints: Hamish Hamilton, Michael Joseph, Viking, F. Warne and Blackie; Chair. and Chief Exec. DAVID WAN; Man. Dir (UK) ANTHONY FORBES-WATSON.

Phaidon Press Ltd: Regent's Wharf, All Saints St, London, N1 9PA; tel. (20) 7843-1000; internet www.phaidon.com; art, architecture, contemporary culture, design, decorative arts, fashion, photography and music, film, fine art; Chair. RICHARD SCHLAGMAN.

Philip's: 1 Marlin House, Marlin's Meadow, Croxley Business Park, Watford, WD18 8TA; tel. (1923) 819423; fax (1923) 819541; e-mail george.philip@philips-maps.co.uk; internet www.philips-maps.co .uk; imprint of Octopus Publishing Group; maps, atlases, globes, astronomy, encyclopaedias; Publr JOHN GAISFORD.

Pluto Press: 345 Archway Rd, London, N6 5AA; tel. (20) 8348-2724; fax (20) 8348-9133; e-mail beech@plutobooks.com; internet www .plutobooks.com; academic, scholarly, current affairs and reference; Man. Dir ROGER VAN ZWANENBERG; Editorial Dir ANNE BEECH.

Proquest Information and Learning: The Quorum, Barnwell Rd, Cambridge, CB5 8SW; tel. (1223) 215512; fax (1223) 215513; e-mail mailmarketing@proquest.co.uk; internet www.proquest.co.uk; f. 1973 as Chadwyck-Healy Ltd; changed name to above in 2001; academic; Gen. Man. STEVEN HALL.

The Random House Group: Random House, 20 Vauxhall Bridge Rd, London, SW1V 2SA; tel. (20) 7840-8400; fax (20) 7233-6115; internet www.randomhouse.co.uk; imprints: Arrow Books Ltd, Jonathan Cape (imprint Yellow Jersey Press), Century Publishing, Chatto & Windus, William Heinemann, Hutchinson, Random House Business Books, Secker and Warburg, Pimlico, Vintage, Random House Children's, Red Fox, Ebury Press (imprints: Rider, Vermilion); Chair. and Chief Exec. GAIL REBUCK.

Reader's Digest Association Ltd: 11 Westferry Circus, Canary Wharf, London, E14 4HE; tel. (20) 7715-8000; fax (20) 7715-8181; internet www.readersdigest.co.uk; various non-fiction, condensed and series fiction; Man. Dir ANDREW LYNAM-SMITH.

Reed Business Information: Quadrant House, The Quadrant, Sutton, Surrey, SM2 5AS; tel. (20) 8652-3500; fax (20) 8652-8932; e-mail information@reedinfo.co.uk; internet www.reedbusiness .com; f. 1866; business directories and online services; Man. Dir JOHN MINCH.

Reed Educational and Professional Publishing Ltd: Halley Court, Jordan Hill, Oxford, OX2 8EJ; tel. (1865) 314691; fax (1865) 314641; e-mail john.philbin@repp.co.uk; part of Reed Elsevier UK Ltd; imprints: Ginn & Co, Heinemann Educational, Butterworth-Heinemann, Rigby, Focal Press, Newnes; Chief Exec. JOHN PHILBIN.

Reed Elsevier plc: 25 Victoria St, London, SW1H 0EX; tel. (20) 7222-8420; fax (20) 7227-5799; internet www.r-e.com; f. 1992; Chief Exec. CRISPIN DAVIS.

Routledge: 11 New Fetter Lane, London, EC4P 4EE; tel. (20) 7583-9855; fax (20) 7583-0701; e-mail info@routledge.co.uk; internet www .routledge.com; f. 1988; imprint of Taylor and Francis (Books) Ltd; professional, academic, reference; Chief Exec. DAVID SMITH; Man. Dir R. HORTON.

Sage Publications Ltd: 6 Bonhill St, London, EC2A 4PU; tel. (20) 7374-0645; fax (20) 7374-8741; e-mail info@sagepub.co.uk; internet www.sagepub.co.uk; f. 1971; academic and professional social sciences, sciences and humanities; Man Dir STEPHEN BARR.

W. B. Saunders Co Ltd: 32 Jamestown Rd, London, NW1 7BY; tel. (20) 7424-4200; fax (20) 7482-2293; internet www .harcourt-international.com; f. 1900; inc. 1919; division of Harcourt Brace and Co; medical, veterinary and scientific; Div. Man. Dir ANDREW STEVENSON.

Schofield and Sims Ltd: Dogley Mill, Penistone Rd, Fenay Bridge, Huddersfield, West Yorks., HD8 0NQ; tel. (1484) 607080; fax (1484) 606815; e-mail schofield_and_sims@compuserve.com; internet www .schofieldandsims.co.uk; f. 1901; educational; Chair. J. STEPHEN PLATTS.

Scholastic Ltd: Villiers House, Clarendon Ave, Leamington Spa, Warwickshire, CV32 5PR; tel. (1926) 887799; fax (1926) 883331;

internet www.scholastic.co.uk; f. 1964; direct marketing, educational and children's books; Man. Dir IAN RONALD; Dir of Publishing ANNE PEEL.

SCM-Canterbury Press Ltd: 9–17 St Alban's Pl., London, N1 0NX; tel. (20) 7359-8033; fax (20) 7359-0049; e-mail admin@ scm-canterburypress.co.uk; internet www.scm-canterburypress.co .uk; f. 1929; religious, theological; Man. Dir GORDON KNIGHTS.

Scripture Union: 207–209 Queensway, Bletchley, Milton Keynes, Bucks, MK2 2EB; tel. (1908) 856000; fax (1908) 856111; e-mail info@ scriptureunion.org.uk; internet www.scriptureunion.org.uk; f. 1867; Christian education and Bible reading aids.

Martin Secker and Warburg Ltd: Random House, 20 Vauxhall Bridge Rd, London, SW1V 2SA; tel. (20) 7840-8400; fax (20) 7233-6117; internet www.randomhouse.co.uk; imprint of Random House Group Ltd; f. 1936; history, music, political, biography, art, criticism, science, fiction; Editorial Dir GEOFFREY MULLIGAN.

Sheed and Ward Ltd: 4 Rickett St, London, SW6 1RU; tel. (20) 7610-2722; fax (20) 7610-3373; e-mail sheed@breathemail.net; internet www.sheed.co.uk; f. 1926; theology, philosophy, church history and spiritual questions; mainly Catholic authors; Man. Dir MARTIN REDFERN.

Sidgwick and Jackson Ltd: 20 New Wharf Rd, London, N1 9RR; tel. (20) 7014-6000; fax (20) 7014-6001; internet www.panmacmillan .com; f. 1908; popular non-fiction, biography, autobiography, military history, music and popular culture, history; Publisher GORDON SCOTT WISE.

Simon and Schuster: Africa House, 64–78 Kingsway, London, WC2B 6AH; tel. (20) 7316-1900; fax (20) 7316-0331; e-mail enquiries@simonandschuster.co.uk; internet www.simonsays.com; f. 1986; owned by Gy Viacom; fiction, non-fiction, music, travel; imprints: Pocket Books, Touchstone, Scribner, Earthlight, Free Press; Man. Dir IAN S. CHAPMAN.

Society for Promoting Christian Knowledge: Holy Trinity Church, Marylebone, London, NW1 4DU; tel. (20) 7643-0382; fax (20) 7643-0391; e-mail spck@spck.org.uk; internet www.spck.org.uk; f. 1698; religious; imprints: SPCK, Triangle, Azure, Sheldon Press; Publishing Dir SIMON KINGSTON.

Souvenir Press Ltd: 43 Great Russell St, London, WC1B 3PD; tel. (20) 7580-9307; fax (20) 7580-5064; e-mail souvenirpress@ukonline .co.uk; general; Man. Dir ERNEST HECHT.

The Stationery Office: St Crispins, Duke St, Norwich, NR3 1PD; tel. (1603) 622211; e-mail book.enquiries@tso.co.uk; internet www .tso.co.uk; f. 1786 as His Majesty's Stationery Office (govt publishing house); privatized (acquired by National Publishing Group consortium) in 1996; business and publishing services; publishes *Hansard, Highway Code, British Pharmacopoeia*; Chair. RUPERT PENNANT-REA; Chief Exec. IAIN BURNS.

Sweet and Maxwell Ltd: 100 Avenue Rd, London, NW3 3PF; tel. (20) 7393-7000; fax (20) 7393-7010; e-mail customer.services@ sweetandmaxwell.co.uk; internet www.smlawpub.co.uk; f. 1799; imprints: Stevens and Sons Ltd, W. Green, Round Hall, ESC Publishing, the European Law Centre; holding co the Thomson Corporation; law books; Man. Dir WENDY BEECHAM.

Taylor and Francis (Books) Ltd: 11 New Fetter Lane, London, EC4P 4EE; tel. (20) 7583-9855; fax (20) 7842-2298; e-mail info@ tandf.co.uk; internet www.tandf.co.uk; division of Taylor and Francis Group plc; imprints: Taylor and Francis, Brunner-Routledge, Europa Publications, Garland, Garland Science, Martin Dunitz, Curzon Press, Psychology Press, Routledge, Routledge-Falmer, UCL Press, Spon Press; professional, academic, scientific, technical, reference; Chief Exec. DAVID SMITH; Man. Dir R. HORTON.

Thames and Hudson Ltd: 181A High Holborn, London, WC1V 7QX; tel. (20) 7845-5000; fax (20) 7845-5050; e-mail sales@ thameshudson.co.uk; internet www.thamesandhudson.com; art, archaeology, history, etc.; Man. Dir T. NEURATH.

Thorsons: 77–85 Fulham Palace Rd, London, W6 8JB; tel. (20) 8741-7070; fax (20) 8307-4440; internet www.thorsons.com; Proprs HarperCollins Publishers Ltd; Man. Dir BELINDA BUDGE.

Time Warner Books UK: Brettenham House, Lancaster Pl., London, WC2E 7EN; tel. (20) 7911-8000; fax (20) 7911-8100; e-mail email.uk@timewarnerbooks.co.uk; internet www.timewarnerbooks .co.uk; subsidiary of AOL Time-Warner; imprints: Time-Warner, Abacus, Virago, Orbit, Little, Brown, Atom; Chief Exec. DAVID YOUNG.

Times Books: 77–85 Fulham Palace Rd, London, W6 8JB; tel. (20) 8741-7070; fax (20) 8307-4037; Proprs HarperCollins Publishers Ltd; atlases, maps and general reference; Man. Dir SARAH BAILEY.

Transworld Publishers Ltd: 61–63 Uxbridge Rd, London, W5 5SA; tel. (20) 8579-2652; fax (20) 8579-5479; e-mail info@ transworld-publishers.co.uk; internet www.booksattransworld.co .uk; imprints: Corgi Books, Bantam Books, Black Swan, Bantam

Press, Partridge Press, Doubleday, Doubleday (Childrens), Expert Books, IDG, Young Corgi, Picture Corgi, Yearling, Bantam Young Adult; all types of fiction and non-fiction; Chair. MARK BARTY-KING.

University of Wales Press: 10 Columbus Walk, Brigantine Pl., Cardiff, CF10 4UP; tel. (29) 2049-6899; fax (29) 2049-6108; e-mail press@press.wales.ac.uk; internet www.wales.ac.uk/press; f. 1922; academic and educational (Welsh and English); Dir SUSAN JENKINS.

Usborne Publishing: Usborne House, 83–85 Saffron Hill, London, EC1N 8RT; tel. (20) 7430-2800; fax (20) 7430-1562; e-mail mail@usborne.co.uk; internet www.usborne.com; f. 1973; educational and children's publishing; Man. Dir T. P. USBORNE.

Viking: 80 Strand, London, WC2R 0RL; tel. (20) 7416-3000; fax (20) 7416-3099; literary imprint of Penguin Books; fiction, general non-fiction, biography, history, art, literature, science, popular culture; Publishing Dir JULIET ANNAN.

Virgin Books: Thames Wharf Studios, Rainville Rd, London, W6 9HT; tel. (20) 7386-3300; fax (20) 7386-3360; e-mail info@virgin-books.co.uk; internet www.virgin.com/books; W. H. Allen and Co. f. before 1800; general, popular culture, film, music, humour, biography, fiction, non-fiction, erotica; imprints: Virgin, Black Lace and Nexus; Chair. MARK FISHER; Man. Dir K. T. FORSTER.

Frederick Warne (Publishers) Ltd: 80 Strand, London, WC2R 0RL; tel. (20) 7010-3000; fax (20) 7010-6060; internet www .peterrabbit.com; f. 1865; a division of Penguin Books since 1983; classic illustrated children's books (including Beatrix Potter); Man. Dir SALLY FLOYER.

Weidenfeld and Nicolson Ltd: Orion House, 5 Upper St Martin's Lane, London, WC2H 9EA; tel. (20) 7240-3444; fax (20) 7240-4822; f. 1947; imprint of Orion Publishing Group (see above); fiction and non-fiction covering wide range of subjects, biography, belles-lettres and art books; Chair. Lord WEIDENFELD; Man. Dir Adrian BOURNE.

J. Whitaker and Sons Ltd: 189 Shaftsbury Ave, London, WC2H 8TJ; tel. (20) 7420-6000; fax (20) 7836-6781; e-mail sales@teleord.co .uk; f. 1841; part of VNU Entertainment Media UK Ltd; *The Bookseller*, information service provider for the book industry; Man. Dir JOHNATHON NOWELL.

The Women's Press: 34 Great Sutton St, London, EC1V 0LQ; tel. (20) 7251-3007; fax (20) 7608-1938; e-mail carolineb@the-womens-press.com; internet www.the-womens-press.com; f. 1978; feminist; Man. Dir CHARLOTTE GASCOIGNE.

Zed Books Ltd: 7 Cynthia Rd, London, N1 9JF; tel. (20) 7837-4014; fax (20) 7833-3960; e-mail zedbooks@zedbooks.demon.co.uk; internet www.zedbooks.demon.co.uk; f. 1983; academic, scholarly, current affairs; Editor ROBERT MOLTENO.

A. Zwemmer Ltd: 24 Litchfield St, London, WC2H 9NJ; tel. (20) 7240-4180; fax (20) 7836-7049; e-mail zwemmer.co@btinternet.com; internet www.zwemmer.com; f. 1921; architecture, visual arts, applied arts.

PUBLISHERS' ORGANIZATIONS

Booktrust: Book House, 45 East Hill, London, SW18 2QZ; tel. (20) 8516-2977; fax (20) 8516-2998; e-mail info@booktrust.org.uk; internet www.booktrust.org.uk; non-profit-making organization funded by voluntary donations and membership fees; f. 1945; originally f. 1925 as The National Book Council to extend the use and enjoyment of books; renamed Book Trust 1986; publishes annotated book lists; postal book information service; organizes book prizes, including the Booker Prize for Fiction; Young Book Trust inc. the Centre for Children's Books (reference collection of the current two years' children's books); Chair. TREVOR GLOVER; Exec. Dir CHRIS MEAD.

Publishers' Association: 29B Montague St, London, WC1B 5BH; tel. (20) 7691-9191; fax (20) 7691-9199; e-mail mail@publishers.org .uk; internet www.publishers.org.uk; f. 1896; represents book and journal publishers in the UK and seeks to promote the sales of British books; Pres. ROB HAMADI; Chief Exec. RONNIE WILLIAMS; 180 mems.

Scottish Publishers' Association: Scottish Book Centre, 137 Dundee St, Edinburgh, EH11 1BG; tel. (131) 228-6866; fax (131) 228-3220; e-mail carol.lothian@scottishbooks.org; internet www .scottishbooks.org; f. 1973; assists member publishers in the promotion and marketing of their books; offers export services, consultancy and training; Chair. TIMOTHY WRIGHT; Dir LORRAINE FANNIN.

Broadcasting and Communications

TELECOMMUNICATIONS

Office of Telecommunications (Oftel): 50 Ludgate Hill, London, EC4M 7JJ; tel. (20) 7634-8700; fax (20) 7634-8845; e-mail infocent@oftel.gov.uk; internet www.oftel.org; f. 1984; under Tele-

communications Act as an independent regulatory body responsible for monitoring and enforcing the conditions of telecommunications licences; contributes to the development of policy to expand the existing regulatory framework in order to reflect the increasing convergence of telecommunications, information technology and broadcasting suppliers; to be replaced by Ofcom in 2003; Dir-Gen. DAVID EDMONDS.

Office of Communications (Ofcom): Riverside House, 2A Southwark Bridge Rd, London, SE1 9HA; tel. (20) 7981–3000; fax (20) 7981–3333; e-mail wwwenq@ofcom.org.com; internet www.ofcom .org.uk; will come into existence in late 2003 following the amalgamation of the Office of Telecommunications, the Broadcasting Standards Commission, the Radio Authority, the Independent Television Commission and the Radiocommunications Agency; Chair. Lord CURRIE OF MARYLEBONE; Chief Exec. STEPHEN CARTER.

British Telecommunications PLC: BT Centre, 81 Newgate St, London, EC1A 7AJ; tel. (20) 7356-5000; fax (20) 7356-5520; internet www.bt.com; wholly-owned subsidiary of BT Group PLC; Chair. Sir CHRISTOPHER BLAND; Chief Exec. BEN VERWAAYEN.

Crown Castle UK Ltd: Warwick Technology Park, Heathcote Lane, Warwick, CV34 6TN; tel. (1926) 416000; fax (20) 416600; e-mail marketinguk@crowncastle.com; internet www.crowncastle .com; Pres and Man. Dir PETER ABERY.

Cable and Wireless PLC: Caxton Way, Watford Business Park, Watford, WD1 8XH; tel. (20) 7528-2000; fax (20) 7528-2181; internet www.cwcom.co.uk; Chair. RICHARD LAPTHORNE; CEO FRANCESCO CAIO.

Energis: Crosby Ct, Bishopsgate, London, EC2N 4AF; tel. (20) 7360-5500; fax (20) 7360-5599; e-mail marta.judge@energis.com; internet www.energis.com; Chair. ARCHIE NORMAN; CEO DAVID WICKHAM.

Kingston Communications: Telephone House, Carr Lane, Hull, HU1 3RE; tel. (1482) 602100; fax (1482) 320652; e-mail publicrelations@kingston-comms.co.uk; internet www.kcom.com; Chair. MICHAEL ABRAHAMS; Chief Exec. STEVE MAINE.

NTL UK: NTL Bldg, 280 Barclay Wood Business Park, Barclay Way Hook, Reading, RG27 9XA; tel. (1256) 752000; fax (1256) 752100; internet www.ntl.com; Chair. and Chief Exec. BARCLAY KNAPP.

O2: 260 Bath Rd, Slough, Berks, SL1 4DX; tel. (1753) 504000; fax (1752) 565010; e-mail feedback@o2.com; internet www.o2.co.uk; formerly BT Cellnet; demerged from BT Group in October 2002 and part of the mmO$_2$ group; Group Chair. DAVID VARNEY.

Orange: 50 George St, London, W1U 7DZ; tel. (20) 7984-1600; fax (20) 7984-1601; internet www.orange.co.uk; f. 1994; acquired by France Telecom in 2000; part of the Orange SA (France) group; Chief Exec. SOLOMON TRUJILLO.

T-Mobile UK: Unit 3, Imperial Pl., Maxwell Rd, Borehamwood, Herts, WD6 1EA; tel. (20) 8214-2121; internet www.t-mobile.co.uk; owned by Deutsche Telekom AG; formerly One2One; Man. Dir BRIAN McBRIDE.

TeleWest Communications PLC: Export House, Causeway, Woking, Surrey, GU21 1QX; tel. (1483) 750900; fax (1483) 750901; internet www.telewest.co.uk; Chair. COB STENHAM; Man. Dir CHARLES BURDICK.

THUS plc: 1/2 Berkeley Sq., 99 Berkeley St, Glasgow, G3 7HR; tel. (141) 567-1234; fax (141) 566-3035; e-mail thus.enquiries@thus.net; internet www.thus.co.uk; f. 1994 as Scottish Telecom; changed name as above in 1999; Chief Exec. BILL ALLAN.

Vodafone Group PLC: The Courtyard, 2–4 London Rd, Newbury, Berks, RG14 1JX; tel. (1635) 33251; fax (1635) 45713; internet www .vodafone.co.uk; Chair. Lord MACLAURIN OF KNEBWORTH; Chief Exec. ARUN SARIN.

BROADCASTING

British Broadcasting Corporation (BBC): Broadcasting House, London, W1A 1AA; tel. (20) 7580-4468; fax (20) 7637-1630; internet www.bbc.co.uk; f. 1922; operates under Royal Charter. It is financed by the television licence fees; Chair. GAVYN DAVIES; Vice Chair. RICHARD RYDER; Dir-Gen. GREG DYKE; Dir of Drama, Entertainment and Children ALAN YENTOB; Dir of Television JANA BENNETT; Dir of Finance, Property and Business Affairs JOHN SMITH; Dir of Marketing and Communications ANDY DUNCAN; Dir of Nations and Regions PAT LOUGHREY; Chief Exec. BBC Ventures Group ROGER FLYNN; Dir of Human Resources and Internal Communications STEPHEN DANDO; Dir of Public Policy CAROLINE THOMSON; Dir of BBC News RICHARD SAMBROOK; Chief Exec. of BBC Worldwide RUPERT GAVIN; Dir of BBC World Service MARK BYFORD; Dir of Radio JENNY ABRAMSKY; Dir of Strategy CAROLYN FAIRBAIRN; Dir of Sport PETER SALMON; Dirs of Factual and Learning MICHAEL STEVENSON, GLENWYN BENSON; Dir of New Media ASHLEY HIGHFIELD.

Broadcasting Standards Commission: 7 The Sanctuary, London, SW1P 3JS; tel. (20) 7808-1000; fax (20) 7233-0397; e-mail bsc@bsc.org.uk; internet www.bsc.org.uk; f. 1997; by merger of the Broadcasting Standards Council and the Broadcasting Complaints Commission; statutory body under the 1996 Broadcasting Act, with a remit to research and monitor broadcasting standards in the United Kingdom, with respect to the broadcast portrayal of violence, sexual conduct and matters of taste and decency; considers and adjudicates on complaints from the public; produces a broadcasting Code of Practice; to be replaced by Ofcom in 2003; Chair. Lord DUBS OF BATTERSEA; Dir PAUL BOLT.

Radio

British Broadcasting Corporation

BBC Radio provides a service of five national networks throughout the United Kingdom, 38 local radio stations in England and the Channel Islands, Radio Scotland, Radio Wales, Radio Cymru, broadcasting in Welsh, and Radio Ulster; it also offers a number of specialist digital services; Dir of Radio JENNY ABRAMSKY.

Radio 1: broadcasts 24 hours a day of contemporary music programmes; Controller ANDREW PARFITT.

Radio 2: broadcasts popular music and culture; Controller JAMES MOIR.

Radio 3: provides 24-hour broadcasts of classical music, drama, talks and documentaries; Controller ROGER WRIGHT.

Radio 4: broadcasts news and current affairs and also provides a wide range of features, drama and discussions; Controller HELEN BOADEN.

Radio Five Live: began broadcasting in March 1994, replacing Radio 5; provides a 24-hour service of news and sports programmes; Controller BOB SHENNAN.

   Five Live Sports Extra: part-time digital network for sports events not broadcast elsewhere on BBC Radio.

6 Music: began broadcasting in 2002, digital station playing pop and rock music; Controller JAMES MOIR.

1Xtra: began broadcasting in 2002; digital station playing contemporary black music for a young audience; Controller ANDY PARFITT.

Asian Network: began broadcasting in 2002, digital station aimed at the Asian communities in the United Kingdom.

BBC7: digital radio station featuring archive material, began broadcasting in 2002; Editor MARY KALEMKERIAN.

BBC World Service: Bush House, Strand, London, WC2B 4PH; tel. (20) 7240-3456; fax (20) 7557-1258; e-mail worldservice.letters@bbc.co.uk; internet www.bbc.co.uk/worldservice; the World Service in English is broadcast for 24 hours daily and directed to all areas of the world. In addition, there are special services to: the Far East (in Mandarin, Cantonese, Indonesian, Thai and Vietnamese); the Indian sub-continent (in Bengali, Burmese, Hindi, Nepali, Pashto, Persian, Sinhala, Tamil and Urdu); the Caucasus and Central Asia (in Azeri, Kazakh, Kyrgyz, Uzbek and Russian); the Middle East and North Africa (in Arabic and French); Central, East, West and South Africa (in English, French, Hausa, Kinyarwanda/Kirundi, Portuguese, Somali and Swahili); and the Western Hemisphere (in Portuguese for Brazil and Spanish for Latin America). Services in the following languages are transmitted for listeners in Europe: Albanian, Bulgarian, Croatian, Czech and Slovak, Greek, Hungarian, Macedonian, Polish, Romanian, Russian, Serbian, Slovene and Turkish; Dir MARK BYFORD.

Independent National Radio

Radio Authority: Holbrook House, 14 Gt Queen St, London, WC2B 5DG; tel. (20) 7430-2724; fax (20) 7405-7064; e-mail info@radioauthority.org.uk; internet www.radioauthority.org.uk; f. 1991; regulatory body responsible for advertising and awarding licences to three national commercial radio channels (INR—Independent National Radio) and 260 local radio stations. Will be replaced by Ofcom in 2003. In August 1991 Classic FM was awarded the national franchise for INR-1, which began broadcasting in late 1992. In May 1992 Virgin Radio was awarded the franchise for INR-2, which began broadcasting in April 1993. The third national franchise was awarded in June 1994 to Talk Radio, which commenced broadcasts in February 1995. Talk Radio was relaunched as Talk Sport in January 2000 with a sports-focused service. A national licence to operate a multi-channel digital service was awarded in 1998 to Digital One, which began broadcasting in November 1999; to be replaced by Ofcom in late 2003; Chair. RICHARD HOOPER; Chief Exec. TONY STOLLER.

Radiocommunications Agency: Wyndham House, 189 Marsh Wall, London, E14 9SX; tel. (20) 7211-0211; fax (20) 7211-0507; internet www.radio.gov.uk; f. 1990 as executive agency of the Department of Trade and Industry; responsible for managing most non-military radio spectrum in the UK and representing the UK in

international discussions on radio spectrum; to be replaced by Ofcom in 2003; Chief Exec. ROLANDE ANDERSON.

Classic FM: Classic FM House, 7 Swallow Pl., London, W1B 2AG; tel. (20) 7343-9000; fax (20) 7344-2700; e-mail enquiries@classicfm.com; internet www.classicfm.com; began broadcasting September 1992; popular classical music; Chair. Sir PETER MICHAEL; Man. Dir ROGER LEWIS.

Independent Radio News (IRN): 200 Gray's Inn Rd, London, WC1X 8XZ; tel. (20) 7430-4814; e-mail news@irn.co.uk; internet www.irn.co.uk; f. 1973; produced by ITN Radio; news agency for the independent local radio network; Man. Dir JOHN PERKINS.

TalkSport UK: POB 1089, London, SE1 8WQ; tel. (20) 7959-7800; internet www.talksport.co.uk; began broadcasting February 1995 as Talk Radio UK; name changed as above January 2000; Propr The Wireless Group; Chair. and Chief Exec. KELVIN MACKENZIE.

Virgin Radio (Virgin 1215): 1 Golden Sq., London, W1R 4DJ; tel. (20) 7434-1215; fax (20) 7434-1197; e-mail reception@ginger.com; internet www.virginradio.co.uk; began broadcasting April 1993; popular music; Propr Ginger Media Group; Chief Exec. JOHN PEARSON.

Television

British Broadcasting Corporation

BBC Television: Television Centre, Wood Lane, London, W12 7RJ; tel. (20) 8743-8000; internet www.bbc.co.uk/tv; operates two terrestrial services, BBC-1 and BBC-2, and six digital channels, BBC Choice, BBC-4, CBeebies, CBBC, BBC News 24 and BBC Parliament; Dir of Television ALAN YENTOB.

   BBC-1: internet www.bbc.co.uk/bbcone; provides a coverage of over 99% of the population of the United Kingdom. Colour service began in 1969; a breakfast-time television service began in 1983; Controller LORRAINE HEGGESSEY.

   BBC-2: internet www.bbc.co.uk/two; opened in 1964, and is available to 99% of the population. Colour service began in 1967; Controller JANE ROOT.

   BBC-3: internet www.bbc.co.uk/choice; digital entertainment channel; Controller STUART MURPHY.

   BBC-4: internet www.bbc.co.uk/bbcfour; digital channel showing in-depth cultural programmes; Controller ROLY KEATING.

   CBeebies: digital service aimed at under-fives.

   CBBC: Room E917 BBC TV Centre, Wood Lane, London, W12 7RJ; e-mail cbbc.online@bbc.co.uk; internet www.bbc.co.uk/cbbc; digital service for children aged six to 13.

   BBC News 24: 24 hour digital news service.

   BBC Parliament: 4 Millbank, London SW1P 3JA; tel. (20) 7973-6216; internet www.bbc.co.uk/bbcparliament; provides coverage from the Houses of Parliament and the devolved Parliament and Assemblies in Scotland Wales and Northern Ireland.

Independent Television

Independent Television Commission (ITC): 33 Foley St, London, W1W 7TL; tel. (845) 601-3608; fax (20) 7306-7800; e-mail publicaffairs@itc.org.uk; internet www.itc.org.uk; f. 1954 as the Independent Television Authority, renamed Independent Broadcasting Authority 1972 and Independent Television Commission 1991; public body responsible for licensing and regulating all commercially-funded television in the United Kingdom, including Independent Television (ITV—which was renamed Channel 3 from 1 Jan. 1993), Channel 4, Channel 5, cable, satellite and digital services, public teletext and certain other text and data services; The ITC has a duty, under the Broadcasting Act of 1990, to ensure the variety and quality of programme services and to ensure that there is effective competition in the provision of such services. The ITC has the statutory powers to impose penalties on licensees if they do not comply with their licence conditions; in late 2003 the ITC will become part of Ofcom (see above).

In October 1991 the ITC, in accordance with the provisions of the Broadcasting Act of 1990, awarded the 16 licences that constituted the renamed Channel 3 (ITV 1). The franchises were allocated by a system of competitive tendering, although the ITC was empowered to select a company presenting a lower bid in 'exceptional circumstances'. The new licences came into force on 1 January 1993, when Channel 4 (q.v.) also became an ITC licensee. By the end of 1995 the ITC had also issued 183 non-domestic satellite and licensable programme service licences. In October 1995 the ITC awarded the licence for the fifth terrestrial channel to Channel 5 Broadcasting; broadcasting commenced in March 1997. In June the ITC awarded the British Digital Broadcasting consortium (ONdigital, later renamed ITV Digital) three licences to operate digital terrestrial television (DTT) services in the United Kingdom. Following the collapse of ITV Digital in April 2002, the ITC withdrew the consortium's licences and in May it announced that they were to be retendered; in August one licence was awarded to the BBC and two to Crown Castle. DTV Services Ltd, a consortium of the BBC, Crown View and BSkyB, subsequently announced its plans to launch Freeview, which would provide a wide range of free-to-view digital television channels. Freeview commenced broadcasting in late 2002; Chair. Sir ROBIN BIGGAM; Chief Exec. PATRICIA HODGSON.

Channel Four Television Corpn: 124 Horseferry Rd, London, SW1P 2TX; tel. (20) 7396-4444; internet www.channel4.com; f. 1980; began broadcasting 1982; national television service; available to 97% of the population; financed by advertising; in accordance with the Broadcasting Act (1990), Channel Four became a public corporation and ITC licensee, responsible for selling its own advertising, from January 1993; Chair. VANNI TREVES; Chief Exec. MARK THOMPSON.

five: 22 Long Acre, London, WC2E 9LY; tel. (20) 7550-5555; internet www.channel5.co.uk; awarded licence for fifth national terrestrial channel in October 1995; commenced broadcasting on 30 March 1997 as Channel 5; renamed as above in 2002; owned by United Business Media and RTL; Chair. REMY SAUTTER; Chief Exec. JANE LIGHTING.

Independent Television News Ltd (ITN): 200 Gray's Inn Rd, London, WC1X 8XZ; tel. (20) 7833-3000; internet www.itn.co.uk; f. 1955; Granada Media Group, Daily Mail and General Trust PLC, Carlton Communications, Reuters Holdings and United Business Media each hold a 20% stake; provides all national and international news bulletins for the ITV network and news programming for Channel 4 and five; became a profit-making company in 1993; Chair. MARK WOOD; Chief Exec. STEWART PURVIS.

S4C Welsh Fourth Channel Authority (Awdurdod Sianel Pedwar Cymru): Parc Ty Glas, Llanishen, Cardiff, CF4 5DU; tel. (29) 2074-7444; fax (29) 2075-4444; e-mail s4c@s4c.co.uk; internet www.s4c.co.uk; f. 1982; television service for Wales; Chair. ELAN CLOSS STEPHENS; Chief Exec. HUW JONES.

Independent Television (ITV—Channel 3) Companies

Independent Television Association Ltd (ITV): ITV Network Centre, 200 Grays Inn Rd, London, WC1X 8HF; tel. (20) 7843-8000; fax (20) 7843-8158; e-mail info@itv.co.uk; internet www.itv.co.uk; f. 1956; from 1992 the central co-ordinating body for Channel 3 (ITV 1); the Asscn's Council comprises the Managing Directors of all Channel 3 companies; Chair. LESLIE HILL; Joint Chief Execs MICK DESMOND, CLIVE JONES.

Anglia Television Ltd: Anglia House, Norwich, NR1 3JG; 48 Leicester Sq., London, WC2H 7FB; tel. (1603) 615151; fax (1603) 631032; tel. (20) 7389-8555; e-mail angliatv@angliatv.co.uk; internet www.anglia.tv.com; East of England; Propr Granada Media Group; Chair. CHARLES ALLEN; Man. Dir GRAHAM CREELMAN.

Border Television PLC: Television Centre, Carlisle, CA1 3NT; tel. (1228) 525101; fax (1228) 541384; internet www.border-tv.com; Borders and the Isle of Man; acquired by Granada Media Group in July 2001; Chair. JAMES L. GRAHAM; Chief Exec. PAUL CORLEY.

Carlton Broadcasting: 101 St Martin's Lane, London, WC2N 4AZ; tel. (20) 7240-4000; fax (20) 7615-1775; internet www.carlton.com; London area, Monday to Thursday, Friday to 5.15 p.m. began broadcasting in January 1993 (replacing Thames Television Ltd); licensee of Carlton Television Ltd; Chair. MICHAEL GREEN; Chief Exec. GERALD MURPHY.

Carlton Broadcasting, Westcountry Region: Western Wood Way, Langage Science Park, Plymouth PL7 5BQ; tel. (1752) 333333; fax (1752) 333444; e-mail dutyofficewestcountry@carltontv.co.uk; internet www.carlton.com; south-west England; began broadcasting in January 1993; licensee of Carlton Television Ltd; Chair. MICHAEL GREEN; Man. Dir MARK HASKELL.

Carlton Broadcasting, Central Region: Central House, Gas St, Birmingham, B1 2JT; tel. (121) 643-9898; fax (121) 643-4740; internet www.centraltv.co.uk; South, East and West Midlands; licensee of Carlton Television Ltd; Chair. MICHAEL GREEN; Man. Dir IAN SQUIRES.

Channel Television Ltd: The Television Centre, St Helier, Jersey, JE1 3ZD; tel. (1534) 816816; fax (1534) 816817; e-mail broadcast@channeltv.co.uk; internet www.channeltv.co.uk; Chair. FRANCIS HAMON; Chief Exec. HUW DAVIES.

Good Morning TV (GMTV): c/o London TV Centre, London, SE1 9TT; tel. (20) 7827-7000; fax (20) 7827-7249; internet www.gmtv.co.uk; nationwide breakfast-time service; began broadcasting in January 1993 (replacing TV-am PLC); Chair. CHARLES ALLEN; Man. Dir CHRISTOPHER STODDART.

Grampian Television Ltd: Queen's Cross, Aberdeen, AB15 4XJ; tel. (1224) 846846; fax (1224) 846800; e-mail gtv@grampiantv.co.uk; internet www.grampiantv.co.uk; north Scotland; acquired by Scot-

tish Media Group in June 1997; Chair. Dr CALUM A. MACLEOD; Man. Dir DERRICK THOMSON.

Granada Television Ltd: Granada TV Centre, Quay St, Manchester, M60 9EA; tel. and fax (161) 832-7211; internet www.granadatv.co.uk; north-west England; Chairman CHARLES ALLEN; Chief Exec. STEVE MORRISON.

HTV Ltd: HTV Wales, Television Centre, Culverhouse Cross, Cardiff, CF5 6XJ; HTV West, The Television Centre, Bath Rd, Bristol, BS4 3HG; tel. (29) 2059-0590; fax (29) 2059-7183; e-mail htv@htv-wales.co.uk; internet www.htv-wales.co.uk; tel. (1179) 722722; fax (1179) 722400; e-mail htv@htv.co.uk; internet www.htv-west.com; fmrly Harlech Television; Wales and the West of England; acquired by Carlton Communications in October 2000; Chief Exec., United Broadcasting and Entertainment MALCOLM WALL.

London Weekend Television Ltd (LWT): The London Television Centre, Upper Ground, London, SE1 9LT; tel. (20) 7620-1620; fax (20) 7261-1290; e-mail feedback@lwt.co.uk; internet www.lwt.co.uk; London area and the South East, 5.15 p.m. Friday to closedown on Sunday; Propr Granada Media Group; Chief Exec. STEVE MORRISON.

Meridian Broadcasting Ltd: Television Centre, Northam, Southampton, Hants, SO14 0PZ; tel. (23) 8022-2555; fax (23) 8033-5050; internet www.meridiantv.com; south and south-east England; began broadcasting in January 1993; Propr Granada Media Group; Chair. Sir WILLIAM (BILL) COTTON; Man. Dir LYNDSAY CHARLTON.

Scottish Television PLC: Cowcaddens, Glasgow, G2 3PR; tel. (141) 300-3000; fax (141) 300-3030; internet www.scottishtv.co.uk; f. 1957; central Scotland; Propr Scottish Media Group; Chair. DONALD CRUICKSHANK; Chief Exec. ANDREW FLANAGAN.

Tyne Tees Television Ltd: Television Centre, City Rd, Newcastle upon Tyne, NE1 2AL; tel. (191) 261 0181; fax (191) 261-2302; e-mail tyne.tees@granadamedia.com; internet www.tynetees-tv.co.uk; North-east England; acquired by Granada Media Group in 1997; Man. Dir MARGARET FAY; Dir of Broadcasting GRAEME THOMPSON.

Yorkshire Television Ltd: Television Centre, Leeds, LS3 1JS; tel. (113) 243-8283; fax (113) 244-5107; internet www.yorkshire-tv.co.uk; acquired by Granada Media Group in 1997; Man. Dir DAVID M. B. CROFT.

Satellite and Cable Broadcasting

There were 5,498,000 households in the United Kingdom subscribing to digital satellite television in September 2001 with a further 3,680,000 households subscribing to cable television (digital 1,860,000; analogue 1,820,000). The major satellite and cable television companies are listed below.

BBC Worldwide Television: Woodlands, 80 Wood Lane, London W12 0TT; tel. (20) 8576-2700; fax (20) 8576-2782; began broadcasting in 1991; part of BBC Worldwide Ltd; broadcasts 24-hour news and information ('BBC World') and light entertainment programmes to Europe ('BBC Prime'); other news programmes broadcast to Africa, Asia (including a Japanese-language service to Japan), the Middle East, Australia and New Zealand; Chief Exec. RUPERT GAVIN.

British Sky Broadcasting Group PLC: Grant Way, Isleworth, Middlesex, TW7 5QD; tel. (870) 240-3000; fax (870) 240-3060; internet www.sky.com; f. 1990; by merger of British Satellite Broadcasting (BSB) and Sky TV PLC (a subsidiary of News International); satellite broadcaster and programme provider; multi-channel digital television service SkyDigital (see below); Chair. RUPERT MURDOCH; CEO and Man. Dir TONY BALL.

Cable News Network Inc (CNN): 16 Great Marlborough St., London, W1F 7HS; tel. (20) 7693-1000; fax (20) 7693-1550; internet www.cnn.com; Senior Vice Pres. Europe, Middle East and Africa TONY MADDOX.

Eurosport UK: 55 Drury Lane, London, WC2B 5SQ; tel. (20) 7468-7777; fax (20) 7468-0023; e-mail network@eurosport.co.uk; internet www.eurosport.co.uk; began broadcasting in 1989; Dir E. FLORENT.

MTV Networks Europe: 180 Oxford St, London, W1D 1DS1; tel. (20) 7284-7777; fax (20) 7284-7788; internet www.mtv.co.uk; began broadcasting in 1987; popular music; Pres. BRENT HANSEN.

NTL: NTL Bldg, 280 Barclay Wood Business Park, Barclay Way Hook, Reading, RG27 9XA; tel. (118) 9544000; internet www.ntl.com; Chair GEORGE BLUMENTHAL; Chief Exec. BARCLAY KNAPP.

UK TV: 2nd Floor, 160 Great Portland St, London, W1W 5QA; tel. (20) 7299-5000; fax (20) 7299-6000; internet www.flextech.co.uk; began broadcasting 1992; satellite, cable and DTT; Chief Exec. RICHARD EMERY.

Digital Television

The first digital television services became available in 1998. Digital television is envisaged as a replacement to existing analogue frequencies, available by cable, satellite and terrestrial operators. In

April 2002, following the collapse of ITV Digital, the Independent Television Committee (ITC) invited tenders for the licences to operate digital terrestrial television services in the United Kingdom. In August the ITC awarded one licence to the BBC and two to Crown Castle, who combined to provide Freeview.

Freeview: 2nd Floor, 85 Tottenham Court Rd, London, W1T 4DU; tel. (8708) 809980; internet www.freeview.co.uk; f. 2002; a consortium of the BBC, Crown Castle and BSkyB providing Freeview, a digital service offering 28 television station and additional interactive services; commenced transmission in late 2002.

SkyDigital: 6 Centaurs Business Park, Grant Way, Isleworth, Middlesex, TW7 5QD; tel. (20) 7705-3000; fax (20) 7705-3030; internet www.sky.com; owned by British Sky Broadcasting Group PLC; Chief Exec. TONY BALL.

Finance

The United Kingdom's central bank is the Bank of England, which was established by Act of Parliament and Royal Charter in 1694 and nationalized under the Bank of England Act 1946. The Scottish and Northern Ireland banks issue their own notes but these are largely covered by holdings of Bank of England notes.

The Bank of England holds the main government accounts, acts as registrar of government stocks and as agent of the Government for a number of financial operations. It is also banker to a number of commercial banks. The London clearing banks maintain a substantial proportion of their total cash holdings in the form of balances at the Bank and these are used in the settlement of daily cheque and credit clearings. The Bank has traditionally been responsible for advising the Government on the formulation of monetary policy and for its subsequent execution. In May 1997 the newly-elected Labour Government announced its intention to introduce legislation to amend the 1946 Bank of England Act in order to accord the Bank statutory operational independence for monetary policy, within agreed government economic targets. The new Bank of England Act received Royal Assent in April 1998, and entered into force on 1 June. The Act provided for the establishment of a Monetary Policy Committee (MPC), with responsibility for analysing and formulating monetary policy within the framework of maintaining price stability and supporting the Government's economic policies. The Treasury was to reserve the right to direct the Bank with respect to monetary decisions in extreme circumstances. The MPC was to comprise the Governor of the Bank, the two newly-created Deputy-Governors, two other Bank officials and four members appointed by the Chancellor of the Exchequer. The Bank's Court of Directors was to review the MPC's procedures and produce an annual report, to be presented to Parliament, under new measures to promote greater accountability and transparency of the Bank's operations. The 1998 Act also transferred, to the Financial Services Authority, the Bank's functions with regard to the supervision of banks.

The commercial banks may be divided into two broad categories: clearing banks and other banks. Clearing banks play the main part in operating the money transmission system throughout the UK. The other banks comprise accepting houses (taking their name from their business of accepting bills of exchange for payment) and other UK-owned banks, overseas-owned banks and consortium banks. As the use of bills of exchange has declined, all accepting houses have assumed the specialist financial services of merchant banks, which include the management of investment trusts, foreign currency trading and company mergers and acquisitions. Since the late 1980s several merchant banks have been incorporated into larger banking organizations to provide a full range of financial, including retail, banking services.

Consortium banks have been formed in the UK by groups of banks, mostly from overseas, but including some British clearing banks. Initially they were set up to afford shareholders access to the Eurocurrency markets. More recently consortia have been formed as a means of combining institutions from similar geographical areas, when a London operation would be uneconomic for individual banks. Consortium banks are important participants in the major interbank markets in sterling and currency deposits and certificates of deposit.

The discount houses are a specialized group of institutions peculiar to London. They raise the greater part of their funds from within the banking sector. These funds are borrowed by the houses at call or short notice (thereby providing the lending banks with a highly liquid interest-bearing investment) and are used to purchase correspondingly liquid assets—mainly Treasury and commercial bills, short-dated government stocks, certificates of deposit, local authority debt, etc. The discount houses are now more generally incorporated as part of the group of banks authorized by the Bank as listed money market institutions under the 1986 Financial Services Act. The United Kingdom's official reserves, comprising gold, convertible currencies and special drawing rights on the International Monetary Fund, are held in the Exchange Equalization Account operated since 1932 by the Bank of England as agent for the Treasury.

The London Gold Market engages in the trading, transporting, refining, melting, assaying and vaulting of gold. The unique feature of the London market is the 'fixing', which determines the price of gold on a twice-daily basis by matching orders from customers and markets throughout the world. In September 1996 the London Commodity Exchange merged with the London International Financial Futures and Options Exchange (LIFFE), which has since become unique as an exchange trading options on individual equities and on financial, agricultural, soft commodity and equity index products. In October 2001 the French-based Euronext security market acquired LIFFE for a sum of £555m.

The building society movement is important both as a medium of savings (the largest in the United Kingdom) and for the finance of house purchase in a country where more than two-thirds (67% in 1995) of dwellings are owner-occupied. The expansion of building societies into banking was a characteristic of the late 1980s. This trend was furthered in the 1990s with several large building societies converting to banks through public share offers or opting to merge with similar institutions or with retail banks in order to provide a comprehensive range of financial services. In 2001 there were 48 societies registered in the United Kingdom, compared with 190 in 1984.

National Savings are administered by the Department for National Savings and the Trustee Savings Banks. Through the Department for National Savings the Government administers the National Savings Bank 'investment' and 'ordinary' accounts, National Savings certificates, Premium bonds and other securities, all aimed primarily at the small saver. The outlets for these services are some 20,000 post offices in the United Kingdom.

There are certain institutions set up to provide finance for specific purposes; the more important of these are the 3i Group PLC (which provides investment capital to companies which do not have ready access to capital markets) and the Agricultural Mortgage Corporation (loans against mortgages on agricultural property).

The main capital market is the London Stock Exchange, and since October 1986 the volume of business transacted has greatly expanded with the introduction of the Stock Exchange Automated Quotations system (SEAQ), an electronic trading system which allows off-floor trading. The process of automating trading was completed in October 1997 when the Stock Exchange Electronic Trading Service (Sets) became operational.

The United Kingdom has a highly developed insurance market, located primarily in London. Lloyd's, with its unique system of underwriting syndicates (of which there are about 230) has an international reputation for marine, aviation and reinsurance, as well as a significant share of the British motor insurance market. Almost two-thirds of Lloyd's premium income comes from outside the United Kingdom through Lloyd's 219 accredited brokers. There are over 800 authorized insurance companies in the United Kingdom, dealing with life and general insurance, as well as international reinsurance.

BANKING

(cap. = capital; p.u. = paid up; auth. = authorized; m. = million; dep. = deposits; res = reserves; subs. = subscribed; brs = branches; amounts in pounds sterling)

The 1987 Banking Act replaced the Banking Act of 1979 under which a statutory framework for the supervision of the banking sector was established. The 1987 Act defines new criteria by which an institution can be authorized to accept deposits. The administrative authority for the Act is the Bank of England. In February 1997 the Bank of England recorded 554 authorized banking institutions in the United Kingdom.

The Financial Ombudsman Service: South Quay Plaza, 183 Marsh Wall, London, E14 9SR; tel. (20) 7964-1000; fax (20) 7405-5052; e-mail enquiries@financial-ombudsman.org.uk; internet www.financial-ombudsman.org.uk; f. 2001 to replace The Personal Investment Authority Ombudsman Bureau, The Insurance Ombudsman Bureau, The Office of the Banking Ombudsman, The Office of the Building Societies Ombudsman, The Office of the Investment Ombudsman, The Securities and Futures Authority Complaints Bureau, The Financial Services Authority Complaints Unit and The Personal Insurance Arbitration Service; Chair. SUE SLIPMAN; Chief Ombudsman WALTER MERRICKS.

Central Bank

Bank of England: Threadneedle St, London, EC2R 8AH; tel. (20) 7601-4444; fax (20) 7601-4771; e-mail enquiries@bankofengland.co.uk; internet www.bankofengland.co.uk; inc. by Royal Charter in 1694, and nationalized by Act of Parliament on 1 March 1946; amended by 1998 Bank of England Act (see above); the Government's banker and on its behalf manages the note issue; also the bankers' bank; mem. of the Clearing House; br. at Leeds; agencies in Belfast, Birmingham, Bristol, Cambridge, Cardiff, Glasgow, Leeds, Liverpool, Manchester, Newcastle upon Tyne, Nottingham and Southampton; capital stock amounting to 14.6m. is held by the Treasury; res 242m., dep. 21,972m. (Feb. 2001); Gov. Sir EDWARD (EDDIE) GEORGE; (from July 2003 Prof. Mervyn King); Deputy Govs Sir ANDREW LARGE, Prof. MERVYN KING.

Principal Banks Incorporated in Great Britain

Abbey National PLC: Abbey National House, 2 Triton Sq., Regent's Place, London, NW1 3AN; tel. (20) 7612-4000; fax (20) 7612-4010; internet www.abbeynational.co.uk; f. 1944 as Abbey National Building Society; current status assumed in 1989; total assets 214,906m. (Dec. 2001); Chair. Lord BURNS; Chief Exec. LUQMAN ARNOLD; 793 brs.

Alliance & Leicester PLC: Carlton Park, Narborough, Leicester, LE19 0AL; tel. (116) 201-1000; fax (116) 200-4040; internet www.alliance-leicester.co.uk; fmrly a building society; assumed banking status in 1997; broad-based financial services provider incl. business banking services through wholly-owned subsidiary, Girobank; dep. 35,000m., total assets 39,000m. (Dec. 2001); Chief Exec. RICHARD PYM; 309 brs.

Barclays Bank PLC: 54 Lombard St, London, EC3P 3AH; tel. (20) 7699-5000; fax (20) 7699-2460; internet www.barclays.co.uk; inc. 1896; clearing bank; principal operating co of Barclays PLC (group holding co); cap. 1,668m., res 6,028m., dep. 274,591m. (Dec. 2001); Group Chair. Sir PETER MIDDLETON; Chief Exec. MATTHEW BARRETT; 3,500 brs in 76 countries.

Cheltenham and Gloucester PLC: Barnett Way, Gloucester, GL4 3RL; tel. (1452) 372372; fax (1452) 373955; e-mail general-enquiries@cgdirect.demon.co.uk; internet www.cheltglos.co.uk; f. 1850 as Cheltenham and Gloucester Benefit Building Society; current name and status assumed in 1995; mem. of the Lloyds TSB Group; cap. 508.3m., res 1,084.6m., dep. 45,979.4m. (Dec. 2000); Chair. ALAN E. MOORE; Man. Dir ROGER F. BURDEN.

Clydesdale Bank PLC: 30 St Vincent Pl., Glasgow, G1 2HL; tel. (141) 248-7070; fax (141) 204-0828; internet www.cbonline.co.uk; f. 1838; wholly-owned by National Australia Bank Ltd; clearing bank; cap. 204.8m., res 50.0m., dep. 8,299.2m. (Sept. 2001); Chair. Lord SANDERSON OF BOWDEN; Chief Executive STEVE TARGETT; COO DAVID THORBURN; 307 brs.

The Co-operative Bank PLC: POB 101, 1 Balloon St, Manchester, M60 4EP; tel. (161) 832-3456; fax (161) 829-4475; e-mail jennie@co-operativebank.co.uk; internet www.co-operativebank.co.uk; f. 1872; clearing bank; cap. 95m., dep. 6,940.8m., total assets 7,826.2m. (Jan. 2002); Chair. G. R. BENNETT; Chief Exec. MERVYN PEDELTY; 158 brs.

Coutts and Co: 440 Strand, London, WC2R 0QS; tel. (20) 7753-1000; fax (20) 7649-4600; internet www.coutts.com; f. 1692; private clearing bank and asset management; parent co Royal Bank Of Scotland Group PLC; cap. 41.3m., dep. 7,390.8m. (Dec. 1996); Chair. EARL OF HOME; Chief Exec. ANDREW FISHER; 22 brs.

HBOS PLC: The Mound, Edinburgh, EH1 1YZ; tel. (131) 442-7777; fax (131) 243-5537; e-mail pressoffice@hbosplc.com; internet www.hbosplc.com; f. 2001; following merger between Bank of Scotland and Halifax PLC; cap. 449m., res 10m., dep. 133,935m. (Dec. 2000); Chair. Lord STEVENSON; Chief Exec. JAMES CROSBY.

HSBC Bank PLC: 27–32 Poultry, London, EC2P 2BX; tel. (20) 7260-8000; fax (20) 7260-7065; internet www.hsbc.co.uk; f. 1836; from 1992 subsidiary of HSBC Holdings PLC; clearing bank; cap. 797m., res 12,175m., dep. 157,678m. (Dec 2001); Chair. Sir JOHN BOND; Chief Exec. STEPHEN GREEN; 1,700 brs.

Lloyds TSB Bank PLC: 71 Lombard St, London, EC3P 3BS; tel. (20) 7626-1500; internet www.lloydstsb.co.uk; f. 1995 by merger of Lloyds Bank PLC (f. 1765) and TSB Group (f. 1973), name changed as above June 1999; clearing bank; cap. 1,411m. (Dec. 2001); Chair. MAARTEN VAN DEN BERGH; Chief Exec. ERIC DANIELS; 2,500 brs.

Lloyds TSB Scotland PLC: POB 177, Henry Duncan House, 120 George St, Edinburgh, EH2 4TS; tel. (131) 225-4555; fax (131) 220-4217; internet www.lloydstsbscotland.com; f. 1983 as TSB Bank Scotland PLC following merger of four Scottish TSBs; wholly-owned subsidiary of Lloyds TSB Group PLC; cap. 75m., dep. 3,947.4m. (Dec. 2001); Chair. Prof. EWAN BROWN; Chief Exec. S. RICE; 186 brs.

National Westminster Bank PLC: 135 Bishopsgate, London, EC2M 3UR; tel. (20) 7375-5000; fax (20) 7375-5050; internet www.natwest.co.uk; f. 1968; clearing bank; acquired by The Royal Bank of Scotland Group PLC in 2000; cap. 2,187m., dep. 150,137m., total assets 186,233m. (Dec. 2000); Chair. Sir GEORGE ROSS MATHEWSON; Group Chief Exec. FRED GOODWIN; 2,416 brs.

Northern Rock PLC: Northern Rock House, Gosforth, Tyne and Wear, NE3 4PL; tel. (191) 285-7191; fax (191) 284-8470; internet www.northernrock.co.uk; current status assumed in 1997; cap.

123.9m., res 314.1m., dep. 23,797.6m. (Dec. 2001); Chair. Sir JOHN RIDDELL; Chief Exec. ADAM APPLEGARTH.

The Royal Bank of Scotland PLC: POB 31, 42 St Andrew Sq., Edinburgh, EH2 2YE; tel. (131) 556-8555; fax (131) 557-6565; internet www.rbs.co.uk; f. 1985 as result of merger of Royal Bank of Scotland and Williams & Glyn's Bank. The Royal Bank of Scotland (est. by Royal Charter in 1727) merged with National Commercial Bank of Scotland in 1969. Williams & Glyn's Bank was result of merger of Glyn Mills & Co (est. 1753) and Williams Deacon's Bank (est. 1771); subsidiary of The Royal Bank of Scotland Group PLC; clearing bank; cap. 893m., res 20,654m., dep. 271,811m. (Sept. 2001); Chair. Sir GEORGE ROSS MATHEWSON; Group Chief Exec. FRED GOODWIN; 680 brs.

Standard Chartered Bank: 1 Aldermanbury Sq., London, EC2V 7SB; tel. (20) 7280-7500; fax (20) 7280-7791; internet www.standardchartered.com; f. 1853; holding co Standard Chartered PLC; cap. US $861m., res US $2,811m., dep. US $83,249m. (Dec. 2001); Chair. Sir PATRICK GILLAM; Chief Exec. MERVYN DAVIES; 570 brs.

Woolwich PLC: Watling St, Bexleyheath, Kent, DA6 7RR; tel. (20) 8298-5000; fax (1322) 555621; internet www.woolwich.co.uk; f. 1847 as Woolwich Building Society; assumed present status in July 1997, acquired by Barclays PLC in October 2000; res 58.2m., dep. 32,072.7m. (Dec. 2000); Chair. Sir PETER MIDDLETON; Chief Exec. LYNNE M. PEACOCK; 402 brs.

Yorkshire Bank PLC: 56–58 Cheapside, London, EC2P 2BA; Regd Office: 20 Merrion Way, Leeds, LS2 8NZ; tel. (20) 7248-1791; tel. (113) 247-2000; fax (113) 242-0733; internet www.ybonline.co.uk; f. 1859; wholly-owned by National Australia Bank Ltd; cap. 251.1m., res 88.4m., dep. 7,066.8m. (Sept. 2001); Chief Executive STEVE TARGETT; COO PAUL FEGAN; 260 brs.

Principal Merchant Banks

Ansbacher & Co Ltd: 1 Mitre Sq., London, EC3A 5AN; tel. (20) 7283-2500; fax (20) 7626-0839; e-mail info@ansbacher.com; internet www.ansbacher.com; f. 1894; cap. 50.0m., res 0.9m., dep. 787.5m. (June 2001); Man. Dir S. F. JENNINGS.

Banc of America Securities Ltd: 1 Alie St, POB 407, London, E1 8DE; tel. (20) 7634-4000; fax (20) 7634-4334; internet www.bankofamerica.com; f. 1971; cap. US $426.9m., res US $333.5m., dep. US $6,346.3m. (Dec. 2000); Pres. WILLIAM FALL; Man. Dir JOHN WEGUELIN.

Barclays Capital: 5 The North Colonnade, Canary Wharf, London, E14 4BB; tel. (20) 7623-2323; e-mail publisher@barclayscapital.com; internet www.barcap.com; investment banking division of Barclays PLC; Chief Exec. ROBERT E. DIAMOND, Jnr.

Brown, Shipley & Co Ltd: Founders Court, Lothbury, London, EC2R 7HE; tel. (20) 7606-9833; fax (20) 7282-3274; e-mail marketing@brownshipley.com; internet www.brownshipley.com; f. 1810; acquired by Kredietbank SA Luxembourgeoise in 1992; cap. issued 86.4m., dep. 573.7m. (Dec. 2001); Chair. RICHARD MANSELL-JONES; Man. Dir PATRICK MOORSOM.

Cater Allen Ltd: 20 Birchin Lane, London, EC3V 9HN; tel. (20) 7623-2070; fax (20) 7645-6587; e-mail info@caterallen.co.uk; internet www.caterallen.co.uk; f. 1981; by merger of Cater Ryder and Co Ltd (f. 1816) and Allen Harvey and Ross Ltd (f. 1888); acquired by Abbey National Treasury Services in 1997; cap. 30m., dep. 15,969.9m. (Dec. 1997); Chair. MALCOLM MILLINGTON; Man. Dir RICHARD J. WISE.

Citibank International PLC: 336 Strand, POB 242, London, WC2R 1HB; tel. (20) 7500-5000; fax (20) 7500-1695; f. 1972; cap. 393.6m., res 246.9m., dep. 9,209.3m. (Dec. 2000); Chair. and Chief Exec. FRANCESCO VANNI D'ARCHIRAFI.

Citigroup: Victoria Plaza, 111 Buckingham Palace Rd, London, SW1W 0SB; tel. (20) 7721-2000; fax (20) 7222-7062; f. 2000; by merger of J. Henry Schroder & Co Ltd and Salomon Smith Barney, changed name to above in 2001; Chairs CHARLES McVEIGH, DAVID CHALLEN.

Close Brothers Ltd: 10 Crown Pl., London, EC2A 4FT; tel. (20) 7655-3100; fax (20) 7426-4044; e-mail enquiries@closebrothers.co.uk; internet www.closebrothers.co.uk; cap. 82.5m., res 109.4m., dep. 1,881.3m. (Dec. 2001); Chair. R. D. KENT; Man. Dir S. R. HODGES.

Dresdner Kleinwort Wasserstein Ltd: 20 Fenchurch St, London, EC3P 3DB; tel. (20) 7623-8000; fax (20) 7623-4069; e-mail website@drkw.com; internet www.dresdnerkb.com; wholly-owned subsidiary of Kleinwort Benson Group; ultimate holding co Dresdner Bank AG; share cap. 243.5m., res 72.6m., dep. 2,503.5m. (Dec. 2000); Chair. TIMOTHY SHACKLOCK.

Robert Fleming & Co Ltd: 10 Aldermanbury, London, EC2V 7RF; tel. (20) 7742-4000; fax (20) 7742-8000; internet www.flemings.co.uk; f. 1932; cap. 142.7m., dep. 6,721.7m. (March 2000); Chair. MARK GARVIN.

HSBC Investment Bank PLC: Thames Exchange, 10 Queen St Pl., London, EC4R 1BL; tel. (20) 7260-9000; fax (20) 7621-0496; internet www.hsbcib.com; wholly-owned subsidiary of HSBC Holdings PLC (parent co of Hongkong and Shanghai Banking Corpn); incorporates James Capel and Co Ltd (f. 1775) and Samuel Montagu and Co Ltd (f. 1853); cap. 205.0m., dep. 6,740.1m. (Dec. 2000); Chair. S. K. GREEN.

Investec Bank (UK) Ltd: 2 Gresham St, London, EC2V 7QP; tel. (20) 7597-4000; fax (20) 7597-4070; internet www.investec.com; f. 1977 as Allied Arab Bank Ltd, name changed as above 1997; acquired Guinness Mahon & Co Ltd 1998; cap. 292.0m. res 37.4m. dep. 7,366.6m. (March 2000); Chair. B. KARDOL; CEO ALAN TAPNACK.

Leopold Joseph and Sons Ltd: 29 Gresham St, London, EC2V 7EA; tel. (20) 7588-2323; fax (20) 7726-0105; e-mail ljlondon@ leopoldjoseph.com; internet www.leopoldjoseph.com; f. 1919; wholly-owned by Leopold Joseph Holdings PLC; cap. 5.4m., res 13.0m., dep. 495.5m. (March 2001); Chair. ROBIN HERBERT; Chief Exec. MICHAEL QUICKE.

Morgan Grenfell & Co Ltd: 23 Great Winchester St, London, EC2P 2AX; tel. (20) 7545-8000; fax (20) 7545-6155; f. 1838; acquired by Deutsche Bank Group in 1989; cap. p.u. 175m., total assets 8,615.3m. (Dec. 1996); Chair. P. I. ESPENHAHN; Chief Exec. D. H. THOMAS.

Rea Brothers Ltd: Alderman's House, Alderman's Walk, London, EC2M 3XR; f. 1919 as Rea, Warren and McLennan Ltd; subsidiary of Rea Brothers Group PLC; cap. 12.4m., dep. 352.9m. (Dec. 1998); Man. Dir R. W. PARSONS.

N M Rothschild & Sons Limited: New Court, St Swithin's Lane, London, EC4P 4DU; tel. (20) 7280-5000; fax (20) 7929-1643; internet www.nmrothschild.com; f. 1804; cap. 50.0m., res 86.2m., dep. 2,782.3m. (March 2002); Chair. Sir EVELYN DE ROTHSCHILD.

Singer & Friedlander Ltd: 21 New St, Bishopsgate, London, EC2M 4HR; tel. (20) 7623-3000; fax (20) 7623-2122; internet www .singer-friedlander.com; f. 1907; cap. 50m., res 2.9m., dep. 1,593.3m. (Dec. 2001); Chair. JOHN HODSON; Chief Exec. MICHAEL GIBBINS; 11 brs.

UBS Warburg: 1/2 Finsbury Ave, London, EC2M 2PP; tel. (20) 7567-8000; fax (20) 7568-4800; internet www.ubswarburg.com; Chair. and CEO MARKUS GRANZIOL.

West Merchant Bank Ltd: 33–36 Gracechurch St, London, EC3V 0AX; tel. (20) 7623-8711; fax (20) 7626-1610; f. 1964 as Standard Chartered Merchant Bank Ltd; renamed Chartered West LB Ltd in 1990; present name adopted 1993; subsidiary of Westdeutsche Landesbank Girozentrale; cap. 90.0m., res 7.3m., dep. 5,148.4m. (Dec. 1997); Chief Exec. RICHARD BRIANCE.

Consortium Banks

Joint ventures are recognized banks or licensed deposit-taking institutions which are registered in the United Kingdom and which have more than one bank among their principal shareholders, a majority of which are foreign.

Anglo-Romanian Bank: 3 Finsbury Sq., London EC2A 1AE; tel. (20) 7826-4200; fax (20) 7628-1274; e-mail enquiries@anglorom.co .uk; internet www.anglorom.co.uk; f. 1973; owned by Banca Comerciala Romana; cap. 22.2m., dep. 27.9m. (Dec. 2000); Chair. M.G. WOOD; Man. Dir M. RADOI.

British Arab Commercial Bank Ltd: 8–10 Mansion House Pl., London, EC4N 8BJ; tel. (20) 7648-7777; fax (20) 7600-3318; internet www.bacb.co.uk; f. 1972; owned by HSBC Bank Middle East, Libyan Arab Foreign Bank (Libya), Bank Al-Maghrib (Morocco), Central Bank of Egypt, Banque Extérieure d'Algérie, Rafidain Bank (Iraq); cap. 83.6m., dep. 1,406.6m. (Dec. 2001); Chair. JOHN A. P. HILL; Chief Exec. MICHAEL PARR.

Saudi International Bank (Al-Bank Al-Saudi Al-Alami Ltd): 1 Knightsbridge, London, SW1X 7XS; tel. (20) 7259-3456; fax (20) 7259-6060; f. 1975; total assets 2,991m. (Dec. 1998); Chair. Dr KHALED AL-FAYEZ; CEO MATTHEW C. SNYDER.

United Bank of Kuwait: 7 Baker St, London, W1M 1AB; tel. (20) 7487-6500; fax (20) 7487-6808; internet www.ubk-plc.co.uk; f. 1966; owned by 11 Kuwaiti banks; cap. 125.9m., dep. 1,258.2m. (Dec. 1999); Chair. FAHAD MAZIAD AL-RAJAAN; Group Chief Exec. ADEL EL-LABBAN.

Savings Organization

National Savings & Investments: 375 Kensington High St, London, W14 8SD; tel. (845) 964-50000; e-mail pressoffice@ nationalsavings.co.uk; internet www.nsandi.com; govt department and Executive Agency of the Chancellor of the Exchequer; money placed in National Savings and Investments is used by the Treasury to help cost-effectively manage the national debt and contribute towards the Government's financing needs; Chief Exec. ALAN COOK.

National Savings regional offices: Glasgow, G58 1SB; Durham, DH99 1NS; Blackpool, FY3 9ZW; Lytham St Annes, Lancs., FY0 1YN; f. 1861; Chief Exec. PETER BAREAU.

Credit Institutions

ECI Ventures: 1st Floor, Brettenham House, Lancaster Pl., London, WC2E 7EN; tel. (20) 7606-1000; fax (20) 7240-5050; e-mail ecivmail@eciv.co.uk; internet www.eciv.co.uk; f. 1976; advises and manages ECI5 (£78m. UK Ltd Partnership), ECI6 (£100m. UK Ltd Partnership) and EC17 (£175m. UK Ltd Partnership) to provide equity capital, mainly for management buyouts; Man. Dir PAUL THOMAS.

3i Group PLC: 91 Waterloo Rd, London, SE1 8XP; tel. (20) 7928-3131; fax (20) 7928-0058; internet www.3i.com; f. 1945 as the Industrial and Commercial Finance Corpn Ltd by the English and Scottish clearing banks, renamed Finance for Industry PLC, renamed Investors in Industry Group PLC in 1983, and renamed as above in 1988; provides long-term and permanent financial and advice; cap. 292.1m., res 1,757.1m., dep. 1,385.0m. (March 1995); Chair. Sir GEORGE RUSSELL; Chief Exec. BRIAN LARCOMBE; Sec. TONY BRIERLY.

Banking and Finance Organizations

Association of Foreign Banks (AFB): 1 Bengal Ct, London, EC3V 9DD; tel. (20) 7283–8300; fax (20) 7283–8302; e-mail secretariat@ foreignbanks.org.uk; internet www.foreignbanks.org.uk; f. 1947; in 1996 incorporated mems of the British Overseas and Commonwealth Banks' Association (f. 1917); changed name as above in 2002; approx. 185 mem. banks; Chair. ANGUS MACLENNAN; Dir and Sec. JAMES TREE.

Banking Code Standards Board: 33 St James's Sq., London, SW1Y 4JS; tel. (20) 7661-9694; fax (20) 7661-9784; e-mail helpline@ bcsb.org.uk; internet www.bankingcode.org.uk; fmrly Independent Review Body; enforces voluntary code of practice; Chair. RICHARD FARRANT; Chief Exec. SEYMOUR FORTESCUE.

British Bankers' Association: Pinners Hall, 105–108 Old Broad St, London, EC2N 1EX; tel. (20) 7216-8800; fax (20) 7216-8811; internet www.bba.org.uk; f. 1919; Pres. Sir GEORGE ROSS MATHEWSON; Chief Exec. IAN MULLEN.

The Chartered Institute of Bankers in Scotland: Drumsheugh House, 38B Drumsheugh Gardens, Edinburgh, EH3 7SW; tel. (131) 473-7777; fax (131) 473-7788; e-mail info@ciobs.org.uk; internet www.ciobs.org.uk; f. 1875; professional examinations, courses and publications; approx. 13,000 mems; Pres. BILL BLACK; Chief Exec. Prof. CHARLES W. MUNN.

Institute of Financial Services: 90 Bishopsgate, London, EC2N 4DQ; tel. (20) 7444-7111; fax (20) 7444-7115; e-mail customerservices@ifslearning.com; internet www.ifslearning.com; f. 1879 as the Chartered Institute of Bankers, current name adopted 2001; association for financial services professionals; Pres. JOHN STEWART; Chief Exec. GAVIN SHREEVE.

Investment Management Association: 65 Kingsway, London, WC2B 6TD; tel. (20) 7831-0898; fax (20) 7831-9975; e-mail ima@ investmentuk.org; internet www.investmentfunds.org.uk; f. 2002; following merger of the Association of Unit Trusts and Investment Funds and the Fund Managers Association; represents the UK unit trust and investment management industry; Dir-Gen. RICHARD SAUNDERS.

London Investment Banking Association: 6 Frederick's Pl., London, EC2R 8BT; tel. (20) 7796-3606; fax (20) 7796-4345; e-mail liba@liba.org.uk; internet www.liba.org.uk; mems c. 50 British and foreign banks and securities houses; Chair. Sir DAVID WALKER; Dir-Gen. Sir ADAM RIDLEY.

London Money Market Association: 2 Gresham St, London, EC2V 7QP; tel. (20) 7597-4485; fax (20) 7597-4491; e-mail rvardy@ investec.co.uk; f. 1998; mems include international banks, securities houses, building societies; 22 mems; Chair. IAN MAIR; Hon. Sec. R. J. VARDY.

STOCK EXCHANGE

The London Stock Exchange: Old Broad St, London, EC2N 1HP; tel. (20) 7797-1000; fax (20) 7334-8916; internet www .londonstockexchange.com; had its origins in the coffee houses of 17th-century London, when those wishing to invest or raise money bought and sold shares in joint-stock companies; formally constituted in 1802. By 1890 an association of stock exchanges had been formed. In 1965 a process of federation began which led to the amalgamation of all stock exchanges in the UK and Ireland in 1973. The Irish Stock Exchange officially ended its 200-year-old association with the London Stock Exchange in December 1995. In November 1986, the Exchange became a private limited company and member firms became shareholders of the Exchange with one vote each. In 1991, the 1875 Deed of Settlement was superseded as the Exchange's constitutional document by a Memorandum and Articles of Association. The governing council of the Exchange was replaced with a Board of Directors drawn from the Exchange's executive and from its customer and user base. In October 1996 an electronic quotation and trading system was introduced, which allowed for off-floor trading and direct global access to share price information. The old mandatory separation of the functions of brokers and jobbers and the system of fixed minimum commissions were then abolished. The Exchange regulates the operation of the market-place as a Recognised Investment Exchange and also regulates listed companies as the United Kingdom's Competent Authority for Listing. The Official List is the Exchange's main market. In June 1995 an Alternative Investment Market (AIM) was established to accommodate smaller and expanding companies. In March 2000 the member institutions voted to end 199 years of mutual status and convert the London Stock Exchange into a public limited company. Its own shares were fully listed from July 2001. In September 2000 plans for the proposed merger with its German counterpart, Deutsche Börse, were abandoned following a hostile takeover bid for the Exchange by the Swedish technology company Om Gruppen. The bid was rejected by shareholders in November. In October 2002 the London Stock Exchange opened a new derivatives trading platform, which would enable investors to purchase covered warrants. In mid-2002 there were 2,200 companies listed on the main market and 640 companies on AIM. At March 1999 the total securities quoted on the Stock Exchange had a combined market value of £4,781,450m. Chair. DONALD CRUICKSHANK; Chief Exec. CLARA FURSE.

SUPERVISORY BODIES

In May 1997 the Government announced its intention to establish a single statutory supervisory authority for the financial services sector. Accordingly, in November the then Securities and Investment Board was transformed into a new Financial Services Authority (FSA). From 1 June 1998, when the new Bank of England Act entered into force, the FSA incorporated the Board of Banking Supervision, which advises on supervision policy. The FSA also assumed responsibility for the supervision of insurance companies from the Department of Trade and Industry. On 1 December 2001 the FSA formally incorporated the activities of the existing regulatory bodies as well as the Building Societies Commission, the Registry of Friendly Societies and the Friendly Societies Commission following the enactment of the 2000 Financial Services and Markets Act.

The Financial Ombudsman Service: (see p. 4300).

Financial Services Authority: 25 The North Colonnade, Canary Wharf, London, E14 5HS; tel. (20) 7676-1000; fax (20) 7676-1099; internet www.fsa.gov.uk; f. 1998 to undertake supervision, regulation and market surveillance of all areas of financial activity as defined under the 2000 Financial Services and Markets Act; single statutory regulator responsible for regulating deposit taking, insurance and investment business, promoting public understanding of the financial system and reducing financial crime; Chair. Sir HOWARD DAVIES; Man. Dirs MICHAEL FOOT, JOHN TINER, CAROL SERGEANT.

Securities Institute: Centurion House, 24 Monument St, London, EC3R 8AQ; tel. (20) 7645-0600; fax (20) 7645-0601; internet www.securities-institute.org.uk; f. 1992; aims to promote professional standards and ethics in the securities industry; Chair. SCOTT DOBBIE; Chief Exec. GEOFFREY TURNER.

INSURANCE

Lloyd's: 1 Lime St, London, EC3M 7HA; tel. (20) 7327-1000; fax (20) 7626-2389; internet www.lloydsoflondon.com; had its origins in the coffee house opened c. 1688 by Edward Lloyd and was incorporated by Act of Parliament (Lloyd's Acts 1871–1982); an international insurance market and Society of Underwriters, consisting of about 3,317 individual and (since January 1994) corporate members grouped into syndicates who accept risks on the basis of unlimited and limited liability respectively; business is effected through about 133 firms of accredited Lloyd's brokers who alone are permitted to place insurances either directly or by way of reinsurance, and some three-quarters of the annual premium income (about £6,000m.) is from overseas business. Lloyd's accounts for approximately half of all international insurance premiums underwritten in the London market. The Lloyd's market is administered by the Corporation of Lloyd's through an 18-member Council, mostly elected by and from the underwriting membership. Lloyd's currently operates under a system of self-regulation, introduced by the Lloyd's Act of 1982. A regulatory board was established in October 1993. Council Chair. PETER LEVENE; CEO NICK PRETTEJOHN.

Principal Insurance Companies

Abbey Life Assurance Co Ltd: Abbey Life Centre, 100 Holdenhurst Rd, Bournemouth, Dorset, BH8 8AL; tel. (1202) 292373; fax (1202) 551236; internet www.abbeylife.co.uk; f. 1961; part of Lloyds TSB Group; Man. Dir MICHAEL GREEN.

Allied Dunbar Assurance PLC: UK Life Centre, Station Rd, Swindon, SN1 1EL; tel. (1793) 514514; internet www.allieddunbar.co.uk; f. 1971; subsidiary of BAT Industries; Chair. and CEO SANDY LEICH.

AMP NPI Ltd: NP House, 55 Calverly Rd, Tunbridge Wells, Kent, TN1 2UE; tel. (1892) 515151; fax (1892) 704607; internet www.amp-npi.co.uk; f. 1835 as NPI Ltd; acquired by AMP Group (Australia) January 2000; present name adopted November 2000; Chair. PETER MORGAN; Man. Dir TREVOR THOMPSON.

AMP Pearl Assurance PLC: AMP, Lynch Wood, Peterborough, Cambridgeshire, PE2 6FY; tel. (1733) 470470; fax (1733) 472300; internet www.pearl.co.uk; f. 1864; acquired by AMP Group (Australia) 1990; present name adopted Dec. 2001; Chair. Sir MALCOLM BATES.

AVIVA PLC: POB 420, St Helen's, 1 Undershaft, London, EC3P 3DQ; tel. (20) 7283-2000; internet www.cgnu-group.com; formed by merger of Commercial Union and General Accident in 1998; merged with The Norwich Union PLC in 2000; renamed as above in 2002; Chair. PEHR GYLLENHAMMAR; Group Chief Exec. RICHARD HARVEY.

AXA Insurance PLC: 1 Aldgate, London, EC3N 1RE; tel. (20) 7702-3109; fax (20) 7369-3909; internet www.axa-insurance.co.uk; f. 1903; CEO PETER HUBBARD.

AXA Sun Life PLC: POB 1810, Bristol, BS99 5SN; tel. (117) 989-9000; fax (117) 989-1810; internet www.sunlife.co.uk; f. 1810; Chair. ANTHONY HAMILTON; Chief Exec. PAUL EVANS.

Britannic Assurance PLC: 1 Wythall Green Way, Wythall, Birmingham, B47 6WG; tel. (870) 887-0001; fax (870) 887-0002; e-mail ask@britannic.co.uk; internet www.britannic.co.uk; f. 1866; Chair. and acting CEO HAROLD COTTAM.

Century Life PLC: Century House, 5 Old Bailey, London, EC4M 7BA; tel. (20) 7332-5000; fax (20) 7332-5030; internet www.adeptaonline.com; CEO CHRIS LITTLE.

Co-operative Insurance Society Ltd: Miller St, Manchester, M60 0AL; tel. (161) 832-8686; fax (161) 837-4048; e-mail cis@cis.co.uk; internet www.cis.co.uk; f. 1867; Chair. WILLIAM TUCKER; Chief Gen. Man. DAVID HOLLAS.

Cornhill Insurance Co PLC: 32 Cornhill, London, EC3V 3LJ; tel. (20) 7626-5410; fax (20) 7929-3562; internet www.cornhill.co.uk; part of the Allianz Group (Germany); f. 1905; Chair. Lord WALKER OF WORCESTER; Chief Exec. RAY TREEN.

Direct Line Group: 3 Edridge Rd, Croydon, Surrey, CR9 1AG; tel. (20) 8686-3313; fax (20) 8681-0512; internet www.directline.com; wholly owned by The Royal Bank of Scotland; Group CEO ANNETTE COURT.

Eagle Star Insurance Co Ltd: 60 St Mary Axe, London, EC3A 8JQ; tel. (20) 7929-1111; fax (20) 7626-1266; internet www.eaglestardirect.co.uk; f. 1904; subsidiary of Zurich Insurance; CEO PATRICK O'SULLIVAN.

Ecclesiastical Insurance Office PLC: Beaufort House, Brunswick Rd, Gloucester, GL1 1JZ; tel. (1452) 528533; fax (1452) 423557; internet www.eigonline.co.uk; f. 1887; Chair. M. R. CORNWALL-JONES; Man. Dir G. V. DOSWELL.

Equitable Life Assurance Society: Walton St, Aylesbury, Buckinghamshire, HP21 7QW; tel. (870) 901-0052; fax (1296) 386383; internet www.equitable.co.uk; f. 1762; Chair. VANNI TREVES; Chief Exec. CHARLES THOMSON; Man. Dir ALAN NASH.

Friends' Provident PLC: Pixham End, Dorking, Surrey, RH4 1QA; tel. (870) 6083678; fax (1306) 740150; e-mail diana.monger@friendsprovident.co.uk; internet www.friendsprovident.co.uk; f. 1832; Chair. DAVID K. NEWBIGGING; Group CEO KEITH SATCHELL.

Iron Trades Insurance Co Ltd: Corn Exchange, 55 Mark Pl., London, EC3R 7NE; tel. (20) 7235-6033; fax (20) 7680-1962; f. 1990; Chair. BEN STRICKLAND.

Legal and General Group PLC: Temple Court, 11 Queen Victoria St, London, EC4N 4TP; tel. (20) 7528-6200; fax (20) 7528-6222; internet www.legalandgeneral.com; f. 1836; Group CEO DAVID J. PROSSER; Group Chair. ROB MARGETTS; Sec. DAVID BINDING.

Gresham Insurance Society Ltd: Temple Court, 11 Queen Victoria St, London, EC4N 4TP; tel. (20) 7528-6200; fax (20) 7528-6222; f. 1910; Chair. DAVID J. PROSSER; Sec. ELIZABETH HODSON.

Legal and General Insurance Ltd: Temple Court, 11 Queen Victoria St, London, EC4N 4TP; tel. (20) 7528-6200; fax (20) 7528-6222; f. 1946 as British Commonwealth Insurance Co; Chair. ROBIN PHIPPS; Sec. CLARE CARSON.

Liverpool Victoria Friendly Society Ltd: County Gates, Bournemouth, BH1 2NF; tel. (1202) 292333; fax (1202) 292253; internet www.liverpool-victoria.co.uk; f. 1843; Chair. STEPHEN MARAN; Sec. D. NICHOLLS.

MGM Assurance (Marine and General Mutual Life Assurance Society): MGM House, Heene Rd, Worthing, Sussex, BN11 2DY; tel. (1903) 836000; fax (1903) 836001; internet www.mgm-assurance .co.uk; f. 1852; CEO G. P. N. HEALY.

National Farmers' Union Mutual & Avon Group: Tiddington Rd, Stratford upon Avon, Warwicks., CV37 7BJ; tel. (1789) 204211; fax (1789) 298992; internet www.nfumutual.co.uk; f. 1910; Chair. RICHARD CARTER; Man. Dir I. S. GEDEN.

The Prudential Assurance Co Ltd: 250 Euston Rd, London, NW1 2PQ; tel. (20) 7405-9222; fax (20) 7548-3465; internet www .prudentialcorp.com; f. 1848; holding co: Prudential Corpn PLC; Chair. (vacant); CEO MARK WOOD.

Royal and Sun Alliance Insurance Group PLC: 30 Berkeley Sq., London, W1J 6EW; tel. (20) 7636-3450; fax (20) 7569-6280; internet www.royalsunalliance.com; f. 1996; by merger of Royal Insurance Holdings PLC (f. 1845) and Sun Alliance Group PLC; Chair. Sir PATRICK GILLAM; CEO BOB GUNN.

Royal Liver Assurance Ltd: Royal Liver Bldg, Pier Head, Liverpool, L3 1HT; tel. (151) 236-1451; fax (151) 236-2122; internet www .royal-liver.com; f. 1850; Chair. BRIAN BARNACLE; Sec. KEVIN DOBSON.

The Royal London Mutual Insurance Society Ltd: Royal London House, Alderley Rd, Wilmslow, Cheshire, SK9 1PF; tel. (1625) 605040; fax (1625) 605400; e-mail info@royal-london.co.uk; internet www.royal-london.co.uk; f. 1861; Chair. HUBERT REID; CEO MIKE YARDLEY.

  Scottish Life: POB 54, 19 St Andrew Sq., Edinburgh, EH2 1YE; tel. (131) 456-7777; fax (131) 456-7880; e-mail enquiries@ scottishlife.co.uk; internet www.scottishlife.co.uk; f. 1881; re-inc. as a Mutual Company 1968; became part of Royal London Mutual Insurance Society in July 2001; Chief Exec. BRIAN DUFFIN.

Scottish Amicable Life PLC: POB 25, Craigforth, Sterling, FK9 4UE; tel. (1786) 448844; fax (1786) 462134; internet www .scottishamicable.co.uk; f. 1826; Chair. SANDY STEWART; Sec. DAVID GREEN.

Scottish Mutual Assurance PLC: 301 St Vincent St, Glasgow, G2 5HN; tel. (141) 248-6321; fax (141) 275-9230; internet www .scottishmutual.co.uk; f. 1883; acquired by Abbey National PLC in 1992; Chair. C. N. VILLIERS; CEO G. R. POTTINGER.

The Scottish Provident Institution: 7–11 Melville St, Edinburgh, EH3 7YZ; tel. (131) 527-1100; fax (131) 527-1111; internet www.scotprov.co.uk; f. 1837; acquired by Abbey National PLC in 2000; Chair. JOHN FODEN; Man. Dir D. E. WOODS.

Scottish Widows' PLC: POB 902, 15 Dalkeith Rd, Edinburgh, EH16 5BU; tel. (131) 655-6000; fax (131) 662-4053; internet www .scottishwidows.co.uk; f. 1815 as Scottish Widows' Fund and Life Assurance Society; name changed as above March 2000 following acquisition by Lloyds TSB; Chair. GAVIN GEMMELL; Group CEO MICHAEL D. ROSS.

Standard Life Assurance Co: Standard Life House, 30 Lothian Rd, Edinburgh, EH1 2DH; tel. (845) 606-0100; fax (131) 245-7990; e-mail info@standardlife.com; internet www.standardlife.co.uk; f. 1825; assets £60,000m. Chair. J. TROTT; Group CEO IAIN LUMSDEN.

Swiss Life (UK) PLC: Swiss Life House, 24–26 South Park, Sevenoaks, Kent, TN13 1BG; tel. (1732) 582000; fax (1732) 582001; e-mail swisslife@swisslife.co.uk; internet www.swisslife.co.uk; CEO STEVE BURNETT.

Swiss Re UK Ltd: Swiss Re House, 71–77 Leadenhall St, London, ECA 3DE; tel. (20) 7628-7070; fax (20) 7814-3000; internet www .swissre.com; CEO (life and health) MARTYN HARKER; CEO (property and casualty) MARTIN ALBERS.

  Mercantile and General Reinsurance Co PLC: Moorfields House, Moorfields, London, EC2Y 9AL; tel. (20) 7628-7070; fax (20) 78143000; acquired by Swiss Reinsurance Group in 1996; currently in run-off.

Wesleyan Assurance Society: Colmore Circus, Birmingham, B4 6AR; tel. (121) 200-3003; fax (121) 200-2971; internet www.wesleyan .co.uk; f. 1841; Chair. L. D. MACLEAN; Vice-Chair. and Man. Dir PETER MCNAMARA.

Western Provident Association: Rivergate House, Blackbrook Park, Taunton, Somerset, TA1 2PE; tel. (1823) 625000; fax (1823) 623050; internet www.upa.org.uk; specialists in medical insurance; CEO JULIAN STAINTON.

Zurich Insurance: Zurich House, Stanhope Rd, Portsmouth, Hants, PO1 1DU; tel. (23) 9282-2200; internet www.zurich.co.uk; f. 1872; CEO ROLF HÜPPI.

Insurance Associations

Associated Scottish Life Offices: POB 25, Craigforth, Stirling, FK9 4UE; tel. (1786) 448844; fax (1786) 450427; constituted 1841 as an Association of General Managers of Scottish Offices transacting life assurance business; 7 full mems; Chair. MICHAEL D. ROSS; Sec. G. E. SPENCE.

Association of British Insurers: 51 Gresham St, London, EC2V 7HQ; tel. (20) 7600-3333; fax (20) 7696-8999; e-mail info@abi.org.uk; internet www.abi.org.uk; f. 1985; principal trade association for insurance companies; protection, promotion, and advancement of the common interests of all classes of insurance business; c. 420 mems; Chair. MICHAEL D. ROSS; Dir-Gen. MARY FRANCIS.

British Insurance Brokers' Association (BIBA): BIBA House, 14 Bevis Marks, London, EC3A 7NT; tel. (20) 7623-9043; fax (20) 7626-9676; e-mail enquiries@biba.org.uk; internet www.biba.org .uk; Chair. HAMISH RITCHIE; Chief Exec. MICHAEL WILLIAMS.

Chartered Insurance Institute: 20 Aldermanbury, London, EC2V 7HY; tel. (20) 8989-8464; fax (20) 8530-3052; e-mail customer .serv@cii.co.uk; internet www.cii.co.uk; f. 1897; inc. 1912; approx. 68,000 mems; Pres. MICHAEL BRIGHT; Dir-Gen. Dr A. SCOTT.

Fire Protection Association: Bastille Ct, 2 Paris Garden, London SE1 8ND; tel. (20) 7902-5300; fax (20) 7902-5301; e-mail fpa@thefpa .co.uk; internet www.thefpa.co.uk; f. 1946; Man. Dir JON O'NEILL.

Fire and Risk Services: BRE Garston, Watford, Herts., WD25 9XX; tel. (1923) 664700; fax (1923) 664910; e-mail frsenquiries@bre .co.uk; internet www.bre.co.uk/frs; f. 1986; incorporates the Loss Prevention Council, fire division of the Building Research Establishment; Dir CHRIS BROADBENT.

Insurance Institute of London: 20 Aldermanbury, London, EC2V 7HY; tel. (20) 7600-1343; fax (20) 7600-6857; e-mail iil.london@cii.co .uk; internet www.iilondon.co.uk; f. 1907; Pres. DENNIS MAHONEY.

International Underwriting Association (IUA): London Underwriting Centre, 3 Minster Ct, Mincing Ln, London, EC3R 7DD; tel. (20) 7617-4444; fax (20) 7617-4440; e-mail info@iua.co.uk; internet www.iua.co.uk; f. 1998 by merger of the Institute of London Underwriters and London International Insurance and Reinsurance Market Association; Chair. STEPHEN CANE; CEO MARIE-LOUISE ROSSI.

Advisory Body

The Financial Ombudsman Service: see p. 717. (see p. 4300).

Associations of Actuaries

Faculty of Actuaries: 18 Dublin St, Edinburgh, EH1 3PP; tel. (131) 240-1300; fax (131) 240-1313; e-mail faculty@actuaries.org.uk; internet www.actuaries.org.uk; f. 1856; 1080 Fellows, 8 Honorary Fellows; Pres. T. M. ROSS; Sec. R. MACONACHIE.

Institute of Actuaries: Staple Inn Hall, High Holborn, London, WC1V 7QJ; tel. (20) 7632-2100; fax (20) 7632-2111; e-mail institute@ actuaries.org.uk; internet www.actuaries.org.uk; f. 1848; Royal Charter 1884; 11,817 mems; Pres. JEREMY GOFORD; Sec.-Gen. CAROLINE INSTANCE.

Trade and Industry

GOVERNMENT AGENCIES

Advisory, Conciliation and Arbitration Service (ACAS): Brandon House, 180 Borough High St, London, SE1 1LW; tel. (20) 7210-3613; fax (20) 7210-3708; internet www.acas.org.uk; f. 1974; an independent organization, under the management of a council comprising employers, trade union representatives and independent members, appointed by the Sec. of State for Trade and Industry. The service aims to promote good industrial relations in an impartial and confidential manner. ACAS provides collective conciliation, arbitration, mediation, advisory and information services, and conciliates in individual employment rights issues; Chair. RITA DONAGHY; Chief Exec. JOHN TAYLOR.

Central Arbitration Committee: 3rd Floor, Discovery House, 28–42 Banner St, London, EC1Y 8QE; tel. (20) 7251-9747; fax (20) 7251-3114; internet www.cac.gov.uk; f. 1976 as an independent body under the 1975 Employment Protection Act, in succession to Industrial Court/Industrial Arbitration Board; arbitrates on trade disputes; adjudicates on disclosure of information complaints; determines claims for statutory trade union recognition under the 1999 Employment Relations Act and certain issues relating to the implementation of the European Works Council; Chair. Sir MICHAEL BURTON.

Charity Commission for England and Wales: Harmsworth House, 13–15 Bouverie St, London, EC4Y 8DP; tel. (870) 333-0123; fax (20) 7674-2300; e-mail kevin.snow@charitycommission.gsi.gov

.uk; internet www.charity-commission.gov.uk; statutory organization responsible for the regulation of charities; Chief Commissioner JOHN STOKER.

Competition Commission: New Court, 48 Carey St, London, WC2A 2JT; tel. (20) 7271-0243; fax (20) 7271-0367; e-mail info@competition-commission.org.uk; internet www.competition-commission.org.uk; f. 1948 as Monopolies and Restrictive Practices Commission which was replaced by Monopolies and Mergers Commission in 1973; present name adopted 1999; investigates, and reports on, matters referred to it by the Sec. of State for Trade and Industry and by the Dir-Gen. of Fair Trading under the Fair Trading Act of 1973 and the Competition Act of 1980; other references may be made under the Telecommunications Act of 1984, the Airports Act of 1986, the Gas Act of 1986, the Electricity Act of 1989, the Broadcasting Act of 1990, the Water Industry Act of 1991, the Railways Act of 1993; hears appeals against certain decisions of the Dir-Gen. of Fair Trading under the Competition Act of 1998; Chair. Sir DEREK MORRIS; Chief Exec. and Sec. ROBERT FOSTER.

Countryside Agency: John Dower House, Crescent Pl., Cheltenham, Gloucestershire GL50 3RA; tel. (1242) 521381; fax (1242) 584270; e-mail info@countryside.gov.uk; internet www.countryside.gov.uk; f. 1999; advises Government and acts on issues relating to the environmental, economic and social well-being of the English countryside; Chair. EWEN CAMERON; Chief Exec. RICHARD WAKEFORD.

Learning and Skills Council: Cheylesmore House, Quinton Road, Coventry, CV1 2WT; tel. (24) 7682–3501; fax (24) 7682-3675; e-mail info@lsc.gov.uk; internet www.lsc.gov.uk; Chair. BRYAN SANDERSON; Chief Exec. JOHN HARWOOD.

Environment Agency: Rio House, Waterside Drive, Almondsbury, Bristol, BS32 4UD; tel. (1454) 624400; fax (1454) 624409; e-mail enquiries@environment-agency.gov.uk; internet www.environment-agency.gov.uk; f. 1996; incorporated former National Rivers Authority; Chair. of Board Sir JOHN HARMAN; Chief Exec. BARONESS YOUNG OF OLD SCONE.

Food Standards Agency: Aviation House, 125 Kingsway, London, WC2B 6NH; tel. (20) 7276-8000; fax (20) 7276-8004; internet www.food.gov.uk; f. 2000; Chair. Sir JOHN KREBS; Chief Exec. GEOFFREY PODGER.

Forestry Commission: Silvan House, 231 Corstorphine Rd, Edinburgh, EH12 7AT; tel. (131) 334-0303; fax (131) 334-3047; e-mail enquiries@forestry.gsi.gov.uk; internet www.forestry.gsi.gov.uk; government department responsible for protecting and expanding Britain's forest and woodlands and increasing their value to society and the environment; implements the Government's forestry policy within the framework of the Forestry Acts, administers the Woodland Grant Scheme, controls tree-felling through the issue of licences, administers plant health regulations to protect woodlands against tree-pests and diseases, and conducts research; has two executive agencies (1) Forest Enterprise, the agency responsible for the management of the national forests (Chief Exec. Dr Bob McIntosh) and, (2) Forest Research (Acting Chief Exec. Dr Peter Freer-Smith), which conducts research, development and surveys, and provides advice to the Commission and forestry industries; Chair. Lord CLARK OF WINDEMERE; Dir-Gen. D. J. BILLS.

National Audit Office: 157–197 Buckingham Palace Rd, London, SW1W 9SP; tel. (20) 7798-7000; fax (20) 7828-3774; e-mail enquiries@nao.gsi.gov.uk; internet www.nao.gov.uk; audits the financial statements of all government departments and agencies, certain public bodies and international organizations; the Comptroller and Auditor-General is responsible for controlling receipts into, and issues from, the Consolidated and National Loans Funds and reports to Parliament on value for money issues or on important issues arising from the financial statements; Comptroller and Auditor-General Sir JOHN BOURN.

National Consumer Council: 20 Grosvenor Gdns, London, SW1W 0DH; tel. (20) 7730-3469; fax (20) 7730-0191; e-mail info@ncc.org.uk; internet www.ncc.org.uk; f. 1975; 12 mems; Chair. DEIRDRE HUTTON.

Office of Fair Trading: Fleetbank House, 2–6 Salisbury Sq., London, EC4Y 8JX; tel. (20) 7211-8000; fax (20) 7211-8800; internet www.oft.gov.uk; f. 1973; monitors consumer affairs, competition policy, consumer credit, estate agencies, etc. Dir-Gen. JOHN VICKERS.

oneLondon: 28 Park St, London, SE1 9EQ; tel. (20) 7403-0300; fax (20) 7248-8877; e-mail info@one-london.com; internet www.one-london.com; f. 2001; following merger between London Enterprise Agency and Greater London Enterprise; Chair. AMANDA JORDAN.

Postal Services Commission (Postcomm): Hercules House, Hercules Rd, London, SE1 7DB; tel. (20) 7593-2100; fax (20) 7593-2142; e-mail info@psc.org.uk; internet www.psc.gov.uk; f. 2000; under the Postal Services Act of 2000 to regulate Consignia PLC (formerly the Post Office, but due to be renamed Royal Mail Group PLC by late 2002); duties include the introduction of competition, ensuring a universal postal service and licensing Royal mail and controlling its

uniformity of postal tariffs; Chair. GRAHAM CORBETT; Chief Exec. MARTIN STANLEY.

Statistics Commission: 10 Great George St, London, SW1P 3AE; tel. (20) 7273-8008; fax (20) 7273-8019; e-mail statscom@statscom.org.uk; internet www.statscom.org.uk; f. 2000 to advise on the quality, quality assurance and priority-setting for National Statistics and on the procedures designed to deliver statistical integrity, to ensure National Statistics are trustworthy and responsive to public needs; Chair. DAVID RHIND; Chief Exec. GILL EASTABROOK.

United Kingdom Atomic Energy Authority: Harwell, Oxfordshire, OX11 0RA; tel. (1235) 820220; fax (1235) 436401; internet www.ukaea.org.uk; f. 1954 to take responsibility for UK research and development into all aspects of atomic energy; separated into AEA Technology, which operated as the Authority's commercial division, and UKAEA; AEA Technology transferred to the private sector in 1996. UKAEA's core task is to manage the decommissioning of reactors and other facilities used for the nuclear research and development programme. It also carries out fusion research. These activities are conducted at sites at Windscale (Cumbria), Dounreay (Caithness), Harwell and Culham (Oxfordshire) and Winfrith (Dorset); Chair. DENNIS TUNNICLIFFE; Chief Exec. JOHN McKEOWN.

DEVELOPMENT ORGANIZATIONS

London First: 1 Hobhouse Court, Suffolk St, London, SW1Y 4HH; tel. (20) 7665-1500; fax (20) 7665-1501; e-mail staff@london-first.co.uk; internet www.london-first.co.uk; promotes London as a business centre; Chair. LORD SHEPPARD OF DIDGEMERE; Chief Exec. STEPHEN O'BRIEN.

Overseas Development Institute: 111 Westminster Bridge Rd, London, SE1 7JD; tel. (20) 7922-0300; fax (20) 7922 0399; e-mail odi@odi.org.uk; internet www.odi.org.uk; Dir SIMON MAXWELL.

Scottish Enterprise: 120 Bothwell St, Glasgow, G2 7JP; tel. (141) 248-2700; fax (141) 221-3217; e-mail scotentcsd@scotent.co.uk; internet www.scotent.co.uk; economic development agency for Scotland; Chair. Sir IAN ROBINSON; Chief Exec. ROBERT CRAWFORD.

Welsh Development Agency: Principality House, The Friary, Cardiff, CF10 3FE; tel. (1443) 845500; fax (1443) 845589; e-mail enquiries@wda.co.uk; internet www.wda.co.uk; Chief Exec. GRAHAM HAWKER.

CHAMBERS OF COMMERCE

British Chambers of Commerce (BCC): Manning House, 22 Carlisle Pl., London, SW1P 1JA; tel. (20) 7565-2000; fax (20) 7565-2049; e-mail info@britishchambers.org.uk; internet www.chamberonline.co.uk; f. 1860; in January 1993 subsumed National Chamber of Trade (f. 1897); represents the new Approved Chamber Network in the United Kingdom (comprising 58 Chambers at April 1997); Pres. ISABELLA MOORE; Dir-Gen. DAVID FROST.

International Chamber of Commerce (ICC) United Kingdom: 14–15 Belgrave Sq., London, SW1X 8PS; tel. (20) 7823-2811; fax (20) 7235-5447; e-mail richardbate@iccorg.co.uk; f. 1920; British affiliate of the world business org. Chair. PHIL WATTS; Dir R. C. I. BATE.

London Chamber of Commerce and Industry: 33 Queen St, London, EC4R 1AP; tel. (20) 7248-4444; fax (20) 7489-0391; e-mail lc@londonchamber.co.uk; internet www.londonchamber.co.uk; Pres. Sir GULAM NOON; Chief Exec. COLIN STANBRIDGE.

INDUSTRIAL AND TRADE ASSOCIATIONS

Aluminium Federation: Broadway House, Calthorpe Rd, Five Ways, Birmingham, B15 1TN; tel. (121) 456-1103; fax (121) 456-2274; e-mail alfed@alfed.org.uk; internet www.alfed.org.uk; f. 1962; Pres. J. MORRISON; Sec.-Gen. Dr D. A. HARRIS.

Association of the British Pharmaceutical Industry: 12 Whitehall, London, SW1A 2DY; tel. (20) 7930-3477; fax (20) 7747-1414; e-mail abpi@abpi.org.uk; internet www.abpi.org.uk; f. 1930; Pres. Dr J. PATTERSON; Dir-Gen. Dr T. M. JONES.

Association of Manufacturers of Domestic Appliances: Lamb's Conduit St, London, WC1N 3NW; tel. (20) 7405-0666; fax (20) 7405-6609; e-mail info@amdea.org.uk; f. 1969; c. 70 mem. cos; Dir-Gen. PETER CARVER.

BFM (British Furniture Manufacturers): 30 Harcourt St, London, W1H 2AA; tel. (20) 7724-0851; fax (20) 7706-1924; e-mail info@bfm.org.uk; internet www.bfm.org.uk; merged in January 1993 with BFM Exhibitions and BFM Exports; Man. Dir ROGER MASON.

British Beer and Pub Association: Market Towers, 1 Nine Elms Ln., London, SW8 5NQ; tel. (20) 7627-9191; fax (20) 7627-9123; e-mail enquiries@beerandpub.com; internet www.beerandpub.com; f. 1904; 76 mems; trade association for UK brewing industry and multiple pub chains; Chief Exec. ROB HAYWARD.

British Cable Association: 37A Walton Rd, East Molesey, Surrey, KT8 0DH; tel. (20) 8941-4079; fax (20) 8783-0104; e-mail admin@bcauk.org; f. 1958; fmrly British Cable Makers' Confederation; Sec.-Gen. P. M. A. SMEETH.

British Carpet Manufacturers' Association: POB 1155, MFC Complex, 60 New Rd, Kidderminster, Worcs., DY10 1WW; tel. (1562) 747351; fax (1562) 747359; e-mail bcma@clara.net; 18 mems. Pres. and Chair. M. A. C. BRINTON; Exec. Dir. H. G. W. WILSON.

British Cement Association: Century House, Telford Ave, Crowthorne, Berks, RG45 6YS; tel. (1344) 762676; fax (1344) 761214; e-mail library@bca.org.uk; internet www.bca.org.uk; Chair. Sir GEOFFREY CHIPPERFIELD; Chief Exec. MIKE GILBERT.

British Ceramic Confederation: Federation House, Station Rd, Stoke-on-Trent, Staffs., ST4 2SA; tel. (1782) 744631; fax (1782) 744102; e-mail bcc@ceramfed.co.uk; internet www.ceramfed.co.uk; f. 1984; 225 mems; Chief Exec. K. C. FARRELL.

British Clothing Industry Association: 5 Portland Pl., London, W1B 1PW; tel. (20) 7636-7788; fax (20) 7636-7515; e-mail bcia@dial.pipex.com; f. 1980; Chair. JAMES MCADAM; Dir JOHN R. WILSON.

British Electrotechnical and Allied Manufacturers' Association (BEAMA Ltd): Westminster Tower, 3 Albert Embankment, London, SE1 7SL; tel. (20) 7793-3000; fax (20) 7793-3003; e-mail info@beama.org.uk; internet www.beama.org.uk; f. 1905 as British Electrical and Allied Manufacturers' Association Ltd, present name from 2002; 460 mems; Pres. M. GALLEY.

British Exporters' Association: Broadway House, Tothill St, London, SW1H 9NQ; tel. (20) 7222-5419; fax (20) 7799-2468; e-mail bexamail@aol.com; internet www.bexa.co.uk; Pres. Sir RICHARD NEEDHAM; Chair. JOHN TYLER.

British Footwear Association: 5 Portland Pl., London, W1B 1PW; tel. (20) 7580-8687; fax (20) 7580-8696; e-mail bfa@easynet.co.uk; internet www.britfoot.com; Chief Exec. NIALL CAMPBELL.

British Glass Manufacturers' Confederation: Northumberland Rd, Sheffield, S10 2UA; tel. (114) 268-6201; fax (114) 268-1073; e-mail info@britglass.co.uk; internet www.britglass.co.uk; over 100 mems; Company Sec. D. K. BARLOW.

British Hospitality Association: Queen's House, 55/56 Lincoln's Inn Fields, London, WC2A 3BH; tel. (20) 7404-7744; fax (20) 7404-7799; e-mail bha@bha.org.uk; internet www.bha-online.org.uk; f. 1907; Pres. RAMON PAJARES; Chief Exec. R. G. COTTON.

British Non-Ferrous Metals Federation: 10 Greenfield Cres., Birmingham, B15 3AU; tel. (121) 456-3322; fax (121) 456-1394; e-mail copperuk@compuserve.com; Dir SIMON PAYTON.

The British Precast Concrete Federation Ltd: 60 Charles St, Leicester, LE1 1FB; tel. (116) 253-6161; fax (116) 251-4568; e-mail info@britishprecast.org; internet www.britishprecast.org.uk; f. 1918; approx. 125 mems; Chief Exec. MARTIN A. CLARKE; Sec. DAVID J. ZANKER.

British Printing Industries Federation: Farringdon Point, 29–35 Farringdon Rd, London, EC1M 3JF; tel. (870) 240-4085; fax (20) 7405-7784; e-mail cicely.brown@bpif.org.uk; internet www.britishprint.com; f. 1900; 3,500 mems; Pres. PETER YATES; Chief Exec. MICHAEL JOHNSON.

British Rubber Manufacturers' Association: 6 Bath Pl., Rivington St, London, EC2A 3JE; tel. (20) 7457-5040; fax (20) 7972-9008; e-mail mail@brma.co.uk; internet www.brma.co.uk; f. 1968; Pres. D. E. P. OWEN; Dir A. J. DORKEN.

CBI (The Voice of Business): Centre Point, 103 New Oxford St, London, WC1A 1DU; tel. (20) 7395-8247; fax (20) 7240-1578; internet www.cbi.org.uk; f. 1965 as the Confederation of British Industry, name changed as above in 2001; acts as a national point of reference for all seeking views of industry and is recognized internationally as the representative organization of British industry and management; advises the Government on all aspects of policy affecting the interests of industry; has a direct corporate membership employing more than 4m., and a trade association membership representing more than 6m. of the workforce; Pres. Sir JOHN EGAN; Dir-Gen. DIGBY JONES.

Chemical Industries Association: King's Buildings, Smith Sq., London SW1P 3JJ; tel. (20) 7834-3399; fax (20) 7834-4469; e-mail enquiries@cia.org.uk; internet www.cia.org.uk; Dir-Gen. JUDITH HACKITT.

Construction Confederation: Construction House, 56–64 Leonard St, London, EC2A 4JX; tel. (20) 7608-5000; fax (20) 7608-5001; e-mail enquiries@thecc.org.uk; internet www.thecc.org.uk; f. 1878; 5,000 mems; Pres. JOHN GAINS; Chief Exec. STEPHEN RATCLIFFE.

Dairy Industry Association Ltd (DIAL): 19 Cornwall Terrace, London, NW1 4QP; tel. (20) 7467-2659; fax (20) 7935-3920; e-mail info@dia-ltd.org.uk; internet www.dia-ltd.org.uk; f. 1933; Pres. ALAN HINTON; Dir-Gen. JIM BEGG.

Electrical Contractors' Association: ESCA House, 34 Palace Court, London, W2 4HY; tel. (20) 7313-4800; fax (20) 7221-7344; e-mail electricalcontractors@eca.co.uk; internet www.eca.co.uk; f. 1901; Pres. I. R. HARRIS; Dir DAVID R. J. POLLOCK.

Electricity Association Services Ltd: 30 Millbank, London, SW1P 4RD; tel. (20) 7963-5712; fax (20) 7963-5998; e-mail enquiries@electricity.org.uk; internet www.electricity.org.uk; f. 1990 as a trade asscn for the new electricity companies in England, Wales, Scotland and Northern Ireland, and to provide them with various services. Assoc. mems. include CEPS, ESB Ireland, ESKOM, Jersey Electricity Co, States of Guernsey Electricity Board, Manx Electricity Authority, ChubuElectric Power Co, Tokyo Electric Power Co; Pres. MIKE HUGHES; Chief Exec. JENNY KIRKPATRICK.

Engineering Employers' Federation: Broadway House, Tothill St, London, SW1H 9NQ; tel. (20) 7222-7777; fax (20) 7222-2782; e-mail enquiries@eef-fed.org.uk; internet www.eef.org.uk; f. 1896; 5,700 mems through 14 associations; Pres. PAUL LESTER; Dir-Gen. MARTIN TEMPLE.

Farmers' Union of Wales: Llys Amaeth, Plas Gogerddan, Aberystwyth, Ceredigion, SY23 3BT; tel. (1970) 820820; fax (1970) 820821; e-mail head.office@fuw.org.uk; internet www.fuw.org.uk; f. 1955; 14,000 mems; Pres. BOB PARRY.

Food and Drink Federation: 6 Catherine St, London, WC2B 5JJ; tel. (20) 7836-2460; fax (20) 7836-0580; e-mail generalenquiries@fdf.org.uk; internet www.fdf.org.uk; Dir-Gen. SYLVIA JAY.

Glass and Glazing Federation: 44–48 Borough High St, London, SE1 1XB; tel. (20) 7403-7177; fax (20) 7357-7458; e-mail info@ggf.org.uk; internet www.ggf.org.uk; f. 1977; trade organization for employers and cos in the flat glass, glazing, home improvement, plastic and film industries; Chief Exec. NIGEL REES.

Institute of Export: Export House, Minerva Business Park, Lynch Wood, Peterborough, PE2 6FT; tel. (1733) 404400; fax (1733) 404444; e-mail institute@export.org.uk; internet www.export.org.uk; f. 1935 as a professional educational organization devoted to the development of British export trade and the interests of those associated with it; more than 6,000 mems; Pres. Sir MARTIN LAING.

National Association of British and Irish Millers Ltd: 21 Arlington St, London, SW1A 1RN; tel. (20) 7493-2521; fax (20) 7493-6785; e-mail info@nabim.org.uk; trade assoc. of the UK flour milling industry; f. 1878; Dir-Gen. A. WAUGH; Sec. N. F. BENNETT.

National Farmers' Union: Agriculture House, 164 Shaftesbury Ave, London, WC2H 8HL; tel. (20) 7331-7200; fax (20) 7331-7313; e-mail nfu@nfu.org.uk; internet www.nfu.org.uk; f. 1904 as Lincolnshire Farmers' Union, adopted present name in 1908; Pres. BEN GILL; Dir-Gen. RICHARD MACDONALD.

National Metal Trades Federation: Savoy Tower, 77 Renfrew St, Glasgow, G2 3BZ; tel. (141) 332-0826; fax (141) 332-5788; e-mail gmcfall@nmtf.org.uk; internet www.metcom.org.uk/memdetails/nmtf.htm; Sec. ALEX SHAW.

Producers Alliance for Cinema and Television (PACT) Ltd: 45 Mortimer St, London, W1W 8HJ; tel. (20) 7331-6000; fax (20) 7331-6700; e-mail enquiries@pact.co.uk; internet www.pact.co.uk; film and TV producers; represents 1,400 companies; Chief Exec. JOHN McVAY.

Quarry Products Association: 156 Buckingham Palace Rd, London, SW1W 9TR; tel. (20) 7730-8194; fax (20) 7730-4355; e-mail info@qpa.org; internet www.qpa.org; fmrly British Ready Mixed Concrete Assoc., and the British Aggregate Construction Materials Industry Ltd; Dir SIMON VANDERBYL.

Scottish Building: Carron Grange, Carrongrange Ave, Stenhousemuir, FK5 3BQ; tel. (1324) 555550; fax (1324) 555551; e-mail info@scottish-building.co.uk; internet www.scottish-building.co.uk; Pres. DREW CONNELL; Chief Exec. S. C. PATTEN.

Scottish Textile Association: Apex House, 99 Haymarket Terrace, Edinburgh, EH12 5HD; tel. (131) 313-4000; fax (131) 313-4231; e-mail scottish.textiles@scotent.co.uk; internet www.scottish-textiles.com; present name since 1991; Chair. TONY TAYLOR.

Sea Fish Industry Authority (Seafish): 18 Logie Mill, Logie Green Rd, Edinburgh, EH7 4HG; tel. (131) 558-3331; fax (131) 558-1442; e-mail seafish@seafish.co.uk; internet www.seafish.co.uk; serves all sectors of the UK seafood industry; services include business development, training, commodity quality research, finfish and shellfish aquaculture, economic and statistical analysis, generic promotion of consumption of fish, and market reasearch; Chair. ANDREW DEWAR-DURIE; Chief Exec. JOHN RUTHERFORD.

Society of British Aerospace Companies Ltd: Duxbury House, 60 Petty France, London, SW1H 9EU; tel. (20) 7227-1000; fax (20) 7227-1067; e-mail post@sbac.co.uk; internet www.sbac.co.uk; f. 1916; national trade association for the UK aerospace industry; Dir Gen. DAVID MARSHALL.

Society of Motor Manufacturers and Traders: Forbes House, Halkin St, London, SW1X 7DS; tel. (20) 7235-7000; fax (20) 7235-7112; e-mail smmt@smmt.co.uk; internet www.smmt.co.uk; Pres. MIKE BAUNTON; Chief Exec. CHRISTOPHER MACGOWAN.

The Sugar Bureau: Duncan House, Dolphin Sq., London, SW1V 3PW; tel. (20) 7828-9465; fax (20) 7821-5393; e-mail info@sugar-bureau.co.uk; internet www.sugar-bureau.co.uk; represents sugar companies in the UK, provides technical, educational and consumer information about sugar and health; Dir Dr R. C. COTTRELL.

Timber Trade Federation: Clareville House, 26–27 Oxendon St, London, SW1Y 4EL; tel. (20) 7839-1891; fax (20) 7930-0094; e-mail ttf@ttf.co.uk; internet www.ttf.co.uk; Dir-Gen. PAUL MARTIN.

United Kingdom Petroleum Industry Association: 9 Kingsway, London, WC2B 6XH; tel. (20) 7240-0289; fax (20) 7379-3102; e-mail ukpia@aol.com; internet www.ukpia.com; Pres. GARY JONES; Dir-Gen. Dr MALCOLM WEBB.

EMPLOYERS' ASSOCIATIONS

British Retail Consortium: 2nd Floor, 21 Dartmouth St, London, SW1H 9BP; tel. (20) 7854-8900; fax (20) 7854-8901; e-mail info@brc.org.uk; internet www.brc.org.uk; f. 1975; represents retailers; Dir-Gen. WILLIAM MOYES.

Chartered Management Institute: 3rd Floor, 2 Savoy Ct, Strand, London, WC2R 0EZ; tel. (20) 7497-0496; fax (20) 7497-0463; e-mail press.office@managers.org.uk; internet www.managers.org.uk; f. 1992 as the Institute of Management by amalgamation of British Institute of Management (f. 1947) and Institution of Industrial Managers (f. 1931); changed name as above in 2002; represents 89,000 individual mems and 520 corporate members; Pres. JOHN ROBINSON; Dir-Gen. MARY CHAPMAN.

Federation of Small Businesses: 2 Catherine Pl., London, SW1E 6HF; tel. (20) 7592-8100; fax (20) 7233-7899; e-mail london@fsb.org.uk; internet www.fsb.org.uk; f. 1974; represents the interests of UK small businesses and the self employed; 170,000 mems; Head of Parliamentry Affairs STEPHEN ALAMBRITIS.

Institute of Directors: 116 Pall Mall, London, SW1Y 5ED; tel. (20) 7839-1233; fax (20) 7930-8040; e-mail enquiries@iod.com; internet www.iod.com; f. 1903; 60,000 mems, including 10,000 overseas; Pres. Lord YOUNG OF GRAFFHAM; Dir-Gen. GEORGE COX.

UTILITIES

Electricity

Regulatory Authority

Office of Gas and Electricity Markets (Ofgem): 9 Millbank, London, SW1P 3GE; tel. (20) 7901-7000; fax (20) 7901-7066; internet www.ofgem.gov.uk; f. 1999 following merger of Offer and Ofgas; regulates the gas and electricity industries in England, Scotland and Wales and aims to promote the interests of all gas and electricity customers by promoting competition and regulating monopolies; Chair. and CEO CALLUM MCCARTHY.

Principal Electricity Companies

Aquila: Whittington Hall, Whittington, Worcester, WR5 7RB; tel. (8457) 353637; fax (1905) 761464; internet www.aquila.com; formerly GPU Power UK; present name adopted May 2002; Chief Operating Officer ROGER MURRAY.

British Energy PLC: 3 Redwood Crescent, Peel Park, East Kilbride, G74 5PR; tel. (1355) 262000; fax (1355) 262626; internet www.british-energy.com; Chief Exec. MIKE ALEXANDER.

East Midlands Electricity PLC: Herald Way, Pegasus Business Park, East Midlands Airport, Castle Donnington, DE74 2TU; tel. (1332) 393415; e-mail info@eme.co.uk; internet www.eme.co.uk; Propr Eon; Man. Dir BOB TAYLOR.

Innogy Holdings PLC: Windmill Hill Business Park, Whitehill Way, Swindon, Wiltshire, SN5 6PB; tel. (1793) 877777; fax (1793) 892525; internet www.innogy.com; Chair. Dr D. KUHNT; CEO Dr BRIAN COUNT.

London Electricity PLC: Templar House, 81–87 High Holborn, London, WC1V 6NU; tel. (20) 7242-9050; fax (20) 7331-3108; internet www.legroup.co.uk; owned by Electricité de France; Chair. BO KÄLLSTRAND; CEO VINCENT DE RIVAZ.

Manweb Scottish Power PLC: Wilderspool Causeway, Warrington, WA4 6QD; tel. (845) 272-1212; fax (1978) 832162; internet www.manweb.co.uk; owned by Scottish Power Co; Chair. KEN VOWLES; CEO IAN RUSSELL.

National Grid Transco PLC: 1–3 Strand, London, WC2N 5EH; tel. (20) 7004-3000; fax (20) 7004-3004; internet www.ngtgroup.com; Chair. Sir JOHN PARKER; CEO ROGER URWIN.

Northern Electric PLC: Carliol House, Market St, Newcastle upon Tyne, NE1 6NE; tel. (191) 210-2000; fax (191) 210-2001; internet www.northern-electric.co.uk; Propr MidAmerican Energy Holdings Company; Pres. and CEO ERIC CONNOR.

Norweb PLC: Talbot Rd, Manchester, M16 0HQ; tel. (161) 873-8000; fax (161) 875-7360; internet www.energi.co.uk; Propr TXU Europe; Man. Dir JOHN BECKETT.

Powergen UK : Westwood Way, Westwood Business Park, Coventry, CV4 8LG; tel. (24) 7642-4000; fax (24) 7642-5432; internet www.powergenplc.com; CEO Dr PAUL GOLBY.

Scottish and Southern Energy PLC: Inveralmond House, 200 Dunkeld Rd, Perth, PH1 3AQ; tel. (1738) 455154; fax (1738) 455281; internet www.scottish-southern.co.uk; Chair. Dr BRUCE FARMER; CEO IAN MARCHANT.

ScottishPower PLC: Corporate Office, 1 Atlantic Quay, Glasgow, G2 8SP; tel. (141) 248-8200; fax (141) 248-8300; internet www.scottishpower.plc.uk; Chair. CHARLES MILLER SMITH; CEO Sir IAN RUSSELL.

Seeboard PLC: Forest Gate, Brighton Rd, Crawley, West Sussex, RH11 9BH; tel. (1293) 565888; fax (1293) 657327; internet www.seeboard.co.uk; acquired by Electricité de France in 2002; Chair. JIM ELLIS.

South Wales Electricity PLC: Newport Rd, St Mellons, Cardiff, CF3 9XW; tel. (29) 2079-2111; fax (29) 2077-7759; internet www.swalec.co.uk; CEO JOHN ROBINS.

SWEB (Board): 300 Park Ave, Aztec West, Almondsbury, Bristol, BS32 4SE; tel. (1454) 452200; internet www.sweb.co.uk; owned by Electricité de France; CEO VINCENT DE RIVAZ.

TXU Energi: Wherstead Park, POB 40, Wherstead, Ipswich, Suffolk, IP9 2AQ; tel. (1473) 552224; internet www.eastern.co.uk; formerly Eastern Energy; owned by TXU-Europe; CEO PHILIP TURBERVILLE.

Yorkshire Electricity Group PLC: Wetherby Rd, Scarcroft, Leeds, LS14 3HS; tel. (113) 289-2123; fax (113) 289-5611; e-mail customer.services@yeg.co.uk; internet www.yeg.co.uk; Propr Eon; Man. Dir STEVE FLETCHER.

Gas

Regulatory Authority

Office of Gas and Electricity Markets (Ofgem): see Electricity, above.

Principal Gas Suppliers

Beacon Gas: POB 421, Wellesley Rd, Croydon, CR9 2YA; tel. (20) 8585-5000; fax (20) 8253-2245; Man. Dir ALAN LIAS.

British Gas Trading: 17 London Rd, Staines, Middx, TW18 4AE; tel. (1784) 645000; fax (1784) 645404; internet www.britishgas.co.uk; Man. Dir MARK CLARE.

Calortex: Dorcan House, Eldene Drive, Dorcan, Swindon, Wilts, SN3 3SH; tel. (1793) 555800; fax (1793) 555944; owned by Innogy Holdings.

CPL British Fuels Gas: Mill Lane, Winderworth, Chesterfield, Derbyshire, S42 6NG; tel. (1246) 277001; fax (1246) 212212; internet www.cplbritishfuels.co.uk; part of CPL Industries Ltd; CEO ANDREW GLASGOW.

London Electricity PLC: See Electricity, above.

Midlands Gas Ltd: Birchfield House, Joseph St, Oldbury, West Midlands, B69 2AQ; tel. (121) 244-2988; fax (121) 544-2985; subsidiary co of Midland Electricity PLC; Man. Dir PETER WEBSTER.

North Wales Gas: Packsaddle, Wrexham Rd, Rhostyllen, Wrexham, LL14 4EH; tel. (1978) 833233; fax (1978) 844586; e-mail north-wales-energy@btconnect.com; internet www.north-wales-energy.co.uk; CEO Dr STEWART HOWARTH.

Northern Electric PLC: See Electricity, above.

Norweb Gas (Energi): Talbot Rd, Manchester, M16 0HQ; tel. (161) 873-8000; e-mail info@energi.co.uk; internet www.norweb.co.uk; Man. Dir JOHN BECKETT.

ScottishPower: Energy Supply Division, Cathcart House, Spean St, Glasgow, G44 4BE; tel. (141) 568-2000; fax (141) 568-2016; internet www.scottishpower.plc.uk.

Southern Electric Gas Ltd: Westacott Way, Littlewick Green, Maidenhead, Berks, SL6 3QB; tel. (1628) 822166; fax (1628) 584400; internet www.scottish-southern.co.uk; CEO JIM FORBES.

SWEB Gas: 300 Park Ave, Aztec West, Almondsbury, Bristol, BS12 4SE; tel. (345) 652652; fax (1392) 448859.

Yorkshire Electricity Gas Ltd: Wetherby Rd, Scarcroft, Leeds, LS14 3HS; tel. (113) 289-2123; fax (113) 289-5150; internet www.yeg .co.uk.

Water

Regulatory Authority

Office of Water Services (Ofwat): Centre City Tower, 7 Hill St, Birmingham, B5 4UA; tel. (121) 625-1300; fax (121) 625-1400; e-mail enquiries@ofwat.gsi.gov.uk; internet www.ofwat.gov.uk; independent economic regulator of the water and sewerage cos in England and Wales; ensures compliance with the functions specified in the Water Industry Act of 1991; protects consumer interests through 10 regional WaterVoice Committees, which represent the interests of water customers and investigate customer complaints, and a WaterVoice Council (ONCC); Dir-Gen. of Water Services PHILIP FLETCHER.

Principal Companies

Albion Water Ltd: Riverview House, Beavor Lane, Hammersmith, London W6 9AR; tel. (20) 8748-9991; fax (20) 8741-6060; e-mail info@enviro-logic.com; internet www.enviro-logic.com; part of Enviro-Logic; Man. Dir Dr JEREMY BRYAN.

Anglian Water Services Ltd: Henderson House, Ermine Business Park, Lancaster Way, Huntingdon, Cambridgeshire, PE29 6XQ; tel. (1480) 323000; fax (1480) 326981; internet www.anglianwater.co.uk; Chair. ROBIN GORLAYE; Man. Dir ROY POINTER.

Mid-Kent Water PLC: Rocfort Rd, Snodland, Kent, ME6 5AH; tel. (1634) 240313; fax (1634) 242764; internet www.midkent.co.uk; Chair. KEITH TOZZI; Gen. Man. PAUL BUTLER.

Northumbrian Water Ltd: Abbey Rd, Pity Me, Durham, DH1 5FJ; tel. (191) 383-2222; fax (191) 301-6202; internet www.nwl.co.uk; owned by Suez; Chair. Prof. Sir FREDERICK HOLLIDAY; Man. Dir JOHN CUTHBERT.

Severn Trent Water Ltd: 2297 Coventry Rd, Birmingham, B26 3PU; tel. (121) 722-4000; fax (121) 722-4800; internet www .severn-trent.com; Propr Bouygues; Chair. VIC COCKER; Man. Dir BRIAN DUCKWORTH.

South East Water PLC: 3 Church Rd, Haywards Heath, West Sussex, RH16 3NY; tel. (1444) 448200; fax (1444) 413200; internet www.southeastwater.co.uk; Chair. J-F TALBOT; Man. Dir MARGARET DEVLIN.

South Staffordshire Water PLC: Green Lane, Walsall, West Midlands, WS2 7PD; tel. (1922) 638282; internet www .south-staffs-water.co.uk; Man. Dir DAVID PENNA; CEO BRIAN WHITTY.

South West Water Ltd: Peninsula House, Rydon Lane, Exeter, EX2 7HR; tel. (1392) 446688; fax (1392) 434966; internet www .south-west-water.co.uk; part of Pennon Group; Chair. KENNETH HARVEY; CEO ROBERT BATY.

Southern Water PLC: Southern House, Yeoman Rd, Worthing, West Sussex, BN13 3NX; tel. (1903) 264444; fax (1903) 691435; internet www.southernwater.co.uk; Man. Dir STEWART DERWENT.

Thames Water Utilities Ltd: Clearwater Court, Vastern Rd, Reading, RG1 8DB; tel. (118) 373-8000; internet www.thames-water .com; Propr RWE; CEO BILL ALEXANDER; Man. Dir TREVOR JONES.

Three Valleys Water PLC: POB 48, Bishops Rise, Hatfield, Herts, AL10 9HL; tel. (1707) 268111; fax (1707) 277333; internet www .3valleys.co.uk; Chair. Sir ALAN THOMAS; Man. Dir DAVID ALEXANDER.

United Utilities PLC: Dawson House, Great Sankey, Warrington, WA5 3LW; tel. (1925) 234000; fax (1925) 2360932; internet www .uuplc.co.uk; Chair. JOHN ROBERTS; Man. Dir LES DAWSON.

Welsh Water (Glas Cymru Cyfyngedig): Pentwyn Rd, Nelson, Treharris, Mid Glamorgan, CF46 6LY; tel. (1443) 452300; fax (1443) 452323; e-mail enquiries@glascymru.com; internet www.glascymru .com; f. 1989; Chair. Lord BURNS.

Wessex Water Services Ltd: Claverton Down Rd, Bath, BA2 7WW; tel. (1225) 536-000; fax (1225) 528-000; e-mail info@ wessexwater.co.uk; internet www.wessexwater.co.uk; Propr YTL (Malaysia); Chair. and CEO COLIN SKELLETT.

Yorkshire Water Services Ltd: Western House, Western Way, Halifax Rd, Bradford, BD6 2LZ; tel. (1274) 691111; fax (1274) 604764; internet www.yorkshirewater.com; Chair. JOHN NAPIER; CEO KEVIN WHITEMAN.

CO-OPERATIVE ORGANIZATIONS

Co-operative Union Ltd (incorporating ICOM the worker co-op federation): Holyoake House, Hanover St, Manchester, M60 0AS; tel. (161) 246-2900; fax (161) 831-7684; e-mail pgreen .coopunion@co-op.co.uk; f. 1869; co-ordinates, informs and advises the 45 retail consumer co-operative societies and 700 worker co-operatives and employee-owned businesses; Chair. BOB BURLTON; Chief Exec. and Gen. Sec. PAULINE GREEN.

Co-operative Group (CWS) Ltd: New Century House, Manchester, M60 4ES; tel. (161) 834-1212; fax (161) 834-4507; f. 1863; Chair. KEITH DARWIN; Chief Exec. GRAHAM J. MELMOTH; Sec. NICHOLAS A. EYRE.

National Association of Co-operative Officials: 6A Clarendon Pl., Hyde, Cheshire, SK14 2QZ; tel. (161) 351-7900; fax (161) 366-6800; Gen. Sec. L. W. EWING.

TRADE UNIONS

Central Organizations

Trades Union Congress (TUC): Congress House, 23–28 Great Russell St, London, WC1B 3LS; tel. (20) 7636-4030; fax (20) 7636-0632; e-mail info@tuc.org.uk; internet www.tuc.org.uk; f. 1868; a voluntary association of trade unions, the representatives of which meet annually to consider matters of common concern to their members. A General Council of 57 members is elected at the annual Congress to keep watch on all industrial movements, legislation affecting labour and all matters touching the interest of the trade union movement, with authority to promote common action on general questions and to assist trade unions in the work of organization. Through the General Council and its Executive Committee, the TUC campaigns on issues of concern to employees and provides services for affiliated unions. It also makes nominations to various bodies such as the Health and Safety Commission, the Equal Opportunities Commission and the Advisory, Conciliation and Arbitration Service Council. In late 2001 69 unions, with a total membership of over 6.7m. were affiliated to the TUC. The TUC is affiliated to the International Confederation of Free Trade Unions and the European Trade Union Confederation, and nominates the British Workers' Delegate to the International Labour Organization; Chair. General Council TONY YOUNG; Gen. Sec. BRENDAN BARBER.

Scottish Trades Union Congress: 333 Woodlands Rd, Glasgow, G3 6NG; tel. (141) 337-8100; fax (141) 337-8101; e-mail info@stuc .org.uk; f. 1897; 626,816 Scottish trade unionists affiliated through 47 trade unions and 30 trades councils (2002); Gen. Sec. BILL SPEIRS.

Wales Trades Union Council: 1 Cathedral Rd, Cardiff; tel. (29) 2034-7014; fax (29) 2022-1940; e-mail wtuc@tuc.org.uk; internet www.wtuc.org.uk; f. 1973; Gen. Sec. DAVID JENKINS.

General Federation of Trade Unions: Central House, Upper Woburn Pl., London, WC1H 0HY; tel. (20) 7388-0852; fax (20) 7383-0820; e-mail gftuhq@gftu.org.uk; internet www.gftu.org.uk; f. 1899 by the TUC; 36 affiliated organizations, with a total membership of 269,949; Sec. MICHAEL BRADLEY.

Principal Trade Unions Affiliated to the TUC

Includes all affiliated unions whose membership is in excess of 10,000.

ACCORD: Simmons House, 46 Old Bath Rd, Charvil, Reading, Berks, RG10 9QR; tel. (118) 934-1808; fax (118) 932-0208; e-mail info@accordhq.org; internet www.accord-myunion.org; Gen. Sec. GED NICHOLS; 23,995 mems.

Amicus (Amalgamated Engineering and Electrical Union—AEEU —section) (Manufacturing, Science, Finance—MSF—section): Hayes Court, West Common Rd, Bromley, Kent, BR2 7AU; MSF Centre, 33–37 Moreland St, London, EC1V 8HA; tel. (20) 8462-7755; fax (20) 8315-8234; e-mail r.fulham@headoffice.aeeu.org.uk; internet www.aeeu.org.uk; tel. (20) 7505-3000; fax (20) 7505-3030; e-mail info@msf.org.uk; internet www.msf.org.uk; f. 2002 by merger of AEEU and MSF; Joint Gen. Secs DEREK SIMPSON, ROGER LYONS; 1,146,000 mems.

Associated Society of Locomotive Engineers and Firemen (ASLEF): 9 Arkwright Rd, London, NW3 6AB; tel. (20) 7317-8600; fax (20) 7794-6406; e-mail info@aslef.org.uk; internet www.aslef.org .uk; f. 1880; Gen. Sec. MICK RIX; 15,790 mems.

Association of Teachers and Lecturers (ATL): 7 Northumberland St, London WC2N 5RD; tel. (20) 7930-6441; fax (20) 7930-1359; e-mail info@atl.org.uk; internet www.askatl.org.uk; f. 1978; Pres. MIKE MOORE; Gen. Sec. PETER SMITH; 160,000 mems.

Association of University Teachers (AUT): Egmont House, 25–31 Tavistock Place, London, WC1H 9UT; tel. (20) 7670-9700; fax (20) 7670-9799; e-mail hq@aut.org.uk; internet www.aut.org.uk; f. 1919; Pres. JANE McADOO; Gen. Sec. SALLY HUNT; 45,350 mems.

Bakers, Food and Allied Workers' Union (BFAWU): Stanborough House, Great North Rd, Stanborough, Welwyn Garden City, Herts., AL8 7TA; tel. (1707) 260150; fax (1707) 261570; e-mail bfawho@aol.com; internet www.bfawu.org.uk; f. 1861; Pres. RONNIE DRAPER; Gen. Sec. JOSEPH MARINO; 29,489 mems.

British Actors' Equity Association: Guild House, Upper St Martin's Lane, London, WC2H 9EG; tel. (20) 7379-6000; fax (20) 7379-7001; e-mail info@equity.org.uk; internet www.equity.org.uk; Pres. FREDERICK PAYNE; Gen. Sec. IAN MCGARRY; 35,246 mems.

Broadcasting, Entertainment, Cinematograph and Theatre Union (BECTU): 373–377 Clapham Rd, London, SW9 9BT; tel. (20) 7346-0900; fax (20) 7346-0901; e-mail info@bectu.org.uk; internet www.bectu.org.uk; f. 1991 as a result of merger between Asscn of Cinematograph, Television and Allied Technicians (f. 1933) and the Broadcasting and Entertainment Trades Alliance (f. 1984); Pres. TONY LENNON; Gen. Sec. ROGER BOLTON; 24,631 mems.

Ceramic and Allied Trades Union (CATU): Hillcrest House, Garth St, Hanley, Stoke-on-Trent, Staffs., ST1 2AB; tel. (1782) 272755; fax (1782) 284902; e-mail enquiries@catu.org.uk; internet www.catu.org.uk; f. 1825; Pres. J. ALCOCK; Gen. Sec. GEOFF BAGNALL; 16,168 mems.

Chartered Society of Physiotherapy (CSP): 14 Bedford Row, London WC1R 4ED; tel. (20) 7306-6666; fax (20) 7306-6611; e-mail csp@csphysio.org.uk; internet www.csp.org.uk; Chief Exec. PHIL GRAY; 32,576 mems.

Communication Managers' Association (CMA): CMA House, Ruscombe Business Park, Twyford, Berks, RG10 9JD; tel. (118) 934-2300; fax (118) 934-2087; e-mail reception@cma.org.uk; internet www.amicus-cma.org.uk; Gen. Sec. PETER SKYTE; 14,300 mems.

Communications Workers' Union (CWU): 150 The Broadway, Wimbledon, London, SW19 1RX; tel. (20) 8971-7200; fax (20) 8971-7300; e-mail info@cwu.org; internet www.cwu.org; f. 1995 by merger of the National Communications Union and the Union of Communication Workers; Pres. ANDY KERR; Gen. Sec. BILLY HAYES; 284,422 mems.

Connect: 30 St George's Rd, Wimbledon, London, SW19 4BD; tel. (20) 8971-6000; fax (20) 8971-6002; e-mail union@connectuk.org; internet www.connectuk.org; trade union for professionals in the communications industry; fmrly Society of Telecom Executives, name changed as above Jan. 2000; Pres. DENISE MCGUIRE; Gen. Sec. ADRIAN ASKEW; 19,000 mems.

Educational Institute of Scotland (EIS): 46 Moray Pl., Edinburgh, EH3 6BH; tel. (131) 225-6244; fax (131) 220-3151; e-mail enquiries@eis.org.uk; internet www.eis.org.uk; f. 1847; professional and trade union org. for teachers and lecturers in schools, colleges and universities; Pres. ALANA ROSS; Gen. Sec. RONALD A. SMITH; 54,663 mems.

FDA: 2 Caxton St, London, SW1H 0QH; tel. (20) 7343-1111; fax (20) 7343-1105; e-mail head-office@fda.org.uk; internet www.fda.org.uk; Pres. CHARLES PITT; Gen. Sec. JONATHAN BAUME; 10,010 mems.

Fire Brigades Union (FBU): Bradley House, 68 Coombe Rd, Kingston upon Thames, Surrey, KT2 7AE; tel. (20) 8541-1765; fax (20) 8546-5187; e-mail office@fbu-ho.org.uk; internet www.fbu.org.uk; f. 1918; Pres. RUTH WINTERS; Gen. Sec. ANDY GILCHRIST; 51,558 mems.

GMB: 22–24 Worple Rd, Wimbledon, London, SW19 4DD; tel. (20) 8947-3131; fax (20) 8944-6552; e-mail john.edmonds@gmb.org.uk; internet www.gmb.org.uk; f. 1982; Pres. MARY TURNER; Gen. Sec. KEVIN CURRAN; 692,147 mems.

Graphical, Paper and Media Union (GPMU): 63–67 Bromham Rd, Bedford, MK40 2AG; tel. (1234) 351521; fax (1234) 270580; e-mail general@gpmu.org.uk; internet www.gpmu.org.uk; f. 1991; trade union for print, paper, packaging, publishing and new media employees; Pres. RAY WILLIAMS; Gen. Sec. TONY DUBBINS; 203,229 mems.

Iron and Steel Trades Confederation (ISTC): Swinton House, 324 Gray's Inn Rd, London, WC1X 8DD; tel. (20) 7239-1200; fax (20) 7278-8378; e-mail istc@istc-tu.org; internet www.istc-tu.org; f. 1917; Gen. Sec. MICHAEL J. LEAHY; 51,400 mems.

Musicians' Union (MU): 60–62 Clapham Rd, London, SW9 0JJ; tel. (20) 7582-5566; fax (20) 7582-9805; e-mail info@musiciansunion.org.uk; internet www.musiciansunion.org.uk; f. 1893; Gen. Sec. JOHN F. SMITH; 31,500 mems.

NATFHE (The University & College Lecturers' Union) (formerly National Association of Teachers in Further and Higher Education): 27 Britannia St, London, WC1X 9JP; tel. (20) 7837-3636; fax (20) 7837-4403; e-mail hq@natfhe.org.uk; internet www.natfhe.org.uk; f. 1976; Pres. GERARD KELLY; Gen. Sec. PAUL MACKNEY; 65,031 mems.

National Association of Schoolmasters Union of Women Teachers (NASUWT): 5 King St, London, WC2E 8SD; tel. (20) 7420-9670; fax (20) 7420-9679; e-mail nasuwt@nasuwt.org.uk; internet www.teachersunion.org.uk; f. 1919; merged with UWT 1976; Pres. PETER BUTLER; Gen. Sec. EAMONN O'KANE; 200,257 mems.

National Union of Journalists (NUJ): Acorn House, 314–320 Gray's Inn Rd, London, WC1X 8DP; tel. (20) 7278-7916; fax (20) 7837-8143; e-mail acorn.house@nuj.org.uk; internet www.nuj.org

.uk; f. 1907; Pres. RORY MACLEOD; Gen. Sec. JEREMY DEAR; 22,930 mems.

National Union of Knitwear, Footwear and Apparel Trades (KFAT): 55 New Walk, Leicester, LE1 7EA; tel. (116) 255-6703; fax (116) 254-4406; e-mail head-office@kfat.org.uk; internet www.kfat.org.uk; f. 1991; Sec.-Gen. PAUL GATES; Dep. Gen. Sec. BARRY MORRIS; 16,000 mems.

National Union of Marine Aviation and Shipping Transport Officers (NUMAST): Oceanair House, 750–760 High Rd, Leytonstone, London, E11 3BB; tel. (20) 8989-6677; fax (20) 8530-1015; e-mail info@numast.org; internet www.numast.org; f. 1936; Sec. BRIAN ORRELL; 18,812 mems.

National Union of Rail, Maritime and Transport Workers (RMT): 39 Chalton Rd, London, NW1 1JD; tel. (20) 7387-4771; fax (20) 7387-4123; e-mail info@rmt.org.uk; internet www.rmt.org.uk; f. 1990; through merger of National Union of Railwaymen (f. 1872) and National Union of Seamen (f. 1887); Pres. JOHN COGGER; Gen. Sec. BOB CROW; 60,200 mems.

National Union of Teachers (NUT): Hamilton House, Mabledon Pl., London, WC1H 9BD; tel. (20) 7388-6191; fax (20) 7387-8458; internet www.teachers.org.uk; Pres. LESLEY AUGER; Gen. Sec. DOUG MCAVOY; 220,000 mems.

Nationwide Group Staff Union (NGSU): Middleton Farmhouse, 37 Main Rd, Middleton Cheney, Banbury, OX17 2QT; tel. (1295) 710767; fax (1295) 712580; e-mail ngsu@ngsu.org.uk; internet www.ngsu.org.uk; Gen. Sec. TIM POIL; 11,025 mems.

Prison Officers' Association (POA): Cronin House, 245 Church St, London, N9 9HW; tel. (20) 8803-0255; fax (20) 8803-1761; internet www.poauk.org.uk; f. 1939; Chair. COLIN MOSES; Gen. Sec. BRIAN CATON; 30,200 mems.

Prospect: 75–79 York Rd, London, SE1 7AQ; tel. (20) 7902-6600; fax (20) 7902-6667; e-mail ipmshq@ipms.org.uk; internet www.ipms.org.uk; f. 1919 as the Institution of Professionals, Managers and Specialists; changed name as above in 2001; Pres. DOUGLAS BOYD; Gen. Sec. PAUL NOON; 75,086 mems.

> **Prospect (Engineers' and Managers' Association Sector):** Flaxman House, Gogmore Lane, Chertsey, Surrey, KT16 9JS; tel. (1932) 577007; fax (1932) 567707; e-mail chertsey@prospect.org.uk; internet www.prospect.org.uk; f. 1913; Pres. DAVID SIMPSON; Gen. Sec. PAUL NOON; 28,776 mems.

Public and Commercial Services Union (PCS): 160 Falcon Rd, London, SW11 2LN; tel. (20) 7924-2727; fax (20) 7924-1847; internet www.pcs.org.uk; f. 1998 by merger of Civil and Public Services Asscn (f. 1903) and Public Services, Tax and Commerce Union (f. 1996); Pres. JANICE GODRICH; Gen. Sec MARK SERWOTKA; 267,644 mems.

Society of Radiographers (SoR): 207 Providence Sq., Mill St, London, SE1 2EW; tel. (20) 7740-7200; fax (20) 7740-7204; e-mail info@sor.org; internet www.sor.org; Pres. CHARLOTTE BEARDSMORE; Chief Exec. ANN CATTELL; 18,210 mems.

Transport and General Workers' Union (TGWU): Transport House, 128 Theobalds Rd, London, WC1X 8TN; tel. (20) 7611-2500; fax (20) 7611-2555; e-mail tgwu@tgwu.org.uk; internet www.tgwu.org.uk; Gen. Sec. WILLIAM (BILL) MORRIS; 871,512 mems.

Transport Salaried Staffs' Association (TSSA): Walkden House, 10 Melton St, London, NW1 2EJ; tel. (20) 7387-2101; fax (20) 7383-0656; e-mail enquiries@tssa.org.uk; internet www.tssa.org.uk; f. 1897; Pres. DAVID PORTER; Gen. Sec. RICHARD ROSSER; 31,494 mems.

UNIFI: Sheffield House, 1B Amity Grove, Raynes Park, London, SW20 0LG; tel. (20) 8946-9151; fax (20) 8879-7916; e-mail info@unifi.org.uk; internet www.unifi.org.uk; banking and other financial institutions; Gen. Sec. ED SWEENEY; 171,249 mems.

Union of Construction, Allied Trades and Technicians (UCATT): UCATT House, 177 Abbeville Rd, Clapham, London, SW4 9RL; tel. (20) 7622-2442; fax (20) 7720-4081; e-mail info@ucatt.org.uk; internet www.ucatt.org.uk; f. 1921; Pres. JOHN THOMPSON; Gen. Sec. GEORGE BRUMWELL; 123,000 mems.

Union of Shop, Distributive and Allied Workers (USDAW): Oakley, 188 Wilmslow Rd, Fallowfield, Manchester, M14 6LJ; tel. (161) 224-2804; fax (161) 257-2566; e-mail enquiries@usdaw.org.uk; internet www.usdaw.org.uk; Pres. MARGE CAREY; Gen. Sec. WILLIAM CONNOR; 316,000 mems.

UNISON: 1 Mabledon Pl., London, WC1H 9AJ; tel. (845) 355-0845; fax (20) 7387-6692; e-mail direct@unison.co.uk; internet www.unison.org.uk; f. 1993; through merger of Confederation of Health Service Employees (COHSE—f. 1910), National and Local Government Officers Asscn (NALGO—f. 1905) and National Union of Public Employees (NUPE—f. 1888); Pres. NANCY COULL; Gen. Sec. DAVE PRENTIS; 1,272,470 mems.

Unions not affiliated to the TUC

National Farmers' Union (NFU): (see p. 4306).

Union of Democratic Mineworkers (UDM): Berry Hill, Mansfield, Notts, NG18 4JU; tel. (1623) 626094; fax (1623) 642300; f. 1986; Pres. and Gen. Sec. NEIL GREATREX; c. 4,000 mems.

United Road Transport Union: 76 High Lane, Manchester, M21 9EF; tel. (161) 881-6245; fax (161) 861-0976; e-mail info@urtu.com; internet www.urtu.com; f. 1890; Gen. Sec. ROBERT MONKS; 16,800 mems.

National Federations

Confederation of Shipbuilding and Engineering Unions: 140/142 Walworth Rd, London, SE17 1JW; tel. (20) 7703-2215; fax (20) 7252-7397; 1,093,001 mems in 10 affiliated trade unions; Gen. Sec. ALAN ROBSON.

Federation of Entertainment Unions: 1 Highfield, Twyford, Hampshire, SO21 1QR; tel. (1962) 713134; fax (1962) 713134; e-mail harris@interalpha.co.uk; Sec. STEVE HARRIS.

National Federation of Furniture Trade Unions: 22–24 Worple Rd, London, SW19 4DD; tel. (20) 8947-3131; fax (20) 8944-6552; National Sec. PHIL DAVIES.

Transport

RAILWAYS

The Railways Act 1993, providing for a process of rail privatization, received royal assent in November 1993. A separate, government-owned company, Railtrack, was set up on 1 April 1994 to take responsibility for infrastructure (track, signals and stations) and levy charges on train operators for track access. British Rail was to remain in control of all businesses (except Railtrack) until their transfer to the private sector. As a result of the 1993 Railways Act, 25 Train Operating Units (TOUs) came into being on 1 April 1994. The Director of Passenger Rail Franchises was responsible for awarding franchises for the 25 TOUs as early as practicable and was to monitor the franchises to ensure compliance with the agreed contracts. The first passenger train franchises were awarded in December 1995, and two TOUs were transferred to private operators in February 1996; the final TOU transferred to private sector at the end of March 1997. Railtrack was transferred to the private sector in May 1996. In October 2001 the Government placed the heavily-indebted Railtrack in administration. In March 2002 Network Rail, a 'not-for-profit' Government-supported company, offered £500m. for Railtrack, and in July Railtrack shareholders voted to accept Network Rail's offer. Railtrack remained in administration until October 2002, when the final takeover by National Rail proceeded.

In July 1987 the Channel Tunnel Treaty was signed between the Governments of France and the United Kingdom, providing the constitutional basis for the construction of a cross-channel tunnel between the two countries, comprising a fixed link of two rail tunnels and one service tunnel, at an estimated cost of £4,700m. Of the total length of 31 miles (50 km), 23 miles are under the seabed. The tunnel was opened in May 1994. Plans to construct a 68-mile fast rail link between the tunnel and London, estimated to cost £5,800m., have been extensively delayed.

Office of the Rail Regulator: 1 Waterhouse Sq., 138–142 Holborn, London, EC1N 2TQ; tel. (20) 7282-2000; fax (20) 7282-2040; e-mail rail.library@orr.gsi.gov.uk; internet www.rail-reg.gov.uk; Rail Regulator TOM WINSOR.

British Railways Board: 55 Victoria St, London, SW1H 0EU; tel. (20) 7654-6201; fax (20) 7654-6010; internet www.brb.gov.uk; Chair. TERRENCE JENNER.

Network Rail Ltd: 40 Melton St, London, NW1 2EE; e-mail enquiries@networkrail.com; f. 2002 as a 'not-for-profit' company by train operators, rail unions and passenger groups to take over responsibility for running the UK rail network from Railtrack PLC; Chair. IAN MCALLISTER.

Strategic Rail Authority (SRA): 55 Victoria St, London, SW1H 0EU; tel. (20) 7654-6000; fax (20) 7654-6010; e-mail mckie@sra.gov.uk; internet www.sra.gov.uk; f. 1999 as the Shadow Strategic Rail Authority to provide strategic direction for Great Britain's railways, encourage investment and manage passenger rail franchises; formally came into being in February 2001; includes functions of Office of Passenger Rail Franchising f. 1993 to monitor and manage the 25 passenger train franchises operating on the national railway network in Great Britain; Chair. RICHARD BOWKER.

Channel Tunnel

Eurotunnel Group: Admin. Bldg, Cheriton Parc, Cheriton High St, Folkestone, Kent, CT19 4QS; tel. (8000) 969992; fax (1303) 288698; e-mail press.uk@eurotunnel.com; internet www.eurotunnel.com; customer information; Anglo-French consortium contracted to design, finance and construct the Channel Tunnel under a concession granted for a period up to 2052 (later extended to 2086); receives finance exclusively from the private sector, including international commercial banks; the Channel Tunnel was formally opened in May 1994; operates a service of road vehicle 'shuttle' trains and passenger and freight trains through the Channel Tunnel; Group Chair. CHARLES MACKAY; Chief Exec. RICHARD SHIRREFS.

Eurostar UK Ltd: Eurostar House, Waterloo Station, London, SE1 8SE; tel. (20) 7922-6180; fax (20) 7922-4499; internet www.eurostar.co.uk; division of London and Continental Railways, an international consortium which, in February 1996, was awarded the British operating contract for Eurostar, providing direct passenger rail services from London and Ashford, in Kent, to Paris and to Brussels; Man. Dir RICHARD BROWN.

Metropolitan Transport

London Underground: 55 Broadway, London, SW1H 0BD; tel. (20) 7222-5600; internet www.thetube.com; f. 1985; however, dates back to 1863; responsible for providing and securing the services of underground rail in Greater London; Chair. EDMUND WALLIS; Dir of Communications TONY MAGUIRE.

Docklands Light Railway: POB 154, Castor Lane, London, E14 0DX; tel. (20) 7363-9898; fax (20) 7363-9708; e-mail hsmith@dlr.co.uk; internet www.dlr.co.uk; opened Sep. 1987; in 1992 responsibility for the Railway was transferred from London Transport to the London Docklands Development Corporation; in 1998 the Railway was again transferred to the Dept for Environment, Transport and the Regions and in July 2000 the Railway became part of Transport for London; franchised to a private co, Docklands Railway Management, in March 1997; comprises a 36-station system bounded by Bank, Tower Gateway, Beckton, Stratford, Island Gardens (Isle of Dogs) and Lewisham; Chair. IAN BROWN; Gen. Man. HOWARD SMITH.

Transport for London (TFL): Windsor House, 42–50 Victoria St, London, SW1H 0TL; tel. (20) 7941-4500; fax (20) 7941-4605; e-mail enquire@tfl.gov.uk; internet www.tfl.gov.uk; f. 2000; executive arm of Greater London Authority responsible for activities of former London Transport; London's integrated transport body, responsible for all modes of transport, TFL is an executive arm of the Greater London Authority (GLA); Chair. KEN LIVINGSTONE; Commissioner ROBERT KILEY.

Associations

Railway Industry Association: 22 Headfort Pl., London, SW1X 7RY; tel. (20) 7201-0777; fax (20) 7235-5777; e-mail ria@riagb.org.uk; internet www.riagb.org.uk; f. 1875; represents UK-based railway suppliers, with a free sourcing service for products and services; Chair. J. COTTON; Dir-Gen. J. CANDFIELD.

Association of Train Operating Companies: 3rd Floor, 40 Bernard St, London, WC1N 1BY; tel. (20) 7904-3000; e-mail ewers@atoc.org; internet www.atoc.org; f. 1994; Chief Exec. GEORGE MUIR.

ROADS

Total road length in Great Britain in 2001 was 392,408 km (243,883 miles), of which 3,47265 km (2,158 miles) was motorway.

Passenger traffic is handled by London Regional Transport, municipal companies, Passenger Transport Executives, private bus companies, the Scottish Bus Group, and private coach companies. Under The Transport Act 1985, 75% of local bus services were deregulated in October 1986.

Highways Agency: St Christopher House, Southwark St, London, SE1 0TE; tel. (345) 504030; fax (20) 7921-4899; e-mail ha_info@highways.gov.uk; internet www.highways.gov.uk; executive agency of the Department for Transport; responsible for maintaining, operating and improving the trunk road network in England; Chief Exec. TIM MATTHEWS.

Exel PLC: Ocean House, The Ring, Bracknell, RG12 1AW; tel. (1344) 302000; fax (1344) 710031; internet www.exel.com; f. 1969 as the National Freight Corpn, a statutory body responsible to the Minister for Transport; became a limited company in 1980; bought by consortium of employees and former employees 1982; changed name from National Freight Consortium PLC 1989; merged with Ocean Group in 2000; Chair. J. DEVANEY; Chief Exec. JOHN ALLAN.

INLAND WATERWAYS

There are some 3,200 km (2,000 miles) of inland waterways in Great Britain under the control of the British Waterways Board, varying from the river navigations and wide waterways accommodating commercial craft to canals taking small holiday craft.

British Waterways: Willow Grange, Church Rd, Watford, Herts. WD17 4QA; tel. (1923) 226422; fax (1923) 201400; e-mail enquiries

.hq@britishwaterways.co.uk; internet www.britishwaterways.co.uk; f. 1963; Chair. Dr GEORGE GREENER; Chief Exec. Dr DAVID FLETCHER.

SHIPPING

There are more than 400 ports in the United Kingdom, of which London (Tilbury), Milford Haven, the Tees and Hartlepool ports, the Forth ports, Grimsby and Immingham, Southampton, Sullom Voe, the Medway ports, Dover, Felixstowe and Liverpool are the largest (in terms of the tonnage of goods traffic handled). Twenty-two ports, including Southampton, Grimsby and Immingham, Hull and five ports in South Wales, are owned and administered by Associated British Ports. The majority of the other large ports are owned and operated by public trusts, including London, which is administered by the Port of London Authority, and Belfast, administered by the Belfast Harbour Commission. Under the Ports Act (1991), trust ports were permitted to become private, commercial enterprises. By mid-1995 five major trust ports, including the Port of London Authority and the Medway Ports Authority, had been transferred to the private sector. Sullom Voe, Bristol and a number of smaller ports are under the control of local authorities, and there are more than 100 ports owned and administered by statutory or private companies; of these, Felixstowe, Liverpool (owned by Mersey Docks and Harbour Company) and Manchester are the largest.

Britain is linked to the rest of Europe by an extensive passenger and vehicle ship ferry service. There are also hovercraft services to Belgium and France for passengers and vehicles.

Associated British Ports: 150 Holborn, London, EC1N 2LR; tel. (20) 7430-1177; fax (20) 7430-1384; e-mail mcollins@abports.co.uk; internet www.abports.co.uk/; f. 1983; controls 21 UK ports; Chief Exec. BO LERENIUS.

The Baltic Exchange Ltd: 38 St Mary Axe, London, EC3A 8BH; tel. (20) 7623-5501; fax (20) 7369-1622; e-mail enquiries@balticexchange.co.uk; internet www.balticexchange.com; world market for chartering ships, charters aircraft, buys and sells ships and aircraft; Chair. PETER KITCHING; Chief Exec. JAMES BUCKLEY.

British Ports Association: Africa House, 64–78 Kingsway, London, WC2B 6AH; tel. (20) 7242-1200; fax (20) 74305-7474; e-mail info@britishports.org.uk; internet www.britishports.org.uk; promotes and protects the general interests of port authorities, comments on proposed legislation and policy matters; Dir D. WHITEHEAD.

Port of London Authority: Bakers' Hall, 7 Harp Lane, London, EC3R 6LB; tel. (20) 7743-7900; internet www.portoflondon.co.uk; Chair. SIMON SHERRARD.

Principal Shipping Companies

Bibby Line Ltd: 105 Duke St, Liverpool, L1 5JQ; tel. (151) 708-8000; fax (151) 794-1000; f. 1807; operates chemical carriers and shallow water accommodation units; Chair. S. P. SHERRARD.

Boyd Line Management Services Ltd: Albert Dock, Hull, HU1 2DH; tel. (1482) 324024; fax (1482) 323737; e-mail blms@boydline.co.uk; internet www.boydline.co.uk; vessel owners and managers; Man. Dir S. HARALDSSON; 2 vessels.

BP Shipping Ltd: Breakspear Park, Breakspear Way, Hemel Hempstead, Herts, HP2 4UL; tel. (1442) 232323; fax (1442) 255893; f. 1915; division of British Petroleum Ltd; Chief Exec. R. PANIGUIAN; 28 vessels.

Caledonian MacBrayne Ltd: The Ferry Terminal, Gourock, Renfrewshire, PA19 1QP; tel. (1475) 650100; fax (1475) 637607; e-mail mike.blair@calmac.co.uk; internet www.calmac.co.uk; state-owned ferry co; extensive car and passenger services on Firth of Clyde, to Western Isles of Scotland and a service between Ballycastle, in Northern Ireland, and Rathlin Island; 29 roll-on/roll-off vessels; Man. Dir LAWRIE SINCLAIR.

The China Navigation Co Ltd: Swire House, 59 Buckingham Gate, London, SW1E 6AJ; tel. (20) 7834-7717; fax (20) 7630-0353; f. 1872; wholly-owned subsidiary of John Swire & Sons Ltd; diversified fleet operating throughout the Pacific; Chair. J. W. J. HUGHES-HALLETT; 18 vessels.

Crescent Shipping Ltd: Brunswick House, 8–13 Brunswick Pl., Southampton, SO15 2AP; tel. (23) 8063-9777; fax (23) 8023-2208; internet www.crescentplc.com; Man. Dir J STEWART.

Exel PLC: (see p. 4310).

F. T. Everard & Sons Ltd: Candlewick House, 120 Cannon St, London, EC4N 6AS; tel. (20) 7398-4450; fax (20) 7398-4480; shipowners; forestry products service between Sweden, the UK and Ireland, tanker and dry cargo in Europe; 45 vessels.

Frontline Management (UK) Ltd: 12 Grosvenor Pl., London, SW1X 7HH; tel. (20) 7235-0500; fax (20) 7245-0768; e-mail frontuk@frontuk.co.uk; ship owners; Man. Dir MARTIN BENNY.

Furness, Withy & Co Ltd: Furness House, 53 Brighton Rd, Redhill, Surrey, RH1 6YL; tel. (1737) 771122; fax (1737) 761234; Man. Dirs PAUL EDWARDS, A. MOUZOUROPOULOS.

Fyffes Group Ltd: Houndmills Rd, Houndmills Industrial Estate, Basingstoke, Hampshire, RG21 6XL; tel. (1256) 383200; fax (1256) 383259; f. 1901; Chair. A. J. ELLIS; Sec. NIALL QUIGLEY.

Geest Line: POB 154, Windward Terminal, Herbert Walker Ave, Southampton, SO15 1AJ; tel. (23) 8033-3388; fax (23) 8071-4050; e-mail freight@geestline.co.uk; internet www.geestline.co.uk; Man. Dir W. SALMOND.

Gibson Gas Tankers Ltd: 1A Commercial Quay, 86 Commercial St, Leith, Edinburgh, EH6 6LX; tel. (131) 554-4466; fax (131) 554-3843; f. 1966; Man. Dir C. SPENCER.

Goulandris Bros Ltd: 34A Queen Anne's Gate, London, SW1H 9AB; tel. (20) 7222-5244; fax (20) 7222-6817; tankers and bulk carriers; Man. Dir N. G. KAIRIS.

Thos. & Jas. Harrison Ltd: Mersey Chambers, Covent Garden, Liverpool, L2 8UF; tel. (151) 236-5611; fax (151) 236-1200; e-mail mailroom@harrisons.co.uk; f. 1853; liner operators and UK agency, principally to the Caribbean and South America; Chair. MICHAEL A. SEAFORD.

Holbud Ship Managment Ltd: Hydery House, 66 Leman St, London, E1 8EU; tel. (20) 7488-4901; fax (20) 7265-0654; ship agents; Dir B. D. SABARWAL.

Kvaerner: Kvaerner House, 68 Hammersmith Rd, London, W14 8YW; tel. (20) 7339-1000; fax (20) 7339-1100; internet www.kvaerner.com; Group Chair. KJELL E. ALMSKOG.

Mobil Shipping Co Ltd: Mobil Court, 3 Clements Inn, London, WC2A 2EB; tel. (20) 7412-4000; fax (20) 7430-2150; tanker services; Man. Dir JOHN ENSTON.

Peninsular and Oriental Steam Navigation Co: 79 Pall Mall, London, SW1Y 5EJ; tel. (20) 7930-4343; fax (20) 7925-0384; e-mail communications@pogroup.com; internet www.pogroup.com; f. 1837; ferry operators; worldwide container shipping services; port management and development; also engaged in non-shipping activities incl. cold storage and road haulage; Chair. Lord STERLING OF PLAISTOW; Man. Dir Sir BRUCE MACPHAIL.

P & O North Sea Ferries Ltd: King George Dock, Hedon Rd, Hull, HU9 5QA; tel. (1482) 795141; fax (1482) 706438; internet www.ponsf.com; car and passenger services; Chair. G. D. S. DUNLOP; Man. Dir PETER VAN DER BRANDHOF.

P & O Nedlloyd Container Line: Beagle House, Braham St, London, E1 8EP; tel. (20) 7441-1000; fax (20) 7441-1500; f. 1996; by the merger of the container shipping units of the Peninsular and Oriental Steam Navigation Co and the Royal Nedlloyd Group NV; worldwide transport container services; Chair. HADDO MEIJER; Group Man. Dir ROBERT WOODS.

P & O: Channel House, Channel View Rd, Dover, Kent, CT17 9TJ; tel. (1304) 863833; fax (1304) 863223; e-mail customer.services@posl.com; internet www.posl.com; Man. Dir RUSS PETERS.

Shell International Trading and Shipping Co Ltd: Shell-Mex House, Strand, London, WC2R 0ZA; tel. (20) 7546-5000; fax (20) 7546-2200; worldwide operations trading and transporting crude petroleum and supplying petroleum products; incorporates Shell Tankers (UK) Ltd; Pres. R. J. W. WALLIS.

Souter Shipping Ltd: Clayton House, Regent Centre, Gosforth, Newcastle upon Tyne, NE3 3HW; tel. (191) 285-0621; bulk carriers, parcels tankers, conventional tankers; Man. Dir R. I. D. SOUTER.

Stena Line: Charter House, Park St, Ashford, Kent, TN24 8EX; tel. (1233) 647022; parent co Stena AB; services to Ireland and the Netherlands; CEO BO SEVERED.

Stephenson Clarke Shipping Ltd: Eldon Court, Percy St, Newcastle upon Tyne, NE99 1TD; tel. (191) 232-2184; fax (191) 261-1156; f. 1730; Man. Dir G. WALKER.

Andrew Weir & Co Ltd: Dexter House, 2 Royal Mint Court, London, EC3N 4XX; tel. (20) 7265-0808; fax (20) 7956-1178; f. 1885; shipowners, ship managers, intermodal transport operators, hotels, forestry and land, rubber dealers; Chair. Lord RUNCIMAN; Chief Exec. A. R. C. B. COOKE.

Shipping Associations

Chamber of Shipping Ltd: Carthusian Court, 12 Carthusian St, London, EC1M 6EZ; tel. (20) 7417-2800; fax (20) 7726-2080; e-mail postmaster@british-shipping.org; internet www.british-shipping.org; Pres. ROBERT WOODS (2003); Dir-Gen. MARK BROWNRIGG.

Passenger Shipping Association Ltd: Walmar House, 4th Floor, 288-292 Regent St, London, W1R 5HE; tel. (20) 7436-2449; fax (20) 7636-9206; formerly Ocean Travel Development (f. 1958); 50 mems; Chair. ERIC PHIPPIN; Dir and Sec. WILLIAM GIBBONS.

CIVIL AVIATION

In addition to many international air services into and out of the country, an internal air network operates from more than 20 main commercial airports.

The principal airports are Heathrow and Gatwick serving London, and Manchester, Birmingham and Glasgow, which in 2001 handled 60.5m., 31.1m., 19.1m., 7.7m. and 7.2m. passengers respectively. In March 1991 a new development was opened at Stansted, including a new terminal, cargo centre and rail link to central London. In 2001 Stansted handled 13.7m. passengers. In March 1988 a new £250m. passenger terminal was opened at Gatwick to increase capacity to 25m. passengers a year. A new £30m. London City Airport, in the Docklands, opened in October 1987, providing domestic and international flights to and from city centres for business travellers. In March 1993 a second terminal was opened at Manchester Airport. In November 2001 plans for the construction of a fifth terminal at Heathrow were approved by the Government. The first phase is scheduled for completion in 2007 and will increase capacity at the airport to some 90m. passengers a year.

BAA PLC: 130 Wilton Rd, London, SW1V 1LQ; tel. (20) 7932-6654; fax (20) 7932-6699; e-mail newsdesk@baa.com; internet www.baa.com; f. 1966 as British Airports Authority; privatized in 1987; propr of Heathrow, Stansted, Gatwick, Southampton, Glasgow, Aberdeen and Edinburgh airports; Chair. MARCUS AGIUS; Chief Exec. MIKE CLASPER.

Civil Aviation Authority: CAA House, 45–59 Kingsway, London, WC2B 6TE; tel. (20) 7379-7311; fax (20) 7240-1153; internet www.caa.co.uk; f. 1972; public service enterprise and a regulatory body responsible for economic and safety regulation of civil aviation; advises Government on aviation issues; conducts economic and scientific research; produces statistical data; regulates British airspace; represents consumer interests and manages airspace users' needs; Chair. Sir ROY McNULTY.

National Air Traffic Services (NATS) Ltd: 1 Kemble Street, London, WC2B 4AP; internet www.nats.co.uk; public private partnership between the Airline Group (a consortium of British Airways, BMI, Virgin Atlantic, Britannia, Monarch, easyJet and Airtours) Nats employees and the British Government; provides air traffic control services at 14 UK airports and operates and maintains a nationwide communications, surveillance and navigation network; Chair. CHRIS GIBSON-SMITH; CEO RICHARD EVERITT.

Principal Private Airlines

Air 2000 Ltd: First Choice House, London Rd, Crawley, West Sussex, RH10 2GX; tel. (1293) 518966; fax (1293) 524642; internet www.air2000.com; f. 1987; wholly-owned subsidiary of First Choice Holidays; operates charter flights from 22 UK airports to 69 destinations worldwide and a scheduled service to Cyprus; Man. Dir KEN SMITH.

Britannia Airways: Britannia House, London Luton Airport, Luton, LU2 9ND; tel. (1582) 424155; fax (1582) 428272; e-mail webrelations@uk.britanniaairways.com; internet www.britanniaairways.com; f. 1962; propr TUI AG; acquired Orion Airways in 1988; charter and inclusive tour operations; services from 20 UK airports to more than 100 destinations; Man. Dir KEVIN HATTON.

British Airways PLC: Waterside, Harmondsworth, POB 365, Middx, UB7 0GB; tel. (845) 779-9977; internet www.britishairways.com; f. 1972; operates extensive domestic, European and worldwide services, scheduled services to more than 250 destinations in 99 countries; Chair. Lord MARSHALL OF KNIGHTSBRIDGE; Chief Exec. RODERICK EDDINGTON.

British Mediterranean Airways Ltd: Cirrus House, Bedfont Rd, London Heathrow Airport, Staines, Middlesex, TW19 7NL; tel. (1784) 266300; fax (1784) 266353; internet www.britishmediterranean.com; f. 1994; scheduled passenger services to destinations in the Middle East, Africa and Central Asia; Chair. Lord HESKETH; Chief Exec. DES HETHERINGTON.

BMI: Donington Hall, Castle Donington, Derby, DE74 2SB; tel. (1332) 854000; fax (1332) 854662; internet www.flybmi.com; f. 1938; scheduled services to 25 destination in the UK, mainland Europe and North America; cargo and charter flights; Chair. Sir MICHAEL BISHOP; CEO A. REID.

BmiBaby: Donington Hall, Castle Donington, Derby, DE74 2SB; tel. (1332) 854990; e-mail babytalk@bmi-email.com; internet www.bmibaby.com; f. 2002; low-cost passenger services to 20 European destinations; Man. Dir TONY DAVIS.

Caledonian Airways: Caledonian House, Gatwick Airport, West Sussex, RH6 0LF; tel. (1293) 536321; fax (1293) 668353; f. 1988; as subsidiary of British Airways; acquired by Inspirations Ltd in 1995; operates charter passenger services to the USA, Canada, the Caribbean, Africa and the Far East; Chief Exec. TERRY SOULT.

easyJet Airline: London Luton Airport, Easy Land, Luton, LU2 9LS; tel. (1582) 445566; fax (1582) 443355; internet www.easyjet.co.uk; f. 1995; low-cost scheduled domestic and European passenger services from 8 UK airports; Chair. Sir COLIN CHANDLER; Man. Dir RAY WEBSTER.

Go: Enterprise House, London Stansted Airport, Stansted, Essex, CM24 1SB; tel. (1279) 666333; fax (1279) 681762; internet www.go-fly.com; f. 1998; low-cost passenger services to European destinations; acquired by 3i Group PLC in 2001; acquired by easyJet in 2002; Chair. KEITH HAMILL; Man. Dir BARBARA CASSANI.

KLM UK: Endeavour House, London Stansted Airport, Stansted, Essex, CM24 1RS; tel. (1279) 660400; fax (1279) 660330; internet www.klmuk.com; f. 1980 as Air UK; wholly-owned subsidiary of KLM Royal Dutch Airlines since 1997; serves Amsterdam from 15 UK regional airports; Chief Exec. FLORIS J. van PALLANDT.

Loganair Ltd: St Andrews Drive, Glasgow Airport, Abbotsinch, Paisley, Renfrewshire, PA3 2TG; tel. (141) 848-7594; fax (141) 887-6020; internet www.loganair.co.uk; f. 1962; operating as British Airways franchisee; Scottish domestic services; Chair. SCOTT GRIER; Chief Exec. JIM CAMERON.

Monarch Airlines: London Luton Airport, Luton, LU2 9NU; tel. (1582) 400000; fax (1582) 411000; internet www.monarchairlines.com; f. 1967; scheduled and charter services to the Mediterranean, the Caribbean, Africa and the Far East; Man. Dir D. L. BERNSTEIN.

MyTravel: Parkway Three, 300 Princess Rd, Manchester, M14 7LU; tel. (161) 232-6600; fax (161) 232-6610; internet www.uk/mytravel.com; world-wide charter operations; operates scheduled, chartered and low-cost passenger service to European destinations; Chair ERIC SANDERSON; CEO PETER McHUGH.

MyTravelLite: Parkway One, 300 Princess Rd, Manchester, M14 7QU; tel. (8701) 564564; internet www.mytravellite.com; low-cost passenger services to five European destinations; Man. Dir TIM JEANS.

Virgin Atlantic Airways: Manor Royal, Crawley, West Sussex, RH10 2NU; tel. (1293) 562345; fax (1293) 561721; internet www.virgin-atlantic.com; f. 1984; operates services to destinations in the USA, the Caribbean and the Far East; Chair. Sir RICHARD BRANSON.

Tourism

In 2001 there were an estimated 22.8m. arrivals by foreign visitors to the United Kingdom, generating £11,306m. in revenue.

British Tourist Authority: Thames Tower, Black's Rd, London, W6 9EL; tel. (20) 8846-9000; fax (20) 8563-0302; internet www.visitbritain.com; responsible for promoting the UK as a destination for visitors from overseas; Chair. DAVID QUARMBY; Chief Exec. TOM WRIGHT.

English Tourism Council: Thames Tower, Black's Rd, London, W6 9EL; tel. (20) 8563-3000; fax (20) 8563-0302; internet www.englishtourism.org.uk; Chair. ALAN BRITTEN; Chief Exec. MARY LYNCH.

visitscotland: 23 Ravelston Terrace, Edinburgh, EH4 3TP; tel. (131) 332-2433; fax (131) 315-2906; internet www.visitscotland.com; Chair. PETER LEDERER; Chief Exec. PHILIP RIDDLE.

Wales Tourist Board: Brunel House, 2 Fitzalan Rd, Cardiff, CF2 1UY; tel. (29) 2049-9909; fax (29) 2048-5031; e-mail philip.evans@tourism.wales.gov.uk; Chair. PHILIP EVANS; Chief Exec. JONATHAN JONES.

Northern Ireland Tourist Board: see under Northern Ireland (see p. 4330).

NORTHERN IRELAND

Introductory Survey

Location, Climate, Language, Religion, Flag, Capital

Northern Ireland is situated in the north-east of Ireland and forms part of the United Kingdom of Great Britain and Northern Ireland. It comprises six of the nine counties in the Irish province of Ulster: Antrim, Armagh, Down, Fermanagh, Londonderry and Tyrone. The rest of the island comprises the Republic of Ireland. The climate is mild and free from extremes of temperature. The language is English. Almost all the inhabitants profess Christianity: about 58% are Protestants and 42% Roman Catholics. The flag is the union flag of the United Kingdom. The capital is Belfast.

Recent History

The sectarian tension that has characterized Ireland's history began with the first major settlement by British Protestants in the 17th century. The main area of Protestant colonization in Ireland was the province of Ulster, comprising nine counties in the north-east of the island, in much of which Protestant supremacy was gradually established over the indigenous Roman Catholic population. In 1801 Ireland became part of the new United Kingdom, but throughout the 19th century there were demands for Irish independence, and an organized movement seeking Home Rule emerged. In the north, however, an Ulster Unionist Council was established in 1911, with Protestant support, to resist Irish nationalist demands and to campaign for the continuation of union with Great Britain.

The resentment of Irish nationalists culminated in 1916 with the Easter rising in Dublin. The rebellion was suppressed, but a clandestine organization, the Irish Republican Army (IRA), continued to wage a guerrilla campaign against the British administration in an attempt to force British withdrawal from Ireland. Faced with mounting popular support for independence, the British Government conceded to the demand for Home Rule, but only to a limited extent, since this was strongly opposed by Protestants in Ulster, who did not wish to become part of a Catholic-dominated all-Ireland state. The Government of Ireland Act (1920) provided for two parliaments in Ireland: one in Dublin, for 26 of the 32 counties, and one in Belfast, for the remaining six (mainly Protestant-populated) counties, which collectively became known as Northern Ireland and stayed within the United Kingdom. Although most of Ireland's political leaders initially rejected proposals for the division of the island, agreement was eventually reached on partition: in 1922 the 26 counties obtained dominion status as the Irish Free State, now the Republic of Ireland (q.v.).

With the support of the Protestant majority in Northern Ireland, the Unionists retained permanent control of the Belfast Parliament. The province was governed by a one-party administration, with an all-Unionist Cabinet headed by a provincial Prime Minister. The British monarch was represented by a Governor. Since the Catholics were not only effectively excluded from political power, but also suffered discrimination in civil matters, a state of tension continued.

During the late 1960s an active civil rights movement emerged, which sought to end the Catholics' grievances by non-violent means. However, Protestant extremists viewed the movement as a republican threat, and resorted to violence against Catholic activists. The IRA was originally a small element in the civil rights movement, but, after the increasingly serious disturbances of 1968–69, a breakaway group, calling itself the Provisional IRA, embarked on a campaign of violence with the aim of reuniting Ireland on its own terms. In April 1969 the Northern Ireland Government requested that British army units be assigned to protect important installations and in August the British and Northern Ireland Governments agreed that all security forces in the province would be placed under British command. In March 1972, as a result of increased violence, the British Government assumed direct responsibility for law and order. Finding this unacceptable, the Northern Ireland Government resigned. The British Government prorogued the Northern Ireland Parliament and introduced direct rule from London, thus alienating many Protestants.

In 1973 new legislation abolished the office of Governor and the Northern Ireland Parliament, and provided for new constitutional arrangements. In June elections were conducted for a 78-member Northern Ireland Assembly, and an Executive was subsequently constituted from its members. An important part of this new 'power-sharing' arrangement was the establishment of a limited role for the Irish Government in Northern Ireland's affairs. Accordingly, in December, at Sunningdale (in southern England), the British and Irish Governments and the Northern Ireland Executive finalized an agreement to form a Council of Ireland (with members drawn from the Governments of Northern Ireland and the Republic), which would have a range of economic and cultural responsibilities in both parts of Ireland. However, the 'Sunningdale Agreement' and the new devolved authority in Northern Ireland were rejected by many Protestants, and led, in 1974, to a general strike. A state of emergency was declared and the Executive was forced to resign. The Assembly was prorogued, and the province returned to direct rule by the British Government. The collapse of the Sunningdale Agreement led to a rise in popularity of the more extreme Democratic Unionist Party (DUP—founded in 1971, and led by Ian Paisley), which established itself as the main rival to the previously dominant Ulster Unionist Party (UUP—the 'official' Unionists).

Throughout the 1970s the Provisional IRA and the Irish National Liberation Army (INLA, which emerged in 1975) continued their terrorist attacks on both British military and civilian targets, while Protestant 'loyalist' paramilitary groups engaged in indiscriminate bombings and killings of Roman Catholics.

Discussions between the Governments of the United Kingdom and the Republic of Ireland in 1984–85 culminated in the signing of the Anglo-Irish Agreement in November 1985. The Agreement, which was subject to review after three years, established the Intergovernmental Conference, through which British and Irish ministers were to meet regularly to discuss political, security, legal and cross-border matters relating to Northern Ireland. While giving the Irish Government a formal consultative role in the affairs of Northern Ireland, the Agreement recognized that the constitutional status of Northern Ireland remained unchanged and would not be altered without the consent of a majority of the province's population. The Agreement had the support of the predominantly Catholic Social Democratic and Labour Party (SDLP), and was approved by the Irish and British Parliaments. However, it was strongly opposed by most Unionist politicians, who organized mass demonstrations and violent protests against the agreement, and in November 15 Unionist MPs resigned their seats at Westminster. In the ensuing by-elections 14 Unionists were returned to Parliament, while one seat was won by the SDLP. In June 1986 the Northern Ireland Assembly was dissolved.

In December 1987 the Irish Government agreed to ratify the European Convention on the Suppression of Terrorism, which would facilitate the extradition of suspected IRA terrorists from the Irish Republic to the United Kingdom. Ratification was, however, accompanied by a provision that extradition was only to be granted subject to certification by the British Attorney-General that suspects against whom extradition warrants were issued (by the Irish Attorney-General) had a case to answer. In July 1988 the first Irishman was extradited from Ireland to the United Kingdom under the provisions of the European Convention: the defendant was, however, acquitted of charges of conspiracy to cause explosions in October 1991.

The Provisional IRA's campaign of violence in Northern Ireland escalated during 1987 and in 1988 IRA members conducted a successful campaign against British military targets, particularly in Western Europe. Between late 1988 and early 1991 a series of terrorist attacks took place against British Army personnel and politicians in both mainland Britain and in continental Europe.

In September 1989 the Irish Government demanded a review of the Ulster Defence Regiment (UDR), the main security force in the province, following allegations that intelligence documents had been passed to loyalist paramilitary groups by the UDR, and subsequently used by the organizations to target and murder members of the IRA. In May 1990 an inquiry into the alleged breaches of security confirmed the allegations, although it was emphasized that the practice was not widespread. Some 59 people were charged as a result of the investigations. Fresh evidence of collusion between the security forces and loyalist paramilitary organizations emerged during the case, heard in January 1992, of a member of the Ulster Defence Association (UDA) who was prosecuted as a result of the inquiry. The defendant, who was subsequently sentenced to 10 years' imprisonment on several charges of terrorist offences, continued to reveal his involvement with army intelligence, and in particular details of events leading to the murder by the UDA in 1989 of a republican lawyer, Patrick Finucane. In June 1999 a former British soldier, William Alfred Stobie, was charged with Finucane's murder. He subsequently claimed that he had been working as a police informer at the time and had warned them of the impending killing. Furthermore, it was revealed that Stobie had confessed to his involvement in the murder to Royal Ulster Constabulary (RUC—the Northern Ireland police force) detectives nine years earlier. The revelation prompted calls for a judicial inquiry into the original investigation of the killing. In September 2000 it was reported that an investigation into Finucane's murder, which had been established in April 1999 and was led by Sir John Stevens, the Commissioner of the Metropolitan Police Force, had revealed evidence of what it termed 'institutional collusion' between undercover army agents and loyalist paramilitaries. Earlier in September 2000 the British Prime Minister, Tony Blair, had given an undertaking to consider instituting an independent judicial inquiry into Finucane's murder upon the completion of the Stevens investigation and of the pending court cases. In late November 2001 Stobie was acquitted of any involvement in Finucane's murder, after it was ruled that, owing to medical reasons, the main prosecution witness was incapable of giving evidence to the court. The British Government subsequently stated that a judge of international standing would decide whether an independent public judicial inquiry into the murder would be held, and in August 2002 a former Canadian supreme court judge, Peter Cory, began investigating whether six cases where collusion between the security forces and paramilitary organizations had been alleged (including the Finucane murder) would be subject to public inquiries. Meanwhile, in mid-December 2001 Stobie was assassinated near his home in Belfast by loyalist paramilitaries.

In April 1991 the major loyalist paramilitary groups announced a new combined command structure and their intention to implement a cease-fire to coincide with formal discussions on the future of Northern Ireland (see below). However, following the collapse of the negotiations in early July, the paramilitary groups announced an end to their cease-fire and in August there was an intensification of sectarian violence. In an attempt to contain the conflict, three additional army battalions were deployed in Northern Ireland, bringing the total number of soldiers there to its highest level since 1979. In August 1992 the British Government announced the proscription of the UDA under the Emergency Provisions Act, a measure that was widely regarded as long overdue in the light of the UDA's paramilitary activities from the early 1970s onwards (some committed under the name of Ulster Freedom Fighters, or UFF).

In January 1990 the British Government launched an initiative to convene meetings between representatives from the major political parties in Northern Ireland and the British and Irish Governments to discuss devolution in Northern Ireland and the future of its relations with the Republic of Ireland. Sinn Féin (the political wing of the Provisional IRA) was to be excluded from the talks because of its refusal to denounce the IRA's campaign of violence. Lengthy negotiations ensued, and in June plans were announced for a three-tiered structure of interlocking talks. Bilateral discussions between the British Government and the DUP, the UUP, the SDLP and the Alliance Party began in April 1991. In mid-June all the parties approved the appointment of Sir Ninian Stephen, a former governor-general of Australia, to chair discussions between all the Northern Ireland parties and the Irish Government.

The principal point of contention of the talks was the Unionists' demand that Ireland hold a referendum on Articles 2 and 3 of its Constitution, which lay claim to the territory of Northern Ireland. The Irish Government, however, remained unwilling to make such a concession except as part of an overall settlement. With no progress made on the constitutional question, nor on the

subject of Ireland's role in the administration of Northern Ireland, the negotiations formally ended in early November 1992, and the Anglo-Irish Conference resumed.

In the general election to the United Kingdom Parliament in April 1992 nine of the then 17 seats contested in Northern Ireland were won by the UUP, four by the SDLP, three by the DUP and one by the Ulster Popular Unionist Party. Sinn Féin lost its seat in west Belfast (which had been held by the party's President, Gerry Adams, who had declined to take up his seat at Westminster) to the SDLP, apparently as a result of tactical voting on the part of Protestants in the constituency.

At the end of October 1993 the British and Irish Prime Ministers, John Major and Albert Reynolds, issued a joint statement setting out the principles on which future negotiations were to be based. The statement emphasized the precondition that Sinn Féin permanently renounce violence before being admitted to the negotiations. In mid-December the Prime Ministers made a joint declaration, known as the 'Downing Street Declaration', which provided a specific framework for a peace settlement. The initiative, which was widely supported by opposition parties in Britain and Ireland, referred to the possibility of a united Ireland and, for the first time in a joint statement, accepted the legitimacy of self-determination, while insisting on majority consent within Northern Ireland. Sinn Féin demanded further clarification of the Declaration before expressing a definitive stance on the proposals. However, at a meeting between Reynolds and Major in February 1994, the leaders insisted that inter-party talks on Northern Ireland would resume, based on the principles of the Declaration, even without the participation of Sinn Féin or the DUP (which had already rejected the document). In March the UUP condemned the Declaration, which effectively removed any confidence of achieving an imminent peace settlement. In May a written statement issued by the British Government to Sinn Féin, clarifying 20 specific questions on the Downing Street Declaration, marked a possible breakthrough in the peace process. However, in late July at a specially convened party conference Sinn Féin delegates rejected elements of the Declaration, in particular the commitment to the consent of the majority in Northern Ireland. The British and Irish Governments reiterated their intention to pursue the peace process in spite of Sinn Féin's stance.

On 31 August 1994 the IRA announced 'a complete cessation of violence' with effect from midnight that day. The announcement was widely welcomed, yet, while the Irish Government and the SDLP accepted that statement as a declaration of a permanent end to hostilities, the British Government insisted that the IRA should confirm that this was indeed the intention. Immediately following the announcement, loyalist paramilitaries conducted an indiscriminate killing in a Catholic area of Belfast. On 13 October the loyalist paramilitary groups declared a suspension of military activity, which was effectively to be linked to that of the IRA. Although the loyalist announcement was welcomed as a means of stimulating efforts to complete a peace settlement, the Irish Government urged a substantive response from the British to the IRA cease-fire, owing to fears that 'hard-line' republicans would advocate a return to violence in the absence of peace negotiations. Later that month Major announced new measures to reassert the peace process, including the removal of all security blocks on border roads, while adopting the 'working assumption' that the IRA cease-fire was permanent, and exclusion orders preventing Sinn Féin leaders from visiting Britain were removed. The first public meeting between Sinn Féin and government officials was held in December, marking the start of exploratory talks between the two sides. In February 1995 John Major and the new Irish Prime Minister, John Bruton, presented a Framework Document, together with a separate British government paper on a new Northern Ireland Assembly. The Framework Document reaffirmed the principles of the Downing Street Declaration, and included provisions for the co-operation and involvement of both Governments in the peace settlement, as well as guarantees of civil, political and human rights in the north and south of Ireland. In addition, the Document proposed the establishment of a cross-border body in which elected representatives of the Irish Parliament and a Northern Ireland Assembly might create and implement policy on issues agreed by the two Governments, in consultation with the Northern Irish parties. The proposals for the Northern Ireland Assembly envisaged an elected authority with wide legislative and executive responsibility (except, initially, over taxation, and law and order), although it was to be monitored by a three-member elected panel as part of a series of measures to verify the impartiality of, and maintain confidence in, the institution. Both Governments emphasized that the proposals were to form the basis of negotiations and public consideration, and any final agreement was to be subject to parliamentary approval and popular consent by means of a referendum.

Despite a positive Sinn Féin response to the Framework Document, the issue of decommissioning paramilitary weapons remained the major obstacle to the opening of peace negotiations. The Government repeatedly objected to Sinn Féin's linking of IRA decommissioning with the demilitarization of Northern Ireland. In May 1995, having agreed that these would be discussed as separate issues the Secretary of State for Northern Ireland, Sir Patrick Mayhew, and the Sinn Féin President, Gerry Adams, met (the highest-level encounter of the two sides in 20 years) at an investment conference for Northern Ireland, held in Washington, DC. Further political dialogue was hindered by Sinn Féin's opposition to the British Government's insistence that decommissioning of armaments by paramilitary organizations be a precondition to initiating all-party negotiations for the formulation of a peaceful settlement. In September the persisting differences between the British and Irish Governments were revealed when Bruton unexpectedly postponed a meeting with Major, at which the leaders were scheduled to announce a further peace initiative, when it became evident that no agreement satisfactory to all sides could be reached on the timing and other practicalities of the decommissioning of weaponry.

In June 1995 a by-election to the House of Commons was won by Robert McCartney, standing as an independent United Kingdom Unionist Party (UKUP) candidate. The result was considered to be a significant reverse for the mainstream Unionist parties and further undermined James Molyneaux's standing as leader of the UUP (which had been adversely affected by a challenge to his leadership in March). In August Molyneaux resigned from his position, with the declared intention of enabling his successor to prepare sufficiently for the next general election to the House of Commons. In September David Trimble was elected the new UUP leader.

Throughout November 1995 the British and Irish Governments pursued intensive efforts to conclude a substantial agreement on the future of the peace process prior to a visit by the US President, Bill Clinton, at the end of that month; however, these revealed further tensions between the two sides. Finally, the Prime Ministers announced their agreement to initiate preliminary talks involving all the parties in Northern Ireland with the British and Irish Governments, which were provisionally scheduled to commence in February 1996, and to establish an international commission to assess the practicalities of the decommissioning of armaments and other aspects of the peace process. This 'twin-track' initiative was strongly endorsed by Clinton, whose administration was considered to be an important element in the region's political manoeuvrings. The three-member commission, which was chaired by one of Clinton's advisers, George Mitchell, began meetings with all sides involved in the peace process in December 1995. Disciplinary beatings and killings remained a source of concern for both communities, and in late 1995 and early 1996 a spate of drugs-related murders, thought to have been perpetrated by the IRA, attracted widespread condemnation.

The final report of the international commission was issued in January 1996, and recommended proceeding with all-party talks on the condition that all sides endorse the eventual, complete disarmament of paramilitary organizations, the renunciation of violence and the cessation of all paramilitary 'punishment' attacks. According to the report, the issue of arms decommissioning was to be considered in parallel with the negotiations, while the eventual surrender of weaponry was to be conducted under international supervision, with those involved free from prosecution. The report was generally supported by all sides.

In February 1996 the IRA cease-fire was abruptly terminated with the explosion of a large bomb in London. The organization blamed the British Government for the resumption of hostilities, citing its inflexible response to the Mitchell report. Bruton and Major declared that they would suspend all ministerial dialogue with Sinn Féin, but would intensify efforts to achieve a peaceful settlement. At the end of the month the leaders announced an initiative to pursue the peace process, incorporating nationalist and Unionist demands. Consultations were to commence immediately on an electoral format to establish a forum for intersectoral dialogue, while 10 June was announced as the firm date for the initiation of comprehensive political negotiations, to be based on the 1995 Framework Document. In March the British Cabinet approved a 'hybrid' electoral system for the Northern Ireland forum, in an attempt to accommodate demands from all sides and to ensure a wide representation of the region's political groupings: of the 110 seats in the proposed body, five were to be elected from each of the 18 local constituencies, chosen on a party-list system, while the remaining 20 seats were to be taken by two representatives of each of the 10 most successful parties in the poll, on the basis of the total votes cast throughout the region. Participants in the all-party negotiations were to be selected from among the forum members. In the election, held on 30 May, the UUP secured 24% of the votes cast and the largest number of seats (30), while the DUP and SDLP took 21 and 17 seats respectively. Sinn Féin's 15% share of the votes, which was higher than had been anticipated, secured the party 17 seats. In addition, seven seats were won by the Alliance Party, three by the UKUP and two each by the Progressive Unionist Party (PUP), the Ulster Democratic Party (UDP), the Women's Coalition of Northern Ireland and representatives of Labour (a coalition of left-wing individuals and associations). The multi-party discussions, which commenced, as previously scheduled, on 10 June, were immediately undermined by Sinn Féin's exclusion, in the absence of a new IRA cease-fire declaration, and by Unionist opposition to the appointment of George Mitchell as Chairman of the plenary session of the proceedings, which they claimed was part of a nationalist agenda. An interim proposal, under which the UUP agreed to confirm Mitchell's appointment while a sub-committee was to be established to review procedural aspects of his role, secured the discussions temporarily, despite the continued opposition of the DUP and the UKUP. At the same time all the parties confirmed their commitment to the Mitchell principles. The first meeting of the forum was conducted a few days later. Despite the tentative progress in the peace discussions, further political uncertainty followed the explosion of a massive IRA bomb in Manchester, England, in June 1996 and both the British and Irish Governments undertook to review their relations with Sinn Féin.

In early July 1996 political events in Northern Ireland were dominated by sectarian disputes regarding the organization of traditional Protestant marches. The decision by the RUC to prohibit some 4,000 marchers from proceeding through the mainly Catholic area of Drumcree, in Portadown, Co Armagh, provoked widespread protests and was the focus of unionist demonstrations. Sectarian violence escalated and following five days of confrontation at Drumcree, the RUC, in an apparent attempt to prevent further disorder, decided to allow the march to proceed along its original route, despite the hostility of local residents. The reversal of policy was widely condemned and aggravated a deterioration in relations between the British and Irish Governments. The increasingly precarious peace process suffered a further set-back when the SDLP announced that it was to withdraw from the recently-elected forum, owing to the British Government's management of the crisis.

In October 1996 the UUP and the SDLP agreed on a draft agenda, based on the provisions of the Mitchell report (see above), to enable substantive multi-party talks to proceed without being dominated by the issue of decommissioning of paramilitary weapons. In November Sinn Féin revealed a set of proposals, formulated with the SDLP in order to bolster the peace process, which included the implementation by the British Government of confidence-building measures, such as the release of IRA prisoners, and a guarantee that Sinn Féin would be admitted to the talks in the event of a renewed IRA cease-fire. In response, John Major defined the terms by which the party could join the talks, namely, a credible and lasting restoration of the IRA cease-fire and an end to all paramilitary training activities and punishment beatings. However, the issue remained a source of contention with the Irish Government, which urged a more flexible response to any eventual IRA cease-fire announcement. At the end of December a car-bombing incident against a leading member of the republican movement generated fears that the loyalist cease-fire had been terminated. The attack followed an IRA shooting of a guard accompanying a DUP official at a Belfast hospital. While Unionist officials reasserted their support for the cease-fire, and in the absence of any formal declaration from the Combined Loyalist Military Command, the UDP and the PUP (both parties with alleged links to loyalist paramilitary organizations) were permitted to continue their participation in the political negotiations, which resumed in mid-January 1997. Nevertheless, a disintegration of the cease-fire remained a possibility, with a further car-bombing incident in January. In March an attack on a Sinn Féin office and a failed car-bomb attack were both suspected to have been conducted by loyalist paramilitaries. In early January the IRA launched two attacks against RUC targets. In February a British soldier was killed by an IRA sniper, confirming an IRA statement, issued a few days earlier to mark the first anniversary of the resumption of hostilities, that the campaign of violence was to be maintained alongside its political interest in securing a peaceful settlement. In March the all-party talks were suspended until after the general election in the United Kingdom, scheduled to be held on 1 May. In the weeks preceding the poll the IRA initiated a campaign in mainland Britain, causing considerable economic disruption. Within Northern Ireland sectarian tensions increased and there were incidents of arson attacks on Catholic churches and rioting by loyalists in a Catholic area of north Belfast.

In the general election to the United Kingdom Parliament, held on 1 May 1997, the UUP secured 10 seats with 32.7% of the votes cast in Northern Ireland. Sinn Féin regained a parliamentary mandate, winning two seats (with 16.1% of the votes), one of which was at the expense of the SDLP candidate, following the disintegration at the beginning of the year of an electoral pact between the two parties jointly to contest constituencies against Unionist candidates. The SDLP won three seats, with 24.1% of the votes. The DUP lost two of its previously held seats, securing two seats (13.6%), and the UKUP won its first seat in a general election (1.6%).

The newly elected Labour Government immediately undertook to demonstrate its commitment to the peace process, and, with its sizeable parliamentary majority (in contrast to the previous Conservative administration, which had relied on the Unionist MPs for a majority), generated renewed optimism that a settlement could be achieved. Prime Minister Anthony (Tony) Blair aimed to focus political deliberations by proposing a timetable for the talks, and reiterated that he envisaged their conclusion no later than May 1998—when the results were to be put to a popular referendum. In late June 1997 the British and Irish Governments announced a new initiative to accelerate the peace process, according to which the decommissioning of paramilitary weapons, together with other confidence-building measures, would be undertaken concurrently with political negotiations, in an attempt to facilitate Sinn Féin's participation in the process, and clarified that Sinn Féin would be eligible to join substantive negotiations six weeks after a new IRA cease-fire announcement. The conduct of sectarian marches once again aggravated tensions between the communities in Northern Ireland, and dominated the first meeting between Blair and the newly-elected Irish Prime Minister, Bertie Ahern, in early July. The new Secretary of State for Northern Ireland, Dr Marjorie (Mo) Mowlam, was severely criticized by nationalists when, after negotiations with local residents and organizers of the most contentious march at Drumcree failed to secure a compromise, the loyalist parade was permitted to proceed through the Catholic area of Portadown, albeit under heavy security. The incident prompted widespread protests and unrest in nationalist areas. However, a few days later members of the Protestant Orange Order agreed to alter the traditional route of four other processions, diminishing the prospect of more serious violence.

On 19 July 1997 the IRA announced a restoration of its cease-fire. A few days later the Irish and British Governments issued a joint statement that the all-party negotiations would commence on 15 September, with the participation of Sinn Féin. At the same time, however, the Unionist parties rejected the measures for weapons' decommissioning that had been formulated by the two Governments. At the end of August Mowlam concluded that the restoration of the IRA cease-fire was 'unequivocal' and invited Sinn Féin to join the inter-party talks. Accordingly, in September Sinn Féin endorsed the so-called Mitchell principles, which committed participants in the negotiations to accepting the outcome of the peace process and renouncing violence as a means of punishment or resolving problems, providing for the party's inclusion in the talks. The UUP, together with the DUP and UKUP which had already declared their boycott of any discussions with Sinn Féin, and other loyalist representatives, failed to attend the opening session of the talks when they resumed in mid-September, owing partly to a statement by the IRA that undermined Sinn Féin's endorsement of the Mitchell principles. The talks were further jeopardized by the explosion of a republican bomb in Co Armagh. The dissident paramilitary faction, the Community Army Council, which along with the Loyalist Volunteer Force (LVF) had been proscribed in June, claimed responsibility for the attack. The UUP consented to rejoin the peace negotiations a few days later, but the incident strengthened opposition within the Unionist movement towards Sinn Féin's participation in the political discussions. (Opposition within the republican movement towards Sinn Féin's acceptance of the Mitchell principles was also apparent, and culminated in December in the formation, by dissident republican supporters, of a 32-County Sovereignty Committee to focus on the objective of a united Ireland.) In late September all eight parties to the talks signed a procedural agreement to pursue substantive negotiations. At the same time the Independent International Commission on Decommissioning (IICD) was inaugurated, under the chairmanship of the former head of the Canadian armed forces, Gen. John de Chastelain. The first meeting between a British Prime Minister and Sinn Féin leaders in more than 70 years took place at the session of the talks in October, when Blair held private discussions with Adams and Martin McGuinness. During December the loyalist cease-fire, which had been undermined since October, came under increased pressure by activists who accused the Irish and British Governments of appeasing nationalists by accelerating the transfer and release of republican prisoners. At the end of December the murder of the convicted LVF leader, Billy Wright, by INLA prisoners prompted immediate retaliation and an escalation of sectarian violence throughout Northern Ireland. In early January 1998 Mowlam took the unprecedented action of meeting loyalist paramilitary prisoners within Belfast's Maze prison, which secured their continued endorsement of PUP and UDP participation in the peace discussions.

In mid-January 1998 Blair and Ahern published a document outlining a framework for negotiations. The so-called Propositions on Heads of Agreement envisaged 'balanced constitutional change' by both Governments and proposed wide-ranging institutional reform providing for a devolved form of government within Northern Ireland. At the end of January the two Governments resolved temporarily to expel the UDP, owing to its close relationship with the UDF/UFF—which the RUC stated had been involved in the murder of three Catholic Northern Ireland citizens since the start of the year, in violation of their declared cease-fire. In February Sinn Féin was suspended from the talks for a two-week period, following RUC claims that the IRA was responsible for two recent murders in Belfast. Unionist attempts to expel Sinn Féin permanently from the peace process because of ongoing extremist violence were rejected, owing to the RUC's insistence that recent nationalist acts of terrorism had not been sanctioned by the IRA leadership. On 25 March, with all eight parties having rejoined the proceedings, George Mitchell announced that the multi-party peace talks were to be concluded by 9 April. The deadline, which aimed to focus the determination of all parties towards achievement of a positive outcome to the peace process, was preceded by an intensive period of negotiations. Finally, on 10 April a settlement was announced. The so-called Good Friday Agreement envisaged radical reform of the political structures of Northern Ireland, its relations with Ireland, and its constitutional standing within the United Kingdom. The main provisions of the Agreement were as follows: the establishment of a 108-member elected Northern Ireland Assembly, with authority to legislate on all domestic matters currently administered by the Northern Ireland Office; an Executive Committee, to be elected by the Assembly and headed by a First Minister and Deputy First Minister; an obligation that the Assembly establish, within one year, a North/South Ministerial Council (which had been one of the most contentious issues of the talks) at which representatives of the Irish Government and the executive authority in Northern Ireland might consider issues of cross-border concern; regular meetings of representatives of the Irish Government with members of the British Parliament, the Northern Ireland Assembly and other regional assemblies of the United Kingdom, under a new British-Irish Council, with the objective of promoting co-operation, information exchange and agreement on issues of mutual interest; amendment of Articles 2 and 3 of the Irish Constitution; replacement of the 1985 Anglo-Irish agreement with a new bilateral accord, incorporating a British-Irish Intergovernmental Council to oversee the Assembly and North/South Council; and a commitment by all parties to achieve the decommissioning of paramilitary weapons within two years. In addition, the agreement incorporated guarantees of respect for human rights and equal opportunities, a review of criminal justice procedures, and a restructuring of security arrangements in Northern Ireland. Furthermore, both Governments pledged to accelerate the release of prisoners convicted of terrorist offences, but only of members of paramilitary organizations maintaining the cease-fire. Popular referendums to ensure all-island approval of the settlement were to be held in Northern Ireland and the Republic of Ireland in May. (Voters in the Republic would notably be asked whether they approved amendment of their Constitution to revoke the claim to the six counties.) In mid-April Trimble secured the critical support of his party; however, several dissident UUP politicians later joined the DUP and UKUP in their rigorous campaign to prevent an endorsement of the accord. In May the decision of the Protestant Orange Order to propose that its 80,000 members oppose the settlement contributed to growing concerns that a significantly divided Unionist vote could make the arrangements unworkable, even with the support of the majority of the electorate. A special conference of Sinn Féin members approved the accord and amended party rules to enable Sinn Féin politicians to take up seats in a Northern Ireland Assembly. In the referendums, conducted on 22 May, some 71.1% of voters in Northern Ireland and 94.4% of voters in the Republic approved the proposed peace settlement, securing its immediate future. Parties in Northern Ireland began almost immediately to prepare for the elections to the Northern Ireland Assembly, which were scheduled to be held on 25 June. Voting was to be conducted using the single transferable vote system of proportional representation, providing for six members to be elected from each of the 18 Westminster parliamentary constituencies, with a broad representation of political preferences. The outstanding political problems remained the decommissioning of weapons, with some Unionists insisting that the process be initiated before Sinn Féin members be permitted to participate in any 'power-sharing' arrangements, the reform of policing and management of the forthcoming sectarian marching season.

In the elections to the Northern Ireland Assembly, conducted on 25 June 1998, the UUP won 28 of the 108 seats, while the SDLP took 24, despite having won the largest share of first-preference votes under the new voting system. Sinn Féin won 18 Assembly seats. Those opposed to the Good Friday Agreement secured a total of 28 seats, including 20 representatives of the DUP, five of the UKUP and three dissident UUP politicians. The remaining seats were won by the Alliance Party (six), the PUP (two) and the Women's Coalition (two). Following the election, Lord Alderdice resigned as leader of the Alliance Party, owing to its decline in popular support, and was subsequently appointed as the presiding officer of the New Assembly. At the inaugural meeting of the Assembly, on 1 July, David Trimble was elected as First Minister of the executive body, while Seamus Mallon of the SDLP was elected as Deputy First Minister. However, that month sectarian violence threatened to disrupt the peace process following confrontations between the security forces and members of the Orange Order who, in defiance of the newly-established Parades Commission, sought to march its traditional route along the predominantly Roman Catholic Garvaghy Road in Drumcree. Tension mounted throughout Northern Ireland during early July as an impasse developed between the security forces and loyalists who, having established an encampment, continued to demand access to the Garvaghy Road. However, following an atrocity in Ballymoney, Co Antrim, involving the deaths of three young Roman Catholics in a petrol bomb attack on their home, in mid-July the majority of the loyalists in Drumcree abandoned their protest. In August the peace process again came under threat following a further atrocity in Omagh, Co Tyrone. In the worst single incident in Northern Ireland since the beginning of the conflict, 29 people were killed when an explosive device, planted by a republican splinter group, the Real IRA, was detonated. Later that month Ahern announced a series of anti-terrorist measures, including restrictions on the right to silence, in an effort to facilitate convictions against terrorists based in the Republic of Ireland. Similarly, Blair announced legislation, which was approved in September, including heightened powers to convict anyone conspiring within the United Kingdom to commit terrorist offences.

Progress in the peace process continued to be obstructed throughout late 1998 by a dispute between Unionists and Sinn Féin concerning the decommissioning of paramilitary weapons, with Trimble insisting that the admittance of Sinn Féin representatives to the Executive Committee be conditional on progress in the demilitarization of the IRA. (Under the electoral system, by which parties are allocated portfolios according to their strength in the legislative assembly, Sinn Féin was to have two representatives in the Executive Committee.) For its part, Sinn Féin insisted that the Good Friday Agreement did not specify when decommissioning should begin, only that it should be completed by May 2000. As a result of the dispute the deadline for the formation of the Executive Committee and the North/South bodies, specified as 21 October 1998 by the Good Friday Agreement, was not met. In November Blair held talks with Sinn Féin and the UUP in an effort to end the deadlock, and in December he asserted that the release of convicted terrorists under the accelerated prisoner release programme, which began in September, would continue despite demands made by Unionists for the release of nationalist prisoners to be linked with progress on decommissioning by the IRA. In mid-December agreement was finally reached on the responsibilities of the 10 government departments of the Executive Committee and of six North/South 'implementation' bodies. This was endorsed by the Northern Ireland Assembly in February 1999. However, the decommissioning dispute remained unresolved and Unionists continued to demand Sinn Féin's exclusion from the Executive Committee until the IRA had begun disarming.

In early March 1999 the date for the devolution of powers to the new Northern Ireland institutions, envisaged as 10 March in the Good Friday Agreement, was postponed until 2 April (Good Friday). However, despite strenuous efforts by Blair and Ahern to end the impasse, the April deadline was not met. An 'absolute deadline' for devolution was subsequently set for 30 June 1999, after which date, Blair asserted, he would suspend the Northern Ireland Assembly if agreement had not been reached. On 25 June the two Prime Ministers presented a compromise plan which envisaged the immediate establishment of the Executive Committee prior to the surrender of paramilitary weapons, with the condition that Sinn Féin guarantee that the IRA complete decommissioning by May 2000. Negotiations continued beyond the June deadline but collapsed in mid-July when Trimble announced that the UUP would not participate in a devolved administration with Sinn Féin until some decommissioning had taken place. Consequently the devolution of powers from Westminster was postponed until after the summer recess. A review of the peace process, headed by George Mitchell, began in early September. That month the former Chairman of the Conservative Party, Chris Patten, who had been appointed in April 1998 to head an independent commission charged with conducting a review of policing in Northern Ireland, published his report. Among the changes to the RUC recommended in the report was the establishment of an elected body of representatives drawn from all sections of the community to which the new force would be accountable. Roman Catholic officers were also to be aggressively recruited in order that the force should achieve a balanced representation from across the community, while the number of serving officers was to be reduced from 13,500 to 7,500, subject to the successful conclusion of the peace process. The report provoked anger from Unionists who particularly objected to plans to change the force's name, oath and symbols. Sinn Féin, meanwhile, renewed its demand that the force be disbanded.

In early October 1999 Peter Mandelson succeeded Mowlam as the British Secretary of State for Northern Ireland. In November Mitchell concluded the review of the peace process and succeeded in producing an agreement providing for the devolution of powers to the Executive Committee. The agreement followed a statement by the IRA that it would appoint a representative to enter discussions with the IICD. At a meeting of the ruling council of the UUP held in late November, Trimble persuaded his party to vote in favour of the agreement. However, the council was to meet again on 12 February 2000 to review the decommissioning process, when it was expected that the UUP would withdraw from the executive if the IRA had failed to begin submitting its weapons. On 29 November 1999 the Northern Ireland Assembly convened to appoint the 10-member Executive Committee. On 2 December power was officially transferred from Westminster to the new Northern Ireland executive at Stormont Castle. On the same day, in accordance with the Good Friday Agreement, the Irish Government removed from the Republic's Constitution its territorial claim over Northern Ireland. In mid-December the inaugural meeting was held, in Armagh, of the North/South Ministerial Council. The British-Irish Council met for the first time later that month. In late December Mandelson announced a review of security procedures in Northern Ireland and the withdrawal of some 2,000 troops from the province. In January 2000 Mandelson announced his decision to adopt the majority of the recommendations contained in the Patten report, provoking an angry response from Unionists. That month Adams dismissed the possibility of immediate IRA decommissioning, and a report by the IICD confirmed that there had been no disarmament. With the prospect of the collapse of the peace process the British and Irish Governments engaged in intensive negotiations. On 1 February the IRA released a statement giving assurances that its cease-fire would not be broken and expressing support for the peace process. On 4 February the IRA were given until 11 February to begin decommissioning. However, it failed to comply and legislation came into effect on that day suspending the new executive, legislative and co-operative institutions and returning Northern Ireland to direct rule. The IRA subsequently announced its withdrawal from discussions with the IICD, raising serious doubts about the future of its cease-fire. In addition, Adams refused to participate in any further review of the peace process until the suspended institutions had been restored. At a republican rally held at the end of February Adams announced that Sinn Féin had abandoned its special role of attempting to persuade the IRA to decommission.

Direct talks between the British and Irish Governments and the principal parties resumed in early May 2000 with the Government promising to restore the Northern Ireland institutions on 22 May and postpone the deadline for decommissioning until June 2001 subject to a commitment by the IRA on the arms issue. On 6 May the IRA responded by offering to 'initiate a process that will completely and verifiably put arms beyond use'. Under the offer a number of IRA arms depositories were to be regularly inspected by two independent international figures, Martii Ahtisaari, the former President of Finland, and Cyril Ramaphosa, a principal figure in the South African peace process. Trimble succeeded in securing the approval of the UUP, albeit by a narrow majority, of a return to power sharing and on 30 May power was once again transferred from Westminster to the new Northern Ireland institutions. In accordance with their continued policy of attempting to impede the functioning of the Assembly, DUP ministers agreed to retake their places in the Assembly but announced their intention to periodically resign their posts in order to disrupt parliamentary business.

In early June 2000, in an attempt to secure republican support for the Northern Ireland Policing Bill, Mandelson announced a number of amendments to the policing legislation, the most notable of which was the extension of arrangements to secure equal recruitment of Roman Catholics and Protestants to the new police force beyond the ten years originally envisaged. Later in June the IRA allowed three of its arms depositories to be inspected by Ramaphosa and Ahtisaari and announced that it had also resumed contact with the IICD. The two inspectors affirmed that the arms they had seen were 'safely and adequately stored' and that they had installed devices at the depositories, which would enable them to detect if the weapons were subsequently tampered with. Despite Ahern's optimism that the arms issue was close to settlement Blair, whilst acknowledging the moves as an important breakthrough for the peace process, displayed considerable caution.

In July 2001 the decision to once again prohibit the loyalist Orange Order from marching along the predominantly Roman Catholic Garvaghy Road in Drumcree provoked a renewed outburst of sectarian violence and numerous attacks on the security forces. Members of the RUC came under fire from loyalist demonstrators in the Shankhill Road area of Belfast and much of Northern Ireland was brought to a standstill as roads across the province were blocked. Later that month, under the terms of the Good Friday Agreement, the final group of 86 convicted terrorists was freed from prison in Northern Ireland. The British Government's decision was widely criticized as the release of the prisoners had been conditionally linked to the commencement of IRA arms decommissioning, which had yet to begin. In late August Mandelson warned feuding loyalist paramilitary groups that they risked further delaying IRA decommissioning if they continued their retaliatory attacks: three people had been killed and numerous others injured in a series of incidents suspected to be related to the trade in illicit drugs. In an attempt to quell unrest troops were once again deployed on the streets of Belfast and John Adair, the leader of the UFF, who was widely believed to be responsible for many of the incidents, was arrested and imprisoned; he had been released under the provisions of the Good Friday Agreement in September 1999. Nevertheless, unrest continued throughout late 2000 and a further four people were killed in a series of revenge attacks. In

mid-December, however, the feud was declared to be at an end by three of the four groups involved.

Meanwhile, in late August 2000 the SDLP leader, John Hume, announced his resignation from the Northern Ireland Assembly, owing to ill health, though he confirmed that he would retain his seat at Westminster and remain party leader. A by-election to the House of Commons in South Antrim in late September, precipitated by the death of the incumbent MP, resulted in the DUP winning what was regarded as a safe UUP seat by a margin of just 822 votes. The defeat was regarded as a significant reverse for Trimble and his policy of power sharing with Sinn Féin and prompted calls from his opponents in the UUP for the party to withdraw from the Northern Ireland Executive.

In mid-November 2000 Unionist attempts to postpone the passing of the Northern Ireland Policing Bill, by proposing an amendment to the element of it that would ensure equal recruitment of both Protestants and Roman Catholics, were narrowly defeated in the House of Lords. They had also argued that the planned reform of the RUC should only proceed 'after the Secretary of State has made a decision that all terrorism in Northern Ireland has ended'. Nevertheless the following week the bill received royal assent and later that month the House of Lords approved controversial legislation, which would enable members of the Irish Parliament to stand for election to the Northern Ireland Assembly as well as to the British Parliament.

The issue of IRA weapons decommissioning continued to severely threaten the peace process during late 2000 and early 2001 as Trimble came under increasing pressure from those opposed to the Good Friday Agreement within his own party to withdraw from the Assembly. In late October 2000 the UUP's ruling council narrowly defeated a motion tabled by an anti-Agreement MP, Jeffrey Donaldson, which had called for the party to withdraw from the Northern Ireland Executive unless the IRA commenced decommissioning of its weapons by the end of November. Trimble, however, announced he would take measures to exclude Sinn Féin ministers from attending North/South ministerial meetings as a result of the IRA's 'failure' to meet its commitments regarding the decommissioning of arms.

In late January 2001 Mandelson resigned from his position as Secretary of State for Northern Ireland (see chapter on Great Britain); Dr John Reid, hitherto Secretary of State for Scotland, was appointed to succeed Mandelson and became the first Roman Catholic to assume the Northern Ireland portfolio.

In early March 2001 the IRA unexpectedly announced that it had re-established contact with the IICD. Following talks with Ahern in Belfast Blair maintained that whilst a comprehensive settlement to the decommissioning issue remained some distance away the differences between the two sides were 'narrowing'. Both Ahern and Blair stressed the need for further talks to resolve the outstanding issues although these were not expected to commence until after local and general elections in the United Kingdom, which were to be held on 7 June. Earlier in March a bomb, suspected to have been planted by the Real IRA, intent on further disrupting peace negotiations, exploded outside the British Broadcasting Corporation building in London. The incident was widely condemned by all parties democratically involved in the peace process. A further bombing took place in mid-April at a post-office sorting depot in the British capital. The Real IRA had also been responsible for four previous attacks on mainland Britain during 2000 and early 2001. In May 2001 the US Government designated the Real IRA as a foreign terrorist organization and froze the group's assets in the USA. The US administration also took measures to prohibit US citizens from raising funds for the organization.

In May 2001 the Minister of Education, Martin McGuinness, survived a motion of 'no confidence', tabled in the Northern Ireland Assembly by the DUP, after he admitted in a written statement presented to the Saville inquiry (see below) that he was the IRA's adjutant (effectively second-in-command) in Londonderry in January 1972. McGuinness, however, denied that IRA gunmen had been involved in the exchanges of fire with security forces and rejected the claim of an eyewitness that he had fired the first shot.

The peace process suffered a major setback in early May 2001 when Trimble announced his intention to resign as First Minister on 1 July if the IRA had not commenced a process of putting its weapons beyond use by that date. He stressed, however, that the three UUP ministers would continue to serve in the Executive. Later that month Ramaphosa and Ahtisaari announced that they had again inspected the IRA arms depositories and confirmed that the weapons stored there had not been tampered with and remained secure.

At the general election to the British Parliament held on 7 June 2001 the UUP won six seats (compared with 10 in 1997) with 26.8% of the votes cast in Northern Ireland. The DUP secured five seats, gaining three at the expense of the UUP, with 22.5% of the votes cast. Sinn Féin increased its parliamentary representation, winning four seats with 21.7% of the votes, while the SDLP took only three seats with 21.0% of the votes. Voter participation in Northern Ireland was significantly higher than in the United Kingdom as a whole, with 68.0% of the electorate casting their ballot. The UUP's loss of seats to the anti-agreement DUP provoked concern among the parties working towards the full implementation of the Good Friday Agreement, and the UUP suffered a further significant reverse at local elections held in Northern Ireland later in June with Sinn Féin and the DUP making substantial gains at the UUP's expense.

In mid-June 2001 Blair and Ahern held emergency talks with representatives from the UUP, Sinn Féin and the SDLP in London, however, Trimble announced that he would not retract his threat to step down and, despite further discussions between the parties in Belfast later that month, on 1 July Trimble duly resigned. The administrative functions of the office of the First Minister were assumed on a caretaker basis by the Minister of Enterprise, Trade and Investment, Sir Reg Empey. (Mallon's position of Deputy First Minister became vacant, although he continued to exercise the functions of his office.) Trimble's resignation triggered a six-week period at the end of which, barring the resolution of the impasse between the parties and the election of a First Minister and Deputy First Minister, new elections to the Assembly would have to be held. Days later the IICD stated that the IRA had yet to decommission a single weapon, nor had it outlined how it intended to put its arms beyond use.

The prospects of a resolution to the continuing deadlock over the issues of decommissioning of arms, police reform and demilitarization deteriorated further during mid-2001 following the outbreak of renewed violent, sectarian clashes in the Ardoyne area of north Belfast in June, during which some 50 police officers were injured. The rioting continued into July and early that month a Catholic youth was killed by loyalist paramilitaries. Later in July at least 10 civilians and 113 police officers were injured after nationalists staged a series of protests to coincide with holding of traditional Orange Order celebrations. The RUC subsequently claimed that the IRA was responsible for fomenting the unrest.

In early August 2001, following several weeks of intensive discussions, the British and Irish Governments unveiled their joint 'Proposals for the Implementation of the Good Friday Agreement' which they maintained were non-negotiable, and granted the parties involved in the peace process five days in which to respond to them. The proposals stipulated that while decommissioning was not a precondition of the agreement, it remained indispensable to a political resolution and must be resolved in a manner 'acceptable to and verified by the IICD'. Furthermore, the package pledged new policing legislation, which would reflect more fully the recommendations of the Patten report; the introduction of a rolling programme to reduce the number of troops and army installations in the province; a review of the Parades Commission and the legislation under which it was established; the lifting of the ban on Sinn Féin ministers attending North/South Ministerial Council meetings; the appointment of an international judge to investigate controversial murder cases where security force collusion had been alleged; the introduction of a general amnesty for members of paramilitary organizations that had announced a cease-fire and against whom there are outstanding prosecutions; and the establishment of a new implementation group to oversee the workings of the Good Friday Agreement. However, while Trimble stated that he would 'carefully consider' the proposals, he remained adamant that in the continued absence of IRA decommissioning of weapons there would be no progress and no UUP member would stand for election as First Minister. Although the five-day deadline for responding to the proposals was not met, on 8 August both the IICD and the IRA issued statements confirming that they had agreed upon a confidential decommissioning scheme, and De Chastelain announced that he was satisfied that the IRA had begun a process that would put arms 'completely and verifiably' beyond use. Trimble described the announcement as a 'step forward', but insisted that it was

not sufficient for him to retract his resignation and demanded evidence of the actual physical destruction of weapons. Faced with the impending collapse of the Northern Irish institutions, on 10 August the British Government temporarily suspended the Northern Ireland institutions for a 24-hour period. Under a legal loophole contained within the Good Friday Agreement this decision allowed for a six-week extension to the previously imposed deadline for the election of a First Minister and Deputy. In response to the suspension the IRA announced that it had withdrawn the offer to commence the process of decommissioning. Notably, the declaration was issued just hours after the arrest of three suspected IRA members in Columbia on suspicion of collaborating with the left-wing guerrilla movement, Fuerzas Armadas Revolucionarias de Colombia (FARC), on illegal paramilitary training methods and bomb-making techniques. The DUP unsuccessfully tabled a motion to have Sinn Féin members excluded from the Assembly, although it was claimed that two of the men had previously been members of Sinn Féin but had no current links with the party, while the third man had never been a member of the party. Later in August, in response to allegations made by the Cuban authorities that one of the men detained in Columbia was Sinn Féin's Latin American representative, Adams stated that the men had not been representing Sinn Féin and had no authorization to represent the party. The three men were subsequently charged with training guerrillas to construct bombs and travelling on false documents, and were transferred to high security jail in Bogotá. Although the men refuted the charges and insisted that they had merely been studying the Colombian peace process, forensic tests indicated that there were traces of explosives on their clothing.

Also in August 2001 speculation that the RUC (which was renamed the Police Service of Northern Ireland—PSNI—in November) had ignored warnings of an imminent bomb attack in Omagh, prior to the atrocity in August 1998 (see above), prompted an inquiry by the Police Ombudsman for Northern Ireland, Nuala O'Loan, into the police force's investigation of the bombing. O'Loan's report, which was published in mid-December 2001, stated that the RUC's Special Branch had failed to pass on two separate warnings from informants to police officers on the ground, and that a number of serious mistakes were made during the subsequent police investigation into the attack. Furthermore, O'Loan maintained that the Chief Constable of the PSNI, Sir Ronnie Flanagan, had displayed 'defective leadership, poor judgement, and a lack of urgency', which had significantly reduced the chances of detaining and convicting those responsible for the bombing. She was also critical of the fact that five people mentioned in the two warnings had not been questioned by investigating officers. The report, nevertheless, concluded that it could never be known if the atrocity could have been prevented had the RUC heeded the warnings. Flanagan announced that he was considering legal action to have the O'Loan's report quashed, and days later Flanagan issued a formal response to the O'Loan report on behalf of the PSNI in which he maintained that the criticisms of the force were 'unfounded' and that, while some mistakes were made, nothing could have been done to prevent the bomb attack. In mid-August the British Government had announced revised policing proposals to bring the scheduled reforms to the Northern Ireland police force more in line with the suggestions contained within the Patten report. Under the revised proposals recruitment to the PSNI was to be divided equally between Protestants and Roman Catholics and they also allowed for the possibility of ex-paramilitary prisoners sitting on the 29 District Police Partnership Boards, providing they vowed to relinquish their support for terrorist organizations. Sinn Féin had rejected the proposals before their publication and insisted that they would refuse to nominate members to the new 19-member Northern Ireland Policing Board (NIPB), which would be responsible for overseeing the PSNI. The package was endorsed later that month by the SDLP and the Roman Catholic Church, and in September the UUP and the DUP agreed to appoint members to the board. On 4 November the RUC was officially renamed the PNSI and three days later the NIPB held its inaugural meeting. The two vacant Sinn Féin seats on the board were allocated to the DUP and the UUP. In early February 2002 the NIPB announced that it had decided to appoint a senior police officer from outside Northern Ireland to oversee the ongoing investigation into the Omagh bombing. The Chairman of the NIPB also issued a joint statement on behalf of the NIPB, O'Loan and Flanagan, which recognized that 'on the basis of the information available the Omagh bombing could not have been prevented'. Later that month Flanagan announced his resignation as Chief Constable of the PSNI but agreed to remain in his post until the end of April. Meanwhile, in late January Colm Murphy, the only person to have been charged in relation to the bomb attack, was sentenced to 14 years' imprisonment by the Special Criminal Court in Dublin for conspiracy to cause an explosion. In April Colin Cramphorn replaced O'Flanaghan in an acting capacity and in September Hugh Orde was appointed Chief Constable of the PSNI.

In early September 2001 violence again broke out in the Ardoyne area of Belfast as Roman Catholic children and their parents came under attack from loyalist protesters as they attempted to make their way to the Holy Cross Girls' Primary School, situated on the outskirts of a loyalist enclave in the predominantly nationalist area. The incidents were fiercely condemned by politicians of all parties and security forces were deployed to escort the children and their parents to the school. Days later four police officers were injured when an incendiary device was thrown at their protective security cordon. Despite pleas from numerous senior British and Irish politicians, the loyalist refused to cease their protest and disturbances continued in the area for several months, necessitating a permanent police presence outside the school. In late November, following negotiations between representatives of the Northern Ireland Executive and the two communities, the loyalists agreed to call off their protests after the two sides agreed a package of community safety measures for the area.

Meanwhile, in mid-August 2001 John Hume announced his intention to resign the leadership of the SDLP, owing to ill health; in November Mark Durkan, was elected to replace him. In early September the Alliance Party leader, Sean Neeson, also resigned from his post; he was succeeded that month by David Ford.

On 20 September 2001, as the six-week deadline neared expiry, the IRA stated that it was prepared to renew and intensify talks with IICD. Despite this move, two days later Reid announced a further 24-hour suspension of the Assembly, thus granting the parties a further six weeks in which to overcome the continuing impasse. Trimble subsequently announced that the UUP would table a motion in the Assembly to exclude the two Sinn Féin ministers from the Executive, and that if, as was almost certain, the motion was defeated and there was still no progress on the decommissioning issue by the IRA, UUP ministers would begin to withdraw from the Executive, thus precipitating its collapse. As sectarian clashes continued in Belfast in late September, resulting in the injury of some 30 police officers, Reid warned the UDA (which he held responsible for orchestrating the violence) that he would declare their cease-fire at an end if it continued to organize violent attacks. The UDA issued a statement in which it pledged to halt all attacks, however, following a series of further incidents and the murder of a journalist in Co. Armagh, for which the LVF claimed responsibility, Reid announced that the British Government no longer recognized the UDA/UFF and LVF cease-fires.

On 8 October 2001 the UUP exclusion motion was defeated and on 18 October the three UUP ministers along with the two DUP ministers resigned, thus increasing the likelihood of the province's return to direct British rule. However, the following day the IRA offered to intensify contacts with the IICD and McGuinness and Adams announced that they had asked the IRA to make a 'groundbreaking move' on the arms issue. This was, notably, the first time that Sinn Féin had appealed directly to the IRA to begin the decommissioning of weapons. On 23 October the IRA and the IICD issued separate statements, which confirmed that the IRA had taken the hitherto unprecedented step of putting a significant quantity of arms, ammunition and explosives beyond use. The move prevented the imminent collapse of the Northern Irish institutions and was widely welcomed by all pro-agreement parties. Trimble immediately announced that he would reappoint the three UUP ministers to the Executive and seek re-election to the post of First Minister. On 24 October the UUP ministers reassumed their posts and the following day the DUP reassumed its two portfolios, although as part of its policy of rotating ministers different members to those who stood down were appointed. Later in October Trimble received approval from the UUP Executive to retake his post as First Minister with the SDLP leader-elect, Mark Durkan, announcing his intention to stand for the position of Deputy First Minister. Their appointment was, however, subject to the securing of a majority of both nationalist and unionist members in the Assembly, and it was anticipated that a number of anti-

agreement unionists from within the UUP intended to vote against Trimble's re-election. Immediately following the IRA's decommissioning of arms the British Government commenced a rolling security reduction programme, including the dismantling of two army observation towers in South Armagh, and pledged a further reduction in the number of British troops based in the province.

Nevertheless, on 2 November 2001 Trimble was unsuccessful in his attempt to be re-elected as First Minister. Although, he secured 70.6% of the total votes cast (including all 38 nationalist votes), two anti-agreement members of the UUP voted against Trimble, thus preventing him from obtaining the constitutionally required majority of unionists in favour of his re-election. Following intensive negotiations three members of the independent Alliance Party and one member of the Women's Coalition agreed to temporarily redesignate themselves as unionists and on 6 November Trimble finally regained the post of First Minister. Durkan was returned as Deputy First Minister. The election was, however, marred by scuffles, which broke out between politicians outside the Assembly building.

In December 2001 the British Government provoked considerable controversy when it announced that it had agreed to grant Sinn Féin MPs access to the facilities of the House of Commons and that they would receive their full parliamentary allowances and travel expenses, despite the fact that they still refused to take their seats in Parliament or participate in debates, and would not swear their allegiance to the Queen. In January 2002 Sinn Féin MPs occupied offices in the House of Commons for the first time. In March 2002 Trimble provoked outrage in the Irish Republic when, during a speech at the UUP's annual conference, he described that country as a 'pathetic sectarian state'. Earlier that month Trimble had called for a referendum on the constitutional future of the province to be held concurrently with elections to the Northern Ireland Assembly, which were scheduled for May 2003.

In mid-2002, despite the announcement in April that the IRA had put a further quantity of arms, ammunition and explosives beyond use, the fragile state of the peace process was underscored by the unprecedented levels of street violence in North and East Belfast and by the ongoing detention and investigation of three Irishmen in Colombia accused of collaborating with the left-wing guerrilla movement, Fuerzas Armadas Revolucionarias de Colombia (FARC), on illegal paramilitary training methods and bomb-making techniques. The three detainees were subsequently discovered to have strong links with Sinn Féin, and in April a US congressional investigation heard testimonies of further evidence of current IRA links to left-wing rebels in Colombia. Adams' refusal to testify before the US investigation allied with the alleged IRA involvement in the theft of documents from PNSI Special Branch offices in Belfast in March and the discovery, in June, of an IRA intelligence database listing details of more than 200 judges, politicians and members of the security forces provoked Unionist demands that Sinn Féin ministers be removed from the power-sharing Executive and further 'crisis' meetings between the British and Irish Governments.

In mid-July 2002 the IRA issued an apology for the deaths and injuries of 'non-combatants' caused as a result of its actions over the previous 30 years. The sincerity of the apology was questioned by Trimble and senior Unionists were sceptical that the IRA remained committed to the peace process in the light of continued sectarian violence in Belfast, for which the UUP maintained that the IRA was primarily responsible. Earlier in July during talks between the British and Irish Governments and the pro-Agreement parties in Belfast, Trimble had implied that UUP ministers would resign from the Executive by the end of that month if the IRA did not clearly demonstrate its commitment to a 'full transition from violence to democracy'. He had also appealed to the British and Irish Governments to take sterner action against paramilitary groups and warned that the British Government risked losing public support for the Good Friday Agreement unless the ever-deteriorating situation in the province was resolved. In late July the British Government outlined new conditions for judging whether paramilitary organizations were observing their cease-fires, which would give 'particular weight' to intelligence that paramilitaries were engaged in training, targeting or acquiring weapons. Furthermore, Reid stated that he would use existing powers to ask the Assembly to exclude any party related to paramilitary organizations deemed to have breached the cease-fire.

Nevertheless, violent sectarian disturbances continued in Belfast during August 2002. Early that month the Real IRA was suspected to have been responsible for the detonating of a bomb which killed a Protestant man—the first fatality caused by the organization since the Omagh bombing in August 1998—and in mid-August a Roman Catholic was murdered in an apparent revenge act for the earlier wounding of a young Protestant. In September in his first report to the NIPB Orde stated that loyalists had been responsible for the majority of the recent violence in Belfast and again admitted that the PSNI's resources were being stretched to their limits in their attempts to address the ongoing violence. The situation was further exacerbated by the escalation of a feud between rival loyalist paramilitary groups, which resulted in a number of shootings, and Unionists called for the establishment of an independent body to monitor the paramilitary cease-fires. Later that month the UUP Council announced that it would withdraw UUP ministers from the Northern Ireland Executive on 18 January 2003 if the IRA and Sinn Féin had not demonstrated a complete transition to democracy and non-violence.

In early October 2002 Northern Ireland was once again plunged into political crisis after Sinn Féin's offices at the Northern Ireland Assembly were raided by police, who, as part of a major investigation into intelligence-gathering by Republicans, suspected that the IRA had infiltrated the Northern Ireland Office (NIO) and gained access to large numbers of confidential documents, including Reid's correspondence, highly sensitive intelligence material and details of members of the security forces and the prison service. Among a number of people detained by the police was Sinn Féin's Head of Administration, who was charged with possession of documents likely to be of assistance to terrorist organizations. Trimble accused Sinn Féin of a 'massive political conspiracy' and threatened to withdraw from the Executive unless the British Government proposed the expulsion of Sinn Féin from the Assembly. Emergency talks between the British and Irish Governments and the Northern Ireland political leaders followed; however, Blair's demands for IRA concessions on the arms issue were not met. On 11 October the two DUP ministers resigned from the Executive, and on 14 October Reid suspended the Assembly and returned Northern Ireland to direct rule. In a joint statement, Blair and Ahern announced that the devolved institutions would only be restored if Sinn Féin ended its link with paramilitary organizations and Blair subsequently called on the IRA to disband itself. Later that month the IRA announced that it had suspended all contact with the IICD and claimed that the British Government was to blame for the current crisis, having failed to honour its commitments under the Good Friday Agreement. Days earlier, following a cabinet reshuffle, Paul Murphy, hitherto Secretary of State for Wales, had assumed the Northern Ireland portfolio.

Also in October 2002 the trial commenced in Bogotá of the three suspected IRA members who were charged with 'instructing guerillas in the manufacture of bombs, detonation of explosive artefacts and the planning of terrorist attacks'. However, the three accused refused to attend the hearing claiming they would not receive a fair trial. Upon resumption of the trial in early December the Irishmen did not appear in court, asserting their right to remain silent and the trial was again adjourned after two key witnesses failed to attend the hearing. The trial resumed in March 2003.

Talks aimed at resolving the impasse continued between the major parties during late 2002 and early 2003, however, relations between Unionists and Nationalists were further strained in November 2002 by the arrest of a Roman Catholic civil servant, who had worked in the offices of both Trimble and Durkan, in connection with the earlier suspected IRA infiltration of the NIO. In December Trimble walked out of multi-party talks in Belfast in protest at the leaking of a confidential Irish government document that stated that the IRA was still 'actively engaged in training, targeting, recruiting and acquiring small quantities of weapons'. Further talks in January and February 2003 were overshadowed by a severe escalation of the feud between rival loyalist paramilitary organizations in Belfast, in which two senior members of the UDA were killed and in March Ahern and Blair announced that the elections to the Northern Ireland Assembly would be postponed until 29 May. In April US President George W. Bush met with Blair in the province to discuss the progress of the US-led military campaign to oust the regime of Saddam Hussein in Iraq and subsequently held talks with Ahern and the pro-Agreement parties at which he urged their leaders to 'seize the opportunity

for peace'. Despite these efforts, plans to publish proposals for reinstating the Northern Ireland institutions were abandoned just days later, after the British Government claimed that the IRA had failed to respond to its demand for a definitive cessation of paramilitary activities. In early May Blair postponed the elections until late 2003.

In November 1988 the European Court of Human Rights ruled in favour of four men who were protesting against being detained without charge for more than four days, under the Prevention of Terrorism Act (which allows detention for up to seven days). In December the Government responded to the ruling by announcing a derogation from the European Convention for the Protection of Human Rights. In November 1991 the UN Committee Against Torture expressed concern over cases of alleged ill-treatment of terrorist suspects in detention and other abuses of human rights in Northern Ireland, which had been detailed in a report compiled by a prominent human rights organization, Amnesty International. In September 1995 the European Court of Human Rights unexpectedly overturned an earlier decision of the European Commission of Human Rights and ruled that the killing of three IRA activists in Gibraltar, in 1988, was in breach of Article 2 of the Convention, defining the 'right of life'. While clearing the Government of operating a 'shoot-to-kill' policy, the Court insisted that excessive and unlawful force had been used. In July 1997 the newly-elected Labour Government confirmed that the European Convention was to be incorporated into United Kingdom law and applied in full in Northern Ireland. In April 1998 a report of a special inquiry of the United Nations Human Rights Commission, initiated in October 1997, upheld complaints by human rights groups regarding the RUC's intimidation of lawyers defending terrorist suspects and the failure to extend adequate legal rights to those detained under emergency legislation. In particular, the report recommended a new inquiry into the allegations that the RUC failed to prevent the murder, by UDA activists, of a republican lawyer, Patrick Finucane, in Belfast, in 1989 (see above); however, the Government rejected the proposal in the absence of any new evidence. In early May 2001 the European Court of Human Rights awarded compensation to the families of ten IRA members killed by security forces in Northern Ireland during the 1980s and 1990s, after it agreed that the Government had breached Article 2 of the Convention. It also criticized the investigation into the shootings of eight of those ten IRA members for its lack of independence.

In April 1998 representatives of civil rights groups and the Irish Government commended the British Government for initiating a new official inquiry into the 1972 fatal shooting of 14 republican demonstrators by the security forces in Derry (Londonderry). The inquiry, conducted by Lord Saville of Newdigate, began hearing evidence in March 2000 although it was not expected to conclude before 2004. The destruction by the British army, prior to the inquiry, of rifles required as evidence prompted lawyers representing the families of the victims to accuse the Minister of Defence of deliberately attempting to frustrate the process. In mid-November 2000 the Saville inquiry reopened following a three-month delay, which had been precipitated by the resignation of one of the two tribunal judges. In a significant development later that month the lawyer acting for the 440 soldiers involved in the case accepted, in contrast to the findings of the original inquiry, that none of the civilians officially listed as killed or wounded in the incident had been armed. He did, however, maintain that a second list of at least 34 'untraced or unidentified casualties' who were never publicly acknowledged as injured in the incident could have included in their number gunmen who had fired on the soldiers. In January 2003 Sir Edward Heath, British Prime Minister in 1972, appeared before the Saville inquiry and dismissed allegations that the shootings had been premeditated as 'absurd'.

Under new 'emergency powers' legislation, presented to Parliament in October 1997 as part of confidence-building measures to secure nationalist support for the peace process (see above), the Government announced an end to the practice of internment and consideration of a radical reform of the RUC (see above). The Government also confirmed its support of a report of the Standing Advisory Committee on Human Rights which urged greater equality of opportunity within Northern Ireland and criticized the procedure of issuing certificates against people deemed to be a security risk, preventing their employment in certain public sectors.

Government

The Northern Ireland Act 1974 made the Secretary of State for Northern Ireland and his ministers answerable to Parliament at Westminster for the government of Northern Ireland, under a parliamentary order which is renewable annually. In October 1982 a 78-member Northern Ireland Assembly was elected, in accordance with the Northern Ireland Act 1982: its role was primarily consultative, pending the devolution of executive power. The 1985 Anglo-Irish Agreement, signed by the Prime Ministers of the United Kingdom and of the Republic of Ireland in November, left the constitutional status of Northern Ireland unaltered, but gave the Republic of Ireland a consultative role in Northern Irish affairs, through an Intergovernmental Conference. In June 1986 the British Government announced the dissolution of the Northern Ireland Assembly, four months before the end of its four-year term, following a boycott of meetings by some members, in protest at the Anglo-Irish Agreement. Elections to a new 108-member Assembly were held on 25 June 1998, as part of the multi-party agreement on the future governance of Northern Ireland, approved by a popular referendum in May. An Executive Committee, headed by a First Minister, was constituted from among the legislative members. Responsibility for all matters formerly implemented by the Northern Ireland Office was transferred to the devolved authority under new parliamentary legislation implemented in December 1999. The 1998 Agreement also provided for the establishment of a North/South Ministerial Council, to facilitate co-operation between the Irish Government and representatives of the Northern Ireland executive on specific cross-border and all-island concerns, and of a British-Irish Council, comprising representatives of British and Irish Governments, members of the devolved authorities in Northern Ireland, Scotland and Wales, and representatives of the Isle of Man and the Channel Islands. The arrangements of the Anglo-Irish Agreement were replaced by a British-Irish Intergovernmental Conference, with responsibility to oversee the new political institutions. The new Northern Ireland institutions were suspended in February 2000, owing to a political impasse concerning the decommissioning of paramilitary weapons and Northern Ireland was returned to direct rule. On 30 May, following an agreement on the issue of decommissioning, power was once again transferred from Westminster to the new Northern Ireland institutions. The Northern Ireland Executive was suspended again on 14 October 2002 and Northern Ireland was returned to direct rule from Westminster.

Northern Ireland returns 18 members to the United Kingdom Parliament at Westminster.

Defence

All matters of defence come under the jurisdiction of the United Kingdom Parliament.

Economic Affairs

In 1997 Northern Ireland's gross domestic product (GDP) amounted to £15,468m., and GDP per head amounted to £9,235.

Agriculture (including hunting, forestry and fishing) contributed 3.9% of GDP in 1998, and engaged 5.5% of the employed labour force at mid-2000. The principal crops include barley, potatoes and wheat. Livestock-rearing (particularly poultry) and animal products are also important, as is fishing.

Industry (including mining, manufacturing, construction and power) contributed 27.1% of GDP in 1998, and at mid-2000 engaged 22.7% of the employed labour force.

Mining contributed 0.5% of GDP in 1998. The principal minerals are basalt, gritstone, limestone, and sand and gravel. Northern Ireland also possesses 1,200m. metric tons of recoverable reserves of lignite and two deposits of gold.

Manufacturing contributed 18.5% of GDP in 1998, and engaged 19.8% of the employed labour force in 1990. Among the principal manufacturing sectors are food products, beverages and tobacco, textiles and clothing, and pharmaceuticals. The sector is dependent on export markets for the majority of its sales.

Energy is principally derived from petroleum and coal. In 1989 coal was used by 71% of domestic consumers for main heating. In 1996 the construction of a pipeline linking Northern Ireland to the natural gas transmission system on mainland Britain was completed. The Northern Ireland Electricity Company (NIE) is linked to the Irish state power grid; in early 1998 the Government approved the construction of an electricity interconnector between NIE and the Scottish regional power company. Northern Ireland is heavily reliant on imports of mineral fuels.

Services accounted for 69.1% of GDP in 1998, and engaged 71.7% of the employed labour force at mid-2000. Financial and business services alone accounted for 16.4% of GDP in 1998. Tourism represents a small but expanding sector of the economy. Telephone-based services are also an increasingly important sector of the service industry.

Traditionally trade in Northern Ireland is dependent on mainland Britain, which is both the principal market for exports and the main source of imports. However, by 1998/99 exports to the rest of the world had increased considerably and sales outside Europe accounted for almost half of the total of £3,400m. Basic manufactures, especially textiles, and machinery and transport equipment are the main sources of export earnings. The principal import is petroleum.

According to official estimates, in the financial year ending 31 March 1999 budgetary revenue and expenditure were balanced at £7,167.2m. The budget included a grant-in-aid of £1,661.2m. towards revenue. In 1996 public expenditure was equivalent to 45.2% of GDP. An estimated 7.2% of the labour force were unemployed in April 1999.

For membership of economic groupings, see the preceding Great Britain chapter.

Northern Ireland's economy is closely linked to that of mainland Britain. However, GDP per head is substantially below that of the rest of the United Kingdom and unemployment, particularly the level of long-term unemployed, is traditionally higher than in any other region. None the less, Northern Ireland's rate of economic growth during the early 1990s exceeded that of Great Britain. The resumption of violence and an escalation of civil unrest in 1996–97 undermined the steady expansion of the Northern Ireland economy that had followed the cessation of sectarian conflict in 1994, and necessitated increased expenditure on security measures. With the endorsement of the peace settlement, in May 1998, Northern Ireland's economic prospects improved considerably. Prior to the referendum the Government had announced additional economic aid of £315m. to enhance the development of small businesses, transport infrastructure and employment in Northern Ireland. In addition, a new regional development strategy was to be implemented to ensure that the economic benefits of peace would be extended across both communities. However, investor confidence was largely dependent on the progress of the new Northern Ireland institutions, which resumed operating in May 2000 following a suspension of some four months (see Recent History). In addition, there was concern throughout the business community at the continuing strong value of sterling and its detrimental effects on export trade. The diversification away from traditional low-profit, low-skill sectors, which are particularly vulnerable to foreign competition, in favour of the higher value-added sectors of information technology and pharmaceuticals was identified as a principal means of sustaining economic development, and large investment was made in this sector in the late 1990s and early 2000s. By early 2002 the rate of unemployment in Northern Ireland had declined to its lowest level form more than 25 years while growth in industrial GDP was the highest of all regions in the United Kingdom. The province's first budget for some 30 years was announced in October 2000 and the budget for the 2002–03 financial year, announced in September 2001, made provisions for further increases in expenditure on health, social services and education. In mid-2002 the British Government announced an ambitious investment and reconstruction initiative for the province, and approved the establishment of a strategic investment body that would oversee the rebuilding of Northern Ireland's infrastructure and public services. Funding totalling £200m. was immediately made available to the Northern Ireland Executive as part of the arrangement.

Education

Education is compulsory between the ages of four and 16 years, and is available free of charge in primary, secondary (intermediate) and special schools. Fees are payable in all grammar schools but the great majority of the pupils in their secondary departments receive non-fee-paying places on the basis of their performance in Transfer Procedure Tests. In 1993/94 a new examination system was to be introduced (replacing the Transfer Procedure Tests), whereby pupils were to be tested at the ages of eight, 11 and 14. Children receiving education in the preparatory departments of grammar schools are charged fees. Schools are divided largely on a sectarian basis, although integrated education is increasingly favoured. Northern Ireland has two main institutions of higher education: Queen's University of Belfast (QUB) and the University of Ulster (UU), formed in 1984, with campuses in Belfast, Coleraine, Jordanstown and Londonderry. In the budget for 1998/99 £1,495.0m. was allocated to education, libraries, science and the arts (20.9% of the total expenditure).

Teacher training is catered for by two general Colleges of Education, and by departments of education at the QUB and the UU.

Public Holidays

The main public holidays are the same as for Great Britain, with the addition of 17 March (St Patrick's Day) and 12 July (Battle of the Boyne).

Weights and Measures

The Imperial system of weights and measures is gradually being replaced by the metric system (see under Great Britain).

Statistical Survey

Source: Northern Ireland Statistics and Research Agency, McAuley House, 2–14 Castle St, Belfast, BT1 1SA; tel. (28) 9034-8100; fax (28) 9034-8106; e-mail info.nisra@dfpni.gov.uk; internet www.nisra.gov.uk.

Area and Population

AREA, POPULATION AND DENSITY

Area (sq km)	13,576*
Population (census results)	
21 April 1991	1,577,800
29 April 2001	
Males	821,449
Females	863,818
Total	1,685,267
Population (official estimates at mid-year)	
1999	1,679,006
2000	1,682,944
2001	1,689,319
Density (per sq km) at April 2001	124.1

* 5,242 sq miles.

Capital: Belfast, estimated population 282,500 at mid-2000.

BIRTHS, MARRIAGES AND DEATHS

	Registered live births Number	Rate (per 1,000)	Registered marriages Number	Rate (per 1,000)	Registered deaths Number	Rate (per 1,000)
1996 . .	24,382	14.6	8,297	5.0	15,218	9.1
1997 . .	24,087	14.3	8,071	4.8	14,971	8.9
1998 . .	23,668	14.0	7,826	4.6	14,993	8.9
1999 . .	22,957	13.6	7,628	4.5	15,663	9.3
2000 . .	21,512	12.7	7,584	4.5	14,903	8.8

WORKFORCE JOBS
('000 at June 2000)*

Agriculture, hunting, forestry, fishing	40.1
Industry	164.3
Services	519.0
Sub-total	723.4
Government-supported trainees	10.6
Total	733.9
Males	397.8
Females	336.1

* Excluding HM Forces.

Agriculture

PRINCIPAL CROPS
('000 metric tons)

	1999	2000	2001
Wheat	22.3	36.2	25.6
Barley	167.6	179.1	167.9
Oats	12.3	14.2	12.8
Potatoes†	287.6	258.9	236.9

† Figures are for all marketable production, both maincrop and earlies.

LIVESTOCK
('000 head)

	1999	2000	2001
Cattle	1,718.5	1,676.5	1,679.1
Sheep	2,908.9	2,740.6	2,525.6
Pigs	490.3	413.5	385.6
Poultry	15,047.9	15,375.9	14,347.5

Fishing

(metric tons, live weight)

	1997	1998	1999
Herring	7,241	4,713	3,851
Mackerel	1,063	3,711	3,200
Horse mackerel	1,817	758	951
Cod	2,325	2,205	1,665
Hake	709	624	640
Prime*	71	98	78
Whiting	3,139	1,722	1,180
Other sea fish†	3,791	3,865	5,369
Shell-fish	7,839	7,261	7,499
Total catch	27,995	24,957	24,433

* Prime fish: turbot, brill, sole.

† Other sea fish: dabs, haddock, coalfish, skate, dogfish, pollack, sprats, roe, gurnard, conger eel, angler, ling, pout, megrims, plaice, witches, and other demersal fish.

Mining and Quarrying

('000 metric tons)

	1996	1997	1998
Basalt	6,974	6,286	6,107
Sandstone	4,941	6,042	6,584
Limestone	4,122	3,500	3,892
Sand and gravel	7,684	5,138	5,300

Finance

CURRENCY AND EXCHANGE RATES

Monetary Units
  100 pence (pennies) = 1 pound sterling (£)

Dollar and Euro Equivalents (31 December 2002)
  US $1 = 62.04 pence
  €1 = 65.06 pence
  £100 = $161.18 = €153.70

Average Exchange Rate (US $ per pound)
  2000   1.5161
  2001   1.4400
  2002   1.5013

BUDGET
(£ million, year ending 31 March)

Revenue	1997/98	1998/99	1999/2000
Northern Ireland share of UK taxes (net)	4,721.1	4,709.3	3,104.4
Adjustment for previous years . .	−139.6	—	—
Northern Ireland Office (grant-in-aid)	1,536.4	1,475.0	3,745.0
Regional and district rates . . .	277.2	324.3	503.5
Interest on advances. . . .	189.9	270.7	103.0
Other receipts	245.3	335.0	177.2
Excess of expenditure over revenue	32.3	—	—
Total	6,862.6	7,114.3	7,633.1

Expenditure	1996/97	1997/98	1998/99
Interest on borrowing	178.7	181.0	173.7
District rates	180.6	190.9	203.6
Supply services	6,338.2	6,490.0	6,570.7
of which:			
Agriculture, fisheries and forestry	163.8	189.1	165.7
Trade, industry, energy and employment	448.3	456.3	448.1
Roads, ports and transport . .	167.1	198.7	175.8
Housing.	217.0	237.8	265.2
Other environmental services .	212.8	195.5	167.8
Education, libraries, science and arts	1,431.9	1,438.2	1,495.0
Health and personal social services	1,508.0	1,639.2	1,695.1
Social security	1,965.8	1,936.0	2,113.3
Total (incl. others)	6,728.8	6,862.6	7,167.2

NATIONAL ACCOUNTS

Gross Domestic Product by Economic Activity[*]
(provisional figures, £ million at current factor cost)

	1997	1998
Agriculture, hunting, forestry and fishing . .	741	653
Mining and quarrying of energy-producing materials	9	10
Other mining and quarrying	72	77
Manufacturing	3,109	3,135
Electricity, gas and water supply	428	354
Construction	915	1,001
Wholesale and retail trade (including motor trade)	1,983	2,085
Hotels and restaurants	459	505
Transport, storage and communication . . .	900	938
Financial intermediation	583	591
Real estate, renting and business activities .	1,869	2,175
Public administration and defence[†] . . .	1,969	1,966
Education	1,252	1,367
Health and social work	1,373	1,380
Other services	650	672
Sub-total	16,314	16,907
Adjustment for financial services	−362	−406
Total	15,952	16,501

[*] Estimates of GDP in this table are on a residence basis, where the income of commuters is allocated to where they live rather than their place of work.
[†] Public administration, national defence and compulsory social security.
1999 (£ million): Total GDP 17,003.

Transport

RAILWAYS
(year ending 31 March)

	1999/2000	2000/01	2001/02
Passenger journeys ('000) . .	5,900	5,900	6,200
Passenger-km (million) . . .	221.7	227.1	239.7

ROAD TRAFFIC
(motor vehicles in use, at 31 March)

	1999	2000	2001
Private light goods vehicles . .	608,316	615,180	644,968
General goods vehicles (HGVs)	17,075	17,864	19,415
Buses	2,204	2,266	2,315
Agricultural tractors, etc. . . .	5,505	5,048	4,901
Motorcycles	13,087	14,116	15,205
Other vehicles	74,458	76,256	80,501

CIVIL AVIATION
(traffic)

	1999	2000	2001
Passengers ('000).	4,398	4,604	4,982
Freight (metric tons).	27,086	31,419	33,052

Tourism

VISITORS BY COUNTRY OF PERMANENT RESIDENCE
('000)

	1999	2000	2001
Great Britain	1,002	950	1,053
England and Wales . . .	726	681	739
Scotland.	276	681	314
Ireland.	384	380	365
Europe	92	126	106
France	13	23	17
Germany	23	29	23
Italy	11	15	8
Netherlands	11	14	21
Scandinavia	n.a.	n.a.	11
Other Europe	35	46	26
North America	123	148	102
USA	93	110	75
Canada	30	38	27
Australia and New Zealand . .	35	42	30
Other areas	19	25	20
Total	1,655	1,672	1,676

Communications Media

(at 31 March)

	1995	1996	1997
Television licences	373,990	395,018	406,222

Households with a telephone: 92% in 1997/98.

Education

(2000/01)

	Institutions	Students (Full-time)	Teachers (Full-time)
Pre-primary	95	4,635	190
Primary	924	179,077	8,911
Secondary	238	155,553	10,747
Special	48	4,674	795
Institutions of further education[*]	17	24,128	2,031
University colleges[*] . . .	2	1,362	108
Universities[*]	2	26,920	2,719

[*] Figures are for 1999/2000.

Directory

The Constitution

Following the prorogation of the Northern Ireland Parliament in 1972, responsibility for the Government of Northern Ireland rested with the Secretary of State for Northern Ireland. Direct rule continued until 1973, when the Northern Ireland Executive was established under the provisions of the Northern Ireland Constitution Act (1973). The Northern Ireland Executive assumed responsibility for the administration of Northern Ireland and was answerable to the Northern Ireland Assembly, elected in June 1973. The Executive collapsed in May 1974, and the Secretary of State resumed control of the Northern Ireland departments.

In October 1982 a new Northern Ireland assembly was elected under the provisions of the Northern Ireland Act 1982. Under the Act, the Assembly was eventually to resume legislative and executive functions, provided that it produced proposals for the resumption of its powers, deemed to be acceptable to the people of Northern Ireland by Parliament. In June 1986 the Assembly was dissolved.

In November 1985 the Anglo-Irish Agreement was signed by the Prime Ministers of the United Kingdom and the Republic of Ireland, leaving the status of Northern Ireland unaltered and confirming that the status of Northern Ireland would not be altered without the consent of a majority of its inhabitants. The Agreement provided for the establishment of an intergovernmental conference, through which the Government of the Republic of Ireland was permitted to make proposals on matters relating to Northern Irish affairs.

New constitutional arrangements for Northern Ireland were agreed by the leaders of Northern Ireland's political parties (with the exception of the Democratic Unionist Party and the United Kingdom Unionist Party) and by the British and Irish Governments in April 1998, and were approved in a popular referendum conducted in May. Accordingly, legislation was introduced into the United Kingdom Parliament to provide for the transfer of responsibility for the administration of Northern Ireland to an elected Assembly and Executive. A North/South Ministerial Council was established by the Assembly to undertake consideration of all-Ireland issues. Representatives of the Irish and British Governments, of the devolved authorities in Northern Ireland, Scotland and Wales and of the Channel Islands and Isle of Man were to convene under a British-Irish Council, to consider the development of the islands and formulate common policies, although with no legislative or administrative powers. A new bilateral agreement between the United Kingdom and the Republic of Ireland subsumed the 1985 accord and established a new British-Irish Intergovernmental Conference.

Northern Ireland returns 18 members to the United Kingdom Parliament at Westminster.

NORTHERN IRELAND EXECUTIVE

On 14 October 2002 the Executive was suspended and Northern Ireland was returned to direct rule from Westminster.

Secretary of State for Northern Ireland: PAUL MURPHY (responsible for the overall conduct of the Northern Ireland political process, policing, security policy, prisons, criminal justice and international relations for which the British Government remains responsible; also represents Northern Ireland's interest in the British Cabinet).

Minister of State: JANE KENNEDY (responsible for security, policing and prisons; following the suspension of the Northern Ireland Assembly, assumed responsibility for the Department of Education and the Department for Employment and Learning).

Parliamentary Under-Secretary of State: DESMOND BROWNE (responsible for relations with, and policy on, the institutions created by the Good Friday Agreement—Assembly, Executive, British-Irish Council; criminal justice; victims; elections; and equality and human rights issues; following the suspension of the Northern Ireland Assembly, assumed responsibility for the Department of Social Development, The Department of Health, Social Services and Public Sector and equality, human rights and community relations).

Parliamentary Under-Secretary of State: IAN PEARSON (following the suspension of the Northern Ireland Assembly assumed responsibility for the Department of Finance and Personnel, the Department of Enterprise, Trade and Investment, the Department of Agriculture and Rural Development, the Economic Policy Unit and European affairs).

Parliamentary Under-Secretary of State: ANGELA SMITH (following the suspension of the Northern Ireland Assembly assumed responsibility for the Department of the Environment, the Department for Regional Development and the Department of Culture, Arts and Leisure).

MINISTRIES

Following the suspension of the Northern Ireland Executive on 14 October 2002, responsibility for the ministries listed below was transferred to the Northern Ireland Office.

Office of the First Minister and Deputy First Minister: Block A, Castle Buildings, Stormont Estate, Belfast, BT4 3SR; tel. (28) 9052-8400; internet www.ofmdfmni.gov.uk.

Department of Agriculture and Rural Development: Dundonald House, Upper Newtownards Rd, Belfast, BT4 3SB; tel. (28) 9052-4999; fax (28) 9052-5003; e-mail library.dardni@nics.gov.uk; internet www.dardni.gov.uk.

Department of Culture, Arts and Leisure: 3rd Floor, Interpoint, 20–24 York St, Belfast, BT15 1AQ; tel. (28) 9025-8825; e-mail dcal@decalni.gov.uk; internet www.dcalni.gov.uk.

Department of Education: Rathgael House, 43 Balloo Rd, Bangor, Co Down, BT19 7PR; tel. (28) 9127-9279; fax (28) 9127-9100; e-mail deni@nics.gov.uk; internet www.deni.gov.uk.

Department for Employment and Learning: Adelaide House, 39–49 Adelaide St, Belfast, BT2 8FD; tel. (28) 9025-7493; fax (28) 9025-7555; e-mail employment.rights@delni.gov.uk; internet www.delni.gov.uk.

Department of Enterprise, Trade and Investment: Netherleigh, Massey Ave, Belfast, BT4 2JP; tel. (28) 9052-9900; e-mail information@detini.gov.uk; internet www.detini.gov.uk.

Department of the Environment: Clarence Court, 10–18 Adelaide St, Belfast, BT1 2GB; tel. (28) 9054-0540; e-mail cmb@doeni.gov.uk; internet www.northernireland.gov.uk/env.htm.

Department of Finance and Personnel: Rathgael House, Balloo Rd, Bangor, Co Down, BT19 7NA; tel. (28) 9127-9279; e-mail dfpni@nics.gov.uk; internet www.northernireland.gov.uk/dfp.htm.

Department of Health, Social Services and Public Safety: Castle Buildings, Stormont Estate, Belfast, BT4 3PP; tel. (28) 9052-0500; fax (28) 9052-0572; e-mail webmaster@dhsspsni.gov.uk; internet www.dhsspsni.gov.uk.

Department for Regional Development: Clarence Court, 10–18 Adelaide St, Belfast, BT1 2GB; tel. (28) 9054-0540; e-mail cmb@drdni.gov.uk; internet www.drdni.gov.uk.

Department for Social Development: Churchill House, Victoria Sq., Belfast, BT1 4SD; tel. (28) 9056-9100; fax (28) 9056-9240; e-mail ops@dsdni.gov.uk; internet www.dsdni.gov.uk.

Legislature

NORTHERN IRELAND ASSEMBLY*

On 14 October 2002 the Assembly was suspended and Northern Ireland was returned to direct rule from Westminster. Elections, scheduled to have taken place in May 2003, were subsequently postponed until the end of that year.

Presiding Officer: Lord ALDERDICE.

Election, 25 June 1998

	% of votes	Seats
Ulster Unionist Party	21.3	28
Social Democratic and Labour Party	22.3	24
Democratic Unionist Party	18.1	20
Sinn Féin	17.6	18
Alliance Party	6.5	6
United Kingdom Unionist Party	4.5	5
Independent Unionists	n.a.	3
Progressive Unionist Party	2.5	2
Northern Ireland Women's Coalition	1.6	2
Total (incl. others)	100.0	108

* In September 1998 the three independent Unionists formed the United Unionist Assembly Party. In January 1999 four assembly members resigned from the United Kingdom Unionist Party to form the Northern Ireland Unionist Party (NIUP). In December 1999 one of these members was expelled from the NIUP and became an independent Unionist.

Political Organizations

Alliance Party: 88 University St, Belfast, BT7 1HE; tel. (28) 9032-4274; fax (28) 9033-3147; e-mail alliance@allianceparty.org; internet www.allianceparty.org; f. 1970; non-sectarian and non-doctrinaire party of the centre, attracting support from within both Catholic and Protestant sections of the community; 5,000 mems; Leader DAVID FORD; Gen. Sec. STEPHEN FARRY.

Conservative and Unionist Party: (for headquarters in London, see Great Britain chapter) 2 May Ave, Bangor, Co Down, BT20 4JT; tel. (28) 9146-9210; f. 1870 as Conservative Central Office; organized in Northern Ireland since 1990.

Democratic Unionist Party: 91 Dundela Ave, Belfast, BT4 3BU; tel. (28) 9047-1155; fax (28) 9047-1797; e-mail info@dup.org.uk; internet www.dup.org.uk; f. 1971; pro-British; Leader Rev. Dr IAN R. K. PAISLEY; Party Sec. NIGEL DODDS.

Labour: 84–86 Main St, Killough, Downpatrick, Co Down, BT30 7QD; tel. and fax (28) 4484-1858; e-mail socialistni@online.pednet.co.uk; internet www.labourni.org; f. 1996; coalition of individuals, councillors and left-wing organizations representing non-sectarian trade union interests.

Northern Ireland Unionist Party: Room 358, Parliament Bldgs, Stormont, Belfast, BT4 3XX; tel. (28) 9052-1901; fax (28) 9052-1845; e-mail info@niup.org; internet www.niup.org; f. 1999; breakaway faction of United Kingdom Unionist Party; Leader CEDRIC WILSON.

Northern Ireland Womens' Coalition: 50 University St, Belfast, BT7 1HB; tel. and fax (28) 9068-1118; e-mail info@niwc.org; internet www.niwc.org; non-partisan coalition; aims to promote peace and greater female political representation in Northern Ireland; Elected reps MONICA WILLIAMS, JANE MORRICE.

Progressive Unionist Party: 182 Shankhill Rd, Belfast, BT13 2BL; tel. (28) 9032-6233; fax (28) 9024-9602; e-mail central@pup-ni.org.uk; internet www.pup-ni.org.uk; loyalist party; Leader DAVID ERVINE.

Sinn Féin ('Ourselves Alone'): 51–55 Falls Rd, Belfast, BT12; tel. (28) 9032-3214; fax (28) 9023-1723; e-mail sinnfein@iol.ie; internet www.sinnfein.ie; f. 1905; political wing of the Provisional IRA; seeks the reunification of Ireland and the establishment of a 32-county democratic socialist state; engages in community politics; Chair. MITCHELL MCLAUGHLIN; Pres. GERARD (GERRY) ADAMS.

Social Democratic and Labour Party (SDLP): 121 Ormeau Rd, Belfast, BT7 1SH; tel. (28) 9024-7700; fax (28) 9023-6699; e-mail sdlp@indigo.ie; internet www.sdlp.ie; f. 1970; radical, left-of-centre principles with a view to the eventual re-unification of Ireland by popular consent; Leader MARK DURKAN.

Ulster Unionist Party: Cunningham House, 429 Holywood Rd, Belfast, BT4 2LN; tel. (28) 9076-5500; fax (28) 9076-9419; e-mail uup@uup.org; internet www.uup.org; f. 1905; governed Northern Ireland 1921–72; largest political party in Northern Ireland; supports parity and equality for Northern Ireland within the United Kingdom; Pres. Rev. MARTIN SMYTH; Leader DAVID TRIMBLE.

United Kingdom Unionist Party: Parliament Bldgs, Stormont, Belfast; tel. (28) 9052-1482; fax (28) 9052-1483; e-mail info@ukup.org; internet www.ukup.org; Leader ROBERT MCCARTNEY.

United Unionist Assembly Party (UUAP): f. 1998 by independent Unionist members of Northern Ireland Assembly.

The Workers' Party: 6 Springfield Rd, Belfast, BT12; tel. (28) 9022-8663; fax (28) 9033-3475; present name adopted 1978; democratic socialist party; aims to win state power for the working class and to establish a democratic, secular, socialist and unitary republic in Ireland; Chair. (Northern Ireland) GERRY GRAINGER; Gen. Sec. PAT QUEARNEY.

The following paramilitary organizations are proscribed under Schedule 2 of the Emergency Provisions Act 1978: (nationalist) the Irish Republican Army, the Irish National Liberation Army, Cumann na mBan (women's section of the IRA), Fianna na hEireann (youth section of the IRA), Saor Eire and the Irish People's Liberation Organization; (loyalist) the Ulster Freedom Fighters, the Ulster Volunteer Force and the Red Hand Commandos. In August 1992 the loyalist Ulster Defence Association (UDA) was proscribed by the British Government. The Loyalist Volunteer Force (LVF) and the Continuity Army Council (CAC) were proscribed in 1997.

Judicial System

The judicial system of Northern Ireland, so far as the Supreme Court is concerned, is a miniature of the English system, and is based on the Judicature (Northern Ireland) Act 1978. It consists, as in England, of the High Court, the Court of Appeal, and the Crown Court (which has jurisdiction in criminal matters). The county court system corresponds to its English counterpart, but there is no system of pleadings, as is found in the English county court. There are also variations in jurisdiction levels. County court judges share with the judges of the High Court the exercise of the jurisdiction of the Crown Court. The jurisdiction of the Magistrates' Courts (Courts of Summary Jurisdiction) is exercised by a permanent judiciary of legally qualified resident magistrates.

The Lord Chief Justice of Northern Ireland: Sir ROBERT CARSWELL, Royal Courts of Justice, Belfast, BT1 3JF; tel. (28) 9072-4603.

COURT OF APPEAL

President: The Lord Chief Justice of Northern Ireland.

Judges: Sir WILLIAM (LIAM) MCCOLLUM, Sir MICHAEL NICHOLSON, Sir ANTHONY CAMPBELL.

HIGH COURT

President: The Lord Chief Justice of Northern Ireland.

Judges: Sir JOHN SHEIL, Sir BRIAN KERR, Sir MALACHY HIGGINS, Sir PAUL FREDERICK GIRVAN, Sir PATRICK COGHLIN, Sir JOHN GILLEN, Sir RICHARD MCLAUGHLIN.

COUNTY COURT

Recorders: Belfast ANTHONY R. HART, Londonderry THOMAS A. BURGESS.

Judges: J. J. CURRAN, G. P. H. GIBSON, D. KENNEDY, J. A. H. MARTIN, D. W. SMYTH, P. MARKEY, R. MCKAY, J. BRADY, J. FOOTE, R. RODGERS, C. E. M. PHILPOTT, D. N. LOCKIE, D. K. MCFARLAND.

Religion

CHRISTIANITY

The organization of the churches takes no account of the partition of the island of Ireland into two separate political entities. Thus the Republic of Ireland and Northern Ireland are subject to a unified jurisdiction for ecclesiastical purposes. The Roman Catholic and Church of Ireland Primates of All Ireland both have their seats in Northern Ireland, at Armagh, while Belfast is the headquarters of the Presbyterians and Methodists. In Northern Ireland the religious affiliations recorded at the 2001 census were:

	% of population
Catholic*	40.26
Presbyterian	20.69
Church of Ireland	15.30
Methodist	3.51
Other denominations	6.37
No religion or religion not stated	13.88
Total	100.00

* The term Catholic includes those residents who gave their religion as Catholic or Roman Catholic.

The Irish Council of Churches: Inter-Church Centre, 48 Elmwood Ave, Belfast, BT9 6AZ; tel. (28) 9066-3145; fax (28) 9066-4160; e-mail icpep@email.com; internet www.irishchurches.org; f. 1922 (present name adopted 1966); 12 mem. churches; Pres. Rev. Canon R. HERRON; Gen. Sec. Dr DAVID STEVENS.

The Roman Catholic Church

Ireland (including Northern Ireland) comprises four archdioceses and 22 dioceses. The dioceses of Down and Connor and Dromore are completely in Northern Ireland, while the archdiocese of Armagh and the dioceses of Derry and Clogher are partly in Northern Ireland and partly in the Republic of Ireland.

Archbishop of Armagh and Primate of All Ireland: Most Rev. SEÁN BRADY, Ara Coeli, Armagh, BT61 7QY; tel. (28) 3752-2045; fax (28) 3752-6182; e-mail admin@aracoeli.com; internet www.archdioceseofarmagh.org.

The Church of Ireland
(The Anglican Communion)

Ireland (including Northern Ireland) comprises two archdioceses and 10 dioceses.

Archbishop of Armagh and Primate of All Ireland: Most Rev. Lord EAMES, The See House, Cathedral Close, Armagh, BT61 7EE; tel. (28) 3752-2851; fax (28) 3752-7823; e-mail archbishop@armagh.anglican.org.

Protestant Churches

Association of Baptist Churches in Ireland: 19 Ballinderry Rd, Lisburn, BT28 2SA; tel. (28) 9266-9366; fax (28) 9266-9377; e-mail abcini@aol.com; 111 churches; 93 ministers; 8,446 mems; Pres. S. WEIR; Sec. W. COLVILLE.

Congregational Union of Ireland: 1 Bradford Heights, Carrickfergus, Co Antrim, BT38 9EB; Irish Union 1829; 26 churches; 33 ministers; 10,000 adherents; 25 Sunday Schools; Chair. Rev. C. MCFARLAND; Sec. Rev. M. COLES.

Methodist Church in Ireland: 1 Fountainville Ave, Belfast, BT9 6AN; tel. (28) 9032-4554; fax (28) 9023-9467; e-mail secretary@irishmethodist.org; 222 churches; 197 ministers; 55,585 mems; Sec. Rev. EDMUND T. I. MAWHINNEY.

Moravian Church in Ireland: Moravian House, 25 Church Rd, Gracehill, Ballymena, BT42 2NL; tel. (28) 2566-6314; f. 1749; Chair. of Conf. Rev. V. D. LAUNDER.

Non-Subscribing Presbyterian Church of Ireland: Central Hall, 41 Rosemary St, Belfast; tel. (28) 9084-3592; Clerk to Gen. Synod Rev. T. N. PLAYFAIR.

Presbyterian Church in Ireland: Church House, Fisherwick Pl., Belfast, BT1 6DW; tel. (28) 9032-2284; fax (28) 9023-6609; e-mail info@presbyterianireland.org; internet www.presbyterianireland.org; 560 churches; 624 ministers; 279,961 mems, 32,098 in 550 Sunday Schools; Moderator of the Gen. Assembly Rt Rev. Dr R. I. BIRNEY; Clerk of Assembly and Gen. Sec. Very Rev. Dr SAMUEL HUTCHINSON.

The Press

DAILIES

Belfast Telegraph: 124–144 Royal Ave, Belfast, BT1 1EB; tel. (28) 9026-4000; fax (28) 9024-2287; e-mail editor@belfasttelegraph.co.uk; internet www.belfasttelegraph.co.uk; f. 1870; independent; evening; Proprs Independent News and Media PLC; Editor EDMUND CURRAN; circ. 111,682.

Irish News: 113–117 Donegall St, Belfast, BT1 2GE; tel. (28) 9032-2226; fax (28) 9033-7505; e-mail newsdesk@irishnews.com; internet www.irishnews.com; f. 1855; Irish nationalist; morning; Editor NOEL DORAN; circ. 50,747.

News Letter: 45–56 Boucher Crescent, Belfast, BT12 6QY; tel. (28) 9068-0000; fax (28) 9066-4412; e-mail newsletter@mgn.co.uk; internet www.newsletter.co.uk; f. 1737; pro-Union; morning; Editor (vacant); circ. 32,128.

WEEKLIES

An Phoblacht (Republican News): 535 Falls Rd, Belfast, BT11; tel. (28) 9060-0279; fax (28) 9060-0207; internet www.irlnet.com/aprn; party newspaper of Sinn Féin.

Armagh Observer: Observer Newspapers (NI) Ltd, Ann St, Dungannon, Co Tyrone; tel. (28) 8772-2557; fax (28) 8772-7334; f. 1930; Wednesday; nationalist; Editor DESMOND MALLON.

Ballymena Guardian: Northern Newspapers Ltd, 20 Railway Rd, Coleraine, Co Londonderry, BT52 1PD; tel. (28) 7034-3344; fax (28) 7034-3606; f. 1970; Wednesday; Editor MAURICE O'NEILL; circ. 24,000.

Ballymena Times: 22 Ballymoney St, Ballymena, Co Antrim, BT43 6AL; tel. (28) 2565-3300; fax (28) 2564-1517; f. 1855; Wednesday; independent; mem. of Morton Newspapers Ltd; Editor DESSIE BLACK-ADDER; circ. 8,000.

Banbridge Chronicle: 14 Bridge St, Banbridge, Co Down, BT32 3JS; tel. (28) 4066-2322; fax (28) 4062-4397; e-mail banbridgechronicle@btinternet.com; internet www.banbridgechronicle.com; f. 1870; Thursday; independent; Editor BRYAN HOOKS; circ. 6,102.

Carrickfergus Advertiser: 31A High St, Carrickfergus, Co Antrim, BT38 7AN; tel. (28) 9336-3651; fax (28) 9336-3092; internet www.ulsternet-ni.co.uk; f. 1883; Wednesday; Editor STEPHEN KERNOHAN; circ. 2,307.

Coleraine Chronicle: 20 Railway Rd, Coleraine, Co Londonderry, BT52 1PD; tel. (28) 7034-3344; fax (28) 7034-3606; f. 1844; Thursday; Editor ANTHONY TONER; circ. 23,000.

Community Telegraph: 124–144 Royal Ave, Belfast, BT1 1EB; tel. (28) 9026-4396; fax (28) 9055-4585; f. 1984; Wednesday and Thursday; Editor ROBIN YOUNG; circ. 142,148.

County Down Spectator: 109 Main St, Bangor, Co Down, BT20 4AF; tel. (28) 9127-0270; fax (28) 9127-1544; e-mail spectator@dial-pipex.com; f. 1904; Thursday; independent; Editor PAUL FLOWERS; circ. 12,372.

Derry Journal: Buncrana Rd, Londonderry, BT48 8AA; tel. (28) 7127-2200; fax (28) 7127-2260; e-mail derryj.editorial@mgn.co.uk; internet www.derryjournal.com; f. 1772; Tuesday and Friday; Editor P. MCART; circ. Tuesday 24,802, Friday 24,859.

Down Recorder: W. Y. Crichton & Co Ltd, 2–4 Church St, Downpatrick, Co Down, BT30 6EJ; tel. (28) 4461-3711; fax (28) 4461-4624; f. 1836; Wednesday; Editor P. SYMINGTON; circ. 12,535.

Fermanagh News: Observer Newspapers (NI) Ltd, Ann St, Dungannon, Co Tyrone; tel. (28) 8772-2557; fax (28) 8772-7334; f. 1967; Saturday; nationalist; Editor DESMOND MALLON.

Impartial Reporter & Farmers' Journal: 8–10 East Bridge St, Enniskillen, Co Fermanagh, BT74 7BT; tel. (28) 6632-4422; fax (28) 6632-5047; e-mail info@impartialreporter.com; internet www.impartialreporter.com; f. 1825; Thursday; independent; Editor DENZIL MCDANIEL; circ. 13,970.

Larne Gazette: c/o Carrickfergus Advertiser, 31A High St, Carrickfergus, Co Antrim, BT38 7AN; tel. (28) 9336-3651; fax (28) 9336-3092; internet www.ulsternet-ni.co.uk; Wednesday; Editor STEPHEN KERNOHAN; circ. 4,956.

Londonderry Sentinel: Suite 3, Spencer House, Spencer Rd, Londonderry, BT47 6AA; tel. (28) 7134-8889; fax (28) 7134-1175; f. 1829; Wednesday; Editor C. MCNABB; circ. 5,277.

Lurgan and Portadown Examiner: Observer Newspapers (NI) Ltd, Ann St, Dungannon, Co Tyrone; tel. (28) 8772-2557; fax (28) 8772-7334; f. 1930; Saturday; nationalist; Editor DESMOND MALLON.

Mid-Ulster Mail: 52 Oldtown St, Cookstown, Co Tyrone, BT80 8BB; tel. (28) 8676-2288; fax (28) 8676-4295; internet www.mortonnewspapers.com; f. 1891; Thursday; Editor JOHN FILLIS; circ. 11,930.

Mid-Ulster Observer: Observer Newspapers (NI) Ltd, Ann St, Dungannon, Co Tyrone; tel. (28) 8772-2557; fax (28) 8772-7334; f. 1952; Wednesday; Nationalist; Editor DESMOND MALLON.

Mourne Observer and Co Down News: The Roundabout, Castlewellan Rd, Newcastle, Co Down, BT33 0JX; tel. (28) 4372-2666; fax (28) 4372-4566; e-mail mourneobserver@btinternet.com; f. 1949; Wednesday; independent; Man. Dir D. J. HAWTHORNE; Editor T. BOWMAN; circ. 12,032.

Newtownards Chronicle: 25 Frances St, Newtownards, Co Down, BT23 7DT; tel. (28) 9181-3333; fax (28) 9182-0087; e-mail news@ardschronicle.co.uk; f. 1873; Thursday; independent; Editor JOHN SAVAGE; circ. 10,572.

Newtownards Spectator: 109 Main St, Bangor, Co Down, BT20 4AF; tel. (28) 9127-0270; fax (28) 9127-1544; e-mail spectator@dial.pipex.com; f. 1904; Thursday; independent; Editor PAUL FLOWERS; circ. 1,656.

North West Echo: Suite 3, Spencer House, Spencer Rd, Londonderry, BT47 6AA; tel. (28) 7134-2226; fax (28) 7134-1175; f. 1991; Tuesday; Editor C. MCNABB; circ. 31,200.

Northern Constitution: 20 Railway Rd, Coleraine, Co Londonderry, BT52 1PD; tel. (28) 7034-3344; fax (28) 7034-3606; f. 1875; Friday; independent; Editor MAURICE ALEESE; circ. 8,500.

The Outlook: Castle St, Rathfriland, Co Down, BT34 5QR; tel. (28) 4063-0202; fax (28) 4063-1022; f. 1939; Wednesday; independent; Editor STEPHEN PATTON; circ. 7,500.

Portadown Times (incorporating Craigavon News): 14 Church St, Portadown, Co Armagh, BT62 3LN; tel. (28) 3833-6111; fax (28) 3835-0203; e-mail edpt@mortonnewspapers.com; f. 1859; Friday; Editor DAVID ARMSTRONG; circ. 11,037.

Strabane Chronicle: 15 Main St, Strabane, Co Tyrone, BT82 8AS; tel. (28) 7188-2100; fax (28) 7188-3199; Proprs North-West of Ireland Printing and Publishing Co Ltd; Thursday; Editor DARACH MCDONALD; circ. 5,141.

Strabane Weekly News: 54–56 Main St, Strabane, Co Tyrone, BT82 8AX; tel. (28) 7188-6869; fax (28) 7188-6867; e-mail editor@tyroneconstitution.com; f. 1908; f. 1908; Friday; Unionist; Editor WESLEY ATCHISON; circ. 2,463.

Sunday Life: 124–144 Royal Ave, Belfast, BT1 1EB; tel. (28) 9026-4300; fax (28) 9054-4507; e-mail betty.arnold@belfasttelegraph.co.uk; internet www.sundaylife.co.uk; f. 1988; Editor MARTIN LINDSAY; circ. 94,747.

Tyrone Constitution: 25–27 High St, Omagh, Co Tyrone, BT78 1BD; tel. (28) 8224-2721; fax (28) 8224-3549; e-mail editor@tyroneconstitution.com; f. 1844; Thursday; Unionist; Editor WESLEY ATCHISON; circ. 11,864.

Tyrone Times and Dungannon Gazette: Unit B, Buttermarket Centre, Thomas St, Dungannon, BT70 1JH; tel. (28) 8775-2801; fax (28) 8775-2819; Editor PAUL MCCREARY; circ. 7,500.

Ulster Gazette: 56 Scotch St, Armagh, BT61 7DQ; tel. (28) 3752-2639; fax (28) 3752-7029; internet www.ulsternet-ni.co.uk; f. 1844; Thursday; Editor RICHARD STEWART; circ. 10,496.

Ulster Herald: 10 John St, Omagh, Co Tyrone, BT78 1DW; tel. (28) 8224-3444; fax (28) 8224-2206; e-mail editor@ulsterherald.com; internet www.ulsterherald.com; f. 1901; Proprs North-West of Ireland Printing and Publishing Co Ltd; Thursday; nationalist; Editor DARACH MCDONALD; circ. 11,787.

Ulster Star: 12A Bow St, Lisburn, Co Antrim, BT28 1BN; tel. (28) 9267-9111; fax (28) 9260-2904; f. 1957; Friday; Unionist; Editor DAVID FLETCHER; circ. 11,907.

Association

Associated Northern Ireland Newspapers: c/o W. Trimble Ltd, 8–10 East Bridge St, Enniskillen, Co Fermanagh, BT74 7BT; tel. (28) 6632-4422; fax (28) 6632-5047; Chair. N. ARMSTRONG; Sec. J. MCVEY.

Broadcasting and Communications

TELECOMMUNICATIONS

Northern Ireland Advisory Committee on Telecommunications: Chamber of Commerce House, 22 Gt Victoria St, Belfast, BT2 7QA; tel. (28) 9024-2631; e-mail niact@acts.org.uk; internet www.acts.org.uk; Dir FRANK HEWITT.

British Telecommunications: Riverside Tower, 5 Lanyon Place, Belfast, BT1 3BT; tel. (28) 9032-7327; e-mail marnie.oneill@bt.com; internet www.bt.com.

BROADCASTING

British Broadcasting Corporation (BBC): Broadcasting House, 22–27 Ormeau Ave, Belfast, BT2 8HQ; tel. (28) 9033-8000; fax (28) 9033-8800; National Gov. for Northern Ireland Prof FABIAN MONDS; Controller, Northern Ireland ANNA CARRAGHER.

Radio

Northern Ireland relays all national BBC radio programmes broadcast throughout the United Kingdom and two regional services, BBC Radio Ulster and BBC Radio Foyle in the north-west.

Cool FM: POB 974, Belfast, BT1 1RT; tel. (28) 9081-7181; fax (28) 9081-4974; f. 1990; independent music radio station; Chair. J. T. DONNELLY; Man. Dir. G. D. SLOAN.

Downtown Radio: Newtownards, Co Down, BT23 4ES; tel. (28) 9181-5555; fax (28) 9181-8913; f. 1976; independent local radio station; Chair. J. T. DONNELLY; Man. Dir G. D. SLOAN.

Television

The BBC has two colour TV studios in Belfast and a full-scale colour outside broadcast unit. A wide range of programmes is made for broadcasting in Northern Ireland, and for the BBC-1 and BBC-2 UK networks. The BBC has 44 television transmitting stations and 11 radio transmitting stations in Northern Ireland.

The main television transmitters at Divis, Limavady, Brougher Mountain and Londonderry serve most of Northern Ireland on BBC-1 and BBC-2 625-line colour television.

Independent Television Commission (ITC): Albany House, 75 Great Victoria St, Belfast, BT2 7AF; tel. (28) 9024-8733; fax (28) 9032-2828; e-mail denis.wolinski@itc.org.uk; internet www.itc.org.uk; Chief Exec. PATRICIA HODGSON; Head (Northern Ireland) DENIS WOLINSKI.

Ulster Television PLC: Havelock House, Ormeau Rd, Belfast, BT7 1EB; tel. (28) 9032-8122; fax (28) 9024-6695; internet www.utvlive.com; started transmission 1959; Chair. JOHN B. MCGUCKIAN; Man. Dir JOHN MCCANN.

Finance

(cap. = capital; res = reserves; dep. = deposits; m. = million; br.(s) = branch(es); amounts in pounds sterling, unless otherwise indicated)

BANKS

AIB Group (UK) plc: Belfast; tel. (28) 9023-3439; fax (28) 9024-8505; subsidiary of Allied Irish Banks; cap. 165m., dep 2,836m. (Dec. 1997); Chair. WILLIAM CARSON; Sec. TIANA PECK; 31 brs (Northern Ireland).

Bank of Ireland: Belfast Office: POB 482, 54 Donegall Pl., Belfast, BT1 1DR; Head Office: Lower Baggot St, Dublin 2; tel. (28) 9023-4334; fax (28) 9023-8705; f. 1783; cap. €679m., res €3,521m., dep. €63,694m. (March 2002); mem. of Associate Banks; Gov. LAURENCE CROWLEY; Group Chief Exec. MICHAEL SODEN; Gen. Man. (Northern Ireland) GERRARD MCGUNN; 45 brs (Northern Ireland).

Northern Bank Executor and Trustee Co Ltd: POB 183, Donegall Sq. West, Belfast, BT1 6JS; tel. (28) 9024-5277; fax (28) 9024-1790; f. 1960; owned by the Northern Bank Ltd; Sen. Man. C.W. DUNCAN.

Ulster Bank Ltd: 11–16 Donegall Sq. East, Belfast, BT1 5UB; tel. (28) 9027-6000; fax (28) 9027-5661; e-mail morrow@ulsterbank.com; internet www.ulsterbank.com; f. 1836; mem. of Royal Bank of Scotland Group; cap. 203m., total assets 12,071m. (Dec. 2000); Chair. Dr ALAN GILLESPIE; Group Chief Exec. MARTIN WILSON; 224 brs.

Banking Association

Northern Ireland Bankers' Asscn: Stokes House, 17–25 College Sq. East, Belfast BT1 6DE; tel. (28) 9032-7551; fax (28) 9033-1449; e-mail sharon@niba.demon.co.uk; Chair. DON PRICE; Sec. W. A. MCALISTER.

STOCK EXCHANGE

Stock Exchange: 10 High St, Belfast BT1 2BP; Head Office: London; tel. (28) 9032-1094; fax (28) 9032-8149; see under Great Britain.

Trade and Industry

DEVELOPMENT ORGANIZATIONS

Foyle Development Organization: c/o Derry City Council, 98 Strand Rd, Londonderry, BT48 7NN; tel. (28) 7136-5151; fax (28) 7136-8536; f. 1979 as a forum for issues relating to the economic, industrial and commercial development of the area; represents management, labour and city council interests; Sec. KAREN MCELHINNEY.

Industrial Development Board for Northern Ireland: IDB House, 64 Chichester St, Belfast, BT1 4JX; tel. (28) 9023-3233; fax (28) 9054-5000; e-mail idbni@detini.gov.uk; internet www.idbni.co.uk; established under the Industrial Development (NI) Order 1982 as an executive body of the Dept of Economic Development; aims to encourage greater sustainable growth by locally and externally owned internationally competitive companies in the manufacturing and tradeable service sectors in Northern Ireland and attract new foreign direct investment contributing to growth in sustainable employment; Chair. ALAN GILLESPIE; Chief Exec. BRUCE ROBINSON.

Invest Northern Ireland (INI): LEDU House, Upper Galwally, Belfast, BT8 6TB; tel. (28) 9049-1031; fax (28) 9069-1432; e-mail ebic@investni.com; internet www.investni.com; f. 2001 to assume responsibility for the activities of the Industrial Development Board for Northern Ireland, the Local Enterprise Development Unit, the Industrial Research and Technology Unit, the Company Development Programme and the business support activities of the Northern Irish Tourist Board; aims to accelerate economic development in Northern Ireland; Chair. Prof. FABIAN MONDS; Chief Exec. LESLIE MORRISON.

Northern Ireland Economic Council: Pearl Assurance House, 1–3 Donegall Sq. East, Belfast, BT1 5HB; tel. (28) 9023-2125; fax (28) 9033-1250; e-mail info@niec.org.uk; internet www.niec.org.uk; f. 1977; provides independent advice to the First Minister and Deputy First Minister on the development of economic policy for Northern Ireland; 15 mems representing trade union, employer, and independent interests; Chair. JANET M. TREWSDALE (acting).

CHAMBERS OF COMMERCE

Northern Ireland Chamber of Commerce and Industry: Chamber of Commerce House, 22 Great Victoria St, Belfast, BT2 7BJ; tel. (28) 9024-4113; fax (28) 9024-7024; e-mail nicham@dial-pipex.com; internet www.nicci.co.uk; f. 1783; Pres. OWEN LAMONT; Chief Exec. JOHN STRINGER; 1,200 mems.

Northern Ireland Chamber of Trade: POB 444, Belfast, BT1 1DY; tel. and fax (28) 9023-0444; Sec. J. ROBERTS.

INDUSTRIAL AND TRADE ASSOCIATIONS

Confederation of British Industry (CBI): Fanum House, 108 Great Victoria St, Belfast, BT2 7PD; tel. (28) 9032-6658; fax (28) 9032-5915; Chair CHRIS GIBSON; Dir NIGEL SMYTH.

Northern Ireland Certification Office for Trade Unions and Employers' Associations: 27–29 Gordon St, Belfast, BT1 2LG; tel.

(28) 9023-7773; fax (28) 9023-2271; e-mail certoffice@nicertoffice .fsnet.co.uk; internet www.nicertoffice.com.

EMPLOYERS' ORGANIZATIONS

Belfast Shipbuilders' Asscn: c/o Harland and Wolff Holdings PLC, Queen's Island, Belfast, BT3 9DU; tel. (28) 9045-8456; fax (28) 9045-8515; f. 1989.

Construction Employers' Federation Ltd: 143 Malone Rd, Belfast, BT9 6SU; tel. (28) 9087-7143; fax (28) 9087-7155; e-mail mail@ cefni.co.uk; internet www.cefni.co.uk; f. 1945; Man. Dir W. A. DORAN.

Electrical Contractors' Asscn (Northern Ireland Regional Office): 17 Farm Lodge Drive, Upper Rd, Greenisland, Carrickfergus, Co Antrim, BT38 8XN; tel. (28) 9085-4553; fax (28) 9085-1528; Reg. Officer I. BROWNLEES.

Engineering Employers' Federation, NI Asscn: 2 Greenwood Ave, Belfast, BT4 3JJ; tel. (28) 9067-2490; fax (28) 9065-8571; f. 1866; Dir PETER BLOCH.

Northern Ireland Hotels Federation: Midland Bldgs, Whitla St, Belfast, BT15 1JP; tel. (28) 9035-1110; fax (28) 9035-1509; internet www.nihf.co.uk; Chief Exec. JANICE GAULT.

Northern Ireland Textiles and Apparel Asscn: 5C The Square, Hillsborough, BT26 6AG; tel. (28) 9268-9999; fax (28) 9268-9968; e-mail info@nita.co.uk; internet www.nita.co.uk; f. 1993; Dir LINDA MACHUGH; 70 mems.

Northern Ireland Trade Asscns Ltd: Belfast; Secretariat to 14 Trade Asscns; Dir HAMILTON MARTIN.

Ulster Chemists' Asscn: 73 University St, Belfast, BT7 1HL; tel. (28) 9032-0787; e-mail adrienne@ulster-chemists.abelgratis.com; f. 1901; promotion and protection of interests of community pharmacies in Northern Ireland; Contact ANDRENNE CLUGSTON.

Ulster Farmers' Union: Dunedin, 475 Antrim Rd, Belfast, BT15 3DA; tel. (28) 9037-0222; fax (28) 9037-0739; e-mail info@ufuhq.com; internet www.ufuni.org; f. 1918; Pres. JOHN GILLILAND; Dir-Gen. CLARK BLACK; 12,500 mems.

UTILITIES

Electricity

Office for the Regulation of Electricity and Gas (Ofreg): Brookmount Bldgs, 42 Fountain St, Belfast, BT1 5EE; tel. (28) 9024-4113; e-mail ofreg@nics.gov.uk; internet www.ofreg.nics.gov.uk; independent public body to regulate the electricity and natural gas industries in Northern Ireland; Dir DOUGLAS MCILDOON.

Northern Ireland Electricity PLC: 120 Malone Rd, Belfast, BT9 5HT; tel. (28) 9066-1100; internet www.nie.co.uk; holding co Viridian Group; Chair. PHILIP ROGERSON; Man. Dir HARRY MCCRACKEN.

Gas

See above for regulatory body.

Phoenix Natural Gas Ltd: 197 Airport Rd West, Belfast, BT3 9ED; tel. (28) 9055-5555; fax (28) 9055-5500; e-mail info@ phoenix-natural-gas.com; internet www.phoenix-natural-gas.com; f. 1997.

Water

Department for Regional Development, Water Service: Northland House, 3 Frederick St, Belfast, BT1 2NR; tel. (28) 9024-4711; fax (28) 9035-4888; e-mail water.service@nics.gov.uk; internet www .waterni.gov.uk; Chief Exec. ROBERT MARTIN.

TRADE UNIONS

The organization of trade unions in Northern Ireland is a similar system to that in Great Britain. Below are some of the major organizations in Northern Ireland, some of which are affiliated to corresponding unions in Great Britain and the Republic of Ireland. Many of the large unions in Great Britain are represented by branches in Northern Ireland. Membership figures are for Northern Ireland only.

Irish Congress of Trade Unions (NI Committee): 3 Crescent Gardens, Belfast, BT7 1NS; tel. (28) 9024-7940; fax (28) 9024-6181; e-mail info@ictuni.org; Gen. Sec. DAVE BEGG.

Amalgamated Transport and General Workers' Union: Transport House, 102 High St, Belfast, BT1 2DL; tel. (28) 9023-2381; fax (28) 9024-0133; Irish Regional Sec. M. O'REILLY; 33,484 mems.

Amicus (AEEU): Unit 1, Citylink Business Park, 8 Albert St, Belfast, BT12 4HB; tel. (28) 9024-5785; fax (28) 9024-5939; e-mail p .williamson@aeeu.org.uk; internet www.aeeu.org.uk; f. 2002 by merger of Amalgamated Engineering and Electrical Union and MSF; c. 30,000 mems; Regional Sec P. A. WILLIAMSON.

Communication Workers's Union: 22 Croob Park, Ballynahinch, Co Down, BT24 8BB; f. 1995 by merger of Union of Communication Workers and National Communications Union; Irish Rep. I. BURROWS; 6,365 mems.

Confederation of Shipbuilding and Engineering Unions: Unit 1, Citylink Business Park, 8 Albert St, Belfast, BT12 4HB; tel. (28) 9024-5785; fax (28) 9024-5939; District Sec. P. WILLIAMSON.

General, Municipal, Boilermakers and Allied Trades Union: 3/4 Donegall Quay, Belfast, BT1 3EA; tel. (28) 9031-2111; fax (28) 9031-2333; Regional Sec. B. SMITH; 20,427 mems.

Irish National Teachers' Organization: 23 College Gardens, Belfast, BT9 6BS (headquarters in Dublin); tel. (28) 9038-1455; fax (28) 9066-2803; e-mail info@ni.into.ie; internet www.into.ie; f. 1868; Northern Sec. F. BUNTING; 6,300 mems.

Northern Ireland Musicians' Asscn: Unit 4, Fortwilliam Business Park, Dargan Rd, Belfast, BT3 9JZ; tel. and fax (28) 9037-0037; Sec. H. HAMILTON; 1,003 mems.

Northern Ireland Public Service Alliance: Harkin House, 54 Wellington Park, Belfast, BT9 6DP; tel. (28) 9066-1831; fax (28) 9066-5847; e-mail info@nipsa.org.uk; Gen. Sec. J. MCCUSKER; 36,473 mems.

Services Industrial Professional Technical Union: 3 Antrim Rd, Belfast, BT15 2BE; tel. (28) 9031-4000; fax (28) 9031-4044; Gen. Sec. JOHN MCDONNELL; Regional Sec. GEORGE HUNTER; 7,001 members.

Ulster Teachers' Union: 94 Malone Rd, Belfast, BT9 5HP; tel. (28) 9066-2216; fax (28) 9066-3055; e-mail office@utu.edu; internet www .utu.edu/home.html; f. 1919; Gen. Sec. RAY CALVIN; Asst Gen. Sec. AVRIL HALL-CALLAGHAN; 6,081 mems.

UCATT: The Midland Building, Whitla St, Belfast; BT15 1JP; tel. (28) 9077-7045; Regional Sec. J. CROOKS; 2,140 mems.

Union of Shop, Distributive and Allied Workers: 40 Wellington Park, Belfast, BT9 6DN; tel. (28) 9066-3773; fax (28) 9066-2133; Area Organizers ALAN WHITE, ROBERT GOURLEY, KIERAN SMYTH; 7,500 mems.

UNISON: Unit 4, Fortwilliam Business Park, Dargan Rd, Belfast, BT3 9JZ; tel. (28) 9077-0813; fax (28) 9077-9772; f. 1993 by amalgamation of Confederation of Health Service Employees (COHSE), Nat. and Local Government Officers Asscn (NALGO) and Nat. Union of Public Employees (NUPE); Regional Sec. INEZ MCCORMACK; 26,088 mems.

Transport

RAILWAYS

Northern Ireland Railways Co Ltd: Central Station, East Bridge St, Belfast, BT1 3PB; tel. (28) 9089-9400; fax (28) 9089-9401; f. 1967; subsidiary of Northern Ireland Transport Holding Co (see below); operates rail services for passenger traffic over 336 km and for freight traffic over 268 km of railway track; a high-speed passenger service between Belfast and Dublin, launched, in co-operation with Irish Rail, began operations in 1997; Man. Dir E. HESKETH.

ROADS

In 1997 there were 24,350 km (15,130 miles) of roads of all classes including some 110 km (68 miles) of motorway.

Northern Ireland Transport Holding Co: Chamber of Commerce House, 22 Great Victoria St, Belfast, BT2 7LX; tel. (28) 9024-3456; fax (28) 9033-3845; publicly-owned; three subsidiaries.

  Citybus Ltd: Milewater Rd, Belfast, BT3 9BG; tel. (28) 9035-1201; fax (28) 9035-1474; responsible for operating municipal transport in the City of Belfast; Man. Dir TED HESKETH.

  Ulsterbus Ltd: Milewater Rd, Belfast, BT3 9BG; Central Station, Belfast, BT1 3PB; tel. (28) 9035-1201; fax (28) 9035-1473; tel. (28) 9089-9400; fax (28) 9035-1474; responsible for almost all bus transport in Northern Ireland, except Belfast city; services into the Republic of Ireland; assoc. co Flexibus Ltd (minibus contract hire); Man. Dir TED HESKETH.

SHIPPING

There are regular freight services from Belfast, Warrenpoint and Larne to ports in Great Britain and Europe; freight services also operate from Londonderry and Coleraine. Passenger services operate daily between Belfast and Stranraer and between Larne and Cairnryan. With major financial assistance from the EU, Northern Ireland has undertaken a major programme of upgrading its harbour facilities. At the port of Belfast three 'roll on, roll off' terminals and two large container terminals are now operational. In May 1998 the Government announced that the port was to be transferred to the private sector. The port of Londonderry was transferred to a new location at Lishally with 200 m of quay in February 1993. The port of Larne has modernized a 'roll on, roll off' terminal.

B.G. Freightline: c/o T.R. Shipping Services, Victoria Terminal 3, West Bank Rd, Belfast, BT3 9JL; tel. (28) 9077-7968; fax (28) 9077-4299; container service to Rotterdam.

Belfast Freight Ferries Ltd: Victoria Terminal 1, Dargan Rd, Belfast, BT3 9LJ; tel. (28) 9077-0112; fax (28) 9078-1217; roll-on, roll-off service to Heysham; Chair. ANGUS FRASER; Man. Dir ALAN PEACOCK.

Coastal Container Line Ltd: Coastal House, Victoria Terminal 3, West Bank Rd, Belfast, BT3 9JL; tel. (28) 9037-3200; fax (28) 9037-1444; container services to Liverpool and Cardiff.

Dragon Shipping Line Ltd: York Dock Terminal, Dufferin Rd, Belfast, BT3 9AA; tel. (28) 9035-1513; fax (28) 9035-1521; container service to Swansea.

Heyn Group Ltd: 1 Corry Pl., Belfast Harbour, Belfast, BT3 9AH; tel. (28) 9035-0000; fax (28) 9035-0011; e-mail info@heyn.co.uk; internet www.heyn.co.uk; Man. Dir M. W. S. MACLARAN.

John Kelly Ltd: 1 Lombard St, Belfast, BT1 1BN; tel. (28) 9026-1500; fax (28) 9033-0032; internet www.kellyfuels.co.uk; f. 1840; coal and petroleum distributors, shipping agent; Chair. and Man. Dir R. REIHILL.

Norse Irish Ferries: Victoria Terminal 2, West Bank Rd, Belfast, BT3 9JN; tel. (28) 9077-9090; fax (28) 9077-5520; internet www.Norse-Irish-Ferries.co.uk; roll-on, roll-off freight, car and passenger services to Liverpool.

P & O European Ferries (Irish Sea) Ltd: The Harbour, Larne, Co Antrim, BT40 1AW; tel. (28) 2887-2200 (freight); tel. (0870) 2424777 (passenger); fax (28) 2887-2129 (freight); fax (28) 2887-2195 (passenger); e-mail callcentre@poefis.com; internet www.poirishsea.com; subsidiary of P & O Group; Gen. Man. G. McCULLOUGH.

P & O Ferrymasters Ltd: Redlands Estate, Larne Harbour, Larne, Co Antrim, BT40 1AX; tel. (28) 2887-1500; fax (28) 2887-1536; e-mail harry.mcveigh@pofm.com; internet www.po-transeuropean.com; freight services twice daily to Fleetwood and daily to Troon; Gen. Man. HARRY McVEIGH.

Stena Line Ltd: Group Travel and Short Breaks Department, Corry Rd Terminal Bldg, Belfast BT3 9SS; tel. (28) 2874-8748; fax (28) 2888-4091; 'roll-on, roll-off' car and passenger services Belfast–Stranraer.

CIVIL AVIATION

Belfast International Airport at Aldergrove handled 3.7m. passengers in 2001 and 45,000 metric tons of freight during 2000. There are daily scheduled flights to one destination in Europe and nine in Great Britain and regular charter flights to cities in Europe and North America. There are also direct services from Belfast City Airport at Sydenham to 19 destinations in Great Britain. In 2001 Belfast City Airport handled 1.7m. passengers. From City of Derry Airport, in Co Londonderry, there are direct services to three United Kingdom destinations. In 2001 City of Derry Airport handled 200,000 passengers.

Belfast International Airport Ltd: Belfast International Airport, Belfast, BT29 4AB; tel. (28) 9448-4848; fax (28) 9448-4849; e-mail info.desk@bial.co.uk; internet www.bial.co.uk; f. 1961 as Northern Ireland Airports Ltd; transferred to private ownership in 1994; propr TBI plc; Man. Dir JAMES MAIRS.

City of Derry Airport: Airport Rd, Eglington, Co Derry, BT47 3GY; tel. (28) 7181-0784; fax (28) 7181-1426; e-mail info@cityofderryairport.com; internet www.cityofderryairport.com.

Tourism

Tourist attractions include unspoilt beaches, the Giant's Causeway, in Co Antrim, the Mourne mountains, in Co Down, and a range of new indoor attractions developed with assistance from EU funds. In 2001 1.7m. tourists visited Northern Ireland.

Northern Ireland Tourist Board: St. Anne's Court, 59 North Street, Belfast, BT1 1NB; tel. (28) 9023-1221; fax (28) 9024-0960; e-mail info@nitb.com; internet www.nitb.com; Chair. ROY BAILIE; Chief Exec. IAN HENDERSON.

UNITED KINGDOM CROWN DEPENDENCIES

The Channel Islands and the Isle of Man lie off shore from the United Kingdom but are not integral parts of the country. They are dependencies of the British Crown and have considerable self-government in internal affairs.

THE CHANNEL ISLANDS

The Channel Islands lie off the north-west coast of France and are the only portions of the Duchy of Normandy now belonging to the Crown of England, to which they have been attached since 1106. They do not, however, form part of the United Kingdom. The islands have their own legislative assemblies and legal and administrative systems, their laws depending for their validity on Orders made by the Queen in Council. Her Majesty's Government in the United Kingdom is responsible for the defence and international relations of the islands, and the Crown is ultimately responsible for their good government.

Exports are protected by British tariff barriers. The citizens of the Channel Islands enjoy tax sovereignty and imports are free of British purchase tax. Income tax is low. Jersey and Guernsey, especially the former, are being developed as finance centres, and Jersey's commercial laws have encouraged the founding of several merchant banks, mainly subsidiaries of London banks, which benefit the economy, otherwise largely based on tourism and agriculture.

In addition to the British public holidays, the Channel Islands also celebrate 9 May (Liberation Day).

GUERNSEY

Introduction

The civil flag of Guernsey is white, bearing a red cross of St George, with a yellow couped cross superimposed on the cross. The capital is St Peter Port. English is the language in common use, but the Norman *patois* is spoken in some rural parishes. Dependencies of Guernsey are Alderney, Brecqhou, Sark, Herm, Jethou and Lihou.

Statistical Survey

(including Herm and Jethou)

Source (unless otherwise stated): Advisory and Finance Committee, POB 43, St Peter Port, Guernsey GY1 1FH; tel. (1481) 717000; fax (1481) 717157; internet www.gov.gg/esu.

AREA, POPULATION AND DENSITY

Area: 63.1 sq km (24.3 sq miles).

Population (census of 29 April 2001): 59,807 (males 29,138, females 30,669).

Density (per sq km, 2001): 947.8.

Principal Towns (2001): St Peter Port 16,488; Vale 9,573; Castel 8,975; St Sampson 8,592, St Martin 6,267.

Births and Deaths (2000): Live births 644; Deaths 565.

Employment (September 2000): Total employed 31,347 (males 17,516, females 13,831).

AGRICULTURE

The principal crops are flowers, much of which are grown under glass. About 16.3 sq km (6.2 sq miles) are cultivated.

FINANCE

Currency and Exchange Rates: 100 pence = 1 pound sterling (£). *Dollar and Euro Equivalents* (31 December 2002): US $1 = 62.04 pence; €1 = 65.06 pence; £100 = $161.18 = €153.70.
Note: Guernsey is in monetary union with the United Kingdom. It has its own coins and notes but United Kingdom coins and notes are also legal tender.

Budget (£ '000, 1999): *Revenue:* General revenue income: 238,216; *Expenditure:* General revenue expenditure: 190,847.

Cost of Living: (Retail price index; base: 1999 = 100) All items 103.9 in 2000.

EXTERNAL TRADE

Principal Commodities: *Imports* (1999): Petroleum and oil 168,026,000 litres. *Exports* (1998, £ million): Light industry 47; Total flowers 34.0; Total vegetables 5.0.

TRANSPORT

Road Traffic (vehicles registered, 1999): Cars 34,460, Motorcycles 4,208; Commercial vehicles 7,247.

Shipping (2000): Passenger arrivals 345,923.

Civil Aviation (2000): Passenger movements 884,284.

TOURISM

Number of Visitors (2000): 421,000.

COMMUNICATIONS MEDIA

Telephones (2001): 55,000 main lines in use.

Mobile Cellular Telephones (2001): 31,500.

Internet Users (2001): 20,000.
Source: International Telecommunication Union.

EDUCATION

Primary (2000): 4,977 pupils.

Secondary (2000): 3,900 pupils.

Directory

The Constitution

The Lieutenant-Governor and Commander-in-Chief of Guernsey is the personal representative of the Sovereign and the channel of communication between the Crown and the Insular Government. He is appointed by the Crown. He is entitled to sit and speak in the Assembly of the States, but not to vote.

The Bailiff is appointed by the Crown and is President both of the Assembly of the States (the insular legislature), where he has a casting vote, and of the Royal Court of Guernsey.

The government of the island is conducted by committees appointed by the States.

The States of Deliberation is composed of the following members:

(*a*) The Bailiff, who is President *ex officio*.

(*b*) HM Procureur (Attorney-General) and HM Comptroller (Solicitor-General) Law Officers of the Crown, who are appointed by the Crown. They are entitled to sit in the States and to speak, but not to vote.

(c) The 45 People's Deputies elected by popular franchise.

(d) The 10 Douzaine Representatives elected by their respective Parochial Douzaines.

(e) The two Alderney Representatives elected by the States of Alderney.

Projets de Loi (Permanent Laws) require the sanction of Her Majesty in Council.

The function of the States of Election is to elect persons to the office of Jurat. It is composed of the following members:

(a) The Bailiff (President *ex officio*).

(b) The 12 Jurats or 'Jures-Justiciers'.

(c) The 10 Rectors of the Parishes.

(d) HM Procureur and HM Comptroller.

(e) The 45 People's Deputies.

(f) The 34 Douzaine Representatives.

Meetings of the States and of the Royal Court, formerly conducted in French, are now conducted in English, but the proceedings in both are begun and ended in French.

The Government

(April 2003)

Lieutenant-Governor and Commander-in-Chief of the Bailiwick of Guernsey: Lt-Gen. Sir JOHN FOLEY.

Secretary and ADC to the Lieutenant-Governor: Col. R. H. GRAHAM.

Bailiff of Guernsey: Sir DE VIC GRAHAM CAREY.

Deputy Bailiff: ANDREW CHRISTOPHER KING DAY.

HM Procureur (Attorney-General): JOHN NIKOLAS VAN LEUVEN.

HM Comptroller (Solicitor-General): HOWARD EDWARD ROBERTS.

States Supervisor: M. BROWN.

Judicial System

Justice is administered in Guernsey by the Royal Court, which consists of the Bailiff and the 12 Jurats. The Royal Court also deals with a wide variety of non-contentious matters. A Stipendiary Magistrate deals with minor civil and criminal cases. The Guernsey Court of Appeal deals with appeals from the Royal Court.

Religion

CHRISTIANITY

The Church of England

The Church of England in Guernsey is the established church. The Deanery includes the islands of Alderney, Sark, Herm and Jethou; it forms part of the diocese of Winchester.

Dean of Guernsey: Very Rev. Canon F. MARC TRICKEY, L'Espérance, Route des Camps, St Martin's, GY4 6AD; tel. (1481) 238441; fax (1481) 231018.

The Roman Catholic Church

The diocese of Portsmouth includes the Channel Islands and part of southern England. In Guernsey there are five Roman Catholic churches, of which the senior is St Joseph and St Mary, Cordier Hill, St Peter Port.

Catholic Dean of Guernsey: Canon GERARD HETHERINGTON, St Peter Port; tel. (1481) 720196.

Other Christian Churches

The Presbyterian Church and the Church of Scotland are represented by St Andrew's Church, The Grange, St Peter Port. The Baptist, Congregational, Elim and Methodist Churches are also represented in the island.

The Press

Guernsey Press and Star: The Guernsey Press Co, POB 57, Braye Rd, Vale; tel. (1481) 240240; fax (1481) 240235; e-mail newsroom@guernsey-press.com; internet www.guernsey-press.com; f. 1897; daily; independent; Editor RICHARD DIGARD; circ. 16,189.

Guernsey Weekly Press: The Guernsey Press Co, POB 57, Braye Rd, Vale; tel. (1481) 240240; fax (1481) 240235; e-mail newsroom@guernsey-press.com; internet www.guernsey-press.com; f. 1902; independent; Thursday; Editor RICHARD DIGARD.

Publisher

Toucan Press: The White Cottage, route de Carteret, Castel; tel. (1481) 257017; f. 1850; history, Thomas Hardy, Channel Islands; Man. Dir G. STEVENS COX.

Broadcasting and Communications

TELECOMMUNICATIONS

Guernsey Telecoms Ltd: Telecoms House, Upland Rd, St Peter Port, GY1 3AB; tel. (1481) 700700; fax (1481) 724640; e-mail contact@guernseytelecoms.com; internet www.guernsey telecomslimited.com; Chief Exec. TONY MULLEE.

BROADCASTING

Radio

BBC Radio Guernsey: Commerce House, St Peter Port; tel. (1481) 728977; fax (1481) 713557; e-mail radio.guernsey@bbc.co.uk; internet www.bbc.co.uk/radioguernsey; f. 1982; Man. ROBERT WALLACE.

Island FM: 12, Westerbrook, St Sampson's, GY2 4QQ; tel. (1481) 242000; fax (1481) 249676; e-mail nick@islandfm.guernsey.net; internet www.islandfm.guernsey.net.

Television

Channel Television: Television House, Bulwer Ave, St Sampsons, GY2 4LA; tel. (1481) 241888; fax (1481) 241889; e-mail broadcast@channeltv.co.uk; internet www.channeltv.co.uk; Chair. FRANCIS HAMON; Chief Exec. HUW DAVIES.

(See also under Jersey).

Finance

(cap. = capital; dep. = deposits; res = reserves; brs = branches; amounts in pounds sterling, unless otherwise indicated.)

Guernsey Financial Services Commission: La Plaiderie Chambers, La Plaiderie, St Peter Port, GY1 1WG; tel. (1481) 712706; fax (1481) 712010; e-mail info@gfsc.guernseyci.com; internet www.gfsc .guernseyci.com; regulates banking, investment, insurance and fiduciary activities; Dir-Gen. PETER NEVILLE.

BANKING

In 2000 total bank deposits in Guernsey were £76,847m. in 77 financial institutions.

British Clearing Banks

The banks listed below are branches of British banks, and details concerning directors, capital, etc. of the parent bank will be found under the appropriate section in the pages dealing with Great Britain.

Barclays Bank PLC: POB 41, Le Marchant House, Le Truchot, St Peter Port, GY1 3BE; tel. (1481) 705600; fax (1481) 713712; e-mail guernsey.internationalcorporateservice@barclays.co.uk; internet www.internationalbanking.barclays.com; Dir STEPHEN JONES; 2 brs.

HSBC Bank PLC: POB 31, HSBC House, Lefebre St, St Peter Port, GY1 3AT; tel. (1481) 717717; fax (1481) 717700; Area Man. G. JOHN DAVIES; 5 brs.

Lloyds TSB Bank (Guernsey) Ltd: POB 13, 24 High St Peter Port, GY1 4BD; tel. (1481) 724061; fax (1481) 717468; Island Dir P. NIVEN; 5 brs.

National Westminster Bank PLC: 35 High St, St Peter Port GY1 4BE; tel. (1481) 703800; fax (1481) 727019; Dir PETER MARCHANT.

Other Banks

Adam and Company International Ltd: POB 402, St Andrew's House, Le Bordage, St Peter Port, GY1 3GB; tel. (1481) 715055; fax (1481) 726919; e-mail adamint@guernsey.net; internet www .adamandcompany.plc.uk; f. 1990; cap. 0.5m., res 0.5m., dep. 111.7m. (Dec. 2001); Chair. SIMON MILLER; Man. Dir BARRY JOHN MILDON.

Banca Monte dei Paschi (Channel Islands) Ltd: St Julian's Court, St Julian's Ave, St Peter Port, GY1 4HA; tel. (1481) 723776; fax (1481) 728628; e-mail admin@bmpci.co; internet www.bmpci .com; f. 1973; cap. 1.0m., res 5.6m., dep. 93.2m. (Dec. 2000); Man. Dir I. C. LACEY.

Banco Santander Central Hispano (Guernsey) Ltd: St Andrew's House, Le Bordage, St Peter Port, GY1 1BR; tel. (1481) 715424; fax (1481) 715432; Man. JOSE REY.

Bank of Bermuda (Guernsey) Ltd: POB 208, Bermuda House, St Julian's Ave, St Peter Port, GY1 3NF; tel. (1481) 707000; fax (1481) 726987; internet www.bankofbermuda.com; f. 1973; cap. 14.0m., res 21.4m., dep. 666.4m., (Dec. 2000); Gen. Man. KEN A. GIBBS; Man. Dir PETER LE NOURY.

Bank of Butterfield International (Guernsey) Ltd: POB 25, Roseneath, The Grange, St Peter Port, GY1 3AP; tel. (1481) 711521; fax (1481) 714533; e-mail mark.stevens@butterfield.gg; internet www.bankofbutterfield.com; Man. Dir BOB MOORE.

Bank Hoffman: POB 147 Helvetia Ct, St Peter Port, GY1 3JA; tel. (1481) 715090; fax (1481) 715037; Man. Dir. A. F. GOOD.

Barclays Finance Co (Guernsey) Ltd: POB 269, Cambria House, New St, St Peter Port; tel. (1481) 723223; Man. Dir W. ALLAN.

Barclays Private Bank and Trust Ltd: POB 184, Barclays Court, Les Echelons, South Esplanade, St Peter Port; tel. (1481) 724706; fax (1481) 728376; Chief Man. S. K. OLIPHANT.

Barings (Guernsey) Ltd: POB 71, Trafalgar Ct, Les Banques, St Peter Port, GY1 3DA; tel. (1481) 745000; fax (1481) 745050; e-mail enquiry@bam-fsg.com; internet www.barings-guernsey.com; member of ING Group; cap. 10.0m., res 50.6m., dep. 911.6m. (Dec. 2001); Chair. D. J. BRENNAN; Man. Dir J. L. BURTON.

BNP Paribas Guernsey Ltd: POB 224, La Plaiderie House, St Peter Port, GY1 3NU; tel. (1481) 712171; fax (1481) 712172; f. 1987; cap. Swiss francs; total assets 1,694.6m Swiss francs; Chair. J-P DELCROIX.

Bristol and West International Ltd: POB 611, Old Bank, St Peter Port, GY1 4NY; tel. (1481) 720609; fax (1481) 711658; e-mail info@bwi.co.gg; internet www.bwi.co.gg; f. 1964; cap. 6.2m., res 25.2m., dep. 730.6m. (March 2001); Chair. JEFF WARREN.

BSI (Channel Islands) Ltd: POB 619, Lefebvre Ct, St Peter Port, GY1 4PQ; tel. (1481) 714444; fax (1481) 734649; f. 1989; Chair. Dr ALFREDO GYSI.

Clariden Bank: POB 581, Helvetia Ct, South Esplanade, St Peter Port, GY1 6LJ; tel. (1481) 715333; fax (1481) 716569; internet www.clariden.com; cap. 7.0m., res 3.0m., dep. 445.0m. (Dec. 2000); CEO A. F. GOOD.

Close Bank Guernsey Ltd: POB 116, Admiral Park, St Peter Port, GY1 3EZ; tel. (1481) 726014; fax (1481) 726645; e-mail banking@closeipb.com; internet www.closeipb.com; cap. 1.0m., dep. 247.5m. (Dec. 2001); Chair. S. R. HODGES.

Coutts (Guernsey) Ltd: POB 16, Le Truchot, St Peter Port, GY1 4AH; tel. (1481) 726101; fax (1481) 728272; internet www.coutts.com; cap. 0.5m., res 3.5m., dep. 10.4m. (Dec. 2000); Gen. Man. M. J. CROCKER.

Crédit Suisse (Guernsey) Ltd: POB 368, Helvetia Court, South Esplanade, St Peter Port, GY1 3JY; tel. (1481) 719000; fax (1481) 724676; e-mail csguernsey.info@cspb.com; internet www.cspb.com/guernsey; f. 1986; cap. 4.0m., res 101.6m., dep. 1,087.3m. (Dec. 2000); CEO A. F. GOOD.

EFG Private Bank (Channel Islands) Ltd: POB 603, EFG House, St Julian's Ave, St Peter Port, GY1 4NN; tel. (1481) 723432; fax (1481) 723488; internet www.efggroup.com; cap. 5.0m., res 19,600m., dep. 201.0m. (Dec. 2001); Man. Dirs M. J. DE JERSEY, J. A. BOTTOMLEY.

SG Hambros Bank and Trust (Guernsey) Ltd: POB 6, Hambro House, St Julian's Ave, St Peter Port, GY1 3AE; tel. (1481) 726521; fax (1481) 727139; f. 1967 (present name from 1998); merchant bankers; called-up share capital 2.5m., dep. 441.9m. (March 1994); Chair. W. J. NEWBURY; Man. Dir R. A. OLLIVER.

HSBC Republic Bank (Guernsey) Ltd: HSBC Republic Bldg, Rue du Pré, St Peter Port, GY1 1LU; tel. (1481) 710901; fax (1481) 711824; internet www.hsbcrepublic.com; f. 1985; cap. US $22.0m., res US $462.7m., dep. US $7,973.0m. (Dec. 2001); CEO GARY MILLER; COO KULVINDER SINGH.

Investec Bank (Channel Islands) Ltd: POB 188, La Vieille Cour, St Peter Port, GY1 3LP; tel. (1481) 723506; fax (1481) 741147; e-mail enquiries@investec.com; internet www.investec.com; f. 1977 as Guinness Mahon Guernsey Ltd, name changed as above in 1999; cap. 7.0m., res 6.1m., dep. 166.5m. (March 2000); Chair. H. HERMAN; Gen. Man. MORT MIRGHAVAMEDDIN.

Leopold Joseph & Sons (Guernsey) Ltd: POB 244, Albert House, South Esplanade, St Peter Port, GY1 3QB; tel. (1481) 712771; fax (1481) 727025; e-mail info@leopoldjoseph.com; internet www.leopoldjoseph.com; f. 1972; private bankers; wholly-owned indirect subsidiary of Leopold Joseph & Sons Ltd, London; cap. 2.0m., res 9.5m., dep. 272.2m. (March 2001); Man. Dir M. C. FORNARA.

Lloyds TSB Offshore Private Banking (Guernsey) Ltd: POB 136, Sarnia House, Le Truchot, St Peter Port, GY1 4EN; tel. (1481) 708000; fax (1481) 727416; e-mail pvtbankingg@lloydstsb-offshore.com; internet www.privatbanking.lloydstsb-offshore.com; cap. 2m., res 51m. (Dec. 2000); Head of Sales and Relationships B. G. ACTON.

MeesPierson (CI) Ltd: POB 253, Bordage House, Le Bordage, St Peter Port, GY1 3QJ; tel. (1481) 733733; fax (1481) 733650; e-mail relationship.managers@meespierson.co.gg; internet www.meespiersonci.com; cap. 65m. (2001); Man. Dir NICK FERRIS.

Rabobank Guernsey Ltd: POB 348, Holland House, St Julian's Ave, St Peter Port, GY1 3UY; tel. (1481) 725147; fax (1481) 725157; e-mail rabobank@guernsey.net; f. 1992; cap. 6.0m., res 0.9m., dep. 331.5m. (Dec. 2001); Man. Dir R. E. VAN BEEK.

N. M. Rothschild & Sons (CI) Ltd: POB 58, St Julian's Court, St Julian's Ave, St Peter Port; tel. (1481) 713713; fax (1481) 727705; e-mail private.banking@rothschild.co.uk; internet www.rothschild.gg; f. 1967; subsidiary of N. M. Rothschild & Sons Ltd, London; cap. 5m., res 69.8m., dep. 1,011m. (March 2002); Chair. PETER JOHNS; Man. Dir PETER ROSE.

Rothschilds Bank Switzerland (CI) Ltd: POB 330, St Julian's Court, St Julian's Ave, St Peter Port, GY1 3UA; tel. (1481) 710521; fax (1481) 711272; e-mail paul.meader@rothschildbank.com; internet www.rothschildbank.com; Man. Dir P. J. MEADER.

Royal Bank of Canada (Channel Islands) Ltd: POB 48, Canada Court, St Peter Port, GY1 3BQ; tel. (1481) 723021; fax (1481) 723524; e-mail info@royalbankci.com; internet www.rbcprivatebanking.com; f. 1973; wholly-owned subsidiary of Royal Bank of Canada; cap. 5m., res 89.5m., dep. 201.7m. (Oct. 2000); Chair. M. LAGOPOULOS; Man. Dir P. E. BREWSTER.

Sabanci Bank (Guernsey) Ltd: 4 North Quay, St Peter Port, GY1 2NB; tel. (1481) 716035; fax (1481) 726675; e-mail info@sabancibank-guernsey.net; internet www.sabancibank-guernsey.net; f. 1994.

Schroders (CI) Ltd: POB 334, Sarnia House, Le Truchot, St Peter Port, GY1 3UF; tel. (1481) 703600; fax (1481) 703700; internet www.schroders.com/ci; cap. 0.5m., res 20.0m., dep. 443.0m. (Dec. 2001); Man. Dir C. W. SHERWELL.

SG Hambros Bank & Trust (Guernsey) Ltd: POB 6, Hambros House, St Julian's Ave, St Peter Port, GY1 3AE; tel. (1481) 7276521; fax (1481) 727139; e-mail richard.olliver@sghambros.com; internet www.sghambros.com; f. 1967; cap. 2.5m., res 43.4m., dep. 441.7m. (Dec. 2000); Man. Dir RICHARD OLLIVER.

Banking Organization

Association of Guernsey Banks: c/o N. M. Rothschild & Sons (CI) Ltd, POB 58, St Julian's Court, St Julian's Ave, St Peter Port; tel. (1481) 713713; fax (1481) 727705; e-mail peter.rose@rothschild.co.uk; internet www.agb.org.gg; f. 1988; Chair. PETER ROSE.

STOCK EXCHANGE

The Channel Islands Stock Exchange, LBG: 1 Lefebvre St, St Peter Port, GY1 4PJ; tel. (1481) 713831; fax (1481) 714856; e-mail info@cisx.com; internet www.cisx.com; 31 cos listed.

INSURANCE

There were 380 insurance companies with offices in Guernsey in 1996.

Britannic Assurance PLC: 7 Berthelot St, St Peter Port, GY1 1JS; tel. (1481) 720907.

Eagle Star Life Assurance Co Ltd: POB 155, Hirzel St, St Peter Port, GY1 4ET; tel. (1481) 726277; fax (1481) 726196.

Eagle Star Trust Co (Guernsey) Ltd: POB 155, Block F, Hirzel Court, St Peter Port, GY1 4ET; tel. (1481) 726277; fax (1481) 726196.

Generali International Ltd: POB 613, Les Echelons Court, South Esplanade, St Peter Port, GY1 4PA; tel. (1481) 714108; fax (1481) 712424; e-mail enquiries@generali-guernsey.com; internet www.generali-guernsey.com.

Insurance Corpn of the Channel Islands Ltd: POB 160, Dixcart House, St Peter Port, GY1 4EY; tel. (1481) 713322; fax (1481) 729189; mem. of the Royal Sun Alliance Group.

Islands' Insurance Co Ltd: Invicta House, Candie Rd, St Peter Port, GY1 1UQ; tel. (1481) 710731.

Norwich Union Insurance Group: Hirzel Court, St Peter Port; tel. (1481) 724864.

Polygon Insurance Co Ltd: POB 225, Polygon Hall, Le Marchant St, St Peter Port, GY1 4HY; tel. (1481) 716000; fax (1481) 728452; e-mail info@heritage.co.gg; internet www.heritage.co.gg.

Prudential Assurance Co Ltd: Prudential Chambers, 39–41 High St, St Peter Port, GY1 2JT.

United Friendly Insurance Co Ltd: Block A5, Hirzel Court, St Peter Port; tel. (1481) 723858.

Trade and Industry

CHAMBER OF COMMERCE

Guernsey Chamber of Commerce: Suite 3, 16 Glategny Esplanade, St Peter Port, GY1 1WN; tel. (1481) 727483; fax (1481) 710755; e-mail director@chamber.guernsey.net; internet chamber.guernsey.net; f. 1808; Dir RODNEY REED.

UTILITIES

Electricity

Guernsey Electricity: POB 4, Electricity House, North Side, Vale, GY1 3AD; tel. (1481) 246931; fax (1481) 246942; e-mail admin@electricity.gg; internet www.electricity.gg; Chair. KEN GREGSON; Man. Dir IAN WATSON.

Gas

Guernsey Gas: POB 70, Rue du Commerce, St Peter Port, GY1 3BZ; tel. (1481) 724811; internet www.gsygas.com; Dir PAUL GARLICK.

Water

States of Guernsey Waterboard: POB 30, South Esplanade, St Peter Port, GY1 3AS; tel. (1481) 724552; Chief Exec. COLIN GAUDION.

Transport

SHIPPING

Alderney Shipping Co Ltd: White Rock, St Peter Port, GY1 2LN; tel. (1481) 724810; fax (1481) 712081; e-mail alderneyshipping@aldshp.co.uk; internet www.aldshp.co.uk.

Commodore Ferries (C.I.) Ltd: POB 10, New Jetty Offices, White Rock, St Peter Port, GY1 3AF; tel. (1481) 728620; fax (1481) 728521; e-mail jvidamour@comferries.com; internet www.comferries.com; regular ro-ro freight services between Portsmouth, Guernsey, Jersey and St Malo; Man. Dir J. VIDAMOUR.

Condor Ferries Ltd: New Jetty, White Rock, St Peter Port; tel. (1481) 726121; fax (1481) 712555; internet www.condorferries.co.uk; f. 1964; regular passenger service operating between the Channel Islands and St Malo, and between the Channel Islands and Poole, Weymouth and Portsmouth; Man. Dir ROBERT PROVAN; Gen. Man. NICK DOBBS.

Emerande Lines: New Jetty, White Rock, St Peter Port, GY1 2LL; tel. (1481) 711414; fax (1481) 715272; car carrying service between Guernsey, Jersey and St Malo.

Herm Seaway Express: Albert Pier, St Peter Port, Guernsey; tel. (1481) 724161; fax (1481) 700226; Contact PETER WILCOX.

Isle of Sark Shipping Co Ltd: The White Rock, St Peter Port, Guernsey, GY1 2LN; tel. (1481) 724059; fax (1481) 713999; e-mail info@sarkshipping.guernsey.net; internet www.sarkshipping.guernsey.net; operates daily services between Guernsey and Sark.

Trident Charter Co Ltd: Woodville, Les Dicqs, Vale, Guernsey, GY6 8JW; tel. (1481) 245253; fax (1481) 700226; Contact PETER WILCOX.

CIVIL AVIATION

Aurigny Air Services Ltd: States Airport, La Planque Lane, Forest, GY8 0DT; tel. (1481) 266444; fax (1481) 266446; e-mail marketing@aurigny.com; internet www.aurigny.com; f. 1968; scheduled passenger services from Guernsey to Alderney, Jersey, London, Dinard, Amsterdam, Manchester, East Midlands; freight services, tour operation, ambulance charters and third party handling; Man. Dir MALCOLM HART.

Tourism

A total of 421,000 tourists visited Guernsey during 2000.

Guernsey Tourist Board: POB 23, St Peter Port, GY1 3AN; tel. (1481) 723552; fax (1481) 714951; e-mail enquiries@guernseytouristboard.com; internet www.guernseytouristboard.com; Chief Exec. (vacant).

Islands of the Bailiwick of Guernsey

Alderney

The area of Alderney is 7.9 sq km (3.1 sq miles) and in 2001 the population was about 2,294. The principal town is St Anne's.

The President is the civic head of Alderney and has precedence on the island over all persons except the Lieutenant-Governor of Guernsey, and the Bailiff of Guernsey or his representative. He presides over meetings of the States of Alderney, which are responsible for the administration of the Island with the exception of police, public health and education, which are administered by the States of Guernsey. The States consist of 10 members who hold office for four years and are elected by universal suffrage of residents.

President of the States: Sir NORMAN BROWSE.

Clerk of the States: DAVID JENKINS.

Clerk of the Court: S. KELLY.

Brecqhou and Lihou

Brecqhou (measuring 1.2 km by 0.5 km) is a dependency of Sark. Lihou (area 0.2 sq km) is, for administrative purposes, part of Guernsey.

Herm

Herm is a tourist and farming island and is held on long lease from the States of Guernsey by Wood of Herm Island Ltd, with a duty to preserve the island's outstanding natural beauty and peacefulness. The island has an area of 2.0 sq km (0.8 sq miles). In 2001 the combined population of Herm and Jethou was 97.

Tenant: Wood of Herm Island Ltd.

Herm Island Administration Office: tel. (1481) 722377; internet www.herm-island.com; Island Man. A. G. HEYWORTH.

Jethou

Jethou has an area of 0.2 sq km (0.07 sq mile) and is leased by the Crown to a tenant who has no official functions.

Sark

The area of the island is 5.5 sq km (2.1 sq miles) and in 1996 the population was about 550. No motor vehicles are permitted apart from a small number of tractors. In summer a daily boat service runs between Guernsey and Sark, and in winter a limited service is provided. There are two harbours on the island.

The Seigneur of Sark is the hereditary civic head of the island and thereby entitled to certain privileges. The Seigneur is a member of the Chief Pleas of Sark, the island's parliament, and has a suspensory veto on its ordinances. The Seigneur has the right, subject to the approval of the Lieutenant-Governor of Guernsey, to appoint the Seneschal of Sark, who is President of the Chief Pleas and Chairman of the Seneschal's Court, which is the local Court of Justice.

Seigneur of Sark: Lt-Col. R. J. GUILLE.

Seneschal: L. P. DE CARTERET.

Greffier: J. P. HAMON.

Sark Committee Office: La Chasse Marette, GY9 0SF; tel. (1481) 832118.

Sark Tourism: Harbour Hill, Sark, GY9 0SB; tel. (1481) 832345; fax (1481) 832483; e-mail office@sark.info; internet www.sark.info.

JERSEY

Introduction

Jersey, the largest of the Channel Islands, is situated to the south-east of Guernsey, from which it is separated by 27 km (17 miles) of sea. The official language of Jersey is English (since 1960), although French is still used in the courts. The state and civil flag is white with a red saltire and coat of arms bearing three yellow lions and surmounted by a yellow crown. The capital is St Helier.

Statistical Survey

Source (unless otherwise stated): States Greffe, States of Jersey; tel. (1534) 502000; fax (1534) 502098; internet www.gov.je.

AREA, POPULATION AND DENSITY

Area: 116.2 sq km (44.9 sq miles).

Population (census of 11 March 2001): 87,186 (males 42,485, females 44,701).

Density (per sq km, 2001): 750.3.

Principal Towns (2001): St Helier 28,310; St Saviour 12,491; St Brelade 10,134; St Clement 8,196.

Births and Deaths (2001): Live births 973; Deaths 784.

Economically Active Population (census of 11 March 2001): Total 48,104 (males 25,983, females 22,121).

AGRICULTURE

There are 34,890 vergees of land under cultivation and 2,490 vergees under glasshouses (1 vergee = 2,200 sq yards). The principal crops are potatoes, cauliflowers and tomatoes. Dairy and cattle farming are important activities.

FINANCE

Currency and Exchange Rates: 100 pence = 1 pound sterling (£). *Dollar and Euro Equivalents* (31 December 2002): US $1 = 62.04 pence; €1 = 65.06 pence; £100 = $161.18 = €153.70.
Note: Jersey is in monetary union with the United Kingdom. It has its own coins and notes but United Kingdom coins and notes are also legal tender.

Budget (£ million, 2002): Revenue 417; Expenditure 424.

Cost of Living (Retail Price Index; base 2000 = 100): Food 105.1; All items 103.9 in 2001.

EXTERNAL TRADE

Exports (£ '000, 2000): Agricultural products 1,651,903.

TRANSPORT

Road Traffic (vehicles registered during 2000): Auto cycles and scooters 235; Motorcycles 529; Private cars 9,880 (incl. taxis and hire cars); Buses and minibuses 35; Tractors 44; Vans 624; Lorries and trucks 189; Others 108.

Shipping (2001): *Vessels Using St Helier Port:* Commercial vessel arrivals 2,048; Passenger arrivals 450,195.

Civil Aviation (2001): Aircraft movements 80,562; Total passengers carried 1,574,566.

COMMUNICATIONS MEDIA

Telephones (2001): 73,900 main lines in use.

Mobile Cellular Telephones (2001): 61,400.

Internet Users (2001): 8,000.
Source: International Telecommunication Union.

Directory

The Constitution

The Lieutenant-Governor and Commander-in-Chief of Jersey is the personal representative of the Sovereign, the Commander of the Armed Forces of the Crown, and the channel of communication between the Crown and the Insular Government. He is appointed by the Crown, and is entitled to sit and speak in the Assembly of the States of Jersey, but not to vote. He has a veto on certain forms of legislation.

The Bailiff is appointed by the Crown, and is President both of the Assembly of the States (the insular legislature) and the Royal Court of Jersey. In the States, he has a right of dissent, and a casting vote.

The Deputy Bailiff is appointed by the Crown and, when authorized by the Bailiff to do so, he may discharge any function appertaining to the office of Bailiff.

The government of the island is conducted by Committees appointed by the States. The States consist of 12 Senators (elected for six years, six retiring every third year), 12 Constables (triennial), and 29 Deputies (triennial). They are elected by universal suffrage. The Dean of Jersey, the Attorney-General and Solicitor-General are appointed by the Crown and are entitled to sit and speak in the States, but not to vote. Permanent laws passed by the States require the sanction of Her Majesty in Council, but Triennial Regulations do not.

The Government

(April 2003)

Lieutenant-Governor and C-in-C Jersey: Air Chief Marshal Sir JOHN CHESHIRE.

Secretary to the Lieutenant-Governor and ADC: Lt-Col A. J. C. WOODROW.

Bailiff: Sir PHILIP MARTIN BAILHACHE.

Deputy Bailiff: MICHAEL CAMERON ST JOHN BIRT.

Dean of Jersey: Very Rev. JOHN N. SEAFORD.

Attorney-General: WILLIAM JAMES BAILHACHE.

Solicitor-General: STEPHANIE CLAIRE NICOLLE.

Greffier of the States: MICHAEL NELSON DE LA HAYE.

Judicial System

Justice is administered in Jersey by the Royal Court, which consists of the Bailiff or Deputy Bailiff and 12 Jurats elected by an Electoral College. There is a Court of Appeal, which consists of the Bailiff (or Deputy Bailiff) and two Judges, selected from a panel appointed by the Crown. A final appeal lies to the Privy Council in certain cases.

A Stipendiary Magistrate deals with minor civil and criminal cases. He also acts as an Examining Magistrate in some criminal matters.

Religion

CHRISTIANITY

The Church of England

The Church of England is the established church. The Deanery of Jersey is an Ecclesiastical Peculiar, governed by its own canons, the Dean being the Ordinary of the Island; it is attached to the diocese of Winchester for episcopal purposes.

Dean of Jersey: Very Rev. JOHN N. SEAFORD, The Deanery, David Place, St Helier, JE2 4TE; tel. (1534) 720001; fax (1534) 617488; e-mail deanofjersey@jerseymail.co.uk.

The Roman Catholic Church

The diocese of Portsmouth includes the Channel Islands and part of southern England. The Episcopal Vicar for the Channel Islands resides at St Peter Port, Guernsey. In Jersey there are 12 Roman Catholic churches, including St Mary and St Peter's, Wellington Rd (English), and St Thomas, Val Plaisant, St Helier (French).

Other Christian Churches

The Baptist, Congregational New Church, Methodist and Presbyterian churches are also represented.

The Press

Jersey Evening Post: POB 582, JE4 8XQ; tel. (1534) 611611; fax (1534) 611622; e-mail editorial@jerseyeveningpost.com; internet www.thisisjersey.com; f. 1890; independent; progressive; Editor C. BRIGHT; Man. Dir J. RAMSDEN; circ. 22,897.

Jersey Weekly Post: POB 582, JE4 8XQ; tel. (1534) 611611; fax (1534) 611622; e-mail editorial@jerseyeveningpost.com; internet www.thisisjersey.com; Thursday; Editor C. BRIGHT; circ. 1,800.

Publishers

Anson & Co Ltd: 8 Vine St, Royal Sq., St Helier, JE2 4WB; tel. (1534) 722572; fax (1534) 723439.

Ashton & Denton Publishing Co (CI) Ltd: 3 Burlington House, St Saviour's Rd, St Helier, JE2 4LA; tel. (1534) 735461; fax (1534) 875805; e-mail asden@supanet.com; f. 1957; local history, holiday guides, financial; Man. Dir A. MACKENZIE.

Broadcasting and Communications

TELECOMMUNICATIONS

Jersey Telecom: POB 53, No 1 The Forum, Grenville Street, St Helier, JE4 8PB; tel. (1534) 882882; fax (1543) 882883; e-mail enquiries@jerseytelecoms.com; internet www.jerseytelecoms.com; Pres. PAUL ROUTIER.

BROADCASTING

Radio

BBC: Radio and Television (see Great Britain).

BBC Radio Jersey: 18 Parade Rd, St Helier, JE2 3PL; tel. (1534) 870000; fax (1534) 732569; e-mail radio.jersey@bbc.co.uk; internet www.bbc.co.uk/jersey; f. 1982; broadcasts 77 hours a week; Senior Broadcast Journalist JAMES FILLEUL; Editor DENZIL DUDLEY.

A new local radio station, Channel 103 FM, began broadcasting in 1992.

Television

Channel Television: Television Centre, St Helier, JE1 3ZD; tel. (1534) 816816; fax (1534) 816817; e-mail broadcast@channeltv.co.uk; internet www.channeltv.co.uk; f. 1962; daily transmissions; Chair. FRANCIS HAMON; Group Chief Exec. HUW DAVIES.

Programmes are also received from the BBC, Channel 4 and Channel 5 in the United Kingdom and also from France.

Finance

Jersey Financial Services Commission: POB 267, Nelson House, David Pl., St Helier, JE4 8TP; tel. (1534) 822000; fax (1534) 822001; e-mail info@jerseyfsc.org; internet www.jerseyfsc.org; f. 1998; financial services regulator; Dir-Gen. RICHARD PRATT.

BANKING

(cap. = capital; auth. = authorized; m. = million; dep. = deposits; res = reserves; br./brs = branch(es); amounts in pounds sterling, unless otherwise indicated.)

In May 2002 total bank deposits in Jersey were more than £135,000m. in 61 institutions.

British Clearing Banks

The banks listed below are branches of British banks, and details concerning directors, capital, etc. of the parent bank will be found under the appropriate section in the pages dealing with Great Britain.

Barclays Bank PLC: POB 8, 13 Library Place, St Helier, JE4 8NE; tel. (1534) 812000; fax (1534) 813500; Jersey Man. MARTYN SCRIVEN; 4 brs.

Lloyds TSB Bank PLC: POB 70, 23 New St, St Helier, JE4 8PL; tel. (1534) 503000; fax (1534) 503099; Island Dir M. SMITH; 3 brs.

National Westminster Bank PLC: POB 11, 16 Library Pl., St Helier, JE4 8NH; tel. (1534) 282828; fax (1534) 282730; Man. P. TAYLOR; 6 brs.

Other Banks

ABN AMRO Trust Company (Jersey) Ltd: POB 255, 7 Castle St, St Helier JE4 8TB; tel. (1534) 604000; fax (1534) 735552; internet www.abnamrotrust.je; f. 1991; Man. Dir XAVIER ISAAC.

AIB Bank (CI) Ltd: POB 468, AIB House, Grenville St, St Helier, JE4 8WT; tel. (1534) 883000; fax (1534) 883112; e-mail one@aib offshore.com; internet www.alliedirishoffshore.com; f. 1981; cap. and res 58.3m. (Dec. 2001); Man. Dir J. F. LYNES.

Ansbacher (Channel Islands) Ltd: POB 393, 7–11 Britannia Pl., Bath St, St Helier, JE4 8US; tel. (1534) 504504; fax (1534) 504575; e-mail info@ansbacher.co.je; internet www.ansbacher.com; f. 1984 as Westpac Banking Corpn (Jersey) Ltd; acquired by Henry Ansbacher Group 1995; cap. 1.0m., res 9.1m., dep. 264.0. (Sept. 2000); Man. Dir ANDREW EVANS.

ANZ Grindlays Bank (Jersey) Ltd: POB 80, West House, West Centre, Peter St, St Helier, JE4 8PT; tel. (1534) 607200; fax (1534) 607250; f. 1969; subsidiary of ANZ Grindlays Bank PLC, London; cap. 2m., res 52.5m., dep. 984.7m. (Sept. 1998); Chair. B. R. LE MARQUAND; Man. Dir B. J. HUMAN.

Bank of Ireland (Jersey) Ltd: POB 416, Bank of Ireland House, Francis St, St Helier, JE4 9WD; tel. (1534) 638600; fax (1534) 737916; e-mail info@boijersey.com; internet www.boijersey.com; Man. Dir D. M. COSGRAVE.

Bank Leumi (Jersey) Ltd: POB 528, 47–49 La Motte St, St Helier, JE4 5UL; tel. (1534) 617445; fax (1534) 617446; f. 1993; cap. 2.5m., res 1.4m., dep. 110.0m. (Dec. 2001).

Bank of Nova Scotia Channel Islands Ltd: POB 60, Kensington Chambers, 46–50 Kensington Pl., St Helier, JE4 9PE; tel. (1534) 789898; fax (1534) 873327; e-mail mailbox@scotia-offshore.com; f. 1972; cap. US $1.3m., dep. US $345.9m. (Sept. 2000); Chair. J. R. MACDONALD; Man. Dir K. C. BRIERLY.

Bank of Scotland Offshore Ltd: Eagle House, 4 Don Rd, St Helier, JE4 8XU; tel. (1534) 825000; fax (1534) 738633; e-mail offshore_enquiries@bankofscotland.co.uk; internet www .bankofscotland.co.uk; cap. 15.0m., dep. 822.8m. (Feb. 2001); f. 1986; Man. Dir WILLIE A. RAEBURN.

Banque Transatlantique (Jersey) Ltd: POB 206, 19–21 Broad St, St Helier, JE4 0XR; tel. (1534) 283190; fax (1534) 283191; e-mail btjersey@psilink.co.je.

BBVA Privanza Bank (Jersey) Ltd: 2 Mulcaster St, St Helier, JE2 3NJ; tel. (1534) 511200; fax (1534) 511201; e-mail bvbj@itl.net; cap. 6.5m., res 48.2m., dep. 976.9m. (Dec. 2000); Man. M. LOPEZ.

BHF-Bank (Jersey) Ltd: 6 Wests Centre, St Helier, JE2 4ST; tel. (1534) 879044; fax (1534) 879246; f. 1981; cap. euro 4m., res 6.7m., dep. 880.9m. (Dec. 2000); Man. J. M. ALCOCK.

Cantrade Private Bank Switzerland (CI) Ltd: POB 350, Cantrade House, 24 Union St, St Helier, JE4 8UJ; tel. (1534) 611200; fax (1534) 611209; f. 1979; subsidiary of UBS AG; cap. and res 40m. (Dec. 1998); Man. Dir J. G. BAERLOCHER.

Chase Bank & Trust Co (CI) Ltd: POB 127, Chase House, Grenville St, St Helier; tel. (1534) 626262; fax (1534) 626300; cap. US $30m. Chair. T. TODMAN; Man. Dir L. C. WORTHAM.

Chase Manhattan Bank N.A.: POB 127, Chase House, Grenville St, St Helier, JE4 8QH; tel. (1534) 626262; fax (1534) 626301; Gen. Man. L. C. WORTHAM.

Citibank (Channel Islands) Ltd: POB 104, 38 The Esplanade, St Helier, JE4 8QB; tel. (1534) 608000; fax (1534) 608190; f. 1969; cap. US $0.9m., res US $7.6m., dep. US $1,353.8m. (Dec. 2000); Chair. CLIVE JONES.

Citicorp Banking Corporation Jersey: 38 The Esplanade, St Helier, JE4 8QB; tel. (1534) 608000; fax (1534) 608290; Man. CLIVE JONES.

Coutts (Jersey) Ltd: POB 6, 23/25 Broad St, St Helier, JE4 8ND; tel. (1534) 282345; fax (1534) 282400; internet www.coutts.com; f. 1969; cap. 0.5m., dep. 18.5m. Man. Dir GERRY WILLIAMS.

Deutsche Bank International Ltd: POB 727, St Paul's Gate, New St, St Helier, JE4 8ZB; tel. (1534) 889900; fax (1534) 889911; internet www.dboffshore.com; f. 1972; cap. 15.0m., res 112.1m., dep. 2,685.5m. (Dec. 2000); Man. Dir P. J. PICHLER.

Dexia Private Bank Jersey Ltd: POB 12, Victoria Chambers, Liberation Sq., St Helier, JE4 9NE; tel. (1534) 834400; fax (1534) 834411; e-mail dexiapbjsy@localdial.com; internet www.dexia.com; Man. Dir DAVID G. SMITH.

Gerrard Private Bank (Jersey) Ltd: 28 New St, St Helier, JE2 3TE; tel. (1534) 887889; fax (1534) 509725; e-mail jer@gerrardpb .com; internet www.gerrardpb.com; f. 1994 as Flemings (Jersey) Ltd, changed name as above in 2001; cap. 0.4m., res 23.8m., dep. 572.8m. (March 2001); Man. Dir G. J. H. TITCOMB.

SG Hambros Bank and Trust (Jersey) Ltd: POB 78, 13 Broad St, St Helier, JE4 8PR; tel. (1534) 815555; fax (1534) 815560; internet www.sghambros.com; f. 1967; subsidiary of SG Hambros Bank and Trust Ltd, London; cap. 2.6m., dep. 738.8m. (Dec. 1999); Chair. W. J. NEWBURY; Man. Dir RICHARD OLLIVER.

Hill Samuel Bank (Jersey) Ltd: POB 63, 7 Bond St, St Helier, JE4 8PH; tel. (1534) 604604; fax (1534) 604606; e-mail hsj@hillsamjsy.co .uk; internet www.hillsamjsy.co.uk; f. 1961; private bank; ultimate parent co Lloyds TSB Group PLC; cap. 1.0m., res 0.2m., dep. 528.2m. (Dec. 2000); Man. Dir TOM SLATTERY.

HSBC Bank International Ltd: POB 26, 28–34 Hill St, St Helier, JE4 8NR; tel. (1534) 606000; fax (1534) 606097; e-mail offshore@ hsbc.com; internet www.offshore.hsbc.com; cap. 1.3m., res. 91.1m. dep. 3,704.4m. (Dec. 1998); Man. Dir B. McDONAGH.

HSBC Bank Middle East: 1 Grenville St, St Helier, JE4 8UB; tel. (1534) 606511; fax (1534) 606149; e-mail mem.bpa@hsbc.com; internet www.hsbc.com; cap. US $331.3m., res US $260.8m., dep. US $7,756.4m. (Dec. 2001); Chair. Sir JOHN BOND.

HSBC Republic Bank (Jersey) Ltd: POB 88, 1 Grenville St, St Helier, JE4 9PF; tel. (1534) 606500; fax (1534) 606504; cap. 1.1m., res 29.5m., dep. 1,368.5m. (Dec. 2001); CEO JONATHAN WATSON.

ING Banque Bruxelles Lambert (Jersey) Ltd: Huguenot House, 28 La Motte St, St Helier, JE4 4SZ; tel. (1534) 880888; fax (1534) 880777; f. 1988; name changed as above in 2001; Man. J. FAVRE.

Kleinwort Benson (Channel Islands) Ltd: POB 76, Wests Centre, St Helier, JE4 8PQ; tel. (1534) 613000; fax (1534) 613141; f. 1962; mem. of the Dresdner Bank Group; cap. and res 138.2m., dep. 2.5m. (Feb. 2002); Man. Dir R. F. ROBINS.

Lloyds TSB Bank (Jersey) Ltd: POB 160, 25 New St, St Helier, JE4 8RG; tel. (1534) 503000; fax (1534) 503047; e-mail leg&secjsy@ lloydstsb-offshore.com; part of Lloyds TSB banking group; cap. 7.6m., res 62.1m., dep. 1,112.2m. (Dec. 2001); Chair. A. R. JESSEMAN; 4 brs.

Lloyds TSB Offshore Treasury Ltd: POB 351, 25 New St, St Helier, JE4 9YT; tel. (1534) 284100; fax (1534) 284481; internet www.treasury.lloydstsb-offshore.com; f. 1969; cap. 4.0m., res 187.6m., dep. 3,721.1m. (Dec. 2001); Chief Exec. MARTIN F. FRICKER.

RBSI Custody Bank Ltd: POB 451, Liberté House, 19–23 La Motte St, St Helier, JE4 5RL; tel. (1534) 286000; fax (1534) 286071; internet www.rbs.co.uk; cap. 4.0m., res 23.3m., dep. 1,408.0m. (Dec. 2000); Man. Dir D. GILLESPIE.

Royal Bank of Canada (CI) Ltd: POB 194, 19–21 Broad St, St Helier, JE4 8RR; tel. (1534) 283000; fax (1534) 283801; internet www.rcbprivatebanking.com; cap. 3.5m., res 45.6m., dep. 1,276.1m. (Oct. 1999); Chair M. J. LAGAPOLOUS.

The Royal Bank of Scotland International Ltd: POB 64, 71 Bath St, St Helier, JE4 8PJ; tel. (1534) 285200; fax (1534) 285222; internet www.rbsint.com; cap. 86.5m., res 180.9m., dep. 8,096.2m. (Dec. 2000); Chief Exec. JIM PATON.

Standard Bank Jersey Ltd: POB 583, Standard Bank House, 47–49 La Motte St, St Helier, JE4 8XR; tel. (1534) 881188; fax (1534) 881199; e-mail sbj@sboff.com; internet www.sboff.com; f. 1977; fmrly Brown Shipley (Jersey); cap. 5.0m., res 4.5m., dep. 688.1m. (Sept. 2000); Man. Dir P. R. WILLIAMS.

Standard Chartered Grindlays (Offshore) Ltd: 13–15 Castle St, St Helier, JE4 8PT; tel. (1534) 704000; fax (1534) 704111; e-mail info .offshore@uk.standardchartered.com; internet www.standard chartered.com/je; f. 1966; name changed as above in 2001; cap. 3.6m., res 131.1m., dep. 3,900m. (Dec. 2001); CEO ANDREW HUNTER; Man. Dir C. DICKINSON.

INSURANCE

Jersey Mutual Insurance Soc., Inc: 74 Halkett Pl., St Helier, JE1 1BT; tel. (1534) 734246; fax (1534) 733381; e-mail info@jersey mutual.com; internet www.jerseymutual.com; f. 1869; fire; Pres. P. F. HANNING; Sec. S. J. MOREL.

Trade and Industry

CHAMBER OF COMMERCE

Chamber of Commerce: 19 Royal Sq., St Helier, JE1 4HF; tel. (1534) 724536; fax (1534) 734942; e-mail admin@jersey-chamber .co .uk; internet www.jerseychamber.com; f. 1768; Pres. MARTIN BRALSFORD; Chief Exec. CLAIRE LE MONNIER; 700 mems.

UTILITIES

Electricity

Jersey Electricity Co Ltd: POB 45, Queen's Rd, St Helier, JE4 8NY; tel. (1534) 505000; fax (1534) 505011; internet www.jec.co.uk; f. 1924; Chair. DEREK MALTWOOD; Man. Dir MIKE LISTON.

Gas

Jersey Gas Co Ltd: POB 169, Thomas Edge House, Tunnell St, St Helier, JE4 8RE; tel. (1534) 633400; fax (1534) 769822; e-mail jerseygas@jsy-gas.com; Man. Dir ROBERT STADDON.

Water

Jersey New Waterworks Co Ltd: Mulcaster House, West Mount Rd, St Helier, JE1 1DG; tel. (1534) 509999; fax (1534) 509666.

Transport

SHIPPING

The harbour of St Helier has 1,400 m of cargo working quays, with 10 berths in dredged portion (2.29 m) and eight drying berths. Range of tide 2.7 m–12.2 m. Unloading facilities include 14 electric cranes of three to 30 metric tons, two Scotch Derricks of 32 tons and 35 tons and two 15-ton mobile cranes.

Condor Jersey Ltd: POB 25, Elizabeth Terminal and Albert Quay, St Helier; tel. (1534) 607080; fax (1534) 280767; head office in Poole, England; daily services to mainland Britain; also regular services to Guernsey and St Malo (France); Gen. Man. NICK DOBBS.

CIVIL AVIATION

The States of Jersey Airport is at St Peter, Jersey.

Airline

British European Airways: States Airport, St Peter; tel. (1534) 45661; internet www.flybe.com; f. 1983 as Jersey European Airways, changed name as above in 2000; services between Jersey and Guernsey, London, Exeter, Blackpool, Bristol, Leeds/Bradford, Birmingham, the Isle of Man, Belfast, Dublin, Derry, Amsterdam, Marseilles and Dinard; Chief Exec. BARRY PERROTT.

Tourism

In 2000 some 609,000 tourists stayed in Jersey.

Jersey Tourism: Liberation Sq., St Helier, JE1 1BB; tel. (1534) 500700; fax (1534) 500808; e-mail info@jersey.com; internet www .jersey.com; CEO ELIZABETH JEFFREYS.

THE ISLE OF MAN

Introduction

The Isle of Man lies in the Irish Sea between the Cumbrian coast of England and Northern Ireland. It is a dependency of the Crown and does not form part of the United Kingdom. It has its own legislative assembly and legal and administrative systems, its laws depending for their validity on Orders made by the Queen in Council. Her Majesty's Government in the United Kingdom is responsible for the defence and international relations of the island, and the Crown is ultimately responsible for its good government. However, control of direct taxation is exercised by the Manx Government and, although most rates of indirect taxation are the same on the island as in the United Kingdom, there is some divergence of rates. The capital is Douglas. In addition to the British public holidays, the Isle of Man also celebrates 5 July (Tynwald Day).

Statistical Survey

Source: Economic Affairs Division, Government Offices, Douglas.

AREA, POPULATION AND DENSITY

Area: 572 sq km (221 sq miles).

Population (census, 29–30 April 2001): 76,315 (males 37,372, females 38,943).

Density (per sq km, 2001): 133.4.

Principal Towns (2001): Douglas (capital) 25,347; Onchan 8,803; Ramsey 7,322; Peel 3,785; Port Erin 3,351; Castletown 3,100.

Births and Deaths (2001): Live births 863 (birth rate 11.3 per 1,000); Deaths 855 (death rate 11.2 per 1,000).

Employment (29–30 April 2001): 39,050 (males 21,299, females 17,751): Agriculture, etc. 543; Manufacturing 3,185; Construction 2,512; Transport and communication 2,970; Retail distribution 3,644; Banking and finance 8,959; Professional and scientific services 7,356; Public administration 3,105.

AGRICULTURE, ETC.

Crops (area in acres, 2001): Cereals and potatoes 11,028; Grass 65,265; Rough grazing 35,978.

Livestock (2001): Cattle 33,354; Sheep 166,894; Pigs 3,053; Poultry 11,466.

Fishing: *Amount Landed* (metric tons, 2001): Scallops 1,116; Queen scallops 1,749; *Value of Landings* (2001): Scallops £1.6m.; Queen scallops £0.6m.; Total firsthand sale value of all landings (2001): £2.2m.

FINANCE

Currency and Exchange Rates: 100 pence = 1 pound sterling (£). *Dollar and Euro Equivalents* (31 December 2002): US $1 = 62.04 pence; €1 = 65.06 pence; £100 = $161.18 = €153.70. Note: The Isle of Man is in monetary union with the United Kingdom. It has its own coins and notes, but United Kingdom coins and notes are also legal tender.

Budget: (projections, year ending 31 March 2003): *Revenue* (major items) Customs duties £251.6m.; Income tax £149.5m. *Expenditure* (major items) Social security £148.2m.; Health services £105.9m.; Education £71.0m.

TRANSPORT

Road Traffic (registered vehicles, 2001): Private 45,195; Engineering 385; Goods 4,489; Agricultural 931; Hackney 790; Public service 146; Motorcycles, scooters and tricycles 4,519.

Shipping (2000/01): Passengers handled 567,323; Registered merchant vessels 258; Total displacement ('000 grt) 5,944.

Civil Aviation (2001): Passengers handled 701,980; Freight unloaded 4,863 metric tons (2001).

TOURISM

Tourist Arrivals (2001): Staying visitors 201,300; Day visitors 9,500; Business travellers 76,300.

COMMUNICATIONS MEDIA

Telephone Connections (2001): Fixed 56,000; Mobile 32,000.
Television Licences (2000): 28,601.

EDUCATION

State Primary (2001): 32 schools, 6,611 students.
State Secondary (2001): 5 schools, 5,374 students.
College (2001): 1.
There are, in addition, two private schools.

Directory

The Constitution

The legislature is Tynwald, comprising two branches, the Legislative Council and the House of Keys, sitting together as one body, but voting separately on all questions except in certain eventualities. The House of Keys has 24 members elected by adult suffrage for five years. The Legislative Council is composed of a President, the Lord Bishop of Sodor and Man, the Attorney-General and eight members elected by the House of Keys. The Head of State of the Isle of Man is the British monarch. The Lieutenant-Governor, who is the Crown's personal representative on the island, is appointed by the Head of State for a five-year term.

The Government

(April 2003)

HEAD OF STATE

Lord of Mann: HM Queen ELIZABETH II.
Lieutenant-Governor: Air Marshal IAN MACFADYEN.

COUNCIL OF MINISTERS

Chief Minister: RICHARD CORKHILL.

GOVERNMENT OFFICES

Isle of Man Government: Bucks Rd, Douglas; tel. (1624) 685685; fax (1624) 685710; e-mail chiefsecs@gov.im; internet www.gov.im.
External Relations Division: Government Office, Bucks Rd, Douglas, IM1 3PN; tel. (1624) 685202; fax (1624) 685710; e-mail anne.shimmin@chiefsecs.gov.im.

Legislature

TYNWALD

President: NOEL QUAYLE CRINGLE.
Deputy President: JAMES ANTHONY BROWN.

Legislative Council (Upper House)

President of the Council: NOEL QUAYLE CRINGLE.
Lord Bishop of Sodor and Man: Rt Rev. NOEL DEBROY JONES.
Attorney-General: WILLIAM JOHN HOWARTH CORLETT.
Members appointed by the House of Keys: G. H. WAFT, D.J. GELLING, D. F. K. DELANEY, L.I. SINGER, E. G. LOWEY, C. M. CHRISTIAN, J. R. KNIVETON, P.M. CROWE.
Clerk: MARYLIN CULLEN.

House of Keys (Lower House)

Speaker: JAMES ANTHONY BROWN.
Deputy Speaker: DONALD JAMES GELLING.
Clerk of Tynwald, Secretary of the House and Counsel to the Speaker: MALACHY CORNWELL-KELLY.

The House of Keys consists of 24 members, elected by adult suffrage —eight for Douglas, two for Ramsey, one each for Peel and Castletown, and 12 for rural districts. The last general election was held in November 2001. There are no political parties as such on the Isle of Man.

Judicial System

The Isle of Man is, for legal purposes, an autonomous sovereign country under the British Crown, with its own legislature and its own independent judiciary administering its own common or customary and statute law. The law of the Isle of Man is, in most essential matters, the same as the law of England and general principles of equity administered by the English Courts are followed by the Courts of the Isle of Man unless they conflict with established local precedents. Her Majesty's High Court of Justice of the Isle of Man is based upon the English system but modified and simplified to meet local conditions. Justices of the Peace are appointed by the Lord Chancellor of England usually on the nomination of the Lieutenant-Governor. The Deemsters (see below), the High Bailiff, the Mayor of Douglas, and the Chairmen of the Town and Village Commissioners are *ex-officio* JPs. The Manx Court of Appeal consists of the Deemsters and the Judge of Appeal.

First Deemster and Clerk of the Rolls: T. W. CAIN.

Second Deemster: J. M. KERRUÍSH.

Judge of Appeal: G. F. TATTERSALL.

Religion

CHRISTIANITY

The Church of England

The Isle of Man forms the diocese of Sodor and Man, comprising 27 parishes. The parish church at Peel was designated a cathedral in 1980.

Lord Bishop of Sodor and Man: Rt Rev. NOEL DEBROY JONES,, Bishop's House, Quarterbridge Rd, Douglas, IM2 3RF; tel. (1624) 622108; fax (1624) 672890.

Roman Catholic Church

The deanery of the Isle of Man is part of the archdiocese of Liverpool. There are eight Catholic churches on the island.

Dean of the Isle of Man: Very Rev. Canon BRENDAN ALGER, St Mary of the Isle, Douglas, IM1 3EG; tel. (1624) 675509.

Other Churches

There are also congregations of the following denominations: Baptist, Bethel Non-Denominational, Christadelphian, Congregational, Greek Orthodox, Independent Methodist, Methodist, Presbyterian, Elim Pentecostal, United Reform, and Society of Friends; also Christian Science, Jehovah's Witnesses and the Church of Jesus Christ of Latter-day Saints.

There are small Bahá'í, Jewish and Muslim communities on the island.

The Press

Isle of Man Church Leader: POB 9, Peel, IM99 9XA; tel. (1624) 843102; e-mail faulds@mcb.net; monthly; Editor IAN FAULDS; circ. 15,000.

Isle of Man Courier: Publishing House, Peel Rd, Douglas, IM1 5PZ; tel. (1624) 695695; fax (1624) 661041; e-mail enquiries@isle-of-man-newspapers.com; internet www.iomonline.co.im; f. 1884; weekly; Editor LIONEL COWIN; circ. 34,931.

Isle of Man Examiner: Publishing House, Peel Rd, Douglas, IM1 5PZ; tel. (1624) 695695; fax (1624) 661041; e-mail enquiries@isle-of-man-newspapers.com; internet www.iomonline.co.im; f. 1880; weekly; Editor LIONEL COWIN; circ. 15,269.

The Manx Independent: Publishing House, Peel Rd, Douglas, IM1 5PZ; tel. (1624) 695695; fax (1624) 661041; e-mail enquiries@isle-of-man-newspapers.com; internet www.iomonline.co.im; f. 1987; Friday; Editor LIONEL COWIN; circ. 12,660.

Manx Post: Ballafodda Farm, Ballabeg, Arbory; tel. (1624) 823355.

Manx Tails Magazine: Unit 21, Spring Valley Industrial Estate, Braddan, IM2 2QT; tel. (1624) 677173; fax (1624) 625623; e-mail execpubs@manninmedia.co.im; internet www.manninmedia.co.im; Editor SIMON RICHARDSON.

Sea Breezes Magazine: Unit 28-30, Spring Valley Industrial Estate, Braddan, IM2 2QS; tel. (1624) 626018; fax (1624) 661655; e-mail seabreezes@manninmedia.co.im; internet www.enterprise .net/manninmedia/; Editor ANDREW DOUGLAS.

Publishers

Amulree Publications: Glen Rd, Laxey, IM4 7AJ; tel. (1624) 862238.

Electrochemical Publications Ltd: Asahi House, Church Rd, Port Erin, IM99 8HD; tel. (1624) 834941; fax (1624) 835400; e-mail wela@enterprise.net; internet www.elchempub.com.

Executive Publications: Unit 21, Spring Valley Industrial Estate, Braddan, IM2 2QS; tel. (1624) 677173; fax (1624) 625623; e-mail execpubs@manninmedia.co.im; internet www.manninmedia.co.im.

Grove Publishing Co: The Ballacrosha, Ballaugh; tel. (1624) 897355.

Lily Publications Ltd: POB 33, Ramsey, IM99 4LP; tel. (1624) 898446; e-mail lilypubs@aol.com.

Mannin Media Group Ltd: Units 28–30, Spring Valley Industrial Estate, Braddan, IM2 2QS; tel. (1624) 626018; fax (1624) 661655; e-mail manninmedia@enterprise.net; internet www.enterprise.net/manninmedia.

Mansk Svenska Publishing Co Ltd: 17 North View, Peel, IM5 1DQ; tel. (1624) 842855.

The Manx Experience: 45 Slieau Dhoo, Tremode Park, Douglas; tel. (1624) 627727; fax (1624) 663627.

Pines Press: The Pines, Ballelin, Maughold, Ramsey, IM7 1HJ; tel. (1624) 862030.

Keith Uren Publishing: 12 Manor Lane, Farmhill, Braddan, IM2 2NX; tel. and fax (1624) 611100; e-mail portfolio@enterprise.net; internet www.iom-portfolio.co.uk.

Broadcasting and Communications

TELECOMMUNICATIONS

Manx Telecom Ltd: Isle of Man Business Park, Cooil Road, Braddan, IM99 1HX; tel. (1624) 633633; fax (1624) 634050; e-mail mail@manx-telecom.com; internet www.manx-telecom.com.

BROADCASTING

Isle of Man Communications Commission: Winchester Court, Second Ave, Onchan, IM3 4LT; tel. (1624) 677022; fax (1624) 626499; e-mail margaret.king@cc.gov.im; internet www.gov.im/deptindex/comminfo.asp; appointed by the Isle of Man Government to represent the Island's interests in all matters of radio and television; Chair. of Comm. R. P. BRAIDWOOD; Dir A. R. HEWITT.

Radio and Television

Manx Radio: POB 1368, Broadcasting House, Douglas, IM99 1SW; tel. (1624) 682600; fax (1624) 682604; e-mail postbox@manxradio .com; internet www.manxradio.com; commercial station operated (by agreement with the Isle of Man Government) by Radio Manx Ltd; Chair. J. C. FARGHER; Man. Dir STEWART WATTERSON.

Border Television PLC: Television Centre, Carlisle, CA1 3NT; tel. (1228) 525101; fax (1228) 541384; internet www.border-tv.com; Borders and the Isle of Man; Chair. JAMES L. GRAHAM; Chief Exec. PAUL CORLEY.

The Isle of Man also receives television programmes from the BBC, Channel 4 and five.

Finance

Isle of Man Government Financial Supervision Commission: POB 58, Finch Hill House, Bucks Rd, Douglas, IM99 1DT; tel. (1624) 689300; fax (1624) 629342; e-mail fsc@gov.im; internet www.fsc.gov .im; responsible for the licensing, authorization and supervision of banks, building societies, investment businesses, collective investment schemes and corporate service providers; also responsible for the Companies Registry; Chief Exec. JOHN ASPDEN.

Treasury: Government Offices, Buck's Rd, Douglas, IM1 3PU; tel. (1624) 685586; fax (1624) 685662; e-mail treasuryadmin@gov.im; internet www.gov.im/treasury; Minister ALLAN BELL; Chief Financial Officer P. M. SHIMMIN.

BANKING

(cap. = capital; res = reserves; dep. = deposits; m. = million; brs = branches; amounts in pounds sterling)

At 31 December 2000 total bank deposits in the Isle of Man amounted to some £24,690m. and there were 62 licensed banks and two building societies. The Financial Supervision Commission may allow a major bank to establish a presence on the island on a managed bank basis, by awarding an offshore banking licence.

AIB Bank (Isle of Man) Ltd: POB 186, 10 Finch Rd, Douglas, IM99 1QE; tel. (1624) 639639; fax (1624) 639636; e-mail one@aiboffshore .com; internet www.alliedirishoffshore.com; f. 1977; cap. 7.5m., dep. 615.4m. (Dec. 2000); Chair. J. C. FARGHER; Man. Dir S. K. DOWLING.

Alliance & Leicester (International) Ltd: POB 226, 19–21 Prospect Hill, Douglas, IM99 1RY; tel. (1624) 663566; fax (1624) 663577; e-mail marketing@alil.co.im; internet www.alil.co.im; Man. Dir SIMON HULL.

Allied Dunbar Bank International Ltd: POB 78, 43–51 Athol St, Douglas; tel. (1624) 661551; fax (1624) 662183; internet www .allieddunbarint.com; cap. 5m., res 2.8m., dep. 114.2m. (Dec. 2000); Man. IAN CRAWFORD.

Anglo Irish Bank Corpn (IOM) PLC: St George's Ct, Upper Church St, Douglas, IM1 1EE; tel. (1624) 698000; e-mail iom@ angloirishbank.ie; internet www.angloirishbank.ie; CEO MICHAEL McGEE.

Bank of Bermuda (IOM) Ltd: 12/13 Hill Street, Douglas, IM99 1BW; tel. (1624) 637777; fax (1624) 637778; e-mail bobman@ enterprise.net; internet www.bankofbermuda.com; cap. 5.0m., dep. 548.5m. (June 2000); Man. Dir A. SMITH.

Bank of Ireland (IOM) Ltd: POB 246, Christian Rd, Douglas, IM99 1XF; tel. (1624) 644200; fax (1624) 644298; e-mail info@boiiom .com; internet www.boiiom.com; cap. 5m., dep. 635m. (March 1997); Man. Dir R. ALDEN.

Barclays Bank PLC: POB 213, Eagle Court, 25 Circular Rd, Douglas, IM99 1RH; tel. (1624) 684000; fax (1624) 684321; international banking services; Man. E. SHALLCROSS; 6 brs.

Barclays Finance Co (IOM) Ltd: POB 9, Barclays House, Victoria St, Douglas, IM99 1AJ; tel. (1624) 684567; fax (1624) 684593; e-mail finco.iom@barclays.co.uk; cap. and res 26.3m. Man. L. E. BENNETT.

Barclays Private Bank and Trust (Isle of Man) Ltd: POB 48, Queen Victoria House, Victoria St, Douglas, IM99 1DF; tel. (1624) 682828; fax (1624) 620905; Man. Dir COLIN JONES.

Britannia International Ltd: Britannia House, Victoria St, Douglas, IM99 1SD; tel. (1624) 681100; fax (1624) 681105; e-mail britannia@mcb.net; internet www.britanniainternational.com; offshore subsidiary of Britannia Building Society; Man. Dir D. P. WADDINGHAM.

Caymanx Trust Co Ltd: 34 Athol St, Douglas, IM1 1RD; tel. (1624) 646900; fax (1624) 662192; e-mail mail@cnciom.com; internet www .cnciom.com; Man. Dir E. HARKIN.

Celtic Bank Ltd: POB 114, Celtic House, Victoria St, Douglas, IM99 1JW; tel. (1624) 622856; fax (1624) 620926; f. 1977; issued cap. 6.8m., res 2.0m., dep. 144.9m. (March 2001); Chair. RICHARD G. DANIELSON; Man. Dir SIMON YOUNG.

Close Bank (Isle of Man) Ltd: POB 203, St George's Ct, Upper Church St, Douglas, IM99 1RB; tel. (1624) 643200; fax (1624) 622039; e-mail info@close.co.im; internet www.close.co.im; f. 1976; merchant bank; cap. 5.0m., res 1.5m., dep. 160.0m. (July 2000); Man. Dir IAN BANCROFT.

Conister Trust PLC: POB 17, Conister House, 16–18 Finch Rd, Douglas, IM99 1AR; tel. (1624) 694694; fax (1624) 624278; e-mail info@conistertrust.com; internet www.conistertrust.com; f. 1935; specializes in asset finance; cap. and res 8m., dep. 33m. Man. Dir E. J. THORN; 1 br.

Duncan Lawrie (IOM) Ltd: 14–15 Mount Havelock, Douglas IM1 2QG; tel. (1624) 620770; fax (1624) 676315; e-mail priv_bank@iom .duncanl.co.uk; internet www.duncan-lawrie.co.uk; cap. 5.0m., dep. 91.1m. (Dec. 2001); Chair. D. A. REEVES; Man. Dir A. M. MOLLOY.

Gerrard Private Bank (IOM) Ltd: 5 Mount Pleasant, Douglas, IM1 2PU; tel. (1624) 645000; fax (1624) 627218; e-mail iom@ gerrardpb.com; internet www.gerrardpb.com; Dir G. HORTON.

Habib European Bank Ltd: St James's House, Market St, Douglas, IM1 2PQ; tel. (1624) 622554; fax (1624) 627135; wholly-owned subsidiary of Habib Bank AG Zurich; cap. 5.0m., dep. 66.2m. (Dec. 2001); Sr Vice-Pres. A. SHAIKH.

Lloyds TSB Bank (Isle of Man) Ltd: Peveril Bldg, Peveril Sq., Douglas, IM99 1JJ; tel. (8457) 301280; fax (1624) 626003; 5 brs.

Lloyds Private Banking (Isle of Man) Ltd: POB 111, Peveril Bldg, Peveril Sq., Douglas, IM99 1JJ; tel. (1624) 638200; fax (1624) 676289; Dir and Man. T. P. WILD.

Meghraj Bank (IOM) Ltd: POB 3, Meghraj Centre, Upper Church St, Douglas, IM99 1AE; tel. (1624) 620848; fax (1624) 677318; e-mail bank@meghrajiom.co.im; cap. 5m., dep. 85.5m. (June 1998); Chair. WILFRED COTTON; Sec. DAVID MOORHOUSE.

Nationwide International Ltd: POB 217, 5–11 St Georges St, Douglas, IM99 1RN; tel. (1624) 696000; fax (1624) 696001; internet www.nationwideinternational.com; Man. Dir C. GANDY.

Northern Offshore Banking and Financial Services: POB 113, 49 Victoria St, Douglas, IM99 1JN; tel. (1624) 629106; fax (1624) 627508; mem. of National Australia Bank Group; Man. ALASTAIR CLARKE.

Singer & Friedlander (Isle of Man) Ltd: Samuel Harris House, 5–11 St George's St, Douglas, IM99 1SN; tel. (1624) 699222; fax (1624) 699200; e-mail info@iom.singer-friedlander.com; internet www.singers-iom.co.im; f. 1971; merchant bank; cap. 5.0m., res 25.3m., dep. 326.0m. (Dec. 2001); Man. Dir R. JAMES.

Standard Bank Isle of Man Ltd: Standard Bank House, 1 Circular Rd, Douglas, IM1 1SB; tel. (1624) 643643; fax (1624) 643800; e-mail sbiom@sboff.com; internet www.sboff.com; cap. 5.0m., res 2.6m., dep. 367.0m. (Dec. 2000); Man. Dir K. J. FODEN.

Ulster Bank (IOM) Ltd: 45 Victoria St, Douglas, IM1 1UB; tel. (1624) 672221; fax (1624) 661276; e-mail clientservices@ubiom.com; internet www.ulsterbank.com; f. 1979; cap. 5.0m., res 5.5m., dep. 306.2m. (Nov. 1996); Chief Exec. M. P. SALLEY.

'Offshore' Banks

Abbey National Offshore: POB 150, Carrick House, Circular Road, Douglas, IM99 1NH; tel. (1624) 644800; fax (1624) 644691; Man. Dir P. BRACKPOOL.

Bank of Scotland International: POB 19, Prospect Hill, Douglas IM99 1AT; tel. (1624) 644000; fax (1624) 644090; e-mail enquiries@ bankof scotland.co.uk; internet www.bankofscotlandoffshore.co.uk; f. 1976; cap. 5m.

Bradford & Bingley International Ltd: 30 Ridgeway St, Douglas, IM1 1TA; tel. (1624) 695000; fax (1624) 695001; e-mail enquiries@bbi.co.im; internet www.bbi.co.im; f. 1989; wholly-owned subsidiary of Bradford & Bingley PLC, UK; cap. and res 185m. Gen. Man. JOHN SHEATH.

Clydesdale Bank PLC: POB 113, 49 Victoria St, Douglas, IM86 1PX; tel. (1624) 672592; fax (1624) 627508; mem. of National Australia Bank Group; Man. R. I. MONTGOMERY.

Coutts (IOM) International Ltd: Coutts House, Summerhill Rd, Onchan, IM3 1RB; tel. (1624) 632222; fax (1624) 620988; Gen. Man. P. WEYNANDT.

The Derbyshire (Isle of Man) Ltd: POB 136, HSBC House, Ridgeway St, Douglas, IM99 1LR; tel. (1624) 663432; fax (1624) 615133; e-mail info@derbyshire.co.im; internet www.derbyshire .co .im; Man. Dir CLIVE D. PARRISH.

Lloyds TSB Offshore Private Banking (Isle of Man) Ltd: Peveril Bldgs, Peveril Sq., Douglas, IM99 2RZ; tel. (1624) 638030; fax (1624) 676289; Gen. Man. A. E. HULL.

National Irish Bank Ltd: POB 113, 49 Victoria St, Douglas, IM86 1PX; tel. (1624) 628314; mem. of National Australia Bank Group; Man. ALASTAIR CLARKE.

NatWest Offshore Ltd: POB 13, 2 Athol St, Douglas IM99 1AN; tel. (1624) 637100; fax (1624) 624686; internet www.natwestoffshore .com; f. 1865; cap. 7.5m., res 531.7m., dep. 7,993.2m. (Dec. 2000); bankers to Isle of Man Government; mem. of the Royal Bank of Scotland Group; Chair. C. McPHAIL; 12 brs.

The Royal Bank of Scotland International Ltd: POB 151, Royal Bank House, 2 Victoria St, Douglas, IM99 1NJ; tel. (1624) 646464; fax (1624) 646453; e-mail marketingiom@rbsint.com; Dir WILLIAM Mc KAY.

Restricted Banks

Bermuda Trust (Isle of Man) Ltd: POB 34, 12/13 Hill St, Douglas, IM99 1BW; tel. (1624) 637777; Man. Dir A. SMITH.

HSBC Trust Corpn (Isle of Man) Ltd: POB 32, HSBC House, Ridgeway St, Douglas, IM99 1US; tel. (1624) 684800; fax (1624) 684879; Man. Dir G. R. DRINKWATER.

Irish Permanent (IOM) Ltd: St James's Chambers, 64A Athol St, Douglas; tel. (1624) 676726; fax (1624) 676795; e-mail mail@irish -permanent.co.im; Man. Dir PHILIP MURRAY.

Merrill Lynch Bank and Trust Co (Cayman) Ltd: Belgravia House, 34–44 Circular Rd, Douglas, IM1 1QW; tel. (1624) 688600; fax (1624) 688601; Man. N. ORDERS.

Nedcor Bank Ltd: Nedcor House, 29–33 Bucks Rd, Douglas, IM1 3DD; tel. (1624) 612893; fax (1624) 612836; e-mail nedbank@nib-int .com.

INSURANCE

There were 196 authorized insurance companies in the Isle of Man in 1998, including:

Albany International Assurance Ltd: St Mary's, The Parade, Castletown, IM9 1RJ; tel. (1624) 823262; Man. Dir SUE CORLETT.

AXA Equity and Law International Life Assurance Co Ltd: Victory House, Prospect Hill, Douglas, IM1 1QP; tel. (1624) 683683; fax (1624) 672700.

CMI Insurance Co Ltd: Clerical Medical House, Victoria Rd, Douglas, IM99 1LT; tel. (1624) 638888.

Friends Provident International Ltd: Royal Court, Castletown, IM9 1RA; tel. (1624) 821212; fax (1624) 824405; e-mail service desk@ rsaifs.com; internet www.rsaifs.com; Man. Dir PAUL QUIRK.

Hansard International Ltd: POB 192, Anglo International House, Bank Hill, North Quay, Douglas, IM99 1QL; tel. (1624) 688000; fax (1624) 688008; internet www.hftrust.com.

Isle of Man Assurance Ltd: IOMA House, Hope St, Douglas, IM1 1AP; tel. (1624) 681200; fax (1624) 681390; e-mail ioma@ioma .co.im; internet www.ioma.co.im.

Prudential Assurance Co Ltd: 19–21 Circular Rd, Douglas; tel. (1624) 675393; fax (1624) 662606.

Royal Insurance Service Co (IOM) Ltd: POB 27, Atlantic House, Circular Rd, Douglas, IM99 1BF; tel. (1624) 620625; fax (1624) 620934; Man. DAVID STACEY.

Royal Skandia Life Assurance Ltd: POB 159, Skandia House, King Edward Rd, Onchan, IM99 1NU; tel. (1624) 655555; fax (1624) 611715; internet www.royalskandia.com.

Scottish Provident International Life Assurance Ltd: Provident House, Ballacottier Business Park, Cooil Rd, Douglas, IM2 2SP; tel. (1624) 681681; fax (1624) 677336; internet www. spila.com; f. 1991; Man. Dir A. A. WHYTE.

Tower Insurance Co Ltd: POB 27, Jubilee Bldgs, 1 Victoria St, Douglas, IM99 1BF; tel. (1624) 673446; fax (1624) 663864; subsidiary of Royal Insurance Services Co Ltd; Dir DAVID STACEY.

Zurich International Life Ltd: 45–51 Athol St, Douglas, IM99 1EF; tel. (1624) 662266; fax (1624) 662038; internet www.zurich intlife.com.

Insurance Association

Insurance and Pensions Authority: HSBC House, Ridgeway St, Douglas, IM1 1ER; tel. (1624) 646000; fax (1624) 646001; e-mail ipa .admin@ipa.gov.im; internet www.gov.im/ipa; Chief Exec. DAVID VICK.

Trade and Industry

CHAMBER OF COMMERCE

Isle of Man Chamber of Commerce: 17 Drinkwater St, Douglas, IM1 1PP; tel. (1624) 674941; fax (1624) 663367; e-mail enquiries@ iomchamber.org.im; 450 mems.

UTILITIES

Electricity

Manx Electricity Authority: POB 177, Douglas, IM1 1EW; tel. (1624) 687687; fax (1624) 687612; Chief Exec. MICHAEL J. PROFFITT.

Gas

Manx Gas Ltd: Murdoch House, South Quay, Douglas, IM1 5PA; tel. (1624) 644444; fax (1624) 626528; Man. Dir C. J. SIDLEY.

Water

Isle of Man Water Authority: Drill Hall, Tromode Rd, Douglas, IM2 5PA; tel. (1624) 695949; fax (1624) 695956; e-mail water@gov .im; internet www.gov.im/water.

TRADE UNIONS

In 1991 the Trade Union Act was approved by Tynwald, providing for the registration of trade unions. Although trade unions had been active previously on the Isle of Man, they had not received legal recognition.

Isle of Man Fisherman's Association Ltd: Heritage Centre, The Quay, Peel, IM5 1TA; tel. (1624) 842144; fax (1624) 844395; e-mail manx.fa@lineone.net.

Manx National Farmers' Union: Agriculture House, Ground Floor, Tromode, IM4 4QE; tel. (1624) 674191; fax (1624) 662204.

Transport and General Workers' Union: 25 Fort St, Douglas, IM1 2LJ; tel. (1624) 621156; fax (1624) 673115; District Sec. J. B. MOFFATT.

Transport

RAILWAYS

Isle of Man Transport: Transport Headquarters, Bank Circus, Douglas, IM1 5PT; tel. (1624) 663366; fax (1624) 663637; e-mail businfo@busandrail.gov.im; 29 km (18 miles) of electric track; also 25 km (16 miles) of steam railway track, and Snaefell Mountain Railway (7 km of electric track); Dir of Public Transport DAVID R. HOWARD.

ROADS

There are over 640 km (400 miles) of country roads, excluding streets and roads in the four towns; about one-half are main roads. Some roads form the course for the International TT races.

Dept of Transport: Sea Terminal, Douglas, IM1 2RF; tel. (1624) 686600; fax (1624) 686617; Chief Exec. A. J. BELL.

Isle of Man Transport: see above.

SHIPPING

Isle of Man Steam Packet Co Ltd: PO Box 5, Imperial Bldgs, Douglas, IM1 2BY; tel. (1624) 645645; fax (1624) 645609; internet www.steam-packet.com; f. 1830; daily services operate all the year round between Heysham and Douglas; during the summer there are frequent services between the Island and Dublin, Belfast and Liverpool; during the winter there is a weekend service to Liverpool; Chair. JUAN KELLY; Man. Dir HAMISH ROSS; fleet of 1 passenger/car ferry, 1 roll-on/roll-off passenger/freight ferry and 2 Seacat Fastcraft.

Maersk Co (IOM) Ltd: Portland House, Station Rd, Ballasalla, IM9 2RB; tel. (1624) 822667; fax (1624) 822618.

Mezeron Ltd: East Quay, Ramsey, IM8 1BG; tel. (1624) 812302; fax (1624) 815613; f. 1983; cargo services; Man. Dir N. A. LEECE.

Ramsey Steamship Co Ltd: 13 North Quay, Douglas, IM1 4LE; tel. (1624) 673557; fax (1624) 620460; e-mail tony@ramsey -steamship.com; internet www.ramsey-steamship.com; f. 1913; cargo services; Sec. and Man. A. G. KENNISH.

Tufton Oceanic Investments Ltd: 9 Myrtle St, Douglas, IM1 1ED; tel. (1624) 663616; fax (1624) 663918; e-mail tufton@ tuftonoceanic.com.

CIVIL AVIATION

British European Airways: Ronaldsway Airport, Ballasalla, IM9 2AS; tel. (1624) 824354; fax (1624) 825822; e-mail rod.breheny@ british-european.com; internet www.british-european.com; daily services to London, Bristol and Belfast.

Emerald Airways Ltd: Ronaldsway Airport, Ballasalla; tel. (1624) 825608; fax (1624) 825723; daily cargo services to Liverpool.

Island Aviation and Travel Ltd: Ronaldsway Airport, Ballasalla, IM9 2AS; tel. (1624) 824300; fax (1624) 824946; e-mail enquiries@ iaat.co.uk; internet www.iaat.co.uk; provides executive charters to worldwide destinations, runs air-ambulance services, aircraft management, handling.

Manx Airlines Ltd: Ronaldsway Airport, Ballasalla, IM9 2JE; tel. (1624) 826000; fax (1624) 826001; e-mail enquiries@manx-airlines .com; internet www.manx-airlines.com; f. 1982 by British Midland Airways and Air UK; parent co British Regional Airlines Group PLC; scheduled passenger and freight services throughout the UK; Chair. Sir MICHAEL BISHOP; CEO T. R. P. LIDDIARD.

Tourism

Dept of Tourism and Leisure, Tourism Division: Sea Terminal Buildings, Douglas, IM1 2RG; tel. (1624) 686801; fax (1624) 686800; e-mail tourism@gov.im; internet www.visitisleofman.com; responsibilities of tourist board, also operates modern and vintage transport systems, a Victorian theatre and an indoor and outdoor sport and leisure complex; f. 1896; CEO T. P. TOOHEY.

UNITED KINGDOM OVERSEAS TERRITORIES

From February 1998 the British Dependent Territories were referred to as the United Kingdom Overseas Territories, following the announcement of the interim findings of a British government review of the United Kingdom's relations with the Overseas Territories. In March 1999 draft legislation confirming this change was published by the British Government; under the proposed legislation, the citizens of Overseas Territories would be granted the rights, already enjoyed by the citizens of Gibraltar and the Falkland Islands, to British citizenship and of residence in the United Kingdom. These entitlements were not reciprocal, and British citizens would not enjoy the same rights with regard to the Overseas Territories. The British Overseas Territories Act entered into effect in May 2002. The British Government meanwhile announced its determination to ensure that legislation in the Overseas Territories adhered to British and European Union standards, particularly in the areas of financial regulation and human rights.

ANGUILLA

Introductory Survey

Location, Climate, Language, Religion, Flag, Capital

Anguilla, a coralline island, is the most northerly of the Leeward Islands, lying 113 km (70 miles) to the north-west of Saint Christopher (St Kitts) and 8 km (5 miles) to the north of St Maarten/St Martin. Also included in the Territory are the island of Sombrero, 48 km (30 miles) north of Anguilla, and several other uninhabited small islands. The climate is sub-tropical, the heat and humidity being tempered by the trade winds. Temperatures average 27°C (80°F) and mean annual rainfall is 914 mm (36 ins), the wettest months being September to December. English is the official language. Many Christian churches are represented, the principal denominations being the Anglican and Methodist Churches. The flag (proportions 3 by 5 on land, 1 by 2 at sea) has a dark blue field with the Union flag in the upper hoist corner and, in the centre of the fly, a white shield bearing three orange circling dolphins above a light blue base. The capital is The Valley.

Recent History

Anguilla, previously inhabited by Arawaks and Caribs, was a British colony from 1650 until 1967. From 1825 the island became increasingly associated with Saint Christopher (St Kitts) for administrative purposes (also see chapter on Saint Christopher and Nevis). The inhabitants of Anguilla petitioned for separate status in 1875 and 1958. In February 1967, however, St Christopher-Nevis-Anguilla assumed the status of a State in Association with the United Kingdom, as did four other former British colonies in the Eastern Caribbean. These Associated States became independent internally, while the British Government retained responsibility for external affairs and defence.

In May 1967 the Anguillans, under the leadership of Ronald Webster, a local businessman and head of the only political party, the People's Progressive Party (PPP), repudiated government from Saint Christopher. After attempts to repair the breach between Saint Christopher and Anguilla had failed, British security forces were deployed in Anguilla in March 1969 to install a British Commissioner. Members of London's Metropolitan Police Force remained on the island until the Anguilla Police Force was established in 1972. In July 1971 the British Parliament approved the Anguilla Act, one clause of which stipulated that, should Saint Christopher-Nevis-Anguilla decide to end its associated status, Anguilla could be separated from the other islands. In August the British Government's Anguilla Administration Order 1971 determined that the British Commissioner would continue to be responsible for the direct administration of the island, with the co-operation of a local elected council. The terms of this Order were superseded by the introduction of a new Constitution in February 1976. Anguilla formally separated from Saint Christopher-Nevis-Anguilla on 19 December 1980, assuming the status of British Dependent Territory. In accordance with the terms of the British Government's Anguilla Constitution Order of 1982, a new Constitution came into operation in Anguilla on 1 April 1982.

Legislative elections were held in March 1976, and Webster was appointed Chief Minister. In February 1977, following his defeat on a motion of confidence, he was replaced by Emile Gumbs as Chief Minister and as leader of the PPP (renamed the Anguilla National Alliance—ANA—in 1980). Webster was returned to power, to lead the recently-formed Anguilla United Party (AUP), at a general election in May 1980. The dismissal of the Minister of Agriculture in May 1981 led to serious divisions within the Government, and the resignation in sympathy of another minister precipitated the collapse of Webster's administration. Webster subsequently formed a new political party, the Anguilla People's Party (APP), which won five of the seven seats in a general election in June. An early general election in March 1984 resulted in a conclusive defeat for the APP, including the loss of Webster's own seat. Gumbs became Chief Minister, and pursued a policy of revitalizing the island's economy, mainly through tourism and attracting foreign investment. Webster resigned from the leadership of the APP, which was renamed the Anguilla Democratic Party (ADP).

The majority of the population expressed no desire for independence, but the new Government appealed for wider powers for the Executive Council, and for more aid and investment from the United Kingdom in the island's economy and infrastructure. In October 1985 the Governor appointed a committee to review the Constitution, in response to an earlier unanimous request from the House of Assembly for modifications, particularly concerning the status of women and of persons born overseas of Anguillan parents. The amendments, which provided for the appointment of a Deputy Governor and designated international financial affairs (the 'offshore' banking sector) as the Governor's responsibility, came into effect in May 1990.

Gumbs remained Chief Minister following a general election in February 1989. The ANA won only three seats in the House of Assembly but was supported by the independent member, Osbourne Fleming, who retained his cabinet portfolio. The ADP secured one seat and the revived AUP won two.

In May 1991 the British Government abolished capital punishment for the crime of murder in Anguilla (as well as in several other British Dependent Territories). The announcement by the Governor in late 1991 that a number of professionals from overseas were to be appointed to help in the management of the island's administration provoked widespread criticism, both from Anguillans resident in the Territory and from those abroad. In August 1992 Alan Shave assumed office as Governor of Anguilla (replacing Brian Canty).

A general election in March 1994 failed to produce a clear majority for any one party, and a coalition was subsequently formed by the ADP and the AUP, which had each won two seats and, respectively, secured 31.2% and 11.4% of total votes cast. The ANA, under the leadership of Eric Reid, won two seats with 35.7% of the vote, while the remaining seat was secured by Fleming. A newly-formed party, Anguillans for Good Government (whose candidates included Webster), failed to win any seats, despite attaining 11.6% of total votes cast. The AUP leader, Hubert Hughes, was subsequently appointed Chief Minister, replacing Sir Emile Gumbs (as he had become).

On becoming Chief Minister, Hughes stated that he might seek Anguilla's independence from the United Kingdom. The appointment of one of the nominated members of the House of

Assembly in May 1994 led to a dispute between the Governor and Hughes: the latter strongly disapproved of the nomination of David Carty, a leading member of the ANA who had failed to win a parliamentary seat in March, and alleged that he had not been consulted regarding the appointment, a charge strenuously denied by the Governor. Debate surrounding the issue intensified following a High Court declaration in December 1995 that upheld Carty's appointment as constitutionally valid, the Speaker refused to swear him in as a member of the House of Assembly. Protests ensued, in which Osbourne Fleming, who had become the leader of the ANA and Leader of the Opposition, was removed from the House for disorderly conduct and two other opposition members walked out in support of Carty.

In October 1995 the island suffered severe damage from 'Hurricane Luis'. Destruction of buildings and infrastructure, as well as damage to the agricultural sector, was estimated to be worth some EC $72m. Hughes was highly critical of the British Government's response to the hurricane, which he alleged was inadequate. In May 1997 Robert Harris, hitherto Deputy Governor, assumed office as Governor.

The announcement by the British Government in January 1997 that it was considering the extension of its powers in the Dependent Territories of the Caribbean attracted further criticism from Hughes. The proposed reintroduction of reserve powers, whereby the Governor (with the consent of the British Government) can amend, veto or introduce legislation without the agreement of the local legislature, provoked accusations from Hughes that the United Kingdom hoped to create a situation in which Territories would be forced to seek independence. The British Government, however, maintained that the initiative had been prompted largely by a desire to secure Anguilla's financial services sector from exploitation by criminal organizations, particularly drugs-traffickers (which had remained a problem, owing to the territory's bank secrecy laws).

In September 1997 Hughes publicly denounced Robert Harris for being oblivious to his country's needs, and, furthermore, made allegations of corruption within the Civil Service Association (CSA). The CSA denied the claim and immediately requested a public apology. Meanwhile Osbourne Fleming pressed for Hughes' resignation, claiming that the remarks were unjustified and jeopardized public and investor confidence in the Government.

In May 1998 Hughes announced that public consultations would be undertaken on a proposal to reform Anguilla's constitutional status in the hope that a reformed Constitution could be in place before the general election, scheduled for March 1999. Hughes criticized the current Constitution for vesting executive authority in the Governor rather than in locally-elected ministers. Hughes ruled out any prospect of creating a Senate on the grounds of the cost involved. In September 1998, however, the British Government announced that its Overseas Dependencies were to be renamed United Kingdom Overseas Territories. In March 1999 the British Government issued a policy document confirming the change of name, and guaranteeing citizens of Overseas Dependencies the right to British citizenship. The proposals also included the requirement that the Constitutions of Overseas Territories should be revised in order to conform to British and international standards. The process of revision of the Anguillan Constitution began in September 1999.

Legislative elections were held on 4 March 1999. Sixteen candidates, including four independents, contested the seven seats in the House of Assembly; the Government campaigned on its record of encouraging the development of the tourist and offshore financial services sectors. At the elections, the AUP and the ADP both retained their two seats, securing 1,579 and 704 votes, respectively. The opposition ANA also retained its three seats, securing 2,053 votes. The AUP-ADP coalition therefore kept control of the House of Assembly, and the four members of the Executive Council retained their portfolios.

In May 1999 the two ADP ministers threatened to withdraw from the coalition Government, accusing Hughes of excluding them from the decision-making process, and in June the ADP leader, Victor Banks, resigned his post as Minister of Finance and Economic Development, and withdrew from the ruling coalition. The other ADP minister, Edison Baird, refused, however, to resign his post, and was subsequently expelled from the party. Although Banks' resignation deprived the AUP-ADP coalition of its majority in the House of Assembly, Hughes announced that he did not intend to resign his position. Banks and the three members of the opposition ANA therefore withdrew from the House, demanding that fresh elections be held. Lacking the necessary quorum in the legislature, the Government was unable to implement policy or to introduce a budget for 1999/2000.

In January 2000 legal proceedings begun by Hughes, in an attempt to compel the Speaker to convene the House of Assembly, were rejected by the High Court. Hughes therefore announced that he would hold legislative elections in March 2000. At the elections, held on 3 March, the ANA won three seats, the AUP two, and the ADP one, while Edison Baird was elected as an independent. The ANA and the ADP, which had formed an electoral alliance, known as the United Front, prior to the elections, therefore gained control of the House of Assembly. The leader of the ANA, Osbourne Fleming, was subsequently appointed the Chief Minister of an Executive Council, which included two other ANA ministers, while Victor Banks was again appointed Minister of Finance, Economic Development, Investment and Commerce.

In February 2000 the Governor, Robert Harris, departed the island. Harris, who had reportedly been extremely frustrated by the island's political crisis, suggested that he had found it very difficult to work closely with the Government of Anguilla, and described his period in office 'as a waste of my professional time'. Peter Johnstone replaced him as Governor.

Following Anguilla's inclusion on an Organisation for Economic Co-operation and Development (OECD) blacklist of tax 'havens' in 2000, the Government introduced a number of articles of legislation to combat money-laundering on the island, including the establishment of a 'Money Laundering Reporting Authority'. OECD removed Anguilla from the list in March 2002, declaring that the Government had made sufficient commitments to improve transparency and effective exchange of information on tax matters by the end of 2005. In late 2002, however, the burgeoning financial sector faced further disruption when the United Kingdom, under pressure from the European Union (EU), as part of its effort to investigate tax evasion, demanded that Anguilla disclose the identities and account details of Europeans holding private savings accounts on the island. Anguilla, along with some other British Overseas Territories facing similar demands, claimed it was being treated unfairly compared with more powerful European countries, such as Switzerland and Luxembourg.

In January 2001, following the United Kingdom's incorporation of the European Union's Convention on Human Rights, homosexuality was legalized in Anguilla.

In June 2001 the Government officially approved the draft of its National Telecommunications Policy, which would liberalize the sector. Although the legislation still needed to pass through parliament, in April 2003 Cable and Wireless, the country's sole telecommunications provider, signed an agreement with the Government to open the market for competition. The opposition argued that a single operator was more suitable in a country as small as Anguilla, where economies of scale were not achievable. It was argued that the proposed legislation could lead to a reduction in investment and consequent job losses.

In May 2002 the British Overseas Territories Act, having received royal assent in the United Kingdom in February, came into force and granted British citizenship to the people of its Overseas Territories, including Anguilla. Under the new law Anguillans would be able to hold British passports and work in the United Kingdom and anywhere else in the EU.

Government

The Constitution vests executive power in a Governor, appointed by the British monarch. The Governor is responsible for external affairs, international financial affairs, defence and internal security. In most other matters the Governor acts on the advice of the Executive Council, led by the Chief Minister. Legislative power is held by the House of Assembly, comprising 11 members: two *ex officio*, two nominated by the Governor, and seven elected for five years by universal adult suffrage. The Executive Council is responsible to the House.

Economic Affairs

In 2001, according to estimates, the gross national income (GNI) of Anguilla, measured at current prices, was EC $295.38m., equivalent to EC $25,552 per head. During 1990–2001, it was estimated, the population increased at an average annual rate of 2.6%, while gross domestic product (GDP) per head increased, in real terms, by an average of 1.6% per year. Overall GDP increased, in real terms, at an average annual rate of 4.3% in 1990–2001; growth in 2001 was 1.3%.

Agriculture (including fishing) contributed 2.5% to GDP in 2001 and agriculture, fishing and mining engaged 3.3% of the employed labour force in the same year. Smallholders grow vegetables and fruit for domestic consumption; the principal crops are pigeon peas, sweet potatoes and maize. Livestock-rearing traditionally supplies significant export earnings, but the principal productive sector is the fishing industry (which is also a major employer). Real agricultural GDP decreased by an annual average of 1.6% during 1990–2001; growth was an estimated 3.9% in 2001.

Industry (including mining, manufacturing, construction, and power), which accounted for 16.1% of GDP and (not including the small mining sector) engaged 18.8% of the employed labour force in 2001, is traditionally based on salt production and shipbuilding. Real industrial GDP increased by an annual average of 1.4% in 1990–2001, but decreased by an estimated 12.3% in 2001, primarily owing to a reversal, from 1999, in the hitherto sharp expansion of construction activity.

The mining and quarrying sector, contributed only 0.8% of GDP in 2001 and engaged only 0.2% of the working population in 1992. Anguilla's principal mineral product is salt. Mining GDP increased by an annual average of 8.9% during 1990–2001, in real terms, but decreased by an estimated 10.1% in 2001.

The manufacturing sector, accounting for 2.4% of employment and for 1.2% of GDP in 2001, consists almost entirely of boat-building and fisheries processing. Real manufacturing GDP increased by an annual average of 9.4% in 1990–2001. GDP in the sector increased by 2.1% in 2001, in real terms.

The construction industry, which engaged 14.9% of the employed labour force in 2001, accounted for 10.9% of GDP in the same year. Growth in the construction industry remained high, owing to reconstruction work necessitated by the effects of 'Hurricane Luis'. Imported hydrocarbon fuels meet most energy needs. GDP in the construction sector decreased at an annual average of 0.7% during 1990–2001, in real terms, and by 19.1% in 2001.

The services sector accounted for 81.4% of GDP and engaged 77.9% of the employed labour force in 2001. Tourism is increasingly the dominant industry of the economy, and is a catalyst for growth in other areas. The hotel and restaurant sector is the largest contributor to GDP, accounting for 26.5% of GDP in 2001. The contribution to GDP from the hotel and restaurant sector increased by 9.5% in 2001. In 2002 tourist expenditure totalled US $55.3m. The USA provided 53.6% of visitors in 2002. The offshore financial institutions are also important contributors to the GDP of the service industry, with the banking and insurance sector contributing 14.0% of GDP in 2001. The real GDP of the services sector increased at an annual average of 5.4% in 1990–2002. GDP in services increased by 5.6% in 2001, in real terms.

In 2001 Anguilla recorded a merchandise trade deficit of EC $174.1m., and a deficit on the current account of the balance of payments of EC $95.1m. The trade deficit was partly offset by receipts from the 'invisibles' sector: tourism, financial services, remittances from Anguillans abroad and official assistance. The principal sources of imports are the USA and Puerto Rico, Trinidad and Tobago and the European Union (EU), mainly the United Kingdom. The principal markets for exports are the USA and St Maarten/St Martin. The main commodity exports are lobsters, fish, livestock and salt. Imports, upon which Anguilla is highly dependent, consist of foodstuffs, construction materials, manufactures, machinery and transport equipment.

In 2001, according to preliminary figures from the Eastern Caribbean Central Bank (ECCB, see p. 343), a budgetary deficit of EC $11.7m. was recorded. Anguilla's external public debt totalled an estimated US $9.5m. in 2000. Development assistance was estimated to total US $3.1m. in 1998. Consumer prices decreased by an annual average of 3.0% in 1991–2000; the average annual rate of inflation increased by 2.4% in 2000 and decreased by 0.7% in 2001. Some 7.8% of the labour force were unemployed in July 2002 (compared with 26% in 1985).

In April 1987 Anguilla became the eighth member of the ECCB and in 2001 joined the regional stock exchange, the Eastern Caribbean Securities Exchange (based in Saint Christopher and Nevis), established in the same year. The Territory is also a member of the Organisation of Eastern Caribbean States (OECS, see p. 341), an associate member of the Association of Caribbean States (ACS, see p. 338) and the Economic Community for Latin America and the Caribbean (ECLAC, see p. 31). As a dependency of the United Kingdom, Anguilla has the status of Overseas Territory in association with the EU (see p.

199). In 1999 Anguilla was granted associate membership of the Caribbean Community and Common Market (CARICOM, see p. 155).

Since its reversion to dependency on the United Kingdom, as a separate unit, the island has developed its limited resources. Tourism has become the dominant industry, resulting in a high level of tourism-related activity in the construction industry during the late 1980s and 1990s. Since the early 1980s the offshore financial sector has grown rapidly, while the computerization of the operations of the financial services department in the offshore sector, allowing for on-line registration of companies 24 hours a day, has attracted further investment. Both tourism and the international financial sector have apparently benefited from the perceived stability of dependent status. However, Anguilla remains particularly vulnerable to adverse climatic conditions, as was demonstrated in October 1995, when Hurricane Luis devastated the island, and again in November 1999, when damage caused by Hurricane Lenny forced the temporary closure of the island's two largest tourist resorts. According to preliminary figures, real GDP decreased by 0.7% in 2000, compared with an increase of 8.6% in 1999; a decline, in part, attributed to the effects of Hurricane Lenny. The economy recovered in 2001 to record estimated growth of 3.9%, despite the decline in the tourist sector following the September 2001 terrorist attacks in the USA. The new Government in 2000 committed itself to increased expenditure and increased state investment in tourism, financial services and fisheries. The Government also hoped to establish the island as a centre for information technology and electronic commerce, and to raise revenue from the sale and leasing of internet domain names. In June the Government launched an internet service which would facilitate the incorporation of offshore companies into the Anguilla tax system; the system is quick and cost-effective, and a total of 1,021 new International Business Companies were registered in 2001. In June 2002 the ECCB predicted an expansion in economic activity, led by a recovery in the construction sector. However, given the importance of tourists to the island, the performance of Anguilla's economy in 2003 would depend on the reaction of the global economy to the US-led military campaign to remove the regime of Saddam Hussain in Iraq.

Education

Education is free and compulsory between the ages of five and 16 years. Primary education begins at five years of age and lasts for six years. Secondary education, beginning at eleven years of age, lasts for a further six years. There are six government primary schools and one government secondary school. A 'comprehensive' secondary school education system was introduced in September 1986. Post-secondary education is undertaken abroad.

Public Holidays

2003: 1 January (New Year's Day), 18 April (Good Friday), 21 April (Easter Monday), 1 May (Labour Day), 30 May (Anguilla Day), 9 June (Whit Monday), 16 June (Queen's Official Birthday), 7 July (CARICOM Day), 4 August (August Monday), 7 August (August Thursday), 8 August (Constitution Day), 19 December (Separation Day), 25–26 December (Christmas).

2004: 1 January (New Year's Day), 9 April (Good Friday), 12 April (Easter Monday), 1 May (Labour Day), 29 May (Anguilla Day), 31 May (Whit Monday), 21 June (Queen's Official Birthday), 1 July (CARICOM Day), 2 August (August Monday), 5 August (August Thursday), 6 August (Constitution Day), 19 December (Separation Day), 25–26 December (Christmas).

Weights and Measures

The metric system has been adopted, although imperial weights and measures are also used.

Statistical Survey

Source: Government of Anguilla, The Secretariat, The Valley; tel. 497-2451; fax 497-3389; e-mail stats@gov.ai; internet www.gov.ai.

AREA AND POPULATION

Area (sq km): 96 (Anguilla 91, Sombrero 5).

Population: 11,430 (males 5,628; females 5,802) at census of 9 May 2001.

Density (at census of May 2001): 119.1 per sq km.

Principal Towns (population at 2001 census): South Hill 1,495; North Side 1,195; The Valley (capital) 1,169; Stoney Ground 1,133. Source: Gwillim Law (internet www.mindspring .com/~gwil/uai.html).

Births, Marriages and Deaths (2001): Registered live births 184; Birth rate 15.9 per 1,000; Registered marriages 181; Marriage rate 15.7 per 1,000; Registered deaths 66; Death rate 5.7 per 1,000.

Expectation of Life (official estimates, years at birth): 77.94 (males 77.90; females 78.02) in 2001.

Economically Active Population (persons aged 15 years and over, census of 9 May 2001): Agriculture, fishing and mining 183; Manufacturing 135; Electricity, gas and water 81; Construction 830; Trade 556; Restaurants and hotels 1,587; Transport, storage and communications 379; Finance, insurance, real estate and business services 433; Public administration, social security 662; Education, health and social work 383; Other community, social and personal services 164; Private households with employed persons 164; Activities not stated 871; *Total employed* 5,644 (males 3,014; females 2,630); Unemployed 406 (males 208; females 198); *Total labour force* 6,050 (males 3,222; females 2,828).

HEALTH AND WELFARE

Under-5 Mortality Rate (per 1,000 live births, 1997): 34.0.

Physicians (per 1,000 head, 1997): 1.75.

Health Expenditure: % of GDP (1995): 5.1. Source: Pan American Health Organization. For definitions see explanatory note on p. vi.

AGRICULTURE, ETC.

Fishing (metric tons, live weight, 2000, estimates): Marine fishes 180, Caribbean spiny lobster 60, Stromboid conchs 10; Total catch 250. Source: FAO, *Yearbook of Fishery Statistics*.

INDUSTRY

Electric Energy (million kWh): 45.85 in 2000; 53.60 in 2001; 55.33 in 2002.

FINANCE

Currency and Exchange Rates: 100 cents = 1 Eastern Caribbean dollar (EC $). *Sterling, US Dollar and Euro Equivalents* (31 December 2002): £1 sterling = EC $4.352; US $1 = EC $2.700; €1 = EC $2.831; EC $100 = £22.98 = US $37.04 = €35.32. *Exchange Rate:* Fixed at US $1 = EC $2.70 since July 1976.

Budget (Preliminary, EC $ million, 2001): *Current revenue* Tax revenue 58.3 (Taxes on domestic goods and services 23.1, Taxes on international trade and transactions 34.6); Non-tax revenue 14.3; Capital grants 6.2; Total 78.9. *Current expenditure* Personal emoluments 39.6, Other goods and services 34.1, Transfers and subsidies 2.6, Interest payments 1.8; Capital expenditure 12.4; Total 90.6. Source: Eastern Caribbean Central Bank, *Report and Statement of Accounts*.

Cost of Living (Consumer Price Index; base: 2000 = 100): 102.4 in 2001; 101.7 in 2002.

Expenditure on the Gross Domestic Product (EC $ million at current prices, 2000): Government final consumption expenditure 57.06; Private final consumption expenditure 286.90; Gross fixed capital formation 93.72; *Total domestic expenditure* 437.68; Export of goods and services 175.27; *Less* Import of goods and services 322.43; *GDP in purchasers' values* 290.52.

Gross Domestic Product by Economic Activity (Preliminary, EC $ million at current prices, 2001): Agriculture, hunting, forestry and fishing 6.76; Mining and quarrying 2.25; Manufacturing 3.40; Electricity, gas and water 8.78; Construction 29.78; Wholesale and retail 18.97; Hotels and restaurants 72.54; Transport 14.86; Communications 23.01; Banks and insurance 38.27; Real estate and housing 8.02; Government services 41.72; Other services 5.02; Subtotal 273.38; *Less* Imputed bank service charge 33.49; *GDP at factor cost* 239.89.

Balance of Payments (EC $ million, 2001): Export of goods f.o.b. 10.84; Imports of goods f.o.b. –184.94; *Trade balance* –174.10; Exports of services 190.74; Imports of services –102.66; *Balance on goods and services* –86.02; Other income received 5.00; Other income paid –14.47; *Balance on goods, services and income* –95.49; Current transfers received 20.96; Current transfers paid –20.59; *Current balance* –95.12; Capital account (net) 18.93; Direct investment (net) 88.13; Portfolio investment (net) 2.72; Other investment (net) –40.11; Net errors and omissions 35.97; *Overall balance* 10.52.

EXTERNAL TRADE

Principal Commodities (EC $ million, 2002): *Imports:* Food and live animals 34.4; Beverages and tobacco 16.9; Crude materials, inedible, except fuels 5.8; Mineral fuels, lubricants, etc. 18.3; Chemicals and related products 12.8; Basic manufactures 35.9; Machinery and transport equipment 42.9 ; Miscellaneous manufactured articles 20.8; Total (incl. others) 188.7. *Exports* (2001, incl. re-exports): Prepared foodstuffs; beverages, spirits and vinegar; tobacco and manufactured substitutes 0.7 (Beverages, spirits and vinegar 0.3); Articles of stone, plaster, cement, asbestos, mica, etc.; ceramic products; glass and glassware 1.0 (Articles of stone, plaster, cement, asbestos, mica, etc. 1.0); Base metals and articles thereof 0.3; Machinery and mechanical appliances; electrical equipment; sound and television apparatus 1.7 (Nuclear reactors, boilers, machinery and mechanical appliances; parts thereof 1.1; Electrical machinery, equipment and parts; sound and television apparatus, parts and accessories 0.6); Vehicles, aircraft, vessels and associated transport equipment 3.3 (Vehicles other than railway or tramway rolling-stock, and parts and accessories 3.2); Works of art, collectors' pieces and antiques 0.3; Total (incl. others) 8.6.

Principal Trading Partners (EC $ million, 2002): *Imports:* Canada 3.9; France 2.2; Guadeloupe 3.7; Guyana 2.1; Netherlands Antilles 15.2; Puerto Rico 17.7; Trinidad and Tobago 11.0; United Kingdom 5.8; USA 94.1; US Virgin Islands 11.4; Total (incl. others) 188.7. *Exports:* Barbados 0.1; Guadeloupe 0.7; Guyana 0.3; Italy 0.2; Netherlands Antilles 2.3; Puerto Rico 0.1; Trinidad and Tobago 0.2; United Kingdom 0.4; USA 6.4; US Virgin Islands 0.2; Total (incl. others) 11.7.

TRANSPORT

Road Traffic (motor vehicles licensed, 2002): Private cars 2,937; Hired cars 830; Buses/trucks/jeeps/pickups 1,962; Motorcycles 66; Tractors 2; Heavy equipment 175; Other 6.

Shipping: *Merchant Fleet* (registered at 31 December 2001): 3; Total displacement 701 grt. Source: Lloyd's Register-Fairplay, *World Fleet Statistics*.

TOURISM

Visitor Arrivals: 112,469 (Stop–overs 43,789, Excursionists 68,680) in 2000; 104,974 (Stop–overs 47,965, Excursionists 57,009) in 2001; 111,118 (Stop–overs 43,969, Excursionists 67,149) in 2002.

Visitor Arrivals by Country of Residence (2002): Canada 4,425; Caribbean 10,449; Germany 1,376; Italy 1,903; United Kingdom 4,847; USA 59,561; *Total* (incl. others) 111,118.

Tourism Receipts (US $ million): 55.2 in 2000; 61.0 in 2001; 55.3 in 2002.

COMMUNICATIONS MEDIA

Radio Receivers (1997): 3,000 in use.

Television Receivers (1999): 1,000 in use.

Telephones (2002): 5,796 main lines in use.

Facsimile Machines (1993): 190 in use.

Mobile Cellular Telephones (2000): 15,000 subscribers.

Internet Connections (1999): 659. Sources: mostly UN, *Statistical Yearbook*; International Telecommunication Union.

EDUCATION

Pre-primary (2001/02): 11 schools; 38 teachers; 438 pupils.

Primary (2001/02): 6 schools; 90 teachers; 1,427 pupils.

General Secondary (2001/02): 1 school; 86 teachers; 1,147 pupils.

Adult Literacy Rate (UNESCO estimates): 95.4% (males 95.1%; females 95.7%) in 1995. (Source: UNESCO, *Statistical Yearbook*).

Directory

The Constitution

The Constitution, established in 1976, accorded Anguilla the status of a British Dependent Territory. It formally became a separate dependency on 19 December 1980, and is administered under the Anguilla Constitution Orders of 1982 and 1990. British Dependent Territories were referred to as United Kingdom Overseas Territories from February 1998 and draft legislation confirming this change and granting citizens rights to full British citizenship and residence in the United Kingdom was published in March 1999. The British

Overseas Territories Act entered effect in May 2002. The British Government proposals also included the requirement that the Constitutions of Overseas Territories should be revised in order to conform to British and international standards. The process of revision of the Anguillan Constitution began in September 1999.

The British monarch is represented locally by a Governor, who presides over the Executive Council and the House of Assembly. The Governor is responsible for defence, external affairs (including international financial affairs), internal security (including the police), the public service, the judiciary and the audit. The Governor appoints a Deputy Governor. On matters relating to internal security, the public service and the appointment of an acting governor or deputy governor, the Governor is required to consult the Chief Minister. The Executive Council consists of the Chief Minister and not more than three other ministers (appointed by the Governor from the elected members of the legislative House of Assembly) and two *ex-officio* members (the Deputy Governor and the Attorney-General). The House of Assembly is elected for a maximum term of five years by universal adult suffrage and consists of seven elected members, two *ex-officio* members (the Deputy Governor and the Attorney-General) and two nominated members who are appointed by the Governor, one upon the advice of the Chief Minister, and one after consultations with the Chief Minister and the Leader of the Opposition. The House elects a Speaker and a Deputy Speaker.

The Governor may order the dissolution of the House of Assembly if a resolution of 'no confidence' is passed in the Government, and elections must be held within two months of the dissolution.

The Constitution provides for an Anguilla Belonger Commission, which determines cases of whether a person can be 'regarded as belonging to Anguilla' (i.e. having 'belonger' status). A belonger is someone of Anguillan birth or parentage, someone who has married a belonger, or someone who is a citizen of the United Kingdom Overseas Territories from Anguilla (by birth, parentage, adoption or naturalization). The Commission may grant belonger status to those who have been domiciled and ordinarily resident in Anguilla for not less than 15 years.

The Government

Governor: PETER JOHNSTONE (appointed February 2000).

EXECUTIVE COUNCIL
(April 2003)

Chief Minister and Minister of Home Affairs, Tourism, Agriculture, Fisheries and Environment: OSBOURNE FLEMING (ANA).

Minister of Finance, Economic Development, Investment and Commerce: VICTOR F. BANKS (ADP).

Minister of Education, Health, Social Development and Lands: ERIC REID (ANA).

Minister of Infrastructure, Communications, Public Utilities, Transportation and Housing: KENNETH HARRIGAN (ANA).

Attorney-General: RONALD SCIPIO.

Deputy Governor: HENRY MCCRORY.

MINISTRIES

Office of the Governor: Government House, POB 60, The Valley; tel. 497-2622; fax 497-3314; e-mail govthouse@anguillanet.com.

Office of the Chief Minister: The Secretariat, The Valley; tel. 497-2518; fax 497-3389; e-mail chief-minister@gov.ai.

All ministries are based in The Valley, mostly at the Secretariat (tel. 497-2451; internet www.gov.ai).

Legislature

HOUSE OF ASSEMBLY

Speaker: LEROY ROGERS.

Clerk to House of Assembly: Rev. JOHN A. GUMBS.

Election, 3 March 2000

Party	% of votes	Seats
Anguilla National Alliance (ANA)*	34.1	3
Independents	30.8	1
Anguilla United Party (AUP)	12.1	2
Anguilla Democratic Party (ADP)*	10.8	1
Anguilla Patriotic Movement (APM)	3.9	—
Movement for Grassroots Democracy (MFGR)	3.6	—
Total (incl. others)	100.0	7

* The ANA and the ADP formed an electoral alliance, the United Front.

There are also two ex-officio members and two nominated members.

Political Organizations

Anguilla Democratic Party (ADP): The Valley; f. 1981 as Anguilla People's Party; name changed 1984; Leader VICTOR F. BANKS.

Anguilla National Alliance (ANA): The Valley; f. 1980 by reconstitution of People's Progressive Party; Leader OSBOURNE FLEMING.

Anguilla Patriotic Movement (APM): The Valley; f. 2000; Leaders QUINCEY GUMBS, FRANKLIN RICHARDSON.

Anguilla United Party (AUP): The Valley; f. 1979; revived 1984; Leader HUBERT B. HUGHES.

Movement for Grassroots Democracy (MFGR): The Valley; f. 2000; Leaders JOHN BENJAMIN, JOYCE KENTISH.

Judicial System

Justice is administered by the High Court, Court of Appeal and Magistrates' Courts. During the High Court sitting, the Eastern Caribbean Supreme Court provides Anguilla with a judge.

Religion

CHRISTIANITY

The Anglican Communion

Anglicans in Anguilla are adherents of the Church in the Province of the West Indies, comprising nine dioceses. Anguilla forms part of the diocese of the North Eastern Caribbean and Aruba.

Bishop of the North Eastern Caribbean and Aruba: Rt Revd LEROY ERROL BROOKS, St Mary's Rectory, POB 180, The Valley; fax 497-3012; e-mail diocesnesca@candw.ag.

The Roman Catholic Church

The diocese of St John's-Basseterre, suffragan to the archdiocese of Castries (Saint Lucia), includes Anguilla, Antigua and Barbuda, the British Virgin Islands, Montserrat and Saint Christopher and Nevis. The Bishop resides in St John's, Antigua.

Roman Catholic Church: St Gerard's, POB 47, The Valley; tel. 497-2405.

Protestant Churches

Methodist Church: South Hill; Minister (vacant).

The Seventh-day Adventist, Baptist, Church of God, Pentecostal, Apostolic Faith and Jehovah's Witnesses Churches and sects are also represented.

The Press

Anguilla Life Magazine: Caribbean Commercial Centre, POB 109, The Valley; tel. 497-3080; fax 497-2501; 3 a year; circ. 10,000.

The Light: POB 1373, The Valley; tel. 497-5058; fax 497-5795; e-mail thelight@anguillanet.com; internet www.thelight-anguilla.com; f. 1993; weekly; newspaper; Editor GEORGE HODGE.

Official Gazette: The Valley; tel. 497-5081; monthly; government news-sheet.

What We Do in Anguilla: POB 1373, The Valley; tel. 497-5641; fax 497-5795; e-mail thelight@anguillanet.com; internet www.anguillatourguide.com; f. 1987; monthly; tourism; Editor GEORGE HODGE; circ. 50,000.

Broadcasting and Communications

TELECOMMUNICATIONS

Cable & Wireless Anguilla: POB 77, The Valley; tel. 497-3100; fax 497-2501; internet www.anguillanet.com; Gen. Man. SUTCLIFFE HODGE.

Eastern Caribbean Cellular: POB 1000, George Hill; tel. 497-2100; internet www.easterncaribbeancellular.com; f. 1989.

BROADCASTING

Radio

Caribbean Beacon Radio: POB 690, Long Rd, The Valley; Head Office: POB 7008, Columbus, GA 31908, USA; tel. 497-4340; fax 497-4311; f. 1981; privately owned and operated; religious and commercial; broadcasts 24 hours daily; Pres. Dr GENE SCOTT; CEO B. MONSELL HAZELL.

Radio Anguilla: Department of Information and Broadcasting, The Valley; tel. 497-2218; fax 497-5432; f. 1969; owned and operated by the Govt of Anguilla since 1976; 250,000 listeners throughout the north-eastern Caribbean; broadcasts 17 hours daily; Dir of Information and Broadcasting NAT HODGE; News Editor WYCLIFFE RICHARDSON.

ZJF FM: The Valley; tel. 497-3157; f. 1989; commercial.

Television

All Island Cable Television Service Ltd: POB 336, George Hill, The Valley; tel. 497-3600; fax 497-3602.

Network Community Television Ltd: POB 333, Sachasses; tel. 497-3919; fax 497-3909.

Finance

(cap. = capital; dep. = deposits; res = reserves; m. = million; amounts in EC dollars)

CENTRAL BANK

Eastern Caribbean Central Bank: Fairplay Commercial Complex, The Valley; tel. 497-5050; fax 497-5150; e-mail eccbaxa@anguillanet.com; HQ in Basseterre, Saint Christopher and Nevis; bank of issue and central monetary authority for Anguilla, Antigua and Barbuda, Dominica, Grenada, Montserrat, Saint Christopher and Nevis, Saint Lucia and Saint Vincent and the Grenadines; Gov. Sir K. DWIGHT VENNER.

COMMERCIAL BANKS

Caribbean Commercial Bank (Anguilla) Ltd: POB 23, The Valley; tel. 497-2571; fax 497-3570; e-mail ccbaxa@anguillanet.com; internet www.ccb.ai; f. 1976; Chair. OSBOURNE B. FLEMING; Man. Dir PRESTON B. BRYAN.

FirstCaribbean International Bank Ltd: The Valley; internet www.firstcaribbeaninternational.com; f. 2002 following merger of Caribbean operations of Barclays Bank PLC and CIBC; Exec. Chair. MICHAEL MANSOOR; CEO CHARLES PINK.

National Bank of Anguilla Ltd: POB 44, The Valley; tel. 497-2101; fax 497-3310; e-mail nbabankl@anguillanet.com; internet www.nba.ai; f. 1985; cap. and res 28.0m., dep. 244.0m. (Mar. 2001); Chair. JOSEPH N. PAYNE; CEO E. VALENTINE BANKS.

Scotiabank Anguilla Ltd: Fairplay Commercial Centre, POB 250, The Valley; tel. 497-3333; fax 497-3344; e-mail scotia@anguillanet.com; Man. WALTER MACCALMAN.

There are 'offshore', foreign banks based on the island, but most are not authorized to operate in Anguilla. There is a financial complex known as the Caribbean Commercial Centre in The Valley.

Anguilla Offshore Financial Centre: POB 60, The Valley; tel. 497-5881; fax 497-5872; internet www.anguillaoffshore.com.

TRUST COMPANIES

Codan Trust Co (Anguilla) Ltd: c/o Intertrust Offices, POB 147, The Valley; tel. 497-2189; fax 497-5007; e-mail djastwood@cdp.bm; internet www.cdp.bm.

Emerald Trust International Ltd: POB 645, The Valley; tel. 497-5342; fax 497-5812; e-mail emerald@offshore.com.ai; Man. THOMAS PEACOCK.

Financial Services Co Ltd: POB 58, The Valley; tel. 497-3777; fax 497-5377; e-mail firstanguilla@anguillalaw.com.

First Anguilla Trust Co Ltd: Victoria House, POB 58, The Valley; tel. 497-2060; fax 497-3096; e-mail information@firstanguilla.com; internet www.firstanguilla.com; Mans JOHN DYRUD, PALMAVON WEBSTER.

Hansa Bank and Trust Co Ltd: Hansa Bank Bldg, POB 213, The Valley; tel. 497-3802; fax 497-3801; e-mail hansa@attglobal.net; internet www.hansa.net.

Intertrust (Anguilla) Ltd: POB 1388, The Valley; tel. 497-2189; fax 497-5007; e-mail anguilla@intertrustgroup.com; internet www.intertrust-group.com.

HWR Services (Anguilla) Ltd: Harlaw Chambers, POB 1026, The Valley; tel. 498-5000; fax 498-5001; e-mail hwr@anguillanet.com; internet www.harneys.com.

Renaissance International Trust: POB 687, The Valley; tel. 498-7878; fax 498-7872; e-mail renaissance@anguillanet.com.

Sinel Trust (Anguilla) Ltd: Sinel Chambers, POB 1269, The Valley; tel. 497-3311; fax 497-5659; e-mail jbrice@sineltrust.com; internet www.sineltrust-anguilla.com.

STOCK EXCHANGE

Eastern Caribbean Securities Exchange: based in Basseterre, Saint Christopher and Nevis; e-mail info@ecseonline.com; internet www.ecseonline.com; f. 2001; regional securities market designed to facilitate the buying and selling of financial products for the eight member territories—Anguilla, Antigua and Barbuda, Dominica, Grenada, Montserrat, Saint Christopher and Nevis, Saint Lucia and Saint Vincent and the Grenadines; Gen. Man. BALJIT VOHRA.

INSURANCE

Anguilla Mutual Assurance Co Ltd: Stony Ground, The Valley; tel. 497-2246.

Anguilla National Insurance Co Ltd: Airport Rd, POB 44, The Valley; tel. 497-5280; fax 497-3870.

British American Insurance Co Ltd: Herbert's Commercial Centre, POB 148; tel. 497-2653; fax 497-5933.

D-3 Enterprises Ltd: Herbert's Commercial Centre, POB 1377, The Valley; tel. 497-3525; fax 497-3526; Man. CLEMENT RUAN.

Gulf Insurance Ltd: Blowing Point; tel. 497-6613.

Malliouhana Insurance Co Ltd: Herbert's Commercial Centre, POB 492, The Valley; tel. 497-3710; fax 497-3712; Man. MONICA HODGE.

Nagico Insurance: POB 79, The Valley; tel. 497-2976; fax 497-3303.

National Caribbean Insurance Co Ltd: Herbert's Commercial Centre, POB 323, The Valley; tel. 497-2865; fax 497-3783.

Trade and Industry

DEVELOPMENT ORGANIZATION

Anguilla Development Board: POB 285, Wallblake Rd, The Valley; tel. 497-3690; fax 497-2959.

CHAMBER OF COMMERCE

Anguilla Chamber of Commerce: POB 321, The Valley; tel. 497-2701; fax 497-5858; Exec. Dir PAULA MACK; Pres. SUTCLIFFE HODGE.

INDUSTRIAL AND TRADE ASSOCIATION

Anguilla Financial Services Association: POB 1071, The Valley; e-mail arichardson@anguillanet.com; Pres. ALEX RICHARDSON; Vice-Pres. JOSEPH BRICE.

UTILITIES

Electricity

Anguilla Electricity Co Ltd: POB 400, The Valley; tel. 497-5200; fax 497-5440; operates a power-station and generators.

Transport

ROADS

Anguilla has 140 km (87 miles) of roads, of which 100 km (62 miles) are tarred.

SHIPPING

The principal port of entry is Sandy Ground on Road Bay. There is a daily ferry service between Blowing Point and Marigot (St Martin).

Link Ferries: Little Harbour; tel. 497-2231; fax 497-3290; e-mail fbconnor@anguillanet.com; internet www.link.ai; f. 1992; daily services to Julianna International Airport (St Martin) and charter services; Owner FRANKLYN CONNOR.

CIVIL AVIATION

Wallblake Airport, 3.2 km (2 miles) from The Valley, has a bitumen-surfaced runway with a length of 1,100 m (3,600 ft). In 1996 Anguilla signed an agreement with the Government of Aruba providing for the construction of a new jet airport on the north coast of the island, with finance of some US $30m. from the Aruba Investment Bank. In 1998 construction of a new airport with a 1,833 m-long (6,000 ft) runway, to replace Wallblake Airport, was begun. The US $25m. construction was due for completion in 2000.

Air Anguilla: POB 110, Wallblake; tel. 497-2643; fax 497-2982; scheduled services to St Thomas, St Maarten/St Martin, Saint Christopher and Beef Island (British Virgin Islands); Pres. RESTORMEL FRANKLIN.

American Eagle: POB 659, Wallblake Airport; tel. 497-3131; fax 497-3502; operates scheduled flights from Puerto Rico three times a day (December to April) and once daily (May to November).

Tyden Air: POB 107, Wallblake Airport; tel. 497-2719; fax 497-3079; charter company servicing whole Caribbean.

Tourism

Anguilla's sandy beaches and unspoilt natural beauty attract tourists and also day visitors from neighbouring St Maarten/St Martin. The tourist sector was damaged by the effects of Hurricane Luis in 1995, but had recovered to pre-hurricane levels by 1997. In November 1999 'Hurricane Lenny' badly affected Anguilla, forcing the temporary closure of the island's two largest hotels. 53.6% of visitors were from the USA, 9.4% were from other Caribbean countries, while most of the remainder were from the United Kingdom, Canada, Italy and Germany. In 2001 there were some 1,069 hotel rooms on the island and tourist receipts totalled US $55.3m. in 2002.

Anguilla Tourist Board: POB 1388, The Valley; tel. 497-2759; fax 497-2710; e-mail atbtour@anguillanet.com; internet www .anguilla-vacation.com.

Anguilla Hotel and Tourism Association: POB 1388, Old Factory Plaza, The Valley; tel. 497-2944; fax 497-3091; e-mail ahta@ anguillanet.com; f. 1981; Exec. Dir MIMI GRATTON.

BERMUDA

Introductory Survey

Location, Climate, Language, Religion, Flag, Capital

The Bermudas or Somers Islands are an isolated archipelago, comprising about 138 islands, in the Atlantic Ocean, about 917 km (570 miles) off the coast of South Carolina, USA. Bridges and causeways link seven of the islands to form the principal mainland. The climate is mild and humid. Temperatures are generally between 8°C (46°F) and 32°C (90°F), with an average annual rainfall of 1,470 mm (58 ins). The official language is English, but there is a small community of Portuguese speakers. Most of the inhabitants profess Christianity, and numerous denominations are represented, the principal one being the Anglican Church. The flag (proportions 1 by 2) is the British 'Red Ensign' (this usage being unique among the British colonies), with, in the fly, the colony's badge: a seated red lion holding a shield (with a gold baroque border), which depicts the wreck off Bermuda of the ship of the first settlers. The capital is Hamilton.

Recent History

Bermuda was first settled by the British in 1609. It has had a representative assembly since 1620 (and thus claims one of the oldest parliaments in the world), and became a British crown colony in 1684. Bermuda was granted internal self-government by the Constitution introduced in 1968, although the British Government retains responsibility in certain matters. Various amendments to the 1968 Constitution were made in 1973, the most important being the establishment of the Governor's Council, through which the Governor exercises responsibility for external affairs, defence, internal security and the police. In 1974 the Government Leader was restyled Premier and the Executive Council became the Cabinet.

The first general election under the new Constitution, which took place in May 1968 against a background of rioting and racial tension (some 60% of the population are of African origin, the rest mostly of European extraction), was won by the United Bermuda Party (UBP), a moderate, multi-racial party whose policies were based on racial co-operation and continued support for dependent status. The underlying racial tensions were emphasized in 1972 and 1973 by shooting incidents which resulted in the deaths of the Governor, the Commissioner of Police and three others. In December 1977 the Governor's assassin and another convicted murderer were executed, and further rioting and arson ensued. A state of emergency was

declared, and British troops were flown to Bermuda to restore order.

At the general election of May 1976, the UBP was returned to power with a decreased majority, winning 26 of the 40 seats in the House of Assembly. The remaining seats were won by the mainly black, left-wing Progressive Labour Party (PLP), which campaigned for independence. In August 1977 Sir John Sharpe, Premier and leader of the UBP since December 1975, resigned both posts and was succeeded by David Gibbons, the Minister of Finance.

In February 1978 a Royal Commission was established to investigate the causes of racial violence, and in August the Commission published a report which suggested the redrawing of constituency boundaries to improve the PLP's prospects for winning seats. Despite this, the UBP won the December 1980 election, securing 22 seats in the House of Assembly. Gibbons resigned as Premier and UBP leader in January 1982 and was succeeded by John Swan, the Minister of Home Affairs. At a general election in February 1983, the UBP gained a further four seats in the House of Assembly. Internal divisions within the PLP led to the expulsion from the party of four PLP members of the House of Assembly. The four members, after sitting as independents, formed a new centre party, the National Liberal Party (NLP), in August 1985. In October Swan called an early general election, hoping to take advantage of the divided opposition. The UBP was decisively returned to power, securing 31 of the 40 seats in the House of Assembly, while the PLP retained only seven seats and the NLP won two. Following a general election in February 1989, the UBP remained in power, but with a reduced representation in the House of Assembly of only 23 seats. By contrast, the PLP increased its representation to 15 seats.

Constitutional amendments introduced in 1979 included provision for closer consultation between the Premier and the Leader of the Opposition on the appointment of members of the Public Service Commission and the Boundaries Commission, and on the appointment of the Chief Justice. The 1978 Royal Commission recommended early independence for Bermuda, but the majority of the population at that time seemed to oppose such a policy. Swan had declared himself in favour of eventual independence for the colony, but only with the support of the Bermudian people.

In August 1992 Lord Waddington (former leader of the British House of Lords) replaced Sir Desmond Langley as Governor. Waddington remained in office until June 1997, when he was succeeded by Thorold Masefield.

During 1992 and 1993 the Government attracted international criticism for its refusal to amend legislation criminalizing homosexual activities. However, in May 1994 legislation was approved in the House of Assembly, by 22 votes to 16, to legalize homosexual acts between consenting adults (with 18 years as the age of consent).

At a general election on 5 October 1993 (the first to be held since the voting age was lowered from 21 to 18 years in 1990), the UBP was returned to power, winning 22 seats in the House of Assembly, while the PLP secured 18. In February 1994 legislation providing for the organization of a referendum on independence for Bermuda was narrowly approved in the House of Assembly. The debate on independence was believed to have intensified as a result of the announcement in late 1993 that British and US forces would close their facilities and withdraw permanently from the island by April 1995 and September 1995, respectively. The PLP, which advocates independence for Bermuda, consistently opposed the organization of a referendum on the subject, believing that the independence issue should be determined by a general election. In May 1994 a PLP motion to reject a proposed government inquiry into the possibilities for independence was approved by 18 votes to 17 in the House of Assembly, effectively halting further progress towards a referendum. However, the debate continued, and in October a government delegation travelled to London for official discussions on the subject. Further legislation regarding the proposed referendum was narrowly approved in March 1995, and it was subsequently announced that a vote would be held in August. The PLP encouraged its supporters to boycott the poll, which required not only a majority of votes, but also the approval of 40% of eligible voters in order to achieve a pro-independence result.

The referendum, which was delayed briefly owing to the passage of 'Hurricane Felix', took place on 16 August 1995. Some 58.8% of eligible voters participated in the poll (a relatively low level for Bermuda) in which 16,369 citizens (equivalent to 73.6% of those voting) registered their opposition to independence from the United Kingdom, and 5,714 voters (25.7% of those participating) expressed their support for independence. The following day Swan resigned as Premier and as leader of the UBP. Factions within the governing party were perceived to have become considerably polarized during the independence debate, which had resulted in the division of opinion along racial lines. The Minister of Finance, Dr David Saul (who had remained neutral on the independence issue), was subsequently elected leader of the UBP, and Saul was therefore sworn in as Premier on 25 August. Saul stated that his principal objectives were to re-establish a climate of political stability (thus reassuring the international business community), to encourage the continued development of the financial services and tourism sectors and to reunite the UBP. However, under Saul's leadership divisions within the party appeared to deepen, culminating in June 1996 in the approval of a motion of censure against him in the House of Assembly. The motion, which was supported by five UBP members, had been prompted by disagreement with Saul's decision to authorize the establishment of a foreign-owned restaurant in the Territory, in contravention of a ruling by the Bermuda Monetary Authority regarding the granting of franchises to such businesses.

In August 1996 the Leader of the Opposition, Frederick Wade, died. At a by-election in October Wade's former seat was retained by the PLP, and in the following month the party's Deputy Leader, Jennifer Smith, was elected to the leadership of the organization.

In an attempt to restore a measure of unity within the UBP, Saul announced a reallocation of cabinet portfolios in January 1997. In the reorganization three of the five party members who had supported a motion of censure against Saul in June of the previous year were appointed to positions in the Cabinet. In March, however, Saul announced his resignation as Premier, as a member of the House of Assembly and as the leader of the party. He was replaced by Pamela Gordon, who was elected to the party leadership (and thus as Premier) unopposed.

In May 1997 by-elections were held for those legislative seats vacated by Swan and Saul. Both were retained by the UBP. In that month the Minister of Legislative Affairs and Women's Issues, Senator Lynda Milligan-Whyte, resigned from the Cabinet and the Senate, having failed to win the UBP nomination to contest the by-election in the constituency vacated by Swan. A cabinet reshuffle ensued, and E. T. (Bob) Richards was appointed to replace Milligan-Whyte in the Senate. In October a PLP deputy, Trevor Woolridge, resigned from the party following his conviction for sexual assault, although the Court of

Appeal later overturned the conviction. The legislative seat vacated by Woolridge was retained by the PLP in a by-election held in February 1998.

In March 1998 it was confirmed that the British-based telecommunications company Cable & Wireless had initiated legal proceedings against the Government. Cable & Wireless had been the sole operator of Bermuda's international telecommunications until 1997 when the Government granted a licence to a new company, Tele-Bermuda International, to operate in competition with the British company. Compensation sought by Cable & Wireless, which claimed that it should have been given three years' notice of the loss of its monopoly, amounted to US $100m. (equivalent to almost one-fifth of the Government's annual budget). In August Cable & Wireless agreed to a settlement with the Government, in which the Government agreed to offer the company a new 15-year licence, and to end the 'start-up' protection that Tele-Bermuda International had enjoyed.

In May 1998 Pamela Gordon effected a major re-organization of the Cabinet with the expressed aim of making the Government 'more efficient and effective'. In the following month the Court of Appeal upheld the constitutionality of the Prohibited Restaurants Act, passed by the House of Assembly in response to a further attempt by a group of Bermudan entrepreneurs, including Sir John Swan, to introduce fast-food franchises to Bermuda. The debate on the bill in the House of Assembly had been highly contentious, and was reported to have caused deep divisions within the ruling UBP. The Supreme Court had previously ruled that the Act was contrary to the provisions of the Constitution, as it made no provision for compensation. In July 1999 the Judicial Committee of the Privy Council upheld the constitutionality of the Prohibited Restaurants Act, rejecting a final appeal by the consortium.

Elections to the House of Assembly took place on 9 November 1998. The PLP won 54.2% of the vote, taking 26 seats, its first ever majority in the House of Assembly, while the UBP obtained 44.1% of the vote and 14 seats. The NLP obtained 0.8% of the vote, and independent candidates won a similar figure. Turn-out was estimated at 81.4%. On 10 November a new Cabinet was appointed and Jennifer Smith was sworn in as Bermuda's first PLP Premier. In her subsequent public address she sought to reassure the international business community that her Government would seek to enhance Bermuda's attraction as an international business centre, and that she would resist any attempts to alter the island's tax status. Smith further promised that, although independence for Bermuda remained a stated aim of her party, no immediate moves towards independence were planned.

In February 1999 Smith met members of the Organisation for Economic Co-operation and Development (OECD, see p. 341) to reassure them that Bermuda was determined to improve regulation of the 'offshore' financial services sector. In March the British Government published draft legislation re-designating its Dependencies as United Kingdom Overseas Territories, and guaranteeing their citizens' rights to a British passport and to residence in the United Kingdom. The document also stated, however, that the Overseas Territories would be obliged to reform their legislation to ensure compliance with European standards on human rights and on financial regulation. In October it was announced that in accordance with the proposed reforms, corporal and capital punishment were to be removed from the statute book.

A report by the Financial Action Task Force on Money Laundering (see p. 343) concluded in June 2000 that Bermuda appeared 'to have effective regulations and supervision' in place in its financial services sector. In the same month the Government agreed to co-operate with OECD in an international effort to reduce tax evasion, promising to end within five years the 'harmful' practices that had given the island a reputation as a tax 'haven'. Measures included a pledge to exchange information about tax in Bermuda with other nations, the introduction of legislation for companies to audit accounts and for these to be made available to the Bermudian authorities, and in the opening up of previously sheltered sectors of the economy to international companies. The Government had, however, pledged to maintain its existing tax system, which included no income tax. In December the members of the House of Assembly agreed, for the first time, to declare their assets and financial interests.

In October 2000 the opposition UBP boycotted the opening of parliament in protest at government plans to reduce the number of seats in the House of Assembly. Pamela Gordon claimed that there had not been adequate public consultation on the matter. Premier Smith had rejected calls for a constitutional conference or a referendum on the proposals, which included replacing the two-member constituencies with single-member ones, although she did announce that the Government would hold a public meeting to discuss the issue. The PLP believed that the existing system was weighted in favour of the UBP, which was considered the party of the white population. The UBP claimed that changes made without proper consultation and a referendum would mean a move towards a 'black dictatorship'. In December the House of Assembly approved a motion requesting the British Government to approve the establishment of a boundaries commission, which would recommend the size of the island's constituencies. Any changes would be subject to ratification by the United Kingdom's Foreign and Commonwealth Office (FCO). In January 2001 the UBP submitted a 8,500-signature petition to the British Government, demanding a constitutional conference or referendum before any changes were made. Gordon also claimed that some Bermudians had refused to sign the petition fearing recriminations. The FCO, however, stated that a constitutional conference was unnecessary, and in April it began consultations over the proposed changes. The commission recommended reducing the number of seats in the House of Assembly by four, to 36. In addition, whereas deputies had previously been elected from 20 two-member constituencies, under the proposed scheme each member of parliament would be elected by a separate constituency. It was expected that the FCO would approve the changes before the forthcoming general election, which must take place by November 2003.

In October 2001 the former Prime Minister, Pamela Gordon, resigned as leader of the UBP. The party elected Grant Gibbons as her successor. In the same month Smith reshuffled her Cabinet. The main surprise was the retention of the heavily-criticized Minister of Tourism, David Allen. The only new appointment was David Burch, who joined the Cabinet as the Minister without Portfolio. In November Sir John Vereker succeeded Sir Thorold Masefield as Governor of Bermuda.

In May 2002 the British Overseas Territories Act, having received royal assent in the United Kingdom in February, came into force and granted British citizenship to the people of its Overseas Territories, including Bermuda. Under the new law Bermudians would be able to hold British passports and work in the United Kingdom and anywhere else in the European Union.

In mid-2002 the issue of financial transparency and corporate governance in Bermuda re-emerged following the disastrous collapse of the US energy concern Enron and several other multinationals in late 2001 and early 2002. The indictment on tax-evasion charges of Dennis Kozlowski, the former CEO of Tyco International Ltd, a manufacturer of electronic security systems with a nominal headquarters on the island, fuelled a growing campaign in the US media and the US Congress against the perceived lack of financial regulation and scrutiny in Bermuda. In February 2003 three US congressmen introduced a bill in the House of Representatives that sought to force corporations that had moved their headquarters from the USA to offshore sites, such as Bermuda, to re-incorporate back in the USA. The legislation, if approved by the US Congress, would apply to those companies that had moved to so-called tax 'havens' after 11 September 2001. Since 1997, it was reported, nine major US companies had re-incorporated in Bermuda and the Cayman Islands.

In September 2002 David Allen, the Minister of Tourism, died. The tourism portfolio was passed to the Minister of Telecommunications and E-Commerce, Maurine Webb. Following allegations of corruption at the Bermuda Housing Corporation (BHC), in October Premier Smith transferred responsibility for housing from the Minister of Health and Family Services, Nelson Bascombe, to David Burch, who gained the position of Minister of Housing. Neletha Butterfield replaced Burch as Minister without Portfolio. In August the General Manager of the BHC, Raymonde Dill, was fired after a government investigation into mismanagement and overpayments to contractors at the authority.

In November 2002 Smith and the entire national executive of the PLP were re-appointed at the party's annual conference, ahead of the forthcoming general election, due by November 2003.

Following increased drugs smuggling and immigration violations by Jamaican nationals, in January 2003 it was announced that Jamaican visitors to Bermuda would henceforth require visas.

Government

Bermuda is a crown colony of the United Kingdom, with a wide measure of internal self-government. An appointed Governor, responsible for external affairs, defence and internal security, represents the British monarch. The bicameral legislature comprises the Senate (11 nominated members) and the House of Assembly, with 40 members elected for five years by universal adult suffrage. The Governor appoints the majority leader in the House as Premier, and the latter nominates other ministers. The Cabinet is responsible to the legislature. For the purposes of local government, the island has long been divided into nine parishes (originally known as 'tribes', except for the 'public land' of St George's, the capital until 1815). The town of St George's and the city of Hamilton constitute the two municipalities of the Territory.

Defence

The local defence force is the Bermuda Regiment, with a strength of some 700 men and women in 1993. The Regiment employs selective conscription.

Economic Affairs

In 1997, according to estimates by the World Bank, Bermuda's gross national income (GNI), measured at average 1995–1997 prices, was US $2,128m. During 1991–2001, it was estimated, the population increased at an average annual rate of 0.6%, while overall gross domestic product (GDP) increased, in real terms, at an average annual rate of 2.0% in 1990–1998 and of 4.2% in 1996/97–1999/2000; growth was estimated at 1% in 2002. In 2000 GDP per head was estimated to be equivalent to some US $34,600, one of the highest levels in the world.

Agriculture (including fishing and quarrying) engaged only an estimated 1.5% of the employed labour force in 2000, and the sector makes a minimal contribution to GDP. The principal crops were potatoes, tomatoes, carrots, bananas, citrus fruits and cabbage. Flowers (notably lilies) are grown for export. Other vegetables and fruit are also grown, but Bermuda remains very dependent upon food imports, which, with beverages and tobacco, accounted for 19.0% of total imports in 1999. Livestock-rearing includes cattle and goats (both mainly for dairy purposes), pigs and poultry. There is a small fishing industry, mainly for domestic consumption.

Industry (including mining, manufacturing, construction and public utilities) contributed about 10.2% of GDP in 1993 and engaged an estimated 11.4% of the employed labour force in 2000. The main activities include ship repairs, boat-building and the manufacture of paints and pharmaceuticals. The principal industrial sector is construction (in which an estimated 6.9% of the total labour force were engaged in 2000). Most of Bermuda's water is provided by privately-collected rainfall. Energy requirements are met mainly by the import of mineral fuels (fuels accounted for 3.8% of total imports in 1999).

Bermuda is overwhelmingly a service economy, with service industries engaging 87.1% of the employed labour force in 2000. In 1995, despite the growth of financial services, it was estimated that tourism still accounted for almost one-half of foreign exchange earnings. Visitor expenditure accounted for 19.1% of GDP in 1999/2000. In 2000 an estimated 13.8% of the employed labour force worked in restaurants and hotels, but tourism is estimated to account for some 60% of all employment, directly and indirectly. The sector earned an estimated B $349.7m. in 2001. The total number of tourists, particularly of cruise-ship passengers, is strictly controlled, in order to maintain Bermuda's environment and its market for wealthier visitors. Plans were approved in early 1999 for an eco-tourism development, the first major hotel development for more than 25 years. Most tourists come from the USA (some 46.4% of total arrivals in 2001). In 2001 454,444 tourists visited Bermuda, a decrease of 15.5% on the 2000 figure.

There is a significant commercial and 'offshore' financial sector, and in 2000 Bermuda was the world's third-largest insurance market, having doubled in size during the 1990s. In late 2001 the industry was under huge pressure from claims made in connection to the September terrorist attacks in the USA, although increased demand for insurance and reinsurance services led to a number of new companies being formed at the same time. In March 2002 the US Department of the Treasury began an investigation into the reasons why many formerly US-based firms had relocated to the island. It was estimated that, in

1995, the entire financial sector contributed more than one-third of foreign exchange earnings. An estimated 18.7% of the employed labour force were engaged directly in the finance, insurance, real estate and business sectors in 2000. International business was estimated to account for 15.3% of GDP in 2002, when the number of companies registered in Bermuda totalled 13,318 (compared with 13,286 in 2001). The sector's real GDP was reported to have increased by some 0.9% in 2002. Another important source of income is the 'free-flag' registration of shipping, giving Bermuda the fifth largest such fleet in the world in 1995. In 1999 Bermuda passed the Electronic Transactions Act, designed to create an infrastructure to support the country's burgeoning 'e-commerce' sector, which was intended to become Bermuda's third major service industry, alongside financial services and tourism.

Bermuda is almost entirely dependent upon imports, has very few commodity exports and, therefore, consistently records a large visible trade deficit (B $668m. in 2000). Receipts from the service industries normally ensure a surplus on the current account of the balance of payments (B $197m. in 2000). The USA is the principal source of imports (72.8% of total imports in 1999) and the principal market for exports. Other important trading partners include the United Kingdom, Canada and France. The main exports are rum, flowers, medicinal and pharmaceutical products and the re-export of petroleum products. The principal imports are machinery and food, beverages and tobacco.

In 2000 Bermuda recorded a provisional budgetary surplus of some B $21.7m. A deficit of some $78.9m. was forecast for the 2003/04 financial year. The average annual rate of inflation was 2.6% in 1990–2001. The rate was estimated at 2.3% in 2002. Some 1.5% of the labour force were registered unemployed in 1995, although unofficial sources estimated that the rate might be as high as 15%. In February 2001 the government figures indicated that unemployment had fallen for the first time since 1993. In 2000 foreign workers comprised some 19.5% of those employed in the Territory.

Bermuda, the oldest colony of the United Kingdom, has the status of Overseas Territory in association with the EU and has also been granted Designated Territory status by the British Government (this allows Bermudian-based funds and unit trusts access to the British market). Bermuda's financial services also benefit from a special tax treaty with the USA. In 2000 Bermuda joined the Caribbean Tourism Organization. In 2003 Bermuda was expected to upgrade its observer status in the Caribbean Community and Common Market (CARICOM, see p. 155) to full membership.

Bermudians enjoy a high standard of living, although addressing the inequality of the distribution of wealth is a key objective of the Smith Government, as is local disquiet at the cost of property. Proximity to the USA and the parity of the US and Bermuda dollars help both tourist and financial industries, and Bermuda's status as a United Kingdom Overseas Territory remains a perceived contributor to political stability and financial integrity. The Territory's insurance industry has experienced a period of rapid expansion and remains the most important component of the financial sector. Another rapidly growing sector in Bermuda are trust funds. Measures to assist the tourist industry (including a reduction in customs duties on certain goods) were introduced in budgets during the late 1990s, following a slight decline in the sector in 1995 and 1996. The ongoing decline in the tourist sector, the island's biggest employer, was likely to also affect the retail sector, and to lead to an overall increase in unemployment. Although the number of cruise-ship passengers increased in 1998, 1999 and 2000, there was a large decrease (14.4%) in 2001, partly owing to the repercussions of the terrorist attacks on the USA in September. The number of air arrivals fell consistently during 1998–2001. In late 2002, in an effort to halt the consequent decline in tourist receipts, the Bermuda Alliance for Tourism launched a rebranding of Bermuda as a luxury destination, in order to attract higher-spending visitors. In August 2002 it was reported that visitor arrivals increased by 2.7% in the first half of the year. Bermuda received some 215,618 visitors during January–June, compared with 209,927 in the corresponding period of 2001. Air arrivals, however, regarded as a more accurate measure of the state of the tourist sector, decreased by 6.4%. Between 1980 and 2000 the number of hotel rooms on Bermuda fell from 9,298 to 6,586, and in that period no new hotels were built. In August 2000, however, the Smith Government granted tax concessions for hotel construction. The measure was intended to create a better climate for investment in the sector.

In the long-term, the Government will need to address the differences between the requirements of the international businesses domiciled on Bermuda and the needs of Bermudians employed in other sectors. In particular, concerns were raised over how much further the international business sector could expand without putting excessive strain on the local infrastructure.

Education

There is free compulsory education in government schools between the ages of five and 16 years, and a number of scholarships are awarded for higher education and teacher training. There are also seven private secondary schools which charge fees. The Bermuda College, founded in 1972, accepts students over the age of 16, and is the only post-secondary educational institution. Extramural degree courses are available through Queen's University, Canada, and Indiana and Maryland Universities, USA. A major programme to upgrade the education system, involving the establishment of five new primary and two secondary schools, was to be implemented between 1996 and 2002.

Public Holidays

2003: 1 January (New Year's Day), 18 April (Good Friday), 24 May (Bermuda Day), 16 June (Queen's Official Birthday), 31 July (Cup Match), 1 August (Somers' Day), 8 September (Labour Day), 11 November (Remembrance Day), 25–26 December (Christmas).

2004: 1 January (New Year's Day), 9 April (Good Friday), 24 May (Bermuda Day), 14 June (Queen's Official Birthday), 30 July (Cup Match), 31 July (Somers' Day), 6 September (Labour Day), 11 November (Remembrance Day), 25–26 December (Christmas).

Weights and Measures

The metric system has been widely adopted but imperial and US weights and measures are both used in certain fields.

Statistical Survey

Source: Department of Information Services, Global House, 43 Church St, Hamilton HM 12; tel. 292-6384; fax 295-5267.

AREA AND POPULATION

Area: 53 sq km (20.59 sq miles).

Population (excluding visitors): 58,460 (males 28,345; females 30,115) at census of 20 May 1991; 62,000 (estimate) at mid-2001 (Source: UN, *Population and Vital Statistics Report*).

Density (mid-2001, estimate): 1,169.8 per sq km.

Principal Towns (population at 1991 census): St George's 1,648; Hamilton (capital) 1,100.

Births, Marriages and Deaths (2000): Live births 838 (birth rate 13.3 per 1,000); Marriage rate 17.8 per 1,000 (1999); Deaths 473 (death rate 7.5 per 1,000). Source: partly, UN, *Population and Vital Statistics Report*.

Expectation of Life (years at birth, official estimates in 2000): Males 71.1; Females 77.8.

Employment (excluding unpaid family workers, 2000): Agriculture, fishing and quarrying 561; Manufacturing 1,211; Electricity, gas and water 447; Construction 2,601; Wholesale and retail trade 5,090; Restaurants and hotels 5,175; Transport and communications 2,918; Financial intermediation and real estate 3,423; Business activities 3,568; Public administration 4,259; Education, health and social services 2,796; Other community, social and personnel services 2,207; International business activity 3,216; Total 37,472.

HEALTH AND WELFARE

Physicians (per 1,000 head, 1999): 2.15.

Health Expenditure: % of GDP (1997): 4.2.

Health Expenditure: public (% of total, 1995): 53.2.
Source: Pan American Health Organization.
For definitions, see explanatory note on p. vi.

AGRICULTURE, ETC.

Principal Crops (FAO estimates, metric tons, 2001): Potatoes 615; Vegetables and melons 2,855; Bananas 330. Source: FAO.

Livestock (FAO estimates, '000 head, 2001): Cattle 1; Horses 1; Pigs 1. Source: FAO.

Livestock Products (FAO estimates, metric tons, 2001): Cows' milk 1,350; Hen eggs 280. Source: FAO.

Fishing (metric tons, live weight, 2000): Groupers 27, Snappers and jobfishes 23, Wahoo 61, Yellowfin tuna 31, Carangids 30, Sharks, rays, skates, etc. 10, Caribbean spiny lobster 29; Total catch 286. Source: FAO, *Yearbook of Fishery Statistics*.

INDUSTRY

Electric Energy (production, million kWh): 615.0 in 2001. Source: BELCO Holdings Limited, *2001 Annual Report*.

FINANCE

Currency and Exchange Rates: 100 cents = 1 Bermuda dollar (B $). *Sterling, US Dollar and Euro Equivalents* (31 December 2002): £1 sterling = B $1.6118; US $1 = B $1.000; €1 = B $1.0487; B $100 = £62.04 = US $100.00 = €95.36. *Exchange Rate:* The Bermuda dollar is at par with the US dollar. Note: US and Canadian currencies are also accepted.

Budget (B $ million, 2000, provisional): *Total revenue* 588.8 (Customs duties 168.7; Payroll tax 164.5; Hotel occupancy tax 12.4; Passenger tax 24.9; Land tax 32.9; International company tax 39.1; Stamp duties 24.7; Telecommunications tax 7.6; Other taxes 96.9). *Total expenditure* 567.1 (Salaries and wages 242.1; Other goods and services 133.8; Grants and contributions 121.2; Public debt 11.5; Capital expenditure 58.5.

Cost of Living (Consumer Price Index; base: 1990 = 100): 126.0 in 1999; 129.4 in 2000; 133.1 in 2001. Source: ILO.

Expenditure on the Gross Domestic Product (B $ million at current prices, year ending 31 March 2000): Government final consumption expenditure 325.4; Private final consumption expenditure 1,654.3; Gross fixed capital formation 413.2; *Total domestic expenditure* 2,392.9; Exports of goods and services 1,549.2; *Less* Imports of goods and services 1,318.2; *GDP in purchasers' values* 2,623.9.

Balance of Payments (B $ million, 2001, estimates): Payments (gross) 1,713 (Imports 720); Receipts (gross) 1,856 (Tourism 350, Professional services 986); *Overall balance* (net) −47. Source: Bermuda Monetary Authority.

EXTERNAL TRADE

Principal Commodities (US $ million, 1999): *Imports:* Food, beverages and tobacco 135.0; Clothing 40.7; Fuels 27.2; Chemicals 75.1; Basic material and semi-manufacturing 115.1; Machinery 154.8; Transport equipment 54.7; Finished equipment 109.3; Miscellaneous 170; Total (incl. others) 712.1. *Exports:* Total 50.8.

Principal Trading Partners (US $ million): *Imports* (1999): Canada 40.2; United Kingdom 34.5; USA 518.3; Total (incl. others) 712.1. *Exports* (1995): France 7.5; United Kingdom 3.9; USA 31.3; Total (incl. others) 62.9.
Source: partly UN, *International Trade Statistics Yearbook*.

TRANSPORT

Road Traffic (vehicles in use, 1999): Private cars 22,567; Motor cycles 24,927; Buses, taxis and limousines 723; Trucks and tank wagons 3,492; Other 723; Total 52,432.

Shipping: *Ship arrivals* (1999): Cruise ships 140; Cargo ships 171; Oil and gas tankers 17. *Merchant Fleet** (registered at 31 December 2001): 121; Total displacement 5,312,780 grt. *International Freight Traffic†* ('000 metric tons, 1990): Goods loaded 130; Goods unloaded 470.
* Source: Lloyd's Register-Fairplay, *World Fleet Statistics*.
† Source: UN, *Monthly Bulletin of Statistics*.

Civil Aviation (1999): Aircraft arrivals 6,024; passengers 354,026; air cargo 4,761,444 kg; air mail 422,897 kg.

TOURISM

Visitor Arrivals: 549,612 (arrivals by air 354,026; cruise-ship passengers 195,586) in 1999; 538,059 (arrivals by air 328,332; cruise ship passengers 209,727) in 2000; 454,444 (arrivals by air 275,009; cruise-ship passengers 179,435) in 2001.

Tourism Receipts (B $ million, estimated): 349.7 in 2001.

COMMUNICATIONS MEDIA

Radio Receivers (1997): 82,000 in use.

Television Receivers (1999): 70,000 in use.

Telephones (2001): 56,300 main lines in use.

Mobile Cellular Telephones (2001): 13,300 subscribers.

Personal Computers (2001): 32,000 in use.

Internet Users (1999): 25,000.

Daily Newspapers (2000): 1 (estimated circulation 17,700).

Non-daily Newspapers (2000): 2 (estimated circulation 11,600). Sources: mainly UNESCO, *Statistical Yearbook*; UN, *Statistical Yearbook*; International Telecommunication Union.

EDUCATION

Pre-primary (1999): 12 schools; 191 teachers; 429 pupils.

Primary (1999): 25 schools; 368 teachers; 4,980 pupils.

Senior (1999): 18 schools; 399 teachers; 2,335 pupils*.

Higher (1999): 1 institution; 628 students.
* Including six private schools.

Adult Literacy Rate (UNESCO estimates): 99% (males 98%; females 99%) in 1998 (Source: UNESCO, *Statistical Yearbook*).

Directory

The Constitution

The Constitution, introduced on 8 June 1968 and amended in 1973 and 1979, contains provisions relating to the protection of fundamental rights and freedoms of the individual; the powers and duties of the Governor; the composition, powers and procedure of the Legislature; the Cabinet; the judiciary; the public service and finance.

The British monarch is represented by an appointed Governor, who retains responsibility for external affairs, defence, internal security and the police.

The Legislature consists of the monarch, the Senate and the House of Assembly. Three members of the Senate are appointed at the Governor's discretion, five on the advice of the Government leader and three on the advice of the Opposition leader. The Senate elects a President and Vice-President. The House of Assembly, consisting of 40 members elected under universal adult franchise from 20 constituencies, elects a Speaker and a Deputy Speaker, and sits for a five-year term.

The Cabinet consists of the Premier and at least six other members of the Legislature. The Governor appoints the majority leader in the House of Assembly as Premier, who in turn nominates the other members of the Cabinet. They are assigned responsibilities for government departments and other business and, in some cases, are assisted by Permanent Cabinet Secretaries.

The Cabinet is presided over by the Premier. The Governor's Council enables the Governor to consult with the Premier and two other members of the Cabinet nominated by the Premier on matters for which the Governor has responsibility. The Secretary to the Cabinet, who heads the public service, acts as secretary to the Governor's Council.

Voters must be British subjects aged 18 years or over (lowered from 21 years in 1990), and, if not possessing Bermudian status, must have been registered as electors on 1 May 1976. Candidates for election must qualify as electors, and must possess Bermudian status.

Under the British Overseas Territories Act, which entered into effect in May 2002, Bermudian citizens have the right to United Kingdom citizenship and the right of abode in the United Kingdom. British citizens do not enjoy reciprocal rights.

The Government

Governor and Commander-in-Chief: Sir JOHN VEREKER (took office 21 November 2001).

Deputy Governor: TIM GURNEY.

CABINET
(April 2003)

Premier: JENNIFER M. SMITH.

Deputy Premier, Minister of Finance: C. EUGENE COX.

Minister of Legislative Affairs and Attorney-General: Dame LOIS BROWNE-EVANS.

Minister of the Environment: DENNIS P. LISTER.

Minister of Education: PAULA A. COX.

Minister of Health and Family Services: NELSON B. A. BASCOMBE.

Minister of Labour, Home Affairs and Public Safety: TERRY E. LISTER.

Minister of Tourism, Telecommunications and E-Commerce: MAURINE (RENEE) WEBB.

Minister of Housing: David Burch.

Minister of Transport: Dr Ewart F. Brown.

Minister of Works and Engineering: W. Alex Scott.

Minister of Youth Development, Parks, Sports and Recreation: Terry E. Lister.

Minister without Portfolio: Neletha Butterfield.

MINISTRIES

Office of the Governor: Government House, 11 Langton Hill, Pembroke HM 13; tel. 292-3600; fax 295-3823; e-mail depgov@ibl.bm.

Office of the Premier: Cabinet Office, Cabinet Bldg, 105 Front St, Hamilton HM 12; tel. 292-5502; fax 292-8397; e-mail premier@bdagov.bm.

Ministry of Youth Development, Parks, Sport and Recreation: Old Fire Station Bldg, 81 Court St, Hamilton HM 12; tel. 295-0855; fax 295-6292.

Ministry of Education: 2nd Floor, 7 Point Finger Rd, Paget DV 04, POB HM 1185, Hamilton HM EX; tel. 236-6904; fax 236-4006.

Ministry of the Environment: Government Administration Bldg, 30 Parliament St, Hamilton HM 12; tel. 297-7590; fax 292-2349; e-mail browlinson@gov.bm.

Ministry of Finance: Government Administration Bldg, 30 Parliament St, Hamilton HM 12; tel. 295-5151; fax 295-5727.

Ministry of Health and Family Services: 7 Point Finger Rd, Paget DV 04, POB HM 380, Hamilton HM BX; tel. 236-0224; fax 236-3971; e-mail ejjoell@gov.bm.

Ministry of Housing: Hamilton.

Ministry of Labour, Home Affairs and Public Safety: Government Administration Bldg, 30 Parliament St, POB HM 1364, Hamilton HM 12; tel. 295-5151; fax 295-4780.

Ministry of Legislative Affairs, Attorney-General's Chambers: Global House, 43 Church St, Hamilton HM 12; tel. 293-2463; fax 292-3608; e-mail govtlaur@ibl.bm.

Ministry of Tourism, Telecommunications and E-Commerce: F. B. Perry Bldg, 2nd Floor, 40 Church St, Hamilton HM 12; tel. 292-4595; fax 296-9444; internet www.mtec.bm.

Ministry of Transport: Global House, 43 Church St, Hamilton HM 12; tel. 295-3130; fax 295-1013.

Ministry of Works and Engineering: Post Office Bldg, 56 Church St, POB HM 525, Hamilton HM 12; tel. 295-5151; fax 295-0170.

Legislature

SENATE

President: Alfred Oughton.

Vice-President: Dr Idwal Wyn (Walwyn) Hughes.

There are 11 nominated members.

HOUSE OF ASSEMBLY

Speaker: Stanley W. Lowe.

Deputy Speaker: W. M. Lister.

There are 40 elected members. Two candidates are elected by each constituency. The House of Assembly meets on Fridays when in session, and on Mondays, Wednesdays and Fridays during the period that the annual budget is debated.

Clerk to the Legislature: Y. Muriel Roach; (The Legislature, Hamilton tel. 292-7408; fax 292-2006; e-mail mroach@gov.bm).

General Election, 9 November 1998

Party	% of votes	Seats
Progressive Labour Party	54.2	26
United Bermuda Party	44.1	14
National Liberal Party	0.8	—
Independents	0.8	—
Total	100.0	40

Political Organizations

National Liberal Party (NLP): 53 Church St, Hamilton HM 12, POB HM 1794, Hamilton HM FX; tel. 292-8587; f. 1985; Leader Dessaline Waldron; Chair. Graeme Outerbridge.

Progressive Labour Party (PLP): Alaska Hall, 16 Court St, POB 1367, Hamilton HM 12; tel. 292-2264; fax 295-7890; e-mail plp@plp.bm; internet www.plp.bm; f. 1963; advocates the 'Bermudianization' of the economy, more equitable taxation, a more developed system of welfare and preparation for independence; Leader Jennifer M. Smith; Deputy Leader C. Eugene Cox; Chair. Neville Tyrrell.

United Bermuda Party (UBP): Central Office, 87 John F. Burrows Bldg, Chancery Lane, Hamilton HM 12, POB HM 715, Hamilton HM CX; tel. 295-0729; fax 292-7195; e-mail info@ubp.bm; internet www.ubp.bm; f. 1964; policy of participatory democracy, supporting system of free enterprise; Leader Grant Gibbons; Chair. Austin B. Woods.

Judicial System

Chief Justice: Austin Ward.

President of the Court of Appeal: Sir James Astwood.

Registrar of Supreme Court and Court of Appeal: Charlene Scott (acting).

Attorney-General: Dame Lois Browne-Evans.

Director of Public Prosecutions: Khamisi Tokumbo.

Solicitor-General: William Pearce.

The Court of Appeal was established in 1964, with powers and jurisdiction of equivalent courts in other parts of the Commonwealth. The Supreme Court has jurisdiction over all serious criminal matters and has unlimited civil jurisdiction. The Court also hears civil and criminal appeals from the Magistrates' Courts. The three Magistrates' Courts have jurisdiction over all petty offences, and have a limited civil jurisdiction.

Religion

CHRISTIANITY

In 1991 it was estimated that 28% of the population were members of the Anglican Communion, 15% were Roman Catholics, 12% were African Methodist Episcopalians, 6% were Seventh-day Adventists and 5% were Wesleyan Methodists. The Presbyterian Church, the Baptist Church and the Pentecostal Church are also active in Bermuda.

The Anglican Communion

The Anglican Church of Bermuda consists of a single, extra-provincial diocese, directly under the metropolitan jurisdiction of the Archbishop of Canterbury, the Primate of All England. There are about 23,000 Anglicans and Episcopalians in Bermuda.

Bishop of Bermuda: Rt Rev. Ewen Ratteray, Bishop's Lodge, 18 Ferrar's Lane, Pembroke HM 08, POB HM 769, Hamilton HM CX; tel. 292-6987; fax 292-5421; e-mail bishopratteray@ibl.bm; internet www.anglican.bm.

The Roman Catholic Church

Bermuda forms a single diocese, suffragan to the archdiocese of Kingston in Jamaica. At 31 December 2001 there were an estimated 9,300 adherents in the Territory. The Bishop participates in the Antilles Episcopal Conference (currently based in Port of Spain, Trinidad and Tobago).

Bishop of Hamilton in Bermuda: Robert Joseph Kurtz, 2 Astwood Rd, POB HM 1191, Hamilton HM EX; tel. 232-4414; fax 232-4447; e-mail rjkurtz@northrock.bm.

Protestant Churches

Baptist Church: Emmanuel Baptist Church, 35 Dundonald St, Hamilton HM 10; tel. 295-6555; fax 296-4461; Pastor Ronald K. Smith.

Wesley Methodist Church: 41 Church St, POB HM 346, Hamilton HM BX; tel. 292-0418; fax 295-9460; e-mail info@wesley.bm; internet www.wesley.bm.

The Press

Bermuda Magazine: POB HM 2032, Hamilton HM HX; tel. 292-7279; e-mail cbarclay@ibl.bm; f. 1990; quarterly; Editor-in-Chief Charles Barclay.

The Bermuda Sun: 41 Victoria St, POB HM 1241, Hamilton HM FX; tel. 295-3902; fax 292-5597; e-mail bdasun@ibl.bm; internet www.bermudasun.bm; f. 1964; 2 a week; official government gazette; Editor Tony McWilliam; circ. 12,500.

The Bermuda Times: 9 Burnaby St, Hamilton HM 12; tel. 292-2596; fax 295-8771.

The Bermudian: 13 Addendum Lane, Pitt's Bay Rd, Pembroke HM07; POB HM 283, Hamilton HM AX; tel. 295-0695; fax 295-8616;

e-mail berpub@ibl.bm; f. 1930; monthly; pictorial and resort magazine; Editor MEREDITH EBBIN; circ. 7,500.

Cable TV Guide: 41 Victoria St, Hamilton HM 12; tel. 295-3902; fax 295-5597.

The Mid-Ocean News: 2 Par-la-Ville Rd, POB HM 1025, Hamilton HM DX; tel. 295-5881; f. 1911; weekly with *TV Guide*; Editor TIM HODGSON; Gen. Man. KEITH JENSEN; circ. 14,500.

The Royal Gazette: 2 Par-la-Ville Rd, POB HM 1025, Hamilton HM DX; tel. 295-5881; internet www.theroyalgazette.com; f. 1828; morning daily; Editor WILLIAM J. ZUILL; Gen. Man. KEITH JENSEN; circ. 17,500.

TV Week: 2 Par-la-Ville Rd, Hamilton HM 08; tel. 295-5881.

The Worker's Voice: 49 Union Sq., Hamilton HM 12; tel. 292-0044; fax 295-7992; e-mail biu@ibl.bm; fortnightly; organ of the Bermuda Industrial Union; Editor Dr B. B. BALL.

Publisher

Bermudian Publishing Co: POB HM 283, Hamilton HM AX; tel. 295-0695; fax 295-8616; social sciences, sociology, sports; Editor KEVIN STEVENSON.

Broadcasting and Communications

TELECOMMUNICATIONS

Bermuda Telephone Co (BTC): 30 Victoria St, POB 1021, Hamilton HM DX; tel. 295-1001; fax 295-1192; internet www.btc.bm; f. 1987; Pres. FRANCIS R. MUSSENDEN.

Bermuda Digital Communications: 22 Reid St, Hamilton HM 11; tel. 296-4010; fax 296-4020; e-mail info@bdc.bm; internet www.bdc.bm; mobile cellular telephone operator; Chair. and CEO KURT EVE.

Cable & Wireless (Bermuda) Ltd: 1 Middle Rd, Smith's FL 03, POB HM 151, Hamilton HM AX; tel. 297-7000; fax 295-7909; e-mail helpdesk@bda.cwplc.com; internet www.cwbda.net.bm; Gen. Man. EDDIE SAINTS.

TeleBermuda International (TBI) Ltd: Bermuda Commercial Bank Bldg, 2nd Floor, 43 Victoria St, Hamilton HM 12; tel. 296-9000; e-mail 292.save@telebermuda.com; internet www.telebermuda.com; f. 1997; a division of GlobeNet Communications, provides an international service; owns a fibre-optic network connecting Bermuda and the USA; Gen. Man. JAMES FITZGERALD.

BROADCASTING

Radio

Bermuda Broadcasting Company: POB HM 452, Hamilton HM BX; tel. 295-2828; fax 295-4282; e-mail zbmzfb@bermudabroadcasting.com; internet www.bermudabroadcasting.com; f. 1982 as merger of ZBM (f. 1943) and ZFB (f. 1962); operates 4 radio stations; CEO ULRIC P. RICHARDSON; Operations Man. E. DELANO INGHAM.

DeFontes Broadcasting Co Ltd (VSB): POB HM 1450, Hamilton HM FX; tel. 295-1450; fax 295-1658; e-mail vsbnews@ibl.bm; f. 1981 as St George's Broadcasting Co; commercial; 4 radio stations; Pres. KENNETH DEFONTES; Station Man. MIKE BISHOP.

Television

Bermuda Broadcasting Company: see Radio; operates 2 TV stations (Channels 7 and 9).

Bermuda Cablevision Ltd: 19 Laffan St, Hamilton; tel. 292-5544; fax 296-3023; e-mail info@cablevision.bm; f. 1988; 61 channels; Pres. DAVID LINES; Gen. Man. JEREMY ELMAS.

DeFontes Broadcasting Co Ltd (VSB): see Radio; operates 1 TV station.

Finance

(cap. = capital; dep. = deposits; res = reserves; m. = million; br. = branch; amounts in Bermuda dollars)

BANKING

Central Bank

Bermuda Monetary Authority: Burnaby House, 26 Burnaby St, POB HM 2447, Hamilton HM JX; tel. 295-5278; fax 292-7471; e-mail info@bma.bm; internet www.bma.bm; f. 1969; central issuing and monetary authority; cap. 10.6m., res 13.5m., total assets 110.9m. (Dec. 2000); Chair., CEO and Controller of Foreign Exchange CHERYL-ANN LISTER.

Commercial Banks

Bank of Bermuda Ltd: 6 Front St, POB HM 1020, Hamilton HM DX; tel. 295-4000; fax 295-7093; e-mail corpcom@ibl.bm; internet www.bankofbermuda.com; f. 1889; cap. 23.9m., res 182.0m., dep. 9,478.6m. (June 2000); Chair. JOSEPH C. H. JOHNSON; Pres. and CEO HENRY B. SMITH; 6 brs.

Bank of N. T. Butterfield & Son Ltd: 65 Front St, POB HM 195, Hamilton HM AX; tel. 295-1111; fax 292-4365; e-mail contact@bntb.bm; internet www.bankofbutterfield.com; f. 1858; inc. 1904; cap. 19.4m., res 90.8m., dep. 4,756.1m. (June 2001); Chair. Dr JAMES A. C. KING; CEO ALAN THOMPSON; 4 domestic brs.

Bermuda Commercial Bank Ltd: Bermuda Commercial Bank Bldg, 43 Victoria St, Hamilton HM 12; tel. 295-5678; fax 295-8091; e-mail enquiries@bcb.bm; internet www.bermuda-bcb.com; f. 1969; 32%-owned by First Curaçao International Bank NV; cap. 10.3m., res 12.6m., dep. 522.6m. (Sept. 2000); Pres. JOHN CHR M. A. M. DEUSS; CEO TIMOTHY ULRICH.

STOCK EXCHANGE

Bermuda Stock Exchange: 3rd Floor, Washington Mall, Church St, Hamilton HM FX; tel. 292-7212; fax 292-7619; e-mail info@bsx.com; internet www.bsx.com; f. 1971; 380 listed equities, funds, debt issues and depositary programs; Pres. and CEO GREG WOJCIECHOWSKI.

INSURANCE

Bermuda had a total of some 1,500 registered insurance companies in 2001, the majority of which are subsidiaries of foreign insurance companies, or owned by foreign industrial or financial concerns. Many of them have offices on the island.

Insurance Information Office: Cedarpark Centre, 48 Cedar Ave, POB HM 2911, Hamilton HM LX; tel. 292-9829; fax 295-3532; e-mail biminfo@ibl.bm; internet www.bermuda-insurance.org.

Major Companies

ACE Bermuda: ACE Bldg, 30 Woodbourne Ave, POB HM 1015, Hamilton HM DX; tel. 295-5200; fax 295-5221; e-mail info@mail.ace.bm; internet www.ace.bm; total revenues US $3,017.0m. (Dec. 1999); Chair. and CEO BRIAN DUPERREAULT.

Argus Insurance Co Ltd: Argus Insurance Bldg, 12 Wesley St, POB HM 1064, Hamilton HM EX; tel. 295-2021; fax 292-6763; e-mail insurance@argus.bm; internet www.argus.bm; Man. Dir and CEO E. JOHN SAINSBURY.

Bermuda Insurance Management Association (BIMA): POB HM 1752, Hamilton HM GX; tel. 295-4864; fax 292-7375.

Paumanock Insurance Co Ltd: POB HM 2267, Hamilton HM JX; tel. 292-2404; fax 292-2648.

X. L. Insurance Co Ltd: Cumberland House, 1 Victoria St, Hamilton; tel. 292-8515; fax 292-7524; e-mail info@xl.bm; Pres. ROBERT J. COONEY; Chief Exec. BRIAN O'HARA.

Trade and Industry

GOVERNMENT AGENCY

Bermuda Registrar of Companies: Government Administration Bldg, 30 Parliament St, Hamilton HM 12; tel. 297-7574; fax 292-6640; internet www.roc.bdagov.bm.

DEVELOPMENT ORGANIZATION

Bermuda Small Business Development Corpn: POB HM 637, Hamilton HM CX; tel. 292-5570; fax 295-1600; e-mail bsbdc@ibl.bm; internet www.bsbdc.bm; f. 1980; funded jointly by the Government and private banks; guarantees loans to small businesses; assets B $500,000; Gen. Man. WILLIAM SPRIGGS.

CHAMBER OF COMMERCE

Bermuda Chamber of Commerce: 1 Point Pleasant Rd, POB HM 655, Hamilton HM CX; tel. 295-4201; fax 292-5779; e-mail bcc@ibm.bm; internet www.bermudacommerce.com; f. 1905; Pres. CHARLES GOSLING; Exec. Vice-Pres. DIANE GORDON; 750 mems.

INDUSTRIAL AND TRADE ASSOCIATION

Bermuda International Business Association (BIBA): 1 Washington Mall, Hamilton HM 11; tel. 292-0632; fax 292-1797; e-mail webinfo@biba.org; internet www.biba.org; Chair. JEFF CONYERS.

EMPLOYERS' ASSOCIATIONS

Bermuda Employers' Council: 304 Mechanics Bldg, 12 Church St, Hamilton HM 11; tel. 295-5070; fax 295-1966; e-mail emp.org@bec.bm; internet www.bec.bm; f. 1960; advisory body on employment and labour relations; Pres. GERALD SIMONS; Exec. Dir ANDREA MOWBRAY; 347 mems.

Construction Association of Bermuda: POB HM 238, Hamilton HM AX; tel. 291-4784; fax 293-3514; e-mail caob@ibl.bm; internet www.constructionbermuda.com; f. 1968; Pres. T. BERRY; 65 mems.

Hotel Employers of Bermuda: c/o Bermuda Hotel Association, 'Carmel', 61 King St, Hamilton HM 19; tel. 295-2127; fax 292-6671; e-mail johnh@ibl.bm; internet www.bermudahotels.com; f. 1968; Pres. DENNIS TUCKER; Exec. Dir JOHN HARVEY; 7 mems.

UTILITY

BELCO Holdings Ltd: 27 Serpentine Rd, POB HM 1026, Hamilton HM DX; tel. 295-5111; fax 292-8975; e-mail webmaster@belco.bhl.bm; internet www.belcoholdings.bm; f. 1908; holding co for Bermuda Electric Light Co Ltd, Bermuda Gas and Utility Co Ltd, and BELCO Energy Services Co; Chair. MILES E. OUTERBRIDGE; Pres. and CEO GARRY A. MADEIROS.

TRADE UNIONS

In 1997 trade union membership was estimated at 8,859. There are nine registered trade unions, the principal ones being:

Bermuda Federation of Musicians and Variety Artists: Reid St, POB HM 6, Hamilton HM AX; tel. 291-0138; Sec.-Gen. LLOYD H. L. SIMMONS; 318 mems.

Bermuda Industrial Union: 49 Union Sq., Hamilton HM 12; tel. 292-0044; fax 295-7992; e-mail biu@ibl.bm; f. 1946; Pres. DERRICK BURGESS; Gen. Sec. HELENA BURGESS; 5,202 mems.

Bermuda Public Services Union: POB HM 763, Hamilton HM CX; tel. 292-6985; fax 292-1149; e-mail infor@bpsu.bm; re-formed 1961; Pres. NIGEL A. D. PEMBERTON; Gen. Sec. EDWARD G. BALL, Jr; 3,190 mems.

Bermuda Union of Teachers: POB HM 726, Hamilton HM CX; tel. 292-6515; fax 292-0697; e-mail butunion@ibl.bm; f. 1919; Pres. ANTHONY E. WOLFFE; Gen. Sec. MICHAEL A. CHARLES; 700 mems.

Transport

ROADS

There are some 240 km (150 miles) of well-surfaced roads, with almost 6 km (4 miles) reserved for cyclists and pedestrians. Each Bermudian household is permitted only one passenger vehicle, and visitors may only hire mopeds, to limit traffic congestion.

SHIPPING

The chief port of Bermuda is Hamilton, with a secondary port at St George's. Both are used by freight and cruise ships. There is also a 'free' port, Freeport, on Ireland Island. In 2000 it was proposed to enlarge Hamilton docks in order to accommodate larger cruise ships. There remained, however, fears that such an enlargement would place excessive strain on the island's environment and infrastructure. Bermuda is a free-flag nation, and at December 2001 the shipping register comprised 121 vessels totalling 5,312,780 grt. In 1995 Bermuda had the fifth largest free-flag merchant fleet in the world.

Department of Marine and Ports Services: POB HM 180, Hamilton HM AX; tel. 295-6575; fax 295-5523; e-mail marineports@bolagov.bm; Dir of Marine and Ports Services RONALD D. ROSS; Deputy Dir and Habour Master MICHAEL DOLDING.

Bermuda Registry of Shipping: POB HM 1628, Hamilton HM GX; tel. 295-7251; fax 295-3718.

Principal Shipping Companies

A. M. Services Ltd: 10 Queen St, Hamilton HM 11; tel. 295-0850; fax 292-3704.

Atlantic Marine Limited Partnership: Richmond House, 12 Par-la-Ville Rd, POB HM 2089, Hamilton HM HX; tel. 295-0614; fax 292-1549; e-mail amlp@amlp.bm; internet www.amlp.bm; f. 1970; Pres. JENS ALERS.

B & H Ocean Carriers Ltd: 3rd Floor, Par-la-Ville Place, 14 Par-la-Ville Rd, POB HM 2257 HM JX, Hamilton; tel. 295-6875; fax 295-6796; f. 1987; Chair. MICHAEL S. HUDNER.

Benor Tankers Ltd: Cedar House, 41 Cedar Ave, HM 12 Hamilton; Pres. CARL-ERIK HAAVALDSEN; Chair. HARRY RUTTEN.

Bermuda International Shipping Ltd: POB GE 4, St George's GE BX; tel. 297-2303; fax 292-1583; Dir J. HENRY HAYWARD.

Container Ship Management Ltd: 14 Par-la-Ville Rd, Hamilton HM 08; tel. 295-1624; fax 295-3781.

Gearbulk Holding Ltd: Par-la-Ville Place, 14 Par-la-Ville Rd, HM JX Hamilton; tel. 295-2184; fax 295-2234.

Globe Forwarding Co: 32 Parliament St, Hamilton; tel. 292-3218; fax 295-3502.

Golden Ocean Management: Clarendon House, 2 Church St West, POB 1022, Hamilton; Man. Dir ROBERT J. KNUTZEN.

Norwegian Cruise Line: 3rd Floor, Reid House, Church St, POB 1564, Hamilton; Chair. EINAR KLOSTER.

Red Rose Ltd: Clarendon House, Church St, Hamilton; Pres. FRANK MUTCH; Sec. ALAN L. BROWN.

Shell Bermuda (Overseas) Ltd: Shell House, Ferry Reach, POB 2, St George's 1.

Unicool Ltd: POB HM 1179, HM EX Hamilton; tel. 295-2244; fax 292-8666; Pres. MATS JANSSON.

Worldwide Shipping Managers Ltd: Suite 402, 7 Reid St, POB HM 1862, HM 11 Hamilton; tel. 295-3770; fax 295-3801.

CIVIL AVIATION

The former US Naval Air Station (the only airfield) was returned to the Government of Bermuda in September 1995, following the closure of the base and the withdrawal of US forces from the islands.

Department of Civil Aviation: Channel House, Longfield Rd, Southside, St David's; tel. 293-1640; fax 293-2417; e-mail info@bdagov.bm; internet www.dca.gov.bm; responsible for all civil aviation matters; Dir of Civil Aviation IAN MACINTYRE.

Bermuda International Airport: 3 Cahow Way, St George's GE CX; e-mail dao@bdagov.bm; internet www.bermudaairport.com; Gen. Man. (vacant).

Delta Airlines: Kindley Field; tel. 293-2050; passenger and air cargo service.

Tourism

Tourism is the principal industry of Bermuda and is government-sponsored. The great attractions of the islands are the climate, scenery, and facilities for outdoor entertainment of all types. In 2001 a total of 454,444 tourists (including 179,435 cruise-ship passengers) visited Bermuda. In 2001 the industry earned B $349.7m. In 2000 there were 3,400 hotel rooms. A large proportion of visitors (46.4% of total arrivals) are from the USA.

Department of Tourism: Global House, 43 Church St, Hamilton HM 12; tel. 292-0023; fax 292-7537; internet www.bermudatourism.org; Dir of Tourism RICHARD CALDERON.

Bermuda Hotel Association: 'Carmel', 61 King St, Hamilton HM 19; tel. 295-2127; fax 292-6671; e-mail johnh@ibl.bm; internet www.bermudahotels.com; Chair. WILLIAM GRIFFITH; CEO JOHN HARVEY; Pres. NORMAN MASTALIR; 35 mem. hotels.

THE BRITISH ANTARCTIC TERRITORY

The British Antarctic Territory lies within the Antarctic Treaty area (i.e. south of latitude 60° S). The Territory, created by an Order in Council which came into force on 3 March 1962, consists of all islands and territories south of latitude 60° S, between longitudes 20° and 80° W, and includes the South Orkney Islands, the South Shetland Islands, the Antarctic Peninsula and areas south and east of the Weddell Sea. With the island of South Georgia and the South Sandwich Islands (now forming a separate territory, q.v.), this area had been constituted by the United Kingdom as the Falkland Islands Dependencies in 1908. The flag of the British Antarctic Territory (proportions 1 by 2) has a white field bearing the union flag of the United Kingdom in the canton and, in the centre of the fly half of the flag, the arms of the territory, which consists of a white shield with three wavy blue horizontal lines at the top overlapped by a red triangle, apex downwards, bearing a brown and yellow torch with red-bordered yellow flames framed by golden rays, the shield supported by a golden lion and a black and white penguin with a yellow throat, both supporters surmounted by a scroll of yellow and light blue with a red reverse and the red inscription 'Research and Discovery'; above the shield, a helmet of grey, light blue and white supporting a torse, alternately of white and light blue, is depicted below a sailing ship of black flying the British Blue Ensign at the gaff.

Area: Land covers about 1,709,400 sq km (660,003 sq miles).

Population: There is no permanent population, but scientists and support personnel (some 40 in the Antarctic winter, rising to about 400 in summer) staff the British Antarctic Survey stations.

Commissioner: ALAN HUCKLE, Polar Regions Section, Overseas Territories Dept, Foreign and Commonwealth Office, Whitehall, London, SW1A 2AH, United Kingdom; tel. (20) 7270-2616.

Administrator: Dr MICHAEL G. RICHARDSON, Polar Regions Section, Overseas Territories Dept, Foreign and Commonwealth Office, Whitehall, London, SW1A 2AH, United Kingdom; tel. (20) 7270-2616.

British Antarctic Survey: High Cross, Madingley Rd, Cambridge, CB3 0ET, United Kingdom; tel. (1223) 221400; fax (1223) 362616; e-mail information@bas.ac.uk; internet www.antarctica.ac.uk; f. 1962 to replace Falkland Islands Dependencies Survey; responsible for almost all British scientific activities in Antarctica; operates two ice-strengthened ocean-going vessels, four de Havilland Twin Otter and one Dash-7 aircraft; the Survey's total expenditure for 2001/02 was £32,692,000; Dir Prof. C. G. RAPLEY.

RESEARCH STATIONS

	Latitude	Longitude
Halley	75° 36′ S	26° 32′ W
Rothera	67° 34′ S	68° 07′ W
Signy (summer only)	60° 43′ S	45° 36′ W

THE BRITISH INDIAN OCEAN TERRITORY (BIOT)

The British Indian Ocean Territory (BIOT) was formed in November 1965, through the amalgamation of the former Seychelles islands of Aldabra, Desroches and Farquhar with the Chagos Archipelago, a group of islands 1,930 km north-east of Mauritius, and previously administered by the Governor of Mauritius. Aldabra, Desroches and Farquhar were ceded to Seychelles when that country was granted independence in June 1976. Since then BIOT has comprised only the Chagos Archipelago, including the coral atoll Diego Garcia, with a total land area of 60 sq km (23 sq miles), together with a surrounding area of some 54,400 sq km (21,000 sq miles) of ocean.

BIOT was established to meet British and US defence requirements in the Indian Ocean. Previously, the principal economic function of the islands was the production of copra: the islands, together with the coconut plantations, were owned by a private company. The copra industry, however, went into decline after the Second World War, and, following the purchase of the islands by the British Crown in 1967, the plantations ceased to operate and the inhabitants were offered the choice of resettlement in Mauritius or in Seychelles. The majority (which numbered about 1,200) went to Mauritius, the resettlement taking place during 1969–73, prior to the construction of the military facility. Mauritius subsequently campaigned for the immediate return of the Territory, and received support from the Organization of African Unity (now the African Union) and from India. The election victory of the left-wing Mouvement Militant Mauricien in 1982 led to an intensification of these demands. Mauritius supported the former island population in a protracted dispute with the United Kingdom over compensation for those displaced, which ended in 1982 when the British Government agreed to an *ex gratia* payment of £4m. In early 1984, however, it was reported that people who had been displaced from Diego Garcia were seeking US $6m. from the US Government to finance their resettlement in Mauritius. The US Administration declined to accept any financial responsibility for the population. In March 1999 a former resident of BIOT obtained leave from the High Court in London to seek a judicial review of the validity of the Immigration Ordinance of 1971, under which the islanders were removed from BIOT, and which continued to prevent them from resettling in the Territory; a review was instigated in July 2000. Later in March 1999 it was disclosed that the displaced islanders and their families, now estimated to number up to 4,000, were not to be included in the offer of full British citizenship, with the right of abode in the United Kingdom, that was to be extended to residents of other United Kingdom Overseas Territories by legislation pending in the British Parliament. In April 2001 the islanders demanded British citizenship for themselves and their direct descendants.

In November 2000 the High Court ruled that the Chagos islanders (Ilois) had been illegally evicted from the Chagos Archipelago, and quashed Section 4 of the 1971 Ordinance, which prevented the return of the Ilois to BIOT. During the case it became known that the British Government had received a subsidy of US $11m. on the purchase of Polaris submarines in the 1960s from the USA, in return for the lease of Diego Garcia for the US military. Furthermore, the Government had apparently termed the Ilois 'contract workers' in order to persuade the UN that the islanders were not an indigenous population with democratic rights. However, memos of the Foreign and Commonwealth Office revealed government knowledge of some of the Ilois living in the Chagos Archipelago for two generations. Robin Cook, the British Secretary of State for Foreign and Commonwealth Affairs, declined an appeal, thereby granting the islanders an immediate right to return to BIOT. Despite this, a new ordinance, issued in January 2001, allowed the residents to return to any of the islands in the Archipelago, except Diego Garcia, easing US fears of a population near its military base. The cost of the resettlement was to be paid by the British Government. In November 2001 an estimated 200 exiled Chagos islanders staged a demonstration at the British High Commission in Port Louis, Mauritius, in protest at the lack of progress in their demands for compensation and repatriation. The British Overseas Territories Act came into effect in May 2002, having received royal assent in February, allowing the displaced islanders to apply for British citizenship. At that time the British Government was also examining the feasibility of a return to the Chagos Archipelago for the islanders, who continued to seek compensation. (However, a report had concluded that resettlement on the atolls of Salomon and Peros Banhos was logistically possible, if not necessarily economically viable.) Eight islanders testified before the British High Court in October–November 2002 on their conditions in exile in connection with claims for compensation. Meanwhile, a meeting of the Chagos Social Committee in November 2000 unanimously resolved to oppose any idea of independence for the Chagos Islands. One month later the Ilois announced their intention to sue the US Government for $6,000m. in compensation. The hearing of the case, in which the Ilois alleged genocide, torture and forced relocation, opened in a US District Court in December 2001. In mid-2002 the Chagos islanders intiated legal action against the recruitment consultancy that supplies civilian employees for the US naval base on Diego Garcia, alleging that the company had discriminated against them when appointing staff to the base; the consultancy was the first of 12 entities that the islanders intended to sue in the USA.

A 1966 agreement between the United Kingdom and the USA provided for BIOT to be used by both countries over an initial period of 50 years, with the option of extending this for a further 20 years. The United Kingdom undertook to cede the Chagos Archipelago to Mauritius when it was no longer required for defence purposes. Originally the US military presence was limited to a communications centre on Diego Garcia. In 1972, however, construction of a naval support facility was begun, apparently in response to the expansion of the Soviet maritime presence in the Indian Ocean. This plan was expanded in 1974, the agreement being formalized by an 'exchange of notes' in 1976, and again following Soviet military intervention in Afghanistan in December 1979. Facilities on Diego Garcia include a communications centre, a runway with a length of 3,650 m, anchorage, refuelling and various ancillary services. During the 1980s the US Government undertook a programme of expansion and improvement of the naval support facility, which was to include a space-tracking station. In August 1987 the US navy began to use Diego Garcia as a facility for minesweeping helicopters taking part in operations in the Persian (Arabian) Gulf. Following Iraq's invasion of Kuwait in August 1990, Diego Garcia was used as a base for US B-52 aircraft, which were deployed in the Gulf region. Runway facilities on Diego Garcia were again used in September 1996 and December 1998 as a base for US support aircraft during US missile attacks on Iraq. In October 2001 US forces used the Diego Garcia base to launch strikes on Afghanistan with B-52 aircraft. In March–April 2003 the base was again used by the US military, to launch bombing raids on Saddam Hussain's regime in Baghdad, Iraq, using B-2 aircraft.

In January 1988 Mauritius renewed its campaign to regain sovereignty over the Chagos Archipelago, and reiterated its support for a 'zone of peace' in the Indian Ocean. In November 1989, following an incident in which a military aircraft belonging to the US air force accidentally bombed a US naval vessel near Diego Garcia, a demonstration was held outside the US embassy in Mauritius, demanding the withdrawal of foreign military forces from the area. The Mauritius Government announced that it would draw the attention of the UN Security Council to the dangers that it perceived in the execution of US military air exercises. However, the US Assistant Secretary of State for African Affairs reiterated during an official visit to Mauritius, in the same month, that the USA would maintain its military presence in the Indian Ocean. In December 2000, following the High Court's ruling, Mauritius once again staked its claim for sovereignty over the Chagos Archipelago.

In January 1994 arrangements were agreed for the establishment of a joint British-Mauritius fisheries' commission to promote and coordinate conservation and scientific research within the territorial waters of Mauritius and BIOT.

The civil administration of BIOT is the responsibility of a non-resident commissioner in the Foreign and Commonwealth Office in London, represented on Diego Garcia by a Royal Naval commander and a small British naval presence. A chief justice, a senior magistrate and a principal legal adviser (who performs the functions of an attorney-general) are resident in the United Kingdom.

Land Area: about 60 sq km.

Population: There are no permanent inhabitants. In 2001 there were about 3,200 US and British military personnel and civilian support staff stationed in the Territory.

Currency: The US dollar is used.

Commissioner: ALAN HUCKLE, Head of Overseas Territories Dept, Foreign and Commonwealth Office, King Charles St, London SW1A 2AH, United Kingdom; tel. (20) 7270-3000.

Administrator: CHARLES HAMILTON, Overseas Territories Dept, Foreign and Commonwealth Office, King Charles St, London SW1A 2AH, United Kingdom; tel. (20) 7270-3000.

Commissioner's Representative: Commdr ADAM PETERS, RN, Diego Garcia, c/o BFPO Ships.

THE BRITISH VIRGIN ISLANDS

Introductory Survey

Location, Climate, Language, Religion, Flag, Capital

The British Virgin Islands consist of more than 60 islands and cays, of which only 16 are inhabited. The islands, most of which are mountainous and of volcanic origin (the only exception of any size is the coralline island of Anegada), lie at the northern end of the Leeward Islands, about 100 km (62 miles) to the east of Puerto Rico and adjoining the United States Virgin Islands. The climate is sub-tropical but extremes of heat are relieved by the trade winds. The average annual rainfall is 1,000 mm (39 ins). The official language is English. Most of the inhabitants profess Christianity. The flag is the British 'Blue Ensign', with the Territory's badge (a green shield, with a white-clad virgin and 12 oil lamps, above a scroll bearing the motto 'vigilate') in the fly. The capital, Road Town, is situated on the island of Tortola.

Recent History

Previously peopled by Caribs, and named by the navigator Christopher Colombus after St Ursula and her 11,000 fellow-martyrs, the islands were settled by buccaneers and the Dutch, but were finally annexed by the British in 1672. In 1872 they became part of the British colony of the Leeward Islands, which was administered under a federal system. The federation was dissolved in July 1956, but the Governor of the Leeward Islands continued to administer the British Virgin Islands until 1960, when an appointed Administrator (restyled Governor in 1971) assumed direct responsibility. Unlike the other Leeward Islands, the British Virgin Islands did not join the Federation of the West Indies (1958–62), preferring to develop its links with the US Virgin Islands.

A new Constitution was introduced in April 1967, when H. Lavity Stoutt became the islands' first Chief Minister. He was later replaced by Willard Wheatley. At an election in September 1975 Stoutt's Virgin Islands Party (VIP) and the United Party (UP) each won three of the seven elective seats on the Legislative Council. Wheatley, sitting as an independent member, held the balance of power and he continued in office, with Stoutt as Deputy Chief Minister.

An amended Constitution took effect in June 1977, giving more extensive internal self-government; some electoral changes were also made (see Constitution, below). In the first election to the enlarged Legislative Council to take place under the new Constitution, in November 1979, independent candidates won five of the nine elective seats, with the VIP winning the remainder. Stoutt secured enough support to be reinstated as Chief Minister. In the November 1983 election the VIP and the UP each secured four seats. The one successful independent candidate, Cyril Romney, became Chief Minister and formed a coalition Government with members of the UP.

In August 1986 the Governor dissolved the Legislative Council, six days before a scheduled council debate on a motion of 'no confidence' against Romney (who had allegedly been involved with a company under investigation by the British police and the US Department of Justice's Drug Enforcement Administration—DEA). At a general election in the following month the VIP won five of the nine elective seats, with the UP and independent candidates (including Romney) taking two seats each. Stoutt was appointed Chief Minister.

The Deputy Chief Minister, Omar Hodge, was dismissed from the Executive Council in March 1988, following an official inquiry into allegations of financial malpractice (he continued to protest his innocence, and won a libel suit in January 1990). Hodge was replaced by Ralph O'Neal, formerly leader of the UP, who joined the VIP. In March 1989 Hodge formed a new political party, the Independent People's Movement (IPM), together with the Director of Tourism, who complained of a lack of government support for the industry.

At a general election in November 1990 the VIP increased its majority to six seats, while the IPM secured one seat and independent candidates won two; the UP lost both its seats. Stoutt retained the post of Chief Minister.

The principal concern of the Stoutt administration in the early 1990s was the trade in, and increasing local use of, illicit drugs. In late 1990 the Stoutt administration introduced legislation to impose more stringent regulations governing the 'offshore' financial sector, while plans to review immigration policy were under discussion, in an attempt to reduce the number of illegal immigrants entering the Territory. Both areas had previously been considered to be insufficiently protected from exploitation by traffickers seeking to introduce illicit drugs into the islands or to divert funds from their sale through the financial sector. In December 1991 the DEA paid the Government of the British Virgin Islands US $0.6m. and in May 1992 a further US $1.8m. in assets confiscated from drugs-traffickers convicted in the USA.

In August 1993 the British Government appointed three commissioners to review the Territory's Constitution at the request of the Legislative Council. Proposed changes included the introduction of direct elections for the position of Chief Minister, the enlargement of the Legislative Council and the adoption of a bill of rights. The British Government's decision in early 1994 to accept the commission's proposal to enlarge the Legislative Council to 13 seats (by the creation of four seats representing the Territory 'at large') was strongly criticized by Stoutt. His opposition to the changes intensified in July, when he failed to obtain a deferral of the decision in order that the Legislative Council could debate the issue. Discussions on various recommendations in the review continued in 1995 and 1996.

At elections to the newly-enlarged legislature on 20 February 1995 the VIP won six seats, the UP and the Concerned Citizens' Movement (CCM—formerly IPM) each secured two seats and independent candidates won three seats. One of the successful independents, Alvin Christopher, subsequently gave his support to the VIP, thus providing the party with the majority required to form a Government. Stoutt retained the post of Chief Minister, and Christopher was appointed Minister of Communications, Works and Public Utilities in the new Government.

In May 1995 the Deputy Chief Minister, Ralph O'Neal, was appointed Chief Minister, following the sudden death of Stoutt. At a by-election held in July for the vacant seat, the VIP candidate was successful.

In June 1995 David Mackilligin replaced Peter Alfred Penfold as Governor of the Territory. In July of the following year the Governor recommended that there should be a public debate on the continued use of judicial corporal punishment in the Territory (the British Virgin Islands being the only British Dependent Territory in which the practice remained in force). The issue was raised owing to concern that, as a signatory to the European Convention on Human Rights, the United Kingdom was potentially in violation of the accord every time that a sentence of corporal punishment was passed in the islands.

In May 1998 Frank Savage was appointed Governor. In September the Governments of the United Kingdom and of the British Virgin Islands signed a Memorandum of Co-operation and Partnership. The Memorandum was intended to foster a closer working relationship between the two countries, in particular in relation to the execution of public works and services.

In March 1999 the Government of the United Kingdom published draft legislation pertaining to its relationship with its Overseas Dependencies, which were to be renamed United Kingdom Overseas Territories (and had been referred to as such since February 1998). The legislation proposed the extension of British citizenship to the citizens of Overseas Territories, although it also required its Territories to amend their legislation on human rights and on the regulation of the financial services sector to meet international standards. In July the British Government appointed a consultant, Alan Hoole, a former Governor of Anguilla, to review the Constitution of the British Virgin Islands. In September Hoole proposed several changes to the Constitution, including the introduction of more frequent meetings of the Legislative Council and the removal of the Governor's powers to veto legislation. Under the terms of the proposed changes, the Governor was also to be obliged to consult with the Executive Council before implementing policy in his areas of special responsibility (foreign affairs, the civil service and defence). It was also suggested that members of the Legislative Council and senior civil servants should be obliged to declare their interests. In August the Governor outlined the Government's legislative programme. The main aim of the proposed legislation was to ensure that the regulation of the financial services sector conformed to international standards. Savage, who also announced the introduction of a comprehensive review of the education system, announced that the drafting of the proposed amendments to the Constitution would continue throughout the year.

Elections to the Legislative Council took place on 17 May 1999. The VIP retained control of the legislature, increasing its representation to seven seats. The recently-founded National Democratic Party (NDP) performed particularly well, taking five seats, while the CCM retained one of the two seats it had previously held. The UP and several independent candidates also contested the elections. O'Neal subsequently re-appointed the members of the previous Executive Council.

In July 2000 O'Neal dismissed the Deputy Chief Minister, Eileene Parsons. O'Neal claimed that Parsons had been planning a coup against his administration because of his intention to replace Parsons as Minister for Education and Culture with Andrew Fahie (Parsons would have retained the health and welfare portfolios). Fahie's appointment was the result of the British Government's decision to allow the number of ministers to be increased to five. Following her dismissal, Parsons left the governing VIP and joined the NDP. Alvin Christopher, the Minister for Communications, Works and Public Utilities, was appointed the new Deputy Chief Minister.

In September 2000 the Legislative Council passed legislation abolishing judicial corporal punishment on the British Virgin Islands, in keeping with the United Kingdom's acceptance of the European Convention of Human Rights. In November the Legislative Council voted in favour of making 7 March, the birth date of Lavity Stoutt, a public holiday; this was to replace, from 2002, the public holiday of 14 November, the birthday of the Prince of Wales.

In January 2002 O'Neal announced that, in order for the Government to exert greater control over immigration, visitors from Cuba, Jamaica and Saint Vincent and the Grenadines might soon require entry visas.

The Organisation for Economic Co-operation and Development (OECD, see p. 277) announced in April 2002 that the British Virgin Islands had made sufficient commitments to improve the transparency of its tax and regulatory systems to be removed from an updated list of un-co-operative tax 'havens', first published in 2000. Also in April, a tax information exchange agreement, designed to reduce the potential for abuse of the tax system, was signed with the USA. In the same month, the financial secretary, L. Allen Wheatley, was arrested in connection with the mishandling of government contracts relating to the Beef Island Airport development project, and in May the Government survived a motion of 'no confidence' brought against it in connection with the airport development project. In November 2002 some of the charges against Wheatley were dropped because the prosecution were unable to provide sufficient evidence of fraud or breach of trust; however, the presiding magistrate said there was enough evidence for Wheatley to answer related charges of theft and corruption.

In late 2002 the recovering financial sector faced further disruption when the United Kingdom, under pressure from a European Union (EU, see p. 199) investigation into tax evasion, demanded that the British Virgin Islands disclose the identities and account details of Europeans holding private savings accounts on the islands. The British Virgin Islands, along with some other British Overseas Territories facing similar demands, claimed it was being treated unfairly compared with more powerful European countries, such as Switzerland and Luxembourg.

In May 2002 the British Overseas Territories Act, having received royal assent in the United Kingdom in February, came into force and granted British citizenship to the people of its Overseas Territories, including the British Virgin Islands. Under the new law British Virgin Islanders would be able to hold British passports and work in the United Kingdom and anywhere else in the EU. Meanwhile, in the same month, Julian Frazer was appointed Deputy Chief Minister and Minister of Communications and Works in succession to J. Alvin Christopher. Although O'Neal denied the claims, it was reported that Christopher had been removed from office because of his support for corruption allegations against the Government in connection with the airport development project. Rieal George replaced Frazer as Minister for Natural Resources and Labour.

In October 2002 Tom Macan succeeded Frank Savage as Governor. The new Governor immediately announced his intention to try to reduce corruption and maintain economic growth on the islands. In late April 2003 the Chief Minister asked Macan to dissolve the Legislative Council in preparation for elections, to be held on 16 June.

Government

Under the provisions of the 1977 Constitution, the Governor is appointed by the British monarch and is responsible for external affairs, defence and internal security. The Governor is also Chairman of the Executive Council, which comprises five other members. The Legislative Council comprises 15 members: a Speaker, one *ex-officio* member, and 13 members elected by universal adult suffrage.

Defence

The United Kingdom is responsible for the defence of the islands. In September 1999 it was announced that Royal Air Force patrols were to be undertaken from the islands in order to intercept drugs-traffickers. Central government expenditure on defence totalled US $0.4m. in 1997.

Economic Affairs

In 2000, according to estimates by the Caribbean Development Bank (CDB), the British Virgin Islands' gross domestic product (GDP) was US $682.9m., equivalent to some $33,640 per head. The population doubled during 1984–94 to 17,903, primarily owing to a large influx of immigrants from other Caribbean Islands, the United Kingdom and the USA. During 1991–2001, it was estimated, the population increased at an average annual rate at 2.1%, while GDP increased, in real terms, by some 4% per year during 1995–1999, according to reports.

Agriculture (including forestry and fishing) contributed 1.7% of GDP in 2001, and engaged 1.9% of those in paid employment in 1996. The Territory produces fruit and vegetables for domestic consumption or export to the US Virgin Islands, and some sugar cane (for the production of rum). Food imports accounted for 18.9% of total import costs in 1997. In November 1999 the Government announced that it intended to raise the level of agricultural production, through the revision of legislation and policy relating to the sector, in order to ensure self-sufficiency in agriculture and a limited level of exports. The fishing industry caters for local consumption and export, and provides a sporting activity for tourists, although the Government was looking to develop deep-sea fishing commercially for domestic and export markets.

Industry (including mining, manufacturing, construction and public utilities) accounted for 5.5% of GDP in 2001 and engaged 21.3% of the employed labour force in 1996. The mining sector is small, consisting of the extraction of materials for the construction industry and of some salt. Manufacturing, which provided 0.9% of GDP in 2001, consists mainly of light industry; there is one rum distillery, two factories for the production of ice, some plants producing concrete blocks and other construction materials, small boat manufacture and various cottage industries. A water desalination plant began operations on Virgin Gorda in 1994 and another was opened later in the year. Construction of a further plant was planned in 2001. Construction activity accounted for 2.6% of GDP in 2001. Most energy requirements must be imported (mineral fuels accounted for an estimated 8.5% of total imports in 1997).

Services, primarily tourism and financial services, constitute the principal economic sector of the British Virgin Islands, contributing 92.8% of GDP in 2001. The tourist industry earned some US $292.1m. in 2000, and employed one-third of the working population, directly or indirectly, in 1995. The British Virgin Islands is the largest 'bareboat' chartering centre in the Caribbean, and approximately 60% of stop-over visitors stay aboard yachts. Nevertheless, in 1997 the restaurants and hotels sector contributed 14.0% of GDP. The number of stop-over visitors increased by an average of 13.6% per year in 1992–99, reaching 303,600 in 2000 (most of whom were from the USA); the ratio of tourists to local population is therefore higher than at any other Caribbean destination. The 2001 budget included $53m. to be spent on renovations to the Beef Island airport, in addition to further investment to the country's infrastructure.

Financial services expanded rapidly as a result of legislative measures adopted in 1984, and in 2000 the 'offshore' sector contributed over half of direct government revenue (some US $100m.). There were a cumulative total of 476,000 International Business Company (IBC) registrations in the islands 1984–2001. The islands have also recorded significant growth in the establishment of mutual funds and of insurance companies. In January 2002 the Government created the Financial Services Commission, an independent regulatory authority for the sector, in order to meet international demands for a clear separation between the Government and financial services regulation.

In 1999 the British Virgin Islands recorded a trade deficit of US $206.3m. (exports were worth some 1.0% of imports); the deficit was estimated to have increased to 224.7m. in 2001. The trade deficit is normally offset by receipts from tourism, development aid, remittances from islanders working abroad (many in the US Virgin Islands) and, increasingly, from the offshore financial sector. The principal sources of imports (most of the islands' requirements must be imported) are the USA (which provided 56.9% of imports in 1997), Trinidad and Tobago, Antigua and Barbuda, and also the United Kingdom. The principal markets for the limited amount of exports are the US Virgin Islands and the USA and Puerto Rico; rum is exported to the USA. Machinery and transport equipment are the main import (accounting for 28.3% of total imports in 1997), and fruit and vegetables, rum, sand and gravel the main exports.

In the financial year ending 30 June 1999 there was an estimated recurrent budgetary surplus of US $26.9m. Estimated recurrent expenditure for 1999 was US $116.1m. The budget for 2001 projected revenue of US $186.6m. against recurrent expenditure of US $145.3m., amounting to a projected surplus of US $41.3m. The surplus was to be allocated to capital expenditure and the national relief fund. In 1995/96 there was a deficit of US $22m. on the current account of the balance of payments. British budgetary support ceased in 1977, but the United Kingdom grants assistance for capital development. In the period ending 31 December 1998 the total public debt was estimated to be $61,386,788, a decrease of 3.3% from 1997. In 1998 the territory received $1.2m. in development assistance. Central Government debt to GDP ratio was estimated at 10.0%. The average annual rate of inflation was 4.1% in 1990–2001; consumer prices increased by an average of 3.1% in 2001. Unemployment is negligible.

The British Virgin Islands became an associate member of the Caribbean Community and Common Market (CARICOM, see p. 155) in 1991; it is a member of CARICOM's Caribbean Development Bank (CDB, see p. 159) and an associate member of the Organisation of Eastern Caribbean States (OECS, see p. 341). In economic affairs the Territory has close affiliations with the neighbouring US Virgin Islands, and uses US currency. As a dependency of the United Kingdom, the islands have the status of Overseas Territory in association with the EU (see p. 199).

The economy of the British Virgin Islands is largely dominated by tourism and by the provision of international financial services. The 'offshore' financial sector, which developed rapidly in the last two decades of the 20th century, is an important source of employment and provided 51% of direct government revenue in 1998. The islands are the world centre for the registration of IBCs, and some 476,000 IBCs were estimated to have been established in the islands between 1984, when the International Business Companies Act was put in place, and early 2000. Despite ongoing efforts to attract insurance and trust companies to the islands, it was estimated that in early 2000 IBCs still accounted for around 90% of government revenues from financial services. International attempts, notably by the OECD, to encourage the reform of offshore financial centres are therefore of great concern to the British Virgin Islands, particularly as IBCs, which are not taxed and which are not obliged to disclose their directors or shareholders, have been singled out for particular criticism. Nevertheless, revenues from annual licence fees paid by offshore companies continued to grow in 2000/01. Despite the importance of the financial sector, tourism remains the most important sector of the economy, as the construction and retail sectors, amongst others, are to a certain extent dependent on its performance. In the long-term, however, the Government hoped to encourage greater diversification of the economy, in order to reduce reliance on tourism and financial services, both of which remained vulnerable to external pressures. According to the CDB, the economy performed strongly in 2000; growth in tourism and in the offshore financial sector remained solid. The number of registered IBCs increased by 19%, and the number of mutual funds increased by 400, to a total of over 2,000. However, the aftermath of the September 2001 terrorist attacks in the USA adversely affected tourism revenues in 2001 and 2002, which was only partially offset by increased activity in the offshore banking sector. In March 2003 the Chief Minister announced a proposed reduction in government expenditure in the 2003/04 budget; in 2002/03 the Government collected some US $183m., compared with predicted revenues of US $201m.

Education

Primary education is free, universal and compulsory between the ages of five and 11. Secondary education is also free and lasts from 12 to 16 years of age. In 1997 some 206 pupils were enrolled in pre-primary schools and in 2001 there were 2,226 pupils attending primary schools. In 2001 some 1,572 were enrolled in secondary education. Higher education is available at the University of the Virgin Islands (St Thomas, US Virgin Islands) and elsewhere in the Caribbean, in North America and in the United Kingdom. In 1990 only 0.7% of the adult population had received no schooling. Central government expenditure on education in 1997 was US $17.1m.

Public Holidays

2003: 1 January (New Year's Day), 3 March (Lavity Stoutt's birthday), 10 March (Commonwealth Day), 18 April (Good Friday), 21 April (Easter Monday), 9 June (Whit Monday), 14 June (Queen's Official Birthday), 1 July (Territory Day), 4–6 August (Festival Monday, Tuesday and Wednesday), 21 October (Saint Ursula's Day), 25–26 December (Christmas).

2004: 1 January (New Year's Day), 1 March (Lavity Stoutt's Birthday), 8 March (Commonwealth Day), 9 April (Good Friday), 12 April (Easter Monday), 31 May (Whit Monday), 12 June (Queen's Official Birthday), 1 July (Territory Day), 2–4 August (Festival Monday, Tuesday and Wednesday), 21 October (Saint Ursula's Day), 25–26 December (Christmas).

Weights and Measures

The imperial system is used.

Statistical Survey

Source: Development Planning Unit, Central Administrative Complex, Road Town, Tortola; tel. 494-3701; fax 494-3947; e-mail dpu@dpu.org; internet www.dpu.org.

AREA AND POPULATION

Area: 153 sq km (59 sq miles). *Principal islands* (sq km): Tortola 54.4; Anegada 38.8; Virgin Gorda 21.4; Jost Van Dyke 9.1.

Population: 16,644 (males 8,570; females 8,074) at census of 12 May 1991; 19,864 (males 10,234; females 9,630) in 1999; 21,000 (UN estimate) at mid-2001; *By island* (1980): Tortola 9,119; Virgin Gorda 1,412; Anegada 164; Jost Van Dyke 134; Other islands 156; (1991) Tortola 13,568. Source: partly UN, *Population and Vital Statistics Report.*

Density (mid-2001): 137.3 per sq km.

Principal Town: Road Town (capital), population 11,000 (UN estimate, incl. suburbs, mid-2001). Source: UN, *World Urbanization Prospects: The 2001 Revision.*

Births, Marriages and Deaths (registrations, 2001): 318 live births (birth rate 15.4 per 1,000); (1988) 176 marriages (marriage rate 14.2 per 1,000); 101 deaths (death rate 4.9 per 1,000). Sources: UN, *Population and Vital Statistics Report*; UN, *Demographic Yearbook.*

Expectation of Life (years at birth, estimates): 75.6 (males 74.7; females 76.6) in 2001. Source: US Census Bureau.

Employment (1996): Agriculture, hunting and forestry 110; Fishing 84; Mining and quarrying 26; Manufacturing 573; Electricity, gas and water supply 176; Construction 1,349; Wholesale and retail trade 1,270; Hotels and restaurants 2,118; Transport, storage and communications 734; Financial intermediation 377; Real estate, renting and business activities 704; Public administration and defence 945; Education 373; Health and social work 296; Other community, social and personal service activities 297; Private households with employed persons 458; Not classifiable by economic activity 59; Total 9,949 (males 5,635, females 4,314).

HEALTH AND WELFARE

Physicians (per 1,000 head, 1999): 1.15.

Health expenditure (% of GDP, 1995): 3.9.

Health Expenditure (public, % of total, 1995): 36.5 (Source: Pan American Health Organization).

For definitions, see explanatory note on p. vi.

AGRICULTURE, ETC.

Livestock (FAO estimates, '000 head, 2001): Cattle 2.4; Sheep 6.1; Goats 10.0; Pigs 1.5. Source: FAO.

Fishing (metric tons, live weight, 2000): Swordfish 2, Caribbean spiny lobster 3, Stromboid conchs 6; Total catch 43. Source: FAO, *Yearbook of Fishery Statistics.*

INDUSTRY

Electric Energy (production, million kWh): 43 in 1988; 44 in 1989; 45 in 1990. 1991–98 annual production as in 1990 (UN estimates). Source: UN, *Industrial Commodity Statistics Yearbook.*

FINANCE

Currency and Exchange Rate: United States currency is used: 100 cents = 1 US dollar ($). *Sterling and Euro Equivalents* (31 December 2002): £1 sterling = US $1.6118; €1 = US $1.0487; US $100 = £62.04 = €95.36.

Budget (estimates, $ million, 2001/02): Recurrent revenue 195.1; Recurrent expenditure 142.2; Capital expenditure 47.1. Source: Caribbean Development Bank, *Social and Economic Indicators 2001.*

Cost of Living (Consumer Price Index; base: 1990 = 100): 146.3 in 1999; 150.3 in 2000; 155.0 in 2001. Source: ILO.

Gross Domestic Product ($ million, at market prices): 611.7 in 1998; 651.1 in 1999; 682.9 in 2000.

Gross Domestic Product by Economic Activity (Current prices, $ million, 1997): Agriculture, hunting and forestry 3.5; Fishing 5.2; Mining and quarrying 3.5; Manufacturing 6.0; Electricity, gas and water 11.2; Construction 36.0; Wholesale and retail trade 110.0; Hotels and restaurants 87.8; Transport, storage and communications 47.0; Financial intermediation 151.7; Real estate, renting and business services 48.0; Public administration 30.1; Education 10.4; Health and social work 7.3; Other community, social and personal services 10.2; Private households with employed persons 3.8; Sub-total 571.7; Import duty 17.0; *Less* imputed service charges 15.0; GDP in purchasers' values 573.7.

EXTERNAL TRADE

Principal Commodities ($ '000): *Imports c.i.f.* (1997): Food and live animals 31,515; Beverages and tobacco 8,797; Crude materials (inedible) except fuels 1,168; Mineral fuels, lubricants, etc. 9,847; Chemicals 8,816; Basic manufactures 31,715; Machinery and transport equipment 47,019; Total (incl. others) 116,379. *Exports f.o.b.* (1996): Food and live animals 368; Beverages and tobacco 3,967; Crude materials (inedible) except fuels 1,334; Total (incl. others) 5,862. *1999* ($ '000): Total imports 208,419; Total exports 2,081.

Principal Trading Partners ($ '000): *Imports c.i.f.* (1997): Antigua and Barbuda 1,807; Trinidad and Tobago 2,555; United Kingdom 406; USA 94,651; Total (incl. others) 166,379. *Exports f.o.b.* (1996): USA and Puerto Rico 1,077; US Virgin Islands 2,001; Total (incl. others) 5,862.

1999 ($ '000): Imports 208,419; Exports 2,081.
Source: mainly UN, *International Trade Statistics Yearbook.*

TRANSPORT

Road Traffic (motor vehicles in use): 6,900 in 1992; 6,700 in 1993; 7,000 in 1994. *1997* (motor vehicles registered and licenced): 7,944. Source: mainly UN, *Statistical Yearbook.*

Shipping: *International Freight Traffic* ('000 metric tons, 1997): Goods unloaded 102.6. *Cargo Ship Arrivals* (1988): 1,139. *Merchant Fleet* (vessels registered, at 31 December 2001): 15; Total displacement 3,255 grt. (Source: Lloyd's Register-Fairplay, *World Fleet Statistics*).

Civil Aviation (aircraft arrivals): 8,972 in 1985; 9,854 in 1986.

TOURISM

Visitor Arrivals ('000): 279.1 stop-over visitors, 105.1 cruise-ship passengers in 1998; 285.9 stop-over visitors, 180.7 cruise-ship passengers in 1999; 303.6 stop-over visitors, 188.5 cruise-ship passengers in 2000.

Visitor Expenditure (estimates, US $ million): 253.9 in 1998; 279.0 in 1999; 292.1 in 2000 (Source: Caribbean Development Bank, *Social and Economic Indicators 2001*).

COMMUNICATIONS MEDIA

Radio Receivers (1997): 9,000 in use.

Television Receivers (1999): 4,000 in use.

Telephones (1996): 10,000 main lines in use.

Facsimile Machines (1996): 1,200 in use.

Non-daily Newspapers (1996): 2 (estimated circulation 4,000).
Sources: UNESCO, *Statistical Yearbook*; UN, *Statistical Yearbook.*

EDUCATION

Pre-primary: 5 schools (1994/95); 52 teachers (1994/95); 206 pupils (1997).

Primary: 20 schools (1993/94); 169 teachers (1994/95); 2,226 pupils (2001).

Secondary: 4 schools (1988); 115 teachers (1994/95); 1,572 pupils (2001).

Source: partly Caribbean Development Bank, *Social and Economic Indicators 2001*.

Directory

The Constitution

The British Virgin Islands have had a representative assembly since 1774. The present Constitution took effect from June 1977. Under its terms, the Governor is responsible for defence and internal security, external affairs, terms and conditions of service of public officers, and the administration of the Courts. The Governor also possesses reserved legislative powers in respect of legislation necessary in the interests of his special responsibilities. There is an Executive Council, with the Governor as Chairman, one *ex-officio* member (the Attorney-General), the Chief Minister (appointed by the Governor from among the elected members of the Legislative Council) who has responsibility for finance, and three other ministers (appointed by the Governor on the advice of the Chief Minister); and a Legislative Council consisting of a Speaker, chosen from outside the Council, one *ex-officio* member (the Attorney-General) and 13 elected members (nine members from one-member electoral districts and four members representing the Territory 'at large').

The division of the islands into nine electoral districts, instead of seven, came into effect at the November 1979 general election. The four 'at large' seats were introduced at the February 1995 general election. The minimum voting age was lowered from 21 years to 18 years.

Under the British Overseas Territories Act, which entered into effect in May 2002, British Virgin Islanders have the right to United Kingdom citizenship and the right of abode in the United Kingdom. British citizens do not enjoy reciprocal rights.

The Government

Governor: TOM MACAN (assumed office October 2002).

Deputy Governor: ELTON GEORGES.

EXECUTIVE COUNCIL
(April 2003)

Chairman: The Governor.

Chief Minister and Minister for Finance: RALPH T. O'NEAL.

Deputy Chief Minister and Minister for Communications, Works and Public Utilities: JULIAN FRAZER.

Minister for Natural Resources and Labour: RIEAL GEORGE.

Minister for Education and Culture: ANDREW FAHIE.

Minister for Health and Welfare: ETHLYN SMITH.

Attorney-General: CHERNO JALLOW.

MINISTRIES

Office of the Governor: Government House, Road Town, Tortola; tel. 494-2345; fax 494-5790; e-mail bvigovernor@bvigovernment.com; internet www.bvigovernment.org/governor.

Office of the Deputy Governor: Central Administration Bldg, Road Town, Tortola; tel. 494-3701; fax 494-6481; e-mail egeorges@bvigovernment.org; internet www.bvi.gov.vg.

Office of the Chief Minister: Road Town, Tortola; tel. 494-3701; fax 494-4435; e-mail pcsmo@bvigovernment.org.

Ministry of Communications and Works: Road Town, Tortola; tel. 494-3701; e-mail mcw@bvigovernment.org.

Ministry of Finance: Pasea Estate, Road Town, Tortola; tel. 494-3701; fax 494-6180; e-mail finance@mail.caribsurf.com.

Ministry of Health, Education, Culture and Welfare: Road Town, Tortola; tel. 494-3887.

Ministry of Natural Resources and Labour: Road Town, Tortola; tel. 494-3614.

All ministries are based in Road Town, Tortola, mainly at the Central Administration Building (fax 494-4435; e-mail tsm@bvigovernment.org; internet www.bvigovernment.org).

LEGISLATIVE COUNCIL

Speaker: REUBEN VANTERPOOL.

Clerk: JULIA LEONARD-MASSICOTT.

General Election, 17 May 1999

Party	% of vote	Seats
Virgin Islands Party	38.0	7
National Democratic Party	36.9	5
Concerned Citizens' Movement	4.0	1
United Party	7.7	—
Independent	13.4	—
Total	100.0	13

Political Organizations

Concerned Citizens' Movement (CCM): Road Town, Tortola; f. 1994 as successor to Independent People's Movement; Leader WALWYN BREWLEY.

National Democratic Party (NDP): Road Town, Tortola; f. 1998; Chair. RUSSELL HARRIGAN; Leader ORLANDO SMITH.

United Party (UP): Road Town, Tortola; Chair. ROY PICKERING; Leader CONRAD MADURO.

Virgin Islands Party (VIP): Road Town, Tortola; Leader RALPH T. O'NEAL.

Judicial System

Justice is administered by the Eastern Caribbean Supreme Court, based in Saint Lucia, which consists of two divisions: The High Court of Justice and the Court of Appeal. There are two resident High Court Judges, and a visiting Court of Appeal which is comprised of the Chief Justice and two Judges of Appeal and which sits twice a year in the British Virgin Islands. There is also a Magistrates' Court, which hears prescribed civil and criminal cases. The final Court of Appeal is the Privy Council in the United Kingdom.

Resident Judges: STANLEY MOORE, KENNETH BENJAMIN.

Magistrate: DORIEN TAYLOR.

Registrar: GAIL CHARLES.

Religion

CHRISTIANITY

The Roman Catholic Church

The diocese of St John's-Basseterre, suffragan to the archdiocese of Castries (Saint Lucia), includes Anguilla, Antigua and Barbuda, the British Virgin Islands, Montserrat and Saint Christopher and Nevis. The Bishop is resident in St John's, Antigua.

The Anglican Communion

The British and US Virgin Islands form a single, missionary diocese of the Episcopal Church of the United States of America. The Bishop of the Virgin Islands is resident on St Thomas in the US Virgin Islands.

Protestant Churches

Various Protestant denominations are represented, principally the Methodist Church. Others include the Seventh-day Adventist, Church of God and Baptist Churches.

The Press

The BVI Beacon: POB 3030, Road Town, Tortola; tel. 494-3767; fax 494-6267; e-mail bvibeacn@surfbvi.com; internet www.bvibeacon.com; f. 1984; Thursdays; covers local and international news; Editor LINNELL M. ABBOTT; circ. 3,400.

BVI Pennysaver: POB 3892, Lower Estate, Road Town, Tortola; tel. 494-8106; fax 494-8647.

The Island Sun: 112 Main St, Road Town, Tortola; tel. 494-2476; fax 494-7789; e-mail issun@candwbvi.net; internet www.islandsun.com; f. 1962; Fridays; Editor VERNON PICKERING; circ. 2,850.

The BVI StandPoint: POB 3892, Sea Cows Bay, Tortola; tel. 494-8106; fax 494-8647; e-mail bvistandpoint@surfbvi.com; internet www.bvistandpoint.com; Tuesdays; covers local and international news; Editor SUSAN HENIGHAN.

The Welcome: POB 133, Road Town, Tortola; tel. 494-2413; fax 494-4413; e-mail paul@bviwelcome.com; internet www.bviwelcome .com; f. 1971; every 2 months; general, tourist information; Publr PAUL BACKSHALL; Editor CLAUDIA COLLI; annual circ. 165,000.

Publishers

Caribbean Publishing Co (BVI) Ltd: Alcedo Hodge Bldg, 1 Wickhams Cay, POB 266, Road Town, Tortola; tel. 494-2060; fax 494-3060.

Island Publishing Co: POB 133, Road Town, Tortola; tel. 494-2413; fax 494-4413; e-mail iponline@caribsurf.com; internet www .bviwelcome.com; publishes *The British Virgin Islands Welcome Tourist Guide.*

Broadcasting and Communications

TELECOMMUNICATIONS

Telephone Services Management: Central Administration Building, Road Town, Tortola; tel. 494-4728; fax 494-6551; e-mail tsmu@caribsurf.com; internet www.bvigovernment.org/tsmu/index .htm; government agency.

Cable & Wireless (WI) Ltd: Cutlass Bldg, Wickhams Cay 1, POB 440, Road Town, Tortola; tel. 494-6092; fax 494-6967; e-mail laverne .hodge@cwbvi.cwplc.com; internet www.candw.vg; f. 1967; Gen. Man. KEITH LOWE.

CCT Boatphone Ltd: Town Office, Mill Mall, POB 267, Road Town, Tortola; tel. 494-3825; fax 494-4933; e-mail boatphon@caribsurf .com; internet www.britishvirginislands.com/boatphone; mobile cellular telephone operator.

BROADCASTING

Radio

Caribbean Broadcasting System: POB 3049, Road Town, Tortola; tel. 494-4990; commercial; Gen. Man. ALVIN KORNGOLD.

Virgin Islands Broadcasting Ltd—Radio ZBVI: Baughers Bay, POB 78, Road Town, Tortola; tel. 494-2430; fax 494-2010; e-mail zbvi@caribsurf.com; internet www.zbvi.com; f. 1965; commercial; Gen. Man. HARVEY HERBERT; CEO OLIN HESTER.

Television

BVI Cable TV: Fishlock Rd, POB 694, Road Town, Tortola; tel. 494-3205; fax 494-2952; programmes from US Virgin Islands and Puerto Rico; 53 channels; Man. Dir TODD KLINDWORTH.

Television West Indies Ltd (ZBTV): Broadcast Peak, Chawell, POB 34, Tortola; tel. 494-3332; commercial.

Finance

BANKING

Regulatory Authority

Financial Services Commission: f. 2002; independent financial services regulator; Chair. MICHAEL RIEGELS; CEO ROBERT MATHAVIOUS.

Commercial Banks

Banco Popular de Puerto Rico: POB 67, Road Town, Tortola; tel. 494-2117; fax 494-5294; Man. SANDRA SCATLIFFE.

Bank of East Asia (BVI) Ltd: POB 901, Road Town, Tortola; tel. 495-5588; fax 494-4513; Man. ELIZABETH WILKINSON.

Bank of Nova Scotia (Canada): Wickhams Cay 1, POB 434, Road Town, Tortola; tel. 494-2526; fax 494-4657; e-mail terry.bell@ scotiabankbvi.com; f. 1967; Man. TERRY C. BELL.

Chase Manhattan Bank: Wickhams Cay 1, POB 435, Road Town, Tortola; tel. 494-2662; fax 494-5106; f. 1968; Man. MARGUERITE D. HODGE.

Citco Bank (BVI) Ltd: Citco Bldg, Wickhams Cay, POB 662, Road Town, Tortola; tel. 494-2217; fax 494-3917; e-mail info@citco.com; internet www.citco.com; f. 1978; Man. RENE ROMER.

Croreridge Bank Ltd: POB 71, Road Town, Tortola; tel. 494-2233; fax 494-3547; Man. RICHARD A. PETERS.

DISA Bank (BVI) Ltd: POB 985, Road Town, Tortola; tel. 494-6036; fax 494-4980; Man. ROSA RESTREPO.

FirstCaribbean International Bank Ltd: Wickhams Cay 1, POB 70, Road Town, Tortola; tel. 494-2171; fax 494-4315; internet www .firstcaribbeanbank.com; f. 2003 following merger of Caribbean operations of Barclays Bank PLC and CIBC; CEO CHARLES PINK; Exec. Dir SHARON BROWN.

HSBC Guyerzeller Bank (BVI) Ltd: POB 3162, Road Town, Tortola; tel. 494-5416; fax 494-5417; e-mail rhbvi@surfbvi.com; Dir KENNETH W. MORGAN.

Rathbone Bank (BVI) Ltd: POB 986, Road Town, Tortola; tel. 494-6544; fax 494-6532; e-mail rathbone@surfbvi.com; Man. CORNEL BAPTISTE.

VP Bank (BVI) Ltd: POB 3463, Road Town, Tortola; tel. 494-1100; fax 494-1199; internet www.vpbankbvi.com; Gen-Man. PETER REICHENSTEIN.

Development Bank

Development Bank of the British Virgin Islands: Wickhams Cay 1, POB 275, Road Town, Tortola; tel. 494-3737; fax 494-3119; state-owned; Chair. MEADE MALONE.

INSURANCE

Caribbean Insurance Ltd: POB 129, Road Town, Tortola; tel. 494-2728; fax 494-4394; Man. JOHN WILLIAMS.

Marine Insurance Office (BVI) Ltd: POB 874, Road Town, Tortola; tel. 494-3795; fax 494-4540; Man. WESLEY WOODHOUSE.

Several US and other foreign companies have agents in the British Virgin Islands.

Trade and Industry

GOVERNMENT AGENCY

Trade and Investment Promotion Department: Office of the Chief Minister, Road Town, Tortola; tel. 494-3701; fax 494-6413.

CHAMBER OF COMMERCE

British Virgin Islands Chamber of Commerce and Hotel Association: James Fretzt Bldg, Wickhams Cay 1, POB 376, Road Town, Tortola; tel. 294-2947; fax 494-6179; e-mail bviccha@surfbvi.com; internet www.bvihotels.org; f. 1986; Chair. KEDRICK MALONE; Exec. Dir NADINE BATTLE.

UTILITIES

Electricity

British Virgin Islands Electricity Corpn (BVIEC): Long Bush, POB 268, Road Town, Tortola; tel. 494-3911; fax 494-4291; e-mail bviecce@caribsurf.com; f. 1979; state-owned, privatization pending in 2002; Chair. ALEXANDER SHIRLEY.

Transport

ROADS

There are about 160 km (100 miles) of motorable roads, and in 1997 there were about 8,000 motor vehicles in use. In 1996 work began on a dual carriageway road in the Road Town area, at a cost of US $4.8m.

Public Works Department: Baughers Bay, Tortola; tel. 468-2722; fax 468-4740; e-mail pwd@mailbvigovernment.com; responsible for road maintenance.

SHIPPING

There are two direct steamship services, one from the United Kingdom and one from the USA. Motor launches maintain daily mail and passenger services with St Thomas and St John, US Virgin Islands. A new cruise-ship pier, built at a cost of US $6.9m. with assistance from the Caribbean Development Bank, was opened in Road Town in 1994 and work on its expansion was begun in 1998.

British Virgin Islands Port Authority: Port Purcell, POB 4, Road Town, Tortola; tel. 494-3435; fax 494-2642; e-mail bviports@ candwbvi.net; internet www.bviports.org; Man. Dir GENE E. CREQUE (acting).

Tropical Shipping: POB 250, Pasea Estate, Road Town, Tortola; tel. 494-5288; fax 494-3505; e-mail vgonzalez@tropical.com; internet www.tropical.com; Man. VINCE GONZALEZ.

CIVIL AVIATION

Beef Island Airport, about 16 km (10 miles) from Road Town, has a runway with a length of 1,100 m (3,700 ft). A new US $65m. airport terminal was opened at the airport in March 2002. In February 2000 work began to lengthen the runway to 1,500 m (4,700 ft). Upon completion of the renovation, scheduled for late 2003, the airport was to be renamed Terrence B. Lettsome Airport. Captain Auguste George Airport on Anegada has been designated an international point of entry and was resurfaced in the late 1990s. The airport runway on Virgin Gorda was to be extended to 1,200 m (4,000 ft) to allow larger aircraft to land.

Director of Civil Aviation: MILTON CREQUE, tel. 494-3701.

Tourism

The main attraction of the islands is their tranquillity and clear waters, which provide excellent facilities for sailing, fishing, diving and other water sports. In 1998 there 1,231 hotel rooms in the islands and 365 rooms in guest-houses and rented apartments. There are also many charter yachts offering overnight accommodation. There were some 303,600 stop-over visitors and 188,500 cruise-ship passengers in 2000. The majority of tourists are from the USA (59.6% of stop-over tourists in 1999). Some 146 cruise ships called at the islands in 1998. Receipts from tourism totalled US $292.1m. in 2000.

British Virgin Islands Tourist Board: Social Security Bldg, Waterfront Dr., POB 134, Road Town, Tortola; tel. 494-3134; fax 494-3866; e-mail bvitourb@caribsurf.com; internet www .bvitouristboard.com; Dir of Tourism ANNE LENNARD (acting).

British Virgin Islands Chamber of Commerce and Hotel Association: see Chamber of Commerce.

THE CAYMAN ISLANDS

Introductory Survey

Location, Climate, Language, Religion, Flag, Capital

The Cayman Islands lie about 290 km (180 miles) west-north-west of Jamaica and consist of three main islands: Grand Cayman and, to the north-east, Little Cayman and Cayman Brac. The climate is tropical but is tempered by the trade winds, with a cool season between November and March, when temperatures average 24°C (75°F). The rainy season lasts from May until October. Mean annual rainfall is 1,524 mm (60 ins). The official language is English. Many Christian churches are represented. The flag is the British 'Blue Ensign', with the islands' coat of arms (a golden lion on a red background above three stars in green, representing the three main islands, superimposed on wavy lines of blue and white, the shield surmounted by a torse of white and blue bearing a yellow pineapple behind a green turtle, and with the motto 'He hath founded it upon the seas' on a scroll beneath) on a white roundel in the fly. The capital is George Town, on the island of Grand Cayman.

Recent History

The Cayman Islands came under acknowledged British rule in 1670 and were settled mainly from Jamaica and by privateers and buccaneers. The islands of Little Cayman and Cayman Brac were permanently settled only in 1833, and until 1877 there was no administrative connection between them and Grand Cayman. A representative assembly first sat in 1832. The islands formed a dependency of Jamaica until 1959, and the Governor of Jamaica held responsibility for the Cayman Islands until Jamaican independence in 1962, when a separate administrator was appointed (the title was changed to that of Governor in 1971). The 1959 Constitution was revised in 1972, 1992 and 1994 (see below).

For many years there have been no formal political parties on the islands, despite the emergence of a nascent party political system during the 1960s with the formation, in 1961, of the National Democratic Party (NDP), as part of a campaign for self-government. The Christian Democratic Party was formed as a conservative opposition. Both parties disappeared within a few years despite the electoral success of the NDP, largely owing to the system of gubernatorial nomination to the Executive Council. In the 1970s elections for the 12 elective seats in the Legislative Assembly came to be contested by 'teams' of candidates, as well as by independents. Two such teams were formed, Progress and Dignity (the more conservative) and Unity, but all candidates were committed to augmenting the economic success of the Caymans, and favoured continued dependent status. There are no plans for independence, and the majority of the population wish to maintain the islands' links with the United Kingdom.

At elections in November 1980 the Unity team, led by Jim Bodden, took eight of the 12 seats. In the November 1984 elections opposition independents won nine seats, aided by public disquiet at the rapid growth of the immigrant work-force, and the implications of the recent US challenges to the Cayman Islands' bank secrecy laws. In 1987 the Legislative Assembly successfully sought stricter regulations of status and residency for those able to participate in elections, in an attempt to protect the political rights of native Caymanians (in view of the very large immigrant population). At a general election in November 1988 seven of the existing members were returned, and five new members were elected. Prior to the election the teams had regrouped into more informal coalitions, indicating the primacy of personal over 'party' affiliations.

In July 1990 the Legislative Assembly approved proposals to review the Constitution, and in January 1991 the British Government sent two commissioners to the Territory to discuss possible amendments. The implementation of most recommendations, including the appointment of a Chief Minister, was postponed pending a general election to be held in 1992. One of the amendments, however, which involved increasing the number of elective seats in the Legislative Assembly to 15, was adopted in March 1992. The proposed reforms had prompted the formation, in mid-1991, of the Territory's first political organization since the 1960s, the Progressive Democratic Party (PDP). During 1992 the organization developed into a coalition and was renamed the National Team. At the general election in November 1992 National Team members secured 12 of the elective seats in the newly-enlarged Legislative Assembly, while independent candidates won the remaining three. The three elected members of the Executive Council who stood for re-election were defeated, while the fourth did not contest the seat. The new Government opted to revoke the provisions in the Constitution for a Chief Minister; however, it decided to introduce a ministerial system and to create a fifth ministerial portfolio. The amendments took effect on 1 February 1994. In November of that year James Ryan was appointed Chief Secretary, following the retirement of Lemuel Hurlston.

At a general election on 20 November 1996 the governing National Team remained in power, although with a reduced majority, winning nine seats in the Legislative Assembly. Two new groupings, the Democratic Alliance and Team Cayman (which had formed in opposition to the Government's alleged mismanagement of the public debt and of Cayman Airways) secured two seats and one seat, respectively. Independent candidates won three seats.

In October 1997 the National Team in the Legislative Assembly urged the resignation of the Minister of Community Development, Sport, Youth Affairs and Culture, McKeeva Bush, after it was alleged that a bank of which he was a director had authorized fraudulent loans totalling some US $1.1m. Bush (who denied any knowledge of the alleged corruption) was dismissed from his ministerial post later in the month, and replaced by Julianna O'Connor Connolly, the first woman minister on the island.

In March 1999 the Government of the United Kingdom published draft legislation pertaining to its relationship with its Overseas Dependencies, which were to be renamed United Kingdom Overseas Territories (and had been referred to as such since February 1998). The legislation proposed the extension of British citizenship to the citizens of Overseas Territories, although it also required its Territories to amend their legislation on human rights and on the regulation of the financial services sector to meet international standards. The Cayman Islands were praised for the introduction in 1998 of laws on tax evasion, and for strengthening the regulatory powers of the

Monetary Authority, although concern was expressed that homosexuality remained a criminal offence in the islands. The issue of the legal status of homosexuality in the Cayman Islands had been highlighted in January 1998 by the authorities' refusal to permit a stopover by a US cruise liner whose 900 passengers were homosexual men.

In late April 1999 representatives of the European Union held meetings with the overseas territories of member states to discuss proposed reforms of legislation relating to the financial services sector. The Cayman Islands delegation defended the islands' standards of regulation, arguing that the islands had implemented some of the toughest laws in the world against money-laundering, and that proposals to abolish the Cayman Islands' laws on banking secrecy would place the islands at a disadvantage, compared with the financial centres of Switzerland and Luxembourg. In early June the Cayman Islands announced that it was to seek certification under the UN's Offshore Initiative, and that consequently a UN agency, the Global Programme against Money Laundering, was to undertake a review of the Territory's financial systems and regulations. In the same month, however, the Cayman Islands was one of the four countries accused by the French Government of engaging in 'modern-day piracy' and of possessing faulty banking controls. In July two Caymanian citizens and a US citizen were arrested in connection with suspected money-laundering at the Eurobank offshore bank, which was subsequently liquidated.

In August 1999 an American citizen, John Matthewson, was sentenced to five years' probation by a US court on charges of money-laundering in the Cayman Islands. Matthewson had reportedly escaped a prison sentence by revealing to US investigators the extent of his activities in the Cayman Islands and the extent to which the islands' financial system benefited those seeking to evade US taxation. The US Government subsequently charged several of Matthewson's clients with tax evasion, and it was widely believed that the case had seriously damaged the islands' reputation both for secrecy and as a reputable financial centre. However, the island authorities claimed that the Royal Cayman Islands Police had co-operated fully with the US investigators, and also observed that in 1998 the islands' policy of co-operation with US investigators in their efforts to prevent money-laundering had been singled out for praise in the US *International Narcotics Control Strategy Report*.

In October 1999 several buildings in the Northward Prison compound were destroyed during a serious prison riot. Overcrowded conditions were reported to have been the cause of the disturbances; the prison, which had been designed to hold 168 people, in fact contained 308 prisoners. Several prisoners were subsequently transferred to prisons in the United Kingdom, while later in the month a group of British police officers arrived in the Cayman Islands to assist local police with security duties.

Drugs-related crime continued to be a serious problem in the 1990s, when an estimated 75% of all thefts and burglaries in the islands were attributed, directly or indirectly, to the drugs trade. The Mutual Legal Assistance Treaty (signed in 1986, and ratified by the US Senate in 1990) between the Cayman Islands and the USA provides for the mutual exchange of information for use in combating crime (particularly drugs-trafficking and the diversion of funds gained illegally from the drugs trade). Further legislation relating to the abuse of the financial sector by criminal organizations was approved in November 1996.

In a general election held on 8 November 2000 the governing National Team suffered a heavy defeat, losing six of its nine seats, including that held by Truman Bodden, the Leader of Government Business. The Minister of Agriculture, John McLean, lost his seat to his cousin, Arden McLean. The newly elected Legislative Assembly appointed Kurt Tibbets of the Democratic Alliance as Leader of Government Business. Important issues in the election campaign included the islands' constitutional status, immigration, housing and environmental protection.

In an unprecedented development in November 2001, several members of the Legislative Assembly, dissatisfied with the Government's leadership during the economic slowdown, formed the United Democratic Party (UDP). McKeeva Bush, the leader of the new party and Deputy Leader of Government Business and Minister of Tourism, Environment and Transport, claimed that at least 10 members of the 15-member Assembly were UDP supporters. Subsequently, the passing of a motion of 'no confidence' (by nine votes to five, with one abstention)

against the Leader of Government Business resulted in Tibbets and Edna Moyle, the Minister of Community Development, Women's Affairs, Youth and Sport, leaving the Executive Council. Bush became the new Leader of Government Business, whilst two other legislators, Gilbert McLean and Frank McField, both members of the UDP, joined the cabinet. Also in November, the Concerned Caymanians group was established; the group planned a petition to force an early general election following the removal of Tibbets. In May 2002, at the UDP's inaugural convention, Bush was formally elected leader of the party. In the same month it was announced that the five opposition members of the legislative assembly had formed a new political party, the People's Progressive Movement, led by Tibbets.

In March 2002 the three-member Constitutional Review Commission, appointed by the Governor in May 2001, submitted a new draft constitution. The proposed constitution had to be debated by the Legislative Assembly and then approved by the British Parliament before being formally adopted. The draft constitution, made public in April, included the creation of the office of Chief Minister, proposed a full ministerial government, and incorporated a bill of rights. The opposition demanded a referendum on the recommendations, on the grounds that the UDP had rejected several of the proposals, despite strong public support for the changes, but Bush forwarded the proposals to the British Foreign and Commonwealth Office (FCO), via the Governor's office. In December Bush and the leader of the opposition, Tibbets, travelled to the United Kingdom in order to review the proposed constitution with FCO officials. Consensus, however, proved impossible to achieve, and the FCO was expected to produce a revised draft constitution for public discussion and debate in early 2003.

In May 2002 the British Overseas Territories Act, having received royal assent in the United Kingdom in February, came into force and granted British citizenship to the people of its Overseas Territories, including the Cayman Islands. Under the new law Caymanians would be able to hold British passports and work in the United Kingdom and elsewhere in the European Union. Also in May, the Cayman Islands became an associate member of the Caribbean Community and Common Market (CARICOM, see p. 155). In the same month Bruce Dinwiddy succeeded Peter Smith as Governor.

In January 2003 Bush accused the United Kingdom of undermining the course of Cayman Islands' justice, after a routine money-laundering case was dismissed amid allegations of espionage and obstruction of justice by British intelligence agents. The trial collapsed after it was alleged that the Director of the Cayman Islands Financial Reporting Unit and a key witness in the trial, had passed information about the case to an unnamed agency of the British Government, understood to be the Secret Intelligence Service (MI6). It was claimed that MI6 wished to protect the names of its sources within the Caribbean offshore banking community. Bush demanded the British Government pay for the failed trial, estimated to cost some US $5m., and for any negative repercussions the affair might have for the reputation of the territory's banking sector. The United Kingdom, however, refused to compensate the Cayman Islands and maintained that although its intelligence agencies might have helped in the investigation, they had never interfered in the case. In March the Attorney-General, David Ballantyne, resigned amid accusations that he was aware that British intelligence agents were working covertly in the Cayman Islands; Samuel Bulgin, the Solicitor-General, replaced Ballantyne on a temporary basis.

Government

Under the revised Constitution of 1994, the Governor, who is appointed by the British monarch, is responsible for external affairs, defence, internal security and the public service. The Governor is Chairman of the Executive Council, comprising three members appointed by the Governor and five members elected by the Legislative Assembly. The Legislative Assembly comprises three official members and 15 members elected by universal adult suffrage for a period of four years.

Defence

The United Kingdom is responsible for the defence of the Cayman Islands.

Economic Affairs

In 2000, according to estimates by the Caribbean Development Bank (CDB), the Cayman Islands' gross domestic product (GDP) was US $1,773.8m., equivalent to some $43,369 per head. During 1989–1995, according to estimates, the population increased at an average annual rate of 4.8%, while GDP increased, in real terms, by 4.1% per year during 1990–2001; growth in 2001 was estimated at 1.5%.

Agriculture (which engaged only 1.4% of the employed labour force in 1995 and provided some 0.5% of GDP in 1997) is limited by infertile soil, low rainfall and high labour costs. The principal crops are citrus fruits and bananas, and some other produce for local consumption. Flowers (particularly orchids) are produced for export. Livestock-rearing consists of beef cattle, poultry (mainly for eggs) and pigs. The traditional activity of turtle-hunting has virtually disappeared; the turtle farm (the only commercial one in the world) now produces mainly for domestic consumption (and serves as a research centre), following the imposition of US restrictions on the trade in turtle products in 1979. Fishing is mainly for lobster and shrimp.

Industry, engaging 12.6% of the employed labour force in 1995 and providing some 15.5% of GDP in 1997, consists mainly of construction and related manufacturing, some food-processing and tourist-related light industries. The construction sector contributed an estimated 9.3% of GDP in 1999, while manufacturing activities accounted for only about 2.3% of the total in that year. Energy requirements are satisfied by the import of mineral fuels and related products (10.9% of total imports in 1996).

Service industries dominate the Caymanian economy, accounting for 86.0% of employment in 1995 and contributing 83.9% of GDP in 1999. The tourist industry is the principal economic activity, and in 1991 accounted for 22.9% of GDP and employed, directly and indirectly, some 50% of the working population. The industry earned an estimated US $559.2m. in 2000. Most visitors are from the USA (71.0% of tourist arrivals in 1999). The Cayman Islands is one of the largest 'offshore' financial centres in the world; in July 2002 there were 527 banks and trust companies and 4,077 mutual funds on the islands, according to the Caribbean Development Bank. In 1995 the financial services sector engaged 18.9% of the working population, and in 1999 contributed about 36.0% of GDP.

In 2001 the Cayman Islands recorded an estimated trade deficit of US $645.1m. (commodity exports represented less than 1% of the value of total imports). Receipts from tourism and the financial sector, remittances and capital inflows normally offset the trade deficit. The principal source of imports is the USA (which provided some 76.7% of total imports in 1996), which is also one of the principal markets for exports (34.6% in 1994). Other major trading partners in 1996 included the United Kingdom, Japan and the Netherlands Antilles (which received 10.6% of total exports in that year). The principal exports in the 1980s were meat (mainly turtle meat, the export of which was subsequently banned under international treaty) and chemical products (in the late 1980s and early 1990s second-hand cars were a significant export). Principal exports in the 1990s were fish and cut flowers. The principal imports are machinery and transport equipment (26.0% of total imports in 1996), foodstuffs (18.6%), manufactured articles (18.5%) and basic manufactures (13.6%).

A government surplus in its recurrent operations of US $58m. was recorded in 1999. Capital development aid from the United Kingdom ceased in 1982. In 1998 official development assistance totalled US $0.2m. At the end of 1999 the public debt stood at US $114.8m. The average annual rate of inflation was 3.4% in 1990–2001 and stood at an estimated 1.2% in 2001. According to official census figures, only 63% of the resident population of the islands were Caymanian in 1994 (compared with 79% in 1980). At the census of October 1999 some 5.3% of the labour force were unemployed.

The United Kingdom is responsible for the external affairs of the Cayman Islands, and the dependency has the status of Overseas Territory in association with the European Union (EU, see p. 199). The Cayman Islands has associate-member status in the CARICOM (see p. 155) and was expected to become a full member in 2003. The Cayman Islands is also a member of CARICOM's Caribbean Development Bank (see p. 159).

Both the principal economic sectors, offshore finance and tourism, benefit from the Cayman Islands' political stability, good infrastructure and extensive development. The financial sector, which benefits from an absence of taxation and of foreign exchange regulations, recorded consistently high levels of growth during the 1990s, and provided an estimated 30% of GDP in 1998. The banking sector was reckoned to be the world's

fifth largest in 2000, owing to the absence of direct taxation, lenient regulation and strict confidentiality laws. The Cayman Islands have a policy of openly confronting the issues of financial transparency and of money-laundering, and an information exchange treaty with the USA was ratified in 1990. However, despite the efforts of the authorities, the vulnerability of the islands' financial services sector to exploitation by criminal organizations continued to cause concern, and it was feared that if the Government did not impose further controls, then the United Kingdom Government would be obliged to impose more stringent regulatory measures in response to international pressure. Indeed, in June 2000 the Cayman Islands were included on a list of harmful tax regimes compiled by an agency of the Organisation for Economic Co-operation and Development (OECD) and were urged to make legislative changes, introducing greater legal and administrative transparency. The Government said that it would seek to be removed from the list as swiftly as possible and pledged to adopt international standards of legal and administrative transparency by 2005. In 2001, following stricter regulation of the private banking sector, the Cayman Islands were removed from the blacklist. In November, in a further move to increase international confidence in its financial regulation, the Government signed a tax information exchange agreement with the USA, designed to reduce the potential for abuse of the tax system. Tourism continued to expand in the 1990s, although the Government attempted to limit tourist numbers in order to minimize damage to the environment, particularly the coral reef, and to preserve the islands' reputation as a destination for visitors of above-average wealth. Although the economy continued to grow in the late 1990s, consultant economic advisers warned the Government that increases in public spending, and the increased subsidization of Cayman Airways, were unsustainable, while fears remained that reforms to the financial services sector would reduce the islands' ability to attract international business. Indeed, in October 2001 the Chamber of Commerce linked an economic downturn to the negative impact of OECD pressure on the financial services sector, although the global economic slowdown and the adverse affects on the tourism industry of the September 2001 terrorist attacks in the USA were also regarded as factors in the economic decline. In late 2002 the financial sector faced further disruption when the United Kingdom, under pressure from an EU investigation into tax evasion, demanded that the Cayman Islands disclose the identities and account details of Europeans holding private savings accounts on the islands. The Cayman Islands, along with some other British Overseas Territories facing similar demands, claimed it was being treated unfairly compared with more powerful European countries, such as Switzerland and Luxembourg, and refused to make any concessions.

Education

Schooling is compulsory for children between the ages of five and 15 years. It is provided free in 10 government-run primary schools, and there are also three state secondary schools, as well as six church-sponsored schools (five of which offer secondary as well as primary education). Primary education, from five years of age, lasts for six years. Secondary education is for seven years. Government expenditure on education in 1994 was CI $31.5m. (20.9% of total spending). Some CI $17.7m. (9.9% of total expenditure) was allocated for education in 1995.

Public Holidays

2003: 1 January (New Year's Day), 5 March (Ash Wednesday), 18 April (Good Friday), 21 April (Easter Monday), 19 May (Discovery Day), 9 June (Whit Monday), 16 June (Queen's Official Birthday), 7 July (Constitution Day), 11 November (Remembrance Day), 25–26 December (Christmas).

2004: 1 January (New Year's Day), 25 February (Ash Wednesday), 9 April (Good Friday), 12 April (Easter Monday), 17 May (Discovery Day), 31 May (Whit Monday), 14 June (Queen's Official Birthday), 5 July (Constitution Day), 11 November (Remembrance Day), 25–26 December (Christmas).

Weights and Measures

The imperial system is in use.

Statistical Survey

Source: Government Information Services, Cricket Square, Elgin Avenue, George Town, Grand Cayman; tel. 949-8092; fax 949-5936.

AREA AND POPULATION

Area: 262 sq km (102 sq miles). The main island of Grand Cayman is about 197 sq km (76 sq miles), about one-half of which is swamp Cayman Brac is 39 sq km (15 sq miles); Little Cayman is 26 sq km (11 sq miles).

Population: 39,410 (males 19,311; females 20,099) at census of 10 October 1999: Grand Cayman 37,473; Cayman Brac 1,822; Little Cayman 115. *Mid-2001* (estimate): Population 41,000 (Source: UN, *Population and Vital Statistics Report*).

Density (mid-2001): 156.5 per sq km.

Principal Towns (population at 1999 census): George Town (capital) 20,626; West Bay 8,243; Bodden Town 5,764. *2001:* George Town 21,000 (Source: UN, *World Urbanization Prospects: The 2001 Revision*).

Births, Marriages and Deaths (estimates, 2001): Live births 622 (birth rate 15.0 per 1,000); Marriage rate 9.7 per 1,000 (2000); Deaths 132 (death rate 3.2 per 1,000).

Expectation of Life (years at birth): 77 in 2000.

Economically Active Population (sample survey, persons aged 15 years and over, October 1995): Agriculture, hunting, forestry and fishing 270; Manufacturing 320; Electricity, gas and water 245; Construction 1,805; Trade, restaurants and hotels 5,555; Transport, storage and communications 1,785; Financing, insurance, real estate and business services 3,570; Community, social and personal serv-ices 5,295; Total employment 18,845 (males 8,930, females 9,910. Figures exclude persons seeking work for the first time, totalling 100 (males 60, females 40), and other unemployed persons, totalling 900 (males 455, females 445) (Source: ILO). *1999* (census of 10 October): Total employed 25,459 (males 12,949, females 12,510); Unemployed 1,341; Total labour force 26,800.

HEALTH AND WELFARE

Physicians (per 1,000 head, 1999): 2.15.

Health expenditure: % of GDP (1997): 4.2.

Health expenditure: public (% of total, 1995): 53.2.
Source: Pan American Health Organization.
For definitions see explanatory note on p. vi.

AGRICULTURE, ETC.

Livestock ('000 head, FAO estimates, 2001): Cattle 1.3; Goats 0.3; Pigs 0.4; Chickens 6. Source: FAO.

Fishing (metric tons, live weight, 2000): Total catch 125 (marine fishes). Source: FAO, *Yearbook of Fishery Statistics*.

INDUSTRY

Electric Energy (consumption, million kWh): 347.0 in 1999; 369.4 in 2000; 393.3 in 2001. Source: Caribbean Utilities Company Ltd.

FINANCE

Currency and Exchange Rates: 100 cents = 1 Cayman Islands dollar (CI $). *Sterling, US Dollar and Euro Equivalents* (31 December 2002): £1 sterling = CI $1.3432; US $1 = 83.33 CI cents; €1 = 87.39 CI cents; CI $100 = £74.45 = US $120.00 = €114.43. *Exchange rate:* Fixed at CI $1 = US $1.20.

Budget (CI $ million, 1999): *Revenue:* Import duties 133.9; Fees 71.1; Licences 26.3; Tax revenue 20.9; Other current revenue 27.4; Total 279.6. *Expenditure:* Health, social welfare, drug abuse prevention and rehabilitation 52.7; Tourism, commerce, transport and works 41.8; Education, aviation and planning 39.0; Internal and external affairs 32.7; Finance and economic development 30.4; Agriculture, communication, environment and natural resources 23.1; Community affairs, sports, women, youth and culture 12.9; Governor's office 4.5; Legal affairs 2.7; Total 239.8.

Cost of Living (Consumer Price Index; base: 1990 = 100): 139.7 in 1999; 143.4 in 2000; 145.1 in 2001. Source: ILO.

Gross Domestic Product (estimates, CI $ million in current prices): 1,414 in 1999; 1,490 in 2000; 1,550 in 2001.

Gross Domestic Product by Economic Activity (CI $ million in current prices, 1991): Primary industries 5; Manufacturing 9; Electricity, gas and water 19; Construction 54; Trade, restaurants and hotels 138; Transport, storage and communications 65; Finance, insurance, real estate and business services 210; Community, social and personal services 42; Government services 63; Statistical discrepancy 1; Sub-total 606; Import duties less imputed bank service charge 11; GDP in purchasers' values 617.

EXTERNAL TRADE

Principal Commodities (US $ million): *Imports c.i.f.* (1996): Food and live animals 70.3; Beverages and tobacco 15.2; Mineral fuels, lubricants, etc. 41.2 (Refined petroleum products 39.8); Chemicals 22.2; Basic manufactures 51.3; Machinery and transport equipment 98.4; Miscellaneous manufactured articles 69.9; Total (incl. others) 377.9. *Exports f.o.b.* (1996): Total 3.96.

Principal Trading Partners (US $ million): *Imports c.i.f.* (1996): Japan 8.2; Netherlands Antilles 40.1; United Kingdom 6.8; USA 289.7; Total (incl. others) 377.9. *Exports f.o.b.* (1994): USA 0.9; Total 2.6.
Source: mainly UN, *International Trade Statistics Yearbook*.

TRANSPORT

Road Traffic (2000): Motor vehicles in use 24,791.

Shipping: *International Freight Traffic* ('000 metric tons, 1995): Goods loaded 735 (1990); Goods unloaded 239,138 (2000). *Cargo Vessels* (1995): Vessels 15, Calls at port 266. *Merchant Fleet* (vessels registered at 31 December 2001): 144; Total displacement 2,053,934 grt. (Source: Lloyd's Register-Fairplay, *World Fleet Statistics*).

TOURISM

Visitor Arrivals: 1,214,397 (arrivals by air 342,993, cruise-ship passengers 871,404) in 1998; 1,358,217 (arrivals by air 322,695, cruise-ship passengers 1,035,522) in 1999; 1,346,886 (arrivals by air 316,029, cruise-ship passengers 1,030,857) in 2000.

Visitor Expenditure (estimates, US $ million): 502.0 in 1998; 494.0 in 1999; 559.2 in 2000 (Source: Caribbean Development Bank, *Social and Economic Indicators 2001*).

COMMUNICATIONS MEDIA

Radio Receivers: 36,000 in use in 1997.

Television Receivers: 23,239 in use in 1999.

Telephones: 34,702 main lines in use in 2000.

Facsimile Machines: 116 in use in 1993.

Mobile Cellular Telephones (subscribers): 11,370 in 2000.

Internet Users: 14,908 (4,259 households) in 1999.

Daily Newspapers: 1 (circulation 10,500) in 2000.

EDUCATION

Institutions (2001): 10 state primary schools (with 2,246 pupils); 9 private primary and secondary schools (2,238 pupils); 3 state high schools (1,750 pupils); 1 community college; 1 private college (519 pupils.

Directory

The Constitution

The Constitution of 1959 was revised in 1972, 1992 and 1994. Under its terms, the Governor, who is appointed for four years, is responsible for defence and internal security, external affairs, and the public service. The Executive Council comprises the Chief Secretary, the Financial Secretary, the Attorney-General and five other Ministers elected by the Legislative Assembly from their own number. The Governor assigns ministerial portfolios to the elected members of the Executive Council. The office of Administrative Secretary was abolished in April 1992 and replaced by the re-established post of Chief Secretary. There are 15 elected members of the Legislative Assembly (elected by direct, universal adult suffrage for a term of four years) and three official members appointed by the Governor. The Speaker presides over the Assembly. The United Kingdom retains full control over foreign affairs. In May 2001 the Governor appointed a Constitutional Review Commission to make recommendations on changes to the Cayman Islands' political structure and processes.

The Government

Governor: BRUCE DINWIDDY (assumed office May 2002).

EXECUTIVE COUNCIL
(April 2003)

Chairman: The Governor.

Chief Secretary*: JAMES RYAN.

Attorney-General*: SAMUEL BULGIN (acting).

Financial Secretary*: GEORGE MCCARTHY.

Leader of Government Business and Minister of Tourism, Environment and Transport: W. MCKEEVA BUSH.

Deputy Leader of Government Business and Minister of Planning, Communications, Works and Information Technology: LINFORD PIERSON.

Minister of Community Services and Youth and Women's Affairs: FRANK MCFIELD.

Minister of Education, Human Resources and Culture: ROY BODDEN.

Minister of Health, District Administration and Agriculture: GILBERT MCLEAN.

A District Commissioner, Jenny Manderson, represents the Governor on Cayman Brac and Little Cayman.

* Appointed by the Governor.

LEGISLATIVE ASSEMBLY

Members: The Chief Secretary, the Financial Secretary, the Attorney-General, and 15 elected members. The most recent general election to the Assembly was on 8 November 2000. In February 1991 a Speaker was elected to preside over the Assembly (despite provision for such a post in the Constitution, the functions of the Speaker had hitherto been assumed by the Governor).

Speaker: JULIANA O'CONNOR-CONNOLLY.

Leader of Government Business: W. MCKEEVA BUSH.

GOVERNMENT OFFICES

Office of the Governor: Government Administration Bldg, Elgin Ave, George Town, Grand Cayman; tel. 949-7900; fax 949-7544; e-mail staffoff@candw.ky.

All official Government offices and Ministries are located in the Government Administration Bldg, Elgin Ave, George Town, Grand Cayman.

Political Organizations

People's Progressive Movement: Grand Cayman; f. 2002; Leader KURT TIBBETTS.

United Democratic Party (UDP): Grand Cayman; f. 2001; Leader W. MCKEEVA BUSH; Deputy Leader LINFORD PIERSON; Chair. BILLY REID.

Judicial System

There is a Grand Court of the Islands (with Supreme Court status), a Summary Court, a Youth Court and a Coroner's Court. The Grand Court has jurisdiction in all civil matters, admiralty matters, and in trials on indictment. Appeals lie to the Court of Appeal of the Cayman Islands and beyond that to the Privy Council in the United Kingdom. The Summary Courts deal with criminal and civil matters (up to a certain limit defined by law) and appeals lie to the Grand Court.

Chief Justice: ANTHONY SMELLIE.

President of the Court of Appeal: EDWARD ZACCA.

Solicitor-General: SAMUEL BULGIN.

Registrar of the Grand Court of the Islands: DELENE M. BODDEN, Court's Office, George Town, Grand Cayman; tel. 949-4296; fax 949-9856.

Religion

CHRISTIANITY

The oldest-established denominations are (on Grand Cayman) the United Church of Jamaica and Grand Cayman (Presbyterian), and (on Cayman Brac) the Baptist Church. Anglicans are adherents of the Church in the Province of the West Indies (Grand Cayman forms part of the diocese of Jamaica). Within the Roman Catholic Church, the Cayman Islands forms part of the archdiocese of Kingston in Jamaica. Other denominations include the Church of God, Church of God (Full Gospel), Church of Christ, Seventh-day Adventist, Wesleyan Holiness, Jehovah's Witnesses, Church of the Latter Day Saints, Bahá'í and Church of God (Universal). In 1999 there were an estimated 90 churches in the Cayman Islands, including seven churches on Cayman Brac, and a Baptist Church on Little Cayman.

The Press

Cayman Islands Journal: POB 173, George Town, Grand Cayman; tel. 949-5111; fax 949-7033; monthly; broadsheet business newspaper; Publr BRIAN UZZELL.

Chamber in Action: POB 1000, George Town, Grand Cayman; tel. 949-8090; fax 949-0220; e-mail info@caymanchamber.ky; internet www.caymanchamber.ky; f. 1965; monthly; newsletter of the Cayman Islands Chamber of Commerce; Editor WIL PINEAU; circ. 5,000.

The Daily Caymanian Compass: POB 1365, Grand Cayman; tel. 949-5111; fax 949-7033; f. 1965; 5 a week; Publr BRIAN UZZELL; circ. 9,500.

The New Caymanian: POB 1139, George Town, Grand Cayman; tel. 949-7414; fax 949-0036; weekly; Publr and Editor-in-Chief PETER JACKSON.

Publishers

Caribbean Publishing Co (Cayman) Ltd: Paddington Place, Suite 306, POB 688, George Town, Grand Cayman; tel. 949-7027; fax 949-8366; f. 1978.

Cayman Free Press Ltd: POB 1365, Shedden Rd, George Town, Grand Cayman; tel. 949-5111; fax 949-7033.

Cayman Publishing Co: POB 173, George Town, Grand Cayman; tel. 949-5111; fax 949-7033.

Progressive Publications Ltd: Economy Printers Bldg, POB 764, George Town, Grand Cayman; tel. 949-5780; fax 949-7674.

Broadcasting and Communications

TELECOMMUNICATIONS

Cable and Wireless (Cayman Islands) Ltd: Anderson Sq., POB 293, George Town, Grand Cayman; tel. 949-7800; fax 949-7962; e-mail cs@candw.ky; internet www.candw.ky; f. 1966; Man. Dir TONEY HEART; Gen. Man. TIMOTHY ADAM.

BROADCASTING

Radio

Radio Cayman: Elgin Ave, POB 1110, George Town, Grand Cayman; tel. 949-7799; fax 949-6536; e-mail radiocym@candw.ky; started full-time broadcasting 1976; govt-owned commercial radio station; service in English; Dir LOXLEY E. M. BANKS.

Radio Heaven 97 FM: POB 31481 SMB, Industrial Park, George Town, Grand Cayman; tel. 945-2797; fax 945-2707; e-mail heaven97@candw.ky; f. 1997; Christian broadcasting, music and news; commercial station.

Radio ICCI-FM: International College of the Cayman Islands, Newlands, Grand Cayman; tel. 947-1100; fax 947-1210; e-mail icci@candw.ky; f. 1973; educational and cultural; Pres. Dr ELSA M. CUMMINGS.

Radio Z99.9 FM: POB 30110, Grand Cayman; tel. 945-1166; fax 945-1006; internet www.z99.ky; Gen. Man. RANDY MERREN.

Reggae 97.3 FM: Grand Cayman; internet www.reggae973fm.com; commercial music station.

Television

Cayman Adventist Network (CATN/TV): George Town, Grand Cayman; tel. 949-2739; f. 1996; local and international programmes, mainly religious.

Cayman Christian TV Ltd: George Town, Grand Cayman; relays Christian broadcasting from the Trinity Broadcasting Network (USA).

Cayman International Television Network (CITN): POB 55G, Sound Way, George Town, Grand Cayman; tel. 945-2739; fax 945-1373; f. 1992; 24 hrs daily; local and international news and US entertainment; 10-channel cable service of international programmes by subscription; Mans COLIN WILSON, JOANNE WILSON.

Cayman Television Service (CTS): George Town, Grand Cayman; f. 1993; 24 hrs daily; local and international news from a regional perspective; Mans COLIN WILSON, JOANNE WILSON.

Finance

Banking facilities are provided by commercial banks. The islands have become an important centre for 'offshore' companies and trusts. At the end of 1999 there were 50,951 companies registered in the Cayman Islands. At the end of July 2002 there were 527 licensed banks, 32 of which were licensed to transact local business. The number of insurance companies totalled 590 and some 4,077 mutual funds were registered in the Cayman Islands in the same month. The islands were well-known as a tax haven because of the absence of any form of direct taxation. In 1997 assets held by banks registered in the Cayman Islands totalled some US $504,000m.

Cayman Islands Monetary Authority: POB 10052, Elizabethan Sq., George Town, Grand Cayman; tel. 949-7089; fax 945-1145; e-mail admin@cimoney.com.ky; internet www.cimoney.com.ky; f. 1997; responsible for managing the Territory's currency and reserves and for regulating the financial services sector; cap. CI $4.3m., res 6.8m., dep. 40.5m. (Dec. 1997); Chair. G. A. McCarthy; Man. Dir Cindy Scotland.

PRINCIPAL BANKS AND TRUST COMPANIES

AALL Trust and Banking Corpn Ltd: AALL Bldg, POB 1166, George Town, Grand Cayman; tel. 949-5588; fax 949-8265; Chair. Eric Monsen; Man. Dir Kevin Doyle.

Ansbacher (Cayman) Ltd: POB 887, George Town, Grand Cayman; tel. 949-8655; fax 949-7946; e-mail info@ansbacher.com.ky; internet www.ansbacher.com; f. 1971; Chair. H. C. Hart; Man. Dir J. B. Bothwell.

Arab Commerce Bank Ltd: POB 309, George Town, Grand Cayman; tel. 949-8066; fax 949-8080; f. 1976 as Arab Caribbean Bank Ltd, name changed as above in 1991; Chair. C. N. Nasser; Dir Sheikh Hani Al Emam.

Atlantic Security Bank: George Town, Grand Cayman; Chair. Dionisio Romero; Pres. Carlos Muñoz.

Julius Baer Bank and Trust Co Ltd: Windward Bldg 3, Safe Haven Corporate Centre, West Bay Rd, POB 1100, George Town, Grand Cayman; tel. 949-7212; fax 949-0993; f. 1974; Man. Dir Charles Q. Farrington.

Banca Unione di Credito (Cayman) Ltd: POB 10182 APO, George Town, Grand Cayman; tel. 949-7129; fax 949-2168; cap. Sw Fr 10m., dep. Sw Fr 573.7m., total assets Sw Fr 591.3m. (Dec. 1999); Gen. Man. Urs Frei.

Banco Português do Atlântico: POB 30124, Grand Cayman; tel. 949-8322; fax 949-7743; Gen. Man. Helena Soares Carneiro.

Banco Safra (Cayman Islands) Ltd: c/o Bank of Nova Scotia, POB 501, George Town, Grand Cayman; tel. 949-2001; fax 949-7097; f. 1993; cap. US $60.0m., res US $124.5m., dep. US $97.3m. (Dec. 2000).

BANIF-Banco Internaçional do Funchal (Cayman) Ltd: POB 32338 SMB, George Town, Grand Cayman; tel. 945-8060; fax 945-8069; e-mail banifcay@candw.ky; Chair. and CEO Dr Joaquim Filipe Marques dos Santos; Gen. Man. Valdemar B. Lopes.

Bank America Trust and Banking Corpn (Cayman) Ltd: Fort St, POB 1092, George Town, Grand Cayman; tel. 949-7888; fax 949-7883; f. 1999; Man. Dir Charles Farrington.

Bank of Bermuda (Cayman) Ltd: POB 513, 3rd Floor, British American Tower, George Town, Grand Cayman; tel. 949-9898; fax 949-7959; internet www.bankofbermuda.com; f. 1968 as a trust; converted to a bank in 1988; total assets US $1,041m. (July 2001); Chair. Henry B. Smith; Man. Dir Allen Bernardo.

Bank of Butterfield International (Cayman) Ltd: Butterfield House, 68 Fort St, POB 705, Grand Cayman; tel. 949-7055; fax 949-7004; e-mail info@bankofbutterfield.ky; internet www.bankofbutterfield.ky; f. 1967; subsidiary of N. T. Butterfield & Son Ltd, Bermuda; cap. US $16.5m., res US $35.0m., dep. US $846.1m. (June 2000); Chair. J. M. Calum Johnston; Man. Dir Conor J. O'Dea; 3 brs.

Bank of Nova Scotia: Cardinall Ave, POB 689, George Town, Grand Cayman; tel. 949-7666; fax 949-0020; also runs trust company; Man. A. Brodie.

Bank of Novia Scotia Trust Company (Cayman) Ltd: POB 501, George Town, Grand Cayman; tel. 949-2001; fax 949-7097; e-mail cayman@bnstrust.com; internet www.scotiabank.com; Man. Dir Steve J. Grainger.

BankBoston Trust Co (Cayman Islands) Ltd: c/o Maples and Calder, POB 309, George Town, Grand Cayman; tel. 949-8066; fax 949-8080; e-mail info@maples.candw.ky; f. 1997.

Bermuda Trust (Cayman) Ltd: Floor 5, Bermuda House, POB 513, George Town, Grand Cayman; tel. 949-9898; fax 949-7959; f. 1968 as Arawak Trust Co; became subsidiary of Bank of Bermuda in 1988; bank and trust services; Chair. Joseph Johnson; Man. Dir Kenneth Gibbs.

BFC Bank (Cayman) Ltd: POB 1765, Trafalgar Pl., George Town, Grand Cayman; tel. 949-8748; fax 949-8749; e-mail bfc@candw.ky; internet www.bfc.ch; f. 1985; Chair. Simon C. Tay; Resident Man. Cherrylee Bush.

BII Creditanstalt International Bank Ltd: POB 1043, George Town, Grand Cayman; f. 1999.

British American Bank Ltd: POB 914, George Town, Grand Cayman; tel. 949-7822; fax 949-6064; Pres. and CEO Leonard Ebanks.

Caledonian Bank and Trust Ltd: POB 1043, George Town, Grand Cayman; tel. 949-0050; fax 949-8062; e-mail info@caledonian.com; internet www.caledonian.com; f. 1970; Chair. William S. Walker; Man. Dir David S. Sargison.

Cayman National Bank Ltd: 4th Floor, Cayman National Bldg, 200 Elgin Ave, POB 1097, George Town, Grand Cayman; tel. 949-4655; fax 949-7506; e-mail cnb@candw.ky; f. 1974; subsidiary of Cayman National Corporation; cap. CI $2.4m., res. 41.2m., dep 448.0m. (Oct. 1999); Chair. Eric J. Crutchley; Pres. David McConney; 6 brs.

Coutts (Cayman) Ltd: Coutts House, West Bay Rd, POB 707, George Town, Grand Cayman; tel. 945-4777; fax 945-4799; internet www.coutts.com; f. 1967; fmrly NatWest International Trust Corpn (Cayman) Ltd; Chair. Gerald C. Williams; Man. Dir Andrew Galloway.

Deutsche Bank (Cayman) Ltd: Elizabethan Sq., POB 1984, George Town, Grand Cayman; tel. 949-8244; fax 949-8178; e-mail dmg-cay@candw.ky; cap. US $5.0m., res 20.3m., dep. 129.3m. (Dec. 1998); Chair. P. E. Smith; Exec. Dir T. Godber.

Deutsche Bank International Trust Co (Cayman) Ltd: POB 1967, George Town, Grand Cayman; tel. 949-8244; fax 949-7866; f. 1999.

Deutsche Girozentrale Overseas Ltd: POB 852, George Town, Grand Cayman; tel. 914-1066; fax 9144-060.

FirstCaribbean International Bank Ltd: Grand Cayman; internet www.firstcaribbeaninternational.com; f. 2002 following merger of Caribbean operations of Barclays Bank PLC and CIBC; Exec. Chair. Michael Mansoor; CEO Charles Pink.

Fortis Bank (Cayman) Ltd: POB 2003, George Town, Grand Cayman; tel. 949-7942; fax 949-8340; internet www.fortis.com; f. 1984 as Pierson Heldring & Pierson (Cayman) Ltd; name changed to Mees Pierson (Cayman) Ltd in 1993; present name adopted in June 2000; Man. Dir Roger Hanson.

Habib Bank Zurich (International) Ltd: c/o Caledonian Bank and Trust Ltd, POB 1043, George Town, Grand Cayman; tel. 949-0050; fax 949-8062; f. 1976; Chair. Wolfgang E. Seeger; Gen. Man. S. Mazhar Ali Kazmi.

HSBC Financial Services (Cayman) Ltd: POB 1109, Mary St, George Town, Grand Cayman; tel. 949-7755; fax 949-7634; e-mail tom.clark@ky.hsbc.com; internet www.hsbc.ky; f. 1982; Dirs Tom Clark, David A. Whitefield.

IBJ Whitehall Bank and Trust Co: West Wind Bldg, POB 1040, George Town, Grand Cayman; tel. 949-5566; Man. Roger Healy.

Intesa Bank Overseas Ltd: c/o Coutts (Cayman) Ltd, Coutts House, West Bay Rd, POB 707, George Town, Grand Cayman; tel. 945-4777; fax 945-4799; f. 1994 as Ambroveneto International Bank; name changed as above in March 1999; cap. US $10.0m., total assets US $1,339.8m. (Dec. 1999); Chair. Francesco de Vecchi; Man. Dirs Richard Austin, Andrew Galloway.

Leumi Cayman Finance and Trust Corpn: c/o Fortis Bank (Cayman) Ltd, POB 2003, George Town, Grand Cayman; tel. 949-7942; fax 949-8340; f. 1979.

LGT Bank in Liechtenstein (Cayman) Ltd: POB 852, George Town, Grand Cayman; tel. 949-7676; fax 949-8512.

Lloyds TSB Bank and Trust (Cayman) Ltd: c/o CIBC Bank and Trust Co (Cayman) Ltd, POB 694, George Town, Grand Cayman; tel. 949-7854; fax 949-0090; Man. Roger C. Barker.

Mercury Bank and Trust Ltd: POB 2424, George Town, Grand Cayman; tel. 949-0800; fax 949-0295; Man. Volker Mergenthaler.

Merrill Lynch Bank and Trust Co (Cayman) Ltd: POB 1164, George Town, Grand Cayman; tel. 949-8206; fax 949-8895.

Royal Bank of Canada: POB 245, Grand Cayman; tel. 949-4600; fax 949-7396; Man. Harry C. Chisholm.

Royal Bank of Canada Trust Co (Cayman) Ltd: POB 1586; tel. 949-9107; fax 949-5777.

UBS (Cayman Islands) Ltd: POB 852G, UBS House, 227 Elgin Ave, George Town, Grand Cayman; tel. 914-1000; fax 914-4000; CEO WALTER EGGENSCHWILER.

Banking Association

Cayman Islands Bankers' Association: POB 676, Macdonald Sq., Fort St, George Town, Grand Cayman; tel. 949-0330; fax 945-1448; e-mail ciba@candw.ky; Pres. TIMOTHY GODBER.

STOCK EXCHANGE

Cayman Islands Stock Exchange (CSX): POB 2408, George Town, Grand Cayman; tel. 945-6060; fax 945-6061; e-mail csx@csx.com.ky; internet www.csx.com.ky; f. 1997; some 400 companies registered, including over 300 hedge funds (April 2002); CEO VALIA THEODORAKI.

INSURANCE

Several foreign companies have agents in the islands. A total of 590 companies were registered in July 2002. Local companies include the following:

British Caymanian Insurance Agency Ltd: Elizabethan Sq., POB 74, Grand Cayman; tel. 949-8699; fax 949-8411.

Capital Life Insurance: Capital Life Bldg, Eastern Ave, POB 1816, George Town, Grand Cayman; tel. 949-7717; fax 949-8741.

Caribbean Home Insurance: POB 931, Commerce House 7, Genesis Close, George Town, Grand Cayman; tel. 949-7788; fax 949-8422.

Cayman General Insurance Co Ltd: Cayman National Bank Bldg, 200 Elgin Ave, POB 2171, George Town, Grand Cayman; tel. 949-7028; fax 949-7457; e-mail cay_gen@candw.ky; Chair. BENSON O. EBANKS; Pres. DANNY A. SCOTT.

Global Life Assurance Co Ltd: Global House, POB 1087, North Church St, Grand Cayman; tel. 949-8211; fax 949-8262; f. 1992; Man. WINSOME RUDDOCK.

Trade and Industry

DEVELOPMENT ORGANIZATION

Agricultural and Industrial Development Board: 3rd Floor, Tower Bldg, POB 1271, George Town, Grand Cayman; tel. 949-5277; fax 949-6168; e-mail aidb@gov.ky; development loans organization; Gen. Man. ANGELA MILLER.

CHAMBER OF COMMERCE

Cayman Islands Chamber of Commerce: Macdonald Sq., Fort St, POB 1000, George Town, Grand Cayman; tel. 949-8090; fax 949-0220; e-mail info@caymanchamber.ky; internet www.caymanchamber.ky; f. 1965; Pres. CONOR O'DEA; Man. WIL PINEAU; 730 local mems.

EMPLOYERS' ORGANIZATION

Labour Office: Tower Bldg, 4th Floor; tel. 949-0941; fax 949-6057; Dir DALE M. BANKS.

The Cayman Islands have had a labour law since 1942, but only three trade unions have been registered.

UTILITIES

Electricity

Caribbean Utilities Co. Ltd (CUC): Corporate HQ & Plant, North Sound Rd, POB 38, George Town, Grand Cayman; tel. 949-5200; fax 949-4621; e-mail sparky@cuc-cayman.com; internet www.cuc-cayman.com; Pres. and CEO PETER A. THOMSON; Chair. JOSEPH IMPARATO; Gen. Man. RICHARD HEW.

Cayman Brac Power and Light Co. Ltd: Stake Bay Point, POB 95, Stake Bay, Cayman Brac; tel. 948-2224; fax 948-2204.

West Indies Power Corpn Ltd: CUC Corporate Centre, North Sound Rd, POB 38, George Town, Grand Cayman; tel. 949-2250.

Water

Cayman Islands Water Authority: 13G Red Gate Rd, POB 1104, George Town, Grand Cayman; tel. 949-6352; fax 949-0094; e-mail wac@candw.ky.

Cayman Water Co. Ltd. (CWC): Trafalgar Pl., West Bay Rd, POB 1114, George Town, Grand Cayman; tel. 945-4277; fax 945-4191.

Transport

ROADS

There are some 406 km (252 miles) of motorable roads, of which 304 km (189 miles) are surfaced with tarmac. The road network connects all districts on Grand Cayman and Cayman Brac (which has 76 km (47 miles) of motorable road), and there are 27 miles of motorable road on Little Cayman (of which about 11 miles are paved). During 1996 work began on the construction of a major new road linking the important tourist area of West Bay with the airport industrial park area on Grand Cayman.

SHIPPING

George Town is the principal port and a new port facility was opened in July 1977. Cruise liners, container ships and smaller cargo vessels ply between the Cayman Islands, Florida, Jamaica and Costa Rica. There is no cruise-ship dock in the Cayman Islands. Ships anchor off George Town and ferry passengers ashore to the North or South Dock Terminals in George Town. In February 2002 the Florida Caribbean Cruise Ship Association agreed to provide up to US $10m. for improvements to the port's cruise-ship facilities. In 1993 the Government limited the number of cruise-ship passengers to 6,000 per day. The port of Cayman Brac is Creek; there are limited facilities on Little Cayman.

Port Authority of the Cayman Islands: Harbour Dr., POB 1358, George Town, Grand Cayman; tel. 949-2055; fax 949-5820; e-mail ebush@caymanport.com; Port Dir ERROL BUSH.

Cayman Islands Shipping Registry: Elizabethan Sq., 3rd Floor, Phase Four, POB 2256, George Town, Grand Cayman; tel. 949-8831; fax 949-8849; e-mail cisr@candw.ky; internet www.caymarad.org; Dir PETER GIBBS.

Cayman Brac Shipping Corporation: Banksville Ave, Stake Bay, POB 25, Cayman Brac; tel. 948-2221; fax 948-2289.

Cayman Freight Shipping Ltd: 2nd Floor, Micro Centre, Industrial Park, POB 1372, George Town, Grand Cayman; tel. 949-4977; fax 949-8402; e-mail caribbean@seaboardmarine.com; internet www.seaboardmarine.com; Man. Dir ROBERT FOSTER.

Thompson Shipping Co Ltd: POB 188, Terminal Eastern Ave, George Town, Grand Cayman; tel. 949-8044; fax 949-8349; f. 1977.

CIVIL AVIATION

There are two international airports in the Territory: Owen Roberts International Airport, 3.5 km (2 miles) from George Town, and Gerrard Smith Airport on Cayman Brac. Both are capable of handling jet-engined aircraft. Edward Bodden Airport on Little Cayman can cater for light aircraft. Several scheduled carriers serve the islands.

Civil Aviation Authority: Beacon House, POB 10277 APO, George Town, Grand Cayman; tel. 949-7811; fax 949-0761; e-mail rs_caa@candw.ky; f. 1987; Dir RICHARD SMITH.

Cayman Airways Ltd: POB 1101, George Town, Grand Cayman; tel. 949-8200; fax 949-7607; internet www.caymanairways.com; f. 1968; wholly govt-owned since 1977; operates local services and scheduled flights to Jamaica, Honduras and the USA; Chair. ROY McTAGGART; Exec. Vice-Pres. MIKE ADAM.

Island Air: POB 2433, Airport Rd, George Town, Grand Cayman; tel. 949-0241; fax 949-7044; operates daily scheduled services between Grand Cayman, Cayman Brac and Little Cayman.

Tourism

The Cayman Islands are a major tourist destination, the majority of visitors coming from North America. The beaches and opportunities for diving in the offshore reefs form the main attraction for most tourists. Major celebrations include Pirates' Week in October and the costume festivals on Grand Cayman (Batabano), at the end of April, and, one week later, on Cayman Brac (Brachanal). In 1995 there were an estimated 7,648 hotel beds. In 2000 there were 316,029 arrivals by air and 1,030,857 cruise visitors. In 2000 the tourist industry earned an estimated US $559.2m.

Cayman Islands Department of Tourism: Cricket Sq., POB 67, George Town, Grand Cayman; tel. 949-0623; fax 949-4053; internet www.divecayman.ky; f. 1965; Dir ANGELA MARTINS.

Cayman Islands Hotel and Condominium Association (CIHCA): West Bay Rd, POB 1367, George Town; tel. 947-4057; fax 947-4143; Pres. WILLI GIGER; Sec. L. EBANKS.

Sister Islands Tourism Association: Stake Bay, POB 187, Cayman Brac; tel. and fax 948-1345.

THE FALKLAND ISLANDS

Introductory Survey

Location, Climate, Language, Religion, Flag, Capital

The Falkland Islands, comprising two large islands and about 200 smaller ones, are in the south-western Atlantic Ocean, about 770 km (480 miles) north-east of Cape Horn, South America. The climate is generally cool, with strong winds (mainly westerly) throughout the year. The mean annual temperature is 6°C (42°F), while average annual rainfall is 635 mm (25 ins). The language is English. Most of the inhabitants profess Christianity, with several denominations represented. The flag is the British 'Blue Ensign', with the colony's coat of arms (a shield showing a white and violet ram standing in green grass, on a blue background, above a sailing ship bearing red crosses on its pennants and five six-pointed stars on its central sail, on three white horizontal wavy lines, with the motto 'Desire the Right' on a scroll beneath) on a white disc in the centre of the flag. The capital is Stanley, on East Falkland Island.

Recent History

The first recorded landing on the islands was made from a British ship in 1690, when the group was named after Viscount Falkland, then Treasurer of the Royal Navy. French sailors named the islands 'Les Malouines' (after their home port of Saint-Malo), from which the Spanish name 'Islas Malvinas' is derived. A French settlement was established in 1764 on the island of East Falkland, but in 1767 France relinquished its rights to the territory to Spain, which then ruled the adjacent regions of South America. Meanwhile, a British expedition annexed West Falkland in 1765, and a garrison was established. The British settlement, formed in 1765–66, was recognized by Spain in 1771 but withdrawn in 1774. The Spanish garrison was withdrawn in 1811.

When the United Provinces of the River Plate (now Argentina) gained independence from Spain in 1816, the Falkland Islands had no permanent inhabitants, although they provided temporary bases for sealing and whaling activities by British and US vessels. In 1820 an Argentine ship was sent to the islands to proclaim Argentine sovereignty as successor to Spain. An Argentine settlement was founded in 1826 but most of its occupants were expelled by a US warship in 1831. The remaining Argentines were ejected by a British expedition in 1832, and British sovereignty was established in 1833.

The islands became a Crown Colony of the United Kingdom, administered by a British-appointed Governor. However, Argentina did not relinquish its claim, and negotiations to resolve the dispute began in 1966 at the instigation of the UN. The inhabitants of the islands, nearly all British by descent, consistently expressed their desire to remain under British sovereignty.

After routine talks between delegations of the British and Argentine Governments in New York in February 1982, the Argentine Foreign Ministry announced that it would seek other means to resolve the dispute. Rumours of a possible invasion had begun in the Argentine press in January, and Argentina's military regime took advantage of a British protest at the presence of a group of Argentine scrap merchants, who had made an unauthorized landing on South Georgia (q.v.) in March and had raised an Argentine flag, to invade the Falkland Islands on 2 April. A small contingent of British marines was overwhelmed, the British Governor, Rex (later Sir Rex) Hunt, was expelled and an Argentine military governorship was established. Although the Argentine Government promised to respect the rights of the islanders, some property was damaged, stolen or destroyed, and livestock was lost. The USA and the UN attempted (unsuccessfully) to mediate, in an effort to prevent military escalation. British forces, which had been dispatched to the islands immediately after the Argentine invasion, recaptured South Georgia on 25 April. The Argentine forces on the Falklands formally surrendered on 14 June, after a conflict in the course of which about 750 Argentine, 255 British and three Falklanders' lives were lost.

The Governor returned to the islands as Civil Commissioner on 25 June 1982, and Britain established a 'protection zone' around the islands, extending 150 nautical miles (278 km) off shore, as well as a garrison of about 4,000 troops. The British Government began an investigation into the possibilities of developing the islands' economy, and in November agreed to grant the Falkland Islanders full British citizenship. In November 1983 the post of Chief Executive of the Falkland Islands Government was created, in combination with the executive vice-chairmanship of the newly-formed Falkland Islands Development Corporation. The Civil Commissioner, Sir Rex Hunt, retired in September 1985, whereupon a new Governor was appointed.

The issue of the sovereignty of the Falkland Islands remained a major impediment to the normalization of relations between Argentina and the United Kingdom. The Argentine Government refused to agree to a formal declaration that hostilities were ended until the United Kingdom agreed to participate in negotiations over sovereignty, while the United Kingdom refused to negotiate until Argentina had formally ended hostilities.

Following the return to civilian rule in Argentina in December 1983, the newly-elected President, Dr Raúl Alfonsín, stated his Government's desire to seek a negotiated settlement to the dispute over the Falkland Islands. In October 1984 the Argentine Government removed restrictions on British companies and interests in Argentina as a possible prelude to resuming negotiations.

The British Government's refusal to discuss the issue of sovereignty, and its insistence on the paramountcy of the Falkland Islanders' wishes, were reflected in the new Constitution for the Falklands (approved by the islands' Legislative Council in January 1985), which guaranteed the islanders' right to self-determination.

The number of British troops stationed on the islands was reduced, following the opening, in mid-1985, of a new military airport at Mount Pleasant, about 30 km south-west of Stanley, enabling rapid reinforcement of the garrison, if necessary. In July the British Government ended its ban on Argentine imports, which had been in force since 1982. In October elections took place on the Falklands for a new Legislative Council. In the same month, South Georgia and the South Sandwich Islands (see separate section) ceased to be dependencies of the Falkland Islands, although the Governor of the Falkland Islands was to be (*ex officio*) Commissioner for the territories.

In 1986 parliamentary delegations from the United Kingdom and Argentina conducted exploratory talks. However, the British Government remained intransigent on the issue of the sovereignty of the islands. In early 1986 Argentina's continued claim to the naval 'protection zone' was manifested in attacks on foreign fishing vessels by Argentine gunboats. In October Britain unilaterally declared a fisheries conservation and management zone extending 150 nautical miles (278 km) around the islands, with effect from February 1987, to prevent the overfishing of the waters. The imposition of this zone, whose radius coincided with that of the naval protection zone, was condemned by the majority of UN members, as was Britain's rejection, in November 1986, of an offer by Argentina to declare a formal end to hostilities in exchange for the abolition of the protection zone. The resignation, in June 1989, of three members of the Legislative Council, in protest against a proposed agricultural grants scheme, prompted the dissolution of the legislative body. In the ensuing parliamentary elections in October, eight independent candidates, all of whom vigorously opposed renewing links, at any level, with Argentina, defeated 10 other candidates to take all the elective seats. Three representatives of a recently-formed political organization, the Desire the Right Party, which advocated a policy of limited *rapprochement* with Argentina, received little support.

In October 1993 25 independent candidates contested elections to the eight elective seats of the Legislative Council. The successful candidates had all expressed a reluctance to develop closer contacts with Argentina as long as the Argentine Government continued to claim sovereignty over the islands.

At elections to the Legislative Council held on 9 October 1997, the eight elective seats were secured by independent candidates, all of whom expressed their determination not to enter into negotiations with Argentina regarding the islands' sovereignty.

Beginning in 1982 the UN General Assembly voted annually, by an overwhelming majority, in favour of the resumption of negotiations between Argentina and the United Kingdom. The British Government consistently declined to engage in such dialogue. However, relations between Argentina and the United Kingdom improved, following the election, in May 1989, of a new Argentine President, Carlos Saúl Menem, who initially indicated that his country would be willing to suspend temporarily its demand that the issue of the sovereignty of the Falkland Islands be discussed, in the interests of the restoration of full diplomatic and commercial relations with the United Kingdom. In October a meeting of British and Argentine representatives, which took place in Madrid, Spain, culminated in the formal cessation of all hostilities, and the re-establishment of diplomatic relations at consular level. Restrictions on Argentine merchant vessels with regard to the naval protection zone around the Falkland Islands were also eased. In the following month, however, the United Kingdom announced that it was to increase the extent of its territorial waters around the islands from three to 12 nautical miles, in spite of protests from the Argentine authorities. In February 1990 Argentina and the United Kingdom conducted further negotiations in Madrid, as a result of which the two countries re-established full diplomatic relations. It was also announced that the naval protection zone around the Falkland Islands was to be modified in March, and that mutually-agreed military procedures, that would ensure the security of the region, would take effect. In mid-1993 the further reduction of military restrictions around the islands was announced by both Governments.

Following successful negotiations between Argentina and the United Kingdom in Madrid in November 1990, an agreement regarding the protection and conservation of the South Atlantic fishing area was announced, whereby a temporary ban on fishing was to be extended, from late December, to an area incorporating an additional 50-mile (93-km) semicircular region to the east of the islands, beyond the existing 150-mile fishing zone. (The agreement was renewed in December 1991 and 1992.) The two sides also agreed to establish a South Atlantic Fisheries Commission, which was to meet at least twice in every year that the ban remained in place, in order to discuss fishing activity and conservation in the region. Throughout 1990 the Falkland Islands Government had appealed to the British Government to exercise its legal right under international law to extend the fisheries conservation and management zone, claiming that over-fishing of the previously well-stocked waters just beyond the 150-mile limit by vessels from Taiwan and the Republic of Korea (ignoring previously agreed voluntary restraints on fishing in the area) had seriously depleted stocks and posed a threat to the islands' lucrative squid-fishing industry.

In May 1993 the British Government's announced that it would extend from 12 to 200 nautical miles its territorial jurisdiction in the waters surrounding South Georgia and the South Sandwich Islands. In December the Argentine Government indicated its acceptance of the United Kingdom's proposed extension of fishing rights around the Falkland Islands from 150 to 200 miles, in order to allow the islanders to fulfil an annual squid-fishing quota of 150,000 metric tons (effective from January 1994). The Argentine quota was agreed at 220,000 tons (compared with an estimated catch of 130,000 tons in 1992). In August 1994 the British Government unilaterally decided to extend its fisheries conservation zone north of the islands, thereby annexing a small but lucrative fishing ground (not previously protected by British or Argentine legislation) that was being plundered by foreign fishing vessels. In January 1997 the United Kingdom and Argentina agreed to resume negotiations on a long-term fisheries agreement that would include the disputed waters around the islands. Following the release of a Joint Declaration between the two Governments on 14 July 1999, both Governments agreed to co-operate to combat illegal fishing in the South West Atlantic and to ensure the sustainability of fish stocks in the region.

In November 1991 the Governments of both Argentina and the United Kingdom claimed rights of exploration and exploitation of the sea-bed and the subsoil of the continental shelf around the Falkland Islands (which are believed to be rich in petroleum reserves). In April 1992 the Falkland Islands Government invited tenders for seismic reports of the region. In December 1993 the British Geological Survey reported that preliminary seismic investigations indicated deposits in excess of those located in British North Sea oilfields. A bilateral agreement on petroleum and gas exploration in an area of 18,000 sq

km, south-west of the islands, was concluded in New York in September 1994. A joint hydrocarbons commission would regulate licensing in the area, examining bids from Anglo-Argentine joint ventures (in which case taxes would be levied on operators by the respective Governments) or by third countries (from which royalties on revenues would be exacted by the Falkland Islands Government at a rate expected to approach 9%). The successful conclusion of the agreement appeared to dissipate Argentine objections, voiced earlier in the year, to the Falkland Islands' unilateral offer of rights to drill in 19 areas (comprising 44,000 sq km not covered by the Anglo-Argentine agreement) to the north and south of the islands. Licences to explore for hydrocarbons were awarded to five international consortia in October 1996. The possibility that commercial quantities of petroleum might be discovered prompted renewed discussion as to the amount of any future royalties exacted by the Falkland Islands Government that should be returned to the Government of the United Kingdom. In early 1997 the British Government indicated that it expected to benefit considerably from any such royalties, while the Falkland Islands administration proposed that some of the revenue could be used to finance the islands' defence expenditure (currently funded by the United Kingdom). Meanwhile, the Argentine Government claimed that it should be entitled to benefit from the discovery of petroleum in the region: draft legislation presented to Congress provided for the imposition of sanctions on petroleum companies and fishing vessels operating in Falkland Islands waters without Argentine authorization, in addition to the levying of 3% royalties from the sale of petroleum discovered in the area.

In late 1996 the Argentine Government suggested, for the first time, that it might consider shared sovereignty of the Falkland Islands with the United Kingdom. The proposal was firmly rejected by the British Government and by the Falkland Islanders, who reiterated their commitment to persuading the UN Special Political and Decolonization Committee to adopt a clause granting the islanders the right to self-determination.

In May 1999 Richard Ralph was succeeded as Governor by Donald Lamont. Later that month formal negotiations between the Falkland Islands and Argentina took place in the United Kingdom, under the auspices of Robin Cook, the British Secretary of State for Foreign and Commonwealth Affairs. Issues under discussion included co-operation in fishing and petroleum exploration, Argentine access to the islands and the resumption of air links with mainland South America. (In March Chile had ended its country's regular air services to the islands in protest at the British Government's continued detention of Gen. Pinochet; Uruguay subsequently agreed not to establish an air link with the islands unless flights were routed via the Argentine capital.) The sovereignty of the Falkland Islands was not scheduled for discussion. Four of the islands' councillors also attended the three days of talks, thereby occasioning the first direct talks between Falkland Islanders and the Argentine Government. The dialogue continued in July in New York and London. On 14 July a joint Argentine-British declaration was issued that eliminated the restrictions on travel by Argentine citizens to the Falkland Islands and re-established airline services by the Chilean carrier LanChile between South America and the Falkland Islands (with a stop-over in Argentina). It was also agreed to increase bilateral co-operation between Argentina and the Falkland Islands on combating illegal fishing and conservation of fish stocks. Symbolic gestures included allowing the construction of a monument to the Argentine war dead at their cemetery on the islands (permission was finally granted in March 2002), while in return the Argentine Government would cease to use the Spanish names given to Falklands locations during the 1982 occupation. The agreement did not affect claims to sovereignty. Even so, the round of talks provoked demonstrations by an estimated 500 people on the Falkland Islands. The protests resumed on 16 October when the first flights carrying Argentine visitors arrived in the Falklands.

The Argentine President, Fernando de la Rua, in a meeting with British Prime Minister Tony Blair in late January 2000, reiterated Argentina's claim to sovereignty over the Falkland Islands. His Government indicated a less friendly attitude to the Falkland islanders, in contrast to the previous administration, when it announced in July that it would not engage in any dialogue with Falkland Island councillors that involved the British Government. In the same month the Anglo-Argentine dialogue on joint petroleum and gas exploration was suspended by mutual agreement for an indefinite period of time.

On 22 November 2001 a general election took place to elect members to a new Legislative Council. Of the eight elected, only three members had not served on the Legislative Council before. In a concurrent referendum the electorate voted against changing the two-constituency system (the Stanley constituency and the Camp constituency) to a single constituency for legislative elections.

On the 20th anniversary of the landing of Argentine troops on the Falkland Islands in April 2002, the new Argentine President, Eduardo Duhalde, promised to recover the Falkland Islands by non-violent means. On 3 December Howard Pearce succeeded Donald Lamont as Governor of the Falkland Islands and Commissioner of South Georgia and the Sandwich Islands. In March 2003 Chris Simpkins became the new Chief Executive; he replaced Michael Blanch who had reached the end of his three-year contract.

Government

Administration is conducted by the appointed Governor (who is the personal representative of the British monarch), aided by the Executive Council, comprising two *ex-officio* members and three members elected by the Legislative Council. The Legislative Council is composed of two *ex-officio* members and eight elected members. Voting is by universal adult suffrage.

Defence

In August 2002 there were approximately 1,300 British troops stationed on the islands. The total cost of the conflict in 1982 and of building and maintaining a garrison for four years was estimated at £2,560m. The current annual cost of maintaining the garrison is approximately £68m. There is a Falkland Islands Defence Force, composed of islanders.

Economic Affairs

Most of the agricultural land on the Falkland Islands is devoted to the rearing of sheep. However, the land is poor and more than four acres are required to support one animal. In the late 1990s annual exports of wool were valued at some £3.5m. Some vegetables are produced (notably in a hydroponic market garden), and there are small dairy herds. From 1987, when a licensing system was introduced for foreign vessels fishing within a 150-nautical-mile conservation and management zone (see Recent History), the economy was diversified and the islands' annual income increased considerably. Revenue from the sale of licences totalled £25m. in 1991, but subsequently declined (following the Argentine Government's commencement of the sale of fishing licences in 1993), and totalled some £23m. in 1998/99. In the late 1980s about one-third of the world's total catch of *Illex* and *Loligo* squid was derived from this fishing zone. However, over-fishing in the area surrounding the conservation zone had a detrimental effect on stocks of fish in the islands' waters, and frequently the Government has been obliged to call an early halt to the exploitation of both squid types.

Manufacturing activity on the islands reflects the predominance of the agricultural sector: a wool mill on West Falkland produces yarns for machine knitting, hand knitting and weaving. Several small companies in the Falklands produce garments for local and export sales. Some fish-processing also takes place on East Falkland.

The Falkland Islands are heavily dependent on imports of all fuels, except peat. Wind power is used in many remote locations to offset this dependence and reduce pollution of the atmosphere. The Falkland Islands Government licensed five consortia to explore for hydrocarbons in waters north of the islands in October 1996. These companies, including Shell, Amerada Hess and LASMO, drilled six exploration wells in 1998. Five of the six wells had minor traces of hydrocarbons present, but no commercial quantities of petroleum were found in the initial phase of drilling. A British prospecting company has been granted an exploration licence to search for minerals on the islands. Mineral sands including garnet and rutile were being appraised, while more valuable minerals such as gold were being sought. In July 2002 the Falkland Islands Government granted 10 petroleum exploration licences to the Falklands Hydrocarbon Consortium (comprising Global Petroleum Ltd, Hardman Resources Ltd and Falkland Islands Holdings) for an area covering 57,700 sq km to the south of the islands.

The Falkland Islands Development Corporation oversees the islands' economic development on behalf of the Government. Since the 1980s the Government has sought to promote the development of the tourism sector. Tourism, and in particular eco-tourism, was developing rapidly in 2002, and the number of visitors staying on the Falklands Islands had grown to some 3,000 a year, while around 40,000 tourists were expected to sail through Stanley harbour on their way to Antarctica and sub-antarctic islands such as South Georgia. The sale of postage stamps and coins represents a significant source of income; the value of sales of the former was £296,229 in 1996/97, while the value of sales of the latter totalled £49,351 in 1995/96.

In 2000 the islands recorded an estimated trade surplus of £28,041,897. Fish, most of which is purchased by the United Kingdom, Spain and Chile, is the islands' most significant export. The principal imports are fuel, provisions, alcoholic beverages, building materials and clothing. In early 2001 the Government brought 100 reindeer from the South Georgia Islands (with the aim of increasing the number to 10,000 over the next 20 years) in order to export venison to Scandinavia and Chile.

Ordinary budget estimates for the financial year 1999/2000 envisaged revenue of £52,339,241 and expenditure of £40,449,156. The annual rate of inflation averaged 4.5% in 1990–98; consumer prices increased by 6.2% in 2000, and by 0.8% in 2001. There is a significant shortage of local labour on the islands.

Since 1982 the economy of the Falkland Islands has enjoyed a period of strong and sustained growth, partly owing to substantial investment by the British Government during the 1980s, but primarily as a result of the introduction of the fisheries licensing scheme in 1987. It was anticipated that royalties derived from the sale of licences for the exploration and exploitation of hydrocarbons would strengthen the economy further; however, the Falkland Islands Government was expected to utilize such revenue to finance the islands' defence expenditure, and possibly to reimburse the British Government for part of the cost of the 1982 conflict. The services sector expanded rapidly during the late 1990s, while the importance of the agricultural sector has decreased, not least because of its reliance on direct and indirect subsidies. The revenues from the sale of fishing licences, fund social provisions and economic development programmes, including subsidies to the wool industry, which is in long-term decline, owing to the oversupply of that commodity on the international market. The Government's development plan for 2001–03 emphasized agricultural diversification and the promotion of tourism as its main economic aims.

Education

Education is compulsory, and is provided free of charge, for children between the ages of five and 16 years. Facilities are available for further study beyond the statutory school-leaving age. In 2000 195 pupils were instructed by 18 teachers at the primary school in Stanley, while 140 pupils received instruction from 18 teachers at the secondary school in the capital; a further 36 pupils received education from 12 teachers in rural districts. Total expenditure on education and training was estimated at £3,337,000 for 1999/2000.

Public Holidays

2003: 1 January (New Year's Day), 18 April (Good Friday), 21 April (HM the Queen's Birthday), 16 June (Liberation Day), 6 October (Spring Holiday), 8 December (Anniversary of the Battle of the Falkland Islands in 1914), 25–29 December (Christmas).

2004: 1 January (New Year's Day), 9 April (Good Friday), 21 April (HM the Queen's Birthday), 14 June (Liberation Day), 4 October (Spring Holiday), 8 December (Anniversary of the Battle of the Falkland Islands in 1914), 25–29 December (Christmas).

Weights and Measures

Both the imperial and metric systems are in general use.

Statistical Survey

Source (unless otherwise stated): The Treasury of the Falkland Islands Government, Stanley; tel. 27143; fax 27144.

AREA AND POPULATION

Area: approx. 12,173 sq km (4,700 sq miles): East Falkland and adjacent islands 6,760 sq km (2,610 sq miles); West Falkland and adjacent islands 5,413 sq km (2,090 sq miles).

Population: 2,913 at 2001 census .

Density (2001): 0.24 per sq km.

Principal Town (2001 census): Stanley (capital), population 1,981.

Births and Deaths (2000): Live births 27; Deaths 6.

Economically Active Population (persons aged 15 years and over, 2001 census): 2,475 (males 1,370; females 1,105).

AGRICULTURE, ETC.

Livestock (FAO estimates, 2001): Sheep 690,000; Cattle 4,100; Horses 1,188. Source: FAO.

Livestock Products (FAO estimates, metric tons, 2001): Mutton and lamb 774; Cow's milk 1,500; Wool (greasy) 2,339. Source: FAO.

Fishing ('000 metric tons, live weight, 2000): Southern blue whiting 2.7; Patagonian grenadier 3.4; Patagonian squid 50.3; Total catch 62.9. Source: FAO, *Yearbook of Fishery Statistics.*

FINANCE

Currency and Exchange Rates: 100 pence (pennies) = 1 Falkland Islands pound (FI £). *Sterling, Dollar and Euro Equivalents* (31 December 2002): £1 sterling = FI £1.0000; US $1 = 62.04 pence; €1 = 65.06 pence; FI £100 = £100.00 sterling = $161.18 = €153.70. *Average Exchange Rate* (US $ per FI £): 1.5161 in 2000; 1.4400 in 2001; 1.5013 in 2002. Note: The Falkland Islands pound is at par with the pound sterling.

Budget (1999/2000 estimates): Ordinary Revenue £52,339,241; Ordinary Expenditure £40,449,156.

Cost of Living (Retail Price Index for Stanley; base: 1999 = 100): 106.2 in 2000; 107.1 in 2001.

EXTERNAL TRADE

2000 (estimates): *Imports:* £18,958,103, *Exports:* £47,000,000. Fish is the principal export. Trade is mainly with the United Kingdom, Spain and Chile.

TRANSPORT

Shipping: *Merchant Fleet* (at 31 December 2001): Vessels 31; Displacement 54,707 grt. Source: Lloyd's Register-Fairplay, *World Fleet Statistics.*

Road Traffic: 3,065 vehicles in use in 1995.

EDUCATION

2000 (Stanley): *Primary:* Teachers 18; Pupils 195, *Secondary:* Teachers 18; Pupils 140.

Directory

The Constitution

The present Constitution of the Falkland Islands came into force on 3 October 1985 (replacing that of 1977) and was amended in 1997. The Governor, who is the personal representative of the British monarch, is advised by the Executive Council, comprising six members: the Governor (presiding), three members elected by the Legislative Council, and two *ex-officio* members, the Chief Executive and the Financial Secretary of the Falkland Islands Government, who are non-voting. The Legislative Council is composed of eight elected members and the same two (non-voting) *ex-officio* members. One of the principal features of the Constitution is the reference in the preamble to the islanders' right to self-determination. The separate post of Chief Executive (responsible to the Governor) was created in 1983. The electoral principle was introduced, on the basis of universal adult suffrage, in 1949. The minimum voting age was lowered from 21 years to 18 years in 1977.

The Government

(April 2003)

Governor: HOWARD J. S. PEARCE (took office 3 December 2002).

Chief Executive of the Falkland Islands Government: CHRIS SIMPKINS.

Government Secretary: PETER T. KING.

Financial Secretary: DEREK F. HOWATT.

Attorney-General: DAVID G. LANG.

Military Commander: Cdre RICHARD IBBOTSON.

EXECUTIVE COUNCIL

The Council consists of six members (see Constitution, above).

LEGISLATIVE COUNCIL

Comprises the Governor, two *ex-officio* (non-voting) members and eight elected members.

GOVERNMENT OFFICES

Office of the Governor: Government House, Stanley; tel. 27433; fax 27434; e-mail gov.house@horizon.co.fk.

General Office: Secretariat, Stanley; tel. 27242; fax 27109; e-mail govsec.fig@horizon.co.fk; internet www.falklandislands.com.

London Office: Falkland Islands Government Office, Falkland House, 14 Broadway, London, SW1H 0BH, United Kingdom; tel. (020) 7222-2542; fax (020) 7222-2375; e-mail rep@figo.u-net.com; internet www.falklandislands.com; f. 1983.

Judicial System

The judicial system of the Falkland Islands is administered by the Supreme Court (presided over by the non-resident Chief Justice), the Magistrate's Court (presided over by the Senior Magistrate) and the Court of Summary Jurisdiction. The Court of Appeal for the Territory sits in England and appeals therefrom may be heard by the Judicial Committee of the Privy Council.

Chief Justice of the Supreme Court: JAMES WOOD.

Acting Judge of the Supreme Court and Senior Magistrate: KEITH WATSON.

Courts Administrator: LESLEY TITTERINGTON.

Registrar-General: JOHN ROWLAND.

FALKLAND ISLANDS COURT OF APPEAL

President: Sir LIONEL BRETT.

Registrar: MICHAEL J. ELKS.

Religion

CHRISTIANITY

The Anglican Communion, the Roman Catholic Church and the United Free Church predominate. Also represented are the Evangelist Church, Jehovah's Witnesses, the Lutheran Church, Seventh-day Adventists and the Bahá'í faith.

The Anglican Communion

The Archbishop of Canterbury, the Primate of All England, exercises episcopal jurisdiction over the Falkland Islands and South Georgia.

Rector: Rev. ALISTAIR MCHAFFIE, The Deanery, Christ Church Cathedral, Stanley; tel. 21100; fax 21842; e-mail deanery@horizon.co.fk.

The Roman Catholic Church

Prefect Apostolic of the Falkland Islands: MICHAEL BERNARD MCPARTLAND, St Mary's Presbytery, 12 Ross Rd, Stanley; tel. 21204; fax 22242; e-mail stmarys@horizon.co.fk; f. 1764; 230 adherents (2001).

The Press

The Falkland Islands Gazette: Stanley; tel. 27242; fax 27109; e-mail govsec.fig@horizon.co.fk; internet www.falklands.gov.fk; govt publication.

Falkland Islands News Network: Stanley; tel. 21182; e-mail finn@horizon.co.uk; relays news daily via fax; Man. JUAN BROCK; publishes:

  Teaberry Express: Stanley; tel. 21182; weekly.

Penguin News: Ross Rd, Stanley; tel. 22684; fax 22238; e-mail pnews@horizon.co.fk; f. 1979; weekly; publicly-supported newspaper; Man. Editor LISA RIDDELL; circ. 1,460.

Broadcasting and Communications

TELECOMMUNICATIONS

In 1989 Cable & Wireless PLC installed a £5.4m. digital telecommunications network covering the entire Falkland Islands. The Government contributed to the cost of the new system, which provides international services as well as a new domestic network. Further work to improve the domestic telephone system was completed in the late 1990s at a cost of £3,286,000.

BROADCASTING

Radio

Falkland Islands Broadcasting Station (FIBS): Broadcasting Studios, Stanley; tel. 27277; fax 27279; e-mail fibs.fig@horizon.co.fk; 24-hour service, financed by local Govt in association with SSVC of London, United Kingdom; broadcasts in English; Broadcasting Officer Tony Burnett (acting); Asst Producer Corina Goss.

British Forces Broadcasting Service (BFBS): BFBS Falkland Islands, Mount Pleasant, BFPO 655; tel. 32179; fax 32193; e-mail chris.pearson@bfbs.com; internet www.bfbs.com; 24-hour satellite service from the United Kingdom; Station Man. Chris Pearson; Sr Engineer Adrian Almond.

Television

British Forces Broadcasting Service: BFBS Falkland Islands, Mount Pleasant, BFPO 655; tel. 32179; fax 32193; daily four-hour transmissions of taped broadcasts from BBC and ITV of London, United Kingdom; Sr Engineer Colin McDonald.

KTV: Stanley; tel. and fax 21049; satellite television broadcasting services; Man. Mario Zuvic Bulic.

Finance

BANK

Standard Chartered Bank: POB 597, Ross Rd, Stanley; tel. 21352; fax 22219; branch opened in 1983; Man. N. P. Hutton.

INSURANCE

The British Commercial Union, Royal Insurance and Norman Tremellen companies maintain agencies in Stanley.

Consultancy Services Falklands Ltd: 44 John St, Stanley; tel. 22666; fax 22639; e-mail consultancy@horizon.co.uk; Man. Alison Baker.

Trade and Industry

DEVELOPMENT ORGANIZATION

Falkland Islands Development Corporation (FIDC): Stanley; tel. 27211; fax 27210; e-mail reception@fidc.org.fk; internet www.fidc.org.fk; f. 1983; provides loans and grants; encourages private-sector investment, inward investment and technology transfer; Gen. Man. Hugh Normand.

CHAMBER OF COMMERCE

Chamber of Commerce: POB 378, Stanley; tel. 22264; fax 22265; e-mail commerce@horizon.co.uk; f. 1993; promotes private industry; operates DHL courier service; runs an employment agency; Pres. Hamish Wylie; 100 mems.

TRADING COMPANY

Falkland Islands Co Ltd (FIC): Crozier Pl., Stanley; tel. 27600; fax 27603; e-mail fic@horizon.co.fk; f. 1851; part of Falkland Islands Holding PLC; the largest trading co; retailing, wholesaling, shipping, insurance and Land Rover sales and servicing; operates as agent for Lloyd's of London and general shipping concerns; travel services and hoteliers; wharf owners and operators; Dir and Gen. Man. Roger Kenneth Spink.

EMPLOYERS' ASSOCIATION

Sheep Owners' Association: Coast Ridge Farm, Fox Bay; tel. 42094; fax 42084; e-mail n.knight.coastridge@horizon.co.fk; asscn for sheep-station owners; Sec. N. Knight.

TRADE UNION

Falkland Islands General Employees Union: Ross Rd, Stanley; tel. 21151; f. 1943; Sec. C. A. Rowlands; 100 mems.

CO-OPERATIVE SOCIETY

Stanley Co-operative Society: Stanley; f. 1952; open to all members of the public; Man. Norma Thom.

Transport

RAILWAYS

There are no railways on the islands.

ROADS

There are 29 km (18 miles) of paved road in and around Stanley. There are 54 km (34 miles) of all-weather road linking Stanley and the Mount Pleasant airport (some of which has been surfaced with a bitumen substance), and a further 37 km of road as far as Goose Green. There are 300 km of arterial roads in the North Camp on East Falkland linking settlements, and a further 197 km of road on West Falkland. An ongoing roads network project to link remote farms is in progress. Where roads have still not been built, settlements are linked by tracks, which are passable by all-terrain motor vehicle or motor cycle except in the most severe weather conditions.

SHIPPING

There is a ship on charter to the Falkland Islands Co Ltd which makes the round trip to the United Kingdom four or five times a year, carrying cargo. A floating deep-water jetty was completed in 1984. The British Ministry of Defence charters ships, which sail for the Falkland Islands once every three weeks. There are irregular cargo services between the islands and southern Chile and Uruguay.

The Falkland Islands merchant fleet numbered 31 vessels, with a total displacement of 54,707 grt, at December 2001; the majority of vessels registered are deep-sea fishing vessels.

Stanley Port Authority: c/o Department of Fisheries, POB 598, Stanley; tel. 27260; fax 27265; e-mail fish.fig@horizon.co.fk; Harbour Master J. Clark.

Private Companies

Byron Marine Ltd: 3 'H' Jones Rd, Stanley; tel. 22245; fax 22246; e-mail byron@horizon.co.fk.

Darwin Shipping Ltd: Stanley; tel. 27629; fax 27603; e-mail darwin@horizon.co.fk.

European South Atlantic Line (ESAL): Stanley; tel. 22622; fax 22623.

Sulivan Shipping Services Ltd: Stanley; tel. 22626; fax 22625; e-mail sulivan@horizon.co.fk.

CIVIL AVIATION

There are airports at Stanley and Mount Pleasant; the latter has a runway of 2,590 m, and is capable of receiving wide-bodied jet aircraft. The British Royal Air Force operates three weekly flights from the United Kingdom. The Chilean carrier LanChile operates weekly return flights from Punta Arenas.

Falkland Islands Government Air Service (FIGAS): Stanley Airport, Stanley; tel. 27219; fax 27309; f. 1948 to provide social, medical and postal services between the settlements and Stanley; aerial surveillance for Fishery Dept since 1990; Gen. Man. Vernon R. Steen.

Tourism

Approximately 3,000 shore-based and 40,000 cruise-ship tourists visit the islands each year. Wildlife photography, bird-watching and hiking are popular tourist activities. The Falkland Islands Development Corpn plans to develop the sector, which currently generates some £3m. in turnover annually.

Falkland Islands Tourist Board: Shackleton House, West Hillside, Stanley; tel. 22215; fax 22619; e-mail manager@tourism.org.fk; internet www.tourism.org.fk; Man. John A. T. Fowler.

GIBRALTAR

Introductory Survey

Location, Climate, Language, Religion, Flag

The City of Gibraltar lies in southern Europe. The territory consists of a narrow peninsula of approximately 4.8 km (3 miles) in length, running southwards from the south-west coast of Spain, to which it is connected by an isthmus. About 8 km (5 miles) across the bay, to the west, lies the Spanish port of Algeciras, while 32 km (20 miles) to the south, across the Strait of Gibraltar, is Morocco. The Mediterranean Sea lies to the east. The climate is temperate, and snow or frost are extremely rare. The mean minimum and maximum temperatures during the winter are 13°C (55°F) and 18°C (65°F), respectively, and during the summer they are 13°C (55°F) and 29°C (85°F) respectively; the average annual rainfall is 890 mm (35 ins). The official language is English, although most of the population are bilingual in English and Spanish. More than three-quarters of the population are Roman Catholic. The flag (proportions 1 by 2) bears the arms of Gibraltar (a red castle with a pendant golden key) on a background, the upper two-thirds of which are white and the lower one-third red.

Recent History

Since the Second World War, this Overseas Territory has achieved considerable social and economic progress, through intensive development of its social and economic infrastructure, and by the expansion of commerce and the encouragement of tourism. Gibraltar has exercised control over most internal matters since 1969.

The Spanish Government lays claim to Gibraltar as a part of its territory, while the United Kingdom maintains that the Treaty of Utrecht (1713) granted sovereignty over Gibraltar to the United Kingdom in perpetuity (with the stipulation that, if the United Kingdom relinquished the colony, it would be returned to Spain). In 1963 the Spanish Government began a campaign, through the UN, for the cession of Gibraltar to Spain. It also imposed restrictions against Gibraltar, culminating in the closure of the frontier in 1969, the withdrawal of the Spanish labour force, and the severing of transport and communication links with Spain.

Following a referendum held in the territory in 1967, in which the overwhelming majority voted in favour of retaining British sovereignty, a new Constitution, promulgated in 1969, contained a provision that the British Government undertook never to enter into arrangements whereby the people of Gibraltar would pass under the sovereignty of another state against their freely and democratically expressed wishes. Gibraltar joined the European Community (EC, now European Union—EU, see p. 199) with the United Kingdom in 1973, under the provisions of the Treaty of Rome that relate to European territories for whose external relations a member state is responsible.

By 1977, a more flexible attitude by Spain towards Gibraltar became apparent. At talks held between Spanish and British ministers in November representatives of the Gibraltar Government were included for the first time as part of the British delegation. In December 1979 Spain requested new negotiations, and at meetings in April 1980 it was agreed, in principle, to reopen the frontier by June. However, the reopening was delayed by the Spanish Government's insistence that Spanish workers in Gibraltar should be allowed equal status with nationals of EC countries. In October the British Parliament granted Gibraltarians the right to retain full British citizenship. Negotiations for the full opening of the frontier continued in 1982, but a change of attitudes in both countries, following the war between the United Kingdom and Argentina over the sovereignty of the Falkland Islands (q.v.), resulted in an indefinite postponement. In December Spain reopened the border to pedestrians of Spanish nationality and to British subjects resident in Gibraltar.

In a general election held in January 1984, the Gibraltar Labour Party–Association for the Advancement of Civil Rights (GLP–AACR), led by Sir Joshua Hassan, retained a majority of one seat in the House of Assembly. The Gibraltar Socialist Labour Party (GSLP), led by Joseph Bossano, secured the remaining seven seats, replacing the Democratic Party of British Gibraltar as the opposition party in the House of Assembly. (Under the terms of the Constitution, the party with the largest share of the vote obtains a maximum of eight seats in the House of Assembly.)

In November 1984 the British and Spanish Governments agreed to provide equal rights for Spaniards in Gibraltar and for Gibraltarians in Spain; to allow free movement for all traffic between Gibraltar and Spain; and to conduct negotiations on the future of the territory, including (for the first time) discussions on sovereignty. Border restrictions were finally ended in February 1985, and negotiations took place between the British and Spanish Governments to improve cross-border co-operation, especially in tourism and civil aviation. In December, however, Spanish proposals for an interim settlement of the territory's future were rejected by the British Government as unacceptable since they implied the eventual automatic cession of Gibraltar to Spain. Subsequent discussions concerning principally Spain's demands for access to the Gibraltar airport (which the Spanish Government claimed was situated on land not covered by the terms of the Treaty of Utrecht) were inconclusive, owing to the Gibraltar Government's insistence that the airport remain exclusively under the control of the British and Gibraltar authorities. In December 1987 negotiators concluded an agreement that recommended increased co-operation between Spain and Gibraltar in the area of transport, in particular the joint administration of Gibraltar's airport, which would exempt passengers travelling to and from Spain from Gibraltar frontier controls. It was announced that Gibraltar's inclusion in an EC directive concerning air transport regulation was subject to the Gibraltar Government's approval of the Anglo-Spanish agreement. However, Gibraltar's House of Assembly rejected the agreement, on the grounds that it would represent an infringement of British sovereignty, and voted unanimously to contest Gibraltar's exclusion from the EC directive. The Spanish Government announced that, if Gibraltar continued to reject the agreement, it would consider the construction of its own airport on the Spanish side of the border.

In December 1987 Hassan resigned as Chief Minister and leader of the GLP–AACR and was succeeded by Adolfo Canepa, the Deputy Chief Minister. At a general election held in March 1988, the GSLP received 58.2% of the votes cast, obtaining eight seats in the House of Assembly, and the GLP–AACR received 29.3% of the vote, securing seven seats. The newly formed Independent Democratic Party failed to obtain parliamentary representation. Bossano replaced Canepa as Chief Minister, at the head of Gibraltar's first socialist Government. Bossano announced that he would not participate in Anglo-Spanish negotiations concerning Gibraltar, on the grounds that the territory's sovereignty was not a matter for negotiation between Spain and the United Kingdom, and that the December 1987 agreement would, in his view, result in the absorption of Gibraltar into Spain.

In January 1989, in an unprecedented gesture of co-operation between Gibraltar and Spain, Bossano met the mayor of La Línea, the Spanish town bordering Gibraltar, and offered to assist in financing an economic revival in the region. In February 1990 the British and Spanish Governments agreed to contest a legal action that was to be brought by Gibraltar in the European Court of Justice against Gibraltar's exclusion from measures adopted to liberalize European air transport, which prevented the territory from expanding its air links with Europe. The decision to contest the action was considered to be a further attempt by the United Kingdom to persuade Gibraltar to co-operate with Spain. In March 1991 the United Kingdom withdrew the majority of British army personnel from Gibraltar, although the Royal Navy and Royal Air Force detachments remained.

In May 1991 the Spanish Prime Minister made an official visit to the United Kingdom, and was reported to have proposed a plan for joint sovereignty over Gibraltar, whereby the dependency would become effectively autonomous, with the British and Spanish monarchs as joint heads of state. Although it represented a significant concession by the Spanish Government (which had hitherto demanded full sovereignty over Gibraltar), the plan was rejected by the Gibraltar Government in July. At the EC summit meeting at Maastricht in December, Spain continued to refuse to recognize Gibraltar's status as a member of the EC, and remained determined to exclude it from the External Frontiers Convention (EFC), which was designed to strengthen common controls on entry into countries belonging to the EC. The Spanish Government opposed the inclusion of Gibraltar in the EFC on the grounds that it did not recognize Gibraltar as part of the EC. It was asserted by the Spanish Government that the inclusion of Gibraltar had to be subject to a separate bilateral agreement between the United Kingdom and Spain.

At a general election held in January 1992 the GSLP retained eight seats in the House of Assembly, and Bossano was returned for a second term as Chief Minister. The Gibraltar Social Democrats, an organization founded in 1989 that supported Gibraltar's participation in Anglo-Spanish negotiations, secured the remaining seven seats. In February, prior to discussions with British ministers in London, Bossano announced that Gibraltar was to attempt to obtain a revision of the 1969 Constitution, with the aim of achieving self-determination within four years. The British Government, however, stated that it would not consider granting independence to Gibraltar, unless the Spanish Government was prepared to accept the agreement, and excluded the possibility of formal negotiations on the issue.

In May 1992 Spain announced that it would continue to exclude Gibraltar from the EFC, unless there was progress in the Anglo-Spanish negotiations regarding the restoration of Spain's sovereignty over Gibraltar. Further Anglo-Spanish negotiations, which were to take place in November, were postponed, however, and the continued failure to reach an agreement on the issue of the administration of Gibraltar airport prevented the ratification of the EFC.

In January 1993 Gibraltarians formally protested, after increasingly stringent monitoring of vehicles by Spanish customs officials resulted in severe delays at the border with Spain. In March an official meeting between the foreign ministers of the United Kingdom and Spain achieved little progress; it was agreed, however, that contacts between British and Spanish officials were to be maintained. In early 1994 Bossano accused the British Government of subordinating the interests of Gibraltar to the promotion of harmonious relations with Spain, and demanded a renegotiation of the 1987 airport agreement on the grounds that its provisions were redundant and contrary to EU law, following the implementation of the Third Air Liberalization Directives in 1993.

In September 1994 the Gibraltar Government began to come under pressure from the United Kingdom to implement EU directives governing health and safety regulations, public procurement procedures, environmental matters and the regulation of the banking and financial services sectors. In addition, it was alleged by Spain that insufficient action was being taken by Gibraltar to curtail the smuggling of tobacco from Gibraltar to Spain and of drugs between Morocco and Spain by Gibraltar-based fast launches. The imposition in October of stringent border inspections by Spain, leading to lengthy delays in commercial and visitor traffic, prompted a protest by the British Government. These border checks were eased following assurances that measures were being taken to curtail the activities of the fast launches operating from Gibraltar.

Spain reimposed frontier controls in March 1995 and was again criticized by the British Government. In May, however, it emerged that the Gibraltar Government had brought into effect only about one-quarter of the relevant EU directives, and Gibraltar was warned by the British Government that substantial progress must be made by late June. Bossano, however, declared that the House of Assembly had the right to interpret EU legislation as it saw fit, and that any interference by the United Kingdom would be challenged in the British courts. In July 1996 the Gibraltar administration extended money-laundering offences from drugs-trafficking to all crimes.

In July 1995, following the confiscation of more than 60 speed launches, alleged to be used in the transport of contraband, the Spanish Government eased the frontier controls imposed 16 months earlier. The seizures provoked two days of riots and looting in the City, followed, however, by a peaceful mass demonstration, organized by Gibraltar business interests and trade unions, in support of the continuing implementation of anti-smuggling measures.

Although the British and Spanish Governments jointly agreed in September 1995 that the anti-smuggling measures were proving effective, the death of a Spanish civil guard in pursuit of

smugglers in April 1996 led to the renewal of border controls by Spain, and in the following month the newly-elected Spanish Government, alleging a resurgence of smuggling activity, threatened to impose a total closure of the frontier. In April Bossano announced that legislative elections would take place in May. Campaign debates focused on the single issue of the territory's external relations. Bossano and the GSLP proposed that Gibraltar's colonial status be replaced before the year 2000 by a form of 'free association' with the United Kingdom, while the GSD declared as its aims the achievement of improved relations both with Spain and the United Kingdom and the modernization of Gibraltar's Constitution. The GSD also stated its willingness to participate in negotiations with Spain on matters of mutual co-operation, excluding the issue of sovereignty. The election attracted an unusually high turn-out (88% of eligible voters), and resulted in the GSD, led by Peter Caruana, receiving 48% of the vote and the maximum of eight seats in the House of Assembly. The GSLP received 39% of the vote and the Gibraltar National Party obtained 13%.

In November 1996 the Spanish Government lodged a complaint with the EU Commission over a private visit to Gibraltar by the EU Commissioner responsible for Immigration and Home and Judicial Affairs to view the operation of Spanish border controls. In the same month Caruana renewed his demand that Gibraltar be accorded equal status with the United Kingdom in future negotiations concerning the territory's interests. On a visit to the EU Commission in January 1997, the Chief Minister cited a number of alleged abuses by Spain of EU treaty arrangements, including its imposition of a ban on maritime and air links and its refusal to recognize identity cards issued in Gibraltar. Caruana indicated that legal action would be instituted against the Spanish Government where violations of EU regulations could be established. In the same month Caruana refused to attend discussions on Gibraltar, held in Madrid, between the United Kingdom and Spain, on the grounds that Gibraltar would not be granted power of veto. A suggestion by Spain that sovereignty over Gibraltar be shared between Spain and the United Kingdom for a 100-year period, with full control then passing to Spain, was rejected by the British Government. In September the Government of Gibraltar opened an office in Brussels, Belgium, to promote the territory's financial services and tourism and to facilitate liaison with British representation in the EU.

In October 1997 Caruana informed the Decolonization Committee of the UN General Assembly that he was to seek from the British Government an extensive review of the territory's 1969 Constitution. It was to be proposed that Gibraltar would obtain additional autonomy in the conduct of its affairs while remaining in a close political and constitutional relationship to the United Kingdom, similar to that held by the Channel Islands and the Isle of Man (qq.v.). The Chief Minister stated his belief that such an arrangement would 'strengthen and modernize' Gibraltar's relationship to the United Kingdom, and that these proposals would, if accepted by the people of Gibraltar in a referendum, create a non-colonial relationship and constitute an effective and valid exercise of self-determination.

During 1997 new tensions arose between the United Kingdom and Spanish Governments over the long-standing refusal by Spain to permit military aircraft from the United Kingdom and the North Atlantic Treaty Organization (NATO, see p. 271) to cross Spanish air space on their approach to Gibraltar airport. In July the British Secretary of State for Foreign and Commonwealth Affairs, Robin Cook, indicated that the United Kingdom would oppose the full incorporation of Spain into NATO unless the ban were lifted. An indication by Spain of its willingness to open its airspace to these flights in return for joint military control of the airport was strongly opposed by Caruana and rejected by the British Government. In July 1998 Spain reversed its long-standing refusal to participate in military manoeuvres by NATO that were based in, or passing through, Gibraltar. In that month the Spanish Government unsuccessfully requested the British Government to consider a revived proposal for the shared sovereignty of Gibraltar for a period of 50 years, to be followed by the territory's full integration into Spain.

In November 1998 complaints by the Gibraltar Government arose over the conduct of Spanish fishing vessels in the Bay of Gibraltar, which were stated to be operating in violation of the territory's nature protection ordinance. In January 1999 a Spanish trawler was arrested by the Gibraltar authorities, and Spain began to intensify delays in motor traffic crossing the frontier. An agreement reached in February between the

Gibraltar authorities and the Spanish fishermen (at the Gibraltar Government's initiative) was not recognized by the Spanish Government. Border crossing delays were intensified, and Spain indicated that it was considering withdrawing its recognition of driving licences and other legal documents issued by the Gibraltar Government. Although relations with Spain were further complicated in March by an announcement that the British Government wished to obtain the right for Gibraltar residents to vote in EU elections, negotiations between the two countries continued through 1999.

At the general election held in February 2000, the GSD secured 58.7% of the vote, against 40.8% obtained by an electoral coalition of the GSLP and the Gibraltar Liberal Party. Caruana was reconfirmed as Chief Minister, again commanding eight seats in the House of Assembly, while opposition representation was unchanged at seven seats. Immediately following the election, Caruana expressed his wish for improved relations with Spain. In April David Durie was appointed Governor and Commander-in-Chief.

The extended negotiations between the Spanish and British Governments were concluded in April 2000 with a compromise agreement, whereby Spain was to recognize the validity of Gibraltar identity cards and of the Territory's financial institutions, provided that the 'competent authority' responsible for their supervision was the United Kingdom rather than the Gibraltar Government. It was also agreed that the British authorities would provide a facility, based in London, through which the Spanish and Gibraltar administrations could have indirect communication. An incidental effect of the agreement was to terminate the long-standing refusal by Spain to adopt any legislation by the EU that might have required it to deal directly with Gibraltar's police or financial regulatory authorities.

In February 2001 the Spanish Government issued a statement attacking British sovereignty over Gibraltar, criticizing the island's monetary system and accusing the island of being an 'economic parasite' financed by Spain. In March the Gibraltar political parties reached an agreement to request the previously proposed reforms to the 1969 Constitution, allowing self-determination, and to hold a referendum on decolonization. However, the move was condemned by Spain as a breach of the Treaty of Utrecht. Owing to the continuing delays in crossing the border, in April the British Foreign Affairs Committee suggested that legal action be taken against the Spanish Government, through the European Court of Justice.

In July 2001 the British and Spanish Governments renewed discussions on Gibraltar's future status for the first time since 1998. In response, the Gibraltarian legislature requested that a UN decolonization mission visit the territory. At a subsequent meeting in October, the British Secretary of State for Foreign and Commonwealth Affairs, Jack Straw, and his Spanish counterpart, Josep Piqué I Camps, agreed to work towards achieving a settlement on the issue by December 2002 (this was later modified to September 2002). Amid public criticism of proposals of joint British-Spanish sovereignty, Caruana rebuffed an invitation to attend the next round of negotiations in November, claiming that he would not be accorded equal status in the discussions. The Chief Minister also stated that the territory would not accept any change in sovereignty, the sharing of responsibility for its external affairs between Spain and the United Kingdom, nor Spanish military presence.

At the negotiations in November 2001, Piqué announced that Spain was prepared to increase the number of telephone lines available to Gibraltar from 35,000 to 100,000 and provide greater access to the Spanish health care system. However, the issue of the right of the citizens of Gibraltar to vote on the terms of an agreement regarding the future status of the territory remained one of the main points of contention between Spain and the United Kingdom. At the end of the month the British Government announced that Gibraltarians would be given the right to vote in elections to the EU Parliament, but ruled out the possibility of the territory's further integration into the United Kingdom. Caruana continued to voice Gibraltar's opposition to a transfer of sovereignty and asserted its citizens' rights to self-determination. In an open letter published in the local press, Piqué attempted to allay Gibraltarians' fears of the implications of Spanish rule and urged Caruana to attend the negotiations. The following month, however, most of the territory's 300,000 citizens took part in a public demonstration against the proposals. Following further public protests in March 2002, EU leaders agreed to a joint British-Spanish request for a grant of £37m. to fund the development of Gibraltar's port, infrastructure and airport. Caruana rejected the proposals and threatened to organize a referendum.

Shortly before negotiations on the sovereignty issue were due to resume in May 2002, the Spanish Prime Minister, José María Aznar, asserted that Spain would never withdraw its territorial claim to Gibraltar. During a subsequent visit, Straw's efforts to persuade Gibraltar of the benefits of joint sovereignty and to reassure its residents that any agreement would be subject to a referendum, were met with scepticism. Also in May, the Overseas Territories Act, having received royal assent in the United Kingdom in February, came into force and granted British citizenship rights to the people of its Overseas Territories, including Gibraltar. Under the new law Gibraltarians would be able to hold British passports and work in the United Kingdom and other EU countries.

Negotiations between the Spanish and UK Governments progressed in mid-2002, although discussions stalled over Spain's claims to eventual sovereignty rather than permanent co-sovereignty and its refusal to allow British control over the military base. In response, Caruana called a referendum for November 2002. Talks recommenced in late September, but with no certain deadline. The referendum held on 7 November, in which 87.9% of the electorate voted, demonstrated overwhelming (98.97%) opinion against joint-sovereignty with Spain; it was, however, not recognized, by either Spain or the United Kingdom, and the British Prime Minister, Anthony (Tony) Blair, refused to abandon discussions regarding joint sovereignty. Relations were strained in late November 2002 when the Spanish Minister of Foreign Affairs claimed that Gibraltar was partly responsible for the sinking of the oil tanker *Prestige* off the coast of Galicia in Spain, as Gibraltarian maritime officials had allegedly failed properly to examine the vessel when it had docked near the enclave in June. The British Government refuted these accusations, as the tanker had docked outside the port, and confirmed further that the final destination of the ship had been Singapore, and not Gibraltar as Spain claimed. In January 2003 Caruana proposed plans for constitutional reform which would establish a decolonized status for the enclave, but maintain its links with the United Kingdom. Further discussions between Spain and the United Kingdom were scheduled for 2003, although the accession of a military expert, Sir Francis Richards, to the governorship of Gibraltar in May 2003, and the proposed visit to the colony by the British monarch, Queen Elizabeth II, in 2004, appeared to make the attainment of a swift resolution unlikely.

Government

Gibraltar is a United Kingdom Overseas Territory. Executive authority is exercised by the Governor, who is advised by the Gibraltar Council, which comprises four *ex-officio* members and five elected members of the Gibraltar House of Assembly. The Council of Ministers, which is presided over by the Chief Minister, is responsible for domestic affairs, excluding defence and internal security. The House of Assembly comprises the Speaker (who is appointed by the Governor after consultation with the Chief Minister), two *ex-officio* members, and 15 members who are elected for a four-year term. The party obtaining the largest share of the vote at a general election is restricted to a maximum of eight seats in the Assembly.

Defence

There is a local defence force, the Gibraltar Regiment, which, following the abolition of conscription, was reorganized as a predominantly volunteer reserve unit (comprising 175 members in August 2002). In August 2002 British army personnel stationed in Gibraltar numbered 60, while the Royal Navy and Royal Marines detachment numbered 235. Royal Air Force personnel stationed in the territory numbered about 105.

Economic Affairs

In 1995/96 Gibraltar's gross domestic product (GDP), measured at current prices, was £327.7m., equivalent to £11,680 per head. Gibraltar's population totalled some 27,000 in mid-2001, according to UN estimates.

Gibraltar lacks agricultural land and natural resources, and the territory is dependent on imports of foodstuffs and fuels. Foodstuffs were estimated to account for 12% of total imports (excluding petroleum products) in 1997.

The industrial sector (including manufacturing, construction and power) employed 16.6% of the working population in 1997.

Manufacturing employed 3.3% of the working population in 1997. The most important sectors are shipbuilding and ship-repairs, and small-scale domestic manufacturing (mainly bottling, coffee-processing, pottery and handicrafts).

Gibraltar is dependent on imported petroleum for its energy supplies. Mineral fuels (excluding petroleum products) accounted for about 41.0% of the value of total imports in 1997.

Tourism and banking make a significant contribution to the economy. In 1997 revenue from tourism was estimated at US $300m. In that year the financial sector employed about 12% of the working population. Several Spanish banks have established offices in Gibraltar, encouraging the growth of the territory as an 'offshore' banking centre, while the absence of taxes for non-residents has also encouraged the use of Gibraltar as a financial centre. The value of bank deposits increased by more than 480% in the period 1987–95. In November 2002, however, the European Commission (EC) ruled that Gibraltar's tax-free status was illegal and ordered Gibraltar to close its tax 'haven', which was unique in the European Union (EU, see p. 199). Tax reforms subsequently negotiated with the Organisation for Economic Co-operation and Development (OECD, see p. 277) were awaiting approval by the EC in 2003.

In 1997 Gibraltar recorded a visible trade deficit of £173m. In that year the principal source of imports was the United Kingdom (accounting for 57% of the total). Other major trading partners included Spain, Japan and the Netherlands. The principal imports in 1997 were mineral fuels and manufactured goods. The principal re-exports in that year were petroleum products, manufactured goods and wines, spirits, malt and tobacco.

In the year ending 31 March 1999 there was a budgetary deficit of £30.7m. The annual rate of inflation averaged 2.7% during 1990–2001. The average annual rate was 1.1% in 2000 and 1.8% in 2001. An estimated 4.0% of the labour force were unemployed in 1998.

Gibraltar joined the European Community (EC—now EU, see p. 199) with the United Kingdom in 1973.

The Gibraltar economy is based on revenue from the British defence forces, tourism, shipping, and banking and finance. In 1988 the Gibraltar Government declared its aim to develop the territory as an 'offshore' financial centre, to stimulate private investment, and to promote the tourism sector. A project to build a new financial and administrative centre on land reclaimed from the sea commenced in 1990, and in the same year a Financial Services Commission was appointed to regulate financial activities in Gibraltar. In 1994, following the reduction in British military personnel in Gibraltar, revenue from the British defence forces (which had accounted for some 60% of the economy in 1985) contributed only 10% to total government revenue. In 1999 there was a sudden increase in gambling outlets in Gibraltar, as leading operations transferred from the United Kingdom. By mid-2000 the Government had issued seven new licences.

Education

Education is compulsory between the ages of five and 15 years, and is provided free in government schools. The language of instruction is English. There are four nursery schools, 11 primary schools (of which one is private), one Service school (administered by the Ministry of Defence for the children of military personnel) and two secondary comprehensive schools—one for boys and one for girls. Scholarships for students in higher education are provided by both government and private sources. There is also one college providing technical and vocational training, and a special school for handicapped children. Government expenditure on education in the year ending 31 March 1999 was G£14.5m.

Public Holidays

2003: 1 January (New Year's Day), 10 March (Commonwealth Day), 18 April (Good Friday), 21 April (Easter Monday), 1 May (May Day), 5 May (Spring Bank Holiday), 16 June (Queen's Official Birthday), 25 August (Late Summer Bank Holiday), 10 September (Gibraltar National Holiday), 25–26 December (Christmas).

2004: 1 January (New Year's Day), 8 March (Commonwealth Day), 9 April (Good Friday), 12 April (Easter Monday), 3 May (Spring Bank Holiday), 14 June (Queen's Official Birthday), 30 August (Late Summer Bank Holiday), 10 September (Gibraltar National Day), 27–28 December (for Christmas).

Weights and Measures

Imperial weights and measures are in use, but the metric system is gradually being introduced.

Statistical Survey

Source: Government Secretariat, No. 6 Convent Place, Gibraltar; tel. 70071; fax 74524.

AREA AND POPULATION

Area: 6.5 sq km (2.5 sq miles).

Population (1998): 27,025: 20,921 Gibraltarians; 3,825 other British; 2,279 non-British. Figures exclude visitors and transients. *Mid-2001* (estimate): 27,000 (Source: UN, *Population and Vital Statistics Report*).

Births, Marriages and Deaths (1998): Live births 411; marriages 639; deaths 267. Figures exclude members of the armed forces.

Expectation of Life (years at birth): 78.95 (males 76.09; females 81.96) in 2001.

Employment (April 1997): Manufacturing 432; Construction 1,486; Electricity and water 242; Trade, restaurants and hotels 3,060; Community, social and personal services 6,171; Total (incl. others) 13,000 (males 8,199; females 6,171). Figures cover only non-agricultural activities, excluding mining and quarrying.

FINANCE

Currency and Exchange Rates: 100 pence (pennies) = 1 Gibraltar pound (G£). *Sterling, Dollar and Euro Equivalents* (31 December 2002): £1 sterling = G£1.0000; US $1 = 62.04 pence; €1 = 65.06 pence; G£100 = £100.00 sterling = $161.18 = €153.70. *Average Exchange Rate* (US $ per G£): 1.5161 in 2000; 1.4400 in 2001; 1.5013 in 2002. Note: The Gibraltar pound is at par with sterling.

Budget (G£ '000, year ending 31 March 1999): *Revenue:* Income tax 47,000; General rates 10,900; Total (incl. Import duties and others) 82,800. *Expenditure:* Education, youth, culture and consumer affairs 14,500; Electricity 9,300; Police 6,900; Support services 3,300; Environment and health 13,600; Fire service 2,300; Customs 2,600; Tourism and transport 6,200; Consolidated fund charges 19,600; Total (incl. others) 113,500.

Cost of Living (Consumer Price Index; base: 1990 = 100): 130.8 in 1999; 132.2 in 2000; 134.6 in 2001. Source: ILO.

EXTERNAL TRADE

Principal Commodities (G£ '000, 1997): *Imports* (excl. petroleum products): Foodstuffs 26,397, Manufactured goods 22,825, Fuels n.a.; Total (incl. others) 300,210. *Re-exports* (excl. petroleum products): Machinery and transport equipment 30,330; Total (incl. others) 49,528.

Principal Trading Partner (G£ '000, 1997): *Imports* (excl. petroleum products): United Kingdom 190,507; Total (incl. others) 300,210.

TRANSPORT

Road Traffic (registered motor vehicles, 1999): Cars and taxis 2,532, Commercial vehicles 184, Motorcycles 986.

Shipping (1999): Tonnage entered ('000 grt) 105,800; Vessels entered 5,376.

Civil Aviation (1999): Passenger arrivals 98,200; Passenger departures 97,700; Freight loaded 77 metric tons; Freight unloaded 433 metric tons. Figures exclude military passengers and freight.

TOURISM

Tourist Arrivals ('000, excl. excursionists): 72 in 1995; 66 in 1996; 72 in 1997.

Tourism Receipts (US $ million): 215 in 1995; 282 in 1996; 300 in 1997 (Source: World Tourism Organization, *Yearbook of Tourism Statistics*).

COMMUNICATIONS MEDIA

Radio Receivers (1997): 37,000 in use (Source: UNESCO, *Statistical Yearbook*).

Television Licences (2000): 7,789*.

Daily Newspapers (1999): 1.

Telephones (2000): 23,541*.

Facsimile Machines (1997): 322 in use (Source: UN, *Statistical Yearbook*).

Mobile Cellular Telephones (2000): 5,558 subscribers*.

*Source: International Telecommunication Union.

EDUCATION

Primary (1999): 11 schools, 3,181 pupils.

Secondary (1999): 2 schools, 1,807 pupils.

Total Teaching Staff at Primary and Secondary Schools (1996): 309.

Technical and Vocational (1999): 1 college, 201 full-time students.

Directory

The Constitution

Gibraltar is a United Kingdom Overseas Territory, and the supreme authority is vested in the Governor and Commander-in-Chief, who is the representative of the British monarch. Relations with the British Government are maintained through the Foreign and Commonwealth Office.

Gibraltar controls the majority of its domestic affairs, while the United Kingdom is responsible for matters of external affairs, defence and internal security. Following the referendum of 10 September 1967 (in which the people of Gibraltar voted in favour of retaining British sovereignty), a new Constitution was introduced on 11 August 1969. This Constitution contains a code of human rights and provides for its enforcement by the Supreme Court of Gibraltar. The other main provisions are as follows:

BRITISH SOVEREIGNTY

The Preamble to the Gibraltar Constitution Order contains assurances that Gibraltar will remain part of the dominions of the British Crown (unless these provisions are amended by further legislation adopted by the British Parliament), and that the United Kingdom will never enter into arrangements under which the people of Gibraltar would pass under the sovereignty of another State against their freely and democratically expressed wishes.

THE GOVERNOR AND COMMANDER-IN-CHIEF

As a representative of the British monarch, the Governor and Commander-in-Chief is responsible for matters which directly relate to external affairs, defence and internal security and certain other matters not specifically defined as domestic matters. The Governor is also head of the executive and administers Gibraltar, acting generally on the advice of the Gibraltar Council. In exceptional circumstances, the Governor has special powers to refuse any advice from the Gibraltar Council which, in the Governor's opinion, may not be in the interests of maintaining financial and economic stability. The Governor's formal assent, on behalf of the Crown, is required for all legislation. In some cases, the prior concurrence of the Crown, conveyed through the Secretary of State for Foreign and Commonwealth Affairs, is also required. The Crown may, through the Governor and Commander-in-Chief, disband the House of Assembly, introduce direct rule and enact legislation for the 'peace, order and good government of Gibraltar'.

THE GIBRALTAR COUNCIL

The Council consists of the Deputy Governor, the Land Forces Commander, the Attorney-General, the Financial and Development Secretary, ex officio, the Chief Minister, who is appointed by the Governor as the elected member of the House of Assembly most likely to command the confidence of the other elected members, and four other ministers designated by the Governor after consultation with the Chief Minister. The Council advises the Governor, who usually acts on its advice.

COUNCIL OF MINISTERS

The Council of Ministers comprises the Chief Minister and between four and eight other ministers appointed from the elected members of the Assembly by the Governor, in consultation with the Chief Minister. It is presided over by the Chief Minister and deals with domestic matters which have been defined as such by the Constitution. The Chief Minister is constitutionally responsible for the economy. Individual ministers may be given responsibility for specific business. Heads of Departments and other government officials appear before it when required.

HOUSE OF ASSEMBLY

The House of Assembly is composed of the Speaker, 15 elected members and two ex-officio members (the Attorney-General and the Financial and Development Secretary). The Financial and Development Secretary is appointed by the Governor, normally after consultation with the Chief Minister. The Speaker is appointed by the Governor, after consultation with the Chief Minister and the Leader of the Opposition.

The normal term of the House of Assembly is four years. Elections are open to all adult British subjects and citizens of the Republic of Ireland who have been ordinarily resident in Gibraltar for a continuous period of six months prior to the date for registration as an elector. The minimum voting age is 18 years. The system of proportional representation, which was formerly used for elections to the Legislative Council, has been abandoned in favour of a new system, whereby each elector may vote for a maximum of eight candidates, and the party with the largest share of the vote is restricted to a maximum of eight seats.

The elected members of the House of Assembly elect the Mayor from among their number, and he carries out ceremonial and representational functions on behalf of the City of Gibraltar.

The Government

(May 2003)

Governor and Commander-in-Chief: Sir FRANCIS RICHARDS (took office 27 May 2003).

GIBRALTAR COUNCIL

President: Sir FRANCIS RICHARDS (The Governor).

Ex-Officio Members: PAUL SPELLER (Deputy Governor), Cdre A. WILLMETT (Commander British Forces), TIMOTHY BRISTOW (Financial and Development Secretary), R. RHODA (Attorney-General).

Elected Members: PETER CARUANA, KEITH AZZOPARDI, Dr BERNARD LINARES, ERNEST BRITTO, JOE HOLLIDAY.

COUNCIL OF MINISTERS

Chief Minister: PETER CARUANA.

Deputy Chief Minister and Minister for Trade, Industry and Telecommunications: KEITH AZZOPARDI.

Minister for Education, Training, Culture and Health: Dr BERNARD LINARES.

Minister for Public Services, the Environment, Sport and Leisure: ERNEST BRITTO.

Minister for Tourism and Transport: JOE HOLLIDAY.

Minister for Housing: JAIME NETTO.

Minister for Employment and Consumer Affairs: HUBERT CORBY.

Minister for Social Affairs: Y. DEL AGUA.

GOVERNMENT OFFICES

Office of the Governor: The Convent, Main St; tel. 45440; fax 47823; e-mail convent@gibnet.gi.

Office of the Chief Minister: 6 Convent Pl.; tel. 70071; fax 76396; e-mail govsec@gibnet.gi.

Department of Education and Training: 40 Town Range; tel. 77486; fax 71564; e-mail teachers@gibnynex.gi.

Employment and Training Board: Unit 76–77, New Harbours; tel. 40408; fax 73981.

Ministry for the Environment: Joshua Hassan House, Secretary's Lane; tel. 59833; fax 71143; e-mail environ@gibnynex.gi.

Income Tax Office: St Jago's Stone Block, 331 Main St; tel. 74889; fax 42398.

Department of Personnel: St Jago's Stone Block, 331 Main St; tel. 71911; fax 79689.

Post Office: 104 Main St; tel. 75714; fax 72476.

Ministry of Social Affairs: 14 Governor's Parade; tel. 78566; fax 42509; e-mail dssgibmg@gibnynex.gi.

Ministry for Tourism and Transport: Duke of Kent House, Cathedral Sq.; tel. 79336; fax 70029; e-mail tourism@gibraltar.gi; internet www.gibraltar.gi.

Ministry for Trade, Industry and Telecommunications: Suite 771, Europort; tel. 52052; fax 71406; e-mail finance@dtti.gov.gi; internet www.gibraltar.gov.gi.

Legislature

HOUSE OF ASSEMBLY

156 Main St; tel. 78420; fax 42849.

Speaker: JOHN E. ALCANTARA.

General Election, 10 February 2000

Party	% of votes cast	Seats
Gibraltar Social Democrats	58.7	8
Gibraltar Socialist Labour Party	} 40.8	7
Gibraltar Liberal Party		
Other	0.5	—
Total	**100.0**	**15**

In addition to the 15 elected members, the House of Assembly has an appointed Speaker and two *ex-officio* members (the Attorney-General and the Financial and Development Secretary). A Mayor of Gibraltar, with ceremonial and representational functions, is chosen from among their number by the elected members of the Assembly.

Political Organizations

All political organizations in Gibraltar advocate self-determination for the territory.

Gibraltar Labour Party–Association for the Advancement of Civil Rights (GLP-AACR): e-mail ISM@Marrache.com; internet pirelec@gibnet.gi; Pres. ISAAC MARRACHE; Gen. Sec. JOHN PIRIS.

Gibraltar Liberal Party (GLP): 93 Irish Town, POB 225; tel. 76959; fax 74664; e-mail libparty@gibnet.gi; internet www.gibraltar.gi/liberalparty; f. 1991 as the Gibraltar National Party; Leader Dr JOSEPH GARCÍA.

Gibraltar Social Democrats (GSD): 5/7 Horse Barrack Lane; tel. and fax 70786; internet www.gibnynex.gi; f. 1989; holds a majority of seats in the House of Assembly; Leader PETER CARUANA; Gen. Sec. LAURA V. CORREA.

Gibraltar Socialist Labour Party (GSLP): Suite 16, Block 3, Watergardens; tel. 50700; fax 78983; e-mail gslp@gibnet.gi; f. 1976; Leader JOSEPH BOSSANO.

Judicial System

The 1969 Gibraltar Constitution provides for the protection of the fundamental rights and freedoms of the individual and the maintenance of a Supreme Court with unlimited jurisdiction to hear and determine any civil or criminal proceedings under any law. The Courts of Law of Gibraltar comprise a Court of Appeal, the Supreme Court, the Court of First Instance and the Magistrates' Court.

The substantive law of Gibraltar is contained in Orders in Council which apply to Gibraltar, enactments of the Parliament of the United Kingdom which apply to or have been extended or applied to Gibraltar, locally enacted ordinances and subsidiary legislation, and common law and the rules of equity from time to time in force in the United Kingdom so far as they may be applicable and subject to all necessary modification.

COURT OF APPEAL

277 Main St; the Court of Appeal holds three sessions each year. The Justices of Appeal are drawn from the English Court of Appeal.

President: Sir BRIAN NEILL.

Justices of Appeal: Sir JOHN WAITE, Sir IAN GLIDEWELL, PHILIP CLOUGH.

SUPREME COURT

277 Main St; the Supreme Court includes the office of Admiralty Marshal.

Chief Justice: DEREK SCHOFIELD.

Justice: FELIX E. PIZZARELLO.

COURT OF FIRST INSTANCE

Judge: ANTHONY E. DUDLEY.

MAGISTRATES' COURT

Stipendiary Magistrate: ANTHONY E. DUDLEY.

Religion

At the 1991 census 76.9% of the population were Roman Catholic, 6.9% Muslim, 6.9% Church of England and 2.3% Jewish.

CHRISTIANITY

The Roman Catholic Church

Gibraltar forms a single diocese, directly responsible to the Holy See. At 31 December 2001 there were an estimated 23,000 adherents in the territory.

Bishop of Gibraltar: Rt Rev. CHARLES CARUANA, 215 Main St; e-mail epis.carroca@gibnynex.gi; tel. 76688; fax 43112.

The Church of England

The diocese of Gibraltar in Europe, founded in 1980, has jurisdiction over the whole of continental Europe, Turkey and Morocco.

Bishop of Gibraltar in Europe: Rt Rev. Dr GEOFFREY ROWELL, Bishop's Lodge, Church Rd, Worth, RH10 7RT, United Kingdom; tel. (1293) 883051; fax (1293) 884479; e-mail bishop@eurobish.clara.co.uk; internet europe.anglican.org; in Gibraltar: Cathedral of the Holy Trinity, Cathedral Sq., Main St; tel. 75745; fax 78463.

Other Christian Churches

Church of Scotland (St Andrew's Presbyterian): Governor's Parade; tel. 77040; fax 40852; e-mail macross@gibnynex.gi; f. 1800; Locum Minister Rev. STEWART LAMONT (St Andrew's Manse, 29 Scud Hill); 50 mems.

Methodist Church: Wesley House, 297 Main St; tel. and fax 40870; e-mail widor@gibnetmail.gi; Rev. WILF PEARCE; f. 1769; 49 mems.

ISLAM

A mosque to serve the Islamic community in Gibraltar and financed by the Government of Saudi Arabia was under construction in 1999. It will have a capacity for 1,000 worshippers.

JUDAISM

Jewish Community: Managing Board, 10 Bomb House Lane, POB 318; tel. 72606; fax 40487; Pres. H. J. M. LEVY; Hon. Sec. M. BENADY; Admin. Sec. E. BENADY; 600 mems.

The Press

Gibraltar Chronicle: 2 Library Gardens, POB 27; tel. 78589; fax 79927; e-mail gibchron@gibnet.gi; internet www.chronicle.gi; f. 1801; daily (except Sunday); English; Man. Editor D. SEARLE; circ. 6,000.

Gibraltar Gazette: 6 Convent Pl.; tel. 47932; fax 74524; e-mail legisunit@gibnynex.gi; f. 1949; weekly; publ. by *Gibraltar Chronicle*; official notices; circ. 375.

Gibraltar Magazine: Suite 6377, Imossi House, Irish Town; tel. and fax 77748; e-mail gibmag@gibnet.gi; internet www.thegibraltarmagazine.com; f. 1995; monthly; English.

Panorama: 93–95 Irish Town; tel. 79797; fax 74664; e-mail gibnet@gibnews.gi; internet www.panorama.gi; f. 1975; weekly, on Monday; English; Editor JOE GARCÍA; circ. 4,000.

The New People: 6B Portland House, Glacis Rd, POB 484; tel. 79018; fax 50349; weekly; English with Spanish section; Editor C. GOLT; circ. 1,000.

Vox: Unit 101, Harbours Walk, New Harbours, POB 306; tel. 77414; fax 72531; e-mail vox@gibnynex.gi; f. 1955; weekly; bilingual (English and Spanish); Editor E. J. CAMPELLO; circ. 1,800.

Broadcasting and Communications

TELECOMMUNICATIONS

Gibraltar Nynex Communications Ltd (Gibtelecom): Suite 942, Europort; tel. 52200; fax 71673; e-mail headoffice@gibtele.gi; internet www.gibtele.gi; f. 1990; jointly owned by Govt and Verizon Inc (USA); operates local and international telephone and telecommunications services; provides range of digital, satellite, mobile and internet services.

Gibraltar Telecommunications International Ltd (Gibtel): Mount Pleasant, 25 South Barrack Rd; tel. 75687; operates telegraph facilities and international telephone service; provides range of digital, satellite, mobile and internet services; jointly owned by Govt and British Telecom (United Kingdom).

BROADCASTING

Gibraltar Broadcasting Corporation (GBC): Broadcasting House, 18 South Barrack Rd; tel. 79760; fax 78673; e-mail gbc@gibraltar.gi; internet www.gbc.gi; f. 1963; responsible for television and radio broadcasting; Gen. Man. G. J. VALARINO.

Radio

GBC–Radio (Radio Gibraltar): 24 hours daily in English and Spanish, including commercial broadcasting. In addition to local programmes, the BBC World Service programme is relayed.

Television

GBC–TV: operates in English for 24 hours daily.

GBC and relayed BBC programmes are transmitted.

Finance

(cap. = capital; res = reserves; dep. = deposits; m. = million; brs = branches; amounts in G£)

BANKING

There were 19 banks operating in Gibraltar in March 2001.

Regulatory Authority

Financial Services Commission: Suite 943, Europort, POB 940; tel. 40283; fax 40282; e-mail info@fsc.gi; internet www.fsc.gi; f. 1989; regulates the activities of the financial sector; Chair. MARTIN FUGGLE.

Banks

Abbey National Treasury International Ltd: 237/239 Main St; tel. 76090; fax 72028; cap. and res 93.7m., dep. 2,172.5m. (Dec. 1996); Man. BOB WARNE.

ABN AMRO Bank (Gibraltar) Ltd: 2–6 Main St, POB 100; tel. 79220; fax 78512; e-mail private.banking@gi.abnamro.com; internet www.abnamro.gi; f. 1964; cap. and res 1.8m., dep. 148m. (Dec. 1995); Chair. J. J. W. ZWEEGERS; Man. Dir A. H. MEULENBERG.

Banco Atlantico (Gibraltar) Ltd: Eurolife Bldg, 1 Corral Rd, POB 561; tel. 40117; fax 40110; Man. CARLOS DEL CASTILLO.

BBVA Privanza International (Gibraltar) Ltd: 260–262 Main St, POB 488; tel. 79420; fax 73870; Man. ALFONSO RAMOS.

Barclays Bank PLC: Regal House, 3 Queensway, POB 187; tel. 78565; fax 795069; Chief Man. DOUGLAS REYES.

Crédit Agricole Indosuez (Gibraltar): 206/210 Main St, POB 26; tel. 75090; fax 79618; e-mail caigib@indosuez.gi; internet www.gi.ca-indosuez.com; f. 1875; Man. BERTRAND LEPISSIER.

Credit Suisse (Gibraltar) Ltd: Neptune House, 1st Floor, Marina Bay, POB 556; tel. 78399; fax 76027; f. 1987; Man. Dir PETER SCHUSTER.

S.G. Hambros Bank & Trust (Gibraltar) Ltd: Hambro House, 32 Line Wall Rd, POB 375; tel. 74850; fax 79037; e-mail franco.cassar@sghambros.com; internet www.sghambros.com; est. 1981; cap.1.5m. res 1.1m., dep. 89.6m. (Dec. 1999); Chair. W. J. NEWBURY; Man. Dir F. CASSAR.

Hispano Commerzbank (Gibraltar) Ltd: Don House, Suite 14, 30/38 Main St; tel. 74199; fax 74174; e-mail hcg@gibnynex.gi; f. 1991; cap. and res 5.0m., dep. 3.8m. (Dec. 2000); CEO BERND VON OELFFEN.

Jyske Bank (Gibraltar) Ltd: 76 Main St, POB 143; tel. 72782; fax 72732; e-mail jyskebank@jyskebank.ltd.gi; internet www.jbpb.com; cap.and res 26.5m., dep. 1,077.7m. (Dec. 2000); Man. Dir PETTER BLONDEAU.

Lloyds TSB Bank PLC: 323 Main St, POB 482; tel. 77373; fax 70023; Man. ALBERT DOUGLAS LANGSTON.

Lombard Odier Private Bank (Gibraltar) Ltd: Suite 921, Europort, POB 407.

NatWest Offshore Ltd: NatWest House, 57/63 Line Wall Rd, POB 707; tel. 77737; fax 74557; f. 1988; Chief Man. PETE YEOMAN.

Royal Bank of Scotland (Gibraltar) Ltd: 1 Corral Rd.

Turicum Private Bank Ltd: Turicum House, 315 Main St, POB 619; tel. 44144; fax 44145; e-mail turicum@gibnet.gi; f. 1993; cap. and res €5.0m., dep. €13.7m. (Dec. 2000); Gen. Man. FRIEDRICH STUCKI.

Savings Bank

Gibraltar Government Savings Bank: Gibraltar Post Office, 104 Main St; tel. 75624; fax 72476; f. 1882; dep. 102.3m. (March 2000); Dir D. D. TIRATHDAS.

Association

Gibraltar Bankers' Association: c/o S.G. Hambros Bank & Trust (Gibraltar) Ltd, 32 Line Wall Rd; tel. 74850; fax 79037; f. 1982; Pres. RAY LANGHAM; 20 mem. banks.

INSURANCE

There were 17 licensed insurance companies operating in Gibraltar in March 2001.

AXA Insurance PLC: 20 Line Wall Rd, POB 130; tel. 40850; fax 40851; e-mail info@axa-insurance.gi; internet www.axa-insurance.gi.

BMI Insurance Services Limited: Unit 7, Portland House, Glacis Rd, POB 469; tel. 51010.

Capurro Insurance and Investments Ltd: 20 Line Wall Rd, POB 130; tel. 40850; fax 40851; e-mail info@capurroinsurance.com; internet www.capurroinsurance.com.

Castiel Winser Insurance and Financial Consultants: Natwest House, 57/63 Line Wall Rd, POB 464; tel. 77723.

Eurolife Assurance (International) Ltd: Eurolife Bldg, 1 Corral Rd, POB 233; tel. 73495; fax 73120; Man. A. SMITH.

Eurolinx (Gibraltar) Ltd: Suites 21–22, Victoria House, 26 Main St, POB 671; tel. 40240; fax 40241; e-mail eurolinx@gibnet.gi.

Gibro Insurance Services Ltd: Gibro House, 4 Giros Passage, POB 693; tel. 43777.

Middle Sea Insurance PLC: Suite 1A, 143 Main St, POB 502; tel. 76434.

Norwich Union International Insurance Ltd: Regal House, 3 Queensway, POB 45; tel. 79520; fax 70942; e-mail nugib@gibnet.gi; f. 1984; cap. 1,600,000; CEO. ERIC D. CHALONER; Chair. PAUL L. SAVIGNON.

Ophir Insurance Services Ltd: 123 Main St, POB 914; tel. 73871.

Association

Gibraltar Insurance Association: c/o NatWest House, 57/63 Line Wall Rd, POB 464; tel. 77723; fax 79257; f. 1995.

Trade and Industry

At 31 December 1991 there were 16 registered unions (total membership 7,602). Of these, eight, including the Chamber of Commerce, were employers' associations, and eight were unions of employees. Two of the employees' unions are branches of British unions.

CHAMBER OF COMMERCE

Gibraltar Chamber of Commerce: Watergate House, Casemates, POB 29; tel. 78376; fax 78403; e-mail gichacom@gibnet.gi; internet www.gibraltarchamberofcommerce.com; f. 1882; Pres. PETER ISOLA; 300 mems.

EMPLOYERS' ORGANIZATIONS

Gibraltar Hotel Association: c/o Caleta Hotel; tel. 76501; fax 71050; e-mail caleta@gibynex.gi; internet www.caletahotel.com; f. 1960; Chair. FRANCO OSTUNI; 7 mems.

Gibraltar Licensed Victuallers' Association: c/o Watergate Restaurant, Queensway Quay; tel. 74195; f. 1976; Chair. M. OTON; 120 mems.

Gibraltar Motor Traders' Association: POB 167; tel. 79004; f. 1961; Gen. Sec. G. BASSADONE; 6 mems.

Hindu Merchants' Association: POB 82; tel. 73521; fax 79895; e-mail budlaw@gibynex.gi; f. 1964; Pres. H. K. BUDHRANI; 125 mems.

PRINCIPAL TRADE UNIONS

Gibraltar Taxi Association: 19 Waterport Wharf; tel. 70052; fax 76986; f. 1957; Pres. CLIVE ZAMMIT; 100 mems.

Gibraltar Trades Council: c/o 25 Antwerp Court, Harbour View; tel. 76308; fax 77608; e-mail alraphil@gibynex.gi; comprises unions representing 70% of the working population; affiliated to the United Kingdom Trades Union Congress; Pres. EDWIN J. REYES.

Affiliated unions:

Gibraltar Teachers' Association: 40 Town Range; tel. 76308; fax 77608; e-mail gtateachers@gibnyex.gi; f. 1962; Pres. EDWIN J. REYES; 350 mems.

Prospect/GGCA Branch: 7 Hargrave's Ramp, POB 279; tel. 76930; e-mail ggca.prospect@gibnynex.gi; internet www.prospectbranches

.org.uk/gibraltar; f. 1967; Pres. JOSE LUIS GARCIA; Br. Sec. MICHAEL J. A. TAMPIN; c. 750 mems.

Transport & General Workers' Union (United Kingdom) (Gibraltar District): tel. 74185; fax 71596; f. 1924; Dist. Officer LUIS MONTIEL; 4,239 mems.

UTILITIES
Electricity

Gibraltar Electricity Department: Waterport Power Station, North Mole; govt-owned; generation, distribution and supply of electricity.

Water

Lyonnais des Eaux (Gibraltar) Ltd: Leanse Pl., Suite 10B, 50 Town Range; tel. 40880; fax 40881; e-mail water@gibnet.gi; internet www.lyonnaise.gi; Man. Dir M. PÉREZ.

Transport

There are no railways in Gibraltar. There are 12.9 km of highways in the City, and a total road length of 53.1 km, including 6.8 km of footpaths.

ROADS

Ministry for Tourism and Transport (Roads Department): British Lines Depot; tel. 77506; fax 42659; responsible for the maintenance of all public highways.

SHIPPING

The Strait of Gibraltar is a principal ocean route between the Mediterranean and Black Sea areas and the rest of the world.

Gibraltar is used by many long-distance liners, and has dry dock facilities and a commercial ship-repair yard. Tax concessions are available to ship-owners who register their ships at Gibraltar. At 31 December 2001 79 vessels, with a combined total displacement of 816,323 grt, were registered at Gibraltar.

Office of the Maritime Administrator: Registry of Ships, Duke of Kent House, Cathedral Sq.; tel. 47771; fax 47770; e-mail shipregistry@gibnynex.gi.

Gibraltar Port Authority: Port Office, North Mole; tel. 77254; fax 51513; e-mail Davis.GPA@gibnyex.gi; administers the Port of Gibraltar; part of the Ministry for Tourism and Transport; CEO TONY DAVIES.

Cammell Laird (Gibraltar) Ltd: Main Wharf Rd, The Dockyard, POB 858; tel. 59400; fax 44404; e-mail mail@lairds.gi; drydock facilities and general ship repairing; Man. Dir MEL SMITH.

M. H. Bland & Co Ltd: Cloister Bldg, Market Lane, POB 554; tel. 75009; fax 71608; f. 1810; ship agents, salvage and towage contractors; Chair. JOHN G. GAGGERO.

Association

Gibraltar Shipping Association: 47 Irish Town, POB 9; tel. 78646; fax 77838; f. 1957; Sec. P. L. IMOSSI; 11 mems.

CIVIL AVIATION

The airport is at North Front, on the isthmus, 2.5 km from the City centre.

Gibraltar Civil Aviation Advisory Board: Air Terminal, Winston Churchill Ave; tel. 73026; fax 73925; e-mail airport@gibnet.gi; Sec. JOHN GONÇALVES.

Tourism

Gibraltar's tourist attractions include its climate, beaches, and a variety of amenities. Following the reopening of the border with Spain in February 1985, the resumption of traffic by day-visitors contributed to the expansion of the tourist industry. In 1997 visitor arrivals were estimated at 72,000, while revenue from this source totalled about US $300m. There are an estimated 2,000 hotel beds in Gibraltar.

Gibraltar Tourist Board: Duke of Kent House, Cathedral Sq.; tel. 74950; fax 74943; e-mail tourism@gibraltar.gi; internet www.gibraltar.gov.uk; CEO P. R. CANESSA.

MONTSERRAT

Introductory Survey

Location, Climate, Language, Religion, Flag, Capital

Montserrat is one of the Leeward Islands in the West Indies. A mountainous, volcanic island, it lies about 55 km (35 miles) north of Basse-Terre, Guadeloupe, and about 43 km (27 miles) south west of Antigua. The climate is generally warm, with a mean maximum temperature of 30°C (86°F) and a mean minimum of 23°C (73°F), but the island is fanned by sea breezes for most of the year. The average annual rainfall is about 1,475 mm (58 ins), although there is more rain in the central and western areas. English is the official language. Many Christian churches are represented, but the principal denominations are the Anglican, Roman Catholic and Methodist Churches. The flag is the British 'Blue Ensign', with the island's badge (a shield depicting a woman dressed in green holding a harp and a cross) on a white roundel in the fly. The capital is Plymouth.

Recent History

Montserrat was first settled by the British (initially Roman Catholic exiles) in 1632, by which time the few original Carib inhabitants had disappeared. It formed part of the federal colony of the Leeward Islands from 1871 until 1956, when the federation was dissolved and the presidency of Montserrat became a separate colony. Montserrat participated in the short-lived Federation of the West Indies (1958–62) and, from 1960, the island had its own Administrator (the title was changed to that of Governor in 1971). The Constitution (see below) came into force in 1960.

The first priority of successive legislatures has been to improve infrastructure and maintain a healthy economy. Between 1952 and 1970 William Bramble dominated island politics. His son, Austin Bramble, leader of the Progressive

Democratic Party (PDP), opposed and succeeded him as Chief Minister. In November 1978 the People's Liberation Movement (PLM) won all seven elective seats in the Legislative Council, and the PLM's leader, John Osborne, became Chief Minister. In the general election of February 1983 the PLM was returned to government with five seats. The remainder were won by the PDP, whose commitment to development projects, agriculture and education complemented those of the PLM.

Attempts to form an opposition alliance between the PDP and the National Development Party (NDP—formed by business interests and former members of the PDP) were unsuccessful. Against a divided opposition, the PLM won four of the seven elective seats in the Legislative Council at an early general election in August 1987. The NDP won two seats, and the PDP one (Bramble lost his seat and announced his retirement from politics). Osborne was returned to office as Chief Minister.

Osborne was an advocate of independence from the United Kingdom, despite the apparent lack of popular support for this policy. A referendum on the issue was planned for 1990, but the devastation caused by 'Hurricane Hugo' in September 1989, meant that any plans for independence were postponed. Furthermore, the Osborne Government and the British authorities were embarrassed by controversy surrounding the hitherto lucrative 'offshore' financial sector. In early 1989 the Governor's office announced that the British police were investigating serious allegations against certain banks (involving the processing of illegal funds from a variety of criminal activities). Registration was suspended, several people were charged with criminal offences and, at the end of 1989, most banking licences were revoked. The Montserrat Government agreed to introduce recommended provisions for the regulation of the financial services industry, but Osborne objected strongly to a proposed amendment to the Constitution which transferred responsibility for the sector from the Chief Minister to the Governor. Agreement was subsequently reached, however, when Osborne acknowledged that offshore finance was part of the British Government's responsibility for external affairs.

In late 1990 a dispute arose between the Chief Minister and his deputy, Benjamin Chalmers, who was reported to have accused Osborne of dishonesty in his relations with the Executive Council. Allegations of corruption continued in 1991, and in June an inquiry was undertaken by the British police to investigate the possible involvement of members of the Executive Council in the 1989 banking scandal, as well as in fraudulent land transfers.

The resignation of Chalmers in September 1991, following a further dispute with Osborne, resulted in the loss of the Government's majority in the Legislative Council. This prompted an early election in the following month, when the National Progressive Party (NPP), which had been formed only two months prior to the election, secured four seats. The PLM and the NDP retained one seat each, while an independent candidate won the remaining seat. The leader of the NPP, Reuben Meade, became Chief Minister.

In December 1991 the Legislative Council approved legislation allowing the re-establishment of a comprehensive offshore financial centre. Despite considerably improved regulation, more than 90% of the island's offshore and commercial banks were again closed down, following further investigations by British inspectors in mid-1992.

The eruption of Chance's Peak volcano in July 1995, which had been dormant for more than 100 years, caused severe disruption to the island and threatened to devastate Plymouth and surrounding areas in southern Montserrat. In late August the threat of a more serious eruption prompted the evacuation of some 5,000 people to the north of the island, and the declaration by the Government of a state of emergency and a night curfew. As volcanic activity subsided in September, evacuated islanders returned to Plymouth and villages near the volcano. However, by December the area was again deemed to be unsafe, and 4,000 people were evacuated for a further period of several weeks. The Governor and Chief Minister secured an agreement from the British Government for the provision of assistance with evacuation and rehabilitation programmes. A third evacuation took place in April 1996, following a further series of eruptions, and it was announced that some 5,000 evacuees living in 'safe areas' would remain there at least until the end of the year. In that month the British Government announced that Montserratians would be granted residency and the right to work in the United Kingdom for up to two years. In August the British Government announced that it was to provide assistance worth £25m. to finance housing construction projects, infrastructure development, the provision of temporary health and education facilities and other public services in the northern 'safe areas' of the island. By the end of 1996 it was estimated that some 5,000 islanders had left the Territory since the onset of volcanic activity in mid-1995.

In September 1996 the Government announced that the general election would take place, despite the continued disruption in the Territory. The Deputy Chief Minister, Noel Tuitt, resigned from his post and from the NPP later that month, stating that he was disillusioned with Meade's leadership. Disagreement over the Government's management of the volcano crisis and its handling of aid funds led to the proposal, by an opposition member in early October, of a motion of 'no confidence' in the Chief Minister. Meade, however, avoided a vote on the motion by dissolving the Legislative Council. A second member of the Executive Council, Lazelle Howes, also subsequently resigned from the Government, and stated her intention to contest the election as an independent candidate.

No party won an overall majority at the election on 11 November 1996. The NPP secured only one seat (won by Meade). The recently-formed People's Progressive Alliance (PPA), led by John Osborne, secured two seats, as did both the Movement for National Reconstruction (MNR), led by Austin Bramble, and independent candidates. A four-member coalition cabinet (which included Meade, but did not include either PPA member) was subsequently formed under the leadership of Bertrand Osborne, who was sworn in as Chief Minister on 13 November. Meanwhile, volcanic activity intensified, and in January 1997 Osborne and the Governor made an official visit to Britain for further discussions with government representatives on the volcano crisis.

In June 1997 the scale of volcanic activity on the island increased dramatically with the eruption of the Soufrière Hills volcano which left some two-thirds of the island uninhabitable, destroyed the capital and resulted in the deaths of 19 people. Islanders were evacuated to 'safe areas' in the north of the country. The British Government responded to the crisis by releasing emergency aid in order to finance the construction of emergency shelters for evacuees, and for repairs to temporary hospital facilities. In July it was announced that a package of options for Montserratians was being formulated, which would offer islanders resettlement grants and assisted passage either to other islands within the Caribbean or to the United Kingdom. The 'safe area' in the north was to be developed for those wishing to remain on the island. By the end of July the population of Montserrat was estimated to have declined to 5,800; in the month since the eruption of the Soufrière Hills volcano some 800 islanders had moved to Antigua, bringing the total number who had moved there since the onset of volcanic activity in 1995 to some 3,000. Many more had resettled on other Caribbean islands or in the United Kingdom.

On 21 August 1997 Bertrand Osborne resigned as Chief Minister following four days of public demonstrations in protest at his handling of the volcano crisis, in particular at uncertainty surrounding the future of the islanders and at poor conditions in emergency shelters. On the same day the British Government announced the financial details of its voluntary evacuation scheme for those wishing to leave Montserrat. The offer, which comprised a relocation grant of £2,400 for adults and £600 for minors, in addition to travel costs, provoked an angry response from islanders, who protested that the grants were severely inadequate. Osborne's successor as Chief Minister, David Brandt, an independent member of the Legislative Council, criticized the British Government's offer whilst also accusing it of attempting to depopulate Montserrat by showing insufficient commitment to the redevelopment of the island. The British Secretary of State for International Development, Clare Short, denied that the United Kingdom was encouraging people to leave Montserrat. However, accusations made by Short, to the effect that the island's leaders were making unreasonable demands, caused considerable offence to the island Government and the controversy was assuaged only when the British Secretary of State for Foreign and Commonwealth Affairs, Robin Cook, announced, on 25 August, the formation of a special interdepartmental committee charged with co-ordinating assistance to Montserrat. At the end of August George Foulkes, the Under-Secretary of State for International Development, visited the island for discussions with the Montserrat Government, during which he announced a five-year sustainable development plan for the north of the island, to include finance for new housing, social services and improved infrastructure. In September Tony Abbott was inaugurated as Governor of Montserrat, replacing Frank Savage.

In January 1998 Brandt renewed his accusations that the British Government was attempting to depopulate Montserrat by delaying the release of development funds. Prompted by these accusations, in February Cook made a formal visit to Montserrat and it was subsequently announced that the United Kingdom would provide further finance of £4.8m. for housing on the island. The new funding brought the total amount committed by the British Government since the beginning of the volcano crisis in 1995 to £55m.

In May 1998 the British Government announced that all citizens of Montserrat, except those already resident in other countries, would be entitled to settle in the United Kingdom. The estimated 3,500 refugees already in the United Kingdom on temporary visas were to be allowed to apply for permanent residency. In early July, to the surprise of monitoring scientists, the Soufrière Hills volcano erupted again, covering much of the island in ash, and postponing plans to re-open parts of Plymouth to residents. In August part of the central zone of Montserrat was re-opened, following operations to remove ash and debris. Also in August a committee of British MPs investigating the situation in Montserrat criticized the Government's handling of the crisis, noting that neither the Foreign and Commonwealth Office nor the Department for International Development had taken full responsibility for the situation. In September the Chief Minister and the Governor met Baroness Symons, Under-Secretary of State in the Foreign and Commonwealth Office, to discuss the current aid package and the speed of aid delivery.

In January 1999 an inquest into the 19 deaths during the eruptions found that in nine cases, the British Government was in part to blame for the deaths. The jury criticized the public shelters provided, where conditions were described as 'deplorable', and the Government's failure to provide farming land in the 'safe area', which had led to some farmers' choosing to risk their lives rather than abandon their farms. The Department for International Development, which was accused of providing 'unimaginative, grudging and tardy' long-term aid, denied culpability for the deaths, and announced that it was to spend a further £75m. on a three-year redevelopment programme in the north of the island.

In February 1999 studies were published confirming that the volcanic ash covering much of Montserrat contained significant amounts of silica, the cause of the lung disease silicosis. It was suggested that the threat to health from long-term exposure to the ash might further limit the number of areas of the island suitable for redevelopment. In July a bulletin from the Montserrat Volcano Observatory noted that there were no signs of decline in residual volcanic activity, warning that it would take decades for the lava still present to cool to ambient temperatures. Further explosions of ash and minor eruptions of lava continued throughout the rest of the year.

In September 1999 public consultations took place to discuss government proposals to establish a new capital at Little Bay, in the north-west of the island. The new town would take an estimated 10 years to construct. In the same month, Baroness Scotland, the British Government Under-Secretary for Overseas Territories, visited Montserrat. She announced further assistance for the construction of housing and expressed support for Government plans to establish Montserrat as a centre for international financial services. In March 2000 the dome of lava, which had been covering the Soufrière Hills volcano collapsed, producing lava flows and mudslides in the west of the island, and covering much of the 'safe zone' with ash.

In May 2000 an advisory commission on electoral reform recommended the replacement of the constituency system, which was deemed to be redundant following the abandonment of much of the island, by a nine-member single constituency. It was intended that the new system would be in place prior to the general election, scheduled for late 2001. In June the Organisation for Economic Co-operation and Development (OECD) published a list, on which Montserrat was included, of countries which it believed were taking insufficient action against money-laundering. Brandt subsequently called Montserrat's inclusion an 'affront' and stated that he would provide the OECD with no further information unless it could point to illegal activities on the island. In December Brandt declared his wish for responsibility for managing and monitoring Montserrat's financial services sector to be transferred to the Eastern Caribbean Central Bank, and for policy matters to fall under the Ministry of Finance portfolio. In March 2002 OECD declared that the Government had made sufficient commitments improve transparency and effective exchange of information on tax matters with OECD countries by 2005, and removed Montserrat from its blacklist.

In July 2001 there was a further partial collapse of the dome of lava covering the Soufrière Hills volanco. Hot ash and volcanic pebbles affected the communities of Salem and Olveston, and ash clouds severely disrupted air travel in the north-eastern Caribbean. In the following month Montserrat signed up to a British mortgage assistance programme, which would provide housing subsidies and loans to residents who had been made homeless as a result of volcanic activity. Many residents were still paying mortgages on homes in an off-limits zone of the island as well as paying rent for new accommodation. At a conference in October in Anguilla, the Chief Minister called for the right for each of the United Kingdom's Overseas Territories to have a representative in the British Parliament to represent each territory's particular concerns. There was, however, no immediate reaction from the British Government.

In February 2001 Chief Minister Brandt's coalition Government collapsed following the resignations of Adelina Tuitt, the Minister of Education, Health and Community Services, and Rupert Weekes, the Deputy Chief Minister and Minister of Communications, Works and Sports. The two accused Brandt of making decisions, in particular about a proposed new airport, without consulting other ministers. Their resignations forced Brandt to dissolve the Executive Council and announce that an early general election would be held on 2 April, under the new system of the nine-member single constituency (see above). The main contestants in the election were former Chief Minister Reuben Meade's NPP, and former Chief Minister John Osborne's newly-formed New People's Liberation Movement (NPLM). Brandt was not seeking re-election. There was anger

following the announcement that Montserratians who had left the island following the volcanic eruptions would not be entitled to vote. At the elections the NPLM won seven of the nine seats and 52% of the votes cast. The NPP won the remaining two seats. Turn-out was put at 77.6% of the 2,955 islanders registered to vote. Osborne was sworn in as Chief Minister on 5 April and an Executive Council was subsequently formed. One of Osborne's first statements as Chief Minister called on the United Kingdom to increase its grants to the island.

In May 2001 Anthony Longrigg was inaugurated as Governor of Montserrat, replacing Tony Abbott.

In February 2002 the Organisation of Eastern Caribbean States (OECS) countries, including Montserrat, agreed to allow nationals of member states to travel freely within the OECS area and to remain in a foreign territory within the area for up to six months. It was also planned to introduce a common OECS passport by 2003. In May the British Overseas Territories Act, having received royal assent in the United Kingdom in February, came into force and granted British citizenship to the people of its 14 Overseas Territories, including Montserrat. Under the new law Montserratians would be able to hold British passports and work in the United Kingdom and anywhere else in the European Union.

In March 2003 the Minister of Communications and Works, Lowell Lewis, resigned, pre-empting moves by Chief Minister Osborne to dismiss him; he was replaced by John Wilson. Lewis, who also resigned from the NPLM, challenged the leadership of Osborne earlier in the month and regarded his position as untenable after he considered supporting a vote of 'no confidence' in the Government, proposed by the leader of the opposition.

Government

Under the provisions of the 1960 Constitution and subsequent legislation, the Governor is appointed by the British monarch and is responsible for defence, external affairs and internal security. The Governor is President of the seven-member Executive Council. The Legislative Council comprises 12 members: a Speaker, two official members, two nominated and seven elected by universal adult suffrage.

Economic Affairs

In 2001, according to figures from the Eastern Caribbean Central Bank (ECCB), Montserrat's gross domestic product (GDP) at market prices was an estimated EC $82.6m., equivalent to EC $16,767 per head. In 1990–2001 real GDP decreased by an annual average of 9.0%; real GDP contracted by 3.7% in 2001.

Agriculture (including forestry and fishing) contributed an estimated 1.1% of GDP in 2001, and engaged 6.6% of the employed labour force in 1992. The sector was almost destroyed by the volcanic eruptions of 1997, which caused an 81.3% decline in agricultural production, and a return to subsistence farming. The sector's GDP contracted by a further 33.3% in 1998, in real terms, but increased by 7.6% in 1999 and by 36.6% in 2000. Prior to the volcanic eruption the principal crops grown were white potatoes, onions, rice and sea-island cotton. Cattle, goats, sheep and poultry were also farmed. Montserrat's fisheries are underexploited, owing to the absence of a sheltered harbour.

Industry (including mining, manufacturing, construction and public utilities) contributed some 20.1% to GDP in 2001, and engaged some 30.9% of the employed labour force in 1987. Mining and quarrying contributed 1.1% of GDP in 1996, but only 0.1% in 2001. Manufacturing contributed 0.8% of GDP in 2001, engaged 5.6% of the employed labour force (together with mining) in 1992, and accounted for about 70% of exports in the early 1990s. Many industrial sites were destroyed in 1997, causing a decline in real manufacturing GDP of 45.2% in that year and of 85.0% in 1998. In 1999 the sector's GDP improved by 10.6%, but growth was static in 2000. Light industries comprise the processing of agricultural produce (also cotton and tropical fruits), as well as spring-water bottling and the manufacture of garments and plastic bags. The assembly of electrical components, which accounted for 69% of export earnings in 1993, ceased in 1998, following further volcanic activity.

Construction contributed an estimated 12.5% of GDP in 2001 and employed 17.5% of the working population in 1988. The sector enjoyed growth in the early 1990s, owing to reconstruction programmes in response to the devastation caused by 'Hurricane Hugo' in 1989. Activity in the sector declined in the mid-1990s, before increasing in the middle of the decade, owing to reconstruction work following the volcanic eruptions. In 1999, however, real construction GDP fell by 13.5%, and it decreased by a further 36.0% in 2000. However, according to official data, the contribution of the construction industry to Montserrat's GDP in 2001 was more than double the 2000 figure. Energy requirements are dependent upon the import of hydrocarbon fuels (7.3% of total imports in 1998).

It is hoped to re-establish Montserrat as a data-processing centre, and as a centre for financial services, which previously provided an important source of government revenue. The tourism sector, which, in 2001, contributed some EC $19.3m. in gross visitor expenditure, remains important to the island, and it is hoped to establish Montserrat as a centre for environmental tourism with the volcano itself as the premier attraction. Output from the hotel and restaurant sector decreased by an annual average of 26.6% between 1994–2000, but most dramatically in 1996 and 1997, when revenues declined by 78.2% and 42.9%, respectively, although increases of 8.3%, 7.7% and 4.3% were recorded in 1998, 1999 and 2000, respectively. The real GDP of the services sector decreased by an annual average of 13.6% during 1994–2000, but increased by 7.3% in 2000. Services contributed some 78.8% of GDP in 2001.

In 2001 Montserrat recorded an estimated visible trade deficit of EC $44.1m. Earnings from the services sector—mainly tourist receipts and net transfers (in particular, the remittances from Montserratians abroad and the income of foreign retired people), generally offset persistent trade deficits. There was an estimated deficit on the current account of the balance of payments of EC $19.7m. in 2001. The principal trading partner is the USA (47.4% of imports in 1998 and 56.3% of exports in 1996). Other trading partners include the United Kingdom, Trinidad and Tobago and Saint Vincent and the Grenadines. The export of rice and of electrical components, previously the most important of the island's few exports, ceased in 1998 following further volcanic activity. Food imports constituted 10.8% of total imports in 1997; the principal imports are basic manufactures, machinery and transport equipment and construction materials.

In 2000, according to preliminary figures, there was a budgetary surplus of EC $2.9m. The capital budget is funded almost entirely by overseas aid, notably from the United Kingdom and Canada. The United Kingdom provided aid worth £14.5m. for 1995–98 (additional assistance for emergency housing and other services necessitated by continued volcanic activity had brought this total to £55m. by early 1998). In 1999 official development assistance totalled US $65.6m. Montserrat's total external public debt was estimated to be equivalent to 23.2% of GDP in 2000. The average annual rate of inflation was static in 1999 and 0.9% in 2000. According to official data, the rate stood at 4.9% in 2001. Unemployment was estimated at some 6% of the labour force in 1995.

Montserrat is a member of the ECCB (see p. 344), the Caribbean Community and Common Market (CARICOM, see p. 155), the Organisation of Eastern Caribbean States (OECS, see p. 341) and, as a dependency of the United Kingdom, has the status of Overseas Territory in association with the European Union (EU, see p. 199). The territory is also a member of the regional stock exchange, the Eastern Caribbean Securities Exchange (based in Saint Christopher and Nevis), established in 2001.

The eruption of the Soufrière Hills volcano in June 1997, and subsequent volcanic activity, rendered the southern two-thirds of Montserrat, including the capital, Plymouth, uninhabitable. Much of the country's infrastructure, including the main port and airport, was destroyed, and the island's agricultural heartland devastated. The implications for the island's principal industry, tourism, were extremely severe. In August the British Government announced a five-year reconstruction programme for the development of the 'safe areas' in the north of the island. However, by mid-February 1998 the population of Montserrat had declined to just 2,850 (the population was an estimated 11,581 in 1994) owing to the lack of employment prospects and to poor living conditions. Of the remaining work-force, some 25% were employed by the Government or statutory bodies. The population was believed to total some 35,000 by mid-2001, and it was hoped that a reduction in volcanic activity would encourage Montserratians resident abroad to return home, thereby stimulating the economy. It is hoped that the ongoing reconstruction efforts and the development of the island as a centre for environmental tourism will stimulate short-term economic growth, while in the long-term it is hoped to re-establish Montserrat as a centre for international financial services. However, the Territory's economic prospects depend

entirely on the activity of the volcano, and although reconstruction work is in progress, other areas of the economy are likely to remain at extremely low levels of output for some years. In September 2000 the EU allocated EC $19m. for infrastructural and development projects to Montserrat. In December one of Montserrat's main hotels, which was forced to close following the eruption of the Soufrière Hills volcano in 1997, reopened. In 2002 a further £10m. of aid from the United Kingdom over five years was announced, for new housing projects and the privatization of the island's fuel operations. In total the United Kingdom was due to provide a total aid package worth £17m. for 2002/03. The major projects in progress in 2003 were a new port and an airstrip of at least 600 m, capable of taking small aircraft for flights to neighbouring islands. Both are due for completion in 2004, funded by the European Union and the United Kingdom. The repercussions of the September 2001 terrorist attacks in the USA adversely affected tourism on the island in 2001 and 2002, providing a further blow to the economy.

Education

Education, beginning at five years of age, is compulsory up to the age of 14. In 1993 there were 11 primary schools, including 10 government schools. Secondary education begins at 12 years of age, and comprises a first cycle of five years and a second, two-year cycle. In 1989 there was one government secondary school and one private secondary school. In addition, in 1993 there were 12 nursery schools, sponsored by a government-financed organization, and a Technical College, which provided vocational and technical training for school-leavers. There was also an extra-mural department of the University of the West Indies in Plymouth. Current expenditure on education totalled EC $7m. in 1993, equivalent to 18.8% of total current expenditure. In 2002 the European Union (EU) and the United Kingdom contributed a total of EC $6m. to the construction of a further education college, which is expected to be completed in late 2003. A nursery school was also being built in mid-2002.

Public Holidays

2003: 1 January (New Year's Day), 17 March (St Patrick's Day), 18 April (Good Friday), 21 April (Easter Monday), 5 May (Labour Day), 9 June (Whit Monday), 4 August (August Monday), 23 November (Liberation Day), 25–26 December (Christmas), 31 December (Festival Day).

2004: 1 January (New Year's Day), 17 March (St Patrick's Day), 9 April (Good Friday), 12 April (Easter Monday), 3 May (Labour Day), 31 May (Whit Monday), 2 August (August Monday), 23 November (Liberation Day), 25–26 December (Christmas), 31 December (Festival Day).

Weights and Measures

The imperial system is in use but the metric system is being introduced.

Statistical Survey

Sources (unless otherwise stated): Government Information Service, Media Centre, Chief Minister's Office, Old Towne; tel. 491-2702; fax 491-2711; Eastern Caribbean Central Bank, POB 89, Basseterre, Saint Christopher OECS Economic Affairs Secretariat, *Statistical Digest*.

AREA AND POPULATION

Area: 102 sq km (39.5 sq miles).

Population: 10,639 (males 5,290; females 5,349) at census of 12 May 1991; 3,000 (UN estimate) at mid-2001. Source: partly UN, *Population and Vital Statistics Report*.

Density (mid-2001): 29.4 per sq km.

Principal Towns: Plymouth, the former capital, was abandoned in 1997. Brades is the interim capital.

Births and Deaths (1986): 200 live births (birth rate 16.8 per 1,000); 123 deaths (death rate 10.3 per 1,000). *1996:* Crude death rate 12.6 per 1,000 (Source: Pan American Health Organization).

Expectation of Life (years at birth, estimates): 78.0 (males 76.0; females 80.2) in 2001. Source: US Census Bureau.

Employment (1992): Agriculture, forestry and fishing 298; Mining and manufacturing 254; Electricity, gas and water 68; Wholesale and retail trade 1,666; Restaurants and hotels 234; Transport and communication 417; Finance, insurance and business services 242; Public defence 390; Other community, social and personal services 952; Total 4,521 (Source: *The Commonwealth Yearbook*). *1998* (estimate): Total labour force 1,500.

HEALTH AND WELFARE

Physicians (per 1,000 head, 1999): 0.18.

Health Expenditure: % of GDP (1995): 6.2.

Health Expenditure: public (% of total, 1995): 67.0.

Access to Water (% of persons, 1998): 100.
Source: Pan American Health Organization.
For definitions, see explanatory note on p. vi.

AGRICULTURE, ETC.

Principal Crops (FAO estimate, metric tons, 2001): Vegetables 475; Fruit (excl. melons) 710. Source: FAO.

Livestock (FAO estimates, '000 head, 2001): Cattle 10; Sheep 5; Goats 7; Pigs 1. Source: FAO.

Livestock Products (FAO estimates, '000 metric tons, 2001): Beef and veal 1; Cows' milk 2. Source: FAO.

Fishing (FAO estimates, metric tons, live weight, 2000): Total catch 50 (marine fishes). Source: FAO, *Yearbook of Fishery Statistics*.

INDUSTRY

Electric Energy (estimated production, million kWh): 17 in 1996; 18 in 1997; 18 in 1998. Source: UN, *Industrial Commodity Statistics Yearbook*.

FINANCE

Currency and Exchange Rates: 100 cents = 1 East Caribbean dollar (EC $). *Sterling, US Dollar and Euro Equivalents* (31 December 2002): £1 sterling = EC $4.352; US $1 = EC $2.700; €1 = EC $2.831; EC $100 = £22.98 = US $37.04 = €35.32. *Exchange Rate*: Fixed at US $1 = EC $2.70 since July 1976.

Budget (EC $ million, preliminary figures, 2001): *Revenue*: Revenue from taxation 23.0 (Taxes on income and profits 11.0, Taxes on domestic goods and services 3.1, Taxes on international trade and transactions 8.4); Non-tax revenue 1.7; Grants 76; Total 100.7. *Expenditure*: Current expenditure 51.2 (Personal emoluments 22.9, Goods and services 22.2, Transfers and subsidies 6.0); Capital expenditure 46.6; Total 97.8. Source: Eastern Caribbean Central Bank, *Report and Statement of Accounts*.

Cost of Living (consumer price index; base: previous year = 100): 100.8 in 1998; 100.8 in 1999; 101.7 in 2000.

Expenditure on the Gross Domestic Product (EC $ million at current prices, 2000): Government final consumption expenditure 54.46; Private final consumption expenditure 51.36; Gross fixed capital formation 47.37; *Total domestic expenditure* 153.19; Export of goods and services 60.16; *Less* Imports of goods and services 122.84; *GDP in purchasers' values* 90.51. Source: Eastern Caribbean Central Bank, *National Accounts*.

Gross Domestic Product by Economic Activity (EC $ million at current factor cost, 2000): Agriculture, forestry and fishing 1.03; Mining and quarrying 0.07; Manufacturing 0.62; Electricity, gas and water 3.45; Construction 11.74; Wholesale and retail trade 3.97; Restaurants and hotels 0.78; Transport 7.28; Communications 5.41; Banks and insurance 7.00; Real estate and housing 9.87; Government services 25.37; Other services 5.82; Sub-total 82.41; *Less* Imputed service charge 6.45; GDP at factor cost 75.96. Source: Eastern Caribbean Central Bank, *National Accounts*.

Balance of Payments (EC $ million, 1999): Exports of goods f.o.b. 3.41; Imports of goods f.o.b. −64.91; *Trade balance* −61.50; Exports of services 53.81; Imports of services −57.98; *Balance on goods and services* −65.67; Other income received 3.21; Other income paid −10.77; *Balance on goods, services and income* −73.23; Current transfers received 65.67; Current transfers paid −7.26; *Current balance* −14.82; Capital account (net) 4.25; Direct investment (net) 22.18; Other investment (net) −38.11; Net errors and omissions −2.53; *Overall balance* −29.03. Source: Eastern Caribbean Central Bank, *Balance of Payments*.

EXTERNAL TRADE

Principal Commodities (EC $ '000): *Imports c.i.f. (1998)*: Food and live animals 6,960; Beverages and tobacco 3,171; Crude materials (inedible) except fuels 4,404; Mineral fuels, lubricants, etc. 4,714; Chemicals 3,779; Basic manufactures 13,691; Machinery and transport equipment 13,372; Miscellaneous manufactured articles 14,137; Total (incl. others) 64,335. *Exports f.o.b. (1997)*: Food and live animals 8,221; Basic manufactures 8,362; Machinery and transport equipment 6,719; Miscellaneous manufactured articles 1,749; Total (incl. others) 29,939.

Principal Trading Partners (EC $ '000): *Imports c.i.f. (1998)*: Canada 775; Jamaica 772; Saint Vincent and the Grenadines 1,279; Trinidad and Tobago 8,150; United Kingdom 8,977; USA 30,505; Total (incl. others) 64,335. *Exports f.o.b. (1996)*: Antigua and Barbuda 1,294; Belgium 5,442; Ireland 3,683; Martinique 2,104; Spain 7,519; United Kingdom 27,000; USA 62,789; Total (incl. others) 111,597.
Source: OECS, *External Merchandise Trade Annual Report*.

TOURISM

Visitor Arrivals: 7,467 in 1998; 9,900 in 1999; 14,356 (excursionists 4,019; stay-over visitors 10,337) in 2000. Sources: World Tourism Organization, *Yearbook of Tourism Statistics*, and Ministry of Fi-nance, Economic Development and Trade, *Budget Statement 2001*.

Tourism Receipts (EC $ million): 22.0 in 1999; 24.0 in 2000; 19.3 in 2001(preliminary figure). Source: Eastern Caribbean Central Bank, *Report and Statement of Accounts*.

TRANSPORT

Road Traffic (vehicles in use, 1990): Passenger cars 1,823; Goods vehicles 54; Public service vehicles 4; Motorcycles 21; Miscellaneous 806.

Shipping: ('000 metric tons, 1990): *International Freight Traffic*: Goods loaded 6; Goods unloaded 49. Source: UN, *Monthly Bulletin of Statistics*.

Civil Aviation (1985): Aircraft arrivals 4,422; passengers 25,380; air cargo 132.4 metric tons.

COMMUNICATIONS MEDIA

Radio Receivers (1997): 7,000 in use.

Television Receivers (1999): 3,000 in use.

Telephones (2000): 2,811 main lines in use.

Mobile Cellular Telephones (2000): 489 subscribers.

Non-daily Newspapers (1996): 2 (estimated circulation 3,000).
Sources: UNESCO, *Statistical Yearbook*; International Telecommunication Union.

EDUCATION

Pre-primary (1993/94): 12 schools; 31 teachers; 407 pupils.

Primary (1993/94): 11 schools; 85 teachers; 1,453 pupils (1995).

Secondary (1995): 2 schools (1989); 80 teachers (1993/94); 925 pupils.
Sources: UNESCO, *Statistical Yearbook*; Caribbean Development Bank, *Social and Economic Indicators 2001*.

Directory

The eruption in June 1997 of the Soufrière Hills volcano, and subsequent volcanic activity, rendered some two-thirds of Montserrat uninhabitable and destroyed the capital, Plymouth. Islanders were evacuated to a 'safe zone' in the north of the island.

The Constitution

The present Constitution came into force on 19 December 1989 and made few amendments to the constitutional order established in 1960. The Constitution now guarantees the fundamental rights and freedoms of the individual and grants the Territory the right of self-determination. Montserrat is governed by a Governor and has its own Executive and Legislative Councils. The Governor retains responsibility for defence, external affairs (including international financial affairs) and internal security. The Executive Council consists of the Governor as President, the Chief Minister and three other Ministers, the Attorney-General and the Financial Secretary. The Legislative Council consists of the Speaker (chosen from outside the Council), nine elected, two official and two nominated members.

The Government

Governor: ANTHONY LONGRIGG (took office 17 May 2001).

EXECUTIVE COUNCIL
(April 2003)

President: The Governor.

Official Members:

Attorney-General: BRIAN COTTLE.

Financial Secretary: JOHN SKERRIT.

Chief Minister and Minister of Finance, Economic Development, Trade, Tourism and Media: JOHN A. OSBORNE.

Minister of Agriculture and the Environment: MARGARET DYER-HOWE.

Minister of Communications and Works, Land, Housing and Disaster Mitigation: JOHN WILSON.

Minister of Education, Health, Community Services, Sports and Culture: IDABELLE MEADE.

Clerk to the Executive Council: CLAUDETTE WEEKES.

MINISTRIES

Office of the Governor: Lancaster House, Olveston; tel. 491-2688; fax 491-8867; e-mail govoff@candw.ag; internet www.montserrat-newsletter.com.

Office of the Chief Minister: Government Headquarters, POB 292; tel. 491-3463; fax 491-6780.

Ministry of Agriculture, Land, Housing and the Environment: tel. 491-2075; fax 491-9275.

Ministry of Communications and Works, Land, Housing and Disaster Mitigation: tel. 491-2521; fax 491-4534.

Ministry of Education, Health, Community Services, Sports and Culture: Government Headquarters, POB 24; tel. 491-2880; fax 491-3131.

Ministry of Finance, Economic Development, Trade, Tourism and Media: POB 292; tel. 491-2066; fax 491-4632.

LEGISLATIVE COUNCIL

Speaker: Dr HOWARD A. FERGUS (acting).

Election, 2 April 2001

Party	Seats
New People's Liberation Movement (NPLM)	7
National Progressive Party (NPP)	2

There are also two *ex-officio* members (the Attorney-General and the Financial Secretary), and two nominated members.

Political Organizations

Movement for National Reconstruction (MNR): f. 1996; Leader AUSTIN BRAMBLE.

National Progressive Party (NPP): POB 280; tel. 491-2444; f. 1991; Leader REUBEN T. MEADE.

New People's Liberation Movement (NPLM): f. 2001 as successor party to People's Progressive Alliance; Leader JOHN A. OSBORNE.

Judicial System

Justice is administered by the Eastern Caribbean Supreme Court (based in Saint Lucia), the Court of Summary Jurisdiction and the Magistrate's Court.

Puisne Judge (Montserrat Circuit): NEVILLE L. SMITH.

Magistrate: ANNA B. RYAN.

Registrar: EULALIE GREENAWAY.

Religion

CHRISTIANITY

The Montserrat Christian Council: St Peter's, POB 227; tel. 491-4864; fax 491-2813; e-mail 113057.1074@compuserve.com.

The Anglican Communion

Anglicans are adherents of the Church in the Province of the West Indies, comprising eight dioceses. Montserrat forms part of the diocese of the North Eastern Caribbean and Aruba. The Bishop is resident in The Valley, Anguilla.

The Roman Catholic Church

Montserrat forms part of the diocese of St John's-Basseterre, suffragan to the archdiocese of Castries (Saint Lucia). The Bishop is resident in St John's, Antigua.

Other Christian Churches

There are Baptist, Methodist, Pentecostal and Seventh-day Adventist churches and other places of worship on the island.

The Press

Montserrat Newsletter: e-mail monmedia@candw.ag; internet www.montserrat-newsletter.com; government information publication.

The Montserrat Reporter: POB 306, Olveston; tel. 491-4715; fax 491-2430; e-mail editor@montserratreporter.org; internet www.montserratreporter.org; weekly on Fridays; circ. 2,000; Editor BENNETTE ROACH.

The Montserrat Times: POB 28; tel. 491-2501; fax 491-6069; weekly on Fridays; circ. 1,000.

Broadcasting and Communications

TELECOMMUNICATIONS

Cable & Wireless: POB 219, Sweeney's; tel. 491-1000; fax 491-3599; e-mail venus.george@cwni.cwplc.com.

BROADCASTING

Prior to the volcanic eruption of June 1997 there were three radio stations operating in Montserrat. Television services can also be obtained from Saint Christopher and Nevis, Puerto Rico, and from Antigua (ABS).

Radio

Family FM: f. 2002; locally-owned station.

Gem Radio Network: Barzey's, POB 488; tel. 491-5728; fax 491-5729; f. 1984; commercial; Station Man. KEVIN LEWIS; Man. Dir KENNETH LEE.

Radio Antilles: POB 35/930; tel. 491-2755; fax 491-2724; f. 1963; in 1989 the Govt of Montserrat, on behalf of the OECS, acquired the station; has one of the most powerful transmitters in the region; commercial; regional; broadcasts in English and French; Chair. Dr H. FELLHAUER; Man. Dir KRISTIAN KNAACK; Gen. Man. KEITH GREAVES.

Radio Montserrat (ZJB): POB 51, Sweeney's; tel. 491-2885; fax 491-9250; e-mail online@candw.ag; internet www.mratgov.com/zjb.htm; f. 1952; first broadcast 1957; govt station; Station Man. ROSE WILLOCK; CEO LOWELL MASON.

Television

Antilles Television Ltd: POB 342; tel. 491-2226; fax 491-4511; 2 channels for region; Gen. Man. KARNEY OSBORNE; Technical Dir Z. A. JOSEPH.

Cable Television of Montserrat Ltd: POB 447, Olveston; tel. 491-2507; fax 491-3081; Man. SYLVIA WHITE.

Montserrat Television Foundation: POB 447; tel. 491-7767; fax 491-3081.

Finance

The Eastern Caribbean Central Bank (see p. 343), based in Saint Christopher and Nevis, is the central issuing and monetary authority for Montserrat.

Financial Services Centre: POB 292; tel. 491-3057; fax 491-3757; e-mail minfin@candw.ag.

BANKING

Bank of Montserrat Ltd: POB 10, St Peters; tel. 491-3843; fax 491-3163; e-mail bom@candw.ag; Man. ANTON DOLDRON.

Barclays Bank PLC: POB 131; tel. 491-2501; fax 491-3801; Man. NORRIS VIDAL.

Government Savings Bank: 2,026 depositors (March 1998).

Royal Bank of Canada: tel. 491-2426; fax 491-3991; Man. J. R. GILBERT.

STOCK EXCHANGE

Eastern Caribbean Securities Exchange: based in Basseterre, Saint Christopher and Nevis; e-mail info@ecseonline.com; internet www.ecseonline.com; f. 2001; regional securities market designed to facilitate the buying and selling of financial products for the eight member territories—Anguilla, Antigua and Barbuda, Dominica, Grenada, Montserrat, Saint Christopher and Nevis, Saint Lucia and Saint Vincent and the Grenadines; Gen. Man. BALJIT VOHRA.

INSURANCE

Insurance Services (Montserrat) Ltd: POB 185, Sweeney's; tel. 491-2103; fax 491-6013.

United Insurance Co Ltd: Jacquie Ryan Enterprises Ltd, Woodlands; tel. 491-2055; fax 491-3257.

Trade and Industry

CHAMBER OF COMMERCE

Montserrat Chamber of Commerce and Industry: POB 384, Olveston; tel. 491-3640; fax 491-6602; refounded 1971; 22 company mems, 8 individual mems; Pres. BRUCE FARARA.

UTILITIES

Electricity

Montserrat Electricity Services Ltd (MONLEC): POB 16; tel. 491-3148; fax 491-3143; e-mail monlec@candw.ag; domestic electricity generation and supply.

Gas

Grant Enterprises and Trading: Brades, POB 350; tel. 491-9654; fax 491-4854; e-mail granten@candw.ag; domestic gas supplies.

Water

Montserrat Water Authority: POB 324; tel. 491-2527; fax 491-4904; e-mail mwa@candw.ag; f. 1972; domestic water supplies; Chair. ALIC TAYLOR; Gen. Man. EMILE DUBERRY.

TRADE UNIONS

Montserrat Allied Workers' Union (MAWU): Banks; tel. 491-2919; f. 1973; private-sector employees; Gen. Sec. HYLROY BRAMBLE; 1,000 mems.

Montserrat Seamen's and Waterfront Workers' Union: tel. 491-6335; fax 491-6335; f. 1980; Sec.-Gen. CHEDMOND BROWNE; 100 mems.

Montserrat Union of Teachers: POB 460; tel. 491-7034; fax 491-5779; e-mail hcb@candw.ag; f. 1978; Pres. GREGORY JULIUS (acting); Gen. Sec. HYACINTH BRAMBLE-BROWNE; 46 mems.

Transport

The eruption in June 1997 of the Soufrière Hills volcano, and subsequent volcanic activity, destroyed much of the infrastructure in the southern two-thirds of the island, including the country's principal port and airport facilities, as well as the road network.

ROADS

Prior to the volcanic eruption of June 1997 Montserrat had an extensive and well-constructed road network. There were 203 km (126 miles) of good surfaced main roads, 24 km (15 miles) of secondary unsurfaced roads and 42 km (26 miles) of rough tracks.

SHIPPING

The principal port at Plymouth was destroyed by the volcanic activity of June 1997. An emergency jetty was constructed at Little Bay in the north of the island. Regular transhipment steamship services are provided by Harrison Line and Nedlloyd Line. The Bermuth Line and the West Indies Shipping Service link Montserrat with Miami, USA and with neighbouring territories. A twice-daily ferry service is in operation between Montserrat and Antigua.

Port Authority of Montserrat: Little Bay; tel. 491-2791; fax 491-8063.

Montserrat Shipping Services: POB 46, Carr's Bay; tel. 491-3614; fax 491-3617.

CIVIL AVIATION

The main airport, Blackburne at Trants, 13 km (8 miles) from Plymouth, was destroyed by the volcanic activity of June 1997. The airport is to be rebuilt, and it was hoped to complete the renovation work in 2001. A helicopter port at Gerald's in the north of the island was completed in 2000. In 2002 there were plans to build a new, temporary, international airport at Gerald's, although opponents of the scheme considered Blake's Estate to be a superior alternative. In the longer term, the Government intended to construct a permanent international airport at Thatch Valley. Montserrat is linked to Antigua by a helicopter service, which operates three times a day. Montserrat is a shareholder in the regional airline, LIAT (based in Antigua and Barbuda).

Montserrat Airways Ltd: tel. 491-6494; fax 491-6205; charter services.

Montserrat Aviation Services Ltd: Nixon's, POB 257; tel. 491-2533; fax 491-7186; f. 1981; handling agent.

Tourism

Since the 1997 volcanic activity, Montserrat has been marketed as an eco-tourism destination. Known as the 'Emerald Isle of the Caribbean', Montserrat is noted for its Irish connections, and for its range of flora and fauna. In 2000 there were 14,356 visitor arrivals. In 1997 some 44% of tourist arrivals were from Caribbean countries, 24% from the USA, 19% from the United Kingdom and 5% from Canada. A large proportion of visitors are estimated to be Montserrat nationals residing overseas. In 2000 earnings from the sector amounted to an estimated EC $24m.

Montserrat Tourist Board: POB 7; tel. 491-2230; fax 491-7430; e-mail mrattouristboard@candw.ag; internet www.visitmontserrat.com; f. 1961; Chair. JOHN RYAN; Dir of Tourism ERNESTINE CASSELL.

PITCAIRN ISLANDS

Introduction

The Pitcairn Islands consist of Pitcairn Island and three uninhabited islands, Henderson, Ducie and Oeno. Pitcairn, situated at 25°04' S, and 130°06' W, and about midway between Panama and New Zealand, has an area of 4.5 sq km (1.75 sq miles) and had a population of 44 in March 2003.

Discovered in 1767 and first settled by the British in 1790, Pitcairn officially became a British settlement in 1887. In 1893 a parliamentary form of government was adopted, and in 1898 responsibility for administration was assumed by the High Commissioner for the Western Pacific. Pitcairn came under the jurisdiction of the Governor of Fiji in 1952, and, from 1970 onwards, of the British High Commissioner in New Zealand acting as Governor, in consultation with an Island Council, presided over by the Island Magistrate (who is elected trien-

nially) and comprising one *ex-officio* member (the Island Secretary), five elected and three nominated members. In 1987 the British High Commissioner in Fiji, acting on behalf of Pitcairn, the United Kingdom's last remaining dependency in the South Pacific, joined representatives of the USA, France, New Zealand and six South Pacific island states in signing the South Pacific Regional Environment Protection Convention, the main aim of which is to prevent the dumping of nuclear waste in the region.

In 1989 uninhabited Henderson Island was included on the UNESCO 'World Heritage List'. The island, 168 km (104 miles) east-north-east of Pitcairn, is to be preserved as a bird sanctuary. There are five species of bird unique to the island: the flightless rail or Henderson chicken, the green Henderson fruit dove, the Henderson crake, the Henderson warbler and the Henderson lorikeet. However, concern was expressed in 1994 following claims by scientists studying the island that its unique flora and fauna were threatened by the accidental introduction of foreign plant species by visitors and by an increase in the rat population.

Following some structural changes in the local government of Pitcairn, Steve Christian was elected to the position of Mayor in December 1999, presiding over the Island Council (a role previously fulfilled by the Island Magistrate).

In early 2000 British detectives began an investigation into an alleged rape case on the island. The British team was joined by the New Zealand police force in early 2001, when the case was widened to include 15 alleged sexual assaults, amid reports claiming that sexual abuse, particularly of children, was commonplace on the island. The trial, which was expected to take place in Auckland, New Zealand, would represent the first significant criminal case on Pitcairn since a murder trial in 1897. In November 2000 Auckland's Crown Solicitor, Simon Moore, was appointed Pitcairn's first Public Prosecutor, with the task of deciding whether to bring charges against 20 Pitcairn islanders. His decision was delayed by the fact that many of the complainants now lived in New Zealand and by the logistical problems of a trial that could potentially involve the entire populace. However, in April 2003 a judicial delegation of eight people visited Pitcairn and nine men on the island were charged with a total of 64 offences, some of which dated back about 40 years. Many islanders expressed serious concern that their community would not be able to manage if the men (who constituted virtually the entire male work-force) were extradited to New Zealand to stand trial.

The British Overseas Territories Act, which entered effect in May 2002, granted citizenship rights in the United Kingdom to residents of the Overseas Territories, including Pitcairn. The legislation also entitled Pitcairn Islanders to hold British passports and to work in the United Kingdom and elsewhere in the European Union.

The economy has been based on subsistence gardening, fishing, handicrafts and the sale of postage stamps. Attempts to increase revenue from the island's agricultural output by producing dried fruits (notably bananas, mangoes and pineapples) began in 1999. Diversification of this sector to include production of jam, dried fish and coffee was subsequently under consideration. In early 1999 the Pitcairn Island police and customs office requested that no honey or beeswax be sent to the Island in order to protect from disease the island's growing honey industry, which was being developed as a source of foreign exchange. Pitcairn honey, which was pronounced to be 'exceptionally pure' by the New Zealand Ministry of Agriculture, began to be exported, largely through internet sales, in late 1999. A new stamp was issued to commemorate the launch of the industry.

A reafforestation scheme, begun in 1963, concentrated on the planting of miro trees, which provide a rosewood suitable for handicrafts. In 1987 the Governor of the islands signed a one-year fishing agreement with Japan, whereby the Japan Tuna Fisheries Co-operative Association was granted a licence to operate vessels within Pitcairn's EEZ. The agreement was subsequently renewed, but lapsed in 1990. In 1992 an exclusive economic zone (EEZ), designated in 1980 and extending 370 km (200 nautical miles) off shore, was officially declared.

In early 1992 it was reported that significant mineral deposits, formed by underwater volcanoes, had been discovered within the islands' EEZ. The minerals, which were believed to include manganese, iron, copper, zinc, silver and gold, could (if exploited) dramatically affect the Territory's economy.

New Zealand currency is used. There is no taxation (except for small licensing fees on guns and vehicles), and government revenue has been derived mainly from philatelic sales (one-half of current revenue in 1992/93), and from interest earned on investments. In 1998/99 revenue totalled $NZ492,000, and expenditure $NZ667,000. Capital assistance is received from the United Kingdom. Exports from the Pitcairn Islands to Australia totalled $A21,000 in 2000/01, while imports from Australia totalled $A7,000 in that year, consisting mainly of food. Pitcairn's imports from the USA totalled US $5.5m. in 2001, while exports to the USA were worth US $0.2m. Hopes that Pitcairn might find an additional source of revenue through the sale of website addresses were boosted in early 2000 when the island won a legal victory to gain control of its internet domain name suffix '.pn'.

Development projects have been focused on harbour improvements, power supplies, telecommunications and road-building. Pitcairn's first radio-telephone link was established in 1985, and a modern telecommunications unit was installed in 1992. A new health clinic was established, with British finance, in 1996.

A steady decline in the population, due mainly to emigration to New Zealand, is the island's main problem. In March 2001 a New Zealand company expressed an interest in acquiring development rights on Pitcairn with the aim of establishing fishing and tourism projects. The company claimed that if the islands achieved self-sufficiency through the proposals within five years then Pitcairn could become an independent state within the Commonwealth. In May 2002 the company's director reportedly announced that the development would begin within the next 12 months, describing plans for a lodge on Pitcairn and for a floating hotel off Oeno Island. The British High Commission in Wellington, however, emphasized that any such developments remained subject to the approval of Pitcairn Island Council, but that the company was welcome to submit proposals.

Statistical Survey

Source: Office of the Governor of Pitcairn, Henderson, Ducie and Oeno Islands, c/o British Consulate-General, Pitcairn Islands Administration, Private Box 105-696, Auckland, New Zealand; tel. (9) 366-0186; fax (9) 366-0187; e-mail pitcairn@iconz.co.nz.

AREA AND POPULATION

Area: 35.5 sq km. *By island*: Pitcairn 4.35 sq km; Henderson 30.0 sq km; Oeno is less than 1 sq km and Ducie is smaller.

Population: 44 (March 2003).

Density (Pitcairn only, August 2002): 9.9 per sq km.

Employment (able-bodied men, 2002): 9.

FINANCE

Currency and Exchange Rates: 100 cents = 1 Pitcairn dollar. The Pitcairn dollar is at par with the New Zealand dollar ($NZ). New Zealand currency is usually used.

Budget ($NZ, 1998/99): Revenue 492,000; Expenditure 667,000.

TRANSPORT

Road Traffic (motor vehicles, 2002): Passenger vehicles 29 (two-wheeled 1, three-wheeled 6, four-wheeled 23); Tractors 3; Bulldozer 1; Digger 1.

Shipping: *Local vessels* (communally-owned open surf boats, 2000): 3. *International Shipping Arrivals* (visits by passing vessels, 1996): Ships 51; Yachts 30.

COMMUNICATIONS

Telephones (2002): a party-line service with 15 telephones in use; 2 public telephones; 2 digital telephones. Most homes also have VHF radio.

Directory

The Constitution and Government

Pitcairn is a British settlement under the British Settlements Act 1887, although the islanders reckon their recognition as a colony from 1838, when a British naval captain instituted a Constitution with universal adult suffrage and a code of law. That system served as the basis of the 1904 reformed Constitution and the wider reforms of 1940, effected by Order in Council. The Constitution of 1940 provides for a Governor of Pitcairn, Henderson, Ducie and Oeno Islands (who, since 1970, is concurrently the British High Commissioner in New Zealand), representing the British monarch. A Mayor is elected every three years to preside over the Island Council. The Local Government Ordinance 1964 constituted an Island Council of 10 members: in addition to the Mayor, five members are elected annually; three are nominated for terms of one year (the Governor appoints two of these members at his own discretion); and the Island Secretary is an *ex-officio* member. In addition to the Island Council there is an Island Magistrate who presides over the Magistrate's Court of Pitcairn, and is appointed by the Governor. Liaison between the Governor and the Island Council is conducted by a Commissioner, usually based in the Office of the British Consulate-General in Auckland, New Zealand.

Customary land tenure provides for a system of family ownership (based upon the original division of land in the 18th century). Alienation to foreigners is not forbidden by law, but in practice this is difficult. There is no taxation, and public works are performed by the community.

Governor of Pitcairn, Henderson, Ducie and Oeno Islands: RICHARD FELL (British High Commissioner in New Zealand—took office December 2001).

Office of the Governor of Pitcairn, Henderson, Ducie and Oeno Islands: c/o British High Commission, 44 Hill St, POB 1812, Wellington, New Zealand; tel. (4) 924-2888; fax (4) 473-4982; e-mail bhc.wel@xtra.co.nz; internet www.britain.org.nz; Gov. RICHARD FELL; Deputy Gov. MATTHEW FORBES; Commissioner LEON SALT.

Pitcairn Islands Administration: Private Box 105-696, Auckland, New Zealand; tel. (9) 366-0186; fax (9) 366-0187; e-mail admin@pitcairn.gov.pn; internet www.government.pn.

ISLAND COUNCIL
(April 2003)

Mayor: STEVE CHRISTIAN.

Island Secretary (ex officio): BETTY CHRISTIAN.

Government Treasurer: OLIVE CHRISTIAN.

Island Auditor: MIKE CHRISTIAN.

Chairman of Internal Committee: JAY WARREN.

Other Members: LEA BROWN, BRENDA CHRISTIAN, TOM CHRISTIAN, ROBERT MCDONALD, JOHN O'MALLEY, MERALDA WARREN, NOLA WARREN.

Elections to the Island Council take place each December. Meetings are held at the Court House in Adamstown.

Office of the Island Secretary: The Square, Adamstown.

Judicial System

Chief Justice: CHARLES BLACKIE.

Island Magistrate: LEA BROWN.

Public Prosecutor: SIMON MOORE.

Public Defender: PAUL DACRE.

Religion

CHRISTIANITY
Since 1887 many of the islanders have been adherents of the Seventh-day Adventist Church.

Pastor: JOHN O'MALLEY, SDA Church, The Square, POB 24, Adamstown; fax 872-7620/9763.

The Press

Pitcairn Miscellany: monthly four-page mimeographed news sheet; f. 1959; edited by the Education Officer; circulation 1,400 in 2002; Editor P. FOLEY.

Finance, Trade and Industry

There are no formal banking facilities. A co-operative trading store was established in 1967. Industry consists of handicrafts, honey and dried fruit.

Transport

ROADS
There are approximately 14 km (9 miles) of dirt road suitable for two-, three- and four-wheeled vehicles. In 2002 there was one conventional motor cycle, six three-wheelers and 22 four-wheeled motor cycles, one four-wheel-drive motor car, three tractors, a five-ton digger and a bulldozer; traditional wheelbarrows are used occasionally. In late 1995 a total of £79,000 was received from individual donors for work to improve the road leading to the jetty at Bounty Bay. Additional funding from the United Kingdom and the European Union was suspended in 2001, and the project remained incomplete.

SHIPPING
No passenger ships have called regularly since 1968, and sea communications are restricted to cargo vessels operating between New Zealand and Panama, which make scheduled calls at Pitcairn three times a year, as well as a number of unscheduled calls. There are also occasional visits by private yachts. The number of cruise ships calling at Pitcairn increased in the late 1990s, and 10 such vessels visited the island in 2000 (compared with just two or three annually in previous years). Bounty Bay, near Adamstown, is the only possible landing site, and there are no docking facilities. In 1993 the jetty derrick was refitted with an hydraulic system. The islanders have three aluminium open surf boats.

ST HELENA AND DEPENDENCIES

St Helena

Introduction

St Helena lies in the South Atlantic Ocean, about 1,930 km (1,200 miles) from the south-west coast of Africa. Governed by the British East India Co from 1673, the island was brought under the direct control of the British Crown in 1834. The present Constitution (see p. 4392) came into force in 1989. At general elections held in September 1976, the St Helena Progressive Party, advocating the retention of close economic links with the United Kingdom, won 11 of the 12 elective seats in the Legislative Council. This policy has been advocated by almost all members of the Legislative Council brought to office at subsequent general elections (normally held every four years) up to and including that held in June 2001.

In October 1981 a commission was established by the Governor to review the island's constitutional arrangements. The commission reported in 1983 that it was unable to identify any proposal for constitutional change that would command the support of the majority of the islanders. In 1988, however, a formal Constitution was introduced to replace the Order in

Council and Royal Instructions under which St Helena had been governed since 1967. The Constitution entered into force on 1 January 1989.

Owing to the limited range of economic activity on the island (see below), St Helena is dependent on development and budgetary aid from the United Kingdom. Since 1981, when the United Kingdom adopted the British Nationality Act, which effectively removed the islanders' traditional right of residence in Britain, opportunities for overseas employment have been limited to contract work, principally in Ascension and the Falkland Islands. In 1992 an informal 'commission on citizenship' was established by a number of islanders to examine St Helena's constitutional relationship with the United Kingdom, with special reference to the legal validity of the 1981 legislation as applied to St Helena. In April 1997 the commission obtained a legal opinion from a former Attorney-General of St Helena to the effect that the application of the Act to the population of St Helena was in contravention of the Royal Charter establishing British sovereignty in 1673. The commission indicated that it intended to pursue the matter further. In July 1997 private legislation was introduced in the British Parliament to extend full British nationality to 'persons having connections with' St Helena. In the following month the British Government indicated that it was considering arrangements under which islanders would be granted employment and residence rights in the United Kingdom. In February 1998, following a conference held in London of representatives of the British Dependent Territories, it was announced that a review was to take place of the future constitutional status of these territories, and of means whereby their economies might be strengthened. It was subsequently agreed that the operation of the 1981 legislation in relation to St Helena would also be reviewed. As an immediate measure to ameliorate the isolation of St Helena, the British Government conceded permission for civilian air landing rights on Ascension Island, which, with the contemplated construction of a small airstrip on St Helena, could facilitate the future development of the island as a tourist destination. In March 1999 the British Government published draft legislation proposing that full British nationality, including the right of abode in the United Kingdom, was to be restored to the population of St Helena and its dependencies, under the reorganization of the British Dependent Territories as the United Kingdom Overseas Territories. However, this had still not been implemented by July 2000, when the citizens took their case to the UN Committee on Decolonization, seeking British passports, a new Constitution and administration as a Crown dependency rather than as a colony. In May 2002 the British Overseas Territories Act, which granted British citizenship to the people of the Overseas Territories, including St Helena and dependencies, came into effect, having received royal assent in February. Under the new legislation these citizens acquired the right to hold a British passport and to work in the United Kingdom, but not the other benefits of citizenship (such as reduced fees for education). The Act restored those rights removed by the British Nationality Act of 1981. In September 2002 an independent constitutional adviser visited St Helena and consulted extensively with the island's residents on the options for future constitutional development.

On 4 February 2002 a referendum was held by the Government in St Helena, Ascension Island, the Falkland Islands and on RMS *St Helena* on future access to the island; 71.6% of votes cast were in favour of the construction of an airport (28.4% opting for a shipping alternative). Plans for the airport and associated commercial developments were cancelled in February 2003, on the grounds of unprofitability and environmental concerns; however, following protests by islanders, in April the Executive Council invited tenders for the construction of the airport. The project was expected to cost some £40m., of which the British Government was reported to have agreed to contribute some £26.3m., approximately equal to the cost of replacing the mail ship in 2010. The airport was scheduled to be completed by 2008.

The economy of St Helena is heavily reliant on British aid. In 1996 the St Helena Government undertook a strategic review, which formed the basis of a three-year country policy plan, committing the British Government to provide a package of development assistance totalling some £26m. over the period 1997/98–1999/2000. The assistance consisted of direct budgetary aid (approximately £3.2m. a year), an annual subsidy for the operation of the RMS *St Helena* (approximately £1.3m.) and support for bilateral development assistance. In 1999/2000 the island received about £8.9m. in British aid. Budget revenue (including budgetary aid of £3.18m.) totalled £10.56m. in 1999/2000, and expenditure in that year was £10.48m. The annual rate of inflation averaged 3.7% in 1990–2000. Consumer prices increased by an average of 2.1% in 1999 and by 1.5% in 2000.

St Helena's persistently high rate of unemployment has resulted in widespread reliance on welfare benefit payments and a concurrent decline in living standards for the majority of the population. Evidence of underlying social discontent emerged in April 1997, when minor public disorders broke out in Jamestown following the refusal of the Governor (who exercises full executive and legislative authority in St Helena) to accept the nomination of a prominent critic of government policy to the post of Director of the Department of Social Welfare. Two members of the Executive Council (which acts in an advisory capacity) resigned in protest at the action of the Governor, who subsequently announced that elections to the Legislative Council were to take place in July. Following the elections, held on 9 July, the Governor agreed to the nomination as Chairman

of the Education Committee of the candidate he had previously refused to nominate to the Social Welfare Directorate. The newly elected Legislative Council became the first in which members were to receive a fixed salary to serve on a full-time basis, relinquishing any other employment during their term of office.

At the 1998 census 10.2% of the employed labour force were engaged in agriculture and fishing, 19.7% in industry (predominantly construction), 65.6% in services and 4.5% in unspecified activities. Employment in the public sector was estimated to be at 45% of the working population in 1999. St Helena's unemployment rate was 18.1% at the 1998 census. In 2000 exports of fish (which, apart from a small quantity of coffee, is the only commodity exported) totalled 43.1 metric tons (compared with 27.2 tons in 1985) and export earnings from this source amounted to £113,000. Timber production is being developed, with sales amounting to 390 cu m in 1999. However, a large proportion of the labour force (approximately 1,000) must seek employment overseas, principally on Ascension and the Falkland Islands. In March 2001 551 St Helenians were working on Ascension, and in December 1999 371 were working on the Falkland Islands; approximately 1,400 members of the work-force were employed offshore at the end of 2001.

St Helena is of interest to naturalists for its rare flora and fauna. The island has about 40 species of flora that are unique to St Helena.

Statistical Survey

Source: Development and Economic Planning Dept, Government of St Helena, St Helena Island, STHL 1ZZ; e-mail depd@helanta.sh.

AREA AND POPULATION

Area: 122 sq km (47 sq miles).

Population: 5,147 (males 2,514; females 2,633) at census of 31 October 1976; 5,644 (males 2,769; females 2,875) at census of 22 February 1987; 4,913 (males 2,481; females 2,432) at census of 8 March 1998; 4,647 in 2000 (official estimate).

Density (1998 census): 40.0 per sq km.

Principal Town (1998 census): Jamestown (capital), population 850.

Births and Deaths (2000): Registered live births 56; Registered deaths 53.

Economically Active Population (1998 census): Agriculture, hunting and related activities 187; Fishing 20; Manufacturing 87; Electricity, gas and water 48; Construction 267; Wholesale and retail trade 344; Hotels and restaurants 24; Transport, storage and communications 181; Financial intermediation 17; Real estate, renting and business activities 7; Public administration and defence 293; Education 187; Health and social work 196; Other community services 87; Private household 74; Extra-territorial organizations 11; Total employed 2,037 (males 1,146, females 891); Unemployed 449 (males 290, females 159); Total labour force 2,486 (males 1,436, females 1,050).

AGRICULTURE, ETC.

Livestock (2000): Cattle 535; Sheep 777; Pigs 503; Goats 1,224; Donkeys 150; Poultry 6,082.

Fishing (metric tons, live weight, including Ascension and Tristan da Cunha): Skipjack tuna 64, Albacore 58, Yellowfin tuna 136, Tristan da Cunha rock lobster 316, Octopuses, etc. 24; Total catch 658. Figures include catches of rock lobster from Tristan da Cunha during the 12 months ending 30 April of the year stated. Source: FAO, *Yearbook of Fishery Statistics*.

FINANCE

Currency and Exchange Rate: 100 pence (pennies) = 1 St Helena pound (£). *Sterling, Dollar and Euro Equivalents* (31 December 2002): £1 sterling = St Helena £1; US $1 = 62.04 pence; €1 = 65.06 pence; £100 = $161.18 = €153.70. *Average Exchange Rate* (US $ per £): 1.5161 in 2000; 1.4400 in 2001; 1.5013 in 2002. Note: The St Helena pound is at par with the pound sterling.

Budget (1999/2000): *Revenue* £10.56m. (including budgetary aid of £3.18m.); *Expenditure* £10.48m.

Cost of Living (Consumer Price Index; base: 1990 = 100): 139.1 in 1998; 142.0 in 1999; 144.1 in 2000. Source: ILO.

EXTERNAL TRADE

Principal Commodities: *Imports* (1994/95, £ '000): Total 5,076 (Food and live animals 27.9%; Beverages and tobacco 8.5%; Mineral fuels, lubricants, etc. 8.5%; Chemicals and related materials 11.4%; Basic manufactures 12.7%; Machinery and transport equipment 11.7%; Miscellaneous manufactured articles 13.0%; Other commodities and transactions 3.3%); *Exports* (2000): fish £113,000; coffee n.a. Trade is mainly with the United Kingdom and South Africa. *1998* (trade with UK): Imports £0.65m.; Exports £6.99m. (Source: Foreign and Commonwealth Office).

TRANSPORT

Road Traffic (1999): 1,516 licensed vehicles.

Shipping (1999): Vessels entered 214; Merchant fleet (31 December 2001): 1 vessel (displacement 789 grt).

COMMUNICATIONS MEDIA

Radio Receivers ('000 in use, 1997): 3. Source: UNESCO, *Statistical Yearbook*.

Television Receivers ('000 in use, July 2001): 1.

Telephones ('000 main lines in use, July 2001): 2.

EDUCATION

Primary (1999/2000): 4 schools; 30 teachers; 262 pupils.

Intermediate (1999/2000): 3 schools; 26 teachers; 271 pupils.

Secondary (1999/2000): 1 school; 31 teachers; 327 pupils.

Directory

The Constitution

The St Helena Constitution Order 1988, which entered into force on 1 January 1989, replaced the Order in Council and Royal Instructions of 1 January 1967. Executive and legislative authority is reserved to the British Crown, but is ordinarily exercised by others in accordance with provisions of the Constitution. The Constitution provides for the office of Governor and Commander-in-Chief of St Helena and its dependencies (Ascension Island and Tristan da Cunha). The Legislative Council for St Helena consists of the Speaker, three *ex-officio* members (the Chief Secretary, the Financial Secretary and the Attorney-General) and 12 elected members; the Executive Council is presided over by the Governor and consists of the above *ex-officio* members and five of the elected members of the Legislative Council. The elected members of the legislature choose from among themselves those who will also be members of the Executive Council. Although a member of both the Legislative Council and the Executive Council, the Attorney-General does not vote on either. Members of the legislature provide the Chairmen and a majority of the members of the various Council Committees. Executive and legislative functions for the dependencies are exercised by the Governor (although an advisory Island Council was inaugurated on Ascension in November 2002).

The Government

(April 2003)

Governor and Commander-in-Chief: DAVID J. HOLLAMBY.

Chief Secretary: JOHN M. STYLES.

Financial Secretary: ROBERT DOLAN.

Chairmen of Council Committees:

Agriculture and Natural Resources: MERVYN ROBERT YON.

Education: WILLIAM E. DRABBLE.

Employment and Social Services: CYRIL KEITH GUNNELL.

Public Health: MARGARET A. C. HOPKINS.

Public Works and Social Services: ERIC W. GEORGE.

Speaker of the Legislative Council: JOHN WAINWRIGHT NEWMAN.

GOVERNMENT OFFICES

Office of the Governor: The Castle, Jamestown; tel. 2555; fax 2598; e-mail ocs@helanta.sh.

Office of the Chief Secretary: The Castle, Jamestown; tel. 2555; fax 2598; e-mail ocs@helanta.sh.

Political Organizations

There are no political parties in St Helena. Elections to the Legislative Council, the latest of which took place in June 2001, are conducted on a non-partisan basis.

Judicial System

The legal system is derived from English common law and statutes. There are four Courts on St Helena: the Supreme Court, the Magistrate's Court, the Small Debts Court and the Juvenile Court. Provision exists for the St Helena Court of Appeal, which can sit in Jamestown or London.

Chief Justice: B. W. MARTIN (non-resident).

Attorney-General: KURT DE FREITAS.

Sheriff: G. P. MUSK.

Magistrates: J. BEADON, D. BENNETT, D. CLARKE, R. COLEMAN, J. CORKER, L. CROWIE, J. FLAGG, P. FRANCIS, B. GEORGE, E. W. GEORGE, I. GEORGE, H. LEGG, V. MARCH, G. P. MUSK, R. PRIDHAM, G. SIM, S. STROUD, D. WADE, C. YON, P. YON, S. YOUDE.

Religion

The majority of the population belongs to the Anglican Communion.

CHRISTIANITY

The Anglican Communion

Anglicans are adherents of the Church of the Province of Southern Africa. The Metropolitan of the Province is the Archbishop of Cape Town, South Africa. St Helena forms a single diocese.

Bishop of St Helena: Rt Rev. JOHN SALT, Bishopsholme, POB 62, St Helena; tel. 4471; fax 4330; e-mail bishop@helanta.sh; diocese f. 1859; has jurisdiction over the islands of St Helena and Ascension.

The Roman Catholic Church

The Church is represented in St Helena, Ascension and Tristan da Cunha by a Mission, established in August 1986. There were an estimated 87 adherents in the islands at 31 December 2000.

Superior: Rev. Fr MICHAEL MCPARTLAND (also Prefect Apostolic of the Falkland Islands); normally visits Tristan da Cunha once a year and Ascension Island two or three times a year; Vicar Delegate Rev. Fr JOSEPH WHELAN, Sacred Heart Church, Jamestown; tel. and fax 2535.

Other Christian Churches

The Salvation Army, Seventh-day Adventists, Baptists, New Apostolics and Jehovah's Witnesses are active on the island.

BAHÁ'Í FAITH

There is a small Bahá'í community on the island.

The Press

St Helena News Media: St Helena News Media Board, Broadway House, Jamestown; tel. 2612; fax 2802; e-mail sthelena.news@helanta.sh; internet www.news.co.sh; f. 1986; govt-sponsored, independent; weekly; includes the *St Helena Herald* and St Helena Radio; Chief Exec. MIKE OLSSON; Editor JOHN DRUMMOND; circ. 1,450.

Broadcasting and Communications

TELECOMMUNICATIONS

Cable & Wireless PLC: POB 2, The Briars, Jamestown; tel. 2200; fax 2206; e-mail webmaster@helanta.sh; internet www.cwsthelena.sh.

BROADCASTING

Cable & Wireless PLC: The Moon, Jamestown; tel. 2200; provides a two channel television service 24 hours daily from five satellite channels.

St Helena Radio: St Helena Information Office, Broadway House, Jamestown; tel. 4669; fax 4542; e-mail radio.sthelena@helanta.sh; independent service; providing broadcasts for 24 hours per day; local programming and relays of British Broadcasting Corporation World Service programmes; Station Man. ANTHONY D. LEO.

Finance

BANK

Government Savings Bank: Jamestown; tel. 2345; total deposits £8,782,269 (31 March 1996).

INSURANCE

Royal and SunAlliance Insurance Group PLC: Agents: Solomon & Co (St Helena) PLC, Jamestown; tel. 2380; fax 2423; e-mail solco@helanta.sh.

Trade and Industry

GOVERNMENT AGENCY

St Helena Development Agency: POB 117, Jamestown; tel. 2920; fax 2166; e-mail global@shda.helanta.sh; internet www.shda .helanta.sh.

CHAMBER OF COMMERCE

St Helena Chamber of Commerce: Jamestown.

CO-OPERATIVE

St Helena Growers' Co-operative Society: Jamestown; tel. and fax 2511; vegetable marketing; also suppliers of agricultural tools, seeds and animal feeding products; 108 mems (1999); Chair. STEDSON FRANCIS; Sec. PETER W. THORPE.

Transport

There are no railways or airfields in St Helena. In April 2003 St Helena sought tenders for the construction of an airport, which was scheduled to be completed by 2008 and was likely to be situated on Prosperous Bay Plain.

ROADS

In 2002 there were 118 km of bitumen-sealed roads, and a further 20 km of earth roads, which can be used by motor vehicles only in dry weather. All roads have steep gradients and sharp bends.

SHIPPING

St Helena Line Ltd: Andrew Weir Agencies, Lancaster House, Mercury Court, Tithebarn St, Liverpool, L2 2QP, United Kingdom; tel. (151) 479-5555; fax (151) 236-2644; internet www.aws.co.uk; awarded the five-year government contract in May 2001; service subsidized by the British Government by £1.5m. annually; operates two-monthly passenger/cargo services by the RMS *St Helena* to and from the United Kingdom and Cape Town, South Africa, calling at the Canary Islands, Ascension Island and Vigo, Spain, and once a year at Tristan da Cunha; also operates programme of shuttle services between St Helena and Ascension Island and the St Helena Liner Shipping Service.

Tourism

Although St Helena possesses flora and fauna of considerable interest to naturalists, as well as the house (now an important museum) in which the French Emperor Napoleon I spent his final years in exile, the remoteness of the island, which is a two-day sea voyage from Ascension Island, has inhibited the development of tourism. Following the opening of air facilities on Ascension Island to civilian visitors, it is hoped that proposals to construct a small airfield on St Helena will proceed, thus increasing the island's accessibility to the limited number of visitors that can currently be accommodated. A total of 8,968 tourists visited St Helena in 1997. There are three hotels and a range of self-catering facilities.

St Helena Tourist Office: Canister Bldg, Main St, Jamestown; tel. 2158; fax 2159; e-mail sthelena.tourism@helanta.sh; internet www .sthelenatourism; Dir PAMELA YOUNG.

Ascension

The island of Ascension lies in the South Atlantic Ocean, 1,131 km (703 miles) north-west of St Helena, of which it is a dependency. Discovered by Portuguese navigators in 1501, the island is a semi-barren, rocky peak of purely volcanic origin. Britain took possession of Ascension in 1815, in connection with Napoleon's detention on St Helena. The island is famous for green turtles, and is also a breeding ground for the sooty tern. Under an agreement with the British Government, US forces occupy Wideawake Airfield, which is used as a tracking station for guided missiles. Ascension has no indigenous population, being inhabited by British and US military personnel, *émigré* workers and government administrative staff from St Helena, together with expatriate civilian personnel of Merlin Communications International (MCI), which operates the British Broadcasting Corporation (BBC) Overseas World Service Atlantic relay station, Cable and Wireless PLC, which provides international communications services and operates the 'Ariane' satellite tracking station of the European Space Agency, and staff providing the island's common services. The island is an important communications centre. The BBC operates a relay station on the island. Ascension does not raise its own finance; the costs of administering the island are borne collectively by the user organizations, supplemented by income from philatelic sales. The island is developing a modest eco-tourism sector. Some revenue, which is remitted to the St Helena administration, is derived from fishing licences (estimated to be around £1m. in 1999). Facilities on Ascension underwent rapid development in 1982 to serve as a major staging post for British vessels and aircraft on their way to the Falkland Islands (q.v.), and the island has continued to provide a key link in British supply lines to the South Atlantic. On 31 March 2001 the joint venture between the BBC and Cable and Wireless to provide public services to the island was dissolved. The Ascension Island Government took over responsibility for health and education, the Ascension Island Works and Services Agency, a statutory body, was established to maintain transport and infrastructure, and any remaining services were taken over by the new Ascension Island Commercial Services Ltd (AICS) company. AICS was jointly owned by the Ascension Islands Government, the BBC and Cable and Wireless and had the declared aim of privatizing the new enterprises by April 2002. This develop-ment was regarded as reorientating public-service provision towards the demands of the resident population rather than the needs of those organizations using the island.

Dissent developed among the resident population in June 2002, following the decision of the Foreign and Commonwealth Office to impose taxes for the first time on the island (including income tax, property tax and tax on alcohol and tobacco). The primary objection of the population was that this was 'taxation without representa-tion', as the islanders do not possess the right to vote, to own property or even to live on the island. (Protests took the form of a petition and the threat of legal action under the European Con-vention on Human Rights.) The Governor responded with plans to introduce a democratically elected council that would have a purely advisory function and no decision-making powers, claiming that the islanders initially needed to acquire experience of governance. On 22–23 August a vote on the democratic options took place on the island, with 95% of the votes cast being in favour of an Island Council, rather than an Inter-Island Council plus Island Council structure; 50% of those eligible to vote did so. The Council was to be chaired by the Administrator, on behalf of the Governor, and was to comprise seven elected members, the Attorney-General, the Director of Finance and one or two appointed members. Elections for coun-cillors took place in October, and the Island Council was inaugurated in the following month. A joint consultative council was also to be established, with representatives from both Ascension and St Helena, in order to develop policy relating to economic development and tourism common to both islands.

Area: 88 sq km (34 sq miles).

Population: (March 2001): 982 (St Helenians 760, UK nationals 150, US nationals 65).

Budget: (estimates for year ending 31 March 2002): Net expenditure £2,085,000.

Government: The Governor of St Helena, in his capacity as Gov-ernor of Ascension Island, is represented by an Administrator. Two advisory groups, one comprising senior managers of resident organ-izations, and one comprising their employees' representatives, assist the Administrator, who also has professional financial and technical advisers. In November 2002 an advisory Island Council, chaired by the Administrator and comprising seven elected members, the Attorney-General, the Director of Finance and one or two appointed members, was inaugurated.

Administrator: ANDREW MICHAEL KETTLEWELL, The Residency, Georgetown, Ascension; tel. 6311; fax 6152; e-mail administrator@atlantis.co.ac; internet www.ascension-island.gov.ac.

Magistrate: ANDREW MICHAEL KETTLEWELL.

Justices of the Peace: G. F. THOMAS, A. FOWLER, J. PETERS, C. PARKER-YON.

Religion: Ascension forms part of the Anglican diocese of St Helena, which normally provides a resident chaplain who is also available to minister to members of other denominations. There is a Roman Catholic chapel served by visiting priests, as well as a small mosque.

Transport: (1998): *Road vehicles*: 830. *Shipping*: ships entered and cleared 105. The St Helena Line Ltd (q.v.) serves the island with a two-monthly passenger/cargo service between Cardiff, in the United Kingdom, and Cape Town, in South Africa. A vessel under charter to the British Ministry of Defence visits the island monthly on its United Kingdom–Falkland Islands service. A US freighter from Cape Canaveral calls at three-month intervals. *Air services*: A twice-weekly Royal Air Force Tristar service between the United Kingdom and the Falkland Islands transits Ascension Island both southbound and northbound. There is a weekly US Air Force military service linking the Patrick Air Force Base in Florida, USA, with Ascension Island, via Antigua.

Tourism: Small-scale eco-tourism is encouraged, although accommodation on the island is limited and all visits require written permission from the Administrator. Access is available by twice-weekly flights operated from the United Kingdom by the Royal Air Force (see above), and by the RMS *St Helena* (see St Helena—Shipping).

Tristan da Cunha

The island of Tristan da Cunha lies in the South Atlantic Ocean, 2,800 km (1,740 miles) west of Cape Town, South Africa. It comes under the jurisdiction of St Helena, 2,300 km (1,430 miles) to the north-east. Also in the group are Inaccessible Island, 37 km (23 miles) west of Tristan; the three Nightingale Islands, 37 km (23 miles) south; and Gough Island (Diego Álvarez), 425 km (264 miles) south. Tristan da Cunha was discovered in 1506, but remained uninhabited until occupied by US whalers during 1790–1811. The British Navy took possession of the island in 1817. Tristan's population was evacuated in 1961, after volcanic eruptions, but was resettled in 1963. The island's major source of revenue derives from a royalty for a crayfishing concession, supplemented by income from the sale of postage stamps and other philatelic items, and handicrafts. The fishing industry and the administration employ all of the working population. Some 20 power boats operating from the island land their catches to a fish-freezing factory built by the Atlantic Islands Development Corpn, whose fishing concession was transferred in January 1997 to a new holder, Premier Fishing (Pty) Ltd., of Cape Town. Premier also operates two large fishing vessels exporting the catch to the USA, France and Japan. A substantial budget deficit, of £158,345, was forecast in 1999/2000, owing to a decline in demand in the international crayfish market. Budget estimates for 2000/01 projected a deficit of £90,251. Development aid from the United Kingdom ceased in 1980; since then the island has financed its own projects. In June 2001 a hurricane in the main settlement of Edinburgh of the Seven Seas destroyed the hospital, community centre and numerous homes, and also killed many cattle; the satellite phone link was lost and the island was without electricity for one week, although no serious injuries were sustained. The British Department for International Development granted a £75,000 emergency aid package in response to the disaster.

Area: Tristan da Cunha 98 sq km (38 sq miles); Inaccessible Island 10 sq km (4 sq miles); Nightingale Islands 2 sq km (¾ sq mile); Gough Island 91 sq km (35 sq miles).

Population: (December 2000): 290 (including 11 expatriates) on Tristan; there is a small weather station on Gough Island, staffed, under agreement, by personnel employed by the South African Government.

Fishing: (catch, metric tons, year ending 30 April): Tristan da Cunha rock lobster 376 in 1997/98; 336 in 1998/99; 316 in 1999/2000. Source: FAO, *Yearbook of Fishery Statistics*.

Budget: (estimates for 2000/01): Revenue £672,166; Expenditure £762,417.

Government: The Administrator, representing the Governor of St Helena, is assisted by an Island Council of eight elected members (of whom at least one must be a woman) and three appointed members, which has advisory powers in legislative and executive functions. The member receiving the largest number of votes at elections to the Council is appointed Chief Islander. The Council's advisory functions in executive matters are performed through 11 committees of the Council dealing with the separate branches of administration. Elections are held every three years.

Administrator: BRIAN P. BALDWIN, The Residency, Tristan da Cunha; tel. (satellite) 874-1445434; fax (satellite) 874-1445435; e-mail hmg@cunha.demon.co.uk.

Legal System: The Administrator is also the Magistrate and Coroner.

Religion: Adherents of the Anglican church predominate on Tristan da Cunha, which is within the Church of the Province of Southern Africa, and is under the jurisdiction of the Archbishop of Cape Town, South Africa. There is also a small number of Roman Catholics.

Transport: The St Helena Line Ltd (q.v.), the MV *Hanseatic*, and MS *Explorer* and the SA *Agulhas* each visit the island once each year, and two lobster concession vessels each make three visits annually, remaining for between two and three months. Occasional cruise ships also visit the island. There is no airfield.

Tourism: Permission from the Administrator and the Island Council is required for visits to Tristan da Cunha. Facilities for tourism are limited, although some accommodation is available in island homes.

SOUTH GEORGIA AND THE SOUTH SANDWICH ISLANDS

South Georgia, an island of 3,592 sq km (1,387 sq miles), lies in the South Atlantic Ocean, about 1,300 km (800 miles) east-south-east of the Falkland Islands. The South Sandwich Islands, which have an area of 311 sq km (120 sq miles), lie about 750 km (470 miles) south-east of South Georgia.

The United Kingdom annexed South Georgia and the South Sandwich Islands in 1775. With a segment of the Antarctic mainland and other nearby islands (now the British Antarctic Territory), they were constituted as the Falkland Islands Dependencies in 1908.

Argentina made formal claim to South Georgia in 1927, and to the South Sandwich Islands in 1948. In 1955 the United Kingdom unilaterally submitted the dispute over sovereignty to the International Court of Justice (based in the Netherlands), which decided not to hear the application in view of Argentina's refusal to submit to the Court's jurisdiction. South Georgia was the site of a British Antarctic Survey base (staffed by 22 scientists and support personnel) until it was invaded in April 1982 by Argentine forces, who occupied the island until its recapture by British forces three weeks later. The

South Sandwich Islands were uninhabited until the occupation of Southern Thule in December 1976 by about 50 Argentines, reported to be scientists. Argentine personnel remained until removed by British forces in June 1982.

In mid-1989 it was reported that the British Government was considering the imposition of a conservation zone extending to 200 nautical miles (370 km) around South Georgia, similar to that which surrounds the Falkland Islands, in an attempt to prevent the threatened extinction of certain types of marine life.

Under the provisions of the South Georgia and South Sandwich Islands Order of 1985, the islands ceased to be governed as dependencies of the Falkland Islands on 3 October 1985. The Governor of the Falkland Islands is, *ex officio*, Commissioner for the territory.

In May 1993, in response to the Argentine Government's decision to commence the sale of fishing licences for the region's waters, the British Government announced an extension, from 12 to 200 nautical miles, of its territorial jurisdiction in the waters surrounding the islands, in order to conserve crucial fishing stocks.

In September 1998 the British Government announced that it would withdraw its military detachment from South Georgia in 2000, while it would increase its scientific presence on the island with the installation of a permanent team from the British Antarctic Survey to investigate the fisheries around the island for possible exploitation. The small military detachment finally withdrew in March 2001. The British garrison stationed in the Falkland Islands would remain responsible for the security of South Georgia and the South Sandwich Islands. On 3 December 2002 Howard Pearce succeeded Donald Lamont as Commissioner.

Commissioner: HOWARD PEARCE (assumed office 3 December 2002).

Assistant Commissioner and Director of Fisheries: ROSS T. JARVIS (Stanley, Falkland Islands).

THE TURKS AND CAICOS ISLANDS

Introductory Survey

Location, Climate, Language, Religion, Flag, Capital

The Turks and Caicos Islands consist of more than 30 low-lying islands forming the south-eastern end of the Bahamas chain of islands, and lying about 145 km (90 miles) north of Haiti. Eight islands are inhabited: Grand Turk and Salt Cay (both in the smaller Turks group to the east of the Caicos), South Caicos, Middle (Grand) Caicos, North Caicos, Providenciales (Provo), Pine Cay and Parrot Cay. The climate is warm throughout the year but tempered by constant trade winds. The average annual temperature is 27°C (82°F) and rainfall ranges from 530 mm (21 ins) in the eastern islands to 1,000 mm (40 ins) in the west. The official language is English, though some Creole is spoken by Haitian immigrants. Many Christian churches are represented, the largest denomination being the Baptist Union (25.5% of the population at the census of May 1990). The flag is the British 'Blue Ensign', with the shield from the islands' coat of arms, bearing a shell, a lobster and a cactus, in the fly. The capital is Cockburn Town, on Grand Turk island.

Recent History

The Turks and Caicos Islands were first settled by Amerindian peoples. The islands were then inhabited by privateers, and were settled from Bermuda and by exiled 'Loyalists' from the former British colonies in North America. A Jamaican dependency from 1874 to 1959, the Turks and Caicos Islands became a separate colony in 1962, following Jamaican independence. After an administrative association with the Bahamas, the islands received their own Governor in 1972. The first elections under the present Constitution took place in 1976, and were won by the pro-independence People's Democratic Movement (PDM). In 1980 an agreement was made with the United Kingdom whereby, if the governing PDM won the 1980 elections, the islands would receive independence and a payment of £12m. However, lacking the leadership of J. A. G. S. McCartney, the Chief Minister, (who had been killed in an aircraft accident in May 1980), the PDM lost the election in November to the Progressive National Party (PNP), which is committed to continued dependent status. At a subsequent general election, in May 1984, the PNP, led by the Chief Minister, Norman Saunders, won eight of the 11 elective seats.

In March 1985 the Chief Minister, the Minister for Development and Commerce and a PNP member of the Legislative Council were arrested in Miami, Florida, on charges involving illicit drugs and violations of the US Travel Act. All three men were subsequently convicted and imprisoned (with Saunders receiving an eight-year sentence). Saunders resigned and was replaced as Chief Minister by Nathaniel Francis, hitherto the Minister of Public Works and Utilities. Emily Saunders won the by-election for her husband's constituency in December, and PNP candidates were returned unopposed in the other two vacant seats.

In April 1986 a commission of inquiry was appointed to investigate allegations of arson and administrative malpractice, following the destruction by fire of a government building in December 1985. The commission's report, published in July, concluded that Francis and two of his ministers were unfit for ministerial office, accusing them of unconstitutional behaviour and ministerial malpractice; all three ministers subsequently resigned. Two members of the PDM were also deemed to be unfit for public office. In the same month the Governor dissolved the Government, and the Executive Council was replaced by an interim advisory council, comprising the Governor and four members of the former Executive Council. A constitutional commission was appointed in September to review the future administration of the islands. In July 1987 a deportation order was served on Terence Donegan, Attorney-General in 1980–82, after a commission of inquiry revealed that he had committed 'various acts of misfeasance' while in public office.

Three of the four members of the advisory council resigned from the PNP in February 1987 and subsequently formed a new party, the National Democratic Alliance. All four members resigned from the council in May, to enable the appointment of a new council that would be more representative of the balance of parties in the Legislative Council.

A general election, preceding the return to ministerial rule, took place in March 1988, following the British Government's acceptance of the principal recommendations of the constitutional commission in the previous year. Under a new multi-member system of representation (see Constitution, below), the PDM won 11 of the 13 seats on the Legislative Council, and the PNP won the remaining two. Oswald O. Skippings, the leader of the PDM, was appointed Chief Minister. The new Constitution strengthened the reserve powers of the Governor, but otherwise the form of government was similar to the provisions of the 1976 Constitution.

In April 1991 a general election took place, at which the PNP secured eight seats, defeating the PDM (which won the remaining five). Skippings was replaced as Chief Minister by C. Washington Misick, the leader of the PNP.

Following his expulsion from the PDM, the former Minister of Social Services, Wendal Swann, founded a new party in 1993, the United Democratic Party (UDP). In June of that year Martin Bourke was appointed Governor of the Territory.

At a general election in January 1995 the PDM secured eight seats, while the PNP won four. Norman Saunders, who had failed to secure nomination as a candidate for the PNP, won his seat as an independent. The UDP fielded three candidates but failed to win a seat. Derek Taylor, leader of the PDM, was appointed Chief Minister. The PDM's victory was largely attributed to widespread popular discontent with the previous Government's policies of economic austerity, which included severe reductions in the number of public service employees.

A serious dispute arose between the Legislative Council and the Governor in August 1995, following the latter's decision to reappoint Kipling Douglas to the position of Chief Justice. Taylor, who claimed that Douglas did not enjoy the confidence of his Government, described the decision as provocative and disrespectful. Relations deteriorated in subsequent months, and in February 1996 a petition requesting the immediate removal of the Governor, signed by all members of the Government and opposition, was presented to the British Foreign and Commonwealth Office. The signatories accused Bourke of abusing his position, and were particularly angered by remarks he had made in an interview that portrayed the islands as lawless and unstable, with drugs-related crime and corruption at unprecedented levels. A delegation of politicians from the Territory travelled to the United Kingdom to reinforce the views of the Legislative Council, which were believed to be shared by a majority of islanders. In the following month, however, their demands were rejected by the British Government, which deployed a frigate in the islands' waters and ordered 100 police officers to prepare for immediate transfer to the Territory in the event of civil disturbance. A climate of animosity between the Governor and the islanders persisted during 1996, and in September Bourke departed from the Territory, without formal ceremony, following the expiry of his term of office. He was replaced by John Kelly.

At legislative elections, held on 4 March 1999, the PDM won 52.2% of the vote. Norman Saunders, who had secured nomination as a PDM candidate, retained the seat that he had held as an independent, increasing the PDM's representation in the Legislative Council to nine seats. The PNP won the other four seats, with 40.9% of the vote.

In June 2000 the Turks and Caicos Islands were included on a list of territories regarded as operating harmful tax regimes. The Organisation for Economic Co-operation and Development (OECD), which compiled the list, urged the Government to make legislative changes, in order to introduce greater legal and administrative transparency to prevent companies using the country's tax system for money-laundering or tax-avoidance purposes. OECD removed the Turks and Caicos Islands from the list in March 2002, declaring that the Government had made sufficient commitments to improve transparency and effective exchange of information on tax matters by the end of 2005. In late 2002, however, the recovering financial sector faced further disruption when the United Kingdom, under pressure from a European Union (EU) investigation into tax evasion, demanded that the Turks and Caicos Islands disclose the identities and account details of Europeans holding private savings accounts on the islands. The Turks and Caicos Islands, along with some other British Overseas Territories facing similar demands, claimed it was being treated unfairly compared with more powerful European countries, such as Switzerland and Luxembourg.

In May 2002 the British Overseas Territories Act, having received royal assent in the United Kingdom in February, came into force and granted British citizenship rights to the people of its Overseas Territories, including the Turks and Caicos Islands. Under the new law Turks and Caicos Islanders would be able to hold British passports and work in the United Kingdom and anywhere else in the EU.

In October 2002 capital punishment for treason and piracy, the only remaining capital crime in the British Overseas Territories, was abolished in the Turks and Caicos Islands. In December James Poston replaced Mervyn Jones as Governor.

In March 2003 Chief Minister Taylor, seeking an unprecedented third consecutive term in office, announced that a general election would be held on 24 April. He added that the PDM had fulfilled all of its promises and that the opposition would find no issues to contest. Misick, however, dismissed the Government's claims of economic progress, arguing the strong growth had benefited expatriates rather than Turks and Caicos 'belongers'. In the same month, following the repatriation of more than 400 Haitian 'boat people', a spokesman for the Ministry of Immigration criticized Haiti for not doing enough to stop illegal migration and raised the possibility of cancelling all work permits for Haitians.

At the general election of 24 April 2003 the PDM won seven of the 13 seats in the Legislative Council, two fewer than in 1999. The PNP took the remaining six seats, but challenged the results in two of the more closely-fought constituencies. Following the election, Governor Poston appointed Delroy Williams (as Minister of Home Affairs and Local Government) and Sean Astwood (as Minister of Natural Resources, Planning, Heritage, Agriculture and Fisheries and Environmental and Coastal Resources) to the Executive Council, to replace the retiring Hilly Ewing and Larry Coalbrook, respectively. In addition, Clarence Selver, the Minister of Education, Health, Youth, Sports, Social Welfare and National Insurance, became Deputy Prime Minister.

Government

Under the provisions of the 1976 Constitution (amended in 1988), executive power is vested in the Governor, appointed by the British monarch. The Governor is responsible for external affairs, internal security, defence and the appointment of public officers. The Governor is President of the Executive Council, which comprises nine members: three *ex officio* and six appointed by the Governor from among the elected members of the Legislative Council. The Legislative Council comprises the Speaker, three nominated members, the *ex-officio* members of the Executive Council and 13 members elected by universal adult suffrage.

Economic Affairs

In 2000, according to estimates by the Caribbean Development Bank (CDB), the Turks and Caicos Islands' gross domestic product (GDP) was US $230.8m., equivalent to some $9,051 per head. During 1990–98, it was estimated, the population increased at an average annual rate of 3.5%, while GDP increased, in real terms, by 7.9% per year during 1990–2000; growth in 2000 was 4.9%.

Agriculture is not practised on any significant scale in the Turks Islands or on South Caicos (the most populous island of the Territory). The other islands of the Caicos group grow some beans, maize and a few fruits and vegetables. There is some livestock-rearing, but the islands' principal natural resource is fisheries, which account for almost all commodity exports, the principal species caught being the spiny lobster (an estimated 230 metric tons in 2000) and the conch (an estimated 770 metric tons in that year). Conchs are now being developed commercially (on the largest conch farm in the world), and there is potential for larger-scale fishing. Exports of lobster and conch earned $3.4m. in 1995, which constituted an increase of more than 14% compared with the previous year's earnings.

Industrial activity consists mainly of construction (especially for the tourist industry) and fish-processing. The islands possess plentiful supplies of aragonite. The Territory is dependent upon the import of mineral fuels to satisfy energy requirements.

The principal economic sector is the service industry. This is dominated by tourism, which is concentrated on the island of Providenciales. The market is for wealthier visitors, most of whom come from the USA. Tourist arrivals increased from 120,898 in 1999 to 152,211 in 2000. However, a decline in the number of tourist arrivals was expected in 2001–03, owing to the weakening of demand in the aftermath of the September 2001 terrorist attacks on the USA and the US-led military campaign to remove the regime of Saddam Hussein in Iraq in 2003. An 'offshore' financial sector was encouraged in the 1980s, and new regulatory legislation was ratified at the end of 1989. In 2000 there were some 8,000 overseas companies registered in the islands. Earnings from some 2,858 new registrations totalled US $2.3m. in 1995.

In 1994 the Turks and Caicos Islands recorded a trade deficit of US $94.7m. (exports were 3.6% of the value of imports). This deficit is normally offset by receipts from tourism, aid from the United Kingdom and revenue from the offshore financial sector. The USA is the principal trading partner, but some trade is conducted with the United Kingdom and with neighbouring nations.

In the financial year ending 31 March 2001 the Government estimated an overall budgetary deficit of US $0.06m. The islands received a total of $8.2m. in British development assistance in 1999/2000. The total public debt was reduced to $1.4m. by March 1990. The rate of inflation, which stood at about 4% in 1995, is dependent upon the movement of prices in the USA, the Territory's principal trading partner, and the currency of which it uses. Unemployment increased to an estimated 10% in the late 1990s. A large number of Turks and Caicos 'belongers' have emigrated, many to the Bahamas, especially in search of skilled labour (there is no tertiary education in the Territory). In July 2000 the CDB announced a loan to the Government of some US $4m. to assist the Turks and Caicos Investment Agency.

The Turks and Caicos Islands, as a dependency of the United Kingdom, have the status of Overseas Territory in association with the European Union. The Territory is also a member of the CDB (see p. 159) and an associate member of the Caribbean Community and Common Market (CARICOM, see p. 155).

The economy, and also the population, of the Turks and Caicos Islands were estimated to have doubled in size during the 1990s, making the islands one of the region's most dynamic economies. The remarkable economic growth experienced by the islands was chiefly owing to the increasing significance of the tourism and international financial services sectors, both of which bene-fited from the perceived stability of United Kingdom Overseas Territory status. In the late 1990s the offshore financial sector successfully rehabilitated its international reputation through the introduction of a supervisory body, the Financial Services Commission, and the implementation of more stringent regu-latory legislation based on the maxim of 'privacy not secrecy'. Tourism also grew steadily in the late 1990s, and as a result many new hotels and resorts have been developed. Concern has, however, been expressed that the islands are in danger of becoming overdeveloped and thereby of damaging their reputa-tion as an unspoilt tourist location. A further source of disquiet is the exclusion of many inhabitants from the benefits of eco-nomic growth; it is estimated that the economic situation of the majority of 'belongers' has improved only marginally during the 1990s, as newly-created jobs were often taken by low-wage migrant workers or by highly-skilled expatriate workers. It has also been noted that the Territory's growth, which is driven more by inward investment than by domestic production, is highly dependent on exterior factors, and international pro-posals to force comprehensive reforms of offshore financial serv-ices centres are therefore of particular concern. Growth in 2002, after a decline in regional tourism, was reported to have slowed.

Education

Primary education, beginning at seven years of age and lasting seven years, is compulsory, and is provided free of charge in government schools. Secondary education, from the age of 14, lasts for five years, and is also free. In 1997 there were 21 primary schools, and in 1990 one private secondary school and four government secondary schools. In 1997 the Caribbean Development Bank approved a loan of just under US $4m. to fund the establishment of a permanent campus for the Turks and Caicos Community College.

Public Holidays

2003: 1 January (New Year's Day), 10 March (Commonwealth Day), 18 April (Good Friday), 21 April (Easter Monday), 19 May (National Heroes' Day), 6 June (J. A. G. S. McCartney Memorial Day), 14 June (Queen's Official Birthday), 28 July (Emanci-pation Day), 30 August (Constitution Day), 30 September (National Youth Day), 13 October (for Columbus Day), 10 December (International Human Rights Day), 25–26 December (Christmas).

2004: 1 January (New Year's Day), 11 March (Commonwealth Day), 9 April (Good Friday), 12 April (Easter Monday), 17 May (National Heroes' Day), 6 June (J. A. G. S. McCartney Memorial Day), 12 June (Queen's Official Birthday), 26 July (Emancipa-tion Day), 30 August (Constitution Day), 30 September (National Youth Day), 11 October (for Columbus Day), 10 December (International Human Rights Day), 25–26 December (Christmas).

Weights and Measures

The imperial system is in use.

Statistical Survey

Source: Chief Secretary's Office, Grand Turk; tel. 946-2300; fax 946-2886.

AREA AND POPULATION

Area: 430 sq km (166 sq miles).

Population: 7,435 (males 3,602; females 3,833) at census of 12 May 1980; 12,350 (males 6,289; females 6,061) at census of 31 May 1990; 17,000 (estimate) at mid-2001 (Source: UN, *Population and Vital Statistics Report*). *By island* (1980): Grand Turk 3,098; South Caicos 1,380; Middle Caicos 396; North Caicos 1,278; Salt Cay 284; Provi-denciales 977. (1990): Grand Turk 3,761; Providenciales 5,586.

Density: 39.5 per sq km (mid-2001).

Principal Towns: Cockburn Town (capital, on Grand Turk), pop-ulation 2,500 (estimate, 1987); Cockburn Harbour (South Caicos), population 1,000. *Mid-2001* (UN estimate, incl. suburbs): Grand Turk 5,000 (Source: UN, *World Urbanization Prospects: The 2001 Revision*).

Births and Deaths (registrations, 1990): Live births 240; Deaths 37; (rates per 1,000, 1998) Births 27.14; Deaths 4.98.

Expectation of Life (years at birth, 1998): Males 70.21; Females 74.20.

Economically Active Population (1990 census): 4,848 (males 2,306; females 2,542).

HEALTH AND WELFARE

Under-5 Mortality Rate (per 1,000 live births, 1997): 22.0.

Physicians (per 1,000 head, 1997): 0.73.
Source: Pan American Health Organization.
For definitions see explanatory note on p. vi.

AGRICULTURE, ETC.

Fishing (FAO estimates, metric tons, live weight, 2000): Capture 1,300 (Marine fishes 300, Caribbean spiny lobster 230, Stromboid conchs 770); Aquaculture 5; Total catch 1,305. Figures exclude aquatic plants and mammals. Source: FAO, *Yearbook of Fishery Statistics*.

INDUSTRY

Electric Energy (estimated production, million kWh): 5 in 1996; 5 in 1997; 5 in 1998. Source: UN, *Industrial Commodity Statistics Yearbook*.

FINANCE

Currency and Exchange Rate: United States currency is used: 100 cents = 1 US dollar ($). *Sterling and Euro Equivalents* (31 December 2002): £1 sterling = US $1.6118; €1 = US $1.0487; $100 = £62.04 = €95.36.

Budget (provisional, US $ million, 2000/01): Total revenue 67.05; Total expenditure 67.11.

Gross Domestic Product (US $ million at current prices): 171.7 in 1998; 200.0 in 1999; 230.8 in 2001. Source: Caribbean Development Bank.

EXTERNAL TRADE

2000 (US $ million): *Imports:* 216.4. *Exports:* 169.2. Source: Car-ibbean Development Bank.

TRANSPORT

Road Traffic (1984): 1,563 registered motor vehicles.

Shipping: : *International Freight Traffic* (estimates in '000 metric tons, 1990) Goods loaded 135; Goods unloaded 149. *Merchant Fleet* (vessels registered at 31 December 2001): 6; Total displacement 1,095 grt. Sources: UN, *Monthly Bulletin of Statistics*; Lloyd's Register-Fairplay, *World Fleet Statistics*.

TOURISM

Tourist Arrivals: 110,855 in 1998; 120,898 in 1999; 152,211 in 2000. Source: World Tourism Organization, *Yearbook of Tourism Statistics*.

Tourism Receipts (US $ million): 196 in 1998; 246 in 1999; 329 in 2000 (estimate). Source: World Tourism Organization.

COMMUNICATIONS MEDIA

Radio Receivers (1997): 8,000 in use.

Telephones (1994): 3,000 main lines in use.

Facsimile Machines (1992): 200 in use.

Non-daily Newspapers (1996): 1 (estimated circulation 5,000).
Sources: UNESCO, *Statistical Yearbook*; UN, *Statistical Yearbook*.

EDUCATION

Pre-primary (1996/97): 21 schools; 797 pupils.

Primary (1999): 21 schools (1996/97); 86 teachers (1993/94); 1,921 pupils.

General Secondary (1999): 5 schools (1990); 101 teachers (1993/94); 1,018 pupils.

Vocational Education (1993/94): 0 teachers; 89 pupils.

Adult Literacy Rate (UNESCO estimates): 99% (males 99%; females 98%) in 1998.
Sources: UNESCO, *Statistical Yearbook*; Caribbean Development Bank, *Social and Economic Indicators 2001*.

Directory

The Constitution

The Order in Council of July 1986 enabled the Governor to suspend the ministerial form of government, for which the Constitution of 1976 made provision. Ministerial government was restored in March 1988, following amendments to the Constitution, recommended by a constitutional commission.

The revised Constitution of 1988 provides for an Executive Council and a Legislative Council. Executive authority is vested in the British monarch and is exercised by the Governor (the monarch's appointed representative), who also holds responsibility for external affairs, internal security, defence, the appointment of any person to any public office and the suspension and termination of appointment of any public officer.

The Executive Council comprises: three *ex-officio* members (the Financial Secretary, the Chief Secretary and the Attorney-General); a Chief Minister (appointed by the Governor) who is, in the judgement of the Governor, the leader of that political party represented in the Legislative Council which commands the support of a majority of the elected members of the Council; and four other ministers, appointed by the Governor, on the advice of the Chief Minister. The Executive Council is presided over by the Governor.

The Legislative Council consists of the Speaker, the three *ex-officio* members of the Executive Council, 13 members elected by residents aged 18 and over, and three nominated members (appointed by the Governor, one on the advice of the Chief Minister, one on the advice of the Leader of the Opposition and one at the Governor's discretion).

For the purposes of elections to the Legislative Council, the islands are divided into five electoral districts. In 1988 and 1991 a multiple voting system was used, whereby three districts elected three members each, while the remaining five districts each elected two members. However, from the 1995 election a single-member constituency system was used.

The Government

Governor: JAMES POSTON (sworn in 9 December 2002).

EXECUTIVE COUNCIL
(April 2003)

President: The Governor.

Ex-Officio Members:

Financial Secretary: AUSTIN ROBINSON.

Attorney-General: DAVID J. JEREMIAH.

Chief Secretary: CYNTHIA ASTWOOD.

Chief Minister and Minister of Finance, Development and Commerce: HUGH DEREK TAYLOR.

Deputy Prime Minister and Minister of Education, Health, Youth, Sports, Social Welfare and National Insurance: CLARENCE WESLEY SELVER.

Minister of Home Affairs and Local Government: DELROY WILLIAMS.

Minister of Transport, Communications, Tourism, Information, Immigration, Labour and CARICOM Affairs: OSWALD O'NEAL SKIPPINGS.

Minister of Natural Resources, Planning, Heritage, Agriculture and Fisheries and Environment and Coastal Resources: SEAN ASTWOOD.

Minister of Public Works and Utilities: NOEL TERRANCE SKIPPINGS.

GOVERNMENT OFFICES

Office of the Governor: Government House, Waterloo, Grand Turk; tel. 946-2308; fax 946-2903; e-mail governoroffice@tciway.tc.

Office of the Chief Minister: Government Compound, Grand Turk; tel. 946-2801; fax 946-2777; e-mail unfptc@tciway.tc.

Chief Secretary's Office: Government Secretariat, Grand Turk; tel. 946-2702; fax 946-2886.

Office of the Permanent Secretary: Finance Department, Chief Minister's Office, Government Buildings, Front St, Grand Turk; tel. 946-1115; fax 946-2777.

LEGISLATIVE COUNCIL

Speaker: WINSTON R. OUTTEN.

Election, 24 April 2003

Party	Seats
People's Democratic Movement	7
Progressive National Party	6
Total	13

There are three *ex-officio* members (the Chief Secretary, the Financial Secretary and the Attorney-General), three appointed members, and a Speaker chosen from outside the Council.

Political Organizations

People's Democratic Movement (PDM): POB 38, Grand Turk; favours internal self-government and eventual independence; Leader DEREK TAYLOR.

Progressive National Party (PNP): Grand Turk; tel. 941-4663; fax 946-3673; e-mail info@votepnp.com; internet www.votepnp.com; supports full internal self-government; Chair. N. B. SAUNDERS; Leader C. WASHINGTON MISICK.

United Democratic Party (UDP): Grand Turk; f. 1993; Leader WENDAL SWANN.

Judicial System

Justice is administered by the Supreme Court of the islands, presided over by the Chief Justice. Following the suspension of the Constitution in 1986, an inquiry recommended that the Chief Justice should reside in the Territory. There is a Chief Magistrate resident on Grand Turk, who also acts as Judge of the Supreme Court. There are also three Deputy Magistrates.

The Court of Appeal held its first sitting in February 1995. Previously the islands had shared a court of appeal in Nassau, Bahamas. In certain cases, appeals are made to the Judicial Committee of the Privy Council (based in the United Kingdom).

Judicial Dept: Grand Turk; tel. 946-2114; fax 946-2720.

Chief Justice: DAVID HALLCHURCH.

Magistrate: DEREK REDMAN.

Attorney-General's Chambers: Grand Turk; tel. 946-2096; fax 946-2588; e-mail attorneygeneral@tciway.tc.

Religion

CHRISTIANITY

The Anglican Communion

Within the Church in the Province of the West Indies, the territory forms part of the diocese of Nassau and the Bahamas. The Bishop is resident in Nassau. According to census results, there were 1,465 adherents in 1990.

Anglican Church: St Mary's Church, Front St, Grand Turk; tel. 946-2289.

The Roman Catholic Church

The Bishop of Nassau, Bahamas (suffragan to the archdiocese of Kingston in Jamaica), has jurisdiction in the Turks and Caicos Islands, as Superior of the Mission to the Territory (founded in June 1984).

Roman Catholic Mission: Leeward Highway, POB 340, Providenciales; tel. and fax 946-1888; e-mail rcmission@tciway.tc; churches on Grand Turk and on Providenciales; 132 adherents in 1990 (according to census results); Superior Archbishop of Newark.

Protestant Churches

The Baptist, Jehovah's Witness, Methodist, Church of God and Seventh-day Adventist faiths are represented on the islands.

Baptist Union of the Turks and Caicos Islands: South Caicos; tel. 946-3220; 3,153 adherents in 1990 (according to census results).

Jehovah's Witnesses: Kingdom Hall, Intersection of Turtle Cove and Bridge Rd, POB 400, Providenciales; tel. 941-5583.

Methodist Church: The Ridge, Grand Turk; tel. 946-2115; 1,238 adherents in 1990 (according to census results).

New Testament Church of God: Orea Alley, Grand Turk; tel. 946-2175.

The Press

Free Press: Caribbean Pl., POB 179, Providenciales; tel. 946-5615; fax 941-3402; e-mail frepress@tciway.tc; internet www.turksandcaicos.tc/freepress; f. 1991; weekly; Man. Editor YASMIN BLUES; Editor FAITH HAMER; circ. 2,000.

Times of the Islands Magazine: Southwind Plaza, POB 234, Providenciales; tel. and fax 946-4788; e-mail timespub@tciway.tc; internet www.timespub.tc; f. 1988; quarterly; circ. 7,000; Editor KATHEY BORSUK.

Turks and Caicos Times: Southern Shores Bldg, Providenciales; tel. 946-4257; e-mail times@tciway.tc.

Turks and Caicos Weekly News: POB 52, Cheshire House, Providenciales; tel. 946-4664; fax 946-4661; e-mail tcnews@tcway.tc.

Where, When, How: POB 192, Providenciales; tel. 946-4815; fax 941-3497; e-mail wwh@provo.net; internet www.wherewhenhow.com; monthly; travel magazine.

Broadcasting and Communications

TELECOMMUNICATIONS

Cable and Wireless (Turks and Caicos) Ltd: Grand Turk; tel. 946-2222; fax 946-2497; e-mail cwtci@tciway.tc; internet www.cw.tc; f. 1973.

Radio

Caribbean Christian Radio: POB 200, Grand Turk; tel. 946-1095; fax 946-1095; operates under licence from West Indies Broadcasting; Gen. Man. REO STUBBS; Station Man. BUDDY TUCKER; CEO JERRY KIEFER.

Radio Providenciales: Leeward Highway, POB 32, Providenciales; tel. 946-4496; fax 946-4108; commercial.

Radio Turks and Caicos (RTC): POB 69, Grand Turk; tel. 946-2007; fax 946-1600; e-mail rtc@tciway.tc; internet www.tcimall.tc; govt-owned; commercial; broadcasts 105 hrs weekly; Man. LYNETTE SMITH.

Radio Visión Cristiana Internacional: North End, South Caicos; tel. 946-6601; fax 946-6600; e-mail radiovision@tciway.tc; internet www.rvci.net; commercial; Man. WENDELL SEYMOUR.

Victory in Christ (VIC) Radio: Butterfield Sq., POB 32, Providenciales; tel. 946-4496; religious.

WIV FM Radio: POB 108, Providenciales.

WPRT Radio: Leeward Highway, POB 262, Providenciales; tel. 946-4267; commercial; Station Man. PETER STUBBS.

Television

Television programmes are available from a cabled network, and broadcasts from the Bahamas can be received in the islands.

Turks and Caicos Television: Pond St, POB 80, Grand Turk; tel. 946-1530; fax 946-2896.

WIV Cable TV: Tower Raza, Leeward Highway, POB 679, Providenciales; tel. 946-4273; fax 946-4790.

Finance

Financial Services Commission (FSC): POB 173, Post Office Bldg, Front St, Grand Turk; tel. 946-2791; fax 946-2821; e-mail fsc@tciway.tc; regulates local and 'offshore' financial services sector; Man. Dir DULCIE JAMES.

BANKING

Bank of Nova Scotia (Canada): Harbour House, Front St, Cockburn Town, POB 132, Grand Turk; tel. 946-2506; fax 946-2667; Man. C. COALBROOKE; br. on Providenciales.

Bordier International Bank and Trust Ltd: Caribbean Pl., Leeward Highway, POB 5, Providenciales; tel. 946-4535; fax 946-4540; e-mail bibt@tciway.tc; Man. ELISE HARTSHORN.

FirstCaribbean International Bank Ltd: Grand Turk; internet www.firstcaribbeaninternational.com; f. 2002 following merger of Caribbean operations of Barclays Bank PLC and CIBC; Exec. Chair. MICHAEL MANSOOR; CEO CHARLES PINK.

First National Bank Ltd: The Arch Plaza, Leeward Highway, POB 58, Providenciales; tel. 946-4060; fax 946-4061; e-mail fnb@tciway.tc.

Turks and Caicos Banking Co Ltd: Duke St North, Cockburn Town, POB 123, Grand Turk; tel. 946-2368; fax 946-2365; e-mail tcbc@tciways.com; internet www.turksandcaicosbanking.tc; f. 1980; cap. $2.7m., dep. $9.7m. Man. Dir ANTON FAESSLER.

INSURANCE

Turks and Caicos Islands National Insurance Board: Church Folly, POB 250, Grand Turk; tel. 946-1045; fax 946-1362; e-mail nib@tciway.tc; 3 brs.

Several foreign (mainly US and British) companies have offices in the Turks and Caicos Islands. Some 1,491 insurance companies were registered at the end of 1993.

Financial Association

United Belongers in Financial Services: Grand Turk; f. 2000.

Trade and Industry

GOVERNMENT AGENCY

Financial Services Commission (FSC): see Finance.

General Trading Company (Turks and Caicos) Ltd: PMBI, Cockburn Town, Grand Turk; tel. 946-2464; fax 946-2799; shipping agents, importers, air freight handlers; wholesale distributor of petroleum products, wines and spirits.

Turks Islands Importers Ltd (TIMCO): Front St, POB 72, Grand Turk; tel. 946-2480; fax 946-2481; f. 1952; agents for Lloyds of London, importers and distributors of food, beer, liquor, building materials, hardware and appliances; Dir H. E. MAGNUS.

DEVELOPMENT ORGANIZATION

Turks and Caicos Islands Investment Agency (TC Invest): Hibiscus Sq., Pond St, POB 105, Grand Turk; tel. 946-2058; fax 946-1464; e-mail TCInvest@caribsurf.com; internet www.tcinvest.tc; f. 1974 as Development Board of the Turks and Caicos Islands; statutory body; development finance for private sector; promotion and management of internal investment; Chair. LILLIAN MISICK; Pres. and CEO COLIN R. HEARTWELL.

CHAMBER OF COMMERCE

Chamber of Commerce: POB 148, Grand Turk; also on Providenciales; tel. 946-2324; fax 946-2714; tel. 946-4650; fax 946-4565; Pres. JENNY SMITH; Exec. Dir GLEN CLARKE.

UTILITIES

Electricity and Gas

Atlantic Equipment and Power (Turks and Caicos) Ltd: New Airport Rd, Airport Area, South Caicos; tel. 946-3201; fax 946-3202.

North Caicos Power Co: Bottle Creek, North Caicos; tel. 946-7234.

PPC Ltd: Town Centre Mall, POB 132, Providenciales; tel. 946-4313; fax 946-4532.

Turks and Caicos Utilities Ltd: Pond St, POB 80, Grand Turk; tel. 946-2402; fax 946-2896.

Water

Provo Water Co: Grace Bay Rd, POB 124, Providenciales; tel. 946-5202; fax 946-5204.

Turks and Caicos Water Co: Provo Golf Clubhouse, Grace Bay Rd, POB 124, Providenciales; tel. 946-5126; fax 946-5127.

TRADE UNION

Turks and Caicos Workers' Labour Trade Union: Grand Turk; all professions; f. 2000; Leader CALVIN HANDFIELD.

Transport

ROADS

There are 121 km (75 miles) of roads in the islands, of which 24 km (15 miles), on Grand Turk, South Caicos and Providenciales, are tarmac.

SHIPPING

There are regular freight services from Miami, Florida. The main sea ports are Grand Turk, Providenciales, Salt Cay and Cockburn Harbour on South Caicos. Harbour facilities on South Caicos and Providenciales are being improved, and there are plans for a new port on North Caicos. Plans are also under way for a deep-water port on East Caicos for cruise liners and a transhipment port on South Caicos.

Cargo Express Shipping Service Ltd: Butterfield Sq., POB 645, Providenciales; tel. 941-3865; fax 941-5062; Man. GRANTLEY HINDS.

Ocean Research and Recovery Ltd: The Mariner, POB 64, Providenciales; tel. 946-4109; fax 946-4939.

Seacair Ltd: Churchill Bldg, POB 170, Grand Turk; tel. 946-2591; fax 946-2226.

Seacorp Shipping Ltd: Grand Turk; tel. 946-2226; fax 946-2226.

Southeast and Caribbean Shipping Co Ltd: Churchill Bldg, Front St, POB 1, Grand Turk; tel. 946-2355.

Tropical Shipping: Butterfield Sq., Providenciales; tel. 941-3865; fax 941-5062; e-mail vgonzalez@tropical.com; internet www.tropical.com; Man. VINCE GONZALEZ.

Turks and Caicos National Shipping and Development Co Ltd: Front St, POB 103, Grand Turk; tel. 946-2194.

CIVIL AVIATION

There are international airfields on Grand Turk, South Caicos, North Caicos and Providenciales, the last being the most important; there are also landing strips on Middle Caicos, Pine Cay, Parrot Cay and Salt Cay.

Department of Civil Aviation: Off Waterloo Rd, Grand Turk; tel. 946-2801; fax 946-1185; e-mail gtws@tciway.tc.

Caicos Caribbean Airlines: South Caicos; tel. 946-3283; fax 946-3377; freight to Miami (USA).

Cairsea Services Ltd: Old Airport Rd, POB 138, Providenciales; tel. 946-4205; fax 946-4504; internet www.cairsea.com.

Flamingo Air Services Ltd: Grand Turk Int. Airport, POB 162, Grand Turk; tel. 946-2109; fax 946-2188.

Inter-Island Airways: POB 191, Providenciales; tel. 946-4181.

SkyKing Ltd: POB 398, Providenciales; tel. 941-5464; fax 941-5127; e-mail king@tciway.tc; internet www.skyking.tc; f. 1985; daily inter-island passenger services, and services to Haiti and the Dominican Republic; CEO HAROLD CHARLES; Gen. Man. MALLORY MCCOMISH.

Turks Air Ltd: Providenciales; Head Office: 7294 NW 41st, Miami, FL 33166, USA; tel. 946-4504; fax 946-4504; tel. 593-8847; fax 871-1622; twice-weekly cargo service to and from Miami; Grand Turk Local Agent CRIS NEWTON.

Turks and Caicos Airways Ltd: Providenciales International Airport, POB 114, Providenciales; tel. 946-4255; fax 946-4438; f. 1976 as Air Turks and Caicos, privatized 1983; scheduled daily inter-island service to each of the Caicos Islands, charter flights; Chair. ALBRAY BUTTERFIELD; Dir-Gen. C. MOSER.

Tourism

The islands' main tourist attractions are the numerous unspoilt beaches, and the opportunities for diving. Salt Cay has been designated a World Heritage site by UNESCO. Hotel accommodation is available on Grand Turk, Salt Cay, South Caicos, Pine Cay and Providenciales. In 2000 there were 152,211 tourist arrivals (an increase of some 26% compared with the previous year). In 2000 73.9% of tourists were from the USA. In 1998 there were 1,522 hotel rooms (some 80% of which were on Providenciales). Revenue from the sector in 2000 totalled an estimated US $329m.

Turks and Caicos Hotel Association: Third Turtle Inn, Providenciales; tel. 946-4230.

Turks and Caicos Hotel and Tourism Association: internet www.tchta.com; Pres. LOU WIZEMAN.

Turks and Caicos Islands Tourist Board: Pond St, POB 128, Grand Turk; tel. 946-2321; fax 946-2833; e-mail tci.tourism@tciway.tc; internet www.turksandcaicostourism.com; f. 1970; Dir JOHN SKIPPINGS.

THE UNITED STATES OF AMERICA

Introductory Survey

Location, Climate, Language, Religion, Flag, Capital

The United States of America comprises mainly the North American continent between Canada and Mexico. Alaska, to the north-west of Canada, and Hawaii, in the central Pacific Ocean, are two of the 50 States of the USA. There is considerable climatic variation, with mean annual average temperatures ranging from 29°C (77°F) in Florida to –13.3°C (10°F) in Alaska. Average annual rainfall ranges from 1,831 mm (72.1 in) in Arkansas to 191 mm (7.5 in) in Nevada. Much of Texas, New Mexico, Arizona, Nevada and Utah is desert. The language is English, although there are significant Spanish-speaking minorities. Christianity is the predominant religion. The national flag (proportions 10 by 19) has 13 alternating stripes (seven red and six white) with a dark blue rectangular canton, containing 50 white five-pointed stars, in the upper hoist. The capital is Washington, DC.

Recent History

Concern at the spread of communist influence in Asia dominated US foreign policy during the 1960s and early 1970s. From 1961, until their termination in 1973 by President Richard Nixon, US military operations against communist forces in South Viet Nam led to considerable political division within the USA and were widely criticized internationally. Following a series of scandals involving Nixon and senior administration officials in allegations of corruption and obstruction of justice, known as the 'Watergate' affair, Nixon resigned in August 1974 and was replaced by the Vice-President, Gerald Ford. In November 1976 Jimmy Carter, a Democrat, was elected President. Efforts by the new Administration to resolve tensions in the Middle East culminated in the signing in 1979 of a peace treaty between Egypt and Israel. In 1978 the USA severed formal links with Taiwan and established diplomatic relations with the People's Republic of China. Domestically, economic recession and inflation preoccupied the Carter Administration, and the President's management of the economy was a decisive factor in his defeat by the Republican candidate, Ronald Reagan, in the 1980 presidential election. Although economic recession and high unemployment persisted in the early period of the new Administration, the Republicans retained their previous level of congressional representation in the November 1982 elections. With the resumption of economic growth in 1983, and its strong resurgence through 1984, unemployment and inflation fell, and in November Reagan was re-elected for a further four-year term, securing the largest majority of electoral votes in US history.

The conservative orientation of the Reagan Administration was expressed domestically in a programme aimed at transferring to the individual states the financial responsibility for many federal social programmes, while expanding expenditure on defence. In foreign affairs, the Government generally pursued a firmly anti-communist line, notably in its active support of right-wing regimes in Latin America, where the US military occupation of Grenada in November 1983 attracted considerable international criticism, and in Africa and the Middle East. Generally friendly relations were, however, maintained with the People's Republic of China. The change of leadership in the USSR in November 1982 was followed by a period of deterioration in contacts between the two countries. Formal disarmament negotiations were renewed following the assumption of leadership in the USSR by Mikhail Gorbachev in 1985. However, US–Soviet relations were overshadowed by Reagan's pursuit of his Strategic Defense Initiative (SDI). Initiated in 1983, this advanced-technology research programme aimed to create a space-based system of defences against nuclear attack. The Reagan Government consistently refused to negotiate the termination of SDI, which was viewed by the USSR as a potential source of arms escalation and a first step in the militarization of space. US–Soviet relations experienced further strain following Soviet military intervention in Afghanistan in 1979.

During the Reagan period the USA adopted a forceful stance (generally welcomed by other Western governments) on international air and sea terrorism. However, in 1985 a ban on trade with Libya, which Reagan alleged to be promoting terrorist activity, received little support from other Western countries. In April 1986, following a terrorist attack on US military personnel in West Berlin, Reagan ordered the selective bombing of government offices and military installations in Tripoli and Benghazi. Direct US military involvement in the Middle East, which had been minimized since its withdrawal in 1984 from peacekeeping operations in Lebanon, was reactivated in July 1987, when Reagan agreed to a request by Kuwait to provide military protection for its petroleum tankers in the Persian (Arabian) Gulf, following attacks on them by Iran. Subsequent incidents in the Gulf brought the USA and Iran into armed confrontations. In April 1988 the USA was a signatory, with the USSR, Afghanistan and Pakistan, of an agreement for the phased withdrawal of Soviet troops from Afghanistan, which was completed in February 1989.

Negotiations on the issue of arms control were maintained between the USA and the USSR during 1986. In November the USA abandoned the weapon deployment limits set by the 1979 Strategic Arms Limitation Treaty (SALT II), which, although never ratified by Congress, had been informally observed by both the USA and the USSR. In March 1987, however, the US Government responded favourably to an indication by the USSR of its willingness to expedite an agreement to eliminate medium-range nuclear missiles from Europe by 1992.

These discussions, which were subsequently extended to include short-range nuclear weaponry, were followed, in September 1987, by an agreement in principle on terms under which both countries would eliminate all stocks of medium- and short-range nuclear missiles. The resultant Intermediate Nuclear Forces (INF) treaty, the first to terminate an entire class of offensive nuclear weapon, was finalized in December, when the two leaders also agreed to pursue negotiations towards a new Strategic Arms Reduction Treaty (START) to reduce long-range nuclear weaponry by up to 50%. The INF treaty was ratified and activated in 1988. The further advancement of SDI, meanwhile, had become increasingly conjectural: the US Congress proved reluctant to allocate its high funding requirements, and during 1988 and 1989 expressed doubts about the feasibility of the project's goals. The USSR, while maintaining its objections to SDI, agreed in 1990 to exclude it from the ambit of negotiations on START.

In November 1986 details began to emerge of covert foreign policy operations by senior members of the Reagan Administration in relation to US contacts with the Government of Iran. The ensuing scandal, known as the 'Irangate' or 'Iran-Contra' affair, developed into a major political embarrassment for the President. Subsequent investigations by an independent commission, and by the US Congress, concluded that secret arms sales had been made to the Iranian Government, in return for an undertaking by Iran to help to secure the release of US hostages held by pro-Iranian Islamic groups in Lebanon, and that Reagan had been misled by officials of the security services into authorizing the arms transactions, and bypassing the required congressional consultative procedures. The report also upheld allegations that funds derived from the arms sales had been secretly diverted into bank accounts held by the Nicaraguan Contra rebels. Reagan, who accepted full personal responsibility for the 'Iran-Contra' affair, was exonerated of any deliberate attempt to misrepresent his role in the events. The closing months of Reagan's presidency were clouded by further political scandals involving senior presidential appointees.

At the November 1988 presidential election, Reagan was succeeded by his Vice-President, George Bush, although the Senate and House of Representatives both retained Democratic majorities. The initial months of the Bush Administration were dominated by concern over the formulation of effective measures to contain the federal budget deficit, and over the future course of arms reduction negotiations with the USSR. In June 1989, following an agreement to resume START discussions, President Bush proposed the initiation of new negotiations aimed at achieving substantial reductions in North Atlantic Treaty Organization (NATO) and Warsaw Pact countries' conventional ground forces in Europe. In September the USA and USSR finalized agreements on the monitoring of chemical weapons and procedures for the verification of limits on strategic forces and nuclear tests. A summit meeting between Bush and Gorbachev followed at Valletta, Malta, in December, which marked the opening of a new era in US–Soviet relations. Under discussion were the prospects for new agreements by the mid-1990s for reductions of 50% in nuclear strategic arms, together with substantial reductions in the size of conventional forces based in Europe.

The withdrawal by the USSR in late 1989 and early 1990 from the exercise of direct political influence on the internal affairs of the countries of Eastern Europe was accompanied by a further improvement in US–Soviet relations, and by the implementation of programmes of US economic aid for several of the former Soviet 'client' states. In September 1990 the USA and USSR, with France and the United Kingdom, the other powers that occupied Germany at the end of the Second World War, formally agreed terms for the unification of the two post-war German states, which took effect in the following month. US-Soviet relations came under some strain, however, following the assertion by Lithuania of independence from the USSR and subsequent Soviet measures to blockade the Lithuanian economy. In July the USA, together with the world's six largest industrial democracies, agreed to provide the USSR with economic and technical assistance in undertaking a change-over to a market economy. In the same month, a summit meeting of NATO members proposed that the USSR and the other members of the Warsaw Pact alliance join in a formal declaration that the two military groupings were no longer adversaries and would refrain from the threat or use of force. This initiative was followed in November by the signing in Paris, by members of NATO and the Warsaw Pact, of a Treaty on Conventional Armed Forces in Europe (CFE), which provided for bilateral limits to be placed on the number of non-nuclear weapons sited between the Atlantic Ocean and the Ural Mountains. Immediately following the signing of the CFE Treaty, Presidents Bush and Gorbachev were present at a meeting of the Conference on Security and Co-operation in Europe (CSCE, now the Organization for Security and Co-operation in Europe—OSCE, see p. 283), at which the USA, the USSR and 32 other countries signed a charter declaring the end of the post-war era of confrontation and division in Europe.

In September 1989 President Bush outlined the terms of a federal programme aimed at combating drug abuse, which in recent years had become a serious social problem in the USA. The initiative received co-operation from the governments of Bolivia, Colombia and Peru, but the activities of drugs-traffickers operating from Panama, allegedly with the collusion of the regime controlled by Gen. Manuel Noriega, had been unaffected by US sanctions. In December 1989, following the failure of an internal coup attempt that received non-military US support, the USA carried out an armed invasion of Panama and subsequently installed an elected government. US troops were withdrawn in February 1990. In Nicaragua the departure of the Sandinista government, as the result of a general election held in February 1990, was followed by the resumption of cordial relations with the US Government.

During 1990 the Bush Administration pursued domestic policy reforms in a number of areas, particularly in education and banking, although tax increases formed an unpopular element in measures aimed at containing persistently heavy deficits in the federal budget. Bush's political prestige, however, was considerably enhanced by his management of the US involvement in an unexpected conflict in the Middle East.

Following the invasion of Kuwait by Iraqi forces on 2 August 1990, and the subsequent annexation of that country by Iraq, the US Government assumed a leading international role in the implementation of political, economic and military measures to bring about an Iraqi withdrawal. The imposition of mandatory economic sanctions against Iraq by the UN Security Council on 6 August was quickly followed by 'Operation Desert Shield', in which US combat troops and aircraft were dispatched to Saudi Arabia, at that country's request, to secure its borders against a possible attack by Iraq. Tensions were heightened in mid-August by Iraq's detention of Western nationals resident in Kuwait and Iraq, and the harassment of Western diplomatic personnel in Kuwait. An offer, subsequently repeated, by President Saddam Hussain of Iraq to link withdrawal from Kuwait with a resolution of other outstanding Middle East problems, was rejected, and in late August the UN Security Council endorsed the use of military action to enforce its economic

sanctions. Despite intense diplomatic activity, in which the USSR was prominent, the crisis deepened. In early September Presidents Bush and Gorbachev jointly demanded an Iraqi withdrawal, although the USSR expressed reluctance to support military operations by the UN. In late September the UN Security Council intensified its economic measures against Iraq. However, the ineffectiveness both of economic sanctions and of diplomatic negotiation had become evident by late November, and the USSR gave its assent to the use of force against Iraq, although it did not participate in the multinational force that was now arrayed in the Gulf region and included, under US command, air, sea and ground forces from the United Kingdom, France, Italy, Egypt, Morocco, Kuwait and the other Arab Gulf states. Jordan, which was active throughout the crisis in seeking to promote a negotiated settlement, was perceived by the US Government as sympathetic to Iraq, and US financial aid programmes to that country were suspended.

On 29 November 1990 the UN Security Council authorized the use of 'all necessary means' to force Iraq to withdraw from Kuwait, unless it did so by 15 January 1991. By early January the USA had established a considerable military presence in the Gulf region, and on 17 January 'Operation Desert Storm' was launched, with massive air and missile attacks against Iraqi positions, both in Iraq and Kuwait. In the course of the conflict, more than 110,000 attacking air missions were flown over Kuwait and Iraq by multinational air forces, while naval support operations were conducted from the Gulf. In the following weeks, severe damage was inflicted on Iraqi military and economic targets, while counter-attacks by its air force, and attempts to draw Israel into the conflict by launching missile attacks on population centres, proved ineffective. A ground offensive by the multinational force was launched on 23–24 February, and Iraqi positions were quickly overrun. Hostilities were suspended on 28 February. The Government of Iraq accepted cease-fire terms on 3 March, leaving the multinational forces in control of Kuwait, together with an area of southern Iraq, comprising about 15% of that country's total national territory. Troop withdrawals from the occupied area of Iraq commenced in March, with the remaining US troops evacuated in early May, to be replaced by a UN peace-keeping force.

Following the termination of hostilities, in which 148 US troops died in combat, internal rebellions broke out within Iraq by groups opposed to President Saddam Hussain. The severity with which these were suppressed, particularly in the northern region among the Kurdish ethnic group, and the subsequent flight of refugees into neighbouring areas of Turkey and Iran, prompted large-scale international relief operations. The US Government was widely criticized for its refusal to support the anti-government insurgents and to take action to depose Saddam Hussain. In May 1991 the USA began airlifting troops to northern Iraq to establish 'safe' enclaves, to which Kurdish refugees were encouraged to return. The US military continued to monitor events in these Kurdish areas from operational bases in Turkey and other strategic points in the region. In September 1996 the USA launched missile strikes from naval vessels in the Gulf at military targets in Iraq, in retaliation for attacks by Iraqi forces against Kurds in northern Iraq.

In the period following the Gulf War, the US Government actively pursued initiatives to convene a regional conference, with joint and Soviet sponsorship, to seek a permanent solution to the wider problems of the Middle East. In August 1991 the US Secretary of State, James Baker, obtained the agreement of Egypt, Israel, Jordan, Lebanon and Syria to take part in such a conference, the opening session of which was convened in October. Successive negotiations failed to make any substantive progress, and traditionally close relations between Israel and the USA subsequently came under strain, following pressure by the US Government on Israel to suspend the construction of Jewish settlements in occupied territories, pending the eventual outcome of the peace negotiations.

During the second half of 1991 there was increasing concern by the US Government at the implications of economic dislocation and political unrest within the USSR. In June President Bush offered the USSR guarantees of up to $1,500m. in loans for grain purchases, together with assistance in restructuring the Soviet food distribution system. In late July the USA and USSR signed START, providing for a 30% reduction in long-range nuclear weapons over a seven-year period. Further moves towards bilateral disarmament followed in September, when the USA announced that it was to begin the phased elimination of sea and air tactical nuclear weapons in Europe and Asia; in

October the USSR offered to reduce its holdings of nuclear weapons to below the levels agreed in START.

In December 1991, following the replacement of the USSR by the Commonwealth of Independent States (CIS) comprising 11 of the republics of the former Soviet Union, the independence of each republic was recognized by the USA. In January 1992 a meeting was held between President Bush and President Yeltsin of Russia, the dominant republic within the CIS. President Bush expressed concern that effective measures should be taken by the Russian Government to ensure that the nuclear weapons and related technical expertise of the former USSR did not become available to countries not in possession of nuclear weapons capability, or to nations in the Middle East or to the Democratic People's Republic of Korea (DPRK—North Korea). At a subsequent meeting held in February, the Russian leader assured President Bush that immediate safeguards were in force, and that all short-range nuclear warheads would be moved into Russia from sites in other CIS republics by July 1992. President Yeltsin also proposed that the USA and Russia should share in the joint future development of the SDI project (see above), and further reductions in nuclear arsenals were agreed by the two leaders.

At a summit meeting held between Presidents Bush and Yeltsin in June 1992 in Washington, DC, agreement was reached on further substantial reductions in nuclear arms, under which, by the year 2003, total holdings of nuclear warheads would be reduced to less than one-half of the quotas contained in START. Agreements covering other areas of co-operation, including the encouragement of US private-sector investment in Russia, arrangements for mutual assistance in the event of accidents in space, and the outline of a joint ballistic missiles protection system, were also signed.

In its relations with the former communist countries in Europe, the USA augmented its commitment to the CSCE with economic support, and promoted the membership of former members of the Warsaw Pact in the North Atlantic Co-operation Council, an offshoot of NATO. Contacts were also revived between the USA and Viet Nam, and in May 1992 there was a partial relaxation of a 19-year trade embargo. Relations with Iraq remained tense following the discovery, made in November 1991 by UN representatives, that President Saddam Hussain's regime was seeking to conceal its continuing development of nuclear weapons capability.

Following the conclusion of the Gulf War in early 1991, Bush's political popularity fell sharply, amid growing public perception that the Government was assigning greater priority to foreign affairs than to addressing the problems of the US economy, which had been in recession since early 1989. Criticism was also directed at the Administration's alleged neglect of other domestic issues, particularly in the areas of social welfare, medical costs and health care, and the interrelated issues of urban poverty and civil rights. In 1990 Bush vetoed legislation providing financial compensation for those victimized by discrimination in employment, although a compromise version was eventually approved in November 1991. In April 1992 serious rioting broke out in Los Angeles and spread briefly to several other cities. The underlying causes of the disorders were widely ascribed to the worsening economic and social plight of the impoverished urban black minority.

The 1992 presidential election campaign, in which Bush was opposed by Bill Clinton, a Democrat state governor, and Ross Perot, a populist independent, was dominated by social and economic issues. The problems of health care, urban crime and the legal status of abortion were major topics of debate, although Bush's record of economic management, particularly in relation to the persistence of federal budget deficits, provided the major line of attack by the opposing candidates. The perception of the electorate that the Bush presidency had neglected urgent domestic problems in its concentration on foreign affairs proved to be the decisive factor: the turn-out of voters, at 55.2%, was the highest at any presidential election since 1968, and gave a decisive majority, of 43.0% to 37.4%, to Clinton. Perot, whose campaign had concentrated on the question of federal deficit spending, obtained almost 19% of the popular vote.

Foreign affairs dominated the final months of the Bush Administration. In July 1992 contention arose between the Government of Iraq and the UN over the rights of UN observers to inspect Iraqi nuclear facilities, and in the following month the US Government sought to limit internal military operations by the Iraqi Government by imposing an air exclusion zone south of latitude 32°N. This was followed, in January 1993, by US participation in selective bombings of Iraqi missile sites. In December 1992 relations with the People's Republic of China, which had been strained since 1989 by the Chinese Government's persistent suppression of political dissent, were revived by the removal of a US embargo on sales of military equipment. In the same month President Bush launched 'Operation Restore Hope', under which 24,000 US troops were sent to Somalia, as part of an international force under US command, to protect shipments of food aid and to assist in the restoration of civil order. (In May 1993 the USA transferred command of operations in Somalia to the UN, although about 4,000 US troops remained until the termination of the peace-keeping operation in March 1994.)

Shortly before the transfer of the presidency to Bill Clinton in January 1993, Presidents Bush and Yeltsin met in Moscow to sign a second Nuclear Arms Reduction Treaty (START II), which provided for the elimination by 2003 of almost 75% of all US and CIS-held nuclear warheads. The implementation, however, of START I and START II could not begin until Belarus, Kazakhstan and Ukraine, the other former republics of the USSR which hold stocks of nuclear weapons, had endorsed START I. Ukraine was the last of these republics (in December 1994) to ratify the START arrangements, and in March 1995 undertook that the transfer of its stocks of nuclear weapons to Russia would be completed by 1997. Clinton announced the termination of SDI, although there was subsequent discussion within the USA of its possible reactivation (see below). Although ratified by the US Senate in 1993, START II remained unratified by the Russian legislature until April 2000. However, arrangements agreed in late 1997 by the US and Russian Governments had extended by five years the period allowed for the elimination of Russia's long-range nuclear missiles.

The initial preoccupation of the Clinton Administration was the formulation of an economic recovery plan, to be phased over a five-year period, to reduce the federal budget deficit by means of increased taxation and economies in the cost of government, rather than by reduced levels of federal spending. Military expenditure was a particular area in which economies were proposed, while additional spending was planned for infrastructural projects and measures to stimulate economic activity. A major restructuring of the US health care system was also planned, and a commission to formulate proposals was placed under the chairmanship of President Clinton's wife, Hillary. Certain aspects of the economic recovery plan, particularly those relating to higher income tax and a new energy tax, encountered initial opposition in the Democrat-controlled Congress, but were eventually approved, in a modified form, by the House of Representatives in May 1993. Approval by the Senate, following further amendments, took place in June. By mid-1993, however, the President's initial popularity had fallen sharply, owing in part to perceptions of indecisiveness by Clinton in formulating effective policies. There was also widespread criticism of the competence of some of his advisers and appointees.

By mid-1993 the crisis in former Yugoslavia had assumed increased importance as a foreign policy issue, leading to disagreements between the USA and the Western European powers, which opposed US proposals to launch direct air strikes against military positions held by Bosnian Serbs. The US Administration, while avoiding any direct military commitment, gave its support, through NATO, to peace-keeping operations in Bosnia and Herzegovina. Clinton was unsuccessful, however, in efforts to secure the removal of the international embargo on arms sales to the Bosnian Muslims. In June 1994 the US Government endorsed proposals by the European Union (EU) countries for the tripartite partition of Bosnia and Herzegovina.

Although the Clinton Administration chose not to pursue an initiative in August 1993 by Cuba to normalize its economic and diplomatic relations with the USA (see below), renewed efforts were made to restore to power Fr Jean-Bertrand Aristide, the first democratically elected President of Haiti, who had taken refuge in the USA following his overthrow by a military junta in 1991. An economic embargo imposed by the Organization of American States (OAS, see p. 288), together with implied threats of military intervention by the US Government, had failed to displace the military regime, and conditions within Haiti had led large numbers of refugees to seek asylum in the USA, many of whom were forcibly repatriated by the US authorities. In June 1994, following the imposition in the previous month of international sanctions against Haiti by the UN Security Council, Clinton announced the suspension of all commercial and financial transactions with Haiti. In September, following a diplomatic mission led by former President Carter, a UN-sponsored multinational force, composed almost entirely of US troops, arrived in Haiti with the agreement of the military junta, which relinquished power in October. US troops were withdrawn from the UN force in March 1995.

In late June 1993 the US Government launched a missile attack against the headquarters of Iraqi military intelligence in Baghdad, in retaliation for an alleged plot by Iraq to assassinate former President Bush in Kuwait in April. Nevertheless, during 1993 the Clinton Administration continued to foster efforts to promote a general resolution of tensions in the Middle East. With US assistance, but as a direct result of secret diplomatic mediation by Norway, the Palestine Liberation Organization (PLO) and the Government of Israel signed an agreement providing for Palestinian self-government in the Occupied Territories and for mutual recognition by Israel and the PLO. In January 1994, following a meeting held in Geneva, Switzerland, between Clinton and President Assad of Syria, negotiations were initiated for a settlement between Israel and Syria.

Political and economic contacts with Russia continued on a cordial level, with the two countries adopting a co-operative stance in many areas of foreign policy. In February 1994 the US Government lifted its embargo on trade with Viet Nam, in force since 1975, and in the following July the USA established full diplomatic relations with that country. Relations with the People's Republic of China improved in 1994, following a controversial decision by Clinton to extend enhanced trading privileges to that country until June 1995, despite China's continued suppression of free political debate. Little progress, however, was made in the resolution of the persistently adverse US balance of trade with Japan, despite an agreement between the two countries in July 1993 to implement measures to reduce the trade deficit. In March 1994 the US Government assumed reserve powers to impose high retaliatory tariffs on Japanese imports; following unsuccessful attempts to resolve the disagreement, the US Government announced that a tariff of 100% was to be levied on certain Japanese motor vehicles in June 1995. However, an agreement between the two Governments was finalized a few hours before the trade sanctions were due to take effect.

In March 1994 the USA extended its ban on nuclear testing until September 1995. The prevention of nuclear proliferation, which has remained a prime objective of US foreign policy, led in 1993 and early 1994 to a serious confrontation between the USA and North Korea. In March 1993 the DPRK, which is a signatory of the Nuclear Non-Proliferation Treaty (NPT) and is subject, by virtue of its membership of the International Atomic Energy Agency (IAEA, see p. 80), to the monitoring of its nuclear installations, refused to grant the IAEA inspectorate full access to its nuclear power facility. It cited as its reasons the existence of joint military exercises between the Republic of Korea (South Korea) and the USA and 'unjust acts' by the IAEA. The US Government stated that it had reason to suspect that the DPRK had been diverting nuclear plant material for the development of atomic weapons. In July Clinton visited South Korea, and warned the DPRK that any use of nuclear weapons by them would be met with military force. He reiterated that the USA would maintain its military presence in the Republic of Korea. Despite increasing international pressure (from which the People's Republic of China remained aloof), and attempts at mediation by the UN, the DPRK repeatedly asserted its refusal to comply with the treaty's inspection requirements. The crisis steadily worsened during early 1994, and in June the US Government, after seeking unsuccessfully to offer the DPRK economic aid, investment and diplomatic recognition, began to seek support for the imposition of UN economic sanctions. Later in the same month, following a visit to the DPRK by former President Carter (acting as an unofficial representative of the Government), the DPRK agreed to a temporary suspension of its nuclear programme, pending formal discussions with the US Government. These meetings were convened in July. Negotiations aimed at improving relations between the USA and the DPRK, and at fostering a political settlement between the DPRK and the Republic of Korea, were pursued throughout both Clinton Administrations. In March 1999 the US and DPRK Governments agreed on terms whereby US officials would receive unrestricted access to inspect DPRK nuclear facilities.

In September 1993 Clinton announced his proposals for the reform of health care, under which universal coverage was to be available for medical and hospital care. The plan, which was estimated to cost $350,000m. over a seven-year period, was opposed by the American Medical Association, the private health insurance sector and by many employers, who, under its provisions, were to be responsible for 80% of employees' insurance premiums. Congressional opposition to the plan, however, re-sulted in substantial amendments to the Clinton proposals, and to the effective removal of provisions for federal subsidies. Efforts to formulate compromise legislation were eventually abandoned in September 1994.

During 1993 and 1994 the personal integrity of both the President and his wife was challenged by accusations of financial irregularities in their alleged involvement in a savings bank and property development company that collapsed in 1989, during Clinton's tenure as Governor of Arkansas. These allegations, which came to be known as the 'Whitewater' affair, were strenuously denied by the Clintons, and were made the subject of official investigations. Related allegations of involvement in the 'Whitewater' affair, however, led to the resignations of five senior presidential appointees during 1993 and 1994, and proved politically damaging to Clinton. In October 1994 a sixth official, the Secretary of Agriculture, resigned following accusations of unethical financial dealings during Clinton's state governorship. In May 1996 Clinton's successor as Governor of Arkansas resigned following his conviction for fraud in connection with the 'Whitewater' affair. In the following month a Senate committee alleged that Mrs Clinton and certain officials in the President's office had acted to obstruct a federal investigation into the Whitewater Corporation. These findings, however, were challenged by Democrat members of the committee.

The collapse of plans for health care reform, together with increasing public concern about the domestic economy and the effectiveness of Clinton's policies on social issues (notably in the areas of welfare expenditure, law enforcement and the protection of traditional social values), led in 1994 to a sharp rise in support for the conservative doctrines of politicians representing the right wing of the Republican Party. At congressional elections held in November, the Republicans gained control both of the Senate (for the first time since 1986) and the House of Representatives (which had been controlled by the Democrats since 1954).

The new congressional leadership declared its intention of implementing a 'Contract with America', which encompassed a series of measures aimed at narrowing the range of federal social programmes, reducing taxation and balancing the federal budget by 2002. In its social policies, the 'Contract' proposed substantial reductions in welfare programmes and the transfer to state governments of responsibilities for many federally-funded services. Clinton, in an attempt to reach a consensus with the Republicans, proposed a 'New Covenant', promoting increased individual responsibility, less involvement by federal government, and agreeing to co-operate in an overhaul of the welfare system. However, during 1995 serious divisions began to emerge between President and Congress. In February Clinton threatened to veto foreign policy legislation on the grounds that it violated the President's constitutional prerogatives in foreign relations and defence. In June 1995 further tensions arose over proposals to achieve a balanced federal budget. Negotiations proved inconclusive, and in November Clinton, in an effort to resolve the deadlock, refused to renew the temporary funding arrangements, causing an eight-day shutdown of all non-essential operations of the federal government. Agreement on the 1995/96 budget was eventually reached in April, although disagreements on the timetable for, and the method of achieving, a balanced budget remained unresolved.

The interlinked issues of political terrorism and the private possession of firearms (which is constitutionally guaranteed) came to the fore in April 1995, when 168 lives were lost in the terrorist bombing of a federal building in Oklahoma City. Subsequent investigations suggested the involvement of sympathizers of paramilitary groups whose supporters accused the federal Government of conducting a conspiracy to deprive them of individual and constitutional freedoms. One such sympathizer, Timothy McVeigh, was eventually convicted of the attack and was executed in June 2001.

Robert Dole, a long-serving senator who had resigned from the Senate in May to concentrate on the campaign, contested the 1996 presidential election as the Republican nominee. Ross Perot, who had contested the previous election as a populist independent candidate, was nominated by the Reform Party, an organization founded by him to seek radical reductions in federal government spending. Clinton, whose campaign was based on his record of economic management (particularly in relation to job creation, health insurance reform, and reductions in the rates of inflation and unemployment), was decisively re-elected in November, obtaining 49.3% of the popular vote, compared with 43% in the 1992 election. Dole obtained 40.7% of the votes, and Perot 8.4%. The Republicans retained control of the Senate and House of Representatives.

Following his inauguration for a second term in January 1997, Clinton declared the enhancement of educational standards to be a primary aim of his second term. Proposals were also announced to achieve further reductions in welfare dependency, by providing tax credits and other incentives to employers. Financial savings were to be achieved by further reductions in defence expenditure, and by the implementation of further cuts in spending on health care for the elderly. Clinton reiterated his intention, however, of seeking improved provisions for insured health care, and of achieving a balanced federal budget by 2002. Agreement between Clinton and the Republican congressional leadership on the general terms of these budgetary measures was reached in May 1997. The President, however, in the first exercise of selective veto powers granted in January (when he had obtained the right to veto individual provisions in fiscal legislation without being obliged to reject the entire bill), subsequently struck out three of the 79 measures contained in the balanced budget legislation enacted in July.

In foreign affairs, the Clinton Administration continued to support economic reform in Russia and the successor states of the former USSR, with particular emphasis on fostering the change-over from defence to consumer production. Prior to the cease-fire declared in August 1996, the US Government expressed disapproval of the scale of Russian military operations in Chechnya, and in May 1995 the Clinton Administration was refused Russian co-operation in its ban on US trade and investment in Iran, in retaliation for that country's alleged involvement in international terrorism. Concerns expressed by Russia at the proposed enlargement of NATO were addressed at a summit meeting of Presidents Yeltsin and Clinton in Helsinki, Finland, in March 1997. (See the chapter on Russia for details of the subsequent agreement between NATO and Russia.)

The reluctance of the Clinton Administration to participate directly in UN military operations in Bosnia and Herzegovina was modified in June 1995 with a statement by Clinton that US ground troops would be sent to Bosnia and Herzegovina in 'emergency' circumstances on a 'limited basis' if required to assist in the redeployment of existing UN forces, or to participate in monitoring an eventual peace settlement. In November, following US-sponsored negotiations held in Dayton, Ohio, a peace agreement was reached by the opposing sides. As part of its implementation, the US Government agreed to contribute 20,000 troops to a multinational supervisory force of 60,000 troops under the command of NATO. The USA committed about 8,500 troops in an extended NATO peace-keeping operation in Bosnia and Herzegovina from January 1997 until mid-1998. US troops remained on duty in Bosnia in early 2002.

Relations with China pursued an uneven course under the Clinton Administration, owing to disagreements over trade matters and criticism by the USA of alleged abuses by the Chinese Government of human rights. Relations between the two countries declined sharply in February 1996, following US protests over Chinese military operations near Taiwan. Following the settlement in June of a dispute over infringements of US copyright and other intellectual property rights, enhanced trading privileges were extended for a further year and were granted permanent status in May 2000, opening the way for the People's Republic of China to join the World Trade Organization (WTO, see p. 323).

Successive US Governments remained unwilling to restore relations with Cuba. Relations between the two countries deteriorated in March 1996, after two civilian aircraft carrying Cuban exiles protesting against the Castro Government were shot down by the Cuban air force over international waters. In response, Clinton acceded to congressional demands to strengthen the US commercial and economic embargo that has been in force since 1962. Under the new measure, known as the Helms-Burton Act, the USA was to penalize foreign investors whose business in any way involves property in Cuba that was confiscated from US citizens following the 1959 revolution. This measure, which was initially intended to enter into operation in August 1996, attracted strong protests from the EU, and from Mexico and Canada, which have substantial trading links with Cuba. In June legislation was approved by Congress to impose penalties on foreign companies investing in Iran and Libya, both of which have been accused by the US Government of sponsoring international terrorism. In July a number of Canadian, Mexican and Italian companies were informed that sanctions were to be imposed on them under the Helms-Burton legislation, barring their senior executives and certain shareholders from visiting the USA. In response to intense international pressure, Clinton declared a six-month moratorium on certain provisions of the Helms-Burton Act. This was renewed in January 1997, and in April the US Government and the EU, which had referred its complaint to the WTO, announced that a compromise had been agreed, subject to the abandonment by the US Government of certain sections of the Act. The moratorium on Title IV of the Act was subsequently extended at six-monthly intervals and remained in operation in early -2002. In March 1998 the US Government lifted bans (imposed in 1996) on civilian aircraft services to Cuba and on financial remittances to Cuba from the USA. In April 1998 the UN Commission on Human Rights defeated a US resolution criticizing human rights policies of the Cuban Government. (However, a UN motion, supported by the USA, condemning Cuba for human rights violations, was approved in April 2001.) During 1999 and 2000 the Clinton Administration introduced further modest relaxations of travel and commercial embargoes against Cuba. In 2000 US–Cuban relations were dominated by the decision of the Department of Justice to return to his family in Cuba a six-year-old boy, Elián González, who had been shipwrecked on a vessel carrying Cuban refugees to the USA. In late 2001 the USA lifted temporarily the trade embargo against Cuba to allow the purchase of food and medicines necessary for the reconstruction and aid effort following the devastation caused by 'Hurricane Michelle'. In January 1995 the USA led an international financial consortium to provide substantial loan guarantees to resolve a major financial crisis in Mexico. In the previous month President Clinton proposed the formation, by 2006, of a 'Free Trade Area of the Americas', comprising 34 countries of the Western Hemisphere. Proposals for the new free-trade area were pursued by Clinton at a second 'Summit of the Americas' held in Santiago, Chile, in April 1998, at which it was agreed to begin negotiations for a trade treaty. A third Summit of the Americas was held in Québec, Canada, in April 2001, at which a timetable for the establishment of the Free Trade Area, to take effect by 2005, was agreed upon. Negotiations were scheduled to conclude by January 2005.

At the end of 1998 President Clinton and the President of Colombia, Andrés Pastrana Arango, signed a Counter-Narcotics Alliance, in an attempt to address the ongoing war against drugs-trafficking. In January 2000 the Clinton Administration announced an aid package for the Andean region worth $1,300m., the largest ever aid programme for Latin America. The main portion of the programme, which became known as the 'Plan Colombia', was some $860m. to Colombia, three-quarters of which was allocated to the security forces in that country. The size of the military component of the Plan caused controversy internationally, as did the proposed aerial destruction of crops in the region. As a result, in 2001 the incoming Administration of George W. Bush proposed a modified Plan Colombia, to be known as the Andean Regional Initiative, the focus of which would be on improving social and economic conditions in the region. Nevertheless, the objective remained the same: to reduce significantly the flow of drugs from the Andean region into the USA.

International concern at the effects on world climate of emissions of carbon dioxide and other gases that have a warming effect on the atmosphere ('greenhouse gases') has, in recent years, brought the USA and other industrialized countries under pressure to implement measures to reduce the use of these substances. In December 1997, at the third Conference of the Parties to the Framework Convention on Climate Change (UN Environment Programme, see p. 49), held in Kyoto, Japan, the USA undertook to implement reductions of its emissions of 'greenhouse gases' to 7% below 1990 levels by the year 2012. However, in view of the problems inherent in the cost-effective phasing-out of these substances, ratification of the Kyoto arrangements encountered strong opposition in Congress and among business leaders.

Relations between the USA and the People's Republic of China were enhanced in October 1997 by a state visit to the USA by President Jiang Zemin, following which the US Government revoked a ban, in force since 1989, on the export of US nuclear technology to China. China, together with Russia and the USA, refused in December 1997 to sign an international treaty banning the manufacture and use of anti-personnel land-mines; the US Government based its objection to the arrangements on its requirement for land-mines to protect its troops stationed in the Republic of Korea. It was stated that the USA proposed to develop an alternative weapons technology to replace land-mines by 2003. In mid-1998 President Clinton made a state visit to the People's Republic of China, the first to be undertaken by a US President since that country's violent suppression of political dissent in 1989.

In November 1997 the Government of Iraq demanded the immediate removal of US inspectors working in the UN Special Commission (UNSCOM, see p. 14) (see also the chapter on Iraq) carrying out the identification and elimination of biological, chemical and other weapons of mass destruction allegedly held by Iraq. This action was strongly resisted by the UN, amid increasing concern in the USA and internationally at subsequent actions by Iraq to disrupt the weapons inspection programme. Following repeated threats of military action by the USA against Iraq to enforce the inspections arrangements, substantial US military forces were dispatched to the Gulf region. Following extended negotiations, culminating in a meeting in February 1998 between President Saddam Hussain and the UN Secretary-General, Kofi Annan, the Government of Iraq agreed to restore unrestricted access to UN inspectors, and to withdraw its objection to the presence of US personnel. The US Government accepted the agreement, but warned of 'serious consequences' in the event of future violations by Iraq.

The Clinton Administration acted to assist in the resolution of serious financial crises in Thailand, Indonesia, Malaysia and the Republic of Korea in late 1997 and early 1998. US policy also continued to encourage political reform and economic development in the former communist countries of Eastern Europe, and in 1998 the Senate gave formal approval for the accession to NATO membership in 1999 of the Czech Republic, Hungary and Poland. Foreign policy concerns involving South Asia were revived in June, when successive tests of nuclear weapons were carried out by the Governments of India and Pakistan. The tests, which were condemned by the five states with nuclear armaments (the USA, France, Russia, The United Kingdom and the People's Republic of China), prompted Clinton to impose economic sanctions on both countries, while pursuing efforts to obtain their accession to the NPT.

During his second term as President, Clinton was confronted by a number of other allegations, which he consistently denied, dating from prior to 1992 and extending through his presidency, of perjury and obstruction of justice arising from accusations of sexual harassment. These matters, which related to Clinton's period as a state official in Arkansas, were brought within the ambit of a congressionally mandated independent counsel, Kenneth Starr, who began in 1994 to examine the legal ramifications of the 'Whitewater' affair. In January 1998 a former junior employee on the presidential staff, Monica Lewinsky, was required to give evidence in a civil action by Paula Jones, who had alleged that she had been sexually harassed by Clinton in 1991. In mid-January 1998 Starr was authorized by the Attorney-General to investigate whether a sexual relationship alleged by Lewinsky had taken place with the President in 1995. Clinton vehemently denied any improper conduct with Lewinsky, and, following his private testimony to a grand jury, declared in late January 1998 that he had made no attempt to induce Lewinsky or others to give perjured testimony.

As the Starr investigation continued, public opinion remained generally supportive of Clinton. In August 1998, however, following an offer of immunity from prosecution by Starr to Lewinsky, the President submitted new testimony to the grand jury; he subsequently made a public statement to the effect that an inappropriate relationship had taken place with Lewinsky, and asked for forgiveness of his behaviour, although insisting that he had at no time sought to obstruct legal processes. The President's admission provoked an indignant response from socially conservative supporters of the Republicans, who believed that his conduct had seriously undermined the dignity and authority of the presidency, and that Clinton should resign or face removal from office. Many Democrats, while accepting the President's statements and endorsing his wish that national attention should return to important domestic and foreign policy issues, were none the less concerned that the scandal would adversely affect the party's performance in the state and congressional elections due to take place in November 1998. Clinton's public credibility was widely perceived to be in decline, and

his political prospects apparently worsened in September, when Congress received the completed Starr report, making public intimate details of the President's relationship with Lewinsky, and alleging that Clinton had committed 11 offences of perjury and obstruction of justice, constituting grounds for his removal from office. No evidence, however, was offered of wrongdoing by Clinton in relation to the 'Whitewater' affair.

In October 1998 the House of Representatives voted by 258–176 votes to commence an impeachment inquiry against the President. Following extensive committee hearings, the case was referred in late December to the Senate, which is constitutionally empowered to remove the President from office, subject to a majority vote of two-thirds (67 of 100 seats). However, ahead of the impeachment proceedings, which began in January 1999, it had become clear that the electorate was satisfied with the Clinton Administration's conduct of government, and largely indifferent to any personal shortcomings of the President. In the November 1998 elections, at which the voter turn-out was only 36%, the lowest figure since 1942, the Republicans, while retaining control of the Congress, sustained a net loss of five seats in the House of Representatives and made no gains in the Senate. The party also lost one state governorship.

In mid-February 1999 the Senate acquitted Clinton by 55 votes to 45 on the first article of impeachment, alleging perjury before a grand jury, and by 50 votes to 50 on the second article, relating to alleged obstruction of justice. Following the verdict, Clinton reiterated his regret for his actions and their consequences for government administration and national life. A subsequent attempt in the Senate to obtain a vote of censure on Clinton was unsuccessful. (In January 2001, shortly before he left office, Clinton agreed to admit giving misleading testimony to an Arkansas court regarding his relationship with Lewinsky and to make a contribution towards the cost of the investigation into his alleged obstruction of justice in the matter. In return, the investigation was discontinued.)

International terrorist activity provided a major focus of US foreign policy during 1998 and early 1999. In August 1998 bomb attacks on US embassy buildings in Nairobi, Kenya, and Dar es Salaam, Tanzania, claimed 258 lives, and were followed by US air missile attacks on a factory site in Khartoum, Sudan (which was alleged to be a manufactory of chemicals for use in toxic gases), and on targets in Afghanistan, which were stated by the US Government to be operational centres for Osama bin Laden, a fugitive Saudi Arabian-born Islamist activist whom the USA believed to be responsible for past assaults on US forces and facilities in Somalia, Yemen and Saudi Arabia. Bin Laden was also held responsible for terrorist operations within the USA, including the 1993 bombing of the World Trade Center in New York. In October 2001 four associates of bin Laden were sentenced to life imprisonment by a US court for their involvement in the bomb attacks in Nairobi and Dar es Salaam.

In December 1998, following the termination by Iraq of international weapons inspections in its territory, the USA and the United Kingdom conducted a series of missile raids on Iraqi military sites. In March 1999 the US Government initiated and led, under NATO auspices, a sustained campaign of missile raids on military and related installations in Serbia and Montenegro, in support of international demands that the President of the Federal Republic of Yugoslavia, Slobodan Milošević, desist from the mass expulsion of members of the ethnic Albanian population of the Serbian province of Kosovo. NATO air attacks on Belgrade during May resulted in the accidental bombing by US aircraft of the diplomatic mission in the Yugoslav capital of the People's Republic of China, which, despite a subsequent apology and the payment of compensation by the US Government, led to a period of strained relations between the two countries. Following the military withdrawal of Serbian forces from Kosovo in June, US forces have taken a leading role in subsequent UN peace-keeping operations in the region.

Throughout Clinton's presidency the USA continued to pursue an active role in efforts to secure the settlement of conflicts in the Middle East, with particular reference to matters at issue between Israel, Syria and Lebanon, and in December 1999, under Clinton's auspices, the first substantive negotiations since 1996 between the Governments of Israel and Syria took place in Washington, DC. In March 2000 the US Government sought to move towards a *rapprochement* with Iran with the announcement that it was to ease some of the trade sanctions against Iran that had been in force since 1979. The USA, and Clinton personally, was also active in the Irish peace process.

In January 1999 the Clinton Administration indicated that it was considering an allocation of $7,000m. over a three-year period from 2000 for new research into the SDI programme (see above), which had been initiated by President Reagan in 1983 and on which an estimated $55,000m. had been spent prior to its termination by Clinton in 1995. Under the new proposals, which attracted considerable congressional support from Republicans, the original concept of a space-based missile defence system was to be replaced by a network of ground- or sea-based interceptor rockets with the capability of destroying intercontinental ballistic missiles either accidentally launched or fired by a hostile power. This modification of the SDI, which was redesignated as the National Missile Defence (NMD) system, would require the agreement of Russia to amend prior anti-nuclear treaties, and has been widely criticized as posing a possible threat to efforts to achieve further reductions in nuclear arms world-wide. In May 2000 the USA, together with the United Kingdom, France, Russia and the People's Republic of China, announced a commitment to global nuclear disarmament, although no timetable was set out for the eventual elimination of stockpiles of these weapons.

Following the contests for the nominations within the two major parties, Vice-President Al Gore was selected as the Democratic Party candidate in the presidential election that was scheduled for November 2000, with George W. Bush, the Governor of Texas and a son of former President Bush, as the Republican contender. Following voting on 7 November, it emerged that the possession of an overall majority in the presidential Electoral College would depend on the 25 college mandates from the state of Florida, where the result of the ballot was in dispute. The state was initially declared in favour of Governor Bush by some 1,600 votes, giving him 271 of the 538 Electoral-College mandates, pending the result of a mandatory automated recount of the votes; however, the Democrats challenged the declaration (and the state government's refusal to permit the ballots to be recounted by electoral staff following the automated recount) in the Florida Supreme Court, claiming that a significant number of votes in certain counties had been incorrectly registered by the automated voting and counting system. The Court ruled that the ballots in the counties concerned should be recounted by electoral staff and allowed an additional 12 days for this process to be completed. The US Supreme Court disallowed this ruling, however, and returned the matter to the Florida Supreme Court for further consideration. Only one county completed its 'manual' recount and the result remained in Governor Bush's favour (by 537 votes).

The Democrats began further legal action, claiming that the recounting of all disputed ballots transcended time limits. A Florida judge rejected the claim, but the Florida Supreme Court upheld an appeal and ordered the recounting of some 45,000 disputed ballots. The Republicans challenged the verdict, claiming that no provision for such 'manual' recounts was made in the electoral legislation. The US Supreme Court upheld the Republican appeal, by a margin of five judges to four. With all legal recourses exhausted, and with the Florida legislature having voted to endorse a list of Republican electors irrespective of the outcome of further legal action, Vice-President Gore conceded defeat in Florida (and thereby nationally) on 13 December 2000.

Final results subsequently indicated that Vice-President Gore obtained 48.4% of the valid votes cast, compared with 47.9% obtained by Governor Bush. Thus, the latter became the first contender since 1876 to win a majority in the Electoral College while losing the national popular ballot. In the concurrently held elections to the Senate, the Democrats made a net gain of five seats, resulting in both parties holding 50 of the 100 seats (Hillary Rodham Clinton, the wife of President Clinton, was elected as a Democratic Senator representing New York). The Republicans retained their effective majority in the chamber, however, owing to the casting vote of the President of the Senate, the incoming Vice-President, Dick Cheney. In May 2001 Senator James Jeffords of Vermont left the Republican Party to sit in the Senate as an Independent, thus establishing a Democratic majority of one in the chamber; the Democrats assumed formal control of the Senate in early June, with Thomas Daschle as Majority Leader. The Democrats also made net gains of three seats in the House of Representatives and one state governorship.

Governor Bush was inaugurated as President on 20 January 2001—his first Cabinet contained several individuals who had served in his father's Administration, as well as one member of Clinton's Cabinet. His Administration immediately suspended the implementation of a number of environmental regulations issued by Clinton shortly before his departure from office. The Administration's first budget, presented in February, included provisions for reductions in levels of personal taxation. Environmental campaigners (who had expressed reservations over President Bush's attitude to environmental issues) and numerous foreign governments and international organizations strongly criticized the new President in March when his Administration withdrew support for the ratification process of the Kyoto Protocol on climate change, claiming it would be detrimental to US economic interests. In February 2002 Bush proposed voluntary, less far-reaching, measures to reduce emissions of 'greenhouse gases'. The Bush Administration published a report on energy policy in May 2001, which included a proposal to introduce legislation authorizing exploratory drilling for oil in the Arctic National Wildlife Refuge in Alaska. The plan prompted criticism from the environmental lobby. In August 2001 the House of Representatives voted in favour of the proposal by a narrow majority; however, the proposed legislation was rejected by the Senate in April 2002. The Administration subsequently introduced a provision to allow drilling to start in 2004, whereby federal revenue would be raised from the sale of leases to petroleum companies; however, in March 2003 Congress passed an amendment to remove the provision.

President Bush's strong personal support for the NMD programme, expressed throughout the electoral campaign and in the period after his inauguration, caused further concern both within the USA and abroad. In November 2001, following a summit meeting in Washington, DC, President Bush and the Russian President, Vladimir Putin, both pledged to reduce their nation's nuclear arsenals by approximately two-thirds over the following decade; a formal agreement was signed in May 2002. (Bush also pledged to repeal the Jackson–Vanik Amendment of 1974, which imposed trade sanctions on the former USSR). Despite this measure, in December 2001 President Bush announced that the USA was to formally withdraw, in June 2002, from the Anti-Ballistic Missile Treaty (ABM), signed with the USSR in 1972, claiming that its adherence prevented the development of NMD. He emphasized that the USA's withdrawal from the ABM would not undermine US–Russian relations. Putin described the withdrawal as a mistake, but insisted it would not damage Russian security. Also in December 2001, the USA received fierce criticism from EU member states after forcing the collapse of an international conference convened to reinforce the terms of the Biological and Toxic Weapons Convention, signed in 1972; the USA opposed plans which would have allowed international inspectors to monitor its military and industrial facilities. The USA attracted further international criticism by its refusal to sign up to the terms of the International Criminal Court (ICC), established to try war criminals, which was inaugurated at The Hague, Netherlands, in March 2003. The USA defended its position by claiming that members of its military could be put on trial on political grounds, and, in response, in the same month, Congress passed the American Servicemember and Citizen Protection Act, which would enable the USA to free, by force if necessary, any member of its military arrested by the ICC.

In February 2001 US and British aircraft were involved in the bombardment of a number of targets in Iraq, ostensibly to maintain the 'no-fly' zones imposed on that country. The action was condemned by numerous countries. A further bombardment took place in April, the USA stating that the missions were in response to anti-aircraft fire in the southern zone. Further bombardments were reported in June, August, September and October, during which three unmanned US surveillance planes were reportedly shot down over the 'no-fly' zones.

Relations with the People's Republic of China were strained in April 2001 when a US Navy aircraft, claimed by the USA to have been on a reconnaissance mission in international airspace over the South China Sea, was involved in a collision with one of two Chinese aircraft monitoring its movements. The US aircraft was forced to make an emergency landing at a military airbase on the Chinese island of Hainan; it was subsequently impounded by the Chinese authorities and its 24-strong crew detained. (The Chinese aircraft involved and its pilot were lost). The crew was released following 11 days of intensive negotiations, when the USA expressed regret for the presumed death of the Chinese pilot and for entering Chinese airspace in order to make its landing. However, the USA did not admit responsibility for the incident, as the Chinese Government had demanded. Following the return of the aircraft's crew to the USA, the US Government claimed that the Chinese pilots had been responsible for the collision. In late May the Chinese Government announced that the aircraft would be dismantled and returned to the USA. Tensions increased shortly after the crew's return when the US Government approved the sale of defence equipment to Taiwan. In May it was announced that the USA was to suspend all bilateral military co-operation with China, although this announcement was immediately rescinded, President Bush stating that such contacts were 'under review'. In early September 2001, in return for China's acceptance of NMD, the USA pledged to keep China informed of its development and agreed to recognize that the Chinese might, in the future, want to resume nuclear weapons testing. The USA also urged China not to transfer ballistic missile technology to countries which the USA considered to be 'rogue states' (deemed by the Department of State to be those countries with the capabilities to use weapons of mass destruction without adherence to traditional international conventions). In January 2002 it was reported that a US-built aeroplane destined to serve as Chinese President Jiang Zemin's official aircraft had been fitted with more than 20 surveillance devices; the Chinese dismissed the incident, however, in an apparent attempt to maintain cordial relations with the USA.

On 11 September 2001 four commercial passenger aircraft were hijacked shortly after take-off from Boston, New York and Washington, DC. The two aircraft originating in Boston, both bound for Los Angeles, were diverted to New York and each was flown into the two towers of the World Trade Center, both of which subsequently collapsed. The third aircraft was flown into the Pentagon building (the headquarters of the Department of Defense) in Washington, DC, and the fourth aircraft, also apparently heading for Washington, DC, crashed in farmland near Pittsburgh, Pennsylvania. The death toll was estimated to be approximately 3,300, including 266 passengers and crew (including the hijackers) on the four aircraft, 190 at the Pentagon, and the remainder in New York, principally those unable to escape from the towers before they collapsed, and members of the emergency services. (In January 2003 2,738 death certificates had been issued, and 59 persons were still unaccounted for, in New York—these figures excluded the hijackers.) On 13 September the Secretary of State, Gen. Colin Powell, identified bin Laden and his al-Qa'ida (Base) organization, a network of fundamentalist Islamist militants, as responsible for the attacks. However, bin Laden, who was believed to be in Afghanistan, where he was harboured by the extremist Islamist Taliban regime, had already denied accusations that he had ordered the hijackings, although he expressed his approval of the attacks.

In the immediate wake of the attacks, President Bush declared that those responsible should be captured 'dead or alive'. Both houses of Congress unanimously approved emergency anti-terrorism legislation, which made provision for increased military spending and US $20,000m. for reconstruction in New York, and approved a resolution authorizing the President to use 'all necessary and appropriate force' against those who organized the attacks. The Government began to form an international coalition against terrorism, for which most Western Governments pledged their support. NATO invoked Article Five of the NATO Charter (which states that an attack on a member state is an attack on all 19 members), which required members to assist the USA, according to judgement and resources; the Governments of the United Kingdom, France and Germany, among others, offered military and financial assistance. The Taliban regime in Afghanistan denied involvement in the terrorist attacks, and warned that it would retaliate if attacked. On 17 September the USA issued an ultimatum to the Taliban, via Pakistan (the only state with diplomatic links to the regime), to surrender bin Laden or face an imminent military assault. Several weeks of intense diplomatic activity ensued, during which time international support for the USA's so-called 'Global Coalition Against Terror' increased, and the US Government reportedly was able to gather further evidence of the al-Qa'ida network's involvement in the attacks. The Taliban reportedly requested to see evidence of bin Laden's involvement in the attacks, a request rejected by the USA. In the meantime, US military forces increased their presence in the region around Afghanistan. Pakistan and Uzbekistan agreed to grant the US-led forces access to their air bases for emergency operations and Russia allowed access to its airspace for humanitarian missions. Saudi Arabia, although it refused to allow the USA to use its military bases, granted access to its airspace.

On 2 October 2001 NATO declared that it had received evidence from the USA that confirmed bin Laden's responsibility for the terrorist attacks. On the evening of 7 October US and British armed forces commenced military operations ('Operation Enduring Freedom') against Taliban military targets and suspected al-Qa'ida training camps in Afghanistan. In addition to military strikes, aircraft released food and medicine parcels to Afghan civilians; leaflets were also dropped offering protection and a reward in return for information on the whereabouts of al-Qa'ida leaders. On 14 October a senior Taliban official offered to surrender bin Laden to a third country in return for a cessation of US bombing, if the USA provided evidence of his involvement in the terrorist attacks, an offer the USA rejected. The US-led forces co-ordinated operations with the military wing of the exiled Afghanistani Government, the United National Islamic Front for the Salvation of Afghanistan (UIFSA—also known as the Northern Alliance). During November the latter made substantial territorial gains in northern and western Afghanistan, including the Afghan capital, Kabul, and Mazar-i-Sharif, a strategically important town in the north. In late November US ground forces were deployed for the first time, near the southern city of Kandahar, in an attempt to locate bin Laden. Kandahar fell to the US-led forces in early December, leaving only pockets of Taliban resistance; US forces subsequently intensified their search for bin Laden, who was believed to be in the Tora Bora caves near Jalalabad, in the east of the country. US-led ground forces were still deployed in Afghanistan in May 2002, attempting to overcome a small number of Taliban and al-Qa'ida members who had not surrendered; bin Laden remained at large. The USA refused, however, to deploy peace-keeping troops in Afghanistan to support the interim administration of Hamid Karzai, which had replaced the Taliban regime in early December 2001, although it released previously withheld assets to his Government, and pledged financial aid to rebuild the country's infrastructure. In January 2002 the Bush Government pledged some $296.8m. in funds for the reconstruction of Afghanistan.

In mid-January 2002 the US military began transferring members of the Taliban and al-Qa'ida, who had been captured in battle, to the US naval base in Guantánamo Bay in Cuba. Initially, the USA refused to grant the detainees (numbering almost 300) prisoner-of-war status under the Geneva Convention of 1949 (which guaranteed trial by court martial or a civilian court, as opposed to a military tribunal), prompting criticism from its coalition partners, which intensified following the publication of photographs showing prisoners shackled and blindfolded. In February, following pressure from the British and French Governments, President Bush accorded partial protection of the Convention to captured Taliban fighters (he stopped short of full protection, however, claiming that the soldiers were members of an irregular militia); al-Qa'ida captives were offered no protection, as they were considered to be terrorists with no allegiance to any specific state or government. President Bush also abandoned an earlier demand to make the final judgement on a detainee's guilt or innocence.

In late September 2001 the Bush Administration established the Office of Homeland Security, under Thomas J. Ridge, to develop and implement a strategy to prevent future terrorist attacks against the USA. In the following month traces of anthrax (a toxic biological agent) were discovered in items of post sent to government buildings and media organizations in Washington, DC, New York and Florida. Letters containing anthrax were sent to the Majority Leader in the Senate, Tom Daschle, and other senior members of Congress, and the House of Representatives was closed for several days in late October as a precautionary measure. Responsibility for the contamination was initially attributed to al-Qa'ida, although it was subsequently reported that the anthrax had originated in the USA; however, the perpetrators remained unknown. Items of post containing traces of anthrax were subsequently discovered in Missouri, and sent to the US embassies in Lithuania and Peru and the US consulate in Yekaterinburg, Russia. In total, five people died from exposure to anthrax spores (all in mainland USA), and some 300,000 postal workers and civil servants were given precautionary medical treatment in October and November.

In his State of the Union address in January 2002, President Bush described Iran, Iraq and North Korea as forming an 'axis of evil' that supported international terrorism and sought to develop weapons of mass destruction, and hinted that the USA was considering pre-emptive strikes against them. US allies warned against attacking states unless firm evidence of a link to terrorism could be found. In February Bush faced protests on a visit to South Korea, and members of South Korean President Kim Dae-Jung's ruling party accused Bush of damaging the so-called 'sunshine policy' of reconciliation with North Korea. In the same month Secretary of State Powell made specific mention of removing Saddam Hussain from power in Iraq. In January it was announced that US troops were to be sent to the Philippines to fight against the Abu Sayyaf guerrilla group, which was believed to have links with al-Qa'ida network. In May the 'axis of evil' was extended to include Cuba, Libya and Syria. The Bush Administration accused Cuba of maintaining a biological warfare programme and offering weapons technology to 'rogue states', and claimed that Libya and Syria had violated international weapons treaties.

In January 2002, following an escalation in the ongoing conflict in the Middle East, President Bush sent US special envoy Anthony Zinni on a four-day visit to the region in an unsuccessful attempt to secure a cease-fire agreement between Israel and the Palestinians. In March Zinni returned to Jerusalem in a renewed attempt to broker a cease-fire. Following discussions between Zinni and the Palestinian leader, Yasser Arafat, and US-brokered talks between Israeli and Palestinian security officials in Jerusalem, the Israeli Prime Minister, Ariel Sharon, agreed to redeploy some Israeli troops from Palestinian areas. However, in early April, following a further escalation in the conflict, President Bush urged Sharon to withdraw Israeli forces from Palestinian towns and to adhere to the cease-fire recommendations proposed by former Senator George Mitchell and the Central Intelligence Agency (CIA) Director George Tenet in 2001. In mid-April Powell visited Israel and held separate talks with Sharon and with Arafat in his besieged headquarters, in an attempt to bring an end to the crisis. However, the mission failed to bring about a cease-fire or the withdrawal of Israeli forces from Palestinian areas.

In December 2001 Enron Corporation, the largest energy company in the USA, filed for bankruptcy. This was the largest ever bankruptcy in US history, with the immediate loss of 4,000 jobs. It subsequently emerged that Enron's accounts had been falsified over several years, possibly with the approval of the Corporation's accountancy firm, Arthur Andersen. The firm was found guilty of obstructing justice in June 2002, and ceased operations at the end of August. Furthermore, it was revealed that Enron had donated more than $500,000 to Bush's presidential campaign, and that Vice-President Cheney had met senior Enron executives on several occasions in 2001 while drafting the proposed national energy plan. An investigation into the bankruptcy was begun by the Department of Justice in early 2002. It was also reported that senior members of the Bush Administration had refused requests from Enron for financial assistance in 2001. In June Worldcom, the second largest long-distance telecommunications company in the USA, revealed that it too had manipulated its accounts to show figures for cashflow and profits that were higher than in reality; the disclosure prompted the Securities and Exchange Commission to announce that the regulation of listed companies and subsequent penalties would become more stringent.

Reform of electoral campaign financing was finally approved by the House of Representatives in February 2002 (after being rejected in July 2001). The proposal banned unregulated, or so-called 'soft money' donations to political parties from individuals, businesses and unions, which were ostensibly used only for general activities, but were often used to support the campaigns of particular candidates. At mid-term elections held on 5 November, at which voter participation was 39%, the Republicans assumed control of the Senate and increased its majority in the House of Representatives. The Democrats gained three state governorships overall. Later that month, President Bush signed legislation establishing the federal Department of Homeland Security at cabinet level, with Ridge as its Secretary. Earlier in the year the Federal Bureau of Investigation (FBI), which had been criticized since September 2001 for overlooking information which could have prevented the terrorist attacks, announced measures to prioritize and extend its counter-terrorism activities.

In September 2002 the Bush Administration issued a National Security Strategy for the United States, which set out the new threats faced by the USA internationally, and outlined the policies adopted to meet these challenges. In the same month the Republicans submitted a draft resolution to Congress which would authorize President Bush to use 'any means neces-

sary' to enforce existing UN resolutions against the regime of Saddam Hussain in Iraq and to defend US national interests by depriving Iraq of weapons of mass destruction. It was the first tangible evidence that the Administration was willing to deploy unilateral military action if the UN Security Council did not pass a new resolution authorizing military action against the Iraqi regime. The resolution was approved in October by both houses of Congress, with the provision that the Administration should first exhaust all available channels at the UN and other diplomatic means. As a result of US-led pressure, in November the UN passed unanimously Resolution 1441, which obliged Iraq, *inter alia*, to declare all weapons of mass destruction within 30 days, to comply with the UN Monitoring, Verification and Inspection Commission (UNMOVIC—the UN weapons inspectors, and successor to UNSCOM), to allow UNMOVIC to resume its work within 45 days (UNSCOM had been expelled from Iraq in 1998—see above), and to allow inspectors unrestricted access within Iraq, including Saddam Hussain's palaces. Later that month UNMOVIC resumed its operations and reported that the Iraqi Government was prepared to comply with Resolution 1441. In December Iraq presented its report on weapons of mass destruction to UNMOVIC; however, US officials declared Iraq to be in 'material breach' of Resolution 1441, for failing to comply with the demand for an accurate and complete account of its weapons programmes, and for resubmitting information that it had previously given to the UN. Following this development, the US and British Governments drew up a timetable to allow UNMOVIC to carry out intensified searches in early 2003, with the threat of military action against Saddam's regime for non-compliance.

In January 2003 some 70,000 US servicemen and -women joined the 60,000 troops already stationed in the Persian (Arabian) Gulf, and military exercises intensified. The French and German Governments expressed their opposition to any eventual conflict and called for a resolution to the problem by diplomatic means. In response, President Bush stated that the USA would lead a 'coalition of the willing' if support was withheld by other UN Security Council members and its traditional allies. The Administration took an increasingly uncompromising stance; the Secretary of Defense, Donald Rumsfeld, described France and Germany as 'old Europe' (as opposed to other more pro-US states in Southern and Eastern Europe), and the Secretary of State, Colin Powell, excluded the possibility of extending the time allocated to inspectors to find prohibited weapons in Iraq. However, Rumsfeld had also suggested the possibility of granting senior Iraqi leaders amnesty and avoiding conflict if they chose exile in a third country. In late January UNMOVIC reported that it had discovered substances and missiles which could be in contravention of UN resolutions. In February the USA, together with the United Kingdom, intensified its efforts to secure a second UN resolution which would authorize military intervention in Iraq; on 5 February Powell presented evidence of, *inter alia*, the alleged existence of weapons of mass destruction in Iraq, and possible links between Saddam Hussain's regime and al-Qa'ida. However, in mid-February UNMOVIC reported greater co-operation on the part of the Iraqi Government and that it had thus far failed to find any weapons of mass destruction. (On 13 February Saddam Hussain issued a presidential decree prohibiting weapons of mass destruction, although some al-Samoud missiles were found with a greater range than permitted under UN resolutions.) On 24 February the USA, with the United Kingdom and Spain, presented a draft resolution, reiterating that Iraq had been warned it would face serious consequences if it failed to disarm, and that it had failed to comply with Resolution 1441. In an effort to win the support of the 10 non-permanent members of the UN Security Council, the draft resolution contained no ultimatum to Iraq or explicit threat of attack. A few days later, however, President Bush insisted that only full disarmament could prevent war. In early March diplomatic efforts to resolve the crisis showed signs of breaking down when Russia and then France declared that they would employ their veto on any resolution leading to conflict, while the UN Secretary-General, Kofi Annan, questioned the legitimacy of a conflict in Iraq without UN approval. Nevertheless, Powell stated that the USA could go to war without a second UN resolution. UNMOVIC, meanwhile, reported that Iraq had destroyed part of its stock of al-Masoud missiles. An amended version of the draft for a second resolution was issued in mid-March and a deadline of 17 March given for Iraq to demonstrate full compliance with Resolution 1441. On 16 March President Bush, the

British Prime Minister, Tony Blair, and the Spanish premier, José María Aznar, held an emergency summit in the Azores, Portugal, at the end of which the three leaders issued an ultimatum giving Saddam Hussain and his two sons 48 hours to leave Iraq or face invasion. The following day the USA, the United Kingdom and Spain decided not to seek a second UN resolution and condemned France for obstructing diplomatic efforts to reach a peaceful outcome. The President of France, Jacques Chirac, responded by criticizing the USA and the United Kingdom for making an 'unjustified' decision to resort to war, and for gravely undermining the UN. The USA announced that some 30 countries had expressed support for its 'coalition of the willing', although only the United Kingdom, Australia, the Czech Republic and Slovakia provided troops.

Shortly after the expiry of President Bush's 48-hour deadline, on 19 March 2003 US and British armed forces launched 'Operation Iraqi Freedom' to oust the regime of Saddam Hussain. A first wave of air-strikes against targets in the southern suburbs of Baghdad, apparently aimed at leading members of the Iraqi regime (including the President himself), failed to achieve their target. Soon afterwards British and US forces crossed into Iraq from Kuwait and generally made a swift advance towards the capital. At the same time, a concerted campaign of massive air-strikes was launched by US-led forces against the key symbols of the Iraqi regime in and around Baghdad, including selected military bases, communications sites, government buildings and broadcasting headquarters. Government and military sites in other prominent Iraqi cities were targeted by the US-led coalition in subsequent days. The US and British forces adopted a simultaneous campaign of issuing leaflets and broadcasting radio messages, in an attempt to persuade Iraqi citizens to abandon their support for Saddam Hussain: their declared intention was that Operation Iraqi Freedom would precipitate the disintegration of the regime 'from within'. Some criticism was made within the US Administration of senior military officials for underestimating the determination of the Iraqi forces. However, by 9 April US forces reached the centre of Baghdad and the Iraqi regime appeared to have collapsed. Although the whereabouts of Saddam Hussain and his sons was unknown, a number of senior Iraqi officials had been captured by late April. US military fatalities in late April numbered 132. Sporadic fighting was ongoing in parts of Iraq in late April, despite the arrival, earlier in the month, of US Gen. (retd) Jay Garner, as Civil Administrator, with the intention of overseeing the peaceful transition to civilian rule by Iraqi nationals. Garner claimed that appointments to a new Government would begin in May; the US Administration favoured Ahmed Chalabi of the Iraqi National Congress, who had been in exile in the USA, to eventually lead the country. In early May a US diplomat, Paul Bremer, succeeded Garner as Civil Administrator in Iraq.

Meanwhile, relations with Turkey were strained in early 2003 following pressure from the USA to allow some 60,000 of its troops to use its military bases and territory for an eventual assault on northern Iraq. In February the USA offered the Turkish Government a financial package worth US $26,000m., which the Turks rejected as too little. In March the Turkish National Assembly rejected a motion allowing the US military to use its bases and territory, and restricted it to using Turkish airspace. In early April, however, the USA offered reduced financial renumeration of up to $8,500m. to restore bilateral relations and secured the use of Turkey as a route to transport humanitarian supplies and logistical aid to the US military in Iraq. Earlier in the year the issue of Turkey's role in an eventual conflict had led to a division within NATO, when France, Germany and Belgium opposed US attempts to engage NATO in reinforcing Turkish military forces in the event of an Iraqi attack. A compromise proposed by the three European countries to provide only defensive, rather than offensive, support was accepted by NATO in March.

Relations with the DPRK were severely strained in late 2002 when it emerged that the DPRK Government had resumed its nuclear energy programme, effectively breaking the accord signed with the USA in 1994. In October the DPRK demanded a treaty of non-agression with the USA and asserted its right to possess nuclear weapons. In the following month the USA, South Korea, Japan and the EU suspended their supply of petroleum to the DPRK until its Government promised to terminate its nuclear weapons programme, although the DPRK denied it operated such a programme. However, in December it announced it would resume operations at a nuclear plant capable of producing weapons-grade plutonium (although

whether it had done so by April 2003 was unclear). The USA considered that economic sanctions would be an effective means of containing North Korea, although this led to a more uncompromising stance from the DPRK, which said it would consider UN sanctions an 'act of war', and subsequently withdrew from the NPT in January 2003. The USA, the DPRK and the People's Republic of China were engaged in tentative talks in mid-2003 to resolve the impasse.

Government

The USA is a federal republic. Each of the 50 constituent states and the District of Columbia exercises a measure of internal self-government. Defence, foreign affairs, coinage, posts, the higher levels of justice, and internal security are the responsibility of the federal government. The President is head of the executive and is elected for a four-year term by a college of representatives elected directly from each state. The President appoints the other members of the executive, subject to the consent of the Senate. The Congress is the seat of legislative power and consists of the Senate (100 members) and the House of Representatives (435 members). Two senators are chosen by direct election in each state, to serve a six-year term, and one-third of the membership is renewable every two years. Representatives are elected by direct and universal suffrage for a two-year term. The number of representatives of each state in Congress is determined by the size of the state's population. Ultimate judicial power is vested in the Supreme Court, which has the power to disallow legislation and to overturn executive actions which it deems unconstitutional.

Defence

In August 2002 US armed forces totalled 1,414,000: army 485,500, air force 369,700, navy 385,400 and 173,400 marine corps. There are also active reservists numbering 1,259,300. Military conscription ended in 1973. The Strategic Air Command and Polaris nuclear submarines are equipped with nuclear weapons. The USA is a member of the NATO alliance. Federal defence expenditure for 2001/02 totalled $362,106m., and proposed expenditure for 2002/03 was $382,681m. (some 17.8% of total federal budgetary expenditure).

Economic Affairs

In 2001, according to estimates by the World Bank, the USA's gross national income (GNI), measured at average 1999–2001 prices, was US $9,900,724m., equivalent to $34,870 per head. During 1990–2001, it was estimated, the population increased at an annual average rate of 1.2%, while gross domestic product (GDP) per head increased, in real terms, by an average of 1.9% per year. Overall GDP increased, in real terms, at an average annual rate of 3.1%; growth in 2001 was 0.3%.

Agriculture (including forestry and fishing) contributed 1.4% of GDP in 2001. About 2.4% of the working population were employed in this sector in that same year. The principal crops are hay, potatoes, sugar beet and citrus fruit, which, together with cereals, cotton and tobacco, are important export crops. The principal livestock are cattle, pigs and poultry. Food and live animals provided 5.4% of total exports in 2000. The GDP of the sector increased, in real terms, by an average of 2.7% per year in 1994–2001. Real agricultural GDP increased by 7.8% in 2000, but declined by 1.7% in 2001.

Industry (including mining, manufacturing, construction and utilities) provided 22.2% of GDP in 2001 and employed 22.6% of the civilian working population in that same year. Industrial GDP increased, in real terms, at an average annual rate of 2.6% in 1994–2001. Real industrial GDP increased by 3.4% in 2000, but decreased by 5.1% in 2001.

Mining and quarrying contributed 1.4% of GDP in 2001, and employed 0.4% of the civilian working population in that year. The USA's principal mineral deposits are of petroleum, natural gas, coal, copper, iron, silver and uranium. The mining sector accounted for 3.9% of total exports in 2000. In real terms, the GDP of the sector decreased at an average annual rate of 0.2% during 1994–2001. Real mining GDP decreased by 11.2% in 2000 before increasing by 4.8% in 2001.

Manufacturing contributed 14.0% of GDP in 2001, when the sector employed 14.0% of the civilian working population. In 1994 the principal branches (measured by value of output) were transport equipment (14.4% of the total), food products (11.3%), non-electrical machinery (10.3%), chemical products (10.2%), electrical machinery, printing and publishing and metal products. Manufacturing provided 74.5% of total exports in 2000. Manufacturing GDP increased, in real terms, by an average of

3.1% per year in 1994–2001. Sectoral GDP increased by 4.7% in 2000, but decreased by 6.0% in 2001.

Energy is derived principally from domestic and imported hydrocarbons. In 1999 51.8% of total electricity production was provided by coal, 15.7% was derived from natural gas, and 19.9% was provided by nuclear power. In 2000 fuel imports amounted to 11.1% of total merchandise import costs.

Services provided 76.4% of GDP and 75.0% of total civilian employment in 2001. The combined GDP of all service sectors rose, in real terms, at an average rate of 4.3% per year during 1994–2001. Services GDP increased by 5.2% in 2000 and by 2.1% in 2001.

In 2001 the USA recorded a visible trade deficit of $424,230m. (excluding military transactions), and there was a deficit of $294,450m. on the current account of the balance of payments. The USA's principal export market and main source of imports in 2002 was Canada, with which a free-trade agreement came into force in January 1989, providing for the progressive elimination, over a 10-year period, of virtually all trade tariffs between the two countries. In 2002 Canada accounted for 23.2% of total US exports and 18.1% of total imports. Mexico was the second-largest trading partner, providing 11.6% of US imports in 2002. Other major trading partners include Japan, the United Kingdom, Germany and other members of the European Union (EU), and the People's Republic of China. In 2000 machinery and transport equipment constituted the principal category of exports (accounting for 51.4% of the total) and of imports (44.8%).

In the financial year ending 30 September 2002 there was an estimated federal budget deficit of $236,884m. The annual rate of inflation averaged 2.8% per year in 1990–2001. The average rate was 2.8% in 2001 and 1.6% in 2002. The rate of unemployment averaged 4.0% of the labour force in 2000 (its lowest level since 1969); this figure rose to 4.8% in 2001 and stood at 5.8% in January 2003.

The US economy grew strongly throughout the 1990s, despite the persistence of many of the factors that had inhibited growth in the previous decade. The Federal Government's level of foreign debt continued to increase until 1998, its reduction being a priority of the second Clinton Administration. The deficits in trade and on the current account of the balance of payments increased throughout the decade. Trade with Canada, and particularly with Mexico, was facilitated by the North American Free Trade Agreement (NAFTA, see p. 270), which entered into operation in January 1994 and provided for the progressive abolition (over a 15-year period) of tariffs between the three countries. In the second half of the decade the US dollar appreciated considerably in value against many major world currencies, enabling the Federal Reserve System to maintain low interest rates, thus stimulating growth, led by developments in the telecommunications and information-technology sectors. However, growth in these sectors began to decelerate in 2000, provoking fears of a recession in the economy as a whole. Under President Clinton the country's budget deficit was reduced and, from 1998–2001, a budget surplus was operated. Pledges to reduce levels of personal taxation were a prominent feature of the presidential campaign of George W. Bush, and his Administration's first budget included the largest single cut in federal taxation since 1981, amounting to $1,350,000m. Concerns of a significant recession, after the sustained growth of previous years, dominated the US economy in 2001; interest rates were cut sharply in this year, in an effort to sustain economic activity. The events of 11 September 2001 further undermined confidence in the US economy, which was officially in recession in the third quarter of 2001, although growth was recorded in the final quarter, and further growth was forecast in 2002–03, according to the IMF. In March 2002 the Government imposed tariffs on steel imported from the EU, Russia and Japan, among other countries (Canada, Mexico and some developing countries were exempt); the measure was taken as a response to cheap exports from those countries, which the USA claimed were damaging the domestic steel industry. The countries affected appealed to the WTO to overturn the decision and demanded compensation from the USA. The Government enacted legislation in May which provided for large agricultural subsidies over a period of 10 years; the move was criticized by EU countries, which claimed that they would be obliged to increase subsidies to protect their own farmers. In January 2003 the Administration presented plans to reduce taxes worth some $726,000m. over 10 years; however, in March Congress voted to reduce the cuts to $350,000m., owing partly to concerns about the cost of the US-led military conflict against the regime of Saddam Hussain in Iraq and the eventual reconstruction of that country. The federal budget for 2004 included relatively small increases in all areas except defence and homeland security, and forecast a budget deficit for the third successive year.

Education

Education is primarily the responsibility of state and local governments, but some federal funds are available to help meet special needs at primary, secondary and higher education levels. Public education is free in every state from elementary school through high school. The period of compulsory education varies among states, but most states require attendance between the ages of seven and 16 years. At the beginning of the 2001/02 academic year there were an estimated 33.6m. pupils enrolled in public primary schools and 13.6m. in public secondary schools. Private school enrolment was approximately 4.6m. at primary level and about 1.3m. at secondary level. In 1998/99 there were almost 4,000 two-year and four-year universities and colleges, with a total enrolment of an estimated 15.3m. students at the beginning of the 2001/02 academic year. Federal government expenditure on education (including training and employment programmes) totalled $79,861m. in 2002. Spending on education by all levels of government in 1999/2000 was $521,612m. (29.9% of total public expenditure).

Public Holidays*

2003: 1 January (New Year's Day), 20 January (Martin Luther King Day), 17 February (Presidents' Day), 26 May (Memorial Day), 4 July (Independence Day), 1 September (Labor Day), 11 November (Veterans' Day), 27 November (Thanksgiving Day), 25 December (Christmas Day).

2004: 1 January (New Year's Day), 19 January (Martin Luther King Day), 16 February (Presidents' Day), 31 May (Memorial Day), 4 July (Independence Day), 6 September (Labor Day), 11 November (Veterans' Day), 25 November (Thanksgiving Day), 25 December (Christmas Day).

* Federal legal public holidays are designated by presidential proclamation or congressional enactment, but need not be observed in individual states, which have legal jurisdiction over their public holidays.

Weights and Measures

With certain exceptions, the imperial system is in force. One US billion equals 1,000 million; one US cwt equals 100 lb; long ton equals 2,240 lb; short ton equals 2,000 lb. A policy of gradual voluntary conversion to the metric system is being encouraged.

Statistical Survey

Area and Population

Source (unless otherwise stated): Statistical Information Office, Population Division, Bureau of the Census, US Department of Commerce, Washington, DC 20233-0001; internet www.census.gov.

AREA, POPULATION AND DENSITY

Area (sq km)	9,809,155*
Population (census results)†	
1 April 1990	248,709,873
1 April 2000	
Males	138,053,563
Females.	143,368,343
Total	281,421,906
Population (official estimates at mid-year)‡	
2000	282,124,631
2001	284,796,887
2002	288,368,698
Density (per sq km) at mid-2002	29.40

* This is the official US equivalent of 3,787,319 sq miles, assuming a conversion factor of 1 sq mile = 2.59 sq km, a rounded version of the internationally accepted standard of 1 sq mile = 2.5899881 sq km.
† Excluding adjustment for underenumeration.
‡ Estimates of the resident population, based on 2000 census results (excluding adjustment for underenumeration).

RACES
(2000 census)

	Number	%
White	211,460,626	75.14
Black	34,658,190	12.32
Asian	10,242,998	3.64
American Indian and Alaska Native . .	2,475,956	0.88
Native Hawaiian and Pacific Islander .	398,835	0.14
Others*	22,185,301	7.88
Total	281,421,906	100.00

* Includes those of two or more races.

Hispanic or Latino population (all races): 35,305,818 (12.6%).

STATES

State	Gross area (land and water, sq km)	Resident population* (2000 census, '000)	Capital
Alabama	135,775	4,447	Montgomery
Alaska	1,700,138	627	Juneau
Arizona. . . .	295,276	5,131	Phoenix
Arkansas . . .	137,742	2,673	Little Rock
California . . .	424,002	33,872	Sacramento
Colorado . . .	269,618	4,301	Denver
Connecticut . .	14,358	3,406	Hartford
Delaware . . .	6,448	784	Dover
District of Columbia .	177	572	Washington
Florida	170,314	15,982	Tallahassee
Georgia. . . .	153,952	8,186	Atlanta
Hawaii	28,313	1,212	Honolulu
Idaho	216,456	1,294	Boise
Illinois	150,007	12,419	Springfield
Indiana. . . .	94,328	6,080	Indianapolis
Iowa	145,754	2,926	Des Moines
Kansas	213,111	2,688	Topeka
Kentucky . . .	104,665	4,042	Frankfort
Louisiana . . .	134,275	4,469	Baton Rouge
Maine	91,653	1,275	Augusta
Maryland . . .	32,134	5,296	Annapolis
Massachusetts. .	27,337	6,349	Boston
Michigan . . .	250,465	9,938	Lansing
Minnesota . . .	225,182	4,919	St Paul
Mississippi. . .	125,443	2,845	Jackson
Missouri . . .	180,546	5,595	Jefferson City
Montana . . .	380,850	902	Helena
Nebraska . . .	200,358	1,711	Lincoln
Nevada	286,367	1,998	Carson City
New Hampshire . .	24,219	1,236	Concord
New Jersey . .	22,590	8,414	Trenton
New Mexico . .	314,939	1,819	Santa Fe
New York . . .	141,080	18,976	Albany
North Carolina .	139,397	8,049	Raleigh
North Dakota . .	183,123	642	Bismarck
Ohio	116,103	11,353	Columbus
Oklahoma . . .	181,048	3,451	Oklahoma City
Oregon	254,819	3,421	Salem
Pennsylvania . .	119,291	12,281	Harrisburg
Rhode Island . .	4,002	1,048	Providence
South Carolina . .	82,902	4,012	Columbia
South Dakota . .	199,744	755	Pierre
Tennessee . . .	109,158	5,689	Nashville
Texas	695,676	20,852	Austin
Utah	219,902	2,233	Salt Lake City
Vermont . . .	24,903	609	Montpelier
Virginia . . .	110,792	7,079	Richmond
Washington . .	184,672	5,894	Olympia
West Virginia . .	62,759	1,808	Charleston
Wisconsin . . .	169,643	5,364	Madison
Wyoming . . .	253,349	494	Cheyenne
Total	9,809,155	281,422	

* Includes armed forces residing in each State.

PRINCIPAL TOWNS
(population at census of 1 April 2000)

New York	8,008,278	Oklahoma City	506,132
Los Angeles	3,694,820	Tucson	486,699
Chicago	2,896,016	New Orleans	484,674
Houston	1,953,631	Las Vegas	478,434
Philadelphia	1,517,550	Cleveland	478,403
Phoenix	1,321,045	Long Beach, CA	461,522
San Diego	1,223,400	Albuquerque	448,607
Dallas	1,188,580	Kansas City, MO	441,545
San Antonio	1,114,646	Fresno	427,652
Detroit	951,270	Virginia Beach, VA	425,257
San Jose	894,943	Atlanta	416,474
Indianapolis	791,926	Sacramento	407,018
San Francisco	776,733	Oakland	399,484
Jacksonville	735,617	Mesa City, AZ	396,375
Columbus, OH	711,470	Tulsa	393,049
Austin	656,562	Omaha	390,007
Baltimore	651,154	Minneapolis	382,618
Memphis	650,100	Honolulu	371,657
Milwaukee	596,974	Colorado Springs	360,980
Boston	589,141	St Louis	348,189
Washington, DC (capital)	572,059	Wichita	344,284
Nashville-Davidson	569,891	Santa Ana, CA	337,977
El Paso	563,662	Pittsburgh	334,563
Seattle	563,374	Arlington, TX	332,969
Denver	554,636	Cincinnati	331,285
Charlotte	540,828	Anaheim	328,014
Fort Worth	534,694	Toledo, OH	313,619
Portland, OR	529,121	Tampa	303,447

BIRTHS, MARRIAGES, DEATHS

	Registered live births Number ('000)	Rate (per 1,000)	Registered marriages Number ('000)	Rate (per 1,000)	Registered deaths Number ('000)	Rate (per 1,000)
1994	3,953	15.2	2,362	9.1	2,279	8.8
1995	3,900	14.8	2,358	9.0	2,312	8.8
1996	3,891	14.7	2,344	8.8	2,315	8.7
1997	3,881	14.5	2,384	8.9	2,314	8.6
1998	3,944	14.6	2,244	7.0	2,338	8.7
1999	3,959	14.5	2,358*	8.6*	2,391	8.8
2000	4,059	14.7	2,398*	8.7*	2,403	8.7
2001*	4,040	14.5	2,344	8.5	n.a.	n.a.

* Provisional figure(s).

Source: National Center for Health Statistics, US Department of Health and Human Services.

Expectation of life (WHO estimates, years at birth): 77.0 (males 74.3; females 79.5) in 2001 (Source: WHO, *World Health Report*).

IMMIGRATION
(year ending 30 September)*

Country of last permanent residence	1999	2000	2001
Europe	94,373	133,362	177,833
USSR (former)	32,740	43,807	55,099
Asia	193,061	255,860	337,566
China (incl. Taiwan)	29,579	41,861	50,821
India	28,355	39,072	65,916
Korea, Repub.	12,301	15,214	19,933
Philippines	29,590	40,587	50,870
Viet Nam	19,164	25,340	34,648
North and South America	312,324	397,201	473,351
Canada	12,948	21,475	30,203
Colombia	9,769	14,191	16,333
Cuba	13,289	19,322	26,073
Dominican Repub.	17,745	17,441	21,256
Ecuador	8,903	7,658	9,694
El Salvador	14,416	22,332	31,054
Haiti	16,459	22,004	22,535
Jamaica	14,449	15,654	15,099
Mexico	146,436	171,748	204,844
Africa	33,740	40,969	50,209
Total (incl. others)	646,568	849,807	1,064,318

* Figures include immigrant aliens granted permanent resident status.

Source: Immigration and Naturalization Service, US Department of Justice.

ECONOMICALLY ACTIVE POPULATION
(annual averages, civilian labour force, '000 persons aged 16 years and over)

	1999	2000	2001
Agriculture, forestry and fisheries	3,416	3,457	3,277
Mining	565	521	567
Manufacturing	20,070	19,940	18,970
Electricity, gas and water	1,468	1,447	1,408
Construction	8,987	9,433	9,581
Wholesale and retail trade	27,572	27,832	27,672
Transport, storage and communications	8,086	8,294	8,330
Finance, insurance, real estate and business services	16,054	16,515	16,669
Community, social and personal services*	47,271	47,770	48,599
Civilian employment	133,488	135,208	135,073
Unemployed	5,880	5,655	6,742
Civilian labour force	139,368	140,863	141,815

* Including hotels.

Source: ILO.

Health and Welfare

KEY INDICATORS

Total fertility rate (children per woman, 2001)	2.0
Under-5 mortality rate (per 1,000 live births, 2000)	8
HIV/AIDS (% of persons aged 15–49, 2001)	0.61
Physicians (per 1,000 head, 2000)	2.88
Hospital beds (per 1,000 head, 1999)	3.6
Health expenditure (2000): US $ per head (PPP)	4,499
Health expenditure (2000): % of GDP	13.0
Health expenditure (2000): public (% of total)	44.3
Access to water (% of persons, 2000)	100
Access to sanitation (% of persons, 2000)	100
Human Development Index (2000): ranking	6
Human Development Index (2000): value	0.939

For sources and definitions, see explanatory note on p. vi.

Agriculture

PRINCIPAL CROPS

('000 metric tons)

	1999	2000	2001
Wheat	62,567	60,757	53,262
Rice (paddy)	9,344	8,658	9,664
Barley	6,103	6,939	5,430
Maize	238,549	251,854	241,485
Rye	280	213	177
Oats	2,122	2,171	1,699
Sorghum	15,118	11,952	13,070
Other cereals	469	231	502
Potatoes	21,692	23,297	19,862
Dry beans	1,501	1,198	886
Soybeans	72,223	75,055	78,671
Cottonseed	9,458	9,580	11,186
Tomatoes	13,311	11,270	10,250*
Onions (dry)	3,337	3,248	3,060
Carrots	1,989	1,941	1,900†
Other vegetables	12,910	17,916	17,473
Almonds	378	319	376
Sugar beet	30,318	29,521	23,394
Apples	4,822	4,830	4,363
Peaches	1,394	1,422	1,355
Pears	921	877	912
Grapes	5,658	6,947	5,944
Oranges	8,912	11,791	11,087
Grapefruit	2,280	2,506	2,233
Other fruits	7,272	6,039	7,065
Tobacco (leaves)	586	478	450
Cotton (lint)	3,694	3,742	4,420

* Unofficial figure.
† FAO estimate.

Source: FAO.

LIVESTOCK

('000 head at 1 January)

	1999	2000	2001
Cattle	99,115	98,198	97,277
Pigs	62,206	59,342	59,138
Sheep	7,215	7,032	6,965
Chickens (million)*	1,785	1,816	1,830

* Unofficial figures.

Source: FAO.

LIVESTOCK PRODUCTS

('000 metric tons)

	1999	2000	2001
Beef and veal	12,123	12,298	11,983
Lamb and mutton	113	106	103
Pork	8,758	8,597	8,691
Eggs (million)	4,912	4,998	5,083

Source: FAO.

Forestry

ROUNDWOOD REMOVALS

('000 cubic metres)

	1999	2000	2001
Sawlogs and veneer logs	246,241	248,241	230,126
Pulp wood	164,518	164,513	164,430
Other industrial wood	14,900	14,900	13,734
Fuel wood	71,982	72,520	72,803
Total	497,641	500,174	481,093

Source: FAO.

SAWNWOOD PRODUCTION

('000 cubic metres)

	1999	2000	2001
Coniferous	62,343*	61,144	59,350
Broadleaved	30,272	29,932	27,985
Total	92,615	91,076	87,335

* Unofficial figure.

Source: FAO.

Fishing

(million lb, live weight)*

	1998	1999	2000
Capture	7,494.4	7,532.8	7,788.0
Pacific cod	252.2	237.7	240.6
Atlantic menhaden	276.2	208.0	207.1
Gulf menhaden	497.5	694.2	591.4
Walleye pollock	1,232.2	1,055.0	1,182.4
Aquaculture	445.1	478.7	428.3
Channel catfish	226.0	270.6	269.3
Total catch	7,939.5	8,011.5	8,216.3

* Figures refer to the total catch (excl. weight of mollusc shells) by US flag vessels, wherever landed.

Source: FAO, *Yearbook of Fishery Statistics*.

Mining

('000 metric tons, unless otherwise indicated)

	2000	2001	2002*
Phosphate rock	38,600	31,900	35,800
Sulphur	10,300	9,250	9,280
Gypsum	19,500	16,300	16,100
Lead†	465	466	450
Zinc†	852	842	740
Copper†	1,450	1,340	1,130
Gold (metric tons)†	353	335	300
Silver (metric tons)†	1,860	1,740	1,470
Uranium (metric tons)‡	1,456	1,000	1,456
Molybdenum (metric tons)†	40,900	37,600	32,600
Natural gas ('000 million cubic feet)§	24,150	2,450	n.a.
Crude petroleum ('000 barrels per day)§	5,822	5,853	n.a.
Iron ore‖	63,100	46,200	50,000
Coal§	1,073.6	1,121.3	n.a.

* Provisional.
† Figures refer to the metal content of ores and concentrates.
‡ Uranium content (Source: World Nuclear Association).
§ Source: Energy Information Administration, US Department of Energy.
‖ Figures refer to the gross weight of usable ore. The average iron content is about 63%.

Source (unless otherwise stated): US Geological Survey, US Department of the Interior.

Industry

PRINCIPAL MANUFACTURES
(value added in $ million)

	1998	1999	2000
Food	173,416.4	176,778.1	183,482.0
Beverages and tobacco products	62,444.9	68,379.3	71,763.3
Textile mills	23,782.1	22,760.9	21,428.5
Textile product mills	13,265.7	14,336.7	13,796.7
Apparel	31,778.1	30,370.1	28,210.0
Leather and allied products	5,015.8	4,562.8	4,510.0
Wood products	34,469.5	37,957.4	36,093.4
Paper	72,879.0	74,119.1	78,166.3
Printing and related activities	60,247.7	61,937.1	63,446.3
Petroleum and coal products	31,649.2	38,718.9	45,747.7
Petroleum refineries	24,023.6	31,516.3	38,584.0
Chemicals	230,218.8	228,395.8	235,614.0
Basic Chemicals	53,041.9	48,098.7	47,671.2
Pharmaceuticals and medicines	70,763.1	76,274.2	85,231.2
Plastics and rubber products	85,541.9	91,276.4	92,333.3
Nonmetallic mineral products	52,851.2	55,635.5	55,721.9
Primary metal industries	69,139.2	66,314.8	66,095.5
Fabricated metal products	139,741.1	142,248.7	149,449.3
Architectural and structural products	28,291.4	30,307.2	32,245.2
Machinery	141,268.8	139,610.6	148,798.1
Computer and electronic products	252,515.8	270,706.6	291,124.9
Computer and peripheral equipment	50,015.1	47,056.6	43,380.1
Communications equipment	48,255.6	55,867.7	66,812.7
Semiconductors and components	89,078.0	101,734.0	111,624.7
Navigational, measuring, medical and control instruments	61,438.6	58,304.9	59,915.9
Electric equipment	59,124.4	59,544.2	62,990.6
Transportation equipment	245,618.7	263,782.9	240,988.9
Motor vehicles	66,288.7	77,424.7	61,680.5
Motor vehicle parts	77,370.5	85,426.3	85,458.4
Aerospace products and parts	76,049.0	72,547.7	64,863.1
Furniture and related products	37,810.3	40,290.2	42,267.0
Miscellaneous manufactures	64,874.5	66,772.4	70,621.5

Source: Bureau of the Census, US Department of Commerce, *Annual Survey of Manufactures*.

Finance

CURRENCY AND EXCHANGE RATES

Monetary Units
100 cents = 1 United States dollar ($)

Sterling and Euro Equivalents (31 December 2002)
£1 sterling = US $1.6118
€1 = $1.0487
US $100 = £62.04 = €95.36

FEDERAL BUDGET
($ '000 million, year ending 30 September)

Revenue*	2002	2003†	2004†
Individual income taxes	858,345	849,053	849,880
Corporation income taxes	148,044	143,186	169,060
Social insurance taxes and contributions	700,760	726,593	764,548
Excise taxes	66,989	68,416	70,905
Estate and gift taxes	26,507	20,209	23,379
Customs duties and fees	18,602	19,052	20,713
Miscellaneous receipts	−33,926	−34,709	−38,540
Total	1,853,173	1,836,218	1,922,025

Expenditure‡	2002	2003†	2004†
National defence	362,106	382,681	399,683
International affairs	25,144	20,511	23,791
General science, space research and technology	22,016	22,360	23,500
Energy	400	675	887
Natural resources and environment	31,126	29,357	30,400
Agriculture	23,821	20,050	21,139
Commerce and housing credit	11,298	8,542	9,575
Transportation	68,887	63,575	63,828
Community and regional development	23,061	15,377	13,616
Education, training, employment and social services	79,861	88,484	86,002
Health	206,080	228,644	247,281
Medicare	234,428	245,021	258,642
Income security	309,667	326,498	322,891
Social security	462,363	479,913	498,844
Veterans' benefits and services	52,095	57,724	61,556
Administration of justice	36,177	35,984	38,756
General government	18,384	18,292	20,190
Net interest	170,949	161,441	176,396
Allowances	—	−400	−288
Undistributed offsetting receipts	−47,806	−50,286	−53,668
Total	2,090,057	2,154,443	2,243,021

* Including social security receipts, which are extrabudgetary.
† Forecasts published in February 2002.
‡ Including social security and Postal Service outlays, which are extra-budgetary.

Source: Office of Management and Budget, Executive Office of the President.

STATE AND LOCAL GOVERNMENT FINANCES
($ million, year ending 30 June)

Revenue	1997/98	1998/99	1999/2000
From Federal Government	255,048	270,628	291,950
From State and Local Governments	1,465,841	1,523,929	n.a.
General Revenue from own sources	1,110,714	1,163,401	1,249,373
Taxes	773,963	815,341	872,351
Property	230,150	239,672	249,178
Sales and gross receipts	274,883	290,993	309,290
Individual income	175,630	189,309	211,661
Corporation income	34,412	33,922	36,059
Other	44,004	46,104	49,763
Charges and miscellaneous	336,751	348,060	377,022
Utility and liquor stores	81,127	86,125	89,546
Insurance Trust Revenue	274,001	273,968	311,460
Unemployment compensation	23,153	22,234	23,366
Employee retirement	237,472	236,527	273,881
Other	13,376	15,207	14,212
Total	1,720,889	1,794,557	1,942,328

Expenditure	1997/98	1998/99	1999/2000
General Expenditure	1,314,496	1,398,533	1,502,768
Education	450,365	483,259	521,612
Elementary and secondary .	318,065	339,871	365,181
Institutions of higher education	112,874	122,716	134,352
Other	19,426	20,672	22,080
Libraries	6,569	6,840	7,155
Public welfare	204,640	215,190	233,350
Hospitals	69,633	71,733	75,976
Health	44,391	47,628	51,366
Social insurance administration	4,133	4,130	4,178
Veterans' services	288	283	357
Highways	87,214	93,018	101,336
Other transportation . . .	14,612	17,145	17,638
General public building . .	7,626	8,853	9,319
Housing and community development	24,697	25,234	26,590
Police	50,475	53,367	56,798
Fire protection	20,269	21,262	23,102
Correction	42,479	45,598	48,805
Protective inspection . . .	7,958	8,516	9,104
Parks and recreation . . .	22,365	23,417	25,038
Sewerage and sanitation . .	25,647	26,980	28,052
Natural resources	17,492	18,232	20,235
General control	37,187	40,253	43,041
Financial administration . .	25,914	27,593	29,300
Interest on general debt . .	64,554	67,294	69,814
Other and unallocable . .	69,871	76,640	83,005
Utility and liquor stores. . .	102,865	108,398	114,916
Insurance Trust Expenditure . .	108,400	115,172	125,230
Unemployment compensation .	17,779	19,223	18,648
Employee retirement . . .	80,222	85,318	95,679
Other	10,399	10,631	10,902
Total *	1,529,308	1,625,939	1,746,943

* Including intergovernmental expenditure ($ million): 3,546 in 1997/98; 3,836 in 1998/99; 4,029 in 1999/2000.

Source: Governments Division, Bureau of the Census, US Department of Commerce, *Government Finances*.

INTERNATIONAL RESERVES
($ million at 31 December)

	2000	2001	2002
Gold*	11,045.7	11,045.0	11,043.0
IMF special drawing rights .	10,538.5	10,783.3	12,165.7
Reserve position in IMF. . .	14,823.6	17,869.4	21,978.7
Foreign exchange.	31,238.2	28,981.0	33,818.0
Total	67,646.1	68,678.7	79,005.3

* National valuation.

Source: IMF, *International Financial Statistics*.

CURRENCY AND COIN IN CIRCULATION*
($ million at 31 December)

	2000	2001	2002
Total	593,874	643,328	687,530

* Currency outside Treasury and Federal Reserve banks, including currency held by commercial banks.

Source: Financial Management Service, US Department of the Treasury.

COST OF LIVING
(Consumer Price Index for all urban consumers, average of monthly figures. Base: 1982–84 = 100, unless otherwise indicated)

	2000	2001	2002
Food and beverages	168.4	173.6	176.8
Housing	169.6	176.4	180.3
Shelter	193.4	200.6	208.1
Fuels and utilities	137.9	150.2	143.6
Household furnishings and operations	128.2	129.1	128.3
Clothing	129.6	127.3	124.0
Transport	153.3	154.3	152.9
Medical care	260.8	272.8	285.6
Recreation*	103.3	104.9	106.2
Education and communication*	102.5	105.2	107.9
Other goods and services . .	271.1	282.6	293.2
All items	172.2	177.1	179.9

* Base: December 1997 = 100.

Source: Bureau of Labor Statistics, US Department of Labor.

NATIONAL ACCOUNTS
($ '000 million at current prices)

National Income and Product
(provisional)

	1997	1998	1999
Compensation of employees. . .	4,656.2	4,994.6	5,315.8
Operating surplus	2,016.8	2,050.1	2,128.4
Domestic factor incomes. .	6,673.0	7,044.7	7,444.2
Consumption of fixed capital . .	951.5	1,010.7	1,089.7
Statistical discrepancy . . .	−18.8	−34.0	−39.7
Gross domestic product (GDP) at factor cost	7,605.7	8,021.4	8,494.2
Indirect taxes, *less* subsidies .	613.2	644.6	674.1
GDP in purchasers' values . .	8,218.9	8,666.0	9,168.3
Factor income received from abroad	281.3	286.1	313.8
Less Factor income paid abroad	274.2	289.6	320.5
Gross national product (GNP) .	8,226.0	8,662.5	9,161.6
Less Consumption of fixed capital	951.5	1,010.7	1,089.7
National income in market prices	7,274.5	7,651.8	8,071.9
Other current transfers received from abroad	12.3	15.6	15.5
Less Other current transfers paid abroad	53.4	60.6	65.3
National disposable income. .	7,233.4	7,606.8	8,022.1

Source: UN, *National Accounts Statistics*.

Expenditure on the Gross Domestic Product

	1999	2000	2001
Government final consumption expenditure*	1,641.0	1,751.0	1,858.0
Private final consumption expenditure.	6,246.5	6,683.8	6,987.0
Increase in stocks	59.5	63.6	−60.3
Gross fixed capital formation* . .	1,577.2	1,691.8	1,646.3
Total domestic expenditure. .	9,524.2	10,190.2	10,431.0
Exports of goods and services . .	989.3	1,101.1	1,034.1
Less Imports of goods and services	1,239.2	1,466.6	1,383.0
GDP in purchasers' values . .	9,274.3	9,824.6	10,082.2
GDP at constant 1996 prices .	8,859.0	9,191.4	9,214.5

* Government investment is included in final consumption expenditure and excluded from gross fixed capital formation.

Source: IMF, *International Financial Statistics*.

Gross Domestic Product by Economic Activity*

	1999	2000	2001
Agriculture, hunting, forestry and fishing	127.7	134.3	140.7
Mining and quarrying . . .	104.1	133.1	139.0
Manufacturing	1,481.3	1,520.3	1,423.0
Electricity, gas and water . . .	211.0	216.5	221.9
Construction	425.5	461.3	480.0
Trade, restaurants and hotels . .	1,557.0	1,671.5	1,700.9
Transport, storage and communications	559.1	592.8	597.6
Finance, insurance, real estate and business services	2,299.8	2,511.1	2,621.0
Government enterprises. . . .	127.8	135.5	141.5
Government services.	1,023.5	1,082.2	1,139.8
Other community, social and personal services	1,383.5	1,481.0	1,582.2
Private households	12.7	13.6	11.9
Sub-total	9,313.0	9,953.2	10,199.5
Statistical discrepancy†	−38.8	−128.5	−117.3
GDP in purchasers' values . .	9,274.3	9,824.6	10,082.2

* The distribution is based on the US Standard Industrial Classification, which differs from the ISIC. The contribution of the various industries excludes the activities of government enterprises, listed separately.
† Referring to an adjustment to the consumption of fixed capital.

Source: Bureau of Economic Analysis, US Department of Commerce.

BALANCE OF PAYMENTS
($ million)*

	1999	2000	2001
Exports of goods f.o.b.	686,280	774,640	721,750
Imports of goods f.o.b.	−1,029,980	−1,224,430	−1,145,980
Trade balance	−343,700	−449,790	−424,230
Exports of services	270,900	289,630	276,280
Imports of services	−189,470	−218,520	−210,340
Balance on goods and services.	−262,270	−378,680	−358,290
Other income received	290,560	353,030	283,760
Other income paid	−272,390	−331,220	−269,390
Balance on goods, services and income	−244,100	−356,870	−343,920
Current transfers received . . .	9,570	10,650	10,470
Current transfers paid	−58,330	−64,080	−59,940
Current balance	−292,860	−410,300	−294,450
Capital account (net)	−3,390	840	830
Direct investment abroad . . .	−188,910	−178,290	−127,840
Direct investment from abroad. .	289,440	307,740	130,800
Portfolio investment assets . . .	−128,440	−127,450	−94,660
Portfolio investment liabilities . .	285,590	419,900	426,060
Other investment assets . . .	−169,000	−300,400	−143,540
Other investment liabilities . .	167,430	288,360	195,970
Net errors and omissions . . .	31,410	−50	10,700
Overall balance	−8,730	300	4,930

* Figures are rounded to the nearest $10 million.

Source: IMF, *International Financial Statistics*.

FOREIGN AID
($ million, year ending 30 September)

	1998/99	1999/2000	2000/01
Multilateral assistance	1,588.3	1,298.6	1,329.9
Bilateral assistance	9,402.8	9,336.2	8,438.9
Military assistance	3,450.0	4,988.1	3,752.6

Source: US Agency for International Development.

External Trade

The customs territory of the USA includes Puerto Rico and the US Virgin Islands. Figures exclude trade with other US possessions.

PRINCIPAL COMMODITIES
(distribution by SITC, $ million)

Imports c.i.f.	1998	1999	2000
Food and live animals . . .	35,806.6	37,662.7	39,547.3
Mineral fuels, lubricants, etc.	62,224.1	79,347.8	139,705.8
Petroleum, petroleum products, etc.	53,696.5	69,779.8	122,908.9
Crude petroleum oils, etc. . .	40,734.1	53,425.2	93,939.3
Chemicals and related products	55,480.7	62,947.8	74,561.9
Basic manufactures	118,509.9	124,099.7	142,245.3
Machinery and transport equipment.	431,318.0	488,840.4	563,304.3
Power-generating machinery and equipment	28,516.3	32,021.8	34,369.4
General industrial machinery, equipment and parts	29,973.3	32,461.4	35,963.7
Office machines and automatic data-processing machines . .	78,070.5	86,033.0	94,193.5
Automatic data-processing machines and units. . . .	44,825.0	50,115.2	57,064.7
Parts and accessories for office machines, etc.	28,665.1	32,468.4	34,122.1
Telecommunications and sound equipment	43,118.9	51,941.1	71,769.0
Other electrical machinery, apparatus, etc..	81,340.1	90,952.4	17,552.6
Thermionic valves, tubes, etc.	34,718.7	38,866.2	49,581.3
Road vehicles (incl. air-cushion vehicles) and parts*	123,588.0	148,971.3	164,473.3
Passenger motor vehicles (excl. buses)	82,430.3	98,328.7	110,919.9
Miscellaneous manufactured articles.	168,880.2	184,729.8	210,503.1
Clothing and accessories (excl. footwear)	55,920.1	58,962.5	67,325.9
Total (incl. others)	944,350.1	1,059,220.1	1,258,080.3

* Excluding tyres, engines and electrical parts.

Exports f.o.b.	1998	1999	2000
Food and live animals	38,295.3	38,216.6	40,242.1
Crude materials (inedible) except fuels	26,235.9	24,162.4	29,014.5
Chemicals and related products	67,245.0	69,818.6	80,021.3
Basic manufactures	62,926.1	63,248.7	73,265.0
Machinery and transport equipment	357,786.5	368,881.4	382,362.5
Power-generating machinery and equipment	29,962.5	32,380.2	34,345.3
Machinery specialized for particular industries	27,604.1	25,323.4	31,400.8
General industrial machinery, equipment and parts	32,252.6	31,695.0	35,667.8
Office machines and automatic data-processing machines	47,759.3	48,603.9	57,361.1
Automatic data-processing machines and units	25,834.6	26,714.9	30,929.3
Parts and accessories for office machines, etc.	20,692.7	20,810.8	25,304.2
Telecommunications and sound equipment	25,977.9	27,709.4	27,898.0
Other electrical machinery, apparatus, etc.	76,702.9	88,436.4	90,299.5
Thermionic valves, tubes, etc.	40,156.0	49,350.9	47,761.9
Electronic microcircuits	32,828.1	41,156.7	77,360.0
Road vehicles (incl. air-cushion vehicles) and parts*	56,468.7	56,640.4	56,873.4
Parts and accessories for cars, buses, lorries, etc.*	28,324.9	29,397.9	30,499.8
Other transport equipment*	55,724.2	52,741.7	42,240.6
Aircraft (incl. spacecraft), associated equipment and parts*	52,366.7	49,610.7	39,918.3
Miscellaneous manufactured articles	77,738.6	80,166.4	86,191.3
Professional, scientific and controlling instruments, etc.	25,832.5	27,708.8	32,404.9
Total (incl. others)	680,434.7	692,783.9	743,404.0

* Excluding tyres, engines and electrical parts.

Source: UN, *International Trade Statistics Yearbook*.

PRINCIPAL TRADING PARTNERS
($ million)

Imports (customs value)	2000	2001	2002
Brazil	13,853	14,466	15,812
Canada	230,838	216,268	210,590
China, People's Repub.	100,018	102,278	125,168
France	29,800	30,408	28,408
Germany	58,512	59,077	62,480
Hong Kong	11,449	9,646	9,328
Israel	12,964	11,959	12,442
Italy	25,043	23,790	24,290
Japan	146,479	126,473	121,494
Korea, Repub.	40,308	35,181	35,575
Malaysia	25,568	22,340	24,010
Mexico	135,926	131,338	134,732
Philippines	13,935	11,325	10,985
Saudi Arabia	14,365	13,272	13,143
Singapore	19,178	15,000	14,793
Taiwan	40,503	33,375	32,199
Thailand	16,385	14,727	14,799
United Kingdom	43,345	41,369	40,870
Venezuela	18,623	15,251	15,109
Total (incl. others)	1,218,022	1,140,999	1,163,561

Exports f.a.s.	2000	2001	2002
Australia	12,482	10,931	13,084
Belgium-Luxembourg	13,926	13,502	13,343
Brazil	15,321	15,880	12,409
Canada	178,941	163,424	160,829
China, People's Repub.	16,185	19,182	22,053
France	20,362	19,865	19,019
Germany	29,448	29,995	26,628
Hong Kong	14,582	14,028	12,617
Israel	7,746	7,475	7,039
Italy	11,060	9,916	10,089
Japan	64,924	57,452	51,440
Korea, Repub.	27,830	22,181	22,596
Malaysia	10,938	9,358	10,348
Mexico	111,349	101,297	97,531
Netherlands	21,836	19,485	18,335
Philippines	8,799	7,660	7,270
Saudi Arabia	6,234	5,958	4,779
Singapore	17,806	17,652	16,221
Switzerland	9,954	9,807	7,782
Taiwan	24,406	18,122	18,394
United Kingdom	41,570	40,714	33,253
Total (incl. others)	781,918	729,100	693,302

Source: Foreign Trade Division, Bureau of the Census, US Department of Commerce.

Transport

RAILWAYS

	1998	1999	2000
Passenger-miles (million)	5,304	5,330	5,498
Freight revenue ($ million)*	32,247	32,680	n.a.
Passenger revenue ($ million)*	61	61	n.a.

* Excluding Amtrak.

Source: Bureau of Transportation Statistics, US Department of Transportation.

Passengers carried (million): 373 in 1996; 382 in 1997.

ROAD TRAFFIC
('000 motor vehicles registered at 31 December)

	1998	1999	2000
Passenger cars and vans	203,656	132,432*	133,621*
Buses and coaches	718	729	746
Lorries (Trucks)	7,244	83,148†	87,108†
Motorcycles	3,879	4,111	4,346

* Excludes vans.
† Includes vans.

Source: Federal Highway Administration, US Department of Transportation, *Highway Statistics 2000*.

INLAND WATERWAYS
(freight traffic in million ton-miles)

	1998	1999	2000
Coastal waterways	314,864	292,730	283,871
Lake waterways	61,654	57,045	57,879
Internal waterways	294,896	304,724	302,558
Local waterways	1,381	1,362	1,490
Total	672,795	655,861	645,799

Source: Maritime Administration, US Department of Transportation.

OCEAN SHIPPING
Sea-going Merchant Vessels

	2000	2001	2002
Number:			
combination passengers/cargo .	11	n.a.	n.a.
freighters	147	n.a.	n.a.
bulk carriers	14	15	17
tankers	154	142	130
Total	463	454	443
Capacity ('000 dwt):			
combination passengers/cargo .	99	n.a.	n.a.
freighters	4,292	n.a.	n.a.
bulk carriers	579	605	707
tankers	9,373	8,438	7,529
Total	16,747	15,769	14,968

Source: Maritime Administration, US Department of Transportation.

Vessels Entered and Cleared in Foreign Trade in all Ports

	1998	1999	2000
Entered:			
number	61,417	58,374	60,064
displacement ('000 net tons) . .	619,071	621,204	672,834
Cleared:			
number	60,711	56,599	57,864
displacement ('000 net tons) . .	630,816	618,990	670,855

Source: Maritime Administration, US Department of Transportation.

CIVIL AVIATION
Ceritificated Air Carriers
(traffic, million)

	2000	2001	2002
Passengers	689	640	944
Passenger-miles	725,095	677,988	992,849
Freight ton-miles.	30,221	44,399	54,302

Source: Bureau of Transportation Statistics, US Department of Transportation.

Tourism
FOREIGN VISITORS BY COUNTRY OF NATIONALITY
('000)

	1998	1999	2000
Canada	13,422	14,110	14,594
France	1,013	1,059	1,087
Germany	1,902	1,985	1,786
Japan	4,885	4,826	5,061
Mexico	9,276	9,915	10,322
United Kingdom	3,975	4,252	4,703
Total (incl. others)	46,396	48,491	50,891
Tourist receipts ($ million) . . .	71,286	74,881	85,153

Source: Tourism Industries, International Trade Administration, US Department of Commerce.

Tourism receipts ($ million): 71,286 in 1998; 74,881 in 1999; 85,153 in 2000 (Source:: World Tourism Organization).

Communications Media

	1999	2000	2001
Telephones ('000 main lines in use)	183,521	192,519	190,000
Mobile cellular telephones ('000 subscribers) . .	86,047	109,478	127,000
Personal computers ('000 in use)	141,000	161,000	178,000
Internet users ('000) . . .	74,100	95,354	142,823
Daily newspapers: number .	1,483	1,480	n.a.
Daily newspapers: circulation ('000)	55,979	55,773	n.a.

Radio receivers ('000 in use): 570,000 in 1996*.

Television receivers ('000 in use): 217,000 in 1996*.

Facsimile machines ('000 in use): 21,000 in 1997*.

Books published (titles): 64,711 in 1997†.

* Estimates.

† Figure covers only the commercial production of the book trade (other than pamphlets), excluding government publications, university theses and other non-trade book production.

Sources: International Telecommunication Union; UN, *Statistical Yearbook*.

Education

('000, academic year 2001/02, projections)

	Teachers*	Students
Public:		
elementary	1,899	33,587
secondary	1,220	13,626
higher†	721	11,775
Private:		
elementary	307	4,576‡
secondary	121	1,276
higher†	291	3,525

* Figures for teachers refer to 2000.

† Includes students in colleges, universities, and professional schools, and two-year colleges.

‡ Includes some pre-primary students.

Source: National Center for Education Statistics, US Department of Education.

Directory

The Constitution

Adopted 4 March 1789.

PREAMBLE

We, the people of the United States, in order to form a more perfect Union, establish justice, insure domestic tranquillity, provide for the common defence, promote the general welfare, and secure the blessings of liberty to ourselves and our posterity, do ordain and establish this Constitution for the United States of America.

ARTICLE I

Section 1

All legislative powers herein granted shall be vested in a Congress of the United States, which shall consist of a Senate and House of Representatives.

Section 2

1. The House of Representatives shall be composed of members chosen every second year by the people of the several States and the electors in each State shall have the qualifications requisite for electors of the most numerous branch of the State Legislature.

2. No person shall be a Representative who shall not have attained to the age of 25 years, and been seven years a citizen of the United States and who shall not, when elected, be an inhabitant of that State in which he shall be chosen.

3. Representatives and direct taxes shall be apportioned among the several States which may be included within this Union according to their respective numbers, which shall be determined by adding to the whole number of free persons, including those bound to service for a term of years, and excluding Indians not taxed, three-fifths of all other persons. The actual enumeration shall be made within three years after the first meeting of the Congress of the United States, and within every subsequent term of 10 years, in such manner as they shall by law direct. The number of Representatives shall not exceed one for every 30,000, but each State shall have at least one Representative; and until such enumeration shall be made, the State of New Hampshire shall be entitled to choose 3; Massachusetts 8; Rhode Island and Providence Plantations 1; Connecticut 5; New York 6; New Jersey 4; Pennsylvania 8; Delaware 1; Maryland 6; Virginia 10; North Carolina 5; South Carolina 5; and Georgia 3.*

4. When vacancies happen in the representation from any State, the Executive Authority thereof shall issue writs of election to fill such vacancies.

5. The House of Representatives shall choose their Speaker and other officers and shall have the sole power of impeachment.

*See Amendment XIV.

Section 3

1. The Senate of the United States shall be composed of two Senators from each State, chosen by the Legislature thereof, for six years; and each Senator shall have one vote.

2. Immediately after they shall be assembled in consequence of the first election, they shall be divided as equally as may be into three classes. The seats of the Senators of the first class shall be vacated at the expiration of the second year, of the second class at the expiration of the fourth year, and of the third class at the expiration of the sixth year, so that one-third may be chosen every second year, and if vacancies happen by resignation or otherwise, during the recess of the Legislature or of any State, the Executive therefore may make temporary appointment until the next meeting of the Legislature, which shall then fill such vacancies.

3. No person shall be a Senator who shall not have attained to the age of 30 years, and been nine years a citizen of the United States, and who shall not, when elected, be an inhabitant of that State for which he shall be chosen.

4. The Vice-President of the United States shall be President of the Senate, but shall have no vote unless they be equally divided.

5. The Senate shall choose their other officers, and also a President *pro tempore*, in the absence of the Vice-President, or when he shall exercise the office of the President of the United States.

6. The Senate shall have the sole power to try all impeachments. When sitting for that purpose, they shall be on oath or affirmation. When the President of the United States is tried, the Chief Justice shall preside; and no person shall be convicted without the concurrence of two-thirds of the members present.

7. Judgment of case of impeachment shall not extend further than to removal from office, and disqualification to hold and enjoy any office of honour, trust, or profit under the United States; but the party convicted shall nevertheless be liable and subject to indictment, trial, judgment, and punishment, according to law.

Section 4

1. The times, places and manner of holding elections for Senators and Representatives shall be prescribed in each State by the Legislature thereof; but the Congress may at any time by law make or alter such regulations, except as to places of choosing Senators.

2. The Congress shall assemble at least once in every year, and such meeting shall be on the first Monday in December, unless they shall by law appoint a different day.

Section 5

1. Each House shall be the judge of the elections, returns, and qualifications of its own members, and a majority of each shall constitute a quorum to do business; but a smaller number may adjourn from day to day, and may be authorized to compel the attendance of absent members in such manner and under such penalties as each House may provide.

2. Each House may determine the rules of its proceedings, punish its members for disorderly behaviour, and with the concurrence of two-thirds, expel a member.

3. Each House shall keep a journal of its proceedings, and from time to time publish the same, excepting such parts as may in their judgment require secrecy; and the yeas and nays of the members of either House on any question shall, at the desire of one-fifth of those present, be entered on the journal.

4. Neither House, during the session of Congress shall, without the consent of the other, adjourn for more than three days, nor to any other place than that in which the two Houses shall be sitting.

Section 6

1. The Senators and Representatives shall receive a compensation for their services to be ascertained by law, and paid out of the Treasury of the United States. They shall in all cases, except treason, felony, and breach of the peace, be privileged from arrest during their attendance at the session of their respective Houses, and in going to and returning from the same; and for any speech or debate in either House they shall not be questioned in any other place.

2. No Senator or Representative shall, during the time for which he was elected, be appointed to any civil office under the authority of the United States which shall have been created, or the emoluments whereof shall have been increased during such time; and no person holding any office under the United States shall be a member of either House during his continuance in office.

Section 7

1. All bills for raising revenue shall originate in the House of Representatives, but the Senate may propose or concur with amendments, as on other bills.

2. Every bill which shall have passed the House of Representatives and the Senate shall, before it becomes a law, be presented to the President of the United States; if he approve, he shall sign it, but if not he shall return it, with his objections to that House in which it shall have originated, who shall enter the objections at large on their journal and proceed to reconsider it. If after such reconsideration two-thirds of that House shall agree to pass the bill, it shall be sent, together with the objections, to the other House, by which it shall likewise be reconsidered; and if approved by two-thirds of that House it shall become a law. But in such cases the votes of both Houses shall be determined by yeas and nays, and the names of the persons voting for and against the bill be entered on the journal of each House respectively. If any bill shall not be returned by the President within 10 days (Sundays excepted) after it shall have been presented to him the same shall be a law in like manner as if he had signed it, unless the Congress by their adjournment prevent its return; in which case it shall not be a law.

3. Every order, resolution, or vote to which the concurrence of the Senate and House of Representatives may be necessary (except on a question of adjournment) shall be presented to the President of the United States, and before the same shall take effect shall be approved by him, or being disapproved by him shall be repassed by two-thirds of the Senate and the House of Representatives, according to the rules and limitations prescribed in the case of a bill.

Section 8

1. The Congress shall have power

To lay and collect taxes, duties, imposts, and excises, to pay the debts and provide for the common defence and general welfare of the

United States; but all duties, imposts, and excises shall be uniform throughout the United States.

2. To borrow money on the credit of the United States.

3. To regulate commerce with foreign nations; and among the several States and with the Indian tribes.

4. To establish a uniform rule of naturalization and uniform laws on the subject of bankruptcies throughout the United States.

5. To coin money, regulate the value thereof, and of foreign coin, and fix the standard of weights and measures.

6. To provide for the punishment of counterfeiting the securities and current coin of the United States.

7. To establish post-offices and post-roads.

8. To promote the progress of science and useful arts by securing for limited times to authors and inventors the exclusive rights to their respective writings and discoveries.

9. To constitute tribunals inferior to the Supreme Court.

10. To define and punish piracies and felonies committed on the high seas, and offences against the law of nations.

11. To declare war, grant letters of marque and reprisal, and make rules concerning captures on land and water.

12. To raise and support armies, but no appropriation of money to that use shall be for a longer term than two years.

13. To provide and maintain a navy.

14. To make rules for the government and regulation of the land and naval forces.

15. To provide for calling forth the militia to execute the laws of the Union, suppress insurrections, and repel invasions.

16. To provide for organizing, arming and disciplining the militia, and for governing such part of them as may be employed in the service of the United States, reserving to the States respectively the appointment of the officers, and the authority of training the militia according to the discipline prescribed by Congress.

17. To exercise exclusive legislation in all cases whatsoever over such district (not exceeding 10 miles square) as may, by cession of particular States and the acceptance of Congress, become the seat of Government of the United States and to exercise like authority over all places purchased by the consent of the Legislature of the State in which the same shall be, for the erection of forts, magazines, arsenals, dry-docks, and other needful buildings.

18. To make all laws which shall be necessary and proper for carrying into execution the foregoing powers and all other powers vested by this Constitution in the Government of the United States, or in any department or officer thereof.

Section 9

1. The migration or importation of such persons as any of the States now existing shall think proper to admit shall not be prohibited by the Congress prior to the year 1808, but a tax or duty may be imposed on such importations, not exceeding 10 dollars for each person.

2. The privilege of the writ of habeas corpus shall not be suspended, unless when in cases of rebellion or invasion the public safety may require it.

3. No bill or attainder or *ex post facto* law shall be passed.

4. No capitation or other direct tax shall be laid, unless in proportion to the census or enumeration hereinbefore directed to be taken.

5. No tax or duty shall be laid on articles exported from any State.

6. No preference shall be given by any regulation of commerce or revenue to the ports of one State over those of another, nor shall vessels bound to or from one State be obliged to enter, clear, or pay duties to another.

7. No money shall be drawn from the Treasury but in consequence of appropriations made by law; and a regular statement and account of the receipts and expenditures of all public money shall be published from time to time.

8. No title of nobility shall be granted by the United States. And no person holding any office of profit or trust under them shall, without the consent of the Congress, accept of any present, emolument, office, or title of any kind whatever from any king, prince, or foreign state.

Section 10

1. No State shall enter into any treaty, alliance or confederation, grant letters of marque and reprisal, coin money, emit bills of credit, make anything but gold and silver coin a tender in payment of debts, pass any bill of attainder, *ex post facto* law, or law impairing the obligation of contracts, or grant any title of nobility.

2. No State shall, without the consent of the Congress, lay any impost or duties on imports or exports, except what may be absolutely necessary for executing its inspection laws, and the net produce of all duties and imposts, laid by any State on imports or exports, shall be for the use of the Treasury of the United States; and all such laws shall be subject to the revision and control of the Congress.

3. No State shall, without the consent of Congress, lay any duty of tonnage, keep troops or ships of war in time of peace, enter into agreement or compact with another State, or with a foreign power, or engage in war, unless actually invaded, or in such imminent danger as will not admit of delay.

ARTICLE II

Section 1

1. The Executive power shall be vested in a President of the United States of America. He shall hold his office during the term of four years, and, together with the Vice-President chosen for the same term, be elected as follows

2. Each State shall appoint, in such manner as the Legislature thereof may direct, a number of electors equal to the whole number of Senators and Representatives to which the State may be entitled in the Congress; but no Senator or Representative or person holding an office of trust or profit under the United States shall be appointed an elector.

3. The electors shall meet in their respective States and vote by ballot for two persons, of whom one at least shall not be an inhabitant of the same State with themselves. And they shall make a list of all the persons voted for, and of the number of votes for each, which list they shall sign and certify and transmit, sealed, to the seat of the Government of the United States, directed to the President of the Senate. The President of the Senate shall, in the presence of the Senate and House of Representatives, open all the certificates, and the votes shall then be counted. The person having the greatest number of votes shall be the President, if such number be a majority of the whole number of electors appointed, and if there be more than one who have such a majority, and have an equal number of votes, then the House of Representatives shall immediately choose by ballot one of them for President; and if no person have a majority, then from the five highest on the list the said House shall in like manner choose the President. But in choosing the President, the vote shall be taken by States, the representation from each State having one vote. A quorum, for this purpose, shall consist of a member or members from two-thirds of the States, and a majority of all the States shall be necessary to a choice. In every case, after the choice of the President, the person having the greatest number of votes of the electors shall be the Vice-President. But if there should remain two or more who have equal votes, the Senate shall choose from them by ballot the Vice-President.*

4. The Congress may determine the time of choosing the electors and the day on which they shall give their votes, which day shall be the same throughout the United States.

5. No person except a natural born citizen, or a citizen of the United States, at the time of the adoption of the Constitution, shall be eligible to the office of President; neither shall any person be eligible to that office who shall not have attained to the age of 35 years and been 14 years a resident within the United States.

6. In case of the removal of the President from office, or of his death, resignation, or inability to discharge the powers and duties of the said office, the same shall devolve on the Vice-President, and the Congress may by law provide for the case of removal, death, resignation, or inability, both of the President and Vice-President, declaring what officer shall then act as President, and such officer shall act accordingly until the disability be removed or a President shall be elected.†

7. The President shall, at stated times, receive for his services a compensation which shall neither be increased nor diminished during the period for which he shall have been elected, and he shall not receive within that period any other emolument from the United States, or any of them.

8. Before he enter on the execution of his office he shall take the following oath or affirmation:

'I do solemnly swear (or affirm) that I will faithfully execute the office of President of the United States, and will, to the best of my ability, preserve, protect, and defend the Constitution of the United States.'

* This clause is superseded by Amendment XII.
† This clause is amended by Amendments XX and XXV.

Section 2

1. The President shall be Commander-in-Chief of the Army and Navy of the United States, and of the militia of the several States when called into the actual service of the United States; he may require the opinion, in writing, of the principal officer in each of the executive departments upon any subject relating to the duties of their respective offices, and he shall have the power to grant reprieves and pardons for offences against the United States except in cases of impeachment.

2. He shall have power by and with the advice and consent of the Senate to make treaties, provided two-thirds of the Senators present concur; and he shall nominate and by and with the advice and consent of the Senate shall appoint ambassadors, other public ministers and consuls, judges of the Supreme Court, and all other officers of the United States whose appointments are not herein

otherwise provided for, and which shall be established by law; but the Congress may by law vest the appointment of such inferior officers as they think proper in the President alone, in the courts of law, or in the heads of departments.

3. The President shall have power to fill up all vacancies that may happen during the recess of the Senate by granting commissions, which shall expire at the end of their next session.

Section 3

He shall from time to time give to the Congress information of the state of the Union, and recommend to their consideration such measures as he shall judge necessary and expedient; he may, on extraordinary occasions, convene both Houses, or either of them, and in case of disagreement between them with respect to the time of adjournment, he may adjourn them to such time as he shall think proper; he shall receive ambassadors and other public ministers; he shall take care that the laws be faithfully executed, and shall commission all the officers of the United States.

Section 4

The President, Vice-President, and all civil officers of the United States shall be removed from office on impeachment for conviction of treason, bribery or other high crimes and misdemeanours.

ARTICLE III

Section 1

The judicial power of the United States shall be vested in one Supreme Court, and in such inferior courts as the Congress may from time to time ordain and establish. The judges, both of the Supreme and inferior courts, shall hold their offices during good behaviour, and shall at stated times receive for their services a compensation which shall not be diminished during their continuance in office.

Section 2

1. The judicial power shall extend to all cases in law and equity arising under this Constitution, the laws of the United States, and treaties made, or which shall be made, under their authority; to all cases affecting ambassadors, other public ministers and consuls; to all cases of admiralty and maritime jurisdiction; to controversies to which the United States shall be a party; to controversies between two or more States, between a State and citizens of another State, between citizens of different States, between citizens of the same State claiming lands under grants of different States, and between a State, or the citizens thereof, and foreign States, citizens, or subjects.

2. In all cases affecting ambassadors, other public ministers, and consuls, and those in which a State shall be party, the Supreme Court shall have original jurisdiction. In all the other cases before mentioned the Supreme Court shall have appellate jurisdiction both as to law and fact, with such exceptions and under such regulations as the Congress shall make.

3. The trial of all crimes, except in cases of impeachment, shall be by jury, and such trials shall be held in the State where the said crimes shall have been committed; but when not committed within any State the trial shall be at such place or places as the Congress may by law have directed.

Section 3

1. Treason against the United States shall consist only in levying war against them, or in adhering to their enemies, giving them aid and comfort. No person shall be convicted of treason unless on the testimony of two witnesses to the same overt act, or on confession in open court.

2. The Congress shall have power to declare the punishment of treason, but no attainder of treason shall work corruption of blood, or forfeiture except during the life of the person attained.

ARTICLE IV

Section 1

Full faith and credit shall be given in each State to the public acts, records, and judicial proceedings of every other State. And the Congress may by general laws prescribe the manner in which such acts, records, and proceedings shall be proved, and the effect thereof.

Section 2

1. The citizens of each State shall be entitled to all privileges and immunities of citizens in the several States.

2. A person charged in any State with treason, felony, or other crime, who shall flee from justice, and be found in another State, shall, on demand of the Executive authority of the State from which he fled, be delivered up, to be removed to the State having jurisdiction of the crime.

3. No person held to service or labour in one State, under the laws thereof, escaping into another shall in consequence of any law or regulation therein, be discharged from such service or labour, but shall be delivered up on claim of the party to whom such service or labour may be due.

Section 3

1. New States may be admitted by the Congress into this Union; but no new State shall be formed or erected within the jurisdiction of any other State, nor any State be formed by the junction of two or more States, or parts of States, without the consent of the Legislatures of the States concerned, as well as of the Congress.

2. The Congress shall have the power to dispose of and make all needful rules and regulations respecting the territory or other property belonging to the United States; and nothing in this Constitution shall be so construed as to prejudice any claims of the United States, or of any particular State.

Section 4

The United States shall guarantee to every State in this Union a Republican form of government, and shall protect each of them against invasion, and on application of the Legislature, or of the Executive (when the Legislature cannot be convened) against domestic violence.

ARTICLE V

The Congress, whenever two-thirds of both Houses shall deem it necessary, shall propose amendments to this Constitution, or, on the application of the Legislature of two-thirds of the several States, shall call a convention for proposing amendments, which in either case, shall be valid to all intents and purposes, as part of this Constitution, when ratified by the Legislature of three-fourths of the several States, or by conventions in three-fourths thereof, as the one or the other mode of ratification may be proposed by the Congress, provided that no amendment which may be made prior to the year 1808 shall in any manner affect the first and fourth clauses in the Ninth Section of the First Article; and that no State, without its consent, shall be deprived of its equal suffrage in the Senate.

ARTICLE VI

1. All debts contracted and engagements entered into before the adoption of this Constitution shall be as valid against the United States under this Constitution as under the Confederation.

2. This Constitution and the laws of the United States which shall be made in pursuance thereof and all treaties made, or which shall be made, under the authority of the United States, shall be the supreme law of the land, and the judges in every State shall be bound thereby, anything in the Constitution or laws of any State to the contrary notwithstanding.

3. The Senators and Representatives before mentioned, and the members of the several State Legislatures, and all executives and judicial officers, both of the United States and of the several States, shall be bound by oath or affirmation to support this Constitution; but no religious test shall ever be required as a qualification to any office or public trust under the United States.

ARTICLE VII

The ratification of the Conventions of nine States shall be sufficient for the establishment of this Constitution between the States so ratifying the same.

Amendments to the Constitution

Ten Original Amendments, in force 15 December 1791:

AMENDMENT I

Congress shall make no law respecting an establishment of religion, or prohibiting the free exercise thereof; or abridging the freedom of speech or of the Press; or the right of the people peaceably to assemble and to petition the Government for a redress of grievances.

AMENDMENT II

A well-regulated militia being necessary to the security of a free State, the right of the people to keep and bear arms shall not be infringed.

AMENDMENT III

No soldier shall, in time of peace, be quartered in any house without the consent of the owner, nor in time of war but in a manner to be prescribed by law.

AMENDMENT IV

The right of the people to be secure in their persons, houses, papers, and effects, against unreasonable searches and seizures, shall not be violated, and no warrants shall issue but upon probable cause, supported by oath or affirmation, and particularly describing the place to be searched, and the persons or things to be seized.

AMENDMENT V

No person shall be held to answer for a capital or other infamous crime unless on a presentment or indictment of a Grand Jury, except in cases arising in the land or naval forces, or in the militia, when in actual service, in time of war or public danger; nor shall any person be subject for the same offense to be twice put in jeopardy of life or limb; nor shall be compelled in any criminal case to be a witness against himself, nor be deprived of life, liberty, or property, without due process of law; nor shall private property be taken for public use without just compensation.

AMENDMENT VI

In all criminal prosecutions, the accused shall enjoy the right to a speedy and public trial, by an impartial jury of the State and district wherein the crime shall have been committed, which districts shall have been previously ascertained by law, and to be informed of the nature and cause of the accusation; to be confronted with the witnesses against him; to have compulsory process for obtaining witnesses in his favour, and to have the assistance of counsel for his defense.

AMENDMENT VII

In suits at common law, where the value in controversy shall exceed 20 dollars, the right of trial by jury shall be preserved, and no fact tried by a jury shall be otherwise re-examined in any court of the United States than according to the rules of the common law.

AMENDMENT VIII

Excessive bail shall not be required, nor excessive fines imposed, nor cruel and unusual punishments inflicted.

AMENDMENT IX

The enumeration in the Constitution of certain rights shall not be construed to deny or disparage others retained by the people.

AMENDMENT X

The powers not delegated to the United States by the Constitution, nor prohibited by it to the States, are reserved to the States respectively, or to the people.
  Subsequent Amendments:

AMENDMENT XI
(became part of the Constitution February 1795)

The judicial power of the United States shall not be construed to extend to any suit in law or equity, commenced or prosecuted against one of the United States, by citizens of another State, or by citizens or subjects of any foreign State.

AMENDMENT XII
(ratified June 1804)

The Electors shall meet in their respective States, and vote by ballot for President and Vice-President, one of whom at least shall not be an inhabitant of the same State with themselves; they shall name in their ballots the person voted for as President, and in distinct ballots the person voted for as Vice-President; and they shall make distinct list of all persons voted for as President, and of all persons voted for as Vice-President, and of the number of votes for each, which list they shall sign and certify, and transmit, sealed, to the seat of the Government of the United States, directed to the President of the Senate; the President of the Senate shall, in the presence of the Senate and House of Representatives, open all the certificates and the votes shall then be counted; the person having the greatest number of votes for President shall be the President, if such number be a majority of the whole number of Electors appointed; and if no person have such majority, then from the persons having the highest number, not exceeding three, on the list of those voted for as President, the House of Representatives shall choose immediately, by ballot, the President. But in choosing the President, the votes shall be taken by States, the representation from each State having one vote; a quorum for this purpose shall consist of a member or members from two-thirds of the States, and a majority of all the States shall be necessary to a choice. And if the House of Representatives shall not choose a President, whenever the right of choice shall devolve upon them, before the fourth day of March next following, then the Vice-President shall act as President, as in the case of the death or other constitutional disability of the President. The person having the greatest number of votes as Vice-President

shall be the Vice-President if such number be a majority of the whole number of Electors appointed, and if no person have a majority, then, from the two highest numbers on the list the Senate shall choose the Vice-President; a quorum for the purpose shall consist of two-thirds of the whole number of Senators, and a majority of the whole number shall be necessary to a choice. But no person constitutionally ineligible to the office of President shall be eligible to that of Vice-President of the United States.

AMENDMENT XIII
(ratified December 1865)

1. Neither slavery nor involuntary servitude, except as a punishment for crime whereof the party shall have been duly convicted, shall exist within the United States, or any place subject to their jurisdiction.
2. Congress shall have the power to enforce this article by appropriate legislation.

AMENDMENT XIV
(ratified July 1868)

1. All persons born or naturalized in the United States, and subject to the jurisdiction thereof, are citizens of the United States and of the State wherein they reside. No State shall make or enforce any law which shall abridge the privileges or immunities of citizens of the United States, nor shall any State deprive any person of life, liberty, or property without due process of law, nor deny to any person within its jurisdiction the equal protection of the laws.
2. Representatives shall be apportioned among the several States according to their respective numbers, counting the whole number of persons in each State excluding Indians not taxed. But when the right to vote at any election for the choice of Electors for President and Vice-President of the United States, Representatives in Congress, the executive and judicial officers of a State, or the members of the Legislature thereof, is denied to any of the male inhabitants of such State, being 21 years of age, and citizens of the United States, or in any way abridged, except for participation in rebellion, or other crime, the basis of representation therein shall be reduced in the proportion which the number of such male citizens shall bear to the whole number of male citizens 21 years of age in such State.
3. No person shall be a Senator or Representative in Congress, or Elector of President and Vice-President or hold any office, civil or military, under the United States, or under any State, who, having previously taken an oath as member of Congress or as an officer of the United States, or as a member of any State Legislature, or as an executive or judicial officer of any State, to support the Constitution of the United States, shall have engaged in insurrection or rebellion against the same, or given aid and comfort to the enemies thereof. But Congress may, by vote of two-thirds of each House, remove such disability.
4. The validity of the public debt of the United States, authorized by law, including debts incurred for payment of pensions and bounties for services in suppressing insurrection and rebellion, shall not be questioned. But neither the United States nor any State shall assume or pay any debt or obligation incurred in aid of insurrection or rebellion against the United States, or any claim for the loss or emancipation of any slave; but all such debts, obligations, and claims shall be held illegal and void.
5. The Congress shall have power to enforce by appropriate legislation the provisions of this article.

AMENDMENT XV
(ratified March 1870)

1. The right of the citizens of the United States to vote shall not be denied or abridged by the United States or by any State on account of race, colour, or previous condition of servitude.
2. The Congress shall have power to enforce the provisions of this article by appropriate legislation.

AMENDMENT XVI
(ratified February 1913)

The Congress shall have power to lay and collect taxes on incomes, from whatever sources derived, without apportionment among the several States, and without regard to any census or enumeration.

AMENDMENT XVII
(ratified May 1913)

1. The Senate of the United States shall be composed of two Senators from each State, elected by the people thereof, for six years; and each Senator shall have one vote. The electors in each State shall have the qualifications requisite for electors of the most numerous branch of the State Legislature.
2. When vacancies happen in the representation of any State in the Senate, the executive authority of such State shall issue writs of election to fill such vacancies: Provided that the Legislature of any State may empower the Executive thereof to make temporary

appointment until the people fill the vacancies by election as the Legislature may direct.

3. This amendment shall not be so construed as to affect the election or term of any Senator chosen before it becomes valid as part of the Constitution.

AMENDMENT XVIII
(ratified January 1919*)

1. After one year from the ratification of this article the manufacture, sale, or transportation of intoxicating liquors within, the importation thereof into, or the exportation thereof from the United States, and all territory subject to the jurisdiction thereof for beverage purposes is hereby prohibited.

2. The Congress and the several States shall have concurrent power to enforce this article by appropriate legislation.

3. This article shall be inoperative unless it shall have been ratified as an amendment to the Constitution by the Legislatures of the several States, as provided in the Constitution, within seven years from the date of the submission hereof to the States by the Congress.

* Repealed by Amendment XXI.

AMENDMENT XIX
(ratified August 1920)

1. The right of citizens of the United States to vote shall not be denied or abridged by the United States or by any State on account of sex.

2. Congress shall have power, by appropriate legislation to enforce the provisions of this article.

AMENDMENT XX
(ratified January 1933)

Section 1

The terms of the President and Vice-President shall end at noon on the 20th day of January, and the terms of Senators and Representatives at noon on the third day of January, of the years in which such terms would have ended if this article had not been ratified; and the terms of their successors shall then begin.

Section 2

The Congress shall assemble at least once in every year, and such meetings shall begin at noon on the third day of January, unless they shall by law appoint a different day.

Section 3

If, at the time fixed for the beginning of the term of the President, the President elect shall have died, the Vice-President elect shall become President. If a President shall not have been chosen before the time fixed for the beginning of his term, or if the President elect shall have failed to qualify, then the Vice-President elect shall act as President until a President shall have qualified; and the Congress may by law provide for the case wherein neither a President elect nor a Vice-President elect shall have qualified, declaring who shall then act as President, or the manner in which one who is to act shall be selected, and such person shall act accordingly until a President or Vice-President shall have qualified.

Section 4

The Congress may by law provide for the case of the death of any of the persons from whom the House of Representatives may choose a President whenever the right of choice shall have devolved upon them, and for the case of the death of any of the persons from whom the Senate may choose a Vice-President whenever the right of choice shall have devolved upon them.

Section 5

Sections 1 and 2 shall take effect on the 15th day of October following the ratification of this article.

Section 6

This article shall be inoperative unless it shall have been ratified as an amendment to the Constitution by the legislature of three-fourths of the several States within seven years from the date of its submission.

AMENDMENT XXI
(ratified December 1933)

Section 1

The 18th article of amendment to the Constitution of the United States is hereby repealed.

Section 2

The transportation or importation into any State, Territory or Possession of the United States for delivery or use therein of intoxicating liquors, in violation of the laws thereof, is hereby prohibited.

Section 3

This article shall be inoperative unless it shall have been ratified as an amendment to the Constitution by conventions in the several States, as provided in the Constitution, within seven years from the date of the submission hereof to the States by the Congress.

AMENDMENT XXII
(ratified February 1951)

No person shall be elected to the office of President more than twice, and no person who has held the office of President, or acted as President, for more than two years of a term to which some other person was elected President shall be elected to the office of President more than once. But this article shall not apply to any person holding the office of President when this Article was proposed by Congress, and shall not prevent any person who may be holding the office of President, or acting as President, during the term within which this Article becomes operative from holding the office of President or acting as President during the remainder of such term.

AMENDMENT XXIII
(ratified March 1961)

Section 1

The District constituting the seat of Government of the United States shall appoint in such manner as the Congress may direct:

A number of electors of President and Vice-President equal to the whole number of Senators and Representatives in Congress to which the District would be entitled if it were a State, but in no event more than the least populous State; they shall be in addition to those appointed by the States, but they shall be considered, for the purposes of the election of President and Vice-President, to be electors appointed by a State; and they shall meet in the District and perform such duties as provided by the 12th article of amendment.

Section 2

The Congress shall have power to enforce this article by appropriate legislation.

AMENDMENT XXIV
(ratified January 1964)

Section 1

The right of citizens of the United States to vote in any primary or other election for President or Vice-President, for electors for President or Vice-President, or for Senator or Representative in Congress, shall not be denied or abridged by the United States or any State by reason of failure to pay any poll tax or other tax.

Section 2

The Congress shall have power to enforce this article by appropriate legislation.

AMENDMENT XXV
(ratified February 1967)

Section 1

In the case of the removal of the President from office or of his death or resignation, the Vice-President shall become President.

Section 2

Whenever there is a vacancy in the office of the Vice-President, the President shall nominate a Vice-President who shall take office upon confirmation by a majority vote of both Houses of Congress.

Section 3

Whenever the President transmits to the President *pro tempore* of the Senate and the Speaker of the House of Representatives his written declaration that he is unable to discharge the powers and duties of his office, and until he transmits to them a written declaration to the contrary, such powers and duties shall be discharged by the Vice-President as Acting President.

Section 4

Whenever the Vice-President and a majority of either the principal officers of the executive departments or of such other body as Congress may by law provide, transmit to the President *pro tempore* of the Senate and the Speaker of the House of Representatives their written declaration that the President is unable to discharge the powers and duties of his office, the Vice-President shall immediately assume the powers and duties of the office as Acting President.

Thereafter, when the President transmits to the President *pro tempore* of the Senate and the Speaker of the House of Representatives his written declaration that no inability exists, he shall resume the powers and duties of his office unless the Vice-President and a majority of either the principal officers of the executive department or of such other body as Congress may by law provide, transmit within four days to the President *pro tempore* of the Senate and the Speaker of the House of Representatives their written declaration that the President is unable to discharge the powers and duties of his office. Thereupon Congress shall decide the issue, assembling within 48 hours for that purpose if not in session. If the Congress, within 21 days after receipt of the latter written declaration, or, if Congress is not in session, within 21 days after Congress is required to assemble, determines by two-thirds vote of both Houses that the President is unable to discharge the powers and duties of his office, the Vice-President shall continue to discharge the same as Acting President; otherwise, the President shall resume the powers and duties of his office.

AMENDMENT XXVI
(ratified July 1971)

Section 1
The right of citizens of the United States, who are 18 years of age or older, to vote shall not be denied or abridged by the United States or by any State on account of age.

Section 2
The Congress shall have power to enforce this article by appropriate legislation.

AMENDMENT XXVII
(ratified May 1992)
No law, varying the compensation for the services of the Senators and Representatives, shall take effect, until an election of Representatives shall have intervened.

By Article IV, Section 3 of the Constitution, implemented by vote of Congress and referendum in the territory concerned, Alaska was admitted into the United States on 3 January 1959, and Hawaii on 21 August 1959.

The Executive

HEAD OF STATE

President: GEORGE W. BUSH (took office 20 January 2001).
Vice-President: RICHARD B. CHENEY.

THE CABINET
(April 2003)

Secretary of State: COLIN POWELL.
Secretary of the Treasury: JOHN SNOW.
Secretary of Defense: DONALD RUMSFELD.
Attorney-General: JOHN ASHCROFT.
Secretary of the Interior: GALE NORTON.
Secretary of Agriculture: ANN VENEMAN.
Secretary of Commerce: DON EVANS.
Secretary of Labor: ELAINE CHAO.
Secretary of Health and Human Services: TOMMY THOMPSON.
Secretary of Homeland Security: THOMAS J. RIDGE.
Secretary of Housing and Urban Development: MEL MARTINEZ.
Secretary of Transportation: NORMAN MINETA.
Secretary of Energy: SPENCER ABRAHAM.
Secretary of Education: ROD PAIGE.
Secretary of Veterans Affairs: ANTHONY PRINCIPI.

Officials with Cabinet Rank

Vice-President: RICHARD B. CHENEY.
Chief of Staff to the President: ANDREW H. CARD, Jr.
Director of the Office of Management and Budget: MITCHELL E. DANIELS.
US Trade Representative: ROBERT B. ZOELLICK.
Administrator of the Environmental Protection Agency: (vacant).
Director of the Office of National Drug Control Policy: JOHN WALTERS.

GOVERNMENT DEPARTMENTS

Department of Agriculture: 1400 Independence Ave, SW, Washington, DC 20250; tel. (202) 720-2791; internet www.usda.gov; f. 1889.

Department of Commerce: 14th St and Constitution Ave, NW, Washington, DC 20230-0001; tel. (202) 219-3605; fax (202) 219-4247; internet www.doc.gov; f. 1913.

Department of Defense: The Pentagon, Washington, DC 20301; tel. (703) 697-5737; fax (703) 695-1149; internet www.defenselink.mil; f. 1947.

Department of Education: 400 Maryland Ave, SW, Washington, DC 20202; tel. (202) 401-2000; fax (202) 401-0596; internet www.ed.gov; f. 1979.

Department of Energy: Forrestal Bldg, 1000 Independence Ave, SW, Washington, DC 20585; tel. (202) 586-5000; internet www.energy.gov; f. 1977.

Department of Health and Human Services: 200 Independence Ave, SW, Washington, DC 20201; tel. (202) 690-6343; internet www.os.dhhs.gov; f. 1980.

Department of Homeland Security: 1600 Pennsylvania Ave, NW, Washington, DC 20500; tel. (202) 456-1700; internet www.whitehouse.gov/homeland/.

Department of Housing and Urban Development: 451 Seventh St, SW, Washington, DC 20410; tel. (202) 708-0980; fax (202) 708-0299; internet www.hud.gov; f. 1965.

Department of the Interior: 1849 C St, NW, Washington, DC 20240; tel. (202) 208-3171; fax (202) 208-5048; internet www..doi.gov; f. 1849.

Department of Justice: 10th St and Constitution Ave, NW, Washington, DC 20530; tel. (202) 514-2007; fax (202) 514-4371; internet www.usdoj.gov; f. 1870.

Department of Labor: 200 Constitution Ave, NW, Washington, DC 20210; tel. (202) 219-5000; fax (202) 219-7312; internet www.dol.gov; f. 1913.

Department of State: 2201 C St, NW, Washington, DC 20520; tel. (202) 647-6575; fax (202) 647-6738; internet www.state.gov/index.html; f. 1789.

Department of Transportation: 400 Seventh St, SW, Washington, DC 20590; tel. (202) 366-5580; fax (202) 366-7202; internet www.dot.gov; 4508; f. 1967.

Department of the Treasury: 1500 Pennsylvania Ave, NW, Washington, DC 20220; tel. (202) 622-2970; fax (202) 622-0073; internet www.ustreas.gov; f. 1789.

Department of Veterans Affairs: 810 Vermont Ave, NW, Washington, DC 20420; tel. (202) 273-5700; internet www.va.gov; f. 1989.

EXECUTIVE OFFICE OF THE PRESIDENT

The White House Office: 1600 Pennsylvania Ave, NW, Washington, DC 20500; tel. (202) 456-1414; fax (202) 456-2461; e-mail president@whitehouse.gov; internet www.whitehouse.gov; co-ordinates activities relating to the President's immediate office; Chief of Staff to the Pres. ANDREW H. CARD, Jr.

Central Intelligence Agency: Washington, DC 20505; tel. (703) 482-7677; internet www.cia.gov; f. 1947; Dir GEORGE J. TENET.

Council of Economic Advisers: Eisenhower Executive Office Bldg, 17th St and Pennsylvania Ave, NW, Washington, DC 20502; tel. (202) 395-5042; fax (202) 395-6958; internet www.whitehouse.gov/cea; Chair. GLENN HUBBARD.

Council on Environmental Quality: 722 Jackson Pl., Washington, DC 20503; tel. (202) 395-5750; fax (202) 456-6546; internet www.whitehouse.gov/ceq/; Chair. JAMES LAURENCE CONNAUGHTON.

National Security Council: Eisenhower Executive Office Bldg, 17th St and Pennsylvania Ave, NW, Washington, DC 20504; tel. (202) 456-9371; internet www.whitehouse.gov/nsc; Asst to the Pres. for Nat. Security Affairs CONDOLEEZZA RICE.

Office of Administration: Eisenhower Executive Office Bldg, 17th St and Pennsylvania Ave, NW, Washington, DC 20503; tel. (202) 395-7235; fax (202) 456-6512; internet www.whitehouse.gov/oa; Dir MICHAEL J. LYLE.

Office of Management and Budget: Eisenhower Executive Office Bldg, 17th St and Pennsylvania Ave, NW Washington, DC 20503; tel. (202) 395-3000; fax (202) 395-3888; internet www.whitehouse.gov/omb; Dir MITCHELL E. DANIELS.

Office of National Drug Control Policy: 750 17th St, NW, Washington, DC 20006; tel. (202) 395-6700; fax (202) 395-6708; internet www.whitehousedrugpolicy.gov/; Dir JOHN WALTERS.

Office of Policy Development: Executive Office of the President, 1600 Pennsylvania Ave, NW, Washington, DC 20500; tel. (202) 456-6515; fax (202) 456-2878; internet www.whitehouse.gov/dpc; Asst to the Pres. for Domestic Policy MARGARET LA MONTAGNE; Asst to Pres. for Economic Policy LARRY LINDSEY.

Office of Science and Technology Policy: Eisenhower Executive Office Bldg, 17th St and Pennsylvania Ave, NW, Washington, DC, 20502; tel. (202) 456-7116; fax (202) 456-6022; internet www.ostp .gov; Dir JOHN H. MARBURGER, III.

Office of the United States Trade Representative: Winder Bldg, 600 17th St, NW, Washington, DC 20508; tel. (202) 395-3230; fax (202) 395-3911; internet www.ustr.gov; US Trade Rep. ROBERT B. ZOELLICK.

United States Mission to the United Nations: 799 United Nations Plaza, New York, NY 10017; tel. (212) 415-4404; fax (212) 415-4303; e-mail usa@un@.int; internet www.un.int/usa; US Ambassador to the United Nations JOHN D. NEGROPONTE.

Presidential Election, 7 November 2000

	Popular votes	% of Popular votes	Electoral College votes
George W. Bush (Republican) .	50,456,167	47.88	271
Albert A. Gore, Jr (Democrat) .	50,996,064	48.39	266
Ralph Nader (Green Party) . .	2,864,810	2.72	—
Others	1,063,888	1.01	—
Total	105,380,929	100.00	537*

*There are 538 Electoral College mandates. However, one elector mandated to support Gore abstained from the Electoral College's vote.

Legislature

CONGRESS

Senate
(April 2003)

The Senate comprises 100 members. Senators' terms are for six years, one-third of the Senate being elected every two years.

President of the Senate: Vice-President RICHARD B. CHENEY.

President Pro Tempore: TED STEVENS.

Democrats: 51 seats.

Republicans: 48 seats.

Independent: 1 seat.

Majority Leader: BILL FRIST.

Minority Leader: THOMAS A. DASCHLE.

Members
With political party and year in which term expires, on 3 January in all cases.

Alabama
| Richard C. Shelby | Rep. | 2005 |
| Jeff Sessions | Rep. | 2009 |

Alaska
| Lisa Murkowski | Rep. | 2005 |
| Ted Stevens | Rep. | 2009 |

Arizona
| John McCain, III | Rep. | 2005 |
| Jon Kyl | Rep. | 2007 |

Arkansas
| Blanche Lambert Lincoln | Dem. | 2005 |
| Mark Pryor | Dem. | 2009 |

California
| Barbara Boxer | Dem. | 2005 |
| Dianne Feinstein | Dem. | 2007 |

Colorado
| Ben Nighthorse Campbell | Rep. | 2005 |
| Wayne Allard | Rep. | 2009 |

Connecticut
| Christopher J. Dodd | Dem. | 2005 |
| Joseph I. Lieberman | Dem. | 2007 |

Delaware
| Thomas Carper | Dem. | 2007 |
| Joseph R. Biden, Jr | Dem. | 2009 |

Florida
| D. Robert Graham | Dem. | 2005 |
| Bill Nelson | Dem. | 2007 |

Georgia
| Zell Miller | Dem. | 2005 |
| Saxby Chambliss | Rep. | 2009 |

Hawaii
| Daniel K. Inouye | Dem. | 2005 |
| Daniel K. Akaka | Dem. | 2007 |

Idaho
| Mike Crapo | Rep. | 2005 |
| Larry E. Craig | Rep. | 2009 |

Illinois
| Peter G. Fitzgerald | Dem. | 2005 |
| Richard J. Durbin | Rep. | 2009 |

Indiana
| Evan Bayh | Dem. | 2005 |
| Richard G. Lugar | Rep. | 2007 |

Iowa
| Charles E. Grassley | Rep. | 2005 |
| Tom Harkin | Dem. | 2009 |

Kansas
| Sam Brownback | Rep. | 2005 |
| Pat Roberts | Rep. | 2009 |

Kentucky
| Jim Bunning | Rep. | 2005 |
| A. Mitchell McConnell | Rep. | 2009 |

Louisiana
| John B. Breaux | Dem. | 2005 |
| Mary L. Landrieu | Dem. | 2009 |

Maine
| Olympia J. Snowe | Rep. | 2007 |
| Susan M. Collins | Rep. | 2009 |

Maryland
| Barbara A. Mikulski | Dem. | 2005 |
| Paul S. Sarbanes | Dem. | 2007 |

Massachusetts
| Edward M. Kennedy | Dem. | 2007 |
| John F. Kerry | Dem. | 2009 |

Michigan
| Debbie Stabenow | Dem. | 2007 |
| Carl Levin | Dem. | 2009 |

Minnesota
| Mark Dayton | Dem. | 2007 |
| Norm Coleman | Rep. | 2009 |

Mississippi
| Trent Lott | Rep. | 2007 |
| Thad Cochran | Rep. | 2009 |

Missouri
| Christopher S. Bond | Rep. | 2005 |
| Jean Carnahan | Dem. | 2007 |

Montana
| Conrad Burns | Rep. | 2007 |
| Max Baucus | Dem. | 2009 |

Nebraska
| Ben Nelson | Dem. | 2007 |
| Chuck Hagel | Rep. | 2009 |

Nevada
| Harry M. Reid | Dem. | 2005 |
| John Ensign | Rep. | 2007 |

New Hampshire
| Judd Gregg | Rep. | 2005 |
| John Sununu | Rep. | 2009 |

New Jersey		
Jon S. Corzine	Dem.	2007
Frank Lautenberg	Dem.	2009

New Mexico		
Jeff Bingaman	Dem.	2007
Pete V. Domenici	Rep.	2009

New York		
Charles E. Schumer	Dem.	2005
Hillary Clinton	Dem.	2007

North Carolina		
John Edwards	Dem.	2005
Elizabeth Dole	Rep.	2009

North Dakota		
Byron L. Dorgan	Dem.	2005
Kent Conrad	Dem.	2007

Ohio		
Gorge V. Voinovich	Rep.	2005
Mike DeWine	Rep.	2007

Oklahoma		
Don Nickles	Rep.	2005
James M. Inhofe	Rep.	2009

Oregon		
Ronald L. Wyden	Rep.	2005
Gordon Smith	Rep.	2009

Pennsylvania		
Arlen Specter	Rep.	2005
Rick Santorum	Rep.	2007

Rhode Island		
Lincoln Chafee	Rep.	2007
John F. Reed	Dem.	2009

South Carolina		
Ernest F. Hollings	Dem.	2005
Lindsey Graham	Rep.	2009

South Dakota		
Thomas A. Daschle	Dem.	2005
Tim Johnson	Dem.	2009

Tennessee		
Bill Frist	Rep.	2007
Lamar Alexander	Rep.	2009

Texas		
Kay Bailey Hutchison	Rep.	2007
John Cornyn	Rep.	2009

Utah		
Robert F. Bennett	Rep.	2005
Orrin G. Hatch	Rep.	2007

Vermont		
Patrick J. Leahy	Dem.	2005
James M. Jeffords	Ind.	2007

Virginia		
George Allen	Rep.	2007
John W. Warner	Rep.	2009

Washington		
Patty Murray	Dem.	2005
Maria Cantwell	Dem.	2007

West Virginia		
Robert C. Byrd	Dem.	2007
John D. Rockefeller, IV	Dem.	2009

Wisconsin		
Russell D. Feingold	Dem.	2005
Herbert H. Kohl	Dem.	2007

Wyoming		
Craig Thomas	Rep.	2007
Michael B. Enzi	Rep.	2009

House of Representatives
(April 2003)

A new House of Representatives, comprising 435 members, is elected every two years.

Speaker: Dennis Hastert.

Republicans: 229 seats.

Democrats: 205 seats.

Independent: 1 seat.

Majority Leader: Tom DeLay.

Minority Leader: Nancy Pelosi.

Independent Agencies

African Development Foundation: 1400 Eye St, NW, 10th Floor, Washington, DC 20005-2248; tel. (202) 673-3916; fax (202) 673-3810; e-mail info@adf.gov; internet www.adf.gov; Chair. Ernest G. Green.

American Battle Monuments Commission: Courthouse Plaza II, Suite 500, 2300 Clarendon Blvd, Arlington, VA 22201-3367; tel. (703) 696-6900; fax (703) 696-6666; internet www.abmc.gov; f. 1923; Chair. Gen. (retd) Paul X. Kelley.

Appalachian Regional Commission: 1666 Connecticut Ave, NW, Washington, DC 20235; tel. (202) 884-7660; fax (202) 884-7682; e-mail crea@arc.gov; internet www.arc.gov; f. 1965; Fed. Co-Chair. Jesse L. White, Jr; States' Co-Chair. Gov. Don Sundquist (Tennessee).

Commission on Civil Rights: 624 Ninth St, NW, Washington, DC 20425; tel. (202) 376-8312; fax (202) 376-7672; internet www.usccr.gov; f. 1957; Chair. Mary Frances Berry.

Commission of Fine Arts: National Building Museum Bldg, Suite 312, 401 F St, NW, Washington, DC 20001; tel. (202) 504-2200; fax (202) 504-2195; e-mail staff@cfa.gov; internet www.cfa.gov; f. 1910; Chair. Harry G. Robinson, III.

Commodity Futures Trading Commission: Three Lafayette Centre, 1155 21st St, NW, Washington, DC 20581; tel. (202) 418-5080; fax (202) 418-5521; internet www.cftc.gov; f. 1974; Chair. James E. Newsome (designate).

Consumer Product Safety Commission: 4330 East-West Hwy, Bethesda, MD 20814; tel. (301) 504-0580; fax (301) 504-0124; internet www.cpsc.gov; f. 1972; Chair. Ann Brown.

Corporation for National Service: 1201 New York Ave, NW, Washington, DC 20525; tel. (202) 606-5000; fax (202) 565-2784; internet www.nationalservice.org; CEO Stephen Goldsmith.

Defense Nuclear Facilities Safety Board: 625 Indiana Ave, NW, Washington, DC 20004–2901; tel. (202) 694-7088; fax (202) 208-6518; internet www.dnfsb.gov/; Chair. John T. Conway.

Environmental Protection Agency: 401 M St, SW, Washington, DC 20460; tel. (202) 260-2090; internet www.epa.gov; f. 1970; Admin. (vacant).

Equal Employment Opportunity Commission: 1801 L St, NW, Washington, DC 20507; tel. (202) 663-4900; internet www.eeoc.gov; f. 1965; Chair. Cari M. Dominguez.

Export-Import Bank of the United States (Ex-Im Bank): see Finance—Banking.

Farm Credit Administration: 1501 Farm Credit Dr., McLean, VA 22102–5090; tel. (703) 883-4056; fax (703) 734-5784; e-mail info-line@fca.gov; internet www.fca.gov; Chair. and CEO Michael M. Reyna.

Federal Communications Commission: see Radio and Television.

Federal Deposit Insurance Corporation: 550 17th St, NW, Washington, DC 20429; tel. (202) 393-8400; internet www.fdic.gov/; f. 1933; Chair. Donald E. Powell.

Federal Election Commission: 999 E St, NW, Washington, DC 20463; tel. (202) 694-1100; fax (202) 219-3880; e-mail webmaster@fec.gov; internet www.fec.gov; f. 1974; Chair. Danny Lee McDonald.

Federal Emergency Management Agency: Federal Center Plaza, 500 C St, SW, Washington, DC 20472; tel. (202) 646-4600; fax (202) 646-2531; internet www.fema.gov/; f. 1979; Dir Joe M. Allbaugh.

Federal Housing Finance Board: 1777 F St, NW, Washington, DC 20006; tel. (202) 408-2500; fax (202) 408-1435; internet www.fhfb.gov; Chair. Bruce A. Morrison.

Federal Labor Relations Authority: 607 14th St, NW, Washington, DC 20424-0001; tel. (202) 482-6560; fax (202) 482-6659; internet www.flra.gov; f. 1978; Chair. Dale Cabaniss.

Federal Maritime Commission: see Transport—Ocean Shipping.

Federal Mediation and Conciliation Service: 2100 K St, NW, Washington, DC 20427; tel. (202) 606-8080; fax (202) 606-4251; internet www.fmcs.gov; f. 1947; Dir Charles Richard Barnes.

Federal Reserve System: see Finance—Banking.

Federal Retirement Thrift Investment Board: 1250 H St, NW, Washington, DC 20005; tel. (202) 942-1600; fax (202) 942-1676; internet www.tsp.gov; Exec. Dir ROGER W. MEHLE.

Federal Trade Commission: 600 Pennsylvania, NW, Washington, DC 20580; tel. (202) 326-2222; fax (202) 326-2396; internet www.ftc.gov; f. 1914; Chair. TIMOTHY J. MURIS.

General Services Administration: 18th and F Sts, NW, Washington, DC 20405; tel. (202) 501-1231; fax (202) 501-1489; internet www.gsa.gov/; f. 1949; Admin. STEPHEN A. PERRY.

Inter-American Foundation: 901 North Stuart St, Arlington, VA 22203; tel. (703) 306-4301; fax (703) 306-4369; e-mail info@iaf.gov; internet www.iaf.gov/; f. 1969; Chair. FRANK D. YTURRIA.

Merit Systems Protection Board: 1615 M St, NW, Washington, DC 20419; tel. (202) 653-7200; fax (202) 653-7130; e-mail mspb@mspb.gov; internet www.mspb.gov; f. 1883; Chair. BETH S. SLAVET.

National Aeronautics and Space Administration: Two Independence Sq., 300 E St, SW, Washington, DC 20546; tel. (202) 358-2345; fax (202) 358-2810; internet www.hq.nasa.gov/; f. 1958; Admin. SEAN O'KEEFE.

National Archives and Records Administration: 8601 Adelphi Rd, College Park, MD 20740-6001; tel. (301) 837-2000; fax (301) 837-0483; internet www.archives.gov; f. 1934; Archivist of the US JOHN W. CARLIN.

National Capital Planning Commission: 401 Ninth St, NW North Lobby, Suite 500, Washington, DC 20576; tel. (202) 482-7200; fax (202) 482-7272; e-mail info@ncpc.gov; internet www.ncpc.gov; f. 1924; Chair. JOHN V. COGBILL III.

National Commission on Libraries and Information Science: 1110 Vermont Ave, NW, Washington, DC 20005; tel. (202) 606-9200; fax (202) 606-9203; internet www.nclis.gov; Chair. MATHA B. GOULD.

National Council on Disability: 1331 F St, NW, Washington, DC 20004-1107; tel. (202) 272-2004; fax (202) 272-2022; internet www.ncd.gov; Chair. LEX FRIEDEN.

National Credit Union Administration: 1775 Duke St, Alexandria, VA 22314-3428; tel. (703) 518-6330; fax (703) 518-6319; e-mail boardmail@ncua.gov; f. 1970; Chair. DENNIS E. DOLLAR.

National Endowment for the Arts: 1100 Pennsylvania Ave, NW, Washington, DC 20506; tel. (202) 682-5400; fax (202) 682-5617; internet www.arts.endow.gov; f. 1965; Chair. MICHAEL HAMMOND.

National Endowment for the Humanities: 1100 Pennsylvania Ave, NW, Room 402, Washington, DC 20506; tel. (202) 606-8400; e-mail info@neh.gov; f. 1965; Chair. BRUCE COLE.

National Labor Relations Board: 1099 14th St, NW, Washington, DC 20570; tel. (202) 273-1991; fax (202) 273-4266; internet www.nlrb.gov; f. 1935; Chair. PETER J. HURTGEN.

National Mediation Board: 1301 K St, NW, Washington, DC 20572; tel. (202) 692-5000; fax (202) 523-5082; internet www.nmb.gov; f. 1934; Chair. FRANCIS J. DUGGAN.

National Science Foundation: 4201 Wilson Blvd, Arlington, VA 22230; tel. (703) 306-1234; internet www.nsf.gov; f. 1950; Dir RITA R. COLWELL.

National Transportation Safety Board: see Transport.

Nuclear Regulatory Commission: 1 White Flint North Bldg, 11555 Rockville Pike, Rockville, MD 20852; tel. (301) 415-8200; internet www.nrc.gov; Chair. RICHARD A. MESERVE.

Occupational Safety and Health Review Commission: 1 Lafayette Centre, 1120 20th St, NW, Washington, DC 20036-3419; tel. (202) 606-5398; fax (202) 606-5050; e-mail lwhitsett@oshrc.gov; internet www.oshrc.gov; f. 1970; Chair. THOMASINA V. ROGERS.

Office of Government Ethics: 1201 New York Ave, NW, Washington, DC 20005; tel. (202) 208-8000; fax (202) 208-8037; internet www.usoge.gov; Dir AMY L. COMSTOCK.

Office of Personnel Management: Theodore Roosevelt Federal Bldg, 1900 E St, NW, Washington, DC 20415; tel. (202) 606-1212; fax (202) 606-2573; internet www.opm.gov; f. 1979; Dir KAY COLES JAMES.

Peace Corps: 1111 20th St, NW, Washington, DC 20526; tel. (202) 692-2100; fax (202) 692-2101; e-mail webmaster@peacecorps.gov; internet www.peacecorps.gov; f. 1961; Dir CHARLES R. 'CHUCK' BAQUET, III (acting).

Pension Benefit Guaranty Corporation: 1200 K St, NW, Washington, DC 20005-4026; tel. (202) 326-4000; fax (202) 326-4153; f. 1974; Chair. ELAINE L. CHAO.

Postal Rate Commission: 1333 H St, NW, Washington, DC 20268-0001; tel. (202) 789-6800; fax (202) 789-6861; internet www.prc.gov; f. 1970; Chair. GEORGE OMAS.

Railroad Retirement Board: 844 North Rush St, Chicago, IL 60611-2092; tel. (312) 751-4777; fax (312) 751-7154; e-mail opa@rrb.gov; internet www.rrb.gov; f. 1935; Chair. CHERRYL T. THOMAS.

Securities and Exchange Commission: 450 Fifth St, NW, Washington, DC 20549; tel. (202) 942–8088; fax (202) 942–9646; internet www.sec.gov; f. 1935; Chair. WILLIAM DONALDSON.

Selective Service System: 1515 Wilson Blvd, Arlington, VA 22209-2425; tel. (703) 605-4000; fax (703) 605-4133; internet www.sss.gov; f. 1940; Dir ALFRED V. RASCON.

Small Business Administration: 409 Third St, SW, Washington, DC 20416; tel. (202) 205-6740; fax (202) 205-7064; internet www.sba.gov; f. 1953; Admin. HECTOR V. BARRETO.

Smithsonian Institution: 1000 Jefferson Dr., SW, Washington, DC 20560-0001; tel. (202) 357-2700; fax (202) 357-2116; internet www.si.edu; f. 1846; Sec. LAWRENCE M. SMALL.

Social Security Administration: 6401 Security Blvd, Baltimore, MD 21235; tel. (410) 965-3120; fax (410) 966-1463; internet www.ssa.gov; Commr JO ANNE B. BARNHART.

Tennessee Valley Authority: 400 West Summit Hill Dr., Knoxville, TN 37902; tel. (865) 632-2531; fax (865) 632-6634; internet www.tva.gov; f. 1933; Chair. GLENN L. MCCULLOUGH, Jr.

United States Agency for International Development: Ronald Reagan Bldg, 1300 Pennsylvania Ave, NW, Washington, DC 20523-6100; tel. (202) 712-4810; fax (202) 216-3524; e-mail pinquiries@usaid.gov; internet www.usaid.gov; f. 1961; Dir ANDREW S. NATSIOS.

United States International Trade Commission: 500 E St, SW, Washington, DC 20436; tel. (202) 205-1819; fax (202) 205-2798; internet www.usitc.gov; f. 1916; Chair. STEPHEN KOPLAN.

United States Postal Service: 475 L'Enfant Plaza, SW, Washington, DC 20260-0010; tel. (202) 268-2000; fax (202) 268-4860; internet www.usps.com; f. 1970; Postmaster-Gen. and CEO JOHN E. 'JACK' POTTER.

United States Trade and Development Agency: 1621 North Kent St, Suite 300, Arlington, VA 22209-2131; tel. (703) 875-4357; fax (703) 875-4009; e-mail info@tda.gov; internet www.tda.gov; Dir THELMA J. ASKEY.

State Governments

(with expiration date of Governors' current term of office; legislatures at April 2003)

Alabama: Governor BOB RILEY; Rep.; Jan. 2007. Senate: Dem. 25, Rep. 10. House: Dem. 62, Rep. 43.

Alaska: Governor FRANK MURKOWSKI; Rep.; Dec. 2006. Senate: Dem. 8, Rep. 12. House: Dem. 13, Rep. 27.

Arizona: Governor JANET NAPOLITANO; Dem.; Jan. 2007. Senate: Dem. 13, Rep. 17. House: Dem. 20, Rep. 35, Ind. 1.

Arkansas: Governor MIKE D. HUCKABEE; Rep.; Jan. 2007. Senate: Dem. 27, Rep. 8. House: Dem. 70, Rep. 30.

California: Governor GRAY DAVIS; Dem.; Jan. 2007. Senate: Dem. 25, Rep. 15. Assembly: Dem. 48, Rep. 32.

Colorado: Governor BILL OWENS; Rep.; Jan. 2007. Senate: Dem. 18, Rep. 18. House: Dem. 28, Rep. 37.

Connecticut: Governor JOHN G. ROWLAND; Rep.; Jan. 2007. Senate: Dem. 21, Rep. 15. House: Dem. 94, Rep. 57.

Delaware: Governor RUTH ANN MINNER; Dem.; Jan. 2004. Senate: Dem. 13, Rep. 8. House: Dem. 12, Rep. 29.

Florida: Governor JEB BUSH; Rep.; Jan. 2007. Senate: Dem. 14, Rep. 26. House: Dem. 39, Rep. 81.

Georgia: Governor SONNY PERDUE; Rep.; Jan. 2007. Senate: Dem. 26, Rep. 30. House: Dem. 106, Rep. 72, 1 Ind.

Hawaii: Governor LINDA LINGLE; Rep.; Dec. 2006. Senate: Dem. 20, Rep. 5. House: Dem. 36, Rep. 15.

Idaho: Governor DIRK KEMPTHORNE; Rep.; Jan. 2007. Senate: Dem. 37, Rep. 28. House: Dem. 16, Rep. 54.

Illinois: Governor ROD R. BLAGOJEVICH; Dem.; Jan. 2007. Senate: Dem. 32, Rep. 26, 1 Ind. House: Dem. 66, Rep. 52.

Indiana: Governor FRANK O'BANNON; Dem.; Jan. 2005. Senate: Dem. 18, Rep. 32. House: Dem. 51, Rep. 49.

Iowa: Governor TOM VILSACK; Dem.; Jan. 2007. Senate: Dem. 21, Rep. 29. House: Dem. 46, Rep. 54.

Kansas: Governor KATHLEEN SIBELIUS; Dem.; Jan. 2007. Senate: Dem. 10, Rep. 30. House: Dem. 45, Rep. 80.

Kentucky: Governor PAUL E. PATTON; Dem.; Dec. 2003. Senate: Dem. 16, Rep. 22. House: Dem. 65, Rep. 35.

Louisiana: Governor MIKE J. FOSTER; Rep.; Jan. 2004. Senate: Dem. 24, Rep. 15. House: Dem. 70, Rep. 34, 1 Ind.

Maine: Governor JOHN BALDACCI, Jr; Dem.; Jan. 2007. Senate: Dem. 18, Rep. 17. House: Dem. 80, Rep. 67, Ind. 4.

Maryland: Governor ROBERT EHRLICH, Jr; Rep.; Jan. 2007. Senate: Dem. 33, Rep. 14. House: Dem. 97, Rep. 44.

Massachusetts: Governor W. MITT ROMNEY; Rep.; Jan. 2007. Senate: Dem. 34, Rep. 6. House: Dem. 134, Rep. 22, 4 vacancies.

Michigan: Governor JENNIFER M. GRANHOLM; Dem.; Jan. 2007. Senate: Dem. 16, Rep. 22. House: Dem. 47, Rep. 63.

Minnesota: Governor TIM PAWLENTY; Rep.; Jan. 2007. Senate: Dem. Farm. Lab. 35, Rep. 31, Ind. 1. House: Dem. Farm. Lab. 52, Rep. 82.

Mississippi: Governor RONNIE MUSGROVE; Dem.; Jan. 2004. Senate: Dem. 28, Rep. 24. House: Dem. 79, Rep. 39, Ind. 3.

Missouri: Governor BOB HOLDEN; Dem.; Jan. 2005. Senate: Dem. 14, Rep. 20. House: Dem. 73, Rep. 90.

Montana: Governor JUDY MARTZ; Rep.; Jan. 2005. Senate: Dem. 21, Rep. 29. House: Dem. 47, Rep. 53.

Nebraska: Governor MIKE JOHANNS; Rep.; Jan. 2007. Legislature: unicameral body comprising 49 members elected on a non-partisan ballot and classed as senators.

Nevada: Governor KENNY GUINN; Rep.; Jan. 2007. Senate: Dem. 8, Rep. 13. Assembly: Dem. 23, Rep. 19.

New Hampshire: Governor CRAIG BENSON; Rep.; Jan. 2005. Senate: Dem. 11, Rep. 13. House: Dem. 140, Rep. 249, Ind. 1, 10 vacancies.

New Jersey: Governor JAMES MCGREEVEY; Dem.; Jan. 2006. Senate: aDem. 20, Rep. 20. Assembly: Dem. 41, Rep. 38, 1 Ind.

New Mexico: Governor BILL RICHARDSON; Dem.; Jan. 2007. Senate: Dem. 24, Rep. 18. House: Dem. 40, Rep. 30.

New York: Governor GEORGE E. PATAKI; Rep.; Jan. 2007. Senate: Dem. 24, Rep. 37. Assembly: Dem. 99, Rep. 51.

North Carolina: Governor MIKE EASLEY, Jr; Dem.; Jan. 2005. Senate: Dem. 35, Rep. 15. House: Dem. 62, Rep. 58.

North Dakota: Governor JOHN HOEVEN; Rep.; Jan. 2005. Senate: Dem. 16, Rep. 33. House: Dem. 27, Rep. 71.

Ohio: Governor BOB TAFT; Rep.; Jan. 2007. Senate: Dem. 11, Rep. 22. House: Dem. 40, Rep. 59.

Oklahoma: Governor BRAD HENRY; Dem.; Jan. 2007. Senate: Dem. 27, Rep. 21. House: Dem. 52, Rep. 49.

Oregon: Governor TED KULONGOSKI; Dem.; Jan. 2007. Senate: Dem. 14, Rep. 16. House: Dem. 28, Rep. 32.

Pennsylvania: Governor ED RENDELL; Dem.; Jan. 2007. Senate: Dem. 21, Rep. 29. House: Dem. 94, Rep. 109.

Rhode Island: Governor DONALD L. CARCIERI; Rep.; Jan. 2007. Senate: Dem. 44, Rep. 6. House: Dem. 85, Rep. 15.

South Carolina: Governor MARK SANFORD; Rep. Jan. 2007. Senate: Dem. 21, Rep. 24, 1 vacancy. House: Dem. 51, Rep. 72, 1 vacancy.

South Dakota: Governor M. MICHAEL ROUNDS; Rep.; Jan. 2007. Senate: Dem. 9, Rep. 26. House: Dem. 21 Rep. 49.

Tennessee: Governor PHIL BREDESEN; Dem.; Jan. 2007. Senate: Dem. 18, Rep. 15. House: Dem. 54, Rep. 45.

Texas: Governor RICK PERRY; Rep.; Jan. 2007. Senate: Dem. 12, Rep. 19. House: Dem. 62, Rep. 88.

Utah: Governor MICHAEL O. LEAVITT; Rep.; Jan. 2005. Senate: Dem. 7, Rep. 22. House: Dem. 19, Rep. 56.

Vermont: Governor JIM DOUGLAS; Rep.; Jan. 2005. Senate: Dem. 19, Rep. 11. House: Dem. 69, Rep. 73, Prog. 4, Ind. 2.

Virginia: Governor MARK R. WARNER; Dem.; Jan. 2006. Senate: Dem. 17, Rep. 23. House: Dem. 34, Rep. 64, Ind. 2.

Washington: Governor GARY LOCKE; Dem.; Jan. 2005. Senate: Dem. 24, Rep. 25. House: Dem. 52, Rep. 46.

West Virginia: Governor ROBERT E. WISE; Dem.; Jan. 2005. Senate: Dem. 28, Rep. 6. House: Dem. 75, Rep. 25.

Wisconsin: Governor JAMES E. DOYLE; Dem.; Jan. 2007. Senate: Dem. 18, Rep. 13, 2 vacancies. Assembly: Dem. 40, Rep. 58, 1 vacancy.

Wyoming: Governor DAVE FREUDENTHAL; Dem.; Jan. 2007. Senate: Dem. 10, Rep. 20. House: Dem. 15, Rep. 45.

Political Organizations

Communist Party USA: 235 West 23rd St, 7th Floor, New York, NY 10011; tel. (212) 989-4994; fax (212) 229-1713; e-mail cpusa@cpusa.org; internet www.cpusa.org; f. 1919; 40 state groups; Chair. SAM WEBB.

Democratic National Committee: 430 South Capitol St, SE, Washington, DC 20003; tel. (202) 863-8000; fax (202) 863-8174; internet www.democrats.org; f. 1848; Nat. Chair. TERRY MCAULIFFE; Sec. KATHLEEN M. VICK; Treas. ANDREW TOBIAS.

The Greens/Green Party USA: POB 1406, Lawrence, MA 60690; tel. (978) 682-4353; e-mail gpusa@igc.org; internet www.greenparty.org; f. 1984; 22 state groups.

International Green Party: 461 North Lake, Apt 209, Aurora, IL 60506; tel. (630) 896-2075; f. 1973 to promote ecological issues; 500,000 mems; Spokesperson RANDY TOLER.

Libertarian Party: 2600 Virginia Ave, NW, Suite 100, Washington, DC 20037; tel. (202) 333-0008; fax (202) 333-0072; e-mail hq@lp.org; internet www.lp.org; opposes govt regulation of individual rights; f. 1971; Chair. STEVE DASBACH.

Prohibition National Committee: POB 2635, Denver, CO 80201; tel. (303) 572-0646; fax (303) 237-4947; internet www.prohibition.org; f. 1869; opposes the manufacture and sale of alcoholic drinks; opposes abortion, drug abuse and euthanasia; Nat. Chair. EARL F. DODGE; Nat. Sec. RACHEL MITCHELL.

Reform Party of the USA: 9219 E Shonto LN, Tucson, AZ 85749; tel. (520) 394-7180; internet www.reformparty.org; f. 1996 as populist movement supporting presidential candidature of Ross Perot; Nat. Chair. GERRY MOAN; Sec. FRANK REED (acting).

Republican National Committee: 310 First St, SE, Washington, DC 20003; tel. (202) 863-8500; fax (202) 863-8820; e-mail info@mc.org; internet www.rnc.org; f. 1854; Chair. Nat. Cttee MARC RACICOT; Sec. LINDA SHAW; Treas. MIKE DUNCAN.

Social Democrats, USA: 815 15th St, NW, Washington, DC 20005; tel. (202) 638-1515; fax (202) 347-5585; f. 1972 to succeed Socialist Party est. in 1901; Pres. DONALD SLAIMAN; Exec. Dir RITA FREEDMAN.

Socialist Labor Party: POB 218, Mountain View, CA 94042; tel. (408) 280-7226; fax (408) 280-6964; e-mail socialists@slp.org; internet www.slp.org; f. 1877; Nat. Sec. ROBERT BILLS.

Socialist Party USA: 339 Lafayette St, Suite 303, New York, NY 10012; tel. and fax (212) 982-4586; e-mail SocialistParty@sp-usa.org; internet www.sp-usa.org; f. 1901; Nat. Co-Chair. DONALD DOUMAKES, KATHERINE NICEWANDER; Nat. Sec. GREG PASON.

Socialist Workers Party: 406 West St, New York, NY 10014; tel. (212) 242-5530; fax (212) 727-3107; f. 1938; Nat. Sec. JACK BARNES.

Diplomatic Representation

EMBASSIES IN THE UNITED STATES

Albania: 2100 S St, NW, Washington, DC 20008; tel. (202) 223-4942; fax (202) 628-7342; Ambassador FATOS TARIFA.

Algeria: 2118 Kalorama Rd, NW, Washington, DC 20008; tel. (202) 265-2800; fax (202) 667-2174; e-mail embalgous@verizon.net; internet www.algeria-us.org; Ambassador IDRISS JAZAIRY.

Andorra: 2 United Nations Plaza, 25th Floor, New York, NY 10017; tel. (212) 750-8064; fax (212) 750-6630; Ambassador JULI MINOVES TRIQUELL.

Angola: 2108 16th St, NW, Washington, DC 20009; tel. (202) 785-1156; fax (202) 785-1258; e-mail angola@angola.org; internet www.angola.org; Ambassador JOSEFINA PITRA DIAKITE.

Antigua and Barbuda: 3216 New Mexico Ave, NW, Washington, DC 20016; tel. (202) 362-5122; fax (202) 362-5225; Ambassador LIONEL A. HURST.

Argentina: 1600 New Hampshire Ave, NW, Washington, DC 20009; tel. (202) 238-6424; fax (202) 332-3171; e-mail argentina@veriomail.com; internet www.embassyofargentina-usa.org; Ambassador DIEGO RAMIRO GUELAR.

Armenia: 2225 R St, NW, Washington, DC 20008; tel. (202) 319-1976; fax (202) 319-2982; internet www.armeniaemb.org; Ambassador ARMAN J. KIRAKOSSIAN.

Australia: 1601 Massachusetts Ave, NW, Washington, DC 20036; tel. (202) 797-3000; fax (202) 797-3168; e-mail library.washington@dfat.gov.au; internet www.austemb.org; Ambassador MICHAEL THAWLEY.

Austria: 3524 International Court, NW, Washington, DC 20008-3022; tel. (202) 895-6700; fax (202) 895-6750; internet www.embassy.org/embassies/at.html; Ambassador PETER MOSER.

Azerbaijan: 927 15th St, NW, Suite 700, POB 28790, Washington, DC 20038; tel. (202) 842-0001; fax (202) 842-0004; internet www

.ourworld.compuserv.com/homepages/Azerbaijan; Ambassador HAFIZ MIR JALAL OGLU PASHAYEV.

Bahamas: 2220 Massachusetts Ave, NW, Washington, DC 20008; tel. (202) 319-2660; fax (202) 319-2668; Chargé d'affaires a.i. SHEILA GWENETH CAREY.

Bahrain: 3502 International Dr., NW, Washington, DC 20008; tel. (202) 342-0741; fax (202) 362-2192; e-mail info@bahrainembassy .org; internet www.bahrainembassy.org; Ambassador SHEIKH KHALIFA BIN AL-KHALIFA.

Bangladesh: 3510 International Dr., NW 20008; tel. (202) 244-0183; fax (202) 244-5366; Ambassador SYED HASAN AHMAD.

Barbados: 2144 Wyoming Ave, NW, Washington, DC 20008; tel. (202) 939-9200; fax (202) 332-7467; e-mail barbados@oas.org; internet www.barbados.org; Ambassador MICHAEL IAN KING.

Belarus: 1619 New Hampshire Ave, NW, Washington, DC 20009; tel. (202) 986-1604; fax (202) 986-1805; e-mail usa@belarusembassy .org; internet www.belarusembassy.org; Ambassador MIKHAIL KHVASTOU.

Belgium: 3330 Garfield St, NW, Washington, DC 20008; tel. (202) 333-6900; fax (202) 333-3079; e-mail washington@diplobel.org; internet www.belgium-emb.org/usa; Ambassador FRANS VAN DAELE.

Belize: 2535 Massachusetts Ave, NW, Washington, DC 20008; tel. (202) 332-9636; fax (202) 332-6888; e-mail ambassador@ embassyofbelize.org; internet www.embassyofbelize.org; Ambassador LISA SHOMAN.

Benin: 2737 Cathedral Ave, NW, Washington, DC 20008; tel. (202) 232-6656; fax (202) 265-1996; Ambassador CYRILLE OGUIN.

Bolivia: 3014 Massachusetts Ave, NW, Washington, DC 20008; tel. (202) 483-4410; fax (202) 328-3712; Ambassador JAIME APARICIO.

Bosnia and Herzegovina: 2109 E St, NW, Washington, DC 20037; tel. (202) 337-1500; fax (202) 337-1502; e-mail info@bosnianembassy .org; internet www.bosnianembassy.org; Ambassador IGOR DAVIDOVIĆ.

Botswana: 1531-1533 New Hampshire Ave, NW, Washington, DC 20036; tel. (202) 244-4990; fax (202) 244-4164; Ambassador KGOSI SEEPAPITSO, IV.

Brazil: 3006 Massachusetts Ave, NW, Washington, DC 20008; tel. (202) 238-2700; fax (202) 238-2827; internet www.brasilemb.org; Ambassador RUBENS BARBOSA.

Brunei: 3520 International Court, NW, Washington, DC 20008; tel. (202) 237-1838; fax (202) 885-0560; e-mail info@bruneiembassy.org; internet www.bruneiembassy.org; Ambassador PENGIRAN ANAK DATO PUTEH.

Bulgaria: 1621 22nd St, NW, Washington, DC 20008; tel. (202) 387-0174; fax (202) 234-7973; internet www.bulgaria-embassy.org; Ambassador ELENA POPTODOROVA.

Burkina Faso: 2340 Massachusetts Ave, NW, Washington, DC 20008; tel. (202) 332-5577; fax (202) 667-1882; e-mail ambawdc@rcn .com; internet www.burkinaembassy-usa.org; Ambassador TERTIUS ZONGO.

Burundi: 2233 Wisconsin Ave, NW, Suite 212, Washington, DC 20007; tel. (202) 342-2574; fax (202) 342-2578; e-mail burundiembassy@erols.com; Ambassador THOMAS NDIKUMANA.

Cambodia: 4500 16th St, NW, Washington, DC 20011; tel. (202) 726-7742; fax (202) 726-8381; e-mail Cambodia@embassy.org; internet www.embassy.org/cambodia; Ambassador ROLAND ENG.

Cameroon: 2349 Massachusetts Ave, NW, Washington, DC 20008; tel. (202) 265-8790; fax (202) 387-3826; Ambassador JEROME MENDOUGA.

Canada: 501 Pennsylvania Ave, NW, Washington, DC 20001; tel. (202) 682-1740; fax (202) 682-7726; internet www.nstn.ca/wshde; Ambassador MICHAEL FREDERICK KERGIN.

Cape Verde: 3415 Massachusetts Ave, NW, Washington, DC 20007; tel. (202) 965-6820; fax (202) 965-1207; e-mail ambacvus@ sysnet.net; internet www.capeverdeusembassy.org; Ambassador JOSÉ BRITO.

Central African Republic: 1618 22nd St, NW, Washington, DC 20008; tel. (202) 483-7800; fax (202) 332-9893; e-mail centafremb@ starpower.net; Ambassador EMMANUEL TOUABOY.

Chad: 2002 R St, NW, Washington, DC 20009; tel. (202) 462-4009; fax (202) 265-1937; Ambassador HASSABALLAH AHMAT SOUBIANE.

Chile: 1732 Massachusetts Ave, NW, Washington, DC 20036; tel. (202) 785-1746; fax (202) 887-5579; e-mail embassy@embassyofchile .org; internet www.embassyofchile.org; Ambassador ANDRÉS BIANCHI.

China, People's Republic: 2300 Connecticut Ave, NW, Washington, DC 20008; tel. (202) 328-2500; fax (202) 232-7855; internet www.china-embassy.org; Ambassador YANG JIECHI.

Colombia: 2118 Leroy Pl., NW, Washington, DC 20008; tel. (202) 387-8338; fax (202) 232-8643; internet www.colombiaemb.org; Ambassador LUIS ALBERTO MORENO.

Comoros: 336 East 45th St, 2nd Floor, New York, NY 10017; tel. (212) 972-8010; fax (212) 983-4712; e-mail comun@undp.org; Ambassador (vacant).

Congo, Democratic Republic: 1800 New Hampshire Ave, NW, Washington, DC 20009; tel. (202) 234-7690; fax (202) 237-0748; Ambasssador FAIDA MITIFU.

Congo, Republic: 4891 Colorado Ave, NW, Washington, DC 20011; tel. (202) 726-5500; fax (202) 726-1860; Ambassador SERGE MOMBOULI.

Costa Rica: 2114 S St, NW, Washington, DC 20008; tel. (202) 234-2945; fax (202) 265-4795; Ambassador JAIME DAREMBLUM.

Côte d'Ivoire: 2424 Massachusetts Ave, NW, Washington, DC 20008; tel. (202) 797-0300; fax (202) 462-9444; Ambassador YOUSSOUFOU BAMBA.

Croatia: 2343 Massachusetts Ave, NW, Washington, DC 20008; tel. (202) 588-5899; fax (202) 588-8936; e-mail webmaster@croatiaemb .org; Ambassador IVAN GRDEŠIĆ.

Cuba: 'Interests section' in the Embassy of Switzerland, 2630 16th St, NW, Washington, DC 20009; tel. (202) 797-8518; fax (202) 797-8521; Counselor DAGOBERTO RODRÍGUEZ BARRERA.

Cyprus: 2211 R St, NW, Washington, DC 20008; tel. (202) 462-5772; fax (202) 483-6710; Ambassador Dr ERATO KOZAKOU MARCOULLIS.

Czech Republic: 3900 Spring of Freedom St, NW, Washington, DC 20008; tel. (202) 274-9100; fax (202) 966-8540; e-mail washington@ embassy.mzv.cz; internet www.czech.cz/washington; Ambassador MARTIN PALOUS.

Denmark: 3200 Whitehaven St, NW, Washington, DC 20008-3683; tel. (202) 234-4300; fax (202) 328-1470; e-mail wasamb@wasamb.um .dk; internet www.denmarkemb.org; Ambassador ULRIK ANDREAS WEDERSPIEL.

Djibouti: 1156 15th St, NW, Suite 515, Washington, DC 20005; tel. (202) 331-0270; fax (202) 331-0302; Ambassador ROBLÉ OLHAYE.

Dominica: 3216 New Mexico Ave, NW, Washington, DC 20016; tel. (202) 364-6781; fax (202) 364-6791; Ambassador Dr NICHOLAS J. O. LIVERPOOL.

Dominican Republic: 1715 22nd St, NW, Washington, DC 20008; tel. (202) 332-6280; fax (202) 265-8057; e-mail embdomrepusa@msn .com; internet www.domrep.org; Ambassador HUGO GUILIANI CURY SELIN.

Ecuador: 2535 15th St, NW, Washington, DC 20009; tel. (202) 234-7200; fax (202) 667-3482; e-mail mecuawaa@erols.com; internet www.ecuador.org/ecuador; Chargé d'affaires a.i. CARLOS JÁTIVA.

Egypt: 3521 International Court, NW, Washington, DC 20008; tel. (202) 895-5400; fax (202) 244-4319; e-mail egypt-embassy@usa.net; internet www.mfa.gov.eg; Ambassador NABIL FAHMY.

El Salvador: 2308 California St, NW, Washington, DC 20008; tel. (202) 265-9671; Ambassador RENÉ A. LEÓN.

Equatorial Guinea: 2020 16th St, NW, Washington, DC 20009; tel. (202) 518-5700; fax (202) 518-5252; Ambassador TEODORO BIYOGO NSUE.

Eritrea: 1708 New Hampshire Ave, NW, Washington, DC 20009; tel. (202) 319-1991; fax (202) 319-1304; Ambassador GIRMA ASMEROM.

Estonia: 2131 Massachusetts Ave, NW, Washington, DC 20008; tel. (202) 588-0101; fax (202) 588-0108; e-mail info@estemb.org; internet www.estemb.org; Ambassador SVEN JÜRGENSON.

Ethiopia: 3506 International Dr., NW, Washington, DC 20008; tel. (202) 364-1200; fax (202) 364-6387; Ambassador KASAHUN AYELE.

Fiji: 2233 Wisconsin Ave, NW, Suite 240, Washington, DC 20007; tel. (202) 337-8320; fax (202) 337-1996; Ambassador ANARE JALE.

Finland: 3301 Massachusetts Ave, NW, Washington, DC 20008; tel. (202) 298-5800; fax (202) 298-6030; e-mail info@finland.org; internet www.finland.org; Ambassador JUKKA VALTASAARI.

France: 4101 Reservoir Rd, NW, Washington, DC 20007; tel. (202) 944-6000; fax (202) 944-6072; e-mail info-washington@diplomatie .gouv.fr; internet www.ambafrance-us.org; Ambassador JEAN-DAVID LEVITTE.

Gabon: 2034 20th St, NW, Suite 200, Washington, DC 20009; tel. (202) 797-1000; fax (202) 332-0668; Ambassador JULES MARIUS OGOUEBANDJA.

Gambia: 1156 15th St, NW, Suite 905, Washington, DC 20005; tel. (202) 785-1399; fax (202) 785-1430; Ambassador ESSA BOKARR SEY.

Georgia: 1511 K St, NW, Suite 424, Washington, DC 20005; tel. (202) 393-5959; fax (202) 393-6060; Ambassador Dr TEDO DJAPARIDZE.

Germany: 4645 Reservoir Rd, NW, Washington, DC 20007-1998; tel. (202) 298-4000; fax (202) 298-4249; e-mail ge-embus@ix.netcom.com; internet www.germany-info.org; Ambassador WOLFGANG FRIEDRICH ISCHINGER.

Ghana: 3512 International Dr., NW, Washington, DC 20008; tel. (202) 686-4520; fax (202) 686-4527; Ambassador ALAN JOHN KYEREMATEN.

Greece: 2221 Massachusetts Ave, NW, Washington, DC 20008; tel. (202) 939-1300; fax (202) 939-1324; e-mail greece@greekembassy.org; internet www.greekembassy.org; Ambassador GEORGE SAVVAIDES.

Grenada: 1701 New Hampshire Ave, NW, Washington, DC 20009; tel. (202) 265-2561; fax (202) 265-2468; Ambassador DENIS G. ANTOINE.

Guatemala: 2220 R St, NW, Washington, DC 20008; tel. (202) 745-4952; fax (202) 745-1908; Ambassador ARIEL RIVERA IRIAS.

Guinea: 2112 Leroy Pl., NW, Washington, DC 20008; tel. (202) 483-9420; fax (202) 483-8688; Ambassador MAMADOU ALIMOU DIALLO.

Guinea-Bissau: POB 33813, Washington, DC 20033-3813; tel. (301) 947-3958; fax 301-947-3958; Ambassador HENRIQUE ADRIANO DA SILVA.

Guyana: 2490 Tracy Pl., NW, Washington, DC 20008; tel. (202) 265-6900; fax (202) 232-1297; e-mail guyanaembassy@hotmail.com; Ambassador Dr MOHAMMED ALI ODEEN ISHMAEL.

Haiti: 2311 Massachusetts Ave, Washington, DC 20008; tel. (202) 332-4090; fax (202) 745-7215; Chargé d'affaires a.i. HARRY FRANZ LÉO.

Holy See: 3339 Massachusetts Ave, NW, Washington, DC 20008; tel. (202) 333-7121; fax (202) 337-4036; Apostolic Nuncio Most Rev. GABRIEL MONTALVO (Titular Archbishop of Celene).

Honduras: 3007 Tilden St, NW, Suite 4-M, Washington, DC 20008; tel. (202) 966-7702; fax (202) 966-9751; e-mail embhonduras@aol.com; internet www.hondurasemb.org; Ambassador MARIO M. CANAHUATI.

Hungary: 3910 Shoemaker St, NW, Washington, DC 20008; tel. (202) 362-6730; fax (202) 966-8135; internet www.huembwas.org; Ambassador Dr ANDRÁS SIMONYI.

Iceland: 1156 15th St, NW, Suite 1200, Washington, DC 20005; tel. (202) 265-6653; fax (202) 265-6656; e-mail icemb.wash@utn.stjr.is; internet www.iceland.org; Ambassador JÓN BALDVIN HANNIBALSSON.

India: 2107 Massachusetts Ave, NW, Washington, DC 20008; tel. (202) 939-7000; fax (202) 483-3972; internet www.india.bgsm.edu/dc/emb.html; Ambassador LALIT MANSINGH.

Indonesia: 2020 Massachusetts Ave, NW, Washington, DC 20036-1084; tel. (202) 775-5200; fax (202) 775-5365; Chargé d'affaires a.i. SOEMADI D. M. BROTODININGRAT.

Iran: 'Interests section' in the Embassy of Pakistan, 2209 Wisconsin Ave, NW, Washington DC 20007; tel. (202) 965-4990; internet www.daftar.org; Director of Section FARIBORZ JAHANSOOZAN.

Iraq: 'Interests section' in the Embassy of Algeria, 1801 P St, NW, Washington, DC 20036; tel. (202) 483-7500; fax (202) 462-5066.

Ireland: 2234 Massachusetts Ave, NW, Washington, DC 20008; tel. (202) 462-3939; fax (202) 232-5993; e-mail embirlus@aol.com; Ambassador NOEL FAHEY.

Israel: 3514 International Dr., NW, Washington, DC 20008; tel. (202) 364-5500; fax (202) 364-5610; e-mail dcisrael@ix.netcom.com; internet www.israelemb.org; Ambassador DANNY AYALON.

Italy: 1601 Fuller St, NW, Washington, DC 20009; tel. (202) 328-5500; fax (202) 483-2187; e-mail itapress@ix.netcom.com; internet www.italyemb.nw.dc.us/italy/index.html; Ambassador FERDINANDO SALLEO.

Jamaica: 1520 New Hampshire Ave, NW, Washington, DC 20006; tel. (202) 452-0660; fax (202) 452-0081; e-mail contactus@jamaicaembassy.com; internet www.jamusa.org; Ambassador SEYMOUR MULLINGS.

Japan: 2520 Massachusetts Ave, NW, Washington, DC 20008-2869; tel. (202) 238-6700; fax (202) 238-2187; Ambassador RYOZO KATO.

Jordan: 3504 International Dr., NW, Washington, DC 20008; tel. (202) 966-2664; fax (202) 966-3110; Ambassador KARIM KAWAR.

Kazakhstan: 1401 16th St, NW, Washington, DC 20036; tel. (202) 232-5488; fax (202) 232-5845; Ambassador KANAT SAUDABAYEV.

Kenya: 2249 R St, NW, Washington, DC 20008; tel. (202) 387-6101; fax (202) 462-3829; e-mail info@kenyaembassy.com; internet www.kenyaembassy.com; Ambassador Dr YUSUF A. NZIBO.

Korea, Republic: 2450 Massachusetts Ave, NW, Washington, DC 20008; tel. (202) 939-5600; fax (202) 387-0205; internet www.korea.emb.washington.dc/us; Ambassador SUNG-JOO HAN.

Kuwait: 2940 Tilden St, NW, Washington, DC 20008; tel. (202) 966-0702; fax (202) 966-0517; Ambassador Dr MOHAMMED SABAH AS-SALIM AS-SABAH.

Kyrgyzstan: 1732 Wisconsin Ave, NW, Washington, DC 20007; tel. (202) 338-5141; fax (202) 338-5139; e-mail embassy@kyrgyzstan.org; internet www.kyrgyzstan.org; Ambassador BAKTYBEK ABDRISSAEV.

Laos: 2222 S St, NW, Washington, DC 20008; tel. (202) 332-6416; fax (202) 332-4923; Ambassador PHANTONG PHOMMAHAXAY.

Latvia: 4325 17th St, NW, Washington, DC 20011; tel. (202) 726-8213; fax (202) 726-6785; e-mail latvia@ambergateway.com; internet www.latvia-usa.org; Ambassador AIVIS RONIS.

Lebanon: 2560 28th St, NW, Washington, DC 20008; tel. (202) 939-6300; fax (202) 939-6324; e-mail emlebanon@aol.com; internet www.emboleb.org; Ambassador FARID ABBOUD.

Lesotho: 2511 Massachusetts Ave, NW, Washington, DC 20008; tel. (202) 797-5533; fax (202) 234-6815; e-mail Lesotho@Afrika.com; Ambassador Prof. MOLELEKENG E. RAPOLAKI.

Liberia: 5201 16h St, Washington, DC 20011; tel. (202) 723-0437; fax (202) 723-0431; e-mail liberia-embassy@msn.com; Ambassador WILLIAM V. S. BULL.

Lithuania: 2622 16th St, NW, Washington, DC 20009; tel. (202) 234-5860; fax (202) 328-0466; Ambassador VYGAUDAS USACKAS.

Luxembourg: 2200 Massachusetts Ave, NW, Washington, DC 20008; tel. (202) 265-4171; fax (202) 328-8270; e-mail info@luxembourg-usa.org; internet www.luxembourg-usa.org; Ambassador ARLETTE CONZEMIUS-PACCOUD.

Macedonia: 1101 30th St, NW, Suite 302, 20007; tel. (202) 337-3063; fax (202) 337-3093; e-mail rmacedonia@aol.com; Ambassador NIKOLA DIMITROV.

Madagascar: 2374 Massachusetts Ave, NW, Washington, DC 20008; tel. (202) 265-5525; e-mail malagasy@embassy.org; internet www.embassy.org/madagascar; Ambassador ZINA ANDRIANARIVELO RAZAFY.

Malawi: 2408 Massachusetts Ave, NW, Washington, DC 20008; tel. (202) 797-1007; fax (202) 265-0976; Ambassador TONY KANDIERO.

Malaysia: 2401 Massachusetts Ave, NW, Washington, DC 20008; tel. (202) 328-2700; fax (202) 483-7661; e-mail mwwashdc@erols.com; Ambassador Dato' GHAZZALI SHEIKH ABDUL KHALID.

Mali: 2130 R St, NW, Washington, DC 20008; tel. (202) 332-2249; fax (202) 332-6603; Ambassador CHEICK OUMAR DIARRAH.

Malta: 2017 Connecticut Ave, NW, Washington, DC 20008; tel. (202) 462-3611; fax (202) 387-5470; e-mail gbsaliba@aol.com; Ambassador GEORGE SALIBA.

Marshall Islands: 2433 Massachusetts Ave, NW, Washington, DC 20008; tel. (202) 234-5414; fax (202) 232-3236; e-mail info@rmiembassyus.org; Ambassador BANNY DE BRUM.

Mauritania: 2129 Leroy Pl., NW, Washington, DC 20008; tel. (202) 232-5700; fax (202) 319-2623; Ambassador ABAL ABASS BASS.

Mauritius: 4301 Connecticut Ave, NW, Suite 441, Washington, DC 20008; tel. (202) 244-1491; fax (202) 966-0983; Ambassador Dr USHA JEETAH.

Mexico: 1911 Pennsylvania Ave, NW, Washington, DC 20006; tel. (202) 728-1600; fax (202) 234-7739; Ambassador JUAN JOSÉ BREMER MARTINO.

Micronesia: 1725 N St, NW, Washington, DC 20036; tel. (202) 223-4383; fax (202) 223-4391; internet fsmembassy.org; Ambassador JESSE B. MAREHALAU.

Moldova: 2101 S St, NW, Suite 329, Washington, DC 20008; tel. (202) 667-1130; fax (202) 667-1204; Chargé d'affaires a.i. VSEVOLOD GRIGORE.

Mongolia: 2833 M St, NW, Washington, DC 20007; tel. (202) 333-7117; fax (202) 298-9227; e-mail monemb@aol.com; Ambassador JALBUU CHOINKHOR.

Morocco: 1601 21st St, NW, Washington, DC 20009; tel. (202) 462-7979; fax (202) 265-0161; Chargé d'affaires a.i. ABDALLAH EL MAAROUFI.

Mozambique: 1990 M St, NW, Suite 570, Washington, DC 20036; tel. (202) 293-7146; fax (202) 835-0245; e-mail embamoc@aol.com; internet www.embamoc-usa.org; Ambassador ARMANDO A. PANGUENE.

Myanmar: 2300 S St, NW, Washington, DC 20008; tel. (202) 332-9044; fax (202) 332-9046; Ambassador U TIN WIN.

Namibia: 1605 New Hampshire Ave, NW, Washington, DC 20009; tel. (202) 986-0540; fax (202) 986-0443; e-mail embnamibia@aol.com; Ambassador LEONARD N. IIPUMBU.

Nepal: 2131 Leroy Pl., NW, Washington, DC 20008; tel. (202) 667-4550; fax (202) 667-5534; e-mail nepali@erols.com; Ambassador JAI PRATAP RANA.

Netherlands: 4200 Linnean Ave, NW, Washington, DC 20008; tel. (202) 244-5300; fax (202) 362-3430; e-mail was@minbuza.nl; internet www.netherlands-embassy.org; Ambassador BOUDEWIJN VAN EENENNAAM.

New Zealand: 37 Observatory Circle, NW, Washington, DC 20008; tel. (202) 328-4848; fax (202) 667-5227; e-mail nzemb@dc.infi.net; internet www.nzemb.org; Ambassador JAMES B. BOLGER.

Nicaragua: 1627 New Hampshire Ave, NW, Washington, DC 20009; tel. (202) 939-6570; fax (202) 939-6542; Ambassador CARLOS J. ULVERT.

Niger: 2204 R St, NW, Washington, DC 20008; tel. (202) 483-4224; fax (202) 483-3169; Ambassador JOSEPH DIATTA.

Nigeria: 1333 16th St, NW, Washington, DC 20036; tel. (202) 986-8400; fax (202) 775-1385; Ambassador Prof. JIBRIL MUHAMMED AMINU.

Norway: 2720 34th St, NW, Washington, DC 20008; tel. (202) 333-6000; fax (202) 337-0870; internet www.norway.org; Ambassador KNUT VOLLEBAEK.

Oman: 2535 Belmont Rd, NW, Washington, DC 20008; tel. (202) 387-1980; fax (202) 745-4933; Ambassador MOHAMED ALI AL KHU-SAIBY.

Pakistan: 2315 Massachusetts Ave, NW, Washington, DC 20008; tel. (202) 939-6200; fax (202) 387-0484; e-mail info@pakistan-embassy.com; internet www.imran.com/Pakistan; Ambassador ASHRAF JAHANGIR QAZI.

Palau: 1150 18th St, NW, Suite 750, Washington, DC 20036; tel. (202) 452-6814; fax (202) 452-6281; Ambassador HERSEY KYOTA.

Panama: 2862 McGill Terrace, NW, Washington, DC 20008; tel. (202) 483-1407; fax (202) 483-8413; e-mail iga@panaembadc.org; Ambassador GUILLERMO A. FORD BOYD.

Papua New Guinea: 1779 Massachusetts Ave, NW, Suite 805, Washington, DC 20036; tel. (202) 745-3680; fax (202) 745-3679; e-mail kunduwash@aol.com; Ambassador NAGORA Y. BOGAN.

Paraguay: 2400 Massachusetts Ave, NW, Washington, DC 20008; tel. (202) 483-6960; fax (202) 234-4508; Ambassador LEILA TERESA RACHID COWLES.

Peru: 1700 Massachusetts Ave, NW, Washington, DC 20036; tel. (202) 833-9860; fax (202) 659-8124; Ambassador ALLAN WAGNER.

Philippines: 1600 Massachusetts Ave, NW, Washington, DC 20036-2274; tel. (202) 467-9300; fax (202) 328-7614; e-mail USWashpe@aol.com; internet www.philippineembassy-usa.org; Ambassador ALBERTO F. DEL ROSARIO.

Poland: 2640 16th St, NW, Washington, DC 20009; tel. (202) 234-3800; fax (202) 328-6271; e-mail information@ioip.com; internet www.polandembassy.org; Ambassador PRZEMYSLAW GRUDZINSKI.

Portugal: 2125 Kalorama Rd, NW, Washington, DC 20008; tel. (202) 328-8610; fax (202) 462-3726; e-mail embportwash@mindspring.com; internet www.portugalemb.org; Ambassador PEDRO CATARINO.

Qatar: 4200 Wisconsin Ave, NW, Washington, DC 20016; tel. (202) 274-1600; Ambassador BADA OMAR AL DAFA.

Romania: 1607 23rd St, NW, Washington, DC 20008; tel. (202) 232-3694; fax (202) 232-4748; e-mail romania@embassy.org; internet www.embassy.org/romania; Ambassador DUMITRU SORIN DUCARU.

Russia: 2650 Wisconsin Ave, NW, Washington, DC 20007; tel. (202) 298-5700; fax (202) 298-5735; e-mail rusembus@erols.com; internet www.russianembassy.org; Ambassador YURII VIKTOROVICH USHAKOV.

Rwanda: 1714 New Hampshire Ave, NW, Washington, DC 20009; tel. (202) 232-2882; fax (202) 232-4544; Ambassador Maj. Dr RICHARD SEZIBERA.

Saint Christopher and Nevis: 3216 New Mexico Ave, NW, Washington DC 20016; tel. (202) 686-2636; fax (202) 686-5740; Ambassador Dr OSBERT LIBURD.

Saint Lucia: 3216 New Mexico Ave, NW, Washington, DC 20016; tel. (202) 364-6792; fax (202) 364-6723; Ambassador SONIA M. JOHNNY.

Saint Vincent and the Grenadines: 3216 New Mexico Ave, NW, Washington, DC 20016; tel. (202) 364-6730; fax (202) 364-6736; e-mail ejohn@embvsg.com; internet www.embvsg.com; Ambassador ELLSWORTH I. A. JOHN.

Samoa: 800 Second Ave, Suite 800D, New York, NY 10017; tel. (212) 599-6196; fax (212) 599-0797; internet www.interwebinc.com/samoa/missus.html; Ambassador TUILOMA NERONI SLADE.

Saudi Arabia: 601 New Hampshire Ave, NW, Washington, DC 20037; tel. (202) 342-3800; fax (202) 944-5983; e-mail info@saudiembassy.net; internet www.saudiembassy.net; Ambassador HRH Prince BANDAR BIN SULTAN.

Senegal: 2112 Wyoming Ave, NW, Washington, DC 20008; tel. (202) 234-0540; fax (202) 352-6315; Ambassador MAMADOU MANSOUR SECK.

Serbia and Montenegro: 2410 Kalorama Rd,NW, Washington, DC 20008; tel. (202) 332-0333; fax (202) 332-3933; e-mail info@yuembusa.org; internet www.yuembusa.org; Ambassador IVAN VUKACIC.

Seychelles: 820 Second Ave, Suite 900F, New York, NY 10017; tel. (212) 687-9766; fax (212) 922-9177; Ambassador CLAUDE S. MOREL.

Sierra Leone: 1701 19th St, NW, Washington, DC 20009; tel. (202) 939-9261; fax (202) 483-1793; e-mail sierrale@UMBC7.UMBC.edu; Ambassador (vacant).

Singapore: 3501 International Pl., NW, Washington, DC 20008; tel. (202) 537-3100; fax (202) 537-0876; e-mail singemb@bellatlantic.net; Ambassador HENG CHEE CHAN.

Slovakia: 3523 International Court, NW, Suite 250, Washington, DC 20008; tel. (202) 237-1054; fax (202) 237-6438; e-mail info@slovakembassy-us.org; internet www.slovakembassy-us.org; Ambassador MARTIN BUTORA.

Slovenia: 1525 New Hampshire Ave, NW, Washington, DC 20036-1203; tel. (201) 667-5363; fax (202) 667-4563; Ambassador Dr DAVORIN KRAČUN.

Solomon Islands: 800 Second Ave, Suite 400-L, B, New York, NY 10017; tel. (212) 599-6192; fax (212) 661-8925; e-mail simny@solomons.com; Chargé d'affaires a.i. BERAKI JINO.

South Africa: 3051 Massachusetts Ave, NW, Washington, DC 20008; tel. (202) 232-4400; fax (202) 232-3402; e-mail safrica@southafrica.net; internet www.southafrica.net; Ambassador (vacant).

Spain: 2375 Pennsylvania Ave, NW, Washington, DC 20037; tel. (202) 452-0100; fax (202) 833-5670; e-mail embespus@mail.mae.us; internet www.spainemb.org; Ambassador JAVIER RUPEREZ.

Sri Lanka: 2148 Wyoming Ave, NW, Washington, DC 20008; tel. (202) 483-4025; fax (202) 232-7181; e-mail slembassy@clark.net; Chargé d'affaires a.i. Dr J. D. A. WIJEWARDENA.

Sudan: 2210 Massachusetts Ave, NW, Washington, DC 20008; tel. (202) 338-8565; fax (202) 667-2406; Chargé d'affaires a.i. KHIDIR HAROUN AHMED.

Suriname: 4301 Connecticut Ave, NW, Suite 460, Washington, DC 20008; tel. (202) 244-7488; fax (202) 244-5878; e-mail embsur@erols.com; internet www.surinameembassy.org; Ambassador HENRY LOTHAR ILLES.

Swaziland: 3400 International Dr., NW, Washington, DC 20008; tel. (202) 362-6683; fax (202) 244-8059; e-mail 723451.2752@compuserve.com; Ambassador MARY M. KANYA.

Sweden: 1501 M St, NW, Washington, DC 20005; tel. (202) 467-2600; fax (202) 467-2699; internet www.globescope.com/sweden; Ambassador JAN ELIASSON.

Switzerland: 2900 Cathedral Ave, NW, Washington, DC 20008; tel. (202) 745-7900; fax (202) 387-2564; e-mail vertretung@was.rep.admin.ch; internet www.swissemb.org; Ambassador CHRISTIAN BLICKENSDORFER.

Syria: 2215 Wyoming Ave, NW, Washington, DC 20008; tel. (202) 232-6313; fax (202) 234-9548; Ambassador ROSTOM AZ-ZOUBI.

Tanzania: 2139 R St, NW, Washington, DC 20008; tel. (202) 939-6125; fax (202) 797-7408; Ambassador MUSTAFA SALIM NYANG'ANYI.

Thailand: 1024 Wisconsin Ave, NW, Washington, DC 20007; tel. (202) 944-3600; fax (202) 944-3611; internet www.thaiembdc.org; Ambassador SAKTHIP KRAIRIKSH.

Togo: 2208 Massachusetts Ave, NW, Washington, DC 20008; tel. (202) 234-4212; fax (202) 232-3190; Ambassador AKOUSSOULELOU BODJONA.

Tonga: 800 Second Ave, Suite 400B, New York, NY 10017; tel. (917) 369-1025; fax (917) 369-1024; Ambassador SONATANE TUA TAUMOE-PEAU TUPOU.

Trinidad and Tobago: 1708 Massachusetts Ave, NW, Washington, DC 20036; tel. (202) 467-6490; fax (202) 785-3130; e-mail embttgo@erols.com; Chargé d'affaires a.i. MACKISACK ADRIAN LOGIE.

Tunisia: 1515 Massachusetts Ave, NW, Washington, DC 20005; tel. (202) 862-1850; fax (202) 862-1858; Ambassador HATEM ATALLAH.

Turkey: 2525 Massachusetts Ave, NW, Washington, DC 20008; tel. (202) 612-6700; fax (202) 612-6744; internet www.turkey.org/turkey; Ambassador OSMAN FARUK LOGOGLU.

Turkmenistan: 2207 Massachusetts Ave, NW, Washington, DC 20008; tel. (202) 588-1500; fax (202) 588-0697; e-mail embassy@dc

.infi.net; internet www.infi.net/~embassy/; Ambassador MERET BAIR-AMOVICH ORAZOV.

Uganda: 5911 16th St, NW, Washington, DC 20011; tel. (202) 726-7100; fax (202) 726-1727; Ambassador EDITH GRACE SSEMPALA.

Ukraine: 3350 M St, NW, Washington, DC 20007; tel. (202) 333-0606; fax (202) 333-0817; e-mail emb_usa@mfa.gov.ua; internet www.ukremb.com; Ambassador KOSTYANTYN HRYSHCHENKO.

United Arab Emirates: 3522 International Court NW, Washington, DC 20008; tel. (202) 243-2400; fax (202) 243-2432; Ambassador AL ASRI S. A. AL DHAHRI.

United Kingdom: 3100 Massachusetts Ave, NW, Washington, DC 20008; tel. (202) 588-6500; fax (202) 588-7870; internet www.britainusa.com/bis/embassy/embassy.stm; Ambassador Sir DAVID MANNING.

Uruguay: 1913 Eye St, NW, Washington, DC 20006; tel. (202) 331-1313; fax (202) 331-8142; e-mail uruwashi@uruwashi.org; internet www.embassy.org/uruguay; Ambassador Dr HUGO FERNÁNDEZ FAINGOLD.

Uzbekistan: 1746 Massachusetts Ave, NW, Washington, DC 20036; tel. (202) 887-5300; fax (202) 293-6804; internet www.uzbekistan.org; Ambassador SHAVKAT KHAMRAKULOV.

Venezuela: 1099 30th St, NW, Washington, DC 20007; tel. (202) 342-2214; fax (202) 342-6820; e-mail embavene@dgsys.com; internet www.venezuela.mit.edu/embassy; Ambasador LUIS HERRERA MARCANO.

Viet Nam: 1233 20th St, NW, Suite 400, Washington, DC 20036; tel. (202) 861-0737; fax (202) 861-0917; e-mail vietnamembassy@msn.com; internet www.vietnamembassy-usa.com; Ambassador CHIEN TAM NGUYEN.

Yemen: 2600 Virginia Ave, NW, Suite 705, Washington, DC 20037; tel. (202) 965-4760; fax (202) 337-2017; Ambassador ALI ABDULLAH SALEH.

Zambia: 2419 Massachusetts Ave, NW, Washington, DC 20008; tel. (202) 265-9717; fax (202) 332-0826; Ambassador ATAN SHANSONGA.

Zimbabwe: 1608 New Hampshire Ave, NW, Washington, DC 20009; tel. (202) 332-7100; fax (202) 483-9326; Ambassador SIMBI VEKE MUBAKO.

Judicial System

Each state has a judicial system structured similarly to the Federal system, with a Supreme Court and subsidiary courts, to deal with cases arising under State Law. These courts have jurisdiction in most criminal and civil actions. Each state has its own bar association of lawyers and its own legal code.

SUPREME COURT OF THE UNITED STATES
Supreme Court Bldg, 1 First St, NE, Washington, DC 20543; tel. (202) 479-3000; fax (202) 479-2971; internet www.supremecourtus.gov.

The Supreme Court is the only Federal Court established by the Constitution. It is the highest court in the nation, comprised of a Chief Justice and eight Associate Justices. Appointments, which are for life or until voluntary retirement, are made by the President, subject to confirmation by the US Senate.

Chief Justice: WILLIAM H. REHNQUIST (appointed Associate Justice 1971, Chief Justice 1986).

Associate Justices: JOHN PAUL STEVENS (1975), SANDRA DAY O'CONNOR (1981), ANTONIN SCALIA (1986), ANTHONY M. KENNEDY (1988), DAVID H. SOUTER (1990), CLARENCE THOMAS (1991), RUTH BADER GINSBURG (1993), STEPHEN G. BREYER (1994).

US COURTS OF APPEAL
Administrative Office of the US Courts, Washington, DC 20544; tel. (202) 273-1120; internet www.uscourts.gov.

The USA is divided into 12 judicial circuits, in each of which there is one Court of Appeals. The Court of Appeals for the Federal Circuit has nation-wide specialized jurisdiction.

Federal Courts hear cases involving federal law, cases involving participants from more than one state, crimes committed in more than one state and civil or corporate cases that cross state lines. Federal District Courts, of which there are 94, are the courts of first instance for most federal suits.

Federal Circuit: H. ROBERT MAYER (Chief Judge), PAUL R. MICHEL, S. JAY PLAGER, ALAN D. LOURIE, PAULINE NEWMAN, RANDALL R. RADER, RAYMOND C. CLEVENGER, III, ALVIN A. SCHALL, WILLIAM C. BRYSON, ARTHUR J. GAJARSA, RICHARD LINN, TIMOTHY B. DYK, WILSON COWEN, DANIEL M. FRIEDMAN, SHARON PROST, BYRON G. SKELTON, GLENN LEROY ARCHER, Jr.

District of Columbia Circuit: DOUGLAS H. GINSBURG (Chief Judge), STEPHEN F. WILLIAMS, DAVID B. SENTELLE, KAREN LeCRAFT HENDERSON, LAURENCE H. SILBERMAN, A. RAYMOND RANDOLPH, JUDITH W. ROGERS, DAVID S. TATEL, MERRICK B. GARLAND, HARRY T. EDWARDS.

First Circuit (Maine, Massachusetts, New Hampshire, Rhode Island, Puerto Rico): MICHAEL BOUDIN (Chief Judge), JUAN R. TORRUELLA, BRUCE M. SELYA, SANDRA L. LYNCH, KERMIT V. LIPEZ, JEFFREY R. HOWARD.

Second Circuit (Connecticut, New York, Vermont): JOHN M. WALKER, Jr (Chief Judge), AMALYA LYLE KEARSE, SONIA SOTOMAYOR, DENNIS G. JACOBS, GUIDO CALABRESI, JOSE A. CABRANES, FRED I. PARKER, CHESTER J. STRAUB, ROBERT D. SACK, ROSEMARY S. POOLER, ROBERT A. KATZMANN, BARRINGTON D. PARKER, REENA RAGGI.

Third Circuit (Delaware, New Jersey, Pennsylvania, Virgin Islands): EDWARD R. BECKER (Chief Judge), DOLORES K. SLOVITER, ANTHONY J. SCIRICA, RICHARD L. NYGAARD, SAMUEL A. ALITO, Jr, JANE R. ROTH, THEODORE A. McKEE, MARJORIE O. RENDELL, MARYANNE TRUMP BARRY, THOMAS L. AMBRO, JULIO M. FUENTES, D. BROOKS SMITH.

Fourth Circuit (Maryland, North Carolina, South Carolina, Virginia, West Virginia): WILLIAM W. WILKINS, Jr (Chief Judge), J. HARVIE WILKINSON, III, PAUL V. NIEMAYER, E. EMORY WIDENER, Jr, J. MICHAEL LUTTIG, WILLIAM B. TRAXLER, Jr, KAREN J. WILLIAMS, M. BLANE MICHAEL, DIANA GRIBBON MOTZ, ROBERT B. KING, ROGER L. GREGORY, DENNIS W. SHEDD.

Fifth Circuit (Louisiana, Mississippi, Texas): CAROLYN DINEEN KING (Chief Judge), EDITH HOLLAN JONES, RHESA H. BARKSDALE, JACQUES L. WIENER, Jr, W. EUGENE DAVIS, PATRICK E. HIGGINBOTHAM, E. GRADY JOLLY, JERRY E. SMITH, EMILIO M. GARZA, HAROLD R. DEMOSS, Jr, CARL E. STEWART, FORTUNATO P. BENAVIDES, ROBERT M. PARKER, JAMES L. DENNIS, EDITH BROWN CLEMENT, JOHN M. DUHÉ, Jr, WILL GARWOOD, THOMAS M. REAVLEY, HENRY A. POLITZ.

Sixth Circuit (Kentucky, Michigan, Ohio, Tennessee): BOYCE F. MARTIN, Jr (Chief Judge), GILBERT S. MERRITT, ALAN E. NORRIS, RICHARD F. SUHRHEINRICH, DANNY J. BOGGS, EUGENE E. SILER, Jr, ALICE M. BATCHELDER, MARTHA CRAIG DAUGHTREY, KAREN NELSON MOORE, RANSEY GUY COLE, Jr, ERIC L. CLAY, RONALD LEE GILMAN, ALBERT J. ENGEL, DAMON J. KEITH, CORNELIA G. KENNEDY, ROBERT B. KRUPANSKY, RALPH B. GUY, DAVID A. NELSON, JAMES L. RYAN, JULIA SMITH GIBBONS.

Seventh Circuit (Illinois, Indiana, Wisconsin): JOEL M. FLAUM (Chief Judge), RICHARD A. POSNER, THOMAS E. FAIRCHILD, DANIEL A. MANION, KENNETH F. RIPPLE, FRANK H. EASTERBROOK, MICHAEL S. KANNE, JOHN L. COFFEY, ILANA DIAMOND ROVNER, DIANE P. WOOD, TERENCE T. EVANS, ANN C. WILLIAMS, HARLINGTON WOOD, Jr, WILLIAM J. BAUER.

Eighth Circuit (Arkansas, Iowa, Minnesota, Missouri, Nebraska, North Dakota, South Dakota): DAVID R. HANSEN (Chief Judge), JAMES B. LOKEN, THEODORE McMILLIAN, PASCO M. BOWMAN, II,, MORRIS S. ARNOLD, DIANA E. MURPHY, ROGER L. WOLLMAN, KERMIT E. BYE, WILLIAM J. RILEY, MICHAEL J. MELLOY, LAVENSKI R. SMITH.

Ninth Circuit (Alaska, Arizona, California, Guam, Hawaii, Idaho, Montana, Nevada, Northern Mariana Islands, Oregon, Washington): MARY M. SCHROEDER (Chief Judge), HARRY PREGERSON, STEPHEN REINHARDT, ALEX KOZINSKI, DIARMUID F. O'SCANNLAIN, STEPHEN S. TROTT, PAMELA ANN RYMER, THOMAS G. NELSON, ANDREW J. KLEINFELD, MICHAEL DALY HAWKINS, A. WALLACE TASHIMA, SIDNEY R. THOMAS, BARRY G. SILVERMAN, SUSAN B. GRABER, MARGARET M. McKEOWN, KIM McLANE WARDLAW, WILLIAM A. FLETCHER, RAYMOND C. FISHER, RONALD M. GOULD, RICHARD A. PAEZ, MARSHA S. BERZON, RICHARD C. TALLMAN, JOHNNIE RAWLINSON.

Tenth Circuit (Colorado, Kansas, New Mexico, Oklahoma, Utah, Wyoming): DEANELL R. TACHA (Chief Judge), STEPHANIE K. SEYMOUR, HARRIS L. HARTZ, TERRENCE O'BRIEN, DAVID M. EBEL, PAUL J. KELLY, Jr, ROBERT H. HENRY, MARY BECK BRISCOE, CARLOS LUCERO, MICHAEL R. MURPHY, MICHAEL W. McCONNELL.

Eleventh Circuit (Alabama, Florida, Georgia): J. L. EDMONSON (Chief Judge), GERALD B. TJOFLAT, R. LANIER ANDERSON, JOEL F. DUBINA, STANLEY F. BIRCH, Jr, SUSAN H. BLACK, STANLEY MARCUS, EDWARD E. CARNES, ROSEMARY BARKETT, FRANK MAYS HULL, CHARLES R. WILSON.

UNITED STATES COURT OF FEDERAL CLAIMS
717 Madison Pl., NW, Washington, DC 20005; tel. (202) 219-9657; fax (202) 219-9593; internet www.uscfc.uscourts.gov.

Judges: EDWARD J. DAMICH (Chief Judge), LAWRENCE M. BASKIR, DIANE GILBERT SYPOLT, CHRISTINE O. C. MILLER, BOHDAN A. FUTEY, JAMES T. TURNER, ROBERT H. HODGES, Jr, LYNN JEANNE BUSH, FRANCIS M. ALLEGRA, NANCY B. FIRESTONE, EMILY C. HEWITT, LAWRENCE J. BLOCK.

US COURT OF INTERNATIONAL TRADE
1 Federal Plaza, New York, NY 10278-0001; tel. (212) 264-2800; fax (212) 264-1085; internet www.uscit.gov.

Judges: GREGORY W. CARMAN (Chief Judge), JANE A. RESTANI, THOMAS J. AQUILINO, Jr, DONALD C. POGUE, EVAN J. WALLACH, JUDITH M. BARZILAY, DELISSA A. RIDGWAY, RICHARD K. EATON, TIMOTHY C. STANCEU.

Senior Judges: RICHARD W. GOLDBERG, NICHOLAS TSOUCALAS, R. KENTON MUSGRAVE.

Religion

Christianity is the predominant religion. The largest single denomination is the Roman Catholic Church. Other major groups in terms of membership are the Baptist, Methodist, Lutheran and Orthodox churches. Numerous other beliefs are represented, the largest in terms of adherents being Judaism, Islam and Buddhism.

CHRISTIANITY

National Council of the Churches of Christ in the USA: 475 Riverside Dr., Rm 880, New York, NY 10115-0050; tel. (212) 870-2511; fax (212) 870-3112; e-mail webmaster@ncccusa.org; internet www.ncccusa.org; f. 1950; an ecumenical org. of 36 Protestant and Orthodox denominations, representing *c.*52m. mems; Pres. ELENIE HUSZAGH; Gen. Sec. Dr ROBERT EDGAR.

The Anglican Communion

The Episcopal Church in the USA: 815 Second Ave, New York, NY 10017-4564; tel. (212) 867-8400; fax (212) 490-6684; internet www.episcopalchurch.org; f. 1789; 7,342 churches (2000); 2.3m. mems (2000); Presiding Bishop and Pres. Exec. Council Most Rev. FRANK TRACY GRISWOLD , III; Exec. Officer Gen. Convention and Sec. Exec. Council Rev. ROSEMARI SULLIVAN.

The Baptist Church

Members (1998 estimate): 33.1m., in 15 bodies, of which the following have the greatest number of members:

American Baptist Association: 4605 North State Line Ave, Texarkana, TX 75503-2928; tel. (903) 792-2783; e-mail bssc@abaptist.org; internet www.abaptist.org; f. 1905; 1,760 churches; 275,000 mems; Pres. GEORGE RALEY.

American Baptist Churches in the USA: POB 851, Valley Forge, PA 19482-0851; tel. (610) 768-2000; fax (610) 768-2320; e-mail richard.schramm@abc-usa.org; internet www.abc-usa.org; f. 1907; 5,775 churches; 1.5m. mems; Pres. TINETTE V. MCCRAY.

Conservative Baptist Association of America: 1501 West Mineral Ave, Suite B, Littleton, CO 80120; tel. (720) 283-3030; fax (720) 283-3333; e-mail cba@cbamerica.org; internet www.CBAmerica.org; f. 1947; 1,200 churches; 200,000 mems; Exec. Admin. Rev. ED MITCHELL.

General Association of Regular Baptist Churches: 1300 North Meacham Rd, Schaumburg, IL 60173-4806; tel. (847) 843-1600; fax (847) 843-3757; e-mail garbc@garbc.org; internet www.garbc.org; 1,417 churches; Nat. Rep. Rev. JOHN GREENING.

National Baptist Convention, USA: 1700 Baptist World Center Dr., Nashville, TN 37207-4948; tel. (615) 228-6292; fax (615) 226-5935; internet www.nationalbaptist.org; f. 1880; 2,500 churches; 3.5m. mems; Pres. Dr. WILLIAM J. SHAW; Gen. Sec. Rev. ROSCOE COOPER.

Southern Baptist Convention: 901 Commerce St,, Nashville, TN 37203-3629; tel. (615) 244-2355; fax (615) 742-8919; internet www.sbc.net; f. 1845; 42,000 churches; 15.8m. mems; Pres. Dr. JAMES MERRITT; Pres. Exec. Cttee Dr MORRIS H. CHAPMAN.

The Lutheran Church

Members (1998 estimate): 8.3m., in 10 bodies, of which the following have the greatest number of members:

Evangelical Lutheran Church in America: 8765 West Higgins Rd, Chicago, IL 60631; tel. (773) 380-2700; fax (773) 380-1465; e-mail info@elca.org; internet www.elca.org; f. 1988; 10,851 churches; 5.1m. mems; Bishop Rev. Dr H. GEORGE ANDERSON; Sec. Rev. Dr LOWELL G. ALMEN.

Lutheran Church—Missouri Synod: 1333 South Kirkwood Rd, St Louis, MO 63122-7295; tel. (314) 965-9000; e-mail infocenter@lcms.org; internet www.lcms.org; f. 1847; 6,220 churches; 2.6m. mems; Pres. Dr ALVIN L. BARRY; Sec. Dr RAYMOND HARTWIG.

The Methodist Church

Members (1998 estimate): 13.4m. in eight bodies, of which the following have the greatest number of members:

African Methodist Episcopal Church: 1134 11th St, NW, Washington, DC 20001; tel. (202) 371-8700; f. 1816; 86,200 churches, 2.5m. mems; Sr Bishop JOHN H. ADAMS; Gen. Sec. Dr CECIL W. HOWARD.

African Methodist Episcopal Zion Church: POB 32843, Charlotte, NC 28232; tel. (704) 333-1769; f. 1796; 3,098 churches; 1.3m. mems; Pres. SAMUEL CHUKA EKENAM, Sr.

The United Methodist Church: POB 320, Nashville, TN; tel. 37202; e-mail infoserve@umcom.umc.org; f. 1968; 35,609 pastoral charges and 8.4m. mems (in USA); Presiding Bishop GEORGE W. BASHORE; Sec. Gen. Conf. CAROLYN M. MARSHALL.

The Orthodox Churches

Members (1998 estimate): 5.1m. in 12 bodies, of which the following have the greatest number of members:

Antiochian Orthodox Christian Archdiocese of North America (Greek Orthodox Patriarchate of Antioch and all the East): 358 Mountain Rd, Englewood, NJ 07631-3798; tel. (201) 871-1355; fax (201) 871-7954; e-mail archdiocese@antiochian.org; internet www.antiochian.org; f. 1895; 235 churches; 350,000 mems; Primate Metropolitan PHILIP (SALIBA).

Armenian Apostolic Church of America: Eastern Prelacy: 138 East 39th St, New York, NY 10016; Western Prelacy: 4401 Russell Ave, Los Angeles, CA 90027; tel. (212) 689-7810; fax (212) 689-7168; e-mail prelacy@gis.net; internet www.armprelacy.org; tel. (323) 663-8273; fax (323) 663-0438; e-mail prelacy@aol.com; f. 1887; 32 churches; 150,000 mems; Prelate (Eastern Prelacy) Archbishop OSHAGAN CHOLOYAN; Prelate (Western Prelacy) Bishop MOUSHEGH MARDIROSIAN.

Armenian Church of America: Eastern Diocese, 630 Second Ave, New York, NY 10016; Western Diocese, 3325 North Glenoaks Blvd, Burbank, CA 91504; tel. (212) 686-0710; e-mail pri@armeniandiocese.org; internet www.armeniandiocese.org; tel. (818) 558-7474; fax (818) 558-6333; f. 1889; 94 churches; 660,000 mems; Primate (Eastern Diocese) Archbishop KHAJAG BARSAMIAN; Primate (Western Diocese) Archbishop VATCHÉ HOVSEPIAN.

Greek Orthodox Archdiocese of North and South America: 10 East 79th St, New York, NY 10021-0191; tel. (212) 570-3500; fax (212) 861-8060; e-mail archdiocese@goarch.org; internet www.goarch.org; inc 1922; 600 churches; 2.5m. mems; Primate Archbishop DIMITRIOS; Chancellor Very Rev. GEORGE PASSIAS.

Orthodox Church in America: POB 675, Syosset, NY 11791; tel. (516) 922-0550; fax (516) 922-0954; e-mail info@oca.org; internet www.oca.org; f. 1794; fmrly Russian Orthodox Greek Catholic Church of North America; 700 churches; 600,000 mems; Primate Metropolitan HERMAN; Chancellor Archpriest ROBERT S. KONDRATICK; Dir of Communications Archpriest JOHN MATUSIAK.

The Albanian, Bulgarian, Coptic, Romanian, Russian, Serbian, Syrian and Ukrainian Orthodox Churches are also represented.

The Presbyterian Church

Members (1998 estimate): 4.1m. in nine bodies, of which the following have the greatest number of members:

Presbyterian Church in America: 1852 Century Pl., NE, Atlanta, GA 30345-4305; tel. (404) 320-3366; fax (404) 329-1275; e-mail ac@pcanet.org; internet www.pcanet.org; f. 1973; 1,340 churches; 280,000 mems; Moderator Rev. KENNEDY SMARTT; Stated Clerk Dr L. ROY TAYLOR.

Presbyterian Church (USA): 100 Witherspoon St, Louisville, KY 40202-1396; tel. (502) 569-5000; fax (502) 569-5018; e-mail presytel@pcusa.org; internet www.pcusa.org; f. 1983; 11,328 churches; 3.6m. mems; Moderator SYNGMAN RHEE; Stated Clerk Rev. CLIFTON KIRKPATRICK.

The Roman Catholic Church

In 2000 there were 22,592 parishes in 152 dioceses and 33 archdioceses; 62.0m. mems.

National Conference of Catholic Bishops: 3211 Fourth St, NE, Washington, DC 20017; tel. (202) 541-3193; internet www.nccbuscc.org; Pres. Mgr WILTON D. GREGORY (Bishop of Belleville); Gen. Sec. Mgr WILLIAM P. FAY.

Archbishops

Anchorage: ROGER L. SCHWIETZ.

Atlanta: JOHN F. DONOGHUE.

Baltimore: Cardinal WILLIAM H. KEELER.

Boston: (vacant).

Chicago: Cardinal FRANCIS E. GEORGE.

Cincinnati: DANIEL E. PILARCZYK.

Denver: CHARLES J. CHAPUT.

Detroit: Cardinal ADAM J. MAIDA.

Dubuque: JEROME G. HANUS.

Hartford: DANIEL A. CRONIN.

Indianapolis: DANIEL M. BUECHLEIN.

Kansas City in Kansas: JAMES P. KELEHER.

Los Angeles: Cardinal ROGER M. MAHONY.

Louisville: THOMAS C. KELLY.

Miami: JOHN C. FAVALORA.

Milwaukee: REMBERT G. WEAKLAND.

Mobile: OSCAR H. LIPSCOMB.

Newark: JOHN JOSEPH MYERS.

New Orleans: FRANCIS B. SCHULTE.

New York: Cardinal EDWARD MICHAEL EGAN.

Oklahoma City: EUSEBIUS J. BELTRAN.

Omaha: ELDEN F. CURTISS.

Philadelphia: Cardinal ANTHONY J. BEVILACQUA, STEFAN SOROKA (Ukrainian, Byzantine Rite).

Pittsburgh: DONALD WILLIAM WUERL (Ruthenian, Byzantine Rite).

Portland in Oregon: JOHN G. VLAZNY.

Saint Louis: JUSTIN F. RIGALI.

Saint Paul and Minneapolis: HARRY J. FLYNN.

San Antonio: PATRICK F. FLORES.

San Francisco: WILLIAM J. LEVADA.

Santa Fe: MICHAEL J. SHEEHAN.

Seattle: ALEXANDER J. BRUNETT.

Washington: Cardinal THEODORE E. MCCARRICK.

Other Christian Churches

Assemblies of God: 1445 Boonville Ave, Springfield, MO 65802-1894; tel. (417) 862-2781; fax (417) 863-6614; e-mail info@ag.org; internet www.ag.org; f. 1914; 12,082 churches in USA; 2.6m. mems in USA; Gen. Supt THOMAS E. TRASK; Gen. Sec. GEORGE O. WOOD.

Christian Church (Disciples of Christ): 130 East Washington St, Indianapolis, IN 46204; tel. (317) 635-3100; fax (317) 635-3700; internet www.disciples.org; f. 1809; 3,873 congregations; 910,000 mems; Gen. Minister and Pres. Dr RICHARD L. HAMM.

Christian Reformed Church in North America: 2850 Kalamazoo Ave, SE, Grand Rapids, MI 49560; tel. (616) 224-0744; fax (616) 224-5895; e-mail engelhad@crcna.org; internet www.crcna.org; f. 1857; 995 churches; 278,798 mems (USA and Canada); Gen. Sec. Dr DAVID H. ENGELHARD.

Church of Christ: POB 472, Independence, MO 64051; f. 1830; 13,013 churches; 1.7m. mems; Sec. Council of Apostles Apostle SMITH N. BRICKHOUSE.

Church of Christ, Scientist: 175 Huntington Ave, Boston, MA 02115; tel. (617) 450-2000; fax (617) 450-3554; internet www.tfccs.com; f. 1879; 2,400 congregations world-wide; Pres. JEAN STARK HEBENSTREIT; Clerk OLGA M. CHAFFEE.

Church of God in Christ: Mason Temple, 939 Mason St, Memphis, TN 38126; f. 1907; 15,300 churches; 5.5m. mems; Presiding Bishop CHANDLER D. OWENS.

Church of Jesus Christ of Latter-day Saints (Mormon): 47 East South Temple St, Salt Lake City, UT 84150-0001; tel. (801) 240-1000; fax (801) 240-2033; internet www.lds.org; f. 1830; 10,811 wards and branches (congregations) in USA; 4.9m. mems in USA; Pres. GORDON B. HINCKLEY.

Church of the Nazarene: 6401 The Paseo, Kansas City, MO 64131-1284; tel. (816) 333-7000; fax (816) 361-4983; f. 1908; 12,977 churches; 1.5m. mems (world-wide); Gen. Sec. JACK STONE.

Friends United Meeting: 101 Quaker Hill Dr., Richmond, IN 47374-1980; tel. (765) 962-7573; fax (765) 966-1293; e-mail fum@fum.org; internet www.fum.org; f. 1902; 44,000 mems (USA and Canada); Presiding Clerk STAN BAUER; Gen. Sec. RETHA MCCUTCHEN.

Mariavite Old Catholic Church—Province of North America: 2803 10th St, Wyandotte, MI 48192-4994; tel. and fax (734) 281-3082; e-mail mariaviteocc@hotmail.com; f. 1930; 158 churches; 357,100 mems; Prime Bishop Most Rev. Archbishop Dr ROBERT R. J. M. ŽABOROWSKI.

Reformed Church in America, General Synod: 475 Riverside Dr., New York, NY 10115-0001; tel. (212) 870-3071; fax (212) 870-2499; internet www.rca.org; f. 1628; 949 churches; 305,000 mems; Pres. FREDERICK KRUITHIG; Gen. Sec. Rev. WESLEY GRANBERG-MICHAELSON.

Seventh-day Adventists: 12501 Old Columbia Pike, Silver Spring, MD 20904-6600; tel. (301) 680-6000; fax (301) 680-6090; internet www.adventist.org; f. 1863; 4,933 churches; 955,076 mems (USA and Canada); Pres. JAN PAULSEN; Sec. MATTHEW A. BEDIAKO.

United Church of Christ: 700 Prospect Ave, Cleveland, OH 44115; tel. (216) 736-2100; fax (216) 736-2120; e-mail langa@ucc.org; internet www.ucc.org; f. 1957; 5,961 churches; 1.4m. mems; Moderator Rev. NANCY TAYLOR.

United Pentecostal Church International: 8855 Dunn Rd, Hazelwood, MO 63042-2212; tel. (314) 837-7300; fax (314) 837-4503; e-mail upcimain@aol.com; internet www.upci.org; f. 1945; 3,790 churches (USA and Canada); 500,000 mems; Gen. Supt Rev. NATHANIEL A. URSHAN.

BAHÁ'Í FAITH

National Spiritual Assembly: 536 Sheridan Rd, Wilmette, IL 60091; tel. (847) 869-9039; fax (847) 869-0247; e-mail usopi-ny@bic.org; f. 1844; in Persia (Iran); 143,000 mems residing in over 7,000 localities; Chair. WILLIAM E. DAVIS; Sec.-Gen. Dr ROBERT C. HENDERSON.

BUDDHISM

There are an estimated 780,000 Buddhists in the USA.

American Buddhist Movement: 301 West 45th St, New York, NY 10036; tel. (212) 489-1075; f. 1980; 15 regional groups; Pres. Dr KEVIN R. O'NEIL.

Buddhist Churches of America: 1710 Octavia St, San Francisco, CA 94109-4341; tel. (415) 776-5600; fax (415) 771-6293; e-mail bcahq@pacbell.net; f. 1899; Hongwanji-ha Jodo Shinshu denomination; c.230,000 mems; Presiding Bishop HAKUBUN WATANABE.

HINDUISM

There are an estimated 1.3m. Hindus in the USA.

Ramakrishna–Vivekananda Center: 17 East 94th St, New York, NY 10128; tel. (212) 534-9445; internet www.ramakrishna.org; teachings based on the system of Vedanta; Minister SWAMI ADISWARANANDA.

ISLAM

There are an estimated 4.0m. Muslims in the USA, of whom African-American Muslims are estimated to number 1.3m.

Council of Masajid of United States (CMUS): 45 Lilac St, Edison, NJ 08817; tel. (732) 985-3304; f. 1978; educational agency representing 650 local groups; Pres. DAWUD ASSAD.

Federation of Islamic Associations in the US and Canada: 25351 Five Mile and Aubery Rd, Redford Township, MI 48239; tel. (313) 534-3295; fax (313) 534-1474; f. 1951; co-ordinating agency for 45 affiliated orgs; Gen. Sec. NIHAD HAMED.

Islamic Center of New York: 1711 Third Ave, New York, NY 10029-7303; tel. (212) 722-5234; fax (212) 722-5936; f. 1966; Sr Imam Dr ABDEL-RAHMAN OSMAN.

Islamic Mission of America: 143 State St, Brooklyn, NY 11201; tel. (718) 875-6607; f. 1938; maintains an educational and training inst. 15,000 mems; Chair. MOHAMED KABBAJ.

JUDAISM

There are an estimated 6.0m. Jews in North America.

American Jewish Congress: 15 East 84th St, New York, NY 10028-0458; tel. (212) 879-4500; fax (212) 249-3672; f. 1918; Exec. Dir PHIL BAUM; 50,000 mems.

Central Conference of American Rabbis: 355 Lexington Ave, New York, NY 10017; tel. (212) 972-3636; e-mail info@ccarnet.org; internet www.ccarnet.org; f. 1889; Reform; Pres. MARTIN S. WIENER; 1,650 mems.

The Rabbinical Assembly: 3080 Broadway, New York, NY 10027-4650; tel. (212) 280-6000; fax (212) 749-9166; internet www.rabassembly.org; f. 1901; Pres. Rabbi REUVEN HAMMER; Exec. Vice-Pres. Rabbi JOEL H. MEYERS; 1,500 mems.

Union of American Hebrew Congregations: 633 Third Ave, New York, NY 10017-6778; tel. (212) 650-4000; fax (212) 650-4169; e-mail uahc@uahc.org; internet www.uahcweb.org; f. 1873; Reform; Pres. Rabbi ERIC H. YOFFIE; Vice-Pres. Rabbi LEONARD R. THAL; 889 affiliated congregations representing c. 1.5m. mems.

Union of Orthodox Jewish Congregations of America: 11 Broadway, New York, NY 10004; tel. (212) 563-4000; fax (212) 564-9058; e-mail info@ou.org; internet www.ou.org; f. 1898; Pres. HARVEY BLITZ; Exec. Vice-Pres. Rabbi Dr TZVI HERSH WEINVEB; 1,200 affiliated congregations representing c. 1m. mems.

United Synagogue of Conservative Judaism: 155 Fifth Ave, New York, NY 10010-6802; tel. (212) 533-7800; fax (212) 353-9439; e-mail info@uscj.org; internet www.uscj.org; f. 1913; Pres. JUDY YUDOF; Exec. Vice-Pres. Rabbi JEROME EPSTEIN; 760 affiliated congregations in North America representing c.1.5m. mems.

SIKHISM

There are an estimated 498,000 Sikhs in North America.

International Sikh Organization: 2025 Eye St, NW, Suite 922, Washington, DC 20006; tel. (202) 833-3262; fax (202) 452-9161; Pres. Dr GURMIT SINGH AULAKH.

The Press

The USA publishes more newspapers and periodicals than any other country. Most dailies give a greater emphasis to local news because of the strong interest in local and regional affairs and the decentralized structure of many government services. These factors, together with the distribution problem inherent in the size of the country, are responsible for the lack of national newspapers. In 1998 almost 123m. people, representing 59.0% of the adult population, read a daily newspaper.

Most influential and highly respected among the few newspapers with a national readership are the *New York Times* (which introduced a national edition in 1980), the *Washington Post, Los Angeles Times* and *The Wall Street Journal* (the financial and news daily with editions in New York City, California, Illinois and Texas, and a European and an Asian edition). In 1982 the first national general interest newspaper, *USA Today*, was introduced by Gannett. An international edition was launched in 1984.

In 1999 34 daily newspapers had circulations of over 250,000 copies. Among the largest of these, in order of daily circulation, were *The Wall Street Journal, USA Today, Los Angeles Times, The New York Times, The Washington Post, New York Daily News, Chicago Tribune, Newsday, The Houston Chronicle, The Chicago Sun-Times* and *The Dallas Morning News*.

In late 2000 there were 1,480 English language daily newspapers. In 2000 average total daily newspaper circulation was 55,773,000 copies per day. The Sunday edition is an important and distinctive feature of US newspaper publishing; many Sunday newspapers run to over 300 pages. In 2000 there were 917 Sunday newspapers, with a total circulation of 59,214,000. In 2000 there were 7,594 weekly newspapers.

The famous tradition of press freedom in the USA is grounded in the First Amendment to the Constitution which declares that 'Congress shall make no law . . . abridging the freedom of speech or of the Press . . .' and confirmed in the legislations of many states which prohibit any kind of legal restriction on the dissemination of news.

Legislation affecting the Press is both state and federal. A source of controversy between the Press and the courts has been the threat of the encroachment by judicial decrees on the area of courtroom and criminal trial coverage. In 1972 the Supreme Court ruled that journalists were not entitled to refuse to give evidence before grand juries on information they have received confidentially. Since then the frequent issuing of subpoenas to journalists and the jailing of several reporters for refusing to disclose sources has led to many 'shield' bills being put before Congress and state legislatures calling for immunity for journalists from both federal and state jurisdiction.

In recent years, increased production costs have subjected the industry to considerable economic strain, resulting in mergers and take-overs, a great decline in competition between dailies in the same city, and the appearance of inter-city dailies catering for two or more adjoining centres. A consequence of these trends has been the steady growth of newspaper groups or chains.

The following are among the principal daily newspaper groups:

Dow Jones & Co Inc: New York, NY 10281; tel. (212) 416-2000; fax (212) 416-3478; internet www.bis.dowjones.com; Chair. and CEO PETER R. KANN; 20 daily newspapers, including *The Wall Street Journal*.

Gannett Co Inc: 1100 Wilson Blvd, 10th Floor, Arlington, VA 22234; tel. (703) 284-6000; fax (703) 247-3294; internet www .gannett.com; f. 1906; Chair. JOHN J. CURLEY; Pres. DOUGLAS MCCORKINDALE; largest US newspaper group in terms of total circulation; 74 daily newspapers, including *USA Today* and *The Detroit News*.

Hearst Corpn: 959 Eighth Ave, New York, NY 10019; tel. (212) 649-2000; fax (212) 262-2680; internet www.hearstcorp.com; Pres. and CEO FRANK A. BENNACK, Jr; 12 daily newspapers, including *San Francisco Examiner*.

Knight Ridder Inc: 1 Herald Plaza, 6th Floor, Miami, FL 33132-1693; tel. (305) 376-3800; fax (305) 376-3865; internet www.kri.com; Chair. and CEO P. ANTHONY RIDDER; 33 daily newspapers, including *Miami Herald, Philadelphia Enquirer*.

Newhouse Newspapers: 140 East 45th St, New York, NY 10017; tel. (212) 697-8020; fax (212) 972-3146; Pres. DONALD E. NEWHOUSE; 23 daily newspapers.

E. W. Scripps Co: POB 5380, Cincinnati, OH 45201; tel. (513) 977-3000; fax (513) 977-3721; e-mail corpcomm@scripps.com; internet www.scripps.com; Chair. and CEO WILLIAM R. BURLEIGH; Pres. KENNETH W. LOWE; 19 daily newspapers.

Thomson Newspapers Inc: Metro Centre, 1 Station Pl., Stamford, CT 06902; tel. (203) 969-8700; fax (203) 977-8354; e-mail generalinfo@thomson.com; internet www.thomson.com; Pres. S. M. GARNER; 50 daily newspapers in USA.

Tribune Co: 435 North Michigan Ave, Chicago, IL 60611; tel. (312) 222-9100; fax (312) 222-4760; internet www.tribune.com; 9205; Chair. and CEO JOHN W. MADIGAN; Pres. DENNIS J. FITZSIMMONS; 15 daily newspapers, including *Chicago Tribune, Los Angeles Times, Newsday* and *Baltimore Sun*.

PRINCIPAL DAILY AND SUNDAY NEWSPAPERS
(m = morning; e =evening; d = all day; s = Sunday)

In general, only newspapers with circulations exceeding 50,000 are included, except in Wyoming, where the newspaper with the largest circulation is listed.

Alabama

Birmingham News: 2200 North Fourth Ave, POB 2553, Birmingham, AL 35202-2553; tel. (205) 325-2222; fax (205) 325-2410; internet www.bhamnews.com; f. 1888; Publr V. H. HANSON, II; Editor THOMAS SCARRITT; circ. 152,000 (e), 186,000 (s).

Huntsville Times: 2317 Memorial Parkway, Huntsville, AL 35801-5623; tel. (205) 532-4000; fax (205) 532-4420; internet www.htimes .com; f. 1910; Publr BOB LUDWIG; Editor JOE DISTELHEIM; circ. 60,000 (d), 67,000 (s).

Mobile Register, Mobile Press-Register: 304 Government St, POB 2488, Mobile, AL 36630; tel. (334) 433-1551; fax (334) 434-8662; e-mail gtab@dibbs.net; internet www.al.com; f. 1813; Publr HOWARD BRONSON; Editor MICHAEL MARSHALL; circ. 100,000 (m, Mobile Register), 120,000 (s, Mobile Press Register).

Montgomery Advertiser: 200 Washington Ave, POB 1000, Montgomery, AL 36101-1000; tel. (334) 262-1611; fax (334) 261-1521; e-mail advertiser@compuserve.com; internet www .montgomeryadvertiser.com; f. 1828; Publr SCOTT M. BROWN; Exec. Editor PAULA MOORE; circ. 59,000 (m), 73,000 (s).

Alaska

Anchorage Daily News: 1001 Northway Dr., POB 149001, Anchorage, AK 99514-9001; tel. (907) 257-4200; fax (907) 258-2157; e-mail subscription@adn.com; internet www.adn.com; f. 1946; Publr MICHAEL SEXTON; Editor W. PATRICK DOUGHERTY; circ. 71,400 (m), 85,800 (s).

Arizona

Arizona Daily Star: 4850 South Park Ave, POB 26807, Tucson, AZ 85726-6807; tel. (520) 573-4220; fax (520) 573-4107; internet www .azstarnet.com; f. 1877; Publr MICHAEL E. PULITZER; Editor STEPHEN AUSLANDER; circ. 101,000 (m), 185,000 (s).

Arizona Republic: 120 East Van Buren St, Phoenix, AZ 85001; tel. (602) 271-8000; fax (602) 271-8044; internet www.azcentral.com; f. 1890; Editor TOM CALLINAN; circ. 500,000 (m), 600,000 (s).

Tucson Citizen: 4850 South Park Ave, POB 26807, Tucson, AZ 85726-6807; tel. (520) 573-4561; fax (520) 573-4569; f. 1870; Publr and Editor C. DONALD HATFIELD; circ. 51,000 (e).

Arkansas

Democrat-Gazette: POB 2221, Little Rock, AR 72203; tel. (501) 378-3400; fax (501) 372-3908; e-mail news@ardemgaz.com; internet www.ardemgaz.com; f. 1819; Publr WALTER E. HUSSMAN, Jr; Exec. Editor GRIFFIN SMITH, Jr; circ. 172,223 (m), 285,731 (s).

California

Bakersfield Californian: POB 440, Bakersfield, CA 93302-0440; tel. (805) 395-7500; fax (805) 395-7519; internet www.bakersfield .com; f. 1866; Publr GINGER MOORHOUSE; Exec. Editor RICHARD BEENE; circ. 77,000 (m), 92,000 (s).

Daily Breeze: Copley Los Angeles Newspapers, 5215 Torrance Blvd, Torrance, CA 90509; tel. (310) 540-5511; f. 1894; Mon. to Sat. evening, Sun. morning; Publr BERTRAM E. WINROW; Exec. Editor JAMES M. BOX (Rep.); circ. 82,372 (e), 120,302 (s).

Daily News: 21221 Oxnard St, Woodland Hills, CA 91367; tel. (818) 713-3000; fax (818) 713-0057; f. 1911; morning; Publr DAVID J. AUGER; Editor ROBERT W. BURDICK (Ind.); circ. 207,421 (m), 192,326 (Sat.), 226,294 (s).

Fresno Bee: 3425 North First St, Suite 201, Fresno, CA 93726-6819; tel. (209) 441-6111; fax (209) 441-6436; f. 1922; Publr J. KEITH MOYER; Exec. Editor CHARLIE WATERS; circ. 155,000 (m), 192,000 (s).

Investor's Business Daily: 12655 Beatrice Ave, Los Angeles, CA 90066; tel. (310) 448-6000; fax (310) 577-7350; e-mail ibdcust@investors.com; internet www.investors.com; f. 1984; morning; Publr W. SCOTT O'NEILL; Editor WESLEY F. MANN; circ. 233,000.

Los Angeles Times: 202 West First St, Los Angeles, CA 90012-3645; tel. (213) 237-5000; fax (213) 237-4712; internet www.latimes.com; f. 1881; Pres. and Publr JOHN PUERNER; Editor JOHN CARROLL; circ. 1,111,000 (m), 1,384,000 (s).

Modesto Bee: 1325 H St, Modesto, CA 95354; tel. (209) 578-2000; fax (209) 578-2207; internet www.modbee.com; f. 1884; Publr ORAGE QUARLES, III; Editor-in-Chief SANDERS LAMONT; circ. 83,023 (m), 90,341 (s).

Oakland Tribune: 116 West Wenton Ave., Oakland, CA 94540; tel. (510) 208-6300; fax (510) 208-6477; internet www.cyberia-ang.com; f. 1874; Editor TIM GRAHAM; circ. 77,000 (m), 75,000 (s).

Orange County Register: 625 North Grand Ave, POB 11626, Santa Ana, CA 92701-4347; tel. (714) 767-7000; fax (714) 796-3681; e-mail register_customer_service@link.freedom.com; internet www.ocregister.com; Publr CHRISTIAN ANDERSON; Editor TONNIE KATZ; circ. 353,812 (d), 412,553 (s).

Press Democrat: 427 Mendocino Ave, Santa Rosa, CA 95402; tel. (707) 546-2020; fax (707) 521-5330; internet www.pressdemo.com; f. 1857; Publr MICHAEL PARMAN; Exec. Editor CATHERINE BARNETT; circ. 93,363 (m), 102,985 (s).

Press Enterprise: 3512 14th St, POB 792, Riverside, CA 92501; tel. (714) 684-1200; fax (714) 782-7630; f. 1878; morning; Publr WILLIAM D. RICH; Exec. Editor MARCIA McQUERN; circ. 154,790 (m), 162,940 (s).

Press-Telegram: 604 Pine Ave, Long Beach, CA 90844-0001; tel. (562) 435-1161; fax (562) 437-7892; e-mail ptconnect@infi.net; internet www.ptconnect.com; Pres. and Publr RICK SADOWSKI; Exec. Editor JIM CRUTCHFIELD; circ. 106,000 (d), 125,000 (s).

Sacramento Bee: 2100 Q St, POB 15779, Sacramento, CA 95852; tel. (916) 321-1000; fax (916) 321-1306; e-mail jheapy@sacbee.com; internet www.sacbee.com; f. 1857; Pres. and Publr JANIS HEAPHY; Exec. Editor RICK RODRIGUEZ; circ. 293,973 (m), 352,629 (s).

San Bernardino County Sun: 399 North D St, San Bernardino, CA 92401-1518; tel. (909) 889-9666; fax (909) 381-3976; f. 1894; Publr MARK ADKINS; Editor RICARDO PIMENTEL; circ. 82,000 (m), 91,000 (s).

San Diego Union-Tribune: 350 Camino de la Renta, San Diego, CA 92112; tel. (619) 299-3131; fax (619) 293-1896; e-mail letters@uniontrib.com; internet www.uniontrib.com; f. 1868; Publr HELEN K. COPLEY; Editor KARIN WINNER; circ. 376,500 (d), 453,900 (s).

San Francisco Chronicle: 901 Mission St, San Francisco, CA 94103; tel. (415) 777-1111; fax (415) 896-1107; e-mail chronletters@sfgate.com; internet www.sfgate.com/chronicle; f. 1865; Publr, Chair and CEO JOHN OPPEDAHL; Editor PHIL BRONSTEIN; circ. 600,000 (m), 704,000 (s).

San Francisco Examiner: 988 Market St, San Francisco, CA 94103-2918; tel. (415) 359-2767; fax (415) 359-2766; e-mail sfexaminer@examiner.com; internet www.examiner.com; f. 1887; Publr TED FANG; Editor ZORAN BASICH; circ. 70,000 (m), 90,000 (s).

San Jose Mercury News: 750 Ridder Park Dr., San Jose, CA 95190-0001; tel. (408) 920-5000; fax (408) 288-8060; e-mail sjmercury@aol.com; internet www.bayarea.com; Publr JOSEPH T. NATOLI; Editor DAVID YARNOLD; circ. 288,212 (m), 326,839 (s).

Stockton Record: 530 East Market St, POB 900, Stockton, CA 95202-3009; tel. (209) 943-6397; fax (209) 943-8246; e-mail newsroom@recordnet.com; internet www.recordnet.com; f. 1895; Publr VIRGIL SMITH; Man. Editor JIM GOLD; circ. 54,000 (m), 60,000 (s).

Colorado

Denver Post: 1560 Broadway, Denver, CO 80202; tel. (303) 820-1010; fax (303) 820-1369; e-mail newsroom@denverpost.com; internet www.denverpost.com; f. 1892; Publr DEAN SINGLETON; Editor GLENN GUZZO; circ. 370,423 (m), 523,324 (s).

The Gazette: 30 South Prospect, Colorado Springs, CO 80903; tel. (719) 632-5511; fax (719) 636-0202; e-mail gtnews@usa.net; internet www.gazette.com; f. 1872; Publr SCOTT A. FISCHER; Editor STEVEN A. SMITH; circ. 104,000 (m), 125,000 (s).

Rocky Mountain News: 400 West Colfax Ave, POB 719, Denver, CO 80201; tel. (303) 892-5000; fax (303) 892-5081; e-mail subscribe@rockymountainnews.com; internet www.rockymountainnews.com; f. 1859; Publr, Pres. and Editor JOHN R. TEMPLE; circ. 394,000 (m), 504,000 (s).

Connecticut

Connecticut Post: 410 State St, Bridgeport, CT 06604-4501; tel. (203) 333-0161; fax (203) 366-3373; e-mail ctnews@snet.net; internet www.connpost.com; f. 1883; Publr DUDLEY THOMAS; Editor RICK SAYERS; circ. 78,255 (m), 90,217 (s).

Hartford Courant: 285 Broad St, Hartford, CT 06115; tel. (860) 241-6200; fax (860) 520-3176; e-mail letters@courant.com; internet www.courant.com; f. 1764; Publr and CEO JACK DAVIS; Editor BRIAN P. TOOLAN; circ. 211,866 (m), 298,143 (s).

New Haven Register: 40 Sargent Dr., New Haven, CT 06511; tel. (203) 789-5200; fax (203) 865-7894; internet www.ctcentral.com; f. 1812; Publr THOMAS RICE; Editor JACK KRAMER; circ. 100,000 (m), 114,000 (s).

Waterbury Republican-American: American-Republican, Inc, 389 Meadow St, POB 2090, Waterbury, CT 06722-3636; tel. (203) 574-3636; fax (203) 754-0644; f. 1844; morning; Publr WILLIAM J. PAPE, II; circ. 60,202 (m), 77,682 (s).

Delaware

News Journal: 950 West Basin Rd, New Castle, DE 19720; tel. (302) 324-2617; fax (302) 324-5518; e-mail newsroom@newsjournal.com; internet www.newszap.com; f. 1871; Publr SAL DE VIVO; Editor J. DONALD BRANDT; circ. 126,000 (d), 140,000 (s).

District of Columbia

Washington Post: 1150 15th St, NW, Washington, DC 20071; tel. (202) 334-6000; fax (202) 334-5693; internet www.washingtonpost.com; f. 1877; Chair. DONALD E. GRAHAM; Publr and CEO BOISFEUILLET JONES; Exec. Editor LEONARD DOWNIE, Jr; Man. Editor STEVE COLL; circ. 802,594 (m), 1,070,809 (s).

Washington Times: 3600 New York Ave, NE, Washington, DC 20002; tel. (202) 636-3000; fax (202) 529-2471; e-mail general@washtimes.com; internet www.washingtontimes.com; f. 1982; Man. Editor WILLIAM GILES; circ. 110,000 (m), 65,000 (s).

Florida

Daytona Beach News-Journal: 901 Sixth St, Daytona Beach, FL 32120-2831; tel. (904) 252-1511; fax (904) 258-8470; internet www.n-jcenter.com; f. 1904; morning; Publr HERBERT M. DAVIDSON (Dem.); circ. 99,556 (m), 117,571 (s).

Diario Las Américas: 2900 NW 39th St, Miami, FL 33142-5419; tel. (305) 633-3341; fax (305) 635-7668; internet www.diariolasamericas.com; f. 1953; Spanish; Publr and Editor HORACIO AGUIRRE; circ. 66,000 (m), 70,000 (s).

Florida Times-Union: 1 Riverside Ave, Jacksonville, FL 32202-4904; tel. (904) 359-4111; fax (904) 359-4478; internet www.jacksonville.com; f. 1864; Publr CARL N. CANNON; Exec. Editor PAT YACK; circ. 197,706 (m), 251,216 (s).

Florida Today: Cape Publs, Inc, POB 419000, Melbourne, FL 32941-9000; tel. (407) 242-3500; fax (407) 242-6618; f. 1966; morning; Publr MICHAEL J. COLEMAN; Exec. Editor BENNIE IVORY; circ. 83,502 (m), 111,674 (s).

Ledger: POB 408, Lakeland, FL 33802; tel. (813) 687-7000; fax (813) 687-7090; f. 1924; morning; Publr and Pres. DON R. WHITWORTH; Exec. Editor LOUIS MICHAEL PEREZ (Ind.); circ. 81,325 (m), 99,143 (s).

Miami Herald: 1 Herald Plaza, Miami, FL 33132-1609; tel. (305) 350-2111; fax (305) 376-5287; internet www.herald.com; f. 1910; Publr ALBERTO IBARGUEN; Exec. Editor TOM FIEDLER; circ. 367,029 (m), 482,149 (s).

News-Press: 2422 Dr Martin Luther King, Jr Blvd, Fort Myers, FL 33901-3987; tel. (941) 335-0200; fax (941) 332-7581; e-mail chudlerpress@news-press.com; internet www.news-press.com; f. 1884; morning; Publr CAROL HUDLER; Editor KATE MARYMONT (Ind.); circ. 93,769 (m), 116,944 (s).

Orlando Sentinel: 633 North Orange Ave, Orlando, FL 32801-1300; tel. (407) 420-5000; fax (407) 420-5661; internet www.orlandosentinel.com; f. 1876; Publr, Pres. and CEO KATHLEEN WALTZ; Editor TIM FRANKLIN; circ. 260,367 (d), 382,439 (s).

Palm Beach Post: 2751 South Dixie Hwy, West Palm Beach, FL 33405; tel. (561) 820-4100; fax (561) 820-4136; e-mail letters@pbpost.com; internet www.pbpost.com; f. 1916; Publr TOM GIUFFRIDA; Editor EDWARD M. SEARS; circ. 187,000 (m), 237,000 (s).

Pensacola News Journal: 1 News-Journal Plaza, Pensacola, FL 32501-5670; tel. (850) 435-8500; fax (850) 435-8633; e-mail pns@gulfsurf.infi.net; internet www.gulfcoastgateway.com; f. 1889; Publr KENNETH W. ANDREWS; Exec. Editor ANNE SAUL; circ. 62,000 (m), 85,000 (s).

Sarasota Herald-Tribune: 801 South Tamiami Trail, Sarasota, FL 34236; tel. (941) 953-7755; fax (941) 957-5276; f. 1925; Publr DIANE McFARLIN; Exec. Editor JANET WEAVER; circ. 120,000 (m), 149,000 (s).

St Petersburg Times: 490 First Ave South, POB 1121, St Petersburg, FL 33701; tel. (813) 893-8111; fax (813) 893-8675; e-mail letters@sptimes.com; internet www.sptimes.com; f. 1894; CEO ANDREW BARNES; Pres., Editor PAUL TASH; circ. 351,110 (m), 431,320 (s).

Sun-Sentinel: 200 East Las Olas Blvd, Fort Lauderdale, FL 33301-2293; tel. (954) 356-4000; fax (954) 356-4559; internet www .sun-sentinel.com; f. 1960; Publr ROBERT GREMILLION; Editor EARL MAUKER; circ. 276,000 (m), 390,000 (s).

Tampa Tribune: 200 Parker St, Tampa, FL 33606; tel. (813) 259-7600; fax (813) 254-4952; internet www.tampatrib.com; f. 1893; morning; Editor GIL THELEN (Ind.); circ. 252,000 (m), 350,000 (s).

Georgia

Atlanta Constitution: 72 Marietta St, POB 4689, Atlanta, GA 30302-4689; tel. (404) 526-5151; fax (404) 526-5746; e-mail constitution@ajc.com; internet www.ajc.com/cox/ajc.htm; f. 1950; Sun. morning; Publr ROGER KINTZEL; Editor RON MARTIN; circ. 703,590.

Augusta Chronicle: 725 Broad St, POB 1928, Augusta, GA 30913-1928; tel. (706) 724-0851; fax (706) 722-5746; internet www .augustachronicle.com; Publr W. S. MORRIS, III; Exec. Editor DENNIS SODOMKA; circ. 75,000 (m), 100,000 (s).

Chronicle Herald: 725 Broad St, POB 1928, Augusta, GA 30903-1928; tel. (706) 724-0851; fax (706) 722-7403; Sun. Publr W. S. MORRIS, III; Exec. Editor DENNIS SODOMKA (Ind.); circ. 103,000.

Macon Telegraph: 120 Broadway, Macon, GA 31201-3444; tel. (912) 744-4200; fax (912) 744-4269; e-mail metro@mto.infi.net; internet www.macontel.com; f. 1826; Publr ED OLSON; Editor RICK THOMAS; circ. 77,000 (m), 106,000 (s).

Savannah Morning News: POB 1088, Savannah, GA 31402-1088; tel. (912) 236-9511; fax (912) 234-6522; internet www.savanews .com; f. 1850; Publr FRANK ANDERSON; Editor WALLACE M. DAVIS, Jr; circ. 56,000 (m), 82,000 (s).

Hawaii

Honolulu Advertiser, Honolulu Star-Bulletin, Honolulu Star-Bulletin & Advertiser: 605 Kapiolani Blvd, Honolulu, HI 96802; tel. (808) 525-8000; fax (808) 525-8037; e-mail editor@starbulletin .com; internet www.starbulletin.com; f. 1856; f. 1882; f. 1962; Editors JIM GATTI (Advertiser), JOHN FLANAGAN (Star-Bulletin); circ. 106,000 (m, Advertiser), 66,000 (e, Star-Bulletin), 197,000 (s, Star-Bulletin & Advertiser).

Idaho

Idaho Statesman: 1200 North Curtis Rd, POB 40, Boise, ID 83707; tel. (208) 377-6200; fax (208) 377-6309; e-mail news@idstates.com; internet www.idahostatesman.com; f. 1864; Publr MARGARET BUCHANAN; Man. Editor CAROLYN WASHBURN; circ. 66,730 (m), 88,542 (s).

Illinois

Bloomington Pantagraph: 301 West Washington, Bloomington, IL 61701-3803; tel. (309) 829-9411; fax (309) 829-9104; internet www .pantagraph.com; f. 1837; Publr DONALD SKAGGS; Man. Editor JAN DENNIS; circ. 51,000 (m), 56,000 (s).

Chicago Sun-Times: 401 North Wabash Ave, Chicago, IL 60611-3593; tel. (312) 321-3000; fax (312) 321-3084; e-mail letters@ suntimes.com; internet www.suntimes.com; f. 1948; Publr F. DAVID RADLER; Editor-in-Chief MICHAEL COOKE; circ. 496,000 (m), 445,000 (s).

Chicago Tribune: 435 North Michigan Ave, Chicago, IL 60611-4022; tel. (312) 222-3232; fax (312) 222-3162; internet www.chicago .tribune.com; f. 1847; Publr SCOTT SMITH; Editor ANN MARIE LIPINSKI; circ. 675,000 (m), 1,001,000 (s).

Daily Herald: POB 280, Arlington Heights, IL 60006; tel. (847) 427-4300; fax (847) 427-1301; internet www.dailyherald.com; f. 1872; Exec. Editor JOHN LAMPINEN; circ. 149,882 (m), 152,323 (s).

Journal Star: 1 News Plaza, Peoria, IL 61643; tel. (309) 686-3000; fax (309) 686-3296; internet www.pjstar.com; f. 1855; Publr JOHN T. MCCONNELL; Editor JACK BRIMEYER; circ. 81,000 (m), 108,000 (s).

Rockford Register Star: 99 East State St, Rockford, IL 61104; tel. (815) 987-1200; fax (815) 987-6578; e-mail rrslibrary@smtp .registerstartower.com; internet www.rrstar.com; f. 1888; Publr MARY P. STIER; Exec. Editor LINDA G. CUNNINGHAM; circ. 78,000 (m), 90,000 (s).

State Journal-Register: 1 Copley Plaza, POB 219, Springfield, IL 62705-0219; tel. (217) 788-1300; fax (217) 788-1551; e-mail sjr@sj-r .com; internet www.sj-r.com; f. 1831; Publr PATRICK COBURN; Editor BARRY J. LOCHER; circ. 59,597 (m), 68,577 (s).

Indiana

Evansville Courier: 300 Walnut St, Evansville, IN 47713; tel. (812) 424-7711; fax (812) 422-8196; e-mail courierpress@evansville .net; internet www.courierpress.com; f. 1845; Publr and Pres. VINCE VAWTER; Editor PAUL MCAULIFFE; circ. 73,000 (m), 107,000 (s).

Indianapolis News: 307 North Pennsylvania St, Indianapolis, IN 46204; tel. (317) 633-1240; fax (317) 633-1038; f. 1869; Mon. to Sat. evening; Publr EUGENE S. PULLIAM; Editor RUSSEL B. PULLIAM (Ind.); circ. 93,000 (e).

Indianapolis Star: 307 North Pennsylvania St, Indianapolis, IN 46204; tel. (317) 633-1240; fax (317) 633-1038; internet www .indystar.com; Publr and Pres. BARBARA HENRY; Editor TERRY R. EBERLE; circ. 272,483 (m), 371,684 (s).

Journal-Gazette: 600 West Main St, Fort Wayne, IN 46802; tel. (219) 461-8444; fax (219) 461-8648; e-mail jgnews@jg.netr; internet www.journalgazette.net; f. 1863; Publr JULIE INSKEEPWALDA; Editor CRAIG KLUGMAN; circ. 62,000 (m), 134,000 (s).

News-Sentinel: 600 West Main St, Fort Wayne, IN 46802; tel. (219) 461-8444; fax (219) 461-8817; internet www.fortwayne.com/ns; f. 1833; Publr SCOTT MCGHEE; Exec. Editor JOSEPH A. WEILER; circ. 54,000 (e).

Post-Tribune: 1065 Broadway, Gary, IN 46402-2907; tel. (219) 881-3000; fax (219) 881-3232; f. 1907; Publr SCOTT BOSLEY; Editor MARK LETT; circ. 64,000 (m), 72,000 (s).

South Bend Tribune: 225 West Colfax Ave, South Bend, IN 46626; tel. (219) 235-6161; fax (219) 236-1765; e-mail mclein@sbt.sbtinfo .com; internet www.sbtinfo.com; f. 1872; Publr and Editor DAVID C. RAY; circ. 72,000 (e), 102,000 (s).

The Times: 601 45th Ave, Munster, IN 46325; tel. (219) 932-3100; fax (219) 933-3332; f. 1906; morning; Publr WILLIAM E. HOWARD; Exec. Editor WILLIAM NANGLE (Ind.); circ. 65,494 (m), 63,896 (Sat.), 72,740 (s).

Iowa

Cedar Rapids Gazette: 500 Third Ave SE, Cedar Rapids, IA 52401; tel. (319) 398-8211; fax (319) 398-5846; e-mail gazette@ fyiowa.infi.net; internet www.GazetteOnline.com; f. 1883; Publr and Editor J. F. HLADKY, III; Man. Editor MARK BOWDEN; circ. 71,000 (m), 85,000 (s).

Des Moines Register: 715 Locust St, POB 957, Des Moines, IA 50304; tel. (515) 284-8530; fax (515) 286-2511; e-mail newssub@ dmreg.com; internet www.DesMoinesRegister.com; f. 1849; Publr MARY STIER; Editor DENNIS RYERSON; circ. 174,412 (m), 294,794 (S).

Quad-City Times: 500 East Third St, POB 3828, Davenport, IA 52801-1708; tel. (319) 383-2200; fax (319) 383-2433; f. 1855; Publr ROBERT A. FUSIE; Editor DANIEL K. HAYES; circ. 54,000 (d), 85,000 (s).

Sioux City Journal: 515 Pavonia St, Sioux City, IA 51102; tel. (712) 279-5026; fax (712) 279-5059; e-mail scjournal@pronet.net; internet www.siouxcityjournal.com; f. 1864; Publr DEAN A. KRENZ; Editor LARRY MYHRE; circ. 50,000 (m).

Kansas

Topeka Capital-Journal: 616 SE Jefferson St, Topeka, KS 66607-1120; tel. (785) 295-1111; fax (785) 295-1230; e-mail state@ cjnetworks.com; internet www.cjonline.com; f. 1879; Publr JOHN FISH; Exec. Editor PETE GOERING; circ. 59,000 (m), 65,000 (s).

Wichita Eagle: 825 East Douglas Ave, POB 820, Wichita, KS 67201; tel. (316) 268-6000; fax (316) 268-6627; e-mail wenews@ wichitaeagle.com; internet www.wichitaeagle.com; f. 1872; Publr PETER PITZ; Editor RICK THAMES, Jr; circ. 91,943 (m), 168,974 (s).

Kentucky

Courier-Journal: 525 West Broadway St, Louisville, KY 40202-2137; tel. (502) 582-4011; fax (502) 582-4075; internet www .courier-journal.com; f. 1868; Publr EDWARD MANASSAH; Editor DAVID V. HAWPE; circ. 228,809 (m), 301,426 (s).

Lexington Herald-Leader: 100 Midland Ave, Lexington, KY 40508; tel. (606) 231-3100; fax (606) 254-9738; internet www .kentuckyconnect.com; f. 1860; Publr TIM KELLY; Man. Editor AMANDA BENNETT; circ. 121,034 (m), 165,352 (s).

Louisiana

Advocate: POB 588, Baton Rouge, LA 70821; tel. (504) 383-1111; fax (504) 388-0348; e-mail comments@theadvocate.com; internet www.theadvocate.com; f. 1904; Publr DOUGLAS L. MANSHIP; Editor LINDA C. LIGHTFOOT; circ. 92,524 (m), 124,589 (s).

The Times: 222 Luke St, POB 30222, Shreveport, LA 71130; tel. (318) 459-3200; fax (318) 459-3301; f. 1872; Publr RICHARD STONE; Editor MIKE WHITEHEAD; circ. 77,000 (m), 94,000 (s).

Times-Picayune: 3800 Howard Ave, New Orleans, LA 70125-1429; tel. (504) 826-3279; fax (504) 826-3636; internet www.nola.com; f. 1880; Publr Ashton Phelps, Jr; Editor Jim Amoss; circ. 268,000 (d), 324,000 (s).

Maine

Bangor Daily News: 491 Main St, POB 1329, Bangor, ME 04402-1329; tel. (207) 990-8000; fax (207) 941-0885; internet www.bangornews.com; f. 1834; Publr and Editor Richard J. Warren; circ. 72,000 (m).

Maine Sunday Telegram: 390 Congress St, POB 1460, Portland, ME 04104; tel. (207) 780-9000; fax (207) 791-6920; f. 1887; Publr Jean Gannett Hawley; Exec. Editor Louis A. Ureneck (Ind.); circ. 145,000.

Portland Press Herald, Maine Sunday Telegram: 390 Congress St, POB 1460, Portland, ME 04104; tel. (207) 791-6650; fax (207) 791-6920; e-mail herald@portland.com; internet www.portland.com; f. 1862; f. 1887; Publr Jean Gannett Hawley; Editor Jeannine Guttman; circ. 76,000 (m, Press Herald), 140,000 (s, Telegram).

Maryland

Baltimore Sun: 501 North Calvert St, Baltimore, MD 21278-0001; tel. (410) 332-6000; fax (410) 752-6049; e-mail imogene.lambie@baltsun.com; internet www.sunspot.net; f. 1837; Man. Editor Tony Barbieri; Editor Wiliam Marimow; circ. 320,000 (m), 490,692 (s).

Massachusetts

Boston Globe: POB 2378, Boston, MA 02107-2000; tel. (617) 929-2000; fax (617) 929-3192; e-mail news@globe.com; internet www.boston.com; f. 1872; Publr Richard Gilman; Editor Martin D. Baron; circ. 464,472 (m), 721,859 (s).

Boston Herald: 1 Herald Sq., POB 2096, Boston, MA 02106-2096; tel. (617) 426-3000; fax (617) 426-1869; e-mail library@bostonherald.com; internet www.bostonherald.com; f. 1825; Publr Patrick Purcell; Editor Andrew F. Costello; circ. 301,797 (m), 206,996 (s).

Christian Science Monitor: 1 Norway St, Boston, MA 02115-3195; tel. (617) 450-2000; fax (617) 450-7575; internet www.csmonitor.com; f. 1908; Mon.–Fri. Editor Paul Van Slambrouck; circ. 90,000.

Lowell Sun: 15 Kearney Sq., Lowell, MA 01853; tel. (978) 458-7100; fax (978) 970-4800; internet www.newschoice.com; f. 1878; Pres. and Sr Editor John H. Costello, Jr; circ. 55,000 (e), 57,000 (s).

Patriot Ledger: POB 9159, Quincy, MA 02269-9159; tel. (617) 786-7000; fax (617) 786-7298; e-mail chazy@ledger.com; internet www.southofboston.com; f. 1837; Publr James Plugh; Editor Chazy Dowaliby; circ. 77,000 (e).

Springfield Union-News, Sunday Republican: 1860 Main St, Springfield, MA 01101; tel. (413) 788-1000; fax (413) 788-1301; e-mail unews-news@union-news.com; internet www.masslive.com; f. 1864; f. 1824; Publr Larry McDermott; Editor Wayne E. Phaneuf; circ. 100,000 (m, Union News), 150,000 (s, Republican).

Worcester Telegram & Gazette: 20 Franklin St, POB 15012, Worcester, MA 01615-0012; tel. (508) 793-9100; fax (508) 793-9281; internet www.telegram.com; f. 1866; Publr Bruce S. Bennett; Editor Harry T. Within; circ. 112,000 (d), 142,000 (s).

Michigan

Detroit Free Press: 600 West Fort St, Detroit, MI 48226; tel. (313) 222-6400; fax (313) 222-5981; e-mail merriwe@freepress.com; internet www.freep.com; f. 1831; Publr Heath J. Merriweather; Editor Carole Leigh Hutton; circ. 362,841 (m), 1,173,000 (s).

Detroit News: 615 West Lafayette Blvd, Detroit, MI 48226-3197; tel. (313) 222-2300; fax (313) 222-2335; e-mail msilverman@detnews.com; internet www.detnews.com; f. 1873; Publr and Editor Mark Silverman; circ. 246,638 (e), 830,000 (s).

Flint Journal: 200 East First St, Flint, MI 48502; tel. (810) 766-6100; fax (810) 767-7518; e-mail fj@flintj.com; f. 1876; Publr Danny R. Gaydou; Editor Tom Lindley; circ. 102,000 (m), 124,000 (s).

Grand Rapids Press: 155 Michigan St, NW, Grand Rapids, MI 49503-2302; tel. (616) 459-1400; fax (616) 459-1502; f. 1890; Editor Michael S. Lloyd; circ. 139,000 (e), 190,000 (s).

Kalamazoo Gazette: 401 South Burdick St, Kalamazoo, MI 49007-5279; tel. (616) 345-3511; fax (616) 345-0583; f. 1883; Publr Daniel M. Ryan; Editor James R. Mosby, Jr; circ. 60,000 (e), 76,000 (s).

Lansing State Journal: 120 East Lenawee St, Lansing, MI 48919-0001; tel. (517) 377-1000; fax (517) 377-1298; f. 1855; Publr Michael Kane; Exec. Editor Michael Hirten; circ. 70,260 (m), 92,041 (s).

Oakland Press: 48 West Huron St, POB 436009, Pontiac, MI 48343; tel. (248) 332-8181; fax (248) 332-8294; f. 1843; Publr Bruce H. McIntyre; Editor William Thomas; circ. 86,000 (m), 103,000 (s).

Saginaw News: 203 South Washington Ave, Saginaw, MI 48607-1283; tel. (517) 752-7171; fax (517) 752-3115; internet www.sa.mlive.com; f. 1859; Publr H. Renee Hampton; Editor Paul Chaffee; circ. 57,333 (e), 67,739 (s).

Minnesota

Duluth News-Tribune: 424 West First St, POB 169000, Duluth, MN 55816-9000; tel. (218) 723-5281; fax (218) 723-5339; f. 1869; morning; Publr James V. Gels; Editor Vicki Gowler (Ind.); circ. 58,565 (d), 84,518 (s).

Star Tribune: 425 Portland Ave South, Minneapolis, MN 55488; tel. (612) 673-4000; fax (612) 673-7138; e-mail roberts@startribune.com; internet www.startribune.com; f. 1920; Publr Keith Moyer; Editor Tim McGuire; circ. 374,570 (m), 678,001 (s).

St Paul Pioneer Press: 345 Cedar St, St Paul, MN 55101; tel. (612) 222-5011; fax (612) 228-5500; e-mail feedback@pioneerplanet.infi.net; internet www.pioneerpress.com; f. 1849; Pres. Rick Sadowski; Editor Walker Lundy; circ. 207,624 (m), 275,057 (s).

Mississippi

Clarion-Ledger: 201 South Congress St, Jackson, MS 39201; tel. (601) 961-7000; fax (601) 961-7211; e-mail homesub@jackson-gannett.com; internet www.clarionledger.com; f. 1954; Publr and Pres. William W. Hunsberger; Editor Shawn McIntosh; circ. 112,000 (e), 130,000 (s).

Missouri

Kansas City Star: 1729 Grand Blvd, Kansas City, MO 64108; tel. (816) 234-4280; fax (816) 234-4926; e-mail subscriptions@kansascity.com; internet www.kansascity.com; f. 1880; Publr Arthur S. Brisbane; Editor Mark Zieman; circ. 291,000 (m), 434,000 (s).

News-Leader: 651 Boonville Ave, Springfield, MO 65806; tel. (417) 836-1100; fax (417) 836-1147; f. 1933; morning; Publr Fritz Jacobi; Editor Andy McMills (Ind.); circ. 61,623 (m), 101,612 (s).

St Louis Post-Dispatch: 900 North Tucker Blvd, St Louis, MO 63101; tel. (314) 340-8000; fax (314) 340-3050; e-mail post@postnet.com; internet www.postnet.com; f. 1878; Publr Terrence Egger (Editor Ellen Soeteber); circ. 324,059 (d), 520,635 (s).

Montana

Billings Gazette: POB 36300, Billings, MT 59101; tel. (406) 657-1200; fax (406) 657-1345; internet www.bigskywire.com/gazette/; f. 1885; Publr Wayne Schile; Editor Richard J. Wesnick; circ. 54,000 (m), 63,000 (s).

Nebraska

Lincoln Star: Journal Star Printing Co, 926 P St, POB 81609, Lincoln, NE 68501; tel. (402) 475-4200; fax (402) 473-7291; e-mail feedback@journalstar.com; internet www.journalstar.com; f. 1867; morning; Publr Bill Johnston; Editor David Stoeffler (Ind.); circ. 40,093 (m), 79,210 (Sat.), 84,699 (s).

Omaha World-Herald: 1334 Dodge St, Omaha, NE 68102-1122; tel. (402) 444-1000; fax (402) 345-0183; internet www.omaha.com; f. 1885; Publr and Pres. John Gottschalk; Editor Deanna Sands; circ. 229,418 (d), 277,970 (s).

Nevada

Las Vegas Review-Journal: 1111 West Bonanza Rd, Las Vegas, NV 89106; tel. (702) 383-0211; e-mail webmaster@lvrj.com; internet www.lvrj.com; f. 1908; Publr Sherman Frederick; Editor Thomas Mitchell; circ. 172,352 (m), 223,151 (s).

Reno Gazette-Journal: POB 22000, Reno, NV 89520-2000; tel. (702) 788-6397; fax (702) 788-6458; e-mail rgjmail@nevadanet.com; internet www.nevadanet.com/RGJ.html; f. 1870; Publr Sue Clark-Johnson; Editor Ward Bushee; circ. 67,000 (m), 84,000 (s).

New Hampshire

Union Leader, New Hampshire Sunday News: POB 9555, Manchester, NH 03108-9555; tel. (603) 668-4321; fax (603) 668-0382; e-mail theul@aol.com; internet www.theunionleader.com; f. 1863; f. 1946; Pres. and Publr Joseph W. McQuaid; Editor Charles Perkins; circ. 65,250 (m, Union Leader), 88,000 (s, Sunday News).

New Jersey

Asbury Park Press: 3601 Highway 66, POB 1550, Neptune, NJ 07754-1550; tel. (732) 922-6000; fax (732) 918-9144; e-mail custer@app.com; internet www.app.com; f. 1879; Publr and Pres. Robert T. Collins; Editor W. Raymond Ollwerther; circ. 161,929 (d), 224,800 (s).

Courier-News: 1201 Highway 22 West, POB 6600, Bridgewater, NJ 08807; tel. (908) 722-8800; fax (908) 707-3252; e-mail cneditor@

c-n.com; internet www.c-n.com; f. 1884; Publr Charles W. Nutt; Editor James A. Flachsenhaar; circ. 42,000 (e), 43,000 (s).

Courier-Post: POB 5300, Cherry Hill, NJ 08034; tel. (856) 663-3000; fax (856) 663-2831; f. 1875; Publr Dan A. Martin; Exec. Editor William C. Hidlay; circ. 87,000 (m), 99,000 (s).

Home News and Tribune: 3601 Highway 66, POB 1550, Neptune, NJ 07754-1550; tel. (732) 922-6000; fax (732) 918-9144; e-mail letter@thnt.com; f. 1879; Publr Robert T. Collins; Editor Richard Hughes; circ. 70,000 (m), 77,500 (s).

Jersey Journal: 30 Journal Sq., Jersey City, NJ 07306; tel. (201) 217-2455; fax (201) 653-1414; internet www.nj.com/jjournal; f. 1867; Editor Judith Locorriere; circ. 55,000 (e).

The Press: 1000 West Washington Ave, Pleasantville, NJ 08232-3816; tel. (609) 272-7000; fax (609) 272-7059; f. 1895; morning; Publr James W. Hopson; Exec. Editor Paul A. Merkoski (Ind.); circ. 80,417 (m), 102,544 (s).

The Record: 150 River St, Hackensack, NJ 07601-7172; tel. (201) 646-4000; fax (201) 646-4135; e-mail newsroom@northjersey.com; internet www.newjersey.com; f. 1895; Pres. Jon Markey; Editor Vivien Waixel; circ. 158,000 (m), 213,000 (s).

Star-Ledger: 1, Star-Ledger Plaza, Newark, NJ 07101; tel. (973) 877-4141; fax (973) 877-5845; e-mail metro@starledger.com; internet www.nj.com; f. 1917; Publr Linda Dennery; Editor Jim Willse; circ. 407,537 (m), 608,015 (s).

The Times: 500 Perry St, Trenton, NJ 08605; tel. (609) 396-5454; fax (609) 396-3633; e-mail news@njtimes.com; internet www.nj.com/times; f. 1882; Publr Richard Bilotti; Exec. Editor Brian S. Malone; circ. 80,000 (m), 90,000 (s).

Trentonian: 600 Perry St, Trenton, NJ 08602; tel. (609) 989-7800; fax (609) 394-1358; internet www.trentonian.com; f. 1945; Publr David Bonfield; Editor Paul Mickle; circ. 54,595 (m), 43,749 (s).

The Wall Street Journal: 4300 North Route 1, South Brunswick, NJ 08852; tel. (609) 520-5542; internet www.wsj.com; f. 1889; morning; Chair. and Publr Peter R. Kann; Man. Editor Paul E. Steiger; circ. 1,800,000.

New Mexico

Albuquerque Journal: 7777 Jefferson NE, NM 87109; tel. (505) 823-3393; fax (505) 823-3369; e-mail journal@abqjournal.com; internet www.abqjournal.com; f. 1880; Publr T. H. Lang; Editor Kent Walz; circ. 116,134 (m), 168,818 (s).

New York

Albany Times Union: News Plaza, POB 15000, Albany, NY 12212; tel. (518) 454-5694; fax (518) 454-5514; e-mail tuletters@timesunion.com; internet www.timesunion.com; f. 1856; Publr David White; Exec. Editor Jeff Cohen; circ. 100,401 (m), 146,723 (s).

Buffalo News: 1 News Plaza, POB 100, Buffalo, NY 14203-2930; tel. (716) 849-3434; fax (716) 849-3409; internet www.buffalonews.com; f. 1880; Publr Stanford Lipsey; Editor Margaret M. Sullivan; circ. 240,000 (d), 340,000 (s).

Daily Gazette: POB 1090, Schenectady, NY 12301-1090; tel. (518) 374-4141; fax (518) 395-3089; e-mail gazette@dailygazette.com; internet www.dailygazette.com; f. 1894; Publr and Editor John E. N. Hume, II; circ. 57,000 (m), 59,000 (s).

Democrat and Chronicle: 55 Exchange Blvd, Rochester, NY 14614-2001; tel. (716) 232-7100; fax (716) 258-3027; internet www.rochesterdandc.com; f. 1833; Publr David L. Hunke; Editor Karen Magnuson; circ. 177,747 (m), 239,822 (s).

Newsday: 235 Pinelawn, Melville, NY 11747-4250; tel. (516) 843-2020; fax (516) 843-2953; e-mail delivery@newsday.com; internet www.newsday.com; f. 1940; Publr Raymond A. Jansen; Editor Anthony Marro; circ. 571,283 (m), 657,559 (s).

Post-Standard, Herald-Journal: Clinton Sq., POB 4915, Syracuse, NY 13221; tel. (315) 470-0011; fax (315) 470-3081; e-mail linhorst@syracuse.com; internet www.syracuse.com; f. 1877; Publr Stephen A. Rogers; Exec. Editor Michael J. Connor; circ. 87,000 (m, Post-Standard), 83,000 (e, Herald-Journal).

Press & Sun-Bulletin: 4421 Vestal Pkwy East, POB 1270, Binghamton, NY 13850; tel. (607) 798-1234; fax (607) 798-0261; Publr Bernie Griffin; Editor Rick Jensen; circ. 65,000 (m), 80,000 (s).

Rochester Democrat and Chronicle: 55 Exchange Blvd, Rochester, NY 14614; tel. (716) 232-7100; fax (716) 232-3027; f. 1826; Mon. to Fri. evening; Publr Steven R. Brandt; Editor Tom Callinan (Ind.); circ. 142,649 (e), 206,780 (Sat.), 251,307 (s).

Syracuse Herald Journal: Clinton Sq., POB 4915, Syracuse, NY 13221-4915; tel. (315) 470-0011; fax (315) 470-3030; f. 1877; Mon. to Sat. evening; Exec. Editor Timothy D. Bunn (Ind.); circ. 88,565 (e).

Times Herald-Record, Record: 40 Mulberry St, Middletown, NY 10940; tel. (914) 343-2181; fax (914) 343-2170; f. 1956; Publr John M. Szefc; Editor Gary Grossman; circ. 86,000 (m, Times Herald-Record), 102,000 (s, Record).

New York City

New York Daily News: 450 West 33rd St, New York, NY 10001; tel. (212) 210-2100; fax (212) 682-4953; internet www.nydailynews.com; f. 1919; Publrs Fred Drasner, Mortimer B. Zuckerman; Editor-in-Chief Edward Kosner; circ. 727,089 (m), 851,921 (s).

New York Post: 1211 Ave of the Americas, New York, NY 10036; tel. (212) 930-8000; e-mail letters@nypost.com; internet www.nypost.com; f. 1801; Chair. and Pres. Rupert Murdoch; Publr Lachlan Murdoch; Editor-in-Chief Col Allan; circ. 437,467 (m), 382,000 (s).

New York Sun: 105 Chambers St, 2nd Floor, New York, NY 10007; tel. (212) 406-2000; internet www.nysun.com; f. 2002; Editor and Pres. Seth Lipsky.

New York Times: 229 West 43rd St, New York, NY 10036; tel. (212) 556-1234; internet www.nytimes.com; f. 1851; Chair and Publr Arthur Ochs Sulzberger, Jr; Exec. Editor Howell Raines; circ. 1,159,954 (m), 1,698,281 (s).

Staten Island Advance: 950 Fingerboard Rd, Staten Island, New York, NY 10305; tel. (718) 981-1234; fax (718) 981-5679; internet www.silive.com; f. 1886; Publr Richard E. Diamond; Editor Brian J. Laline; circ. 78,000 (e), 95,000 (s).

North Carolina

Charlotte Observer: 600 South Tryon St, POB 32188-28232, Charlotte, NC 28202-1842; tel. (704) 358-5840; fax (704) 358-5036; internet www.charlotte.com/observer; f. 1886; Publr Peter Ridder; Editor Jennie Buckner; circ. 242,000 (m), 295,000 (s).

Citizen-Times: 14 O'Henry Ave, POB 2090, Asheville, NC 28802; tel. (704) 252-5611; fax (704) 251-2659; f. 1870; morning; Publr James B. Banks; Exec. Editor Larry Pope (Ind.); circ. 66,564 (m), 79,302 (s).

Fayetteville Observer-Times: Fayetteville Publishing Co, 458 Whitfield St, POB 849, Fayetteville, NC 28302; tel. (919) 323-4848; fax (919) 486-3531; f. 1816; morning; Publr Ramon L. Yarborough; Exec. Editor J. Michael Rouse (Ind.); circ. 71,361 (m), 80,511 (s).

Greensboro News and Record: 200 East Market St, POB 20848, Greensboro, NC 27401-2910; tel. (919) 373-7000; fax (919) 373-7043; internet www.triadonline.com; f. 1890; Publr Carl Magnum, Jr; Exec. Editor Ben J. Bowers; circ. 91,000 (m), 119,000 (s).

News and Observer: 215 South McDowell St, POB 191, Raleigh, NC 27602; tel. (919) 829-4500; fax (919) 829-4529; e-mail naostaff@nando.com; internet www.news-observer.com; f. 1865; Publr Orage Quarles, III; Sr Man. Editor Anders Gyllenhaal; circ. 161,604 (m), 208,676 (s).

Winston-Salem Journal: 418 North Marshall St, Winston-Salem, NC 27102-3159; tel. (336) 727-7211; fax (336) 727-7315; e-mail news@journalnow.com; internet www.wsjournal.com; Publr Jon Witherspoon; Man. Editor Jim Laughrun; circ. 90,344 (m), 102,878 (s).

North Dakota

The Forum: 401 Fifth St North, Box 2020, Fargo, ND 58102-4826; tel. (701) 235-7311; fax (701) 241-5487; internet www.in-forum.com; f. 1878; Publr William C. Marcil; Editor Joseph Dill; circ. 53,634 (m), 67,750 (s).

Ohio

Akron Beacon Journal: 44 East Exchange St, POB 640, Akron, OH 44328-0001; tel. (330) 996-3000; fax (330) 376-9235; internet www.ohio.com; f. 1839; Publr James N. Crutchfield; Editor Janet Leach; circ. 146,838 (m), 209,038 (s).

The Blade: 541 North Superior St, Toledo, OH 43660; tel. (419) 245-6000; fax (419) 245-6191; f. 1835; morning; Publr John Robinson Block; Editor Thomas Walton (Ind.); circ. 146,334 (m), 207,352 (s).

Canton Repository: 500 Market Ave South, Canton, OH 44711-2112; tel. (330) 454-5611; fax (330) 454-5610; internet www.cannet.com/~therep/; f. 1815; Publr David Greenfield; Editor Michael E. Hanke; circ. 61,000 (e), 80,000 (s).

Cincinnati Enquirer: 312 Elm St, Cincinnati, OH 45202; tel. (513) 721-2700; fax (513) 721-2703; internet www.enquirer.com; f. 1841; Publr Harry M. Whipple; Editor Ward Bushee; circ. 204,388 (m), 351,898 (s).

Cincinnati Post: 125 East Court St, Cincinnati, OH 45202; tel. (513) 352-2000; fax (513) 621-3962; internet www.cincypost.com; f. 1881; Publr Alan Horton; Editor Mike Philipps; circ. 55,800 (m).

Cleveland Plain Dealer: 1801 Superior Ave East, Cleveland, OH 44114; tel. (216) 344-4600; fax (216) 344-4620; e-mail circhepl@plaind.com; internet www.plaindealer.com; f. 1842; Publr ALEX MACHASKEE; Editor DOUGLAS C. CLIFTON; circ. 382,933 (m), 492,337 (s).

Columbus Dispatch: 34 South Third St, Columbus, OH 43215-4241; tel. (614) 461-5000; fax (614) 461-7580; e-mail letters@dispatch.com; internet www.dispatch.com; f. 1871; Publr JOHN F. WOLFE; Editor BEN MARRISON; circ. 258,297 (m), 393,757 (s).

Dayton Daily News: 45 South Ludlow St, Dayton, OH 45402; tel. (937) 225-2321; fax (937) 225-2334; internet www.daytondailynews.com; Publr BRAD TILSON; Editor JEFF BRUCE; circ. 162,537 (m), 212,128 (s).

Dayton Journal Herald: 45 South Ludlow St, Dayton, OH 45402; tel. (937) 225-2321; fax (937) 225-2334; Sun. Publr BRAD TILSON; Editor MAX JENNINGS; circ. 225,000.

News-Herald: 38879 Mentor Ave, Willoughby, OH 44094; tel. (216) 951-0000; fax (216) 951-0917; f. 1880; Mon. to Sat. evening, Sun. morning; Publr JOSEPH A. COCOZZO; Editor JAMES K. COLLINS (Ind.); circ. 56,332 (e), 66,668 (s).

Toledo Blade: 541 North Superior St, Toledo, OH 43660-1000; tel. (419) 245-6000; fax (419) 245-6439; internet www.toledoblade.com; f. 1835; Editor THOMAS WALTON; circ. 147,635 (e), 200,547 (s).

The Vindicator: Vindicator Sq., POB 780, Youngstown, OH 44501-0780; tel. (330) 747-1471; fax (330) 747-6712; Publr BETTY H. BROWN JAGNOW; Editor PAUL C. JAGNOW; circ. 82,000 (e), 120,000 (s).

Oklahoma

Daily Oklahoman: 9000 North Broadway, POB 25125, Oklahoma City, OK 73114; tel. (405) 475-3311; fax (405) 475-3970; internet www.newsok.com; f. 1894; Publr EDWARD L. GAYLORD; Editor SUE HALE; circ. 213,722 (m), 395,775 (s).

Tulsa Tribune: 315 South Boulder Ave, POB 1770, Tulsa, OK 74103; tel. (918) 581-8400; fax (918) 584-1037; f. 1904; evening; Publr JENKIN L. JONES; Editor JENK JONES, Jr (Ind.); circ. 67,000.

Tulsa World: 315 South Boulder Ave, POB 1770, Tulsa, OK 74103; tel. (918) 581-8300; fax (918) 581-8353; e-mail tulsaworld@tulsaworld.com; internet www.tulsaworld.com; f. 1906; Publr ROBERT E. LORTON; Editor JOE WORLEY; circ. 142,000 (m), 207,000 (s).

Oregon

The Oregonian: 1320 SW Broadway, Portland, OR 97201-3469; tel. (503) 221-8327; fax (503) 227-5306; internet www.oregonian.com; f. 1850; Publr. FRED A. STICKEL; Editor SANDRA M. ROWE; circ. 356,000 (d), 440,000 (s).

The Register-Guard: 3500 Chad Dr., Eugene, OR 97408; tel. and fax (541) 485-1234; fax (541) 683-7631; internet www.registerguard.com; f. 1867; Publr and Editor ALTON F. BAKER, III; circ. 75,510 (m), 78,903 (s).

Statesman Journal: POB 13009, Salem, OR 97309; tel. (503) 399-6611; fax (503) 399-6808; e-mail newsroom@statesmanjournal.com; internet www.statesmanjournal.com; f. 1851; Publr SARAH M. BENTLEY; Exec. Editor STEVEN A. SMITH; circ. 57,000 (m), 66,000 (s).

Pennsylvania

Bucks County Courier Times: 8400 Route 13, Levittown, PA 19057-5198; tel. (215) 949-4000; fax (215) 949-4177; internet www.phillyburbs.com; f. 1910; Editor PAT WALKER; circ. 71,000 (m), 77,000 (s).

Call Chronicle: POB 1260, Allentown, PA 18105; tel. (610) 820-6500; fax (610) 820-6693; f. 1921; Sun. Publr GARY K. SHORTS; Exec. Editor LAWRENCE H. HYMANS; circ. 189,000.

Harrisburg Patriot: 812 Market St, POB 2265, Harrisburg, PA 17105; tel. (717) 255-8100; fax (717) 257-4796; f. 1854; daily (except Sat.) morning; Publr JOHN A. KIRKPATRICK (Ind.); circ. 100,208 (d), 154,543 (s).

The Morning Call: POB 1260, Allentown, PA 18101-1403; tel. (610) 820-6500; fax (610) 820-6617; internet www.mcall.com; Publr SUSAN HUNT; Exec. Editor ARDITH HILLIARD; circ. 129,574 (m), 182,907 (s).

Patriot-News: 812 Market St, Harrisburg, PA 17105; tel. (717) 255-8100; fax (717) 255-8450; e-mail newsroom@patriot.microserve.com; f. 1854; Publr JOHN KIRKPATRICK; Editor THOMAS BADEN; circ. 99,690 (m), 158,009 (s).

Philadelphia Daily News: 400 North Broad St, POB 8623, Philadelphia, PA 19101; tel. (215) 854-2000; fax (215) 854-4794; e-mail dailynews.opinion@phillynews.com; internet www.philly.com; f. 1925; Editor ZACHARY STALBERG; circ. 161,755 (e).

Philadelphia Inquirer: 400 North Broad St, POB 8623, Philadelphia, PA 19101; tel. (215) 854-2000; fax (215) 854-4794; e-mail inquirer.opinion@phillynews.com; internet www.philly.com; f. 1829; Editor ROBERT ROSENTHAL; circ. 414,815 (m), 838,296 (s).

Pittsburg Post-Gazette: POB 957, Pittsburgh, PA 15230-0957; tel. (412) 263-1100; fax (412) 391-8452; f. 1786; Publrs WILLIAM BLOCK, Jr, JOHN ROBINSON BLOCK; Editor JOHN G. CRAIG, Jr; circ. 244,000 (m), 431,000 (s).

Sunday News: Lancaster Newspapers, Inc, 8 West King St, Lancaster, PA 17603; tel. (717) 291-8733; fax (717) 399-6506; f. 1923; Editor DAVID HENNIGAN (Ind.); circ. 105,000.

Tribune-Democrat: 425 Locust St, Johnstown, PA 15907; tel. (814) 532-5199; fax (814) 539-1409; f. 1853; Publr PAMELA MAYER; Editors ARLENE MCLAREN, STEVE LIEBMAN; circ. 50,000 (m), 56,000 (s).

Rhode Island

Providence Journal-Bulletin: 75 Fountain St, Providence, RI 02902-0050; tel. (401) 277-7000; fax (401) 277-7889; e-mail letters@projo.com; internet www.projo.com; f. 1829; Publr HOWARD G. SUTTON; Exec. Editor JOEL RAWSON; circ. 165,000 (d), 250,000 (s).

South Carolina

Greenville News, News-Piedmont: 305 South Main St, POB 1688, Greenville, SC 29601-2605; tel. (864) 298-4100; fax (864) 298-4805; e-mail NewsLetters@greenville.ifni.net; internet www.greenvilleonline.com; f. 1874; Publr STEVEN BRANDT; Editor JOHN S. PITTMAN; circ. 97,000 (m, Greenville News), 145,000 (s, News-Piedmont).

News-Piedmont: 305 South Main St, POB 1688, Greenville, SC 29602-1688; tel. (864) 298-4100; fax (864) 298-4395; f. 1874; Sun. Publr STEVEN R. BRANDT; Editor JOHN S. PITTMAN (Ind.); circ. 145,000.

The Post and Courier: 134 Columbus St, Charleston, SC 29403-4800; tel. (843) 577-7111; fax (843) 937-5579; e-mail seima@postandcourier.com; internet www.charleston.net; f. 1803; Publr LARRY TARLETON, Jr; Editor BARBARA WILLIAMS; circ. 110,000 (m), 122,000 (s).

State Record: POB 1333, Columbia, SC 29202; tel. (803) 771-6161; fax (803) 771-8430; e-mail state@thestate.com; internet www.thestate.com; f. 1891; Publr FRED MOTT; Exec. Editor MARK LETT; circ. 135,000 (m), 175,000 (s).

South Dakota

Argus Leader: POB 5034, Sioux Falls, SD 57117-5034; tel. (605) 331-2200; fax (605) 331-2294; e-mail editor@argusleader.com; f. 1881; Publrs MARY DEVISH, JACK MARSH; Editor RICHARD SOMERVILLE; circ. 51,000 (m), 73,000 (s).

Tennessee

Chattanooga Times-Free Press: 400 East 11th St, POB 1447, Chattanooga, TN 37401-1447; tel. (423) 756-6900; fax (423) 757-6383; e-mail editor@chatfreepress.com; internet www.chattimes.com; f. 1888; Publr WALTER E. HUSSMAN; Man. Editor BOB LUTGEN; circ. 82,000 (m), 110,000 (s).

The Commercial Appeal: 495 Union Ave, Memphis, TN 38103; tel. (901) 529-2322; fax (901) 529-5833; internet www.gomemphis.com; f. 1841; Pres. ANGUS MCEACHRAN; Man. Editor HENRY STOKES; circ. 182,978 (m), 253,982 (s).

Knoxville News-Sentinel: 208 West Church Ave, POB 59038, Knoxville, TN 37902-1683; tel. (865) 523-3131; fax (865) 521-8186; e-mail kns@knoxnews.com; internet www.knoxnews.com; f. 1886; Editor HARRY MOSKOS; circ. 117,948 (m), 168,075 (s).

The Tennessean: 1100 Broadway St, Nashville, TN 37203; tel. (615) 259-8800; fax (615) 259-8093; internet www.tennessean.com; f. 1812; Publr CRAIG MOON; Editor FRANK SUTHERLAND; circ. 190,000 (m), 285,000 (s).

Texas

Austin American-Statesman: POB 670, Austin, TX 78767; tel. (512) 445-3500; fax (512) 445-3800; e-mail editors@statesman.com; internet www.austin360.com; f. 1871; Publr MICHAEL LAOSA; Editor RICH OPPEL; circ. 185,000 (m), 245,000 (s).

Beaumont Enterprise: 380 Main St, POB 3071, Beaumont, TX 77701-2331; tel. (409) 833-3311; fax (409) 838-2857; internet www.ent-net.com; f. 1880; Publr GEORGE B. IRISH; Editor BEN HANSEN; circ. 61,000 (m), 74,000 (s).

Caller-Times: 820 North Lower Broadway, POB 9136, Corpus Christi, TX 78469; tel. (512) 884-2011; fax (512) 886-3732; e-mail cteds@caller.com; internet www.caller.com; f. 1883; Publr STEPHEN W. SULLIVAN; Exec. Editor DAVID A. HOUSE; circ. 70,000 (m), 92,000 (s).

Dallas Morning News: POB 655237, Dallas, TX 75265; tel. (214) 977-8222; fax (214) 977-8638; internet www.dallasnews.com; f. 1885; Editor ROBERT MONG; circ. 536,002 (m), 809,552 (s).

El Paso Times: Times Plaza, El Paso, TX 79901-1470; tel. (915) 546-6104; fax (915) 546-6496; f. 1881; Publr and Editor TOM FENTON; circ. 66,000 (m), 97,000 (s).

Express-News: POB 2171, San Antonio, TX 78297-2171; tel. (210) 225-7411; fax (210) 225-8351; internet www.express-news.net; f. 1865; Publr W. LAWRENCE WALKER, Jr; Exec. Editor JIM MOSS; circ. 216,000 (m), 375,000 (s).

Fort Worth Star-Telegram: POB 1870, Fort Worth, TX 76101; tel. (817) 390-7400; fax (817) 390-7789; e-mail newsroom@star-telegram .com; internet www.star-telegram.com; f. 1909; Publr WES TURNER; Exec. Editor JIM WITT; circ. 240,136 (d), 341,893 (s).

Houston Chronicle: 801 Texas Ave, Houston, TX 77002; tel. (713) 220-7171; fax (713) 220-6677; e-mail hci@HoustonChronicle.com; internet www.chron.com; f. 1901; Publr JACK SWEENEY; Editor JACK LOFTUS; circ. 553,462 (m), 747,803 (s).

Houston Post: 4747 Southwest Freeway, POB 4747, Houston, TX 77210-4747; tel. (713) 840-5600; f. 1885; morning; Publr IKE MASSEY; Editor GERALD GARCIA (Ind.); circ. 300,121 (m), 348,676 (s).

Lubbock Avalanche-Journal: 710 Ave J, POB 491, Lubbock, TX 79401-1808; tel. (806) 762-8844; fax (806) 744-9603; internet www .lubbockonline.com; f. 1900; Publr DAVID C. SHARP; Editor JAY HARRIS; circ. 65,000 (m), 75,000 (s).

San Antonio Express-News: Ave E and Third St, POB 2171-7297, San Antonio, TX 78297-2171; tel. (210) 250-3000; fax (210) 250-3105; internet www.expressnews.com; f. 1864; Mon. to Fri. all day, Sat. and Sun. morning; Publr W. LAWRENCE WALKER, Jr; Exec. Editor ROBERT RIVARD (Ind.); circ. 218,661 (Mon. to Thurs.), 273,889 (Fri.), 267,051 (Sat.), 366,402 (s).

San Antonio Light: 420 Broadway, San Antonio, TX 78205; tel. (512) 271-2700; fax (512) 271-2770; f. 1881; Mon. to Fri. all day, Sat. and Sun. morning; Publr GEORGE B. IRISH; Exec. Editor ED RADE-MAEKERS (Ind.); circ. 166,722 (d), 233,268 (s).

Utah

Deseret News: 30 East First St South, POB 1257, Salt Lake City, UT 84110; tel. (801) 237-2188; fax (801) 237-2121; e-mail letters@ desnews.com; internet www.desnews.com; f. 1850; Pres. and Publr JIM WALL; Editor JOHN HUGHES; circ. 62,410 (e), 67,574 (s).

Salt Lake Tribune: 143 South Main St, POB 867, Salt Lake City, UT 84111; tel. (801) 257-8742; fax (801) 257-8525; internet www .sltrib.com; f. 1871; Publr DOMINIC WELCH; Editor JAMES SHELLEDY; circ. 117,858 (m), 150,146 (s).

Standard-Examiner: 455 23rd St, POB 951, Ogden, UT 84401-1507; tel. (801) 625-4200; fax (801) 625-4508; internet www .standard.net; f. 1888; Editor RANDY HATCH; circ. 60,000 (e), 61,000 (s).

Vermont

Burlington Free Press: 191 College St, Burlington, VT 05402-0010; tel. (802) 863-3441; fax (802) 660-1802; e-mail bfreepress@aol .com; internet burlingtonfreepress.com; f. 1827; Publr JAMES CAREY; Editor MIKE TOWNSEND; circ. 53,171 (m), 66,855 (s).

Virginia

Daily Press: POB 746, Newport News, VA 23607; tel. (757) 247-4600; fax (757) 245-8618; e-mail dpedit@aol.com; internet www .dailyxpress.com; f. 1896; Publr JOSEPH D. CANTRELL; Editor JACK DAVIS; circ. 104,000 (m), 127,000 (s).

Richmond Times-Dispatch: 300 East Franklin St, POB 85333, Richmond, VA 23293; tel. (804) 649-6000; fax (804) 775-8059; internet www.timesdispatch.com; f. 1850; Publr J. STEWART BRYAN, III; Man. Editor LOUISE SEALS; circ. 194,625 (m), 230,299 (s).

Roanoke Times: POB 2491, Roanoke, VA 24010-2491; tel. (540) 981-3100; fax (540) 981-3171; e-mail roatimes@infi.net; internet www.roanoke.com; Publr WENDY ZOMPARELLI; Exec. Editor MIKE RILEY; circ. 115,000 (m), 127,000 (s).

USA Today: 1100 Wilson Blvd, Arlington, VA 22234-0011; tel. (703) 276-3400; fax (703) 558-4646; internet www.usatoday.com; f. 1982; Publr TOM CURLEY; Editor KAREN JURGENSEN; circ. 2,300,000 (m).

Virginian-Pilot: 150 West Brambleton Ave, POB 449, Norfolk, VA 23501; tel. (757) 446-2000; fax (757) 446-2983; e-mail pilot@infi.net; internet www.pilotonline.com; f. 1876; Publr BRUCE BRADLEY; Editor KAY TUCKER ADDIS; circ. 219,000 (e), 230,000 (s).

Washington

The Herald: Grand and California Sts, POB 930, Everett, WA 98206; tel. (425) 339-3000; fax (425) 339-3049; f. 1891; Publr ALLEN B. FUNK; Exec. Editor STAN STRICK; circ. 53,000 (m), 64,000 (s).

News Tribune: POB 11000, Tacoma, WA 98411-0008; tel. (253) 597-8742; fax (253) 597-8266; internet www.tribnet.com; f. 1883;

Publr KELSO GILLENWATER; Exec. Editor DAVID ZEECK; circ. 128,000 (m), 148,000 (s).

Seattle Post-Intelligencer: 101 Elliott Ave West, Seattle, WA 98119-4220; tel. (206) 448-8000; fax (206) 448-8292; e-mail editor@ seattlep-i.com; internet www.seattlep-i.com; f. 1863; Publr and Editor ROGER OGLESBY; circ. 168,951 (m), 482,978 (s).

Seattle Times: POB 70, Seattle, WA 98111-0070; tel. (206) 464-2111; fax (206) 464-2261; e-mail opinion@seattletimes.com; internet www.seattletimes.com; f. 1896; Publr FRANK A. BLETHEN; Editor MICHAEL R. FANCHER; circ. 225,222 (e), 482,978 (s).

Spokesman-Review: 999 West Riverside, POB 2160, Spokane, WA 99210; tel. (509) 459-5000; fax (509) 459-5234; e-mail editor@ spokesman.com; internet www.spokane.net; f. 1883; Publr W. STANLEY COWLES; Editor CHRISTOPHER PECK; circ. 150,550 (m), 137,568 (s).

Tacoma Morning News Tribune: 1950 South State St, POB 11000, Tacoma, WA 98411; tel. (206) 597-8742; fax (206) 597-8263; f. 1883; morning; Publr KELSO GILLENWATER; Editor JOHN D. KOMEN (Ind.); circ. 126,303 (d), 140,033 (s).

West Virginia

Charleston Daily Mail: 1001 Virginia St East, POB 2993, Charleston, WV 25301-2895; tel. (304) 348-5110; fax (304) 348-5133; e-mail dmnews@dailymail.com; internet www.dailymail.com; f. 1973; Publr SAMUEL E. HINDMAN; Editor NANYA FRIEND; circ. 40,000 (e), 95,000 (s).

Wisconsin

Green Bay Press-Gazette: 435 East Walnut St, POB 19430, Green Bay, WI 54307-5001; tel. (920) 435-4411; fax (920) 431-8499; f. 1915; Publr W. T. NUSBAUM; Editor JOHN D. GIBSON; circ. 58,000 (m), 86,000 (s).

Milwaukee Journal Sentinel: 333 West State St, Milwaukee, WI 53203-1305; tel. (414) 224-2000; fax (414) 224-2469; internet www .jsonline.com; f. 1837; Publr KEITH SPORE; Editor MARTIN KAISER; circ. 266,590 (m), 443,411 (s).

Post-Crescent: POB 59, Appleton, WI 54912; tel. (920) 733-4411; fax (920) 733-1983; e-mail pcnews@athenet.net; f. 1920; Publr PAUL P. SEVESKA; Editor WILLIAM HARKE; circ. 58,000 (e), 76,000 (s).

Wisconsin State Journal: 1901 Fish Hatchery Rd, POB 8058, Madison, WI 53708; tel. (608) 252-6100; fax (608) 252-6119; e-mail wsjcity@madison.com; internet www.madison.com/wsj/; f. 1839; Publr JAMES HOPSON; Editor FRANK DENTON; circ. 94,000 (m), 158,000 (s).

Wyoming

Star-Tribune: POB 80, Casper, WY 82602; tel. (307) 266-0500; fax (307) 266-0501; internet www.trib.com; f. 1891; Publr ROB HURLESS; Editor DAN NEAL; circ. 33,500 (m), 38,000 (s).

SELECTED PERIODICALS
(q = quarterly; m = monthly; f = fortnightly; w = weekly)

Affirmative Action Register: 8356 Olive Blvd, St Louis, MO 63132; tel. (314) 991-1335; fax (314) 997-1788; e-mail aareeo@ concentric.net; internet www.aar-eeo.com; f. 1974; recruitment; Editor JOYCE R. GREEN; circ. 67,000 (m).

American Heritage: 90 Fifth Ave, New York, NY 10011-8882; tel. (212) 367-3100; fax (212) 367-3149; e-mail mail@americanheritage .com; internet www.americanheritage.com; f. 1954; Editor RICHARD F. SNOW; circ. 330,000 (8 a year).

American Historical Review: 914 Atwater, Indiana University, Bloomington, IN 47401; tel. (812) 855-7609; fax (812) 855-5827; e-mail ahr@indiana.edu; internet www.indiana.edu/~ahr; f. 1895; Editor MICHAEL GROSSBERG; circ. 19,000 (5 a year).

American Hunter: c/o National Rifle Asscn, 11250 Waples Mill Rd, Fairfax, VA 22030-9400; tel. (703) 267-1300; fax (703) 267-3971; e-mail publications@nrahq.org; internet nra.org; f. 1973; Editor-in-Chief JOHN ZENT; circ. 1,059,000 (m).

American Journal of Psychiatry: American Psychiatric Asscn, 1400 K St, NW, Washington, DC 20005-2403; tel. (202) 682-6020; fax (202) 682-6016; e-mail ajp@psych.org; internet www.ajp .psychiatryonline.org; f. 1844; Editor Dr NANCY C. ANDREASEN; circ. 40,000 (m).

American Legion Magazine: 700 North Pennsylvania St, POB 1055, Indianapolis, IN 46206-1055; tel. (317) 630-1200; fax (317) 630-1280; e-mail magazine@legion.org; internet www.legion.org; f. 1919; organ of the American Legion; Editor JOHN B. RAUGHTER; circ. 2,650,000 (m).

American Motorcyclist: 33 Collegeview Rd, Westerville, OH 43081-1484; tel. (614) 891-2425; fax (614) 891-5012; e-mail letters@

ama_cycle.org; f. 1947; Exec. Editor GREG HARRISON; circ. 225,000 (m).

American Political Science Review: 1527 New Hampshire Ave, NW, Washington, DC 20036; tel. (202) 483-2512; fax (202) 483-2657; e-mail apsr@ssc.msu.edu; f. 1906; Editor ADA W. FINIFTER; circ. 16,000 (q).

American Teacher: 555 New Jersey Ave, NW, Washington, DC 20001-2079; tel. (202) 879-4430; fax (202) 783-2014; e-mail online@aft.org; internet www.aft.org; f. 1916; Editor ROGER GLASS; circ. 950,000 (8 a year).

Architectural Digest: The Condé Nast Publications Inc, 6300 Wilshire Blvd, Los Angeles, CA 90048; tel. (213) 965-3700; fax (213) 937-1458; internet www.archdigest.com; f. 1920; Publr AMY CHURGIN; Editor PAIGE RENSE; circ. 850,000 (m).

Architectural Record: 2 Penn Plaza, New York, NY 10021; tel. (212) 904-2594; fax (212) 904-4256; internet www.archrecord.com; f. 1891; Publr ELAINE SHUSTERMAN; Editor ROBERT IVY; circ. 95,000 (m).

Aviation Week & Space Technology: 2 Penn Plaza, 5th Floor, New York, NY 10021; tel. (212) 904-2000; fax (212) 904-6068; internet www.awstonline.com; f. 1916; Editor-in-Chief DAVID M. NORTH, Jr; circ. 107,353 (w).

Barron's The Dow Jones Business & Financial Weekly: 4300 North Route 1, South Brunswick, NJ; tel. 6092) 520-5542; e-mail editors@barrons.com; internet www.barrons.com; f. 1921; Editor EDWIN A. FINN, Jr; circ. 300,158 (w).

Better Homes and Gardens: 1716 Locust St, Des Moines, IA 50309-3023; tel. (515) 284-3000; fax (515) 284-3684; internet www.bhg.com; f. 1922; Publr JEANNINE SHAO; Editor-in-Chief KAREL DE WULF NICKELL; circ. 7,600,000 (m).

Better Living: 80 Central Park West, Suite 16B, New York, NY 10023; tel. (212) 581-2000; f. 1980; Editor JOSEPH QUEENAN; circ. 200,000 (q).

Boating Magazine: 122 E 42nd St, Suite 2211, New York, NY 10168; tel. (212) 455-1651; fax (212) 953-6420; internet boatingmag.com; f. 1956; Editor RANDY STEELE; circ. 200,152 (m).

Bon Appetit: 6300 Wilshire Blvd, 10th Floor, Los Angeles, CA 90048; tel. (323) 965-3600; fax (323) 937-1206; internet www.bonappetit.com; f. 1955; Publr LYNN W. HEILER; Editor-in-Chief BARBARA FAIRCHILD; circ. 1,280,105 (m).

Boys' Life: 1325 West Walnut Hill Lane, POB 152079, Irving, TX 75015-2079; tel. (972) 580-2366; fax (972) 580-2079; f. 1911; Editor J. D. OWEN; circ. 1,300,000 (m).

Bride's Magazine: 4 Times Sq., 6th Floor, New York, NY 10036; tel. (212) 286-2860; fax (212) 286-8831; e-mail letters@brides.com; internet www.brides.com; f. 1934; Editor MILLIE BRATTEN; circ. 475,013 (6 a year).

Broadcasting & Cable: 245 West 17th St, 7th Floor, New York, NY 10011; tel. (212) 645-0067; fax (212) 337-6948; f. 1931; Publr PEGGY CONLON; Editor HARRY A. JESSELL; circ. 36,194 (w).

Business Week International: 1221 Ave of the Americas, 39th Floor, New York, NY 10020-1095; tel. (212) 512-2511; fax (212) 512-4464; internet www.businessweek.com; f. 1929; Editor-in-Chief STEPHEN B. SHEPARD; circ. 1,008,000 (w).

Capper's: 1503 SW 42nd St, Topeka, KS 66609-1265; tel. (785) 274-4300; fax (785) 274-4305; e-mail cappers@kspress.com; f. 1879; Editor ANN GRAHAM; circ. 210,000 (f).

Car and Driver: 2002 Hogback Rd, Ann Arbor, MI 48105; tel. (734) 971-3600; fax (734) 971-9188; e-mail editors@caranddriver.com; internet www.caranddriver.com; f. 1956; Editor-in-Chief CSABA CSERE; circ. 1,365,195.

Catholic Digest: POB 64090, St Paul, MN 55164-0090; tel. (612) 962-6739; fax (612) 962-6725; e-mail cdigest@stthomas.edu; internet www.catholicdigest.org; f. 1936; Editor RICHARD REECE; circ. 509,000 (m).

Chemical and Engineering News: American Chemical Society, 1155 16th St, NW, Washington, DC 20036-4800; tel. (202) 872-4600; fax (202) 872-8727; e-mail edit.cen@acs.org; internet www.pubs.acs.org/cen; f. 1923; Editor MADELEINE JACOBS; circ. 156,000 (w).

Children's Digest: 1100 Waterway Blvd, POB 567, Indianapolis, IN 46206; tel. (317) 636-8881; fax (317) 637-0126; internet www.childrensdigestmag.org; f. 1950; Editor LISE HOFFMAN; circ. 91,000 (8 a year).

Christianity Today: 465 Gundersen Dr., Carol Stream, IL 60188-2498; tel. (630) 260-6200; fax (630) 260-0014; e-mail ctedit@aol.com; internet www.christianitytoday.net; f. 1956; Exec. Editor DAVID NEFF; circ. 174,000 (14 a year).

Civil Engineering: 345 East 47th St, 16th Floor, New York, NY 10017-2398; tel. (212) 705-7463; fax (212) 705-7712; e-mail cemag@ny.asce.org; f. 1930; Editor VIRGINIA FAIRWEATHER; circ. 95,000 (m).

Congressional Digest: 3231 P St, NW, Washington, DC 20007-2772; tel. (202) 333-7332; fax (202) 625-6670; e-mail cdeditor@aol.com; internet www.congressionaldigest.com; f. 1921; Publr PAGE B. ROBINSON; 10 a year.

Consumer Reports: 101 Truman Ave, Yonkers, NY 10703-1057; tel. (914) 378-2000; fax (914) 378-2900; internet www.consumerreports.org; f. 1936; Editor JULIA KAGAN; circ. 4,500,000 (m).

Consumers Digest: 8001 North Lincoln Ave, 6th Floor, Skokie, IL 60077-3657; tel. (847) 763-9200; fax (847) 763-0200; f. 1959; Editor RANDY WEBER; circ. 1,000,000 (6 a year).

Cosmopolitan: 224 West 57th St, New York, NY 10019-3203; tel. (212) 649-2000; fax (212) 207-5363; e-mail cosmo_letters@hearst.com; internet www.cosmomag.com; f. 1886; women's; Publr SUSAN PLAGEMANN; Editor KATE WHITE; circ. 2,800,000 (m).

Country Living: 224 West 57th St, New York, NY 10019-3203; tel. (212) 649-2000; fax (212) 956-3857; e-mail countryliving@hearst.com; internet www.countryliving.com; f. 1978; Publr STEVEN GRUNE; Editor NANCY MERNIT SORRIANO; circ. 1,600,000 (m).

CQ Researcher: 1255 22nd St, 4th Floor, NW, Washington, DC 20037; tel. (202) 729-1800; fax (202) 729-1807; e-mail cqresearch@cqpress.com; internet www.cqpress.library.com; f. 1923; publ. by Congressional Quarterly Inc; politics and government; Editor THOMAS COLIN; circ. 5,000 (w).

Ebony: 820 South Michigan Ave, Chicago, IL 60605-2191; tel. (312) 322-9200; fax (312) 322-9375; internet www.ebony.com; f. 1945; African-American general interest; Publr and CEO JOHN H. JOHNSON; Exec. Editor LERONE BENNETT; circ. 1,800,000 (m).

Editor & Publisher—The Fourth Estate: 770 Broadway, 7th Floor, New York, NY 10003-9595; tel. (646) 654-5270; fax (646) 654-4370; e-mail edpub@editorandpublisher.com; internet www.editorandpublisher.com; f. 1884; Exec. Editor SID HOLT; circ. 19,689 (w).

Elks Magazine: 425 West Diversey Pkwy, Chicago, IL 60614-6196; tel. (773) 755-4894; e-mail elksmag@elks.org; f. 1922; Publr FRED D. OAKES; circ. 1,116,000 (m).

Entertainment Weekly: 1675 Broadway, 29th Floor, New York, NY 10019; tel. (212) 522-5600; fax (212) 522-0074; internet www.ew.com; f. 1990; Man. Editor JAMES W. SEYMORE, Jr; circ. 1,518,763.

Episcopal Life: 815 Second Ave, New York, NY 10017; tel. (800) 334-7626; fax (212) 949-8059; internet www.episcopalchurch.org/episcopal-life/; Editor JERROLD HAMES; circ. 285,000 (m).

Esquire: 250 West 55th St, New York, NY 10019-3203; tel. (212) 649-2000; fax (212) 977-3158; e-mail esquire@hearst.com; internet www.esquire.com; f. 1933; Editor-in-Chief DAVID GRANGER; circ. 672,073 (m).

Essence: 1500 Broadway, 6th Floor, New York, NY 10036-4071; tel. (212) 642-0600; fax (212) 921-5173; e-mail info@essence.com; internet www.essence.com; f. 1970; Editor-in-Chief DIANE MARIE WEATHERS; circ. 950,000 (m).

Family Circle: 375 Lexington Ave, New York, NY 10017-5514; tel. (212) 499-2000; fax (212) 499-6740; f. 1932; Editor-in-Chief SUSAN KELLIHER UNGARO; circ. 5,213,000 (every 3 weeks).

Family Handyman: 7900 International Dr., Suite 950, Bloomington, MN 55425-1510; tel. (612) 854-3000; fax (612) 854-8009; f. 1951; Editor GARY HAVENS; circ. 1,123,000 (10 a year).

Farm Journal: 1818 Market St, 31st Floor, Philadelphia, PA 19103; tel. (215) 557-8922; fax (215) 568-3989; internet www.agweb.com; f. 1877; Editor SONJA HILLGREN; circ. 650,000 (m).

Field & Stream: 2 Park Ave, New York, NY 10016-5601; tel. (212) 779-5000; fax (212) 779-5114; e-mail fsmagazine@aol.com; internet www.fieldandstream.com; f. 1895; Editor SID EVANS; circ. 1.5m. (m).

Flower & Garden Magazine: 4645 Belleview, Kansas City, MO 64112; tel. (816) 531-5730; fax (816) 531-3873; internet www.flowerandgardenmag.com; f. 1957; Sr Editor ANGELA M. HUGHES; circ. 300,000 (6 a year).

Forbes: 60 Fifth Ave, New York, NY 10011-8802; tel. (212) 620-2200; fax (212) 620-1875; internet www.forbes.com; f. 1917; Pres. and Editor-in-Chief STEVE FORBES; Editor WILLIAM BALDWIN; circ. 900,000 (f).

Foreign Affairs: 58 East 68th St, New York, NY 10021-5987; tel. (212) 434-9400; fax (212) 861-2759; e-mail foraff@cfr.org; internet www.foreignaffairs.org; f. 1922; Editor JAMES F. HOGE, Jr; circ. 110,000 (6 a year).

Fortune: 1271 Ave of the Americas, New York, NY 10020; tel. (212) 522-1212; fax (212) 246-3375; internet www.fortune.com; f. 1930; Man. Editor RICHARD I. KIRKLAND; circ. 933,000.

Glamour: 4 Times Sq., 16th Floor, New York, NY 10036; tel. (212) 286-2860; fax (212) 286-6922; e-mail letters@glamour.com; internet www.glamour.com; f. 1939; Editor CYNTHIA LEIVE; circ. 2,132,000 (m).

Golf Digest: 5520 Park Ave, Trumbull, CT 06611-3426; tel. (203) 373-7000; fax (203) 371-2162; e-mail editor@golfdigest.com; internet www.golfdigest.com; f. 1950; Editor JERRY TARDE; circ. 1,500,000 (m).

Golf Magazine: 2 Park Ave, New York, NY 10016-5601; tel. (212) 779-5000; fax (212) 779-5522; e-mail letters@golfonline.com; internet www.golfonline.com; f. 1959; Editor-in-Chief GEORGE PEPER; circ. 1,400,000 (m).

Good Housekeeping: 959 Eighth Ave, New York, NY 10019-5203; tel. (212) 649-2000; fax (212) 265-3307; internet www.goodhousekeeping.com; f. 1885; Editor-in-Chief ELLEN LEVINE; circ. 5,032,901 (m).

Gourmet—The Magazine of Good Living: 4 Times Sq., 9th Floor, New York, NY 10036; tel. (212) 286-2860; fax (212) 753-2596; internet www.gourmet.com; f. 1941; Editor RUTH REICHL; circ. 855,000 (m).

Grit: 1503 SW 42nd St, Topeka, KS 66609-1214; tel. (913) 274-4300; fax (913) 274-4305; e-mail grit@cjnetwors.com; internet www.grit.com; f. 1882; Editor-in-Chief DONNA DOYLE; circ. 150,000 (f).

Harper's Bazaar: 1700 Broadway, New York, NY 10019-5970; tel. (212) 903-5000; fax (212) 262-7101; e-mail bazaar@hearst.com; internet www.bazaar411.com; Editor-in-Chief GLENDA BAILEY; circ. 746,000 (m).

Harper's Magazine: 666 Broadway, New York, NY 10012-2317; tel. (212) 614-6500; fax (212) 228-5889; e-mail letters@harpers.org; internet www.harpers.org; f. 1850; Editor LEWIS H. LAPHAM; circ. 205,000 (m).

Harvard Business Review: 300 North Beacon St, Watertown, MA 02472; tel. (617) 783-7400; fax (617) 783-7493; e-mail hbr_editorial@hbsp.harvard.edu; internet www.hbsp.harvard.edu; f. 1922; Publr WALTER KIECHEL; Editor SUZY WETLAUFER; circ. 249,100 (6 a year).

Highlights for Children: 803 Church St, Honesdale, PA 18413; tel. (717) 253-1080; fax (717) 253-0179; f. 1946; Editor CHRISTINE FRENCH CLARK; circ. 2,500,000 (m).

Hot Rod Magazine: 6420 Wilshire Blvd, Los Angeles, CA 90048; tel. (332) 782-2000; fax (323) 782-2223; e-mail hotrod@primediacmmg.com; f. 1948; Editor DAVID FREIBURGER; circ. 780,000 (m).

House Beautiful: 1700 Broadway, New York, NY 10019-5970; tel. (212) 903-5000; fax (212) 765-8292; f. 1896; Editor MARIAN MCEVOY; circ. 850,000 (m).

Industry Week: 1300 East Ninth St, Cleveland, OH 44114-1503; tel. (216) 696-1503; fax (216) 696-7000; e-mail ppanchak@industryweek.com; internet www.industryweek.com; f. 1970; Editor-in-Chief PATRICIA PANCHAK; circ. 233,000 (12 a year).

Information Outlook: Special Libraries Asscn, 1700 18th St, NW, Washington, DC 20009-2514; tel. (202) 234-4700; fax (202) 265-9317; e-mail magazine@sla.org; f. 1910; Editor SUSAN WRIGHT; circ. 15,000 (m).

Jet: 820 South Michigan Ave, Chicago, IL 60605-2191; tel. (312) 322-9200; fax (312) 322-0951; internet www.jetmag.com; f. 1951; African-American general interest; Man. Editor MALCOLM R. WEST; circ. 1,000,000 (w).

Journal of Accountancy: Harborside Financial Center, Plaza III, Jersey City, NJ 07311; tel. (312) 938-3292; fax (312) 938-3714; e-mail journal@AICPA.org; f. 1905; Editor COLLEEN KATZ; circ. 370,000 (m).

Journal of the American Medical Association (JAMA): 515 North State St, Chicago, IL 60610-4319; tel. (312) 464-2400; fax (312) 464-5824; f. 1883; Editor Dr CATHERINE DEANGELIS; circ. 333,000 (w).

Junior Scholastic: 555 Broadway, New York, NY 10012; tel. (212) 343-6295; fax (212) 343-6333; e-mail junior@scholastic.com; f. 1937; Editor LEE BAIER; circ. 615,000 (18 a year).

Kiplinger's Personal Finance Magazine: 1729 H St, NW, Washington, DC 20006-3904; tel. (202) 887-6400; fax (202) 331-1206; e-mail magazine@kiplinger.com; internet www.kiplinger.com; f. 1947; Editor FRED FRAILEY; circ. 1,400,000 (m).

Ladies' Home Journal: 125 Park Ave, New York, NY 10017-5599; tel. (212) 557-6600; fax (212) 455-1010; f. 1883; Editor-in-Chief MYRNA BLYTH; circ. 4,500,000 (m).

Lion Magazine: 300 22nd St, Oak Brook, IL 60523; tel. (630) 571-5466; fax (630) 571-8890; e-mail rkleinsfe@lionsclubs.org; f. 1918; business and professional; Editor ROBERT KLEINFELDER; circ. 600,000 (m).

Mademoiselle: 4 Times Sq., New York, NY 10036; tel. (212) 286-2860; fax (212) 286-7778; e-mail mllemag@aol.com; internet www.mademoiselle.com; f. 1935; Editor-in-Chief MANDI NORWOOD; circ. 1,233,160 (m).

Management Review: American Management Asscn, 1601 Broadway, New York, NY 10019-7420; tel. (212) 903-8393; fax (212) 903-8083; e-mail mgmtreview@amanet.org; f. 1917; Editor BARBARA ETTORRE; circ. 67,000 (m).

McCall's Magazine: 110 Fifth Ave, New York, NY 10011; tel. (212) 463-1000; fax (212) 463-1403; f. 1876; women's; Editor SALLY KOSLOW; circ. 4,200,000 (m).

Marie Claire: 1790 Broadway, 3rd Floor, New York, NY 10019; tel. (212) 649-5000; fax (212) 501-5050; e-mail marieclaire@hearst.com; internet www.marieclaire.com; f. 1994; Editor LESLIE JANE SEYMOUR; circ. 903,000 (m).

Metropolitan Home: 1633 Broadway, New York, NY 10019-6741; tel. (212) 767-4500; fax (212) 767-5636; f. 1981; Editor-in-Chief DONNA WARNER; circ. 600,000 (6 a year).

Money: 1271 Ave of the Americas, New York, NY 10020-1301; tel. (212) 522-1212; fax (212) 522-0189; internet www.money.com; f. 1972; Man. Editor ROBERT SAFIAN; circ. 1,929,347 (m).

Motor Trend: 6420 Wilshire Blvd, Los Angeles, CA 90048; tel. (323) 782-2220; fax (323) 782-2355; e-mail motortrend@emapusa.com; internet www.motortrend.com; f. 1949; Editor-in-Chief C. VAN TUNE; circ. 1,285,178 (m).

The Nation: 33 Irving Pl., 8th Floor, New York, NY 10003; tel. (212) 209-5400; fax (212) 982-9000; e-mail info@thenation.com; internet www.thenation.com; f. 1865; Editor KATRINA VANDEN HEUVEL; politics and the arts; circ. 100,000 (w).

Nation's Business: US Chamber of Commerce, 1615 H St, NW, Washington, DC 20062-0002; tel. (202) 659-6000; fax (202) 463-5928; f. 1912; Editor MARY MCELVEEN; circ. 858,000 (m).

National Enquirer: 600 SE Coast Ave, Lantana, FL 33462-0001; tel. (561) 586-1111; fax (561) 540-1010; e-mail letters@nationalenquirer.com; internet www.nationalenquirer.com; f. 1926; Editor IAIN CALDER; circ. 2,717,000 (w).

National Geographic Magazine: 1145 17th St, NW, Washington, DC 20036-4701; tel. (202) 857-7000; fax (202) 775-6141; e-mail ngm@nationalgeographic.com; internet www.nationalgeographic.com; f. 1888; Editor WILLIAM L. ALLEN; circ. 8,974,000 (m).

National Review: 215 Lexington Ave, 4th Floor, New York, NY 10016; tel. (212) 679-7330; fax (212) 696-0309; internet www.nationalreview.com; f. 1955; Editor RICHARD LOWRY; circ. 150,000 (f).

New Republic: 1331 H St, NW, Suite 700, Washington, DC 2005; tel. (202) 508-4444; fax (202) 628-9383; e-mail tnr@aol.com; internet www.tnr.com; f. 1914; Editor PETER BEINART; circ. 60,000 (w).

New York Review of Books: 1755 Broadway, 5th Floor, New York, NY 10019-3780; tel. (212) 757-8070; fax (212) 333-5374; e-mail nyrev@nybooks.com; internet www.nybooks.com; f. 1963; Editor BARBARA EPSTEIN; circ. 130,000 (20 a year).

The New Yorker: 4 Times Sq., New York, NY 10036-7448; tel. (212) 286-2860; fax (212) 536-5735; e-mail themail@newyorker.com; internet www.newyorker.com; f. 1925; Editor DAVID REMNICK; circ. 850,081 (w).

Newsweek: Newsweek Bldg, 251 West 57th St, New York, NY 10019-1894; tel. (212) 445-4000; fax (212) 445-5068; f. 1933; Man. Editors MARK WHITAKER; circ. 3,156,000 (w).

Organic Gardening: 33 East Minor St, Emmaus, PA 18098-0001; tel. (610) 967-8363; fax (610) 967-7722; e-mail organicgardening@vodale.com; internet www.organicgardening.com; f. 1942; Editor SCOTT MEYER; circ. 350,000 (6 a year).

Outdoor Life: 2 Park Ave, New York, NY 10016-5601; tel. (212) 779-5000; fax (212) 779-5366; e-mail olmagazine@aol.com; internet www.outdoorlife.com; f. 1898; Editor TODD SMITH; circ. 1,350,000 (m).

Parents' Magazine: 685 Third Ave, New York, NY 10017; tel. (212) 878-8700; fax (212) 986-2656; f. 1926; Editor-in-Chief ANN PLESHETTE MURPHY; circ. 1,740,000 (m).

Partisan Review: 236 Bay State Rd, Boston, MA 02215; tel. (617) 353-4260; fax (617) 353-7444; e-mail partisan@bu.edu; internet www.webdelsol.com/Partisan–Review; f. 1934; Editor WILLIAM PHILLIPS; circ. 8,000 (q).

PC Magazine: 1 Park Ave, New York, NY 10016-5802; tel. (212) 503-5255; fax (212) 503-5799; internet www.pcmag.com; f. 1981; personal computer industry; Editors MICHAEL MILLER, ROBIN RASKIN; circ. 1,154,000 (f).

Penthouse: 277 Park Ave, 4th Floor, New York, NY 10172-0003; tel. (212) 702-6000; fax (212) 702-6262; e-mail webmaster@penthousemag.com; internet www.penthousemag.com; f. 1969; Editor PETER BLOCH; circ. 884,000 (m).

People Weekly: 1271 Ave of the Americas, New York, NY 10020-1300; tel. (212) 522-1212; fax (212) 522-0331; internet www.people.com; f. 1974; Man. Editor CAROL WALLACE; circ. 3,703,922 (w).

Playboy: 680 North Lake Shore Dr., Chicago, IL 60611-4402; tel. (312) 751-8000; fax (312) 751-2818; e-mail edit@playboy.com; internet www.playboy.com/magazine-toc.html; f. 1953; men's interest; Publr MARIANNE HOWATSON; Editor-in-Chief HUGH M. HEFNER; circ. 3,172,000 (m).

Political Science Quarterly: 475 Riverside Dr., Suite 1274, New York, NY 10115-1274; tel. (212) 870-2500; fax (212) 870-2202; e-mail aps@psqonline.org; internet www.epn.org/psq.html; f. 1886; Editor DEMETRIOS CARALEY; circ. 8,000 (q).

Popular Mechanics: 224 West 57th St, New York, NY 10019; tel. (212) 649-2000; fax (212) 586-5562; internet www.popularmechanics.com; f. 1902; Editor JOE OLDHAM; circ. 1,239,654 (m).

Popular Photography: 1633 Broadway, New York, NY 10019-6741; tel. (212) 767-6578; fax (212) 767-5602; e-mail popeditor@aol.com; f. 1937; Editor JASON SCHNEIDER; circ. 454,122 (m).

Popular Science: 2 Park Ave, 9th Floor, New York, NY 10016; tel. (212) 779-5000; fax (212) 481-8062; e-mail PSletters@aol.com; internet www.popsci.com; f. 1872; Editor-in-Chief CECILIA WESSNER; circ. 1,550,000 (m).

Prevention: 33 East Minor St, Emmaus, PA 18098-0001; tel. (610) 967-5171; fax (610) 967-7654; e-mail preventiondm@aol.com; internet www.prevention.com; f. 1950; Editor-in-Chief CATHERINE CASSIDY; circ. 3,221,000 (m).

Progressive Farmer: 2100 Lakeshore Dr., Birmingham, AL 35202; tel. (205) 445-6000; fax (205) 445-6860; e-mail ProgressiveFarmer@timeinccom; internet www.progressivefarmer.com; f. 1886; Editor JACK ODLE; circ. 600,000 (m).

Publishers Weekly: 360 Park Ave, South, New York NY 10010; tel. (212) 746-6758; fax (646) 746-6631; internet www.publishersweekly.com; f. 1872; Editor NORA RAWLINSON; circ. 32,863 (w).

QST: American Radio Relay League, 225 Main St, Newington, CT 06111-1494; tel. (860) 594-0200; fax (860) 594-0259; e-mail qst@arrl.org; f. 1915; Editor MARK WILSON; circ. 172,000 (m).

Reader's Digest: Reader's Digest Rd, Pleasantville, NY 10570-7000; tel. (914) 238-1000; fax (914) 238-4559; internet www.readersdigest.com; f. 1922; Editor JACQUELINE LEO; circ. 16,262,000 (m).

Redbook Magazine: 224 West 57th St, 6th Floor, New York, NY 10019-3203; tel. (212) 649-2000; fax (212) 581-8114; internet www.redbookmag.com; f. 1903; Editor-in-Chief ELLEN KUNES; circ. 2,250,000 (m).

Road & Track: 1499 Monrovia Ave, Newport Beach, CA 92663-2752; tel. (949) 720-5300; fax (949) 631-2757; f. 1947; Editor THOMAS L. BRYANT; circ. 742,000 (m).

Rolling Stone: 1290 Ave of the Americas, 2nd Floor, New York, NY 10104; tel. (212) 484-1616; fax (212) 767-8209; e-mail feedback@rollingstone.com; internet www.rollingstone.com; f. 1967; Man. Editor JANN S. WENNER; circ. 1,229,000 (f).

The Rotarian: Rotary International, 1 Rotary Center, 1560 Sherman Ave, Evanston, IL 60201-3698; tel. (847) 866-3000; fax (847) 866-9732; e-mail 75457.3577@compuserve.com; f. 1911; Editor-in-Chief WILLMON L. WHITE; circ. 521,000 (m).

Saturday Evening Post: 1100 Waterway Blvd, Indianapolis, IN 46202-2174; tel. (317) 634-1100; fax (317) 637-0126; e-mail satevepsteaol.com; internet www.satevepost.com; f. 1728; Editor CORY J. SERVASS; circ. 350,000.

Science: 1200 New York Ave, NW, Washington, DC 20005; tel. (202) 326-6500; fax (202) 371-9227; e-mail scinews@scisvc.org; internet www.sciencemag.org; f. 1880; publ. by the American Asscn for the Advancement of Science; Editor-in-Chief DON KENNEDY; circ. 155,000 (w).

Science News: 1719 N St, NW, Washington, DC 20036-2890; tel. (202) 785-2255; fax (202) 659-0365; e-mail scinews@sciserv.org; internet www.sciencenews.org; f. 1926; Editor JULIE ANN MILLER; circ. 200,000 (w).

Scientific American: 415 Madison Ave, New York, NY 10017-1179; tel. (212) 754-0550; fax (212) 755-1976; e-mail editors@sciam.com; internet www.sciam.com; f. 1845; Editor JOHN RENNIE; circ. 666,631 (m).

Scouting Magazine: 1325 West Walnut Hill Lane, POB 152079, Irving, TX 75015-2079; tel. (972) 580-2000; fax (972) 580-2079; internet www.bsa.scouting.org/mags/scouting/index.html; f. 1913; publ. by Boy Scouts of America; Editor JON C. HALTER; circ. 1,000,000 (6 a year).

SELF Magazine: 4 Times Sq., 5th Floor, New York, NY 10036; tel. (212) 286-2860; fax (212) 286-8110; e-mail comments@self.com; internet www.self.com; f. 1979; Editor-in-Chief LUCY DANZIGER; circ. 1,111,000 (m).

Seventeen: 850 Third Ave, 9th Floor, New York, NY 10022; tel. (212) 407-9700; fax (212) 935-4237; e-mail seventeenm@ad.com; internet www.seventeen.com; f. 1944; Editor-in-Chief ANNEMARIE IVERSON; circ. 2,350,000 (m).

Smithsonian Magazine: 750 Ninth St, SW, Washington, DC 20560-0951; tel. (202) 275-2072; e-mail articles@simag.si.com; internet www.smithsonianmag.si.edu; f. 1970; Editor CAREY WINFREY; circ. 2,100,000 (m).

Soap Opera Digest: 261 Madison Ave, New York, NY 10010-2754; tel. (212) 716-2100; fax (212) 661-2560; internet www.soapdigest.com; f. 1975; Editor LYNN LEAHEY; circ. 1,361,293 (f).

Southern Living: 2100 Lakeshore Dr., Birmingham, AL 35209-6721; tel. (205) 877-6000; fax (205) 877-6085; internet www.southernliving.com; f. 1966; Editor JOHN ALEX FLOYD, Jr; circ. 2,300,000 (m).

Sport Magazine: 437 Madison Ave, 4th Floor, New York, NY 10022; tel. (212) 888-9133; fax (212) 593-5447; internet www.petersenpub.com; f. 1946; Editor NORB GARRETT; circ. 780,000 (m).

Sporting News: 10176 Corporate Sq. Dr., Suite 200, St Louis, MO 63132; tel. (314) 997-7111; fax (314) 997-0765; e-mail tsnmail@aol.com; internet www.sportingnews.com; f. 1886; Editor JOHN RAWLINGS; circ. 600,000 (w).

Sports Illustrated: Sports Illustrated Bldg, 135 west 50th St, New York, NY 10020-1393; tel. (212) 522-1212; fax (212) 977-4540; internet www.cnssi.com; f. 1954; Editor BILL COLSON; circ. 3,220,000 (w).

Star: 660 White Plains Rd, Tarrytown, NY 10591; tel. (914) 332-5000; fax (914) 332-5044; f. 1974; Editor-in-Chief PHIL BUNTON; circ. 1,984,000 (w).

Sunset Magazine: 80 Willow Rd, Menlo Park, CA 94025-3691; tel. (650) 321-3600; fax (650) 327-5737; internet www.sunset.com; f. 1898; Editor KATIE TAMONY; circ. 1,500,000 (m).

'TEEN: 6420 Wilshire Blvd, Los Angeles, CA 90048-5515; tel. (323) 782-2000; fax (323) 782-2660; e-mail teen@emapusa.com; internet www.teenmag.com; f. 1957; Editor TOMMI LEWIS; circ. 2,100,000 (m).

Time: Time-Life Bldg, Rockefeller Center, 1271 Ave of the Americas, New York, NY 10020-1393; tel. (212) 522-1212; fax (212) 522-0323; e-mail Letters@time.com; internet www.time.com; f. 1923; Man. Editor JAMES KELLY; circ. 4,500,000 (w).

Travel Holiday: 1633 Broadway, 43rd Floor, New York, NY 10019; tel. (212) 767-5126; fax (212) 767-5115; e-mail travelhol@aol.com; internet www.travelholiday.com; f. 1901; Editor JOHN OWENS; circ. 650,000 (m).

Travel & Leisure: 1120 Ave of the Americas, 10th Floor, New York, NY 10036-6770; tel. (212) 382-5600; fax (212) 382-5877; e-mail tlquery@amexpub.com; internet www.travelandleisure.com; f. 1971; Editor-in-Chief NANCY NOVOGROD; circ. 960,485 (m).

True Story: 333 Seventh Ave, 11th Floor, New York, NY 10003; tel. (212) 979-4800; fax (212) 979-7342; f. 1919; Editors HEATHER DALTON, TINA PAPPALARDO; circ. 825,000 (m).

TV Guide: 1211 Ave of the Americas, New York, NY 10036; tel. (212) 852-7500; fax (212) 852-7470; internet www.tvguide.com; f. 1953; Editor-in-Chief STEVEN REDDICLIFFE; circ. 13,077,000 (w).

Us Weekly: 1290 Ave of the Americas, 2nd Floor, New York, NY 10104-0002; tel. (212) 484-1616; fax (212) 484-1621; f. 1977; Editor TERRY McDONELL; circ. 850,000 (m).

US News & World Report: 1050 Thomas Jefferson St, NW, Washington, DC 20007; tel. (202) 955-2000; fax (202) 955-2049; e-mail letters@usnews.com; internet www.usnews.com; f. 1933; Editor MORTIMER B. ZUCKERMAN; circ. 2,000,000 (w).

Vanity Fair: 4 Times Sq., 7th Floor, New York, NY 10036; tel. (212) 286-8180; fax (212) 286-6707; e-mail vfmail@vf.com; internet www.vanityfair.com; f. 1983; Editor GRAYDON CARTER; circ. 1,120,000 (m).

Variety: 5700 Wilshire Blvd, Suite 120, Los Angeles, CA 90036; tel. (213) 857-6600; fax (213) 857-0494; f. 1905; Editor PETER BART; circ. 30,000 (w).

VFW Magazine: 406 West 34th St, Kansas City, MO 64111-2736; tel. (816) 756-3390; fax (816) 968-1169; internet www.vfw.org; e-mail pbrown@vfw.org; f. 1912; Editor RICHARD K. KOLB; circ. 1,813,000 (11 a year).

VIA: 150 Van Ness Ave, San Francisco, CA 94102-5208; tel. (415) 565-2451; fax (415) 863-4726; f. 1917; motoring; Editor BRUCE ANDERSON; circ. 2,585,000 (6 a year).

Village Voice: 36 Cooper Sq., New York, NY 10003-7149; tel. (212) 475-3300; fax (212) 475-8944; internet www.villagevoice.com; f. 1955; Editor DONALD FORST; circ. 230,000 (w).

Vogue: 4 Times Sq., 12th Floor, New York, NY 10036; tel. (212) 286-7351; fax (212) 286-8593; e-mail voguemail@aol.com; internet www .vogue.com; f. 1892; Editor ANNA WINTOUR; circ. 1,250,000 (m).

Weight Watchers Magazine: 360 Lexington Ave, 11th Floor, New York, NY 10017; tel. (212) 370-0644; fax (212) 687-4398; f. 1968; Editor KATE GREER; circ. 1,060,000 (m).

Working Woman Magazine: 230 Park Ave, 7th Floor, New York, NY 10169; tel. (212) 551-9500; fax (212) 599-4763; e-mail wwedit@ womwet.com; f. 1976; Editor-in-Chief NANCY F. SMITH; circ. 764,000 (m).

Yale Review: Box 208243 Yale Station, New Haven, CT 06520; tel. (203) 432-0499; fax (203) 432-0510; e-mail bianconi@yale.edu; f. 1911; Man. Editor SUSAN BIANCONI; circ. 6,000 (q).

Yankee Magazine: Main St, Dublin, NH 03444; tel. (603) 563-8111; fax (603) 563-8252; e-mail dearyank@yankeepub.com; internet www .newengland.com; f. 1935; Editor JUDSON D. HALE; circ. 500,000 (m).

YM: 375 Lexington Ave, 8th Floor, New York, NY 10017; tel. (212) 499-1000; fax (212) 499-1698; f. 1940; women's interest; Publr LAURA MCEWEN; Editor CHRISTINA KELLY; circ. 2,200,000 (10 a year).

NEWS AGENCIES

Associated Press (AP): 50 Rockefeller Plaza, New York, NY 10020-1666; tel. (212) 621-1500; fax (212) 621-1679; internet www .ap.org; f. 1848; Pres. and Gen. Man. LOUIS D. BOCCARDI; c. 1,700 newspaper mems in the US, 6,000 broadcast mems and over 8,500 subscribers abroad.

Bloomberg Business News: 499 Park Ave, 15th Floor, New York, NY 10022; tel. (212) 318-2000; fax (212) 893-5999; internet www .bloomberg.com; Editor-in-Chief MATTHEW WINKLER.

Dow-Jones News Service: Harborside Financial Center, 600 Plaza II, Jersey City, NJ 07311-3992; tel. (201) 938-5400; fax (201) 938-5600; Pres. PAUL INGRASSIA; Man. Editor RICK STINE.

Jewish Telegraphic Agency, Inc (JTA): 330 Seventh Ave, 17th Floor, New York NY 10001; tel. (212) 643-1890; fax (212) 643-8498; e-mail info@jta.org; internet www.jta.org; f. 1917; world-wide coverage of Jewish news; offices in Washington, DC, and Jerusalem; Exec. Editor and Publr MARK J. JOFFE.

Religion News Service: 1101 Connecticut Ave, NW, Suite 350, Washington, DC 20036; tel. (202) 463-8777; fax (202) 463-0033; e-mail info@religionnews.com; internet www.religionnews.com; Editor DAVID E. ANDERSON.

United Media (UM): 200 Madison Ave, 4th Floor, New York, NY 10016; tel. (212) 293-8500; fax (212) 293-8717; internet www .unitedfeatures.com; f. 1978; licensing and syndication of news features; Pres. and CEO DOUGLAS R. STERN.

United Press International (UPI): 1400 I St, Suite 800, NW, Washington, DC 20005; tel. (202) 898-8000; fax (202) 898-8057; internet www.upi.com; f. 1907; Pres. and CEO DOUGLAS JOO; Editor-in-Chief JOHN O'SULLIVAN; serves c.1,000 newspaper clients world-wide.

WorldWide Media: 27324 Camino Capistrano, Suite 211, Laguna Niguel, CA 92677; tel. (949) 582-6995; fax (949) 582-7009; e-mail wwm@wwmedia.net; news and features services in 20 countries; Dirs HELEN J. LEE, MAYRA A. GOMEZ.

Foreign Bureaux

Agence France-Presse (AFP): 1015 15th St, NW, Suite 500, Washington, DC 20005; tel. (202) 289-0700; fax (202) 414-0525; Bureau Chief GEORGES BIANNIC; also office in New York.

Agencia EFE (Spain): 25 West 43rd St, Suite 1512, New York, NY 10036; tel. (212) 867-5757; fax (212) 867-9074; e-mail efe@efenews .com; Rep. RAFAEL MORENO; also offices in Washington, DC, and Miami.

Agenzia Nazionale Stampa Associata (ANSA) (Italy): National Press Bldg, Suite 1285, Washington, DC 20045; tel. (202) 628-3317; fax (202) 638-1792; e-mail ansaws@natonalpress.com; Bureau Chief GIAMPIERO GRAMAGLIA; also offices in New York and San Francisco.

Allgemeiner Deutscher Nachrichtendienst (ADN) (Germany): UN Secretariat Bldg, Room 482, UN Plaza, New York, NY 10017; tel. (212) 421-5876; fax (212) 832-5140; Bureau Chief ANDREAS LINDNER.

Canadian Press (Canada): 1331 Pennsylvania Ave, NW, Suite 524, Washington, DC 20004; tel. (202) 638-3367; fax (202) 638-3369; Bureau Chief BOB RUSSO.

Central News Agency (CNA) (Taiwan): 1173 National Press Bldg, Washington, DC 20045; tel. (202) 628-2738; fax (202) 637-6788; e-mail cnausa@aol.com; Bureau Chief NELSON CHUNG; also offices in New York, San Francisco and Los Angeles.

Deutsche Presse-Agentur (dpa) (Germany): National Press Bldg, Suite 969, Washington, DC 20045; tel. (202) 662-1220; fax (202) 662-

1270; e-mail wshdesk@dpa-us.com; Bureau Chief HERBERT WINKLER; also office in New York.

Informatsionnoye Telegrafnoye Agentstvo Rossii—Telegrafnoye Agentstvo Suverennykh Stran (ITAR—TASS) (Russia): 50 Rockefeller Plaza, Suite 501, New York, NY 10020-1605; tel. (212) 245-4250; fax (212) 245-4258; e-mail itar@aol.com; Bureau Chief ALEX BEREZHKOV; also office in Washington, DC.

Inter Press Service (IPS) (Italy): United Nations Bldg, Room 485, New York, NY 10017; tel. (212) 963-6156; e-mail ipsun@aol.com; internet www.ipsdailyjournal.org; Bureau Chief THALIF DEEN; also office in Washington, DC.

Jiji Tsushin (Japan): 120 West 45th St, 14th Floor, New York, NY 10036; tel. (212) 575-5830; fax (212) 764-3950; f. 1945; Chief Rep. SUGURU SASAKI; also offices in Washington, DC, Los Angeles, San Francisco and Chicago.

Kyodo Tsushin (Japan): 50 Rockefeller Plaza, Suite 816, Washington, DC 1002020045; tel. (202) 347-5767; fax (202) 393-2342; Bureau Chief HIRISHI OSHIMA; also offices in New York and Los Angeles.

Magyar Távirati Iroda (MTI) (Hungary): 8515 Farrell Dr., Chevy Chase, MD 20815; tel. (301) 565-2221; fax (301) 589-6907; e-mail karpmti@aol.com; Bureau Chief JÁNOS KÁRPÁTI.

Reuters (United Kingdom): 1333 H St, NW, Suite 600, Washington, DC 20005; tel. (202) 898-0056; fax (202) 898-1237; Editor ROBERT DOHERTY; also offices in New York, Chicago, San Francisco and five other cities.

Tlačová agentúra Slovenskej republiky (TASR) (Slovakia): 4501 Connecticut Ave, Apt 713, NW, Washington, DC 20008; tel. (202) 686-4710; fax (202) 537-0574; f. 1992; Chief Officer OTAKAR KOŘINEK.

Xinhua (New China) News Agency (People's Republic of China): 40-35 72nd St, Woodside, NY 11377; tel. (718) 335-8388; fax (718) 335-8778; Bureau Dir HONGQI LI; also office in Washington, DC.

Agence Belga (Belgium), **PAP** (Poland), **RIA—Novosti** (Russia), **Middle East News Agency** (Egypt), **Press Trust of India**, **Česká tisková kancelář** (Czech Republic), **Kuwait News Agency**, **SPA** (Saudi Arabia) and **Notimex** (Mexico) are also represented.

NATIONAL ASSOCIATIONS

American Business Press: 675 Third Ave, Suite 415, New York, NY 10017; tel. (212) 661-6360; fax (212) 370-0736; e-mail abp2@aol .com; f. 1906; mems: 160 publrs, 900 periodicals, 35 associates (suppliers); Pres. GORDON T. HUGHES, III.

American Society of Magazine Editors: 919 Third Ave, New York, NY 10022; tel. (212) 872-3700; fax (212) 906-0128; e-mail asme@magazine.org; internet asme.magazine.org; Exec. Dir MARLENE KAHAN; 900 mems.

Audit Bureau of Circulations: 900 North Meacham Rd, Schaumburg, IL 60173-4968; tel. (847) 605-0909; fax (847) 605-0483; internet www.accessabc.com; f. 1914; Chair. and Sec. ANTHONY M. GASPARRO; Pres. and Man. Dir MICHAEL J. LAVERY; 4,500 mems.

Council of Literary Magazines and Presses (CLMP): 154 Christopher St, Suite 3c, New York, NY 10014-2839; tel. (212) 741-9110; fax (212) 741-9112; e-mail info@clmp.org; internet www.clmp .org; f. 1967; provides services to non-commercial US literary magazines and presses; Exec. Dir PEGGY RANDALL; 350 mems.

Magazine Publishers of America: 919 Third Ave, 22nd Floor, New York, NY 10022; tel. (212) 872-3700; fax (212) 888-4217; internet www.magazine.org; f. 1919; Chair. DANIEL B. BREWSTER, Jr; Pres. NINA B. LINK; 380 mems.

National Newspaper Association: 1525 Wilson Blvd, Suite 550, Arlington, VA 22209; tel. (703) 907-7900; fax (703) 907-7901; f. 1885; CEO KENNETH B. ALLEN; 4,000 mems.

Newspaper Association of America: 1921 Gallows Rd, Suite 600, Vienna, VA 22182-3900; tel. (703) 902-1600; fax (703) 917-0636; internet www.naa.org; f. 1992; Chair. ORAGE QUARLES, III; Pres. and CEO JOHN F. STURM; more than 2,000 mems in USA and Canada accounting for over 87% of US daily newspaper circulation.

The Newspaper Guild: 501 Third St, NW, Washington, DC 20001-2760; tel. (202) 434-7177; fax (202) 434-1472; internet www .newsguild.org; f. 1933; journalists' org., organ of the Communications Workers of America trade union; Pres. LINDA K. FOLEY; 36,000 mems.

Periodical & Book Association of America Inc: 475 Park Ave South, 8th Floor, New York, NY 10016-6989; tel. (212) 689-4952; fax (212) 545-8328; e-mail pbaa@aol.com; Exec. Dir RICHARD BROWNE; 60 mems.

Publishers

Abaris Books: 64 Wall St, Norwalk, CT 06850; tel. (203) 838-8402; fax (203) 857-0730; e-mail abaris@abarisbooks.com; f. 1973; division of Opal Publishing Corpn; Publr ANTHONY S. KAUFMANN; Gen. Man. J. C. WEST; scholarly, fine art reference, philosophy.

Abbeville Publishing Group: 22 Cortland St, 32nd Floor, New York, NY 10007; tel. (212) 577-5555; fax (212) 577-5579; internet www.abbeville.com; f. 1977; fine arts and illustrated books; Pres. and Publr ROBERT E. ABRAMS.

Abingdon Press: 201 Eighth Ave South, Nashville, TN 37202; tel. (615) 749-6403; fax (615) 749-6512; e-mail holson@ampublishing .org; internet www.abingdon.org; f. 1789; religious; Gen. Man. HARRIET JANE OLSON.

Harry N. Abrams, Inc: 100 Fifth Ave, New York, NY 10011; tel. (212) 206-7715; fax (212) 645-8437; internet www.abramsbooks.com; division of Times Mirror Co; art, architecture, natural history, popular culture; Pres., CEO and Editor-in-Chief PAUL GOTTLIEB.

Addison-Wesley-Longman Publishing Co: 1 Jacob Way, Reading, MA 01867-3999; tel. (617) 944-3700; fax (617) 944-9338; internet www.awl.com; f. 1988; educational, trade, scientific, engineering, and language teaching materials; Chair. and CEO J. LARRY JONES.

Andrews & McMeel: 4520 Main St, Suite 700, Kansas City, MO 64112; tel. (816) 932-6700; fax (816) 932-6706; f. 1933; humour, general trade; Pres. KATHLEEN W. ANDREWS.

Jason Aronson, Inc: 230 Livingston St, Northvale, NJ 07647; tel. (201) 767-4093; fax (201) 767-4330; e-mail editor@aronson.com; internet www.psychotherapylibrary.com; f. 1965; psychiatry, psychoanalysis and behavioural sciences; Judaica; Pres. JASON ARONSON.

Augsburg Fortress, Publishers: 100 South Fifth St, POB 1209, Minneapolis, MN 55440; tel. (612) 330-3300; fax (612) 330-3455; e-mail info@augsburgfortress.org; internet www.augsburgfortress .org; f. 1890; religious; Pres. MARVIN ROLOFF.

August House Inc, Publishers: POB 3223, Little Rock, AR 72203; tel. (501) 372-5540; fax (501) 372-5579; e-mail ahinfo@augusthouse .com; internet www.augusthouse.com; f. 1979; Southern regional, history, humour and folklore; Pres. TED PARKHURST.

Avery Publishing Group, Inc: 120 Old Broadway, Garden City Park, NY 11040; tel. (516) 741-2155; fax (516) 742-1892; e-mail info@ averypublishing.com; internet www.averypublishing.com; f. 1976; college textbooks, trade books specializing in childbirth, child care, health, cookery, nutrition; Pres. RUDY SHUR.

Avon Books: 10 East St, New York, NY 10022; tel. (212) 207-7000; fax (212) 207-7203; internet www.harpercollins.com; f. 1941; division of HarperCollins; reprints and originals; Pres. JANE FRIEDMAN.

Baker Book House: POB 6287, Grand Rapids, MI 49516; tel. (616) 676-9185; fax (616) 676-9573; internet www.bakerbooks.com; f. 1939; Pres. DWIGHT BAKER; religious (Protestant).

Barron's Educational Series, Inc: 250 Wireless Blvd, Hauppauge, NY 11788; tel. (516) 434-3311; fax (516) 434-3723; e-mail info@barronseduc.com; f. 1945; general non-fiction, educational, juvenile; Pres. MANUEL H. BARRON.

Beacon Press: 25 Beacon St, Boston, MA 02108; tel. (617) 742-2110; fax (617) 723-3097; internet www.beacon.org; f. 1854; world affairs, religion, general non-fiction; Dir HELENE ATWAN.

The Borgo Press: POB 2845, San Bernardino, CA 92406; tel. (909) 884-5813; fax (909) 888-4942; e-mail borgopr@gte.net; internet www .borgopress.com; f. 1975; Publrs ROBERT REGINALD, MARY A. BURGESS; academic and scholarly.

R. R. Bowker: 121 Chanlon Rd, New Providence, NJ 07974; tel. (908) 464-6800; fax (908) 464-3553; e-mail info@bowker.com; internet www.bowker.com; f. 1872; Publr CHARLES HALPIN; reference, bibliographies.

Braille Inc: 65B Town Hall Sq., Falmouth, MA 02540-2754; tel. (508) 540-0800; fax (508) 548-6116; e-mail brailleinc@capecod.net; internet www.capecod.net/braillinc; f. 1971; Pres. JOSIE P. LITTLE; fiction, non-fiction, mathematics, science, foreign languages, educational and computer materials in Braille transcription.

George Braziller, Inc: 171 Madison Ave, New York, NY 10016; tel. (212) 889-0909; fax (212) 689-5405; f. 1955; fiction and non-fiction, art; Publr GEORGE BRAZILLER.

Broadman and Holman Publishers: 127 North Ninth Ave, Nashville, TN 37234-0198; tel. (615) 251-5003; fax (615) 251-5004; e-mail kstephe@bssb.com; internet www.broadmanholman.com; f. 1891; religious (Protestant), fiction, non-fiction, juvenile; Publr KENNETH H. STEPHENS.

Brookings Institution Press: 1775 Massachusetts Ave, NW, Washington, DC 20036-2188; tel. (202) 797-6000; fax (202) 797-6004; e-mail bibooks@brook.edu; internet www.brookings.edu; f. 1927; economics, government, foreign policy; Dir ROBERT L. FAHERTY.

Burnham Publishers: 111 North Canal St, Chicago, IL 60606; tel. (312) 930-9446; fax (312) 930-5903; e-mail publishers@burnhaminc .com; f. 1909; Pres. and Publr KATHLEEN KUSTA; general interest non-fiction and educational.

Cambridge University Press: 40 West 20th St, New York, NY 10011-4211; tel. (212) 924-3900; fax (212) 691-3239; internet www .cup.org; Dir RICHARD ZIEMACKI.

Catholic University of America Press: 620 Michigan Ave, NE, Washington, DC 20064; tel. (202) 319-5052; fax (202) 319-4985; e-mail cua-press@cua,edu; internet www.cuapress.cua.edu; f. 1939; scholarly; Dir DAVID J. MCGONAGLE.

Caxton Printers Ltd: 312 Main St, Caldwell, ID 83605; tel. (208) 459-7421; fax (208) 459-7450; e-mail publish@caxtonprinters.com; internet www.caxtonprinters.com; f. 1903; Western Americana; Pres. GORDON GIPSON.

Columbia University Press: 61 West 62nd St, New York, NY 10023; tel. (212) 459-0600; fax (212) 316-9422; e-mail mm441@ columbia.edu; internet www.cc.columbia.edu/cu/wp; f. 1893; trade, educational, scientific, reference; Pres. and Dir WILLIAM B. STRACHAN.

Concordia Publishing House: 3558 South Jefferson Ave, St Louis, MO 63118; tel. (314) 268-1000; fax (314) 268-1329; internet www.cpn.org; f. 1869; religious (Protestant) children's books, devotionals, bulletins, curriculum music; Pres. STEPHEN J. CARTER.

Congressional Quarterly Books: 1414 22nd St, NW, Washington, DC 20037; tel. (202) 887-8500; fax (202) 887-6706; f. 1945; business, education and government; directories; Publr ROBERT MERRY.

Cornell University Press: Sage House, 512 East Seneca St, POB 250, Ithaca, NY 14851; tel. (607) 257-2338; fax (607) 277-2374; e-mail cupressinfo@cornell.edu; internet www.cornellpress.cornell .edu; f. 1869; scholarly, non-fiction; Dir JOHN G. ACKERMAN.

Creative Co: 123 South Broad St, POB 227, Mankato, MN 56001; tel. (507) 388-6273; fax (507) 388-2746; e-mail creativeco@aol.com; f. 1932; juvenile; Pres. TOM PETERSON.

F. A. Davis Co: 1915 Arch St, Philadelphia, PA 19103; tel. (215) 568-2270; fax (215) 568-5065; e-mail info@fadavis.com; f. 1879; Pres. ROBERT H. CRAVEN, Jr; medical, nursing and allied health textbooks.

Marcel Dekker, Inc: 270 Madison Ave, New York, NY 10016; tel. (212) 696-9000; fax (212) 685-4540; e-mail marketing@dekker.com; internet www.dekker.com; f. 1963; textbooks and reference; Pres. and CEO MARCEL DEKKER.

Dover Publications, Inc: 31 East Second St, Mineola, NY 11501; tel. (516) 294-7000; fax (516) 742-5049; internet www .doverpublications.com; f. 1941; trade, reprints, scientific, classics, language, arts and crafts; Pres. CLARENCE STROWBRIDGE.

Dufour Editions, Inc: POB 7, Chester Springs, PA 19425-0007; tel. (610) 458-5005; fax (610) 458-7103; e-mail info@dufoureditions.com; internet www.dufoureditions.com; f. 1946; literary, political science, humanities, music, history; Pres. CHRISTOPHER MAY.

Duke University Press: POB 90660, Duke University, Durham, NC 27708-0660; tel. (919) 687-3600; fax (919) 688-4574; internet www.dukeupress.edu; f. 1921; scholarly; Editor-in-Chief PETER GUVVARDI.

Duquesne University Press: 600 Forbes Ave, Pittsburgh, PA 15282; tel. (412) 396-6610; fax (412) 396-5984; internet www.duq .edu/dupress; f. 1927; Dir SUSAN WADSWORTH-BOOTH; scholarly.

Ediciones Universal: 3090 SW Eighth St, Miami, FL 33135; tel. (305) 642-3234; fax (305) 642-7978; e-mail ediciones@ediciones.com; internet www.ediciones.com; f. 1965; Man. JUAN MANUEL SALVAT; Spanish language fiction and non-fiction.

Elsevier Science, Inc: 655 Ave of the Americas, New York, NY 10010; tel. (212) 989-5800; fax (212) 633-3990; f. 1962; scientific, medical, technical, multilingual technical journals; Publr GLEN CAMPELL.

Encyclopaedia Britannica, Inc: 310 South Michigan Ave, Chicago, IL 60604; tel. (312) 347-7000; fax (312) 294-2108; f. 1768; encyclopaedias, atlases, dictionaries; CEO DON YANNIAS.

M. Evans & Co, Inc: 216 East 49th St, New York, NY 10017; tel. (212) 688-2810; fax (212) 486-4544; e-mail editorial@mevans.com; f. 1960; Pres. GEORGE C. DE KAY; adult fiction and non-fiction.

Facts On File Inc: 11 Penn Plaza, New York, NY 10001-2006; tel. (212) 967-8800; fax (212) 967-9196; internet www.factsonfile.com; f. 1940; division of Infobase Holdings, Inc; non-fiction, reference, electronic data bases; Publr MARK MCDONNELL.

Farrar, Straus & Giroux, Inc: 19 Union Sq. West, New York, NY 10003; tel. (212) 741-6900; fax (212) 633-9385; f. 1946; general trade; Chair. ROGER W. STRAUS; Pres. JONATHAN GALASSI.

Ferguson Publishing Co: 200 West Madison St, Chicago, IL 60606; tel. (312) 580-5480; fax (312) 580-7215; internet www.fergpubco.com; f. 1907; children's, encyclopedias; Pres. PETER EWING.

Fordham University Press: University Box L, Bronx, NY 10458-5172; tel. (718) 817-4780; fax (718) 817-4785; e-mail mnoonan@fordham.edu; f. 1907; scholarly; Dir SAVERIO PROCARIO.

W. H. Freeman & Co, Publishers: 41 Madison Ave, New York, NY 10010; tel. (212) 576-9400; fax (212) 689-2383; internet www.whfreeman.com; f. 1946; textbooks; Pres. ELIZABETH WIDDICOMBE.

Samuel French, Inc: 45 West 25th St, New York, NY 10010; tel. (212) 206-8990; fax (212) 206-1429; f. 1830; plays; Man. Dir CHARLES R. VAN NOSTRAND.

Futura Publishing Co Inc: 135 Bedford Rd, POB 418, Armonk, NY 10504; tel. (914) 273-1014; fax (914) 273-1015; e-mail pub@futuraco; internet www.futuraco.com; f. 1970; medical and scientific; Chair. and Publr STEVEN E. KORN.

Gale: 27500 Drake Rd, Farmington Hills, MI 48331-3535; tel. (248) 669-4253; fax (248) 669-8064; e-mail galeord@galegroup.com; internet www.galegroup.com; f. 1954; reference; Pres. and CEO DEDRIA BRYFONSKI.

Garland Publishing Inc: 29 West 35th St, New York, NY 10001; tel. (212) 751-7447; fax (212) 584-7854; e-mail info@garland.com; internet www.garlandpub.com; division of Taylor and Francis Group; f. 1969; reprints, reference, college textbooks, law; Publr K. WRIGHT.

Bernard Geis Associates: 500 Fifth Ave, Suite 3600, New York, NY 10110; tel. (212) 730-4730; fax (212) 730-4464; f. 1958; Pres. BERNARD GEIS; general fiction and non-fiction.

Genealogical Publishing Co: 1001 North Calvert St, Baltimore, MD 21202; tel. (410) 837-8271; fax (410) 752-8492; f. 1959; genealogy, immigration studies, heraldry, local history; Editor-in-Chief MICHAEL TEPPER.

The K. S. Giniger Co, Inc: 250 West 57th St, Suite 414, New York, NY 10107; tel. (212) 570-7499; fax (212) 369-6692; f. 1965; Pres. KENNETH S. GINIGER; general non-fiction.

Warren H. Green, Inc: 8356 Olive Blvd, St Louis, MO 63132; tel. (314) 991-1335; fax (314) 997-1788; e-mail whgreen@inlink.com; internet www.whgreen.com; f. 1966; medical, science, technology, philosophy; Pres. JOYCE R. GREEN.

Greenwood Publishing Group: 88 Post Rd West, POB 5007, Westport, CT 06881; tel. (203) 226-3571; fax (203) 222-1502; e-mail bookinfo@greenwood.com; internet www.greenwood.com; f. 1967; division of Reed Elsevier; business reference and non-fiction; Pres. WAYNE SMITH.

Grolier Publishing Co, Inc: 90 Sherman Turnpike, Danbury, CT 06816; tel. (203) 797-3500; fax (203) 797-3720; internet www.publishing.grolier.com; f. 1946; juvenile educational; Pres. JOSEPH TESSITORE.

Grove/Atlantic: 841 Broadway, New York, NY 10003-4793; tel. (212) 614-7850; fax (212) 614-7886; e-mail mentrekin@groveatlantic.com; Pres. MORGAN ENTREKIN; fiction, non-fiction and poetry.

Hammond World Atlas Corpn: 95 Progress St, Union, NJ 07083; tel. (908) 206-1300; fax (908) 206-1104; e-mail chuck@hammondmap.com; internet www.hammondmap.com; f. 1900; maps, atlases, cartography; Chair. and CEO STUART DOLGINS.

Harcourt Inc: 6277 Sea Harbor Dr., Orlando, FL 32887; tel. (407) 345-2000; fax (407) 352-3445; f. 1919; fiction, textbooks, general; Pres. and CEO JAMES LEVY.

HarperCollins Publishers: 10 East 53rd St, New York, NY 10022; tel. (212) 207-7000; fax (212) 207-7759; internet www.harpercollins.com; f. 1817; fiction, non-fiction, religious, children's, medical, general; Pres. and CEO JANE FRIEDMAN.

Harvard University Press: 79 Garden St, Cambridge, MA 02138; tel. (617) 495-2600; fax (617) 495-5898; internet www.hup.harvard.edu; f. 1913; classics, fine arts, philosophy, science, medicine, law, literature, political science, religion, history and government; Dir WILLIAM P. SISLER.

Hastings House, Book Publishers: 9 Mott Ave, Suite 203, Norwalk, CT 06850; tel. (203) 838-4083; fax (203) 838-4084; e-mail hhousebks@aol.com; internet www.hastingshousebooks.com; f. 1936; communication, arts, media, travel, children's; Pres. PETER LEES.

Holiday House, Inc: 425 Madison Ave, New York, NY 10017; tel. (212) 688-0085; fax (212) 421-6134; f. 1935; juvenile; Pres. JOHN H. BRIGGS, Jr.

Holloway House Publishing Co: 8060 Melrose Ave, Los Angeles, CA 90046-7082; tel. (323) 653-8060; fax (323) 655-9452; e-mail psi@loop.com; f. 1960; Pres. BENTLEY MORRISS; African-American and American Indian literature, games and gambling.

Holmes & Meier Publishers, Inc: East Bldg, 160 Broadway, New York, NY 10038; tel. (212) 374-0100; fax (212) 374-1313; e-mail holmesandmeier.com; f. 1969; history, political science, area studies, Judaica, foreign literature in translation, college texts and scholarly; Publr MIRIAM H. HOLMES.

Hoover Institution Press: Stanford University, Stanford, CA 94305-6010; tel. (650) 723-3373; fax (650) 723-8626; e-mail presley@hoover.stanford.edu; internet www.hoover.org; f. 1962; scholarly; Exec. Editor PATRICIA A. BAKER.

Houghton Mifflin Co: 222 Berkeley St, Boston, MA 02116; tel. (617) 351-5000; fax (617) 351-3604; internet www.hcmo.com; f. 1832; general and educational; Chair., Pres. and CEO NADER F. DARESHORI.

Indiana University Press: 601 North Morton St, Bloomington, IN 47404-3796; tel. (812) 855-8817; fax (812) 855-8507; e-mail iupress@indiana.edu; internet iupress.indiana.edu; f. 1950; Dir PETER-JOHN LEONE; trade and scholarly non-fiction.

International Universities Press, Inc: 59 Boston Post Rd, Madison, CT 06443; tel. (203) 245-4000; fax (203) 245-0775; e-mail orders@iup.com; internet www.iup.com; f. 1943; psychology, psychiatry, medicine, social sciences and journals; Pres. MARTIN V. AZARIAN; Exec. Vice-Pres. Dr MARGARET EMERY.

Iowa State University Press: 2121 State Ave, Ames, IA 50014-8300; tel. (515) 292-0140; fax (515) 292-3348; e-mail marketing@iowastatepress.com; internet www.iowastatepress.com; f. 1924; Publishing Dir PAUL BECKER; textbooks, reference.

Islamic Books/Tahrike Tarsile Qur'ān, Inc: POB 731115, Elmhurst, NY 11373-0115; tel. (718) 446-6472; fax (718) 446-4370; internet www.koranusa.org; f. 1978; Pres. AUNALI KHALFAN; Koran and Islamic religious texts.

Jewish Publication Society: 2100 Arch St, 2nd Floor, Philadelphia, PA 19103; tel. (215) 832-0600; fax (215) 568-2017; f. 1888; Pres. ELLEN FRANKEL.

Johns Hopkins University Press: 2715 North Charles St, Baltimore, MD 21218-4319; tel. (410) 516-6900; fax (410) 516-6998; f. 1878; social and physical sciences, humanities, health sciences, economics, literary criticism, history.

Augustus M. Kelley, Publishers: POB 1048, Fairfield, NJ 07004-1048; tel. (212) 685-7202; f. 1947; reprints of economic classics; Editor FREDERICK S. CHEESMAN.

Kendall/Hunt Publishing Co: POB 1840, Dubuque, IA 52004-1840; tel. (563) 589-1000; fax (563) 589-1046; internet www.kendallhunt.com; f. 1944; COO MARK FALB; business and educational.

Kluwer Academic Publishers: 101 Philip Dr., Norwell, MA 02061; tel. (617) 871-6600; fax (617) 871-6528; e-mail kluwer@wkap.com; internet www.wkap.nl; f. 1978; scientific, technical, medical, scholarly and professional books and journals; Pres. JAY LIPPENCOTT.

Krieger Publishing Co: POB 9542, Melbourne, FL 32902-9542; tel. (321) 724-9542; fax (321) 951-3671; e-mail info@krieger-pubishing.com; internet www.krieger-publishing.com; f. 1970; Pres. DONALD E. KRIEGER; scientific and technical originals and reprints.

Lippincott, Williams & Wilkins: 351 West Camden St, Baltimore, MD 21201-2436; tel. (410) 528-4000; fax (410) 528-5897; f. 1792; medical, dental, veterinary, scientific; Pres. Education TIM SATTERFIELD.

Loyola Press: 3441 North Ashland Ave, Chicago, IL 60657; tel. (773) 281-1818; fax (773) 281-0885; e-mail lane@loyolapress.com; internet www.loyolapress.org; f. 1912; Dir GEORGE A. LANE (sj).

McGraw-Hill, Inc: 1221 Ave of the Americas, New York, NY 10020; tel. (212) 512-2000; fax (212) 512-2821; internet www.mcgraw-hill.com; f. 1888; information texts and services for business, industry, government and the general public; Chair. and CEO HAROLD McGRAW, III.

Macmillan USA: 201 West 103rd St, Indianapolis, IN 46290; tel. (317) 581-3500; fax (317) 581-4657; internet www.mcp.com; scientific, technical and medical; Pres. SCOTT N. FLANDERS.

Michigan State University Press: 1405 South Harrison Rd, Suite 25, East Lansing, MI 48823-5202; tel. (517) 355-9543; fax (517) 432-2611; e-mail msupress@msu.edu; internet www.msupress.msu.edu; f. 1947; scholarly; Dir FRED C. BOHM.

The MIT Press: 5 Cambridge Centre, Cambridge, MA 02142; tel. (617) 253-5646; fax (617) 258-6779; internet www.mitpress.mit.edu; f. 1932; computer sciences, architecture, design, linguistics, economics, philosophy, general science, neuroscience, cognitive science and engineering; Dir FRANK URBANOWSKI.

Moody Press: 820 North LaSalle Blvd, Chicago, IL 60610; tel. (312) 329-2101; fax (312) 329-2144; e-mail gthornto@moody.edu; f. 1894; Man. GREG THORNTON; religious.

William Morrow & Co Inc: 1350 Ave of the Americas, New York, NY 10019; tel. (212) 261-6500; fax (212) 261-6595; f. 1926; division of HarperCollins; fiction, non-fiction, juveniles; Pres. and CEO ALLEN MARCHIONI.

National Academy Press: 2101 Constitution Ave, NW, POB 285, Washington, DC 20055; tel. (202) 334-3313; fax (202) 334-2451; internet www.nap.edu; f. 1863; division of National Academy of Sciences; scientific and technical reports, abstracts, bibliographies, catalogues; Dir SCOTT LUBECK.

National Learning Corpn: 212 Michael Dr., Syosset, NY 11791; tel. (516) 921-8888; fax (516) 921-8743; internet www.passbooks .com; f. 1967; professional and vocational study guides; Pres. MICHAEL P. RUDMAN.

New Directions Publishing Corpn: 80 Eighth Ave, 19th Floor, New York, NY 10011; tel. (212) 255-0230; fax (212) 255-0231; e-mail nd@ndbooks.com; internet www.ndpublishing.com; f. 1936; modern literature, poetry, criticism, belles-lettres; Pres. and Publr GRISELDA J. OHANNESSIAN.

New York University Press: 838 Broadway, New York, NY 10012; tel. (212) 998-2575; fax (212) 995-3833; internet www.nyupress.nyu .edu; f. 1916; scholarly, non-fiction, general; Dir NIKO PFUND; Man. Editor DESPINA GIMBEL.

Northwestern University Press: 625 Colfax St, Evanston, IL 60208-4210; tel. (847) 491-5313; fax (847) 491-8150; e-mail nupress@ northwestern.edu; internet http://nupress.northwestern.edu; f. 1958; Dir SUSAN HARRIS; scholarly and trade.

W. W. Norton & Co Inc: 500 Fifth Ave, New York, NY 10110; tel. (212) 354-5500; fax (212) 869-0856; internet www.wwnorton.com; f. 1924; general fiction and non-fiction, college textbooks, paperbacks; Chair. DONALD S. LAMM; Pres. DRAKE McFEELY.

NOVA Publications: 7342 Lee Hwy, No. 201, Falls Church, VA 22046; tel. and fax (703) 280-5383; e-mail novapublic@aol.com; internet www.members.aol.com/novapublic/index.htm; f. 1993; military history, political science, Russian and Middle Eastern studies; Publr ARNOLD C. DUPUY.

Oceana Publications Inc: 75 Main St, Dobbs Ferry, NY 10522-1632; tel. (914) 693-5956; fax (914) 693-0402; e-mail info@oceanalaw .com; internet www.oceanalaw.com; f. 1957; international law and trade; Pres. DAVID R. COHEN.

Ohio State University Press: 1070 Carmack Rd, Columbus, OH 43210; tel. (740) 292-6930; fax (740) 292-2065; e-mail mbucy@ magnus.acs.ohio-state.edu; f. 1957; general scholarly non-fiction; Dir MALCOM LITCHFIELD.

Ohio University Press: Scott Quadrangle 220, Ohio University, Athens, OH 45701; tel. (740) 593-1154; fax (740) 593-4536; e-mail gilbert@ohio.edu; internet www.ohiou.edu/oupress/; f. 1964; Dir DAVID SANDERS; scholarly, regional studies.

Open Court Publishing Co: 332 South Michigan Ave, Suite 2000, Chicago, IL 60604; tel. (312) 939-1500; fax (312) 939-8150; e-mail opencourt@caruspub.com; internet www.opencourtbooks.com; f. 1887; general non-fiction; Pres. and Publr ANDRE CARUS.

Orbis Books: Walsh Bldg, POB 308, Maryknoll, NY 10545-0308; tel. (914) 941-7590; fax (914) 945-0670; e-mail orbisbooks@ maryknoll.org; internet www.orbisbooks.com; f. 1970; theology, religion and social concerns; Exec. Dir MICHAEL LEACH.

Oxford University Press Inc: 198 Madison Ave, New York, NY 10016; tel. (212) 726-6000; fax (212) 725-2972; internet www.oup .com; f. 1896; non-fiction, trade, religious, reference, bibles, college textbooks, medical, music; Pres. EDWARD W. BARRY.

Paladin Press: POB 1307, Boulder, CO 80306; tel. (303) 443-7250; fax (303) 442-8741; e-mail service@paladin-press.com; internet www .paladin-press.com; f. 1970; military science and history; Chair. and Pres. PEDER C. LUND.

Paragon House: 2700 University Ave, Suite 200, St Paul, MN 55114; tel. (651) 644-3087; fax (651) 644-0997; e-mail paragon@ paragonhouse.com; internet www.paragonhouse.com; f. 1982; general trade non-fiction, university texts, reference; Vice-Pres. and Dir MICHAEL GIAMPAOLI.

Penguin Putnam Inc: 375 Hudson St, New York, NY 10014; tel. (212) 366-2000; fax (212) 366-2666; e-mail online@penguinputnam .com; internet www.penguinputnam.com; f. 1925; Pres. DAVID WAN.

Pennsylvania State University Press: University Support Bldg I, Suite C, 820 North University Dr., University Park, PA 16802; tel. (814) 865-1327; fax (814) 863-1408; internet www.psupress.org; f. 1956; scholarly non-fiction; Dir SANFORD G. THATCHER.

Praeger Publishers/Greenwood Publishing Group: 88 Post Rd West, POB 5007, Westport, CT 06881; tel. (203) 226-3571; fax (203) 222-1502; f. 1950; general non-fiction, reference, scholarly, academic; Pres ROBERT HAGELSTEIN; Vice-Pres. CAROLE BRONSON.

Princeton University Press: 41 William St, Princeton, NJ 08540; tel. (609) 452-4900; fax (609) 258-0825; f. 1905; scholarly; Dir WALTER H. LIPPINCOTT, Jr; Editor-in-Chief TERRY VAUGHN.

Quite Specific Media Group Ltd: 260 Fifth Ave, New York, NY 10001; tel. (212) 725-5377; fax (212) 725-8506; e-mail info@ quitespecificmedia.com; internet www.quitespecificmedia.com; f. 1967; costume, design, fashion, performing arts; Publr RALPH PINE.

Rand McNally: 8255 Central Park Ave, Skokie, IL 60076; tel. (847) 329-8100; fax (847) 673-0539; internet www.randmcnally.com; f. 1856; maps, atlases, travel guides; Chair. ANDREW McNALLY, III; Pres. RICHARD DAVIS.

Random House Inc: 299 Park Ave, New York, NY 10170; tel. (212) 751-2600; fax (212) 572-8026; internet www.randomhouse.com; f. 1925; originals, reprints, paperbacks, juvenile, series, textbooks; Chair. and CEO PETER OLSON.

Reader's Digest Association, Inc: Reader's Digest Rd, Pleasant-ville, NY 10570-7000; tel. (914) 238-1000; fax (914) 238-4559; internet www.readersdigest.com; reference and non-fiction; Chair. and CEO THOMAS RYDER.

Rizzoli International Publications Inc: 300 Park Ave South, New York, NY 10010-5399; tel. (212) 387-3400; fax (212) 3873535; f. 1975; fine arts, performing arts, architecture; Pres., CEO and Publr MARTA HALLETT.

Routledge: 29 West 35th St, New York, NY 10001-2299; tel. (212) 244-3336; fax (212) 563-2269; internet www.routledge-ny.com; f. 1977; division of Taylor and Francis Group; scholarly, professional, trade, humanities, social sciences; Pres. KEVIN BRADLEY.

Rutgers University Press: 100 Joyce Kilmer Ave, Piscataway, NJ 08854; tel. (732) 445-7762; fax (732) 445-7039; internet www .rutgerspress.rutgers.edu; scholarly and regional; Editor-in-Chief MARLIE WASSERMAN.

William H. Sadlier Inc: 9 Pine St, New York, NY 10005; tel. (212) 227-2120; fax (212) 267-8696; e-mail wsd@sadlier.com; internet www.sadlier.com; f. 1832; textbooks; Pres. WILLIAM SADLIER DINGER.

St Martin's Press Inc: 175 Fifth Ave, New York, NY 10010; tel. (212) 674-5151; fax (212) 420-9314; e-mail inquiries@stmartins.com; internet www.stmartins.com; f. 1952; general, scholarly, college textbooks, reference; Pres. JOHN SARGENT.

Scarecrow Press, Inc: 4720 Boston Way, Lanham, MD 20706; tel. (301) 459-3366; fax (301) 459-2118; internet www.scarecrowpress .com; f. 1950; reference, textbooks, library science; Pres. JAMES E. LYONS.

Scholastic, Inc: 555 Broadway, New York, NY 10012; tel. (212) 343-6100; fax (212) 343-6930; internet www.scholastic.com/; f. 1920; children's periodicals, textbooks, educational materials; Chair., Pres. and CEO M. RICHARD ROBINSON.

Shoe String Press Inc: 2 Linsley St, North Haven, CT 06473; tel. (203) 239-2702; fax (203) 239-2568; e-mail books@shoestringpresss .com; internet www.shoestringpress.com; f. 1952; scholarly, children's and general non-fiction; Pres. and Editorial Dir DIANTHA THORPE.

Silhouette Books: 233 Broadway, New York, NY 10017; tel. (212) 553-4200; fax (212) 227-8969; internet www.eharlequin.com; f. 1979; Pres. DONNA HAYES; romantic fiction.

Simon & Schuster, Inc: 1230 Ave of the Americas, New York, NY 10020; tel. (212) 698-7000; fax (212) 698-7007; internet www .simonsays.com; f. 1924; trade, juvenile, reference, educational, elementary and secondary school textbooks, business and professional; Chair. and CEO JONATHAN NEWCOMB.

Peter Smith Publisher, Inc: 5 Lexington Ave, Magnolia, MA 01930; tel. (978) 525-3562; fax (978) 525-3674; Pres. MARY ANN LASH; reprints.

Smithsonian Institution Press: 750 Ninth St NW, Suite 4300, Washington, DC 20560-0950; tel. (202) 275-2243; fax (202) 275-2243; e-mail phernandez@sipress.si.edu; internet www.si.edu; f. 1848; Dir PETER F. CANNELL; scholarly and general interest in American studies and culture, anthropology, archaeology, natural science, museum studies; Dir PROSPERO HERNANDEZ (acting).

Southern Illinois University Press: POB 3697, Carbondale, IL 62902-3697; tel. (618) 453-2281; fax (618) 453-1221; e-mail jstetter@ siu.edu; internet www.siu.edu/~siupress; f. 1953; scholarly non-fiction; Dir JOHN F. STETTER.

Springer-Verlag New York, Inc: 175 Fifth Ave, 19th Floor, New York, NY 10010; tel. (212) 460-1500; fax (212) 473-6272; internet www.springer-ny.com; f. 1964; scientific, technical and medical; Exec. Vice-Pres. and Publr RÜIDIGER GEBAUER.

Stanford University Press: Stanford, CA 94305; tel. (415) 723-9434; fax (415) 725-3457; internet www.sup.org; f. 1925; Man. Dir GEOFFREY BURN.

State University of New York Press: 90 State St, Suite 700, Albany, NY 12207-1707; tel. (518) 472-5000; fax (518) 472-5038; e-mail info@sunypress.edu; internet www.sunypress.edu; f. 1966; Dir PRISCILLA ROSS; scholarly.

Sterling Publishing Co, Inc: 387 Park Ave South, New York, NY 10016; tel. (212) 532-7160; fax (212) 213-2495; f. 1949; non-fiction; Chair. BURTON H. HOBSON.

Summy–Birchard Inc: 15800 NW 48th Ave, Miami, FL 33014; tel. (305) 620-1500; fax (305) 621-1094; e-mail judi.gowe@warnerchappell.com; f. 1872; educational music, methods and texts; Dir JUDI GOWE.

Syracuse University Press: Suite 110, 621 Skytop Rd, Syracuse, NY 13244-5290; tel. (315) 443-5534; fax (315) 443-5545; internet sumweb.syr.edu/su_press/; f. 1943; Dir JOHN FRUEHWIRTH (acting); scholarly.

Taplinger Publishing Co Inc: POB 175, Marlboro, NJ 07746; tel. (201) 432-3257; fax (201) 432-3708; f. 1955; general fiction and non-fiction; Pres. LOUIS STRICK.

Taylor & Francis Inc: 1900 Frost Rd, Suite 101, Bristol, PA; tel. (215) 785-5800; fax (215) 785-5515; e-mail info@taylorandfrancis.com; internet www.taylorandfrancis.com; f. 1972; scientific, technical and reference; Pres. KEVIN BRADLEY.

Charles C. Thomas, Publisher: 2600 South First St, Springfield, IL 62794-9265; tel. (217) 789-8980; fax (217) 789-9130; e-mail books@ccthomasa.com; f. 1927; textbooks and reference on education, medicine, psychology and criminology; Pres. MICHAEL P. THOMAS.

Time-Life Books Inc: 2000 Duke St, Alexandria, VA 22314; tel. (703) 838-7000; fax (703) 838-7474; f. 1961; general non-fiction; Pres. and CEO JIM NELSON.

Tuttle Publishing: 153 Milk St, 5th Floor, Boston, MA 02109; tel. (617) 951-4080; fax (617) 951-4045; e-mail info@tuttlepublishing.com; internet www.tuttlepublishing.com; f. 1832; Publishing Dir EDWARD WALTERS; the Far East, particularly Japan, languages, art, literature, culture, juveniles, cookery.

United Nations Publications: United Nations Plaza, Room DC2-0853, New York, NY 10017; tel. (212) 963-8302; fax (212) 963-3489; e-mail publications@un.org; internet www.un.org; f. 1946; world and national economies, international trade, social questions, human rights, international law; Chief of Section CHRISTOPHER WOODTHORPE.

University of Alabama Press: POB 870380, Tuscaloosa, AL 35487; tel. (205) 348-5180; fax (205) 348-9201; f. 1945; scholarly non-fiction; Dir DANIEL J. J. ROSS.

University of Alaska Press: 104 Eielson Bldg, Salcha Lane, POB 756240, University of Alaska, Fairbanks, AK 99775-6240; tel. (907) 474-5831; fax (907) 474-5502; e-mail fypress@aurora.alaska.edu; internet www.uaf.edu/press; f. 1967; scholarly regional non-fiction; Dir CLAUS M. NASKE.

University of Arizona Press: 355 South Euclid, Suite 103, Tucson, AZ 85719; tel. (520) 621-1441; fax (520) 621-8899; e-mail uapress@arizona.edu; internet www.uapress.arizona.edu; f. 1959; Dir CHRISTINE SZUTER; scholarly, popular, regional, non-fiction.

University of Arkansas Press: McIlroy House, 201 Ozark Ave, Fayetteville, AR 72701; tel. (479) 575-3246; fax (479) 575-6044; e-mail uaprinfo@uark.edu; internet www.uapress.com; f. 1980; Dir LARRY MALLEY; general humanities, literature, regional studies, natural history, Middle Eastern studies, poetry, civil rights studies, American history.

University of California Press: 2120 Berkeley Way, Berkeley, CA 94720; tel. (510) 642-4247; fax (510) 643-7127; e-mail ucpress@ucop.edu; internet www.ucpress.edu; f. 1893; academic, scholarly; Dir JAMES H. CLARK.

University of Chicago Press: 1427 East 60th St, Chicago, IL 60637; tel. (773) 702-7700; fax (773) 702-2705; e-mail general@press.uchicago.edu; internet www.press.uchicago.edu; f. 1891; Dir PAULA BARKER DUFFY; scholarly books and journals, general.

University of Georgia Press: Athens, GA 30602; tel. (706) 369-6130; fax (706) 369-6131; f. 1938; academic, scholarly, poetry, fiction, non-fiction, literary trade; Dir NICOLE MITCHELL.

University of Hawaii Press: 2840 Kolowalu St, Honolulu, HI 96822; tel. (808) 956-8255; fax (808) 988-6052; e-mail uhpbooks@hawaii.edu; internet www.uhpress.hawaii.edu; f. 1947; Asian, Pacific and Hawaiian studies; Dir WILLIAM H. HAMILTON.

University of Idaho Press: POB 4416, Moscow, ID 83844-4416; tel. (208) 885-3300; fax (208) 885-3301; e-mail uipress@uidaho.edu; internet www.uidaho.edu/uipress; f. 1972; Dir IVAR NELSON; scholarly, regional studies, folklore, natural history, literary criticism, native American studies, journals, *Hemingway Review* and *Native Plant Journal*, biannuals.

University of Illinois Press: 1325 South Oak St, Champaign, IL 61820; tel. (217) 333-0950; fax (217) 244-8082; e-mail uipress@uillinois.edu; internet www.uillinois.edu; f. 1918; scholarly and poetry; Dir WILLIAM REGIER.

University of Massachusetts Press: POB 429, Amherst, MA 01004-0429; tel. (413) 545-2217; fax (413) 545-1226; e-mail umpress@umass.edu; internet www.umass.edu/umpress; f. 1964; scholarly non-fiction; Dir BRUCE G. WILCOX.

University of Michigan Press: 839 Greene St, POB 1104, Ann Arbor, MI 48106; tel. (313) 734-4388; fax (313) 734-0456; e-mail um.press.bus@umich.edu; internet www.press.umich.edu; f. 1930; academic, textbooks, paperbacks; Dir PHILIP POCHODA.

University of Minnesota Press: 111 Third Ave South, Suite 290, Minneapolis, MN 55401-5250; tel. (612) 627-1970; fax (612) 627-1980; internet www.upress.umn.edu; f. 1927; scholarly, general; Dir DOUGLAS M. ARMATO.

University of Missouri Press: 2910 LeMone Blvd, Columbia, MO 65201; tel. (573) 882-7641; fax (573) 884-4498; internet www.system.missouri.edu/upress; scholarly; Dir BEVERLY JARRETT.

University of Nebraska Press: 233 North 8th St, Lincoln, NE 68588-0255; tel. (402) 472-3581; fax (402) 472-0308; e-mail pressmail@unl.edu; internet www.nebraskapress.unl.edu; f. 1941; general interest and scholarly; Dir PAUL ROYSTER.

University of New Mexico Press: 1720 Lomas Blvd, NE, Albuquerque, NM 87131-1591; tel. (505) 277-2346; fax (505) 277-9270; e-mail unmpress@unm.edu; internet www.unmpress.com; f. 1929; scholarly, regional studies; Dir LUTHER WILSON.

University of North Carolina Press: POB 2288, Chapel Hill, NC 27515-2288; tel. (919) 966-3561; fax (919) 966-3829; e-mail uncpress@unc.edu; internet www.uncpress.unc.edu; f. 1922; biographical, regional, scholarly non-fiction; Dir KATE D. TORREY.

University of Notre Dame Press: Notre Dame, IN 46556; tel. (219) 631-6346; fax (219) 631-8148; e-mail undpress.1@nd.edu; internet www.undpress.nd.edu; f. 1949; humanities and social sciences; Dir BARBARA J. HANRAHAN.

University of Oklahoma Press: 1005 Asp Ave, Norman, OK 73019; tel. (405) 325-2000; fax (405) 325-4000; internet www.oupress.com; f. 1928; scholarly; Dir JOHN DRAYTON.

University of Pennsylvania Press: 4200 Pine St, Philadelphia, PA 19104-4011; tel. (215) 898-6261; fax (215) 898-0404; e-mail custserve@pobox.upenn.edu; internet www.upenn.edu/pennpress; scholarly; Dir ERIC HALPERN.

University of Pittsburgh Press: 3400 Forbes Ave, 5h Floor, Pittsburgh, PA 15260; tel. (412) 383-2456; fax (412) 383-2466; e-mail press@pitt.edu; internet www.pitt.edu/~press; f. 1936; Dir CYNTHIA MILLER; scholarly.

University of South Carolina Press: 937 Assembly St, 8th Floor, Columbia, SC 29208; tel. (803) 777-5245; fax (803) 777-0160; e-mail gsauer@sc.edu; internet www.gopher.press.sc.edu; scholarly, regional studies; Dir CATHERINE FRY.

University of Tennessee Press: 293 Communications Bldg, Knoxville, TN 37996-0325; tel. (423) 974-3321; fax (423) 974-3724; e-mail gadair@utk.edu; internet www.sunsite.utk.edu/utpress; f. 1940; scholarly and regional; Editor JOYCE HARRISON.

University of Texas Press: POB 7819, Austin, TX 78713-7819; tel. (512) 471-7233; fax (512) 320-0668; internet www.utexas.edu/utpress; f. 1950; general scholarly non-fiction; Dir JOANNA HITCHCOCK.

University of Utah Press: 1795 East South Campus Dr., 101, Salt Lake City, UT 84112; tel. (801) 581-6771; fax (801) 581-3365; e-mail info@upress.utah.edu; internet www.media.utah.edu/upress/; f. 1949; scholarly, regional and Middle East studies; Dir JEFF GRATHWOHL.

University of Virginia Press: POB 400318, Charlottesville, VA 22904-4318; tel. (804) 924-3468; fax (804) 982-2655; internet www.upress.virginia.edu; f. 1963; Dir PENELOPE KAISERLIAN; scholarly non-fiction, literarature, history, Victorian, African and Afro-American studies.

University of Washington Press: POB 50096, Seattle, WA 98145-5096; tel. (206) 543-4050; fax (206) 543-3932; e-mail uwpord@u.washington.edu; f. 1920; general, scholarly, non-fiction, reprints; Dir PAT SODEN.

University of Wisconsin Press: 2537 Daniels St, Madison, WI 53718-6772; tel. (608) 224-3900; fax (608) 224-3897; e-mail uwiscpress@uwpress.wisc.edu; internet www.wisc.edu/wisconsinpress; f. 1936; scholarly non-fiction, trade; Dir DAVID BETHEA.

University Press of America, Inc: 4720 Boston Way, Lanham, MD 20706; tel. (301) 459-3366; fax (301) 459-2118; internet www.univpress.com; f. 1974; scholarly; Publr JAMES E. LYONS.

University Press of Florida: 15 North-West 15th St, Gainesville, FL 32611-2079; tel. (352) 392-1351; fax (352) 392-7302; e-mail info@upf.com; internet www.upf.com; f. 1945; general, scholarly, regional; Dir KENNETH J. SCOTT.

University Press of Kansas: 2501 West 15th St, Lawrence, KS 66049-3905; tel. (785) 864-4154; fax (785) 864-4586; e-mail upress@ku.edu; internet www.kansaspress.ku.edu; f. 1946; Dir FRED M. WOODWARD; scholarly.

University Press of Kentucky: 663 South Limestone St, Lexington, KY 40508-4008; tel. (606) 257-2951; fax (606) 257-2984; internet www.uky.edu/universitypress; f. 1943; non-fiction, scholarly, regional.

University Press of Mississippi: 3825 Ridgewood Rd, Jackson, MS 39211; tel. (601) 432-6205; fax (601) 432-6217; e-mail press@ihl.state.ms.us; internet www.upress.state.ms.us; f. 1970; scholarly, non-fiction, regional; Dir SEETHA SRINIVASAN.

University Press of New England: 23 South Main St, Hanover, NH 03755-2048; tel. (603) 643-7100; fax (603) 643-1540; internet www.upne.com; f. 1970; general scholarly; Dir RICHARD ABEL.

Vanderbilt University Press: VU Station B 351813, Nashville, TN 37235; tel. (617) 322-3585; fax (617) 343-8823; Dir MICHAEL AMES.

Warner Books Inc: 1271 Ave of the Americas, New York, NY 10020; tel. (212) 522-7200; fax (212) 522-7991; f. 1961; reprints, fiction and non-fiction, trade; Pres. MAUREEN EGEN.

Wayne State University Press: 4809 Woodward Ave, Detroit, MI 48201; tel. (313) 577-4600; fax (313) 577-6131; internet wsupress.wayne.edu; f. 1941; Dir JANE HOEHNER.

Westminster John Knox Press: 100 Witherspoon St, Louisville, KY 40202-1396; tel. (502) 569-5043; fax (502) 569-5113; e-mail wjk@ctr.pcusa.org; f. 1938; religious and scholarly Pres. and Publr DAVIS PERKINS.

Westview Press Inc: 5500 Central Ave, Boulder, CO 80301; tel. (303) 444-3541; fax (303) 449-3356; e-mail westview.press@perseusbooks.com; scholarly, academic, general interest and scientific; Publr MARCUS BOGGS.

John Wiley and Sons, Inc: 111 River St, Hoboken, NJ 07030; tel. (201) 748-6000; fax (201) 748-6088; internet www.wiley.com; f. 1807; higher education, scientific, technical, medical and social science; Chair. PETER BOOTH WILEY, II; Pres. and CEO WILL PESCE.

H. W. Wilson Co: 950 University Ave, Bronx, NY 10452; tel. (718) 588-8400; fax (718) 538-2716; internet www.hwwilson.com; f. 1898; book and periodical indices, reference; Pres. and CEO HAROLD REGAN.

Yale University Press: 302 Temple St, New Haven, CT 06511; tel. (203) 432-0960; fax (203) 432-0948; internet www.yale.edu/yup; f. 1908; scholarly; Dir JOHN DONATICH.

Government Publishing House

Government Printing Office: North Capitol and H Sts, NW, Washington, DC 20401; tel. (202) 512-1991; fax (202) 512-1293; internet www.access.gpo.gov; Public Printer MICHAEL F. DiMARIO.

ORGANIZATIONS AND ASSOCIATIONS

American Booksellers' Association (ABA): 828 South Broadway, Tarrytown, NY 10591; tel. (914) 591-2665; fax (914) 591-2720; e-mail editorial@bookweb.org; internet www.bookweb.org; f. 1900; 8,000 mems; CEO AVIN MARK DOMNITZ.

American Medical Publishers' Association: c/o Jill G. Rudansky, 14 Fort Hill Rd, Huntingdon, NY 11743; tel. (516) 423-0075; fax (516) 423-0075; e-mail jillrudansky-ampa@msn.com; internet www.ampaonline.org; f. 1960; 75 mems; Pres. MEG WHITE.

Association of American University Presses, Inc: 584 Broadway, Suite 410, New York, NY 10012; tel. (212) 941-6610; fax (212) 941-6618; internet www.aaupnet.org; f. 1937; 116 mems; Exec. Dir PETER J. GIVLER.

The Children's Book Council, Inc: 12 West 37th St, New York, NY 10018; tel. (212) 966-1990; fax (212) 966-2073; e-mail staff@cbcbooks.org; internet www.cbcbooks.org; f. 1945; 75 mems; Chair. BRENDA BOWEN; Pres. PAULA QUINT.

Music Publishers' Association of the US: 711 Third Ave, New York, NY 10017; tel. (212) 370-5330; fax (212) 953-2384; 60 mems; Pres. EDWARD P. MURPHY.

National Association of Independent Publishers: POB 430, Highland City, FL 33846-0430; tel. (836) 648 4420; fax (836) 647-5951; e-mail naip@aol.com; internet www.publishersreport.com; f. 1985; 500 mems; Exec. Dir BETSY A. LAMPE.

Publishers' Marketing Association (PMA): 627 Aviation Way, Manhattan Beach, CA 90266; tel. (310) 372-2732; fax (310) 374-3342; e-mail naip@aol.com; internet www.pma-online.org; 1,600 mems; Exec. Dir JAN NATHAN.

Broadcasting and Communications

Federal Communications Commission (FCC): 445 12th St, SW, Washington, DC 20554; tel. (202) 418-0200; fax (202) 418-0232; e-mail fccinfo@fcc.gov; internet www.fcc.gov; f. 1934; regulates interstate and foreign communications by radio, television, wire and cable; Chair. MICHAEL K. POWELL.

TELECOMMUNICATIONS

Principal Telecommunications Networks

Ameritech (American Information Technologies Corporation): 30 South Wacker Dr., Chicago, IL 60606; tel. (312) 750-5000; fax (312) 906-4197; internet www.ameritech.com; serves *c.*13m. customers in 50 states and 40 overseas countries; Chair. and CEO RICHARD C. NOTEBAERT.

AT&T (American Telegraph and Telephone Corporation): 32 Ave of the Americas, New York, NY 10013; tel. (212) 387-5400; fax (212) 226-4935; internet www.att.com; f. 1885; Chair. and CEO MICHAEL ARMSTRONG.

Bell Atlantic Corporation: 1717 Arch St, Philadelphia, PA 19103; tel. (215) 963-6000; fax (215) 563-8934; e-mail info@bell-atl.com; internet www.bell-atl.com; f. 1983; fmrly Bell operating cos; serves six states and the District of Columbia; agreed merger with Nynex Corpn in 1997; Chair. and CEO (vacant).

BellSouth Corporation: 1155 Peachtree St, NE, Atlanta, GA 30309; tel. (404) 249-2000; fax (404) 249-5599; internet www.bellsouth.com; f. 1983; serves 18.7m. customers in nine states; Pres. DUANE ACKERMAN.

C-Tec Corporation: DPA Bldg, Suite 5, Route 209, Dallas, PA 18612-1015; tel. (717) 675-5822; *c.*196,000 telephone customers and c. 200,000 cable television customers; Pres. and CEO CHARLES E. PARENTE.

GE American Communications, Inc (GE Americom): 4 Research Way, Princeton, NJ 08540-6684; tel. (609) 987-4000; Chair. and CEO JOHN F. CONNELLY.

GTE Spacenet Corporation: 1700 Old Meadow Rd, McLean, VA 22102; tel. (703) 848-1000; fax (703) 848-0004; f. 1981; comprehensive satellite-based transmission services.

MCI Inc: Ashburn, VA; internet www.mci.com; f. 1968; long-distance carrier serving *c.* 10m. customers; Pres. and CEO MICHAEL D. CAPELLAS.

Nynex Corporation: 1095 Ave of the Americas, New York, NY 10036; tel. (212) 395-2121; internet www.nynex.com; f. 1984; serves c. 12m. customers in the north-eastern USA; agreed merger with Bell Atlantic Corpn in 1997; Chair. and CEO WILLIAM C. FERGUSON.

SBC Communications: 175 East Houston St, San Antonio, TX 78205; tel. (210) 821-4105; fax (210) 351-2274; internet www.sbc.com; f. 1997; by merger of SBC Corpn (fmrly Southwestern Bell Corpn) and Pacific Telesis Group (PacTel); Chair. EDWARD E. WHITACRE, Jr; Pres. and CEO ROBERT G. POPE.

US West, Inc: 7800 East Orchard Rd, Englewood, CO 80111; tel. (303) 793-6500; fax (303) 793-6654; internet www.uswest.com; f. 1983; main operating subsidiary comprises the fmr Mountain Bell, Northwestern Bell and Pacific Northwest Telephone cos; provides telecommunications services in 14 Western states; Chair. and CEO RICHARD D. McCORMICK.

Associations

US Telephone Association: 1401 H St, NW, Suite 600, Washington, DC 20005; tel. (202) 326-7300; fax (202) 326-7333; e-mail supervisor@usta.org; internet www.usta.org.

UTC–The United Telecom Council: 1140 Connecticut Ave, NW, Suite 1140, Washington, DC 20036; tel. (202) 872-0030; fax (202) 872-1331; e-mail utc@utc.org; internet www.utc.org; f. 1948; non-profit asscn representing telecommunications and information interests of public utilities, natural gas pipelines and other infrastructure cos and their strategic business partners.

RADIO

In June 2001 there were 12,932 licensed commercial radio stations operating in the USA.

Principal Domestic Networks

American Broadcasting Companies Radio Networks (ABC/SMN): 13725 Montfort Dr., Dallas, TX 75240; tel. (214) 991-9200; fax (214) 991-1071; internet www.abc.com; f. 1986; Pres. LYN ANDREWS; serves more than 3,400 radio stations broadcasting six full service line networks.

Columbia Broadcasting System Radio Division (CBS): 524 West 57th St, New York, NY 10019-6165; tel. (212) 975-3615; fax (212) 975-6347; internet www.cbs.com; subsidiary of Viacom, Inc; Pres. DANIEL MASON; 175 owned radio stations.

National Broadcasting Co, Inc (NBC): 30 Rockefeller Plaza, New York, NY 10112-0100; tel. (212) 664-4444; fax (212) 765-1478; internet www.nbc.com; f. 1926; Pres. and CEO ROBERT C. WRIGHT; Pres. NBC Radio Network WILLIAM J. BATTISON; 8 owned stations, 206 affiliated stations.

National Public Radio (NPR): 635 Massachusetts Ave, NW, Washington, DC 20001; tel. (202) 513-2000; fax (202) 513-3329; e-mail www-info@npr.org; internet www.npr.org; Pres. and CEO KEVIN KLOSE; private non-profit corpn providing programmes and support facilities to over 600 mem. stations nation-wide; also operates a global programme distribution service by radio, cable and satellite.

Premier Radio Newtwork: POB 3130, Central Point, OR 97502; tel. (541) 664-8829; fax (541) 664-8261; Sr Vice-Pres. ALAN CORBETH; syndicated radio broadcasts to c. 450 affiliated stations throughout North America.

USA Radio Networks: 2290 Springlake Rd, Dallas, TX 75234; tel. (972) 484-3900; fax (972) 243-3489; e-mail tradup@usaradio.com; internet www.usaradio.com; Pres. MARLIN MADDOUX; news and information programmes carried by 1,200 affiliates; also broadcasts on short-wave and to US Armed Forces Radio.

Westwood One Inc: 8403 Colesville Rd, Suite 1500, Silver Spring, VA 20910; tel. (301) 628-2300; internet www.westwoodone.com; f. 1934; Pres. and CEO JOEL HOLLANDER.

Principal External Radio Services

Armed Forces Radio and Television Service Broadcast Center (AFRTS–BC): 1363 Z St, Suite 2730, March Air Force Base, CA 92518-2717; f. 1945; operated by Dept of Defense; provides US radio and TV programming in English by satellite and mail for use by US military personnel and their families overseas; c. 750 outlets in more than 130 countries, US territories and aboard US Navy ships-at-sea; Commdr Capt. C. L. HANEY; Dir of Programming GERALD M. FRY.

RFE/RL (Radio Free Europe/Radio Liberty): 1201 Connecticut Ave, NW, Suite 1100, Washington, DC 20036; tel. (202) 457-6900; fax (202) 457-6913; internet www.rferl.org; f. 1950; private non-profit corpn financed by the fed. govt; Dir of Broadcasting JEFF TRIMBLE; broadcasts from Prague, Czech Republic, to Central and Eastern Europe and Eurasia 900 hours weekly in 26 languages.

Voice of America: 330 Independence Ave, SW, Washington, DC 20237; tel. (202) 619-2538; fax (202) 619-1241; internet www.voa .gov; f. 1942; govt-controlled; broadcasts in 52 languages to all areas of the world; Program Dir MYRNA WHITWORTH.

TELEVISION

In December 1998 there were an estimated 98m. households owning one or more television receivers.

In 1998 there were an estimated 67.0m. households receiving commercial cable TV. There were 10,700 cable systems in operation in January 1999.

Principal Networks

Capital Cities/American Broadcasting Companies, Inc: 77 West 66th St, New York, NY 10023; tel. (212) 456-7777; fax (212) 887-7168; internet www.abctelevision.com; f. 1986; Pres. and CEO THOMAS S. MURPHY; Pres., Radio Network ROBERT F. CALLAHAN.

CNN (Cable News Network): 1 CNN Center, Atlanta, GA 30303; tel. (404) 827-1500; fax (404) 827-1784; internet www.cnn.com; subsidiary of Time Warner; Chair. and CEO WALTER ISAACSON.

Columbia Broadcasting System Radio Division (CBS): 524 West 57th St, New York, NY 10019-6165; tel. (212) 975-3615; fax (212) 975-6347; internet www.cbs.com; subsidiary of Viacom, Inc; 175 owned radio stations; Pres. DANIEL MASON.

C-SPAN–Cable-Satellite Public Affairs Network: 400 North Capitol St, Suite 650, Washington, DC 20001; tel. (2) 737-3200; internet www.c-span.org.

FoxNet: 11833 Mississippi Ave, Los Angeles, CA 90025; tel. (310) 477-7300; fax (310) 447-7315; internet www.fox.com; CEO DAN KENDALL; cable and satellite programmes; more than 900 cable affiliates.

Multimedia Cablevision, Inc: 701 East Douglas, POB 3027, Wichita, KS 67201; tel. (316) 262-4270; fax (316) 262-2309; cable television system serving more than 400,000 subscribers; Pres. MICHAEL BURRUS.

National Broadcasting Co, Inc: 30 Rockefeller Plaza, New York, NY 10112; tel. (212) 664-4444; fax (212) 664-5830; internet www.nbc

.com; Pres. and CEO ROBERT C. WRIGHT; 5 owned and 214 affiliated stations.

Public Broadcasting Service (PBS): 1320 Braddock Pl., Alexandria, VA 22314-1698; tel. (703) 739-5000; fax (703) 739-8689; internet www.pbs.org; f. 1969; non-profit-making; financed by private subscriptions and federal govt funds; provides programming to 350 independent non-commercial TV stations; Pres. and CEO PAT MITCHELL.

Time Warner Cable (TWC): 290 Harbor Dr., Stamford, CT 06902; tel. (203) 328-0600; fax (203) 328-0690; Chair. and CEO JOSEPH J. COLLINS; Pres. GLENN BRITT; cable television system serving c.12.6m. subscribers.

USA Network (Cable): 1230 Ave of the Americas, 8th Floor, New York, NY 10020; tel. (212) 408-9100; fax (212) 408-3600; internet www.usanetwork.com; Pres. and CEO KAY KOPLOVITZ; cable television network with 12,500 affiliates.

Associations

National Association of Broadcasters (NAB): 1771 N St, NW, Washington, DC 20036; tel. (202) 429-5300; fax (202) 429-5406; internet www.nab.org; f. 1922; Pres. and CEO EDWARD O. FRITTS; trade asscn of radio and TV stations and networks; 7,500 mems.

National Cable Television Association (NCTA): 1724 Massachusetts Ave, NW, Washington, DC 20036-1905; tel. (202) 775-3550; fax (202) 775-3695; f. 1952; Pres. and CEO S. DECKER ANSTROM; c.3,100 mems.

Finance

BANKING

Commercial Banking System

The US banking system is the largest and, in many respects, the most comprehensive and sophisticated in the world. Banking has, however, been largely subject to state rather than federal jurisdiction, and this has created a structure very different from that in other advanced industrial countries. In general, no bank may open branches or acquire subsidiaries in states other than that in which it is based, although in June 1985 the US Supreme Court ruled that federal legislation prohibiting interstate banks does not preclude state governments from permitting regional interstate banking. A number of such mergers have followed, although some states continue to restrict banks to a single branch, or to operating only in certain counties of the state. Federal anti-trust laws also limit mergers of banks within a state. The effect of these measures has been to preserve the independence of a very large number of banks: 8,080 in 2001. Nevertheless, the dominant banks are the main banks in the big industrial states; of the 10 largest in 2002, three were based in New York, two in North Carolina and two in Illinois. The influence of these banks, however, has been increasingly challenged by the formation of several groupings of regional banks. Federal legislation permitting the operation of interstate branch banking networks and the provision of non-banking financial services was enacted in November 1999.

During the late 1980s there was a weakening of public confidence in the banking system, and many small banks became insolvent after the failure of investments or the withdrawal of deposits by investors. The Federal Deposit Insurance Corporation, a government-sponsored body which insures deposits in banks and acts as receiver for national and state banks that have been placed in receivership, was obliged to provide assistance for a large number of institutions. Such bank failures, which seldom exceeded 10 annually between 1955–81, rose sharply during the 1980s, reaching a record of 221 institutions in 1988. These insolvencies, however, declined each year until 1997, when they were reduced to only one. The number of insolvencies then gradually increased: seven were recorded in the first half of 2002. Many banks, meanwhile, have expanded their 'fee income' activities (such as sales of mutual fund investments) to offset declines in customer borrowing, particularly from the industrial and commercial sectors.

The possession of bank accounts and the use of banking facilities are perhaps more widespread among all regions and social groups in the USA than in any other country. This has influenced the formulation of monetary theory and policy, as bank credit has become a more important factor than currency supply in the regulation of the economy. The use of current accounts and credit cards is so common that many authorities claim that the USA can be regarded as effectively a cashless society.

Bank Holding Companies

Since 1956 bank holding companies, corporations that control one or more banks in the USA, have become significant elements in the banking system. These organizations control commercial banks which, at the end of 1989, held 93.4% of the total assets of insured commercial banks in the USA.

Banking Activities Overseas

From the mid-1960s, the leading banks rapidly expanded their overseas interests. At the end of 1960 there were only eight US banks operating foreign branches, mostly in Latin America and the Far East. The main factors behind this expansion were the geographical limitations imposed by law at home; the rapid expansion of US business interests abroad; the faster economic growth of certain foreign markets; and finally the profitability of the 'Euro-dollar' capital markets. The expansion in the overseas activities of US banks reached a high point in 1984. Subsequently declining levels of profitability in this area have resulted in the closure of some overseas offices, although the aggregate total of assets held has continued to rise.

In 1981 the Federal Reserve Board sanctioned the establishment of domestic International Banking Facilities (IBF), permitting commercial banks within the US (including US branches and agencies of foreign banks) to transact certain types of foreign deposit and loan business free of reserve requirements and, in most cases, state income tax liability.

Federal Reserve System: 20th St and Constitution Ave, NW, Washington, DC 20551; tel. (202) 452-3000; fax (202) 452-3819; internet www.federalreserve.gov.

The Federal Reserve System, founded in 1913, comprises the Board of Governors, the Federal Open Market Committee, the Federal Advisory Council, the Consumer Advisory Council, the Thrift Institutions Advisory Council, the 25 branches of the 12 Federal Reserve Banks, together with all member banks.

The Board of Governors is composed of seven members appointed by the President of the United States with the advice and consent of the Senate.

The Reserve Banks are empowered to issue Federal Reserve notes fully secured by the following assets, alone or in any combination: (i) Gold certificates; (ii) US Government and agency securities; (iii) Other eligible assets as described by statute; and (iv) Special Drawing Rights certificates. The Reserve Banks may discount paper for depository institutions and make properly secured advances to depository institutions. Federal Reserve Banks were established by Congress as the operating arms of the nation's central banking system. Many of the services performed by this network for depository institutions and for the Government are similar to services performed by banks and thrifts for business customers and individuals. Reserve Banks hold the cash reserves of depository institutions and make loans to them. They move currency and coin into and out of circulation, and collect and process millions of cheques each day. They provide banking services for the Treasury, issue and redeem government securities on behalf of the Treasury, and act in other ways as fiscal agent for the US Government. The Banks also take part in the primary responsibility of the Federal Reserve System, the setting of monetary policy, through participation on the Federal Open Market Committee.

The Comptroller of the Currency (see below) has primary supervisory authority over all federally chartered banks, and the banking supervisors of the States have similar jurisdiction over banks organized under State laws. State member banks are examined by the Federal Reserve.

At 30 June 2002 2,268 of the nation's 7,966 banks were members of the Federal Reserve System.

Board of Governors

Chairman: ALAN GREENSPAN.

Vice-Chairman: ROGER W. FERGUSON, Jr.

Governors: SUSAN SCHMIDT BIES, EDWARD M. GRAMLICH, MARK W. OLSON, BEN S. BERNANKE, DONALD L. KOHN.

Secretary of the Board: JENNIFER J. JOHNSON.

Federal Reserve Banks

	Chairman	President
Boston	William C. Brainard	Cathy E. Minehan
New York	Peter G. Peterson	William J. McDonough
Philadelphia	Charisse R. Lillie	Anthony Santomero
Cleveland	David H. Hoag	Jerry L. Jordan
Richmond	Jeremiah J. Smeehan	J. Alfred Broaddus, Jr
Atlanta	John F. Wieland	Jack Guynn
Chicago	Arthur C. Martinez	Michael H. Moskow
St Louis	Charles W. Mueller	William Poole
Minneapolis	James J. Howard	Gary H. Stern
Kansas City	Terrence P. Dunn	Thomas M. Hoenig
Dallas	Roger M. Hemminghaus	Robert D. McTeer, Jr
San Francisco	Nelson C. Rising	Robert T. Parry

Comptroller of the Currency

250 E St, SW, Washington, DC 20219; tel. (202) 874-4900; internet www.occ.treas.gov.

The Comptroller of the Currency has supervisory control over all federally chartered banks (see Federal Reserve System).

Comptroller: JOHN D. HAWKE, Jr.

Principal Commercial Banks

(cap. = total capital and reserves; dep. = deposits; m. = million; amounts in US dollars)

In general, only banks with a minimum of $2,000m. deposits are listed. In states where no such bank exists, that with the largest deposits is listed.

Alabama

AmSouth Bank NA: POB 11007, Birmingham, AL 35288; tel. (205) 801-0359; fax (205) 326-5015; e-mail 10312,1342@compuserve.com; internet www.amsouth.com; f. 1873; cap. 10,000, dep. 34,326.4m. (Dec. 2000); Chair., Pres. and CEO C. DOWD RITTER.

Regions Bank: 417 North 20th St, POB 10247, Birmingham, AL 35202-0247; tel. (205) 326-7697; fax (205) 326-7779; internet www.regionsbank.com; f. 1928; cap. 0.1m., dep. 39,797.6m. (Dec. 2000); Chair. and CEO CARL E. JONES, Jr.

SouthTrust Bank NA: 420 North 20th St, POB 2554, Birmingham, AL 35290; tel. (205) 254-5000; fax (205) 254-5656; f. 1887; cap. 9,007.0m., dep. 40,309.0m. (Dec. 2000); Chair., Pres. and CEO JULIAN W. BANTON.

Alaska

National Bank of Alaska: 301 West Northern Lights Blvd, Anchorage, AK 99503; tel. (907) 522-8888; fax (907) 267-5448; e-mail questions@nbak.com; internet www.nbak.com; f. 1916; cap. 270.8m., dep. 2,157.8m. (Dec. 1999); Chair. EDWARD B. RASMUSON; Pres. RICHARD STRUTZ.

Arizona

Bank One, Arizona NA: 201 North Central Ave, 11th Floor, Phoenix, AZ 85004; tel. (602) 221-2900; fax (602) 221-4993; internet www.bankone.com; f. 1899; cap. 1,435.2m., dep. 18,215.2m. (Dec. 1998); CEO R. MICHAEL WELBORN.

Norwest Bank Arizona NA: 3300 North Central Ave, Phoenix, AZ 85012; tel. (602) 504-1234; cap. 226.9m., dep. 3,908.3m. (Dec. 1997).

Arkansas

First Commercial Bank NA: 400 West Capitol St, POB 1471, Little Rock, AR 72201; tel. (501) 371-7000; fax (501) 371-7413; cap. 138.4m., dep. 1,726.1m. (Dec. 2000).

California

Bank of the West: 180 Montgomery St, San Francisco, CA 94104; tel. (415) 765-4800; fax (415) 434-3470; internet www.bankofthewest.com; f. 1874; cap. 9.1m., dep. 9,305.1m. (Dec. 2000); Chair. WALTER A. DODS, Jr; Pres. and CEO DON J. MCGRATH.

California Bank and Trust: 4320 La Jolla Village Dr., Suite 355, San Diego, CA 92122; tel. (619) 623-3190; fax (619) 552-0463; internet www.calbanktrust.com; f. 1998; cap. 17.6m., dep. 6,057.9m. (Dec. 2000); Chair. and CEO DAVID BLACKFORD.

City National Bank: 400 Roxbury Dr., North, Beverly Hills, CA 90210; tel. (310) 888-6000; fax (310) 888-6045; e-mail contact@cityntl.com; internet www.cityntl.com; f. 1954; cap. 541.4m., dep. 5,500m. (Oct. 2001); Chair. and CEO RUSSELL GOLDSMITH; Pres. GEORGE H. BENTER, Jr; 49 brs.

Comerica Bank–California: 333 West Santa Clara St, San Jose, CA 95113; tel. (408) 244-1700; fax (408) 286-5242; f. 1955; cap. 2.5m., dep. 3,194.8m., (Dec. 2000); Pres. and CEO CHARLES L. GUMMER.

Union Bank of California NA: 350 California St, 6th Floor, San Francisco, CA 94104; tel. (415) 705-7000; internet www.uboc.com; f. 1996; cap. 604.6m., dep. 30,549.5m. (Dec. 2000); Pres. and CEO TAKAHIRO MORIGUCHI.

Wells Fargo Bank NA: 420 Montgomery St, San Francisco, CA 94163; tel. (415) 477-1000; fax (415) 975-6847; internet www.wellsfargo.com; f. 1852; cap. 520.0m., dep. 88,766.0m. (Dec. 2000); Chair. PAUL HAZEN; Pres. and CEO RICHARD KOVACEVICH.

Colorado

Bank One, Colorado NA: 1125 17th St, POB 5586, Denver, CO 80202-2025; tel. (303) 759-0111; fax (303) 297-4462; internet www.bankone.com; cap. 345m., dep. 2,600m. (Dec. 1999); Chair. and CEO WAYNE HUTCHENS.

Colorado National Bank: 1515 Arapahoe St, POB 5548, Denver, CO 80217; tel. (303) 585-5000; fax (303) 585-7346; f. 1862; cap.

453m., dep. 6,078.8m. (Dec. 1996); Chair. ROBERT MALONE; Pres. DANIEL QUINN.

Connecticut

Citizens Bank of Connecticut: 63 Eugene O'Neill Dr., New London, CT 06320; tel. (860) 638-4419; fax (860) 638-4444; e-mail intbank@citizensbank.com; internet www.citizensbank.com; f. 1996; dep. 2,006.2m., total assets 2,248.1m. (Dec. 2000); Pres. and CEO JOSEPH R. MARCAURELE.

Delaware

Chase Manhattan Bank USA NA: 802 Delaware Ave, Wilmington, DE 19801; tel. (302) 575-5000; fax (302) 575-5024; internet www.chase.com; cap. 3,542.4m., dep. 29,514m. (Dec. 1999).

First USA Bank: 201 North Walnut St, Wilmington, DE 19801; tel. (302) 594-4000; cap. 2,878.7m., dep. 13,666.0m. (Dec. 1999).

MBNA America Bank NA: 1100 North King St, Wilmington, DE 19801; tel. (302) 453-9930; fax (302) 456-8541; cap. 400.0m., dep. 29,211.7m. (Dec. 2000); President CHARLES M. CAWLEY.

PNC Bank, Delaware: 300 Delaware Ave, POB 791, Wilmington, DE 19899; tel. (302) 429-1011; fax (302) 429-1206; f. 1952; cap. 202.5m., dep. 2,232.1m. (Dec. 1999); Chair., Pres. and CEO CALVERT A. MORGAN, Jr.

District of Columbia

Riggs Bank NA: 1503 Pennsylvania Ave, Washington, DC 20005; tel. (301) 887-6000; fax (301) 887-8983; f. 1836; cap. 20.8m., dep. 4,676.7m. (Dec. 2000); Pres. and CEO LARRY HEBERT.

Florida

Northern Trust Bank of Florida: 700 Brickell Ave, Miami, FL 33131; tel. (305) 372-1000; fax (305) 789-1106; internet www.northerntrust.com; f. 1982; cap. 18.6m., dep. 3,787.4m. (Dec. 2000); CEO WILLIAM L. MORRISON.

Ocean Bank: 780 Northwest 42nd Ave, Miami, POB 441140, FL 33126; tel. (305) 442-2660; fax (305) 444-8153; internet www.oceanbank.com; f. 1982; dep. 3,055.7m. (Dec. 2000); Pres. and CEO JOSE A. CONCEPCION.

Republic Bank: 111 Second Ave, NE, Suite 211, POB 33008, St Petersburg, FL 33701; tel. (727) 823-7300; f. 1973; dep. 2,158.9m. (Dec. 2000); Pres. WILLIAM R. KLICH.

Georgia

SunTrust Bank: 25 Park Pl., POB 4418, Atlanta, GA 30302; tel. (404) 588-7785; fax (404) 302-4782; internet www.suntrust.com; f. 1891; assumed all SunTrust Banks 2000; cap. 21.6m., dep. 87,013.2m. (Dec. 2000); Chair. and Pres. PHILLIP HUMANN.

Hawaii

Bank of Hawaii: 111 South King St, Honolulu, HI 96813; tel. (808) 537-8111; internet www.boh.com; f. 1897; cap. 14,908.0m., dep. 10,944.3m. (Dec. 2000); Chair. and CEO MICHAEL E. O'NEILL; Pres. RICHARD J. DAHL.

First Hawaiian Bank: 999 Bishop St, Honolulu, HI 96813; tel. (808) 525-7000; fax (808) 525-8182; internet www.fhb.com; f. 1858; cap. 16.2m., dep. 6,207.2m. (Dec. 2000); Chair. and CEO WALTER A. DODS, Jr; Pres. JOHN K. TSUI.

Idaho

West One Bank, Idaho, NA: 101 South Capitol Blvd, POB 8247, Boise, ID 83733; tel. (208) 383-7000; fax (208) 383-7563; f. 1891; cap. 231.4m., dep. 3,502.5m. (Dec. 1996); Chair. DANIEL R. NELSON; Pres. and CEO ROBERT LANE.

Illinois

Bank One NA: 1 Bank One Plaza, Chicago, IL 60670; tel. (312) 732-7053; fax (312) 732-5466; internet www.bankone.com; f. 1863; merged with American National Bank in Nov. 2002; cap. 200.9m., dep. 89,852.3m. (Dec. 2000); Chair. and CEO JAMES DIMON; Pres. VERNE G. ISTOCK.

First Midwest Bank: 506 15th St, Moline, IL 61265; internet www.firstmidwest.com; cap. 40.0m., dep. 5,435.3m. (Dec. 2000); Chair. and CEO JOHN O'MEARA.

Harris Trust and Savings Bank: 111 West Monroe St, Chicago, IL 60603; tel. (312) 845-2028; fax (312) 845-2199; internet www.harrisbank.com; f. 1882; cap. 100.0m., dep. 19,262.5m. (Dec. 2000); Chair. and CEO ALAN G. MCNALLY.

LaSalle Bank NA: 135 South LaSalle St, Chicago, IL 60603; tel. (312) 904-2000; fax (312) 904-2819; internet www.lasallebank.com; f. 1927; cap. 176.6m., dep. 43,914.4m. (Dec. 2000); Chair., Pres. and CEO NORMAN BOBINS.

Northern Trust Co: 50 South LaSalle St, Chicago, IL 60675; tel. (312) 630-6000; fax (312) 444-5244; internet www.northerntrust.com; f. 1889; cap. 213.8m., dep. 26,457.6m. (Dec. 2000); Chair. WILLIAM A. OSBORN; Pres. BARRY G. HASTINGS.

Indiana

Bank One, Indiana, NA: 111 Monument Circle, Indianapolis, IN 46277-0188; tel. (317) 321-3000; fax (317) 321-7965; f. 1839; cap. 609.1m., dep. 6,991.2m. (Dec. 1998); Chair. and CEO JOSEPH D. BARNETTE, Jr.

National City Bank of Indiana: 1, Merchants Plaza, Indianapolis, IN 46255; tel. (317) 267-7147; fax (317) 267-7152; internet www.national-city.com; f. 1865; cap. 21.3m., dep. 18,457.0m. (Dec. 2000); Chair., Pres. and CEO STEPHEN A. STITLE.

NBD Bank NA: 1 Indiana Sq., Indianapolis, IN 46266; tel. (317) 266-6000; fax (317) 266-6379; f. 1834; cap. 632.6m., dep. 8,746.6m. (Dec. 1998); Pres. ANDREW J. PAINE, Jr.

Iowa

Norwest Bank Iowa, NA: POB 837, Des Moines, IA 50304; tel. (515) 245-8212; fax (515) 245-3139; f. 1929; cap. 341.3m., dep. 4,944.6m. (Dec. 1997); Chair. and CEO H. LYNN HORAK; Pres. J. SCOTT JOHNSON.

Kansas

Bank IV Kansas, NA: POB 4, Wichita, KS 67201; tel. (316) 261-4444; fax (316) 261-2243; f. 1887; cap. 367.6m., dep. 3,905m. (Dec. 1994); Chair. and Pres. K. GORDON GREER.

Kentucky

Bank One, Kentucky NA: POB 32500, Louisville, KY 40202; tel. (502) 566-2000; fax (502) 566-2016; internet www.bankone.com; f. 1935; cap. 345.1m., dep. 4,799.3m. (Dec. 1998); Chair. WILLIAM HARTMAN.

National City Bank of Kentucky: 3700 National City Tower, 101 South Fifth St, Louisville, KY 40202; tel. (502) 581-4200; fax (502) 581-7909; f. 1863; cap. 21.0m., dep. 7,848.2m. (Dec. 2000); Chair. LEONARD V. HARDIN; Pres. and CEO FREDERICK W. SCHANTZ.

Louisiana

First National Bank of Commerce: 201 Baronne St, POB 60279, New Orleans, LA 70160; tel. (504) 561-1371; fax (504) 561-7082; f. 1933; cap. 422.3m., dep. 5,447.1m. (Dec. 1997); Chair. HOWARD C. GAINES; Pres. and CEO ASHTON J. RYAN, Jr.

Hibernia National Bank: 313 Carondelet St, New Orleans, LA 70130; tel. (504) 533-3333; fax (504) 533-5739; internet www.hiberniabank.com; f. 1933; cap. 1,246.2m., dep. 13,937.1m. (Dec. 1999); Chair. ROBERT H. BOH; Pres. STEPHEN A. HANSEL.

Whitney National Bank: 228 St Charles Ave, New Orleans, LA 70130; tel. (504) 586-7272; fax (504) 586-7412; e-mail rchamberlin@whitneybank.com; internet www.whitneybank.com; f. 1883; cap. 3.4m., dep. 5,534.0m. (Dec. 2000); Chair. and CEO WILLIAM L. MARKS; Pres. R. KING MILLING.

Maine

Fleet Bank of Maine: 2 Portland Sq., Portland, ME 04104-5091; tel. (207) 874-5000; fax (617) 874-5117; internet www.fleet.com; f. 1991; cap. 118.5m., dep. 1,855.7m. (Dec. 1999); Chair. LEO BREITMAN; Pres. and CEO DAVID OTT.

Maryland

Allfirst Bank: 25 South Charles St, Baltimore, MD 21201; tel. (410) 244-4000; fax (410) 244-4026; internet www.allfirst.com; f. 1806; cap. 18.4m., dep. 14,542.6m. (Dec. 2000); Chair. FRANK P. BRAMBLE; Pres. SUSAN C. KEATING.

Provident Bank: 114 East Lexington St, Baltimore, MD 21202-1725; tel. (410) 277-7000; fax (410) 576-2747; internet www.provident-bank.com; f. 1951; cap. 50.0m., dep. 11,956.9m. (Dec. 2000).

Massachusetts

Citizens Bank of Massachusetts: 28 State St, Boston, MA 02109; tel. (617) 725-5500; fax (617) 725-5877; e-mail intbank@citizensbank.com; internet www.citizensbank.com; f. 1825; dep. 13,177.5m., total assets 16,145.4m. (Dec. 2000); Pres. and CEO THOMAS J. HOLLISTER.

State Street Bank and Trust Co: 225 Franklin St, POB 351, Suffolk, MA 02101; tel. (617) 786-3000; internet www.statestreet.com; f. 1955; cap. 2,683.8m., dep. 39,327.4m. (Dec. 1998); Chair. and CEO MARSHALL N. CARTER; Pres. DAVID A. SPINA.

Michigan

Citizens Bank: 328 South Saginaw St, Flint, MI 48502; tel. (313) 766-7500; fax (313) 768-6948; f. 1871; cap. 12.5m., dep. 4,977.2m. (Dec. 2000).

Comerica Bank: 500 Woodward Ave, Detroit, MI 48226; tel. (313) 222-3300; fax (313) 961-7349; f. 1849; cap. 2,863.4m., dep. 26,834.6m. (Dec. 1999); Chair. and CEO EUGENE A. MILLER; Pres. MICHAEL T. MONAHAN.

National City Bank of Michigan/Illinois: 211 South Rose St, Kalamazoo, MI 49007; tel. (313) 396-4480; fax (313) 396-4496; f. 1949; cap. 198.6m., dep. 15,486.0m. (Dec. 2000); Chair., Pres. and CEO RICHARD F. CHORMANN.

Minnesota

US Bank NA: 601 Second Ave South, Minneapolis, MN 55402-4302; tel. (612) 973-0728; fax (612) 973-0838; internet www.usbank.com; f. 1929; cap. 310.0m., dep. 67,108.8m. (Dec. 2000); Chair. JOHN F. GRUNDHOFER; Pres. and CEO JERRY F. GRUNDHOFER.

Wells Fargo Bank Minnesota NA: Norwest Center, Sixth St and Marquette Ave, Minneapolis, MN 55479; tel. (612) 667-8110; fax (612) 667-5185; internet www.wellsfargo.com; f. 1872; cap. 100.0m., dep. 49,247.9m. (Dec. 2000); Chair. JAMES R. CAMPBELL; Pres. and CEO ROBERT KOVACEVICH.

Mississippi

Trustmark National Bank: 248 Capitol St, Jackson, MS 39205; tel. (601) 354-5863; fax (601) 949-2387; internet www.trustmark .com; f. 1889; cap. 13.4m., dep. 6,198.7m. (Dec. 2000); Chair. T. H. KENDALL, III.

Missouri

Commerce Bank NA: 1000 Walnut St, Mailstop KCIN, Kansas City, MO 64106; tel. (816) 234-2000; fax (816) 234-2799; e-mail mymoney@commercebank.com; internet www.commercebank.com; f. 1865; cap. 10.0m., dep. 8,495.5m. (Dec. 2000); Chair. JOHN O. BROWN; Pres. and CEO JONATHAN KEMPER.

Montana

First Interstate Bank of Montana NA: 2 Main St, POB 7130, Kalispell, MT 59901; tel. (406) 752-5001; f. 1891; cap. 35m., dep. 257.1m. (Dec. 1996); Chair. JAMES CURRAN; Pres. DEAN A. NELSON.

Nebraska

First National Bank of Omaha: 1 First National Center, Omaha, NE 68103; tel. (402) 341-0500; fax (402) 633-3518; f. 1857; cap. 240.0m., dep. 4,016.1m. (Dec. 1999); Chair. F. PHILLIPS GILTNER; Pres. BRUCE R. LAURITZEN.

Norwest Bank Nebraska NA: 1919 Douglas St, POB 3408, Omaha, NE 68103; tel. (402) 536-2420; fax (402) 536-2531; cap. 127.9m., dep. 2,065.8m. (Dec. 1997).

Nevada

Citibank (Nevada) NA: 8725 West Sahara, POB 6800, Las Vegas, NV 89109; cap. 75.0m., dep. 9,364.3m. (Dec. 2000).

Wells Fargo Bank Nevada NA: 3800 Howard Hughes Pkwy, Las Vegas, NV 89109; tel. (702) 791-6500; internet www.wellsfargo.com; dep. 4,400m. (July 1999); Pres. and CEO LAURA SCHULTE.

New Hampshire

Citizens Bank New Hampshire: 875 Elm St, Manchester, NH 03101; tel. (603) 634-7418; fax (603) 634-7481; e-mail intbank@ citizensbank.com; internet www.citizensbank.com; f. 1853; cap. 0.8m., dep. 4,913.1m. (Dec. 2000); Pres. and CEO KIM A. MEADER.

New Jersey

Summit Bank: 301 Carnegie Center, POB 2066, Princeton, NJ 08543-2066; tel. (609) 987-3200; internet www.summitbank.com; f. 1996; cap. 2,150.9m., dep. 28,569.7m. (Dec. 1999); Chair., Pres. and CEO T. JOSEPH SEMROD.

Trust Co of New Jersey: 35 Journal Sq., Jersey City, NJ 07306; tel. (201) 420-2500; fax (201) 420-2516; f. 1896; cap. 173.0m., dep. 3,327.3m. (Dec. 2000); Chair. and CEO SIGGI B. WILZIG.

New Mexico

First Security Bank of New Mexico NA: 40 First Plaza, POB 1305, Albuquerque, NM 87103; tel. (505) 765-4000; fax (505) 766-9571; internet www.firstsecuritybank.com; f. 1933; cap. 206.3m., dep. 2,578.8m. (Dec. 1999); Pres. and CEO EDWARD T. O'LEARY.

New York

American Express Bank Ltd: American Express Tower, 200 Vesey St, 23rd Floor, New York, NY 10285-2300; tel. (212) 640-5000; fax (212) 693-1721; internet www.americanexpress.com; f. 1919; cap. 121.0m., dep. 8,620.0m. (Dec. 2000); Chair. and CEO W. RICHARD HOLMES.

Bank of New York: 1 Wall St, New York, NY 10286; tel. (212) 495-1784; fax (212) 495-1398; internet www.bankofny.com; f. 1784; cap. 1,135.3m., dep. 61,147.2m. (Dec. 2000); Chair. and CEO THOMAS A. RENYI; Pres. GERALD C. HASSELL.

Bank of Tokyo–Mitsubishi Trust Co: 1251 Ave of the Americas, New York, NY 10020-1104; tel. (212) 782-4000; fax (212) 782-6415; internet www.btmna.com; f. 1955; cap. 444.4m., dep. 1,792.4m. (Dec. 2002); Chair. NAOTAKA OBATA; Pres. and CEO NOBORU TAKEUCHI.

Bankers' Trust Co: New York, NY; tel. (212) 250-2500; fax (212) 250-4429; internet www.deutsche-bank.com; f. 1903; cap. 3,627.0m., dep. 33,721.0m. (Dec. 2000); Chair. and CEO JOSEF ACKERMAN; Pres. JOHN A. ROSS.

Chase Manhattan Bank: 270 Park Ave, New York, NY 10017; tel. (212) 270-6000; fax (212) 682-3761; internet www.chase.com/; f. 1955; cap. 1,211.0m., dep. 333,684.0m. (Dec. 2000); Chair. and CEO WILLIAM B. HARRISON, Jr.

Citibank NA: 399 Park Ave, New York, NY 10043; tel. (212) 559-1000; fax (212) 223-2681; internet www.citibank.com; f. 1812; cap. 751.0m., dep. 328,178.0m. (Dec. 2000); Chair. and CEO JOHN S. REED; Pres. VICTOR J. MENEZES.

Citibank (New York State): 99 Garnsey Rd, Pittsburg, NY 14538; tel. (716) 248-7378; fax (716) 248-7722; cap. 14.0m., dep. 15,864.4m. (Dec. 2000).

European American Bank: 1 EAB Plaza, Uniondale, NY 11555; tel. (516) 296-5000; fax (516) 296-6768; internet www.eab.com; f. 1950; cap. 891.6m., dep. 13,353.4m. (Dec. 1999); Chair. and CEO EDWARD TRAVAGLIANTI; Pres. BRENDAN J. DUGAN.

HSBC Bank USA: 1 HSBC Center, Buffalo, NY 14203; tel. (716) 841-2424; fax (716) 841-5391; internet www.marinemidland.com; f. 1999 following acquisition of Marine Midland Bank by Hongkong & Shanghai Banking Corpn; acquired Republic National Bank of New York 2000; cap. 205.0m., dep. 68,729.1m. (Dec. 2000); Pres. and CEO YOUSSEF A. NASR.

Manufacturers' and Traders' Trust Co—M & T Bank: 1 M & T Plaza, Buffalo, NY 14203-2399; tel. (716) 842-4200; fax (716) 842-5021; internet www.mandtbank.com; f. 1856; cap. 120.6m., dep. 23,906.3m. (Dec. 2000); Chair. and CEO ROBERT G. WILMERS.

Morgan Guaranty Trust Co of New York: 60 Wall St, New York, NY 10260-0060; tel. (212) 483-2323; fax (212) 233-2623; internet www.jpmorgan.com; f. 1959; cap. 265.0m., dep. 161,606.0m. (Dec. 2000); Chair., Pres. and CEO DOUGLAS A. WARNER, III.

National Bank of Geneva: 2 Seneca St, Geneva, NY 14456; tel. (315) 789-2300; fax (315) 789-0381; internet www.nbgeneva.com; f. 1817; cap. 39.3m., dep. 411.0mm. (Dec. 2000); Pres. THOMAS L. KIME; 5 brs.

Trustco Bank NA: 192 Erie Blvd, POB 1082, Schenectady, NY 12301-1082; tel. (518) 377-3311; fax (518) 381-3668; cap. 29.4m., dep. 2,202.7m. (Dec. 2000); Pres. ROBERT A. McCORMICK.

United States Trust Co of New York: 114 West 47th St, New York, NY 10036; tel. (212) 852-1000; fax (212) 995-5642; f. 1853; cap. 15.0m., dep. 3,274.1m. (Dec. 2000); Chair. and CEO H. MARSHALL SCHWARZ; Pres. JEFFREY S. MAURER.

North Carolina

Bank of America NA: Bank of America Corporate Center, 100 North Tryon St, Charlotte, NC 28255; tel. (704) 386-5000; fax (704) 386-0981; internet www.bankamerica.com; f. 1904; cap. 2,833.0m., dep. 502,938m. (Dec. 2000); Chair. and CEO HUGH L. McCOLL, Jr; Pres. KENNETH D. LEWIS.

First Union Corporation: 1 First Union Center, Charlotte, NC 28288-0570; tel. (704) 374-6161; fax (704) 374-3420; internet www .firstunion.com; f. 1908; cap. 17,135m., dep. 200,262.0m. (Dec. 1999); Chair. and CEO EDWARD E. CRUTCHFIELD, Jr; Pres. and CEO KEN THOMPSON.

Wachovia Bank NA: 100 North Main St, Winston-Salem, NC 27150; tel. (336) 732-5000; fax (336) 770-5931; internet www .wachovia.com; f. 1866; cap. 51.4m., dep. 58,717.7m. (Dec. 2000); Chair. and CEO L. M. BAKER, Jr.

North Dakota

Norwest Bank North Dakota NA: 406 Main Ave, Fargo, ND 58126; tel. (701) 293-4200; fax (701) 280-8821; cap. 77.4m., dep. 1,249.9m. (Dec. 1997).

Ohio

Bank One NA: 100 East Bond St, Columbus, OH 43215; tel. (614) 248-5931; fax (614) 248-5518; internet www.bankone.com; f. 1868;

cap. 1,945.9m., dep. 26,976.9m. (Dec. 1998); Chair. and CEO FRED-ERICK CULLEN.

Fifth Third Bank: 38 Fountain Sq. Plaza, Cincinnati, OH 45263; tel. (513) 579-5300; fax (513) 579-4185; internet ww.53.com; f. 1927; cap. 4.5m., dep. 28,236.6m. (Dec. 2000); Pres. and CEO GEORGE A. SCHAEFER, Jr.

FirstMerit Bank NA: 3 Cascade Plaza, Akron, OH 44308; tel. (330) 996-6300; fax (330) 384-7008; internet www.firstmerit.com; cap. 837.6m., dep. 9,081.2m. (Dec. 1999); Chair. and CEO JOHN R. COCHRAN; Pres. SID A. BOSTIC.

Huntington National Bank: 17 South High St, Columbus, OH 43287; tel. (614) 480-8300; fax (614) 480-3537; internet www .huntington.com; f. 1866; cap. 40.0m., dep. 24,441.1m. (Dec. 2000); Chair. FRANK WOBST.

KeyBank NA: 127 Public Sq., Cleveland, OH 44114; tel. (216) 689-3000; fax (216) 689-3683; internet www.key.com; f. 1849; cap. 50.0m., dep. 67,117.6m. (Dec. 2000); Chair. and CEO ROBERT W. GILLESPIE.

National City Bank: 1900 East Ninth St, POB 94750, Cleveland, OH 44114-3484; tel. (216) 575-2000; fax (216) 575-9263; internet www.national-city.com; f. 1845; cap. 7.3m., dep. 31,249.6m. (Dec. 2000); Chair. GARY A. GLASER; Pres. and CEO WILLIAM E. MACDONALD, III.

Oklahoma

Bank of Oklahoma NA: Bank of Oklahoma Tower, POB 2300, Tulsa, OK 74192; tel. (918) 588-6829; fax (918) 588-6026; internet www.bankofoklahoma.com; f. 1933; cap. 52.9m., dep. 7,151.3m. (Dec. 2000); Chair. GEORGE B. KAISER; Pres. and CEO STANLEY A. LY-BARGER.

Oregon

United States National Bank of Oregon: 321 SW Sixth Ave, Portland, OR 97204; tel. (503) 275-6111; fax (503) 275-5132; f. 1891; cap. 1,095m., dep. 12,225m. (Dec. 1996); Chair. ROGER BREEZLEY; CEO GERRY CAMERON; Pres. JOHN ESKILDSEN.

Pennsylvania

Mellon Bank, NA: 1 Mellon Bank Center, Pittsburgh, PA 15258-0001; tel. (412) 234-5000; fax (412) 234-4025; internet www.mellon .com; f. 1869; cap. 169.3m., dep. 35,268.6m. (Dec. 2000); Chair., Pres. and CEO MARTIN G. MCGUINN.

PNC Bank, NA: 1 PNC Plaza, 249 Fifth Ave, Pittsburgh, PA 15222-2707; tel. (412) 762-2000; fax (412) 762-5022; internet www.pnc.com; f. 1959; cap. 218.9m., dep. 39,236.1m. (Dec. 2000); Chair., Pres. and CEO JAMES E. ROHR.

Rhode Island

Citizens Bank of Rhode Island: 1 Citizens Plaza, Providence, RI 02903; tel. (401) 454-2441; fax (401) 455-5859; e-mail intbank@ citizensbank.com; internet www.citizensbank.com; f. 1996; cap. 1.0m., dep. 6,975.0m. (Dec. 2000); Chair. ROBERT M. MAHONEY; Pres. and CEO JOSEPH J. MARCAURELE.

Fleet National Bank: 111 Westminster St, Providence, RI 02903; tel. (401) 278-6000; internet www.fleet.com; f. 1996; cap. 126.0m., dep. 138,629.0m. (Dec. 2000); Chair. and CEO TERRENCE MURRAY; Pres. CHARLES K. GIFFORD.

South Carolina

Carolina First Bank: 102 South Main St, POB 1029, Greenville, SC 29602; tel. (864) 255-7900; fax (864) 239-6401; internet www .carolinafirst.com; cap. 7.9m., dep. 4,140.9m. (Dec. 2000); Chair. MACK I. WHITTLE, Jr; Pres. JAMES W. TERRY, Jr.

South Dakota

Citibank (South Dakota): 701 East 60th St, North, POB 6000, Sioux Falls, SD 57117; tel. (605) 331-2626; internet www.citibank .com; f. 1981; cap. 113.0m., dep. 15,035.9m. (Dec. 2000); Chair. KEVIN KESSINGER; Pres. KENDALL E. STORK.

Norwest Bank South Dakota NA: 101 North Phillips Ave, Sioux Falls, SD 57117; tel. (605) 575-7300; fax (605) 575-4815; cap. 233.5m., dep. 3,717.2m. (Dec. 1997); Pres. and CEO GARY G. OLSON.

Tennessee

First Tennessee Bank NA: 165 Madison Ave, 9th Floor, POB 84, Memphis, TN 38101-0084; tel. (901) 523-4444; fax (901) 523-4267; internet www.ftb.com; f. 1864; cap. 72.5m., dep. 15,083.7m. (Dec. 2000); Chair. and CEO RALPH HORN; Pres. JOHN KELLEY.

Union Planters Bank NA: 6200 Poplar, POB 387, Memphis, TN 38147; tel. (901) 580-5970; fax (901) 580-5958; f. 1869; cap. 18.0m., dep. 30,349.3m. (Dec. 2000); Chair. and CEO BEN RAWLINS, Jr.

Texas

Bank One, Texas NA: 1717 Main St, Dallas, TX 75201; tel. (214) 290-4130; fax (214) 290-2090; internet www.bankone.com; cap. 1,661.2m. dep. 22,626.1m. (Dec. 1998); Chair. and CEO TERRY KELLEY.

Comerica Bank–Texas: Thanksgiving Tower, 1601 Elm St, Dallas, TX 75201; tel. (214) 841-1400; fax (214) 841-9298; internet www .comerica.com; f. 1988; cap. 2.5m., dep. 3,194.8m. (Dec. 2000); Pres. and CEO CHARLES L. GUMMER.

Frost National Bank: 100 West Houston St, POB 1600, San Antonio, TX 78296; tel. (210) 220-4011; f. 1899; cap. 8.5m., dep. 6,987.6m. (Dec. 2000); Chair. and CEO T. C. FROST.

Wells Fargo Bank of Texas: POB 3326, Houston, TX 77253-3326; internet www.wellsfargo.com; f. 1996; cap. 21.0m., dep. 18,445.9m. (Dec. 2000).

Utah

First Security Bank NA: 79 South Main St, Salt Lake City, UT 84111; tel. (801) 246-6000; fax (801) 246-5992; e-mail amanbei@ fscnet.com; internet www.firstsecuritybank.com; f. 1996; acquisiton by Wells Fargo Bank NA pending in 2000; cap. 1,428.3m., dep. 15,517.2m. (Dec. 1999); Chair. SPENCER ECCLES; Pres. SCOTT NELSON.

Vermont

Howard Bank: 111 Main St, Burlington, VT 05402; tel. (802) 658-3400; fax (802) 865-1891; f. 1870; cap. 45m., dep. 470m. (Sept. 1991); Chair. RICHARD MALLARY; Pres. JOSEPH L. BOUTIN.

Virginia

Branch Banking and Trust Co of Virginia: 823 East Main St, Richmond, VA 23219; tel. (757) 823-7890; fax (704) 954-1117; internet www.bbandt; f. 1978; cap. 10.8m., dep. 4,725.8m. (Dec. 2000).

Chevy Chase Bank, FSB: 7926 Jones Branch Dr., Mclean, VA 22101; internet www.chevychasebank.com; f. 1955; dep. 7,189.5m. (Dec. 2000).

Washington

Seafirst Bank: 701 Fifth Ave, POB 3586, Seattle, WA 98124; tel. (206) 358-3000; fax (206) 358-3771; f. 1870; cap. 1,681m., dep. 14,375m. (Dec. 1996); CEO JOHN V. RINDLAUB.

Washington Mutual Bank: 1201 Third Ave, Suite 1000, Seattle, WA 98101; tel. (206) 490-8625; internet www.wamu.com; dep. 32,213.0m., total assets 34,715.0m. (Dec. 2000); Pres. and Chair. KERRY KILLINGER.

West Virginia

Bank One, West Virginia NA: 1000 Fifth Ave, Huntington, WV 25701; tel. (304) 526-4336; internet www.bankone.com; f. 1872; cap. 140.9m., dep. 1,637.3m. (Dec. 1998); Chair. and CEO A. MICHAEL PERRY.

Wisconsin

Bank One, Wisconsin: 111 East Wisconsin Ave, Milwaukee, WI 53202; tel. (414) 765-3000; fax (414) 765-0553; internet www .bankone.com; f. 1930; cap. 552.1m., dep. 7,521.5m. (Dec. 1997); Chair. RONALD C. BALDWIN; Pres. and CEO WILLIAM E. READ.

Firstar Bank NA: 777 East Wisconsin Ave, Milwaukee, WI 53202; tel. (414) 765-5705; fax (414) 765-6207; f. 1853; cap. 6,303m., dep. 49,889m. (June 2000); CEO JERRY GRUNDHOFER.

Wyoming

Norwest Bank Wyoming NA: POB 2799, Casper, WY 82601; tel. (307) 266-1100; fax (307) 235-7626; cap. 176.3m., dep. 2,709.6m. (Dec. 1997).

Co-operative Bank

CoBank: POB 5110, Denver, CO 80217; tel. (303) 740-4000; fax (303) 740-4366; internet www.cobank.com; f. 1933; provides loan finance and domestic and international banking services for agricultural and farmer-owned co-operatives; cap. 1,664.9m., dep. 21,997.5m. (Dec. 1999); Chair. OTIS H. MOLZ; CEO DOUGLAS D. SIMS; Pres. JAMES A. PIERSON.

Trade Bank

Export-Import Bank of the United States (Ex-Im Bank): 811 Vermont Ave, NW, Washington, DC 20571; tel. (202) 565-3946; fax (202) 565-3380; internet www.exim.gov; f. 1934; independent agency since 1945; cap. subscribed by the US Treasury; finances and facilitates US external trade, guarantees payment to US foreign traders and banks, extends credit to foreign governmental and private concerns; cap. 1,973.2m. (Dec. 1996); Chair. and Pres. PHILIP MERRIL.

BANKING ASSOCIATIONS

There is a State Bankers Association in each state.

American Bankers Association: 1120 Connecticut Ave, NW, Washington, DC 20036; tel. (202) 663-5000; fax (202) 828-4547; e-mail custserv@aba.com; internet www.aba.com; f. 1875; Pres.-elect AUBREY B. PATTERSON Jr.

America's Community Bankers: 900 19th St, NW, Suite 400, Washington, DC 20006; tel. (202) 857-3100; fax (202) 296-8716; e-mail info@acbankers.org; f. 1992; 2,000 mems; Pres. and CEO DIANE M. CASEY.

Bank Administration Institute (BAI): 1 North Franklin St, Suite 1000, Chicago, IL 60606; tel. (312) 553-4600; fax (312) 683-2426; e-mail info@bai.org; internet www.bai.org; f. 1924; Pres. and CEO THOMAS P. JOHNSON, Jr.

Independent Community Bankers of America: 1 Thomas Circle, NW, Suite 400, Washington, DC 20005; tel. (202) 659-8111; e-mail info@icba.org; internet www.icba.org; f. 1930; Pres. and CEO KENNETH A. GUENTHER; 5,000 banks.

Mortgage Bankers Association of America: 1919 Pennsylvania Ave, Washington, DC 20006; tel. (202) 557-2700; internet www.mbaa.org; f. 1914; Chair. JAMES M. MURPHY; 2,800 mems.

PRINCIPAL STOCK EXCHANGES

American Stock Exchange: 86 Trinity Pl., New York, NY 10006; tel. (212) 306-1000; fax (212) 306-1152; internet www.amex.com; f. 1849; Chair. SALVATORE SODANO; Pres. PETER QUICK; mems: 661 regular, 160 associate, 203 option principal, 13 limited-trading permitholders.

Boston Stock Exchange Inc: 1 Boston Pl., Boston, MA 02108; tel. (617) 723-9500; fax (617) 723-2474; f. 1834; Chair. and CEO WILLIAM G. MORTON, Jr; 190 mems.

Chicago Stock Exchange: 440 South LaSalle St, Chicago, IL 60605; f. 1882; Chair. DAVID W. FOX; Pres. and CEO ROBERT H. FORNEY, Jr; 445 mems.

Cincinnati Stock Exchange: 36 Fourth St, Suite 906, Cincinnati, OH 45202; tel. (513) 786-8898.

Nasdaq Stock Market Inc: 2500 Sand Hill Rd, Suite 220, Menlo Park, CA 94025; tel. (650) 233-2000; fax (650) 233-2099; internet www.nasdaq.com; f. 1998 by the American Stock Exchange and the Nat. Asscn of Securities Dealers (NASD); world-wide electronic trading market.

New York Stock Exchange Inc: 11 Wall St, New York, NY 10005; tel. (212) 656-3000; fax (212) 656-5646; f. 1792; Chair. and CEO RICHARD A. GRASSO; 1,366 mems.

Pacific Exchange Inc: 301 Pine St, San Francisco, CA 94104; tel. (415) 393-4000; fax (415) 393-5964; internet www.pacificex.com; f. 1882; Chair. and CEO PHILIP D. DEFEO; 552 mems.

Philadelphia Stock Exchange Inc: Stock Exchange Bldg, 1900 Market St, Philadelphia, PA 19103; tel. (215) 496-5000; fax (215) 496-5460; e-mail info@phlx.com; f. 1790; Chair. (vacant); Pres. (vacant); 505 mems.

INSURANCE

Principal Companies

Acacia Mutual Life Insurance Co: 51 Louisiana Ave, NW, Washington, DC 20001-2176; tel. (202) 628-4506; fax (202) 783-0403; f. 1869; Chair., Pres. and CEO CHARLES T. NASON.

Allstate Corporation: 2775 Sanders Rd, Northbrook, IL 60062-6127; tel. (708) 402-5000; fax (708) 402-2351; e-mail allstate@digiplanet.com; internet www.allstate.com; f. 1931; CEO JERRY CHOATE.

American National Insurance Co: 1 Moody Plaza, Galveston, TX 77550-7999; tel. (409) 763-4661; f. 1905; Chair., Pres. and CEO R. L. MOODY.

American United Life Insurance Co: 1 American Sq., POB 368, Indianapolis, IN 46206-0368; tel. (317) 285-1877; internet www.aul.com; f. 1877; Chair., Pres. and CEO JERRY D. SEMLER.

AmerUS Life: 611 Fifth Ave, Des Moines, IA 50309; tel. (515) 283-2371; fax (515) 242-4692; f. 1896; Pres. D. T. DOAN.

Baltimore Life Insurance Co: 10075 Red Run Blvd, Owings Mills, MD 21117-4871; tel. (410) 581-6600; fax (410) 581-6602; internet www.baltlife.com; f. 1882; Chair. J. E. BLAIR, Jr; Pres. and CEO L. J. PEARSON.

Bankers' Life & Casualty Co: 222 Merchandise Mart Plaza, Chicago, IL 60654; tel. (312) 396-6000; fax (312) 685-4296; f. 1880; Chair. and CEO R. T. SHAW; Pres. J. W. GARDINER.

Business Men's Assurance Co of America: BMA Tower, 700 Karnes Blvd, POB 419458, Kansas City, MO 64141; tel. (816) 753-8000; fax (816) 751-5717; f. 1909; Chair. and CEO GIORGIO BALZER; Pres. R. T. RAKICH, Jr.

Central United Life Insurance Co: 4301 Sergeant Rd, Sioux City, IA 51106; tel. (712) 276 8000; Chair F. W. PURMORT, Jr.

CIGNA Property and Casualty Insurance Co: 2 Liberty Pl., 31st Floor, Philadelphia, PA 19192; tel. (215) 761-4555; fax (215) 761-5588; f. 1982; Chair. and CEO WILSON H. TAYLOR.

Combined Insurance Co of America: 5050 North Broadway St, Chicago, IL 60640; tel. (773) 275-8000; fax (773) 769-8705; f. 1949; Chair. and CEO P. G. RYAN.

Commercial Union Insurance Companies (CGU): 1 Beacon St, Boston, MA 02108-3106; tel. (617) 725-6000; fax (617) 725-6702; internet www.cgu-insurance.net; f. 1861; Pres. and CEO ROBERT C. GOWDY.

Commonwealth Life Insurance Co: 680 Fourth Ave, Louisville, KY 40202; tel. (502) 587-7371; fax (502) 560-3295; f. 1904; Chair., Pres. and CEO THOMAS H. SCHNICK.

Continental American Life Insurance Co: 300 Continental Dr., Newark, DE 19713-4399; tel. (302) 454-5000; fax (302) 731-1101; f. 1907; Chair. WILLIAM G. COPELAND; Pres. and CEO JOHN T. UNIPAN.

Continental Assurance Co/Continental Casualty Co: CNA Plaza, 333 South Wabash Ave, Chicago, IL 60685-0001; tel. (312) 822-5000; fax (312) 822-6419; Chair. and CEO DENNIS H. CHOOKASZIAN.

The Continental Insurance Co: 180 Maiden Lane, New York, NY 10038-4925; tel. (212) 440-3000; fax (212) 440-3857; f. 1853; Chair. and CEO J. P. MASCOTTE.

The Equitable Companies Inc: 787 Seventh Ave, New York, NY 10019; tel. (212) 554-1234; fax (212) 262-9019; f. 1859; Chair. CLAUDE BEBEAR; Pres. and CEO JOSEPH J. MELLONE.

Farmers Insurance Exchange: 4680 Wilshire Blvd, Los Angeles, CA 90010-3807; tel. (213) 930-3200; fax (213) 932-3101; Pres. and CEO MARTIN D. FERNSTEIN.

Federal Insurance Co: POB 1615, Warren, NJ 07061; tel. (908) 903-2000; internet www.chubb.com; CEO DEAN R. O'HARE.

Fidelity and Guaranty Life Insurance Co: 6225 Smith Ave, Baltimore, MD 21209; tel. (410) 547-3000; fax (410) 205-0321; CEO IHOR HRON.

Franklin Life Insurance Co: 1 Franklin Sq., Springfield, IL 62713; tel. (217) 528-2011; fax (217) 528-9106; f. 1884; Chair., Pres. and CEO WILLIAM A. SIMPSON (acting).

General American Life Insurance Co: 13045 Tesson Ferry Rd, St Louis, MO 63128; tel. (314) 231-1700; fax (314) 444-0486; internet www.genam.com; f. 1933; Chair., Pres. and CEO RICHARD A. LIDDY.

Great Southern Life Insurance Co: POB 219040, Dallas, TX 75221; tel. (972) 954-8100; fax (972) 954-8148; f. 1909; Pres. and CEO GARY L. MULLER.

Guarantee Mutual Life Insurance Co: 8801 Indian Hills Dr., Omaha, NE 68114-4066; tel. (402) 390-7300; fax (402) 390-7577; f. 1901; Pres. ROBERT D. BATES.

The Guardian Life Insurance Co of America: 201 Park Ave South, New York, NY 10003-1605; tel. (212) 598-8000; fax (212) 533-5156; internet www.theguardian.com; f. 1860; Pres. and CEO JOSEPH D. SARGENT.

Hanover Insurance Co: 100 North Parkway, Worcester, MA 01605; tel. (508) 853-7200; fax (508) 856-9092; f. 1973; Chair. JOHN F. O'BRIEN; Pres. and CEO T. J. RUPLEY.

Home Beneficial Life Insurance Co: POB 27572, Richmond, VA 23261; tel. (804) 358-8431; fax (804) 254-9601; f. 1899; Pres. and CEO R. W. WILTSHIRE, Jr.

Indianapolis Life Insurance Co: 2960 North Meridian St, Indianapolis, IN 46206; tel. (317) 927-6500; fax (317) 927-3326; f. 1905; Pres. and CEO EUGENE M. BUSCHE.

Integon Corpn: 500 West Fifth St, Winston-Salem, NC 27102-3199; tel. (910) 770-2000; fax (910) 770-2122; f. 1920; Pres. and CEO JAMES T. LAMBIE.

John Hancock Life Insurance Co: POB 111, Boston, MA 02117; tel. (617) 572-6000; fax (617) 572-4539; CEO DAVID F. D'ALESSANDRO.

Kansas City Life Insurance Co: 3520 Broadway, Kansas City, MO 64141-6139; tel. (816) 753-7000; f. 1895; Chair. and Pres. JOSEPH R. BIXBY.

Lamar Life Insurance Co: POB 880, Jackson, MS 39205; tel. (601) 949-3100; fax (601) 355-8733; f. 1906; Pres. JACK P. DEAN.

Liberty Life Insurance Co: POB 789, Greenville, SC 29602; tel. (864) 609-8111; fax (864) 292-4390; f. 1905; Chair. W. HAYNE HIPP; Pres. RONALD F. LOEWEN.

Liberty Mutual Insurance Group: 175 Berkeley St, Boston, MA 02117-0140; tel. (617) 357-9500; fax (617) 350-7648; Chair. and CEO GARY L. COUNTRYMAN.

Liberty National Life Insurance Co: POB 2612, Birmingham, AL 35202; tel. (205) 325-2722; fax (205) 325-2520; f. 1900; Pres. ANTHONY L. MCWHORTER.

Life Insurance Co of Virginia: 6610 West Broad St, Richmond, VA 23230; tel. (804) 281-6000; fax (804) 281-6929; f. 1871; CEO PAUL RUTLEDGE.

Lincoln American Life Insurance Co: 11815 North Pennsylvania St, Carmel, IN 46032; tel. (317) 817-6300; fax (317) 817-6102; f. 1957; Pres. D. F. GONGAWARE; CEO S. C. HILBERT.

Manhattan Life Insurance Co: 111 West 57th St, New York, NY 10019-2211; tel. (212) 484-9300; fax (212) 484-9541; f. 1850; Chair. and CEO D. M. FORDYCE.

Massachusetts Mutual Life Insurance Co: 1295 State St, Springfield, MA 01111-0001; tel. (413) 788-8411; fax (413) 744-6005; internet www.massmutual.com; f. 1851; Chair. THOMAS B. WHEELER; Pres. and CEO ROBERT J. O'CONNELL.

Metropolitan Life Insurance Co: 1 Madison Ave, New York, NY 10010-3681; tel. (212) 578-2211; fax (212) 689-1980; internet www .metlife.com; f. 1868; Chair., Pres. and CEO ROBERT G. SCHWARTZ.

Minnesota Life Insurance Co: 400 Robert St North, St Paul, MN 55101; tel. (651) 665-3500; fax (651) 665-4488; internet www .minnesotamutual.com; f. 1880; Chair., Pres. and CEO ROBERT L. SENKLER.

Monarch Life Insurance Co: 1 Monarch Pl., Springfield, MA 01144-1001; tel. (413) 784-2000; fax (413) 784-6271; f. 1901; CEO ROGER T. SERVISON.

Mutual Life Insurance Co of New York (MONY): 1740 Broadway, New York, NY 10019; tel. (212) 708-2000; fax (212) 708-2056; f. 1842; Chair. and CEO MICHAEL I. ROTH.

Mutual of Omaha Insurance Co: Mutual of Omaha Plaza, Omaha, NE 68175; tel. (402) 342-7600; internet mutualofomaha .com; f. 1909; operating in 50 states, the District of Columbia, the US Virgin Is, Puerto Rico and Guam; Chair. and CEO JOHN W. WEEKLY; Pres. and COO JOHN A. STURGEON.

National Home Life Assurance Co: 20 Moores Rd, Frazer, PA 19355; tel. (610) 648-5000; fax (610) 648-5308; CEO DONALD D. KENNEDY, Jr.

Nationwide Insurance Enterprise: 1 Nationwide Plaza, Columbus, OH 43215-2220; tel. (614) 249-7111; internet www .nationwide.com; f. 1925; Chair. and CEO DIMON R. MCFERSON.

New York Life Insurance Co: 51 Madison Ave, New York, NY 10010-1603; tel. (212) 576-7000; fax (212) 576-6794; e-mail infonyl@ e-mail.com; internet www.newyorklife.com; f. 1845; CEO HARRY G. HOHN.

Niagara Fire Insurance Co: 180 Maiden Lane, New York, NY 10038-4925; tel. (212) 440-3000; fax (212) 440-7130; f. 1850; Chair. J. P. MASCOTTE.

Northwestern Mutual Life Financial Network: 720 East Wisconsin Ave, Milwaukee, WI 53202-4797; tel. (414) 271-1444; internet www.northwesternmutual.com; f. 1857; Chair. and CEO JAMES D. ERICSON.

Old Line Life Insurance Co of America: POB 401, Milwaukee, WI 53201; tel. (414) 271-2820; fax (414) 283-5556; f. 1910; Pres. and CEO JAMES A. GRIFFIN.

Pacific Life Insurance Co: 700 Newport Center Dr., Newport Beach, CA 92660-6397; tel. (949) 219-3011; fax (949) 219-7614; e-mail info@pacificlife.com; internet www.pacificlife.com; f. 1868; Chair. and CEO THOMAS C. SUTTON.

Penn Mutual Life Insurance Co: Independence Sq., Philadelphia, PA 19172; tel. (215) 956-8000; fax (215) 956-7508; f. 1847; Chair. JOHN E. TAIT.

Phoenix Companies Inc: 1 American Row, Hartford, CT 06115; tel. (860) 403-5000; f. 1851; operating in all states, the District of Columbia, Puerto Rico, the US Virgin Is and Canada; Chair., Pres. and CEO ROBERT W. FIONDELLA.

Principal Financial Group: 711 High St, Des Moines, IA 50392; tel. (515) 247 5111; CEO BARRY GRISWELL.

Protective Life Insurance Co: 2801 Hwy 280 South, Birmingham, AL 35223-2488; tel. (205) 879-9230; fax (205) 868-3196; f. 1907; Chair. DRAYTON NABERS, Jr.

Provident Life and Accident Insurance Co of America: 1 Fountain Sq., Chattanooga, TN 37402-1389; tel. (423) 755-1011; fax (423) 755-7013; f. 1887; Pres. and CEO WINSTON W. WALKER.

Provident Mutual Life Insurance Co: Westlake Dr., Berwyn, PA 19312-2419; tel. (610) 407-1717; internet www.providentmutual .com; f. 1865; Pres. and CEO ROBERT W. KLOSS.

The Prudential Insurance Co of America: 751 Broad St, Newark, NJ 07102-3714; tel. (973) 802-6000; fax (973) 802-7277; internet www.prudential.com; f. 1875; Chair. and CEO ARTHUR F. RYAN; Pres. RONALD D. BARBARO.

SAFECO Property and Casualty Insurance Cos: Safeco Plaza, 4333 Brooklyn Ave, NE, Seattle, WA 98185-0001; tel. (206) 545-5000; fax (206) 548-7117; tel. (206) 545-5000; f. 1929; Chair. ROGER EIGSTI; Pres. BOH DICKEY.

Security Mutual Life Insurance Co of New York: Court House Sq., POB 1625, Binghamton, NY 13902; tel. (607) 723-3551; internet www.smlny.com; f. 1886; operating in all states; Pres. and Chair. and CEO B. W. BOYEA.

Southwestern Life Insurance Co: POB 2699, Dallas, TX 752221; tel. (972) 954-7111; fax (972) 954-7717; f. 1903; Pres. THOMAS J. BROPHY.

Standard Insurance Co: POB 711, Portland, OR 97207; tel. (503) 248-2700; fax (503) 321-7757; f. 1906; Pres. and CEO RONALD E. TIMPE.

State Farm Life Insurance Co: 1 State Farm Plaza, Bloomington, IL 61710-0001; tel. (309) 766-2311; fax (309) 766-6169; internet www .statefarm.com; f. 1929; Chair. MARVIN D. BOWER; Pres. EDWARD B. RUST, Jr.

State Life Insurance Co: 141 East Washington St, Indianapolis, IN 46204-3649; tel. (317) 681-5300; fax (317) 681-5492; f. 1894; Chair. and Pres. ARTHUR L. BRYANT.

Sun Life Insurance Co of America: 11601 Wilshire Blvd, Los Angeles, CA 90025; tel. (213) 312-5000; f. 1897; operating in 48 states and the District of Columbia; Chair. ELI BROAD; Pres. and CEO ROBERT P. SALTZMAN.

Transamerica Occidental Life Insurance Co: 1150 South Olive St, Los Angeles, CA 90015-2290; tel. (213) 741-7629; fax (213) 742-5280; f. 1906; Pres. RON WAGLEY; COO KAREN MCDONAL.

Travelers/Aetna Property & Casualty Corporation: 1 Tower Sq., Hartford, CT 06183-0001; tel. (860) 277-0111; fax (860) 277-1970; internet www.travelers.com; f. 1893; Chair. THOMAS H. MCABOY; Pres. and CEO RICHARD W. MCLAUGHLIN.

Unigard Security Insurance Co: 15805 NE 24th St, POB 90701, Bellevue, WA 98008; tel. (425) 641-4321; fax (425) 562-5256; internet www.unigard.com; f. 1901; Pres. and CEO PETER CHRISTEN.

Union Central Life Insurance Co: POB 40888, Cincinnati, OH 45240; tel. (513) 595-2200; fax (513) 595-2888; internet www .unioncentral.com; f. 1867; Pres and CEO JOHN H. JACOBS.

United Insurance Co of America: 1 East Wacker Dr., Chicago, IL 60601-1883; tel. (312) 661-4500; fax (312) 661-4731; f. 1955; Pres. RICHARD C. VIE; Chair. J. V. JEROME.

United States Fidelity & Guaranty Co: 100 Light St, Baltimore, MD 21202-1036; tel. (410) 547-3000; fax (410) 625-2829; f. 1896; Chair. and CEO JACK MOSELEY; Pres. PAUL SCHEEL.

UNUM Life Insurance Co of America: 2211 Congress St, Portland, ME 04122-0001; tel. (207) 770-2211; internet www.unum.com/ UNUMAmer/; f. 1848; Chair. and CEO JAMES F. ORR, III.

Washington National Corporation: 300 Tower Pkwy, Lincolnshire, IL 60069; tel. (847) 793-3000; fax (847) 793-3737; f. 1911; Chair. and CEO ROBERT PATIN.

Western National Life Insurance Co: 5555 San Felipe Rd, Suite 900, Houston, TX 77056; tel. (713) 888-7800; fax (713) 888-7893; CEO J. K. CLAYTON.

Western & Southern Life Insurance Co: 400 Broadway, Cincinnati, OH 45202-3341; tel. (513) 629-1800; fax (513) 629-1050; f. 1888; operating in 44 states; Chair. W. J. WILLIAMS; Pres. and CEO JOHN F. BARRETT.

Wisconsin National Life Insurance Co: 220 Washington Ave, Oshkosh, WI 54901-5030; tel. (414) 235-0800; f. 1908; operating in 33 states and the District of Columbia; Pres. A. DEAN.

Zenith National Insurance Corpn: 21255 Califer St, Woodland Hills, CA 91367; tel. (818) 894-5297; fax (818) 713-0177; Chair. and Pres. S. R. ZAX.

INSURANCE ORGANIZATIONS

American Council of Life Insurance: 1001 Pennsylvania Ave, NW, Washington, DC 20004-2599; tel. (202) 624-2000; fax (202) 624-2319; f. 1976; 493 mem. cos; Pres. and CEO CARROLL A. CAMPBELL, Jr.

American Institute of Marine Underwriters: 14 Wall St, 21st Floor, New York, NY 10005-2145; tel. (212) 233-0550; fax (212) 227-5102; f. 1898; 105 mems; Pres. WALTER M. CRAMER.

American Insurance Association: 1130 Connecticut Ave, NW, Suite 1000, Washington, DC 20036; tel. (202) 828-7100; fax (202) 293-1219; internet www.aiadc.org; f. 1964; 300 mems; Chair. DEAN O'HARE; Pres. ROBERT E. VAGLEY.

Casualty Actuarial Society: 1100 North Glebe Rd, Suite 600, Arlington, VA 22201; tel. (703) 276-3100; fax (703) 276-3108; e-mail office@casact.org; internet www.casact.org; f. 1914; 3,012 mems; Exec. Dir JAMES H. TINSLEY.

Life Insurance Marketing and Research Association International, Inc (LIMRA Inc): 300 Day Hill Rd, Windsor, CT 06095; tel. (860) 688 3358; fax (860) 298 9555; internet www.limra.com; f. 1916; 850 mems; Chair. J. TORAN; Pres. RICHARD A. WECKER.

LOMA (Life Office Management Association): 2300 Windy Ridge Pkwy, Suite 600, Atlanta, GA 30339-8443; tel. (770) 951-1770; fax (770) 984-6417; internet www.loma.org; f. 1924; 1,230 mem. cos; Chair. HOWARD R. FRICKE; Pres. THOMAS P. DONALDSON.

National Association of Health Underwriters: 1000 Connecticut Ave, NW, Suite 810, Washington, DC 20036; tel. (202) 223-5533; fax (202) 785-2274; e-mail dsaltz@lx.netcom.com; internet www.nahu.org.

National Association of Life Underwriters: 1922 F St, NW, Washington, DC 20006-4387; tel. (202) 331-6000; fax (202) 331-2179; internet www.agents-online.com/NALU/NALUhome.html; 108,000 mems; CEO WILLIAM V. REGAN, III.

National Association of Mutual Insurance Cos: 3601 Vincennes Rd, POB 68700, Indianapolis, IN 46268-0700; tel. (317) 875-5250; fax (317) 879-8408; e-mail info@namic.org; internet www.namic.org; 1,290 mems; Pres. LARRY L. FORRESTER.

Reinsurance Association of America: 1301 Pennsylvania Ave, NW, Suite 900, Washington, DC 20004; tel. (202) 638-3690; fax (202) 638-0936; internet www.reinsurance.org; f. 1969; 29 mems; Pres. FRANKLIN W. NUTTER.

Trade and Industry

CHAMBER OF COMMERCE

Chamber of Commerce of the USA: 1615 H St, NW, Washington, DC 20062-2000; tel. (202) 659-6000; fax (202) 463-5836; f. 1912; mems: c. 215,000 cos, professional asscns and chambers of commerce; Pres. RICHARD L. LESHER.

EMPLOYERS' ORGANIZATIONS

Chemicals

American Chemistry Council: 1300 Wilson Blvd, Arlington, VA 22202; tel. (703) 741-5000; fax (703) 741-6000; f. 1872; c. 185 mems; Pres. and CEO FREDERICK L. WEBBER; Sec. JOHN P. CONNELLY.

American Pharmaceutical Association: 2215 Constitution Ave, NW, Washington, DC 20037; tel. (202) 628-4410; fax (202) 783-2351; f. 1852; 40,000 mems; Exec. Vice-Pres. Dr JOHN A. GANS.

Chemical Specialities Manufacturers Association: 1913 I St, NW, Washington, DC 20006; tel. (202) 872-8110; fax (202) 872-8114; f. 1914; 440 mems; Pres. RALPH ENGEL.

Drug, Chemical and Allied Trades Association, Inc: 2 Roosevelt Ave, 3rd Floor, Syosset, NY 11791; tel. (516) 496-3317; fax (516) 496-2231; 500 mems; Exec. Dir RICHARD J. LERMAN.

The Fertilizer Institute: The Fertilizer Institute: Union Center Plaza 820 First St, NE, Washington, DC 20002; tel. (202) 962-0490; fax (202) 962-0577; internet www.tfi.org; f. 1883; 300 mems; Pres. GARY D. MYERS.

National Community Pharmacists Association: 205 Daingerfield Rd, Alexandria, VA 22314; tel. (703) 683-8200; fax (703) 683-3619; f. 1898; fmrly Nat. Asscn of Retail Druggists; 30,000 mems; Exec. Vice-Pres. CALVIN J. ANTHONY.

Pharmaceutical Research & Manufacturers of America: 1100 15th St, NW, Suite 900, Washington, DC 20005-1797; tel. (202) 835-3400; fax (202) 785-4834; internet www.pharma.org; f. 1958; 87 mems; Pres. GERALD J. MOSSINGHOFF.

Soap and Detergent Association: 1500 K St, NW, Suite 300, Washington, DC, 20005; tel. (202) 347-2900; fax (202) 347-4110; e-mail info@cleaning101.com; internet www.cleaning101.com; f. 1926; 100 mems; Pres. ERNIE ROSENBERG.

Construction
(see also Electricity, and Engineering and Machinery)

American Institute of Constructors: 466 94th Ave North, St Petersburg, FL 33702; tel. (727) 578-0317; fax (727) 578-9982; internet www.aicnet.org; f. 1971; 1,600 mems; Exec. Dir CHERYL P. HARRIS.

Associated Builders and Contractors, Inc (ABC): 1300 North 17th St, Rosslyn, VA 22209; tel. (703) 812-2000; fax (703) 812-8235; internet www.abc.org; f. 1950; 20,000 mems; Exec. Vice-Pres. ROBERT P. HEPNER.

Associated General Contractors of America: 1957 E St, NW, Washington, DC 20006-5107; tel. (202) 393-2040; fax (202) 347-4004; e-mail cinmaster@agc.org; internet www.agc.org; f. 1918; 33,000 mems; Exec. Vice-Pres. and CEO STEPHEN SANDHERR.

Associated Specialty Contractors: 3 Bethesda Metro Center, Suite 1100, Bethesda, MD 20814-5372; tel. (301) 657-3110; fax (310) 215-4500; f. 1950; 7 mem. asscns; Pres. DANIEL G. WALTER.

Building Stone Institute: POB 5047, White Plains, NY 10602-5047; tel. (914) 232-5725; fax (914) 232-5259; f. 1919; 400 mems; Exec. Vice-Pres. DOROTHY KENDER.

Construction Specifications Institute: 99 Canal Center Plaza, Suite 300, Alexandria, VA 22314; tel. (703) 706-4781; fax (703) 684-0465; e-mail csimail@csinet.org; internet www.csinet.org; f. 1948; 17,300 mems; Exec. Dir GREG BALESTRERO.

Mechanical Contractors Association of America, Inc: 1385 Piccard Dr., Rockville, MD 20850-4329; tel. (301) 869-5800; fax (301) 990-9690; e-mail postmaster@mcaa.org; internet www.mcaa.org; f. 1889; 1,400 mems; Exec. Vice-Pres. JOHN R. GENTILLE.

National Association of Home Builders of the US: 15th and M Sts, NW, Washington, DC 20005; tel. (202) 822-0200; f. 1942; 153,000 mems; Exec. Vice-Pres. KENT W. COLTON.

National Association of Plumbing-Heating-Cooling Contractors: 180 South Washington St, POB 6808, Falls Church, VA 22046; tel. (703) 237-8100; fax (703) 237-7442; e-mail naphcc@naphcc.org; internet www.naphcc.org; f. 1883; 5,100 mems; CEO ALLEN INLOW.

National Ready-Mixed Concrete Association: 900 Spring St, Silver Spring, MD 20910; tel. (301) 587-1400; fax (301) 585-4219; f. 1930; 1,000 mems; Pres. VINCENT P. AHEARN, Jr.

Tile Council of America Inc: 100 Clemson Research Blvd, Anderson, SC 29625; tel. (864) 646-8453; fax (864) 646-2821; e-mail literature@tileusa.com; internet www.tileusa.com; f. 1946; 85 mems; Exec. Dir ROBERT E. DANIELS.

Electricity
(see also Construction, Engineering and Machinery, and Trade and Industry—Utilities)

American Electronics Association: 5201 Great America Parkway, Suite 520, Santa Clara, CA 95054; tel. (408) 987-4200; fax (408) 970-8565; f. 1943; 3,000 mems; CEO and Pres. WILLIAM T. ARCHEY.

Edison Electric Institute: 701 Pennsylvania Ave, NW, Washington, DC 20004-2696; tel. (202) 508-5000; fax (202) 508-5360; f. 1933; mems: 208 investor-owned electric utility cos, 31 int. affiliates; Pres. THOMAS R. KUHN.

Electronic Industries Alliance: 2500 Wilson Blvd, Arlington, VA 22201-3834; tel. (703) 907-7500; fax (703) 907-7501; internet www.eia.org; f. 1924; over 2,100 mems; Pres. DAVE MCCURDY.

National Association of Electrical Distributors: 45 Danbury Rd, Wilton, CT 06897; tel. (203) 834-1908; fax (203) 834-1555; internet www.naed.org; f. 1908; 2,900 mems; Pres. RICHARD A. COLDRICK.

National Electrical Contractors Association: 3 Bethesda Metro Center, Suite 1100, Bethesda, MD 20814-5372; tel. (301) 657-3110; fax (301) 215-4500; internet www.necanet.org; f. 1901; 4,200 mems; Exec. Vice-Pres. and CEO JOHN M. GRAU.

National Electrical Manufacturers Association: 1300 North 17th St, Suite 1847, Rosslyn, VA 22209; tel. (703) 841-3200; fax (703) 841-5900; internet www.nema.org; f. 1926; 650 mems; Pres. MALCOLM E. O'HAGAN.

Engineering and Machinery
(see also Electricity and Construction)

Air-Conditioning and Refrigeration Institute: 4301 North Fair Dr., Suite 425, Arlington, VA 22203; tel. (703) 524-8800; fax (703) 528-3816; internet www.ari.org; f. 1953; 220 mems; Pres. CLIFFORD H. (TED) REES, Jr.

American Council of Engineering Companies: 1015 15th St, NW, Washington, DC 20005-2670; tel. (202) 347-7474; fax (202) 898-

0068; e-mail acec@acec.org; internet www.acec.org; f. 1973; 5,800 mem cos; Pres. DAVID A. RAYMOND.

American Institute of Chemical Engineers: 345 East 47th St, 11th Floor, New York, NY 10017-2395; tel. (212) 705-7338; fax (212) 705-8400; e-mail xpress@aiche.org; f. 1908; 58,000 mems; Exec. Dir GLENN TAYLOR.

American Institute of Mining, Metallurgical and Petroleum Engineers, Inc: 345 East 47th St, 14th Floor, New York, NY 10017-2330; tel. (212) 705-7695; f. 1871; four constituent socs representing 79,000 mems; Exec. Dir ROBERT H. MARCRUM.

American Railway Engineering Association: 50 F St, NW, Suite 7702, Washington, DC 20001; tel. (202) 639-2190; fax (202) 639-2183; f. 1899; 4,000 mems; Exec. Dir L. T. CERNY.

American Society of Civil Engineers: c/o Jane Howell, 1015 15th St, NW, Suite 600, Washington, DC 20005; tel. (703) 295-6000; fax (703) 295-6222; f. 1852; 120,000 mems; Exec. Dir JAMES E. DAVIS.

American Society of Heating, Refrigerating and Air Conditioning Engineers: 1791 Tullie Circle, NE, Atlanta, GA 30329; tel. (404) 636-8400; fax (404) 321-5478; e-mail ashrae@ashrae.org; internet www.ashrae.org; f. 1894; 58,000 mems; Sec. FRANK M. CODA.

American Society of Mechanical Engineers (ASME): 345 East 47th St, New York, NY 10017-2392; tel. (212) 705-7722; fax (212) 705-7675; f. 1880; 125,000 mems; Exec. Dir Dr DAVID BELDEN.

American Society of Naval Engineers Inc: 1452 Duke St, Alexandria, VA 22314-3458; tel. (703) 836-6727; fax (703) 836-7491; e-mail asnehq@navalengineers; internet www.navalengineers.org; f. 1888; 6,000 mems; Exec. Dir Capt. (retd) DENNIS K. KRUSE.

AMT (Association for Manufacturing Technology): 7901 Westpark Dr., McLean, VA 22102-4269; tel. (703) 893-2900; fax (703) 893-1151; e-mail amt@mfgtech.org; internet www.mfgtech.org; f. 1902; 370 mems; Pres. DON F. CARLSON.

ASME International (American Society of Mechanical Engineers): 3 Park Ave, New York, NY 10016-5990; tel. (212) 591-7000; fax (212) 882-1717; e-mail infocentrale@asme.org; f. 1880; 125,000 mems; Exec. Dir Dr DAVID BELDEN.

Engineering Foundation: 345 East 47th St, Suite 303, New York, NY 10017; tel. (212) 705-7837; fax (212) 705-7441; e-mail engfnd@aol.com; internet www.engfnd.org; f. 1914; Dir Dr CHARLES V. FREIMAN.

Institute of Electrical and Electronics Engineers: 445 Hoes Lane, Piscataway, NJ 08854-1331; tel. (732) 981-0060; fax (732) 981-9667; internet www.ieee.org; f. 1963; 366,000 mems; Exec. Dir DANIEL J. SENESE.

Manufacturers' Alliance for Productivity and Innovation: 1200 18th St, NW, Washington, DC 20036; tel. (202) 331-8430; fax (202) 331-7160; f. 1933; 500 companies; Pres. KENNETH McLENNAN.

Petroleum Equipment Institute: POB 2380, Tulsa, OK 74101; tel. (918) 494-9696; fax (918) 491-9895; e-mail info@pei.org; internet www.pei.org; f. 1951; 1,560 mems; Exec. Vice-Pres. ROBERT N. RENKES.

SAE (Society of Automotive Engineers), International: 400 Commonwealth Dr., Warrendale, PA 15096-0001; tel. (724) 776-4841; fax (724) 772-1851; internet www.sae.org; f. 1905; 75,000 mems; Exec. Vice-Pres. RAYMOND A. MORRIS.

Society of Naval Architects and Marine Engineers: 601 Pavonia Ave, Suite 400, Jersey City, NJ 07306-2907; tel. (201) 798-4800; fax (201) 798-4975; internet www.sname.org; f. 1893; 13,000 mems; Exec. Dir PHILIP KIMBALL.

Food

American Farm Bureau Federation: 225 West Touhy Ave, Park Ridge, IL 60068-4202; tel. (847) 685-8680; fax (847) 685-8896; internet www.fb.com; f. 1919; 3.3m. mems; Pres. BOB STALLMAN.

American Meat Institute: 1700 North Moore St, Suite 1600, Arlington, VA 22209; tel. (703) 841-2400; fax (703) 527-0938; f. 1906; 1,175 mems; Pres. J. PATRICK BOYLE.

Association of Sales & Marketing Companies: 2100 Reston Pkwy, Suite 400, Reston, VA 20191-1218; tel. (703) 758-7790; fax (703) 758-7787; e-mail info@asmc.org; internet www.asmc.org; f. 1904; 1,000 corporate and 40,000 individual mems; Pres. and CEO MARK W. BAUM.

DFA of California: 710 Striker Ave, Sacramento, CA 95834; tel. (916) 561-5900; fax (916) 561-5906; e-mail rnovy@dfaofca.com; f. 1908; 42 mems; Pres. RICHARD W. NOVY.

Distilled Spirits Council of the US, Inc (DISCUS): 1250 Eye St, NW, Suite 400, Washington, DC 20005; tel. (202) 628-3544; fax (202) 682-8888; internet www.discus.health.org; f. 1973; 14 active mems and 23 affiliates; Pres. and CEO Dr. PETER H. CRESSY.

Food Distributors International: 201 Park Washington Court, Falls Church, VA 22046; tel. (703) 532-9400; fax (703) 538-4673;

e-mail staff@fdi.org; internet www.fdi.org; f. 1906; 242 mems; Pres. JOHN R. BLOCK.

Food Marketing Institute: 655 15th St, NW, Suite 700, Washington, DC 20005; tel. (202) 452-8444; fax (202) 429-4519; e-mail fmi@fmi.org; internet www.fmi.org; f. 1977; 1,500 mems; Pres. TIMOTHY M. HAMMONDS.

Grocery Manufacturers of America, Inc: 1010 Wisconsin Ave, NW, Suite 900, Washington, DC 20007-3603; tel. (202) 337-9400; fax (202) 337-4508; internet www.gmabrands.com; f. 1908; 130 mems; Pres. and CEO C. MANLY MOLPUS.

Millers' National Federation: 600 Maryland Ave, SW, Suite 305-W, Washington, DC 20024; tel. (202) 484-2000; f. 1902; 44 mems, accounting for 90% of flour and milled grains produced in the USA; Pres. BETSY FAGA.

National Association of Wheat Growers: 412 Second St, NE, Suite 300, Washington, DC 20002; tel. (202) 547-7800; fax (202) 546-2638; e-mail wheatworld@wheatworld.org; internet www.wheatworld.org.

National Cattlemen's Beef Association: 5420 South Quebec St, Greenwood Village, CO 80111; tel. (303) 694-0305; internet www.beef.org; f. 1922; CEO CHUCK SCHROEDER.

National Confectioners Association of the US: 7900 Westpark Dr., Suite A-320, McLean, VA 22102-0000; tel. (703) 790-5750; fax (703) 790-5752; e-mail info@candyusa.org; internet www.candyusa.org; f. 1884; 340 mems; Pres. RICHARD T. O'CONNELL.

National Dairy Council: 10255 West Higgins Rd, Suite 900, Rosemount, IL 60018; tel. (847) 803-2000; fax (847) 803-2077; internet www.realbutter.com; f. 1915; 600 mems; Pres. M. F. BRINK.

National Farmers Organization: 2505 Elwood Dr., Ames, IA 50010-2000; tel. (515) 292-2000; fax (515) 292-7106; e-mail NFO@netins.net; internet www.nfo.org; f. 1955; Pres. EUGENE F. PAUL.

National Farmers Union: 11900 East Cornell Ave, Aurora, CO 80014-3194; tel. (303) 337-5500; fax (303) 368-1390; e-mail nfu@nfu.org; f. 1902; 300,000 mems; Pres. LELAND H. SWENSON.

National Grain Trade Council: 1300 L St, NW, Suite 925, Washington, DC 20005; tel. (202) 842-0400; fax (202) 789-7223; f. 1930; 64 mems; Pres. ROBERT PETERSEN.

National Grocers Association: 1005 N. Glebe Rd, Suite 250, Arlington, VA 22201; tel. (703) 516 0700; fax (703) 516 0115; internet www.nationalgrocers.org; f. 1982; 3,000 mems; Pres and CEO THOMAS K. ZAUCHA.

National Soft Drink Association: 1101 16th St, NW, Washington, DC 20036-4803; tel. (202) 463-6732; fax (202) 463-8178; f. 1919; 1,700 mems; Pres. WILLIAM L. BALL, III.

North American Millers' Association: 600 Maryland Ave, SW, Washington, DC 20024; tel. (202) 484-2200; fax (202) 488-7416; e-mail bfaga@mamamillers.org; internet www.namamillers.org; f. 1902; 44 mems, accounting for 90% of flour produced in the USA; Pres. BETSY FAGA.

United Fresh Fruit & Vegetable Association: 727 North Washington St, Alexandria, VA 22314; tel. (703) 836-3410; fax (703) 836-2049; e-mail united@uffva.org; internet www.uffva.org; f. 1904; c. 2,000 mems; Pres. and CEO THOMAS E. STENZEL.

US Dairy Export Council: 2300 Clarendon Blvd, Suite 306, Arlington, VA 22201; tel. (703) 528-3049; fax (703) 528-3705; f. 1995; 55 mems; Exec. Dir TOM SUBER.

Iron and Steel

American Hardware Manufacturers Association: 801 North Plaza Dr., Schaumburg, IL 60173-4977; tel. (847) 605-1025; fax (847) 605-1093; e-mail rarredia@ahma.org; internet www.ahma.org; f. 1901; 1,000 mems; Pres. and CEO WILLIAM P. FARRELL.

American Iron and Steel Institute: 1101 17th St, NW, Suite 1300, Washington, DC 20036-4700; tel. (202) 452-7100; fax (202) 463-6573; internet www.steel.org; f. 1908; 50 producer mems, 132 assoc. mems, 19 affiliated mems; Pres. and CEO ANDREW G. SHARKEY, III.

Steel Founders' Society of America (SFSA): Cast Metals Federation Bldg, 455 State St, Des Plaines, IL 60016; tel. (847) 299-9160; fax (847) 299-3105; e-mail monroe@scra.org; internet www.sfsa.org; f. 1902; 80 mems; Exec. Vice-Pres. RAYMOND W. MONROE.

Leather

Leather Apparel Association: 19 West 21st St, Suite 403, New York, NY 10010; tel. (212) 924-8895; fax (212) 727-1218; e-mail info@leatherassociation.com; internet www.leatherassociation.com; f. 1990; c. 100 mems; Dir LILI KASDAN.

Leather Industries of America: 1000 Thomas Jefferson St, NW, Suite 515, Washington, DC 20007-3835; tel. (202) 342-8086; fax (202) 342-9063; f. 1917; 250 mems; Pres. CHARLES S. MYERS.

Luggage and Leather Goods Manufacturers of America: 350 Fifth Ave, Suite 2624, New York, NY 10118-0110; tel. (212) 695-2340; fax (212) 643-8021; f. 1938; 240 mems; Exec. Vice-Pres. ROBERT K. ERMATINGER.

Lumber
(see also Paper)

American Forest and Paper Association: 1111 19th St, NW, Suite 700, Washington, DC 20036; tel. (202) 463-2700; fax (202) 463-2785; internet www.afandpa.org; f. 1932; 850 mems; Pres. REDD CARANEY.

APA–The Engineered Wood Association: POB 11700, Tacoma, WA 98411-0700; tel. (253) 565-6600; fax (253) 565-7265; internet www.apawood.org; 109 mems; Pres. D. L. ROGOWAY.

Forest Resources Association Inc: 600 Jefferson Plaza, Suite 350, Rockville, MD 20852-1150; tel. (301) 838-9385; fax (301) 838-9481; e-mail fra@forestresources.org; internet www.forestresources.org; f. 1934; 1,300 mems; Pres. R. LEWIS.

National Lumber and Building Material Dealers Association: 40 Ivy St, SE, Washington, DC 20003; tel. (202) 547-2230; f. 1915; 23 mems; Exec. Vice-Pres. HARLAN W. HUMMEL.

National Wooden Pallet and Container Association: 1800 North Kent St, Suite 911, Arlington, VA 22209-2109; tel. (703) 527-7667; fax (703) 527-7717; f. 1967; 687 mems; Pres. JOSEPH N. SCHOLNICK.

Southern Forest Products Association: POB 641700, Kenner, LA 70064; tel. (504) 443-4464; fax (504) 443-6612; f. 1915; 220 mems; Pres. KARL W. LINDBERG.

Western Forest Industries Association: 14780 SW Osprey Dr., Suite 270, Beaverton, OR 97007-8424; f. 1947; 125 mems; Pres. DAVID A. FORD.

Wood Products Manufacturers Association: 175 State Rd East, Westminster, MA 01473; tel. (978) 874-5445; fax (978) 874-9946; e-mail woodprod@wpma.org; f. 1929; 664 mems; Exec. Dir ALBERT J. BIBEAU.

Metals

Aluminum Association, Inc: 900 19th St, NW, Suite 300, Washington, DC 20006-2168; tel. (202) 862-5100; fax (202) 862-5164; internet www.aluminium.org; f. 1933; 53 mems; Pres. J. STEPHEN LARKIN.

ASM International: 9639 Kinsman, Materials Park, OH 44073; tel. (440) 338-5151; fax (440) 338-4634; e-mail cust-serv@po.asm-intl.org; internet www.asm-intl.org; f. 1920; 43,000 mems; Man. Dir Dr MICHAEL J. DETTAEMER.

Copper and Brass Fabricators Council Inc: 1050 17th St, NW, Suite 440, Washington, DC 20036; tel. (202) 833-8575; f. 1964; Pres. JOSEPH L. MAYER.

Copper Development Association Inc: 260 Madison Ave, New York, NY 10016; tel. (212) 251-7200; fax (212) 251-7234; e-mail staff@cda.copper.org; internet www.copper.org; f. 1963; 65 mems; Pres. ANDREW G. KIRETA, Sr.

Gold Institute: 1112 16th St, NW, Suite 240, Washington, DC 20036; tel. (202) 835-0185; fax (202) 835-0155; internet www.goldinstitute.com; f. 1976; 50 mems; Pres. JOHN H. LUTLEY.

Manufacturing Jewelers and Silversmiths of America, Inc: 1 State St, 6th Floor, Providence, RI 02908; tel. (401) 274-3840; fax (401) 274-0265; f. 1903; 1,800 mems; Pres. and CEO JAMES F. MARQUART.

Metal Powder Industries Federation: 105 College Rd East, 1st Floor, Princeton, NJ 08540-6692; tel. (609) 452-7700; fax (609) 987-8523; e-mail info@mpif.org; internet www.mpif.org/mpif/; f. 1944; 303 corporate mems; Exec. Dir DONALD G. WHITE.

Mining and Metallurgical Society of America: 476 Wilson Ave, Novato, CA 94947-4236; tel. (415) 897-1380; fax (415) 899-0262; e-mail akburton@worldnet.att.net; internet www.mmsa.net; f. 1908; 340 mems; Exec. ALAN K. BURTON.

National Mining Association: 1130 17th St, NW, Washington, DC 20036; tel. (202) 463-2625; fax (202) 463-6152; e-mail nma@planetcom.com; internet www.nma.org.

Silver Institute: 1112 16th St, NW, Suite 240, Washington, DC 20036; tel. (202) 835-0185; fax (202) 835-0155; e-mail info@silverinstitute.org; f. 1971; 53 mems; Exec. Dir PAUL BATEMAN.

Paper
(see also Lumber)

National Paper Box Association: 801 North Fairfax, Suite 211, Alexandria, VA 22314; tel. (703) 684-2212; fax (703) 683-6920; e-mail boxmaker@paperbox.org; internet www.paperbox.org.

National Paper Trade Association, Inc: 111 Great Neck Rd, Great Neck NY 11021; tel. (516) 829-3070; fax (516) 829-3074; e-mail info@60NPTA.com; internet www.60NPTA.com; f. 1903; 2,250 mems; Pres. JOHN J. BUCKLEY.

Paperboard Packaging Council: 888 17th St, NW, Suite 900, Washington, DC 20006; tel. (202) 289-4100; fax (202) 289-4243; f. 1964; Pres. JOHN A. MCINTYRE.

Petroleum and Fuel

American Association of Petroleum Landmen: 4100 Fossil Creek Blvd, Fort Worth, TX 76137-2791; tel. (817) 847-7700; fax (817) 847-7704; f. 1955; 8,500 mems; Exec. Vice-Pres. JACK E. DEETER.

American Gas Association: see Trade and Industry—Utilities.

American Gas Association: 1515 Wilson Blvd, Arlington, VA 22209; tel. (703) 841-8400; fax (703) 841-8406; internet www.aga.com; f. 1918; 350 assoc. mems; Pres. MICHAEL BALY, III.

American Petroleum Institute: 1220 L St NW, Washington, DC 20005; tel. (202) 682-8000; fax (202) 682-8232; internet www.api.org; f. 1919; 400 corporate mems; Chair. H. LAWRENCE FULLER; Pres. RED CAVANEY.

Coal Exporters' Association of the US, Inc: 1130 17th St, NW, Washington, DC 20036; tel. (202) 463-2639; fax (202) 833-9636; e-mail cea@nma.org; f. 1945; 35 mems; Exec. Dir MOYA PHELLEPS.

Independent Petroleum Association of America: 1101 16th St, NW, Washington, DC 20036; tel. (201) 857-4722; fax (202) 857-4799; internet www.ipaa.org; f. 1929; 6,000 mems; Pres. DENISE A. BODE.

National Mining Association: 1130 17th St, NW, Washington, DC 20036; tel. (202) 463-2625; fax (202) 463-6152; e-mail nma@planetcom.com; internet www.nma.org; f. 1995; by merger; 395 mems; Pres. JACK N. GERARD.

National Petrochemical and Refiners Association: 1899 L St, NW, Suite 1000, Washington, DC 20036; tel. (202) 457-0480; fax (202) 457-0486; e-mail npra1@cais.com; internet www.hpradc.org; f. 1902; 420 mems; Pres. URVAN R. STERNFELS.

Petroleum Marketers Association of America: 1901 North Fort Myer Dr., Suite 1200, Arlington, VA 22209; tel. (703) 351-8000; fax (703) 351-9160; e-mail info@pmaa.org; internet www.pmaa.org.

Western States Petroleum Association: 505 North Brand Blvd, Suite 1400, Glendale, CA 91203-1925; tel. (818) 545-4105; fax (818) 545-0954; f. 1907; 60 mems; Exec. Dir DOUGLAS F. HENDERSON.

Printing and Publishing
(see also Publishers)

Association for the Suppliers of Printing and Publishing Technologies: 1899 Preston White Dr., Reston, VA 22091-4367; tel. (703) 264-7200; fax (703) 620-0994; e-mail mhurley@npes.org; internet www.npes.org; 315 mems; Pres. REGIS J. DELMONTAGNE.

Binding Industries Association International: 70 East Lake St, Suite 300, Chicago, IL 60601-5907; tel. (312) 372-7606; fax (312) 704-5025; e-mail bia1@ixnetcom.com; internet www.bindingindustries.org; f. 1955; 340 mems; Exec. Dir DON DUNHAM.

National Association of Printers & Lithographers: 780 Palisade Ave, Teaneck, NJ 07666-3129; tel. (201) 342-7000; fax (201) 692-0286; 3,700 mems; Pres. I. GREGG VAN WERT.

Printing Industries of America, Inc: 100 Daingerfield Rd, Alexandria, VA 22314; tel. (703) 519-8100; fax (703) 548-3227; f. 1887; 13,000 mems; Pres. MICHAEL MAKIN.

Public Utilities
(See also Trade and Industry—Utilities)

American Public Works Association: 2345 Grand Blvd, Suite 500, Kansas City, MO 64108-2641; tel. (816) 472-6100; fax (816) 472-1610; e-mail apwa@apwa.net; f. 1894; 27,000 mems; Exec. Dir PETER B. KING.

Rubber

Rubber Manufacturers Association: 1400 K St, NW, Suite 900, Washington, DC 20005-2043; tel. (202) 682-4800; fax (202) 682-4854; f. 1915; 130 mems; Pres. and CEO DONALD B. SHEA.

Rubber Trade Association of North America, Inc: 220 Maple Ave, POB 196, Rockville Centre, NY 11571-0196; tel. (516) 536-7228; fax (516) 536-2251; f. 1914; 39 mems; Sec. F. B. FINLEY.

Stone, Clay and Glass Products

Glass Association of North America: 2045 SW Wanamaker Dr., Suite A, Topeka, KS 66614-5321; tel. (785) 271-0208; fax (785) 271-0166; e-mail stan@glasswebsite.com; internet www.glasswebsite.com/gana; f. 1949; 130 mems; Exec. Vice-Pres. STANLEY L. SMITH.

National Aggregates Association: 900 Spring St, Silver Spring, MD 20910; tel. (301) 587-1400; fax (301) 585-4219; f. 1911; 500 mems; Exec. Vice-Pres. CRAIG G. THIBAUDEAU.

National Glass Association: 8200 Greensboro Dr., Suite 302, McLean, VA 22102-3881; tel. (703) 442-4890; fax (703) 442-0630; f. 1948; 4,400 mems. Pres. and CEO PHILIP J. JAMES.

National Stone, Sand and Gravel Association: 2101 Wilson Blvd, Suite 100, Arlington, VA 22201; tel. (703) 525-8788; fax (703) 525-7782; internet www.nssga.org; f. 2000; by merger of National Aggregates Asscn and National Stone Asscn; 950 mems; Pres. and CEO JENNIFER JOY WILSON.

Textiles

American Apparel Manufacturers Association: 2500 Wilson Blvd, Suite 301, Arlington, VA 22201; tel. (703) 524-1864; fax (703) 522-6741; f. 1962; 815 mems; Pres. LARRY K. MARTIN.

American Fiber Manufacturers Association Inc: 1530 Wilson Blvd, NW, Suite 390, Washington, DC 20036; tel. (703) 875–1032; fax (703) 875–0907; e-mail oday@afma.org; internet www.fibersource.com; 17 mems; Pres. PAUL T. O'DAY.

Apparel Retailers of America: 325 Seventh St, Suite 1000, NW, Washington, DC 20004-2801; tel. (202) 347-1932; fax (202) 457-0386; f. 1916; 1,200 mems; Exec. Dir DOUGLAS W. WIEGAND.

Knitted Textile Association: 386 Park Ave South, Suite 901, New York, NY 10016; tel. (212) 689-3807; fax (212) 889-6160; e-mail kta386@aol.com; f. 1965; 140 mems; Exec. Dir PETER ADELMAN.

Knitwear Employers Association: 75 Livingston St, Brooklyn, NY 11201; tel. (718) 875-2300; fax (718) 875-1598; f. 1959; 40 mems.

National Knitwear and Sportswear Association: 386 Park Ave South, New York, NY 10016; tel. (212) 683-7520; fax (212) 532-0766; f. 1918; 600 mems; Exec. Dir SETH M. BODNER.

Northern Textile Association: 230 Congress St, Boston, MA 02110; tel. (617) 542-8220; fax (617) 542-2199; e-mail textilenta@aol.com; f. 1854; 300 mems; Pres. KARL SPILHAUS.

United Infants' and Children's Wear Association Inc: 1430 Broadway, Suite 1603, New York, NY 10018; tel. (212) 244-2953; f. 1933; 50 mems; Pres. ALAN D. LUBELL.

Tobacco

Tobacco Associates: 1725 K St, NW, Suite 512, Washington, DC 20006; tel. (202) 828-9144; fax (202) 828-9149; e-mail taw@tobaccoassociatesinc.org; internet www.tobaccoassociatesinc.org; f. 1947; Pres. C. N. WAYNE, Jr.

Tobacco Merchants Association of the United States: POB 8019, Princeton, NJ 08543-8019; tel. (609) 275-4900; fax (609) 275-8379; f. 1915; 130 mems; Pres. FARRELL DELMAN.

Transport

Aerospace Industries Association of America, Inc: 1250 Eye St, NW, Suite 1200, Washington, DC 20005; tel. (202) 371-8400; fax (202) 371-8470; internet www.aia-aerospace.org/; f. 1919; 50 mems; Pres. DON FUQUA.

Air Transport Association of America: see Civil Aviation—Association.

American Bureau of Shipping: see Ocean Shipping—Associations.

American Bus Association: 1100 New York Ave, NW, Suite 1050, Washington, DC 20005-2934; tel. (202) 842-1645; fax (202) 842-0850; e-mail abainfo@buses.org; internet www.buses.org; f. 1926; 3,000 mems; Pres. and CEO PETER J. PANTUSO.

American Institute of Merchant Shipping: see Ocean Shipping—Associations.

American Public Transportation Association: 1201 New York Ave, NW, Suite 400, Washington, DC 20005-6141; tel. (202) 898-4000; fax (202) 898-4070; e-mail info@apta.com; internet www.apta.com; f. 1974; 1,200 mems; Pres. WILLIAM W. MILLAR.

American Short Line Railroad Association: see Principal Railways—Associations.

American Trucking Associations: 2200 Mill Rd, Alexandria, VA 22314-4654; tel. (703) 838-1955; fax (703) 684-5751; e-mail membership@trucking.org; internet www.truckline.com; f. 1933; 3,000 mems; Pres. and CEO WALTER B. McCORMICK, Jr.

Association of American Railroads: see Principal Railways—Associations.

Independent Truck Owner/Operator Association: POB 621, Stoughton, MA 02072; tel. (617) 828-7200; fax (617) 828-6606; f. 1981; 10,000 mems; Pres. MARSHALL SIEGEL.

National Automobile Dealers Association: 8400 Westpark Dr., McLean, VA 22102-3522; tel. (703) 827-7407; fax (703) 821-7075; e-mail nada@nadanet.com; internet www.nadanet.com; f. 1917; 19,500 mems; Pres. PHILLIP D. BRADY.

Shipbuilders Council of America: 4301 North Fairfax Dr., Suite 330, Arlington, VA 22203; tel. (703) 276-1700; fax (703) 276-1707; f. 1921; 70 mems; Pres. JOHN J. STOCKER.

Miscellaneous

American Advertising Federation: 1101 Vermont Ave, NW, Suite 500, Washington, DC 20005; tel. (202) 898-0089; fax (202) 898-0159; e-mail aaf@aaf.org; internet www.aaf.org; f. 1967; 48,000 mems; Pres. and CEO WALLY SNYDER.

American Association of Exporters and Importers: 11 West 42nd St, 30th Floor, New York, NY 10036-8002; tel. (212) 944-2230; fax (212) 382-2606; f. 1921; 1,200 mems; Pres. EUGENE J. MILOSH.

American Marketing Association: 250 South Wacker Dr., Suite 200, Chicago, IL 60606-5834; tel. (312) 648-0536; fax (312) 993-7542; internet www.ama.org; f. 1915; 53,000 mems; CEO DENNIS JORGENSEN.

American Society of Association Executives: 1575 Eye St, NW, Washington, DC 20005-1103; tel. (202) 626-2723; fax (202) 371-8825; e-mail info@asaenet.org; internet www.asaenet.org; f. 1920; 25,000 mems; Pres.and CEO MICHAEL S. OLSON.

Institute for Supply Management: 2055 East Centennial Circle, POB 22160, Tempe, AZ 85285-2160; tel. (408) 752-6276; fax (408) 752-7890; internet www.ism.ws; f. 1915; 49,000 mems; CEO PAUL NOVAK.

Motion Picture Association of America, Inc: 1600 Eye St, NW, Washington, DC 20006; tel. (202) 293-1966; fax (202) 293-7674; e-mail pegge@mpaa.org; internet www.mpaa.org; f. 1922; 7 mems; Pres. JACK J. VALENTI.

National Association of Manufacturers: 1331 Pennsylvania Ave, NW, Suite 600, Washington, DC 20004-1790; tel. (202) 637-3000; fax (202) 637-3182; f. 1895; 14,000 mems; Pres. JERRY J. JASINOWSKI.

National Association of Realtors: 430 North Michigan Ave, Suite 500, Chicago, IL 60611-4087; tel. (312) 329-8200; fax (312) 329-8576; f. 1908; 750,000 mems; Exec. Vice-Pres. ALMON R. SMITH.

National Cooperative Business Association: 1401 New York Ave, NW, Suite 1100, Washington, DC 20005-2160; tel. (202) 638-6222; fax (202) 638-1374; e-mail ncba@ncba.org; internet www.ncba.org; f. 1916; 350 mems; Pres. and CEO PAUL HAZEN.

National Retail Federation: 325 7th St, NW, Suite 1000, Washington, DC 20004-2802; tel. (202) 783-7941; fax (202) 737-2849; internet www.nrf.com; f. 1911; 55,000 mems; Pres. TRACY MULLIN.

UTILITIES

Electricity

American Electric Power (AEP): 1 Riverside Plaza, Columbus, OH 43215-2373; tel. (614) 223-1000; internet www.aep.com; f. 1906 as the American Gas and Electricity Co., present name adopted 1958; electricity supplier to Arkansas, Indiana, Kentucky, Louisiana, Michigan, Ohio, Oklahoma, Tennessee, Texas, Virginia and West Virginia; Chair., Pres. and CEO E LINN DRAPER, Jr.

American Public Power Association: 2301 M St, NW, 3rd Floor, Washington, DC 20037-1484; tel. (202) 467-2900; fax (202) 467-2910; internet www.appanet.org; f. 1940; 1,750 mems; Exec. Dir ALAN H. RICHARDSON.

Association of Edison Illuminating Companies: 6000 North 18th St, POB 2641, Birmingham, AL 35291-0992; tel. (205) 250-2530; fax (205) 250-2540; f. 1885; mems comprise 78 investor-owned public utilities; Exec. Dir W. O. WHITT.

Edison Electric Institute: 701 Pennsylvania Ave, NW, Washington, DC 2004-2696; tel. (202) 508-5000; fax (202) 508-5794; internet www.eei.org; f. 1933; mems comprise 190 investor-owned electric utility cos in the USA and 26 foreign mems; Pres. THOMAS R. KUHN.

Electrification Council: 701 Pennsylvania Ave, NW, Washington, DC 20004; tel. (202) 508-5900; fax (202) 508-5335; f. 1951; electricity industry trade partnership; 50 mems; Man. STEVEN KOEP.

Energy Telecommunications and Electrical Association: POB 79, 5038, Dallas, TX 75379; tel. (214) 235-0655; fax (214) 235-0653; f. 1928; 170 mems; Exec. Man. MARTHA G. FIKE.

National Rural Electric Co-operative Association: 4301 Wilson Blvd, Arlington, VA 22203; tel. (703) 907-5500; fax (703) 907-5528; e-mail nreca@nreca.org; internet www.nreca.org; f. 1942; rural electric co-operative systems, public power, and public utility distribution in 46 states; 1,000 mems; Exec. Vice-Pres. BOB BERGLAND.

Gas

American Gas Association: 1515 Wilson Blvd, Arlington, VA 22209; tel. (703) 841-8400; fax (703) 841-8406; internet www.aga.com; f. 1918; 350 assoc. mems; Pres. MICHAEL BALY, III.

American Public Gas Association: 11094DLee Hwy, Suite 102, Fairfax, VA 22030; tel. (703) 352-3890; fax (703) 352-1271; f. 1961; promotes efficiency among public gas systems; 430 mems; Exec. Dir ROBERT S. CAVE.

Gas Research Institute: 8600 West Bryn Mawr Ave, Chicago, IL 60631; tel. (312) 399-8100; fax (312) 399-8170; internet www.gri.org; f. 1976; 255 mems; Pres. and CEO STEPHEN D. BAN.

Natural Gas Supply Association: 805 15th St, NW, Suite 510, Washington, DC 20005-2207; tel. (202) 331-8900; internet www.ngsa.org; f. 1967; monitors legislation and economic issues affecting natural-gas producers; Pres. R. SKIP HORVATH.

Water

American Water Works Association: 6666 West Quincy Ave, Denver, CO 80235-3098; tel. (303) 794-7711; fax (303) 794-7310; internet www.awwa.org; f. 1881; 54,000 mems; Exec. Dir JACK W. HOFFBUHR.

Association of Metropolitan Water Agencies: 1717 K St, NW, Suite 1102, Washington, DC 20036; tel. (202) 331-2820; fax (202) 842-0621; f. 1981; 63 mems; Exec. Dir DIANE VAN DE HEI.

National Association of Water Companies: 1725 K St, NW, Suite 1212, Washington, DC 20006; tel. (202) 833-8383; fax (202) 331-7442; internet www.nawc.org; f. 1895; privately- and commercially-owned water cos, and individuals; 500 mems; Exec. Dir PETER COOK.

National Rural Water Association: POB 1428, Duncan, OK 73534; tel. (405) 252-0629; fax (405) 255-4476; e-mail NRWAinfo@NRWA.org; internet www.cais.com/nrwainfo.

TRADE UNIONS

In 1999 there were approximately 16.5m. union members in the USA, representing 13.9% of the civilian labour force.

Many trade unions based in the USA have members throughout North America. More than 29% of Canada's trade union members belong to unions having headquarters in the USA.

American Federation of Labor and Congress of Industrial Organizations (AFL-CIO): 815 16th St, NW, Washington, DC 20006; tel. (202) 637-5000; fax (202) 637-5058; internet www.aflcio.org; f. 1955; Pres. JOHN J. SWEENEY; Sec.-Treas. RICHARD L. TRUMKA; 68 affiliated unions with total membership of 13.1m. (1999).

AFL-CIO Affiliates
(with 50,000 members and over)

Aluminum, Brick and Glass Workers International Union: 3362 Hollenberg Dr., Bridgeton, MO 63044; tel. (314) 739-6142; fax (314) 739-1216; f. 1982; 51,800 mems; Pres. ERNIE J. LaBAFF.

Amalgamated Clothing and Textile Workers' Union: 15 Union Sq. West, New York, NY 10003; tel. (212) 242-0700; fax (212) 255-7230; f. 1976; 273,000 mems; Pres. JACK SHEINKMAN; Sec.-Treas. ARTHUR L. LOEVY.

Amalgamated Transit Union: 5025 Wisconsin Ave, NW, Washington, DC 20016; tel. (202) 537-1645; fax (202) 244-7824; f. 1892; 165,000 mems; Int. Pres. JOHN W. ROWLAND.

American Federation of Government Employees: 80 F St, NW, Washington, DC 20001; tel. (202) 639-6419; fax (202) 639-6441; f. 1932; 210,000 mems; Nat. Pres. BOBBY L. HARNAGE.

American Federation of Musicians of the United States and Canada: Paramount Bldg, Suite 600, 1501 Broadway, New York, NY 10036; tel. (212) 869-1330; fax (212) 764-6134; internet www.afm.org; f. 1896; 120,000 mems; Pres. THOMAS F. LEE; Sec.-Treas. FLORENCE NELSON.

American Federation of State, County and Municipal Employees: 1625 L St, NW, Washington, DC 20036; tel. (202) 429-1000; fax (202) 429-1293; f. 1936; 1.3m. mems; Pres. GERALD W. McENTEE; Sec.-Treas. WILLIAM LUCY.

American Federation of Teachers: 555 New Jersey Ave, NW, Washington, DC 20001; tel. (202) 879-4400; fax (202) 879-4545; f.

1916; 800,000 mems; Pres. ALBERT SHANKER; Sec.-Treas. EDWARD J. McELROY.

American Federation of Television and Radio Artists: 260 Madison Ave, 7th Floor, New York, NY 10016-2401; tel. (212) 532-0800; fax (212) 921-8454; f. 1937; 80,000 mems; Exec. Dir BRUCE A. YORK.

American Postal Workers' Union: 1300 L St, NW, Washington, DC 20005; tel. (202) 842-4200; fax (202) 842-4297; f. 1971; 320,000 mems; Pres. MORRIS BILLER.

Associated Actors and Artistes of America: 165 46th St West, New York, NY 10036; tel. (212) 869-0358; fax (212) 869-1746; f. 1919; 7 nat. unions representing 125,000 mems; Pres. THEODORE BIKEL.

Automobile, Aerospace and Agricultural Implement Workers of America, United: 8000 East Jefferson Ave, Detroit, MI 48214; tel. (313) 926-5000; fax (313) 823-6016; internet www.uaw.org; f. 1935; Pres. STEPHEN P. YOKICH; Sec.-Treas. RUBEN BURKS; 1.3m. mems (1999).

Bakery, Confectionery, Tobacco Workers' and Grain Millers International Union: 10401 Connecticut Ave, Kensington, MD 20895; tel. (301) 933-8600; fax (301) 946-8452; f. 1886; Pres. FRANK HURT; Sec.-Treas. DAVID B. DURKEE; 125,000 mems (1999).

Boilermakers, Iron Ship Builders, Blacksmiths, Forgers and Helpers, International Brotherhood of: 753 State Ave, Suite 570, Kansas City, KS 66101; tel. (913) 371-2640; fax (913) 281-8101; e-mail pamd@boilermakers.org; f. 1880; Pres. CHARLES W. JONES; Sec.-Treas. JERRY Z. WILLBURN; 80,000 mems (1999).

Bricklayers and Allied Craftsmen, International Union of: 815 15th St, NW, Washington, DC 20005; tel. (202) 783-3788; fax (202) 393-0219; f. 1865; Pres. JOHN J. FLYNN; Sec.-Treas. L. GERALD CARLISLE; 100,000 mems (1999).

Bridge, Structural, Ornamental and Reinforcing Iron Workers, International Association of: 1750 New York Ave, NW, Suite 400, Washington, DC 20006; tel. (202) 383-4810; fax (202) 638-4856; f. 1896; Pres. JAKE WEST; Gen. Sec. LEROY E. WORLEY; 120,000 mems (1997).

Carpenters and Joiners of America, United Brotherhood of: 101 Constitution Ave, NW, Washington, DC 20001; tel. (202) 546-6206; fax (202) 543-5724; f. 1881; Pres. DOUGLAS J. McCARRON; Sec.-Treas. DOUG BANES; 509,000 mems (1999).

Communications Workers of America: 501 Third St, NW, Washington, DC 20001; tel. (202) 434-1100; fax (202) 434-1279; e-mail cwa@capcon.net; internet www.cwa-union.org/home; f. 1939; Pres. MORTON BAHR; Sec.-Treas. BARBARA J. EASTERLING; 630,000 mems (1999).

Electrical Workers, International Brotherhood of: 1125 15th St, NW, Washington, DC 20005; tel. (202) 833-7000; fax (202) 467-6316; e-mail journalmedia@compuserve.com; f. 1891; Pres. J. J. BARRY; Sec.-Treas. EDWIN D. HILL; 750,000 mems (1999).

Electronic, Electrical, Salaried, Machine and Furniture Workers, International Union of (IUE): 1126 16th St, NW, Washington, DC 20036; tel. (202) 785-7200; fax (202) 785-4563; f. 1949; Pres. EDWARD FIRE; Sec.-Treas. THOMAS REBMAN; 120,000 mems (1999).

Fire Fighters, International Association of: 1750 New York Ave, NW, 3rd Floor, Washington, DC 20006-5395; tel. (202) 737-8484; fax (202) 737-8418; f. 1918; Pres. ALFRED K. WHITEHEAD; Sec.-Treas. VINCENT J. BOLLON; 250,000 mems (1999).

United Food and Commercial Workers International Union: 1775 K St, NW, Washington, DC 20006; tel. (202) 223-3111; fax (202) 466-1562; internet www.ufcw.org; f. 1979; Int. Pres. DOUGLAS H. DORITY; Int. Sec.-Treas. JOSEPH T. HANSEN; 1.4m. mems (1999).

Glass Molders, Pottery, Plastics & Allied Workers International Union, AFL-CIO, CLC: 608 East Baltimore Pike, POB 607, Media, PA 19063; tel. (610) 565-5051; fax (610) 565-0983; f. 1842; Pres. JAMES H. RANKIN; Sec.-Treas. JOSEPH MITCHELL, Sr; 68,000 mems (1999).

Government Employees, American Federation of: 80 F St, NW, Washington, DC, 20001; tel. (202) 737-8700; fax (202) 639-6441; e-mail communications@afge.org; internet www.afge.org; f. 1932; Nat. Pres. BOBBY L. HARNAGE, Sr; Nat. Sec.-Treas JIM DAVIS; 200,000 mems (2000).

Graphic Communications International Union: 1900 L St, NW, Washington, DC 20036; tel. (202) 462-1400; fax (202) 721-0600; internet www.gciu.org; f. 1983; Pres. GEORGE TEDESCHI; Sec.-Treas. GERALD DENEAU; 125,000 mems (2003).

Hotel Employees & Restaurant Employees International Union: 1219 28th St, NW, Washington, DC 20007; tel. (202) 393-4373; fax (202) 333-0468; f. 1891; Pres. JOHN W. WILHELM; Sec.-Treas. TED HANSEN; 350,000 mems (1999).

International Association of Fire Fighters: 1750 New York Ave, NW, Washington, DC 20006-5395; tel. (202) 737-8484; f. 1918; 195,000 mems; Pres. ALFRED K. WHITEHEAD; Sec.-Treas. VINCENT J. BOLLON.

International Longshoremen's Association: 17 Battery Pl., Rm 1530, New York, NY 10004; tel. (212) 425-1200; fax (212) 425-2928; f. 1892; Pres. JOHN BOWERS; Sec.-Treas. HARRY R. HASSELGREN; 65,000 mems (1999).

International Union of Painters and Allied Trades: 1750 New York Ave, NW, Washington, DC 20006; tel. (202) 637-0700; f. 1887; Gen. Pres. MICHAEL E. MONROE; Sec.-Treas. JAMES A. WILLIAMS.

International Union of Electronic, Electrical, Salaried, Machine and Furniture Workers (IUE): 1275 K St, NW, Suite 600, Washington, DC 20005; tel. (202) 513 6357; fax (202) 513 6357; f. 1949; 125,000 mems. Pres. EDWARD FIRE.

Laborers' International Union of North America: 905 16th St, NW, Washington, DC 20006; tel. (202) 737-8320; fax (202) 737-2754; f. 1903; Pres. TERENCE M. O'SULLIVAN; Gen. Sec.-Treas. ARMAND E. SABATONI; 820,000 mems (1999).

Letter Carriers, National Association of: 100 Indiana Ave, NW, Washington, DC 20001; tel. (202) 393-4695; fax (202) 737-1540; e-mail nalcinf@access.digex.net; internet www.nalc.org; f. 1889; Pres. VINCENT R. SOMBROTTO; Sec.-Treas. WILLIAM R. YATES; 315,000 mems (2000).

Machinists and Aerospace Workers, International Association of: 9000 Machinists Pl., Upper Marboro, MD 20772; tel. (301) 967-4500; fax (301) 967-4588; internet www.iamaw.org; f. 1888; Int. Pres. R. THOMAS BUFFENBARGER; Gen. Sec.-Treas. DONALD WHARTON; 780,000 mems (1999).

Maintenance of Way Employees, Brotherhood of: 26555 Evergreen Rd, Suite 200, Southfield, MI 48076-4225; tel. (248) 948-1010; fax (248) 948-7150; f. 1887; Pres. MAC A. FLEMING; Sec.-Treas. WILLIAM E. LaRUE; 50,000 mems (1999).

Marine Engineers' Beneficial Association: 444 North Capitol St, NW, Suite 800, Washington, DC 20001; tel. (202) 638-5355; fax (202) 638-5369; e-mail mebahq@d1meba.org; f. 1988; 50,000 mems; Pres. C. E. DeFRIES.

United Mine Workers of America, International Union: 900 15th St, NW, Washington, DC 20005; tel. (202) 842-7200; fax (202) 842-7227; internet www.access.digex.net/~miner; f. 1890; Int. Pres. CECIL ROBERTS; Sec.-Treas. JERRY D. JONES; 130,000 mems (1999).

Musicians of the United States and Canada, American Federation of: 1501 Broadway, Suite 600, New York, NY 10036; tel. (212) 869-1330; fax (212) 764-6134; e-mail info@afm.org; internet www.afm.org; f. 1896; Pres. STEVE YOUNG; Sec.-Treas. THOMAS LEE; 125,000 mems (1999).

Needletrades, Industrial, and Textile Employees, AFL–CIO, United: 1710 Broadway, New York, NY 10019-5299; tel. (212) 265-7000; fax (212) 265-3415; e-mail jmortzzz@aol.org; internet www.uniteunion.org; f. 1900; Pres. JAY MAZUR; 250,000 mems (1999).

Office and Professional Employees International Union: 265 West 14th St, Suite 610, New York, NY 10011; tel. (212) 675-3210; fax (212) 727-3466; f. 1945; Int. Pres. MICHAEL GOODWIN; Sec.-Treas. GILLES BEAUREGARD; 130,000 mems (1999).

Operating Engineers, International Union of: 1125 17th St, NW, Washington, DC 20036; tel. (202) 429-9100; fax (202) 778-2616; f. 1896; Gen. Pres. FRANK HANLEY; 360,000 mems (1999).

PACE International Union: POB 1475, Nashville, TN 37202; tel. (615) 834-8590; fax (615) 831-6791; internet www.paceunion.org; f. 1999 by merger of United Paperworkers' International Union and Oil, Chemical and Atomic Workers' International Union; Pres. BOYD YOUNG; Sec.-Treas. JAMES DUNN; 320,000 mems (1999).

Painters and Allied Trades, International Union of: 1750 New York Ave, NW, 8th Floor, Washington, DC 20006; tel. (202) 637-0700; fax (202) 637-0771; f. 1887; Gen. Pres. MICHAEL E. MONROE; Gen. Sec.-Treas. JAMES A. WILLIAMS; 133,000 mems (2000).

Journeymen and Apprentices of the Plumbing and Pipe Fitting Industry of the United States and Canada, United Association of: 901 Massachusetts Ave, NW, Washington, DC 20001; tel. (202) 628-5823; fax (202) 628-5024; internet www.ua.org; f. 1889; Pres. MARTIN J. MADDALONI; Sec.-Treas. MARION A. LEE; 304,000 mems (1999).

International Union of Police Associations: 1421 Prince St, Suite 330, Alexandria, VA 22314; tel. (703) 549-7473; fax (703) 683-9048; Pres. SAM A. CABRAL; 50,000 mems (1999).

Postal Workers Union, American: 1300 L St, NW, Washington, DC 20005; tel. (202) 842-4200; fax (202) 842-4297; internet www.apwu.org; f. 1971; Pres. MORRIS BILLER; Sec.-Treas. DOUGLAS C. HOLBROOK; 350,000 mems (1999).

Retail, Wholesale and Department Store Union: 30 East 29th St, New York, NY 10016; tel. (212) 684-5300; fax (212) 779-2809; internet www.atbs.com/rwdsu.html; f. 1937; Pres. STUART APPELBAUM; Sec.-Treas. CHARLIE N. HALL, Sr; 100,000 mems (1997).

Screen Actors Guild: 5757 Wilshire Blvd, Los Angeles, CA 90036; tel. (323) 954-1600; fax (323) 549-6656; internet www.sag.org; f. 1933; Pres. MELISSA GILBERT; Nat. Exec. Dir and CEO A. ROBERT PISANO; 98,000 mems (March 2002).

Seafarers International Union of North America: 5201 Auth Way, Camp Springs, MD 20746; tel. (301) 899-0675; fax (301) 899-7355; f. 1938; Pres. MICHAEL SACCO; Sec.-Treas. JOHN FAY; 85,000 mems (1999).

Service Employees' International Union (SEIU): 1313 L St, NW, Washington, DC 20005; tel. (202) 898-3200; fax (202) 898-3304; internet www.seiu.org; f. 1921; Pres. ANDREW L. STERN; Sec.-Treas. BETTY BEDNARCZYK; 1.3m. mems (1999).

Sheet Metal Workers' International Association: 1750 New York Ave, NW, Washington, DC 20006; tel. (202) 783-5880; fax (202) 662-0894; e-mail smwia@compuserve.com; internet www.smwia.org; f. 1888; Gen. Pres. MICHAEL J. SULLIVAN; Sec.-Treas. TED ZLOTOPOLSKI; 150,000 mems (1999).

State, County and Municipal Employees, American Federation of: 1625 L St, NW, Washington, DC 20036; tel. (202) 452-4800; fax (202) 429-1293; internet www.afscme.org; f. 1936; Pres. GERALD W. McENTEE; Sec.-Treas. WILLIAM LUCY; 1.3m. mems (1999).

United Steelworkers of America: 5 Gateway Center, Rm 802, Pittsburgh, PA 15222; tel. (412) 562-2400; fax (412) 562-2445; internet www.uswa.org; f. 1936; Int. Pres. GEORGE BECKER; Int. Sec.-Treas. LEO GERARD; 700,000 mems (1999).

Teachers, American Federation of: 555 New Jersey Ave, NW, Washington, DC 20001; tel. (202) 879-4400; fax (202) 879-4556; internet www.aft.org; f. 1916; Pres. SANDRA FELDMAN; Sec.-Treas. EDWARD J. McELROY; 1.0m. mems (1999).

Teamsters, International Brotherhood of: 25 Louisiana Ave, NW, Washington, DC 20001; tel. (202) 624-6800; fax (202) 624-6918; internet www.teamster.org; f. 1903; Pres. JAMES P. HOFFA; Gen. Sec.-Treas. TOM KEEGAL; 1.4m. mems (1999).

Television and Radio Artists, American Federation of: 260 Madison Ave, 7th Floor, New York, NY 10016-2401; tel. (212) 532-0800; fax (212) 545-1238; e-mail nyfilm@ios.com; internet www.ios.com/~nyfilm/union/aftra.html; f. 1937; Pres. SHELBY SCOTT; 75,000 mems (1999).

Theatrical Stage Employees, Moving Picture Technicians, Artists and Allied Crafts of the US, its Territories and Canada, International Alliance of: 1515 Broadway, Suite 601, New York, NY 10036; tel. (212) 730-1770; fax (212) 921-7699; internet www.iatse.lm.com; f. 1893; Int. Pres. THOMAS C. SHORT; Gen. Sec.-Treas. MICHAEL W. PROSCIA; 100,000 mems (2000).

Amalgamated Transit Union: 5025 Wisconsin Ave, NW, Washington, DC 20016; tel. (202) 537-1645; fax (202) 244-7824; f. 1892; Int. Pres. JAMES LaSALA; 165,000 mems (1999).

Transport Workers Union International: 80 West End Ave, 5th Floor, New York, NY 10023; tel. (212) 873-6000; fax (212) 721-1431; e-mail twu@twu.com; internet www.twu.com; f. 1934; Int. Pres. SONNY HALL; Sec.-Treas. GEORGE LEITZ; 125,000 mems (1999).

Transportation-Communications International Union: 3 Research Pl., Rockville, MD 20850; tel. (301) 948-4910; fax (301) 948-1369; f. 1899; Pres. ROBERT A. SCARDELLETTI; Sec.-Treas. L.E. BOSHER; 87,800 mems (2001).

United Food and Commercial Workers International Union: 1775 K St, NW, Washington, DC 20006; tel. (202) 223-3111; f. 1979; 1.3m. mems; Int. Pres. DOUGLAS H. DORITY; Int. Sec.-Treas. JOSEPH HANSEN.

United Paperworkers International Union: 3340 Perimeter Hill Dr., POB 1475, Nashville, TN 37202; tel. (615) 834-8590; fax (615) 834-7741; f. 1884; 230,000 mems; Pres. BOYD YOUNG; Sec.-Treas. JAMES H. DUNN.

United Rubber, Cork, Linoleum and Plastic Workers of America: 570 White Pond Dr., Akron, OH 44320; tel. (330) 869-0320; fax (330) 869-5627; f. 1935; 100,000 mems; Pres. KENNETH L. COSS; Sec.-Treas. GLENN ELLISON.

United Steelworkers of America: 5 Gateway Center, Pittsburgh, PA 15222; tel. (412) 562-2400; fax (412) 562-2445; f. 1936; 750,000 mems; Int. Pres. LEO W. GERARD; Sec.-Treas. JAMES D. ENGLISH.

United Transportation Union: 14600 Detroit Ave, Lakewood, OH 44107; tel. (216) 228-9400; fax (216) 228-5755; internet www.utu.org; f. 1969; Pres. CHARLES L. LITTLE; Sec.-Treas. ROGER D. GRIFFETH; 140,000 mems (1999).

Utility Workers Union of America: 815 16th St, NW, Washington, DC 20006; tel. (202) 974-8200; fax (202) 974-8201; internet www.uwua.org; f. 1945; Pres. DONALD E. WIGHTMAN; Sec.-Treas. GARY M. RUFFNER; 50,000 mems (1999).

Independent Unions
(with 50,000 members and over)

National Education Association of the United States: 1201 16th St, NW, Washington, DC 20036; tel. (202) 833-4000; fax (202) 822-7974; internet www.nea.org; f. 1857; Pres. BOB CHASE; Exec. Dir JOHN WILSON; 2.6m. mems (2001).

National Federation of Federal Employees: 1016 16th St, NW, Suite 300, Washington, DC 20036; tel. (202) 862-4400; fax (202) 862-4432; internet www.nffe.org; f. 1917; Pres. ALBERT SCHMIDT; Sec.-Treas. R. JOYCE JAMES; 120,000 mems (1999).

International Brotherhood of Locomotive Engineers: 1370 Ontario St, Mezzanine, Cleveland, OH 44113-1702; tel. (216) 241-2630; fax (216) 241-6516; e-mail webmaster@ble.org; internet www.ble.org; f. 1863; Pres. DON M. HAHS; Sec.-Treas. WILLIAM C. WALPERT; 58,000 mems (2002).

Longshore and Warehouse Union, International: 1188 Franklin St, San Francisco, CA 94109; tel. (415) 775-0533; fax (415) 775-1302; f. 1937; Pres. BRIAN MCWILLIAMS; Sec.-Treas. JOE IBARRA; 60,000 mems (1999).

American Nurses Association: 600 Maryland Ave, SW, Suite 100-W, Washington, DC 20024-2571; tel. (202) 651-7000; fax (202) 651-7001; e-mail ana@ana.org; internet www.nursingworld.org; f. 1896; Pres. MARY E. FOLEY; Exec. Dir LINDA STIERLE; 53 constituent state asscns comprising 180,000 mems (1999).

National Fraternal Order of Police: 1410 Donelson Pike, A-17, Nashville, TN 37217-2933; Nat. Pres. GILBERT G. GALLEGOS; Nat. Sec. JERRY W. ATNIP; 280,000 mems (1999).

National Rural Letter Carriers' Association: 1630 Duke St, 4th Floor, Alexandria, VA 22314-3465; tel. (703) 684-5545; fax (703) 548-8735; f. 1903; Pres. STEVEN SMITH; 98,000 mems (1999).

Treasury Employees Union, National: 901 E St, NW, Suite 600, Washington, DC 20004; tel. (202) 783-4444; fax (202) 783-4085; internet www.nteu.org; f. 1938; Nat. Pres. ROBERT M. TOBIAS; 155,000 mems (1999).

Transport

Federal Railroad Administration: US Dept of Transportation, 1120 Vermont Ave, NW, Washington, DC 20005; tel. (202) 493-6000; internet www.fra.dot.gov; formulates federal railway policies and administers and enforces safety regulations; Admin. ALLAN RUTTER.

Federal Transit Administration: US Dept of Transportation, 400 Seventh St, SW, Washington, DC 20590; tel. (202) 366-4043; fax (202) 366-9854; internet www.fta.dot.gov; Admin. JENNIFER L. DORN.

National Transportation Safety Board: 490 L'Enfant Plaza East, SW, Washington, DC 20594; tel. (202) 314-6000; fax (202) 314-6148; internet www.ntsb.gov; f. 1967; seeks to ensure that all types of transportation in the USA are conducted safely; carries out studies and accident investigations; Chair. ELLEN G. ENGLEMAN.

Surface Transportation Board: Mercury Bldg, 1925 K St, NW, Washington, DC 20423; tel. (202) 565-1500; fax (202) 565-9016; internet www.stb.dot.gov; f. 1995; exercises regulatory authority over domestic surface common carriers; jurisdiction extends over rail, inland waterways and motorized traffic; Chair. ROGER NOBER.

PRINCIPAL RAILWAYS

Alaska Railroad Corporation: POB 107500, Anchorage, AK 99510-7500; tel. (907) 265-2414; fax (907) 265-2312; e-mail reservations@akrr.com; f. 1912; independent corpn owned by the State of Alaska; year-round freight service and summer passenger service; Pres. and CEO PATRICK GAMBLE; 846 track-km.

AMTRAK (National Railroad Passenger Corpn): 60 Massachusetts Ave, NE, Washington, DC 20002; tel. (202) 906-3860; fax (202) 906-3306; internet www.amtrak.com; f. 1970; govt-funded private corpn operating inter-city passenger services over 33,600 track-km in 45 states; Chair. TOMMY THOMPSON; Pres. and CEO GEORGE D. WARRINGTON.

Burlington Northern Santa Fe Corporation: 2650 Lou Menk Dr., Fort Worth, TX 76131; tel. (817) 333-7000; Chair., Pres. and CEO ROBERT D. KREBS; 49,879 track-km.

Conrail (Consolidated Rail Corporation): 2001 Market St, POB 41419, Philadelphia, PA 19101-1419; tel. (215) 209-2000; fax (215) 209-4822; e-mail info@conrail.com; internet www.conrail.com; f. 1975 by fed. govt merger of six bankrupt freight carriers; transfer of most operations to CSX Transportation Inc and Norfolk Southern Railway Co completed in June 1999; Chair. DAVID M. LEVAN; 19,040 track-km (1998).

CSX Transportation Inc (Rail Transport): 500 Water St, Jacksonville, FL 32202; tel. (904) 359-3100; fax (904) 359-1832; f. 1980; by merger; Pres. JOHN SNOW; 30,248 track-km.

Guilford Rail Systems: Iron Horse Park, North Billerica, MA 01862; tel. (508) 663-1130; fax (508) 663-1143; Pres. D. A. FINK; 3,516 track-km.

Illinois Central Railroad: 455 North Cityfront Plaza Dr., Chicago, IL 60611; tel. (312) 755-7500; fax (312) 755-7920; f. 1851; Pres. and CEO JOHN D. MCPHERSON; 4,452 track-km.

Kansas City Southern Railway Co: 114 West 11th St, Kansas City, MO 64105; tel. (816) 983-1537; fax (816) 983-1418; internet www.kcsi.com; Chair. L. H. ROWLAND; Pres. MICHAEL R. HAVERTY; 2,561 track-km.

Long Island Rail Road Co: Jamaica Station, Jamaica, NY 11435; tel. (718) 558-7400; fax (718) 558-6824; f. 1834; Pres. THOMAS PRENDERGAST; 435 track-km.

Norfolk Southern Railway Co: NS Tower, Three Commercial Pl., Norfolk, VA 23510-2191; tel. (757) 629-2600; fax (757) 629-2345; f. 1982; Chair., Pres. and CEO D. R. GOODE; 35,084 track-km.

Union Pacific Railroad Co: 1416 Dodge St, Omaha NE 68179; tel. (402) 271-5000; fax (402) 271-2256; internet www.uprr.com; f. 1897; division of Union Pacific Corpn; Chair. and CEO RICHARD DAVIDSON; Pres. JERRY DAVIS; 57,833 track-km.

Associations

American Short Line and Regional Railroad Association: 1120 G St, NW, Suite 520, Washington, DC 20005; tel. (202) 628-4500; fax (202) 628-6430; f. 1913; Pres. FRANK K. TURNER; 760 mems.

Association of American Railroads: 50 F St, NW, Washington, DC 20001; tel. (202) 639-2100; fax (202) 639-2558; e-mail information@aar.org; internet www.aar.org; f. 1934; Pres. EDWARD R. HAMBERGER; 71 mems, representing virtually all major railroads in the USA, Canada and Mexico.

ROADS

In 2000 there were 3,936,229 miles of roads, of which 388,726 miles were classified as arterial systems and 2,707,940 miles were local roads. In 1999 an estimated 58.8% of all roads were paved.

Federal Highway Administration: US Dept of Transportation, 400 Seventh St, SW, Washington, DC 20590; tel. (202) 366-4000; fax (202) 366-3244; internet www.fhwa.dot.gov; implements federal highway policy and promotes road safety; Admin. MARY E. PETERS.

INLAND WATERWAYS

St Lawrence Seaway Development Corporation: US Dept of Transportation, 400 Seventh St, SW, Rm 5424, Washington, DC 20590; tel. (202) 366-0091; fax (202) 366-7147; internet www.dot.gov/slsdc; responsible for the operations and maintenance of sections of the St Lawrence Seaway within the territorial limits of the USA; Admin. ALBERT S. JACQUEZ.

Principal Companies

American Commercial Lines Inc: 1701 East Market St, Jeffersonville, IN 47130; tel. (812) 288-0100; fax (812) 288-1664; operates barge services along c. 24,000 km of the Mississippi and Ohio rivers and tributaries to the Gulf Intracoastal Waterway; Pres. and CEO H. JOSEPH BOBIZEN, Jr; fleet of 2,400 barges and 96 towboats.

Great Lakes Dredge & Dock Co: 2122 York Rd, Oak Brook, IL 60521; tel. (630) 574-3000; fax (630) 574-2909; f. 1890; dredging, marine construction and reclamation; operates tugboats, drillboats, carfloats, barges and dredges; Man. (International Business) WILLIAM HANNUM; 149 vessels.

Great Lakes Fleet, Inc: 227 West First St, Suite 400, Duluth, MN 55802-1990; tel. (218) 723-2401; fax (218) 723-2455; Gen. Man. ELLIOTT M. HUGHES, III; 8 vessels.

Midland Enterprises Inc: 580 Walnut St, POB 5323, Cincinnati, OH 45201; tel. (513) 943-7100; fax (513) 943-1502; river and inter-coastal transportation, towing and tugboat service and marine cargo handling; ship and barge building and repairing; Pres. C. F. RASKIN.

Oglebay Norton Co Marine Transportation Division: 1100 Superior Ave, Cleveland, OH 44114-2598; tel. (216) 861-8700; fax (216) 861-2315; services on the Great Lakes; Gen. Man. MICHAEL J. SIRAGUSA; 12 vessels.

Associations

American Waterways Operators: 1600 Wilson Blvd, Suite 1000, Arlington, VA 22209; tel. (703) 841-9300; fax (703) 841-0389;

internet www.americanwaterways.com; f. 1944; 386 mems; Pres. THOMAS A. ALLEGRETTI.

Lake Carriers' Association: 915 Rockefeller Bldg, Cleveland, OH 44113-1383; tel. (216) 621-1107; fax (216) 241-8262; e-mail ryan@lcaships.com; f. 1892; 11 mem cos; Pres. GEORGE J. RYAN.

National Waterways Conference: 1130 17th St, NW, Suite 200, Washington, DC 20036-4676; tel. (202) 296-4415; fax (202) 835-3861; e-mail hcook@waterways; internet www.waterways.org; f. 1960; 500 mems; Pres. HARRY N. COOK.

OCEAN SHIPPING

At 31 December 2001 5,284 vessels, with a total displacement of 10,907,179 grt, were registered in the USA.

Federal Maritime Commission: 800 North Capitol St, NW, Washington, DC 20573; tel. (202) 523-5725; fax (202) 523-3782; internet www.fmc.gov; f. 1961 to regulate the waterborne foreign commerce of the USA; comprises 5 mems; Chair. STEVEN R. BLUST, Jr.

Maritime Administration: 400 Seventh St, SW, Washington, DC 20590; tel. (202) 366-5812; fax (202) 366-3890; internet www.marad .dot.gov; concerned with promoting the US Merchant Marine; also administers subsidy programme to ship operators; Admin. CLYDE J. HART, Jr.

Principal Ports

The three largest ports in the USA, in terms of traffic handled, are the Port of South Louisiana, handling 245m. tons in 2000, Houston (194m. tons in 2001) and New York (135m. tons in 1997). Many other large ports serve each coast, 24 of them handling between 25m. and 89m. tons of traffic annually. The deepening of channels and locks on the St Lawrence–Great Lakes Waterway, allowing the passage of large ocean-going vessels, has increased the importance of the Great Lakes ports, of which the largest, Duluth-Superior, handled an average annual 40m. tons.

Principal Companies

Alcoa Steamship Co, Inc: 1501 Alcoa Bldg, 24th Floor, Pittsburgh, PA 15219; tel. (412) 553-2545; fax (412) 553-2624; bulk services world-wide; Pres. R. S. HOSPODAR; 5 vessels.

American President Lines Ltd: 1111 Broadway, Oakland, CA 94607; tel. (510) 272-8000; fax (510) 272-7941; f. 1929; serves east and west coasts of North America, Mexico, Caribbean Basin, Middle East and Far East; Chair. G. HAYASHI; Pres. and CEO TIMOTHY J. RHEIN; 19 vessels.

Amoco Corpn: 200 East Randolph Dr., Chicago, IL 60601; tel. (312) 856-4511; fax (312) 856-2460; Pres. C. D. PHILLIPS.

Central Gulf Lines, Inc: 650 Poydras St, Suite 1700, POB 53366, New Orleans, LA 70153; tel. (504) 529-5461; fax (504) 529-5745; Chair. N. M. JOHNSEN; Pres. E. L. JOHNSEN; 8 vessels.

Chevron Shipping Co: 555 Market St, Suite 2025, San Francisco, CA 94105-2870; tel. (415) 894-7700; fax (415) 894-5659; world-wide tanker services; Pres. THOMAS R. MOORE; 37 tankers.

Colonial Marine Industries, Inc: 26 East Bryan St, POB 9981, Savannah, GA 31412; tel. (912) 233-7000; fax (912) 232-8216; e-mail administrator@colonialmar.com; internet www.colonialmar.com; Exec. Vice-Pres. RICHARD C. WIGGER; 7 vessels.

Coscol Marine Corpn: 9 Greenway Plaza, Houston, TX 77046; tel. (713) 877-3370; tel. 49616712; fax (713) 877-3433; e-mail edward .knutsen@coastalcorp.com; Pres. EDWARD W. KNUTSEN; 4 tankers.

Crowley Maritime Corpn: 155 Grand Ave, Oakland, CA 94612; tel. (510) 251-7500; fax (510) 251-7625; internet www.crowley.com; f. 1895; Chair., Pres. and CEO TOM CROWLEY, Jr; 200 vessels.

Energy Transportation Corpn: 1185 Ave of the Americas, 24th Floor, New York, NY 10036; tel. (212) 642-9800; fax (212) 642-9890; Pres. K. C. CHEN; 8 vessels.

Farrell Lines Inc: 1 Whitehall St, New York, NY 10004; tel. (212) 440-4200; fax (212) 440-4645; internet www.farrell-lines.com; f. 1925; freight services from US Atlantic to west Africa, Mediterranean, Middle East and Black Sea; Chair. and CEO JOHN M. WILSON, Jr; Pres. RICHARD GRONDA.

Lasco Shipping Co: 3200 NW Yeon Ave, Portland, OR 97210; tel. (503) 323-2700; fax (503) 323-2794; e-mail lasco@schn.com; Pres. A. L. THEOHARIS; 25 vessels.

Lykes Lines Ltd: 401 East Jackson St, Suite 3300, POB 31244, Tampa, FL 33631-3244; tel. (813) 276-4600; fax (813) 276-4873; f. 1997; routes from US Gulf and Atlantic ports to United Kingdom and northern Europe, Mediterranean and Africa; Pres. and CEO FRANK J. HALLIWELL.

Maritime Overseas Corpn: 511 Fifth Ave, New York, NY 10017; tel. (212) 953-4100; fax (212) 536-3735; manages *c.*60 tankers and dry bulk carriers.

Matson Navigation Co: 333 Market St, POB 7452, San Francisco, CA 94120; tel. (415) 957-4000; fax (415) 957-4559; e-mail matson-info@matson.com; internet www.matson.com; f. 1901; container and other freight services between US west coast and Hawaii; container leasing world-wide; Chair. R. J. PFEIFFER; Pres. C. B. MULHOLLAND.

Mobil Oil Corpn: 3225 Gallows Rd, Fairfax, VA 22037; tel. (703) 846-1520; fax (703) 846-3180; Chair. and CEO L. A. NOTO; 29 vessels.

OMI Corpn: 90 Park Ave, New York, NY 10016-1302; tel. (212) 602-6700; fax (212) 602-6701; e-mail info@omnicorp.com; internet www .omnicorp.com; Chair. J. GOLDSTEIN; Pres. and CEO C. STEVENSON; 32 vessels.

Sea-Land Service, Inc: 6000 Carnegie Blvd, Charlotte, NC 28209-4613; tel. (704) 571-2000; largest US-flag container shipping co; 100 vessels providing containerized services to 80 ports in 120 countries and territories; Pres. and CEO JOHN P. CLANCEY.

SeaRiver Maritime, Inc: POB 1512, Houston, TX 77251-1512; tel. (713) 758-5000; fax (713) 758-5091; Pres. A. ELMER; 9 tankers.

Stolt-Nielsen Transportation Group: Stolt-Nielsen Bldg, 8 Sound Shore Dr., POB 2300, Greenwich, CT 06836; tel. (203) 625-9400; fax (203) 661-7695; Chair. SAMUEL L. COOPERMAN; CEO REGINALD J. R. LEE; 142 tankers.

Waterman Steamship Corpn: 1 Whitehall St, New York, NY 10004; tel. (212) 747-8550; fax (212) 747-8588; e-mail waterman@intship.com; internet www.waterman-steamship.com; f. 1919; services to the Middle East and South-East Asia; Chair. C. S. WALSH; Pres. N. M. JOHNSEN.

Associations

American Bureau of Shipping: 16855 Northchase Dr., Houston, TX 77060; tel. (281) 877-6000; fax (281) 877-5801; f. 1862; Chair. FRANK J. IAROSSI; Pres. ROBERT D. SOMERVILLE; 710 mems.

American Maritime Congress: Franklin Sq., 1300 Eye St, Suite 250 West, NW, Washington, DC 20005-3314; tel. (202) 842-4900; fax (202) 842-3492; e-mail gloriatosi@americanmaritime.org; f. 1977; mems represent major US-flag ship operating cos; Exec. Dir GLORIA CATANEO TOSI.

Chamber of Shipping of America: 1730 M St, NW, Suite 407, Washington, DC 20036-4517; tel. (202) 775-4399; fax (202) 659-3795; e-mail kjmetcalf@msn.com; Pres. JOSEPH J. COX; represents 19 US-based cos.

CIVIL AVIATION

Federal Aviation Administration: 800 Independence Ave, SW, Washington, DC 20591; tel. (202) 366-4000; internet www.faa.gov; f. 1958; promotes safety in the air, regulates air commerce and assists in development of an effective national airport system; Admin. JANE F. GARVEY.

Principal Scheduled Companies

Alaska Airlines: POB 68900, Seattle, WA 98168-0900; tel. (206) 433-3200; fax (206) 433-7253; internet www.alaskaair.com; f. 1932; Chair. and CEO JOHN KELLY; scheduled services to 35 US destinations as well as Canada, the former USSR, the Far East and Mexico.

American Airlines Inc: POB 619616, Dallas/Fort Worth Airport, TX 75261-9616; tel. (817) 967-1577; fax (817) 967-4162; internet www.aa.com; f. 1934; Chair. and CEO DONALD CARTY; coast-to-coast domestic routes and services to Canada, Hawaii, Mexico, the Caribbean, South America, Europe and the Far East; acquired Trans World Airlines in 2001.

Continental Airlines Inc: 2929 Allen Pkwy, POB 4607, Houston, TX 77210-4607; tel. (713) 324-5000; fax (713) 523-2831; internet www.continental.com; f. 1934; Chair. and CEO GORDON M. BETHUNE; serves 139 US destinations and 85 points in Mexico, Canada, Europe and the Far East.

Delta Air Lines Inc: Hartsfield Atlanta International Airport, Atlanta, GA 30320-9998; tel. (770) 715-2600; fax (770) 715-5494; internet www.delta-air.com; f. 1929; Chair., Pres. and CEO LEO F. MULLIN; domestic and international services to 208 cities in 32 countries.

Hawaiian Airlines Inc: 30008, Honolulu International Airport, Honolulu, HI 96820; tel. (808) 835-3700; fax (808) 835-3690; internet www.hawaiianair.com; f. 1929; Pres. and CEO PAUL J. CASEY; inter-island, US mainland and South Pacific services.

Northwest Airlines, Inc: Minneapolis-St Paul International, MN 55111-3075; tel. (612) 726-2111; fax (612) 726-0622; internet www .nwa.com; f. 1926; Chair. GARY L. WILSON; 113 domestic destinations and 42 points in Canada, Europe and the Far East.

Southwest Airlines: POB 36611, Love Field, Dallas, TX 75235; tel. (214) 904-4000; fax (214) 792-4011; internet www.southwest.com; CEO HERBERT D. KELLEHER; scheduled domestic carrier.

United Airlines Inc: POB 66100, Chicago, IL 60666-0100; tel. (847) 700-4000; fax (847) 700-7347; internet www.ual.com; f. 1934; Chair. and CEO JOHN W. CREIGHTON, Jr; Pres. RONO DUTTA; domestic and international services to 139 destinations in 26 countries.

US Airways, Inc: 2345 Crystal Dr., Arlington, VA 22227; tel. (703) 872-7000; fax (703) 872-7304; internet www.usairways.com; f. 1939; Chair. and acting CEO STEPHEN M. WOLF; scheduled passenger services to 210 points in the USA and world-wide.

Associations

Air Freight Association of America: 1220 19th St, NW, Suite 400, Washington, DC 20036; tel. (202) 293-1030; fax (202) 293-4377; f. 1948; Exec. Vice-Pres. STEPHEN A. ALTERMAN; 27 mems.

Air Transport Association of America, Inc: 1301 Pennsylvania Ave, NW, Suite 1100, Washington, DC 20004-1707; tel. (202) 626-4000; fax (202) 626-4181; internet www.airlines.org; f. 1936; Pres. CAROL HALLETT; mems: 22 US airlines, 4 non-US assoc. mems.

National Air Carrier Association: 910 17th St, NW, Suite 800, Washington, DC 20006; tel. (202) 833-8200; e-mail naca@erols.com; f. 1962; Pres. RONALD N. PRIDDY; 7 mems.

National Air Transportation Association: 4226 King St, Alexandria, VA 22302; tel. (703) 845-9000; fax (703) 845-8176; e-mail info@ nata-online.org; internet www.nata.online.org; f. 1940; Pres. JAMES. E. COYNE.

Regional Airline Association: 1200 19th St, NW, Suite 300, Washington, DC 20036; tel. (202) 857-1170; fax (202) 429-5113; e-mail raa@sba.com; internet www.raa.org; Pres. WALTER S. COLEMAN.

Tourism

American Society of Travel Agents Inc: 1101 King St, Alexandria, VA 22314; tel. (703) 739-2782; fax (703) 684-8319; internet www.astanet.com; f. 1931; Pres. and CEO RICHARD M. COPLAND; Exec. Vice-Pres. WILLIAM A. MALONEY; 27,000 mems.

Office of Travel and Tourism Industries: International Trade Administration, US Department of Commerce, Rm 7025, Washington, DC 20230; tel. (202) 482-0140; fax (202) 482-2887; internet www.tinet.doc.gov; f. 1996; fed. govt agency; collects and analyses data and develops US tourism policy; Dep. Asst Sec. for Service Industries, Tourism and Finance DOUGLAS B. BAKER.

Travel Industry Association of America: 1100 New York Ave, NW, Suite 450, Washington, DC 20005; tel. (202) 408-8422; fax (202) 255-1225; internet www.tia.org; f. 1941; Pres. and CEO WILLIAM NORMAN.

US National Tourism Organization: 1100 New York Ave, NW, Suite 450, Washington, DC 20005; tel. (202) 408-8686; fax (202) 255-1225; f. 1996; promotes travel within the USA; Exec. Dir MARK HOY.

UNITED STATES COMMONWEALTH TERRITORIES

There are two US Commonwealth Territories, the Northern Mariana Islands, in the Pacific Ocean, and Puerto Rico, in the Caribbean Sea. A Commonwealth is a self-governing incorporated territory that is an integral part of, and in full political union with, the USA.

THE NORTHERN MARIANA ISLANDS

Introductory Survey

Location, Climate, Language, Religion, Flag, Capital

The Commonwealth of the Northern Mariana Islands comprises 14 islands (all the Marianas except Guam) in the western Pacific Ocean, about 5,300 km (3,300 miles) west of Honolulu (Hawaii). The temperature normally ranges between 24°C (75°F) and 30°C (86°F) in June–November, but is generally cooler and drier from December to May. The average annual rainfall is about 2,120 mm (84 ins). English, Chamorro and Carolinian are the official languages. The population is predominantly Christian, mainly Roman Catholic. The national flag of the United States of America (q.v.) is used by the Northern Mariana Islands. Six islands, including the three largest (Saipan, Tinian and Rota), are inhabited; the principal settlement and the administrative centre are on Saipan.

Recent History

The islands which comprise the Northern Mariana Islands were first sighted by Europeans during the 1520s, and were claimed for Spain in 1565. They were sold to Germany in 1899, but control was transferred to Japan, which had taken the islands from Germany in 1914, by the League of Nations in 1921. The USA captured Saipan and Tinian from the Japanese after fierce fighting in 1944, and the Northern Mariana Islands became a part of the Trust Territory of the Pacific Islands in 1947. (See the chapter on the Marshall Islands.)

In June 1975 the Northern Mariana Islands voted for separate status as a US Commonwealth Territory, and in March 1976 US Presid-ent Ford signed the Northern Marianas Commonwealth Covenant. In October 1977 President Carter approved the Constitution of the Northern Mariana Islands, which provided that, from January 1978, the former Marianas District was internally self-governing. In December 1977 elections took place for a bicameral legislature, a Governor and a Lieutenant-Governor. In July 1984 it was reported that the US President, Ronald Reagan, had signed a proclamation giving residents of the Northern Mariana Islands a broad range of civil and political rights in the USA, including equal employment opportunities within the federal government, civil service and armed forces. The Northern Marianas were formally admitted to US Commonwealth status in November 1986, after the ending of the Trusteeship in the Territory. At the same time a proclamation, issued by Reagan, conferred US citizenship on the islands' residents.

At elections in 1989 Republicans retained control of the governorship and ousted a Democrat from the position of Washington Representative. Larry Guerrero was elected Governor after Pedro Tenorio had decided to stand down. Democrat candidates, however, won a majority of seats in the House of Representatives.

In December 1990 the UN Security Council voted to end the Trusteeship of the Northern Marianas, as well as that of two other Pacific Trust Territories. Although the decision to terminate the relationship had been taken in 1986, voting had been delayed. Guerrero, however, opposed the termination on the grounds that the new relationship would leave the islands subject to US law while remaining unrepresented in the US Congress.

At elections to the House of Representatives (which had been enlarged by three seats) in 1991 Republicans regained a majority. Similarly, the party increased the number of its senators to eight. Republicans retained their majority at elections

to the House of Representatives in 1993. However, in the gubernatorial election a Democrat, Froilan Tenorio, was successful. Similarly, a Democrat candidate, Jesús Borja, was elected as Lieutenant-Governor, while Juan Babauta remained as Washington Representative.

In January 1995 the minimum wage was increased by 12.2%, in accordance with the Governor's stated objectives; however, five days later Tenorio signed legislation that effectively reversed the decision. This prompted several members of the House of Representatives to demand that the US Federal Bureau of Investigations (FBI) conduct an investigation into the incident and the allegations of bribery surrounding the Governor's actions. The Territory's reputation deteriorated further in April when the Government of the Philippines introduced a ban on its nationals accepting unskilled employment in the islands, because of persistent reports of abuse and exploitation of immigrant workers. Meanwhile, the US Congress announced that it was to allocate US $7m. towards the enforcement of the islands' labour and immigration laws, following the publication of a report in late 1994 that alleged the repeated violations of these regulations, as well as widespread corruption among immigration officials and business leaders.

At legislative elections in November 1995 Republican candidates won a convincing majority, securing 14 seats in the House of Representatives and six seats in the Senate.

In May 1997 the US President, Bill Clinton, informed Tenorio of his intention to apply US immigration and minimum wage laws to the Territory, stating that labour practices in the islands were inconsistent with US values. In the previous month Democrat congressman George Miller had proposed legislation in the US House of Representatives (the Insular Fair Wage and Human Rights Act) that would equalize the minimum wage level in the islands with that of the US mainland by 1999. The Territory's Government, which denied many of the claims of exploitation of immigrant workers, responded to the proposed legislation by initiating a public relations campaign that persuaded the Republican majority in the US House of Representatives to oppose the bill. The issue dominated the election campaign during late 1997, with Willie Tan (a major entrepreneur who had been fined several million dollars for failing to comply with US Labour Department health and safety standards in his garment factories) providing considerable financial support towards Froilan Tenorio's efforts to remain in office.

In January 1999 the Office of Insular Affairs (OIA) published a report in which it concluded that the Government's attempts to eradicate abuses of labour and immigration laws had been unsuccessful. In particular, it had failed to reduce the Territory's reliance on alien workers, to enforce US minimum wage laws and to curb evasions of trade legislation governing the export of garments to the USA. In the same month former employees of 18 US clothing retailers initiated legal action against the companies, which were accused of failing to comply with US labour laws in Saipan. In April 2000 a settlement was reached with the garment manufacturers, providing some US $8m. in compensation for the workers. The companies also agreed to conform to regulations established by an independent monitoring system in Saipan.

At legislative elections on 1 November 1997 Republican candidates won 13 of the 18 seats in the House of Representatives and eight of the nine seats in the Senate. At the gubernatorial election, held concurrently, Pedro Tenorio was successful, securing 46% of total votes. Opponents of Pedro Tenorio subsequently initiated a legal challenge to his election on the grounds that it constituted his third term as Governor, thereby violating the Constitution, which states that a maximum of two gubernatorial terms may be served by any one individual (although the Constitution had been amended to include this provision only during Pedro Tenorio's second term in office).

Following legislative elections on 6 November 1999, Democrat candidates held two of the nine seats in the Senate and six of the 18 seats in the House of Representatives.

In late 1999 it was announced that legal action was to be taken against the US Government following revelations that traces of a toxic chemical had been found in a village near the capital, Saipan. It was alleged that the chemicals had been abandoned by the US army in the 1960s. It was subsequently announced, in November 2000, that the Government of the Northern Marianas was to claim US $1m. from the USA, to repay the costs of a screening programme, established to test the villagers for traces of the chemicals.

In February 2000 the US Senate approved a bill granting permanent residency in the Northern Marianas to some 40,000 immigrant workers. However, the bill also included provisions for limiting the stay of all future guest workers. In December 2000 Governor Tenorio announced that he was to oppose the decision by the US Government to bring the Northern Marianas' labour and immigration laws under federal control; Tenorio argued that this might have a negative impact on the Northern Marianas' economy. In May 2001, following intense lobbying by the Northern Marianas Government, the US Congress abandoned the bill.

Legislative elections were held on 3 November 2001, at which the Republican Party secured 12 seats in the House of Representatives, the Democratic Party won five and the Covenant Party took one. The Republican Party won six seats in the Senate, the Democratic Party two and the Covenant Party one. Gubernatorial elections were held concurrently, at which Juan Nekai Babauta, the Republican Party candidate and former Representative to Washington, won a convincing victory, securing 42.8% of the votes cast. Benigno Fitial, of the Covenant Party, received 24.4%. Babauta was inaugurated as Governor in January 2002, while Diego Benavente, his running mate and the former Speaker of the House of Representatives, became Lieutenant-Governor.

In January 2002 the Supreme Court suspended deportation proceedings against an immigrant labourer working in the Northern Marianas illegally, after he appealed to the office of the UN High Commissioner for Refugees. The Court warned the Government that it might not be able to order the deportation of up to 10,000 of the Chinese, Sri Lankan and Bangladeshi workers in the Northern Marianas.

In May 2002 the issue of the Northern Marianas' working conditions was raised again by US Senator Edward Kennedy, who proposed a bill that would incrementally increase the minimum wage. The first increase would occur 60 days after the bill's implementation, should it be successful, although Kennedy invited the Northern Marianas to contribute to discussions. In late September 2002 seven further major US clothing retailers agreed to pay US $11.25m. in compensation to employees alleged to have suffered intolerable working conditions and poor rates of pay. The funds also included sponsorship of independent monitoring of labour conditions in the islands. In late 2002 the Government successfully resisted an attempt by the US Administration to place the Northern Mariana Islands' immigration and labour legislation under direct federal control.

A US court order filed by the Center for Biological Diversity, an environmental group, forced military training on the island of Farallon de Medinilla to be suspended for 30 days in mid-2002. Despite environmentalists' concerns about the impact and legality of US military activity—in particular the testing of ordnances—upon the island's wildlife, the Northern Marianas Chamber of Commerce feared that the substantial revenue generated by the visiting US military might be jeopardized. In early 2003 the US Military apologized for damage to property caused by low-flying aircraft.

In May 2002 the Government 'froze' the assets of the Bank of Saipan, pending auditing of its accounts, after the institution's former Chairman was arrested for allegedly attempting to defraud the bank of more than US $6.6m. The bank was placed in receivership and remained closed for 11 months. Following the bank's reopening in April 2003 with assets of some $12m., customers were permitted to retrieve a limited monthly quota of savings deposits.

In September 2002 Babauta proposed reforms to reduce government expenditure. This and immigration issues were reported to be the subject of tension between the Governor and the Speaker of the House of Representatives, Heinz Hofschneider. In November 2002 the Government announced plans for a US $40m. bond issue to cover the cost of compensating traditional landowners for the loss of property expropriated for government use, and in April 2003 draft legislation was proposed that would substantially reduce government personnel costs.

In December 2002 the Northern Marianas island of Rota was devastated by Typhoon Pongsona. President George W. Bush of the USA declared the affected area a federal disaster zone, and authorized relief funding to repair damaged property and infrastructure (there were no confirmed fatalities caused by the storm). In late 2002, following the suspension of Northern Mariana islanders' access to medical facilities in Hawaii, islanders became legally obliged to contribute to the rising costs of their health care, although in March 2003 the Bush Administration pledged US $15m. to assist the development of adequate healthcare infrastructure in the US Pacific territories. None the less, the health and welfare of the population remained a cause for concern in 2002 and 2003, following the publication of independent surveys that claimed that the Northern Marianas registered the world's third highest incidence of diabetes and a child poverty rate of some 38%.

Government

Legislative authority is vested in the Northern Marianas Commonwealth Legislature, a bicameral body consisting of the Senate and the House of Representatives. There are nine senators, elected for four-year terms, and 18 members of the House of Representatives, elected for two-year terms. Executive authority is vested in the Governor, who is elected by popular vote.

Defence

The USA is responsible for the defence of the Northern Marianas.

Economic Affairs

The Commonwealth of the Northern Mariana Islands' gross national income (GNI) was estimated by the Bank of Hawaii (BOH) to be US $696.3m. in 1999. GNI per head was estimated at $8,582. The population increased at an estimated annual rate of more than 7.2% during 1990–99.

Agriculture is concentrated in smallholdings, important crops being coconuts, breadfruit, tomatoes and melons. Cattle-ranching is practised on Tinian. Vegetables, beef and pork are produced for export. There is little commercial fishing in the islands, although there is a major transhipment facility at Tinian harbour. Imports of fish products increased from 1990; fishing remains a potentially valuable but as yet unrealized commercial resource. Agriculture (including forestry, fishing and mining) engaged 1.5% of the employed labour force in 2000, and its commercial value as a sector is minimal. In the same year it accounted for only 0.1% of gross business revenues (total revenues generated by business transactions; the Government does not calculate gross domestic product figures).

Industry (including manufacturing and construction) engaged 47.2% of the employed labour force in 2000. Manufacturing alone engaged 40.7% of workers, while construction employed 6.5%. The principal manufacturing activity is the garment industry, which grew rapidly after its establishment in the mid-1980s to become the islands' chief export sector. Manufacturers benefit from US regulations that permit duty-free and quota-free imports from the Commonwealth. Garment manufacturing accounted for 34.7% of gross business revenues in 2000, and overall exports of garments were worth US $925.7m. in 2001, compared with $1,017m. in 2000. Other small-scale manufacturing activities include handicrafts and the processing of fish and copra. Construction is very closely related to the tourist industry and demand for additional hotel capacity. However, the number of building permits sold, both commercial and residential, declined each year during 1997–2001.

Service industries dominate the economy, particularly tourism. In 2000 services (including utilities) engaged 51.3% of the employed labour force, whilst accounting for 29.2% of gross business revenues. Japan provided the majority (75.5%) of the islands' visitors in 2001. Other significant sources of tourists were the Republic of Korea, Guam and the USA. Tourist arrivals increased steadily in the early 1990s, reaching 736,117 in 1996, but declined considerably in 1997–98, before increasing by 2.4% in 1999 and by 5.3% in 2000, when a total of 528,597 visitors travelled to the islands. Tourist receipts were worth an estimated US $430m. in 2000. In mid-1995, meanwhile, a US company opened the Territory's first casino on Tinian. The islands were expected to receive some $12m. annually in revenue from the casino. Owing to the limited hotel accommodation on Tinian, the company arranged for chartered aircraft to transport tourists to the island from Saipan and Guam. Tourism in the Northern Marianas was severely affected by the repercussions of the terrorist attacks on the USA on 11 September 2001. The number of tourist arrivals by air decreased sharply in late 2001–early 2002, while the hotel occupancy rate declined to only 35% in December 2001. Total visitor arrivals in 2001 declined to 442,466. In 2001 remittances from overseas workers and investments reached $76.7m.

The Northern Marianas are dependent on imports, the value of which totalled US $836.2m. in 1997. The principal imports in that year were foodstuffs (9.6% of the total), petroleum products (8.2%), clothing (7.1%), automobiles and parts (5.0%), and construction materials (4.1%). In 1991 there was a trade deficit of $126.9m. The annual rate of inflation averaged 3.6% in 1990–98. Consumer prices decreased by 0.3% in 1999, increased by 2.0% in 2000 and declined by 0.8% in 2001.

Under the Covenant between the Commonwealth of the Northern Mariana Islands and the USA, the islands receive substantial annual development grants. Budget estimates envisaged total revenue of US $297.2m. in the financial year ending 30 September 2000, federal contributions accounting for $52.9m. Total expenditure of $225.5m. was projected for that year. Loans from the Commonwealth Development Authority totalled more than $0.5m. in 2001. The Territory is a member of the Pacific Community (see p. 304) and an associate member of the UN Economic and Social Commission for Asia and the Pacific (ESCAP, see p. 28).

Continued economic problems in the Territory have been largely attributed to the dramatic increase in the Northern Marianas' population (from some 17,000 in 1979 to 69,221 in 2000). The main restraint on development is the need to expand the islands' infrastructure, coupled with the problem of a labour shortage and the dependence on foreign workers. Rapid economic expansion in the 1980s led to a shortage of local labour and an increase in non-resident alien workers. However, owing to the resulting excess of immigrant workers (whose numbers increased by 655% between 1980 and 1989 and exceeded the permanent population by the early 1990s), wages remained relatively low, and there were widespread complaints of poor working conditions. Increasing concern over the alleged exploitation of foreign workers in the islands' garment factories led to the proposal in April 1997 of legislation in the US House of Representatives to increase the minimum wage to parity with the mainland level. In September 2002 a judgment on a lawsuit against garment manufacturers in Saipan awarded compensation to the affected workers and provided for independent monitoring of labour practices in the Northern Marianas (see Recent History). A total of 22,560 permits were issued to non-resident workers in the islands in 1994, 67.2% of which were for Filipino nationals. The islands have long benefited from their political association with the USA. In late 2000 the Northern Marianas' House of Representatives requested that the USA cancel some US $3.2m. in debt, incurred following the drilling of a number of water wells between 1990 and 1997. The Territory received a total of some $13m. of US federal funding and development assistance in 2001/02. The islands' Republican administration, inaugurated in 2002, pledged to prioritize economic reform by promoting free, competitive markets with a minimum of government interference. It outlined an environmental rehabilitation programme in an effort to raise the Territory's tourism profile. None the less, incidents of contamination by crude petroleum and lead continued to be reported in 2002 and 2003. In March 2002 the Government introduced tax incentives for new businesses and developers, worth a potential 100% abatement of local taxes, or a 95% rebate of federal taxes. However, despite improved expenditure controls, the continued recession in the islands was estimated to have led to a deterioration in the Government's fiscal position in 2003; the 2004 budget envisaged increasing revenues and allocated some $4.2m. towards debt repayments. Moreover, in response to declining demand among tourists for air travel to the islands, Korean Air suspended services to Saipan in March 2003. In the following month a major development project to generate 10 MW of electric power per day using thermal technology appeared to have been cancelled, following a dispute between investors and a member of the Northern Mariana Islands Senate.

Education

School attendance is compulsory from six to 16 years of age. In 1999/2000 there were 11 state primary schools, with a total of 5,651 pupils enrolled, and there were six state secondary schools, with a total enrolment of 3,942 pupils. In 1996/1997 there was a total of 13 private schools, with a total enrolment of 2,699 pupils. There was one college of further education in 1993/94 with 3,051 students. Budgetary expenditure on education totalled US $49.6m. in 2000, equivalent to 22.0% of total government expenditure.

Public Holidays

2003: 1 January (New Year's Day), 8 January (Commonwealth Day), 17 February (Presidents' Day), 24 March (Covenant Day), 18 April (Good Friday), 26 May (Memorial Day), 4 July (US Independence Day), 1 September (Labor Day), 13 October (Columbus Day), 5 November (Citizenship Day), 11 November (Veterans Day), 27 November (Thanksgiving Day), 9 December (Constitution Day), 25 December (Christmas Day).

2004: 1 January (New Year's Day), 8 January (Commonwealth Day), 16 February (Presidents' Day), 24 March (Covenant Day), 9 April (Good Friday), 31 May (Memorial Day), 4 July (US Independence Day), 6 September (Labor Day), 11 October (Columbus Day), 5 November (Citizenship Day), 11 November (Veterans Day), 25 November (Thanksgiving Day), 9 December (Constitution Day), 25 December (Christmas Day).

Weights and Measures

With certain exceptions, the imperial system is in force. One US cwt equals 100 lb; one long ton equals 2,240 lb; one short ton equals 2,000 lb. A policy of gradual voluntary conversion to the metric system is being encouraged by the Federal Government.

Statistical Survey

Source: (unless otherwise stated): Department of Commerce, Central Statistics Division, POB 10007, Saipan MP, 96950; tel. 664-3000; fax 664-3001; internet www.commerce.gov.mp.

AREA AND POPULATION

Area: 457 sq km (176.5 sq miles). *By island*: Saipan 120 sq km (46.5 sq miles); Tinian 102 sq km (39.2 sq miles); Rota 85 sq km (32.8 sq miles); Pagan 48 sq km (18.6 sq miles); Anatahan 32 sq km (12.5 sq miles); Agrihan 30 sq km (11.4 sq miles).

Population: 43,345 at census of 1 April 1990; 69,221 (males 31,984, females 37,237) at census of 1 April 2000. *By island*: Saipan 62,392; Rota 3,283; Tinian 3,540; Northern Islands 6.

Density (2000 census): 151 per sq km (392 per sq mile).

Ethnic Groups (2000 census): Filipino 18,141; Chinese 15,311; Chamorro 14,749; part-Chamorro 4,383; Total (incl. others) 69,221.

Principal Towns (2000 census): San Antonio 4,741; Garapan (capital) 3,588; Koblerville 3,543; San Vincente 3,494; Tanapag 3,318; Chalan Kanoa 3,108; Kagman 3,026. Source: Thomas Brinkhoff, *City Population* (internet www.citypopulation.de).

Births and Deaths (2000): Birth rate 20.7 per 1,000; Death rate 2.2 per 1,000.

Employment (2000 census, persons aged 16 years and over): Agriculture, forestry, fisheries and mining 623; Manufacturing 17,398; Construction 2,785; Transport, communication and utilities 1,449; Trade, restaurants and hotels 9,570; Financing, insurance and real estate 1,013; Community, social and personal services 9,915; Total employed 42,753 (males 19,485; females 23,268); Unemployed 1,712 (males 888; females 824); Total labour force 44,465 (males 20,373; females 24,092).

AGRICULTURE, ETC.

Fishing (metric tons, live weight, 2000): Total catch 189 (Skipjack tuna 56). Source: FAO, *Yearbook of Fishery Statistics*.

FINANCE

Currency and Exchange Rates: 100 cents = 1 United States dollar (US $). *Sterling and Euro Equivalents* (31 December 2002): £1 sterling = US $1.6118; €1 = US $1.05; US $100 = £62.04 = €95.36.

Budget (estimates, US $ million, year ending 30 September 2000): Total Revenue 297.2 (Taxes 247.7, Federal Contributions 52.9); Total Expenditure 225.5 (General Government 36.0, Education 49.6, Health and social welfare 43.6, Public safety 21.6, Public works 9.9).

Cost of Living (Consumer Price Index for Saipan; base: 1977, third quarter = 100): 267.8 in 1999; 273.2 in 2000; 271.0 in 2001.

Gross National Product (US $ million in current prices): 696 in 1999. Source: Bank of Hawaii, *Commonwealth of the Northern Mariana Islands: An Economic Report* (August 2001).

EXTERNAL TRADE

Principal Commodities (f.o.b., US $ million, 1997): *Imports*: Food items 80.1; Construction materials 35.1; Automobiles (incl. parts) 42.1; Petroleum products 68.5; Clothing 59.0; Total (incl. others) 836.2; *Exports* (1991): Total 258.4. Source: partly, UN, *Statistical Yearbook for Asia and the Pacific*.

Principal Trading Partners (US $ million, 1997): *Imports*: Guam 298.0; Hong Kong 200.5; Japan 118.3; Korea, Republic 80.6; USA 63.3; Total (incl. others) 836.2.

TRANSPORT

International Sea-borne Shipping (freight traffic, '000 short tons, 1997): Goods loaded 184.1; Goods unloaded 425.9.

Civil Aviation (Saipan Int. Airport, year ending September 1999): 23,853 aircraft landings; 562,364 boarding passengers. Source: Commonwealth Ports Authority.

Road Traffic (Registered motor vehicles, 2000): 17,616.

TOURISM

Visitor Arrivals: 501,788 in 1999; 528,597 in 2000; 442,466 in 2001.

Visitor Arrivals by Country (2001): Guam 17,989; Japan 333,917; Korea, Republic 54,992; USA 17,229.

Tourism Receipts (US $million): 394 in 1998; 407 in 1999; 430 in 2000. Source: Bank of Hawaii, *Commonwealth of the Northern Mariana Islands: An Economic Report* (August 2001).

COMMUNICATIONS MEDIA

Radio Receivers (estimate, 1987): 15,350 in use.

Television Receivers (estimate, 1995): 15,460 in use.

Telephones (2001): 25,306 main lines in use.

Mobile Cellular Telephones (2000): 3,000 subscribers†.

TeleStations (1996): 1,200 in use*.

* Source: UN, *Statistical Yearbook*.

† Source: International Telecommunication Union.

EDUCATION

Primary (1999/2000, state schools): 11 schools 279 teachers; 5,651 students; 7,884 students (public and private schools) at 2000 census.

Secondary (1999/2000, state schools): 6 schools; 193 teachers; 3,492 students; 2,750 students (public and private schools) at 2000 census.

Higher (1993/94): 1 college; 3,051 students.

Private Schools (1999/2000): 17 schools; 196 teachers; 2,842 students.

Directory

The Government

(April 2003)

Governor: JUAN NEKAI BABAUTA (took office January 2002).

Lieutenant-Governor: DIEGO TENORIO BENAVENTE.

GOVERNMENT OFFICES

Office of the Governor: Caller Box 10007, Capitol Hill, Saipan, MP 96950; tel. 664-2200; fax 664-2211; internet www.cnmi.gov.mp.

Office of the Resident Representative to the USA, Commonwealth of the Northern Mariana Islands: 2121 R St, NW, Washington, DC 20008; tel. (202) 673-5869; fax (202) 673-5873; the Commonwealth Govt also has liaison offices in Hawaii and Guam.

Department of the Interior, Office of Insular Affairs (OIA): Field Office of the OIA, Dept of the Interior, POB 502622, Saipan, MP 96950; tel. 234-8861; fax 234-8814; e-mail jeff.schorr@saipan.com; OIA representation in the Commonwealth; Field Representative JEFFREY SCHORR.

Legislature

Legislative authority is vested in the Northern Marianas Commonwealth Legislature, a bicameral body consisting of the Senate and the House of Representatives. There are nine senators, elected for four-year terms, and 18 members of the House of Representatives, elected for two-year terms. The most recent elections took place on 3 November 2001, following which the Republicans held six of the nine seats in the Senate, the Democratic Party two seats and the Covenant Party one seat. The Republican Party held 12 of the 18 seats in the House of Representatives, the Democrat Party five seats and the Covenant Party one seat.

Senate President: PAUL A. MANGLONA.

Speaker of the House: HEINZ S. HOFSCHNEIDER.

Commonwealth Legislature: Capitol Hill, Saipan, MP 96950; tel. 664-7757; fax 322-6344.

Political Organizations

Covenant Party: c/o Commonwealth Legislature, Capitol Hill, Saipan MP 96950; Leader BENIGNO R. FITIAL; Chair. ELOY INOS.

Democratic Party of the Commonwealth of the Northern Mariana Islands, Inc: POB 500676, Saipan, MP 96950-0676; tel. 234-7497; fax 233-0641; Pres. Dr CARLOS S. CAMACHO; Chair. LORENZO CABRERA.

Republican Party: c/o Commonwealth Legislature, Capitol Hill, Saipan MP 96950; Chair. JOSEPH REYES.

Judicial System

The judicial system in the Commonwealth of the Northern Mariana Islands (CNMI) consists of the Superior Court, the Commonwealth Supreme Court (which considers appeals from the Superior Court) and the Federal District Court. Under the Covenant, federal law applies in the Commonwealth, apart from the following exceptions: the CNMI is not part of the US Customs Territory; the federal minimum wage provisions do not apply; federal immigration laws do not apply; and the CNMI may enact its own taxation laws.

Religion

The population is predominantly Christian, mainly Roman Catholic. There are small communities of Episcopalians (Anglicans—under the jurisdiction of the Bishop of Hawaii, in the USA) and Protestants.

CHRISTIANITY

The Roman Catholic Church

The Northern Mariana Islands comprise the single diocese of Chalan Kanoa, suffragan to the archdiocese of Agaña (Guam). The Bishop participates in the Catholic Bishops' Conference of the Pacific, based in Fiji. At 31 December 2000 there were 53,066 adherents in the Northern Mariana Islands, including temporary residents.

Bishop of Chalan Kanoa: Most Rev. TOMAS AGUON CAMACHO, Bishop's House, Chalan Kanoa, POB 500745, Saipan, MP 96950; tel. 234-3000; fax 235-3002; e-mail tcamacho@vzpacifica.net.

The Press

The weekly *Focus on the Commonwealth* is published in Guam, but distributed solely in the Northern Mariana Islands.

Marianas Observer: POB 502119, Saipan, MP 96950; tel. 233-3955; fax 233-7040; weekly; Publr JOHN VABLAN; Man. Editor ZALDY DANDAN; circ. 2,000.

Marianas Review: POB 501074, Saipan, MP 96950; tel. 234-7160; f. 1979 as The Commonwealth Examiner; weekly; English and Chamorro; independent; Publr LUIS BENAVENTE; Editor RUTH L. TIGHE; circ. 1,700.

Marianas Variety News and Views: POB 500231, Saipan, MP 96950; tel. 234-6341; fax 234-9271; Mon.–Fri. English and Chamorro; independent; Mans ABED YOUNIS, PAZ YOUNIS; circ. 5,500.

North Star: Chalan Kanoa, POB 500745, Saipan, MP 96950; tel. 234-3000; fax 235-3002; e-mail north.star@saipan.com; internet www.cnmicatholic.org/north.htm; weekly; English and Chamorro; Roman Catholic; Publr BISHOP TOMAS A. CAMACHO; Editor RUY VALENTE M. POLISTICO.

Pacific Daily News (Saipan bureau): POB 500822, Saipan, MP 96950; tel. 234-6423; fax 234-5986; Publr LEE WEBBER; circ. 5,000.

Pacific Star: POB 505815 CHRB, Saipan, MP 96950; tel. 288-0746; fax 288-0747; weekly; Operational Man. NICK LEGASPI; circ. 3,000.

Pacifica: POB 502143, Saipan, MP 96950; monthly; Editor MIKE MALONE.

Saipan Tribune: POB 10001, PMB 34, Saipan, MP 96950-8901; tel. 235-8747; fax 235-3740; e-mail editor.tribune@saipan.com; internet www.tribune.co.mp; 2 a week; Editor-in-Chief MARK M. BROADHURST; Publr REX I. PALACIOS; circ. 3,500.

Broadcasting and Communications

TELECOMMUNICATIONS

Micronesian Telecommunications Corpn: Saipan, MP 96950.

BROADCASTING

Radio

Inter-Island Communications Inc: POB 500914, Saipan, MP 96950; tel. 234-7239; fax 234-0447; f. 1984; commercial; station KCNM-AM, or KZMI-FM in stereo; Gen. Man. HANS W. MICKELSON; Programme Dir KEN WARNICK; CEO ANGEL OCAMPO.

Far East Broadcasting Co: POB 500209, Saipan, MP 96950; tel. 322-9088; fax 322-3060; e-mail saipan@febc.org; internet www.febc.org; f. 1946; non-commercial religious broadcasts; Dir ROBERT SPRINGER; Pres. JIM R. BOWMAN.

> **KSAI-AM:** tel. 234-6520; fax 234-3428; e-mail ksai@febc.org; f. 1978; local service; Station Man. HARRY BLALOCK.

> **KFBS-SW:** tel. 322-9088; e-mail saipan@febc.org; international broadcasts in Chinese, Indonesian, Russian, Vietnamese, Burmese, Mongolian; Chief Engineer ROBERT SPRINGER.

Station KHBI-SW: POB 501837, Saipan, MP 96950; tel. 234-6515; fax 234-5452; fmrly KYOI; non-commercial station owned by the *Christian Science Monitor* (USA); Gen. Man. DOMINGO VILLAR.

Station KPXP: PMB 415, Box 10000, Saipan, MP 96950; tel. 235-7996; fax 235-7998; e-mail power99@saipan.com; internet www.radiopacific.com/p99/; f. 1981; acquired Station KRSI in 2000, which also broadcasts on Saipan; Gen. Man. CURTIS DANCOE.

Television

Marianas CableVision: Saipan, MP 96950; tel. 235-4628; fax 235-0965; e-mail mcv@saipan.com; internet www.kmcv.co.mp; 55-channel cable service provider, broadcasting US and Pacific Rim programmes.

Tropic Isles Cable TV Corpn: POB 501015, Saipan, MP 96950; tel. 234-7350; fax 234-9828; 33-channel commercial station, with 5 pay channels, broadcasting 24 hours a day; US programmes and local and international news; 5,000 subscribers; Gen. Man. FRED LORD.

KMCV-TV: POB 501298, Saipan, MP 96950; tel. 235-6365; fax 235-0965; f. 1992; 52-channel commercial station, with 8 pay channels, broadcasting 24 hours a day; US programmes and local and international news; 5,650 subscribers; Gen. Man. WAYNE GAMBLIN.

Finance

BANKING

Bank of Guam (USA): POB 678, Saipan, MP 96950; tel. 234-6467; fax 234-3527; Gen. Man. JAMES LYNN; brs on Tinian and Rota.

Bank of Hawaii: Bank of Hawaii Bldg, El Monte Ave, Garapan, POB 566, Saipan, MP 96950; tel. 234-6673; fax 234-3478; Vice-Pres. DAVID BUEHLER; 2 brs.

Bank of Saipan: POB 500690, Saipan, MP 96950; tel. 234-6260; fax 235-1802; e-mail bankofsaipan@gtepacifica.net.

City Trust Bank: Qualo Rai, POB 501867, Saipan, MP 96950; tel. 234-7773; fax 234-8664; Gen. Man. MARIA LOURDES JOHNSON.

First Savings and Loan Asscn of America (USA): Beach Rd, Susupe, POB 500324, Saipan, MP 96950; tel. 234-6617; Man. SUZIE WILLIAMS.

Guam Savings and Loan Bank: POB 503201, Saipan, MP 96950; tel. 233-2265; fax 233-2227; Gen. Man. GLEN PEREZ.

HSBC Ltd (Hong Kong): Middle Rd, Garapan, Saipan, MP 96950; tel. 234-2468; fax 234-8882.

Union Bank of California: Oleai Centre, Beach Rd, Chalan Laulau, POB 501053, Saipan, MP 96950; tel. 234-6559; fax 234-7438; Gen. Man. KEN KATO.

INSURANCE

Associated Insurance Underwriters of the Pacific Inc: POB 501369, Saipan, MP 96950; tel. 234-7222; fax 234-5367; Gen. Man. MAGGIE GEORGE.

General Accident Insurance Asia Ltd (Microl Insurance): POB 502177, Saipan, MP 96950; tel. 234-2811; fax 234-5462; Man. Dir ANDREW M. HOWLETT.

Marianas Insurance Co Ltd: POB 502505, Saipan, MP 96950-2505; tel. 234-5091; fax 234-5093; e-mail mic@itecnmi.com; Gen. Man. ROSALIA S. CABRERA.

Mitsui Marine and Fire Insurance Co Ltd: POB 502177, Saipan, MP 96950; tel. 234-2811; fax 234-5462; Man. Dir ANDREW M. HOWLETT.

Moylan's Insurance Underwriters (Int.) Inc: POB 500658, Saipan, MP 96950; tel. 234-6442; fax 234-8641; e-mail moylan70@ite.net.

Pacifica Insurance Underwriters Inc: POB 500168, Saipan, MP 96950; tel. 234-6267; fax 234-5880; e-mail norten@netpci.com; Pres. NORMAN T. TENORIO.

Primerica Financial Services: POB 500964, Saipan, MP 96950; tel. 235-2912; fax 235-7910; Gen. Man. JOHN SABLAN.

Staywell: POB 2050, Saipan, MP 96950; tel. 235-4260; fax 235-4263; Gen. Man. LARRY LAVEQUE.

Trade and Industry

GOVERNMENT AGENCIES

Commonwealth Development Authority: POB 502149, Wakins Bldg, Gualo Rai, Saipan, MP 96950; tel. 234-7145; e-mail cda@itecnmi.com; internet www.cda.gov.mp; govt lending institution; funds capital improvement projects and private enterprises; offers tax incentives to qualified investors; Chair. JUAN S. TENORIO.

Office of Public Lands, Board of Public Lands Management: POB 500380, Saipan, MP 96950; tel. 234-3751; fax 234-3755; e-mail opl@vzpacifica.net; manages public land, which constitutes 82% of total land area in the Commonwealth (14% on Saipan).

CHAMBER OF COMMERCE

Saipan Chamber of Commerce: Chalan Kanoa, POB 500806 CK, Saipan, MP 96950; tel. 233-7150; fax 233-7151; e-mail saipanchamber@saipan.com; internet www.saipanchamber.com; Pres. RICHARD A. PIERCE; Exec. Dir CARLENE REYES-TENORIO; Co-ordinator JADENE A. VILLAGOMEZ.

EMPLOYERS' ASSOCIATIONS

Association of Commonwealth Teachers (ACT): POB 5071, Saipan, MP 96950; tel. and fax 256 7567; e-mail cnmiteachers@netscape.net; internet http://silkleaf.tripod.com/cnmi-act; supports the teaching profession and aims to improve education in state schools.

Saipan Garment Manufacturers' Association (SGMA): Saipan, MP 96950; e-mail sgmacs@gtepacifica.net; internet www.sgma-saipan.org; Chair. RICHARD A. PIERCE (acting).

UTILITIES

Commonwealth Utilities Corpn: POB 501220, Saipan, MP 96950; tel. 235-7025; fax 235-6145; e-mail cucedp@gtepacifica.net.

TRADE UNION AND CO-OPERATIVES

International Brotherhood of Electrical Workers: c/o Micronesian Telecommunications Corpn, Saipan, MP 96950; Local 1357 of Hawaii branch of US trade union based in Washington, DC.

The Mariana Islands Co-operative Association, Rota Producers and Tinian Producers Associations operate in the islands.

Transport

RAILWAYS

There have been no railways operating in the islands since the Japanese sugar industry railway, on Saipan, ceased operations in the Second World War.

ROADS

In 1991 there were 494 km (307 miles) of roads on the islands, 320 km (199 miles) of which are on Saipan. First grade roads constitute 135 km (84 miles) of the total, 99 km (62 miles) being on Saipan. There is no public transport, apart from a school bus system.

SHIPPING

The main harbour of the Northern Mariana Islands is Port of Saipan, which underwent extensive renovation in the mid-1990s. There are also two major harbours on Rota and one on Tinian. Several shipping lines link Saipan, direct or via Guam, with ports in Japan, Asia, the Philippines, the USA and other territories in the Pacific.

Commonwealth Ports Authority: POB 501055, Saipan, MP 96950; tel. 664-3500; fax 234-5962; e-mail cpa.admin@saipan.com; internet www.cpa.gov.mp; Exec. Dir CARLOS H. SALAS; Chair. JOSE R. LIFOFOI.

Mariana Express Lines: POB 501937,CTS Building, Saipan, MP 96950; tel. 322-1690; fax 323-6355; e-mail ctsispn@aol.com; services between Saipan, Guam, Japan and Hong Kong.

Saipan Shipping Co Inc (Saiship): Saiship Bldg, Charlie Dock, POB 8, Saipan, MP 96950; tel. 322-9706; fax 322-3183; weekly barge service between Guam, Saipan and Tinian; monthly services to Japan and Micronesia.

Westpac Freight: POB 2048, Puerto Rico, Saipan, MP 96950; tel. 322-8798; fax 322-5536; e-mail westpac@gtepacifica.net; internet www.westpacfreight.com; services between Saipan, Guam and the USA; Man. MICHIE CAMACHO.

CIVIL AVIATION

Air services are centred on the main international airport, Isley Field, on Saipan. There are also airports on Rota and Tinian.

Continental Micronesia: POB 508778, A.B. Won Pat International Airport, Tamuning, MP 96911; tel. 647-6595; fax 649-6588; internet www.continental.com; f. 1968, as Air Micronesia, by Continental Airlines (USA); name changed 1992; wholly owned subsidiary of Continental Airlines; hub operations in Saipan and Guam; services throughout the region and to destinations in the Far East and the mainland USA; Pres. BILL MEEHAN.

Freedom Air: POB 500239 CK, Saipan, MP 96950; tel. and fax 288-5663; scheduled internal flights.

Pacific Island Aviation: PPP 318, POB 10,000, Saipan, MP 96950; tel. 234-3600; fax 234-3604; e-mail piasaipan@saipan.com; internet www.pacificislandaviation.com; f. 1987; scheduled services to Rota and Guam; repair station; flight instruction; Pres. ROBERT F. CHRISTIAN; Gen. Man. FELICIDAD BODDY; Vice-Pres. PAZ PABALINAS.

Tourism

Tourism is one of the most important industries in the Northern Mariana Islands, earning US $430m. in 2001. In 1998 there were 3,942 hotel rooms. Most of the islands' hotels are Japanese-owned, and in 2001 75.5% of tourists came from Japan. The Republic of Korea and the USA are also important sources of tourists. The islands received a total of 442,466 visitors in 2001 (a decrease of some 16.3% on the figure for the previous year). The islands of Asuncion, Guguan, Maug, Managaha, Sariguan and Uracas (Farallon de Pajaros) are maintained as uninhabited reserves. Visitors are mainly attracted by the white, sandy beaches and the excellent diving conditions. There is also interest in the *Latte* or *Taga* stones (mainly on Tinian), pillars carved from the rock by the ancient Chamorros, and relics from the Second World War.

Hotel Association of the Northern Mariana Islands: POB 501983, Saipan, MP 96950; tel. 234-3455; fax 234-3411; e-mail rds@itecnmi.com; internet www.marianashotels.org; f. 1985; Chair. RONALD D. SABLAN.

Marianas Visitors Authority: POB 500861 CK, Saipan, MP 96950; tel. 664-3200; fax 664-3237; e-mail mva@saipan.com; internet www.visit-marianas.com; f. 1976; responsible for the promotion and development of tourism in the Northern Mariana Islands; Man. Dir PERRY JOHN TENORIO.

PUERTO RICO

Introductory Survey

Location, Climate, Language, Religion, Flag, Capital

The Commonwealth of Puerto Rico comprises the main island of Puerto Rico, together with the small offshore islands of Vieques and Culebra and numerous smaller islets, lying about 80 km (50 miles) east of Hispaniola (Haiti and the Dominican Republic) in the Caribbean Sea. The climate is maritime-tropical, with an average annual temperature of 24°C (75°F) and a normal range between 17°C (63°F) and 36°C (97°F). The official languages are Spanish and English. Christianity is the dominant religion, and about 74% of the population are Roman Catholics. The flag (proportions 3 by 5) has five alternating red and white horizontal stripes of equal width, with a blue triangle, in the centre of which is a five-pointed white star, at the hoist. The capital is San Juan.

Recent History

Puerto Rico, also known as Borinquen (after the original Arawak Indian name Boriquen), was ruled by Spain from 1509 until 1898, when it was ceded to the USA at the conclusion of the Spanish–American war, and administered as an 'unincorporated territory' of the USA. In 1917 Puerto Ricans were granted US citizenship, and in 1947 Puerto Rico obtained the right to elect its own Governor. A Constitution, promulgated in 1952, assigned Puerto Rico the status of a self-governing 'Commonwealth', or 'Estado Libre Asociado', in its relation to the USA.

The Partido Popular Democrático (PPD) held a majority in both chambers of the Legislature from 1944 until 1968, when, following a split within the party, the Partido Nuevo Progresista (PNP), an advocate of statehood, won the governorship and legislative control. This followed a plebiscite in 1967, when 60.5% of voters had ratified a continuation of Commonwealth status in preference to independence (0.6%) or incorporation as a State of the USA (38.9%). In the general elections of 1972 the PPD, under the leadership of Rafael Hernández Colón, regained the governorship and legislative control from the PNP, only to

lose them again in 1976. The victorious PNP was led by Carlos Romero Barceló, who became Governor in January 1977.

Romero Barceló, who had promised a referendum on statehood if re-elected for a further term in 1980, abandoned this plan following the election, in which he narrowly defeated former Governor Hernández Colón. The PPD, however, gained control of the Legislature. The 1984 gubernatorial election which was contested mainly on economic issues, was won by Hernández Colón by only 50,000 votes, with the PPD retaining substantial majorities in both legislative chambers. In September 1985 Romero Barceló was succeeded as leader of the PNP by Baltasar Corrada del Río.

Gubernatorial elections, held in November 1988, resulted in the re-election of Hernández Colón, who obtained 48.7% of the popular vote, compared with 45.8% for Corrada del Río and 5.5% for Rubén Berríos Martínez of the pro-independence Partido Independentista Puertorriqueño (PIP). Electoral participation was unusually high, at almost 90%.

The question of eventual independence for Puerto Rico has been a politically sensitive issue for over 50 years. With the PPD supporting the continuation and enhancement of Commonwealth status and the PNP advocating Puerto Rico's inclusion as a State of the USA, mainstream party encouragement of independence aims has come mainly from the PIP and other left-wing groups. There are two small, and occasionally violent, terrorist factions, the Ejército Popular Boricua (Macheteros), which operates in Puerto Rico, and the Fuerzas Armadas de Liberación Nacional (FALN), functioning principally on the US mainland.

In the 1988 election campaign, Corrada del Río, whose campaign was endorsed by the successful US presidential candidate, George Bush, advocated the admission of Puerto Rico as the 51st State of the USA, while Hernández Colón reiterated the traditional PPD policy of 'maximum autonomy' for Puerto Rico 'within a permanent union with the USA'. President Bush's open support of the statehood option was criticized by Hernández Colón and the PPD. In January 1989 Hernández Colón promised that a further plebiscite would be held. Although it was initially planned to hold this referendum in June 1991, in February the proposed legislation to make its result binding on the US Government failed to obtain sufficient support in the US Senate to allow it to proceed to full consideration by the US Congress.

In December 1991 the PPD Government organized a referendum on a proposal to adopt a charter of 'democratic rights', which included guarantees of US citizenship regardless of future change in Puerto Rico's constitutional status, and the maintenance of Spanish as the official language. The proposed charter was rejected by a margin of 53% to 45%. This result was widely interpreted as an indication that the majority of voters wished to retain Puerto Rico's Commonwealth status. Hernández Colón announced in January 1992 that he would not seek re-election in the gubernatorial election in November, and in the following month resigned as leader of the PPD. His successor as party leader, Victoria Muñoz Mendoza, was defeated in the election by the PNP candidate, Pedro Rosselló, by a margin of 49.9% of the popular vote to 45.9% for the PPD. The leadership of the PPD subsequently passed to Héctor Luis Acevedo.

Rosselló, who took office in January 1993, announced that a further referendum on Puerto Rico's future constitutional status would be held during the year. The Government proceeded with legislation rescinding the removal, in 1991, of English as an official language of the island. The referendum, which took place in November 1993, resulted in a 48% vote favouring the retention of Commonwealth status, with 46% of voters supporting accession to statehood and 4% advocating full independence.

In July 1996 a committee of the US House of Representatives unanimously recommended that Puerto Rican voters be given an opportunity, before 1998, to choose whether to retain the island's present status, or to proceed to statehood or full self-government. A preference for change would be followed by a 10-year 'Transition Plan' based on the result, during which time ballots would be held periodically to confirm the direction of the Plan. These proposals, however, were opposed by the Resident Commissioner representing the Puerto Rican Government in the House of Representatives, and were withdrawn in late 1996.

At elections held in November 1996 Rosselló was re-elected as Governor, receiving 51% of the votes, as against 45% obtained by Acevedo, representing the PPD. The PNP retained control of both chambers of the Legislature. During the campaign, the levels of minimum wages on the island, together with the recent abolition by US President, Bill Clinton, of federal tax exemptions for US companies establishing plants in Puerto Rico, formed the main political issues.

Debate on the territory's constitutional future intensified during 1997. In November, following a decision by the US Supreme Court expressly recognizing Puerto Rican citizenship as distinct from US citizenship, a new political movement, the Pro Patria National Union, was formed to encourage Puerto Ricans formally to renounce their US nationality. In March 1998, by a majority of only one vote, the US House of Representatives passed legislation providing for a referendum to determine the island's future status. Under the referendum plan, a vote in favour of statehood would oblige the US Congress to legislate for a 51st state during 1999, with Puerto Rico's admission to the union following within a 10-year period. In December 1998, however, the Puerto Rican electorate rejected the statehood proposal by a margin of 50.2% to 46.5%; 71% of eligible voters participated in the referendum. Rosselló, however, described the result as a reflection of the PNP Government's decline in popularity over domestic issues, and indicated that he was to petition the US Congress to implement measures to facilitate the island's transition to statehood. In June 1999, however, Rosselló unexpectedly announced that he would not seek re-election in the gubernatorial elections scheduled to take place in November 2000. In July 2001 the new Governor, María Sila Calderón, voiced support for a further referendum on the island's status during 2002. In July 2002 Calderón announced the creation of a 'Status Committee' to resolve the status issue; the Committee was to consist of representatives of the PPD, PNP and PIP, including Colón and Barceló.

An extended period of public protest followed the accidental death, in April 1999, of a civilian security guard during routine US military exercises on the small offshore island of Vieques, the eastern section of which, covering a coastline of 32 km, is used by the US Navy as an ammunition testing range. With support from the PIP, groups of protesters promptly established camps on the firing range, compelling the US Navy temporarily

to suspend these operations. Following extended negotiations between the Puerto Rican and US Governments, in January 2000 Rosselló and President Clinton announced a compromise plan to end the protesters' occupation by undertaking that, in return for the resumption of naval exercises in which only dummy ammunition would be used, the US Administration would provide immediate development aid to Vieques of $40m., rising to $90m. if residents of the island would agree in a referendum (provisionally scheduled for November 2001 but subsequently cancelled—see below) to allow the US Navy to resume live ammunition testing, in which event the Navy would undertake to leave Vieques permanently by 2003. In May 2000, prior to a proposed unilateral resumption of naval exercises (using dummy ammunition), protests on Vieques intensified, and several hundred Federal Government agents were sent to remove the protesters forcibly. The US Navy subsequently declared a 5-km land and sea 'security area' around the island.

Gubernatorial and legislative elections were held on 7 November 2000. Sila María Calderón of the PPD won 48.65% of the votes cast and was elected Governor; Carlos Pesquera of the PNP obtained 45.68% of the ballot and Rubén Berríos Martínez of the PIP 5.20%. The PPD secured 19 of the 28 seats in the Senate, its net gain of 12 being equivalent to the net loss of the PNP, which secured eight seats. The PPD also became the largest party grouping in the House of Representatives, securing 27 of the 51 seats, compared with 23 of the 54 in the previous legislature. The PNP won 23 seats, compared with 36 at the previous election. The PIP's representation was unchanged, with one member in each chamber of the legislature.

Upon taking office, Calderón announced her administration's repudiation of the agreement on military activity on Vieques signed in January 2000 by Clinton and Rosselló. Military exercises on the island were resumed in April 2001, despite legal challenges and protests. Operations were suspended in May, but resumed in mid-June. In the days following the resumption of exercises on Vieques (amid further protests), the new US President, George W. Bush, announced that the US Navy would end military activity on the island by May 2003. The Mayor of Vieques was sentenced to four months' imprisonment in August for trespassing on US Navy property during a protest. Exercises ceased temporarily from September 2001. Meanwhile, Calderón announced plans for a referendum on US military activity on Vieques to be held in late July; it was postponed until November, but was subsequently cancelled by the US Congress, which ordered the US military to remain on Vieques until an alternative location was found. The US Congress claimed that on-going tests were necessary as part of the US war on terrorism following the terrorist attacks on Washington, DC, and New York in September. (A non-binding referendum had been held in July, in which 68% of voters were in favour of the immediate departure from the island of the US Navy.) Tests resumed in early April 2002, amid protests from members of the PIP. In mid-2002 the PIP threatened to call a general strike and instigate a campaign of civil disobedience if the US Navy failed to leave the island by May 2003. The final scheduled bombing exercises took place in February 2003, and the US Navy withdrew from the island on 1 May; the withdrawal was marked by both celebrations and protests, during which demonstrators destroyed vehicles belonging to the US Navy. The firing range was to become a wildlife reserve.

In early 2002 Calderón proposed legislation to combat corruption, including the creation of a public fund to finance election campaigns. However, in March the PNP alleged that Calderón had used public funds to finance her gubernatorial campaign in 2000, while mayor of San Juan; an investigation into the charges by the Office of the Comptroller was subsequently launched. Several prominent PNP officials who had served in the Rosselló administration went on trial in 2002, and in December former education secretary Victor Fajardo was sentenced to 12 years' imprisonment after being convicted of diverting state funds to the PNP. In January 2003 the former Speaker of the House of Representatives under the Roselló administration, Edison Misla Aldorano, was found guilty of extortion, money laundering and perverting the course of justice; a former member of Rosselló's staff was sentenced to 18 months' imprisonment in the same month.

Government

Executive power is vested in the Governor, elected for a four-year term by universal adult suffrage. The Governor is assisted by an appointed Cabinet. Legislative power is held by the bicameral Legislative Assembly, comprising the Senate (with 28 members) and the House of Representatives (51 members). Additional members may be assigned in each chamber to ensure adequate representation of minority parties. The members of both chambers are elected by direct vote for four-year terms. The Resident Commissioner, also elected for a four-year term, represents Puerto Rico in the US House of Representatives, but is permitted to vote only in committees of the House. Puerto Ricans are citizens of the USA, but those resident in Puerto Rico, while eligible to participate in national party primary elections, may not vote in presidential elections.

Defence

The USA is responsible for the defence of Puerto Rico. The US Navy maintains a base in eastern Puerto Rico, which includes large sections of the island of Vieques. Puerto Rico has a paramilitary National Guard numbering about 11,000, which is funded mainly by the US Department of Defense.

Economic Affairs

In 1993, according to estimates by the World Bank, Puerto Rico's gross national income (GNI), measured at average 1991–93 prices, was equivalent to US $7,000 per head. In 1989–99, it was estimated, GNI per head increased, in real terms, at an average rate of 1.3% per year. During 1990–2001, it was estimated, the population increased at an average annual rate of 1.0%, while gross domestic product (GDP) per head increased, in real terms, by an average of 1.9% per year in 1990–97; GDP increased by 7.2% in 1998/99, by an estimated 3.6% in 1999/2000, and by a preliminary 2.2% in 2000/01.

Agriculture, forestry and fishing contributed 0.7% of GDP in 2000 and employed 2.0% of the working population in 2001. Dairy produce and other livestock products are the mainstays of the agricultural sector. The principal crops are sugar cane, plantains, bananas and pineapples. Cocoa cultivation has been successfully introduced, and measures to improve agricultural land use have included the replanting of some sugar-growing areas with rice and the cultivation of plantain trees over large areas of unproductive hill land. Commercial fishing is practised on a small scale. The GDP of the agricultural sector increased, in real terms, at an average rate of 2.1% per year between 1980/81 and 1990/91. Agricultural GDP rose by approximately 1.5% in 1993/94.

Industry (including manufacturing, construction and mining) provided 52.7% of GDP in 2000 and employed 21.6% of the working population in 2001. Industrial GDP increased, in real terms, at an average annual rate of 2.9% between 1980/81 and 1990/91. It rose by 3.3% in 1993/94.

Quarrying was estimated to provide about 0.1% of GDP on average and employed 0.2% of the working population in 2001. Otherwise, Puerto Rico has no commercially exploitable mineral resources, although deposits of copper and nickel have been identified.

Manufacturing is the main source of income, accounting for an estimated 43.3% of GDP in 2000 and employing 12.8% of the working population in 2001. From 1996 employment in the manufacturing sector declined at an average annual rate of 6%. The principal branch of manufacturing in 2000, based on the value of output, was chemical products (accounting for 34.7% of the total sector), mainly drugs and medicines. Other important products were electrical machinery (11.2%) and food products (8.4%). The GDP of the manufacturing sector increased, in real terms, by 2.9% per year between 1980/81 and 1990/91. The rate of advance was 3.5% in 1993/94. In 2000/01 total electricity production stood at 22,132.2m. kWh.

Services (including electricity, gas and water) provided 46.6% of GDP in 2000 and engaged 76.4% of the employed labour force in 2001. In real terms, the GDP of all service sectors increased at an average rate of 4.9% per year between 1980/81 and 1990/91, and by 4.4% in 1993/94. Tourism is of increasing importance, although GDP from the tourist sector declined in 1998/99, mainly owing to the effects of 'Hurricane Georges', which hit the island in late 1998. In 1999/2000, however, tourist arrivals were estimated at a record 4,566m. visitors, attracting revenue totalling $2,388m. Visitors from the US mainland comprised more than 54% of the total.

In 2000/01 Puerto Rico recorded a budget surplus of US $841,660m. Puerto Rico's total public debt at the end of the fiscal year to June 2000 was US $23,821.6m. US federal aid programmes are of central importance to the Puerto Rican economy, and the island has also received disaster relief in respect of hurricanes that widely disrupt the Puerto Rican economy intermittently. In 1999/2000 Puerto Rico recorded a

visible trade surplus of $6,734m., but there was a deficit of $7,173m. on the current account of the balance of payments. Mainland USA is the island's dominant trading partner, providing 60.7% of Puerto Rico's recorded imports and absorbing 90.5% of its recorded exports in 1997/98. Japan, the Dominican Republic, the United Kingdom and Venezuela are also significant in Puerto Rico's foreign trade. The principal category of recorded exports in 1999/2000 was chemical products (accounting for 58.9% of the total), mainly drugs and pharmaceutical preparations. Other major exports were machinery (mainly computers) and food. The main imports were also chemical products, food and machinery.

The annual inflation rate averaged 4.7% in 1990–2001. Consumer prices increased by an average of 6.4% in 2000 and by an average of 7.0% in 2001. Puerto Rico is very densely populated, and unemployment has been a persistent problem, although assisted by the growth in the tourist industry, the jobless rate declined during the 1990s. The average rate of unemployment fell from 16.8% of the labour force in 1992/93 to 10.5% in 2000/01.

Puerto Rico holds associate status in the UN Economic Commission for Latin America and the Caribbean (ECLAC, see p. 31) and has observer status in the Caribbean Community and Common Market (CARICOM, see p. 155). Puerto Rico declined to accept associate status in the Association of Caribbean States (ACS), formed in 1994, on the grounds of opposition by the US Government to the inclusion of Cuba. In July 2001 Puerto Rico applied for associate membership of CARICOM; the USA criticized the move, emphasizing that it had authority over the island's foreign policy as long as Puerto Rico held Commonwealth status.

Puerto Rico's economic growth has been inhibited by the lack of an adequate infrastructure. Government programmes of industrial and taxation incentives, aimed at attracting US and foreign investors and encouraging domestic reinvestment of profits and long-term capital investment, have generated growth in the manufacturing and services sectors. However, in 1996 the US Government announced that it was to progressively withdraw a number of important tax exemptions (collectively known as Section 936) enjoyed by US and foreign investors. The Government of Puerto Rico attempted to counteract the economic impact of their removal by seeking to establish the island as a centre for the finishing of Latin American manufactured goods destined for member states of the North American Free Trade Agreement (NAFTA, see p. 270). Approximately US $4,200m. was needed to repair damage from Hurricane Georges (see above), of which $2,700m. was disbursed in 1999/2000, largely from the US Federal Emergency Management Agency (FEMA) and private insurance companies. Economic growth slowed in 2000/01: preliminary figures recorded GDP growth of 2.2%. This figure was forecast to contract further in 2001/02, to 0.3%, partly owing to the economic slowdown in the USA. However, GDP growth was predicted to recover in 2002/03, to 2.7%, but this would be dependent on economic recovery in the USA, as well as continuing low fuel prices and low rates of interest.

Education

The public education system is centrally administered by the Department of Education. Education is compulsory for children between six and 16 years of age. In the academic year 2000/01 there were 606,487 pupils attending public day schools and 128,961 pupils attending private schools. The 12-year curriculum, beginning at five years of age, is subdivided into six grades of elementary school, three years at junior high school and three years at senior high school. Vocational schools at the high-school level and kindergartens also form part of the public education system. Instruction is conducted in Spanish, but English is a required subject at all levels. In 2002 there were five universities. The State University system consists of three principal campuses and six regional colleges. In 1999/2000 there were 174,550 students enrolled in public and private universities and colleges. In 2000/01 US $2,308,479m. of general government expenditure was allocated to education (22.3% of total expenditure).

Public Holidays

2003: 1 January (New Year), 6 January (Epiphany), 11 January (Birthday of Eugenio María de Hostos), 20 January (Martin Luther King Day), 17 February (Presidents' Day), 18 March (Good Friday), 22 March (Emancipation of the Slaves), 16 April (Birthday of José de Diego), 26 May (Memorial Day), 24 June

(Feast of St John the Baptist), 4 July (US Independence Day), 17 July (Birthday of Luis Muñoz Rivera), 24 July (Birthday of José Celso Barbosa), 25 July (Constitution Day), 1 September (Labor Day), 13 October (Columbus Day), 11 November (Veterans' Day), 19 November (Discovery of Puerto Rico Day), 27 November (US Thanksgiving Day), 25 December (Christmas Day).

2004: 1 January (New Year), 6 January (Epiphany), 11 January (Birthday of Eugenio María de Hostos), 19 January (Martin Luther King Day), 16 February (Presidents' Day), 22 March (Emancipation of the Slaves), 9 April (Good Friday), 16 April (Birthday of José de Diego), 31 May (Memorial Day), 24 June (Feast of St John the Baptist), 4 July (US Independence Day), 17 July (Birthday of Luis Muñoz Rivera), 24 July (Birthday of José Celso Barbosa), 25 July (Constitution Day), 6 September (Labor Day), 11 October (Columbus Day), 11 November (Veterans' Day), 19 November (Discovery of Puerto Rico Day), 25 November (US Thanksgiving Day), 25 December (Christmas Day).

Weights and Measures

The US system is officially in force. Some old Spanish weights and measures, as well as the metric system, are used in local commerce.

Statistical Survey

Source (unless otherwise stated): Puerto Rico Planning Board, POB 41119, San Juan, 00940-1119; tel. (787) 723-6200; internet www.jp.gobierno.pr.

Area and Population

AREA, POPULATION AND DENSITY

Area (sq km)	8,959*
Population (census results)	
1 April 1990	3,522,037
1 April 2000	
Males	1,833,577
Females	1,975,033
Total	3,808,610
Population (official estimates at mid-year)	
2000	3,815,893
2001	3,839,810
Density (per sq km) at mid-2001	428.6

* 3,459 sq miles.

PRINCIPAL TOWNS

(population at census of 1 April 2000)

San Juan (capital)	421,958	Caguas	88,680
Bayamón	203,499	Guaynabo	78,806
Carolina	168,164	Mayagüez	78,647
Ponce	155,038	Trujillo Alto	50,841

Source: Bureau of the Census, US Department of Commerce.

BIRTHS, MARRIAGES AND DEATHS*

	Registered live births		Registered marriages		Registered deaths	
	Number	Rate (per 1,000)	Number	Rate (per 1,000)	Number	Rate (per 1,000)
1996	63,259	16.9	32,572	8.7	29,871	8.0
1997	64,214	16.8	31,493	8.2	29,119	7.6
1998	60,518	15.7	26,390	6.8	29,990	7.8
1999	59,684	15.3	26,687	6.9	29,145	7.5
2000	59,333	15.5	26,151†	6.9	28,550†	7.5

* Prior to 2000, rates are based on unrevised population estimates.
† Provisional.

2001 (provisional): Registered live births 55,371 (birth rate 14.4 per 1,000).

Expectation of life (UN estimates, years at birth): 74.9 (males 70.4; females 79.6) in 1995–2000 (Source: UN, *World Population Prospects: The 2000 Revision*).

ECONOMICALLY ACTIVE POPULATION

('000 persons aged 16 years and over)

	1999	2000	2001
Agriculture, hunting, forestry and fishing	25	22	23
Mining and quarrying	1	1	2
Manufacturing	157	164	147
Electricity, gas and water	13	14	15
Construction	84	83	85
Trade and restaurants	231	246	238
Transport, storage and communications	44	41	41
Financing, insurance, real estate and business services	42	41	45
Community, social and personal services (incl. hotels)	552	562	555
Total employed (incl. others)	1,149	1,174	1,151
Unemployed	153	132	147
Total labour force	1,302	1,306	1,297

Source: ILO, *Yearbook of Labour Statistics*.

Health and Welfare

KEY INDICATORS

Total fertility rate (children per woman, 2001)	2.1
Under-5 mortality rate (per 1,000 live births, 1999)	13.7
Physicians (per 1,000 head, 1999)	1.75
Health expenditure (1994): % of GDP	6.0

Source: Pan American Health Organization.
For definitions see explanatory note on p. vi.

Agriculture

PRINCIPAL CROPS

('000 metric tons)

	1997	1998	1999*
Sugar cane	307.4	244.4	320.0
Tomatoes	9.9	4.2	5.0
Pumpkins, squash and gourds	14.0*	11.1	11.0
Bananas	38.2	49.3	50.0
Plantains	76.0*	92.5	82.0
Oranges	16.1	25.7	25.7
Mangoes	17.4	17.4*	17.4
Pineapples	19.2	14.2	15.0
Coffee (green)	11.6	13.4	12.8

* FAO estimate(s).

2000–2001 (FAO estimates): data assumed to be unchanged from 1999.

Source: FAO.

LIVESTOCK

('000 head, year ending September)

	1998	1999*	2000*
Cattle	387.0	390.0	390.0
Sheep	16.4	16.0	16.0
Goats	9.2	9.0	9.0
Pigs	114.8	118.0	118.0
Horses	25.0*	25.0	26.0
Poultry	12,487	12,500	12,500

* FAO estimate(s).

2001 (FAO estimates): Data assumed to be unchanged from 2000.

Source: FAO.

Fishing

(metric tons, live weight)

	1998	1999	2000
Capture	3,006	3,020	4,154
Snappers and jobfishes	n.a.	566	762
Seerfishes	109	123	145
Tuna-like fishes	121	99	111
Marine fishes	50	264	298
Caribbean spiny lobster	n.a.	209	212
Stromboid conchs	1,025	1,025	1,710
Aquaculture	164	138	154
Penaeus shrimps	158	128	127
Total catch	3,170	3,358	4,308

Source: FAO, *Yearbook of Fishery Statistics*.

Industry

SELECTED PRODUCTS
(year ending 30 June)

	1995/96	1996/97	1997/98*
Distilled spirits ('000 proof gallons)	25,343	36,292	33,471
Beer ('000 wine gallons)	7,923	6,973	5,784

* Preliminary.

Cement ('000 metric tons): 1,590 in 1998; 1,600 in 2000 (Source: US Geological Survey).

Electricity (million kWh): 20,140.8 in 1998/99; 21,459.8 in 1999/2000; 22,132.2 in 2000/01.

Finance

CURRENCY AND EXCHANGE RATES

Monetary Units
  United States currency: 100 cents = 1 US dollar (US $)

Sterling and Euro Equivalents (31 December 2002)
  £1 sterling = US $1.6118
  €1 = 1.0487 US cents
  $100 = £62.04 = €95.36.

BUDGET
(US $ '000, year ending 30 June)

Revenue	1998/99	1999/2000	2000/01
Taxation	6,136,230	6,791,200	6,417,856
Income taxes	4,413,860	4,967,138	4,536,840
Excise taxes	1,714,444	1,736,539	1,788,992
Service charges	457,454	617,020	645,806
Intergovernmental transfers	3,435,765	2,971,528	3,807,049
Other receipts	162,228	383,548	270,711
Total *	10,360,557	10,854,821	11,208,442

* Including interest payments (US $ '000): 97,880 in 1998/99; 91,525 in 1999/2000; 67,020 in 2000/01.

Expenditure	1998/99	1999/2000	2000/01
General government	526,629	853,040	739,009
Public safety	1,103,606	1,310,322	1,623,362
Health	625,475	972,757	954,563
Public housing and welfare	2,485,092	2,102,410	2,315,899
Education	2,272,903	2,436,267	2,308,479
Economic development	314,897	337,255	170,937
Aid to municipalities	318,664	373,016	222,721
Capital outlays	642,016	853,597	1,020,344
Debt service	794,336	860,964	1,011,468
Total	9,083,618	10,079,628	10,366,782

Source: Department of the Treasury, Commonwealth of Puerto Rico.

COST OF LIVING
(Consumer Price Index; base: 1990 = 100)

	1999	2000	2001
Food (incl. beverages)	215.2	234.6	267.8
Fuel and light	101.9	117.8	119.2
Rent	124.1	125.4	128.7
Clothing (incl. footwear)	85.5	85.2	83.6
All items (incl. others)	146.1	155.5	166.4

Source: ILO, *Yearbook of Labour Statistics*.

NATIONAL ACCOUNTS
(US $ million at current prices, year ending 30 June)

Expenditure on the Gross Domestic Product

	1997/98	1998/99	1999/2000*
Government final consumption expenditure	7,098.9	7,486.3	7,208.2
Private final consumption expenditure	32,194.2	34,620.1	36,592.7
Increase in stocks	31.2	484.5	347.2
Gross fixed capital formation	9,293.7	12,057.0	12,560.6
Total domestic expenditure	48,618.0	54,647.9	56,708.7
Exports of goods and services			
Less Imports of goods and services	5,515.1	5,391.4	6,441.0
GDP in purchasers' values	54,133.1	60,039.3	63,149.7
GDP at constant 1954 prices	9,252.1	9,915.8	10,276.8

* Preliminary.

Gross Domestic Product by Economic Activity

	1997/98	1998/99	1999/2000*
Agriculture	436.6	335.8	449.7
Manufacturing	22,976.0	26,636.8	27,441.9
Construction and mining†	1,482.5	1,645.0	1,862.7
Transportation and public utilities‡	3,978.5	3,951.1	4,057.4
Trade	7,287.4	7,896.3	8,437.3
Finance, insurance and real estate	7,672.4	8,327.2	8,920.2
Services	5,762.9	6,109.0	6,678.9
Government§	5,251.3	5,525.7	5,477.8
Sub-total	54,847.6	60,426.9	63,325.9
Statistical discrepancy	−714.5	−387.6	−176.1
Total	54,133.1	60,039.3	63,149.7

* Preliminary.
† Mining includes only quarries.
‡ Includes radio and television broadcasting.
§ Includes public enterprises not classified elsewhere.

BALANCE OF PAYMENTS
(US $ million, year ending 30 June)

	1997/98	1998/99	1999/2000
Merchandise exports f.o.b.	33,137.7	37,985.7	41,804.6
Merchandise imports f.o.b.	−27,296.3	−31,916.8	−35,070.8
Trade balance	5,841.4	6,068.9	6,733.8
Investment income received	1,088.0	1,050.9	1,049.3
Investment income paid	−20,824.3	−23,606.6	−23,741.7
Services and other income (net)	524.9	644.3	824.9
Unrequited transfers (net)	7,456.4	9,024.3	8,230.3
Net interest of Commonwealth and municipal governments	−251.7	−292.3	−269.2
Current balance	−6,165.3	−7,110.5	−7,172.6

External Trade

PRINCIPAL COMMODITIES
(US $ million, year ending 30 June)*

Imports	1997/98	1998/99	1999/2000
Mining products	133.3	92.5	458.4
Manufacturing products . . .	21,165.6	24,495.5	26,069.9
Food	2,226.5	2,301.1	2,182.1
Clothing and textiles . .	915.9	1,003.6	1,038.5
Paper, printing and publishing .	531.5	599.8	572.1
Chemical products . . .	5,842.0	7,306.4	9,037.6
Drugs and pharmaceutical			
preparations	3,644.2	4,646.9	5,840.4
Petroleum refining and related			
products	1,579.2	1,379.5	1,993.3
Rubber and plastic products . .	508.6	606.6	570.3
Primary metal products . .	490.0	537.0	424.2
Machinery, except electrical .	1,489.6	2,101.1	1,848.6
Electronic computers . .	375.6	695.2	522.5
Electrical machinery . . .	2,578.8	2,808.9	2,920.9
Transport equipment . . .	2,097.2	2,678.5	2,332.1
Professional and scientific			
instruments	876.2	863.9	933.5
Total (incl. others)	21,797.5	25,299.4	27,042.8

Exports	1997/98	1998/99	1999/2000
Manufacturing products . . .	30,108.7	34,767.0	38,305.1
Food	3,645.3	4,218.8	3,854.1
Clothing and textiles . .	805.1	728.5	695.1
Chemical products . . .	15,748.9	19,551.1	22,644.7
Drugs and pharmaceutical			
preparations	13,203.6	17,330.0	20,763.1
Machinery, except electrical . .	3,997.8	3,966.2	4,608.5
Electronic computers . . .	3,290.2	3,385.2	3,899.0
Electrical machines . . .	2,380.6	2,422.9	2,841.6
Professional and scientific			
instruments	1,682.8	2,054.7	1,800.5
Total (incl. others)	30,272.9	34,901.8	38,465.7

* Figures refer to recorded transactions only. Adjusted totals (in US $ million) are: Imports f.o.b. 27,296.3 in 1997/98; 31,916.8 in 1998/99; 35,070.8 in 1999/2000; Exports f.o.b. 33,137.7 in 1997/98; 37,985.7 in 1998/99; 41,804.6 in 1999/2000.

PRINCIPAL TRADING PARTNERS
(US $ million)*

	1994/95		1995/96	
	Imports	Exports	Imports	Exports
Belgium	53.2	165.2	122.9	205.9
Canada	187.5	74.2	197.8	75.5
Dominican Repub. . .	664.2	693.7	768.1	677.4
France	130.3	86.1	194.1	103.6
Germany	207.0	280.8	175.7	233.8
Ireland	180.8	27.4	278.8	19.6
Italy	203.8	58.3	279.0	56.7
Japan	1,278.5	91.1	1,222.8	184.5
Korea, Repub. . . .	216.8	43.8	236.7	61.1
Mexico	202.2	90.7	181.3	106.0
Netherlands . . .	93.1	157.2	100.2	119.1
United Kingdom . .	708.3	178.0	560.8	159.0
USA	12,158.1	21,106.9	11,909.3	20,148.6
US Virgin Islands . .	307.0	164.8	366.8	137.3
Venezuela	424.0	43.1	509.5	35.8
Total (incl. others) . .	18,816.6	23,811.3	19,060.9	22,944.4

* Recorded trade only.

1996/97 (US $ million): Imports: USA 13,317.8; Total (incl. others) 21,387.4. Exports: USA 21,187.3; Total (incl. others) 23,946.8.

1997/98 (US $ million): Imports: USA 13,225.9; Total (incl. others) 21,797.5. Exports: USA 27,397.4; Total (incl. others) 30,272.9.

Transport

ROAD TRAFFIC
(vehicles in use)

	1987/88	1988/89	1989/90
Cars: private	1,322,069	1,289,873	1,305,074
Cars: for hire	14,814	11,033	10,513
Trucks: private	15,790	13,273	12,577
Trucks: for hire	4,131	3,933	3,283
Light trucks	176,583	174,277	189,705
Other vehicles	75,155	74,930	60,929
Total	1,608,542	1,567,319	1,582,081

1996 (estimates): Passenger cars 878,000; Lorries and vans 190,000.

SHIPPING
(year ending 30 June)

	1985/86	1986/87	1987/88
Passengers arriving	29,559	59,089	33,737
Passengers departing	33,683	63,987	35,627
Cruise visitors	448,973	584,429	723,724

1988/89: Cruise visitors: 777,405.

1989/90: Cruise visitors: 866,090.

1990/91: Cruise visitors: 891,348.

Source: Puerto Rico Ports Authority.

CIVIL AVIATION
(year ending 30 June)

	1988/89	1989/90	1990/91
Passengers arriving	4,064,762	4,282,324	4,245,137
Passengers departing . . .	4,072,828	4,297,521	4,262,154
Freight (tons)*	173,126	208,586	222,172

* Handled by the Luis Muñoz Marin International Airport.

Source: Puerto Rico Ports Authority.

Tourism
(year ending 30 June)

	1997/98	1998/99	1999/2000*
Total visitors ('000)† . . .	4,670.8	4,221.3	4,566.0
From USA‡	2,544.4	2,265.0	2,479.4
From US Virgin Islands‡ . .	25.2	19.1	21.4
From other countries‡ . . .	826.5	740.0	840.6
Expenditure ($ million)	2,232.9	2,138.5	2,387.9

* Figures are preliminary.
† Including cruise-ship visitors and transient military personnel ('000): 1,274.7 in 1997/98; 1,197.2 in 1998/99; 1,224.6 (preliminary) in 1999/2000.
‡ Excluding cruise-ship visitors.

Communications Media

	1999	2000	2001
Television receivers ('000 in use)	1,270	1,290	n.a.
Telephones ('000 main lines in use)	1,294.7	1,299.3	1,329.5
Mobile cellular telephones ('000			
subscribers)	813.8	926.4	1,211.1
Internet users ('000)	200	400	600

Radio receivers ('000 in use): 2,840 in 1997.

Facsimile machines ('000 in use): 543 in 1993.

Daily newspapers (1996): 3; average circulation ('000 copies) 475.

Non-daily newspapers (1988 estimates): 4; average circulation ('000 copies) 106.

Sources: UNESCO, *Statistical Yearbook*; UN, *Statistical Yearbook*; International Telecommunication Union.

Education

	1993/94	1994/95	1995/96
Total number of students . . .	933,183	934,406	947,249
Public day schools	631,460	621,370	627,620
Private schools (accredited)*. .	140,034	145,864	148,004
University of Puerto Rico† . .	53,935	54,353	62,341
Private colleges and universities .	107,754	112,819	109,284
Number of teachers‡	39,816	40,003	39,328

* Includes public and private accredited schools not administered by the Department of Education.
† Includes all university-level students.
‡ School teachers only.

2000: Students at public day schools 606,487; Total number of students 909,998.

Adult literacy rate (UNESCO estimates): 93.8% (males 93.7%; females 94.0%) in 2000 (Source: UNESCO, *Statistical Yearbook*).

Directory

The Constitution

RELATIONSHIP WITH THE USA

On 3 July 1950 the Congress of the United States of America adopted Public Law No. 600, which was to allow 'the people of Puerto Rico to organize a government pursuant to a constitution of their own adoption'. This Law was submitted to the voters of Puerto Rico in a referendum and was accepted in the summer of 1951. A new Constitution was drafted in which Puerto Rico was styled as a commonwealth, or estado libre asociado, 'a state which is free of superior authority in the management of its own local affairs', though it remained in association with the USA. This Constitution, with its amendments and resolutions, was ratified by the people of Puerto Rico on 3 March 1952, and by the Congress of the USA on 3 July 1952; and the Commonwealth of Puerto Rico was established on 25 July 1952.

Under the terms of the political and economic union between the USA and Puerto Rico, US citizens in Puerto Rico enjoy the same privileges and immunities as if Puerto Rico were a member state of the Union. Puerto Rican citizens are citizens of the USA and may freely enter and leave that country.

The Congress of the USA has no control of, and may not intervene in, the internal affairs of Puerto Rico.

Puerto Rico is exempted from the tax laws of the USA, although most other federal legislation does apply to the island. Puerto Rico is represented in the US House of Representatives by a non-voting delegate, the Resident Commissioner, who is directly elected for a four-year term. The island has no representation in the US Senate.

There are no customs duties between the USA and Puerto Rico. Foreign products entering Puerto Rico—with the single exception of coffee, which is subject to customs duty in Puerto Rico, but not in the USA—pay the same customs duties as would be paid on their entry into the USA.

The US social security system is extended to Puerto Rico, except for unemployment insurance provisions. Laws providing for economic co-operation between the Federal Government and the States of the Union for the construction of roads, schools, public health services and similar purposes are extended to Puerto Rico. Such joint programmes are administered by the Commonwealth Government.

Amendments to the Constitution are not subject to approval by the US Congress, provided that they are consistent with the US Federal Constitution, the Federal Relations Act defining federal relations with Puerto Rico, and Public Law No. 600. Subject to these limitations, the Constitution may be amended by a two-thirds vote of the Puerto Rican Legislature and by the subsequent majority approval of the electorate.

BILL OF RIGHTS

No discrimination shall be made on account of race, colour, sex, birth, social origin or condition, or political or religious ideas. Suffrage shall be direct, equal and universal for all over the age of 18. Public property and funds shall not be used to support schools other than State schools. The death penalty shall not exist. The rights of the individual, of the family and of property are guaranteed. The Constitution establishes trial by jury in all cases of felony, as well as the right of habeas corpus. Every person is to receive free elementary and secondary education. Social protection is to be afforded to the old, the disabled, the sick and the unemployed.

THE LEGISLATURE

The Legislative Assembly consists of two chambers, whose members are elected by direct vote for a four-year term. The Senate is composed of 27 members, the House of Representatives of 51 members. Senators must be over 30 years of age, and Representatives over 25 years of age. The Constitution guarantees the minority parties additional representation in the Legislature, which may fluctuate from one quarter to one third of the seats in each House.

The Senate elects a President and the House of Representatives a Speaker from their respective members. The sessions of each house are public. A majority of the total number of members of each house constitutes a quorum. Either house can initiate legislation, although bills for raising revenue must originate in the House of Representatives. Once passed by both Houses, a bill is submitted to the Governor, who can either sign it into law or return it, with his reasons for refusal, within 10 days. If it is returned, the Houses may pass it again by a two-thirds majority, in which case the Governor must accept it.

The House of Representatives, or the Senate, can impeach one of its members for treason, bribery, other felonies and 'misdemeanours involving moral turpitude'. A two-thirds majority is necessary before an indictment may be brought. The cases are tried by the Senate. If a Representative or Senator is declared guilty, he is deprived of his office and becomes punishable by law.

THE EXECUTIVE

The Governor, who must be at least 35 years of age, is elected by direct suffrage and serves for four years. Responsible for the execution of laws, the Governor is Commander-in-Chief of the militia and has the power to proclaim martial law. At the beginning of every regular session of the Assembly, in January, the Governor presents a report on the state of the treasury, and on proposed expenditure. The Governor chooses the Secretaries of Departments, subject to the approval of the Legislative Assembly. These are led by the Secretary of State, who replaces the Governor at need.

LOCAL GOVERNMENT

The island is divided into 78 municipal districts for the purposes of local administration. The municipalities comprise both urban areas and the surrounding neighbourhood. They are governed by a mayor and a municipal assembly, both elected for a four-year term.

The Government

HEAD OF STATE

Governor: SILA MARÍA CALDERÓN (took office 2 January 2001).

EXECUTIVE
(April 2003)

Secretary of State: FERNANDO MERCADO RAMOS.

Secretary of Justice: ANABELLE RODRÍGUEZ.

Secretary of the Treasury: JUAN A. FLORES GALARZA.

Secretary of Education: CÉSAR REY HERNÁNDEZ.

Secretary of Labor and Human Resources: VICTOR RIVERA HERNÁNDEZ.

Secretary of Transportation and Public Works: FERNANDO E. FAGUNDO.

Secretary of Health: JOHNNY RULLÁN.

Secretary of Agriculture: FERNANDO TOLEDO.

Secretary of Housing: ILEANA ECHEGOYEN.

Secretary of Natural and Environmental Resources: LUIS RODRIGUEZ RIVERA.

Secretary of Consumer Affairs: FERNANDO TORRES RAMÍREZ.

Secretary of Recreation and Sports: JORGE L. ROSARIO.

Secretary of Economic Development and Commerce: MILTON SEGARRA.

Secretary of Prisons and Rehabilitation: MIGUEL PEREIRA.

Secretary of the Family: YOLANDA ZAYAS.

Resident Commissioner in Washington: ANÍBAL ACEVEDO VILÁ.

GOVERNMENT OFFICES

Office of the Governor: La Fortaleza, POB 9020082, PR 00909-0082; tel. (787) 721-7000; fax (787) 724-0942; internet www.fortaleza.gobierno.pr.

Department of Agriculture: POB 10163, San Juan, PR 00908-1163; tel. (787) 721-2120; fax (787) 723-9747.

Department of Consumer Affairs: POB 41059, San Juan, PR 00940-1059; tel. (787) 722-7555; fax (787) 726-6576; internet www.daco.prstar.net.

Department of Economic Development and Commerce: POB 4435, San Juan, PR 00902-4435; tel. (787) 721-2400; fax (787) 725-4417.

Department of Education: POB 190759, San Juan, PR 00919; tel. (787) 758-4949; fax (787) 250-0275; internet www.de.prstar.net.

Department of the Family: POB 11398, Santurce, San Juan, PR 00910; tel. (787) 722-7400; fax (787) 722-7910.

Department of Health: POB 70184, San Juan, PR 00936; tel. (787) 766-1616; fax (787) 250-6547.

Department of Housing: POB 21365, San Juan, PR 00928-1365; tel. (787) 274-2004; fax (787) 758-9263; internet www.vivienda.prstar.net.

Department of Justice: POB 192, San Juan, PR 00902; tel. (787) 721-2900; fax (787) 724-4770; internet www.justicia.prstar.net.

Department of Labor and Human Resources: 505 Muñoz Rivera Ave, San Juan, PR 00918; tel. (787) 754-5353; fax (787) 753-9550; internet www.dtrh.prstar.net.

Department of Natural and Environmental Resources: POB 9066600, San Juan, PR 00906-6600; tel. (787) 724-8774; fax (787) 723-4255.

Department of Recreation and Sports: POB 3207, San Juan, PR 00904; tel. (787) 721-2800; fax (787) 722-3382.

Department of State: POB 3271, San Juan, PR 00902-3271; tel. (787) 722-2121; fax (787) 725-7303; internet www.estado.prstar.net.

Department of Transportation and Public Works: POB 41269, San Juan, PR 00940; tel. (787) 722-2929; fax (787) 728-8963; internet www.dtop.prstar.net.

Department of the Treasury: POB 4515, San Juan, PR 009012; tel. (787) 721-2020; fax (787) 723-6213; internet www.hacienda.prstar.net.

Gubernatorial Election, 7 November 2000

Candidate	Votes	%
Sila María Calderón (PPD)	978,860	48.65
Carlos I. Pesquera (PNP)	919,194	45.68
Rubén Berríos Martínez (PIP)	104,705	5.20
Others†	9,376	0.47
Total	2,012,135	100.00

† Including 4,103 blank votes and 4,564 invalid votes.

Legislature

LEGISLATIVE ASSEMBLY

Senate
(28 members)

President of the Senate: Antonio J. Fas Alzamora.

Election, 7 November 2000

Party	Seats
PPD	19
PNP	8
PIP	1

House of Representatives
(51 members)

Speaker of the House: Carlos Vizcarrondo Irrizarry.

Election, 7 November 2000

Party	Seats
PPD	27
PNP	23
PIP	1

Political Organizations

Alliance for a Better Puerto Rico: San Juan; pro-statehood party.

Partido Comunista Puertorriqueño (PCP) (Puerto Rican Communist Party): f. 1934; seeks full independence and severance of ties with the USA.

Partido Independentista Puertorriqueño (PIP) (Puerto Rican Independence Party): 963 F. D. Roosevelt Ave, Hato Rey, San Juan PR 00918; e-mail jrbas@independencia.net; internet www.independencia.net; f. 1946; advocates full independence for Puerto Rico as a socialist-democratic republic; c. 60,000 mems; Leader Rubén Berríos Martínez.

Partido Nuevo Progresista (PNP) (New Progressive Party): POB 1992, Fernández Zuncos Station, San Juan 00910-1992; tel. (787) 289-2000; e-mail susanag@coqui.net; internet www.pnp.org; f. 1967; advocates eventual admission of Puerto Rico as a federated state of the USA; Pres. Leo Díaz Urbina; Sec.-Gen. Hugo Pérez; c. 225,000 mems.

Partido Popular Democrático (PPD) (Popular Democratic Party): 403 Ponce de León Ave, POB 5788, Puerta de Tierra, San Juan, PR 00906; f. 1938; supports continuation and improvement of the present Commonwealth status of Puerto Rico; Pres. and Leader Sila María Calderón; c. 660,000 mems.

Partido Socialista Puertorriqueño (PSP) (Puerto Rican Socialist Party): f. 1971; seeks the establishment of an independent socialist republic; Pres. and Leader Carlos Gallisá; c. 6,000 mems.

Pro Patria National Union: seeks independence for Puerto Rico; encourages assertion of distinct Puerto Rican citizenship as recognized by US Supreme Court in Nov. 1997; Leader Fufi Santori.

Puerto Rican Republican Party: POB 366108, San Juan, PR 00936-6108; tel. (787) 793-4040; Chair. Luis A. Ferré.

Puerto Rico Democratic Party: POB 5788, San Juan, PR 00906; tel. (787) 722-4952; Pres. William Miranda Marín.

The Fuerzas Armadas de Liberación Nacional Puertorriqueña (FALN—Puerto Rican National Liberation Armed Forces) and the Ejército Popular Boricua (Macheteros; f. 1978; Leader Filiberto Ojeda Ríos), which seek to attain independence through non-electoral means, are not incorporated or registered as political parties.

Judicial System

The Judiciary is vested in the Supreme Court and other courts as may be established by law. The Supreme Court comprises a Chief Justice and six Associate Justices, appointed by the Governor with the consent of the Senate. The lower Judiciary consists of Superior and District Courts and Municipal Justices equally appointed.

There is also a US Federal District Court, whose judges are appointed by the President of the USA. Judges of the US Territorial District Court are appointed by the Governor.

SUPREME COURT OF PUERTO RICO

POB 2392, Puerta de Tierra, San Juan, PR 00902-2392; tel. (787) 724-3551; fax (787) 725-4910; e-mail buzon@ribunales.gobierno.pr; internet www.tribunalpr.org.

Chief Justice: José A. Andréu García.

Justices: Federico Hernández Denton, Francisco Rebollo López, Jaime B. Fuster Berlingeri, Baltasar Corrada del Río, Efraín E. Rivera Pérez, Miriam Naveira Merly.

US TERRITORIAL DISTRICT COURT FOR PUERTO RICO

Federico Degetau Federal Bldg, Carlos Chardón Ave, Hato Rey, PR 00918; tel. (787) 772-3011; e-mail prdinfo@prd.uscourts.gov; internet www.prd.uscourts.gov.

Judges: Héctor M. Laffitte (Chief Judge), Juan M. Pérez-Giménez, José A. Fusté, Salvador E. Casellas, Daniel R. Domínguez, Carmen C. Cerezo, Jay A. García-Gregory, Jaime Pieras, Gilberto Gierbolini, Raymond L. Acosta.

Religion

About 72% of the population belonged to the Roman Catholic Church at the end of 2000. The Protestant churches active in Puerto Rico include the Episcopalian, Baptist, Presbyterian, Methodist, Seventh-day Adventist, Lutheran, Mennonite, Salvation Army and Christian Science. There is a small Jewish community.

CHRISTIANITY

The Roman Catholic Church

Puerto Rico comprises one archdiocese and four dioceses. At 31 December 2000 there were an estimated 2,738,000 adherents.

Bishops' Conference of Puerto Rico

POB 40682, San Juan, PR 00940-0682; tel. (787) 728-1650; fax (787) 728-1654.

f. 1966; Pres. Rt Rev. ROBERTO OCTAVIO GONZÁLEZ NIEVES (Archbishop of San Juan de Puerto Rico).

Archbishop of San Juan de Puerto Rico: ROBERTO OCTAVIO GONZÁLEZ NIEVES, Arzobispado, Calle San Jorge 201, San Juan, POB 902-1967; tel. (787) 725-4975; fax (787) 723-4040; internet www.arquidiocesisdesanjuan.org.

Other Christian Churches

Episcopal Church of Puerto Rico: POB 902, St Just, PR 00978; tel. (787) 761-9800; fax (787) 761-0320; e-mail iep@spiderlink.net; internet www.iepanglicom.org; diocese of the Episcopal Church in the USA, part of the Anglican Communion; Bishop Rt Rev. DAVID ANDRÉS ALVAREZ.

Evangelical Council of Puerto Rico: Calle El Roble 54, Apdo 21343, Río Piedras, San Juan, PR 00928; tel. (787) 765-6030; fax (787) 765-5977; f. 1954; 6 mem. churches; Pres. Rev. HARRY DEL VALLE; Exec. Sec. Rev. MOISÉS ROSA-RAMOS.

BAHÁ'Í FAITH

Spiritual Assembly: POB 11603, San Juan, PR 00910-2703; tel. (787) 763-0982; fax (787) 753-4449; e-mail bahaispr@caribe.net.

JUDAISM

Jewish Community Center: 903 Ponce de León Ave, San Juan, PR 00907; tel. (787) 724-4157; fax (787) 722-4157; e-mail rgtrydman@hotmail.com; f. 1953; conservative congregation with 250 families; Rabbi GABRIEL TRYDMAN.

There is also a reform congregation with 60 families.

The Press

Puerto Rico has high readership figures for its few newspapers and magazines, as well as for mainland US periodicals. Several newspapers have large additional readerships among the immigrant communities in New York.

DAILIES

(m = morning; s = Sunday)

El Nuevo Día: 404 Ponce de León Ave, POB S-297, San Juan, PR 00902; tel. (787) 793-7070; fax (787) 793-8850; internet www.endi.com; f. 1970; Publr and Editor ANTONIO LUIS FERRÉ; circ. 220,000 (m), 223,000 (s).

The San Juan Star: POB 364187, San Juan, PR 00936-4187; tel. (787) 782-4200; fax (787) 749-8840; internet www.thesanjuanstar.com; f. 1959; English; Publr GERARD ANGULO; Editor ANDY VIGLUCCI; circ. 100,000.

El Vocero de Puerto Rico: 206 Ponce de León Ave, POB 3831, San Juan, PR 00902-3831; tel. (787) 721-2300; fax (787) 725-8422; internet www.vocero.com; f. 1974; Publr and Editor GASPAR ROCA; circ 259,000 (m).

PERIODICALS

Buena Salud: 1700 Fernández Juncos Ave, San Juan, PR 00909; tel. (787) 728-7325; f. 1990; monthly; Editor IVONNE LONGUEIRA; circ. 59,000.

Caribbean Business: 1700 Fernández Juncos Ave, San Juan, PR 00909; tel. (787) 728-3000; fax (787) 728-7325; e-mail editor@casiano.com; internet www.casiano.com/html/cb.html; f. 1973; weekly; business and finance; Man. Editor MANUEL A. CASIANO, Jr; circ. 45,000.

Educación: c/o Dept of Education, POB 190759, Hato Rey Station, San Juan, PR 00919; f. 1960; 2 a year; Spanish; Editor JOSÉ GALARZA RODRÍGUEZ; circ. 28,000.

La Estrella de Puerto Rico: 165 Calle París, Urb. Floral Park, Hato Rey, PR 00917; tel. (787) 754-4440; fax (787) 754-4457; internet www.estrelladepr.com; f. 1983; weekly; Spanish and English; Editors-in-Chief FRANK GAUD, JAVIER MEDINA MÉNDEZ; circ. 123,500.

Imagen: 1700 Fernández Juncos Ave, Stop 25, San Juan, PR 00909-2999; tel. (787) 728-4545; fax (787) 728-7325; e-mail imagen@casiano.com; internet www.casiano.com/html/imagen.html; f. 1986; monthly; women's interest; Editor LIZZY FONFRÍAS; circ. 70,000.

Qué Pasa: Loiza St Station, POB 6338, San Juan, PR 00914; tel. (787) 728-3000; fax (787) 728-1075; e-mail quepasa@casiano.com; internet www.casiano.com/html/quepasa.html; f. 1948; quarterly; English; publ. by Puerto Rico Tourism Co; official tourist guide; Editor YAHIRA CARO; circ. 120,000.

Revista Colegio de Abogados de Puerto Rico: POB 9021900, San Juan, PR 00902-1900; tel. (787) 721-3358; fax (787) 725-0330; e-mail abogados@prtc.net; f. 1914; quarterly; Spanish; law; Editor Lic. ALBERTO MEDINA; circ. 10,000.

Revista del Instituto de Cultura Puertorriqueña: POB 9024184, San Juan, PR 00902-4184; tel. (787) 721-0901; e-mail revista@icp.gobierno.pr; internet icp.prstar.net; f. 1958; biannual; Spanish; arts, literature, history, theatre, Puerto Rican culture; Editor GLORIA TAPIA; circ. 3,000.

La Semana: Calle Cristóbal Colón, Esq. Ponce de León, Casilla 6527, Caguas 00725; tel. (787) 743-6537; e-mail lasemana@lasemana.com; internet www.lasemana.com/principal; weekly; f. 1963; Spanish; Gen. Man. MARJORIE M. RIVERA RIVERA.

La Torre: POB 23322, UPR Station, San Juan, PR 00931-3322; tel. (787) 758-0148; fax (787) 753-9116; e-mail ydef@hotmail.com; f. 1953; publ. by University of Puerto Rico; quarterly; literary criticism, linguistics, humanities; Editor J. MARTÍNEZ; circ. 1,000.

Vea: POB 190240, San Juan, PR 00919-0240; tel. (787) 721-0095; fax (787) 725-1940; e-mail editor@veavea.com; f. 1969; weekly; Spanish; TV, films and celebrities; Editor ENRIQUE PIZZI; circ. 92,000.

El Visitante: POB 41305, San Juan, PR 00940-1305; tel. (787) 728-3710; fax (787) 268-1748; e-mail elvisitante@pucpr.edu; internet www.elvisitante.com; f. 1975; weekly; publ. by the Puerto Rican Conf. of Roman Catholic Bishops; Dir JOSÉ R. ORTIZ VALLADARES; Editor Rev. EFRAÍN ZABALA; circ. 64,000.

FOREIGN NEWS BUREAUX

Agencia EFE (Spain): Cobian's Plaza, Suite 214, Santurce, PR 00910; tel. (787) 723-6023; fax (787) 725-8651; Dir ELÍAS GARCÍA.

Associated Press (USA): Metro Office Park 8, 1 St 108, Guaynabo, PR 00968.

Publishers

Ediciones Huracán Inc: González 1002, Río Piedras, San Juan, PR 00925; tel. (787) 763-7407; fax (787) 763-7407; f. 1975; textbooks, literature, social studies, history; Dir CARMEN RIVERA-IZCOA.

Editorial Académica, Inc: 67 Santa Anastacia St, El Vigía, Río Piedras, PR 00926; tel. (787) 760-3879; f. 1988; regional history, politics, government, educational materials, fiction; Dir FIDELIO CALDERÓN.

Editorial Coquí: POB 21992, UPR Station, San Juan, PR 00931.

Editorial Cordillera, Inc: POB 192363, San Juan, PR 00919-2363; tel. (787) 767-6188; fax (787) 767-8646; e-mail info@editorialcordillera.com; internet www.editorialcordillera.com; f. 1962; Pres. and Treas. CARLOS E. SERRANO.

Editorial Cultural Inc: POB 21056, Río Piedras, San Juan, PR 00928; tel. (787) 765-9767; e-mail cultural@editorialcultural.com; f. 1949; general literature and political science; Dir FRANCISCO M. VÁZQUEZ.

Editorial Edil, Inc: POB 23088, UPR Station, Río Piedras, PR 00931; tel. (787) 753-9381; fax (787) 250-1407; e-mail editedil@coqui.net; internet www.editorialedil.com; f. 1967; university texts, literature, technical and official publs; Man. Dir CONSUELO ANDINO ORTIZ.

Librería y Tienda de Artesanias Instituto de Cultura Puertorriqueña: POB 9024184, San Juan, PR 00902-4184; tel. (787) 724-4295; fax (787) 723-0168; e-mail tienda@icp.gobierno.pr; internet www.icp.gobierno.pr; f. 1955; literature, history, poetry, music, textbooks, arts and crafts; Man. Dir MAIRA PIAZZA.

University of Puerto Rico Press (EDUPR): POB 23322, UPR Station, Río Piedras, San Juan, PR 00931-3322; tel. (787) 250-0550; fax (787) 753-9116; f. 1932; general literature, children's literature, Caribbean studies, law, philosophy, science, educational; Dir CARLOS D'ALZINA.

Broadcasting and Communications

TELECOMMUNICATIONS

Junta Reglamentadora de Telecomunicaciones de Puerto Rico: Edif. Capital Center, Ave Arterial Hostos 235, Torre II, 9° Norte, Hato Rey, PR 00918; tel. (787) 756-0803; fax (787) 756-0814; e-mail correspondenci@jrtpr.gobierno.pr; internet www.jrtpr.gobierno.pr; Pres. PHOEBE FORSYTHE ISALES.

Puerto Rico Telephone Co (PRTC): GPO Box 360998, San Juan, PR 00936-0998; tel. (787) 782-8282; fax (787) 774-0037; e-mail telefonicapr@prtc.net; internet www.telefonicapr.com; provides all telecommunications services in Puerto Rico; majority control transferred from govt to private-sector GTE Corpn in March 1999; Pres. and CEO JON E. SLATER.

RADIO AND TELEVISION

There were 120 radio stations and 15 television stations operating in early 2002. The only non-commercial stations are the radio station and the two television stations operated by the Puerto Rico Department of Education. The US Armed Forces also operate a radio station and three television channels. All television services are in colour.

Asociación de Radiodifusores de Puerto Rico (Puerto Rican Radio Broadcasters' Asscn): Caparra Terrace, Delta 1305, San Juan, PR 00920; tel. (787) 783-8810; fax (787) 781-7647; e-mail prbroadcasters@centennialpr.net; f. 1947; 90 mems; Pres. EFRAÍN ARCHILLA DIEZ; Exec. Dir JOSÉ A. RIBAS DOMINICCI.

Finance

(cap. = capital; res = reserves; dep. = deposits; brs = branches; amounts in US dollars)

BANKING

Government Bank

Government Development Bank for Puerto Rico: POB 42001, San Juan, PR 00940-2001; tel. (787) 728-9200; fax (787) 268-5496; e-mail gdbcomm@prstar.net; internet www.gdb-pur.com; f. 1942; an independent govt agency; acts as fiscal (borrowing) agent to the Commonwealth Govt and its public corpns and provides long- and medium-term loans to private businesses; cap. 20.5m., res 46.8m., dep. 5,816.5m. (June 2001); Pres. JUAN AGUSTO-ALICEA.

Commercial Banks

Banco Bilbao Vizcaya Argentaria Puerto Rico: 258 Muñoz Rivera Ave, POB 364745, San Juan, PR 00936-4745; tel. (787) 777-2000; internet www.bbvapr.com; Pres. ANTONIO UGUINA.

Banco Popular de Puerto Rico: Banco Popular Centre, 209 Muñoz Rivera Ave, San Juan, PR 00918; tel. (787) 765-9800; fax (787) 758-2714; internet www.bpprcom; f. 1893; cap. and res 1,380m., dep. 12,836m. (Dec. 2002); Chair., Pres. and CEO RICHARD L. CARRIÓN; 195 brs.

Banco Santander Puerto Rico: 207 Ponce de León Ave, Hato Rey, PR 00918; tel. (787) 759-7070; fax (787) 767-7913; e-mail bspr@santanderpr.com; internet www.santanderpr.com; f. 1976; cap. 171.5m., res 225.5m., dep. 6,949.0m. (Dec. 2001); Chair. and CEO MONICA APARICIO; 64 brs.

Banco de la Vivienda: POB 213365, Hato Rey, San Juan, PR 00928-1365; tel. (787) 274-0000; fax (787) 764-8680; f. 1961; housing bank and finance agency; helps low-income families to purchase houses; Pres. MILDRED GOYCO; 7 brs.

Scotiabank de Puerto Rico: Plaza Scotiabank, 273 Ponce de León Ave, Hato Rey, PR 00918; tel. (787) 758-8989; fax (787) 766-7879; f. 1910; cap. 23.2m., res 128.0m., dep. 915.8m. (Dec. 2000); Chair. BRUCE R. BIRMINGHAM; Pres. I. A. MÉNDEZ; 13 brs.

Savings Banks

FirstBank Puerto Rico: First Federal Bldg, 1519 Ponce de León Ave, POB 9146, Santurce, PR 00908-0146; tel. (787) 729-8200; fax (787) 729-8139; internet www.firstbankpr.com; f. 1948; cap. and res 368.3m., dep. 3,363.0m. (Dec. 2000); Pres. ANGEL ALVAREZ-PÉREZ; 40 brs.

Oriental Bank and Trust: Ave Fagot, Esq. Obispado M-26, Ponce; tel. (787) 259-0000; fax (787) 259-0700; e-mail jllantin@orientalfg .com; internet www.orientalonline.com; total assets 2,039m. (June 2001); Chair., Pres. and CEO JOSÉ ENRIQUE FERNÁNDEZ.

Ponce Federal Bank, FSB: Villa esq. Concordia, POB 1024, Ponce, PR 00733; tel. (787) 844-8100; fax (787) 848-5380; f. 1958; Pres. and CEO HANS H. HERTELL; 19 brs.

R & G Corporation: POB 2510, Guaynabo, PR 00970; tel. (787) 766-6677; fax (787) 766-8175; internet www.rgonline.com; total assets 4,676m. (Dec. 2001); Chair., Pres. and CEO VÍCTOR J. GALÁN.

US Banks in Puerto Rico

Chase Manhattan Bank NA: 254 Muñoz Rivera Ave, Hato Rey, PR 00918; tel. (787) 753-3400; fax (787) 766-6886; Man. Dir and Gen. Man. ROBERT C. DÁVILA; 1 br.

Citibank NA: 252 Ponce de León Ave, San Juan, PR 00918; tel. (787) 753-5619; fax (787) 766-3880; Gen. Man. HORACIO IGUST; 14 brs.

SAVINGS AND LOAN ASSOCIATIONS

Caguas Central Federal Savings of Puerto Rico: POB 7199, Caguas, PR 00626; tel. (787) 783-3370; f. 1959; assets 800m. Pres. LORENZO MUÑOZ FRANCO.

Westernbank Puerto Rico: 19 West McKinley St, Mayagüez, PR 00680; tel. (787) 834-8000; fax (787) 831-5958; internet www.wbpr

.com; cap. and res 250.6m. dep. 2,610.4m. (Dec. 2000); Chair. and CEO Lic. FRANK C. STIPES; 31 brs.

Banking Organization

Puerto Rico Bankers' Association: Suite 1014, 208 Ponce de León Ave, San Juan, PR 00918; tel. (787) 753-8630; fax (787) 754-6077; e-mail info@abpr.com; internet www.abpr.com; Pres. JUAN A. NET; Exec. Vice-Pres. ARTURO L. CARRIÓN.

INSURANCE

Atlantic Southern Insurance Co: POB 362889, San Juan, PR 00936-2889; tel. (787) 767-9750; fax (787) 764-4707; internet www .atlanticsouthern.com; f. 1945; Chair. DIANE BEAN SCHWARTZ; Pres. RAMÓN L. GALANES.

Caribbean American Life Assurance Co: Suite 1300, 273 Ponce de Léon Ave, Scotiabank Plaza, San Juan, PR 00917; tel. (787) 250-1199; fax (787) 250-7680; e-mail cservice@calac.com; internet www .calac.com; Pres. IVÁN C. LOPÉZ.

Caribbean Bankers Life Insurance Co: POB 7145, Ponce, PR 00732-7145.

Cooperativa de Seguros Multiples de Puerto Rico: POB 3846, San Juan, PR 00936; internet www.segurosmultiples.com; general insurance; Pres. EDWIN QUIÑONES SUÁREZ.

La Cruz Azul de Puerto Rico: Road 1, Río Piedras, San Juan, PR 00927; tel. (787) 272-9898; fax (787) 272-7867; e-mail sclientes@ cruzazul.com; internet www.cruzazul.comhealth; Exec. Dir MARKS VIDAL.

Great American Life Assurance Co of Puerto Rico: POB 363786, San Juan, PR 00936-3786; tel. (787) 758-4888; fax (787) 766-1985; known as General Accident Life Assurance Co until 1998; Pres. ARTURA CARIÓN; Sr Vice-Pres. EDGARDO DIAZ.

Pan American Life Insurance Co: POB 364865, San Juan, PR 00936-4865; tel. (787) 724-5354; fax (787) 722-0253; e-mail palicpr@ prtc.net; Man. MAITE MUÑOZGUREN.

Puerto Rican–American Insurance Co: POB 70333, San Juan, PR 00936-8333; tel. (787) 250-5214; fax (787) 250-5371; f. 1920; total assets 119.9m. (1993); Chair. and CEO RAFAEL A. ROCA; Pres. RODOLFO E. CRISCUOLO.

Security National Life Insurance Co: POB 193309, Hato Rey, PR 00919; tel. (787) 753-6161; fax (787) 758-7409; Pres. CARLOS FERNÁNDEZ.

There are numerous agents, representing Puerto Rican, US and foreign companies.

Trade and Industry

DEVELOPMENT ORGANIZATION

Puerto Rico Industrial Development Co (PRIDCO): POB 362350, San Juan, PR 00936-2350; 355 Roosevelt Ave, Hato Rey, San Juan, PR 00918; tel. (787) 758-4747; fax (787) 764-1415; internet www.pridco.com; public agency responsible for the govt-sponsored industrial development programme; Exec. Dir WILLIAM RIEFKOHL.

CHAMBERS OF COMMERCE

Chamber of Commerce of Puerto Rico: 100 Calle Tetuán, POB 9024033, San Juan, PR 00902-4033; tel. (787) 721-6060; fax (787) 723-1891; f. 1913; 1,800 mems; Pres. RICARDO D'ACOSTA; Exec. Vice-Pres. EDGARDO BIGAS.

Chamber of Commerce of Bayamón: POB 2007, Bayamón, PR 00619; tel. (787) 786-4320; 350 mems; Pres. IVÁN A. MARRERO; Exec. Sec. ANGELICA B. DE REMÍREZ.

Chamber of Commerce of Ponce and the South of Puerto Rico: POB 7455, Ponce, PR 00732-7455; tel. (787) 844-4000; fax (787) 844-4705; f. 1885; 500 mems; Pres. CÁNDIDO R. RIVERA TOLL-INCHE.

Chamber of Commerce of Río Piedras: San Juan; f. 1960; 300 mems; Pres. NEFTALÍ GONZÁLEZ PÉREZ.

Chamber of Commerce of the West of Puerto Rico Inc: POB 9, Mayagüez, PR 00681; tel. (787) 832-3749; fax (787) 832-4287; e-mail ccopr@coqui.net; f. 1962; 220 mems; Pres. RAFAEL MOLINA.

Official Chamber of Commerce of Spain: POB 894, San Juan, PR 00902; tel. (787) 725-5178; fax (787) 724-0527; f. 1966; promotes Spanish goods; provides information for Spanish exporters and Puerto Rican importers; 300 mems; Pres. MANUEL GARCÍA; Gen. Sec. ANTONIO TRUJILO.

INDUSTRIAL AND TRADE ASSOCIATIONS

Home Builders' Association of Puerto Rico: 1605 Ponce de León Ave, Condominium San Martín, Santurce, San Juan, PR 00909; tel. (787) 723-0279; 150 mems; Pres. FRANKLIN D. LÓPEZ; Exec. Dir WANDA I. NAVAJAS.

Puerto Rico Farm Bureau: Cond. San Martín, 16054 Ponce de León Ave, Suite 403, San Juan, PR 00909-1895; tel. (787) 721-5970; fax (787) 724-6932; f. 1925; over 1,500 mems; Pres. ANTONIO ALVAREZ.

Puerto Rico Manufacturers' Association (PRMA): POB 195477, San Juan, PR 00919-5477; tel. (787) 759-9445; fax (787) 756-7670; e-mail prma@i-lan.com.

Puerto Rico United Retailers Center: POB 190127, San Juan, PR 00919-0127; tel. (787) 759-8405; fax (787) 763-9494; e-mail cud@centrounido.org; internet www.centrounido.org; f. 1891; 20,000 mems; Pres. RICARDO CALERO; Exec. Dir RUTH GRACIA.

UTILITIES

Electricity

Autoridad de Energía Eléctrica de Puerto Rico: POB 364267, San Juan, PR 00936-4267; tel. (787) 289-3434; fax (787) 289-4690; e-mail director@prepa.com; internet www.aeepr.com; govt-owned electricity corpn, opened to private co-generators in the mid-1990s; installed capacity of 4,389 MW; Dir HÉCTOR ROSARIO.

TRADE UNIONS

American Federation of Labor–Congress of Industrial Organizations (AFL–CIO): San Juan; internet www.afl-cio.org; c. 60,000 mems; Regional Dir AGUSTÍN BENÍTEZ.

Central Puertorriqueña de Trabajadores (CPT): POB 364084, San Juan, PR 00936-4084; tel. (787) 781-6649; fax (787) 277-9290; f. 1982; Pres. FEDERICO TORRES MONTALVO.

Confederación General de Trabajadores de Puerto Rico: 620 San Antonio St, San Juan, PR 00907; f. 1939; Pres. FRANCISCO COLÓN GORDIANY; 35,000 mems.

Federación del Trabajo de Puerto Rico (AFL-CIO): POB S-1648, San Juan, PR 00903; tel. (787) 722-4012; f. 1952; Pres. HIPÓLITO MARCANO; Sec.-Treas. CLIFFORD W. DEPIN; 200,000 mems.

Puerto Rico Industrial Workers' Union, Inc: POB 22014, UPR Station, San Juan, PR 00931; Pres. DAVID MUÑOZ HERNÁNDEZ.

Sindicato Empleados de Equipo Pesado, Construcción y Ramas Anexas de Puerto Rico, Inc (Construction and Allied Trades Union): Calle Hicaco 95–Urb. Milaville, Río Piedras, San Juan, PR 00926; f. 1954; Pres. JESÚS M. AGOSTO; 950 mems.

Sindicato de Obreros Unidos del Sur de Puerto Rico (United Workers' Union of South Puerto Rico): POB 106, Salinas, PR 00751; f. 1961; Pres. JOSÉ CARABALLO; 52,000 mems.

Unión General de Trabajadores de Puerto Rico: Apdo 29247, Estación de Infantería, Río Piedras, San Juan, PR 00929; tel. (787) 751-5350; fax (787) 751-7604; f. 1965; Pres. JUAN G. ELIZA-COLÓN; Sec.-Treas. OSVALDO ROMERO-PIZARRO.

Unión de Trabajadores de la Industría Eléctrica y Riego de Puerto Rico (UTIER): POB 13068, Santurce, San Juan, PR 00908; tel. (787) 721-1700; e-mail utier@coqui.net; internet www.utier.org; Pres. RICARDOS SANTOS RAMOS; Sec.-Treas. IRIS DELIA MATOS RIVERA; 6,000 mems.

Transport

There are no passenger railways in Puerto Rico, although in 1996 construction began of a 16.6-km (10.3-mile) urban rail system in greater San Juan. The system, which would cost US $1,200m., was under construction in 2002.

Ponce and Guayama Railway: Aguirre, PR 00608; tel. (787) 853-3810; owned by the Corporación Azucarera de Puerto Rico; transports sugar cane over 96 km of track route; Exec. Dir A. MARTÍNEZ; Gen. Supt J. RODRÍGUEZ.

ROADS

The road network totalled 14,400 km (8,950 miles) in 1999. A modern highway system links all cities and towns along the coast and cross-country. A highways authority oversees the design and construction of roads, highways and bridges. In April 2002 it was announced that some US $585.6m. was to be invested in projects to improve or expand the road network.

Autoridad de Carreteras: Centro Gubierno Minillas, Edif. Norte, Ave de Diego 23, POB 42007, Santurce, San Juan, PR 00940-2007; tel. (787) 721-8787; fax (787) 727-5456; internet www.dtop.gov.pr/ACT/actmain.html; Dir Dr FERNANDO FACUNDO.

SHIPPING

There are nine major ports in the island, the principal ones being San Juan, Ponce and Mayagüez. Other ports include Guayama, Guayanilla, Guánica, Yabucoa, Aguirre, Aguadilla, Fajardo, Arecibo, Humacao and Arroyo. San Juan, one of the finest and longest all-weather natural harbours in the Caribbean, is the main port of entry for foodstuffs and raw materials and for shipping finished industrial products. In 1992 it handled 14.3m. tons of cargo. Passenger traffic is limited to tourist cruise vessels.

Autoridad de los Puertos: POB 362829, San Juan, PR 00936-2829; tel. (787) 729-8805; fax (787) 722-7867; manages and administers all ports and airports; Exec. Dir JOSÉ GUILLERMO VAQUERO.

CIVIL AVIATION

The principal airports are at San Juan (Carolina), Ponce, Mayagüez and Aguadilla.

Tourism

An estimated 4,566,000 tourists visited Puerto Rico in 1999/2000, when revenue from this source was estimated at US $2,388m. More than one-half of all tourist visitors were from the mainland USA. In 2001 there were approximately 12,353 hotel rooms in Puerto Rico, with an occupancy rate of 67%. In April 2002 several major tourist projects were announced, with the aim of increasing the number of hotel rooms to 13,795 by 2004.

Compañía de Turismo: Edif. La Princesa Bldg, 2 Paseo La Princesa, POB 9023960, San Juan, PR 00902-3960; tel. (787) 721-2400; fax (787) 722-6238; internet www.prtourism.com; Dir MILTON E. SEGARRA PANCORBO.

UNITED STATES EXTERNAL TERRITORIES

The External or Unincorporated Territories of the USA comprise the Pacific Territories of American Samoa and Guam, the Caribbean Territory of the US Virgin Islands, and a number of smaller islands.

AMERICAN SAMOA

Introductory Survey

Location, Climate, Language, Religion, Flag, Capital

American Samoa comprises the seven islands of Tutuila, Ta'u, Olosega, Ofu, Aunu'u, Rose and Swains. They lie in the southern central Pacific Ocean, along latitude 14°S at about longitude 170°W, about 3,700 km (2,300 miles) south-west of Hawaii. The temperature normally ranges between 21°C (70°F) and 32°C (90°F), and the average annual rainfall is 5,000 mm (197 ins), the greatest precipitation occurring between December and March. English and Samoan, a Polynesian language, are spoken. The population is largely Christian, more than 50% being members of the Christian Congregational Church. The flag has a dark blue field, on which is superimposed a red-edged white triangle (with its apex at the hoist and its base at the outer edge of the flag), containing an eagle, representing the USA, grasping in its talons a yellow *fue* (staff) and *uatogi* (club), Samoan symbols of sovereignty. The capital is Pago Pago, on Tutuila (the officially designated seat of government is the village of Fagatogo).

Recent History

The Samoan islands were first visited by Europeans in the 1700s, but it was not until 1830 that missionaries from the London Missionary Society settled there. In 1878 the Kingdom of Samoa, then an independent state, gave the USA the right to establish a naval base at Pago Pago. The United Kingdom and Germany were also interested in the islands, but the United Kingdom withdrew in 1899, leaving the western islands for Germany to govern. The chiefs of the eastern islands ceded their lands to the USA in 1904, and the islands officially became an Unincorporated Territory of the USA in 1922.

Until 1978 American Samoa was administered by a Governor, appointed by the US Government, and a legislature comprising the Senate and the House of Representatives. In November 1977 the first gubernatorial elections took place and, in January 1978, Peter Coleman was inaugurated as Governor. He was re-elected for a second term in November 1980, after three years in office instead of four, to allow synchronization with US elections in 1980. At elections in November 1984 A. P. Lutali was elected Governor and Eni Hunkin (who subsequently adopted the use of his chiefly name, Faleomavaega) was elected Lieutenant-Governor. The High Court of American Samoa had ruled earlier that Coleman was ineligible to stand for a third successive term as Governor, because a law restricted tenure by any individual to two successive terms. In July 1988 the Territory's delegate to the US House of Representatives, Fofō Sunia, announced that he would not seek re-election, as he was then the subject of an official investigation for alleged financial mismanagement. In October he received a prison sentence for fraud. Eni F. H. Faleomavaega replaced Sunia as delegate in November. At gubernatorial elections, which took place in November, Coleman was elected Governor for a third term, while Galea'i Poumele replaced Faleomavaega as Lieutenant-Governor.

At gubernatorial elections in November 1992 Peter Coleman was defeated by A. P. Lutali. At elections to the House of Representatives in November 1994 about one-third of those members who sought re-election was defeated. Faleomavaega was re-elected as non-voting delegate.

In late 1994 and early 1995 American Samoa was one of a number of Pacific islands to express concern at the proposed passage through their waters of regular shipments of pluto-nium, *en route* from Europe to Japan. Moreover, the decision by France to resume nuclear-testing in the South Pacific in September 1995 was fiercely criticized by Lutali, who described the action as an affront to the entire Pacific community.

Gubernatorial and legislative elections took place in November 1996. An estimated 87% of eligible voters participated in the election, at which only eight of the 18 members seeking re-election to the Fono were successful. At a second round of voting the incumbent Lieutenant-Governor, the Democrat Tauese Sunia, was elected Governor with 51.3% of the vote, defeating Leala Peter Reid, Jr, who secured 48.7% of votes. Faleomavaega was re-elected as delegate to the US House of Representatives, with 56.5% of the vote, defeating Gus Hannemann, who won 43.5% of votes.

The decision in July 1997 by the Government of neighbouring Western Samoa to change the country's name to simply Samoa caused some controversy in the Territory. Legislation approved in March 1998 in the House of Representatives stated that American Samoa should not recognize the new name, which was viewed by many islanders as serving to undermine their own Samoan identity. Similarly, legislation prohibiting citizens of Samoa (formerly Western Samoa) from owning land in American Samoa was approved in response to the change of name.

In September 1998 a motion to impeach the Governor was introduced in the House of Representatives. Tauese Sunia was alleged to have used public funds allocated for school building repairs to purchase and install a sauna at his home.

In November 1998 Faleomavaega was re-elected as delegate to the US House of Representatives. In the same month, following a dispute lasting several years, a legal settlement was reached between the five leading US tobacco companies and the 46 US states and several of its territories, including American Samoa. It was agreed that between 1998 and 2025 American Samoa was to receive a total of some US$29m. in compensation for the harmful effects of cigarette smoking suffered by its inhabitants.

In March 1999 legislation was adopted introducing capital punishment (by lethal injection) for murder convictions; it was intended that this would act as a deterrent to drug dealers and users. However, the decision was reversed when, in mid-2000, the Territory's House of Representatives enacted legislation to abolish capital punishment; the legislation was to be presented to the Senate for approval. In April 2000 the Territory's House of Representatives rejected a bill proposing the legalization of gambling on the grounds that this would foster social problems.

At elections held on 7 November 2000, Tauese Sunia was narrowly re-elected as Governor, receiving 50.7% of votes cast, compared with 47.9% for opposition candidate, Senator Lealaifuaneva. However, following the Chief Electoral Officer's refusal to allow a recount, as requested by Lealaifuaneva (who claimed that absentee ballots had not been properly handled), Lealaifuaneva filed a lawsuit against the Government, but this was dismissed by the High Court in early December. At congressional elections, held concurrently, no candidate received the necessary 50% majority, Faleomavaega winning 45.7% of votes cast, compared with 30.3% for Hanneman. A second round of polling took place on 21 November, when Faleomavaega won a reported 61.1% of the votes and Hanneman received 38.9%. Faleomavaega therefore returned to the US House of Representatives for a seventh two-year term.

The issue of US jurisdiction in the Territory was raised once more in September 2001, when the Senate approved a resolution urging discussion with the US Government regarding the conferral of limited federal jurisdiction to the High Court of American Samoa, the only US territory without a sitting federal judge. A congressional public survey, conducted in the same month, registered wide popular support for a Federal Court and Public Prosecutor. At a meeting of the UN General Assembly in January 2002, the UN accepted American Samoa's proposal of May 2001 to be removed from the list of colonized territories. The Governor had sent a resolution to the UN Committee on Decolonization affirming American Samoa's wish to remain a US territory.

In May 2002 a lawsuit seeking eviction from its premises for rent arrears was filed in the High Court against Starkist Samoa, a tuna producer and the territory's largest private employer (with some 2,500 workers).

In mid-September 2002 the Territory's immigration procedures were amended to give the Attorney-General, rather than the Immigration Board, the ultimate authority to grant permanent residency status to aliens. The House of Representatives also approved a resolution to repeal legislation automatically conferring US citizenship in the Territory to foreign parents. In the same month the Territory's intelligence agencies claimed that the Speaker of the House of Representatives, Tuanaitau Tuia, had used public funds to purchase a car and to finance private travel for his wife. Meanwhile, in early June, a former president of the Amerika Samoa Bank (now ANZ Amerika Samoa Bank), Will Cravens, was convicted of fraud for his involvement in a scheme that had misappropriated US $75m. of investors' money.

The authorities were forced to introduce petrol rationing in October 2002 after a shipment of fuel was turned away from Pago Pago when it was discovered that its contents did not meet the specifications of the Environmental Protection Agency. Emergency supplies were delivered from neighbouring Samoa, pending the arrival of the next shipment.

In elections for American Samoa's delegate to the Federal Congress on 6 November 2002, Faleomavaega won 41.3% of votes cast, Fagafaga Daniel Langkilde secured 32.1% and Aumua Amata Coleman won 26.6%. Since none of the candidates secured the 50% of votes required, Faleomavaega and Langkilde entered a second round of voting on 19 November, at which Faleomavaega secured an eighth term in office.

In mid-December 2002 legislation was introduced that prohibited nationals of 23 countries thought to present a terrorist threat from entering the Territory, unless they were granted special permission. Opposition groups in Fiji expressed their displeasure at the neighbouring islands' inclusion on the list of countries, owing to its large Muslim population. In late March 2003 airlines also complained that the strict security measures introduced at the airport were damaging business.

In late January 2003 the Senate approved a motion to begin expulsion hearings against Senator Faamausili Pola. Members had already voted to remove Faamausili Pola in September 2002 when it was alleged that he had not been elected according to Samoan tradition. In March 2003 it was reported that the South Korean owner of the Daewoosa Samoa clothing factory had been convicted by a US court of human trafficking. The mainly Vietnamese and Chinese factory employees received very low wages and suffered appalling working conditions. The American Samoan High Court had previously ordered Daewoosa to pay workers US $3.5m. in compensation and fined the company an additional $290,000 in April 2002.

On 26 March 2003 Tauese Sunia died whilst travelling to Hawaii for medical treatment. Lieutenant-Governor Togiola Tulafono became acting Governor and appointed Aitofele Sunia as his deputy.

Government

Executive power is vested in the Governor, who is elected by popular vote and has authority which extends to all operations within the Territory of American Samoa. He has the power of veto with respect to legislation approved by the Fono (Legislature). The Fono consists of the Senate and the House of Representatives, with a President and a Speaker presiding over their respective divisions. The Senate is composed of 18 members, elected, according to Samoan custom, from local chiefs, or Matai, for a term of four years. The House of Representatives consists of 20 members who are elected by popular vote for a term of two years, and a non-voting delegate from Swains Island. The Fono meets twice a year, in January and July, for not more than 45 days, and at such special sessions as the Governor may call. The Governor has the authority to appoint heads of government departments with the approval of the Fono. Local government is carried out by indigenous officials.

Defence

The USA is responsible for the defence of American Samoa.

Economic Affairs

In 1985, according to estimates by the World Bank, American Samoa's gross national income (GNI), measured at average 1983–85 prices, was about US $190m., equivalent to $5,410 per head. GNI per head was estimated at some $8,000 in 1992. Between 1973 and 1985, it was estimated, GNI increased, in real terms, at an average rate of 1.7% per year, with real GNI per head rising by only 0.1% per year. In 1990–2000 the population increased by an average of 3.3% per year. An estimated 91,000 American Samoans live on the US mainland or Hawaii.

Agriculture, hunting, forestry, fishing and mining engaged only 3.1% of the employed labour force in 2000. Agricultural production provides little surplus for export. Major crops are coconuts, bananas, taro, pineapples, yams and breadfruit. Local fisheries are at subsistence level, but tuna-canning plants at Pago Pago process fish from US, Taiwanese and South Korean vessels. Canned tuna constituted some 96.8% of export revenue in 1998/99, when earnings reached US $334.2m.

Within the industrial sector, manufacturing activities engaged 35.3% of the employed labour force in 2000. Fish-canning is the dominant industry, and in 2001 some 70% of those employed in these factories were guest workers from Samoa (formerly Western Samoa). Other manufacturing activities include meat-canning, handicrafts, dairy farming, orchid farming and the production of soap, perfume, paper products and alcoholic beverages. A garment factory began operations at Tafuna in 1995 and in the following year employed more than 700 people (although almost one-half of these employees were foreign workers). However, the island's garment manufacturing industry was adversely affected following a riot between local workers and Vietnamese employees at a clothing factory, during which a number of people were injured. The incident was widely condemned, and Governor Tauese Sunia stated that the future of the garment industry in American Samoa would require consideration. Exports of finished garments declined from US $15.4m. in 1997/98 to $4.6m. in 1998/99. In 2002 the management of the Daewoosa clothing manufacturer was ordered by the authorities to pay compensation to its employees owing to the poor working conditions at the factory, and in early 2003 the factory's South Korean owner was convicted of human trafficking. The construction sector engaged 6.4% of the employed labour force in 2000.

Service industries engage a majority of the employed labour force in American Samoa (55.2% in 2000). The Government alone employs almost one-third of workers, although in the mid-1990s a series of reductions in the number of public-sector employees were introduced. The tourist industry is developing slowly, and earned some US $10m. in 1998. The number of tourist arrivals rose from 41,050 in 1998 to 49,060 in 1999.

The visible trade deficit rose from US $83.4m. in the year ending September 1998 to $107.5m. in 1999, when imports (including items imported by the Government and goods by the fish-canning sector) totalled $452.6m. and exports reached $345.1m. Most of American Samoa's trade is conducted with the USA. Other trading partners in 1998/99 included New Zealand, which supplied 9.2% of total imports, Australia (8.6%) and Fiji (5.6%). The UN estimated that, during 1990–2000, the Territory's exports increased at an average annual rate of 2.4%, while imports increased at a rate of 3.2% per year. Imports decreased by 1.0% in 2000 compared with the previous year. In 2000 the trade deficit was equivalent to the value of 22.9% of imports.

In 2001 a fiscal surplus of US$200,000 was recorded, the Territory's first budgetary surplus in more than 20 years. Government revenues in 2001 surpassed budgeted expectations by more than $4.2m. Annual inflation averaged 2.8% in 1990–96. Consumer prices rose by 1.7% in 1998 and by 0.9% in 1999. An inflation rate of 2.5% was recorded in the final quarter of 2002. An estimated 5.2% of the total labour force were unemployed in 2000.

American Samoa is a member of the Pacific Community (see p. 304), and is an associate member of the UN Economic and Social Commission for Asia and the Pacific (ESCAP, see p. 28).

The issue of American Samoa's minimum wage structure has caused considerable controversy. The situation (in which American Samoa has a lower minimum wage than the rest of the USA) has been largely attributed to the presence of the two tuna-canning plants on the islands, which employ almost half of the labour force, and consequently exert substantial influence over the setting of wage levels. In 1991, while the minimum wage on the US mainland increased by some 12%, the rate in American Samoa remained unchanged (leaving the Territory's minimum wage level some 50% below that of the mainland). A US recommendation for modest increases in wage levels, implemented in mid-1996, was strongly opposed by the American Samoan Government, which argued that, with higher costs, the Territory's tuna-canning industry would be unable to compete with other parts of the world. American Samoa's continued financial problems have been compounded by the high demand for government services from an increasing population, the limited economic and tax base and natural disasters. Attempts to reduce the persistent budget deficit and achieve a greater measure of financial security for the islands have included severe reductions in the number of public-sector employees, increased fees for government services and plans to diversify the economy by encouraging tourism and expanding manufacturing activity. Economic development, however, is hindered by the islands' remote location, the limited infrastructure and lack of skilled workers. In February 1998 the American Samoa Economic Advisory Commission was established, to help the Territory attain self-sufficiency and reduce its budget deficit. Its task was facilitated in November of that year, when the so-called 'tobacco settlement' (see Recent History) was reached. In late 1999 the Government opted to negotiate a loan of US $18.6m. from the US Department of the Interior, which was to be repaid from the proceeds of the 'tobacco settlement'. The money allowed the Government to pay outstanding debts—settlement of health care and utility bills were a condition stipulated by the USA— and to launch a programme of fiscal reforms. This was bolstered by an insurance settlement for damages sustained during Hurricane Val, in 1991, worth $47.9m. In April 2002 the American Samoan Economic Advisory Commission published a report, amended in July of that year, outlining proposals for the development of a more diverse market economy in the Territory. The Commission identified four sectors—fisheries and agriculture, telecommunications and information technology, manufacturing and tourism—as industries with the most potential for further development. The plan aimed to implement initiatives over a period of five to 10 years, leading ultimately to the creation of new enterprises and of more small to medium-sized businesses. In May 2001, meanwhile, the Government waived the provision requiring foreign employees to perform domestic duties for a year prior to progressing to other work. The move was welcomed by the tuna canneries, which were experiencing difficulties in recruiting sufficient workers. In 2002 the tuna-canning companies expressed concern that an impending US free trade agreement with Central American countries, which included the removal of tariffs on canned tuna, would threaten their exports to the USA. Nevertheless, in March 2003 the Senate approved a bill to levy tax on foreign tuna meat sold to the Territory's canneries. In the same month preliminary figures indicated that there had been a $121m. surplus on the balance of payments in 2002.

Education

Education is officially compulsory for 12 years between six and 18 years of age. Primary education begins at six years of age and lasts for eight years. Secondary education, beginning at the age of 14, lasts for a further four years. In 1996 there were 59 pre-primary schools, with 3,349 pupils, 32 primary schools, with 9,971 pupils, and nine secondary schools, with 3,624 pupils. There is also a community college of further education, with 1,049 students in 1996. Expenditure on education and culture in 1988/89 was US $30.4m., or 25.3% of total government expenditure.

Public Holidays

2003: 1 January (New Year's Day), 20 January (Martin Luther King Day), 17 February (Presidents' Day), 17 April (Flag Day, commemorating the first raising of the US flag in American Samoa), 27 May (Memorial Day), 4 July (US Independence Day), 1 September (Labor Day), 27 November (Thanksgiving Day), 25 December (Christmas Day).

2004: 1 January (New Year's Day), 19 January (Martin Luther King Day), 16 February (Presidents' Day), 17 April (Flag Day, commemorating the first raising of the US flag in American Samoa), 31 May (Memorial Day), 4 July (US Independence Day), 6 September (Labor Day), 25 November (Thanksgiving Day), 25 December (Christmas Day).

Weights and Measures

With certain exceptions, the imperial system is in force. One US cwt equals 100 lb; one long ton equals 2,240 lb; one short ton equals 2,000 lb. A policy of gradual voluntary conversion to the metric system is being encouraged by the Federal Government.

Statistical Survey

Source (unless otherwise indicated): Statistics Division, Department of Commerce, Pago Pago, AS 96799; tel. 633-5155; fax 633-4195; internet www.amsamoa.com.

AREA AND POPULATION

Area: 201 sq km (77.6 sq miles); *By island* (sq km): Tutuila 137; Ta'u 46; Ofu 7; Olosega 5; Swain's Island (Olohenga) 3; Aunu'u 2; Rose 1.

Population: 46,773 at census of 1 April 1990; 57,291 (males 29,264, females 28,027) at census of 1 April 2000. *By island* (2000): Tutuila 55,400; Manu'a District (Ta'u, Olosega and Ofu islands) 1,378; Aunu'u 476; Swain's Island (Olohenga) 37.

Density (2000): 285.0 per sq km.

Ethnic Groups (2000 census): Samoan 50,545; part-Samoan 1,991; Asian 1,631; Tongan 1,598; Total (incl. others) 57,291.

Principal Towns (population at 2000 census): Tafuna 8,409; Nu'uuli 5,154; Pago Pago (capital) 4,278; Leone 3,568; Fagatogo 2,096.

Births, Marriages and Deaths (1999): Registered live births 1,736; Registered marriages 272; Registered deaths 249.

Expectation of Life (years at birth): Males 68.0; Females 76.0 in 1995. Source: UN Economic and Social Commission for Asia and the Pacific.

Economically Active Population (persons aged 16 years and over, 2000 census): Agriculture, hunting, forestry, fishing and mining 517; Manufacturing 5,900; Construction 1,066; Trade, restaurants and hotels 2,414; Transport, storage, communications and utilities 1,036; Financing, insurance, real estate and business services 311; Community, social and personal services 5,474; Total employed 16,718 (males 9,804, females 6,914); Unemployed 909 (males 494, females 415); Total labour force 17,627 (males 10,298, females 7,329). Source: US Department of Commerce, *2000 Census of Population and Housing*.

AGRICULTURE, ETC.

Principal Crops (FAO estimates, '000 metric tons, 2001): Coconuts 5; Taro 2; Bananas 1. Source: FAO.

Livestock (FAO estimates, 2001): Pigs 10,700; Cattle 103; Chickens 37,000. Source: FAO.

Fishing (metric tons, live weight, 2000): Total catch 866 (Albacore 658). Source: FAO, *Yearbook of Fishery Statistics*.

INDUSTRY

Production (1994): Tinned fish 211,600 metric tons; Electric energy 158.60 million kWh (year ending September 1999). Source: partly Bank of Hawaii.

FINANCE

Currency and Exchange Rates: United States currency is used. For details, see section on the Northern Mariana Islands.

Budget (US $ '000, year ending September 1997): *Revenue:* Local revenue 47,151 (Taxes 34,105, Charges for services 7,099); Grants from US Department of Interior 97,287 (Operating grant 23,056, Capital projects 4,015, Special revenue 70,216); Total 144,438. *Expenditure:* General government 21,615; Public safety 10,558; Public works 19,580; Health and recreation 41,706; Education and culture 43,533; Economic development 9,344; Capital projects 5,221; Debt-servicing 1,356; Total 152,912.

Cost of Living (Consumer Price Index; annual averages; base: July-Sept. 1997 = 100): 99.6 in 1997; 101.3 in 1998; 102.2 in 1999.

EXTERNAL TRADE

Principal Commodities (US $ million, year ending September 1999): *Imports:* Food 47.7 (Fish 13.1); Fuel and oil 49.0 (Diesel fuel 37.7); Textiles and clothing 7.1; Machinery and transport equipment 19.3 (Road motor vehicles and parts 12.5); Miscellaneous manufactured articles 44.9 (Tin plates 13.3); Construction materials 15.3; Total (incl. others) 187.8. *Exports:* Canned tuna 334.2; Total (incl. others) 345.1. Note: Figures for imports exclude the value of goods imported by the American Samoa Government ($5.0 million) and by the fish-canning sector ($259.9 million).

Principal Trading Partners (US $ million, year ending September 1999): *Imports:* Australia 16.1; Fiji 10.4; Japan 3.6; Korea, Republic 2.7; New Zealand 17.2; Samoa 5.2; Taiwan 2.0; USA 124.8; Total (incl. others) 187.7. *Exports:* Total 345.1 (almost entirely to the USA). Note: Figures for imports exclude the value of goods imported by the American Samoa Government and by the fish-canning sector. The total value of imports was $452.6 million in 1998/99.

TRANSPORT

Road Traffic ('000 motor vehicles in use, 1999): Passenger cars 6.2; Commercial vehicles 0.7. Source: UN, *Statistical Yearbook*.

International Sea-borne Shipping (estimated freight traffic, '000 metric tons, 2001): Goods loaded 257; Goods unloaded 272.

Civil Aviation (Pago Pago Int. Airport, 2001): Flights 7,263; Passengers 154,185 (Boarding 81,669, Disembarking 70,421, Transit 2,095); Freight and mail ('000 lb) 4,500 (Loaded 1,604, Unloaded 2,896).

TOURISM

Tourist Arrivals: 29,997 in 1997; 41,050 in 1998; 49,060 in 1999.

Tourist Arrivals by Country (1996): Australia 1,469; China 669; Germany 785; India 466; New Zealand 4,032; Philippines 671; Tonga 790; United Kingdom 1,514; USA 8,778; Total (incl. others) 21,366 Figures exclude arrivals from Samoa (formerly Western Samoa). Source: World Tourism Organization, *Yearbook of Tourism Statistics*.

Tourism Receipts (US $ million): 9 in 1996; 10 in 1997; 10 in 1998. Source: World Tourism Organization.

COMMUNICATIONS MEDIA

Daily Newspapers (1996): 2; estimated circulation 5,000*.

Non-daily Newspapers (1996): 1; estimated circulation 3,000*.

Radio Receivers (1997): 57,000* in use.

Television Receivers (1999): 15,000* in use.

Telephones (2000): 14,300† main lines in use.

Facsimile Machines (1999): 563 subscribers.

Mobile Cellular Telephones (1999): 2,377† subscribers.
* Source: UNESCO, *Statistical Yearbook*.
† Source: International Telecommunication Union.

EDUCATION

Pre-primary: 60 schools (1998); 123 teachers (1991/92); 3,293 pupils (2000).

Primary: 32 schools (1998); 524 teachers (1991/92); 11,418 pupils (2000).

Secondary: 10 high schools (1998); 266 teachers (1991/92); 4,645 pupils (2000).

Higher (2000): American Samoa Community College 1,474 students.
Source: mainly UN, *Statistical Yearbook for Asia and the Pacific* and US Department of Commerce, *2000 Census of Population and Housing*.

Directory

The Constitution

American Samoa is an Unincorporated Territory of the USA. Therefore not all the provisions of the US Constitution apply. As an unorganized territory it has not been provided with an organic act by Congress. Instead the US Secretary of the Interior, on behalf of the President, has plenary authority over the Territory and enabled the people of American Samoa to draft their own Constitution.

According to the 1967 Constitution, executive power is vested in the Governor, whose authority extends to all operations within the Territory of American Samoa. The Governor has veto power with respect to legislation passed by the Fono (Legislature). The Fono consists of the Senate and the House of Representatives, with a President and a Speaker presiding over their respective divisions. The Senate is composed of 18 members, elected, according to Samoan custom, from local chiefs, or Matai, for a term of four years. The House of Representatives consists of 20 members who are elected by popular vote for a term of two years, and a non-voting delegate from Swain's Island. The Fono meets twice a year, in January and July, for not more than 45 days and at such special sessions as the Governor may call. The Governor has the authority to appoint heads of government departments with the approval of the Fono. Local government is carried out by indigenous officials. In August 1976 a referendum on the popular election of a Governor and a Lieutenant-Governor resulted in an affirmative vote. The first gubernatorial elections took place on 8 November 1977 and the second occurred in November 1980; subsequent elections were to take place every four years.

American Samoa sends one non-voting delegate to the US House of Representatives, who is popularly elected every two years.

The Government

(April 2003)

Governor: Togiola Tulafono (acting).

Lieutenant-Governor: Aitofele Sunia.

GOVERNMENT OFFICES

Governor's Office: Executive Office Building, Third Floor, Utulei, Pago Pago, AS 96799; tel. 633-4116; fax 633-2269; e-mail governorsoffice@asg-gov.com.

Department of the Interior, Office of Insular Affairs (OIA): Field Office of the OIA, Dept of the Interior, POB 1725, Pago Pago, AS 96799; tel. 633-2800; fax 633-2415; Field Representative Lydia Faleafine Nomura.

Office of the Representative to the Government of American Samoa: Amerika Samoa Office, 1427 Dillingham Blvd, Suite 210, Honolulu HI 96817, USA; tel. (808) 847-1998; fax (808) 847-3420; Representative Soloali'i Faalepo, Jr.

Department of Administrative Services: American Samoa Government, Executive Office Building, Utulei, Pago Pago, AS 96799; tel. 633-4156; fax 633-1814.

Department of Agriculture: American Samoa Government, Executive Office Building, Utulei, Pago Pago, AS 96799; tel. 699-1497; fax 699-4031.

Department of Commerce: American Samoa Government, Executive Office Building, POB 1147, Utulei, Pago Pago, AS 96799; tel. 633-1092; fax 633-2092.

Department of Education: American Samoa Government, Executive Office Building, Utulei, Pago Pago, AS 96799; tel. 633-5237; fax 633-4240.

Department of Legal Affairs: American Samoa Government, Executive Office Building, Utulei, Pago Pago, AS 96799; tel. 633-4163; fax 633-1838.

Department of Local Government: American Samoa Government, Pago Pago, AS 96799; tel. 633-5201; fax 633-5590.

Department of Health: American Samoa Government, Pago Pago; tel. 633-4606; fax 633-5379.

Department of Human Resources: American Samoa Government, Executive Office Building, Utulei, Pago Pago, AS 96799; tel. 633-4485; fax 633-1139.

Department of Human and Social Services: American Samoa Government, Pago Pago, AS 96799; tel. 633-1187; fax 633-7449.

Department of Marine and Wildlife Resources: American Samoa Government, Executive Office Building, Utulei, Pago Pago, AS 96799; tel. 633-4456; fax 633-5590.

Department of Parks and Recreation: American Samoa Government, Pago Pago, AS 96799; tel. 699-9614; fax 699-4427.

Department of Port Administration: American Samoa Government, Pago Pago, AS 96799; tel. 633-4251; fax 633-5281.

Department of Public Safety: American Samoa Government, Pago Pago, AS 96799; tel. 633-1111; fax 633-7296.

Department of Public Works: American Samoa Government, Executive Office Building, Utulei, Pago Pago, AS 96799; tel. 633-4141; fax 633-5958.

Department of Treasury: American Samoa Government, Executive Office Building, Utulei, Pago Pago, AS 96799; tel. 633-4155; fax 633-4100.

Department of Youth and Women's Affairs: American Samoa Government, Executive Office Building, Utulei, Pago Pago, AS 96799; tel. 633–2835; fax 633–2875.

Legislature

FONO

Senate

The Senate has 18 members, elected, according to Samoan custom, from local chiefs, or Matai, for a term of four years.

President: LUTU TENARI S. FUIMAONO.

House of Representatives

The House has 20 members who are elected by popular vote for a term of two years, and a non-voting delegate from Swain's Island.

Speaker: MATAGI MAILO RAY MCMOORE.

CONGRESS

Since 1980 American Samoa has been able to elect, for a two-year term, a delegate to the Federal Congress, who may vote in committee but not on the floor of the House of Representatives. Elections to the post took place in November 2000.

Delegate of American Samoa: ENI F. H. FALEOMAVAEGA (November 2002), US House of Representatives, 2422 Rayburn House Office Bldg, Washington, DC 20515, USA; tel. (202) 225-8577; fax (202) 225-8757; e-mail faleomavaega@mail.house.gov.

Judicial System

The judicial system of American Samoa consists of the High Court, presided over by the Chief Justice and assisted by Associate Justices (all appointed by the Secretary of the Interior), and a local judiciary in the District and Village Courts. The judges for these local courts are appointed by the Governor, subject to confirmation by the Senate of the Fono. The High Court consists of three Divisions: Appellate, Trial, and Land and Titles. The Appellate Division has limited original jurisdiction and hears appeals from the Trial Division, the Land and Titles Division and from the District Court when it has operated as a court of record. The Trial Division has general jurisdiction over all cases. The Land and Titles Division hears cases involving land or Matai titles.

The District Court hears preliminary felony proceedings, misdemeanours, infractions (traffic and health), civil claims less than US $3,000, small claims, Uniform Reciprocal Enforcement of Support cases, and *de novo* trials from Village Courts. The Village Courts hear matters arising under village regulations and local customs.

Chief Justice: MICHAEL KRUSE.

Associate Justice: LYLE L. RICHMOND.

Attorney-General: MALAETASI M. TOGAFAU.

High Court

Office of the Chief Justice, High Court, Pago Pago, AS 96799; tel. 633-1261; e-mail Hcourt@samoatelco.com.

Judge of the District Court: JOHN L. WARD II, POB 427, Pago Pago, AS 96799; tel. 633-1101.

Judge of the Village Court: FAISIOTA TAUANU'U, Pago Pago, AS 96799; tel. 633-1102.

Religion

The population is largely Christian, more than 50% being members of the Congregational Christian Church and about 20% being Roman Catholics.

CHRISTIANITY

American Samoa Council of Christian Churches: c/o CCCAS Offices, POB 1637, Pago Pago, AS 96799; f. 1985; six mem. churches; Pres. Cardinal PIO TAOFINU'U (Roman Catholic Archbishop of Samoa-Apia and Tokelau); Gen. Sec. Rev. ENOKA L. ALESANA (Congregational Christian Church in American Samoa).

The Roman Catholic Church

American Samoa comprises the single diocese of Samoa-Pago Pago, suffragan to the archdiocese of Samoa-Apia and Tokelau. At 31 December 2000 there were 12,000 adherents in the islands. The Bishop participates in the Catholic Bishops' Conference of the Pacific, based in Fiji.

Bishop of Samoa-Pago Pago: Rev. JOHN QUINN WEITZEL, Diocesan

Pastoral Center, POB 596, Fatuoaiga, Pago Pago, AS 96799; tel. 699-1402; fax 699-1459; e-mail QUINN@samoatelco.com.

The Anglican Communion

American Samoa is within the diocese of Polynesia, part of the Church of the Province of New Zealand. The Bishop of Polynesia is resident in Fiji.

Protestant Churches

Congregational Christian Church in American Samoa (CCCAS): POB 1637, Pago Pago, AS 96799; 34,000 mems (22,000 in American Samoa) in 1985.

Other active Protestant groups include the Baptist Church, the Christian Church of Jesus Christ, the Methodist Church, Assemblies of God, Church of the Nazarene and Seventh-day Adventists. The Church of Jesus Christ of Latter-day Saints (Mormon) is also represented.

The Press

News Bulletin: Office of Public Information, American Samoa Government, Utulei; tel. 633-5490; daily (Mon.–Fri.); English; non-commercial; Editor PHILIP SWETT; circ. 1,800.

Samoa Journal and Advertiser: POB 3986, Pago Pago, AS 96799; tel. 633-2399; weekly; English and Samoan; Editor MICHAEL STARK; circ. 3,000.

Samoa News: POB 909, Pago Pago, AS 96799; tel. 633-5599; fax 633-4864; e-mail samoanews@samoatelco.com; 5 a week; English and Samoan; Publr LEWIS WOLMAN; circ. 4,500.

Broadcasting and Communications

TELECOMMUNICATIONS

American Samoa Telecommunications Authority: Box M, Pago Pago, AS 96799; tel. 633-1211; internet www.samoatelco.com.

BROADCASTING

Radio

KSBS-FM: POB 793, Pago Pago, AS 96799; tel. 633-7000; fax 622-7839; internet www.samoanet.com/ksbsfm; commercial.

WVUV: POB 4894, Pago Pago, AS 96799; tel. 688-7397; fax 688-1545; fmr govt-administered station leased to Radio Samoa Ltd in 1975; commercial; English and Samoan; 24 hours a day; Man. VINCENT IULI.

Television

KVZK-TV: Office of Public Information, POB 3511, Pago Pago, AS 96799; tel. 633-4191; fax 633-1044; f. 1964; govt-owned; non-commercial; English and Samoan; broadcasts 18 hours daily on two channels; Gen. Man. VAOITA SAVALI; Technical Dir CARL SEVERA.

Finance

(cap. = capital; dep. = deposits; m. = million; amounts in US dollars)

BANKING

Commercial Banks

ANZ Amerika Samoa Bank: POB 3790, Pago Pago, AS 96799; tel. 633-5053; fax 633-5057; e-mail decourtb@samoatelco.com; internet www.anz.com.au/americansamoa; f. 1979; fmrly Amerika Samoa Bank; joined ANZ group in April 2001; cap. 6.6m., dep. 45.3m. (June 1995); Pres. and CEO HAROLD P. FIELDING; 4 brs.

Bank of Hawaii (USA): POB 69, Pago Pago, AS 96799; tel. 633-4226; fax 633-7197; f. 1897; total assets 12,674.6m. (Mar. 1993); Man. BRENT A. SCHWENKE.

Development Bank

Development Bank of American Samoa: POB 9, Pago Pago, AS 96799; tel. 633-4031; fax 633-1163; f. 1969; govt-owned and non-profit-making; cap. 6.4m. (1989); Chair. EUGENE G. C. H. REID; Pres. MANUTAFEA E. MEREDITH.

INSURANCE

American International Underwriters (South Pacific) Ltd: Pago Pago, AS 96799; tel. 633-4845.

National Pacific Insurance Ltd: Lumana'i Bldg, POB 1386, Pago Pago, AS 96799; tel. 633-4266; fax 633-2964; e-mail npi@samoatelco .com; f. 1977; Man. PETER MILLER.

Oxford Pacific Insurance Management: POB 1420, Pago Pago, AS 96799; tel. 633-4990; fax 633-2721; e-mail progressive_oxford@ yahoo.com; f. 1977; represents major international property and life insurance cos; Pres. JULIAN E. ASHBY.

Trade and Industry

DEVELOPMENT ORGANIZATIONS

American Samoa Development Corporation: Pago Pago, AS 96799; tel. 633-4241; f. 1962; financed by private Samoan interests.

American Samoa Economic Advisory Commission: Pago Pago; Chair. JOHN WAIHEE.

Department of Commerce: Government of American Samoa, Pago Pago, AS 96799; tel. 633-5155; fax 633-4195; Dir ALIIMAU H. SCANLAN, Jr.

UTILITIES

American Samoa Power Authority: Pago Pago, AS 96799; tel. 644-2772; fax 644-5005; e-mail abe@aspower.com; supplies water and electricity throughout the islands; also manages sewer and solid waste collection.

Transport

ROADS

There are about 150 km (93 miles) of paved and 200 km (124 miles) of secondary roads. Non-scheduled commercial buses operate a service over 350 km (217 miles) of main and secondary roads. There were an estimated 5,900 registered motor vehicles in the islands in 1996.

SHIPPING

There are various passenger and cargo services from the US Pacific coast, Japan, Australia (mainly Sydney) and New Zealand, that call at Pago Pago, which is one of the deepest and most sheltered harbours in the Pacific. Inter-island boats provide frequent services between Samoa and American Samoa.

Polynesia Shipping: POB 1478, Pago Pago AS 96799; tel. 633-1211; fax 633-1265; e-mail polyship@samoatelco.com.

CIVIL AVIATION

There is an international airport at Tafuna, 11 km (7 miles) from Pago Pago, and smaller airstrips on the islands of Ta'u and Ofu.

Samoa Aviation: POB 280, Pago Pago Int. Airport, Pago Pago, AS 96799; tel. 699-9106; fax 699-9751; e-mail samoaair@aol.com; f. 1986; operates service between Pago Pago and Samoa, Tonga and Niue; Pres. and Chair. JAMES PORTER.

Tourism

The tourist industry is encouraged by the Government, but suffers from the cost and paucity of air services linking American Samoa with its main sources of custom, particularly the USA. Pago Pago is an important mid-Pacific stop-over for large passenger aircraft. An estimated 21,366 tourists visited the islands in 1996. In that year 41.1% of tourists came from the USA, 18.9% from New Zealand, 7.1% from the United Kingdom, 6.9% from Australia, 3.7% from both Germany and Tonga, 3.1% from both China and the Philippines and 2.2% from India. In 1992 there were some 542 hotel beds available in the islands. The industry earned an estimated US $10m. in 1998. Tourist arrivals totalled 49,060 in 1999.

Office of Tourism: Convention Center, POB 1147, Pago Pago, AS 96799; tel. 633-1091; fax 633-2092; e-mail amsamoa@amsamoa.com; internet www.amsamoa.com/tourism; Dir SINIRA T. LUTU FUIMAONO.

GUAM

Introductory Survey

Location, Climate, Language, Religion, Flag, Capital

Guam is the southernmost and largest of the Mariana Islands, situated about 2,170 km (1,350 miles) south of Tokyo (Japan) and 5,300 km (3,300 miles) west of Honolulu (Hawaii). The temperature normally ranges between 24°C (75°F) and 30°C (86°F) in June–November, but is generally cooler and drier from December to May. The average annual rainfall is about 2,000 mm (79 ins). English is the official language, but Japanese and Chamorro, the local language, are also spoken. The principal religion is Christianity, about 90% of the population being Roman Catholics. The national flag of the United States of America (q.v.) is used by Guam. The capital is Hagåtña (formerly Agaña).

Recent History

Members of a Spanish expedition, under the Portuguese navigator, Fernão Magalhães (Ferdinand Magellan), were the first Europeans to discover Guam, visiting the island in 1521, during a voyage that accomplished the first circumnavigation of the globe. The island was claimed by Spain in 1565, and the first Jesuit missionaries arrived three years later. The native Micronesian population is estimated to have fallen from 100,000 in 1521 to fewer than 5,000 in 1741, owing largely to a combination of aggression by the Spaniards and exposure to imported diseases. The intermarrying of Micronesians, Spaniards and Filipinos resulted in the people now called Chamorros. Guam was ceded to the USA after the Spanish–American War of 1898, but was invaded by Japan in 1941. Fierce fighting took place before the island was recaptured by US forces in 1944.

Guam became an Unincorporated Territory of the USA, under the jurisdiction of the US Department of the Interior, in 1950. In 1970 the island elected its first Governor, and in 1972 a new law gave Guam one Delegate to the US House of Representatives.

The Delegate may vote in committee but not on the floor of the House. In 1976 an island-wide referendum decided that Guam should maintain close ties with the USA, but that negotiations should be held to improve the island's status. In a further referendum, in 1982, in which only 38% of eligible voters participated, the status of a Commonwealth, in association with the USA, was the most favoured of six options, supported by 48% of the votes cast. In 1987, in a referendum on the provisions of a draft law aimed at conferring the status of Commonwealth on the Territory, voters approved the central proposal, while rejecting articles empowering the Guam Government to restrict immigration and granting the indigenous Chamorro people the right to determine the island's future political status. In a further referendum in late 1987 both outstanding provisions were approved. Negotiations between the Guam Commission for Self Determination and the USA continued throughout the late 1980s and early 1990s. As well as demands for greater autonomy, the Commission raised the issue of military bases on the island, particularly the US Naval Air Station, which the Republican Governor and leader of the Commission, Joseph Ada, requested should be returned to civilian use. This finally occurred in March 1995.

In February 1987 the former Governor of Guam, Ricardo Bordallo, was found guilty of charges of bribery, extortion and conspiracy to obstruct justice, and was sentenced to 30 years' imprisonment (later reduced to nine years) in April. In November Bordallo's wife, Madeleine, was elected to replace him in the Guam Legislature, and in October 1988 Bordallo won an appeal and his sentence was cancelled. Bordallo was liable for imprisonment in the USA on charges of obstruction and attempting to influence witnesses, but he committed suicide at the end of January 1990. Madeleine Bordallo was the Democrat candidate at gubernatorial elections in November 1990, when Ada was re-elected. Concurrent elections to the Guam Legislature resulted in a Democrat majority of one seat.

At legislative elections in November 1992 the Democrats increased their representation to 14 seats, while the Republicans secured only seven. Robert Underwood was elected as the new Democrat Delegate to the US House of Representatives, replacing the Republican, Ben Blaz.

In January 1994 the US Congress approved legislation providing for the transfer of 3,200 acres of land on Guam from federal to local control. This was a significant achievement for the Government of Guam, which had campaigned consistently for the return of 27,000 acres (some 20% of Guam's total area), appropriated by US military forces after the Second World War. Chamorro rights activists, however, opposed the move, claiming that land should not be transferred to the Government of Guam, but rather to the original landowners.

At gubernatorial elections in November 1994 the Democrat Carl Gutierrez, defeated his Republican opponent, Tommy Tanaka, winning 54.6% of total votes cast, while Madeleine Bordallo was elected to the position of Lieutenant-Governor. Legislative elections held concurrently also resulted in a Democrat majority, with candidates of the party securing 13 seats, while the Republicans won eight. Robert Underwood was re-elected unopposed as Delegate to the US House of Representatives.

Reports that Chamorro rights activists had initiated a campaign for independence from the USA were denied by the Governor in July 1995. In September, however, at the Fourth World Conference on Women in Beijing, People's Republic of China, the Lieutenant-Governor, Madeleine Bordallo, expressed her support for the achievement of full autonomy for Guam and for the Chamorro people's desire for decolonization.

It was reported in 1995 that the US President, Bill Clinton, had appointed a team of Commonwealth negotiators to review the draft Guam Commonwealth Act. However, in mid-2001 the proposals were still awaiting a hearing in the US Congress, despite considerable pressure from the Democrat Governor, Carl Gutierrez, for a serious debate on Guam's political status. Reports in mid-1996 that the US Government was seeking to have Guam removed from the UN's list of Non Self-Governing Territories prompted representatives of the Guam Landowners' Association to warn that consideration of the Commonwealth Act should not be viewed as a full debate on self-determination, and reiterated their belief in the Chamorro people's right to autonomy. Guam's self-styled Commission on Decolonization was established in 1997, headed by the Governor.

At elections in November 1996 Republican members regained a majority in the Legislature, winning 11 seats, while Democrat candidates secured 10 seats. In a referendum held concurrently voters approved a proposed reduction in the number of Senators from 21 to 15 (effective from November 1998), and plans to impose an upper limit (2.5% of total budgetary expenditure) on legislative expenses. However, a proposal to restrict the number of terms that Senators can seek to serve in the Legislature was rejected by voters. Guam's Delegate to the US House of Representatives, Robert Underwood, was re-elected unopposed.

In March 1998 delegates from several Pacific island nations and territories met in Hawaii to discuss possible methods of controlling the increasing population of brown tree snakes in Guam. The reptile, which was accidentally introduced to the island from New Guinea after the Second World War, has been responsible for severe power cuts, as a result of climbing electricity lines, as well as major environmental problems (including the decimation of native bird populations); it was feared that, if left unchecked, the snakes could spread to other islands in the region. In 2002 government researchers from the US Department of Agriculture announced plans to poison the snakes using dead mice filled with Tylenol (a household painkiller), and measures to improve detection of the snakes at points of entry on other Pacific islands were discussed.

In June 1998 Underwood secured approval from the US authorities to change the spelling of Guam's capital from Agaña to Hagåtña. The change was effected in order to reflect more accurately the original Chamorro language name for the town.

Robert Underwood was re-elected, with 70.2% of the total votes cast, as Guam's Delegate to the US House of Representatives on 4 November 1998, defeating Manuel Cruz, who secured 20.1% of the votes. Concurrent gubernatorial and legislative elections resulted in the return to office, as Governor, of Carl Gutierrez, and, as Lieutenant-Governor, of Madeleine Bordallo. (In December former Governor Joseph Ada alleged that Gutierrez's victory had been achieved by fraudulent means, and later in the month a Guam court invalidated the election result and

ordered a new poll to be held. In February 1999, however, the Superior Court of Guam found that there had been no electoral malpractice and confirmed the appointments of Gutierrez and Bordallo.) In elections to the legislature, where the number of seats had been reduced from 21 to 15, 12 candidates of the Republican Party and three candidates of the Democratic Party were returned as Senators.

US President Clinton visited Guam in November 1998. During his visit President Clinton approved the transfer of some 1,300 ha of federal land to the local administration and undertook to hasten the transfer of a further 2,020 ha of former US air force and navy land. In August 2001 the US Army announced plans to move some combat weaponry and equipment from Europe to storage bases in Guam, as well as in Taiwan and Hawaii.

In mid-1999 it was announced that Guam was no longer able to support the growing numbers of illegal immigrants from the People's Republic of China, some 500 having arrived between April and June alone, seeking refugee status. The immigrants were to be diverted to and detained in the nearby Northern Mariana Islands, the immigration laws of which differ from those of Guam.

At elections held on 7 November 2000, Underwood was re-elected as Guam's delegate to the US House of Representatives, winning 78.1% of votes cast. At legislative elections, held concurrently, eight candidates of the Republican Party and seven candidates of the Democratic Party were returned as senators. In July 2002 Marilyn Manibusan, a former Senator, and another former government official were indicted by a federal grand jury. They were charged with conspiring to extort real estate developers. Manibusan and his co-defendant, James Sablan, were convicted of the charges in May 2003.

Robert Underwood secured the Democrat nomination for the gubernatorial elections of 5 November 2002, but was defeated by the Republican candidate, Felix Camacho, who received 55.4% of the votes cast. (Madeleine Z. Bordallo was designated Guam's delegate to the US Congress.) In the legislature, nine Democrat-candidates were elected as senators, while the Republican party's representation decreased to six seats. Governor Camacho pledged to halt the widely-perceived rise in corruption and misallocation of public funds on Guam, and to improve public finances (see Economic Affairs). On 15 December President George W. Bush of the USA announced the creation of a new five-member panel to examine the issue of compensation for events on the island following its occupation by the Japanese during the Second World War.

Meanwhile, the island remained vulnerable to the impact of extreme weather formations during the second half of 2002. President George W. Bush declared the island a federal disaster area on two occasions, following Typhoon Chata'an in July and Supertyphoon Pongsona in early December 2002. Although no loss of life was reported as a direct consequence of the severe storms, some 35,000 islanders remained homeless in early 2003. The US Government granted some $10m. towards the recruitment of 4,000 largely unemployed islanders to assist in the recovery effort, and Governor Camacho retained several members of the former administration in order to ensure the provision of essential services during his transition to office.

In April 2003 a former Republican senator, Thomas Tanaka, pleaded guilty to charges of misprision of felony, which related to his alleged involvement in a fraudulent government contract. In the same month Joseph Mafnas, a former chief of the Guam police department, was indicted on forgery and financial fraud charges.

Government

Guam is governed under the Organic Act of Guam of 1950, which gave the island statutory local power of self-government and made its inhabitants citizens of the United States, although they are not permitted to vote in national elections. Guam's non-voting Delegate to the US House of Representatives is elected every two years. Executive power is vested in the civilian Governor, who is elected by popular vote every four years. The Government has 48 executive departments, whose heads are appointed by the Governor with the consent of the Guam Legislature. The Legislature consists of 21 members elected by popular vote every two years. It is empowered to enact legislation on local matters, including taxation and fiscal appropriations. In a referendum in November 1996 voters approved a reduction in the size of the Legislature from 21 to 15 members, effective from November 1998.

Defence

Guam is an important strategic military base for the USA, with 1,580 members of the Air Force, 1,850 naval personnel and 30 army personnel stationed there in August 2002.

Economic Affairs

In 2000, according to estimates by the Bank of Hawaii (BOH), Guam's gross national income (GNI), at current prices, was US $2,772.8m., equivalent to $16,575 per head. Between 1988 and 1993, it was estimated, GNI increased, in real terms, at an average rate of some 10% per year, and by 3.9% in 1994. In 1990–2001, according to World Bank figures, the population increased at an average annual rate of 1.5%.

Agriculture (including forestry, fishing and mining) engaged only 0.5% of the employed labour force in 2000. The principal crops cultivated on the island include watermelons, cucumbers, bananas, runner beans, aubergines, squash, tomatoes and papaya. Livestock reared includes pigs, cattle, goats and poultry.

The industrial sector accounted for some 15% of gross domestic product (GDP) in 1993. Construction and manufacturing engaged an estimated 10.0% of the employed labour force in 2000. Construction is the dominant industrial activity and is closely related to the increasingly important tourist industry. Construction engaged 9.7% of the employed labour force in 2000. Manufacturing industries, including textile and garment production and boat-building, engaged an estimated 2.0% of the employed labour force in 2000. Guam is a duty-free port and an important distribution point for goods destined for Micronesia. Re-exports constitute a high proportion of Guam's exports, major commodities being petroleum and petroleum products, iron and steel scrap, and eggs.

Service industries dominate the economy, engaging 87.8% of the employed labour force in 2000. The federal and territorial Governments alone employed 27.0% of workers in that year. Tourism is an increasingly important industry, providing 18% of GDP in 1994. In 2001 some 1,159,426 tourists (of whom almost 78% were Japanese) visited the island, a decline of 10% compared with the previous year. In 1999 tourism earned an estimated US $1,908m.; the sector engaged an estimated 21.4% of the employed labour force in 1994.

The Territory consistently records a visible trade deficit. Total exports were valued at US $75.7m. in 1999, compared with $47.9m. in 1994, in which year imports of petroleum and petroleum products alone cost $163.7m. In 1999 total imports (excluding petroleum and petroleum products) were valued at $38.7m. Japan provided an estimated 53.9% of total imports in 1999.

In 1998 total budgetary operational expenditure stood at US $206.1m. and revenue at $503.7m. In 2000 federal expenditure on the territory totalled $888m., comprising military spending of $451m., non-defence expenditure of $388m. and other federal assistance of $49m. Guam's unemployment rate stood at 13.0% in 2001. The annual average rate of inflation was 10.1% in 1990–95 and stood at 5.3% in 1995. Consumer prices decreased by 0.5% in 1998 and by 0.3% in 1999.

Guam is a member of the Pacific Community (see p. 304) and an associate member of the UN's Economic and Social Commission for Asia and the Pacific (ESCAP, see p. 28). In early 1996 Guam joined representatives of the other countries and territories of Micronesia at a meeting in Hawaii, at which a new regional organization, the Council of Micronesian Government Executives, was established. The body aimed to facilitate discussion of economic developments in the region and to examine possibilities for reducing the considerable cost of shipping essential goods between the islands.

In the 1990s Guam's economy benefited from increased foreign investment, notably from Japan and the Republic of Korea. Much of this investment resulted in the rapid expansion of the tourist industry. Guam continues to receive considerable financial support from the USA (direct federal grants totalled US $143m. in 1997) in addition to revenue from US military installations on the island (which accounts for some $400m. annually). In July 1999 it was announced that Guam was to receive a further US $5m. in funding from the USA. Considerable interest in establishing an 'offshore' financial centre on Guam was expressed in 1992. The development of such a centre, however, was dependent upon Guam's achievement of Commonwealth status, which would allow the introduction of new tax laws. The announcement by the National Space Development Agency of Japan in mid-2001 that it was to build a rocket-tracking station on Guam was expected to enhance the territory's attraction to international investors. The tourism sector was badly affected by the repercussions of the terrorist attacks on the USA in September 2001, compounded by the continued economic difficulties in Japan (the principal source of the island's visitors). In early 2003 the consequences of the war in Iraq, combined with the outbreak of the illness identified as Severe Acute Respiratory Syndrome (SARS) in China and then elsewhere, also affected Guam's tourist industry. Despite an increase in US military spending on the island in 2002 and early 2003 (when US bomber aircraft were deployed on Guam), the decline in tourism revenues led the Government to report substantial fiscal deficits and to reduce public expenditure. In April 2003 the legislature approved the issuance of some $246m. in new debt aimed at refinancing the Government's pensions and public service provision system.

Education

School attendance is compulsory from six to 16 years of age. There were 24 public elementary schools, six junior high and five senior high schools, as well as a number of private schools operating on the island in 1997/98. Total secondary enrolment in public schools in 1998/99 was 15,758 students. Some 3,748 students were enrolled in tertiary education in that year. In 1990 the rate of adult illiteracy was 1.0%. Government expenditure on education was US $8.7m. in 1998 (equivalent to 4.2% of total expenditure).

Public Holidays

2003: 1 January (New Year's Day), 20 January (Martin Luther King Day), 17 February (Presidents' Day), 3 March (Guam Discovery Day), 18 April (Good Friday), 26 May (Memorial Day), 4 July (US Independence Day), 21 July (Liberation Day), 1 September (Labor Day), 13 October (Columbus Day), 2 November (All Souls Day), 11 November (Veterans Day), 27 November (Thanksgiving Day), 8 December (Immaculate Conception), 25 December (Christmas Day).

2004: 1 January (New Year's Day), 19 January (Martin Luther King Day), 16 February (Presidents' Day), 1 March (Guam Discovery Day), 9 April (Good Friday), 31 May (Memorial Day), 4 July (US Independence Day), 21 July (Liberation Day), 6 September (Labor Day), 11 October (Columbus Day), 2 November (All Souls Day), 11 November (Veterans Day), 25 November (Thanksgiving Day), 8 December (Immaculate Conception), 25 December (Christmas Day).

Weights and Measures

With certain exceptions, the imperial system is in force. One US cwt equals 100 lb; one long ton equals 2,240 lb; one short ton equals 2,000 lb. A policy of gradual voluntary conversion to the metric system is being encouraged by the Federal Government.

Statistical Survey

Sources (unless otherwise stated): Department of Commerce, Government of Guam, 102 M St, Tiyan, GU 96913; tel. 475-0321; fax 477-9031; e-mail commerce@ns.gov.gu; internet www.admin.gov.gu/commerce/economy.

AREA AND POPULATION

Area: 549 sq km (212 sq miles).

Population: 133,152 at census of 1 April 1990; 154,805 (males 79,181, females 75,624) at census of 1 April 2000.

Density (2000): 282.0 per sq km.

Ethnic Groups (2000 census): Chamorro 57,297; Filipino 40,729; White 10,509; Other Asian 9,600; part-Chamorro 7,946; Chuukese 6,229; Total (incl. others) 154,805.

Principal Towns (population at 2000 census): Tamuning 10,833; Mangilao 7,794; Yigo 6,391; Astumbo 5,207; Barrigada 4,417; Hagåtña (capital) 1,122.

Births, Marriages and Deaths (2000, unless otherwise indicated): Registered live births 3,766 (birth rate 24.4 per 1,000); Registered marriages (1998) 1,514; Registered deaths 648 (death rate 4.2 per 1,000). Sources: National Center for Health Statistics, US Department of Health and Human Services; Office of Vital Statistics, Department of Public Health and Social Services, Government of Guam.

Expectation of Life (UN estimates, years at birth): 78.0 (males 75.5; females 80.4) in 2000. Source: UN, *Statistical Yearbook for Asia and the Pacific*.

Economically Active Population (persons aged 16 and over, excl. armed forces, 2000 census): Agriculture, forestry, fishing and mining 296; Manufacturing 1,155; Construction 5,532; Transport, storage and utilities 4,319; Wholesale and retail trade 9,506; Arts, entertainment, recreation, accommodation and food services 10,278; Finance, insurance and real estate 3,053; Public administration 6,527; Education, health and social services 8,412; Professional, scientific, management and administrative services 4,277; Other services 3,698; Total employed 57,053 (males 31,609, females 25,444); Unemployed 7,399 (males 4,097, females 3,302); Total labour force 64,452 (males 35,706, females 28,746). Source: US Department of Commerce, *2000 Census of Population and Housing*.

AGRICULTURE, ETC

Principal Crops ('000 lb, 1999): Aubergines 172; Tomatoes 128; Cucumbers 671; Runner beans 419; Watermelons 1,200; Bittermelon 213; Bananas 97; Pepino 79; Papaya 128; Squash 80.

Livestock (head, 1998): Chickens 12,791; Pigs 3,025; Cattle 206; Goats 359; Horses 64; Water buffalo 43. Source: Department of Agriculture, Government of Guam.

Livestock Products ('000 lb, 1997): Poultry meat 2,683; Hen eggs 40,057. *2000* ('000 metric tons, FAO estimate): Hen eggs 1. Source: FAO.

Fishing (metric tons, live weight, 2000): Capture 275 (Common dolphinfish 34, Wahoo 20, Skipjack tuna 61, Yellowfin tuna 18, Indo-Pacific blue marlin 30); Aquaculture (estimate) 232(Mozambique tilapia 150, Philippine catfish 20, Milkfish 30, Banana prawn 25); Total catch 507. Source: FAO, *Yearbook of Fishery Statistics*.

INDUSTRY

Electric Energy (million kWh, estimates): 825 in 1996; 825 in 1997; 830 in 1998. Source: UN, *Industrial Commodity Statistics Yearbook*.

FINANCE

Currency and Exchange Rates: US currency is used. For details, see section on the Northern Mariana Islands.

Budget (estimates, US $ million, 1998): *Expenditure*: General Government 55.3; Defence 71.8; Community services 19.8; Recreation 5.9; Public health 3.3; Transportation 10.1; Environmental Protection 5.2; Economic development 5.8; Transfers to persons 17.7; Total (incl. others) 206.1. *Revenue*: Taxes 451.1; Federal contributions 2.9; Interest received 46.1; Total (incl. others) 503.7.

Cost of Living (Consumer Price Index; base: July–September 1996 = 100): 100.5 in 1999; 104.4 in 2000; 102.6 in 2001. Source: Cost of Living Office, Economic Research Center, Department of Commerce, Government of Guam.

Gross Domestic Product (US $ million at current prices): 3,020.5 in 1998; 2,718.5 in 1999; 2,772.8 in 2000. Source: Office of Insular Affairs, US Department of the Interior.

EXTERNAL TRADE

Principal Commodities (US $ '000, 1999): *Imports**: Travel goods, handbags, etc. 7,607; Meat, prepared or preserved 1,043; Bakery products 804; Watches 1,558. Jewellery articles 1,392; Meat and edible offals (beef, pork and poultry) 2,475; Fruits (incl. nuts) and vegetables 1,335; Passenger motor cars 2,767; Non-alcoholic beverages 1,304; Beer 1,516; Cigars and cigarettes 830; Total (incl. others) 38,709. *Exports*: Fish (chilled, fresh, frozen, dried and salted) 40,720; Tobacco, cigars, etc. 5,123; Petroleum oils and gases 15,183; Perfumes and toilet waters 2,726; Passenger motor cars 2,367; Total (incl. others) 75,748.

* Does not include figures for imports of petroleum and petroleum products (totalling US $163,685,000 in 1994).

Principal Trading Partners (US $ '000): *Imports (1991)*: Hong Kong 7,977.3; Japan 42,357.4; Korea, Republic 5,357.5; Philippines 3,281.3; Singapore 1,622.0; USA 59,837.8; Total (incl. others) 134,231.0. *Exports (1999)*: Hong Kong 1.5; Japan 40.8; Federated States of Micronesia 18.6; Palau 4.7; Papua New Guinea 0.9; Singapore 0.8; Taiwan 1.5; Thailand 1.4; USA 1.4. Total (incl. others) 75.7. Source: UN, *Statistical Yearbook for Asia and the Pacific*, and Economic Research Center, Department of Commerce, Government of Guam.

TRANSPORT

Road Traffic (registered motor vehicles, 1999): Private cars 65,887, Taxis 537, Buses 627, Goods vehicles 26,220, Motorcycles 633, Total (incl. others) 99,618. Source: Department of Revenue and Taxation, Government of Guam.

International Sea-borne Shipping (estimated freight traffic, '000 metric tons, 1991): Goods loaded 195.1; Goods unloaded 1,524.1; Goods transhipped 314.7. *Merchant Fleet* (total displacement, '000 grt at 31 December 1992): 1 (Source: Lloyd's Register-Fairplay, *World Fleet Statistics*).

Air Cargo ('000 lb): 36,691 in 1998.

TOURISM

Foreign Tourist Arrivals: 1,155,517 in 1999; 1,279,243 in 2000; 1,124,198 in 2001.

Tourist Arrivals by Country of Residence (2001): Japan 901,536; Korea, Republic 89,655; Taiwan 31,539; USA 41,875; Total (incl. others) 1,124,198. Note: Figures refer to air arrivals only. Arrivals by sea totalled 35,327 in 2001. Source: Guam Department of Commerce.

Tourism Receipts (US $ million): 2,361 in 1998; 1,908 in 1999. Source: World Tourism Organization.

COMMUNICATIONS MEDIA

Radio Receivers (1997): 221,000 in use*.

Television Receivers (1997): 106,000 in use*.

Telephones (2000): 80,300 main lines in use†.

Mobile Cellular Telephones (2000): 27,200 subscribers†.

Internet Users (estimate, 1999): 5,000†.

Daily Newspapers (1997): 1 (circulation 24,457).

Non-daily Newspapers (1988): 4 (estimated circulation 26,000)*.

* Source: UNESCO, *Statistical Yearbook*.
† Source: International Telecommunication Union.

EDUCATION

Institutions (public schools only, 1997/98): Elementary 24; Middle school 6; Senior high 5; Business colleges (private) 1; Guam Community College; University of Guam.

Teachers (public schools only, 1998/99): Elementary 1,063; Secondary 1,010.

Enrolment (public schools only, 1998/99): Elementary 16,102; Middle school 7,205; Senior high 8,364; Guam Community College 189; University of Guam 3,748.
Source: Department of Education, Government of Guam, and University of Guam.

Directory

The Constitution

Guam is governed under the Organic Act of Guam of 1950, which gave the island statutory local power of self-government and made its inhabitants citizens of the United States, although they cannot vote in presidential elections. Their Delegate to the US House of Representatives is elected every two years. Executive power is vested in the civilian Governor and the Lieutenant-Governor, first elected, by popular vote, in 1970. Elections for the governorship occur every four years. The Government has 48 executive departments, whose heads are appointed by the Governor with the consent of the Guam Legislature. The Legislature consists of 15 members elected by popular vote every two years (members are known as Senators). It is empowered to pass laws on local matters, including taxation and fiscal appropriations.

The Government

(April 2003)

Governor: Felix Camacho (Republican—took office January 2003).

Lieutenant-Governor: Kaleo Moylan.

GOVERNMENT OFFICES

Government offices are located throughout the island.

Office of the Governor: POB 2950, Adelup, Hagåtña, GU 96932; tel. 475-8931; fax 477-4826; e-mail governor@mail.gov.gu; internet ns.gov.gu.

Department of the Interior, Office of Insular Affairs (OIA): Hagåtña, GU 96910; tel. 472-7279; fax 472-7309; Field Representative KEITH A. PARSKY.

Department of Administration: POB 884, Hagåtña, GU 96932; tel. 475-1101; fax 475-6788; e-mail doa@ns.gov.gu.

Department of Agriculture: 192 Dairy Rd, Mangilao, GU 96923; tel. 734-3942; fax 734-6569; e-mail agr@ns.gov.gu.

Department of Commerce: 102 M St, Tiyan, GU 96913; tel. 475-0321; fax 477-9031; e-mail commerce@mail.gov.gu; internet www .admin.gov.gu/commerce.

Department of Corrections: POB 3236, Hagåtña, GU 96932; tel. 734-4668; fax 734-4990; e-mail doc@mail.gov.gu.

Department of Customs and Quarantine: 1503 Central Ave Tiyan, Barrigada, GU 96921; tel. 475-6202; fax 475-62207; e-mail iperedo@ns.gov.gu.

Department of Education: POB DE, Hagåtña, GU 96932; tel. 475-0457; fax 472-5003; e-mail rtainato@doe.edu.gu; internet www.doe .edu.gu.

Department of Labor: POB 9970, Tamuning, GU 96931; tel. 475-0101; fax 477-2988; e-mail labor@ns.gov.gu; internet www.labor.gov .gu.

Department of Land Management: POB 2950, Hagåtña, GU 96932; tel. 475-5252; fax 477-0883; e-mail dlm@mail.gov.gu; internet www.gov.gu/dlm.

Department of Law: Suite 2-200E, Judicial Ctr. building, 120 West O'Brien Drive, Hagåtña, GU 96910; tel. 475-3324; fax 475-2493; e-mail law@ns.gov.gu; internet www.justice.gov.gu/dol.

Department of Parks and Recreation: POB 2950, 13-8 Seagull Ave, Tiyan, Hagåtña, GU 96932; tel. 475-6296; fax 472-9626; e-mail dpr@gov.gu; internet www.gov.gu/dpr.

Department of Public Health and Social Services: POB 2816, Hagåtña, GU 96932; tel. 735-7102; fax 734-5910; e-mail dennisr@ mail.gov.gu; internet www.admin.gov.gu/pubhealth.

Department of Public Works: 542 North Marine Drive, Tamuning, GU 96911; tel. 646-4388; fax 649-6178; e-mail dpwdir@ ns.gov.gu.

Department of Revenue and Taxation: POB 23607, Guam Main Facility, 13-1 Mariner Drive, Tiyan, Hagåtña, GU 96921; tel. 475-1817; fax 472-2643; e-mail revtax@ns.gov.gu; internet www.gov.gu/ revtax.

Department of the Treasury: PDN Bldg, Suite 404, 238 Archbishop Flores St, Hagåtña, GU 96910.

Department of Youth Affairs: POB 23672, Guam Main Facility, GU 96921; tel. 734-2597; fax 734-7536; e-mail ddell@ns.gov.gu.

Legislature

GUAM LEGISLATURE

The Guam Legislature has 15 members, directly elected by popular vote for a two-year term. Elections took place in November 2002, when the Democratic Party won nine seats and the Republican Party six.

Speaker: VICENTE PANGELINAN.

CONGRESS

Guam elects a Delegate to the US House of Representatives. An election was held in November 2002, when the Democrat candidate, Madeleine Z. Bordallo, was elected as Delegate.

Delegate: MADELEINE BORDALLO, US House of Representatives, 2428 Rayburn HOB, Washington, DC 20515, USA; fax (202) 226-0341.

Judicial System

Attorney-General: DOUGLAS B. MOYAN.

US Attorney: FREDERICK BLACK.

Supreme Court of Guam: Suite 300, Guam Judicial Center, 120 West O'Brien Drive, Hagåtña, GU 96910; tel. 475-3162; fax 475-3140; e-mail justice@guamsupremecourt.com; internet www .guamsupremecourt.com.

District Court of Guam
4th floor, US Courthouse, 520 West Soledad Ave, Hagåtña, GU 96910.

Judge appointed by the President of the USA. The court has the jurisdiction of a Federal district court and of a bankruptcy court of the United States in all cases arising under the laws of the United States. Appeals may be made to the Court of Appeals for the Ninth Circuit and to the Supreme Court of the United States.

Presiding Judge: JOHN S. UNPINGCO.

Superior Court of Guam
120 West O'Brien Drive, Hagåtña, GU 96910; tel. 475-3544; internet www.justice.gov.gu/superior.

Judges are appointed by the Governor of Guam for an initial eight-year term and are thereafter retained by popular vote. The Superior Court has jurisdiction over cases arising in Guam other than those heard in the District Court.

Presiding Judge: ALBERTO C. LAMORENA III.

There are also Probate, Traffic, Domestic, Juvenile and Small Claims Courts.

Religion

About 90% of the population are Roman Catholic, but there are also members of the Episcopal (Anglican) Church, the Baptist churches and the Seventh-day Adventist Church. There are small communities of Muslims, Buddhists and Jews.

CHRISTIANITY

The Roman Catholic Church
Guam comprises the single archdiocese of Agaña. The Archbishop participates in the Catholic Bishops' Conference of the Pacific, based in Fiji, and the Federation of Catholic Bishops' Conferences of Oceania, based in New Zealand.

At 31 December 2000 there were 150,563 adherents in Guam.

Archbishop of Agaña: Most Rev. ANTHONY SABLAN APURON, Chancery Office, Cuesta San Ramón 196B, Hagåtña, GU 96910; tel. 472-6116; fax 477-3519; e-mail arch@ite.net.

BAHÁ'Í FAITH

National Spiritual Assembly: POB 20280, Guam Main Facility, Hagåtña, GU 96921; tel. 828-8639; fax 828-8112; mems resident in 19 localities in Guam and 10 localities in the Northern Mariana Islands.

The Press

NEWSPAPERS AND PERIODICALS

Bonita: POB 11468, Tumon, GU 96931; tel. 632-4543; fax 637-6720; f. 1998; monthly; Publr IMELDA SANTOS; circ. 3,000.

Directions: POB 27290, Barrigada, GU 96921; tel. 635-7501; fax 635-7520; f. 1996; monthly; Publr JERRY ROBERTS; circ. 3,800.

Drive Guam: POB 3191, Hagåtña, GU 96932; tel. 649-0883; fax 649-8883; e-mail glimpses@kuentos.guam.net; internet www .glimpsesofguam.com; f. 1991; quarterly; Publr STEPHEN V. NYGARD; circ. 20,000.

Guam Business News: POB 3191, Hagåtña, GU 96932; tel. 649-0883; fax 649-8883; e-mail glimpses@kuentos.guam.net; internet www.glimpsesofguam.com; f. 1983; monthly; Publr STEPHEN V. NYGARD; Editor MAUREEN MARATITA; circ. 2,600.

Guam Tribune: POB EG, Hagåtña, GU 96910; tel. 646-5871; fax 646-6702; Tue. and Fri.; Publr MARK PANGILINAN; Man. Editor ROBERT TEODOSIO.

Hospitality Guahan: POB 8565, Tamuning, GU 96931; tel. 649-1447; fax 649-8565; e-mail ghra@ghra.org; internet www.ghra.org; f. 1996; quarterly; circ. 3,000.

Latte Magazine: Tamuning, GU 96911; tel. 649-7736; fax 649-7737; e-mail editor@lattemag.com; internet www.lattemagazine .com; f. 1995; quarterly; Publr Manny Crisostomo Publications, Inc; circ. 40,000.

Pacific Daily News and Sunday News: POB DN, Hagåtña, GU 96932; tel. 471-9711; fax 472-1512; e-mail news@pdnguam.com; internet www.pdnguam.com; f. 1944; Publr LEE P. WEBBER; Man. Editor RINDRATY LIMTIACO; circ. 26,999 (weekdays), 25,115 (Sunday).

The Pacific Voice: POB 2553, Hagåtña, GU 96932; tel. 472-6427; fax 477-5224; f. 1950; Sunday; Roman Catholic; Gen. Man. TEREZO MORTERA; Editor Rev. Fr HERMES LOSBANES; circ. 6,500.

TV Guam Magazine: 237 Mamis St, Tamuning, GU 96911; tel. 646-4030; fax 646-7445; f. 1973; weekly; Publr DINA GRANT; Man. Editor EMILY UNTALAN; circ. 15,000.

NEWS AGENCY

United Press International (UPI) (USA): POB 1617, Hagåtña, GU 96910; tel. 632-1138; Correspondent Dick Williams.

Broadcasting and Communications

TELECOMMUNICATIONS

Guam Educational Telecommunication Corporation (KGTF): POB 21449, Guam Main Facility, Barrigada, GU 96921; tel. 734-2207; fax 734-5483; e-mail kgtfl2@ite.net.

Guam Telephone Authority: POB 9008, Tamuning, GU 96931; tel. 646-1427; fax 649-4821; e-mail gtagm@ite.net; internet www.gta .guam.net; Chair. Pedro R. Martinez; Gen. Man. Ralph Taitano.

BROADCASTING

Radio

K-Stereo: POB 20249, Guam Main Facility, Barrigada, GU 96921; tel. 477-9448; fax 477-6411; operates on FM 24 hours a day; Pres. Edward H. Poppe; Gen. Man. Frances W. Poppe.

KGUM/KZGZ: 111 Chalan Santo, Hagåtña, GU 96910; tel. 477-5700; fax 477-3982; e-mail rex@spbguam.com; internet www .radiopacific.com; Chair. and CEO Rex Sorensen; Pres. Jon Anderson.

KOKU-FM: 508 West O'Brien Drive, Hagåtña, GU 96910; tel. 477-5658; fax 472-7663; operates on FM 24 hours a day; Pres. Lee M. Holmes; Gen. Man. Ernie A. Galito.

Radio Guam (KUAM): POB 368, Hagåtña, GU 96910; tel. 637-5826; fax 637-9865; e-mail kellykel@94jam2.com; internet www .kuam.com; f. 1954; operates on AM and FM 24 hours a day; Pres. Paul M. Calvo; Gen. Man. Joey Calvo.

Trans World Radio Pacific (TWR): POB CC, Hagåtña, GU 96932; tel. 477-9701; fax 477-2838; e-mail ktwr@twr.org; internet www .guam.net/pub/twr; f. 1975; broadcasts Christian programmes on KTWR and one medium-wave station, KTWG, covering Guam and nearby islands, and operates five short-wave transmitters reaching most of Asia, Africa and the Pacific; Pres. Thomas Lowell; Station Dir Michael Davis.

Television

Guam Cable TV: 530 West O'Brien Drive, Hagåtña, GU 96910; tel. 477-7815; fax 477-7847; f. 1987; Pres. Lee M. Holmes; Gen. Man. Harrison O. Flora.

KGTF—TV: POB 21449 Guam Main Facility, Barrigada, GU 96921; tel. 734-3476; fax 734-5483; e-mail kgtfl2@ite.net; f. 1970; cultural, public service and educational programmes; Gen. Man. Geraldine 'Ginger' S. Underwood; Operations Man. Benny T. Flores.

KTGM—TV: 692 Marine Dr, Tamuning 96911; tel. 649-8814; fax 649-0371.

KUAM—TV: POB 368, Hagåtña, GU 96932; tel. 687-5826; fax 637-9865; internet www.kuam.com; f. 1956; operates colour service; Gen. Man. Joey Calvo.

Finance

(cap. = capital; res = reserves; = dep. = deposits; m. = million; brs = branches; amounts in US dollars)

BANKING

Commercial Banks

Allied Banking Corpn (Philippines): POB CT, Hagåtña, GU 96932; tel. 646-9143; fax 649-5002; e-mail abcguam@kuentos.guam .net; Man. Noel L. Cruz; 1 br.

Bank of Guam: POB BW, 134 W. Soledad Ave, Hagåtña, GU 96932; tel. 472-5300; fax 477-8687; e-mail customerservice@bankofguam .com; internet www.bankofguam.com; f. 1972; cap. 89m., res 11.3m., dep. 592m. (1998); Chair. Anthony A. Leon Guerrero; Chair. Jesus S. Leon Guerrero; 23 brs.

Bank of Hawaii (USA): POB BH, Hagåtña, GU 96932; tel. 479-3603; fax 479-3777; Exec. Vice-Pres. Ron Leach; Vice-Pres. Thomas Michels; 3 brs.

BankPacific, Ltd: 151 Aspinall Ave, POB 2888, Hagåtña, GU 96932; tel. 477-2671; fax 477-1483; e-mail philipf@bankpacific.com; internet www.bankpacific.com; f. 1954; Pres. and CEO Philip J. Flores; Exec. Vice-Pres. Mark O. Fish; 4 brs in Guam, 1 br. in Palau; 1 br. in Northern Mariana Islands.

Citibank NA (USA): 402 East Marine Drive, POB FF, Hagåtña, GU 96932; tel. 477-2484; fax 477-9441; Vice-Pres. Rashid Habib; 2 brs.

Citizens Security Bank (Guam) Inc: POB EQ, Hagåtña, GU 96932; tel. 479-9000; fax 479-9090; Pres. and CEO Daniel L. Webb; 4 brs.

First Commercial Bank (Taiwan): POB 2461, Hagåtña, GU 96932; tel. 472-6864; fax 477-8921; Gen. Man. Yao Der Chen; 1 br.

First Hawaiian Bank (USA): POB AD, 194 Hernan Cortes Ave, Hagåtña, GU 96910; tel. 477-8811; fax 472-3284; Vice-Pres. and Man. (Hagåtña) John K. Lee; 2 brs.

First Savings and Loan Association (FSLA): 140 Aspinal Street, Hagåtña, GU 96910; affiliated to Bank of Hawaii; 6 brs.

HSBC Ltd (Hong Kong): POB 27c, Hagåtña, GU 96932; tel. 647-8588; fax 646-3767; CEO Guy N. de B. Priestley; 2 brs.

Metropolitan Bank and Trust Co (Philippines): GCIC Bldg, 414 W Soledad Ave, Hagåtña, Guam 96913; tel. 477-9554; fax 477-8834; e-mail mbguam@metrobank.com.ph; f. 1975; Sen. Man. Benneth A. Reyes.

Union Bank of California (USA): 194 Hernan Cortes Ave, POB 7809, Hagåtña, GU 96910; tel. 477-8811; fax 472-3284; Man. Kinji Suzuki; 2 brs.

CHAMBER OF COMMERCE

Guam Chamber of Commerce: Ada Plaza Center, Suite 102, 173 Aspinall Ave, POB 283, Hagåtña, GU 96932; tel. 472-6311; fax 472-6202; e-mail gchamber@guamchamber.com.gu; Pres. Eloise R. Baza; Chair. Carl Peterson.

Trade and Industry

DEVELOPMENT ORGANIZATION

Guam Economic Development Authority (GEDA): Guam International Trade Center Bldg, Suite 511, 590 South Marine Drive, Tamuning, GU 96911; tel. 647-4332; fax 649-4146; e-mail gedamp@ iftech.net; internet www.investguam; f. 1965; Administrator Edward G. Untalan.

EMPLOYERS' ORGANIZATION

Guam Employers' Council: 718 North Marine Drive, Suite 201, East-West Business Center, Upper Tumon, GU 96913; tel. 649-6616; fax 649-3030; e-mail tecinc@netpci.com; internet www.ecouncil.org; f. 1966; private, non-profit asscn providing management development training and advice on personnel law and labour relations; Exec. Dir Joseph Borja.

UTILITIES

Electricity

Guam Energy Office: 1504 East Sunset Boulevard, Tiyan, GU 96913; tel. 477-0538; fax 477-0589; e-mail guamenergy@kuentos .guam.net.

Guam Power Authority: POB 2977, Hagåtña, GU 96932; tel. 649-6818; fax 649-6942; e-mail gpa@ns.gov.gu; autonomous government agency; supplies electricity throughout the island.

Water

Guam Waterworks Authority: POB 3010, Hagåtña, GU 96932; tel. 479-7823; fax 649-0158.

Public Utility Agency of Guam: Hagåtña, GU 96910; supplies the majority of water on the island.

TRADE UNIONS

Many workers belong to trade unions based in the USA such as the American Federation of Government Employees and the American Postal Workers' Union. About 4,000 of the island's working population of 65,380 (in 1991) belong to unions.

Guam Federation of Teachers (GFT): Local 1581, POB 2301, Hagåtña, GU 96932; tel. 735-4390; fax 734-8085; e-mail gft@netpci .com; f. 1965; affiliate of American Federation of Teachers; Pres. John T. Burch; Vice-Pres. Barbara M. Blas; 2,000 mems.

Guam Landowners' Association: Hagåtña; Sec. Ronald Teehan.

Transport

ROADS

There are 885 km (550 miles) of public roads, of which some 675 km (420 miles) are paved. A further 685 km (425 miles) of roads are classified as non-public, and include roads located on federal government installations.

SHIPPING

Apra, on the central western side of the island, is one of the largest protected deep-water harbours in the Pacific.

Port Authority of Guam: 1026 Cabras Highway, Suite 201, Piti, GU 96925; tel. 477-5931; fax 477-2689; e-mail pag4@netpci.com; internet www.netpci.com/~pag4; Gen. Man. FRANCISCO P. CAMACHO.

Ambyth, Shipping and Trading Inc: PAG Bldg, Suite 205, 1026 Cabras Highway, Piti, GU 96925; tel. 477-8000; fax 472-1264; agents for all types of vessels and charter brokers; Vice-Pres. GREGORY R. DAVID.

Atkins, Kroll Inc: 443 South Marine Drive, Tamuning, GU 96911; tel. 646-1866; f. 1914; Pres. ALBERT P. WERNER.

COAM Trading Co Ltd: PAG Bldg, Suite 110, 1026 Cabas Highway, Piti, GU 96925; tel. 477-1737; fax 472-3386.

Interbulk Shipping (Guam) Inc: Bank of Guam Bldg, Suite 502, 111 Chalan Santo Papa, Hagåtña, GU 96910.

Maritime Agencies of the Pacific Ltd: Piti, GU 96925; tel. 477-8500; fax 477-5726; e-mail rehmapship@kuentos.guam.net; f. 1976; agents for fishing vessels, cargo, dry products and construction materials; Pres. ROBERT E. HAHN.

Pacific Navigation System: POB 7, Hagåtña, GU 96910; f. 1946; Pres. KENNETH T. JONES, Jr.

Tucor Services: Tamuning, GU 96931; tel. 646-6947; fax 646-6945; e-mail tucor@tucor.com; general agents for numerous dry cargo, passenger and steamship cos; Pres. MICHELLE BOLL.

CIVIL AVIATION

Guam is served by the A. B. Won Pat International Airport. Work to triple the size of the airport terminal, at a cost of US $253m., was completed in late 1996.

Guam International Airport Authority: POB 8770, Tamuning, GU 96931; tel. 646-0300; fax 646-8823; e-mail rolendal@guamcell .net; internet www.airport.guam.net.

Continental Airlines: POB 8778, Tamuning, GU 96931; tel. 649-6594; fax 649-6588; internet www.continental.com; f. 1968, as Air Micronesia, by Continental Airlines (USA); name changed 1992; hub operations in Guam and Saipan (Northern Mariana Islands); services throughout the region and to destinations in the Far East and the mainland USA; Pres. BILL MEEHAN; Chair. D. BREEDING.

Freedom Air: POB 1578, Hagåtña, GU 96932; tel. 472-8009; fax 4728080; e-mail freedom@ite.net; f. 1974; Man. Dir JOAQUIN L. FLORES Jr.

Tourism

Tourism is the most important industry on Guam. In 2000 there were 1,288,002 visitor arrivals (including 8,759 arrivals by sea), compared with 769,876 in 1990. In 2000 some 82.0% of arrivals by air were visitors from Japan, 6.8% from the Republic of Korea, 3.3% from the USA and 3.1% from Taiwan. Most of Guam's hotels are situated in, or near to, Tumon, where amenities for entertainment are well-developed. Numerous sunken wrecks of aircraft and ships from Second World War battles provide interesting sites for divers. There were 10,110 hotel rooms on Guam at March 2001. A total of US $20.6m. was collected in hotel occupancy taxes in 2000. The industry as a whole earned some US $1,908m. in 1999.

Guam Visitors Bureau: 401 Pale San Vitores Rd, Tumon, GU 96911; tel. 646-5278; fax 646-8861; e-mail guaminfo@visitguam.org; internet www.visitguam.org; Gen. Man. JAMES E. NELSON III.

THE UNITED STATES VIRGIN ISLANDS

Introductory Survey

Location, Climate, Language, Religion, Flag, Capital

The Territory consists of three main inhabited islands (St Croix, St Thomas and St John) and about 50 smaller islands, mostly uninhabited. They are situated at the eastern end of the Greater Antilles, about 64 km (40 miles) east of Puerto Rico in the Caribbean Sea. The climate is tropical, although tempered by the prevailing easterly trade winds. The temperature averages 26°C (79°F), with little variation between winter and summer. The humidity is low for the tropics. English is the official language, but Spanish and Creole are also widely used. The people of the US Virgin Islands are predominantly of African descent. There is a strong religious tradition, and most of the inhabitants are Christians, mainly Protestants. The flag (proportions 2 by 3) is white, with a modified version of the US coat of arms (an eagle holding an olive branch in one foot and a sheaf of arrows in the other, with a shield, comprising a small horizontal blue panel above vertical red and white stripes, superimposed), between the letters V and I, in the centre. The capital is Charlotte Amalie, on the island of St Thomas.

Recent History

The Virgin Islands, originally inhabited by Carib and Arawak Indians, were discovered by Europeans in 1493. The group subsequently passed through English, French, and Dutch control, before the western islands of St Thomas and St John, colonized by Denmark after 1670, and St Croix, purchased from France in 1733, became the Danish West Indies. In 1917 these islands, which are strategically placed in relation to the Panama Canal, were sold for US $25m. by Denmark to the USA. They now form an unincorporated territory of the USA. Residents of the US Virgin Islands are US citizens, but cannot vote in presidential elections, if resident in the islands. The US Virgin Islands is represented in the US House of Representatives by one popularly-elected Delegate, who is permitted to vote only in committees of the House.

The inhabitants of the islands were granted a measure of self-government by the Organic Act, as revised in 1954, which created the elected 15-member Senate. Since 1970, executive authority has been vested in the elected Governor and Lieutenant-Governor. In the first gubernatorial election, in 1970, the Republican incumbent, Melvin Evans, retained office. In 1974 Cyril E. King, leader of the Independent Citizens Movement (a breakaway faction of the Democratic Party), was elected Governor. On King's death in 1978, the former Lieutenant-Governor, Juan Luis, was elected Governor. He was returned to power in the 1982 election. The governorship passed to the Democratic Party with the election of Alexander Farrelly in 1986. Farrelly was re-elected Governor in 1990, and in the 1994 elections was succeeded by an Independent, Dr Roy Schneider. The governorship was regained by a Democrat, Charles Turnbull, in the 1998 elections. Turnbull was re-elected to the post in 2000 and 2002.

Since 1954 there have been five attempts to redraft the Constitution to give the US Virgin Islands greater autonomy. Each draft has, however, been rejected by a referendum. The US Government has expressed the view that it would welcome reform, if approved by the residents, as long as it were economically feasible and did not affect US national security. A non-binding referendum on the islands' future status, which was to take place in November 1989, was postponed following the disruption caused by 'Hurricane Hugo' (see Economic Affairs). Voting, which eventually took place in October 1993, produced support of 80.3% for retaining the islands' existing status, with 14.2% favouring full integration with the USA and 4.8% advocating the termination of US sovereignty. The result of the referendum was, however, invalidated by the low turn-out: only 27.4% of registered voters took part, falling short of the 50% participation required for the referendum to be valid. Subsequent legislation to create a constitutional convention was presented to the US Virgin Islands Senate, and in May 2000 a committee of the US House of Representatives began consideration of a range of measures to enlarge the scope of local self-government in the Territory.

In March 2002 the Territory was removed from the Organisation for Economic Co-operation and Development's list of tax 'havens', after pledging to improve the transparency of its financial services sector by the end of 2005.

Economic Affairs

According to estimates by the Territorial Government, the islands' gross national income (GNI) in 1989 was US $1,344m., equivalent to about $13,100 per head. Average personal income in that year was $11,052 per head, or about 62.6% of the US mainland average. GNI increased, in real terms, at an average rate of 2.5% per year during 1980–89. In 1990–2000 the population increased by an annual average of 0.6%.

Most of the land is unsuitable for large-scale cultivation, but tax incentives have encouraged the growing of vegetables, fruit and cereals, which are produced for local consumption. According to the 2000 census figures, 0.7% of the economically active population were engaged in agriculture, forestry, fishing and mining.

The islands are heavily dependent on links with the US mainland. There are no known natural resources, and, because of limited land space and other factors, the islands are unable to produce sufficient food to satisfy local consumption. Most goods are imported, mainly from the mainland USA.

Industry (comprising manufacturing and construction, but excluding mining) engaged 16.4% of the labour force, according to 2000 census figures. Only an estimated 0.1% of the labour force were in the mining sector, while 5.9% were in manufacturing. The main branch of manufacturing is petroleum-refining.

Services employed 82.9% of the labour force in 2000, according to census figures. Tourism, which is estimated to account for more than 60% of gross domestic product (GDP), is the mainstay of the islands' income and employment, and provides the major source of direct and indirect revenue for other service sectors (including trade and transport). The emphasis is on the visiting cruise-ship business, and the advantages of duty-free products for tourist visitors. The total number of visitors declined by 9.7% in 1995, when the islands experienced severe storm damage (see below), but increased steadily during 1996–98. In 2000 tourist arrivals (those staying in hotels) totalled 496,349.

St Croix has one of the world's largest petroleum refineries, with a capacity of 550,000 barrels per day (b/d). However, it operates at reduced levels of throughput. An alumina processing plant, closed down in 1994, was acquired in 1995 by Alcoa, which intended to rehabilitate the plant, which has an annual throughput capacity of 600,000 metric tons. The plant was reopened in the late 1990s, but in November 2000 it was announced that it would close again in January 2001, with the loss of 350 jobs. Efforts have been made to introduce labour-intensive and non-polluting manufacturing industries. Rum is an important product. This industry, however, was expected to encounter increased competition from Mexico as a result of the North American Free Trade Agreement (NAFTA, see p. 270), which entered into operation in January 1994.

The population increased dramatically from the 1960s. This inflow included people from neighbouring Caribbean countries, together with wealthy white settlers from the US mainland, attracted by the climate and the low taxes. At the 2000 census, 31% of the population originated from other Caribbean islands, and 14.5% from the mainland USA.

Throughout the 1990s the budget deficit of the Territorial Government increased. By December 1999, the deficit was estimated to have risen to $305m., and in that year the Territorial Government introduced a Five-Year Strategic and Financial Operating Plan to reduce government expenditure and enhance the effectiveness of procedures for revenue collection. However, the islands were expected in the foreseeable future to continue to receive grants and other remittances from the US Government. The Government forecast that the budget would record a surplus of $19m. in the year ending 30 September 2001. The rate of unemployment averaged 6.1% of the labour force in 1997.

In 1995 the Territory recorded a trade deficit of $174m. In that year the USA provided 34.5% of imports and took 92.7% of exports. Other major sources of imports included the United Arab Emirates, the Republic of the Congo and Nigeria. Of total exports to the USA in 1993, 90.6% was refined petroleum products. Crude petroleum accounted for 68.6% of the islands' total imports in that year.

Owing to the islands' heavy reliance on imported goods, local prices and inflation are higher than on the mainland, and the islands' economy, in contrast to that of the USA, remained in recession for most of the 1990s. 'Hurricane Hugo', which struck the islands in September 1989, was estimated to have caused $1,000m. in property damage, although subsequent work on rebuilding temporarily revitalized employment in the construction sector, where the demand for labour rose to between two and three times normal levels. 'Hurricane Marilyn' caused considerable damage in September 1995, destroying an estimated 80% of houses on St Thomas. Serious storm damage was again experienced in July 1996, from 'Hurricane Bertha', and in September 1998 from 'Hurricane Georges'. In August 2000 'Hurricane Debby' caused less serious damage. It was hoped that the successful implementation of the Government's five-year plan in 1999–2004 would reverse the economy's decline.

The Territory is an associate member of the UN Economic Commission for Latin America and the Caribbean (ECLAC, see p. 31).

Education

Education is compulsory up to the age of 16 years. It generally comprises eight years at primary school and four years at secondary school. In 2000 there were 32,119 elementary and secondary students at public and private schools. The University of the Virgin Islands, with campuses on St Thomas and St Croix, had 2,610 students in 2000.

Public Holidays

2003: 1 January (New Year's Day), 6 January (Three Kings' Day), 20 January (Martin Luther King Day), 17 February (Presidents' Day), 31 March (Transfer Day), 18–21 April (Easter), 26 May (Memorial Day), 16 June (Organic Act Day), 3 July (Danish West Indies Emancipation Day), 4 July (US Independence Day), 28 July (Hurricane Supplication Day), 1 September (Labor Day), 13 October (for Columbus Day), 17 October (Puerto Rico Friendship Day), 20 October (Virgin Islands Thanksgiving Day), 1 November (Liberty Day), 11 November (Veterans' Day), 27 November (US Thanksgiving Day), 25–26 December (Christmas).

2004: 1 January (New Year's Day), 6 January (Three Kings' Day), 19 January (Martin Luther King Day), 16 February (Presidents' Day), 29 March (Transfer Day), 9–12 April (Easter), 31 May (Memorial Day), 21 June (Organic Act Day), 3 July (Danish West Indies Emancipation Day), 4 July (US Independence Day), 26 July (Hurricane Supplication Day), 6 September (Labor Day), 12 October (Columbus Day), 17 October (Puerto Rico Friendship Day), 21 October (Virgin Islands Thanksgiving Day), 1 November (Liberty Day), 11 November (Veterans' Day), 25 November (US Thanksgiving Day), 25–26 December (Christmas).

Statistical Survey

Sources (unless otherwise stated): Office of Public Relations, Office of the Governor, Charlotte Amalie, VI 00802; tel. (340) 774-0294; fax (340) 774-4988; Bureau of Economic Research, Department of Economic Development and Agriculture, POB 6400, Charlotte Amalie, VI 00804; tel. (340) 774-8784.

AREA AND POPULATION

Area: 347.1 sq km (134 sq miles): St Croix 215 sq km (83 sq miles) St Thomas 80.3 sq km (31 sq miles); St John 51.8 sq km (20 sq miles).

Population: 101,809 at census of 1 April 1990; 108,612 (males 51,684, females 56,748) at census of 1 April 2000. *Distribution by island* (2000 census): St Croix 53,234, St Thomas 51,181, St John 4,197. Source: US Bureau of the Census.

Density (at 2000 census): 312.9 per sq km.

Principal Towns (population at census of 1 April 2000): Charlotte Amalie (capital) 11,004; Christiansted 2,637; Frederiksted 732. Source: Thomas Brinkhoff, *City Population* (internet www.citypopulation.de).

Births and Deaths (2001): Birth rate 15.9 per 1,000; Death rate 5.5 per 1,000. Source: US Bureau of the Census.

Expectation of Life (estimates, years at birth): 78.3 (males 74.4; females 82.4) in 2001. Source: US Bureau of the Census.

Economically Active Population (persons aged 16 years and over, 2000 census): Agriculture, forestry, fishing, hunting and mining 324; Manufacturing 2,754; Construction 4,900; Wholesale trade 912; Retail trade 6,476; Transportation, warehousing and utilities 3,321; Information 931; Finance, insurance, real estate, rental and leasing 2,330; Professional, scientific, management, administrative and waste management services 3,058; Educational, health, and social services 6,742; Arts, entertainment, recreation, accommodation and food services 7,351; Public administration 4,931; Other services 2,535; Total employed 46,565. Source: US Bureau of the Census.

HEALTH AND WELFARE

Under-5 Mortality Rate (per 1,000 live births, 1997): 15.0.

Physicians (per 1,000 head, 1999): 1.65 (Source: Pan American Health Organization).
For definitions, see explanatory note on p. vi.

AGRICULTURE, ETC

Livestock (estimates, 2001): Cattle 8,000; Sheep 3,200; Pigs 2,600; Goats 4,000; Chickens 35,000. Source: FAO.

Fishing: Total catch 300* in 1998; 263 in 1999; 300* in 2000.
* FAO estimate. Source: FAO, *Yearbook of Fishery Statistics*.

INDUSTRY

Production (estimates, '000 metric tons, unless otherwise indicated, 1998): Jet fuels 1,595; Motor spirit (petrol) 2,325; Kerosene 65; Gas-diesel (distillate fuel) oil 2,895; Residual fuel oils 3,818; Liquefied petroleum gas 146; Electric energy 1,082 million kWh. Source: UN, *Industrial Commodity Statistics Yearbook*.

FINANCE

Currency and Exchange Rates: 100 cents = 1 United States dollar (US $). *Sterling and Euro Equivalents* (31 December 2002): £1 sterling = US $1.6118; €1 = 1.0487 US cents; $100 = £62.04 = €95.36.

Budget (projection US $ million, year ending 30 September 2001): Total revenue 522.4; Total expenditure 503.9.

EXTERNAL TRADE

Total (US $ million): *Imports*: 2,625.6 in 1993; 3,108.4 in 1994; 3,200.3 in 1995. *Exports*: 2,191.4 in 1993; 2,847.7 in 1994; 3,026.3 in 1995. The main import is crude petroleum ($1,802.1m. in 1993), while the principal exports are refined petroleum products.

Trade with the USA (US $ million): *Imports*: 976.5 in 1993; 1,021.4 in 1994; 1,045.0 in 1995. *Exports*: 2,014.7 in 1993; 2,666.9 in 1994; 2,805.8 in 1995.

TRANSPORT

Road Traffic (registered motor vehicles, 1993): 63,332.

Shipping (2000): Cruise-ship arrivals 1,014; Passenger arrivals 1,768,402.

Civil Aviation (2000): Visitor arrivals 629,760.

TOURISM

Tourist Arrivals (tourists staying in hotels): 480,064 in 1998; 484,156 in 1999; 496,349 in 2000.

Tourism Receipts (US $ million): 965 in 2000 (Source: World Tourism Organization, *Yearbook of Tourism Statistics*).

COMMUNICATIONS MEDIA

Radio Receivers (1997): 107,100 in use.

Television Receivers (1999): 71,000 in use.

Telephones (2000): 69,000 main lines in use.

Mobile Cellular Telephones (2000): 35,000 subscribers.

Internet Users (1999): 12,000.

Daily Newspapers (1996): 3; average circulation 42,000 copies.

Non-daily Newspapers (1988 estimates): 2; average circulation 4,000 copies.
Sources: UNESCO, *Statistical Yearbook*; International Telecommunication Union.

EDUCATION

Pre-primary (1992/93): 62 schools; 121 teachers; 4,714 students (2000).

Elementary (1992/93): 62 schools; 790 teachers (public schools only); 16,858 students (2000).

Secondary: 541 teachers (public schools only, 1990); 7,440 students (2000).

Higher Education: 266 teachers (1992/93); 3,107 students (2000).
Sources: UNESCO, *Statistical Yearbook*; US Bureau of the Census.

Directory

The Constitution

The Government of the US Virgin Islands is organized under the provisions of the Organic Act of the Virgin Islands, passed by the Congress of the United States in 1936 and revised in 1954. Subsequent amendments provided for the popular election of the Governor and Lieutenant-Governor of the Virgin Islands in 1970, and, since 1973, for representation in the US House of Representatives by a popularly-elected Delegate. The Delegate has voting powers only in committees of the House. Executive power is vested in the Governor, who is elected for a term of four years by universal adult suffrage and who appoints, with the advice and consent of the Legislature, the heads of the executive departments. The Governor may also appoint administrative assistants as his representatives on St John and St Croix. Legislative power is vested in the Legislature of the Virgin Islands, a unicameral body comprising 15 Senators, elected for a two-year term by popular vote. Legislation is subject to the approval of the Governor, whose veto can be overridden by a two-thirds vote of the Legislature. All residents of the islands, who are citizens of the United States and at least 18 years of age, have the right to vote in local elections but not in national elections. In 1976 the Virgin Islands were granted the right to draft their own constitution, subject to the approval of the US President and Congress. A Constitution permitting a degree of autonomy was drawn up in 1978 and gained the necessary approval, but was then rejected by the people of the Virgin Islands in a referendum in March 1979. A fourth draft, providing for greater autonomy than the 1978 draft, was rejected in a referendum in November 1981.

The Government

EXECUTIVE
(April 2003)

Governor: CHARLES WESLEY TURNBULL.

Lieutenant-Governor: GERARD AMWUR 'LUZ' JAMES, II.

Commissioner of Agriculture: HENRY SCHUSTER, Jr.

Commissioner of Education: RUBY SIMMONDS.

Commissioner of Finance: BERNICE TURNBULL.

Commissioner of Health: MAVIS MATTHEW.

Commissioner of Housing, Parks and Recreation: IRA M. HOBSON.

Commissioner of Human Services: SEDONIE HALBERT.

Commissioner of Labor: CARMELO RIVERA.

Commissioner of Licensing and Consumer Affairs: ANDREW RUTNIK.

Commissioner of Planning and Natural Resources: DEAN C. PLASKETT.

Commissioner of Police: FRANZ CHRISTIAN, Sr.

Commissioner of Property and Procurement: MARC BIGGS.

Commissioner of Public Works: WAYNE D. CALLWOOD.

Commissioner of Tourism: PAMELA C. RICHARDS.

Attorney-General: IVER A. STRIDIRON.

US Virgin Islands Delegate to the US Congress: DONNA M. CHRISTIAN CHRISTENSEN.

GOVERNMENT OFFICES

Office of the Governor: Government House, 21–22 Kongens Gade, Charlotte Amalie, VI 00802; tel. (340) 774-0001; fax (340) 774-1361.

Office of the Lieutenant-Governor: Government Hill, 18 Kongens Gade, Charlotte Amalie, VI 00802; tel. (340) 774-2991; fax (340) 774-6953; e-mail admin@ltg.gov.vi; internet www.ltg.gov.vi.

Department of Agriculture: Estate Lower Love, Kingshill, St Croix, VI 00850; tel. (340) 774-0997; fax (340) 774-5182; e-mail agriculture@usvi.org; internet www.usvi.org/agriculture/.

Department of Economic Development: 81 AB Kronprindsens Gade, POB 6400, Charlotte Amalie, VI 00801; tel. (340) 774-8784; fax (340) 774-4390.

Department of Education: 44–46 Kongens Gade, Charlotte Amalie, VI 00802; tel. (340) 774-0100; fax (340) 779-7153; e-mail education@usvi.org; internet www.education.usvi.org.

Department of Finance: GERS Bldg, 2nd Floor, 76 Kronprindsens Gade, Charlotte Amalie, VI 00802; tel. (340) 774-4750; fax (340) 776-4028; internet www.usvi.org/finance.

Department of Health: 48 Sugar Estate, Charlotte Amalie, VI 00802; tel. (340) 774-0117; fax (340) 777-4001; internet www.usvi.org/health/.

Department of Housing, Parks and Recreation: Property & Procurement Bldg No. 1, Sub Base, 2nd Floor, Rm 206, Charlotte Amalie, VI 00802; tel. (340) 774-0255; fax (340) 774-4600.

Department of Human Services: Knud Hansen Complex Bldg A 1303, Hospital Ground, Charlotte Amalie, VI 00802; tel. (340) 774-0930; fax (340) 774-3466; e-mail humanservices@usvi.org; internet www.usvi.org/humanservices/.

Department of Justice: GERS Bldg, 2nd Floor, 48B–50C Kronprindsens Gade, Charlotte Amalie, VI 00802; tel. (340) 774-5666; fax (340) 774-9710; e-mail justice@usvi.org; internet www.usvi.org/justice.

Department of Labor: 21–31 Hospital St, Christiansted, St Croix, VI 00802; tel. (340) 774-3700; fax (340) 776-0529; e-mail labor@usvi.org; internet www.usvi.org/labor.

Department of Licensing and Consumer Affairs: Property & Procurement Bldg No. 1, Sub Base, RM 205, Charlotte Amalie, VI 00802; tel. (340) 774-3130; fax (340) 776-0675; internet www.usvi.org/dlca.

Department of Planning and Natural Resources: 396-1 Anna's Retreat–Foster Bldg, Charlotte Amalie, VI 00802; tel. (340) 774-3320; fax (340) 775-5706.

Department of Police: 8172 Sub Base, St Thomas, VI 00802; tel. (340) 774-2211; fax (340) 778-2211; e-mail police@usvi.org; internet www.usvi.org/police.

Department of Property and Procurement: Property & Procurement Bldg No. 1, Sub Base, 3rd Floor, Charlotte Amalie, VI 00802; tel. (340) 774-0828; fax (340) 774-9704; e-mail pnp@usvi.org; internet www.usvi.org/pnp.

Department of Public Works: No. 8 Sub Base, Charlotte Amalie, VI 00802; tel. (340) 773-1290; fax (340) 774-5869; e-mail publicworks@usvi.org; internet www.usvi.org/publicworks.

Department of Tourism: 78-123 Estate Contant, POB 6400, Charlotte Amalie, VI 00802; tel. (340) 774-8784; fax (340) 774-4390; e-mail info@usvitourism.vi; internet www.usvi.org/tourism/index.html.

Legislature

LEGISLATIVE ASSEMBLY

Senate
(15 members)

President of the Senate: ALMANDO LIBURD.

Election, 5 November 2002

Party	Seats
Democrats	8
Independent Citizens Movement	2
Independent	5

Political Organizations

Democratic Party of the Virgin Islands: POB 2033, St Thomas Democratic District, VI 00803; e-mail videms@email.com; affiliated to the Democratic Party in the USA; Chair. ARTURO WATLINGTON, Jr.

Independent Citizens Movement: Charlotte Amalie, VI 00801; Chair. USIE RICHON.

Republican Party of the Virgin Islands: Charlotte Amalie, VI 00801; tel. (340) 776-7660; affiliated to the Republican Party in the USA; Chair. GARRY SPRAUVE.

Judicial System

US Federal District Court of the Virgin Islands: Federal Bldg and US Courthouse, 5500 Veteran's Dr., Charlotte Amalie, VI 00802; tel. (340) 774-0640; internet www.vid.uscourts.gov/; jurisdiction in civil, criminal and federal actions; the judges are appointed by the President of the United States with the advice and consent of the Senate.

US Territorial District Court of the Virgin Islands: Alexander A. Farrelly Justice Center, POB 70, Charlotte Amalie, VI 00802; tel. (340) 774-6680; internet www.vid.uscourts.gov/; exclusive jurisdiction in violations of police and executive regulations; original jurisdiction over all local criminal matters and civil actions, regardless of the amount in controversy; and concurrent jurisdiction with the US Federal District Court of the Virgin Islands over federal question and diversity cases, and over local Virgin Islands criminal offences based on the same act or transaction if the act or transaction also constitutes an offence against federal law. The Court is also vested with jurisdiction to promulgate rules and regulations governing its practice and procedure, and to regulate the admission of attorneys to the Virgin Islands Bar.

Judges: RAYMOND L. FINCH (Chief Judge), THOMAS K. MOORE.

Religion

The population is mainly Christian. The main churches with followings in the islands are the Roman Catholic (with an estimated 30,000 adherents in 2000), Episcopalian, Lutheran, Methodist, Moravian and Seventh-day Adventist. There is also a small Jewish community.

CHRISTIANITY

The Roman Catholic Church

The US Virgin Islands comprise a single diocese, suffragan to the archdiocese of Washington, DC, USA. At 31 December 2000 there were an estimated 30,000 adherents in the territory.

Bishop of St Thomas: Most Rev. GEORGE V. MURRY, Bishop's Residence, 68 Kronprindsens Gade, POB 301825, Charlotte Amalie, VI 00803; tel. (340) 774-3166; fax (340) 774-5816; e-mail chancery@islands.vi.

The Anglican Communion

Episcopal Church of the Virgin Islands: Bishop: Rt Rev. THEODORE A. DANIELS, POB 10437, St Thomas. VI 00801; fax (340) 777-8485; e-mail tad@aol.com.

The Press

Pride Magazine: 22A Norre Gade, POB 7908, Charlotte Amalie, VI 00801; tel. (340) 776-4106; f. 1983; monthly; Editor JUDITH WILLIAMS; circ. 4,000.

St Croix Avis: La Grande Princesse, Christiansted, St Croix, VI 00820; tel. (340) 773-2300; f. 1944; morning; independent; Editor RENA BROADHURST-KNIGHT; circ. 10,000.

Tradewinds: POB 1500, Cruz Bay, St John, VI 00831; tel. (340) 776-6496; fax (340) 693-8885; e-mail editor@tradewinds.vi; internet www.stjohntradewindsnews.com; f. 1972; fortnightly; Editor THOMAS C. OAT; circ. 2,000.

Virgin Islands Business Journal: 69 Kronprindsens Gade, POB 1208, Charlotte Amalie, VI 00804; tel. (340) 776-2874; fax (340) 774-3636; internet www.vibj.com; f. 1986; weekly; independent; Man. Editor CARTER HAGUE; circ. 10,000.

Virgin Islands Daily News: 49 and 52A Estate Thomas, POB 7760, Charlotte Amalie, VI 00801; tel. (340) 774-8772; fax (340) 776-0740; internet www.dailynews.vi; f. 1930; morning; CEO RON DILLMAN; Publr and Editor ARIEL MELCHIOR, Jr; circ. 17,000.

Broadcasting and Communications

TELECOMMUNICATIONS

Virgin Islands Telephone Corporation (Vitelco): POB 1141, Charlotte Amalie, VI 00801; tel. (340) 774-5555; internet www.vitelco.com; owned by Atlantic Tele-Network; provides telephone services throughout the islands.

RADIO

WAVI—FM: POB 25016, Gallows Bay Station, St Croix, VI 00824; tel. (340) 773-3693; commercial; Gen. Man. DOUG HARRIS.

WGOD: Crown Mountain, POB 5012, Charlotte Amalie, VI 00803; tel. (340) 774-4498; fax (340) 776-0877; commercial; Gen. Man. PETER RICHARDSON.

WJKC—FM: 5020 Anchor Way, POB 25680, Christiansted, St Croix, VI 00824-1680; tel. (340) 773-0995; e-mail jkc95@aol.com; internet www.wjkcisle95.com; commercial; Gen. Man. JONATHAN COHEN.

WSTA: Sub Base 121, POB 1340, St Thomas, VI 00804; tel. (340) 774-1340; fax (340) 776-1316; e-mail addie@wsta.com; internet www .wsta.com; commercial; Gen. Man. ATHNIEL C. OTTLEY.

WVWI, WVJZ, WWKS (Knight Quality Stations): 13 Crown Bay Fill, POB 305678, Charlotte Amalie, VI 00803-5678; tel. (340) 776-1000; fax (340) 776-5357; e-mail kqs@viaccess.net; f. 1962; commercial; Pres. and Gen. Man. RANDOLPH H. KNIGHT.

TELEVISION

Caribbean Communications Corporation: 1 Beltjen Pl., Charlotte Amalie, VI 00802-6735; tel. (340) 776-2150; fax (340) 774-5029; f. 1966; cable service, 72 channels; Gen. Man. ANDREA L. MARTIN.

St Croix, VI Cable TV: Heron Commercial Park, POB 5968, Sunny Isle, St Croix, VI 00823; f. 1981; 32 channels; Gen. Man. JACK WHITE.

WSVI—TV: Sunny Isle, POB 8ABC, Christiansted, St Croix, VI 00823; tel. (340) 778-5008; fax (340) 778-5011; f. 1965; one channel and one translator; Gen. Man. BARAKAT SALEH.

WTJX—TV (Public Television Service): Barbel Plaza, POB 7879, Charlotte Amalie, VI 00801; tel. (340) 774-6255; fax (340) 774-7092; e-mail lelskoe@wtjx.org; internet www.wtjx.org; one channel; Gen. Man. LORI E. RAWLINGS.

Finance

BANKING

Banco Popular of the Virgin Islands: 193 Altonad and Welgunst, Charlotte Amalie, VI 00802; tel. (340) 693-2702; fax (340) 693-2702; Regional Man. VALENTINO I. McBEAN; 7 brs.

Bank of Nova Scotia (Canada): 214c Altona and Welgunst, POB 420, Charlotte Amalie, VI 00804; tel. (340) 774-6393; fax (340) 693-5994; Man. R. HAINES; 10 brs.

Bank of St Croix: POB 24240, Gallows Bay, St Croix 00824; tel. (340) 773-8500; fax (340) 773-8508; Man. JAMES BRISBOIS; 1 br.

Chase Manhattan Bank, NA (USA): Waterfront, Charlotte Amalie, POB 6620, VI 00801; tel. (340) 776-2222; Gen. Man. WARREN BEER; brs in St Croix and St John.

Citibank, NA (USA): Grand Hotel Bldg, 43–46 Norrie Gade, POB 5167, Charlotte Amalie, VI 00801; tel. (340) 776-353; fax (340) 774-6609; Vice-Pres. KEVIN SZOT.

First Bank of Puerto Rico: POB 3126, St Thomas; tel. (340) 774-2022; fax (340) 776-1313; Pres. and CEO JAMES E. CRITES; 4 brs.

First Federal Savings Bank: Veterans Dr., Charlotte Amalie, VI; tel. (340) 774-2022; fax (340) 776-1313; Man. ALFRED LESLIE; br. in St Croix.

Virgin Islands Community Bank: 12–13 King St, Christiansted, St Croix, VI 00820; tel. (340) 773-0440; fax (340) 773-4028; Pres. and CEO MICHAEL J. DOW; 2 brs.

INSURANCE

A number of mainland US companies have agencies in the Virgin Islands.

Trade and Industry

GOVERNMENT AGENCY

US Virgin Islands Industrial Development Commission: Government Development Bank Bldg, 1050 Norre Gade, POB 305038, St Thomas, VI 00803; tel. (340) 774-8104; e-mail idc@usvi.org; internet www.usvi.org/idc; govt agency; offices in St Thomas and St Croix.

CHAMBERS OF COMMERCE

St Croix Chamber of Commerce: POB 4369, Kings Hill, St Croix, VI 00851; tel. and fax (340) 773-1435; e-mail info@stcroixchamber .org; internet www.stcroixchamber.org; f. 1925; 450 mems; Exec. Dir RACHEL HAINES.

St Thomas–St John Chamber of Commerce: 6–7 Dronning Gade, POB 324, Charlotte Amalie, VI 00804; tel. (340) 776-0010; fax (340) 776-0588; e-mail chamber@islands.vi; internet www .usvichamber.com; Pres. JOHN DE JONGH, Jr; Exec. Dir JOSEPH S. AUBAIN.

UTILITIES

Electricity

Virgin Islands Energy Office: 45 Mars Hill, Frederiksted, St Croix, VI 00840; tel. (340) 773-3450; e-mail vieo0441@viaccess.net; internet www.vienergy.com; Dir VICTOR SOMME, III.

Water

Virgin Islands Water and Power Authority: POB 1450, Charlotte Amalie, VI 00804; tel. (340) 774-3552; fax (340) 774-3422; f. 1964; public corpn; manufactures and distributes electric power and desalinated sea water; Exec. Dir RAYMOND GEORGE.

Transport

ROADS

The islands' road network totals approximately 855.5 km (531.6 miles).

SHIPPING

The US Virgin Islands are a popular port of call for cruise ships. The bulk of cargo traffic is handled at a container port on St Croix. A ferry service provides frequent daily connections between St Thomas and St John and between St Thomas and Tortola (British Virgin Islands).

Virgin Islands Port Authority: POB 301707, Charlotte Amalie, VI 00803; also at POB 1134, Christiansted, St Croix, VI 00821; tel. (340) 774-1629; fax (340) 774-0025; tel. (340) 778-1012; fax (340) 778-1033; e-mail info@viport.com; internet www.viport.com; f. 1968; semi-autonomous govt agency; maintains, operates and develops marine and airport facilities; Exec. Dir GORDON A. FINCH.

CIVIL AVIATION

There are airports on St Thomas and St Croix, and an airfield on St John. Seaplane services link the three islands. The runways at Cyril E. King Airport, St Thomas, and Alexander Hamilton Airport, St Croix, can accommodate intercontinental flights.

Tourism

The islands have a well-developed tourist infrastructure, offering excellent facilities for fishing, yachting and other aquatic sports. A National Park covers about two-thirds of St John. There were 5,148 hotel rooms in 1995. In 2000 some 496,349 tourists stayed in hotels on the islands. Tourist expenditure in that year totalled US $965m.

St Croix Hotel Association: POB 24238, St Croix, VI 00824; tel. (340) 773-7117; fax (340) 773-5883.

St Thomas–St John Hotel and Tourism Association: POB 2300, Charlotte Amalie, VI 00803; tel. (340) 774-6835; fax (340) 774-4993; e-mail stha@viaccess.net; internet www.sttstjhta.com.

OTHER TERRITORIES

Baker and Howland Islands

The Baker and Howland Islands lie in the Central Pacific Ocean, about 2,575 km (1,600 miles) south-west of Honolulu, Hawaii; they comprise two low-lying coral atolls without lagoons, and are uninhabited. Both islands were mined for guano in the late 19th century. Settlements, known as Meyerton (on Baker) and Itascatown (on Howland), were established by the USA in 1935, but were evacuated during the Second World War, owing to Japanese air attacks. The islands are national wildlife refuges and since 1974 have been administered by the US Fish and Wildlife Service. In 1990 legislation before Congress proposed that the islands be included within the boundaries of the State of Hawaii. The islands are administered by the **US Department of the Interior**, US Fish and Wildlife Service, 1849 C St NW, Washington, DC 20240, USA; tel. (202) 208-3171; fax (202) 208-3171; internet www.doi.gov.

Jarvis Island

Jarvis Island lies in the Central Pacific Ocean, about 2,090 km (1,300 miles) south of Hawaii. It is a low-lying coral island and is uninhabited. The island was mined for guano in the late 19th century. A settlement, known as Millersville, including a weather station for the benefit of trans-Pacific aviation, was established by the USA in 1935, but was evacuated during the Second World War. Legislation before Congress in 1990 proposed that the island be included within the State of Hawaii. The island is a national wildlife refuge and is administered by the US Department of the Interior, US Fish and Wildlife Service (address as above, under Baker and Howland Islands).

Johnston Atoll

Johnston Atoll lies in the Pacific Ocean, about 1,319 km (820 miles) west-south-west of Honolulu, Hawaii. It comprises Johnston Island, Sand Island (uninhabited) and two man-made islands, North (Akua) and East (Hikina); area 2.6 sq km (1 sq mile). In 1985 construction of a chemical weapons disposal facility began on the atoll, and by 1990 it was fully operational. In 1989 the US Government agreed to remove artillery shells containing more than 400 metric tons of nerve gas from the Federal Republic of Germany, and destroy them on Johnston Island. In late 1991, following expressions of protest to the US Government by the nations of the South Pacific Forum (now Pacific Islands Forum, see p. 306), together with many environmental groups, a team of scientists visited the chemical disposal facility to monitor the safety and environmental impact of its activities. In January 1995, following a series of accidents, the US army announced that it was to seek an extension to the 30 August 1995 deadline, the date by which the 400,000 weapons stored on the island were due to be destroyed. A facility capable of performing atmospheric tests of nuclear weapons remains operational on the atoll. In May 1996 it was reported that all nerve gases stored on the atoll had been destroyed. However, 1,000 tons of chemical agents remained contained in land mines, bombs and missiles at the site. In December 2000 it was announced that the destruction of the remaining stock of chemical weapons had been completed, and that the facility was to close. Clean-up operations, however, were expected to continue until 2004. The US Fish and Wildlife Service has reported its intention eventually to create a nature reserve on the atoll. Johnston Atoll has been designated a Naval Defense Sea Area and Airspace Reservation, and is closed to public access. The atoll had an estimated population of 173 in 1990, although this increased to approximately 1,000, mainly military, personnel during weapons disposal operations in previous years. Johnston Atoll is administered jointly by the Department of the Interior, US Fish and Wildlife Service (address as above, under Baker and Howland Islands), and the **US Department of Defense**, Commander, Johnston Atoll (FCDNA), APO San Francisco, CA 96035, USA.

Kingman Reef

Kingman Reef lies in the Pacific Ocean, about 1,500km (925 miles) south-west of Hawaii and comprises a reef and shoal measuring about 8 km (5 miles) by 15 km (9.5 miles). In 2000 administrative control was transferred from the US Navy to the Department of the Interior. In 2001 the waters around the reef were designated a National Wildlife Refuge, under the jurisdiction of the US Fish and Wildlife Service (for address see above, under Baker and Howland Islands).

Midway Island

Midway Island lies in the northern Pacific Ocean, about 1,850 km (1,150 miles) north-west of Hawaii. A coral atoll, it comprises Sand Island, Eastern Island and several small islets within the reef, has a total area of about 5 sq km (2 sq miles) and a population 2,200 in 1983, although by 1990 this had declined to 13. Since the transfer of the island's administration from the US Department of Defense to the Department of the Interior in October 1996 limited tourism is permitted. There is a national wildlife refuge on the Territory, which is home to many species of birds. Legislation before Congress in 1990 proposed the inclusion of the Territory within the State of Hawaii. The islands are administered by the US Department of the Interior, US Fish and Wildlife Service (see above, under Baker and Howland Islands).

Navassa Island

Navassa Island lies in the Caribbean Sea, about 160 km (100 miles) south of Guantánamo Bay, Cuba, and 65 km (40 miles) west of Haiti. It is a raised coral island with a limestone plateau and has an area of 5.2 sq km (2 sq miles). The island is uninhabited. Navassa became a US Insular Area in 1857, and was mined throughout the late 19th century, under the Navassa Phosphate Co. All mining activities were terminated in 1898. In 1996 the US Coast Guard ceased operations of the island's lighthouse, and in January 1997 the Office of Insular Affairs (under the control of the US Department of the Interior) assumed control of the island. A research expedition, undertaken in mid-1998, revealed the presence of numerous undiscovered plant and animal species, many of which were thought to be unique to the island. Visits to the island and its surrounding waters were subsequently prohibited, pending further assessment of the island's environment. In December 1999 administrative responsibility for Navassa passed to the US Department of the Interior, US Fish and Wildlife Service (see above, under Baker and Howland Islands); however, control over political matters was retained by the Office of Insular Affairs.

Palmyra

Palmyra lies in the Pacific Ocean, about 1,600 km (1,000 miles) south of Honolulu, Hawaii. It comprises some 50 low-lying islets, has a total area of 100 ha, is uninhabited and is privately owned. Since 1961 the Territory has been administered by the US Department of the Interior. In 1990 legislation before Congress proposed the inclusion of Palmyra within the boundaries of the State of Hawaii. In mid-1996 it was announced that the owners (the Fullard-Leo family in Hawaii) were to sell the atoll to a US company, which, it was believed, planned to establish a nuclear waste storage facility in the Territory. The Government of neighbouring Kiribati expressed alarm at the proposal, and reiterated its intention to seek the reinclusion of the atoll within its own national boundaries. However, in June one of the Hawaiian Representatives to the US Congress proposed legislation in the US House of Representatives to prevent the establishment of such a facility, and a US government official subsequently announced that the atoll would almost certainly not be used for that purpose. In May 2000 it was announced that the island was to be purchased by The Nature Conservancy (internet www.tnc.org); the sale, for some US $30m., was confirmed in November 2000. The lagoons and surrounding waters within the 12 nautical mile zone of US territorial seas were transferred to the US Fish and Wildlife Service in January 2001, and designated a National Wildlife Refuge.

Wake Island

Wake Island lies in the Pacific Ocean, about 2,060 km (1,280 miles) east of Guam. It is a coral atoll comprising the three islets of Wake, Wilkes and Peale, with an area less than 8 sq km (3 sq miles) and a population estimated to be almost 2,000 in 1988. Legislation before Congress in 1990 proposed the inclusion of the islands within the Territory of Guam. However, the Republic of the Marshall Islands, some 500 km (310 miles) south of Wake, exerted its own claim to the atoll (known as Enenkio to the Micronesians), which is a site of great importance for the islands' traditional chiefly rituals. Plans by a US company, announced in 1998, to establish a large-scale nuclear waste storage facility on the atoll were condemned by environmentalists and politicians in the region. Since 1972 the group has been administered by the **US Department of Defense**, Department of the Air Force, The Pentagon, Washington, DC 20330, USA; tel. (202) 697-6061; fax (703) 696-7273; internet www.af.mil.

URUGUAY

Introductory Survey

Location, Climate, Language, Religion, Flag, Capital

The Eastern Republic of Uruguay lies on the south-east coast of South America, with Brazil to the north and Argentina to the west. The climate is temperate, with an average temperature of 14°C–16°C (57°F–61°F) in winter and 21°C–28°C (70°F–82°F) in summer. The language is Spanish. There is no state religion but Roman Catholicism is predominant. The national flag (proportions 2 by 3) has nine horizontal stripes (five white and four blue, alternating), with a square white canton, containing a yellow sun with 16 alternating straight and wavy rays, in the upper hoist. The capital is Montevideo.

Recent History

Since independence from Spain, gained in 1825, domestic politics in Uruguay traditionally has been dominated by two parties: the Colorados ('reds' or Liberals) and the Blancos ('whites' or Conservatives, subsequently also known as the Partido Nacional). Their rivalry resulted in frequent outbreaks of civil war in the 19th century: the names derive from the flags of the 1836 civil war. From 1880 to 1958 the governing Partido Colorado was led by the Batlle family. Owing to the progressive policies of José Batlle y Ordóñez, Colorado President in 1903–07 and in 1911–15, Uruguay became the first welfare state in Latin America. During 1951–66 the presidency was in abeyance, being replaced by a collective leadership.

In December 1967 Jorge Pacheco Areco assumed the presidency. His period in office was notable for massive increases in the cost of living, labour unrest and the spectacular exploits of the Tupamaro urban guerrilla movement. In March 1972 Pacheco was succeeded by Juan María Bordaberry Arocena, a Colorado, who won the presidential election in November 1971. The army took complete control of the campaign against the Tupamaros, and by late 1973 had suppressed the movement. Military intervention in civilian affairs led, in 1973, to the closure of the Congress and its replacement by an appointed 25-member Council of State (subsequently increased to 35 members). The Partido Comunista and other left-wing groups were banned; repressive measures, including strict press censorship, continued. In September 1974 army officers were placed in control of the major state-owned enterprises.

President Bordaberry was deposed by the army in June 1976 because of his refusal to countenance any return, however gradual, to constitutional rule. In July the recently formed Council of the Nation elected Dr Aparicio Méndez Manfredini to the presidency for five years. Despite the Government's announcement that there would be a return to democracy, persecution of political figures continued, and the number of political prisoners held in 1976 was thought to have reached 6,000. Although the decision taken by the USA in 1979 to restore a fraction of its former military aid to Uruguay was governed by an easing of repression, according to humanitarian organizations some 1,100 political prisoners remained in detention in 1981.

President Méndez introduced constitutional amendments, known as Institutional Acts, to consolidate the internal situation and to create a 'new order'. By 1980 severe economic problems made the army anxious to return executive responsibility to civilian politicians. A new constitution, under which the armed forces would continue to be involved in all matters of national security, was drafted and submitted to a plebiscite in November 1980, but was rejected by 57.8% of voters. The military leadership was therefore forced to amend the draft document in consultation with leaders of the recognized political parties, and, in September 1981, a retired army general, Gregorio Alvarez Armellino, was appointed by the Joint Council of the Armed Forces to serve as President during the transition period to full civilian government.

The Government's reluctance to permit greater public freedom and to improve observance of human rights caused serious unrest throughout 1983. Popular discontent was further aroused by the rapid deterioration of the economy and by the effect of events in Argentina. In August the authorities suspended all public political activity and reserved the right to impose a new constitution without consultation, insisting, however, that the original electoral timetable would be maintained. The political opposition responded by threatening to boycott the elections and by uniting with proscribed opposition groups to hold a national day of protest. In September the first organized labour protest for 10 years was supported by 500,000 workers.

Political agitation increased during 1984, and the Government threatened to postpone the elections, planned for 25 November 1984, unless the political parties agreed to its proposals for constitutional reform. Tensions increased in June, following the return from exile and the subsequent arrest of Ferreira Aldunate, the proposed presidential candidate of the Partido Nacional. Talks between the Government, the Partido Colorado and the Unión Cívica (a Christian democratic party) resumed in July; the parties obtained several important concessions, including the right to engage in political activity. In August, encouraged by the Government's commitment to the restoration of the democratic process, the parties (with the exception of the Partido Nacional) agreed to the Government's proposals, including a transitional set of laws and the formation of the National Security Council. The Government confirmed that elections would take place, and all restrictions on political activity were withdrawn.

At the elections in November 1984 the Partido Colorado, led by Dr Julio María Sanguinetti Cairolo, secured a narrow victory over the opposition. In February 1985 the military regime relinquished power, one month earlier than originally planned. President Sanguinetti was inaugurated on 1 March, as was a Government of national unity, incorporating representatives of the other parties. Concurrently, various outlawed organizations, including the Partido Comunista, were legalized. All political prisoners were released under an amnesty law later in the month.

The new Government announced its commitment to reversing the economic recession; however, its efforts to address the crisis were hampered by frequent industrial stoppages. Discussions between the administration and trade union and business leaders began in August 1985. Although the Government suspended negotiations following another series of strikes, discussions were resumed in September.

A major political issue in 1986 was the investigation into alleged violations of human rights by the armed forces during the military dictatorship. In August the Government proposed legislation that would offer an amnesty for all military and police personnel accused of this type of crime, in accordance with a pact made with the armed forces that human rights trials would not take place. In October the draft legislation was rejected by opposition parties, but in December a revised law (the 'punto final') was approved, which, while its sponsors insisted that it was not an amnesty law, brought an end to current military trials and made the President responsible for any further investigations. The law was widely opposed, particularly by left-wing political parties, trade unions and student groups. In February 1987 a campaign was initiated to organize a petition containing the signatures of at least 25% of the registered electorate in order to force a referendum on the issue. (The Constitution specifies that, if such a petition is successfully produced, a referendum must be held within 60 days.) The campaign was supported principally by human rights groups, trade unions and the centre-left coalition, the Frente Amplio. By late 1988 the required number of signatures had been collected, and a referendum took place in April 1989, at which a total of 52.6% of the votes were cast in favour of maintaining the amnesty law.

Industrial unrest, which had re-emerged earlier in 1989 in response to price increases, intensified as the presidential and legislative elections approached. In October the trade union confederation, the Plenario Intersindical de Trabajadores—Convención Nacional de Trabajadores (PIT—CNT), organized two 24-hour general strikes, in support of a teachers' pay dispute and to protest against the strict conditions stipulated by the World Bank upon granting a new structural adjustment loan. The presidential and legislative elections in November resulted in victory (for the first time since 1962) for the Partido Nacional. In the presidential election, Luis Alberto Lacalle, the party's main candidate (the electoral code permitted each party to present more than one candidate), received 37% of the votes, while his closest rival, Jorge Batlle Ibáñez of the Partido Colorado, won 30%. However, the Partido Nacional failed to obtain an overall majority in Congress, thus compelling the President-elect to seek support from a wider political base. Immediately before taking office, in March 1990, he announced the conclusion of an agreement, the 'coincidencia nacional', between the two principal parties, whereby the Partido Colorado undertook to support proposed legislation on economic reform, in return for the appointment of four of its members to the Council of Ministers.

Labour unrest intensified during the early 1990s. The PIT—CNT organized a series of general strikes in support of demands for wage increases and in opposition to government austerity measures and plans for the transfer to private ownership of state-owned companies. Opposition from within the coalition Government to the planned privatization of state enterprises became apparent in May 1991, when former President Sanguinetti, the leader of the Foro Batllista faction of the Partido Colorado, withdrew his support from the Government, thus forcing the resignation of the Minister of Public Health, the faction's sole representative in the Council of Ministers. Reservations about the proposed privatization law were also expressed by elements of the Partido Nacional. In September, none the less, the legislation was narrowly approved by Congress. In response, the opposition Frente Amplio (FA), with the support of another political organization, Nuevo Espacio, and the trade unions, began a campaign to overrule the legislature by way of a referendum. In October 1992, in a special poll, some 30% of the electorate voted for a full referendum to be held on the partial amendment of the Government's privatization legislation. At the referendum, held in December, 71.6% of voters supported the proposal for a partial repeal of the legislation. The vote was also widely recognized as a vote of censure against the President's economic policy, and in particular his determination to keep public-sector wage increases to a minimum. While the result of the referendum did not affect all planned divestments, it was considered to be a serious reverse and served to undermine confidence in government economic policy. Notwithstanding, President Lacalle indicated that he would continue to pursue the privatization programme.

Industrial unrest in the public sector intensified in 1992, owing primarily to the Government's refusal to grant wage increases in line with inflation. In November, however, following a four-day strike by the police, the Government was forced to concede wage increases of up to 50% to the security forces. Encouraged by this concession, transport and public health workers initiated strikes in support of demands for wage increases.

In January 1993 President Lacalle reorganized the Council of Ministers, but made no attempt to reconstruct the coalition with the Partido Colorado. (The 'coincidencia nacional', agreed in 1990, had failed to ensure the Government a majority in the legislature on important economic reforms.) In March the President's failure to accede to demands for the dismissal of the Minister of Economy and Finance, and for a change in economic policy, led to the withdrawal of legislative support by two influential factions of the Partido Nacional, the Movimiento Nacional de Rocha—Corriente Popular Nacionalista, led by Carlos Julio Pereyra, and Renovación y Victoria, led by Vice-President Aguirre. Consequently, the Minister of Public Works and Transport, a member of the Movimiento Nacional de Rocha, resigned. He was replaced by a member of Lacalle's own Consejo Nacional Herrerista faction.

In mid-1993 revelations implicating members of the Uruguayan armed forces in the abduction of a former employee of the Chilean secret service, Eugenio Berríos Sagredo, had serious political repercussions for the Government, creating diplomatic tension between Uruguay and Chile, and prompting concern at the Government's lack of control over the armed forces. Reportedly, Berríos, who was to give testimony in Chile at various legal proceedings concerning alleged human rights violations which took place during the period of military rule in that country, had been abducted and transferred via Argentina to Uruguay by units of the armed forces of the three countries acting in secret co-operation. In Uruguay Berríos had escaped detention but had been returned to his captors by a local police chief, Col (retd) Ramón Rivas. Rivas's subsequent dismissal by the Ministry of

the Interior for his involvement in the affair provoked criticism from senior military leaders, and a confrontation occurred when the Commander-in-Chief of the Armed Forces, Lt-Gen. Juan Modesto Rebollo, attempted to assume responsibility for the actions of all his subordinates implicated in the affair. Following conciliatory discussions between President Lacalle and the military leadership, it was agreed that those charged with involvement in the abduction were to be tried by military tribunal rather than by the civilian courts. Lacalle was obliged to relieve the head of army intelligence, Gen. Mario Aguerrondo (purportedly a close associate of the President), of his position; subsequently Aguerrondo was appointed director of a military academy. In August, however, it emerged that Aguerrondo had been responsible for placing an illicit electronic listening device in the office of a senior military official. Rebollo was dismissed for demanding that Lacalle force Aguerrondo into retirement. Lacalle later removed Aguerrondo from his post and also dismissed the Minister of National Defence for his involvement in the internal espionage, in order to avoid a motion of censure by the Senate.

In October 1994 Vice-President Aguirre announced his withdrawal from the presidential election that was due to be held in the following month, after a claim by former President Sanguinetti that Aguirre's candidacy was in violation of the Constitution, which stated that anyone holding presidential office within three months of a presidential election was not eligible to contest it; Aguirre had been acting President during Lacalle's absence abroad in September. It was widely believed that Sanguinetti's intervention was a retaliatory action prompted by an earlier request by the Partido Nacional that the Electoral Commission annul the candidacy of a member of the Partido Colorado for the mayorship of Montevideo.

The presidential and legislative elections of 27 November 1994 were notable for the emergence of a third political force to rival the traditional powers of the Partido Nacional and the Partido Colorado. The Encuentro Progresista (EP)—a predominantly left-wing alliance principally comprising the parties of the FA, as well as dissidents of the Partido Nacional and other minor parties—secured 30.8% of the votes, while the Partido Nacional obtained 31.4% and the Partido Colorado won a narrow victory with 32.5% of the vote. Subsequently, the leading presidential candidate of the Partido Colorado, Sanguinetti, was pronounced President-elect (to be inaugurated in March 1995). Sanguinetti indicated that he planned to appoint a broadly-based Council of Ministers in order to ensure legislative support for his administration. Two plebiscites, concerning education and social security, were conducted concurrently with the presidential and legislative elections. The education proposal, which was promoted by the teachers' unions, sought to have 27% of the national budget allocated to education. The social security proposal, which was supported by pensioners' organizations, sought the repeal of social security legislation enacted under the Lacalle administration. The education proposal was rejected by the electorate, while the social security proposal received approval. A resolution of the latter issue was later identified by the Sanguinetti administration as its main priority.

In early 1995, following talks with opposition parties, the Partido Colorado established a 'governability pact' with the Partido Nacional, providing for a coalition Government. In February President Sanguinetti announced the appointment of the Council of Ministers, allocating six portfolios to members of the Partido Colorado, four to the Partido Nacional, one to the Unión Cívica, and one to the Partido por el Gobierno del Pueblo (Lista 99), which had contested the elections in alliance with Sanguinetti's Foro Batllista faction of the Partido Colorado, and whose leader, Hugo Batalla, had been elected as Sanguinetti's Vice-President. The EP remained in opposition to the Government, but the principal member of the alliance, the FA, was reported to have agreed to co-operate with the administration in return for government consideration of its views when determining social policy.

Despite popular opposition and resistance in the legislature from the FA, the proposed legislation to restructure the social security system was approved in August 1995. The measure provided for the introduction of a mixed public and private pension scheme, replacing the existing system of state provision whereby the contributions of those in employment financed payments to current pensioners. This system had proved an increasing burden on state finances; in 1994 there were some 700,000 pensioners supported by an economically active population of only 1.3m., and the resultant shortfall in funding (some US $500m.) was financed directly from the state budget. The reform of the social security system, which provided for a gradual increase in the retirement age and introduced compulsory personal savings plans for those earning more than 5,000 pesos per month, aimed to eliminate the system's structural deficit within 10 years.

In July 1995 the Government and the legislative opposition reached an agreement providing for the reform of the electoral system. Under the existing system, known as the Ley de Lemas, parties were permitted to present more than one presidential candidate, with the leading candidate in each party assuming the total number of votes for candidates in that party. According to the proposed reform, each party would present one candidate, selected by means of an internal election, and, in the event of no candidate securing an absolute majority, a second round of voting would be conducted. In March 1996 draft legislation for the reform was submitted to the legislature. However, certain details of the bill were opposed by elements of the FA. In February Gen. (retd) Líber Seregni Mosquera resigned as President of the FA, owing to the party's inability to reach a consensus on the issue; members of the Partido Comunista, the Partido Socialista del Uruguay and the Movimiento de Liberación Nacional—Tupamaros opposed the proposal providing for a second round of presidential elections, which, they contended, would allow supporters of the Partido Nacional and the Partido Colorado to unite in order to deny the presidency to the FA. Supporters of Seregni preferred to endorse the proposal and thereby ensure the abolition of the prevailing multi-candidate system.

In October 1996 President Sanguinetti secured the necessary two-thirds' support in the legislature for the reform of the Constitution. Besides abolishing the Ley de Lemas and introducing provision for second-round presidential elections (see above), the reform also accorded greater autonomy to municipal administrations, and established a framework for environmental protection. The amendments were approved by 50.5% of voters in a plebiscite held in December, and came into effect in January 1997.

In October 1996 a judge ordered the imprisonment of the former Minister of Economy and Finance, Braga, and of Daniel Cambón (an erstwhile adviser to Lacalle), on charges concerning irregularities in their management of the privatization of the Banco Pan de Azúcar in 1994. Investigations into alleged corrupt practices involving members of the former Lacalle administration had been under way since 1995.

In March 1997 Congress approved legislation to establish a 'citizens' police force, led by 200 retired police-officers, to counteract a dramatic increase in violent crime in the country. The integrity of the police had been undermined by reports of numerous instances in which serving and retired police-officers had colluded with criminal groups.

In May 1997 some 20,000 civilians staged a rally in the capital to demand that the Government and the armed forces provide information on the whereabouts of as many as 140 people who had 'disappeared' during the military dictatorship. The demonstrators' cause appeared to have been advanced in April by a judicial ruling that facilitated the investigation of allegations that 32 people had been interred in two clandestine cemeteries in army barracks during the dictatorship, and that their remains had been covertly removed from the burial sites in 1985–86. However, in June the ruling was revoked by a court of appeal, on the grounds that it contravened the 'punto final' amnesty law (see above). Notwithstanding, human rights organizations welcomed a decree announced by President Sanguinetti in December that granted an amnesty to 41 former army officers who had been dismissed from service during the dictatorship, owing to their political beliefs. Lt-Gen. Raúl Mermot, the Commander-in-Chief of the Armed Forces, resigned from his post one month ahead of schedule, in protest at the decision. In May 1999 some 15,000 people participated in a further march in support of demands that the authorities account for the disappearance of friends and relatives during the military dictatorship.

In mid-1998 serious divisions emerged within the Partido Nacional as rival factions prepared for the party's forthcoming internal elections for a presidential candidate. In August the Movimiento Nacional de Rocha—Corriente Popular Nacionalista and the Consejo Nacional Herrerista withdrew from the Partido Nacional's executive committee after a bitter dispute concerning the apparent suicide of the party's controversial

mayor of Cerro Largo. Earlier Lacalle's Herrerista faction had demanded unsuccessfully that the executive committee take disciplinary action against the mayor, who had stated publicly that the armed forces should seize power if Lacalle won the presidential election; rumours circulated subsequently that Herrerista sympathizers were implicated in the mayor's death.

In late April 1999, in the first primary elections to be held in Uruguay, Lacalle, Batlle and Tabaré Vázquez were selected as the presidential candidates for the Partido Nacional, the Partido Colorado and the EP (subsequently known as Encuentro Progresista—Frente Amplio, EP—FA), respectively. Vázquez, a former mayor of Montevideo, won a particularly convincing victory, securing 82% of the votes of his party's supporters, while Batlle defeated Sanguinetti's favoured candidate, Luis Hierro López, who was later nominated as the Partido Colorado's candidate for the vice-presidency.

As Uruguay suffered the adverse effects of slowing economic activity in the region, notably in Brazil and Argentina, the PIT—CNT organized a 24-hour general strike in May 1999 to protest against rising unemployment. In August the Minister of Livestock, Agriculture and Fishing resigned amid a crisis in the farming sector. Farmers, who had accumulated debts estimated at some US $1,200m., had been demanding government assistance.

The presidential and legislative elections of 31 October 1999 confirmed the end of the traditional dominance of the Partido Colorado and the Partido Nacional. The EP—FA became the largest single party in both the Chamber of Deputies and the Senate, winning 40 and 12 seats, respectively. The Partido Colorado largely maintained its representation, securing 33 and 10 seats, while support for the Partido Nacional declined considerably, with the party winning only 22 seats in the Chamber of Deputies and seven in the Senate, having held a combined total of 41 seats in the outgoing legislature. Vázquez gained 38.5% of the vote, compared with 31.3% for Batlle and 21.3% for Lacalle. Despite the convincing success of the EP—FA in the first round, Jorge Batlle defeated Vázquez in a second round of voting on 28 November, with 51.6% of the vote, aided by the support of the Partido Nacional (under a formal accord). Following his inauguration on 1 March 2000, President Batlle appointed a new Council of Ministers, allocating eight portfolios to the Partido Colorado and five to the Partido Nacional. Batlle retained the four ministers responsible for the interior, foreign affairs, planning and the budget, and transport and public works (all from the Partido Colorado), and moved Luis Brezzo from the agriculture portfolio to defence.

In early 2000 Batlle held several meetings with Vázquez, in an apparent attempt to achieve a degree of rapprochement with the left, and also committed himself to resolving the issue of the 'disappeared', in marked contrast to his predecessor, Sanguinetti, who had consistently resisted pressure to investigate their fate. In April 2000 Batlle dismissed Gen. Manuel Fernández, one of the country's most senior army officials, after he sought to justify the military repression of the 1970s and suggested that sooner or later the armed forces would again have to fight against left-wing extremists. In August Batlle announced the formation of a commission, composed of representatives from the Government, the opposition, the Church and the victims' families, to investigate the fate of 164 people who disappeared during the military dictatorship. The unexpected dismissal in January 2001 of Gen. Juan Geymonat, Commander-in-Chief of the Armed Forces, was interpreted as a first step in a military reform programme advocated by Batlle. In May as many as 70,000 people participated in a march in Montevideo to demand a full investigation into the fate of those who disappeared during the military dictatorship. In late October 2002 the Commission reported its preliminary findings that 26 of the 33 'disappeared' Uruguayan citizens under its investigation had been murdered by Argentine and Uruguayan military officers. In November new legislation confirming the legal status of the victims as deceased was rejected by relatives, who requested that victims be reclassified as 'missing through enforced absence'.

The Partido Nacional performed well in local and regional elections in May 2000, securing control of 13 of the 19 departments, while the Partido Colorado won five. The EP—FA retained control of Montevideo, but was disappointed by defeats in three other departments where it had made advances in the October 1999 elections (notably Canelones).

Against a background of ongoing economic recession, the Batlle administration encountered opposition to its policies from organized labour groups from 2000. In June 2000 a general strike was organized by the PIT—CNT to demand increased action on unemployment and more finance for education and health care, as well as to protest against emergency legislation, passed that month, which would allow the partial privatization of some public services, including the railways and the ports. A more widespread strike was held in December to protest at the same issues. However, an attempt by the EP—FA to force a referendum on the controversial law in February 2001 failed, owing to a lack of public support. Although public opinion continued to be supportive of public ownership of state industries, it was also becoming increasingly opposed to monopolies and, therefore, more receptive to the Government's proposals to allow private companies to compete with the state concerns, or bid to operate their services under contract. Nevertheless, the PIT—CNT led a further general strike in July 2001.

In April 2001 the farming sector suffered a further set-back when Uruguayan exports of beef were suspended following the discovery of cattle infected with foot-and-mouth disease near the border with Argentina. The country's entire herd was vaccinated and the Government declared that the epidemic had ended in September. Exports to the European Union resumed in November; it was estimated that the epidemic had cost the country US $250m. in lost exports.

The financial crisis in neighbouring Argentina of December 2001–January 2002 caused additional economic hardship in Uruguay, with continued rural unrest and political and trade-union opposition to the austerity measures introduced by the Government. There was an unprecedented rise in street violence and organized crime, along with accelerated rates of emigration. In May the Argentine Government's imposition of severe restrictions on bank withdrawals prompted many Argentine citizens holding assets in Uruguay to access their funds, precipitating a crisis in Uruguay's financial system. In late June, the Government was forced to abandon exchange rate controls in order to maintain the peso uruguayo's competitiveness against the devalued Argentine and Brazilian currencies. However by late July, following a 30% decline in the peso's value in relation to the US dollar and rising concerns over the viability and transparency of the banking sector, substantial numbers of Uruguayans also began to withdraw their deposits. In an attempt to avert a major financial collapse, the Government instructed all banking institutions in Uruguay to close for a period of four days and introduced emergency economic measures, which included an increase in taxation on salaries and pensions. Moreover, three state-owned banks were placed under direct government administration, and restrictions were imposed on their customers' access to long-term foreign exchange deposits. The Government successfully sought an immediate loan of $1,500m. from the USA to prevent a severe deterioration in international reserves and in November agreement was reached with the IMF on stand-by loans totalling some US $2,800m., to be disbursed in 2002 and 2003. Also, notably, the Batlle administration was swift to restore public order following the looting of some commercial premises in the immediate aftermath of the bank closures. Nevertheless, as a result of the financial crisis, in late July Alberto Bensión, the Minister of Economy and Finance, was forced to resign, having lost the support of the Partido Nacional. He was succeeded by Alejandro Atchugarry, a prominent member of the Partido Colorado. At the same time, President Batlle replaced César Rodríguez Batlle as Central Bank President with Julio de Brun.

The financial crisis, as well as popular resentment towards the Government's economic strategy and unprecedentedly high levels of unemployment in mid-2002, contributed to the growing political isolation of President Batlle in that year, and created a greater willingness within the Partido Nacional to reconsider its association with the Partido Colorado. In November the Partido Nacional terminated discussions on a new 'governability pact' between the two parties, removed its five ministers from the Government and withdrew from the ruling coalition, leaving the Frente Amplio as the largest political bloc in the Congreso. President Batlle subsequently appointed non-partisan ministers to the vacant posts and a limited rationalization of ministries was effected.

In September 2002 the Congreso approved new legislation, proposed by the Partido Nacional, which authorized the payment of 20% of public-sector salaries in the form of transport tokens. The legislation prompted a series of one-day strikes by transport workers in January 2003. In November 2002 it was announced that the three suspended state-run banks were to be merged into one: in March 2003 the Nuevo Banco Comercial

began operations (see Economic Affairs, below). The incorporation of the new bank coincided with the resumption of IMF disbursements, suspended in November owing to the Government's perceived lack of progress on the restructuring of the banking sector.

Following a summit conference in Paraguay in March 1991, the Governments of Argentina, Brazil, Paraguay and Uruguay agreed to create a common market of the 'Southern Cone' countries, the Mercado Común del Sur (Mercosur, see p. 316). The Treaty of Asunción allowed for the dismantling of trade barriers between the four countries, and entered full operation in 1995. However, in February 2002 President Batlle, during a visit to the US capital, Washington, DC, declared that Uruguay would begin bilateral free trade negotiations with the USA because of the drastic reduction in exports to other Mercosur member states (particularly Argentina and Brazil) as a result of the devaluation of the Argentine peso at the beginning of that year. A series of trade agreements between Chile and overseas nations in 2002 and 2003 also prompted Uruguay to seek international commercial agreements on a unilateral basis.

In May 1991 Uruguay and the USA signed an agreement facilitating joint investigations into the diversion of illicit proceeds from drugs-trafficking in Uruguay. The accord, which came in response to an acknowledged increase in such money-laundering activities in Uruguay's 'offshore' banking system, permitted more rapid access to suspect accounts.

In January 1999 Uruguay's security forces announced that they had arrested an Egyptian national (suspected of affiliation to a proscribed Islamist group responsible for the massacre of foreign tourists in Egypt), who allegedly was planning a campaign of terrorist attacks on British diplomatic facilities in Europe. The Governments of Uruguay, Argentina, Brazil, the USA and the United Kingdom subsequently pledged to implement an agreement on co-ordinating intelligence operations in order to curb the activities of radical Islamist groups within Mercosur.

In April 2002 Uruguay severed diplomatic relations with Cuba, citing insults by the Cuban Government after Uruguay sponsored a motion, which was passed by the UN Human Rights Commission, calling on Cuba to improve its civil and political rights record.

In May 2002 relations with Argentina were strained by resentment in Uruguay over the consequences of the Argentine financial crisis. Uruguayan displeasure was reflected in apparent remarks by President Batlle characterizing the Argentines as 'a bunch of thieves.' However President Batlle subsequently visited Argentina and apologized for his comments, leading to the restoration of cordial relations between the two countries.

Government

Uruguay is a republic comprising 19 departments. Under the 1966 Constitution, executive power is held by the President, who is directly elected by universal adult suffrage for a five-year term. The President is assisted by the Vice-President and the appointed Council of Ministers. Legislative power is vested in the bicameral Congress, comprising the Senate and the Chamber of Representatives, also directly elected for five years. The President, the Vice-President, the Senators (who number 31, including the Vice-President, who is automatically allocated a seat as President of the Senate) and the 99 Deputies are elected nationally.

Defence

In August 2002 Uruguay's active armed forces comprised an army of 15,200, a navy of 5,700 and an air force of 3,000. Paramilitary forces numbered 920 men. The defence expenditure in 2001 was 3,272m. pesos uruguayos.

Economic Affairs

In 2001, according to estimates by the World Bank, Uruguay's gross national income (GNI), measured at average 1999–2001 prices, was US $19,036m., equivalent to $5,670 per head (or $8,710 per head on an international purchasing-power parity basis). During 1990–2001, it was estimated, the population increased by an annual average of 0.7%, while gross domestic product (GDP) per head increased, in real terms, by an annual average of 1.7% per year. Overall GDP increased, in real terms, at an average annual rate of 2.5% in 1990–2001; GDP decreased by 3.1% in 2001.

Agriculture (including forestry and fishing) contributed an estimated 6.0% of GDP in 2001. Some 4.0% of the labour force were employed in the sector in 2000. The principal crops are rice, sugar cane, wheat, barley, potatoes, sorghum and maize. Live-stock-rearing, particularly sheep and cattle, is traditionally Uruguay's major economic activity. Exports of live animals, animal products, skins and hides provided 42.0% of export revenue in 2000. According to the Central Bank, agricultural GDP increased by an annual average of 1.5% per year in 1990–2001. Agricultural GDP declined by an estimated 3.0% in 2000, and by a further estimated 5.1% in 2001. Exports of beef to the USA were suspended from October to December 2000, owing to a suspected outbreak of foot-and-mouth disease, and from April to November 2001, owing to an actual outbreak of the disease.

Industry (including mining, manufacturing, construction and power) contributed an estimated 25.0% of GDP in 2001, and employed 24.5% of the working population in 2000. According to the Central Bank, industrial GDP increased by an annual average of 0.2% in 1990–2001. Industrial GDP decreased by an estimated 2.3% in 2000, and by an estimated 5.6% in 2001.

Although there is believed to be considerable potential for the mining sector, mining and quarrying contributed an estimated 0.3% of GDP in 2001, and employed 0.2% of the working population in 2000. Apart from the small-scale extraction of building materials, industrial minerals and semi-precious stones, there has been little mining activity, although gold deposits are currently being developed. Uruguay has no known petroleum resources. According to figures from the central bank, the GDP of the mining sector increased by an annual average of 9.1% in 1990–2001. Mining GDP decreased by an estimated 8.8% in 2000 and by an estimated 11.2% in 2001.

Manufacturing contributed an estimated 15.6% of GDP in 2001 and employed 14.8% of the working population in 2000. Measured by the value of output, the principal branches of manufacturing in 2000 were food products, beverages and tobacco (accounting for an estimated 45.4% of the total), chemicals (22.8%), metal products, machinery and equipment, and textiles, clothing and leather products. According to figures from the Central Bank, manufacturing GDP decreased by an annual average of 1.1% in 1990–2001. Manufacturing GDP decreased by an estimated 2.1% in 2000, and by a further estimated 6.2% in 2001.

Energy is derived principally from hydroelectric power (76.5% of total electricity production in 1999) and mineral fuels (23.0% in 1999). There were plans to increase the use of natural gas as an energy resource; the first natural gas pipeline between Uruguay and Argentina began operating in late 1998. Imports of mineral products (including fuels) comprised 15.8% of the value of total imports in 2000.

The services sector contributed an estimated 69.0% of GDP in 2001, and engaged 71.4% of the working population in 2000. Tourism is a significant source of foreign exchange, earning US $652m. in 2000. According to the Central Bank, the GDP of the services sector increased by an annual average of 3.1% in 1990–2001. The GDP of the services sector decreased by an estimated 0.2% in 2000, and by a further 0.6% in 2001.

In 2001 Uruguay recorded a visible trade deficit of US $770.9m., and there was a deficit of $512.5m. on the current account of the balance of payments. In 2000 the principal source of imports was Argentina (24.1%); other major suppliers were Brazil (19.2%) and the USA. Brazil was the principal market for exports (23.1%) in that year; other major recipients were Argentina and the USA. The main exports in 2000 were live animals and animal products, vegetable products, textiles, hides and skins, and foodstuffs, beverages and tobacco. The principal imports in that year were machinery and appliances, chemical products, mineral products, transport equipment, foodstuffs, beverages and tobacco, and synthetic plastics, resins and rubber.

In 2001 there was a budgetary deficit of 11,554m. pesos uruguayos, equivalent to 4.6% of GDP. At the end of 2000 Uruguay's total external debt was US $8,196m., of which $6,131m. was long-term public debt. In that year the cost of debt-servicing was equivalent to 29.2% of the value of exports of goods and services. The average annual rate of inflation was 32.0% in 1990–2001. Consumer prices increased by 4.8% in 2000 and by 4.4% in 2001. An estimated 14.4% of the urban labour force were unemployed in February 2002.

Uruguay is a member of the Inter-American Development Bank (IDB, see p. 239), the Asociación Latinoamericana de Integración (ALADI, see p. 259), the Sistema Económico Latinoamericano (SELA, see p. 340) and the Mercado Común del Sur (Mercosur, see p. 316).

Uruguay's economy was in recession from 1999, largely owing to external factors, notably the negative impact of the recession in Argentina and Brazil, the devaluation of the Brazilian currency at the beginning of 1999 and low world prices for its principal export products. GDP declined by 2.7% in 1999. In May 2000 the IMF approved a 22-month stand-by credit worth US $197m. to support the new Batlle administration's economic programme, which included plans to implement significant cuts in public expenditure, with the aim of reducing the fiscal deficit, as well as structural reforms to make state enterprises more competitive. However, the economic decline continued in 2000 (a decrease in GDP of 1.4%), owing to high oil prices and low agricultural commodity prices. Industrial unrest greeted the Government's proposals to deregulate public services in 2000 and 2001. In 2001 GDP declined for the third consecutive year, by an estimated 3.1%. In January 2002, in response to the financial crisis in Argentina, which adversely affected Uruguay's exports (already damaged by the outbreak of foot-and-mouth disease in 2001—see above), as well as its tourist industry, the Government announced a fiscal adjustment plan. In an attempt to contain the fiscal deficit to 2.5% of GDP, it was proposed that taxes would be increased and some state-owned real estate be sold off (although progress on privatization was subsequently stalled in 2002 and 2003). In the following month, after international credit agencies had downgraded Uruguay's investment grade rating, Congress approved measures that extended the scope of value-added tax, and introduced an additional levy on high salaries for government officials, as well as a tax on international telephone calls and a 4% increase in fuel prices. In March the IMF approved a new stand-by credit, worth about $743m., intended to support the country's economic programme in 2002–04. The programme was extended by a further year in March 2003, although the Government confirmed that its fiscal target for that year would be revised from 4% to 3.2% of GDP. In the wake of the crisis in the banking sector in mid-2002 (see Recent History, above), new legislation was introduced in early 2003 enhancing the supervisory powers of the Central Bank and reforming state-controlled lending. Moreover, the new laws authorized the merger of the three state-owned banks placed under government administration in late 2002, thus reducing the risk posed by further insolvencies in the banking system. However, in March a lack of investors obliged the Government to use IMF funds to capitalize the new bank, to be known as Nuevo Banco Comercial. Following a further downgrading of Uruguay's debt by international credit agencies in early 2003, measures to restructure the country's heavy debt burden were announced. In April the Government confirmed that new bonds, which carried extended terms of repayment and a cash incentive of 15% on face value, would be offered to commercial holders of Uruguay's short-term debt, pending the consent of some 75% of investors. In the same month, the World Bank pledged further loans, totalling US $252m., to finance infrastructure and social-welfare projects. The funds would complement previous assistance from the IDB and other institutions. Nevertheless, the overall economic outlook remained poor in mid-2003, with unemployment of around 20% and annual inflation averaging some 30%. In 2002 there was an estimated contraction in the economy of 10.5%. However, although the devaluation of the currency in mid-2002 did not result in an immediate improvement in Uruguay's trade position (owing to competitive currencies in Argentina and Brazil), notably in March 2003 the country reported its first quarterly trade surplus since 1990. Furthermore, international lending agencies were encouraged by the Government's apparent willingness to resolve the crisis, and regarded the country's democratic credentials as a necessary asset in any future economic recovery.

Education

All education, including university tuition, is provided free of charge. Education is officially compulsory for six years between six and 14 years of age. Primary education begins at the age of six and lasts for six years. Secondary education, beginning at 12 years of age, lasts for a further six years, comprising two cycles of three years each. In 1996 the total enrolment at primary and secondary schools was equivalent to 97% of the school-age population. In that year primary enrolment included 93% of children in the relevant age-group (males 92%; females 93%), while secondary enrolment was equivalent to 85% of the population in the appropriate age-group (males 77%; females 92%). The programmes of instruction are the same in both public and private schools, and private schools are subject to certain state controls. There are two universities. Central government expenditure on education in 2000 was an estimated 5,429m. pesos uruguayos (7.1% of central government spending).

Public Holidays

2003: 1 January (New Year's Day), 6 January (Epiphany), 19 April (Landing of the 33 Patriots), 1 May (Labour Day), 18 May (Battle of Las Piedras), 19 June (Birth of General Artigas), 18 July (Constitution Day), 25 August (National Independence Day), 12 October (Discovery of America), 2 November (All Souls' Day), 8 December (Blessing of the Waters), 25 December (Christmas Day).

2004: 1 January (New Year's Day), 6 January (Epiphany), 19 April (Landing of the 33 Patriots), 1 May (Labour Day), 18 May (Battle of Las Piedras), 19 June (Birth of General Artigas), 18 July (Constitution Day), 25 August (National Independence Day), 12 October (Discovery of America), 2 November (All Souls' Day), 8 December (Blessing of the Waters), 25 December (Christmas Day).

Many businesses close during Carnival week (3–7 March 2003 and 23–27 February 2004) and Tourist week (Easter).

Weights and Measures

The metric system is in force.

Statistical Survey

Sources (unless otherwise stated): CENCI-Uruguay, Misiones 1361, Casilla 1510, Montevideo; tel. (2) 9152930; fax (2) 9154578; e-mail cenci@adinet.com .uy; Banco Central del Uruguay, Avda Juan P. Fabini, esq. Florida 777, Casilla 1467, 11100 Montevideo; tel. (2) 9017112; fax (2) 9021634; e-mail info@ bcu.gub.uy; internet www.bcu.gub.uy; Cámara Nacional de Comercio y Servicios del Uruguay, Edif. Bolsa de Comercio, Rincón 454, 2°, Casilla 1000, 11000 Montevideo; tel. (2) 9161277; fax (2) 9161243; e-mail canadeco@adinet.com.uy; internet www.davanet.com.uy/canadeco.

Area and Population

AREA, POPULATION AND DENSITY*

Area (sq km)	
Total	176,215†
Population (census results)	
23 October 1985	2,955,241
22 May 1996	
Males	1,532,288
Females	1,631,475
Total	3,163,763
Population (official estimates at mid-year, preliminary figures)	
1999	3,302,843
2000	3,322,141
2001	3,341,521
Density (per sq km) at mid-2001	19.0

* Census results exclude, and estimates include, adjustment for under-enumeration, estimated at 2.6% at 1985 census.
† 68,037 sq miles.

DEPARTMENTS

(estimated population at mid-2001)

	Area (sq km)	Population	Density (per sq km)	Capital
Artigas . . .	11,928	78,075	6.5	Artigas
Canelones .	4,536	503,359	11.0	Canelones
Cerro Largo .	13,648	85,881	6.3	Melo
Colonia . . .	6,106	125,946	20.6	Colonia del Sacramento
Durazno . .	11,643	57,561	4.9	Durazno
Flores . . .	5,144	25,471	5.0	Trinidad
Florida . . .	10,417	68,562	6.6	Florida
Lavalleja . .	10,016	62,552	6.3	Minas
Maldonado .	4,793	148,313	30.9	Maldonado
Montevideo .	530	1,381,542	2,606.7	Montevideo
Paysandú . .	13,922	117,595	8.4	Paysandú
Río Negro . .	9,282	54,563	5.9	Fray Bentos
Rivera . . .	9,370	104,843	11.2	Rivera
Rocha . . .	10,551	72,463	6.9	Rocha
Salto . . .	14,163	126,625	8.9	Salto
San José . .	4,992	104,635	20.1	San José de Mayo
Soriano . .	9,008	84,098	9.3	Mercedes
Tacuarembó .	15,438	87,658	5.7	Tacuarembó
Treinta y Tres	9,529	51,779	5.4	Treinta y Tres
Total . . .	175,016	3,341,521	19.1	

PRINCIPAL TOWNS

(population at 22 May 1996 census)

Montevideo (capital) . . .	1,378,707	Rivera	63,370
Salto . . .	93,420	Mercedes . . .	50,800
Paysandú . .	84,160	Maldonado . .	50,420
Las Piedras . .	66,100	Melo	47,160
		Tacuarembó . .	42,580

2000 (estimate): Montevideo 1,324,000 (Source: UN, *World Urbanization Prospects: The 2001 Revision*.

BIRTHS, MARRIAGES AND DEATHS

	Registered live births*		Registered deaths	
	Number	Rate (per 1,000)	Number	Rate (per 1,000)
1993 . . .	55,958	17.8	31,547	10.0
1994 . . .	55,990	17.7	30,122	9.5
1995 . . .	55,664	17.5	31,525	9.9
1996 . . .	56,928	17.8	31,108	9.5
1997 . . .	58,032	18.0	30,459	9.3
1998 . . .	54,760	16.6	32,082	9.8
1999 . . .	54,055	16.3	32,430	9.8
2000 . . .	52,720	15.9	30,456†	9.2

* Data are tabulated by year of registration rather than by year of occurrence (Source: mainly UN, *Demographic Yearbook*).
† Preliminary.

Registered marriages: 13,888 (marriage rate 4.2 per 1,000) in 2000.

Expectation of life (WHO estimates, years at birth): 75.0 (males 70.9; females 79.2) in 2001 (Source: WHO, *World Health Report*).

ECONOMICALLY ACTIVE POPULATION

(ISIC major divisions, '000 persons aged 14 years and over, urban areas)

	1998	1999	2000
Agriculture, hunting, forestry and fishing	43.2	41.8	42.4
Mining and quarrying	1.6	1.4	1.7
Manufacturing (incl. electricity, gas and water)	177.9	170.5	158.2
Electricity, gas and water	10.9	10.2	13.1
Construction	82.5	90.5	88.7
Trade, restaurants and hotels	223.6	214.3	214.1
Transport, storage and communications	66.9	66.2	61.5
Financing, insurance, real estate and business services	70.4	71.9	72.0
Community, social and personal services	426.8	415.4	415.5
Activities not adequately defined	—	—	0.4
Total employed	1,103.7	1,082.1	1,067.6
Males	635.3	623.7	613.4
Females	468.4	458.4	454.2
Unemployed	123.8	137.7	167.7
Total labour force	1,227.5	1,219.8	1,235.3

Source: ILO.

2001 ('000 persons aged 14 years and over, urban areas): Total employed 1,076.2 (males 617.7; females 458.5); Unemployed 193.2; Total labour force 1,269.4 (males 698.2; females 571.2).

Health and Welfare

KEY INDICATORS

Total fertility rate (children per woman, 2001)	2.3
Under-5 mortality rate (per 1,000 live births, 2001)	16
HIV/AIDS (% of persons aged 15–49, 2001)	0.30
Physicians (per 1,000 head, 1996)	3.7
Hospital beds (per 1,000 head, 1996)	4.39
Health expenditure (2000): US $ per head (PPP)	1,005
Health expenditure (2000): % of GDP	10.9
Health expenditure (2000): public (% of total)	46.5
Access to water (% of persons, 2000)	98
Access to sanitation (% of persons, 2000)	95
Human Development Index (2000): ranking	40
Human Development Index (2000): value	0.831

For sources and definitions, see explanatory note on p. vi.

Agriculture

PRINCIPAL CROPS

('000 metric tons)

	1999	2000	2001
Wheat	383.9	324.4	143.6
Rice (paddy)	1,328.2	1,209.1	1,030.2
Barley	109.9	228.8	117.7
Maize	242.5	64.7	266.8
Oats*	45.0	45.0	45.0
Sorghum	106.1	19.9	158.9
Potatoes	159.4	108.6	121.1
Sweet potatoes	60.0	62.0*	63.0*
Sugar cane	160.0	160.0*	160.0*
Sunflower seed	160.7	33.3	57.1
Tomatoes	40.0	36.0	37.0
Dry onions	30.0	20.0	20.5*
Carrots*	19.0	20.0	20.5
Oranges	170.4	150.0	155.0*
Tangerines, mandarins, clementines and satsumas	99.1	60.0	29.3*
Lemons and limes	46.8	48.0	48.5*
Apples	73.7	59.9	53.8
Pears	12.8	18.1	17.7
Peaches and nectarines	23.5	24.6	13.7
Grapes	140.0*	140.0	160.0*

* FAO estimate(s).

Source: FAO.

LIVESTOCK

('000 head, year ending September)

	1999	2000	2001
Cattle	10,504	10,800	10,595
Sheep	14,409	13,032	13,033*
Pigs*	360	380	385
Horses*	500	501	501
Chickens*	13,000	13,000	13,500

* FAO estimate(s).

Source: FAO.

LIVESTOCK PRODUCTS

('000 metric tons)

	1999	2000	2001
Beef and veal	457.7	453.1	317.0*
Mutton and lamb	51.0*	51.0*	51.2†
Pigmeat	27.0	26.0	26.5†
Poultry meat	57.7	52.7	53.2†
Cows' milk	1,479.4	1,421.7	1,422.0†
Poultry eggs	37.0	37.0	37.0†
Wool: greasy	60.3	54.8	53.2†
Cattle hides†	58.0	60.5	41.0
Sheepskins	16.5	15.4	15.4†

* Unofficial figure.
† FAO estimate(s).

Source: FAO.

Forestry

ROUNDWOOD REMOVALS

('000 cubic m, FAO estimates)

	1999	2000	2001
Sawlogs, veneer logs and logs for sleepers	1,374	1,374	1,374
Pulpwood	380	380	380
Other industrial wood	74	74	74
Fuel wood	3,807	3,894	3,984
Total	5,635	5,722	4,612

Source: FAO.

SAWNWOOD PRODUCTION

('000 cubic m, incl. railway sleepers)

	1990	1991	1992
Coniferous (softwood)	77	67	84
Broadleaved (hardwood)	152	138	185
Total	229	205	269

1993–2001: Annual production as in 1992 (FAO estimates).

Source: FAO.

Fishing

('000 metric tons, live weight)

	1998	1999	2000
Argentine hake	49.1	32.0	27.7
Striped weakfish	15.3	8.5	13.4
Whitemouth croaker	22.3	14.7	24.2
Castaneta	9.7	3.1	1.4
Argentine shortfin squid	13.2	13.7	12.1
Total catch	140.6	103.0	116.6

Source: FAO, *Yearbook of Fishery Statistics*.

Mining

('000 metric tons, unless otherwise indicated)

	1999	2000*	2001
Gold (kg)	2,400*	2,300	2,083*
Gypsum	1,050	1,040	1,050
Feldspar (metric tons)	1,556	1,600	1,500

* Estimate(s).

Source: US Geological Survey.

Industry

SELECTED PRODUCTS

('000 metric tons, unless otherwise indicated)

	1998	1999	2000
Raw sugar*	12	8	7
Wine†	105	105	105
Cigarettes (million)	9,209	n.a.	n.a.
Motor spirit (petrol) ('000 barrels) .	2,100	2,150	2,200
Kerosene ('000 barrels)	500	525	500
Distillate fuel oils ('000 barrels) .	4,200	4,150	4,100
Residual fuel oils ('000 barrels) .	3,600	3,620	3,600
Cement	750	720	n.a.
Electric energy (million kWh) . .	9,570	n.a.	n.a.

2001 ('000 metric tons): Raw sugar 7*; Wine 110†.

* Unofficial figures.
† FAO estimates.

Sources: mainly FAO; US Geological Survey; UN, *Industrial Commodity Statistics Yearbook*.

Finance

CURRENCY AND EXCHANGE RATES

Monetary Units
100 centésimos = 1 peso uruguayo

Sterling, Dollar and Euro Equivalents (31 December 2002)
£1 sterling = 43.841 pesos
US $1 = 27.200 pesos
€1 = 28.525 pesos
1,000 pesos uruguayos = £22.81 = $36.77 = €35.06

Average Exchange Rate (pesos per US $)
2000   12.0996
2001   13.3191
2002   21.2570

Note: On 1 March 1993 a new currency, the peso uruguayo (equivalent to 1,000 former new pesos), was introduced.

BUDGET*
(million pesos uruguayos)

Revenue†	1999	2000	2001
Tax revenue	59,033	60,303	57,823
Taxes on income, profits, etc. .	9,945	10,194	9,540
Individual taxes	4,296	4,502	4,198
Corporate taxes	5,416	5,468	5,149
Social security contributions . .	17,482	19,711	14,655
Employees	8,036	9,390	5,656
Employers	8,872	9,754	8,500
Taxes on payroll and work-force .	—	441	254
Taxes on property	3,884	3,765	3,940
Recurrent taxes on net wealth	3,099	3,015	3,526
Domestic taxes on goods and services	27,909	23,198	24,289
General sales, take-over or value-added tax	20,536	14,959	15,442
Excises	6,524	7,518	7,982
Taxes on international trade and transactions	2,353	1,894	1,796
Import duties	2,079	1,838	1,756
Other taxes	184	1,263	938
Adjustment to tax revenue . . .	-2,794	-163	2,411
Other current revenue	6,571	7,853	4,544
Entrepreneurial and property income	2,875	3,779	2,425
Administration fees, charges and non-industrial sales	1,671	951	427
Capital revenue	1,593	11	341
Total	67,197	68,167	62,708

Expenditure	1999	2000	2001
General public services	5,076	2,808	3,548
Defence	3,115	2,734	3,272
Public order and safety	3,409	2,845	3,631
Education	5,902	5,429	5,854
Health	4,459	4,428	5,080
Social security and welfare . . .	45,115	46,554	43,803
Housing and community amenities	1,258	1,302	1,233
Recreational, cultural and religious affairs	523	884	474
Economic affairs and services . .	4,305	4,101	4,465
Agriculture, fishing, forestry and hunting	1,150	934	955
Transport and communications .	2,498	2,184	2,265
Total	76,079	76,489	77,487
Current‡	71,840	73,246	74,428
Capital	4,239	3,243	3,059

* Figures represent the consolidated accounts of the central Government, which include social security revenue and expenditure.

† Excluding grants received (million pesos uruguayos): 3,225 in 2001.

‡ Including interest payments (million pesos uruguayos): 4,720 in 1999; 5,307 in 2000; 6,062 in 2001.

INTERNATIONAL RESERVES
(US $ million at 31 December)

	2000	2001	2002
Gold	295	2	3
IMF special drawing rights . .	—	2	6
Reserve position in the IMF .	46	45	—
Foreign exchange	2,432	3,050	763
Total	2,773	3,099	772

Source: IMF, *International Financial Statistics*.

MONEY SUPPLY
(million pesos uruguayos at 31 December)

	1999	2000	2001
Currency outside banks . . .	7,639.0	7,284.0	7,095.1
Demand deposits at commercial banks	7,216.6	7,053.7	6,641.0
Total money (incl. others) . . .	14,873.9	14,355.8	13,755.2

Source: IMF, *International Financial Statistics*.

COST OF LIVING

(Consumer Price Index for Montevideo; base: 1990 = 100)

	1999	2000	2001
Food	1,497.5	1,582.2	1,630.9
Clothing and footwear	1,435.8	1,384.4	1,386.3
Rent	3,317.1	3,412.4	3,477.3
All items	1,943.5	2,036.1	2,125.0

Source: ILO.

NATIONAL ACCOUNTS

(million pesos uruguayos at current prices)

Expenditure on the Gross Domestic Product

	1999	2000	2001
Government final consumption expenditure	30,871	32,070	33,413
Private final consumption expenditure	173,360	179,327	184,905
Increase in stocks	1,536	1,891	3,233
Gross fixed capital formation	34,377	32,029	30,191
Total domestic expenditure	240,144	245,317	251,742
Exports of goods and services	42,758	48,703	46,324
Less Imports of goods and services	45,758	50,993	49,446
GDP in purchasers' values	237,143	243,027	248,619
GDP at constant 1983 prices	291	287	278

Source: mainly IMF, *International Financial Statistics.*

Gross Domestic Product by Economic Activity

	1999	2000*	2001*
Agriculture	13,029.1	14,650.4	15,461.6
Fishing	320.2	438.3	402.7
Mining and quarrying	814.9	766.8	730.0
Manufacturing	39,545.6	41,036.4	40,988.1
Electricity, gas and water	9,393.8	9,997.2	10,514.4
Construction	15,108.5	14,369.4	13,418.3
Trade, restaurants and hotels	33,258.6	32,356.8	31,977.8
Transport, storage and communications	20,942.1	22,013.4	23,143.7
Finance and insurance	23,065.9	24,901.5	29,318.0
Real estate and business services	41,389.4	42,688.8	43,784.9
General government services	22,726.6	23,592.5	24,580.5
Other community, social and personal services	27,157.9	27,966.0	28,714.1
Sub-total	246,752.7	254,777.7	263,034.0
Import duties	9,545.3	9,544.6	10,911.6
Less Imputed bank service charges	19,154.9	21,295.2	25,326.1
GDP in purchasers' values	237,143.0	243,027.1	248,619.4

* Preliminary figures.

BALANCE OF PAYMENTS

(US $ million)

	1999	2000	2001
Exports of goods f.o.b.	2,290.6	2,383.8	2,143.6
Imports of goods f.o.b.	−3,187.2	−3,311.1	−2,914.5
Trade balance	−896.6	−927.3	−770.9
Exports of services	1,261.6	1,275.7	1,132.2
Imports of services	−802.3	−881.8	−803.2
Balance on goods and services	−437.3	−533.4	−441.9
Other income received	735.5	781.5	827.3
Other income paid	−879.3	−841.8	−941.1
Balance on goods, services and income	−581.1	−593.7	−555.7
Current transfers received	78.4	48.0	48.0
Current transfers paid	−4.9	−20.5	−4.8
Current balance	−507.6	−566.2	−512.5
Direct investment abroad	—	0.6	1.1
Direct investment from abroad	235.3	273.5	318.2
Portfolio investment assets	−44.3	−98.1	249.8
Portfolio investment liabilities	128.2	289.5	281.3
Other investment assets	−119.3	−690.4	−1,991.1
Other investment liabilities	−52.8	1,004.2	1,940.3
Net errors and omissions	250.9	−46.6	16.5
Overall balance	−109.6	166.5	303.6

Source: IMF, *International Financial Statistics.*

External Trade

PRINCIPAL COMMODITIES

(US $ '000)

Imports c.i.f.	1998	1999	2000
Vegetable products	118,507	97,086	126,127
Prepared foodstuffs; beverages, spirits and vinegar; tobacco and manufactured substitutes	256,523	239,528	244,463
Mineral products	242,355	390,387	546,772
Products of chemical or allied industries	512,390	489,681	462,474
Plastics, rubber and articles thereof	257,900	234,869	248,344
Paper-making material; paper paperboard and articles thereof	144,840	136,664	140,467
Textiles and textile products	207,023	155,389	159,685
Base metals and articles thereof	226,769	161,743	154,942
Machinery and mechanical appliances; electrical equipment; sound and television apparatus	852,797	745,254	669,284
Vehicles, aircraft, vessels and associated transport equipment	553,394	304,256	303,270
Total (incl. others)	3,810,501	3,356,770	3,465,809

Exports f.o.b.	1998	1999	2000
Live animals and animal products	823,147	673,221	699,808
Vegetable products	439,875	353,608	255,130
Prepared foodstuffs; beverages spirits and vinegar; tobacco and manufactured substitutes	149,238	120,801	114,733
Products of chemical or allied industries	120,743	97,095	106,334
Plastics, rubber and articles thereof	97,005	88,924	95,195
Raw hides and skins, leather, furskins and articles thereof; saddlery and harness; travel goods, handbags, etc.	249,123	218,347	263,668
Paper-making material; paper paperboard and articles thereof	68,457	62,776	73,961
Textiles and textile articles	356,521	264,599	269,624
Vehicles, aircraft, vessels and associated transport equipment	178,706	130,236	161,603
Total (incl. others)	2,768,737	2,236,798	2,294,557

2001 (US $ '000, provisional): Total imports c.i.f. 3,060,843; Total exports f.o.b. 2,060,391.

PRINCIPAL TRADING PARTNERS

(US $ '000)

Imports c.i.f.	1998	1999	2000
Argentina	839,336	795,491	836,061
Brazil	793,379	651,638	666,515
Chile	59,136	54,828	59,355
China, People's Republic	78,717	89,020	112,154
Ecuador	39,786	9,985	11,031
France	177,525	140,400	145,407
Germany	125,098	97,852	105,357
Hong Kong	44,718	31,422	29,277
Italy	176,473	123,760	110,029
Japan	92,662	69,445	57,296
Korea, Republic	81,680	54,954	44,880
Mexico	43,427	38,682	38,428
Nigeria	27,120	3	65,484
Spain	140,655	113,340	113,677
Taiwan	44,056	27,496	23,705
United Kingdom	58,950	45,602	63,754
USA	459,750	375,428	336,217
Venezuela	38,113	124,315	149,859
Total (incl. others)	3,808,151	3,356,770	3,465,809

Exports f.o.b.	1998	1999	2000
Argentina	513,192	368,614	410,600
Brazil	935,246	557,119	530,030
Canada	24,351	44,985	60,196
Chile	73,382	46,499	55,966
China, People's Republic . .	76,466	61,860	91,204
Germany	112,123	110,955	89,960
Hong Kong	46,348	35,057	23,396
Iran	3,574	52,002	38,221
Israel	75,943	69,215	64,475
Italy	78,740	72,109	69,160
Japan	21,874	23,544	34,614
Mexico	25,812	43,417	87,785
Netherlands	53,750	49,468	32,970
Nigeria.	1	267	23,712
Paraguay	83,860	81,139	82,063
Peru	32,962	17,524	17,507
Spain	55,226	69,545	59,527
United Kingdom	94,034	80,452	71,596
USA	158,424	140,767	179,613
Venezuela	27,716	27,994	15,184
Total (incl. others)	2,768,737	2,236,798	2,294,557

Transport

RAILWAYS
(traffic)

	1996	1997	1998
Passenger-km (million) . . .	n.a.	17	14
Freight ton-km (million) . .	182	204	244

Source: UN, *Statistical Yearbook*.

ROAD TRAFFIC
(motor vehicles in use at 31 December)

	1995	1996	1997
Passenger cars	464,547	485,109	516,889
Buses and coaches . . .	4,409	4,752	4,984
Lorries and vans	41,417	43,656	45,280
Road tractors	12,511	14,628	15,514
Motorcycles and mopeds . .	300,850	328,406	359,824

Source: International Road Federation: *World Road Statistics*.

2000: Passenger cars 647,310; Buses and coaches 6,851; Lorries and vans 49,236; Road tractors 15,125; Motorcycles and mopeds 439,578; Taxis 4,986.

SHIPPING

Merchant Fleet
(registered at 31 December)

	1999	2000	2001
Number of vessels	90	88	90
Total displacement ('000 grt) . .	61.8	67.5	72.8

Source: Lloyd's Register-Fairplay, *World Fleet Statistics*.

CIVIL AVIATION
(traffic on scheduled services)

	1996	1997	1998
Kilometres flown (million) . . .	5	6	7
Passengers carried ('000) . . .	504	544	557
Passenger-km (million)	640	627	642
Total ton-km (million)	62	57	70

Source: UN, *Statistical Yearbook*.

Communications Media

	1999	2000	2001
Television receivers ('000 in use)	1,760	1,770	n.a.
Telephones ('000 main lines in use)	896.8	929.1	950.9
Mobile cellular telephones ('000 subscribers).	316.1	440.2	520.0
Personal computers ('000 in use) .	330	n.a.	370
Internet users ('000)	330	370	400

Radio receivers (1997): 1,970,000 in use.

Book production (1996): 934 titles.

Daily newspapers (1996): 36 (estimated average circulation 950,000).

Facsimile machines (1995): 11,000 in use.

Sources: UNESCO, *Statistical Yearbook*; UN, *Statistical Yearbook*; International Telecommunication Union.

Tourism

ARRIVALS BY NATIONALITY*
('000)

	1998	1999	2000
Argentina	1,513.6	1,532.7	1,510.4
Brazil	212.2	153.7	140.9
Total (incl. others)	2,324.0	2,273.2	2,235.9

* Figures refer to arrivals at frontiers of visitors from abroad.

Sources: World Tourism Organization, *Yearbook of Tourism Statistics* ; and Ministerio de Turismo.

Tourism receipts (million US $): 695 in 1998; 653 in 1999; 652 in 2000 (Source: mainly World Bank).

Education

(2000)

	Institutions	Teachers	Students
Pre-primary	1,422	3,207*	108,396
Primary	2,409	17,311	351,525
Secondary: general	400	20,476†	210,208
Secondary: vocational . . .	106	n.a.	59,716
University and equivalent institutions†	6	6,887	69,827

* 1999 figure.
† Public education only.

Adult literacy rate (UNESCO estimates): 97.7% (males 97.3%; females 98.1%) in 2000 (Source: UN Development Programme, *Human Development Report*).

Directory

The Constitution

The Constitution of Uruguay was ratified by plebiscite, on 27 November 1966, when the country voted to return to the presidential form of government after 15 years of 'collegiate' government. The main points of the Constitution, as amended in January 1997, are as follows:

General Provisions

Uruguay shall have a democratic republican form of government, sovereignty being exercised directly by the Electoral Body in cases of election, by initiative or by referendum, and indirectly by representative powers established by the Constitution, according to the rules set out therein.

There shall be freedom of religion; there is no state religion; property shall be inviolable; there shall be freedom of thought. Anyone may enter Uruguay. There are two forms of citizenship: natural, being persons born in Uruguay or of Uruguayan parents, and legal, being people established in Uruguay with at least three years' residence in the case of those with family, and five years' for those without family. Every citizen has the right and obligation to vote.

Legislature

Legislative power is vested in the Congreso (Congress or General Assembly), comprising two houses, which may act separately or together according to the dispositions of the Constitution. It elects in joint session the members of the Supreme Court of Justice, of the Electoral Court, Tribunals, Administrative Litigation and the Accounts Tribunal.

Elections for both houses, the President and the Vice-President shall take place every five years on the last Sunday in October; sessions of the Assembly begin on 1 March each year and last until 15 December (15 September in election years, in which case the new Congress takes office on 15 February). Extraordinary sessions can be convened only in case of extreme urgency.

Chamber of Representatives

The Chamber of Representatives has 99 members elected by direct suffrage according to the system of proportional representation, with at least two representatives for each Department. The number of representatives can be altered by law by a two-thirds' majority in both houses. Their term of office is five years and they must be over 25 years of age and be natural citizens or legal citizens with five years' exercise of their citizenship. Representatives have the right to bring accusations against any member of the Government or judiciary for violation of the Constitution or any other serious offence.

Senate

The Senate comprises 31 members, including the Vice-President, who sits as President of the Senate, and 30 members elected directly by proportional representation on the same lists as the representatives, for a term of five years. They must be natural citizens or legal citizens with seven years' exercise of their rights, and be over 30 years of age. The Senate is responsible for hearing cases brought by the representatives and can deprive a guilty person of a post by a two-thirds' majority.

The Executive

Executive power is exercised by the President and the Council of Ministers. There is a Vice-President, who is also President of the Congress and of the Senate. The President and Vice-President are directly elected by absolute majority, and remain in office for five years. They must be over 35 years of age and be natural citizens.

The Council of Ministers comprises the office holders in the ministries or their deputies, and is responsible for all acts of government and administration. It is presided over by the President of the Republic, who has a vote.

The Judiciary

Judicial power is exercised by the five-member Supreme Court of Justice and by Tribunals and local courts; members of the Supreme Court must be over 40 years of age and be natural citizens, or legal citizens with 10 years' exercise and 25 years' residence, and must be lawyers of 10 years' standing, eight of them in public or fiscal ministry or judicature. Members serve for 10 years and can be re-elected after a break of five years. The Court nominates all other judges and judicial officials.

The Government

HEAD OF STATE

President: JORGE LUIS BATLLE IBÁÑEZ (took office 1 March 2000).
Vice-President: LUIS HIERRO LÓPEZ.

COUNCIL OF MINISTERS
(April 2003)

The Council of Ministers is composed of members of the Partido Colorado (PC) and Independents.

Minister of the Interior: GUILLERMO STIRLING (PC).
Minister of Foreign Affairs: Dr DIDIER OPERTTI (PC).
Minister of National Defence: YAMANDÚ FAU (Ind.).
Minister of Economy and Finance: ALEJANDRO ATCHUGARRY (PC).
Director of Planning and Budget Office: ARIEL DAVRIEUX (PC).
Minister of Industry, Energy, Mining and Tourism: JUAN PEDRO BORDABERRY (PC).
Minister of Livestock, Agriculture and Fishing: GONZALO GONZÁLEZ (Ind.).
Minister of Transport and Public Works: LUCIO CÁCERES BEHRENS (PC).
Minister of Labour and Social Security: SANTIAGO PÉREZ DEL CASTILLO (Ind.).
Minister of Education, Culture, Youth and Sport: LEONARDO GUZMÁN (Ind.).
Minister of Public Health: CONRADO BONILLA (PC).
Minister of Housing, Territorial Regulation and the Environment: SAUL MARVA IRURETA SARALEGUI (Ind.).

MINISTRIES

Office of the President: Casa de Gobierno, Edif. Libertad, Avda Luis Alberto de Herrera 3350, Montevideo; tel. (2) 4872110; fax (2) 4809397.

Ministry of Economy and Finance: Colonia 1089, 3°, 11100 Montevideo; tel. (2) 9021017; fax (2) 9021277; internet www.dgi.gub.uy.

Ministry of Education, Culture, Youth and Sport: Reconquista 535, 11000 Montevideo; tel. (2) 9150103; fax (2) 9162632; e-mail webmaster@mec.gub.uy; internet chana.mec.gub.uy.

Ministry of Foreign Affairs: Avda 18 de Julio 1205, 11100 Montevideo; tel. (2) 9021007; fax (2) 9021327; e-mail webmaster@mrree.gub.uy; internet www.mrree.gub.uy.

Ministry of Housing, Territorial Regulation and the Environment: Zabala 1427, 11000 Montevideo; tel. (2) 9150211; fax (2) 9162914; e-mail computos@mvotma.gub.uy; internet www.mvotma.gub.uy.

Ministry of Industry, Energy, Mining and Tourism: Rincón 723, 11000 Montevideo; tel. (2) 9000231; fax (2) 9021245.

Ministry of the Interior: Mercedes 993, 11100 Montevideo; tel. (2) 9089024; fax (2) 9020716; internet www.minterior.gub.uy.

Ministry of Labour and Social Security: Juncal 1511, 4°, 11000 Montevideo; tel. (2) 9162681; fax (2) 9162708; e-mail webmtss@mtss.gub.uy; internet www.mtss.gub.uy.

Ministry of Livestock, Agriculture and Fishing: Avda Constituyente 1476, 11900 Montevideo; tel. (2) 4004155; fax (2) 4099623; e-mail informatica@mgap.gub.uy; internet www.mgap.gub.uy.

Ministry of National Defence: Edif. General Artigas, Avda 8 de Octubre 2628, Montevideo; tel. (2) 4809707; fax (2) 4809397.

Ministry of Public Health: Avda 18 de Julio 1892, 11100 Montevideo; tel. (2) 4000101; fax (2) 4088676; e-mail msp@msp.gub.uy; internet www.msp.gub.uy.

Ministry of Transport and Public Works: Rincón 575, 4° y 5°, 11000 Montevideo; tel. (2) 9150509; fax (2) 9162883; e-mail info@dnt.gub.uy; internet www.dnt.gub.uy.

Office of Planning and Budget: Fondo de las Americas, Convención 1366, 11100 Montevideo; tel. (2) 9000461; fax (2) 2099730; e-mail diropp@presidencia.gub.uy.

President and Legislature

PRESIDENT

Election, 31 October and 28 November 1999

Candidate	First ballot % of vote	Second ballot % of vote
Jorge Luis Batlle Ibáñez (Partido Colorado)	31.32	51.59
Tabaré Vázquez (Encuentro Progresista— Frente Amplio)	38.51	44.07
Luis Alberto Lacalle (Partido Nacional)	21.29	—
Rafael Michelini (Nuevo Espacio)	4.36	—
Luis Pieri (Unión Cívica)	0.23	—
Invalid votes	4.29	4.34
Total	100.00	100.00

CONGRESO

Senate

Election, 31 October 1999

Party	Seats
Encuentro Progresista—Frente Amplio	12
Partido Colorado	10
Partido Nacional	7
Nuevo Espacio	1
Total*	30

*An additional seat is reserved for the Vice-President, who sits as President of the Senate.

Chamber of Representatives

Election, 31 October 1999

Party	Seats
Encuentro Progresista—Frente Amplio	40
Partido Colorado	33
Partido Nacional	22
Nuevo Espacio	4
Total	99

Political Organizations

Alianza Libertadora Nacionalista: Montevideo; extreme right-wing; Leader OSVALDO MARTÍNEZ JAUME.

Encuentro Progresista—Frente Amplio (EP—FA): Colonia 1367, 2°, 11100 Montevideo; tel. (2) 9022176; f. 1971; left-wing grouping; Pres. TABARÉ VÁZQUEZ; members include:

> **Frente Izquierda de Liberación (FIDEL):** Montevideo; f. 1962; socialist; Leader ADOLFO AGUIRRE GONZÁLEZ.

> **Grupo Pregón:** Montevideo; left-wing liberal party; Leaders SERGIO PREVITALI, ENRIQUE MORAS.

> **Movimiento de Acción Nacionalista (MAN):** Montevideo; left-wing nationalist org. Leader JOSÉ DURÁN MATOS.

> **Movimiento Blanco Popular y Progresista (MBPP):** Montevideo; moderate left-wing; Leader A. FRANCISCO RODRÍGUEZ CAMUSSO.

> **Movimiento de Liberación Nacional (MLN)—Tupamaros:** Montevideo; f. 1962; radical socialist; during 1962–73 the MLN, operating under its popular name of the **Tupamaros,** conducted a campaign of urban guerrilla warfare until it was defeated by the Armed Forces in late 1973; following the return to civilian rule, in 1985, the MLN announced its decision to abandon its armed struggle; legally recognized in May 1989; Sec.-Gen. JOSÉ MUJICA.

> **Movimiento 26 de Marzo:** Durazno 1118, 11200 Montevideo; tel. (2) 9011584; f. 1971; socialist; Pres. EDUARDO RUBIO; Sec.-Gen. FERNANDO VÁZQUEZ.

> **Partido Comunista:** Río Negro 1525, 11100 Montevideo; tel. (2) 9017171; fax (2) 9011050; f. 1920; Sec.-Gen. MARINA ARISMENDI; 42,000 mems (est.).

> **Partido de Democracia Avanzada:** Montevideo; Communist.

> **Partido Socialista del Uruguay:** Casa del Pueblo, Soriano 1218, 11100 Montevideo; tel. (2) 9013344; fax (2) 9032226; e-mail

ps@chasque.apc.org; internet www.chasque.apc.org/ps; f. 1910; Pres. REINALDO GARGANO; Sec.-Gen. ROBERTO CONDE.

Nuevo Espacio: Eduardo Acevedo 1615, 11200 Montevideo; tel. (2) 4026989; fax (2) 4026991; e-mail larosa@adinet.com.uy; internet www.nuevoespacio.org.uy; f. 1989 by parties withdrawing from the Frente Amplio; moderate left-wing; Leader RAFAEL MICHELINI; Pres. HÉCTOR PÉREZ PIERA; Sec. EDGARDO CARVALHO; members include:

> **Partido Demócrata Cristiano (PDC):** Aquiles Lanza 1318 bis, Montevideo; tel. and fax (2) 9030704; e-mail pdc@chasque.apc.org; internet www.chasque.apc.org/pdc; fmrly Unión Cívica del Uruguay; f. 1962; Pres. Dr HÉCTOR LESCANO; Sec.-Gen. FRANCISCO OTTONELLI.

> **Unión Cívica:** Montevideo; tel. (2) 9005535; e-mail info@unioncivica.com; internet www.unioncivica.com; f. 1912; recognized Christian Democrat faction which split from the Partido Demócrata Cristiano in 1980; Leader ALDO LAMORTE.

Partido Azul (PA): Paul Harris 1722, Montevideo; tel. and fax (2) 6016327; f. 1993; Leader Dr ROBERTO CANESSA; Gen. Sec. Ing. ARMANDO VAL.

Partido Colorado: Andrés Martínez Trueba 1271, 11100 Montevideo; tel. (2) 4090180; f. 1836; Sec.-Gen. JORGE BATLLE IBÁÑEZ; Leader JOSÉ LUIS BATLLE; factions include:

> **Batllismo Radical:** Leader JORGE BATLLE IBÁÑEZ.

> **Cruzada 94:** Leader PABLO MILLOR.

> **Foro Batllista:** Colonia 1243, 11100 Montevideo; tel. (2) 9030154; Leader Dr JULIO MARÍA SANGUINETTI CAIROLO.

> **Unión Colorada y Batllista (Pachequista):** Buenos Aires 594, 11000 Montevideo; tel. (2) 9164648; right-wing.

Partido Justiciero: Montevideo; extreme right-wing; Leader BOLÍVAR ESPÍNDOLA.

Partido Nacional (Blanco): Juan Carlos Gómez 1384, Montevideo; tel. (2) 9163831; fax (2) 9163758; e-mail partidonacional@partidonacional.com.uy; internet www.partidonacional.com.uy; f. 1836; Exec. Pres. LUIS ALBERTO LACALLE; Sec.-Gen. ALBERTO ZUMARÁN; tendencies within the party include:

> **Alianza Nacional:** Leader JORGE LARRAÑAGA.

> **Consejo Nacional Herrerista:** Leader LUIS ALBERTO LACALLE.

> **Desafío Nacional:** Leader JUAN ANDRÉS RAMÍREZ.

> **Linea Nacional de Florida:** Leader ARTURO HEBER.

> **Manos a la Obra:** Plaza Cagancha 1145, 11100 Montevideo; tel. (2) 9028149; Leader ALBERTO VOLONTÉ.

> **Movimiento Nacional de Rocha—Corriente Popular Nacionalista:** Avda Uruguay 1324, Montevideo; tel. (2) 9027502; Leader CARLOS JULIO PEREYRA.

Partido del Sol: Peatonal Yi 1385, 11000 Montevideo; tel. (2) 9001616; fax (2) 9006739; e-mail sol@adinet.com.uy; ecologist, federal, pacifist; Leader HOMERO MIERES.

Partido de los Trabajadores: Convención 1196, 11100 Montevideo; tel. (2) 9082624; f. 1980; extreme left-wing; Leader JUAN VITAL ANDRADE.

Diplomatic Representation

EMBASSIES IN URUGUAY

Argentina: Cuareim 1470, 11800 Montevideo; tel. (2) 9028166; fax (2) 9028172; e-mail emargrou@adinet.com.uy; internet emb-uruguay.mrecic.gov.ar; Ambassador HERNÁN MARÍA PATIÑO MEYER.

Bolivia: Dr Prudencio de Pena 2469, 11300 Montevideo; tel. (2) 7083573; fax (2) 7080066; e-mail repbol@adinet.com.uy; Ambassador ARMANDO LOAYZA MARIACA .

Brazil: Blvr Artigas 1328, 11300 Montevideo; tel. (2) 7072119; fax (2) 7072086; e-mail montevideu@brasemb.org.uy; internet www.brasmont.org.uy; Ambassador FRANCISCO THOMPSON-FLÔRES.

Bulgaria: Rambla Mahatma Gandhi 647, 5°, Casilla 502, 11300 Montevideo; tel. (2) 7111627; Ambassador LIUBOMIR ILIEV IVANOV.

Canada: Plaza Independencia 749, Of. 102, 11100 Montevideo; tel. (2) 9022030; fax (2) 9022029; Ambassador SUSAN HARPER.

Chile: Andes 1365, 1°, 11100 Montevideo; tel. (2) 9009273; fax (2) 9021649; Ambassador AUGUSTO BERMÚDEZ ARANCIBIA.

China, People's Republic: Miraflores 1508, Casilla 18966, Montevideo; tel. (2) 6016126; fax (2) 6018508; e-mail embchina@adinet.com.uy; Ambassador YONGZHAN WANG.

Colombia: Juncal 1305, 18°, 11000 Montevideo; tel. (2) 9154434; fax (2) 9161594; e-mail euruguay@minrelext.gov.co; Ambassador CLAUDIA TURBAY QUINTERA.

Costa Rica: José Martí 3295, Apt 102, Casilla 12242, Montevideo; tel. (2) 7083645; fax (2) 7089714; e-mail embarica@netgate.com.uy; Ambassador ALEXANDER SALAS ARAYA.

Czech Republic: Luis B. Cavia 2996, Casilla 12262, 11300 Montevideo; tel. (2) 7087808; fax (2) 7096410; Ambassador PAVEL ZRUST.

Dominican Republic: T. de Tezanos 1186, 11300 Montevideo; tel. (2) 6287766; fax (2) 6289655; e-mail embajadomuruguay@hotmail.com; Ambassador JEANNETTE GUZMÁN SÁNCHEZ.

Ecuador: Guayaquí 3428, 11300 Montevideo; tel. (2) 7076463; fax (2) 7076466; Ambassador EDUARDO CABEZAS MOLINA.

Egypt: Avda Brasil 2663, 11300 Montevideo; tel. (2) 7096412; fax (2) 7080977; e-mail boustanemontevideo@netgate.com.uy; Ambassador AMINA HUSSEIN FARID.

El Salvador: M. González 1157, Montevideo; tel. (2) 6222005; fax (2) 622 6842; Ambassador ERNESTO FERREIRO RUSCONI.

France: Avda Uruguay 853, Casilla 290, 11100 Montevideo; tel. (2) 9020077; fax (2) 9023711; e-mail ambfra@adinet.com.uy; internet www.amb-montevideo.fr; Ambassador JOSEPH RAPIN.

Germany: La Cumparsita 1435, Casilla 20014, 11200 Montevideo; tel. (2) 9025222; fax (2) 9023422; e-mail deubot@montevideo.com.uy; internet www.emb-alemania.com; Ambassador JÜRGEN KRIEGHOFF.

Guatemala: General French 1695, Montevideo; tel. (2) 6287880; fax (2) 6287568; Ambassador GUILLERMO ESTRADA STRECKER.

Holy See: Blvr Artigas 1270, Casilla 1503, Montevideo (Apostolic Nunciature); tel. (2) 7072016; fax (2) 7072209; Apostolic Nuncio Most Rev. JANUSZ BOLONEK (Titular Archbishop of Madaurus).

Hungary: Dr Prudencio de Pena 2469, Montevideo; tel. (2) 7086173; Ambassador Dr BÉLA SZABÓ.

Iran: Blvr Artigas 449, Montevideo; tel. (2) 7116657; fax (2) 7116659; Ambassador KAMBIZ JALALI.

Israel: Blvr Artigas 1585, Montevideo; tel. (2) 4004164; Ambassador AVRAHAM TOLEDO.

Italy: José B. Lamas 2857, Casilla 268, 11300 Montevideo; tel. (2) 7080542; fax (2) 7084148; e-mail amburuit@netgate.com.uy; internet www.ambitalia.com.uy; Ambassador GIORGIO MALFATTI DI MONTE TRETTO.

Japan: Blvr Artigas 953, 11300 Montevideo; tel. (2) 4187645; fax (2) 4187980; Ambassador KATSUHIKO TSUNODA.

Lebanon: Avda Gral Rivera 2278, Montevideo; tel. (2) 4086365; fax (2) 4086640; Ambassador AZIZ GEORGES AZZI.

Mexico: Andes 1365, 7°, 11100 Montevideo; tel. (2) 9020791; fax (2) 9021232; e-mail embmexur@netgate.com.uy; internet www.rau.edu.uy/embamex; Ambassador JESÚS PUENTE.

Netherlands: Leyenda Patria 2880/202, Casilla 1519, 11300 Montevideo; tel. (2) 7112956; fax (2) 7113301; e-mail embajada@holanda.org.uy; internet www.holanda.org.uy; Ambassador J. W. C. ZANDVLIET.

Panama: Juan Benito Blanco 3388, 11300 Montevideo; tel. (2) 6224713; fax (2) 6230300; Ambassador LUIS MARIO CUESTAS GÓMEZ.

Paraguay: Blvr Artigas 1256, Montevideo; tel. (2) 7072138; fax (2) 7083682; Ambassador RAÚL SILVA VELAZQUEZ.

Peru: Soriano 1124, Casilla 126, 11100 Montevideo; tel. (2) 9012079; fax (2) 9021194; e-mail embaperu@multi.com.uy; Ambassador WILLIAM BELEVAN MCBRIDE.

Poland: Jorge Canning 2389, Casilla 1538, 11600 Montevideo; tel. (2) 4801313; fax (2) 4873389; e-mail ambmonte@netgate.com.uy; Ambassador JAROSLAVW GUGALA.

Portugal: Avda Dr Francisco Soca 1128, Casilla 701, 11300 Montevideo; tel. (2) 7084061; fax (2) 7096456; Ambassador Dr DOMINGOS GARRIDO SERRA.

Romania: Echevarriarza 3452, 11300 Montevideo; tel. (2) 6220876; fax (2) 6220135; e-mail ambromvd@adinet.com.uy; Ambassador VASILE MACOVEI.

Russia: Blvr España 2741, 11300 Montevideo; tel. (2) 7081884; fax (2) 7086597; e-mail embaru@montevideo.com.uy; internet www.rusiaoficial.org.uy; Ambassador YAN A. BURLIAI.

South Africa: Echevarriarza 3335, Casilla 498, 11300 Montevideo; tel. (2) 6230161; fax (2) 6230066; e-mail safem@netgate.com.uy; Ambassador Prof. M. W. MAKALIMA (resident in Argentina).

Spain: Avda Libertad 2738, 11300 Montevideo; tel. (2) 7086010; fax (2) 7083291; e-mail embespuy@correo.mae.es; Ambassador JOAQUÍN MARÍA DE ARÍSTEGUI.

Switzerland: Ing. Federico Abadie 2936/40, 11°, Casilla 12261, 11300 Montevideo; tel. (2) 7104315; fax (2) 7115031; e-mail swissmtv@multi.com.uy; Ambassador URS STEMMLER.

United Kingdom: Marco Bruto 1073, Casilla 16024, 11300 Montevideo; tel. (2) 6223650; fax (2) 6227815; e-mail bemonte@internet.com.uy; internet www.britishembassy.org.uy; Ambassador JOHN EVERARD.

USA: Lauro Muller 1776, 11200 Montevideo; tel. (2) 4187777; fax (2) 4188611; internet www.embeeuu.gub.uy; Ambassador MARTIN J. SILVERSTEIN.

Venezuela: Iturriaga 3589, Montevideo; tel. (2) 6221140; fax (2) 6018608; e-mail embaven@adinet.com.uy; Chargé d'affaires a.i. CARLOS LONGA GONZÁLEZ.

Judicial System

The Supreme Court of Justice comprises five members appointed at the suggestion of the executive, for a period of five years. It has original jurisdiction in constitutional, international and admiralty cases, and hears appeals from the appellate courts, of which there are seven, each with three judges.

Cases involving the functioning of the state administration are heard in the ordinary Administrative Courts and in the Supreme Administrative Court, which consists of five members appointed in the same way as members of the Supreme Court of Justice.

In Montevideo there are 19 civil courts, 10 criminal and correctional courts, 19 courts presided over by justices of the peace, three juvenile courts, three labour courts and courts for government and other cases. Each departmental capital, and some other cities, have a departmental court; each of the 224 judicial divisions has a justice of the peace.

The administration of justice became free of charge in 1980, with the placing of attorneys-at-law in all courts to assist those unable to pay for the services of a lawyer.

Supreme Court of Justice

Pasaje de los Derechos Humanos 1310, 11100 Montevideo; tel. (2) 9081435; fax (2) 9087018; e-mail secparga@poderjudicial.gub.uy; internet www.poderjudicial.gub.uy.

President of the Supreme Court of Justice: Dr GERVASIO GUILLOT MARTÍNEZ.

Supreme Administrative Court: Mercedes 961, 11100 Montevideo; tel. (2) 9008047; fax (2) 9080539.

Religion

Under the Constitution, the Church and the State were declared separate and toleration for all forms of worship was proclaimed. Roman Catholicism predominates.

CHRISTIANITY

Federación de Iglesias Evangélicas del Uruguay: Estero Bellaco 2676, 11600 Montevideo; tel. (2) 4873375; fax (2) 4872181; f. 1956; eight mem. churches; Pres. LUIS ROSSO; Sec. ALFREDO SERVETTI.

The Roman Catholic Church

Uruguay comprises one archdiocese and nine dioceses. At 31 December 2000 there were an estimated 2,360,291 adherents in the country, representing about 74% of the total population.

Bishops' Conference

Conferencia Episcopal Uruguaya, Avda Uruguay 1319, 11100 Montevideo; tel. (2) 9002642; fax (2) 9011802; e-mail ceusecre@adinet.com.uy; internet www.iglesiauruguaya.com.

f. 1972; Pres. Rt Rev. CARLOS MARÍA COLLAZZI IRAZÁBAL (Bishop of Mercedes).

Archbishop of Montevideo: Most Rev. NICOLÁS COTUGNO FANIZZI, Arzobispado, Treinta y Tres 1368, Casilla 356, 11000 Montevideo; tel. (2) 9158127; fax (2) 9158926; e-mail arzmvdeo@sicoar.com.uy; internet www.iglesia-mvdo.org.

The Anglican Communion

Uruguay is the newest diocese in the Province of the Southern Cone of America, having been established in 1988. The presiding Bishop of the Iglesia Anglicana del Cono Sur de América, is the Bishop of Northern Argentina.

Bishop of Uruguay: Rt Rev. MIGUEL TAMAYO ZALDÍVAR, Centro Diocesano, Reconquista 522, Casilla 6108, 11000 Montevideo; tel. (2) 9159627; fax (2) 9162519; e-mail mtamayo@netgate.com.uy.

Other Churches

Baptist Evangelical Convention of Uruguay: Mercedes 1487, 11100 Montevideo; tel. and fax (2) 2167012; e-mail suspasos@adinet .com.uy; f. 1948; Pres Dr JUAN CARLOS OTORMÍN.

Iglesia Adventista (Adventist Church): Castro 167, Montevideo; f. 1901; 4,000 mems; Principal officers Dr GUILLERMO DURÁN, Dr ALEXIS PIRO.

Iglesia Evangélica Metodista en el Uruguay (Evangelical Methodist Church in Uruguay): Estero Bellaco 2678, 11600 Montevideo; tel. (2) 4800984; fax (2) 4872181; e-mail iemu@adinet.com.uy; f. 1878; 1,193 mems (1997); Pres. BEATRIZ FERRARI.

Iglesia Evangélica Valdense (Waldensian Evangelical Church): Avda 8 de Octubre 3039, 11600 Montevideo; tel. and fax (2) 4879406; e-mail ievm@internet.com.uy; f. 1952; 15,000 mems; Pastor ALVARO MICHELIN SALOMÓN.

Iglesia Pentecostal Unida Internacional en Uruguay (United Pentecostal Church International in Uruguay): Helvecia 4032, Piedras Blancas, 12200 Montevideo; tel. (2) 5133618; e-mail lrodrigu@montevideo.com.uy; internet members.tripod.com/ ~lrodrigu; Pastor LUIS RODRÍGUEZ.

Primera Iglesia Bautista (First Baptist Church): Avda Daniel Fernández Crespo 1741, Casilla 5051, 11200 Montevideo; tel. (2) 4098744; fax (2) 4002694; f. 1911; 350 mems; Pastor LEMUEL J. LARROSA.

Other denominations active in Uruguay include the Iglesia Evangélica del Río de la Plata and the Iglesia Evangélica Menonita (Evangelical Mennonite Church).

BAHÁ'Í FAITH

National Spiritual Assembly of the Bahá'ís: Blvr Artigas 2440, 11600 Montevideo; tel. (2) 4875890; fax (2) 4802165; e-mail bahai@ multi.com.uy; f. 1938; mems resident in 140 localities.

The Press

DAILIES

Montevideo

El Diario: Rincón 712, 11000 Montevideo; tel. (2) 9030465; fax (2) 9030637; e-mail joterom@adinet.com.uy; f. 1923; evening; independent; Editor JORGE OTERO; circ. 80,000.

El Diario Español: Cerrito 551–555, Casilla 899, 11000 Montevideo; tel. (2) 9159481; fax (2) 9159545; f. 1905; morning (except Monday); newspaper of the Spanish community; Editor CARLOS REINANTE; circ. 20,000.

Diario Oficial: Florida 1178, Montevideo; f. 1905; morning; publishes laws, official decrees, parliamentary debates, judicial decisions and legal transactions; Dir Sra ZAIN NASSIF DE ZARUMBE.

Gaceta Comercial: Juncal 1391, 11000 Montevideo; tel. (2) 9165618; fax (2) 9165619; f. 1916; morning (Mon.–Fri.); Dir MILTON SANS; Editor PABLO SANS; circ. 4,500.

La Mañana: Paysandú 926, Montevideo; tel. (2) 9029055; fax (2) 9021326; f. 1917; supports the Partido Colorado; Editor Dr SALVADOR ALABÁN DEMARE; circ. 40,000.

Mundocolor: Cuareim 1287, 11800 Montevideo; f. 1976; evening (except Sunday); Dir DANIEL HERRERA LUSSICH; circ. 4,500.

El Observador: Cuareim 2052, 11800 Montevideo; tel. (2) 9247000; fax (2) 9248698; e-mail elobservador@observador.com.uy; internet www.observador.com.uy; f. 1991; morning; Editor RICARDO PEIRANO; circ. 26,000.

Observador Económico: Soriano 791, 11100 Montevideo; tel. (2) 9030690; fax (2) 9030691.

El País: Zelmar Michelini 1287, 11100 Montevideo; tel. (2) 9020115; fax (2) 9020464; e-mail cartas@elpais.com.uy; internet www3 .diarioelpais.com/edicion; f. 1918; morning; supports the Partido Nacional; Editor MARTÍN AGUIRRE; circ. 106,000.

La República: Avda Gral Garibaldi 2579, 11600 Montevideo; tel. (2) 4873565; fax (2) 4872419; internet www.multi.com.uy/republica; f. 1988; morning; Editor FEDERICO FASANO MERTENS.

Ultimas Noticias: Paysandú 1179, 11100 Montevideo; tel. (2) 9020452; fax (2) 9024669; f. 1981; evening (except Saturday); owned by Impresora Polo Ltd; Publr Dr ALPHONSE EMANUILOFF-MAX; circ. 25,000.

Florida

El Heraldo: Independencia 824, 94000 Florida; tel. (35) 22229; fax (35) 24546; e-mail heraldo@adinet.com.uy; f. 1919; morning; independent; Dir ALVARO RIVA REY; circ. 1,800.

Minas

La Unión: Florencio Sánchez 569, Minas; tel. (442) 2065; fax (442) 4011; e-mail union@chasque.apc.org; f. 1877; evening (except Sunday); Dir LAURA PUCHET MARTÍNEZ; Editor ALEJANDRO MAYA SOSA; circ. 2,600.

Maldonado

Correo de Punta del Este: Michelini 815 bis, 20000 Maldonado; tel. and fax (42) 35633; e-mail gallardo@adinet.com.uy; f. 1993; morning; Editor MARÍA P. RODRÍGUEZ ZANONI; circ. 2,500.

Paysandú

El Telégrafo: 18 de Julio 1027, 60000 Paysandú; tel. (722) 2314; fax (722) 7999; e-mail correo@eltelegrafo.com; internet www.eltelegrafo .com; f. 1910; morning; independent; Dir FERNANDO M. BACCARO; circ. 10,000.

Salto

Tribuna Salteña: Joaquín Suárez 71, Salto; f. 1906; morning; Dir MODESTO LLANTADA FABINI; circ. 3,000.

PERIODICALS

Montevideo

Aquí: Zabala 1322, Of. 102, 11000 Montevideo; weekly; supports the Encuentro Progresista—Frente Amplio; Dir FRANCISCO JOSÉ O'HONELLI.

Brecha: Avda Uruguay 844, 11100 Montevideo; tel. (2) 9025042; fax (2) 9020388; e-mail brecha@brecha.com.uy; internet www.brecha .com.uy; f. 1985; weekly; politics, current affairs; circ. 14,500; Dir GUILLERMO GONZÁLEZ; Editor-in-Chief DANIEL GATTI.

Búsqueda: Avda Uruguay 1146, 11100 Montevideo; tel. (2) 9021300; fax (2) 9022036; e-mail busqueda@adinet.com.uy; f. 1972; weekly; independent; politics and economics; Dir DANILO ARBILLA FRACHIA; circ. 25,000.

Charoná: Gutiérrez Ruiz 1276, Of. 201, Montevideo; tel. (2) 9086665; f. 1968; fortnightly; children's; Dir SERGIO BOFFANO; circ. 25,000.

Colorín Colorado: Dalmiro Costa 4482, Montevideo; f. 1980; monthly; children's; Dir SARA MINSTER DE MURNINKAS; circ. 3,000.

Crónicas Económicas: Avda Libertador Brig.-Gen. Lavalleja 1532, Montevideo; tel. (2) 9004790; f. 1981; weekly; independent; economics; Dirs JULIO ARIEL FRANCO, WALTER HUGO PAGÉS, JORGE ESTELLANO.

La Democracia: Colonia 1308, 11100 Montevideo; f. 1981; weekly; organ of the Partido Nacional; Editor ALBERTO ZUMARÁN; circ. 17,000.

La Gaceta Militar Naval: Montevideo; monthly.

Indice Industrial-Anuario de la Industria Uruguaya: Sarandí 456, 11000 Montevideo; tel. (2) 9151963; f. 1957; annually; Dir W. M. TRIAS; circ. 6,000.

La Justicia Uruguaya: 25 de Mayo 555, 11000 Montevideo; tel. (2) 9157587; fax (2) 9159721; e-mail justicia@isoft.com.uy; internet www.lajusticiauruguaya.com.uy; f. 1940; bimonthly; jurisprudence; Dirs EDUARDO ALBANELL, ADOLFO ALBANELL, SUSANA ARIAS; circ. 3,000.

La Juventud: Durazno 1118, 11200 Montevideo; tel. (2) 9011584; weekly; supports the Movimiento 26 de Marzo.

Marketing Directo: Mario Cassinoni 1157, 11200 Montevideo; tel. (2) 4012174; fax (2) 4087221; e-mail consumo@adinet.com.uy; f. 1988; monthly; Dir EDGARDO MARTÍNEZ ZIMARIOFF; circ. 9,500.

Mate Amargo: Tristán Narvaja 1578 bis, Montevideo; f. 1986; organ of the Movimiento de Liberación Nacional; circ. 22,500.

Opción: J. Barrios Amorín 1531, Casilla 102, 11100 Montevideo; f. 1981; weekly; Dir FRANCISCO JOSÉ OTTONELLI; circ. 15,000.

Patatín y Patatán: Montevideo; f. 1977; weekly; children's; Dir JUAN JOSÉ RAVAIOLI; circ. 3,000.

Revista Naval: Soriano 1117, 11100 Montevideo; tel. (2) 9087884; f. 1988; 3 a year; military; Editor GUSTAVO VANZINI; circ. 1,000.

PRESS ASSOCIATIONS

Asociación de Diarios del Uruguay: Río Negro 1308, 6°, 11100 Montevideo; f. 1922; Pres. BATLLE T. BARBATO.

Asociación de la Prensa Uruguaya: Avda Uruguay 1255, Montevideo; tel. and fax (2) 9013695; e-mail apu@adinet.com.uy; f. 1944; Pres. GUSTAVO AGUIRRE.

PRESS AGENCIES

Foreign Bureaux

Agence France-Presse (AFP): Plaza Independencia 831, 11100 Montevideo; tel. (2) 9005095; Chief JUPITER PUYO.

Agencia EFE (Spain): Wilson Ferreira Aldunate 1294, Of. 501, 11200 Montevideo; tel. (2) 9020322; fax (2) 9026726; e-mail efeuru@adinet.com.uy; Correspondent ANA ROSA MENGOTTI MEAURIO.

Agenzia Nazionale Stampa Associata (ANSA) (Italy): Florida 1408, Montevideo; tel. (2) 9011032; fax (2) 9081950; Bureau Chief JUAN ATELLA.

Associated Press (AP) (USA): Avda 18 de Julio 1076, Montevideo; tel. (2) 9018291; Correspondent DANIEL GIANELLI.

Deutsche Presse-Agentur (dpa) (Germany): Avda 18 de Julio 994, 4°, Montevideo; tel. (2) 9028052; fax (2) 9022662; e-mail dpaurc@montevideo.com.uy; Correspondent MARÍA ISABEL RIVERO DE LOS CAMPOS.

Inter Press Service (IPS) (Italy): Juan Carlos Gómez 1445, Of. 102, 1°, 11000 Montevideo; tel. (2) 9164397; fax (2) 9163598; e-mail ips@tips.org.uy; internet www.ips.org; f. 1964; Dir MARIO LUBETKIN.

Reuters (United Kingdom): Plaza Independencia 831, Of. 907-908, 11100 Montevideo; tel. (2) 9020336; fax (2) 9027912; Correspondent ANAHI RAMA.

Prensa Latina (Cuba): Montevideo; tel. (2) 7092955; Correspondent OSVALDO BURGOS.

Publishers

Editorial Arca: Ana Monterroso 2231, Montevideo; tel. (2) 4099796; fax (2) 4099788; f. 1963; general literature, social science and history; Man. Dir ENRIQUE PIQUÉ.

Ediciones de la Banda Oriental: Gaboto 1582, 11200 Montevideo; tel. (2) 4083206; fax (2) 4098138; e-mail ebo@chasque.net; general literature; Man. Dir HEBER RAVIOLO.

CENCI—Uruguay (Centro de Estadísticas Nacionales y Comercio Internacional): Misiones 1361, Casilla 1510, 11000 Montevideo; tel. (2) 9152930; fax (2) 9154578; e-mail cenci@adinet.com.uy; f. 1956; economics, statistics; Dirs CRISTINA Z. DE VERTESI, KENNETH BRUNNER.

Editorial y Librería Jurídica Amalio M. Fernández SRL: 25 de Mayo 589, 11000 Montevideo; tel. and fax (2) 9151782; f. 1951; law and sociology; Man. Dir CARLOS W. DEAMESTOY.

Fundación de Cultura Universitaria: 25 de Mayo 568, Casilla 1155, 11000 Montevideo; tel. (2) 9161152; fax (2) 9152549; e-mail ventas@fcu.com.uy; internet www.fcu.com.uy; f. 1968; law and social sciences; Man. Dir NELSON ROJAS.

Hemisferio Sur: Buenos Aires 335, Casilla 1755, 11000 Montevideo; tel. (2) 9164515; fax (2) 9164520; e-mail librperi@adinet.com.uy; f. 1951; agronomy and veterinary science.

Editorial Idea: Misiones 1424, 5°, 11000 Montevideo; tel. (2) 9165456; fax (2) 9150868; e-mail vescovi@fastlink.com.uy; law; Dir Dr GUILLERMO VESCOVI.

Librería Linardi y Risso: Juan C. Gómez 1435, 11000 Montevideo; tel. (2) 9157129; fax (2) 9157431; e-mail lyrbooks@linardiyrisso.com.uy; internet www.linardiyrisso.com.uy; f. 1944; general; Man. Dirs ALVARO RISSO, ANDRÉS LINARDI.

Editorial Medina SRL: Gaboto 1521, Montevideo; tel. (2) 4085800; f. 1933; general; Pres. MARCOS MEDINA VIDAL.

A. Monteverde & Cía, SA: Treinta y Tres 1475, Casilla 371, 11000 Montevideo; tel. (2) 9152939; fax (2) 9152012; f. 1879; educational; Man. Dir LILIANA MUSSINI.

Mosca Hermanos SA: Avda 18 de Julio 1578, 11300 Montevideo; tel. (2) 4093141; fax (2) 4088059; e-mail mosca@attmail.com.uy; f. 1888; general; Pres. Lic. ZSOLT AGARDY.

Librería Selecta Editorial: Guayabo 1865, 11200 Montevideo; tel. (2) 4086989; fax (2) 4086831; f. 1950; academic books; Dir FERNANDO MASA.

PUBLISHERS' ASSOCIATION

Cámara Uruguaya del Libro: Juan D. Jackson 1118, 11200 Montevideo; tel. (2) 4015732; fax (2) 4011860; e-mail camurlib@adinet.com.uy; f. 1944; Pres. ERNESTO SANJINÉS; Man. ANA CRISTINA RODRÍGUEZ.

Broadcasting and Communications

TELECOMMUNICATIONS

Administración Nacional de Telecomunicaciones (ANTEL): Avda Daniel Fernández Crespo 1534, 9°, 11200 Montevideo; tel. (2) 4083629; fax (2) 4082672; e-mail kely@adinet.com.uy; internet www.antel.com.uy; f. 1974; state-owned; Pres. GABRIEL GURMÉNDEZ ARMAND-UGÓN; Gen. Man. JORGE HENÓN.

ANCEL: Pablo Galarza 3537, Montevideo; internet www.ancel.com.uy; f. 1994; state-owned mobile telephone co; pending partial (40%) privatization.

Unidad Reguladora de Servicios de Comunicaciones (URSEC): Uruguay 988, Casilla 11100, Montevideo; tel. (2) 9028082; fax (2) 9005708; internet www.uyweb.com.uy; regulates telecommunications and postal sectors; Pres. Dr FERNANDO OMAR PÉREZ TABÓ.

BROADCASTING

Regulatory Authority

Asociación Nacional de Broadcasters Uruguayos (ANDEBU): Yi 1264, 11100 Montevideo; tel. (2) 9000053; internet www.andebu.com.uy; f. 1933; 101 mems; Pres. MARÍA CELIA FOUNTAINA; Vice-Pres. CÉSAR LASSUS.

Radio

El Espectador: Río Branco 1481, 11100 Montevideo; tel. (2) 9023531; fax (2) 9083044; e-mail am810@espectador.com.uy; internet www.espectador.com; f. 1923; commercial; Pres. MARÍA A. MASTRÁNGELO; Dir-Gen. JAVIER MASSA.

Radio Carve: Mercedes 973, 11100 Montevideo; tel. (2) 9020911; fax (2) 9022839; e-mail carve@portalx.com.uy; internet www.carve.portalx.com.uy; f. 1928; commercial; Dir PABLO FONTAINA MINELLI.

Radio Montecarlo: Avda 18 de Julio 1224, 1°, 11100 Montevideo; tel. (2) 9014433; fax (2) 9017762; e-mail cx20@netgate.comintur.com.uy; internet netgate.comintur.com.uy/x20; f. 1928; commercial; Dir DANIEL ROMAY.

Radio Sarandí: Enriqueta Compte y Riqué 1250, 11800 Montevideo; tel. (2) 2082612; fax (2) 2036906; e-mail sarandi@netgate.com.uy; internet isa.isa.com.uy/sarandi; f. 1931; commercial; Pres. RAMIRO RODRÍGUEZ VALLAMIL RIVIERE.

Radio Universal: Avda 18 de Julio 1220, 3°, 11100 Montevideo; tel. (2) 9032222; fax (2) 9026050; f. 1929; commercial; Pres. OSCAR IMPERIO.

Radiodifusión Nacional SODRE: Sarandí 430, 11000 Montevideo; tel. (2) 957865; fax (2) 9161933; internet www.sodre.gub.uy; f. 1929; state-owned; Pres. JULIO CÉSAR OCAMPOS.

In 2002 there were some 16 AM and six FM radio stations in the Montevideo area. In addition, there were approximately 41 AM and 56 FM radio stations outside the capital.

Television

Canal 4 Monte Carlo: Paraguay 2253, 11800 Montevideo; tel. (2) 9244444; fax (2) 9242001; e-mail secretarias@montecarlotv.com.uy; f. 1961; Dir HUGO ROMAY SALVO.

SAETA TV—Canal 10: Dr Lorenzo Carnelli 1234, 11200 Montevideo; tel. (2) 4002120; fax (2) 4009771; internet www.canal10.com.uy; f. 1956; Pres. JORGE DE FEO.

SODRE (Servicio Oficial de Difusión Radiotelevisión y Espectáculos): Blvr Artigas 2552, 11600 Montevideo; tel. (2) 4806448; fax (2) 4808515; internet www.sodre.gub.uy; f. 1963; Dir. Dr RAMIRO RODRÍGUEZ VILLAMIL.

Teledoce Televisora Color—Canal 12: Enriqueta Compte y Riqué 1276, 11800 Montevideo; tel. (2) 2035856; fax (2) 2037623; internet www.teledoce.com; f. 1962; Dir ALEJANDRA MORGAN; Gen. Man. HORACIO SCHECK.

In 1999 there were 21 television stations outside the capital.

Finance

BANKING

(cap. = capital; res = reserves; dep. = deposits; m. = million; amounts in pesos, unless otherwise indicated)

State Banks

Banco Central del Uruguay: Avda Juan P. Fabini 777, Casilla 1467, 11100 Montevideo; tel. (2) 9085629; fax (2) 9021634; e-mail secgral@bcu.gub.uy; internet www.bcu.gub.uy; f. 1967; note-issuing bank, also controls private banking; Pres. JULIO DE BRUN; Gen. Man. GUALBERTO DE LEÓN.

Banco Hipotecario del Uruguay (BHU): Avda Daniel Fernández Crespo 1508, Montevideo; tel. (2) 4090000; fax (2) 4005675; e-mail info@bhu.net; internet www.bhu.com.uy; f. 1892; state mortgage bank; in 1977 assumed responsibility for housing projects in Uruguay; Pres. ARIEL LAUSAROT; Gen. Man. ENRIQUE RUÍZ CORBO.

Banco de la República Oriental del Uruguay (BROU): Cerrito 351, 11000 Montevideo; tel. (2) 9150157; fax (2) 9162064; internet www.brounet.com.uy; f. 1896; a state institution; cap. and res 8,149.0m., dep. 45,263.1m. (Dec. 1999); Pres. DANIEL CAIRO VILA; Vice-Pres. MILKA BARBATO; 107 brs.

Nuevo Banco Comercial (NBC): Montevideo; f. 2003 by merger of Banco Comercial, Banco La Caja Obrera and Banco de Montevideo; state-run; dep. US $667m., assets US $882m.; 46 brs.

Principal Commercial Banks

Banco Bilbao Vizcaya Argentaria Uruguay SA (BBVA): 25 de Mayo 401, 11000 Montevideo; tel. (2) 9161444; fax (2) 9162821; f. 1968; formerly Unión de Bancos del Uruguay, and later Banesto Banco Uruguay, SA and Banco Francés Uruguay, SA; adopted current name in 2000 following merger with Banco Exterior de América, SA; cap. 70m., res 451.6m., dep. 4,769.4m. (Dec. 1997); Pres. RODOLVO CORVI; Gen. Man. JORGE LUNA; 14 brs.

Banco Santander Uruguay, SA: Cerrito 449, 11000 Montevideo; tel. (2) 9160656; fax (2) 9163685; e-mail santander@santander.com .uy; internet www.santander.com.uy; 100% owned by Banco Santander (Spain); cap. 161.1m., res. 477.9m., dep. 9,283.8m. (Dec. 2000); Vice-Pres. MIGUEL ESTRUGO SANTAEUGENIA; Dir JORGE JOURDÁN PEYRONEL; 28 brs.

Banco Surinvest SA: Rincón 530, 11000 Montevideo; tel. (2) 9160177; fax (2) 9160241; e-mail surinves@netgate.com.uy; f. 1981 as Surinvest Casa Bancaria, name changed as above 1991; cap. 35.2m., res 85.6m., dep. 1,709.6m. (Dec. 1999); Chair. and Gen. Man. JUAN MARTÍN ETCHEGOYHEN.

Foreign Banks

ABN AMRO Bank NV (Netherlands): Avda 18 de Julio 999, Casilla 888, 11100 Montevideo; tel. (2) 9009799; fax (2) 9009798; internet www.abnamro.com.uy; f. 1952; Gen. Man. ERIC SIMON; 23 brs.

American Express Bank, SA (USA): Rincón 477, 8°, 11000 Montevideo; tel. (2) 9160103; fax (2) 9162245; e-mail aeburuguay@amex .com.uy; Pres. SERGIO J. MASVIDAL; Gen. Man. MARA MATTOZO; 1 br.

Banco de la Nación Argentina: Juan C. Gómez 1372, 11000 Montevideo; tel. (2) 9158760; fax (2) 9160078; Gen. Man. JORGE HUMBERTO ROSSI; 2 brs.

Banco Sudameris (France): Rincón 500, 11000 Montevideo; tel. (2) 9150095; fax (2) 9162509; Pres. Dr SAGUNTO PÉREZ FONTANA; Gen. Man. IGNACIO JAQUOTOT; 6 brs.

BankBoston NA (USA): Zabala 1463, 11000 Montevideo; tel. (2) 9160127; fax (2) 9162209; took over Banco Internacional in 1978; cap. US $10.8m., dep. $179.9m. (May 1990); Gen. Man. HORACIO VILARÓ; 11 brs.

Citibank NA (USA): Cerrito 455, Casilla 690, 11000 Montevideo; tel. (2) 91550374; fax (2) 9163665; Dir-Gen. GUSTAVO CARDONI; 3 brs.

Discount Bank (Latin America), SA (USA): Rincón 390, 11000 Montevideo; tel. (2) 9164848; fax (2) 9160890; e-mail mensajes@ discbank.com.uy; internet www.discbank.com.uy; f. 1958; cap. 46.0m., res 204.6m., dep. 3,047.1m. (Dec. 2000); Pres. and Chair. ARIE SHEER; Gen. Man. BITOUSH MENAHEM; 4 brs.

HSBC Banco Roberts (Uruguay) SAIFE (Argentina): Rincón 477, Of. 201, 11000 Montevideo; tel. (2) 9164802; fax (2) 9164805; e-mail roberts@adinet.com.uy; f. 1995; cap. US $18.0m., res $16.6m., dep. $311.9m. (June 1998); Pres. and Chair. ANTONIO M. LOSADA; Gen. Man. LEONEL JUAN PUPPO.

Leumi (Latin America) SA: 25 de Mayo 549, 11000 Montevideo; tel. (2) 9160223; fax (2) 9170673; e-mail leumont@montevideo.com .uy; f. 1980; Chair. Dr ZALMAN SEGAL; Gen. Man. MORDECHAI KESSOUS; 2 brs.

Lloyds TSB Bank PLC (United Kingdom): Zabala 1500, Casilla 204, 11000 Montevideo; tel. (2) 9160976; fax (2) 9161262; e-mail lloydsm@adinet.com.uy; internet www.lloydstsb.com.uy; f. 1862; fmrly Bank of London and South America; Man. CHRISTOPHER D. GOLBY.

Bankers' Association

Asociación de Bancos del Uruguay (Bank Association of Uruguay): Rincón 468, 2°, 11000 Montevideo; tel. (2) 9162342; fax (2) 9162329; e-mail uy340424@adinet.com.uy; internet www.abu.org .uy; f. 1945; 15 mem. banks; Pres. Dr CARLOS GARCÍA AROCENA.

STOCK EXCHANGE

Bolsa de Valores de Montevideo: Edif. Bolsa de Comercio, Misiones 1400, 11000 Montevideo; tel. (2) 9165051; fax (2) 9161900; e-mail bvm@netgate.com.uy; internet www.bvm.com.uy; f. 1867; 75 mems; Pres. IGNACIO ROSPIDE.

INSURANCE

From mid-1994, following the introduction of legislation ending the state monopoly of most types of insurance, the Banco de Seguros del Estado lost its monopoly on all insurance except life, sea transport and fire risks, which have been traditionally open to private underwriters.

Banco de Seguros del Estado: Mercedes 1051, Montevideo; tel. (2) 9089303; fax (2) 9017030; e-mail directorio@bse.com.uy; internet www.bse.com.uy; f. 1912; state insurance org. all risks; Pres. ALBERTO IGLESIAS; Vice-Pres. ENRIQUE ROIG CURBELO.

Real Seguros SA: 18 de Julio 988, Montevideo; tel. (2) 9025858; fax (2) 9024515; e-mail realseg@realseguros.com.uy; f. 1900; life and property; part of the ABN AMRO Group (Netherlands); Pres. PAUL ELBERSE; Gen. Man. EIJI AJIMURA.

Trade and Industry

GOVERNMENT AGENCY

Oficina de Planeamiento y Presupuesto de la Presidencia de la República: Fondo de las Americas, Convención 1366, Montevideo; tel. (2) 9000461; fax (2) 2099730; f. 1976; responsible for the implementation of devt plans; co-ordinates the policies of the various ministries; advises on the preparation of the budget of public enterprises; Sub-Dir MARCELO BRASCA SARLO.

DEVELOPMENT ORGANIZATION

Corporación Nacional para el Desarrollo: Rincón 528, 7°, Casilla 977, 11000 Montevideo; tel. (2) 9155764; fax (2) 9159662; e-mail cnd01@adinet.com.uy; internet www.cnd.org.uy; f. 1985; national devt corpn; mixed-capital org. obtains 60% of funding from state; Vice-Pres. JULIO GEMELLI; Dir CARLOS GARAT.

CHAMBERS OF COMMERCE

Cámara de Industrias del Uruguay (Chamber of Industries): Avda Libertador Brig.-General Lavalleja 1672, 11100 Montevideo; tel. (2) 9023402; fax (2) 9022567; e-mail ciu@ciu.com.uy; internet www.ciu.com.uy; f. 1898; Pres. GUALBERTO ROCCO.

Cámara Nacional de Comercio y Servicios del Uruguay (National Chamber of Commerce): Edif. Bolsa de Comercio, Rincón 454, 2°, Casilla 1000, 11000 Montevideo; tel. (2) 9161277; fax (2) 9161243; e-mail canadeco@adinet.com.uy; internet www.davanet .com.uy/canadeco; f. 1867; 1,500 mems; Pres. Dr JORGE PEIRANO BASSO; Sec. and Man. Dr CLAUDIO PIACENZA.

Cámara Mercantil de Productos del País (Chamber of Commerce for Local Products): Avda General Rondeau 1908, 11800 Montevideo; tel. (2) 9240644; fax (2) 9240673; e-mail cmpp@davanet .com.uy; internet www.davanet.com.uy/cmpp; f. 1891; 180 mems; Pres. CHRISTIAN BOLZ; Gen. Man. GONZALO GONZÁLEZ PIEDRAS.

EMPLOYERS' ORGANIZATIONS

Asociación de Importadores y Mayoristas de Almacén (Importers' and Wholesalers' Asscn): Edif. Bolsa de Comercio, Of. 317/319, Rincón 454, 11000 Montevideo; tel. (2) 9156103; fax (2) 9160796; f. 1926; 52 mems; Pres. FERNANDO MELISSARI.

Asociación Rural del Uruguay: Avda Uruguay 864, 11100 Montevideo; tel. (2) 9020484; fax (2) 9020489; e-mail aru@netgate.com .uy; internet www.aru.org.uy; f. 1871; 1,800 mems; Pres. ALBERTO PEREIRA MICOUD; Vice-Pres. JULIO BONOMI.

Comisión Patronal del Uruguay de Asuntos Relacionados con la OIT (Commission of Uruguayan Employers for Affairs of the ILO): Edif. Bolsa de Comercio, Rincón 454, 2°, Casilla 1000, 11000 Montevideo; tel. (2) 9161277; fax (2) 9161243; e-mail canadeco@ adinet.com.uy; internet www.davanet.com.uy/canadeco; f. 1954; mem. of Cámara Nacional de Comercio y Servicios del Uruguay; Sec. and Man. Dr CLAUDIO PIACENZA.

Federación Rural del Uruguay: Avda 18 de Julio 965, 1°, Montevideo; tel. (2) 9005583; fax (2) 9004791; e-mail fedrural@adinet.com .uy; f. 1915; 2,000 mems; Pres. ARTIGAS DELCUADRO.

Unión de Exportadores del Uruguay (Uruguayan Exporters' Asscn): Edif. Bolsa de Comercio, Of. 401, 4°, Rincón 454, 11000 Montevideo; tel. (2) 9170105; fax (2) 9161117; e-mail ueu@adinet .com.uy; Pres. DANIEL SOLODUCHO; Exec. Sec. TERESA AISHEMBERG.

UTILITIES

Electricity

Administración Nacional de Usinas y Transmisiones Eléctricas (UTE): Paraguay 2431, 11100 Montevideo; tel. (2) 2097685; fax (2) 2080708; e-mail ute@ute.com.uy; internet www.ute.com.uy; f. 1912; autonomous state body; sole purveyor of electricity; Pres. RICARDO SCAGLIA; Gen. Man. CARLOS POMBO.

Gas

Gaseba Uruguay (Gaz de France): 25 de Mayo 702, 11000 Montevideo; tel. (2) 9017454; internet www.gaseba.com.uy; gas producers and service providers.

Water

Obras Sanitarias del Estado (OSE): Carlos Roxlo 1275, 11200 Montevideo; tel. (2) 4001151; fax (2) 4088069; e-mail oserou@adinet .com.uy; f. 1962; processing and distribution of drinking water, sinking wells, supplying industrial zones of the country; Pres. JUAN JUSTO AMARO.

TRADE UNIONS

All trade-union activity was under strict control during 1973–85. On taking office in March 1985, President Julio María Sanguinetti ordered the restoration of the legal status of the principal workers' and university students' federations.

Plenario Intersindical de Trabajadores—Convención Nacional de Trabajadores (PIT—CNT): Avda 18 de Julio 2190, Montevideo; tel. (2) 4096680; fax (2) 4004160; f. 1966; org. comprising 83 trade unions, 17 labour federations; 320,000 mems; Pres. JOSÉ D'ELÍA; Exec.-Sec. JUAN CASTILLO.

Transport

Dirección Nacional de Transporte: Rincón 575, 5°, 11000 Montevideo; tel. (2) 9162940; fax (2) 9163122; e-mail info@dnt.gub.uy; internet www.dnt.gub.uy; co-ordinates national and international transport services.

RAILWAYS

Administración de los Ferrocarriles del Estado (AFE): La Paz 1095, Casilla 419, Montevideo; tel. (2) 9240805; fax (2) 9240847; e-mail affegg@adinet.com.uy; f. 1952; state org. 3,002 km of track connecting all parts of the country; there are connections with the Argentine and Brazilian networks; passenger services ceased in 1988; passenger services linking Montevideo with Florida and Canelones were resumed in mid-1993; Pres. JORGE GARCÍA CARRERE; Gen. Man. MARÍA ANASTASIA.

ROADS

In 1999 Uruguay had an estimated 8,983 km of motorways (forming the most dense motorway network in South America), connecting Montevideo with the main towns of the interior and the Argentine and Brazilian frontiers. There was also a network of approximately 40,000 km of paved roads under departmental control.

INLAND WATERWAYS

There are about 1,250 km of navigable waterways, which provide an important means of transport.

Nobleza Naviera, SA: Avda General Rondeau 2257, Montevideo; tel. (2) 9243222; fax (2) 9243218; e-mail nobleza@netgate.com.uy; operates cargo services on the River Plate, and the Uruguay and Paraná rivers; Chair. AMÉRICO DEAMBROSI; Man. Dir DORIS FERRARI.

SHIPPING

Administración Nacional de Combustibles, Alcohol y Portland (ANCAP): Paraguay 1598, 11100 Montevideo; tel. (2) 9024192; fax (2) 9021136; e-mail webmaster@ancap.com.uy; internet www .ancap.com.uy; f. 1931; deals with transport, refining and sale of petroleum products, and the manufacture of alcohol, spirit and cement; tanker services, also river transport; Pres. JORGE SANGUINETTI; CEO BENITO E. PIÑEIRO.

Administración Nacional de Puertos (ANP): Rambla 25 de Agosto de 1825 160, Montevideo; tel. (2) 91664747; fax (2) 9161704; e-mail presidencia@anp.com.uy; internet www.anp.gub.uy; f. 1916; national ports admin. Pres. JOSÉ AGUSTÍN AGUERRE.

Prefectura Nacional Naval: Edif. Comando General de la Armada, 5°, Rambla 25 de Agosto de 1825 s/n, esq. Maciel, Montevideo; tel. (2) 9160741; fax (2) 9163969; internet www.armada.gub .uy/prena; f. 1829; maritime supervisory body, responsible for rescue services, protection of sea against pollution, etc. Commdr Rear-Adm. OSCAR OTERO IZZI.

Navegación Atlántida, SA: Río Branco 1373, 11100 Montevideo; tel. (2) 9084449; f. 1967; ferry services for passengers and vehicles between Argentina and Uruguay; Pres. H. C. PIETRANERA.

Transportadora Marítima de Combustibles, SA (TRAMACO, SA): Treinta y Tres 1383, 1°, 11000 Montevideo; tel. (2) 9165754; fax (2) 9165755; Pres. J. FERNÁNDEZ BAUBETA.

CIVIL AVIATION

Civil aviation is controlled by the Dirección General de Aviación Civil and the Dirección General de Infraestructura Aeronáutica. The main airport is at Carrasco, 21 km from Montevideo, and there are also airports at Paysandú, Rivera, Salto, Melo, Artigas, Punta del Este and Durazno.

Primeras Líneas Uruguayas de Navegación Aérea (PLUNA): Puntas de Santiago 1604, Casilla 1360, 11500 Montevideo; tel. (2) 6042244; fax (2) 6042247; e-mail pumkt@adinet.com.uy; internet www.pluna.com.uy; f. 1936; nationalized 1951; in 1994 a 49% stake was acquired by a consortium led by Varig, SA (Brazil); operates international services to Argentina, Brazil, Chile, El Salvador, Paraguay, Spain and the USA; Man. NERY TROIS.

Tourism

The sandy beaches and woodlands on the coast and the grasslands of the interior, with their variety of fauna and flora, provide the main tourist attractions. About 80% of tourists come from Argentina, and 10% from Brazil. Uruguay received 2.2m. visitors in 2000. Revenue from the sector amounted to US $652m. that year.

Asociación Uruguaya de Agencias de Viajes (AUDAVI): Río Branco 1407, Of. 205, 11100 Montevideo; tel. (2) 9012326; fax (2) 9021972; e-mail audavi@k-bell.com.uy; f. 1951; 100 mems; Pres. FEDERICO GAMBARDELLA; Man. MÓNICA W. DE RAIJ.

Cámara Uruguaya de Turismo: Martín C. Martínez 1865, Montevideo; tel. (2) 4016404; fax (2) 4016013.

Uruguayan Hotel Association: Gutiérrez Ruiz 1213, Montevideo; tel. (2) 4080139; fax (2) 9082317; e-mail ahru@montevideo.com.uy.

UZBEKISTAN

Introductory Survey

Location, Climate, Language, Religion, Flag, Capital

The Republic of Uzbekistan (formerly the Uzbek Soviet Socialist Republic) is located in Central Asia. It is bordered by Kazakhstan to the north, Turkmenistan to the south, Kyrgyzstan to the east, Tajikistan to the south-east and Afghanistan to the south. The climate is marked by extreme temperatures and low levels of precipitation. Summers are long and hot with average temperatures in July of 32°C (90°F); daytime temperatures often exceed 40°C (104°F). During the short winter there are frequent severe frosts, and temperatures can fall as low as –38°C (–36°F). The official language is Uzbek. Islam is the predominant religion. Most Uzbeks are Sunni Muslims (Hanafi school), but there are small communities of Wahhabis; Sufism is relatively well established in southern Uzbekistan. There are also Orthodox Christians among the Slavic communities, and an estimated 65,000 European Jews and 28,000 Central Asian Jews. The national flag (proportions 1 by 2) consists of five unequal horizontal stripes of (from top to bottom) light blue, red, white, red and light green, with a white crescent and 12 white stars near the hoist on the top stripe. The capital is Tashkent.

Recent History

Soviet power was first established in parts of Uzbekistan in November 1917. In April 1918 the Turkestan Autonomous Soviet Socialist Republic (ASSR), a vast region in Central Asia including Uzbekistan, was proclaimed, but Soviet forces then withdrew against opposition from the nationalist *basmachi* movement, the White Army and a British expeditionary force. Soviet power was re-established in September 1919, although armed opposition continued until the early 1920s. The khanates of Bukhara and Khiva became nominally independent Soviet republics in 1920, but were incorporated into the Turkestan ASSR by 1924. On 27 October 1924 the Uzbek Soviet Socialist Republic (SSR) was established (including, until 1929, the Tajik ASSR). In May 1925 the Uzbek SSR became a constituent republic of the Union of Soviet Socialist Republics (USSR, which had been established in December 1922). In 1936 Karakalpakstan was transferred from the Russian Federation to the Uzbek SSR, retaining its autonomous status.

The National Delimitation of the Central Asian republics of 1924–25 established an Uzbek nation-state for the first time. Its formation was accompanied by the creation of corresponding national symbols, including the development of a new literary language (the ancient Uzbek literary language, Chatagai, was accessible only to a small minority of the population). Campaigns promoting literacy were an integral part of the establishment of Soviet ideology, and the level of literacy rose from 3.8% at the 1926 census to 52.5% in 1932. There was an increase in the provision of educational facilities, which played a crucial role in the policy of secularization in the region. The campaign against religion, initially promoted by educational means, became a repressive policy against all who admitted their adherence to Islam. Muslim schools, courts and mosques were closed, and Muslim clergy were subject to persecution.

There had been little industrial development in Central Asia under the Tsarist regime, other than the extraction of raw materials. Under the first two Five-Year Plans (1928–33 and 1933–38), however, there was considerable economic growth, aided by the immigration of skilled workers from other republics of the USSR. Although economic expansion continued at a significant rate after the Second World War (during which Uzbekistan's industrial base was enlarged by the transfer of industries from the war-zone), most Uzbeks continued to lead a traditional rural life-style, affected only by the huge increase in the amount of cotton grown in the republic.

There was a greater measure of freedom of the press in the late 1980s, facilitated by the policies of the Soviet leader, Mikhail Gorbachev, which allowed discussion of previously unexamined aspects of Uzbek history and contemporary ecological and economic problems. The poor condition of the environment was a major source of popular discontent. The over-irrigation of land to feed the vast cotton-fields had caused both salination of the soil and, most importantly, the desiccation of the Aral Sea, which is a vital element in the ecology of the entire region. By the early 1980s it was evident that excessive drainage of the Amu-Dar'ya and Syr-Dar'ya rivers was resulting in dangerously low levels of water reaching the Aral Sea.

Environmental problems and the status of the Uzbek language were among the issues on which Uzbekistan's first major non-communist political movement, Birlik (Unity), campaigned. It was formed in 1988 by a group of intellectuals in Tashkent, but quickly grew to be the main challenger to the ruling Communist Party of Uzbekistan (CPU). However, the movement was not granted official registration, and its attempts to nominate a candidate in the 1989 elections to the USSR's Congress of People's Deputies were unsuccessful. Nevertheless, its campaign led to the adoption of legislation, declaring Uzbek to be the official language of the republic, in October of that year.

On 18 February 1990 elections were held to the 500-seat Uzbek Supreme Soviet (legislature). Members of Birlik were not permitted to stand as candidates, and many leading members of the CPU stood unopposed. The new Supreme Soviet convened in March and elected Islam Karimov, the First Secretary (leader) of the CPU, to the newly created post of executive President. Shakurulla Mirsaidov was elected Chairman of the Council of Ministers (premier). In November, however, the Council of Ministers was abolished and replaced by a Cabinet of Ministers, subordinate to the President of the Republic. At the same time Mirsaidov was appointed Vice-President.

In April 1991 Uzbekistan agreed, together with eight other Soviet republics, to sign a new Union Treaty to redefine the state structure of the USSR. However, on 19 August, the day before the signing was to take place, a State Committee for the State of Emergency (SCSE) attempted to stage a *coup d'état* in Moscow. President Karimov did not initially oppose the coup, and some opposition leaders in Uzbekistan were temporarily detained. However, once it became clear that the coup had failed, Karimov declared that the orders of the SCSE were invalid. On 31 August an extraordinary session of the Supreme Soviet voted to declare the republic independent, and it was renamed the Republic of Uzbekistan. The CPU voted to dissociate itself from the Communist Party of the Soviet Union, and in November 1991 the party was restructured as the People's Democratic Party of Uzbekistan (PDPU), with Karimov retaining the leadership.

On 21 December 1991 Karimov agreed, together with 10 other republican leaders, to dissolve the USSR and formally establish the Commonwealth of Independent States (CIS, see p. 172). On 29 December direct presidential elections were held for the first time in Uzbekistan, which were won by Karimov with a reported 86% of the total votes cast. His sole rival (winning 12% of the votes) was the poet Muhammad Solikh, the leader of the Erk (Freedom) opposition party, which had been established as an offshoot of Birlik in 1990. (Birlik was banned from contesting the election, as it had still not been granted official registration as a political party.) A referendum was held simultaneously, in which 98.2% of participants endorsed Uzbekistan's independence. In January 1992 the post of Vice-President was abolished and Mirsaidov was thereby removed from office.

The PDPU remained dominant both in the Supreme Soviet and the Cabinet of Ministers. Under Karimov's increasingly authoritarian leadership, there was widespread repression of opposition and Islamist groups, prompting strong criticism from international human rights organizations. In order to justify its oppressive measures, the Government used the example of neighbouring Tajikistan, where religious, ethnic and ideological conflicts had combined to provoke a violent civil war (see below). Uzbekistan's new Constitution, adopted on 8 December 1992, firmly enshrined the concept of state secularism. It also guaranteed a democratic multi-party system, freedom of expression and the observance of human rights. In addition, the Constitution provided for a new, smaller legislature, the 250-member Oly Majlis (Supreme Assembly). However, until the election of the Majlis in late 1994, the Supreme Soviet was to be retained as the republican parliament.

Despite the Constitution's provisions, on the day of its adoption three leading opposition members who were attending an international conference on human rights in the Kyrgyz capital, Bishkek, were seized by Uzbek security police on charges of sedition. (One of their number was put on trial.) On the following day Birlik was banned for its allegedly subversive activities. Restriction of the media also intensified: in mid-1993 the Government instructed all newspapers and periodicals to be re-registered with the State Committee for the Press; only organs of state and government were permitted official registration. In October Erk failed to receive registration as a political party and was subsequently banned.

Although Karimov pledged that all political parties would be free to contest the election to the Oly Majlis in 1994, in the event only the PDPU and its ally, Progress of the Fatherland (PF), were permitted to register. At the election, held on 25 December (with a second round of voting in January 1995), the PDPU won 69 of the 250 seats, while the PF secured 14. The remaining 167 deputies elected had been nominated by local councils rather than by political parties; however, the overwhelming majority of these deputies (some 120) were members of the PDPU, and thus the party's domination of the Majlis was retained. Some 94% of eligible voters were reported to have participated in the election.

In January 1995 Karimov announced that the Government would welcome a diversification of opinions in the Oly Majlis and that it would permit the formation of blocs within the Assembly. In February a new political party, the Adolat (Justice) Social Democratic Party of Uzbekistan, was registered, and immediately declared its intention to establish such a parliamentary faction (it claimed to have the support of some 47 deputies within the Majlis). A referendum held in March produced a 99.6% vote in favour of extending Karimov's presidential term from 1997 to 2000, ostensibly to coincide with parliamentary elections. In April 1995 several members of Erk were imprisoned for allegedly attempting to provide military training abroad for Uzbek citizens in preparation for a *coup d'état*. In May two new political formations emerged: the Milli Tiklanish (National Revival) Democratic Party and the Khalk Birliki (People's Unity) Movement. Both were reported to be pro-Government, and were officially registered in June. In December 1995 Otkir Sultanov, hitherto the Minister of Foreign Economic Relations, replaced Abdulkhashim Mutalov as Prime Minister. His removal was believed to have been prompted by the country's economic difficulties, principally the decline in value of the national currency. In June 1996 Karimov resigned from his position as Chairman of the PDPU.

During 1996 Karimov began to advocate the creation of a political opposition to the PDPU, and in December a new law on political parties was approved by the Oly Majlis. The legislation prohibited the organization of parties on a religious or ethnic basis and compelled prospective parties to provide evidence of some 5,000 members drawn from at least eight of Uzbekistan's 12 administrative regions. Parties were to be permitted to publish newspapers and participate in local and general elections. In November an international human rights conference was held in Tashkent, under the auspices of the UN, despite a report critical of the human rights situation in Uzbekistan published earlier in the year by a US-based monitoring organization.

There was an upsurge of violence in eastern Uzbekistan in late 1997: in November the deputy head of the local administration of Namangan region was assassinated, and in the following month four police officers were killed. The Government attributed the unrest to groups of Islamist activists (belonging to the Wahhabi sect), which, it claimed, was operating in the region, and in mid-December government troops were dispatched to the area, resulting in hundreds of arrests. Unofficial sources suggested that the assassination of the administrative official, in November, might have been related to the illegal drugs-trafficking trade, but that it had been exploited by the Government as a pretext to repress the Islamist movement in the region.

The Government's campaign against alleged Islamist fundamentalism intensified in early 1998. In February the Uzbek Ministry of Foreign Affairs appealed to the Pakistani Government to extirpate military camps where Uzbeks were allegedly being trained in dissident activities by illegal Pakistani religious groups. (Pakistan denied the existence of any such camps.) In May a rigorous new law on religion—which severely limited the activities of Uzbek religious organizations—was adopted by the Oly Majlis. The new legislation was supposedly designed to counter the 'threat of aggressive Wahhabi activism' in Uzbekistan. Karimov declared to the Majlis that he would be prepared

personally to execute members of Islamist fundamentalist groups found guilty of terrorism. In May–July prison sentences were given against several suspected militant Islamists, and a member of an Islamist organization was sentenced to death after having been found guilty of the murder of five people and of involvement in the training of Wahhabi militants in Afghanistan. Human rights groups in Uzbekistan claimed that the Government was attempting to create fear within the religious opposition prior to the forthcoming legislative and presidential elections. In January 1999, in a further high-profile trial of alleged Wahhabi activists, five men allegedly linked with a former *imam* of Tashkent's Tokhtoboy mosque, who had been in hiding since early 1998, were found guilty of attempting to overthrow the Government and establish an Islamic state. The independent Human Rights Organization of Uzbekistan, however, described the charges as a 'fabrication'.

Meanwhile, in January 1998, on the occasion of Karimov's 60th birthday, the Oly Majlis conferred on the President the Amir Timur (Tamerlane) decoration for his services to Uzbekistan. In March Shakurulla Mirsaidov announced the disintegration of the Democratic Opposition Co-ordinating Council, which had been established in October 1995 in an attempt to unite Uzbek opposition groups. In June 1998 new legislation was passed regarding land ownership. The law, which was to take effect from July, stated that land was the property of the state and included a ban on its purchase, sale or exchange. At the end of December 1998 the founding congress of the Fidokorlar (Self-Sacrificers') National Democratic Party was held, with the support of President Karimov; Erkin Norbotayev was elected as the party's leader.

In mid-February 1999 a series of bombs exploded in the centre of Tashkent, killing an estimated 15 people. Government officials claimed that the explosions had been carried out in an attempt to assassinate President Karimov and destabilize the country. In April the President announced that a number of people had come forward, as a result of his recent plea that religious extremists hand themselves over to the authorities in order to avoid prosecution. In mid-May the Government announced legislation imposing harsher punishment for members of 'religious, extremist, separatist and fundamentalist organizations', under an amendment to the Criminal Code. Following the trial, in June, of 22 people suspected of involvement in the bomb attacks in Tashkent earlier that year, six of the accused were sentenced to death, and the other defendants received lengthy prison sentences. In mid-August six members of the banned Erk party were also given prison sentences of between eight and 15 years for their alleged involvement in the bombings; it was reported that two of the defendants were brothers of Muhammad Solikh, the leader of Erk. The sentence handed out to one of the alleged militants, a well-known Uzbek writer, was strongly criticized by human rights organizations, which alleged that the authorities had used torture during their investigation. Meanwhile, in late August it was announced that elections to the Oly Majlis, as well as to municipal and local councils, would be held in December, while presidential elections were to take place in January 2000. In mid-November 1999 the Tashkent region was infiltrated by a group of about 15 armed militants, resulting in the shooting of three police officers and three civilians. (It was alleged that the group, who were subsequently killed by security forces, had been trained in the separatist Russian republic of Chechnya and had entered the country from Kyrgyzstan.) Following the violence, President Karimov demanded a tightening of security in the capital and appealed to the Organization of Security and Co-operation in Europe (OSCE, see p. 283) to assist Uzbekistan in the fight against international terrorism.

At elections to the Oly Majlis, held on 5 and 19 December 1999, the PDPU was reported to have secured the largest representation of any single party in the legislature, winning 48 seats. Non-partisan local council nominees, however, obtained a combined total of 110 seats. The Fidokorlar National Democratic Party was the second largest party, with 34 seats, while the Progress of the Fatherland (PF), the Adolat Social Democratic Party and the Milli Tiklanish Democratic Party also achieved representation in the Oly Majlis, winning 20, 11 and 10 seats, respectively. Of the 250 seats, only 184 were filled at the first round, on 5 December, which necessitated a second round of voting ('run-off' elections) on 19 December, at which all but one deputy was elected. The rate of voter participation at the first round was reported to be some 93.5%. The OSCE had sent only a limited number of observers to the elections, claiming that

Uzbekistan had reneged on earlier commitments to make them free and fair, since all of the parties participating were pro-Government and two opposition parties had been prevented from contesting the poll.

President Karimov reportedly secured 91.9% of the votes cast at the presidential election held on 9 January 2000, compared with only 4.2% for his sole opponent, the leader of the PDPU, Abdulkhafiz Jalolov. He was duly inaugurated for another five-year term on 22 January. An estimated 95% of the registered electorate participated in the poll. However, both the OSCE and the US Government criticized the elections as undemocratic, owing to the fact that opposition parties had been barred from nominating candidates. Meanwhile, on the day prior to the election, it was reported that President Karimov had offered an invitation to the exiled former Muslim leader, Sheikh Muhammad Sadeq, to return to Uzbekistan. The President's offer was widely interpreted as an attempt to counter the increasing influence of Islamist organizations. In early 2000 the regime's suppression of religious extremism continued, with dozens of arrests being made and reports of excessive violence being used against those in custody.

At the end of September 2000 Yurii Agzamov, the Minister of Defence, was dismissed; he was replaced by Khodir Gulomov. Later that month by-elections were held for six seats in the Oly Majlis. In November Rustam Azimov, hitherto Deputy Prime Minister and Minister of Finance, was appointed First Deputy Prime Minister and Minister of Macroeconomics and Statistics. Mamarizo Normurodov was appointed Minister of Finance in the same month. Meanwhile, the trial of 12 defendants accused of involvement in the bomb attacks of February 1999 opened in October 2000. In mid-November the spiritual leader of the banned militant group, the Islamist Movement of Uzbekistan (IMU), Takhir Yoldoshev, and his field commander, Jumaboy Khojiyev (known as Juma Namangoniy), were sentenced to death, *in absentia*. The remaining 10 defendants, including, *in absentia*, the leader of Erk, Muhammad Solikh, were sentenced to between 12 and 20 years' imprisonment. In June 2001 a further 10 Islamist militants were reported to have received prison sentences for attempting to overthrow the Government. In early December it was reported that Karimov had requested the extradition of Solikh from Prague, the Czech Republic. However, in mid-December Solikh was released by a Czech court. Meanwhile, in September Kozim Tulyaganov, hitherto Mayor of Tashkent, was appointed First Deputy Prime Minister.

The Government's repression of minorities continued in 2001. During March, in the towns of Samarkand and Bukhara, which had been incorporated into Uzbekistan at the formation of the SSRs, books in the Tajik language were removed from libraries and schools. At the end of April it was reported that a human rights group alleged the Ministry of Education to have commanded the destruction of books in the Tajik language elsewhere in the country, including areas with large ethnic Tajik populations.

The threat posed by the Islamist militant movement intensified in the latter half of 2001, following the terrorist attacks on the USA on 11 September (see below). There were reported to be concerns among the Uzbek population that co-operation with the USA in its attempts to form an international coalition to combat the al-Qa'ida (Base) organization (harboured by Afghanistan's Taliban regime), which the USA held responsible for the attacks on its territory, would lead to an increase in terrorist activity by the IMU. However, it was widely believed that Karimov expected to reap strategic benefits from such co-operation, notably the suppression of the IMU and the moderation of international criticism of his Government's position on economic reforms and human rights. Indeed, the US Government identified the IMU as a terrorist target prior to the initiation of air-strikes against Afghanistan. None the less, the Chairman of the OSCE warned President Karimov that human rights abuses would not be ignored. In the mean time, further restrictions were placed on the media, in an attempt to limit public reprisals against the country's co-operation with the USA. There were frequent allegations of the torture and arrest of suspected members of the IMU and Hizb-ut-Tahrir al-Islami (the Party of Islamic Liberation), which seeks to establish an Islamic state through peaceful means. In mid-October an estimated 5,000–7,000 members of the IMU were reported to be fighting alongside forces of Afghanistan's Taliban regime. The UN had also included the IMU on its list of terrorist organizations.

On 27 January 2002 a referendum on extending the President's term of office for a further two years and changing the legislative structure took place. Some 91.6% of the electorate voted, of whom 93.7% approved the establishment of a bicameral legislature and 91.8% endorsed the extension of the presidential term to seven years. The legitimacy of the referendum was questioned by both the USA and human rights groups. Some observers also queried whether the extension of the presidential term applied to the current term or the next, and the OSCE expressed hope that Uzbekistan would wait until the next presidential elections before implementing the extension. However, in early April the Oly Majlis approved a resolution delaying the next presidential elections by two years, until 2007. The legislature also endorsed a resolution on the election of a new, bicameral legislature in December 2004; the upper chamber, the Senate, was to be composed of members of local councils and 16 presidentially appointed citizens. In the same month Nosirjon Yusupov succeeded Turop Holtoyev as Deputy Prime Minister and Minister of Agriculture and Water Resources.

In early March 2002 the Uzbek Government registered the country's first domestic human rights group. Some observers considered this development to result from the country's improved relations with the USA. None the less, in May the international human rights organization, Human Rights Watch, alleged that the Government had authorized the detention of women and children in its campaign to suppress Hizb-ut-Tahrir, and many suspected members of Hizb-ut-Tahrir were reported to have been subjected to torture and imprisonment.

In October 2002 Deputy Prime Minister Valerii Otayev was dismissed and replaced by Elyor Ganiyev. In the same month Bahrom Kurbanov was appointed as Minister of Culture, in place of Hayrulla Jurayev. Pursuant to the referendum held in January, in December the Oly Majlis passed legislation on the formation of the bicameral legislature; Karimov announced that the new Senate would assume some of the duties formerly performed by the President. In February 2003 Bakhtiyor Subanov was approved as Minister for Emergency Situations, and in March Sodyk Safayev was appointed as Minister of Foreign Affairs, replacing Abdulaziz Komilov, who became an adviser to the President. In April the Oly Majlis approved constitutional amendments permitting the redistribution of authority within the Government with effect from the next legislative election, which were to separate responsibility for leading the cabinet from the role of the President; the right to occupy simultaneously the roles of president and prime minister was to be removed. In addition, a law granting former presidents lifelong immunity from prosecution, as well as permanent membership of the Senate, was endorsed, and restructuring of the judiciary was implemented.

Uzbekistan's closest relations are with the neighbouring Central Asian republics—Kazakhstan, Kyrgyzstan, Tajikistan and Turkmenistan—also CIS members. In January 1994 the five republics established a joint fund and a permanent committee to attempt to redress the ecological damage to the Aral Sea, and also to improve health standards in the region. In the same year Uzbekistan formed, with Kazakhstan and Kyrgyzstan, a trilateral economic area, creating in 1995 an Interstate Council to supervise their closer economic integration. In 1997 the Presidents of the three countries agreed to establish an interparliamentary council to promote the harmonization of legislation among them, which, in turn, would accelerate economic integration. In September a Central Asian peace-keeping battalion participated, with troops from the USA and other countries, in military manoeuvres, which were held in Uzbekistan and elsewhere in the region under the auspices of NATO's 'Partnership for Peace' programme (see p. 273) of military co-operation. (Uzbekistan had joined the programme in 1994.) In October 1998 Uzbekistan and Kazakhstan signed a Treaty of Eternal Friendship and agreed on a seven-year programme of bilateral economic co-operation. In November 2001 Uzbekistan and Kazakhstan signed a treaty on demarcating most of their border. However, the demarcation of areas including the villages of Bagys and Turkestanets remained unresolved. The majority of citizens in Bagy were ethnic Kazakhs, and it had been hoped that the land, hitherto leased to Uzbekistan, would be returned to Kazakhstan following independence. However, Uzbekistan had been reluctant to cede the land, and Kazakhstan did not pursue the issue, in order to maintain good diplomatic relations. As a sign of their frustration, in December residents declared an Independent Kazakh Republic of Bagys, and elected a president and legislature. The Uzbek security forces subsequently arrested a number of activists, and in late April 2002 it was reported that troops had barricaded the villages, after virtual martial law had been established in Bagys. In September a final agreement delimiting the Kazakh–Uzbek border was signed by the Presidents of both countries; a declaration enhancing the bilateral agreement of 1998 was also signed. However, at the end of 2002 Uzbekistan unexpectedly closed its border with Kazakhstan, allegedly as a protective measure to prevent hard currency from leaving the country by that route, following the introduction of new import taxes (see Economy).

In mid-1990 there was inter-ethnic tension in connection with clashes in Osh, a region in Kyrgyzstan with an ethnic Uzbek majority (see chapter on Kyrgyzstan). Border crossings were closed to prevent up to 15,000 armed Uzbek citizens from joining the Uzbeks in Kyrgyzstan, while President Karimov declared a state of emergency in Andizhan region (which borders Osh region). Relations were adversely affected in September 2000, when Uzbek government forces reportedly planted landmines along the Kyrgyz–Uzbek border, in order to prevent insurgents from entering Uzbekistan, without informing Kyrgyz border guards. Although it was announced in June 2001 that the mines were to be removed, there were claims in September that the laying of mines was continuing. As a result, the Kyrgyz Legislative Assembly refused to ratify an agreement with Uzbekistan on arms' supplies. Border tension increased in April, following unsuccessful attempts by the two Governments to resolve land disputes surrounding four enclaves, in particular Sokh and Barak. In March 2002 Uzbekistan agreed to supply natural gas to Kyrgyzstan in return for deliveries of water.

In September 2000 Turkmenistan and Uzbekistan signed a treaty demarcating their 1,867 km border. Tighter control of the border, however, exacerbated tension (see Turkmenistan chapter). In mid-December 2003 Turkmen special forces entered the Uzbek embassy in the Turkmen capital, Ashgabat, purportedly in order to investigate reports that it was harbouring Boris Shikhmuradov, who the Turkmen authorities blamed for an assassination attempt against that country's President, Saparmyrat Niyazov. Uzbekistan's ambassador to Turkmenistan was subsequently declared *persona non grata*, on the grounds that he had offered support to Shikhmuradov. The Uzbek authorities denied the allegations and reacted with hostility; open confrontation rapidly led to the deployment of troops from both countries along their mutual border, and an associated increase in border security.

In April 2001, at a meeting of leaders of the Turkic-speaking countries, the Presidents of Azerbaijan, Kazakhstan, Kyrgyzstan, Turkey and Turkmenistan, and the Chairman of the Uzbek legislature signed an agreement on regional co-operation to combat terrorism and drugs-trafficking, to revive the old 'Silk Road' trade route between the People's Republic of China and Europe, and to ensure further protection of the environment.

Uzbekistan dispatched troops to neighbouring Tajikistan in 1992, as part of a CIS peace-keeping contingent, and it tightened border controls with Tajikistan in an attempt to prevent the Tajik civil conflict from extending into Uzbekistan (see chapter on Tajikistan). It was reported that the Uzbek Government actively supported the communist regime in Tajikistan in its efforts to suppress opposition Islamist and democratic forces. This was attributed, in part, to Uzbek concerns for their co-nationals in Tajikistan (who form that republic's largest ethnic minority, numbering more than 1m. people). Following the signature, in June 1997, of a peace accord between the Tajik Government and opposition forces, Uzbekistan did not agree to act as one of the guarantor states of the accord until August. This delay was attributed to Uzbekistan's concern that some of Tajikistan's opposition groups had been excluded from the peace process. During a visit to Uzbekistan in January 1998 President Rakhmonov of Tajikistan met Karimov, and the two leaders voiced their opposition to religious extremism and to Tajikistan becoming an Islamist state. In the following month an intergovernmental agreement on restructuring Tajikistan's debt to Uzbekistan was agreed. In mid-1998 Tajikistan joined the trilateral economic area established by Uzbekistan, Kazakhstan and Kyrgyzstan, and known as the Central Asian Co-operation Organization from March 2002. In November 1998 Uzbekistan denied reports of its involvement with a rebel uprising launched against the Tajik Government (see chapter on Tajikistan). In February 1999 Uzbekistan announced its intention to withdraw from the CIS Collective Security Treaty, owing to its opposition to Russia's attempts at closer integration within the CIS and, in particular, Russia's military presence in Tajikistan. In August the Uzbek Government accused Tajikistan of allowing militant

groups to operate from its territory. Meanwhile, the Tajik leadership was angered by Uzbekistan's admittance that its forces might have accidentally bombed Tajik villages during a military operation to assist Kyrgyzstan to repel armed militants from the nearby Kyrgyz region of Osh. From August 2000 armed Islamist militants made a series of incursions into Uzbekistan from Tajikistan, leading to armed conflict with government forces; the insurgents reportedly came within 100 km of Tashkent. By mid-September, however, the remaining militants were reported to have been killed by government troops. In the mean time, Uzbekistan, which had begun laying landmines along its border with Tajikistan from mid-2000, in an effort to prevent cross-border incursions by Islamist insurgents, officially informed Tajikistan of its actions only in early May 2001 (see chapter on Tajikistan). However, despite the tensions between the two countries, the increased threat of terrorism in late 2001 led to an improvement in bilateral relations. President Rakhmonov met President Karimov in Uzbekistan in December; although no border agreement was reached, it was announced that the crossing between the Penjakent district in Tajikistan and Uzbekistan's Samarkand district was to reopen. The leaders also agreed to collaborate to combat terrorism, crime and the illegal drugs trade. At a meeting of the Tajik and Uzbek Prime Ministers in February 2002, an agreement on border-crossing procedures was reached. However, reports continued to emerge in early 2002 of obstruction to the free movement of people and goods by Uzbek border guards. The continued influx of illegal drugs from Tajikistan also threatened relations. In March 2001 the Uzbek authorities evicted a number of Tajik citizens who had fled across the border during the civil war. However, following a summit of the Central Asian Co-operation Organization in October 2002 the Presidents of the two countries agreed on the demarcation of over 85% of their shared border.

Uzbekistan's concerns for the security of the Central Asian region, and its conviction of the instability caused by Islamist extremism, were augmented by a second conflict on its southern border: the long-standing civil war in Afghanistan. In the early 1990s President Rabbani of Afghanistan claimed that Uzbekistan was providing military and financial assistance to the Afghan militia leader, Gen. Abdul Rashid Dostam (an ethnic Uzbek), whose forces controlled parts of northern Afghanistan. In October 1994 the Uzbek Government denied any military involvement in Afghanistan and declared that only humanitarian aid had been given; in 1994 and 1995, however, Rabbani reiterated his allegations. At a summit meeting attended by representatives of Russia and the Central Asian republics in October 1996, Karimov confirmed that no military assistance would be accorded to Gen. Dostam, but declared that Dostam's forces provided the only defence for the Central Asian republics against the Taliban militant Islamist grouping. Following the defeat of Dostam's forces in May 1997, troop deployment on the Uzbekistan–Afghanistan border was intensified. In the following month Karimov urged Taliban leaders not to retain absolute power, but to form a broadly-based coalition government. The Uzbek authorities expressed outrage in August, when hostilities in northern Afghanistan resulted in missiles falling on the Uzbek border town of Termez. There were also reports of Taliban incursions into Uzbek territory. In late 1997 the Uzbek Government denied having facilitated the return of Gen. Dostam to Afghanistan from exile in Turkey. In October 2000 Gen. Dostam rejected allegations that his troops fought alongside Uzbek government forces in August–September to repel incursions by Islamist militants. At the same time, the Uzbek authorities confirmed that informal dialogue had taken place between the Uzbek and Afghan ambassadors to Pakistan; the Uzbek Government stated that it would recognize the legitimacy of any government in Afghanistan that had the support of the majority of that country's population, and the two sides pledged non-interference in each other's internal affairs. However, relations deteriorated after the Taliban granted political asylum to Juma Namangoniy, the field commander of the rebel IMU. In January 2001 the Uzbek Minister of Foreign Affairs met the Afghan ambassador to Pakistan to discuss security concerns. Relations worsened further following reports in late August 2001 that Namangoniy had been appointed the deputy Commander-in-Chief of the Taliban forces. At the same time there were reports of the appointment of the Saudi-born al-Qa'ida leader, Osama bin Laden, to the post of Commander-in-Chief of the Taliban forces. The Islamist militant threat intensified following the terrorist attacks on the USA of 11 September (see chapter on the USA). At the same time, Uzbekistan's relationship with the USA became closer. (Relations had already improved noticeably in the latter half of the 1990s, and during a visit to Tashkent in April 2000, the US Secretary of State had affirmed the USA's willingness to assist Uzbekistan in combating the spread of Islamist extremism.) Uzbekistan's decision to support the US-led coalition against global terrorism was of great strategic importance to the US Government, which hoped to benefit from access to the country's transportation facilities. On 23 September the Uzbek Government confirmed that US military aircraft had landed at an airfield near Tashkent. On 7 October Uzbekistan and the USA signed a co-operation agreement, whereby Uzbekistan agreed to make its airbases available for use in humanitarian and 'search-and-rescue' operations during the US-led aerial bombardment of Taliban and terrorist bases in Afghanistan. The USA also agreed to enter into urgent negotiations, should Uzbekistan's security be threatened. Uzbekistan emphasized that it would not conduct military operations against Afghanistan, but would assist with the activities of those countries involved in the retaliatory attacks. In mid-October a UN official confirmed that US troops were deployed in Uzbekistan and would not be permitted to launch attacks from Uzbek bases.

In October 2001 Uzbekistan commenced the deployment of its troops on the Uzbek–Afghan border. The Uzbek Government was reluctant to accept refugees from Afghanistan, even though 1.5m. of them were ethnic Uzbeks, citing security concerns. Initially, the Government also refused to open the border to allow humanitarian aid to reach Afghanistan. Following the military successes of the anti-Taliban forces in November, however, the Government was persuaded to open the 'Friendship Bridge', the only transit point into Afghanistan, in early December. In November the death of Namangoniy was reported and later confirmed. Karimov, however, requested proof of his death.

In late November 2001 Uzbekistan and the USA signed a number of agreements pledging to improve bilateral relations and to increase economic co-operation. The USA agreed to donate more than US $150m. in aid towards improving Uzbekistan's security and economic development. Disagreements over Uzbekistan's pace of democratization, however, remained. Further bilateral agreements on political, economic and military co-operation were signed in January and March 2002, and Karimov visited the USA in March.

At an official summit of the heads of the Central Asian states in Tashkent in late December 2001 (Turkmenistan was not represented), the leaders declared their support for the new Afghan Interim Administration, which was established following the defeat of the Taliban regime. In March 2002 the leaders of Uzbekistan and Afghanistan pledged jointly to combat terrorism and the drugs trade; the IMU, for example, continued to be a threat to both countries. The 'Friendship Bridge' remained open in 2002, but the rest of the border was closed and heavily guarded.

Relations with Russia, the most influential member state of the CIS, have been intermittently strained by the issue of Uzbekistan's large ethnic Russian population. Uzbekistan has repeatedly refused to grant dual citizenship to its Russian minority, and since independence many thousands of these Russians have emigrated. This, in turn, has adversely affected Uzbekistan's economic and cultural life, as Russians are believed to form the best-educated and most highly-skilled social group. In October 1998 Russia, Uzbekistan and Tajikistan signed a pact offering mutual military assistance, especially against 'the threat of religious extremism'; at the same time Russia and Uzbekistan signed a number of inter-governmental agreements. Relations with the People's Republic of China improved in the 1990s, and in July 1996 Jiang Zemin became the first Chinese President to visit Uzbekistan; a joint declaration on bilateral relations and co-operation was signed. Further co-operation agreements were signed between China and Uzbekistan in November 1999, including a joint communiqué on the future development of bilateral relations. In October 2000 the two countries signed an agreement on combating terrorism. In June 2001 Uzbekistan joined the Shanghai Co-operation Organization (see p. 351), hitherto the Shanghai Forum—comprising China, Russia, Kazakhstan, Kyrgyzstan and Tajikistan, and signed the Shanghai Convention on Combating Terrorism, Separatism and Extremism. At an emergency meeting, in October, members agreed to establish an anti-terrorism centre.

Government

Under the terms of the Constitution of 8 December 1992, Uzbekistan is a secular, democratic presidential republic. The directly elected President is Head of State and also holds supreme executive power; he may serve for no more than two consecutive five-year terms. In April 2002 the Oly Majlis adopted a resolution extending the presidential term to seven years, with immediate effect. The Government (Cabinet of Ministers) is subordinate to the President, who appoints its Chairman (Prime Minister), Deputy Chairmen and Ministers (subject to the approval of the legislature). The highest legislative body is the 250-member Oly Majlis (Supreme Assembly), elected for a five-year term. Eighty-three members are directly elected, while the remaining 167 are appointed by local councils. The Majlis may be dissolved by the President (with the approval of the Constitutional Court). In April 2002 the Oly Majlis approved a resolution to create a new, bicameral legislature, to be elected in December 2004. For administrative purposes, Uzbekistan is divided into 12 oblasts (regions) and one autonomous republic (Karakalpakstan), with a directly elected President.

Defence

Prior to independence, Uzbekistan had no armed forces separate from those of the USSR. The establishment of Uzbek national armed forces was initiated in 1992 and, by August 2002, these comprised approximately 50,000–55,000, including an army of 40,000 and an air force of some 10,000–15,000. There were also paramilitary forces numbering an estimated 18,000–20,000 (comprising a 1,000-strong National Guard attached to the Ministry of Defence and some 17,000–19,000 troops attached to the Ministry of Internal Affairs). Compulsory military service lasts for 18 months. In April 2003 the Government pledged to reduce the size of the armed forces by 15,000 by 2005. The budget for 2000 allocated an estimated US $300m. to defence. In July 1994 Uzbekistan joined NATO's 'Partnership for Peace' programme of military co-operation. In April 1999 Uzbekistan did not renew its membership of the Collective Security Treaty of the Commonwealth of Independent States.

Economic Affairs

In 2001, according to the World Bank, Uzbekistan's gross national income (GNI), measured at average 1999–2001 prices, was US $13,780m., equivalent to $550 per head (or $2,470 per head on an international purchasing-power parity basis). During 1990–2001, it was estimated, the population increased by an annual average of 1.9%, while gross domestic product (GDP) per head decreased, in real terms, at an average annual rate of 1.9%. Overall GDP declined, in real terms, by an average of 0.04% per year in 1990–2001; growth increased steadily from 1996, however, and it grew by 4.0% in both 2000 and 2001.

In 2001 agriculture (including forestry) contributed an estimated 35.9% of GDP, and it employed 34.3% of the working population in 2000. Some 60% of the country's land is covered by desert and steppe, while the remainder comprises fertile valleys watered by two major river systems. The massive irrigation of arid areas has greatly increased production of the major crop, cotton, but has caused devastating environmental problems (most urgently the desiccation of the Aral Sea). Uzbekistan is among the five largest producers of cotton in the world, and the crop accounts for about 30% of the value of total exports. Other major crops include grain, rice, vegetables and fruit. Since independence the Government has striven to reduce the area under cultivation of cotton in order to produce more grain. Harvests of grain have improved since 1990, but in 1997 only some 70% of the official target for the grain harvest was met. In 1998, despite a greater harvest than in 1997, most regions still failed to meet their production targets. Private farming was legalized in 1992. In 1996 more than 98% of agricultural production originated in the non-state sector. During 1990–2001 agricultural GDP increased, in real terms, by an annual average of 0.8%. Agricultural GDP increased by 3.2% in both 2000 and 2001, largely owing to a 10% rise in crop yields.

In 2001 industry (including mining, manufacturing, construction, power and fishing) contributed an estimated 21.4% of GDP, and in 2000 the sector provided 20.3% of employment. During 1990–2001 industrial GDP declined by an average of 1.9% annually, in real terms. However, the real GDP of the sector increased by 1.9% in 2000 and by 6.4% in 2001.

Uzbekistan is well endowed with mineral deposits, in particular gold, natural gas, petroleum and coal. It is estimated that Uzbekistan has sufficient reserves of crude petroleum to maintain output at mid-1990s levels for 30 years, and enough natural gas for 50 years. There are large reserves of silver, copper, lead, zinc and tungsten, and Uzbekistan is one of the world's largest producers of uranium and gold. The Navoi mine produced an estimated 2,000 metric tons of uranium in 1999; all uranium mined is exported. The Murantau mine, in the Kyzylkum desert, is reportedly the world's largest single open-cast gold mine, producing some 70% of Uzbekistan's average annual output of 80 tons in the mid-1990s. Gold-mines at Amantaytau and Daugistau, reportedly containing reserves of 280 tons, were under development in 1996. Annual output of gold was consequently expected to reach 126 tons by 2005. Gold production in 2000 was some 86 tons, compared with 70 tons in 1995.

The manufacturing sector contributed 9.3% of GDP in 2001. Manufacturing activity in that year focused largely on the machine-building and metal-working sub-sectors. This was owing, in part, to the development of an automobile-manufacturing plant. Production of consumer goods (such as textiles and rugs) declined in the late 1990s. However, significant investment has been directed to the expansion of the raw-materials processing industry.

Uzbekistan is self-sufficient in natural gas, crude petroleum and coal, and became a net exporter of crude petroleum in 1995. The opening of two petroleum refineries, which had a total refining capacity of 173,000 barrels per day, significantly increased Uzbekistan's hydrocarbons capacity. In 2000 the country's total petroleum production reached an estimated 175,000 barrels per day. In the same year natural gas production was an estimated 52,000m. cu m, thereby making Uzbekistan the 10th-largest producer world-wide. In 1999 71.3% of electricity was generated by natural gas, 12.5% was produced by hydroelectric power and 11.4% by petroleum.

The services sector contributed an estimated 42.7% of GDP in 2001 and employed 45.4% of the working population in 2000. During 1990–2001 the GDP of the services sector increased, in real terms, by an average of 0.7% annually. However, from 1996 there was strong growth in services GDP, particularly in the catering sector, and in financial and legal services. From the late 1990s small-scale privatization also contributed to growth in the services sector. Services GDP increased by 6.0% in 2000 and by 7.6% in 2001.

In 2001 Uzbekistan recorded a visible trade surplus of US $128m., and in 2000 there was a surplus of $184m. on the current account of the balance of payments. In 2000 the principal source of imports was Russia (accounting for 15.8% of the total value of imports). Other major suppliers were the Republic of Korea, the USA and Germany. The main market for exports in that year was Russia (16.7% of the total value of exports); other important purchasers were Switzerland, the United Kingdom and Ukraine. The principal exports in 2000 were cotton fibre (27.5% of the total value of exports), energy products, metals, and food products. The main imports in that year were machinery and equipment (38.7% of the total value of imports), chemicals and plastics, food products, and metals. By 2000 trade with republics of the former USSR had decreased to some 35% of Uzbekistan's total trade, compared with about 83% in 1990.

Uzbekistan's overall budget deficit (including extrabudgetary operations) in 2000 was 35,700m. sum (equivalent to 1.0% of GDP). At the end of 2000 Uzbekistan's total external debt was US $4,340m., of which $3,578m. was long-term public debt. In that year the cost of debt-servicing was equivalent to 26.3% of the value of exports of goods and services. The average annual rate of inflation declined from 1,568% in 1994 to 29% in 1999. The rate of inflation continued to decline, to 28.3% in 2000, and to an estimated 26.6% in 2001. In 2001 38,000 people (0.4% of the economically active population) were officially registered as unemployed, although the true level was believed to be considerably higher.

In 1992 Uzbekistan became a member of the IMF and the World Bank, also joining, as a 'Country of Operations', the European Bank for Reconstruction and Development (EBRD, see p. 193). In the same year Uzbekistan was admitted to the Economic Co-operation Organization (ECO, see p. 192). In 1995 Uzbekistan became a member of the Asian Development Bank (ADB, see p. 143). Uzbekistan is pursuing membership of the World Trade Organization (WTO, see p. 323).

Following the collapse of the USSR in December 1991, in 1992 GDP declined sharply and inflation increased rapidly. Measures to effect a gradual transition to a market economy, announced in 1994, included price liberalization and the privatization of

selected state enterprises, and the trade and currency-exchange systems were liberalized in 1995. The economy returned to growth in 1996, when the pace of structural reform was accelerated, supported by loans from international financial organizations. However, a poor cotton harvest resulted in a weakening of monetary policy, and a significant depreciation of the national currency, the sum, as well as the introduction of restrictions on access to foreign-currency reserves, led to the withdrawal of many international investments. The economy achieved sustained growth in the late 1990s; however, it was adversely affected by the Russian financial crisis from mid-1998, as well as by a poor cotton harvest and low market prices for both cotton and gold, which led to a decline in export earnings. None the less, the industrial sector benefited from a successful Uzbek-South Korean automobile venture, and the services sector also registered strong growth, largely as a result of small-scale privatization. In early 2002 Uzbekistan agreed to implement a structural-reform programme, with the objective of achieving currency convertibility and unifying the country's various official exchange rates. In 2002 new taxes on imports were introduced, apparently in an attempt to protect the economy from the loss of hard currency, prior to the planned introduction of measures to make the sum freely convertible; unemployment increased as a result, and there were indications that the new tax had served to encourage illegal transactions. Privatization revenues increased significantly in 2002, the budgetary deficit was reduced, and inflation declined. The Government's priorites for 2003 included efforts to strengthen the position of the private sector, to curb unauthorized imports, to liberalize the foreign-currency market and to further stabilize the som. None the less, in early 2003 the EBRD warned that its programme of lending to Uzbekistan would be restrained if significant progress in political and economic reform was not recorded in that year. (The continued lack of reform, and the maintenance of restrictions on the convertibility of the som, had led to the permanent withdrawal of the IMF's representative to Uzbekistan in April 2001.) Foreign investment declined significantly in 2002 and, despite Uzbekistan's self-sufficiency in mineral fuels and the expansion of its energy-export capacity, there remained international concern that its economic policies served to further its economic isolation.

Education

Primary education, beginning at six years of age, lasts for four years. Secondary education, beginning at 10 years of age, lasts for seven years, comprising a first cycle of five years and a second cycle of two years. In 1994 total enrolment at primary and secondary schools was equivalent to 87% of the school-age population (91% of males; 83% of females). The gross primary enrolment ratio in 1999, according to the Asian Development Bank, was equivalent to 85% of females and 86% of males in the relevant age-group, while the comparable ratio for secondary enrolment in 1994 was 94%. In the 1994/95 academic year 5.0m. pupils were enrolled in general primary and secondary schools. In the same year there were 214,500 students in vocational schools. In 2000 6.0m. pupils were enrolled in general secondary schools. Higher education was provided in 61 institutes in the same year, with a total enrolment of 183,600 students. In 1992–93 a number of religious schools (*madrassas*) of the Wahhabi branch of Islam were established with Saudi Arabian financial assistance, providing education free of charge. In 1993 construction of a Saudi-financed university at Margilan began; when completed it was to offer places for 5,000 students. However, legislation adopted in May 1993 banned private educational establishments in Uzbekistan; those already in existence were reportedly to be transferred to state control. In April 1999 the establishment of the Tashkent Islamic University was agreed. In 1999 government expenditure on education was an estimated 171,376m. sum (27.1% of total budgetary expenditure).

Public Holidays

2003: 1 January (New Year's Day), 12 February* (Kurban Hayit, Id al-Adha or Feast of the Sacrifice), 8 March (International Women's Day), 21 March (Navruz Bairam, Uzbek New Year), 9 May (Victory Day), 1 September (Independence Day), 26 November* (Ruza Hayit, Id al-Fitr or end of Ramadan), 10 December (Constitution Day).

2004: 1 January (New Year's Day), 2 February* (Kurban Hayit, Id al-Adha or Feast of the Sacrifice), 8 March (International Women's Day), 21 March (Navruz Bairam, Uzbek New Year), 9 May (Victory Day), 1 September (Independence Day), 14 November* (Ruza Hayit, Id al-Fitr or end of Ramadan), 10 December (Constitution Day).

*These holidays are dependent on the Islamic lunar calendar and may vary by one or two days from the dates given.

Weights and Measures

The metric system is in force.

Statistical Survey

Principal sources (unless otherwise indicated): IMF, *Republic of Uzbekistan—Recent Economic Developments* (March 2000), IMF, *Uzbekistan, Economic Review*; IMF, *Republic of Uzbekistan—Background Paper and Statistical Appendix*; World Bank, *Statistical Handbook: States of the Former USSR*; World Bank, *Uzbekistan: An Agenda for Economic Reform*.

Area and Population

AREA, POPULATION AND DENSITY

Area (sq km)	447,400*
Population (census results)†	
17 January 1979	15,389,307
12 January 1989	
Males	9,784,156
Females	10,025,921
Total	19,810,077
Population (official estimates at mid-year)	
1999	24,410,000
2000	24,752,000
2001	25,068,000
Density (per sq km) at mid-2001	56.0

* 172,740 sq miles.

† Figures refer to *de jure* population. The *de facto* total at the 1989 census was 19,905,158.

POPULATION BY ETHNIC GROUP
(census of 12 January 1989)

	%
Uzbek	71.4
Russian	8.3
Tajik	4.7
Kazakh	4.1
Tatar	2.4
Others*	9.1
Total	100.0

* Including Karakalpaks, Crimean Tatars, Koreans, Kyrgyz, Ukrainians, Turkmen and Turks.

PRINCIPAL TOWNS
(estimated population at 1 January 1999)

Tashkent (capital)	2,142,700	Chirchik . . .	145,600
Namangan . .	376,600	Margilan . . .	143,600
Samarkand . .	362,300	Urgench . . .	139,100
Andizhan . .	323,900	Angren . . .	128,600
Bukhara . .	237,900	Jizak . . .	126,400
Nukus . . .	199,000	Navoi . . .	117,600
Karshi . . .	197,600	Almalyk . . .	115,100
Kokand . . .	192,500	Termez . . .	111,500
Fergana . .	182,800		

Source: UN, *Demographic Yearbook*.

Mid-2001 (UN estimate, incl. suburbs): Tashkent 2,157,000 (Source: UN, *World Urbanization Prospects: The 2001 Revision*).

BIRTHS, MARRIAGES AND DEATHS

	Registered live births		Registered marriages		Registered deaths	
	Number	Rate (per 1,000)	Number	Rate (per 1,000)	Number	Rate (per 1,000)
1994 . .	657,725	29.5	176,287	7.9	148,423	6.7
1995 . .	677,999	29.9	170,828	7.5	145,439	6.4
1996 . .	634,842	27.4	171,662	7.4	144,829	6.3
1997 . .	602,694	25.6	181,126	7.7	137,331	5.8
1999*† . .	553,745	23.1	170,525	7.1	140,526	5.9

* Provisional figures.

† Figures for 1998 are not available.

Source: UN, *Demographic Yearbook*.

2001 (provisional figures): Registered live births 512,800 (birth rate 20.5 per 1,000); Registered deaths 131,740 (death rate 5.3 per 1,000) (Source: UN, *Population and Vital Statistics Report*).

Expectation of life (WHO estimates, years at birth): 65.5 (males 62.7; females 68.5) in 2001 (Source: WHO, *World Health Report*).

EMPLOYMENT
(annual averages, '000 persons)

	1998	1999	2000
Agriculture*	3,467	3,213	3,083
Industry†	1,114	1,124	1,145
Construction	573	640	676
Transport and communications .	362	370	382
Trade and catering‡	717	735	754
Other services	1,976	2,042	2,042
Housing, public utilities and personal services . . .	235	240	246
Health care, social security, physical culture and sports . .	502	538	567
Education, culture and art . .	1,073	1,094	1,120
Banking and insurance . . .	50	48	51
General administration . . .	111	122	126
Information and computer services	5	—	—
Total (incl. others)	8,800	8,885	8,983

* Including forestry.

† Comprising manufacturing (except printing and publishing), mining and quarrying, electricity, gas, water, logging and fishing.

‡ Including material and technical supply.

Source: *Uzbek Economic Trends*.

2001 (provisional figures, 000 persons): Total employed 9,136 (Agriculture 3,088; Mining 70; Manufacturing 545; Other 5,433) (Source: Asian Development Bank, *Key Indicators of Developing Asian and Pacific Countries*).

Health and Welfare

KEY INDICATORS

Total fertility rate (children per woman, 2001) . . .	2.5
Under-5 mortality rate (per 1,000 live births, 2001) . .	68
HIV/AIDS (% of persons aged 15–49, 2001)	<0.10
Physicians (per 1,000 head, 1998)	3.09
Hospital beds (per 1,000 head, 1999)	8.31
Health expenditure (2000): US $ per head (PPP) . . .	86
Health expenditure (2000): % of GDP	3.7
Health expenditure (2000): public (% of total) . . .	77.5
Access to water (% of persons, 2000)	85
Access to sanitation (% of persons, 2000)	100
Human Development Index (2000): ranking	95
Human Development Index (2000): value	0.727

For sources and definitions, see explanatory note on p. vi.

Agriculture

PRINCIPAL CROPS

('000 metric tons)

	1999	2000	2001
Wheat	3,601.8	3,521.7	3,786.0
Rice (paddy)	420.8	154.8	81.6
Barley*	84.5	80.0	58
Maize	167.9	131.4	100.0*
Sorghum*	21	20	15
Potatoes	657.8	731.1	735.5
Sugar beet	225	215*	104*
Dry broad beans*	16	14	12
Cottonseed	3,600	3,002	3,275
Other oilseeds†	22.1	41.6	35.5
Cabbages*	900	878	921
Tomatoes*	1,020	994	1,040
Cucumbers and gherkins* . .	278	271	284
Dry onions*	151	146	154
Garlic*	27	25	26
Carrots*	35	34	40
Other vegetables* . . .	270	299	313
Apples*	342	549	555
Pears*	13.9	22.3	22.6
Apricots*	11	17	18
Peaches and nectarines* . .	29.0	47.0	47.5
Plums*	62	99.5	101.0
Grapes	344.0	624.2	573.8
Watermelons‡	517.6	451.4	459.9
Other fruits and berries* . .	19	32	33
Tobacco (leaves)*	19	19	19
Jute†	21	20	21
Cotton (lint)	1,021	1,000*	1,015

* Unofficial figure(s).
† FAO estimates.
‡ Including melons, pumpkins and squash.

Source: FAO.

LIVESTOCK

('000 head at 1 January)

	1999	2000	2001
Horses*	155	155	150
Asses*	165	160	165
Cattle	5,225	5,268	5,344
Camels*	28	25	28
Pigs	80	80	89
Sheep†	7,840	8,000	8,100
Goats†	884	886	830
Chickens	13,935	14,407	14,420
Turkeys*	400	380	380
Rabbits*	90,000	80,000	90,000

* FAO estimates.
† Unofficial figure(s).

Source: FAO.

LIVESTOCK PRODUCTS

('000 metric tons)

	1999	2000	2001
Beef and veal*	372	390	398
Mutton, lamb and goat meat* . .	73.0	79.4	81.0
Pig meat*	19.8	14.6	14.7
Poultry meat*	16.3	16.1	16.4
Other meat†	1.4	1.9	1.9
Cows' milk	3,543	3,633	3,667
Sheep's milk*	20	24	24
Goats' milk*	63	66	63
Cheese†	16.1	17.1	16.8
Butter	3.0†	2.2	3.0†
Hen eggs*	68.1	68.9	72.1
Other poultry eggs* . . .	1.5	1.5	1.7
Honey†	2.4	2.3	2.4
Raw silk (incl. waste) . . .	0.9*	1.0†	1.2†
Wool: greasy	15.7	15.8	15.9
Wool: scoured	9.4	9.5	9.5
Cattle hides (fresh)	40.9	43.1	43.9
Sheepskins (fresh)	8.8	9.1	9.3

* Unofficial figure(s).
† FAO estimate(s).

Source: FAO.

Fishing

(metric tons, live weight)

	1998	1999	2000
Capture	2,799	2,871	3,387
Freshwater bream	387	353	335
Common carp	804	826	617
Goldfish	300	300	400
Roach	392	613	1,035
Silver carp	249	322	586
Aquaculture	6,966	5,665	5,142
Common carp	858	674	592
Silver carp	3,570	2,899	2,576
Bighead carp	2,381	1,933	1,717
Total catch	9,765	8,536	8,529

Source: FAO, *Yearbook of Fishery Statistics*.

Mining

(metric tons, unless otherwise indicated)

	1998	1999	2000*
Coal ('000 metric tons)† . . .	2,950	3,033	2,556
Crude petroleum ('000 metric tons)‡	8,100	8,100	7,500
Natural gas (million cu metres) .	54,800	55,600	55,600
Copper ore§	n.a.	91,600	91,800
Tungsten ore§‖	200	0	0
Molybdenum ore§‖	350	350	350
Silver ore (kilograms)§ . . .	70,000‖	88,700	89,900
Uranium ore§	2,000	2,159	2,054
Gold (kilograms)§	80,000	66,028	62,276
Kaolin ('000 metic tons)‖ . .	5,500	5,500	5,333
Fluorspar	80,000‖	0	0
Feldspar	n.a.	300	4,300

* Preliminary figures.
† Including lignite and brown coal.
‡ Including gas condensate.
§ Figures refer to the metal content of ores.
‖ Estimated production.

Source: mainly US Geological Survey.

Gold (metric tons): 85.4 in 2001 (Source: Gold Fields Mineral Services, *Gold Survey 2002*).

Industry

SELECTED PRODUCTS
('000 metric tons, unless otherwise indicated)

	1995	1996	1997
Ethyl alcohol ('000 hectolitres) . .	181	247	357
Wine ('000 hectolitres)	801	848	794
Beer ('000 hectolitres)	724	677	619
Cigarettes (million)	2,742	5,172	8,521
Wool yarn (pure and mixed) . .	3.3	2.7	2.3
Cotton yarn (pure and mixed) . .	103.2	105.2	114.3
Woven cotton fabrics (million sq m)	456	445	425
Woven silk fabrics ('000 sq m) . .	43,980	28,144	16,369
Woven jute fabrics ('000 sq m) . .	4,759	447	346
Knotted wool carpets and rugs ('000 sq m)	1,982	1,555	1,241
Footwear, excl. rubber ('000 pairs)	5,654	5,591	5,547
Sulphuric acid	1,016	984	870
Nitric acid	10	17	17
Phosphoric acid	149.0	179.7	113.6
Nitrogenous fertilizers (a)* . . .	775	835†	826†
Phosphate fertilizers (b)* . . .	168	194†	129†
Motor spirit (petrol)	1,213	1,202	1,344
Gas-diesel (distillate fuel) oils . .	2,105	1,861	2,035
Residual fuel oils	2,082	2,181	1,979
Lubricating oils	208	267	231
Rubber footwear ('000 pairs) . .	2,102	3,584	4,810
Clay building bricks (million) . .	1,185	1,038	969
Quicklime	241	227	185
Cement	3,419	3,277	3,286
Domestic refrigerators ('000) . .	19	13	13
Domestic washing machines ('000)	14	4	4
Television receivers ('000) . .	65	140	269
Electric energy (million kWh) . .	47,453	45,418	46,054

* Production in terms of (a) nitrogen; (b) phosphoric acid.
† Official figure.

Source: UN, *Industrial Commodity Statistics Yearbook.*

1998 ('000 metric tons, unless otherwise indicated): Footwear, excl. rubber ('000 pairs) 5,000; Phosphate fertilizers 141; Motor spirit (petrol) 1,406*; Gas-diesel (distillate fuel) oils 2,318*; Residual fuel oils 1,801*; Lubricating oils 229*; Cement 3,358; Domestic refrigerators ('000) 16; Television receivers ('000) 192; Electric energy (million kWh) 45,935.
* Provisional or estimated figure.

1999 ('000 metric tons, unless otherwise indicated): Phosphate fertilizers 147; Cement 3,331; Electric energy (million kWh) 45,372.

2000: Cement ('000 metric tons) 3,284; Electric energy (million kWh) 46,839.

2001: Cement ('000 metric tons, estimate) 3,722; Electric energy (million kWh) 47,979.

Sources (1998–2001): partly UN, *Industrial Commodity Statistics Yearbook* and Asian Development Bank, *Key Indicators of Developing Asian and Pacific Countries.*

Finance

CURRENCY AND EXCHANGE RATES

Monetary Units
100 teen = 1 sum

Sterling, Dollar and Euro Equivalents (31 December 2002)
£1 sterling = 1,454.9 sum
US $1 = 902.7 sum
€1 = 946.6 sum
10,000 sum = £6.873 = $11.078 = €10.564

Average Exchange Rate (sum per US $)
1997   66.26
1998   94.48
1999   124.64

Note: Prior to the introduction of the sum (see below), Uzbekistan used a transitional currency, the sum-coupon. This had been introduced in November 1993 to circulate alongside (and initially at par with) the Russian (formerly Soviet) rouble. Following the dissolution of the USSR in December 1991, Russia and several other former Soviet republics retained the rouble as their monetary unit. The Russian rouble ceased to be legal tender in Uzbekistan from 15 April 1994.
On 1 July 1994 a permanent currency, the sum, was introduced to replace the sum-coupon at 1 sum per 1,000 coupons. The initial exchange rate was set at US $1 = 7.00 sum. Sum-coupons continued to circulate, but from 15 October 1994 the sum became the sole legal tender.

STATE BUDGET
(million sum*)

Revenue	1997†	1998*	1999‖
Taxes on income and profits . .	109,142	138,674	186,729
Enterprise profit tax . . .	70,177	83,001	99,114
Individual income tax . . .	38,965	50,569	77,511
Taxes on domestic goods and services	132,289	216,205	306,928
Value-added tax	73,339	133,076	167,334
Excises	58,950	83,128	139,595
Property, mining and land taxes .	23,528	52,558	73,838
Customs duties and export taxes .	3,104	5,519	7,489
Total (incl. others)	293,676	440,140	611,897

Expenditure	1997†	1998†‡	1999‖
National economy	39,898	54,700	67,834
Social and cultural services . .	111,180	167,100	240,416
Education	69,267	107,484	171,376
Health and sports	31,907	44,649	53,510
Other subsidies and transfers to population	31,064	44,990	68,500
Services	6,121	15,003	19,345
Allowances	23,354	26,887	42,240
Public transfers	1,590	3,100	4,916
State authority and administration	7,951	11,000	14,457
Other purposes§	55,087	90,268	107,065
Investments	72,170	94,600	122,347
Total	317,350	472,244	633,085

* Excluding the accounts of extrabudgetary funds.
† Including the former external sector budget.
‡ Excluding net lending (million sum): 16,052 in 1998.
§ Including defence, public order and safety.
‖ IMF estimates.

MONEY SUPPLY
(million sum at 31 December)

	1997	1998	1999
Currency outside banks	71,639	101,709	137,306
Demand deposits at deposit money banks	53,728	65,698	91,009
Total money	125,367	167,407	228,315

Source: Asian Development Bank, *Key Indicators of Developing Asian and Pacific Countries.*

COST OF LIVING
(Consumer Price Index; base: December 1994 = 100)

	1998	1999	2000
Food	492.5	619.0	737.4
Other goods	372.6	493.2	667.1
Services	1,124.2	1,615.3	2,382.1
All items	508.3	655.9	819.6

Source: *Uzbek Economic Trends.*

NATIONAL ACCOUNTS
(million sum at current prices)

Expenditure on the Gross Domestic Product

	1998	1999	2000
Government final consumption expenditure	303,604.5	460,089.5	656,230.1
Private final consumption expenditure	831,104.7	1,301,277.5	2,008,769.3
Increase in stocks	−123,315.8	−214,509.2	−291,424.1
Gross fixed capital formation . .	421,083.5	578,685.4	797,785.8
Total domestic expenditure	1,430,476.9	2,125,543.2	3,171,361.1
Exports of goods and services *Less* Imports of goods and services	−14,319.6	3,116.5	23,143.1
GDP in purchasers' values	1,416,157.3	2,128,659.7	3,194,504.2

Source: *Uzbek Economic Trends.*

Gross Domestic Product by Economic Activity

	1999	2000	2001
Agriculture and forestry . . .	617,746	978,507	1,471,675
Industry*	304,744	462,423	690,014
Construction	143,298	196,180	286,646
Trade	192,348	315,556	492,001
Transport and communications	147,187	250,565	379,542
Other services	437,511	644,694	945,928
GDP at factor cost . . .	1,842,834	2,847,925	4,265,805
Indirect taxes . . . . }	285,826	407,641	602,608
Less Subsidies			
GDP in purchasers' values .	2,128,660	3,255,567	4,868,413

* Comprising manufacturing (except printing and publishing), mining and quarrying, electricity, gas, water, logging and fishing.

Source: Asian Development Bank, *Key Indicators of Developing Asian and Pacific Countries*.

BALANCE OF PAYMENTS
(US $ million)

	1996	1997	1998
Exports of goods f.o.b. . . .	3,534	3,695	2,888
Imports of goods f.o.b. . . .	−4,240	−3,767	−2,717
Trade balance	−706	−72	171
Services and other income (net) .	−272	−540	−252
Balance on goods, services and income .	−978	−612	−81
Current transfers (net) . . .	−2	29	43
Current balance	−980	−584	−39
Direct investment (net) . . .	90	167	176
Other capital (net)	80	−507	−802
Net errors and omissions . .	296	−185	—
Overall balance	−50	−480	1

External Trade

PRINCIPAL COMMODITIES
(US $ million)

Imports f.o.b.	1998	1999	2000
Chemicals and plastics . . .	407.2	363.0	399.5
Metals	303.6	245.4	253.5
Machinery and equipment . .	1,553.7	1,393.5	1,044.1
Food products.	512.2	408.1	361.1
Energy products	16.3	66.6	112.7
Total (incl. others)	3,288.7	3,110.7	2,696.4

Exports f.o.b.	1998	1999	2000
Cotton fibre	1,361.0	883.7	897.1
Chemicals and plastics . . .	51.7	101.8	93.4
Metals	180.7	138.9	216.7
Machinery and equipment . .	146.6	103.2	111.8
Food products.	111.9	206.7	176.4
Energy products	277.8	371.5	335.2
Total (incl. others)	3,528.2	3,235.8	3,264.7

Source: *Uzbek Economic Trends*.

PRINCIPAL TRADING PARTNERS
(US $ million)

Imports f.o.b.	1998	1999	2000
France	156.1	72.9	84.6
Germany	272.2	332.1	255.5
Kazakhstan	162.6	126.3	215.6
Korea, Republic	375.0	404.4	287.5
Russia	527.2	432.1	464.8
Turkey.	198.0	148.0	97.1
Ukraine	148.8	130.4	178.4
United Kingdom	133.1	94.2	58.9
USA	298.2	237.0	256.5
Total (incl. others)	3,288.7	3,110.7	2,947.1

Exports f.o.b.	1998	1999	2000
Belgium	149.4	82.0	36.8
Iran	31.2	40.1	72.2
Italy	117.6	45.4	70.9
Kazakhstan	122.0	148.7	100.8
Korea, Republic	258.7	122.4	106.4
Netherlands	61.2	98.1	84.6
Russia	526.2	432.7	545.5
Switzerland	362.5	307.7	272.3
Turkey.	45.3	66.1	99.3
Ukraine	33.3	122.4	153.5
United Kingdom	353.1	310.6	236.1
Total (incl. others)	3,528.2	3,235.9	3,264.7

Source: *Uzbek Economic Trends*.

Transport

CIVIL AVIATION
(estimated traffic on scheduled services)

	1997	1998	1999
Kilometres flown (million) . . .	23	33	37
Passengers carried ('000) . . .	1,566	1,401	1,658
Passenger-km (million) . . .	3,460	2,609	3,328
Total ton-km (million) . . .	321	284	370

Source: UN, *Statistical Yearbook*.

Tourism

FOREIGN VISITOR ARRIVALS
('000, incl. excursionists)

	1996	1997	1998
Total	174	253	272

Tourism receipts (US $ million): 15 in 1996; 19 in 1997; 21 in 1998.

Source: World Tourism Organization.

Communications Media

	1999	2000	2001
Television receivers ('000 in use)	6,700	6,800	n.a.
Telephones ('000 main lines in use)	1,599.4	1,655	1,663.0
Facsimile machines (number in use)	2,245	2,720	n.a.
Mobile cellular telephones ('000 subscribers)	40.4	53.1	62.8
Internet users ('000)	7.5	120.0	150.0

Source: International Telecommunication Union.

Book production (1,003 titles and 30,914,000 copies in 1996): (Source: UNESCO, *Statistical Yearbook*).

Daily newspapers: 3 titles and 75,000 copies (average circulation) in 1996 (Source: UNESCO, *Statistical Yearbook*).

Non-daily newspapers: 350 titles and 1,404,000 copies (average circulation) in 1996 (Source: UNESCO, *Statistical Yearbook*).

Other periodicals: 81 titles and 684,000 copies (average circulation) in 1996 (Source: UNESCO, *Statistical Yearbook*).

Radio receivers ('000 in use): 10,800 in 1997 (Source: UNESCO, *Statistical Yearbook*).

Education

(1994/95, unless otherwise indicated)

	Institutions	Teachers	Students
Pre-primary	n.a.	96,100	1,071,400
Primary	} 9,726	92,400	1,905,693
Secondary:			
general		454,200*	6,037,400*
teacher training	n.a.	2,464†	35,411†
vocational	440‡	7,900	214,500
Higher	61	18,400	183,600

* 2000.

† 1993.

‡ 1992/93.

Sources: UNESCO, *Statistical Yearbook*; and *Uzbek Economic Trends*.

Adult literacy rate (UNESCO estimates): 99.2% (males 99.6%; females 98.8%) in 2000 (Source: UN Development Programme, *Human Development Report*).

Directory

The Constitution

A new Constitution was adopted by the Supreme Soviet on 8 December 1992. It declares Uzbekistan to be a secular, democratic and presidential republic. Basic human rights are guaranteed.

The highest legislative body is the Oly Majlis (Supreme Assembly), comprising 250 deputies. It is elected for a term of five years. Parliament may be dissolved by the President (by agreement with the Constitutional Court). The Oly Majlis enacts normal legislation and constitutional legislation, elects its own officials, the judges of the higher courts and the Chairman of the State Committee for Environmental Protection. It confirms the President's appointments to ministerial office, the procuracy-general and the governorship of the Central Bank. It must ratify international treaties, changes to borders and presidential decrees on emergency situations. Legislation may be initiated by the deputies, by the President, by the higher courts, by the Procurator-General and by the Autonomous Republic of Karakalpakstan.

The President of the Republic, who is directly elected by the people for a five-year term, is Head of State and holds supreme executive power. An individual may be elected President for a maximum of two consecutive terms. The President is required to form and supervise the Cabinet of Ministers, appointing the Prime Minister and Ministers, subject to confirmation by the Oly Majlis. The President also nominates the candidates for appointment to the higher courts and certain offices of state, subject to confirmation by the Oly Majlis. The President appoints the judges of the lower courts and the khokims (governors) of the regions. Legislation may be initiated, reviewed and returned to the Oly Majlis by the President, who must promulgate all laws. The President may dissolve the Oly Majlis. The President is also Commander-in-Chief of the Armed Forces and may declare a state of emergency or a state of war (subject to confirmation by the Oly Majlis within three days).

The Cabinet of Ministers is the Government of the republic; it is subordinate to the President, who appoints its Prime Minister, Deputy Prime Ministers and Ministers, subject to the approval of the legislature. Local government is carried out by elected councils and appointed khokims, the latter having significant personal authority and responsibility.

The exercise of judicial power is independent of government. The higher courts, of which the judges are nominated by the President and confirmed by the Oly Majlis, consist of the Constitutional Court, the Supreme Court and the High Economic Court. There is also a Supreme Court of the Autonomous Republic of Karakalpakstan. Lower courts, including economic courts, are based in the regions, districts and towns. The Procurator-General's office is responsible for supervising the observance of the law.

Note: In accordance with the outcome of a referendum held in January 2002, in April the Oly Majlis approved a resolution to extend immediately the presidential term of office from five years to seven, and adopted a resolution stipulating the procedure for the election in December 2004 of a new, bicameral legislature. It was agreed that the lower legislative chamber would consist of elected deputies; the upper chamber would comprise members of local councils and 16 'widely respected' citizens. Further constitutional amendments were adopted in April 2003.

The Government

HEAD OF STATE

President of the Republic: ISLAM A. KARIMOV (elected 24 March 1990; re-elected, by direct popular vote, 29 December 1991; term of office extended to 2000, by popular referendum, 27 March 1995; re-elected, by direct popular vote, 9 January 2000).

CABINET OF MINISTERS
(April 2003)

Prime Minister: OTKIR S. SULTANOV.

First Deputy Prime Minister: KOZIM N. TULYAGANOV.

Deputy Prime Minister and Minister of Economics: RUSTAM S. AZIMOV.

Deputy Prime Minister and Minister of Agriculture and Water Resources: NOSIRJON S. YUSUPOV.

Deputy Prime Minister and Minister of Energy and Electrification: VALERII Y. OTAYEV.

Deputy Prime Minister and Chairman of the State Committee for Women's Affairs: DILBAR GHULOMOVA.

Deputy Prime Minister and Chairman of the Agency for Foreign Economic Relations at the Cabinet of Ministers: ELYOR GANIYEV.

Deputy Prime Ministers: ANATOLII N. ISAYEV, KHAMIDULLO S. KARAMATOV, MIRABROR Z. USMONOV.

Minister of Defence: Maj.-Gen. KHODIR GUFUROVICH GULOMOV.

Minister of Foreign Affairs: SODYK SAFAYEV.

Minister of Justice: ABDUSAMAD A. POLVONZODA.

Minister of Labour and Social Security: OKILJON OBIDOV.

Minister of Internal Affairs: ZOKIRJON A. ALMATOV.

Minister of Finance: MAMARIZO B. NORMURODOV.

Minister of Culture: BAHROM KURBANOV.

Minister of Higher Education and Specialized Secondary Education: Dr SAIDAHROR GULYAMOV.

Minister of Health: FERUZ G. NAZIROV.

Minister for Emergency Situations: BAKHTIYOR SUBANOV.

Minister of Education: RISBOY HAYDAROVICH JORAYEV.

Minister of Utilities: GAFUR MUKHAMEDOV.

MINISTRIES

Office of the President: 700163 Tashkent, pr. Uzbekistanskii 43; tel. (71) 139-54-04; fax (71) 139-53-25; e-mail presidents_office@press-service.uz; internet www.press-service.uz.

Office of the Cabinet of Ministers: 700008 Tashkent, Government House; tel. (71) 139-82-95; fax (71) 139-86-01.

Ministry of Agriculture and Water Resources: 700128 Tashkent, ul. Abdulla Qodyri 5A; tel. (712) 41-46-60; fax (712) 41-49-24.

Ministry of Communication: Tashkent.

Ministry of Culture: 700129 Tashkent, ul. Navoi 30; tel. (71) 139-49-57.

Ministry of Defence: 700000 Tashkent, ul. Academician Abdullayev 100; tel. (71) 133-66-67; fax (712) 68-48-67.

Ministry of Economics: 700066 Tashkent, ul. Uzbekistanskii 45A; tel. (712) 45-82-37; fax (71) 139-86-39; internet www.gov.uz/government/minmacro/index.html.

Ministry of Education: 700078 Tashkent, pl. Mustakillik 5; tel. (71) 139-42-14; fax (71) 139-11-73.

Ministry for Emergency Situations: Tashkent.

Ministry of Finance: 700008 Tashkent, pl. Mustakillik 5; tel. (71) 139-19-43; fax (71) 144-56-43.

Ministry of Foreign Affairs: 700029 Tashkent, pr. Uzbekistanskii 9; tel. (71) 133-64-75; fax (71) 139-15-17; e-mail root@relay.tiv.uz; internet www.tiv.uz.

Ministry of Health: 700000 Tashkent, ul. Navoi 12; tel. (71) 144-10-40; fax (712) 41-16-41.

Ministry of Higher and Specialized Secondary Education: 700078 Tashkent, Mustakillik maidony 5; tel. (71) 139-15-00; fax (71) 139-12-71.

Ministry of Internal Affairs: 700029 Tashkent, ul. Yunus Rajaby 1; tel. (71) 133-63-77; fax (71) 133-89-34.

Ministry of Justice: 700047 Tashkent, ul. Sailgokh 5; tel. (71) 133-13-05; fax (71) 133-50-39; e-mail adliya@mail.uznet.net; internet www.minjust.uz.

Ministry of Labour and Social Security: 700100 Tashkent, ul. Abdulla Avloni 20A; tel. (71) 139-41-24; fax (71) 139-41-56.

Principal State Committees

National Information Agency: 700000 Tashkent, ul. Khamza 38; tel. (71) 133-16-22; fax (71) 133-24-45; Dir MAMATSKUL KHAZRATSKULOV.

National Security Service: Tashkent; tel. (712) 33-56-48; Chair. Col-Gen. RUSTAM INOYATOV.

Uzbek Association of Utilities Services: Tashkent; Chair. UKTUR KHOLMUKHAMEDOV.

State Committee for Architecture and Engineering: 700011 Tashkent, Abay 6; tel. (71) 144-07-00; fax (71) 144-02-61; e-mail gkas@uzpak.uz; internet www.uzgkas.com; f. 1959; Chair. AZAMAT R. TOHTAYEV.

State Committee for Border Protection: Tashkent; Chair. GOFURJON TISHAYEV.

State Committee for Forecasting and Statistics: 700003 Tashkent, pr. Uzbekistanskii 45A; tel. (712) 39-82-16; fax (712) 39-86-39; Chair. RIM A. GINIYATULLIN.

State Committee for Geology and Mineral Resources: 700060 Tashkent, ul. Shevchenko 11; tel. (71) 133-46-03; fax (71) 133-18-01; e-mail gicenter@online.ru; f. 1926; Chair. NURMUKHAMMAD AKHMEDOV.

State Committee for State Property Management and Entrepreneurship Support: 700003 Tashkent, ul. Uzbekistanskii 55; tel. (71) 139-44-46; fax (71) 139-14-84; e-mail askarov@spc.gov.uz; internet www.spc.gov.uz; f. 1994; Chair. UKTAM K. ISMOILOV; First Dep. Chair. MAKHMUDJON A. ASKAROV.

State Committee for Nature Protection: 700128 Tashkent, ul. A. Kadiry 7; tel. (712) 41-04-42; fax (712) 41-39-90; e-mail uznature@gimli.com; Chair. ASKHAT SH. KHABIBULLAYEV.

State Committee for Precious Metals: 700019 Tashkent, pr. Turakorgan 26; tel. (712) 48-07-20; fax (712) 44-26-03; Chair. SH. NAZHIMOV.

State Committee for Science and Technology: 700017 Tashkent, Hadicha Suleymonova 29; tel. (71) 139-18-43; fax (71) 139-12-43; Chair. POLAT K. HABIBULLAYEV.

State Committee for Women's Affairs: Tashkent; Chair. DILBAR GHULOMOVA.

State Customs Committee: 700100 Tashkent, ul. Usmon Nasir 62; tel. (71) 136-07-55; fax (712) 53-39-40; Chair. BOTIR PARPIYEV.

State Sports Committee: Tashkent; Chair. BOKHODIR MAKHSITOV.

State Statistics Committee: Tashkent; Chair GHOFURJON QUDRATOV.

State Taxation Committee: 700195 Tashkent, ul. Abai 4; tel. (712) 41-78-70; Chair. JAMSHID SAYFIDDINOV.

Legislature

OLY MAJLIS
(Supreme Assembly)

Supreme Assembly

700008 Tashkent, pl. Mustakillik 5; tel. (71) 139-87-49; fax (71) 139-41-51; internet www.gov.uz/oliy.

Chairman: ERKIN KH. KHALILOV.

Deputy Chairmen: UBBINIYAZ ASHIRBEKOV, BORIS BUGROV, BORITOSH SHODIYEVA, AKMOLZHON KHOSIMOV, MUSA T. ERNIYAZOV.

General Election, 5 December and 19 December 1999*

Parties, etc.	Seats
People's Democratic Party of Uzbekistan (PDPU) . .	48
Fidokorlar National Democratic Party	34
Progress of the Fatherland	20
Adolat Social Democratic Party of Uzbekistan . . .	11
Milli Tiklanish Democratic Party	10
Citizens' groups	16
Local council nominees†	110
Vacant	1
Total	**250**

* Five parties were permitted to contest the election; however, two opposition parties (Birlik and Erk) were refused permission to put forward candidates.

† The overwhelming majority of local council nominees were members of the PDPU.

Political Organizations

Following Uzbekistan's independence (achieved in August 1991), the ruling People's Democratic Party of Uzbekistan (PDPU) took increasingly repressive measures against opposition and Islamist parties; all religious political parties were banned in 1991, and in 1992 and 1993 the leading opposition groups, Birlik and Erk, were likewise outlawed. In October 1995 several opposition groups, including Birlik, Erk and Adolat, established a joint centre in Tashkent—the Democratic Opposition Co-ordinating Council—in united opposition to the Government (the Council ceased to function in March 1998). A new law on political parties was approved in 1996; among other provisions, the law prohibited the establishment of parties on a religious or ethnic basis and stipulated a minimum membership, per party, of 5,000 people (representing at least eight of the republic's 12 regions). Since independence a number of opposition elements have been based in Russia, in particular in Moscow.

Adolat (Justice) Social Democratic Party of Uzbekistan: Tashkent; f. 1995; advocates respect of human rights, improvement of social justice and consolidation of democratic reform; First Sec. ANWAR JURABAYEV; 6,000 mems.

Birlik (Unity): c/o Union of Writers of Uzbekistan, 700000 Tashkent, ul. Javakharlara Neru 1; tel. (712) 33-63-74; e-mail webmaster@birlik.net; internet www.birlik.net; f. 1988; leading opposition group, banned in 1992; registered as a social movement; Chair. Prof. ABDURAKHIM PULATOV.

Erk (Freedom): Tashkent; f. 1990; banned in 1993; Chair. MUHAMMAD SOLIKH (based in Russia); Sec.-Gen. OTANAZAR ORIPOV; 5,000 mems (1991).

Fidokorlar (Self-Sacrificers') National Democratic Party: Tashkent; f. 1998; merged with Watan Taraqqioti (Progress of the Fatherland) in Apr. 2000; pro-Government; First Sec. AHTAM TURSUNOV; 30,000 mems.

Ishtiqlal Yoli (Independence Path): Tashkent; f. 1994; Leader SHADI KARIMOV.

Islamic Renaissance Party: Tashkent; banned in 1991; advocates introduction of a political system based on the tenets of Islam; Leader ABDULLAH UTAYEV.

Khalk Birliki (People's Unity) Movement: Tashkent; f. 1995; pro-Government; Chair. TURABEK DOLIMOV.

Milli Tiklanish (National Revival) Democratic Party: Tashkent; f. 1995; pro-Government; Chair. AZIZ KAYUMOV.

People's Democratic Party of Uzbekistan: 700029 Tashkent, pl. Mustakillik 5/1; tel. (71) 139-83-11; fax (71) 133-59-34; f. 1991; successor of Communist Party of Uzbekistan; Leader ABDULKHAFIZ JALOLOV; c. 570,000 mems (Jan. 2002).

Diplomatic Representation

EMBASSIES IN UZBEKISTAN

Afghanistan: Tashkent, ul. Gogolya 73; tel. (712) 33-91-76.

Algeria: Tashkent, ul. Murtozayeva 6; Ambassador LASKRI KHASEN.

Bangladesh: Tashkent; Ambassador A. B. M. ABDUS SALAM.

Belarus: 700031 Tashkent, ul. Vakhidova 53; tel. (71) 120-72-52; fax (712) 120-72-53; Ambassador Dr NIKOLAI N. DEMCHUK.

China, People's Republic: 700047 Tashkent, ul. Yahyo Gulomoy 79; tel. (71) 136–08–51; fax (71) 133-47-35; e-mail chinaemb@bcc .com.uz; internet www.chinaembassy.uz; Ambassador ZHANG ZHIMING.

Egypt: Tashkent, ul. Chilanzarskaya 53; Ambassador JAMIL FAYID SAID IBRAHIM.

France: Tashkent, ul. Akhunbabayeva 25; Ambassador JACQUES-ANDRÉ COSTILHES.

Germany: 700017 Tashkent, pr. Sharaf-Rashidov 15; tel. (71) 120-84-40; fax (71) 120-66-93; e-mail gerembuz@online.ru; internet www .germanembassy.uz; Ambassador MARTIN HECKER.

India: Tashkent, ul. A. Tolstogo 3; tel. (712) 33-82-67; fax (712) 36-19-76; Ambassador M. K. BHADRAKUMAR.

Indonesia: Tashkent, ul. Murtozayeva 6; tel. (712) 34-23-60; fax (712) 89-15-40.

Iran: Tashkent, ul. Parkentskaya 20; tel. (712) 68-69-68; Ambassador HOSSEIN NARAGHIAN.

Israel: Tashkent, ul. Abdulla Kakhara 3; tel. (71) 120-58-08; fax (71) 120-58-12; e-mail isremb@online.ru; Ambassador ZVI COHEN LITANT.

Italy: 700031 Tashkent, ul. Yusuf Xos Xojib 40; tel. (71) 152-11-19; fax (71) 120-66-06; e-mail ambital@online.ru; Ambassador LEOPOLDO FERRI DE LAZARA.

Japan: 700047 Tashkent, ul. Sadyk/Azimov 52/1; tel. (712) 33-51-42; fax (712) 89-15-14; Ambassador KIOKO NAKAYAMA.

Kazakhstan: 700015 Tashkent, ul. Chekhov 23; tel. (71) 152-16-54; fax (71) 152-16-50; e-mail kzembuz@silk.org.

Korea, Democratic People's Republic: Tashkent; Ambassador KIM THAE SAM.

Korea, Republic: Tashkent, ul. Afrosiab 7; tel. (71) 152-31-51; fax (71) 120-62-48; Ambassador CHOI YOUNG-HA.

Kyrgyzstan: Tashkent, ul. Samatova 30; tel. and fax (712) 33-08-93; e-mail krembas@globalnet.uz.

Latvia: Tashkent, ul. Murtazayeva 6, Apt 115–17; tel. (712) 234-92-13; fax (71) 120-70-36; e-mail amblatv@bcc.com.uz; Ambassador IGORS APOKINS.

Lithuania: Tashkent; Ambassador KHALINA KOBETSKAITE.

Malaysia: Tashkent; Ambassador MOHAMAD REDZUAN MOHAMMAD.

Moldova: Tashkent; Ambassador EFIM KILAR.

Pakistan: 700115 Tashkent, ul. Abdurakhmonov 15; tel. (712) 48-25-60; fax (71) 144-79-43; e-mail parepuzb@online.ru; Ambassador MOHAMMAD AKHTAR TUFAIL.

Poland: 700084 Tashkent, ul. Firdavsiy 66; tel. (71) 120-86-50; fax (71) 120-86-51; e-mail zkuchciak@bcc.com.uz; Ambassador ZENON KUCHCIAK.

Russia: 700015 Tashkent, ul. Nukusskaya 83; tel. (71) 152-62-80; fax (71) 152-21-43; e-mail rusemb@albatros.uz; Ambassador DMITRII B. RYURIKOV.

Sri Lanka: Tashkent; Ambassador NAGURPITCHAI SIKKANDER.

Switzerland: Tashkent, ul. Usmon Nosyr, Tupik 1/4; tel. (71) 120-67-38; e-mail vertretung@tas.rep.admin.ch; Ambassador WILHELM MEIER.

Turkey: Tashkent, ul. Gogolya 87; tel. (712) 33-21-07; fax (712) 33-13-58; Ambassador ERDOGAN AYTUN.

Turkmenistan: Tashkent; Ambassador SOLTAN PIRMUHAMEDOV.

Ukraine: 700000 Tashkent, ul. Gogolya 68; tel. and fax (71) 136-08-12; e-mail emb_uz@mfa.gov.ua; Ambassador ANATOLIY KASIANENKO.

United Kingdom: 700000 Tashkent, ul. Gulyamova 67; tel. (71) 120-62-88; fax (71) 120-65-49; e-mail brit@emb.uz; internet www .britain.uz; Ambassador CRAIG MURRAY.

USA: 700115 Tashkent, ul. Chilanzarskaya 82; tel. (71) 120-54-50; fax (71) 120-63-35; e-mail consul_tashkent@yahoo.com; internet www.usis.uz; Ambassador (vacant).

Viet Nam: Tashkent, ul. Rashidova 100; tel. (712) 34-45-36; fax (71) 120-62-65; e-mail dsqvntas@online.ru; Ambassador NGUYEN QUOC BAO.

Judicial System

Chairman of the Supreme Court: FARUHA FAHRUDDINOVA MUHIDDINOVA (desig.).

Judges of the Supreme Court: KH. B. YODGOROV, N. S. NORMURODOV, H. B. KHOLMIRZAYEV, O. KH. KHOLIQOV, VOKHID NAZAROV, DILBAR SUYUNOVA, DILMIR KHALILOV, BAKHTIYOR DJAMALOV, SOBIR SALIKHOVICH.

Procurator-General: RASHIDJON QODIROV.

Chairman of the Constitutional Court: BURITOSH MUSTAFAYEV.

Chairman of the Higher Economic Court: MIRZOULUGHBEK ABDUSALOMOV.

Religion

The Constitution of 8 December 1992 stipulates that, while there is freedom of worship and expression, there may be no state religion or ideology. A new law on religion was adopted in May 1998, which severely restricted the activities of religious organizations. The Government stated that the legislation was designed to curb the recent increase in militant Islamist activity (including terrorism) in Uzbekistan.

The most widespread religion in Uzbekistan is Islam; the majority of ethnic Uzbeks are Sunni Muslims (Hanafi school), but the number of Wahhabi communities is increasing. Most ethnic Slavs in Uzbekistan are adherents of Orthodox Christianity. In the early 1990s there were reported to be some 65,000 European Jews and 28,000 Central Asian Jews.

State Committee for Religious Affairs: 700028 Tashkent, pl. Mustakillik 5; tel. (71) 139-10-14; fax (71) 139-17-63; e-mail uzreligion@vodiy.com; internet www.uzreligion.vodiy.com; Chair. SHAAZIM SH. MINAVAROV.

ISLAM

Muslim Board of Central Asia: Tashkent, Zarkainar 103; tel. (712) 40-39-33; fax (712) 40-08-31; f. 1943; has spiritual jurisdiction over the Muslims in the Central Asian republics of the former USSR; Chair. ABDURASHID QORI BAKROMOV (Chief Mufti of Mowarounnahr (Central Asia)).

CHRISTIANITY

Roman Catholic Church

The Church is represented in Uzbekistan by a Mission, established in September 1997. There were an estimated 3,000 adherents at 31 December 2000.

Superior: Fr KRZYSZTOF KUKUŁKA, 700015 Tashkent, ul. Vtoraya Sapiyornaya 13; tel. and fax (712) 56-30-10; e-mail misio@silk.org.

The Press

In 1997, according to official statistics, there were 495 newspapers published in Uzbekistan, including 385 published in Uzbek. The average daily circulation was 1,844,200 copies. There were 113 periodicals published, including 90 in Uzbek. Newspapers and periodicals were also published in Russian, Kazakh, Tajik, Korean, Arabic, English and Karakalpak.

The publications listed below are in Uzbek, unless otherwise stated.

Uzbek Agency for Press and Information: 700129 Tashkent, ul. Navoi 30; tel. (71) 144-32-87; fax (71) 144-14-84; Gen. Dir RUSTAM SH. SHAGULYAMOV.

PRINCIPAL NEWSPAPERS

Adolat: Tashkent; f. 1995; organ of the Adolat (Justice) Social Democratic Party of Uzbekistan; Editor TOHTAMUROD TOSHEV; circ. 5,900.

Biznes-vestnik Vostoka (Business Bulletin of the East): 700000 Tashkent, ul. Matbuotchilar 32; tel. (71) 133-95-93; e-mail info@bvv .uz; internet www.bvv.uz; f. 1991; weekly; in Russian and Uzbek; economic and financial news; Editor VADIM SIROTIN; circ. 20,000.

Delovoy Partner: Tashkent; tel. (71) 139-17-31; internet hamkor .uzpak.uz; f. 1991; in Russian and English; Editor Ismat Hushev; circ. 20,000.

Fidokor: Tashkent; tel. (712) 34-87-74; f. 1999; weekly; organ of the Fidokorlar National Democratic Party; Editor Jaloliddin Safayev; circ. 32,000.

Golos uzbekistana: Tashkent; tel. (71) 133-11-49; f. 1918; in Russian; Editor Andrei Orlov; circ. 40,000.

Hurriyat: Tashkent; tel. (71) 144-25-06; fax (71) 144-36-16; e-mail amir@uzpac.uz; f. 1996; independent; Editor Amirkul Karimov; circ. 5,000.

Khalk suzi (People's Word): 700000 Tashkent, ul. Matbuotchilar 32; tel. (71) 133-15-22; f. 1991; 5 a week; organ of the Oly Majlis and the Cabinet of Ministers; in Uzbek and Russian; Editor Abbaskhon Usmanov; circ. 41,580 (Uzbek edn), 12,750 (Russian edn).

Kommercheskiy Vestnik: Tashkent; f. 1992; in Russian; Editor Valerii Niyazmatov; circ. 22,000.

Ma'rifat (Enlightenment): 700000 Tashkent, ul. Matbuotchilar 32; tel. (71) 133-50-55; f. 1931; 2 a week; Editor Khalim Saidov; circ. 21,500.

Menejer (Manager): 700000 Tashkent, ul. Buyuk Turon 41; tel. (71) 136-58-85; f. 1997; weekly; in Russian and Uzbek; commercial information and advertising; Editor Khotam Abduraimov; circ. 15,000.

Molodiozh Uzbekistana (Youth of Uzbekistan): 700000 Tashkent, ul. Matbuotchilar 32; tel. (71) 133-72-77; fax (71) 133-41-52; e-mail pressa@online.ru; f. 1926; weekly; in Russian; economic and social news; Editor-in-Chief Ivan N. Kasachev; circ. 6,000.

Mulkdor (Property Owner): 700000 Tashkent, pr. Uzbekistanskii 53; tel. (71) 139-21-96; f. 1994; weekly; Editor Mirodil Abdurakhmanov; circ. 21,000.

Na postu/Postda: Tashkent; f. 1930; in Russian and Uzbek; Editor Z. Atayev.

Narodnoye Slovo (People's Word): 700000 Tashkent, ul. Matbuotchilar 19; tel. (71) 133-15-22; e-mail slovo@uzpak.uz; internet hc .uzpak.uz; f. 1991; govt newspaper; weekly; in Russian and Uzbek; Editor Abbos Usmonov; circ. 50,000.

Pravda Vostoka (Truth of the East): 700000 Tashkent, ul. Matbuotchilar 32; tel. (71) 133-56-33; fax (71) 133-70-98; e-mail pvostok@mail.tps.uz; internet pravdavostoka.intal.uz; f. 1917; 5 a week; organ of the Cabinet of Ministers; in Russian; Editor Bakhtiyor Khasanov; circ. 12,000.

Savdogar: Tashkent; f. 1992; Editor Muhammad Orazmetov; circ. 17,000.

Soliqlar va Bojhona Habarlari/Nalogovie I Tamojennie Vesti: Tashkent; f. 1994; Editor Mikhail Perper; circ. 45,000.

Sport: Tashkent; f. 1932; Editor Haydar Akbarov; circ. 8,490.

Tashkentskaya Pravda (Tashkent Truth): 700000 Tashkent, ul. Matbuotchilar 32; tel. (71) 133-90-82; f. 1954; 2 a week; in Russian; Editor Fatkhiddin Mukhitdinov; circ. 6,400.

Toshkent Khakikati (Tashkent Truth): 700000 Tashkent, ul. Matbuotchilar 32; tel. (71) 133-64-95; f. 1954; 2 a week; Editor Fatkhiddin Mukhitdinov; circ. 19,000.

Turkiston (Turkestan): 700000 Tashkent, ul. Matbuotchilar 32; tel. (71) 136-56-58; f. 1925 as *Yash Leninchy* (Young Leninist), renamed as above 1992; 2 a week; organ of the Kamolot Asscn of Young People of Uzbekistan; Editor Gafar Khatomov; circ. 12,580.

Uzbekiston adabiyoti va san'ati (Literature and Art of Uzbekistan): 700000 Tashkent, ul. Matbuotchilar 32; tel. (71) 133-52-91; f. 1956; weekly; organ of the Union of Writers of Uzbekistan; Editor Akhmajon Meliboyev; circ. 10,300.

Uzbekiston ovizi (Voice of Uzbekistan): 700000 Tashkent, ul. Matbuotchilar 32; tel. (71) 133-65-45; Editor Azim Suiuk; circ. 40,000.

PRINCIPAL PERIODICALS

Monthly, unless otherwise indicated.

Fan va turmush (Science and Life): 700000 Tashkent, ul. Gulyamova 70; tel. (71) 133-07-05; f. 1933; every 2 months; publ. by the Fan (Science) Publishing House; popular scientific; Editor Murad Sharifkhojayev; circ. 28,000.

Gulistan (Flourishing Area): 700000 Tashkent, ul. Buyuk Turon 41; tel. (71) 136-78-90; f. 1925; every 2 months; socio-political; Editor Tilab Makhmudov; circ. 4,000.

Gulkhan (Bonfire): 700000 Tashkent, ul. Buyuk Turon 41; tel. (71) 136-78-85; f. 1929; illustrated juvenile fiction; Editor Safar Barnoyev; circ. 26,000.

Guncha (Small Bud): 700000 Tashkent, ul. Buyuk Turon 41; tel. (71) 136-78-80; f. 1958; illustrated; literary, for pre-school-age children; Editor Erkin Malikov; circ. 35,000.

Jakhon adabiyoti (World Literature): 700129 Tashkent, ul. Navoi 30; tel. (71) 144-41-60; f. 1997; Editor Ozod Sharafiddinov; circ. 2,000.

Mushtum (Fist): 700000 Tashkent, ul. Buyuk Turon 41; tel. (71) 133-99-72; f. 1923; fortnightly; satirical; Editor Ashurali Jurayev; circ. 10,650.

Obshchestvennye Nauki v Uzbekistane (Social Sciences in Uzbekistan): 700047 Tashkent, ul. Gulyamova 70; tel. (71) 136-73-29; f. 1957; publ. by the Fan (Science) Publishing House of the Academy of Sciences of Uzbekistan; history, oriental studies, archaeology, economics, ethnology, etc. in Russian and Uzbek; Editor A. Mukhamejanov; circ. 500.

Saodat (Happiness): 700083 Tashkent, ul. Buyuk Turon 41; tel. (71) 133-68-10; f. 1925; twice every 3 months; women's popular; Editor Oidin Khajiyeva; circ. 70,000.

Sharq yulduzi (Star of the East): 700000 Tashkent, ul. Buyuk Turon 41; tel. (71) 133-09-18; f. 1932; monthly; journal of the Union of Writers of Uzbekistan; fiction; Editor Utkur Khashimov; circ. 10,000.

Sikhat salomatlik (Health): 700000 Tashkent, ul. Parkentskaya 51; tel. (712) 68-17-54; f. 1990; every 2 months; Editor Damin Abdurakhimovich Asadov; circ. 36,000.

Tong yulduzi (Morning Star): 700129 Tashkent, ul. Navoi 30; tel. (71) 144-62-34; e-mail ijod@uzpak.uz; f. 1929; weekly; children's; Editor Umida Abduazimova; circ. 60,000.

Uzbek tili va adabiyoti (Uzbek Language and Literature): 700000 Tashkent, ul. Muminova 9; tel. (712) 62-42-47; f. 1958; every 2 months; publ. by the Fan (Science) Publishing House; journal of the Academy of Sciences of Uzbekistan; history and modern development of the Uzbek language, folklore, etc. Editor Azim Khajiyev; circ. 3,700.

Yoshlik (Youth): 700000 Tashkent, ul. Buyuk Turon 41; tel. (71) 133-09-18; f. 1932; monthly; literature and arts for young people; Editor Sabir Unarov; circ. 10,000.

Zvezda Vostoka (Star of the East): 700129 Tashkent, ul. Navoi 30; tel. (71) 144-11-49; f. 1932; monthly; journal of the Union of Writers of Uzbekistan; fiction; translations into Russian from Arabic, English, Hindi, Turkish, Japanese, etc. Editor Nikolai Krasilnikov; circ. 3,000.

NEWS AGENCY

Information Agency of the Ministry of Foreign Affairs of the Republic of Uzbekistan—'Jakhon' ('World'): 700029 Tashkent, pr. Uzbekistanskii 9; tel. (71) 133-65-91; fax (71) 120-64-43; e-mail jahon@tiv.uz; internet www.jahon.tiv.uz; Dir Abror Gulyamov.

Turkiston Press: Tashkent; tel. (71) 136-11-45; Dir-Gen. Zafar Roziyev.

UzA (Uzbek Information Agency): Tashkent, ul. Khamza 2; tel. (71) 133-16-22; fax (71) 133-24-45; Dir-Gen. Murod Muhammad.

Foreign Bureaux

Agence France-Presse (AFP): Tashkent; tel. (71) 132-02-93; e-mail galima@bcc.com.uz; Correspondent Galima Burharbayeva.

Associated Press (AP) (USA): Tashkent; tel. (71) 136-19-58; Correspondent Timofey Zhukov.

Interfax (Russia): Tashkent; tel. (71) 133-70-69; Correspondent Bakhtiyor Khasanov.

Reuters (United Kingdom): Tashkent; tel. (71) 120-73-66; e-mail shamil.baygin@reuters.co.uz; Correspondent Shamil Baygin.

Publishers

In 1997 there were approximately 1,000 book titles published in Uzbekistan, of which some 70% were in Uzbek.

Uzbek Agency for Press and Information: 700129, Tashkent, ul. Navoi 30; tel. (71) 144-32-87; fax (71) 144-14-84; f. 2002; mass media, press and information exchange; printing, publishing and distribution of periodicals; Gen. Dir Rustam Sh. Shagulyamov.

Abdulla Kadyri Publishers: 700129 Tashkent, ul. Navoi 30; tel. (71) 144-61-51; f. 1992; history, culture, literature; Dir D. I. Ikramova.

Abu Ali ibn Sino Publishers: Tashkent, ul. Navoi 30; tel. (71) 144-51-72; f. 1958; medical sciences; Dir Akmal Kamalov (acting).

Chulpon (Morning Star): 700129 Tashkent, ul. Navoi 30; tel. (71) 139-13-75; Dir N. Kholbutayev.

Fan (Science Publishing House): 700047 Tashkent, ul. Gulyamova 70, kv. 102; tel. (71) 133-69-61; scientific books and journals; Dir N. T. KHATAMOV.

Gafur Gulyam Publishers: 700129 Tashkent, ul. Navoi 30; tel. (71) 144-22-53; fax (71) 41-35-47; f. 1957; refounded in 2002; fiction, the arts; books in Uzbek, Russian and English; Dir RIKHSITILLA N. KHAKIMOV.

Izdatelstvo Literatury i Iskusstva (Literature and Art Publishing House): 700129 Tashkent, ul. Navoi 30; tel. (71) 144-51-72; f. 1926; literature, literary criticism and essays; Dir SH. Z. USMANKHOJAYEV; Editor-in-Chief H. T. TURABEKOV.

Izdatelstvo Uzbekistan (Uzbekistan Publishing House): 700129 Tashkent, ul. Navoi 30; tel. (71) 144-38-10; fax (71) 144-11-35; f. 1924; politics, economics, law, history and art; illustrated; manuals for schools and higher educational institutes; Dir SHUKHRAT YA. AKHMEDOV; Editor-in-Chief SHOMUKHITDIN SH MANSUROV.

Mekhnat (Labour): 700129 Tashkent, ul. Navoi 30; tel. (71) 144-22-27; Dir O. I. MIRZAYEV.

Sharq Publishing House: 700000 Tashkent, ul. Buyuk Turon 41; tel. (71) 133-47-86; fax (71) 133-18-58; largest publishing house; govt-owned.

Ukituvchi (Teacher): 700129 Tashkent, ul. Navoi 30; tel. (71) 144-23-86; fax (71) 144-30-94; f. 1936; literary textbooks, education manuals, scientific literature, juvenile; Dir M. IKROMOVA.

Uzbekiston millii entsiklopediyasi (Uzbekistan National Encyclopaedia): 700129 Tashkent, ul. Navoi 30; tel. (71) 144-34-38; f. 1997; encyclopedias, dictionaries and reference books; Dir N. TUKHLIYEV.

Yozuvchi (Writer): 700129 Tashkent, ul. Navoi 30; tel. (71) 144-29-97; f. 1990; Dir M. U. TOICHIYEV.

WRITERS' UNION

Union of Journalists of Uzbekistan: 700129 Tashkent, ul. Navoi 30; tel. and fax (71) 144-19-79; e-mail jorn@online.ru; Pres. LUTFULLA KABIROV.

Union of Writers of Uzbekistan: 700000 Tashkent, ul. Javakharlara Neru 1; tel. (71) 133-63-74; Chair. ABDULLA ARIPOV.

Broadcasting and Communications

TELECOMMUNICATIONS

Communications and Information Agency of Uzbekistan: 700000 Tashkent, ul. A. Tolstogo 1; tel. (71) 133-65-03; fax (71) 139-87-82; internet www.uzapt.uzpak.uz; Dir-Gen. ABDULLA ARIPOV.

Daewoo Unitel: Tashkent; country's largest provider of global mobile cellular telecommunications services.

JSC Uzbektelecom: 700000 Tashkent, ul. Amir Temur 24; tel. (71) 133-42-59; fax (71) 136-01-88; e-mail uztelecom@intal.uz; internet www.uztelecom.uz; f. 2000; comprises 14 regional and four specialized brs; provides local, regional and international telecommunications services; Gen. Dir KH. A. MUKHITDINOV.

Uzdunrobita: 700000 Tashkent, ul. Amir Temur 24; tel. (71) 130-01-01; fax (71) 130-01-05; e-mail office@uzdunrobita.com.uz; internet www.uzdunrobita.uz; f. 1991 as an Uzbek-US joint venture; provides mobile cellular telecommunications services; Gen. Dir BEKHZOD AKHMEDOV.

BROADCASTING

State Television and Radio Broadcasting Company of Uzbekistan (UZTELERADIO): 700011 Tashkent, ul. Navoi 69; tel. (71) 133-81-06; fax (71) 144-16-60; e-mail uztrcint@tkt.uz; internet www.teleradio.uz; local broadcasts, as well as relays from Egypt, France, India, Japan, Russia and Turkey; Dir-Gen. ABUSAID KUCHIMOV.

Radio

Uzbek Radio: 700047 Tashkent, ul. Khorezmskaya 49; tel. (71) 133-89-20; fax (71) 133-60-68; e-mail uzradio@eanetways.com; f. 1947; broadcasts in Uzbek, Russian, English, Urdu, Hindi, Farsi, Dari, Pushtu, Turkish, Tajik, Kazakh, Crimean Tatar, German, Arabic, Chinese and Uigur; Dir BARNO RAJABOV.

Television

Uzbek Television: 700011 Tashkent, ul. Navoi 69; tel. (71) 133-81-06; fax (712) 41-39-81; e-mail uzteee@uzpak.uz; four local programmes as well as relays from Russia, Kazakhstan, Egypt, India and Turkey; Chair. ABUSAID KUCHIMOV.

Kamalak Television: 700084 Tashkent, ul. Amir Temur 109; tel. (71) 137-51-77; fax (71) 120-62-28; e-mail kam.tv@kamalak.co.uz; f. 1992; joint venture between State Television and Radio Broadcasting Company and a US company; satellite broadcasts; relays from France, Germany, India, Russia, the United Kingdom and the USA; Gen. Dir PULAT UMAROV.

Finance

(cap. = capital; res = reserves; dep. = deposits; m. = million; amounts in Uzbek sum, unless otherwise stated; brs = branches)

BANKING

A reform of the banking sector was begun in 1994. A two-tier system was introduced, consisting of the Central Bank and about 30 commercial banks. An association of commercial banks was established in 1995 to co-ordinate the role of commercial banks in the national economy. In October 2001 there were reported to be 38 commercial banks, of which 16 were under private ownership.

Central Bank

Central Bank of the Republic of Uzbekistan: 700001 Tashkent, pr. Uzbekistanskii 6; tel. (71) 133-68-29; fax (71) 140-65-58; e-mail turgun@cbu.gov.uz; internet www.gov.uz/government/cbu/cbu_0e .htm; f. 1991; Chair. of Bd FAIZULLA M. MULLAJONOV; Vice-Chair. MAMARIZO B. NURMURODOV.

State Commercial Banks

Asaka—Specialized State Joint-Stock Commercial Bank: 700015 Tashkent, ul. Nukus 67; tel. (71) 120-81-11; fax (712) 54-06-59; e-mail contact@asakabank.com; internet www.asakabank.com; f. 1995; cap. US $150m., res $4.7m., dep. $99.6m. (Dec. 2001); Chair. SAIDOKHMAD B. RAKHIMOV; 22 brs.

National Bank for Foreign Economic Activity of the Republic of Uzbekistan: 700194 Tashkent, ul. Amir Temur 101; tel. (71) 137-59-70; fax (71) 133-32-00; e-mail webmaster@central.nbu.com; internet www.nbu.com; f. 1991; cap. US $364m., res $20m., dep. $1,746m. (Dec. 2000); due to be privatized; Chair. ZAINIDDIN S. MIRKHOJAYEV; 99 brs.

State Joint-Stock Commercial Banks

Halk Bank (State Commercial People's Bank of the Republic of Uzbekistan): 700096 Tashkent, Katortol 46; tel. (71) 278-59-44; fax (71) 173-69-13; e-mail farhod_azizov@yahoo.com; internet www .halkbank.uz; f. 1995; fmrly Savings Bank of Uzbekistan; cap. 5,720m., res 519.9m., dep. 43,900m. (Jan. 2003); Chair. ADHAM HAYDAROV; 2,849 brs.

Uzbek State Joint-Stock Housing Savings Bank: 700000 Tashkent, ul. Pushkina 17; tel. (71) 133-29-57; fax (71) 133-30-89; Chair. TIMUR S. AZIMOV.

Zaminbank: 700015 Tashkent, ul. Rzhevskaya 3; tel. (712) 55-82-59; fax (712) 55-77-49; e-mail zamin@albatros.uz; internet www .zaminbank.uz; f. 1995; Chair. of Bd ODLI O. MAVLANOV.

Other Joint-Stock Commercial Banks

Alokabank: 700000 Tashkent, ul. A. Tolstogo 1; tel. (71) 133-62-54; fax (71) 136-36-22; e-mail alokauz@uzpak.uz; f. 1995; cap. 2,500m., res 429m., dep. 10,182m. (2002); Chair. FAKHRIDDIN T. YULDASHEV; 9 brs.

Avia Bank: 700015 Tashkent, ul. Nukus 86A; tel. (71) 254-75-75; fax (71) 254-79-53; e-mail aviabank2002@mail.ru; f. 1989; cap. 1,700m., res 732.1m., dep. 3,205.8m. (Jan. 2003); Chair. SHUKURULLO IMAMALIYEV.

Gala Bank: 700060 Tashkent, ul. Lakhuti 38; tel. and fax (71) 133-42-25; Chair. YULDASHBAI E. ERGASHEV.

HamkorBank: 710011 Andizhan, ul. Babura 85; tel. and fax (74) 24–70–39; e-mail hamkorbank@mail.ru; f. 1991; Chair. IKRAM IBRAGIMOV; 15 brs.

Ipak Yuli: Tashkent; f. July 2000 by merger with Namanganbank and Umarbank.

Pakhta Bank: 700096 Tashkent, ul. Mukimi 43; tel. (71) 278-21-96; fax (71) 120-88-18; e-mail pahtabnk@sovam.com; internet www .pakhtabank.com; f. 1995; cap. 10,000m., res 13,903.4m., dep. 112,048.6m. (Dec. 2002); Chair. KOBILJON TOSHMATOV; 184 brs.

Parvina Bank: 703001 Samarkand, ul. Uzbekistanskaya 82; tel. (66) 231-05-07; fax (66) 231-02-82; Chair. DILSHOD A. PULATOV.

Sanoatkurilish Bank: 700000 Tashkent, ul. Abdulla Tukai 3; tel. (71) 133-90-61; fax (71) 133-34-26; f. 1922; cap. 2,438m. Russian roubles, dep. 1,287.1m. Russian roubles (Dec. 1997); Chair. UTKUR U. NIGMATOV; 46 brs.

Sarmoyabank: 700011 Tashkent, ul. Navoi 18; tel. (71) 144-08-84; fax (71) 144-07-83; Chair. KOLMAHON E. KURBONBOYEV.

Savdogarbank: 700060 Tashkent, ul. Said Baraka 76; tel. (712) 54-19-91; fax (712) 56-56-71; Chair. MURSURMON N. NURMAMATOV.

Tadbirkor Bank: 700047 Tashkent, ul. S. Azimova 52; tel. (71) 133-18-75; fax (71) 136-88-32; Chair. MUZAFFARBEK SABIROV.

Trustbank: 700038 Tashkent, ul. Navoi 7; tel. (712) 41-23-43; fax (71) 144-76-25; e-mail magnoliya1974@mail.ru; f. 1994; cap. US $2.6m., res $0.2m., dep. $4.2m. Chair. VLADISLAV N. PAK; 2 brs.

Turonbank: 700011 Tashkent, ul. Navoi 44; tel. (71) 42-27-30; fax (71) 144-33-94; Chair. ATKHAM T. ZIYAYEV.

Uzlegkombank: 700031 Tashkent, ul. Baranova 40; tel. and fax (712) 56-05-09; Chair. ZAINUTDIN M. AKROMOV.

Uzmevasabzavotbank: 700015 Tashkent, ul. Lakhuti 16A; tel. and fax (71) 133-83-96; Chair. ISLOM T. SALOMOV.

Uzsayokharinvestbank: 700047 Tashkent, ul. Khorezmskaya 47; tel. and fax (71) 136-23-30.

Joint-Venture Banks

ABN-AMRO Bank NB Uzbekistan AO: 700000 Tashkent, pl. Khamid Alimzhan (West Side), Business Complex, 4th Entrance; tel. (71) 120-61-41; fax (71) 120-63-67; e-mail aziz.mirjuraev@abnamro.com; internet www.abnamro.com; f. 1996 as joint venture between European Bank for Reconstruction and Development, ABN-AMRO (the Netherlands), the World Bank and the Uzbek National Bank for Foreign Economic Relations; universal commercial bank; cap. US $8.5m. Chair. and Gen. Man. HUGO MINDERHOUD.

Uzbek-Turkish UT Bank: 700043 Tashkent, ul. Xalger Dostligi 15; tel. (71) 173-83-25; fax (71) 120-63-62; e-mail utbank@main.utbk .com; f. 1993; cap. 1,131.6m., res 360.9m., dep. 4,698.9m. (Dec. 2001); Chair. MUHAMMADJAN A. SUKURALIYEV.

UzDaewoo Bank: 700000 Tashkent, ul. Pushkina; tel. (71) 120-80-00; fax (71) 120-69-70; e-mail office@daewoobank.com; internet www .daewoobank.com; f. 1997; total assets US $20m. Chair. TAE YOUNG JUAG.

Uzprivatbank (Uzbek International Bank): 700003 Tashkent, pr. Uzbekistanskii 51; tel. (71) 120-63-08; fax (71) 120-63-07; e-mail bank@uib.iz; internet www.uzprivatbank.com; f. 1994; cap. US $5.5m. Chair. A. A. ERGASHEV.

INSURANCE

Uzbekinvest National Export–Import Insurance Co: 700017 Tashkent, ul. Suleimanova 49; tel. (71) 133-05-56; fax (71) 133-07-04; e-mail root@unic.gov.uz; internet www.unic.gov.uz; f. 1994 restructured 1997; joint venture with American International Group (AIG); cap. US $60m. Dir-Gen. SUNNAT A. UMAROV; Chief Exec. NODIR KALANDAROV.

Uzbekinvest International Insurance Co: Tashkent; e-mail nodir.kalandarov@aig.com; f. 1994; Chief Exec. NODIR KALANDAROV.

COMMODITY EXCHANGE

Tashkent Commodity Exchange: 700003 Tashkent, ul. Uzbekistanskii 53; tel. (71) 139-83-77; fax (71) 139-83-85; Chair. of Bd SHUKHRAT MUKHAMEDOV.

STOCK EXCHANGE

Uzbekistan Stock Exchange 'Toshkent' (UZSE): 700047 Tashkent, ul. Bukhara 10; tel. (71) 136-07-40; fax (71) 133-32-31; e-mail info@uzse.com; internet www.uzse.com; f. 1994; stocks and securities; Chair. TAKHIR R. TOKHTABAYEV.

Trade and Industry

GOVERNMENT AGENCIES

Foreign Investment Agency: 700077 Tashkent, ul. Buyuk Ipak Yuli 75; tel. (712) 68-77-05; fax (712) 67-07-52; e-mail afi@mail.uznet .net; internet www.gov.uz/fia; Gen. Dir SHAZIYATOV SHOAZIZ.

State Committee for the Management of State Property and for Privatization: 700008 Tashkent, pl. Mustakillik 6; tel. (71) 139-82-03; fax (71) 139-46-66; Chair. UKTAM K. ISMOILOV.

CHAMBER OF COMMERCE

Chamber of Commodity Producers and Entrepreneurs of Uzbekistan: 700047 Tashkent, ul. Bukhoro 6; tel. (71) 139-18-83;

fax (71) 132-09-03; e-mail info@maroqand.uz; internet www .maroqand.uz; f. 1996; provides assistance, consulting and support for businesses; Chair. MUZAFFARBEK A. SABIROV.

EMPLOYERS' ORGANIZATIONS

Employers' Association of Uzbekistan: 700017 Tashkent, ul. A. Kadiry 2; tel. (712) 34-06-71; fax (712) 34-13-39.

STATE HYDROCARBONS COMPANY

Uzbekneftegaz: 700047 Tashkent, ul. Akhunbabayeva 21; tel. (712) 32-02-10; fax (712) 32-10-62; national petroleum and gas corpn; Chair. KAIM ZALILOVICH KHAKKULOV; 90,000 employees.

TRADE UNIONS

Federation of Trade Unions of Uzbekistan: Tashkent; Chair. of Council KHULKAR DZHAMALOV.

Transport

RAILWAYS

Uzbekistan's railway network is connected to those of the neighbouring republics of Kazakhstan, Kyrgyzstan, Tajikistan and Turkmenistan. In 1994 Uzbekiston Temir Yollari (the Uzbekistan State Railway Company) was established on the basis of the existing facilities of its predecessor, the Central Asian Railway. There were 3,656 km of standard-gauge track in 1999, of which 489 km was electrified. Another line, connecting central Uzbekistan with the north-western part of the country, was brought into operation in March 2001.

Uzbekiston Temir Yollari (Uzbekistan State Railway Company): 700060 Tashkent, ul. Shevchenko 7; tel. (712) 32-44-00; fax (712) 47-39-58; f. 1994 to replace the Central Asian Railway's operations in Uzbekistan; state-owned joint-stock co; Pres. NORMAT ERMETOV.

City Underground Railway

Tashgorpasstreans (Tashkent Metro): 700027 Tashkent, pr. Uzbekistanskii 93A; tel. (712) 32-38-52; f. 1977; 2 lines of 30 km open, third line under construction; Chair. R. FAYZULLAYEV.

ROADS

In 1997 Uzbekistan's road network totalled 43,463 km, of which 3,237 km were main or national roads, 18,767 km were secondary roads and 21,459 km were other roads. In 1999 an estimated 87.3% of roads were paved.

INLAND WATERWAYS

The extensive use of the waters of the Amu-Dar'ya and Syr-Dar'ya for irrigation lessened the flow of these rivers and caused the desiccation of the Aral Sea. This reduced a valuable transport asset. However, the Amu-Dar'ya Steamship Co still operates important river traffic.

CIVIL AVIATION

Proposals to construct a new airport, 45 km from Tashkent, first discussed in 1991, were rejected in 1995 in favour of modernizing the capital's existing airport. In 1996 it was announced that the airports at Samarkand, Urgench and Bukhara would be upgraded to stimulate tourism.

Uzbekistan Airways (Uzbekiston Havo Yollari): 700061 Tashkent, ul. Proletarskaya 41; tel. (712) 91-14-90; fax (712) 32-73-71; e-mail info@uzbekistan-airways.com; internet www.uzbekistan-airways .com; f. 1992; operates flights to Central Asia, South-East Asia, the USA, the Middle East and Europe; Dir-Gen. RAFIKOV GANIY; Gen. Dir VALERIY TYAN.

Tourism

Since independence Uzbekistan has sought to promote tourism as an important source of revenue. The republic has more than 4,000 historical monuments, many of which are associated with the ancient 'Silk Route', particularly the cities of Samarkand (Tamerlane's capital), Khiva and Bukhara, as well as other historical sites. Infrastructural limitations, however, have constrained development. In 1998 Uzbekistan received an estimated 272,000 foreign visitors (including excursionists), and tourism receipts totalled some US $21m.

Uzbektourism: 700027 Tashkent, ul. Khorezmskaya 47; tel. (71) 133-54-14; fax (71) 136-79-48; f. 1992; Chair. BAKHTIYOR M. HUSANBAYEV.

VANUATU

Introductory Survey

Location, Climate, Language, Religion, Flag, Capital

The Republic of Vanuatu comprises an irregular archipelago of 83 islands in the south-west Pacific Ocean, lying about 1,000 km (600 miles) west of Fiji and 400 km (250 miles) north-east of New Caledonia. The group extends over a distance of about 1,300 km (808 miles) from north to south. The islands have an oceanic tropical climate, with a season of south-east trade winds between May and October. Winds are variable, with occasional cyclones for the rest of the year, and annual rainfall varies between 2,300 mm (90 ins) in the south and 3,900 mm (154 ins) in the north. In Port Vila, in the centre of the group, mean temperatures vary between 22°C (72°F) and 27°C (81°F). The national language is Bislama, ni-Vanuatu pidgin. There are many Melanesian languages and dialects. English, French and Bislama are the official languages. Most of the inhabitants (about 80%) profess Christianity, of which a number of denominations are represented. The national flag (proportions 3 by 5) consists of two equal horizontal stripes, red above green, on which are superimposed a black-edged yellow horizontal 'Y' (with its base in the fly) and, at the hoist, a black triangle containing two crossed yellow mele leaves encircled by a curled yellow boar's tusk. The capital is Port Vila, on the island of Efate.

Recent History

During the 19th century the New Hebrides (now Vanuatu) were settled by British and French missionaries, planters and traders. The United Kingdom and France established a Joint Naval Commission for the islands in 1887. The two countries later agreed on a joint civil administration, and in 1906 the territory became the Anglo-French Condominium of the New Hebrides (Nouvelles-Hébrides). Under this arrangement, there were three elements in the structure of administration: the British National Service, the French National Service and the Condominium (Joint) Departments. Each power was responsible for its own citizens and other non-New Hebrideans who chose to be 'ressortissants' of either power. Indigenous New Hebrideans were not permitted to claim either British or French citizenship. This resulted in two official languages, two police forces, three public services, three courts of law, three currencies, three national budgets, two resident commissioners in Port Vila (the capital) and two district commissioners in each of the four Districts.

Local political initiatives began after the Second World War, originating in New Hebridean concern over the alienation of native land. More than 36% of the New Hebrides was owned by foreigners. Na-Griamel, one of the first political groups to emerge, had its source in cult-like activities. In 1971 the leaders of Na-Griamel petitioned the UN to prevent further sales of land at a time when areas were being sold to US interests for development as tropical tourist resorts. In 1972 the New Hebrides National Party was formed, with support from Protestant missions and covert support from British interests. In response, French interests formed the Union des Communautés Néo-Hébridaises in 1974. Discussions in the United Kingdom in 1974 resulted in the replacement of the Advisory Council, established in 1957, by a Representative Assembly of 42 members, of whom 29 were directly elected in November 1975. The Assembly did not hold its first full working session until November 1976, and it was dissolved in early 1977, following a boycott by the National Party, which had changed its name to the Vanuaaku Pati (VP) in 1976. However, the VP reached an agreement with the Condominium powers on new elections for the Representative Assembly, based on universal suffrage for all seats.

In 1977 it was announced, at a conference in France between British, French and New Hebrides representatives, that the islands would become independent in 1980, following a referendum and elections. The VP boycotted this conference, as it demanded immediate independence. The VP also boycotted the elections in November 1977, and declared a 'People's Provisional Government'. Nevertheless, a reduced Assembly of 39 members was elected, and a measure of self-government was introduced in early 1978. A Council of Ministers and the office of Chief Minister (occupied by Georges Kalsakau) were created, and the French, British and Condominium Services began to be replaced by a single New Hebrides Public Service. In December a Government of National Unity was formed, with Fr Gérard Leymang as Chief Minister and Fr Walter Lini (the VP President) as Deputy Chief Minister.

At elections in November 1979 the VP won 26 of the 39 seats in the Assembly. The outcome of the election led to rioting by supporters of Na-Griamel on the island of Espiritu Santo, who threatened non-Santo 'foreigners'. However, the new Assembly elected Lini as Chief Minister.

In June 1980 Jimmy Stevens, the leader of Na-Griamel, declared Espiritu Santo independent of the rest of the New Hebrides, styling it the 'Independent State of Vemarana'. Members of his movement, allegedly assisted by French colons and supported by private US business interests, moved to the coast and imprisoned government officers and police, who were later released together with other European and indigenous public servants. British Royal Marines were deployed as a peace-keeping force, prompting strong criticism by the French, who would not permit Britain's unilateral use of force on Espiritu Santo.

In mid-July 1980, however, agreement was reached between the two Condominium powers and Lini, and the New Hebrides became independent within the Commonwealth, under the name of Vanuatu, as planned, on 30 July. The first President was the former Deputy Chief Minister, George Kalkoa, who adopted the surname Sokomanu ('leader of thousands'), although the post is largely ceremonial. Lini became Prime Minister. The Republic of Vanuatu signed a defence pact with Papua New Guinea, and in August units of the Papua New Guinea Defence Force replaced the British and French troops on Espiritu Santo and arrested the Na-Griamel rebels.

At a general election in November 1983 the VP retained a majority in Parliament, taking 24 of the 39 seats. Sokomanu remained as President. Parliament was expanded to 46 seats for the general election held in December 1987. Of these, the VP won 26 seats, the Union of Moderate Parties (UMP) 19, and the Fren Melanesia one.

In May 1988 a government decision to abolish a local land corporation, which had been a principal source of patronage for Sope, prompted a demonstration in Port Vila by Sope's supporters. Serious rioting ensued, in which one person was killed and several others injured. Lini accused Sope of being instrumental in provoking the riots, and subsequently dismissed him from the Council of Ministers. In July Sope and four colleagues resigned from the VP, and were subsequently dismissed from Parliament at Lini's behest. In addition, 18 members of the UMP were dismissed after they had boycotted successive parliamentary sittings in protest at the expulsions. In September Sope and his colleagues announced the formation of a new political party, the Melanesian Progressive Pati (MPP), and in October the VP expelled 128 of its own members for allegedly supporting the new party. In October the Court of Appeal ruled as unconstitutional the dismissal from Parliament of Sope and his colleagues, and reinstated them, but upheld the expulsion of the 18 members of the UMP. In November Sope resigned from Parliament, citing loss of confidence in its Speaker. In December President Sokomanu dissolved Parliament and announced that Sope would act as interim Prime Minister, pending a general election scheduled to be held in February 1989. Lini immediately denounced Sokomanu's actions, and the Governments of Australia, New Zealand and Papua New Guinea refused to recognize the interim Government. The islands' police force remained loyal to Lini, and later in December Sokomanu, Sope and other members of the interim Government were arrested and charged with treason. In 1989 Sokomanu was sentenced to six years' imprisonment, and Sope and the then leader of the parliamentary opposition, Maxime Carlot Korman, were jailed for five-year terms, for seditious conspiracy and incitement to mutiny. However, representatives of the International Commission of Jurists, who had been present at the trials, criticized the rulings, and in April the Court of Appeal overturned the original judgment, citing insufficient evidence for the convictions. Fred Timakata, the former Minister of Health, replaced Sokomanu as President in January 1989.

Diminishing support for Lini's leadership led to the approval in August 1991 of a motion of 'no confidence' in Lini as party leader at the VP's congress. Donald Kalpokas, the Secretary-General of the VP, was unanimously elected to replace Lini as President of the party. In September a motion of 'no confidence' in the premiership of Lini was narrowly approved in Parliament, and Kalpokas was elected Prime Minister. Subsequently, Lini, with the support of a substantial number of defectors from the VP, formed the National United Party (NUP). At a general election in December the UMP secured 19 seats, while the VP and NUP each won 10 seats, the MPP four and Tan Union, Fren Melanesia and Na-Griamel one each. The leader of the UMP, Maxime Carlot Korman, was appointed Prime Minister, and a coalition Government was formed between the UMP and the NUP.

At a presidential election in February 1994 neither the UMP's candidate, Fr Luc Dini, nor Fr John Bani, who was supported by the opposition, attained the requisite two-thirds of total votes cast. The election was rescheduled for March. The VP subsequently agreed to vote with the ruling UMP, in return for a guaranteed role in a future coalition government. As a result of this agreement, the UMP's candidate, Jean-Marie Leye, was elected to the presidency with 41 votes. The VP subsequently withdrew its support for the UMP when Carlot refused to offer the party more than one ministerial post; the VP had requested three.

In May 1994 Regenvanu, Tabisari and Sinker were expelled from the NUP. They subsequently formed a new grouping, the People's Democratic Party (PDP), and later that month signed an agreement with the UMP to form a new coalition Government, the third since the election of December 1991. The UMP-PDP coalition held a total of 26 legislative seats.

In October 1994 the Supreme Court granted the Government a restraining order against further actions by the President, pending the hearing of an application to the Supreme Court to overrule several of the President's recent decisions. Members of the Government and judiciary had become increasingly alarmed by Leye's exercise of his presidential powers, which had included orders to free 26 criminals (many of whom had been convicted on extremely serious offences) and to appoint a convicted criminal to the position of Police Commissioner (on the recommendation of the Prime Minister).

In April 1995 Carlot attracted severe criticism from the Vanuatu-based regional news agency, Pacnews, when he dismissed two senior government officials for making comments critical of the Government; moreover, the journalists who reported the comments were threatened with dismissal. The Prime Minister's increasing reputation for intolerance of criticism was compounded by allegations that, as part of his Government's policy of reducing the number of employees in the public service, civil servants believed to be opposition sympathizers were among the first to lose their jobs.

At a general election held in November 1995, the Unity Front coalition won 20 of the 50 seats in the newly enlarged Parliament and the UMP secured 17 seats. A period of intense political manoeuvring followed the election, as the two main parties sought to form coalitions with other members in an attempt to secure a parliamentary majority. The situation was compounded by the emergence of two factions within the UMP, one comprising the supporters of Carlot and another led by Vohor (the party's President). The Carlot faction of the UMP and the Unity Front both sought the political allegiance of the NUP. The latter's decision to accept the offer of a coalition with the UMP effectively excluded the Unity Front (the grouping with the largest number of seats) from Government, and, in protest, its members boycotted the opening of Parliament in December, thus preventing a vote on the formation of a new government taking place. At a subsequent parliamentary session Vohor was elected as Prime Minister, despite continuing allegations of irregularities in the election of senior members of Government.

In early February 1996 seven dissident UMP members of Parliament proposed a motion of 'no confidence' in Vohor, supported by 22 other opposition members. However, Vohor announced his resignation as Prime Minister, thus preventing the vote from taking place. A parliamentary session to elect a new premier was abandoned as a result of a boycott by supporters of Vohor, who was reported to have retracted his resig-

nation. However, at a further sitting, Carlot was elected Prime Minister.

In July 1996 a report published by the national ombudsman revealed that a serious financial scandal had occurred in the country, involving the issuing of 10 bank guarantees with a total value of US $100m. The Minister of Finance, Barak Sope, who had issued the guarantees in April, had been persuaded by an Australian financial adviser, Peter Swanson, that the scheme could earn the country significant revenue. Swanson, who left Vanuatu after securing the guarantees, was subsequently traced and charged with criminal offences relating to his dealings with Sope. (In February 1998 the Supreme Court found Swanson guilty on seven charges arising from the scandal, sentencing him to 18 months' imprisonment.) Carlot, meanwhile, rejected demands for his resignation for his compliance with the scheme and resisted considerable pressure to dismiss Sope and the Governor of the Reserve Bank of Vanuatu. In the following month, however, Sope was dismissed following his defection to the opposition.

In an attempt to restore a measure of political stability, Carlot appealed for reconciliation among the various political groups in the country in August 1996 and invited members of the opposition to join the Government. The opposition responded by reiterating its demand for Carlot's resignation, and in September a motion of 'no confidence' in the Government was approved and Vohor was elected Prime Minister. Vohor's coalition Government comprised the pro-Vohor faction of the UMP, the NUP, the MPP, Tan Union and Fren Melanesia. A new Council of Ministers, in which Sope was appointed Deputy Prime Minister, was announced in mid-October.

A dispute over unpaid allowances, dating from 1993, led members of the 300-strong Vanuatu Mobile Force (VMF—the country's paramilitary force) briefly to abduct the President and Deputy Prime Minister to demand a settlement. Both Leye and Sope expressed sympathy for the VMF members. Sope was replaced as Deputy Prime Minister by Donald Kalpokas, and Fr Walter Lini was appointed Minister of Justice. Following a further incident in November in connection with the pay dispute, in which an official from the Department of Finance was abducted and allegedly assaulted, Lini ordered the arrest of more than half of the members of the VMF. About 30 members were detained and charged with criminal offences. In June 1999 18 VMF members were charged with the alleged kidnapping of a number of government officers in 1996. One was found guilty and was to be referred to a court martial for sentencing.

In March 1997 a memorandum of agreement was signed between the VP, the NUP and the UMP, the three parties of the newly formed governing coalition. The defection in May, however, of five NUP members of Parliament, including two cabinet ministers, to the VP led to the party's expulsion from the Government. As a result, a new coalition, comprising the UMP, the MPP, Tan Union and Fren Melanesia, was formed. The subsequent designation of a new Cabinet was controversial for the appointment of Sope to the position of Deputy Prime Minister and Minister of Commerce, Trade and Industry. Sope had been described in January (in a further report on the financial scandal of the previous year), as unfit for public office. Ferrieux-Patterson also criticized the recent appointment of Willie Jimmy as Minister of Finance.

In July 1997 legal action was initiated to recover the estimated US $300,000 of public funds paid in 1993 by Jimmy, together with Carlot, as compensation to the 23 members dismissed from Parliament following their boycott of the legislature in 1988. In the same month it was reported that the Government was preparing to amend legislation governing the powers of the ombudsman, in an attempt to contain her increasingly vociferous criticism of certain public figures.

In September 1997 Vohor dismissed Jimmy from his position as Minister of Finance, apparently owing to a dispute between Jimmy and the Prime Minister over the latter's decision to remove several areas of responsibility from the Finance portfolio. Meanwhile, further allegations of financial impropriety were published by the ombudsman, this time concerning the illegal sale of ni-Vanuatu passports to foreign nationals. In September the Prime Minister ordered an investigation into the matter. With both Vohor and Jimmy alleging the involvement of the other, the dispute intensified the disunity within the UMP, which had now come to comprise three factions, led respectively by Vohor, Carlot and Jimmy.

In November 1997 Parliament approved legislation to repeal the Ombudsman Act and the Government announced that it was to establish a commission of inquiry to determine if the ombudsman had exceeded her constitutional powers. However, President Leye refused to promulgate the new law on the grounds that it was unconstitutional, and he referred it to the Supreme Court. Later in the month Carlot filed a motion of 'no confidence' in Vohor's Government. When Vohor attempted to withdraw all proposed legislation in order to prevent debate on the motion, Leye announced the dissolution of Parliament. However, the Supreme Court revived the parliamentary session in December. The matter was referred to the Court of Appeal, and Vohor and Carlot agreed to co-operate temporarily pending its judgment, which was eventually delivered in January 1998 and which once again ordered the immediate dissolution of Parliament. Following Leye's announcement of a forthcoming general election, Carlot announced the formation of the Vanuatu Republikan Pati (VRP). Meanwhile, Ferrieux-Patterson released a report in December 1997 in which she recommended that Vohor be investigated for offences relating to the illegal sale of ni-Vanuatu passports. The release of outspoken reports by the ombudsman continued into early 1998 and was widely believed to have contributed significantly to the domination of the election campaign by allegations of government corruption.

At a general election held on 6 March 1998, the VP won 18 of the 52 seats in the newly enlarged Parliament, the UMP secured 12, the NUP won 11, the MPP obtained six, the John Frum Movement secured two, the VRP obtained one, and independent candidates won two seats. In mid-March the VP and the NUP agreed to form a coalition Government, with the support of Carlot (the VRP's sole representative) and one independent member. At the end of the month Kalpokas was elected Prime Minister with 35 parliamentary votes, defeating Vohor (who secured 17). Kalpokas also assumed three ministerial portfolios, including that for Foreign Affairs, while Lini, who was appointed to the revived post of Deputy Prime Minister, also became Minister of Justice and Internal Affairs.

In June 1998, despite strong opposition, notably from the UMP, Parliament approved a new 'leadership code'. Regarded as a key element in ensuring greater accountability and transparency in public life, the code defined clear guidelines for the conduct of state officials (including a requirement that all public figures submit an annual declaration of assets to Parliament), and laid down strict penalties for those convicted of corruption. Shortly before, the Supreme Court upheld the repeal of the Ombudsman Act, as approved by Parliament in November 1997. The Kalpokas Government emphasized its commitment to strengthening the role of the ombudsman, stating that new legislation governing the office would be prepared. Although the ombudsman was to continue to function in the mean time, in early August 1998 Ferrieux-Patterson issued a statement in which she expressed concern that her powers of jurisdiction had been diminished.

In October 1998 Kalpokas expelled the NUP from the governing coalition, following reports that Lini (who died in February 1999), the party's leader, had organized a series of meetings with prominent members of the opposition, with the aim of forming a new coalition government which would exclude the VP. NUP ministers were largely replaced by members of the UMP faction led by Jimmy, which included the Deputy President of the party, Vincent Boulekone, and its Secretary-General, Henri Taga; one ministerial post was allocated to the John Frum Movement. In March 1999 Fr John Bani was chosen by the electoral college to succeed Jean-Marie Leye as President of Vanuatu.

The issue of press freedom returned to the fore in May 1999 when the Pacific Islands News Association expressed concern at the alleged assault on a local newspaper publisher by an associate of the Deputy Prime Minister, Willie Jimmy. Jimmy was reportedly displeased with the newspaper's coverage of an election campaign. The news association urged the Government to act against the increasing number of cases of media intimidation on the island.

The governing coalition was threatened in August 1999 by a decision by the National Council of the UMP to oppose participation in the Government. The Council issued a directive to the 17 members of Jimmy's faction to resign from the Kalpokas administration. Following their refusal to comply with the directive, the National Council acted to suspend the members in October. However, later that month the suspensions were over-

ruled by the Supreme Court. The two factions of the UMP had previously attempted reunification but negotiations had stalled over the demands of Vohor's faction for two of the four ministerial positions held by Jimmy's faction. (The UMP achieved reunification in November 2000.)

At the end of August 1999 four by-elections took place, three of which were won by opposition parties, thus eliminating the Government's majority in Parliament. In November the Government staged a boycott of Parliament to avoid a proposed vote of 'no confidence' by opposition parties against the Kalpokas administration. However, the subsequent defection to the opposition of an independent representative, followed by that of the Minister of Health, forced the resignation of Kalpokas prior to a 'no confidence' motion on 25 November. The Speaker, Edward Natapei, announced his resignation shortly afterwards and Paul Ren Tari of the NUP was elected as his replacement. The leader of the MPP, Sope, was elected to lead a new Government the same day; he secured 28 votes compared with the 24 votes gained by Natapei as the newly appointed President of the VP. Sope formed a five-party coalition Government, comprising the MPP, the NUP, the Vohor faction of the UMP, the VRP and the John Frum Movement. The composition of the new Council of Ministers was swiftly announced; it included Vohor as Minister of Foreign Affairs and Carlot as Minister of Lands and Mineral Resources, both of whom, with Sope, had been the subject of critical reports by the ombudsman. The new Government pledged to reduce the country's dependence on foreign advisers, review the recently introduced value-added tax and ensure that adequate services were delivered to rural communities.

In May 2000 Parliament approved controversial legislation (the Public Services Amendment Bill and the Government Amendment Bill) giving the Government direct power to appoint and dismiss public servants. The opposition criticized the changes, claiming that they contravened the principles of the Comprehensive Reform Programme (a range of economic measures supported by the Asian Development Bank—ADB). President John Bani subsequently referred both pieces of legislation to the Supreme Court, which, in August, ordered that he approve them. The ADB reacted angrily to the development, arguing that it allowed for political bias in the public sector, and threatened to withhold further funds from Vanuatu. The bank's stance served to perpetuate an ongoing dispute between the organization and the Vanuatu Government, which had often expressed the view that the bank imposed harsh conditions in return for its finance.

An incident in August 2000 in which the Deputy Prime Minister, Reginald Stanley, was allegedly involved in the serious assault of two people and in causing criminal damage to property while under the influence of alcohol led to Stanley's dismissal from the post. He was replaced by the Minister of Trade Development, James Bule.

In September 2000 the opposition leader, Edward Natapei, invited the Vohor faction of the UMP to join the opposition and form a new government. Vohor declined the offer, saying that his priority was the stability of the current Government. The resignation of a VP member in October prevented the success of a motion of 'no confidence' in the Prime Minister. (A further planned motion of 'no confidence' in the Prime Minister was withdrawn in December.) Also in October the Government was forced to defend a controversial plan, which allowed a Thai company, Apex, to pay off a portion of government debt, allegedly in return for tax-haven privileges. The President of Apex, Amarendra Nath Ghosh, was also Vanuatu's recently appointed honorary consul to Thailand. In January 2001 the Government deported Mark Neil-Jones, the publisher of the independent newspaper, *Trading Post*, on the grounds of instigating instability in the country. (The *Trading Post* had recently published several critical articles about the Government, including reports on the Government's financial dealings with Nath Ghosh.) However, the Supreme Court reversed the decision, declaring that the deportation order was illegal, and Neil-Jones was allowed to return to the country. An investigation was subsequently launched into the circumstances of the deportation.

In late January 2001 three members of the UMP resigned from the party, further reducing the Government's majority. The Government's problems intensified in March after the withdrawal of the UMP from the ruling coalition. Opposition attempts to vote on a motion of 'no confidence' were delayed as Sope initiated legal action against the motion, and the Speaker, Paul Ren Tari, refused to allow the vote while legal action was pending. The Chief Justice, however, ordered the vote to proceed, and after further postponements by the Speaker, the Sope Government was voted out of office on 13 April. A new Government, led by Edward Natapei of the VP, was elected. The incoming administration, a coalition of the VP and UMP, was sworn in on 17 April and pledged to continue the reform programme and to restore investor confidence. One of the Government's first acts was to remove Nath Ghosh from his diplomatic position. Vohor was appointed Deputy Prime Minister. In early May Parliament held an extraordinary session to debate a motion to remove Ren Tari as Speaker because of his conduct during the political crisis. Ren Tari responded by suspending Natapei, along with five other Members of Parliament who held cabinet posts, for breaching parliamentary procedure. Despite an order by the Chief Justice that they be allowed to return to Parliament to continue the extraordinary session, Ren Tari refused to open the legislature while he appealed to the Supreme Court against the order. In response, Ren Tari and his two deputies were arrested and charged with sedition. A new Speaker, Donald Kalpokas, President of the UMP, was elected, thus reducing Matapei's majority in Parliament to one. In September 2001 opposition leader Sope tabled a motion of 'no confidence' against the ruling coalition but was defeated.

In November 2001 Sope was ordered to appear in court to answer charges that he had forged two government-supported Letters of Guarantee, worth US $23m., while he was Prime Minister. It was reported that police were also investigating the activities of the former Minister of Finance, Morkin Steven, whose signature appeared on the documents. Meanwhile, Sope was under investigation for possible involvement in the illegal issuing of diplomatic passports and in connection with allegations of bribery. The preliminary hearing of the forgery charges was postponed until February 2002, enabling Sope to contest the general election due to take place later in that year.

In March 2002 Parliament was dissolved after the Supreme Court ruled that its four-year term had expired. Prime Minister Natapei remained in charge of a 'caretaker' Government until the general election, scheduled for 2 May 2002. Also in March it was announced that the newly established People's Progressive Party (PPP) and Fren Melanesia were to form a coalition with the ruling NUP to contest the forthcoming election. The announcement contradicted a statement issued earlier in the same month by the NUP, in which the party had declared that it would stand independently. Meanwhile, the Government dismissed the board of the Vanuatu Broadcasting and Television Corporation (VBTC), claiming that the organization had failed to consult with it over a number of important decisions and that it had incurred unnecessary costs. Later in March 27 VBTC employees returned to work, having been dismissed in October 2001 for participating in a strike. They claimed to have been reinstated by the newly appointed government board—a claim denied by the board—and refused to leave. The individuals alleged to be responsible for the reinstatement subsequently resigned. Negotiations to settle the ongoing disputes began in April amid allegations of political interference into the affairs of the company by government appointees. It was reported that the general election was to be monitored by an independent group of observers. The future of the Comprehensive Reform Programme was widely perceived to be the main issue at stake in the electoral campaign.

The general election was held on 2 May 2002. A total of 327 candidates contested the 52 seats available in Parliament. A record 138 candidates stood as independents, prompting Natapei to comment prior to the election that if Vanuatu were to attain political stability the electoral constituency should vote only for party candidates. Bad weather and problems with ballot papers delayed voting in some constituencies. The two ruling coalition parties secured a sufficient number of seats in the new Parliament to claim victory. The NUP came third. After some initial uncertainty, it was announced that the UMP had won 15 seats in the new Parliament and that the VP had secured 14. In accordance with the terms of the coalition agreement, however, the VP was permitted to nominate the next Prime Minister. The new Government was formed on 3 June 2002, with Natapei duly re-elected Prime Minister.

In July 2002 former Prime Minister Barak Sope was convicted of fraud by the Supreme Court and sentenced to three years' imprisonment. It was alleged soon afterwards that New Zealand had interfered in Vanuatu's internal affairs by funding the investigation that had led to Sope's conviction. In early August, following the controversial appointment of Mael Apisai as Vanuatu's new Police Commissioner, disaffected police officers

staged a raid during which they arrested Apisai, Attorney-General Hamilton Bulu and 14 other senior civil servants on charges of seditious conspiracy. Following an investigation, the charges were abandoned owing to a lack of evidence. Prime Minister Natapei subsequently assumed the police and VMF portfolios from the Minister of Internal Affairs, Joe Natuman, in what was thought to be an attempt to distance Natuman from some members of the police force, with whom he had reportedly become too closely involved. Later in the month members of the VMF surrounded the police headquarters in Port Vila to serve arrest warrants on 27 of those who had been involved in the raid, including the acting police commissioner, Holis Simon, and the commander of the VMF, Api Jack Marikembo. Shortly afterwards, in an attempt to bring an end to hostilities, the Government signed an agreement with representatives from the police department and the VMF during a traditional Melanesian reconciliation ceremony. The police officers involved, who had been suspended from their posts, were reinstated, the police and the VMF pledged to make no further arrests and it was agreed that Apisai's appointment would be reviewed by a newly appointed police services commission. At the same time it was decided that the allegations of conpsiracy that had been brought against the 15 officials initially arrested would be considered by the judicial authorities. A new acting police commissioner, Lt-Gen. Arthur Coulton, was then appointed. In early October 2002 it was announced that the charges against 18 of those arrested in connection with the August raid would be abandoned, leaving eight senior officers to face trial on charges of mutiny and incitement to mutiny. Meanwhile, the UMP urged the removal of the Australian High Commissioner, Steve Waters, while reportedly accusing Australia of interference in Vanuatu's internal affairs and of destabilizing the coalition Government by communicating solely with the VP at the expense of the UMP. Deputy Prime Minister Serge Vohor alleged that the Australian Federal Police (AFP) had been engaged in the surveillance of government ministers and other officials in Vanuatu. The AFP denied the charges. In early December four of the eight senior police officers tried were found guilty by the Supreme Court on charges of mutiny, incitement to mutiny, kidnapping and false imprisonment and were given suspended two-year prison sentences. In the same month police intervened to prevent the former Prime Minister Barak Sope from reclaiming his seat in the National Assembly, claiming that this was nullified by his conviction for fraud in July, despite receiving a pardon in November from President Bani. The pardon, which Bani stated he had made on the grounds of Sope's poor health, provoked widespread public opposition and led the Government to announce the appointment of a commission of inquiry to investigate the President's decision.

In April 2003 the election of Ham Lini (brother of Walter Lini, the late founder of the NUP) as President of the NUP, led to the signing of a memorandum of understanding inviting that party to join the coalition Government. The NUP was expected to assume three ministerial portfolios (including finance) in a development which observers believed could signify the possible reunification of the NUP with the VP (which had been a single political organization until their split in 1991). However, in late April the NUP rejected the VP's offer and announced its intention to remove the Government in a motion of 'no confidence'.

Meanwhile, Vanuatu has had an uneasy relationship with France. In 1981 the French Ambassador to Vanuatu was expelled, following the deportation from New Caledonia of the VP Secretary-General, who had been due to attend an assembly of the New Caledonian Independence Front. France immediately withdrew aid to Vanuatu but this was subsequently restored and a new Ambassador appointed. However, the French Ambassador was expelled again in 1987, for allegedly providing 'substantial financial assistance' to Vanuatu's opposition parties. In response to the expulsion, the French Government again announced that it would withdraw aid to Vanuatu. Carlot, Vanuatu's first francophone Prime Minister, made an official visit to France in May 1992, and the two countries fully restored diplomatic relations in October. In July, however, the Carlot Government reaffirmed its support for the Kanak independence movement on the French Territory of New Caledonia, following threats by Lini to withdraw from the Government unless Carlot's pro-French policies were modified. Improved relations with France were confirmed in 1993 with the signing of a bilateral co-operation agreement. In mid-1995 the Carlot Government was virtually alone in the region in failing to condemn France's resumption of nuclear tests in French Polynesia. The opposition criticized the Government's stance as not reflecting the views of the vast majority of ni-Vanuatu.

In March 1988 Vanuatu signed an agreement with Papua New Guinea and Solomon Islands to form the 'Spearhead Group', which aimed to preserve Melanesian cultural traditions and to lobby for independence for New Caledonia. In 1994 the group concluded an agreement regarded as the first step towards the establishment of a free-trade area between the three countries. Fiji joined the group in early 1996.

Government

Vanuatu is a republic. Legislative power is vested in the unicameral Parliament, with 52 members who are elected by universal adult suffrage for four years. The Head of State is the President, elected for a five-year term by an electoral college consisting of Parliament and the Presidents of the Regional Councils. Executive power is vested in the Council of Ministers, appointed by the Prime Minister and responsible to Parliament. The Prime Minister is elected by and from members of Parliament. Legislation enacted in 1994 resulted in the replacement of the 11 local government councils by six provincial bodies, with greater executive powers. The six provincial authorities are Malampa, Penama, Sanma, Shefa, Tafea and Torba.

Economic Affairs

In 2001, according to estimates by the World Bank, Vanuatu's gross national income (GNI), measured at average 1999–2001 prices, was US $212m., equivalent to $1,050 per head (or $2,710 per head on an international purchasing-power parity basis). During 1990–2001, it was estimated, the population increased at an average annual rate of 2.9%, while gross domestic product (GDP) per head decreased, in real terms, by an average of 0.9% per year. Overall GDP increased, in real terms, at an average annual rate of 2.0% in 1990–2001; GDP contracted by 4.0% in 2001.

The agricultural sector (including forestry and fishing) contributed 13.4% of GDP in 2001, compared with some 40% in the early 1980s. According to figures from the Asian Development Bank (ADB), the GDP of the agricultural sector was estimated to have decreased by an average annual rate of 0.7% in 1990–2001. Compared with the previous year, the sector's GDP decreased by 9.3% in 1999, increased by 2.5% in 2000 but declined by 14.9% in 2001. The performance of the agricultural sector in 2001 was severely affected by the devastation caused by two cyclones that struck Vanuatu early in the year. About 61.4% of the employed labour force were engaged in agricultural activities at the time of the 1989 census. Coconuts, cocoa and coffee are grown largely for export (copra being the most important of these), while yams, taro, cassava, breadfruit and vegetables are cultivated for subsistence purposes. Cattle, pigs, goats and poultry are the country's principal livestock, and beef is an important export commodity (contributing 7.5% of export earnings in 2001). Vanuatu has encouraged the development of a forestry industry. However, the Government caused considerable controversy in mid-1993, when it granted a Malaysian consortium a licence to log 70,000 cu m of timber annually; previous licences for all operators had permitted total logging of only 5,000 cu m per year. A complete ban on the export of round logs was subsequently introduced. The Government derives substantial revenue from the sale of fishing rights to foreign fleets: sales of licences to Taiwanese and South Korean vessels earned more than $A136,000 in 1997.

The industrial sector (including manufacturing, utilities and construction) contributed about 11.5% of GDP in 2001, although only 3.5% of the employed labour force were engaged in the sector in 1989. Compared with the previous year, according to the ADB, industrial GDP increased by 5.2% in 1999 and by 8.4% in 2000, before declining by 1.1% in 2001. Manufacturing, which contributed about 5.0% of GDP in 2001, is mainly concerned with the processing of agricultural products. In 1990–2001 the GDP of the manufacturing sector increased by an average annual rate of only 1.7%. The country's first kava extraction plant (for the manufacture of alcoholic drink) was opened in 1998. However, it was feared that a ban imposed on kava imports in 2001 by several countries in Europe owing to health concerns would have a detrimental effect upon the kava industry. Construction activity contributed 4.2% of GDP in 2001). In early 1992 an Australian mining company announced plans to mine 60,000 metric tons of manganese per year on the island of Efate for export to Japan and China. In addition, several possibilities for gold- and copper-mining, as well as large deposits of petroleum, were identified in 1994 around the

islands of Malekula and Espiritu Santo. Electricity generation is largely thermal. However, plans to construct hydroelectric power stations on Espiritu Santo and Malekula were announced in the mid-1990s. Imports of mineral fuels comprised 13.7% of the value of total imports in 2001.

The economy depends heavily on the services sector, which accounted for 75.0% of GDP in 2001. According to the ADB, the GDP of the services sector declined by 1.7% in 1999 before rising by 3.3% in 2000 and again by 3.3% in 2001. Tourism, 'offshore' banking facilities and a shipping registry, providing a 'flag of convenience' to foreign-owned vessels, make a significant contribution to the country's income. In 2000 57,364 foreign tourists visited Vanuatu; revenue from tourism was US $58m. in 2000.

In 2001 Vanuatu recorded a visible trade deficit of US $58.07m., and a deficit of $14.53m. on the current account of the balance of payments. In 2001 the principal sources of imports were Japan (26.1%) and Australia (16.9%), while the principal markets for exports were Indonesia (34.8%), Greece (15.5%) and Japan (14.2%). The principal imports in 2001 were machinery and transport equipment (23.8% of total imports), food and live animals (16.6%), mineral fuels (13.7%), and basic manufactures (12.6%). Timber (which provided 10.5% of total export earnings), copra (which provided 10.1%) and beef (7.5%) were the main export commodities in 2001.

Budget estimates for 1999 projected an overall deficit of 375m. vatu, compared with a deficit of 3,057m. vatu in 1998. (However, almost 90% of the projected 1998 budget deficit was an exceptional payment to the Vanuatu National Provident Fund—VNPF, and to the Comprehensive Reform Programme—CRP.) In 2000 Vanuatu received US $45.8m. of official development assistance, of which US $28.3m. was bilateral aid and US $17.5m. was multilateral assistance. Australia, New Zealand, France, the United Kingdom and Japan are significant suppliers of development assistance. In 2002/03 Australia provided aid of some $A22.1m., and development assistance from New Zealand totalled $NZ5.25m. In 1997 the Government asked the UN to reclassify Vanuatu under 'least developed country' status, so that aid in support of the Government's economic reform programme would be more forthcoming. In February 2002 the European Union (EU) allocated Vanuatu 2,000m. vatu of aid to be disbursed over the next five years from the ninth European Development Fund; the aid was to be used principally for the development of education and human resources training. Vanuatu's total external debt was US $68.6m. at the end of 2000, of which $67.2m. was long-term public debt. In that year the cost of debt-servicing was equivalent to 1.4% of the value of exports of goods and services. The annual rate of inflation averaged 2.9% in 1991–2001; consumer prices increased by 2.5% in 2000 and by 3.2% in 2001.

Vanuatu is a member of the Pacific Community (see p. 304), the Pacific Islands Forum (see p. 306), the Asian Development Bank (ADB, see p. 143) and the UN Economic and Social Commission for Asia and the Pacific (ESCAP, see p. 28). The country is also a signatory of the South Pacific Regional Trade and Economic Agreement (SPARTECA, see p. 308) and of the Lomé Conventions and the successor Cotonou Agreement (see p. 235) with the EU.

Vanuatu's economic development has been impeded by its dependence on the agricultural sector, particularly the production and export of copra, which is vulnerable to adverse weather conditions and fluctuations in international commodity prices. Successive administrations, therefore, have attempted to encourage the diversification of the country's economy, notably through the development of the tourism sector. Economic development, however, remains inhibited by a shortage of skilled indigenous labour, a weak infrastructure and frequent foreign exploitation. The new Government's implementation in early 1998 of a Comprehensive Reform Programme (CRP), approved by the ADB in early 1997, was expected to enhance Vanuatu's economic prospects. In mid-1999 the ADB reported that the Government had demonstrated a strong level of commitment to the CRP: the number of ministries had been reduced from 34 to nine, and the number of civil service personnel had been decreased by 7%, creating a more efficient and autonomous public sector; a value-added tax had been introduced; and the National Bank and the Development Bank had been restructured. Development plans, known as the Year 2000 policy statement, placed emphasis on the agricultural and tourism sectors, with the Government planning to establish an Agricultural Development Bank to promote ni-Vanuatu development in the rural sector and envisaging the construction of a new airport capable of handling Boeing 747s. The country's status as an offshore financial centre aroused controversy in June 2000 when the Paris-based Organisation for Economic Co-operation and Development (OECD, see p. 277) listed Vanuatu as one of a number of countries and territories operating as unfair tax havens. It was claimed that the country was being used to 'launder' the proceeds of illegal activities of the Russian mafia and drug cartels. Sanctions were threatened if Vanuatu failed to take action to prevent both 'money-laundering' and international tax evasion. In September 2001 the Minister of Finance rejected demands to provide information on the country's revenue from its international tax haven facility. In February 2002 the Government stated that it would not co-operate with an international initiative intended to eliminate tax evasion by encouraging transparency in world-wide tax policies. Vanuatu thus remained on the OECD's list of unco-operative tax havens. In November 2001, after five years of negotiations, the World Trade Organization (WTO, see p. 323) offered Vanuatu membership. However, the Government rejected the offer on the grounds that it wished to delay its entry while it negotiated a more favourable tariff agreement. Prime Minister Natapei also voiced his concern that the opening of free trade between members of the Melanesian 'Spearhead Group' had proved harmful to businesses in Vanuatu. The economy experienced a deceleration in 2001; GDP contracted by 0.5%. This was mainly attributable to the detrimental effect of adverse weather conditions upon the performance of the agricultural sector (and particularly upon exports of copra, which decreased by nearly 50%) and to the effects of the European ban on kava imports. However, the repercussions of the September 2001 terrorist attacks on the USA also contributed to a decline in tourism, an important source of foreign revenue, in the last months of the year. GDP was forecast to increase by only 0.7% in 2002, as the Government's fiscal position continued to deteriorate.

Education

The abolition of nominal fees for primary education following independence resulted in a significant increase in enrolment at that level. Thus, at the beginning of the 1990s it was estimated that about 85% of children between the ages of six and 11 were enrolled at state-controlled primary institutions (which numbered 267 in 1995). Secondary education begins at 12 years of age, and comprises a preliminary cycle of four years and a second cycle of three years. In 1992 4,269 pupils attended the country's secondary schools (which numbered 27 in 1995). Vocational education and teacher-training are also available. The relatively low level of secondary enrolment is a cause of some concern to the Government, and a major programme for the expansion of the education system, costing US $17.8m., was inaugurated in 1989. The programme aimed to double secondary enrolment by 1996. Literacy rates are another cause of concern; it was estimated in 1997 that 64% of the population was illiterate.

An extension centre of the University of the South Pacific was opened in Port Vila in May 1989. Students from Vanuatu can also receive higher education at the principal faculties of that university (in Suva, Fiji), in Papua New Guinea or in France.

The 1997 budget allocated an estimated 1,396m. vatu to education (21.9% of total recurrent expenditure by the central Government).

Public Holidays

2003: 1 January (New Year's Day), 5 March (Custom Chief's Day), 18–21 April (Easter), 1 May (Labour Day), 29 May (Ascension Day), 24 July (Children's Day), 30 July (Independence Day), 15 August (Assumption), 5 October (Constitution Day), 29 November (Unity Day), 25 December (Christmas Day), 27 December (Family Day).

2004: 1 January (New Year's Day), 5 March (Custom Chief's Day), 9–12 April (Easter), 1 May (Labour Day), 20 May (Ascension Day), 24 July (Children's Day), 30 July (Independence Day), 15 August (Assumption), 5 October (Constitution Day), 29 November (Unity Day), 25 December (Christmas Day), 27 December (Family Day).

Statistical Survey

Source (unless otherwise indicated): Vanuatu Statistics Office, PMB 19, Port Vila; tel. 22110; fax 24583; e-mail stats@vanuatu.com.vu; internet www.spc.int/stats/vanuatu.

AREA AND POPULATION

Area: 12,190 sq km (4,707 sq miles); *By island:* (sq km) Espiritu Santo 4,010; Malekula 2,024; Efate 887; Erromango 887; Ambrym 666; Tanna 561; Pentecost 499; Epi 444; Ambae 399; Vanua Lava 343; Gaua 315; Maewo 300.

Population: 142,419 at census of 16 May 1989; 186,678 (males 95,682, females 90,996) at census of 16–30 November 1999; 192,910 (estimate) at mid-2001. *By island* (mid-1999, official estimates): Espiritu Santo 31,811; Malekula 19,766; Efate 43,295; Erromango 1,554; Ambrym 7,613; Tanna 26,306; Pentecost 14,837; Epi 4,706; Ambae 10,692; Vanua Lava 2,074; Gaua 1,924; Maewo 3,385.

Density (mid-2001): 15.8 per sq km.

Principal Towns (at 1999 census): Port Vila (capital) 29,356; Luganville 10,738. Source: UN, *World Urbanization Prospects: The 2001 Revision.*

Births and Deaths (estimates, 1995–2000): Birth rate 33.7 per 1,000; Death rate 6.1 per 1,000. Source: UN, *World Population Prospects: The 2000 Revision.*

Expectation of Life (WHO estimates, years at birth): 65.6 (males 64.5; females 67.1) in 2001. Source: WHO, *World Health Report.*

Economically Active Population (census of May 1989): Agriculture, forestry, hunting and fishing 40,889; Mining and quarrying 1; Manufacturing 891; Electricity, gas and water 109; Construction 1,302; Trade, restaurants and hotels 2,712; Transport, storage and communications 1,030; Financing, insurance, real estate and business services 646; Community, social and personal services 7,891; Activities not adequately defined 11,126; Total labour force 66,597 (males 35,692; females 30,905).

HEALTH AND WELFARE

Key Indicators

Total Fertility Rate (children per woman, 2001): 4.4.

Under-5 Mortality Rate (per 1,000 live births, 2001): 42.

Physicians (per 1,000 head, 1996): 0.12.

Health Expenditure (2000): US $ per head (PPP): 119.

Health Expenditure (2000): % of GDP: 3.9.

Health Expenditure (2000): public (% of total): 60.9.

Access to Water (% of persons, 2000): 88.

Access to Sanitation (% of persons, 2000): 100.

Human Development Index (2000): ranking: 131.

Human Development Index (2000): value: 0.542.
 For sources and definitions, see explanatory note on p. vi.

AGRICULTURE, ETC.

Principal Crops (FAO estimates, '000 metric tons, 2001): Coconuts 180; Roots and tubers 45; Vegetables and melons 10; Bananas 13; Other fruit 7; Groundnuts (in shell) 2; Maize 1; Cocoa beans 2. Source: FAO.

Livestock (FAO estimates, 2001): Cattle 151,000; Pigs 62,000; Goats 12,000; Horses 3,100; Chickens 340,000. Source: FAO.

Livestock Products (FAO estimates, metric tons, 2001): Beef and veal 5,800; Pig meat 2,805; Cows' milk 3,100; Hen eggs 320; Cattle and buffalo hides 821; Goatskins 6. Source: FAO.

Forestry ('000 cu m, 2001): *Roundwood Removals* (excl. bark): Sawlogs and veneer logs 28; Fuel wood 91; Total 119. *Sawnwood Production* (all broadleaved, incl. railway sleepers): Total 28. Source: FAO.

Fishing ('000 metric tons, 2000): Skipjack tuna 46.5; Yellowfin tuna 17.6; Total catch 73.5. Source: FAO, *Yearbook of Fishery Statistics.*

FINANCE

Currency and Exchange Rates: Currency is the vatu. *Sterling, Dollar and Euro Equivalents* (31 December 2002): £1 sterling = 214.6 vatu; US $1 = 133.17 vatu; €1 = 139.66 vatu; 1,000 vatu = £4.659 = $7.509 = €7.160. *Average Exchange Rate* (vatu per US $): 137.64 in 2000; 145.31 in 2001; 139.20 in 2002.

Budget (estimates, million vatu, 2001): *Revenue:* Tax revenue 5,786 (Taxes on goods and services 3,336, Import duties 2,288); Non-tax revenue 648; Total 6,446, excluding grants from abroad (440). *Expenditure:* Wages and salaries 3,734. Purchases of goods and services 1,840; Interest payments 248; Transfers 800; Total 6,622 (excluding technical assistance). Source: IMF, *Vanuatu: Selected Issues and Statistical Appendix* (December 2000).

International Reserves (US $ million at 31 December 2002): IMF special drawing rights 1.15; Reserve position in IMF 3.39; Foreign exchange 31.98; Total 36.52. Source: IMF, *International Financial Statistics.*

Money Supply (million vatu at 31 December 2002): Currency outside banks 1,916; Demand deposits at banks 9,608; Total money (incl. others) 11,606. Source: IMF, *International Financial Statistics.*

Cost of Living (Consumer Price Index for low-income households in urban areas; base: 1995 = 100): All items 109.3 in 1999; 112.0 in 2000; 116.1 in 2001. Source: IMF, *International Financial Statistics.*

Expenditure on the Gross Domestic Product (million vatu at current prices, 1999): Government final consumption expenditure 8,470; Private final consumption expenditure 17,904; Increase in stocks –55; Gross fixed capital formation 6,537; Statistical discrepancy 528; *Total domestic expenditure* 33,384; Exports of goods and services 14,130; *Less* Imports of goods and services 18,308; *GDP in purchasers' values* 29,206. Source: Asian Development Bank, *Key Indicators of Developing Asian and Pacific Countries.*

Gross Domestic Product by Economic Activity (million vatu at current prices, 2001, estimates): Agriculture, forestry and fishing 4,270; Manufacturing 1,576; Electricity, gas and water 763; Construction 1,334; Wholesale and retail trade, restaurants and hotels 10,867; Transport, storage and communications 3,861; Finance 2,779; Public administration 3,839; Other services (net of imputed bank service charge) 2,542; GDP in purchasers' values 31,831. Source: Asian Development Bank, *Key Indicators of Developing Asian and Pacific Countries.*

Balance of Payments (US $ million, 2001): Exports of goods f.o.b. 19.89; Imports of goods f.o.b. –77.96; *Trade balance* –58.07; Exports of services 119.26; Imports of services –72.99; *Balance on goods and services* –11.80; Other income received 17.23; Other income paid –21.23; *Balance on goods, services and income* –15.80; Current transfers received 39.53; Current transfers paid –38.26; *Current balance* –14.53; Capital account (net) –16.03; Direct investment from abroad 18.00; Portfolio investment assets –4.33; Other investment assets –11.41; Other investment liabilities 10.48; Net errors and omissions 7.55; *Overall balance* –10.27. Source: IMF, *International Financial Statistics.*

EXTERNAL TRADE*

Principal Commodities (million vatu, 2001): *Imports:* Food and live animals 2,240; Mineral fuels, lubricants, etc. 1,859; Chemicals 1,449; Basic manufactures 1,704; Machinery and transport equipment 3,219; Miscellaneous manufactured articles 1,112; Total (incl. others) 13,532. *Exports:* Copra 323; Beef 239; Timber 334; Total (incl. others) 3,192. Source: Asian Development Bank, *Key Indicators of Developing Asian and Pacific Countries.*

Principal Trading Partners (US $ million, 2001): *Imports:* Australia 28.4; Fiji 8.1; France 7.9; Germany 18.4; Hong Kong 1.7; Japan 43.7; New Caledonia 3.1; New Zealand 11.3; Singapore 24.4; USA 0.9; Total (incl. others) 167.7. *Exports:* Bangladesh 1.3; Germany 1.6; Greece 8.3; Indonesia 18.7; Japan 7.6; Korea, Republic 0.6; USA 0.5; Total (incl. others) 53.7. Source: Asian Development Bank, *Key Indicators of Developing Asian and Pacific Countries.*

*Figures refer to domestic imports and exports only.

TRANSPORT

Road Traffic (estimates, '000 motor vehicles in use): 9.2 (Passenger cars 7.4) in 1995; 5.9 (Passenger cars 2.7) in 1996; 6.2 (Passenger cars 2.7) in 1997. Source: UN, *Statistical Yearbook.*

Shipping: *Merchant Fleet* (registered at 31 December 2001): Vessels 316; Total displacement ('000 grt) 1,496 (Source: Lloyd's Register-Fairplay, *World Fleet Statistics*). *International Sea-borne Freight Traffic* (estimates, '000 metric tons, 1990): Goods loaded 80; Goods unloaded 55 (Source: UN, *Monthly Bulletin of Statistics*).

Civil Aviation (traffic on scheduled services, 1999): Kilometres flown (million) 3; Passengers carried ('000) 86; Passenger-km (million) 178; Total ton-km (million) 18. Source: UN, *Statistical Yearbook.*

TOURISM

Foreign Tourist Arrivals: 52,085 in 1998; 50,746 in 1999; 57,364 in 2000.

Tourist Arrivals by Country of Residence (2000): Australia 36,751; New Caledonia 4,114; New Zealand 7,985; Total (incl. others) 57,364.

Tourism Receipts (US $ million): 52 in 1998; 56 in 1999; 58 in 2000 (Source: World Tourism Organization).

COMMUNICATIONS MEDIA

Radio Receivers (1997): 62,000 in use*.

Television Receivers (1999): 2,000 in use†.

Telephones (2001): 6,800 main lines in use‡.

Facsimile Machines (1996): 600 in use†.

Mobile Cellular Telephones (2001): 300 subscribers‡.

Internet Users (2001): 5,500‡.

Non-daily Newspapers (1996): 2 (estimated circulation 4,000)*.

* Source: UNESCO, *Statistical Yearbook.*
† Source: UN, *Statistical Yearbook.*
‡ Source: International Telecommunication Union.

EDUCATION

Pre-primary (1992): 252 schools; 49 teachers (1980); 5,178 pupils.

Primary (1995): 374 schools; 852 teachers (1992); 32,352 pupils.

Secondary (General) (1992): 27 schools (1995); 220 teachers; 4,269 students.

Secondary (Vocational): 50 teachers (1981); 444 students (1992).

Secondary (Teacher Training): 1 college (1989); 13 teachers (1983); 124 students (1991).
Source: mainly UNESCO, *Statistical Yearbook.*

Directory

The Constitution

A new Constitution came into effect at independence on 30 July 1980. The main provisions are as follows:

The Republic of Vanuatu is a sovereign democratic state, of which the Constitution is the supreme law. Bislama is the national language and the official languages are Bislama, English and French. The Constitution guarantees protection of all fundamental rights and freedoms and provides for the determination of citizenship.

The President, as head of the Republic, symbolizes the unity of the Republic and is elected for a five-year term of office by secret ballot by an electoral college consisting of Parliament and the Presidents of the Regional Councils.

Legislative power resides in the single-chamber Parliament, consisting of 39 members (amended to 46 members in 1987, to 50 in 1995 and further to 52 in 1998) elected for four years on the basis of universal franchise through an electoral system that includes an element of proportional representation to ensure fair representation of different political groups and opinions. Parliament is presided over by the Speaker elected by the members. Executive power is vested in the Council of Ministers which consists of the Prime Minister (elected by Parliament from among its members) and other ministers (appointed by the Prime Minister from among the members of Parliament). The number of ministers, including the Prime Minister, may not exceed a quarter of the number of members of Parliament.

Special attention is paid to custom law and to decentralization. The Constitution states that all land in the Republic belongs to the indigenous custom owners and their descendants. There is a National Council of Chiefs, composed of custom chiefs elected by their peers sitting in District Councils of Chiefs. It may discuss all matters relating to custom and tradition and may make recommendations to Parliament for the preservation and promotion of the culture and languages of Vanuatu. The Council may be consulted on any question in connection with any bill before Parliament. Each region may elect a regional council and the Constitution lays particular emphasis on the representation of custom chiefs within each one. (A reorganization of local government was initiated in May 1994, and resulted in September of that year in the replacement of 11 local councils with six provincial governments.)

The Constitution also makes provision for public finance, the Public Service, the Ombudsman, a leadership code and the judiciary (see Judicial System).

The Government

HEAD OF STATE

President: Fr JOHN BANI (took office March 1999).

COUNCIL OF MINISTERS
(April 2003)

A coalition of the Vanuaaku Pati (VP) and the Union of Moderate Parties (UMP).

Prime Minister: EDWARD NIPAKE NATAPEI (VP).

Deputy Prime Minister and Minister of Foreign Affairs, External Trade and Telecommunications: SERGE VOHOR (UMP).

Minister of Agriculture, Livestock, Forestry and Fisheries: STEVEN KALSAKAU (UMP).

Minister of Internal Affairs: JOE NATUMAN (VP).

Minister of Education: JACQUES SESE (UMP).

Minister of Finance: SELA MOLISA (VP).

Minister of Health: DONALD KALPOKAS (VP).

Minister of Infrastructure and Public Utilities: WILLIE POSEN (UMP).

Minister of Lands and Mineral Resources: JACKLYN RUEBEN TITEK (VP).

Minister for ni-Vanuatu Business Development: NICHOLAS BROWN (Independent).

Minister of the Comprehensive Reform Programme: PHILIP BOETORO (VP).

Minister of Industry and Commerce: JEAN ALLAN MAHÉ (UMP).

Minister of Youth and Sports: RAPHAEL WORWOR (VP).

MINISTRIES AND DEPARTMENTS

Prime Minister's Office: PMB 053, Port Vila; tel. 22413; fax 22863; internet www.vanuatu.gov.vu.

Deputy Prime Minister's Office: PMB 057, Port Vila; tel. 22750; fax 27714.

Ministry of Agriculture, Livestock, Forestry and Fisheries: POB 39, Port Vila; tel. 23406; fax 26498.

Ministry of Civil Aviation, Meteorology, Postal Services, Public Works and Transport: PMB 057, Port Vila; tel. 22790; fax 27214.

Ministry of the Comprehensive Reform Programme: POB 110, Port Vila.

Ministry of Culture, Home Affairs and Justice: PMB 036, Port Vila; tel. 22252; fax 27064.

Ministry of Education, Youth and Sports: PMB 028, Port Vila; tel. 22309; fax 24569; e-mail andrews@vanuatu.com.vu.

Ministry of Energy, Lands, Mines and Rural Water Supply: PMB 007, Port Vila; tel. 27833; fax 25165.

Ministry of Finance: PMB 058, Port Vila; tel. 23032; fax 27937.

Ministry of Foreign Affairs, External Trade and Telecommunications: PMB 074, Port Vila; tel. 27045; e-mail depfa@vanuatu.com.vu.

Ministry of Health: PMB 042, Port Vila; tel. 22545; fax 26113.

Ministry of Trade, Industry, Co-operatives and Commerce: PMB 056, Port Vila; tel. 25674; fax 25677.

Ministry of Women's Affairs: PMB 028, Port Vila; tel. 25099; fax 26353.

Legislature

PARLIAMENT

Speaker: HENRI TAGA.

General Election, 2 May 2002 (provisional results)

	Seats
Union of Moderate Parties	15
Vanuaaku Pati	14
National United Party	8
Melanesian Progressive Pati	3
Green Party	3
Vanuatu Republikan Pati	3
Independents and others	6
Total	**52**

Political Organizations

Efate Laketu Party: Port Vila; f. 1982; regional party, based on the island of Efate.

Green Party: Port Vila; f. 2001 by breakaway group of the UMP; Leader GERARD LEYMANG.

Independence Front: Port Vila; f. 1995 by breakaway group of the UMP; Chair. PATRICK CROWBY.

Melanesian Progressive Pati (MPP): POB 39, Port Vila; tel. 23485; fax 23315; f. 1988 by breakaway group from the VP; Chair. BARAK SOPE; Sec.-Gen. GEORGES CALO.

National Democratic Party (NDP): Port Vila; f. 1986; advocates strengthening of links with France and the UK; Leader JOHN NAUPA.

National United Party (NUP): Port Vila; f. 1991 by supporters of Walter Lini, following his removal as leader of the VP; Pres. HAM LINI; Sec.-Gen. WILLIE TITONGOA.

New People's Party (NPP): Port Vila; f. 1986; Leader FRASER SINE.

People's Democratic Party (PDP): Port Vila; f. 1994 by breakaway faction of the NUP.

People's Progressive Party (PPP): Port Vila; f. 2001; formed coalition with National United Party (NUP) and Fren Melanesia to contest 2002 elections; Pres. SATO KILMAN.

Tu Vanuatu Kominiti: Port Vila; f. 1996; espouses traditional Melanesian and Christian values; Leader HILDA LINI.

Union of Moderate Parties (UMP): POB 698, Port Vila; f. 1980; Pres. SERGE VOHOR; the UMP is divided into two factions, one led by SERGE VOHOR and the other by WILLIE JIMMY.

Vanuaaku Pati (VP) (Our Land Party): POB 472, Port Vila; tel. 22584; f. 1971 as the New Hebrides National Party; advocates 'Melanesian socialism'; Pres. EDWARD NATAPEI; First Vice-Pres. IOLU ABBIL; Sec.-Gen. SELA MOLISA.

Vanuatu Independent Alliance Party (VIAP): Port Vila; f. 1982; supports free enterprise; Leaders THOMAS SERU, GEORGE WOREK, KALMER VOCOR.

Vanuatu Independent Movement: Port Vila; f. 2002; Pres. WILLIE TASSO.

Vanuatu Labour Party: Port Vila; f. 1986; trade-union based; Leader KENNETH SATUNGIA.

Vanuatu Republikan Pati (VRP): Port Vila; f. 1998 by breakaway faction of the UMP; Leader MAXIME CARLOT KORMAN.

The **Na-Griamel** (Leader FRANKLEY STEVENS), **Namaki Aute, Tan Union** (Leader VINCENT BULEKONE) and **Fren Melanesia** (Leader ALBERT RAVUTIA) represent rural interests on the islands of Espiritu Santo and Malekula. The **John Frum Movement** represents interests on the island of Tanna.

Diplomatic Representation

EMBASSIES AND HIGH COMMISSIONS IN VANUATU

Australia: KPMG House, POB 111, Port Vila; tel. 22777; fax 23948; e-mail australia_vanuatu@dfat.gov.au; internet www.vanuatu.embassy.gov.au; High Commissioner STEPHEN WATERS.

China, People's Republic: PMB 071, Rue d'Auvergne, Nambatu, Port Vila; tel. 23598; fax 24877; e-mail trade@chinese-embassy.com.vu; Ambassador WU ZURONG.

France: Kumul Highway, POB 60, Port Vila; tel. 22353; fax 22695; Ambassador JEAN GARBE.

New Zealand: BDO House, Lini Highway, POB 161, Port Vila; tel. 22933; fax 22518; e-mail kiwi@vanuatu.com.vu; High Commissioner BRIAN SMYTHE.

United Kingdom: KPMG House, rue Pasteur, POB 567, Port Vila; tel. 23100; fax 23651; e-mail bhcvila@vanuatu.com.vu; High Commissioner MICHAEL HILL.

Judicial System

The Supreme Court has unlimited jurisdiction to hear and determine any civil or criminal proceedings. It consists of the Chief Justice, appointed by the President of the Republic after consultation with the Prime Minister and the leader of the opposition, and three other judges, who are appointed by the President of the Republic on the advice of the Judicial Service Commission.

The Court of Appeal is constituted by two or more judges of the Supreme Court sitting together. The Supreme Court is the court of first instance in constitutional matters and is composed of a single judge.

Magistrates' Courts have limited jurisdiction to hear and determine any civil or criminal proceedings. Island Courts have been established in several Local Government Regions, and are constituted when three justices are sitting together to exercise civil or criminal jurisdiction, as defined in the warrant establishing the court. A magistrate nominated by the Chief Justice acts as Chairman. The Island Courts are competent to rule on land disputes.

In late 2001 legislation was introduced to establish a new Land Tribunal which was intended to expedite the hearing of land disputes. The tribunal was to have three levels, and no cases were to go beyond the tribunal and enter either the Supreme Court or the Island Courts. The tribunal was to be funded by the disputing parties.

In 1986 Papua New Guinea and Vanuatu signed a memorandum of understanding, under which Papua New Guinea Supreme Court judges were to conduct court hearings in Vanuatu, chiefly in the Court of Appeal.

Supreme Court of Vanuatu
PMB 041, rue de Querios, Port Vila; tel. 22420; fax 22692.

Attorney-General: HAMILTON BULU (acting).

Chief Justice: VINCENT LUNABECK (acting).

Chief Prosecutor: HEATHER LINI LEO.

Religion

Most of Vanuatu's inhabitants profess Christianity. Presbyterians form the largest Christian group (with about one-half of the population being adherents), followed by Anglicans and Roman Catholics.

CHRISTIANITY

Vanuatu Christian Council: POB 13, Luganville, Santo; tel. 03232; f. 1967 as New Hebrides Christian Council; five mem. churches, two observers; Chair. Rt Rev MICHEL VISI; Sec. Rev. JOHN LIU.

The Roman Catholic Church

Vanuatu forms the single diocese of Port Vila, suffragan to the archdiocese of Nouméa (New Caledonia). At 31 December 2000 there were an estimated 28,600 adherents in the country. The Bishop participates in the Catholic Bishops' Conference of the Pacific, based in Fiji.

Bishop of Port Vila: Rt Rev. MICHEL VISI, Evêché, POB 59, Port Vila; tel. 22640; fax 25342; e-mail catholik@vanuatu.com.vu.

The Anglican Communion

Anglicans in Vanuatu are adherents of the Church of the Province of Melanesia, comprising eight dioceses: Vanuatu (which also includes New Caledonia), Banks and Torres and six dioceses in Solomon Islands. The Archbishop of the Province is the Bishop of Central Melanesia, resident in Honiara, Solomon Islands. In 1985 the Church had an estimated 16,000 adherents in Vanuatu.

Bishop of Vanuatu: Rt Rev. HUGH BLESSING BOE, Bishop's House, POB 238, Luganville, Santo; tel. 37065; fax 36026.

Bishop of Banks and Torres: Rt Rev. NATHAN TOME, Bishop's House, POB 19, Toutamwat, Torba Province.

Protestant Churches

Presbyterian Church of Vanuatu (Presbitirin Jyos long Vanuatu): POB 150, Port Vila; tel. 23008; fax 26480; f. 1948; 56,000 mems (1995); Moderator Pastor BANI KALSINGER; Assembly Clerk Pastor FAMA RAKAU.

Other denominations active in the country include the Apostolic Church, the Assemblies of God, the Churches of Christ in Vanuatu and the Seventh-day Adventist Church.

BAHÁ'Í FAITH

National Spiritual Assembly of the Bahá'ís of Vanuatu: POB 1017, Port Vila; tel. 22419; e-mail cbpierce@vanuatu.com.vu; f. 1953; Sec. CHARLES PIERCE; mems resident in 191 localities.

The Press

Hapi Tumas Long Vanuatu: POB 1292, Port Vila; tel. 23642; fax 23343; quarterly tourist information; in English; Publr MARC NEIL-JONES; circ. 12,000.

Logging News: Port Vila; environment and logging industry.

Pacific Island Profile: Port Vila; f. 1990; monthly; general interest; English and French; Editor HILDA LINI.

Port Vila Presse: 1st Floor, Raffea House, POB 637, Port Vila; tel. 22200; fax 27999; e-mail marke@presse.com.vu; internet www.presse.com.vu; f. 2000; daily; English and French; Publr MARKE LOWEN; Editor RICKY BINIHI.

The Trading Post: POB 1292, Port Vila; tel. 23111; fax 24111; e-mail tpost@vanuatu.com.vu; 2 a week; English; Publr MARC NEIL-JONES; circ. 2,000.

Vanuatu Weekly: PMB 049, Port Vila; tel. 22999; fax 22026; e-mail vbtcnews@vanuatu.com.vu; f. 1980; weekly; govt-owned; Bislama, English and French; circ. 1,700.

Viewpoints: Port Vila; weekly; newsletter of Vanuaaku Pati; Editor PETER TAURAKOTO.

Wantok Niuspepa: POB 1292, Port Vila; tel. 23642; fax 23343.

Broadcasting and Communications

TELECOMMUNICATIONS

Freedom Telecommunications Company (USA): Santo; f. 2000; provides services on Santo and islands in the north of Vanuatu.

Telecom Vanuatu Ltd (TVL): POB 146, Port Vila; tel. 22185; fax 22628; e-mail telecom@tvl.net.vu; internet www.vanuatu.com.vu; f. 1989 as a joint venture between the Government of Vanuatu, Cable & Wireless Ltd and France Câbles et Radio; operates all national and international telecommunications services in Vanuatu; Man. Dir RICHARD HALL.

BROADCASTING

Radio

Vanuatu Broadcasting and Television Corporation (VBTC): PMB 049, Port Vila; tel. 22999; fax 22026; e-mail vbtcnews@vanuatu .com.vu; internet www.vbtc.com.vu; fmrly Government Media Services, name changed in 1992; Gen. Man. JOE BOMAL CARLO; Chair. PHIL RICHARD; Dir of Programmes A. THOMPSON.

Radio Vanuatu: PMB 049, Port Vila; tel. 22999; fax 22026; f. 1966; govt-owned; broadcasts in English, French and Bislama; Dir JOE BOMAL CARLO.

Television

Vanuatu Broadcasting and Television Corporation (VBTC): see Radio.

Television Blong Vanuatu: PMB 049, Port Vila; f. 1993; govt-owned; French-funded; broadcasts for four hours daily in French and English; Gen. Man. CLAUDE CASTELLY; Programme Man. GAEL LE DANTEC.

Finance

(cap. = capital; res = reserves; dep. = deposits; amounts in vatu unless otherwise indicated)

Vanuatu has no personal income tax nor tax on company profits and is therefore attractive as a financial centre and 'tax haven'.

BANKING

Central Bank

Reserve Bank of Vanuatu: POB 62, Port Vila; tel. 23333; fax 24231; e-mail resrvbnk@vanuatu.com.vu; f. 1981 as Central Bank of Vanuatu; name changed as above in 1989; cap. 100m., res 640.9m., total resources 5,598.1m. (Dec. 1996); Gov. EDWARD NATAPEI.

Development Banks

Development Bank of Vanuatu: rue de Paris, POB 241, Port Vila; tel. 22181; fax 24591; f. 1979; govt-owned; cap. 315m. (Nov. 1988); Man. Dir AUGUSTINE GARAE.

Agence Française de Développement: Kumul Highway, La Casa d'Andrea Bldg, BP 296, Port Vila; tel. 22171; fax 24021; e-mail afd .arep@vanuatu.com.vu; fmrly Caisse Française de Développement; provides finance for various development projects; Man. BERNARD SIRVAIN.

National Bank

National Bank of Vanuatu: POB 249, Air Vanuatu House, rue de Paris, Port Vila; tel. 22201; fax 27227; f. 1991; when it assumed control of Vanuatu Co-operative Savings Bank; govt-owned; cap. 600m., dep. 2,357m. (Dec. 2000); Chair. HAM BULE; Gen. Man. KEN MCARTHUR; 19 brs.

Foreign Banks

ANZ Bank (Vanuatu) Ltd: Lini Highway, POB 123, Port Vila; tel. 22536; fax 23950; e-mail vanuatu@anz.com; internet www.anz.com/vanuatu; f. 1971; cap. 3.7m., res 112.4m., dep. 14,271.2m. (Sept. 1998); Man. Dir MALCOLM TILBROOK; brs in Port Vila and Santo.

European Bank Ltd (USA): International Bldg, Lini Highway, POB 65, Port Vila; tel. 27700; fax 22884; e-mail info@europeanbank .net; internet www.europeanbank.net; cap. US $0.8m., res US $1.3m., dep. US $25.0m. (Dec. 2000); 'offshore' and private banking; Chair. THOMAS MONTGOMERY BAYER; Pres. ROBERT MURRAY BOHN.

Westpac Banking Corporation (Australia): Kumul Highway, POB 32, Port Vila; tel. 22084; fax 24773; e-mail westpacv@vanuatu .com.vu; Man. R. B. WRIGHT; 2 brs.

Financial Institution

The Financial Centre Association: POB 1128, Port Vila; tel. 27272; fax 27272; e-mail fincen@vanuatu.com.vu; f. 1980; group of banking, legal, accounting and trust companies administering 'offshore' banking and investment; Chair. MARK STAFFORD; Sec. ALISTAIR RODGERS.

INSURANCE

Pacific Insurance Brokers: POB 229, Port Vila; tel. 23863; fax 23089.

QBE Insurance (Vanuatu) Ltd: La Casa D'Andrea Bldg, POB 186, Port Vila; tel. 22299; fax 23298; e-mail info.van@qbe.com; Gen. Man. GEOFFREY R. CUTTING.

Trade and Industry

CHAMBER OF COMMERCE

Vanuatu Chamber of Commerce and Industry: POB 189, Port Vila; tel. 27543; fax 27542; e-mail vancci@vanuatu.com.vu; Pres. JOSEPH JACOBE.

MARKETING BOARD

Vanuatu Commodities Marketing Board: POB 268, Luganville, Santo; e-mail vcmb@vanuatu.com.vu; f. 1982; sole exporter of major commodities, including copra, kava and cocoa; Gen. Man. IAN G. BALTOR (acting).

UTILITIES

Electricity

Union Electrique du Vanuatu (Unelco Vanuatu Ltd): POB 26, rue Winston Churchill, Port Vila; tel. 22211; fax 25011; e-mail unelco@unelco.com.vu; private organization contracted for the generation and supply of electricity in Port Vila, Luganville, Tanna and Malekula, and for the supply of water in Port Vila; Dir-Gen. JEAN FRANÇOIS BARBEAU.

Village generators provide electricity in rural areas. The Department of Infrastructure, Utilities and Public Works provides recircu-lated water supplies to about 85% of urban and 30% of rural households.

CO-OPERATIVES

During the early 1980s there were some 180 co-operative primary societies in Vanuatu and at least 85% of goods in the islands were distributed by co-operative organizations. Almost all rural ni-Vanuatu were members of a co-operative society, as were many urban dwellers. By the end of that decade, however, membership of co-operatives had declined, and the organizations' supervisory body, the Vanuatu Co-operative Federation, had been dissolved, after having accumulated debts totalling some $A1m.

TRADE UNIONS

Vanuatu Council of Trade Unions (VCTU): PMB 89, Port Vila; tel. 24517; fax 23679; e-mail synt@vanuatu.com.vu; Pres. OBED MASINGIOW; Sec.-Gen. EPHRAIM KALSAKAU.

National Union of Labour: Port Vila.

The principal trade unions include:

Oil and Gas Workers' Union: Port Vila; f. 1984.

Vanuatu Airline Workers' Union: Port Vila; f. 1984.

Vanuatu Public Service Association: Port Vila.

Vanuatu Teachers' Union: Port Vila; Gen. Sec. CHARLES KALO; Pres. OBED MASSING.

Vanuatu Waterside, Maritime and Allied Workers' Union: Port Vila.

Transport

ROADS

There are about 1,130 km of roads, of which 54 km, mostly on Efate Island, are sealed. In early 1998 Japan granted more than 400m. vatu to finance the sealing of the main road around Efate. In January 2002 an earthquake caused significant damage to the transport infrastructure around Efate. Several foreign donors, including New Zealand, contributed to funding urgent repairs to roads and bridges in the area.

SHIPPING

The principal ports are Port Vila and Luganville.

Vanuatu Maritime Authority: POB 320, Marine Quay, Port Vila; tel. 23128; fax 22949; e-mail vma@vanuatu.com.vu; domestic and international ship registry, maritime safety regulator; Commissioner of Maritime Affairs JOHN T. ROOSEN.

Ports and Marine Department: PMB 046, Port Vila; tel. 22339; fax 22475; Harbour Master Capt. PAUL PETER.

Burns Philp (Vanuatu) Ltd: POB 27, Port Vila.

Ifira Shipping Agencies Ltd: POB 68, Port Vila; tel. 22929; fax 22052; f. 1986; Man. Dir CLAUDE BOUDIER.

Sami Ltd: Kumul Highway, POB 301, Port Vila; tel. 24106; fax 23405.

South Sea Shipping: POB 84, Port Vila; tel. 22205; fax 23304; e-mail southsea@vanuatu.com.vu.

Vanua Navigation Ltd: POB 44, Port Vila; tel. 22027; f. 1977 by the Co-operative Federation and Sofrana Unilines; Chief Exec. GEOFFREY J. CLARKE.

The following services call regularly at Vanuatu: Compagnie Générale Maritime, Kyowa Shipping Co, Pacific Forum Line, Papua New Guinea Shipping Corpn, Sofrana-Unilines, Bank Line, Columbus Line and Bali Hai Shipping. Royal Viking Line, Sitmar and P & O cruises also call at Vanuatu.

CIVIL AVIATION

The principal airports are Bauerfield (Efate, for Port Vila) and Pekoa (Espiritu Santo, for Luganville). There are airstrips on all Vanuatu's principal islands and an international airport at White Grass on Tanna was completed in 1998. The Civil Aviation Corporation Act, approved by Parliament in August 1998, provided for the transfer of ownership of Vanuatu's airports to a commercially-run corporation, in which the Government is to have a majority shareholding. In early 2000 it was announced that a further three airports were to be built on the islands of Pentecost, Malekula and Tanna. Major improvements providing for the accommodation of larger aircraft at both Bauerfield and Pekoa airports began in mid-2000. Moreover, in September 2000 plans for a new international airport at Teouma (Efate) were announced, with finance from a private Thai investor.

In late 2001 plans were also announced for the improvement of the international terminal at Bauerfield airport.

Air Vanuatu (Operations) Ltd: POB 148, Du Vanuatu House, rue de Paris, Port Vila; tel. 23838; fax 23250; e-mail service@airvanuatu .com.vu; internet www.pacificislands.com/airlines/vanuatu.html; f. 1981; govt-owned national carrier since 1987; regular services between Port Vila and Sydney, Brisbane and Melbourne (Australia), Nadi (Fiji), Nouméa (New Caledonia), Auckland (New Zealand), and Honiara (Solomon Islands); Man. Dir and CEO JEAN-PAUL VIRELALA.

Vanair: rue Pasteur, PMB 9069, Port Vila; tel. 22643; fax 23910; e-mail vias@vanuatu.com.vu; internet www.islandsvanuatu.com/vanair.htm; operates scheduled services to 29 destinations within the archipelago; CEO Capt YVES CHEVALIER.

Dovair: Port Vila; privately-owned; operates domestic services.

Tourism

Tourism is an important source of revenue for the Government of Vanuatu. Visitors are attracted by the islands' unspoilt landscape and rich local customs. The establishment of regular air services from Australia and New Zealand in the late 1980s precipitated a significant increase in the number of visitors to Vanuatu. In 2000 there were an estimated 57,364 foreign visitor arrivals in Vanuatu, an increase of 13.0% compared with the previous year. In 1997 passengers on cruise ships visiting the islands numbered 30,530. In 2000 some 64% of visitors were from Australia and 14% were from New Zealand. There was a total of 1,641 hotel beds at the end of 1996. Receipts from tourism totalled some US $58m. in 2000. The development of the tourist industry has hitherto been concentrated on the islands of Efate, Espiritu Santo and Tanna; however, the promotion of other islands as tourist centres is beginning to occur.

National Tourism Office of Vanuatu: Lini Highway, POB 209, Port Vila; tel. 22685; fax 23889; e-mail tourism@vanuatu.com.vu; internet www.vanuatutourism.com; Gen. Man. LINDA KALPOI.

Vanuatu Hotel and Resorts Association: POB 215, Port Vila; tel. 22040; fax 27579; Pres. JOHN GROCOCK.

THE VATICAN CITY

(THE HOLY SEE)

Introductory Survey

Location, Climate, Language, Religion, Flag

The State of the Vatican City is situated entirely within the Italian capital, Rome, on the right bank of the Tiber river. It covers an area of 0.44 sq km (0.17 sq mile). The climate is Mediterranean, with warm summers and mild winters (see Italy). Italian and Latin are the official languages. Roman Catholicism is the official religion. The state flag, which is square, consists of two vertical stripes of yellow and white, with the papal coat of arms superimposed on the white stripe.

History

For a period of nearly 1,000 years, dating roughly from the time of Charlemagne to the year 1870, the Popes ruled much of the central Italian peninsula, including the city of Rome. During the process of unification, the Kingdom of Italy gradually absorbed these States of the Church, the process being completed by the entry into Rome of King Victor Emmanuel's troops in September 1870. From 1860 to 1870 many attempts had been made to induce the Pope, Pius IX, to surrender his temporal possessions. Since, however, he regarded them as a sacred trust from a higher Power, to be guarded on behalf of the Church, he refused to do so. After the entry of the Royal Army into Rome, he retired to the Vatican from where no Pope emerged again until the ratification of the Lateran Treaty of 11 February 1929. By the Law of Guarantees of May 1871, Italy attempted to stabilize the position of the Papacy by recognizing the Pope's claim to use of the Palaces of the Lateran and the Vatican, the Papal villa of Castelgandolfo, and their gardens and annexes, and to certain privileges customary to sovereignty. This unilateral arrangement was not accepted by Pius IX, and his protest against it was repeated constantly by his successors.

In 1929 two agreements were made with the Italian Government—the Lateran Treaty and the Concordat. By the terms of the Lateran Treaty, the Holy See was given exclusive power and sovereign jurisdiction over the State of the Vatican City, which was declared neutral and inviolable territory. Financial compensation was also given for the earlier losses. Under the Concordat, Roman Catholicism became the state religion of Italy, with special privileges defined by law. The new Italian Constitution of 1947 reaffirmed adherence to the Lateran Treaty, but in 1967 negotiations began for a revision of the Concordat. In December 1978 the two sides agreed on a draft plan for a new Concordat, under which Catholicism would cease to be the official Italian state religion and most of the Catholic Church's special privileges in Italy would be removed. The revised version, finally agreed, was signed in February 1984.

In 1917 the first legal code, the Code of Canon Law (Codex Iuris Canonici), was devised for the Catholic Church. In 1963 a pontifical commission was inaugurated to investigate possible reforms to the law, and in 1981 the Pope received more than 70 cardinals and bishops who had prepared the new code's 1,752 rules. Revisions included a reduction in the number of cases meriting excommunication and a general relaxing of penalties, with increased emphasis on the importance of the laity within the church. The code was ratified in January 1983, and came into force in November.

In October 1978 Cardinal Karol Wojtyła (then Archbishop of Kraków in Poland) became the first non-Italian Pope since the 16th century, taking the name John Paul II. Security surrounding the Pontiff was considerably tightened after an attempt on the Pope's life in May 1981 and another in May 1982.

In April 1984 Pope John Paul II announced a major reshuffle of offices in the Roman Curia, which included the delegation of most of his responsibility for the routine administration of the Vatican to the Secretariat of State. In July 1988 a number of reforms to the Curia were introduced. These consolidated the power of the Secretariat of State, as well as reorganizing some of the Congregations and Pontifical Commissions.

In February 1987 Italian judges issued a warrant for the arrest of Archbishop Paul Marcinkus, the Chairman of the Istituto per le Opere di Religione ('Vatican Bank'), and two other bank officials for alleged involvement in the fraudulent bankruptcy of the Banco Ambrosiano in Milan, which collapsed in 1982. In July 1987, however, the Italian Supreme Court cancelled the warrants for the arrest of the three bank officials, stating that the Vatican stood outside Italian jurisdiction and that, according to the Lateran Treaty, Italy did not have the right to interfere in the affairs of the central organs of the Roman Catholic Church. In May 1988, after an appeal, the Archbishop's immunity was endorsed by the Constitutional Court. In March 1989 the Vatican announced a wide-ranging reorganization of the Istituto per le Opere di Religione, by abolishing the post of Chairman, held by Marcinkus, and appointing a commission of five cardinals, nominated by the Pope, to preside over the bank, assisted by a committee of financial experts. Archbishop Marcinkus retired from papal service in October 1990.

In October 1994 Pope John Paul II nominated 30 new cardinals, many from former communist countries, and from regions without a strong tradition of representation in the Roman Catholic hierarchy. The nominations brought the cardinals' conclave close to its maximum size (120 cardinals under the age of 80 are permitted to participate in the election of a new Pope).

In August 1998 the Italian police raided the private apartment of Cardinal Michele Giordano, the Archbishop of Naples, and warned him that he was under investigation for fraud, extortion and usury; Cardinal Giordano strenuously denied any wrongdoing. The cardinal was subsequently acquitted of involvement in a 'loan-sharking' operation, but, in early 2003, remained under trial for tax evasion.

In March 1998 the Vatican released its long-awaited 'definitive statement' condemning anti-Semitism and anti-Judaism, and repenting for Roman Catholic passivity during the Nazi Holocaust. However, a number of high-ranking Jewish officials expressed disappointment in the document and demanded an explicit apology for the attitude of Pope Pius XII and the Roman Catholic Church's failure to speak out, at the time, against Nazi atrocities. In March 2000, during a service in St Peter's Basilica in Rome, despite misgivings expressed by some theologians that such a statement would undermine the Church's authority, the Pope made a comprehensive and unprecedented plea for forgiveness for the 'past sins of the Church', including racial and ethnic discrimination and Christian mistreatment of minorities, women and native peoples. However, in July 2001 a panel of Catholic and Jewish historians was forced to halt its study of the Church's role in the Holocaust when the Vatican refused it access to files on Pope Pius XII; the decision prompted allegations that the Vatican was seeking to conceal potentially damaging evidence. Following further pressure, however, archives covering the years 1922–39 were released in February 2003.

In January 2001 the Pope nominated 44 new cardinals (including three from countries of the former Soviet bloc), and increased the cardinals' conclave to 135, well above the limit of 120 established by Pope Paul VI. In the wake of concern surrounding the Pope's apparently failing health, the appointments were generally regarded as an attempt to strengthen the number of cardinals loyal to his broadly conservative views. Moreover, for the first time ever, a majority of cardinals was non-European, increasing the probability that the Pope's eventual successor would originate from a region other than Europe.

In February 2001 it was announced that the Constitution, dating back to the Lateran Treaty of 1929, was to be replaced by a new Basic Law incorporating a number of constitutional amendments made over the years. The Basic Law improved the distinction between the legislative, executive and judicial branches.

Demonstrations took place outside the offices of Radio Vaticana in April 2001, in protest at the allegedly high rates of electromagnetic radiation emitted by the station's transmitter. These were thought to be linked to an increase in incidences of childhood leukaemia near the transmitter. The radio subsequently pledged to ensure that radiation levels complied with national emission regulations.

In late November 2001 the Pope issued an apology to victims of sexual abuse perpetrated by members of the Catholic clergy. Furthermore, in January 2002 new regulations were published by the Vatican, outlining the appropriate method of dealing with cases of alleged sexual abuse, notably against children, by members of the clergy. However, in mid-2002, in the most significant scandal to affect the Roman Catholic Church in many years, it was revealed that Cardinal Bernard Law, the Archbishop of Boston, USA, had protected a number of priests who faced accusations of sexual misconduct against children. The revelations followed the indictment of Father John Geoghan (also based in Boston) for sexual abuse, and the subsequent accusation by as many as 200 alleged victims that they had suffered sexual abuse involving members of the clergy in the Boston area. Hundreds of priests in the USA resigned or were subsequently suspended or sued in the wake of the allegations. In response, in late April the Pope summoned 13 US cardinals to the Vatican to discuss the crisis. A 'zero tolerance' policy adopted by the US National Conference of Catholic Bishops in June was subsequently rejected by the Vatican; a somewhat altered charter, which provided for the eventual dismissal of any priests found guilty of sexual abuse in a church tribunal, was accepted in December 2002. Victims' groups were disappointed with the revisions, however, which reintroduced a 10-year statute of limitation on accusations. Following the filing of 450 lawsuits against Archbishop Law's diocese and the petition of 58 Boston priests, Law resigned in December 2002.

The publication in March 2003 of a *Lexicon On Ambiguous and Colloquial Terms About Family Life and Ethical Questions* caused controversy by its reaffirmation of the Catholic Church's uncompromising stance regarding birth control and homosexuality.

Meanwhile, in October 2002, the Spanish founder of the conservative 'Opus Dei' movement, Josemaría Escrivá de Balaguer, was canonized only 27 years after his death in 1975.

The Vatican's prominence in international affairs increased from the late 1980s. In July 1989 diplomatic relations with Poland, severed in 1945, were restored. The Vatican had hitherto maintained no diplomatic relations with eastern European Governments under communist rule, except for Yugoslavia. In February 1990 diplomatic relations between the Vatican and Hungary were restored. In the following month permanent official contacts with the USSR were established and a Soviet ambassador to the Vatican was appointed. In April diplomatic relations between the Vatican and Czechoslovakia were restored. By mid-1992, following the collapse of communism in many parts of the world (particularly in eastern Europe) and the disintegration of the USSR in December 1991, the Vatican had established diplomatic relations with the former communist states of Mongolia, Romania, Bulgaria, and with Ukraine and the newly independent Baltic states of Estonia, Latvia and Lithuania. In September 1992 full diplomatic relations were restored, after more than 120 years of discord, between the Vatican and Mexico. In December 1993 the Vatican and Israel signed a mutual-recognition agreement, which led to the establishment of full diplomatic ties and the exchange of ambassadors in September 1994. Meanwhile, in February 1994 the Vatican established diplomatic relations with Jordan, in an apparent move to strengthen links with the Arab world to counterbalance its recent recognition of Israel. Similarly, in October of that year the Vatican instituted 'official relations' with the Palestine Liberation Organization. In 1997 the Vatican established diplomatic relations with Libya and Morocco. By 2002, following the drawing up of an accord with Qatar, the Vatican had diplomatic relations with 176 countries.

Diplomatic relations between the Vatican and China had been severed in 1951 following the communists' accession to power in Beijing. In August 1999 the People's Republic of China vetoed plans for the Pope to visit Hong Kong later that year, owing to the Vatican's diplomatic ties with Taiwan. Any hope of a reconciliation between China and the Vatican looked increasingly unlikely in January 2000, when the state-controlled Patriotic Church in Beijing rebuffed the Pope by ordaining five bishops in a ceremony timed to upstage official papal ordinations in the Vatican City. Relations further deteriorated following the Pope's announcement in September 2000 that he was to canonize 120 western and Chinese Catholics killed in China between 1648 and 1930. The controversy was exacerbated by the decision to

hold the ceremony on China's National Day, the anniversary of the accession to power of communist rule (although the Vatican insisted that the date was merely coincidental). The canonizations were also denounced by Catholic organizations in China. However, in October 2001 the Pope issued an apology to China for the sins committed by Christians against the country; an appeal was also made for diplomatic relations between the two states to be restored. Informal talks recommenced in early 2003, but were somewhat jeopardized by the outspoken anti-Government stance of Hong Kong's Bishop, Joseph Zen Ze-kiun.

In February 2000 the Vatican and the Palestinian (National) Authority signed an historic agreement on joint interests, which appealed for a peaceful solution, through dialogue, to the Israeli-Palestinian conflict and called for an internationally-guaranteed special statute for the city of Jerusalem, which safeguarded freedom of religion and conscience. The Israeli Government criticized the accord as representing unwelcome 'interference' by the Vatican in the ongoing Middle East peace talks. In early 2000 the Pope undertook a millennial pilgrimage to some of the principal biblical sites of the Middle East, including Mount Sinai in Egypt in February (the first ever visit by a pontiff to that country) and Israel, Jordan and the West Bank in March. The Pope's six-day visit to the politically volatile Holy Land constituted the first papal visit to that region for 36 years. In April 2002 an agreement was signed by the Vatican and the Turkish Government, promoting religious dialogue between Muslims and Christians.

In mid-2001 the Pope undertook visits to Greece and Syria, the first of these since the division of Christianity into eastern and western churches. During his visit to Greece, the Pope attempted to heal the historic rift between the Roman Catholic and Orthodox churches by presenting an apology to the Orthodox community for wrongs committed over the centuries by the Roman Catholic Church. The Pope, despite not being granted the consent of the Russian Orthodox Patriarch, also visited Ukraine, where he called for an end to the 1,000-year schism between Roman Catholicism and the Orthodox Church in Ukraine and, by extension, the Russian Orthodox Church. The leaders of the Orthodox Church in Ukraine refused to meet the Pope, although his visit attracted much popular support. In September the Pope visited Armenia, becoming the first ever pontiff to visit the country.

Tensions between the Roman Catholic Church and the Russian Orthodox Church increased in February 2002 when the Vatican announced that the four apostolic administrations in Russia (officially considered to be temporary) had become dioceses. This move was interpreted by representatives of the Russian Orthodox Church as the establishment of an alternative church within the country, and a few days later a visit to Russia by the Head of the Pontifical Council for the Promotion of Christian Unity, Cardinal Walter Kasper, was cancelled by the Russian Orthodox Church. A papal visit to Mongolia planned for late 2003 opened the possibility of a visit to Russia en route, in an attempt to overcome differences between the churches.

In November 2002 Jean-Paul II became the first pontiff to address the Italian Parliament, symbolically closing the Vatican's territorial dispute with Italy. His speech advocated institutional recognition by the EU of Europe's Christian heritage; this followed a call in October that Christianity be enshrined in the proposed EU constitution. During late 2002 and early 2003 the Pope was one of the world leaders most vocal in opposition to possible US-led military invention against the regime of Saddam Hussein in Iraq; he denounced the planned conflict as a 'defeat for humanity', and urged a diplomatic resolution to the crisis. February and March 2003 witnessed much diplomatic activity, the Pope granting a series of private audiences to key international figures, including Tareq Aziz, the Deputy Prime Minister of Iraq, Kofi Annan, the Secretary-General of the UN, the British Prime Minister, Tony Blair, and Prime Minister Silvio Berlusconi of Italy. Papal envoys were also sent to Baghdad and Washington. This was followed in March by an historic five-day meeting with a delegation from Israel's Chief Rabbinate.

The population of the Vatican City was 475 at December 1997. Its inhabitants are of many nationalities, representing the presence of the Roman Catholic Church throughout the world. The papal guards, who number some 110, are of Swiss nationality.

Finance

The Vatican has three main sources of income: the Istituto per le Opere di Religione (see Directory), voluntary contributions to the Church, known as 'Peter's Pence' (Obolo di San Pietro), and interest on financial investments, managed by the Administration of the Patrimony of the Holy See. Italian currency is used. The Vatican first revealed budget figures for the Holy See in 1979, when it disclosed a deficit of US $20.1m. This was incurred through the normal operating expenses of the Vatican bureaucracy, including the newspaper and radio services and overseas diplomatic missions. The alleged mismanagement of investments, banking scandals and the decline in the value of the US dollar contributed to a deficit of $56.7m. in 1986, when annual income reached $57m. The deficit was met by the receipt of $32m. from the 'Peter's pence' levy, and by the withdrawal of $24.7m. from the 'Peter's pence' reserve fund. In March 1988 the Vatican published an independently audited annual balance sheet, thereby, for the first time in its history, revealing the church's financial affairs to public scrutiny. During 1988–1990 the budget deficit continued to grow, and in April 1991 more than 100 representatives of bishops' conferences from around the world attended an unprecedented meeting held in the Vatican City, at which they discussed ways of making local dioceses systematically share the burden of the Vatican's annual budg-

etary deficit. In that year, however, the budgetary deficit reached a peak of $87.5m. The establishment of new diplomatic missions in the late 1980s and early 1990s (see History) entailed considerable capital expenditure for the papacy. However, in 1992 the deficit fell substantially and in 1993, after 23 years of budgetary deficits, a modest surplus, of $1.5m., was recorded (expenditure $167.5m.; income $169m., including $59.9m. in 'Peter's pence' contributions). A small annual budgetary surplus was maintained thoughout the 1990s, cumulating in a surplus of $8.5m. in 2000, a 70% rise compared with 1999, which reflected the greater receipts generated by activities associated with the jubilee year. 'Peter's pence' amounted to $63.6m in 2000. The budget for 2001, in contrast, showed the first deficit since 1993, of $3.1m. (expenditure $177m.; income $174m.), as a result of a slowdown in the global economy; 'Peter's pence' contributions for that year, not included in the consolidated budget, amounted to almost $52m.

The Istituto per le Opere di Religione has consistently returned an operating profit, although much of the revenue generated by it in the 1980s was used to repay the creditors remaining from the collapse of the Banco Ambrosiano in 1982.

Directory

Government

The State of the Vatican City came into existence with the Lateran Treaty of 1929. The Holy See (a term designating the papacy, i.e. the office of the Pope, and thus the central governing body of the Roman Catholic Church) is a distinct, pre-existing entity. Both entities are subjects of international law. Ambassadors and Ministers are accredited to the Holy See, which sends diplomatic representatives (Nuncios and Pro-Nuncios) to more than 120 states, as well as having Delegates or Observers at the UN and other international organizations. The Vatican City is also a member of certain international organizations, including specialized agencies of the UN.

Both entities are indissolubly united in the person of the Pope, the Bishop of Rome, who is simultaneously ruler of the State and visible head of the Roman Catholic Church.

On 1 February 2001 a new Basic Law replaced the former Constitution dating back to the 1929 Lateran Treaty.

THE GOVERNMENT OF THE VATICAN CITY STATE

The Vatican City State is under the temporal jurisdiction of the Pope, the Supreme Pontiff elected for life by a conclave comprising members of the Sacred College of Cardinals. The Pope holds all legislative, executive and judicial power. Legislative power is vested in the Pontifical Commission for the Vatican State, which comprises a Cardinal President and six other Cardinals, nominated by the Pope for a five-year period. Executive power is vested in the President of the Pontifical Commission (who is also the President of the Governorate of the Vatican City State), who is assisted by a Secretary-General. The State Councillors, including one General Councillor and eight other Councillors, are nominated by the Pope for a five-year period, and assist in the drawing-up of laws and report to the Pontifical Commission. Judiciary power is vested in a number of Tribunals and the Apostolic Penitentiary, who exercise their judicial authority in the name of the Pope. The Pontiff exclusively retains the right to grant pardons and amnesties.

Head of State

His Holiness Pope JOHN PAUL II (elected 16 October 1978).

Pontifical Commission for the Vatican City State

Cardinal EDMUND CASIMIR SZOKA (President).

Cardinal ANGELO SODANO.

Cardinal GIOVANNI BATTISTA RE.

Cardinal JOZEF TOMKO.

Cardinal ANDRZEJ MARIA DESKUR.

Cardinal JAN PIETER SCHOTTE.

Cardinal AGOSTINO CACCIAVILLAN.

State Councillors

Marchese Dott. GIULIO SACCHETTI (General Councillor).

There are eight additional councillors.

Governorate of the Vatican City State

President: Cardinal EDMUND CASIMIR SZOKA.

Secretary-General: Rt Rev. GIANNI DANZI (Titular Bishop of Castello).

Vice Secretary-General: Rev. GIORGIO CORBELLINI.

THE SUPREME PONTIFF

His Holiness Pope John Paul II (Karol Wojtyła), Bishop of Rome, Vicar of Christ, Successor of the Prince of the Apostles, Supreme Pontiff of the Universal Church, Patriarch of the West, Primate of Italy, Archbishop and Metropolitan of the Province of Rome, Sovereign of the Vatican City State, Servant of the Servants of God; acceded 16 October 1978, as the 264th Roman Pontiff.

THE SACRED COLLEGE OF CARDINALS AND THE ROMAN CURIA

Members of the Sacred College of Cardinals are created by the Pope. The cardinals are divided into three orders: Bishops (including the Cardinal of Patriarchal Sees of Oriental Rites), Priests and Deacons. Under the decree of November 1970, *Ingravescentem Aetatem* only Cardinals under 80 years of age have the right to enter the conclave for the election of the Pope. Cardinals who reside in Rome, Italy, as the Pope's immediate advisers are styled Cardinals 'in Curia'. The Roman Curia acts as the Papal court and the principal administrative body of the Church. The College of Cardinals derives from the Church's earliest days. At 31 December 2002 there were 171 Cardinals. In March 1973 the Pope announced that the number of Cardinals permitted to participate in the conclave would be limited to 120. This was increased to 135 in February 2001 following the appointment of 44 new cardinals by Pope John Paul II. There are usually six Cardinal Bishops who are in titular charge of suburban sees of Rome—Sabina-Poggio Mirteto and Ostia, Albano, Frascati, Palestrina, Porto and Santa Rufina, and Velletri and Segni. The order of Cardinal Bishops also includes three Cardinals of Patriarchal Sees of Oriental Rites. Cardinal Priests occupy titular churches in Rome, Italy, founded soon after Christianity originated. The administration of the Church's affairs is undertaken through the Secretariat of State and the Council for the Public Affairs of the Church, under the Cardinal Secretary of State, and through a number of Congregations, each under the direction of a Cardinal or senior member of the Church, as well as through Tribunals, Offices, Commissions and Secretariats for special purposes.

The 'Apostolic Constitution' (Regimini Ecclesiae Universae), published in August 1967 and effective from 1 March 1968, reformed the Roman Curia. Among the changes were the creation of new organs and the restructuring of the Secretariat of State. In 1969 the Congregation of Rites was divided into two Congregations—one for Divine Worship and the other for the Causes of Saints. The Congregation for the Discipline of the Sacraments and the Congregation for Divine Worship were amalgamated in 1975, but separated again in 1984.

In July 1988 further reforms of the Curia were introduced. The Secretariat of State was divided into two sections: the first section dealing with 'General Affairs' and the second 'Relations with States'.

The Congregation for Divine Worship was again amalgamated with the Congregation for the Discipline of the Sacraments.

Cardinal Bishops

(Members in order of precedence)

JOSEPH RATZINGER (Germany—Titular Bishop of Velletri-Segni, Prefect of the Congregation for the Doctrine of the Faith, President of the International Theological Commission and of the Pontifical Biblical Commission, and Dean of the College of Cardinals).

ANGELO SODANO (Italy—Titular Bishop of Albano, Secretary of State and Vice-Dean of the College of Cardinals).

BERNARDIN GANTIN (Benin—Titular Bishop of Palestrina and of Ostia).

ROGER ETCHEGARAY (France—Titular Bishop of Porto-Santa Rufina).

ALFONSO LÓPEZ TRUJILLO (Colombia—President of the Pontifical Council for the Family).

GIOVANNI BATTISTA RE (Italy—Prefect of the Congregation for the Bishops and President of the Pontifical Commission for Latin America).

Cardinals of Patriarchal Sees of Oriental Rites

NASRALLAH PIERRE SFEIR (Lebanon—Maronite Patriarch of Antioch).

STÉPHANOS II GHATTAS (Egypt—Coptic Patriarch of Alexandria).

IGNACE MOUSSA I DAOUD (Syria—Prefect of the Congregation of Oriental Churches, Grand Chancellor of the Pontifical Oriental Institute).

Cardinal Priests

FRANZ KÖNIG (Austria).

CORRADO URSI (Italy).

STEPHEN KIM SOU-HWAN (Republic of Korea).

EUGÊNIO DE ARAÚJO SALES (Brazil).

JOHANNES WILLEBRANDS (Netherlands).

LUIS APONTE MARTÍNEZ (Puerto Rico).

RAÚL FRANCISCO PRIMATESTA (Argentina).

SALVATORE PAPPALARDO (Italy).

MARCELO GONZÁLEZ MARTÍN (Spain).

MAURICE MICHAEL OTUNGA (Kenya).

PAULO EVARISTO ARNS (Brazil).

PIO TAOFINU'U (Samoa—Archbishop of Samoa-Apia).

OPILIO ROSSI (Italy).

JUAN CARLOS ARAMBURU (Argentina).

CORRADO BAFILE (Italy).

HYACINTHE THIANDOUM (Senegal).

JAIME L. SIN (Philippines—Archbishop of Manila).

WILLIAM WAKEFIELD BAUM (USA).

ALOÍSIO LORSCHEIDER (Brazil—Archbishop of Aparecida).

GIUSEPPE CAPRIO (Italy).

MARCO CÉ (Italy—Patriarch of Venice).

ERNESTO CORRIPIO AHUMADA (Mexico).

GERALD EMMETT CARTER (Canada).

FRANCISZEK MACHARSKI (Poland—Archbishop of Kraków).

AURELIO SABATTANI (Italy).

MICHAEL MICHAI KITBUNCHU (Thailand—Archbishop of Bangkok).

ALEXANDRE DO NASCIMENTO (Angola).

GODFRIED DANNEELS (Belgium—Archbishop of Mechelen-Brussels).

THOMAS STAFFORD WILLIAMS (New Zealand—Archbishop of Wellington).

CARLO MARIA MARTINI (Italy).

JEAN-MARIE LUSTIGER (France—Archbishop of Paris).

JÓZEF GLEMP (Poland—Archbishop of Warsaw).

JOACHIM MEISNER (Germany—Archbishop of Cologne).

D. SIMON LOURDUSAMY (India).

FRANCIS A. ARINZE (Nigeria—President of the Pontifical Council for Inter-Religious Dialogue and Prefect of the Congregation for Divine Worship and the Discipline of the Sacraments).

JUAN FRANCISCO FRESNO LARRAÍN (Chile).

ANTONIO INNOCENTI (Italy).

MIGUEL OBANDO BRAVO (Nicaragua—Archbishop of Managua).

PAUL AUGUSTIN MAYER (Germany).

ANGEL SUQUÍA GOICOECHEA (Spain).

RICARDO J. VIDAL (Philippines—Archbishop of Cebu).

HENRYK ROMAN GULBINOWICZ (Poland—Archbishop of Wrocław).

PAULOS TZADUA (Ethiopia).

JOZEF TOMKO (Slovakia—President of the Pontifical Committee for International Eucharistic Congresses).

ANDRZEJ MARIA DESKUR (Poland).

PAUL POUPARD (France—President of the Pontifical Council for Culture).

LOUIS-ALBERT VACHON (Canada).

ROSALIO JOSÉ CASTILLO LARA (Venezuela).

FRIEDRICH WETTER (Germany—Archbishop of Munich and Freising).

SILVANO PIOVANELLI (Italy).

ADRIANUS JOHANNES SIMONIS (Netherlands—Archbishop of Utrecht).

EDOUARD GAGNON (Canada).

ALFONS MARIA STICKLER (Austria).

BERNARD FRANCIS LAW (USA).

GIACOMO BIFFI (Italy—Archbishop of Bologna).

EDUARDO MARTÍNEZ SOMALO (Spain—Prefect of the Congregation for Institutes of Consecrated Life and for Societies of Apostolic Life, and Chamberlain of the Holy Roman Church).

ACHILLE SILVESTRINI (Italy).

ANGELO FELICI (Italy).

JOSÉ FREIRE FALCÃO (Brazil—Archbishop of Brasília).

MICHELE GIORDANO (Italy—Archbishop of Naples).

ALEXANDRE JOSÉ MARIA DOS SANTOS (Mozambique—Archbishop of Maputo).

GIOVANNI CANESTRI (Italy).

ANTONIO MARÍA JAVIERRE ORTAS (Spain).

SIMON IGNATIUS PIMENTA (India).

EDWARD BEDE CLANCY (Australia—Archbishop of Sydney).

JAMES ALOYSIUS HICKEY (USA).

EDMUND CASIMIR SZOKA (USA—President of the Pontifical Commission for the Vatican City State, President of the Governorate of the State of the Vatican City).

LÁSZLÓ PASKAI (Hungary—Archbishop of Esztergom-Budapest).

CHRISTIAN WIYGHAN TUMI (Cameroon—Archbishop of Douala).

HANS HERMANN GROËR (Austria).

JEAN MARGÉOT (Mauritius).

PIO LAGHI (Italy—Patron of the Supreme Military Order of Malta).

EDWARD IDRIS CASSIDY (Australia).

FRÉDÉRIC ETSOU-NZABI-BAMUNGWABI (Democratic Republic of the Congo—Archbishop of Kinshasa).

NICOLÁS DE JESÚS LÓPEZ RODRÍGUEZ (Dominican Republic—Archbishop of Santo Domingo).

JOSÉ T. SÁNCHEZ (Philippines).

VIRGILIO NOÈ (Italy—Archpriest of the Vatican Patriarchal Basilica, Vicar-Gen. of His Holiness for the Vatican City and President of the Fabbrica di San Pietro).

FIORENZO ANGELINI (Italy).

ROGER MICHAEL MAHONY (USA—Archbishop of Los Angeles).

ANTHONY JOSEPH BEVILACQUA (USA—Archbishop of Philadelphia).

GIOVANNI SALDARINI (Italy).

CAHAL BRENDAN DALY (Ireland).

CAMILLO RUINI (Italy—Vicar-General of His Holiness for the Diocese of Rome, Archpriest of the Lateran Patriarchal Arcibasilica, and Grand Chancellor of the Lateran Pontifical University).

JÁN CHRYZOSTOM KOREC (Slovakia—Bishop of Nitra).

HENRI SCHWÉRY (Switzerland).

GEORG MAXIMILIAN STERZINSKY (Germany—Archbishop of Berlin).

MILOSLAV VLK (Czech Republic—Archbishop of Prague).

PETER SEIICHI SHIRAYANAGI (Japan).

ADOLFO ANTONIO SUÁREZ RIVERA (Mexico—Archbishop of Monterrey).

JULIUS RIYADI DARMAATMADJA (Indonesia—Archbishop of Jakarta).

JAIME LUCAS ORTEGA Y ALAMINO (Cuba—Archbishop of San Cristóbal de la Habana).

EMMANUEL WAMALA (Uganda—Archbishop of Kampala).

WILLIAM HENRY KEELER (USA—Archbishop of Baltimore).

JEAN-CLAUDE TURCOTTE (Canada—Archbishop of Montreal).

RICARDO MARÍA CARLES GORDÓ (Spain—Archbishop of Barcelona).

ADAM JOSEPH MAIDA (USA—Archbishop of Detroit, and Superior of the Cayman Islands).

VINKO PULJIĆ (Bosnia and Herzegovina—Archbishop of Vrhbosna).

ARMAND GAÉTAN RAZAFINDRATANDRA (Madagascar—Archbishop of Antananarivo).

PAUL JOSEPH PHAM DÌNH TUNG (Viet Nam—Archbishop of Hanoi).

JUAN SANDOVAL IÑIGUEZ (Mexico—Archbishop of Guadalajara).

KAZIMIERZ ŚWIĄTEK (Belarus—Archbishop of Minsk and Mogilev and Apostolic Administrator of Pinsk).

ERSILIO TONINI (Italy).

SALVATORE DE GIORGI (Italy—Archbishop of Palermo).

SERAFIM FERNANDES DE ARAÚJO (Brazil—Archbishop of Belo Horizonte).

ANTONIO MARÍA ROUCO VARELA (Spain—Archbishop of Madrid).

ALOYSIUS MATTHEW AMBROZIC (Canada—Archbishop of Toronto).

DIONIGI TETTAMANZI (Italy—Archbishop of Milan).

POLYCARP PENGO (Tanzania—Archbishop of Dar-es-Salaam).

CHRISTOPH SCHÖNBORN (Austria—Archbishop of Vienna).

NORBERTO RIVERA CARRERA (Mexico—Archbishop of Mexico City).

FRANCIS EUGENE GEORGE (USA—Archbishop of Chicago).

PAUL SHAN KUO-HSI (Taiwan—Bishop of Kaohsiung).

ADAM KOZŁOWIECKI (Zambia).

MARIAN JAWORSKI (Ukraine—Archbishop of Lviv—Latin Rite).

JĀNIS PUJATS (Latvia—Archbishop of Rīga).

ANTONIO JOSÉ GONZÁLEZ ZUMÁRRAGA (Ecuador—Archbishop of Quito).

IVAN DIAS (India—Archbishop of Bombay/Mumbai).

GERALDO MAJELLA AGNELO (Brazil—Archbishop of São Salvador de Bahia).

PEDRO RUBIANO SÁENZ (Colombia—Archbishop of Santafé de Bogotá).

THEODORE EDGAR MCCARRICK (USA— Archbishop of Washington).

DESMOND CONNELL (Ireland—Archbishop of Dublin).

AUDRYS JUOZAS BAČKIS (Lithuania—Archbishop of Vilnius).

FRANCISCO JAVIER ERRÁZURIZ OSSA (Chile—Archbishop of Santiago de Chile).

JULIO TERRAZAS SANDOVAL (Bolivia—Archbishop of Santa Cruz de la Sierra).

WILFRID FOX NAPIER (South Africa—Archbishop of Durban).

OSCAR ANDRÉS RODRÍGUES MARADIAGA (Honduras—Archbishop of Tegucigalpa).

BERNARD AGRÉ (Côte d'Ivoire—Archbishop of Abidjan).

IGNACIO ANTONIO VELASCO GARCÍA (Venezuela—Archbishop of Caracas).

JUAN LUIS CIPRIANI THORNE (Peru—Archbishop of Lima).

FRANCISCO ALVAREZ MARTÍNEZ (Spain—Archbishop of Toledo).

CLÁUDIO HUMMES (Brazil—Archbishop of São Paulo).

VARKEY VITHAYATHIL (India—Major Archbishop of Ernakulam-Angamaly).

JORGE MARIO BERGOGLIO (Argentina—Archbishop of Buenos Aires).

JOSÉ DA CRUZ POLICARPO (Portugal—Patriarch of Lisbon).

SEVERINO POLETTO (Italy—Archbishop of Turin).

CORMAC MURPHY-O'CONNOR (United Kingdom—Archbishop of Westminster).

EDWARD MICHAEL EGAN (USA—Archbishop of New York).

LUBOMYR HUSAR (Ukraine—Archbishop-Major of Lviv—Byzantine Ukrainian Rite).

KARL LEHMANN (Germany—Bishop of Mainz).

JEAN HONORÉ (France).

Cardinal Deacons

LUIGI POGGI (Italy).

CARLO FURNO (Italy—Grand Master of the Equestrian Order of the Holy Sepulchre of Jerusalem and Archpriest of the Patriarchal Liberian Basilica of Santa Maria Maggiore).

JAN PIETER SCHOTTE (Belgium—Secretary-General of the Synod of Bishops and President of the Office of Work of the Apostolic See).

GILBERTO AGUSTONI (Italy).

JORGE ARTURO MEDINA ESTÉVEZ (Chile).

DARÍO CASTRILLÓN HOYOS (Colombia—Prefect of the Congregation for the Clergy, and President of the Pontifical Commission 'Ecclesia Dei').

LORENZO ANTONETTI (Italy—Pontifical Delegate for the Patriarchal Basilica of St Francis in Assisi).

JAMES FRANCIS STAFFORD (USA—President of the Pontifical Council for the Laity).

GIOVANNI CHELI (Italy).

FRANCESCO COLASUONNO (Italy).

DINO MONDUZZI (Italy).

AGOSTINO CACCIAVILLAN (Italy—President of the Administration of the Patrimony of the Holy See).

SERGIO SEBASTIANI (Italy—President of the Prefecture of the Economic Affairs of the Holy See).

ZENON GROCHOLEWSKI (Poland—Prefect of the Congregation for Catholic Education and Grand Chancellor of the Università Gregoriana).

JOSÉ SARAIVA MARTINS (Portugal—Prefect of the Congregation for the Causes of Saints).

CRESCENZIO SEPE (Italy—Prefect of the Congregation for the Evangelization of Peoples and Grand Chancellor of the Università Urbaniana).

JORGE MARÍA MEJÍA (Argentina—Archivist and Librarian for the Holy Roman Church).

MARIO FRANCESCO POMPEDDA (Italy—Prefect of the Supreme Tribunal of the Apostolic Signature).

WALTER KASPER (Germany—President of the Pontifical Council for the Promotion of Christian Unity).

ROBERTO TUCCI (Italy).

LEO SCHEFFCZYK (Poland).

AVERY DULLES (USA).

THE ROMAN CURIA

Secretariat of State: Palazzo Apostolico Vaticano, 00120 Città del Vaticano; tel. (06) 69883913; fax (06) 69885255; e-mail vati026@relstat-segstat.va; Sec. of State Cardinal ANGELO SODANO; divided into two sections:

First Section—General Affairs: Segreteria di Stato, 00120 Città del Vaticano; tel. (06) 69883438; fax (06) 69885088; e-mail vati023@genaff-segstat.va; Asst Sec. of State Most Rev. LEONARDO SANDRI (Titular Archbishop of Cittanova).

Second Section—Relations with States: Palazzo Apostolico Vaticano, 00120 Città del Vaticano; tel. (06) 69883014; fax (06) 69885364; e-mail vati032@relstat-segstat.va; Sec. Most Rev. JEAN-LOUIS TAURAN (Titular Archbishop of Thelepte).

Congregations

Congregation for the Doctrine of the Faith: Palazzo della Congregazione per la Dottrina della Fede, Piazza del S. Uffizio 11, 00193 Rome, Italy; tel. (06) 69883357; fax (06) 69883409; concerned with questions of doctrine and morals; examines doctrines and gives a judgement on them; Prefect Cardinal JOSEPH RATZINGER; Sec. Most Rev. ANGELO AMATO.

Congregation for the Eastern Churches: Palazzo del Bramante, Via della Conciliazione 34, 00193 Rome, Italy; tel. (06) 69884293; fax (06) 69884300; f. 1862; exercises jurisdiction over all persons and things pertaining to the Oriental Rites; Prefect Cardinal IGNACE MOUSSA I DAOUD; Sec. Most Rev. ANTONIO MARIA VEGLIÒ (Titular Archbishop of Eclano).

Congregation for Divine Worship and the Discipline of the Sacraments: Palazzo delle Congregazioni, Piazza Pio XII 10, 00193 Rome, Italy; tel. (06) 69884316; fax (06) 69883499; e-mail cultdiv@ccdds.va; internet www.ccds.va; considers all questions relating to divine worship, liturgy and the sacraments; Prefect Cardinal FRANCIS A. ARINZE; Sec. Most Rev. FRANCESCO PIO TAMBURRINO.

Congregation for the Causes of Saints: Palazzo delle Congregazioni, Piazza Pio XII 10, 00193 Rome, Italy; tel. (06) 69884247; fax (06) 69881935; e-mail vati335@csaints.va; concerned with the proceedings relating to beatification and canonization; Prefect Cardinal JOSÉ SARAIVA MARTINS; Sec. Most Rev. EDWARD NOWAK (Titular Archbishop of Luni).

Congregation for the Bishops: Palazzo delle Congregazioni, Piazza Pio XII 10, 00193 Rome, Italy; tel. (06) 69884217; fax (06) 69885303; e-mail vati076@cbishops.va; designed for the preparation of matters for the erection and division of dioceses and the election of Bishops and for dealing with Apostolic Visitations; Prefect Cardinal GIOVANNI BATTISTA RE; Sec. Most Rev. FRANCESCO MONTERISI (Titular Archbishop of Alba maritima).

Pontifical Commission for Latin America: Palazzo di San Paolo, Via della Conciliazione 1, 00193 Rome, Italy; tel. (06) 69883131; fax (06) 69884260; e-mail pcal@latinamer.va; Pres. Cardinal GIOVANNI BATTISTA RE; Vice-Pres. Rt Rev. CIPRIANO CALDERÓN POLO (Titular Bishop of Thagora).

Congregation for the Evangelization of Peoples: Palazzo di Propaganda Fide, Piazza di Spagna 48, 00187 Rome, Italy; tel. (06) 69879299; fax (06) 69880118; e-mail cepsegreteria@evangel.va; exercises ecclesiastical jurisdiction over missionary countries; Prefect Cardinal CRESCENZIO SEPE; Sec. Most Rev. ROBERT SARAH (Titular Archbishop of Conakry).

Congregation for the Clergy: Palazzo delle Congregazioni, Piazza Pio XII 3, 00193 Rome, Italy; tel. (06) 69884151; fax (06) 69884845; e-mail clero@cclergy.va; internet www.clero.org; controls the life and discipline of the clergy and its permanent formation; parishes, chapters, pastoral and presbyteral councils; promotes catechesis and the preaching of the Word of God; deals with economic questions related to the compensation of the clergy and the patrimony of parishes; Prefect Cardinal DARÍO CASTRILLÓN HOYOS; Sec. Most Rev. CSABA TERNYÁK (Titular Archbishop of Eminentiana).

Congregation for Institutes of Consecrated Life and for Societies of Apostolic Life: Palazzo delle Congregazioni, Piazza Pio XII 3, 00193 Rome, Italy; tel. (06) 69884128; fax (06) 69884526; e-mail civcsva@ccscrlife.va; promotes and supervises practice of evangelical counsels, according to approved forms of consecrated life, and activities of societies of apostolic life; Prefect Cardinal EDUARDO MARTÍNEZ SOMALO; Sec. Most Rev. PIERGIORGIO SILVANO NESTI.

Congregation for Catholic Education: Palazzo delle Congregazioni, Piazza Pio XII 3, 00193 Rome, Italy; tel. (06) 69884167; fax (06) 69884172; concerned with the direction, temporal administration and studies of Catholic universities, seminaries, schools and colleges; Prefect Cardinal ZENON GROCHOLEWSKI; Sec. Most Rev. GIUSEPPE PITTAU (Titular Archbishop of Castro di Sardegna).

Tribunals

Apostolic Penitentiary: Palazzo della Cancelleria, Piazza della Cancelleria 1, 00186 Rome, Italy; tel. (06) 69887603; fax (06) 69887557; Pro Grand Penitentiary Most Rev. LUIGI DE MAGISTRIS (Titular Archbishop of Nova); Regent Most Rev. GIANFRANCO GIROTTI.

Supreme Tribunal of the Apostolic Signature: Palazzo della Cancelleria, Piazza della Cancelleria 1, 00186 Rome, Italy; tel. (06) 69887520; fax (06) 69887553; Prefect Cardinal MARIO FRANCESCO POMPEDDA; Sec. Rt Rev. FRANCESCO SAVERIO SALERNO (Titular Bishop of Cerveteri).

Tribunal of the Roman Rota: Palazzo della Cancelleria, Piazza della Cancelleria 1, 00186 Rome, Italy; tel. (06) 69887502; fax (06) 69887554; Dean Mgr RAFFAELLO FUNGHINI.

Pontifical Councils

Pontifical Council for the Laity: Piazza S. Calisto 16, 00153 Rome, Italy; tel. (06) 69887322; fax (06) 69887214; e-mail vati089@laity.va; advises and conducts research, on lay apostolic initiatives; Pres. Cardinal JAMES FRANCIS STAFFORD; Sec. Rt Rev. STANISŁAW RYŁKO (Titular Bishop of Novica).

Pontifical Council for the Promotion of Christian Unity: Via dell'Erba 1, 00193 Rome, Italy; tel. (06) 69884083; fax (06) 69885365; e-mail office1@chrstuni.va; f. 1964; Pres. Cardinal WALTER KASPER; Sec. Rt Rev. BRIAN FARREL (Titular Bishop of Abitine).

Pontifical Council for the Family: Piazza S. Calisto 16, 00153 Rome, Italy; tel. (06) 69887243; fax (06) 69887272; e-mail pcf@family.va; Pres. Cardinal ALFONSO LÓPEZ TRUJILLO; Sec. Rt Rev. KARL JOSEF ROMER (Titular Bishop of Colonnata).

Pontifical Council for Justice and Peace: Piazza S. Calisto 16, 00153 Rome, Italy; tel. (06) 69879911; fax (06) 69887205; e-mail pcjustpax@justpeace.va; to promote social justice, human rights, peace and development in needy areas; Pres. Rt Rev. RENATO RAFFAELE MARTINO (Titular Bishop of Segerme); Sec. Rt Rev. GIAMPAOLO CREPALDI (Titular Bishop of Bisarcio).

Pontifical Council 'Cor Unum': Piazza S. Calisto 16, 00153 Rome, Italy; tel. (06) 69889411; fax (06) 69887301; e-mail corunum@corunum.va; f. 1971; Pres. Most Rev. PAUL JOSEF CORDES (Titular Archbishop of Naissus); Sec. Rt Rev. Mgr KAREL KASTEEL.

Pontifical Council for the Pastoral Care of Migrants and Itinerant People: Piazza S. Calisto 16, 00153 Rome, Italy; tel. (06) 69887193; fax (06) 69887111; e-mail office@migrants.va; f. 1970; Pres. Most Rev. STEPHEN FUMIO HAMAO; Sec. Most Rev. AGOSTINO MARCHETTO (Titular Archbishop of Astigi).

Pontifical Council for Health Professionals: Via della Conciliazione 3, 00193 Rome, Italy; tel. (06) 69883138; fax (06) 69883139; e-mail opersanit@hlthwork.va; internet www.healthpastoral.org; Pres. Most Rev. JAVIER LOZANO BARRAGÁN; Sec. Rt Rev. JOSÉ LUIS REDRADO MARCHITE (Titular Bishop of Ofena).

Pontifical Council for Legislative Texts: Palazzo delle Congregazioni, Piazza Pio XII 10, 00193 Rome, Italy; tel. (06) 69884008; fax (06) 69884710; f. 1984; Pres. Most Rev. JULIÁN HERRANZ (Titular Archbishop of Vertara); Sec. Rt Rev. BRUNO BERTAGNA (Titular Bishop of Drivasto).

Pontifical Council for Inter-Religious Dialogue: Via dell'Erba 1, 00193 Rome, Italy; tel. (06) 69884321; fax (06) 69884494; e-mail pcid-office@interelg.va; f. 1964; Pres. Most Rev. MICHAEL LOUIS FITZGERALD (Titular Archbishop of Nepte); Sec. Most Rev. PIER LUIGI CELATA (Titular Archbishop of Dolcea).

Pontifical Council for Culture: Piazza S. Calisto 16, 00153 Rome, Italy; tel. (06) 69893811; fax (06) 69887368; e-mail cultura@cultr.va; merged with Pontifical Council for Dialogue with Non-Believers in 1993; promotes understanding and dialogue between the Church and both the arts and non-believers; Pres. Cardinal PAUL POUPARD; Sec. Fr BERNARD ARDURA.

Pontifical Council for Social Communication: Palazzo S. Carlo, 00120 Città del Vaticano; tel. (06) 69883197; fax (06) 69885373; e-mail pccs@vatican.va; f. 1948 to examine the relationship between the media and religious affairs; Pres. Most Rev. JOHN PATRICK FOLEY (Titular Archbishop of Neapolis); Sec. Rt Rev. PIERFRANCO PASTORE (Titular Bishop of Forontoniana).

Pontifical Commissions and Committees

Pontifical Commission for the Cultural Heritage of the Church: Palazzo della Cancelleria, Piazza della Cancellaria 1, 00120 Città del Vaticano; tel. (06) 69887517; fax (06) 69887567; e-mail pcbcc@pcchc.va; f. 1988; Pres. Most Rev. FRANCESCO MARCHISANO (Titular Archbishop of Populonia); Sec. Rev. Prof. CARLO CHENIS.

Pontifical Biblical Commission: Palazzo della Congregazione per la Dottrina della Fede, Piazza del S. Uffizio 11, 00193 Rome, Italy; tel. (06) 69884886; e-mail pcombiblica@cfaith.va; Pres. Cardinal JOSEPH RATZINGER; Sec. Rev. Fr KLEMENS STOCK.

Pontifical Commission of Sacred Archaeology: Palazzo del Pontificio Istituto di Archeologia Cristiana, Via Napoleone III 1, 00185 Rome, Italy; tel. (06) 4465610; fax (06) 4467625; e-mail pcomm.arch@arcsacra.va; internet www.vatican.va/roman_curia; Pres. Most Rev. FRANCESCO MARCHISANO (Titular Archbishop of Populonia); Sec. Prof. FABRIZIO BISCONTI.

Pontifical Commission for the Revision and Amendment of the Vulgate: Via di Torre Rossa 21, 00165 Rome, Italy; tel. (06) 6638792; Dir Rev. Fr JEAN MALLET.

Pontifical Commission 'Ecclesia Dei': Palazzo della Congregazione per la Dottrina della Fede, Piazza del S. Uffizio 11, 00193 Rome, Italy; tel. (06) 69885213; fax (06) 69883412; e-mail eccdei@ecclsdei.va; Pres. Cardinal DARÍO CASTRILLON HOYOS; Sec. Mgr CAMILLE PERL.

International Theological Commission: Palazzo della Congregazione per la Dottrina della Fede, Piazza del S. Uffizio 11, 00193 Rome, Italy; tel. (06) 69884638; Pres. Cardinal JOSEPH RATZINGER; Sec.-Gen. Rev. Fr GEORGES MARIE MARTIN COTTIER.

Pontifical Committee for International Eucharistic Congresses: Piazza S. Calisto 16, 00153 Rome, Italy; tel. and fax (06) 69887366; e-mail eucharistcongress@org.va; Pres. Cardinal JOZEF TOMKO; Sec. Rev. Fr FERDINAND PRATZNER.

Pontifical Committee of Historical Sciences: Palazzo delle Congregazioni, Piazza Pio XII 3, 00193 Rome, Italy; tel. (06) 69884618; fax (06) 69873014; e-mail vati065@scienstor.va; Pres. Mgr WALTER BRANDMÜLLER; Sec. Rev. SEMERANO COSIMO.

Archives of the Second Vatican Council: c/o Archivio Segreto Vaticano, 00120 Città del Vaticano; tel. (06) 68883314; fax (06) 69885574; Dir Fr SERGIO PAGANO.

Commission for Lawyers: Palazzo della Cancelleria, Piazza della Cancelleria 1, 00186 Rome, Italy; tel. (06) 69887523; fax (06) 698887557; f. 1988; Pres. Cardinal MARIO FRANCESCO POMPEDDA.

Disciplinary Commission of the Roman Curia: 00120 Città del Vaticano; Pres. Most Rev. JULIÁN HERRANZ (Titular Archbishop of Vertara).

Offices

Apostolic Chamber: Palazzo Apostolico, 00120 Città del Vaticano; tel. (06) 69883554; e-mail kkasteel@corunum.va; Chamberlain of the Holy Roman Church Cardinal EDUARDO MARTÍNEZ SOMALO; Vice-Chamberlain Most Rev. ETTORE CUNIAL (Titular Archbishop of Soteropolis); Dean Rt Rev. KAREL KASTEEL.

Administration of the Patrimony of the Holy See: Palazzo Apostolico, 00120 Città del Vaticano; tel. (06) 69893403; fax (06) 69883141; e-mail apsa-ss@apsa.va; f. 1967; Pres. Cardinal NICORA ATTILIO; Sec. Most Rev. CLAUDIO MARIA CELLI (Titular Archbishop of Civitanova).

Labour Office of the Apostolic See: Via della Conciliazione 1, 00193 Rome, Italy; tel. (06) 69884449; fax (06) 69883800; e-mail ulsa1@ulsa.va; internet www.vatican.va/roman_curia/labour_office/index_it.htm; Pres. Cardinal JAN PIETER SCHOTTE.

Prefecture for the Economic Affairs of the Holy See: Palazzo delle Congregazioni, Largo del Colonnato 3, 00193 Rome, Italy; tel. (06) 69884263; fax (06) 69885011; f. 1967; Pres. Cardinal SERGIO SEBASTIANI; Sec. Most Rev. FRANCO CROCI (Titular Bishop of Potenza Picena).

Prefecture of the Papal Household: 00120 Città del Vaticano; tel. (06) 69883114; fax (06) 69885863; f. 1967; responsible for domestic administration and organization; Prefect Rt Rev. JAMES MICHAEL HARVEY (Titular Bishop of Memphis).

Office of the Liturgical Celebrations of the Supreme Pontiff: Palazzo Apostolico, 00120 Città del Vaticano; tel. (06) 69883253; fax (06) 69885412; Master of Pontifical Liturgical Celebrations Rt Rev. PIERO MARINI (Titular Bishop of Martirano).

Holy See Press Office: Via della Conciliazione 54, 00193 Rome, Italy; tel. (06) 698921; fax (06) 69885178; internet www.vatican.va; Dir Dr JOAQUÍN NAVARRO-VALLS; Vice-Dir Fr CIRO BENEDETTINI.

Central Statistical Office of the Church: Palazzo Apostolico, 00120 Città del Vaticano; tel. (06) 69883493; fax (06) 69885088; Dir Mgr VITTORIO FORMENTI.

Pontifical Administration of the Patriarchal Basilica of San Paolo: 00120 Città del Vaticano; tel. (06) 5410194; fax (06) 5409374; Pontifical Administrator Most Rev. FRANCESCO GIOIA; Sec. Rt Rev. LUIGI RUCO.

Diplomatic Representation

DIPLOMATIC MISSIONS IN ROME ACCREDITED TO THE HOLY SEE

Albania: Via Antonio Genovesi 48/12, 00136 Rome, Italy; tel. (06) 39736022; fax (06) 39733150; e-mail ambalbvatican@libero.it; Ambassador ZEF BUSHATI.

Angola: Via Cardinal D. Ferrata 20, 00165 Rome, Italy; tel. and fax (06) 39387255; Ambassador ARMINDO FERNANDES DO ESPÍRITO SANTO VIEIRA.

Argentina: Palazzo Patrizi, Piazza S. Luigi de' Francesi 37, 00186 Rome, Italy; tel. (06) 68801701; fax (06) 6879021; e-mail emba .argentina@flashnet.it; Ambassador VICENTE ESPECHE GIL.

Australia: Via Paola 24/10, 00186 Rome, Italy; tel. (06) 6877688; fax (06) 6896255; Ambassador Dr JOHN HERRON.

Austria: Via Reno 9, 00198 Rome, Italy; tel. (06) 8416262; fax (06) 8543058; e-mail vtikan-ob@bmaa.gv.at; Ambassador WALTER GREINERT.

Belgium: Via Giuseppe de Notaris 6A, 00197 Rome, Italy; tel. (06) 3224740; fax (06) 3226042; e-mail ambelvat@pronet.it; Ambassador BENOÎT CARDON DE LICHTBUER.

Bolivia: Via di Porta Angelica 15/2, 00193 Rome, Italy; tel. (06) 6874191; fax (06) 6874193; e-mail embolvat@rdn.it; Ambassador PEDRO JOSÉ RIVERA SAAVEDRA.

Bosnia and Herzegovina: P. le Clodio 12/11, 00195 Rome, Italy; tel. (06) 39742411; fax (06) 39742484; Ambassador IVAN MIŠIĆ.

Brazil: Via della Conciliazione 22, 00193 Rome, Italy; tel. (06) 6875252; fax (06) 6872540; Ambassador OTO AGRIPINO MAIA.

Bulgaria: Via Ferdinando Galiani 36, 00191 Rome, Italy; tel. (06) 36307712; fax (06) 3292987; Ambassador VLADIMIR NIKOLAEV GRADEV.

Canada: Via della Conciliazione 4D, 00193 Rome, Italy; tel. (06) 68307316; fax (06) 68806283; Ambassador WILFRID-GUY LICARI.

Chile: Piazza Risorgimento 55/20, 00192 Rome, Italy; tel. (06) 6861232; fax (06) 6874992; Ambassador MÁXIMO PACHECO GÓMEZ.

China (Taiwan): Piazza delle Muse 7, 00197 Rome, Italy; tel. (06) 8083166; fax (06) 8085679; e-mail ambacina@tuttopmi.it; Ambassador RAYMOND RUEY-MING TAI.

Colombia: Via Cola di Rienzo 285/12B, 00192 Rome, Italy; tel. (06) 3211681; fax (06) 3211703; Ambassador GUILLERMO LEÓN ESCOBAR HERRÁN.

Congo, Democratic Republic: Via del Castro Pretorio 28/2, 00185 Rome, Italy; tel. and fax (06) 4452359; Chargé d'affaires a.i. EDOUARD KAMBEMBO NGUNZA.

Costa Rica: Via del Corso 47/4, 00186 Rome, Italy; tel. and fax (06) 3215528; e-mail embcr.vaticano@iol.it; Ambassador JAVIER GUERRA LASPIUR.

Côte d'Ivoire: Via Sforza Pallavicini 11, 00193 Rome, Italy; tel. (06) 6877503; fax (06) 6867925; Ambassador LOUIS ESMEL.

Croatia: Via della Conciliazione 44, 00193 Rome, Italy; tel. (06) 6877000; fax (06) 6877003; e-mail velrhvat@tin.it; Ambassador FRANJO ZENKO.

Cuba: Via Aurelia 137/5A, 00165 Rome, Italy; tel. (06) 39366680; fax (06) 636685; e-mail cuba.ssede@libero.it; Ambassador ISIDRO GÓMEZ SANTOS.

Czech Republic: Via Crescenzio 91/1B, 00193 Rome, Italy; tel. (06) 6874694; fax (06) 6879731; Chargé d'affaires a.i. VLADIMÍR NÉMEC.

Dominican Republic: Lungotevere Marzio 3/6, 00186 Rome, Italy; tel. and fax (06) 6864084; e-mail embajada.rd@tiscalinet.it; Ambassador VÍCTOR A. HIDALGO JUSTO.

Ecuador: Via di Porta Angelica 63, 00193 Rome, Italy; tel. (06) 6897179; fax (06) 68892786; Ambassador MARCELO FERNÁNDEZ DE CÓRDOBA PONCE.

Egypt: Piazza della Città Leonina 9, 00193 Rome, Italy; tel. (06) 6865878; fax (06) 6832335; Ambassador FAROUK HUSSEIN RAAFAT.

El Salvador: Via Panama 22/2, 00198 Rome, Italy; tel. (06) 8540538; fax (06) 85301131; e-mail embasalssede@iol.it; Ambassador ROBERTO JOSÉ SIMÁN JACIR.

Finland: Villa Lante, Passeggiata del Gianicolo 10, 00165 Rome, Italy; tel. (06) 68804604; fax (06) 68802349; Ambassador ANTTI HYNNINEN.

France: Villa Bonaparte, Via Piave 23, 00187 Rome, Italy; tel. (06) 42030900; fax (06) 42030968; e-mail ambfrssg@tin.it; Ambassador PIERRE MOREL.

Gabon: Piazzale Clodio 12, 00195 Rome, Italy; tel. (06) 39721584; fax (06) 39724847; Ambassador DÉSIRÉ KOUMBA.

Germany: Via di Villa Sacchetti 4-6, 00197 Rome, Italy; tel. (06) 809511; fax (06) 80951227; Ambassador Dr GERD WESTDICKENBERG.

Greece: Via Giuseppe Mercalli 6, 00197 Rome, Italy; tel. (06) 8070786; fax (06) 8079862; e-mail grembvat@m.tin.it; Ambassador CHRISTOS BOTZIOS.

Guatemala: Piazzale Gregorio VII 65/A, 00165 Rome, Italy; tel. (06) 6381632; fax (06) 39376981; e-mail embaguate.santasede@tin.it; Ambassador ACISCLO VALLADARES MOLINA.

Haiti: Via di Villa Patrizi 5B, 00161 Roma, Italy; tel. (06) 44242749; fax (06) 44236637; Ambassador CARL HENRI GUITEAU.

Honduras: Via Boezio 45, 00192 Rome, Italy; tel. and fax (06) 6876051; e-mail honvati@tin.it; Ambassador ALEJANDRO EMILIO VALLADARES LANZA.

Hungary: Piazza Girolamo Fabrizio 2, 00161 Rome, Italy; tel. (06) 4402167; fax (06) 4402312; Ambassador PÁL TAR.

Indonesia: Piazzale Roberto Ardigò 42, 00142 Rome, Italy; tel. (06) 5940441; fax (06) 5417934; Ambassador WIDODO SUYIYO.

Iran: Via Bruxelles 57, 00198 Rome, Italy; tel. (06) 8552494; fax (06) 8547910; e-mail chalac@libero.it; Ambassador MOSTAFA BOROUJERDI.

Iraq: Via della Camilluccia 355, 00135 Rome, Italy; tel. (06) 3011140; fax (06) 35506416; e-mail iraqscv@tin.it; Ambassador ABD AL-AMIR AL-ANBARI.

Ireland: Villa Spada al Gianicolo, Via Giacomo Medici 1, 00153 Rome, Italy; tel. (06) 5810777; fax (06) 5895709; Ambassador BERNARD DAVENPORT.

Israel: Via Michele Mercati 12, 00197 Rome, Italy; tel. (06) 36198690; fax (06) 36198626; e-mail info-vat@holysee.mfa.gov.il; Ambassador YOSEF LAMDAN.

Italy: Palazzo Borromeo, Piazzale delle Belle Arti 2, 00196 Rome, Italy; tel. (06) 3264881; fax (06) 3201801; e-mail amb.scv@esteri.it; Ambassador RANIERO AVOGADRO.

Japan: Via Virgilio 30, 00193 Rome, Italy; tel. (06) 6875828; fax (06) 68807543; Ambassador MITSUHIRO NAKAMURA.

Korea, Republic: Via della Mendola 109, 00135 Rome, Italy; tel. (06) 3314505; fax (06) 3314522; Ambassador HYUN-SEOP SEO.

Lebanon: Via di Porta Angelica 15, 00193 Rome, Italy; tel. (06) 6833512; fax (06) 6833507; Ambassador FOUAD AOUN.

Libya: Via Archimede 144, 00197 Rome, Italy; tel. (06) 8073485; fax (06) 8078003; Ambassador HUSEIN-FUAD MUSTAFA KABAZI.

Lithuania: Via G.G. Porro 4, 00197 Rome, Italy; tel. (06) 8078259; fax (06) 8078291; Ambassador KAZYS LOZORAITIS.

Luxembourg: Via Casale di S. Pio V 20, 00165 Rome, Italy; tel. (06) 660560; fax (06) 66056309; Ambassador JEAN WAGNER (resident in Luxembourg).

Macedonia, former Yugoslav Republic: Via di Porta Cavalleggeri 143, 00165 Rome, Italy; tel. (06) 635878; fax (06) 634826; Ambassador IVAN ANGELOV.

Mexico: Via Ezio 49, 00192 Rome, Italy; tel. (06) 3230360; fax (06) 3230361; e-mail embamex-s.sede@mclink.it; Ambassador FERNANDO ESTRADA SAMANO.

Monaco: Largo Nicola Spinelli 5, 00198 Rome, Italy; tel. (06) 8414357; fax (06) 8414507; e-mail ambmonacovat@virgilio.it; Ambassador JEAN-CLAUDE MICHEL.

Morocco: Via delle Fornaci 203, 00165 Rome, Italy; tel. (06) 39388367; fax (06) 6374459; e-mail sifamavat@pronet.it; Ambassador MOHAMED SBIHI.

Netherlands: Piazza della Città Leonina 9, 00193 Rome, Italy; tel. (06) 6868044; fax (06) 6879593; Ambassador Baron HENDRIK V. BENTINCK VAN SCHOONHETEN.

Nicaragua: Via Luigi Luciani 42/1, 00197 Rome, Italy; tel. (06) 36000880; fax (06) 3207249; e-mail embanicsantasede@tin.it; Ambassador LUVY SALERNI NAVAS.

Panama: Largo di Torre Argentina 11/28, 00186 Rome, Italy; tel. (06) 68809764; fax (06) 68809812; e-mail embapass@tiscalinet.it; Ambassador EDDA VICTORIA MARTINELLI DE DUTARI.

Paraguay: Via dell' Alpinismo 24/9A, 00194 Rome, Italy; tel. (06) 36300559; fax (06) 36300260; e-mail pyssede@mclink.it; Ambassador BLANCA ELIDA ZUCCOLILLO DE RODRÍGUEZ ALCALÁ.

Peru: Via di Porta Angelica 63, 00193 Rome, Italy; tel. (06) 68308535; fax (06) 6896059; e-mail emperu.ssede@flashnet.it; Ambassador ALBERTO MONTAGNE VIDAL.

Philippines: Via Paolo VI 29, 00193 Rome, Italy; tel. (06) 68308020; fax (06) 6834076; e-mail philamsee@theta.it; Ambassador FRANCISCO A. ALBA.

Poland: Via dei Delfini 16/3, 00186 Rome, Italy; tel. (06) 6990958; fax (06) 6990978; e-mail polamb.wat@agora.stm.it; Ambassador HANNA SUCHOCKA.

Portugal: Villa Lusa, Via S. Valentino 9, 00197 Rome, Italy; tel. (06) 8077012; fax (06) 8084634; e-mail embportugalvatican@tiscalinet.it; Ambassador PEDRO JOSÉ RIBEIRO DE MENEZES.

Romania: Via Panama 92, 00198 Rome, Italy; tel. (06) 8541802; fax (06) 8554067; e-mail ambvatican@libero.it; Ambassador MIHAIL DOBRE.

Russia: Via della Conciliazione 10/2, 00193 Rome, Italy; tel. (06) 6877078; fax (06) 6877168; Ambassador VITALY LITVIN.

San Marino: Piazza G. Winckelmann 14, 00162 Rome, Italy; tel. (06) 86321798; fax (06) 8610814; Ambassador Prof. GIOVANNI GALASSI.

Senegal: Via dei Monti Parioli 51, 00197 Rome, Italy; tel. (06) 3218892; fax (06) 3203624; e-mail hturpin@iol.it; Ambassador HENRI ANTOINE TURPIN.

Serbia and Montenegro: Via dei Monti Parioli 20, 00197 Rome, Italy; tel. (06) 3200099; fax (06) 3204530; e-mail sveta.stolica@flashnet.it; Ambassador Dr DARKO TANASKOVIĆ.

Slovakia: Via dei Colli della Farnesina 144/6B, 00194 Rome, Italy; tel. (06) 36715234; fax (06) 3296507; e-mail slovakemvat@libero.it; Ambassador DAGMAR BABČANOVÁ.

Slovenia: Via della Conciliazione 10, 00193 Rome, Italy; tel. (06) 6833009; fax (06) 68307942; e-mail VVA@mzz-dkp.gov.si; Ambassador Dr LUDWIG TOPLAK.

Spain: Palazzo di Spagna, Piazza di Spagna 57, 00187 Rome, Italy; tel. (06) 6784351; fax (06) 6784355; e-mail ambespvat@mail.mae.es; Ambassador CARLOS JUSTO ABELLA Y RAMALLO.

Turkey: Via Lovanio 24/1, 00198 Rome, Italy; tel. (06) 8550454; fax (06) 8543986; Ambassador FILIZ DINÇMEN.

Ukraine: Via Guido d'Arezzo 9, 00198 Rome, Italy; tel. and fax (06) 8413345; fax (06) 8547539; e-mail ucraina.ssede@tin.it; Ambassador BORYS HUDYMA.

United Kingdom: Via Condotti 91, 00187 Rome, Italy; tel. (06) 69923561; fax (06) 69940684; Ambassador KATHYRN FRANCES COLVIN.

USA: Villa Domiziana, Via delle Terme Deciane 26, 00153 Rome, Italy; tel. (06) 46741; fax (06) 5758346; e-mail embassyvatican@libero.it; internet www.usembassy.it/usembvat; Ambassador JIM NICHOLSON.

Uruguay: Via Antonio Gramsci 9/14, 00197 Rome, Italy; tel. (06) 3218904; fax (06) 3613249; e-mail uruvati@tin.it; Ambassador DANIEL PÉREZ DE CASTILLO.

Venezuela: Via Antonio Gramsci 14, 00197 Rome, Italy; tel. (06) 3225868; fax (06) 36001505; e-mail evidano@iol.it; Chargé d'affaires a.i. PABLO HERRERA MALDONADO.

Ecclesiastical Organization

The organization of the Church consists of:
(1) Patriarchs, Archbishops and Bishops in countries under the common law of the Church.
(2) Abbots and Prelates 'nullius dioceseos'.
(3) Vicars Apostolic and Prefects Apostolic in countries classified as Missionary and under Propaganda, the former having Episcopal dignity.
The population of the world adhering to the Roman Catholic faith was estimated in 1994 at 958m., about 17% of the total.
Among the Pope's titles is that of Patriarch of the West. There are five other Patriarchates of the Latin Rite—Jerusalem, the West

Indies, the East Indies, Lisbon and Venice. The Eastern Catholic Churches each have Patriarchs: Alexandria for the Coptic Rite, Babylon for the Chaldean Rite, Cilicia for the Armenian Rite, and Antioch for the Syrian, Maronite and Melkite Rites.
At 31 December 2002 there were 2,722 residential sees—13 patriarchates, 2 senior archbishoprics, 516 metropolitan archbishoprics, 78 archbishoprics and 2,113 bishoprics. Of the 2,053 titular sees (92 metropolitan archbishoprics, 91 archbishoprics and 1,870 bishoprics), 974 are filled by bishops who have been given these titles, but exercise no territorial jurisdiction. Other territorial divisions of the Church include 49 prelacies, 13 territorial abbacies, 9 apostolic administrations, 25 exarchates of the Eastern Church, 79 apostolic vicariates, 45 apostolic prefectures and 11 missions 'sui iuris'.

The Press

Acta Apostolicae Sedis: The Secretariat of State, Palazzo Apostolico, 00120 Città del Vaticano; tel. (06) 69883693; f. 1909; official bulletin issued by the Holy See; monthly, with special editions on special occasions; the record of Encyclicals and other Papal pronouncements, Acts of the Sacred Congregations and Offices, nominations, etc. circ. 6,000.

Annuario Pontificio: Palazzo Apostolico, 00120 Città del Vaticano; tel. (06) 69883493; fax (06) 69885088; official year book edited by Central Statistical Office; Dir Mgr VITTORIO FORMENTI.

L'Osservatore Romano: Via del Pellegrino, 00120 Città del Vaticano; tel. (06) 69883461; fax (06) 69883675; e-mail ornet@ossrom.va; internet www.vatican.va/news_services/or/home_ita.html; f. 1861; an authoritative daily newspaper in Italian; its special columns devoted to the affairs of the Holy See may be described as semi-official; the news service covers religious matters and, in a limited measure, general affairs; weekly editions in Italian, French, Spanish, Portuguese, German, English, monthly edition in Polish; Editor-in-Chief Prof. MARIO AGNES; Man. Editor CARLO DE LUCIA; circ. (Italian daily) 20,000.

Pro Dialogo: Via dell' Erba 1, 00193 Rome, Italy; tel. (06) 69884321; fax (06) 69884494; e-mail pcid-office@interelg.va; three per year; publ. by the Pontifical Council for Inter-Religious Dialogue; Editor Most Rev. FELIX A. MACHADO.

Statistical Yearbook of the Church: c/o Secretariat of State, 00120 Città del Vaticano; tel. (06) 69883655; fax (06) 69885088; Dir Mgr VITTORIO FORMENTI.

NEWS AGENCY

Agenzia Internazionale FIDES: Palazzo di 'Propaganda Fide', Via di Propaganda 1C, 00187 Rome, Italy; tel. (06) 69880115; fax (06) 69880107; e-mail fides@fides.va; internet www.fides.org; f. 1926; handles news of missions throughout the world and publishes a weekly bulletin in six languages (circ. 3,000), provides a daily news service by e-mail; Dir LUCA DE MATA.

Publishers

Biblioteca Apostolica Vaticana: 00120 Città del Vaticano; tel. (06) 69879437; fax (06) 69884795; e-mail bav@vatlib.it; internet www.vatican.va/library_archives/vat_library/index_it.htm; f. 1451; philology, classics, history, catalogues; Librarian of the Holy Roman Church Cardinal JORGE MARÍA MEJÍA; Prefect Rev. RAFFAELE FARINA.

Libreria Editrice Vaticana: Via della Tipografia, 00120 Città del Vaticano; tel. (06) 69885003; fax 69884716; e-mail lev@publish.va; internet www.libreriaeditricevaticana.com; f. 1926; religion, philosophy, literature, art, Latin philology, history; Pres. Most Rev. GIOVANNI DE ANDREA (Titular Archbishop of Acquaviva); Dir Rev. CLAUDIO ROSSINI.

Tipografia Vaticana (Vatican Press): Via della Tipografia, 00120 Città del Vaticano; tel. (06) 69883506; fax (06) 69884570; e-mail tipvat@tipografia.va; f. 1587; religion, theology, education, juveniles, natural and social sciences; prints *Acta Apostolicae Sedis* and *L'Osservatore Romano*; Dir-Gen. Rev. ELIO TORRIGIANI; Admin. Dir MARIO ERCOLE.

Broadcasting and Communications

RADIO

Radio Vaticana was founded in 1931 and situated within the Vatican City. A transmitting centre, inaugurated by Pius XII in 1957, is located at Santa Maria di Galeria, about 20 km north-west of the Vatican. Under a special treaty between the Holy See and Italy, the site of this centre, which covers 420 ha, enjoys the same extra-territorial privileges as are recognized by international law for the diplomatic headquarters of foreign states.

The station operates an all-day service, normally in 37 languages, but with facilities for broadcasting liturgical and other religious services in additional languages, including Latin.

The purpose of the Vatican Radio is to broadcast Papal teaching, to provide information on important events in the Catholic Church, to express the Catholic point of view on problems affecting religion and morality, but above all to form a continuous link between the Holy See and Catholics throughout the world.

Radio Vaticana: Palazzo Pio, Piazza Pia 3, 00193 Rome, Italy; tel. (06) 69883551; fax (06) 69883237; e-mail dirgen@vatiradio.va; internet www.vaticanradio.org; f. 1931; Dir-Gen. Rev. Fr PASQUALE BORGOMEO (SJ); Tech. Dir Rev. Fr LINO DAN (SJ); Dir of Programmes Rev. Fr FEDERICO LOMBARDI (SJ).

TELEVISION

Centro Televisivo Vaticano (Vatican Television Centre): Via del Pellegrino, 00120 Città del Vaticano; tel. (06) 69885467; fax (06) 69885192; e-mail ctv@ctv.va; f. 1983; produces and distributes religious programmes; Pres. Dott. EMILIO ROSSI; Dir-Gen. Fr FREDERICO LOMBARDI.

Finance

Istituto per le Opere di Religione (IOR): 00120 Città del Vaticano; tel. (06) 69883354; fax (06) 69883809; f. 1887; and renamed in 1942; oversees the distribution of capital designated for religious works; its assets are believed to lie between US $3,000m. and $4,000m. it takes deposits from religious bodies and Vatican residents; administrative changes, announced in 1989, involved the appointment of a commission of five cardinals and of a Board of Superintendence comprising five financial experts; Pres. Prof. ANGELO CALOIA; Dir-Gen. Comm. LELIO SCALETTI; Commission mems Cardinals ANGELO SODANO, JOZEF TOMKO, ADAM JOSEPH MAIDA, JUAN SANDOVAL IÑIGUEZ, EDUARDO MARTÍNEZ SOMALO.

Lay Employees' Association

In 1989 the Pope agreed to establish a Labour Council to settle any disputes between the Holy See and its lay employees.

Associazione Dipendenti Laici Vaticani (Association of Vatican Lay Workers): Arco del Belvedere, 00120 Città del Vaticano; tel. (06) 69885343; fax (06) 69884400; f. 1979; aims to safeguard the professional, legal, economic and moral interests of its members; Sec.-Gen. ALESSANDRO CANDI; mems 2,000.

Transport

There is a small railway (862 m) which runs from the Vatican into Italy. It began to operate in 1934 and now carries supplies and goods. There is also a heliport used by visiting heads of state and Vatican officials.

VENEZUELA

Introductory Survey

Location, Climate, Language, Religion, Flag, Capital

The Bolivarian Republic of Venezuela lies on the north coast of South America, bordered by Colombia to the west, Guyana to the east and Brazil to the south. The climate varies with altitude from tropical to temperate; the average temperature in Caracas is 21°C (69°F). The language is Spanish. There is no state religion, but some 92% of the population is Roman Catholic. The national flag (proportions 2 by 3) has three horizontal stripes of yellow, blue and red, with seven five-pointed white stars, arranged in a semi-circle, in the centre of the blue stripe. The state flag has, in addition, the national coat of arms (a shield bearing a gold wheat sheaf, a panoply of swords, flags and a lance, and a white running horse in its three divisions, flanked by branches of laurel and palm and with two cornucopias at the crest) in the top left-hand corner. The capital is Caracas.

Recent History

Venezuela was a Spanish colony from 1499 until 1821 and, under the leadership of Simón Bolívar, achieved independence in 1830. The country was governed principally by dictators until 1945, when a military-civilian coup replaced Isaías Medina Angarita by Rómulo Betancourt as head of a revolutionary junta. Col (later Gen.) Marcos Pérez Jiménez seized power in December 1952 and took office as President in 1953. He remained in office until 1958, when he was overthrown by a military junta under Adm. Wolfgang Larrazábal. Betancourt was elected President in the same year.

A new Constitution was promulgated in 1961. Three years later President Betancourt became the first Venezuelan President to complete his term of office. Dr Raúl Leoni was elected President in December 1963. Supporters of former President Pérez staged an abortive military uprising in 1966. Dr Rafael Caldera Rodríguez became Venezuela's first Christian Democratic President in March 1969. He achieved some success in stabilizing the country politically and economically, although political assassinations and abductions committed by underground organizations continued into 1974. At elections in December 1973 Carlos Andrés Pérez Rodríguez, candidate of Acción Democrática (AD), the main opposition party, was chosen to succeed President Caldera. The new Government invested heavily in agriculture and industrial development, creating a more balanced economy, and also undertook to nationalize important sectors. The presidential election of December 1978 was won by the leader of the Partido Social-Cristiano (Comité de Organización Política Electoral Independiente—COPEI), Dr Luis Herrera Campíns, who took office in March 1979.

In 1981 a deteriorating economic situation provoked social unrest and a succession of guerrilla attacks. At a presidential election conducted in December 1983, Dr Jaime Lusinchi, the candidate of the AD, was elected with 56.8% of the votes cast. The AD also won the majority of seats in the Congreso Nacional; Lusinchi assumed power in February 1984.

At presidential and legislative elections conducted in December 1988, AD candidate Carlos Andrés Pérez Rodríguez became the first former President to be re-elected (he previously held office in 1974–79). However, the AD lost its overall majority in the Congreso Nacional. Following his inauguration in February 1989, President Pérez implemented a series of adjustments designed to halt Venezuela's economic decline. These measures, which included increases in the prices of petrol and public transport, provoked rioting throughout the country in late February. The Government introduced a curfew and suspended various constitutional rights in order to quell the disturbances, but it was estimated that some 246 people had died during the protests. In early March the curfew was revoked, and all constitutional rights were restored, after wages had been increased and the prices of some basic goods were 'frozen'.

In May 1989 popular opposition to the Government's austerity programme became co-ordinated by the country's largest trade union, the Confederación de Trabajadores de Venezuela (CTV), which organized a 24-hour general strike (the first for 31 years) in favour of the introduction of pro-labour reforms. In June several thousand protesters marched through Caracas to demonstrate against official corruption. In July, despite its growing dissatisfaction with the stabilization plan then in progress, the CTV signed an agreement with the Government and the business sector to promote national harmony and to support the continuation of economic adjustment policies that had been agreed with the IMF in June.

In December 1989 State Governors were selected by direct election for the first time. There was a high degree of abstention (estimated at around 70%), and significant gains were made by left-wing parties, which had campaigned energetically against the corruption allegedly rife in the main parties.

In November 1990 a controversial new labour law was adopted by the Congreso Nacional, provoking fears that the resulting additional costs for employers would lead to redundancies and an increase in inflation. The law, which came into effect in May 1991, included provision for a severance benefit scheme and a social security system. A series of widespread demonstrations and strikes followed the introduction, in August 1991, of monthly increases in the price of petrol. Opposition to the increases and protests against other measures in the Government's economic programme escalated during October, and in November trade union organizations staged a 12-hour general strike in support of various demands, including wage increases, the reintroduction of price controls on basic goods, and the suspension of government plans to dismiss some 300,000 public-sector employees. The trade unions also appealed for an end to the increases in petrol prices. Clashes between demonstrators and the security forces resulted in several fatalities, provoking further demonstrations which continued into December.

On 4 February 1992 an attempt to overthrow the President by rebel army units was defeated by armed forces loyal to the Government. The rebels, identified as members of the 'Movimiento Bolivariano Revolucionario 200' (MBR-200), attempted to occupy the President's office, the Miraflores Palace, and his official residence but were forced to capitulate. Simultaneous rebel action in the cities of Maracay, Valencia and Maracaibo ended when one of the leaders of the coup, Lt-Col Hugo Chávez Frías, broadcast an appeal for their surrender. More than 1,000 soldiers were arrested, and 33 officers were subsequently charged. A number of constitutional guarantees were immediately suspended, and press and television censorship was imposed to exclude coverage of Chávez, who had received considerable passive popular support. The rebels' stated reasons for staging the insurrection were the increasing social divisions and uneven distribution of wealth resulting from government economic policy, and widespread corruption in public life. President Pérez's public recognition, in January, of Colombia's claims to territorial rights in the Gulf of Venezuela had also angered the rebels. In what was widely perceived as an attempt to appease disaffected sectors of society, immediately following the attempted coup Pérez authorized a 50% increase in the minimum wage and a 30% increase in the pay of middle-ranking officers of the armed forces. He also announced plans to bring forward a US $4,000m. social project, aimed at improving health care, social welfare and education.

In March 1992 Pérez announced a series of proposed political and economic reforms, including the introduction of legislation for immediate reform of the Constitution. In addition, the President announced the suspension of increases in the price of petrol and electricity, and the reintroduction of price controls on a number of basic foodstuffs and on medicine. In that month, in an effort to broaden the base of support for his Government, Pérez appointed two members of COPEI to the Council of Ministers. Social unrest, however, continued in March with a series of demonstrations calling for the resignation of Pérez. Full constitutional rights were finally restored in April. In June, following the withdrawal of the COPEI members from the Council of Ministers, Pérez effected a minor reshuffle.

The climate of political instability intensified in September and October 1992, with widespread protests against government austerity measures and alleged official corruption. A series of bomb attacks, attributed to the rebel movements Los

Justicieros de Venezuela and the Fuerzas Bolivarianos de Liberación (an organization claiming to have links with MBR-200), were directed at the residences of allegedly corrupt senior politicians.

On 27 November 1992 a further attempt by rebel members of the armed forces to overthrow the President was suppressed by forces loyal to the Government. The attempted coup, led by senior air force and navy officers, was reported to have been instigated by members of MRB-200. A videotaped statement by the imprisoned Lt-Col Chávez, transmitted from a captured government-owned television station, urged Venezuelans to stage public demonstrations in support of the rebels. Principal air force bases were seized, and rebel aircraft attacked the presidential palace and other strategically important installations. The Government introduced a state of emergency and suspended the Constitution. Sporadic fighting continued into the following day, but by 29 November order had been restored and some 1,300 rebel members of the armed forces had been arrested. President Pérez rejected demands from the press and opposition parties for his resignation. The curfew imposed during the coup was ended at the beginning of December, and further constitutional rights were restored later in the month.

Popular discontent with the Government was reflected further in regional and municipal elections held on 6 December 1992, which resulted in significant gains for COPEI as well as revealing increasing support for the left-wing Movimiento al Socialismo (MAS) and La Causa Radical (La Causa R), whose candidate, Aristóbulo Istúriz, was elected mayor of Caracas. In March 1993 the Supreme Court annulled the rulings of an extraordinary summary court martial, which had been established by presidential decree to try those implicated in the attempted coup of November 1992, on the grounds that the court was unconstitutional. Those sentenced by the court were to be retried by an ordinary court martial.

In May 1993 an extraordinary joint session of the Congreso Nacional voted to endorse a Supreme Court ruling that sufficient evidence existed for Pérez to be brought to trial on corruption charges. The charges concerned allegations that Pérez, and two former government ministers, had, in 1989, embezzled US $17m. from a secret government fund. Pérez was subsequently suspended from office and, in accordance with the terms of the Constitution, replaced by the President of the Senado, Octavio Lepage, pending the election by the Congreso Nacional of an interim President who would assume control until the expiry of the presidential term in February 1994, should Pérez be found guilty. On 5 June the Congreso Nacional elected Ramón José Velásquez, an independent senator, as interim President. By mid-June Velásquez had completed a broad-ranging reorganization of the Council of Ministers, replacing 14 ministers, creating a new portfolio with responsibility for decentralization, and upgrading the Instituto de Comercio Exterior (ICE—foreign trade institute) to the status of ministry. In the same month the founder of the COPEI, former President Dr Rafael Caldera Rodríguez, was expelled from the party. Caldera was accused of contravening the interests and by-laws of the party by announcing his independent candidacy, in opposition to the party's official candidate, for the forthcoming presidential elections, held in conjunction with legislative elections in December 1993.

In August 1993 the Congreso Nacional approved legislation enabling Velásquez to introduce urgent economic and financial measures by decree in order to address the growing economic crisis. In late August a special session of the Congreso Nacional voted in favour of the permanent suspension from office of Pérez, regardless of the outcome of the legal proceedings being conducted against him. (In May 1994 Pérez was arrested and imprisoned, pending trial by the Supreme Court on charges of corruption.) At the same session, Velásquez was ratified as interim President.

On 5 December 1993 the presidential and legislative elections proceeded peacefully. Dr Rafael Caldera Rodríguez, the candidate of a newly-formed party, the Convergencia Nacional (CN), was elected President (having previously held office in 1969–74), winning 30.46% of the votes cast. However, the CN and its electoral ally, the MAS, secured only minority representation in the Congreso Nacional. Caldera took office in February 1994 and installed a Council of Ministers, including new portfolios with responsibility for economic reform, youth affairs, and higher education, science and technology. In that month the AD and the COPEI established a legislative pact using their combined majority representation in the Congreso Nacional in order to

gain control of the major legislative committees. In response, Caldera warned that he would dissolve the legislature and organize elections to a Constituent Assembly should the government programme encounter obstructions in the Congreso Nacional. Also in February, in an attempt to consolidate relations with the armed forces, Caldera initiated proceedings providing for the release and pardon of all those charged with involvement in the coup attempts of February and November 1992.

In June 1994 the Government announced that it was to assume extraordinary powers, in view of the deepening economic crisis and the virtual collapse of the banking sector. Six articles of the Constitution were suspended concerning guarantees including freedom of movement and freedom from arbitrary arrest and the right to own property and to engage in legal economic activity. The Government also announced the introduction of price controls and a single fixed exchange rate, in order to address the problems of a rapidly depreciating currency and depleted foreign exchange reserves. Later in the month Caldera issued a decree placing the financial system under its control. Of those banks affected by the crisis, 10 were closed permanently; the majority of those still operational were to be returned to private control. In July a confrontation between the legislature and the presidency developed when the Congreso Nacional voted to restore five of the six constitutional guarantees suspended by the Government in June. Despite protest, the Government promptly reintroduced the suspensions. Later that month, however, the legislative opposition, with the exception of La Causa R, which withdrew from the legislature in protest, endorsed emergency financial measures, including an extension of price controls and the strengthening of finance-sector regulation, which were presented by the Government as a precursor to the restoration of full constitutional guarantees. In the same month former President Lusinchi, who had been indicted on corruption charges in 1993, was acquitted.

In March 1995 the arrest of some 500 alleged subversives (including activists of the MBR-200) by the security forces prompted demonstrations in the capital in support of demands for the release of those detained and in opposition to the deployment of the National Guard to patrol Venezuela's cities. Protesters also demanded the restoration of the constitutional guarantees suspended in June 1994. In July 1995, with the promulgation of legislation allowing for government intervention in the economy without recourse to further emergency measures, the constitutional guarantees were restored. However, in the light of continued criminal activity along the borders with Colombia and Brazil, the constitutional guarantees remained suspended in those areas. In that month a joint session of the Congreso Nacional approved legislation permitting the participation of foreign multinational companies in the petroleum sector. The legislation enabled the state petroleum company, Petróleos de Venezuela, SA (PDVSA), to offer exploration contracts for 10 petroleum fields covering a total area of 18,000 sq km. Under the terms of the contracts foreign concerns would be permitted to undertake exploration at their own risk; discovery of commercially viable deposits of petroleum would then be developed in joint ventures with the PDVSA and its affiliates, which would assume a share of up to 35%.

At regional and municipal elections conducted in December 1995 the CN suffered a considerable political set-back, obtaining only one of the total of 22 state governorships. Conversely, the AD won 11 governorships as well as securing the mayorship of Caracas. The elections were marked by particularly low voter participation, which, at less than 40%, was widely interpreted as reflecting the general disillusionment of the electorate with the political parties.

In May 1996 former President Pérez was found guilty by the Supreme Court of misuse of public funds, although he was acquitted of charges of embezzlement. He was sentenced to two years and four months under house arrest, of which he had already served two years. In July the Senado voted to deny Pérez the seat-for-life in that chamber to which former Presidents of the country are normally entitled. In April 1998 Pérez was charged with misappropriation of public funds during his time in office, and was placed under house arrest pending full investigation of the charges. At legislative elections conducted in November (see below), however, he was successfully elected to the Senado, and was therefore entitled to parliamentary immunity from prosecution.

In July 1997 the leader of the attempted coup of February 1992, Lt-Col (retd) Hugo Chávez Frías, founded his own political party, Movimiento V República (MVR), and expressed his intention to contest the forthcoming presidential election. In early May 1998 COPEI announced that it would support the presidential election campaign of independent candidate, Irene Sáez (a former beauty pageant winner). Legislative and regional elections were scheduled for 8 November, while the presidential poll was to be conducted on 6 December. In early June the MAS announced that it would support Chávez's presidential aspirations. This decision led to some dissent among prominent MAS members, and to the departure from the party of Minister of Planning, Teodoro Petkoff, co-founder of the MAS. Meanwhile, as the country's economic crisis (exacerbated by a sustained decline in world prices for petroleum) worsened, the Minister of Finance, Freddy Rojas Parra, resigned at the end of June and was replaced by Maritza Izaguirre Porras. In September the Congreso conferred extraordinary powers to enact legislation by 'enabling law' ('ley habilitante') on President Caldera, in order to facilitate the implementation of emergency economic measures designed to reduce the huge fiscal deficit and to accelerate social security reforms.

The legislative elections of 8 November 1998 were won by the Polo Patriótico, an alliance of small, mainly left-wing parties led by Chávez's MVR in a development widely considered to reflect the popular rejection of apparent corruption in the country's major political parties. The parties of the Polo secured more than 34% of votes to the Cámara (the MVR alone won 21.3%), although the most successful single party was AD, with 21.7% of the votes. Proyecto Venezuela (PRVZL), the party created to support the presidential candidacy of the independent Henrique Salas Römer, also performed well, securing 12.3% of the votes. Disappointing results were recorded by the CN (with 2.42%) and Irene Sáez's Integración, Renovación y Nueva Esperanza (IRENE—1.48%). AD was more successful in elections to the Senado, where they secured 19 seats (with 24.4% of the votes) compared with 12 seats (and 19.8% of the votes) won by the MVR. Success at the concurrent gubernatorial elections was shared equally between the Polo Patriótico and AD, who each secured approximately one-third of the governorships.

In the light of the MVR's success in the legislative poll, prior to the presidential election AD and COPEI withdrew their support for their respective candidates (Luis Alfaro Ucero—who refused to withdraw from the contest and was promptly expelled by the AD, and Sáez—who also refused to have her name removed from the ballots) and united in support of Salas Römer, hoping to forestall the loss of their long-standing political predominance. However, Chávez, who had styled himself as a radical left-wing populist—with promises of social revolution and constitutional reform—had engaged the popular imagination, and was elected President on 6 December 1998, with 56.2% of the votes cast, ahead of Salas Römer, who received the support of some 40% of voters.

Chávez immediately announced plans for elections to a Constituent Assembly to draft a new constitution, and requested congressional permission to employ the 'enabling law' to implement an extensive restructuring of public administration and a comprehensive economic recovery programme. Chávez was inaugurated as President on 2 February 1999 and a new Council of Ministers was installed. At the end of February Chávez announced details of an ambitious emergency social improvement plan (the Plan Bolívar 2000) to rehabilitate public property and land through voluntary civil and military action. Such pledges (together with a promise that the armed forces would not be used against the civilian population) prompted a series of rural and urban public land occupations, none of which was forcibly ended.

In April 1999, following prolonged negotiation and compromise, Chávez received congressional endorsement of his proposed use of the 'enabling law'. On 25 April a national referendum, organized to ascertain levels of popular support for the convening of a Constituent Assembly and the regulations governing the election of such a body, demonstrated 81.5% support for the Assembly and 80.0% support for Chávez's proposals for electoral procedures. (The success of the referendum was somewhat marred by the 60% rate of voter abstention.) Elections to the National Constituent Assembly (ANC) took place on 25 July 1999 and resulted in an outright victory for Polo Patriótico, which won 120 out of the 131 seats. The leadership of COPEI and of Acción Democrática subsequently resigned. The ANC was formally inaugurated on 3 August. Luis Miquelena, the former Minister of the Interior and Justice, was elected Assembly President with Isaias Rodríguez (MAS) as First Deputy Presi-

dent and Aristobulo Isturiz as Second. By late August the ANC had assumed most functions of the opposition-controlled Congreso and the Congreso itself was put into recess indefinitely. In response, the opposition accused the Government of establishing a *de facto* dictatorship. There were also complaints about the increasing military presence in the Government, as former military officers held positions in the Council of Ministers and 19 of them had been elected to the ANC. Clashes between the supporters and the opponents of the Government occurred outside the Congreso building, which left at least 30 people injured. Chávez justified the control of the legislature, executive and judiciary as necessary in order to eradicate corruption and implement social reforms. A Judicial Emergency Commission was appointed in August with the task of investigating the notoriously corrupt judicial system. (By November 1999, 200 judges had been dismissed or suspended.) In response, the Supreme Court President resigned. On 9 September, the ANC and the Congreso signed an agreement of political coexistence, which was mediated by the Catholic Church, that guaranteed the full functioning of the legislative branch from 2 October until a new constitution entered into force. However, relations between the Government and the Congreso were further strained when Chávez ignored congressional objections to the 2000 budget proposal and asked the ANC to approve it instead.

The draft of the new Constitution was signed by the ANC on 19 November 1999 and was approved by 71.21% of the popular vote in a referendum held on 15 December. The low rate of voter participation (only 46%) was largely blamed on torrential rain in much of the country (which killed 30,000 and left a further 200,000 homeless in the central state of Vargas). The 350-article Constitution, which renamed the country the Bolivarian Republic of Venezuela, was promulgated on 30 December. It extended the President's term from five to six years, eliminated the Senate, permitted more state intervention in the economy, reduced civilian supervisory powers over the military, guaranteed the Government's oil monopoly and strengthened minority rights. The Government's political opponents opposed the Constitution because of its centralization of power in the executive branch. The Constitution also promoted public participation by giving the electorate the right to remove elected officials from office by referendum and to annul all but a handful of key laws with an absolute majority. It granted far-reaching social security and labour benefits, including the reduction of the working week to 44 hours, which was strongly opposed by business leaders. An article, which required the media to provide 'truthful information', caused concern amongst journalists that it could be used as a pretext for censorship. The Congreso of the Republic was officially dissolved on 4 January 2000. A new post of executive Vice-President was created and on 24 January Chávez appointed Isaias Rodríguez (ANC Vice-President) to the position. In the same month the ANC appointed many of Chávez's nominees to head state institutions, ranging from the Tribunal Supremo de Justicia to the Central Bank, and including the Ombudsman, the Attorney-General and the Comptroller-General (national auditor). There was criticism that they were appointed without wider consultation and that they were all close associates of the President. The ANC also approved a decree to reinstate the soldiers that participated in the 1992 coup attempts into the armed forces.

New elections for the President, governors, legislators and mayors, as stipulated under the new Constitution, were scheduled for 28 May 2000. The ANC was dissolved in January after it formally delegated its powers to a newly-created 21-member Legislative Commission, which was designated as an interim body until the formation of a new Asamblea National. For the first time in the country's history, the military were authorized to vote. Francisco Arias Cádenas, Governor of the state of Zulia, and one of the four commanders who had led the abortive coup against President Carlos Andrés Pérez, was the main presidential challenger to Chávez. In April Chávez announced a 20% increase in public-sector pay and a 44% pension increase. Arias denounced the move as a populist ploy that would create mass unemployment.

On 25 May 2000, three days before voting was scheduled to take place, the Tribunal Supremo de Justicia suspended the elections, citing technical faults with the electronic voting system. Elections for the President, national legislators and governors were eventually held on 30 July 2000, separate from the local elections, which were postponed until December. Despite the poor economic situation, popular support for the President, especially from the poorest sections of society, remained strong: Chavez won 59.7% of the valid votes cast in the presidential poll, compared with the 37.5% of the ballot polled by Arias and the 2.7% secured by Claudio Fermín (a former mayor of Caracas and ANC member). In the concurrently-held elections to the new, 165-seat Asamblea Nacional, the ruling MVR secured a majority of 93 seats. The AD came second with 32 seats, Salas Römer's PRVZL gained eight seats, MAS won six seats, while the once powerful COPEI secured only five seats. However, the MVR's 93 seats fell short of the three-fifths' majority required to appoint members of the judiciary and the Fiscal- and Comptroller-General. In gubernatorial elections the MVR-led Polo Patriótico alliance dominated, narrowly gaining control of 14 regional executives. Chávez was sworn in as President on 16 August. His new administration was largely unchanged from the previous one. The Asamblea Nacional was convened for the first time in the same month.

In November 2000 Chávez's powers were further enhanced when the Asamblea approved (despite all opposition parties voting against it) an 'enabling law', allowing the President to decree, without legislative debate, a wide range of laws (from public finance to land reform) for one year. In the same month the legislature also passed controversial legislation that assigned the power to appoint important government posts, such as Attorney-General, public ombudsman and senior judges, to a 15-member congressional committee that was dominated by members of the ruling party. Also in November, a government proposal to hold a referendum on whether the opposition-controlled CTV trade union should be suspended until new leadership elections could be held, also received parliamentary approval. Chávez accused the CTV leadership of corruption and undemocratic behaviour while his critics accused him of simply trying to eradicate a powerful opposition faction. In the previous month members of Fedepetrol, the petroleum workers' union, had gone on strike to demand a higher daily rate of pay. Their action proved successful and strikes by other unionized professions swiftly followed. The trade unions, with support from the International Labour Organization, declared the proposed referendum to be unconstitutional, but the Tribunal Supremo de Justicia rejected their arguments and the referendum proceeded on 3 December. In the event, the proposal to suspend trade union leaders for 180 days was approved by 65% of the vote, but the result was undermined by a very low rate of voter participation (23%). The MVR also performed well in municipal elections, held on the same day, although these were also affected by a high abstention rate.

In late December 2000 a new Vice-President, Adina Bastidas, was appointed to replace Isaias Rodríguez who, in the previous month, had been appointed Attorney-General by the congressional committee. The committee appointed Chávez supporters to the remaining important government posts. A few days later Alvaro Silva Calderón was appointed Minister of Energy and Mines, succeeding Alí Rodríguez Araque, who became the Secretary-General of the Organization of the Petroleum Exporting Countries (OPEC, see p. 298).

In early February 2001 José Vicente Rangel became the first civilian to be appointed Minister of National Defence to the consternation of many within the armed forces. However, tensions were eased the following day, when the President appointed Gen. Luis Amaya Chacón to the newly created post of Commander of the Armed Forces, effectively removing Rangel from the chain of military command.

From February to May 2001 public school teachers organized numerous strikes to demand better pay and to protest at government educational reforms. In March a preliminary report by the Comptroller-General alleged widespread corruption within the Chávez administration's social programme, the Plan Bolívar 2000. In May Chávez generated intense constitutional debate when he announced that he was considering emergency powers to attempt to resolve the problems of corruption and crime. The proposal was criticized by MAS members, partners with the MVR in the Polo Patriótico, which prompted Chávez to exclude MAS from the ruling alliance. Chávez, however, did not pursue the proposal and turned his attention to reforming his organizational base. Concerned by mounting allegations of corruption within the military and his own MVR, in June the President announced his intention to relaunch MBR-200 and to create neighbourhood groups of ideologically committed activists, called Círculos Bolivarianos (Bolivarian Circles), in June.

In May 2001 thousands of petroleum and steel workers went on strike to demand recognition of trade union rights. By late November the Chávez administration had antagonized both the labour and business sectors sufficiently for them to find common cause. Earlier that month it was confirmed, amid government allegations of fraud and electoral malpractice, that Carlos Ortega had won the CTV leadership election, thus frustrating Chávez's efforts to establish a pro-government trade union umbrella organization. The CTV allied itself with the country's largest business association, Fedecámaras (Federación Venezolana de Cámaras y Asociaciones de Comercio y Producción), to call for a nation-wide general strike. Fedecámaras was protesting against a recently decreed series of 49 laws (passed using the 'enabling law', thereby bypassing legislative scrutiny); these measures included land reform legislation allowing the Government to expropriate land it deemed unproductive, and a hydrocarbons law, which increased royalties on the petroleum industry. The CTV leaders objected to the hydrocarbons law, claiming that it threatened foreign investment and jobs. In the same month thousands of AD supporters marched on the Asamblea Nacional to demand the resignation of the President. A one-day general strike paralysed the country on 11 December and garnered support from a broad range of sectors.

In January 2002 Chávez replaced his Vice-President, Adina Bastidas, with his co-conspirator in the 1992 military coup attempt, Diosdado Cabello. Later that month, in the midst of further popular demonstrations, including a march in the capital attended by more than 70,000 people demanding that the President either resign or modify his policies, Bastidas was named Minister of Production and Trade. Another participant in the 1992 coup attempt, Rámon Rodríguez Chacín, was appointed Minister of the Interior and Justice, replacing Luis Miquilena following the latter's resignation. The cabinet reshuffle was interpreted by many as a move to the left that would increase political instability in the country. Also in February, four military officials, in separate statements, publicly demanded that Chávez resign, leading to further anti-Government protests and counter-demonstrations in support of the Government. In the same month, in the face of increasing economic uncertainty, the Government abandoned the fixed currency exchange regime and allowed the bolívar to float freely, in an attempt to halt mass capital flight. The bolívar subsequently lost nearly 19% of its value against the US dollar. In late February Chávez replaced the Minister of Finance with another former army colleague, Francisco Usón.

In early March 2002 business leaders, trade union leaders and representatives of the Catholic Church signed a pact calling for the installation of a government of national unity, and more transparency in government, as well as action against poverty and corruption. At the same time, industrial unrest continued to escalate. Following the appointment of a new management board of the state petroleum company PDVSA, several thousand PDVSA managers marched through Caracas in protest; the managers claimed that the appointments were politically motivated. The demonstrators were supported by Fedepetrol, the petroleum workers' trade union, as well as by Fedecámaras. As petroleum production and exports began to be severely affected by a five-week slow-down staged by managers and workers (the reduction in supply was exacerbated by Iraq's concurrent decision to suspend petroleum exports for 30 days as a gesture of support for the Palestinians), on 9 April a 48-hour general strike was organized by the CTV and Fedecámaras. It was subsequently announced that the strike would continue indefinitely, and on 11 April more than 150,000 people marched on the presidential palace to demand Chávez's resignation. In the subsequent clashes outside the Miraflores palace between protesters, government supporters and the security forces, 20 people were killed and more than 100 injured.

On 12 April 2002 a group of senior military officers announced that President Chávez had resigned amid allegations that pro-Government loyalists had fired on opposition protesters. It later emerged that Chávez had, in fact, refused to resign and that, in effect, a military coup had taken place. The military conspirators appointed Pedro Carmona, the President of Fedecámaras, interim President, while Chávez was held incommunicado. On assuming power, Carmona immediately dissolved the Asamblea Nacional, the Tribunal Suprema de Justicia and pronounced Chávez's Bolivarian Constitution to be null and void. The removal from office by the military of an elected Head of State was immediately condemned by many Governments in the region; however, in contrast, the US Administration of George W. Bush blamed the crisis on Chávez and refused to call his ousting from power a coup (see below). Thousands of pro-Chávez and pro-democracy supporters immediately took to the streets to demand Chávez's reinstatement, while many senior military officers also expressed their continued loyalty to the deposed President. In the face of threats by officers loyal to Chávez to attack the presidential palace, Carmona immediately resigned; Vice-President Cabello was sworn in as interim President on 13 April, and Chávez returned to the Miraflores presidential palace within hours and, in a televised ceremony, resumed his presidential powers, less than two days after his ouster.

On reassuming the presidency, as a gesture of reconciliation, Chávez announced the resignation of the disputed PDVSA board of directors (Alí Rodríguez Araque, the Secretary-General of OPEC and former Minister of Energy and Mines, was subsequently appointed President of PDVSA). He also declared that there would be no persecution of those who had supported his removal from office. Nevertheless, Carmona and 100 military personnel were arrested. (Carmona escaped from house arrest and was subsequently granted asylum in Colombia.) In late April the Asamblea Nacional approved the establishment of a Truth Commission to investigate the events surrounding the coup attempt.

In early May 2002 a cabinet reshuffle was implemented, which was interpreted as a further gesture to appease Chávez's opponents. Gen. Lucas Rincón, the Commander of the Armed Forces who had announced Chávez's resignation one month earlier, was appointed Minister of Defence (to replace José Vicente Rangel who was named Vice-President), while both the new Minister of Finance, Tobias Nobrega, and the new Minister of Planning and Development, Felipe Pérez, were members of the business community. Later that month Roy Chaderton Matos was appointed Minister of Foreign Affairs and Ramón Rosales was named Minister of Production and Trade. In late June it was announced that the Minister of Energy and Mines, Alvaro Silva Calderón, would replace Rodríguez Araque as OPEC Secretary-General on 1 July.

In July 2002 former US President Jimmy Carter visited Caracas in an attempt to promote dialogue between the Government and the opposition. Carter was, however, unable to persuade the two sides to meet face-to-face and the country's political and economic situation continued to worsen throughout mid-2002. In late October the opposition and its allies in the CTV labour union and Fedecámaras called a one-day strike, intended to force President Chávez to accept early presidential and legislative elections. The strike brought much of Venezuela to a halt, although the country's important oil industry was not seriously affected. The Government dismissed the industrial action as a failure, while the President also claimed that the intelligence services had foiled a recent attempt to assassinate him. On 23 October a group of 14 senior military officers declared themselves in rebellion against the Chávez Government. The men, many of whom had been involved in April's failed coup, occupied a square in eastern Caracas, where they were joined by hundreds of opposition activists. More than 100 junior officers later also expressed their rejection of Chávez's policies and joined the protest. All of the officers involved were subsequently dismissed from the armed forces. In an attempt to find a constitutional solution to the ongoing political crisis, 12 representatives of the opposition and the Government began round-table discussions in early November 2002. The negotiations were chaired by the Secretary-General of the Organization of American States (OAS, see p. 288), César Gaviria Trujillo, and were also attended by representatives of the Carter Center. The talks failed to make any progress, however, and in late November the opposition, the CTV and Fedecámaras announced that they would call a general strike to force President Chávez to call fresh elections or submit to a referendum. The general strike began on 2 December 2002 and continued for a further nine weeks. The vast majority of large businesses and international companies observed the stoppage, although small shopkeepers and the public-transport sector continued to operate throughout. The strike had a particularly severe impact on Venezuela's crucial oil industry. The majority of managers and administrative staff at PDVSA staged a walk-out, and the company was obliged to declare *force majeure* on its exports of crude petroleum and petroleum products. The President of PDVSA, Alí Rodríguez, sought to restart the industry by replacing the strikers with new staff, contract workers and retired employees. He eventually dismissed 18,000 of PDVSA's previous 33,000 full-time work-force for observing the strike, and production recovered to pre-strike levels by late March. The strike caused enormous difficulties for the Venezuelan Government, which saw oil revenues collapse, while ordinary Venezuelans suffered from severe shortages of food and other basic products.

In mid-January 2003 President Chávez suspended trading in the national currency, the bolívar, in response to the economic crisis. Nonetheless, the Government refused to negotiate on the issue of early elections, although discussions between the two sides, suspended at the start of the strike, began once more in late January. The general strike focused international attention on the ongoing crisis in Venezuela, and in late January six countries formed the 'Group of Friends of Venezuela', to support a peaceful solution to the crisis. The Group was composed of the USA, Brazil, Chile, Mexico, Portugal and Spain, despite President Chávez's call for the inclusion of countries more sympathetic to his revolutionary project, such as Cuba.

In early February 2003 the opposition parties, CTV and Fedecámaras announced an end to the two-month general strike after failing to secure any concessions from the Government. The opposition announced that they would instead begin a 'new phase' of their campaign to force the President to resign, and on 2 February they collected an estimated four million signatures in support of early elections. The Government did not respond to the petition, and several days later the Venezuelan authorities announced new exchange rate rules, which critics alleged were designed to punish companies that had participated in the recent strike. On 18 February the Government and opposition representatives at the OAS-sponsored negotiations signed an agreement to seek to reduce political tension in Venezuela. The pact was immediately thrown into question, however, when the following day police arrested the President of Fedecámaras, Carlos Fernández Pérez, on the orders of President Chávez. Fernández was charged with a number of offences, including treason, relating to his role in organizing the recent general strike. A warrant was also issued for his fellow strike leader, the President of the CTV, Carlos Ortega, who went into hiding and later sought political asylum in the Costa Rican Embassy. The opposition immediately accused President Chávez of authoritarianism and observers expressed fears that a further deterioration in the political situation was likely. These predictions seemed to be borne out when bombs exploded on 25 February outside a Colombian Consulate in Caracas and diplomatic offices belonging to the Spanish Embassy. No one was killed in the blasts, which occurred just days after President Chávez had criticized the two countries for intervening in Venezuela's internal affairs. The Government and opposition each blamed the other's supporters for the explosions. Later that week arrest warrants were issued for six senior PDVSA managers who had backed the strike, but an appeals court later struck these down.

Hopes of a constitutional settlement to the Venezuelan crisis improved on 11 April 2003, when the Government and opposition agreed to hold a referendum on the Chávez Government later in the year. The referendum was to take place after 18 August, the mid-way point in the President's six-year mandate, according to provisions established in the Constitution. President Chávez promised his supporters that he would defeat his opponents in the ballot, although opinion polls suggested that his approval rating had fallen to around 30%.

In 1982 Venezuela refused to renew the 1970 Port of Spain Protocol, declaring a 12-year moratorium on the issue of Venezuela's claim to a large area of Guyana to the west of the Essequibo river, which expired in that year. Venezuela's border garrisons were strengthened and border violations were reported. In 1985 Venezuela and Guyana requested UN mediation in an attempt to resolve their dispute over the Essequibo region. A UN mediator was appointed in late 1989; however, negotiations remained deadlocked and the dispute resurfaced in 1999 when Guyana granted offshore oil concessions in the disputed waters to foreign oil firms. In October Chávez renewed Venezuela's claim to the Essequibo region. The tension escalated in March 2000 when Guyana gave preliminary approval to the installation of a US satellite-launching facility in the disputed area.

Venezuela also has a claim to some islands in the Netherlands Antilles, and a territorial dispute with Colombia concerning maritime boundaries in the Gulf of Venezuela. In March 1989 an agreement was reached with Colombia on the establishment of a border commission to negotiate a settlement for the territorial dispute. In March 1990 President Virgilio Barco of Colombia and President Pérez signed the 'San Pedro Alejandrino' document, by which they pledged to implement the commission's proposals. At a meeting of the Presidents of Colombia and Venezuela in Caracas in January 1992, Pérez publicly recognized that

Colombia had legitimate territorial rights in the Gulf of Venezuela. In late 1994 a series of incursions by Colombian guerrillas resulted in the deaths of several Venezuelan soldiers, and prompted the Government to deploy reinforcements to secure the border with Colombia. Despite assurances of increased vigilance by the Colombian Government, attacks by the guerrillas in February and May 1995 resulted in the deaths of a further 16 Venezuelan soldiers. Confrontations between the Venezuelan armed forces and Colombian guerrillas and other criminal elements continued in late 1995 and early 1996 prompting further bilateral discussions concerning the demarcation and control of the border with Colombia, although Venezuelan demands for permission to enter Colombian territory in pursuit of suspected criminals were continually resisted by the Colombian authorities. In February 1997, following a succession of violent incidents on the countries' joint border, Venezuela and Colombia signed an accord creating a bilateral verification commission, comprising diplomatic and military representatives of both countries, to conduct investigations into border incidents. Colombia also agreed to increase its military presence on the border. During 1999 there was a steady increase of guerrilla fighting in border areas. Chávez was accused of interfering in Colombia's domestic affairs when he offered to mediate in the conflict with the Revolutionary Armed Forces of Colombia (FARC). However, relations were improved by the signing on 15 February 2000 of the Guasdualito Declaration, which included a commitment to joint border area development work, and co-operation on other bilateral issues. Nevertheless, later that year tensions resurfaced, owing to Chávez's opposition to the military component of the 'Plan Colombia' (Colombia's US-supported anti-drugs strategy) and accusations by Colombia that Venezuela was covertly aiding the guerrilla forces. In November 2000 Colombia briefly recalled its ambassador to Venezuela after a representative of FARC was allowed to speak in the Venezuelan Asamblea Nacional. Tensions were exacerbated further in March 2001 after Venezuela refused to extradite to Colombia a member of a guerrilla group accused of hijacking an aircraft in 1999. Relations with Colombia continued to deteriorate after the election of Alvaro Uribe Vélez, a hard-line independent candidate, to the Colombian presidency in May 2002. In late 2002 the Uribe Government repeatedly criticized President Chávez for failing to label the FARC as a terrorist organization. The two Governments also continued to clash over rebel activities in the border area, with Venezuela accusing Colombia of failing to patrol its border properly, while the Colombian Government accused its Venezuelan counterpart of sheltering terrorist bases.

Following his election in December 1998, President Chávez announced that his administration would seek greater integration in large regional organizations such as CARICOM (see p. 155) and Mercosur (see p. 316). (In May 2001 Venezuela officially submitted an application to become an associate member of Mercosur.) He also made closer relations with Cuba a priority and in October 2000 Chávez and Cuba's Fidel Castro Ruz signed a co-operation agreement allowing the export of oil to Cuba on the same preferential terms enjoyed by a number of Central American and Caribbean countries. In August 2000 Chávez became the first elected head of state to meet President Saddam Hussein of Iraq since sanctions were imposed on that country following the war in the region of the Persian (Arabian) Gulf in 1991. The meeting was condemned by the USA.

The relationship between Venezuela and the USA (the main purchaser of Venezuelan crude petroleum) deteriorated following the election of Chávez. In 2000 Chávez refused to authorize US drugs surveillance flights over Venezuela. Furthermore, the President's close relationship with Fidel Castro, his visit to Iraq and his populist rhetoric led to further estrangement from the USA. The Venezuelan Government also signed a number of bilateral trade and cultural agreements with the People's Republic of China, India, Iran and Russia in mid-2001. Following Chávez's criticisms of the US-led bombing of Afghanistan in October and November 2001, the US Ambassador to Venezuela was briefly recalled for consultations. The relationship reached a nadir after the US Administration of George W. Bush refused to condemn the short-lived military ouster of Chávez in April 2002. It was subsequently revealed that US officials had met with opposition figures shortly before the failed coup; however, the US Government denied it had encouraged or supported the coup. The USA participated in the 'Group of Friends of Venezuela' in January 2003, but the relationship between the US Government and President Chávez did not improve. Venezuela was highly critical of the US-led military campaign against the regime of Saddam Hussain in Iraq in March 2003, although the Government continued to supply the USA with petroleum.

Venezuela has observer status in the Non-aligned Movement (see p. 350).

Government

Venezuela is a federal republic comprising 22 states, a Federal District (containing the capital) and 72 Federal Dependencies. Under the 1999 Constitution, legislative power is held by the unicameral Asamblea Nacional (National Assembly). Executive authority rests with the President. The President is elected for six years by universal adult suffrage. The President has extensive powers, and is assisted by a Council of Ministers. Each state has a directly-elected executive governor and an elected legislature.

Defence

Military service is selective for two years and six months between 18 and 45 years of age. In August 2002 the armed forces numbered 82,300 men: an army of 34,000, a navy of 18,300 (including 7,800 marines), an air force of 7,000 and a National Guard of 23,000. The defence budget for 2002 was 1,326,000m. bolívares.

Economic Affairs

In 2001, according to estimates by the World Bank, Venezuela's gross national income (GNI), measured at average 1999–2001 prices, was US $117,169m., equivalent to $4,760 per head (or $5,890 per head on an international purchasing-power parity basis). During 1990–2001, it was estimated, the population increased by an annual average of 2.1%, while gross domestic product (GDP) per head decreased, in real terms, by an average of 0.1% per year. Overall GDP increased, in real terms, by an average annual rate of 2.1% in 1990–2001; growth in 2001 was an estimated 2.8%.

Agriculture (including hunting, forestry and fishing) contributed 4.4% of GDP in 2001, and engaged 10.6% of the employed labour force in 2000. The principal crops are sugar cane, bananas, maize, rice, plantains, oranges, sorghum and cassava. Cattle are the principal livestock, but the practice of smuggling cattle across Venezuela's border into Colombia has had a severe effect on the livestock sector. According to the World Bank, agricultural GDP increased by an estimated annual average of 1.4% during 1990–2001. The sector's GDP increased, in real terms, by 2.4% in 2000 and by an estimated 2.6% in 2001.

Industry (including mining, manufacturing, construction and power) contributed 34.7% of GDP in 2001, and engaged 22.8% of the employed labour force in 2000. According to the World Bank, industrial GDP increased by an annual average of 2.7% during 1990–2001. Sectoral GDP increased, in real terms, by 2.8% in 2000 and by an estimated 1.9% in 2001.

Mining and quarrying contributed 15.0% of GDP in 2001, but engaged only 0.6% of the employed labour force in 2000. Petroleum production is the most important industry in Venezuela, providing some 85.6% of export revenue in 2000. In 2000 proven reserves totalled 76.9m. barrels. Aluminium and iron ore are also major sources of export revenue. Venezuela also has substantial deposits of natural gas, coal, diamonds, gold, zinc, copper, lead, silver, phosphates, manganese and titanium. The GDP of the mining sector increased by an average of 2.5% per year in 1995–2001; by 4.7% in 2000 and by an estimated 1.1% in 2001.

Manufacturing contributed 12.4% of GDP in 2001, and engaged 13.3% of the employed labour force in 2000. The most important sectors in 1998, measured by gross value of output, were refined petroleum products (24.3%), food products, transport equipment, industrial chemicals and iron and steel. Manufacturing GDP decreased by an annual average of 0.1% during 1995–2001. The sector's GDP increased, in real terms, by 2.1% in 2000, but decreased by an estimated 0.2% in 2001.

Energy is derived principally from domestic supplies of petroleum and coal, and from hydroelectric power. Hydroelectric power provided 75.1% of electricity production in 1999, with natural gas supplying a further 17.8%. Imports of mineral fuels comprised 3.7% of the total value of merchandise imports in 2000.

The services sector contributed 60.9% of GDP in 2001, and engaged 66.5% of the employed labour force in 2000. GDP growth of the services sector was stagnant during 1994–2001.

Sectoral GDP increased, in real terms, by 3.4% in 2000 and by an estimated 3.2% in 2001.

In 2001 Venezuela recorded a visible trade surplus of US $9,335m., and there was a surplus of $3,931m. on the current account of the balance of payments. In 2001 the principal source of imports (33.8%) was the USA; other major suppliers were other countries of the Andean Community of Nations (CAN, see p. 133), Brazil, Mexico and Japan. The USA was also the principal market for exports (50.0%) in 2000; other major purchasers were other members of the CAN, Brazil and the Netherlands Antilles. The principal exports in 2000 were petroleum and related products (85.6%), steel, aluminium and chemical products. The principal imports in 2001 were electrical and transport equipment (41.9%), basic manufactures, and chemicals.

There was an estimated budgetary deficit of 5,433,887m. bolívares in 2001 (equivalent to 6.0% of GDP). Venezuela's total external debt was US $38,196m. at the end of 2000, of which $27,628m. was long-term public debt. In that year the cost of servicing the debt was equivalent to 15.3% of the value of exports of goods and services. The average annual rate of inflation was 39.8% in 1991–2001. Consumer prices increased by an annual average of 12.5% in 2001 and by 22.4% in 2002. An estimated 18.0% of the labour force were unemployed in September 2002.

Venezuela is a member of the CAN (see p. 133), the Inter-American Development Bank (IDB, see p. 239), the Latin American Integration Association (Asociación Latinoamericana de Integración—ALADI, see p. 259), the Organization of the Petroleum Exporting Countries (OPEC, see p. 298), the Latin American Economic System (Sistema Económico Latinoamericano—SELA, see p. 340) and the Group of Three (G3, see p. 340). In April 2003 President Chávez appeared to discount the possibility of Venezuela joining the planned Free Trade Area of the Americas (FTAA) during his term of office.

Venezuela's economy is largely dependent on the petroleum sector, which provides some 80% of government revenue, and is therefore particularly vulnerable to fluctuations in the world petroleum market. The Chávez administration, inaugurated in 1999, introduced new pension benefits and health programmes, to be financed by surplus petroleum profits, known as the oil stabilization fund. High petroleum prices in 2000 allowed for an estimated 40% increase in government spending. Pensions increased by 20% and there was a large increase in public sector pay. However, the non-petroleum sector stagnated, partly because of an overvalued currency. Economic growth slowed in 2001, owing to lower petroleum prices and the consequent decrease in the value of exports and increase in the fiscal deficit. In an attempt to reduce the deficit, planned government spending was reduced by 7% in the 2002 budget and a 49-point series of economic measures was approved by decree in November 2001. However, the controversial measures contained in the package (most notably, a hydrocarbons law that increased royalty taxes on the petroleum sector from 16.6% to 30%) led to widespread industrial unrest and political instability, which severely affected petroleum production rates in early 2002. The situation was compounded in February after a controlled devaluation plan (initiated by the Government to make domestic products more competitive) was abandoned in favour of a floating exchange rate, in a bid to halt the flight of capital caused by the continuing political unrest. The bolívar immediately depreciated by as much as 19% against the US dollar; nevertheless, a subsequent increase in the price of petroleum helped to stabilize the currency. Investor confidence in Venezuela continued to deteriorate following the attempted coup against President Chávez in April 2002. The protracted industrial and social unrest in early 2003 (see Recent History, above) was estimated to have reduced GDP in the first quarter of the year by some 25%. A further rapid decline in the value of the bolívar in January 2003 prompted the Central Bank to suspend currency trading. After the collapse of the general strike in February 2003, it was announced that the bolívar would be pegged to the US dollar, although at a reduction of some 17% in relation to its value prior to the suspension of trading. (In a further effort to support the weakening currency in the same month the Chávez administration announced price controls on basic foodstuffs.) The outlook for the country's external debt also deteriorated in 2002 and 2003, as international credit ratings agencies continued to downgrade Venezuelan bonds. In mid-2002 investors were further discouraged not only by revelations that the Government had spent its monthly obligations under the government debt-reduction mechanism (known as the Fondo de Inversión para la Estabilidad Macroeconómica—FIEM) on the public-sector payroll, but also by an outright ban on local trading in US-dollar-denominated Brady bonds. In 2003, however, despite the apparently ambivalent attitude of President Chávez towards the multilateral lending agencies, and the severe domestic liquidity and interest rate problems provoked by the growing burden of short-term debt, it appeared that the Government at least intended to honour its commitments. Nevertheless, a substantial restructuring of Venezuela's external debt seemed increasingly likely in 2003. Moreover, the two-month general strike which began in early December 2002 was estimated to have increased the Government's annual budget deficit by some $6,000m.; oil revenues did not return to previous levels until mid-2003. None the less, despite the country's high proportion of short-term debt, Venezuela's overall level of indebtedness remained comparatively low in relation with some other Latin American nations, and although the economic outlook in mid-2003 remained dominated by the continued lack of genuine political stability, investor confidence did improve after the collapse of the strike in February 2003. Estimated annual economic growth declined sharply in 2002, by approximately 8.9%.

Education

Education is officially compulsory for 10 years, to be undertaken between six and 15 years of age. Primary education, which is available free of charge, begins at six years of age and lasts for nine years. Secondary education, beginning at the age of 15, lasts for a further two years. In 1996 the total enrolment at primary and secondary schools was equivalent to 83% of the school-age population (males 80%; females 85%). Of children in the relevant age-groups, primary enrolment in 1996 was equivalent to 91% (males 90%; females 93%), while secondary enrolment in that year was equivalent to 40% (males 33%; females 41%). In 2001 there were 20 universities. Expenditure on education by the central Government was 3.8% of GDP in 1998.

Public Holidays

2003: 1 January (New Year's Day), 3–4 March (Carnival), 10 March (La Guaira only), 18–21 April (Easter), 19 April (Declaration of Independence), 1 May (Labour Day), 24 June (Battle of Carabobo), 5 July (Independence Day), 24 July (Birth of Simón Bolívar and Battle of Lago de Maracaibo), 4 September (Civil Servants' Day), 12 October (Discovery of America), 24 October (Maracaibo only), 24–25 December (Christmas), 31 December (New Year's Eve).

2004: 1 January (New Year's Day), 20–25 February (Carnival), 10 March (La Guaira only), 9–12 April (Easter), 19 April (Declaration of Independence), 1 May (Labour Day), 24 June (Battle of Carabobo), 5 July (Independence Day), 24 July (Birth of Simón Bolívar and Battle of Lago de Maracaibo), 4 September (Civil Servants' Day), 12 October (Discovery of America), 24 October (Maracaibo only), 24–25 December (Christmas), 31 December (New Year's Eve).

Banks and insurance companies also close on: 6 January (Epiphany), 19 March (St Joseph), Ascension Day (29 May 2003, 20 May 2004), 29 June (SS Peter and Paul), 15 August (Assumption), 1 November (All Saints' Day), and 8 December (Immaculate Conception).

Weights and Measures

The metric system is in force.

Statistical Survey

Sources (unless otherwise stated): Oficina Central de Estadística e Informática (formerly Dirección General de Estadística y Censos Nacionales), Edif. Fundación La Salle, Avda Boyacá, Caracas 1050; tel. (212) 782-1133; fax (212) 782-2243; e-mail ocei@platino.gov.ve; internet www.ocei.gov.ve; Banco Central de Venezuela, Avda Urdaneta esq. de las Carmelitas, Caracas 1010; tel. (212) 801-5111; fax (212) 861-0048; e-mail mbatista@bcv.org.ve; internet www.bcv.org.ve.

Area and Population

AREA, POPULATION AND DENSITY

Area (sq km)	
Land	882,050
Inland waters.	30,000
Total	912,050*
Population (census results)†	
20 October 1990	18,105,265
20 October 2001 (preliminary results)	
Males	11,244,160
Females.	11,444,643
Total	22,688,803
Population (official estimates at mid-year)†	
1998	23,242,000
1999	23,706,711
2000	24,169,744
Density (per sq km) at census of 2001	24.8

* 352,144 sq miles.

† Excluding Indian jungle inhabitants, estimated at 140,562 in 1982. Census results also exclude an adjustment for underenumeration, estimated at 6.7% in 1990.

ADMINISTRATIVE DIVISIONS

(1 July 2000)

	Area (sq km)	Population Density (per (estimates)	sq km)	Capital
Federal				
District . .	1,930	2,284,921	1,183.9	Caracas
Amazonas . .	175,750	100,325	0.6	Puerto Ayacucho
Anzoátegui. .	43,300	1,140,369	26.3	Barcelona
Apure . .	76,500	466,931	6.1	San Fernando
Aragua . .	7,014	1,481,453	211.2	Maracay
Barinas. .	35,200	583,521	16.6	Barinas
Bolívar . .	238,000	1,306,651	5.5	Ciudad Bolívar
Carabobo . .	4,650	2,106,264	453.0	Valencia
Cojedes . .	14,800	262,154	17.7	San Carlos
Delta Amacuro	40,200	137,939	3.4	Tucupita
Falcón . .	24,800	747,672	30.1	Coro
Guárico. .	64,986	638,638	9.8	San Juan de los Morros
Lara. . .	19,800	1,581,121	79.9	Barquisimeto
Mérida . .	11,300	744,986	65.9	Mérida
Miranda .	7,950	2,607,163	327.9	Los Teques
Monagas . .	28,900	599,764	20.8	Maturín
Nueva Esparta	1,500	377,701	328.4	La Asunción
Portuguesa. .	15,200	830,441	54.6	Guanare
Sucre . .	11,800	824,764	69.9	Cumaná
Táchira . .	11,100	1,031,158	92.9	San Cristóbal
Trujillo . .	7,400	587,280	79.4	Trujillo
Yaracuy. .	7,100	518,902	73.1	San Felipe
Zulia . .	63,100	3,209,626	50.9	Maracaibo
Federal				
Dependencies	120	—	—	—
Total . . .	912,050	24,169,744	26.5	

PRINCIPAL TOWNS

(city proper, estimated population at 1 July 2000)

Caracas (capital). .	1,975,787	Mérida	230,101
Maracaibo. . . .	1,764,038	Barinas	228,598
Valencia	1,338,833	Turmero	226,084
Barquisimeto . .	875,790	Cabimas	214,000
Ciudad Guayana .	704,168	Baruta	213,373
Petare	520,982	Puerto la Cruz . .	205,635
Maracay	459,007	Los Teques . . .	183,142
Ciudad Bolívar . .	312,691	Guarenas	170,204
Barcelona . . .	311,475	Puerto Cabello . .	169,959
San Cristóbal . .	307,184	Acarigua . . .	166,720
Maturín	283,318	Coro	158,763
Cumaná	269,428		

BIRTHS, MARRIAGES AND DEATHS*

	Registered live births		Registered marriages		Registered deaths	
	Number	Rate (per 1,000)	Number	Rate (per 1,000)	Number	Rate (per 1,000)
1993 . .	524,387	25.1	100,042	4.8	92,273	4.4
1994 . .	547,819	25.6	97,674	4.6	98,911	4.6
1995 . .	520,584	24.1	83,735	3.9	n.a.	n.a.
1996 . .	595,816†	26.2†	73,064†	3.2†	93,839	4.2
1997 . .	575,832	25.3	n.a.	n.a.	n.a.	n.a.
1998 . .	501,808	24.7	n.a.	n.a.	98,624	4.7
1999 . .	527,888	24.3	90,220	3.8	101,907	4.6
2000 . .	544,416	23.9	91,088	3.8	103,255	4.6

* Excluding Indian jungle population.

† Provisional.

Expectation of life (WHO estimates, years at birth): 73.6 (males 70.7; females 76.5) in 2001 (Source: WHO, *World Health Report*).

ECONOMICALLY ACTIVE POPULATION

(household surveys, '000 persons aged 15 years and over, July–December)*

	1998	1999	2000†
Agriculture, hunting, forestry and fishing	881	890	950
Mining and quarrying	83	57	53
Manufacturing	1,226	1,202	1,191
Electricity, gas and water . . .	58	59	58
Construction	772	665	741
Transport, storage and communications	574	604	608
Financing, insurance, real estate business services and trade . .	2,687	2,742	2,752
Community, social and personal services	2,516	2,514	2,598
Activities not adequately defined .	19	7	10
Total employed.	8,816	8,742	8,961
Unemployed	1,091	1,483	1,366
Total labour force	9,907	10,225	10,327

* Figures exclude members of the armed forces.

† Provisional.

Health and Welfare

KEY INDICATORS

Total fertility rate (children per woman, 2001)	2.8
Under-5 mortality rate (per 1,000 live births, 2000) . . .	23
HIV/AIDS (% of persons aged 15–49, 2001). . . .	0.50
Physicians (per 1,000 head, 1997)	2.36
Hospital beds (per 1,000 head, 1996)	1.47
Health expenditure (2000): US $ per head (PPP) . . .	280
Health expenditure (2000): % of GDP	4.7
Health expenditure (2000): public (% of total) . . .	57.4
Access to water (% of persons, 2000).	84
Access to sanitation (% of persons, 2000)	74
Human Development Index (2000): ranking	69
Human Development Index (2000): value	0.770

For sources and definitions, see explanatory note on p. vi.

Agriculture

PRINCIPAL CROPS
('000 metric tons)

	1999	2000	2001
Rice (paddy)	720	677	690†
Maize	1,149	1,690	1,200†
Sorghum	364	582	390†
Potatoes	384	342	342
Cassava (Manioc)	594	571	571
Yautia (Cocoyam)	63	63	63
Yams	70	88	88
Sugar cane	8,501	8,832	8,856
Coconuts	128	111	111
Oil palm fruit	336	373	380†
Cabbages	61	55	55
Tomatoes	221	213	215
Chillies and green peppers . . .	87	78	80
Dry onions	200	175	180
Carrots	213	184	200
Other vegetables	150	209	140
Bananas	788	1,100	1,050
Plantains	615	684	700
Oranges	463	497	500
Tangerines, mandarins, clementines and satsumas . .	68	69	69
Watermelons	249	200	200
Cantaloupes and other melons .	126	113	115
Mangoes	132	132	132
Avocados	41	52	50
Pineapples	299	351	300
Papayas	99	114	105
Other fruit*	41	41	41
Coffee (green)	80	78	69†

* FAO estimates.
† Provisional figure.

Source: FAO.

LIVESTOCK
('000 head, year ending September)

	1999	2000	2001
Horses*	500	500	500
Asses*	440	440	440
Cattle	15,778	14,084	16,000*
Pigs	5,355	5,655	5,655*
Sheep	705	815	820*
Goats	3,392	4,015	4,000*
Chickens*	105,000	110,000	115,000

* FAO estimate(s).

Source: FAO.

LIVESTOCK PRODUCTS
('000 metric tons)

	1999	2000	2001
Beef and veal	391	429	365†
Pig meat	114	117	118†
Poultry meat	505	588	550†
Cows' milk	1,352	1,415	1,400*
Cheese	89	97	89*
Hen eggs	169	175	180*
Cattle hides (fresh)*	45	50	43

* FAO estimate(s).
† Provisional figure.

Source: FAO.

Forestry

ROUNDWOOD REMOVALS
('000 cubic metres, excl. bark)

	1999	2000	2001
Sawlogs, veneer logs and logs for sleepers	1,620	848	737
Pulpwood	181	255	233
Fuel wood*	3,517	3,605	3,650
Total	5,318	3,944	4,620

* FAO estimates.

Source: FAO.

SAWNWOOD PRODUCTION
('000 cubic metres, incl. railway sleepers)

	1999	2000	2001
Total (all broadleaved)	174	175	211

Source: FAO.

Fishing

('000 metric tons, live weight)

	1998	1999	2000
Capture	505.7	412.8	391.3
Prochilods	15.7	9.3	9.6
Round sardinella	186.1	126.5	73.5
Atlantic thread herring . . .	10.6	14.8	9.9
Skipjack tuna	10.1	17.6	8.2
Yellowfin tuna	76.6	69.2	80.3
Ark clams	28.0	38.6	44.7
Aquaculture	9.7	10.9	12.7
Total catch	516.2	422.6	404.0

Source: FAO, *Yearbook of Fishery Statistics*.

Mining

('000 metric tons, unless otherwise indicated)

	1998	1999	2000
Hard coal	6,458	6,593	7,844
Crude petroleum ('000 barrels).	1,215,120	1,077,352	1,117,475
Natural gas (million cu metres)* .	62,167	58,744	60,000†
Iron ore: gross weight	16,553	14,051	17,353
Iron ore: metal content . . .	5,424	5,071	6,412
Nickel ore (metric tons)‡ . .	—	—	2,472
Bauxite	4,826	4,166	4,361
Gold (kilograms)‡	6,740	5,946	7,332
Phosphate rock§	322	366	389
Salt (evaporated)†	350	350	350
Gypsum	72	42	25
Diamonds (carats): Gem. . .	80,033	59,446	65,000†
Diamonds (carats): Industrial . .	16,778	35,968	44,600†

* Figures refer to the gross volume of output. Marketed production (in million cu metres) was: 39,005 in 1998; 36,000 in 1999 (estimate); 37,000 in 2000 (estimate).

† Estimated production.

‡ Figures refer to the metal content of ores and concentrates.

§ Figures refer to gross weight. The phosphoric acid content (in '000 metric tons) was: 87 in 1998; 99 in 1999.

Source: US Geological Survey.

Industry

PETROLEUM PRODUCTS

('000 barrels)

	1998	1999*	2000*
Motor spirit (petrol)	70,956	63,600	65,400
Kerosene	766	687	706
Jet fuel	32,551	29,200	30,000
Distillate fuel oils	120,815	108,300	111,400
Residual fuel oils.	80,957	72,600	74,700

* Estimates.

Source: US *Geological Survey*.

SELECTED OTHER PRODUCTS

('000 metric tons, unless otherwise indicated)

	1997	1998	1999
Raw sugar*	614	564	629
Fertilizers† ‡	5,717	468	450
Cement*	8,145	8,202	8,500§
Crude steel‖	3,986	3,553	3,261
Aluminium‖	634	585	570
Electric energy (million kWh)† . .	78,066	80,904	n.a.

2000 ('000 metric tons): Raw sugar 673*; Crude steel 3,835‖; Cement 8,600*‡

2001 ('000 metric tons): Raw sugar 800*§.

* FAO figure(s).

† Data from UN Economic Commission for Latin America and the Caribbean.

‡ Including phosphatic, nitrogenous and potassic fertilizers, year beginning July 1.

§ Estimate.

‖ Data from US Geological Survey.

Finance

CURRENCY AND EXCHANGE RATES

Monetary Units
100 céntimos = 1 bolívar

Sterling, Dollar and Euro Equivalents (31 December 2002)
£1 sterling = 2,258.53 bolívares
US $1 = 1,401.25 bolívares
€1 = 1,469.49 bolívares
10,000 bolívares = £4.428 = $7.136 = €6.805

Average Exchange Rate (bolívares per US dollar)
2000	679.960
2001	723.666
2002	1,160.953

BUDGET

(million bolívares)

Revenue	1999	2000*	2001†
Petroleum revenue	4,459,534	8,687,534	6,120,702
Non-petroleum revenues . . .	5,433,973	5,976,052	8,882,491
Taxes on income	1,159,184	1,318,062	1,650,960
Value-added tax	1,496,709	2,532,420	4,488,974
Sales tax	941,481	0	0
Import duties	927,893	1,070,552	1,260,575
Total revenue (incl. others)‡ . .	9,895,524	14,664,587	15,036,493

Expenditure	1999	2000*	2001†
Current expenditure. . . .	10,122,636	14,535,550	16,316,235
Wages and salaries . . .	2,062,142	3,293,810	3,793,166
Interest payments. . . .	1,643,607	2,004,259	1,983,174
Goods and services . . .	560,114	472,408	1,233,522
Transfers	5,369,733	8,699,497	8,972,564
Extrabudgetary expenditure .	162,288	307,880	333,809
Capital expenditure	1,785,753	2,499,416	3,988,157
Capital transfers	1,668,728	2,368,336	3,264,571
Total expenditure§	11,981,396	17,238,854	20,503,680

* Estimates.

† Projections.

‡ Excluding lending and other extraordinary revenues: 3,167,513 in 1999; 5,886,143 in 2000; 8,337,810 in 2001. Including revenue from iron: 2,017 in 1999; 876 in 2000; 33,300 in 2001.

§ Including net lending: 73,006 in 1999; 203,889 in 2000; 199,289 in 2001.

Source: Central Office of Budget.

CENTRAL BANK RESERVES

(US $ million at 31 December)

	2000	2001	2002
Gold*	2,794	3,056	3,043
IMF special drawing rights. . .	28	8	11
Reserve position in IMF. . . .	419	405	438
Foreign exchange.	12,633	8,825	8,143
Total	15,874	12,294	11,635

* Valued at $300 per troy ounce.

Source: IMF, *International Financial Statistics*.

MONEY SUPPLY

(million bolívares at 31 December)*

	2000	2001	2002
Currency outside banks. . . .	1,997,610	2,286,880	3,795,870
Demand deposits at commercial banks	5,743,230	6,821,990	7,029,870
Total (incl. others)	8,037,220	9,287,010	10,973,460

* Figures rounded to the nearest 10m. bolívares.

Source: IMF, *International Financial Statistics*.

COST OF LIVING
(Consumer Price Index; Base: 1990 = 100)

	1997	1998	1999
Food	1,585.4	2,181.5	2,516.3
Fuel and light	1,793.5	2,903.0	3,663.9
Clothing	1,313.6	1,590.7	1,864.6
Rent	1,946.5	2,568.8	3,143.8
All items (incl. others)	1,818.8	2,447.8	2,986.4

Source: ILO, *Yearbook of Labour Statistics*.

All items (base: 1995 = 100): 584.7 in 2000; 658.0 in 2001; 805.6 in 2002 (Source: IMF, *International Financial Statistics*).

NATIONAL ACCOUNTS

National Income and Product
(million bolívares at current prices)

	1998	1999	2000
Compensation of employees	17,107,333	19,912,227	23,943,843
Operating surplus	26,542,365	32,281,004	46,079,386
Domestic factor incomes	43,649,698	52,193,231	70,023,229
Consumption of fixed capital	4,068,958	4,777,728	5,868,469
Gross domestic product (GDP) at factor cost	47,718,656	56,970,959	75,891,698
Indirect taxes	4,916,808	5,742,479	6,201,398
Less Subsidies	152,998	136,399	168,903
GDP in purchasers' values	52,482,466	62,577,039	81,924,193
Less Net factor income paid abroad	1,061,873	928,812	792,228
Gross national product	51,420,593	61,648,227	81,131,965
Less Consumption of fixed capital	4,068,958	4,777,728	5,868,469
National income in market prices	47,351,635	56,870,499	75,263,496
Other net current transfers from abroad	−59,237	41,638	−97,601
National disposable income	47,292,398	56,912,137	75,165,895

Source: UN Economic Commission for Latin America and the Caribbean.

Expenditure on the Gross Domestic Product
('000 million bolívares at current prices)

	1999	2000	2001
Government final consumption expenditure	4,700.3	5,958.9	7,846.7
Private final consumption expenditure	43,236.9	52,295.1	61,107.9
Increase in stocks	1,477.2	2,475.0	3,057.0
Gross fixed capital formation	9,850.6	11,719.0	14,952.6
Total domestic expenditure	59,265.0	72,448.0	86,964.2
Exports of goods and services	13,546.0	23,457.0	20,320.2
Less Imports of goods and services	10,233.9	13,454.3	15,959.6
GDP in purchasers' values	62,577.0	82,450.7	91,324.8
GDP at constant 1984 prices	565.9	584.2	600.5

Source: IMF, *International Financial Statistics*.

Gross Domestic Product by Economic Activity
(million bolívares at current prices)

	1999	2000	2001
Agriculture, hunting, forestry and fishing	2,880,633	3,258,018	3,872,766
Mining and quarrying*	8,321,318	15,917,745	13,212,095
Manufacturing†	8,204,542	10,621,524	10,952,067
Electricity and water	931,608	1,137,058	1,355,214
Construction	3,400,092	3,842,038	5,032,111
Trade, restaurants and hotels	9,794,983	11,688,516	13,477,347
Transport, storage and communications	5,716,383	6,920,770	8,063,945
Finance, insurance, real estate and business services	6,543,918	7,893,992	9,780,679
Government services	3,378,833	4,247,454	5,572,100
Other services	11,164,145	14,213,174	16,724,866
Sub-total	60,336,461	79,740,289	88,043,190
Import duties	4,037,065	4,562,028	5,372,789
Less Imputed bank service charge	1,796,487	1,851,643	2,091,206
Total	62,577,039	82,450,674	91,324,773

* Includes crude petroleum and natural gas production.
† Includes petroleum refining.
‡ Preliminary figures.

BALANCE OF PAYMENTS
(US $ million)

	1999	2000	2001
Exports of goods f.o.b.	20,819	33,035	26,726
Imports of goods f.o.b.	−13,213	−15,491	−17,391
Trade balance	7,606	17,544	9,335
Exports of services	1,310	1,237	1,280
Imports of services	−3,772	−4,255	−4,614
Balance on goods and services	5,144	14,526	6,001
Other income received	2,157	2,915	2,495
Other income paid	−3,684	−4,119	−3,948
Balance on goods, services and income	3,617	13,322	4,548
Current transfers received	191	222	196
Current transfers paid	−251	−433	−813
Current balance	3,557	13,111	3,931
Direct investment abroad	−501	−107	−148
Direct investment from abroad	3,290	4,464	3,448
Portfolio investment assets	372	−905	−340
Portfolio investment liabilities	1,565	−1,512	936
Other investment assets	−6,371	−4,920	−4,414
Other investment liabilities	635	196	−293
Net errors and omissions	−1,508	−4,502	−5,183
Overall balance	1,039	5,825	−2,063

Source: IMF, *International Financial Statistics*.

External Trade

PRINCIPAL COMMODITIES
(US $ million)

Imports f.o.b.	1998	1999	2000
Food and live animals	1,342.7	1,387.6	1,327.7
Cereals and cereal preparations	434.1	476.1	446.4
Crude materials (inedible) except fuels	370.4	317.7	387.9
Mineral fuels	288.1	345.8	538.6
Petroleum and products	275.9	339.3	526.3
Chemicals and related products	1,603.8	1,595.9	2,010.4
Organic chemicals	426.0	390.8	449.5
Basic manufactures	2,256.9	2,160.0	2,276.4
Iron and steel	686.5	545.7	516.7
Other metal manufactures	385.6	470.1	467.6
Machinery and transport equipment	6,755.6	5,847.2	6,059.7
Machinery specialized for particular industries	643.3	399.1	418.3
General industrial machinery equipment and parts	1,698.2	1,883.2	1,450.3
Heating and cooling equipment and parts	575.8	719.6	488.2
Machinery, plant and laboratory equipment for heating and cooling	362.6	566.2	346.9
Pumps, compressors, centrifuges and filtering apparatus	257.7	443.4	297.1
Office machines and automatic data-processing equipment	391.5	408.2	387.8
Telecommunications and sound recording and reproducing equipment	682.6	684.6	760.3
Telecommunications equipment parts and accessories	575.0	551.6	617.0
Other electrical machinery apparatus, etc.	806.3	737.2	852.9
Road vehicles	1,908.8	1,116.9	1,453.5
Passenger motor vehicles (except buses)	984.9	573.8	893.0
Lorries and special purpose motor vehicles	407.9	186.4	224.5
Miscellaneous manufactured articles	1,278.7	1,567.5	623.5
Total (incl. others)	14,250.4	13,554.0	14,584.2

Exports f.o.b.	1998	1999	2000
Mineral fuels, lubricants and related materials . . .	12,047.5	16,343.2	26,642.5
Petroleum, petroleum products and related materials . . .	11,906.6	16,230.8	26,487.8
Crude petroleum	7,788.1	16,214.9	18,238.0
Petroleum products, refined . .	4,111.6	11.8	8237.1
Chemicals and related products . . .	999.8	712.4	861.5
Basic manufactures . . .	2,076.8	1,845.1	2,177.3
Iron and steel.	695.2	649.5	822.8
Non-ferrous metals	704.1	663.1	786.2
Aluminium	688.3	653.1	770.4
Machinery and transport equipment. . .	591.2	301.4	352.0
Total (incl. others)	17,054.1	20,076.3	30,948.1

Source: UN, *International Trade Statistics Yearbook*.

PRINCIPAL TRADING PARTNERS
(US $ million)

Imports f.o.b.	1999	2000*	2001*
Bolivia	n.a.	n.a.	183
Brazil	457	725	976
Canada	290	307	n.a.
Chile	198	248	n.a.
Colombia	739	1,088	1,432
France	n.a.	247	303
Germany	604	503	579
Italy	n.a.	620	551
Japan	388	463	750
Mexico	486	596	774
Netherlands	186	261	n.a.
Netherlands Antilles . . .	163	339	n.a.
Spain	406	373	n.a.
United Kingdom	209	301	n.a.
USA	5,351	5,756	5,549
Total (incl. others)	13,213	15,491	16,435

Exports f.o.b.	1998	1999*	2000*
Brazil	700	901	1,231
Canada	366	559	400
Chile	189	193	181
Colombia	1,427	798	867
Germany	227	204	291
Japan	209	236	239
Mexico	226	185	335
Netherlands	173	200	343
Netherlands Antilles	1,152	959	2,492
United Kingdom	355	168	79
USA	7,999	9,748	16,533
Total (incl. others)	17,576	20,819	33,035

* Provisional.

Transport

RAILWAYS
(traffic)

	1994	1995	1996
Passenger-kilometres (million) . .	31.4	12.5	0.1
Freight ton-kilometres (million) .	46.8	53.3	45.5

Freight ton-kilometres (million): 54.5 in 1997; 79.5 in 1998.

Source: UN Economic Commission for Latin America and the Caribbean.

ROAD TRAFFIC
('000 motor vehicles in use at 31 December)

	1991	1992	1993
Passenger cars	1,540	1,566	1,579
Buses and coaches	18	20	20
Goods vehicles	431	436	440
Motorcycles, scooters and mopeds	295	298	301

1994–96 (estimates, '000 motor vehicles in use): 1,520 passenger cars; 434 commercial vehicles (Source: IRF, *World Road Statistics*).

SHIPPING

Merchant Fleet
(registered at 31 December)

	1999	2000	2001
Number of vessels	250	262	268
Total displacement ('000 grt) . .	657.4	666.6	872.2

Source: Lloyd's Register-Fairplay, *World Fleet Statistics*.

CIVIL AVIATION
(traffic on scheduled services)

	1996	1997	1998
Kilometres flown (million) . . .	80	63	52
Passengers carried ('000) . . .	4,487	4,020	3,720
Passenger-km (million) . . .	5,800	4,444	3,133
Total ton-km (million)	639	483	332

Source: UN, *Statistical Yearbook*.

Tourism

ARRIVALS BY NATIONALITY

	1998	1999	2000
Argentina	41,534	30,553	9,538
Brazil	28,125	20,213	7,984
Canada	33,034	27,191	38,045
Chile	16,346	16,198	4,234
Colombia	26,245	24,543	8,902
Denmark	15,575	4,871	10,645
France	27,841	25,617	20,417
Germany	67,063	52,783	80,286
Italy	43,540	48,277	19,681
Mexico	18,774	14,572	7,569
Netherlands	46,931	49,667	71,310
Spain	15,345	29,628	14,803
United Kingdom	35,570	27,369	33,308
USA	158,265	128,545	74,124
Total (incl. others)	685,429	586,900	469,047

Source: World Tourism Organization, *Yearbook of Tourism Statistics*.

Tourism receipts (US $ million): 1,086 in 1997; 961 in 1998; 656 in 1999 (Source: World Development Indicators).

Communications Media

	1999	2000	2001
Telephones ('000 main lines in use)	2,550.8	2,605.6	2,758.3
Mobile cellular telephones ('000 subscribers)	3,784.7	5,256.0	6,489.0
Television receivers ('000 in use) .	4,386	4,471	n.a.
Personal computers ('000 in use) .	1,000	1,100	1,300
Internet users ('000)	525	950	1,300

Facsimile machines ('000 in use, 1997): 70.

Radio receivers ('000 in use, 1997, estimate): 10,750.

Book production (titles, 1996): 3,468*.

Daily newspapers: 86 (estimated average circulation 4,600,000).

* First editions only.

Sources: UNESCO, *Statistical Yearbook*; UN, *Statistical Yearbook*; International Telecommunication Union.

Education

(1998/99)

	Institutions	Teachers	Students
Pre-primary	11,414	49,977*	737,967
Primary	17,372	186,658*	4,299,671
Secondary .	2,524	61,761*	400,794
Higher	99†	43,883‡	550,783‡

* 1997/98 figure, refers to teaching posts.
† 1990/91 figure.
‡ 1991/92 figure.

Source: partly UNESCO, *Statistical Yearbook*.

Adult literacy rate (UNESCO estimates): 92.6% (males 92.1%; females 93.1%) in 2000 (Source: UN Development Programme, *Human Development Report*).

Directory

The Constitution

The Bolivarian Constitution of Venezuela was promulgated on 30 December 1999.

The Bolivarian Republic of Venezuela is divided into 23 States, one Federal District and 72 Federal Dependencies. The States are autonomous but must comply with the laws and Constitution of the Republic.

LEGISLATURE

Legislative power is exercised by the unicameral National Assembly (Asamblea Nacional). This replaced the bicameral Congreso Nacional (National Congress) following the introduction of the 1999 Constitution.

Deputies are elected by direct universal and secret suffrage, the number representing each State being determined by population size on a proportional basis. A deputy must be of Venezuelan nationality and be over 21 years of age. Indigenous minorities have the right to select three representatives. Ordinary sessions of the Asamblea Nacional begin on the fifth day of January of each year and continue until the fifteenth day of the following August; thereafter, sessions are renewed from the fifteenth day of September to the fifteenth day of December, both dates inclusive. The Asamblea is empowered to initiate legislation. The Asamblea also elects a Comptroller-General to preside over the Audit Office (Contraloría General de la República), which investigates Treasury income and expenditure, and the finances of the autonomous institutes.

GOVERNMENT

Executive power is vested in a President of the Republic elected by universal suffrage every six years, who may serve one additional term. The President is empowered to discharge the Constitution and the laws, to nominate or remove Ministers, to take supreme command of the Armed Forces, to direct foreign relations of the State, to declare a state of emergency and withdraw the civil guarantees laid down in the Constitution, to convene extraordinary sessions of the Asamblea Nacional and to administer national finance.

JUDICIARY

Judicial power is exercised by the Supreme Tribunal of Justice (Tribunal Suprema de Justicia) and by the other tribunals. The Supreme Tribunal forms the highest court of the Republic and the Magistrates of the Supreme Tribunal are appointed by the Asamblea Nacional following recommendations from the Committee for Judicial Postulations, which consults with civil society groups. Magistrates serve a maximum of twelve years.

The 1999 Constitution created two new elements of power. The Moral Republican Council (Consejo Moral Republicano) is comprised of the Comptroller-General, the Attorney-General and the Peoples' Defender (or ombudsman). Its principle duty is to uphold the Constitution. The National Electoral Council (Consejo Nacional Electoral) administers and supervises elections.

The Government

HEAD OF STATE

President of the Republic: Lt-Col (retd) HUGO CHÁVEZ FRÍAS (took office 2 February 1999; re-elected 30 July 2000).

COUNCIL OF MINISTERS
(April 2003)

Vice-President: JOSÉ VICENTE RANGEL.

Minister of Finance: TOBÍAS NÓBREGA.

Minister of the Interior and Justice: Gen. (retd) LUCAS RINCÓN.

Minister of National Defence: Gen. (retd) JOSÉ LUIS PRIETO.

Minister of Energy and Mines: RAFAEL RAMÍREZ.

Minister of Foreign Affairs: ROY CHADERTON MATOS.

Minister of Labour: MARÍA CRISTINA IGLESIAS.

Minister of Production and Trade: RAMÓN ROSALES.

Minister of Education, Culture and Sport: ARISTÓBULO ISTÚRIZ.

Minister of Health and Social Development: MARÍA DE LOURDES URBANEJA.

Minister of Infrastructure: DIOSDADO CABELLO.

Minister of the Environment and Natural Resources: ANA ELISA OSORIO GRANADOS.

Minister of Agriculture and Lands: EFRÉN ANDRADE.

Minister of Planning and Development: JORGE GIORDANI.

Minister of Science and Technology and of Social and Economic Development: NELSON MERENTES.

Minister of Communications and Information: NORA URIBE.

MINISTRIES

Ministry of Agriculture and Lands: Caracas.

Ministry of Communications and Information: Edif. Administrativo, 1°, Palacio de Miraflores, Caracas; tel. (212) 806-3702; fax (212) 806-3244; e-mail miraflores@hotmail.com; internet www.venezuela.gov.ve.

Ministry of Economic and Social Development: Caracas.

Ministry of Education, Culture and Sport: Edif. Ministerio de Educación, Mezzanina, esq. de Salas, Parroquia Altogracia, Caracas 1010; tel. (212) 564-0025; fax (212) 562-1096; e-mail prensa@gov.me; internet www.me.gov.ve.

Ministry of Energy and Mines: Edif. Petróleos de Venezuela, Torre Oeste, Avda Libertador, La Campiña, Apdo 169, Caracas 1010-A; e-mail dazaroy@hotmail.com.

Ministry of the Environment and Natural Resources: Torre Sur, 19°, Centro Simón Bolívar, Caracas 1010; tel. (212) 481-7008; fax (212) 483-8765.

Ministry of Finance: Edif. Ministerio de Finanzas, esq. de Carmelitas, Avda Urdaneta, Caracas; tel. (212) 802-1404; fax (212) 802-1413.

Ministry of Foreign Affairs: Torre MRE, esq. Carmelitas, Avda Urdaneta, Caracas 1010; tel. (212) 862-1085; fax (212) 864-3633; e-mail criptogr@mre.gov.ve; internet www.mre.gov.ve.

Ministry of Health: Torre Sur, 9°, Centro Simón Bolívar, Caracas 1010; tel. (212) 484-3725; fax (212) 484-3725.

Ministry of Infrastructure: Torre Este, 50°, Parque Central, Caracas 1010; tel. (212) 509-1076; fax (212) 509-3682.

Ministry of the Interior and Justice: Edif. Ministerio del Interior y Justicia, esq. de Platanal, Avda Urdaneta, Caracas 1010; tel. (212) 506-1101; fax (212) 506-1559; internet www.minjusticia.gov.ve.

Ministry of Labour: Torre Sur, 5°, Centro Simón Bolívar, Caracas 1010; tel. (212) 481-1368; fax (212) 483-8914.

Ministry of National Defence: Edif. 17 de Diciembre, planta baja, Base Aérea Francisco de Miranda, La Carlota, Caracas; tel. (212) 908-1264; fax (212) 237-4974; e-mail prensa@ven.net; internet www.mindefensa.gov.ve.

Ministry of Planning and Development: Torre Oeste, 22°, Avda Lecuna, Parque Central, Caracas 1010; tel. (212) 507-7645; fax (212) 573-3076.

Ministry of Production and Trade: Torre Este, 13°, Avda Lecuna, Parque Central, Caracas; tel. (212) 509-0241; fax (212) 574-0454.

Ministry of Science and Technology: Edif. Maploca 1, planta baja, Final Avda Principal de los Cortijos de Lourdes, Caracas; tel. (212) 239-6475; fax (212) 239-6056; e-mail mct-info@conicit.gov.ve.

State Agencies

Consejo de Defensa de la Nación (Codena): Palacio Blanco, 3°, Avda Urdaneta frente del Palacio Miraflores, Caracas; tel. (212) 806-3104; fax (212) 806-3151; national defence council.

Consejo Nacional Electoral (CNE): Centro Simón Bolívar, Nivel Avenida, El Silencio, Caracas; tel. (212) 484-4145; fax (212) 484-5269; national electoral council.

Contraloría General de la República (CGR): Edif. Contraloría, Avda Andrés Bello, Guaicaipuro, Caracas; tel. (212) 481-3437; fax (212) 571-8131; national audit office; investigates Treasury income and expenditure, and the finances of the autonomous institutes.

Defensoría del Pueblo: Edif. Defensoría del Pueblo, Plaza Morelos, Los Caobos, Caracas; tel. (212) 578-3862; fax (212) 578-3862; e-mail prensadefensoria@hotmail.com; acts as an ombudsman and investigates complaints between citizens and the authorities.

Procuraduría General de la República: Paseo Los Ilustres con Avda Lazo Martí, Santa Mónica, Caracas; tel. (212) 693-0911; fax (212) 693-4657; e-mail procuraduria@platino.gov.ve.

President

Presidential Election, 30 July 2000

Candidates	% of valid votes
Lt-Col (retd) Hugo Chávez Frías (MVR)	59.7
Francisco Arias Cárdenas (Causa R)	37.5
Claudio Fermín (EN)	2.7
Others	0.1
Total	100.0

Legislature

ASAMBLEA NACIONAL
(National Assembly)

President: FRANCISCO AMELIACH.

First Vice-President: RICARDO GUTIÉRREZ.

Second Vice-President: NOEMI POCATIERRA.

Election, 30 July 2000

Party	Seats
Movimiento V República (MVR)	93
Acción Democrática (AD)	32
Proyecto Venezuela (PRVZL)	8
Movimiento al Socialismo (MAS)	6
Partido Social-Cristiano (COPEI)	5
Primero Justicia (PJ)	5
Causa Radical (Causa R)	3
Indigenous groups	3
Others	10
Total	**165**

Political Organizations

Acción Democrática (AD): Casa Nacional Acción Democrática, Calle Los Cedros, La Florida, Caracas 1050; internet www.ad.org.ve; f. 1936 as Partido Democrático Nacional; adopted present name and obtained legal recognition in 1941; social democratic; Leader HENRY RAMOS ALLUP.

Bandera Roja: Caracas; f. 1968; Marxist-Leninist grouping.

La Causa Radical (La Causa R): Caracas; tel. (212) 541-2412; f. 1971; radical democratic; Leader ANDRÉS VELÁSQUEZ.

Convergencia Nacional (CN): Edif. Tajamar, 2°, Of. 215, Parque Central, Avda Lecuna, El Conde, Caracas 1010; tel. (212) 578-1177; fax (212) 578-0363; e-mail convergeprensa@cantv.net; internet www.convergencia.org.ve; f. 1993; Leader Dr RAFAEL CALDERA RODRÍGUEZ; Gen. Co-ordinator JUAN JOSÉ CALDERA.

Movimiento Electoral del Pueblo (MEP): Caracas; f. 1967 by left-wing AD dissidents; 100,000 mems; Pres. Dr LUIS BELTRÁN PRIETO FIGUEROA; Sec-Gen. Dr JESÚS ÁNGEL PAZ GALARRAGA.

Movimiento Al Socialismo (MAS): Quinta Alemar, Avda Valencia, Las Palmas, Caracas 1050; tel. (212) 793-7800; fax (212) 761-9297; e-mail asamblea07@cantv.net; f. 1971 by PCV dissidents; democratic-socialist party; split in 1997 over issue of support for Hugo Chávez's presidential campaign; Pres. FELIPE MÚJICA; Sec.-Gen. LEOPOLDO PUCHI.

Movimiento de Integración Nacional (MIN): Edif. José María Vargas, 1°, esq. Pajarito, Caracas; tel. (212) 563-7504; fax (212) 563-7553; f. 1977; Sec.-Gen. GONZALO PÉREZ HERNÁNDEZ.

Movimiento de Izquierda Revolucionaria (MIR): c/o Fracción Parlamentaria MIR, Edif. Tribunales, esq. Pajaritos, Caracas; f. 1960 by splinter group from AD; left-wing; Sec.-Gen. MOISÉS MOLEIRO.

Movimiento V República (MVR): Calle Lima, cruce con Avda Libertador, Los Caobos, Caracas; tel. (212) 782-3808; fax (212) 782-9720; f. 1998; promotes Bolivarian revolution; Leader Lt-Col (retd) HUGO CHÁVEZ FRÍAS.

Partido Comunista de Venezuela (PCV): Edif. Cantaclaro, esq. San Pedro, San Juan, Apdo 20428, Caracas; tel. (212) 484-0061; fax (212) 481-9737; f. 1931; Sec.-Gen. OSCAR FIGUERA.

Partido Social-Cristiano (Comité de Organización Política Electoral Independiente) (COPEI): esq. San Miguel, Avda Panteón cruce con Fuerzas Armadas, San José, Caracas 1010; f. 1946; Christian Democratic; more than 1,500,000 mems; Leader ENRIQUE MENDOZA.

Partido Unión: Caracas; f. 2001; Leader FRANCISCO ARIAS CÁRDENAS.

Patria Para Todos (PPT): Caracas; tel. (212) 577-4545; e-mail ppt@cantv.net; internet www.patriaparatodos.org/index.htm; f. 1997; breakaway faction of La Causa Radical; revolutionary humanist party; Leaders ARISTÓBULO ISTÚRIZ, PABLO MEDINA.

Polo Patriótico: f. 1998; grouping of small, mainly left-wing and nationalist political parties, including the MVR, in support of presidential election campaign of; Lt-Col (retd) HUGO CHÁVEZ FRÍAS.

Primero Justicia: Planta de Oficinas, Centro Comercial Chacaito, Chacaito, Caracas; f. 2000; no fixed ideological stance; Leader JULIO BORGES.

Proyecto Venezuela (PRVZL): internet www.proyectovenezuela.org.ve; f. 1998; humanist party; ended alliance with govt in Jan. 2002; Leader HENRIQUE SALAS RÖMER.

Diplomatic Representation

EMBASSIES IN VENEZUELA

Algeria: Transversal con Avda San Juan Bosco Quinta Tatau, Altamira, Caracas 1060; tel. (212) 263-9771; fax (212) 263-8482; e-mail ambalgcar@ccs.fast-link.net; Ambassador MOHAMMED GHALIB NEDJARI.

Argentina: Edif. Fedecámaras, 3°, Avda El Empalme, El Bosque, Apdo 569, Caracas; tel. (212) 731-3311; fax (212) 731-2659; Ambassador EDUARDO ALBERTO SADOUS.

Australia: Quinta Yolanda, Avda Luis Roche entre 6 y 7 transversales, Apdo 61123, Caracas 1060-A; tel. (212) 263-4033; fax (212) 261-3448; e-mail ausembcrcs@cantv.net; Ambassador JOHN WOODS.

Austria: Edif. Torre Las Mercedes, 4°, Of. 408, Avda La Estancia, Chuao, Apdo 61381, Caracas 1060-A; tel. (212) 991-3863; fax (212) 959-9804; e-mail e.austria@cantv.net; internet www.internet.ve/austria; Ambassador Dr ERICA LIEBENWIEN.

Barbados: Edif. Los Frailes, 5°, Of. 501, Calle La Guairita, Chuao, Caracas; tel. (212) 992-0545; fax (212) 991-0333; e-mail caracas@foreign.gov.bb; Ambassador SONJA P. J. WELCH.

Belgium: Quinta la Azulita, Avda 11, entre 6 y 7 transversales, Apdo del Este 61550, Altamira, Caracas 1060; tel. (212) 263-3334; fax (212) 261-0309; e-mail ambelven@sa.omnes.net; Ambassador Baron ANDRE DE VIRON.

Bolivia: Avda Luis Roche con 6 transversal, Altamira, Caracas; tel. (212) 263-3015; fax (212) 261-3386; e-mail embabolivia@cantv.net; Chargé d'affaires a.i. JOSÉ GUILLERMO LORIA GONZÁLEZ.

Brazil: Avda Mohedano con Calle Los Chaguaramos, Centro Gerencial Mohedano, 6°, La Castellana, Caracas; tel. (212) 261-5505; fax (212) 261-9601; e-mail brasembcaracas@cantv.net; internet www.brasil-ve.org; Ambassador RUY NUNES PINTO NOQUEIRA.

Bulgaria: Quinta Sofia, Calle Las Lomas, Urb. Las Mercedes, Apdo 68389, Caracas; tel. (212) 993-2714; fax (212) 993-4839; e-mail embulven@cantv.net.

Canada: Avda de Altamira 6 entre 3 y 5 transversal, Altamira, Caracas 1062; tel. (212) 264-0833; fax (212) 261-8741; e-mail embajada.canada@crcas01.X400.gc.ca; Ambassador ALLAN CULHAM.

Chile: Edif. Torre La Noria, 10°, Calle Paseo Enrique Eraso, Las Mercedes, Caracas; tel. (212) 991-1967; fax (212) 991-1621; e-mail echileve@cantv.net; Ambassador FABIO VÍO UGARTE.

China, People's Republic: Prados del Este, Apdo 80665, Caracas 1080-A; tel. (212) 977-4949; fax (212) 978-0876; e-mail embcnven@att.com.ven; Ambassador WANG ZHEN.

Colombia: Torre Credival, 11°, 2a Calle de Campo Alegre con Avda Francisco de Miranda, Apdo 60887, Caracas; tel. (212) 261-6592; fax (212) 261-1358; e-mail colombia@telcel.net.ve; Ambassador MARÍA ANGELA HOLGUÍN.

Costa Rica: Edif. For You P.H., Avda San Juan Bosco, entre 1 y 2 transversal, Altamira, Apdo 62239, Caracas; tel. (212) 267-1104; fax (212) 262-0038; e-mail embcostar@cantv.net; Ambassador RICARDO LIZANO CALZADA.

Cuba: Calle Roraima e Río de Janeiro y Choroni, Chuao, Caracas 1060; tel. (212) 991-6611; fax (212) 993-5695; Ambassador GERMÁN SÁNCHEZ OTERO.

Czech Republic: Calle Los Cedros, Quarta Isobel, Urb. Country Club, Altamira, Caracas 1060; tel. (212) 261-1746; fax (212) 266-3987; e-mail caracas@embassy.mzv.cz; internet www.mfa.cz/caracas; Ambassador ANTONÍN BLAŽEK.

Denmark: Torre Centuria, 7°, Avda Venezuela con Calle Mohedano, El Rosal, Caracas 1060-A; tel. (212) 951-4618; fax (212) 951-5278; e-mail danmark@cantv.net; internet www.dinamarca.com; Ambassador JENS PETER LARSEN.

Dominican Republic: Edif. Humboldt, 6°, Of. 26, Avda Francisco de Miranda, Altamira, Caracas; tel. (212) 284-2443; fax (212) 283-3965; e-mail embaredo@telcel.net.ve; Ambassador RICARDO A. DE MOYA DESPRADEL.

Ecuador: Centro Andrés Bello, Torre Oeste, 13°, Avda Andrés Bello, Maripérez, Apdo 62124, Caracas 1060; tel. (212) 781-3180; fax (212) 782-7978; e-mail embajado@viptel.com; Ambassador MARCELO FERNÁNDEZ DE CÓRDOBA PONCE.

Egypt: Quinta Maribel, Calle Guaicaipuro, Las Mercedes, Caracas; tel. (212) 992-6259; fax (212) 993-1555; e-mail egyptianembassy@cantv.net; Ambassador MOHAMED FADEL EL-KADI.

El Salvador: Quinta Cuzcatlán, Calle Amazonas, final Avda Principal de Prados del Este, Caracas; tel. (212) 959-0817; fax (212) 959-3920; Ambassador ERNESTO ARRIETA PERALTA.

Finland: Edif. Atrium, 1°, Calle Sorocaima, entre Avdas Venezuela y Tamanaco, El Rosal, Apdo 61118-A, Caracas 1060; tel. (212) 952-4111; fax (212) 952-7536; e-mail finland@viptel.com; internet www.finlandia-caracas.com; Ambassador ORA MERES-WUORI.

France: Calle Madrid con Avda Trinidad-las-Mercedes, Apdo 60385, Caracas 1060; tel. (212) 993-6666; fax (212) 993-3483; e-mail consulat@telul.net.ve; internet www.ambafrance.org.ve; Ambassador PIERRE-JEAN VANDOORNE.

Germany: Edif. Panavén, 2°, Avda San Juan Bosco, esq. 3 transversal, Altamira, Apdo 2078, Caracas; tel. (212) 261-0181; fax (212) 261-0641; Ambassador HERMANN ERATH.

Greece: Quinta Maryland, Avda Papal del Avila, Alta Florida, Caracas 1050; tel. (212) 730-3833; fax (212) 731-0429; e-mail embgrccs@cantv.net; Ambassador ATHANASSIOS M. VALASSIDIS.

Grenada: Edif. Los Frailes, 3°, Of. 34, Calle La Guairita, Chuao, Caracas; tel. (212) 991-0933; fax (212) 991-8907; e-mail egrenada@cantv.net; Ambassador MARGARET HARRIS.

Guatemala: Avda de Francísco de Miranda, Torre Dozsa, Urb. El Rosal, Caracas; tel. (212) 952-1166; fax (212) 952-1992; e-mail guateven@ven.net; Ambassador LUIS PEDRO QUEZADA CÓRDOVA.

Guyana: Quinta 'Roraima', Avda El Paseo, Prados del Este, Apdo 51054, Caracas 1050; tel. (212) 978-2781; fax (212) 977-1158; fax (212) 976-3765; e-mail embaguy@caracas-office.org.ve; Ambassador BAYNEY RAM KARRAN.

Haiti: Quinta Flor 59, Avda Las Rosas, La Florida, Caracas; tel. (212) 730-7220; fax (212) 730-4605; Chargé d'affaires a.i. MARIO BRIERRE.

Holy See: Avda La Salle, Los Caobos, Apdo 29, Caracas 1010-A (Apostolic Nunciature); tel. (212) 781-8939; fax (212) 793-2403; e-mail nunapos@cantv.net; Apostolic Nuncio Most Rev. ANDRÉ DUPUY (Titular Archbishop of Selsea).

Honduras: Edif. Excelsior, Avda San Juan Bosco, 5°, Altamira, Apdo 68259, Caracas; tel. (212) 284-5593; fax (212) 266-1935; e-mail embhondv@truevision.net; Ambassador CARLOS ALBERTO TURCIOS.

Hungary: Caracas; tel. (212) 209-3511; fax (212) 209-3722.

India: Apdo 61585, Chacao, Caracas 1060-A, Caracas; tel. (212) 285-7887; fax (212) 286-5131; e-mail embindia@eldish.net; Ambassador N. N. DESAI.

Indonesia: Quinta La Trinidad, Avda El Paseo, Prados del Este, Apdo 80807, Caracas 1080; tel. (212) 976-2725; fax (212) 976-0550; Ambassador GHAFFAR FADYL.

Iran: Quinta Ommat, Calle Kemal Ataturk, Valle Arriba, Caracas; tel. (212) 992-3575; fax (212) 992-9989; e-mail kesmavrz@sa.omnes.net; Ambassador MOHAMMAD KESHAVARZZADEH.

Iraq: Quinta Babilonia, Avda Nicolas Cópernico con Calle Los Malabares, Valle Arriba, Caracas; tel. (212) 991-1627; fax (212) 992-0268; Ambassador GHAZI KARIM KHALIFA.

Israel: Centro Empresarial Miranda, 4°, Avda Principal de los Ruices cruce con Francisco de Miranda, Apdo 70081, Los Ruices, Caracas; tel. (212) 239-4511; fax (212) 239-4320; e-mail embajo01@cantv.net; Ambassador ARIE TENNE.

Italy: Edif. Atrium, Calle Sorocaima, entre Avdas Tamanaco y Venezuela, El Rosal, Apdo 3995, Caracas; tel. (212) 952-7311; fax (212) 952-7120; e-mail ambcara@italamb.org.ve; internet www.italamb.org.ve; Ambassador ADRIANO BENEDETTI.

Jamaica: Edif. Los Frailes, 5°, Calle La Guairita, Urb. Chuao, Caracas 1062; tel. (212) 991-6955; fax (212) 991-5798; e-mail embjaven@cantv.net; Ambassador PAUL A. ROBOTHAM.

Japan: Quinta Sakura, Avda San Juan Bosco, entre 8a y 9a transversales, Altamira, Apdo 68790, Caracas 1062; tel. (212) 261-8333; fax (212) 261-6780; Ambassador MASATERU ITO.

Korea, Democratic People's Republic: Caracas; tel. (212) 256-3905; fax (212) 256-3905; Ambassador PAK TONG CHUN.

Korea, Republic: Edif. Atrium, 3°, Avda Sorocaima con Avda Venezuela, El Rosal, Apdo 80671, Caracas; tel. (212) 954-1270; fax (212) 954-0619; e-mail venadmi@viptel.com; Ambassador DONG-CHUL CHANG.

Kuwait: Quinta El-Kuwait, Avda Las Magnolias con Calle Los Olivos, Los Chorros, Caracas; tel. (212) 235-1257; fax (212) 239-3127; Ambassador YOUSUF AL-ONAIZI.

Lebanon: Quinta el Cedro del Lebanon, Avda Primera, Colinas Bello Monte, Calle Motatán, Caracas 1050; tel. (212) 751-5943; fax (212) 753-0726; e-mail embajada@libano.org.ve; Ambassador MUSTAPHA HRAIBEH.

Libya: 3a Avda entre 9a y 10a transversales, Quinta Los Leones, Altamira, Apdo 68946, Caracas 1060; tel. (212) 261-1290; fax (212) 261-7271; Ambassador AHMED TAHER TABIB.

Lithuania: Centro Plaza, Torre A, Avda Francisco de Miranda, 9°, Apdo 62818, Caracas; tel. (212) 286-2649; fax (212) 286-1268; e-mail lrambven@sa.omnes.net; Ambassador VYTAUTAS A. DAMBRAVA.

Malaysia: Centro Profesional Eurobuilding, 6°, Ofs 6F–G, Calle La Guairita, Apdo 65107, Chuao, Caracas 1060; tel. (212) 992-1011; fax (212) 992-1277; e-mail mwcaracas@malaysia.org.ve; Ambassador Datuk JOHN TENEWI NUEK.

Mexico: Edif. Forum, Calle Guaicaipuro con Principal de las Mercedes, 5°, El Rosal, Apdo 61371, Caracas; tel. (212) 952-5777; fax (212) 952-3003; e-mail mexico@embamex.com.ve; internet www .embamex.com.ve; Ambassador ENRIQUE M. LOAEZA Y TOVAR.

Morocco: Torre Multinvest, Plaza Isabel La Católica, Avda Eugenio Mendoza, piso 2, La Castellana, Caracas; tel. (212) 266-7543; fax (212) 266-4681; Ambassador HOUSSEIN MOUSSA.

Netherlands: Edif. San Juan Bosco, 9°, San Juan Bosco con 2 transversal de Altamira, Caracas; tel. (212) 263-3622; fax (212) 263-0462; e-mail nlgovcar@internet.ve; Ambassador N. P. VAN ZUTPHEN.

Nicaragua: Quinta Teocal, Calle Codazzi, Prados del Este, Caracas; tel. (212) 977-2459; fax (212) 979-9167; e-mail embnicve@mail.lat .net; Ambassador JULIO ALEJANDRO ESPINAL SANDINO.

Nigeria: Quinta Leticia, Calle Chivacoa cruce con Calle Taría, San Román, Caracas; tel. (212) 263-4816; fax (212) 263-4635; Ambassador ADEYOMBO OLUBONMI OYESOLA.

Norway: Centro Lido, Torre A-92A, Avda Francisco de Miranda, El Rosal, Apdo 60532, Caracas 1060-A; tel. (212) 953-0671; fax (212) 953-6877; e-mail emb.caracas@mfa.no; Ambassador DAG MORK-ULNES.

Panama: Edif. Los Frailes, 6°, Calle La Guairita, Chuao, Apdo 1989, Caracas; tel. (212) 992-9093; fax (212) 992-8107; Ambassador CARMEN MENÉNDEZ.

Paraguay: Quinta Paraguay, Avda Principal Macaracuay 1960, entre Avda Cuicas y Carretera del Este, Caracas; tel. (212) 257-2747; fax (212) 257-2256; e-mail embaparven@cantv.net; Ambassador EUGENIO MOREL GARAY.

Peru: Edif. San Juan, Avda San Juan Bosco, 5°, Altamira, Apdo 1947, Carmelitas 1010, Caracas; tel. (212) 264-1483; fax (212) 265-7592; e-mail leprucaracas@cantv.net; Ambassador JULIO BALBUENA LÓPEZ-ALFARO.

Philippines: Quinta Taray, Avda Tropical, La Floresta, Caracas; tel. (212) 284-2006; Ambassador RONALD ALLAREY.

Poland: Quinta Ambar, Final Avda Nicolás Copérnico, Sector Los Naranjos, Las Mercedes, Apdo 62293, Caracas; tel. (212) 991-1461; fax (212) 992-2164; e-mail ambcarac@ven.net; Ambassador (vacant).

Portugal: Edif. Fedecámaras, 1°, Avda El Empalme, El Bosque, Caracas 1062; tel. (212) 731-0539; fax (212) 731-0543; e-mail embport@etheron.net; Ambassador VASCO BRAMÃO RAMOS.

Romania: Calle El Pedregal (Alto), La Castellana, Caracas; tel. (212) 261-2769; fax (212) 263-7594; e-mail ambarove@infoline.wtfe .com; Ambassador PETRU PEPELEA.

Russia: Quinta Soyuz, Calle Las Lomas, Las Mercedes, Caracas; tel. (212) 993-4395; fax (212) 993-6526; e-mail emruscar@cantv.net; Ambassador VALERII MOROZOV.

Saudi Arabia: Calle Andrés Pietri, Los Chorros, Caracas 1071; tel. (212) 239-0290; fax (212) 239-6494; e-mail arabsaudi@eldish.net; Ambassador MARWAN BIN BASHIR AL-ROUMI.

South Africa: Centro Profesional Eurobuilding, 4°, Of. 4B-C, Calle La Guairita, Chuao, Apdo 2613, Caracas 1064; tel. (212) 991-6822; fax (212) 991-5555; e-mail rsaven@ifxnw.com.ve; Chargé d'affaires a.i. J. SWANEPOEL.

Spain: Avda Mohedano entre la y 2a transversal, La Castellana, Caracas; tel. (212) 263-2855; fax (212) 261-0892; Ambassador MIGUEL ANGEL FERNÁNDEZ MAZARAMBROZ Y BERNABEU.

Suriname: 4a Avda entre 7a y 8a transversal, Quinta 41, Altamira, Caracas; Apdo 61140, Chacao, Caracas; tel. (212) 261-2724; fax (212) 263-9006; e-mail emsurl@contv.net; Chargé d'affaires a.i. LAURENCE E. NEEDE.

Switzerland: Centro Letonia, Torre Ing-Bank, 15°, La Castellana, Apdo 62555, Chacao, Caracas 1060-A; tel. (212) 267-8501; fax (212) 267-7745; e-mail vertretung@car.rep.admin.ch; Ambassador PIERRE MONOD.

Syria: Quinta Damasco, Avda Casiquare, Colinas de Bello Monte, Caracas; tel. (212) 752-6687; fax (212) 751-6146; Chargé d'affaires a.i. NADER NADER.

Trinidad and Tobago: Quinta Serrana, 4a Avda entre 7 y 8 transversales, Altamira, Caracas; tel. (212) 261-4772; fax (212) 261-9801; e-mail embtt@caracas.c-com.net; Ambassador PHILIP SEALY.

Turkey: Calle Kemal Atatürk, Quinta Turquesa 6, Valle Arriba, Apdo 62078; Caracas 1060-A; tel. (212) 991-0075; fax (212) 992-0442; e-mail turkishemb@cantv.net; Ambassador TANJU ÜLGEN.

United Kingdom: Torre La Castellana, 11°, Avda Principal La Castellana, Caracas 1061; tel. (212) 263-8411; fax (212) 267-1275; e-mail britishembassy@internet.ve; internet www.britain.org.ve; Ambassador JOHN HUGHES.

USA: Calle Suapure con Calle F, Colinas de Valle Arriba, Caracas; tel. (212) 975-6411; fax (212) 975-9429; e-mail embajada@usia.gov; internet embajadausa.org.ve; Ambassador CHARLES S. SHAPIRO.

Uruguay: Torre Delta, 8°, Of. A y B, Avda Francisco de Miranda, Altamira Sur, Apdo 60366, Caracas 1060-A; tel. (212) 261-5352; fax (212) 266-9233; Ambassador JUAN SAENZ DE ZUMARÁN.

Judicial System

The judicature is headed by the Supreme Tribunal of Justice, which replaced the Supreme Court of Justice after the promulgation of the December 1999 Constitution. The judges are divided into penal and civil and mercantile judges; there are military, juvenile, labour, administrative litigation, finance and agrarian tribunals. In each state there is a superior court and several secondary courts which act on civil and criminal cases. A number of reforms to the judicial system were introduced under the Organic Criminal Trial Code of March 1998. The Code replaced the inquisitorial system, based on the Napoleonic code, with an adversarial system in July 1999. In addition, citizen participation as lay judges and trial by jury was introduced, with training financed by the World Bank.

SUPREME TRIBUNAL OF JUSTICE

The Supreme Tribunal comprises 20 judges appointed by the Asamblea Nacional for 12 years. It is divided into five courts, each with three judges: political-administrative; civil, electoral, social and criminal. When these act together the court is in full session. It has the power to abrogate any laws, regulations or other acts of the executive or legislative branches conflicting with the Constitution. It hears accusations against members of the Government and high public officials, cases involving diplomatic representatives and certain civil actions arising between the State and individuals.

Tribunal Supremo de Justicia

Final Avda Baralt, esq. Dos Pilitas, Foro Libertador, Caracas 1010; tel. (212) 563-9555; fax (212) 563-8481; e-mail rrpp@csj.gov.ve.

President: IVÁN GUILLERMO RINCÓN URDANETA.

First Vice-President: FRANKLIN ARRIECHE GUTIÉRREZ.

Second Vice-President: OMAR ALFREDO MORO DÍAZ.

Attorney-General: ISAÍAS RODRÍGUEZ.

Religion

Roman Catholicism is the religion of the majority of the population, but there is complete freedom of worship.

CHRISTIANITY

The Roman Catholic Church

For ecclesiastical purposes, Venezuela comprises nine archdioceses, 22 dioceses and four Apostolic Vicariates. There is also an apostolic exarchate for the Melkite Rite. At 31 December 2000 adherents, of whom 48,000 were of the Melkite rite, accounted for about 90% of the total population.

Latin Rite

Bishops' Conference

Conferencia Episcopal de Venezuela, Prolongación Avda Páez, Montalbán, Apdo 4897, Caracas 1010; tel. (212) 471-6284; fax (212) 472-7029; e-mail prensa@cev.org.ve; internet www.cev.org.ve.

f. 1985; statutes approved 2000; Pres. Most Rev. BALTAZAR ENRIQUE PORRAS CARDOZO (Archbishop of Mérida).

Archbishop of Barquisimeto: Most Rev. TULIO MANUEL CHIRIVELLA, Varela, Arzobispado, Calle 23 con Carrera 16, Barquisimeto 3001; tel. (251) 231-3446; fax (251) 231-3724; e-mail arquibarqui@cantv .net.

Archbishop of Calabozo: Most Rev. ANTONIO JOSÉ LÓPEZ CASTILLO, Arzobispado, Calle 4, N. 11–82, Apdo 954, Calabozo; tel. (246) 871-0483; fax (246) 871-0483.

Archbishop of Caracas (Santiago de Venezuela): Cardinal IGNACIO ANTONIO VELASCO GARCÍA, Arzobispado, Plaza Bolívar, Apdo 954, Caracas 1010-A; tel. (212) 542-1611; fax (212) 542-0297; e-mail arzobispado@cantv.net.

Archbishop of Ciudad Bolívar: Most Rev. MEDARDO LUIS LUZARDO ROMERO, Arzobispado, Avda Andrés Eloy Blanco con Calle Naiguatá, Apdo 43, Ciudad Bolívar; tel. (285) 6544-960; fax (285) 6540-821; e-mail arzcb@cantv.net.

Archbishop of Coro: Most Rev. ROBERTO LÜCKERT LEÓN, Arzobispado, Calle Palmasola, Apdo 7342, Coro; tel. (268) 251-7024; fax (268) 251-8868; e-mail dioceco@funflc.org.ve.

Archbishop of Cumaná: Most Rev. DIEGO RAFAEL PADRÓN SÁNCHEZ, Arzobispado, Calle Bolívar con Catedral 34, Apdo 134, Cumaná 6101-A; tel. (293) 431-4131; fax (293) 433-3413; e-mail dipa@cantv .net.

Archbishop of Maracaibo: Most Rev. UBALDO RAMÓN SANTANA SEQUERA, Arzobispado, Calle 95, entre Avdas 2 y 3, Apdo 439, Maracaibo; tel. (261) 722-5351; fax (261) 721-0805; e-mail ubsa@ telcel.net.ve.

Archbishop of Mérida: Most Rev. BALTAZAR ENRIQUE PORRAS CARDOZO, Arzobispado, Avda 4, Plaza Bolívar, Apdo 26, Mérida 5101; tel. (274) 252-5786; fax (274) 252-1238; e-mail bepor@latinmail.com.

Archbishop of Valencia: Most Rev. JORGE LIBERATO UROSA SAVINO, Arzobispado, Avda Urdaneta 100-54, Apdo 32, Valencia 2001-A; tel. (241) 858-5865; fax (241) 857-8061; e-mail arqui_valencia@cantv .net.

Melkite Rite

Apostolic Exarch: Rt. Rev. GEORGES KAHHALE ZOUHAÏRATY, Iglesia San Jorge, Final 3a Urb. Montalbán II, Apdo 20120, Caracas; tel. (212) 443-3019; fax (212) 443-0131; e-mail georges@cev.org.ve.

The Anglican Communion

Anglicans in Venezuela are adherents of the Episcopal Church in the USA, in which the country forms a single, extra-provincial diocese attached to Province IX.

Bishop of Venezuela: Rt Rev. ORLANDO DE JESÚS GUERRERO, Avda Caroní 100, Apdo 49-143, Colinas de Bello Monte, Caracas 1042-A; tel. (212) 753-0723; fax (212) 751-3180; e-mail iglanglicanavzla@ cantv.net.

Protestant Churches

Iglesia Evangélica Luterana en Venezuela: Apdo 68738, Caracas 1062-A; tel. and fax (212) 264-1868; e-mail ielv@telcel.net .ve; Pres. AKOS V. PUKY; 4,000 mems.

The National Baptist Convention of Venezuela: Avda Santiago de Chile 12–14, Urb. Los Caobos, Caracas 1050; Apdo 61152, Chacao, Caracas 1060-A; tel. (212) 782-2308; fax (212) 781-9043; e-mail cnbv@telcel.net.ve; f. 1951; Pres. Rev. ENRIQUE DÁMASO; Gen. Man. Rev. DANIEL RODRÍGUEZ.

ISLAM

Mezquita Sheikh Ibrahim bin-Abdulaziz bin-Ibrahim: Calle Real de Quebrada Honda, Los Caobos, Caracas; tel. (212) 577-7382; internet www.mezquitaibrahim.org; f. 1994; Leader OMAR KADWA.

BAHÁ'Í FAITH

National Spiritual Assembly of the Bahá'ís: Colinas de Bello Monte, Apdo 49133, Caracas; tel. and fax (212) 751-7669; f. 1961; mems resident in 954 localities.

The Press

DAILIES

Caracas

Abril: Edif. Bloque DeArmas, final Avda San Martín cruce con Avda La Paz, Caracas; tel. (212) 406-4111; e-mail abril@dearmas.com; internet www.abril.org; f. 1997; independent; morning; Mon. to Sat. Dir APOLINAR MARTÍNEZ; Chief Editor MANUEL MÁRQUEZ.

Así es la Noticia: Maderero a Puente Nuevo, Caracas; tel. (212) 408-3444; fax (212) 408-3911; e-mail ipacheco@el-nacional.com; f. 1996; morning; Editor IBÉYISE PACHECO.

The Daily Journal: Avda Principal de Boleíta Norte, Apdo 76478, Caracas 1070-A; tel. (212) 237-9644; fax (212) 232-6831; e-mail thedailyjournal@cantv.net; f. 1945; morning; in English.

Diario 2001: Edif. Bloque DeArmas, final Avda San Martín cruce con Avda La Paz, Caracas; tel. (212) 406-4111; fax 443-4961; e-mail 2001@dearmas.com; f. 1973; Dir ISRAEL MÁRQUEZ.

El Globo: Avda Principal de Maripérez, transversal Colón con Avda Libertador, Apdo 16415, Caracas 1010-A; tel. (2) 576-4111; fax (212) 574-4353; e-mail elglobo@wtfe.com; f. 1990; Pres. and Dir ANÍBAL J. LATUFF.

Meridiano: Edif. Bloque DeArmas, final Avda San Martín cruce con Avda La Paz, Caracas 1010; tel. (212) 406-4040; fax (212) 406-4162; e-mail meridian@dearmas.com; internet www.meridiano.com.ve; f. 1969; morning; sports; Dir Dr ANDRÉS DE ARMAS.

El Mundo: Torre de la Prensa, 4°, Plaza del Panteón, Apdo 1192, Caracas; tel. (212) 596-1911; fax (212) 596-1478; e-mail elmundo@ la-cadena.com; f. 1958; evening; independent; Dir RAFAEL DEL NARRANCO; Chief Editor CARLOS ORTEGA.

El Nacional: Edif. El Nacional, Puente Nuevo a Puerto Escondido, El Silencio, Apdo 209, Caracas; tel. (212) 408-3111; fax (212) 481-0548; e-mail mhotero@el-nacional.com; internet www.el-nacional .com; f. 1943; morning; independent; Pres. and Editor MIGUEL HENRIQUE OTERO; Asst. Editor SERGIO DAHBAR.

El Nuevo País: Pinto a Santa Rosalía 44, Caracas; tel. (212) 541-5211; fax (212) 545-9675; e-mail enpais1@telcel.net.ve; f. 1988; Dir and Editor RAFAEL POLEO.

Puerto: Avda Soublette, Maiquetia, Caracas; tel. (212) 331-2275; fax (212) 331-0886; e-mail diariopuerto@telcel.net.ve; f. 1975; Pres. CARLOS PARMIGIANI.

La Religión: Edif. Juan XXIII, Torre a Madrices, Caracas; tel. (212) 563-0600; fax (212) 563-5583; e-mail religion@cantv.ve; f. 1890; morning; independent; Dir ENNIO TORRES.

Reporte (Diario de la Economia): Torre Británica, 12°, Of. B, Avda Luis Roche, Altamira Sur, Caracas; tel. (212) 264-0591; fax (212) 264-6023; e-mail reporte2000@hotmail.com; f. 1988; Pres. TANNOUS GERGES; Editor MIGUEL LÓPEZ TROCELT.

Tal Cual: Galpón 3, 1°, Avda Principal de Boleíta Norte, Caracas 1070-A; tel. (212) 237-5711; fax (212) 232-9377; e-mail tpekoff@ talcualdigital.com; internet www.talcualdigital.com; f. 2000; morning; Dir TEODORO PETKOFF; Editor-in-Chief ROGER SANTODOMINGO.

Ultimas Noticias: Torre de la Prensa, 3°, Plaza del Panteón, Apdo 1192, Caracas; tel. (212) 596-1911; fax (212) 596-1433; e-mail fmayorga@la-cadena.com; f. 1941; morning; independent; Dir ELEAZAR DÍAZ RANGEL.

El Universal: Edif. El Universal, Avda Urdaneta esq. de Animas, Apdo 1909, Caracas; tel. (212) 561-7511; fax (212) 505-3710; e-mail diario@eluniversal.com; internet www.eluniversal.com; f. 1909; morning; Pres. ANDRÉS MATA OSORIO; Editor ELIDES ROJAS.

La Voz: C. C. Nueva Guarenas, Mezzanina, Urb. Trapichito, Sector 2, Caracas; tel. (212) 362-9702; fax (212) 362-0851; e-mail diariolavoz@cantv.net; morning; Exec. Dir FREDDY BLANCO; Editor ALEXIS CASTRO BLANDÍN.

Barcelona

El Norte: Avda Intercomunal Andrés Bello, Sector Colinas del Neverí, Barcelona; tel. (281) 286-2933; fax (281) 286-2484; e-mail diarioelnorte@telcel.net.ve; f. 1989; morning; Dir and Editor ALBERTINA DE PETRICCA.

Barquisimeto

El Impulso: Avda Los Comuneros, entre Avda República y Calle 1a, Urb. El Parque, Apdo 602, Barquisimeto; tel. (251) 250-2222; fax (251) 250-2129; e-mail reaccion@elimpulso.com; f. 1904; morning; independent; Dir and Editor JUAN MANUEL CARMONA PERERA.

El Informador: Carrera 21, esq. Calle 23, Barquisimeto; tel. (251) 231-1811; fax (251) 231-0624; e-mail informad@telcel.net.ve; f. 1968; morning; Dir ALEJANDRO GÓMEZ SIGALA.

Ciudad Bolívar

El Bolivarense: Calle Igualdad 26, Apdo 91, Ciudad Bolívar; tel. (285) 632-2378; fax (285) 632-4878; e-mail abi28@unete.com.ve; f. 1957; morning; independent; Dir ALVARO NATERA.

El Expreso: Paseo Gáspari con Calle Democracia, Ciudad Bolívar; tel. (285) 632-0334; fax (285) 632-0334; e-mail expresobol@cantv.net; f. 1969; morning; independent; Dir LUIS ALBERTO GUZMÁN.

Maracaibo

Panorama: Avda 15 No 95–60, Apdo 425, Maracaibo; tel. (261) 725-6888; fax (261) 725-6911; e-mail panorama@cantv.net; f. 1914; morning; independent; Pres. ESTEBAN PINEDA BELLOSA; Editor ROBERTO BAITTINER.

Maracay

El Aragueño: Calle 3a Oeste con Avda 1 Oeste, Urb. Ind. San Jacinto, Maracay; tel. (243) 235-9018; fax (243) 235-7866; e-mail aragueno@telcel.net.ve; f. 1972; morning; Editor EVERT GARCÍA.

El Siglo: Edif. 'El Siglo', Avda Bolívar Oeste 244, La Romana, Maracay; tel. (243) 554-9265; fax (243) 554-5910; e-mail elsiglo@telcel.net.ve; f. 1973; morning; independent; Editor TULIO CAPRILES.

Puerto la Cruz

El Tiempo: Avda Constitución, Paseo Miranda 39, Apdo 4733, Puerto la Cruz; tel. (281) 265-4344; fax (281) 269-9224; e-mail buzon@eltiempo.com.ve; internet www.eltiempo.com.ve; f. 1958; independent; Pres. MARÍA A. MÁRQUEZ; Editor Dr GIOCONDA DE MÁRQUEZ.

San Cristóbal

Diario Católico: Carrera 4a No 3–41, San Cristóbal; tel. (276) 343-2819; fax (276) 343-4683; e-mail catolico@truevision.net; f. 1924; morning; Catholic; Man. Dir Mgr NELSON ARELLANO.

Diario de la Nación: Edif. La Nación, Calle 4 con Carreras 6 bis, La Concordia, Apdo 651, San Cristóbal; tel. (276) 346-2367; fax (276) 346-5178; f. 1968; morning; independent; Editor JOSÉ RAFAEL CORTEZ.

El Tigre

Antorcha: Torre Alcabala, 5°, Of. 53-A, Alcabala a Peligro, El Tigre; tel. (283) 235-2383; fax (283) 235-3923; f. 1954; morning; independent; Pres. and Editor ANTONIO BRICEÑO AMPARÁN.

Valencia

El Carabobeño: Edif. El Carabobeño, Avda Universidad, Urb. La Granja, Naguanagua, Valencia; tel. (241) 867-2918; fax (241) 867-3450; e-mail general@el-carabobeno.com; internet www.el-carabobeno.com; f. 1933; morning; Dir EDUARDO ALEMÁN PÉREZ.

PERIODICALS

Ambiente: Edif. Sur, Nivel Plaza Caracas, Local 9, Centro Simón Bolívar, Caracas; tel. (212) 484-0664; e-mail fundam@marnr.gov.ve; environmental issues; Gen. Man. OLGA URIBE.

Artesania y Folklore de Venezuela: C. C. Vista Mar, Local 20, Urbaneja, Lecherías, Estado Anzoátegui; tel. and fax (212) 286-2857; e-mail ismandacorrea@cantv.net; handicrafts and folklore; Dir ISMANDA CORREA.

Automóvil de Venezuela: Avda Caurimare, Qta Expo, Colinas de Bello Monte, Caracas 1050; tel. (212) 751-1355; fax (212) 751-1122; e-mail ortizauto@cantv.net; f. 1961; monthly; automotive trade; Editor ARMANDO ORTIZ.

Bohemia: Edif. Bloque DeArmas, Final Avda San Martín cruce con Avda La Paz, Apdo 575, Caracas; tel. (212) 406-4040; fax (212) 451-0762; e-mail bohemia@dearmas.com; f. 1966; weekly; general interest; Dir PEDRO RAMÓN ROMERA.

Business Venezuela: Torre Credival, Avda de Campo Alegre, Apdo 5181, Caracas 1010-A; tel. (212) 263-0833; fax (212) 263-2060; e-mail bramirez@venancham.org; every 2 months; business and economics journal in English published by the Venezuelan-American Chamber of Commerce and Industry; Gen. Man. ANTONIO HERRERA.

Computer World: Edif. MaryStella, Avda Carabobo, El Rosal, Caracas; tel. (212) 952-7427; fax (212) 953-3950; e-mail cernic@cwv.com.ve; Editor CLELIA SANTAMBROGIO.

Contrapunto: Edif. Unión, 1°, Of. 2, Avda El Parque, Las Acacias Sur, Caracas; tel. (212) 690-0431; Dir VÍCTOR VERA MORALES.

El Corresponsal: Conj. Residencial El Naranjal, Torre D, 8°, No 82-D, Urb. Los Samanes, Caracas; tel. and fax (212) 941-0409; Editor DOMINGO GARCÍA PÉREZ.

Convenciones: Torre Nonza, 4°, Plaza Venezuela, Caracas; tel. (212) 793-1962; e-mail redacta@tutopia.com; Dir MARIO ERNESTO ARBELÁEZ.

Dinero: Edif. Aco, Entrada A, 7°, Avda Principal Las Mercedes, Caracas; tel. (212) 993-5633; fax (212) 991-3132; e-mail lotitto@gep.com.ve; business and finance; Pres. and Editor RAÚL LOTITTO.

Gerente Venezuela: Torre Banco Provincial, Entrada B, 15°, Avda Francisco de Miranda, Chacao, Caracas; tel. (212) 267-3733; fax (212) 267-6583; e-mail itmedia@america.com; business and management; Dir LUIS RODÁN; Editor INGRID RODRÍGUEZ.

El Mirador: Edif. Pascal, Torre A, 1°, Of. 12-A, Avda Rómulo Gallegos, Santa Eduvigis, Caracas; tel. (212) 286-1661; fax (212) 283-5823; e-mail diarioelmirador@cantv.net; Dir JESÚS COUTO.

Mujer-Mujer: Centro Banaven, Nivel Sótano, No 13-A, Avda La Estancia, Chuao, Caracas; tel. (212) 959-5393; fax (212) 959-7864;

e-mail ceciliapicon@hotmail.com.ve; women's interest; Dir and Editor CECILIA PICÓN DE TORRES.

Primicia: Edif. El Nacional, 4°, Puente Nuevo a Puerto Escondido, Caracas; tel. (212) 408-3434; fax (212) 408-3485; e-mail primicia@el-nacional.com; current affairs and business; Editor FRANCHESCA CORDIDO.

La Razón: Edif. Valores, Sótano 'A', Avda Urdaneta, esq. de Urapal, Apdo 16362, La Candelaria, Caracas; tel. (212) 578-3143; fax (212) 578-2397; e-mail larazon@internet.ve; internet www.razon.com; weekly on Sundays; independent; Dir PABLO LÓPEZ ULACIO.

Reporte Petrolero: Torre Británica, 12°, Of. B, Altamira Sur, Caracas; tel. (212) 264-6023; fax (212) 266-9991; e-mail reporte2002@hotmail.com; journal of the petroleum industry; Dir ENRIQUE ROMAI; Editor MIGUEL LÓPEZ TROCELT.

Sic: Edif. Centro de Valores, esq. de Luneta, Centro Gumilla, Caracas; tel. (212) 564-9803; fax (212) 564-7557; e-mail rsic@gumilla.org.ve; monthly; liberal Jesuit publication; Dir MERCEDES PULIDO DE BRICEÑO.

Variedades: Edif. Bloque DeArmas, final Avda San Martín cruce con Avda La Paz, Caracas 1020; tel. (212) 406-43-90; fax (212) 451-0762; e-mail mgonzalez@dearmas.com; women's weekly; Dir GLORIA FUENTES DE VALLADARES.

Venezuela Gráfica: Torre de la Prensa, Plaza del Panteón, Apdo 2976, Caracas 101; tel. (212) 81-4931; f. 1951; weekly; illustrated news magazine, especially entertainment; Dir DIEGO FORTUNATO; Editor MIGUEL ANGEL CAPRILES.

Zeta: Pinto a Santa Rosalía 44, Apdo 14067, Santa Rosalía, Caracas; tel. (212) 541-5211; fax (212) 545-9675; e-mail enpaiscolumna@hotmail.com; f. 1974; weekly; politics and current affairs; Dir JURATE ROSALES; Editor RAFAEL POLEO.

Zulia Deportivo: Torre Luali, 5°, Of. 3, Piñango a Muñoz, Avda Baralt, Maracaibo; tel. (261) 787-2809; sports; Dir MANUEL COLINA HIDALGO.

PRESS ASSOCIATIONS

Asociación de Prensa Extranjera en Venezuela (APEX): Hotel Caracas Hilton, Avda México, Torre Sur, 3°, Of. 301, Caracas; tel. (212) 503-5301; fax (212) 576-9284; e-mail caracashilton@hotmail.com; Pres. PHIL GUNSON.

Bloque de Prensa Venezolano (BEV): Edif. El Universal, Avda Urdaneta, 5°, Of. C, Caracas; tel. (212) 561-7704; fax (212) 561-9409; e-mail luichi@telcel.net.ve; asscn of newspaper owners; Pres. MIGUEL ANGEL MARTÍNEZ.

Colegio Nacional de Periodistas (CNP): Casa Nacional del Periodista, Avda Andrés Bello, 2°, Caracas; tel. and fax (212) 781-7601; e-mail cnpjdn@cantv.net; journalists' asscn; Pres. LEVY BENSHIMOL; Sec.-Gen. NOEL MOLINA.

PRESS AGENCIES

Agence France-Presse (AFP): Torre Provincial, Torre A, 14°, Of. 14-1, Avda Francisco de Miranda, Chacao, Caracas; tel. (212) 264-2945; fax (212) 267-2773; e-mail jorge.calmet@afp.com; Bureau Chief JACQUES THOMET.

Agencia EFE (Spain): Calle San Cristóbal, Quinta Altas Cumbres, Urb. Las Palmas, Caracas 1050; tel. (212) 793-7118; fax (212) 793-4920; e-mail efered1@cantv.net; Bureau Chief JESÚS MARÍA ALONSO GIL.

Agenzia Nazionale Stampa Associata (ANSA) (Italy): Centro Financiero Latino, piso 7, Of. 2, Animas a Plaza España, Avda Urdaneta, Caracas; tel. (212) 564-2059; fax (212) 564-2516; e-mail ansaven@infoline.wtfe.com; Dir NATACHA SALAZAR.

Associated Press (AP) (USA): Edif. El Universal, Avda Urdaneta, esq. Animas, 2°, Of. D, Caracas; tel. (212) 564-1834; fax (212) 564-7124; e-mail janderson@ap.org; Chief JAMES ANDERSON.

BBC Latin Service: Res. Los Tulipanes, Torre A, 6°, No 6-B, Urb. Guaicai, Los Samanes; tel. (212) 941-7564; e-mail mariusareyes@hotmail.com; Correspondent MARIUSA REYES.

Bloomberg: Torre Edicampo, 5°, Of. 1-2, Avda Francisco de Miranda, Caracas; tel. (212) 263-3355; fax (212) 264-2171; e-mail pewilson@bloomberg.net; Chief Correspondent PETER WILSON.

Deutsche Presse-Agentur (dpa) (Germany): Edif. El Universal, 4°, Of. 4-E, Avda Urdaneta, Caracas; tel. (212) 561-9776; fax (212) 562-9017; e-mail dpacaracas@tutopia.com; Correspondent NÉSTOR ROJAS.

Inter Press Service (IPS) (Italy): Edif. El Universal, 8°, Of. 3, Avda Urdaneta Caracas; tel. (212) 564-6386; fax (212) 564-6374; e-mail caracas@ipsenespanol.org; Dir ANDRÉS CAÑIZÁLEZ.

Prensa Latina (Cuba): Edif. Fondo Común, Torre Sur, Of. 20-D, Avda de las Fuerzas Armadas y Urdaneta, Apdo 4400, Carmelitas,

Caracas; tel. (212) 561-9733; fax (212) 564-7960; e-mail prelaccs@telcel.net.ve; Correspondent JAVIER RODRÍGUEZ.

Reuters (United Kingdom): Torre la Castellana, 4°, Avda Principal La Castellana, Caracas; tel. (212) 277-2700; fax (212) 277-2664; e-mail caracas.newsroom@reuters.com; Chief Correspondent PASCAL FLETCHER.

Xinhua (New China) News Agency (People's Republic of China): Qta Xinjua, Avda Maracaibo, Prados del Este, Apdo 80564, Caracas; tel. (212) 8977-2489; fax (212) 978-1664; e-mail xinhua@c-com.ve; Bureau Chief QUANFU WUANC.

Publishers

Alfadil Ediciones: Edif. Alfa, Calle Los Mangos, Las Delicias de Sabana Grande, Apdo 50304, Caracas 1050-A; tel. (212) 762-3036; fax (212) 762-0210; f. 1980; general; Pres. LEONARDO MILLA A.

Armitano Editores, CA: Centro Industrial Boleíta Sur, 1°, 4a Transversal de Boleíta, Sabana Grande, Apdo 50853, Caracas 1070; tel. (212) 234-2565; fax (212) 234-1647; e-mail armiedit@telcel.net.ve; internet www.armitano.com; art, architecture, ecology, botany, anthropology; Dir ERNESTO ARMITANO.

Bienes Lacónica, CA: Avda Orinoco, Quinta Praga, Las Mercedes, Apdo 69732, Caracas 1063-A; tel. (212) 752-2111; fax (212) 751-8363; f. 1977; philosophy; Gen. Man. DIEGO GIL VELUTINI.

Colegial Bolivariana, CA: Edif. COBO, 1°, Avda Diego Cisneros (Principal), Los Ruices, Apdo 70324, Caracas 1071-A; tel. (212) 239-1433; f. 1961; Dir ANTONIO JUZGADO ARIAS.

Editorial El Ateneo, CA: Complejo Cultural, Plaza Morelos, Los Caobos, Apdo 662, Caracas; tel. (212) 573-4622; f. 1931; school-books and reference; Pres. MARÍA TERESA CASTILLO; Dir ANTONIO POLO.

Ediciones Ekaré: Edif. Banco del Libro, Final Avda Luis Roche, Altamira Sur, Apdo 68284, Caracas 1062; tel. (212) 263-0091; fax (212) 263-3291; f. 1978; children's literature; Pres. CARMEN DIANA DEARDEN; Exec. Dir ELENA IRIBARREN.

Editora Ferga, CA: Torre Bazar Bolívar, 5°, Of. 501, Avda Francisco de Miranda, El Marqués, Apdo 16044, Caracas 1011-A; tel. (212) 239-1564; fax (212) 234-1008; e-mail ddex1@ibm.net; internet www.ddex.com; f. 1971; Venezuelan Exporters' Directory; Dir NELSON SÁNCHEZ MARTÍNEZ.

Fondo Editorial Común: Edif. Royal Palace, Of. 401, Avda El Bosque, Chacaíto, Apdo 50992, Caracas 1050; Pres. ALBA ILLARAMENDI; Dir PETER NEUMANN.

Fundación Biblioteca Ayacucho: Centro Financiero Latino, 12°, Of. 1, 2 y 3, Avda Urdaneta, Animas a Plaza España, Apdo 14413, Caracas 1010; tel. (212) 561-6691; fax (212) 564-5643; e-mail biblioayacucho@telcel.net.ve; f. 1974; literature; Pres. ALFREDO CHACON.

Fundarte: Edif. Tajamar, P. H., Avda Lecuna, Parque Central, Apdo 17559, Caracas 1015-A; tel. (212) 573-1719; fax (212) 574-2794; f. 1975; literature, history; Pres. ALFREDO GOSEN; Dir ROBERTO LOVERA DE SOLA.

Editorial González Porto: Sociedad a Traposos 8, Avda Universidad, Caracas; Pres. Dr PABLO PERALES.

Ediciones IESA: Edif. IESA, 3°, Final Avda IESA, San Bernardino, Apdo 1640, Caracas 1010-A; f. 1984; economics, business; Pres. RAMÓN PIÑANGO.

Editorial Cincel Kapelusz Venezolana, SA: Avda Cajigal, Quinta K No 29, entre Avdas Panteón y Roraima, San Bernardino, Apdo 14234, Caracas 1011-A; f. 1963; school-books; Pres. DANTE TONI; Man. MAYELA MORGADO.

Ediciones La Casa Bello: Mercedes a Luneta, Apdo 134, Caracas 1010; tel. (212) 562-7100; f. 1973; literature, history; Pres. OSCAR SAMBRANO URDANETA.

Ediciones María Di Mase: Caracas; f. 1979; children's books; Pres. MARÍA DI MASE; Gen. Man. ANA RODRÍGUEZ.

Monte Avila Editores Latinoamericana, CA: Avda Principal La Castellana, Quinta Cristina, Apdo 70712, Caracas 1070; tel. (212) 265-6020; fax (212) 263-8783; e-mail maelca@telcel.net.ve; f. 1968; general; Pres. MARIELA SÁNCHEZ URDANETA.

Ediciones Panamericanas EP, SRL: Edif. Freites, 2°, Avda Libertador cruce con Santiago de Chile, Apdo 14054, Caracas; tel. (212) 782-9891; Man. JAIME SALGADO PALACIO.

Editorial Salesiana, SA: Paradero a Salesianos 6, Apdo 369, Caracas; tel. (212) 571-6109; fax (212) 574-9451; e-mail e.salesiana@unete.com.ve; internet www.salesiana.com.ve; f. 1960; education; Man. P. CLARENCIO GARCÍA S.

Nueva Sociedad: Edif. IASA, 6°, Of. 606, Plaza La Castellana, Apdo 61712, Chacao, Caracas 1060-A; tel. (212) 265-0593; fax (212)

267-3397; e-mail nuso@nuevasoc.org.ve; f. 1972; social sciences; Dir DIETMAR DIRMOSER.

Oscar Todtmann Editores: Avda Libertador, Centro Comercial El Bosque, Local 4, Caracas 1050; tel. (212) 763-0881; fax (212) 762-5244; science, literature, photography; Dir CARSTEN TODTMANN.

Vadell Hermanos Editores, CA: Edif. Tacarigua, 6°, Calle Montes de Oca, Valencia; f. 1973; science, social science; Gen. Man. MANUEL VADELL GRATEROL.

Ediciones Vega S.R.L.: Edif. Odeon, Plaza Las Tres Gracias, Los Chaguaramos, Caracas 1050-A; tel. (212) 662-2092; fax (212) 662-1397; f. 1965; educational; Man. Dir FERNANDO VEGA ALONSO.

ASSOCIATION

Cámara Venezolana del Libro: Centro Andrés Bello, Torre Oeste, 11°, Of. 112-0, Avda Andrés Bello, Caracas 1050-A; tel. (212) 793-1347; fax (212) 793-1368; f. 1969; Pres. HANS SCHNELL; Sec. ISIDORO DUARTE.

Broadcasting and Communications

TELECOMMUNICATIONS

Regulatory Authority

Comisión Nacional de Telecomunicaciones (CONATEL): Ministerio de Transportes y Comunicaciones, Torre Este, 35°, Parque Central, Caracas; tel. (212) 993-5389; regulatory body for telecommunications; Dir JESSE CHACÓN.

Service Providers

Compañía Anónima Nacional Teléfonos de Venezuela (CANTV): Edif. NEA, 20, Avda Libertador, Caracas 1010-A; tel. (212) 500-3016; fax (212) 500-3512; e-mail amora@cantv.com.ve; internet www.cantv.net; privatized 1991; 49% state-owned, 40% owned by Venworld Consortium; 11% owned by employees; Pres. GUSTAVO ROOSEN; Gen. Man. EDUARDO MENASCÉ.

Movilnet: Edif. NEA, 20, Avda Libertador, Caracas 1010-A; tel. (202) 705-7901; e-mail info@movilnet.com.ve; internet www.movilnet.com.ve; f. 1992; mobile cellular telephone operator; owned by CANTV; Pres. GUILLERMO OLAIZOLA.

Digitel: Caracas; internet www.digitel.com.ve; mobile cellular telephone operator.

Intercable: Caracas; internet www.intercable.com; cable, internet and telecommunications services; Pres. EDUARDO STIGOL.

NetUno: Caracas; f. 1995; voice, data and video transmission services; Pres. GILBERT MINIONIS.

TelCel Bellsouth: Edif. Parque Cristal, Torre Este, 14°, Avda Francisco de Miranda, Caracas; tel. (212) 200-8201; internet www.telcel.net.ve; mobile cellular telephone operator; Pres. ENRIQUE GARCIA.

BROADCASTING

Regulatory Authorities

Cámara Venezolana de la Industria de Radiodifusión: Avda Antonio José Istúriz entre Mohedano y Country Club, La Castellana, Caracas; tel. (212) 263-2228; fax (212) 261-4783; e-mail camradio@camradio.org.ve; internet www.camradio.org.ve; Pres. MIGUEL ANGEL MARTÍNEZ.

Cámara Venezolana de Televisión: Edif. Venevisión, 4°, Colinas de Los Caobos, Caracas; tel. (212) 708-9223; fax (212) 708-9146; e-mail esalinas@cisneros.com; regulatory body for private stations; Pres. EDUARDO SALINAS.

Radio

Radio Nacional de Venezuela (RNV): Final Calle las Marías, El Pedregal, Chapellín, POB 3979, Caracas 1050; tel. (212) 730-6022; fax (212) 731-1457; e-mail rnv2000@hotmail.com; internet www.rnv-web.com; f. 1936; state broadcasting organization; 15 stations; Dir-Gen. ROBERTO RUIZ TOVAR.

There are also 20 cultural and some 500 commercial stations.

Television

Government Stations

Venezolana de Televisión (VTV)—Canal 8: Edif. VTV, Avda Principal Los Ruices, Caracas; tel. (212) 239-4870; fax (212) 239-8102; 26 relay stations; Pres. JOSÉ VICENTE RODRÍGUEZ.

Private Stations

Corporación Televén—Canal 10: Edif. Televén, 4ta Transversal con Avda Rómulo Gallegos, Urb. Horizonte, Apdo 1070, Caracas; tel. (212) 239-7211; fax (212) 280-0204; e-mail abenavides@televen.com; internet www.televen.com; Pres. OMAR CAMERO ZAMORA.

Corporación Venezolana de Televisión (Venevisión)—Channel 4: Edif. Venevisión, Final Avda La Salle, Colinas de los Caobos, Apdo 6674, Caracas; tel. (212) 708-9444; fax (212) 708-9114; e-mail mcastro@venevision.com.ve; internet www.venevision.net; f. 1961; commercial; Pres. GUSTAVO CISNEROS.

Globovisión—Channel 33: Quinta Globovisión, Avda Los Pinos, Urb. Alta Florida, Caracas; tel. (212) 706-2600; fax (212) 730-3606; e-mail info@globovision.com; internet www.globovision.com; 24-hour news and current affairs channel; Pres. GUILLERMO ZULOAGA; Gen. Man. ALBERTO FEDERICO RAVELL.

Radio Caracas Televisión (RCTV)—Channel 2: Edif. RCTV, Dolores a Puente Soublette, Quinta Crespo, Caracas; tel. (212) 401-2222; fax (212) 401-2647; e-mail marriaga@rctv.net; f. 1953; commercial station; station in Caracas and 13 relay stations throughout the country; Pres. MARCEL GRANIER.

Televisora Andina de Mérida (TAM)—Channel 6: Edif. Imperador, Entrada Independiente, Avda 6 y 7, Calle 23, Mérida 5101; tel. and fax (274) 251-0660; f. 1982; Pres. Most Rev. BALTAZAR ENRIQUE PORRAS CARDOZO.

VALE TV (Valores Educativos)—Channel 5: Quinta VALE TV, Final Avda La Salle, Colinas de los Caobos, Caracas 1050; tel. (212) 793-9215; fax (212) 708-9743; e-mail webmaster@valetv.com; internet www.valetv.com; Pres. Cardinal IGNACIO ANTONIO VELASCO GARCÍA; Gen. Man. MARÍA EUGENIA MOSQUERA.

Zuliana de Televisión—Channel 30: Edif. 95.5 América, Avda 11 (Veritas), Maracaibo; tel. (265) 641-0355; fax (265) 641-0565; e-mail elregionalredac@iamnet.com; Pres. GILBERTO URDANETA FIDOL.

Finance

(cap. = capital; res = reserves; dep. = deposits; m. = million; brs = branches; amounts in bolívares unless otherwise indicated)

BANKING

Regulatory Authority

Superintendencia de Bancos (SUDEBAN): Edif. SUDEBAN, Avda Universidad, Apdo 6761, Caracas 1010; tel. (212) 505-0933; e-mail sudeban@sudeban.gov.ve; internet www.sudeban.gov.ve; regulates banking sector; Pres. IRVING OCHOA.

Central Bank

Banco Central de Venezuela: Avda Urdaneta esq. de las Carmelitas, Caracas 1010; tel. (212) 801-5111; fax (212) 861-0048; e-mail tlashera@bcv.org.ve; internet www.bcv.org.ve; f. 1940; bank of issue and clearing house for commercial banks; granted autonomy 1992; controls international reserves, interest rates and exchange rates; cap. 10.0m., res 3,969,340.0m., dep. 4,465,022.0m. (Dec. 1998); Pres. DIEGO LUIS CASTELLANOS ESCALONA.

Commercial Banks, Caracas

Banco del Caribe, SACA: Edif. Banco del Caribe, Dr Paúl a esq. Salvador de León, Apdo 6704, Carmelitas, Caracas 1010; tel. (212) 505-5511; fax (212) 562-0460; e-mail producto@bancaribe.com.ve; internet www.bancaribe.net; f. 1954; cap. 10,666.7m., res 12,831.3m., dep. 425,340.7m. (Dec. 1999); Pres. EDGAR A. DAO; Vice-Pres. and Gen. Man. Dr LUIS E. DE LLANO M; 70 brs and agencies.

Banco de Comercio Exterior (Bancoex): Central Gerencial Mohedano, 1°, Calle Los Chaguaramos, La Castellana, Caracas 1060; tel. (212) 265-1433; fax (212) 265-6722; e-mail exports@bancoex.com; internet www.bancoex.com; f. 1997; principally to promote non-traditional exports; state-owned; cap. US $200m. Pres. LIÉBER PATIÑO.

Banco de Desarrollo Económico y Social de Venezuela (BANDES): Torre Bandes, Avda Universidad, Traposos a Colón, Caracas 1010; tel. (212) 505-8010; fax (212) 505-8030; e-mail apublicos@bandes.gov.ve; internet www.bandes.gov.ve; state-owned development bank; Pres. (vacant) (Minister of Planning and Development); Gen. Man. ANGELA FLORES.

Banco de los Trabajadores de Venezuela (BTV) CA: Edif. BTV, Avda Universidad, esq. Colón a esq. Dr Díaz, Caracas; tel. (212) 541-7322; f. 1968 to channel workers' savings for the financing of artisans and small industrial firms; came under state control in

1982; Pres. JOSÉ SÁNCHEZ PIÑA; Man. SILVERIO ANTONIO NARVÁEZ; 11 agencies.

Banco Exterior, CA, Banco Universal: Edif. Banco Exterior, Avda Urdaneta, Urapal a Río, Apdo 14278, Caracas 1010; tel. (212) 501-0111; fax (212) 501-0612; e-mail presidencia@bancoexterior.com; internet www.bancoexterior.com; f. 1958; cap. 45,360m., res 12,173m., dep. 356,564m. (Dec. 2000); Pres. SERGIO SANNIA ANDREOZZI; Gen. Man. EMILIO DURAN CEBALLOS; 72 brs.

Banco Industrial de Venezuela, CA: Torre Financiera BIV, Avda Las Delicias,Sabana Grande, Caracas 1010; tel. (212) 901-1282; fax (212) 952-7361; e-mail webmaster@biv.com.ve; internet www.biv.com.ve; f. 1937; state-owned; cap. 100,000m. (Dec. 2001); Pres. JORGE CASTILLO; 60 brs.

Banco Internacional, CA: Edif. Banco Internacional, esq. de Animas, Avda Urdaneta, Carmelitas, Apdo 6688, Caracas 101; tel. (212) 506-2111; f. 1971 to take over brs. of Royal Bank of Canada, as Banco Royal Venezolano, CA; cap. 129.3m., res 422.9m. (Dec. 1986); Pres. JOSÉ LUIS RAVENGA; Exec. Dir JAIME SILVEIRA; 9 brs.

Banco Latino, SACA: Centro Financiero Latino, Mezzanina, Avda Urdaneta, de Animas a Plaza España, Apdo 2026, Caracas 1010-A; tel. (212) 562-7555; fax (212) 502-5093; f. 1950; cap. 20,000m., dep. 205,194.6m. (Dec. 1995); placed under government control following collapse in January 1994, 54% privatized in mid-1996, privatization of remaining 46% pending; 106 brs.

Banco Mercantil, CA: Edif. Torre Mercantil, 35°, Avda Andrés Bello 1, San Bernardino, Apdo 789, Caracas 1010-A; tel. (212) 503-1112; fax (212) 575-1461; e-mail mercan24@bancomercantil.com; internet www.bancomercantil.com; f. 1925; cap. 81,812.0m., res 43,821.0m., dep. 1,689,825.0m. (Dec. 1999); Chair. and CEO Dr GUSTAVO A. MARTURET; Exec. Vice-Pres. ALFREDO RODRÍGUEZ G; 285 brs.

Banco Metropolitano, CA: Edif. Banco Hipotecario de Crédito Urbano, 10°, Avda Universidad esq. Traposos, Caracas 1010-A; tel. (212) 545-6022; fax (212) 545-9574; f. 1953; Pres. J. DAVID BRILLEMBOURG; Vice-Pres. UMBERTO PETRICCA.

Banco Nacional de Ahorro y Préstamo (BANAP): Torre Banap, Avda Venezuela, El Rosal, Caracas 1060; tel. (212) 951-6222; fax (212) 951-6532; e-mail banap@banap.com; f. 1966; Pres. OSWALDO RAMÍREZ BRICEÑO.

Banco del Pueblo Soberano CA: Edif. Banco del Pueblo Soberano, Gradillas a San Jacinto Parroquia Catedral, Caracas; tel. (212) 505-2800; fax (212) 505-2995; e-mail abarrera@bancodelpueblo.com.ve; internet www.bancodelpueblo.com.ve.

Banco República, CA: Edif. EDSAM, Madrices a San Jacinto No 6, Caracas 1010-A; tel. (212) 564-8265; fax (212) 563-4090; f. 1958; placed under government control in 1994, scheduled for reprivatization; cap. 4,243m., res 482m., dep. 78,718m. (Dec. 1996); Pres. OLGA FERRER DE HERNÁNDEZ; Exec. Vice-Pres. CAROLINA ALBANELL; 39 brs.

Banco Standard Chartered: Edif. Banaven, Torre D, 5°, Avda la Estancia A, Chuao, Caracas 1060; tel. (212) 901-0149; fax (212) 951-3397; f. 1980 as Banco Exterior de los Andes y de España, current name adopted in 1998 following acquisition by Standard Chartered Bank (UK); cap. US $94m., res $38.9m., dep. $943.5m. (Dec. 1996); Chair. DAVID LORETTA; CEO FRANK D. ROBLETON.

Banco Venezolano de Crédito, SACA: Edif. Banco Venezolano de Crédito, Avda Alameda, San Bernadino, Caracas 1011; tel. (212) 806-6111; fax (212) 541-2757; e-mail jurbano@venezolano.com; internet www.venezelano.com; f. 1925; cap. 25,272.0m., res 55,685.6m., dep. 304,902.9m. (Dec. 2000); Pres. Dr OSCAR GARCÍA MENDOZA; 59 brs.

Banco de Venezuela (Grupo Santander): Torre Banco de Venezuela, Avda Universidad, esq. Sociedad a Traposos, Apdo 6268, Caracas 1010-A; tel. (212) 501-3333; fax (212) 501-2546; internet www.bancodevenezuela.com; f. 1890; frmly Banco de Venezuela CA, 93.38% share purchased by Banco Santander (Spain) in Dec. 1996; changed name to above in 1998; acquired Banco Caracas, CA in Dec. 2000; cap. 5,000.0m., res 56,401.2m., dep. 1,408,337.7m. (Dec. 1999); Pres. MICHEL J. GOGUIKIAN; 202 brs and agencies.

Banesco: Torre Banesco, Avda Guaicaipuro con Avda Principal de Las Mercedes, Caracas; tel. (212) 952-4972; fax (212) 952-7124; e-mail atcliente@banesco.com; internet www.banesco.com; began merger talks with Unibanca in March 2002; Exec. Pres. LUIS XAVIER LUJÁN.

BBVA Banco Provincial, SA: Centro Financiero Provincial, Avda Vollmer con Avda Este O, San Bernardino, Apdo 1269, Caracas 1011; tel. (212) 504-5111; fax (212) 504-4313; internet www.provincial.com; f. 1952; cap. 89,461.6m., res 301,350.7m., dep. 2,857,727.7m. (Dec. 2000); Pres. HERNAN ANZOLA.

Corp Banca, CA: Torre Corp Banca, Plaza la Castellana, Chacao, Caracas 1060; tel. (212) 206-3333; fax (212) 206-1298; e-mail calidad@corpbanca.com.ve; internet www.corpbanca.com.ve; f. 1969; frmly Banco Consolidado, current name adopted in 1997; cap.

16,633.3m., res 22,244,4m., dep. 560,177.0m. (Dec. 1999); Chair. RODRIGO ERRAZURIZ; Exec. Pres. LAUTARO AGUILAR.

Unibanca: Torre Grupo Unión, Avda Universidad, esq. El Chorro, Apdo 2044, Caracas; tel. (212) 501-7111; fax (212) 501-7068; internet www.unibanca.com; f. 2001; by merger of Banco Unión (f. 1943) and Caja Familia; began merger talks with Banesco March 2002; Pres. Dr IGNACIO SALVATIERRA; Vice-Pres. JOSÉ Q. SALVATIERRA; 174 brs.

Barquisimeto, Lara

Banco de Lara: Edif. Torre Lara, Avda 20, entre Calles 27 y 28, Apdo 545, Barquisimeto, Lara; tel. (251) 31-5211; fax (251) 31-6820; f. 1953; cap. 4,000m., res 4,830m., dep. 87,887m. (Jan. 1996); Pres. ARTURO GANTEAUME; Exec. Vice-Pres. CÉSAR ARISTIMUÑO; 44 agencies.

Banco Capital, CA: Carrera 17 Cruce con Calle 26, Frente a La Plaza Bolívar, Barquisimeto, Lara; tel. (251) 31-4979; fax (251) 31-1831; e-mail eximport@bancocapital.net; internet www.bancocapital .net; f. 1980; cap. 1,500.0m., res 1,854.7m., dep. 60,428.3m. (Dec. 1997); Chair. and Pres. JOSÉ REINALDO FURIATI; Gen. Man. VICENTE M. FURIATI; 13 brs.

Ciudad Guayana, Bolívar

Banco Caroní: Edif. Multicentro Banco Caroní, Vía Venezuela, Puerto Ordaz, Estado Bolívar; tel. (286) 23-2230; fax (286) 22-0995; e-mail carupsis@telcel.net.ve; Pres. ARISTIDES MAZA TIRADO.

Banco Guayana, CA: Edif. Banguayana, Prolongación Paseo Orinoco, Apdo 156, Ciudad Bolívar, Bolívar; tel. (285) 25511; f. 1955; state-owned; cap. 80m., dep. 683.2m. (Feb. 1988); Pres. ANDRÉS E. BELLO BILANCIERI; Gen. Man. OMAIRA UNCEIN DE NATERA.

Banco del Orinoco, SACA: Edif. Seguros Orinoco, Avda Cuchivero con Calle Caruachí, Alta Vista, Apdo 143, Ciudad Guayana, Bolívar; tel. (285) 61-2311; fax (285) 62-2645; f. 1980; cap. 4,800.0m., res 5,353.2m., dep. 121,862.7m. (Dec. 1997); Pres. ALFONSO TREDINIK BRUSCO; Gen. Man. HUGO CHÁVEZ O; 48 brs.

Coro, Falcón

Banco Federal, CA: Avda Manaure, cruce con Avda Ruiz Pineda, Coro, Falcón; tel. (268) 51-4011; f. 1982; cap. 50m., dep. 357m. (Dec. 1986); Pres. BERNARDO PAUL; Vice-Pres. JOSÉ TOMÁS CANIELO BATALLA.

Banco de Fomento Regional Coro, CA: Avda Manaure, entre Calles Falcón y Zamora, Coro, Falcón; tel. (268) 51-4421; f. 1950; transferred to private ownership in 1994; Pres. ABRAHAM NAÍN SENIOR URBINA; Gen. Man. DIMAS BUENO ARENAS.

Maracaibo, Zulia

Banco Occidental de Descuento, SACA: Avda 5 de Julio esq. Avda 17, Apdo 695, Maracaibo 4001-A, Zulia; tel. (261) 59-3044; fax (261) 59-4981; e-mail atclient@bodinternet.com; internet www .bodinternet.com; f. 1957; transferred to private ownership in 1991; cap. 5,000.0m., res 8,743.4m., dep. 125,544.3m. (Dec. 1997); Pres. VÍCTOR VARGAS IRASUSQUIN; Exec. Dir CÁNDIDO RODRÍGUEZ; 17 brs.

Nuevo Esparta

Banco Confederado: Edif. Centro Financiero Confederado, Blvd Gómez, Porlamar, Estado Nuevo Esparta; tel. (95) 65-4230; fax (95) 63-7033; internet www.bancoconfederado.com; Pres. HASSAN SALEH SALEH.

San Cristóbal, Táchira

Banco de Fomento Regional Los Andes, CA: Carrera 6, esq. Calle 5, San Cristóbal, Táchira; tel. (276) 43-1269; f. 1951; cap. 20m., res 18.8m., dep. 796.2m. (Dec. 1985); Pres. EDGAR MORENO MÉNDEZ; Exec. Vice-Pres. PEDRO ROA SÁNCHEZ.

Mortgage and Credit Institutions Caracas

Banco Hipotecario de la Vivienda Popular, SA: Intersección Avda Roosevelt y Avda Los Ilustres, frente a la Plaza Los Símbolos, Caracas; tel. (212) 62-9971; f. 1961; cap. 100m., res 68.2m., dep. 259.3m. (Dec. 1987); Pres. HELY MALARET M; First Vice-Pres. ALFREDO ESQUIVAR.

Banco Hipotecario Unido, SA: Edif. Banco Hipotecario Unido, Avda Este 2, No 201, Los Caobos, Apdo 1896, Caracas 1010; tel. (212) 575-1111; fax (212) 571-1075; f. 1961; cap. 230m., res 143m., dep. 8,075m. (May 1990); Pres. ARTURO J. BRILLEMBOURG; Gen. Man. ALFONSO ESPINOSA M.

Maracaibo, Zulia

Banco Hipotecario del Zulia, CA: Avda 2, El Milagro con Calle 84, Maracaibo, Zulia; tel. (261) 91-6055; f. 1963; cap. 120m., res 133.5m., dep. 671.5m. (Nov. 1986); Pres. ALBERTO LÓPEZ BRACHO.

Foreign Banks

ABN AMRO Bank NV (Netherlands): Edif. Centro Seguros Sud América, 1°, Avda Francisco de Miranda, El Rosal, Apdo 69179, Caracas 1060; tel. (212) 957-0300; fax (212) 953-5758.

Banco do Brasil SA (Brazil): Edif. Centro Lido, 9°, Avda Francisco de Miranda, El Rosal, Apdo 52023, Caracas; tel. (212) 952-2674; fax (212) 952-5251.

Citibank NA (USA): Edif. Citibank, esq. de Carmelitas a esq. de Altagracia, Apdo 1289, Caracas; tel. (212) 81-9501; fax (212) 81-6493; cap. 40m., res 203.8m., dep. 677.6m. (Dec. 1986); Pres. THOMAS J. CHARTERS; Vice-Pres. JOSÉ L. GARCÍA M; 4 brs.

Banking Association

Asociación Bancaria de Venezuela: Torre Asociación Bancaria de Venezuela, Avda Venezuela, 1°, El Rosal, Caracas; tel. (212) 951-4711; fax (212) 951-3696; e-mail abvinfo@asobanca.com.ve; internet www.asobanca.com.ve; f. 1959; 79 mems; Pres. IGNACIO SALVATIERRA; Exec. Dir. LAURY DE CRACCO.

STOCK EXCHANGE

Bolsa de Valores de Caracas, CA: Edif. Atrium, Nivel C-1, Calle Sorocaima entre Avdas Tamanaco y Venezuela, Urbanización El Rosal, Apdo 62724-A, Caracas 1060-A; tel. (212) 905-5511; fax (212) 952-2640; e-mail bvc@caracasstock.com; internet www.caracasstock .com; f. 1947; 65 mems; Pres. ALEJANDRO SALCEDO THIELEN.

INSURANCE

Supervisory Board

Superintendencia de Seguros: Torre Metálica, 1°–4°, Avda Francisco de Miranda, cruce con Avda Loyola, Chacao, Caracas 1061; tel. (212) 263-1344; Superintendent Dr MORELIA CORREDOR OCHOA.

Principal Insurance Companies

All companies must have at least 80% Venezuelan participation in their capital. The following list comprises the most important companies on the basis of revenue from premiums.

Adriática, CA de Seguros: Edif. Adriática de Seguros, Avda Andrés Bello, Apdo 1928, Caracas; tel. (212) 571-6422; fax (212) 571-5546; e-mail adriatica@adriatica; internet www.adriatica.com.ve; f. 1952; cap. 27m. Pres. JEAN MARIE MONTEIL; Gen. Man. FRANCIS DESMAZES.

Avila, CA de Seguros: Torre Fondo Común, Avda Urdaneta Candilito a Platanal, 8°–13°, Apdo 1007, Caracas 1010; tel. (212) 507-0111; fax (212) 507-0175; f. 1936; cap. 30m. Pres. RAMÓN RODRÍGUEZ; Vice-Pres JUAN LUIS CASAÑAS.

Carabobo, CA de Seguros: Edif. Seguros Carabobo, Calle Rondón, cruce con Avda Díaz Moreno, Apdo 138, Valencia; tel. (241) 88601; e-mail walvarez@seguroscarabobo.com; f. 1955; cap. 75m. Pres. PAUL FRAYNO; Gen. Man. WILLIAM ALVAREZ Y.

Latinoamericana de Seguros, CA: Centro Comercial Concresa, Avda Humboldt, Nivel TD, Prados del Este, Caracas 1080; tel. (212) 979-3511; f. 1974; cap. 25m. Pres. JOAQUÍN SILVEIRA ORTIZ; Exec. Pres. Lic. LUIS XAVIER LUJAN.

Pan American, CA de Seguros: Edif. Panavén, 1° y 4°–9°, Avda San Juan Bosco, cruce con 3 transversal, Urb. Altamira, Apdo 6166, Caracas; tel. (212) 261-9655; fax (212) 261-9655; f. 1966; cap. 55m. Pres. VICTORIA GURIDI; Vice-Pres. VICTOR MEINTJES.

Seguros Caracas, CAV: Edif. Seguros Caracas, 1°, Marrón a Cují, Apdo 981, Caracas 1010; tel. (212) 561-6122; f. 1943; cap. 600m. Pres. Dr MOISES BENACERRAF; Exec. Vice-Pres. Dr RICARDO ECHEVERRÍA.

Seguros Catatumbo, CA: Avda 4 (Bella Vista), No 77–55, Apdo 1083, Maracaibo; tel. (261) 700-5555; fax (261) 700-5556; e-mail mercado@seguroscatatumbo.com; f. 1957; cap. 9,300m. Pres. ESTEBAN R. PINEDA B; Dir-Gen. ATENÁGORAS VERGEL RIVERA.

Seguros La Metropolitana, SA: Centro Financiero Metropolitano, Avda Andrés Bello con Avda El Parque, San Bernardino, Caracas 1011; tel. (212) 575-0033; fax (212) 576-5884; f. 1949; cap. 38m. Pres. Dr IMANOL VALDÉS CANTOLLA; Vice-Pres. JOSÉ DÍAZ DEVESA.

Seguros Nuevo Mundo, SA: Edif. Seguros Nuevo Mundo, Avda Luis Roche con 3 transversal, Altamira, Apdo 2062, Caracas; tel. (212) 263-0333; fax (212) 263-1435; e-mail nmundo01@true.net; f. 1856; cap. 100m. Pres. RAFAEL PEÑA ALVAREZ; Exec. Vice-Pres. RAFAEL VALENTINO.

Seguros Orinoco, CA: Esq. de Socarrás, Avda Fuerzas Armadas, Edificio Seguros Orinoco, piso 7, Caracas 1010; tel. (212) 596-4371; fax (212) 596-4070; internet www.seguros-orinoco.com; f. 1957; cap. 300m. Pres. PAUL REIMPELL; Exec. Pres. GREGORIO SCHARIFKER.

Seguros La Seguridad, CA: Calle 3A, Frente a La Torre Express, La Urbina Sur, Apdo 473, Caracas 1010; tel. (212) 204-8737; fax (212) 204-8890; e-mail reasas@la-seguridad.com; f. 1943; cap. 5,438.5m. Pres. ALBERTO SOSA SCHLAGETER; Vice-Pres. RAFAEL CASAS GUTIÉRREZ.

Insurance Association

Cámara de Aseguradores de Venezuela: Torre Taeca, 2°, Avda Guaicaipuro, El Rosal, Apdo 3460, Caracas 1010; tel. (212) 952-4411; fax (212) 951-3268; e-mail cavrelpublicas3@eldish.net; internet www.camaraseg.org; f. 1942; 50 mems; Pres. JUAN BLANCO URIBE.

Trade and Industry

GOVERNMENT AGENCIES

Corporación de Mercadeo Agrícola (Corpomercadeo): Edif. Torre Industrial, Calle Vargas-Boleíta, Caracas; tel. (212) 35-8044; responsible for marketing agricultural products; Pres. Dr ALBERTO SILVA GUILLÉN.

Corporación Venezolana de Guayana (CVG): Edif. General, 2°, Avda La Estancia, Apdo 7000, Caracas; tel. (212) 991-2157; fax (212) 991-9235; f. 1960 to organize development of Guayana area, particularly its iron ore and hydroelectric resources; Pres. Gen. FRANCISCO RANGEL GÓMEZ.

Dirección General Sectorial de Hidrocarburos: Torre Oeste, 12°, Parque Central, Caracas 1010; tel. (212) 507-6201; division of Ministry of Energy and Mines responsible for determining and implementing national policy for the exploration and exploitation of petroleum reserves and for the marketing of petroleum and its products; Dir-Gen. MANUEL ALAYETO E.

Dirección General Sectorial de Minas y Geología: Torre Oeste, 4°, Parque Central, Caracas; tel. (212) 507-5401; fax (212) 575-2497; division of Ministry of Energy and Mines responsible for formulating and implementing national policy on non-petroleum mineral reserves; Dir MIGUEL H. CANO DE LOS RÍOS.

Instituto Agrario Nacional (IAN): Quinta Barrancas, La Quebradita, Caracas; f. 1945; under Agrarian Law to assure ownership of the land to those who worked on it; now authorized to expropriate and redistribute idle or unproductive lands; Pres. Dr ANTONIO JOSÉ ALVAREZ FERNÁNDEZ.

Instituto de Crédito Agrícola y Pecuario: 40–44 Salvador de León a Socarras, Caracas; formerly the Banco Agrícola y Pecuario; administers the government crop credit scheme for small farmers; Dir-Gen. Dr ANTONIO JOSÉ ALVAREZ FERNÁNDEZ.

Instituto Nacional de la Vivienda: Caracas; f. 1975; administers government housing projects; Pres. Dr LEANDRO QUINTA.

Palmaven: Edif. PDVSA La Floresta, Torre Palmaven, Avda Principal Urb. La Floresta, Caracas; tel. (212) 208-0309; fax (212) 208-0212; promotes agricultural development, provides agricultural and environmental services and technical assistance to farmers; Man. Dir EDDIE RAMÍREZ.

Superintendencia de Inversiones Extranjeras (SIEX): Edif. La Perla, Bolsa a Mercaderes, 3°, Apdo 213, Caracas 1010; tel. (212) 483-6666; fax (212) 41-4368; f. 1974; supervises foreign investment in Venezuela; Supt. Dr ANSELMO CHUECOS PÉREZ.

DEVELOPMENT ORGANIZATIONS

Corporación de Desarrollo de la Pequeña y Mediana Industria (Corpoindustria): Aragua; tel. (243) 23459; promotes the development of small and medium-sized industries; Pres. Dr CARLOS GONZÁLEZ-LÓPEZ.

CVG Bauxita Venezolana (Bauxivén): Caracas; f. 1978 to develop the bauxite deposits at Los Pijiguaos; financed by the FIV and the CVG which has a majority holding; Pres. JOSÉ TOMÁS MILANO.

CHAMBERS OF COMMERCE AND INDUSTRY

Federación Venezolana de Cámaras y Asociaciones de Comercio y Producción (Fedecámaras): Edif. Fedecámaras, Avda El Empalme, Urb. El Bosque, Apdo 2568, Caracas; tel. (212) 731-1711; fax (212) 745-040; e-mail direje@fedecameras.org; internet www.fedecamaras.org; f. 1944; 307 mems; Pres. CARLOS FERNÁNDEZ PÉREZ.

Cámara de Comercio de Caracas: Edif. Cámara de Comercio de Caracas, Avda Andrés Eloy Blanco 215, 8°, Los Caobos, Caracas; tel. (212) 571-3222; fax (212) 571-0050; e-mail comercio@ccc.com.ve; f. 1893; 650 mems; Pres. RAFAEL ALFONZO HERNÁNDEZ.

Cámara de Industriales de Caracas: Edif. Cámara de Industriales, 3°, Avda Las Industrias esq. Pte Anauco, La Candelaria, Apdo

14255, Caracas 1011; tel. (212) 571-4224; fax (212) 571-2009; e-mail ciccs@telcel.net.ve; internet www.cic.org.ve; f. 1939; Pres. JORGE JEZERSKAS; 550 mems.

Cámara Venezolano-Americana de Industria y Comercio (Venamcham): Torre Credival, 10°, Of. A, 2a Avda Campo Alegre, Apdo 5181, Caracas 1010-A; tel. (212) 263-0833; fax (212) 263-1829; e-mail venam@venamcham.org; internet www.venamcham.org; f. 1950; Pres. ANDRÉS MATA OSORIO; Gen. Man. ANTONIO HERRERA VAILLANT.

There are chambers of commerce and industry in all major provincial centres.

EMPLOYERS' ORGANIZATIONS

Caracas

Asociación Nacional de Comerciantes e Industriales: Plaza Panteón Norte 1, Apdo 33, Caracas; f. 1936; traders and industrialists; Pres. Dr HORACIO GUILLERMO VILLALOBOS; Sec. R. H. OJEDA MAZZARELLI; 500 mems.

Asociación Nacional de Industriales Metalúrgicos y de Minería de Venezuela: Edif. Cámara de Industriales, 9°, Puente Anauco a Puente República, Apdo 14139, Caracas; metallurgy and mining; Pres. JOSÉ LUIS GÓMEZ; Exec. Dir LUIS CÓRDOVA BRITO.

Asociación Textil Venezolana: Edif. Karam, 5°, Of. 503, Avda Urdaneta, Ibarras a Pelota, Caracas; tel. (212) 561-6851; fax (212) 562-8197; f. 1957; textiles; Pres. JACK LEVI; Exec. Dir AGUILES ORTÍZ; 68 mems.

Asociación Venezolana de Exportadores (AVEX): Centro Comercial Coneresa, Redoma de Prados del Este 435, 2°, Prados del Este, Caracas; tel. (212) 979-0824; fax (212) 979-4542; e-mail avex@telcel.net.ve; Pres. FRANCISCO MENDOZA.

Cámara Petrolera: Torre Domus, 3°, Of. 3-A, Avda Abraham Lincoln con Calle Olimpo, Sabana Grande, Caracas; tel. (212) 794-1222; fax (212) 794-0068; e-mail informaciones@camarapetrolera.org; internet www.camarapetrolera.org; f. 1978; association of petroleum-sector companies; Pres. HENRIQUE RODRÍGUEZ GUILLÉN.

Consejo Venezolano de la Industria—Conindustria: Centro Empresarial Los Ruices, Avda Diego Cisneros 302, 3°, Caracas; tel. (212) 991-2116; fax (212) 991-7737; e-mail coindustria@coindustria.org; internet www.coindustria.org; association of industrialists; Pres. JUAN CALVO; Dir GERARDO LUCAS.

Confederación Nacional de Asociaciones de Productores Agropecuarios—Fedeagro: Edif. Casa de Italia, planta baja, Avda La Industria, San Bernardino, Caracas 1010; tel. (212) 571-4035; fax (212) 573-4423; f. 1960; agricultural producers; 133 affiliated associations; Pres. FERNANDO CAMINO PEÑALVER; Exec. Sec. IVÁN LÓPEZ GONZÁLEZ.

Consejo Venezolano de la Industria: Edif. Cámara de Industriales, esq. de Puente Anauco, Caracas; industry council; Pres. GUSTAVO PÉREZ MIJARES; Co-ordinator Ing. ISRAEL DÍAZ VALLES.

Federación Nacional de Ganaderos de Venezuela: Edif. Casa de Italia, 7°, Avda La Industria, San Bernardino, Caracas; cattle owners; Dir ELÍAS CASTRO CORREAS; Sec. MIGUEL A. GRANADOS.

Unión Patronal Venezolana del Comercio: Edif. General Urdaneta, 2°, Marrón a Pelota, Apdo 6578, Caracas; trade; Sec. H. ESPINOZA BANDERS.

Other Towns

Asociación de Comerciantes e Industriales del Zulia (ACIZ): Edif. Los Cerros, 3°, Calle 77 con Avda 3C, Apdo 91, Maracaibo, Zulia; tel. (261) 91-7174; fax (261) 91-2570; f. 1941; traders and industrialists; Pres. JORGE AVILA.

Asociación Nacional de Cultivadores de Algodón (National Cotton Growers' Association): Planta Desmotadora, Carretera Guanare, Zona Industrial Acarigua; Sec. LEOPOLD BAPTISTA.

Asociación Nacional de Empresarios y Trabajadores de la Pesca: Cumaná; fishermen.

Unión Nacional de Cultivadores de Tabaco: Urb. Industrial La Hamaca, Avda Hustaf Dalen, Maracay; tobacco growers.

STATE HYDROCARBONS COMPANIES

Petróleos de Venezuela, SA (PDVSA): Edif. Petróleos de Venezuela, Torre Este, Avda Libertador, La Campiña, Apdo 169, Caracas 1010-A; tel. (212) 708-4111; fax (212) 708-4661; e-mail webmaster@pdvsa.com.ve; internet www.pdvsa.com.ve; f. 1975; holding company for national petroleum industry; responsible for petrochemical sector since 1978 and for development of coal resources in western Venezuela since 1985; plans pending in 2003 to divide the company into two divisions, PDVSA Occidente and PDVSA Oriente; Pres. ALÍ RODRÍGUEZ ARAQUE; Gen. Man PDVSA

Occidente Félix Rodríguez; Gen. Man. PDVSA Oriente Luis Marín; The following are subsidiaries of PDVSA:

Bariven, SA: Edif. PDVSA Los Chaguaramos, Avda Leonardo Da Vinci, 6°, Urb. Los Chaguaramos, Apdo 1889, Caracas 1010-A; tel. (212) 606-4060; fax (212) 606-2741; handles the petroleum, petrochemical and hydrocarbons industries' overseas purchases of equipment and materials.

Bitúmenes Orinoco, SA (BITOR): Edif. PDVSA Exploración, Producción y Mejoramiento, 9°, Avda Ernesto Blohm, La Estancia, Chuao, Apdo 3470, Caracas 1010-A; tel. (212) 908-2811; fax (212) 908-3982; e-mail abreuew@pdvsa.com; plans, develops and markets the bitumen resources of the Orinoco belt; produces Venezuela's trademark boiler fuel Orimulsion.

Carbozulia, SA: Edif. PDVSA Exploración, Producción y Mejoramiento, Avda 5 de Julio, esq. Avda 11, Apdo 1200, Maracaibo CP 4001; tel. (261) 806-8600; fax (261) 806-8790; f. 1978; responsible for the commercial exploitation of the Guasare coalfields in Zulia.

Deltaven: Edif. PDVSA Deltaven, Avda Principal de La Floresta, La Floresta, Caracas 1060; tel. (212) 208-1111; markets PDVSA products and services within Venezuela.

Interven, SA: Edif. Petróleos de Venezuela, Torre Oeste, 11°, Avda Libertador, La Campiña, Apdo 2103, Caracas 1010-A; tel. (212) 708-1111; fax (212) 706-6621; f. 1986; to manage PDVSA's joint ventures overseas.

Intevep: Edif. Sede Central, Urb. Santa Rosa, Sector El Tambor, Los Teques, Apdo 76343, Caracas 1070-A; tel. (212) 908-6111; fax (212) 908-6447; e-mail webmaster@intevep.com; internet www.intevep.pdv.com; f. 1979; research and development branch of PDVSA; undertakes applied research and development in new products and processes and provides specialized technical services for the petroleum and petrochemical industries.

PDV Marina: Edif. Petróleos de Venezuela Refinación, Suministro y Comercio, Torre Oeste, 9°, Avda Libertador, La Campiña, Apdo 2103, Caracas 1010-A; tel. (212) 708-1111; fax (212) 708-2200.

PDVSA Gas: Edif. Sucre, Avda Francisco de Miranda, La Floresta, Caracas; tel. (212) 208-6212; fax (212) 208-6288; e-mail messina@pdvsa.com; internet www.pdvsa.com/gas; Pres. Nelson Nava.

Petroquímica de Venezuela, SA (Pequiven): Torre Pequiven, Avda Francisco de Miranda, Chacao, Apdo 2066, Caracas 1010-A; tel. (212) 201-4011; fax (212) 201-3189; e-mail wensmasterp@pdvsa.com; internet www.pequiven.pdv.com; f. 1956 as Instituto Venezolano de Petroquímica; became Pequiven in 1977; involved in many joint ventures with foreign and private Venezuelan interests for expanding petrochemical industry; active in regional economic integration; an affiliate of PDVSA from 1978; Pres. Aires Barreto.

Productos Especiales C.A. (Proesca): Torre Pequiven, 13°, Avda Francisco de Miranda, Chacao, Apdo 2066, Caracas 1060-A; tel. (212) 201-3152; fax (212) 201-3008.

UTILITIES

Electricity

La Electricidad de Caracas (EDC): Edif. La Electricidad de Caracas, Avda Vollmer, San Bernadino, Caracas; tel. (212) 502-2111; internet www.edc-ven.com; supplies electricity to capital; owned by AES Corpn; Pres. Andrés Gluski.

Electrificación del Caroní, CA (Edelca): Edif. General, planta baja, Avda La Estancia, Chuao, Caracas; tel. (212) 950-2111; fax (212) 950-2808; e-mail wriera@edelca.com.ve; state-owned electricity co. supplies some 70% of country's electricity.

Sistema Eléctrico de Nueva Esparta (Seneca): electricity co; privatized in October 1998.

Water

Compañía Anónima Hidrológica de la Región Capital (Hidrocapital): Edif. Hidroven, Avda Augusto César Sandino con 9a Transversal, Maripérez, Caracas; tel. (212) 793-1638; fax (212) 793-6794; e-mail 73070.2174@compuserve.com; internet www.hidrocapital.com.ve; f. 1992; owned by Hidroven; operates water supply in Federal District and States of Miranda and Vargas; Pres. Jacqueline Faria Pineda.

Hidroven: Edif. Hidroven, Avda Augusto César Sandino con 9a Transversal, Maripérez, Caracas; tel. (212) 781-4778; fax (212) 781-6424; national water co. owns Hidroandes, Hidrocapital, Hidrocaribe, Hidrofalcon, Hidrolago, Hidrollanos, Hidropaez, Hidrosuroeste, Aguas de Monagas, Aguas de Ejido, Hidrolara, Aguas de Anaco, Aguas de Cojedes, Aguas de Mérida, Aguas de Apure, Aguas

de Yaracuy, Aguas de Portuguesa; Pres. Cristóbal Francisco Ortiz; Vice-Pres. Reinaldo Bravo.

Instituto Nacional de Obras Sanitarias (INOS): Edif. La Paz, Caracas; autonomous government institution; administers water supply and sewerage projects; privatization plans announced in April 1990; Pres. Dr Alexis Carstens Ramos.

TRADE UNIONS

About one-quarter of the labour force in Venezuela belongs to unions, more than one-half of which are legally recognized. Venezuela's union movement is strongest in the public sector.

Confederación de Trabajadores de Venezuela (CTV) (Confederation of Venezuelan Workers): Edif. José Vargas, 17°, Avda Este 2, Los Caobos, Caracas; tel. (212) 575-1105; f. 1936; largest trade union confederation; principally active in public sector; Chávez Govt disputes legitimacy of election of CTV leadership; Pres. Carlos Ortega; Sec.-Gen. Manuel Cova; 1,000,000 mems from 24 regional and 16 industrial federations.

Fedepetrol: union of petroleum workers; Pres. Rafael Rosales.

Federación Campesina (FC): peasant union; CTV affiliate; Leader Rubén Lanz.

Fetrametal: union of metal workers; CTV affiliate; Leader José Mollegas.

Fuerza Bolivariana de Trabajadores (FBT): f. 2000; pro-Govt union.

Movimiento Nacional de Trabajadores para la Liberación (MONTRAL): Edif. Don Miguel, 6°, esq. Cipreses, Caracas; f. 1974; affiliated to CLAT and WFTU; Pres. Laureano Ortiz Braeamonte; Sec.-Gen. Dagoberto González; co-ordinating body for the following trade unions:

Central Nacional Campesina (CNC): Pres. Reinaldo Vásquez.

Cooperativa Nacional de Trabajadores de Servicios Múltiples (CNTSM).

Federación Nacional de Sindicatos Autónomos de Trabajadores de la Educación de Venezuela (FENASATREV): Pres. Luis Efraín Orta.

Federación de los Trabajadores de Hidrocarburos de Venezuela (FETRAHIDROCARBUROS).

Frente de Trabajadores Copeyanos (FTC): Sec.-Gen. Dagoberto González.

Movimiento Agrario Social-Cristiano (MASC): Sec.-Gen. Gustavo Mendoza.

Movimiento Magisterial Social-Cristiano (MMSC): Sec.-Gen. Felipe Montilla.

Movimiento Nacional de Trabajadores de Comunicaciones (MONTRAC).

Movimiento Nacional de Trabajadores Estatales de Venezuela (MONTREV).

Transport

RAILWAYS

In 1999 work began on lines linking Acarigua and Turén (45 km) and Morón and Riecito (100 km). Construction of the first section (Caracas–Cúa) of a line linking the capital to the existing network at Puerto Cabello (219 km in total) was also begun. Services on the underground system began in 1983 on a two-line system: east to west from Palos Verdes to Propatria; north to south from Capitolio/El Silencio to Zoológico. A southern extension from Plaza Venezuela to El Valle opened in 1995. Further extensions to the lines were under way in 2002.

CVG Ferrominera Orinoco, CA: Vía Caracas, Puerto Ordaz, Apdo 399, Bolívar; tel. (286) 30-3451; fax (286) 30-3333; e-mail 104721.2354@compuserve.com; f. 1976; state company; operates two lines San Isidro mine–Puerto Ordaz (316 km) and El Pao–Palua (55 km) for transporting iron ore; Pres. Ing. Leopoldo Sucre Figarella; Man. M. Aro G.

Ferrocarril de CVG Bauxilum—Operadora de Bauxita: Caracas; tel. (212) 40-1716; fax (212) 40-1707; f. 1989; state company; operates line linking Los Pijiguaos with river Orinoco port of Gumilla (52 km) for transporting bauxite; Pres. P. Morales.

Instituto Autónomo de Ferrocarriles del Estado (IAFE): Edif. Torre Británica de Seguros, 7° y 8°, Avda José Féliz Sosa, Urb. Altamira, Chacao, Caracas 1062-A; tel. (212) 201-8911; e-mail relacp@cantv.net; state company; 336 km; Pres. Rafael Alvarez; Vice-Pres. Inova Castro Pérez.

CA Metro de Caracas: Multicentro Empresarial del Este, Edif. Miranda, Torre B, 7°, Avda Francisco de Miranda, Apdo 61036, Caracas; tel. (212) 206-7611; fax (212) 266-3346; e-mail mgrp@telcel .net.ve; f. 1976 to supervise the construction and use of the underground railway system; state-owned; Pres. I. COMBELLAS LARES.

ROADS

In 2001 there were an estimated 96,155 km of roads, of which 32,308 km were paved.

Of the three great highways, the first (960 km) runs from Caracas to Ciudad Bolívar. The second, the Pan-American Highway (1,290 km), runs from Caracas to the Colombian frontier and is continued as far as Cúcuta. A branch runs from Valencia to Puerto Cabello. The third highway runs southwards from Coro to La Ceiba, on Lake Maracaibo.

A new 'marginal highway' was under construction along the western fringe of the Amazon Basin in Venezuela, Colombia, Ecuador, Peru, Bolivia and Paraguay. The Venezuelan section now runs for over 440 km and is fully paved.

INLAND WATERWAYS

Instituto Nacional de Canalizaciones: Edif. INC, Calle Caracas, Chuao, al lado de la Torre Diamen, Apdo E.61959, Caracas; f. 1951; semi-autonomous institution connected with the Ministry of Infrastructure; Pres. Rear-Adm. AGUEDO FELIPE HERNÁNDEZ; Vice-Pres. FERNANDO MARTÍ O.

Compañía Anónima La Translacustre: Maracaibo; freight and passenger service serving Lake Maracaibo, principally from Maracaibo to the road terminal from Caracas at Palmarejo.

SHIPPING

There are 13 major ports, 34 petroleum and mineral ports and five fishing ports. Formerly the main port for imports, La Guaira, the port for Caracas, was affected by mudslides caused by heavy rains in November 1999. Venezuela's main port is now Puerto Cabello, which handles raw materials for the industrial region around Valencia. Maracaibo is the chief port for the petroleum industry. Puerto Ordaz, on the Orinoco River, was also developed to deal with the shipments of iron from Cerro Bolívar.

Instituto Nacional de Puertos: Caracas; tel. (212) 92-2811; f. 1976 as the sole port authority; Pres. Vice-Adm. FREDDY J. MOTA CARPIO.

Consolidada de Ferrys, CA: Torre Banhorient, 3°, Avda Las Acacias y Avda Casanova, Apdo 87, Sabana Grande, Caracas 1010-A; tel. (212) 782-8544; fax (212) 793-0739; f. 1970; Pres. RAFAEL TOVAR.

Consorcio Naviero Venezolano (Conavén): Torre Uno, 4°, Avda Orinoco, Las Mercedes, Caracas; tel. (212) 993-2922; fax (212) 993-1505; e-mail conavent@conaven.

Corpoven, SA: Edif. Petróleos de Venezuela, Avda Libertador, La Campiña, Apdo 61373, Caracas 1060-A; tel. (212) 708-1111; fax (212) 708-1833; Pres. Dr ROBERTO MANDINI; Vice-Pres. JUAN CARLOS GÓMEZ; 2 oil tankers.

Lagoven, SA: Edif. Lagovén, Avda Leonardo da Vinci, Los Chaguaramos, Apdo 889, Caracas; tel. (212) 606-3311; fax (212) 606-3637; f. 1978 as a result of the nationalization of the petroleum industry; formerly known as the Creole Petroleum Group; transports crude petroleum and by-products between Maracaibo, Aniba and other ports in the area; Pres. B. R. NATERA; Marine Man. P. D. CAREZIS; 10 tankers.

Tacarigua Marina, CA: Torre Lincoln 7A-B, Avda Lincoln, Apdo 51107, Sabana Grande, Caracas 1050-A; tel. (212) 781-1315; Pres. R. BELLIZZI.

Transpapel, CA: Edif. Centro, 11°, Of. 111, Centro Parque Boyaca, Avda Sucre, Los Dos Caminos, Apdo 61316, Caracas 1071; tel. (212) 283-8366; fax (212) 285-7749; e-mail nmaldonado@cantv.net; Chair. GUILLERMO ESPINOSA F; Man. Dir Capt. NELSON MALDONADO A.

Transporte Industrial, SA: Carretera Guanta, Km 5 Planta Vencemos, Pertigalete-Edif. Anzoátegui, Apdo 4356, Puerto la Cruz; tel. (281) 68-5607; fax (281) 68-5683; f. 1955; bulk handling and cement bulk carrier; Chair. VÍCTOR ROMO; Man. Dir RAFAEL ANEE.

Venezolana de Navegación, CA: Avda Rómulo Gallegos 8007, Sector El Samán, entre Calle El Carmen y 1a Transversal de Monte Cristo, Los Dos Caminos, Apdo 70135, Caracas 1071; tel. (212) 203-6511; fax (212) 35-7185; regular services to US ports and Germany, the Netherlands, France and Spain; associated services from Scandinavian, Baltic, Mediterranean and Japanese ports; Chair. Rear-Adm. CARLOS HERNÁNDEZ F; Man. Dir Capt. L. E. LUGO MARÍN.

CIVIL AVIATION

There are two adjacent airports 13 km from Caracas; Maiquetía for domestic and Simón Bolívar for international services. There are 61 commercial airports, 11 of which are international airports.

National Airlines

Aeropostal (Alas de Venezuela): Torre Polar II, 22°, Plaza Venezuela, Caracas 1051; tel. (212) 708-6211; fax (212) 782-6323; internet www.aeropostal.com; f. 1933; transferred to private ownership in Sept. 1996, acquired by Venezuela/US consortium Corporación Alas de Venezuela; domestic services and flights to destinations in the Caribbean, South America and the USA; Pres. and CEO NELSON RAMIZ.

Aerovías Venezolanas, SA (AVENSA): Edif. 29, 2°, Avda Universidad, esq. El Chorro, Apdo 943, Caracas 101; tel. (212) 562-3022; fax (212) 563-0225; internet www.avensa.com.ve; f. 1943; provides extensive domestic services from Caracas and international services to Europe and the USA; government-owned; Pres. WILMAR CASTRO.

Aserca Airlines: Torre Exterior, 8°, Avda Bolivar Norte, Valencia, Carabobo 2002; tel. (241) 237-111; fax (241) 220-210; e-mail rsv@ asercaairlines.com; internet www.asercaairlines.com; f. 1968; domestic services and flights to Caribbean destinations; CEO SIMEON GARCÍA; Exec. Pres. JULIAN VILLALBA.

LASER (Línea Aérea de Servicio Ejecutivo Regional): Torre Bazar Bolívar, 8°, Avda Francisco de Miranda, El Marqués, Caracas; tel. (212) 235-6181; fax (212) 235-8359; f. 1994; scheduled and charter services to domestic and international destinations, passenger and cargo; Pres. INOCENCIO ALVAREZ.

Línea Turística Aereotuy, CA: Edif. Gran Sabana, 5°, Blvd de Sabana Grande, Apdo 2923, Carmelitas, Caracas 1050; tel. (212) 762-3009; fax (212) 761-1892; e-mail jcmarquez@ethevon.net; internet www.tuy.com; f. 1982; operates on domestic and international routes; Pres. PETER BOTTOME; Gen. Man. JUAN C. MÁRQUEZ.

Santa Barbara Airlines: Avda 3H, No 78-51, Res. República, Local 01, Maracaibo; tel. (261) 922-090; fax (261) 927-977; internet www .sbairlines.com; f. 1995; domestic and international services; Chair. and Pres. HELI S. FERNÁNDEZ; CEO and Gen. Man. FRANCISCO GONZÁLEZ YANEZ.

Tourism

In 2000 Venezuela received 469,000 tourists. In 1999 tourism generated an income of US $656m. Tourist numbers declined in the late 1990s, and were 40% lower in 2001 than in 1997. Venezuela's high crime levels, political instability and high prices relative to regional competitors have deterred tour operators. An estimated 90% of tourists visit the island of Margarita, while only 20% of tourists visit the mainland.

Corporación de Turismo de Venezuela (Corpoturismo): Torre Oeste, 37°, Avda Lecuna, Parque Central, Caracas 1010; tel. (212) 576-5696; fax (212) 574-2679; e-mail corpoturismo@platino.gov.ve; internet www.venetur.com.ve; promotes tourism; Pres. Dr ANGEL NELSON SALVATIERRA.

Departamento de Turismo: c/o Central Information Office of the Presidency, Torre Oeste, 18°, Parque Central, Caracas; Dir Dr JESÚS FEDERICO RAVEL.

Corporación Nacional de Hoteles y Turismo (CONAHOTU): Caracas; f. 1969; government agency; Pres. ERASTO FERNÁNDEZ.

Fondoturismo Venezuela: Hotel Caracas Hilton, Torre Sur, 4°, Of. 424, Caracas; tel. (212) 503-5423; fax (212) 503-5424; e-mail fondoturismo@cantv.net; government tourist development agency; Pres. Dr ANGEL NELSON SALVATIERRA.

VIET NAM

Introductory Survey

Location, Climate, Language, Religion, Flag, Capital

The Socialist Republic of Viet Nam is situated in South-East Asia, bordered to the north by the People's Republic of China, to the west by Laos and Cambodia, and to the east by the South China Sea. The climate is humid during both the hot summer and the relatively cold winter, and there are monsoon rains in both seasons. Temperatures in Hanoi are generally between 13°C (55°F) and 33°C (91°F). The language is Vietnamese. The principal religion is Buddhism. There are also Daoist, Confucian, Hoa Hao, Caodaist and Christian (mainly Roman Catholic) minorities. The national flag (proportions 2 by 3) is red, with a large five-pointed yellow star in the centre. The capital is Hanoi.

Recent History

Cochin-China (the southernmost part of Viet Nam) became a French colony in 1867. Annam and Tonkin (central and northern Viet Nam) were proclaimed French protectorates in 1883. Later all three were merged with Cambodia and Laos to form French Indo-China. Throughout the French colonial period, but especially after 1920, nationalist and revolutionary groups operated in Viet Nam. The best-organized was the Vietnamese Revolutionary Youth League, founded by Ho Chi Minh. The League was succeeded in 1930 by the Communist Party of Indo-China, also led by Ho Chi Minh.

In September 1940 Japanese forces began to occupy Viet Nam, although (Vichy) France retained administrative authority, and in June 1941 the nationalists formed the Viet Nam Doc Lap Dong Minh Hoi (Revolutionary League for the Independence of Viet Nam), or Viet Minh. In March 1945 French control was ended by a Japanese coup. Following Japan's surrender in August, Viet Minh forces entered Hanoi, and on 2 September the new regime proclaimed independence as the Democratic Republic of Viet Nam (DRV), with Ho Chi Minh as President. The Communist Party, formally dissolved in 1945, continued to be the dominant group within the Viet Minh Government. In March 1946, after French forces re-entered Viet Nam, an agreement between France and the DRV recognized Viet Nam as a 'free' state within the French Union. The DRV Government, however, continued to seek complete independence. Negotiations with France broke down, and full-scale hostilities began in December 1946.

In March 1949 the French established the State of Viet Nam in the South. Meanwhile, in the North the Viet Minh was dissolved in 1951, and the Communists formed the Dang Lao Dong Viet Nam (Viet Nam Workers' Party), with Ho Chi Minh as Chairman of the Central Committee. After the defeat of French forces at Dien Bien Phu in May 1954, terms for a cease-fire were settled in Geneva, Switzerland. Agreements signed in July provided for the provisional partition of Viet Nam into two military zones, with French forces south of latitude 17°N and DRV forces in the north. Later in 1954 the French withdrew from South Viet Nam. Ngo Dinh Diem became Prime Minister of the State of Viet Nam, and in 1955, following a referendum, proclaimed himself President of the Republic of Viet Nam. He thereby deposed Bao Dai, Emperor of Viet Nam from 1932 until his forced abdication in 1945, who had become Head of the State of Viet Nam in 1949. (The former Emperor died in exile in France in 1997.) Diem refused to participate in elections envisaged by the Geneva agreement. In the DRV Ho Chi Minh was succeeded as Prime Minister by Pham Van Dong in 1955, but remained Head of State and party Chairman.

The anti-communist Diem regime in the South was opposed by former members of the Viet Minh who became known as the Viet Cong. Diem was overthrown by a coup in November 1963, and a series of short-lived military regimes held power until June 1965, when some stability was restored by the National Leadership Committee, with Lt-Gen. Nguyen Van Thieu as Chairman and Air Vice-Marshal Nguyen Cao Ky as Prime Minister. In 1967 Gen. Thieu was elected President, with Marshal Ky as Vice-President, and in 1971, after splitting with Ky, President Thieu was re-elected unopposed.

From 1959 the DRV actively assisted the insurgent movement in South Viet Nam, supporting the establishment there of the communist-dominated National Liberation Front (NLF) in December 1960. In 1961 the USA joined the war on the side of the anti-communist regime in the South, later bombing the North extensively from 1965 to 1968. In November 1968 peace talks between the four participants in the Viet Nam war began in Paris, France, but remained deadlocked as the fighting continued. In June 1969 the NLF formed the Provisional Revolutionary Government (PRG) in the South. Ho Chi Minh died in September 1969: he was succeeded as Head of State by Ton Duc Thang, while political leadership passed to Le Duan, First Secretary of the Viet Nam Workers' Party since 1960.

In 1972 PRG and North Vietnamese forces launched a major offensive in South Viet Nam, and US bombing of the North was renewed with greater intensity. In January 1973 a peace agreement was finally signed in Paris, providing for a cease-fire in the South, the withdrawal of US forces, the eventual peaceful reunification of the whole country, and US aid to the Government in the North to assist in reconstruction. US troops withdrew, and in December 1974 combined PRG and North Vietnamese forces began a final offensive, taking the southern capital, Saigon, in April 1975. By May the new regime was in complete control of the South.

While South Viet Nam, under the PRG, remained technically separate from the DRV, effective control of the whole country passed to Hanoi. In July 1976 the country's reunification was proclaimed under the name of the Socialist Republic of Viet Nam, and Saigon was renamed Ho Chi Minh City. A new Government was appointed, dominated by members of the former Government of the DRV but including some members of the PRG. In December Le Duan was appointed General Secretary of the Communist Party of Viet Nam (formerly the Viet Nam Workers' Party). President Ton Duc Thang died in March 1980. A new Constitution was adopted in December of that year. Truong Chinh was appointed President of the Council of State (Head of State) in July 1981, but real power remained with Le Duan.

Le Duan died in July 1986, and was succeeded as General Secretary of the Communist Party by Truong Chinh. At the sixth Party Congress, held in December, the country's three most senior leaders, Truong Chinh, Pham Van Dong and Le Duc Tho, announced their retirement from the party Politburo. However, they continued to attend politburo meetings in an advisory capacity. Truong Chinh and Pham Van Dong retained their respective posts as President of the Council of State and Chairman of the Council of Ministers (Prime Minister) until 1987, and Le Duc Tho continued to wield considerable political influence until his death in October 1990. The Congress appointed Nguyen Van Linh, a long-standing party official, as General Secretary of the Party.

In February 1987 an extensive government reshuffle involved the dismissal of 12 ministers, as well as the merger or restructuring of several ministries, apparently with a view to the implementation of economic reforms. An election to the National Assembly took place in April. There were 829 candidates for the 496 seats (compared with 613 candidates at the previous election). In June the new Assembly elected Vo Chi Cong and Pham Hung, both former Vice-Chairmen of the Council of Ministers, to the posts of President of the Council of State and Chairman of the Council of Ministers respectively. Although a veteran of the struggle with the South, and reputedly a strict conservative, Pham Hung gave his support to the programme of economic reform, referred to as *doi moi* (renovation), initiated by Nguyen Van Linh. The new liberalism of the regime was demonstrated by the release in September of 480 political prisoners from 're-education' camps, as part of an amnesty for more than 6,600 prisoners on the anniversary of independence from France in 1945. In February 1988 more than 1,000 political prisoners were released. In March Pham Hung died. The Council of State appointed Vo Van Kiet, a Vice-Chairman of the Council of Ministers and the Chairman of the State Commission for Planning, as acting Chairman of the Council of Ministers until the next session of the National Assembly.

Mismanagement of a food shortage in early 1988 led to a famine in northern Viet Nam during April and May. In a critical gesture, members of the National Assembly, supported by a newly formed pressure group comprising veteran soldiers, demanded the resignation of the Minister of Agriculture. At the meeting of the National Assembly in June, members from the south took the similarly unprecedented step of nominating the reformist Vo Van Kiet to oppose the Central Committee's more conservative candidate, Do Muoi (ranked third in the Politburo), in the election for the chairmanship of the Council of Ministers. Do Muoi was elected to the chairmanship, but Vo Van Kiet received unexpectedly strong support (36% of the votes). Despite his reputation, Do Muoi declared his commitment to the advancement of reform. Widespread dissatisfaction with the condition of the economy and the slow progress of reform (often because of the refusal of officials to implement new policies) led to the removal of hundreds of cadres from government posts in a 'purification' of the party. In an attempt to improve international relations, and thus secure much-needed Western aid, Viet Nam amended its Constitution in December, removing derogatory references to the USA, China, France and Japan. In March 1989 a reshuffle of senior economic ministers adjusted the balance further towards reform and strengthened the position of Nguyen Van Linh.

In August 1989 68 members of a US-based exiles' movement, the National Front for the Liberation of Viet Nam, were arrested while crossing from Thailand into Laos. Viet Nam formally protested to Thailand for supporting the group, which had allegedly attempted to incite a rebellion in southern Viet Nam, although the Thai Government denied involvement. In January 1990 38 suspected rebels were extradited to Viet Nam; they were later charged with attempting to overthrow the Government, and in October were sentenced to long terms of imprisonment.

Municipal elections to provincial and district councils took place in November 1989. Under new legislation adopted during a meeting of the National Assembly in June, candidates who were not members of the Communist Party were allowed to participate for the first time. In December the National Assembly approved legislation imposing new restrictions on the press: the appointment of editors became subject to government approval, and journalists were required to reveal sources of information on request. Open dissension towards Communist Party policy also became a criminal offence. In late 1989 progress towards political reform under *doi moi* was adversely affected by government concern regarding the demise of socialism in Eastern Europe. At a meeting of the Central Committee in March 1990, disagreement on the issue of political pluralism resulted in the dismissal of a member of the Politburo, Tran Xuan Bach, who had openly advocated political reform. In April the Council of State announced an extensive ministerial reshuffle, in which four ministers were dismissed and several portfolios reorganized.

In the second half of 1990 the Government dismissed or brought charges against more than 18,000 officials, in an attempt to eradicate corruption. In December the Central Committee produced draft political and economic reports, reaffirming the party's commitment to socialism and to the process of economic liberalization, which were to be submitted to the next Party Congress. In the same month Bui Tin, the Deputy Editor of the official organ of the Communist Party, *Nhan Dan*, criticized government policy and demanded extensive political reform. He was subsequently expelled from the Politburo and dismissed as Deputy Editor. Following a request by the Central Committee for public comment on the reports, in early 1991 the party journal, *Tap Chi Cong San* (Communist Review), published articles by prominent intellectuals that severely criticized the reports and questioned the effectiveness of a socialist system in Viet Nam. The Communist Party subsequently increased surveillance of dissidents and instructed the press to publish retaliatory articles condemning party critics. In June the Communist Party Congress approved the reports. It elected Do Muoi to replace Nguyen Van Linh as General Secretary of the Party; seven members of the Politburo were removed from their posts, including Nguyen Van Linh, although he, together with Pham Van Dong and the President of the Council of State, Vo Chi Cong, remained in the Central Committee in an advisory capacity. At a session of the National Assembly held in late July and early August, the reformist Vo Van Kiet was elected to replace Do Muoi as Chairman of the Council of Ministers. The

Ministers of Foreign Affairs and of the Interior (both formerly close associates of Le Duc Tho) were dismissed. In addition, the National Assembly studied proposals, made by a constitutional commission, for amendments to the Constitution.

A new draft Constitution was published in December 1991 and, after being reviewed in public discussions and debated in the National Assembly, was adopted by the Assembly in April 1992. Like the previous (1980) Constitution, it emphasized the central role of the Communist Party; however, the new document stipulated that the party must be subject to the law. While affirming adherence to a state-regulated socialist economy, the new Constitution guaranteed protection for foreign investment in Viet Nam, and permitted foreign travel and overseas investment for Vietnamese. Land was to remain the property of the State, although the right was granted to long-term leases, which could be inherited or sold. The National Assembly was to be reduced in number, but was to have greater power. The Council of State was to be replaced by a single President as Head of State, to be responsible for appointing (subject to the approval of the National Assembly) a Prime Minister and senior members of the judiciary. The new Constitution was to enter into effect after the July 1992 general election.

In July 1992 a total of 601 candidates contested 395 seats in the National Assembly. Almost 90% were members of the Communist Party: although independent candidates (i.e. not endorsed by the Viet Nam Fatherland Front—the grouping of mass organizations, such as trade unions, affiliated to the Communist Party) were for the first time permitted to seek election, in the event only two were deemed to qualify, and neither was elected. Of the members of the outgoing National Assembly, only 118 were candidates: more than 100 of these were returned.

At the first session of the new National Assembly, in September 1992, the conservative Gen. Le Duc Anh (a member of the Politburo and a former Minister of Defence) was elected to the new post of executive President. Vo Van Kiet was appointed Prime Minister (the equivalent of his former post) by the Assembly in October. Only four ministers, all of whom had been implicated in corruption scandals, were not reappointed. Vo Van Kiet identified corruption and smuggling as being among the principal problems to be overcome by the new administration. During 1993 the Government emphasized its determination to continue progress towards a market-led economy and to encourage foreign investment. Despite the country's economic liberalization, however, there was no tolerance of political dissent. In August 14 people were sentenced to terms of imprisonment, after having been convicted of conspiring to overthrow the Government, and in November several Buddhist monks were imprisoned for allegedly inciting anti-Government demonstrations. At a Communist Party conference in January 1994 Do Muoi praised the country's recent economic achievements and its widening external relations, but denounced the continuing prevalence of poverty, the increase in corruption and crime, and the inadequacy of the educational system; he also strongly criticized the party for disunity and poor organization. Immediately before the conference four new members were appointed to the Politburo, including the Minister of Foreign Affairs, Nguyen Manh Cam, and during the conference 20 new members (all under the age of 55) were elected to the party's Central Committee. In June the National Assembly approved a labour law that guaranteed the right to strike (providing that the 'social life of the community' was not adversely affected). Strikes followed in some southern provinces, and in August the first incident of industrial action in Hanoi was reported. At a plenum of the party Central Committee, held in late July–early August, Do Muoi reasserted the need to strengthen Viet Nam's 'open-door' policy in order to attract wide foreign investment. At the fourth Congress of the Fatherland Front, in August, a new, 200-member Central Committee was elected, the Presidium of which was headed by the 73-year-old Le Quang Dao, described as a 'veteran revolutionary'. Elections to provincial and district councils took place during December 1994.

In February 1995 a prominent human rights organization, Amnesty International, protested to the Vietnamese Government about the recent arrest and detention of members of the anti-Government Unified Buddhist Church of Viet Nam. In August the People's Court of Ho Chi Minh City sentenced nine political activists, who had attempted to organize pro-democracy conferences, to terms of imprisonment. (Two of those sentenced, who held joint US-Vietnamese nationality, were released in November following a request from the US Government.) Also in

August five members of the Unified Buddhist Church of Viet Nam received custodial sentences for acting in contravention of national solidarity (in 1994 they had organized a relief effort to assist flood victims independently of other religious organizations). Several ministries were merged in a government reorganization in October 1995. Later that month the National Assembly adopted an extensive civil code (drafted over a period of 10 years), guaranteeing the rights of the individual and enshrining existing rights concerning land usage and inheritance of property. In November two former prominent members of the Communist Party, Do Trung Hieu and Hoang Minh Chinh, were sentenced to custodial terms on charges of damaging national security: Hieu had been involved with an organization demanding political pluralism, while Chinh had published articles urging the restoration of senior party officials removed in the 1960s.

In April 1996 the Central Committee of the Communist Party released draft reports on political and economic policy, which were to be submitted to the eighth Communist Party Congress at the end of June, indicating that the party intended to maintain state control of the economy (while remaining committed to economic growth) and to continue to reject political pluralism. Also in April the Vice-Chairman of the National Assembly, who had been regarded as a potential successor to Vo Van Kiet in the forthcoming Party Congress, was dismissed from the Politburo and from the Communist Party; it was reported that he had been accused of treason in connection with the Viet Nam war. In June the Congress elected a new, 170-member Central Committee and an expanded (19-member) Politburo. A five-member Standing Board, which included Do Muoi, Le Duc Anh and Vo Van Kiet, was created. In November 12 ministers were dismissed in an extensive cabinet reorganization. Later in the month Le Duc Anh withdrew temporarily from politics, owing to ill health: this prompted considerable speculation regarding the eventual leadership succession. In subsequent months Lt-Gen. Le Kha Phieu, a member of the new Standing Board, came to the fore as a likely successor to Do Muoi as General Secretary of the Communist Party. Widely seen as a conservative, Le Kha Phieu was expected to seek an increased political role for the military. Le Duc Anh returned to active politics in April 1997.

In November 1996 the National Assembly began drafting amendments to the criminal code that would define specific forms of corruption. In the same month the UN Development Programme agreed financial assistance for the reform of Viet Nam's legal system. In December the Politburo issued a directive requiring the establishment of Communist Party cells in all foreign-invested enterprises, in order to increase party discipline. In January 1997 two business executives were sentenced to death for embezzlement of state funds. Also in January an unprecedentedly high-profile corruption case was brought to trial: the case involved former senior officials of Tamexco (an import-export company owned by the Communist Party), along with officials from Vietcombank (the state foreign trade bank) and the financial sector. The 20 defendants were accused of a range of financial crimes, principally embezzlement of socialist property. In late January four death sentences were pronounced, together with one sentence of life imprisonment, two suspended sentences and a combined total of 103 years' imprisonment for the remaining defendants. The Communist Party newspaper, *Nhan Dan*, subsequently blamed the slow progress of reform in Viet Nam on the prevalence of corruption in the higher echelons of the State. Appeals were lodged by 15 of those convicted in the Tamexco case; however, in March the Supreme People's Court upheld the sentences, and in January 1998 three of those sentenced to death were executed. In February 1997 a judge of the Supreme People's Court was sentenced to two years' imprisonment, having been found to have abused a position of influence for personal gain, and was thus the first member of Viet Nam's judiciary to be convicted of corruption.

In May 1997 substantial amendments to the criminal code were approved by the National Assembly in respect of corruption, bribery, child-abuse and drugs-trafficking. The acceptance of bribes in excess of 50m. dông, and possession of 5 kg of opium or 100 grams of heroin became crimes punishable by death or life imprisonment; increased penalties were introduced for first-time offenders in cases of corruption. In the same month a group of 22 people, including police, customs and border officials, stood trial for drugs-trafficking: all were convicted, with eight sentenced to death and eight to life imprisonment. In mid-July two people were sentenced to death, and three others to life imprisonment, following what was reported as Viet Nam's first ter-

rorism trial, having been convicted of involvement in a bomb attack in Ho Chi Minh City in October 1994. Official reports stated that the defendants were members of the National Resistance Front for the Restoration of Viet Nam, which was alleged to have issued death threats to foreign nationals who had established businesses in Viet Nam.

Elections to the 10th National Assembly took place on 20 July 1997. A record 663 candidates contested 450 seats (expanded from 395 seats under revised electoral legislation). Under a modified selection process, 112 non-Communist Party members registered as potential candidates. However, following rigorous screening procedures, only 11 independent ('self-nominated') candidates qualified to contest the elections, of whom three secured seats in the Assembly. Do Muoi was among senior figures who did not seek re-election, and, in total, fewer than one-third of the members of the outgoing Assembly returned to office. The new National Assembly convened for its first session in late September and elected Tran Duc Luong, hitherto a Deputy Prime Minister, as President in succession to Le Duc Anh, who, owing to continued ill health, had previously announced his intention not to seek re-election. The Assembly subsequently endorsed the appointment of Nguyen Thi Binh as Vice-President, Nong Duc Manh as Chairman of the National Assembly Standing Committee, and Phan Van Khai as Prime Minister. (Vo Van Kiet had also announced his intention to step down.) A reorganization of the Cabinet was approved at the end of September: the new Cabinet included an increased number of Deputy Prime Ministers, each of whom held a wide portfolio of responsibilities, and several new ministers. In October Do Que Luong was appointed acting Governor of the State Bank of Viet Nam (a cabinet post), following the refusal of the National Assembly to re-elect the incumbent Cao Si Kiem, deemed responsible for recent corruption scandals in the banking sector.

Reports emerged during September 1997 of violent unrest in the northern province of Thai Binh. The unrest, which had begun in May and intensified in June as hundreds of farmers protested against taxes and local corruption, had remained largely unreported earlier in the year as the province had been closed to foreign journalists. There was violence in November in the predominantly Roman Catholic province of Dong Nai, in southern Viet Nam, as thousands of protesters demonstrated against corruption in local government and attempts to confiscate church land. At the end of November the Government pledged to provide financial aid to Thai Binh province, and in February 1998 President Luong made an official tour of the province. In July 1998 more than 30 people were sentenced to terms of imprisonment for their involvement in the previous year's violent unrest in Thai Binh.

At the end of December 1997 Le Kha Phieu was elected to succeed Do Muoi as General Secretary of the Central Committee of the Communist Party. At the same time Do Muoi, Le Duch Anh and Vo Van Kiet resigned from the Politburo; all three were subsequently appointed as advisers to the Central Committee. Four new members were elected to the Politburo, and in early January 1998 the election by the Politburo of a new Standing Board, comprising Le Kha Phieu, Tran Duc Luong, Phan Van Khai, Nong Duc Manh and Pham The Duyet, was announced. The new appointments were widely perceived to reflect the consolidation of the conservative tendency within the leadership, and thus a cautious approach to reform, to the detriment of reformists, among them the Prime Minister. Included in further appointments of high-ranking officials announced in early January was that of Maj.-Gen. Dao Trong Lich as Deputy Minister of National Defence and Chief of General Staff. However, in May Dao Trong Lich was killed in an air crash in Laos, along with 13 other senior officers; he was succeeded as Chief of General Staff in September by Lt-Gen. Le Van Dung. In March, in an illustration of the Government's commitment to countering corruption, the Communist Party announced that in 1997 it had disciplined and expelled some 18,000 members, and sentenced 469 to terms of imprisonment. (Further members of the party were subsequently reported to have been disciplined over corruption-related offences in July.) In August it was reported that a group of 11 veteran members of the Communist Party were responsible for a letter sent in May to the party's leadership accusing Pham The Duyet of corruption; the allegations were said to be under investigation by Communist Party leaders. In November it was announced that an investigation into allegations of corruption made against senior government officials had found the accusations to be unfounded; however, corruption among lower-level officials was acknowledged to represent a problem.

In a general amnesty announced by the Government to mark Viet Nam's National Day on 2 September 1998, more than 5,000 prisoners, including four of the country's most prominent dissidents—Doan Viet Hoat, Nguyen Dan Que, Thich Quang Do and Thich Tue Sy—were released from detention; however, the release of at least two of the dissidents was reported to be dependent upon their immediate exile from Viet Nam. (In January 1999 Doan Viet Hoat, in exile in the USA, expressed his intention to establish Viet Nam's first domestic opposition group.) In October 1998 amnesty was granted to a further 2,630 prisoners. Also in October, the former Editor-in-Chief of *Doanh Nghiep*, Nguyen Hoang Linh, was convicted of 'abusing freedom and democratic rights to violate the interests of the state', following the publication in his newspaper of articles detailing alleged government corruption; Nguyen Hoang Linh was sentenced to more than 12 months' imprisonment, but was released almost immediately as his sentence represented the exact time he had served in detention while awaiting trial. In October the Special Rapporteur on religious intolerance of the UN Commission on Human Rights, Abdelfattah Amor, visited Viet Nam to investigate assertions made by the Vietnamese authorities that greater freedom of religious expression was being tolerated in the country. However, at the end of his visit, Amor stated that his investigation had been obstructed by government officials and that he had been prevented from meeting key religious dissidents.

In January 1999 the leadership of the Communist Party announced that it had expelled Gen. (retd) Tran Do from the party in response to his explicit criticism of the establishment in a series of letters to the leadership. The expulsion of Gen. Tran Do caused renewed speculation about divisions within the uppermost level of the leadership of the Communist Party and the Politburo, and also set the precedent for the continued suppression of political dissent by the Communist Party throughout the course of 1999. In March the prominent writer and geophysicist, Nguyen Thanh Giang, whose critiques of the Communist Party were reported to have been widely disseminated both within Viet Nam and abroad, was arrested on the grounds of 'propagandizing against the socialist regime'; Nguyen Thanh Giang was subsequently released in May, but reportedly remained under house arrest. In September the trial opened of 24 members of the dissident People's Action Party, charged with 'exiting the country illegally for the purpose of undermining the people's administration'; all 24 defendants were subsequently convicted and sentenced to terms of imprisonment ranging from two to 20 years. Prior to the trial Le Kha Phieu, speaking at the Seventh Plenum of the Eighth Party Central Committee in August, had emphasized the Communist Party's opposition to 'political pluralism'.

In June 1999 it was reported that the Vietnamese Government was to hold a nation-wide census to assess the health of individuals affected by the chemical defoliant, Agent Orange, sprayed in large quantities over areas of Viet Nam by US forces during the Viet Nam war; the chemical was believed to be responsible for widespread health problems, including genetic damage to unborn children.

In 1999 the issue of corruption remained a major source of concern for the ruling Communist Party. At the Sixth Plenum of the Eighth Party Central Committee, which concluded in January, it was announced that the party was to renew its efforts to eliminate corruption from within its ranks. In the first half of 1999 two major corruption trials opened: the trial of 74 people accused of smuggling (more than one-half of whom were reported to be former government officials) opened in late March, with two of the defendants being subsequently sentenced to death, and the remainder to terms of imprisonment, in April. In the second trial, which opened in May, 77 businessmen, bankers and government officials appeared in court charged with the fraudulent procurement of state loans; in August six of the defendants were sentenced to death (although two of these subsequently had their sentences commuted to life imprisonment), six others to life imprisonment, and the remainder to various other terms of imprisonment. In December, in a further demonstration of the efforts of the Communist Party to address the perceived problem of corruption within the party and the Government itself, Deputy Prime Minister Ngo Xuan Loc was dismissed from the Cabinet; although not publicly accused of corruption, Ngo Xuan Loc was dismissed from the Government following his implication in a corrupt land deal related to a private-sector project. However, in April 2000 he was reinstated to a government post and resumed responsibility for the sectors connected to the initial accusations against him, thus attracting speculation as to the extent of the Government's attempts to eliminate corruption. In September 2001 eight officials were tried on charges of fraud in Hanoi in connection with the land deal. One businessman received a 20-year prison sentence; the remaining defendants were either released or sentenced to prison terms of nine months or less.

In March 2000 Prime Minister Phan Van Khai appointed Deputy Prime Minister Nguyen Tan Dung as deputy head of the Steering Committee for Administrative Reform, with the aim of accelerating the process of decision-making on political reform. On 30 April massive celebrations were held in Ho Chi Minh City to mark the 25th anniversary of the fall of the city and the subsequent reunification of North and South Viet Nam. Some 12,000 prisoners were given an amnesty during the celebrations. In the same month the President's Office promulgated five new laws designed to create more favourable conditions for foreign investment, improve the country's research and development facilities and promote the role of the family in society. In August 2000 President Tran Duc Luong announced an amnesty for 10,693 prisoners, to coincide with the 55th National Day, on 2 September.

Viet Nam experienced its worst flooding in more than 40 years in September 2000, as the Mekong River rose to exceptionally high levels. By late October more than 400 people had been killed, over 760,000 houses had been inundated, 40,000 families evacuated and 500,000 people left in need of emergency aid. Destruction of crops, schools and provincial roads was widespread. Viet Nam invited international relief agencies to help mitigate the disaster, and several western countries provided financial and humanitarian aid.

In October 2000 the Politburo issued orders to develop the country's information technology (IT) capabilities and raise them to a level comparable to other countries in the region by 2010. The order emphasized the application of IT for the development of economics, culture and society, along with defence and security, and aimed to make IT a key sector of the economy. Also in October the Ministry of Public Security announced a nation-wide campaign against the use of illicit drugs. In November Communist Party documents divulged to the US-based human rights group, Freedom House, emphasized the leadership's level of concern regarding the increasing number of ethnic minorities converting to Christianity, and the fear that religion would be used by the USA and other countries to undermine communism in Viet Nam. In December the Minister of National Defence, Lt-Gen. Pham Van Tra, instructed the army not to become depoliticized, and to remain vigilant and safeguard the Communist Party and the socialist system. His directive was reiterated by the Party General Secretary, Le Kha Phieu, who in January 2001 urged the army to preserve political stability and guard against attempts to undermine socialism. The Eighth Session of the National Assembly held in December 2000 discussed the issue of whether or not party members should be allowed to conduct private economic activities as business individuals.

Ethnic violence broke out in the Central Highland provinces of Gia Lai and Dac Lac in February 2001, as local hill minorities (known as Montagnards) protested against perceived injustices caused by the migration of ethnic Vietnamese from the densely populated coastal regions and by the deforestation resulting from the establishment of coffee plantations. Some 5,000 protesters in the provincial capitals of Pleiku and Buon Ma Thuot respectively attacked state offices and blocked roads. The Vietnamese authorities deployed troops, riot police, water cannon and helicopters to quell the unrest, and injuries were reported on both sides. Some 20 people were arrested in connection with instigating the violence, which was attributed to 'extremists' seeking to use religion to foment unrest. The protesters had demanded autonomy, freedom to practise their Protestant religion, the return of ancestral lands confiscated for use as coffee plantations and the right to preserve their traditional way of life. The Ministry of Public Security accused the US-based Montagnard Foundation of organizing the violence, stating that several of those arrested were former members of the United Front for the Liberation of Oppressed Races (FULRO), a guerrilla unit that had close ties to the US Military and Central Intelligence Agency (CIA) during the Viet Nam war. The Vietnamese authorities also stated that during 2000 there had been several incursions into the country by agents of Free Viet Nam, a movement based in Thailand. The unrest coincided with a climate of increasing repression of religion, and it was feared that 'hardliners' in the Communist Party might use the incident to strengthen their position and to delay economic and political reforms. In March the authorities denounced a Catholic priest, Nguyen Van Ly, for writing to the US Congress and urging it not to ratify a bilateral trade agreement, owing to human rights abuses in Viet Nam. Nguyen Van Ly was accused of undermining Viet Nam's independence and was placed under house arrest. In October he was sentenced to 15 years in prison after a court convicted him of undermining national unity and contravening a detention order. Exiled Vietnamese Buddhist leaders also claimed that their followers in Viet Nam were routinely harassed. In September 2001 Ho Tan Anh, leader of the Buddhist Youth Movement, burnt himself to death in protest at the restrictions that had been imposed upon his organization.

The Ninth Party Congress was held in April 2001, and resulted in the election of a new 150-member Central Committee, 15-member Politburo and nine-member Secretariat. Nong Duc Manh was appointed General Secretary, replacing Le Kha Phieu, who was accused of using military intelligence against Party members and slowing the pace of reforms. Phieu had agreed to step down after pressure from the Central Committee. Nong Duc Manh, who was rumoured to be the illegitimate son of Ho Chi Minh, was the first ethnic Tay to attain such a senior position. Some 84 members of the previous Central Committee were re-elected. President Tran Duc Luong and Prime Minister Phan Van Khai retained their party posts. However, former President Le Duc Anh, former Prime Minister Vo Van Kiet and former General Secretary Do Muoi lost their positions as senior advisers to the Central Committee upon the abolition of the posts. Manh was believed to favour economic reforms and greater democracy, the latter a major theme at the Congress. However, the Congress reiterated its commitment to socialism as a means to national industrialization and modernization. In June 2001 Nguyen Van An, a member of the Politburo, was elected to the chairmanship of the National Assembly, succeeding Nong Duc Manh.

In September 2001 14 Montagnards received sentences of between six and 12 years' imprisonment for participating in the protests of February of that year. In October a further six men were convicted of distributing propaganda and inciting ethnic unrest in the city of Buon Ma Thuot during the disturbances. No diplomats or foreign journalists were permitted to attend the trials. A critical report issued by the international organization Human Rights Watch in April 2002 warned of further violence in the Central Highlands if the Government continued to implement its repressive policies towards ethnic minorities. In November 2002 it was alleged that the Government had executed three Montagnards in the previous month, reportedly owing to their involvement in the violence of February 2001. In December a further eight people were convicted of charges of undermining national unity, having allegedly aided people attempting to leave the region following the violence. In January 2003, according to Human Rights Watch, 70 Montagnards were known to be imprisoned in Viet Nam owing to their political or religious beliefs.

In December 2001 the National Assembly gave its approval to several constitutional amendments, including one allowing politicians to instigate mid-term votes of no confidence if they considered any minister to be performing unsatisfactorily. The amendments were intended to encourage the development of Viet Nam's market economy and improve democracy, thus facilitating the country's further integration into the international community.

It was reported in January 2002 that the Communist Party had passed a decree authorizing the police to engage in the destruction of publications that had not been approved by the party. Books written by several leading dissidents, including Gen. Tran Do, had subsequently been destroyed. In March 2002 the Politburo was reported to have established a special investigation into allegations that more than 50 government officials had colluded in organized crime. Several of those accused were reported to have accepted bribes to protect a gang whose alleged leader, Truong Van Cam, also known as Nam Cam, was undergoing investigation on murder charges. As the investigation continued, more than 100 government officials and an estimated 50 police officers were implicated; two members of the Central Committee (the Director-General of the state radio station Voice of Viet Nam, Tran Mai Hanh, and Pham Sy Chien) were expelled from the Communist Party in July owing to their involvement.

In November 2002 the Deputy Minister of Public Security, Maj.-Gen. Haong Ngoc Nhat, was dismissed from his position and demoted in rank, owing to his alleged complicity. In January 2003 the director of the Economic Commission of the Politburo, Truong Tan San, became the most senior member of the Communist Party to be punished in relation to the investigation; he was formally reprimanded for 'dereliction of duty' during his tenure as secretary of the party in Ho Chi Minh City in 1996–2000.

Meanwhile, in March 2002 the Communist Party decided that it would formally permit its members to engage in private business, indicating the Government's desire to encourage the expansion of the role of the private sector within the economy. In April 59 people went on trial in Ho Chi Minh City charged with embezzling state assets and violating commercial law in connection with the Chinese-owned Viet Hoa bank. The case proceeded despite the death of an alleged principal participant in the fraud, Tran Tuan Tai—the head of the bank—in 1997, after which the bank's licence was revoked. In the following month all of those tried were found guilty of the charges against them; 43 were sentenced to prison terms of varying lengths while those remaining were given suspended sentences. The trial was widely perceived to constitute a further attempt on the part of the Government to take firm action against corruption.

Elections to the 11th National Assembly took place on 19 May 2002. The 498 seats available were contested by 759 candidates, only 13 of whom were independent. Non-Communist Party candidates won 51 seats and independents two, the remainder being secured by party members. In July and August the newly elected National Assembly held its first session, during which significant reorganizations of both the Standing Committee and the Cabinet were approved. Three new ministries were created during the extensive reshuffle, in which Vu Khoan, the former Minister of Trade, was promoted to the position of Deputy Prime Minister and former Minister of Public Security Le Minh Huong was replaced by Politburo member Le Hong Anh. President Tran Duc Luong, Prime Minister Phan Van Khai and the Chairman of the National Assembly, Nguyen Van An, were all formally re-elected to their posts, while Truong My Hoa succeeded Nguyen Thi Binh as Vice-President.

In November 2002 Le Chi Quang, a lawyer, was convicted of committing 'acts of propaganda' against the State, following his arrest in February of that year for allegedly publishing material critical of the Government on the internet. He was sentenced to a four-year prison term. In the following month another dissident, Nguyen Khac Toan, was sentenced to 12 years in prison, having been convicted of using the internet for espionage purposes. In March 2003 the dissident Nguyen Dan Que, who had spent over 18 years in prison for campaigning for improved democracy and human rights in Viet Nam, was arrested again, having been freed from prison five years previously. The human rights organization Amnesty International demanded his immediate release. Meanwhile, at the Seventh Plenum of the Central Committee of the Communist Party held in January 2003, a resolution was passed intended to increase the Party's control over religious affairs. At the Plenum Nguyen Van Chi was appointed to the Party Secretariat.

In February 2003 the trial of Nam Cam and 154 other defendants on a number of charges, including murder, organized gambling, bribery, drug-trafficking and extortion, began in Ho Chi Minh City. Amongst the defendants were 21 former state and government officials. The hearings constituted Viet Nam's largest corruption trial to date.

In April 2003 Prime Minister Phan Van Khai held talks with Thich Huyen Quang, leader of the anti-Government Unified Buddhist Church of Viet Nam, who had been held under house arrest since the group was proscribed almost 20 years previously. While the meeting was welcomed by international diplomats, there was speculation that the Communist Party might use it to respond to continued criticism of its human rights record, while avoiding making any more substantial reforms.

By the end of 1976, meanwhile, Viet Nam had established diplomatic relations with many countries, including all of its South-East Asian neighbours. However, tension arose over the growing number of Vietnamese refugees (particularly ethnic Chinese) arriving in Thailand and other nearby countries. In 1979 more than 200,000 fled Viet Nam, and in July an international conference was convened in Geneva to discuss the situation. The Orderly Departure Programme, sponsored by the office of the UN High Commissioner for Refugees (UNHCR), whereby Viet Nam agreed to legal departures, was negotiated, and by the end of 1988 about 140,000 people had left the country in this way. Illegal departures continued, however, and the increasing reluctance of Western countries to provide resettlement opportunities led to a meeting in Malaysia in March 1989, at which representatives of 30 nations were present and a comprehensive programme of action was drafted. Members of the Association of South East Asian Nations (ASEAN, see p. 146) subsequently ceased to accept refugees for automatic resettlement and planned to institute a screening procedure to distinguish genuine refugees from economic migrants. A similar procedure had been in effect since June 1988 in Hong Kong, and an agreement had been signed in November, whereby Viet Nam agreed to accept voluntary repatriation of refugees from Hong Kong, funded by UNHCR and the United Kingdom, with UN supervision to protect the returning refugees from punitive measures by the Vietnamese Government.

In June 1989 a UN-sponsored conference adopted the so-called Comprehensive Action Plan that had been drafted in March, introducing screening procedures to distinguish political refugees from economic migrants (who might be forcibly repatriated if efforts to secure their voluntary return proved unsuccessful). In December the United Kingdom forcibly repatriated a group of 51 Vietnamese from Hong Kong, provoking international criticism; this policy was abandoned as a result both of opposition by the USA and of Viet Nam's refusal to accept further deportations. In July 1990, however, the USA accepted in principle the 'involuntary' repatriation of refugees classed as economic migrants who did not actively oppose deportation. In September the United Kingdom, Viet Nam and UNHCR reached an agreement whereby the Vietnamese Government would no longer refuse refugees who had been repatriated 'involuntarily'. In May 1992 the United Kingdom and Viet Nam signed an agreement providing for the compulsory repatriation of all economic migrants from Hong Kong. In 1991–95 some 66,132 Vietnamese were voluntarily repatriated, while an additional 1,562 were forcibly returned. In January 1996 ASEAN member states, including Viet Nam (see below), agreed that all Vietnamese residing in South-East Asian refugee camps (apart from those in Hong Kong) would be repatriated by the end of June of that year. (The People's Republic of China had already indicated that all Vietnamese refugees in Hong Kong should be returned prior to the transfer of the territory to Chinese sovereignty in June 1997.) In March 1996 UNHCR announced that it would suspend funding of Vietnamese refugee camps from the end of June. Also in March 217 refugees were released from camps in Hong Kong, after Viet Nam refused to accept them on the grounds that they were not Vietnamese nationals. In April a new initiative, proposed by the US Government in an effort to accelerate the repatriation programme, whereby refugees who returned to Viet Nam would be eligible to apply for settlement in the USA under a new screening process, was received with caution by the Vietnamese authorities. In June 1996 both Malaysia and Singapore closed their camps, following the repatriation of all Vietnamese refugees from those countries. In September 1996 and February 1997 respectively Indonesia and Thailand also closed their camps, leaving Hong Kong as the only South-East Asian country with a significant number (12,000 in November 1996) of Vietnamese refugees. In December it was reported that a scheme operated under the aegis of the European Commission, the Returnee Assistance Programme, to assist returning refugees in re-establishing themselves in Viet Nam, was in disarray owing to financial disagreement. The programme had been established in June and was intended to last for three years. (In July 1999 the European Union (EU, see p. 199) announced that it was terminating its support for the programme.) In December 1996 repatriates were prohibited from engaging in any type of political activity, and from January 1997 anti-communist activists and critics of the Government were banned from returning to Viet Nam. In mid-June the main Vietnamese detention centre in Hong Kong was closed. However, the scheduled repatriation of all remaining Vietnamese (estimated at some 1,600 people qualifying as refugees and 700 non-refugees) before the transfer of sovereignty of the territory to the People's Republic of China at the end of the month was not achieved. In January 1998 Hong Kong announced that it was to discontinue its policy of granting a port of first asylum to Vietnamese refugees. However, in July 1999 Hong Kong announced that the Vietnamese that remained in the territory—estimated to number around 1,400, some classed as refugees, others as 'stateless' persons—would be given permanent residency in Hong Kong; the last remaining camp for Vietnamese refugees in Hong Kong was closed in May 2000.

Following the unrest in the Central Highlands in February 2001 (see above), many Montagnards fled over the border into Cambodia, where they were accommodated in two camps situated in the provinces of Mondol Kiri and Rotanak Kiri. By December 2001 the camps housed 805 refugees, who sought a supervised return to the Highlands, accompanied by a guarantee that they would be given permission to reoccupy their ancestral lands. In January 2002 Viet Nam and Cambodia signed a joint repatriation agreement with UNHCR, and in February a total of 15 refugees left the camps to return to their home in Kon Tum province. Later in the same month the Vietnamese Government criticized UNHCR for the delay in the repatriation of the refugees (of whom there were now more than 1,000). It had imposed a deadline of 30 April 2002 for the completion of the repatriation process. The programme was later suspended, as UNHCR claimed that by imposing the deadline the Government was undermining the voluntary nature of returns. In March 2002 UNHCR announced its withdrawal from the agreement, owing to the frequent intimidation of both refugees and UN staff at the camps. Its decision was precipitated by an incident in which more than 400 Vietnamese had crossed the border with Cambodia and threatened inmates and staff at the Mondol Kiri camp. Following the termination of the agreement, the US Government stated that it was prepared to offer asylum to the refugees who remained in Cambodia. The Cambodian Government announced in April that, while it would authorize the resettlement of the Montagnard refugees in the USA, it planned to close down the camps housing the refugees and cease its provision of asylum within one month. In early April 2003 the Cambodian Government also announced its intention to shut the refugee transit centre operated by UNHCR in Phnom-Penh as soon as the remaining refugees housed there had been resettled.

Relations with Kampuchea (known as Cambodia until 1976 and again from 1989) deteriorated during 1977, and in December Viet Nam launched a major offensive into eastern Kampuchea. Sporadic fighting continued, and in December 1978 Viet Nam invaded Kampuchea in support of elements opposed to the regime (see the chapter on Cambodia). By January 1979 the Government of Pol Pot had been overthrown and a pro-Vietnamese regime was installed. The invasion prompted much international criticism, and in February 1979 Chinese forces launched a punitive attack across the border into Viet Nam. Peace talks began in April but made little progress, and in March 1980 they were suspended by the People's Republic of China. In March 1983 Viet Nam rejected a five-point peace plan, proposed by China, aimed at resolving the dispute over Kampuchea. In 1984 Chinese and Vietnamese troops engaged in heavy fighting, accusing each other of persistent border violations. China refused to normalize relations with Viet Nam until the withdrawal of Vietnamese troops from Kampuchea. Throughout 1986 and 1987 further armed clashes between Vietnamese and Chinese soldiers occurred on the Sino-Vietnamese border. Both sides denied responsibility for initiating the attacks. In early 1988 the tension between the two countries was exacerbated by the re-emergence of conflict over the Spratly Islands in the South China Sea, when the Vietnamese Government alleged that China had dispatched warships to the islands. (For many years the sovereignty of the islands had been contested, not only by Viet Nam and China, which engaged in military conflict concerning the islands in 1974, but also by the neighbouring states of Brunei, Malaysia, the Philippines and Taiwan. In November 2002 a declaration was issued to govern the conduct of the parties involved which would, it was hoped, bring an end to the ongoing tensions in the area.)

In March 1984 Viet Nam agreed in principle that it would eventually withdraw its troops from Kampuchea, and in August 1985 it was announced that all Vietnamese troops would be withdrawn by 1990. An eight-point peace plan, proposed by Kampuchean resistance leaders in March 1986 (involving the installation of a quadripartite government in Kampuchea, to be followed by UN-supervised elections), was rejected by Viet Nam. Viet Nam's urgent need of Western aid, together with increasing pressure from the USSR, prompted an announcement in May 1988 that Viet Nam would withdraw 50,000 (of an estimated total of 100,000) troops from Kampuchea by the end of 1988. The Vietnamese military high command left Kampuchea in June, placing the remainder of the Vietnamese forces under Kampuchean control. Viet Nam announced that the withdrawal from Kampuchea would be complete by the end of 1989.

In April 1989 the Vietnamese Government and the Heng Samrin regime in Kampuchea declared that Vietnamese troops would withdraw by September even if a political settlement had not been reached, on condition that military assistance to the three other Kampuchean factions also ceased by that date. The People's Republic of China responded that it would halt military aid to the Khmers Rouges only after a complete withdrawal of Vietnamese troops had been verified. The Vietnamese Government claimed that the withdrawal of troops had been completed by the end of September 1989. However, the absence of a UN commission to verify the troops' departure led to claims by the Government-in-exile of Democratic Kampuchea that a number of troops remained in the country, while China, the ASEAN countries and the USA initially refused to recognize the alleged withdrawal. In July 1990 the USA finally acknowledged that all troops had been withdrawn.

In September 1990 secret negotiations took place between Viet Nam and the People's Republic of China, during which the Vietnamese endorsed a new UN Security Council agreement to resolve the conflict in Cambodia (q.v.). It was widely believed that the Chinese had promised an improvement in Sino-Vietnamese relations in exchange for Vietnamese support for the UN plan. In October 1991 Viet Nam was a signatory to a peace agreement whereby an interim Supreme National Council was established in Cambodia, representing all four factions there, as a prelude to the holding of UN-supervised elections. The agreement allowed immediate progress towards ending Viet Nam's diplomatic and economic isolation (see below). During 1992–93 there were several massacres of civilians of Vietnamese origin living in Cambodia. In January 1995 the First Prime Minister of Cambodia, Prince Norodom Ranariddh, visited Viet Nam for discussions. In November of that year Viet Nam accused the Cambodian Government of supporting a dissident Vietnamese movement, based in Phnom-Penh. In January 1996 it was reported that Cambodian troops had opened fire in a southern border area; Cambodia subsequently claimed that Vietnamese forces had made incursions into Cambodian territory. Discussions between Vietnamese and Cambodian government officials on the border issue took place in April and May. In March 1997 Viet Nam and Cambodia signed an agreement on bilateral co-operation in combating crime and, during 2000, security officials from the two countries signed a number of agreements aimed at combating drug-trafficking and strengthening border controls.

From the mid-1970s Viet Nam developed closer relations with the USSR, and became increasingly dependent on its support. In 1990–91 the USSR substantially reduced financial assistance to Viet Nam. After the dissolution of the USSR, the Vietnamese Government pursued close relations with its successor states. In June 1994 Vo Van Kiet visited Ukraine, Kazakhstan and Russia to discuss economic and defence co-operation issues. During a visit by the Russian Minister of Foreign Affairs in July 1995, it was agreed that Russian vessels would continue to use the former Soviet naval base at Cam Ranh Bay, in central Viet Nam. In February 1997 Russia announced plans further to develop its defence ties with Viet Nam, and in November of that year the Russian Prime Minister, Viktor Chernomyrdin, paid an official visit to Viet Nam; Tran Duc Luong made a reciprocal visit to Russia in August 1998. The Russian Deputy Prime Minister, Viktor Khristenko, visited Viet Nam in July 2000 to discuss Russian involvement in oil and gas development, and Viet Nam's outstanding 11,000m. rouble Soviet-era debt. Agreement on the latter was reached in September, when it was arranged that Viet Nam would repay Russia US $1,700m. over 23 years, mostly in the form of business concessions. A major concern for Russia was its continued use of the naval base at Cam Ranh Bay. Under a 1978 agreement, Russia was to have access to the facilities until 2004. In February–March 2001 the Russian President, Vladimir Putin, became the first Russian (or Soviet) Head of State to visit Viet Nam. The two countries agreed to strengthen co-operation in economic, energy, and military and defence matters, and proclaimed a new 'strategic partnership'. The two leaders also supported non-involvement by other countries in their internal affairs, and expressed their opposition to the USA's planned missile defence shield. In May 2002 control of the naval base at Cam Ranh Bay was formally transferred to the Vietnamese Government, two years ahead of the agreed date. President Tran Duc Luong visited Ukraine in April 2000 and pledged to increase bilateral economic and political co-operation.

Viet Nam also signed a military co-operation agreement with Ukraine in May.

The collapse of communism in Eastern Europe prompted renewed efforts by Viet Nam to restore political and economic links with the People's Republic of China. Relations between Viet Nam and China improved significantly in the second half of 1990, owing to the co-operation of the Vietnamese Government concerning Cambodia. After the conclusion of the Cambodian peace agreement in October 1991, Vo Van Kiet and Do Muoi paid an official visit to China in November, during which normal diplomatic relations were restored and agreements were concluded on trade and on border affairs, while in March 1992 further agreements were signed on the resumption of transport and communications links (severed in 1979), and on the reopening of border posts. In May 1992 Viet Nam protested to China when the latter unilaterally granted exploration rights to a US petroleum company in an area of the South China Sea regarded by Viet Nam as part of its continental shelf. Several more protests were lodged later in the year over the presence of Chinese vessels in disputed areas. In November the Chinese Premier, Li Peng, made an official visit to Viet Nam (the first visit by a Chinese head of government since 1971): new agreements on economic, scientific and cultural co-operation were signed, and the two Governments agreed to accelerate negotiations on disputed territory that had begun in the previous month. In October 1993 Viet Nam and China concluded an agreement to avoid the use of force when resolving territorial disputes. In November 1994 the two countries agreed to co-operate in seeking an early resolution to all border disputes. However, tension remained over the issue of the sovereignty of the Spratly Islands (where significant reserves of petroleum and natural gas were believed to be situated). During an official visit by Do Muoi to China in November 1995, it was agreed that rail links between the two countries would be restored (they were subsequently reopened in February 1996). In April 1996 the state-owned petroleum company, Petrovietnam, signed a joint exploration contract with a US enterprise that covered part of the South China Sea where the Chinese Government had granted exploration rights in May 1992. In May 1996 China agreed to abide by the UN Convention on the Law of the Sea, which provided for international arbitration, but at the same time announced a new delineation of its sea border, attracting criticism from Viet Nam and other nations in the region.

In March 1997 Chinese vessels entered Vietnamese waters around the disputed Spratly Islands and were believed to be carrying out exploratory activities. China defended its actions, declaring a legitimate claim to the territory. In April China agreed to hold talks with Viet Nam over the issue; however, China withdrew the vessels before the discussions took place, stating that its operation in the area had been completed. In May China ratified the opening to traffic of a sea route between north-east Viet Nam and China. In July Do Muoi visited China and met with President Jiang Zemin to discuss the development of bilateral relations. In October 1998 Phan Van Khai made an official visit to China, during which it was agreed that Viet Nam and China would increase efforts to reach a settlement on their various border disputes; in November, however, Viet Nam reiterated its territorial claim to the disputed Spratly Islands. In February 1999 Le Kha Phieu paid an official visit to China, and in December the Chinese Premier, Zhu Rongji, visited Viet Nam. Also in December a formal border treaty was signed by Viet Nam and China. Vietnamese leaders travelled to China in June 2000 to attend an ideological symposium on methods of introducing market reforms without incurring any loss of political control. The visit was regarded as a major improvement in bilateral relations, and was followed by a second symposium in Hanoi in November. The two countries also made further progress in delineating their mutual land border, which took effect from July 2000, and finalized their border in the Gulf of Tonkin in late December, the latter agreement demarcating their economic and fishing zones. Chinese military delegations visited Viet Nam in July 2000 and February 2001 to enhance military co-operation, and President Tran Duc Luong visited China in December 2000 and 2001. In February 2002 Chinese President Jiang Zemin paid an official visit to Viet Nam, his second since the restoration of normal bilateral relations in 1991. His visit coincided with campaigns mounted by several dissidents expressing concern over the agreements that had been signed to demarcate the Sino-Vietnamese border. An ongoing dispute over fishing rights in the Gulf of Tonkin prevented the ratification of any agreement to delineate the shared maritime boundary.

During the Chinese President's visit modest agreements on technical and economic co-operation were signed, and the framework was agreed for a Chinese loan of US $12m. to Viet Nam. In April 2002 it was reported that the two countries had begun the three-year process of demarcating their land border. In November of that year, following an ASEAN summit meeting attended by China, a declaration was issued outlining a code of conduct to be observed by those countries contesting the Spratly Islands. It was hoped that the agreement would end Viet Nam's dispute with China over the issue.

In the late 1990s Viet Nam developed closer links with India, ostensibly because of mutual concerns about China. The Indian Minister of Defence, George Fernandes, visited Viet Nam in March 2000 and signed a wide-ranging defence agreement that would allow Viet Nam to train the Indian army in jungle warfare and counter-insurgency methods, and India to assist in the modernization of the Vietnamese military. The two countries also agreed to take action to combat piracy in the South China Sea. The Indian Minister of External Affairs, Jaswant Singh, and Prime Minister Atal Bihari Vajpayee made separate visits to Viet Nam in November 2000 and January 2001 respectively and agreed to co-ordinate their positions in the Non-Aligned Movement (NAM), South-South Co-operation, and regional forums. India's Oil and Natural Gas Company became an investor in Viet Nam's Nam Con Son gas field in 2000, and India pledged some US $238m. of investment in the Vietnamese petroleum and gas industries. In September 2001 the Minister of Foreign Affairs, Nguyen Dy Nien, visited India, and in March 2002 Vice-President Nguyen Thi Binh also visited the country to discuss the possibility of closer bilateral co-operation.

From 1984 Viet Nam indicated that it would welcome a return to normal diplomatic relations with the USA, but the latter rejected any re-establishment of relations until agreements were made concerning the return to the USA of the remains of US soldiers 'missing in action' (MIA) from Viet Nam, and the proposed resettlement in the USA of some 10,000 Vietnamese 'political prisoners'. A number of senior US officials visited Hanoi during 1985 and 1986 for discussions about missing soldiers (estimated to total 1,797), and Viet Nam arranged for the return of some of the remains. In September 1987 the Vietnamese Government agreed to investigate the fate of some 70 soldiers who were believed to have been captured alive, while the US Government, in turn, agreed to facilitate humanitarian aid for Viet Nam from US charities and private groups, which had hitherto been illegal. In July 1988 Viet Nam agreed in principle to the resettlement of former political detainees in the USA or elsewhere. In early 1991 a US representative was stationed in Hanoi to supervise inquiries into MIA, the first official US presence in Viet Nam since 1975. In April 1991 the USA proposed a four-stage programme for the resumption of normal diplomatic relations with Viet Nam, conditional on Vietnamese co-operation in reaching a diplomatic settlement in Cambodia and in accounting for the remaining MIA. Following the conclusion of the peace agreement on Cambodia in October, Viet Nam made a plea for the removal of the US economic embargo, and in November discussions on the establishment of normal relations began. In early 1992 the US Government agreed to provide humanitarian aid for Viet Nam, but refused to end the economic embargo, reiterating that relations would not fully return to normal until after the UN-supervised elections in Cambodia, due to take place in early 1993. The embargo was renewed for another year in September 1992, although in December the US Government announced that US companies would now be allowed to open offices and sign contracts in Viet Nam, in anticipation of a future removal of the embargo. In July 1993 the new administration of President Bill Clinton revoked the US veto on assistance from the IMF and the World Bank for Viet Nam. In September the USA permitted US companies to take part in projects in Viet Nam that were financed by international aid agencies. The trade embargo was finally removed in February 1994.

In January 1995 Viet Nam and the USA signed an agreement that permitted the two countries to establish liaison offices in each other's capitals (these were opened immediately), and which resolved a long-standing dispute concerning former US diplomatic properties seized by the Vietnamese authorities in 1975. The establishment of full diplomatic relations was announced in July 1995. In May 1996 Clinton formally ended Viet Nam's official classification as a combat zone. In March 1997 military relations were established between the two countries. In April Douglas Peterson was appointed as the first US

ambassador to Viet Nam, and in May Le Van Bang was formally appointed the first Vietnamese ambassador to the USA. Also in April the Vietnamese Government agreed to repay a debt outstanding from the Saigon regime to the US Government. In June 1997 Madeleine Albright was the first US Secretary of State to visit the country since the end of the Viet Nam war. During a visit to Washington, DC, by the Vietnamese Minister of Planning and Investment, Tran Xuan Gia, an agreement was signed to promote greater economic co-operation. This was facilitated in March 1998, when Clinton signed a waiver to the 'Jackson-Vanik amendment' to 1974 US trade legislation, which restricted trade with communist countries. (In August 1999 the US House of Representatives voted in favour of an extension of the waiver of the amendment for Viet Nam.) In September 1998 the Vietnamese Deputy Prime Minister and Minister of Foreign Affairs, Nguyen Manh Cam, made an official visit to the USA at the invitation of the US Secretary of State. In July 1999 Viet Nam and the USA reached agreement in principle on the establishment of normal trade relations between the two countries. Madeleine Albright made another official visit to Viet Nam in September 1999. In March 2000 the US Secretary of Defense, William Cohen, made an official visit to Viet Nam; Cohen's visit represented the first to Viet Nam by a US Secretary of Defense since the end of the Viet Nam war.

Although in early 2000 the US Government continued to refuse to acknowledge the responsibility of the chemical defoliant Agent Orange, sprayed in large quantities over areas of Viet Nam by the USA during the Viet Nam war, for widespread health problems (including birth defects) among the Vietnamese, Cohen, during his visit in March, reportedly indicated that the US Government would be willing to conduct joint research with the Vietnamese Government into the effects of the chemical. In May the US House of Representatives passed a resolution calling for the release of all political and religious prisoners in Viet Nam, a motion that was criticized as 'impudent interference' by Viet Nam. A landmark bilateral trade agreement between the USA and Viet Nam was signed in Washington, DC, in July 2000, paving the way for an increase in exports to, and investment from, the USA. The agreement was subject to an annual review by the US Congress. In September the US State Department released a report on religious freedom in 104 countries, which included strong criticism of Viet Nam. US President Bill Clinton made a highly significant visit to Viet Nam in November 2000, the first since a brief stop-over by Richard Nixon in 1969. Although warmly received by the Vietnamese people, Clinton's calls for greater freedoms were rebuffed by General Secretary Le Kha Phieu, who defended the socialist system. In March 2001 Viet Nam accused US-based groups of fomenting the recent unrest in the Central Highlands (see above). In April a helicopter carrying nine Vietnamese and seven US citizens, searching for the remains of MIA, crashed in the highlands, killing all on board. Some 1,498 US servicemen and 300,000 Vietnamese remained unaccounted for in Viet Nam.

Following the September 2001 attacks on the USA (see the chapter on the USA) the Vietnamese Government expressed its support for the US-led war on terrorism. In October the severe penalty imposed on the dissident Roman Catholic priest Father Nguyen Van Ly (see above) accelerated the passage of the Viet Nam Human Rights Act through the US Congress. The act made US non-humanitarian aid to Viet Nam conditional upon the improvement of its human rights record, thus angering the Vietnamese Government. In November the National Assembly finally ratified the bilateral trade agreement, marking the complete restoration of normal relations between the two countries. In December First Deputy Prime Minister Nguyen Tan Dung led a delegation of senior Vietnamese officials on a visit to the USA. In March 2002 Vietnamese and US scientists attended an unprecedented joint conference in Hanoi, at which the effects of Agent Orange were discussed. As a result, the two countries agreed to conduct joint research into the effects of the defoliant. However, relations with the USA threatened to deteriorate once more when the US Government expressed its concern for the safety of refugees returning to the Central Highlands from Cambodia. In March 2002, following the collapse of Viet Nam's agreement with UNHCR, the USA offered asylum to those refugees who remained in Cambodia. In the same month relations were further strained when the US Government issued a critical report on Viet Nam's human rights record.

Viet Nam's relations with Canada were suspended in late April 2000 following the execution of a Vietnamese-Canadian citizen on drugs-smuggling charges. However, in 2001 the two countries agreed to improve relations. Relations with Australia improved during 2000, with a visit by the Minister of Foreign Affairs, Alexander Downer, and the participation of Australian troops in the delivery of humanitarian aid following the heavy flooding in September 2000.

In October 1990 the European Community (now EU) announced the restoration of diplomatic relations with Viet Nam. In October 1991 a group of industrialized countries, led by France, agreed to assist Viet Nam in paying its arrears to the IMF, thereby enabling it to qualify for future IMF loans (which were, however, still dependent on the approval of the USA, as the IMF's principal vote-holder). In February 1993 President Mitterrand of France made an official visit to Viet Nam (the first Western Head of State to do so since the country's reunification). The President of the French Senate, Christian Poncelet, visited Viet Nam in April 2000, and General Secretary Le Kha Phieu visited Paris and Rome in May. France's Geopetrol oil company formed part of a consortium to develop Vietnamese offshore oil and gas deposits. In October 2002 President Tran Duc Luong paid the first visit to France by a Vietnamese leader since the establishment of diplomatic relations with France in 1973. In January 1992 a Japanese government mission visited Viet Nam to negotiate the repayment of Vietnamese debts, and in November Japan (which—although a principal trading partner —had hitherto imposed a ban on official economic co-operation) began to provide financial assistance to Viet Nam. In March 1999 Prime Minister Phan Van Khai made an official visit to Japan. In August 2000 a Japanese consortium pledged to assist the construction of nuclear power plants in Viet Nam. During 2000 Viet Nam and Japan also strengthened their defence links, with the aim of promoting regional security. In June 2001 Phan Van Khai paid a further visit to Japan.

The Cambodian peace agreement of 1991 allowed Viet Nam to initiate closer relations with ASEAN member states: Vo Van Kiet visited Indonesia, Thailand and Singapore in October and November 1991 and Malaysia, Brunei and the Philippines in early 1992; agreements on economic co-operation were concluded with these countries, including guarantees of protection for future investment by them in Viet Nam. In July 1992 Viet Nam signed the ASEAN agreement (of 1976) on regional amity and co-operation, and in July 1995 became a full member of the organization. In September 1992 an agreement was signed with Singapore on the mutual provision of 'most-favoured nation' trading status. In April 1995 Viet Nam, Thailand, Laos and Cambodia signed an agreement providing for the establishment of the Mekong River Commission (see p. 341), which was to co-ordinate the sustainable development of the resources of the Lower Mekong River basin. In October 1997 Viet Nam and Thailand reached an agreement to demarcate their maritime boundary, following a series of incidents between Vietnamese and Thai fishing vessels. At the 31st annual ASEAN ministerial meeting in July 1998 Viet Nam opposed a Thai initiative to modify ASEAN's long-standing policy of non-interference in the internal affairs of member countries in favour of a policy of 'flexible engagement'. In December 1998 Viet Nam hosted the sixth summit meeting of the heads of state and government of the ASEAN grouping of countries. During 2000 Viet Nam reaffirmed sovereignty over the Spratly and Paracel Islands, but reassured ASEAN that it was committed to a peaceful solution to the territorial dispute through multilateral negotiations. It was hoped that the declaration of November 2002, which established a code of conduct to be adhered to by the claimants of the islands, would provide such a solution. Vietnamese and Laotian officials held several meetings during the course of 2000, and Viet Nam provided assistance to Laos in its fight against ethnic Hmong rebels. In November 2001 President Tran Duc Long held talks with President Gloria Macapagal Arroyo while on an official visit to the Philippines. The two countries agreed to the enhancement of economic relations and to co-operation in trade, investment and tourism. In February 2002 the Prime Minister met with the Prime Ministers of Cambodia and Laos in Ho Chi Minh City. The three countries agreed to boost co-operation in the development of tourism and infrastructure within the 'development triangle'.

In mid-November 1997 Viet Nam hosted the seventh summit meeting of francophone states (La Francophonie), which was attended by representatives of 49 countries. In April 2000 President Tran Duc Luong attended the Group of 77 (G-77) South Summit meeting of developing countries, held in Havana, Cuba.

Government

The 1992 Constitution declares the supremacy of the Communist Party. Legislative power is vested in the National Assembly, which is elected for a five-year term by universal adult suffrage and, from 2002, had 498 members. The President, elected by the National Assembly from among its members, is the Head of State and Commander-in-Chief of the armed forces. The President appoints a Prime Minister (from among the members of the National Assembly, and subject to their approval), who forms a government (again, subject to ratification by the National Assembly). The country is divided into provinces and municipalities, which are subordinate to the central government. Local government is entrusted to locally elected People's Councils.

Defence

In August 2002 the active ('Main Force') armed forces of Viet Nam had an estimated total strength of 484,000: an estimated 412,000 in the army, an estimated 42,000 in the navy, and 30,000 in the air and air defence forces. Military service is compulsory and usually lasts for two years. Paramilitary forces number 4m.–5m. and include the urban People's Self-Defence Force and the rural People's Militia. The defence budget for 2002 was estimated at US $2,400m.

Economic Affairs

In 2001, according to estimates by the World Bank, Viet Nam's gross national income (GNI), measured at average 1999–2001 prices, was US $32,578m., equivalent to $410 per head (or $2,130 per head on an international purchasing-power parity basis). During 1990–2001, it was estimated, the population increased at an average annual rate of 1.7%, while gross domestic product (GDP) per head increased, in real terms, by an average of 5.5% per year. Overall GDP increased, in real terms, at an average annual rate of 7.3% in 1990–2001. According to official estimates, GDP grew by 6.8% in 2001 and by 7.0% in 2002.

Agriculture (including forestry and fishing) contributed an estimated 23.6% of GDP in 2001 and engaged 62.6% of the employed labour force in 2000. The staple crop is rice, which also provided 3.9% of total export earnings in 2001; in that year Viet Nam was the world's second-largest exporter of rice. Other important cash crops include sugar cane, coffee, groundnuts, rubber, tea and cotton. By 2000 Viet Nam had emerged as the world's second-biggest producer of coffee. In 1992, in an attempt to preserve Viet Nam's remaining forests, a ban was imposed on the export of logs and sawn timber, and in March 1997 a 10-year ban on all timber products except wooden artefacts was introduced. (The total forest area declined from 13.5m. ha in 1943 to 9.2m. ha in 1994.) Livestock-rearing and fishing are also important. In 2001 marine products accounted for some 12.0% of export revenues. According to the Asian Development Bank (ADB), agricultural GDP increased by an annual average of 4.2% in 1990–2000. The sector's GDP expanded by an estimated 4.6% in 2000 and by 2.8% in 2001.

In 2001 industry (comprising manufacturing, mining and quarrying, construction and power) contributed an estimated 37.8% of GDP. The industrial sector engaged 13.1% of the labour force in 2000. In 2000 the non-state economic sector accounted for an estimated 22.4% of industrial production. According to the ADB, industrial GDP increased by an annual average of 11.3% per year in 1990–2000. The sector's GDP expanded by 10.1% in 2000 and by 9.7% in 2001.

In 2001 mining and quarrying contributed an estimated 9.2% of GDP. In 2000 the mining sector engaged an estimated 0.6% of the labour force. Viet Nam's principal mineral exports are petroleum and coal. Tin, zinc, iron, antimony, chromium, natural phosphates, bauxite and gold are also mined. Significant reserves of offshore natural gas were discovered in 1993. In 2001 exports of crude petroleum accounted for 21.1% of total merchandise exports. Mining GDP increased by an estimated 7.2% in 2000 and by an estimated 4.1% in 2001.

Manufacturing contributed an estimated 19.6% of GDP in 2001, and accounted for 10.2% of employment in 1996. The main manufacturing sectors in 2000, measured by gross value of output, included food-processing, cigarettes and tobacco, textiles, chemicals, and electrical goods. According to the ADB, manufacturing GDP increased by an annual average of 10.9% in 1990–2000. Manufacturing GDP increased by an estimated 11.7% in 2000 and by an estimated 11.3% in 2001.

Energy is derived principally from hydroelectric installations, petroleum and coal. Although production of petroleum increased in the late 1980s and early 1990s, exports were mainly in the form of crude petroleum, and Viet Nam still relied on the import of refined products. Imports of petroleum products accounted for 11.6% of total imports in 2001. Nuclear power was also being developed from the 1990s onwards.

The services sector contributed an estimated 38.6% of GDP in 2001. Tourism is an important source of foreign exchange; in 2002 about 2.6m. foreign tourists visited Viet Nam and in 1998 receipts from tourism totalled some US $86m. According to the ADB, the GDP of the services sector increased by an average of 7.2% per year in 1990–2000. The sector's GDP rose by an estimated 5.3% in 2000 and by an estimated 6.1% in 2001.

In 2001 Viet Nam recorded a visible trade surplus of US $481m. The surplus on the current account of the balance of payments in that year was an estimated $682m. In 2001 Singapore was Viet Nam's principal source of imports (13.9%); other major sources were the People's Republic of China (12.2%), Japan (11.9%), and the Republic of Korea (11.4%). The principal market for exports in that year was Japan (17.5%); other important purchasers were Australia (9.0%), the People's Republic of China (7.7%), and the USA (7.3%). The principal exports in 2001 were petroleum, agricultural and forestry products (particularly rice and coffee), clothing, marine products and footwear. Principal imports included machinery and equipment, petroleum products, iron and steel, motorcycles and fertilizers. Illegal trade, which is widespread (and was exacerbated by legislation adopted in September 1992 banning the import of 17 commodities), was estimated to be equivalent to 50% of official trade in 1992.

In 2001 there was an estimated budgetary deficit of 14,210,000m. dông. In 2000 Viet Nam's total external debt was US $12,787m., of which $11,546m. was long-term public debt. In that year the cost of debt-servicing was equivalent to 7.5% of the value of exports of goods and services. The annual rate of inflation averaged 2.7% in 1996–2002, reaching 4.1% in 1999. Consumer prices declined by 0.4% in 2001 but increased by 3.9% in 2002. In 2000 about 6.4% of the labour force were officially stated to be unemployed.

Viet Nam is a member of the Asian Development Bank (ADB, see p. 143), the Association of South East Asian Nations (ASEAN, see p. 146), the Asia-Pacific Economic Co-operation (APEC, see p. 139) and the Mekong River Commission (see p. 341). Viet Nam also joined the ASEAN Free Trade Area (AFTA) in 1996 and was granted until 2003 to comply with the tariff reductions (to between 0% and 5%) required. The area was formally established on 1 January 2002.

From 1990 the process of *doi moi* (renovation) aimed to transform Viet Nam from a centralized economy to a market-orientated system. New investment laws allowed the establishment of wholly foreign-owned enterprises; agricultural production was stimulated by the removal of price controls, by a new system of land tenure and, from early 1998, the relaxation of the state monopoly on rice exports, with the result that by the mid-1990s Viet Nam, formerly dependent on rice imports, was among the world's principal rice exporters. The resumption of financing agreements with the IMF and the World Bank after 1993, and the ending of the US trade restriction from 1994, allowed new credits, debt relief and foreign investment. None the less, the country's underdeveloped infrastructure, bureaucratic delays and controls on foreign-exchange transactions, as well as a perceived lack of transparency and the slow pace of economic reform, continued to deter greater foreign investment throughout the 1990s. Despite a decline in performance precipitated by the regional economic crisis that originated in Thailand in mid-1997, from late 1999 the economy showed signs of recovery. The establishment of Viet Nam's first stock exchange in July 2000 was an important fiscal development; by November 2002 a total of 19 companies were listed on the exchange. In 2001 the pace of economic reforms accelerated. The Ninth Communist Party Congress approved a 10-year socio-economic development strategy which enhanced the role of the private sector, while simultaneously affirming the primacy of the State in motivating economic development. The Government also announced a Five-Year (2001–2005) Import-Export regime intended significantly to liberalize trade. In addition, a more flexible exchange rate policy was adopted. In December 2001 the National Assembly approved several amendments to the 1992 Constitution intended principally to encourage the development of the small-owner and foreign investment sectors, indicating its formal recognition of the private sector as an important part of the national economy. The implementation of such measures succeeded in promoting investment and strengthening domestic demand. In the same month a landmark bilateral agreement with the USA came into effect. As a result, in the first nine months of 2002 Vietnamese exports to the USA more than doubled in volume. However, in early 2003 the USA announced a preliminary decision to impose high tariffs on imports of frozen Vietnamese catfish, prompting criticism that the ruling undermined the increasing liberalization of trade between the two countries. Viet Nam recorded the highest regional rate of economic growth in 2002; GDP expanded by an estimated 7.0%. In that year a decline in exports, combined with an increase in demand for imports, contributed to a widening trade deficit. Exports of motorcycles, however, increased significantly, although the Government's decision later in the year to impose strict quotas on imports of the motorcycle kits upon which the industry depended was met with widespread criticism as it forced several companies to cease production. It was expected that a rise in global demand for Vietnamese exports in 2003, combined with an increasingly high level of remittances from Vietnamese workers abroad, would contribute to a recovery in trade and a narrowing of the deficit. In December 2002 revisions to the Budget Law resulted in the delegation of a significant amount of power in budgetary management to provincial and city authorities. Following improvements in legislation governing foreign investment in the country, levels of investment began to increase. However, Viet Nam's continued economic development, as well as its planned accession to the World Trade Organization (WTO) at the end of 2004, remained dependent upon the implementation of further reforms, particularly in state enterprises and the public administration sector. The World Bank forecast GDP growth of 7.0% in 2003.

Education

Primary education, which is compulsory, begins at six years of age and lasts for five years. Secondary education, beginning at the age of 11, lasts for seven years, comprising a first cycle of four years and a second cycle of three years. In 1997 total pre-primary enrolment was equivalent to 40% of children in the relevant age-group. In the same year total enrolment in primary education was equivalent to 113% of children in the relevant age-group (males 115%; females 111%), while total secondary enrolment was equivalent to 57% of children in the relevant age-group. In 1993/94 there were 104 universities and colleges of higher education, with a total enrolment of 509,300 students in 1996/97. In 1989 Viet Nam's first private college since 1954 was opened in Hanoi; Thang Long College was to cater for university students. Of total planned budgetary expenditure by the central Government in 2002, 13,581,000m. dông (11.3%) was allocated to education.

Public Holidays

2003: 1 January (New Year's Day), 1–3 February* (Tet, lunar new year), 3 February (Founding of the Communist Party), 30 April (Liberation of Saigon), 1 May (May Day), 2 September (National Day).

2004: 1 January (New Year's Day), 22–24 January* (Tet, lunar new year), 3 February (Founding of the Communist Party), 30 April (Liberation of Saigon), 1 May (May Day), 2 September (National Day).

*Varies according to the lunar calendar.

Weights and Measures

The metric system is in force.

Statistical Survey

Sources (unless otherwise stated): General Statistical Office of the Socialist Republic of Viet Nam, 2 Hoang Van Thu, Hanoi; tel. (4) 8464385; fax (4) 264345; Communist Party of Viet Nam.

Area and Population

AREA, POPULATION AND DENSITY

Area (sq km)	331,114*
Population (census results)	
1 April 1989	64,411,713
1 April 1999†	
Males	37,519,754
Females	38,804,999
Total	76,324,753
Population (official estimates at mid-year)	
2000	77,635,000
2001	78,686,000
Density (per sq km) at mid-2001	237.6

* 127,844 sq miles.
† Provisional.

ADMINISTRATIVE DIVISIONS
(estimates, 2001)

Provinces and cities	Area (sq km)	Population ('000)	Density (per sq km)
North Mountains and Midlands	104,801	13,423	128
Ha Giang	7,831	626	80
Tuyen Quang	5,801	693	120
Cao Bang	8,445	502	59
Lang Son	8,187	715	87
Lai Chau	17,131	616	36
Lao Cai	8,050	617	77
Yen Bai	6,808	700	103
Bac Can	4,796	283	59
Thai Nguyen	3,541	1,062	300
Son La	14,210	922	65
Hoa Binh	4,612	774	168
Phu Tho	3,465	1,288	372
Vinh Phuc	1,371	1,116	814
Bac Giang	3,817	1,522	399
Bac Ninh	797	958	1,202
Quang Ninh	5,939	1,030	173
Red River Delta	12,521	15,170	1,212
Hanoi	921	2,842	3,086
Haiphong	1,504	1,711	1,138
Hung Yen	895	1,091	1,219
Hai Duong	1,661	1,671	1,006
Ha Tay	2,147	2,432	1,133
Thai Binh	1,509	1,815	1,203
Nam Dinh	1,669	1,916	1,148
Ha Nam	827	800	967
Ninh Binh	1,388	892	643
North Central Coast	46,179	9,110	197
Thanh Hoa	11,168	3,510	314
Nghe An	16,381	2,914	178
Ha Tinh	6,054	1,285	212
Quang Binh	7,984	813	102
Quang Tri	4,592	589	128
South Central Coast	50,247	9,384	187
Thua Thien-Hué	5,009	1,079	215
Quang Nam	10,406	1,403	135
Da Nang	942	715	759
Quang Ngai	5,856	1,206	206
Binh Dinh	6,076	1,492	246
Phu Yen	5,278	811	154
Khanh Hoa	5,258	1,066	203
Ninh Thuan	3,430	532	155
Binh Thuan	7,992	1,080	135
Central Highlands	55,569	4,330	78
Gia Lai	15,662	1,048	67
Kon Tum	9,934	331	33
Dac Lac	19,800	1,901	96
Lam Dong	10,173	1,050	103

Provinces and cities — *continued*	Area (sq km)	Population ('000)	Density (per sq km)
North-East South	23,463	10,750	458
Ho Chi Minh City	2,090	5,378	2,573
Binh Duong	2,718	768	283
Binh Phuoc	6,814	708	104
Tay Ninh	4,020	990	246
Dong Nai	5,864	2,067	353
Ba Ria-Vung Tau	1,957	839	429
Mekong River Delta	39,554	16,519	418
Long An	4,338	1,348	311
Dong Thap	3,276	1,593	486
An Giang	3,424	2,099	613
Tien Giang	2,339	1,636	699
Ben Tre	2,247	1,308	582
Vinh Long	1,487	1,023	688
Tra Vinh	2,369	989	417
Can Tho	2,951	1,852	628
Soc Trang	3,191	1,213	380
Kien Giang	6,243	1,543	247
Bac Lieu	2,485	757	305
Ca Mau	5,204	1,158	223
Total	332,334	76,686	231

PRINCIPAL TOWNS
(estimated population, excl. suburbs, at mid-1992)

Ho Chi Minh City			
(formerly Saigon) .	3,015,743*	Nam Dinh . . .	171,699
Hanoi (capital) .	1,073,760	Qui Nhon . . .	163,385
Haiphong . .	783,133	Vung Tau . . .	145,145
Da Nang . . .	382,674	Rach Gia . . .	141,132
Buon Ma Thuot .	282,095	Long Xuyen . .	132,681
Nha Trang . .	221,331	Thai Nguyen . .	127,643
Hué	219,149	Hong Gai . . .	127,484
Can Tho . . .	215,587	Vinh	112,455
Cam Pha . . .	209,086		

* Including Cholon.

Source: UN, *Demographic Yearbook*.

Mid-2000 (UN estimates, incl. suburbs): Ho Chi Minh City 4,619,000; Hanoi 3,751,000; Haiphong 1,676,000 (Source: UN, *World Urbanization Prospects: The 2001 Revision*).

BIRTHS AND DEATHS
(UN estimates, annual averages)

	1985–90	1990–95	1995–2000
Birth rate (per 1,000) . . .	32.5	28.3	21.5
Death rate (per 1,000) . . .	9.3	8.1	7.0

Source: UN, *World Population Prospects: The 2000 Revision*.

Expectation of life (WHO estimates, years at birth): 69.3 (males 66.9; females 71.8) in 2001 (Source: WHO, *World Health Report*).

EMPLOYMENT
('000 persons)

	1995	1996	1997
Agriculture	24,537	24,543	
Forestry	228	232	24,814
Industry*	3,379	3,442	3,656
Construction	996	975	977
Trade and catering	2,290	2,677	2,672
Transport	512	799	
Communications	56	57	856
Science	38	39	41
Education	973	994	999
Culture, arts and sport	94	96	96
Public health	358	359	296
Other activities	1,128	1,579	2,587
Total employed	34,590	35,792	36,994

* Comprising manufacturing, mining and quarrying, electricity, gas and water.

Source: IMF, *Vietnam: Statistical Appendix* (July 1999).

1998 ('000): Total employment 37,877, of which 26,070 in agriculture, fisheries, and forestry; 3,656 in industry; and 980 in construction (Source: IMF, *Vietnam: Statistical Appendix* (August 2000)).

1999 ('000): Total employment 38,546, of which 26,591 in agriculture, fisheries, and forestry; 3,674 in industry; and 982 in construction (Source: IMF, *Vietnam: Statistical Appendix* (August 2000)).

2000 ('000): Total employment 36,206, of which 22,670 in agriculture, fisheries, and forestry and 4,744 in industry and construction (Source: IMF, *Vietnam: Selected Issues and Statistical Appendix* (January 2002)).

Health and Welfare

KEY INDICATORS

Total fertility rate (children per woman, 2001)	2.3
Under-5 mortality rate (per 1,000 live births, 2001)	38
HIV/AIDS (% of persons aged 15–49, 2001)	0.30
Physicians (per 1,000 head, 1998)	0.48
Hospital beds (per 1,000 head, 1997)	1.67
Health expenditure (2000): US $ per head (PPP)	129
Health expenditure (2000): % of GDP	5.2
Health expenditure (2000): public (% of total)	25.8
Access to water (% of persons, 2000)	56
Access to sanitation (% of persons, 2000)	73
Human Development Index (2000): ranking	109
Human Development Index (2000): value	0.688

For sources and definitions, see explanatory note on p. vi.

Agriculture

PRINCIPAL CROPS
('000 metric tons)

	1999	2000	2001
Rice (paddy)	31,394	32,530	31,970
Maize	1,753	2,006	2,123
Potatoes	330*	316	316*
Sweet potatoes	1,745	1,611	1,655
Cassava (Manioc)	1,801	1,986	2,806
Dry beans	144	145	147
Other pulses*	101	100	100
Cashew nuts†	165	270	272
Soybeans (Soya beans)	147	149	176
Groundnuts (in shell)	318	355	353
Coconuts	1,104	885	978
Dry onions*	184	187	187
Other vegetables*	5,939	6,100	6,824
Bananas	1,288	1,125	1,126
Oranges	384	427	428
Watermelons	200	200	200
Mangoes	175	177	179
Pineapples	256	291	285
Other fruit*	1,943	2,022	2,041
Sugar cane	17,760	16,975	14,326
Coffee (green)	553	803	844
Tea (made)	70	70	83
Tobacco (leaves)	36	27	27
Natural rubber	249	291	291

* FAO estimate(s).
† Unofficial figures.

Source: FAO.

LIVESTOCK
('000 head, year ending September)

	1999	2000	2001
Horses	150	127	121
Cattle	4,064	4,128	3,896
Buffaloes	2,956	2,897	2,819
Pigs	18,886	20,194	21,741
Goats	471	544	561
Chickens†	125,500	137,300	151,000
Ducks	53,800†	54,500*	57,000*

* FAO estimate.
† Unofficial figure(s).

Source: FAO.

LIVESTOCK PRODUCTS
('000 metric tons)

	1999	2000	2001
Beef and veal	88.5	92.3	97.0*
Buffalo meat*	90.3	92.5	96.8
Pig meat	1,318.4	1,409.0	1,415.5
Chicken meat	261.9	295.7	302.0†
Duck meat*	63.6	64.5	69.6
Cows' milk	39.7	54.5	60.0
Buffaloes' milk*	30.0	30.0	30.0
Poultry eggs	179.0†	193.0*	168.0*
Cattle hides (fresh)*	15.1	15.7	15.7
Buffalo hides (fresh)*	16.8	17.2	18.0

* FAO estimate(s).
† Unofficial figure.

Source: FAO.

Forestry

ROUNDWOOD REMOVALS

(FAO estimates, '000 cubic metres, excl. bark)

	1999	2000	2001
Sawlogs, etc.:			
Coniferous	152	184	184
Broadleaved	1,971	2,387	2,387
Other industrial wood	350	350	350
Fuel wood (all broadleaved)	26,695	26,686	26,615
Total	29,168	29,607	29,536

Source: FAO.

SAWNWOOD PRODUCTION

('000 cubic metres, incl. railway sleepers)

	1999	2000	2001
Total (all broadleaved)	2,937	2,950	2,950*

* FAO estimate.

Source: FAO.

Fishing

('000 metric tons, live weight)

	1998	1999	2000
Capture	1,294.0	1,386.3	1,441.6
Freshwater fishes	137.8	168.1	160.0*
Marine fishes	849.3	912.7	1,007.7
Natantian decapods	93.5	91.5	81.7*
Cephalopods*	103.0	120.0	107.0
Aquaculture	413.0	467.3	510.6
Freshwater fishes*	311.3	354.5	381.2
Total catch	1,707.0	1,853.6	1,952.1

* FAO estimate(s).

Source: FAO, *Yearbook of Fishery Statistics*.

Mining

('000 metric tons)

	1999	2000	2001*
Coal	9,629	10,857	12,962†
Chromium ore	59	60	60
Phosphate rock	681	707	750
Salt (unrefined)	653	635	650
Crude petroleum ('000 barrels)	107,767	115,252	119,686†

* Estimates.

† Reported figure.

Source: US Geological Survey.

Industry

SELECTED PRODUCTS

('000 metric tons, unless otherwise indicated)

	1999	2000*	2001*
Raw sugar	947	1,209	1,058
Beer (million litres)	690	779	817
Cigarettes (million packets)	2,147	2,836	3,047
Fabrics (million metres)	322	356	379
Chemical fertilizers	1,143	1,210	1,071
Insecticides	22	20	19
Bricks (million)	7,831	9,087	9,615
Cement	10,489	13,298	15,374
Crude steel	1,375	1,583	1,096
Diesel motors (pieces)	15,347	15,623	53,596
Television receivers ('000)	903	1,013	1,159
Electric engines (pieces)	38,091	45,855	54,125
Bicycle tyres ('000)	18,326	20,675	21,700
Bicycle tubes ('000)	21,544	21,917	18,700
Rice milling equipment (pieces)	12,136	12,484	12,540
Transformers (pieces)	10,264	13,535	17,283
Electric energy (million kWh)	23,599	26,682	30,801

* Preliminary figures.

Finance

CURRENCY AND EXCHANGE RATES

Monetary Units
  100 xu = 1 new dông

Sterling, Dollar and Euro Equivalents (29 November 2002)
  £1 sterling = 23,877.5 dông
  US $1 = 15,385.0 dông
  €1 = 15,272.7 dông
  100,000 new dông = £4.188 = $6.500 = €6.548

Average Exchange Rate (new dông per US $)
  1999   13,943.2
  2000   14,167.7
  2001   14,725.2

Note: The new dông, equivalent to 10 former dông, was introduced in September 1985.

BUDGET

('000 million dông)

Revenue	2000	2001	2002
Tax revenue	72,787	80,305	87,515
Corporate income tax	22,240	25,032	26,060
Individual income tax	1,831	1,930	1,975
Value added tax (VAT)	17,072	18,916	23,015
Special consumption tax	5,250	6,304	6,890
Natural resources tax	7,487	7,558	6,780
Taxes on trade	13,437	16,200	20,000
Non-tax revenue	15,096	14,695	15,015
Fees and charges	4,905	5,250	5,985
Net profit after tax	6,710	6,700	5,903
Other	2,782	3,600	2,410
Capital revenues	838	600	670
Grants	2,028	1,900	2,000
Resources transfer revenue	n.a.	3,400	1,700
Total	90,749	100,900	106,900

Expenditure	2000	2001	2002
Current expenditure.	70,127	77,020	78,784
General administrative services	8,089	7,970	7,210
Economic services	5,796	7,880	6,988
Social services	30,694	35,793	38,460
Education	9,910	12,222	13,581
Training	2,767	3,488	4,034
Health	3,453	4,120	4,460
Pensions and social relief . .	10,739	12,190	12,260
Other services (incl. defence). .	22,034	21,094	19,882
Interest on public debt . .	3,514	4,283	6,244
Expenditure on investment and			
development	29,624	36,390	39,000
Capital expenditure	26,211	32,486	35,050
Others	3,413	3,904	3,950
Others	n.a.	n.a.	2,700
Resource transfer	3,400	1,700	n.a.
Total	103,151	115,110	120,484

Source: Ministry of Finance, Hanoi.

INTERNATIONAL RESERVES
(US $ million at 31 December)

	1999	2000	2001
Gold*	97.3	93.1	90.6
IMF special drawing rights . . .	1.5	0.3	14.6
Foreign exchange.	3,324.7	3,416.2	3,660.0
Total	3,423.5	3,509.6	3,765.2

* National valuation.

Source: IMF, *International Financial Statistics*.

MONEY SUPPLY
('000 million dông at 31 December)

	1999	2000	2001
Currency outside banks	41,254	52,208	66,320
Demand deposits at banks . . .	27,106	38,781	46,089
Total money	68,360	90,989	112,408

Source: IMF, *International Financial Statistics*.

COST OF LIVING
(Consumer Price Index; base: 1990 = 100)

	1999	2000	2001
Food	467.4	449.5	443.2
All items	425.8	419.0	417.7

Source: ILO.

2002 (base: 1995 = 100): All items 123.8 (Source: IMF, *International Financial Statistics*).

NATIONAL ACCOUNTS
('000 million dông at current prices)

Expenditure on the Gross Domestic Product

	1999	2000	2001
Government final consumption			
expenditure.	27,137	28,346	30,463
Private final consumption			
expenditure.	274,553	293,507	312,144
Increase in stocks	7,704	8,970	9,726
Gross fixed capital formation . .	102,799	121,857	139,895
Total domestic expenditure. .	412,193	452,680	492,228
Exports of goods and services . .	199,836	243,049	262,864
Less Imports of goods and services	211,254	253,927	278,628
Sub-total	400,775	441,802	476,464
Statistical discrepancy* . . .	−833	−156	8,028
GDP in purchasers' values . .	399,942	441,646	484,492
GDP at constant 1994 prices .	256,272	273,666	292,535

* Referring to the difference between the sum of the expenditure components and official estimates of GDP, compiled from the production approach.

Source: IMF, *International Financial Statistics*.

Gross Domestic Product by Economic Activity

	1999	2000*	2001*
Agriculture, hunting, forestry and			
fishing	101,723	108,356	114,412
Mining and quarrying	33,703	42,606	44,544
Manufacturing	70,767	81,979	95,129
Electricity, gas and water . . .	11,725	13,993	16,197
Construction	21,764	23,642	27,421
Trade, restaurants and hotels . .	72,796	77,179	83,701
Transport, storage and			
communications	15,546	17,341	19,431
Finance, insurance, real estate and			
business services	27,650	29,666	33,092
Public administration	11,683	12,066	12,645
Other community, social and			
personal services	32,585	34,818	37,921
Total	399,942	441,646	484,493

* Preliminary figures.

BALANCE OF PAYMENTS
(US $ million)

	1999	2000	2001
Exports of goods f.o.b.	11,540	14,448	15,027
Imports of goods f.o.b.	−10,568	−14,073	−14,546
Trade balance	972	375	481
Exports of services	2,493	2,702	2,810
Imports of services	−3,040	−3,252	−3,382
Balance on goods and services	425	−175	−91
Other income received	142	331	318
Other income paid	−571	−782	−795
Balance on goods, services and			
income	−4	−626	−568
Current transfers received . . .	1,181	1,732	1,250
Current balance	1,177	1,106	682
Direct investment from abroad .	1,412	1,298	1,300
Other investment assets . . .	−786	−2,089	−1,197
Other investment liabilities . .	432	475	268
Net errors and omissions . . .	−925	−680	−847
Overall balance	1,310	110	206

Source: IMF, *International Financial Statistics*.

External Trade

SELECTED COMMODITIES
(US $ million)

Imports c.i.f.	1999	2000	2001*
Petroleum products	1,054	2,058	1,871
Fertilizers	464	509	412
Iron and steel	587	812	934
Machinery and equipment . . .	2,005	2,571	2,706
Leather and garment material† .	1,096	1,334	n.a.
Motorcycles	399	787	576
Total (incl. others)	11,742	15,637	16,162

Exports f.o.b.	1999	2000	2001*
Petroleum	2,092	3,503	3,175
Rice	1,025	667	588
Coffee	585	501	385
Marine products	971	1,479	1,800
Clothing	1,747	1,892	2,000
Footwear	1,392	1,465	1,520
Electronic goods and components†	585	783	n.a.
Total (incl. others)	11,540	14,448	15,027

* Preliminary figures.

† Source: IMF, *Vietnam: Selected Issues and Statistical Appendix* (January 2002).

PRINCIPAL TRADING PARTNERS
(US $ million)

Imports c.i.f.	1999	2000	2001
China, People's Republic . . .	673.1	1,691.0	2,032.9
France	309.3	291.9	442.4
Hong Kong	504.7	599.3	602.6
Indonesia	286.8	396.7	428.1
Japan	1,618.3	2,172.2	1,986.2
Korea, Republic	1,485.8	1,854.6	1,904.8
Malaysia	305.0	522.9	523.5
Singapore	1,878.5	2,344.4	2,315.7
Thailand	561.8	921.3	872.2
USA	323.1	381.8	499.6
Total (incl. others)	11,740.9	15,552.3	16,652.7

Exports f.o.b.	1999	2000	2001
Australia	814.6	1,254.8	1,258.8
China, People's Republic . . .	746.4	844.7	1,078.3
France	354.9	463.9	579.7
Germany	654.3	990.5	999.6
Japan	1,786.2	2,397.3	2,447.7
Korea, Republic	319.9	293.7	350.7
Netherlands	342.9	343.5	320.2
Singapore	876.4	745.1	772.5
United Kingdom . . .	421.2	470.9	555.9
USA	504.1	782.0	1,021.3
Total (incl. others)	11,541.3	12,881.3	13,981.4

Source: Asian Development Bank, *Key Indicators of Developing Asian and Pacific Countries*.

Transport

RAILWAYS
(traffic)

	1995	1996*	1997*
Passengers carried (million) .	8.8	8.4	9.3
Passenger-km (million) . . .	2,133.3	2,259.0	2,444.0
Freight carried (million metric tons)	4.5	4.4	4.7
Freight ton-km (million) . . .	1,750.6	1,678.0	1,525.0

* Source: Reed Business Information, *Railway Directory*.

1998: Passenger-km ('000) 2,542; Freight ton-km ('000) 1,369 (Source: UN, *Statistical Yearbook*).

1999: Passenger-km ('000) 2,722; Freight ton-km ('000) 1,446 (Source: UN, *Statistical Yearbook*).

2000: Passenger-km ('000) 3,086; Freight ton-km ('000) 1,921 (Source: UN, *Statistical Yearbook*).

ROAD TRAFFIC

	1993	1994	1995
Passengers carried (million) .	419.2	440.6	472.2
Passenger-km (million). . .	10,601.3	11,150.0	16,757.0
Freight carried (million metric tons).	46.0	49.4	55.9
Freight ton-km (million) . . .	2,437.0	2,645.6	2,967.8

INLAND WATERWAYS

	1993	1994	1995
Passengers carried (million) . .	86.4	104.1	109.8
Passenger-km (million). . . .	1,310.6	1,412.0	1,427.9
Freight carried (million metric tons).	16.8	17.5	20.1
Freight ton-km (million) . . .	2,335.0	1,971.3	2,248.2

SHIPPING

Merchant Fleet
(registered at 31 December)

	1999	2000	2001
Number of vessels	640	691	700
Total displacement ('000 grt) . .	864.7	1,001.5	1,073.6

Source: Lloyd's Register-Fairplay, *World Fleet Statistics*.

International Sea-Borne Shipping
(estimated freight traffic, '000 metric tons)

	1988	1989	1990
Goods loaded	305	310	303
Goods unloaded	1,486	1,510	1,510

Source: UN, *Monthly Bulletin of Statistics*.

CIVIL AVIATION
(traffic on scheduled services)

	1997	1998	1999
Kilometres flown (million) . . .	35	33	31
Passengers carried ('000) . . .	2,527	2,373	2,600
Passenger-km (million) . . .	3,785	3,644	3,831
Total ton-km (million) . . .	448	426	445

Source: UN, *Statistical Yearbook*.

Tourism

TOURIST ARRIVALS BY NATIONALITY
('000)

Country	2000	2001	2002
Australia	68,162	84,085	96,624
Cambodia	124,557	76,620	69,538
China, People's Republic . . .	626,476	672,846	724,385
France	86,492	99,700	111,546
Japan	152,755	204,860	279,769
Korea, Republic	53,452	75,167	105,060
Taiwan.	212,370	200,061	211,072
United Kingdom	56,355	64,673	69,682
USA	208,642	230,470	259,967
Total (incl. others)	2,140,100	2,330,050	2,627,988

Source: Vietnam National Administration of Tourism.

Tourism receipts (US $ million): 88 in 1997; 86 in 1998 (Source: World Bank).

Communications Media

	1999	2000	2001
Television receivers ('000 in use)	14,500	14,750	n.a.
Telephones ('000 main lines in use)	2,105.9	2,542.7	3,049.9
Facsimile machines ('000 in use)	31	n.a.	n.a.
Mobile cellular telephones ('000 subscribers)	328.7	788.6	1,251.2
Personal computers ('000 in use)	600	700	800
Internet users ('000)	100	200	400

Source: International Telecommunication Union.

Radio receivers ('000 in use): 8,200 in 1997.

Book production: 8,186 titles (169,800,000 copies) in 1995.

Daily newspapers: 10 (with estimated circulation of 300,000 copies) in 1996.

Sources: mainly UN, *Statistical Yearbook* and UNESCO, *Statistical Yearbook*.

Education

(1999/2000, '000)

	Teachers	Students
Pre-primary	96.3	2,214.1
Primary	340.9	10,063.0
Secondary	273.9	7,743.6
Higher*	26.1	682.3

* 1998/99.

Source: UN, *Statistical Yearbook for Asia and the Pacific*.

Adult literacy rate (UNESCO estimates): 93.4% (males 95.5%; females 91.4%) in 2000 (Source: UN Development Programme, *Human Development Report*).

Directory

The Constitution

On 15 April 1992 the National Assembly adopted a new Constitution, a revised version of that adopted in December 1980 (which in turn replaced the 1959 Constitution of the Democratic Republic of Viet Nam). The National Assembly approved amendments to 24 articles of the Constitution on 12 December 2001. The main provisions of the Constitution (which originally entered into force after elections in July 1992) are summarized as follows:

POLITICAL SYSTEM

All state power belongs to the people. The Communist Party of Viet Nam is a leading force of the state and society. All party organizations operate within the framework of the Constitution and the law. The people exercise power through the National Assembly and the People's Councils.

ECONOMIC SYSTEM

The State develops a multi-sectoral economy, in accordance with a market mechanism based on state management and socialist orientations. All lands are under state management. The State allots land to organizations and individuals for use on a stabilized and long-term basis: they may transfer the right to the use of land allotted to them. Individuals may establish businesses with no restrictions on size or means of production, and the State shall encourage foreign investment. Legal property of individuals and organizations, and business enterprises with foreign invested capital, shall not be subjected to nationalization.

THE NATIONAL ASSEMBLY

The National Assembly is the people's highest representative agency, and the highest organ of state power, exercising its supreme right of supervision over all operations of the State. It elects the President and Vice-President, the Prime Minister and senior judicial officers, and ratifies the Prime Minister's proposals for appointing members of the Government. It decides the country's socio-economic development plans, national financial and monetary policies, and foreign policy. The term of each legislature is five years. The National Assembly Standing Committee supervises the enforcement of laws and the activities of the Government. Amendments to the Constitution may only be made by a majority vote of at least two-thirds of the Assembly's members.

THE PRESIDENT OF THE STATE

The President, as Head of State, represents Viet Nam in domestic and foreign affairs. The President is elected by the National Assembly from among its deputies, and is responsible to the National Assembly. The President's term of office is the same as that of the National Assembly. He or she is Commander-in-Chief of the people's armed forces, and chairs the National Defence and Security Council. The President asks the National Assembly to appoint or dismiss the Vice-President, the Prime Minister, the Chief Justice of the Supreme People's Court and the Chief Procurator of the Supreme People's Organ of Control. According to resolutions of the National Assembly or of its Standing Committee, the President appoints or dismisses members of the Government, and declares war or a state of emergency.

THE GOVERNMENT

The Government comprises the Prime Minister, the Vice-Prime Ministers, ministers and other members. Apart from the Prime Minister, ministers do not have to be members of the National Assembly. The Prime Minister is responsible to the National Assembly, and the term of office of any Government is the same as that of the National Assembly, which ratifies the appointment or dismissal of members of the Government.

LOCAL GOVERNMENT

The country is divided into provinces and municipalities, which are subordinate to the central Government; municipalities are divided into districts, precincts and cities, and districts are divided into villages and townships. People's Councils are elected by the local people.

JUDICIAL SYSTEM

The judicial system comprises the Supreme People's Court, local People's Courts, military tribunals and other courts. The term of office of the presiding judge of the Supreme People's Court corresponds to the term of the National Assembly, and he or she is responsible to the National Assembly. The Supreme People's Organ of Control ensures the observance of the law and exercises the right of public prosecution. Its Chief Procurator is responsible to the National Assembly. There are local People's Organs of Control and Military Organs of Control.

The Government

HEAD OF STATE

President: TRAN DUC LUONG (elected by the 10th National Assembly on 24 September 1997; re-elected by the 11th National Assembly on 24 July 2002).

Vice-President: TRUONG MY HOA.

CABINET
(April 2003)

Prime Minister: PHAN VAN KHAI.

First Deputy Prime Minister: NGUYEN TAN DUNG.

Deputy Prime Ministers: VU KHOAN, PHAM GIA KHIEM.

Minister of National Defence: Lt-Gen. PHAM VAN TRA.

Minister of Public Security: LE HONG ANH.

Minister of Foreign Affairs: NGUYEN DY NIEN.

Minister of Justice: UONG CHU LUU.

Minister of Finance: NGUYEN SINH HUNG.

Minister of Labour, War Invalids and Social Welfare: NGUYEN THI HANG.

Minister of Education and Training: Prof. Nguyen Minh Hien.

Minister of Public Health: Tran Thi Trung Chien.

Minister of Culture and Information: Pham Quang Nghi.

Minister of Construction: Nguyen Hong Quan.

Minister of Transport and Communications: Dao Dinh Binh.

Minister of Agriculture and Rural Development: Le Huy Ngo.

Minister of Fisheries: Dr Ta Quang Ngoc.

Minister of Industry: Hoang Trung Hai.

Minister of Trade: Truong Dinh Tuyen.

Minister of Planning and Investment: Vo Hong Phuc.

Minister of Internal Affairs: Do Quang Trung.

Minister of Science and Technology: Hoang Van Phong.

Minister of Natural Resources and the Environment: Mai Ai Truc.

Minister of Posts and Telecommunications: Do Trung Ta.

State Inspector-General: Quach Le Thanh.

Minister, Chairman of the Ethnic Minorities and Mountain Region Commission: Ksor Phuoc.

Minister, Head of the Government Office: Doan Manh Giao.

Minister, Chairman of the Committee for Physical Training and Sports: Nguyen Danh Thai.

Minister, Chairman of the Committee for Population, Family and Children: Le Thi Thu.

MINISTRIES AND COMMISSIONS

All ministries are based in Hanoi.

Ministry of Agriculture and Rural Development: 2 Ngoc Ha, Ba Dinh District, Hanoi; tel. (4) 8468161; fax (4) 8454319; e-mail bnn@fpt.vn; internet www.mard.gov.vn.

Ministry of Construction: 37 Le Dai Hanh, Hai Ba Trung District, Hanoi; tel. (4) 9760271; fax (4) 9762153; e-mail bxd-vp@hn.vnn.vn.

Ministry of Culture and Information: 51–53 Ngo Quyen, Hoan Kiem District, Hanoi; tel. (4) 8255349; fax (4) 8267101; internet www.cinet.vnn.vn.

Ministry of Education and Training: 49 Dai Co Viet, Hai Ba Trung District, Hanoi; tel. (4) 8694795; fax (4) 8694085; e-mail intlaff@iupui.edu; internet www.edu.net.vn.

Ministry of Finance: 8 Phan Huy Chu, Hoan Kiem District, Hanoi; tel. (4) 9341540; fax (4) 8262266; e-mail ird-mof@hn.vnn.vn; internet www.mof.gov.vn.

Ministry of Fisheries: 10 Nguyen Cong Hoan, Hanoi; tel. (4) 7716269; fax (4) 7716702; e-mail mofi@mofi.gov.vn; internet www.mofi.gov.vn.

Ministry of Foreign Affairs: 1 Ton That Dam, Ba Dinh District, Hanoi; tel. (4) 1992000; fax (4) 8445905; e-mail bc.mfa@mofa.gov.vn; internet www.mofa.gov.vn.

Ministry of Industry: 54 Hai Ba Trung, Hoan Kiem District, Hanoi; tel. (4) 8258311; fax (4) 8265303; e-mail moi@hn.vnn.vn; internet www.industry.gov.vn.

Ministry of Internal Affairs: 37A Nguyen Binh Khiem, Hanoi; tel. (4) 9780870; fax (4) 9781005; e-mail ngoc-hien@hn.vnn.vn.

Ministry of Justice: 58–60 Tran Phu, Hanoi; tel. (4) 7336213; fax (4) 8431431.

Ministry of Labour, War Invalids and Social Welfare: 12 Ngo Quyen, Hoan Kiem District, Hanoi; tel. (4) 8246137; fax (4) 8248036; e-mail vvnd@fpt.vn.

Ministry of National Defence: 1A Hoang Dieu, Ba Dinh District, Hanoi; tel. (4) 8468101; fax (4) 8265540.

Ministry of Natural Resources and the Environment: 83 Nguyen Chi Thanh, Dong Da District, Hanoi; tel. (4) 8357910; fax (4) 8352191.

Ministry of Planning and Investment: 2 Hoang Van Thu, Ba Dinh District, Hanoi; tel. (4) 8453027; fax (4) 8234453; internet www.mpi.gov.vn.

Ministry of Posts and Telecommunications: 18 Nguyen Du, Hanoi; tel. (4) 9435602; fax (4) 8226590; e-mail nmhong@mpt.gov.vn; internet www.mpt.gov.vn.

Ministry of Public Health: 138A Giang Vo, Ba Dinh District, Hanoi; tel. (4) 8464051; fax (4) 8460701; internet www.moh.gov.vn.

Ministry of Public Security: 44 Yet Kieu, Hanoi; tel. (4) 8226602; fax (4) 8260774.

Ministry of Science and Technology: 39 Tran Hung Dao, Hoan Kiem District, Hanoi; tel. (4) 9439731; fax (4) 8252733; internet www.moste.gov.vn.

Ministry of Trade: 21 Ngo Quyen, Hanoi; tel. (4) 8262538; fax (4) 8264696; e-mail webmaster@mot.gov.vn; internet www.mot.gov.vn.

Ministry of Transport and Communications: 80 Tran Hung Dao, Hoan Kiem District, Hanoi; tel. (4) 8254012; fax (4) 8267291; e-mail tic_mot@hn.vnn.vn; internet www.mt.gov.vn.

National Committee for Population, Family and Children: 12 Ngo Tat To, Hanoi; tel. (4) 8260020; fax (4) 8258993; e-mail htqt@vietnam.org.vn.

State Inspectorate: 28 Tang Bat Ho, Hanoi; tel. (4) 8254497.

NATIONAL DEFENCE AND SECURITY COUNCIL

President: Tran Duc Luong.

Vice-President: Phan Van Khai.

Members: Nguyen Van An, Le Hong Anh, Lt-Gen. Pham Van Tra, Nguyen Dy Nien.

Legislature

QUOC HOI
(National Assembly)

Elections to the 11th National Assembly were held on 19 May 2002. The new Assembly comprised 498 members (compared with 450 in the previous Assembly), elected from among 759 candidates; 51 non-party candidates were elected.

Standing Committee

Chairman: Nguyen Van An.

Vice-Chairmen: Nguyen Van Yeu, Nguyen Phuc Thanh, Truong Quang Duoc.

Political Organizations

Dang Cong San Viet Nam (Communist Party of Viet Nam): 1 Hoang Van Thu, Hanoi; e-mail cpv@hn.vnn.vn; internet www.cpv.org.vn; f. 1976; ruling party; fmrly the Viet Nam Workers' Party, f. 1951 as the successor to the Communist Party of Indo-China, f. 1930; c. 2.2m. mems (1996); Gen. Sec. of Cen. Cttee Nong Duc Manh.

POLITBURO

Nong Duc Manh, Tran Duc Luong, Phan Van Khai, Nguyen Minh Triet, Nguyen Tan Dung, Le Minh Huong, Nguyen Phu Trong, Phan Dien, Le Hong Anh, Truong Tan Sang, Lt-Gen. Pham Van Tra, Nguyen Van An, Truong Quang Duoc, Tran Dinh Hoan, Nguyen Khoa Diem.

SECRETARIAT

Nong Duc Manh, Le Hong Anh, Nguyen Van An, Tran Dinh Hoan, Nguyen Khoa Diem, Le Van Dung, Tong Thi Phong, Truong Vinh Trong, Vu Khoan, Nguyen Van Chi.

Ho Chi Minh Communist Youth Union: 60 Ba Trieu, Hanoi; tel. (4) 9435709; fax (4) 9348439; e-mail cydeco@hn.vnn.vn; f. 1931; 4m. mems; First Sec. Hoang Binh Quan.

People's Action Party (PAP): Hanoi; Leader Le Van Tinh.

Viet Nam Fatherland Front: 46 Trang Thi, Hanoi; f. 1930; replaced the Lien Viet (Viet Nam National League), the successor to Viet Nam Doc Lap Dong Minh Hoi (Revolutionary League for the Independence of Viet Nam) or Viet Minh; in 1977 the original org. merged with the National Front for the Liberation of South Viet Nam and the Alliance of National, Democratic and Peace Forces in South Viet Nam to form a single front; 200-member Cen. Cttee; Pres. Presidium of Cen. Cttee Pham The Duyet; Gen. Sec. Tran Van Dang.

Vietnam Women's Union: 39 Hang Chuoi, Hanoi; tel. (4) 9717225; fax (4) 9713143; e-mail VWUnion@netnam.org.vn; f. 1930; 11.4m. mems; Pres. Ha Thi Khiet.

Diplomatic Representation

EMBASSIES IN VIET NAM

Algeria: 13 Phan Chu Trinh, Hanoi; tel. (4) 8253865; fax (4) 8260830; Ambassador Tewfik Abada.

Argentina: Daeha Business Centre, 360 Kim Ma, Ba Dinh District, Hanoi; tel. (4) 8315262; fax (4) 8315577; e-mail embarg@hn.vnn.vn; internet www.embargentina.org.vn; Ambassador TOMÁS FERRARI.

Australia: 8 Dao Tan, Ba Dinh District, Hanoi; tel. (4) 8317755; fax (4) 8317711; internet www.ausinvn.com; Ambassador JOE THWAITES.

Austria: Prime Centre, 8th Floor, 53 Quang Trung, Hai Ba Trung District, Hanoi; tel. (4) 9433050; fax (4) 9433055; e-mail hanoi-ob@bmaa.gv.at; Ambassador Dr JOSEF MÜLLNER.

Bangladesh: 7th Floor, Daeha Business Centre, 360 Kim Ma, Ba Dinh District, Hanoi; tel. (4) 7716625; fax (4) 7716628; Ambassador SHAMSHER MOBIN CHOWDHURY.

Belarus: 11th Floor, 44B Ly Thuong Kiet, Hanoi; tel. (4) 9344416; fax (4) 9344417; e-mail vietnam@belembassy.org; Ambassador PARHUTA ALEKSANDR.

Belgium: Daeha Business Centre, 5th Floor, 360 Kim Ma, Ba Dinh District, Hanoi; tel. (4) 8315240; fax (4) 8315242; e-mail walbru.hanoi@fpt.vn; internet www.wbri.be/hanoi; Ambassador ZÉNON KOWAL.

Brazil: 14 Thuy Khue, T72 Hanoi; tel. (4) 8430817; fax (4) 8432542; e-mail ambviet@netnam.org.vn; Ambassador CHRISTIANO WHITAKER.

Brunei: 27 Quang Trung, Hoan Kiem District, Hanoi; tel. (4) 9435249; fax (4) 9435201; e-mail bruemviet@hn.vnn.vn; Ambassador Dato' Paduka Haji ALI Haji HASSAN.

Bulgaria: Van Phuc, Nui Truc, Hanoi; tel. (4) 8452908; fax (4) 8460856; e-mail bulemb@hn.vnn.vn; Chargé d'affaires a.i. STANILAV BAEV.

Cambodia: 71 Tran Hung Dao, Hanoi; tel. (4) 9424788; fax (4) 9423225; e-mail arch@fpt.vn; Ambassador VAR SIM SAMRETH.

Canada: 31 Hung Vuong, Hanoi; tel. (4) 8235500; fax (4) 8235333; e-mail hanoi@dfait-maeci.gc.ca; internet www.dfait-maeci.gc.ca/vietnam; Ambassador RICHARD LECOQ.

China, People's Republic: 46 Hoang Dieu, Hanoi; tel. (4) 8453736; fax (4) 8232826; e-mail eossc@hn.vnn.vn; Ambassador QI JIANGUO.

Cuba: 65 Ly Thuong Kiet, Hanoi; tel. (4) 9424775; fax (4) 9422426; Ambassador FREDESMAN TURRÁ GONZÁLEZ.

Czech Republic: 13 Chu Van An, Hanoi; tel. (4) 8454131; fax (4) 8233996; e-mail hanoi@embassy.mzv.cz; internet www.mfa.cz/hanoi; Ambassador LUBOS NOVÝ.

Denmark: 19 Dien Bien Phu, Hanoi; tel. (4) 8231888; fax (4) 8231999; e-mail hanamb@un.dk; internet www.dk-vn.dk; Ambassador BJARNE H. SØRENSEN.

Egypt: 106 Nghi Tam, Quang An, Tay Ho, Hanoi; tel. (4) 8294999; fax (4) 8294997; e-mail arabegypt@ftp.vn; Ambassador MUHAMMAD EL SAYED TAHA.

Finland: 6th Floor, Central Bldg, 31 Hai Ba Trung, Hanoi; tel. (4) 8266788; fax (4) 8266766; e-mail sanomat.han@formin.fi; Ambassador KARI ALANKO.

France: 57 Tran Hung Dao, Hanoi; tel. (4) 9437719; fax (4) 9437236; e-mail ambafrance@hn.vnn.vn; internet www.ambafrance-vn.org; Ambassador ANTOINE POUILLIEUTE.

Germany: 29 Tran Phu, Hanoi; tel. (4) 8453836; fax (4) 8453838; e-mail germanemb.hanoi@fpt.vn; internet www.germanemb.org.vn; Ambassador Dr WOLFGANG MASSING.

Hungary: Daeha Business Centre, 12th Floor, 360 Kim Ma, Ba Dinh District, Hanoi; tel. (4) 7715714; fax (4) 7715716; e-mail hungemb@hn.vnn.vn; Ambassador ERNŐ BOHÁR.

India: 58–60 Tran Hung Dao, Hanoi; tel. (4) 8244990; fax (4) 8244998; e-mail india@netnam.org.vn; Ambassador SAURABH KUMAR.

Indonesia: 50 Ngo Quyen, Hanoi; tel. (4) 8253353; fax (4) 8259274; Ambassador AIYUB MOSHIN.

Iran: 54 Tran Phu, Ba Dinh District, Hanoi; tel. (4) 8232068; fax (4) 8232120; e-mail iriemb@fpt.vn; Ambassador HOSSEIN EBRAHIM KHANI.

Iraq: 66 Tran Hung Dao, Hanoi; tel. (4) 9424141; fax (4) 9424055; Ambassador SALAH AL-MUKHTAR.

Israel: 68 Nguyen Thai Hoc, Hanoi; tel. (4) 8433141; fax (4) 8435760; e-mail hanoi@israel.org; Ambassador WALID MANSOUR.

Italy: 9 Le Phung Hieu, Hanoi; tel. (4) 8256256; fax (4) 8267602; e-mail embitaly@embitaly.org.vn; internet www.embitalyvietnam.org; Ambassador LUIGI SOLARI.

Japan: 27 Lieu Giai, Ba Dinh District, Hanoi; tel. (4) 8463000; fax (4) 8463043; Ambassador NARIO HATTORI.

Korea, Democratic People's Republic: 25 Cao Ba Quat, Hanoi; tel. (4) 8453008; fax (4) 8231221; Ambassador PAK UNG-SOP.

Korea, Republic: 4th Floor, Daeha Business Centre, 360 Kim Ma, Ba Dinh District, Hanoi; tel. (4) 8315111; fax (4) 8315117; e-mail korembviet@mofat.go.kr; Ambassador YOO TAE-HYUN.

Laos: 22 Tran Binh Trong, Hanoi; tel. (4) 9424576; fax (4) 8228414; Ambassador VILAYVANH PHOMKEHE.

Libya: A3 Van Phuc Residential Quarter, Hanoi; tel. (4) 8453379; fax (4) 8454977; e-mail libpbha@yahoo.com; Secretary SALEM ALI SALEM DANNAH.

Malaysia: 16th Floor, Fortuna Tower, 6B Lang Ha, Hanoi; tel. (4) 8313400; fax (4) 8313402; e-mail mwhanoi@hn.vnn.vn; Ambassador Dato' MOHAMED RADZI BIN ABDUL RAHMAN.

Mexico: 14 Thuy Khue, T-11, Hanoi; tel. (4) 8470948; fax (4) 8470949; e-mail embvietnam@sre.gob.mx; Ambassador FEDERICO URRUCHUA DURAND.

Mongolia: 39 Tran Phu, Hanoi; tel. (4) 8453009; fax (4) 8454954; e-mail mongembhanoi@hn.vnn.vn; Ambassador AGVAANDORJIIN TSOLMAN.

Myanmar: A3 Van Phuc Diplomatic Quarter, Hanoi; tel. (4) 8453369; fax (4) 8452404; e-mail myan.emb@fpt.vn; Ambassador U KHIN AUNG.

Netherlands: Daeha Office Tower, 6th Floor, 360 Kim Ma, Ba Dinh District, Hanoi; tel. (4) 8315650; fax (4) 8315655; e-mail han@minbuza.nl; internet www.netherlands-embassy.org.vn; Ambassador GERBEN S. DE JONG.

New Zealand: Level 5, 63 Ly Thai To, Hanoi; tel. (4) 8241481; fax (4) 8241480; e-mail nzembhan@fpt.vn; Ambassador MALCOLM McGOUN.

Norway: 7th Floor, Suite 701–702, Metropole Centre, 56 Ly Thai To, Hanoi; tel. (4) 8262111; fax (4) 8260222; Ambassador PER G. STAVNUM.

Pakistan: 8th Floor, Daeha Business Centre, 360 Kim Ma, Ba Dinh District, Hanoi; tel. (4) 7716420; fax (4) 7716418; e-mail parep-hanoi@hn.vnn.vn; Ambassador MOHAMMAD YOUNIS KHAN.

Philippines: 27B Tran Hung Dao, Hanoi; tel. (4) 9437873; fax (4) 9435760; e-mail phvn@hn.vnn.vn; Ambassador GUILLERMO G. WONG.

Poland: 3 Chua Mot Cot, Hanoi; tel. (4) 8452027; fax (4) 8236914; Ambassador WIESLAW SCHOLZ.

Romania: 5 Le Hong Phong, Hanoi; tel. (4) 8452014; fax (4) 8430922; e-mail romambhan@fpt.vn; Ambassador CONSTANTIN LUPEANU.

Russia: 191 La Thanh, Hanoi; tel. (4) 8336991; fax (4) 8336995; e-mail moscow.vietnam@hn.vnn.vn; Ambassador ANDREI ALEXEEVICH TATARINOV.

Singapore: 41–43 Tran Phu, Hanoi; tel. (4) 8233965; fax (4) 7337627; e-mail singemb@hn.vnn.vn; internet www.mfa.gov.sg/hanoi; Ambassador TAN SENG CHYE.

Slovakia: 6 Le Hong Phong, Hanoi; tel. (4) 8454334; fax (4) 8454145; e-mail zuskemb@hn.vnn.vn; Ambassador ANTON HAJDUK.

Spain: 15th Floor, Daeha Business Centre, 360 Kim Ma, Ba Dinh District, Hanoi; tel. (4) 7715207; fax (4) 7715206; e-mail embespvn@mail.mae.es; Ambassador IGNACIO SAGAZ TEMPRANO.

Sweden: 2 Nui Truc, Van Phuc, Khu Ba Dinh, Hanoi; tel. (4) 8454824; fax (4) 8232195; e-mail ambassaden.hanoi@sida.se; internet www.hanoi.embassy.ud.se; Ambassador MARIE SJÖLANDER.

Switzerland: 44B Ly Thuong Kiet, 15th Floor, Hanoi; tel. (4) 9346589; fax (4) 9346591; e-mail vertretung@han.rep.admin.ch; Ambassador THOMAS FELLER.

Thailand: 63–65 Hoang Dieu, Hanoi; tel. (4) 8235092; fax (4) 8235088; e-mail thaiemhn@netnam.org.vn; Ambassador KRIT KRAICHITTI.

Turkey: 4th Floor, North Star Bldg, 4 Da Truong, Hanoi; tel. (4) 8222460; fax (4) 8222458; e-mail turkeyhn@fpt.vn; Ambassador KAYNA INAL.

Ukraine: 49 Nguyen Dy, Hanoi; tel. (4) 9432764; fax (4) 9432766; e-mail ukraine@hn.vnn.vn; internet webua.net/viet; Ambassador ROSTYSLAV BILODID.

United Kingdom: Central Bldg, 31 Hai Ba Trung, Hanoi; tel. (4) 9360500; fax (4) 9360561; e-mail behanoi@fpt.vn; internet www.uk-vietnam.org; Ambassador WARWICK MORRIS.

USA: 7 Lang Ha, Ba Dinh District, Hanoi; tel. (4) 7721500; fax (4) 7721510; e-mail irchano@pd.state.gov; internet usembassy.state.gov/vietnam; Ambassador RAYMOND BURGHARDT.

Judicial System

Supreme People's Court
48 Ly Thuong Kiet, Hanoi.

The Supreme People's Court in Hanoi is the highest court and exercises civil and criminal jurisdiction over all lower courts. The

Supreme Court may also conduct trials of the first instance in certain cases. There are People's Courts in each province and city which exercise jurisdiction in the first and second instance. Military courts hear cases involving members of the People's Army and cases involving national security. In 1993 legislation was adopted on the establishment of economic courts to consider business disputes. The observance of the law by ministries, government offices and all citizens is the concern of the People's Organs of Control, under a Supreme People's Organ of Control. The Chief Justice of the Supreme People's Court and the Chief Procurator of the Supreme People's Organ of Control are elected by the National Assembly, on the recommendation of the President.

Chief Justice of the Supreme People's Court: NGUYEN VAN HIEN.

Chief Procurator of the Supreme People's Organ of Control: HA MANH TRI.

Religion

Traditional Vietnamese religion included elements of Indian and all three Chinese religions: Mahayana Buddhism, Daoism and Confucianism. Its most widespread feature was the cult of ancestors, practised in individual households and clan temples. In addition, there were (and remain) a wide variety of Buddhist sects, the sects belonging to the 'new' religions of Caodaism and Hoa Hao, and the Protestant and Roman Catholic Churches. The Government has guaranteed complete freedom of religious belief.

BUDDHISM

In the North a Buddhist organization, grouping Buddhists loyal to the Democratic Republic of Viet Nam, was formed in 1954. In the South the United Buddhist Church was formed in 1964, incorporating several disparate groups, including the 'militant' An-Quang group (mainly natives of central Viet Nam), the group of Thich Tam Chau (mainly northern emigrés in Saigon) and the southern Buddhists of the Xa Loi temple. In 1982 most of the Buddhist sects were amalgamated into the state-approved Viet Nam Buddhist Church (which comes under the authority of the Viet Nam Fatherland Front; number of adherents estimated at 7% of total population in 1991). The Unified Buddhist Church of Viet Nam is an anti-Government organization.

Viet Nam Buddhist Church: Pres. Exec. Council Most Ven. THICH TRI TINH; Gen. Sec. THICH MING CHAU.

Unified Buddhist Church of Viet Nam: Patriarch THICH HUYEN QUANG.

CAODAISM

Formally inaugurated in 1926, this is a syncretic religion based on spiritualist seances with a predominantly ethical content, but sometimes with political overtones. A number of different sects exist, of which the most politically involved (1940–75) was that of Tay Ninh. Another sect, the Tien Thien, was represented in the National Liberation Front from its inception. There are an estimated 2m. adherents, resident mainly in the South.

Leader: Cardinal THAI HUU THANH.

CHRISTIANITY

In 1991 the number of Christian adherents represented an estimated 7% of the total population.

The Roman Catholic Church

The Roman Catholic Church has been active in Viet Nam since the 17th century, and since 1933 has been led mainly by Vietnamese priests. Many Roman Catholics moved from North to South Viet Nam in 1954–55, but some remained in the North. The total number of adherents was estimated at 5,301,329 in 2000, representing 6.6% of the population. For ecclesiastical purposes, Viet Nam comprises three archdioceses and 22 dioceses.

Committee for Solidarity of Patriotic Vietnamese Catholics: 59 Trang Thi, Hanoi; Pres. Rev. VUONG DINH AI.

Bishops' Conference

Conférence Episcopal du Viet Nam, 40 Pho Nha Chung, Hanoi; tel. (4) 8254424; fax (4) 8285920; e-mail ttgmhn@hn.vnn.vn. f. 1980; Pres. Most Rev. PAUL NGUYEN VAN HOA (Bishop of Nha Trang).

Archbishop of Hanoi: Cardinal PAUL JOSEPH PHAM DINH TUNG, Archevêché, 40 Pho Nha Chung, Hanoi; tel. (4) 8254424; fax (4) 8285920; e-mail ttgm@fpt.vn.

Archbishop of Ho Chi Minh City: Most Rev. JEAN-BAPTISTE PHAM MINH MÂN, Archevêché, 180 Nguyen Dinh Chieu, Ho Chi Minh City 3; tel. (8) 9303828; fax (8) 9300598.

Archbishop of Hué: Most Rev. ETIENNE NGUYEN NHU THE, Archevêché, 37 Phan Dinh Phung, Hué; tel. (54) 823100; fax (54) 833656; e-mail tgmhue@dng.vnn.vn.

The Protestant Church

Introduced in 1920 with 500 adherents; the total number is estimated at 180,000.

HOA HAO

A new manifestation of an older religion called Buu Son Ky Huong, the Hoa Hao sect was founded by Nguyen Phu So in 1939, and at one time claimed 1.5m. adherents in southern Viet Nam.

ISLAM

The number of Muslims was estimated at 50,000 in 1993.

The Press

The Ministry of Culture and Information supervises the activities of newspapers, news agencies and periodicals.

DAILIES

Hanoi

Le Courrier du Viet Nam: 33 Le Thanh Tong, Hanoi; tel. (4) 9334587; fax (4) 8258368; French; publ. by the Viet Nam News Agency; Editor-in-Chief NGUYEN TUONG.

Hanoi Moi (New Hanoi): 44 Le Thai To, Hanoi; tel. (4) 8253067; fax (4) 8248054; f. 1976; organ of Hanoi Cttee of the Communist Party of Viet Nam; Editor HO XUAN SON; circ. 35,000.

Lao Dong (Labour): 51 Hang Bo, Hanoi; tel. (4) 8252441; fax (4) 8254441; e-mail baolaodong@hn.vnn.vn; internet www.laodong.com.vn; f. 1929; organ of the Viet Nam General Confederation of Labour; Editor-in-Chief PHAM HUY HOAN; circ. 80,000.

Nhan Dan (The People): 71 Hang Trong, Hoan Kiem District, Hanoi; tel. (4) 8254231; fax (4) 8255593; e-mail toasoan@nhandan.org.vn; internet www.nhandan.org.vn; f. 1946; official organ of the Communist Party of Viet Nam; Editor-in-Chief DINH THE HUYNH; circ. 180,000.

Quan Doi Nhan Dan (People's Army): 7 Phan Dinh Phung, Hanoi; tel. (4) 8254118; f. 1950; organ of the armed forces; Editor NGUYEN FHONG HAI; circ. 60,000.

Viet Nam News: 79 Ly Thuong Kiet, Hanoi; tel. (4) 8222884; fax 9424908; e-mail vnnews@vnagency.com.vn; internet www.vietnamnews.vnagency.com.vn; f. 1991; English; publ. by the Viet Nam News Agency; Editor-in-Chief TRAN MAI HUONG; circ. 25,000 (Mon.-Sat.), 20,000 Sun. edn (Viet Nam News Sunday); circ. 60,000.

Ho Chi Minh City

Sai Gon Giai Phong (Saigon Liberation): 432 Nguyen Thi Minh Khai, Ho Chi Minh City; tel. (8) 8395942; fax (8) 8334183; internet www.sggp.org.vn; f. 1975; organ of Ho Chi Minh City Cttee of the Communist Party of Viet Nam; Editor-in-Chief VU TUAT VIET; circ. 100,000.

Saigon Times: 35–37 Nam Ky Khoi Nghia, District 1, Ho Chi Minh City; tel. (8) 8295936; fax (8) 8294294; e-mail sgt@hcm.vnn.vn; internet www.saigontimesweekly.saigonnet.vn; f. 1991; Vietnamese, English and French; business issues; Editor-in-Chief VO NHU LANH.

PERIODICALS

Dai Doan Ket (Great Unity): 66 Ba Trieu, Hanoi; and 176 Vo Thi Sau St, Ho Chi Minh City; tel. (4) 8262420; f. 1977; weekly; organ of the Viet Nam Fatherland Front; Editor NGUYEN QUANG CANH.

Dau Tu: 175 Nguyen Thai Hoc, Hanoi; tel. (4) 8450537; fax (4) 8457937; e-mail vir@hn.vnn.vn; internet www.vir.com.vn; 3 a week business newspaper publ. in Vietnamese; Editor-in-Chief NGUYEN TRI DUNG; circ. 40,000.

Dau Tu Chung Khoan: 175 Nguyen Thai Hoc, Hanoi; tel. (4) 8450537; fax (4) 8457937; e-mail vir@hn.vnn.vn; internet www.vir.com.vn; weekly; stock market news publ. in Vietnamese; Editor-in-Chief NGUYEN TRI DUNG; circ. 40,000.

Giao Thong-Van Tai (Communications and Transport): 1 Nha Tho, Hanoi; tel. (4) 8255387; f. 1962; weekly; Thursday; organ of the Ministry of Transport and Communications; Editor NGO DUC NGUYEN; circ. 10,000.

Giao Duc Thoi Dai (People's Teacher): Le Truc, Hanoi; tel. (4) 8252849; f. 1959; weekly; organ of the Ministry of Education and Training; Editor NGUYEN NGOC CHU.

Hoa Hoc Tro (Pupils' Flowers): 5 Hoa Ma, Hanoi; tel. (4) 8211065; weekly; Editor NGUYEN PHONG DOANH; circ. 150,000.

Khoa Hoc Ky Thuat Kinh Te The Gioi (World Science, Technology and Economy): 5 Ly Thuong Kiet, Hanoi; tel. (4) 8252931; f. 1982; weekly.

Khoa Hoc va Doi Song (Science and Life): 70 Tran Hung Dao, Hanoi; tel. (4) 8253427; f. 1959; weekly; Editor-in-Chief TRAN CU; circ. 30,000.

Nghe Thuat Dien Anh (Cinematography): 65 Tran Hung Dao, Hanoi; tel. (4) 8262473; f. 1984; fortnightly; Editor DANG NHAT MINH.

Nguoi Cong Giao Viet Nam (Vietnamese Catholic): 59 Trang Thi, Hanoi; tel. (4) 8256242; internet www.vietcatholic.org; f. 1984; weekly; organ of the Cttee for Solidarity of Patriotic Vietnamese Catholics; Editor-in-Chief SO CHI.

Nguoi Dai Bieu Nhan Dan (People's Deputy): 35 Ngo Quyen, Hanoi; tel. (4) 08046231; fax (4) 08046659; e-mail ndbnd@hn.vnn.vn; f. 1988; bi-weekly; disseminates resolutions of the National Assembly and People's Council; Editor-in-Chief HO ANH TAI (acting); circ. 2m.

Nguoi Hanoi (The Hanoian): 19 Hang Buom, Hanoi; tel. (4) 8255662; f. 1984; Editor VU QUAN PHUONG.

Nha Bao Va Cong Luan (The Journalist and Public Opinion): 59 Ly Thai To, Hanoi; tel. (4) 8253609; fax (4) 8250797; f. 1985; monthly review; organ of the Viet Nam Journalists' Asscn; Editor-in-Chief PHAN DUOC TOAN; circ. 40,000.

Nong Nghiep Viet Nam (Viet Nam Agriculture): 14 Ngo Quyen, Hanoi; tel. (4) 8256492; fax (4) 8252923; f. 1987; weekly; Editor LE NAM SON.

Phu Nu (Woman): Vietnam Women's Union, International Relations Dept, 39 Hang Chuoi, Hanoi; e-mail VWunion@netnam.org.vn; f. 1997; fortnightly; women's magazine; circ. 100,000.

Phu Nu Thu Do (Capital Woman): 72 Quan Su, Hanoi; tel. (4) 8247228; fax (4) 8223989; f. 1987; weekly; magazine of the Hanoi Women's Union; Editor-in-Chief MAI THUC.

Phu Nu Viet Nam (Vietnamese Women): 39 Hang Chuoi, Hanoi; tel. (4) 8253500; weekly; magazine of the Vietnamese Women's Union; Editor-in-Chief PHUONG MINH.

Suc Khoe Va Doi Song (Health and Life): 138 A Giang Vo, Hanoi; tel. (4) 8443144; weekly; published by the Ministry of Public Health; Editor LE THAU; circ. 20,000.

Tap Chi Cong San (Communist Review): 1 Nguyen Thuong Hien, Hanoi; tel. (4) 9422061; fax (4) 8222846; e-mail bbttccs@hn.vnn.vn; internet www.tapchicongsan.org.vn; f. 1955 as *Hoc Tap*; fortnightly; political and theoretical organ of the Communist Party of Viet Nam; Editor-in-Chief HA DANG; circ. 50,000.

Tap Chi San Khau (Theatre Magazine): 51 Tran Hung Dao, Hanoi; tel. (4) 9434423; fax (4) 9434293; e-mail trongkhoi@hn.vnn.vn; f. 1973; monthly; Editor NGO THAO.

Tap Chi Tac Pham Van Hoc: 65 Nguyen Du, Hanoi; tel. (4) 8252442; f. 1987; monthly; organ of the Viet Nam Writers' Asscn; Editor-in-Chief NGUYEN DINH THI; circ. 15,000.

Tap Chi Tu Tuong Van Hoa (Ideology and Culture Review): Hanoi; f. 1990; organ of the Central Committee Department of Ideology and Culture; Editor PHAM HUY VAN.

Tap Chi Van Hoc (Literature Magazine): 20 Ly Thai To, Hanoi; tel. (4) 8252895; monthly; published by the Institute of Literature; Editor HA MINH DUC.

The Thao Van Hoa (Sports and Culture): 5 Ly Thuong Kiet, Hanoi; tel. (4) 8267043; fax (4) 8264901; f. 1982; weekly; Editor-in-Chief NGUYEN HUU VINH; circ. 100,000.

The Thao Viet Nam (Viet Nam Sports): 5 Trinh Hoai Duc, Hanoi; f. 1968; weekly; Editor NGUYEN HUNG.

Thieu Nhi Dan Toc (The Ethnic Young): 5 Hoa Ma, Hanoi; tel. (4) 9317133; bi-monthly; Editor PHAM THANH LONG; circ. 60,000.

Thieu Nien Tien Phong (Young Pioneers): 5 Hoa Ma, Hanoi; tel. (4) 9317133; three a week; Editor PHAM THANH LONG; circ. 210,000.

Thoi Bao Kinh Te Viet Nam: 175 Nguyen Thai Hoc, Hanoi; tel. (4) 8452411; fax (4) 8432755; f. 1993; 2 a week; Editor-in-Chief PAVEF DAONGUYENCAT; circ. 37,000.

Thoi Trang Tre (New Fashion): 12 Ho Xuan Huong, Hanoi; tel. (4) 8254032; fax (4) 8226002; f. 1993; monthly; Editor VU QUANG VINH; circ. 80,000.

Thuong Mai (Commerce): 100 Lo Duc, Hanoi; tel. (4) 8263150; f. 1990; weekly; organ of the Ministry of Commerce; Editor TRAN NAM VINH.

Tien Phong (Vanguard): 15 Ho Xuan Huong, Hanoi; tel. (4) 8264031; fax (4) 8225032; f. 1953; four a week; organ of the Ho Chi Minh Communist Youth Union and of the Forum of Vietnamese Youth; Editor DUONG XUAN NAM; circ. 165,000.

Tuan Tin Tuc (News Weekly): 5 Ly Thuong Kiet, Hanoi; tel. (4) 8252931; f. 1982; Vietnamese.

Van Hoa (Culture and Arts): 26 Dien Bien Phu, Hanoi; tel. (4) 8257781; f. 1957; fortnightly; Editor PHI VAN TUONG.

Van Nghe (Arts and Letters): 17 Tran Quoc Toan, Hanoi; tel. (4) 8264430; f. 1949; weekly; organ of the Vietnamese Writers' Union; Editor HUU THINH; circ. 40,000.

Van Nghe Quan Doi (Army Literature and Arts): 4 Ly Nam De, Hanoi; tel. (4) 8254370; f. 1957; monthly; Editor NGUYEN TRI HUAN; circ. 50,000.

Viet Nam Business Forum: 9 Dao Duy Anh, Dong Da District, Hanoi; tel. (4) 5743063; fax (4) 5742052; e-mail vbfhn@vnn.vn; fortnightly magazine in English; publ. by the Chamber of Commerce and Industry of Vietnam; Editor-in-Chief VU TIEN LOC.

Viet Nam Courier: 5 Ly Thuong Kiet, Hanoi; tel. (4) 8261847; fax (4) 8242317; weekly; English; publ. by the Viet Nam News Agency; Editor-in-Chief NGUYEN DUC GIAP.

Viet Nam Cultural Window: 46 Tran Hung Dao, Hanoi; tel. (4) 8253841; fax (4) 8269578; e-mail thegioi@hn.vnn.vn; internet www .vnn.vn/english/vncw/; f. 1998; monthly; English; Dir THAN DOAN LAM.

Viet Nam Economic Times: 175 Nguyen Thai Hoc, Hanoi; tel. (4) 8452411; fax (8) 8356716; e-mail dist@vethan.com.vn; internet www .vneconomy.com.vn; f. 1994; twice weekly; in Vietnamese (with bi-monthly circ. 38,900; edn in English); Editor-in-Chief Prof. DAO NGUYEN CAT.

Viet Nam Investment Review (VIR): 175 Nguyen Thai Hoc, Hanoi; tel. (4) 8450537; fax (4) 8457937; e-mail vir@hn.vnn.vn; internet www.vir.com.vn; f. 1990; weekly; business newspaper publ. in English; Editor-in-Chief NGUYEN TRI DUNG; circ 40,000.

Viet Nam Renovation: Hanoi; f. 1994; quarterly magazine on reform of the agricultural sector; in Vietnamese, Chinese and English.

Viet Nam Review: 79 Ly Thuong Kiet, Hanoi; tel. (4) 9422297; fax (4) 8221152; e-mail vnreview@vnagency.com.vn; internet www .vietnam.vnagency.com.vn; f. 1954; monthly online, in Vietnamese, English, French, Chinese, Spanish and Russian; Editor-in-Chief VU KHANH; circ. 138,000.

Viet Nam Social Science: 27 Tran Xuan Soan, Hanoi; tel. (4) 8261578; f. 1984; quarterly; publ. in English, French and Russian; organ of National Centre for Social and Human Sciences; Editor PHAM XUAN NAM.

Vietnamese Studies: 46 Tran Hung Dao, Hanoi; tel. (4) 8253841; fax (4) 8269578; e-mail thegioi@hn.vnn.vn; f. 1964; quarterly; English and French edns; Dir TRAN DOAN LAM.

NEWS AGENCIES

Viet Nam News Agency (VNA): 5 Ly Thuong Kiet, Hanoi; tel. (4) 8255443; fax (4) 8252984; e-mail btk@vnagency.com.vn; internet www.vnagency.com.vn; mem. of Organization of Asian and Pacific News Agencies; Dir-Gen. LE QUOC TRUNG.

Foreign Bureaux

Agence France-Presse (AFP): 76 Ngo Quyen, BP 40, Hanoi; tel. (4) 8252045; fax (4) 8266032; e-mail afphanoi@fpt.vn; Bureau Chief PHILLIPPE PERDRIAU.

Informatsionnoye Telegrafnoye Agentstvo Rossii— Telegrafnoye Agentstvo Suverennykh Stran (ITAR—TASS) (Russia): Trung Tam Da Nganh, Thanh Xuan Bac, Dong Da District, Hanoi; tel. and fax (4) 8541381; e-mail tassvn@mail.ru; Bureau Chief IOURI A. DENISSOVITCH.

Kyodo News Service (Japan): Room 304, 8 Tran Hung Dao, Hanoi; tel. (4) 8259622; fax (4) 8255848; Bureau Chief KAZUHISA MIYAKE.

Polska Agencja Prasowa (PAP) (Poland): B5 Van Phuc Residential Quarter, Hanoi; tel. (4) 8252601; Chief TOMASZ TRZCINSKI.

Prensa Latina (Cuba): 66 Ngo Thi Nham, Hanoi; tel. (4) 9434366; fax (4) 9434866; e-mail plvietnam@hn.vnn.vn; Correspondent FELIX ALBISU CRUZ.

Reuters (UK): Room 402, 8 Tran Hung Dao, Hanoi; tel. (4) 8259623; fax (4) 8268606; e-mail hanoi.newsroom@reuters.com.

Rossiiskoye Informatsionnoye Agentstvo—Novosti (RIA—Novosti) (Russia): 55A Tran Phu, Hanoi; tel. (4) 8431607; fax (4) 8230001; e-mail riahanoi@hn.vnn.vn; internet www.rian.ru; f. 1955; Bureau Chief ANDREI P. SHAMSHIN.

Xinhua (New China) News Agency (People's Republic of China): 6 Khuc Hao, Hanoi; tel. (4) 8232521; fax (4) 8452913; Chief Correspondent Zhang Jiaxiang.

PRESS ASSOCIATION

Viet Nam Journalists' Association: 59 Ly Thai To, Hanoi; tel. (4) 8269747; fax (4) 8250797; e-mail vja@hn.vnn.vn; f. 1950; asscn of editors, reporters and photographers working in the press, radio, television and news agencies; 11,000 mems (2000); Pres. Hong Vinh; Vice-Pres. Dinh Phong.

Publishers

All publishing enterprises are controlled by the Ministry of Culture and Information.

Am Nhac Dia Hat (Music) Publishing House: 61 Ly Thai To, Hoan Kiem District, Hanoi; tel. (4) 8256208; f. 1986; produces cassettes, videocassettes, books and printed music; Dir Pham Duc Loc.

Cong An Nhan Dan (People's Public Security) Publishing House: 167 Mai Hac De, Hai Ba Trung District, Hanoi; tel. (4) 8260910; f. 1981; managed by the Ministry of the Interior; cultural and artistic information, public order and security; Dir Pham Van Tham.

Giao Thong Van Tai (Communications and Transport) Publishing House: 80b Tran Hung Dao, Hanoi; tel. (4) 8255620; f. 1983; managed by the Ministry of Transport and Communications; Dir To Khanh Tho.

Khoa Hoc Va Ky Thuat (Science and Technology) Publishing House: 70 Tran Hung Dao, Hanoi; tel. (4) 9424786; fax (4) 8220658; e-mail todanghai@hn.vnn.vn; internet www.nxbkhkt.com.vn; f. 1960; scientific and technical works, guide books, dictionaries, popular and management books; Dir Prof. Dr To Dang Hai.

Khoa Hoc Xa Hoi (Social Sciences) Publishing House: 61 Phan Chu Trinh, Hanoi; tel. (4) 8255428; f. 1967; managed by the Institute of Social Science; Dir Dr Nguyen Duc Zieu.

Kim Dong Publishing House: 62 Ba Trieu, Hanoi; tel. (4) 9434730; fax (4) 8229085; e-mail kimdong@hn.vnn.vn; internet www.nxbkimdong.com.vn; f. 1957; children's; managed by the Ho Chi Minh Communist Youth Union; Dir Pham Quang Vinh; Editor-in-Chief Le Thi Dat.

Lao Dong (Labour) Publishing House: 54 Giang Vo, Hanoi; tel. (4) 8515380; f. 1945; translations and political works; managed by the Viet Nam General Confederation of Labour; Dir Le Thanh Tong.

My Thuat (Fine Arts) Publishing House: 44b Hamlong, Hanoi; tel. (4) 8253036; f. 1987; managed by the Plastic Arts Workers' Association; Dir Truong Hanh.

Nha Xuat Ban Giao Duc (Education) Publishing House: 81 Tran Hung Dao, Hanoi; tel. (4) 8220554; fax (4) 8262010; f. 1957; managed by the Ministry of Education and Training; Dir Pham Van An; Editor-in-Chief Prof. Nguyen Nhu Y.

Nha Xuat Ban Hoi Nha Van (Writers' Association) Publishing House: 65 Nguyen Du, Hoan Kiem District, Hanoi; tel. and fax (4) 8222135; f. 1957; managed by the Vietnamese Writers' Association; Editor-in-Chief and Dir (acting) Ngo Van Phu.

Nong Nghiep (Agriculture) Publishing House: DH 14, Phoung Mai Ward, Dong Da District, Hanoi; tel. (4) 8523887; f. 1976; managed by the Ministry of Agriculture and Rural Development; Dir Duong Quang Dieu.

Phu Nu (Women) Publishing House: 16 Alexandre De Rhodes, Hanoi; tel. (4) 8294459; f. 1957; managed by the Vietnamese Women's Union; Dir Tran Thu Huong.

Quan Doi Nhan Dan (People's Army) Publishing House: 25 Ly Nam De, Hanoi; tel. (4) 8255766; managed by the Ministry of National Defence; Dir Doan Chuong.

San Khau (Theatre) Publishing House: 51 Tran Hung Dao, Hanoi; tel. (4) 8264423; f. 1986; managed by the Stage Artists' Association.

Su That (Truth) Publishing House: 24 Quang Trung, Hanoi; tel. (4) 8252008; fax (4) 8251881; f. 1945; managed by the Communist Party of Viet Nam; Marxist-Leninist classics, politics and philosophy; Dir Tran Nham.

Thanh Nien (Youth) Publishing House: 270 Nguyen Dinh Chieu, District 3, Hanoi; tel. and fax (4) 8222612; f. 1954; managed by the Ho Chi Minh Communist Youth Union; Dir Bui Van Ngoi.

The Duc The Thao (Physical Education and Sports) Publishing House: 7 Trinh Hoai Duc, Hanoi; tel. (4) 8256155; f. 1974;

managed by the Ministry of Culture and Information; Dir Nguyen Hieu.

The Gioi Publishers: 46 Tran Hung Dao, Hanoi; tel. (4) 8253841; fax (4) 8269578; e-mail thegioi@hn.vnn.vn; f. 1957; foreign language publications; managed by the Ministry of Culture and Information; Dir Mai Ly Quang.

Thong Ke (Statistics) Publishing House: 96 Thuy Khe, Hanoi; tel. (4) 8257814; f. 1980; managed by the Gen. Statistical Office; Dir Nguyen Dao.

Van Hoa (Culture) Publishing House: 43 Lo Duc, Hanoi; tel. (4) 8253517; f. 1971; managed by the Ministry of Culture and Information; Dir Quang Huy.

Van Hoc (Literature) Publishing House: 49 Tran Hung Dao, Hanoi; tel. (4) 8252100; f. 1948; managed by the Ministry of Culture and Information; Dir Lu Huy Nguyen.

Xay Dung (Building) Publishing House: 37 Le Dai Hanh, Hanoi; tel. (4) 8268271; fax (4) 8215369; f. 1976; managed by the Ministry of Construction; Dir Nguyen Luong Bich.

Y Hoc (Medicine) Publishing House: 4 Le Thanh Ton, Phan Chu Trinh, Hoan Kiem District, Hanoi; tel. (4) 8255281; e-mail xuatbanyhoc@netnam.vn; managed by the Ministry of Public Health; Dir Hoang Trong Quang.

Broadcasting and Communications

TELECOMMUNICATIONS

Directorate General for Posts and Telecommunications (DGPT): Department of Science-Technology and International Cooperations, 18 Nguyen Du, Hanoi; tel. (4) 8226580; fax (4) 8226590; industry regulator; Sec.-Gen. Dr Mai Liem Truc.

Board of the Technical and Economic Programme on Information Technology: 39 Tran Hung Dao, Hanoi; e-mail nyenet@itnet.gov.vn; Gen. Dir Dr Do Van Loc.

Army Electronics and Communications Corporation: military-owned communications company; awarded a licence in 1998 to provide national telephone services, including a fixed network and mobile and paging systems.

Saigon Post and Telecommunications Service Corpn: 45 Le Duan, District 1, Ho Chi Minh City; tel. (8) 8220121; fax (8) 8220120; e-mail saigonpostel@saigonpostel.com.vn; internet www.saigonpostel.com.vn; partially owned by the state; granted a licence in 1997 to operate services in southern Viet Nam; Chair. Tran Ngoc Binh; Gen. Dir Nguyen Thanh Van.

Viet Nam Posts and Telecommunications Corporation (VNPT): 18 Nguyen Du, Hai Ba Trung District, Hanoi; tel. (4) 8265104; fax (4) 8255851; e-mail infocen2@hn.vnn.vn; internet www.vnpt.com.vn; f. 1995; state-owned communications company; Chair. Do Trung Ta; Pres. and CEO Dang Dinh Lam.

RADIO

In 1998 there were 390 FM stations, 567 district radio stations and 6,505 commune radio stations in Viet Nam. The Ministry of Culture and Information is responsible for the management of radio services.

Voice of Viet Nam (VOV): 58 Quan Su, Hanoi; tel. (4) 9342456; fax (4) 8266707; e-mail btdn.vov@hn.vnn.vn; internet www.vov.org.vn; f. 1945; five domestic channels in Vietnamese; foreign service in English, Japanese, French, Khmer, Laotian, Spanish, Thai, Cantonese, Mandarin, Indonesian, Vietnamese and Russian; Dir-Gen. Vu Hien.

TELEVISION

At the end of 1994 there were 53 provincial television stations and 232 relay stations in Viet Nam. The Ministry of Culture and Information is responsible for the management of television services.

Viet Nam Television (VTV): 43 Nguyen Chi Thanh, Hanoi; tel. (4) 8318123; fax (4) 8318124; e-mail webmaster@vtv.org.vn; internet www.vtv.org.vn; television was introduced in South Viet Nam in 1966 and in North Viet Nam in 1970; broadcasts from Hanoi (via satellite) to the whole country and Asia region; Vietnamese, French, English; Dir-Gen. Vu Van Hien.

Finance

(cap. = capital; res = reserves; dep. = deposits; m. = million; brs = branches)

BANKING

In early 1990 the Government established four independent commercial banks, several joint-venture banks, and introduced legislation to permit the operation of foreign banks in Viet Nam. At the end of 1998 the Vietnamese banking system comprised six state-owned banks, four joint-venture banks, 24 foreign bank branches, 51 joint-stock commercial banks, 977 People's Credit Funds, two joint-stock finance companies, three corporation-subordinated finance companies and eight leasing companies. At the beginning of 2002 there were 27 foreign bank branches and 42 representative offices of foreign financial institutions in Viet Nam.

Central Bank

State Bank of Viet Nam: 47–49 Ly Thai To, Hanoi; tel. (4) 9342524; fax (4) 8268765; e-mail sf-sbv@hn.hnn.vn; f. 1951; central bank of issue; provides a national network of banking services and supervises the operation of the state banking system; Gov. Le Duc Thuy; 61 brs and sub-brs.

State Banks

Bank for Agriculture and Rural Development: 2 Lang Ha, Hanoi; tel. (4) 8313710; fax (4) 8313717; e-mail qhqt@fpt.vn; f. 1988; Chair. Nguyen Quoc Toan; Gen. Dir Trinh Huu Dan; 1,291 brs.

Bank for Foreign Trade of Viet Nam (Vietcombank): 198 Tran Quang Khai, Hanoi; tel. (4) 8265503; fax (4) 8269067; f. 1963; authorized to deal in foreign currencies and all other international banking business; cap. 1,099,258m. dông, res 780,469m. dông, dep. 58,591,190m. dông (Dec. 2000), total assets 65,633,108m. dông (Dec. 2000); Chair. Le Dac Cu; Dir-Gen. Vu Viet Ngoan; 22 brs.

Bank for Investment and Development of Vietnam (Vietinde Bank): 194 Tran Quang Khai, Hanoi; tel. (4) 8266966; fax (4) 8266959; e-mail bidv@hn.vnn.vn; internet www.bidv.com.vn; Chair. Phung Thi Van Anh; Gen. Dir Trinh Ngoc Ho.

Industrial and Commercial Bank of Viet Nam (VIETINCOMBANK): 108 Tran Hung Dao, Hanoi; tel. (4) 9421066; fax (4) 9421143; e-mail sonbk@fpt.vn; internet www.icb.com.vn; f. 1987; state-owned; authorized to receive personal savings, extend loans, issue stocks and invest in export-orientated cos and jt ventures with foreigners; cap. and res 1,624,210m. dông, dep. 40,745,050m. dông (Dec. 2000); Chair. Nguyen Van Binh; Gen. Dir Phung Khao Ke; 101 brs and 29 sub-brs.

Saigon Bank for Industry and Trade: 18–20 Ton Duc Thang, District 1, Ho Chi Minh City; tel. (8) 8257994; fax (8) 8235668; e-mail saigonbank@hcm.vnn.vn; cap. 145,000m. dông, res 17,492m. dông, dep. 1,152,609m. dông (Dec. 2001); specializes in trade and industry activities; Dir Duong Xuan Minh.

Vietnam Export-Import Commercial Joint-Stock Bank (Vietnam Eximbank): 7 Le Thi Hong Gam, Ho Chi Minh City; tel. (8) 8210055; fax (8) 8216913; e-mail icbr.eximbank@hcm.vnn.vn; f. 1989; authorized to undertake banking transactions for the production and processing of export products and export-import operations; cap. 300,000m. dông (April 2001); res 30,913m. dông, dep. 2,567,279m. dông (Dec. 2000); Chair. Nguyen Thanh Long; Dir-Gen. Truong Van Phuoc; 3 brs.

Viet Nam Technological and Commercial Bank: 24 Ly Thuong Kiet, Hoan Kiem, Hanoi; tel. (4) 8250305; Dir Dang Trong Cuong.

Joint-Stock and Other Banks

CBD (Codo Rural Share Commercial Bank): Co Do, Thoi Dong, O Mon, Can Tho Province; tel. (71) 61642; Dir Tran Ngoc Ha.

Chohung Vina Bank: 3-5 Ho Tung Mau, District 1, Ho Chi Minh City; tel. (8) 8291581; fax (8) 8291583; e-mail hcmc.fvb@hcm.vnn .vn; f. 1993; jt venture between the Bank for Foreign Trade of Viet Nam and Korea First Bank; cap. US $20m. Chair. Viet Ngoan Vu.

DS Bank (Dongthap Commercial Joint-Stock Bank): 48 Rad 30/4, Cao Lanh Town, Dong Thap Province; tel. (67) 51441; fax (67) 51878; Dir Hoang Van Tu.

Ficombank (Denhat Joint-Stock Commercial Bank): 67A Le Quang Sung, District 6, Ho Chi Minh City; tel. (8) 5857089; fax (8) 5557093; Dir Van Duong.

Indovina Bank Ltd: 36 Ton That Dam, District 1, Ho Chi Minh City; tel. (8) 8224995; fax (8) 8230131; e-mail ivbhcm@hcm.vnn.vn; internet www.indovinabank.com.vn; f. 1990; jt venture of the United World Chinese Commercial Bank and the Industrial and Commercial Bank of Viet Nam; also has brs in Hanoi, Haiphong and Can

Tho; cap. US $20m., res US $2.3m., dep. US $61.7m. (2001); Chair. Phung Khac Ke; Gen. Dir Peng Yuo Lung.

Maritime Bank: 5A Nguyen Tri Phuong Hai Phong, Ho Chi Minh City; tel. (8) 31823076; fax (8) 31823063; e-mail maritimebank@fpt .vn; Gen. Dir Tran Van Nghi.

Phuongnam Bank—Phuongnam Commercial Joint-Stock Bank: 258 Minh Phung, District 11, Ho Chi Minh City; tel. (8) 8556050; fax (8) 8556047; commercial bank; Dir Hoang Van Toan.

Quedo Joint-Stock Bank: 1-3-5 Can Giuoc, District 8, Ho Chi Minh City; tel. (8) 8562418; fax (8) 8553596; Dir Bao Lan.

VID Public Bank: Ground Floor, Hanoi Tungshing Square, 2 Ngo Quyen, Hanoi; tel. (4) 8268307; fax (4) 8268228; e-mail vpb.han@hn .vnn.vn; f. 1992; joint venture between the Bank for Investment and Development (Viet Nam) and the Public Bank Berhad (Malaysia); commercial bank; cap. US $20m. (2001); Chair. Trinh Ngoc Ho; Gen. Dir Lee Wing Chew; 4 brs.

VinaSiam Bank: 2 Pho Duc Chinh, District 1, Ho Chi Minh City; tel. (8) 8210557; fax (8) 8210585; e-mail vsb@hcm.vnn.vn; internet www.vinasiambank.com; f. 1995; joint venture between Bank for Agriculture and Rural Development, Siam Commercial Bank (Thailand) and Charoen Pokphand Group (Thailand).

VP Bank (Viet Nam Commercial Joint-Stock Bank for Private Enterprises): 18B Le Thanh Tong, Hanoi; tel. (4) 8245246; fax (4) 8260182; Dir Bui Huy Hung.

Foreign Banks

Australia and New Zealand Banking Group Ltd (Australia): 14 Le Thai To, Hanoi; tel. (4) 8258190; fax (4) 8258188; e-mail ahmada@ anz.com; Gen. Man. Adil Ahmad; also has br. in Ho Chi Minh City.

Bangkok Bank Public Co Ltd (Thailand): Harbour View Tower, 35 Nguyen Hue, District 1, Ho Chi Minh City; tel. (8) 8214396; fax (8) 8213772; e-mail bblhcm@hcm.vnn.vn; Man. Wittaya Supatanakul.

Bank of Tokyo-Mitsubishi Ltd (Japan): The Landmark, 8th Floor, 5B Ton Duc Thang, District 1, Ho Chi Minh City; tel. (8) 8231560; fax (8) 8231559.

BNP Paribas (France): 8 Tran Hung Dao, Hanoi; tel. (4) 8253175; fax (4) 8266982.

Crédit Agricole Indosuez (France): Somerset Chancellor Court, 4th Floor, 21–23 Nguyen Thi Minh Khai, District 1, Ho Chi Minh City; tel. (8) 8295048; fax (8) 8296065; e-mail cai.vietnam@hcm.vnn .vn; Gen. Man. Olivier Prechac.

Crédit Lyonnais SA (France): Han Nam Officetel, 4th Floor, 65 Nguyen Du, District 1, Ho Chi Minh City; tel. (8) 8299226; fax (8) 8296465; e-mail contact_vnhcmc@creditlyonnais.fr; f. 1993; Man. Ngoc Vu Han; also has br. in Hanoi.

Natexis Banques Populaires (France): Rm 16-02, Prime Ctr, 53 Quang Trung, Hanoi; tel. (4) 9433667; fax (4) 9433665; e-mail natexis-vn@hcm.vnn.vn; Rep. Mme Ut.

Shinhan Bank (Republic of Korea): Yoco Bldg, 7th Floor, 41 Nguyen Thi Minh Khai, District 1, Ho Chi Minh City; tel. (8) 8230012; fax (8) 8230009; Gen. Man. Hae-Soo Kim.

STOCK EXCHANGE

Securities Trading Centre: 45–47 Chuong Duong, Ho Chi Minh City; f. July 2000 by the State Securities Commission (see Development Organization).

INSURANCE

In January 1994 it was announced that foreign insurance companies were to be permitted to operate in Viet Nam. In 1995 it was announced that Baoviet's monopoly of the insurance industry was to be ended. A number of new insurance companies were subsequently established, including Bao Minh, Nha Long Co, Pijico, PetroViet Nam Insurance Co and Vinare. In August 1996 Viet Nam's first joint-venture insurance company, Viet Nam International Assurance, was founded. By late 1996 some 30 foreign insurance companies had opened representative offices in Viet Nam.

Baoviet (Viet Nam Insurance Co): Head Office, 35 Hai Ba Trung, Hoan Kiem District, Hanoi; tel. (4) 8262632; fax (4) 8257188; e-mail service@baoviet.com.vn; internet www.baoviet.com.vn; f. 1965; property and casualty, personal accident, liability and life insurance; total assets 3,257,000m. dông (2000); Chair. and CEO Prof. Truong Moc Lam.

Viet Nam International Assurance (VIA): 8th Floor, The Landmark, 5B Ton Duc Thang, District 1, Ho Chi Minh City; tel. and fax (8) 8221340; e-mail hcm@via.com.vn; internet www.via.com.vn; f. 1996; jt-venture co, 51% owned by Baoviet, 24.5% owned by Commercial Union (UK), 24.5% owned by Tokyo Marine and Fire Insurance Co (Japan); non-life insurance and reinsurance for foreign cos.

Bao Long (Nharong Joint-Stock Insurance Co): 185 Dien Bien Phu, District 1, Ho Chi Minh City; tel. (8) 8239219; fax (8) 8239223; internet www.nharong.com; cap. 22,000m. dông (1994); Dir Tran Van Binh.

Inchibrok Insurance: 27 Ly Thai To, Hanoi; tel. (4) 8262686; fax (4) 8243983; f. 1993; 50% joint venture between Baoviet and Inchcape Group.

Thanhhoa Insurance: 666 Ba Trieu, Thanh Hoa City, Thanh Hoa Province; tel. (37) 52347; fax (37) 53007; Dir Nguyen Minh Khan.

Trade and Industry

GOVERNMENT AGENCIES

State Financial and Monetary Council (SFMC): f. 1998; established to supervise, review and resolve matters relating to national financial and monetary policy.

Vinacontrol (Viet Nam Superintendence and Inspection Co): 54 Tran Nhan Tong, Hanoi; tel. (4) 9433840; fax (4) 9433844; e-mail vinacontrolvn@hn.vnn.vn; internet www.vinacontrol.com.vn; f. 1957; brs in all main Vietnamese ports; controls quality and volume of exports and imports and transit of goods, and conducts inspections of deliveries and production processes; price verification, marine survey, damage survey, claim settling and adjustment; Gen. Dir Le Viet Su.

DEVELOPMENT ORGANIZATION

State Securities Commission: Hanoi; internet www.ssc.gov.vn; f. 1997; responsible for developing the capital markets, incl. the establishment of a stock exchange; 14 mems; Chair. Nguyen Duc Quang.

CHAMBER OF COMMERCE

VCCI (Viet Nam Chamber of Commerce and Industry): 9 Dao Duy Anh, Hanoi; tel. (4) 5742022; fax (4) 5742030; e-mail vcci@hn.vnn.vn; internet www.vcci.com.vn; f. 1963; offices in Ho Chi Minh City, Da Nang, Haiphong, Can Tho, Vung Tau, Nha Trang, Nghe An, Thanh Hoa and Vinh; promotes business and investment between foreign and Vietnamese cos; protects interests of businesses; organizes training activities, exhbns and fairs in Viet Nam and abroad; provides information about and consultancy in Viet Nam's trade and industry; represents foreign applicants for patents and trade mark registration; issues certificates of origin and other documentation; helps domestic and foreign businesses to settle disputes by negotiation or arbitration; in 1993 foreign businesses operating in Viet Nam and Vietnamese businesses operating abroad were permitted to become assoc. mems; Pres. and Chair. Doan Duy Thanh; Vice-Pres Doan Ngoc Bong, Pham Chi Lan, Dao Duy Chu, Vu Tien Loc, Hoang Van Dung; Sec.-Gen. Doan Duy Khuong; associated organizations: Viet Nam International Arbitration Centre, Viet Nam General Average Adjustment Committee, Advisory Board.

Viet Nam International Arbitration Centre: 9 Dao Duy Anh, Hanoi; tel. (4) 5742022; fax (4) 5742020; e-mail viac-vcci@hn.vnn .vn; adjudicates in disputes concerning both domestic and international economic relations.

INDUSTRIAL AND TRADE ORGANIZATIONS

Agrexport (Viet Nam National Agricultural Produce Export-Import Corpn): 6 Trang Tien, Hanoi; tel. (4) 8254234; fax (4) 8265550; f. 1958; imports and exports agricultural produce and coffee, natural silk, insecticides and agrochemicals; Gen. Dir Nguyen Viet Van.

Agrimex (Viet Nam National Agricultural Products Corpn): 173 Hai Ba Trung, District 3, Ho Chi Minh City; tel. (8) 8241049; fax (8) 8291349; e-mail agrimex@hcm.fpt.vn; f. 1956; imports and exports agricultural products; Gen. Dir Nguyen Bach Tuyet.

Airimex (General Civil Aviation Import-Export and Forwarding Co): Le Van Kim, Gia Lam District, Hanoi; tel. (4) 8271939; fax (4) 8271925; e-mail airimex@fpt.vn; f. 1989; imports and exports aircraft, spare parts and accessories for aircraft and air communications; Dir Nguyen Chi Can.

An Giang Afiex Co (An Giang Agriculture and Foods Import and Export Co): 34–36 Hai Ba Trung, Long Xuyen Town, An Giang Province; tel. (76) 841021; fax (76) 843199; e-mail xnknstpagg@hcm .vnn.net; f. 1992; mfr and sale of agricultural products, also beverages; Dir Pham Van Bay.

Artexport–Hanoi (Viet Nam Handicrafts and Art Articles Export-Import Corpn): 31–33 Ngo Quyen, Hanoi; tel. (4) 8252760; fax (4) 8259275; e-mail artexport.hn@fpt.vn; internet www.artexport.com .vn; f. 1964; deals in craft products and art articles; Gen. Dir Mai Van Nghiem.

Barotex (Viet Nam National Bamboo and Rattan Export-Import Co): 15 Ben Chuong Duong, District 1, Ho Chi Minh City; tel. (8) 8295544; fax (8) 8295352; e-mail barotexsg@saigonnet.vn; f. 1971; specializes in art and handicrafts made from natural materials, sports shoes, ceramic and lacquer wares, gifts and other housewares, fibres, agricultural and forest products; Gen. Dir Ta Quoc Toan.

Bimson Cement Co: Lam Son Hamlet, Bim Con Town, Thanh Hoa Province; tel. (52) 824242; fax (37) 824046; mfr of cement; Dir Le Van Chung.

Binh Tay Import-Export Co (BITEX): 78–82 Hau Giang, District 6, Ho Chi Minh City; tel. (8) 8559669; fax (8) 8557846; e-mail bitex@ hcm.vnn.vn; trade in miscellaneous goods; Dir Nguyen Van Thien.

B12 Petroleum Co: Cai Lan, Bay Chay Sub-District, Ha Long City, Quang Ninh Province; tel. (33) 846360; fax (33) 846349; distribution of petroleum products; Dir Vu Ngoc Hai.

Centrimex (Viet Nam National General Import-Export Corpn): 48 Tran Phu, Nha Trang City, Khanh Hoa; tel. (58) 821239; fax (58) 821914; e-mail centrimex@dng.vnn.vn; internet www.centrimexhn .com.vn; exports and imports goods for five provinces in the south-central region of Viet Nam; Gen. Dir Le Van Ngoc.

Coalimex (Viet Nam National Coal Export-Import and Material Supply Corpn): 47 Quang Trung, Hanoi; tel. (4) 9423166; fax (4) 9422350; e-mail coalimex@fpt.vn; internet www.coalimex.com.vn; f. 1982; exports coal, imports mining machinery and equipment; Gen. Dir Ninh Xuan Son.

Cocenex (Central Production Import-Export Corpn): 80 Hang Gai, Hanoi; tel. (4) 8254535; fax (4) 8294306; f. 1988; Gen. Dir Bui Thi Thu Huong.

Coffee Supply, Processing and Materials Co: 38B Nguyen Bieu, Nha Trang City, Khanh Hoa Province; tel. (58) 21176; coffee producer.

Cokyvina (Post and Telecommunication Equipment Import-Export Service Corpn): 178 Trieu Viet Vuong, Hanoi; tel. (4) 9782362; fax (4) 9782368; e-mail cokyvina@hn.vnn.vn; f. 1987; imports and exports telecom equipment, provides technical advice on related subjects, undertakes authorized imports, jt ventures, jt co-ordination and co-operation on investment with foreign and domestic economic organizations; Dir Nguyen Kim Ky.

Constrexim (Viet Nam National Construction Materials and Technique Export-Import Corpn): 39 Nguyen Dinh Chieu, Hanoi; tel. (4) 8263448; fax (4) 8262701; e-mail constrexim@fpt.vn; internet www .constrexim.com.vn; f. 1982; exports and imports building materials, equipment and machinery; undertakes construction projects in Viet Nam and abroad, and production of building materials with foreign partners; assists Vietnamese enterprises in forming joint-venture projects with foreign partners; also involved in investment promotion and projects management, real estate development, and human resources development and training; Gen. Dir Nguyen Quoc Hiep.

Culturimex (State Enterprise for the Export and Import of Works of Art and other Cultural Commodities): 22B Hai Ba Trung, Hanoi; tel. (4) 8252226; fax (4) 8259224; f. 1988; exports cultural items and imports materials for the cultural industry; Dir Nguyen Quoc Hiep.

Epco Ltd (Export Import and Tourism Co Ltd): 1 Nyuyen Thuong Hien, District 3, Ho Chi Minh City; tel. (8) 8324392; fax (8) 8324744; f. 1986; processes seafood; tourism and hotel business.

Foocosa (Food Co Ho Chi Min City): 57 Nguyen Thi Minh Khai, District 1, Ho Chi Minh City; tel. (8) 9309070; fax (8) 9304552; e-mail foocosa@hcm.vnn.vn; internet www.foocosa.com.vn; mfr and distributor of food products (rice, instant noodles, porridge, sauces, biscuits); Dir Ngo Van Tan.

Genecofov (General Co of Foods and Services): 64 Ba Huyen Thanh Quan, District 3, Ho Chi Minh City; tel. (8) 9325366; fax (8) 9325428; e-mail gecofov@hcm.fpt.vn; f. 1956; import and export of food products; under the Ministry of Commerce; Dir To Van Phat.

Generalexim (Viet Nam National General Export-Import Corpn): 46 Ngo Quyen, Hoan Kiem, Hanoi; tel. (4) 8264009; fax (4) 8259894; e-mail generalexim@bdvn.vnd.net; f. 1981; export and import on behalf of production and trading organizations, also garment processing for export and manufacture of toys; Gen. Dir Yuong Van Tu.

Generalimex (Viet Nam National General Import-Export Corpn): 66 Pho Duc Chinh, Ho Chi Minh City; tel. (8) 8292990; fax (8) 8292968; e-mail generalimex@hcm.fpt.vn; exports of agricultural products and spices, imports of machinery, vehicles, chemicals and fertilizers; Gen. Dir Nguyen Van Hoang.

Geruco (Viet Nam General Rubber Corpn): 236 Nam Ky Khoi Nghia, District 3, Ho Chi Minh City; tel. (8) 9325235; fax (8) 9327341; e-mail grc-imexdept@hcm.vnn.vn; internet www.vngeruco .com; merged with Rubexim (rubber export-import corpn) in 1991; manages and controls the Vietnamese rubber industry, including the planting, processing and trading of natural rubber and rubber wood products; also imports chemicals, machinery and spare parts for the industry; Dir-Gen. LE QUANG THUNG.

Haprosimex (Hanoi General Production and Import-Export Company): 22 Hang Luoc, Hanoi; tel. (4) 8266601; fax (4) 8264014; e-mail hapro@fpt.vn; internet www.hapro.com.vn; specializes in handicrafts, textiles, clothing and agricultural and forestry products; Gen. Dir NGUYEN CU TAM.

Hatien Cement Co No 1: Km 8 Highway Hanoi, Thu Duc, Ho Chi Minh City; tel. (8) 8966608; fax (8) 8967635; mfr of cement; Dir NGUYEN NGOC ANH.

Hatien Cement Co No 2: Kien Luong Town, Ha Tien, Kien Giang Province; tel. (77) 53004; fax (77) 53005; mfr of cement; Dir NGUYEN MANH.

Haugiang Petrolimex (Haugiang Petrol and Oil Co): 21 Cach Mang Thang 8, Can Tho City, Can Tho Province; tel. (71) 21657; fax (71) 12746; distributor of fuel; Dir TRINH MANG THANG.

Hoang Thach Cement Co: Minh Tan Hamlet, Kim Mon, Hai Hung Province; tel. (32) 821092; fax (32) 821098; sale of construction materials; Dir NGUYEN DUC HOAN.

Machinoimport (Viet Nam National Machinery Export-Import Corpn): 8 Trang Thi, Hoan Kiem, Hanoi; tel. (4) 8253703; fax (4) 8254050; e-mail machino@hn.vnn.vn; internet www.machinoimport .com.vn; f. 1956; imports and exports machinery, spare parts and tools; consultancy, investment, joint-venture, and mfring services; comprises 12 cos; Chair. NGUYEN TRAN DAT; Gen. Dir HO QUANG HIEU.

Marine Supply (Marine Technical Materials Import-Export and Supplies): 276A Da Nang, Ngo Quyen, Haiphong; tel. (31) 847308; fax (31) 845159; f. 1985; imports and exports technical materials for marine transportation industry; Dir PHAN TRANG CHAN.

Mecanimex (Viet Nam National Mechanical Products Export-Import Co): 37 Trang Thi, Hoan Kiem District, Hanoi; tel. (4) 8257459; fax (4) 9349904; e-mail mecahn@fpt.vn; exports and imports mechanical products and hand tools; Gen. Dir TRAN BAO GIOC.

Minexport (Viet Nam National Minerals Export-Import Corpn): 35 Hai Ba Trung, Hanoi; tel. (4) 8253674; fax (4) 8253326; e-mail minexport@fpt.vn; internet www.minexport.com; f. 1956; exports minerals and metals, quarry products, chemical products; imports metals, chemical products, industrial materials, fuels and oils, fertilizers; Gen. Dir VO TRONG CUONG.

Nafobird (Viet Nam Forest and Native Birds, Animals and Ornamental Plants Export-Import Enterprises): 64 Truong Dinh, District 3, Ho Chi Minh City; tel. (8) 8290211; fax (8) 8293735; f. 1987; exports native birds, animals and plants, and imports materials for forestry; Dir VO HA AN.

Naforimex (Hanoi Forest Products Export-Import and Production Corpn): 19 Ba Trieu, Hoan Kiem District, Hanoi; tel. (4) 8261254; fax (4) 8259264; e-mail naforimexhanoi@fpt.vn; f. 1960; imports chemicals, machinery and spare parts for the forestry industry, linseed oil and essences; exports oils, forest products, gum benzoin and resin; Dir PHAM CAO CHINH.

Packexport (Viet Nam National Packaging Technology and Import-Export Co): 31 Hang Thung, Hanoi; tel. (4) 8262792; fax (4) 8269227; e-mail packexport-vn@vnn.vn; f. 1976; manufactures packaging for domestic and export demand, and imports materials for the packaging industry; Gen. Dir TRINH LE KIEU.

Petec-Trading and Investment Corpn: 70 Ba Huyen Thanh Quan, District 3, Ho Chi Minh City; tel. (8) 8299299; fax (8) 8299686; f. 1981; imports equipment and technology for oil drilling, exploration and oil production, exports crude petroleum, rice, coffee and agricultural products; invests in silk, coffee, financial and transport sectors; Gen. Dir TRAN HUU LAC.

Petrol and Oil Co (Zone 1): Duc Gliang Town, Gia Lam, Hanoi; tel. (4) 8271400; fax (4) 8272432; sales of oil and gas; Dir PHAN VAN DU.

Petrolimex (Viet Nam National Petroleum Corpn): 1 Kham Thien, Dong Da District, Hanoi; tel. (4) 8512603; fax (4) 8519203; e-mail xttm@petrolimex.com.vn; internet www.petrolimex.com.vn; f. 1956; import, export and distribution of petroleum products and liquefied petroleum gas; Chair. NGUYEN MANH TIEN.

Petrolimex Saigon Petroleum Co (Zone 2): 15 Le Duan, District 1, Ho Chi Minh City; tel. (8) 8292081; fax (8) 8222082; sales of petroleum products; Dir TRAN VAN THANG.

Petrovietnam (Viet Nam National Petroleum Corpn): 22 Ngo Quyen, Hoan Kiem District, Hanoi; tel. (4) 8252526; fax (4) 8265942; e-mail webmaster@hn.pv.com.vn; internet www.petrovietnam.com .vn; f. 1975; exploration and production of petroleum and gas; Chair. HO SI THOANG; Pres. and CEO NGO THUONG SAN.

Saigon Brewery Co: 187 Nguyen Chi Thanh, District 5, Ho Chi Minh City; tel. (8) 8396342; fax (8) 8296856; producer of beer; Dir HOANG CHI QUY.

Seaco (Sundries Electric Appliances Co): 64 Pho Duc Chinh, District 1, Ho Chi Minh City; tel. (8) 8210961; fax (8) 8210974; deals in miscellaneous electrical goods; Dir MAI MINH CUONG.

Seaprodex Saigon (Ho Chi Minh City Sea Products Import-Export Corpn): 87 Ham Nghi, District 1, Ho Chi Minh City; tel. (8) 8293669; fax (8) 8224951; e-mail seaprodex.saigon@bdvn.vnd.net; internet www.seaprodexsg.com; f. 1978; exports frozen and processed sea products; imports machinery and materials for fishing and processing; Gen. Dir PHUNG QUOC MAN.

Seaprodex Hanoi (Hanoi Sea Products Export-Import Co): 20 Lang Ha, Hanoi; tel. (4) 8344437; fax (4) 8354125; e-mail seaprodexhn@hn.vnn.vn; Dir DANG DINH BAO.

SJC (Saigon Jewellery Co): 2D Nguye Trung Truc, District 1, Ho Chi Minh City; tel. (8) 8222827; fax (8) 8294420; e-mail sjc@hcm.vnn.vn; internet www.sjcvn.com; distributor of jewellery; Dir NGUYEN THANH LONG.

Technimex (Viet Nam Technology Export-Import Corpn): 70 Tran Hung Dao, Hanoi; tel. (4) 8256751; fax (4) 8220377; e-mail hanoi .technimex@bdvn.vnmail.vnd.net; f. 1982; exports and imports machines, equipment, instruments, etc. Dir NGUYEN HUY BINH.

Technoimport (Viet Nam National Complete Equipment and Technics Import-Export Corpn): 16–18 Trang Thi, Hanoi; tel. (4) 8254974; fax (4) 8254059; e-mail technohn@netnam.org.vn; internet www.technoimport.com.vn; f. 1959; imports and exports equipment, machinery, transport equipment, spare parts, materials and various consumer commodities; exports products by co-investment and joint-venture enterprises; provides consulting services for trade and investment, transport and forwarding services; acts as import-export brokering and trading agents; Gen. Dir PHAN MAI PHUONG.

Terraprodex (Corpn for Processing and Export-Import of Rare Earth and Other Specialities): 35 Dien Bien Phu, Hanoi; tel. (4) 8232010; fax (4) 8256446; f. 1989; processing and export of rare earth products and other minerals; Dir TRAN DUC HIEP.

Tocontap Saigon (Viet Nam National Sundries Import-Export Co): 35 Le Quy Don, District 3, Ho Chi Minh City; tel. (8) 9321062; fax (8) 9325963; e-mail tocontapsaigon@hcm.vnn.vn; internet www .tocontapsaigon.com; f. 1956; imports and exports apparel, agricultural products, art and handicrafts and sundries; Gen. Dir LE THI THANH HUONG.

Vegetexco (Viet Nam National Vegetables and Fruit Export-Import Corpn): 2 Trung Tu, Dong Da District, Hanoi; tel. (4) 5740779; fax (4) 8523926; e-mail vegetexcovn@fpt.vn; internet www .vegetexcovn.tripod.com; f. 1971; exports fresh and processed vegetables and fruit, spices and flowers, and other agricultural products; imports vegetable seeds and processing materials; Gen. Dir DINH VAN PHUOC.

Vienametal (Viet Nam National Steel Corpn): D2 Ton That Tung, Dong Da District, Hanoi; tel. (4) 8525537; fax (4) 8262657; distributor of metal products; Dir NGO HUY PHAN.

Vietgoldgem (Viet Nam National Gold, Silver and Gemstone Corpn): 23B Quang Trung, Hoan Kiem District, Hanoi; tel. (4) 8260453; fax (4) 8260405; sales of precious metals and gems; Dir NGUYEN DUY HUNG (acting).

Vietrans (Viet Nam National Foreign Trade Forwarding and Warehousing Corpn): 13 Ly Nam De, Hoan Kiem District, Hanoi; tel. (4) 8457801; fax (4) 8455829; e-mail vietrans@hn.vnn.vn; internet www .vietrans.com.vn; f. 1970; agent for forwarding and transport of exports and imports, diplomatic cargoes and other goods, warehousing, shipping and insurance; Gen. Dir THAI DUY LONG.

Vietranscimex (Viet Nam Transportation and Communication Import-Export Co): 22 Nguyen Van Troi, Phu Nhuan District, Ho Chi Minh City; tel. (8) 8442993; fax (8) 8445240; exports and imports specialized equipment and materials for transportation and communication; Gen. Dir PHAM QUANG VINH.

Viettronimex (Viet Nam Electronics Import-Export Corpn): 74–76 Nguyen Hue, District 1, Ho Chi Minh City; tel. (8) 8298201; fax (8) 8294873; e-mail vtr@hcm.vnn.vn; f. 1981; imports and exports electronic goods; Dir NGUYEN HUU THINH.

Vigecam (Viet Nam General Corpn of Agricultural Materials): 16 Ngo Tat To, Dong Da District, Hanoi; tel. (4) 8231972; fax (4) 7474647; exports and imports agricultural products; Dir HUYNH KY.

Vimedimex II (Viet Nam National Medical Products Export-Import Corpn): 246 Cong Quynh, District 1, Ho Chi Minh City; tel. (8) 8398441; fax (8) 8325953; e-mail vietpharma@hcm.vnn.vn; internet www.vietpharm.com.vn; f. 1984; exports and imports medicinal and pharmaceutical materials and products, medical instruments; Gen. Dir NGUYEN TIEN HUNG.

Vinacafe (Viet Nam National Coffee Import-Export Corpn): 5 Ong Ich Khiem, Ba Dinh District, Hanoi; tel. (4) 8235449; fax (4) 8456422; e-mail vinacafe@hn.vnn.vn; internet www.vinacafe.com

.vn; f. 1995; exports coffee, and imports equipment and chemicals for coffee production; Chair. TRAN KHAI; Pres. and CEO THAI DOAN LAI.

Vinacement (Viet Nam National Cement Corpn): 228 Le Duan, Dong Da District, Hanoi; tel. (4) 8510593; fax (4) 8512778; f. 1980; manufactures and exports cement and clinker; Gen. Dir NGUYEN MAN.

Vinachimex (Viet Nam National Chemicals Import-Export Corpn): 4 Pham Ngu Lao, Hanoi; tel. (4) 8256377; fax (4) 8257727; f. 1969; exports and imports chemical products, minerals, rubber, fertilizers, machinery and spare parts; Dir NGUYEN VAN SON.

Vinafilm (Viet Nam Film Import, Export and Film Service Corpn): 73 Nguyen Trai, Dong Da District, Hanoi; tel. (4) 8244566; f. 1987; export and import of films and video tapes; film distribution; organization of film shows and participation of Vietnamese films in international film festivals; Gen. Man. NGO MANH LAN.

Vinafimex (Viet Nam National Agricultural Produce and Food-stuffs Import and Export Corpn): 58 Ly Thai To, Hanoi; tel. (4) 8255768; fax (4) 8255476; e-mail fime@hn.vnn.vn; f. 1984; exports cashews, peanuts, coffee, rubber and other agricultural products, and garments; imports malt, fertilizer, insecticide, seeds, machinery and equipment, etc. Pres. NGUYEN TOAN THANG; Gen. Dir NGUYEN VAN THANG.

Vinafood Hanoi (Hanoi Food Import-Export Co): 4 Ngo Quyen, Hanoi; tel. (4) 8256771; fax (4) 8258528; f. 1988; exports rice, maize, tapioca; imports fertilizers, insecticides, wheat and wheat flour; Dir NGUYEN DUC HY.

Vinalivesco (Vietnam National Livestock Corporation): 519 Minh Khai, Hanoi; tel. (4) 8626763; fax (4) 8623645; f. 1996; imports and exports animal and poultry products, animal feeds and other agro-products, and foodstuffs; Gen. Dir NGUYEN VAN KHAC.

Vinamilk (Viet Nam Milk Co): 36–38 Ngo Duc Ke, District 1, Ho Chi Minh City; tel. (8) 8298054; fax (8) 8238117; internet www.hcm.fpt .vn/adv/vinamilk/vn; producer of dairy products; Dir MAI TRIUE LIEN.

Vinataba (Viet Nam National Tobacco Corpn): 25A Ly Thuong Kiet, Hoan Kiem District, Hanoi; tel. (4) 8265778; fax (4) 8265777; internet www.vinataba.com.vn; mfr of tobacco products; Dir NGUYEN NAM HAI.

Vinatea (Viet Nam National Tea Development Investment and Export-Import Co): 46 Tang Bat Ho, Hanoi; tel. (4) 8212005; fax (4) 8212663; e-mail thitruong@vinatea.com.vn; exports tea, imports tea-processing materials; Gen. Dir NGUYEN KIM PHONG.

Vinatex (Viet Nam National Textile and Garment Corpn): 25 Ba Trieu, Hoan Kiem District, Hanoi; tel. (4) 8257700; fax (4) 8262269; e-mail vinatexhn@hn.vnn.vn; internet www.vinatex.com; f. 1995; imports textile machinery and materials, spare parts accessories, dyestuffs; exports textiles, garments, handicrafts, carpets, jute, silk; Gen. Dir BUI XUAN KHU.

Vocarimex (National Co for Vegetable Oils, Aromas, and Cosmetics of Viet Nam): 58 Nguyen Binh Khiem, District 1, Ho Chi Minh City; tel. (8) 8294513; fax (8) 8290586; e-mail vocar@hcm.vnn.vn; f. 1976; producing and trading vegetable oils, oil-based products and special industry machinery; packaging; operating port facilities; Gen. Dir DUONG THI NGOC TRINH.

Xunhasaba (Viet Nam State Corpn for Export and Import of Books, Periodicals and other Cultural Commodities): 32 Hai Ba Trung, Hanoi; tel. (4) 8262989; fax (4) 8252860; e-mail xunhasaba@hn.vnn .vn; internet www.xunhasaba.com.vn; f. 1957; exports and imports books, periodicals, postage stamps, greetings cards, calendars and paintings; Dir TRAN PHU SON.

UTILITIES

Electricity

Power Co No 1 (PC1): 20 Tran Nguyen Han, Hoan Kiem, Hanoi; tel. (4) 8255074; fax (4) 8244033; e-mail anhdn@pc1.com.vn; manages the generation, transmission and distribution of electrical power in northern Viet Nam; Dir DO VAN LOC.

Power Co No 2 (PC2): 72 Hai Ba Trung, District 1, Ho Chi Minh City; tel. (8) 8297151; fax (8) 8299680; manages the distribution of electrical power in southern Viet Nam; Dir NGUYEN VAN GIAU.

Power Co No 3 (PC3): 16 Rue Le Thanh Ton, Da Nang; manages the generation, transmission and distribution of electrical power in central Viet Nam.

Viet Nam National Electrical Power Corporation (VNEPC): produces electrical power; Vice-Dir TRAN VIETN NGAI.

Water

Hanoi Water Business Co: 44 Yen Phu, Hanoi; tel. (4) 8292478; fax (4) 8294069; f. 1954; responsible for the supply of water to Hanoi and its five urban and two suburban districts; Dir Gen. BUI VAN MAT.

Ho Chi Minh City Water Supply Co: 1 Cong Truong Quoc Te, District 3, Ho Chi Minh City; tel. (8) 8291974; fax (8) 8241644; e-mail hcmcwater@hcm.vnn.vn; f. 1966; manages the water supply system of Ho Chi Minh City; Dir VO QUANG CHAU.

CO-OPERATIVES

Viet Nam Co-operatives Alliance: Hanoi; f. 1993; fmrly Viet Nam Co-operatives Council; Chair. (vacant).

TRADE UNIONS

Tong Lien doan Lao dong Viet Nam (Viet Nam General Confederation of Labour): 82 Tran Hung Dao, POB 627, Hanoi; tel. and fax (4) 8253781; e-mail doingoaitld@hnn.vnn.vn; f. 1929; merged in 1976 with the South Viet Nam Trade Union Fed. for Liberation; 4,000,000 mems; Pres. CU THI HAU; Vice-Pres NGUYEN AN LUONG, DANG NGOC CHIEN, DO DUC NGO, NGUYEN DINH THANG.

Cong Doan Nong Nghiep Cong Nghiep Thu Pham Viet Nam (Viet Nam Agriculture and Food Industry Trade Union): Hanoi; f. 1987; 550,000 mems.

National Union of Building Workers: 12 Cua Dong, Hoan Kiem, Hanoi; tel. (4) 8253781; fax (4) 8281407; f. 1957; Pres. NGUYEN VIET HAI.

Vietnam National Union of Industrial Workers: 54 Hai Ba Trung, Hanoi; tel. (4) 9344426; fax (4) 8245306; f. 1997; Pres. VU TIEN SAU.

Transport

RAILWAYS

Duong Sat Viet Nam (DSVN) (Viet Nam Railways): 118 Le Duan, Hanoi; tel. (4) 8220537; fax (4) 9424998; e-mail vr.hn.irstd@fpt.vn; 2,600 km of main lines (1996); lines in operation are: Hanoi–Ho Chi Minh City (1,726 km), Hanoi–Haiphong (102 km), Hanoi–Dong Dang (167 km), Hanoi–Lao Cai (296 km), Hanoi–Thai Nguyen (75 km), Thai Nguyen–Kep–Bai Chay (106 km); Gen. Dir Dr NGUYEN HUU BANG.

ROADS

In 1999 there were an estimated 93,300 km of roads, of which 25.1% were paved. In 1995 the Government announced plans to upgrade 430 km of the national highway which runs from Hanoi in the north to Ho Chi Minh City in the south. In 1997 the Government announced plans to build a new 1,880-km north–south highway in the east of the country. In 2001 the Government also announced plans to upgrade the section of the national highway that runs between the northern provinces of Hoa Binh and Son La.

SHIPPING

The principal port facilities are at Haiphong, Da Nang and Ho Chi Minh City. In 2001 the Vietnamese merchant fleet (700 vessels) had a combined displacement totalling 1,073,618 grt. In 1994 there were 150 shipping companies with a combined capacity of 800,000 dwt.

Cong Ty Van Tai Duong Bien Viet Nam (VOSCO) (Viet Nam Ocean Shipping Co): 215 Tran Quoc Toan, Ngo Quyen District, Haiphong; tel. (31) 846951; fax (31) 845107; controlled by the Viet Nam Gen. Dept of Marine Transport; Dir TRAN VAN LAM; Dir-Gen. TRAN XUAN NHON.

Dai Ly Hang Hai Viet Nam (VOSA) (VOSA group of companies): Unit 1003, 10th Floor, Harbour View Tower, 35 Nguyen Hue, District 1, Ho Chi Minh City; tel. (8) 9140422; fax (8) 8211290; e-mail vosagroup@hcm.vnn.vn; internet www.vosagroup.com; f. 1957; fmrly the Viet Nam Ocean Shipping Agency; controlled by the Viet Nam National Shipping Lines (VINALINES); in charge of merchant shipping; arranges ship repairs, salvage, passenger services, air and sea freight forwarding services; main br. office in Haiphong; brs in Hanoi, Da Nang, Ben Thuy, Qui Nhon, Quang Ninh, Nha Trang, Vung Tau and Can Tho; Dir-Gen. HA CAM KHAI (acting).

Transport and Chartering Corpn (Vietfracht): 74 Nguyen Du, Hanoi; tel. (4) 9422355; fax (4) 9423679; e-mail vfhan@hn.vnn.vn; internet www.vietfracht.com.vn; f. 1963; ship broking, chartering, ship management, shipping agency, international freight forwarding; consultancy services, import-export services; Gen. Dir DO XUAN QUYNH.

Viet Nam Sea Transport and Chartering Co (Vitranschart): 428–432 Nguyen Tat Thanh, District 4, Ho Chi Minh City; tel. (8) 9404027; fax (8) 9404711; e-mail vitrans@fmail.vnn.vn; Dir VO PHUNG LONG.

CIVIL AVIATION

Viet Nam's principal airports are Tan Son Nhat International Airport (Ho Chi Minh City) and Thu Do (Capital) International Airport at Noi Bai (Hanoi). They cater for domestic and foreign traffic. Airports at Da Nang, Hué, Nha Trang, Da Lat, Can Tho, Haiphong, Muong Thanh (near Dien Bien Phu), Buon Ma Thuot and Lien Khuong handle domestic traffic. In 1990 a programme to expand Tan Son Nhat, Noi Bai and Da Nang airports was initiated. In 1997 it was announced that numerous abandoned wartime airstrips were to be repaired and returned into service under a programme scheduled for completion in 2010, by which time the Government also aims to expand the annual capacity of Tan Son Nhat to 30m. passengers and 1m. tons of freight.

Viet Nam Airlines: Gialem Airport, Hanoi; tel. (4) 8732732; fax (4) 8272291; internet www.vietnamair.com.vn; fmrly the Gen. Civil Aviation Admin. of Viet Nam, then Hang Khong Viet Nam; wholly state-owned; operates domestic passenger services from Hanoi and from Ho Chi Minh City to the principal Vietnamese cities, and international services to 18 countries; Pres. and CEO NGUYEN XUAN HIEN.

Pacific Airlines: 112 Hong Ha, Tan Binh District, Ho Chi Minh City; tel. (8) 8450090; fax (8) 8450085; f. 1991; operates charter cargo flights, also scheduled passenger and cargo services to Taiwan; Man. Dir DUONG CAO THAI NGUYEN.

Tourism

In the 1990s the Vietnamese Government encouraged tourism as a source of much-needed foreign exchange, with the objective of attracting some 4m. tourists annually by the year 2005. About 2.6m. foreign tourists visited Viet Nam in 2002. In 1998 revenue from tourism totalled US $86m.

Viet Nam National Administration of Tourism (VNAT): 80 Quan Su, Hanoi; tel. (4) 9421061; fax (4) 9424115; e-mail icdvnat@ vietnamtourism.com; internet www.vietnamtourism.com; f. 1960; Gen. Dir NGO HUY PHUONG.

Hanoi Tourism Service Company (HANOI TOSERCO): 8 To Hien Thanh, Hanoi; tel. (4) 9780004; fax (4) 8226055; e-mail hanoitoserco@hn.vnn.vn; internet www.tosercohanoi.com; f. 1998; manages the development of tourism, hotels and restaurants in the capital and other services including staff training; Dir TRAN TIEN HUNG.

Saigon Tourist: 23 Le Loi, District 1, Ho Chi Minh City; tel. (8) 8225887; fax (8) 8291026; e-mail saigontourist@sgtourist.com.vn; internet www.saigon-tourist.com; f. 1975; tour operator; Gen. Dir DO VAN HOANG.

Unitour (Union of Haiphong Tourist Co): 40 Tran Quang Khai, Haiphong; tel. (31) 8247295.

Viet Nam Tourism in Haiphong: 60A Dien Bien Phu, Haiphong; tel. and fax (31) 823651; f. 1960; hotel services, travel arrangements, visa service; Dir NGUYEN HUU BONG.

YEMEN

Introductory Survey

Location, Climate, Language, Religion, Flag, Capital

The Republic of Yemen is situated in the south of the Arabian peninsula, bounded to the north by Saudi Arabia, to the east by Oman, to the south by the Gulf of Aden, and to the west by the Red Sea. The islands of Perim and Kamaran at the southern end of the Red Sea, the island of Socotra, at the entrance to the Gulf of Aden, and the Kuria Muria islands, near the coast of Oman, are also part of the Republic. The climate in the semi-desert coastal strip is hot, with high humidity and temperatures rising to more than 38°C (100°F); inland, the climate is somewhat milder, with cool winters and relatively heavy rainfall in the highlands. The eastern plateau slopes into desert. The language is Arabic. The population is almost entirely Muslim, and mainly of the Sunni Shafi'a sect. The national flag (proportions 2 by 3) has three equal horizontal stripes, of red, white and black. The capital is San'a.

Recent History

The Republic of Yemen was formed in May 1990 by the amalgamation of the Yemen Arab Republic (YAR) and the People's Democratic Republic of Yemen (PDRY). The YAR (from 1967 also known as North Yemen) had formerly been a kingdom. When Turkey's Ottoman Empire was dissolved in 1918, the Imam Yahya, leader of the Zaidi community, was left in control. In 1948 Yahya was assassinated in a palace coup, when power was seized by forces opposed to his feudal rule. However, Yahya's son, Ahmad, defeated the rebel forces to become Imam. In 1958 Yemen and the United Arab Republic (Egypt and Syria) formed a federation called the United Arab States, though this was dissolved in 1961. The Imam Ahmad died in September 1962 and was succeeded by his son, Muhammad. Less than a week later, army officers, led by Col (later Marshal) Abdullah as-Sallal, removed the Imam and proclaimed the YAR. Civil war ensued between royalist forces, supported by Saudi Arabia, and republicans, aided by Egyptian troops. The republicans prevailed and Egyptian forces withdrew in 1967. In November President Sallal was deposed by a Republican Council.

The People's Republic of Southern Yemen, comprising Aden and the former Protectorate of South Arabia, was formed on 30 November 1967. Aden had been under British rule since 1839 and the Protectorate was developed by a series of treaties between the United Kingdom and local leaders. Prior to the British withdrawal, two rival factions, the National Liberation Front (NLF) and the Front for the Liberation of Occupied South Yemen, fought for control. The Marxist NLF eventually prevailed and assumed power as the National Front (NF). The country's first President, Qahtan ash-Sha'abi, was forced out of office in June 1969, when a Presidential Council, led by Salem Rubayi Ali, took power. Muhammad Ali Haitham became Prime Minister. In November 1970, on the third anniversary of independence, the country was renamed the PDRY. In May 1971 a provisional Supreme People's Council (SPC) was established as the national legislature. In August Haitham was replaced as Prime Minister by Ali Nasser Muhammad. Following the introduction of repressive measures against dissidents by the Government after independence, more than 300,000 Southern Yemenis fled to the YAR. Backed by Saudi Arabia and Libya, many of the refugees joined mercenary organizations, aimed at the overthrow of the Marxist regime in Southern Yemen, and conducted cross-border raids.

Intermittent fighting, beginning in early 1971, flared into open warfare between the two Yemens in October 1972, with the YAR receiving aid from Saudi Arabia and the PDRY being supplied with Soviet arms. A cease-fire was arranged in the same month, under the auspices of the League of Arab States (Arab League, see p. 260), and soon afterwards both sides agreed to the union of the two Yemens within 18 months. The union was not, however, implemented.

On 13 June 1974 a 10-member Military Command Council (MCC) seized power in the YAR, under the leadership of the pro-Saudi Lt-Col Ibrahim al-Hamadi. Mohsin al-Aini was appointed Prime Minister, but was replaced by Abd al-Aziz Abd al-Ghani in January 1975. An unsuccessful pro-royalist coup was reported in August 1975. Al-Hamadi subsequently attempted to reduce the influence of the USSR, and endeavoured to re-equip the army with US weapons, making use of financial assistance from Saudi Arabia. In October 1977, however, al-Hamadi was killed by unknown assassins in San'a. Another member of the MCC, Lt-Col Ahmad bin Hussain al-Ghashmi, took over as Chairman, and martial law was imposed. In February 1978 the MCC appointed a Constituent People's Assembly, and in April the Assembly elected al-Ghashmi President of the Republic. The MCC was then dissolved.

In June 1978 the proposed union of the two Yemens was seriously hampered when President al-Ghashmi of the YAR was assassinated by a bomb carried in the suitcase of a PDRY envoy. In the following month the Constituent People's Assembly elected a senior military officer, Lt-Col (later Gen., and subsequently Field Marshal) Ali Abdullah Saleh, as President of the YAR. During recriminations that followed the assassination, President Rubayi Ali of the PDRY was deposed and executed by opponents within the ruling party, which had been known as the United Political Organization—National Front (UPO—NF), since its merger with two smaller parties in October 1975. The Prime Minister, Ali Nasser Muhammad, became interim Head of State. Two days after the overthrow of Rubayi Ali, it was announced that the UPO—NF had agreed to form a Marxist-Leninist 'vanguard' party. At the constituent congress of this Yemen Socialist Party (YSP), held in October 1978, Abd al-Fattah Ismail, who favoured uncompromising Marxist policies, became Secretary-General. A new SPC was elected in December and appointed Ismail to be Head of State. In April 1980 Ali Nasser Muhammad replaced Ismail as Head of State, Chairman of the Presidium of the SPC and Secretary-General of the YSP, while retaining the post of Prime Minister; his posts were confirmed at an extraordinary congress of the YSP in October.

Renewed fighting broke out between the YAR and the PDRY in February and March 1979, when the National Democratic Front (NDF), an alliance of disaffected YAR politicians, won the support of the PDRY and began a revolt. Later in the same month, however, at a meeting between the North and South Yemeni Heads of State in Kuwait, arranged by the Arab League, an agreement was signed pledging unification of the two states. Following a series of meetings, in December 1981 the two sides signed a draft constitution for a unified state and established a joint YAR/PDRY Yemen Council to monitor progress towards unification. NDF forces rebelled again in 1982, but they were defeated and forced over the border into the PDRY.

Abd al-Aziz Abd al-Ghani was replaced as Prime Minister of the YAR in October 1980, but was reappointed in November 1983. Meanwhile, in May 1983 President Saleh submitted his resignation at an extraordinary meeting of the Constituent People's Assembly, declaring his intention to nominate himself for a presidential election. His five-year term of office was due to end in July. However, he was nominated and unanimously re-elected by the Assembly for a further five-year term. Elections to the Assembly itself, scheduled for early 1983, were postponed.

In the PDRY, President Muhammad relinquished the post of Prime Minister in February 1985, nominating the Minister of Construction, Haidar Abu Bakr al-Attas, as his successor (while retaining his other senior posts). The former President, Abd al-Fattah Ismail, returned from exile in the USSR in the same month, and was reappointed to the Secretariat of the YSP's Central Committee. At the party's third General Congress, in October, President Muhammad was re-elected to the posts of Secretary-General of the YSP and of its Political Bureau for a further five years. However, his control over the party was weakened by the enlargement of the Political Bureau from 13 members to 16 (including his rival, Ismail), and by an increase in membership of the Central Committee from 47 to 77, to incorporate a number of his critics.

On 13 January 1986 President Muhammad attempted to eliminate his opponents in the Political Bureau: his personal guard opened fire on six members who had assembled for a meeting with the President. Three were killed, and three escaped, including Ismail (who was, however, officially declared to have been killed in subsequent fighting). Muhammad was reported to have left Aden for his tribal stronghold in Abyan province, to the east of the city. In Aden itself, rival elements of the armed forces fought for control, causing widespread destruction, and the conflict quickly spread to the rest of the country, despite diplomatic efforts by the USSR. Apparently prompted by reports of massacres by President Muhammad's supporters, the army intervened decisively, turning back pro-Muhammad tribesmen from Abyan who were advancing on Aden. On 24 January al-Attas, the Prime Minister, who had been abroad when the troubles began, was named by the YSP Central Committee as head of an interim administration in Aden, and Muhammad was stripped of all his party and state posts; he reportedly fled to Ethiopia. An estimated 5,000 people died in the conflict. A new Government of the PDRY was formed in February. Al-Attas was confirmed as President, Chairman of the Presidium of the SPC and Secretary-General of the YSP Political Bureau. The former Deputy Prime Minister and Minister of Fisheries, Dr Yasin Said Numan, was named as Prime Minister. The new Council of Ministers contained only three members of the previous Government. In March a general amnesty was proclaimed, inviting supporters of Muhammad to return from the YAR, where some 10,000 of them had sought refuge. In October a general election took place for a 111-member SPC. Al-Attas was unanimously elected Chairman of the YSP. In December the Supreme Court sentenced Muhammad to death, *in absentia*, for treason; 34 other men received the same sentence, although it was only carried out in five cases.

In July 1988 the first general election took place in the YAR for 128 seats in the new 159-member Consultative Council, which replaced the non-elected Constituent People's Assembly. The remaining 31 seats were filled by presidential decree. Over one million people registered to vote and more than 1,200 candidates contested the poll. Approximately 25% of the elective seats were won by candidates sympathetic to the Muslim Brotherhood, a militant Islamist organization. Later in the month President Saleh was re-elected by the Consultative Council for a third five-year term, winning 96% of the votes, while the Vice-President, Abd al-Karim al-Arashi, was elected as Speaker of the Consultative Council. Al-Ghani was subsequently reappointed Prime Minister by President Saleh, and a new Council of Ministers was announced.

The first session of the joint YAR/PDRY Yemen Council (which had been established in 1981) was held in San'a in August 1983 and discussed the state of progress towards unification. These sessions were scheduled to take place every six months and to alternate between San'a and Aden. A joint committee on foreign policy met for the first time in March 1984 in Aden. In July 1986 Presidents Saleh of the YAR and al-Attas of the PDRY met for the first time in Libya to discuss unification. In early 1987 Kuwait acted as a mediator between the two Yemens in an effort to solve the problem of the thousands of refugees from the PDRY who had recently sought refuge in the north. In July it was reported that more than 50% of these refugees had returned to the PDRY.

In May 1988 the Governments of the YAR and the PDRY agreed to withdraw troops from their mutual border and to create a demilitarized zone, covering an area of 2,200 sq km, between Marib and Shabwah, where they intended to carry out joint projects involving exploration for petroleum. The movement of citizens between the two states was also to be facilitated. In July a programme of wide-ranging political and economic reforms was introduced in the PDRY, indicating the country's intention to create a free market economy. In November President Saleh and the Secretary-General of the Central Committee of the YSP, Ali Salim al-Baid, signed an agreement to unify the two states. On 1 December a draft constitution for the unified state was published: it was to be ratified by both countries within six months, and was subsequently to be approved by a referendum. At the end of December the Governments of the YAR and the PDRY agreed to release all political prisoners in their respective countries.

The first joint meeting of the two Councils of Ministers was held in San'a in January 1990 and resulted in restrictions on travel between the two countries being rescinded. In February President Saleh held talks with King Fahd of Saudi Arabia, who pledged his official support for the unification of the YAR and the PDRY. The growing atmosphere of democracy in the PDRY gave a large section of the work-force the confidence to stage an unprecedented series of strikes, which led to the granting by the Government of significant wage increases.

Opposition to unification developed in the YAR in early 1990. The Muslim Brotherhood, which believed that *Shari'a* (Islamic) law should be enshrined in the Constitution of the unified state (as in the YAR Constitution), condemned the draft Constitution, which was based principally, but not solely, on *Shari'a* law, and advocated a boycott of the referendum on the Constitution. In the PDRY, meanwhile, there were demonstrations by women, who feared that the increasing influence of Islamic militancy might jeopardize their freedom, and demanded that their existing rights in the secular Republic be guaranteed in the new Constitution.

In May 1990 the armed forces of the YAR and the PDRY were declared to be technically dissolved, prior to their unification, and it was announced that they were to be withdrawn from their respective capitals to designated military zones. In the same month a draft law embodying the freedom of the press was signed.

The unification of the YAR and the PDRY was proclaimed on 22 May 1990, six months ahead of the agreed deadline, apparently in order to counter the threat to the unification process posed by disruption in the north of the YAR. The unification agreement had been ratified on the previous day by both countries' legislatures. The new country was to be known as the Republic of Yemen, with San'a as its political capital and Aden its economic and commercial centre. President Saleh of the YAR became President of the new state, while al-Baid was elected Vice-President. The President of the PDRY, al-Attas, became Prime Minister, leading a transitional coalition Council of Ministers with 39 members, of whom 20 were from the YAR (members of the General People's Congress—GPC—a broad grouping of supporters of President Saleh) and 19 from the PDRY (all members of the YSP, under the continued leadership of al-Baid). A five-member Presidential Council (chaired by Saleh) was formed, together with a 45-member advisory council. The two legislatures were amalgamated to form the House of Representatives, pending elections to be held after a 30-month transitional period; an additional 31 members, including opponents of the YAR and PDRY governments, were nominated by President Saleh. In September it was reported that more than 30 new political parties had been formed since unification. The Yemeni Islah Party (YIP), an Islamic grouping with considerable support in the House of Representatives, was regarded as the most influential of the new parties.

In mid-May 1991 the people of Yemen voted in a referendum on the Constitution for the unified state. A few days earlier, religious fundamentalists and sympathizers, including YIP members, urged a boycott of the referendum, owing to the role of Islam under the proposed Constitution. Those who participated in the referendum approved the new Constitution by a large majority, although less than 50% of the electorate registered to vote. Members of the YIP and other opposition groups claimed that irregularities in the voting procedure had invalidated the result.

During late 1991 and early 1992 the deteriorating economic situation (characterized by large increases in unemployment and consumer prices as well as reductions in public spending by the Government) prompted domestic unrest. A shooting incident in San'a in October 1991 led to two days of rioting, in which nine people were believed to have died. In March 1992 workers in some parts of the country held a one-day strike, in support of demands for salary increases and the establishment of a job-creation programme for the estimated 850,000 returnees from Saudi Arabia (see below). In December riots in San'a, Taiz and Hodeida, apparently caused by a sharp rise in consumer prices, spread rapidly to Aden and other towns. It was officially reported that 15 people had been killed in the disturbances, with 98 injured and 661 arrested. Opposition sources, however, estimated significantly higher figures.

In spite of the unrest, voter registration for the legislative elections, scheduled for 27 April 1993, took place during January and February. An estimated 4,730 candidates were to contest the 301 elective seats in the House of Representatives, of whom approximately 30% were affiliated to political parties. International observers were largely satisfied with the conduct of the elections, although there were reports of disturbances in several towns, and some complaints of irregularities. The GPC secured 123 of the 300 seats for which results were announced. The YIP won 62 seats, and the YSP 56, with independents securing 47 of the remaining seats. In May the two former ruling parties, the GPC and YSP, agreed to merge, thereby creating a single political group with an overall majority in the new House of Representatives. The subsequent election of the YIP's leader, Sheikh Abdullah bin Hussain al-Ahmar, as Speaker of the House was regarded as a concession to his party, whose influence had been weakened by the merger. At the end of the month, however, a 31-member coalition Government was announced, including representatives of all three leading parties. Al-Attas was reappointed Prime Minister.

In August 1993 the YSP leader, al-Baid, ceased to participate in the political process and withdrew from San'a to Aden. This followed a visit to the USA, apparently without the approval of President Saleh, for talks with the US Vice-President, Al Gore. Al-Baid claimed that Saleh had made no attempt to halt the numerous armed attacks by northern officials on southerners, and claimed that as many as 150 YSP members had been assassinated since unification. He also protested at what he perceived to be the increasing marginalization of the south, particularly with regard to the distribution of petroleum revenues. In October the House of Representatives elected a new five-member Presidential Council, and later in the month the Council, in the absence of al-Baid, re-elected Saleh as its Chairman, and, accordingly, as President of the Republic of Yemen, for a further four-year term. Al-Baid was unanimously re-elected as Vice-President, but was not sworn in.

The political deadlock persisted into November 1993, in spite of international mediation efforts. Reports emerged that the armed forces of the former YAR and the PDRY (which had failed to integrate since unification) were being deployed along the former frontier. In December, as a result of Jordanian mediation, GPC and YSP officials commenced negotiations with the aim of resolving the political crisis. In September al-Baid, who remained in Aden, had submitted an 18-point programme of conditions for his return to San'a. Although President Saleh accepted the programme in December, there was no indication of any improvement in the political situation. In January 1994 representatives of the main political parties signed a 'Document of Pledge and Agreement' designed to resolve the crisis. In February President Saleh and Vice-President al-Baid signed the document in Amman, Jordan. The agreement contained certain security guarantees, as well as providing for a degree of decentralization, and for a review of the Constitution and of the country's economic policies. Nevertheless, both leaders remained active in mustering support for their positions throughout the region. At the same time there were reports of clashes between rival army units.

In March 1994 Saleh and al-Baid held talks in Oman, but at the end of the month al-Baid, together with Salim Salih Muhammad, refused to attend a meeting of the Presidential Council, which he had boycotted since August 1993. In the last week of March 1994 two meetings of the Council of Ministers, the first to take place in that year, were held in Aden in an attempt to agree preliminary measures to implement the conciliation agreement. Diplomatic initiatives continued while skirmishes between rival army units persisted. At the end of April the First Deputy Prime Minister, Hassan Muhammad Makki, was wounded during an assassination attempt in San'a. A series of pitched battles followed between battalions stationed in the territory of their former neighbour. On 5 May President Saleh declared a 30-day state of emergency, and dismissed al-Baid from his position as Vice-President, together with four other southern members of the Government, including Salim Muhammad. On the same day missile attacks were launched against economic and military targets, including San'a, Aden and other main airports. On 9 May Saleh announced that al-Attas had been replaced as Prime Minister by the Minister of Industry, Muhammad Said al-Attar, and that the Minister of Petroleum and Minerals had also been replaced. By this time fighting had become concentrated around Aden, and along the former north–south frontier. Several thousand southern reservists were mobilized, as the forces of the former YAR attempted to isolate and capture Aden. Meanwhile, President Saleh rejected appeals for a negotiated settlement to the civil war, and demanded that al-Baid surrender.

On 21 May 1994, the fourth anniversary of the unification of Yemen, al-Baid, in a televised address, declared the independence of a new Democratic Republic of Yemen (DRY), with Aden as its capital. He also announced the formation of a Presidential Council, with himself as President and Abd ar-Rahman al-Jifri, the leader of the League of the Sons of Yemen (LSY), as Vice-President. The composition of the Council reflected al-Baid's

need to achieve a consensus of the different political and tribal groups of the former PDRY in opposition to the forces of President Saleh. Saleh himself immediately denounced the secession as illegitimate, and offered an amnesty to all in the PDRY who rejected it, with the exception of 16 YSP leaders (including al-Baid).

At the end of May 1994, with the northern army attacking Aden on three fronts to the north and east of the city, the UN Security Council met, at the instigation of Egypt and five of the Gulf states, to discuss the conflict. Resolution 924 was subsequently adopted, demanding a cease-fire and the resumption of dialogue in Yemen, and ordering the dispatch of a UN commission of inquiry to the region. Although welcomed by the authorities in Aden, the resolution was initially rejected by the Government in San'a, which urged the Arab League to support the unity of Yemen. Subsequently, however, the San'a Government declared itself positively disposed towards the resolution.

On 1 June 1994 the House of Representatives voted to extend the state of emergency for a further 30 days. On the following day al-Baid announced the composition of a DRY Government, in which al-Attas was to be Prime Minister and Minister of Finance. Although most of the ministers were from the YSP, the Government contained a range of religious, political and tribal representatives. As northern forces made further territorial gains around Aden, it was reported that al-Baid had transferred his centre of operations to Mukalla, east of Aden. Military pressure on Aden was maintained for the remainder of June, and on 7 July the town came under the control of Saleh's troops. Many of the southern secessionist leaders fled to neighbouring Arab states, and it was officially announced that the civil war had ended. Al-Baid was believed to have requested political asylum in Oman. In March 1998 al-Baid, together with al-Attas and three other rebel leaders, were sentenced to death *in absentia*.

According to official sources, 931 civilians and soldiers were killed, and 5,000 wounded, in the civil war, although this was generally regarded as a conservative estimate. President Saleh immediately undertook measures to consolidate his position and bring stability to the country, ending the state of emergency and reiterating the general amnesty; by August 1994, when the amnesty expired, more than 5,000 Yemenis had returned to the country. In the same month, in an attempt to undermine the strength of southern military units loyal to the YSP, President Saleh announced that party membership would no longer be permitted within the armed forces. In September, moreover, Saleh introduced amendments to the Constitution intended to strengthen his position further: the Presidential Council was abolished, and in future the President would be elected by universal suffrage. *Shari'a* would also serve as the basis of all legislation. On 1 October Saleh was re-elected President; he appointed Abd ar-Rabbuh Mansur Hadi as his deputy, and Abd al-Aziz Abd al-Ghani (hitherto a member of the Presidential Council) as Prime Minister. In the new Council of Ministers, announced on 6 October, members of the GPC retained the key portfolios, the YSP was denied representation, and the YIP was rewarded for its allegiance during the civil war by the allocation of nine ministerial posts. In a reorganization of the Council of Ministers in June 1995, the GPC increased its share of portfolios at the expense of independents, leading to a Government composed entirely of GPC and YIP members. Also in June President Saleh was re-elected Chairman of the GPC at the party's first general assembly since 1988.

In July 1994 UN-sponsored negotiations between the Yemeni leadership and the secessionists proved inconclusive. President Saleh announced that any further discussions would have to be conducted in Yemen, effectively terminating dialogue, as the YSP leaders remained in exile. In August a faction of the YSP in Yemen declared itself the new party leadership, and selected a new leader and Political Bureau. In October, nevertheless, exiled leaders of the YSP announced the formation of a coalition, the National Opposition Front, which included former Prime Minister al-Attas and Abd ar-Rahman al-Jifri, leader of the LSY. The role of the YSP in Yemeni politics diminished considerably after the civil war, as it was deprived of military power, experienced leadership in the country, and its role in government. In February 1995 another opposition grouping, the Democratic Coalition of Opposition, was formed, embracing 13 political parties and organizations, including a faction of the YSP and the LSY.

The economic repercussions of the civil war on the population were significant, particularly in the south. During March and

April 1994, following the devaluation of the riyal and the doubling of the price of fuel, demonstrators clashed with police in Aden, San'a and Dhamar, resulting in three deaths and more than 50 arrests. The activities of militant Islamists, meanwhile, posed an additional threat to internal stability. In September hundreds demonstrated in Abyan province to protest at water and electricity shortages and against an increase in the price of basic foodstuffs, while some 20 people were reportedly killed in clashes with the security forces there, following the destruction of three Muslim saints' shrines by Islamists who deemed them idolatrous. In September 1995 security forces arrested six alleged members of the Islamic Jihad group for their apparent involvement in acts of terrorism in Aden.

Tensions between the YIP and the GPC became increasingly evident during 1995. The YIP expressed its opposition to economic reforms recommended by the World Bank, and criticized the GPC for attending an economic summit meeting in Jordan, in October, at which Israeli officials were present. Moreover, in December the YIP Minister of Trade and Supply, Muhammad Ahmad Afandi, resigned from his post, citing political and economic differences with the GPC.

In June 1996 it was reported that the Government was considering a redefinition of the boundaries of several governorates in the former border region, prior to forthcoming parliamentary elections, in order to discourage further factionalism in the area. In December YIP deputies withdrew from parliamentary sessions dedicated to the endorsement of the 1997 budget, citing insufficient opportunity to discuss adequately the provisions of the budget prior to their passage to the House of Representatives for approval. Furthermore, 53 of the YIP's 62 parliamentary deputies boycotted the House of Representatives on 1 January 1997, when the budget was formally approved. There was speculation that the deputies had adopted this confrontational stance as a result of government proposals to merge future budget allocations for religious schools (previously administered by YIP members) with those for general expenditure on education. In April four cabinet ministers tendered their resignation in order to seek election at the forthcoming poll.

The results of elections, conducted on 27 April 1997, demonstrated a decisive victory for the GPC, which increased its parliamentary representation from 123 to 187 seats. The YIP secured 53 seats (compared with 62 seats in 1993), and independent candidates won 54 seats. The remaining seats were shared between Nasserite and Baathist parties. The GPC's position was further consolidated by the stated intention of 39 newly-elected independent deputies to demonstrate parliamentary allegiance to the GPC. Despite the declared parliamentary support for the YIP of six independents, it seemed likely that the party's role in government would be diminished.

Prime Minister al-Ghani presented his own resignation, and that of the Council of Ministers, to President Saleh on 12 May 1997. Two days later Faraj Said bin Ghanim, a political independent, was appointed Prime Minister and entrusted with the formation of a new council of Ministers. All but four members of the new Cabinet, announced the following day, were drawn from the GPC. At the first session of the newly-elected House of Representatives, convened later in May, the Speaker, Sheikh Abdullah bin Hussain al-Ahmar, was re-elected unanimously. At the end of April 1998 bin Ghanim resigned (it was reported that cabinet changes that he had wanted to effect had been rejected). The Deputy Prime Minister and Minister of Foreign Affairs, Abd al-Karim al-Iryani, was appointed Prime Minister, and he announced his new Government in May, in which only three new ministers were appointed.

A substantial increase in the price of petrol and basic foodstuffs in June 1998 led to public demonstrations in which more than 50 people died. Further unrest was reported during 1998 and, in September, a series of explosions in Yemen was attributed by the Government to 'foreign elements'. In that month the Minister of Religious Endowments and Guidance resigned, reportedly owing to political interference which had prevented him from fulfilling his duties.

The suppression of lawlessness, which had been exacerbated by the widespread ownership of weapons dating from the period of internal unrest, was a persistent domestic problem in the late 1990s. A number of armed kidnappings, frequently of tourist visitors, attracted international attention during 1997 and 1998, and in December 1998 16 foreign tourists were taken hostage; four were later killed during an attempt to release them. Yemen was criticized for failing to warn foreign embassies of an increased terrorist threat to tourists and for its precipitate

use of force to free the hostages. The trial of the kidnappers, who belonged to the Islamic Aden-Abyan Army, a small extremist Islamist movement, began in late January 1999. By the end of January 10 men, eight with British citizenship and two Algerians, had been arrested on suspicion of plotting terrorist attacks on British targets in Aden; they were also reported to have links to the Islamic Aden-Abyan Army. At their trial all denied the charges, claiming that their earlier confessions had been obtained under duress and that they had been tortured. Despite having no extradition treaty with the United Kingdom, Yemen also requested the extradition from that country of a prominent Muslim cleric, a relative of two of the defendants, who they claimed had funded and masterminded a series of terrorist incidents in Yemen, including the kidnapping of the tourists in December 1998. Relations with the United Kingdom had deteriorated as a result both of Yemeni actions to end the hostage situation (three of the tourists who died were British) and of Yemeni accusations of British support for international terrorism, which were vehemently denied. The lawyer representing the defendants was himself arrested in February 1999, shortly before he was due to publicize allegations of torture against them; he was subsequently expelled from the country. In May three of the kidnappers were sentenced to death, a fourth defendant received a 20-year prison sentence and the remainder were acquitted. Two of the death sentences were eventually commuted to life imprisonment and in October the leader of the Islamic Aden-Abyan Army, Ziene al-Abidine al-Mihdar, was executed. His was the first execution under legislation, enacted in August 1998, providing for the use of capital punishment in kidnapping cases. In August 1999 verdicts were delivered in the trial of the 10 men on terrorist charges. All 10 were found guilty of the charges; three of the Britons were sentenced to the time they had already served (and were released in September) and the remaining seven defendants were sentenced to between three and seven years' imprisonment. (In October 2002 the Islamic Aben-Abayan Army, using a small boat packed with explosives, attacked a French supertanker transporting crude petroleum off the coast of Yemen. A spokesman for the group declared the attack, which killed a crew member and badly damaged the vessel, to be revenge for the execution of al-Mihdar.)

On 23 September 1999 the first direct presidential elections were held in Yemen. The incumbent President, Field Marshal Ali Abdullah Saleh, was re-elected, gaining 96.3% of the votes; his only opponent, Najib Qahtan ash-Sha'bi, a member of the GPC who stood as an independent, gained 3.7% of the votes. The elections, which were boycotted by the YSP, were criticized for their lack of a credible candidate to oppose President Saleh.

Some internal instability was reported in 1999, with a number of bomb explosions in San'a. In November security forces denied allegations that an assassination attempt had been carried out against the Minister of Culture and Tourism. In February 2000 clashes occurred between members of Islamic Jihad and the security forces, and in that month three soldiers were killed in clashes with tribesmen in ad-Dali governorate, north of Aden. In March a demonstration was held in ad-Dali in protest at the detention of two YSP officials; at the end of April 15 YSP officials were arrested in Abyan governorate and the secretary-general was arrested at San'a airport on his return to the country. Kidnappings continued throughout 1999 and early 2000, involving hostages from a number of Western nations including, in March 2000, the Polish ambassador to Yemen; all were released unharmed. However, in June a Norwegian diplomat was killed during a police operation to release him and his son from kidnappers in San'a. In October Hatim Muhsin bin Farid, the alleged new leader of the Islamic Aden-Abyan Army, was granted a seven-year term of imprisonment, having been convicted of kidnapping charges. Owing to a lack of evidence, he was cleared of charges relating to his leadership of the movement and to the possession of heavy weapons. Meanwhile, clashes were reported in ad-Dali governorate between the police and supporters of the YSP, following a riot organized in protest at economic conditions in the country.

In mid-October 2000 a suicide bomb attack on a US destroyer, the USS *Cole*, in Aden harbour, as a result of which 17 US naval personnel were killed, was linked by many commentators to the escalating crisis in the Middle East. The Yemeni authorities responded by arresting several Islamist militants, including leading members of Islamic Jihad from Yemen, Egypt, Algeria and other Arab states. The USA blamed agents of Osama bin Laden, the Saudi-born fundamentalist Islamist believed to be based in Afghanistan, for the attack, and claimed to have evidence that the two suicide bombers were Saudi nationals. Only days after the USS *Cole* bombing, the British embassy in San'a was the target of an attack, although it was unclear as to whether the two incidents were linked. (In July 2001 four Yemenis were found guilty of plotting and orchestrating the embassy bombing, and sentenced to between four and 15 years' imprisonment.) At the end of November 2000 Yemen and the USA signed an anti-terrorism agreement whereby the Yemeni authorities agreed to allow the US Federal Bureau of Investigation to assist in investigations into the USS *Cole* explosion, and to extradite any persons accused of involvement in terrorism against foreign targets. It was announced in early December that investigations into the bombing had been completed and that six Yemeni nationals were expected to stand trial in early 2001. At the end of January, however, the Yemeni Government agreed to a postponement of the trial, following a request by US officials for more time to gather additional evidence. A further two Yemenis entering the country from Afghanistan were detained in mid-February; another three suspects were reportedly arrested in April. In November 2001 a Yemeni newspaper published claims that the individual suspected of planning the attack had subsequently sought refuge in Afghanistan. The man was named as Muhammad Omar al-Harazi, and was also believed to have been one of the principal organizers of the 1998 attacks on the US embassies in Kenya and Tanzania. In February 2002 it was reported that the trial of eight of the suspects in the bombing of the USS *Cole* had been postponed at the request of the US authorities because of the possibility that new information about the case would be obtained during interrogation of al-Qa'ida (see below) and Taliban prisoners captured by US military forces in Afghanistan in late 2001. (Two senior al-Qa'ida operatives believed to have been responsible for planning the attack on USS *Cole* were arrested by US forces and Pakistani police in November 2002 and April 2003, respectively.)

In January 2001 the formation of a new opposition grouping, the Opposition Co-ordination Council, was announced in Yemen. The bloc, which included the YSP, was created in anticipation of the forthcoming municipal elections, in which it hoped to counter the political dominance of the GPC and the YIP. Meanwhile, earlier in the month the YSP's offices in Shaab, ad-Dali governorate, were the target of a bomb explosion. The attack was reportedly linked with the party's decision to participate in the elections. In late January a pro-Iraqi Yemeni national unsuccessfully attempted to hijack a Yemen Airways flight travelling from San'a to Taiz. The aircraft, which was diverted to Djibouti, had US and Yemeni diplomats among its passengers. The hijacker was detained in Djibouti and extradited to Yemen, while a number of Yemeni officials were arrested in San'a on suspicion of having breached security regulations.

Yemen's first municipal elections since unification were held on 20 February 2001. A national referendum was held concurrently on proposed amendments to the Constitution that would extend the President's term of office from five to seven years and the duration of the House of Representatives from four to six years, abolish the right of the President to issue decree laws when parliament is not in session and provide for the creation of a 111-member Consultative Council. According to official sources, 77.5% of voters endorsed the constitutional changes. There were claims of electoral irregularities and harassment of opposition candidates, and violent clashes were reported prior to and during the vote (principally between supporters of the GPC and those of the YIP) in which, according to certain sources, up to 45 people were killed. The elections were boycotted by some opposition parties and were criticized by human rights groups, who claimed that the President and the GPC were seeking to consolidate their dominant position at the expense of further democratization.

At the end of March 2001 President Saleh dismissed Prime Minister Abd al-Karim al-Iryani and declared the formation of a new Government, to be led by the former Deputy Prime Minister and Minister of Foreign Affairs, Abd al-Qadir Bajammal. The new Council of Ministers was composed exclusively of GPC members; several new ministers were appointed (including Yemen's first female minister), with only 12 remaining from the previous administration. Commentators believed that al-Iryani's dismissal was an attempt to hasten the country's reform programme. At the end of April the President elected a new

Consultative Council, which for the first time included three female politicians.

In early 2003 22 political parties were registered for a parliamentary election, which was held on 27 April. The GPC recorded another decisive victory, winning 238 seats (out of a total of 301 seats); the YSP secured 46 seats (compared with 53 seats in 1997). Voter turnout was reported to total 76% of the electorate. The European Union (EU, see p. 199) expressed its satisfaction with the elections, although the US-based National Democratic Institute, which also monitored the voting, said the electoral process was flawed, and cited instances of underage voting, ballot buying and inappropriate behaviour by security forces. Moreover, opposition parties threatened to boycott the new Parliament after widespread claims of ballot rigging, fraud and intimidation. None the less, on 10 May the President re-appointed Bajammal as Prime Minister and requested that he form a new Government. Bajammal's new Council of Ministers, which was sworn in on 19 May, included 17 new appointees, amongst them a Minister of Human Rights, Amat al-Alim as-Susua. In addition, the culture and tourism ministries were merged and a Ministry of Water and the Environment was created. The key portfolios of defence, the interior, petroleum and foreign affairs, however, remained unchanged.

An agreement on the long-disputed former PDRY–Omani border was signed in San'a in October 1992 and ratified in December. Demarcation was completed in June 1995. Oman withdrew an estimated 15,000 troops from the last of the disputed territories on the Yemeni border in July 1996, in accordance with the 1992 agreement. In May 1997 officials from both countries signed the demarcation maps at a ceremony in Muscat, Oman.

The Iraqi invasion of Kuwait in August 1990 proved problematic for the Yemeni Government, as the economy was heavily dependent on trade with, and aid from, Iraq, and also on aid from Saudi Arabia, which was host to a considerable number of Yemeni expatriate workers. In December Yemen assumed the chair of the UN Security Council (which rotates on a monthly basis), and the Government increased its efforts to mediate in the Gulf crisis. It was, however, unable to prevent the outbreak of war despite a peace plan, presented in January 1991, and further diplomatic initiatives. Following the US-led military offensive against Iraq, Yemen issued a statement condemning the action, and large demonstrations were held in support of Iraq. Later in January it was confirmed that US aid to Yemen was to be suspended indefinitely, apparently as a result of Yemen's policy towards Iraq, although reduced US economic aid was resumed in August. Yemen continued to support Iraq and in December 1998 it requested an Arab League summit on Iraq and called for an end to the sanctions. In April 2000 it was announced that the UN Sanctions Committee on Iraq, which had been considering a request from Yemen to remove, repair or sell eight Iraqi ships stranded at Aden port since 1990, had referred the issue to the International Maritime Organization (IMO, see p. 96). The Yemeni Government expressed its concerns regarding the US-led military operations against Iraqi air defence targets in 1999–2002.

Following the terrorist attacks apparently perpetrated by Osama bin Laden's al-Qa'ida (Base) network against New York and Washington, DC, USA on 11 September 2001, the Yemeni Government arrested a number of suspected Islamist militants and froze the assets of individuals and organizations deemed to have links with al-Qa'ida. In mid-December up to 30 people (including about 19 soldiers) were reportedly killed during clashes in the central Marib governorate when local residents apparently fought to prevent the Yemeni security forces from arresting a group of alleged militants. (President Saleh had, during a visit to Washington in late November, been presented with a list of suspected al-Qa'ida members residing in Yemen.) Meanwhile, at least 100 foreign students enrolled at the country's Islamic institutes were said to have been arrested on charges of violating residency requirements. In mid-January 2002 the US embassy at San'a was closed amid fears of an imminent terrorist attack; two grenades were thrown at the building in March, although no injuries were reported. There were reports in early March that the US administration was considering the deployment of several hundred US troops to Yemen to assist the authorities in their struggle against militant Islamist organizations. In mid-April an explosion was reported close to the home of a leading security official involved in the search for al-Qa'ida militants; a previously unknown group styled the al-Qa'ida Sympathizers was suspected of having carried out the bombing. Despite increasing popular resentment towards US activities in the Middle East among Yemenis, President Saleh continued to co-operate with the USA over anti-terrorism initiatives through 2002, and in November an unmanned US aircraft killed six men in northern Yemen believed to have links with al-Qa'ida. Meanwhile, in December the Spanish navy intercepted a North Korean ship carrying *Scud* missiles, which was bound for Yemen. The vessel was handed over to the US authorities the next day, but, after protests by the Yemeni Government that the missiles were purchased legitimately, the shipment was released. In the same month three US missionaries were murdered by a Yemeni who confessed to having links with bin Laden's network.

In mid-February 2002 President Saleh was reported to have warned the US Government that a US-led attack on the regime of Saddam Hussain in Iraq, as part of its 'war against terror', would jeopardize the continued support of its traditional allies in the Arab region. However, Saleh was careful to emphasize his own ongoing efforts to persuade the Iraqi authorities to accept the return of UN weapons inspectors. When the military campaign in Iraq commenced, in March 2003, some 30,000 protesters, some of them armed, marched on the US embassy in San'a. Public resentment also continued to increase towards President Saleh's regime, as a result of its perceived co-operation with the USA.

Relations with Saudi Arabia deteriorated as a result of Yemen's initially strong opposition to the presence of foreign armed forces in the Gulf and to the ambiguous stance it had subsequently adopted in this respect. In September 1990, apparently in retaliation, Saudi Arabia announced that it had withdrawn the privileges that Yemeni workers had previously enjoyed. This resulted in an exodus from Saudi Arabia of some 850,000 Yemeni workers during October and November, which caused widespread economic and social disruption. The expulsion and consequent return to Yemen of the workers not only caused a reduction in the country's income from remittances, but also led to a serious increase in unemployment. (During 1995, at negotiations proceeding from the February 1995 memorandum of understanding—see below), it was reported that the Saudi authorities had agreed to allow Yemenis sponsored by Saudi nationals to seek employment in the kingdom.) In 1998 Saudi Arabia began issuing visas to Yemeni workers.

The Governments of Yemen and Saudi Arabia held negotiations concerning the demarcation of their common border between 1992 and 1994; however, in December 1994 Yemen accused Saudi Arabia of trespassing on Yemeni territory and alleged that three of its soldiers had been killed during clashes earlier in that month. Further clashes were reported in January 1995 following the failure of the two countries to renew the 1934 Ta'if agreement (renewable every 20 years), which delineated their existing frontier. Intense mediation by Syria culminated in a joint statement in mid-January 1995, in which Yemen and Saudi Arabia pledged to cease all military activity in the border area. It was subsequently announced that the demarcation of the disputed border would be undertaken by a joint committee. In February the Yemeni and Saudi Governments signed a memorandum of understanding that reaffirmed their commitment to the Ta'if agreement and provided for the establishment of six joint committees to delineate the land and sea borders and develop economic and commercial ties. In June President Saleh led a high-ranking delegation to Saudi Arabia, constituting the first official visit to that country since February 1990. The two Governments expressed their satisfaction with the memorandum of understanding and, in addition, pledged their commitment to strengthening economic, commercial and cultural co-operation.

Reports of an attempted incursion into Yemen by Saudi forces in December 1995 were denied by both sides. In July 1996 the two countries signed a bilateral security agreement which included provisions intended to counter the cross-border trafficking of illicit drugs. Friction over border claims, however, was revived in 1997, and in May 1998 it was reported that Saudi Arabia had occupied an uninhabited island in the Red Sea regarded by Yemen as within its national boundaries. In the same month Saudi Arabia sent a memorandum to the UN stating that it did not recognize the 1992 border agreement between Yemen and Oman and claiming that parts of the area involved were Saudi Arabian territory. The Saudi objection to the accord was widely believed to be related to its attempts to gain land access to the Arabian Sea, via a corridor between Yemen and Oman, which it had thus far been denied in its

negotiations with Yemen. In July 1998 Yemen submitted a memorandum to the Arab League refuting the Saudi claim to the land, and stating that the Saudi protests contravened the Ta'if agreement signed by that country. Further clashes were reported close to the land and sea border between Yemen and Saudi Arabia in June, and in July three Yemeni troops were killed during fighting with a Saudi border patrol on the disputed island of Duwaima in the Red Sea; Saudi Arabia claimed its actions on the island were in self-defence and that, under the Ta'if agreement, three-quarters of the island belonged to Saudi Arabia. Meanwhile, bilateral discussions continued and the Saudi Minister of Foreign Affairs visited Yemen at the end of July. In October 1999 the Yemeni Prime Minister cancelled a planned visit to Saudi Arabia, reportedly owing to the failure of the two Governments to agree on the issues to be discussed. Despite reported clashes in the border area during 1999, however, relations continued to improve. In early June 2000, at a ceremony in Riyadh, Saudi Arabia, the Saudi Arabian and Yemeni ministers responsible for foreign affairs signed a final border treaty demarcating their joint land and sea border. The treaty incorporated both the 1934 Ta'if agreement and the 1995 memorandum of understanding, although it failed to define the eastern section of the Saudi–Yemeni land frontier. The two countries also agreed to further economic, commercial and cultural ties, and each pledged not to permit its territory to be used as a base for political or military aggression against the other. In the months following the signing of the treaty, however, clashes were reported between rival tribal groups near the border. In December 2000 a meeting was held of the Saudi-Yemeni Co-operation Council (the first since before the Gulf conflict), at which Saudi officials pledged financial assistance to Yemen for development projects. However, talks concerning the proposed construction of a petroleum pipeline between the two countries had reportedly been unsuccessful. In April 2001 Yemen and Saudi Arabia were said to have agreed on the location of four crossing-points on their joint border. At the same time reports suggested that the withdrawal of Yemeni and Saudi troops from their respective sides of the border was almost complete.

In November 1995 there were reports that Eritrean troops had attempted to land on the Red Sea island of Greater Hanish, one of three islands (the others being Lesser Hanish and Zuqar) claimed by both Yemen and Eritrea. The attempted invasion had apparently been prompted by Yemen's announced intention to develop Greater Hanish as a tourist resort, and its subsequent refusal to comply with an Eritrean demand that the island be evacuated. Negotiations in Yemen and Eritrea in late November and early December failed to defuse the crisis, and on 15 December fighting broke out between the two sides, resulting in the deaths of six Eritrean and three Yemeni soldiers. On 17 December Yemen and Eritrea agreed to a cease-fire, to be monitored by a commission comprising a senior official from each country and two US diplomats. None the less, fighting was renewed the following day and Eritrean forces succeeded in occupying Greater Hanish. The cease-fire was adhered to thenceforth, and some 180 Yemeni soldiers (captured during the fighting) were released at the end of the month. Attempts by the Ethiopian and Egyptian Governments to broker an agreement between the two sides proved unsuccessful. In January 1996 France assumed the mediatory role and in May it announced that Yemen and Eritrea would sign an arbitration agreement in Paris, France, whereby both countries would renounce the use of force and submit their dispute to an international tribunal. France subsequently undertook to observe and supervise military movements in the area around the disputed islands. In mid-August, however, Eritrean troops occupied Lesser Hanish, but these were withdrawn later in the month after representations by France and a UN Security Council edict to evacuate the island forthwith. At a meeting held in Paris in October, representatives of Eritrea and Yemen confirmed that they would submit the dispute to an international tribunal. In October 1998 the tribunal ruled that Yemen had sovereignty over Greater and Lesser Hanish, and all islands to their north-west, while Eritrea had sovereignty over the Mohabaka islands. The court recommended that the fishing traditions around the islands be maintained, thereby granting access to the Hanish islands to Eritrean and Yemeni fishermen. Both countries accepted the ruling, and shortly afterwards they agreed to establish a joint committee to strengthen bilateral co-operation. In May 1999 the Presidents of Eritrea and Yemen held talks to discuss bilateral relations. A final ruling on the Hanish islands, issued by the tribunal in December, delineated the joint maritime border as the median line between their mainland coastlines. This was welcomed by both countries and in January 2000 the Yemeni Vice-President made an official visit to Eritrea where he held talks with President Afewerki. In March Eritrea denied reports that it had appealed against the tribunal's decision on the islands.

Since the mid-1990s President Saleh has increasingly sought to widen the range of Yemen's international contacts, particularly in relation to aid and co-operation agreements. In November 1997 an accord was reached with the 'Paris Club' of official creditors for the amelioration of Yemen's burden of external debt. In the same month, on an official visit to the United Kingdom (during which a co-operation agreement was signed with the EU), President Saleh made a formal application for Yemen to join the Commonwealth (see p. 164). Saleh made a state visit to the People's Republic of China in February 1998, during which extensive agreements were negotiated for Yemen to receive technical and economic assistance. In early 2000 Saleh made official visits to Canada, the USA, Italy and Iran; at the same time Yemen repeatedly denied reports that it had had secret contacts with Israel and that it was seeking to normalize relations with that country.

Government

Legislative power is vested in the House of Representatives, with 301 members directly elected by universal adult suffrage. Under the revised Constitution, the President of the Republic (Head of State) is to be elected directly by voters for a period of seven years, renewable once. The President appoints a Council of Ministers, headed by a Prime Minister.

Defence

In August 2002 total armed forces of the Republic of Yemen were estimated to number 66,500 (including conscripts): 60,000 were in the army, 1,500 in the navy and 5,000 in the air force. There was a paramilitary force with an estimated strength of 70,000. Tribal levies numbered at least 20,000. Military conscription was ended in May 2001. The defence budget for 2002 was forecast at 90,000m. riyals.

Economic Affairs

In 2001, according to estimates by the World Bank, Yemen's gross national income (GNI), measured at average 1999–2001 prices, was US $8,304m., equivalent to $460 per head (or $770 per head on an international purchasing-power parity basis). During 1990–2001, it was estimated, the population increased at an average annual rate of 3.8%, while gross domestic product (GDP) per head increased, in real terms, by an average of 1.2% per year. Overall GDP increased, in real terms, at an average annual rate of 5.1% in 1990–2001; GDP growth in 2001 was 1.8%.

Agriculture (including forestry and fishing) contributed an estimated 15.5% of GDP in 2001, and the sector engaged some 48.5% of the working population in 1999. The principal cash crops are coffee, cotton and fruits. Subsistence crops include sorghum, potatoes, wheat and barley. Livestock-rearing (particularly in the east and north) and fishing are also important activities. Livestock, hides and skins and fish are all exported on a small scale. World Bank estimates indicated growth averaging 4.3% annually in 1990–2001. Real agricultural GDP increased by 3.7% in 2000 and by 2.4% in 2001.

Industry (including mining, manufacturing, construction and power) contributed an estimated 43.0% of GDP in 2001, and an estimated 15.1% of the working population were employed in the sector in 1999. According to World Bank estimates, industrial GDP increased at an average annual rate of 6.0% in 1990–2001. Real growth in industrial GDP was estimated at 7.0% in 2000 and 0.7% in 2001.

Mining and quarrying contributed some 31.5% of GDP in 2001, and employed an estimated 0.3% of the working population in 1999. Yemen's proven petroleum reserves totalled 4,000m. barrels at the end of 2001, sufficient to maintain production at that year's levels for 24 years. Petroleum production averaged 458,000 barrels per day (b/d) during 2001, but the Government planned to increase output to 548,000 b/d by 2002. The value of exports of mineral fuels and lubricants accounted for 94.35% of the value of total exports in 2001. There are also significant reserves of natural gas: proven reserves at the end of 2001 were 480,000m. cu m. Salt and gypsum are also exploited on a large scale. In addition, there are deposits of copper, lead, zinc, gold, sulphur and molybdenum. GDP of the mining sector increased at an average annual rate of 6.8% in 1990–2001; real mining GDP rose by 7.2% in 2000 and by 0.6% in 2001.

The manufacturing sector contributed an estimated 6.8% of GDP in 2001; in 1999 some 5.0% of the working population were employed in the sector. The most important branches of manufacturing are food-processing, petroleum refining, construction materials (particularly cement and iron and steel), paper and paper products and traditional light industries (including textiles, leather goods and jewellery). The Aden oil refinery recommenced operations in 1994 and was being prepared for privatization in early 2001; some imported crude oil is also refined. Real growth in manufacturing GDP was estimated at an average of 3.9% annually in 1990–2001, at 6.1% in 2000 and at 0.9% in 2001.

Some domestic energy requirements are served by locally-produced petroleum, but the country is somewhat reliant on fuel imports (particularly petroleum from other producers in the region). Imports of fuel and energy comprised an estimated 12.0% of the value of total imports in 2001. The northern and southern electricity grids were linked in mid-1997.

The services sector contributed some 41.5% of GDP in 2001, and employed some 36.4% of the working population in 1999. A free-trade zone at Aden was inaugurated in May 1991, and was projected to be self-financing by its seventh year of operations. According to World Bank estimates, the real GDP of the services sector increased at an average annual rate of 5.0% in 1990–2001. Real services GDP was estimated to have increased by 4.6% in 2000 and by 2.1% in 2001.

In 2001 Yemen recorded an estimated visible trade surplus of US $546.2m., and there was a deficit of $477.7m. on the current account of the balance of payments. In 2001 the principal source of imports (12.5%) was the United Arab Emirates. Other major suppliers were Saudi Arabia, India, Kuwait and the USA. In that year the main export destination (18.3%) was India. Other important export markets were Thailand, the Republic of Korea and the People's Republic of China. The principal exports in 2000 were petroleum and petroleum products (96.1%). The main imports in that year were food and live animals (especially cereals and cereal preparations), machinery and transport equipment, and basic manufactures. In 2001 exports and petroleum and petroleum products were estimated to have decreased to 94.3% of total exports, after a fall in petroleum prices. Food and live animals, followed by machinery and transport equipment were estimated to have remained the principal imports.

Yemen's budget for 2000 forecast a surplus of 163,494m. riyals. Total external debt at the end of 2000 was estimated to be US $5,616m., of which $4,525m. was long-term public debt. In that year the cost of debt-servicing was equivalent to 3.8% of the value of exports of goods and services. The annual rate of inflation averaged 29.3% in 1990–98 and 10.9% in 1999–2002. Consumer prices increased by 22.3% in 2001 and by 4.3% in 2002. The rate of unemployment is estimated to be as high as 25% of the labour force.

Yemen is a member of the Arab Fund for Economic and Social Development (AFESD, see p. 136), the Council of Arab Economic Unity (see p. 178) and the Arab Co-operation Council (see p. 338).

Between the establishment of the Republic of Yemen in 1990 and the civil war of 1994, the economy declined substantially and in 1994 the annual rate of inflation averaged an estimated 55%, the budget deficit stood at 16.7% of GDP and the cost of servicing Yemen's external debt was equivalent to 186% of GNP. A programme of economic reform, implemented in 1995, achieved some success, particularly with regard to economic diversification, and Yemen's external debt was reduced by almost 50% following agreements with the 'Paris Club' of official creditors in 1996 and 1997. However, further problems were posed in 1998 both by the decline in international petroleum prices and by a lack of political consensus, which affected the Government's ability to implement economic reform. In order to minimize the effect of low petroleum prices on government revenue, budget expenditure was restricted and a number of government subsidies were reduced or abolished. The Government also encouraged the privatization of small state enterprises. Petroleum prices recovered strongly in late 1999, and Yemen's petroleum production capacity was increased, resulting in a more favourable environment for the Government to implement economic reforms. By 1999, inflation had been reduced, the budget deficit had declined and, according to the IMF, non-petroleum sector growth, in real terms, was an estimated 3.2% in that year. However, during 2000–2002, the country's petroleum production declined, severely affecting the Government's main source of revenues. Nevertheless, GDP was projected to increase by 3.5% in 2002 and by 3.0% in 2003. The Government's five-year development plan for 2001–05 aimed to increase overall growth in the non-petroleum sectors to some 5%, tighten monetary policy in order to maintain single-digit inflation, implement tax reforms (including the introduction of a value added tax) and pursue structural reforms. The Government's budget for 2003 forecast an increased deficit, owing to an expected continuing decline in petroleum revenues, and increased spending on infrastructure projects and attempts at economic diversification. Following a notable decline in foreign visitors to Yemen in 1999 and 2000 (owing to fears regarding tourists' security), in August 2000 the EU granted financial aid to Yemen in support of a development programme to revive growth in tourism. It was expected that, following the terrorist attacks against the USA in September 2001 and the continuing US-led 'war against terror', tourism and international trade in Yemen would continue to suffer in 2001–2003. In October 2002 the World Bank agreed to provide Yemen with loans and grants worth US $2,300m. to support an anti-poverty campaign during 2003–2005; in part the funds were to be used to support plans to diversify the country's economic base away from petroleum.

Education

Primary education, between the ages of six and 15, is compulsory. Secondary education, beginning at 15, lasts for a further three years. In 1996 enrolment at primary schools was equivalent to 70% of children in the relevant age-group (boys 100%; girls 40%). Enrolment at secondary schools, in the same year, was equivalent to just 34% of students in the appropriate age-group (males 53%; females 14%). In 2001/02 some 184,072 students were enrolled at seven state-controlled institutions of higher education. In 2000 public expenditure on education was forecast at 90,054m. riyals, equivalent to 21.3% of total government spending.

Public Holidays

2003: 1 January (New Year's Day), 12 February* (Id al-Adha, Feast of the Sacrifice), 5 March* (Muharram, Islamic New Year), 8 March (International Women's Day), 14 March* (Ashoura), 1 May (Labour Day), 14 May* (Mouloud, Birth of the Prophet), 13 June (Corrective Movement Anniversary), 24 September* (Leilat al-Meiraj, Ascension of the Prophet), 14 October (National Day), 27 October* (Ramadan begins), 26 November* (Id al-Fitr, end of Ramadan).

2004: 1 January (New Year's Day), 2 February* (Id al-Adha, Feast of the Sacrifice), 22 February* (Muharram, Islamic New Year), 2 March* (Ashoura), 8 March (International Women's Day), 1 May (Labour Day), 2 May* (Mouloud, Birth of the Prophet), 13 June (Corrective Movement Anniversary), 12 September* (Leilat al-Meiraj, Ascension of the Prophet), 14 October (National Day), 15 October* (Ramadan begins), 14 November* (Id al-Fitr, end of Ramadan).

* These holidays are dependent on the Islamic lunar calendar and may vary by one or two days from the dates given.

Weights and Measures

Local weights and measures are used, and vary according to location.

Statistical Survey

Sources (unless otherwise indicated): Republic of Yemen Central Statistical Organization, POB 13434, San'a; tel. (1) 250619; fax (1) 250664; Central Bank of Yemen, POB 59, Ali Abd al-Mughni St, San'a; tel. (1) 274310; fax (1) 274360; e-mail info@centralbank.gov.ye; internet www.centralbank.gov.ye.

Area and Population

AREA, POPULATION AND DENSITY

Area (sq km)	536,869*
Population (census results)†	
16 December 1994	
Males	7,473,540
Females.	7,114,267
Total	14,587,807
Population (official estimates at mid-year)	
1999	17,671,000
2000	18,261,000
2001	18,863,000
Density (per sq km) at mid-2001	35.1

* 207,286 sq miles.
† Excluding adjustment for underenumeration.

PRINCIPAL TOWNS
(population at 1994 census)

San'a (capital) . .	954,400	Damar. . . .	82,900
Aden	398,300	Sayyan . . .	58,400
Taiz	317,600	Jaar	50,300
Hodeida . . .	298,500	ash-Shahir .	48,600
Mukalla . . .	122,400	Zabid . . .	44,200
Ibb	103,300	Bajil	40,600

Source: Stefan Helders, *World Gazetteer* (internet www.world-gazetteer.com).

Mid-2001 (UN estimate, incl. suburbs): San'a 1,410,000 (Source: UN, *World Urbanization Prospects: The 2001 Revision*).

BIRTHS, MARRIAGES AND DEATHS
(UN estimates, annual averages)

	1985–90	1990–95	1995–2000
Birth rate (per 1,000)	49.3	52.6	51.4
Death rate (per 1,000)	13.8	12.5	9.9

Source: UN, *World Population Prospects: The 2000 Revision*.

2000: Registered live births 252,895; Birth rate (per 1,000) 38.9; Registered deaths 18,441; Death rate (per 1,000) 11.2; Marriages 1,834.

Expectation of life (WHO estimates, years at birth): 60.0 (males 58.4; females 61.4) in 2001 (Source: WHO, *World Health Report*).

ECONOMICALLY ACTIVE POPULATION
(ISIC major divisions, '000 persons aged 15 years and over)

	1998	1999
Agriculture, forestry and fishing	1,928	1,996
Mining and quarrying	13	13
Manufacturing	188	206
Electricity, gas and water	21	21
Construction	341	382
Trade, restaurants and hotels	415	440
Transport, storage and communication . . .	196	210
Finance, insurance and real estate	47	49
Social and community services	365	412
Public administration	405	389
Total labour force	3,919	4,119

Source: IMF, *Republic of Yemen: Selected Issues* (April 2001).

Health and Welfare

KEY INDICATORS

Total fertility rate (children per woman, 2001)	7.6
Under-5 mortality rate (per 1,000 live births, 2001)	107
HIV/AIDS (% of persons aged 15–49, 2001)	0.12
Physicians (per 1,000 head, 1996)	0.23
Hospital beds (per 1,000 head, 1998)	0.6
Health expenditure (2000): US $ per head (PPP)	21
Health expenditure (2000): % of GDP	5
Health expenditure (2000): public (% of total)	32
Access to water (% of persons, 2000)	69
Access to sanitation (% of persons, 2000)	45
Human Development Index (2000): ranking	144
Human Development Index (2000): value	0.479

For sources and definitions, see explanatory note on p. vi.

Agriculture

PRINCIPAL CROPS
('000 metric tons)

	1999	2000	2001
Wheat	140	142	153
Barley	43	42	46
Maize	47	48	50
Millet	65	65	69
Sorghum	399	375	382
Potatoes	211	210	209
Chick-peas	38	37	37
Other pulses	25	26	27*
Sesame seed	18	18	18*
Cottonseed	25	28	28*
Tomatoes	240	251	262
Cucumbers and gherkins	14	14	15
Chillies and green peppers	10	11	12
Dry onions	68	75	79
Garlic	11*	12	12*
Green beans	11	11	11
Okra	20	20	22
Other vegetables*	74	75	79
Bananas	89	90	90*
Oranges	156	158	158*
Tangerines, mandarins, etc.	21	23	23*
Grapes	156	156	156*
Watermelons	83	78	85
Melons	36	36	36
Mangoes	20	23	23*
Dates	29	30	30*
Papayas	67	68	68*
Other fruit	42	43	43*
Coffee (green)	11	11	11*
Tobacco (leaves)	11	12	12*

* FAO estimate(s).

Source: FAO.

LIVESTOCK
('000 head, year ending September)

	1999	2000	2001*
Horses*	3	3	3
Asses*	500	500	500
Cattle	1,282	1,339	1,339
Camels	185	190	190
Sheep	4,667	4,804	4,804
Goats	4,204	4,252	4,252
Chickens (million)*	28	30	30

* FAO estimates.

Source: FAO.

LIVESTOCK PRODUCTS
('000 metric tons)

	1999	2000	2001*
Beef and veal	47	52	52
Mutton and lamb*	24	24	24
Goat meat*	22	22	22
Poultry meat	63	67	67
Camel's milk*	9	9	9
Cows' milk	177	180	180
Sheep's milk*	16	16	16
Goats' milk*	20	20	20
Cheese*	11	11	11
Butter*	4	5	5
Hen eggs	31†	31†	31
Wool (greasy)	4†	4†	4
Cattle hides*	9	10	10
Goatskins (fresh)*	4	4	4

* FAO estimates.
† Unofficial figure.

Source: FAO.

Forestry

ROUNDWOOD REMOVALS
('000 cubic metres, excl. bark, estimates)

	1999	2000	2001
Total (all fuel wood)	290	302	314

Source: FAO.

Fishing

('000 metric tons, live weight)

	1998	1999	2000
Demersal percomorphs*	14.1	6.1	6.1
Indian oil sardine*	4.9	4.7	4.3
Narrow-barred Spanish mackerel	3.6	3.6*	3.6*
Pelagic percomorphs*	67.6	74.0	63.9
Sharks, rays and skates, etc.*	5.8	5.6	5.0
Cuttlefish and bobtail squids	5.1	5.3	8.9
Total catch (incl. others)	127.6	124.4	114.7

* Estimate(s).

Source: FAO, *Yearbook of Fishery Statistics*.

Mining

(Estimates, '000 metric tons, unless otherwise indicated)

	1999	2000	2001
Crude petroleum ('000 barrels)	149,000	167,000	165,000
Natural gas (million cu m)	16,000	18,000	18,000
Salt	149	150	150
Gypsum (crude)	103	100	100

Source: US Geological Survey.

Industry

SELECTED PRODUCTS
('000 barrels, unless otherwise indicated)

	1997	1998*	1999*
Motor spirit (petrol)	8,803	9,100	9,100
Kerosene	4,073	3,700	3,700
Distillate fuel oils	10,530	6,900	6,900
Residual fuel oils*	10,300	10,600	10,600
Cement ('000 metric tons)	1,235	1,201	1,454
Electricity (million kWh)*	2,482	2,633	2,633

* Estimates.
Source: mainly US Geological Survey.

Finance

CURRENCY AND EXCHANGE RATES

Monetary Units
100 fils = 1 Yemeni riyal

Sterling, Dollar and Euro Equivalents (29 November 2002)
£1 sterling = 275.73 riyals
US $1 = 177.66 riyals
€1 = 176.36 riyals
1,000 Yemeni riyals = £3.627 = $5.629 = €5.670

Average Exchange Rate (Yemeni riyals per US $)
2000   161.718
2001   168.672
2002   175.625

Note: The exchange rate of US $1 = 9.76 Yemeni riyals, established in the YAR in 1988, remained in force until February 1990, when a new rate of $1 = 12.01 riyals was introduced. Following the merger of the two Yemens in May 1990, the YAR's currency was adopted as the currency of the unified country. In March 1995 the official exchange rate was amended from 12.01 to 50.04 riyals per US dollar. The rate has since been adjusted. From mid-1996 data refer to a market-determined exchange rate, applicable to most private transactions.

GENERAL BUDGET

(million riyals)

Revenue	1998	1999	2000*
Taxation	80,832	89,745	102,611
Direct	28,868	32,139	44,025
Indirect	51,081	59,414	58,586
Other current revenue . . .	140,890	236,244	482,257
Capital revenue . . .	439	427	677
Loans and aids	22,409	34,375	198
Total	244,570	360,791	585,743

Expenditure	1999	2000*
Services sector	99,977	142,642
General administration	47,147	90,048
Government subsidies . . .	26,930	25,068
Security and internal order	25,900	36,526
Defence	67,602	75,508
Education	66,128	90,054
Health	13,897	18,611
Social services	7,722	10,055
Social insurance and labour. . .	2,338	3,945
Youth and sports . . .	686	747
Culture, information and tourism . . .	4,699	5,363
Economic services	40,119	30,748
Construction and housing . . .	16,640	19,266
Agriculture and fishing . . .	7,581	9,274
Mining	1,150	788
Electricity	12,752	205
Communication	73	52
Transportation	738	273
Economy and commerce	1,185	890
Public sector debt	47,489	54,631
Total	342,934	422,249

* Provisional.

INTERNATIONAL RESERVES

(US $ million at 31 December)

	2000	2001	2002
Gold*	14.4	14.6	18.4
IMF special drawing rights . . .	84.6	18.5	44.9
Foreign exchange. . . .	2,815.6	3,639.6	4,365.6
Total	2,914.6	3,672.7	4,428.9

* National valuation.

Source: IMF, *International Financial Statistics*.

MONEY SUPPLY

(million riyals at 31 December)

	2000	2001	2002
Currency outside banks . . .	197,123	212,795	239,329
Demand deposits at commercial banks	41,004	48,992	49,819
Total money (incl. others) . .	247,248	282,683	306,450

Source: IMF, *International Financial Statistics*.

COST OF LIVING

(Consumer price index; base: November 1999 = 100)

	2000	2001	2002
Food and non-alcoholic beverages .	107.66	128.68	136.22
Housing and related items . . .	104.61	115.95	122.10
Clothing and footwear	104.62	114.38	118.44
All items (incl. others)	108.10	132.26	137.99

NATIONAL ACCOUNTS

(million riyals at current prices)

National Income and Product

	1999	2000*	2001*
Domestic factor incomes† . . .	1,005,980	1,289,893	1,362,033
Consumption of fixed capital . .	97,648	126,473	139,120
Gross domestic product (GDP) at factor cost	1,103,628	1,416,366	1,501,153
Indirect taxes, *less* subsidies . .	59,248	67,749	63,537
GDP in purchasers' values . .	1,162,876	1,484,115	1,564,690
Net factor income from abroad . .	−74,262	−125,716	−116,515
Gross national income (GNI) . .	1,088,614	1,358,399	1,488,175
Less Consumption of fixed capital .	97,648	126,473	139,120
National income in market prices	990,966	1,231,926	1,349,055
Other current transfers received from abroad	226,398	237,981	226,815
Less Other current transfers paid abroad	4,782	11,665	11,987
National disposable income. .	1,212,582	1,458,242	1,523,883

* Preliminary.

† Compensation of employees and the operating surplus of enterprises.

Expenditure on the Gross Domestic Product

	1999	2000*	2001*
Government final consumption expenditure.	156,273	194,133	220,146
Private final consumption expenditure.	755,777	908,963	1,085,050
Increase in stocks	13,122	12,590	13,894
Gross fixed capital formation . .	265,371	251,684	263,994
Total domestic expenditure	1,190,543	1,367,370	1,583,034
Exports of goods and services . .	414,527	645,230	593,139
Less Imports of goods and services	442,194	528,485	611,533
GDP in purchasers' values . .	1,162,876	1,484,115	1,564,690
GDP at constant 1990 prices .	207,672	216,854	223,571

* Preliminary.

Gross Domestic Product by Economic Activity

	1999	2000*	2001*
Agriculture, hunting, forestry and fishing	193,992	216,194	243,044
Mining and quarrying	331,246	550,772	492,753
Manufacturing	91,481	95,886	106,175
Electricity, gas and water	11,822	10,899	11,656
Construction	53,385	54,585	61,681
Trade, restaurants and hotels	119,103	149,134	181,958
Transport, storage and communications	127,880	144,153	169,381
Finance, insurance, real estate and business services	103,756	110,361	119,590
Government services	119,113	141,397	166,129
Other community, social and personal services	10,375	11,270	12,255
Private non-profit services to households	257	285	310
Sub-total	1,162,410	1,484,906	1,564,934
Import duties	28,701	28,348	28,416
Less Imputed bank service charge	28,235	29,139	28,660
GDP in purchasers' values	1,162,876	1,484,115	1,564,690

* Preliminary.

BALANCE OF PAYMENTS
(US $ million)

	1999	2000*	2001*
Exports of goods f.o.b.	2,478.3	3,797.2	3,317.3
Imports of goods f.o.b.	−2,120.4	−2,484.4	−2,771.1
Trade balance	357.8	1,312.8	546.2
Exports of services	183.2	210.9	202.0
Imports of services	−718.7	−809.4	−852.6
Balance on goods and services	−177.7	714.3	−104.4
Other income received	94.1	149.6	178.5
Other income paid	−570.9	−926.7	−869.4
Balance on goods, services and income	−654.5	−62.8	−795.3
Current transfers received	1,453.6	1,471.9	1,344.4
Current transfers paid	−30.7	−72.4	−71.4
Current balance	768.5	1,336.6	477.7
Direct investment from abroad	−194.3	6.4	97.3
Portfolio investment (net)	4.1	0.1	−1.4
Other investment assets	−358.1	−177.9	5.6
Other investment liabilities	22.2	−62.2	−62.8
Net errors and omissions	26.5	305.4	152.9
Overall balance	268.9	1,408.3	669.3

* Preliminary.

External Trade

PRINCIPAL COMMODITIES
(distribution by SITC, million riyals at current prices)

Imports c.i.f.	1998	1999	2000
Food and live animals	83,667.5	103,400.2	111,136.6
Dairy products and birds' eggs	11,395.3	11,106.9	13,973.0
Cereals and cereal preparations	34,520.0	52,771.9	50,596.6
Sugar, sugar preparations and honey	13,399.5	14,618.3	17,454.6
Beverages and tobacco	5,920.6	6,304.5	6,297.4
Mineral fuels, lubricants, etc.	18,977.1	25,165.1	44,930.5
Petroleum, petroleum products, etc.	44,912.3	25,147.4	18,943.9
Animal and vegetable oils and fats	11,274.0	10,435.0	14,612.1
Vegetable oils and fats	13,553.6	9,482.7	11,139.7
Chemicals and related products	28,690.1	29,123.4	36,406.8
Medical and pharmaceutical	12,482.3	11,677.0	12,058.5
Basic manufactures	50,936.9	47,848.1	55,190.2
Iron and steel	15,738.1	14,978.2	16,193.8
Machinery and transport equipment	71,357.0	67,250.9	78,332.0
Machinery specialized in particular industries	13,620.1	16,474.3	14,193.5
Road vehicles	14,473.5	14,959.7	28,071.1
Miscellaneous manufactured articles	15,541.7	16,524.7	16,883.3
Total (incl. others)	294,509.7	312,749.4	375,782.9

Exports f.o.b.*	1998	1999	2000
Crude materials (inedible) except fuels	3,357.9	2,221.9	3,030.9
Mineral fuels, lubricants, etc.	186,151.9	359,104.7	636,503.1
Petroleum, petroleum products, etc.	185,611.0	358,153.0	633,745.5
Total (incl. others)	203,480.3	380,010.2	659,609.0

* Including re-exports (24,362.5 in 1998; 28,385.2 in 1999; 45,671.9 in 2000).

PRINCIPAL TRADING PARTNERS*
(million riyals at current prices)

Imports c.i.f.	1999	2000	2001†
Argentina	1,929.8	4,032.1	6,699.5
Australia	13,144.3	9,456.9	7,474.4
Brazil	8,722.0	9,276.7	15,970.1
China, People's Republic	9,226.4	13,179.8	16,533.4
Djibouti	5,089.9	6,125.2	8,558.9
France (incl. Monaco)	13,108.0	17,118.1	19,407.8
Germany	9,358.1	11,474.3	8,888.6
India	8,213.4	9,570.3	22,799.1
Italy	11,048.0	10,003.4	6,018.4
Japan	8,213.4	11,941.4	11,332.1
Kuwait	17,834.4	17,555.1	21,622.6
Malaysia	10,563.9	12,671.8	11,097.1
Netherlands	4,635.3	6,022.3	8,342.9
Oman	5,958.2	11,778.8	13,557.3
Saudi Arabia	36,424.7	51,737.1	51,611.3
Singapore	10,588.5	11,823.9	5,751.4
Switzerland	6,832.5	17,476.2	8,104.4
Thailand	5,814.8	12,287.4	6,932.8
Turkey	6,860.6	8,328.4	8,607.6
United Arab Emirates	37,962.1	37,385.7	51,896.7
United Kingdom	12,972.8	11,970.9	16,658.9
USA	18,550.0	16,682.4	20,559.8
Total (incl. others)	312,749.4	375,782.9	415,899.0

Exports f.o.b.‡	1999	2000	2001†
China, People's Republic . . .	107,936.5	125,219.8	54,365.2
India	26,412.5	99,070.0	104,327.1
Italy	658.8	5,228.2	12,182.3
Korea, Republic	51,238.6	114,021.7	75,121.8
Malaysia§	0.6	11,759.9	36,816.7
Saudi Arabia	6,657.7	7,746.9	11,449.2
Singapore	30,538.6	12,013.8	53,434.9
South Africa	0.3	4,903.5	18,808.3
Thailand	95,457.9¶	113,226.4	102,161.0
USA	2,284.6	40,551.7	23,442.0
Total (incl. others)	380,010.2	659,609.0	569,007.5

* Imports by country of first consignment; exports by country of last consignment.
† Preliminary.
‡ Including re-exports.
§ Excluding domestic exports.
¶ Excluding re-exports.

Transport

ROAD TRAFFIC
(vehicles in use at 31 December)

	1994	1995	1996
Passenger cars	227,854	229,084	240,567
Buses and coaches	2,712	2,835	3,437
Goods vehicles	279,154	279,780	291,149

Source: IRF, *World Road Statistics*.

SHIPPING

Merchant Fleet
(registered at 31 December)

	1999	2000	2001
Number of vessels	48	46	44
Total displacement ('000 grt) . .	30.9	28.3	73.8

Source: Lloyd's Register-Fairplay, *World Fleet Statistics*.

International Sea-borne Freight Traffic
('000 metric tons)

	1988	1989	1990
Goods loaded	1,836	1,883	1,936
Goods unloaded	7,189	7,151	7,829

Source: UN, *Monthly Bulletin of Statistics*.

CIVIL AVIATION
(traffic on scheduled services)

	1997	1998	1999
Kilometres flown (million) . .	12	11	13
Passengers carried ('000) . .	408	462	480
Passenger-km (million) . .	987	1,017	960
Total ton-km (million) . . .	106	111	107

Source: UN, *Statistical Yearbook*.

Tourism

TOURISM ARRIVALS

	1998	1999	2000
Africa	2,696	4,312	5,658
Sudan	1,858	2,310	2,288
Americas	5,585	6,732	8,161
Asia	6,743	4,444	8,342
Europe	54,164	22,201	24,825
France	11,590	4,500	4,535
Germany	11,109	5,810	4,194
Italy	7,006	2,572	4,748
Netherlands	3,864	976	1,014
Switzerland	2,742	368	502
United Kingdom . . .	6,626	2,759	4,342
Middle East	17,746	20,263	25,404
Egypt	1,990	2,632	3,355
Iraq	2,121	2,250	2,543
Jordan	2,263	2,744	2,352
Saudi Arabia	6,087	7,533	9,842
Syria	1,070	1,574	2,278
Total (incl. others)	87,628	58,370	72,836

Tourism receipts (US $ million): 84 in 1998; 61 in 1999; 76 in 2000.

Source: General Tourism Authority.

Communications Media

	1999	2000	2001
Television receivers ('000 in use)	5,000	5,200	n.a.
Telephones ('000 main lines in use)*	372.0	417.1	423.1
Mobile cellular telephones ('000 subscribers)*	27.7	32.0	152.0
Personal computers ('000 in use)* .	30	35	37
Internet users ('000)*	10	15	17
Daily newspapers:			
number	n.a.	3	n.a.
circulation ('000 copies) . . .	n.a.	50	n.a.

* Source: International Telecommunication Union.

Radio receivers ('000 in use): 1,050 in 1997.

Facsimile machines ('000 in use, estimate): 2,784 in 1995.

Sources: UN, *Statistical Yearbook*; UNESCO, *Statistical Yearbook*.

Education

(2001/02, unless otherwise indicated)

	Schools	Teachers†	Students Males	Students Females	Total
Pre-primary*† . .	42	532	3,274	2,822	6,156
Primary . . .	11,013‡	113,812	2,185,278	1,216,230	3,401,508
Secondary . .	n.a.†	14,063	354,743	129,830	484,573
Higher* . . .	7†	3,429	138,291	45,781	184,072

* Public education only.
† 1999/2000.
‡ 1993/94 (Source: UNESCO, *Statistical Yearbook*).

Adult literacy rate (UNESCO estimates): 46.3% (males 67.5%; females 25.2%) in 2000 (Source: UNDP, *Human Development Report*).

Directory

The Constitution

A draft constitution for the united Republic of Yemen (based on that endorsed by the Yemen Arab Republic (YAR) and the People's Democratic Republic of Yemen (PDRY) in December 1981) was published in December 1989, and was approved by a popular referendum on 15–16 May 1991.

On 29 September 1994 52 articles were amended, 29 added and one cancelled, leaving a total of 159 articles in the Constitution. Further amendments to the Constitution were adopted by the House of Representatives in late November 2000 and approved in a national referendum on 20 February 2001.

The Constitution defines the Yemeni Republic as an independent and sovereign Arab and Islamic country. The document states that the Republic 'is an indivisible whole, and it is impermissible to concede any part of it. The Yemeni people are part of the Arab and Islamic nation.' The Islamic *Shari'a* is identified as the basis of all laws.

The revised Constitution provides for the election, by direct universal suffrage, of the President of the Republic; the President is elected for a seven-year term (increased from five years by the amendments approved in 2001). The President is empowered to appoint a Vice-President. The President of the Republic is, *ex officio*, Supreme Commander of the Armed Forces. The Constitution as amended in 2001 requires presidential candidates to obtain the endorsement of 5% of a combined vote of the appointed Consultative Council and the elected House of Representatives (in place of 10% of the latter chamber alone).

Legislative authority is vested in the 301-member House of Representatives, which is elected, by universal suffrage, for a six-year term (increased from four years by amendment in 2001). The role of the House of Representatives is defined as to 'monitor' the executive. The President is empowered to dissolve the legislature and call new elections within a period of 60 days.

The upper house of the legislature, the Consultative Council, has 111 members (increased from 59 by amendment in 2001), nominated by the President.

The President of the Republic appoints the Prime Minister and other members of the Government on the advice of the Prime Minister.

The Constitution delineates the separation of the powers of the organs of State, and guarantees the independence of the judiciary. The existence of a multi-party political system is confirmed. Serving members of the police and armed forces are banned from political activity.

The Government

HEAD OF STATE

President: Field Marshal ALI ABDULLAH SALEH (took office 24 May 1990) (re-elected 1 October 1994, 23 September 1999).

Vice-President: Maj.-Gen. ABD AR-RABBUH MANSUR HADI.

COUNCIL OF MINISTERS
(May 2003)

Prime Minister: ABD AL-QADIR BAJAMMAL.

Deputy Prime Minister and Minister of Finance: ALAWI SALIH AS-SALAMI.

Deputy Prime Minister and Minister of Planning and International Co-operation: AHMAD MUHAMMAD SUFAN.

Minister of Foreign Affairs: ABU BAKR AL-KURBI.

Minister of Defence: Gen. ABDULLAH ELEWA.

Minister of the Interior: Gen. RASHID AL-ALIMI.

Minister of Education: ABD AS-SALAM AL-JUFI.

Minister of Petroleum and Mineral Resources: RASHID BARBAA.

Minister of Religious Endowments and Guidance: HAMOUD MUHAMMAD ABAD.

Minister of Transport: OMAR MOHSEN AL-AMUDI.

Minister of Fisheries: ALI MUHAMMAD MAJUR.

Minister of Industry and Commerce: KHALID RAJEH SHEIKH.

Minister of Public Works and Roads: ABDULLAH HUSSAIN AD-DAFI.

Minister of Communications and Information Technology: ABD AL-MALIK AL-MAALAMI.

Minister of Culture and Tourism: KHALID ABDULLAH AR-RUWEISHAN.

Minister of Higher Education and Scientific Research: ABD AL-WAHAB ABD AR-RAWEH.

Minister of Agriculture and Water Resources: HASSAN OMAR SUWAID.

Minister of Immigrants' Affairs: ABDO QUBATI.

Minister of Technical Education and Vocational Training: ALI MANSOUR SAFA'A.

Minister of Local Government: SADIQ AMIN ABDURAS.

Minister of Legal Affairs: RASHID AHMAD AR-RUSSAS.

Minister of Youth and Sports: ABD AR-RAHMAN AL-AKWAA.

Minister of the Civil Service and Social Security: HAMOUD KHALID AS-SUFI.

Minister of Water and the Environment: MUHAMMAD LUTF AL-IRYANI.

Minister of Labour and Social Affairs: ABD AL-KARIM AL-ARHABI.

Minister of Information: HUSSAIN AL-AWADHI.

Minister of Justice: ADNAN OMAR AL-JIFRI.

Minister of Public Health and Demography: MUHAMMAD YEHYA AN-NAAMI.

Minister of Electricity: ABD AR-RAHMAN TARMUM.

Minister of Human Rights: AMAT AL-ALIM AS-SUSUA.

Minister of State for Parliamentary Affairs: MUHAMMAD YEHYA ASH-SHERFI.

Ministers of State: QASSIM AHMAD AL-AAJAM, AHMAD MUHAMMAD AL-KAHLANI (also Mayor of San'a), MUHAMMAD YASSER.

Secretary-General for the Presidential Office: ABDULLAH AL-BASHIRI.

MINISTRIES

All ministries are in San'a.

Ministry of Communications and Information Technology: Airport Rd, al-Jiraf, POB 25237, San'a; tel. (1) 331456; fax (1) 331457.

Ministry of Immigrants' Affairs: San'a; internet www.y-mia.net.

Ministry of Industry and Commerce: POB 22210, San'a; tel. (1) 252363; fax (1) 252337; e-mail most@y.net.ye; internet www.most.org.ye.

Ministry of Information: San'a; tel. (1) 274008; fax (1) 282004; e-mail yemen-info@y.net.ye; internet www.yemeninfo.gov.ye.

Ministry of Oil and Mineral Resources: POB 81, San'a; tel. (1) 202313; internet www.momr.gov.ye.

Ministry of Planning and International Co-operation: POB 175, San'a; tel. (1) 250101; fax (1) 251503.

President and Legislature

PRESIDENT

Presidential Election, 23 September 1999

Candidates	Votes	% of votes
Field Marshal Ali Abdullah Saleh	3,445,608	96.3
Najib Qahtan ash-Sha'bi	132,532	3.7
Total	3,577,960	100.0

THE HOUSE OF REPRESENTATIVES

Speaker: Sheikh ABDULLAH BIN HUSSAIN AL-AHMAR.

General Election, 27 April 2003

Party	Seats
General People's Congress (GPC)	238
Yemeni Islah Party (YIP)	46
Yemeni Socialist Party (YSP)	8
Independents	4
Nasserite Unionist Popular Organization	3
Arab Socialist Baath Party	2
Total	301

Political Organizations

In the former PDRY the YSP was the only legal political party until December 1989, when the formation of opposition parties was legalized. There were no political parties in the former YAR. The two leading parties that emerged in the unified Yemen were the GPC and the YSP. During 1990 an estimated 30 to 40 further political parties were reported to have been formed, and in 1991 a law was passed regulating the formation of political parties. Following the civil war from May to July 1994, President Saleh excluded the YSP from the new Government formed in October 1994. In 1995 43 parties were known to be in existence. There were 22 registered political parties in April 2003.

Al-Haq: San'a; conservative Islamic party; Sec.-Gen. Sheikh AHMAD ASH-SHAMI.

Democratic Coalition of Opposition: San'a; f. 1995 as a coalition of 13 political parties and organizations, including a splinter faction of the YSP and the LSY.

General People's Congress (GPC): San'a; e-mail gpc@y.net.ye; internet www.gpc.org.ye; a broad grouping of supporters of President Saleh; Chair. Field Marshal ALI ABDULLAH SALEH; Vice-Chair. Maj.-Gen. ABD AR-RABBUH MANSUR HADI; Sec.-Gen. Dr ABD AL-KARIM AL-IRYANI.

League of the Sons of Yemen (LSY): Aden; represents interests of southern tribes; Leader ABD AR-RAHMAN AL-JIFRI; Sec.-Gen. MOHSEN FARID.

Nasserite Unionist Popular Organization: Aden; f. 1989 as a legal party.

National Opposition Co-ordination Council: San'a; f. 2001 as a coalition of opposition parties, including the YSP.

Yemen Socialist Party (YSP): San'a; f. 1978 to succeed the United Political Organization—National Front (UPO—NF); fmrly Marxist-Leninist 'vanguard' party based on 'scientific socialism'; has Political Bureau and Cen. Cttee; Sec.-Gen. ALI SALEH OBAD.

Yemeni Islah Party (YIP): POB 23090, San'a; tel. (1) 213281; fax (1) 213311; internet www.yemeniislahparty.com; f. 1990 by mems of the legislature and other political figures, and tribal leaders; seeks constitutional reform based on Islamic law; Leader Sheikh ABDULLAH BIN HUSSAIN AL-AHMAR; Sec.-Gen. Sheikh MUHAMMAD ALI AL-YADOUMI.

Yemeni Unionist Rally Party: Aden; f. 1990 by intellectuals and politicians from the fmr YAR and PDRY to safeguard human rights; Leader OMAR AL-JAWI.

Other parties in Yemen include the **Arab Socialist Baath Party;** the **Federation of Popular Forces;** the **Liberation Front Party;** the **Nasserite Democratic Party;** the **National Democratic Front;** the **National Social Party;** the **Popular Nasserite Reformation Party;** the **Social Green Party** and the **Yemen League.**

Diplomatic Representation

EMBASSIES IN YEMEN

Algeria: POB 509, 67 Amman St, San'a; tel. (1) 209689; fax (1) 209688; Ambassador BEN HADID CHADLI.

Bulgaria: POB 1518, St No. 22, San'a; tel. (1) 207924; Chargé d'affaires ALEXI ALAXIEV.

China, People's Republic: az-Zubairy St, San'a; tel. (1) 275337; Ambassador GAO YUSHENG.

Cuba: POB 15256, St No. 6B, San'a; tel. (1) 217304; fax (1) 217305; Ambassador HÉCTOR ARGILES PÉREZ.

Czech Republic: POB 2501, Safiya Janoobia, San'a; tel. (1) 247946; fax (1) 244418; Ambassador ILJA MAZANEK.

Egypt: POB 1134, Gamal Abd al-Nasser St, San'a; tel. (1) 275948; fax (1) 274196; Ambassador Dr MAHMOUD MURTADA.

Eritrea: POB 11040, Western Safia Bldg, San'a; tel. (1) 209422; fax (1) 214088; Ambassador MAHMOUD ALI JABRA.

Ethiopia: POB 234, Al-Hamadani St, San'a; tel. (1) 208833; fax (1) 213780; e-mail ethoembs@y.net.ye; Ambassador TEKETEL FORSIDO.

France: POB 1286, Cnr Sts 2/21, San'a; tel. (1) 268888; fax (1) 269160; internet www.y.net.ye/ambafrancesanaa; Ambassador PIERRE BOILLOT.

Germany: POB 2562 + 41, Hadda, San'a; tel. (1) 413174; fax (1) 413179; e-mail germembasanaa@y.net.ye; internet www .germanembassysanaa.org; Ambassador Dr WERNER ZIMPRICH.

Hungary: POB 11558, As-Safiya Al-Gharbiyya, St No. 6B, San'a; tel. (1) 216250; fax (1) 216251; Ambassador TIBOR SZATMARI.

India: POB 1154, San'a; tel. (1) 508084; fax (1) 508105; e-mail indiaemb@y.net.ye; Ambassador M. S. SUMAN.

Indonesia: POB 19873, No. 15, St No. 16, Sixty Rd, Hadda Area, San'a; tel. (1) 217388; fax (1) 414383; Ambassador AHMAD NOOR.

Iran: POB 1437, Haddah St, San'a; tel. (1) 413552; Chargé d'affaires ABBAS ETRY.

Iraq: POB 498, South Airport Rd, San'a; tel. (1) 269574; Ambassador MUHSIN KHALIL.

Italy: POB 1152, No. 5 Bldg, St No. 29, San'a; tel. (1) 265616; fax (1) 266137; e-mail italianembassy@y.net.ye; internet www .ambitaliasanaa.org.ye; Ambassador GIACOMO FELICE DI MONTEFORTE.

Japan: POB 817, San'a; tel. (1) 207356; fax (1) 209531; Ambassador SUSUMU AKIYAMA.

Jordan: POB 2152, San'a; tel. (1) 413279; Ambassador FOUAD BATAYNEH.

Korea, Democratic People's Republic: POB 1209, al-Hasaba, Mazda Rd, San'a; tel. (1) 232340; Ambassador CHANG MYONG SON.

Korea, Republic: San'a; tel. (1) 245959; Ambassador PAK HI-JOO.

Kuwait: POB 3746, South Ring Rd, San'a; tel. (1) 268876; fax (1) 268875; Chargé d'affaires MANSOUR AL-AWADI.

Lebanon: POB 2283, Haddah St, San'a; tel. (1) 203459; fax (1) 201120; Ambassador HASSAN BERRO.

Libya: POB 1506, Ring Rd, St No. 8, House No. 145, San'a; Secretary of Libyan Brotherhood Office A. U. HEFIANA.

Mauritania: POB 19383, No. 6, Algeria St, San'a; tel. (1) 216770; fax (1) 215926; Ambassador AHMED OULD SIDY.

Morocco: POB 10236, West Safiya, San'a; tel. (1) 247964; fax (1) 247793; Ambassador LAHCEN AZOULAY.

Netherlands: POB 463, off 14th October St, San'a; tel. (1) 421000; fax 421035; e-mail holland@y.net.ye; internet www.holland.com.ye; Ambassador B. J. RONHAAR.

Oman: POB 105, Aser area, az-Zubairy St, San'a; tel. (1) 208933; Ambassador ABDULLAH BIN HAMAD AL-BADI.

Pakistan: POB 2848, Ring Rd, San'a; tel. (1) 248814; fax (1) 248866; e-mail pakemb@y.net.ye; Ambassador M. ASGHAR AFRIDI.

Poland: POB 16168, Hadda St, San'a; tel. (1) 412243; fax (1) 413647; Ambassador KRZYSZTOF SUPROWICZ.

Romania: POB 2169, No. 22, St No. 21, Nouakchott Rd, San'a; tel. (1) 209003; fax (1) 214100; e-mail a.romana-sanaa@y.net.ye; Chargé d'affaires GHEORGHE VILCU.

Russia: POB 1087, 26 September St, San'a; tel. (1) 278719; fax (1) 283142; Ambassador IGOR G. IVASHENKO.

Saudi Arabia: POB 1184, Zuhara House, Hadda Rd, San'a; tel. (1) 240429; Ambassador MUHAMMAD AL-QAHTANI.

Somalia: San'a; tel. (1) 208864; Ambassador ABD AS-SALLAM MU'ALLIM ADAM.

Sudan: POB 2561, 82 Abou al-Hassan al-Hamadani St, San'a; tel. (1) 265231; fax (1) 265234; Ambassador OMAR AS-SAID TAHA.

Syria: POB 494, Hadda Rd, Damascus St 1, San'a; tel. (1) 414891; Ambassador Dr FAROUK TAHA.

Tunisia: POB 2561, Diplomatic area, St No. 22, San'a; tel. (1) 240458; Ambassador ABBÈS MOHSEN.

Turkey: POB 18371, as-Safiya, San'a; tel. and fax (1) 241395; Ambassador SANLI TOPÇUOĞLU.

United Arab Emirates: POB 2250, Ring Rd, San'a; tel. (1) 248777; Ambassador SAIF BIN MAKTOOM AL-MANSOORY.

United Kingdom: POB 1287, 129 Hadda Rd, San'a; tel. (1) 264081; fax (1) 263059; Ambassador FRANCES GUY.

USA: POB 22347, Sheraton Hotel District, San'a; tel. (1) 238843; fax (1) 251563; e-mail usembassy08@y.net.ye; internet www.usembassy .ye; Ambassador EDMUND J. HULL.

Religion

ISLAM

The majority of the population are Muslims. Most are Sunni Muslims of the Shafi'a sect, except in the north-west of the country, where Zaidism (a moderate sect of the Shi'a order) is the dominant persuasion.

CHRISTIANITY

The Roman Catholic Church

Apostolic Vicariate of Arabia: POB 54, Abu Dhabi, United Arab Emirates; tel. (2) 4461895; fax (2) 4465177; e-mail apvicar@emirates .net.ae; responsible for a territory comprising most of the Arabian peninsula (including Saudi Arabia, the UAE, Oman, Qatar, Bahrain and Yemen), containing an estimated 1,300,000 Roman Catholics (31 December 2001); Vicar Apostolic Giovanni Bernardo Gremoli (Titular Bishop of Masuccaba, resident in the UAE); Vicar Delegate for Yemen Rev. George Pudussery.

The Anglican Communion

Within the Episcopal Church in Jerusalem and the Middle East, Yemen forms part of the diocese of Cyprus and the Gulf. The Anglican congregations in San'a and Aden are entirely expatriate; the Bishop in Cyprus and the Gulf is resident in Cyprus, while the Archdeacon in the Gulf is resident in Qatar.

HINDUISM

There is a small Hindu community.

Judicial System

Yemen's Constitution guarantees the independence of the judiciary and identifies Islamic (*Shari'a*) as the basis of all laws.

Yemen is divided into 18 Governorates, each of which is further divided into Districts. Each District has a Court of First Instance in which all cases are heard by a single magistrate. Appeals against decisions of the Courts of First Instance are referred to a Court of Appeal. Each Governorate has a Court of Appeal with four divisions: Civil, Criminal, Matrimonial and Commercial, each of which consists of three judges.

The Supreme Court of the Republic, which sits in San'a, rules on matters concerning the Constitution, appeals against decisions of the Courts of Appeal and cases brought against members of the Legislature. The Supreme Court has eight divisions, each of which consists of five judges.

The Supreme Judicial Council supervises the proper function of the courts and its Chairman is the President of the Republic.

The Press

Legislation embodying the freedom of the press in the unified Republic of Yemen was enacted in May 1990. The lists below include publications which appeared in the YAR and the PDRY prior to their unification in May 1990.

DAILIES

Al-Jumhuriya: Taiz Information Office, Taiz; tel. (4) 216748; Arabic; circ. 100,000.

Ar-Rabi' 'Ashar Min Uktubar (14 October): POB 4227, Crater, Aden; f. 1968; not published on Saturdays; Arabic; Editorial Dir Farouq Mustafa Rifat; Chief Editor Muhammad Hussain Muhammad; circ. 20,000.

Ash-Sharara (The Spark): 14 October Corpn for Printing, Publishing, Distribution and Advertising, POB 4227, Crater, Aden; Arabic; circ. 6,000.

Ath-Thawra (The Revolution): POB 2195, San'a; tel. (1) 262626; fax (1) 274139; e-mail editor@althawra.gov.ye; internet www.althawra .gov.ye; Arabic; govt-owned; Editor Muhammad az-Zorkah; circ. 110,000.

WEEKLIES AND OTHERS

Attijarah (Trade): POB 3370, Hodeida; tel. (3) 213784; fax (3) 211528; e-mail hodcci@y.net.ye; monthly; Arabic; commercial.

Al-Ayyam: POB 648, al-Khalij al-Imami, Crater, Aden; tel. (2) 255170; fax (2) 255692; e-mail editor@al-ayyam-yemen.com; Editor Hisham Bashraheel.

Al-Bilad (The Country): POB 1438, San'a; weekly; Arabic; centre-right.

Dar as-Salam (Peace): POB 1790, San'a; tel. (1) 272946; f. 1948; weekly; Arabic; political, economic and general essays; Editor Abdullah Mukbool as-Sicgul.

Al-Fanoon: Ministry of Culture and Tourism, POB 1187, Tawahi 102, Aden; tel. (2) 23831; f. 1980; Arabic; monthly arts review; Editor Faisal Sofy; circ. 15,500.

Al-Gundi (The Soldier): Ministry of Defence, Madinat ash-Sha'ab; fortnightly; Arabic; circ. 8,500.

Al-Hares: Aden; fortnightly; Arabic; circ. 8,000.

Al-Hikma (Wisdom): POB 4227, Crater, Aden; monthly; Arabic; publ. by the Writers' Union; circ. 5,000.

Al-Ma'in (Spring): Ministry of Information, San'a; monthly; general interest.

Majallat al-Jaish (Army Magazine): POB 2182, San'a; tel. (1) 231181; monthly; publ. by Ministry of Defence.

Al-Maseerah (Journey): Ministry of Information, POB 2182, San'a; tel. (1) 231181; monthly; general interest.

Al-Mithaq (The Charter): San'a; internet www.gpc.org.ye/mathak; weekly; organ of the General People's Congress.

Ar-Ra'i al-'Am (Public Opinion): POB 293, San'a; tel. (1) 242090; weekly; independent; Editor Ali Muhammad al-Olafi.

Ar-Risalah: POB 55777, 26 September St, Taiz; tel. (4) 214215; fax (4) 221164; e-mail alaws@y.net.ye; f. 1968; weekly; Arabic.

As-Sahwa (Awakening): POB 11126, Hadda Road, San'a; tel. (1) 247892; fax (1) 269218; weekly; Islamic fundamentalist; Editor Muhammad al-Yaddoumi.

As-Salam (Peace): POB 181, San'a; tel. (1) 272946; weekly.

San'a: POB 193, San'a; fortnightly; Arabic; inclined to left.

Sawt al-'Ummal (The Workers' Voice): POB 4227, Crater, Aden; weekly; Arabic.

Sawt al-Yemen (Voice of Yemen): POB 302, San'a; weekly; Arabic.

Ash-Shura: POB 15114, San'a; tel. (1) 213584; fax (1) 213468; e-mail shoura@y.net.ye; Editor Abdallah Sa'ad; circ. 15,000.

At-Ta'awun (Co-operation): at-Ta'awun Bldg, az-Zubairy St, San'a; weekly; Arabic; supports co-operative societies.

Ath-Thawri (The Revolutionary): POB 4227, Crater, Aden; weekly; published on Saturday; Arabic; organ of Cen. Cttee of YSP; Editor Dr Ahmad Abdullah Salih.

26 September: 26 September Publishing, POB 17, San'a; tel. (1) 262626; fax (1) 234129; e-mail webmaster@26september.com; internet www.y.net.ye/26september; armed forces weekly; circ. 25,000.

Al-Wahda al-Watani (National Unity): Al-Baath Printing House, POB 193, San'a; tel. (1) 77511; f. 1982; fmrly *Al-Omal*; monthly; Editor Muhammad Salem Ali; circ. 40,000.

Al-Yemen: Yemen Printing and Publishing Co, POB 1081, San'a; tel. (1) 72376; f. 1971; weekly; Arabic; centre-right; Editor Muhammad Ahmad as-Sabagh.

The Yemen Times: POB 2579, Hadda St, San'a; tel. (1) 268661; fax (1) 268276; e-mail editor@yementimes.com; internet www .yementimes.com; f. 1991; independent weekly; English; Editor-in-Chief Walid al-Saqqaf; circ. 30,000.

Yemen Observer: POB 19183, Algeria St, Sana'a; tel. (1) 203393; fax (1) 207239; e-mail faris@yobserver.com; internet www .yobserver,com; f. 1996; independent weekly; English; Editor-in-Chief Faris Sanabani.

Yemeni Women: POB 4227, Crater, Aden; monthly; circ. 5,000.

NEWS AGENCIES

Aden News Agency (ANA): Ministry of Culture and Tourism, POB 1187, Tawahi 102, Aden; tel. (2) 24874; f. 1970; govt-owned; Dir-Gen. Ahmad Muhammad Ibrahim.

Saba News Agency: POB 881, San'a; tel. (1) 250078; fax (1) 250078; e-mail sabanews@y.net.ye; internet www.sabanews.gov.ye; f. 1970; Editor Husein al-Awadi.

Publishers

Armed Forces Printing Press: POB 17, San'a; tel. (1) 274240.

14 October Corpn for Printing, Publishing, Distribution and Advertising: POB 4227, Crater, Aden; under control of the Ministry of Information; Chair. and Gen. Man. Salih Ahmad Salah.

26 September Publishing: POB 17, San'a; tel. (1) 274240.

Ath-Thawrah Corpn: POB 2195, San'a; fax (1) 251505; Chair. M. R. AZ-ZURKAH.

Yemen Printing and Publishing Co: POB 1081, San'a; Chair. AHMAD MUHAMMAD HADI.

Broadcasting and Communications

TELECOMMUNICATIONS

Public Telecommunications Corpn: POB 17045, Airport Rd, al-Jiraf, San'a; tel. (1) 250040; Dir-Gen. MUHAMMAD AL-KASSOUS.

BROADCASTING

Yemen Radio and Television Corpn: POB 2182, San'a; tel. (1) 230654; fax (1) 230761; state-controlled; Gen. Man. AHMED T. SHAYANY.

Finance

(cap. = capital; res = reserves; dep. = deposits; m. = million; brs = branches; amounts in Yemeni riyals, unless otherwise indicated)

BANKING

Central Bank

Central Bank of Yemen: POB 59, Ali Abd al-Mughni St, San'a; tel. (1) 274310; fax (1) 274360; e-mail info@centralbank.gov.ye; internet www.centralbank.gov.ye; f. 1971; merged with Bank of Yemen in 1990; cap. 1,000.0m., res 32,698.8m., dep. 240,028.5m. (Dec. 2000); Gov. AHMAD ABD AR-RAHMAN AS-SAMAWI; Dep. Gov. SALEM MUHAMMAD AL-ASHWALI; 20 brs.

Principal Banks

Arab Bank PLC (Jordan): POB 475, az-Zubairy St, San'a; tel. (1) 276585; fax (1) 276583; e-mail arabbank@y.net.ye; internet www.arabbank.com; f. 1972; Man. MAHDI ALAWI; 5 brs.

Co-operative and Agricultural Credit Bank: POB 2015, Banks Complex, az-Zubairy St, San'a; tel. (1) 220090; fax (1) 220088; e-mail cacbank@y.net.ye; f. 1976; cap. 293m., total assets 4,930m. (Dec. 2000); Chair. Dr MUHAMMAD H. AL-WADAN; Dir-Gen. YAHIA AS-SABRI; 27 brs.

Crédit Agricole Indosuez (France): POB 651, az-Zubairy St, San'a; tel. (1) 274370; fax (1) 274501; e-mail caindosuezye@y.net.ye; Regional Man. FRANÇOIS RIVIER; 6 brs.

Industrial Bank of Yemen: POB 323, Banks Complex, az-Zubairy St, San'a; tel. (1) 207381; fax (1) 207379; f. 1976; industrial investment; cap. 100m., total assets 269.8m. (1987); Chair. and Man. Dir ABBAS ABDU MUHAMMAD AL-KIRSHY; Gen. Man. ABD AL-KARIM ISMAIL AL-ARHABI.

International Bank of Yemen YSC: POB 4444, 106 az-Zubairy St, San'a; tel. (1) 273273; fax (1) 274127; e-mail a.t.alabsi@y.net.ye; internet www.ibyemen.com; f. 1980; commercial bank; cap. 1,001.9m., res 70.8m., dep. 13,250.3m. (Dec. 2000); Chair. ABDULLAH A. WALI NASHER; Gen. Man. MUHAMMAD ABDULLAH M. AL-AMERY; 4 brs.

Islamic Bank of Yemen for Finance and Investment: POB 18452, Mareb Yemen Insurance Co Bldg, az-Zubairy St, San'a; tel. (1) 206117; fax (1) 205679; e-mail ibr-islbk-yesan@y.net.ye; internet www.islamicbankymn.com; f. 1996; commercial, investment and retail banking; cap. 1,250.0m., res 151.8m., dep. 6,753.9m. (Dec. 2001); Chair. A. KARIM AR-RAHMAN AL-ASWADI.

National Bank of Yemen: POB 5, Arwa Rd, Crater, Aden; tel. and fax (2) 253484; e-mail nby.ho@y.net.ye; internet www.natbankofyemen.com; f. 1970 as National Bank of South Yemen; reorg. 1971; cap. 1,600.0m., res 1,256.1m., dep. 33,921.3m. (Dec. 2001); Chair. and Gen. Man. ABD AR-RAHMAN MUHAMMAD AL-KUHALI; 28 brs.

Tadhamon International Islamic Bank: POB 2411, as-Saeed Commercial Bldg, az-Zubairy St, San'a; f. 1995 as Yemen Bank for Investment and Development; became Tadhamon Islamic Bank in 1996, name changed as above in 2002; cap. 2,250.0m., res 855.6m., dep. 34,219.0m. (Dec. 2001); Chair. ABD AL-GABBAR HAYEL SAEED; Gen. Man. TAWFIQ JAMIL ABU DABASAH.

United Bank Ltd (Pakistan): POB 1295, Ali Abd al-Mughni St, San'a; tel. (1) 272424; fax (1) 274168; e-mail ublsana@y.net.ye; Vice-Pres. and Gen. Man. INAYATULLAH BUTT; 1 br.

Watani Bank for Trade and Investment: POB 3058, az-Zubairy St, San'a; tel. (1) 206613; fax (1) 205706; e-mail watanibank@y.net .ye; internet www.watanibank.com; f. 1998; cap. 1,113.0m., res 19.3m., dep. 9,464.6m. (Dec. 2000); Chair. Dr AHMAD ALI AL-HAMDANI; Gen. Man. SHABIH MEHDI NAQVI.

Yemen Bank for Reconstruction and Development (YBRD): POB 541, 26 September St, San'a; tel. (1) 270481; fax (1) 271684; e-mail ybrdho@y.net.ye; internet www.ybrd.com.ye; f. 1962; cap. 1,250.0m., res 571.0m., dep. 27,629.7m. (Dec. 2000); Chair. ABDULLAH SALIM AL-GIFRI; Gen. Man. HUSSAIN FADHLE MUHAMMAD; 13 brs.

Yemen Commercial Bank: POB 19845, az-Zubairy St, San'a; tel. (1) 284272; fax (1) 284656; e-mail ycbho@y.net.ye; internet www .ycbank.com; f. 1993; cap. 993.7m., res 191.2m., dep. 25,470.1m. (Dec. 2001); Chair. Sheikh MUHAMMAD BIN YAHYA AR-ROWAISHAN; Chief Exec. and Gen. Man. SIKANDER MAHMOUD; 8 brs.

INSURANCE

Aman Insurance Co (YSC): POB 1133, San'a; tel. (1) 214104; fax (1) 209452; e-mail aman-ins@y.net.ye; internet www.y.net.ye/amaninsurance; all classes of insurance; Gen. Man. AKIL AS-SAKKAF.

Mareb Yemen Insurance Co: POB 2284, az-Zubairy St, San'a; tel. (1) 206115; fax (1) 206114; e-mail maryinsco74@y.net.ye; internet www.marebinsurance.com.ye; f. 1974; all classes of insurance; cap. 150m. Chair. and Gen. Man. ALI M. HASHIM.

National Insurance and Re-insurance Co: POB 456, Aden; tel. (2) 51464; f. 1970; Lloyd's Agents; cap. 5m. Yemeni dinars; Gen. Man. ABUBAKR S. AL-QOTI.

Saba Yemen Insurance Co: POB 19214, San'a; tel. (1) 240908; fax (1) 240943; e-mail sabains@yenet.com; internet www.sabainsurance .com; f. 1990; all classes of insurance; Gen. Man. SABAH HADDAD.

Trust Yemen Insurance and Reinsurance Co: POB 18392, San'a; tel. (1) 264263; fax (1) 263234; all classes of insurance; Gen. Man. HUSSAIN AYYOUR.

United Insurance Co: POB 1883, az-Zubairy St, San'a; tel. (1) 214232; fax (1) 214012; e-mail unitedinsurance@y.net.ye; internet www.unitedinsuranceyemen.com; f. 1981; all classes of general insurance and life; cap. 100m. Gen. Man. TAREK A. HAYEL SAEED.

Al-Watania Insurance Co (YSC): POB 15497, San'a; tel. (1) 272874; fax (1) 272924; e-mail alwatania@yenet.com; all classes of insurance.

Yemen General Insurance Co (SYC): POB 2709, YGI Bldg, 25 Algiers St, San'a; tel. (1) 442489; fax (1) 442492; e-mail ygi-san@y .net.ye; f. 1977; all classes of insurance; cap. 300m. Chair. ABD AL-GABBAR THABET; Gen. Man. MUN'EM AL-KHAFAJI.

Yemen Insurance Co: POB 8437, San'a; tel. (1) 272805; fax (1) 274177; e-mail yemeninsurance@yenet.com; f. 1990; all classes of insurance; Deputy Gen. Man. KHALID BASHIR TAHIR.

Trade and Industry

GOVERNMENT AGENCIES

General Corpn for Foreign Trade and Grains: POB 77, San'a; tel. (1) 202345; fax (1) 209511; f. 1976; Dir-Gen. ABD AR-RAHMAN AL-MADWAHI.

General Corpn for Manufacturing and Marketing of Cement: POB 1920, San'a; tel. (1) 215691; fax (1) 263168; Chair. AMIN ABD AL-WAHID AHMED.

National Co for Foreign Trade: POB 90, Crater, Aden; tel. (2) 42793; fax (2) 42631; f. 1969; incorporates main foreign trading businesses (nationalized in 1970) and arranges their supply to the National Co for Home Trade; Gen. Man. AHMED MUHAMMAD SALEH (acting).

National Co for Home Trade: POB 90, Crater, Aden; tel. (2) 41483; fax (2) 41226; f. 1969; marketing of general consumer goods, building materials, electrical goods, motor cars and spare parts, agricultural machinery etc. Man. Dir ABD AR-RAHMAN AS-SAILANI.

National Dockyards Co: POB 1244, Tawahi, Aden; tel. (2) 23837; Man. Dir SALEH AL-MUNTASIR MEHDI.

National Drug Corpn: Aden; tel. (2) 04912; fax (2) 21242; f. 1972; import of pharmaceutical products, chemicals, medical supplies, baby foods and scientific instruments; Chair. and Gen. Man. Dr AWADH SALAM ISSA BAMATRAF.

Public Corpn for Building and Housing: POB 7022, al-Mansoura, Aden; tel. (2) 342296; fax (2) 345726; f. 1973; govt contractors and contractors of private housing projects; Dir-Gen. HUSSAIN MUHAMMAD AL-WALI.

Public Corpn for Maritime Affairs (PCMA): POB 19396, San'a; tel. (1) 414412; fax (1) 414645; f. 1990; protection of the marine environment; registration of ships; implementation of international maritime conventions; Chair. SAEED YAFAI.

Yemen Co for Industry and Commerce Ltd: POB 5423, Taiz; tel. (4) 218058; fax (4) 218054; Chair. ALI MUHAMMAD SAID.

Yemen Co for Investment and Finance Ltd: POB 2789, San'a; tel. (1) 276372; fax (1) 274178; f. 1981; cap. 100m. Chair. and Gen. Man. ABDULLAH ISHAQ.

Yemen Drug Co for Industry and Commerce: POB 40, San'a; tel. (1) 234250; fax (1) 234290; Chair. MUHAMMAD ALI MUQBIL; Man. Dir ABD AR-RAHMAN A. GHALEB.

Yemen Economical Corpn: POB 1207, San'a; tel. (1) 262501; fax (1) 262508; e-mail info@yecoyemen.com; internet www.yecoyemen.com; f. 1973; Commercial Man. A. KARIM SAYAGHI.

Yemen Land Transport Corpn: POB 279, Taiz St, San'a; tel. (1) 268307; f. 1961; Chair. ABD AL-KADOOS AL-MASSRY; Gen. Man. SALEH ABDULLAH ABD AL-WALI.

Yemen Trading and Construction Co: POB 1092, San'a; tel. (1) 264005; fax (1) 240624; e-mail ytcc@y.net.ye; f. 1979; intial cap. 100m. riyals.

DEVELOPMENT ORGANIZATIONS

Agricultural Research and Extension Authority: POB 87148 Dhamar; e-mail muharram@y.net.ye.

General Board for Development of Eastern Region: San'a.

General Board for Development of Tihama: San'a.

Yemen Free Zone Public Authority: Aden; tel. (2) 241210; fax (2) 221237; supervises creation of a free zone for industrial investment; Chair. ABD AL-QADIR BA-JAMMAL.

CHAMBERS OF COMMERCE

Chamber of Commerce and Industry—Aden: POB 473, Crater 101, Aden; tel. (2) 257376; fax (2) 255660; e-mail cciaden@y.net.ye; f. 1886; 5,000 mems; Pres. MUHAMMAD OMER BAMASHMUS; Dir G. AHMAD HADI SALEM.

Federation of Chambers of Commerce: POB 16992, San'a; tel. (1) 211765; Dir JAMAL SHARHAN.

Hodeida Chamber of Commerce: POB 3370, 20 az-Zubairy St, Hodeida; tel. (3) 217401; fax (3) 211528; e-mail hodcci@y.net.ye; internet www.hodcci.com.ye; f. 1960; 6,500 mems; cap. 10m. riyals; Dir NABIL AL-WAGEEH.

San'a Chamber of Commerce and Industry: Airport Rd, al-Hasabah St, POB 195, San'a; tel. (1) 232361; fax (1) 232412; f. 1963; Pres. Al-Haj HUSSAIN AL-WATARI; Gen. Man. ABDULLAH H. AR-RUBAIDI.

Taiz Chamber of Commerce: POB 5029, Chamber St, Taiz; tel. (4) 210580; fax (4) 212335; e-mail taizchamber@y.net.ye; Dir MOFID A. SAIF.

Yemen Chamber of Commerce and Industry: POB 16690, San'a; tel. (1) 223539; fax (1) 251555.

STATE HYDROCARBONS COMPANIES

General Corpn for Oil and Mineral Resources: San'a; f. 1990; state petroleum co; Pres. AHMAD BARAKAT.

Ministry of Oil and Mineral Resources: POB 81, San'a; tel. (1) 202313; internet www.momr.gov.ye; responsible for the refining and marketing of petroleum products, and for prospecting and exploitation of indigenous hydrocarbons and other minerals; subsidiaries include:

  Aden Refinery Co: POB 3003, Aden 110; tel. (2) 76234; fax (2) 76600; f. 1952; operates petroleum refinery; capacity 8.6m. tons per year; output 4.2m. tons (1990); operates 1 oil tanker; Exec. Dir MUHAMMAD HUSSEIN AL-HAJ; Refinery Man. AHMAD HASSAN AL-GIFRI.

  Yemen National Oil Co: POB 5050, Maalla, Aden; sole petroleum concessionaire, importer and distributor of petroleum products; Gen. Man. MUHAMMAD ABD HUSSEIN.

UTILITIES

Electricity

Public Electricity Corpn: POB 11422, Government Complex, Haddah Rd, San'a; tel. (1) 264131; fax (1) 263115; Man. Dir AHMAD AL-AINI.

Water

National Water and Sanitation Authority (NWSA): (Taiz Branch) POB 5283, Taiz; tel. (4) 222628; fax (4) 212323.

TRADE UNIONS

Agricultural Co-operatives Union: POB 649, San'a; tel. (1) 270685; fax (1) 274125.

General Confederation of Workers: POB 1162, Maalla, Aden; f. 1956; affiliated to WFTU and ICFTU; 35,000 mems; Pres. RAJEH SALEH NAJI; Gen. Sec. ABD AR-RAZAK SHAIF.

Trade Union Federation: San'a; Pres. ALI SAIF MUQBIL.

Transport

RAILWAYS

There are no railways in Yemen.

ROADS

In 1996 Yemen had a total road network of 64,725 km, including 5,234 km of main roads and 2,474 km of secondary roads. In 1999 there were an estimated 6,000 km of roads, 11.5% of which were paved.

General Corpn for Roads and Bridges: POB 1185, az-Zubairy St, Asir Rd, San'a; tel. (1) 202278; fax (1) 209571; e-mail gcrb@y.net.ye; responsible for maintenance and construction.

Yemen Land Transport Co: Aden; f. 1980; incorporates fmr Yemen Bus Co and all other public transport of the fmr PDRY; Chair. ABD AL-JALIL TAHIR BADR; Gen. Man. SALEH AWAD AL-AMUDI.

SHIPPING

Aden is the main port. Aden Main Harbour has 28 first-class berths. In addition there is ample room to accommodate vessels of light draught at anchor in the 18-foot dredged area. There is also 800 feet of cargo wharf accommodating vessels of 300 feet length and 18 feet draught. Aden Oil Harbour accommodates four tankers of 57,000 tons and up to 40 feet draught. In March 1999 work was completed on a US \$580m. programme to expand container handling facilities at Aden, with the aim of establishing the port as a major transhipment centre. Hodeida port, on the Red Sea, was expanded with Soviet aid and now handles a considerable amount of traffic; there are also ports at Maalla, Mocha, Nishtun and Salif.

At 31 December 2001 Yemen's merchant fleet comprised 44 vessels, with a combined displacement of 73,757 grt.

Yemen Ports Authority: POB 1316, Steamer Point, Aden; tel. (2) 203521; fax (2) 202850; e-mail roy@y.net.ye; f. 1888; Harbour Master Capt. BARAKAT ALI DARWISH.

Principal Shipping Companies

Aden Refinery Co: POB 3003, Aden 110; tel. (2) 430743; fax (2) 376600; 2 general tankers and 1 chemical tanker; Exec.-Dir MUHAMMAD HUSSAIN AL-HAJ.

Arabian Gulf Navigation Co (Yemen) Ltd: POB 3740, Hodeida; tel. (3) 2442; 1 general cargo vessel.

Al-Katiri Shipping Corpn: POB 716, Aden; tel. (2) 255538; fax (2) 251152; 1 general cargo vessel.

Elkirshi Shipping and Stevedoring Co: POB 3813, al-Hamdi St, Hodeida; tel. (3) 224263; operates at ports of Hodeida, Mocha and Salif.

Hodeida Shipping and Transport Co Ltd: POB 3337, Hodeida; tel. (3) 238130; fax (3) 211533; e-mail hodship_1969@y.net.ye; internet www.hodship.com; shipping agents, stevedoring, Lloyd's agents; clearance, haulage land transportation, cargo and vessel surveys.

Middle East Shipping Co Ltd: POB 3700, Hodeida; tel. (3) 217276; fax (3) 211529; e-mail mideast@mideastshipping.com; internet www.mideastshipping.com; f. 1962; Chair. ABD AL-WASA HAYEL SAEED; Gen. Man. SAMEER AL-GALIL GAZEM; brs in Mocha, Aden, Taiz, Mukalla, San'a, Salif, Ras Isa, ash-Shihr.

National Shipping Co: POB 1228, Steamer Point, Aden; tel. (2) 204861; fax (2) 202644; shipping, bunkering, clearing and forwarding, and travel agents; Gen. Man. MUHAMMAD OTHMAN.

Yemen Navigation Line: POB 4190, Aden; tel. (2) 24861; fleet of 3 general cargo vessels.

Yemen Shipping Development Co Ltd: POB 3686, Hodeida; tel. (3) 224103; fax (3) 211584; 1 general cargo vessel; Shipping Man. FAHDLE A. KARIM.

Yeslam Salem Alshagga: POB 778, Aden; 1 general cargo vessel.

CIVIL AVIATION

There are six international airports—San'a International (13 km from the city), Aden Civil Airport (at Khormaksar, 11 km from the port of Aden), al-Ganad (at Taiz), Mukalla (Riyan), Seyoun and Hodeida Airport.

Yemen Airways (Yemenia): POB 1183, Airport Rd, San'a; tel. (1) 232380; fax (1) 252991; e-mail yemenia@y.net.ye; internet www .yemenia.com.ye; f. 1961 as Yemen Airlines; nationalized as Yemen Airways Corpn 1972; present name adopted 1978; merged with airlines of fmr PDRY in 1996; owned 51% by Yemeni Govt and 49% by Govt of Saudi Arabia; scheduled for privatization; supervised by a ministerial cttee under the Ministry of Transport; internal services and external services to more than 25 destinations in the Middle East, Asia, Africa, Europe and the USA; Chair. HASSAN ABDO SOHBI.

Tourism

The former YAR formed a joint tourism company with the PDRY in 1980. Yemen boasts areas of beautiful scenery, a favourable climate and towns of historic and architectural importance. UNESCO has named San'a and Shibam as World Heritage sites. However, the growth of tourism has, in recent years, been hampered by political instability. In 2000 some 72,836 tourists visited Yemen; tourist receipts for that year were estimated at US $76m.

Association of Yemen Tourism and Travel Agencies: San'a; internet www.aytta.org; Chair. YAHAYA M. A. SALEH.

General Authority of Tourism: POB 129, San'a; tel. (1) 252319; fax (1) 252316; e-mail mkt@yenet.com; Chair. ABD AR-RAHMAN MAHYOUB.

Yemen Tourism Promotion Board: POB 5607, 48 Amman St, San'a; tel. (1) 264057; fax (1) 264284; e-mail yementpb@y.net.ye; Man. ABDU LUTF.

ZAMBIA

Introductory Survey

Location, Climate, Language, Religion, Flag, Capital

The Republic of Zambia is a land-locked state in southern central Africa, bordered to the north by Tanzania and the Democratic Republic of the Congo, to the east by Malawi and Mozambique, to the south by Zimbabwe, Botswana and Namibia, and to the west by Angola. The climate is tropical, modified by altitude, with average temperatures from 18°C to 24°C (65°F–75°F). The official language is English. The principal African languages are Nyanja, Bemba, Tonga, Lozi, Lunda and Luvale. Christians comprise an estimated 50% of the population and are roughly divided between Protestants and Roman Catholics. A sizeable proportion of the population follow traditional animist beliefs. Most Asians are Muslims, although some are Hindus. The national flag (proportions 2 by 3) is green, with equal red, black and orange vertical stripes in the lower fly corner, and an orange eagle in flight in the upper fly corner. The capital is Lusaka.

Recent History

In 1924 control of Northern Rhodesia was transferred from the British South Africa Company to the Government of the United Kingdom. In 1953 the protectorate united with Southern Rhodesia (now Zimbabwe) and Nyasaland (now Malawi) to form the Federation of Rhodesia and Nyasaland (also known as the Central African Federation). In 1962, following a campaign of civil disobedience organized by the United National Independence Party (UNIP), in support of demands that Northern Rhodesia be granted independence, the British Government introduced a new Constitution, which provided for a limited African franchise. In December 1963 the Federation was formally dissolved. Following elections in January 1964, the leader of UNIP, Dr Kenneth Kaunda, formed a Government. Northern Rhodesia, which was henceforth known as Zambia, became an independent republic within the Commonwealth on 24 October 1964, with Kaunda as the country's first President.

Following its accession to power, the Kaunda administration supported African liberation groups operating in Southern Rhodesia (then known as Rhodesia) and Mozambique; repeated clashes along the border with both countries were reported, while incidents of internal political violence, particularly in the Copperbelt region, also occurred. In December 1972 Zambia was declared a one-party state. In January 1973 the Rhodesian administration closed the border with Zambia.

Presidential and legislative elections took place in December 1978. Kaunda, who was the sole candidate (after UNIP had approved constitutional changes that effectively eliminated all opposition), was returned for a fourth term as President. In October 1980 a coup was attempted, allegedly involving several prominent business executives, government officials and UNIP members. Kaunda accused South Africa and other foreign powers of supporting the attempt.

Kaunda was re-elected President in October 1983, with 93% of the votes cast. In March 1985 Kaunda adopted emergency powers to prohibit industrial action in essential services, following a series of strikes by public-sector employees and bank staff in support of demands for higher wages. In April several cabinet members and senior party officials were replaced, apparently as part of an ongoing campaign against corruption. During 1985–87 the Government introduced austerity measures in response to increasing economic decline, which precipitated sporadic civil unrest. In December 1986 the Government was forced to reintroduce a subsidy on refined maize meal, the staple food, after its removal prompted rioting in the towns of Kitwe and Ndola in the Copperbelt region, in which at least 15 people died and 450 people were arrested. There were strikes for higher pay in early 1987, and in April of that year the Government cancelled a 70% increase in the price of fuel, following protests in Lusaka. In the same month Kaunda alleged that the South African Government, in collusion with Zambian business executives and military personnel, had conspired to overthrow his administration.

In August 1988 the Central Committee of UNIP was expanded from 25 to 68 members. In October nine people, six of whom were military officers, were arrested and accused of plotting to overthrow the Government. One of the civilians was subsequently released; four of the military officers were convicted of treason in August 1989 (but were released under the terms of a general amnesty in July 1990). Presidential and legislative elections took place later in October 1988. Kaunda, the only candidate, received 95.5% of the votes in the presidential election; however, only 54% of the electorate voted. At the legislative elections four cabinet ministers lost their seats in the National Assembly. In March Kebby Musokotwane, widely considered to be a potential rival to Kaunda, was replaced as Prime Minister.

In July 1989 the introduction of increases in the prices of essential goods provoked rioting in the Copperbelt region. Later that year the Governor of the Bank of Zambia was dismissed and arrested on corruption charges. In June 1990 Frederick Hapunda (believed to be a supporter of multi-party politics) was dismissed as Minister of Defence, and several other prominent state officials were similarly replaced. Later in the month the introduction of austerity measures provoked violent rioting in the capital. At the end of June troops loyal to Kaunda suppressed a revolt by members of the armed forces.

In May 1990 Kaunda announced that a popular referendum on the subject of multi-party politics would take place in October of that year, and that supporters of such a system (which Kaunda and UNIP opposed) would be permitted to campaign and hold public meetings. Accordingly, in July the Movement for Multi-party Democracy (MMD), an unofficial alliance of political opponents of the Government, was formed. The MMD, which was led by a former government minister, Arthur Wina, and the Chairman of the Zambian Congress of Trade Unions (ZCTU), Frederick Chiluba, swiftly gained widespread public support. Later in July Kaunda announced that the referendum was to be postponed until August 1991, to facilitate the registration of a large section of the electorate. In September 1990, however, following the recommendation by Kaunda that a multi-party political system be reintroduced, that multi-party elections be organized by October 1991, that the national referendum be abandoned, and that a commission be appointed to revise the Constitution, the National Council of UNIP endorsed proposals for multi-party legislative and presidential elections, and accepted the recommendations of a parliamentary committee regarding the restructuring of the party.

In December 1990 Kaunda formally adopted constitutional amendments (which had been approved by the National Assembly earlier in the same month) that permitted the formation of other political associations to contest the forthcoming elections. The MMD was subsequently granted official recognition. In early 1991 several prominent members of UNIP resigned from the party and declared their support for the MMD, while the ZCTU officially transferred allegiance to the MMD. Several other opposition movements were also established. In February violent clashes between supporters of the MMD and members of UNIP were suppressed by the security forces.

In June 1991 the constitutional commission presented a series of recommendations, including the creation of the post of Vice-President, the expansion of the National Assembly from 135 to 150 members and the establishment of a constitutional court. Kaunda accepted the majority of the proposed constitutional amendments, which were subsequently submitted for approval by the National Assembly. The MMD, however, rejected the draft, and announced that it would boycott the forthcoming elections if the National Assembly accepted the proposals. In July, following discussions between Kaunda, Chiluba and delegates from seven other political associations, Kaunda agreed to suspend the review of the draft Constitution in the National Assembly pending further negotiations. It was also announced that state subsidies would be granted to all registered political parties. Subsequent discussions between the MMD and UNIP resulted in the establishment of a joint commission to revise the draft Constitution. In late July Kaunda conceded to opposition demands that ministers be appointed only from the National Assembly and that proposals for a constitutional court be abandoned. A provision granting the President the power to impose martial law was also rescinded.

On 2 August 1991 the National Assembly formally adopted the new Constitution. At the UNIP congress in the same month Kaunda was unanimously re-elected as President of the party. However, several prominent party officials, including the incumbent Secretary-General, refused to seek election to a new Central Committee. Kaunda also announced the dissociation of the armed forces from UNIP; senior officers in the armed forces were subsequently obliged to retire from the party's Central Committee. In September 1991 Kaunda officially dissociated UNIP from the State; workers in the public sector were henceforth prohibited from engaging in political activity.

On 31 October 1991 Chiluba, with 75.8% of votes cast, defeated Kaunda in the presidential election. In the concurrent legislative elections, contested by 330 candidates representing six political parties, the MMD secured 125 seats in the National Assembly, while UNIP won the remaining 25 seats; only four members of the previous Government were returned to the National Assembly. Although there had been numerous reports of violence in the pre-election period, international observers reported that the elections had been conducted fairly. Kaunda's failure to secure re-election was attributed to widespread perceptions of economic mismanagement by his administration. On 2 November Chiluba was inaugurated as President. He appointed Levy Mwanawasa, a constitutional lawyer, as Vice-President and Leader of the National Assembly, and formed a new Cabinet. In addition, a government minister was appointed to each of the country's nine provinces, which had hitherto been administered by governors. Chiluba subsequently initiated a major restructuring of the civil service and of parastatal organizations, as part of efforts to reverse the country's significant economic decline. Senior executives in a number of parastatal organizations were dismissed, in an attempt to eradicate widespread corruption among officials.

In December 1991, following a road accident in which Mwanawasa was severely injured, the Minister without Portfolio, Brig.-Gen. Godfrey Miyanda, was accused of attempting to bring about his death. A commission of inquiry was later informed that Miyanda had conspired with members of the former Government to kill Mwanawasa, and subsequently to assume the vice-presidency. In March 1992, however, following an investigation of the incident by detectives from the United Kingdom, Miyanda was exonerated of involvement in the accident.

In mid-1992 widespread opposition to government policies was reported. In May a dissident faction of academics within the MMD, the Caucus for National Unity (CNU), emerged. The CNU, which claimed to have the support of several government members, demanded that Chiluba review procedures for the appointment of cabinet ministers and heads of parastatal organizations, to ensure that all ethnic groups were represented. The CNU, together with other pressure groups, also advocated the establishment of a constitutional commission to curtail the executive power vested in the President and the Cabinet. In July two cabinet ministers (who reportedly supported the CNU) resigned in protest at what they alleged was the Government's failure to suppress corruption and to institute democratic measures, following the refusal of the National Assembly to accept a report that implicated several government members in alleged financial malpractice. Later that month the CNU registered as an independent political party. In September Kaunda formally resigned from active participation in UNIP; Musokotwane was subsequently elected as the party's President. At local government elections in November the MMD won the majority of seats; the high rate of abstention (more than 90% of the registered electorate) was, however, widely attributed to disillusionment with the Chiluba administration.

In March 1993 Chiluba declared a state of emergency, following the discovery of UNIP documents that allegedly revealed details of a conspiracy to destabilize the Government by inciting unrest and civil disobedience. Several prominent members of UNIP, including Kaunda's three sons, were subsequently arrested. Musokotwane admitted the existence of the documents, but denied that UNIP officials were involved in any plot, which he attributed to extreme factions within the party. Kaunda, however, claimed that the conspiracy had been fabricated by Zambian security forces, with the assistance of US intelligence services, in an attempt to undermine the opposition. Later in March diplomatic relations with Iran and Iraq were suspended, following allegations by the Zambian Government that the two countries had funded subversive elements within

UNIP. Shortly afterwards the National Assembly approved the state of emergency, which was to remain in force for a further three months. As a result of pressure from Western Governments, however, Chiluba reduced the maximum period of detention without trial from 28 to seven days.

Divisions within the MMD became apparent in August 1993, when 15 prominent members (11 of whom held seats in the National Assembly) resigned from the party: they accused the Government of protecting corrupt cabinet ministers and of failing to respond to numerous reports linking senior party officials with the illegal drugs trade. Their opposition to the Government was consolidated later in the month by the formation of a new political group, the National Party (NP). In November Chiluba appointed a 22-member commission to revise the Constitution; it was announced that the draft document was to be submitted for approval by a Constituent Assembly, and subsequently by a national referendum.

In January 1994 two senior cabinet ministers announced their resignation, following persistent allegations of their involvement in drugs-trafficking. One of the ministers, Vernon Mwaanga (a founder member of the MMD), who had held the foreign affairs portfolio, had been implicated in the drugs trade by a tribunal in 1985, although he had not been convicted of the alleged offences. Two further ministers were dismissed in an ensuing government reorganization. At partial elections for 10 of the 11 vacated seats in the National Assembly, which took place in November 1993 and April 1994, the MMD regained five seats, while the NP secured four and UNIP took one.

In July 1994 Mwanawasa resigned as Vice-President, citing long-standing differences with Chiluba, and was subsequently replaced by Miyanda. Also in July Kaunda stated that he intended to contest the presidential election due in 1996; however, UNIP officials indicated that he would only be allowed to resume the leadership of the party if he were officially elected by members. (Kaunda's decision to return to active politics subsequently resulted in factional division within UNIP.) In August Kaunda was apparently warned against inciting revolt, after he conducted a number of rallies in the Northern Province (where the MMD traditionally attracted considerable support). Later that month the Government announced that Kaunda had been placed under surveillance in the interests of national security, following reports that he had received support from foreign diplomatic missions in Zambia.

At a by-election in December 1994 UNIP secured the remaining vacant seat in the National Assembly. In February 1995 Chiluba ordered members of the Government immediately to declare their financial assets and liabilities. In the same month Kaunda was charged with convening an illegal political gathering, after he had addressed a public rally. Later in February the Governor of the Bank of Zambia was replaced, following a sharp depreciation in the value of the national currency. In March increasing divisions became evident within the MMD between the Bemba ethnic group (to which Chiluba belonged) and the traditionalist Nsenga; it was reported that MMD factions had circulated tracts criticizing Chiluba and Mwanawasa (who continued to hold the position of MMD Vice-President).

In June 1995 some members of the constitutional review commission rejected a final draft of the Constitution, objecting, in particular, to restrictions on the independent press, and on public gatherings and demonstrations; they claimed that the four members of the commission who had prepared the draft had taken payments from the Government, and accused the Chairman of complicity with the authorities. Later that month, however, the draft Constitution was submitted for approval. At the end of June Kaunda was elected President of UNIP, defeating Musokotwane; he reiterated his intention of seeking re-election to the state presidency, despite provisions in the draft Constitution that effectively debarred his candidature, on the grounds that he had already served two terms of office and that he was not of direct Zambian descent (his parents originated from Malawi). In August, following continued factional violence within UNIP, three parliamentary deputies resigned from the party: among them was the leader of the opposition in the National Assembly, who subsequently joined the MMD. In September a human rights commission, established by Chiluba in 1993, claimed that clandestine underground tunnels, situated beneath the official residence, had been used as torture chambers during Kaunda's tenure in office. At by-elections in 13 constituencies in September–October 1995, the MMD secured seven seats, and UNIP six; it was reported that Kaunda had been placed temporarily under house arrest following incidents of electoral violence. In October the Minister for Legal Affairs announced that Kaunda had not officially relinquished Malawian citizenship until 1970 (and had therefore governed illegally for six years), and that he had not obtained Zambian citizenship through the correct procedures. However, following widespread reports that the authorities intended to deport Kaunda, the Government ordered security forces to suspend investigations into the former President's citizenship (apparently owing to fears of civil unrest).

In January 1996 seven opposition parties, including UNIP and the NP, established an informal alliance to campaign in favour of democratic elections and the establishment of a Constituent Assembly to approve the draft Constitution by a process of national consensus. In early May a cabinet minister resigned, after attracting criticism from other government members for proposing that the constitutional amendments be introduced subsequent to the elections. Opposition parties, moreover, demanded that the Government abandon the draft Constitution and negotiate with them regarding electoral reform. Later that month UNIP deputies withdrew from a parliamentary debate on the draft, which was subsequently approved by a large majority in the National Assembly. On 28 May the Constitution was officially adopted by Chiluba. In early June Western donor Governments suspended aid to Zambia, in protest at the constitutional provisions that effectively precluded Kaunda from contesting the presidency, while Kaunda announced that he intended to defy the ban. In the same month eight senior UNIP officials, including the Vice-President, were arrested and charged in connection with a series of bomb attacks against official buildings, which were attributed to a clandestine anti-Government organization, known as Black Mamba; two of the accused officials were released in September, and the remaining six were acquitted of charges against them in November.

In August 1996 Chiluba and Kaunda met for discussions, as part of a programme of dialogue between the Government and opposition parties. Following Kaunda's decision to boycott a scheduled second round of discussions in September, the Government made minor concessions regarding the conduct of forthcoming elections, including assurances that votes would be counted at polling stations and that the Electoral Commission (appointed by Chiluba) would be independent; UNIP's request that the elections be conducted according to the 1991 Constitution was rejected. In mid-October 1996 Chiluba dissolved the National Assembly and announced that presidential and legislative elections would take place on 18 November. UNIP, still dissatisfied with the electoral system, announced its intention to boycott the elections and organize a campaign of civil disobedience; by early November a further six political parties had also decided to boycott the elections. There was widespread criticism of the voter registration process, in which fewer than one-half of the estimated 4.6m. eligible voters had been listed. The Government ordered the temporary closure of the University of Zambia, after two days of rioting by students who were attempting to force Chiluba to reopen negotiations with the opposition and reach agreement on the electoral process.

Despite appeals for a postponement, the elections were held as planned, and Chiluba and the MMD were returned to power by a large majority. In the presidential election Chiluba defeated the four other candidates with 72.5% of the valid votes cast. His nearest rival (with only 12.5%) was Dean Mung'omba of the Zambia Democratic Congress (ZADECO), an erstwhile opponent of Chiluba within the MMD. The MMD secured 131 of the 150 seats in the National Assembly. Of the eight other parties that contested the elections, only the NP (five seats), ZADECO (two seats) and Agenda for Zambia (AZ—two seats) won parliamentary representation, with independent candidates taking the remaining 10 seats. The rate of participation was low. Despite the Electoral Commission's verdict that the elections had been conducted fairly, allegations of fraud were made by opposition parties and local monitoring groups, which criticized voter registration procedures and accused the MMD of buying votes. The chairmen of two electoral monitoring groups were taken into custody for questioning, but were later released without charge. A former senior official of one of the groups claimed that the monitoring groups had been influenced by donor Governments attempting to discredit the elections, and six journalists working in the state media were suspended for allegedly conspiring to undermine the elections.

Chiluba was inaugurated for a second presidential term on 21 November 1996. Amid demands for his resignation and for fresh

elections to be held, Chiluba dissolved the Cabinet and put the military on alert at the end of the month. In early December a new Government was appointed, although the main portfolios remained largely unchanged. Opposition parties continued their campaign of civil disobedience throughout December, although nation-wide marches of solidarity with the Government were reported to have been widely supported. Four opposition parties filed petitions with the Supreme Court challenging Chiluba's citizenship (and therefore his eligibility as President), and accusing the Electoral Commission of conspiring with the MMD to commit electoral fraud; the petitions were dismissed in early 1997. In response to reports in late December 1996 that a senior army commander had been placed under house arrest as a result of rumours of a military take-over, Chiluba warned the media against attempting to incite the security forces to challenge his leadership.

In February 1997 a human rights report prepared for the US Department of State condemned police brutality and prison conditions in Zambia. In March the Government established a permanent commission to investigate human rights violations, although opposition parties refused to participate. (In October 1996 the human rights commission established by Chiluba in 1993 had presented its final report, disclosing evidence of the violation of the human rights of political detainees under both Kaunda's and Chiluba's Governments.)

Political tension intensified in the second half of 1997. In response to reports in June claiming that Kaunda and Roger Chongwe, the leader of the Liberal Progressive Front, were appealing for international assistance to overcome a political crisis in Zambia, the MMD denied that any such crisis existed. Later that month the MMD's chairman in Lusaka called for the declaration of a state of emergency, on the grounds that the opposition, by refusing to enter into talks with the MDD, were advocating a civil war. The opposition denounced his claims and Chongwe insisted that they would welcome dialogue, but only if the 1996 elections were annulled and the Constitution repealed. Meanwhile, the opposition's campaign of civil disobedience continued, and in late July 1997 security forces dispersed demonstrators at a protest march after government vehicles were stoned. In August Kaunda and Chongwe were shot and wounded (Chongwe seriously) when the security forces opened fire on an opposition gathering in Kabwe, north of Lusaka. Kaunda's subsequent allegation that the shooting was an assassination attempt organized by the Government was strongly denied by Chiluba.

On 28 October 1997 rebel army officers briefly captured the national television and radio station from where they proclaimed the formation of a military regime. The attempted coup was suppressed within a few hours by regular military units; 15 people were arrested during the operation. Allegations by Kaunda that the Government had orchestrated the coup in order to be in a position to detain prominent members of the opposition were repeated by other opposition figures after Chiluba declared a state of emergency on 29 October, providing for the detention for 28 days without trial of people suspected of involvement in the attempted coup. Several non-governmental organizations described the state of emergency as an abuse of human rights. Mung'omba was among 84 people arrested in the immediate aftermath of the coup, and in November the High Court ordered that he undergo a medical examination to investigate injuries allegedly sustained during interrogation by the police.

Chiluba carried out an extensive cabinet reshuffle in early December 1997. Observers interpreted the transfer to lesser cabinet posts of Miyanda and of Benjamin Mwila, hitherto the Minister of Defence, as an attempt to forestall the emergence of potential rivals to Chiluba within the MMD. Lt-Gen. Christon Tembo, hitherto the Minister of Mines and Mineral Development, replaced Miyanda as Vice-President.

On 25 December 1997 Kaunda was arrested under emergency powers and imprisoned, shortly after his return to Zambia from more than two months abroad. Numerous regional and international Governments expressed serious concern at the detention of Kaunda, who refused food until the end of the month when he was visited by Julius Nyerere, the former President of Tanzania. On the following day Kaunda was placed under house arrest at his home in Lusaka. He was arraigned in court in January 1998, and in mid-February he was formally notified that he was to stand trial for 'misprision of treason', on the grounds that he had failed to report in advance to the authorities details allegedly known to him of the attempted coup of October 1997. Meanwhile, in late January the National Assembly voted to extend the state of emergency for a further three months; Chiluba eventually revoked the state of emergency on 17 March, following pressure from external donors. Also in March, Chiluba effected a minor cabinet reshuffle, most notably dismissing the Minister of Finance and Economic Development, Ronald Penza. In late April 80 people who were being detained in connection with the attempted coup, including Kaunda and Mung'omba, were committed to summary trial in the High Court. Kaunda was released from detention in early June, after charges against him were withdrawn, apparently owing to lack of evidence. He subsequently announced his intention to retire from active politics, and his resignation as UNIP President in July created a split within the party over the nomination of a replacement. The MMD was also reported to be divided over an eventual successor to Chiluba, despite a recent ban within the party on presidential campaigning, amid strongly denied suggestions that Chiluba might seek a third term of office in 2001, contrary to the Constitution. In September Chiluba dismissed the Minister of Commerce, Trade and Industry, Enoch Kavindele, following differences over policy. In October two senior UNIP officials resigned from their positions in the party, and it was also reported that Kaunda had reversed his decision to withdraw from active politics. Meanwhile, the MMD announced that 14 political parties had been deregistered for failing to meet the required standards for parties.

In November 1998 Ronald Penza was murdered at his home by a gang of masked men. Shortly afterwards five of the six suspects were shot dead by police-officers, who claimed the motive for Penza's murder was robbery, although it was reported that nothing had been stolen. The police action, and Chiluba's subsequent approval of legislation providing for Zambia's intelligence service to be armed, were of considerable concern to human rights organizations. In mid-December Mung'omba and Princess Nakatindi Wina, a former minister and the MMD's national chairperson for women, were granted bail, as no witnesses had provided evidence against them since their detention on charges of treason following the failed coup attempt of October 1997.

The MMD won the majority of the wards contested at local elections in December 1998, securing 880 of the 1,275 seats, although the rate of participation was reported to be extremely low.

In mid-February 1999 opposition parties demanded the dismissal of Lt-Gen. Christon Tembo, the Vice-President, and Benjamin Mwila, the Minister of Energy and Water Development (previously responsible for defence), who had been implicated, along with Enoch Kavindele, in Angolan claims that Zambia was supporting the Angolan rebel movement, União Nacional para a Independência Total de Angola (UNITA)—allegations that the Zambian authorities strongly denied. In late February a number of bombs exploded in Lusaka, one of which seriously damaged the Angolan embassy, killing a security guard, while several further explosive devices were discovered and defused. The security forces were placed on full alert, and an investigation into the bombings was instigated. In mid-March it was reported that two Zambians had been arrested, and two foreigners deported, in connection with the bombings. Twelve journalists were arrested and charged with espionage in April, after their newspaper printed a report claiming that Zambia's military capacity was inferior to that of Angola. In April the 12 were committed to trial by the High Court (but were all found not guilty in 2000). The Cabinet was reorganized in March 1999.

At the end of March 1999 the High Court delivered its judgment in a case concerning Kaunda's citizenship, declaring him to be a stateless person. The following day Kaunda appealed to the Supreme Court against the ruling, and later that day he escaped a reported assassination attempt, when a group of armed men opened fire on his car. In April five opposition parties, including the AZ and ZADECO, formed a new alliance, the Zambia Alliance for Progress (ZAP). However, the authorities refused to register the ZAP on the grounds that its constituent parties had not been dissolved. The ZAP initially disputed the ruling and announced its intention to appeal to the High Court, but in August ZADECO formally announced its dissolution, thus effectively losing its parliamentary seat. Meanwhile, in June Chiluba effected a minor cabinet reshuffle, notably appointing Katele Kalumba as Minister of Finance and Economic Development.

In September 1999 59 soldiers were sentenced to death for their part in the failed coup against the Chiluba administration

in October 1997. A further soldier was sentenced to 21 years' imprisonment for concealing information regarding the coup attempt from the authorities, while another eight soldiers were acquitted of charges of treason, owing to lack of evidence. In October 1999 55 of the soldiers sentenced to death launched an appeal against the convictions.

In October 1999, on the occasion of the 35th anniversary of Zambian independence, Chiluba pardoned 68 prisoners. In early November Maj. Wezi Kaunda, son of ex-President Kaunda, was shot dead outside his home in Lusaka. According to reports, he was shot several times by four heavily armed men, one of whom was subsequently arrested. Although several UNIP members claimed that there was a political motive behind the murder, police sources indicated that they believed Kaunda had been the victim of an attempted car hijack. Three detectives from the United Kingdom subsequently travelled to Zambia to assist with the investigation into the killing.

In early January 2000 the Zambian Government dismissed all 300 of the country's junior doctors and prohibited them from leaving the country to seek work abroad, following strike action held in protest over the late payment of salaries and shortages of medical equipment. Senior physicians threatened to join the strike if the junior doctors were not reinstated; nevertheless the matter remained unresolved. Also in early January the Minister of the Environment and Natural Resources and MMD National Treasurer, Benjamin Mwila, publicly criticized President Chiluba and denounced his rule as autocratic. Furthermore, he attacked the MMD's economic policies and refused to rule out challenging Chiluba for the MMD's presidential candidacy in 2001. Later in January 2000 Chiluba placed the Minister of Tourism, Anoshi Chipawa, on indefinite forced leave, ostensibly owing to the large number of hunting licences he had granted. However, it was widely suggested that Chiluba's decision was a reaction to Chipawa's support for Mwila.

In March 2000 Kaunda announced his resignation as President of UNIP and his retirement from active politics. At an extraordinary congress, which was convened in Ndola in May, Francis Nkhoma, a former governor of the Bank of Zambia, was elected to replace Kaunda as President of UNIP, while Kaunda's son, Tilyenji, became the party's new Secretary-General.

In May 2000 Mwila announced that he intended to stand in the presidential election scheduled for 2001; Chiluba had previously prohibited members of his Cabinet from publicly discussing their potential candidacy for the presidency upon the expiry of the two terms permitted to him by the Constitution. Mwila was subsequently dismissed from the Government and expelled from the MMD. In July Mwila and a number of other MMD members formed a new political movement, the Republican Party (RP); Mwila reiterated his intention to seek election to the presidency. The RP merged with the ZAP in February 2001, Mwila becoming leader of the new movement, known as the Zambia Republican Party (ZRP).

In early 2001 a number of prominent figures in the MMD publicly advocated Chiluba's election to a third presidential term, despite such an event being prohibited by the Constitution. Chiluba, while declining to reveal his intentions, was reported to have expressed a willingness to listen to the outcome of any public debate on the issue. Opposition parties and some leading MMD members (including Tembo and several ministers) demanded that Chiluba announce that he would not seek re-election. In April, amid increasing controversy, a convention of the MMD approved a motion removing the stipulation that the party's President should serve a maximum of two five-year terms. Vice-President Tembo, Miyanda and seven other ministers expressed their opposition to the convention's decision and were expelled from the party; their supporters subsequently alleged that intimidation by supporters of Chiluba had caused some who opposed the motion not to attend the conference. Several Western donor governments also expressed their opposition to Chiluba's re-election. In April Tilyenji Kaunda was adopted as the President of UNIP.

In May 2001 a motion to impeach Chiluba for misconduct, proposed by two MMD deputies, was signed by more than one-third of the members of the National Assembly. The following day Chiluba ended speculation regarding his potential third term by announcing that he would not seek re-election; he also announced the dissolution of the Cabinet. A new Cabinet was appointed some days later, with the ministers who had opposed Chiluba all being replaced—Tembo was succeeded as Vice-President by Kavindele, the Vice-President of the MMD and hitherto Minister of Health. Mwaanga returned to the Government as Minister of Information and Broadcasting Services. In July Paul Tembo, a former government minister and senior official of the MMD, who had left the party in April to join the newly formed Forum for Democracy and Development (FDD), was shot dead at his home in Lusaka by unknown assailants; he had been expected to give evidence at a tribunal investigating allegations that three cabinet ministers had used state funds to finance the campaign for a third presidential term for Chiluba. (Two of the ministers were found guilty in August, but remained in the Cabinet.) In mid-July the FDD won a by-election in Lusaka, occasioned by the resignation of Christon Tembo after his expulsion from the MMD; violent confrontations between rival supporters from the MMD and FDD were reported. Tembo was elected President of the FDD in October. Meanwhile, Miyanda had established a further opposition party, the Heritage Party (HP).

The MMD adopted former Vice-President Mwanawasa as its presidential candidate in August 2001. Later that month seven opposition parties, including UNIP and the FDD, agreed to form a government of national unity following the forthcoming legislative elections, in order to provide effective opposition in the event of the MMD securing the presidency. Meanwhile, two senior members of the FDD, Edith Nawakwi and Dipak Patel, the editor of *The Post*, Fred M'membe, and one of his reporters, were arrested on charges of defaming Chiluba, after alleging that he had misappropriated state funds allocated for emergency food aid. (Chiluba was scheduled to give evidence at their trial, which was to take place in mid-2002.) In September Michael Sata resigned as Minister without Portfolio and as National Secretary of the MMD, in protest at the nomination of Mwanawasa as presidential candidate. He subsequently formed a new political party, the Patriotic Front (PF). In October Tembo was elected as the FDD's presidential candidate.

The presidential and legislative elections took place on 27 December 2001. On 1 January 2002 (the scheduled date for the announcement of the election results) violent confrontations took place between thousands of anti-Government demonstrators and the security forces in Lusaka and Kitwe, amid allegations that the MMD had engaged in electoral fraud and voter intimidation. Mwanawasa was officially declared President on the following day, with 29.15% of the valid votes cast, narrowly defeating Anderson Mazoka, an economist and leader of the United Party for National Development (UPND, established in 1998), who secured 27.20%, while Tembo won 13.17% and Tilyenji Kaunda 10.12%. The High Court had rejected a petition for the further postponement of the declaration of the results by opposition parties, which were demanding an investigation into their allegations. The MMD secured 69 of the 150 elective seats in the National Assembly (and subsequently all eight of the seats nominated by the President); the UPND became the second largest party in the National Assembly, with 49 seats. Other parties to gain legislative representation were UNIP (with 13 seats), the FDD (12 seats), the HP (four seats), and the PF and the ZRP (one seat each); one independent candidate was also elected. Although the MMD held only 77 of the 158 seats in the National Assembly, Mwanawasa refused to form a coalition with any of the opposition parties to ensure a working majority, and appointed a new Cabinet in early January, retaining many ministers from the previous administration. Kavindele remained Vice-President, and Kalumba was appointed as Minister of Foreign Affairs, while Mwanawasa assumed the defence portfolio himself. A report published in February by an observer mission of the European Union criticized the Electoral Commission of Zambia for misadministration of the recent elections, and later in that month the Supreme Court began hearing a legal challenge to the election results from UNIP, the FDD and the HP, which alleged that the MMD had won the polls fraudulently. Mwaanga was dismissed from the Cabinet in early March, after allegedly undermining Mwanawasa's authority; he was replaced as Minister of Information and Broadcasting Services by Newstead Zimba. Later that month senior members of the FDD expressed their support for the new President, praising his stated commitment to curbing corruption and alleviating poverty.

In July 2002 the Minister of Foreign Affairs and the Chief Justice resigned, apparently in response to pressure from Mwanawasa, exerted in what was regarded as an attempt to rid the administration of corrupt officials. Meanwhile, the Zambian ambassador to the USA and the director of the intelligence service were arrested. Later that month the National Assembly voted to remove Chiluba's immunity from prosecution, pending

a review by the High Court, in order to allow his trial on charges of corruption against him to proceed. Mwanawasa offered Chiluba a full pardon a few days later, on condition that he return the assets he was alleged to have embezzled. The decision to remove his immunity was upheld by the High Court at the end of August, and in early September Mwanawasa ordered Chiluba's house to be searched by the police on suspicion of drugstrafficking. In February 2003 the Supreme Court ruled that Chiluba's immunity could not be restored, and a few days later he was charged with stealing more than US $2m. of public funds while President; he was subsequently released on bail and had his passport seized, and was due to stand trial in mid-2003. Meanwhile, the Minister of Home Affairs, Lackson Mapushi, was killed in a road traffic accident in December 2002; he was replaced by Ronnie Shikapwasha. The Minister of Sports, Youth and Child Development, Levison Mumba, was dismissed in the same month, having testified in court that Mwanawasa had used public funds to finance his presidential campaign. In February 2003 a cabinet reshuffle was effected, in which a number of members of opposition parties assumed ministerial portfolios; observers considered it an attempt to prevent opposition parties from uniting to threaten the MMD's weak position in the National Assembly.

In 1986 South African troops launched attacks on alleged bases of the African National Congress of South Africa (ANC) in Zambia; a number of foreigners and Zambian citizens were subsequently arrested in Zambia on suspicion of spying for South Africa. In August of that year Zambia undertook to impose economic sanctions against South Africa, and the South African Government retaliated by temporarily enforcing trade restrictions on Zambia. Further attacks on ANC targets took place during 1987–89. During the 1980s President Kaunda's support for the Governments of Angola and Mozambique resulted in attacks on Zambian civilians by Angolan rebels (with assistance from the Governments of South Africa and the USA) and by Mozambican rebels (also allegedly supported by South Africa). In September 1992 the Governments of Zambia and Angola signed a security agreement providing for common border controls. In early 1996 Zambia contributed some 1,000 troops to the UN Angola Verification Mission. Zambia consistently denied allegations, made by the Angolan Government in 1997–98, that it was providing military and logistical support to UNITA rebels. In early 1999, however, tension between the two countries intensified, as the accusations resurfaced and a bomb severely damaged the Angolan embassy in Lusaka (see above). Chiluba requested precise details from the Angolan President, José Eduardo dos Santos, regarding Zambia's alleged involvement in the Angolan conflict and invited the international community to send independent missions to investigate the claims. In March 1999 the Angolan Government delivered a letter to the UN explaining its accusations against Zambia. The Zambian Government again refuted all allegations against it. In April, however, relations appeared to have improved, when both countries were reported to have signed an agreement aimed at resolving their differences, under the mediation of Swaziland's King Mswati III. In June the Zambian and Angolan Governments signed a further agreement, which provided for the reactivation of the joint permanent commission on defence and security and the organization of a summit between Chiluba and dos Santos. In December it was reported that Angolan jets had bombed Zambian territory in pursuit of UNITA rebels, and in January 2000 it was announced that some 21,000 Angolan refugees had entered Zambia since October 1999. During January–February 2000 UNITA rebels carried out a series of raids on Zambian villages, which prompted Chiluba to announce that he would not permit UNITA troops to operate from Zambia. In February, following the convention of the joint permanent commission on defence and security to discuss the security situation along the common border, both sides resolved to strengthen measures against UNITA forces operating in the common border area. A further influx of refugees in mid-2000, in addition to further reports of attacks being made on towns in eastern Angola from forces based on Zambian territory, occasioned a further strengthening of border security. In September the Zambian Government declined a request from the Angolan Government for its forces to be allowed to use Zambian territory to attack UNITA positions near the frontier. In February 2001 the Governments of Zambia, Angola and Namibia agreed to establish a tripartite mechanism for political and security co-operation in an attempt to improve security on their joint borders. However, armed Angolans raided three Zambian villages close to the border in November, reportedly abducting some 100 Zambians and subsequently killing seven of them; Zambian forces claimed to have killed 10 Angolans in retaliation. Reports in the Zambian press attributed the attacks on the villages to the Angolan armed forces, which admitted occupying UNITA bases in the area, but claimed to have observed UNITA rebels crossing the border shortly before the attacks. In April 2003 the office of the UN High Commissioner for Refugees oversaw the repatriation of some 40,000 of an estimated total of 200,000 Angolan refugees from Zambia; it was hoped that more would return to Angola later in that year, and that all would be repatriated by 2005.

In early March 1997 the Zambian Government appealed for international assistance in coping with the influx of refugees fleeing the civil conflict in Zaire; by March some 6,000 Zairean refugees had arrived in Zambia. In January 1998 Zambia and the Democratic Republic of the Congo (DRC, formerly Zaire) agreed to establish a joint permanent commission on defence and security. During late 1998 and early 1999 the Zambian Government was involved in regional efforts to find a political solution to the conflict in the DRC, after a rebellion was mounted against the Government in August 1998; President Chiluba was appointed to co-ordinate peace initiatives on the crisis by the Southern African Development Community and the Organization of African Unity (now the African Union). Meanwhile, thousands of Congolese entered Zambia, fleeing the renewed fighting, prompting the Government to appeal to the international community for immediate assistance to cope with the refugees, which, by then, reportedly numbered more than 30,000. In addition, several hundred DRC soldiers crossed into Zambia seeking refuge, but were subsequently repatriated. At a summit held in Lusaka during June–July 1999 a cease-fire document, providing for the withdrawal of foreign forces from the DRC and for political reform in the country, was formulated. The accord was signed by the President of the DRC and the leaders of the five other countries involved in the conflict in July, and by rebel leaders in August. Nevertheless, progress with its implementation was slow. Zambia's involvement in mediation efforts aimed at achieving a definitive end to the conflict in the DRC diminished in the early 2000s, although a number of regional summit meetings were held in Lusaka.

Government

Under the provisions of the Constitution, which was formally adopted in May 1996, Zambia is a multi-party state. Executive power is vested in the President, who is the constitutional Head of State. Legislative power is vested in a National Assembly, which comprises 158 members, of whom 150 are elected by universal adult suffrage, and eight nominated by the President. The President and the National Assembly are elected simultaneously by universal adult suffrage for a five-year term. The maximum duration of the President's tenure of office is limited to two five-year terms. The President governs with the assistance of a Vice-President and a Cabinet, whom he appoints from members of the National Assembly. The Constitution also provides for a 27-member House of Chiefs, which represents traditional tribal authorities. Each of Zambia's nine provinces has a minister, who is appointed by the President.

Defence

The total strength of armed forces at 1 August 2002 was 21,600, with 20,000 in the army and 1,600 in the air force. Paramilitary forces numbered 1,400. Military service is voluntary. There is also a National Defence Force responsible to the Government. The defence budget for 2002 was estimated at K100,000m.

Economic Affairs

In 2001, according to estimates by the World Bank, Zambia's gross national income (GNI), measured at average 1999–2001 prices, was US $3,336m., equivalent to $320 per head (or $790 per head on an international purchasing-power parity basis). During 1990–2001, it was estimated, the population increased at an average annual rate of 2.6%, while gross domestic product (GDP) per head decreased, in real terms, by an average of 1.5% per year. Overall GDP increased, in real terms, at an average annual rate of 1.1% in 1990–2001; growth in 2001 was 5.2%.

Agriculture (including forestry and fishing) contributed 17.0% of GDP in 2001, according to preliminary figures. About 68.6% of the labour force were employed in the sector in 2001. The principal crops are sugar cane, cassava, sweet potatoes, maize, wheat and millet. Rice, cotton, sorghum, tobacco, sunflower seeds, groundnuts and horticultural produce are also cultivated.

Cattle-rearing is important. During 1990–2001, according to the World Bank, agricultural GDP increased by an average of 2.6% per year. Agricultural GDP grew by 1.6% in 2000, but decreased by 2.5% in 2001.

Industry (including mining, manufacturing, construction and power) contributed 27.7% of GDP in 2001, according to preliminary figures, and engaged 22.7% of all wage-earning employees in 1998. According to the World Bank, industrial GDP declined at an average annual rate of 2.2% in 1990–2001. Industrial GDP increased by 9.9% in 2001.

In 2001 mining and quarrying contributed 7.4% of GDP, according to preliminary figures, and engaged 8.5% of wage-earning employees in 1998. Copper is the main mineral export, accounting for some 49.3% of total exports in 1998. Cobalt is also an important export, while coal, gold, emeralds, amethyst, limestone and selenium are also mined. In addition, Zambia has reserves of phosphates, fluorspar and iron ore. In mid-2001 production commenced at a new copper mine near Chibuluma. During 1990–98, according to the IMF, mining GDP declined by an estimated average of 7.7% per year. Mining GDP declined by 24.8% in 1999, but increased by 0.1% in 2000 and, according to preliminary figures, by 14.0% in 2001.

Manufacturing contributed 11.3% of GDP in 2001, according to preliminary figures, and engaged 9.3% of all wage-earning employees in 1998. The principal manufacturing activities are the smelting and refining of copper and other metals, vehicle assembly, petroleum-refining, food-canning and the production of fertilizers, explosives, textiles, bottles, batteries, bricks and copper wire. During 1990–2001, according to the World Bank, manufacturing GDP increased at an average annual rate of 1.6%. Manufacturing GDP increased by 5.9% in 2001.

Energy is derived principally from hydroelectric power, in which Zambia is self-sufficient. Imports of fuel comprised an estimated 13.2% of the value of merchandise imports in 1995. In 1998 agreements were signed that provided for the export of electricity from Zambia to South Africa and Tanzania.

The services sector contributed 55.3% of GDP in 2001, according to preliminary figures, and engaged 64.9% of wage-earning employees in 1998. According to the World Bank, the GDP of the services sector increased by an average of 2.9% per year in 1990–2001. Services GDP increased by 4.9% in 2001.

In 2000 Zambia recorded an estimated trade deficit of US $221m., while there was a deficit of $584m. on the current account of the balance of payments. In 2000 the principal source of imports (55.2%) was the Southern African Customs Union (SACU—Botswana, Lesotho, Namibia, South Africa and Swaziland); other major suppliers were Zimbabwe, the United Kingdom and India. The principal market for exports in 2000 was also SACU (accounting for 45.7% of the total); other significant purchasers were the United Kingdom, Malawi and Switzerland-Liechtenstein. The principal exports in 1998 were copper and cobalt. The principal imports in 1995 were machinery and transport equipment, basic manufactures, chemicals, and mineral fuels and lubricants.

In 2001 there was an estimated overall budgetary deficit of K1,058,000m., equivalent to 8.1% of GDP. Zambia's total external debt was US $5,730m. at the end of 2000, of which US $4,448m. was long-term public debt. In that year the cost of debt-servicing was equivalent to 18.7% of the value of exports of goods and services. In 1990–2000 the average annual rate of inflation was 60.0%. Consumer prices increased by an average of 25.8% in 1999 and by 24.3% in 2000.

Zambia is a member of the Southern African Development Community (see p. 311) and the Common Market for Eastern and Southern Africa (see p. 162).

Zambia's economy is vulnerable to fluctuations in world prices for copper, the country's principal export, and to adverse weather conditions. In December 1995 the IMF approved loans for Zambia under an Enhanced Structural Adjustment Facility. Economic performance was satisfactory in 1996–97, although the value of exports declined substantially (owing to falling prices for copper). By March 1997 more than 60% of state-owned enterprises had been transferred to the private sector. However, concerns about political events in Zambia led to the suspension of aid payments in mid-1996. In mid-1997 aid payments were resumed and later that year the World Bank released further balance-of-payments support. In 1998 Zambia's economic situation was adversely affected by a continued decline in world copper prices, poor weather conditions and delays in the divestiture of Zambia Consolidated Copper Mines (ZCCM)—a precondition for further donor support. The Government implemented an economic programme in the late 1990s, which aimed to achieve GDP growth of 4.5% and to reduce the rate of inflation to below 10% by 2001; in the event, GDP growth for 2001 was 5.2%, although inflation still exceeded 20%. Meanwhile, several countries had announced the partial cancellation of Zambia's debts. It was estimated, however, that the delay in the privatization of ZCCM, which was finally completed in 2000, had stalled the disbursal of some US $130m. in balance-of-payments support. The World Bank granted Zambia development assistance worth some $375m. over three years in February 2000, supporting the Government's priority of increasing investment in the country. The IMF, World Bank and creditor governments pledged a further $3,800m. of debt relief under the Heavily Indebted Poor Countries (HIPC) initiative in December 2000, despite concerns regarding potential irregularities in ZCCM's mineral exports in 1998–99, identified by a panel of auditors. However, the failure to transfer the state-owned Zambia National Commercial Bank to the private sector by early 2002 threatened the implementation of the HIPC programme; the bank's privatization was still pending in early 2003 . The persistent decline in the value of the kwacha has adversely affected the country's economic performance—the currency depreciated by some 20% against the US dollar in October 2000–January 2001, before stabilizing at a slightly higher level throughout February and March; in 2001–02 it depreciated sharply again. Furthermore, in January 2002 the Anglo American mining group, a major shareholder in the Konkola mine (which accounted for approximately two-thirds of Zambian copper production), announced its withdrawal from Zambia, blaming low copper prices; in August Anglo American agreed to pay the Government some $190m. in compensation, and kept the Konkola mine open. Despite steady growth in GDP, President Mwanawasa inherited an economy with serious difficulties on coming to power in 2002: the privatization of numerous state-owned enterprises had been delayed, owing to a shortage of foreign investment, the price of copper continued to fall, and increasing debt repayments threatened the budget for poverty alleviation

programmes, with total external debt estimated to have risen to $7,300m. in March 2002. It was estimated that up to 3m. Zambians were at risk of starvation in 2002, although the Government rejected an offer of genetically modified maize from the USA in October, citing concerns regarding potential health risks.

Education

Between 1964 and 1979 enrolment in schools increased by more than 260%. Primary education, which is compulsory, begins at seven years of age and lasts for seven years. Secondary education, beginning at the age of 14, lasts for a further five years, comprising a first cycle of two years and a second of three years. In 1999/2000 66.4% of children (67.2% of boys; 65.6% of girls) in the relevant age-group attended primary schools, while in 1998/99, according to UNESCO estimates, 20.7% of children (22.5% of boys; 18.9% of girls) in the relevant age-group were enrolled at secondary schools. There are two universities: the University of Zambia at Lusaka, and the Copperbelt University at Kitwe (which is to be transferred to Ndola). There are 14 teacher training colleges. Total budgetary expenditure by the central Government in 1998 on education was projected at K243,500m.

Public Holidays

2003: 1 January (New Year's Day), 11 March (Youth Day), 18–21 April (Easter), 1 May (Labour Day), 25 May (African Freedom Day, anniversary of OAU's foundation), 7 July (Heroes' Day), 8 July (Unity Day), 4 August (Farmers' Day), 24 October (Independence Day), 25 December (Christmas Day).

2004: 1 January (New Year's Day), 11 March (Youth Day), 9–12 April (Easter), 1 May (Labour Day), 25 May (African Freedom Day, anniversary of OAU's foundation), 5 July (Heroes' Day), 6 July (Unity Day), 2 August (Farmers' Day), 24 October (Independence Day), 25 December (Christmas Day).

Weights and Measures

The metric system is in use.

Statistical Survey

Source (unless otherwise indicated): Central Statistical Office, POB 31908, Lusaka; tel. (1) 211231.

Area and Population

AREA, POPULATION AND DENSITY

Area (sq km)	752,614*
Population (census results)	
20 August 1990	7,383,097
25 October 2000	
Males	5,070,891
Females.	5,214,740
Total	10,285,631
Population (official estimates at mid-year)†	
1998	10,096,000
1999	10,407,000
2000	10,723,000
Density (per sq km) at October 2000	13.7

* 290,586 sq miles.

† Figures have not been revised to take account of the 2000 census results.

PRINCIPAL TOWNS
(population at 1990 census)

Lusaka (capital) . .	982,362	Mufulira	152,944
Ndola	370,000*	Luanshya	123,000*
Kitwe	290,000*	Livingstone . . .	82,218
Chingola	167,954	Chililabombwe . .	76,848
Kabwe	159,000*	Kalulushi	75,197

* Estimate.

Source: Thomas Brinkoff, *City Population* (internet www.citypopulation.de).

Mid-2001 (UN projection, including suburbs): Lusaka 1,718,000 (Source: UN, *World Urbanization Prospects: The 2001 Revision*).

BIRTHS AND DEATHS
(UN estimates, annual averages)

	1985–90	1990–95	1995–2000
Birth rate (per 1,000) . . .	44.6	45.0	43.8
Death rate (per 1,000) . . .	14.5	17.8	20.7

Source: UN, *World Population Prospects: The 2000 Revision.*

Expectation of life (WHO estimates, years at birth): 36.8 (males 36.7; females 37.0) in 2001 (Source: WHO, *World Health Report*).

ECONOMICALLY ACTIVE POPULATION
(ILO estimates, '000 persons at mid-1980)

	Males	Females	Total
Agriculture, etc.	959	438	1,398
Industry	174	14	188
Services	257	69	326
Total labour force	**1,390**	**522**	**1,912**

Source: ILO, *Labour Force Estimates and Projections, 1950–2025.*

1980 census (persons aged 12 years and over): Total employed 1,302,944 (males 908,606, females 394,338); Unemployed 492,999 (males 247,013, females 245,986); Total labour force 1,795,943 (males 1,155,619, females 640,324).

Mid-1984 (official estimates): Total labour force 2,032,300 (males 1,464,800; females 567,500).

Mid-2001 (estimates in '000): Agriculture, etc. 3,085; Total 4,498 (Source: FAO).

Health and Welfare

KEY INDICATORS

Total fertility rate (children per woman, 2001)	5.8
Under-5 mortality rate (per 1,000 live births, 2001) . . .	202
HIV/AIDS (% of persons aged 15–49, 2001)	21.52
Physicians (per 1,000 head, 1996)	0.07
Health expenditure (2000): US $ per head (PPP) . . .	49
Health expenditure (2000): % of GDP	5.6
Health expenditure (2000): public (% of total) . . .	62.1
Access to water (% of persons, 2000)	64
Access to sanitation (% of persons, 2000)	78
Human Development Index (2000): ranking	153
Human Development Index (2000): value	0.433

For sources and definitions, see explanatory note on p. vi.

Agriculture

PRINCIPAL CROPS

('000 metric tons)

	1999	2000	2001*
Wheat	90	75	75
Rice (paddy)	15	9	10
Maize	856	882	900
Millet	70	43	55
Sorghum	25	27	27
Sugar cane	1,650	1,600*	1,800
Potatoes	10*	10	11
Sweet potatoes	52*	52	53
Cassava (Manioc)	971	815	950
Pulses	15*	16*	16
Dry onions*	26	27	27
Tomatoes*	24	25	25
Soybeans (Soya beans) . . .	27	30*	30
Sunflower seed	7	7	7
Groundnuts (in shell) . . .	51	55*	55
Cottonseed†	67†	62†	62
Cotton (lint)	24†	22†	22
Tobacco (leaves)	4*	4*	4

* FAO estimate(s).

† Unofficial figure(s).

Source: FAO.

LIVESTOCK

('000 head, year ending September)

	1999	2000	2001*
Cattle	2,273†	2,621	2,400
Sheep	120†	140†	150
Goats	1,069†	1,249†	1,270
Pigs	324†	330	340
Chickens*	28,000	29,000	30,000

* FAO estimates.

† Unofficial figure.

Source: FAO.

LIVESTOCK PRODUCTS

(FAO estimates, '000 metric tons)

	1999	2000	2001
Beef and veal	32	38	38
Pig meat	11	10	10
Poultry meat	34	35	35
Other meat	37	39	39
Cows' milk	62	64	64
Hen eggs	45	46	46
Cattle hides	4	5	5

Source: FAO.

Forestry

ROUNDWOOD REMOVALS

(FAO estimates, '000 cubic metres)

	1997	1998	1999
Sawlogs, veneer logs and logs for sleepers	319	319	319
Other industrial wood	492	504	515
Fuel wood	7,219	7,219	7,219
Total	8,030	8,042	8,053

2000–01: Production as in 1999 (FAO estimates).

Source: FAO.

SAWNWOOD PRODUCTION

(FAO estimates, '000 cubic metres, incl. railway sleepers)

	1995	1996	1997
Coniferous (softwood)	300	230	145
Broadleaved (hardwood)	20	15	12
Total	320	245	157

1998–2001: Annual production as in 1997 (FAO estimates).

Source: FAO.

Fishing

('000 metric tons, live weight)

	1998	1999	2000
Capture	69.9	67.3	66.7
Freshwater fishes	60.1	58.4	57.8
Dagaas	9.8	9.0	8.9
Aquaculture	4.2	4.2*	4.2*
Three-spotted tilapia . . .	2.7	2.7*	2.8*
Total catch	74.1	71.5*	70.9*

* FAO estimate.

Source: FAO, *Yearbook of Fishery Statistics*.

Mining

	1998	1999‡	2000
Coal ('000 metric tons)	50	100	n.a.
Copper ore ('000 metric tons)* . .	315	270	241
Cobalt ore (metric tons)* . . .	11,900	5,640	4,600‡
Silver (kg)*	8,363	5,110	5,000‡§
Gold (kg)*†	765	700	600‡
Amethysts (metric tons)	800	800	n.a.

* Figures refer to the metal content of ore and concentrates. Except for cobalt in 1999 and 2000, data cover production in the 12 months beginning 1 April of the year stated.

† Excluding artisanal production.

‡ Estimated production.

§ Rounded to the nearest metric ton.

Source: US Geological Survey.

Industry

SELECTED PRODUCTS
('000 metric tons, unless otherwise indicated)

	1998	1999	2000
Vegetable oils*	11.5	14.4	14.4
Raw sugar*	184†	197†	189
Cement‡	351	300§	380§
Copper (unwrought): Smelter‡‖	258.6	209.0§	194.5§
Copper (unwrought): Refined‡‖	329.5	233.0§	225.0§
Cobalt (refined, metric tons)‡	4,837‖	4,236	3,342
Electric energy (million kWh)¶	7,603§	n.a.	n.a.

* Source: FAO.
† Unofficial figure.
‡ Source: US Geological Survey.
§ Estimated production.
‖ Data refer to production in 12 months beginning 1 April of year stated.
¶ Net production.
Source: UN, *Industrial Commodity Statistics Yearbook*.

Finance

CURRENCY AND EXCHANGE RATES

Monetary Units
100 ngwee = 1 Zambian kwacha (K)

Sterling, Dollar and Euro Equivalents (31 December 2002)
£1 sterling = 6,986.2 kwacha
US \$1 = 4,334.4 kwacha
€1 = 4,545.5 kwacha
10,000 Zambian kwacha = £1.431 = \$2.307 = €2.200

Average Exchange Rate (Zambian kwacha per US \$)
2000   3,110.84
2001   3,610.93
2002   4,398.59

BUDGET
(K '000 million)

Revenue	1999	2000*	2001*
Tax revenue	1,289	1,931	2,449
Taxes on income, profits and capital gains	483	634	953
Value-added tax	429	575	821
Domestic	248	230	278
Imports	181	345	544
Excises	222	278	366
Customs duty	156	252	285
Clearance of ZESCO† tax arrears	0	191	23
Non-tax revenue	34	22	60
Total‡	1,324	1,953	2,509

Expenditure	1999	2000*	2001*
Current expenditure	1,253	1,701	2,578
Wages and salaries	402	538	888
Public service retrenchment	51	74	19
Recurrent departmental charges	192	300	801
Arrears clearance§	0	0	117
Elections	0	n.a.	110
Transfers and pensions	181	219	353
HIPC-financed	0	0	64
Domestic interest	105	140	207
External interest (paid)	107	167	124
Capital expenditure	789	1,009	1,557
Net transfers to ZCCM¶	152	413	77
Total	2,195	3,122	4,212

* Estimates.
† Zambia Electricity Supply Company.
‡ Excluding grants received (K '000 million): 597 in 1999; 575 in 2000 (estimate); 754 in 2001 (estimate).
§ Classified under recurrent departmental expenditure from 2001.
¶ Zambia Consolidated Copper Mines.

Source: IMF, *Zambia Poverty Reduction Strategy Paper* (March 2002).

INTERNATIONAL RESERVES
(US \$ million at 31 December)

	2000	2001	2002
IMF special drawing rights	22.32	66.92	70.32
Reserve position in IMF	0.02	0.02	0.03
Foreign exchange	222.48	116.50	381.01
Total	244.82	183.45	451.36

Source: IMF, *International Financial Statistics*.

MONEY SUPPLY
(K million at 31 December)

	1999	2000	2001
Currency outside banks	212,163	287,802	373,597
Demand deposits at commercial banks	298,989	471,985	637,143
Total money (incl. others)	513,023	775,851	1,041,400*

* Rounded to the nearest K10 million.

Source: IMF, *International Financial Statistics*.

COST OF LIVING
(Consumer Price Index; low-income group; base: 1990 = 100)

	1998	1999	2000
Food (incl. tobacco)	7,802.6	9,573.7	11,665.8
Clothing and footwear	4,010.0	5,232.5	6,596.3
Rent	11,256.7	14,770.0	19,460.0
All items (incl. others)	7,045.2	8,864.3	11,016.7

Source: ILO.

NATIONAL ACCOUNTS

Expenditure on the Gross Domestic Product
(K million at current prices)

	1996	1997	1998*
Government final consumption expenditure	714,000	857,000	982,000
Private final consumption expenditure	2,894,000	3,895,000	4,923,000
Increase in stocks	16,000	20,000	23,000
Gross fixed capital formation	566,000	681,000	876,000
Total domestic expenditure	4,190,000	5,453,000	6,805,000
Exports of goods and services	1,344,000	1,715,000	1,831,000
Less imports of goods and services	1,590,000	2,000,000	2,395,000
GDP in purchasers' values	3,945,000	5,169,000	6,241,000
GDP at constant 1990 prices	2,334,000	2,412,000	2,364,000

* IMF estimates.

Source: IMF, *Zambia: Statistical Appendix* (May 1999).

Gross Domestic Product by Economic Activity
(K '000 million at constant 1994 prices)

	1999	2000	2001*
Agriculture, forestry and fishing	423.2	429.8	418.9
Mining and quarrying	160.2	160.4	182.9
Manufacturing	254.2	263.2	278.6
Electricity, gas and water	72.1	72.9	82.1
Construction	116.0	123.6	137.8
Wholesale and retail trade, restaurants and hotels	489.0	504.8	544.1
Transport and communications	154.1	157.6	162.1
Finance, insurance, real estate and business services	210.4	443.6	452.2
Community, social and personal services	193.8	192.8	204.0
Sub-total	2,273.2	2,348.7	2,462.7
Import duties	258.9	272.4	291.4
Less imputed bank service charge	−118.8	−121.8	−124.9
GDP in purchasers' values†	2,413.3	2,499.3	2,629.2

* Preliminary.
† Based on unrounded data.

Source: IMF, *Zambia Poverty Reduction Strategy Paper* (March 2002).

BALANCE OF PAYMENTS
(US $ million)

	1998	1999	2000
Exports of goods f.o.b. . . .	818	772	757
Imports of goods c.i.f. . . .	−971	−870	−978
Trade balance	**−153**	**−98**	**−221**
Export of services (net) . . .	−180	−199	−226
Balance on goods and services	**−332**	**−297**	**−447**
Other income (net)	−214	−134	−120
Balance on goods, services and			
income	**−546**	**−431**	**−566**
Transfers (net)	−27	−16	−18
Current account	**−573**	**−447**	**−584**
Official capital (net)	203	196	153
Private capital (net)	−264	−174	−274
Errors and omissions . . .	−37	−229	185
Overall balance	**−671**	**−654**	**−520**

Source: IMF.

External Trade

PRINCIPAL COMMODITIES
(US $ million)

Imports f.o.b.	1985	1986	1995
Food and live animals . .	25.3	n.a.	61.3
Cereals and cereal preparations .	14.3	10.1	45.9
Crude materials (inedible)			
except fuels	10.9	n.a.	29.9
Mineral fuels, lubricants, etc. .	156.1	n.a.	93.4
Petroleum and petroleum products	153.7	80.1	88.7
Crude petroleum	n.a.	71.7	79.9
Chemicals and related			
products	106.0	n.a.	94.1
Fertilizers (manufactured) . . .	29.2	3.0	16.9
Plastic materials, etc. . . .	15.6	9.8	17.7
Basic manufactures . . .	116.0	n.a.	104.8
Rubber manufactures . . .	17.6	16.0	14.0
Textile yarn, fabrics, etc. . .	19.6	14.5	7.5
Iron and steel	25.4	20.6	30.6
Machinery and transport			
equipment	232.1	n.a.	268.5
Power-generating machinery and			
equipment	17.6	18.2	8.9
Machinery specialized for			
particular industries . . .	60.0	46.8	44.9
General industrial machinery,			
equipment and parts . . .	57.8	56.5	62.3
Telecommunications and sound			
equipment	6.5	20.8	16.6
Other electrical machinery,			
apparatus, etc.	21.5	24.1	22.7
Road vehicles and parts . . .	52.3	74.2	68.3
Miscellaneous manufactured			
articles	23.8	n.a.	47.4
Total (incl. others) . . .	713.8	602.8	708.2

Exports f.o.b.	1996	1997	1998*
Copper	567.7	649.4	430.9
Cobalt	186.5	245.6	154.3
Total (incl. others)	993.4	1,190.8	873.6

* IMF estimates.

Total imports (K million, f.o.b.): 6,627.5 in 1987; 6,898.1 in 1988; 10,901.8 in 1989; 37,627.6 in 1990; 59,988.0 in 1991; 172,871.7 in 1992; 553,400.0 in 1993; 805,299.9 in 1994 (Source: UN, *International Trade Statistics Yearbook*).

Source: IMF, *Zambia: Statistical Appendix* (May 1999).

PRINCIPAL TRADING PARTNERS
(US $'000)*

Imports f.o.b.‡	1990	1995	2000
Algeria	20,451	n.a.	n.a.
Belgium-Luxembourg . .	13,694	4,000	14,200
Denmark	11,220	7,400	30,700
Finland	23,184	8,600	n.a.
France	12,471	12,100	27,200
Germany	144,015	18,500	36,300
India	22,930	19,100	229,800
Iran	35,134	11,100	n.a.
Italy	30,289	6,800	21,800
Japan	82,627	45,200	110,200
Kuwait	33,697	14,300	n.a.
Madagascar	66,700	n.a.	n.a.
Mozambique	n.a.	n.a.	58,600
Netherlands	15,472	12,500	18,500
SACU†	224,177	253,900	2,263,700
Sweden	19,213	7,900	8,500
Tanzania	2,247	9,700	192,700
United Kingdom . . .	200,365	71,100	282,600
USA	125,522	19,500	171,100
Zimbabwe	57,866	56,600	295,700
Total (incl. others) . . .	1,237,717	708,200	4,097,600

Exports f.o.b.§	1993	1995	2000
Belgium-Luxembourg . .	99,429	64,800	48,500
Congo, Democratic Repub. . .	11,677	26,700	142,300
France	94,938	23,000	7,700
Germany	2,000	8,100	61,200
Greece	29,367	900	n.a.
Hong Kong	8,600	10,200	46,900
India	52,383	86,800	34,100
Indonesia	28,593	23,200	1,300
Italy	7,638	10,500	83,500
Japan	122,023	163,500	n.a.
Malawi	—	—	240,500
Malaysia	74,058	68,800	n.a.
Netherlands	24,359	8,600	19,900
Pakistan	83,319	45,400	n.a.
SACU†	17,795	23,600	1,376,300
Saudi Arabia	64,017	114,300	n.a.
Singapore	51,504	60,200	n.a.
Switzerland-Liechtenstein . .	2,400	3,600	219,100
Tanzania	1,147	22,000	77,600
Thailand	61,538	128,900	1,300
United Kingdom . . .	14,072	16,800	440,700
USA	3,317	64,500	34,000
Zimbabwe	27,359	31,900	56,800
Total (incl. others) . . .	920,536	1,055,000	3,012,300

* Imports by country of production; exports by country of last consignment.
† Southern African Customs Union, comprising Botswana, Lesotho, Namibia, South Africa and Swaziland.
‡ Figures for 1991–94 and 1996–99 are unavailable.
§ Figures for 1991, 1992, 1994 and 1996–99 are unavailable.

Source: UN, *International Trade Statistics Yearbook*.

Total imports (US $ million): 836 in 1996; 819 in 1997 (Source: UN, *Monthly Bulletin of Statistics*).

Total exports (US $ million): 1,049 in 1996; 914 in 1997 (Source: UN, *Monthly Bulletin of Statistics*).

Transport

ROAD TRAFFIC
(estimates, '000 motor vehicles in use at 31 December)

	1994	1995	1996
Passenger cars	123	142	157
Lorries and vans	68	74	81

Source: International Road Federation, *World Road Statistics*.

CIVIL AVIATION
(scheduled services: Passengers carried—thousands; others—millions)

	1997	1998	1999
Kilometres flown	1	1	1
Passengers carried	50	49	42
Passenger-km	45	44	34
Total ton-km	5	4	3

Source: UN, *Statistical Yearbook*.

Tourism

	1998	1999	2000
Australia	9,234	8,627	15,791
South Africa	71,434	74,157	70,899
Tanzania	16,996	19,188	27,308
United Kingdom	33,755	34,123	51,459
USA	10,688	9,786	17,512
Zimbabwe	113,218	119,108	116,461
Total (incl. others)	362,025	404,247	457,419

Source: World Tourism Organization, *Yearbook of Tourism Statistics*.

Tourism receipts (US $ million): 74.4 in 1998; 85.2 in 1999; 91.2 in 2000 (Source: IMF, *Zambia Poverty Reduction Strategy Paper* (March 2002)).

Communications Media

	1999	2000	2001
Television receivers ('000 in use)	1,300	1,400	n.a.
Telephones ('000 main lines in use)	83.1	83.3	85.4
Mobile cellular telephones ('000 subcribers)	28.2	98.9	98.3
Internet users ('000)	15	20	25

Radio receivers ('000 in use): 1,436 in 1999.

Facsimile machines (number in use): 1,005 (estimate) in year ending 31 March 1999.

Daily newspapers (1996): 3; average circulation: 114,000 copies.

Sources: UNESCO, *Statistical Yearbook*; UN, *Statistical Yearbook*; International Telecommunication Union.

Education

(1998)

	Institutions	Teachers	Pupils/Students		
			Males	Females	Total
Pre-primary . .	443	700	13,737*	16,263*	30,000*
Primary . .	4,221	34,810	810,873	746,384	1,557,257
Secondary . .	n.a.	10,000	164,992	125,093	290,085
Tertiary . .	n.a.	n.a.	14,520	7,181	22,701

* Estimate.

Source: UNESCO Institute for Statistics.

Adult literacy rate (UNESCO estimates): 78.1% (males 85.2%; females 71.5%) in 2000 (Source: UN Development Programme, *Human Development Report*).

Directory

The Constitution

The Constitution for the Republic of Zambia, which was formally adopted on 28 May 1996 (amending the Constitution of 1991), provides for a multi-party form of government. The Head of State is the President of the Republic, who is elected by popular vote at the same time as elections to the National Assembly. The President's tenure of office is limited to two five-year terms. Foreign nationals and those with foreign parentage are prohibited from contesting the presidency. The legislature comprises a National Assembly of 158 members: 150 are elected by universal adult suffrage, while the remaining eight are nominated by the President. The President appoints a Vice-President and a Cabinet from members of the National Assembly.

The Constitution also provides for a House of Chiefs numbering 27: four from each of the Northern, Western, Southern and Eastern Provinces, three each from the North-Western, Luapula and Central Provinces and two from the Copperbelt Province. It may submit resolutions to be debated by the Assembly and consider those matters referred to it by the President.

The Supreme Court of Zambia is the final Court of Appeal. The Chief Justice and other judges are appointed by the President. Subsidiary to the Supreme Court is the High Court, which has unlimited jurisdiction to hear and determine any civil or criminal proceedings under any Zambian law.

The Government

HEAD OF STATE

President: LEVY PATRICK MWANAWASA (took office 2 January 2002).

THE CABINET
(April 2003)

President: LEVY PATRICK MWANAWASA.

Vice-President: ENOCH PERCY KAVINDELE.

Minister of Home Affairs: RONNIE SHIKAPWASHA.

Minister of Foreign Affairs: KALOMBO MWANSA.

Minister of Defence: MICHAEL MABENGA.

Minister of Finance and Economic Development: EMMANUEL KASONDE.

Minister of Commerce, Trade and Industry: DIPAK PATEL.

Minister for Legal Affairs: GEORGE KUNDA.

Minister of Agriculture, Food and Fisheries: MUNDIA SIKATANA.

Minister of Communications and Transport: BATES NAMUYAMBA.

Minister of Energy and Water Development: GEORGE MPOMBO.

Minister of Community Development and Social Welfare: MARINA NSINGO.

Minister of Tourism, the Environment and Natural Resources: PATRICK KALIFUNGWA.

Minister of Education: ANDREW MULENGA.

Minister of Science, Technology and Vocational Training: ABEL CHAMBESHI.

Minister of Health: Brig.-Gen. BRIAN CHITUWO.

Minister of Local Government and Housing: SYLVIA MASEBO.

Minister of Works and Supply: Dr LUDWIG SONDASHI.

Minister of Sports, Youth and Child Development: GLADYS NYIRONGO.

Minister of Lands: JUDITH KAPINGIPANGA.

Minister of Labour and Social Security: MUTALE NALUMANGO.

Minister of Mines and Mineral Development: KAUNDA LEMBA-LEMBA.

Minister of Information and Broadcasting Services: NEWSTEAD ZIMBA.

MINISTRIES

Office of the President: POB 30208, Lusaka; tel. (1) 218282; internet www.statehouse.gov.zm.

Ministry of Agriculture, Food and Fisheries: Mulungushi House, Independence Ave, Nationalist Rd, POB RW50291, Lusaka; tel. (1) 213551; internet www.agriculture.gov.zm.

Ministry of Commerce, Trade and Industry: Kwacha Annex, Cairo Rd, POB 31968, Lusaka; tel. (1) 213767; internet www.commerce.gov.zm.

Ministry of Communications and Transport: Fairley Rd, POB 50065, Lusaka; tel. (1) 251444; fax (1) 253260; internet www.communication.gov.zm.

Ministry of Community Development and Social Welfare: Fidelity House, POB 31958, Lusaka; tel. (1) 228321; fax (1) 225327; internet www.welfare.gov.zm.

Ministry of Defence: POB 31931, Lusaka; tel. (1) 252366; internet www.defence.gov.zm.

Ministry of Education: 15102 Ridgeway, POB RW50093, Lusaka; tel. (1) 227636; fax (1) 222396; internet www.education.gov.zm.

Ministry of Energy and Water Development: Mulungushi House, Independence Ave, Nationalist Rd, POB 36079, Lusaka; tel. (1) 252589; fax (1) 252589; internet www.energy.gov.zm.

Ministry of Finance and Economic Development: Finance Bldg, POB 50062, Lusaka; tel. (1) 253512; fax (1) 251078; internet www.finance.gov.zm.

Ministry of Foreign Affairs: POB RW50069, Lusaka; tel. (1) 213822; fax (1) 222440; e-mail mfalus@zamnet.zm; internet www.foreignaffairs.gov.zm.

Ministry of Health: Woodgate House, 1st–2nd Floors, Cairo Rd, POB 30205, Lusaka; tel. (1) 227745; fax (1) 228385; internet www.health.gov.zm.

Ministry of Home Affairs: POB 32862, Lusaka; tel. (1) 213505; internet www.homeaffairs.gov.zm.

Ministry of Information and Broadcasting Services: Independence Ave, POB 32245, Lusaka; tel. (1) 228202; fax (1) 253457; internet www.information.gov.zm.

Ministry of Labour and Social Security: Lechwe House, Freedom Way, POB 32186, Lusaka; tel. (1) 212020; internet www.labour.gov.zm.

Ministry of Lands: POB 50694, Lusaka; tel. (1) 252288; fax (1) 250120; internet www.lands.gov.zm.

Ministry of Legal Affairs: Fairley Rd, POB 50106, 15101 Ridgeway, Lusaka; tel. (1) 228522; internet www.legalaffairs.gov.zm.

Ministry of Local Government and Housing: Church Rd, POB 34204, Lusaka; tel. (1) 253077; fax (1) 252680; internet www.localgovernment.gov.zm.

Ministry of Mines and Mineral Development: Chilufya Mulenga Rd, POB 31969, 10101 Lusaka; tel. (1) 251402; fax (1) 252095; internet www.mines.gov.zm.

Ministry of Science, Technology and Vocational Training: POB 50464, Lusaka; tel. (1) 229673; fax (1) 252951; internet www.technology.gov.zm.

Ministry of Sport, Youth and Child Development: Memaco House, POB 50195, Lusaka; tel. (1) 227158; fax (1) 223996; internet www.sports.gov.zm.

Ministry of Tourism, the Environment and Natural Resources: Electra House, Cairo Rd, POB 30575, Lusaka; tel. (1) 227645; fax (1) 222189; internet www.tourism.gov.zm.

Ministry of Works and Supply: POB 50003, Lusaka; tel. (1) 253088; fax (1) 253404; internet www.supply.gov.zm.

President and Legislature

PRESIDENT

Presidential Election, 27 December 2001

Candidate	Votes	% of votes
Levy Patrick Mwanawasa (MMD)	506,694	29.15
Anderson Mazoka (UPND)	472,697	27.20
Christon Tembo (FDD)	228,861	13.17
Tilyenji Kaunda (UNIP)	175,898	10.12
Godfrey Miyanda (HP)	140,678	8.09
Benjamin Mwila (ZRP)	85,472	4.92
Michael Sata (PF)	59,172	3.40
Nevers Mumba (NCC)	38,860	2.24
Gwendoline Konie (SDP)	10,253	0.59
Inonge Mbikusita-Lewanika (AZ)	9,882	0.57
Yobert Shamapande (NLD)	9,481	0.55
Total	**1,737,948**	**100.00**

NATIONAL ASSEMBLY

Speaker: AMUSAA KATUNDA MWANAMWAMBWA.

General Election, 27 December 2001

Party	Votes	% of votes	Seats
Movement for Multi-party Democracy (MMD)	490,680	27.48	69
United Party for National Development (UPND)	416,236	23.31	49
Forum for Democracy and Development (FDD)	272,817	15.28	12
United National Independence Party (UNIP)	185,535	10.39	13
Heritage Party (HP)	132,311	7.41	4
Zambia Republican Party (ZRP)	97,010	5.43	1
Independents	59,335	3.32	1
Patriotic Front (PF)	49,362	2.76	1
Others	48,066	2.71	—
Invalid votes	34,133	1.91	—
Total	**1,785,485**	**100.00**	**150**

House of Chiefs

The House of Chiefs is an advisory body which may submit resolutions for debate by the National Assembly. There are 27 Chiefs, four each from the Northern, Western, Southern and Eastern Provinces, three each from the North Western, Luapula and Central Provinces, and two from the Copperbelt Province.

Political Organizations

Agenda for Zambia (AZ): POB 50303, Lusaka; f. 1996 by fmr mems of the NP; Pres. Dr AKASHAMBATWA MBIKUSITA-LEWANIKA.

Democratic Party (DP): Plot C4, President Ave (North), POB 71628, Ndola; f. 1991; Pres. EMMANUEL MWAMBA.

Forum for Democracy and Development (FDD): POB 35868, Lusaka; f. 2001 by expelled mems of the MMD; Pres. CHRISTON TEMBO.

Heritage Party (HP): POB 51055, Lusaka; f. 2001 by expelled mems of the MMD; Pres. Brig.-Gen. GODFREY MIYANDA.

Liberal Progressive Front (LPF): POB 31190, Lusaka; f. 1993; Leader ROGER CHONGWE.

Movement for Democratic Process (MDP): POB 90902, Luanshya; f. 1991.

Movement for Multi-party Democracy (MMD): POB 30708, Lusaka; f. 1990; governing party since Nov. 1991; Pres. LEVY MWANAWASA (acting).

Multi-Racial Party (MRP): POB 30971, Lusaka; tel. (1) 243622; f. 1999; Leader W. LESA.

National Citizens' Coalition (NCC): POB 38796, Lusaka; e-mail sekwila@hotmail.com; internet www.zambiashallbesaved.org; f. 1997; Leader NEVERS MUMBA.

National Democratic Alliance (NADA): Lusaka; f. 1991; deregistered Oct. 1998; Pres. YONAM PHIRI.

National Leadership for Development (NLD): POB 34161, Lusaka; f. 2000; Pres. Dr YOBERT K. SHAMAPANDE.

National Party (NP): POB 37840, Lusaka 10101; tel. (1) 232445; e-mail nationalparty@yahoo.com; f. 1993 by fmr mems of MMD; Pres. Dr SAM CHIPUNGU; Sec.-Gen. Rev. RICHARD KAMBULU.

National People's Salvation Party (NPSP): Lusaka; Pres. LUMBWE LAMBANYA.

New Democratic Party (NDP): Lusaka; f. 1995; Pres. DAVID LIMAKA.

Opposition Party for Progress (OPP): POB 34338, Lusaka; f. 2000; Pres. ESAU TEMBO.

Patriotic Front: f. 2001 by expelled mems of the MMD; Leader MICHAEL SATA.

People Of This Way (POTWAY): POB 80762, Kabwe; f. 1996 as National Salvation Party; Pres. U. B. MUMBA.

Progressive People's Party (PPP): POB Wusakile, Kitwe; f. 1998; Pres. KALUMBA KAPUTO.

Social Democratic Party (SDP): POB 31646, Lusaka; tel. and fax (1) 756485; e-mail gkonie@for-president.com; f. 2000; Pres. GWENDO-LINE CHOMBA KONIE.

United Democratic Congress Party: Lusaka; f. 1992; Leader DANIEL LISULO.

United National Independence Party (UNIP): POB 30302, Lusaka; tel. (1) 221197; fax (1) 221327; f. 1959; sole legal party 1972–90; Pres. TILYENJI KAUNDA.

United Party for National Development (UPND): POB 33199, Lusaka; internet www.upnd.org; f. 1998; Leader ANDERSON MAZOKA.

Unity Party for Democrats (UPD): PB RW 28, Ridgeway, Lusaka; f. 1997; Pres. MATHEW PIKITI.

Zambia Democratic Congress—Popular Front: Lusaka; f. 1998; Chair. EDEN JERRY (acting).

Zambia Democratic Party (ZDP): POB 35856, Lusaka; f. 1998; Pres. SUSAN JERE.

Zambia Progressive Party (ZPP): POB 34927, Lusaka; fax (1) 248818; e-mail zapu@zamnet.zm; f. 1991; Pres. AMBRAM ZAPU.

Zambia Republican Party (ZRP): Lusaka; f. 2001 by merger of Republican Party (f. 2000) and Zambia Alliance for Progress (f. 1999); Leader BENJAMIN MWILA.

Zambia United Development Party: Lusaka; f. 2001; Leader WILSON MUKUPA.

Diplomatic Representation

EMBASSIES AND HIGH COMMISSIONS IN ZAMBIA

Angola: Plot 108, Great East Rd, Northmead, POB 31595, 10101 Lusaka; tel. (1) 34764; fax (1) 221210; Ambassador LOUIS DOUKUI PAULO DE CASTRO.

Botswana: 5201 Pandit Nehru Rd, Diplomatic Triangle, POB 31910, 10101 Lusaka; tel. (1) 250555; fax (1) 250804; High Commissioner LAPOLOGANG CEASAR LEKOA.

Brazil: 74 Anglo-American Bldg, Independence Ave, POB 33300; tel. (1) 250400; fax (1) 251652; Chargé d'affaires a.i. PAULO M. G. DE SOUSA.

Bulgaria: 4045 Lukulu Rd, Lusaka; tel. and fax (1) 263295; Chargé d'affaires a.i. YULI MINCHEV.

Canada: Plot 5199, United Nations Ave, POB 31313, 10101 Lusaka; tel. (1) 250833; fax (1) 254176; e-mail lsaka@dfait-maeci.gc.ca; High Commissioner DAVID M. STOCKWELL.

China, People's Republic: Plot 7430, United Nations Avenue, Longacres, POB 31975, 10101 Lusaka; tel. (1) 253770; fax (1) 251157; e-mail chinaemb@zamnet.zm; Ambassador PENG KEYU.

Congo, Democratic Republic: Plot 1124, Parirenyatwa Rd, POB 31287, 10101 Lusaka; tel. and fax (1) 235679; e-mail congodr@zamnet.zm; Chargé d'affaires a.i. NGOYI NGONGO LUNKAMBA.

Cuba: 5574 Mogoye Rd, Kalundu, POB 33132, 10101 Lusaka; tel. (1) 291308; fax (1) 291586; e-mail sikulem@zamnet.zm; Ambassador NARCISO MARTIN MORA DIAZ.

Denmark: 18 Dunduza Chisidza Crescent, Prospect Hill, POB 50299, Lusaka; tel. (1) 254277; fax (1) 254618; e-mail lunamb@um.dk; Ambassador MADS SANDAU-JENSEN.

Egypt: Plot 5206, United Nations Ave, POB 32428, Lusaka; tel. (1) 253762; Ambassador KHALED M. ALY OSMAN.

Finland: Haile Selassie Ave, opposite Ndeke House, Longacres, POB 50819, 15101 Lusaka; tel. (1) 251988; fax (1) 253783; e-mail finemb@zamnet.zm; internet www.zamnet.zm/zamnet/diplomatic/finland/finhome.htm; Chargé d'affaires a.i. TIMO KARMAKALLIO.

France: Anglo-American Bldg, 4th Floor, 74 Independence Ave, POB 30062, 10101 Lusaka; tel. (1) 251322; fax (1) 254475; e-mail france@zamnet.zm; Ambassador JEAN-PAUL MONCHAU.

Germany: Plot 5209, United Nations Ave, POB 50120, 15101 Ridgeway, Lusaka; tel. (1) 250644; fax (1) 254014; e-mail geremblusaka@zamtel.zm; internet germanembassy-lusaka.org; Ambassador Dr ERICH KRISTOF.

Holy See: 283 Los Angeles Blvd, POB 31445, 10101 Lusaka; tel. (1) 251033; fax (1) 250601; e-mail nuntius@coppernet.zm; Apostolic Nuncio Most Rev. ORLANDO ANTONINI (Titular Archbishop of Formia).

India: 1 Pandit Nehru Rd, POB 32111, 10101 Lusaka; tel. (1) 253159; fax (1) 254118; e-mail hc@india.zm; internet www.india.zm; High Commissioner YOGESH K. GUPTA.

Ireland: 6663 Katima Mulilo Rd, Olympia Park, POB 34923, 10101 Lusaka; tel. (1) 290650; fax (1) 290482; Chargé d'affaires a.i. PATRICK CURRAN.

Italy: Plot 5211, Embassy Park, Diplomatic Triangle, POB 31046, 10101 Lusaka; tel. (1) 250781; fax (1) 254929; e-mail italyzam@zamnet.zm; internet go.to/ambasciatalusaka; Ambassador Dr UMBERTO PLAJA.

Japan: Plot 5218, Haile Selassie Ave, POB 34190, 10101 Lusaka; tel. (1) 251555; fax (1) 254425; e-mail jez@zamnet.zm; internet www.zm.emb-japan.go.jp; Ambassador MITSUHIRO SAOTOME.

Kenya: 5207 United Nations Ave, POB 50298, 10101 Lusaka; tel. (1) 250722; fax (1) 253829; e-mail kenhigh@zamnet.zm; High Commissioner ESTHER MSHAI TOLLE.

Libya: 251 Ngwee Rd, off United Nations Ave, Longacres, POB 35319, 10101 Lusaka; tel. (1) 253055; fax (1) 251239; Ambassador KHALLIFA OMAR S. ALSSAWI.

Malawi: 31 Bishops Rd, Kabulonga, POB 50425, Lusaka; tel. (1) 213750; fax (1) 265765; e-mail mhc@zamnet.zm; High Commissioner Rev. E. CHINKWITA PHIRI.

Mozambique: Kacha Rd, Plot 9592, POB 34877, 10101 Lusaka; tel. (1) 220333; fax (1) 220345; e-mail mozhclsk@zamnet.zm; High Commissioner Dr CRISTOFA INOQUE JAMO.

Namibia: 30B Mutende Rd, Woodlands, POB 30577, 10101 Lusaka; tel. (1) 260407; fax (1) 263858; e-mail namibia@zamtel.zm; High Commissioner FRIEDA NANGULA ITHETE.

Netherlands: 5028 United Nations Ave, POB 31905, 10101 Lusaka; tel. (1) 253819; fax (1) 253733; Ambassador Dr P. SCHÖNHERR.

Nigeria: 5208 Haile Selassie Ave, Longacres, POB 32598, 10101 Lusaka; tel. (1) 253177; fax (1) 253560; High Commissioner: Chief IBIRONKE O. VAUGHAN-ADEFOPE.

Norway: cnr Birdcage Walk and Haile Selassie Ave, Longacres, POB 34570, 10101 Lusaka; tel. (1) 252188; fax (1) 253915; Ambassador JON K. A. LOMOEY.

Portugal: 23 Yotam Muleya Rd, POB 33871, 10101 Lusaka; tel. (1) 253720; fax (1) 253896; e-mail embport@zamnet.zm; Ambassador LAURA C. G. DE SOUSA.

Romania: 2 Leopard's Hill Rd, POB 31944, 10101 Lusaka; tel. (1) 262182; Chargé d'affaires a.i. CORNELIU BALAN.

Russia: Plot 6407, Diplomatic Triangle, POB 32355, 10101 Lusaka; tel. (1) 252120; fax (1) 253582; e-mail embrus@zamnet.zm; Ambassador VLADIMIR L. BOIKO.

Saudi Arabia: 4896 Los Angeles Blvd, Longacres, POB 34411, 10101 Lusaka; tel. (1) 253266; fax (1) 253449; e-mail saudiemb@zamnet.zm; Ambassador TALAT SALEM RADWAN.

Serbia and Montenegro: Plot 5216, Diplomatic Triangle, POB 31180, 10101 Lusaka; tel. (1) 250247; fax (1) 253843; e-mail yuemblus@zamnet.zm; Chargé d'affaires a.i. DUŠAN ZUPAN.

Somalia: G3/377A Kabulonga Rd, POB 34051, Lusaka; tel. (1) 262119; Ambassador Dr OMAN UMAL.

South Africa: D26, Cheetah Rd, Kabulonga, Private Bag W369, Lusaka; tel. (1) 260999; fax (1) 263001; e-mail sahc@zamnet.zm; High Commissioner REDDY JAN MABUSE MAMPANE.

Spain: Lusaka; Ambassador JESÚS CARLOS RIOSALIDO.

Sudan: 31 Ng'umbo Rd, Longacres, POB RW179X, 15200 Lusaka; tel. (1) 215570; fax (1) 40653; Ambassador ABDALLAH KHIDIR BASHIR.

Sweden: Haile Selassie Ave, POB 30788, 10101 Lusaka; tel. (1) 251711; fax (1) 254049; e-mail swedemb@zamnet.zm; internet www.swedemb.org.zm; Ambassador CHRISTINA REHLEN.

Tanzania: Ujamaa House, Plot 5200, United Nations Ave, POB 31219, 10101 Lusaka; tel. (1) 253222; fax (1) 254861; e-mail tzreplsk@zamnet.zm; High Commissioner SHANI OMARI LWENO.

United Kingdom: Plot 5201, Independence Ave, POB 50050, 15101 Ridgeway, Lusaka; tel. (1) 251133; fax (1) 253798; e-mail brithc@ zamnet.zm; High Commissioner THOMAS YOUNG.

USA: cnr Independence and United Nations Aves, POB 31617, Lusaka; tel. (1) 250955; fax (1) 252225; e-mail embpas@zamnet.zm; internet www.usemb.org.zm; Ambassador MARTIN BRENNAN.

Zimbabwe: 11058, Haile Selassie Ave, Longacres, POB 33491, 10101 Lusaka; tel. (1) 254012; fax (1) 227474; High Commissioner TIRIVAFI JOHN KANGAI.

Judicial System

The judicial system of Zambia comprises a Supreme Court, composed of a Chief Justice, a Deputy Chief Justice and five Justices; a High Court comprising the Chief Justice and 30 Judges; Senior Resident and Resident Magistrates' Courts, which sit at various centres; and Local Courts, which deal principally with customary law, but which also have limited criminal jurisdiction.

Supreme Court of Zambia

Independence Ave, POB 50067, Ridgeway, Lusaka; tel. (1) 251330; fax (1) 251743.

Chief Justice: ERNEST L. SAKALA.

Deputy Chief Justice: B. K. BWEUPE.

Supreme Court Judges: M. S. CHAILA, E. K. CHIRWA, W. M. MUZYAMBA, D. M. LEWANIKA.

Religion

CHRISTIANITY

Christian Council of Zambia: Church House, Cairo Rd, POB 30315, Lusaka; tel. (1) 224308; e-mail ccz@zamnet.zm; f. 1945; 19 mem. churches and 18 other Christian orgs; Chair. Rev. THUMA HAMUKANG'ANDU (Brethren in Christ Church); Gen. Sec. VIOLET SAMPA-BREDT.

The Anglican Communion

Anglicans are adherents of the Church of the Province of Central Africa, covering Botswana, Malawi, Zambia and Zimbabwe. The Church comprises 12 dioceses, including four in Zambia. The Archbishop of the Province is the Bishop of Botswana. There are an estimated 40,000 adherents in Zambia.

Bishop of Central Zambia: Rt Rev. G. D. KAMUKWAMBA, POB 70172, Ndola; tel. (2) 612431; e-mail adcznla@zamnet.zm.

Bishop of Eastern Zambia: Rt Rev. JOHN OSMERS, POB 510154, Chipata; tel. and fax (6) 221294; e-mail josmers@zamnet.zm.

Bishop of Lusaka: Rt Rev. LEONARD JAMESON MWENDA, Bishop's Lodge, POB 30183, Lusaka; fax (1) 262379.

Bishop of Northern Zambia: Rt Rev. BERNARD AMOS MALANGO, POB 22317, Kitwe; tel. (2) 223264; fax (2) 224778; e-mail malango@ zamnet.zm.

Protestant Churches

African Methodist Episcopal Church: POB 31478, Lusaka; tel. (1) 264013; 440 congregations, 880,000 mems; Presiding Elder Rev. L. SICHANGWA.

Baptist Church: Lubu Rd, POB 30636, Lusaka; tel. (1) 253620.

Baptist Mission of Zambia: 3061/62 cnr Makishi and Great East Rds, POB 50599, 15101 Ridgeway, Lusaka; tel. (1) 222492; fax (1) 227520; e-mail bmzambia@zamnet.zm.

Brethren in Christ Church: POB 630115, Choma; tel. (3) 20278; fax (3) 20127; e-mail bicczam@zamnet.zm; f. 1906; Bishop Rev. E. SHAMAPANI; 142 congregations, 13,356 communicant mems.

Reformed Church in Zambia: POB 38255, Lusaka; tel. (1) 295369; f. 1899; African successor to the Dutch Reformed Church mission; 147 congregations, 400,000 mems.

Seventh-day Adventist Church: POB 31309, Lusaka; tel. (1) 255197; fax (1) 255191; e-mail zbu@zamnet.zm; 66,408 active mems.

United Church of Zambia: Synod Headquarters, Nationalist Rd at Burma Rd, POB 50122, Lusaka; tel. (1) 250641; fax (1) 252198; e-mail uczsynod@zamnet.zm; f. 1965; c. 1m. mems; Synod Bishop Rev. PATRICE SIYEMETO; Gen. Sec. Rev. SILISHEBO SILISHEBO.

Other denominations active in Zambia include the Assemblies of God, the Church of Christ, the Church of the Nazarene, the Evangelical Fellowship of Zambia, the Kimbanguist Church, the Presby-terian Church of Southern Africa, the Religious Society of Friends (Quakers) and the United Pentecostal Church.

The Roman Catholic Church

Zambia comprises two archdioceses and eight dioceses. At 31 December 2000 there were an estimated 2,302,622 adherents in the country, equivalent to 26.1% of the total population.

Bishops' Conference

Zambia Episcopal Conference, Catholic Secretariat, Unity House, cnr Freedom Way and Katunjila Rd, POB 31965, Lusaka; tel. (1) 227854; fax (1) 220996; e-mail zec@zamnet.zm.

f. 1984; Pres. Most Rev. MEDARDO JOSEPH MAZOMBWE (Archbishop of Lusaka); Sec.-Gen. Rev. IGNATIUS MWEBE.

Archbishop of Kasama: Most Rev. JAMES SPAITA, Archbishop's House, POB 410143, Kasama; tel. (4) 221248; fax (4) 222202.

Archbishop of Lusaka: Most Rev. MEDARDO JOSEPH MAZOMBWE, 41 Wamulwa Rd, POB 32754, Lusaka; tel. (1) 239257; fax (1) 290631; e-mail adl@zamnet.zm.

ISLAM

There are about 10,000 members of the Muslim Association in Zambia.

BAHÁ'Í FAITH

National Spiritual Assembly: Sekou Touré Rd, Plot 4371, Private Bag RW227X, Ridgeway 15102, Lusaka; tel. and fax (1) 254505; e-mail nsa@zamnet.zm; Sec. DAVID SMITH; mems resident in 1,456 localities.

The Press

DAILIES

The Post: 36 Bwinjimfumu Rd, Rhodespark, Private Bag 352, Lusaka; tel. (97) 788200; fax (1) 229271; e-mail post@zamnet.zm; internet www.zamnet.zm/zamnet/post/post.html; f. 1991; independent; Editor-in-Chief FRED M'MEMBE; circ. 29,000.

The Times of Zambia: Kabelenga Ave, POB 70069, Ndola; tel. (2) 621305; fax (2) 617096; e-mail times@zamnet.zm; internet www .times.co.zm; f. 1943; govt-owned; English; Man. Editor CYRUS SIKAZWE; circ. 65,000.

Zambia Daily Mail: Zambia Publishing Company, POB 31421, Lusaka; tel. (1) 225131; fax (1) 225881; internet www.daily-mail.co .zm; f. 1968; govt-owned; English; Man. Editor EMMANUEL NYIRENDA; circ. 40,000.

PERIODICALS

African Social Research: Institute of Economic and Social Research, University of Zambia, POB 32379, Lusaka; tel. (1) 294131; fax (1) 253952; f. 1944; 2 a year; Editor MUBANGA E. KASHOKI; circ. 1,000.

The Challenge: Mission Press, Chifubu Rd, POB 71581, Ndola; tel. (2) 680456; fax (2) 680484; e-mail mpress@zamnet.zm; f. 1999; quarterly; English; social, educational and religious; Roman Catholic; edited by Franciscan friars; circ. 9,000.

Chipembele Magazine: POB 30255, Lusaka; tel. (1) 254226; 6 a year; publ. by Wildlife Conservation Soc. of Zambia; circ. 20,000.

Chronicle: Lusaka; bi-weekly; independent.

Farming in Zambia: POB 50197, Lusaka; tel. (1) 213551; f. 1965; quarterly; publ. by Ministry of Agriculture, Food and Fisheries; Editor L. P. CHIRWA; circ. 3,000.

Imbila: POB RW20, Lusaka; tel. (1) 217254; f. 1953; monthly; publ. by Zambia Information Services; Bemba; Editor D. MUKAKA; circ. 20,000.

Intanda: POB RW20, Lusaka; tel. (1) 219675; f. 1958; monthly; general; publ. by Zambia Information Services; Tonga; Editor J. SIKAULU; circ. 6,000.

Journal of Adult Education: University of Zambia, POB 50516, Lusaka; tel. (1) 216767; f. 1982; Exec. Editor FRANCIS KASOMA.

Leisure Magazine: Farmers House, Cairo Rd, POB 8138, Woodlands, Lusaka; monthly; general interest.

Liseli: POB RW20, Lusaka; tel. (1) 219675; monthly; publ. by Zambia Information Services; Lozi; Editor F. AMNSAA; circ. 8,000.

Lukanga News: POB 919, Kabwe; tel. (5) 217254; publ. by Zambia Information Services; Lenje; Editor J. H. N. NKOMANGA; circ. 5,500.

Mining Mirror: Zambia Consolidated Copper Mines Ltd, PR Dept, POB 71505, Ndola; tel. (2) 640142; f. 1973; monthly; English; Editor G. MUKUWA; circ. 30,000.

National Mirror: Multimedia Zambia, 15701 Woodlands, POB 320199, Lusaka; tel. (1) 263864; fax (1) 263050; f. 1972; fortnightly; news, current affairs and foreign affairs; publ. by Multimedia Zambia; Editor FANWELL CHEMBO; circ. 40,000.

Ngoma: POB RW20, Lusaka; tel. (1) 219675; monthly; Lunda, Kaonde and Luvale; publ. by Zambia Information Services; Editor B. A. LUHILA; circ. 3,000.

Orbit: Printpak Zambia Ltd, POB RW18X, Lusaka; tel. (1) 254915; f. 1971; 9 a year; publ. by Ministry of Education; children's educational magazine; Editor ELIDAH CHISHA; circ. 65,000.

Outlook: TBM Publicity Enterprises Ltd, POB 40, Kitwe; f. 1971; monthly; general interest.

Search Magazine: The Times Newspaper Ltd, POB 70069; tel. (2) 611001; Ndola; monthly; general interest.

Speak Out: POB 70244, Ndola; tel. (2) 612241; fax (2) 620630; e-mail speakout@zamnet.zm; f. 1984; bi-monthly; Christian; aimed at young readership; Man. Editor CONSTANTIA TREPPE; circ. 18,000.

The Sportsman: POB 31762, Lusaka; tel. (1) 214250; f. 1980; monthly; Man. Editor SAM SIKAZWE; circ. 18,000.

The Sun: Lusaka.

Sunday Express: Lusaka; f. 1991; weekly; Man. Editor JOHN MUKELA.

Sunday Times of Zambia: Kabelenga Ave, POB 70069, Ndola; tel. (2) 621305; fax (2) 617096; e-mail times@zamnet.zm; internet www .times.co.zm/sunday/index.html; f. 1965; owned by UNIP; English; Man. Editor ARTHUR SIMUCHOBA; circ. 78,000.

Tsopano: POB RW20, Lusaka; tel. (1) 217254; f. 1958; monthly; publ. by Zambia Information Services; Nyanja; Editor S. S. BANDA; circ. 9,000.

Voters' Voice: Lusaka; monthly; independent.

Weekly Post: Post Newspapers Ltd, Private Bag E352, Lusaka; tel. (1) 293791; fax (1) 293788; f. 1968.

Workers' Challenge: POB 270035, Kitwe; tel. and fax (2) 210904; f. 1981; 2 a month; publ. by the Workers' Pastoral Centre; English and Bemba; Co-Editors Fr MISHECK KAUNDA, JUSTIN CHILUFYA; circ. 16,000.

Workers' Voice: POB 20652, Kitwe; tel. (2) 211999; f. 1972; fortnightly; publ. by Zambia Congress of Trade Unions.

Youth: POB 30302, Lusaka; tel. (1) 211411; f. 1974; quarterly; publ. by UNIP Youth League; Editor-in-Chief N. ANAMELA; circ. 20,000.

Zambia Government Gazette: POB 30136, Lusaka; tel. (1) 228724; fax (1) 224486; f. 1911; weekly; English; official notices.

NEWS AGENCY

Zambia News Agency (ZANA): Mass Media Complex, POB 30007, Lusaka; tel. (1) 219673; e-mail zana@zamnet.zm; internet www .zana.gov.zm; Editor-in-Chief VILLIE LOMBANYA.

Foreign Bureaux

Agence France-Presse: POB 33805, Lusaka; tel. (1) 212959; Bureau Chief ABBE MAINE.

Informatsionnoye Telegrafnoye Agentstvo Rossii—Telegrafnoye Agentstvo Suverennykh Stran (ITAR—TASS) (Russia): POB 33394, Lusaka; tel. (1) 254201; Correspondent ANDREY K. POLYAKOV.

Reuters (UK): 3rd Floor, Woodgate House, Cairo Rd, POB 31685, Lusaka; tel. (1) 253430; fax (1) 235698; e-mail manoah@reuters.com .zm; Senior Correspondent MANOAH ESIPISU.

Rossiiskoye Informatsionnoye Agentstvo—Novosti (RIA-Novosti) (Russia): Lusaka; tel. (1) 252849; Rep. VIKTOR LAPTUKHIN.

Xinhua (New China) News Agency (People's Republic of China): United Nations Ave, POB 31859, Lusaka; tel. (1) 252227; fax (1) 251708; e-mail xinhuana@zamnet.zm; Chief Correspondent CHAI SHIKUAN.

PRESS ASSOCIATION

Press Association of Zambia (PAZA): c/o The Times of Zambia, Kabelenga Ave, POB 70069, Ndola; tel. (2) 621305; fax (2) 617096; f. 1983; Chair. ROBINSON MAKAYI.

Publishers

Africa: Literature Centre, POB 21319, Kitwe; tel. (2) 210765; fax (2) 210716; e-mail alc@zamnet.zm; general, educational, religious; Dir JACKSON MBEWE.

African Social Research: Institute of Economic and Social Research, University of Zambia, POB 32379, Lusaka; tel. (1) 294131; fax (1) 253952; e-mail kashoki@zamnet.zm; internet www.unza.zm; social research in Africa; Editor MUBANGA E. KASHOKI.

Daystar Publications Ltd: POB 32211, Lusaka; f. 1966; religious; Man. Dir S. E. M. PHEKO.

Directory Publishers of Zambia Ltd: Mabalenga Rd, POB 30963, Lusaka; tel. (1) 237915; fax (1) 237912; e-mail dpz@zamtel.zm; f. 1958; trade directories; Gen. Man. W. D. WRATTEN.

Multimedia Zambia: Woodlands, POB 320199, Lusaka; tel. and fax (1) 261193; e-mail nmirror@zamnet.zm; f. 1971; religious and educational books, audio-visual materials; Exec. Dir GOLDEN ZIBA.

University of Zambia Press: POB 32379, 10101 Lusaka; tel. (1) 290740; fax (1) 290409; e-mail press@admin.unza.zm; f. 1938; academic books, papers and journals.

Zambia Educational Publishing House: Chishango Rd, POB 32708, 10101 Lusaka; tel. (1) 222324; fax (1) 225073; f. 1967; educational and general; Man. Dir FINE M. CHILOMO.

Zambia Printing Co Ltd: POB 34798, 10101 Lusaka; tel. (1) 227673; fax (1) 225026; Gen. Man. BERNARD LUBUMBASHI.

Government Publishing Houses

Government Printer: POB 30136, Lusaka; tel. (1) 228724; fax (1) 224486; official documents and statistical bulletins.

Zambia Information Services: POB 50020, Lusaka; tel. (1) 219673; state-controlled; Dir BENSON SIANGA.

PUBLISHERS' ASSOCIATION

Booksellers' and Publishers' Association of Zambia: POB 31838, Lusaka; tel. (1) 222647; fax (1) 225195; Chair. RAY MUNAMWIMBU; Sec. BASIL MBEWE.

Broadcasting and Communications

TELECOMMUNICATIONS

Mobile cellular telephone networks are operated by Telecel Zambia and Zamcell.

Zambia Telecommunications Co Ltd (ZAMTEL): Provident House, POB 71660, Ndola; tel. (2) 611111; fax (2) 611399; internet www.zamtel.zm; transfer to private sector pending; Man. Dir J. M. KATAPA (acting).

BROADCASTING

Radio

Zambia National Broadcasting Corporation: Broadcasting House, POB 50015, Lusaka; tel. (1) 254989; fax (1) 254317; e-mail zambroad@zamnet.zm; f. 1961; state-controlled; radio services in English and seven Zambian languages; Dir-Gen. EDDY MUPESO.

Educational Broadcasting Services: Headquarters: POB 50231, Lusaka; tel. (1) 251724; radio broadcasts from Lusaka; audio-visual aids service from POB 50295, Lusaka; Controller MICHAEL MULOMBE.

Radio Phoenix: Private Bag E702, Lusaka; tel. (1) 226652; fax (1) 226839; e-mail rphoenix@zamnet.zm; commercial; Man. Dir ERROL HICKEY.

Christian Voice (Rlg.): Private Bag E606, Lusaka; tel. (1) 274251; fax (1) 274526; e-mail cvoice@zamnet.zm.

Television

In mid-1997 plans were announced for the transmission of two Egyptian satellite television channels in Zambia.

Zambia National Broadcasting Corporation: (see Radio); television services in English.

Educational Broadcasting Services: POB 21106, Kitwe; television for schools; Controller MICHAEL MULOMBE.

Finance

(cap. = capital; auth. = authorized; res = reserves; dep. = deposits; m. = million; br. = branch; amounts in kwacha)

BANKING

As from 30 June 1996 all banks operating in Zambia were required to have capital of not less than K2,000m. in order to receive a banking licence or to continue to function.

Central Bank

Bank of Zambia: Bank Square, Cairo Rd, POB 30080, 10101 Lusaka; tel. (1) 228888; fax (1) 221722; e-mail pr@boz.zm; internet www.boz.zm; f. 1964; bank of issue; cap. 10m., res 18,765m., dep. 991,774m. (Dec. 2000); Gov. and Chair. Dr CALEB FUNDANGA; br. in Ndola.

Commercial Banks

Finance Bank Zambia Ltd: 2101 Chanik House, Cairo Rd, POB 37102, 10101 Lusaka; tel. (1) 223587; fax (1) 223276; e-mail finance@coppernet.zm; f. 1986; cap. 3,630m., res 7,835m., dep. 91,218m. (Dec. 2000); Chair. T. M. D. MTINE-OGDS; Man. Dir M. WADOOD; 25 brs.

National Savings and Credit Bank of Zambia: Plot 248B, Cairo Rd, POB 30067; Lusaka; tel. (1) 227534; fax (1) 223296; e-mail natsave@zamnet.zm; internet www.webnet.co.zm/nscb.htm; f. 1972; total assets 6,598m. (Dec. 1998); Man. Dir B. K. E. N'GANDU.

New Capital Bank: Lotti House, First Floor, Cairo Rd, POB 36452, Lusaka; tel. (1) 229508; fax (1) 224055; e-mail ncapital@zamnet.zm; f. 1992; cap. 1,000m. (Dec. 1999); Chair. W. D. MUNG'OMBA; CEO G. P. MSISKA; Gen. Man. J. J. DE BEER.

Union Bank Zambia Ltd: Zimco House, Cairo Rd, POB 34940, Lusaka; tel. (1) 229392; fax (1) 221866; e-mail union.lsk@zamnet .zm; cap. and res 3,739.7m., total assets 33,748.9m. (Dec. 1997); Chair. J. R. NAYEE; Man. Dir L. CHONGO.

Zambia National Commercial Bank PLC: POB 33611, Lusaka; tel. (1) 228979; fax (1) 223106; e-mail zncbidf@zamnet.zm; internet www.zanaco.co.zm; f. 1969; govt-controlled; partial transfer to private sector pending; cap. and res 24,443.5m., total assets 364,110.9m. (Dec. 1998); Chair. M. W. LEWANIKA; Man. Dir LIKOLO NDALAMEI; 41 brs.

Foreign Banks

Bank of China (Zambia) Ltd (China): Amandra House, Ben Bella Rd, POB 34550, Lusaka; tel. (1) 238711; fax (1) 235350; cap. and res 4,470.4m., total assets 27,842.2m. (Dec. 1999); Chair. SUN CHANGJI; Gen. Man. JIA ZAISEN.

Barclays Bank of Zambia Ltd (UK): Kafue House, 1 Nairobi Place, POB 31936, Lusaka; tel. (1) 228858; fax (1) 222519; e-mail barclays.zambia@barclays.com; f. 1971; cap. and res 37,666m., dep. 318,363m. (Dec. 1999); Chair. A. BRUCE MUNYAMA; Man. Dir MARGARET MWANAKATWE; 5 brs.

Citibank Zambia Ltd (USA): Citibank House, Cha Cha Cha Rd, POB 30037, Southend, Lusaka; tel. (1) 229025; fax (1) 226264; f. 1979; cap. 521.2m., dep. 237,176m. (Dec. 2001); Man. Dir SURINIVASAN SRIDHAR; 1 br.

Indo-Zambia Bank (IZB): Plot 6907, Cairo Rd, POB 35411, Lusaka; tel. (1) 224653; fax (1) 225090; e-mail izb@zamnet.zm; f. 1984; cap. and res 4,949.6m., dep. 51,229.8m. (March 1999); Chair. Prof. B. MWEENE; Man. Dir A. K. MISRA; 7 brs.

Stanbic Bank Zambia Ltd: Woodgate House, 6th Floor, Nairobi Place, Cairo Rd, POB 31955, Lusaka; tel. (1) 229071; fax (1) 221152; e-mail stanbic@zamnet.zm; internet www.stanbic.co.zm; f. 1971; wholly-owned by Standard Bank Investment Corpn; cap. 7,700.0m., res 21,950.7m., dep. 288,669.6m. (Dec. 2000); Chair. D. A. R. PHIRI; Man. Dir A. H. S. MACLEOD; 7 brs.

Standard Chartered Bank Zambia Ltd (UK): Standard House, Cairo Rd, POB 32238, Lusaka; tel. (1) 229242; fax (1) 222092; e-mail violetsaunders@zm.standardchartered.com; f. 1971; cap. 2,048m., res 75,575m., dep. 450,784m. (Dec. 2001); Chair. A. K. MAZOKA; Man. Dir J. A. H. JANES; 14 brs.

Development Banks

Development Bank of Zambia: Development House, Katondo St, POB 33955, Lusaka; tel. (1) 228576; fax (1) 222426; e-mail dbzcom@zamnet.zm; internet www.dbz.co.zm; f. 1973; 99% state-owned; provides medium- and long-term loans and administers special funds placed at its disposal; cap. and res 7,580.0m., total assets 145,976.6m. (March 1998); Chair. J. M. MTONGA; Man. Dir DIPAK MALIK; 2 brs.

Lima Bank: Kulima House, Cha Cha Cha Rd, POB 32607, Lusaka; tel. (1) 213111; fax (1) 228077; cap. 57m. (March 1986); Chair. N. MUKUTU; Man. Dir K. V. KASAPATU.

Zambia Agricultural Development Bank: Society House, Cairo Rd, POB 30847, Lusaka; tel. (1) 219251; f. 1982; loan finance for development of agriculture and fishing; auth. cap. 75m. Chair. K. MAKASA; Man. Dir AMON CHIBIYA.

Zambia Export and Import Bank Ltd: Society House, Cairo Rd, POB 33046, Lusaka; tel. (1) 229486; fax (1) 222313; f. 1987; cap. 50m. (March 1992), dep. 50.9m. (March 1990); Man. Dir LIKANDO NAWA.

STOCK EXCHANGE

Lusaka Stock Exchange: Farmers House, 3rd Floor, Cairo Rd, POB 34523, Lusaka; tel. (1) 228537; fax (1) 225969; e-mail luse@zamnet.zm; f. 1994; Chair. JOHN JANES; Gen. Man. LLOYD CHINGAMBO.

INSURANCE

Zambia State Insurance Corporation Ltd: Premium House, Independence Ave, POB 30894, Lusaka; tel. (1) 229343; fax (1) 222263; e-mail zsiclsk@zamnet.zm; internet www.zsic.co.zm; f. 1968; took over all insurance business in Zambia in 1971; transfer to private sector pending; Chair. ALBERT WOOD; Man. Dir IRENE MUYENGA.

Trade and Industry

GOVERNMENT AGENCIES

National Import and Export Corporation (NIEC): National Housing Authority Bldg, POB 38282, Lusaka; tel. (1) 2288018; fax (1) 252771; f. 1974.

Zambia Investment Centre: Los Angeles Blvd, POB 34580, 10101 Lusaka; tel. (1) 254214; e-mail invest@zamnet.zm; internet www.zic .org.zm; Dir Gen. KASOTE SINGOGO (acting).

Zambia Privatization Agency: Privatization House, Nasser Rd, POB 30819, Lusaka; tel. (1) 223859; fax (1) 225270; e-mail zpa@zpa .org.zm; internet www.zpa.org.zm; f. 1992; responsible for the divestment of various state-owned enterprises; CEO ANDREW CHIPWENDE (acting).

DEVELOPMENT ORGANIZATIONS

Industrial Development Corporation of Zambia Ltd (INDECO): Indeco House, Buteko Place, POB 31935, Lusaka; tel. (1) 228026; fax (1) 228868; f. 1960; auth. cap. K300m. c. 47 subsidiaries and assoc. cos in brewing, chemicals, property, manufacturing, agriculture and vehicle assembly; Chair. R. L. BWALYA; Man. Dir S. K. TAMELÉ.

Mpongwe Development Company: Block 4450, Mpongwe, POB 90599, Luanshya; tel. (2) 510584; fax (2) 511713; promotes the production of crops for domestic and regional markets; CEO HENK MARMELSTEIN.

Small Industries Development Organization (SIDO): Sido House, Cairo Rd, POB 35373, Lusaka; tel. (1) 229707; fax (1) 224284; e-mail sido@zamnet.zm; f. 1981 to promote development of small and village industries.

CHAMBERS OF COMMERCE

Lusaka Chamber of Commerce and Industry: Business Centre, Farmers House, POB 37887, Lusaka; tel. (1) 221266; fax (1) 224134; f. 1933; Chair. R. D. PENZA; Sec. Dr E. BBENKELE; 400 mems.

Zambia Association of Chambers of Commerce and Industry: Great East Rd, Showgrounds, POB 30844, Lusaka; tel. (1) 253020; fax (1) 252483; e-mail zacci@zamnet.zm; internet www.zacci.org.zm; f. 1938; Chair. A. MKANDAWIRE, CEO P. J. ARMOND.

INDUSTRIAL AND TRADE ASSOCIATIONS

Copper Industry Service Bureau Ltd: POB 22100, Kitwe; tel. (2) 214122; f. 1941 as Chamber of Mines.

The Dairy Produce Board of Zambia: Kwacha House, Cairo Rd, POB 30124, Lusaka; tel. (1) 214770; f. 1964; purchase and supply of dairy products to retailers, manufacture and marketing of milk products.

Metal Marketing Corporation (Zambia) Ltd (MEMACO): Memaco House, Sapele Rd, POB 35570, Lusaka; tel. (1) 228131; fax (1) 223671; f. 1973; sole sales agents for all metal and mineral production; Chair. R. L. BWALYA; Man. Dir U. M. MUTATI.

Tobacco Board of Zambia: POB 31963, Lusaka; tel. (1) 288995; Sec. J. M. Chizuni.

Zambia Association of Manufacturers: POB 240312, Ndola; tel. (2) 619296; fax (2) 619297; e-mail shyams@zamnet.zm; f. 1985; Chair. Richard P. Healey; Sec. Mike G. Purslow; 180 mems.

Zambia Farm Employers' Association: Farmers' Village, Lusaka Agricultural and Commercial Showgrounds, POB 30395, Lusaka; tel. (1) 252649; fax (1) 252648; e-mail znfu@zamnet.zm; Chair. R. Denly; Vice-Chair. D. Mpundu; 350 mems.

Zambia Seed Producers' Association: POB 30013, Lusaka; tel. (1) 223249; fax (1) 223249; f. 1964; Chair. Barry Coxe; 300 mems.

UTILITIES

Electricity

Zambia Electricity Supply Corporation (Zesco): Stand 6949, Great East Rd, POB 33304, Lusaka; tel. (1) 228084; fax (1) 231329; internet www.zesco.co.zm; Man. Dir Robinson Mwansa.

CO-OPERATIVES

Zambia Co-operative Federation Ltd: Co-operative House, Cha Cha Cha Rd, POB 33579, Lusaka; tel. (1) 220157; fax (1) 222516; agricultural marketing; supply of agricultural chemicals and implements; cargo haulage; insurance; agricultural credit; auditing and accounting; property and co-operative development; Chair. B. Teta-mashimba; Man. Dir G. Z. Sibale.

TRADE UNIONS

Zambia Congress of Trade Unions: POB 20652, Kitwe; tel. (2) 211999; e-mail zctu@zamnet.zm; f. 1965; 18 affiliated unions; c. 400,000 mems; Pres. Jackson Shamenda; Sec.-Gen. Alec Chiorma.

Affiliated Unions

Airways and Allied Workers' Union of Zambia: POB 30272, Lusaka; Pres. F. Mulenga; Gen. Sec. B. Chinyanta.

Guards Union of Zambia: POB 21882, Kitwe; tel. (2) 216189; f. 1972; 13,500 mems; Chair. D. N. S. Silungwe; Gen. Sec. Michael S. Simfukwe.

Hotel Catering Workers' Union of Zambia: POB 35693, Lusaka; 9,000 mems; Chair. Ian Mkandawire; Gen. Sec. Stoic Kaputu.

Mineworkers' Union of Zambia: POB 20448, Kitwe; tel. (2) 214022; 50,000 mems; Chair. (vacant); Sec.-Gen. Ernest Mwansa.

National Union of Building, Engineering and General Workers: POB 21515, Kitwe; tel. (2) 213931; 18,000 mems; Chair. Luciano Mutale (acting); Gen. Sec. P. N. Nzima.

National Union of Commercial and Industrial Workers: 87 Gambia Ave, POB 21735, Kitwe; tel. (2) 228607; f. 1982; 16,000 mems; Chair. I. M. Kasumbu; Gen. Sec. G. F. Mwase.

National Union of Communications Workers: POB 70751, Ndola; tel. (2) 611345; fax (2) 614679; e-mail nucw@zamtel.zm; 6,000 mems; Pres. Neddy Nzowa; Gen. Sec. Chella Wellington.

National Union of Plantation and Agricultural Workers: POB 80529, Kabwe; tel. (5) 224548; 15,155 mems; Chair. Alex Msango; Gen. Sec. Bernadette Chimfwembe.

National Union of Public Services' Workers: POB 32523, Lusaka; tel. (1) 215167; Chair. W. Chipasha; Gen. Sec. Willie Mbewe.

National Union of Transport and Allied Workers: Lusaka; tel. (1) 214756; Chair. B. Mulwe; Gen. Sec. L. K. Mabuluki.

Railway Workers' Union of Zambia: POB 80302, Kabwe; tel. (5) 224006; 10,228 mems; Chair. H. K. Ndamana; Gen. Sec. Benson L. Ngula.

University of Zambia and Allied Workers' Union: POB 32379, Lusaka; tel. (1) 213221; f. 1968; Chair. Beriate Sunkutu; Gen. Sec. Saini Phiri.

Zambia Electricity Workers' Union: POB 70859, Ndola; f. 1972; 3,000 mems; Chair. Cosmas Mpampi; Gen. Sec. Adam Kaluba.

Zambia National Farmers' Union: Lusaka Agricultural and Commercial Showgrounds, POB 30395, Lusaka; tel. (1) 252649; fax (1) 252648; e-mail znfu@zamnet.zm; internet www.znfu.org.zm; Exec. Dir Songowayo Zyambo.

Zambia National Union of Teachers: POB 31914, Lusaka; tel. (1) 236670; 2,120 mems; Chair. Richard M. Liywalii; Gen. Sec. Kenneth Kasehela.

Zambia Typographical Workers' Union: Ndola; Chair. R. Shik-wata; Gen. Sec. D. Nawa.

Zambia Union of Financial Institutions and Allied Workers: POB 31174, Lusaka; tel. (1) 219401; Chair. B. Chikoti; Gen. Sec. Geoffrey Alikipo.

Zambia Union of Local Government Officers: f. 1997; Pres. Isaac Mwanza.

Zambia Union of Skilled Mineworkers: f. 1998; Chair. Alex Moloi.

Zambia United Local Authorities Workers' Union: POB 70575, Ndola; tel. (2) 615022; Chair. A. M. Mutakila; Gen. Sec. A. H. Mudenda.

Zambia Union of Journalists: POB 70956, Ndola; tel. (2) 613290; fax (2) 614229; Gen. Sec. Offering Kajimalwendo.

Principal Non-Affiliated Unions

Civil Servants' Union of Zambia: Church House, Cairo Rd, POB 50160, Lusaka; tel. and fax (1) 237578; e-mail csuz@zamnet.zm; f. 1975; 47,000 mems; Chair. L. C. Hikaumba; Gen. Sec. Darison Chaala.

Zambian African Mining Union: Kitwe; f. 1967; 40,000 mems.

Transport

RAILWAYS

Total length of railways in Zambia was 2,162 km (including 891 km of the Tanzania–Zambia railway) in 2000. There are two major railway lines: the Zambia Railways network, which traverses the country from the Copperbelt in northern Zambia and links with the National Railways of Zimbabwe to provide access to South African ports, and the Tanzania–Zambia Railway (Tazara) system, linking New Kapiri-Mposhi in Zambia with Dar es Salaam in Tanzania. The Tazara railway line increased its capacity from 1976, in order to reduce the dependence of southern African countries on trade routes through South Africa. In April 1987 the Governments of Zambia, Angola and Zaire (now the Democratic Republic of the Congo) declared their intention to reopen the Benguela railway, linking Zambian copper-mines with the Angolan port of Lobito, following its closure to international traffic in 1975 as a result of the guerrilla insurgency in Angola. In 1997 a programme of repairs was begun, with the aim of permitting the resumption of freight traffic within a three-year period.

Tanzania–Zambia Railway Authority (Tazara): POB T01, Mpika; Head Office: POB 2834, Dar es Salaam, Tanzania; tel. (4) 370397; fax (4) 370228; tel. 860340; e-mail tazara@zamnet.zm; f. 1975; operates passenger and freight services linking New Kapiri-Mposhi, north of Lusaka, with Dar es Salaam in Tanzania, a distance of 1,860 km, of which 891 km is in Zambia; jtly owned and administered by the Tanzanian and Zambian Govts; a 10-year rehabilitation programme, assisted by the USA and EC countries, began in 1985; it was announced in 1990 that a line linking the railway with the Zambian port of Mpulungu was to be constructed; Chair. Salim H. Msoma; Man. Dir Charles David Phiri.

Zambia Railways Ltd: cnr Buntungwa St and Ghana Ave, POB 80935, Kabwe; tel. (5) 222201; fax (5) 224411; e-mail zamrail@zamnet.zm; f. 1967; management assumed in 1998 by Hifab International AB (Sweden) in consortium with DE Consult (Germany); concession of assets and operations to New Limpopo Bridge Project Investments Ltd agreed in early 2003; Chair. B. Nonde; Man. Dir Göran Malmberg.

ROADS

In 1999 there was a total road network of 66,781 km, including 7,081 km of main roads and 13,700 km of secondary roads. The main arterial roads run from Beit Bridge (Zimbabwe) to Tunduma (the Great North Road), through the copper-mining area to Chingola and Chililabombwe (hitherto the Zaire Border Road), from Livingstone to the junction of the Kafue river and the Great North Road, and from Lusaka to the Malawi border (the Great East Road). In 1984 the 300-km BotZam highway linking Kazungula with Nata, in Botswana, was formally opened. A 1,930-km main road (the TanZam highway) links Zambia and Tanzania. In 1997 the Government initiated a 10-year Road Sector Investment Programme with funding from the World Bank.

Department of Roads: POB 50003, Lusaka; tel. (1) 253088; fax (1) 253404; e-mail roadshq@zamnet.zm; internet www.roads.gov.zm; Dir of Roads T. Ngoma.

SHIPPING

Zambia National Shipping Line: Lusaka; f. 1989; state-owned; cargo and passenger services from Dar es Salaam in Tanzania to northern Europe; Gen. Man. Martin Phiri.

CIVIL AVIATION

In 1984 there were 127 airports, aerodromes and air strips. An international airport, 22.5 km from Lusaka, was opened in 1967.

NAC 2000 Corpn Ltd: Lusaka International Airport, POB 30175, Lusaka; tel. (1) 271281; fax (1) 271292; e-mail naclmd@zamnet.zm; f. 1973; air cargo services; Gen. Man. CHILESHE KAPWEPWE.

Zambia Skyways (Eastern Air): Plot 6, Addis Ababa Rd, POB 32661, Lusaka; tel. (1) 250987; fax (1) 250767; e-mail zskyways@yahoo.com; internet www.zambiatourism.com/zambiaskyways/index.htm; f. 1995; operates scheduled passenger services to domestic destinations and South Africa; Man. Dir YOOSUF ZUMLA.

Zambia Airways: Lusaka International Airport, POB 310277, Lusaka; tel. (1) 271230; fax (1) 271054; e-mail roanhq@zamnet.zm; internet www.zambiaairways.co.zm; f. 1988 as Roanair, changed to current name in 1999; operates domestic and regional routes; CEO STEVE SIMWANZA.

Tourism

Zambia's main tourist attractions are its wildlife, unspoilt scenery and diverse cultural heritage; there are 19 national parks. In 2000 457,419 tourists visited Zambia, and tourism receipts totalled an estimated US $91.2m.

Tourism Council of Zambia: Holiday Inn Cottage, Church Rd, Lusaka; tel. (1) 252859; fax (1) 255337; e-mail tcz@zamnet.zm; internet www.zambiatourism.com/travel/LocalNews/TCZ.htm; Dep. Pres. BRUCE CHAPMAN.

Zambia National Tourist Board: Century House, Lusaka Sq., POB 30017, Lusaka; tel. (1) 229087; fax (1) 225174; e-mail zntb@zamnet.zm; internet www.zambiatourism.com; Chair. GEOFFREY SAMUKONGA; CEO AGNES SEENKA.

ZIMBABWE

Introductory Survey

Location, Climate, Language, Religion, Flag, Capital

The Republic of Zimbabwe is a land-locked state in southern Africa, with Mozambique to the east, Zambia to the north-west, Botswana to the south-west and South Africa to the south. The climate is tropical, modified considerably by altitude. Average monthly temperatures range from 13°C (55°F) to 22°C (72°F) on the highveld, and from 20°C (68°F) to 30°C (86°F) in the low-lying valley of the Zambezi river. The rainy season is from November to March. The official languages are English, Chishona and Sindebele. About 55% of the population are Christians. A large number of the African population follow traditional beliefs, while the Asian minority comprises both Muslims and Hindus. The national flag (proportions 1 by 2) has seven equal horizontal stripes, of green, gold, red, black, red, gold and green, with a white triangle, bearing a red five-pointed star on which a gold 'Great Zimbabwe bird' is superimposed, at the hoist. The capital is Harare.

Recent History

In 1923 responsibility for Southern Rhodesia (now Zimbabwe) was transferred from the British South Africa Company to the Government of the United Kingdom, and the territory became a British colony. It had full self-government (except for African interests and some other matters) under an administration controlled by European settlers. African voting rights were restricted.

In 1953 the colony united with two British protectorates, Northern Rhodesia (now Zambia) and Nyasaland (now Malawi), to form the Federation of Rhodesia and Nyasaland, also known as the Central African Federation. Sir Godfrey Huggins (later Viscount Malvern), the Prime Minister of Southern Rhodesia from 1933 to 1953, became the first Prime Minister of the Federation, being succeeded by Sir Roy Welensky in 1956. In Southern Rhodesia itself, Garfield Todd was Prime Minister from 1953 until 1958, when Sir Edgar Whitehead came to power. A new Constitution, which ended most of the United Kingdom's legal controls and provided for a limited African franchise, came into effect in November 1962. At elections in December Whitehead lost power to the Rhodesian Front (RF), a coalition of white opposition groups committed to maintaining racial segregation. The RF's leader, Winston Field, became Prime Minister.

As a result of pressure from African nationalist movements in Northern Rhodesia and Nyasaland, the Federation was dissolved in December 1963. African nationalists were also active in Southern Rhodesia. The African National Congress, founded in 1934, was revived in 1957, with Joshua Nkomo as President. Following the banning of the Congress in February 1959, some of its members formed the National Democratic Party (NDP) in January 1960. Nkomo, although in exile, was elected President of the NDP in October. When the NDP was banned in December 1961, Nkomo formed the Zimbabwe African People's Union (ZAPU), which was declared an unlawful organization in September 1962. ZAPU split in July 1963, and a breakaway group, led by the Rev. Ndabaningi Sithole, formed the Zimbabwe African National Union (ZANU) in August. Robert Mugabe became Secretary-General of ZANU.

In April 1964 Field was succeeded as Prime Minister of Southern Rhodesia by his deputy, Ian Smith. The new regime rejected British conditions for independence, including acceptance by the whole Rhodesian population and unimpeded progress to majority rule. In August ZANU was banned. After Northern Rhodesia became independent as Zambia in October, Southern Rhodesia became generally (although not officially) known as Rhodesia. At elections in May 1965 the RF won all 50 European seats in the legislature. On 5 November a state of emergency (to be renewed annually) was declared, and on 11 November Smith made a unilateral declaration of independence (UDI) and proclaimed a new Constitution, naming the country Rhodesia. The British Government regarded Rhodesia's independence as unconstitutional and illegal, and no other country formally recognized it. The United Kingdom terminated all relations with Rhodesia, while the UN applied economic sanctions (although it was subsequently revealed that many inter-

national companies had circumvented the restrictions). Both ZAPU and ZANU took up arms against the RF regime, and African guerrilla groups were frequently involved in clashes with Rhodesian security forces.

Following a referendum in June 1969, Rhodesia was declared a republic in March 1970. The 1969 Constitution provided for a bicameral Legislative Assembly, comprising a 23-member Senate and a 66-member House of Assembly (50 Europeans and 16 Africans). The President had only formal powers, and Smith remained Prime Minister. The RF won all 50 European seats in the House of Assembly in 1970, 1974 and 1977.

In November 1971 the British and Rhodesian Governments agreed on draft proposals for a constitutional settlement, subject to their acceptability to the Rhodesian people 'as a whole'. In December the African National Council (ANC), led by Bishop Abel Muzorewa, was formed to co-ordinate opposition to the plan. In December 1974, however, the Rhodesian Government and leaders of four nationalist organizations (including ZAPU, ZANU and the ANC) agreed the terms of a cease-fire, conditional on the release of African political detainees and on the convening of a constitutional conference in 1975. The African organizations agreed to unite within the ANC, with Muzorewa as President. Mugabe opposed the incorporation of ZANU into the ANC, and in mid-1975 left Rhodesia for neighbouring Mozambique, where he took control of ZANU's external wing, and challenged Sithole's leadership of the party. In September the ANC split into rival factions, led by Muzorewa and Nkomo. Constitutional talks between the Government and the Nkomo faction began in December 1975, but were abandoned in March 1976. In September, under pressure from South Africa, Smith announced his Government's acceptance of proposals leading to majority rule within two years. In late 1976 representatives of the RF, the African nationalists and the British Government met to discuss the transition to majority rule. The nationalists were led by Muzorewa, Sithole, Nkomo and Mugabe (by then the recognized leader of ZANU). Nkomo and Mugabe adopted a joint position as the Patriotic Front (PF). The talks were adjourned in December 1976, owing to failure to agree on the composition of the proposed interim government.

In January 1977 negotiations resumed, and Angola, Botswana, Mozambique, Tanzania and Zambia (the 'front-line' states) declared their support for the PF. Smith rejected British proposals for an interim administration, and received a mandate from the RF to repeal racially discriminatory laws and to seek agreement with such African factions as he chose. In July the PF demanded that power be handed directly to them by the Rhodesian Government. In November Smith accepted the principle of universal adult suffrage, and talks on an internal settlement were initiated with Muzorewa's United African National Council (UANC), the Rev. Sithole's faction of the ANC and the Zimbabwe United People's Organization, led by Chief Jeremiah Chirau. These talks led to the signing of an internal settlement on 3 March 1978, providing for an interim power-sharing administration to prepare for independence on 31 December. The proposals were rejected by the PF and by the UN Security Council. In May 1978 the newly created Executive Council, consisting of Smith, Sithole, Muzorewa and Chirau, ordered the release of all political detainees in an attempt to bring about a cease-fire. Frequent clashes between Rhodesian security forces and PF guerrillas resulted in the introduction of selective martial law in September.

In January 1979 a 'majority rule' Constitution, with entrenched safeguards for the white minority, was approved by the House of Assembly and endorsed by a referendum of European voters. In April elections to the new House of Assembly (the first by universal adult suffrage) were held in two stages: for 20 directly elected European members (chosen by non-African voters only) and then for 72 African members (chosen by the whole electorate). The elections were boycotted by the PF. The UANC emerged as the majority party, with 51 seats, while the RF won all 20 seats for whites. In May the new Parliament elected Josiah Gumede as President. Muzorewa became Prime Minister of the country (renamed Zimbabwe Rhodesia) in June.

In accordance with the Constitution, Muzorewa formed a government of national unity, a coalition of parties in the new House, including European members (Smith became Minister without Portfolio). However, international recognition was not forthcoming, and UN sanctions remained in force.

New impetus for a lasting and internationally recognized settlement followed the Commonwealth Conference in Zambia in August 1979. In September a Rhodesian Constitutional Conference was convened at Lancaster House, in London, United Kingdom, under the chairmanship of the British Secretary of State for Foreign and Commonwealth Affairs, and attended by delegations under Muzorewa and the joint leaders of the PF. The PF reluctantly agreed to special representation for the whites under the proposed new Constitution, which was eventually accepted by both parties; complete agreement was reached on transitional arrangements in November, and the details of a cease-fire between the guerrillas of the PF and the Rhodesian security forces were finalized in the following month. On 11 December the Zimbabwe Rhodesia Parliament voted to renounce independence and to revert to the status of a British colony, as Southern Rhodesia. Illegal rule ended on the following day, when Parliament was dissolved, the President, Prime Minister and Cabinet resigned, and the British-appointed Governor, Lord Soames, was vested with full executive and legislative authority for the duration of the transition to legal independence. The United Kingdom immediately revoked economic sanctions.

Lord Soames ended the ban on the two wings of the PF (ZAPU and ZANU) and ordered the release of most of the detainees who were held under the 'emergency powers' laws. Elections to a new House of Assembly proceeded in February 1980 (again in two stages) under the supervision of a British Electoral Commissioner. Mugabe's ZANU—PF emerged as the largest single party, winning 57 of the 80 African seats; Nkomo's PF—ZAPU took 20 seats and the UANC only three. In a separate poll of white voters, Smith's RF secured all 20 reserved seats. The new state of Zimbabwe became legally independent, within the Commonwealth, on 18 April, with Rev. Canaan Banana as President (with largely ceremonial duties) and Mugabe as Prime Minister, at the head of a coalition Government. Some 27,000 people had been killed in the war of independence.

Relations within the Government were strained, particularly between Mugabe and Nkomo. The latter was demoted in a cabinet reshuffle in January 1981, and removed from the Cabinet altogether, with two PF colleagues, in February 1982, under suspicion of plotting against Mugabe. In March 1982 several deputies of the RF, now restyled the Republican Front, resigned from the party over its unwillingness to co-operate with the Government, and sat as independents. By May 1984 the RF retained only seven of the 20 seats reserved for whites, the remaining 13 being held by independents. In July the RF was renamed the Conservative Alliance of Zimbabwe (CAZ), and opened its membership to all races.

Many of the unpopular practices of the Smith regime, including 'emergency powers' and the detention of political opponents, continued after independence. (The state of emergency continued to be renewed at six-monthly intervals until August 1990.) In early 1983 government troops were sent to Matabeleland to quell serious unrest, caused by pro-Nkomo dissidents. In September of that year legislation was introduced providing for increased press censorship and granting the security forces greater powers under the state of emergency. In November Muzorewa was arrested on suspicion of having subversive links with South Africa. He remained in detention, without trial, until September 1984. In February 1984, in a renewed anti-insurgency campaign, an estimated 10,000 troops were again sent into Matabeleland. It was subsequently alleged that some 20,000 civilians were killed during the two campaigns as a result of atrocities perpetrated by the army (see below).

There were several outbreaks of violence prior to a general election in June–July 1985. ZANU—PF was returned to power with an increased majority, winning 63 of the 79 'common roll' seats in the House of Assembly (and an additional seat at a by-election in August). ZAPU won 15 seats, retaining its traditional hold over Matabeleland, and ZANU—Sithole took a single seat. The UANC failed to gain representation. Of the 20 seats reserved for whites, 15 were secured by Smith's CAZ. However, CAZ was not represented in the new Cabinet.

During mid-1985 a large number of ZAPU officials were detained for questioning about dissident activity in Matabeleland. Later in the year, however, ZANU and ZAPU reached broad agreement on the terms of a merger of the two parties, in the interests of national unity; negotiations continued during 1986, but were suspended in April 1987. A resurgence of violence in Matabeleland followed, and in June ZAPU, which was accused of fomenting the unrest, was banned from holding public meetings. The failure, in August, of further talks aimed at uniting ZANU and ZAPU led to renewed rebel activity, whereupon the Government took steps to prevent ZAPU from functioning effectively: in September all offices of the party were closed, six ZAPU-controlled district councils in Matabeleland were dissolved, and a number of prominent ZAPU officers were detained. Furthermore, ZANU declined to endorse seven ZAPU-nominated candidates for the parliamentary seats made vacant in September by the abolition of seats reserved for whites (see below). In November, however, the ban on public meetings by ZAPU was revoked, and the party was permitted to reopen its offices in Harare and Bulawayo. In December Mugabe and Nkomo finally signed an agreement of unity, which was ratified by both parties in April 1988 and implemented in December 1989 (see below). In January 1988 Nkomo was appointed as one of the Senior Ministers in the President's Office, and two other ZAPU officials were given government posts. Following the unity agreement there was a significant improvement in the security situation in Matabeleland. However, the state of emergency remained in force, owing to incursions into eastern Zimbabwe by the Mozambican rebel movement, the Resistência Nacional Moçambicana (Renamo, see below).

Two major constitutional reforms were enacted during 1987. In September the reservation for whites of 20 seats in the House of Assembly and 10 seats in the Senate was abolished, as permitted by the Constitution, subject to a majority vote in the House. (In anticipation of this reform, several white deputies joined ZANU. In May Smith resigned as President of CAZ.) In October the 80 remaining members of the House of Assembly elected 20 candidates, who were nominated by ZANU, including 11 whites, to fill the vacant seats in the House of Assembly until the next general election. In the same month Parliament approved the replacement of the ceremonial presidency by an executive presidency. The post of Prime Minister was to be incorporated into the presidency. President Banana (who, as the only candidate, had been sworn in for a second term of office as President in April 1986) retired in December 1987, and at the end of that month Mugabe (the sole candidate) was inaugurated as Zimbabwe's first executive President.

In October 1988 Edgar Tekere, a former Secretary-General of ZANU, was expelled from the party, having persistently made allegations of corruption involving government members, in addition to criticizing President Mugabe's commitment to the eventual introduction of a one-party state. Nevertheless, in March and April 1989 a number of senior ZANU officials resigned following the release of the findings of a commission set up to investigate reports of illegal financial transactions. During April Tekere founded the Zimbabwe Unity Movement (ZUM), intending to challenge ZANU at the next general election. In November the Government was accused by the Supreme Court of failing to respect judicial decisions. In December ZANU and ZAPU merged to form a single party, named the Zimbabwe African National Union—Patriotic Front (ZANU—PF). The united party aimed to establish a one-party state with a Marxist-Leninist doctrine. Mugabe was appointed President of ZANU—PF, while Nkomo became one of its two Vice-Presidents.

Presidential and parliamentary elections were held concurrently in March 1990; at these elections legislation approved in late 1989 came into effect, abolishing the Senate and increasing the number of seats in the House of Assembly from 100 to 150 (of which 120 were to be directly elected; 12 were to be allocated to presidential nominees, 10 to traditional Chiefs and eight to provincial governors). Mugabe won nearly 80% of all votes cast at the presidential election; his sole opponent was Tekere. At the parliamentary elections ZANU—PF secured 117 of the 120 elective seats in the House of Assembly; the ZUM (which had entered into an informal electoral alliance with CAZ) won only two seats, and the UANC took one seat. Although ZANU—PF won an outright victory, only 54% of the electorate voted, and representatives of the ruling party were accused of intimidating voters. Following the elections Nkomo was appointed as one of two Vice-Presidents (the other being Simon Muzenda, also a Vice-President of ZANU—PF), and remained one of the Senior Ministers in the President's Office. In August 1990 the state of emergency, which had been in force since independence, was revoked.

In March 1992 the House of Assembly approved legislation (the Land Acquisition Act) that permitted the compulsory acquisition of land by the Government; this was intended to facilitate the redistribution of land ownership from Europeans (who owned about one-third of farming land in early 1992) to Africans. In May 1993 the Government published a list of properties allotted for transferral to the State under the Act, provoking a strong protest from the white-dominated Commercial Farmers' Union (CFU). The High Court subsequently ruled against three white farmers who had attempted to prove that the confiscation of their land was unconstitutional. A lack of available funds impeded the progress of the Government's land resettlement programme.

In early July 1992 Mugabe reorganized the Cabinet, reducing the number of ministries in accordance with a policy to restrain public expenditure. Later in July several opposition organizations, including CAZ, the UANC and the ZUM, formed an informal alliance, known as the United Front, which aimed to remove Mugabe from power. In September the House of Assembly approved the Political Parties Finance Act, which granted state funding to any party with at least 15 seats in the Assembly (in effect only ZANU—PF); the fairness of the Act was strongly contested by the opposition. In January 1994 the UANC was incorporated into Tekere's ZUM; later in that year Muzorewa, the former UANC leader, founded a new opposition grouping, the United Parties (UP). In February the Supreme Court ruled that the 34-year-old section of the Law and Order Maintenance Act that prevented opposition members from holding peaceful public demonstrations without prior permission from the authorities was in conflict with the Zimbabwean Bill of Rights and should therefore be repealed.

ZANU—PF won an overwhelming victory at legislative elections in April 1995. The ruling party received more than 82% of the votes cast and secured 118 of the 120 elective seats in the House of Assembly (55 of which were uncontested). The remaining two elective seats were taken by ZANU—Ndonga (formerly ZANU—Sithole). Following the allocation of nominated and reserved seats, ZANU—PF controlled 148 of the total 150 seats. However, only 54% of the electorate voted, and the elections were boycotted by eight opposition groups, including the ZUM and the UP. In mid-April Mugabe appointed a reorganized and enlarged Cabinet; Nkomo and Muzenda remained as Vice-Presidents. Opposition groups accused the Government of electoral malpractice, despite independent observers' verdict that the elections had been free and fair. At local elections in October some 15 independent and dissident ZANU—PF candidates won representation on local councils. During that month Rev. Sithole, the leader of ZANU—Ndonga, was arrested and charged with plotting to assassinate Mugabe, in conspiracy with the Chimwenjes, a group of mainly Zimbabwean dissidents based in Mozambique; Sithole strongly denied the accusation.

Mugabe retained the presidency at an election in March 1996, winning 92.7% of the votes cast. Turn-out was, however, low. The election was also unwillingly contested by Muzorewa (who took 4.7% of the votes) and Sithole, who had been released on bail, (2.4%); they had been denied permission to withdraw their candidacies prior to the ballot. In late March Mugabe was sworn in for a third term as President. He reorganized the Cabinet extensively in May.

Between August and November 1996 there were a number of national strikes by public-sector workers demanding pay increases. In October it was announced that ZANU—PF was abandoning Marxism-Leninism as its guiding principle. In February 1997 a former aide-de-camp to Rev. Banana in the early 1980s, Jefta Dube, made allegations that the then President had sexually assaulted him, and in April Dube lodged a civil suit for damages against Banana. The allegations received considerable international attention, since Mugabe had recently made a number of much-publicized condemnations of homosexual practices. In May a report compiled by the Legal Resources Foundation and the Catholic Commission for Justice and Peace emerged (prior to official publication), detailing atrocities allegedly committed by security forces in Matabeleland in the early 1980s (see above). A reorganization of the Cabinet in July 1997, in which several ministries were merged, was attributed to pressure from international creditors. In August the Government announced that the independence war veterans (an increasingly powerful lobby) were to be awarded a number of substantial, unbudgeted benefits.

In September 1997 the Supreme Court ruled against the Political Parties Finance Act of 1992, decreeing that it was incompatible with a democratic multi-party political system. In December 1997 Rev. Sithole was found guilty of plotting to kill Mugabe and sentenced to two years' imprisonment; he was, however, released on bail, pending an appeal to the Supreme Court, and died in December 2000. In November 1998 Rev. Banana was convicted on 11 charges of sexual assault. However, Banana violated his bail conditions and travelled to Botswana and then South Africa, where he asked for President Mandela's protection. Following Mandela's intervention with Mugabe on Banana's behalf, the former President returned to Zimbabwe in December and was sentenced to 10 years' imprisonment with labour in January 1999. Most of the sentence was conditionally suspended, but Banana was to serve a minimum of one year in prison.

In October 1997 Mugabe announced that the hitherto slow pace of the land resettlement programme would be accelerated, declaring that the constitutional right of white commercial farmers to receive full and fair compensation for confiscated land would not be honoured and (unsuccessfully) challenging the United Kingdom, in its role as former colonial power, to take responsibility for assisting them. A list of 1,503 properties to be reallocated forthwith was published in November. In January 1998, however, the IMF stipulated an assurance from the Mugabe administration that it would respect the Constitution during the land resettlement procedure as a condition for the release of financial assistance; such an assurance was eventually given in March, when it was announced that 120 farms would be acquired in the near future in exchange for full and fair compensation. While the land resettlement programme appeared to command extensive national support, there was also concern that the Government should administer the scheme fairly (without members of the ruling élite becoming beneficiaries) and that the success of the thriving commercial farming sector should not be prejudiced. In June 1998 there was a series of illegal farm occupations by black families. In August Mugabe introduced the second phase of the programme, to resettle 150,000 families on 1m. ha of land each year for the next seven years, and in September Zimbabwe launched an international appeal for Western donors to support its land reform; however, the latter dismissed the scheme as too ambitious and costly. Under pressure, the Government agreed to reduce its plans, and was restricted to using 118 farms that it had already been offered. In November, however, 841 white-owned farms were ordered to be confiscated by the state: compensation was to be deferred. Pressure exerted by the IMF in light of a forthcoming release of aid brought an assurance from Mugabe that his administration would not break agreements for a gradual land reform programme. At the end of March 1999 the President contravened the agreement when he announced a new plan to acquire a further 529 white-owned farms. He accused the USA and the United Kingdom of 'destabilizing' Zimbabwe through their alleged control over the IMF, which was delaying financial assistance to his country. In the following month Mugabe threatened that Zimbabwe would sever its relations with the IMF and the World Bank, although the Minister of Finance continued to hope that further aid would be released shortly. (The IMF approved a US $193m. loan in August.) In May the Government agreed a plan that aimed to resettle 77,700 black families on 1m. ha by 2001. Some of this land was to come from the 118 farms that had already been offered. The remainder would be the result of uncontested acquisitions under the Government's reduced list of 800 farms for compulsory purchase. The plan was to be partially funded by the World Bank, and was broadly accepted by the white landowners' association.

Meanwhile, during 1997 strikes occurred in several sectors of the labour force (including the newspaper industry and agricultural sector). Labour unrest escalated in December, when a general strike was organized by the Zimbabwe Congress of Trade Unions (ZCTU), in protest at the imposition by the Government of three unpopular new taxes in order to finance the provision of benefits to war veterans (see above); the authorities capitulated, withdrawing two of the taxes immediately. Shortly after the demonstrations had subsided, Morgan Tsvangirai, the Secretary-General of ZCTU, was brutally attacked in his office by unknown assailants. The weak Zimbabwe currency and soaring food prices aggravated the nation-wide mood of discontent. In January 1998 riots erupted in most of the country's urban areas in protest at rises in the price of maize meal, the staple food. In response Mugabe agreed to withdraw the most recent price increase. However, the army was deployed to suppress the disturbances and was authorized to open fire on protesters; nine people were reportedly killed and some 800 rioters were arrested. The ZCTU organized a further two-day strike in March, to protest against the continuing rise in living costs; soon afterwards the Congress' Bulawayo office was destroyed in an arson attack.

In September 1998 threats for a five-day stoppage in support of demands for tax cuts resulted in government concessions. Meanwhile, further consumer price increases were followed by renewed rioting. A series of one-day strikes over pay were called by unions, and action took place until banned by Mugabe. In February 1999, however, the ban was ruled to be illegal. In that month growing unrest followed an address to the nation by Mugabe in which he attacked the judiciary, the independent media and 'British agents'. He also accused whites of 'fomenting unrest'. Unrest resulting from declining standards of living continued throughout 1999.

Meanwhile, in October 1998 the Government embarked on discussions on changing Zimbabwe's Constitution with an opposition grouping, known as the National Constitutional Assembly (NCA). The administration affirmed its commitment to an open process that would not allow government domination, and wanted the new Constitution to be in force by the elections due in 2000. However, the opposition withdrew from the negotiations in the following month after about 50 protesters calling for constitutional change were prevented from marching by riot police. In March 1999 Mugabe appointed a commission of inquiry to make recommendations on a new Constitution. The NCA refused to participate, owing to the alleged high risk of presidential manipulation. Joshua Nkomo died in early July 1999. (Joseph Msika, hitherto a minister without portfolio, replaced him as Vice-President in December.) At Nkomo's funeral, Mugabe apologized for the atrocities committed against the Ndebele in Matabeleland in the early 1980s (see above), and issued a call for national unity. Nevertheless, there was a resurgence of ZAPU under new leadership, called ZAPU 2000. This new party declared that it wanted a federal system for Zimbabwe, with considerable powers devolved to Matabeleland and other regions. (In an attempt to win back support, in October the Government announced compensation for the families of those killed in the violence.) Another potentially formidable challenge to ZANU—PF emerged in September with the formation of the Movement for Democratic Change (MDC), led by Morgan Tsvangirai. Administrative chaos and almost total apathy in local elections held in that month humiliated the ruling party and cast severe doubts over the Government's ability to hold general elections due in April or May 2000. Opposition organizations claimed that the perceived apathy was in fact a display of popular displeasure with the ruling élite.

Meanwhile, drafting of the new Constitution continued. An international constitutional conference was held in November 1999, but several experts suspected that the draft had already been created, and that they had been invited to make presentations primarily to give the process global credibility. In late November a document bearing no relation to that prepared by the 400-member constitutional commission, a drafting committee overseen by ZANU—PF having deleted crucial clauses (particularly relating to the reduction of the President's powers and the introduction of a parliamentary system), was declared to have been 'adopted by acclamation', despite vigorous protests. In January 2000 Mugabe announced that a referendum on the new Constitution would take place on 12–13 February. The high level of confusion before the polls over such issues as eligibility to vote and the location of polling stations was believed by the opposition to have been orchestrated by ZANU—PF to maximize Mugabe's chances of victory. The Registrar-General announced that the electoral roll was to be used, which was known to be outdated, 25% of those listed having died and another 30% having changed constituencies. Despite fears that a lack of supervision of the ballot had led to widespread irregularities on ZANU—PF's part, 54.6% of the 26% of the electorate who participated in the polls voted to reject the Constitution. The level of participation was highest in urban areas where MDC support was strong, while voters in the Government's rural strongholds were apathetic, despite promises that the new Constitution would grant them redistributed white land. In a televised address a few days later, Mugabe accepted the result.

Within ZANU—PF, however, there was mounting dissatisfaction with Mugabe's leadership, and, in the wake of the plebiscite defeat, fears grew that he was an electoral liability. The Government embarked on a campaign to restore its popularity to ensure victory over an increasingly confident opposition

in the legislative elections, which, it was announced in March, were to be held in May rather than April. Illegal occupations of white-owned farms by black 'war veterans' (many of whom, too young to have taken part in the war of independence, were suspected of having been paid to participate), which began in late February, were rumoured to have been organized by the Government to in an attempt to regain support through the land issue. The security forces refused to act against the occupiers, declaring that the 'political issue' lay outside their jurisdiction. Occupations increased, and the police also failed to take steps to evict the protesters, following a ruling by the High Court in mid-March in favour of the white farmers (which was ignored by the veterans). Mugabe repeatedly denied that his administration was behind the occupations, but made no secret of his support for them. The invasions became increasingly violent, and two farmers were killed in April. A few days earlier Mugabe had threatened war against farmers who refused to give up their land voluntarily, and following the violence he declared that they were 'enemies of the state'. The international community condemned this increasingly militant stance, which also extended to the treatment of the opposition, in particular the MDC, which was subjected to a campaign of intimidation and aggression. In one of the worst instances a 500-strong mob violently attacked a peace march in Harare in early April. No action was taken against the perpetrators of the attack. A constitutional amendment approved in April stated that white farmers dispossessed of their land would have to apply to the 'former colonial power', the United Kingdom, for compensation (see below). Many farmers were aggrieved, as their land had been purchased under Zimbabwean law. As chaos reigned, following worsening displays of aggression, which had prompted the MDC to threaten to boycott the elections, and amid signs that ZANU—PF had regained its rural support, in mid-May Mugabe called for an end to the violence. He met with war veterans and white farmers and announced the creation of a land commission to redistribute farmland. Shortly afterwards, however, he signed a law allowing the seizure of 841 white-owned farms without compensation. Political violence continued unabated throughout the month. In early June a list was published of 804 farms that were to be confiscated. Ian Smith's farm was among those to be acquired. Farmers were to be granted approximately one month to contest the list. Later in June Mugabe also threatened to seize foreign-owned companies and to nationalize mines. In October Mugabe announced that he intended to seek the arrest and trial of Smith on charges of genocide.

Official manipulation of the media was an important issue in early 2000, as the new Constitution was being drafted and the legislative elections approached. The editor, proprietor and one of the journalists of an independent newspaper were arrested in February, despite a public apology to the Government, and charged with criminal defamation over an article alleging chicanery by the state commission drafting the new Constitution. In March legislation was passed allowing the President to intercept any form of telecommunications. In the following month opposition politicians denounced reports in the state-owned media that they were training guerrilla fighters abroad and that an arms cache found on a white-owned farm belonged to them, accusing ZANU—PF of orchestrating a pre-election campaign to discredit them. Meanwhile, the authorities also strictly controlled reports about losses incurred in the fighting in the Democratic Republic of the Congo (DRC, see below), releasing unfeasibly low figures for deaths and casualties. In December 1998 the same newspaper that printed the article on the Constitution (see above) published a story claiming that 23 disaffected army officers serving in the DRC had been arrested after an attempted coup. In January 1999 the editor of the newspaper and the journalist who wrote the story were arrested, charged with publishing a false news story 'likely to cause fear, alarm and despondency' and held in military custody, arousing widespread protests and controversy; they were released shortly afterwards. In September they appealed to the Supreme Court to compel the authorities to investigate their alleged torture by state investigators. The Commissioner of Police subsequently admitted that the journalists had been handed over to the military, where they had been tortured. In May 2000 the Supreme Court ruled that the charges against the pair were unconstitutional, thereby effectively acquitting them. Meanwhile, in March 1999 three US citizens, who claimed to be missionaries, were charged with being mercenaries involved in terrorism and espionage against Zimbabwe and the DRC. They had been arrested at Harare airport in possession of firearms (which they claimed were for hunting and self-defence). Independent medical reports subsequently confirmed that the men had been tortured while in custody. The charge of terrorism was dropped in June, and in September the men were each sentenced to 27 months' imprisonment with hard labour. In November the three were declared 'prohibited immigrants' and deported.

International aid to Zimbabwe was suspended in October 1999 because the Government had failed to meet reform targets. The IMF was also investigating reports that Zimbabwe had submitted figures to it relating to military expenditure that were substantially lower than those used by the treasury. Zimbabwe denied the allegations. The budget deficit was growing ever larger and huge arrears to overseas suppliers for fuel, partly owing to a desperate shortage of foreign currency reserves, led to the suspension of oil supplies in December. In the following month rationing caused unrest and long queues at petrol stations. In February 2000 the Minister of Transport and Energy, Enos Chikowore, assumed responsibility for the fuel crisis and resigned. The President's office took over the running of the ministry. As reserves fell, so political tensions increased, and Mugabe was forced to look for new suppliers, signing a one-year agreement with Kuwait in March. In April white farmers called for the currency to be substantially devalued and threatened that they would not take their tobacco crop to auction until this happened. The banks agreed that devaluation was needed to avoid mass default. The Government, however, fearing that devaluing the currency might adversely affect its chances of retaining power, refused to act. Meanwhile, in March the Minister of Agriculture, Kumbirai Kangai, appeared in court on charges of manipulating tenders for grain imports. He was the first minister to face corruption charges since Mugabe had come to power. The President had reportedly previously acknowledged that a number of his ministers were corrupt, and it was suspected that, as the legislative elections approached, he wanted to improve ZANU—PF's image by being seen to take a firm stand on the issue. In mid-May Mugabe announced that the elections were to be held on 24–25 June. The MDC obtained a postponement at the High Court to the deadline for nominations until 3 June as ZANU—PF had been given exclusive access to the details of electoral constituency boundaries. The movement feared that the constituencies might have been altered to create more in rural areas where support for the ruling party was strong.

Prior to the elections, which duly took place on 24–25 June 2000, there were reports of violence towards observers, and a UN team, sent to co-ordinate the polls, was recalled following obstruction by the Government. The authorities also refused to permit the accreditation of some 200 foreign monitors. ZANU—PF secured 48.6% of the votes cast and won 62 of the 120 elective seats in the House of Assembly, the MDC received 47.0% of the ballot and 57 seats, while ZANU—Ndonga obtained one seat. Morgan Tsvangirai failed to win his constituency, as did the Ministers of Justice and Home Affairs. There were reports of widespread irregularities in the polls, which international observers declared to have not been free and fair. The MDC announced that it was to submit 10 dossiers listing alleged incidents of electoral fraud to the High Court. In total, the MDC challenged the results in 37 constituencies. In April 2001 the Court announced that results in two constituencies, including that contested by Tsvangirai, were to be nullified and new elections held; the MDC had previously abandoned proceedings relating to two other constituencies, and had been defeated in its challenge to the result in another. In June one more result was nullified, and one upheld.

Political unrest continued after the elections, with a general strike organized by the country's main trade unions in August 2000 being widely observed. Unrest at increases in food and fuel prices continued throughout 2000 and early 2001; the most notable incidents occurred in Harare in October, when police attempted to quell violent demonstrations against increased prices for food and public transport.

In September 2000 the editors of two state-owned newspapers were dismissed, reportedly in connection with falling sales. In October the Government announced an amnesty for all people accused of politically motivated crimes in January–July 2000. The printing presses of *The Daily News*, which was frequently critical of the Government, and whose sales had increased over the previous year, were severely damaged in an explosion in January 2001. The editor of the newspaper (who had alleged

that the security forces had conspired to kill him in 2000) and two journalists were charged with defamation in April, in connection with a report containing allegations of corruption against Mugabe and his associates.

In September 2000 Tsvangirai made a speech to a rally of the MDC in which he urged Mugabe to resign, allegedly predicting that if the President could not be removed by democratic means, the country risked a popular uprising that would remove him by force. In the same month a hand grenade damaged the headquarters of the MDC—the party blamed supporters of ZANU—PF. In October it was announced that Tsvangirai, who was out of the country, would be arrested and charged with incitement to treason upon his return. However, Tsvangirai was able to re-enter the country without attracting the attention of the security forces, and plans to detain him were delayed. The MDC subsequently proposed a motion attempting to impeach the President for misconduct and violations of the Constitution—the motion was unlikely to succeed, given the requirement for a two-thirds' majority in the National Assembly and ZANU—PF's majority in the chamber. In February 2001 Tsvangirai was charged with incitement to violence in connection with the speech. In May the High Court referred Tsvangirai's trial to the Supreme Court, accepting his argument that his constitutional right to free speech was material to the case. In November the Supreme Court withdrew the charges against him; following the ruling, however, the Government announced its intention to replace the Law and Order (Maintenance) Act, under which Tsvangirai had been charged, with a new public order bill, making it an offence to engender hostility to the President.

Shortly after the legislative elections, Mugabe announced that some 500 additional white-owned farms would be appropriated for resettlement. In December 2000 Mugabe declared that whites were the enemy of Zimbabwe; he was criticized by Western governments and by several African leaders. In the same month a court ruling upheld previous opinions that declared the appropriation of white-owned farms without compensation payments to be unlawful, and urged the Government to produce a feasible land-reform programme by June 2001; Mugabe announced that enough white-owned land had been appropriated for resettlement, but repeated his assertion that he would not accept court-imposed impediments to any further land-reform measures. Negotiations between the Government and farmers' representatives resumed in January 2001.

Zimbabwe's Chief Justice, Anthony Gubbay, announced in February 2001 that he would retire, some months ahead of schedule, in June, following allegations of government intimidation. However, he subsequently rescinded this announcement, and stated that he had no intention of retiring early. Following intensive negotiations, Gubbay agreed to retire with immediate effect in March, reportedly in exchange for an agreement by the Government not to seek reprisals against other judges who had opposed his actions. He was succeeded by Godfrey Chidyausiku, a former minister in the justice department, believed to be a close ally of Mugabe. In July 2001 the Government increased membership of the Supreme Court from five to eight judges; opposition groups suggested that the measure was taken in order to increase the number of judges who were sympathetic to the Government. (By April 2002, however, the number of judges was again five, owing to two resignations and the death of one sitting judge.)

In March 2001 the Commonwealth announced that it would send a delegation comprising the foreign ministers of Australia, Barbados and Nigeria to Zimbabwe for discussions with the Government. Mugabe refused to meet the delegation, however, claiming that the decision had been inspired by the United Kingdom. Similar criticisms were made of an attempt by the European Union (EU) to establish a dialogue with Zimbabwe regarding its record on human-rights issues. In April Mugabe dismissed speculation that he would resign and arrange a presidential election for July, by stating that he intended to contest the election in its scheduled time in 2002. In the same month various foreign diplomatic missions in Harare reported receiving threats from war veterans; the Government refused to guarantee the safety of diplomatic personnel if they 'became involved in local politics'. The leader of the veterans' movement, Chenjerai Hunzvi, denied that he had threatened any diplomatic staff or missions. In the same month the Minister of Industry and International Trade, Nkosana Moyo, resigned, stating that he believed Zimbabwe needed to alter its approach to its problems and advocating the formation of a government of national unity. Two cabinet ministers, Border Gezi and Moven

Mahachi, died in road accidents in mid-2001, prompting numerous unsubstantiated reports that their deaths had been brought about deliberately by rival members of ZANU—PF. Hunzvi died in early June; at his funeral, Mugabe urged war veterans to intensify the occupation of white-owned farms, and in the following days attacks against such farms throughout the country were reported to have increased, causing the death of at least one farm worker. The Zimbabwean Government criticized US and British media coverage of the events, and in mid-June it imposed severe restrictions on journalists visiting the country. Later that month the Government listed a further 2,030 farms for compulsory acquisition, and in early August Joseph Made, the Minister of Lands, Agriculture and Rural Development, gave a speech to the CFU, announcing the Government's intention to appropriate 8.3m. ha of commercial farmland. Further unrest occurred later that month in the north of the country, where approximately 100 white-owned farms were reported to have been evacuated following attacks by war veterans. Meanwhile, the ZCTU organized a two-day general strike in early July in protest at a recent increase in the price of fuel. A minor cabinet reshuffle was effected in August.

In early September 2001 a meeting of Commonwealth ministers, including the Zimbabwean Minister of Foreign Affairs, Stan Mudenge, was convened in Abuja, Nigeria, to discuss Mugabe's land resettlement programme; it was agreed that illegal farm seizures would cease and that international donors would compensate white farmers for the distribution of their land to landless black families. The agreement was broadly supported by both ZANU—PF and the MDC. The Government and the CFU held talks on the Abuja agreement throughout September. However, by the end of the month more than 20 new farm invasions were reported to have taken place, resulting in several deaths, and the talks collapsed. Mugabe's intention to disregard the terms of the Abuja agreement became apparent in early October, when he ordered the Supreme Court to recognize the land reform programme as legal, reversing the ruling of December 2000; widespread criticism was directed at the Government for its manipulation of the judiciary. Commonwealth ministers and officials visited Zimbabwe later in October 2001 to monitor the Government's adherence to the Abuja agreement, but failed to persuade the Government to comply with its terms. Government repression intensified in November, when it amended the Land Act by decree. According to the revised legislation, any farm issued with a 'notice of acquisition' would become the property of the state with immediate effect; previously, a farm owner had been served 90 days' notice to leave his land. Meanwhile, the body of a senior war veteran, Cain Nkala, was discovered near Bulawayo; two members of the MDC were detained on suspicion of his murder, and violent confrontations were reported when members of ZANU—PF and war veterans descended on the town. Nkala was given a state funeral, at which Mugabe alleged that the British Government was implicated in the death.

In November 2001 the Government ordered *The Daily News* to close its offices, alleging financial irregularities; it was widely believed, however, that the measure was taken to suppress criticism of the Government. The editor of that newspaper was charged with false reporting and undermining the Government in October 2002, under the Public Order and Security Act (see below), and resigned in December. Meanwhile, also in November 2001, the Government announced plans to make the carrying of national identity cards mandatory. In December Mugabe was nominated as the presidential candidate of ZANU—PF and announced that the election would take place in March 2002; Tsvangirai was arrested twice in December on charges of possessing unlicensed radio equipment, but was released shortly afterwards on both occasions.

International concern about the situation in Zimbabwe intensified at the end of 2001. South African President Thabo Mbeki expressed doubts about whether conditions were suitable for a free and fair election, and the Commonwealth Ministerial Action Group, meeting in London, United Kingdom, in late December, warned the Zimbabwean Government that it risked suspension from the organization unless it ended violent land seizures and political intimidation of the media and opposition groups. Meanwhile, the US Congress approved legislation offering aid and economic incentives to Zimbabwe, on condition that its Government act to create an equitable land reform programme. Despite Zimbabwe's growing isolation in the international community, in January 2002 further controversial legislation, aimed at suppressing opposition to Mugabe, was introduced: the Public

Order and Security Bill prohibited the publication of documents that incited public disorder or undermined the security services, and banned public gatherings that incited rioting; the General Laws Amendment Bill prohibited foreign and independent missions from monitoring the elections, and forbade voter education (the Bill was repealed by the Supreme Court in February, following a challenge from the MDC); and the Access to Information Bill made it an offence for foreign news services to report from Zimbabwe unless they were authorized by the Zimbabwean Government. The EU finally imposed so-called 'smart' sanctions on Zimbabwe in mid-February, after the leader of its electoral observer mission was expelled from the country. (Mugabe had previously attempted to ban certain EU member states, including the United Kingdom, from participating in the mission.) The sanctions included an embargo on the sale of arms to Zimbabwe, the suspension of €128m. worth of aid scheduled to be disbursed during 2002–07, and the freezing of the assets of 19 Zimbabwean officials, including Mugabe, who were also prohibited from visiting any EU state; the USA imposed similar measures several days later. In July the EU applied the sanctions to a further 53 people, including all cabinet members and certain senior officials of ZANU—PF. The EU extended sanctions for a further 12 months in February 2003, although Mugabe attended the Franco-African summit in Paris, France, later that month. The USA also extended its sanctions to more than 70 senior officials in March.

Meanwhile, in late February 2002 Tsvangirai and two other senior members of the MDC were arrested and charged with treason for allegedly plotting to assassinate Mugabe, after an Australian television network broadcast footage that purportedly showed Tsvangirai suggesting the possibility of 'eliminating' Mugabe. (The three men appeared in court in mid-March and were released on bail.) Intimidation of the MDC and election observers occurred across the country during the election campaign. Several members of the MDC were reported to have been killed, and in February police-officers fired at a convoy carrying Tsvangirai near Masvingo in the south-east of the country, while the headquarters of the MDC in Harare were attacked by militant Mugabe supporters.

The presidential election took place on 9–10 March 2002, but voting was extended to 11 March by the High Court, in response to a request from the MDC, which had claimed that the number of polling stations in areas with strong MDC support was inadequate, and that certain stations had closed on 10 March before many people had been able to vote. Mugabe was declared the winner on 13 March, with 56.2% of the valid votes cast; Tsvangirai secured 42.0%. Independent observers were divided in their judgement of whether the election was free and fair; most observers from African countries declared the election result legitimate, while the Norwegian delegation (the only European representatives) and independent Zimbabwean observers condemned the result and reported widespread electoral fraud and intimidation of the electorate and of observers by members of ZANU—PF. The MDC claimed that a number of its agents had been abducted from certain polling stations and detained by the police.

Prior to the presidential election the Commonwealth had nominated the Nigerian President, Olusegun Obasanjo, President Mbeki and the Australian Prime Minister, John Howard, to consider the conduct of the election and to formulate the organization's response. Mbeki and Obasanjo visited Zimbabwe following the election and urged Mugabe and the MDC to form a government of national unity; however, the MDC refused to co-operate unless the election was held again. The Commonwealth suspended Zimbabwe from meetings of the organization for one year in mid-March, stating that the election result had been undermined by politically motivated violence and that conditions did not permit the free will of the electorate to be expressed. (The suspension was extended for a further nine months in March 2003, pending consideration by the next summit of Commonwealth heads of government, scheduled to be held in December, in Abuja, Nigeria.) Meanwhile, the ZCTU organized a three-day general strike in protest at the election result, although participation was low. Immediately after the election the Government enacted the Access to Information and Protection of Privacy Act, which required all journalists reporting in Zimbabwe to be approved by the state; seven journalists had been detained under the Act by early May. In April the NCA organized demonstrations in support of demands for a new constitution and a rerun of the presidential election, at which more than 80 demonstrators were arrested. Violence directed at supporters of the MDC intensified following the election, allegedly committed by ZANU—PF supporters, and more than 50 people were reported to have been killed between the election and the end of April.

Land seizures also escalated, and in late March 2002 the Government listed almost 400 white-owned farms for compulsory acquisition, bringing the total land area scheduled for redistribution to the black population to around 85% of total commercial farmland. In June Mugabe issued an order listing some 2,900 white-owned farms for seizure; farmers were obliged to cease working their land on 25 June, or face up to two years' imprisonment, and to leave their properties by early August. Some 860 farmers had vacated their properties by the deadline, while 1,700 refused to leave. (Some 300 had left their farms temporarily to avoid confrontation.) In a speech in mid-August Mugabe stated that white farmers who were 'loyal' to the Government had the option of staying, although later that month it was reported that almost 200 farmers had been arrested for refusing to leave their properties, while others had gone into hiding. In September the Land Acquisition Act was amended to allow the eviction of white farmers within seven days, as opposed to the 90 days previously required.

In April 2002 ZANU—PF and the MDC engaged in talks in an effort to end the political crisis, but negotiations collapsed in the following month, when ZANU—PF withdrew, citing the MDC's petition to the High Court, seeking to overturn the election results, which ZANU—PF regarded as unlawful. In August Mugabe dissolved his Cabinet and appointed a new Government a few days later, retaining many ministers from the previous administration, although the Minister of Finance and Economic Development, Simba Makoni, who had urged restraint in land seizures, was replaced. Mugabe's failure to appoint a new Cabinet immediately following the election, as prescribed by the Constitution, had been condemned by domestic and international observers. In January 2003 Mugabe dismissed rumours that the Speaker of the National Assembly, Emmerson Mnangagwa, and the Head of the Armed Forces, Gen. Vitalis Zvinavashe, had offered his resignation to the MDC in exchange for the creation of a government of national unity. In the following month the trial of Tsvangirai and two other senior MDC officials for plotting to assassinate Mugabe (see above) began in Harare, but was adjourned until May. In March the MDC led a 'mass action' against the Government, aimed at forcing it to repeal what the party called repressive legislation and to release political prisoners, which resulted in the closure of a large number of factories and businesses throughout the country over two days; the Government claimed that the MDC had detonated bombs in Kadoma, south-west of Harare, and it was reported that up to 500 members of the opposition had been arrested and many more driven from their homes and beaten.

Zimbabwe severed diplomatic relations with South Africa in September 1980 and subsequently played an important role in international attempts to stabilize southern Africa and to end apartheid in South Africa. In July 1987 the Cabinet rejected a proposal by Mugabe to impose sanctions against South Africa, and the Government opted instead for less stringent economic measures. South Africa is believed to have been responsible for intermittent attacks during the 1980s against the then banned African National Congress of South Africa (ANC) in Zimbabwe. A meeting between President Mugabe and a South African government official in April 1991 (following the implementation of a programme of political reforms by President F. W. de Klerk of South Africa in February 1990) constituted the first direct contact between the Zimbabwean and South African Governments since 1980. The two countries re-established diplomatic relations following the holding of the first democratic elections in South Africa in April 1994, and in March 1997 a mutual defence co-operation agreement was concluded. Relations deteriorated in 1998 owing to South Africa's opposition to Zimbabwe's military intervention in the civil war in the DRC (see below). Relations were also strained from 1999, owing to Zimbabwe's increasingly negative economic and political circumstances (see above). In February 2000 South Africa denied reports that it had offered a substantial loan to Zimbabwe to help the country to resolve its financial crisis. However, President Mbeki offered to negotiate on Zimbabwe's behalf with the IMF and the World Bank for emergency aid to prevent the collapse of the economy. By May the increasingly turbulent land reform situation in Zimbabwe had adversely affected South Africa's economy, prompting Mbeki to appeal to foreign donors to fund the transfer of white-owned land to black farmers.

Zimbabwe and South Africa are members of the Southern African Development Community (SADC, see p. 311). However, at a meeting in December 1996 Zimbabwe, together with Malawi, Mozambique and Zambia (also SADC members), formally agreed to establish the Beira Development Corridor, in an effort to develop an alternative trade route to that via South African ports. Zimbabwe was a member of the troika (with Botswana and South Africa) that mediated in the conflict in Lesotho throughout mid-to-late-1998 following elections in May (see chapter on Lesotho). In November 1999 Zimbabwe denied reports that Zimbabwean troops were fighting alongside the Angolan army in that country's civil war.

During the 1980s and early 1990s Zimbabwe provided support to the Mozambican Government against Renamo rebels; in late 1992–early 1993, under the terms of the peace agreement in Mozambique (q.v.), Zimbabwean troops, who had been stationed in Mozambique since 1982, were withdrawn. During the mid-1990s a group of armed Zimbabwean dissidents, known as the Chimwenjes, were reportedly active in western Mozambique (see above). In January 1996 the Mozambican Government announced its intention to expel the rebels, and in January 1997 an accord was signed by representatives of Mozambique and Zimbabwe on the co-ordination of activities against the rebels. Plans for the repatriation of some 145,000 Mozambican refugees were announced in March 1993; this scheme, co-ordinated by the office of the UN High Commissioner for Refugees, was completed by May 1995. In June 1999 Mozambique expressed its displeasure after Zimbabwe forcibly repatriated some 100 Mozambicans without informing their local authorities.

Meanwhile, following an SADC summit in Harare in August 1998, the Zimbabwe Government dispatched troops and arms to the DRC to support the regime of President Laurent-Désiré Kabila against advancing rebel forces. Despite repeated summits attempting to find a peaceful solution to the conflict, by May 1999 it was reported that Zimbabwe had spent at least \$500m. on the continuing unpopular military action. In December 1998 a poll found that 70% of Zimbabweans were opposed to the deployment of the army in the DRC, which placed considerable strain on Zimbabwe's financial and military resources. In mid-1999 all armed forces were put on stand-by and retirements and resignations were banned in an attempt to keep the ranks at full strength. A cease-fire agreement was signed at Lusaka, Zambia, on 10 July and troop withdrawals were to follow within the next few months. However, a few days later, both the rebels and the allies of the DRC were accused of violating the accord. An SADC military commission was formed later that month to monitor the cease-fire. In late September the first observers arrived in the DRC. The cease-fire was in danger of collapse in December as fierce fighting continued. The Zimbabwe and DRC Governments unveiled a plan in September to establish a joint diamond and gold marketing venture to finance the war. However, in early 2000 the Zimbabwean Government was reportedly unable to pay allowances to its troops fighting in the region owing to the critical shortage of foreign currency (see above). Public opinion was further turned against the continuation of the conflict in February when heavy rains and a cyclone struck Mozambique and neighbouring provinces of eastern Zimbabwe. There was a desperate shortage of helicopters, which were needed to bring aid to those affected, owing to their deployment in the DRC. The war also caused tensions between Zimbabwe and the IMF, the latter suspending assistance partly because of Zimbabwe's false accounting of expenses relating to the conflict. In March Congolese rebels breached the cease-fire, capturing a town in the eastern DRC, and continued to advance westwards.

In August 2000 a further conference was held in Lusaka, at which all the governments involved reiterated their support for the accord agreed at the previous meeting; President Kabila subsequently stated that he had no confidence in the process, however. Kabila was assassinated in January 2001 and was succeeded by his son, Joseph. Efforts to agree a solution to the conflict increased, and all countries involved in the conflict agreed to withdraw their forces by May, pending the deployment of a UN force. Nevertheless, in April 2002 the Zimbabwean army announced that some 6,000–7,000 of its troops remained in the DRC, from an initial deployment of around 11,000. However, following a number of positive developments in the peace process, the last Zimbabwean troops withdrew from the DRC in October.

Relations with the United Kingdom centred on land reform in 1999–2001. In November 1999, while on a private visit to

London, Mugabe was assaulted by protesters in support of homosexual rights. The President subsequently alleged at a Commonwealth summit that the British Government had organized the incident to register its disapproval of plans to redistribute land (see above), and declared Prime Minister Tony Blair unfit to govern. Mugabe's anger had been aroused by a speech by Blair criticizing certain African countries' inactivity concerning AIDS. Mugabe repeated his allegations in an outburst in March 2000, also accusing the United Kingdom of orchestrating an international hate campaign against Zimbabwe.

In January 2000 the Blair administration was strongly criticized for selling arms to Zimbabwe in light of the latter's abuses of human rights. The British Government cited contractual obligations. Arms exports were suspended a few months later, as the seizures of farmland became excessively aggressive (see above). Meanwhile, in early April the two sides took part in talks about land reform. Further negotiations later that month followed Zimbabwe's decision that the United Kingdom should pay compensation to white farmers for their land. The 'former colonial power' offered aid towards resettlement, but not in the form of compensation. It also stipulated conditions for its release: illegal farm seizures and political violence must stop, free and fair elections must be held and only the black rural poor should receive redistributed land (there had been reports that thus far close allies of Mugabe had been the principal beneficiaries). The Zimbabwean Government rejected these terms. Meanwhile, relations deteriorated sharply over a diplomatic incident in March concerning the opening of British diplomatic baggage at Harare airport, which resulted in the British Government briefly recalling its High Commissioner to London. Zimbabwe countered by condemning the United Kingdom for smuggling goods into the country.

Relations between the United Kingdom and Zimbabwe remained strained throughout 2000 and deteriorated further in February 2001, when an official at the British Embassy was accused of obstructing the investigation into the activities of a British journalist, who was subsequently expelled from the country. In March a British homosexual-rights activist attempted to 'detain' Mugabe on a visit to Europe and was restrained by presidential guards. Mugabe subsequently accused the activist of being sponsored by the British Government and repeated his demand for the United Kingdom to cease 'interference' in the affairs of Zimbabwe. In September 2002, at the UN World Summit on Sustainable Development in South Africa, tensions increased when Mugabe criticized Blair for his part in imposing EU sanctions on Zimbabwe and for interfering in the country's domestic politics; later that month the Government informed British diplomats that they could not leave Harare without permission from the Ministry of Foreign Affairs. In November Mugabe imposed a ban on senior British officials, including Blair, from travelling to Zimbabwe; the measure was taken in response to the United Kingdom's introduction of a requirement for Zimbabwean nationals to apply for a visa in order to visit that country.

Government

Under the terms of the 1980 Constitution (as subsequently amended), legislative power is vested in a unicameral Parliament, consisting of a House of Assembly, which comprises 150 members, of whom 120 are directly elected by universal adult suffrage, 20 are nominated by the President, 10 are traditional Chiefs and eight are provincial governors. Members of the House of Assembly serve for six years. Executive authority is vested in the President, elected by Parliament for six years. The President appoints, and acts on the advice of, a Cabinet, which comprises two Vice-Presidents and other Ministers and Deputy Ministers. The Cabinet must have the confidence of Parliament, to which it is responsible.

Defence

Total armed forces numbered about 36,000 in August 2002: 32,000 in the army and 4,000 in the air force. Paramilitary forces comprise a police force of 19,500 and a police support unit of 2,300. Defence expenditure was budgeted at Z.$35,000m. for 2002.

Economic Affairs

In 2001, according to the World Bank, Zimbabwe's gross national income (GNI), measured at average 1999–2001 prices, was US $6,164m., equivalent to $480 per head (or $2,340 per head on an international purchasing-power parity basis).

During 1990–2001, it was estimated, the population increased at an average annual rate of 2.1%, while gross domestic product (GDP) per head decreased, in real terms, by an average of 1.4% per year. Overall GDP increased, in real terms, at an average annual rate of 0.6% in 1990–2001; GDP declined by 8.4% in 2001.

Agriculture (including forestry and fishing) contributed 17.6% of GDP and employed 61.9% of the employed labour force in 2001. The principal cash crops are tobacco (which accounted for an estimated 25% of export earnings in 1998), maize, cotton, coffee and sugar. Exports of horticultural produce are expanding rapidly. In addition, wheat, soybeans and groundnuts are cultivated. Beef production is an important activity. Production of tobacco and maize was severely affected by the farm invasions that took place from the late 1990s (see Recent History). During 1990–2001 agricultural GDP increased by an average of 1.7% per year. Agricultural GDP grew by 3.0% in 2000, but decreased by 12.0% in 2001.

Industry (including mining, manufacturing, construction and power) contributed 24.4% of GDP in 2001, and engaged 11.7% of the employed labour force in 1999. During 1990–2001 industrial GDP decreased at an average annual rate of 1.6%. Industrial GDP declined by 9.8% in 2001.

Mining contributed 1.8% of GDP and engaged 1.1% of the employed labour force in 1999. Gold, nickel and asbestos are the major mineral exports. Chromium ore, copper, silver, emeralds, lithium, tin, iron ore, cobalt, magnesite, niobium, tantalum, limestone, phosphate rock, coal and diamonds are also mined. In October 1999 the discovery of significant diamond deposits in Zimbabwe was announced; in December 2000 the development of the site of one such deposit, at Murowa, was announced. Mining of platinum ore at Hartley in central Zimbabwe began in March 1996, reaching full production in June 1997; further platinum deposits are being developed. In June 1999, however, the Hartley Platinum Project was abandoned owing to viability and geological problems. In March 2001 it was announced that a share in the Hartley venture had been sold to a South African company and that the site's viability was under review. In addition, Zimbabwe has large reserves of kyanite and smaller reserves of zinc and lead. Mining GDP declined by an estimated 11.0% in 2000.

Manufacturing contributed 13.9% of GDP in 2001, and engaged 8.1% of the employed labour force in 1999. The most important sectors, measured by gross value of output, are food-processing, metals (mainly ferrochrome and steel), chemicals and textiles. During 1990–2001 manufacturing GDP decreased by an average of 2.7% per year. Manufacturing GDP declined by 19.0% in 2001.

In 1999 58.4% of Zimbabwe's electricity production was derived from coal, and 41.6% from hydroelectric power. In 1998 a new project was introduced to supply electricity to villages by solar energy systems, funded by Italy. The Italian Government cancelled the project in September 1999, however, owing to Zimbabwe's political and economic difficulties. Imports of mineral fuels and lubricants comprised 18.4% of the value of total imports in 2000. In 1999 Zimbabwe purchased 40% of its energy from neighbouring countries.

The services sector contributed 57.9% of GDP in 2001, and engaged 28.3% of the employed labour force in 1999. During 1990–2001 the GDP of the services sector increased at an average annual rate of 1.8%. Services GDP declined by 5.3% in 2001.

In 2000 Zimbabwe had a visible trade surplus of US $272m., while there was a deficit of $101m. on the current account of the balance of payments. South Africa was the principal source of imports in 2000 (38.3%), and, together with the other countries of the Southern African Customs Union (Botswana, Lesotho, Namibia and Swaziland), was the principal market for exports in 1999 (16.0%). Other major trading partners in 2000 were the USA, Germany, Japan and the People's Republic of China. The principal exports in 2000 were tobacco and basic manufactures. The main imports were machinery and transport equipment, mineral fuels and lubricants, chemicals and basic manufactures.

In 2000 there was a budgetary deficit of Z.$67,143m., equivalent to 20.3% of GDP. At the end of 2000 Zimbabwe's external debt totalled US $4,002m., of which $2,948m. was long-term public debt. In that year the cost of debt-servicing was equivalent to 22.1% of the value of exports of goods and services. The rate of inflation averaged 41.6% annually in 1995–2001. Consumer prices increased by an average of 72.0% in 2001.

According to official figures, 6.0% of the total labour force was unemployed in 1999, although the actual percentage was believed to be significantly greater.

Zimbabwe is a member of the Southern African Development Community (see p. 311), which aims to promote closer economic integration among its members, and also belongs to the Common Market for Eastern and Southern Africa (see p. 162).

Zimbabwe has benefited from a well-developed infrastructure, mineral wealth and a highly diversified manufacturing sector. However, in 1999–2002 Zimbabwe suffered its worst economic crisis since 1980. The budget deficit increased, while losses accumulated by state enterprises caused a huge, unbudgeted debt burden. Foreign reserves were at a critically low level. Business and investor confidence fell as a result of Zimbabwe's financial and political problems, notably the issue of enforced land redistribution (see Recent History). International aid was suspended during the latter months of 1999, owing to Zimbabwe's inability to comply with requirements for economic reform. A series of fuel and food crises and ensuing protests contributed to political instability. In April 2000 a number of white farmers refused to participate in the annual tobacco auctions, which were desperately needed to increase Zimbabwe's foreign exchange reserves, until there was a substantial devaluation of the currency. Several banks agreed with their demands. The Government, however, feared that such a move would generally be unpopular and resisted until after its re-election in June—the Zimbabwean dollar was devalued twice in August, by a combined total of over one-quarter. Revenue was also lost by the burning of the tobacco crop on some white-owned farms that had been forcibly occupied, although volumes increased in the tobacco auctions held in late 2000, and prices deteriorated less than had been predicted. In March 2001 the IMF announced that it would not lift its aid suspension; the World Bank had suspended aid in October 2000, and several Western donor Governments suspended payments in 2000–01, in protest at the breakdown of law and order. The IMF removed Zimbabwe from the list of countries eligible to borrow resources under the Poverty Reduction and Growth Facility in September 2001, in response to Zimbabwe's failure to make debt repayments. Political events continued to dominate the economic outlook in 2001–02, as foreign investment remained minimal, domestic and external debt increased, and the shortage of foreign currency grew more significant. In March 2001 the Government obliged one-quarter of all export earnings to be paid into the central bank, in an attempt to improve the country's foreign-currency position; the Government increased the proportion to two-fifths of earnings in June, and to one-half of earnings in November 2002. The shortage of foreign exchange and the weakening of the currency led to a large increase in the price of fuel and public transport in 2001, and measures to prevent rising food costs were opposed by manufacturers. The UN World Food Programme appealed to international donors for emergency supplies to feed more than 500,000 rural Zimbabweans in February 2002, and predicted that food shortages would intensify. However, the maize crop in 2002–03 was better than expected, and the shortfall was expected to be met with imports, although the tobacco crop was forecast to fall by over one-third in 2003, largely as a result of farm occupations. The suspension of aid to Zimbabwe by the international community, the ongoing agricultural crisis caused by the land reform programme, and increasing debt and inflation, exacerbated by Mugabe's refusal to implement policies to stabilize the situation, led some observers to predict widespread civil unrest in Zimbabwe in 2002. Furthermore, the IMF suspended technical assistance in that year, as Zimbabwe had failed to co-operate in meeting its financial obligations. The budget for 2003 provided a bleak outlook for the Zimbabwean economy: GDP was forecast to contract by 11.9% in 2002, and by a further 7.2% in 2003. The Government predicted that the rate of inflation would fall to 96% in 2003 from a peak of 144% in October 2002, although the IMF expected it to exceed 500%. It was reported that the Government had partially devalued the Zimbabwean dollar by 93% in February 2003, pegging the currency for exporters' earnings at Z.$800 = US $1 (although the official exchange rate for other transactions was to remain unchanged, at Z.$55 = US $1).

Education

Primary education, which begins at six years of age and lasts for seven years, has been compulsory since 1987. Secondary education begins at the age of 13 and lasts for six years. In 1999/2000 enrolment at primary schools included 80.2% of children in the relevant age-group (males 79.9%; females 80.5%), while the comparable ratio for secondary enrolment was 42.3% (males 44.4%; females 40.2%). In 1998 some 11,451 students were attending universities, while 36,830 students were enrolled at institutions of higher education. There are two state-run universities, the University of Zimbabwe, which is located in Harare, and the University of Science and Technology, at Bulawayo. There are also two private universities, Africa University in Mutare and Solusi University in Figtree. Education received about 17% of total expenditure by the central Government in the budget for 1999; projected expenditure on education was reported to be 14.9% of the total in 2001.

Public Holidays

2003: 1 January (New Year's Day), 18 April (Independence Day), 18–21 April (Easter), 1 May (Workers' Day), 25 May (Africa Day, anniversary of OAU's foundation), 11 August (Heroes' Day), 12 August (Defence Forces National Day), 22 December (National Unity Day), 25–26 December (Christmas).

2004: 1 January (New Year's Day), 9–12 April (Easter), 18 April (Independence Day), 1 May (Workers' Day), 25 May (Africa Day, anniversary of OAU's foundation), 11 August (Heroes' Day), 12 August (Defence Forces National Day), 22 December (National Unity Day), 25–26 December (Christmas).

Weights and Measures

The metric system is in use.

Statistical Survey

Source (unless otherwise stated): Central Statistical Office, Kaguvi Bldg, Fourth St, POB CY 342, Causeway, Harare; tel. (4) 706681; fax (4) 728529.

Area and Population

AREA, POPULATION AND DENSITY

Area (sq km)	390,757*
Population (census results)	
18 August 1992	10,412,548
18 August 1997	
Males	5,647,090
Females	6,142,184
Total	11,789,274
Density (per sq km) at August 1997	30.2

* 150,872 sq miles.

PRINCIPAL TOWNS
(population at census of August 1992)

Harare (capital) . .	1,189,103		Masvingo	51,743
Bulawayo . . .	621,742		Chinhoyi (Sinoia) .	43,054
Chitungwiza . . .	274,912		Hwange (Wankie) .	42,581
Mutare (Umtali) . .	131,367		Marondera	
			(Marandellas) . .	39,384
Gweru (Gwelo) . .	128,037		Zvishavane	
			(Shabani)	32,984
Kwekwe (Que Que) .	75,425		Redcliff	29,959
Kadoma (Gatooma) .	67,750			

Mid-2001 (UN projection, incl. suburbs): Harare 1,868,000 (Source: UN, *World Urbanization Prospects: The 2001 Revision*).

BIRTHS AND DEATHS
(UN estimates, annual averages)

	1985–90	1990–95	1995–2000
Birth rate (per 1,000)	42.4	40.7	37.4
Death rate (per 1,000)	10.7	14.6	18.0

Source: UN, *World Population Prospects: The 2000 Revision*.

Expectation of life (WHO estimates, years at birth): 36.8 (males 37.1; females 36.5) in 2001 (Source: WHO, *World Health Report*).

ECONOMICALLY ACTIVE POPULATION
(sample survey, persons aged 15 years and over, 1999)

	Males	Females	Total
Agriculture, hunting, forestry and fishing	1,215,661	1,584,839	2,800,500
Mining and quarrying	46,946	3,367	50,313
Manufacturing	283,090	94,667	377,757
Electricity, gas and water . . .	10,158	n.a.	10,158
Construction	98,908	6,659	105,567
Trade, restaurants and hotels . .	154,198	178,341	332,539
Transport, storage and communications	93,289	8,288	101,577
Financing, insurance, real estate and business services	100,425	20,749	121,174
Community, social and personal services	320,020	258,505	578,525
Activities not adequately defined .	63,052	124,286	187,338
Total employed	2,385,747	2,279,701	4,665,448
Unemployed	187,142	110,669	297,811
Total labour force	2,572,889	2,390,370	4,963,259

Mid-2001 (FAO estimates, '000 persons): Agriculture, etc. 3,559; Total labour force 5,749 (Source: FAO).

Health and Welfare

KEY INDICATORS

Total fertility rate (children per woman, 2001)	4.7
Under-5 mortality rate (per 1,000 live births, 2001) . . .	123
HIV/AIDS (% of persons aged 15–49, 2001)	33.73
Physicians (per 1,000 head, 1995)	0.14
Hospital beds (per 1,000 head, 1990)	0.51
Health expenditure (2000): US $ per head (PPP)	171
Health expenditure (2000): % of GDP	7.3
Health expenditure (2000): public (% of total)	62.1
Access to water (% of persons, 2000)	85
Access to sanitation (% of persons, 2000)	68
Human Development Index (2000): ranking	128
Human Development Index (2000): value	0.551

For sources and definitions, see explanatory note on p. vi.

Agriculture

PRINCIPAL CROPS
('000 metric tons)

	1999	2000	2001
Wheat	320	250	275*
Barley	8*	8	10*
Maize	1,520	2,108	1,467
Millet	53	43	43
Sorghum	86	103	103*
Potatoes*	30	31	31
Cassava (Manioc)*	170	175	175
Dry beans*	46	49	49
Sugar cane	4,657†	4,228	4,100*
Soybeans (Soya beans) . . .	107	144	175
Groundnuts (in shell) . . .	113	191	172
Sunflower seed	30†	16	32
Vegetables (incl. melons)* . .	150	147	147
Oranges*	76	80	80
Other citrus fruits* . . .	24	26	27
Bananas*	82	85	85
Coffee (green)	10	9	8†
Tea (made)†	19	22	22
Tobacco (leaves)	193	228	196
Cotton (lint)	104	128	128†

* FAO estimate(s).
† Unofficial figure(s).

Source: FAO.

LIVESTOCK
('000 head, year ending September)

	1999	2000	2001
Horses*	26	26	26
Asses*	106	107	107
Cattle	6,069	5,700*	5,700*
Sheep	640	630*	535*
Pigs	279	600*	604†
Goats	2,910	2,950*	2,970*
Chickens*	15,500	17,500	20,000

* FAO estimate(s).
† Unofficial figure.

Source: FAO.

LIVESTOCK PRODUCTS
(FAO estimates, '000 metric tons)

	1999	2000	2001*
Beef and veal	95	101	101
Goat meat*	13	13	13
Pig meat	13	13	25
Poultry meat*	24	25	27
Other meat	26	27	27
Cows' milk	300	310*	310
Butter*	2	2	2
Cheese*	2	2	2
Poultry eggs*	20	22	22
Cattle hides*	9	9	9

* FAO estimate(s).
Source: FAO.

Forestry

ROUNDWOOD REMOVALS
('000 cubic metres, excl. bark)

	1999	2000	2001
Sawlogs, veneer logs and logs for sleepers	931	773	786
Pulpwood	94	93	94
Other industrial wood . . .	1,137	978	992
Fuel wood	8,115	8,115*	8,115*
Total	10,277	9,959*	9,987*

* FAO estimate.
Source: FAO.

SAWNWOOD PRODUCTION
('000 cubic metres, incl. railway sleepers)

	1999	2000	2001
Coniferous (softwood) . . .	395	343	354
Broadleaved (hardwood). . .	43	43*	43*
Total	438	386	397

* FAO estimate.

Source: FAO.

Fishing

('000 metric tons, live weight)

	1998	1999	2000
Capture	16.4	12.4	13.1
Tilapias	0.4	0.4	0.8
Other freshwater fishes . .	0.7	0.8	1.8
Dagaas	15.3	11.2	10.5
Aquaculture	0.2*	0.2	0.2*
Total catch	16.6*	12.6	13.3*

* FAO estimate.

Source: FAO, *Yearbook of Fishery Statistics.*

Mining

('000 metric tons, unless otherwise indicated)

	1998	1999	2000
Asbestos	123	88	152
Chromium ore	605	653	668
Clay	136	n.a.	n.a.
Coal	5,467	4,977	3,986
Cobalt ore (metric tons)* . .	137	131	79
Copper ore*	4	5	1
Gold (kilograms)* . . .	25,175	27,114	22,007
Iron ore†	372	599	438
Limestone	1,473	1,550	1,979
Magnesite (metric tons) . .	4,321	5,356	4,029
Nickel ore (metric tons)* . .	12,872	9,594	5,968
Phosphate rock† . . .	91	85	78
Silver (kilograms)* . . .	6,681	5,396	3,799
Tin ore (metric tons)* . .	1	—	—

* Figures refer to the metal content of ores and concentrates.

† Figures refer to gross weight. The estimated metal content of iron ore is 50%. The phosphoric acid content of phosphate rock (in '000 metric tons) was: 29 in 1998.

Industry

SELECTED PRODUCTS
('000 metric tons, unless otherwise indicated)

	1995	1996	1997
Raw sugar*	511	337	602
Coke	467	493	540
Cement	948	996	954
Pig-iron‡	209	210	210
Ferro-chromium‡ . . .	212	243	233
Crude steel‡	210	212	240
Refined copper—unwrought† ‡ . .	13.1	20.1	18.8
Nickel—unwrought (metric tons) .	10,863	9,695‡	10,863
Electric energy (million kWh)‖ . .	8,017†	7,819†	7,830

2000 ('000 metric tons, unless otherwise stated): Raw sugar 585*; Ferro-chromium‡ 246; Crude steel‡ 269; Refined copper—unwrought‡ 14; Nickel—unwrought† (metric tons) 8,160.

* Data from the FAO.

† Estimate(s).

‡ Data from the US Geological Survey.

‖ Net production.

Source: mainly UN, *Industrial Commodity Statistics Yearbook.*

Finance

CURRENCY AND EXCHANGE RATES

Monetary Units
100 cents = 1 Zimbabwe dollar (Z.$)

Sterling, US Dollar and Euro Equivalents (31 December 2002)
£1 sterling = Z.$88.71
US $1 = Z.$55.04
€1 = Z.$57.72
Z.$1,000 = £11.27 = US $18.17 = €17.33

Average Exchange Rate (US $ per Zimbabwe dollar)
2000   0.0231
2001   0.0182
2002   0.0182

BUDGET
(Z.$ million, year ending 30 June)

Revenue*	1997/98†	1999‡	2000
Taxation	52,480	55,569	82,275
Taxes on income and profits . .	27,728	29,670	52,189
Personal income . . .	19,491	19,559	35,876
Business profits . . .	5,904	6,772	9,554
Customs duties . . .	8,875	8,507	8,543
Excise duties . . .	2,331	2,926	4,092
Sales tax	11,735	12,340	15,743
Other revenue . . .	4,245	2,995	5,550
Entrepreneurial and property income . .	1,103	528	1,250
Parastatal interest and dividends . . .	825	445	1,135
Total	56,725	58,564	87,825

Expenditure§	1997/98†	1999‡	2000
Recurrent	65,696	72,157	149,353
Goods and services . .	35,072	40,238	74,292
Salaries, wages and allowances	25,450	28,153	54,837
Subsistence and transport . .	939	1,250	2,243
Incidental expenses . .	1,754	2,263	3,665
Other recurrent expenditure .	6,929	8,572	13,547
Transfers: . . .	30,624	31,919	75,061
Interest payments . .	17,699	21,471	55,400
Subsidies and transfers . .	12,925	10,448	19,661
Pensions	7,074	3,957	8,011
Capital	3,789	5,751	5,993
Total	69,485	77,908	155,346

* Excluding grants received (Z.$ million): 1,500 in 1997/98; 2,144 in 1999; 3,517 in 2000.

† Covering the period July 1997 to December 1998.

‡ From January 1999 the financial year corresponds to the calendar year.

§ Excluding lending minus repayments (Z.$ million): 1,200 in 1997/98; 2,469 in 1999; 3,139 in 2000.

Source: IMF, *Zimbabwe: Statistical Appendix* (June 2002).

INTERNATIONAL RESERVES
(US $ million at 31 December)

	2000	2001	2002
Gold*	45.4	27.5	22.7
IMF special drawing rights . .	0.2	—	
Reserve position in IMF . . .	0.4	0.4	0.4
Foreign exchange	192.5	64.3	82.9
Total	238.5	92.2	106.0

* Valued at a market-related price which is determined each month.

Source: IMF, *International Financial Statistics.*

MONEY SUPPLY
(Z.$ million at 31 December)

	1999	2000	2001
Currency outside banks . . .	7,256	9,943	25,642
Demand deposits at deposit money banks . . .	27,804	44,169	106,000
Total money (incl. others) . . .	35,473	54,396	132,093

Source: IMF, *International Financial Statistics.*

COST OF LIVING
(Consumer Price Index; base: 1995 = 100)

	1999	2000	2001
Food	349.4	520.4	833.6
Beverages and tobacco	320.0	524.2	838.9
Clothing and footwear	223.0	358.0	656.9
Rent, fuel and light	229.9	331.9	603.6
All items (incl. others)	301.3	469.6	807.5

NATIONAL ACCOUNTS
(Z.$ million at current prices)

Expenditure on the Gross National Product
(IMF estimates)

	1998	1999	2000
Government final consumption expenditure	23,761	32,025	80,371
Private final consumption expenditure	91,277	145,397	202,498
Increase in stocks	214	2,614	5,822
Gross fixed capital formation	30,590	31,280	45,560
Total domestic expenditure	145,842	211,316	334,251
Exports of goods and services	62,332	97,193	98,487
Less Imports of goods and services	64,814	98,100	102,393
GDP in purchasers' values	143,360	210,409	330,345

Source: IMF, *Zimbabwe: Statistical Appendix* (June 2002).

Gross Domestic Product by Economic Activity
(at factor cost)

	1997	1998	1999
Agriculture, hunting, forestry and fishing	17,042	27,135	35,812
Mining and quarrying	1,400	2,400	3,380
Manufacturing	16,208	20,708	30,538
Electricity and water	2,849	3,139	5,171
Construction	2,544	3,640	5,132
Trade, restaurants and hotels	17,163	22,652	36,261
Transport, storage and communications	5,192	6,712	11,373
Finance, insurance and real estate	9,797	15,679	26,917
Government services	13,640	16,916	22,913
Other services	5,320	6,806	8,273
Sub-total	91,155	125,762	185,770
Less Imputed bank service charges	1,149	1,242	1,357
Total	90,006	124,540	184,413

BALANCE OF PAYMENTS
(US $ million)

	1998	1999	2000
Exports of goods f.o.b.	1,925	1,924	1,791
Imports of goods f.o.b.	−2,020	−1,675	−1,520
Trade balance	−95	249	272
Exports of services	630	621	327
Imports of services	−670	−600	−436
Balance on goods and services	−135	270	163
Investment income (net)	−348	−357	−386
Balance on goods, services and income	−483	−87	−223
Private transfers (net)	128	115	122
Current balance	−355	28	−101
Official transfers (net)	77	101	53
Direct investment (net)	88	50	15
Portfolio investment (net)	11	21	−1
Long-term capital (net)	55	34	−238
Short-term capital (net)	−74	−216	−161
Net errors and omissions	41	0	249
Overall balance	−157	17	−184

Source: IMF, *Zimbabwe: Statistical Appendix* (June 2002).

External Trade

PRINCIPAL COMMODITIES
(distribution by SITC, Z.$'000, excl. stores and bunkers for aircraft)

Imports f.o.b.	1998	1999	2000
Food and live animals	2,917,889	3,915,497	2,621,388
Crude materials (inedible) except fuels	2,278,334	2,754,092	5,017,200
Mineral fuels, lubricants, etc. (incl. electricity)	10,541,459	11,844,855	14,789,458
Chemicals and related products	10,129,763	13,793,057	14,163,719
Basic manufactures	10,992,156	14,117,099	13,360,348
Machinery and transport equipment	22,620,633	28,520,371	23,511,396
Miscellaneous manufactured articles	4,424,665	5,306,680	4,369,886
Total (incl. others)	66,155,618	83,407,196	80,402,591

Exports f.o.b.	1998	1999	2000
Food and live animals	8,233,468	11,478,734	11,447,391
Beverages and tobacco	12,359,452	25,473,731	25,887,652
Crude materials (inedible) except fuels	7,709,872	11,269,773	15,837,440
Chemicals and related products	1,587,175	2,173,610	2,270,814
Basic manufactures	8,468,926	15,140,706	17,455,790
Miscellaneous manufactured articles	5,599,113	4,728,644	5,417,557
Total (incl. others)	46,317,038	73,844,904	81,352,344

PRINCIPAL TRADING PARTNERS*

Imports f.o.b. (Z.$'000)	1998	1999	2000
Australia	737,911	600,291	527,215
Belgium	657,375	1,156,977	1,102,495
Botswana	1,025,360	1,584,015	3,410,314
China, People's Repub.	1,238,415	1,526,088	1,459,298
France (incl. Monaco)	1,856,663	2,388,753	2,157,916
Germany	2,311,973	4,312,856	2,444,840
Hong Kong	537,949	884,152	919,574
India	856,580	1,219,039	839,180
Italy	1,272,769	917,022	1,028,792
Japan	2,958,989	3,346,239	3,302,060
Korea, Repub.	806,017	816,949	597,250
Mozambique	1,825,513	1,870,578	1,877,628
Netherlands	840,556	1,132,831	847,330
South Africa	25,500,255	33,761,192	30,773,742
Switzerland (incl. Liechtenstein)	712,145	1,157,878	941,760
Taiwan	687,806	756,512	727,215
United Kingdom	4,315,836	5,389,697	3,847,382
USA	3,592,318	3,818,991	4,785,660
Total (incl. others)	66,155,618	83,407,196	80,402,591

Exports f.o.b. (US $ '000)	1997	1999†	2000
Belgium-Luxembourg	57,600	n.a.	n.a.
China, People's Repub.	17,800	103,300	99,200
Czech Republic	11,900	7,800	10,100
France (incl. Monaco)	21,700	18,900	17,000
Germany	165,200	149,900	149,700
Greece	7,000	22,700	13,800
Hong Kong	21,700	2,300	2,500
Indonesia	24,800	24,100	13,500
Israel	14,100	4,500	n.a.
Italy	85,400	74,300	67,200
Japan	130,100	134,500	139,800
Malawi	79,100	72,900	48,300
Mozambique	71,100	62,600	37,400
Netherlands	71,800	65,500	62,700
Poland	20,500	15,200	7,400
Portugal	46,400	18,000	8,600
Russian Federation	12,800	15,600	20,900
SACU‡	354,400	301,400	n.a.
Spain	41,900	46,400	32,300
Switzerland (incl. Liechtenstein)	46,400	46,000	76,100
Thailand	24,100	20,000	48,300
United Kingdom	235,500	181,800	0
USA	122,900	109,800	0
Zambia	116,900	69,000	82,800
Total (incl. others)	2,127,700	1,887,200	1,925,000

* Imports by country of production; exports by country of last consignment.
† Figures for 1998 unavailable.
‡ Southern African Customs Union, comprising Botswana, Lesotho, Namibia, South Africa and Swaziland.

Source (for Exports): UN, *International Trade Statistics Yearbook*.

Transport

RAIL TRAFFIC
(National Railways of Zimbabwe, including operations in Botswana)

	1998	1999	2000
Total number of passengers ('000)	1,787	1,896	1,614
Revenue-earning metric tons hauled ('000)	12,421	12,028	9,422
Gross metric ton-km (million)	9,248	8,962	6,953
Net metric ton-km (million)	4,549	4,375	3,326

ROAD TRAFFIC
('000 motor vehicles in use, estimates)

	1998	1999	2000
Passenger cars	540	555	573
Commercial vehicles	37	38	39

CIVIL AVIATION
(traffic on scheduled services)

	1998	1999	2000
Kilometres flown ('000)	13,957	11,532	10,080
Passengers carried ('000)	526	461	409
Passenger-km (million)	95	73	60
Total ton-km (million)	225	292	225

Tourism

	1998	1999	2000
Number of tourist arrivals	1,984,769	2,165,705	705,835
Tourism receipts (Z.$ million)	3,724	7,712	4,811

Communications Media

	1999	2000	2001
Television receivers ('000 in use)	400	410	n.a.
Telephones ('000 main lines in use)	239.0	249.4	253.7
Mobile cellular telephones ('000 subscribers)	174	309	329
Internet users ('000)	20	50	100

Radio receivers ('000 in use): 4,488 in 1999.

Facsimile machines: 4,100 in use in year ending 30 June 1995.

Daily newspapers (1996): 2; average circulation: 209,000 copies.

Sources: UNESCO, *Statistical Yearbook*; UN, *Statistical Yearbook*; International Telecommunication Union.

Education

(1998)

	Schools	Teachers	Students
Primary	4,699	64,538	2,488,939
Secondary	1,539	30,482	829,977
Higher:			
university	5	n.a.	11,451
Other:			
agricultural colleges	7	n.a.	566
technical and vocational centres	11	721	17,891
teachers' colleges	15	907	17,268
nurses	n.a.	n.a.	1,105

Adult literacy rate (UNESCO estimates): 88.7% (males 92.8%; females 84.7%) in 2000 (Source: UN Development Programme, *Human Development Report*).

Directory

The Constitution

The Constitution of the Republic of Zimbabwe took effect at independence on 18 April 1980. Amendments to the Constitution must have the approval of two-thirds of the members of the House of Assembly (see below). The provisions of the 1980 Constitution (with subsequent amendments) are summarized below:

THE REPUBLIC

Zimbabwe is a sovereign republic and the Constitution is the supreme law.

DECLARATION OF RIGHTS

The declaration of rights guarantees the fundamental rights and freedoms of the individual, regardless of race, tribe, place of origin, political opinions, colour, creed or sex.

THE PRESIDENT

Executive power is vested in the President, who acts on the advice of the Cabinet. The President is Head of State and Commander-in-Chief of the Defence Forces. The President appoints two Vice-Presidents and other Ministers and Deputy Ministers, to be members of the Cabinet. The President holds office for six years and is eligible for re-election. Each candidate for the Presidency shall be nominated by not fewer than 10 members of the House of Assembly; if only one candidate is nominated, that candidate shall be declared to be elected without the necessity of a ballot. Otherwise, a ballot shall be held within an electoral college consisting of the members of the House of Assembly.

PARLIAMENT

Legislative power is vested in a unicameral Parliament, consisting of a House of Assembly. The House of Assembly comprises 150 members, of whom 120 are directly elected by universal adult suffrage, 12

4652

are nominated by the President, 10 are traditional Chiefs and eight are Provincial Governors. The life of the House of Assembly is ordinarily to be six years.

OTHER PROVISIONS

An Ombudsman shall be appointed by the President, acting on the advice of the Judicial Service Commission, to investigate complaints against actions taken by employees of the Government or of a local authority.

Chiefs shall be appointed by the President, and shall form a Council of Chiefs from their number in accordance with customary principles of succession.

Other provisions relate to the Judicature, Defence and Police Forces, public service and finance.

The Government

HEAD OF STATE

President: ROBERT GABRIEL MUGABE (took office 31 December 1987; re-elected March 1990, 16–17 March 1996 and 9–11 March 2002).

THE CABINET
(April 2003)

Vice-Presidents: SIMON VENGAYI MUZENDA, JOSEPH MSIKA.

Minister of Special Affairs in the President's Office: JOHN LANDA NKOMO.

Minister of Defence: SYDNEY SEKERAMAYI.

Minister of Home Affairs: KEMBO MOHADI.

Minister of Justice, Legal and Parliamentary Affairs: PATRICK ANTHONY CHINAMASA.

Minister of Finance and Economic Development: HERBERT MURERWA.

Minister of Public Service, Labour and Social Welfare: JULY MOYO.

Minister of Local Government, Public Works and National Housing: Dr IGNATIUS MORGAN CHIMINYA CHOMBO.

Minister of Lands, Agriculture and Rural Resettlement: JOSEPH MADE.

Minister of Industry and International Trade: HERBERT MURERWA.

Minister of Energy and Power Development: AMOS MIDZI.

Minister of the Environment and Tourism: FRANCIS NHEMA.

Minister of Foreign Affairs: Dr I. STANISLAUS GORERAZVO MUDENGE.

Minister of Higher Education and Technology: SIMBARASHE MUMBENGEGWI.

Minister of Education, Sports and Culture: AENEAS CHIGWEDERE.

Minister of Health and Child Welfare: DAVID PARIRENYATWA.

Minister of Transport and Communications: WITNESS MANGWENDE.

Minister of Rural Resources and Water Development: JOYCE MUJURU.

Minister of Youth Development, Gender and Employment Creation: ELLIOT MANYIKA.

Minister of State for Information and Publicity: JONATHAN MOYO.

Minister of State for National Security: NICHOLAS GOCHE.

MINISTRIES

Office of the President: Munhumutapa Bldg, Samora Machel Ave, Private Bag 7700, Causeway, Harare; tel. (4) 707091.

Office of the Vice-Presidents: Munhumutapa Bldg, Samora Machel Ave, Private Bag 7700, Causeway, Harare; tel. (4) 707091.

Ministry of Defence: Defence House, Union Ave/Third St, Private Bag 7713, Causeway, Harare; tel. (4) 700155; fax (4) 727501; e-mail defprot@gta.gov.zw.

Ministry of Education, Sports and Culture: Ambassador House, Union Ave, POB CY121, Causeway, Harare; tel. (4) 734051; fax (4) 734075.

Ministry of Energy and Power Development: Karigamombe Centre, Private Bag 7753, Causeway, Harare; tel. (4) 751720; fax (4) 734075.

Ministry of the Environment and Tourism: Harare.

Ministry of Finance and Economic Development: Munhumutapa Bldg, Samora Machel Ave, Private Bag 7705, Causeway, Harare; tel. (4) 794571; fax (4) 792750.

Ministry of Foreign Affairs: Munhumutapa Bldg, Samora Machel Ave, POB 4240, Causeway, Harare; tel. (4) 727005; fax (4) 705161.

Ministry of Health and Child Welfare: Kaguvi Bldg, Fourth St, POB CY198, Causeway, Harare; tel. (4) 730011; fax (4) 729154.

Ministry of Higher Education and Technology: Old Mutual Centre, Union Ave, POB UA275, Harare; tel. (4) 796441; fax (4) 728730.

Ministry of Home Affairs: Mukwati Bldg, Samora Machel Ave, Private Bag 7703, Causeway, Harare; tel. (4) 703641; fax (4) 726716.

Ministry of Industry and International Trade: Mukwati Bldg, Fourth St, Private Bag 7708, Causeway, Harare; tel. (4) 702731; fax (4) 729311.

Ministry of Information and Publicity: Linquenda House, Baker Ave, POB CY825, Causeway, Harare; tel. (4) 703894; fax (4) 707213.

Ministry of Justice, Legal and Parliamentary Affairs: Corner House, cnr Samora Machel Ave and Leopold Takawira St, Private Bag 7751, Causeway, Harare; tel. (4) 774620; fax (4) 772999.

Ministry of Lands, Agriculture and Rural Resettlement: Ngungunyana Bldg, Private Bag 7701, Causeway, Harare; tel. (4) 792223; fax (4) 734646.

Ministry of Local Government, Public Works and National Housing: Mukwati Bldg, Private Bag 7706, Causeway, Harare; tel. (4) 790601; fax (4) 708848.

Ministry of National Security: Chaminuka Bldg, POB 2278, Harare; tel. (4) 700501; fax (4) 732660.

Ministry of Public Service, Labour and Social Welfare: Compensation House, cnr Central Ave and Fourth St, Private Bag 7707, Causeway, Harare; tel. (4) 790871.

Ministry of Rural Resources and Water Development: Makombe Complex, Private Bag 7701, Causeway, Harare; tel. (4) 706081.

Ministry of Transport and Communications: Kaguvi Bldg, POB CY595, Causeway, Harare; tel. (4) 700991; fax (4) 708225.

Ministry of Youth Development, Gender and Employment Creation: ZANU—PF Bldg, Private Bag 7762, Causeway, Harare; tel. (4) 734691; fax (4) 732709.

PROVINCIAL GOVERNORS

Manicaland: OPPAH MUCHINGURI.

Mashonaland Central: ELLIOT MANYIKA (acting).

Mashonaland East: DAVID ISHEMUNYORO KARIMANZIRA.

Mashonaland West: PETER CHANETSA.

Masvingo: JOSIAH DUNIRA HUNGWE.

Matabeleland North: OBERT MPOFU.

Matabeleland South: (vacant).

Midlands: CEPHAS MSIPA.

President and Legislature

PRESIDENT

Election, 9–11 March 2002

Candidate	Votes	% of votes
Robert Gabriel Mugabe	1,685,212	56.2
Morgan Tsvangirai	1,258,401	42.0
Wilson Kumbala	31,368	1.0
Shakespeare Maya	11,906	0.4
Paul Siwela	11,871	0.4
Total	**2,998,758**	**100.0**

HOUSE OF ASSEMBLY

Speaker: EMMERSON DAMBUDZO MNANGAGWA.

Election, 24–25 June 2000

	Votes	% of votes	Seats*
ZANU—PF	1,212,302	48.6	62†
MDC	1,171,051	47.0	57
Others‡	110,572	4.4	1
Total	**2,493,925**	**100.0**	**120**

* In addition to the 120 directly elective seats, 12 are held by nominees of the President, 10 by traditional Chiefs and eight by Provincial Governors.

† By the end of June 2001 the High Court had annulled the results of the elections held in four constituencies won by ZANU—PF and ordered that the contests be repeated. The results in 26 other constituencies were subsequently challenged.

‡ One seat was won by ZANU—Ndonga.

Political Organizations

Committee for a Democratic Society (CODESO): f. 1993; Kalanga-supported grouping, based in Matabeleland; Leader Soul Ndlovu.

Conservative Alliance of Zimbabwe (CAZ): POB 242, Harare; f. 1962; known as Rhodesian Front until 1981, and subsequently as Republican Front; supported by sections of the white community; Pres. Gerald Smith; Chair. Mike Moroney.

Democratic Party: f. 1991 by a breakaway faction from ZUM; Nat. Chair. Giles Mutsekwa; Pres. Davidson Gomo.

Forum Party of Zimbabwe (FPZ): POB 74, Bulawayo; e-mail trudy@harare.iafrica.com; f. 1993; conservative; Pres. Washington Sansole.

Front for Popular Democracy: f. 1994; Chair. Prof. Austin Chakawodza.

General Conference of Patriots: Harare; f. 1998; anti-Government, aims to organize and direct dissent; Leader Obey Mudzingwa.

Independent Zimbabwe Group: f. 1983 by a breakaway faction from the fmr Republican Front; Leader Bill Irvine.

Movement for Democratic Change (MDC): Harvest House, 6th Floor, cnr Angwa St and Nelson Mandela Ave, Harare; e-mail mdcweb@mdczimbabwe.com; internet www.mdczimbabwe.com; f. 1999; allied to Zimbabwe Congress of Trade Unions; opposes the Govt; Pres. Morgan Tsvangirai; Sec.-Gen. Welshman Ncube.

National Democratic Union: f. 1979; conservative grouping with minority Zezeru support; Leader Henry Chihota.

National Progressive Alliance: f. 1991; Chair. Canciwell Nziramasanga.

United National Federal Party (UNFP): Harare; f. 1978; conservative; seeks a fed. of Mashonaland and Matabeleland; Leader Chief Kayisa Ndiweni.

United Parties (UP): f. 1994; Leader Bishop Abel Muzorewa.

Zimbabwe Active People's Unity Party: Bulawayo; f. 1989; Leader Newman Matutu Ndela.

Zimbabwe African National Union—Patriotic Front (ZANU—PF): ZANU—PF HQ, cnr Rotten Row and Samora Machel Ave, POB 4530, Harare; tel. (4) 753329; e-mail zanupf@africaonline.co.zw; internet www.zanupfpub.co.zw; f. 1989 by merger of PF—ZAPU and ZANU—PF; Pres. Robert Gabriel Mugabe; Vice-Pres. Simon Vengayi Muzenda.

Zimbabwe African National Union—Ndonga (ZANU—Ndonga): POB UA525, Union Ave, Harare; tel. and fax (4) 481180; f. 1977; breakaway faction from ZANU, also includes fmr mems of United African National Council; supports free market economy; Pres. Ndabaningi Sithole; Sec.-Gen. Edwin C. Nguwa.

Zimbabwe Congress Party: Harare; f. 1994; Pres. Kenneth Mano.

Zimbabwe Democratic Party: Harare; f. 1979; traditionalist; Leader James Chikerema.

Zimbabwe Federal Party (ZFPO): Stand 214, Nketa 6, P.O. Nkulumane, Bulawayo; f. 1994; aims to create nat. fed. of five provinces; Leader Richard Ncube.

Zimbabwe Integrated Programme: f. 1999; seeks economic reforms; Pres. Prof. Henedi Dzinochikiweyi.

Zimbabwe National Front: f. 1979; Leader Peter Mandaza.

Zimbabwe Peoples' Democratic Party: f. 1989; Chair. Isabel Pasalk.

Zimbabwe Union of Democrats: Harare; f. 1998; aims to create an effective opposition in the national parliament; Pres. Margaret Dongo.

Zimbabwe Unity Movement (ZUM): f. 1989 by a breakaway faction from ZANU—PF; merged with United African National Council in 1994; Leader Edgar Tekere.

Diplomatic Representation

EMBASSIES AND HIGH COMMISSIONS IN ZIMBABWE

Angola: 26 Speke Ave, POB 3590, Harare; tel. (4) 770075; fax (4) 770077; e-mail 101663.2177@compuserve.com; Ambassador Alberto Ribeiro.

Argentina: Intermarket Life Towers, 15th Floor, 77 Jason Moyo Ave, POB 2770, Harare; tel. (4) 730075; fax (4) 730076; e-mail embassyofargentina@hotmail.com; Ambassador Carlos M. Foradori.

Australia: 29 Mazowe St, The Avenue, POB 4541, Harare; tel. (4) 253661; fax (4) 253678; High Commissioner Jonathan Brown.

Austria: 216 New Shell House, 30 Samora Machel Ave, POB 4120, Harare; tel. (4) 702921; Ambassador Dr Peter Leitenbauer.

Bangladesh: 9 Birchenough Rd, POB 3040, Harare; tel. (4) 727004; High Commissioner Harun Ahmed Chowdhury.

Belgium: Tanganyika House, 5th Floor, cnr 23 Third St and Union Ave, POB 2522, Harare; tel. (4) 793306; fax (4) 703960; e-mail harare@diplobel.org; Ambassador Bénédicte Frankinet.

Botswana: 22 Phillips Ave, Belgravia, POB 563, Harare; tel. (4) 729551; fax (4) 721360; High Commissioner C. Manyeula.

Brazil: Old Mutual Centre, 9th Floor, Jason Moyo Ave, POB 2530, Harare; tel. (4) 790740; fax (4) 790754; e-mail brasemb@ecoweb.co.zw; Chargé d'affaires a.i. Gustavo Martins Nogueira.

Bulgaria: 15 Maasdorp Ave, Alexandra Park, POB 1809, Harare; tel. (4) 730509; Ambassador Christo Tepavitcharov.

Canada: 45 Baines Ave, POB 1430, Harare; tel. (4) 733881; High Commissioner James C. Wall.

China, People's Republic: 30 Baines Ave, POB 4749, Harare; tel. (4) 724572; fax (4) 794959; internet www.chinaembassy.org.zw; Ambassador Hou Qingru.

Congo, Democratic Republic: 5 Pevensey Rd, Highlands, POB 2446, Harare; tel. (4) 481172; fax (4) 796421; Ambassador Dr Kikaya bin Karub (acting).

Cuba: 5 Phillips Ave, Belgravia, POB 4139, Harare; tel. (4) 720256; Ambassador Buenaventura Reyes-Acosta.

Czech Republic: 4 Sandringham Dr., Alexandra Park, POB 4474, Harare; tel. (4) 700636; fax (4) 720930; e-mail czechemb@ecoweb.co.zw; Ambassador Jaroslav Olša Jr.

Denmark: Intermarket Centre, cnr 59 Union Ave and First St, POB 4711, Harare; tel. (4) 758185; fax (4) 758189; e-mail olemoe@um.dk; Ambassador Ole Emil Moesby.

Egypt: 7 Aberdeen Rd, Avondale, POB A433, Harare; tel. (4) 303045; Ambassador Dr Ibrahim Aly Badawi el-Sheik.

Ethiopia: 14 Lanark Rd, Belgravia, POB 2745, Harare; tel. (4) 701514; fax (4) 701516; Ambassador Dina Mufti.

France: 74/76 Samora Machel Ave, Harare; tel. (4) 703216; fax (4) 730078; e-mail fambass@id.co.zw; Ambassador Didier Ferrand.

Germany: 14 Samora Machel Ave, POB 2168, Harare; tel. (4) 705231; fax (4) 708613; e-mail germemb@ecoweb.co.zw; Ambassador Peter Schmidt.

Ghana: 11 Downie Ave, Belgravia, POB 4445, Harare; tel. (4) 738652; fax (4) 738654; e-mail ghcom25@africaonline.co.zw; High Commissioner Kwasi Baah-Boakye.

Greece: 8 Deary Ave, Belgravia, POB 4809, Harare; tel. (4) 793208; fax (4) 703662; e-mail grembha@harare.iafrica.com; Ambassador Athanassios M. Valassidis.

Holy See: 5 St Kilda Rd, Mount Pleasant, POB MP191, Harare (Apostolic Nunciature); tel. (4) 744547; fax (4) 744412; e-mail nunzim@zol.co.zw; Apostolic Nuncio Mgr Leon Kalenga (Titular Archbishop of Tituli in Numidia).

Hungary: 20 Lanark Rd, Belgravia, POB 3594, Harare; tel. (4) 733528; fax (4) 730512; Ambassador Tamás Gás pár Gál.

India: 12 Nathal Rd, Belgravia, POB 4620, Harare; tel. (4) 795955; fax (4) 722324; High Commissioner Amal Krishna Basu.

Indonesia: 3 Duthie Ave, Belgravia, POB 3594, Harare; tel. (4) 251799; fax (4) 796587; Ambassador Dadang Sukandar.

Iran: 8 Allan Wilson Ave, Avondale, POB A293, Harare; tel. (4) 726942; Chargé d'affaires a.i. Alireza Gakarani.

Israel: 54 Jason Moyo Ave, POB CY3191, Harare; tel. (4) 756808; fax (4) 756801; e-mail israel@mweb.co.zw; Ambassador ITZHAK GERBERG.

Italy: 7 Bartholomew Close, Greendale North, POB 1062, Harare; tel. (4) 498190; fax (4) 498199; e-mail segreteria@ambitalia.co.zw; Ambassador Dr GIUSEPPE MARCHINI CAMIA.

Japan: Karigamombe Centre, 18th Floor, 53 Samora Machel Ave, POB 2710, Harare; tel. (4) 757861; fax (4) 757864; Ambassador YUKIO SUGANO.

Kenya: 95 Park Lane, POB 4069, Harare; tel. (4) 790847; fax (4) 723042; High Commissioner C. A. MWAKWERE.

Korea, Democratic People's Republic: 102 Josiah Chinamano Ave, Greenwood, POB 4754, Harare; tel. (4) 724052; Ambassador RI MYONG CHOL.

Kuwait: 1 Bath Rd, Avondale, POB A485, Harare; Ambassador NABILA AL-MULLA.

Libya: 124 Harare St, POB 4310, Harare; tel. (4) 728381; Ambassador M. M. IBN KOURAH.

Malawi: Malawi House, 9–11 Duthie Rd, Alexander Park, POB 321, Harare; tel. (4) 798485; fax (4) 799006; e-mail malahigh@africaonline.co.zw; High Commissioner TUJILANE R. M. CHIZUMILA.

Malaysia: 40 Downie Ave, Avondale, POB 5570, Harare; tel. (4) 334413; fax (4) 334415; e-mail mwharare@africaonline.co.zw; High Commissioner SHAHARUDDIN MOHAMED SOM.

Mozambique: 152 Herbert Chitepo Ave, cnr Leopold Takawira St, POB 4608, Harare; tel. (4) 790837; fax (4) 732898; e-mail embamoc@utande.co.zw; High Commissioner CORREIA FERNANDES SUMBANA.

Netherlands: 2 Arden Rd, Highlands, POB HG601, Harare; tel. (4) 776701; fax (4) 776700; e-mail nlgovhar@samara.co.zw; Ambassador HANS HEINBROEK.

Nigeria: 36 Samora Machel Ave, POB 4742, Harare; tel. (4) 790765; High Commissioner MUHAMMED LAMEEN METTEDEN.

Norway: 5 Lanark Rd, Belgravia, POB A510, Avondale, Harare; tel. (4) 252426; fax (4) 252430; e-mail emb.harare@norad.no; Ambassador KJELL STORLØKKEN.

Pakistan: 11 Van Praagh Ave, Milton Park, POB 3050, Harare; tel. (4) 720293; fax (4) 722446; e-mail pakharare@icon.co.zw; High Commissioner NAWABZADA MEHBOOB ALI KHAN.

Poland: 16 Cork Road, Belgravia, POB 3932, Harare; tel. (4) 253442; fax (4) 253710; e-mail polamb@africaonline.co.zw; Chargé d'affaires a.i. JAN WIELINSKI.

Portugal: 8th Floor, Redbridge, Eastgate, Third St, POB 406, Harare; tel. (4) 706220; fax (4) 722291; e-mail embport@icon.co.zw; Ambassador EURICO J. H. PAES.

Romania: 105 Fourth St, POB 4797, Harare; tel. (4) 700853; fax (4) 725493; e-mail romemb@africaonline.co.zw; Chargé d'affaires LUMINITA FLORESCU.

Russia: 70 Fife Ave, POB 4250, Harare; tel. (4) 720359; fax (4) 700534; e-mail russemb@africaonline.co.zw; Ambassador LEONID A. SAFONOV.

Serbia and Montenegro: 1 Lanark Rd, Belgravia, POB 3420, Harare; tel. (4) 738668; fax (4) 738660; Ambassador LJUBISA KORAC.

Slovakia: 32 Aberdeen Rd, Avondale, POB HG72, Harare; tel. (4) 302636; fax (4) 302236; e-mail slovemba@harare.iafrica.com; Chargé d'affaires a.i. MARTIN PODSTAVEK.

South Africa: 7 Elcombe Rd, Belgravia, POB A1654, Harare; tel. (4) 251851; fax (4) 757908; e-mail sahcomm@ecoweb.co.zw; High Commissioner A. J. D. NDOU.

Spain: 16 Phillips Ave, Belgravia, POB 3300, Harare; tel. (4) 738681; fax (4) 795440; e-mail hararesp@africaonline.co.zw; Ambassador JAVIER SANDOMINGO.

Sudan: 4 Pascoe Ave, Harare; tel. (4) 725240; Ambassador HASSAN GADIR.

Sweden: Pegasus House, 52 Samora Machel Ave, POB 4110, Harare; tel. (4) 790651; fax (4) 754265; Ambassador LENNARTH HJELMÅKER.

Switzerland: 9 Lanark Rd, POB 3440, Harare; tel. (4) 703997; fax (4) 794925; Ambassador CATHERINE KRIEG POLEJACK.

Tunisia: 5 Ashton Rd, Alexandra Park, Harare; tel. (4) 791570; fax (4) 727224; Ambassador HAMID ZAOUCHE.

United Kingdom: Corner House, cnr Leopold Takawira St and Samora Machel Ave, POB 4490, Harare; tel. (4) 772990; fax (4) 774617; High Commissioner BRIAN DONNELLY.

USA: 172 Herbert Chitepo Ave, POB 3340, Harare; tel. (4) 2505931; fax (4) 796488; internet usembassy.state.gov/Zimbabwe; Ambassador JOSEPH G. SULLIVAN.

Zambia: Zambia House, cnr Union and Julius Nyerere Aves, POB 4698, Harare; tel. (4) 790851; fax (4) 790856; High Commissioner NCHIMUNYA SIKAULU.

Judicial System

The legal system is Roman-Dutch, based on the system which was in force in the Cape of Good Hope on 10 June 1891, as modified by subsequent legislation.

The Supreme Court has original jurisdiction in matters in which an infringement of Chapter III of the Constitution defining fundamental rights is alleged. In all other matters it has appellate jurisdiction only. It consists of the Chief Justice and eight Judges of Appeal. A normal bench consists of any five of these.

The High Court consists of the Chief Justice, the Judge President, and 11 other judges. Below the High Court are Regional Courts and Magistrates' Courts with both civil and criminal jurisdiction presided over by full-time professional magistrates.

The Customary Law and Local Courts Act, adopted in 1990, abolished the village and community courts and replaced them with customary law and local courts, presided over by chiefs and headmen; in the case of chiefs, jurisdiction to try customary law cases is limited to those where the monetary values concerned do not exceed Z.$1,000 and in the case of a headman's court Z.$500. Appeals from the Chiefs' Courts are heard in Magistrates' Courts and, ultimately, the Supreme Court. All magistrates now have jurisdiction to try cases determinable by customary law.

Chief Justice: GODFREY CHIDYAUSIKU.

Judges of Appeal: W. SANDURA, ANELE MATIKA, TADIUS KARWI, SUSAN MAVANGIRA, LAVENDER MAKONI.

Judge President: PADDINGTON GARWE.

Attorney-General: ANDREW CHIGOVERA.

Religion

AFRICAN RELIGIONS
Many Africans follow traditional beliefs.

CHRISTIANITY
About 55% of the population are Christians.

Zimbabwe Council of Churches: 128 Mbuya Nehanda St, POB 3566, Harare; tel. (4) 791208; f. 1964; 20 mem. churches, nine assoc. mems; Pres. Rt Rev. JONATHAN SIYACHITEMA (Anglican Bishop of Harare); Gen. Sec. MUROMBEDZI KUCHERA.

The Anglican Communion
Anglicans are adherents of the Church of the Province of Central Africa, covering Botswana, Malawi, Zambia and Zimbabwe. The Church comprises 12 dioceses, including four in Zimbabwe. The Archbishop of the Province is the Bishop of Botswana.

Bishop of Central Zimbabwe: Rt Rev. ISHMAEL MUKUWANDA, POB 25, Gweru; tel. (54) 21030; fax (54) 21097.

Bishop of Harare: Rt Rev. NORBERT KUNONGA, Bishopsmount Close, POB UA7, Harare; tel. (4) 702253; fax (4) 700419; e-mail dioceschre@mango.zw.

Bishop of Manicaland: Rt Rev. Dr SEBASTIAN BAKARE, 115 Herbert Chitepo St, Mutare; tel. (20) 64194; fax (20) 63076; e-mail diomani@syscom.co.zw.

Bishop of Matabeleland: Rt Rev. THEOPHILUS T. NALEDI, POB 2422, Bulawayo; tel. (9) 61370; fax (9) 68353.

The Roman Catholic Church
For ecclesiastical purposes, Zimbabwe comprises two archdioceses and six dioceses. At 31 December 2000 there were an estimated 1,172,169 adherents.

Zimbabwe Catholic Bishops' Conference
General Secretariat, Africa Synod House, 29 Selous Ave, POB 8135, Causeway, Harare; tel. (4) 705368; fax (4) 705369; e-mail zcbc-sec@harare.iafrica.com.

f. 1969; Pres. Mgr ALEXIO MUCHABAIWA (Bishop of Mutare).

Archbishop of Bulawayo: Most Rev. PIUS ALICK NCUBE, cnr Lobenguela St and Ninth Ave, POB 837, Bulawayo; tel. (9) 63590; fax (9) 60359; e-mail archdbyo@acacia.samara.co.zw.

Archbishop of Harare: Most Rev. PATRICK FANI CHAKAIPA, Archbishop's House, 66 Fifth St, POB CY 330, Causeway, Harare; tel. (4) 727386; fax (4) 721598; e-mail hrearch@zol.co.zw.

Other Christian Churches

City Presbyterian Church: 60 Samora Machel Ave, POB 50, Harare; tel. and fax (4) 790366; e-mail cpclight@icon.co.zw; f. 1904; Minister Rev. M. T. CHIGWIDA; Session Clerk A. PHILLIPS; 231 mems.

Dutch Reformed Church (Nederduitse Gereformeerde Kerk): 35 Samora Machel Ave, POB 967, Harare; tel. (4) 442526; fax (4) 774739; e-mail mas@zol.co.zw; f. 1895; 16 parishes; Moderator Rev. A. S. VAN DYK; Gen. Sec. Rev. F. MARITZ; 2,500 mems.

Evangelical Lutheran Church: POB 2175, Bulawayo; tel. (9) 62686; e-mail elczhead@acacia.samara.co.zw; f. 1903; Sec. Rt Rev. Dr AMBROSE MOYO; 57,000 mems.

Greek Orthodox Church: POB 2832, Harare; tel. (4) 744991; Archbishop MAKARIOS.

Methodist Church in Zimbabwe: POB 71, Causeway, Harare; tel. (4) 724069; fax (4) 723709; e-mail methodistzimbabwe@mango.zw; f. 1891; Pres. Bishop CEPHAS Z. MUKANDI; Sec. of Conference Rev. MARGARET M. JAMES; 116,128 mems.

United Congregational Church of Southern Africa: 40 Jason Moyo St, POB 2451, Bulawayo; tel. (9) 63686; e-mail uccsazim@telcomet.co.zw; Chair. Rev. D. SIKHOSANA.

United Methodist Church: POB 3408, Harare; tel. (4) 704127; f. 1890; Bishop of Zimbabwe ABEL TENDEKAYI MUZOREWA; 45,000 mems.

Among other denominations active in Zimbabwe are the African Methodist Church, the African Methodist Episcopal Church, the African Reformed Church, the Christian Marching Church, the Church of Christ in Zimbabwe, the Independent African Church, the Presbyterian Church, the United Church of Christ, the Zimbabwe Assemblies of God and the Ziwezano Church.

JUDAISM

The Jewish community numbered 897 members at 31 December 1997.

Zimbabwe Jewish Board of Deputies: POB 1954, Harare; tel. (4) 702507; fax (4) 702506; e-mail cazo@zol.co.zw; Pres. P. STERNBERG; Sec. E. ALHADEFF.

BAHÁ'Í FAITH

National Spiritual Assembly: POB GD380, Greendale, Harare; tel. (4) 495945; fax (4) 744244; e-mail nsazim@mweb.co.zw; internet www.bahai.co.zw/community.htm; f. 1970; mems resident in more than 3,000 localities.

The Press

DAILIES

The Chronicle: POB 585, Bulawayo; tel. (9) 888871; fax (9) 888884; e-mail editor@chronicle.co.zw; f. 1894; circulates throughout southwest Zimbabwe; English; Editor STEPHEN NDLOVU; circ. 45,000.

The Herald: POB 396, Harare; tel. (4) 795771; fax (4) 700305; internet www.herald.co.zw; f. 1891; English; Chair. THOMAS SITHOLE; circ. 122,077.

WEEKLIES

Business Herald: Harare; weekly; Editor ANDREW RUSINGA.

Financial Gazette: Coal House, 5th Floor, cnr Nelson Mandela Ave and Leopold Takawira St, Harare; tel. (4) 781571; fax (4) 781578; e-mail fimedit@fingaz.co.zw; internet www.fingaz.co.zw; weekly; independent; Editor-in-Chief FRANCIS MDLONGWA; circ. 40,000.

Kwayedza: POB 396, Harare; tel. (4) 795771; fax (4) 791311; internet www.kwayedza.co.zw; weekly; Editor G. M. CHITEWE; circ. 33,944.

Manica Post: POB 960, Mutare; tel. (20) 61212; fax (20) 61149; e-mail manpost@syscom.co.zw; internet www.manicapost.co.zw; f. 1893; weekly; Editor J. GAMBANGA; circ. 20,000.

Masvingo Mirror: POB 1214, Masvingo; tel. (39) 64372; fax (39) 64484; e-mail belpress@mvo.samara.co.zw; weekly; independent.

Midlands Observer: POB 533, Kwekwe; tel. (55) 2248; f. 1953; weekly; English; Editor FELIX MOYO; circ. 5,000.

North Midlands Gazette: POB 222, Kadoma; tel. and fax (68) 3731; e-mail kidia@pci.co.zw; e-mail ckidia@web.co.zw; f. 1912; weekly; Editor C. B. KIDIA.

Sunday Gazette: POB 66070, Kopje, Harare; tel. (4) 738722; weekly; Editor FRANCIS MDLONGWA.

Sunday Mail: POB 396, Harare; tel. (4) 795771; fax (4) 700305; e-mail ronald.imbayago@zimpapers.co.zw; internet www .sundaymail.co.zw; f. 1935; weekly; English; Chair. THOMAS SITHOLE; circ. 159,075.

Sunday News: POB 585, Bulawayo; tel. (9) 540071; fax (9) 540084; f. 1930; weekly; English; Editor E. MACHIRORI; circ. 55,035.

The Times: 71 Seventh St, POB 66, Gweru; tel. (54) 23285; fax (54) 21614; e-mail thetimes@samara.co.zw; f. 1897; weekly; English; Editor SHEPARD SAMASUWO; circ. 5,000.

Zimbabwe Independent: Zimind Publishers (Private) Ltd, Suites 23/24, 1 Union Ave, POB BE 1165, Belvedere, Harare; e-mail tncube@zimind.mweb.co.uk; internet www.theindependent.co.zw; f. 1996; weekly; Editor TREVOR NCUBE; Publr CLIVE WILSON.

Zimbabwean Government Gazette: POB 8062, Causeway, Harare; official notices; weekly; Editor L. TAKAWIRA.

PERIODICALS

Africa Calls Worldwide: POB BW1500, Harare; tel. (4) 728256; fax (4) 792932; f. 1960; travel; 6 a year; Man. Editor DONETTE KRUGER.

Central African Journal of Medicine: POB A195, Avondale, Harare; tel. (4) 791631; f. 1955; monthly; Editor-in-Chief Dr J. A. MATENGA.

Chamber of Mines Journal: POB 1683, Harare; tel. (4) 736835; fax (4) 749803; journal of the Chamber of Mines of Zimbabwe; monthly; Editor M. ZHUWAKINYU.

Chaminuka News: POB 251, Marondera; f. 1988; fortnightly; English and Chishona; Editor M. MUGABE; circ. 10,000.

City Observer: POB 990, Harare; tel. (4) 706536; fax (4) 708544; monthly.

Commerce: POB 1683, Harare; tel. (4) 736835; fax (4) 749803; journal of Zimbabwe Nat. Chambers of Commerce; monthly; Editor I. MILLS; circ. 1,500.

Computer and Telecom News: POB 1683, Harare; tel. (4) 736835; fax (4) 749803; monthly; Editor R. STEWART.

CZI Industrial Review: POB 1683, Harare; tel. (4) 736835; fax (4) 749803; journal of the Confed. of Zimbabwe Industries; monthly; Editor I. MILLS.

Economic Review: c/o Zimbabwe Financial Holdings, POB 3198, Harare; tel. (4) 751168; fax (4) 757497; 4 a year; circ. 3,000.

Executive: Harare; tel. (4) 755084; fax (4) 752162; bi-monthly; Editor MICHAEL J. HAMILTON.

Horizon Magazine: POB UA196, Union Ave, Harare; tel. (4) 704645; e-mail horizon@mango.zw; current affairs; monthly; circ. 40,000.

Hotel and Catering Gazette: POB 2677, Kopje, Harare; tel. (4) 738722; fax (4) 707130; monthly; Editor PAULA CHARLES; circ. 2,000.

Indonsakusa: Hwange; f. 1988; monthly; English and Sindebele; Editor D. NTABENI; circ. 10,000.

Jassa: POB MP203, Mount Pleasant, Harare; tel. (4) 303211; fax (4) 333407; applied science journal of the Univ. of Zimbabwe; 2 a year; Editor Prof. C. F. B. NHACHI.

Just for Me: POB 66070, Kopje, Harare; tel. (4) 704715; f. 1990; family and women's interest; Editor BEVERLEY TILLEY.

Karoi News: POB 441, Karoi; tel. 6216; fortnightly.

Look and Listen: POB UA589, Harare; tel. (4) 752144; fax (4) 752062; e-mail munn@samara.co.zw; f. 1965; radio and TV programmes, cookery, entertainment and reviews; fortnightly; Editor ALASDAIR J. MUNN; circ. 23,000.

Mahogany: POB UA589, Harare; tel. (4) 752063; fax (4) 752062; e-mail munn@samara.co.zw; f. 1980; English; women's interest; 6 a year; Editor TENDAI DONDO; circ. 240,000.

Makoni Clarion: POB 17, Rusape; monthly.

Masiye Pambili (Let Us Go Forward): POB 591, Bulawayo; tel. (9) 75011; fax (9) 69701; f. 1964; English; 2 a year; Editor M. N. NDLOVU; circ. 21,000.

Monthly Bulletin: POB 1283, Harare; tel. (4) 703000; fax (4) 707800; e-mail rbzmail@rbz.co.zw; weekly, monthly and quarterly economic reports; publ. by the Reserve Bank of Zimbabwe.

Moto: POB 890, Gweru; tel. (54) 24886; fax (54) 28194; e-mail moto@telco.co.zw; Roman Catholic; Editor MUNYARADZI MAKONI; circ. 22,000.

Nehanda Guardian: Hwange; f. 1988; monthly; English and Chishona; Editor K. MWANAKA; circ. 10,000.

Nhau Dzekumakomo: POB 910, Mutare; f. 1984; publ. by Mutare City Council; monthly.

On Guard: National Social Security Authority, POB 1387, Causeway, Harare; tel. (4) 728931; fax (4) 796320; Editor P. TAGARA.

The Outpost: POB HG106, Highlands; tel. (4) 724571; f. 1911; English; monthly; Editor ELVIS CHIPUKA; circ. 21,000.

Parade Magazine: POB 3798, Harare; tel. (4) 736837; fax (4) 749803; e-mail tpubl@m-web.co.zw; f. 1953; monthly; English; Editor CHIZA LUSUNGU NGWIRA; circ. 91,000.

Quarterly Guide to the Economy: First Merchant Bank of Zimbabwe, FMB House, 67 Samora Machel Ave, POB 2786, Harare; tel. (4) 703071; fax (4) 738810; quarterly.

RailRoader: POB 596, Bulawayo; tel. (9) 363526; fax (9) 363543; e-mail mgumede@nrz.co.zw; f. 1952; monthly; Editor M. GUMEDE; circ. 10,000.

The Record: POB 179, Harare; tel. (4) 708911; journal of the Public Service Asscn; 6 a year; Editor GAMALIEL RUNGANI; circ. 30,000.

Southern African Political and Economic Monthly: POB MP111, Mt Pleasant, Harare; tel. (4) 252962; fax (4) 252964; e-mail publications@sapes.org.zw; monthly; incorporating Southern African Economist; Editor-in-Chief KHABELE MATLOSA; circ. 16,000.

The Star: POB 138, Chinhoyi; tel. (67) 21656; f. 1989; weekly; English.

Teacher in Zimbabwe: POB 350, Harare; tel. (4) 497548; fax (4) 497554; f. 1981; monthly; circ. 60,000.

Tobacco News: POB 1683, Harare; tel. (4) 736836; fax (4) 749803; monthly; Editor D. MILLER; circ. 2,000.

Vanguard: POB 66102, Kopje; tel. 751193; every 2 months.

The Worker: POB 8323, Causeway, Harare; tel. 700466.

World Vision News: POB 2420, Harare; tel. 703794; quarterly.

Zambezia: POB MP203, Harare; tel. (4) 303211; fax (4) 333407; humanities journal of the Univ. of Zimbabwe; 2 a year; Editor Prof. A. S. MLAMBO.

Zimbabwe Agricultural Journal: POB CY594, Causeway, Harare; tel. (4) 704531; fax (4) 728317; f. 1903; 6 a year; Editor R. J. FENNER; circ. 2,000.

Zimbabwe Defence Forces Magazine: POB 7720, Harare; tel. (4) 722481; f. 1982; 6 a year; circ. 5,000.

Zimbabwe News: POB CY3206, Causeway, Harare; tel. (4) 790148; fax (4) 790483; monthly.

NEWS AGENCIES

Zimbabwe Inter-Africa News Agency (ZIANA): POB CY511, Causeway, Harare; tel. (4) 730151; fax (4) 794336; f. 1981; owned and controlled by Zimbabwe Mass Media Trust; Editor-in-Chief HENRY E. MURADZIKWA.

Foreign Bureaux

Agence France-Presse (AFP): Robinson House, Union Ave, POB 1166, Harare; tel. (4) 758017; fax (4) 753291; e-mail afphre@africaonline.co.zw; Rep. FRANÇOIS-BERNARD CASTÉRAN.

ANGOP (Angola): Mass Media House, 3rd Floor, 19 Selous Ave, POB 6354, Harare; tel. (4) 736849.

Agenzia Nazionale Stampa Associata (ANSA) (Italy): Harare; tel. (4) 723881; Rep. IAN MILLS.

Associated Press (AP) (USA): POB 785, Harare; tel. (4) 706622; fax (4) 703994; Rep. JOHN EDLIN.

Deutsche Presse-Agentur (dpa) (Germany): Harare; tel. (4) 755259; fax (4) 755240; Correspondent JAN RAATH.

Informatsionnoye Telegrafnoye Agentstvo Rossii—Telegrafnoye Agentstvo Suverennykh Stran (ITAR—TASS) (Russia): Mass Media House, 19 Selous Ave, POB 4012, Harare; tel. (4) 790521; Correspondent YURII PITCHUGIN.

Inter Press Service (IPS) (Italy): 127 Union Ave, POB 6050, Harare; tel. (4) 790104; fax (4) 728415; e-mail ipshre@harare.iafrica.com; Rep. KENNETH BLACKMAN.

News Agency of Nigeria (NAN): Harare; tel. (4) 703041.

Pan-African News Agency (PANA) (Senegal): 19 Selous Ave, POB 8364, Harare; tel. (4) 730971; Bureau Chief PETER MWAURA.

Prensa Latina (Cuba): Mass Media House, 3rd Floor, 19 Selous Ave, Harare; tel. (4) 731993; Correspondent HUGO RIUS.

Press Trust of India (PTI): Mass Media House, 3rd Floor, 19 Selous Ave, Harare; tel. (4) 795006; Rep. N. V. R. SWAMI.

Reuters (United Kingdom): 901 Tanganyika Ave, Union Ave, Harare, POB 2987; tel. (4) 724299; Bureau Chief DAVID BLOOM.

Rossiiskoye Informatsionnoye Agentstvo—Novosti (RIA—Novosti) (Russia): 503 Robinson House, cnr Union Ave and Angwa St, POB 3908, Harare; tel. (4) 707232; fax (4) 707233; Correspondent A. TIMONOVICH.

United Press International (UPI) (USA): Harare; tel. (4) 25265; Rep. IAN MILLS.

Xinhua (New China) News Agency (People's Republic of China): 4 Earls Rd, Alexander Park, POB 4746, Harare; tel. and fax (4) 731467; Chief Correspondent LU JIANXIN.

Publishers

Academic Books (Pvt) Ltd: POB 567, Harare; tel. (4) 755408; fax (4) 781913; educational; Editorial Dir IRENE STAUNTON.

Amalgamated Publications (Pvt) Ltd: POB 1683, Harare; tel. (4) 736835; fax (4) 749803; f. 1949; trade journals.

Anvil Press: POB 4209, Harare; tel. (4) 751202; fax (4) 739681; f. 1988; general; Man. Dir PAUL BRICKHILL.

The Argosy Press: POB 2677, Harare; tel. (4) 755084; magazine publrs; Gen. Man. A. W. HARVEY.

Baobab Books (Pvt) Ltd: POB 567, Harare; tel. (4) 665187; fax (4) 665155; e-mail academic@africaonline.co.zw; general, literature, children's.

The Bulletin: POB 1595, Bulawayo; tel. (9) 78831; fax (9) 78835; fmrly Directory Publishers Ltd; education; CEO BRUCE BEALE.

College Press Publishers (Pvt) Ltd: 15 Douglas Rd, POB 3041, Workington, Harare; tel. (4) 754145; fax (4) 754256; f. 1968; educational and general; Man. Dir B. B. MUGABE.

Graham Publishing Co (Pvt) Ltd: POB 2931, Harare; tel. (4) 752437; fax (4) 752439; f. 1967; general; Dir GORDON M. GRAHAM.

Harare Publishing House: Chiremba Rd, Hatfield, POB 4735, Harare; tel. (4) 570613; f. 1984; Dir Dr T. M. SAMKANGE.

HarperCollins Publishers (Zimbabwe) Pvt Ltd: Union Ave, POB UA201, Harare; tel. (4) 721413; fax (4) 732436; Man. S. D. MCMILLAN.

Longman Zimbabwe (Pvt) Ltd: PO Box ST125, Southerton, Harare; tel. (4) 62711; fax (4) 62716; f. 1964; general and educational; Man. Dir N. L. DLODLO.

Mambo Press: Senga Rd, POB 779, Gweru; tel. (54) 24017; fax (54) 21991; e-mail mambo@icon.co.zw; f. 1958; religious, educational and fiction in English and African languages.

Modus Publications (Pvt) Ltd: Modus House, 27–29 Charter Rd, POB 66070, Kopje, Harare; tel. (4) 738722; Man. Dir ELIAS RUSIKE.

Munn Publishing (Pvt) Ltd: POB UA460, Union Ave, Harare; tel. (4) 481048; fax (4) 7481081; e-mail munn@mweb.co.zw; Man. Dir I. D. MUNN.

Standard Publications (Pvt) Ltd: POB 3745, Harare; Dir G. F. BOOT.

Southern African Printing and Publishing House (SAPPHO): 109 Coventry Rd, Workington, POB MP1005, Mt Pleasant, Harare; tel. (4) 621681; fax (4) 666061; e-mail sappho@zimmirror.co.zw; internet www.zimmirror.co.zw; Editor-in-Chief Dr IBBO MANDAZA.

University of Zimbabwe Publications: POB MP203, Mount Pleasant, Harare; tel. (4) 303211; fax (4) 333407; e-mail uzpub@admin.uz.ac.zw; internet www.uz.ac.zw/publications; f. 1969; Dir MUNANI SAM MTETWA.

Zimbabwe Newspapers (1980) Ltd: POB 55, Harare; tel. (4) 704088; fax (4) 702400; e-mail theherald@zimpapers.co.zw; internet www.herald.co.zw; f. 1981; state-owned; controls largest newspaper group; Chair. E. KAMUSHINDA; Man. Dir B. KAMUDYARIWA.

ZPH Publishers Ltd: POB GD 510, Greendale, Harare; tel. (4) 497555; fax (4) 497554; e-mail ndai@zph.co.zw; f. 1982; Chair. B. G. TAFIREYI; Gen. Man. IRENE NYAMAKURA.

Government Publishing House

The Literature Bureau: POB 749, Causeway, Harare; tel. (4) 333812; f. 1954; controlled by Ministry of Education; Dir B. C. CHITSIKE.

Broadcasting and Communications

TELECOMMUNICATIONS

Posts and Telecommunications Corporation (PTC): POB CY331, Causeway, Harare; tel. (4) 728811; fax (4) 731980; e-mail ajchaponda@zptc.co.zw; internet www.zptc.co; Chair. Dr M. MHLOYI; CEO BRIAN MUTANDIRO.

BROADCASTING

Radio

Zimbabwe Broadcasting Corporation: POB HG444, Highlands, Harare; tel. (4) 498610; fax (4) 498613; internet www.zbc.co.zw; f. 1957; Chair. GIDEON GONO; CEO LOVEMORE CHITAPI.

Broadcasts in English, Chishona, Sindebele, Kalanga, Venda, Tonga and Chewa; four programme services comprise a general service (predominantly in English), vernacular languages service, light entertainment, educational programmes.

Television

Zimbabwe Broadcasting Corporation: (see Radio).

The main broadcasting centre is in Harare, with a second studio in Bulawayo; broadcasts on two commercial channels (one of which, Joy TV, serves the Harare area only) for about 95 hours per week.

Finance

(cap. = capital; res = reserves; dep. = deposits; m. = million; brs = branches; amounts in Zimbabwe dollars)

BANKING

Central Bank

Reserve Bank of Zimbabwe: 80 Samora Machel Ave, POB 1283, Harare; tel. (4) 703000; fax (4) 705978; e-mail imabasa@rbz.co.zw; internet www.rbz.co.zw; f. 1964; bank of issue; cap. and res 8m., dep. 35,088m. (Dec. 2001); Gov. Dr LEONARD TSUMBA.

Commercial Banks

Barclays Bank of Zimbabwe Ltd: Barclays House, First St and Jason Moyo Ave, POB 1279, Harare; tel. (4) 758280; fax (4) 752913; e-mail barclays.zimbabwe@barclays.com; internet www.africa .barclays.com/Zimbabwe.htm; cap. and res 4,564m., total assets 33,393m. (Dec. 2001); Chair. D. M. ZAMCHIYA; Man. Dir A. JONGWE; 44 brs.

Commercial Bank of Zimbabwe: Union House, 60 Union Ave, POB 3313, Harare; tel. (4) 758081; fax (4) 758085; e-mail cbzinfo@ africaonline.co.zw; internet www.cbz.co.zw; state-owned; cap. and res 977.2m., dep. 14,350.4m. (Dec. 2000); Chair. R. V. WILDE; Man. Dir GIDEON GONO; 9 brs.

Stanbic Bank Zimbabwe Ltd: Stanbic Centre, 1st Floor, 59 Samora Machel Ave, POB 2700, Harare; tel. (4) 759480; fax (4) 751324; e-mail zimbabweinfo@stanbic.com; f. 1990; cap. and res 368m., total assets 10,600m. (Dec. 2000); Chair. C. M. D. SANYANGA; Man. Dir GREG R. BRACKENRIDGE; 14 brs.

Standard Chartered Bank Zimbabwe Ltd: John Boyne House, 38 Speke Ave, POB 373, Harare; tel. (4) 752852; fax (4) 758560; f. 1983; cap. and res 426m., total assets 48,173m. (Dec. 2001); Chair. H. P. MKUSHI; CEO B. R. HAMILTON; 42 brs and sub-brs; 10 agencies.

Trade and Investment Bank Ltd: Cabs Centre, 10th Floor, 74 Jason Moyo Ave, POB CY1064, Causeway, Harare; tel. (4) 703791; fax (4) 705491; e-mail tib@tibl.co.zw; f. 1997; cap. and res. 32m., total assets 421m. (Dec. 1997); Chair. Dr BERNARD THOMAS CHIDZERO; CEO Dr KOMBO JAMES MOYANA.

Zimbabwe Banking Corporation Ltd (Zimbank): Zimbank House, Speke Ave and First St, POB 3198, Harare; tel. (4) 757471; fax (4) 757497; e-mail finhold@finhold.co.zw; internet www.finhold .co.zw; f. 1951; state-owned; cap. 100m., res 1,292m., dep. 15,305m. (Sept. 2001); Group CEO E. N. MUSHAYAKARARA; 48 brs.

Development Bank

Zimbabwe Development Bank (ZDB): ZDB House, 99 Rotten Row, POB 1720, Harare; tel. (4) 750171; fax (4) 774225; e-mail zdb@ harare.iafrica.com; internet www.zdb.co.zw; f. 1985; 33.3% state-owned; cap. and res 195m., total assets 826m. (June 1997); Chair. Dr T. MASAYA; Man. Dir C. MARIDZA; 3 brs.

Merchant Banks

First Merchant Bank of Zimbabwe Ltd: FMB House, 67 Samora Machel Ave, POB 2786, Harare; tel. (4) 701636; fax (4) 708005; e-mail fmbzau@fmb.finweb.co.zw; internet www.fmb.co.zw; f. 1956; merged with Heritage Investment Bank 1997; cap. 61m., res 1,000m., dep. 2,434m. (Dec. 2001); Chair. P. M. BAUM; Man. Dir R. FELTOE; br. in Bulawayo.

Kingdom Financial Services Merchant Bank: Harare; f. 1998.

Merchant Bank of Central Africa Ltd: Old Mutual Centre, 14th Floor, cnr Third St and Jason Moyo Ave, POB 3200, Harare; tel. (4) 701636; fax (4) 708005; e-mail mbca@bank.co.zw; internet www .mbca.co.zw; f. 1956; cap. 61.2m., res 75.2m., dep. 1,186.5m. (Dec. 2001); Chair. E. D. CHIURA; Man. Dir DAVID T. HATENDI.

NMB Bank Ltd: Unity Court, 1st Floor, cnr Union Ave and First St, POB 2564, Harare; tel. (4) 759651; fax (4) 759648; e-mail enquiries@ nmbz.co.zw; internet www.nmbz.com; f. 1992; fmrly National Merchant Bank of Zimbabwe; cap. and res. 279.1m., dep. 2,799m. (Dec. 2000); Chair. P. T. ZHANDA; CEO Dr JULIUS T. MAKONI; 1 br.

Standard Chartered Merchant Bank Zimbabwe Ltd: Standard Chartered Bank Bldg, cnr Second St and Nelson Mandela Ave, POB 60, Harare; tel. (4) 708585; fax (4) 725667; f. 1971; cap. and res 78m., dep. 83m. (Dec. 1998); Chair. BARRY HAMILTON; Man. Dir EBBY ESSOKA.

Discount Houses

Bard Discount House Ltd: Bard House, 69 Samora Machel Ave, POB 3321, Harare; tel. (4) 752756; fax (4) 790641; e-mail discount@ bard-zim.com; cap. and res 68m. (Dec. 1999); acquisition pending by National Merchant Bank of Zimbabwe; Chair. N. KUDENGA; Man. Dir D. DUBE.

The Discount Co of Zimbabwe (DCZ): 70 Park Lane, POB 3424, Harare; tel. (4) 705414; fax (4) 731670; cap. and res 8.9m., total assets 377.4m. (Feb. 1995); Chair. S. J. CHIHAMBAKWE.

Intermarket Discount House: Unity Court, 5th Floor, Union Ave, POB 3290, Harare; e-mail idh@coldfire.dnet.co.zw.

National Discount House Ltd: MIPF House, 5th Floor, Central Ave, Harare; tel. (4) 700771; fax (4) 792927; e-mail ndhzim@ndf.co .zw; internet www.ndh.co.zw; cap. and res 53m. (Dec. 1997); Man. Dir E. MATIENGA.

udc Holdings Ltd: udc Centre, cnr First St and Union Ave, Private Bag 5550, POB 1685, Mount Pleasant, Harare; tel. (4) 369260; fax (4) 369322; e-mail udc@udc.co.zw; cap. and res 73m. (Dec. 1995); Man. Dir J. W. DICK.

Banking Organization

Institute of Bankers of Zimbabwe: POB UA521, Harare; tel. (4) 752474; fax (4) 750281; e-mail info@iobz.co.zw; f. 1973; Pres. W. MATSAIRA; Dir A. JONGWE.

STOCK EXCHANGE

Zimbabwe Stock Exchange: 65 Samora Machel Ave, 2nd Floor, POB UA234, Harare; tel. (4) 736861; fax (4) 791045; e-mail zse@ econet.co.zw; internet www.zse.co.zw; f. 1946; Chair. G. MHLANGA.

INSURANCE

Commercial Union Insurance Co of Zimbabwe Ltd: POB 1065, Harare; tel. (4) 795840; fax (4) 721241; e-mail cuzimb@harare.iafrica .com; mem. of Commercial Union group; Chair. H. P. MKUSHI.

Diamond Insurance of Zimbabwe Ltd: Harare; Gen. Man. GRACE MURADZIKWA.

Fidelity Life Assurance of Zimbabwe (Pvt) Ltd: 66 Julius Nyerere Way, POB 435, Harare; tel. (4) 750927; fax (4) 704705; Chair. B. KUMALO; Gen. Man. C. CHONZI.

Intermarket Life Assurance Ltd: Intermarket Life Towers, 77 Jason Moyo Ave, POB 969, Harare; tel. (4) 708801; fax (4) 703186; e-mail info@interlife.co.zw; internet www.intermarket.co.zw; life assurance.

National Insurance Co of Zimbabwe (Pvt) Ltd: cnr Baker Ave and First St, POB 1256, Harare; tel. (4) 704911; fax (4) 704134; Man. Dir S. T. MALUMO.

Old Mutual Life Assurance Co: 100 The Chase (West), Emerald Hill, POB 70, Harare; tel. (4) 308400; fax (4) 308467; e-mail info@ oldmutual.co.zw; internet www.oldmutual.co.zw; f. 1845; life assurance; CEO G. D. HOLLICK; Gen. Man. L. E. M. NGWERUME.

RM Insurance Co (Pvt) Ltd: Royal Mutual House, 45 Baker Ave, POB 3599, Harare; tel. (4) 757961; fax (4) 759700; f. 1982; cap. p.u. 2m. Chair. C. WRIGHT; Gen. Man. MIKE GIBSON.

Zimnat Life Assurance Co Ltd: Zimnat House, Nelson Mandela Ave, POB CY1155, Harare; tel. (4) 707581; fax (4) 727214; e-mail info@zimnatlife.co.zw; internet www.zimnat.co.zw; Chair. Dr NKOSANA MOYO; Man. Dir ERIC KAHARI.

Trade and Industry

GOVERNMENT AGENCIES

Privatization Agency of Zimbabwe: Club Chambers, 9th Floor, cnr Nelson Mandela Ave and Third St, Private Bag 7728, Harare;

tel. (4) 251620; fax (4) 253723; internet www.paz.co.zw; CEO Andrew Mvumbe.

Zimbabwe Investment Centre (ZIC): 109 Rotten Row, POB 5950, Harare; tel. (4) 757931; fax (4) 757937; e-mail info@zic.co.zw; internet www.zic.co.zw; promotes domestic and foreign investment.

ZimTrade: 904 Premium Close, Mount Pleasant Business Park, POB 2738, Harare; tel. (4) 369330; fax (4) 369244; e-mail info@zimtrade.co.zw; internet www.zimtrade.co.zw; f. 1991; nat. export promotion org. Chair. E. Matikiti; CEO F. Chawasanra.

DEVELOPMENT ORGANIZATIONS

Industrial Development Corporation of Zimbabwe Ltd: POB CY1431, Causeway, Harare; tel. (4) 706971; fax (4) 796028; e-mail administrator@idc.co.zw; internet www.zimtrade.co.zw/PROFILES/IDC/index.htm/; f. 1963; Chair. P. Chingono; Gen. Man. M. N. Ndudzo.

Zimbabwe Development Corporation (ZDC): Harare; promotes rural devt; CEO A. M. Timbe.

CHAMBERS OF COMMERCE

Manicaland Chamber of Industries: POB 92, Mutare; tel. (20) 62300; f. 1945; Pres. L. Baxter; 60 mems.

Mashonaland Chamber of Industries: POB 3794, Harare; tel. (4) 739833; fax (4) 750953; f. 1922; Pres. A. I. S. Ferguson; Sec. M. Mubataripi; 729 mems.

Matabeleland Chamber of Industries: POB 2317, Bulawayo; tel. (9) 60642; fax (9) 60814; e-mail linksbyo@internet.co.zw; f. 1931; Pres. A. R. Rowland; Sec. N. McKay; about 150 mems.

Midlands Chamber of Industries: POB 213, Gweru; tel. (54) 2812; Pres. J. W. Pringle; 50 mems.

Zimbabwe National Chambers of Commerce (ZNCC): Equity House, Rezende St, POB 1934, Harare; tel. (4) 753444; fax (4) 753450; e-mail info@zncc.co.zw; internet www.zncc.co.zw; f. 1983; Pres. James Sanders; CEO Luckmore Zinyama.

INDUSTRIAL AND TRADE ASSOCIATIONS

Bulawayo Agricultural Society: PO Famona, Bulawayo; tel. and fax (9) 77668; f. 1907; Pres. C. P. D. Goodwin.

Cattle Producers' Association: Harare; e-mail cpa@cfu.co.zw; Pres. G. Franceys.

Chamber of Mines of Zimbabwe: 4 Central Ave, POB 712, Harare; tel. (4) 702841; fax (4) 707983; e-mail chamines@utande.co.zw; f. 1939; Pres. Abel Ntini; CEO David Murangari.

Coffee Growers' Association: Leopold Takawira St, Harare; tel. and fax (4) 750238; Dir Jules Lang.

Commercial Cotton Growers' Association: cnr Adylinn Rd and Marlborough Drive, POB EH191, Harare; tel. (4) 309800; fax (4) 309844; e-mail ccga@samara.co.zw; Administrator M. Bragge.

Confederation of Zimbabwe Industries: 31 Josiah Chinamano Ave, POB 3794, Harare; tel. (4) 251490; fax (4) 252424; e-mail czi@primenet.co.zw; internet www.czi.org.zw; f. 1957; Pres. Z. L. Rusike; CEO M. Rusike.

Construction Industry Federation of Zimbabwe: POB 1502, Harare; tel. (4) 746661; fax (4) 746937; e-mail cifoz@id.co.zw; Pres. C. P. Seager; CEO P. D. Burns.

Horticultural Promotion Council: Harare; represents c. 1,000 producers.

Matabeleland Region of the Construction Industry Federation of Zimbabwe: POB 1970, Bulawayo; tel. (9) 65787; f. 1919; Sec. M. Barron; 124 mems.

Minerals Marketing Corporation of Zimbabwe: 90 Mutare Rd, Msasa, POB 2628, Harare; tel. (4) 486945; fax (4) 487261; f. 1982; sole authority for marketing of mineral production (except gold); Chair. E. Mutowo; Gen. Man. Liz Chitiga.

Tobacco Industry and Marketing Board: POB UA214, Union Ave, Harare; tel. (4) 614431; fax (4) 614430; internet www.timb.co.zw.

Zimbabwe Tobacco Association: POB 1781, Harare; tel. (4) 253610; fax (4) 253738; e-mail fctobacco@zta.co.zw; internet www.zta.co.zw; Pres. Duncan Millar; CEO Chris R. L. Molam; 5,000 mems.

EMPLOYERS' ASSOCIATIONS

Bulawayo Landowners' and Farmers' Association: Bulawayo.

Commercial Farmers' Union: POB WGT390, Westgate, Harare; tel. (4) 309800; fax (4) 309874; e-mail president@cfu.co.zw; internet

www.mweb.co.zw/cfu; f. 1942; Pres. Colin Cloete; Dir H. W. Olivier; 4,348 mems.

Employers' Confederation of Zimbabwe: POB 158, Harare; tel. (4) 739633; fax (4) 739630; Pres. Joshua B. Myoka; Exec. Dir Peter F. Kunjeku.

Employment Council for the Motor Industry: POB 1084, Bulawayo; tel. (9) 78161.

Kadoma Farmers' and Stockowners' Association: Kadoma; tel. (68) 3658; Chair. A. Reed; Sec. P. M. Reed; 66 mems.

Kwekwe Farmers' Association: POB 72, Kwekwe; tel. (55) 247721; f. 1928; Chair. D. Edwards; Sec. J. Tapson; 87 mems.

Mutare District Farmers' Association: POB 29, Mutare; tel. (20) 66614; e-mail mutare@cfu.co.zw; Chair. R. Garvin; Sec. P. Breaks; 45 mems.

National Association of Dairy Farmers: cnr Adylinn Rd and Marlborough Drive, POB WGT390, Harare; tel. (4) 309800; fax (4) 309861; e-mail nadf@cfu.co.zw; f. 1953; Chair. C. Hawgood; CEO R. J. Van Vuuren.

National Employment Council for the Construction Industry of Zimbabwe: St Barbara House, cnr L. Takawira St and N. Mandela Ave, POB 2995, Harare; tel. (4) 773966; fax (4) 773967; e-mail neccon@africaonline.co.zw; CEO S. R. Makoni.

National Employment Council for the Engineering and Iron and Steel Industry: Adven House, 5th Floor, cnr Inez Terrace and Speke Ave, POB 1922, Harare; tel. (4) 775144; fax (4) 775918; f. 1943; Gen. Sec. E. E. Sharpe.

Zimbabwe Farmers' Union: POB 3755, Harare; tel. (4) 704763; fax (4) 700829; Chair. Gary Magadzire.

UTILITIES

Electricity

Zimbabwe Electricity Supply Authority (ZESA): 25 Samora Machel Ave, POB 377, Harare; tel. (4) 774508; fax (4) 774542; state-owned; Chair. Christopher Chetsanga; CEO Simbarashe Mangwengwende.

Gas

BOC Gases: Hull Rd, POB 1282, Harare; tel. (4) 757171; fax (4) 755775; e-mail boczw@ecoweb.co.zw.

Water

Department of Water: City of Harare, POB 1583, Harare.

TRADE UNIONS

All trade unions in Zimbabwe became affiliated to the ZCTU in 1981. The ZCTU is encouraging a policy of union amalgamations.

Zimbabwe Congress of Trade Unions (ZCTU): Chester House, 10th Floor, Speke Ave at Third St, POB 3549, Harare; tel. (4) 794742; fax (4) 728484; f. 1981; co-ordinating org. for trade unions; Pres. Isaac Matongo; Sec.-Gen. Isidore Zindoga; 300,000 mems.

Zimbabwe Federation of Trade Unions: Harare; f. 1996 as alternative to ZCTU; Co-ordinator Cuthbert Chiswa.

Principal Unions

Air Transport Union: POB AP40, Harare Airport, Harare; tel. (4) 575111; fax (4) 575068; f. 1956; Pres. L. S. Kanodereka; Gen. Sec. S. Banda; 400 mems.

Associated Mineworkers' Union of Zimbabwe: POB 384, Harare; tel. (4) 700287; Pres. J. S. Mutandare; Gen. Sec. Edmund Ruzive; 25,000 mems.

Building Workers' Trade Union: St Barbara House, POB 1291, Harare; tel. (4) 720942; Gen. Sec. E. Njekesa.

Commercial Workers' Union of Zimbabwe: Travlos House, 3rd Floor, Harare; tel. (4) 751451; Gen. Sec. S. D. R. Chifamba; 6,000 mems.

Federation of Municipal Workers' Union: Bulawayo; tel. (9) 60506; Gen. Sec. F. V. Ncube.

Furniture and Cabinet Workers' Union: POB 1291, Harare; Gen. Sec. C. Kaseke.

General Agricultural and Plantation Workers' Union: Harare; tel. (4) 792860; Gen. Sec. Philip Munyanye.

Graphical Association: POB 27, Bulawayo; POB 494, Harare; tel. (4) 62477; Gen. Sec. A. Ngwenya; 3,015 mems.

Harare Municipal Workers' Union: Office No 12, Harare Community, Harare; tel. (4) 62343; Gen. Sec. T. G. T. Mapfumo.

National Airways Workers' Union: POB AP1, Harare; tel. (4) 737011; fax (4) 231444; Gen. Sec. B. SPENCER.

National Engineering Workers' Union: POB 4968, Harare; tel. (4) 702963; Pres. I. MATONGO; Gen. Sec. O. KABASA.

National Union of Clothing Industry Workers' Union: POB RY28, Raylton; tel. 64432; Gen. Sec. C. M. PASIPANODYA.

Railways Associated Workers' Union: Bulawayo; tel. (9) 70041; f. 1982; Pres. SAMSON MABEKA; Gen. Sec. A. J. MHUNGU.

Technical & Salaried Staff Association: POB 33, Redcliff; tel. (55) 68798; Gen. Sec. J. DANCAN.

Transport and General Workers' Union: Dublin House, POB 4769, Harare; tel. (4) 793508; Gen. Sec. F. MAKANDA.

United Food and Allied Workers' Union of Zimbabwe: Harare; tel. (4) 74150; f. 1962; Gen. Sec. I. M. NEDZIWE.

Zimbabwe Amalgamated Railwaymen's Union: Unity House, 13th Ave, Herbert Chitepo St, Bulawayo; tel. (9) 60948; Gen. Sec. T. L. SHANA.

Zimbabwe Banks and Allied Workers' Union: POB 966, Harare; tel. (4) 703744; Pres. SHINGEREI MUNGATE; Gen. Sec. C. C. GWIJO.

Zimbabwe Catering and Hotel Workers' Union: Nialis Bldg, POB 3913, Harare; tel. (4) 794627; Gen. Sec. N. E. MUDZENGERERE.

Zimbabwe Chemical & Allied Workers' Union: POB 4810, Harare; Gen. Sec. R. MAKUVAZA.

Zimbabwe Domestic & Allied Workers' Union: Harare; tel. (4) 795405; Gen. Sec. G. SHOKO.

Zimbabwe Educational, Welfare & Mission Workers' Union: St Andrews House, Samora Machel Ave, Harare; Pres. I. O. SAMA-KOMVA.

Zimbabwe Leather Shoe & Allied Workers' Union: Harare; tel. (4) 793173; Gen. Sec. I. ZINDOGA.

Zimbabwe Motor Industry Workers' Union: POB RY00, Bulawayo; tel. (9) 74150; Gen. Sec. M. M. DERAH.

Zimbabwe Posts and Telecommunications Workers' Union: POB 739, Harare; tel. (4) 721141; Gen. Sec. GIFT CHIMANIKIRE.

Zimbabwe Textile Workers' Union: POB UA245, Harare; tel. (4) 705329; Sec. F. C. BHAIKWA.

Zimbabwe Tobacco Industry Workers' Union: St Andrews House, Samora Machel Ave, Harare; Gen. Sec. S. MHEMBERE.

Zimbabwe Union of Musicians: Harare; tel. (4) 708678; Gen. Sec. C. MATEMA.

Transport

In 1986 a Zimbabwe-registered company, the Beira Corridor Group (BCG), was formed to develop the transport system in the Beira corridor as an alternative transport link to those running through South Africa. The transport sector received 4.1% of total expenditure in the government budget for 1991/92. In 1991 National Railways of Zimbabwe (NRZ) announced a Z.\$700m. development programme, which included plans to electrify and extend some railway lines to previously uncovered areas.

RAILWAYS

In 1998 the rail network totalled 2,592 km, of which 313 km was electrified. Trunk lines run from Bulawayo south to the border with Botswana, connecting with the Botswana railways system, which, in turn, connects with the South African railways system; north-west to the Victoria Falls, where there is a connection with Zambia Railways; and north-east to Harare and Mutare connecting with the Mozambique Railways' line from Beira. From a point near Gweru, a line runs to the south-east, making a connection with the Mozambique Railways' Limpopo line and with the Mozambican port of Maputo. A connection runs from Rutenga to the South African Railways system at Beitbridge. A 320-km line from Beitbridge to Bulawayo was opened in 1999.

National Railways of Zimbabwe (NRZ): cnr Fife St and 10th Ave, POB 596, Bulawayo; tel. (9) 363716; fax (9) 363502; f. 1899; reorg. 1967; privatization under way; Chair. S. GEZA; Gen. Man. ALVORD MABENA.

ROADS

In 1999 the road system in Zimbabwe totalled an estimated 18,338 km, of which 6,781 km were main roads and 1,668 km were secondary roads; some 47.4% of the total network was paved.

CIVIL AVIATION

International and domestic air services connect most of the larger towns.

Air Zimbabwe Ltd (AirZim): POB AP1, Harare Airport, Harare; tel. (4) 575111; fax (4) 575068; internet www.airzimbabwe.com; f. 1967; scheduled domestic and international passenger and cargo services to Africa, Australia and Europe; Chair. NICHOLAS NYANDURO; Man. Dir. TICHARWA GARABGA.

Affretair: POB AP13, Harare Airport, Harare; tel. (4) 575000; fax (4) 575011; internet www.sunshinecity.net/affretair/pages; f. 1965; state-owned; freight carrier; scheduled services to Europe and charter services world-wide; Chair. DAVID ZAMCHIYA; Man. Dir GODFREY MANHAMBARA.

Expedition Airline: Harare Airport, Harare; f. 1997; domestic services between Harare and Victoria Falls, Bulawayo, Masvingo and Mutara.

Majestic Air: 106 Lomagund Rd, Avondale West, POB 2426, Harare; f. 2001.

Manicaland Air Charter: f. 1996; operates charter service between Harare and Mutare.

Rhino Airlines: Bulawayo; f. 1997; direct weekly flights between Bulawayo and Moscow; Pres. MILTON THEMBA MHLANGA.

Zimbabwe Express Airlines: Kurima House, Ground Floor, 89 Nelson Mandela Ave, POB 5130, Harare; tel. (4) 729681; fax (4) 737117; e-mail zexpro@samara.co.zw; f. 1995; domestic routes and service to Johannesburg (South Africa); Man. Dir and CEO EVANS NDEBELE.

Tourism

The principal tourist attractions are the Victoria Falls, the Kariba Dam and the Hwange Game Reserve and National Park. Zimbabwe Ruins, near Fort Victoria, and World's View, in the Matapos Hills, are also of interest. There is trout-fishing and climbing in the Eastern Districts, around Umtali. In 2000 705,835 tourists visited Zimbabwe, a sharp decline from previous years, owing to domestic unrest (see Recent History). Revenue from tourism in that year totalled Z.\$4,811m.

Zimbabwe Tourism Authority (ZTA): POB CY286, Causeway, Harare; tel. (4) 758730; fax (4) 758828; internet www.tourismzimbabwe.co.zw; f. 1984; promotes tourism domestically and from abroad; CEO JOSEPH CHIGWEDERE; Gen. Dir N. SAMKANGE.

INDEX OF TERRITORIES IN VOLUMES I AND II

INDEX OF TERRITORIES IN VOLUMES I AND II

INDEX OF TERRITORIES IN VOLUMES I AND II

Greenland
Sea

Denmark Strait

Arctic Circle

*Norwegian
Sea*

Barents
Sea

Kara
Sea

Laptev
Sea

Scandinavia

North
Sea

Baltic Sea

British
Isles

EUROPE

North European Plain

Bay of
Biscay

Alps

Carpathian Mts

Danube

Balkan Mts

El'brus
5642m

Black Sea

Iberian
Peninsula

Mediterranean Sea

Anatolia

Atlas Mts

Tropic of Cancer

Sahara

Hoggar

Tibesti

Libyan Desert

Nile

Red Sea

Sahel

Niger

Lake Chad

Arabian
Peninsula

Ethiopian
Highlands

Gulf of Aden

Horn of
Africa

AFRICA

Adamawa
Highlands

Gulf of
Guinea

Congo
Basin

Congo

Rift Valley

Rift Valley

Red Volta

Lake Victoria

Kilimanjaro
5895m

Lake Tanganyika

Lake Malawi

Equator

ATLANTIC

OCEAN

Zambezi

Mozambique Channel

Tropic of Capricorn

Namib Desert

Kalahari
Desert

Drakensberg

Cape
Basin

Ural Mountains

Volga

West
Siberian
Plain

Ob

Yenisey

Central
Siberian Plain

S i b e r i a

A S I A

Lena

Khrebet Cherskorgo

Lake Balkhash

Lake
Baikal

Aral
Sea

Caspian
Sea

Iranian
Plateau

Zagros Mountains

The Gulf

Pamirs

Hindu Kush

Tien Shan

Altai

Gobi
Desert

Kunlun Mountains

Plateau
of Tibet

Himalayas

Mt Everest
8848m

Thar
Desert

Ganges

Yellow River

Yangtze

Manchurian
Plain

Sea of
Japan

Japan

East
China
Sea

Arabian
Sea

Deccan

Western Ghats

Eastern Ghats

Bay of
Bengal

Sri
Lanka

Mekong

South
China
Sea

Philippine
Sea

Borneo

INDIAN

OCEAN

New
Guinea

Timor
Sea

AUSTRALIA

Great
Sandy Desert

Great Victoria Desert

Nullarbor
Plain

Darling

A n t a r c t i c a

Antarctic Circle